# The Macquarie DICTIONARY

A KEVIN WELDON PRODUCTION

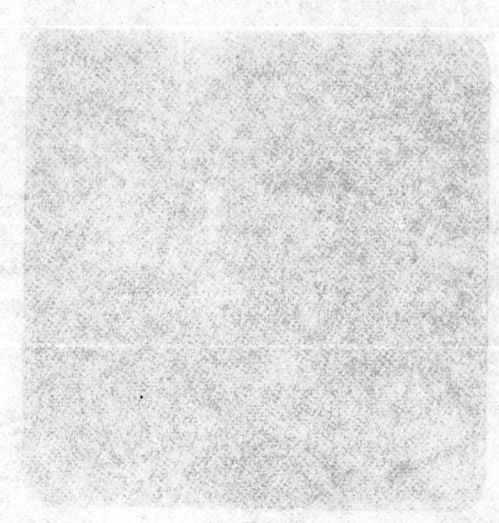

# The Macquarie DICTIONARY

MACQUARIE LIBRARY

Published by Macquarie Library Pty. Ltd.
43 Victoria Street, McMahons Point, NSW, Australia 2060
First published 1981
Reprinted 1982


Produced in Australia for the Publisher
Typeset in Australia by Computer Graphics Corporation Pty. Ltd.

Printed by Griffin Press Limited,
Netley, South Australia

National Library of Australia Cataloguing-in-Publication Data

The Macquarie dictionary

Index
ISBN 0 949757 00 4.

1. English language—Dictionaries. 2. English language in Australia. I. Delbridge, Arthur, 1921–.

423



PUBLISHING DIRECTOR: DANIEL O'KEEFE

Administration Executive: Pamela Seaborn
Limited Edition Consultant: John Reed

A number of words entered in this dictionary are derived from trademarks. However, the presence or absence of this indication of derivation should not be regarded as affecting the legal status of any trademark.

# Contents



Editorial Staff 6

Prefaces:

The English Language 7

Variation in English 10

The History of English Dictionaries 21

Dictionaries and the Problems of Choice 34
J. R. L. Bernard

Explanatory Notes 43

Key to Structure of Entries 45

Pronunciation Key 46

Dictionary 47

Appendixes: 2026

Guide to Usage 2027

Signs and Symbols 2035

Proofreaders' Marks 2040

Weights and Measures 2041

Foreign Alphabets 2046

Ancient Alphabets 2047

Indo-European Languages 2048

Abbreviations used in Etymologies 2049

The Macquarie Dictionary Supplement 2051

# Editorial Staff

EDITORIAL COMMITTEE

Editor-in-Chief: A. Delbridge, M.A.(Lond.), B.A., Dip. Ed.(Syd.),
Professor of Linguistics and
Director of the Speech and Language Research Centre,
Macquarie University.

J. R. L. Bernard, B.Sc., B.A., Ph.D., Dip.Ed.(Syd.),
Associate Professor in Linguistics,
Macquarie University.

D. Blair, M.A.(Syd.),
Senior Tutor in Linguistics,
Macquarie University.

W. S. Ramson, M.A.(N.Z.), Ph.D.(Syd.),
Reader in English,
Australian National University, and
Editor of the Australian National Dictionary.

Executive Editor: Susan Butler, B.A.

# The English Language

The word 'English' or 'Englisc' as it was then spelled first appears in the Old English manuscripts as a word describing the groups of Germanic tribal people who invaded and settled in Britain in the centuries following the collapse of the Roman power there in 410 A.D. This Germanic group included Angles, Saxons, Friesians and the somewhat shadowy Jutes, as well, no doubt, as others. The documentation of their invasions is scant and unreliable but it is here necessary only to point out that they spoke closely related dialects of Germanic and that in the fullness of time they all came to be known as English and spoke what we now call Old English dialects.

From these dialects, after warlike invasions by Dane and Norman, and after peaceful invasions from learned and fashionable languages like Latin and French, and after a hundred and one other vicissitudes, has developed what we now may loosely call the English language.

### *i. English in the World*

It has been estimated that in today's world one person in seven has either inherited English as his or her native tongue, or has learned it as a second language—perhaps as part of a normal pattern of local education as is usual in Sweden, or perhaps in order to be able to function more effectively in some specific sphere of endeavour such as diplomacy, journalism, scientific study, international trade, and so on. For aviators, of course, it is mandatory, being the international language for air control.

It is possibly true that Mandarin Chinese is the inherited language of more people than is English and that Hindustani and Russian could conceivably overtake English in this regard, assuming that they have not as yet already done so. But both of these languages, like Chinese, are confined to a single large area of the world whereas English is spoken throughout the world. Indeed, it is the pre-eminent world language, found more widely spread than any other. Its rivals, Spanish, Portuguese and French, are well behind.

The reasons for this are historical and relate to the roles which English speakers have had as world explorers, world settlers and world leaders in trade and science. English speakers did not always take these pre-eminent roles nor necessarily will they continue to take them in the future. In the days of Elizabeth I for example, English was spoken by only six million people or less, and Richard Mulcaster's often quoted and lugubrious words were quite true. 'The English tongue is of small reach, stretching no further than this island of ours, nay not there overall'.

By 'not there overall' Mulcaster was of course alluding to the areas of his island in which a Celtic language was then spoken—Wales, Cornwall, parts of Devon and parts of Scotland including the Western Islands. English was indeed then of small reach.

Shortly afterwards mercantile adventurers and others began to alter all of this. A settlement was made in Virginia under Captain John Smith in 1608 and the Pilgrim Fathers landed on the Plymouth Rock in Massachusetts in 1620. These two events marked the commencement of the Englishing of North America.

Following the Portuguese and the Dutch, the English began establishing trading posts, and ultimately empire, around the coasts of Africa, in India and in South-East Asia and China.

They captured islands in the Caribbean and territories in many scattered parts of the world. Australia and New Zealand came under their control and ultimately there was no continent over some part of which the English flag did not fly, and in which the English tongue did not begin to take root.

Moreover, the industrial revolution took place first in Great Britain and British-manufactured goods flooded the world. With the goods came new ideas and precepts. The less technologically innovative cultures developed new expectations and began to change, sometimes quite fundamentally. British expertise was brought in to provide the new railways, the new bridges, the new harbour systems and so on and with it the English language. British-style education was sought by many non-British countries and this further expanded the influence of English.

Subsequently the lead, which was first with Britain, passed to the United States and in this century it is the United States that shows the way. But this means that it is still English speakers who set the pace—in the development of technology, in the production of consumer goods, and in providing a model to which numerous non-English speakers, rightly or wrongly, continue to aspire.

It is no wonder then that so many non-English speaking people throughout the world have found it expedient to learn English as a second language. In whatever direction they journey they are likely to encounter it. If they seek to buy manufactured goods, either on their travels or indeed even at home, they are likely to find themselves dealing with English-speaking traders. If they seek to move into any sphere of international activity, they will need it. Their numbers join those of the hundreds of millions for whom English is a first language and swell the ranks of the English speakers.

### *ii. English in Various Lands*

Despite the situation just outlined there are very few countries of the world, in absolute terms perhaps none, in which English is the only language spoken. There are, however, countries like Britain, North America, Australia, New Zealand and certain Caribbean islands, which one may call heartlands of the English tongue, where its future is assured. The language will presumably last as long in them as the descendants of the present populations continue to dominate these areas, despite the presence of sizeable groups among them who do not have it as a first tongue.

In other parts of the world where English is commonly spoken it is not even the majority language. In India and South Africa, in Hong Kong and Singapore, for example, its future is just as uncertain as is its role as a world language in the wider domain.

Its future outside the heartlands depends ultimately on its utility and this will be assessed and reassessed as the centuries unfold and the political and mercantile realities of the world adjust. There it is, and always will be, on trial.

The United Kingdom has about one fifth of the numbers of people who claim English as their mother tongue but has also two communities which still speak a Celtic language—one, relatively small, in the Scottish Highlands speaking Scots Gaelic and the other, about a million strong, in Wales speaking Welsh. Probably both will diminish in numbers, although the force of Welsh nationalism could conceivably reverse the expected pattern. At the moment this seems unlikely if only because Wales itself is not linguistically homogeneous. The Welsh speakers are principally in Glamorganshire and the Western Counties from Anglesey to Carmarthen.

The case of the Republic of Ireland shows linguistic parallels. Despite official encouragement of Irish, another Celtic language, even to the point where children in defined Irish-speaking schools were punished for speaking English, it is still, after many years, in only four of the twenty-six counties of the Republic that Irish is usual in spontaneous conversation. Irish English, of course, reflects some influence from its Celtic bedfellow.

In England itself the regional dialects are numerous and clearly differentiated but those of the South Eastern counties are most influential. They provide now, as they have done for some time, the model for the 'standard grammar', and the forms for most of the words which are in the vast common stock of English vocabulary used throughout the world.

Their spoken accents, too, are caught in the prestigious Received Pronunciation which was said by the originator of this term, Daniel Jones of University College, London, to be the pronunciation 'usually heard in everyday speech in the families of Southern English people who have been educated at the public schools'. By 'public schools' Jones, of course, meant fee-paying upper-class schools like Eton and Harrow. He saw Received Pronunciation therefore as a non-regional accent in the sense that it was likely to appear wherever upper-class English people were to be found, but acknowledges it as a truly South Eastern form. In more or less marked varieties it is the accent in Britain of high prestige and thought most appropriate for high drama, solemn moments of church and parliament and for the serious pronouncements of the BBC.

In many foreign countries English Received Pronunciation is the model taught in the schools and universities. This is especially true in the northern European countries, France, Belgium, Holland, Denmark, Norway, Sweden, Finland, Luxemburg and West Germany where English is the usual second language.

Increasingly, however, the model of American English pronunciation is challenging Received Pronunciation, and in Asian countries and elsewhere the choice of which accent to teach is a vexed one. Some centres like Singapore are close to accepting the idea that a foreign-accented English, that is, their own local variety which is more readily within the grasp of the people, might serve just as well as the standard.

The situation in India is similar in that the distinctively Indian-accented English pronunciation is usual among those who acquire English as a second language there, and is growing in force as a local prestige form.

British English can claim the honour of being the original from which all other offshoots had ultimately to grow and certain of its dialects that of having exerted a greater normative influence than any others but, in its having to rub shoulders with a local foreign language and in showing sharp regional differences, it is like many others. One third or so of Canadians speak French, a French by no means the same as that of Paris, and as well there are minor languages like Eskimo and that of the Algonquian Indians in Canada.

Across the border, the citizens of the United States have regional English dialects which, like those in Britain, ultimately reflect previous patterns of population movement. For example, the north-eastern dialect of the area settled by the Puritans contrasts with the southern dialect of the plantation States settled by a very different group from Britain. Both contrast with dialects in the other parts of the eastern seaboard and with areas further west. Apart from these regional English dialects, there is Black English, which stands apart, and no fewer than twenty-three other languages in significant daily use which between them reflect the successive waves of European and other migration, past and present, which have gone into the vast American melting pot. Among these, Spanish is still constantly fed by legal and illegal migration from the south and leads the field, followed by German, Italian and Polish.

As is usually the case, American English differs least from other sorts of English in its formal and standard guise. The language of the papers of scientists, the columns of serious journals, the considered pronouncements of distinguished citizens is everywhere much the same. The colloquial and lower registers are usually much more typically local, but in the case of American English, because it is the language of the largest single English-speaking political group and of the most dominant country in science and politics and so much else in the twentieth century, even these registers feed significantly into international English and join with standard American terms in providing other forms of modern English.

In these days of near instantaneous telecommunications these terms pass to the world as a whole at great speed. The standard words embed themselves in international English almost at once, terms usually reflecting American expertise or exigencies like *astronaut*, *moonshot*, *escalate* and *Watergate*. The colloquial terms may go into use with cult groups only, but they force at least a nodding familiarity from many English speakers outside these groups who are influenced by American films and television. Only very few non-Americans would say 'man, gimme some skin!' but many non-Americans know what this means. It has become part of their passive language.

Australia and New Zealand are more homogeneous as to English dialect than most countries discussed in that each has in effect one dialect only. But each has some remaining speakers of languages in use before the British settlement began, Aboriginal in Australia and Maori in New Zealand. Australia in particular has sizeable numbers of relatively recently arrived citizens who have a language other than English as their first language and in this regard the Australian society replicates the situation we find in the United States on a smaller scale.

Probably the only political entities in the world within whose margins English is the sole significant language are the island countries of the Caribbean such as Jamaica and Trinidad.

In countries other than the ones so far mentioned English plays various roles. In South Africa it is a minority language, its speakers outnumbered among the white population by those who speak Afrikaans and greatly outnumbered by those among the black population who speak one or the other of the African languages. In India there are numerous speakers of English but few indeed for whom this is their only language. This is also the case in Pakistan, in Singapore, in Hong Kong and most of the territories over which the British once ruled or in the odd case still continue to do. Often English remains as a lingua franca of varying official status in former colonies, but it is very unclear how long this will continue to be the case.

# Variation in English

The preceding discussion will have reminded the reader that English varies from place to place—from city to city in Britain, from region to region in the United States and country to country in the English-speaking world.

It is well to remember that English has always varied and will always vary in time also. The London English of ten centuries ago is quite unintelligible to the usual speaker of London English today. Compare the following extract from the Old English version of the Old Testament with its modern translation.

**Hīe þā hine ā·wurpon intō ānum sēaþe, on þǣm wǣron seofon lēon, þǣm man sealde dæġhwǣmlīċe twā hrīþeru and twā sċēap, ac him wæs þā of·togen ǣlċes fōdan siex dagas, þæt hīe þone Godes mann ā·bītan scolden.**

*Then the King saw that they were unanimous and of necessity gave the prophet into their hands. They then threw him in a hut in which were seven lions, who were given two oxen and two sheep but they had been denied food for six days, so that they would devour the man of God.*

To talk about English as if it is a single entity is to a degree misleading. It is a set of different but related Englishes or dialects and each of these has its own past, present and future.

The whole is not unlike some miraculous multi-stranded cable in each strand of which alterations continuously take place. Sometimes the alterations affect one strand only, sometimes many or all, sometimes strands coalesce or, alternatively, split into new strands, but always there is flux and no strand comes from nothing. Each goes back and back in time, or at least the threads which join to make it do, back past Shakespeare, past the Normans to the Old English period during which English was first written down, then beyond to the primitive Germanic period where our linguistic ancestors lived in Europe and did not write at all and even back beyond them to the primitive Indo-Europeans about whose language we can only guess, and beyond them to the nameless people about whose language we cannot even guess. At no point is there spontaneous generation to any significant degree at all, typically everything comes from something, and everything at any one place or time is changing into something else and always will. The sound system of each form of English, its vocabulary, its grammar and so on, are all being continuously altered but not necessarily all at the same hectic rate.

A cross section through this miraculous cable would give us the picture of world English at any one point in time with all its mind-boggling variations. Yet if one focuses attention on the period since 1608 or so when English began to be exported significantly, it is surprising how few have been the forces at work creating the great variations we see today.

## a. GRAMMAR

The grammar may early and quickly be dismissed in this context because, except in the case of pidgins which will be referred to later on, the grammar of English has not undergone much variation as the language has moved about the world.

It is possible to point to some verb forms which are more or less peculiar to North American English like *gotten* for *got* and *dove* for *dived*, and to some small variations such as *in back of* instead of *at the back of* and *a quarter of five*. These do not amount to much at all and lie in any case in that grey area where grammar, vocabulary and idiom meet.

In the usual case, the morphology and grammar of English exported diverged very little from the pattern of South Eastern English. If Indian English tends to use the continuous tenses in a way which other speakers do not—*I am thinking that it will rain*—the form of the tense itself shows no unusual feature.

## b. THE VOCABULARY

### 1) Why it Extends

A principal underlying reason why vocabulary has altered is simply stated. People who have different experiences develop new words with which to describe them.

This is true whether one makes the focus of one's attention the varieties of English in Britain or out of it and indeed the varieties of any language in any part of the world.

Separation of peoples, whether it is physical or social, is a prime condition for their underlying different experiences and so inevitably those who lose contact with one another begin to drift apart linguistically.

The Germanic peoples who invaded and settled Celtic Britain spoke dialects descended from a common stock but these were already differentiated before they were established in Britain because the tribal groupings wandered and lived substantially apart. The stability of the population once settled in Britain and the difficulty of and restrictions on travel meant that even people in adjacent towns might have little contact and so develop different words. Those more widely separated in different counties certainly did and regional variations proliferated as can still be heard to this day.

When towns became large enough to be significantly stratified socially, the rich and powerful lived differently, apart from the poor and powerless, and so social dialects arose.

The same thing happened again when English speakers began to inhabit isolated pockets of the earth in the territories outside Britain. Indeed there was an intensification of the pattern because the differences in experience undergone by pioneers were inevitably of a dramatic intensity, since the regions they took over were more diverse than any of those in Britain, like for example the snowy wastes of Canada, the jungles of Malaysia and the outback of Australia. New vocabulary was needed and needed quickly if the pioneers were to deal successfully with their new environment, and there was in all such cases an exciting initial burgeoning of new words.

But this was by no means the end of the matter. Once the pioneers were established the societies they had founded went on with a life of their own. Each was in some degree isolated, each had its local problems, and its local characteristics which altered as time went by. In less dramatic ways the new societies then continued, and continue, to develop new vocabularies to cope with their separate physical and social experiences and in Britain the parent society continues to do the same thing.

Everywhere the automatic, self-adjusting miracle of language seems to be able effortlessly to provide new words for particular needs. This is not a feature of English alone but of all languages. Nevertheless, English does seem especially well placed to rise to the challenge of such new needs because it is possessed of word-forming techniques from its Germanic ancestry and also from what one might call its Romance ancestry (which it owes to the Normans and the later fascination of its scholars with Latin and Greek) and because it is so little inflected.

The Germanic pattern of compounding comes easily to English. It has always been able to say directly *moonlight* where French has had to say *clair de lune* (light of moon). The battery of Romance roots has long been available for new coinages and it was easy for the English to name their invention *television*, (*tele*—Greek—distant, *vision*, ultimately Latin) while the Germans preferred native roots and spoke of *Fernsehen* (*far* plus *seeing*). It is true that compoundings are known in French (*gratte-ciel*, skyscraper) and Romance roots in German (*Telefon*, telephone), but neither is as 'ambidextrous' as English and once the coinage has been made the fewness of English inflections allows the same word form to provide related parts of speech with ease. In English the noun *telephone* is the same as the verb *telephone* but in French *téléphone* must become *téléphoner* and in German *telefonieren*.

### 2) How it Extends

#### a. New Applications of Old Words

A little reflection will convince us that in one sense we are each of us creating new words every day. If we think of a word as having a spelling and a meaning, or better, a shape and a content, then, while the shape of a word like *bed* must remain constant, the content will change every time we apply the shape to a piece of furniture of a particular type but which is different. We may at one time in our life be familiar only with a simple wooden bed, but we soon meet more and more elaborate ones, perhaps ultimately electronically controlled plush monsters with built-in television and radio. We still unhesitatingly call them *beds* because we see the essential similarity in function and purpose which links them to our first simple wooden example. Language could not serve us if we did not do this since if we had to have names for every instance of a class of items we would simply not be able to remember them all.

We are thus accustomed to applying an old word shape to a new content and creating, in one sense, a new word. Wherever we see the essential similarity of something new with something old we reach for the sign shape of the something old.

Sometimes the similarity is a bit fanciful yet it is generally accepted. We talk about a *flowerbed.* Is the similarity in the shape or in the fact that the flowers are 'asleep' in it? One does not know, for often the similarity which the coiner of the extended meaning saw is lost. Who now remembers that a lifting *crane* has that name because it has long legs like the bird we call a *crane*, or that *flour* is the *flower* of wheat? A case like the last where even a different spelling has been brought into being is rare but instances where the link is lost to common sight are frequent. *Crane* exemplifies a host of cases thought of as quite unrelated words by most people until they chance to see them in the one entry in a dictionary and learn that they have a common source.

When new experience arises, the most common way of providing words for it is to force old words to take on new meanings as a result of perceived similarity. The similarity may be partial, not real, and may in any case be soon forgotten and never recovered. This does not matter. An old shape has a new content, a new word has been born. There is an enormous chance element in all this, since no two people perceive the world and its patterns in the same way.

In the United States an apartment block in which dwellers own the apartments individually is called a *condominium.* Outside the United States this word has not had this meaning but rather means *joint sovereignty*: Britain and France once ruled the New Hebrides in condominium. The similarity between such a system of political joint ruling and the domestic joint ruling has been seen by the coiner of the American term and it has been taken into general use.

In Australia such a building is called a *home unit.* This is a shortening of *home unit block*, that is, a block of *home units,* since each apartment was viewed as a unit which, when suitably peopled and loved, would be similar to a home in the older sense of a house so peopled and loved.

This term serves to show that contiguity, either of the word shapes or of the word contents, may function like similarity in extending a meaning.

The following are some words of various types of English which have been coined as a result of perceived similarity.

| | *United States* | *Australian* | *New Zealand* |
|---|---|---|---|
| *New Environment* | (prairie) dog | creek | paddock |
| | grizzly (bear) | wattle | birch |
| | meadow | sally (tree) | nugget |
| | panther | bream | honeysuckle |
| | rattler | magpie | missionary |
| *New Society* | turkey | station | graunch |
| | attorney | run | dairy |
| | college | currency | monkey |
| | depot | digger | trundler |
| | nickel | selection | sally |

## b. Compounding Old Words

One of the richest sources of neologisms is to take old words and forge them into new compounds. These are initially like descriptive phrases but typically, as they become established in the language, they take on the stress patterns normal to compounds and people seldom stop to think of their component parts but just accept them as single units in their thought. Who, for example, now stops to consider that a *skyscraper* is so high that it *scrapes* the *sky*.

Some compounds are basically imaginative like *road-runner* and *lyrebird* and highlight the characteristics of the entity they describe. Others are basically dull and mechanical like *native bear* and *native dog* and have very little information built into them.

| | *United States* | *Australian* | *New Zealand* |
|---|---|---|---|
| *New Environment* | nut wood | bentwing swiftmoth | butterfish |
| | copperhead | cherry tree | blue duck |
| | rattlesnake | native pear | hogsback |
| | Red Indian | blackboy | Maori rat |
| | sidewinder | laughing jackass | saddleback |
| *New Society* | fruit machine | bush breakfast | run-off |
| | railroad | bush lawyer | meeting house |
| | grand jury | strata title | state house |
| | ivy league | stickybeak | dairy butter |
| | white trash | government house | ringbolt |

c. Borrowings

*i. From Foreign Languages*

One simple way to gain an extra word is to take it from somebody else's language. English has a long tradition of doing this and has been enriched from many European languages, most noticeably French and Italian. The emotional reaction which some, like the French, show to outside influences is lacking in English speakers and they are not given to pursuing the myth of 'purity'. Not surprisingly, English speakers abroad have found no difficulty in taking in words from foreign languages and many of these have gone into the great central store of international English, for example:

curry (Tamil)
tomato (Nahuatl through Spanish)
chinchilla (Spanish)
budgie (Aboriginal)
commando (Afrikaans)
chutney (Hindi)

In each of the overseas heartlands and many of the other countries where English is an important factor, there have been indigenous languages from which the English speakers have borrowed, usually changing the sound structure of the native words, often quite beyond recognition, so that they sit more comfortably in English-speaking mouths.

The borrowings have not always been as extensive as one might have expected except typically in the case of place names. This is because the new settlers had, as a rule, not regarded the indigenous cultures which they were in the process of mastering or displacing as having a great deal to offer. Names for native landmarks, and for native flora and fauna could be accepted, but usually not very much from the culture itself.

One may see this as an unattractive cultural ethnocentricity if one will, but in fairness it should be pointed out that all language is utilitarian first and foremost and the utility of words borrowed from tribal languages has been limited by the fact that native tribes usually extend over relatively small areas of land, and so words gathered in one region would be of no use in dealing with natives in other regions since the tribes tended to have entirely different languages.

In any case, of course, one does not need words of elements of other people's experience which one has not shared and which under no circumstances will one ever share, such as the complex divisions into moieties and other groups of the Australian Aborigines. Such things develop English names only when English-speaking anthropologists begin to study them.

| *American Indian* | *Aboriginal* | *Afrikaans* |
|---|---|---|
| opossum | quokka | biltong |
| racoon | gang gang | kop |
| skunk | wombat | laager |
| puma | numbat | mealie |
| pow pow | paddymelon | meerkat |

### ii. *From Proper Names*

A second kind of borrowing is from proper names. It is surprising how many new words have arisen from what one might have thought an unlikely source, but after all the English *bobby* is so called because it was Sir *Robert Peel* who created the force in the first place and he was earlier called a *peeler* anyway. The *sandwich* which he eats celebrates the Fourth Earl of *Sandwich* who found this form of food a convenience and the nearby *Belisha beacon*, Leslie Hore-*Belisha*, Minister of Transport in the British Government in the 1930s.

The connection between a generic name like bobby and sandwich and the particular proper name from which it derives is seldom known by those who use it and for most people such a word is just one like any other.

| *United States* | *British* | *Australian* |
|---|---|---|
| Douglas fir | bowdlerise | banksia |
| gerrymander | quisling | boronia |
| oregon | Aunt Sally | bowser |
| Tom and Jerry | Tommy (Atkins) | drongo |
| Jim Crow | blimp | kelpie |

### iii. *Abbreviations and Acronyms*

It is common throughout the whole English-speaking world for the compound names of things like American English son of a bitch *S.O.B.*, and especially organisations, to be referred to by their initials. Thus the British Broadcasting Corporation and the Australian Broadcasting Commission are abbreviated to *BBC* and *ABC*, and in Canada there is the *CBC* and in America the *NBC* and *CBS*, formed on the same principle. These initials act then as the proper names of the entities to which they refer and when they are converted into words, by treating the initials as the letters of a word, the element of vocabulary so formed, that is, the acronym, can be viewed as a form of borrowing. For example, a member of the Australian and New Zealand Army Corps can be referred to as an *Anzac* pronounced /'ænzæk/.

In a similar fashion words like *laser* have been made from selected initials of *light amplification by stimulated emission of radiation*, like the originally U.S. *snafu* which, in a genteel interpretation at least, derives from the initials of *situation normal: all fouled up*. A word like *bumf* represents a sort of half-way house since the first element of *bumfodder* is present in full but only the initial of the second.

## d. Change in Frequency

As societies change, speakers gradually lose touch with words for entities no longer of current interest. More spectacularly, English speakers moved abroad lose contact with old experiences while coming into contact with new experiences and both factors mark their language.

For example, in the harsher environment of Australia words like *meadow*, *copse*, *glen* and even *village*, have little use because the entities they refer to are either missing or vastly different. An English village and a small Australian township are just too dissimilar, apparently, for the word *village* to serve for both in normal use.

Thus some words drop in frequency, while others may become effectively obsolete and fall completely from use, like for example *kelpie* and *gamp*, in their British senses, in the United States. Alternatively, for some speakers at least, they may pass into that curious limbo—the passive vocabulary. This is the collection of words which are known, perhaps through literature or the cinema or television, but are not in daily use in a particular area. Their frequency is, accordingly, minimal but they are not truly dead. The passive vocabularies of the English-speaking communities are in some cases quite large, most contain a large number of Americanisms and a smaller number of Britishisms, but in varying degrees the less influential varieties of world English are referred to also.

Occasionally a dialect word of low frequency in Britain effectively dies while taking on a much wider life in some overseas country. There seems to be a large element of chance in this, for example the north country dialect word *darg* has small use in Britain but was, at one time at least, a very common word of Australian English meaning a portion of work, the daily darg. In South Africa *bioscope* for a cinema lives on having dropped from everyday use elsewhere.

Information about the origins of words is, of course, to be found in their etymologies and some information about their frequency and provenance of use is to be found in the limiting labels such as *Obs.*, *US*, *Brit.*, and so on.

e. Just for Fun

Infants have a very lively interest in patterns in sounds and the books for the very young, as well as their school playground chants, reflect this. The lines of the jingles frequently rhyme and at every turn there is assonance as in *Humpty Dumpty* and alliteration as in *Milly Molly Mandy*.

While it may well be that all this has a serious purpose and is a reflection of the infant's need to practise the material which helps with the assimilation of the complicated sound pattern of the language being learned, there can be no doubt that the very young delight in all of this just the same.

Although their needs are obviously not the same, the not so very young remain responsive at all ages to sound patterns and take pleasure in juggling and creating arrangements which are pleasing to the ear. If at the same time the pattern is thought to be in some way amusing, so much the better.

Numerous words in all forms of English owe their existence to the fact that their users feel that they are funny—either by convention or because they really suggest some of that incongruity which is the basis of most humour—and at the same time because they have an ear-catching sound pattern.

Cockney rhyming slang is a classical case in point. In Britain to call a car a *jam jar* not only tickles the ear but suggests a train of improbable thought. In Australia the name for an archetypal hick township is *Woop Woop*, in New Zealand *Wop Wops*. Both are held to be amusing. So too is the word *jimjams*, an American invention originally used to describe an actor's pre-performance anxieties.

All forms of English have such words built into them. This, with acronyms, is the only area of word coinage where the creation of new word shapes is at all common.

c. PRONUNCIATION

Vocabulary variation is felt only at the points in sentences where a local word shape or meaning chances to be. In many a sentence all over the English-speaking world there may be none of these at all and quite long stretches of writing may contain only words in general use and so no lexical indication of where they have been written.

Accent, however, is all pervasive. A Scot or an American has only to utter a few syllables to be recognised. Accents are very many and very distinctive and how they arise is not quite so simply explained as how new words arise, but at least some of the forces at work in creating accents are apparent.

One must accept that even left to themselves pronunciations tend to drift. The moving parts of the vocal mechanism—the tongue, the jaw, the lips and so on—all have their own inertias and preferred dynamic patterns and these may run counter to the full expression of the sound pattern of a dialect at a given time. Thus short cuts in the mouth are taken, sounds are elided and run together and otherwise modified. It is sometimes possible to see what has happened after the event in this regard but usually not possible to predict where, when or how the resistance of the vocal mechanism will create a permanent change. Words spelt by 'er' in Middle English were pronounced much as the letters would suggest. They included *far* as well as *clerk* and while some have changed since then both in spelling and pronunciation others have changed in pronunciation only and not uniformly in all dialects. American English pronounces *clerk* to rhyme with *jerk*, New Zealand English to rhyme with *ark* and Scottish English as something different again.

There are other imponderable forces at work too. Analogy may occasionally force a word to take a sound shape that joins it to a wider pattern as when *lenger* was made to become *longer*. Or again social considerations may persuade subgroup to adopt a particular set of pronunciations as a sort of badge of identity. By looking at what has happened to the pronunciation of English dialects as they have been exported to countries around the world one can, however, make out some of the forces which seem to have been at work. These are discussed briefly below.

1. Amalgamation

In Britain, the establishment and maintenance of a multiplicity of regional and social dialects was encouraged by the isolation of the speech communities. The one quasi non-regional accent of Britain, namely Received Pronunciation, might possibly be traced back to a bringing together of elements in the population from the West Midlands and East Anglia in London, there to mingle with some local elements, about the time of the first Elizabeth, but in the normal case, populations stayed at home and dialects kept apart, changing, but not with great rapidity.

In the ships of the English adventurers and merchants, going to the corners of the earth to seek profits, and in the ships of the convicts transported as a punishment, the situation was very different. Here folk from many different counties, with many different dialects, might all be immured for long periods together and forced to converse. The situation remained the same when they had landed at their destinations and led ultimately to the amalgamation of the mixed dialects they brought with them.

Amalgamation of dialects is not a process in which adults normally take part. One can readily observe how most adults retain the kind of English which they bring to a new land, be it a British variety like West Country, or a foreign-accented variety such as that spoken by people who are native speakers of Italian or Swedish. There may be some accommodation towards the English of the new land but usually not much, as it is the very exceptional adult who masters the new form of English.

But with children who are young enough and those who are born in the new land, the case is very different. Many people believe that children learn their speech from their parents and there is truth in this in as much that the most basic language skills are, in fact, learnt from the parents. As soon as the child is old enough, however, and has the opportunity to belong to a peer group, the dominant linguistic influence becomes that of the peer group, not the family. If there is a variety of accents in the community the one used by the peer group will become the one adopted by the child, for the desire of the infant to be integrated into the peer group is tremendously strong. Subsequently this speech may be remodelled, but not necessarily. Some speakers are true to their infant peer group for all their lives.

The period of the first decades of the 1800s saw British migration to Australia, New Zealand and South Africa taking place in numbers large enough to be significant. It does not matter whether the migrants were convicts or not in this context since the incentives which urged people towards crime were the same as the incentives which urged people to see if they might improve their lot by migrating and we may regard the migrant population in these three cases as being basically the same blend of imported social and regional dialects with a London bias.

The adults did not change their speech significantly but the children did. The peer groups which formed among the very young, and especially the colonial born, were presumably for a time heterogeneous but very soon created or adopted an accent which owed something to all that could be heard about them, a feature from this dialect, a feature from that, and rather more than a few features from London pronunciation.

There is a basic similarity in the English of Australia, New Zealand and South Africa which derives from the fact that they represent amalgamations of similar groups of dialects at about the same time.

The case of Canada is much more complex. Newfoundland had had English speakers since the Humphrey Gilbert settlement of 1583 and antique forms of the language with West Country overtones are still reported from isolated pockets of settlement, such as *we'm going vishing this zummer*.

Nova Scotia became English after struggles with the French in 1713 but seems to have attracted few, if any, colonists before the American Revolution. The bulk of the English speakers were in Quebec, where a Scottish regiment was discharged and where they were heavily outnumbered by the French, and also in what is now Ontario, where they were few before 1775 but increasing. It is just possible that the dialects of the settlers there were amalgamating in the speech of their children at about this time and a new Canadian accent, like the three above, was being formed.

We shall never know, for with the Revolution of the Thirteen States, forty thousand loyalist Americans shortly settled in Canada, a migration north which continued for quite some time. In 1812, of the hundred thousand English speakers in Canada, eighty thousand were from the United States. Early Canadian English, if it existed, was wiped out by the sheer force of numbers and today Canadian English is clearly of the American family.

English in what is now the United States arrived at various times and with various groups of people. The plantation south with its lordly mansions began in 1608 and came to know indentured labour, convicts and later Negro slaves, supporting an Anglophile aristocracy. The Puritan north started in 1620, a village culture of inbuilt religious intolerance, but independent and hardy, and respecting learning, sobriety and industry. The coastal colonies in between belonged in part to the Dutch, but in 1664 the Dutch lost control of New Jersey and Marylands to the British and New Amsterdam became New York. In 1681 Pennsylvania was wrested from the French and set aside for the Quakers. The central region was thus very mixed in population, there were Swedes, Germans, Ulster Scots and so on also present and the dialects took some time to amalgamate.

The eastern seaboard became British but the populations of the three major areas, north, south and middle, were different. Communications were poor, not least because of the enmity of the Red Indians, and different dialects developed. While the forces of amalgamation operated within their areas no doubt, they could not unite the three parts and in some of them, notably the south, isolative class divisions, as between the aristocracy, the white trash and the black population, were firmly marked and caused further fragmentation.

Many of the features of American English pronunciation reflect linguistic patterns more common in the seventeenth century in Britain than in the twentieth. For example American English *heist* and *pisun* and their rustic pronunciations, /haɪst/ and /ˈpaɪzən/ are in fact older pronunciations of *hoist* and *poison* respectively. The placing of the tongue in a central position in the mouth to create the American quality of the vowel in *hurry* is also a conservative feature once shared by earlier types of British English. Similarly, the general retention of 'r' after a vowel is conservative rather than innovative.

The American dialect scene is immensely complicated. Certain waves of overseas migration bypassed the settled east coast and waves of internal migration drew peoples from it, though not much from the south, so that the central and western States reflect a mosaic of influences. It is not intended to attempt to describe them here but merely to observe that amalgamation of various kinds and in various places has helped shape the complicated end product.

## 2. Self-Image

It seems reasonable to imagine that there are many people who must be blissfully unselfconscious about the way they speak and who do not feel an ego involvement in the nicety with which they choose their speech sounds. Yet it is certain that for millions and millions of people around the world this is not so. It has been written, 'speak that I may see you', and such people are all too aware that as they speak they are revealing themselves, announcing where they have come from, what sort of position they occupy in the economic range, what degree of good taste they have, and so on.

It is most unfortunate that the many different ways of pronouncing English are not all equally valued. As long as they promote communication with equal efficacy, and most of them do, they ought in theory to be held in equal regard. It is not possible for one to *be* more beautiful than another since beauty is not a quality intrinsic to anything but rather a value judgment imposed upon it by the beholder.

The facts are, however, that different pronunciations are differently regarded. Basically they are judged by association. The pronunciations of the poor and uneducated urban dwellers are most reviled, because those who speak them are the least envied, the least thought of as the type of person others would like to be. Rural pronunciations may be 'charming' to those who see rural life romantically or 'coarse' to those whose mind runs to the muck of the cow byre, or 'humorous' to those who see country people as slow and foolish.

The list is unending, but if one thing stands out it is the high if grudging regard given to Received Pronunciation and more recently, to a lesser degree, to its cousins, the prestige dialects around the world. As the pronunciation for so long of the people with money, influence and taste, the very people that others, in their secret hearts, would most like to resemble, Received Pronunciation has enjoyed a supreme position of regard which is only now beginning to weaken.

All of this might only be a sad commentary on human foibles but it is a situation which has effectively changed the pronunciation of millions and millions of English speakers who have with varying degrees of awareness and varying degrees of success modified the pronunciations of their speech away from some natural local form they inherited towards that of the distant, often dimly perceived model provided by Received Pronunciation.

Individuals differ in how far they find it suitable to their own self-image to modify their inherited pronunciation and in any case they differ in their ability to achieve their objective. In countries where this is a significant factor there is thus much variation along what is sometimes called a spectrum, at one end of which is the most local, the most regionally marked form and at the other the least local, the least regionally marked form. How the population is distributed along this spectrum varies from country to country.

In South Africa the pronunciation arising from the amalgamation of the British dialects was modified towards the unmarked end of the spectrum in significant numbers by the fact that the white man, however humble his origin, so often found himself in charge of a number of black or coloured men and so in a position which was managerial and in which therefore it seemed fitting to him to use the pronunciation associated with command. When the diamond industry developed so suddenly and so significantly the need for higher level executives grew rapidly and the incentive to project the total image of the ruling class, even down to the accent, was felt by many. In South Africa elocution classes flourished.

None of this means that South Africans cannot still be heard to be South Africans but only that their speech in many, many cases has less extreme expression of the local hallmarks than might otherwise be the case.

In New Zealand an extremely strong emotional attachment to Britain and British values promoted a significant move away from the most marked New Zealand accent until only very recently. Now, as in South Africa, the speech of the younger people appears to be going strongly in the opposite direction. Whether the world censure of South Africa in the one case and the British defection to the E.E.C. in the other are relevant factors can only be speculated upon at this stage.

In Australia the move from the most marked form resulting from the amalgamation of the dialects brought to the country has caused massive change and responds again to a sense of individual fitness. The marked form, judged harshly by so many because of its association firstly with uneducated convict bastards and subsequently with uncultured roughness, has been repudiated in varying degrees by perhaps seventy percent of the population. Even so, the least marked form of Australian speech as heard in drama and in high officialdom, is still clearly Australian. It would be very much more so without the struggle to 'upgrade'.

In Jamaica too, the ideal Received Pronunciation has had noticeable effect and in the United States the dialect of the New England region has functioned similarly. The prestige universities of that area provided the teachers in the schools, during the great move of population to the west, and their dialect established itself as a local standard of genteelism, not unaided by distant Received Pronunciation.

In the United States, however, the effects of self-image can be seen to be operating in another direction. Studies have shown that people who are in social subsets which feel somehow aggrieved and set apart, will develop, presumably unconsciously for the most part, features of pronunciation which mark them as separate and which they bear as the badges of their difference. Those in the swim of society, the socially upward mobile, adopt its prestige forms, but those seriously alienated from it reject them and seek forms of difference of their own. This can be found in the pronunciation of the Black English of Harlem and in Australia probably in the speech of certain urban Aboriginals. Thus the effect of self image is both unifying and diversifying as circumstances may dictate.

### 3. Language Interference

It is well known that English spoken with a French accent sounds rather different from English spoken with a German accent. The reason is that the intricate speech patterns mastered and inbuilt when the speaker was learning his or her native language interfere with the intricate speech pattern necessary for accentless English. Those of different languages interfere in different ways.

As has been pointed out earlier, English nowhere reigns in isolation and it is not hard to find instances where the speakers of other languages in a given region have been sufficiently numerous to influence the way English is spoken there generally.

South African English is beginning to show small signs of the effects of the propinquity of so many speakers of Afrikaans. Attention has recently been drawn to a new and unusual quality in the vowels found in words like *peat* and *room*.

Indian English is a classical case in point. The consonantal systems of many Indian languages are markedly different from that of English and so too are the speech rhythms. Much of what is characteristic in Indian English pronunciation can be attributed to these two factors, and the speech of those few Indians who are English speakers only is as affected by them as is that of those who are true bi- or polylinguals. The pronunciation resulting in part from interference has become a sort of local standard.

The same situation is to be found among many Black speakers of English in Africa where the influence is coming from the various tribal languages and, on a smaller scale, other parts of the world such as Singapore where Singaporean English probably reflects first language interference from several directions as well as some amalgamation.

### 4. Pidgin

Extreme expressions of language interference are to be found in the pidgin languages. These are languages originally developed in the course of contact between European traders and native peoples in various places around the world.

Although many of the pidgins can never have had physical contact, the fact that they share certain features in common has led to speculations that they may somehow represent a natural basic language to which the traders came intuitively as they tried to make themselves understood. Alternatively, it has been suggested that they continue the basic pattern of the very first pidgins which were worked out by the Portuguese who were the pioneer traders all around the world. To the moulds of language established by them were later inserted significant substitution of Dutch, English or other European words as merchants from these countries displaced the Portuguese from their trading enclaves.

When pidgins become adopted by the native peoples themselves for their own use they become creoles and it is now believed that American Black English which diverges at so many points from American White English, is best to be thought of, not as debased white English, but as a creole formed by the amalgamation of African English pidgins brought with the slaves from Africa and which were used amongst them because the tribal groups could not understand each others' languages. The creole has subsequently become much less marked because of modifications towards prestige American language but nevertheless retains many of its old features.

In Papua New Guinea a creole, which is still called a pidgin, has official status and in it one can see the interference from the native sound system in the pronunciation of the English words embedded in it.

## d. WRITING

(The material in this section was provided by Mrs Pam Peters, Linguistics Department, Macquarie University.)

The urge to represent human events pictorially seems well nigh universal. There are depictions of hunting scenes in aboriginal caves, of conquered warriors bearing tribute on the stones of Persepolis, of great banquets on the walls of Etruscan tombs and so on.

The purposes of such representations have been various—to increase food supply, to glorify kings and to help with a better afterlife. But if a single element is to be seen in common it is that they all attempt to communicate. The representations are made by one person or persons to be seen and understood by someone else, whether human or superhuman or not yet born. The earliest drawings then are a form of writing.

It is a feature of every stable civilisation that its rituals come to be repeated. Thus pictorial propitiations of the gods or pictorial listings of the extent of the year's harvest need to be done over and over again. Inevitably the pictures begin to become conventional, to be made from elements which are simplified and further and further removed from photographic fidelity as time goes on. Ultimately such elements can be called pictographs and they developed in different places at different times—they appear in the Middle East about 3000 B.C., in China about 1300 B.C. and among the Central American peoples about A.D. 300.

Where the pictographs develop to represent ideas, writing becomes ideographic and this would seem to be how Chinese writing started out; but our writing came from the development of pictographs to represent sounds.

In as much as there are so very many more ideas than there are speech sounds in any language, a phonetic system requires the use of very many fewer stylised shapes than an ideographic one and various people around the world have developed systems depicting human events which avail themselves of this advantage.

Most have been *syllabaries.* That is their pictograms have stood for syllables like *ti, to* and *ta* not for individual sounds. Modern Japanese and ancient Hittite are among the many languages in recorded time to rely on such a system. It is perhaps curious that the alphabetic system in which individual sounds are represented has so seldom developed. The alphabets of Arabic, Hebrew, Russian, Greek and other European languages, although so visually different, are all developments of one primitive Phoenician alphabet owing much in shape at least to certain sound-associated Egyptian pictograms. One can still see the yoke of the ox in the shape of the capital A.

When English began to be spelled it was in the characters of this alphabet in shapes which the Romans had given them because those who first wrote it at length were Latin-trained missionaries and scholars. The Germanic people had had an earlier so called Runic alphabet but it was not extensively used being limited mainly to charms and what we would now call graffiti. It did, however, lend one or two letters to the Roman alphabet for the depiction of Old English sounds not found in Latin.

The sounds of Old English appear to have been accurately recorded. When the word for *house* was written *hus* it was because it was pronounced /hus/. Never was the ordinary spelling of English to be so phonetic again.

The reasons are many. The Norman invaders displaced the Anglo-Saxon scholars with their own and Norman scribes took over the depiction of the language. *Hus* became *hous(e)* because *ou* was, and still is, a way of representing /u/ in French. The *cw* of *cwic* became the *qu* of *quick* and so on.

There was less uniformity now than before but the spelling was still more phonetic than it was going to be. One reason for this was that shortly afterwards in the Late Middle and Early Modern English periods the dialects of England underwent convulsive changes in the pronunciations of their vowels—not all dialects in the same way. Thus spellings which correctly indicated their pronunciations before these periods did not do so after them. If we allow that *hous(e)* correctly indicated /hus/ in the Norman phonetic fashion, it now found that it had to indicate /haus/ in accordance with nobody's phonetic fashion. In some parts of the country changes like this took place earlier than in others and writers from different localities trying to spell as they spoke might well use entirely different spellings from one another.

In any case the tradition of scholarship in English was weak before the time of Elizabeth I and there was no central authority and so virtually random spellings, different forms of one word on the one page of the one writer's writing, were quite common.

One does not know how much awkwardness this diversity caused but certainly as time passed the feeling that it was undesirable, clearly expressed for the first time in the sixteenth century, was to grow and grow. Scholars were unagreed on what should be done and bequeathed us such lunacies as *debt* instead of *dette* or *det* so that we may all know that the word descends from the Latin *debitum.* Such 'classical respellings' had some small effect but it was the practicalities of the printers together with a growing feeling that language ought to be 'fixed' which led the ordinary people ultimately to believe in 'correct spelling'.

By the eighteenth century there was no argument about the principle, only the practice. Lord Chesterfield introducing Johnson's Dictionary in 1765 called upon 'my fair countrywomen and . . . fine gentlemen . . . to surrender . . . all their natural rights and privileges of miss-spelling' and exhorts them to spell according to the norm set out by Johnson.

In the main we all continue to spell like him and the system that he bequeaths is not strongly phonetic, very often still betraying Norman influence as in the *wh* of *who* and *what* and generally betraying the chaos of English sound change wherever one looks.

Since Johnson some few simplifications have been achieved—*logick* and such words no longer have their final k and voices such as G. B. Shaw's have from time to time begged us to scrap the whole system and start again. In America Webster gave the matter thought and although he proposed various things at various times, such as *women* as *wimmen, tongue* as *tung* and *reason* as *reezon,* the American spelling which he hoped to reform does not differ so very much from the British. One notes words like *center, dialog, traveler* and *fetal* but in the main it is much the same as British spelling.

While English as a whole presents today a bewildering array of different pronunciations one is at first surprised that so rigid a system can be maintained—a system which, as its detractors would say, requires children to learn the patterns of their words one by one almost as if they lived in a society which used ideographs. But this is to overstate the matter. Even today there is still a great deal of phonetic patterning left in English spelling and many words, once the conventions involved have been mastered, are spelled much as they are said.

In any case the system is maintained and changes to it are very reluctantly accepted. This is because of the widespread, if unthinking, belief that only certain spellings are 'correct' and the eagerness with which we stigmatise other spellings as indicating an inexcusable lack of education.

These social reasons, defensible or not, are the operative ones in maintaining so bizarre a system and are what prevent English from following certain other languages like Polish to a wholesale spelling reform. But there are advantages. The Geordie who can barely be understood in speech by a speaker of Broad Australian becomes immediately intelligible in writing. World Englishes differ at various points in vocabulary, and thoroughly in pronunciation, but the uniformity in their spelling gives them a practical writing system which functions equally well everywhere.

# The History of English Dictionaries

It is today taken for granted that if the correct spelling of a word is sought, if doubt as to its meaning or its origins or its pronunciation is to be dispelled, then the place to look is in a dictionary.

It has not always been thus. The physical nature of dictionaries has been very different in other times and so too have been the functions which have been thought proper for them to perform.

## ANTECEDENTS

In the Middle Ages the learning of Latin was essential for all who wished to be considered educated and sets of *dictiones* or words and phrases in Latin were provided in books for students. Presumably a teacher told them what they meant.

A *liber dictionarius* was a book which contained such a set of *dictiones* and it seemed to be the use of this name which leads on to the modern word *dictionary*.

The first use of the word *dictionarius* by an Englishman dates from the period about 1225 and refers to a book of Latin instruction by Joannes de Garlandia, containing many sentences in that language. Typically the sentence acted as a carrier for a long list of words; thus one sentence read 'in the garden of Master John there are the following plants' and then they were listed one after another, 'sage, parsley, dittany, hissop', and so on.

This association of the *dictionarius* with lists of words was apparently not unusual. Peter Berchorius who died in Paris in 1362 wrote a series of moralisations under this name each based on one of a list of words derived from the Bible.

By the time we find the word Englished and ensconced in that language it has taken on the meaning of a list of words which are useful for instruction in learning a foreign tongue, especially Latin, and thus had a usual meaning which we would give to it now. It appears so in the title of Sir Thomas Elyot's Latin-English dictionary of 1538, and the term was in regular use thereafter.

This is not to suggest that dictionaries as such were not known previously. Though not so called, the earliest English-Latin dictionary dates from about 1440 and has about twelve thousand English entries with their Latin equivalents. A number of early English-Latin dictionaries are known.

Many of them had an organisation which at first glance is surprising. The Latin words ran across the page instead of down it and their English equivalents were printed either above or below them, also across the page. There was no alphabetical arrangement and the best one could hope was that the words were grouped together according to the general area of their meaning. Thus all the words which relate to *fire* or all the words which relate to *ship* might be found together.

This curious arrangement derived from another of the methods of teaching Latin to young students. If one looks back to some of the magnificent illuminated manuscripts of the Old English period which were also invariably in Latin, one is horrified to find that someone in the Old English period itself, perhaps a monk, has written in small writing a translation into Old English. The text had become, as one was later to say, paved.

In later centuries virtue was made of this barbarous practice by providing students with texts which were already in this form, that is to say, the main text was in Latin but a so-called interlinear gloss, that is, a translation running between the lines, was provided. Those dictionaries in which the words ran across the page with their translation between the lines of Latin were following the pattern set out by books of this kind.

A preference for a vertical arrangement began to assert itself during the sixteenth century and although there are some books in which grouping by sense continued to be written, the alphabetical method began to be popular and to be used exclusively as that century advanced.

Although English-Latin and Latin-English dictionaries were the most numerous, in the second half of the sixteenth century a number of dictionaries relating English to the vernacular languages of Europe, especially

French and Italian and Spanish, began to appear. There was need for these because exchange between England and the continent was growing and trade was becoming more international. Italian-English dictionaries appeared in 1567 and in 1598, and a *Dictionarie French and English* was produced by Cotgrave in 1593. Percyvall's *Spanish-English Dictionary* came out in 1591. But still there was no English-English dictionary and this despite the call for it from such eminent teachers as William Bullokar, who in 1580 wrote that he considered a book on spelling and on English grammar and an English dictionary were essential for the study of the English language.

He was not alone, Richard Mulcaster championed the English language as suitable for every scholastic purpose and in his *Elementarie* of 1582 writes 'it were a thing very praiseworthy in my opinion . . . if someone well learned . . . would gather all the words which are used in our English tongue whether natural or incorporate . . . into one dictionary'.

## 'HARD WORDS'

The old argument as to whether Latin or a vernacular tongue like English and French was appropriate for a scholarly purpose had long been decided in favour of the vernacular but for many Englishmen difficulties remained in the fact that English had built into it many recently coined words deriving ultimately from Latin and Greek which were necessary for formal discourse but which were in the main quite unfamiliar to the ordinary speaker of English who had not had the good fortune to enjoy a classical education. These were hard, indeed, incomprehensible words to many Englishmen.

When the first English-English dictionary did appear, it was apparent that it had been written to meet the needs of just such people. This was Robert Cawdrey's *A Table Alphabeticall* of 1604. The use of the word 'alphabetical' reminds us perhaps that it was not for so very long that alphabetical order had been usual and that mention of it was a selling point. The title page of Cawdrey's dictionary speaks of it containing 'the true writing and understanding of hard usual English words borrowed from the Hebrew, Greek, Latin and French, etc., with the interpretation thereof by plain English words gathered for the benefit and help of ladies, gentlewomen and any other unskilful persons'.

It was not an extensive work, containing little over two thousand five hundred words, and many of the definitions were mere synonyms. Thus *mutation* has beside it the one word *change*, *maladie* the one word *disease*, and so on. Nor, in one sense, was it an original work since modern scholars have been able to trace the sources for the material principally to two previous works. One is a Latin-English dictionary possibly published in 1588 by Thomas and the other the *English Schoole-Master* by Coote.

Perhaps Cawdrey was reprehensible in not acknowledging his sources as clearly as he should but at least it may be said that his method of building his dictionary on the work of dictionary workers and others before him sets a pattern which is little changed to this day. If one had the task of writing a dictionary it would obviously be too time consuming to try to think of all the words beginning with A, or with B and so on, and pointless too if a list already assembled was at arm's reach. The long tradition of dictionary writing at the head of which Cawdrey stands and which leads up to this dictionary has always made much use of material written previous to the work in hand.

## GROWING 'APPARATUS'

As the seventeenth century unfolded other English-English dictionaries were written. In 1616 John Bullokar, the son of William, published *An English Expositor*. It may have been based on an incomplete dictionary his father began but certainly it owed a great deal to that Thomas's Latin-English dictionary which Cawdrey had found so useful. He had used Cawdrey also and his book was essentially the same sort of hard-word dictionary which Cawdrey's had been. His definitions, however, were longer and he introduced from time to time *limiting labels* which indicated the area of specialty from which a word had been taken. Thus he begins his definition of *degree* by writing 'a terme often used in astronomie and phisicke'. There were twice as many words as in Cawdrey's.

The word 'dictionary' for an English-English context appeared first on Henry Cockeram's *The English Dictionarie* in 1623 but the next real advance in apparatus was that of Thomas Blount in his *Glossographia* of 1656. Blount again claimed to be interpreting 'all such hard words whether Hebrew, Greek, Latin, Italian, Spanish, French, Teutonick, Belgick, British or Saxon as are now used in our refined English tongue' and he made reference to special fields such as divinity, law and 'phisick', but additionally he provided etymologies. These were very briefly treated. Very often a Latin word follows the English headword without even an indication that it is Latin, and not, for argument's sake, 'Belgick'. Moreover, many of his etymologies appear to have been wrong. He is especially fanciful with words of English origin relating for example the word *honeymoon* to the idea that a marriage may be honey at first but this will change as surely as the moon.

GLOSSOGRAPHIA:
OR A
# DICTIONARY,
Interpreting the
# Hard Words
OF
Whatſoever Language, now uſed
In our refined Engliſh Tongue;
With Etymologies, Definitions,
and Hiſtorical Obſervations on the ſame.
Alſo the terms of Divinity, Law,
Phyſick, Mathematicks, War, Muſic, and other
Arts and Sciences explicated.

*Very uſeful for all ſuch as deſire to underſtand what they read.*

---

The Third EDITION, with ſome Corrections,
and many Additions.

---

By *T. B.* of the Inner-Temple, *Barraſter.*

---

Eraſm Apoph.
*Ut homines, ita libros in dies ſeipſos meliores fieri oportet.*

---

*LONDON,*
Printed by *Tho. Newcomb*, and are to be ſold by
*John Martyn*, at the Bell without *Temple Bar*. 1670.

Title page of the *Glossographia*, a dictionary in the hard word tradition, compiled by Thomas Blount in 1656. 'Blount . . . claimed to be interpreting "all such hard words whether Hebrew, Greek, Latin, Italian, Spanish, French, Teutonick, Belgick, British or Saxon as are now used in our refined English Tongue" and he made reference to special fields such as divinity, law and "phisick", but additionally he provided etymologies.'

THE

# Univerſal Etymological English Dictionary:

CONTAINING

An Additional Collection of Words (not in the firſt Volume) with their Explications and Etymologies from the *Ancient Britiſh*, *Teutonick*, *Dutch*, *Saxon*, *Daniſh*, *French*, *Italian*, *Spaniſh*, *Latin*, *Greek*, *Hebrew*, *Chaldee*, *&c.* each in its proper Character.

ALSO

An Explication of hard and technical Words, or Terms, in all *ARTS* and *SCIENCES*; with *ACCENTS* directing to their proper Pronunciation, ſhewing both the *Orthography* and *Orthoepia* of the *Engliſh Tongue*.

Illuſtrated with above Five Hundred CUTS, giving a clearer Idea of thoſe Figures, not ſo well apprehended by verbal Deſcription.

LIKEWISE

A Collection and Explanation of WORDS and PHRASES us'd in our ancient Charters, Statutes, Writs, Old Records and Proceſſes at Law.

ALSO

The Theogony, Theology, and Mythology of the Egyptians, Greeks, Romans, *&c.* being an Account of their Deities, Solemnities, Divinations, Auguries, Oracles, Hieroglyphicks, and many other curious Matters, neceſſary to be underſtood, eſpecially by the Readers of Engliſh POETRY.

To which is added,

An additional Collection of proper Names of Perſons and Places in *Great Britain*, &c. with their Etymologies and Explications.

The Whole digeſted into an Alphabetical Order, not only for the Information of the Ignorant, but the Entertainment of the Curious; and alſo the Benefit of Artificers, Tradeſmen, Young Students and Foreigners.

*A WORK uſeful for ſuch as would* UNDERSTAND *what they* READ and HEAR, SPEAK *what they* MEAN, *and* WRITE *true* ENGLISH.

VOL. II.

The Third Edition with many Additions,

By N. BAILEY, Φιλόλογος.

*LONDON:*

Printed for THOMAS COX at the *Lamb* under the *Royal Exchange*.

MDCCXXXVII.

Title page of a dictionary by Nathan Bailey published in 1737.
'The importance of this work lies in its implicit picture of a dictionary as a book which describes the words of a language, and which is no longer just a list of hard words, not even such a list with easy words thrown in, but a description of the histories, meanings and all that pertain to all the words of a language.'

An encyclopaedic dictionary of sorts appeared in 1658 in as much that Edward Phillips' *The New World of English Words* included in it proper names and historical and mythological items. (An earlier dictionary by Cockeram had little essays on the crocodile and the armadillo and such like, but is less like the modern encyclopaedic dictionary by far than is Phillips' dictionary.

Phillips owed a great deal to Blount, in fact rather too much and ultimately Blount attacked him in public for his plagiarism pointing out many gross misinterpretations of his, Blount's, own work which appeared in Phillips'. Phillips did not reply but merely corrected the errors which Blount had so kindly pointed out and continued to publish edition after edition.

It is curious to observe that all the English-English dictionaries until Phillips' had either been dedicated to particular women or written for the use of women and sometimes both. But with the Restoration this tradition was to vanish, never to return. Elisha Cole's *An English Dictionary* of 1676 drew very heavily upon Phillips' and is remarkable only for its inclusion of 'canting terms and dialectal words' along with the 'Many thousand of Hard Words'. It would seem therefore to have been the first general dictionary to include words of the non-standard vocabulary. It almost goes without saying that for his canting and dialect material Cole plagiarised the works of other writers. His dictionary was reissued at least ten times and was popular for more than fifty years.

## THE EIGHTEENTH CENTURY

As the seventeenth century gave way to the eighteenth more dictionaries came into being and of these it was the *New English Dictionary*, 1702, by 'J. K.', probably John Kersey, which takes the next major step forward. This dictionary is the first to bring into its pages the ordinary words of everyday English. That is, not only the hard words are to be found in it but also the easy ones. There is also, of course, to be 'a short and clear exposition of difficult words and Terms of Art' and also 'a complete collection of the most proper and significant words commonly used in the Language', but easy words are included expressly so that people might know how to spell them correctly, for the whole was 'designed for the benefit of Young scholars, tradesmen, Artificers and the Female sex who would learn to spell truely'.

During the seventeenth century the idea had grown up that words ought to have a correct spelling, an idea which drew strength from the growing importance of the printers who in the main preferred uniformity. Public opinion also had moved on a great way from its position in pre-Elizabethan days when educated people could spell as they chose. By 1700 the idea that there should be a correct spelling was firmly entrenched and was part of a wider enthusiasm for the idea that English as a whole should in some way be made correct and perfect.

Dictionaries had been getting progressively larger, and J. K.'s dictionary had twenty-eight thousand words or so in it. Because its only interest in easy words was in their spelling, the definitions accorded them were often ludicrous. 'About' is defined by the enigmatic '*as about noon*'; 'and' is defined by the totally incomprehensible '*and if, and not*'; 'apron' is defined as '*for a Woman*', and so on.

It is curious to look back from the safe harbour of the twentieth century to the attitudes of people concerned with the English language in the eighteenth century. Passions ran high but they seem often to have run in contrary directions. On the one hand there was a feeling that the language was in some sense becoming corrupt. In a letter to the *Tatler*, Swift complained of 'the continual corruption of the English tongue which without some timely remedy will suffer more by the false refinements of twenty years past than it hath been improved in the foregoing hundred'. Yet while Sir Thomas More had composed his *Utopia* in Latin, Swift himself wrote in English as did Dryden, Pope, Addison and Steele and there was considerable pride in the excellence of writers of this type. Comparisons were made between the English of the period and the Latin of Cicero's time or the Greek of Aristotle's. Thus while Defoe could speak of the need to 'polish and refine' the English tongue he could also speak of its 'true glory' and of its being 'the noblest and most comprehensive of all the vulgar languages in the world'.

In all the heat of discussion the twin ideas that the language should be corrected and stabilised (they wrote 'ascertained') seem most often to have emerged. For the stabilising to take place there was needed agreement about spelling, an authoritative grammar book, and an authoritative dictionary. In this climate of opinion, dictionaries therefore proliferated, and some of them became very large indeed.

Nathan Bailey was involved with more than one of these and his *Dictionarium Britannicum* of 1730 had about sixty thousand headwords. This was the dictionary upon which Johnson relied most heavily when writing his own and it in turn was an expansion of Bailey's earlier *An Universal Etymological English Dictionary* of 1721. The importance of this work lies in its implicit picture of a dictionary as a book which describes the words of a language, which is no longer just a list of hard words, not even such a list with easy words thrown in, but a description of the histories, meanings and all that pertains to all the words of the language.

Bailey introduced diagrams and proverbs and made a first attempt at indicating pronunciations by showing stress marks. His dictionaries seem to have outsold Dr Johnson until the beginning of the nineteenth century but not to have been accepted as a definitive work by those literary men who were so concerned that the

A

# DICTIONARY

OF THE

# ENGLISH LANGUAGE:

IN WHICH

The WORDS are deduced from their ORIGINALS,

AND

ILLUSTRATED in their DIFFERENT SIGNIFICATIONS

BY

EXAMPLES from the best WRITERS.

TO WHICH ARE PREFIXED,

A HISTORY of the LANGUAGE,

AND

AN ENGLISH GRAMMAR.

BY SAMUEL JOHNSON, A.M.

IN TWO VOLUMES.

VOL. I.

THE SECOND EDITION.

Cum tabulis animum censoris sumet honesti:
Audebit quæcunque parum splendoris habebunt,
Et sine pondere erunt, et honore indigna ferentur,
Verba movere loco; quamvis invita recedant,
Et versentur adhuc intra penetralia Vestæ:
Obscurata diu populo bonus eruet, atque
Proferet in lucem speciosa vocabula rerum,
Quæ priscis memorata Catonibus atque Cethegis,
Nunc situs informis premit et deserta vetustas. HOR.

LONDON,

Printed by W. STRAHAN,

For J. and P. KNAPTON; T. and T. LONGMAN; C. HITCH and L. HAWES; A. MILLAR; and R. and J. DODSLEY.

MDCCLV.

Title page of a second edition of Samuel Johnson's *A Dictionary of the English Language* of 1755.
'In the nineteenth century, for most people, Johnson's was simply *the dictionary.*'

Samuel Johnson, 1709–1784, was born in Lichfield, Staffordshire, the son of a second-hand bookseller. Because of lack of money he was unable to complete his course at Oxford and left in 1731 without a degree, to try his hand, unsuccessfully, at school teaching. In the troubled period that followed he married, happily, in 1735, and came to rely upon his work as a hack writer to support his wife and himself. His earnings were pitiful and they lived in penury. Between his commissioned writings he wrote original material such as a poem called *The Vanity of Human Wishes* and essays to *The Gentleman's Magazine* which gradually began to win for him a literary reputation but no money. While still in abject poverty and subject as ever to melancholia, he published his *Proposal for a New Dictionary* in 1747 and undertook its commission shortly after.

Its success, some of his other writings and the novel *Rasselas*, added to his literary stature, but not till a pension was bestowed by the Crown in 1761 was he free of financial worry.

For the rest of his life he reigned in a circle of sophisticated and admiring friends of like interest, among whom he found his biographer, Boswell.

language be properly 'ascertained'. This accolade they reserved for Samuel Johnson's *A Dictionary of the English Language* which appeared in 1755. It had taken eight and a half years to prepare and cost very much more than the fifteen hundred guineas which the five or six London booksellers who had originally contracted Johnson for the task had been prepared to put up.

Johnson's dictionary had fewer words than Bailey's and it is not difficult to mock many of the entries. Often Johnson was ludicrously verbose. To define a cough as a convulsion . . . *vellicated by some sharp seriosity* or network as '*anything reticulated or decussated* . . .' was hardly helpful. His quotation of authors was occasionally inaccurate. For example, his definition of *instilment* quotes a passage from Hamlet quite wrongly since Shakespeare never ever used that word. His prejudices and wry humour are written into numbers of his entries. Thus his definition for a patron as 'a wretch who supports with insolence and is paid with flattery' reflects his feelings for Lord Chesterfield.

But when all has been said it is a most impressive work. It makes more extensive use of citations than had ever been done before and if this is its only true technical advance its sense of authority and pervading common sense cannot be gainsaid. Revisions of it appeared for almost a century after Johnson's death, notably by Todd in 1818 and by Latham in 1866, and as late as 1900 James Murray could speak of 'the notions of a large number of persons' who thought that ' "the Psalms" were composed by David and "the Dictionary" by Dr Johnson'.

It is immaterial whether all this was because of the excellences of the dictionary itself or because of the perhaps not entirely justified reputation Johnson had as the arbiter of taste and the literary lion of his time—a reputation for which he owed more than something to Boswell. In the nineteenth century, for most people, Johnson's was simply *the dictionary*.

The fuller indication of pronunciation was the last element of the standard apparatus of a dictionary to be added. It appeared in a number of unimportant dictionaries about the 1790s, among the names of the authors of which only that of Thomas Sheridan, the playwright, is remembered. As a dramatist his interest in the spoken word is obvious.

Between 1604 and 1780, then, the dictionary as we most commonly understand it, took its present shape. It grew from being a short, helpful list of hard words to being a comprehensive description of the vocabulary of the language. It was viewed very often, however, not so much as a description but as a prescription.

It is still so today. In the dictionary nominated for the purpose are the meanings of words which courts of law will accept, while in the minds of the ordinary people in almost any dictionary there are the 'correct' meanings of words.

## AMERICA

Probably the first dictionary to be published in the United States was the one by Samuel Johnson Jnr. Whether its writer was truly called or had merely adopted the prestigious name is not known. The work is undated but probably appeared first in 1798 and was a school dictionary of some one hundred and ninety-six pages. Somewhat blatantly it describes itself as being 'a compendium of the latest and most improved dictionaries' and these, at the time, must necessarily have been British. It did have pronunciations but added nothing new.

If there was one innovation still to be made, it probably fell to Noah Webster to make it. As an American patriot he was not happy with the idea that correctness should be enshrined exclusively in British English. His dictionaries included Americanisms and served the sort of function for the American people in the nineteenth century, and indeed later, that Johnson's dictionary alone served for the British in the nineteenth. Indeed Webster's coverage of scientific and other terms caused it to have some impact in Britain too since Johnson did not cover the same ground.

Webster's first attempt at a dictionary, *The Compendious Dictionary of the English Language*, was published in 1806. It did little to advance his cause but Webster was an indefatigable worker, a born definer of words, if a somewhat fanciful etymologist, and he continued at his desk until the important and influential work, *An American Dictionary of the English Language*, was published in 1828.

An abridged version by Joseph Worcester appeared in 1830 and became extremely popular, and the various subsequent editions of Webster have had an acceptance in America and abroad which has made the series one of the most influential of all dictionaries. According to one count, the *New International* second edition had six hundred thousand entries but it is the string of smaller dictionaries which depend from the largest *Webster* which claim the greatest number of sales and it is interesting to observe that one of the strongest rivals to Merriam Webster's desk dictionary, the *Collegiate*, was the *American College Dictionary* of 1947 which is one of the antecedents of the present dictionary.

The publication of Webster's third *New International Dictionary* reminds us that passions about language can still be raised. It made so bold as to include items from the non-standard language for the first time and raised an initial cry of protest from an outraged public.

Noah Webster, 1758–1843, was born in Hartford, Connecticut, and served in the U.S. militia in the War of Independence. He graduated from Yale in 1778 and became a school teacher. He was interested too in the law and practised from time to time. He married and was able to support his family for many years on the prodigious sales of his *Blue-Back Speller* (1783), retiring in 1798 to New Haven where, with small interruption, he spent the rest of his life. He was a man of immense energy and wide-ranging interest. Etymology and spelling reforms seemed especially to interest him although he was often wrong with the former and abandoned many of his first suggestions for the latter (*proov*, *reezon*, *tung*, etc.). It is said that the Rev. Elizar Goodrich first suggested he write a dictionary but the massive collection of linguistic material which he gathered all his life and which he drew into his work was accumulating before this. Before the great dictionary of 1828 was published, he travelled to England and France, financially assisted by his daughter, to check details and afterwards continued to work on the second edition of 1841 in New Haven until shortly before his death.

Noah Webster.

## HISTORICAL DICTIONARIES

At the height of the eighteenth century clamour for the 'ascertainment' of the language even Johnson had to admit that any hopes he may have held for being able to hold back change in language were futile. Like any lexicographer, Johnson became only too aware that the meanings of words are unstable and change with time. Yet most of the dictionaries which are written in the hard word tradition, and that is to say most dictionaries, give scant overt recognition to this fact.

There is, however, a much less numerous group of dictionaries which might be called historical dictionaries. Perhaps one ought to regard the first of these as *A New Dictionary of the English Language* by Charles Richardson, which was published in 1836. Richardson had apparently been impressed by Johnson's use of citations and conceived the idea that if there were sufficient quotations there would be no need for definitions, presumably thereby removing from the dictionary the idiosyncratic intrusions for which Johnson is famous and the inevitable arbitrariness of editorial decision which is reflected in such extrapolations from the original material in any dictionary. His work thus was principally made of citations, but in these he went far beyond Johnson in time, back to Chaucer and Gower, and drew a vast number of carefully documented quotations together from a period of several centuries. The insuperable practical difficulty in his method, as far as the reader is concerned, is that it takes a long time to read through sets and sets of quotations to find the meaning applicable to the text in hand which is being sought.

In any case Richardson's work stands to that of the *New English Dictionary*, later the *Oxford English Dictionary*, as a minnow stands to a whale, and it is the OED which principally comes to mind in any discussion of the historical method. It owes its being, probably, to two papers read by Dr Trench, the Dean of Westminster, to the Philological Society of London in the late 1850s. Dr Trench drew attention to the inadequacies of dictionaries which were then existing and pointed out that the histories of words and relationships between the meanings of words were not usually indicated. Also there was inadequate coverage of the changes in form and in sense which all the words of the English language had experienced. One could not find out how long a word had had its present meaning, how long it had been coined, which of its senses was original, how and when its other senses had developed. If the word was obsolete, one could not find out any information at all in the general case.

It was suggested that material should be gathered together to supplement what could be found in Bailey, Johnson, Todd, Webster, Richardson and the rest. It was seen from the start that the task of reading back through the centuries and assembling all this material was greater than any one person could achieve and so collaborators were envisaged from the first. Ultimately, of course, the idea of a supplement was replaced by the idea of an enormous dictionary. Citations which were eventually to number over five million were collected and the first of the two thousand volunteer readers recruited. In all it took seventy years to bring the work to conclusion and to publish in its ten volumes the *Oxford English Dictionary* with its historical treatment of almost five hundred thousand words. It is without doubt the greatest single achievement of lexicography. Its type placed end to end would extend for almost three hundred kilometres. There are over two hundred and twenty million letters and one million eight hundred thousand quotations.

It was the great good fortune of this enterprise to stem from the enthusiasms of the Philological Society since among its members were people with encyclopaedic knowledge of Old and Middle English and a general approach to the study of language which is entirely modern and surprisingly at variance with that of the eighteenth century and of their own contemporaries.

James Murray, the chief editor, of the dictionary, said of the eighteenth-century idea that a dictionary should stop the corruption and decay in a language that the notion 'seems childlike and pathetic'. His whole approach was descriptive rather than prescriptive. The idea was to record in helpful detail what had happened to words and in no place to imply that one could deduce from the work what should happen to them. The irony of the situation, of course, is that whatever the intention of the writers, the public chooses to regard their work as prescriptive and to hunt in the pages of the *Oxford Dictionary*, as in those of other dictionaries, for that statement of the meaning of a word which cannot be gainsaid.

The editors hoped that their work would be so thorough that, having been done, it would never need to be done again and this seems very likely to be the case. But they knew that 'the structure now reared (would) have to be added to, continued and extended with time'. Accordingly, the enterprise of writing the Oxford Dictionary continues. Shortly after the last letter to be treated was published in 1928 a supplement appeared and even now a newer progressive supplement is being issued to try and keep pace with the changes in the language.

Many smaller dictionaries bear the name Oxford and rely in varying degrees on the main work. Most of these take the form common in those dictionaries in the hard word tradition.

The historical method developed so successfully in the *Oxford English Dictionary* has been applied to other languages and to English in other places. In Australia E. E. Morris in his *Austral English* followed the model as faithfully as he was able, and *The Australian National Dictionary* is currently being prepared under the same pattern.

A NEW

ENGLISH DICTIONARY

ON HISTORICAL PRINCIPLES;

FOUNDED MAINLY ON THE MATERIALS COLLECTED BY

The Philological Society.

EDITED BY

JAMES A. H. MURRAY, LL.D.,

SOMETIME PRESIDENT OF THE PHILOLOGICAL SOCIETY,

*WITH THE ASSISTANCE OF MANY SCHOLARS AND MEN OF SCIENCE.*

PART II. ANT—BATTEN.

OXFORD:

AT THE CLARENDON PRESS,

1885.



**Price Twelve Shillings and Sixpence.**

Title page from Part II of the original part-work edition of *A New English Dictionary*.
'It is without doubt the greatest single achievement of lexicography.'

James Augustus Henry Murray, 1837–1915, was born in Denim, a village of Roxburghshire, the son of a tailor. Despite poverty his schooling was thorough. He left school at 14 and after various jobs became a school teacher at 17. All his life his interests were numerous, but his attention was taken especially by geology and language. He married twice, in 1862 and 1865, and it was because of the illness of his first family that he moved to London as a bank clerk in a vain search for a healthier environment. In London he returned to teaching and became known to the Philological Society. He was able to complete university training with honours from London in 1871 and a doctorate from Edinburgh in 1874. He was made general editor of the *New English Dictionary* beginning in 1876 and working on the task till his death. The 'scriptorium' where he, some of his many children, and many others worked was at first in his house in London and later in his house at Oxford. His knighthood in 1908 honours the part he played in controlling and unifying the vast project.

## DICTIONARIES AND THE COMPUTER

If the twentieth century has, in effect, nothing to add to the shape of the dictionary, it has a great deal to contribute to the technique of compiling it. While few dictionaries, if any, have not looked over their shoulders to the work of dictionaries before them, it is nevertheless true that the better of them have always relied to some great extent on their own original endeavours. This has meant in the main collecting a large number of citations, that is, instances of the words of interest couched in sentences which appeared in the books, newspapers and writings of the public. It does not take much imagination to envisage the physical difficulties of handling thousands upon thousands of these citations. They may be on slips of paper, they may be on filing cards, but, whatever form they take, they provide difficulty of notation, storage, handling and treatment. The computer offers considerable relief in this area. Since it is now possible to hold vast amounts of information in computer storage, the myriad awkward slips of paper with which Murray and Johnson contended are likely to be seen less and less in the offices of dictionary editors henceforth, as material will not be written down at all but fed directly into the storage banks of the computer.

The advantages of this go much further than mere physical convenience. The computer can sort the entries into alphabetical order with total accuracy. It can display on a television screen, or print out in a very short space of time on paper, all the citations which pertain to a particular word which the editor sitting at his or her desk has merely to call up. Decisions as to which quotations will be included or excluded can be made on the spot and the computer will act upon them instantly. If there is need to see how adequate the cover may be in some special area such as music, the computer will obligingly disgorge all the music terms without anyone having the labour of flipping through file box after file box looking desperately for cards which have been labelled *Music.*

Moreover, the bugbear of cross-referencing ceases to be a problem. If *black sauce* is to be cross-referenced to *Worcestershire sauce* then *Worcestershire sauce* must be cross-referenced to *black sauce.* Not only is the tedium of going from the card among the Bs for *black sauce* to the card among the Ws for *Worcestershire sauce* eliminated but the cross-referencing itself can be checked by the computer and, should it be inadequate, attention drawn by the computer to this fact for correction by the editors.

It is possible to prepare computer tapes containing all the dictionary information in a form which can be fed into the typesetting complex which ultimately will produce the book, that is, the computer sidesteps much of the old mechanical labour of assembling the type. This is an advantage enjoyed not only by the writers of dictionaries of course, but by those of all kinds of books, and in as much that many books exist now as computer tapes, it is possible to use these computer tapes for dictionary purposes. They may be rapidly scanned for words which the computer has been programmed to look for because they are of particular interest and because extra citations are needed for them. In other words, the tedium of reading countless books and countless journals may well be reduced for dictionary writers in the future by the ability of computers to scan automatically the tapes prepared for printers of books.

*The Macquarie Dictionary* was prepared in a transitional stage, that is, it started out as a series of cards which were hand-edited but ended up on computer tape with automatic checking of cross-referencing and automatic sorting procedures to make the final stages of preparation more rapid. It was from the final editing of the computer tape which contained all the information in the dictionary, now called its 'database', that the book was directly printed.

# Dictionaries and the Problems of Choice

One is always loath to claim the 'most' of anything for fear of having overlooked someone with a stronger claim to it and seeming foolishly vainglorious, but it is at least reasonable to suggest that English may have the largest vocabulary of any language existing today and the largest vocabulary of any language which has ever existed.

The basic English vocabulary is in some ways an oddity because of what might be termed its two-tiered structure. There are sets of Germanic words like *swine, house* and *board*, which descend from the Anglo-Saxon or Old English pre-1066 stage of its development and these sit beside matching words which are ultimately Latin in origin like *pork, domicile* and *table* which come to us from the Norman invaders and from later continental influences. If Old English *swin, hus* and *bord* were very close in meaning to Latin *porcus, domus* and *tabula* their descendants are certainly nothing like as close. Variations in meaning and overtone have accrued over the centuries and given us subtly or grossly differing words in numbers other languages find hard to match. But it is not so much this which one has in mind when thinking of the richness of the English vocabulary. All languages are the mirrors of their societies. In them can be found the reflections of their attitudes and their interests, their triumphs and their tragedies, their virtues and their vices. Whatever experiences a people have encountered, whatever ideas they have generated, these are likely to be reflected in that automatic self-adjusting miracle which is human language. This will modify itself, will create words, borrow words from other languages and so on, so that almost instantly the speakers of the language will find that they have the means to discuss whatever they wish to discuss. This is not a special feature of English but is true whether the speakers make use of English, Finnish or Patagonian for their purposes. But in the case of speakers of English the experiences, the ideas even, may well have been more numerous and more varied than those of many other language groups.

As explorers and as founders of Empire, the English-speakers have inevitably had experiences far more various than those who never left their ancestral strip of land, and they created new words in which to discuss them. Contact with many other peoples allowed them to borrow countless words from other languages like *veranda, cockatoo* and *curry.* The constant need to extend the basic resources of the language to cope with what they encountered in these travels led them to set old words in new combinations. In Canada they spoke of *corduroy roads*, in Australia of *the outback*, in India of the *hill station*, and so on.

No doubt all this is true in some measure of other European Empire builders like the Portuguese, Spanish, the Dutch and the French. But in addition to this, the English were the explorers of modern technology. The countless inventions of the English-speaking peoples have all called into being new vocabulary, much of which finds its way into other languages. The highly skilled groups of tradespeople who have been involved in new manufactures have all, like special interest groups everywhere, created language of their own—be it technical terminology, jargon or slang.

Probably only those who have set themselves the task of writing a dictionary have any conception of just how gigantic the total vocabulary of the English-speaking peoples really is. If one were to imagine allthe words of this vocabulary somehow in a large hole, this hole, down into which one looks with awe, would be dark and of infinite dimension. The bottom could never be seen. Towards the middle, in the light, there are the thousands and thousands of words which are relatively well known. In the shadows are the more numerous thousands of words which are known less well, being restricted perhaps to some special occupation, some restricted geographical region or some small social group. In the ultimate darkness are the myriads of now unknown words which were coined in other times and which have become obsolete. All the words in the shadows or the darkness are or have been as valid coins of the language as any other, since massive frequency of use has never truly been a criterion for deciding whether a word 'exists' or not. If numbers, even small numbers have used it, it exists.

There is no way that any single person can hope to understand more than a small fraction of the vast mine of words in the imaginary hole in the ground. Various figures are given for the vocabulary of the average person but few of them put it much above twenty thousand items. Among the most highly educated people this number may be thirty-five thousand, perhaps even forty thousand, but this is a small fraction of the number of words in a large dictionary. Yet the number of words in the very largest of our dictionaries is itself only a small fraction of that terrible totality in the fearsome imaginary hole which contains all English words.

If this seems surprising the truth of the statement can easily be demonstrated by taking some specialist book such as a list of the terms commonly used in horticulture or perhaps a small medical dictionary, and seeing just how many entries are missing from the biggest general dictionary one can lay hands on. They are missing in numbers which seldom fail to surprise.

## THE INEVITABLE SELECTIVITY OF DICTIONARIES

It follows that all dictionaries give, and must necessarily give, a partial account only of the total English vocabulary. There can never be sufficient resources to track down all of this vocabulary, and every dictionary is inevitably selective.

To the idealist this is perhaps less than fully satisfactory but it is not a matter for practical concern. Dictionaries are utilitarian books and one way or another the different types of dictionary seem to provide between them for the needs of almost all people.

The largest of dictionaries, while incomplete in the sense just outlined, can be called comprehensive. They are comprehensive in that they seek to give some cover to all sectors of the total vocabulary; they look back in time to include some words from earlier periods, they look across the world to include some words peculiar to the various forms of English outside Great Britain, or, if written outside Great Britain anyway, they look to that country to include some words peculiar to it; they offer words of formal stiffness and words of colloquial overtone, words from the sciences, the arts, the businesses and medicine. In all, they may deal with some hundreds of thousands of words.

The very largest comprehensive dictionaries may run to a number of columns and be physically very heavy books of great cost. To meet the need of those who neither have the space to house them nor the wish to incur so heavy an expense, a series of smaller comprehensive dictionaries usually depends from each of the major larger dictionaries.

These are still comprehensive in the sense that the same areas are covered, but are reduced in scope. The number of words treated becomes fewer and the treatment of individual words becomes shorter. More or less self-explanatory names like *Concise*, *Pocket*, *Little*, *Handy*, *Gem* and so on, are variously applied to smaller and smaller versions of the original master-work.

The smaller derivative dictionaries become less comprehensive since the overall reduction tends to eliminate altogether entries from fields of the more out-of-the-way sort, those which were the least completely covered in the original large work. Terms of medieval fortification or terms for eighteenth-century furniture types may well not be included.

Sometimes specific decisions such as one to exclude all but contemporary usage shapes the smaller dictionary rather than a general shrinkage, and in this case the comprehensive nature is even more violently disturbed.

In comprehensive dictionaries of any size the option to include encyclopaedic material is variously exercised. Encyclopaedic material is that which deals with information about the real world as against lexicographical or dictionary material which deals only with information about words. Thus the birthdate of the French mathematician, Jean Baptiste Joseph Fourier, and the population of Paris at the last census, are both examples of encyclopaedic material, but the words *Fourier analysis* and *Parisian* are lexicographical material. As can readily be seen, the area between the two is a grey one. It is sometimes hard to know which is which and probably there has never been a dictionary written which does not contain some entry which could not be considered, at least by some, as encyclopaedic.

Nevertheless, some dictionaries deliberately include encyclopaedic material and some do not. Some do list Fourier's birthdate and offer a possible biography along with a host of other encyclopaedic material about Paris and other world capitals. It is apparent that in books of comparable size, the encyclopaedic dictionary is likely to contain less lexicographical information than the non-encyclopaedic.

Another family of dictionaries adopts the policy of concentrating on one section of the total vocabulary only, or on one section of the information given at each entry in the comprehensive dictionary.

Thus there are dictionaries containing only medical terms, or containing only words from the study of linguistics, or perhaps even only place names of a particular region. There are others which list only the pronunciation of words or perhaps only their etymologies.

Obviously many of these dictionaries are written for specialist readers—those whose interest in such limited areas is greater than that of the average reader and who do not find the material of their special interest covered with adequate depth or assembled with adequate convenience in the large comprehensive type of dictionary.

Sometimes the specialist dictionary caters not so much for particular interest as particular ability. Dictionaries in extra large type for those who have poor eyesight can be included here along with those written for school children of particular ages in which all the definitions are written in a vocabulary limited to the most frequent—a thousand or two thousand—words of the language. The language in these books is deliberately kept simple to match the limited linguistic abilities of the intended readers.

Dictionaries can also be looked at as belonging to different national categories. Although some very few have, in fact, described themselves as international, none can be said to have been fully so.

At one end of the range one has dictionaries which are international in that they seek to give some cover to the various different regional types of English adequate for the purposes of the readers in one particular country. Thus it may be that a dictionary written in Britain lists some terms from American and Australian and South African and some other forms of overseas English. The main reason for inclusion seems to be that elements of overseas English are likely to find their way to the readers of this British dictionary. Usually only heartland varieties are even considered and such divisions as Indian English, Jamaican English, African Black English and so on are missing entirely or very briefly represented.

The non-British entries are usually in such a case given British pronunciations, thereby, perhaps unconsciously, confirming the British centrality of outlook in the book. The same thing happens again in an American dictionary written for American readers, British and other non-American terms may well be included but the pronunciations given for them will be in terms of American English.

Few indeed are the attempts to list the variant pronunciations of even the different major divisions of heartland English in any one dictionary and practically non-existent are attempts to deal with the dialect divisions within these heartlands, either in terms of meaning or pronunciation. The variations provided by the English of Yorkshire, of Kentucky, of Pitcairn Island and so on find no place. Again, there is an obvious practical impossibility blocking the path to anything like a total international account which would include such small regions, since there is just too much variation to be included in any one book.

At the other end of the range there are specialist dictionaries which list only those words and phrases which are peculiar to some particular regions—what one might term dictionaries of 'isms'. Thus we find a dictionary of Canadianisms containing lexical material which only Canadians use and none of the much more extensive lexical material which Canadians use in common with Britishers, Australians and the rest. Such Dictionaries of Americanisms, South Africanisms and the like are not numerous but are becoming less uncommon.

One may group them with similarly restricted works which take time instead of region as the boundary within which they operate. There are dictionaries of words from the Old English period only and of those from the Middle English period only.

For many, the colloquial strands of language have a particular interest and dictionaries of colloquialisms are also written, limited either by region, as for example a dictionary of Australian colloquialisms would be, or by time, as would be a dictionary of flash language which was the language of the lowest elements of British society around about the eighteenth century.

It is interesting to observe that some acts of selection which shape any particular dictionary, such as choice of typeface and page size, are self-evident, while others, such as headword selection, are usually matters of declared policy which can be read about in the Preface. There are still others which are not so immediately apparent and which, in fact, respond to undeclared prejudice. Sometimes compound words of three or more elements are arbitrarily excluded and thus many terms of modern science like *evoked responsive audiometry* or of military terminology like *intercontinental ballistic missile* are inexplicably missing from the word list.

In many a dictionary, taboo words are not treated, such as those of explicit sexual reference and words which otherwise are simply not approved of, perhaps because they are racially offensive or sexist or whatever. This happens despite the fact that some of them are among the oldest in the language and among the most frequent in current use. This is a perversion of the dictionary's duty to be faithful to the task of recording language as it really is and imposes artificial limits to its scope. At every turn there are options to the dictionary writer in the matter of headword selection but at least the choices which have been made should be spelled out.

Similarly, at every turn, there are choices to be made among the methods of treatment of the headwords chosen but these at least will be apparent from the text of the book itself.

If the treatment is to be historical, the meanings which words have taken over the centuries must be arranged in chronological order. The meaning of *tank* as pond, for example, must precede that of *tank* as military vehicle. The chains of related change in meaning must be disentangled and displayed as clearly as possible; the line which leads from *tank* as a pond to *tank* as a locomotive of a particular type must be separated from that branch which goes on to *tank warfare* and so on. If the treatment is not to be historical perhaps the criterion of frequency will govern the order of entry, although information on frequency is notoriously inaccurate; or perhaps the principle that the most central meaning should precede derived meaning will be adopted, which is perhaps even more difficult to apply.

In any case, the question of whether to include citations, in great or in small numbers, or at all, must be addressed and perhaps it will be decided to fall back on illustrative phrases which have been specially tailored by the editors for the purpose. Further, if one picture is really worth a thousand words, should one include illustrations or not?

The choice of method is among the many which compound the total choices of selection which must be made. All are important to the ultimate utility and impact of the book.

## THIS DICTIONARY

This dictionary is of the larger comprehensive kind. It has rather more than two thousand pages and treats about one hundred and eighty thousand words in greater or less detail in seventeen and a half million characters.

It is large enough to serve the vast majority of readers in most of the areas of their probable interest but of course does not pretend to compete in any one of them with specialist dictionaries dealing with one area only.

It is international in as much that, while the vast majority of the words are drawn from the common pool of words which all speakers of English use, it offers numbers of terms peculiar to various of the heartland areas of English. Those which come from the United States, what may loosely be termed Americanisms, are labelled *U.S.* (the speed with which these tend to move to other forms of English, which has been alluded to above, must of course be borne in mind here and this label may sometimes be superfluous), Britishisms are labelled *Brit.*, New Zealandisms *N.Z.*, and so on.

Like other dictionaries this one does, however, inevitably have a centrality of view and this happens to be Australian. The dictionary was prepared in Australia and is rich in Australian English words, though these are not distinguished by label.

As the preceding chapter on dictionaries has explained, in all the centuries that English dictionaries have existed few indeed have not stood upon the work of earlier dictionaries. In the case of the present dictionary the immediate antecedent was a comprehensive dictionary with a British centrality of view called *The Encyclopedic World Dictionary*. Its editor was the distinguished lexicographer, Patrick Hanks. That dictionary, in turn, derived directly from another earlier and previously mentioned comprehensive dictionary of high repute with an American centrality of view called *The American College Dictionary* with which is associated the name of another distinguished lexicographer, Clarence L. Barnhart.

*The Macquarie Dictionary* is part of a distinguished chain of being, the earlier links of which assure the wideness of its coverage.

### a. THE HEADWORDS

The headwords reflect selection from several of the principal axes of lexical variation—the axes of time, specialty, place and register.

There are words bound to particular periods like *seigneurie* and *bailey*, which derive from medieval contexts, and *video cassette* and *vidicon* which derive from modern ones; many words like *gale* meaning breeze, or *doxy* for a paramour, or *copperhead*, the term for a Confederate sympathiser of the American Civil War, derive from contexts associated with periods in between.

To more than thirty areas of special learning particular editors were freshly appointed and the account of the terms of chemistry, mathematics, music and the like is not only thorough in terms of the general need but contemporary and up to date.

The list of special areas treated is wide indeed, food from *raznici* to *mirepoix*, grape types from *Cabernet Sauvignon* to *Shiraz*, pastimes from *lacrosse* to *curling*, music from *passepied* to *punk rock*, and so on. Much of human learning and interest is reflected in the long list of the headwords which together make a document of social description. Strong evidence for the regional variations of English is wound into the headword list from first to last. The British meaning of *layby* is listed with the Australian meaning and the related United States term *layaway* is also to be found. There are Scots words like *tryst* and *glengarry*, pure Britishisms like *durex* and *paraffin*, Australianisms like *settler's clock* and *Paterson's curse*, New Zealandisms like *capping day* and *patiki*, words from South Africa like *kopje* and *kraal*, from India like *bheestie* and *dhole*, and words acquired from former colonies like *kava* and *bwana*.

The criterion for selection has been the usual one, that is, the likelihood of the regional variant in question being encountered by the general reader in the course of reading novels, current affairs magazines, and so on.

In matters of register the dictionary does not shrink from any level of the language, and *fuck* and *fornicate* are both there. Words of starchy formalism which are used mainly by scholars, like *dekerugmatise* and *fractostratus*, sit beside homely words of the standard range like *seatbelt* and *midday* and both rub shoulders with words of all degree of informality. There are irreverent abbreviations like *deli* for *delicatessen*, and *Poly* for *Polytechnic*, mild colloquialisms like *cop* for *policeman* and *lush* for a *drunk* and newer coinages like *cop-out* and *space shuttle* running through to words like *spick* and *shit*, which for one reason or another, are relegated to the bottom of the range in terms of general acceptability.

The dictionary is especially strong in phrases of colloquial flavour, again ranging from the innocuous, like *spill the beans*, to the extremes like *cream one's jeans*. The dictionary leaves it to its readers to make such judgments as they will about their own use of these terms and act accordingly. It does not see its role as the regulator of language but the recorder.

As we have observed, English has innumerable borrowings from foreign languages. At first these borrowings are clearly felt as foreign. Chaucer pronounced *vertu* much as the French of his day did, and indeed as the French of today continue to do, since in France this word has undergone little change. He did this because it was a word he felt to be French. Its modern form, *virtue*, is unlikely to strike anyone but the student of words as anything but a normal English word.

The naturalising of borrowings is a gradual process and just where a particular word is thought to be in this process is very often an individual matter. To many *chauffeur* and *valet* might as well as have come from Old English or Swahili for all they know or care, rather than from French. Others, however, know only too well that they have come from that language and perhaps even relate *chauffeur* to its basic meaning of one who heats up, the process of getting engines ready for service. For dictionary writers—of all people the ones perhaps most aware of origins—it is very easy to impose an unreal description on words of this nature. This they might do by putting into italics those items which they, the dictionary writers, feel to be foreign in the way that Chaucer felt *vertu* to be foreign, a practice which leads to extraordinary arbitrariness. Thus one dictionary which does this lists *chauffeur* in ordinary print but puts *chateau* into italics. It puts the ordinary terms of music like *allegro* and *andante* and *adagio*, for which English has no practical synonyms, into italics to show their foreignness but leaves *alcade*, *punctilio* and *sombrero*, which to some seem to cry aloud their Spanish ancestry, in ordinary print.

In point of fact, one cannot know how foreign or unforeign people in general think any of the words they use to be and if one is neither to impose one's own impressions, in this case not very typical impressions, nor fall into foolish arbitrariness, it is best to leave the matter alone. Accordingly, the editors of this dictionary do not discriminate between words of native origin, words of foreign origin long naturalised, and words of foreign origin in the process of naturalisation. The origins of all of them are, of course, shown in the etymologies but their degree of foreignness is not commented upon at all and they all appear in the same typeface. The view taken is that if English speakers use a word, then this word is quite simply an English word and this applies as well to *au courant* as to *knowledgable*, to *sangfroid* as to *courage*.

It will be noticed that some headwords have superscript numerals. Each of these is a homograph, that is, one of a group of words which are different both in meaning and origin but which chance to be spelled in the same way. Thus **grave**[1] is the excavation in the ground to receive a dead body and comes from the Old English word, *græf*, of the same meaning; **grave**[2] means dignified and solemn and comes through French from the Latin word *gravis*, heavy, and is thus quite unrelated. There is also **grave**[3] and **grave**[4].

Where one headword is followed by an arrow and a word in bold type instead of a definition, it is to be assumed that the second word is a headword defined fully elsewhere in the dictionary and that its definition applies to the first headword also. Thus, **circumvolve → revolve** means that *circumvolve* has the same meaning as *revolve*, that it is its synonym. In the case of **moveable → movable** the arrow merely links words of variant spelling.

b. SPELLING

The spellings of the headwords in this dictionary are the ones most usual in the firm tradition of British spelling but include some variants such as the last. American variants too have been included in the usual case where they exist. Thus **centre** and **center** both appear, as do **vice** and **vise**, **traveller** and **traveler**, etc.

The spelling of words which derive from headwords in a thoroughly predictable and regular manner are not given. Thus **greater** and **greatest** are not listed with **great** nor are **jumps** and **jumped** with **jump**. Where the slightest doubt can exist or where a change, however obvious, is to be made in deriving one word from another, a full indication is given. Thus the plural of **gravy** is spelt out as **gravies** and the past tense of **travel** as **travelled** (along with its U.S. variant **traveled**). Spellings in **-ise** have generally been preferred but the alternatives in **-ize** have also been indicated where they are current.

c. PRONUNCIATION

It is probably in the pronunciation of words that dictionaries most reveal the lands of their origin. The Australian sound system, as distinct from the Australian accent, is fortunately in a central position in the generality of the spoken forms deriving from South Eastern English. It has the same number and kind of basic units (or phonemes) as South-Eastern British English and thus of many forms of spoken English, such as South African and New Zealand English, especially in their prestige dialects. This statement is perhaps least true for North American English which tends to stand apart from the rest. Individual readers will, of course, express the sound units or phonemes indicated with the pronunciations of them which are normal to them.

It hardly needs to be pointed out that one is called upon to indicate the pronunciation of words in a dictionary only because the traditional spelling of English is so largely unphonetic. The point was earlier made that it is perhaps not as bad as its more violent detractors would have us believe, but it is still sufficiently unsystematic, particularly with regard to the vowels and diphthongs, to be close to useless in cases of real doubt. The reasons for this are partly historical—we are still spelling somewhat like the Normans—and partly inherent—because we use twenty-six letters to grapple with well over forty sounds.

Consider the following series of words, all of which contain the same vowel sound /i/: *police, amoeba, quay, fee, chief, receive, beat, me, people, aegis.* Or consider the famous series, *cough, thought, through, thorough, rough* and *bough,* in which *ough* represents a different sound in each word. Or consider the silent letters of *knight* or the missing letters of *one,* which surely begins with a /w/, and *few,* the second sound of which is the same as the first of *yacht.*

The question then is not whether a second and phonetic spelling of each word must be included, but only in which alphabet it should be written.

On first thoughts the traditional alphabet, judiciously applied, seems to offer certain advantages because of the great familiarity of its characters. But on second thoughts this may well appear as something of a handicap since we are all so used to reading many of these characters as implying a multiplicity of different sounds that a frame of reference in which one sound only is specified is hard to grasp firmly. While we feel we are using the traditional alphabet in any form, the mind is apt to stray into according a pronunciation quite possible in the context of the usual application of this alphabet but not intended by the dictionary editors at all.

Then again, the dictionary use of twenty-six symbols for more than forty sounds generally entails the creation of strange digraphs, and often the use of many diacritics, all of which gives an unsatisfactory, ad hoc and cluttered effect.

Accordingly the editors of this dictionary have decided to use the characters of the alphabet of the International Phonetic Association, or I.P.A., throughout. These characters have a wide, and we believe growing use internationally, being taught for example in Japanese schools and in many countries abroad. They are well differentiated and clear in print, unequivocal in reference, having been assembled specifically for phonetic purposes, and easy to read and use once initial familiarity with them has been achieved. A list of them with key words to show their phonetic value appears on page 46 and they are also listed continuously at the foot of the pages throughout the dictionary.

The total number of characters in the I.P.A. alphabet is very great and there are more ways than one of using them to indicate the pronunciation of English.

In this dictionary we have very largely adopted the selection of characters and the conventions for combining them which were used by A. G. Mitchell in his various books on Australian English pronunciation. The pattern of transcription which these imply already has a certain currency in this country and does not diverge greatly from that which Daniel Jones used to represent upperclass British pronunciation in his English Pronouncing Dictionary, 1917. Perhaps the most eye-catching difference between Mitchell and Jones is in the symbol used to indicate the vowel sound which occurs in words like *car* and *heart.* For this Jones used /ɑ/ and Mitchell /a/.

The editors are aware that current British practice in using the I.P.A. symbols to transcribe English differs more markedly from that of Daniel Jones than does Mitchell's or our own; but they have not been persuaded of any practical or theoretical advantage in this practice which is sufficient to make them wish to adopt it.

Attempts have been made to keep the use of all diacritics to a minimum on the grounds that they of all items are most likely to go astray in the printing process, and that they are found somewhat difficult to interpret by the general reader. Unfortunately, perhaps, they could not be avoided entirely since the description of the pronunciation of a word of more than one syllable is incomplete unless an indication has been made of which syllables have more and which syllables have less prominence when it is uttered in isolation.

Accordingly the I.P.A. diacritics for lexical stress, (ˈ) before a syllable of greatest stress (or primary) prominence and (ˌ) before one of next greatest stress (or secondary) prominence, have been applied throughout. Their application has been relatively sparing, however, both in consideration of the difficulty already mentioned and of the fact that speakers of English are responsive to the relatively few stress patterns which polysyllabic words in that language may have, and do not therefore need to have every syllable precisely labelled.

Most frequently only the syllable of primary stress has been marked; but in words where the hierarchy among the more weakly stressed syllables is less than obvious, the syllable, or syllables, bearing secondary stress have also been marked. The most weakly stressed syllables would in any event by I.P.A. convention be unmarked.

Pains have been taken to use the diacritics to distinguish between word groups which are compounded into one unit in the mind of the speaker, like *black bread* /ˈblæk brɛd/, and those which have more the nature of a phrase sensed as being in two parts, like *black box* /blæk ˈbɒks/.

The stress patterns of compound adjectives such as *well-heeled* and *cold-blooded* call for special consideration. When words of this type are used predicatively or alone, the primary stress they carry most usually falls on the second element. When they are preposed, that is, used before the nouns they qualify, this primary stress most usually falls on the first element. Thus we might say 'he was well héeled' but 'He was a wéll-heeled man'.

This example also demonstrates the spelling convention of hyphenating compound adjectives when they are preposed. It is fairly widely observed.

Now, in as much that the hyphenated form overtly draws attention to the compounded nature of such words and deflects the mind from any attempt to analyse them as phrases, it may be said to provide a more effective visual reference. For this reason the editors have chosen to use hyphenated forms as headwords for the compound adjectives they defined throughout this dictionary.

The pronunciation given for these hyphenated headwords reflects the stress patterns appropriate for compound adjectives in preposed positions. Occasionally the stress pattern appropriate to the predicative position is specified in a separate indication of pronunciation given after the definition, but where this is not the case readers can easily form it by moving the primary stress to the second element.

Although the dictionary offers a wide coverage of colloquialisms it does not seek to record uneducated forms as such, and accordingly the uneducated pronunciations of words which have them, like *dais* /ˈdaɪəs/, *picture* /ˈpɪtʃə/, and so on, do not appear.

Where more than one pronunciation is given, therefore, as for *controversy* /ˈkɒntrəvɜsi, kənˈtrɒvəsi/ or *dance* /dæns, dans/, it is to be assumed that English speakers make use of them both, either as individuals or as a group.

*Dance* is only one of many words the pronunciations of which may involve either the vowel /a/ or the vowel /æ/ . Others are *chance*, *grasp*, *telegraph*, *castle*, etc.

As a rule of thumb it has been decided to place the variant in /æ/ before that in /a/ , except where the editors are convinced that the variant in /a/ is truly the more common overall.

As has been explained when speaking of headwords, the editors treat words of foreign origin as English words if English speakers use them and, consistent with this policy, they have not attempted to indicate how these words are pronounced by the foreigners from whose languages they have come, but only by ordinary English speakers.

For those who seek the native pronunciation of such words, recourse must be had to more specialised dictionaries of the languages in question. It was felt that an apparatus to cope with the original versions of the many foreign words embedded in English, from Italian to Swahili, from German to Hindi, and so on, was quite beyond the scope of this book.

One of the criteria for excluding headwords was that if no English pronunciation could be found the word was left out. One partial exception to this general philosophy was provided by certain French words which have a considerable vogue worldwide. To deal with them English speakers, while not attempting a truly French pronunciation, seem to make use of a sort of omni-purpose nasalised vowel which we have indicated by the symbol "õ". Thus *sangfroid* appears with the pronunciation /sõˈfrwa/, *au courant* with /oʊ kuˈrõ/. *bon voyage* with /bõ vwaˈjaʒ/, and so on.

It should be pointed out finally that, for many speakers of English everywhere, there is a choice of using a neutralised, i.e., an indeterminate vowel, or an unneutralised one of more positive character in many syllables of polysyllabic words. Thus the verb *ferment* might be /fɜˈmɛnt/, or /fəˈmɛnt/. *electric* might be /iˈlɛktrɪk/, or /əˈlɛktrɪk/, or /ɛˈlɛktrɪk/, *roses* might be /ˈroʊzɪz/, or /ˈroʊzəz/, and so on.

Pronunciations with the indeterminate vowel are less characteristic of South-Eastern English than of other British and heartland English dialects, but the dictionary has favoured them to the exclusion of pronunciations in unneutralised vowels.

### d. GRAMMATICAL CATEGORIES

The grammatical category of each headword is indicated and the system adopted is so straight forward as to call for almost no comment. It may be well, however, to point out that transitive uses of verbs marked *v.t.* and intransitive uses marked *v.i.* are kept separate.

This should be borne in mind when reading verb entries of great length as the meaning sought will come more quickly to view if the correct group of entries is being scanned first.

### e. RESTRICTIVE LABELS

Restrictive labels are liberally distributed throughout the dictionary but nevertheless their appearances are not as numerous as they may well have been. The editors have limited the use of diacritics for secondary stress in the indication of pronunciations in this dictionary to cases where they judged the diacritics to be genuinely useful. In the same spirit of trying to keep the apparatus as uncluttered and simple as possible, they have applied the restrictive labels somewhat sparingly.

Thus when a definition given quite obviously comes from an area of particular specialty, like *compound leaf* from botany, or *sonata* from music, it has often been thought unnecessary to apply the restrictive label. Only where economy of expression or genuine additions of information are to be gained has this been done. There are no doubt many cases where one might debate whether there is a slight advantage one way or another but the principle adopted, though difficult always to apply, was to use the label only where it added something.

It may be remarked that the labels *Obscene*, *Taboo*, and such, do not appear. The words and meanings which might have borne them bear simply the label *Colloq*. The decision to adopt this policy was in line with that taken not to indicate degrees of foreignness in foreign borrowings. The point was made in discussing that decision that it is simply not possible to know how foreign any words are to an individual speaker. Similarly, whatever may once have been the case, in days when four-letter words appear regularly in serious books and serious plays and even in films and occasionally on radio, it is hard to know what meaning *Taboo* might have. In the case of *Obscene*, as court action after court action has shown, there is the utmost difficulty in defining what is legally obscene for the very reason that there is so little agreement about it among individuals.

In the fluid and permissive societies of the 1980s there are many significant and very proper citizens who are offended by the idea that they should not use particular words which come spontaneously to mind, just as there are many significant and proper citizens who are still offended when others do.

Where so much depends on individual response, the editors chose not to adjudicate, merely to indicate that terms of this nature are not part of the standard vocabulary and they are accordingly marked *Colloq*.

## f. ETYMOLOGIES

This dictionary attempts to give an account of the origin of words in a form which is most accessible to the general reader. For this reason we have avoided abbreviations and coded information as much as possible, thereby necessarily losing some of the subtleties which a reader would expect to find in an etymological dictionary. For example we do not distinguish between the passage of a word from one language to another and the development of a new form within the same language. All such steps are indicated by the word "from".

The etymology begins with some indication of the age of the word in English. This is not strictly etymological information but it was thought useful to include it at this point in the entry. If the word became current in English in the Middle Ages (between A.D. 1100 and A.D. 1500) it is marked ME (Middle English); if the word was current in an earlier period (before A.D. 1100), it is marked OE (Old English); if the word does not occur in English before the sixteenth century, no indication of its date is set down, thus showing that the word enters the English language after the Middle English period.

Of course in some cases we have unfortunately to record that the origin of a word is not known. This gap in our information can occur with the most recently coined words just as easily as with words which have long been part of the English language. In such cases there is often interesting speculation in the place of definite knowledge, which on the whole we have felt is more suited to an etymological dictionary. Limitations of space in a general dictionary of this size also militate against lengthy discussions of this kind. But within these limits the dictionary does give a most up-to-date account of the origin of the words of our language.

## g. ENCYCLOPAEDIC MATERIAL

This is not an encyclopaedic dictionary and yet despite the earnest endeavours of the editors to keep encyclopaedic material out, certain of the realities of the world as well as the realities of the word, have inevitably impinged upon it.

One obvious place where this is so can be seen in the treatment of weights and measures. In a world where imperial units are by and large giving way to metric units, a coherent policy of metrication was felt appropriate.

*The Macquarie Dictionary* contains a coherent and consistent set of definitions for weights and measures, using the International System of Units (SI) as a base.

Dictionary practice is based on recommendations of the Metric Conversion Board, as found in Australia's Metric System: A Metric Handbook and its Amendment Sheet (February 1977), and in publications of the Standards Association of Australia (specifically AS 1000–1970 and 1376–1973).

The primary statement of equivalence for imperial and other non-SI measures is normally given in SI base or derived units, as recommended in AS 1376–1973. In general, this means that prefixes for units are not used, and that multiples and submultiples involving powers of 1000 ($10^3$) are preferred. The numerical value preceding the multiple is, in general, chosen to lie between 0.1 and 1000. Where helpful, an additional equivalence statement is given in more immediately understandable terms. For example,

inch . . . 1/12 foot or $25.4 \times 10^{-3}$m (25.4 mm).

The dictionary defines fully, and notes as such, the seven base units of the SI system; other SI units are defined in terms of these base units. The two SI supplementary units (the radian and the steradian) are defined, as are the seventeen SI derived units which have special names. All eighteen SI prefixes are also defined. All entries include approved symbols, where appropriate.

At the entry for metric system, the base and supplementary units are listed and the prefixes are given in tabular form. Some examples of derived units are given. Additional material on imperial equivalences and on the style of metric usage is to be found in the endmatter of the dictionary.

The countries of the world are briefly described even though such entries are indeed felt to be encylopaedic by the editors. This is mainly because the adjectives which derive from the names of these countries are felt to be proper dictionary entries and the brief adjacent definition of the country avoids inflating the etymologies of the adjectives in an awkward fashion. Thus for example, *Ireland* as well as *Irish* does appear. *Irish* is needed, as is so often the case with adjectives which derive from the names of countries, because it has many meanings other than the obvious one. The word also makes its contribution to innumerable compounds like *Irish coffee*, *Irish stew*, *Irish setter*, and so on.

In the case of people of distinction and cities of eminence and the like, no entry is usually offered except in the etymologies of the adjectives which such words generate. Thus there is no mention of Paris except in the etymology of the word *Parisian* and the compounds which Paris may inspire.

There are entries like *Mendel's Law* and *Boyle's Law*, which, with certain abbreviations like *I.P.A.* for the International Phonetic Alphabet, belong in the grey area between the encyclopaedic and lexicographical. It has been decided to admit each of these only after careful deliberation and because it was thought helpful to do so.

### h. ILLUSTRATIONS

The dictionary contains over a thousand small illustrations. These have been applied to words where the visual depiction cuts short lengthy written description and makes apparent what is being defined at a glance. All the illustrations have been specially drawn for this dictionary though some of them are based on earlier work found in the antecedent *Encyclopedic World Dictionary*.

# *Explanatory Notes*

## THE ENTRY

All information within one complete entry has been arranged for the convenience of the user. In general, information about spelling and pronunciation comes first, meanings next, etymologies and run-on headwords last.

Abbreviations used in this dictionary have been limited as far as possible to familiar ones. All abbreviations can be found in appropriate tables or in their individual alphabetical places in the dictionary itself.

## HEADWORD

The headword is the word or words which are being defined in a particular entry; it appears in large boldface type at the left, slightly farther into the left margin than the usual line of text.

Separate entries are made for all words which, though spelt identically, are of quite distinct derivation; in such cases, each headword is followed by a small superscript number. (Example: **gum**[1], **gum**[2], **gum**[3] and **gum**[4].) Entries are arranged under headwords in strict alphabetical order. A particular headword can be located by taking each successive letter of the headword in alphabetical order, ignoring hyphens, apostrophes and word spaces. For example, the words **highborn** and **high-class** are found between **high** and **high comedy**.

## PRONUNCIATION

The pronunciation follows the headword within slant brackets. It is given in the International Phonetic Alphabet, for which a key may be found on page 46. A handy guide to the less easily identified symbols can be found at the foot of each page.

For some headwords more than one pronunciation is given, the first of these being the one more widely used.

## PARTS OF SPEECH

The pronunciation is usually followed by an abbreviation in italics which indicates the part of speech of the headword, as *n.*, *adj.*

If the headword is used in more than one grammatical form, the part-of-speech label precedes each set of definitions to which it applies.

## INFLECTED FORMS

If a headword has irregularly inflected forms (any form not made by the simple addition of the suffix to the main entry), the summary of these forms is given immediately after the pronunciation. Regularly inflected forms, not generally shown, include:

1. Nouns forming a plural merely by the addition of *-s* or *-es*, such as *dog* (*dogs*) or *class* (*classes*);
2. Verbs forming the past tense by adding *-ed*, such as *halt* (*halted*);
3. Verbs forming the present tense by adding *-s* or *-es*, such as *talk* (*talks*) or *smash* (*smashes*);
4. Verbs forming the present participle by adding *-ing*, such as *walk* (*walking*);
5. Adjectives forming the comparative and superlative by adding *-er*, *-est*, such as *black* (*blacker*, *blackest*).

Regular forms are given, however, when necessary for clarity or the avoidance of confusion.

The past tense, past participle and present participle are given as the inflected forms of verbs; where, as commonly happens, the past tense and past participle are the same in form, this form is shown once. (Example: the inflected forms indicated for **walk** are **walked**, **walking**, where **walked** is both the past tense and past participle.)

If necessary, variants of inflected forms are labelled as to level of usage or distribution.

## RESTRICTIVE LABELS

Entries that are limited in usage as to level, region, time, or subject, are marked with such labels as: *Colloq.*, *U.S.*, *Obs.*, *Electronics*, etc.

If the restrictive label applies to the entire entry, it appears before the definition(s). If, however, the restrictive label applies to only one grammatical form, it appears after that part-of-speech label but before the definition numbers to which it applies. If the restrictive label applies to only one definition, it appears before that definition, after the definition number.

## DEFINITIONS

Definitions are individually numbered; numbers appear in a single sequence which does not begin afresh with each grammatical form. The central meaning of each part of speech is put first; usually this is also the commonest meaning. The usual order after the central meaning is: figurative or transferred meanings, specialised meanings, obsolete, archaic or rare meanings. However, this order has been broken where, for example, it is desirable to group related meanings together.

In some cases in which two definitions are very closely related, usually within the same field of information, they are marked with bold-face letters of the alphabet under the same definition number.

Special effort has been made to indicate unique grammatical context wherever possible. Thus, the customary prepositional forms following certain words are often shown.

## SECONDARY HEADWORDS

Idiomatic phrases, prepositional verb phrases, etc., are usually listed in secondary bold face alphabetically under main headwords. Such entries are usually placed under the difficult or key word.

Where a secondary headword has more than one meaning, the various meanings are listed after bold-face letters of the alphabet.

## VARIANT SPELLINGS

Definitions always appear under the commonest spelling of a word. Less common variants cross-refer to the main headword. For example, the word *lovable* has a variant *loveable* which appears as a headword followed by **→ lovable**, indicating that the reader should seek information at that headword.

Variants are listed after the definitions at the main headword. They are sometimes labelled as to usage, either within specified fields (as *Law*) or within specific levels, regions or times (as *Colloq.*, *U.S.*, *Archaic*, etc.).

## ETYMOLOGIES

Etymologies appear in square brackets after the definition or definitions of the entry. A key to the symbols used in the etymologies appears on page 2049 of this dictionary.

## RUN-ON HEADWORDS

Words which are derivatives of the headword and which are a simple extension of the meaning are run on after the etymology, or (if there is no etymology) after the last definition in the entry. Such headwords appear in secondary bold-face type, followed by an indication of their grammatical form.

A pronunciation is not usually given for a run-on headword if it is readily predictable given the combination of the main entry and the suffix. This is normally the case whenever the word retains the stress pattern of the main entry. (Example: **bipartite** has one run-on, **bipartitely**, which does not have a pronunciation, and another, **bipartition**, which does.)

## CROSS-REFERENCING

There are several forms of cross-referencing in this dictionary. The arrow → indicates that the headword which precedes it is not defined in this place but that a suitable definition is to be found under the headword which follows the arrow.

The word 'See' directs the reader to information relevant to what he is now reading but to be found in a different part of the dictionary.

The abbreviation 'Cf.' is similar in function but limited to those cases where the information is in some way complementary or matching.

# Key to Structure of Entries

See Explanatory Notes for explanation of terms

valent: *the discontent which abounds in the world.* **2.** to be rich (fol. by *in*): *some languages abound in figurative expressions.* **3.** to be filled; teem (fol. by *with*): *the ship abounds with rats.* [ME *abounde(n)*, from OF *abunder*, from L *abundāre*] –**abounding,** *adj.*
**about** /ə'baʊt/, *prep.* **1.** of; concerning; in regard to: *to talk about secrets.* **2.** connected with: *instructions about the work.* **3.** somewhere near or in: *he is about the house.* **4.** near; close to: *about my height.* **5.** on every side of; around: *the railing about the tower.* **6.** on or near (one's person): *they had lost all they had about them.* **7.** on the point of (fol. by an infinitive): *about to leave.* **8.** here and there in or on: *wander about the place.* **9.** concerned with; engaged in doing. *–adv.* **10.** near in time, number, degree, etc.; approximately: *about a hundred kilometres.* **11.** *Colloq.* nearly; almost: *about ready.* **12.** nearby: *he is somewhere about.* **13.** on every side in every direction: *look about.* **14.** half round; in the reverse direction: *to spin about.* **15.** *Naut.* on the opposite tack. **16.** to and fro; here and there: *move furniture about.* **17.** in rotation or succession; alternately: *turn about is fair play.* **18.** on the move: *be up and about.* **19.** *Archaic.* around. *–adj.* **20. up and about,** astir; active (after sleep). [ME; OE *abūtan*, var. of *onbūtan*, *on būtan* on the outside (of)]
**about-face** /əbaʊt-'feɪs/, *n., v.,* **-faced, -facing.** *–n.* **1.** a complete, sudden change in position, principle, attitude, etc; volte-face. **2.** →**about-turn** (def. 1). *–v.i.* **3.** to turn in the opposite direction.
**about-ship** /əbaʊt-'ʃɪp/, *v.i.,* **-shipped, -shipping.** *Naut.* to tack a ship.
**about-turn** /əbaʊt-'tɜn/, *n., v.,* **-turned, -turning.** *–n.* **1.** the military command to turn to the rear in a prescribed manner. **2.** →**about-face** (def. 1). *–v.i.* **3.** to turn in the opposite direction.
**above** /ə'bʌv/, *adv.* **1.** in or to a higher place; overhead: *the blue sky above.* **2.** higher in rank or power: *appeal to the courts above.* **3.** before in order, esp. in a book or writing: *from what has been said above.* **4.** in heaven. *–prep.* **5.** in or to a higher place than: *fly above the earth.* **6.** more in quantity or number than: *the weight is above a tonne.* **7.** superior to, in rank or authority. **8.** not capable of (an undesirable thought, action, etc.). **9.** in preference to: *to favour one child above another.* **10. above all,** principally; most important of all. **11. above oneself, a.** overexcited; elated. **b.** conceited; smug; self-satisfied. *–adj.* **12.** said, mentioned, or written above; foregoing: *the above explanation.* *–n.* **13. the above,** that which was said, mentioned, or written previously. [ME; OE *abufan*, from A-[1] + *bufan* above]
**aboveboard** /əbʌv'bɔd/, *adv.* **1.** openly; without tricks, deceit or disguise. *–adj.* **2.** open; frank: *open and aboveboard actions.* Also, (*esp. in predicative use*) **above board.**
**ab ovo** /æb 'oʊvoʊ/, from the beginning. [L *ab ōvō usque ad māla* from the beginning to the end (from the Roman habit of beginning a meal with egg and ending it with fruit)]
**abp.,** Archbishop.
**abracadabra** /æbrəkə'dæbrə/, *n.* **1.** a mystical word used in incantations or written in triangular form as a charm on an amulet. **2.** any word charm or empty jingle of words. **3.** gibberish; nonsense. [L]
**abrachia** /eɪ'brækiə, ə'bræk-/, *n.* a total absence of arms due to a developmental anomaly.
**abradant** /ə'breɪdnt/, *adj.* **1.** abrasive. *–n.* **2.** an abrasive.
**abrade** /ə'breɪd/, *v.,* **abraded, abrading.** *–v.t.* **1.** to scrape

run-on
head word
part-of-speech
label
pronunciation
label
inflected forms
secondary headword
variant
abbreviation
etymology
part-of-speech

# International Phonetic Alphabet Symbols for use in Australian English

**(a) Vowels**

i as in "peat" /pit/
ɪ as in "pit" /pɪt/
ɛ as in "pet" /pɛt/
æ as in "pat" /pæt/
a as in "part" /pat/
ɒ as in "pot" /pɒt/
ʌ as in "but" /bʌt/
ɔ as in "port" /pɔt/
ʊ as in "put" /pʊt/
u as in "pool" /pul/
ɜ as in "pert" /pɜt/
ə as in "apart" /əˈpat/
ɒ̃ as in "bon voyage" /bɒ̃ vwaˈjaʒ/

**(b) Diphthongs**

aɪ as in "buy" /baɪ/
eɪ as in "bay" /beɪ/
ɔɪ as in "boy" /bɔɪ/
aʊ as in "how" /haʊ/
oʊ as in "hoe" /hoʊ/
ɪə as in "here" /hɪə/
ɛə as in "hair" /hɛə/
ʊə as in "tour" /tʊə/

**(c) Consonants**

*(i) Plosives*

p as in "pet" /pɛt/
b as in "bet" /bɛt/
t as in "tale" /teɪl/
d as in "dale" /deɪl/
k as in "came" /keɪm/
g as in "game" /geɪm/

*(ii) Fricatives*

f as in "fine" /faɪn/
v as in "vine" /vaɪn/
θ as in "thin" /θɪn/
ð as in "then" /ðɛn/
s as in "seal" /sil/
z as in "zeal" /zil/
ʃ as in "show" /ʃoʊ/
ʒ as in "measure" /ˈmɛʒə/
h as in "heat" /hit/
r as in "rain" /reɪn/

*(iii) Affricatives*

tʃ as in "choke" /tʃoʊk/
dʒ as in "joke" /dʒoʊk/

*(iv) Nasals*

m as in "mile" /maɪl/
n as in "neat" /nit/
ŋ as in "sing" /sɪŋ/

*(v) Semi-vowels*

j as in "you" /ju/
w as in "woo" /wu/

*(vi) Laterals*

l as in "last" /last/

**(d) Stress**

ˈ as in "clatter" /ˈklætə/
ˌ as in "multimillionaire" /ˌmʌltimɪljəˈnɛə/

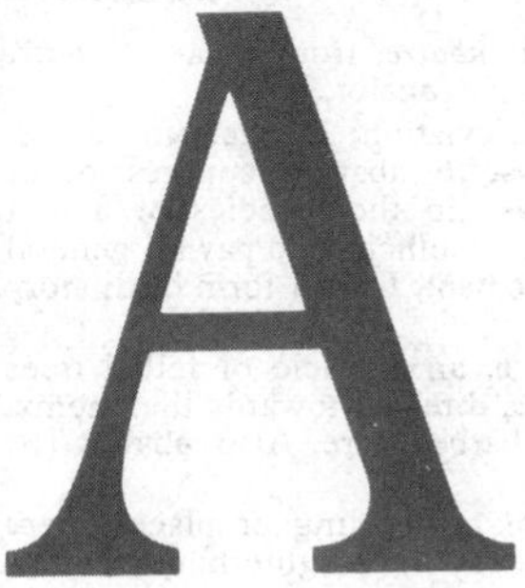

Aa GOUDY **Aa** HELVETICA *Aa* COMMERCIAL SCRIPT Aa UNIVERSITY

*Although there are numerous typefaces in the world they can be divided into four main classifications. These are:*

*ROMAN or SERIF. This typeface came into being from the technique of the Roman masons who, working in stone, finished off each letter with a serif or small stroke projecting from the top or bottom. This was done to correct any feeling of unevenness or imbalance they may have created in cutting the characters in stone.*

*SANS SERIF (without serif). This typeface is geometric in design and has straight-edged characters and lines of a regular thickness.*

*SCRIPT. Based on the movement of the hand, this typeface is often italicised or slanted, as if drawn by a brush or quill pen.*

*DECORATIVE. Any typeface that exaggerates the characteristics of any of the other three classifications to a degree that places it outside of them.*

*The dictionary entries in this book use a SANS SERIF typeface called Helvetica (set in a bold face for the head words) and a SERIF typeface Plantin (used throughout the body of the entries).*

**A, a** /eɪ/, *n., pl.* **A's a's** or **As.** **1.** the first letter of the English alphabet. **2.** the first in any series. **3.** the highest mark for school, college, or university work; alpha. **4.** *Music.* **a.** the sixth degree in the scale of C major, or the first in the relative minor scale (A minor). **b.** a written or printed note representing this tone. **c.** a string, key, or pipe tuned to this note. **d.** (in the fixed system of solmisation) the sixth note of the scale, called **la.** **e.** the note to which concert performers tune their instruments; concert A. **5. from A to Z,** from beginning to end.

**a**$^{1}$ /eɪ/; *weak form* /ə/, *adj. or indef. article.* a word used esp. before nouns beginning with a consonant to mean: **1.** some (indefinite singular referring to one individual of a class): *a man, a house, a star.* **2.** another: *he is a Cicero in eloquence.* **3.** one: *two of a kind, a thousand.* **4.** any (a single): *not a one.* **5.** indefinite plural: *a few, a great many.* Also, *before a vowel,* **an**$^{1}$. [ME, phonetic var. of AN$^{1}$]

**a**$^{2}$ /eɪ/; *weak form* /ə/, *adj. or indef. article.* each; every: *three times a day.* [orig. *a,* prep., OE *an, on,* confused with the indefinite article. See A-$^{1}$]

**a'** /a, ɔ/, *adj. Scot.* all: *for a' that.* Also, **a.**

**a-**$^{1}$, a prefix, a reduced form of Old English prep. *on,* meaning 'on', 'in', 'into', 'to', 'towards', preserved before a noun in a prepositional phrase, forming a predicate adjective or an adverbial element, as in *afoot, abed, ashore, apart, aside,* and in archaic and dialectal use before a present participle in *-ing,* as in *to set the bells aringing.* [ME and late OE *a-*, var. of OE *an, on* at, on. See ON]

**a-**$^{2}$, a prefix, a reduced form of Old English *of,* as in *akin, afresh, anew.* [ME *a-*, OE *of* (prep.) off, of]

**a-**$^{3}$, a prefix indicating **1.** up, out, or away, as in *arise, awake.* **2.** intensified action, as in *abide, amaze.* [ME *a-*, up, out, away, from OE *ā*, reduced form of *ar-*, *or-*, from G]

**a-**$^{4}$, variant of **ab-** before *m, p,* and *v,* as in *amove, aperient, avert.* [ME *a-*, from F, from L *ab-*; or from L, reduced form of *ab-*. See AB-$^{1}$]

**a-**$^{5}$, variant of **ad-**, used: **1.** before *sc, sp, st,* as in *ascend.* **2.** in words of French derivation (often with the sense of increase, addition), as in *amass.* [ME *a-*, from F, from L *ad-*, or assimilated forms of *ad-*, such as *ab-*, *ac-*, *af-*, etc.; or from L, reduced form of *ad-* AD-]

**a-**$^{6}$, variant of **an-**$^{1}$ before consonants, as in *achromatic.* [Gk, called alpha privative, before vowels *an-*; akin to L *in-* not, E UN-$^{1}$]

**a.,** **1.** about. **2.** acre. **3.** adjective. **4.** (of a horse) aged.

**A,** **1.** argon. **2.** ampere.

**A**$^{1}$ /eɪ/, *adj.* **1.** denoting a film, program, etc., on television which is not considered suitable for viewing by children. *–n.* **2.** such a film, program, etc.

**A**$^{2}$ /eɪ/, *n. in the phrase* **give (someone) the big A,** *Colloq. to* reject or rebuff (someone). [standing for *A(rse)*]

**Å,** angstrom.

**A-1** /eɪ-'wʌn/, *adj.* **1.** registered as a first-class vessel in a shipping register, as Lloyd's Register. **2.** *Colloq.* first-class; excellent. Also, **A-one.**

**A4,** an international standard size of paper, 297 x 210 mm, replacing the traditional foolscap and large post quarto.

**A5,** an international standard size of paper, 210 x 148 mm, suitable for personal stationery, business letters, small booklets, etc.

**A6,** an international standard size of paper, 148 x 105 mm, suitable for postcards, invitation cards, and pocket books.

**A7,** an international standard size of paper, 105 x 74 mm, suitable for compliment siips, labels, etc.

**A.A.** /eɪ 'eɪ/, Alcoholics Anonymous.

**A.A.P.** /eɪ eɪ 'pi/, Australian Associated Press.

**aardvark** /'advak/, *n.* a large, nocturnal, burrowing mammal of Africa, subsisting largely on termites, and having a long, extensile tongue, claws, and conspicuously long ears. There is only one genus, *Orycteropus,* constituting a separate order, Tubulidentata. [Afrikaans, *aarde* earth + *vark* pig]

aardvark

**aardwolf** /'adwʊlf/, *n.* a striped, hyena-like African mammal, *Proteles cristatus,* which feeds on carrion and insects. [Afrikaans, *aarde* earth + *wolf* wolf]

**Aaronic** /ɛə'rɒnɪk/, *adj.* priestly; ecclesiastical. Also, **Aaronical.** [from *Aaron,* brother of Moses, the first high priest of the Hebrews]

**Aaron's-rod** /ɛərənz-'rɒd/, *n.* **1.** a widespread biennial plant, *Verbascum thapsus,* densely covered with woolly hairs and having erect spikes of yellow flowers. **2.** *Archit.* a decorative moulding consisting of a tall straight stem with curling foliage.

**A'asia,** Australasia.

**A.A.T.** /eɪ eɪ 'ti/, Australian Antarctic Territory.

i = peat ɪ = pit ɛ = pet æ = pat a = part ɒ = pot ʌ = putt ɔ = port ʊ = put u = pool ɜ = pert ə = apart aɪ = buy eɪ = bay ɔɪ = boy aʊ = how
oʊ = hoe ɪə = here ɛə = hair ʊə = tour g = give θ = thin ð = then ʃ = show ʒ = measure tʃ = choke dʒ = joke ŋ = sing j = you õ = Fr. bon

**ab-**[1], a prefix meaning 'off', 'away', 'from', as in *abduct, abjure*. [L, representing *ab*, prep., from, away; akin to Gk *apó*, Skt *ápa* from]

**ab-**[2], a prefix attached to practical electric units, indicating a centimetre-gram-second electromagnetic unit of measurement: *abvolt is equivalent to* $10^{-8}$ *volts.* [abbrev. of ABSOLUTE]

**ab.**, about.

**a.b.**, able-bodied (seaman).

**Ab**, alabamine.

**aba** /'æbə/, *n.* a sleeveless outer garment, worn by Arabs. [Ar. *'abā'a*]

**abaca** /'æbəkə/, *n.* **1.** a Philippine plant, *Musa textilis.* **2.** the fibre of this plant, Manila hemp, used in making rope. [Sp., from Tagalog]

**aback** /ə'bæk/, *adv.* **1.** with the wind blowing against the forward side of a sail or sails, instead of the after side. **2.** back against the mast, as sails, or with sails so placed. **3.** towards the back. **4. taken aback, a.** suddenly disconcerted. **b.** (of a ship) caught by the wind so as to press the sails back against the mast. **c.** (of sails) caught by a wind on the forward surface. [ME *abak*, OE *on*, prep., + *bæc* on or to the back]

**abacus** /'æbəkəs/, *n., pl.* **-ci** /-si/. **1.** a contrivance for calculating, consisting of beads or balls strung on wires or rods set in a frame. **2.** *Archit.* a slab forming the top or capital of a column. [L, from Gk *ábax*]

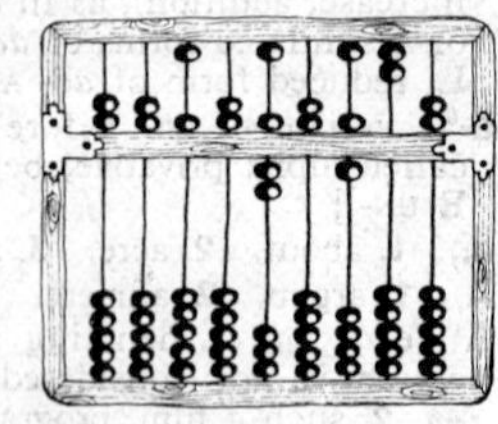

abacus

**abaft** /ə'baft/, *Naut.* *–prep.* **1.** in the rear of; behind. *–adv.* **2.** at or towards the stern; aft. [ME, from A-[1] + *baft*, OE *bæftan, be æftan.* See BY, AFT]

**abalone** /æbə'louni/, *n.* any of the various univalve, marine molluscs of the genus *Haliotis*, having a bowl-like, nacre-lined shell bearing a row of respiratory holes. The flesh is used for food and the shell for mother-of-pearl ornaments; sea-ear; mutton-fish. [Sp.]

**abandon**[1] /ə'bændən/, *v.t.* **1.** to leave completely and finally; forsake utterly; desert: *to abandon one's home.* **2.** to give up all concern in: *to abandon the cares of empire.* **3.** to give up (something begun) without finishing: *to abandon a cricket match because of rain.* **4.** to give up the control of: *to abandon a city to a conqueror.* **5.** to yield (oneself) unrestrainedly: *to abandon oneself to grief.* **6.** *Law.* to cast away or leave personal property with no intention of reclaiming it, thereby making the property available for appropriation by any person. **7.** *Law.* to relinquish insured property to the underwriter in case of partial loss, thereby enabling the insured to claim a total loss. [ME *abandone(n)*, from OF *abandoner*, from the phrase *a bandon* under one's jurisdiction] – **abandoner,** *n.* – **abandonment,** *n.*

**abandon**[2] /ə'bændən/, *n.* a giving up to natural impulses; freedom from constraint or conventionality: *to do something with abandon.* [F]

**abandoned** /ə'bændənd/, *adj.* **1.** forsaken. **2.** unrestrained. **3.** shamelessly and recklessly wicked.

**abandonee** /əbændə'ni/, *n.* an insurer to whom a wreck has been abandoned. Cf. **abandon**[1] (def. 7).

**à bas** /a 'ba/, down with (the person or thing named)! [F]

**abase** /ə'beɪs/, *v.t.*, **abased, abasing. 1.** to reduce or lower, as in rank, office, estimation; humble; degrade. **2.** *Archaic.* to lower; bring down. [b. BASE[2] and ME *abesse(n)* (from OF *abaissier*, from *a-* A-[5] + *baissier* lower, from LL *bassus* low)] – **abasement,** *n.* – **abaser,** *n.*

**abash** /ə'bæʃ/, *v.t.* to destroy the self-possession of; make ashamed or embarrassed: *stand or feel abashed.* [ME *abashe(n)*, from AF *abaiss-*, var. of OF *esbaïss-*, stem of *erbaïr* astonish] – **abashment,** *n.*

**abate** /ə'beɪt/, *v.*, **abated, abating.** *–v.t.* **1.** to reduce in amount, intensity, etc.; lessen; diminish: *to abate a tax, one's enthusiasm, etc.* **2.** *Law.* to put an end to or suppress (a nuisance); suspend or extinguish (an action); annul (a writ). **3.** to deduct or subtract. **4.** to omit. *–v.i.* **5.** to decrease or become less in strength or violence: *the storm has abated.* [ME *abate(n)*, from OF *abatre*, from *a-* A-[5] + *batre* beat] – **abatable,** *adj.* – **abater,** *Law.* **abator,** *n.*

**abatement** /ə'beɪtmənt/, *n.* **1.** alleviation; mitigation. **2.** decrease; reduction. **3.** *Law.* the act of abating; suppression or termination. **4.** *Law.* a decrease in the legacies of a will when the assets of an estate are insufficient to pay all general legacies in full. **5. plea in abatement,** *Law.* a form of dilatory plea, now uncommon.

**abatis** /'æbətəs/; *Mil.* /æbə'ti/, *n.* an obstacle of felled trees with bent or sharpened branches directed towards the enemy, and now often interlaced with barbed wire. Also, **abattis.** [F; akin to ABATE]

**abattoirs** /'æbətwaz, -tɔz/, *n. pl.* a building or place where animals are slaughtered for food; a slaughterhouse. Also, **abattoir.** [F]

**abaxial** /æb'æksiəl/, *adj. Bot.* away from the axis: *the abaxial surface of a leaf.* [AB-[1] + L *axi(s)* axle + -AL[1]]

**abb** /æb/, *n.* **1.** the skirtings and edges of the fleece from a sheep, esp. that which comes from the breech area; the most inferior wool. **2.** a warp yarn made from this. [ME, from OE *āb, āweb, ōweb,* whence WOOF[1]]

**Abba** /'æbə/, *n.* a title of bishops and patriarchs in some Eastern Churches. [ME, from L, from LGk, from Aram.; in Bible, meaning *father* (applied to God)]

**abbacy** /'æbəsi/, *n., pl.* **-cies. 1.** an abbot's office, rights, privileges, or jurisdiction. **2.** the period of office of an abbot. [var. of ME *abbatie*, from LL *abbātia*]

**abbatial** /ə'beɪʃəl/, *adj.* of or pertaining to an abbot, abbess, or abbey. [LL *abbātiālis*]

**abbé** /'æbeɪ/, *n.* **1.** an abbot. **2.** in France, a courtesy title for any ecclesiastic, esp. one who has no other title. [F]

**abbess** /'æbɛs/, *n.* the female superior of a convent, regularly in the same religious orders in which monks are governed by an abbot. [ME *abbesse*, from OF, from LL *abbātissa*]

**Abbevillian** /æbə'vɪliən, -jən/, *adj.* of, pertaining to, or characteristic of a Palaeolithic culture in Europe, marked by the use of crude stone hand axes; Chellean. Also, **Abbevillean.** [named after *Abbeville*, town in France near which such objects were first found]

**abbey** /'æbi/, *n., pl.* **-beys. 1.** the religious body or establishment under an abbot or abbess; a monastery or convent. **2.** the monastic buildings. **3.** the church of an abbey. **4.** *Brit.* a country house that was formerly an abbatial house. [ME *abbeye*, from OF *abaie*, from LL *abbātia*]

**abbot** /'æbət/, *n.* the head or superior of a monastery. [ME, var. of ME and OE *abbod*, from LL *abbās*, from Gk, from Aram. *abbā* father] – **abbotship, abbotric,** *n.*

**abbrev.**, abbreviation. Also, **abbr.**

**abbreviate** /ə'brivieɪt/, *v.t.*, **-ated, -ating.** to make brief; make shorter by contraction or omission: *to abbreviate 'foot' to 'ft'.* [L *abbreviātus*, pp.] – **abbreviator,** *n.*

**abbreviation** /əbrivi'eɪʃən/, *n.* **1.** a shortened or contracted form of a word or phrase, used as a symbol for the whole. **2.** reduction in length; abridgment. **3.** *Music.* any of several signs or symbols used to abbreviate musical notation, as those indicating the repetition of a phrase or a note. [L *abbreviātio*]

**ABC** /eɪ bi 'si/, *n.* **1.** Also, *U.S.*, **ABCs.** the alphabet. **2.** a handbook (on any subject), often arranged alphabetically. **3.** the main or the basic facts, principles, etc. (of any subject). **4.** →**A.B.C.**

**A.B.C.** /eɪ bi 'si/, Australian Broadcasting Commission. Also, **ABC.**

**abdicate** /'æbdəkeɪt/, *v.*, **-cated, -cating.** *–v.i.* **1.** to renounce a throne or some claim; relinquish a right, power, or trust. *–v.t.* **2.** to give up or renounce (office, duties, authority, etc.), esp. in a voluntary, public, or formal manner. [L *abdicātus*, pp.] – **abdicable,** *adj.* – **abdicative** /əb'dɪkətɪv/, *adj.* – **abdicator, abdicant,** *n.*

**abdication** /æbdə'keɪʃən/, *n.* the act of abdicating; renunciation, esp. of sovereign power.

**abdomen** /'æbdəmən, əb'doumən/, *n.* **1.** that part of the body of a mammal between the thorax and the pelvis; the visceral cavity containing most of the digestive organs; the belly. **2.** (in vertebrates below mammals) a region of the body corresponding to but not coincident with the human abdomen. **3.** *Entomol.* the posterior section of the body of an arthropod, behind the thorax or the cephalothorax. [L]

**abdominal** /əb'dɒmənəl, æb-/, *adj.* of, in, or on the abdomen: *abdominal muscles.* – **abdominally,** *adv.*

**abdominous** /əb'dɒmənəs, æb-/, *adj.* pot-bellied.

**abduce** /əb'djus, æb-/, *v.t.,* **-duced, -ducing.** →**abduct** (def. 2). [L *abdūcere*]

**abducent** /əb'djusənt, æb-/, *adj. Physiol.* drawing away (applied to muscles, etc.).

**abduct** /əb'dʌkt, æb-/, *v.t.* **1.** to carry off surreptitiously or by force, esp. to kidnap. **2.** *Physiol.* to draw away from the original position (opposed to *adduct*). [L *abductus,* pp.] – **abductor,** *n.*

**abduction**[1] /əb'dʌkʃən, æb-/, *n.* **1.** the act of fact of abducting. **2.** the state of being abducted. [F, from L *abductus* + -ION]

**abduction**[2] /əb'dʌkʃən, æb-/, *n. Logic.* a syllogism whose major premise is certain but whose minor premise is probable. [NL *abductio*: translation of Gk *apagōgē*]

**abdul** /'æbdʌl/, *v.t.* to erect (a tent) with one side wall extended to form an open shelter.

**Abdul** /'æbdʊl, -dəl/, *n. Colloq.* (*oft. derog.*) **1.** nickname for a Turk. **2.** (collectively) Turks.

**abeam** /ə'bim/, *adv.* at right angles to the keel of a ship; directly opposite the middle part of the ship.

**abecedarian** /eɪbisi'dɛəriən/, *n.* **1.** a pupil who is learning the letters of the alphabet. **2.** a beginner. *–adj.* **3.** alphabetical. **4.** primary; rudimentary. [ML *abecedārius* pertaining to the alphabet, from the first four letters *abcd* + -AN]

**abecedary** /eɪbi'sidəri/, *n., pl.* **-ries.** →**abecedarian.**

**abed** /ə'bɛd/, *adv. Obs.* **1.** in bed. **2.** confined to bed.

**abele** /ə'bil, 'eɪbəl/, *n.* the white poplar tree, *Populus alba.* [D *abeel,* from OF *abel,* from LL *albellus,* diminutive of *albus* white]

**abelia** /ə'biliə/, *n.* any shrub of the genus *Abelia,* esp. *A. grandiflora,* widely grown in gardens for its fragrant pink flowers.

**abelmosk** /'eɪbəlmɒsk/, *n.* a plant, *Abelmoschus moschatus,* of warm countries, cultivated for its musky seed, which is used in perfumery, etc. [NL *Abelmoschus,* from Ar. *habb el mosk* grain of musk]

**Aberdeen Angus** /æbədin 'æŋgəs/, *n.* one of a breed of hornless beef cattle with smooth black hair, originally bred in Scotland.

**Aberdeen sausage** /– 'sɒsɪdʒ/, *n.* a large, home-made beef sausage boiled in a cloth, then untied and rolled in browned breadcrumbs.

**aberrant** /'æbərənt, ə'bɛrənt/, *adj.* **1.** straying from the right or usual course. **2.** deviating from the ordinary or normal type. [L *aberrans,* ppr.] – **aberrance, aberrancy,** *n.*

**aberration** /æbə'reɪʃən/, *n.* **1.** the act of wandering from the usual way or normal course. **2.** deviation from truth or moral rectitude. **3.** lapse from a sound mental state. **4.** *Astron.* apparent displacement of a heavenly body, due to the joint effect of the motion of the rays of light proceeding from it and the motion of the earth. **5.** *Optics.* any disturbance of the rays of a pencil of light such that they can no longer be brought to a sharp focus or form a clear image. **6.** *Genetics.* deviation from type. [L *aberrātio*] – **aberrational,** *adj.*

**abet** /ə'bɛt/, *v.t.,* **abetted, abetting.** to encourage or countenance by aid or approval (used chiefly in a bad sense): *to abet evildoers, to abet a crime or offence.* [ME *abbette(n),* from OF *abeter,* from *a-* A-[5] + *beter* to entice (from Scand. See BAIT)] – **abetment,** *n.*

**abetter** /ə'bɛtə/, *n.* one who abets. Also (*esp. in legal use*), **abettor.**

**abeyance** /ə'beɪəns/, *n.* **1.** temporary inactivity or suspension. **2.** *Law.* a state of waiting for the ascertainment of the person entitled to ownership: *an estate in abeyance.* [AF *abeiance* expectation, from OF *abeer* gape after, from *a-* A-[5] + *beer, baer* gape, from LL *badāre*]

**abeyant** /ə'beɪənt/, *adj.* in abeyance.

**abhor** /əb'hɔ/, *v.t.,* **-horred, -horring.** to regard with repugnance; loathe or abominate. [late ME, from L *abhorrēre*] – **abhorrer,** *n.*

**abhorrence** /əb'hɒrəns/, *n.* **1.** a feeling of extreme aversion. **2.** something detested.

**abhorrent** /əb'hɒrənt/, *adj.* **1.** feeling horror (fol. by *of*): *abhorrent of excess.* **2.** utterly opposed (fol. by *to*): *abhorrent to reason.* **3.** exciting horror; detestable. **4.** remote in character (fol. by *from*): *abhorrent from the principles of law.* – **abhorrently,** *adv.*

**abidance** /ə'baɪdəns/, *n.* **1.** the act of abiding. **2.** conformity (fol. by *by*): *abidance by rules.*

**abide** /ə'baɪd/, *v.,* **abode** /ə'boʊd/ or **abided, abiding.** *–v.i.* **1.** to remain; continue; stay: *abide with me.* **2.** to dwell; reside. **3.** to continue in a certain condition; remain steadfast or faithful. **4. abide by, a.** to stand by: *to abide by a friend.* **b.** to await or accept the consequences of: *to abide by the event.* *–v.t.* **5.** to wait for. **6.** to stand one's ground against; await or sustain defiantly. **7.** *Colloq.* to put up with; tolerate: *I can't abide such people.* [ME *abide(n),* OE *ābīdan.* See A-[3]] – **abider,** *n.*

**abiding** /ə'baɪdɪŋ/, *adj.* continuing; steadfast: *an abiding faith.* – **abidingly,** *adv.* – **abidingness,** *n.*

**abietic acid** /æbi,ɛtɪk 'æsəd/, *n.* a yellow crystalline acid, $C_{19}H_{29}$ COOH, derived from the resin of a species of pine, used in driers, varnishes, and soaps; sylvic acid. [stem of L *abiēs* fir + -IC + ACID[1]]

**abigail** /'æbəgeɪl/, *n.* a lady's maid. [from *Abigail,* the 'waiting gentlewoman', in Beaumont and Fletcher's *The Scornful Lady*]

**ability** /ə'bɪləti/, *n., pl.* **-ties.** **1.** power or capacity to do or act in any relation. **2.** competence in any occupation or field of action, from the possession of capacity, skill, means, or other qualification. **3.** (*pl.*) talents; mental gifts or endowments. [ME *(h)abilite,* from F, from L *habilitas*; replacing ME *ablete,* from OF]

**ab initio** /,æb ɪ'nɪʃioʊ/, from the beginning. [L]

**abiogenesis** /,eɪbaɪoʊ'dʒɛnəsəs/, *n.* **1.** the (hypothetical) production of living things from inanimate matter; spontaneous generation. **2.** the theory, belief, or doctrine that living things can be produced from inanimate matter. [A-[6] + BIO- + GENESIS] – **abiogenist** /eɪbaɪ'ɒdʒənəst/, *n.*

**abiogenetic** /eɪ,baɪoʊdʒə'nɛtɪk/, *adj.* of or pertaining to abiogenesis. – **abiogenetically,** *adv.*

**abirritant** /æb'ɪrətənt/, *Med.* *–n.* **1.** a soothing agent. *–adj.* **2.** reducing irritation.

**abirritate** /æb'ɪrəteɪt/, *v.t.,* **-tated, -tating.** *Med.* to make less irritable. – **abirritation** /æb,ɪrə'teɪʃən/, *n.*

**abject** /'æbdʒɛkt/, *adj.* **1.** utterly humiliating or disheartening: *abject poverty.* **2.** contemptible; despicable: *an abject liar.* **3.** humble; servile: *an abject apology.* **4.** *Obs.* cast aside. [ME, from L *abjectus,* pp., thrown away] – **abjection** /æb'dʒɛkʃən/, *n.* – **abjectly,** *adv.* – **abjectness,** *n.*

**abjuration** /æbdʒə'reɪʃən/, *n.* the act of abjuring; renunciation upon oath.

**abjure** /əb'dʒʊə/, *v.t.,* **-jured, -juring.** **1.** to renounce or repudiate; retract, esp. with solemnity: *to abjure one's errors.* **2.** to forswear: *to abjure allegiance.* [L *abjūrāre*] – **abjuratory,** *adj* – **abjurer,** *n.*

**abl.,** ablative.

**ablactate** /æb'lækteɪt/, *v.t.,* **-tated, -tating.** to wean. [L *ablactātus,* pp.] – **ablactation** /,æblæk'teɪʃən/, *n.*

**ablate** /ə'bleɪt/, *v.,* **-lated, -lating.** *–v.t.* **1.** to remove by ablation. *–v.i.* **2.** to pass directly from a solid state to a gas with no liquid intermediary.

**ablation** /ə'bleɪʃən/, *n.* **1.** *Med.* removal, esp. of organs, abnormal growths, or harmful substances from the body by mechanical, physical or chemical means, as surgery or irradiation. **2.** *Physics, Geol., etc.* erosion of a solid body by a fluid. **3.** the melting or wearing away of some expendable part of a space vehicle upon re-entry into earth's atmosphere. [L *ablatio* a carrying away]

**ablative**[1] /'æblətɪv/, *adj.* **1.** (in some inflected languages) denoting a case which has among its functions the indication of place from which, time when, place in which, manner, means, instrument, agent, etc. *–n.* **2.** the ablative case. **3.** a word in that case, as *Troiā* in Latin *Troiā vēnit,* 'He came from Troy'. [L *ablātīvus* expressing removal; replacing late ME *ablatif,* from F]

**ablative**[2] /ə'bleɪtɪv/, *adj.* **1.** of or pertaining to a substance which ablates. *–n.* **2.** a substance, as iodine, which ablates. **3.** a section of a space vehicle which is made of or coated with an ablative material.

**ablative absolute** /æblətɪv 'æbsəlut/, *n.* (in Latin grammar) a construction not dependent upon any other part of the sentence, consisting of a noun and a participle, noun and adjective, or two nouns, in which both members are in the ablative case, as Latin *viā factā*, 'the road having been made'.

**ablator** /æb'leɪtə/, *n.* **1.** a disposable casing used to protect a spacecraft from excessive heating during re-entry into the earth's atmosphere. **2.** the material of such a casing.

**ablaut** /'æblaut/, *n.* **1.** regular change in the internal structure of roots, particularly in the vowel, showing alteration in function and meaning. **2.** such change in Indo-European languages, as in English *sing, sang, sung, song*; gradation. [G, from *ab* off + *Laut* sound]

**ablaze** /ə'bleɪz/, *adv.* **1.** on fire. *–adj.* **2.** gleaming as if on fire. **3.** excited; eagerly desirous. **4.** very angry.

**able** /'eɪbəl/, *adj.*, **abler, ablest. 1.** having sufficient power, strength, or qualifications; qualified: *a man able to perform military service.* **2.** having unusual intellectual qualifications: *an able minister,* **3.** showing talent or knowledge: *an able speech.* [ME, from OF, from L *habilis* easy to handle, fit]

**-able,** a suffix used to form adjectives, esp. from verbs, to denote ability, liability, tendency, worthiness, or likelihood, as in *teachable, perishable, obtainable*, but also attached to other parts of speech (esp. nouns) as in *objectionable, peaceable,* and even verb phrases, as in *get-at-able.* Many of these adjectives, such as *durable, tolerable,* have been borrowed directly from Latin or French, in which language they were already compounded. However, **-able** is attached freely (now usu. with passive force) to stems of any origin. Also, **-ble, -ible.** [ME, from OF, from L *-ābilis*]

**able-bodied** /'eɪbəl-bɒdid/, *adj.* physically competent.

**able-bodied seaman** /– 'simən/, *n.* an experienced seaman who has passed certain tests in the practice of seamanship.

**ablegate** /'æbləgeɪt/, *n.* a papal envoy to a newly appointed dignitary.

**able seaman** /eɪbəl 'simən/, *n.* →**able-bodied seaman.**

**abloom** /ə'blum/, *adj.* **1.** in blossom. *–adv.* **2.** into blossom.

**abluent** /'æbluənt/, *adj.* **1.** cleansing. *–n.* **2.** a cleansing agent; a detergent. [L *abluens*, ppr.]

**ablution** /ə'bluʃən/, *n.* **1.** a cleansing with water or other liquid, as in ceremonial purification. **2.** the liquid used. **3.** (*pl.*) the act of washing oneself: *do one's ablutions.* [ME, from L *ablūtio*] – **ablutionary,** *adj.*

**ably** /'eɪbli/, *adv.* **1.** competently; well. **2.** with a will; energetically.

**abnegate** /'æbnəgeɪt/, *v.t.*, **-gated, -gating.** to refuse or deny to oneself; reject; renounce. [L *abnegātus*, pp.] – **abnegation** /æbnə'geɪʃən/, *n.* – **abnegator,** *n.*

**abnormal** /æb'nɔməl/, *adj.* not conforming to rule; deviating from the type or standard. [stem of L *abnormis* irregular + -AL[1]; replacing *anormal,* from F, from ML *anormalus* for L *anōmalus*, from Gk *anōmalos.* See ANOMALOUS] – **abnormally,** *adv.*

**abnormality** /æbnɔ'mæləti/, *n., pl.* **-ties. 1.** an abnormal thing, happening, or feature. **2.** deviation from the standard, rule, or type; irregularity.

**abnormal psychology** /ˌæbnɔməl saɪ'kɒlədʒi/, *n.* the study of mental phenomena, behaviour patterns, etc., of individuals who deviate widely from the average.

**abnormity** /æb'nɔməti/, *n., pl.* **-ties. 1.** abnormality; irregularity. **2.** malformation; monstrosity.

**Abo** /'æbou/, *Colloq.* (*oft. derog.*) *–n.* (*also l.c.*) **1.** an Aborigine. *–adj.* **2.** Aboriginal. [shortened form of ABORIGINE]

**aboard** /ə'bɔd/, *adv.* **1.** on board; on or in a ship, train, bus, etc. **2.** alongside. *–prep.* **3.** on board of.

**abode** /ə'boud/, *n.* **1.** a dwelling place; a habitation. **2.** continuance in a place; sojourn; stay. *–v.* **3.** past tense and past participle of **abide.** [ME *abood*, OE *ābād*, pt. of *ābīdan* ABIDE]

**abolish** /ə'bɒlɪʃ/, *v.t.* to do away with; put an end to; annul; destroy: *to abolish slavery.* [F *aboliss-*, stem of *abolir* make perish, from L *abolescere* perish] – **abolishable,** *adj.* – **abolisher,** *n.* – **abolishment,** *n.*

**abolition** /æbə'lɪʃən/, *n.* **1.** utter destruction; annulment; abrogation: *the abolition of laws, customs, debts, etc.* **2.** the termination of convict transportation to Australia. **3.** the legal extinction of Negro slavery. [L *abolitio*] – **abolitionary,** *adj.*

**abolitionism** /æbə'lɪʃənɪzəm/, *n.* the principle or policy of abolition, esp. of convict transportation and of Negro slavery.

**abolitionist** /æbə'lɪʃənəst/, *n.* (formerly) one who espoused or worked for the cessation of convict transportation to Australia; anti-transportationist.

**abomasum** /æbə'meɪsəm/, *n.* the fourth or true stomach of ruminants, lying next to the omasum. Also, **abomasus** /æbə'meɪsəs/. [NL, from L *ab-* AB-[1] + *omāsum* bullock's tripe]

**A-bomb** /'eɪ-bɒm/, *n.* →**atomic bomb.**

**abominable** /ə'bɒmənəbəl, ə'bɒmnəbəl/, *adj.* **1.** detestable; loathsome. **2.** *Colloq.* shocking; unpleasant; bad. [ME, from F, from L *abōminābilis*] – **abominableness,** *n.* – **abominably,** *adv.*

**abominable crime** /– 'kraɪm/, *n.* the felony of buggery which includes sodomy and bestiality.

**abominable snowman** /– 'snoumæn/, *n.* a manlike creature supposed to inhabit the snows of Tibet, a region north of the Himalayas; yeti.

**abominate** /ə'bɒməneɪt/, *v.t.*, **-nated, -nating. 1.** to regard with intense aversion; abhor. **2.** to dislike strongly. [L *abōminātus*, pp., having deprecated as an ill omen]

**abomination** /əbɒmə'neɪʃən/, *n.* **1.** an object greatly disliked or abhorred. **2.** intense aversion; detestation. **3.** a detestable action; shameful vice.

**aborigiana** /ˌæbərɪdʒi'anə/, *n.* Aboriginal artifacts or other items of Aboriginal culture.

**aboriginal** /æbə'rɪdʒənəl/, *adj.* **1.** of or pertaining to an aborigine. **2.** (*usu. cap*) of or pertaining to the Australian Aborigines. *–n.* **3.** (*usu. cap.*) an aborigine (def. 1).

**aboriginality** /ˌæbərɪdʒə'næləti/, *n.* **1.** the qualities inherent in being an aboriginal, relating to heritage, culture, etc. **2.** a colloquial anecdote on Aboriginal or Australian bush subjects in general. [(orig. *pl.*) the title of a former regular feature in the *Bulletin*, a Sydney weekly journal]

**Aboriginal reserve** /ˌæbərɪdʒənəl rə'zɜv/, *n.* →**reserve** (def. 11).

**ab origine** /æb ə'rɪdʒəni/, from the very first; from the source or origin. [L]

**aborigine** /æbə'rɪdʒəni/, *n.* **1.** (*usu. cap.*) one of a race of tribal peoples, the earliest inhabitants of Australia. **2.** a descendant of these people, sometimes of mixed blood. **3.** (*pl.*) (generally) the primitive inhabitants of a country; the people living in a country at the earliest period. **4.** (*pl.*) *Rare.* the original fauna or flora of a region. [L *ab orīgine* from the beginning]

**abort** /ə'bɔt/, *v.i.* **1.** to miscarry before the foetus is viable. **2.** to develop incompletely, remaining in a rudimentary state or degenerating. **3.** to come to nothing; fail. **4.** *Colloq.* to fail to complete a mission, or test of a mechanical device. *–v.t.* **5.** to cause to abort. *–n.* **6.** *Mil.* failure to accomplish a mission for any reason other than enemy action. [L *abortus*, pp., having miscarried]

**aborticide** /ə'bɔtəsaɪd/, *n.* **1.** destruction of a foetus in the uterus; foeticide. **2.** an abortifacient. [L *abortus* miscarriage + -I- + -CIDE]

**abortifacient** /əbɔtə'feɪʃənt/, *adj.* **1.** causing abortion. *–n.* **2.** something used to produce abortion. [L *abortus* miscarriage + -I- + -FACIENT]

**abortion** /ə'bɔʃən/, *n.* **1.** the expulsion or removal of a human foetus before it is viable. **2.** an immature and not viable birth product; miscarriage. **3.** *Biol.* the arrested development of an embryo or an organ at its (more or less) early stage. **4.** anything which fails in its progress before it is matured or perfected, as a design or project. **5.** a total failure. [L *abortio* miscarriage]

**abortionist** /ə'bɔʃənəst/, *n.* (*usu. pejorative*) one who produces or aims to produce an abortion, often a criminal abortion, esp. one who makes a practice of so doing.

**abortive** /ə'bɔtɪv/, *adj.* **1.** failing to succeed; miscarrying: *an abortive scheme.* **2.** born prematurely. **3.** imperfectly developed; rudimentary. **4.** *Med.* **a.** producing or intended to produce abortion; abortifacient. **b.** acting to halt progress of a disease. **5.** *Pathol.* (of the course of a disease) short and mild without the commonly pronounced clinical symptoms. – **abortively,** *adv.* – **abortiveness,** *n.*

**aboulia** /ə'buliə/, *n.* the inability, usu. pathological, to make or to act on decisions. Also, **abulia.** [Gk *aboulía* ill counsel] – **aboulic,** *adj.*

**abound** /ə'baʊnd/, *v.i.* **1.** to be in great plenty; be very prevalent: *the discontent which abounds in the world.* **2.** to be rich (fol. by *in*): *some languages abound in figurative expressions.* **3.** to be filled; teem (fol. by *with*): *the ship abounds with rats.* [ME *abounde(n)*, from OF *abunder,* from L *abundāre*] – **abounding,** *adj.*

**about** /ə'baʊt/, *prep.* **1.** of; concerning; in regard to: *to talk about secrets.* **2.** connected with: *instructions about the work.* **3.** somewhere near or in: *he is about the house.* **4.** near; close to: *about my height.* **5.** on every side of; around: *the railing about the tower.* **6.** on or near (one's person): *they had lost all they had about them.* **7.** on the point of (fol. by an infinitive): *about to leave.* **8.** here and there in or on: *wander about the place.* **9.** concerned with; engaged in doing. *–adv.* **10.** near in time, number, degree, etc.; approximately: *about a hundred kilometres.* **11.** *Colloq.* nearly; almost: *about ready.* **12.** nearby: *he is somewhere about.* **13.** on every side in every direction: *look about.* **14.** half round; in the reverse direction: *to spin about.* **15.** *Naut.* on the opposite tack. **16.** to and fro; here and there: *move furniture about.* **17.** in rotation or succession; alternately: *turn about is fair play.* **18.** on the move: *be up and about.* **19.** *Archaic.* around. *–adj.* **20. up and about,** astir; active (after sleep). [ME; OE *abūtan*, var. of *onbūtan, on būtan* on the outside (of)]

**about-face** /əbaʊt-'feɪs/, *n., v.,* **-faced, -facing.** *–n.* **1.** a complete, sudden change in position, principle, attitude, etc; volte-face. **2.** →**about-turn** (def. 1). *–v.i.* **3.** to turn in the opposite direction.

**about-ship** /əbaʊt-'ʃɪp/, *v.i.,* **-shipped, -shipping.** *Naut.* to tack a ship.

**about-turn** /əbaʊt-'tɜn/, *n., v.,* **-turned, -turning.** *–n.* **1.** the military command to turn to the rear in a prescribed manner. **2.** →**about-face** (def. 1). *–v.i.* **3.** to turn in the opposite direction.

**above** /ə'bʌv/, *adv.* **1.** in or to a higher place; overhead: *the blue sky above.* **2.** higher in rank or power: *appeal to the courts above.* **3.** before in order, esp. in a book or writing: *from what has been said above.* **4.** in heaven. *–prep.* **5.** in or to a higher place than: *fly above the earth.* **6.** more in quantity or number than: *the weight is above a tonne.* **7.** superior to, in rank or authority. **8.** not capable of (an undesirable thought, action, etc.). **9.** in preference to: *to favour one child above another.* **10. above all,** principally; most important of all. **11. above oneself, a.** overexcited; elated. **b.** conceited; smug; self-satisfied. *–adj.* **12.** said, mentioned, or written above; foregoing: *the above explanation.* *–n.* **13. the above,** that which was said, mentioned, or written previously. [ME; OE *abufan*, from A-[1] + *bufan* above]

**aboveboard** /əbʌv'bɔd/, *adv.* **1.** openly; without tricks, deceit or disguise. *–adj.* **2.** open; frank: *open and aboveboard actions.* Also, (*esp. in predicative use*), **above board.**

**ab ovo** /æb 'oʊvoʊ/, from the beginning. [L *ab ōvō usque ad māla* from the beginning to the end (from the Roman habit of beginning a meal with egg and ending it with fruit)]

**abp,** Archbishop.

**abracadabra** /æbrəkə'dæbrə/, *n.* **1.** a mystical word used in incantations or written in triangular form as a charm on an amulet. **2.** any word charm or empty jingle of words. **3.** gibberish; nonsense. [L]

**abrachia** /eɪ'brækiə, ə'bræk-/, *n.* a total absence of arms due to a developmental anomaly.

**abradant** /ə'breɪdnt/, *adj.* **1.** abrasive. *–n.* **2.** an abrasive.

**abrade** /ə'breɪd/, *v.,* **abraded, abrading.** *–v.t.* **1.** to scrape off. *–v.i.* **2.** to wear down by friction. [L *abrādere* scrape off] – **abrader,** *n.*

**abranchiate** /eɪ'bræŋkiət, -eɪt/, *adj. Zool.* without gills. Also, **abranchial** /eɪ'bræŋkiəl/. [A-[6] + Gk *bránchia* gills + -ATE[1]]

**abrasion** /ə'breɪʒən/, *n.* **1.** the result of rubbing or abrading; an abraded spot or place. **2.** the act or process of abrading. [L *abrāsio* a scraping off]

**abrasive** /ə'breɪsɪv, -zɪv/, *n.* **1.** any material or substance used for grinding, polishing, lapping, etc., as emery or sand. *–adj.* **2.** tending to produce abrasion. **3.** (of a personality) irritating; tending to annoy.

**abreact** /ˌæbri'ækt/, *v.t.* to experience an abreaction.

**abreaction** /æbri'ækʃən/, *n.* the release of mental tension due to an unpleasant experience, by reliving the experience in speech and action in the presence of a psychoanalyst. [AB-[1] + REACTION. Cf. G *Abreagierung*]

**abreast** /ə'brɛst/, *adv.* **1.** side by side. **2.** alongside, in progress or attainment; equally advanced (fol. by *of* or *with*): *to keep abreast of the times in science.*

**abridge** /ə'brɪdʒ/, *v.t.,* **abridged, abridging. 1.** to shorten by condensation or omission, or both; rewrite or reconstruct on a smaller scale. **2.** to lessen; diminish. **3.** to deprive; cut off. [ME *abrege(n)*, from OF *abreger*, from L *abbreviāre* shorten] – **abridgeable, abridgable,** *adj.* – **abridged,** *adj.* – **abridger,** *n.*

**abridgment** /ə'brɪdʒmənt/, *n.* **1.** a condensation, as of a book; a reproduction of anything in reduced or condensed form. **2.** the act of abridging. **3.** the state of being abridged. Also, **abridgement.**

**abroad** /ə'brɔd/, *adv.* **1.** in or to a foreign country or countries: *to live abroad.* **2.** out of doors: *the owl ventures abroad at night.* **3.** astir; at large; in circulation: *rumours of disaster are abroad.* **4.** broadly; widely. **5.** wide of the truth. [ME *a brood*; from A-[1] + BROAD[1]. Cf. MnE *at large*]

**abrogate** /'æbrəgeɪt/, *v.t.,* **-gated, -gating.** to abolish summarily; annul by an authoritative act; repeal: *to abrogate a law.* [L *abrogātus*, pp.] – **abrogative,** *adj.* – **abrogator,** *n.* – **abrogable** /'æbrəgəbəl/, *adj.* – **abrogation** /æbrə'geɪʃən/, n.

**abrupt** /ə'brʌpt/, *adj.* **1.** terminating or changing suddenly: *an abrupt turn in a road.* **2.** sudden; unceremonious: *an abrupt entrance.* **3.** lacking in continuity; having sudden transitions from one subject to another: *an abrupt literary style.* **4.** brusque; discourteous: *an abrupt manner.* **5.** steep; precipitous: *an abrupt descent.* **6.** *Bot.* truncated. [L *abruptus*, pp., broken off] – **abruptly,** *adv.* – **abruptness,** *n.*

**abruption** /ə'brʌpʃən/, *n.* a sudden breaking off.

**abs-,** variant of **ab-** before *c, q, t,* as in *abscond, absterge.*

**abs.,** absolute.

**abscess** /'æbsəs/, *n.* a localised collection of pus in a cavity, caused by disintegration of body tissue, often accompanied by swelling and inflammation and usu. caused by bacteria. [L *abscessus* a going away] – **abscessed,** *adj.*

**abscind** /əb'sɪnd/, *v.t.* to cut off; sever.

**abscissa** /æb'sɪsə/, *n., pl.* **-scissas, -scissae** /-'sɪsi/. (in plane Cartesian coordinates) the *x*-coordinate of a point, i.e., its horizontal distance from the *y*-axis measured parallel to the *x*-axis. [L, short for *linea abscissa* line cut off]

abscissa: P, any point; AP or OB, abscissa of P; XX, axis of abscissa; YY axis of the ordinate

**abscission** /əb'sɪʒən/, *n.* the act of cutting off; sudden termination. [L *abscissio*]

**abscond** /æb'skɒnd, əb-/, *v.i.* **1.** to depart in a sudden and secret manner, esp. to avoid legal process. **2.** (formerly) of a convict, to escape. [L *abscondere* put away]

**absconder** /æb'skɒndə, əb-/, *n.* **1.** one who absconds. **2.** Also, **absconder into the woods, absconder from public labour.** (formerly) an escaped convict.

**abseil** /'æbseɪl/, *v.i. Mountaineering.* to lower oneself with a double rope down a rock face. [G *abseilen*]

**absence** /'æbsəns/, *n.* **1.** a state of being away: *speak ill of no-one in his absence.* **2.** a period of being away: *an absence of several weeks.* **3.** lack; non-existence: *the absence of proof.* [ME, from F, from L *absentia*]

**absence of mind,** *n.* inattention; absent-mindedness.

**absent** /'æbsənt/, *adj.*; /əb'sɛnt/, *v.* *–adj.* **1.** not in a certain place at a given time; away (opposed to *present*). **2.** lacking: *revenge is absent from his mind.* **3.** absentminded. *–v.t.* **4.** to take or keep (oneself) away: *to absent oneself from home.* [ME, from L *absens*, ppr.] – **absenter,** *n.* – **absentness,** *n.*

**absentee** /æbsən'ti/, *n.* **1.** one who is absent. **2.** one who habitually lives away from his country, place of work, etc. **3.**

Also, **absentee into the woods, absentee without leave.** (formerly) an escaped convict.

**absenteeism** /æbsən'tiɪzəm/, *n.* **1.** the practice of absenting oneself from duties, studies, employment, etc., often for inadequate reasons. **2.** the practice of living away from one's estates, country, employment, source of income, etc. **3.** (formerly) the state of being an absentee convict.

**absentee landlord** /ˌæbsənti 'lændlɔd/, *n.* an owner, investor, or incumbent who lives in a place, region, or country other than that from which he draws his income.

**absently** /'æbsəntli/, *adv.* inattentively.

**absent-minded** /æbsənt-'maɪndəd/, *adj.* forgetful of one's immediate surroundings; preoccupied. – **absent-mindedly,** *adv.* – **absent-mindedness,** *n.*

**absent without leave,** *adj.* away from military duties without permission, but without the intention of deserting. *Abbrev.:* A.W.L; *U.S.,* A.W.O.L.

**absinth** /'æbsɪnθ/, *n.* **1.** a strong, bitter, green-coloured, aromatic liqueur made with wormwood, anise, and other herbs, having a pronounced liquorice flavour. **2.** →**wormwood** (def. 2). Also, **absinthe.** [F, from L *absinthium,* from Gk *apsínthion* wormwood] – **absinthial** /əb'sɪnθiəl/, **absinthian,** *adj.*

**absolute** /'æbsəlut/, *adj.* **1.** free from imperfection; complete; perfect: *absolute liberty.* **2.** not mixed; pure. **3.** free from restriction or limitation; unqualified: *absolute command.* **4.** arbitrary or despotic: *an absolute monarchy.* **5.** viewed independently; not comparative or relative: *absolute position.* **6.** positive: *absolute in opinion.* **7.** *Gram.* **a.** syntactically independent; not grammatically connected with any other element in the sentence, as *It being Sunday* in *It being Sunday, the family went to church.* **b.** (of a transitive verb) used with no object expressed, as *to give* in *the collectors for the charity asked him to give.* **c.** (of an adjective) having its noun understood, not expressed, as *poor* in *the poor are always with us.* **d.** characterising the phonetic or phonemic form of a word or phrase occurring by itself, not influenced by surrounding forms (distinguished from *sandhi form*). Example: 'not' in 'is not' as opposed to 'isn't', or 'will' in 'they will' as opposed to 'they'll'. **8.** *Physics.* **a.** as nearly independent as possible of arbitrary standards or of properties of special substances or systems: *absolute zero of temperature.* **b.** pertaining to a system of units based on some primary units, esp. units of length, mass, and time: *c.g.s. units are absolute units.* **c.** pertaining to a measurement based on an absolute zero or unit: *absolute pressure.* **9.** *Law.* (of a court order, decree, etc.) unconditional; having full effect immediately (opposed to *nisi*). **10. the Absolute** (*sometimes l.c.*). *Metaphys.* **a.** that which is free from any restriction, or is unconditioned; the ultimate ground of all things. **b.** that which is independent of some or all relations. **c.** that which is perfect or complete. [ME, from L *absolūtus,* pp., loosened from] – **absoluteness,** *n.*

**absolute alcohol** /– 'ælkəhɒl/, *n.* ethyl alcohol containing not more than one per cent by weight of water.

**absolute altitude** /– 'æltətjud/, *n.* the vertical height of an aircraft directly above the surface over which it is flying.

**absolute emancipation** /– əmænsə'peɪʃən/, *n.* →**absolute pardon.**

**absolute humidity** /– hju'mɪdəti/, *n.* →**humidity** (def. 2c).

**absolutely** /'æbsəˌlutli/; *emphatic* /ˌæbsə'lutli/, *adv.* **1.** completely; wholly. **2.** positively. **3.** *Colloq.* yes; certainly. **4.** (of transitive verbs) without an object.

**absolute majority** /ˌæbsəlut mə'dʒɒrəti/, *n.* the number by which votes cast for the leading candidate exceed those cast for all other candidates. Cf. **majority** (def. 3).

**absolute music** /– 'mjuzɪk/, *n.* music whose patterns in sound are not intended to illustrate, or describe (opposed to *program music*).

**absolute pardon** /– 'padn/, *n.* (formerly) a pardon granted to a convict, giving him full restitution of legal rights.

**absolute pitch** /– 'pɪtʃ/, *n.* the ability to sing or recognise the pitch of a note by ear. Also, **perfect pitch.**

**absoluter** /æbsə'lutə/, *n. Bowls.* a bowl which wins the shot when other bowls are very near the jack.

**absolute temperature** /ˌæbsəlut 'tɛmprətʃə/, *n.* thermodynamic temperature; temperature measured in kelvins.

**absolute value** /– 'vælju/, *n.* (of a number) magnitude.

**absolute zero** /– 'zɪəroʊ/, *n.* the lowest possible temperature which the nature of matter admits, or that temperature at which the particles whose motion constitutes heat would be at rest, being defined as **zero kelvin** −273.16 degrees Celsius (or −459.69 degrees Fahrenheit). Cf. **absolute** (def. 8a).

**absolution** /æbsə'luʃən/, *n.* **1.** the act of absolving; release from consequences, obligations, or penalites. **2.** the state of being absolved. **3.** *Rom. Cath. Theol.* **a.** a remission of sin or of the punishment due to sin, which the priest, on the ground of authority received from Christ, makes in the sacrament of penance. **b.** the formula declaring such remission. **4.** *Prot. Theol.* a declaration or assurance of divine forgiveness to penitent believers, made after confession of sins. [L *absolūtio* an acquittal; replacing ME *absolucioun,* from F]

**absolutism** /'æbsəlutˌɪzəm/, *n.* **1.** the principle or the exercise of absolute power in government. **2.** *Philos.* the doctrine of an absolute or non-relative being. – **absolutist,** *n.* – **absolutistic,** *adj.*

**absolutory** /æbsə'lutəri/, *adj.* giving absolution.

**absolve** /əb'zɒlv/, *v.t.,* **-solved, -solving.** **1.** to free from the consequences or penalties of actions (fol. by *from*): *to absolve one from blame.* **2.** to set free or release, as from some duty, obligation, or responsibility (fol. by *from*): *absolved from his oath.* **3.** to grant pardon for. **4.** *Eccles.* **a.** to grant or pronounce remission of sins to. **b.** to remit (sin). **c.** to declare (censure, as excommunication) removed. [L *absolvere* loosen from] – **absolvable,** *adj.* – **absolvent,** *adj., n.* – **absolver,** *n.*

**absonant** /'æbsənənt/, *adj.* **1.** discordant (fol. by *from* or *to*). **2.** abhorrent; unnatural; incompatible (fol. by *from* or *to*). [AB-[1] + L *sonans,* ppr., sounding]

**absorb** /əb'sɔb, -'zɔb/, *v.t.* **1.** to swallow up the identity or individuality of: *the empire absorbed all the small states.* **2.** to engross wholly: *absorbed in a book.* **3.** to suck up or drink in (liquids): *a sponge absorbs water.* **4.** to assimilate (ideas, knowledge, etc.). **5.** to take up or receive in by chemical or molecular action: *carbonic acid is formed when water absorbs carbon dioxide.* **6.** to take in without echo or recoil: *to absorb sound.* **7.** *Obs.* to swallow up. [L *absorbēre* absorb] – **absorbable,** *adj.* – **absorbability** /əbˌsɔbə'bɪləti, -ˌzɔb-/, *n.*

**absorbed** /əb'sɔbd, -'zɔbd/, *adj.* engrossed; preoccupied. – **absorbedly,** *adv.* – **absorbedness,** *n.*

**absorbed dose** /– 'doʊs/, *n.* the amount of energy imparted by nuclear (or ionising) radiation to unit mass of absorbing material. The unit is the **rad.**

**absorbefacient** /əbsɔbə'feɪʃənt, -zɔb-/, *adj.* **1.** causing absorption. –*n.* **2.** a drug or other substance which causes absorption. [L *absorbē(re)* absorb + -FACIENT]

**absorbent** /əb'sɔbənt, -'zɔ-/, *adj.* **1.** capable of absorbing; performing the function of absorption. –*n.* **2.** a thing that absorbs. – **absorbency,** *n.*

**absorber** /əb'sɔbə, -'zɔ-/, *n.* **1.** one who or that which absorbs. **2.** *Nucleonics.* a material which will capture neutrons without generating others.

**absorbing** /əb'sɔbɪŋ, -'zɔ-/, *adj.* engrossing: *an absorbing pursuit.* – **absorbingly,** *adv.*

**absorption** /əb'sɔpʃən, -'zɔp-/, *n.* **1.** assimilation: *the absorption of small farms by a bigger one.* **2.** the sucking up or drawing in of a liquid by a porous substance. **3.** passage of substances to the blood, lymph, and cells, as from the alimentary canal (e.g., digested foods) or from the tissues. **4.** a taking in or reception by molecular or chemical action: *absorption of gases, light, etc.* **5.** preoccupation. [L *absorptio*] – **absorptive,** *adj.* – **absorptiveness,** *n.*

**absorption bands** /'– bændz/, *n.pl.* the dark bands in an absorption spectrum. Also, **absorption lines.**

**absorption factor** /'– fæktə/, *n.* a constant of any material giving its absorption power for light passing through it. Also, **absorption coefficient.**

**absorption spectrum** /– 'spɛktrəm/, *n.* a spectrum containing dark lines or bands which is obtained when the light from a source, itself giving a continuous spectrum, passes through a medium. The dark lines or bands are characteristic of the material of the medium. See **emission spectrum.**

**absorptivity** /ˌæbsɔp'tɪvəti, -zɔp-/, *n.* the ratio between the radiation absorbed by a surface and the total energy striking the surface.

**abstain** /əb'steɪn/, *v.i.* **1.** to refrain voluntarily, esp. from doing or enjoying something (fol. by *from*): *abstain from drinking intoxicants.* **2.** to refrain deliberately from casting one's vote. [ME *absteine(n)*, from F *abstenir*, replacing OF *astenir*, from L *abstinēre*] – **abstainer,** *n.*

**abstemious** /əb'stimiəs/, *adj.* **1.** sparing in diet; moderate in the use of food and drink; temperate. **2.** characterised by abstinence: *an abstemious life.* **3.** sparing: *an abstemious diet.* [L *abstēmius*] – **abstemiously,** *adv.* – **abstemiousness,** *n.*

**abstention** /əb'stɛnʃən/, *n.* **1.** a holding off or refraining; abstinence from action. **2.** a deliberate withholding of one's vote. [L *abstentus*, pp., abstained + -ION] – **abstentious,** *adj.*

**abstergent** /əb'stɜdʒənt/, *adj.* **1.** cleansing; detergent. *–n.* **2.** a cleansing agent; a detergent, as soap. [L *abstergēre* wipe off]

**abstinence** /'æbstənəns/, *n.* **1.** forbearance from any indulgence of appetite, esp. from the drinking of alcohol: *total abstinence.* **2.** self-restraint; forbearance. **3.** *Eccles.* the refraining from certain kinds of food on certain days, as from meat on Fridays. [ME *abstynens*, from L *abstinentia*] Also, **abstinency.** – **abstinent,** *adj.* – **abstinently,** *adv.*

**abstr.,** abstract.

**abstract** /'æbstrækt/, *adj., n.;* /əb'strækt/ *for defs 10-13,* /'æbstrækt/ *for def. 14, v. –adj.* **1.** conceived apart from matter and from special cases: *an abstract number.* **2.** theoretical; not applied: *abstract science.* **3.** difficult to understand; abstruse: *abstract speculations.* **4.** of or pertaining to abstract art. *–n.* **5.** a summary of a statement, document, speech, etc. **6.** that which concentrates in itself the essential qualities of anything more extensive or more general, or of several things; essence. **7.** an idea or term considered apart from some material basis or object. **8. the abstract,** the ideal. **9. in the abstract,** without reference to special circumstances or particular applications. *–v.t.* **10.** to draw or take away; remove. **11.** to withdraw or divert (the attention). **12.** *Colloq.* to steal. **13.** to consider as a general object apart from special circumstances: *to abstract the notions of time, of space, or of matter.* **14.** to summarise. [L *abstractus*, pp., drawn away] – **abstracter** /əb'stræktə/, *n.* – **abstractly,** *adv.* – **abstractness,** *n.*

**abstract art** /– 'at/, *n.* a 20th century concept of art, which rejects the function of art as portraying perceived reality; non-representational art.

**abstracted** /əb'stræktəd/, *adj.* **1.** lost in thought; preoccupied. **2.** withdrawn; removed. – **abstractedly,** *adv.* – **abstractedness,** *n.*

**abstract expressionism** /,æbstrækt ək'sprɛʃənɪzəm/, *n.* abstract art of the post 1950s, mainly of U.S. artists, characterised by rejection of traditional styles and techniques, by non-figurative, non-formal elements and by dynamic qualities of spontaneity and improvisation.

**abstraction** /əb'strækʃən/, *n.* **1.** an abstract or general idea or term. **2.** an idea which cannot lead to any practical result; something visionary. **3.** the act of considering something as a general object apart from special circumstances. **4.** the act of taking away or separating; withdrawal: *the sensation of cold is due to the abstraction of heat from our bodies.* **5.** absent-mindedness; reverie. **6.** *Fine Arts.* **a.** a work of art (**pure abstraction**) using lines, shapes, and colours without reference to natural objects. **b.** a work of art (**near abstraction**) retaining representational characteristics but expressing them through geometrical or generalised forms. [L *abstractio*]

**abstractive** /əb'stræktɪv/, *adj.* **1.** having the power of abstracting. **2.** pertaining to an epitome or summary.

**abstract music** /æbstrækt 'mjuzɪk/, *n.* →**absolute music.**

**abstract noun** /– 'naʊn/, *n.* **1.** a noun having an abstract (as opposed to *concrete*) meaning, as *dread.* **2.** a noun made with an abstract suffix, as *witness.*

**abstract of title,** *n.* a chronological statement of the instruments and events, traced back to the original grant of title, under which a person is currently entitled to property; not applicable to property held under Torrens Title, title to which depends upon registration.

**abstruse** /əb'strus/, *adj.* **1.** difficult to understand; esoteric: *abstruse questions.* **2.** *Obs.* hidden. [L *abstrūsus*, pp., concealed] – **abstrusely,** *adv.* – **abstruseness,** *n.*

**absurd** /əb'sɜd, -'zɜd/, *adj.* **1.** contrary to reason or common sense; obviously false or foolish; logically contradictory; ridiculous: *an absurd statement.* **2.** comical; laughable. [L *absurdus*] – **absurdly,** *adv.* – **absurdness,** *n.*

**absurdity** /əb'sɜdəti, -'zɜd-/, *n., pl.* **-ties. 1.** the state or quality of being absurd. **2.** something absurd.

**abt.,** about.

**abulia** /ə'buliə/, *n.* →**aboulia.**

**abundance** /ə'bʌndəns/, *n.* **1.** an overflowing quantity or supply: *an abundance of grain.* **2.** overflowing fullness: *abundance of the heart.* **3.** affluence; wealth. **4.** *Cards.* (in solo whist) a call of nine tricks. **5.** *Physics.* the ratio of the number of atoms of a certain isotope in a mixture of isotopes to the total number of atoms present, often expressed as a percentage. [ME, from OF, from L *abundantia*]

**abundant** /ə'bʌndənt/, *adj.* **1.** present in great quantity; fully sufficient: *an abundant supply.* **2.** possessing in great quantity; abounding (fol. by *in*): *a river abundant in salmon.* [ME, from OF, from L *abundans*, ppr.] – **abundantly,** *adv.*

**ab urbe condita** /æb ,ɜbi 'kɒndɪtə/, from the founding of the city (Rome, c. 753 B.C.). *Abbrev.:* A.U.C. The year 360 A.U.C. would be the 360th year after the founding of Rome. [L]

**abusage** /ə'bjusɪdʒ/, *n.* improper use of words; unidiomatic or ungrammatical language.

**abuse** /ə'bjuz/, *v.,* **abused, abusing;** /ə'bjus/, *n. –v.t.* **1.** to use wrongly or improperly; misuse: *to abuse authority, to abuse a confidence.* **2.** to do wrong to; act injuriously towards: *to abuse one's wife.* **3.** to revile; malign. **4.** *Archaic.* to deceive. *–n.* **5.** wrong or improper use; misuse: *the abuse of privileges.* **6.** insulting language. **7.** ill treatment of a person. **8.** a corrupt practice or custom; an offence: *the abuses of bad government.* **9.** *Archaic.* deception. [F *abus*, from L *abūsus* a wasting, misuse] – **abuser,** *n.*

**abusive** /ə'bjusɪv/, *adj.* **1.** using harsh words or ill treatment: *an abusive author.* **2.** characterised by or containing abuse: *an abusive satire.* **3.** wrongly used; corrupt: *an abusive exercise of power.* – **abusively,** *adv.* – **abusiveness,** *n.*

**abut** /ə'bʌt/, *v.i.,* **abutted, abutting.** to be adjacent to (oft. fol. by *on, upon,* or *against*): *this piece of land abuts upon a street.* [ME *abutte(n)*, OF: coalescence of *abouter* join end to end (*a-* A-[5] + *bout* end) and *abuter* make contact with one end (*a-* A-[5] + *but* end)] – **abuttal,** *n.*

**abutilon** /ə'bjutələn/, *n.* any plant of the family Malvaceae, genus *Abutilon*; Chinese lantern. [NL, from Ar. *aubūtīlūn*]

**abutment** /ə'bʌtmənt/, *n.* **1.** the state of being adjacent to something. **2.** that on which something abuts, as the part of a pier which receives the thrust of an arch; a part for sustaining or resisting pressure, as the part of a bridge pier exposed to the force of the current or of floating ice, or the structure supporting the shore ends of a bridge and restraining the embankment which supports the approaches. **3.** the place where projecting parts meet; junction.

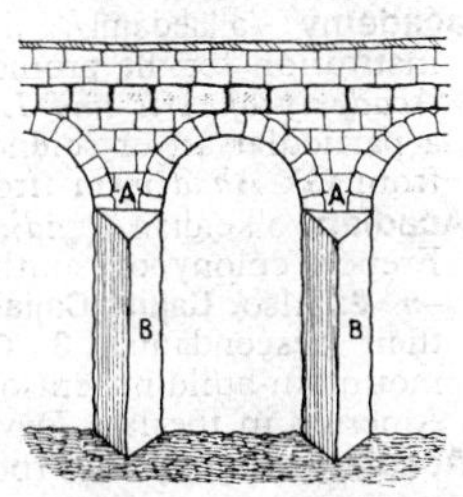

abutment: A, arch abutment; B, current abutment

**abuzz** /ə'bʌz/, *adj.* buzzing.

**abysm** /ə'bɪzəm/, *n. Poetic.* an abyss. [ME *abi(s)me*, from OF, from VL **abyssimus*, superlative of L *abyssus* ABYSS]

**abysmal** /ə'bɪzməl/, *adj.* **1.** of or like an abyss. **2.** immeasurable: *abysmal ignorance.* **3.** immeasurably bad: *an abysmal performance.* – **abysmally,** *adv.*

**abyss** /ə'bɪs/, *n.* **1.** a bottomless gulf; any deep, immeasurable space. **2.** anything profound and unfathomable: *the abyss of time.* **3.** the bottomless pit; hell. [L *abyssus*, from Gk *ábyssos* without bottom]

**abyssal** /ə'bɪsəl/, *adj.* **1.** abysmal. **2.** of or pertaining to the lowest depths of the ocean.

**Abyssinia** /æbə'sɪniə/, *n.* →**Ethiopia.** – **Abyssinian,** *adj.*

**Abyssinian cat** /,æbəsɪniən 'kæt/, *n.* any of a breed of small, slender cats, of African origin, having short greyish or brown hair, darker at the tips and a black stripe along the spine.

**ac-,** variant of **ad-** (by assimilation) before *c* and *qu*, as in *accede, acquire,* etc.

**-ac,** an adjective suffix meaning 'pertaining to', as in *elegiac, cardiac.* [representing Gk adj. suffix *-akos,* whence L *-acus,* F -acque]

**ac.,** acre.

**a.c.,** *Elect.* alternating current.

**Ac,** *Chem.* actinium.

**A/C,** **1.** account. **2.** account current.

**A.C.,** **1.** Companion of the Order of Australia. **2.** alternating current.

**acacia** /əˈkeɪʃə, əˈkeɪsiə/, *n.* **1.** any tree or shrub of the mimosaceous genus *Acacia,* native in warm regions; usu. known as wattle in Australia. **2.** any of certain related plants. **3.** gum arabic. [L, from Gk *akakía* a thorny Egyptian tree]

**Acad.,** **1.** Academic **2.** Academy.

**Academe** /ækəˈdim/, *n. Poetic.* (*oft. l.c.*) **1.** any place of instruction. **2.** the world of scholars; academic life: *the groves of Academe.*

**academic** /ækəˈdɛmɪk/, *adj.* **1.** pertaining to an advanced institution of learning, as a college, university, or academy; relating to higher education. **2.** pertaining to those university subjects which are concerned with the refinement of the mind rather than the learning of skills (opposed to *technical*). **3.** theoretical; not practical. **4.** too much concerned with purely intellectual interests. **5.** conforming to set rules and traditions; conventional. *–n.* **6.** a member of a college or university. **7.** (*pl.*) discussions, arguments, etc., of purely theoretical interest. – **academically,** *adv.*

**academicals** /ækəˈdɛmɪkəlz/, *n. pl.* →**academic dress.**

**academic dress** /ˌækədɛmɪk ˈdrɛs/, *n.* formal university dress, as cap and gown, and sometimes dark suit, etc.

**academic freedom** /– ˈfridəm/, *n.* freedom of a teacher to discuss social, economic, or political problems without interference from university or public officials.

**academician** /əkædəˈmɪʃən/, *n.* a member of a society for promoting literature, art, or science.

**academicism** /ækəˈdɛməsɪzəm/, *n.* traditionalism or conventionalism in art, literature, etc. Also, **academism.**

**academic year** /ˌækədɛmɪk ˈjɪə/, *n.* that part of the calendar year during which the schools, universities, etc. are in session, starting in February or March, but in the Northern Hemisphere in September or October.

**academism** /əˈkædəmɪzəm/, *n.* **1.** →**academicism. 2.** *Philos.* the doctrines of the school founded by Plato.

**academy** /əˈkædəmi/, *n., pl.* **-mies. 1.** an association or institution for the promotion of literature, science, or art: *the Academy of Arts and Letters.* **2.** a school for instruction in a particular art or science: *a military academy.* [L *acadēmia,* from Gk *Akadēmeia* (from *Akádēmos,* an Attic hero)]

**Acadian** /əˈkeɪdiən/, *adj.* **1.** of or pertaining to Acadia, former French colony of south-eastern Canada, or its inhabitants. *–n.* **2.** Also, **Cajun, Cajian.** one of the early French settlers or their descendants. **3.** *Geol.* of or pertaining to the major mountain-building episode which occurred in eastern North America in the late Devonian period.

**Acadian orogeny** /– əˈrɒdʒəni/, *n.* Late Devonian diastrophism.

**acajou** /ˈækəʒu/, *n.* a kind of mahogany. [F *acajou* cashew]

**acalypha** /əˈkæləfə/, *n.* any herb or shrub of the tropical and subtropical genus *Acalypha,* many of which are grown as ornamentals, as *A. wilkesiana* grown for its coloured and often variegated leaves.

**acanthaceous** /ˌækænˈθeɪʃəs/, *adj.* **1.** having prickly growths. **2.** belonging to the Acanthaceae or Acanthus family of plants.

**acantho-,** *Bot.* a word element meaning 'thorn', or 'thorny'. Also, *before vowels,* **acanth-.** [Gk *akantho-,* combining form of *ákantha* thorn]

**acanthocephalan** /əkænθoʊˈsɛfələn/, *n.* any of the worms belonging to a phylum or class of internal parasitic worms, Acanthocephala, having a protrusile proboscis covered with recurved hooks and a hollow body without digestive tract, found in the intestine of vertebrates.

**acanthodian** /ˌækænˈθoʊdiən/, *n.* a spiny-finned sharklike fish of the late Silurian and Devonian periods.

**acanthoid** /əˈkænθɔɪd/, *adj.* spiny; spinous.

**acanthopterygian** /ˌækænˌθɒptəˈrɪdʒiən/, *adj.* **1.** belonging or pertaining to Acanthopterygii, the group of fishes with spiny fins, as the bass and perch. *–n.* **2.** an acanthopterygian fish. [ACANTHO- + Gk *pterýgion* fin + -AN]

**acanthous** /əˈkænθəs/, *adj.* spinous.

**acanthus** /əˈkænθəs/, *n., pl.* **-thuses, -thi** /-θaɪ/. **1.** any herb of the acanthaceous genus *Acanthus,* of the Mediterranean area and tropical Africa and Asia and nearby islands, extending into Australia, having large spiny or toothed leaves; bear's-breech. **2.** an architectural ornament derived from the shape of the leaves of certain southern European plants of this genus, as in the capital of the Corinthian column. [L, from Gk *ákanthos* a thorny tree] – **acanthine,** *adj.*

acanthus: architectural ornament

**a cappella** /a kəˈpɛlə/, *adj., adv.* **1.** without instrumental accompaniment. **2.** in the style of church or chapel music. Also, **alla cappella** /alə kəˈpɛlə/. [It.]

**a capriccio** /a kəˈprɪtʃioʊ/, *adv.* (a musical direction) freely; at the whim of the performer. [It.: according to caprice]

**acariasis** /ækəˈraɪəsəs/, *n.* **1.** infestation with acarids, esp. mites. **2.** a skin disease caused by such infestation. [Gk *akar(í)* mite + -IASIS]

**acaricide** /əˈkærəsaɪd/, *n.* **1.** a substance or preparation used for killing acarids. **2.** the killing of acarids. [ACARI(D) + -CIDE]

**acarid** /ˈækərɪd/, *n.* any animal belonging to the Acari (or Acarida), an order of arachnids including the mites, ticks, etc. [Gk *akar(í)* mite + -ID²]

**acaridan** /əˈkærədən/, *adj.* **1.** belonging to the acarids. *–n.* **2.** an acarid.

**acaroid¹** /ˈækərɔɪd/, *n.* a yellow or reddish resin which exudes from the trunk of the Australian grasstree of the genus *Xanthorrhoea,* and which is used in varnishes, lacquers, and in the manufacture of paper. Also, **accaroid.**

**acaroid²** /ˈækərɔɪd/, *adj.* resembling an acarid.

**acarpellous** /eɪˈkapələs/, *adj. Bot.* having no carpels. Also, *U.S.,* **acarpelous.**

**acarpous** /eɪˈkapəs/, *adj. Bot.* not producing fruit; sterile; barren. [Gk *ákarpos* without fruit]

**acarus** /ˈækərəs/, *n., pl.* **-ri** /-ri/. an animal of the genus *Acarus;* a mite. [NL, from Gk *akarí*]

**acatalectic** /ˌeɪkætəˈlɛktɪk/, *adj.* **1.** not catalectic; complete. *–n.* **2.** a verse having the complete number of syllables in the last foot. See example under **catalectic.**

**acaudal** /eɪˈkɔdl/, *adj. Zool.* tailless. Also, **acaudate** /eɪˈkɔdeɪt/.

**acaulescent** /eɪkɔˈlɛsənt/, *adj.* not caulescent; stemless; without visible stem. Also, **acauline** /eɪˈkɔlaɪn/, **acaulose** /eɪˈkɔloʊs/, **acaulous** /eɪˈkɔləs/.

**acc.,** **1.** accompaniment. **2.** accompanied (by). **3.** according (to). **4.** account. **5.** accusative. **6.** Also, **accom.** accommodation.

**accede** /əkˈsid/, *v.i.,* **-ceded, -ceding. 1.** to give consent; agree; yield: *to accede to terms.* **2.** to attain, as an office or dignity; arrive at (fol. by *to*): *to accede to the throne.* **3.** *Internat. Law.* to become a party (*to*), as a nation signing a treaty. [L *accēdere* go to] – **accedence,** *n.* – **acceder.** *n.*

**accelerando** /əksɛləˈrændoʊ, æk-/, *adv.* (a musical direction) gradually increasing in speed. *Abbrev.*: accel. [It.] – **accelerando,** *n.*

**accelerant** /əkˈsɛlərənt, æk-/, *n.* →**accelerator** (def. 2).

**accelerate** /əkˈsɛləreɪt, æk-/, *v.,* **-rated, -rating.** *–v.t.* **1.** to cause to move or advance faster: *accelerate growth.* **2.** to help to bring about more speedily than would otherwise have been the case: *to accelerate the fall of a government.* **3.** *Physics.* to change the magnitude and or direction of the velocity of a body. *–v.i.* **4.** to become faster; increase in speed. [L *accelerātus,* pp.]

**acceleration** /əksɛləˈreɪʃən, æk-/, *n.* **1.** the act of accelerating; increase of speed or velocity. **2.** *Physics.* **a.** change in velocity. **b.** a measure of the rate of change of velocity. **3.** *Law.* the falling into possession of an interest in remainder or expectancy sooner than normal because the preceding interest is void or comes to an end.

**accelerative** /ək'sɛlərətɪv, æk-/, *adj.* tending to accelerate; increasing the velocity (*of*). Also, **acceleratory.**

**accelerator** /ək'sɛləreɪtə, æk-/, *n.* **1.** one that accelerates. **2.** *Chem.* any substance that increases the speed of a chemical change. **3.** *Motor Vehicles.* a device which increases the speed of the machine by opening and closing the throttle, esp. one operated by the foot. **4.** *Anat.* any muscle, nerve, or activating substance that quickens a movement. **5.** *Physics.* a device for producing high-energy particles, as a cyclotron.

**accelerator principle** /'– prɪnsəpəl/, *n.* an economic principle which states that an increase (or decrease) in the rate of consumer demand will cause an acceleration (or deceleration) in the rate of investment in machines to produce those consumer goods.

**acceleratory** /ək'sɛlərətri, æk-/, *adj.* →**accelerative.**

**accelerometer** /əksɛlə'rɒmətə, æk-/, *n.* an instrument for measuring acceleration, used in aircraft.

**accent** /'æksɛnt/, *n.;* /æk'sɛnt/, *v.* *–n.* **1.** the distinctive character of a vowel or syllable determined by its degree or pattern of stress or musical tone. **2.** any one of the degrees or patterns of stress used in a particular language as essential features of vowels, syllables, or words: *primary accent, falling accent, sentence accent.* **3.** a mark indicating stress, musical tone, or vowel quality. In English the accent mark (') is sometimes used to indicate a syllable which is stressed. French has three accent marks, the acute (´), the grave (`), and the circumflex (ˆ), which indicate vowel quality (or sometimes merely distinguish meaning, as *la* 'the' and *là* 'there'). **4.** *Pros.* **a.** regularly recurring stress. **b.** a mark indicating stress or some other distinction in pronunciation or value. **5.** any one of the musical tones or melodies used in a particular language as essential features of vowels or syllables. **6.** characteristic style of pronunciation: *foreign accent.* **7.** *Music.* **a.** stress or emphasis given to certain notes. **b.** a mark denoting this. **c.** stress or emphasis regularly recurring as a feature of rhythm. **8.** *Maths, etc.* a mark, or one of a number of marks, placed after a letter or figure **a.** to distinguish similar quantities which differ in value, as in b′, b″, b‴, etc. (called *b prime* or *b dash, b double prime* or *b double dash*, etc., respectively). **b.** to indicate a particular unit or measure, as feet (′) or inches (″): 5′3″, meaning *5 feet, 3 inches;* or as minutes (′) or seconds (″) of time or a degree: 18′25″, meaning *18 minutes, 25 seconds.* **c.** to indicate the operation of differentiation in calculus. **9.** words or tones expressive of some emotion. **10.** (*pl.*) *Poetic.* words; language. **11.** distinctive character or tone. *–v.t.* **12.** to pronounce (a vowel, syllable, or word) with one of the distinctive accents of the language, esp. with a stress accent. **13.** to mark with a written accent or accents: *to accent a word to indicate its pronunciation.* **14.** *Chiefly U.S.* to emphasise; accentuate. [L *accentus* tone]

**accentor** /ək'sɛntə/, *n.* a large hedge-sparrow, *Prunella collaris,* with a black-spotted white throat, of European mountainous areas.

**accentual** /ək'sɛntʃuəl/, *adj.* **1.** pertaining to accent; rhythmical. **2.** *Pros.* of, pertaining to, or characterised by syllabic accent (distinguished from *quantitative*). – **accentually,** *adv.*

**accentuate** /ək'sɛntʃueɪt/, *v.t.,* **-ated, -ating. 1.** to emphasise. **2.** to mark or pronounce with an accent. [ML *accentuātus,* pp.] – **accentuation** /əkˌsɛntʃu'eɪʃən/, *n.*

**accept** /ək'sɛpt/, *v.t.* **1.** to take or receive (something offered); receive with approval or favour: *his proposal was accepted.* **2.** to admit and agree to; accede or assent to: *to accept a treaty, an excuse, etc.* **3.** to take with formal acknowledgment of responsibility or consequences: *to accept office.* **4.** to accommodate oneself to: *accept the situation.* **5.** to believe: *to accept a fact.* **6.** to receive as to meaning; understand. **7.** *Comm.* to acknowledge, by signature, as calling for payment, and thus to agree to pay, as a draft. **8.** (in a deliberative body) to receive as an adequate performance of the duty with which an officer or a committee has been charged; receive for further action: *the report of the committee was accepted.* *–v.i.* **9.** *Archaic.* to accept an invitation, gift, position, etc. (fol. by *of*). [ME *accept(en),* from L *acceptāre,* frequentative of *accipere* take] – **accepter,** *n.*

**acceptable** /ək'sɛptəbəl/, *adj.* **1.** capable or worthy of being accepted. **2.** pleasing to the receiver; agreeable; welcome. – **acceptability** /əksɛptə'bɪləti/, **acceptableness,** *n.* – **acceptably,** *adv.*

**acceptance** /ək'sɛptəns/, *n.* **1.** the act of taking or receiving something offered. **2.** favourable reception; favour. **3.** the act of assenting or believing: *acceptance of a theory.* **4.** the fact or state of being accepted or acceptable. **5.** *Comm.* **a.** an engagement to pay an order, draft, or bill of exchange when it becomes due, as by the person on whom it is drawn. **b.** an order, draft, etc., which a person has accepted as calling for payment and has thus promised to pay: *a trade acceptance.* **6.** (*pl.*) *Horseracing.* list of horses for which all dues have been paid to enter a particular race.

**acceptance house** /'– haʊs/, *n.* a bank which specialises in handling bills of exchange for foreign trade.

**acceptant** /ək'sɛptənt/, *adj.* accepting; receptive.

**acceptation** /ˌæksɛp'teɪʃən/, *n.* **1.** favourable regard. **2.** belief. **3.** usual or received meaning.

**accepted** /ək'sɛptəd/, *adj.* customary; established; approved.

**acceptor** /ək'sɛptə/, *n.* **1.** one who or that which accepts. **2.** *Electronics.* a minute impurity introduced into a semiconductor to cause hole conduction. **3.** a horse which has qualified to enter in a race.

**access** /'æksɛs/, *n.* **1.** the act or privilege of coming to; admittance; approach: *to gain access to a person.* **2.** way, means, or opportunity of approach. **3.** *Theol.* approach to God through Jesus Christ. **4.** *Law.* **a.** the opportunity of marital intercourse between husband and wife. **b.** a parent's right to see a child. **5.** an attack, as of disease. **6.** a sudden outburst of passion. **7.** accession. **8.** →**access time.** *–v.t.* **9.** *Computers.* to locate and provide means of getting (information) out of or into a computer storage. *–adj.* **10.** *Radio, T.V., etc.* run by special-interest or minority groups who wish to transmit their own programs.

**accessary** /ək'sɛsəri/, *n.* →**accessory** (def. 3).

**accessible** /ək'sɛsəbəl/, *adj.* **1.** easy of access; approachable. **2.** attainable: *accessible evidence.* **3.** open to the influence of (fol. by *to*): *accessible to bribery.* – **accessibility** /əksɛsə'bɪləti/, *n.* – **accessibly,** *adv.*

**accession** /ək'sɛʃən/, *n.* **1.** the act of coming into the possession of a right, dignity, office, etc.: *accession to the throne.* **2.** an increase by something added: *an accession of territory.* **3.** something added. **4.** *Law.* addition to property by growth or improvement. **5.** consent: *accession to a demand.* **6.** *Internat. Law.* formal acceptance of a treaty, international convention, or other agreement between states. **7.** the act of coming near; approach. *–v.t.* **8.** to record in the order of acquisition, listing essential data, as author, title of a book, etc. [L *accessio* increase] – **accessional,** *adj.*

**accessorise** /ək'sɛsəraɪz/, *v.t.,* **-rised, -rising.** to furnish with accessories.

**accessory** /ək'sɛsəri/, *n., pl.* **-ries,** *adj.* *–n.* **1.** a subordinate part or object; something added or attached for convenience, attractiveness, etc., such as a spotlight, heater, driving mirror, etc., for a vehicle. **2.** (*pl.*) the additional parts of an outfit, as shoes, gloves, hat, handbag, etc. **3.** Also, **accessary.** *Law.* he who is not the chief actor at a felony, nor present at its perpetration, but yet is in some way concerned therein, (either before or after the fact committed). *–adj.* **4.** contributing to a general effect; subsidiary: *accessory sounds in music.* **5.** *Law.* giving aid as an accessory. **6.** *Geol.* denoting minerals present in relatively small amounts in a rock, and not mentioned in its definition, as zircon in granite. [LL *accessōrius*] – **accessorial** /æksɛ'sɔriəl/, *adj.* – **accesssorily,** *adv.* – **accessoriness,** *n.*

**access road** /'æksɛs roʊd/, *n.* a road which allows entry to a group of residences, a rural property, etc.

**access time** /'æksɛs taɪm/, *n.* the time taken to reach information stored in a computer. Also, **access.**

**acciaccatura** /əkætʃə'tjurə/, *n.* **1.** a short appoggiatura. **2.** a short grace-note a semitone above or below, and struck just before (or sometimes simultaneously with) a principal note. [It.]

acciaccatura (def. 2): A, grace-note; B, principal note

**accidence** /'æksədəns/, *n.* **1.** the rudiments of any subject. **2.** *Gram.* **a.** that part of morphology dealing with inflection. **b.** an inflected form of a word. **c.** a property shown by such inflection. [var. of *accidents*, pl. of ACCIDENT (def. 5), or from L *accidentia*, neut. pl. of *accidens*, ppr., striking, happening (as if fem. noun)]

**accident** /'æksədənt/, *n.* **1.** an undesirable or unfortunate happening; casualty; mishap. **2.** anything that happens unexpectedly, without design, or by chance. **3.** the operation of chance: *I was there by accident.* **4.** a non-essential circumstance; occasional characteristic. **5.** *Gram.* an inflectional variation of a word, as *them* (an inflected form of *they*). **6.** *Geol.* an irregularity, generally on a small scale, on a surface, the explanation for which is not readily apparent. [ME, from L *accidens*, ppr., happening]

**accidental** /æksə'dɛntl/, *adj.* **1.** happening by chance or accident, or unexpectedly: *an accidental meeting.* **2.** non-essential; incidental; subsidiary: *accidental gains.* **3.** *Music.* denoting or pertaining to sharps, flats, or naturals not in the key signature. *–n.* **4.** a non-essential or subsidiary circumstance or feature. **5.** *Music.* **a.** a sign placed before a note indicating a sharp, flat, or natural not in the key signature. **b.** the note so indicated. **6.** (*usu. pl.*) *Fine Arts.* striking random effects of light in painting. – **accidentalness,** *n.*

**accidentally** /æksə'dɛntli/, *adv.* **1.** by chance; unexpectedly. **2. accidentally on purpose,** with a hidden purpose.

**accident-prone** /'æksədənt-proun/, *adj.* abnormally susceptible to accidents.

**accidie** /'æksədi/, *n.* →**acedia.**

**accipiter** /æk'sɪpətə/, *n., pl.* **-tres** /-triz/. any bird of the subfamily Accipitrinae and genus *Accipiter*, which comprises short-winged, long-tailed hawks. [L]

**accipitrine** /æk'sɪpətrin/, *adj.* **1.** belonging to the Accipitrinae (see **accipiter**). **2.** raptorial; like, or related to the birds of prey. Also, **accipitral.**

**acclaim** /ə'kleɪm/, *v.t.* **1.** to salute with words or sounds of joy or approval; applaud. **2.** to announce or proclaim by acclamation. *–v.i.* **3.** to make acclamation; applaud. *–n.* **4.** an oral vote, often unanimous, usu. taken after the sense of a meeting is clear and unmistakable. **5.** →**acclamation** (defs 1, 2). [L *acclāmāre*] – **acclaimer,** *n.*

**acclamation** /æklə'meɪʃən/, *n.* **1.** a shout or other demonstration of welcome, goodwill, or applause. **2.** the act of acclaiming. **3.** →**acclaim** (def. 4). – **acclamatory** /ə'klæmətri/, *adj.*

**acclimate** /ə'klaɪmət, 'ækləmeɪt/, *v.t., v.i.,* **-mated, -mating.** *U.S.* →**acclimatise.** – **acclimatable** /ə'klaɪmətəbəl/, *adj.* – **acclimation** /,æklaɪ'meɪʃən/, *n.*

**acclimatise** /ə'klaɪmətaɪz/, *v.,* **-tised, -tising.** *–v.t.* **1.** to habituate to a new climate or environment. *–v.i.* **2.** to become habituated to a new climate or environment. [F *acclimater*, from *à* to + *climat* climate] – **acclimatisable,** *adj.* – **acclimatisation** /əklaɪmətaɪ'zeɪʃən/, *n.* – **acclimatiser,** *n.*

**acclivity** /ə'klɪvəti/, *n., pl.* **-ties.** an upward slope, as of ground; an ascent. [L *acclīvitas* steepness]

**accolade** /'ækəleɪd/, *n.* **1.** a ceremony used in conferring knighthood, consisting at one time of an embrace, and afterwards of giving the candidate a light blow upon the shoulder with the flat of a sword. **2.** the blow itself. **3.** any award; honour. **4.** *Music.* a brace joining several staves. [F, from It. *accollata*, properly fem. pp. of *accollare* embrace about the neck; replacing ME *acolee*, from OF]

**accom.,** accommodation.

**accommodate** /ə'kɒmədeɪt/, *v.,* **-dated, -dating.** *–v.t.* **1.** to do a kindness or a favour to; oblige: *to accommodate a friend.* **2.** to provide suitably; supply (fol. by *with*): *to accommodate a friend with money.* **3.** to provide with room and sometimes with food and entertainment. **4.** to make suitable or consistent; adapt: *to accommodate oneself to circumstances.* **5.** to bring into harmony; adjust; reconcile: *to accommodate differences.* **6.** to find or provide space for (something). *–v.i.* **7.** to become or be conformable; act conformably; agree. [L *accommodātus*, pp., suited] – **accommodator,** *n.*

**accommodating** /ə'kɒmədeɪtɪŋ/, *adj.* easy to deal with; obliging. – **accommodatingly,** *adv.*

**accommodation** /əkɒmə'deɪʃən/, *n.* **1.** the act of accommodating. **2.** the state or process of being accommodated; adaptation. **3.** adjustment of differences; reconciliation. **4.** *Sociol.* a process of mutual adaptation between persons or social groups, usu. through eliminating or lessening of factors of hostility. **5.** anything which supplies a want; a convenience. **6.** lodging, or food and lodging. **7.** a readiness to aid others; obligingness. **8.** a loan or pecuniary favour. **9.** *Physiol.* **a.** the automatic adjustment by which the eye adapts itself to distinct vision at different distances. **b.** in stereoscopy, the ability of the human eye to bring two images into superimposition for stereoscopic viewing.

**accommodation bill** /'- bɪl/, *n.* a bill, draft, note, etc., drawn, accepted or endorsed by one person for another without consideration, to enable the second person to obtain credit or raise money. Also, *U.S.,* **accommodation draft, note, etc.**

**accommodation house** /'- haʊs/, *n.* (formerly) a boarding and lodging house for travellers, esp. stockmen, drovers, etc.

**accommodation ladder** /'- lædə/, *n.* a ladder or stairway hung from a ship's side to connect with boats below.

**accommodation paddock** /'- pædək/, *n.* an area set aside for the overnight pasturing of travelling livestock.

**accommodative** /ə'kɒmədeɪtɪv/, *adj.* tending to accommodate; adaptive. – **accommodativeness,** *n.*

**accompaniment** /ə'kʌmpnimənt/, *n.* **1.** something incidental or added for ornament, symmetry, etc. **2.** *Music.* that part of a composition which provides the harmonic and rhythmic backing to a melodic line, esp. a song.

**accompanist** /ə'kʌmpənəst/, *n.* one who plays an accompaniment.

**accompany** /ə'kʌmpəni, ə'kʌmpni/, *v.t.,* **-nied, -nying.** **1.** to go in company with; join in action: *to accompany a friend on a walk.* **2.** to be or exist in company with: *thunder accompanies lightning.* **3.** to put in company with; associate (fol. by *with*): *he accompanies his speech with gestures.* **4.** *Music.* to play or sing an accompaniment to. [ME *accompanye(n)*, from F *accompagner*, from *à* to + *compagne* COMPANION[1]] – **accompanier,** *n.*

**accomplice** /ə'kʌmpləs, -'kɒm-/, *n.* an associate in a crime; partner in wrongdoing. [earlier *complice*, from F, from ML *complex, complicis* close associate, confederate; the phrase *a complice* became *accomplice* by failure to recognise it as made up of two words]

**accomplish** /ə'kʌmplɪʃ, -'kɒm-/, *v.t.* **1.** to bring to pass; carry out; perform; finish: *to accomplish one's mission.* **2.** to complete (a distance or period of time). **3.** to make complete; equip perfectly. [ME *accomplice(n)*, from OF *acompliss-*, stem of *acomplir*, from LL *accomplēre*] – **accomplishable,** *adj.* – **accomplisher,** *n.*

**accomplished** /ə'kʌmplɪʃt, -'kɒm-/, *adj.* **1.** completed; effected: *an accomplished fact.* **2.** perfected; expert: *an accomplished scholar.* **3.** perfected in the graces and attainments of polite society.

**accomplishment** /ə'kʌmplɪʃmənt, -'kɒm-/, *n.* **1.** the act of carrying into effect; fulfilment: *the accomplishment of our desires.* **2.** anything accomplished; achievement: *the accomplishments of scientists.* **3.** (*oft. pl.*) an acquired art or grace; polite attainment.

**accord** /ə'kɔd/, *v.i.* **1.** to be in correspondence or harmony; agree. *–v.t.* **2.** to make to agree or correspond; adapt. **3.** to grant; concede: *to accord due praise.* **4.** *Archaic.* to settle; reconcile. *–n.* **5.** just correspondence of things; harmony of relation. **6.** a harmonious union of sounds. **7.** consent or concurrence of opinions or wills; agreement. **8.** an international agreement; settlement of questions outstanding between nations. **9. accord and satisfaction,** *Law.* agreement to discharge a right of action which one person has against another; the 'accord' is the agreement that the person released shall do or give something in satisfaction of the right; the 'satisfaction' is the consideration for it. **10. of one's own accord,** voluntarily. **11. with one accord,** with spontaneous agreement. [LL *accordāre*; replacing ME *accorde(n)*, from OF *acorder*] – **accordable,** *adj.* – **accorder,** *n.*

**accordance** /əˈkɔdəns/, *n.* **1.** agreement; conformity. **2.** the act of according.

**accordant** /əˈkɔdənt/, *adj.* agreeing; conformable. – **accordantly,** *adv.*

**according** /əˈkɔdɪŋ/, *adv.* **1. according to, a.** in accordance with: *according to his judgment.* **b.** proportionately. **c.** on the authority of; as stated by. **2. according as,** conformably or proportionately as. –*adj.* **3.** agreeing.

**accordingly** /əˈkɔdɪŋli/, *adv.* **1.** in accordance; correspondingly. **2.** in due course; therefore; so.

**accordion** /əˈkɔdiən/, *n.* **1.** a portable wind instrument with bellows and button-like keys sounded by means of metallic reeds. **2.** a piano accordion. –*adj.* **3.** having folds like the bellows of an accordion: *accordion pleats.* [ACCORD + -ION] – **accordionist,** *n.*

accordion

**accost** /əˈkɒst/, *v.t.* **1.** to approach, esp. with a greeting or remark. **2.** to solicit as a prostitute. [F *accoster*, from LL *accostāre* put side by side]

**accouchement** /əˈkutʃmənt, -ˈkuʃ-/, *n.* period of confinement in childbirth; labour. [F]

**accoucheur** /ækuˈʃɜ/, *n.* a man who acts as a midwife; an obstetrician. [F]

**accoucheuse** /ækuˈʃɜz/, *n.* →**midwife.** [F]

**account** /əˈkaʊnt/, *n.* **1.** a verbal or written recital of particular transactions and events; narrative: *an account of everything as it happened.* **2.** an explanatory statement of conduct, as to a superior. **3.** a statement of reasons, causes, etc., explaining some event. **4.** reason; consideration: *on all accounts.* **5.** consequence; importance: *things of no account.* **6.** estimation; judgment: *to take into account.* **7.** profit; advantage: *to turn anything to account.* **8.** a statement of pecuniary transactions. **9.** *Bookkeeping.* **a.** a formal record of the debits and credits relating to the person named (or caption placed) at the head of the ledger account. **b.** a balance of a specified period's receipts and expenditures. **10. bring** or **call to account,** demand explanation or justification of actions. **11. for the account,** to be paid on the regular settlement day. **12. give a good account of (oneself),** to acquit (oneself) well. **13. go to one's account,** go to the Last Judgment; die. **14. in account with,** having a credit arrangement with. **15. on account of, a.** because of; by reason of. **b.** for the sake of. **16. on** or **to account,** as an interim payment. –*v.i.* **17.** to give an explanation (fol. by *for*): *to account for the accident.* **18.** to answer concerning one's conduct, duties, etc. (fol. by *for*): *to account for shortages.* **19.** to render an account, esp. of money. **20.** to cause death, capture, etc. (fol. by *for*). –*v.t.* **21.** to count; consider as: *I account myself well paid.* **22.** to assign or impute (fol. by *to*). [ME *acunte(n)* from OF *acunter*, from LL *accomptāre*]

**accountable** /əˈkaʊntəbəl/, *adj.* **1.** liable to be called to account; responsible (*to* a person, *for* an act, etc.): *I am not accountable to any man for my deeds.* **2.** that can be explained. – **accountability** /əkaʊntəˈbɪləti/, **accountableness,** *n.* – **accountably,** *adv.*

**accountancy** /əˈkaʊntənsi/, *n.* the art or practice of an accountant.

**accountant** /əˈkaʊntənt/, *n.* a person whose profession is inspecting and auditing business accounts. – **accountantship,** *n.*

**account card** /əˈkaʊnt kad/, *n.* →**credit card.**

**accounting** /əˈkaʊntɪŋ/, *n.* the theory and system of setting up, maintaining, and auditing the books of a firm; the art of analysing the financial position and operating results of a business firm from a study of its sales, purchases, overheads, etc. (distinguished from *bookkeeping* in that a bookkeeper only makes the proper entries in books set up to the accountant's plan).

**accoutre** /əˈkutə/, *v.t.* to equip or array, esp. with military accoutrements. Also, *U.S.,* **accouter.** [F *accoutrer*]

**accoutrements** /əˈkutrəmənts/, *n.pl.* **1.** equipage; trappings. **2.** the equipment of a soldier except arms and clothing. Also, *U.S.,* **accouterments.**

**accredit** /əˈkrɛdət/, *v.t.* **1.** to ascribe or attribute to (fol. by *with*): *he was accredited with having said it.* **2.** to attribute; consider as belonging: *a discovery accredited to Edison.* **3.** to furnish (an officially recognised agent) with credentials: *to accredit an envoy.* **4.** to certify as meeting official requirements. **5.** to bring into credit; invest with credit or authority. **6.** to believe. [F *accréditer*] – **accreditation** /əkrɛdəˈteɪʃən/, *n.*

**accrete** /əˈkrit/, *v.,* **-creted, -creting,** *adj.* –*v.i.* **1.** to grow together; adhere (fol. by *to*). –*v.t.* **2.** to add as by growth. –*adj.* **3.** *Bot.* grown together. [L *accrētus*, pp., increased]

**accretion** /əˈkriʃən/, *n.* **1.** an increase by natural growth or by gradual external addition; growth in size or extent. **2.** the result of this process. **3.** an extraneous addition: *the last part of the legend is a later accretion.* **4.** the growing together of separate parts into a single whole. **5.** *Law.* increase of property by gradual additions caused by acts of nature, as of land by alluvion. **6.** *Pathol.* conglomeration; piling up of substances. [L *accrētio*] – **accretive,** *adj.*

**accrual** /əˈkruəl/, *n.* **1.** the act or process of accruing. **2.** something accrued; accretion.

**accrue** /əˈkru/, *v.i.,* **-crued, -cruing. 1.** to happen or result as a natural growth; arise in due course; come or fall as an addition or increment. **2.** *Law.* to become a present and enforceable right or demand. [from *accrue*, obs. n., from F, orig. fem. pp. of *accroître* increase, from L *accrescere*] – **accruement,** *n.*

**accrued interest** /əkrud ˈɪntrəst/, *n.* the amount of interest accumulated at a given time but not yet paid (or received).

**acct.,** **1.** account. **2.** accountant.

**acculturate** /əˈkʌltʃəreɪt/, *v.,* **-rated, -rating.** –*v.t.* **1.** to cause (a society) to change through the process of acculturation. –*v.i.* **2.** to become changed or modified by acculturation. [backformation from ACCULTURATION]

**acculturation** /əkʌltʃəˈreɪʃən/, *n.* **1.** the process of borrowing between cultures, marked by the continuous transmission of elements and traits between different peoples and resulting in new and blended patterns. **2.** the modification of a primitive culture through direct and prolonged contact with an advanced society, (distinguished from *assimilation*). **3.** the process of socialisation. [AD- + CULTURE + -ATION] – **accultural** /əˈkʌltʃərətɪv/, *adj.*

**accumbent** /əˈkʌmbənt/, *adj.* **1.** reclining: *accumbent posture.* **2.** *Bot.* lying against something, as of cotyledons which have their edges curved against the radicle. [L *accumbere* to recline] – **accumbency,** *n.*

**accumulate** /əˈkjumjəleɪt/, *v.,* **-lated, -lating.** –*v.t.* **1.** to heap up; gather as into a mass; collect: *to accumulate wealth.* –*v.i.* **2.** to grow into a heap or mass; form an increasing quantity: *public evils accumulate.* [L *accumulātus*, pp., heaped up]

**accumulation** /əkjumjəˈleɪʃən/, *n.* **1.** a collecting together. **2.** that which is accumulated. **3.** growth by continuous additions, as of interest to principal. **4.** *Law.* increase of principal by the investment of rents, dividends, etc., and the reinvestment of the interest from them.

**accumulative** /əˈkjumjələtɪv/, *adj.* tending to or arising from accumulation; cumulative. – **accumulatively,** *adv.* – **accumulativeness,** *n.*

**accumulative sentence** /– ˈsɛntns/, *n.* a sentence of imprisonment which is to be served after another sentence already imposed.

**accumulator** /əˈkjumjəleɪtə/, *n.* **1.** one who or that which accumulates. **2.** *Elect.* a secondary cell, or battery of secondary cells connected in series or parallel, used for storing electrical energy; a storage battery. **3.** an electric device in arithmetic machines, as the main register of a digital computer, where the arithmetic operations are performed. **4.** *Brit. Horseracing.* a bet laid on four or more races from which the winnings and the original stake are carried forward to each race in turn. [L]

**accuracy** /ˈækjərəsi/, *n.* the condition or quality of being accurate; precision or exactness; correctness.

**accurate** /ˈækjərət/, *adj.* in exact conformity to truth, to a standard or rule, or to a model; free from error or defect: *an accurate typist.* [L *accūrātus*, pp., exact, cared for] – **accurately,** *adv.* – **accurateness,** *n.*

**accursed** /ə'kɜsəd, ə'kɜst/, *adj.* **1.** subject to a curse; ruined. **2.** worthy of curses; detestable. Also, **accurst.** – **accursedly** /ə'kɜsədli/, *adv.* – **accursedness** /ə'kɜsədnəs/, *n.*

**accusation** /ˌækju'zeɪʃən/, *n.* **1.** a charge of wrongdoing; imputation of guilt or blame. **2.** the specific offence charged: *the accusation is murder.* **3.** the act of accusing or charging. Also, **accusal** /ə'kjuzəl/. [L *accūsātio*]

**accusative** /ə'kjuzətɪv/, *adj.* **1.** (in Greek, Latin, and English grammar) denoting in Latin and Greek by means of its form, in English by means of its form or its position, a case which has as one of its chief functions the indication of the direct object of a finite verb, as in 'the boy loves *the girl*'. **2.** similar to such a case form in function or meaning. *–n.* **3.** the accusative case. **4.** a word in that case: *Latin 'puellam' may be spoken of as an accusative.* **5.** a form or construction of similar meaning. [L *accūsātīvus*, translation of Gk *(ptôsis) aitiātikḗ* (case) pertaining to that which is caused] – **accusatively,** *adv.*

**accusatorial** /əkjuzə'tɔriəl/, *adj.* pertaining to an accuser. – **accusatorially,** *adj.*

**accusatory** /ə'kjuzətəri, -tri/, *adj.* containing an accusation; accusing: *he looked at the jury with an accusatory expression.*

**accuse** /ə'kjuz/, *v.t.,* **-cused, -cusing.** **1.** to bring a charge against; charge with the fault or crime *(of).* **2.** to blame. [L *accūsāre* accuse, blame; replacing ME *acuse*, from OF] – **accuser,** *n.* – **accusable,** *adj.* – **accusingly,** *adv.*

**accused** /ə'kjuzd/, *adj.* **1.** charged with a crime or the like. *–n.* **2.** the defendant or defendants in a criminal law case.

**accustom** /ə'kʌstəm/, *v.t.* to familiarise by custom or use; habituate: *to accustom oneself to cold weather.* [late ME *acustume(n)*, from OF *acostumer*, from *a* to + *costume* custom]

**accustomed** /ə'kʌstəmd/, *adj.* **1.** customary; habitual: *in their accustomed manner.* **2.** in the habit of: *accustomed to doing good.* **3.** habituated; familiar with; used *(to)*: *accustomed to good living.* – **accustomedness,** *n.*

**ac-dc** /ˌeɪˌsi-'diˌsi/, *adj.* **1.** of or pertaining to an electric device, as a radio, which can operate from either an alternating current or direct current power source. **2.** *Colloq.* bisexual; attracted to both males and females as sexual partners.

**ace** /eɪs/, *n.* **1.** a single spot or mark on a card or die. **2.** *Cards.* a playing card marked with a single spot, in most games counting as highest, lowest, or either, in its suit. **3.** *Dice.* a die or the face of a die marked with a single spot. **4.** (in tennis, badminton, etc.) **a.** a serve which the opponent fails to touch. **b.** the point thus scored. **5.** a very small quantity, amount, or degree; a particle: *within an ace of winning.* **6.** a highly skilled person; an adept: *an ace at tap-dancing.* **7.** *Brit.* a fighter pilot officially credited by the RAF with shooting down five or more enemy aeroplanes. **8. on one's ace,** *Colloq.* on one's own; alone. *–adj.* **9.** excellent; first in quality; outstanding. *–v.t.* **10. ace it (up),** *Colloq.* to be quiet; stop it. [ME *as*, from OF, from L, supposedly from d. Gk, var. of Gk *heîs* one]

ace: an ace of spades

**-acea,** a suffix of (Latin) names or classes and orders of animals, as in *Crustacea.* [L, neut. pl. of *-āceus.* See -ACEOUS]

**-aceae,** a suffix of (Latin) names of families of plants, as in *Rosaceae.* [L, fem. pl. of *-āceus.* See -ACEOUS]

**acedia** /ə'sidjə/, *n.* sloth; spiritual apathy. Also, **accidie.** [ML, from Gk *akēdía*]

**acentric** /eɪ'sɛntrɪk/, *adj.* not centred; having no centre.

**-aceous,** a suffix of adjectives used in scientific terminology, indicating: **1.** of or pertaining to, as in *sebaceous.* **2.** of the nature of, or similar to, as in *cretaceous.* **3.** belonging to a scientific grouping, esp. a botanic family, as in *liliaceous, fabaceous.* [NL *-aceus*, from L *-āceus* of a specific kind or group]

**acephalous** /eɪ'sɛfələs, ə-/, *adj.* **1.** headless; lacking a distinct head. **2.** without a leader. [LL *acephalus*, from Gk *aképhalos.* See A-[6], CEPHALOUS]

**ACER** /ˌeɪ si i 'a, 'eɪsə/, Australian Council for Educational Research.

**acerbate** /'æsəbeɪt/, *v.,* **-bated, -bating;** /ə'sɜbət/, *adj.* *–v.t.* **1.** to make sour or bitter. **2.** to exasperate. *–adj.* **3.** embittered. [L *acerbātus*, pp.]

**acerbic** /ə'sɜbɪk/, *adj.* sour; harsh, bitter. [L, from *acerbus* + -IC]

**acerbity** /ə'sɜbəti/, *n., pl.* **-ties.** **1.** sourness, with roughness or astringency of taste. **2.** harshness or severity, as of temper or expression. [F *acerbité*, from L *acerbitas*]

**acerose** /'æsərous/, *adj.* needle-shaped, as the leaves of the pine. Also, **acerous** /'æsərəs/. [L *acerōsus*, from *acus* chaff, but confused with *acus* needle]

**acet-,** variant of **aceto-,** used before vowels, as in *acetaldehyde.*

**acetabulum** /æsə'tæbjələm/, *n., pl.* **-la** /-lə/. the socket of the bone which receives the head of the thighbone. [L: vinegar cup, saucer] – **acetabular,** *adj.*

**acetal** /'æsətl, ə'sitl/, *n.* **1.** a colourless, volatile fluid, $CH_3CH(OC_2H_5)_2$, used as a hypnotic or solvent. **2.** *(pl.)* a class of compounds of aldehydes or ketones with alcohols.

**acetaldehyde** /æsə'tældəhaɪd/, *n.* a volatile, colourless, aromatic liquid, $CH_3CHO$, used commercially in the silvering of mirrors and in organic synthesis.

**acetamide** /ə'sɛtəmaɪd, æsə'tæmaɪd/, *n.* the amide of acetic acid, a white crystalline solid, $CH_3CONH_2$, melting at 80°C. Also, **acetamid** /ə'sɛtəməd, æsə'tæməd/. [ACET(YL) + AMIDE]

**acetanilide** /æsə'tænəlaɪd/, *n.* an organic compound, $C_6H_5NH(COCH_3)$, derived by the action of glacial acetic acid upon aniline, used as a remedy for fever, headache, rheumatism, etc., and in the lacquer industry; antifebrin. Also, **acetanilid.** [ACET(YL) + ANIL(INE) + -IDE]

**acetate** /'æsəteɪt/, *n.* **1.** a salt or ester of acetic acid. **2.** →**acetate fibre.** [ACET- + -ATE[2]] – **acetated,** *adj.*

**acetate fibre** /– 'faɪbə/, *n.* **1.** fibre made by man from pure cellulose. **2.** material made from this fibre.

**acetate rayon** /– 'reɪɒn/, *n.* a rayon made from the acetic ester of cellulose, differing from viscose rayon in having a greater strength when wet and in being more sensitive to high temperature.

**acetic** /ə'sitɪk, ə'sɛtɪk/, *adj.* pertaining to, derived from, or producing vinegar or acetic acid.

**acetic acid** /– 'æsəd/, *n.* a colourless liquid, $CH_3COOH$, the essential constituent of vinegar, used in the manufacture of acetate rayon and the production of numerous esters as solvents and flavouring agents.

**acetic anhydride** /– æn'haɪdraɪd/, *n.* a colourless, pungent fluid, $(CH_3CO)_2O$, the anhydride of acetic acid, used as a reagent and in the production of plastics, film, and fabrics derived from cellulose.

**acetify** /ə'sɛtəfaɪ/, *v.,* **-fied, -fying.** *–v.t.* **1.** to turn into vinegar or make acetous. *–v.i.* **2.** to become acetous. [ACET- + -(I)FY] – **acetification** /əsɛtəfə'keɪʃən/, *n.* – **acetifier,** *n.*

**aceto-,** a word element indicating the presence of acetic acid or the radical acetyl. Also, **acet-.** [combining form representing L *acētum* vinegar]

**acetoacetic acid** /əˌsitouəsitɪk 'æsəd, -əsɛtɪk/, *n.* a carboxylic, $CH_3COCH_2COOH$, distributed widely in nature; excreted in urine and found in abnormal quantities in the urine of diabetics; one of the ketone bodies.

**acetobacter** /ə'sitouˌbæktə/, *n.* the organism which spoils wine by producing acetic acid in it.

**acetone** /'æsətoun/, *n.* a colourless, volatile, inflammable liquid, $(CH_3)_2CO$, formed in the distillation of acetates, etc., used as a solvent and in smokeless powders, varnishes, etc. [ACET- + -ONE]

**acetone bodies** /– 'bɒdiz/, *n.pl.* →**ketone bodies.**

**acetous** /ə'sitəs, 'æsətəs/, *adj.* **1.** containing or producing acetic acid. **2.** sour; vinegary. Also, **acetose** /'æsətous/. [LL *acētōsus* vinegary]

**acetum** /ə'sitəm/, *n.* a preparation made with vinegar or dilute acetic acid as the solvent. [L: vinegar]

**acetyl** /'æsətl, ə'sitl/, *n.* a radical, $CH_3CO$-, in acetic acid. [ACET- + -YL] – **acetylic** /æsə'tɪlɪk/, *adj.*

**acetylate** /ə'sɛtəleɪt/, *v.t.,* **-lated, -lating.** to combine (a compound) with one or more acetyl groups. – **acetylation** /əsɛtə'leɪʃən/, *n.*

**acetylcholine** /ˌæsətaɪl'koulin, əˌsitl-/, *n.* **1.** an ester of acetic acid and choline, $CH_3COOCH_2CH_2N^+(CH_3)_3$, found in animals and some plants; released at parasympathetic nerve endings when they are stimulated, and thought to be responsible for the transmission of nerve impulses across synapses. **2.** this substance prepared from ergot, and used medicinally to decrease the blood pressure or to set up peristalsis.

**acetylcholine esterase** /– 'ɛstəreɪz/, *n.* the enzyme which catalyses the hydrolysis of acetylcholine to acetate and choline; inhibitors of this enzyme are toxic to all animals and are the basis of many poison gases and pesticides.

**acetyl coenzyme A,** *n.* a coenzyme which is a key intermediary metabolite formed by beta-oxidation or by oxidation of pyruvic acid. See **coenzyme A.**

**acetylene** /ə'sɛtəlin, -lən/, *n.* a colourless gas, $C_2H_2$, prepared by the action of water on calcium carbide, used in metal welding and cutting, as an illuminant, and in organic synthesis.

**acetylene lamp** /– 'læmp/, *n.* a lamp burning acetylene.

**acetylsalicylic acid** /ˌæsətlsæləˌsɪlɪk 'æsəd, əˌsitl-/, *n.* →**aspirin.**

**ac.ft,** acre-foot.

**ache** /eɪk/, *v.,* **ached, aching,** *n.* *–v.i.* **1.** to suffer pain; have or be in continuous pain: *his whole body ached.* **2.** to be eager; yearn; long. *–n.* **3.** pain of some duration, in opposition to sudden twinges or spasmodic pain. **4.** a longing. [ME *aken*, v., *ache*, n.; OE *acan*, v., *æce*, n. The MnE word has the spelling of the ME noun with the pronunciation of the ME verb] – **achingly,** *adv.* – **achage,** *n.* – **achey, achy,** *adj.*

**achene** /ə'kin/, *n.* a small, dry, hard, one-seeded, indehiscent fruit. [NL *achaenium*, from Gk *a-* A-[6] + Gk *chainein* gape + *-ium* -IUM] – **achenial** /ə'kiniəl/, *adj.*

**Acheulian** /ə'tʃuliən/, *adj.* of, pertaining to, or characteristic of the lower Palaeolithic culture in Europe, marked by the use of finely made bifacial tools with multiple cutting edges. Also, **Acheulean.** [named after St *Acheul*, village in France where remains were first found]

**achieve** /ə'tʃiv/, *v.,* **achieved, achieving.** *–v.t.* **1.** to bring to a successful end; carry through; accomplish. **2.** to bring about, as by effort; gain or obtain: *to achieve victory.* *–v.i.* **3.** to accomplish some enterprise; bring about a result intended. [ME *acheve(n)*, from OF *achever*, from phrase *(venir) a chief* = LL *ad caput venīre* come to a head] – **achievable,** *adj.* – **achiever,** *n.*

**achievement** /ə'tʃivmənt/, *n.* **1.** something accomplished, esp. by valour, boldness, or superior ability; a great or heroic deed. **2.** the act of achieving; accomplishment: *the achievement of one's object.*

**achievement age** /'– eɪdʒ/, *n.* the age at which, according to an accepted standard of capability, any young person should be able to carry out a selected task successfully.

**achievement quotient** /'– kwouʃənt/, *n.* educational age divided by actual age. Thus a child of 10 years whose educational achievement equals that of the average 12-year-old has an achievement quotient of 1.2 (commonly expressed as 120). *Abbrev.:* AQ Cf. **intelligence quotient.**

**achievement test** /'– tɛst/, *n.* a test designed to measure the results of learning or teaching, as contrasted with tests of native ability or aptitude. Cf. **intelligence test.**

**Achilles heel** /əˌkɪliz 'hil/, *n.* a single major weakness or point of vulnerability. [from the Gk legend of *Achilles*, hero of Homer's *Iliad*, invulnerable except in the heel]

**Achilles tendon** /– 'tɛndən/, *n.* the tendon joining the calf muscles to the heelbone; the hamstring.

**achlamydate** /eɪ'klæmədeɪt/, *adj. Bot.* not chlamydate; having no mantle or pallium.

**achlamydeous** /eɪklə'mɪdiəs/, *adj. Bot.* not chlamydeous; having no floral envelope. [A-[6] + Gk *chlamýs* cloak + -EOUS]

**achondroplasia** /əkɒndrə'pleɪʒə/, *n.* a hereditary form of dwarfism characterised by retarded limb growth, but not usu. affecting the trunk and head. [A-[6] + Gk *chóndros* cartilage + -PLASIA] – **achondroplastic,** *adj.*

**achromatic** /eɪkrə'mætɪk/, *adj.* **1.** of colour perceived to have no saturation, and therefore no hue, such as neutral greys. **2.** *Optics.* free from chromatic aberration. **3.** *Biol.* **a.** containing or consisting of achromatin. **b.** resisting dyes. **4.** *Music.* without accidentals or changes in key. [Gk *achrṓmatos* colourless + -IC] – **achrcmatically,** *adv.*

**achromatin** /ə'kroumətɪn/, *n.* that portion of the nucleus of a cell which is less highly coloured by staining agents than the rest of the cell.

**achromatise** /ə'kroumətaɪz/, *v.t.,* **-tised, -tising.** to make achromatic; deprive of colour. Also, **achromatize.**

**achromatism** /ə'kroumətɪzəm/, *n.* freedom from chromatic aberration. Also, **achromaticity** /əkroumə'tɪsəti/.

**achromatous** /ə'kroumətəs/, *adj.* without colour; of a lighter colour than normal. [Gk *achrṓmatos*]

**achromic** /ə'kroumɪk/, *adj.* colourless; without colouring matter. Also, **achromous.** [A-[6] + Gk *chrôma* colour + -IC]

**acicula** /ə'sɪkjələ/, *n., pl.* **-lae** /-li/. a needle-shaped part or process, as a spine, bristle, or needle-like crystal. [L, diminutive of *acus* needle] – **acicular,** *adj.*

**aciculate** /ə'sɪkjələt, -leɪt/, *adj.* **1.** having aciculae. **2.** marked as with needle scratches. **3.** needle-shaped. Also, **aciculated.**

**aciculum** /ə'sɪkjələm/, *n., pl.* **-lums, -la** /-lə/. **1.** an acicula. **2.** *Zool.* one of the slender sharp stylets embedded in the parapodia of some annelids, as the Polychaeta. [erroneous var. of ACICULA]

**acid**[1] /'æsəd/, *n.* **1.** *Chem.* a compound (usu. having a sour taste and capable of neutralising alkalis and reddening blue litmus paper) containing hydrogen which can be replaced by certain metals or an electropositive radical to form salt. Acids are proton donors, and yield hydronium ions in water solution. **2.** a substance with a sour taste. **3. come the acid over,** *N.Z. Colloq.* to act sharply or viciously towards. **4. put the acid on,** *Colloq.* to ask (something) of (someone) in such a manner that refusal is difficult; pressure (someone). **5. take the acid off,** *Colloq.* to cease to pressure (someone). *–adj.* **6.** *Chem.* **a.** belonging or pertaining to acids or the anhydrides of acids. **b.** having only a part of the hydrogen of an acid replaced by a metal or its equivalent: *an acid phosphate, etc.* **7.** tasting sharp or sour: *acid fruits.* **8.** sour; sharp; ill-tempered: *an acid remark, wit, etc.* **9.** *Geol.* (of igneous rocks) containing 66 per cent or more silica. [L *acidus* sour]

**acid**[2] /æsəd/, *n. Colloq.* **1.** LSD. **2. drop acid,** to take LSD. [from *(lysergic) acid (diethylamide)*]

**acid drop** /'– drɒp/, *n.* a sharp-tasting boiled sweet of sugar and tartaric acid.

**acid dye** /'– daɪ/, *n.* any of a large group of dyes, mostly sodium salts of sulphonic acids, used mainly for cellulosic fibres and those derived from cellulose, as cotton, linen or rayon.

**acid-fast** /'æsəd-fast/, *adj.* resistant to decolourisation by acid after staining.

**acid-forming** /'æsəd-fɔmɪŋ/, *adj.* **1.** yielding acid in chemical reaction; acidic. **2.** (of food) containing a large amount of acid ash after complete oxidisation.

**acidhead** /'æsədhɛd/, *n.* one who often takes LSD.

**acidic** /ə'sɪdɪk/, *adj.* **1.** *Geol.* containing a large amount of silica. **2.** →**acid-forming** (def. 1). **3.** of or pertaining to the nature of an acid. **4.** sour; bitter.

**acidify** /ə'sɪdəfaɪ/, *v.,* **-fied, -fying.** *–v.t.* **1.** to make acid; convert or change into an acid. *–v.i.* **2.** to become acid; turn acidic. [ACID[1] + -IFY] – **acidifiable,** *adj.* – **acidification** /əˌsɪdəfə'keɪʃən/, *n.* – **acidifier,** *n.*

**acidimeter** /æsə'dɪmətə/, *n.* an instrument used to measure the amount of acid present in a solution.

**acidimetry** /æsə'dɪmətri/, *n.* the measurement of the amount of acid present in a solution. – **acidimetric** /əsɪdə'mɛtrɪk/, *adj.* – **acidimetrically,** *adv.*

**acidity** /ə'sɪdəti/, *n., pl.* **-ties.** **1.** the quality or extent of being acid. **2.** sourness; tartness. **3.** excessive acid quality, as of the gastric juice.

**acidometer** /æsə'dɒmətə/, *n.* a type of hydrometer, chiefly used for measuring the specific gravity of the electrolyte in an accumulator.

**acidophil** /ə'sɪdəfɪl/, *n.* an organic cell or cell constituent with selective affinity for acid dyes. Also, **acidophile** /ə'sɪdəfaɪl/. [ACID[1] + -O- + -PHIL]

**acidophilic** /əsɪdə'fɪlɪk/, *adj.* easily stained with acid dyes.

**acidophilus** /æsə'dɒfələs/, *n.* See **lactobacillus.**

**acidophilus milk** /– 'mɪlk/, *n.* a fermented milk which alters the bacterial content of the intestines. The fermenting bacteria are *Lactobacilli acidophili.* See **lactobacillus.**

**acidosis** /æsə'dousəs/, *n.* poisoning by acids formed within the body under morbid conditions. [irregularly from ACID[1] + -OSIS] – **acidotic** /æsə'dɒtɪk/, *adj.*

**acid rock** /æsəd 'rɒk/, *n.* a form of heavy rock music which is often textually based on the content of LSD trips, and which is intended to be listened to by LSD users.

**acid soil** /– 'sɔɪl/, *n.* a soil of acid reaction, or having predominance of hydrogen ions, tasting sour in solution.

**acid test** /– 'tɛst/, *n.* **1.** a test for gold using nitric acid. **2.** a critical test; final analysis.

**acidulate** /ə'sɪdʒəleɪt/, *v.*, **-lated, -lating.** *–v.t.* **1.** to make somewhat acid. **2.** to sour; embitter. *–v.i.* **3.** to become acid. – **acidulation** /əsɪdʒə'leɪʃən/, *n.*

**acidulous** /ə'sɪdʒələs/, *adj.* **1.** slightly sour. **2.** sharp; caustic. **3.** subacid. [L *acidulus,* diminutive of *acidus*]

**aciduric** /æsə'djurɪk/, *adj.* (of bacteria) capable of growth in an acid environment.

**acid value** /'æsəd ˌvælju/, *n.* the number of milligrams of potassium hydroxide neutralised by the free acids present in one gram of a fat, oil, or resin. Also, **acid number.**

**acidy** /'æsədi/, *adj.* of or resembling acid; sour: *an acidy taste.*

**acierate** /'eɪsiəreɪt/, *v.t.*, **-rated, -rating.** to convert (iron) into steel. [F *acier* steel + -ATE[1]] – **acieration** /ˌeɪsiə'reɪʃən/, *n.*

**aciform** /'æsəfɔm/, *adj.* needleshaped; acicular. [L *acus* needle + -I- + -FORM]

**aciniform** /ə'sɪnəfɔm/, *adj.* **1.** clustered like grapes. **2.** acinous. [L *acinus* grape + -I- + -FORM]

**acinous** /'æsənəs/, *adj.* consisting of acini. Also, **acinose** /'æsənous/. [L *acinōsus* like grapes]

**acinus** /'æsənəs/, *n., pl.* **-ni** /-naɪ/. **1.** *Bot.* one of the small drupelets or berries of an aggregate baccate fruit, as the blackberry, etc. **2.** a berry, as a grape, currant, etc. **3.** *Anat.* **a.** a minute rounded lobule. **b.** the smallest secreting portion of a gland. [L: berry, grape]

**-acious,** an adjective suffix made by adding **-ous** to nouns ending in **-acity** (the *-ty* being dropped), indicating a tendency towards or abundance of something, as *audacious.*

**-acity,** a suffix of nouns denoting quality or a state of being, and the like. [F *-acité,* from L *-ācitas,* or directly from L]

**ack-ack** /æk-'æk/, *Colloq. –n.* **1.** anti-aircraft fire. **2.** anti-aircraft arms. *–adj.* **3.** anti-aircraft. [used by radio operators for A.A. (anti-aircraft)]

**ack-emma** /æk-'ɛmə/, *adv. Colloq.* a.m. [used by radio operators]

**acknowledge** /ək'nɒlɪdʒ/, *v.t.*, **-edged, -edging.** **1.** to admit to be real or true; recognise the existence, truth, or fact of: *to acknowledge belief in God.* **2.** to express recognition or realisation of: *to acknowledge an acquaintance by bowing.* **3.** to recognise the authority or claims of: *to acknowledge his right to vote.* **4.** to indicate appreciation or gratitude for. **5.** to admit or certify the receipt of: *to acknowledge a letter.* **6.** *Law.* to own as binding or of legal force: *to acknowledge a deed.* [b. obs. *acknow* (OE *oncnāwan* confess) and *knowledge,* v., admit] – **acknowledgeable,** *adj.* – **acknowledger,** *n.*

**acknowledgment** /ək'nɒlədʒmənt/, *n.* **1.** the act of acknowledging or admitting. **2.** a recognition of the existence or truth of anything: *the acknowledgment of a sovereign power.* **3.** an expression of appreciation. **4.** a thing done or given in appreciation or gratitude. **5.** *Law.* **a.** an admission of a debt or obligation, esp. a written admission that a debt is due. **b.** declaration by a testator before witnesses that he has signed a will. Also, **acknowledgement.**

**ack-willie** /æk-'wɪli/, *adj.* in military jargon, absent without leave. [from the military signalling code in which Ack represented A and Willie represented W, signalling A.W., short for A.W.L.]

**aclinic** /ə'klɪnɪk/, *adj.* free from inclination or dip of the magnetic needle. [Gk *aklinḗs* not bending + -IC]

**aclinic line** /–'laɪn/, *n.* an imaginary line around the earth near the equator where the magnetic needle remains horizontal.

**acme** /'ækmi/, *n.* the highest point; culmination. [Gk *akmḗ*]

**acmite** /'ækmaɪt/, *n.* →**aegerite.**

**acne** /'ækni/, *n.* an inflammatory disease of the sebaceous glands, characterised by an eruption (often pustular) of the skin, esp. of the face. [orig. uncert.]

**acoelomate** /eɪ'siləmeɪt/, *adj.* having no coelom.

**acol** /'ækəl/, *n.* a system of conventions in the game of bridge. [named after *Acol* Road in NW London, where the bridge club in which it was first played is situated]

**acolyte** /'ækəlaɪt/, *n.* **1.** an altar attendant of minor rank. **2.** *Rom. Cath. Ch.* a member of the highest of the four minor orders, ranking next below a subdeacon. **3.** an attendant; an assistant. [ME *acolyt,* from ML *acolitus,* from Gk *akólouthos* follower]

**aconite** /'ækənaɪt/, *n.* **1.** any plant of the genus *Aconitum,* of the family Ranunculaceae, including plants with poisonous and medicinal properties, as monkshood or wolf's-bane. **2.** an extract or tincture made from the root of any of these plants. Also, **aconitum** /ækə'naɪtəm/. [L *aconītum,* from Gk *akóniton*] – **aconitic** /ækə'nɪtɪk/, *adj.*

**acorn** /'eɪkɔn/, *n.* the fruit of the oak, a nut in a hardened scaly cup. [ME *acorne,* replacing ME *akern,* OE *æcern,* c. Icel. *akarn*]

acorn

**acotyledon** /əkɒtə'lidən/, *n.* a plant without cotyledons. [A-[6] + COTYLEDON] – **acotyledonous** /əkɒtə'lidənəs/, adj.

**acouchi** /ə'kuʃi/, *n.* any of the small rodents of the genus *Myoprocta,* of South America. Also, **acouchy.**

**acoustic** /ə'kustɪk/, *adj.* **1.** Also, **acoustical.** pertaining to the sense or organs of hearing, or to the science of sound. **2.** *Music.* of or pertaining to instruments whose sound is not electronically amplified, as acoustic guitar, acoustic bass, opposed to electric guitar and electric bass. *–n.* **3.** a remedy for deafness or imperfect hearing. **4.** →**acoustics** (def. 2). [F *acoustique,* from Gk *akoustikós*] – **acoustically,** *adv.*

**acoustician** /ˌæku'stɪʃən/, *n.* an acoustic engineer.

**acoustic mine** /əˌkustɪk 'maɪn/, *n.* a mine designed to be exploded by vibration, as by that from the propeller of a passing ship.

**acoustic phonetics** /'– fənɛtɪks/, *n.* the branch of phonetics concerned with the physical qualities of speech sounds.

**acoustics** /ə'kustɪks/, *n.* **1.** *Physics.* the science of sound. **2.** (*construed as pl.*) acoustic properties, as of an auditorium. [pl. of ACOUSTIC. See -ICS]

**acoustic tile** /əˌkustɪk 'taɪl/, *n.* a tile of some soft, sound-absorbent material, as cork, used for the interiors of recording studios, concert halls, etc.

**acquaint** /ə'kweɪnt/, *v.t.* **1.** to make more or less familiar or conversant (fol. by *with*): *to acquaint him with our plan.* **2.** to furnish with knowledge; inform: *to acquaint a friend with one's efforts.* [ME *acointe(n),* from OF *acointer,* from LL *adcognitāre* make known]

**acquaintance** /ə'kweɪntəns/, *n.* **1.** a person (or persons) known to one, esp. a person with whom one is not on terms of great intimacy. **2.** the state of being acquainted; personal knowledge. – **acquaintanceship,** *n.*

**acquainted** /ə'kweɪntəd/, *adj.* having personal knowledge; informed (fol. by *with*): *acquainted with law.*

**acquiesce** /ˌækwi'ɛs/, *v.i.*, **-esced, -escing.** to assent tacitly; comply quietly; agree; consent (often fol. by *in*): *to acquiesce in an opinion.* [L *acquiescere*] – **acquiescingly,** *adv.*

**acquiescence** /ˌækwi'ɛsəns/, *n.* **1.** the act or condition of acquiescing or giving tacit assent; a silent submission, or submission with apparent consent. **2.** *Law.* such neglect to take legal proceedings in opposition to a matter as implies consent thereto.

**acquiescent** /ˌækwi'ɛsənt/, *adj.* disposed to acquiesce or yield; submissive. – **acquiescently,** *adv.*

**acquire** /ə'kwaɪə/, *v.t.*, **-quired, -quiring.** **1.** to come into possession of; get as one's own: *to acquire property, a title, etc.* **2.** to gain for oneself through one's actions or efforts:

*to acquire learning, a reputation, etc.* **3.** *Colloq.* to steal. [L *acquīrere*; replacing ME *acquere(n)*, from OF *acquerre*] – **acquirable,** *adj.* – **acquirer,** *n.*

**acquired characteristics** /əˌkwaɪəd kærəktəˈrɪstɪks/, *n. pl.* characteristics that are the results of environment, use or disuse, rather than of heredity.

**acquired taste** /– ˈteɪst/, *n.* **1.** an unusual liking acquired through experience. **2.** the thing so liked.

**acquirement** /əˈkwaɪəmənt/, *n.* **1.** the act of acquiring, esp. the gaining of knowledge or mental attributes. **2.** (*oft. pl*). that which is acquired; attainment.

**acquisition** /ækwəˈzɪʃən/, *n.* **1.** the act of acquiring or gaining possession: *the acquisition of property.* **2.** something acquired: *a valued acquisition.* –*v.t.* **3.** to order and acquire new material, as books for a library. [L *acquīsītio*] – **acquisitionist,** *n.*

**acquisitive** /əˈkwɪzətɪv/, *adj.* tending to make acquisitions; fond of acquiring possessions: *an acquisitive society.* – **acquisitively,** *adv.* – **acquisitiveness,** *n.*

**acquit** /əˈkwɪt/, *v.t.,* **-quitted, -quitting. 1.** to relieve from a charge of fault or crime; pronounce not guilty (fol. by *of*). **2.** to release or discharge (a person) from an obligation. **3.** to settle (a debt, obligation, claim, etc.). **4. acquit oneself, a.** to behave; bear or conduct oneself: *he acquitted himself well in battle.* **b.** to clear oneself: *he acquitted himself of suspicion.* [ME *aquite(n)*, from OF *aquiter.* See AD-, QUIT] – **acquitter,** *n.*

**acquittal** /əˈkwɪtl/, *n.* **1.** the act of acquitting; discharge. **2.** the state of being acquitted; release. **3.** *Law.* judicial deliverance from a criminal charge on a verdict or finding of not guilty.

**acquittance** /əˈkwɪtns/, *n.* **1.** discharge of or from debt or obligation. **2.** a document certifying this; a receipt. **3.** →**acquittal.**

**acr-,** variant of **acro-,** used before vowels.

**acre** /ˈeɪkə/, *n.* **1.** a unit of land measurement in the imperial system, equal to 4840 square yards or 160 perches, and equivalent to 4046.856 422 4 $m^2$ (approx. 0.405 hectares). *Symbol*: ac **2.** (*pl.*) fields or land in general. **3.** (*pl.*) *Colloq.* large quantities: *there were acres of cars.* **4.** *Colloq.* the buttocks. **5.** *Colloq.* the anus. [ME *aker*, OE *æcer*, c. G *Acker*]

**acreage** /ˈeɪkərɪdʒ/, *n.* acres collectively; extent in acres.

**acre-foot** /ˌeɪkə-ˈfʊt/, *n.* a unit of volume of water in irrigation in the imperial system, being the amount covering one acre to a depth of one foot equal to 43 560 cubic feet or 1233.481 837 547 52 $m^3$. *Symbol*: ac.ft

**acrid** /ˈækrəd/, *adj.* **1.** sharp or biting to the taste; bitterly pungent; irritating. **2.** violent; stinging: *acrid remarks.* [L *ācer* sharp + -ID[4]] – **acridity** /əˈkrɪdəti/, **acridness,** *n.* – **acridly,** *adv.*

**acridine** /ˈækrədin, -dən/, *n.* a crystalline substance, $C_{13}H_9N$, part of the anthracene fraction of coal tar. It occurs as needle-shaped crystals and is a source of synthetic dyes and drugs.

**acriflavine** /ˌækrəˈfleɪvin, -vən/, *n.* a derivative of acridine, $C_{14}H_{14}N_3Cl$, used as an antiseptic; trypaflavine.

**acrilan** /ˈækrəlæn/, *n.* an acrylic fibre used in textiles, characterised chiefly by softness, strength, and crease-resistance. [Trademark]

**acrimonious** /ækrəˈmoʊniəs/, *adj.* caustic; stinging; bitter; virulent: *an acrimonious answer.* – **acrimoniously,** *adv.* – **acrimoniousness,** *n.*

**acrimony** /ˈækrəməni/, *n., pl.* **-nies.** sharpness or severity of temper; bitterness of expression proceeding from anger or ill nature. [L *ācrimōnia*]

**acritical** /eɪˈkrɪtɪkəl/, *adj.* **1.** not critical. **2.** *Med.* (of a disease) not showing a crisis.

**acro-,** a word element meaning 'tip', 'top', 'apex', or 'edge', as in *acrogen.* Also, before vowels, **acr-.** [Gk *akro-*, combining form of *ákros* at the top or end]

**acrobat** /ˈækrəbæt/, *n.* **1.** a skilled performer who can walk on a tightrope, perform on a trapeze, or do other similar feats. **2.** one who makes striking changes of opinion, as in politics, etc. [F *acrobate*, from Gk *akróbatos* walking on tiptoe] – **acrobatic** /ækrəˈbætɪk/, *adj.* – **acrobatically** /ækrəˈbætɪkli/, *adv.*

**acrobatics** /ækrəˈbætɪks/, *n.* **1.** (*construed as sing.*) the feats of an acrobat; gymnastics. **2.** (*construed as pl.*) skilled tricks like those of an acrobat. Also, **acrobatism** /ˈækrəˌbætɪzəm/.

**acrocarpous** /ækrəˈkapəs/, *adj. Bot.* having the fruit at the end of the primary axis.

**acrodont** /ˈækrədɒnt/, *adj.* **1.** with rootless teeth fastened to the alveolar ridge of the jaws. **2.** with sharp tips on the crowns of the cheek teeth.

**acrodrome** /ˈækrədroʊm/, *adj.* running to a point; said of a venation with the nerves terminating in, or curving inward to, the point of a leaf. Also, **acrodromous** /əˈkrɒdrəməs/.

**acrogen** /ˈækrədʒən/, *n.* a plant having no proper flowers but a growing point at the end of its perennial stems as a fern or moss. – **acrogenic** /ækrəˈdʒɛnɪk/, **acrogenous** /əˈkrɒdʒənəs/, *adj.* – **acrogenously** /əˈkrɒdʒənəsli/, *adv.*

**acrolein** /əˈkroʊliən/, *n.* a colourless, inflammable pungent liquid, acrylic aldehyde, $CH_2CH\ CHO$, obtained in the decomposition of glycerol. [ACR(ID) + L *olē(re)* smell + -IN[2]]

**acrolith** /ˈækrəlɪθ/, *n.* a sculptured figure having only the head and extremities made of marble or other stone. [L *acrolithus*, from Gk *akrólithos*] – **acrolithic** /ækrəˈlɪθɪk/, *adj.*

**acromegalic** /ˌækroʊməˈgælɪk/, *adj.* **1.** pertaining to or suffering from acromegaly. –*n.* **2.** a person suffering from acromegaly.

**acromegaly** /ˌækroʊˈmɛgəli/, *n.* a chronic disease characterised by excessive growth of the head, feet, hands, and sometimes the chest extremities and other structures, due to overactivity of the pituitary gland. [F *acromégalie.* See ACRO-, MEGALO-]

**acromion** /əˈkroʊmiən/, *n., pl.* **-mia** /-miə/. the outward end of the spine of the scapula or shoulderblade. Also, **acromion process.** [NL, from Gk *akrṓmion*] – **acromial,** *adj.*

**acronychal** /əˈkrɒnɪkəl/, *adj.* occurring at sunset, as the rising or setting of a star. Also, *U.S.*, **acronical.** [Gk *akrónychos* at nightfall + -AL[1]]

**acronym** /ˈækrənɪm/, *n.* a word formed from the initial letters of other words, as *radar* (from *radio detection and ranging*) or *ANZAC* (from *Australian and New Zealand Army Corps*). [ACR(O)- + Gk *ónyma* name (Doric), modelled on HOMONYM]

**acropetal** /əˈkrɒpətl/, *adj. Bot.* (of an inflorescence) developing upwards, towards the apex.

**acrophobia** /ækrəˈfoʊbiə/, *n.* a pathological dread of high places.

**acropolis** /əˈkrɒpələs/, *n.* the citadel of an ancient Greek city. [L, from Gk *akrópolis* the upper city]

**across** /əˈkrɒs/, *prep.* **1.** from side to side of: *a bridge across a river.* **2.** on the other side of: *across the sea.* **3.** so as to meet or fall in with: *we came across our friends.* –*adv.* **4.** from one side to another: *I came across in a steamer.* **5.** on the other side: *we'll soon be across.* **6.** crosswise: *with arms across.* **7.** *Colloq.* so as to pay or own up: *come across.* [A-[1] + CROSS]

**across-the-board** /əˈkrɒs-ðə-bɔd/, *adj.*; /əkrɒs-ðə-ˈbɔd/, *adv.* –*adj.* **1.** embracing all categories; general: *an across-the-board increase.* –*adv.* **2.** generally.

**acrostic** /əˈkrɒstɪk/, *n.* **1.** a series of lines or verses in which the first, last, or other particular letters form a word, phrase, the alphabet, etc. –*adj.* **2.** of or forming an acrostic. [L *acrostichis*, from Gk *akrostichís.* See ACRO-, STICHIC] – **acrostically,** *adv.*

**acrotism** /ˈækrətɪzəm/, *n.* absence or weakness of the pulse. [A-[6] + Gk *krótos* a beat + -ISM] – **acrotic** /əˈkrɒtɪk/, *adj.*

**acryl** /ˈækrəl/, *n.* the hypothetical radical of the allyl series, $C_3H_3O$. [ACR(OLEIN) + -YL]

**acrylate resin** /ˌækrəleɪt ˈrɛzən/, *n.* any of a class of acrylic resins used in adhesives, plastics, emulsion paints, and paper and textile finishes. Also, **acrylate.**

**acrylic** /əˈkrɪlɪk/, *adj.* **1.** of or pertaining to fibres formed by the polymerisation of acrylonitrile, or to fabrics woven from such fibres. –*n.* **2.** such a fabric, as acrilan, orlon. [ACRYL + -IC]

**acrylic acid** /– ˈæsəd/, *n.* one of a series of acids derived from the alkenes, with the general formula, $C_nH_{2n-2}O_2$. It is colourless, corrosive and easily polymerised.

**acrylic aldehyde** /– ˈældəhaɪd/, *n.* →**acrolein.**

**acrylic colour** /– ˈkʌlə/, *n.* artist's colour based on acrylic polymer resin and mixed with water or an acrylic medium. Also, **acrylic paint, acrylic polymer colour, polymer colour.**

**acrylic ester** /– 'ɛstə/, *n.* one of the series of esters derived from the acrylic acids.

**acrylic resin** /– 'rɛzən/, *n.* one of the group of thermoplastic resins formed by polymerising the esters or amides of acrylic acid, used chiefly when transparency is desired. Perspex and plexiglas are in this group.

**acrylonitrile** /əˌkrɪloʊ'naɪtraɪl/, *n.* a colourless toxic organic chemical, $CH_2{\cdot}CHCN$, used in the manufacture of acrylic fibres, thermoplastics, synthetic rubber, etc. [ACRYL(IC) + -O- + NITRILE]

**act** /ækt/, *n.* **1.** anything done or performed; a doing; deed. **2.** the process of doing: *caught in the act.* **3.** a decree, edict, law statute, judgment, resolve, or award: *an act of Parliament.* **4.** a deed of instrument recording a transaction. **5.** one of the main divisions of a play or opera. **6.** an individual performance forming part of a variety show, radio program, etc.: *a juggling act.* **7.** behaviour which is contrived and artificial, somewhat in the manner of a theatrical performance: *he's not really an ocker – it's just an act.* **8.** a display of bad temper. **9. bung (stack) on an act, a.** to display bad temper. **b.** to behave in a manner especially put on for the occasion. *–v.i.* **10.** to do something; exert energy or force; be employed or operative: *his mind acts quickly.* **11.** to be employed or operate in a particular way; perform specific duties or functions: *to act as chairman.* **12.** to produce effect; perform a function: *the medicine failed to act.* **13.** to behave: *to act well under pressure.* **14.** to pretend. **15.** to perform as an actor: *did she ever act on the stage?* **16.** to be capable of being acted on the stage: *his plays don't act well.* **17.** to serve or substitute (fol. by *for*). **18. act on** or **upon, a.** to act in accordance with; follow: *he acted upon my suggestion.* **b.** to affect: *alcohol acts on the brain.* **19. act up,** *Colloq.* **a.** to play up, take advantage of. **b.** (of a car, etc.) to malfunction. **20. act up to,** to come up to a standard set; fulfil. *–v.t.* **21.** to represent (a fictitious or historical character) with one's person: *to act Macbeth.* **22.** to feign; counterfeit: *to act outraged virtue.* **23.** to behave as suitable for: *to act your age.* **24.** to behave as: *he acted the fool.* **25. act out,** to give expression to (an idea, emotion, etc.) by acting or mime, either consciously or unconsciously. **26. act the goat** or **angora,** *Colloq.* to play the fool. **27.** *Obs.* to actuate. [ME, from L *actum* a thing done, and *actus* a doing]

**ACT** /eɪ si 'ti/, Australian Capital Territory. Also, **A.C.T.**

**actable** /'æktəbəl/, *adj.* **1.** capable of being acted on the stage. **2.** capable of being carried out in practice. – **actability** /æktə'bɪləti/, *n.*

**ACTH** /ˌeɪ si ti 'eɪtʃ/, *n.* **1.** a hormone produced by the pituitary gland, which controls the size of the adrenal glands and the production of the corticosteroids. **2.** this hormone extracted from the pituitary of pigs and used medicinally against rheumatic fever, rheumatoid arthritis, and various allergic disorders. [(A)DRENO-(C)ORTICO(T)ROPIC (H)ORMONE]

**actin** /'æktən/, *n.* a globular or fibrous protein present in muscle plasma which, in connection with myosin, plays an important role in muscle contraction.

**actinal** /'æktənəl/, *adj. Zool.* having tentacles or rays. – **actinally,** *adv.*

**acting** /'æktɪŋ/, *adj.* **1.** serving temporarily; substitute: *acting governor.* **2.** that acts; functioning. **3.** provided with stage directions; designed to be used for performance: *an acting version of a play.* *–n.* **4.** performance as an actor. **5.** the occupation of an actor. **6.** pretence; make-believe.

**actinia** /æk'tɪniə/, *n., pl.* **-tiniae** /-'tɪnii/. a sea-anemone of the genus *Actinia.*

**actinic** /æk'tɪnɪk/, *adj.* **1.** pertaining to actinism. **2.** (of radiation) chemically active. – **actinically,** *adv.*

**actinic rays** /– 'reɪz/, *n.pl.* ultraviolet radiation.

**actinide** /'æktənaɪd/, *n.* any of the series of elements with atomic numbers between 89 and 105; analogous to a lanthanide.

**actiniform** /æk'tɪnəfɔm/, *adj. Zool.* having a radiate form.

**actinism** /'æktənɪzəm/, *n.* the action or the property of radiant energy of producing chemical changes.

**actinium** /æk'tɪniəm/, *n.* a radioactive chemical element, an isotope of mesothorium, occurring in pitchblende, and resembling the rare earths in chemical behaviour and valency. *Symbol:* Ac; *at. no.:* 89; *at. wt of most stable isotope:* 227; *radioactive half-life:* 21.7 years. [ACTIN(O)- + -IUM]

**actinium-228** /ækˌtɪniəm-tu tu 'eɪt/, *n.* an isotope of actinium.

**actino-,** **1.** *Chem.* a word element used in compounds relating to actinism or actinic activity, as in *actinotherapy.* **2.** *Zool.* a word element used in compounds relating to radiate structures, as in *actinoid.* Also, **actin-.** [Gk *aktīno-*, combining form of *aktís* ray]

**actinogram** /æk'tɪnəgræm/, *n.* a record made by an actinograph.

**actinograph** /æk'tɪnəgræf, -graf/, *n.* a recording actinometer. – **actinographic** /æktɪnə'græfɪk/, *adj.*

**actinography** /æktə'nɒgrəfi/, *n.* the recording of actinic power by an actinograph.

**actinoid** /'æktənɔɪd/, *adj.* raylike; radiate.

**actinolite** /æk'tɪnəlaɪt/, *n.* calcium magnesium iron silicate which is a variety of amphibole, occurring in greenish bladed crystals or in masses.

**actinomere** /æk'tɪnəmɪə/, *n.* a part corresponding to an opposite or similar part in an organism which is bilaterally or radially symmetrical; antimere. – **actinomeric,** *adj.*

**actinometer** /æktə'nɒmətə/, *n.* an instrument for measuring the intensity of radiation, whether by the chemical effects or otherwise. – **actinometry,** *n.* – **actinometric** /æktənoʊ'mɛtrɪk/, **actinometrical** /æktənoʊ'mɛtrɪkəl/, *adj.*

**actinomorphic** /æktənoʊ'mɔfɪk/, *adj.* **1.** having radial symmetry. **2.** *Bot.* (of certain flowers, as the buttercup) divisible vertically into similar halves by each of a number of planes. Also, **actinomorphous** /æktənoʊ'mɔfəs/.

**actinomycete** /æktənoʊ'maɪsit/, *n.* any member of the Actinomycetes, a group of micro-organisms commonly regarded as filamentous bacteria.

**actinomycosis** /ˌæktənoʊmaɪ'koʊsəs/, *n.* a chronic inflammatory disease of cattle and other animals, sometimes transmitted to man, due to a parasitic fungus and causing lumpy, often suppurative tumours, esp. about the jaws. – **actinomycotic** /ækˌtɪnəmaɪ'kɒtik/, *adj.*

**actinon** /'æktənɒn/, *n.* **1.** an inert gas, an isotope of radon, of mass number 219, produced by the disintegration of actinium. *Symbol:* An **2.** →**actinide.**

**actinopod** /æk'tɪnəpɒd/, *n.* any protozoan of the sub-class Actinopoda, including the heliozoans and radiolarians, having stiff, rodlike, radiating pseudopodia.

**actinozoan** /æktənoʊ'zoʊən/, *n., adj.* →**anthozoan.**

**action** /'ækʃən/, *n.* **1.** the process or state of acting or of being active: *the machine is not now in action.* **2.** something done; an act; deed. **3.** (*pl.*) habitual or usual acts; conduct. **4.** energetic activity. **5.** an exertion of power or force: *the action of wind upon a ship's sails.* **6.** *Physiol.* a change in organs, tissues, or cells leading to performance of a function, as in muscular contraction. **7.** way or manner of moving: *the action of a machine or of a horse.* **8.** the mechanism by which something is operated, as that of a breech-loading rifle or a piano. **9.** *Physics.* **a.** a force exerted by one object on a second object (as opposed to *reaction*, the equal and opposite force exerted by the second object on the first). See **Newton's laws. b.** the product of work and time. **10.** a small battle. **11.** military and naval combat. **12.** the main subject or story, as distinguished from an incidental episode. **13.** *Drama.* **a.** one of the three unities. See **unity** (def. 10). **b.** an event or happening that is part of a dramatic plot: *the action of a scene, a bit of action.* **14.** the gestures or deportment of an actor or speaker. **15.** *Fine Arts.* the appearance of animation, movement, or passion given to figures by their attitude, position, or expression. **16.** *Law.* **a.** a proceeding instituted by one party against another. **b.** the right of bringing it. **c. take action,** to commence legal proceedings. **17.** *Colloq.* a profitable involvement in the enterprise: *a piece of the action.* *–v.t.* **18.** to take action concerning. [L *actio*; replacing ME *accion,* from OF] – **actionless,** *adj.*

**actionable** /'ækʃənəbəl/, *adj.* **1.** furnishing ground for a law suit. **2.** liable to a law suit. – **actionably,** *adv.*

**actionist** /'ækʃənəst/, *n., adj.* →**activist.**

**action painting** /'ækʃən ˌpeɪntɪŋ/, *n.* a form of non-geometric abstract art in which the importance of the physical act of painting as a means of expression is stressed rather than the finished product; both traditional styles and technical procedures are largely ignored.

**action replay** /– 'ripleɪ/, *n.* →**instant replay.**

**action stations** /'– ˌsteɪʃənz/, *n.pl.* **1. a.** *Mil.* stations to be taken up in readiness for or during battle. **b.** *Colloq.* positions taken up preparatory to action. **2. a.** *Mil.* the command to take up action stations. **b.** *Colloq.* a warning or command to get ready for action.

**activate** /'æktəveɪt/, *v.t.*, **-vated, -vating. 1.** to make active. **2.** *Physics.* to render radioactive. **3.** to aerate (sewage) as a purification measure. **4.** *Chem.* **a.** to make more active: *to activate carbon, a catalyst, molecules.* **b.** to hasten (reactions) by various means, such as heating. **5.** *U.S. Mil.* to mobilise. – **activation** /æktə'veɪʃən/, *n.*

**activated charcoal** /ˌæktəveɪtəd 'tʃakoʊl/, *n.* granulated charcoal heated to 800°–1000° C in a current of steam to remove hydrocarbons; highly absorbent to gases and vapours because of its enormous surface area; used in solvent recovery, deodorisation, and as an antidote to certain poisons. Also, **activated carbon, active carbon.**

**activated complex** /– 'kɒmplɛks/, *n.* a short-lived transition state which appears during chemical reactions, when the molecules can no longer be considered as reactants, and are not yet products.

**activated sludge** /– 'slʌdʒ/, *n.* aerated sewage sludge, added to raw sewage to hasten bacterial decomposition.

**activator** /'æktəveɪtə/, *n.* →**catalyst.**

**active** /'æktɪv/, *adj.* **1.** in a state of action; in actual progress or motion: *active hostilities.* **2.** constantly engaged in action; busy: *an active life.* **3.** having the power of quick motion; nimble: *an active animal.* **4.** moving in considerable volume; brisk; lively: *an active market.* **5.** causing change; capable of exerting influence: *active treason.* **6.** *Gram.* denoting a voice of verb inflection, in which the subject is represented as performing the action expressed by the verb (opposed to *passive*). For example: In English, *he writes the letter* (active); *the letter was written* (passive) **7.** requiring action; practical: *the intellectual and the active mental powers.* **8.** *Theol.* devoted to good works (opposed to *contemplative*). **9.** (of a volcano) in eruption. **10.** *Electronics.* (of an electronic component, or a complete circuit) able to amplify or switch a signal. **11.** *Accounting.* profitable; busy: *active accounts* (ones having current transactions). **12.** interest bearing: *active paper.* **13.** *Med.* acting quickly; producing immediate effects: *active remedies.* **14.** capable of acting or reacting, esp. in some specific manner: *active carbon.* **15.** (of a communications satellite) able to retransmit signals. *–n.* **16.** *Gram.* **a.** the active voice. **b.** a form of construction in that voice. [L *actīvus*; replacing ME *actif*, from F] – **actively,** *adv.* – **activeness,** *n.*

**active carbon** /– 'kabən/, *n.* →**activated charcoal.**

**active immunity** /– ə'mjunəti/, *n.* immunity achieved by the manufacture of antibodies within the organism.

**active list** /'– lɪst/, *n.* a list of military officers on full pay available for or engaged in service.

**active service** /– 'sɜvəs/, *n.* **1.** the performance of military duty in the field in time of war. **2.** the state of being on full duty with full pay.

**activist** /'æktəvəst/, *n.* a zealous worker for a cause, esp. a political cause; actionist. – **activism,** *n.*

**activity** /æk'tɪvəti/, *n., pl.* **-ties. 1.** the state of action; doing. **2.** the quality of acting promptly; energy. **3.** a specific deed or action; sphere of action: *social activities.* **4.** an exercise of energy or force; an active movement or operation. **5.** liveliness; agility. **6.** a measure of the rate of spontaneous nuclear transformation of radioactive nuclides; the SI unit is the becquerel. *–adj.* **7.** of or pertaining to educational provision made for slow learners and children with intellectual handicaps, usu. involving methods of learning and teaching associated with activities: *activity class.*

**act of faith,** *n.* **1.** an act which demonstrates or tests the strength of a person's convictions, as a personal sacrifice. **2.** *Colloq.* a risk or gamble, esp. one taken because of a hunch.

**act of God,** *n. Law.* a direct, sudden, and irresistible action of natural forces, such as could not humanly have been foreseen or prevented.

**act of grace,** *n.* **1.** an act of Parliament granting a general pardon. **2.** payment by a government to a citizen with whom it is in dispute to avoid protracted litigation, although the government is not legally liable.

**act of indemnity,** *n.* an act of Parliament passed to exempt persons from punishment for illegal actions undertaken in the public interest, as in wartime.

**act of Parliament,** *n.* a legislative decree passed by Parliament and bearing the Royal assent.

**act of war,** *n.* an illegal act of aggression by a country against another with which it is nominally at peace.

**actomyosin** /æktə'maɪəsən/, *n.* a complex of actin and myosin which is the major constituent of muscle. The shortening of actomyosin fibrils causes muscle contraction.

**actor** /'æktə/, *n.* **1.** one who plays the part of a character in a dramatic performance. **2.** one who acts; doer. Cf. **act** (def. 17). **3.** one who behaves histrionically. **4.** *Colloq.* one whose ordinary behaviour is often ostentatious, bizarre or showy. [L]

**actress** /'æktrəs/, *n.* a female actor.

**A.C.T.U.** /ˌeɪ si ti 'ju/, Australian Council of Trade Unions. Also, **ACTU.**

**actual** /'æktʃuəl/, *adj.* **1.** existing in act or fact; real. **2.** now existing; present: *the actual position of the moon.* **3.** *Obs.* exhibited in action. [LL *actuālis* active, practical; replacing ME *actuel*, from OF] – **actualness,** *n.*

**actual grace** /– 'greɪs/, *n. Rom. Cath. Ch.* supernatural help given by God to enlighten the mind and strengthen the will to do good and avoid evil.

**actual ground zero,** *n.* the point on the earth's surface below, at, or above the centre of a nuclear burst.

**actualise** /'æktʃuəlaɪz/, *v.t.*, **-lised, -lising.** to make actual; realise in action or fact. Also, **actualize.** – **actualisation** /ˌæktʃuəlaɪ'zeɪʃən/, *n.* – **actualisable,** *adj.*

**actuality** /æktʃu'æləti/, *n., pl.* **-ties. 1.** actual existence; reality. **2.** (*pl.*) actual conditions or circumstances; facts: *he had to adjust to the actualities of life.* *–adj.* **3.** of or pertaining to films, television programs, etc., which are of a documentary nature.

**actually** /'æktʃuəli, 'æktʃəli/, *adv.* as an actual or existing fact; really.

**actual sin** /ˌæktʃuəl 'sɪn/, *n.* the sin of an individual, as contrasted with original sin.

**actuary** /'æktʃuəri/, *n., pl.* **-ries. 1.** a statistician who computes risks, rates, etc., according to probabilities indicated by recorded facts. **2.** (formerly) a registrar or clerk. [L *actuārius*] – **actuarial** /æktʃu'ɛəriəl/, *adj.* – **actuarially** /æktʃu'ɛəriəli/, *adv.*

**actuate** /'æktʃueɪt/, *v.t.*, **-ated, -ating. 1.** to incite to action: *actuated by selfish motives.* **2.** to put into action. [ML *actuātus*, pp.] – **actuation** /æktʃu'eɪʃən/, *n.* – **actuator,** *n.*

**acuate** /'ækjueɪt/, *adj.* sharpened; pointed. [ML *acuātus*, pp.]

**acuity** /ə'kjuəti/, *n.* sharpness; acuteness: *acuity of vision.* [ML *acuitas*]

**aculeate** /ə'kjulieɪt/, *adj.* **1.** *Biol.* having or denoting any sharp-pointed structure. **2.** having a slender ovipositor or sting, as the hymenopterous insects. **3.** pointed; stinging. Also, **aculeated.** [L *acūleātus* prickly]

**aculeus** /ə'kjuliəs/, *n.* **1.** a prickle or thorn, esp. one growing from the stem of a rose tree. **2.** an ovipositor or sting.

**acumen** /'ækjəmən/, *n.* quickness of perception; mental acuteness; keen insight. [L] – **acuminous** /ə'kjumənəs/, *adj.*

**acuminate** /ə'kjumənət, -eɪt/, *adj.*; /ə'kjuməneɪt/, *v.*, **-nated, -nating.** *–adj.* **1.** *Bot., Zool., etc.* pointed; tapering to a point. *–v.t.* **2.** to make sharp or keen. [L *acūminātus*, pp.] – **acumination** /əkjumə'neɪʃən/, *n.*

**acupuncture** /'ækjəpʌŋktʃə, 'ækə-/, *n., v.*, **-tured, -turing.** *–n.* **1.** a Chinese medical practice to treat disease, establish diagnosis or relieve pain, by puncturing specific areas of skin with long sharp needles. **2.** *Med.* the puncture of a tissue with a needle

acuminate leaf

as for drawing off fluids or relieving pain. *–v.t.* **3.** to perform an acupunture on. [L *acu(s)* needle + PUNCTURE]

**acupuncturist** /ækjə'pʌŋktʃərəst, ækə-/, *n.* one who practises acupuncture.

**acutance** /ə'kjutəns/, *n.* a measure of the sharpness with which a film can reproduce the edge of an object.

**acute** /ə'kjut/, *adj.* **1.** sharp at the end; ending in a point (opposed to *blunt* or *obtuse*). **2.** sharp in effect; intense; poignant: *acute sorrow.* **3.** severe; crucial: *an acute shortage.* **4.** brief and severe, as disease (opposed to *chronic*). **5.** sharp or penetrating in intellect, insight, or perception: *an acute observer.* **6.** having quick sensibility; susceptible to slight impressions: *acute eyesight.* **7.** high in pitch, as sound (opposed to *grave*). **8.** *Geom., etc.* (of an angle) less than 90°. **9.** *Gram.* designating or having a particular accent (´) indicating: **a.** (orig.) a raised pitch (as in ancient Greek). **b.** (later) stress (as in the Spanish *adiós*), quality of sound (as in the French *résumé*), vowel length (as in Hungarian), etc. *–n.* **10.** the acute accent. [L *acūtus*, pp., sharpened] – **acutely,** *adv.* – **acuteness,** *n.*

**acute dose** /– 'doʊs/, *n.* a total dose of radiation received at one time over a period so short that biological recovery cannot occur.

**-acy** a suffix of nouns of quality, state, office, etc., many of which accompany adjectives in *-acious* or nouns or adjectives in *-ate*, as in *efficacy, fallacy,* etc., *advocacy, primacy,* etc., *accuracy, delicacy,* etc. [representing L *-ācia, -ātia,* and Gk *-áteia*]

**acyclic** /eɪ'saɪklɪk, eɪ'sɪklɪk/, *adj.* **1.** not occurring in cycles; not periodic. **2.** *Chem.* aliphatic. [A-[6] + CYCLIC]

**acyl group** /'æsəl grup/, *n.* any organic acid radical.

**ad**[1] /æd/, *n. Colloq.* advertisement.

**ad**[2] /æd/, *n.* advantage (def. 5).

**ad-,** a prefix of direction, tendency, and addition, attached chiefly to stems not found as words themselves, as in *advert, advent.* Also, **ac-, af-, ag-, al-, an-, ap-, ar-, as-, at-,** and **a-**[5]. [L, representing *ad*, prep., to, towards, at, about]

**-ad,** **1.** a suffix forming nouns denoting a collection of a certain number, as in *triad.* **2.** a suffix found in words and names proper to Greek myth, as in *dryad, Pleiad.* [representing Gk *-áda*, acc. (nom. *-ás*)]

**A.D.,** Australian Democrats.

**A.D.**[1] /eɪ 'di/, Dame of the Order of Australia.

**A.D.**[2] /eɪ 'di/, since Christ was born. From 20 B.C. to A.D. 50 is 70 years. [L *annō Dominī* in the year of our Lord]

**adactylous** /eɪ'dæktələs/, *adj.* without fingers or toes. [A-[6] + DACTYL + -OUS]

**adage** /'ædɪdʒ/, *n.* a proverb. [F, from L *adagium*]

**adagio** /ə'daʒioʊ, -dʒioʊ/, *adv., adj., n., pl.* **-gios.** *–adv.* **1.** (a musical direction) in a leisurely manner; slowly. *–adj.* **2.** slow. *–n.* **3.** an adagio movement or piece. **4.** *Ballet.* a slow dance. [It.]

**Adam** /'ædəm/, *n.* **1.** the name of the first man. **2. the old Adam,** the unregenerate nature of man, the evil inherent in man; human frailty. **3. not to know (someone) from Adam,** *Colloq.* not to know (someone) at all. [See Genesis 2:7] – **Adamic, adamic,** *adj.*

**adamant** /'ædəmənt/, *n.* **1.** (in ancient times) some impenetrably hard substance, variously indentified later as the diamond or the lodestone. **2.** any impenetrably hard substance. *–adj.* **3.** hard as adamant; adamantine. **4.** firm in purpose or opinion; unyielding. [L *adamas*, from Gk; replacing ME *adamaunt* (from OF), and OE *athamans* (representing LL var. of *adamas*)]

**adamantine** /ædə'mæntaɪn/, *adj.* **1.** impenetrable. **2.** like a diamond in lustre.

**Adamite** /'ædəmaɪt/, *n.* **1.** a descendant of Adam; a human being. **2.** a nudist. – **Adamitic** /ædə'mɪtɪk/, *adj.*

**Adam's ale** /ædəmz 'eɪl/, *n. Colloq.* water.

**Adam's apple** /– 'æpəl/, *n.* a projection of the thyroid cartilage at the front of the (male) throat.

**adamsite** /'ædəmzaɪt/, *n.* a yellow irritant smoke, containing a form of arsenic that is poisonous, used as a poison gas. *Symbol:* DM [named after Major Roger *Adams*, U.S. soldier and chemist, b. 1889, who invented it. See -ITE[1]]

**Adam's-needle** /ædəmz-'nidl/, *n.* a species of yucca, *Yucca smalliana*, much cultivated for ornament.

**adapt** /ə'dæpt/, *v.t.* to make suitable to requirements; adjust or modify fittingly. [L *adaptāre*]

**adaptable** /ə'dæptəbəl/, *adj.* **1.** capable of being adapted. **2.** able to adapt oneself easily to new conditions. – **adaptability** /ədæptə'bɪləti/, **adaptableness,** *n.*

**adaptation** /ædæp'teɪʃən, ædæp-/, *n.* **1.** the act of adapting. **2.** the state of being adapted; adjustment. **3.** something produced by adapting. **4.** a literary work rewritten for presentation in a different medium: *an adaptation of a novel for the stage.* **5.** *Biol.* **a.** alteration in the structure or function of organisms which enables them to survive and multiply in a changed environment. **b.** a form or structure modified in response to a changed environment. **6.** *Physiol.* the response of sensory receptor organs, as those of vision, touch, temperature, olfaction, audition, and pain, to constantly applied stimuli from a changing environment. **7.** Also, **adaption** /ə'dæpʃən/. *Sociol.* a slow, usu. unconscious modification of individual and social activity in adjustment to cultural surroundings. – **adaptational,** *adj.*

**adaptive** /ə'dæptɪv/, *adj.* serving to adapt; showing adaptation: *adaptive colouring of a chameleon.* – **adaptively,** *adj.* – **adaptiveness,** *n.*

**adaptor** /ə'dæptə/, *n.* **1.** one that adapts. **2.** a device for fitting together parts having different sizes or designs. **3.** an accessory to convert a machine, tool, etc., to a new or modified use. **4.** *Elect.* an accessory plug for connecting a piece of apparatus fitted with one type of terminals to a supply point with a different type. Also, **adapter.**

**adaxial** /æd'æksiəl/, *adj.* (of a plant) situated on the side towards the axis. [AD- + L *axi(s)* axle + -AL[1]]

**ADC** /eɪ di 'si/, aide-de-camp.

**A-D converter** /eɪ-di kən'vɜtə/, *n.* →**analog-to-digital converter.** Also, **A to D converter.**

**add** /æd/, *v.t.* **1.** to unite or join so as to increase the number, quantity, size, or importance: *to add another stone to the pile.* **2.** to find the sum of (oft. fol. by *up*). **3.** to say or write further. **4.** to include (fol. by *in*). *–v.i.* **5.** to perform the arithmetical operation of addition. **6.** to be or serve as an addition (fol. by *to*): *to add to one's grief.* **7. add up, a.** to amount (*to*): *it adds up to murder.* **b.** to make the desired or expected total: *these figures don't add up.* **c.** *Colloq.* to make sense, be logically consistent: *the facts don't add up.* [ME *adde(n)*, from L *addere*] – **addible, addable,** *adj.* – **adder,** *n.*

**add.,** addendum.

**addax** /'ædæks/, *n.* a large pale-coloured antelope, *Addax nasomaculatus*, of North Africa, with loosely spiral horns. [L; of ancient North African orig.]

addax

**added time** /'ædəd taɪm/, *n.* extra time allowed in a match where the scores are equal at full time.

**added tradesman** /– 'treɪdzmən/, *n.* a person who, though lacking formal trade qualifications, was employed during World War II to do work normally carried out by a tradesman.

**addend** /'ædend/, *n.* any of a set of numbers which are to be added. [short for ADDENDUM]

**addendum** /ə'dendəm/, *n., pl.* **-da** /-də/. **1.** a thing to be added; an addition. **2.** an appendix to a book. **3.** *Mach.* **a.** the distance between the tip of a tooth and the pitch circle or pitch line of a toothed wheel or rack. **b.** Also, **addendum circle.** an imaginary circle touching the ends of the teeth of a toothed wheel. [L, neut. ger. of *addere* add]

**adder** /'ædə/, *n.* **1.** the common European viper, *Vipera berus*, a small venomous snake, widespread in northern Eurasia. **2.** any of various other snakes, venomous or harmless, resembling the viper. [var. of ME *nadder* (*a nadder* being taken as *an adder*), OE *nǣdre*]

**adder's-meat** /'ædəz-mit/, *n.* the greater stitchwort, *Stellaria holostea*.

**adder's-tongue** /'ædəz-tʌŋ/, *n.* a fern of the genus *Ophioglossum*, with a spore-bearing spike.

**addict** /'ædɪkt/, *n.*; /ə'dɪkt/, *v.* *–n.* **1.** one who is addicted to a practice or habit: *a drug addict.* –*v.t.* **2.** to give (oneself) over, as to a habit or pursuit; apply or devote habitually (fol. by *to*): *addict oneself to science.* [L *addictus*, pp., adjudged, devoted]

**addicted** /əˈdɪktəd/, *adj.* devoted or given up (to a practice, habit, or substance) (fol. by *to*): *addicted to drugs.* – **addictedness,** *n.*

**addiction** /əˈdɪkʃən/, *n.* the state of being addicted to some habit, practice, or substance, esp. to narcotics.

**addictive** /əˈdɪktɪv/, *adj.* **1.** (esp. of drugs) causing or tending to cause addiction. –*n.* **2.** an addictive agent.

**adding machine** /ˈædɪŋ məʃin/, *n.* any of various, usu. monetary, calculating machines.

**Addison's disease** /ˈædəsənz dəziz/, *n.* a disease characterised by asthenia, low blood-pressure, and a brownish colouration of the skin, due to progressive destruction of the suprarenal cortex. [named after T. *Addison*, 1793–1860, English physician, who first described it]

**addition** /əˈdɪʃən/, *n.* **1.** the act or process of adding or uniting. **2.** the process of uniting two or more numbers into one sum, denoted by the symbol + . **3.** the result of adding; anything added. **4.** *Obs.* a particularising designation added to a person's name. **5.** (*oft. pl.*) wings, rooms, etc., added to a building, or land added to property already owned. **6. in addition to,** besides; as well as. [L *additio*; replacing ME *addicioun*, from F]

**additional** /əˈdɪʃənəl/, *adj.* added; supplementary: *additional information.* – **additionally,** *adv.*

**addition compound** /əˈdɪʃən ˌkɒmpaʊnd/, *n.* a compound formed by chemical addition.

**additive** /ˈædətɪv/, *adj.* **1.** to be added; of the nature of an addition; characterised by addition: *an additive process.* –*n.* **2.** something added. [L *additīvus*] – **additively,** *adj.*

**addle** /ˈædl/, *v.*, **addled, addling,** *adj.* –*v.t.* **1.** to muddle or confuse. **2.** to spoil or make rotten. –*v.i.* **3.** to become muddled or confused. **4.** to become spoiled or rotten, as eggs. –*adj.* **5.** mentally confused; muddled, as in the combinations **addlebrained, addleheaded, addlepated. 6.** rotten: *addled eggs.* [OE *adela* liquid filth, c. MLG *adele* mud]

**address** /əˈdrɛs, ˈædrɛs/, *n.*; /əˈdrɛs/, *v.* –*n.* **1.** a formal speech or writing directed to a person or a group of persons: *an address on current problems.* **2.** a direction as to name and residence inscribed on a letter, etc. **3.** a place where a person lives or may be reached. **4.** *Computers.* a number or symbol which identifies a particular register in the memory of a digital computer. **5.** manner of speaking to persons; personal bearing in conversation. **6.** skilful management; adroitness: *to handle a matter with address.* **7.** (*usu. pl.*) attentions paid by a lover; courtship. **8.** *Obs.* preparation. –*v.t.* **9.** to make a formal speech to: *the leader addressed the assembly.* **10.** to speak to a person in an official position, as a judge, governor-general, etc., using his formal title: *he began his speech by addressing the governor-general.* **11.** to direct to the ear or attention: *to address a warning to someone.* **12.** to apply in speech (used reflexively, fol. by *to*) : *he addressed himself to the chairman.* **13.** to direct for delivery; put a direction on: *to address a letter.* **14.** to direct the energy or force of (used reflexively, fol. by *to*): *he addressed himself to the work in hand.* **15.** to pay court to; woo; court. **16.** *Golf.* to adjust and apply the club to (the ball) in preparing for a stroke. **17.** *Obs. except in Golf.* to give direction to; aim. **18.** *Obs.* to prepare. –*v.i.* **19.** to make an appeal. **20.** *Obs.* to make preparations. [ME *addresse(n)*, from F *adresser*, earlier *adrecier*, from L *ad* to + *directus* straight] – **addresser, addressor,** *n.*

**addressee** /ədrɛsˈi/, *n.* one to whom anything is addressed.

**address-in-reply** /əˌdrɛs-ɪn-rəˈplaɪ/, *n.* the reply to the speech made by the sovereign's representative at the opening of a parliamentary session.

**addressograph** /əˈdrɛsəgræf, -graf/, *n.* a machine that prints addresses upon envelopes, etc., from stencils. [Trademark]

**adduce** /əˈdjus/, *v.t.*, **-duced, -ducing.** to bring forward in argument; cite as pertinent or conclusive: *to adduce reasons.* [L *addūcere* lead to] – **adducible,** *adj.* – **adducer,** *n.*

**adducent** /əˈdjusənt/, *adj.* drawing towards; adducting. [L *addūcens*, ppr., leading to]

**adduct** /əˈdʌkt/, *v.t. Physiol.* to draw towards the main axis (opposed to *abduct*). [L *adductus*, pp., led to] – **adductive,** *adj.* – **adductor,** *n.*

**adduction** /əˈdʌkʃən/, *n.* **1.** *Physiol.* the action of the adductor or adducent muscles. **2.** the act of adducing.

**-ade**[1], **1.** a suffix found in nouns denoting action or process, product or result of action, person or persons acting, often irregularly attached, as in *blockade, escapade, masquerade.* **2.** a noun suffix indicating a drink made of a particular fruit, as in *orangeade.* [F, from Pr. *-ada*, from L *-āta*; in some words -ADE is for Sp. and Pg. *-ado*, It. *-ato*, from L *-ātus*]

**-ade**[2], a collective suffix, variant of **-ad** (def. 1), as in *decade.*

**Adel.,** Adelaide.

**Adelaidian** /ædəˈleɪdiən/, *n.* **1.** one who was born in Adelaide, the capital city of South Australia, or who has come to regard it as his home town. –*adj.* **2.** of or pertaining to the city of Adelaide.

**Adelie penguin** /əˌdili ˈpɛŋgwən, ˈpɛŋgwən/, *n.* a penguin *Pygoscelis adeliae*, which breeds mainly in Antarctica but is occasionally found on the southern coast of Australia. [named after *Adelie* Land, a French Antarctic territory]

**ademption** /əˈdɛmpʃən/, *n.* revocation; the complete or partial extinction or withholding of a legacy by some act of the testator during his life other than revocation by a testamentary instrument. [L *ademptio*]

Adelie penguin

**adenalgia** /ædəˈnældʒə/, *n.* pain in a gland.

**adenine** /ˈædənin, -naɪn/, *n.* a purine base, $C_5H_5N_5$, present in all living cells, mainly in combined form, as in nucleic acids.

**adeno-,** a word element meaning 'gland'. Also, before vowels, **aden-.** [Gk, combining form of *adēn*]

**adenohypophysis** /ˌædənoʊhaɪˈpɒfəsəs/, *n.* the anterior lobe of the pituitary gland which secretes several hormones, most of which stimulate other endocrine glands. [ADENO- + HYPOPHYSIS]

**adenoid** /ˈædənɔɪd/, *n.* **1.** (*usu. pl.*) an enlarged mass of lymphoid tissue in the upper pharynx, common in children, often preventing nasal breathing. –*adj.* **2.** Also, **adenoidal** /ædəˈnɔɪdl/. pertaining to the lymphatic glands. [Gk *adenoeidēs* glandular]

**adenoidectomy** /ædənɔɪˈdɛktəmi/, *n., pl.* **-mies.** the operation of removing the adenoids.

**adenoma** /ædəˈnoʊmə/, *n., pl.* **-mas, -mata** /-mətə/. **1.** a tumour originating in a gland. **2.** a tumour of glandlike structure. – **adenomatous** /ædəˈnɒmətəs, -ˈnoʊmə-/, *adj.*

**adenosine** /əˈdɛnəsin, ædəˈnoʊsin/, *n.* a nucleoside of adenine and ribose, present in all living cells, mainly in combined form, as in ribonucleic acids.

**adenosine triphosphate** /– traɪˈfɒsfeɪt/, *n.* the triphosphate of adenosine, present in all living cells, which represents a store of chemical energy. *Abbrev.:* ATP.

**adenovirus** /ædənoʊˈvaɪrəs/, *n.* a virus causing infection of the upper respiratory tract. [ADENO- + VIRUS]

**adenyl cyclase** /ˌædənaɪl ˈsaɪkleɪz/, *n.* an enzyme which catalyses the conversion of adenosine triphosphate to cyclic AMP.

**adenylic acid** /ˌædənɪlɪk ˈæsəd/, *n.* the monophosphate of adenosine, present in all living cells, mainly in combined form, as in ribonucleic acids.

**adept** /ˈædɛpt/, *n.*; /əˈdɛpt/, *adj.* –*n.* **1.** one who has attained proficiency; one fully skilled in anything. –*adj.* **2.** highly skilled; proficient; expert. [L *adeptus*, pp., having attained] – **adeptly,** *adv.* – **adeptness,** *n.*

**adequacy** /ˈædəkwəsi/, *n.* the state or quality of being adequate; a sufficiency for a particular purpose.

**adequate** /ˈædəkwət/, *adj.* **1.** equal to the requirement or occasion; fully sufficient, suitable, or fit (oft. fol. by *to* or *for*). **2.** *Law.* reasonably sufficient for starting legal action: *adequate grounds.* [L *adaequātus*, pp., equalised] – **adequately,** *adv.* – **adequateness,** *n.*

**ad eundum (gradum)** /ˌæd eɪʊndəm ˈgradəm/, to the same

(degree). A graduate from one university may be admitted without examination to an *ad eundum* degree in the same subject at another university. [L]

**à deux** /a 'dɜ/, *adv.* of or for two; two at a time. [F]

**ADF** /eɪ di 'ɛf/, automatic direction finder.

**ad fin.**, to the end. [L: *ad fīnem*]

**adhere** /əd'hɪə/, *v.i.*, **-hered, -hering. 1.** to stick fast; cleave; cling (fol. by *to*). **2.** to be devoted; be attached as a follower or upholder (fol. by *to*): *to adhere to a party, a leader, a church, a creed, etc.* **3.** to hold closely or firmly (fol. by *to*): *to adhere to a plan.* **4.** *Obs.* to be consistent. [L *adhaerēre*] – **adherer,** *n.*

**adherence** /əd'hɪərəns/, *n.* **1.** the quality of adhering; fidelity; steady attachment: *adherence to a party, rigid adherence to rules.* **2.** the act or state of adhering; adhesion.

**adherent** /əd'hɪərənt, -'hɛrənt/, *n.* **1.** one who follows or upholds a leader, cause, etc.; supporter; follower (fol. by *of*). *–adj.* **2.** sticking; clinging; adhering. **3.** *Bot.* adnate. **4.** *Gram.* standing before and modifying a noun. – **adherently,** *adv.*

**adhesion** /əd'hiʒən/, *n.* **1.** the act or state of adhering, or of being united: *the adhesion of parts united by growth.* **2.** steady attachment of the mind or feelings; adherence. **3.** *Physics.* the molecular force exerted across the surface of contact between unlike liquids and solids which resists their separation. **4.** *Pathol.* **a.** the abnormal union of adjacent tissues due to inflammation. **b.** the tissue involved. [L *adhaesio*]

**adhesive** /əd'hisɪv, -'hizɪv/, *adj.* **1.** clinging; tenacious; sticking fast. *–n.* **2.** a substance for sticking things together. – **adhesively,** *adv.* – **adhesiveness,** *n.*

**adhesive tape** /– 'teɪp/, *n.* a tape, usu. of plastic or fabric, coated on one side with an adhesive, used for binding, etc.

**ad hoc** /æd 'hɒk/, *adj.* **1.** for this (special purpose); an **ad hoc committee** is one set up to deal with one subject only (opposed to *omnibus*). **2.** impromptu. An **ad hoc decision** is one made with regard to the exigencies of the moment. *–adv.* **3.** with respect to this (subject or thing). [L]

**adhockery** /æd'hɒkəri/, *n.* behaviour influenced by prevailing exigencies without regard for effects over a longer term.

**ad hominem** /æd 'hɒmənəm/, **1.** to the man; personal. An argument *ad hominem* **a.** appeals to a person's prejudices or special interests instead of to his intellect, or **b.** relies on personal attack. [L]

**adiabatic** /ˌædiə'bætɪk/, *adj.* without gain or loss of heat (distinguished from *isothermal*). [Gk *adiábatos* impassable + -IC] – **adiabatically,** *adv.*

**adiaphorous** /ædi'æfərəs/, *adj.* doing neither good nor harm, as a medicine.

**adiathermancy** /ˌædiə'θɜmənsi/, *n.* inability to transmit heat radiation. – **adiathermanous,** *adj.*

**ad idem** /æd 'ɪdəm/, *Law.* of the same mind, used esp. in relation to contracts. [L]

**adieu** /ə'dju, ə'djɜ/, *interj., n., pl.* **adieus** /ə'djuz, ə'djɜz/, **adieux** /ə'dju, ə'djɜ/. *–interj.* **1.** goodbye; farewell. *–n.* **2.** the act of taking one's leave; a farewell. [ME, from F, from L *ad Deum* (I commend you) to God]

**ad inf.**, to infinity. [L *ad infīnītum*]

**ad infinitum** /ˌæd ɪnfə'naɪtəm/, to infinity; endlessly; without limit. [L]

**adios** /'ædiɒs/, *interj.* goodbye; farewell. [Sp.]

**adipocere** /ædəpə'sɪə/, *n.* a waxy substance sometimes formed from dead animal bodies in moist burial places or under water. [*adipo-* (combining form representing L *adeps* fat) + L *cēra* wax] – **adipocerous** /ædə'pɒsərəs/, *adj.*

**adipose** /'ædəpoʊs/, *adj.* fatty; consisting of, resembling, or having relation to fat. [NL *adipōsus* fatty, from L *adeps* fat] – **adiposeness, adiposity** /ædə'pɒsəti/, *n.*

**adipose fin** /– 'fɪn/, *n.* a finlike projection, fleshy and lacking rays, behind the dorsal fin.

**adipose tissue** /– 'tɪʃu/, *n.* specialised cells in animals distributed throughout the body for storage of fats chiefly as triglycerides.

**adit** /'ædət/, *n.* **1.** an entrance or a passage. **2.** *Mining.* a horizontal or nearly horizontal passage leading into a mine used as an entrance or for drainage or ventilation. **3.** access. [L *aditus* approach]

**adj.**, **1.** adjective. **2.** adjectival. **3.** adjustment.

**Adj.**, Adjutant.

**adjacency** /ə'dʒeɪsənsi/, *n., pl.* **-cies. 1.** the state of being adjacent. **2.** (*usu. pl.*) that which is adjacent.

**adjacent** /ə'dʒeɪsənt/, *adj.* lying near, close, or contiguous; adjoining; neighbouring: *a field adjacent to the main road.* [L *adjacens,* ppr.] – **adjacently,** *adv.*

**adjacent angle** /– 'æŋgəl/, *n.* one of two angles having the same vertex and having a common side between them.

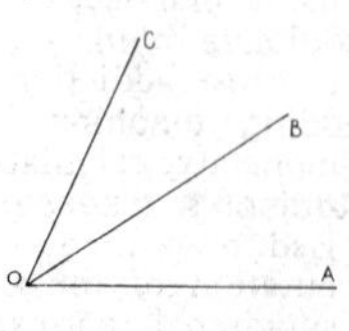

adjacent angles: AOB and BOC are adjacent angles

**adjective** /'ædʒəktɪv/, *n.* **1.** *Gram.* **a.** one of the major parts of speech of many languages, comprising words used to modify or limit a noun. **b.** such a word, as *wise* in *a wise ruler*, or in *he is wise.* **c.** any word or phrase of similar function or meaning. **2. the great Australian adjective,** the adjective *bloody.* *–adj.* **3.** *Gram.* pertaining to an adjective; functioning as an adjective; adjectival: *the adjective use of a noun.* **4.** not able to stand alone; dependent. **5.** *Law.* concerning methods of enforcement of legal rights, as pleading and practice (opposed to *substantive*). **6.** *Dyeing.* (of colours) requiring a mordant or the like to render them permanent (opposed to *substantive*). [L *adjectīvus*] – **adjectival** /ædʒək'taɪvəl/, *adj.* – **adjectivally** /ædʒək'taɪvəli/, **adjectively,** *adv.*

**adjoin** /ə'dʒɔɪn/, *v.t.* **1.** to be in connection or contact with; abut on: *his house adjoins the lake.* *–v.i.* **2.** to lie or be next, or in contact. [ME *ajoine(n)*, from OF *adjoindre*, from L *adjungere* join to]

**adjoining** /ə'dʒɔɪnɪŋ/, *adj.* bordering; contiguous: *the adjoining room.*

**adjourn** /ə'dʒɜn/, *v.t.* **1.** to suspend the meeting of, as a public or private body, to a future day or to another place: *adjourn the court.* **2.** to defer or postpone to a future meeting of the same body: *the court adjourned consideration of the question.* **3.** to put off; defer; postpone. *–v.i.* **4.** to postpone, suspend, or transfer proceedings. [ME *adjourne(n)*, from OF *ajorner*, from phrase *a jorn nome* until an appointed day]

**adjournment** /ə'dʒɜnmənt/, *n.* **1.** the act of adjourning. **2.** a state or period of being adjourned.

**Adjt**, Adjutant.

**adjudge** /ə'dʒʌdʒ/, *v.t.*, **-judged, -judging. 1.** to pronounce formally; decree: *the will was adjudged void.* **2.** to award judicially; assign: *the prize was adjudged to him.* **3.** to decide by a judicial opinion or sentence: *to adjudge a case.* **4.** to sentence or condemn: *he was adjudged to die.* **5.** to deem: *it was adjudged wise to avoid war.* [ME *ajuge(n)*, from OF *ajugier*, from L *adjūdicāre*]

**adjudicate** /ə'dʒudəkeɪt/, *v.*, **-cated, -cating.** *–v.t.* **1.** to pronounce or decree by judicial sentence; settle judicially; pass judgment on; to determine (an issue or dispute) judicially. *–v.i.* **2.** to sit in judgment (fol. by *upon*). **3.** to act as a judge in a competition, esp. a debating competition. [L *adjūdicātus,* pp.] – **adjudicative,** *adj.*

**adjudication** /ədʒudə'keɪʃən/, *n.* **1.** the act of adjudicating. **2.** *Law.* **a.** the act of a court in making an order, judgment, or decree. **b.** a judicial decision or sentence.

**adjudicator** /ə'dʒudəkeɪtə/, *n.* one who adjudicates, esp. in a debate or other competition.

**adjunct** /'ædʒʌŋkt/, *n.* **1.** something added to another thing but not essentially a part of it. **2.** a person joined to another in some duty or service; an assistant. **3.** *Gram.* a modifying form, word, phrase, etc., depending on some other form, word, phrase, etc. **4.** *Logic.* a non-essential attribute. *–adj.* **5.** joined to a thing or person, esp. subordinately; associated; auxiliary. [L *adjunctus,* pp.]

**adjunctive** /ə'dʒʌŋktɪv/, *adj.* forming an adjunct. – **adjunctively,** *adv.*

**adjure** /ə'dʒuə/, *v.t.*, **-jured, -juring. 1.** to charge, bind, or command, earnestly and solemnly, often under oath or the threat of a curse. **2.** to entreat or request earnestly. [ME *adjure(n)*, from L *adjūrāre*] – **adjuration** /ædʒə'reɪʃən/, *n.* – **adjuratory** /ə'dʒuərətri/, *adj.* – **adjurer, adjuror,** *n.*

**adjust** /ə'dʒʌst/, *v.t.* **1.** to fit, as one thing to another, make correspondent or conformable; adapt; accommodate: *to adjust things to a standard.* **2.** to put in working order; regulate; bring to a proper state or position: *to adjust an instrument.* **3.** to settle or bring to a satisfactory state, so that parties are agreed in the result: *to adjust differences.* **4.** *Insurance.* to fix (the sum to be paid on a claim); settle (a claim). **5.** to systematise. **6.** *Mil.* to correct the elevation and deflection of (a gun). *–v.i.* **7.** to adapt oneself; become adapted. [F (obs.) *adjuster,* from ML *adjūstāre,* erroneous Latinisation of OF *ajouster,* from LL *adjuxtāre*] **– adjustable,** *adj.* **– adjustably,** *adv.* **– adjuster, adjustor,** *n.*

**adjustable-pitch** /ədʒʌstəbəl-ˈpɪtʃ/, *adj.* (of a propeller) having blades whose pitch can be changed to suit various conditions of flight.

**adjustment** /əˈdʒʌstmənt/, *n.* **1.** the act of adjusting; act of adapting to a given purpose. **2.** the state of being adjusted; orderly relation of parts or elements. **3.** a means of adjusting: *the adjustment of a microscope.* **4.** *Sociol.* a process of fitting individual or collective patterns of activity to other such patterns carried out with some awareness or purposefulness. **5.** *Insurance.* the act of ascertaining the amount of indemnity which the party insured is entitled to receive under the policy, and of settling the claim. **6.** a settlement of a disputed account or claim.

**adjutant** /ˈædʒətənt/, *n.* **1.** *Mil.* a staff officer who assists the commanding officer. **2.** an assistant. [L *adjūtans,* ppr., aiding] **– adjutancy,** *n.*

**adjutant bird** /ˈ– bɜd/, *n.* a large stork, *Leptoptilus dubius,* of India. Also, **adjutant, adjutant crane, adjutant stork.**

**adjutant general** /– ˈdʒɛnrəl/, *n., pl.* **adjutants general.** *Mil.* **1.** (in the British Army). **a.** the head of a department of the general staff. **b.** an executive officer of a general. **2.** *U.S.* **a. the Adjutant General,** the chief administrative officer of the Army. **b.** a member of the Adjutant General's Department, from which adjutants for higher command are assigned. **3.** *U.S.* a high, often the highest, officer of the National Guard of a state or territory.

**adjuvant** /ˈædʒəvənt/, *adj.* **1.** serving to help or assist. *–n.* **2.** a person or thing aiding or helping. **3.** *Med.* whatever aids in removing or preventing a disease, esp. a substance added to a prescription to aid the operation of the main ingredient. [L *adjuvans,* ppr.]

**ad lib** /æd ˈlɪb/, *adv.* **1.** freely; in an impromptu manner. *–adj.* **2.** of or pertaining to an improvised performance. *–n.* **3.** an improvised performance. Also, **ad-lib.**

**adlib** /ædˈlɪb/, *v.,* **-libbed, -libbing.** *–v.t.* **1.** to improvise and deliver extemporaneously. *–v.i.* **2.** to improvise, as notes, words or business, during rehearsal or performance.

**ad libitum** /æd ˈlɪbətəm/, *adv.* at pleasure; to any extent; without restriction, used in music to indicate that the manner of performance of a passage is left to the discretion of the performer. *Abbrev.*: **ad lib.** [L]

**ad litteram** /æd ˈlɪtəræm/, to the letter; exactly. One cites an author *verbatim* and *ad litteram.* [L]

**ad loc.,** at the place. [L: *ad locum*]

**adman** /ˈædmæn/, *n.* one who takes part in advertising, esp. via the mass media. [short for *advertisement man*]

**admass** /ˈædmæs/, *n.* the consumers who make up the audience of advertising via the mass media. [short for *advertisement mass*]

**admeasure** /ædˈmɛʒə/, *v.t.,* **-ured, -uring.** to measure off or out; apportion. [AD- + MEASURE; replacing ME *amesure,* from OF *amesurer,* from LL *admēnsūrāre*]

**admeasurement** /ædˈmɛʒəmənt/, *n.* **1.** the process of measuring. **2.** the number, dimensions, or measure of anything. **3.** apportionment.

**admin** /ˈædmɪn, ædˈmɪn/, *n.* →**administration.**

**administer** /ædˈmɪnəstə, əd-/, *v.t.* **1.** to manage (affairs, a government, etc.); have charge of the execution of: *to administer laws.* **2.** to bring into use or operation; dispense: *to administer justice.* **3.** to make application of; give: *to administer medicine.* **4.** to tender or impose: *to administer an oath.* **5.** *Law.* to manage or dispose of, as the deceased's estate by an executor or administrator, or a trust estate by a trustee. *–v.i.* **6.** to contribute assistance; bring aid or supplies (fol. by *to*): *to administer to the needs of the poor.* **7.** to perform the duties of an administrator. [L *administrāre;* replacing ME *amynistre,* from OF *aministrer*] **– administrable** /ədˈmɪnəstrəbəl/, *adj.* **– administrant,** *adj., n.*

**administrate** /ædˈmɪnəstreɪt, əd-/, *v.t.,* **-trated, -trating.** to administer.

**administration** /ədmɪnəsˈtreɪʃən/, *n.* **1.** the management or direction of any office or employment. **2.** the function of a political state in exercising its governmental duties. **3.** any body of men entrusted with administrative powers. **4.** the duty or duties of an administrator. **5.** *Chiefly U.S.* the political leaders of a country who wield power; the government. **6.** *Chiefly U.S.* the period of service of a government. **7.** *U.S.* those executive functions of government, both general and local, which are neither legislative nor judicial. **8.** *Law.* management of the estate of a deceased person by an executor or administrator, or of a trust estate by a trustee. **9.** the act of dispensing, esp. formally: *administration of the sacraments.* **10.** the act of tendering: *the administration of an oath.* **11.** the applying of a medicine, etc.

**administrative** /ədˈmɪnəstrətɪv/, *adj.* pertaining to administration; executive: *administrative ability, problems, etc.* **– administratively,** *adv.*

**administrative law** /– ˈlɔ/, *n.* law relating to the powers, duties, and organisation of public administrative authorities.

**administrator** /ədˈmɪnəstreɪtə/, *n.* **1.** one who directs or manages affairs of any kind. **2.** a person with a talent for managing or organising: *she is a born administrator.* **3.** *Law.* a person appointed by a court to take charge of the estate of a person who died without appointing an executor. [L]

**adminstratrix** /ədˈmɪnstrətrɪks/, *n., pl.* **-trices** /-trəˌsiz/. *Law.* a female administrator.

**admirable** /ˈædmərəbəl/, *adj.* worthy of admiration, exciting approval, reverence or affection; excellent. [L *admīrābilis*] **– admirableness,** *n.* **– admirably,** *adv.*

**admiral** /ˈædmərəl/, *n.* **1.** the commander-in-chief of a navy. **2.** a naval officer of the highest rank. **3.** a naval officer of high rank. The grades in the Royal Australian Navy are: **admiral of the fleet, admiral, vice-admiral** and **rear-admiral.** **4.** the ship of an admiral; flagship. **5. a.** the master of a fishing fleet. **b.** the chief ship in such a fleet. **6.** any of various butterflies, as the **Australian admiral,** *Vanessa itea.* [var. of ME *amiral,* from OF, from Ar. *amīr al* (chief of) in various phrases, e.g. *amīr al bahr* commander of the sea; var. *admiral* arose by association with L *admīrābilis* admirable, etc.] **– admiralship,** *n.*

**admiral's walk** /ædmərəlz ˈwɔk/, *n.* →**gallery** (def. 12).

**admiralty** /ˈædmərəlti/, *n., pl.* **-ties,** *adj.* *–n.* **1.** the office or jurisdiction of an admiral. **2.** *Brit.* the officials or the department of state having charge of naval affairs. *–adj.* **3.** pertaining to the sea: *admiralty law.*

**admiration** /ædməˈreɪʃən/, *n.* **1.** a feeling of wonder, pleasure, and approbation. **2.** the act of looking on or contemplating with pleasure: *admiration of a pretty girl.* **3.** an object of wonder or approbation: *she was the admiration of everyone.* **4.** *Archaic.* wonder.

**admire** /ədˈmaɪə/, *v.,* **-mired, -miring.** *–v.t.* **1.** to regard with wonder, pleasure, and approbation. **2.** (usu. ironic) to regard with wonder or surprise: *I admire your audacity.* *–v.i.* **3.** to feel or express admiration. **4.** *U.S.* to like or desire (to do something). [L *admīrārī* wonder at] **– admiringly,** *adv.*

**admirer** /ədˈmaɪərə/, *n.* **1.** one who admires. **2.** a lover.

**admissible** /ədˈmɪsəbəl/, *adj.* **1.** that may be allowed or conceded; allowable. **2.** capable or worthy of being admitted. **3.** *Law.* allowable as evidence. **– admissibility** /ədmɪsəˈbɪləti/, **admissibleness,** *n.* **– admissibly,** *adv.*

**admission** /ədˈmɪʃən/, *n.* **1.** the act of allowing to enter; entrance afforded by permission, by provision or existence of means, or by the removal of obstacles: *the admission of aliens into a country.* **2.** power or permission to enter: *to grant a person admission.* **3.** the price paid for entrance, as to a theatre, etc. **4.** the act or condition of being received or accepted in a position or office; appointment: *admission to the practice of law.* **5.** confession of a charge, an error, or a crime; acknowledgment: *his admission of the theft solved the mystery.* **6.** an acknowledgment of the truth of something. **7.** a point or statement admitted; concession. [L *admissio*]

**admissive** /ədˈmɪsɪv/, *adj.* tending to admit.

**admit** /ədˈmɪt/, *v.,* **-mitted, -mitting.** *–v.t.* **1.** to allow to enter;

grant or afford entrance to: *to admit a student to college.* **2.** to give right or means of entrance to. **3.** to permit; allow. **4.** to permit to exercise a certain function or privilege: *admitted to the bar.* **5.** to allow as valid: *to admit the force of an argument.* **6.** to have capacity for the admission of at one time: *this passage admits two abreast.* **7.** to acknowledge; confess: *he admitted his guilt.* **8.** to grant in argument; concede: *the fact is admitted.* –*v.i.* **9.** to leave room for (fol. by *of*): *this situation admits of no other solution.* **10.** to give access; grant entrance: *this key admits to the garden.* [L *admittere*; replacing late ME *amitte(n)*, from F *amettre*] – **admitter,** *n.*

**admittance** /əd'mɪtns/, *n.* **1.** permission to enter; the power or right of entrance: *admittance into the church.* **2.** the act of admitting. **3.** actual entrance. **4.** *Elect.* the reciprocal of impedance.

**admittedly** /əd'mɪtədli/, *adv.* by acknowledgment; confessedly: *he was admittedly the one who had lost the documents.*

**admix** /əd'mɪks, æd-/, *v.t.* **1.** to mingle or add to. –*v.i.* **2.** to be or become mingled or blended. [backformation from ME *admixt*, from L *admixtus*, pp., mingled with]

**admixture** /'ædmɪkstʃə, əd'mɪkstʃə/, *n.* **1.** the act of mixing. **2.** the state of being mixed. **3.** anything added; any alien element or ingredient.

**admonish** /əd'mɒnɪʃ/, *v.t.* **1.** to counsel against something; caution or advise. **2.** to notify of or reprove for a fault, esp. mildly: *to admonish someone as a brother.* **3.** to recall or incite to duty; remind: *to admonish someone about his obligations.* [backformation from ADMONITION; replacing ME *amonesten*, from OF] – **admonisher,** *n.* – **admonishingly,** *adv.* – **admonishment,** *n.*

**admonition** /ædmə'nɪʃən/, *n.* the act of admonishing; counsel or advice; gentle reproof; caution. [L *admonitio*; replacing ME *amonicioun*, from OF]

**admonitory** /əd'mɒnətri/, *adj.* tending or serving to admonish: *an admonitory gesture.*

**adnate** /'ædneɪt/, *adj.* grown fast to something; congenitally attached. [L *adnātus* born to]

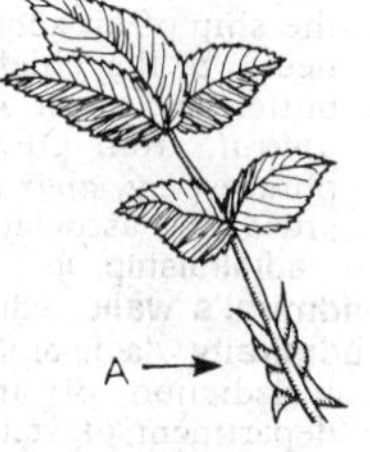

A, adnate stipule

**ad nauseam** /æd 'nɔziəm, -si-/, *adv.* to a sickening or disgusting extent. [L]

**ado** /ə'du/, *n.* **1.** activity; bustle; fuss. **2. much ado about nothing,** a great fuss about very little. [ME *ado*, *at do* to do]

**adobe** /ə'doubi/, *n.* **1.** the sun-dried brick in common use in countries having little rainfall. **2.** a yellow silt or clay, deposited by rivers, used to make bricks. **3.** a building constructed of adobe. **4.** a dark, heavy soil, containing clay. [Sp.]

**adobe flat** /– 'flæt/, *n.* a plain consisting of adobe deposited by short-lived rainfall or thaw streams, usu. having a smooth or unmarked surface.

**adolesce** /ædə'lɛs/, *v.i.*, **-lesced, -lescing.** **1.** to be or become an adolescent. **2.** to behave like an adolescent. [backformation from ADOLESCENT]

**adolescence** /ædə'lɛsəns/, *n.* **1.** the transition period between puberty and adult stages of development; youth. **2.** the quality or state of being adolescent; youthfulness. Also, **adolescency.**

**adolescent** /ædə'lɛsənt/, *adj.* **1.** growing to adulthood: youthful. **2.** having the characteristics of adolescence or of an adolescent. –*n.* **3.** an adolescent person. [L *adolescens*, ppr.]

**Adonic** /ə'dounɪk/, *adj.* **1.** denoting a verse consisting of a dactyl (‒⏑⏑) followed by a spondee (‒‒) or trochee (‒⏑). **2.** of an Adonis. –*n.* **3.** an Adonic verse or line. [ML *adōnicus*]

**Adonis** /ə'dounəs/, *n.* **1.** (*oft. l.c.*) a very handsome young man. **2.** (*l.c.*) a beau or dandy. [in Greek legend *Adonis* was a favourite of Aphrodite, goddess of love]

**adopt** /ə'dɒpt/, *v.t.* **1.** to choose for or take to oneself; make one's own by selection or assent: *to adopt a name or idea.* **2.** to take as one's own child, specifically by a formal legal act. **3.** to vote to accept: *the House adopted the report.* **4.** to receive into any kind of new relationship: *to adopt a person as an heir.* **5.** to nominate (a candidate) for political office. [L *adoptāre*] – **adoptable,** *adj.* – **adopter,** *n.* – **adoption,** *n.*

**adoptive** /ə'dɒptɪv/, *adj.* **1.** related by adoption: *an adoptive father or son.* **2.** tending to adopt. **3.** (of children) for adoption. – **adoptively,** *adv.*

**adorable** /ə'dɔrəbəl/, *adj.* **1.** worthy of being adored. **2.** *Colloq.* arousing strong liking. – **adorableness, adorability** /ədɔrə'bɪləti/, *n.* – **adorably,** *adv.*

**adoration** /ædə'reɪʃən/, *n.* **1.** the act of paying honour as to a divine being; worship. **2.** reverent homage. **3.** fervent and devoted love.

**adore** /ə'dɔ/, *v.*, **adored, adoring.** –*v.t.* **1.** to regard with the utmost esteem, love, and respect. **2.** to honour as divine; worship: *to be adored as gods.* **3.** *Colloq.* to like greatly. –*v.i.* **4.** to worship. [L *adōrāre* address, worship; replacing ME *aoure(n)*, from OF *ao(u)rer*] – **adorer,** *n.* – **adoring,** *adj.* – **adoringly,** *adv.*

**adorn** /ə'dɔn/, *v.t.* **1.** to make pleasing or more attractive; embellish; add lustre to: *the piety which adorns his character.* **2.** to increase or lend beauty to, as by dress or ornaments; decorate: *garlands of flowers adorning her hair.* [L *adornāre*; replacing ME *aourne*, from OF *ao(u)rner*] – **adorner,** *n.* – **adorningly,** *adv.*

**adornment** /ə'dɔnmənt/, *n.* **1.** ornament: *the adornments and furnishings of a room.* **2.** an adorning; ornamentation: *personal adornment.*

**adown** /ə'daʊn/, *adv.* **1.** down. –*prep.* **2.** down.

**ADP** /eɪ di 'pi/, *n.* →**automatic data processing.**

**adpressed** /æd'prɛst/, *adj.* pressed closely against or fitting closely to something. Also, **appressed.**

**ADR,** Australian Design Rules.

**ad rem** /æd 'rɛm/, to the matter or thing. To reply *ad rem* is to keep to the subject being considered. [L]

**adrenal** /ə'drinəl/, *adj.* **1.** situated near or on the kidneys; suprarenal. **2.** of or produced by the adrenal glands. –*n.* **3.** one of the adrenal glands. [AD- + L *rēnēs* kidneys + -AL[1]]

**adrenalectomy** /ədrinə'lɛktəmi/, *n., pl.* **-mies.** the removal of one or both adrenal glands.

**adrenal gland** /ə'drinəl glænd/, *n.* →**suprarenal gland.**

**adrenalin** /ə'drɛnələn, -lin/, *n.* **1.** a white or whitish crystalline compound, $C_9H_{13}NO_3$, a hormone produced by the adrenal medulla; epinephrine. **2.** this substance purified from the suprarenal secretion of animals and used as a drug to speed heart action, contract blood vessels, etc. Also, **adrenaline.**

**adrenocorticotropic hormone** /əˌdrinoukɔtɪkəˌtroupɪk 'hɔmoun/, *n.* →**ACTH.** Also, **adrenocorticotrophic hormone.**

**adrift** /ə'drɪft/, *adj.* **1.** not fastened by any kind of moorings; at the mercy of winds and currents. **2.** swayed by any chance impulse. **3.** *Colloq.* confused; wide of the mark. [A-[1] + DRIFT]

**adroit** /ə'drɔɪt/, *adj.* expert in the use of the hand or mind; possessing readiness of resource; ingenious. [AF, from phrase *à droit* rightly, *droit* from L *dīrectus* straight] – **adroitly,** *adv.* – **adroitness,** *n.*

**adscript** /'ædskrɪpt/, *adj.* written after (distinguished from *subscript, superscript*). [L *adscriptus*, pp.]

**adscription** /æd'skrɪpʃən/, *n.* →**ascription.**

**adsorb** /əd'sɔb/, *v.t.* to gather (a gas, liquid, or dissolved substance) on a surface in a condensed layer, as is the case when charcoal adsorbs gases. [AD- + L *sorbēre* suck in, modelled on ABSORB] – **adsorbent,** *adj., n.* – **adsorption,** *n.* – **adsorptive,** *adj., n.*

**ADT** /eɪ di 'ti/, Automatic Data Transmission.

**adularia** /ædʒə'lɛəriə/, *n.* a transparent or translucent variety of orthoclase, often pearly or opalescent, as the moonstone. [named after the *Adula* mountain group in Switzerland. See -ARIA]

**adulate** /'ædʒəleɪt, 'ædjuleɪt/, *v.t.*, **-lated, -lating.** to show pretended or undiscriminating devotion to; flatter servilely. [L *adūlātus*, pp.] – **adulation** /ædʒə'leɪʃən/, *n.* – **adulater,** *n.* – **adulatory,** *adj.*

**adult** /ə'dʌlt, 'ædʌlt/, *adj.* **1.** having attained full size and strength; grown up; mature. **2.** pertaining to or designed for adults: *adult education.* –*n.* **3.** a person who is grown up or of age. **4.** a full-grown animal or plant. **5. a.** *Common Law.* a person who has attained 18 years of age. **b.** *Civil Law.* a male after attaining 14, or a female after attaining 12 years of age. [L *adultus*, pp.] – **adulthood,** *n.* – **adultness,** *n.*

**adult education** /– ɛdʒəˈkeɪʃən/, *n.* the education of adults beyond the formal schooling system, esp. in non-vocational courses.

**adulterant** /əˈdʌltərənt/, *n.* **1.** a substance used for adulterating. –*adj.* **2.** adulterating.

**adulterate** /əˈdʌltəreɪt/, *v.*, **-rated, -rating;** /əˈdʌltərət, -təreɪt/, *adj.* –*v.t.* **1.** to debase by adding inferior materials or elements; make impure by admixture; use cheaper, inferior, or less desirable goods in the production or marketing of (any professedly genuine article): *to adulterate food.* –*adj.* **2.** adulterated. **3.** adulterous. [L *adulterātus*, pp., defiled] – **adulterator,** *n.*

**adulteration** /ədʌltəˈreɪʃən/, *n.* **1.** the act or process of adulterating. **2.** the state of being adulterated. **3.** something adulterated.

**adulterer** /əˈdʌltərə/, *n.* a person, esp. a man, guilty of adultery. – **adulteress** /əˈdʌltərəs/, *n.fem.*

**adulterine** /əˈdʌltəraɪn/, *adj.* **1.** characterised by adulteration; spurious. **2.** born of adultery. **3.** of or involving adultery. [L *adulterīnus*]

**adulterous** /əˈdʌltərəs/, *adj.* **1.** characterised by, pertaining to, or guilty of adultery. **2.** *Obs.* spurious.

**adultery** /əˈdʌltəri/, *n., pl.* **-teries.** voluntary sexual intercourse between a married person and any other than the lawful spouse. [L *adulterium*; replacing ME *avoutrie*, from OF]

**adumbral** /ædˈʌmbrəl/, *adj.* shadowy; shady.

**adumbrate** /ˈædəmbreɪt/, *v.t.*, **-brated, -brating. 1.** to give a faint shadow or resemblance of; outline or shadow forth. **2.** to foreshadow; prefigure. **3.** to darken or conceal partially; overshadow. [L *adumbrātus*, pp., shadowed] – **adumbration** /ædəmˈbreɪʃən/, *n.*

**adumbrative** /əˈdʌmbrətɪv/, *adj.* shadowing forth; indicative. – **adumbratively,** *adv.*

**adv.,** **1.** adverb. **2.** adverbial.

**ad valorem** /æd vəˈlɔrəm/, *adj.* in proportion to the value. An *ad valorem* duty charged on goods entering a country is fixed at a percentage of the customs value as stated on the invoice. [L]

**advance** /ədˈvæns, -ˈvans/, *v.*, **-vanced, -vancing,** *n., adj.* –*v.t.* **1.** to move or bring forwards in place: *the troops were advanced to the new position.* **2.** to bring to view or notice; propose: *to advance an argument.* **3.** to improve; further: *to advance one's interests.* **4.** to raise in rank; promote. **5.** to raise in rate: *to advance the price.* **6.** to bring forwards in time; accelerate: *to advance growth.* **7.** to supply beforehand; furnish on credit, or before goods are delivered or work is done. **8.** to supply or pay in expectation of reimbursement: *to advance money on loan.* **9.** *Archaic.* to raise, as a banner. –*v.i.* **10.** to move or go forwards; proceed: *the troops advanced.* **11.** to improve or make progress; grow: *to advance in knowledge or rank.* **12.** to increase in quantity, value, price, etc.: *stocks advanced three points.* –*n.* **13.** a moving forwards; progress in space: *advance to the sea.* **14.** advancement; promotion: *an advance in rank.* **15.** a step forwards; actual progress in any course of action: *the advance of knowledge.* **16.** (*usu. pl.*) an effort to bring about acquaintance, accord, understanding, etc. **17.** addition to price; rise in price: *an advance in cottons.* **18.** *Comm.* **a.** a giving beforehand; a furnishing of something before an equivalent is received. **b.** the money or goods thus furnished. **c.** a loan against securities, or in advance of payment due. **19.** *Mil.* (formerly) the order or a signal to advance. **20.** *U.S.* the leading body of an army. **21. in advance, a.** before; in front. **b.** beforehand; ahead of time: *he insisted on paying his rent in advance.* –*adj.* **22.** made or given in advance: *an advance payment.* **23.** issued in advance: *an advance copy.* **24.** advanced; having progressed beyond others or beyond the average: *an advance student.* **25.** going before. [ME *avaunce(n)*, from OF *avancier*, from LL *abanteāre*, from *abante* from before] – **advancer,** *n.*

**advanced** /ədˈvænst, -ˈvanst/, *adj.* **1.** placed in advance: *with foot advanced.* **2.** far on in progress; beyond the average: *an advanced class in French.* **3.** far on in time: *an advanced age.* –*n.* **4.** →**advanced handicap. 5.** →**advanced horse.**

**advanced handicap** /– ˈhændikæp/, *n.* a restricted race for horses which are specified as being in the advanced class in accordance with the rules operating in each State.

**advanced horse** /– ˈhɔs/, *n.* a horse eligible to run in an advanced handicap. Also, **advanced-class horse.**

**advance guard** /ədˈvæns gad/, *n.* a body of troops going before the main force to clear the way, guard against surprise, etc. Also, **advanced guard.**

**advancement** /ədˈvænsmənt, -ˈvans-/, *n.* **1.** the act of moving forwards. **2.** promotion in rank or standing; preferment: *his hopes of advancement failed.* **3.** *Law.* money or property given during his lifetime by a person subsequently dying intestate and deducted from the intestate share of the recipient.

**advantage** /ədˈvæntɪdʒ, -ˈvan-/, *n., v.*, **-taged, -taging.** –*n.* **1.** any state, circumstance, opportunity, or means specially favourable to success, interest, or any desired end: *the advantage of a good education.* **2.** benefit; gain; profit: *it is to his advantage.* **3.** superiority or ascendancy (oft. fol. by *over* or *of*): *to have the advantage of age.* **4.** a position of superiority (oft. fol. by *over* or *of*): *don't let him have the advantage of us.* **5.** *Tennis.* the first point scored after deuce, or the resulting state of the score; vantage. **6. take advantage of, a.** to make use of: *to take advantage of an opportunity.* **b.** to impose upon: *to take advantage of someone.* **7. to advantage,** with good effect; advantageously. –*v.t.* **8.** to be of service to; yield profit or gain to; benefit. [ME *avantage*, from OF *avant* before, forward, from LL *abante.* See ADVANCE]

**advantageous** /ædvənˈteɪdʒəs/, *adj.* of advantage; furnishing convenience or opportunity; profitable; useful; beneficial: *an advantageous position.* – **advantageously,** *adv.* – **advantageousness,** *n.*

**advantage rule** /ədˈvæntɪdʒ rul/, *n. Soccer, Basketball, etc.* the rule which allows the referee or umpire to allow play to continue despite an infringement if the offending team has already been disadvantaged by the play.

**advection** /ədˈvɛkʃən/, *n.* **1.** the transfer of heat by horizontal movements of air; horizontal convection. **2.** the movement of air horizontally. [L *advectio* a carrying]

**advent** /ˈædvɛnt/, *n.* a coming into place, view, or being; arrival: *the advent of death.* [ME, from L *adventus* arrival]

**Adventist** /ˈædvəntəst, ædˈvɛntəst/, *n.* **1.** one who believes that the second coming of Christ is near at hand. **2.** a member of any of certain Christian denominations which maintain that belief. – **Adventism,** *n.*

**adventitia** /ædvɛnˈtɪʃə/, *n.* the outer covering of an organ, esp. a blood vessel derived from adjacent connective tissue. [NL, from L *adventīcius* ADVENTITIOUS]

**adventitious** /ædvɛnˈtɪʃəs/, *adj.* **1.** accidentally or casually acquired; added extrinsically; foreign. **2.** *Bot., Zool.* appearing in an abnormal or unusual position or place, as a root. [L *adventīcius* coming from abroad] – **adventitiously,** *adv.* – **adventitiousness,** *n.*

**adventive** /ədˈvɛntɪv/, *adj.* **1.** not native and usually not yet well established, as exotic plants or animals. –*n.* **2.** an adventive plant or animal.

**adventure** /ədˈvɛntʃə/, *n., v.*, **-tured, -turing.** –*n.* **1.** an undertaking of uncertain outcome; a hazardous enterprise. **2.** an exciting experience. **3.** participation in exciting undertakings or enterprises: *the spirit of adventure.* **4.** a commercial or financial speculation of any kind; a venture. **5.** *Obs.* peril; danger. **6.** *Obs.* chance. –*v.t.* **7.** to risk or hazard. **8.** to take the chance of; dare. –*v.i.* **9.** to take the risk involved. **10.** to venture. [ME *aventure*, from OF, from L (*rēs*) *adventūra*, future p., (a thing) about to happen]

**adventure playground** /– ˈpleɪgraʊnd/, *n.* a children's playground equipped with large artifacts such as pipes, car bodies, etc., or large naturally occurring materials as heavy logs, boulders, etc., the whole being calculated to encourage children to vigorous, imaginative play and the creation of their own adventure.

**adventurer** /ədˈvɛntʃərə/, *n.* **1.** one who adventures. **2.** a seeker of fortune in daring enterprises; a soldier of fortune. **3.** one who undertakes any great commercial risk; a speculator. **4.** a seeker of fortune by underhand or equivocal means.

**adventuresome** /ədˈvɛntʃəsəm/, *adj.* bold; daring; adventurous.

**adventuress** /əd'vɛntʃərɛs/, *n.* **1.** a female adventurer. **2.** a woman who schemes to win social position, money, etc., by equivocal methods.

**adventurism** /əd'vɛntʃərɪzəm/, *n.* recklessness, rash improvisation or experimentation, esp. in politics or finance.

**adventurous** /əd'vɛntʃərəs/, *adj.* **1.** inclined or willing to engage in adventures. **2.** attended with risk; requiring courage. – **adventurously,** *adv.* – **adventurousness,** *n.*

**adverb** /'ædv3b/, *n.* **1.** one of the major parts of speech comprising words used to modify or limit a verb, a verbal noun (also, in Latin, English, and some other languages, an adjective or another adverb), or an adverbial phrase or clause. An adverbial element expresses some relation of place, time, manner, attendant circumstance, degree, cause, inference, result, condition, exception, concession, purpose, or means. **2.** such a word, as *well* in English *she sings well.* **3.** Also, **adverbial.** any word or phrase of similar function or meaning. [L *adverbium*] – **adverbial** /əd'v3biəl/, *adj.* – **adverbially** /əd'v3biəli/, *adv.* – **adverbless,** *adj.*

**ad verbum** /æd 'v3bəm/, *adv.* to the word; exact in wording according to an original. [L]

**adversaria** /ædvə'sɛəriə/, *n. pl.* notes or jottings, as in a commonplace book. [L]

**adversary** /'ædvəsri, -səri/, *n., pl.* **-saries. 1.** an unfriendly opponent. **2.** an opponent in a contest; a contestant. **3. the Adversary,** the Devil; Satan. [ME *adversarie,* from L *adversārius*]

**adversative** /əd'v3sətɪv/, *adj.* **1.** expressing contrariety, opposition, or antithesis: *'but' is an adversative conjunction.* –*n.* **2.** an adversative word or proposition. [LL *adversātīvus*] – **adversatively,** *adv.*

**adverse** /'ædv3s, əd'v3s/, *adj.* **1.** antagonistic in purpose or effect: *adverse criticism, adverse to slavery.* **2.** opposing one's interests or desire: *adverse fate, fortune, influences, or circumstances.* **3.** being or acting in a contrary direction; opposed or opposing: *adverse winds.* **4.** opposite; confronting: *the adverse page.* **5.** *Bot.* turned towards the axis, as a leaf. **6.** *Law.* **a.** opposed to the examining party in a law suit: *an adverse witness.* **b. adverse possession,** an occupation or possession of land by one who has no lawful title to it, which, if unopposed for a certain period, extinguishes the right and title of the true owner. [ME, from L *adversus,* p.p., turned against, turned towards] – **adversely** *adv.* – **adverseness,** *n.*

**adversity** /əd'v3səti/, *n., pl.* **-ties. 1.** adverse fortune or fate; a condition marked by misfortune, calamity, or distress: *his struggles with adversity.* **2.** an unfortunate event or circumstance: *the prosperities and adversities of this life.* [ME *adversite,* from L *adversitas* opposition]

**advert**[1] /əd'v3t/, *v.i.* **1.** to make a remark or remarks (about or in relation to); refer (fol. by *to*): *he adverted briefly to the occurrences of the day.* **2.** to turn the attention (fol. by *to*). [L *advertere* turn to; replacing ME *averte(n),* from OF *avertir*]

**advert**[2] /'ædv3t/, *n. Colloq.* an advertisement. [shortened form of ADVERTISEMENT]

**advertent** /əd'v3tnt/, *adj.* attentive; heedful. – **advertence, advertency,** *n.* – **advertently,** *adv.*

**advertise** /'ædvətaɪz/, *v.,* **-tised, -tising.** –*v.t.* **1.** to give information to the public concerning; make public announcement of, by publication in periodicals, by printed posters, by broadcasting over the radio, television, etc.: *to advertise a reward.* **2.** to praise the good qualities of, in order to induce the public to buy or invest in. **3.** to offer (an article) for sale or (a vacancy) to applicants, etc., by placing an advertisement in a newspaper, magazine, etc.: *he advertised the post of private secretary.* **4.** *Archaic.* to give notice, advice, or information to; inform. **5.** *Obs.* to admonish; warn. –*v.i.* **6.** to ask (*for*) by placing an advertisement in a newspaper, magazine, etc.: *to advertise for a house to rent.* Also, **advertize.** [ME *advertise(n),* from MF *advertiss-,* stem of *advertir,* from L *advertere*] – **advertiser,** *n.*

**advertisement** /əd'v3təsmənt/, *n.* any device or public announcement, as a printed notice in a newspaper, a commercial film on television, a neon sign, etc., designed to attract public attention, bring in custom, etc. Also, *U.S.,* **advertizement.** [ME, from MF *advertissement*]

**advertising** /'ædvətaɪzɪŋ/, *n.* **1.** the act or practice of bringing anything, as one's wants or one's business, into public notice, esp. by paid announcements in periodicals, on hoardings, etc., or on television: *to secure customers by advertising.* **2.** paid announcements; advertisements. **3.** the profession of designing and writing advertisements. Also, *U.S.,* **advertizing.**

**advice** /əd'vaɪs/, *n.* **1.** an opinion recommended, or offered, as worthy to be followed: *I shall act on your advice.* **2.** a communication, esp. from a distance, containing information: *advice from abroad.* **3.** a formal or professional opinion given, esp. by a barrister. [late ME *advyse* (replacing ME *avys,* from OF *avis* opinion), from L *ad-* AD- + *vīsum,* pp. neut., what seems best]

**advisable** /əd'vaɪzəbəl/, *adj.* **1.** proper to be advised or to be recommended. **2.** open to or desirous of advice. – **advisability** /əd,vaɪzə'bɪləti/, **advisableness,** *n.* – **advisably,** *adv.*

**advise** /əd'vaɪz/, *v.,* **-vised, -vising.** –*v.t.* **1.** to give counsel to; offer an opinion to, as worthy or expedient to be followed: *I advise you to be cautious.* **2.** to recommend as wise, prudent, etc.: *he advised secrecy.* **3.** to give (a person, etc.) information or notice (fol. by *of*): *the merchants were advised of the risk.* –*v.i.* **4.** to offer counsel; give advice: *I shall act as you advise.* **5.** *Chiefly U.S.* to take counsel (fol. by *with*): *I shall advise with my friends.* **6.** to ring back on the telephone. [LL *advīsāre*; replacing ME *avise(n),* from OF]

**advised** /əd'vaɪzd/, *adj.* **1.** considered: now chiefly in *ill-advised* or *well-advised.* **2.** informed: *kept thoroughly advised.* – **advisedness** /əd'vaɪzədnəs/, *n.*

**advisedly** /əd'vaɪzədli/, *adv.* after due consideration; deliberately.

**adviser** /əd'vaɪzə/, *n.* **1.** one who gives advice. **2.** a teacher who helps students choose their course of study, etc.

**advisory** /əd'vaɪzəri/, *adj.* of, or giving, advice; having power to advise: *an advisory council.*

**advocaat** /'ædvəka, -kat/, *n.* **1.** a liqueur containing brandy, eggs and flavouring. **2.** *Archaic.* a similar drink used for medicinal purposes. [D, originally *advocatenborrel* the drink of advocates]

**advocacy** /,ædvəkəsi/, *n.* an act of pleading for, supporting, or recommending; active espousal.

**advocate** /'ædvəkeɪt/, *v.,* **-cated, -cating;** /'ædvəkət, -keɪt/, *n.* –*v.t.* **1.** to plead in favour of; support or urge by argument; recommend publicly: *he advocated isolationism.* –*n.* **2.** one who defends, vindicates, or espouses a cause by argument; an upholder; a defender (fol. by *of*): *an advocate of peace.* **3.** one who pleads for or on behalf of another; intercessor. **4.** *Chiefly Scot.* one who pleads the cause of another in a court of law; a barrister. [L *advocātus* (properly pp.) one summoned to help another (in legal case); replacing ME *avocat,* from OF] – **advocator,** *n.*

**advocatory** /əd'vɒkətri/, *adj.* of an advocate or his functions.

**advowson** /əd'vaʊzən/, *n. Law.* the right of presentation to a benefice. [AF; replacing ME *avoweson,* from OF *avoeson,* from L *advocātio*]

**advt,** advertisement.

**adynamia** /,eɪdaɪ'neɪmiə, ædə-/, *n.* weakness; debility; asthenia. [Gk]

**adynamic** /,eɪdaɪ'næmɪk, ædə-/, *adj.* lacking strength; asthenic.

**adytum** /'ædɪtəm/, *n., pl.* **-ta** /-tə/. **1.** (in ancient worship) a sacred place which the public was not allowed to enter; an inner shrine. **2.** the most sacred or reserved part of any place of worship. [L, from Gk *ádyton* (a place) not to be entered]

**adze** /ædz/, *n.* **1.** a heavy chisel-like steel tool fastened at right angles to a wooden handle, used to dress timber, etc. –*v.* **2.** to shape with an adze. Also, *U.S.,* **adz.** [ME *adese,* OE *adesa*]

adze

**æ,** **1.** a digraph or ligature appearing in Latin and Latinised Greek words. In English words of Latin or Greek origin, *æ* is now usu. reduced to *e,* except generally in proper names (*Caesar*), in words belonging to Roman or Greek antiquities (*aegis*), and in modern words of scientific or technical use (*aecium*). **2.** an early English ligature representing a vowel sound like the *a* in modern *bad.* The long *æ* continued in use until about 1250, but was finally replaced by *e.* The short *æ* was given up by 1150, being replaced usu. by *a* but sometimes by *e.*

**ae-,** For words with initial **ae-,** see also **e-.**

**ae.,** at the age of; aged. Also, **aet.** [L: *aetātis*]

**AEC** /eɪ i 'si/, Atomic Energy Commission.

**aecidium** /i'sɪdiəm/, *n., pl.* **-cidia** /-'sɪdiə/. an aecium in which the spores are always formed in chains and enclosed in a cup-shaped peridium. [NL, diminutive of Gk *aikía* injury]

**aeciospore** /'isiəˌspɔ/, *n.* a spore borne by an aecium.

**aecium** /'isiəm/, *n., pl.* **-cia** /-siə/. the sorus of rust fungi which arises from the haploid mycelium, commonly accompanied by spermogonia and bearing chainlike or stalked spores. [NL, from Gk *aikía* an injurious effect + *-ium* -IUM] – **aecial,** *adj.*

**aëdes** /eɪ'idiz/, *n.* **1.** the mosquito, *Aëdes aegypti,* which transmits yellow fever and dengue. **2.** any mosquito of the genus *Aëdes.* [NL, from Gk: unpleasant]

**aedicule** /'idəkjul/, *n.* **1.** a small shrine, esp. one between two pillars. **2.** any small building. [L *aedicula,* diminutive of *aedēs* temple]

**aegerite** /'eɪdʒəraɪt, 'i-/, *n.* a mineral consisting of sodium and iron silicate, $Na_2OFe_2O_3 \cdot 4SiO_2$; acmite. Also, **aegerine.** [*Aegir* (sea-god of Scand. mythology) + -ITE[1]]

**aegis** /'idʒəs/, *n.* protection; sponsorship: *under the imperial aegis.* [L, from Gk *aigís* (a goatskin) the shield of Zeus]

**aegrotat** /'aɪgrətæt, 'i-/, *n.* (in universities) **1.** an official certificate of illness allowing a candidate to pass an examination even though he failed to attend part of it. **2.** the degree thus taken. [L: he is ill]

**-aemia,** a suffix referring to the state of the blood, as in *toxaemia.* Also, **-emia, -haemia, -hemia.** [NL, also *-hemia, -haemia,* from Gk *-aimia* (as in *anaimía* want of blood), from *haíma* blood]

**Aeolian**[1] /i'oʊliən, eɪ-/, *adj.* **1.** belonging to a branch of the Greek race named after Aeolus, the legendary founder. *–n.* **2.** a member of one of the three great divisions of the ancient Greek race, the two other divisions being the Dorian and the Ionian. Also, **Aeolic.** [Gk *Aioleús* Aeolus + -IAN]

**Aeolian**[2] /i'oʊliən, eɪ-/, *adj.* **1.** pertaining to Aeolus, or to the winds in general. **2.** (*l.c.*) due to atmospheric action; wind blown. **3.** (*l.c.*) *Geol.* deposited or formed by wind, as loess or dunes. [Gk *Aíolos* Aeolus (in Gk mythology the ruler of the winds) + -IAN]

**aeolian harp** /iˌoʊliən 'hap/, *n.* a box over which are stretched a number of strings of equal length, tuned in unison and sounded by the wind; wind harp. Also, **aeolian lyre.**

**Aeolian mode** /iˌoʊliən 'moʊd/, *n.* a scale, represented by the white keys of a keyboard instrument, beginning on A.

**aeolipile** /i'ɒləpaɪl/, *n.* an instrument consisting essentially of a round vessel rotated by the force of steam generated within, and escaping through bent arms. Also, **aeolipyle.** [L *aeolipila,* orig. *Aeolī pila* ball of Aeolus, or *Aeolī pylae* doorway of Aeolus]

**aeolotropic** /ˌiəloʊ'trɒpɪk/, *adj.* not isotropic; anisotropic. [Gk *aiólo(s)* changeful + -TROPIC] – **aeolotropy** /iə'lɒtrəpi/, **aeolotropism** /iə'lɒtrəpɪzəm/, *n.*

aeolian harp

**aeon** /'iən/, *n.* **1.** an indefinitely long period of time; an age. **2.** *Geol.* the largest division of geological time, comprising two or more eras. Also, **eon.** [L, from Gk *aiṓn* lifetime, age]

**aeonian** /i'oʊniən/, *adj.* eternal. [Gk *aiṓnios* agelong + -IAN]

**aeq.,** equal [L: *aequālis*]

**aer-,** variant of **aero-** before vowels.

**aerate** /'ɛəreɪt/, *v.t.,* **-rated, -rating.** **1.** to charge or treat with air or a gas, esp. with carbon dioxide. **2.** to expose to the free action of the air: *to aerate milk in order to remove unpleasant smells.* **3.** *Physiol.* to expose (a medium or tissue) to air, as in the oxygenation of the blood in respiration. [AER- + -ATE[1]] – **aeration** /ɛə'reɪʃən/, *n.*

**aerator** /'ɛəreɪtə/, *n.* **1.** an apparatus for aerating water or other fluids. **2.** a contrivance for fumigating wheat and other grain, to bleach it and destroy fungi and insects. **3.** *Agric.* a substance, or mechanical process, which breaks up soil so that air may penetrate. **4.** *Plumbing.* a perforated cap on the end of a tap which disperses water flow.

**aerial** /'ɛəriəl/, *n.* **1.** *Radio.* that part of a radio system designed to radiate or receive electromagnetic waves into or from free space; an antenna. *–adj.* **2.** of, in, or produced by the air: *aerial currents.* **3.** inhabiting or frequenting the air: *aerial creatures.* **4.** reaching far into the air; high; lofty: *aerial spires.* **5.** partaking of the nature of air; airy: *aerial beings.* **6.** unsubstantial; visionary: *aerial fancies.* **7.** having a light and graceful beauty; ethereal: *aerial music.* **8.** *Biol.* growing in the air, as the adventitious roots of some trees. **9.** pertaining to or used for, against, or in aircraft. [L *āerius* airy (from Gk *āérios*) + -AL[1]] – **aerially,** *adv.*

**aerial magnetometer** /– mægnə'tɒmətə/, *n.* a device carried in an aircraft and used to measure variations in the earth's magnetic field. Also, **airborne magnetometer.**

**aerial perspective** /– pə'spɛktɪv/, *n.* that branch of perspective which considers the variations of light, shade, and colour in objects delineated or photographed, according to their distances, the quality of light falling on them, and the medium through which they are seen.

**aerial photograph** /– 'foʊtəgræf/, *n.* a photograph taken from the air. – **aerial photography,** *n.*

**aerial ping-pong** /– 'pɪŋ-pɒŋ/, *n. Colloq.* →**Australian Rules.**

**aerial spraying** /– 'spreɪɪŋ/, *n.* the spreading of weedicides, pesticides, etc., from an aircraft; crop-dusting.

**aerial supering** /– 'supərɪŋ/, *n.* the process of spreading superphosphate over paddocks from an aeroplane.

**aerial top-dressing** /– 'tɒp-drɛsɪŋ/, *n.* the process of spreading top-dressing over paddocks from an aeroplane.

**aerie** /'ɪəri, 'ɛəri/, *n.* eyrie. Also, **aery.** [ML *aeria,* from OF *aire,* from L *ārea* AREA or L *ātrium* ATRIUM]

**aero** /'ɛəroʊ/, *adj.* **1.** of or for aircraft. **2.** of aeronautics.

**aero-,** a word element indicating: **1.** air; atmosphere. **2.** gas. **3.** aeroplane. [Gk, combining form of *āḗr* air]

**aerobatic** /ɛərə'bætɪk/, *adj.* of or pertaining to displays of manoeuvring and other stunts in an aircraft.

**aerobatics** /ɛərə'bætɪks/, *n. pl.* **1.** stunts carried out by aircraft; aerial acrobatics. **2.** (*construed as sing.*) the skill of giving an aerobatic display.

**aerobe** /'ɛəroʊb/, *n.* a bacterium or other micro-organism whose existence requires, or is not destroyed by, the presence of free oxygen (opposed to *anaerobe*). [NL *aerobia,* from Gk *āero-* AERO- + *bíos* life]

**aerobic** /ɛə'roʊbɪk/, *adj.* **1.** (of organisms or tissues) living or active only in the presence of free oxygen. **2.** pertaining to or caused by the presence of oxygen: *aerobic respiration.* **3.** pertaining to or induced by aerobic organisms. Cf. **anaerobic.** – **aerobically,** *adv.*

**aerobics** /ɛə'roʊbɪks/, *n. pl.* physical exercises which stimulate the respiratory and circulatory systems to improve and maintain physical fitness.

**aerobiosis** /ˌɛəroʊbaɪ'oʊsəs/, *n.* existence in the presence of free oxygen. – **aerobiotic,** *adj.*

**aerobridge** /'ɛəroʊbrɪdʒ/, *n.* a covered portable walkway for the transfer of passengers from a departure terminal to an aeroplane.

**aerodonetics** /ɛərədə'nɛtɪks/, *n.* the study of gliding or soaring flight; the science dealing with gliding craft. [Gk *āero-dónētos* air tossed + -ICS]

**aerodrome** /'ɛərədroʊm/, *n.* a landing field for aeroplanes, esp. private aeroplanes, having permanent buildings, equipment, hangars, etc. but usually smaller than an airport; landing strip. Also, *U.S.* **airdrome.**

**aerodynamic missile** /ˌɛəroʊdaɪˌnæmɪk 'mɪsaɪl/, *n.* a missile which uses aerodynamic forces to maintain its flight path, generally employing propulsion guidance.

**aerodynamics** /ˌɛəroʊdaɪ'næmɪks/, *n.* the study of air in motion and of the forces acting on solids in motion relative to the air through which they move. Cf. **aerostatics.** – **aerodynamicist** /ˌɛəroʊdaɪ'næməsəst/, *n.*

**aerodyne** /ˈɛəroudaɪn/, *n.* any heavier-than-air craft.

**aero-elastic** /ˌɛərou-əˈlæstɪk/, *adj.* (of an airframe) deformable by aerodynamic forces. – **aero-elasticity** /ˌɛərou-ilæsˈtɪsəti/, *n.* – **aero-elastician** /ˌɛərou-ilæsˈtɪʃən/, *n.*

**aeroembolism** /ˌɛərouˈɛmbəlɪzəm/, *n.* a morbid condition caused by substantial decrease in atmospheric pressure, as in high-altitude flying, and characterised by the formation of nitrogen bubbles in the blood, pains in the lungs, etc. Cf. **the bends.** See **bend** (def. 21).

**aero-engine** /ˈɛərou-ˌɛndʒən/, *n.* the source of power in an aircraft.

**aerofoil** /ˈɛərəfɔɪl/, *n.* any surface, such as a wing, aileron, or stabiliser, designed to help in lifting or controlling an aircraft or sailing boat by making use of the current of air through which it moves.

**aerogram** /ˈɛərəgræm/, *n.* a sheet of special lightweight airmail paper (sold only by post offices) upon which a letter may be written. The item is then suitably folded, gummed and addressed so as to serve at once as missive and envelope; air letter. Also, **aerogramme.**

**aerograph** /ˈɛərəgræf/, *n.* **1.** a description of the air or atmosphere. **2.** a spray gun for paint, lacquer, etc., used for fine work.

**aerography** /ɛəˈrɒgrəfi/, *n.* description of the air or atmosphere. – **aerographer,** *n.* – **aerographic** /ɛərəˈgræfɪk/, **aerographical** /ɛərəˈgræfɪkəl/, *adj.*

**aerogun** /ˈɛərəgʌn/, *n.* a spray-gun. [Trademark]

**aerolite** /ˈɛərəlaɪt/, *n.* a meteorite consisting mainly of stony matter. Also, **aerolith** /ˈɛərəlɪθ/. – **aerolitic** /ɛərəˈlɪtɪk/, *adj.*

**aerology** /ɛəˈrɒlədʒi/, *n.* the study of the properties of air and of the atmosphere. – **aerologic** /ɛərəˈlɒdʒɪk/, **aerological** /ɛərəˈlɒdʒɪkəl/, *adj.* – **aerologist,** *n.*

**aeromagnetic** /ˌɛəroumægˈnɛtɪk/, *adj.* derived from, or relating to a study from the air of earth's magnetic field: *an aeromagnetic survey of the bauxite field.*

**aeromagnetic prospecting** /– ˈprɒspɛktɪŋ/, *n.* a technique of exploration of an area using an aerial magnetometer.

**aeromancy** /ˈɛərəmænsi/, *n.* divination relating to the air and sky.

**aeromarine** /ˌɛəroumәˈrin/, *adj.* denoting or pertaining to navigation of aircraft above the ocean.

**aeromechanic** /ˌɛəroumәˈkænɪk/, *n.* **1.** an aviation mechanic. *–adj.* **2.** of or pertaining to aeromechanics.

**aeromechanics** /ˌɛəroumәˈkænɪks/, *n.* the mechanics of air or gases. – **aeromechanical,** *adj.*

**aerometer** /ɛəˈrɒmətə/, *n.* an instrument for determining the weight, density, etc., of air or other gases.

**aerometry** /ɛəˈrɒmətri/, *n.* →**pneumatics.** – **aerometric** /ɛərəˈmɛtrɪk/, *adj.*

**aeron.,** aeronautics.

**aeronaut** /ˈɛərənɔt/, *n.* **1.** the pilot of a balloon or other lighter-than-air craft. **2.** a traveller in an airship. [back-formation from AERONAUTICS. Cf. F *aéronaute*]

**aeronautic** /ɛərəˈnɔtɪk/, *adj.* of aeronautics or aeronauts. Also, **aeronautical.** [NL *aeronautica*, neut. pl. adj., pertaining to sailing in the air] – **aeronautically,** *adv.*

**aeronautical engineer** /ɛərəˌnɔtɪkəl ɛndʒəˈnɪə/, *n.* one versed in the design and construction of aeroplanes, etc.

**aeronautical engineering** /– ɛndʒəˈnɪərɪŋ/, *n.* the action, work, or profession of an aeronautical engineer.

**aeronautics** /ɛərəˈnɔtɪks/, *n.* the science or art of flight. [pl. of AERONAUTIC. See -ICS]

**aeropause** /ˈɛərəpɔz/, *n.* a region of the upper atmosphere marking the boundary between the denser portion of the atmosphere and outer space, and in which functional effects of the atmosphere on man and aircraft cease to exist.

**aerophagia** /ɛərəˈfeɪdʒiə, -dʒə/, *n.* morbid swallowing of air due to neurotic gastric disturbances.

**aerophobia** /ɛərəˈfoubiə/, *n.* morbid fear of draughts of air, gases, and airborne noxious influences.

**aerophone** /ˈɛərəfoun/, *n.* an instrument with a tube enclosing a column of air, and with a device for causing the air to vibrate.

**aeroplane** /ˈɛərəpleɪn/, *n.* an aircraft, heavier than air, kept aloft by the upward thrust exerted by the passing air on its fixed wings, and driven by propellers, jet propulsion, etc. Also, *Chiefly U.S.*, **airplane.**

**aeroplane spin** /– ˈspɪn/, *n.* a manoeuvre in which a wrestler hauls his opponent on to his shoulders and spins round to make him giddy.

**aerosol** /ˈɛərəsɒl/, *n.* **1.** *Physics, Chem.* a system consisting of colloidal particles dispersed in a gas; a smoke or fog. **2.** an aerosol container. [AERO- + SOL[2]]

**aerosol bomb** /– ˈbɒm/, *n.* an aerosol container for spraying insecticides on a large scale, esp. agriculturally.

**aerosol container** /– kənˈteɪnə/, *n.* a small metal container for storing under pressure, and subsequently dispensing as a spray, such domestic products in the aerosol form as insecticides, waxes, lacquers, etc. Also, **aerosol pack.**

**aerospace** /ˈɛərouˌspeɪs/, *n.* **1.** the earth's envelope of air and the space beyond it, in which rockets and space vehicles fly. *–adj.* **2.** pertaining to aeronautics and astronautics considered together.

**aerostat** /ˈɛərəstæt/, *n.* a balloon, airship, or any lighter-than-air craft. [AERO- + -STAT]

**aerostatic** /ɛərəˈstætɪk/, *adj.* **1.** of aerostatics. **2.** of, or capable of supporting, aerostats. Also, **aerostatical.**

**aerostatics** /ɛərəˈstætɪks/, *n.* **1.** the science of the equilibrium of air and other gases, and of the equilibrium of bodies sustained in them. **2.** the science of lighter-than-air craft.

**aerostation** /ɛərəˈsteɪʃən/, *n.* the operation of aerostats. [F, *aérostat* AEROSTAT]

**aerotherapeutics** /ˌɛərouθɛrəˈpjutɪks/, *n.* that branch of therapeutics which deals with the curative use of air or of artificially prepared atmospheres. Also, **aerotherapy** /ˌɛərouˈθɛrəpi/.

**aero tow** /ˈɛərou tou/, *n.* (of a glider) a tow by powered aircraft to a prearranged height before the glider is released.

**aertex** /ˈɛətɛks/, *n.* a cellular cotton fabric used for underwear, sports shirts, etc. [Trademark]

**aery**[1] /ˈɛəri/, *adj. Poetic.* ethereal; lofty. [L *āerius* airy]

**aery**[2] /ˈɪəri, ˈɛəri/, *n., pl.* **aeries.** →**eyrie.**

**Aesopian** /iˈsoupiən/, *adj.* pertaining to beast fables. [from *Aesop*, 620?-560? B.C., Greek writer of fables]

**aesthesia** /əsˈθiziə, -ˈθiʒə/, *n.* sensitivity; feeling; perceptibility. Also, *U.S.*, **esthesia.** [NL, from Gk *aisthēsía* perceptive state]

**aesthesis** /əsˈθisəs/, *n.* →**aesthesia.** Also, *U.S.*, **esthesis.** [Gk *aísthēsis* a perceiving]

**aesthete** /əsˈθit, ˈisθit, ˈɛsθit/, *n.* **1.** one who cultivates the sense of the beautiful; one very sensitive to the beauties of art or nature. **2.** one who affects great love of art, music, poetry, etc., and indifference to practical matters. Also, *U.S.*, **esthete.** [Gk *aisthētḗs* one who perceives]

**aesthetic** /əsˈθɛtɪk, is-/, *adj.* **1.** pertaining to the sense of the beautiful or the science of aesthetics. **2.** having a sense of the beautiful; characterised by a love of beauty. Also, *U.S.*, **esthetic.** [Gk *aisthētikós* perceptive]

**aesthetical** /əsˈθɛtɪkəl, is-/, *adj.* of or relating to aesthetics. Also, *U.S.*, **esthetical.**

**aesthetically** /əsˈθɛtɪkli, is-/, *adv.* **1.** according to aesthetics or its principles. **2.** in an aesthetic manner. Also, *U.S.*, **esthetically.**

**aesthetician** /isθəˈtɪʃən/, *n.* one versed in aesthetics. Also, *U.S.*, **esthetician.**

**aestheticism** /əsˈθɛtəsɪzəm, is-/, *n.* **1.** the acceptance of artistic beauty and taste as a fundamental standard, ethical and other standards being secondary. **2.** an exaggerated devotion to art, music, or poetry with indifference to practical matters. Also, *U.S.*, **estheticism.**

**aesthetics** /əsˈθɛtɪks, is-/, *n.* **1.** *Philos.* the science which deduces from nature and taste the rules and principles of art; the theory of the fine arts; the science of the beautiful, or that branch of philosophy which deals with its principles or effects; the doctrines of taste. **2.** *Psychol.* the study of the mind and emotions in relation to the sense of beauty. Also, *U.S.*, **esthetics.** [pl. of AESTHETIC. See -ICS]

**aestival** /ˈɛstəvəl/, *adj.* pertaining or appropriate to summer. Also, *U.S.*, **estival.** [L *aestīvālis*]

**aestivate** /ˈɛstəveɪt/, *v.i.*, **-vated, -vating. 1.** to spend the summer. **2.** *Zool.* to pass the summer in a torpid condition. Also, *U.S.*, **estivate.** – **aestivator,** *n.*

**aestivation** /ɛstəˈveɪʃən/, *n.* **1.** *Zool.* the act of aestivating. **2.**

*Bot.* the arrangement of the parts of a flower in the bud. Also, *U.S.*, **estivation.**

**aetatis suae** /aɪˌtatəs 'suaɪ, iˌtatəs 'sui/, in a certain year of one's age. [L]

**aether** /'iθə/, *n.* →**ether** (defs 2, 3, 4). – **aethereal** /ə'θɪəriəl/, *adj.*

**aetiology** /iti'ɒlədʒi/, *n.* the study of the causes of anything, esp. of diseases. Also, *U.S.*, **etiology.** [L *aetiologia*, from Gk *aitiologia*, from *aitia* cause. See -LOGY] – **aetiological** /itiə'lɒdʒɪkəl/, *adj.* – **aetiologically,** /itiə'lɒdʒɪkli/, *adj.* – **aetiologist,** *n.*

**af-,** variant of **ad-** (by assimilation) before *f*, as in *affect*.

**AF,** Anglo-French. Also, **A.F.**

**A.F.,** audio frequency. Also, **a.f.**

**afar** /ə'fa/, *adv.* **1.** from a distance (usu. prec. by *from*): *he came from afar.* **2.** far away; at or to a distance (oft. fol. by *off*): *he saw the plane afar off.* [ME *a fer.* See A-[1], FAR]

**A.F.C.,** **1.** automatic flight control. **2.** automatic frequency control.

**afeard** /ə'fɪəd/, *adj. Archaic.* afraid. Also, **afeared.** [ME *afered*, OE *āfǣred*]

**afebrile** /eɪ'fibraɪl/, *adj.* without fever; feverless. [A-[6] + FEBRILE]

**affable** /'æfəbəl/, *adj.* **1.** easy to talk to or to approach; polite; friendly: *an affable and courteous gentleman.* **2.** expressing affability, mild; benign: *an affable countenance.* [F, from L *affābilis* able to be spoken to] – **affability** /æfə'bɪləti/, **affableness,** *n.* – **affably,** *adv.*

**affair** /ə'fɛə/, *n.* **1.** anything done or to be done; that which requires action or effort; business; concern: *an affair of great moment, the affairs of state.* **2.** (*pl.*) matters of interest or concern; particular doings or interests: *put your affairs in order.* **3.** an event or a performance; a particular action, operation, or proceeding: *when did this affair happen?* **4.** thing; matter (applied to anything made or existing, with a descriptive or qualifying term): *this machine is a complicated affair.* **5.** a private or personal concern; a special function, business, or duty: *attend to your own affairs.* **6.** → **love affair.** [F *affaire*, from *à faire* to do; replacing ME *afere*, from OF *afaire*]

**affaire de coeur** /əfɛə də 'kɜ/, *n.* an affair of the heart; love affair. [F]

**affaire d'honneur** /əfɛə dɒ'nɜ/, *n.* an affair of honour; a duel. [F]

**affect**[1] /ə'fɛkt/, *v.t.* **1.** to act on; produce an effect or a change in: *cold affects the body.* **2.** to impress; move (in mind or feelings): *the poetry affected me deeply.* **3.** (of pain, disease, etc.) to attack or lay hold of. *–n.* **4.** *Psychol.* feeling or emotion. **5.** *Obs.* affection; passion; sensation; inclination; inward disposition or feeling. [L *affectus*, pp., influenced, attacked]

**affect**[2] /ə'fɛkt/, *v.t.* **1.** to make a show of; put on a pretence of; pretend; feign: *to affect ignorance.* **2.** to make a show of liking or imitating: *to affect an Oxford accent.* **3.** to use or adopt by preference; choose; prefer: *the peculiar costume which he affected.* **4.** to assume the character or attitude of: *to affect the freethinker.* **5.** to tend towards habitually or naturally: *a substance which affects colloidal form.* **6.** (of animals and plants) to inhabit; frequent: *moss affects the northern slopes.* **7.** *Archaic.* to take pleasure in; fancy; like. **8.** *Archaic.* to aim at; aspire to. *–v.i.* **9.** to profess; pretend: *he affected to be wearied.* [F *affecter*, from L *affectāre*] – **affecter,** *n.*

**affectation** /ˌæfɛk'teɪʃən/, *n.* **1.** a striving for the appearance of (a quality not really or fully possessed); pretence of the possession or character; effort for the reputation (fol. by *of*): *an affectation of wit, affectation of great wealth.* **2.** artificiality of manner or conduct; effort to attract notice by pretence, assumption, or any assumed peculiarity: *his affectations are insufferable.* **3.** *Obs.* strenuous pursuit or desire (fol. by *of*). [L *affectātio* a pursuit after]

**affected**[1] /ə'fɛktəd/, *adj.* **1.** acted upon; influenced. **2.** influenced injuriously; impaired; attacked, as by climate or disease. **3.** moved; touched: *she was deeply affected.* [pp. of AFFECT[1]]

**affected**[2] /ə'fɛktəd/, *adj.* **1.** assumed artificially: *affected airs, affected diction.* **2.** assuming or pretending to possess characteristics which are not natural: *an affected lady.* **3.** inclined or disposed: *well affected towards a project.* [pp. of AFFECT[2]] – **affectedly,** *adv.* – **affectedness,** *n.*

**affecting** /ə'fɛktɪŋ/, *adj.* having power to excite or move the feelings; tending to move the affections. – **affectingly,** *adv.*

**affection**[1] /ə'fɛkʃən/, *n.* **1.** a settled goodwill, love, or attachment: *the affection of a parent for his child.* **2.** the state of having one's feelings affected; emotion or feeling: *over and above our reason and affections.* **3.** *Pathol.* a disease, or the condition of being diseased; a morbid or abnormal state of body or mind: *a gouty affection.* **4.** the act of affecting; act of influencing or acting upon. **5.** the state of being affected. **6.** *Philos.* a contingent, alterable, and accidental state or quality of being. **7.** *Psychol.* the affective aspect of a mental process. **8.** *Archaic.* a bodily state due to any influence. **9.** *Obs.* bent or disposition of mind. [L *affectio* influence (active), state of mind, favourable disposition (passive)]

**affection**[2] /ə'fɛkʃən/, *n. Obs.* →**affectation.** [AFFECT[2], *v.* + -ION]

**affectionate** /ə'fɛkʃənət/, *adj.* **1.** characterised by or manifesting affection; possessing or indicating love; tender: *an affectionate embrace.* **2.** having great love or affection; warmly attached: *your affectionate brother.* **3.** *Obs.* strongly disposed or inclined. **4.** *Obs.* biased; partisan. – **affectionately,** *adv.* – **affectionateness,** *n.*

**affective** /ə'fɛktɪv/, *adj.* **1.** pertaining to the affections; emotional. **2.** exciting emotion; affecting. **3.** *Psychol.* pertaining to feeling or emotion, esp. to pleasurable or unpleasurable aspects of mental process. – **affectively,** *adv.* – **affectivity** /ˌæfɛk'tɪvəti/, *n.*

**afferent** /'æfərənt/, *adj.* bringing to or leading towards a central organ or point (opposed to *efferent*): *afferent nerves or veins.* [L *afferens*, ppr., bringing to]

**affetuoso** /əfɛtju'oʊsoʊ, -zoʊ/, *adv.* (a musical direction) with feeling. [It.]

**affiance** /æfi'ɒns, ə'faɪəns/, *v.*, **-anced, -ancing,** *n.* *–v.t.* **1.** to bind by promise of marriage; betroth: *to affiance a daughter.* *–n.* **2.** the pledging of faith, esp. a marriage contract. **3.** trust; confidence; reliance. [ME, from OF *afiance*, from *afier*, from LL *affidāre* pledge]

**affianced** /æfi'ɒnst, ə'faɪənst/, *adj.* betrothed.

**afficionado** /əfɪʃiə'nadoʊ/, *n.* →**aficionado.**

**affidavit** /æfə'deɪvət/, *n.* a written statement on oath, sworn to before an authorised official, often used as evidence in court proceedings. [L: he has made oath]

**affiliate** /ə'fɪlieɪt/, *v.*, **-ated, -ating;** /ə'fɪliət/, *n.* *–v.t.* **1.** to attach as a branch or part; unite; associate (fol. by *with*): *affiliated with the church.* **2.** to bring into association or close connection: *the two banks were affiliated.* **3.** to connect in the way of descent or derivation (fol. by *upon*). **4.** *Law.* **a.** to fix the paternity of, as an illegitimate child. **b.** to refer to as being the child of or belonging to. *–v.i.* **5.** to associate oneself; be intimately united in action or interest. *–n.* **6.** one who or that which is affiliated; associate or auxiliary. [LL *affiliātus*, pp., adopted as a son]

**affiliation** /əfɪli'eɪʃən/, *n.* **1.** the act of affiliating. **2.** the state of being affiliated; association.

**affiliation order** /'– ɔdə/, *n.* an order made by a magistrate making the proven father of an illegitimate child pay maintenance for a specified period.

**affined** /ə'faɪnd/, *adj.* **1.** related; connected. **2.** *Obs.* bound. [F *affiné* related + -ED[2]]

**affinitive** /ə'fɪnətɪv/, *adj.* characterised by affinity; closely related.

**affinity** /ə'fɪnəti/, *n.*, *pl.* **-ties.** **1.** a natural liking for, or attraction to, a person or thing. **2.** inherent likeness or agreement as between things; close resemblance or connection. **3.** relationship by marriage or by ties other than those of blood (distinguished from *consanguinity*). **4.** one for whom such a natural liking or attraction is felt. **5.** *Biol.* the phylogenetic relationship between two organisms or groups of organisms resulting in a resemblance in general plan or structure, or in the essential structural parts. **6.** *Chem.* that force by which the atoms of bodies of dissimilar nature unite in certain definite proportions to form a compound. [ME, from F *af(f)inité*, from L *affinitas*]

**affinity group** /'– grup/, *n.* a group of people united to further a project or purpose they have in common, as obtaining cheap block tickets on an airline, etc.

**affirm** /ə'fɜm/, *v.t.* **1.** to state or assert positively; maintain as true: *to affirm one's loyalty to one's country.* **2.** to establish, confirm, or ratify: *the appellate court affirmed the judgment of the lower court.* **3.** *Logic.* to state in the affirmative. **4.** *Law.* to declare solemnly without oath. *–v.i.* **5.** to declare positively; assert solemnly. **6.** *Law.* to declare solemnly before a court or magistrate, but without oath (a practice allowed where the affirmant has scruples, usually religious, against taking an oath). [L *affirmāre*; replacing ME *afer-me(n)*, from OF *afermer*] – **affirmable,** *adj.* – **affirmably,** *adv.* – **affirmer,** *n.*

**affirmant** /ə'fɜmənt/, *n.* one who affirms.

**affirmation** /æfə'meɪʃən/, *n.* **1.** the assertion that something is, or is true. **2.** that which is affirmed; a proposition that is declared to be true. **3.** establishment of something of prior origin; confirmation; ratification. **4.** *Law.* a solemn declaration accepted instead of a statement under oath. Also, **affirmance** /ə'fɜməns/.

**affirmative** /ə'fɜmətɪv/, *adj.* **1.** giving affirmation or assent; confirmatory; not negative: *an affirmative answer.* **2.** *Logic.* denoting a proposition or judgment that asserts a relation between its terms, or asserts that the predicate applies to the subject. *–n.* **3.** that which affirms or asserts; a positive proposition: *two negatives make an affirmative.* **4.** an affirmative word or phrase, as *yes* or *I do.* **5. the affirmative,** the agreeing or concurring side. Also, **affirmatory** /ə'fɜmətəri, -tri/. [LL *affirmātīvus*; replacing ME *affirmatyff*, from OF] – **affirmatively,** *adj.*

**affix** /ə'fɪks/, *v.*; /'æfɪks/, *n.* *–v.t.* **1.** to fix; fasten, join, or attach (oft. fol. by *to*): *to affix stamps to a letter.* **2.** to impress (a seal or stamp). **3.** to attach (blame, reproach, ridicule, etc.). *–n.* **4.** that which is joined or attached. **5.** *Gram.* any meaningful element (prefix, infix, or suffix) added to a stem or base, as *-ed* added to *want* to form *wanted.* [ML *affixāre*, frequentative of L *affīgere* fasten to] – **affixer** /ə'fɪksə/, *n.*

**affixture** /ə'fɪkstʃə/, *n.* the act of affixing; attachment.

**afflated** /ə'fleɪtəd/, *adj.* inspired.

**afflatus** /ə'fleɪtəs/, *n.* **1.** inspiration; an impelling mental force acting from within. **2.** divine communication of knowledge. Also, **afflation.** [L: *afflātus* a blast]

**afflict** /ə'flɪkt/, *v.t.* **1.** to distress with mental or bodily pain; trouble greatly or grievously: *to be afflicted with the gout.* **2.** *Obs.* to overthrow; rout. [L *afflictus*, pp., thrown down] – **afflicter,** *n.*

**affliction** /ə'flɪkʃən/, *n.* **1.** a state of pain, distress, or grief: *they sympathised with us in our affliction.* **2.** a cause of continual pain of body or mind, as sickness, loss, calamity, persecution, etc. [ME, from L *afflictio*]

**afflictive** /ə'flɪktɪv/, *adj.* characterised by or causing pain; distressing. – **afflictively,** *adv.*

**affluence** /'æfluəns/, *n.* **1.** abundance of material goods; wealth: *to live in great affluence.* **2.** an abundant supply, as of thoughts, words, etc.; a profusion. **3.** a flowing to or towards; afflux. [F, from L *affluentia*]

**affluent** /'æfluənt/, *adj.* **1.** abounding in means; rich: *an affluent person.* **2.** abounding in anything; abundant. **3.** flowing freely: *an affluent fountain.* *–n.* **4.** a tributary stream. [ME, from L *affluens*, ppr., flowing to] – **affluently,** *adv.*

**afflux** /ə'flʌks/, *n.* **1.** that which flows to or towards a point: *an afflux of blood to the head.* **2.** the act of flowing to; a flow. [ML *affluxus*, n., from L *affluere* flow to]

**afford** /ə'fɔd/, *v.t.* **1.** to have the means (oft. prec. by *can* or *may* and fol. by an infinitive): *we can afford to sell cheap.* **2.** to be able to meet the expense of; spare the price of (oft. prec. by *can* or *may*): *he can't afford a car.* **3.** to be able to give or spare (oft. prec. by *can* or *may*): *I can't afford the loss of a day.* **4.** to supply; furnish: *the transaction afforded him a good profit.* **5.** to be capable of yielding or providing: *the records afford no explanation.* **6.** to give or confer upon: *to afford one great pleasure, etc.* [ME *aforthen*, OE *geforthian* further, accomplish] – **affordable,** *adj.*

**afforest** /ə'fɒrəst/, *v.t.* to convert (bare or cultivated land) into forest, originally for the purpose of providing hunting grounds. [ML *afforestāre.* See AD-, FOREST] – **afforestation** /əfɒrəs'teɪʃən/, *n.*

**affranchise** /ə'fræntʃaɪz/, *v.t.*, **-chised, -chising.** to free from a state of dependence, servitude, or obligation. [F (by association with FRANCHISE, n.) *affranchiss-*, stem of *affranchir.* See AD-, FRANK]

**affray** /ə'freɪ/, *n.* **1.** a public fight; a noisy quarrel; a brawl. **2.** *Law.* the fighting of two or more persons in a public place. *–v.t.* **3.** *Archaic.* to frighten. [ME *a(f)fray(en)*, from AF, var. of *effrayer*, OF *effreer*, from LL *exfridāre*, from *ex-* EX[1]- + *-fridāre*, from *fridus* peace (of Gmc origin)]

**affreightment** /ə'freɪtmənt/, *n.* a contract made by a shipowner to carry goods for payment. [obs. *affreight* (from F *affréter*, remodelled on FREIGHT) + -MENT]

**affricate** /'æfrəkeɪt/, *v.*, **-cated, -cating;** /'æfrəkət/, *n.* *–v.t.* **1.** to produce (a sound) with affrication. *–n.* **2.** →**affricative.** [backformation from AFFRICATIVE] – **affrication** /æfrə'keɪʃən/, *n.*

**affricative** /ə'frɪkətɪv/, *n.* a composite speech sound beginning with a stop and ending with a fricative, such as *ch* in *church* (which begins like *t* and ends like *sh*). Also, **affricate.** [L *affricātus*, pp., rubbed on or against]

**affright** /ə'fraɪt/, *Archaic.* *–v.t.* **1.** to frighten. *–n.* **2.** sudden fear or terror; fright. **3.** a source of terror. **4.** the act of terrifying. [ME *afrighten*, OE *āfyrhtan*, from *ā-* (intensive) + *fyrhten* frighten] – **affrightedly,** *adv.*

**affront** /ə'frʌnt/, *n.* **1.** a personally offensive act or word; an intentional slight; an open manifestation of disrespect; an insult to the face: *an affront to the king.* **2.** an offence to one's dignity or self-respect. *–v.t.* **3.** to offend by an open manifestation of disrespect or insolence: *an affronting speech.* **4.** to put out of countenance; make ashamed or confused. **5.** to meet or encounter face to face; confront: *to affront death.* **6.** *Archaic.* to front; face. [ME *afront(en)*, from OF *afronter*, from LL affrontāre] – **affronter,** *n.* – **affrontingly,** *adv.*

**affusion** /ə'fjuʒən/, *n.* the pouring on of water or other liquid, esp. in baptism. [L *affūsus*, pp., poured + -ION]

**afghan** /'æfgæn/, *n.* a kind of woollen blanket, knitted, crocheted, or woven, usu. in a geometric pattern.

**Afghan** /'æfgæn/, *n.* **1.** an inhabitant of Afghanistan. **2.** (formerly) a camel driver from the north-west parts of India, employed in the outback of Australia, and sometimes self-employed as an itinerant merchant. **3.** →**Afghan hound.** *–adj.* **4.** of Afghanistan or its people.

**Afghan hound** /– 'haʊnd/, *n.* a breed of greyhound with a very long silky coat.

**Afghani** /æf'gani, -'gæni/, *n.* **1.** Afghan. **2.** the monetary unit of Afghanistan. *–adj.* **3.** Afghan.

**Afghanistan** /æf'gænəstæn/, *n.* a country in southern Asia.

**aficionado** /əfɪʃiə'nadoʊ/, *n.* an ardent devotee. Also, **afficionado.** [Sp.]

**afield** /ə'fild/, *adv.* **1.** abroad; away from home. **2.** off the beaten path; far and wide: *to stray far afield in one's reading.* **3.** in or to the field or fields.

**afire** /ə'faɪə/, *adj.* **1.** on fire; alight. **2.** involved; enthusiastic.

**aflame** /ə'fleɪm/, *adj.* **1.** on fire; ablaze: *the house was all aflame.* **2.** inflamed; aroused; glowing: *aflame with curiosity.*

**afloat** /ə'floʊt/, *adj.* **1.** borne on the water; in a floating condition: *the ship is afloat.* **2.** on board ship; at sea: *cargo afloat and ashore.* **3.** flooded: *the main deck was afloat.* **4.** moving without guide or control: *our affairs are all afloat.* **5.** passing from place to place; in circulation: *a rumour is afloat.*

**aflutter** /ə'flʌtə/, *adj.* in a flutter.

**afocal** /eɪ'foʊkəl/, *adj.* having no finite focal point, as a telescope.

**afoot** /ə'fʊt/, *adv.* **1.** on foot; walking: *I came afoot.* *–adj.* **2.** astir; in progress: *there is mischief afoot.*

**afore** /ə'fɔ/, *Archaic.* *–adv.* **1.** before. *–prep.* **2.** before. *–conj.* **3.** before. [ME *aforne*, OE *on foran.* See A-[1], FORE[1]]

**aforementioned** /əfɔ'mɛnʃənd/, *adj.* mentioned earlier or previously.

**aforesaid** /ə'fɔsɛd/, *adj.* said or mentioned previously.

**aforethought** /ə'fɔθɔt/, *adj.* **1.** thought of beforehand; premeditated: *malice aforethought.* *–n.* **2.** premeditation; forethought.

---

i = peat ɪ = pit ɛ = pet æ = pat a = part ɒ = pot ʌ = putt ɔ = port ʊ = put u = pool ɜ = pert ə = apart aɪ = buy eɪ = bay ɔɪ = boy aʊ = how oʊ = hoe ɪə = here ɛə = hair ʊə = tour g = give θ = thin ð = then ʃ = show ʒ = measure tʃ = choke dʒ = joke ŋ = sing j = you õ = Fr. bon

**a fortiori** /ˌeɪ fɔti'ɔri/, for a still stronger reason; even more certain; all the more. [L]

**afoul** /ə'faʊl/, *adj.* **1.** in a state of collision or entanglement: *a ship with its shrouds afoul.* *–adv.* **2. run afoul of,** to become entangled with: *run afoul of the law.*

**afraid** /ə'freɪd/, *adj.* **1.** feeling fear; filled with apprehension: *afraid to go.* **2.** reluctantly or regretfully of the opinion (sometimes fol. by *that*). [ME *afraied*, orig. pp. of AFFRAY]

**A-frame** /'eɪ-freɪm/, *adj.* (of a house or other small buildings) built with a steeply pitched roof which forms the walls and extends to the foundations, so as to resemble an A.

**afresh** /ə'frɛʃ/, *adv.* anew; again: *to start afresh.*

**Afric** /'æfrɪk/, *adj. Archaic.* African.

**Africa** /'æfrɪkə/, *n.* the second largest continent, south of Europe and between the Atlantic and Indian Oceans. – **African,** *adj., n.*

**african** /'æfrɪkən/, *n. Colloq.* a cigarette. [rhyming slang, *African nigger* cigger]

**African** /'æfrɪkən/, *adj.* **1.** of or from Africa; belonging to the black race of Africa; Negro. *–n.* **2.** a native of Africa; a member of the black race of Africa; a Negro.

**African boxthorn** /– 'bɒksθɔn/, *n.* a plant, *Lycium ferocissimum,* with orange-red berries and stout spines, found as a weed in pasture areas.

**African lily** /– 'lɪli/, *n.* →**agapanthus.**

**African sleeping sickness,** *n.* a disease, generally fatal, common in parts of Africa, usu. marked by fever, wasting, and progressive lethargy, and caused by a parasitic protozoan, *Trypanosoma gambiense.* It is carried by a tsetse fly, *Glossina palpalis.*

**African violet** /æfrɪkən 'vaɪələt/, *n.* a plant, *Saintpaulia ionantha,* with violet, pink, or white flowers, popular in cultivation.

**Afrikaans** /æfrɪ'kanz, -'kans/, *n.* a language of South Africa, developed out of the speech of 17th-century settlers from Holland and still very like Dutch; South African Dutch; Taal. [var. spelling of D *Afrikaansch*]

**Afrikander** /æfrɪ'kandə/, *n.* →**Afrikaner.**

**Afrikaner** /æfrɪ'kanə/, *n.* an Afrikaans-speaking native of the Republic of South Africa born of white parents of Dutch, German, or Huguenot descent. Also, **Afrikander.** [Afrikaans *Afrikaander*, b. *Afrikaans* and *Hollander*]

**afro** /'æfroʊ/, *n.* a hair-style in which the hair, which is frizzy or frizzed, is allowed to grow to considerable length, then cut to form a large rounded shape.

**Afro-,** a combining form meaning 'African', 'Negro'. [L *Afer* African]

**Afro-American** /ˌæfroʊ-ə'mɛrɪkən/, *adj.* **1.** pertaining to Americans of African origin or descent. *–n.* **2.** an American Negro.

**Afro-Asian** /ˌæfroʊ-'eɪʒən/, *adj.* **1.** consisting of or pertaining to Africa and Asia, or Africans and Asians, considered together. **2.** of Asian descent and African citizenship. **3.** of mixed African and Asian descent. *–n.* **4.** an Asian living in Africa. **5.** one of mixed African and Asian blood.

**afro-rock** /'æfroʊ-rɒk/, *n.* rock music with rhythms, established largely by drumming, which are felt to be black African in character.

**aft** /aft/, *adv. Naut.* **1.** at, in, or towards the stern. *–adj.* **2.** situated in or near the stern. [OE *æftan* from behind (from *æft-* behind + *-an*, suffix marking motion from), c. Goth. *aftana*]

**after** /'aftə/, *prep.* **1.** behind in place; following behind: *men placed in a line one after another.* **2.** in pursuit of; in search of; with or in desire for: *run after him.* **3.** concerning: *to inquire after a person.* **4.** later in time than; in succession to; at the close of: *after supper, time after time I urged him to do it.* **5.** subsequent to and in consequence of: *after what has happened, I can never return.* **6.** below in rank or excellence; next to: *Milton is usually placed after Shakespeare among English poets.* **7.** in imitation of, or in imitation of the style of: *after Raphael, to make something after a model.* **8.** with name of: *he was named after his uncle.* **9.** in proportion to; in accordance with: *after their intrinsic value.* **10.** according to the nature of; in agreement or unison with; in conformity to: *he swore after the manner of his faith.* *–adv.* **11.** behind; in the rear: *Jill came tumbling after.* **12.** later in time; afterwards: *happy ever after.* *–adj.* **13.** later in time; next; subsequent; succeeding: *in after years.* **14.** *Naut.* farther aft, or towards the stern of the ship: *the after sail.* *–conj.* **15.** subsequent to the time that: *after the boys left.* [ME, OE *æfter* (from *æf-* away from + *-ter*, comparative suffix)]

**after-acquired property** /ˌaftər-əkwaɪəd 'prɒpəti/, *n. Law.* property acquired by a bankrupt after sequestration, usu. vested in the trustee.

**afterbirth** /'aftəbɜθ/, *n.* the placenta and foetal membranes expelled from the uterus after parturition.

**afterbrain** /'aftəbreɪn/, *n.* →**metencephalon.**

**afterburner** /'aftəbɜnə/, *n.* a device for reheating, as a ramjet coupled to the exhaust of a jet engine to provide added thrust.

**afterburning** /'aftəbɜnɪŋ/, *n.* **1.** *Astronautics.* the irregular burning of fuel left in the firing chamber of a rocket after main burning has ceased. **2.** combustion in an afterburner.

**after-care** /'aftə-kɛə/, *n.* treatment, supervision, or assistance of convalescents.

**afterdamp** /'aftədæmp/, *n.* an irrespirable mixture of gases, consisting chiefly of carbon dioxide and nitrogen, left in a mine after an explosion or fire; chokedamp.

**afterdeck** /'aftədɛk/, *n.* the weather deck abaft the midship house.

**after-effect** /'aftər-əfɛkt/, *n.* **1.** a delayed effect; effect that follows later. **2.** *Med.* a result appearing after the first effect due to an agent, usu. a drug, has gone.

**afterglow** /'aftəgloʊ/, *n.* **1.** the glow frequently seen in the sky after sunset. **2.** a second or secondary glow. **3.** *Physics.* the persistence of radiation from a gas discharge or luminescent screen after the source of excitation has been removed.

**afterheat** /'aftəhit/, *n.* the heat generated in a nuclear reactor after it has been shut down, due to the radioactive substances formed in the fuel elements.

**afterimage** /'aftərɪmɪdʒ/, *n.* a visual image or other sense impression that persists after the withdrawal of the exciting stimulus.

**afterlife** /'aftəlaɪf/, *n.* **1.** life after death. **2.** later life.

**aftermath** /'aftəmæθ, -maθ/, *n.* resultant conditions, esp. of a catastrophe: *the aftermath of the storm.* [AFTER + *math* a mowing (OE *mæth*)]

**aftermost** /'aftəmoʊst/, *adj.* **1.** *Naut.* farthest aft. **2.** hindmost. [ME *aftermest*, OE *æftemest* last; the *-r-* owing to association with *after.* See AFT, -MOST]

**afternoon** /aftə'nun/, *n.* **1.** the time from noon until evening. **2.** the latter part: *the afternoon of life.* *–adj.* **3.** pertaining to the latter part of the day.

**afternoon tea** /ˌaftənun 'ti/, *n.* **1.** a light but sometimes quite formal meal at which cakes, sandwiches, etc. are served with tea, usu. about three or four o'clock in the afternoon. **2.** any small quantity of food or drink taken after the mid-afternoon, as by children when returning from school.

**afterpains** /'aftəpeɪnz/, *n.pl.* pains, caused by contraction of the uterus, experienced after childbirth.

**after peak** /'aftə pik/, *n.* an enclosed space aft under decks, used as a store or for keeping drinking water.

**afterpiece** /'aftəpis/, *n.* a short dramatic piece performed after a play.

**afters** /'aftəz/, *n.pl. Colloq.* →**dessert.**

**after-sales service** /ˌaftə-seɪlz 'sɜvəs/, *n.* the service given by a company after the sale of goods, esp. during the period of warranty.

**aftershaft** /'aftəʃaft/, *n.* **1.** a supplementary feather, usu. small, arising from the underside of the base of the shafts of certain feathers in many birds. **2.** the shaft of such a feather.

**aftershave** /'aftəʃeɪv/, *adj.* **1.** of or pertaining to skin lotion for use after shaving the face: *aftershave lotion.* *–n.* **2.** the lotion itself.

**aftershock** /'aftəʃɒk/, *n.* a lesser shock after an earthquake, sometimes one of a series occurring over a period of weeks.

**aftertaste** /'aftəteɪst/, *n.* **1.** a taste remaining after the substance causing it is no longer in the mouth. **2.** a slight lingering after-effect, often an unpleasant one.

**afterthought** /'aftəθɔt/, *n.* **1.** reflection after an act; some answer, expedient, or the like, that occurs to one's mind too late, or afterwards. **2.** a later or second thought. **3.** an action, remark, etc., prompted by an afterthought.

**afterwards** /'aftəwədz/, *adv.* in later or subsequent time; subsequently. Also, **afterward** /'aftəwəd/. [OE *æfterweard(es)*, var. of OE *æfteweard(es)*. See AFT, -WARDS; for *-r-*, see AFTERMOST]

**afterworld** /'aftəwɜld/, *n.* the future world.

**aftn,** afternoon.

**afto** /'aftoʊ/, *n.* →**arvo.** Also, **aftie.** [shortened form of AFTERNOON + -O]

**ag-,** variant of **ad-** (by assimilation) before *g*, as in *agglutinate.*

**Ag,** *Chem.* silver. [L *argentum*]

**Ag.,** Agriculture.

**AG,** joint-stock company. [G *Aktiengesellschaft*]

**A.G.** /eɪ 'dʒi/, **1.** Adjutant-General. **2.** Attorney-General. Also, **AG.**

**aga** /'agə/, *n.* (in Turkey) **1.** a title of honour, usu. implying respect for age. **2.** a general. Also, **agha.**

**again** /ə'gɛn, ə'geɪn/, *adv.* **1.** once more; in addition; another time; anew: *he did it all over again.* **2.** in an additional case or instance; moreover; besides; furthermore. **3.** on the other hand: *it might happen and again it might not.* **4.** back; in return; in reply: *to answer again.* **5.** in the opposite direction; to the same place or person: *to return again.* **6. again and again,** often; with frequent repetition. **7. as much again,** twice as much. [ME; OE *ongegn*, adv. and prep., opposite (to), towards, again, from *on* in + *gegn* straight]

**against** /ə'gɛnst, ə'geɪnst/, *prep.* **1.** in an opposite direction to, so as to meet; towards; upon: *to ride against the wind, the rain beats against the window.* **2.** in contact with, or in pressure upon: *to lean against a wall.* **3.** in opposition to; adverse or hostile to: *twenty votes against ten, against reason.* **4.** in resistance to or defence from: *protection against burglars.* **5.** in preparation for; in provision for: *money saved against a rainy day.* **6.** in contrast with; having as background: *the pictures stand out against the dark wall.* **7.** in exchange for; in return for; as a balance to: *draw against merchandise shipped.* **8.** instead of, as an alternative to, in contrast with, (sometimes prec. by *as*): *the advantages of flying against going by train.* **9.** *Obs.* directly opposite; facing; in front of. *–conj.* **10.** *Archaic.* by the time that. [AGAIN + *-(e)s*, adv. gen. suffix + *-t* added later; for this *-t* see WHILST, etc.]

**agalloch** /ə'gælɒk/, *n.* the resinous wood of the eaglewood. [Gk *agállochon*, from Dravidian]

**agama** /'ægəmə, ə'gæmə/, *n.* any lizard of the Old World family Agamidae, allied to the iguanas and including large and brilliantly coloured species. [Carib]

**agamic** /ə'gæmɪk/, *adj.* **1.** *Biol.* **a.** asexual. **b.** occurring without sexual union; germinating without impregnation; not gamic. **2.** *Obs. Bot.* cryptogamic. Also, **agamous.** [Gk *ágamos* unwed + -IC] – **agamically,** *adv.*

**agamid** /'ægəmɪd/, *adj.* of or relating to the Agamidae, a widespread family of lizards, mostly terrestrial, but some arboreal or semi-aquatic, having acrodont dentition and roughened skin, as the bearded lizard or the frill-necked lizard.

**agamogenesis** /ˌægəmoʊ'dʒɛnəsəs/, *n.* asexual reproduction by buds, offshoots, cell division, etc. [Gk *ágamo(s)* unmarried + GENESIS] – **agamogenetic** /ˌægəmoʊdʒə'nɛtɪk/, *adj.*

**agamous** /'ægəməs/, *adj.* →**agamic.**

**agapanthus** /ægə'pænθəs/, *n.* any of several African amaryllidaceous plants constituting the genus *Agapanthus* with umbels of blue or white flowers; African lily. [Gk *agápē* love + *ánthos* flower]

**agape**[1] /ə'geɪp/, *adv.* **1.** in an attitude of wonder or eagerness; with the mouth wide open. *–adj.* **2.** wide open.

**agape**[2] /'ægəpeɪ, ə'gapi/, *n.* **1.** a meal of fellowship originating with the early Christians. **2.** altruistic love. [Gk]

**agar** /'eɪgə/, *n.* **1.** *Biol.* a culture medium with an agar-agar base: *a spore agar.* **2.** →**agar-agar.**

**agar-agar** /eɪgər-'eɪgə/, *n.* a gelatine-like product of certain seaweeds, used to solidify culture media and, esp. in the Orient, for soups, etc. Also, **agar.** [Malay *agar* jelly]

**agaric** /ə'gærɪk, 'ægərɪk/, *n.* an agaricaceous fungus. [L *agaricum*, from Gk *agarikón*; named after *Agaria,* a place in Sarmatia]

**agaricaceous** /əgærə'keɪʃəs/, *adj.* belonging to the Agaricaceae, a family of fungi including mushrooms having blade-shaped gills on the underside of the cap.

**agaristid** /ægə'rɪstɪd/, *adj.* of or pertaining to the Agaristidae, a family of brightly coloured, diurnal moths with clubbed antennae, as the whistling moth.

**agate** /'ægət/, *n.* **1.** a variegated variety of quartz (chalcedony) showing coloured bands or other markings (clouded, moss-like, etc.). **2.** a child's playing marble made of this substance, or of glass in imitation of it. **3.** *U.S.* a printing type; ruby (def. 5). [F *agathe*, from L *achātēs*, from Gk]

**agateware** /'ægətwɛə/, *n.* pottery variegated to resemble agate.

**agaty** /'ægəti/, *adj.* **1.** of or pertaining to agate. **2.** (esp. in Queensland) of potch in which the clay colouring gives a banded effect.

**agave** /ə'geɪvi, 'ægəvi/, *n.* any plant of the American (chiefly Mexican) genus *Agave,* of the family Agavaceae, species of which yield useful fibres, are used in making a fermented beverage, a distilled spirit, or a soap substitute, or are cultivated for ornament, as the century plant. [NL, from Gk *agaué*, fem. of *agauós* noble]

**AGC** /eɪ dʒi 'si/, automatic gain control.

**age** /eɪdʒ/, *n., v.,* **aged, ageing** or **aging.** *–n.* **1.** the length of time during which a being or thing has existed; length of life or existence to the time spoken of or referred to: *his age is 20 years, a tree or building of unknown age.* **2.** the lifetime of an individual, or of the individuals of a class or species on an average: *the age of the horse is from 25 to 30 years.* **3.** a period of human life, usu. marked by a certain stage of physical or mental development, esp. a degree of development, measured by years from birth, which involves legal responsibility and capacity: *the age of discretion, the age of consent.* **4. act** or **be your age,** *Colloq.* to behave in a manner in keeping with that expected of one's age. **5. of age,** *Law.* **a.** being any of several ages, usu. 21 or 18, at which certain legal rights, as voting or marriage, are acquired. **b.** being 18 years old, in possession of full legal rights and responsibilities. **6.** the particular period of life at which one becomes naturally or conventionally qualified or disqualified for anything: *under age or over age for conscription.* **7.** one of the periods or stages of human life: *a person of middle age.* **8.** old age: *his eyes were dim with age.* **9.** a particular period of history, as distinguished from others; a historical epoch: *the age of Pericles, the Stone Age, the Middle Ages.* **10.** the people who live at a particular period. **11.** a generation or a succession of generations: *ages yet unborn.* **12.** *Colloq.* a great length of time: *I haven't seen you for an age* or *for ages.* **13.** *Psychol.* the comparative mental, emotional, or other development of a person expressed by equating performance in various tests to the average age at which the same result is attained. **14.** *Geol.* a long or short part of the world's history distinguished by special features: *the Ice Age.* **15.** any one of the stages in the history of mankind divided, according to Hesiod, into the golden, silver, bronze, heroic, and iron ages. The happiest and best was the first (or golden) age, and the worst the iron age. *–v.i.* **16.** to grow old; develop the characteristics of old age: *he is ageing rapidly.* *–v.t.* **17.** to make old; cause to grow old or to seem old: *fear aged him overnight.* **18.** to bring to maturity or to a state fit for use: *to age wine.* [ME, from OF *aage*, earlier *e(d)age*, from L *aetas* + suffix *-āticum* -AGE]

**-age,** a noun suffix, common in words taken from French, as in *baggage, language, savage, voyage,* etc., now a common English formative, forming: **1.** collective nouns from names of things, as in *fruitage, leafage.* **2.** nouns denoting condition, rank, service, fee, etc., from personal terms, as in *bondage, parsonage.* **3.** nouns expressing various relations, from verbs, as in *breakage, cleavage, postage.* [OF, from L *-āticum*, neut. adj. suffix]

**aged** /'eɪdʒd/, *adj.* **1.** having lived or existed long: *an aged man or tree.* **2.** pertaining to or characteristic of old age: *aged wrinkles.* **3.** of the age of: *a man aged 40 years.* **4.** *Phys. Geog.* old; approaching the state of a peneplain. **5.** (of horses) more than six (or sometimes eight) years old. **6.** of a sheep, usu. five years of age or older, and past the stage of its greatest economic usefulness. – **agedly** /'eɪdʒədli/, *adv.* – **agedness,** *n.*

**aged worker** /– 'wɜkə/, *n.* a worker who is certified as being aged and therefore entitled to earn less than the normal minimum rate prescribed for his classification.

**age-group** /'eɪdʒ-grup/, *n.* a group of persons having similar ages, and sometimes other characteristics in common, as scholastic ability.

**ageing** /'eɪdʒɪŋ/, *adj.* **1.** growing old; elderly. **2.** causing someone or something to grow old. **3.** causing a person to appear old, or older: *an ageing hat.* *–n.* **4.** the process of growing old. **5.** the process of causing someone or something to grow old. **6. the ageing,** elderly people. Also, **aging.**

**ageless** /'eɪdʒləs/, *adj.* never growing old.

**age-long** /'eɪdʒ-lɒŋ/, *adj.* lasting for an age.

**agency** /'eɪdʒənsi/, *n., pl.* **-cies. 1.** a commercial or other organisation furnishing some form of service for the public: *an advertising agency.* **2.** the place of business of an agent. **3.** the office of agent; the business of an agent entrusted with the concerns of another. **4.** the state of being in action or of exerting power; action; operation: *the agency of Providence.* **5.** a mode of exerting power; a means of producing effects; instrumentality: *by the agency of friends.*

**agenda** /ə'dʒɛndə/, *n. pl., sing.* **-dum. 1.** things to be done. **2.** matters to be brought before a committee, council, board, etc., as things to be done. **3.** (construed as *sing.*) a program or list of things to be done, discussed, etc. [L, neut. pl. of gerundive of *agere* do]

**agenda-setting** /ə'dʒɛndə-sɛtɪŋ/, *n.* **1.** the process by which issues which are prominent in the media achieve a corresponding salience in the public mind. *–adj.* **2.** of or pertaining to this process: *the agenda-setting function of the media is to tell people, not what to think, but what to think about.*

**agene** /'eɪdʒin/, *n.* nitrogen trichloride, $NCl_3$, a heavy explosive liquid. It is used in minute quantities as a preservative in bread, and to whiten flour.

**agenise** /'eɪdʒənaɪz/, *v.t.,* **-nised, -nising.** to treat with agene. Also, **agenize.**

**agent** /'eɪdʒənt/, *n.* **1.** a person acting on behalf of another: *my agent has power to sign my name.* **2.** one who or that which acts or has the power to act: *a moral agent.* **3.** a natural force or object producing or used for obtaining specific results; instrumentality: *many insects are agents of fertilisation.* **4.** an active cause; an efficient cause. **5.** one who acts for a buyer or seller of stock or wool, etc. and who usu. represents a firm supplying manufactured rural requirements for the farmer. **6.** an official: *an agent of Dalgety's.* **7.** a representative of a business firm, esp. a commercial traveller; a canvasser; solicitor. **8.** *Chem.* a substance which causes a reaction. **9.** a campaign manager; an election agent. *–adj.* **10.** acting (opposed to *patient* in the sense of sustaining action). [L *agens*, ppr., driving, doing]

**agent blue** /– 'blu/, *n.* a solution of the sodium salt of cacodylic acid, used as a defoliant.

**agential** /eɪ'dʒɛnʃəl/, *adj.* **1.** pertaining to an agent or to an agency. **2.** →**agentive.**

**agentive** /'eɪdʒəntɪv/, *adj.* **1.** pertaining to, or productive of, a form which indicates agent or agency; ergative. *–n.* **2.** an agentive element or formation, as English *-er* in *painter.*

**agent orange** /eɪdʒənt 'ɒrɪndʒ/, *n.* a 50/50 mixture of n-butyl esters of 2,4-D and 2,4,5-T, used as a defoliant.

**agent provocateur** /ˌaʒɔ̃ prəvɒkə'tɜ/, *n., pl.* **agents provocateurs** /ˌaʒɔ̃ prəvɒkə'tɜz/. **1.** a secret agent hired to incite suspected persons to some illegal action, outbreak, etc., that will make them liable to punishment. **2.** any person who tries to incite dissatisfaction or unrest, esp. one who incites to an illegal action. [F]

**agent purple** /eɪdʒənt 'pɜpəl/, *n.* a 50/30/20 mixture, 50% n-butyl ester of 2,4-D, and 30/20 of the n-butyl and isobutyl esters of 2,4,5-T, used as a defoliant.

**agent white** /– 'waɪt/, *n.* a solution containing 2,4-D and picloran, used as a defoliant.

**age of consent,** *n.* the age at which one, esp. a female, is considered by law to be able to give consent to marriage or sexual intercourse.

**age of discretion,** *n.* the age at which a person becomes legally responsible for certain acts and competent to exercise certain powers.

**age-old** /'eɪdʒ-oʊld/, *adj.* very old.

**ageratum** /ædʒə'reɪtəm/, *n.* **1.** any plant of the genus *Ageratum* as *A. houstonianum*, a garden annual with small, dense, blue or white flower heads. **2.** any of various other plants of the family Compositae bearing blue, or sometimes white, flowers. [L, from Gk *agḗraton* kind of plant, properly neut. adj., not growing old]

**agg.,** aggregate.

**aggie** /'ægi/, *n. Colloq.* →**agate** (def. 2).

**aggiornamento** /ədʒɔnə'mɛntoʊ/, *n., pl.* **-ti** /–ti/. the process of bringing customs, institutions, etc., up to date. [It.]

**agglomerate** /ə'glɒməreɪt/, *v.,* **-rated, -rating;** /ə'glɒmərət/, *adj., n.* *–v.t.* **1.** to collect or gather into a mass. *–v.i.* **2.** to take the shape of a mass. *–adj.* **3.** gathered together into a ball or mass. **4.** *Bot.* crowded into a dense cluster, but not cohering. *–n.* **5.** a mass of things clustered together. **6.** a rock formation composed of large angular volcanic fragments. [L *agglomerātus*, pp., wound into a ball] – **agglomerative,** *adj.*

**agglomeration** /əglɒmə'reɪʃən/, *n.* **1.** an indiscriminately formed mass. **2.** the act or process of agglomerating.

**agglutinant** /ə'glutənənt/, *adj.* **1.** uniting, as glue; causing adhesion. *–n.* **2.** an agglutinating agent.

**agglutinate** /ə'glutəneɪt/, *v.,* **-nated, -nating;** /ə'glutənət/ *adj.* *–v.t.* **1.** to unite or cause to adhere, as with glue. *–v.i.* **2.** *Gram.* to form by agglutination. *–adj.* **3.** united by or as by glue. **4.** *Gram.* agglutinative. [L *agglūtinātus*, pp., pasted to]

**agglutinating language** /əˌglutəneɪtɪŋ 'læŋgwɪdʒ/, *n.* a language whose affixes are invariable and are juxtaposed instead of fused. Turkish and Hungarian are agglutinating languages. See **agglutination,** (def. 6).

**agglutination** /əglutə'neɪʃən/, *n.* **1.** the act or process of uniting by glue or other tenacious substance. **2.** the state of being thus united; adhesion of parts. **3.** that which is united; a mass or group cemented together. **4.** *Chem.* the coalescing or clumping of small suspended particles into larger masses. **5.** *Immunol.* the clumping of bacteria, red blood corpuscles, or other cells, due to introduction of an antibody. **6.** *Gram.* a pattern or process of inflection and word formation in some languages, in which the constituent elements of words are relatively distinct and constant in form and meaning, esp. such a process involving the addition of several suffixes to a single root or stem. In Turkish *ev* means 'house', *ev-ler* means 'houses', *ev-den* means 'from a house', and *ev-ler-den* means 'from houses'.

**agglutinative** /ə'glutənətɪv/, *adj.* **1.** tending or having power to agglutinate or unite: *an agglutinative substance.* **2.** *Gram.* (of a language or construction) characterised by agglutination.

**agglutinin** /ə'glutənɪn/, *n.* an antibody which causes agglutination.

**agglutinogen** /ˌæglu'tɪnədʒən/, *n.* an antigen present in a bacterial body which when injected into an animal causes the production of agglutinins.

**aggrade** /ə'greɪd/, *v.t.,* **-graded, -grading.** to raise the grade or level of (a river valley, a stream bed, etc.), as by depositing detritus. [AG- + GRADE, v.] – **aggradation** /ægrə'deɪʃən/, *n.*

**aggrandise** /ə'grændaɪz/, *v.t.,* **-dised, -dising. 1.** to widen in scope; increase in size or intensity; enlarge; extend. **2.** to make great or greater in power, wealth, rank, or honour. **3.** to make (something) appear greater. Also, **aggrandize.** [F *agrandiss-*, stem of *agrandir*, from L *ad-* AD- + *grandīre* make great] – **aggrandisement** /ə'grændəzmənt/, *n.* – **aggrandiser,** *n.*

**aggravate** /'ægrəveɪt/, *v.t.,* **-vated, -vating. 1.** to make worse or more severe; intensify, as anything evil, disorderly, or troublesome: *to aggravate guilt; grief aggravated her illness.* **2.** *Colloq.* to provoke; irritate; exasperate: *threats will only aggravate her.* [L *aggravātus*, pp., added to the weight of] – **aggravated,** *adj.* – **aggravating,** *adj.* – **aggravatingly,** *adv.* – **aggravator,** *n.*

**aggravation** /ægrə'veɪʃən/, *n.* **1.** increase of the intensity or severity of anything; act of making worse: *an aggravation of pain.* **2.** *Colloq.* something that irritates or exasperates.

**aggregate** /'ægrəgət/, *adj., n.;* /'ægrəgeɪt/, *v.,* **-gated, -gating.** *–adj.* **1.** formed by the conjunction or collection of particulars into a whole mass or sum; total; combined: *the aggregate amount of indebtedness.* *–n.* **2.** a sum, or assemblage of particulars; a total or gross amount: *the aggregate of all past* *experience.* **3.** *Cricket.* **a.** the total number of runs scored, or wickets taken, by a player in a season or tour. **b.** the total number of runs scored by a team in a season or tour. **4.** the total number of marks obtained in an examination. **5.** *Geol.* a mixture of different mineral substances separable by mechanical means, as granite. **6.** any hard material added to cement to make concrete. **7.** **in the aggregate,** taken together; considered as a whole; collectively. *–v.t.* **8.** to bring together; collect into one sum, mass, or body. **9.** to amount to (the number of): *the guns captured will aggregate five or six hundred.* *–v.i.* **10.** to combine and form a collection or mass. [L *aggregātus,* pp., added to] – **aggregately,** *adv.* – **aggregative,** *adj.*

**aggregation** /ægrəˈgeɪʃən/, *n.* **1.** a combined whole; an aggregate: *an aggregation of isolated settlements.* **2.** the act of collection into an unorganised whole. **3.** the state of being so collected. **4.** *Ecol.* a group of organisms of the same or different species living closely together but less integrated than a society.

**aggress** /əˈgrɛs/, *v.i.* **1.** to commit the first act of hostility or offence; attack first. **2.** to begin a quarrel.

**aggression** /əˈgrɛʃən/, *n.* **1.** the action of a state in violating by force the rights of another state, particularly its territorial rights. **2.** any offensive action or procedure; an inroad or encroachment: *an aggression upon one's rights.* **3.** the practice of making assaults or attacks; offensive action in general. **4.** *Psychol.* the emotional drive to attack; an offensive mental attitude (rather than defensive). [L *aggressio*]

**aggressive** /əˈgrɛsɪv/, *adj.* **1.** characterised by aggression; tending to aggress; making the first attack: an aggressive foreign policy. **2.** energetic; vigorous. **3.** (of wine), heavy, full-bodied and sometimes harsh. – **aggressively,** *adv.* – **aggressiveness,** *n.*

**aggressor** /əˈgrɛsə/, *n.* a person who attacks first; one who begins hostilities; an assailant or invader. [L]

**aggrieve** /əˈgriv/, *v.t.,* **-grieved, -grieving.** to oppress or wrong grievously; injure by injustice (used now chiefly in the passive). [ME *agreve(n),* OF *agrever,* from L *aggravāre* exasperate]

**aggrieved** /əˈgrivd/, *adj.* **1.** injured; oppressed; wronged: *he felt himself aggrieved.* **2.** *Law.* deprived of legal rights or claims. **3.** *Colloq.* feeling that one has been wronged; hurt; resentful: *an aggrieved expression on someone's face.*

**aggro** /ˈægroʊ/, *adj. Colloq.* aggressive; dominating.

**agha** /ˈagə/, *n.* →**aga.**

**aghast** /əˈgast/, *adj.* struck with amazement; stupefied with fright or horror: *they stood aghast at this unforeseen disaster.* [ME *agast,* pp. of *agasten* terrify. Cf. OE *gæstan* in same sense]

**agile** /ˈædʒaɪl/, *adj.* **1.** quick and light in movement: *a robust and agile frame.* **2.** active; lively: *an agile mind.* [L *agilis*] – **agilely,** *adv.*

**agile wallaby** /– ˈwɒləbi/, *n.* a sandy-coloured wallaby, *Macropus agilis,* with a distinct white stripe on the cheek and hip, which frequents the river country of northern Australia; jungle kangaroo; river wallaby; sandy wallaby.

**agility** /əˈdʒɪləti/, *n.* the power of moving quickly and easily; nimbleness: *agility of the body or mind.* [late ME *agilite,* from F, from L *agilitas*]

**agio** /ˈædʒioʊ/, *n., pl.* **-os.** **1.** a premium on money in exchange. **2.** an allowance for the difference in value of two currencies. **3.** an allowance given or taken on bills of exchange from other countries, to balance out exchange expenses. **4.** →**agiotage.** [It. *aggio* exchange, premium]

**agiotage** /ˈædʒətɪdʒ/, *n.* **1.** the business of exchange. **2.** speculative dealing in securities. Also, **agio.** [F, from It. *aggio* AGIO]

**agist** /əˈdʒɪst/, *v.t.* **1.** to take in and feed or pasture (livestock) for payment. **2.** to lay a public burden, as a tax, on (land or its owner). [ME, from OF *agister,* from *à* to + *giste* resting-place (from L *jacēre* lie)] – **agistor,** *n.*

**agistment** /əˈdʒɪstmənt/, *n.* **1.** the act of agisting. **2.** the price paid for pasturing livestock. **3.** a burden or tax.

**agitate** /ˈædʒəteɪt/, *v.,* **-tated, -tating.** *–v.t.* **1.** to move or force into violent irregular action; shake or move briskly: *the wind agitates the sea.* **2.** to move to and fro; impart regular motion to: *to agitate a fan, etc.* **3.** to disturb, or excite into tumult; perturb: *the mind of man is agitated by various emotions.* **4.** to call attention to by speech or writing; discuss; debate: *to agitate the question.* **5.** *Archaic.* to consider or revolve in the mind. *–v.i.* **6.** to arouse or attempt to arouse public feeling as in some political or social question: *to agitate for the repeal of a tax.* [L *agitātus,* pp., aroused, excited] – **agitatedly,** *adv.*

**agitation** /ædʒəˈteɪʃən/, *n.* **1.** the act of agitating. **2.** a state of being agitated: *she walked away in great agitation.* **3.** persistent urging of a political or social question before the public. – **agitative** /ˈædʒəteɪtɪv/, *adj.*

**agitato** /ædʒəˈtatoʊ/, *adj.* (a musical direction) agitated; restless or hurried in movement or style. [It.]

**agitator** /ˈædʒəteɪtə/, *n.* **1.** one who stirs up others, with a view to strengthening his own cause or that of his party, etc. **2.** a machine for agitating and mixing.

**agitprop** /ˈædʒətprɒp/, *n.* **1.** agitation and propaganda esp. for the cause of communism. **2.** (*oft. cap.*) an agency or department, as of a government, that directs and coordinates agitation and propaganda. **3.** one who is trained or takes part in such activities. *–adj.* **4.** of or pertaining to agitprop. **5.** *Theat.* pertaining to a dramatic style or technique of social protest and Marxist attitudes. [Russ.: b. *agitatsiya* agitation + *propaganda* propaganda]

**agleam** /əˈglim/, *adj.* gleaming.

**aglet** /ˈæglət/, *n.* **1.** a metal tag at the end of a lace. **2.** the points or ribbons generally used in the 16th and 17th centuries to fasten or tie dresses. Also, **aiglet.** [ME, from F *aiguillette* point, from L *acus* needle]

**agley** /əˈgli, əˈglaɪ, əˈgleɪ/, *adv. Chiefly Scot.* off the right line; awry; wrong. [A-[1] + Scot. *gley* squint]

**aglimmer** /əˈglɪmə/, *adj.* glimmering.

**aglitter** /əˈglɪtə/, *adj.* glittering.

**aglossa** /əˈglɒsə/, *n.* any frog of the genus *Aglossa,* family Pipidae, of South America and Africa, which have no tongues; tongueless frog. [A-[6] + Gk *glôssa* tongue]

**aglow** /əˈgloʊ/, *adj.* glowing.

**aglycone** /eɪˈglaɪkoʊn/, *n.* the non-sugar portion of a glycoside, one of the products formed by the hydrolysis of a glycoside.

**AGM** /eɪ dʒi ˈɛm/, Annual General Meeting. Also, **A.G.M.**

**agminate** /ˈægmənət, -neɪt/, *adj.* aggregated or clustered together. Also, **agminated.** [L *agmen* troop + -ATE[1]]

**agnail** /ˈægneɪl/, *n.* →**hangnail.**

**agnate** /ˈægneɪt/, *n.* **1.** a kinsman whose connection is traceable exclusively through males. **2.** any male relation by the father's side. *–adj.* **3.** related or akin through males or on the father's side. **4.** allied or akin. [L *agnātus,* pp., born to] – **agnatic** /ægˈnætɪk/, *adj.* – **agnation** /ægˈneɪʃən/, *n.*

**agnomen** /ægˈnoʊmən/, *n., pl.* **-nomina** /-ˈnɒmənə/. **1.** an additional (fourth) name given to a person by the ancient Romans in allusion to some achievement or other circumstance, as *Africanus* in *Publius Cornelius Scipio Africanus.* **2.** any nickname. [L *ag-* AG- + *nōmen* name] – **agnominal** /ægˈnɒmənəl/, *adj.*

**agnosia** /ægˈnoʊʒə/, *n.* loss or impairment of the ability to recognise objects by any of the various senses. [NL, from Gk *agnōsía* ignorance]

**agnostic** /ægˈnɒstɪk/, *n.* **1.** one who holds that the ultimate cause (God) and the essential nature of things are unknown or unknowable or that human knowledge is limited to experience. *–adj.* **2.** pertaining to the agnostics or their doctrines. **3.** asserting the relativity and uncertainty of all knowledge. [A-[6] + Gk *gnōstikós* knowing. Coined by T. Huxley in 1869] – **agnostically,** *adv.*

**agnosticism** /ægˈnɒstəsɪzəm/, *n.* **1.** the doctrine maintained by agnostics. **2.** an intellectual attitude or doctrine which asserts the relativity and therefore the uncertainty of all knowledge.

**Agnus Dei** /ˌanjʊs ˈdeɪi, ˌægnʊs/, *n.* **1.** *Eccles.* **a.** a figure of a lamb as emblematic of Christ. **b.** such a representation with the nimbus inscribed with the cross about its head, and supporting the banner of the cross. **2.** *Rom. Cath. Ch.* **a.** a wax medallion stamped with this figure and blessed by the pope, or a fragment of such a medallion. **b.** a triple chant, beginning 'Agnus Dei', preceding the communion in the mass. **c.** the music accompanying this prayer. **3. a.** an invocation beginning 'Lamb of God', said or sung in the communion service. **b.** a musical setting for this. [LL: Lamb of God. See John 1:29]

**ago** /ə'gou/, *adv.* in past time; past: *some time ago, long ago.* [ME, var. of *agoon*, OE *āgān*, pp. of *āgān* go by, pass]

**agog** /ə'gɒg/, *adj.* **1.** highly excited by eagerness or curiosity. *–adv.* **2.** in a state of eager desire; with excitement. [F *en gogues* in a merry mood]

**agogic** /ə'gɒdʒɪk/, *adj.* of or relating to variations of tempo in a piece of music. [Gk *agōgḗ* tempo + -IC]

**agogic accent** /– 'æksɛnt/, *n.* an effect similar to an accent produced by sustaining one of a pair of notes slightly beyond its written value.

**-agogue** a word element meaning 'leading' or 'guiding', found in a few agent nouns (often with pejorative value), as in *demagogue, pedagogue.* [Gk *agōgós* leading]

**agonic** /ə'gɒnɪk/, *adj.* not forming an angle. [Gk *ágōnos* without angles + -IC]

**agonic line** /– 'laɪn/, *n.* a line on the earth's surface connecting points at which the declination of the earth's magnetic field is zero.

**agonis** /ə'gounəs/, *n.* any myrtaceous shrub or tree of the western Australian genus *Agonis*, esp. *A. flexuosa*, willow myrtle, which is often planted as an ornamental.

**agonise** /'ægənaɪz/, *v.*, **-nised, -nising.** *–v.i.* **1.** to writhe with extreme pain; suffer violent anguish. **2.** to make great effort of any kind. *–v.t.* **3.** to distress with extreme pain; torture. Also, **agonize.** [ML *agōnizāre*, from Gk *agōnízesthai* contend] **– agonisingly,** *adv.*

**agonist** /'ægənəst/, *n.* an actively contracting muscle considered in relation to its opposing muscle (the antagonist).

**agonistic** /ægə'nɪstɪk/, *adj.* **1.** combative; striving to overcome in argument. **2.** aiming at effect; strained. **3.** pertaining to contests. Also, **agonistical.** [Gk *agōnistikós* fit for contest] **– agonistically,** *adv.* **– agonistics,** *n.*

**agony** /'ægəni/, *n., pl.* **-nies. 1.** extreme, and generally prolonged, pain; intense suffering. **2.** intense mental excitement of any kind. **3.** the struggle preceding natural death: *mortal agony.* **4. put, pile, turn on the agony,** *Colloq.* to exaggerate a story, misfortunes, etc. for effect. **5.** *Rare.* a violent struggle. [ME *agonye*, from LL *agōnia*, from Gk: contest, anguish]

**agony column** /'– kɒləm/, *n. Colloq.* a newspaper column of advertisements, esp. those arising from personal distress; personal column.

**agora** /'ægərə/, *n., pl.* **-rae** /-reɪ/. (in ancient Greece) **1.** a popular political assembly. **2.** the place of such assembly, originally the market place. [Gk]

**agoraphobia** /ægərə'foubiə/, *n.* a morbid fear of being in an open space. [AGORA + PHOBIA]

**agouti** /ə'guti/, *n., pl.* **-tis, -ties. 1.** any of several shorthaired, short-eared, rabbitlike rodents of the genus *Dasyprocta*, of South and Central America and the West Indies, destructive to sugar cane. **2.** an irregularly barred pattern of the fur of certain rodents. **3.** an animal having fur of this pattern. Also, **agouty.** [F, from Sp. *aguti*, from Tupi]

agouti

**ag pipe** /'æg paɪp/, *n.* →**agricultural pipe.**

**agr.,** →**agric.**

**agraffe** /ə'græf/, *n.* **1.** a small cramp iron. **2.** a clasp for hooking together parts of clothing, etc. **3.** Also, **agrafe.** a metal clip used to hold in place the temporary cork used in a champagne bottle during fermentation. [F, var. of *agrafe* hook, from *à* A-$^{5}$ + *grafe* sharp-pointed tool (from L *graphis*, from Gk: pencil); F meaning influenced by *agrappe* hook]

**agranulocytosis** /əˌgrænjəlouˌsaɪ'tousəs/, *n.* a serious, often fatal blood disease, marked by a great reduction in leucocytes, often caused by an idiosyncratic susceptibility to drugs. [NL: *a-* A-$^{6}$ + GRANULE + -CYT(E) + -OSIS]

**agraphia** /ə'græfiə/, *n.* a cerebral disorder marked by total or partial inability to write. [NL, from Gk: *a-* A-$^{6}$ + *graphía* writing] **– agraphic,** *adj.*

**agrarian** /ə'grɛəriən/, *adj.* **1.** relating to land, land tenure, or the division of landed property: *agrarian laws.* **2.** pertaining to the advancement of agricultural groups: *an agrarian experiment.* **3.** rural; agricultural. **4.** growing in fields; wild: *an agrarian plant.* *–n.* **5.** one who favours the equal division of land. [stem of L *agrārius* pertaining to land + -AN] **– agrarianism,** *n.*

**agree** /ə'gri/, *v.*, **agreed, agreeing.** *–v.i.* **1.** to yield assent; consent (oft. fol. by *to*, esp. with reference to things and acts): *he agreed to accompany the ambassador, do you agree to the conditions?* **2.** to be of one mind; harmonise in opinion or feeling (oft. fol. by *with*, esp. with reference to persons): *I don't agree with you.* **3.** to live in concord or without contention; harmonise in action. **4.** to come to one opinion or mind; come to an arrangement or understanding; arrive at a settlement (sometimes fol. by *upon*). **5.** to be consistent; harmonise (fol. by *with*): *this story agrees with others.* **6.** to be applicable or appropriate; resemble; be similar (fol. by *with*): *the picture does not agree with the original.* **7.** to be accommodated or adapted; suit (fol. by *with*): *the same food does not agree with every person.* **8.** *Gram.* to correspond in inflectional form, as in number, case, gender, or person (fol. by *with*). *–v.t.* **9.** to concede; grant (fol. by noun clause): *I agree that he is the ablest of us.* **10.** to determine; settle (usu. fol. by noun clause): *It was agreed that we should meet again.* [ME *agre(en)*, from OF *agréer*, from phrase *a gré* at pleasure]

**agreeable** /ə'griəbəl/, *adj.* **1.** to one's liking; pleasing: *agreeable manners.* **2.** willing or ready to agree or consent: *are you agreeable?* **3.** suitable; conformable (fol. by *to*). **– agreeability** /əgriə'bɪləti/, **agreeableness,** *n.* **– agreeably,** *adv.*

**agreed** /ə'grid/, *adj.* arranged by common consent: *they met at the agreed time.*

**agreement** /ə'grimənt/, *n.* **1.** the act of coming to a mutual arrangement. **2.** the arrangement itself. **3.** unanimity of opinion; harmony in feeling: *agreement among the members.* **4.** the state of being in accord; concord; harmony; conformity: *agreement between observation and theory.* **5.** *Gram.* correspondence in number, case, gender, person, or some other formal category between syntactically connected words, esp. between one or more subordinate words and the word or words upon which they depend. For example: in *the boy runs*, *boy* is a singular noun and *runs* is a distinctively singular form of the verb. **6.** →**consent agreement. 7.** *Law.* **a.** an expression of assent by two or more parties to the same object. **b.** the phraseology, written or oral, of an exchange of promises.

**agribusiness** /'ægribɪznəs/, *n.* business based on primary industry.

**agric., 1.** agricultural. **2.** agriculture. Also, **agr.**

**agricultural** /ægrə'kʌltʃərəl/, *n. Colloq.* (in cricket) a wild stroke without finesse that digs up the turf. Also, **agricultural shot.**

**agricultural college** /'– ˌkɒlɪdʒ/, *n.* a tertiary institution, usu. residential, offering diploma courses in dairying, animal husbandry, food technology, wine-making, etc.

**agricultural high school,** *n.* often with residential facilities, a secondary school which provides general education and also subjects of agricultural importance.

**agricultural holding** /ægrɪˌkʌltʃərəl 'houldɪŋ/, *n. Law.* a form of agricultural lease.

**agriculturalist** /ægrə'kʌltʃərələst/, *n.* **1.** a farmer. **2.** an expert in agriculture. Also, **agriculturist.**

**agricultural pipe** /ægrə'kʌltʃərəl paɪp/, *n.* a pipe, formerly made of porous material but now usu. made from continuous plastic pipe with concentric ridges and slits, used for drainage in agriculture, landscaping, etc. Also, **ag pipe.**

**agriculture** /'ægrəkʌltʃə/, *n.* the cultivation of land, including crop-raising, forestry, stock-raising, etc.; farming. [L *agricultūra*, from *agri*, gen. of *ager* land + *cultūra* cultivation] **– agricultural** /ægrə'kʌltʃərəl/, *adj.* **– agriculturally** /ægrə'kʌltʃərəli/, *adv.*

**agriculturist** /ægrə'kʌltʃərəst/, *n.* →**agriculturalist.**

**agrimony** /'ægrəməni/, *n., pl.* **-nies. 1.** any plant of the rosaceous genus *Agrimonia*, esp. *A. eupatoria*, a perennial herb with pinnate leaves and small yellow flowers. **2.** any of certain other plants, as hemp agrimony or burr-marigold. [L *agrimōnia*, var. of *argemōnia* a plant, from Gk *argemṓnē*; replacing ME *egrimoigne*, from OF *aigremoine*]

**agro-**, a word element meaning 'soil', 'field', as in *agrology*. [Gk, combining form of *agrós*]

**agrobiologic** /ægroubaɪə'lɒdʒɪk/, *adj.* of or pertaining to the science of agrobiology. Also, **agrobiological.** – **agrobiologically,** *adv.*

**agrobiology** /ˌægroubaɪ'ɒlədʒi/, *n.* the quantitative science of plant life and plant nutrition. – **agrobiologist,** *n.*

**agro-dome** /'ægrou-doum/, *n.* a building, originally a dome, in which displays are given of the milking of cows, the shearing of sheep, the feeding of poddy lambs, and other agricultural activities.

**agrology** /ə'grɒlədʒi/, *n.* the applied aspects of soil science. See **pedology**[1]. – **agrologic** /ægrə'lɒdʒɪk/, **agrological** /ægrə'lɒdʒɪkəl/, *adj.*

**agron.**, agronomy.

**agronomics** /ægrə'nɒmɪks/, *n.* the art and science of managing land and crops.

**agronomist** /ə'grɒnəməst/, *n.* a specialist in agronomy.

**agronomy** /ə'grɒnəmi/, *n.* **1.** the applied aspects of both soil science and the several plant sciences, often limited to applied plant sciences dealing with crops. **2.** →**agriculture.** – **agronomic** /ægrə'nɒmɪk/, **agronomical** /ægrə'nɒmɪkəl/, *adj.*

**agro-politician** /ˌægrou-pɒlə'tɪʃən/, *n.* a politician who has a vested interest in promoting the rural sector.

**agrostology** /ægrəs'tɒlədʒi/, *n.* the part of botany that treats of grasses. [Gk *ágrōstis* kind of grass + -O- + -LOGY]

**aground** /ə'graund/, *adv.* on the ground; stranded: *the ship ran aground.*

**ague** /'eɪgju/, *n.* **1.** *Pathol.* a malarial fever characterised by regularly returning paroxysms, marked by successive cold, hot, and sweating fits. **2.** a fit of shaking or shivering as if with cold; a chill. [ME, from OF, from Pr., from L *acūta (febris)* acute (fever)] – **agued,** *adj.* – **aguish,** *adj.* – **aguishly,** *adv.*

**ah** /a/, *interj.* (an exclamation expressing pain, surprise, pity, complaint, dislike, joy, etc., according to the manner of utterance.) [ME]

**a.h.**, after hours. Also, **A.H.**

**A·h**, ampere-hour.

**aha** /a'ha, ə'ha/, *interj.* (an exclamation expressing triumph, contempt, mockery, irony, surprise, etc., according to the manner of utterance.) [ME]

**ahead** /ə'hɛd/, *adv.* **1.** in or to the front; in advance; before. **2.** forward; onward. **3. be ahead,** to be to the good; be winning: *I was well ahead in the deal.* **4. get ahead of,** to surpass. [A-[1] + HEAD]

**ahem** /ə'hɛm/, *interj. but in spontaneous manner* /ə'hm/ *or a throat-clearing sound* (an utterance designed to attract attention, express doubt, etc.)

**ahimsa** /a'hɪmsa/, *n.* the doctrine of refraining from violence to all living things, held by Jainists, Buddhists and Hindus. [Skt]

**ahoy** /ə'hɔɪ/, *interj.* (a call used in hailing, esp. on ships). [*a*, interj. + HOY[2]]

**ahull** /ə'hʌl/, *adv. Naut.* hove to with all canvas furled: *lying ahull in heavy weather.*

**ai** /'aˌi/, *n., pl.* **ais** /'aˌiz/. **1.** a large three-toed sloth, *Bradypus tridactylus*, of Central and South America. [Tupi *(h)aī*, imitation of its cry]

**A.I.** /eɪ 'aɪ/, *n., v.,* **A.I.ed, A.I.ing.** *–n.* **1.** artificial insemination. *–v.t.* **2.** to induce pregnancy in by artificial insemination.

**aid** /eɪd/, *v.t.* **1.** to afford support or relief to; help. **2.** to promote the course of accomplishment of; facilitate. **3.** to give financial support to: *a state-aided school.* *–v.i.* **4.** to give help or assistance. *–n.* **5.** help; support; assistance. **6.** one who or that which aids or yields assistance; a helper; an auxiliary. **7. in aid of,** directed towards; intended to achieve. **8.** a payment made by feudal vassals to their lord on special occasions. **9.** *U.S.* →**aide-de-camp.** [ME *aide(n)*, from OF *aidier*, from L *adjūtāre*] – **aider,** *n.* – **aidless,** *adj.*

**A.I.D.** /eɪ aɪ 'di/, artificial insemination (by) donor.

**aide** /eɪd/, *n.* an aide-de-camp. [F]

**aide-de-camp** /eɪd-də-'kɒ̃/, *n., pl.* **aides-de-camp.** a military or naval officer acting as a confidential assistant to a superior, esp. a general, governor, etc. [F: camp assistant]

**aide-mémoire** /eɪd-mɛm'wa/, *n.* a reminder; a memorandum of discussion, agreement, or action. [F]

**A.I.F.** /eɪ aɪ 'ɛf/, Australian Imperial Forces.

**aiglet** /'eɪglət/, *n.* →**aglet.**

**aigrette** /'eɪgrət, eɪ'grɛt/, *n.* **1.** a plume or tuft of feathers arranged as a head ornament, esp. the back plumes of various herons. **2.** a copy in jewellery of such a plume. **3.** →**egret** (defs 2 and 3).

**aiguille** /eɪ'gwil, 'eɪgwil/, *n.* **1.** a needle-like rock mass or mountain peak. **2.** a slender stone-boring tool. [F, in OF *aguille* needle, from LL diminutive of L *acus* needle]

**aiguillette** /eɪgwə'lɛt/, *n.* an ornamental tagged cord or braid on a uniform. [F, diminutive of *aiguille.* See AGLET]

**A.I.H.** /eɪ aɪ 'eɪtʃ/, artificial insemination (by) husband.

**ail** /eɪl/, *v.t.* **1.** to affect with pain or uneasiness; trouble. *–v.i.* **2.** to feel pain; be ill (usu. in a slight degree); be unwell. [ME *ailen*, OE *eglan*, c. Goth *agljan*]

**ailanthus** /eɪ'lænθəs/, *n.* a tree of the Simaroubaceae, *Ailanthus altissima*, with pinnate leaves and greenish flowers, native to eastern Asia and planted widely as a shade tree; tree of heaven. [NL, from Amboinese (language of people of Amboyna, island in Indonesia) *aylanto* tree of heaven] – **ailanthic,** *adj.*

**aileron** /'eɪlərɒn/, *n.* a hinged, movable flap of an aeroplane wing, usu. part of the trailing edge, used primarily to maintain lateral balance or to bank, roll, etc. [F, diminutive of *aile* wing. See AISLE]

**ailing** /'eɪlɪŋ/, *adj.* sickly.

**ailloli** /eɪ'ouli/, *n.* →**aioli.**

**ailment** /'eɪlmənt/, *n.* a morbid affection of the body or mind; indisposition: *a slight ailment.*

**aim** /eɪm/, *v.t.* **1.** to give a certain direction and elevation to (a gun or the like), for the purpose of causing the projectile, when the weapon is discharged, to hit the object. **2.** to direct or point (something) at something: *the satire was aimed at the Church.* *–v.i.* **3.** to level a gun; give direction to a blow, missile, etc. **4.** to strive; try (fol. by *at* or *to*): *they aim at saving something every month.* **5.** to direct efforts towards an object: *to aim high, at the highest.* **6.** *Colloq.* to intend: *she aims to go tomorrow.* **7.** *Obs.* to estimate; guess. *–n.* **8.** the act of aiming or directing anything at or towards a particular point or object. **9.** the direction in which a missile is pointed; the line of sighting: *to take aim.* **10.** the point intended to be hit; thing or person aimed at. **11.** something intended or desired to be attained by one's efforts; purpose. **12.** *Obs.* conjecture; guess. [ME *ayme(n)*, from OF *(a)esmer*, from L *(ad)aestimāre* estimate] – **aimer,** *n.*

**aimless** /'eɪmləs/, *adj.* without aim; purposeless. – **aimlessly,** *adv.* – **aimlessness,** *n.*

**ain** /eɪn/, *adj. Scot.* own.

**aîné** /eɪ'neɪ/, *adj.* of the greater age; elder; eldest. [F] – **aînée,** *adj. fem.*

**ain't** /eɪnt/, an (uneducated) contraction of *am not*, extended in use as a contraction of *are not*, and *is not*, and also *have not*, or *has not* in auxiliary use: *I ain't seen it.*

**aioli** /eɪ'ouli/, *n.* a thick mayonnaise containing a large amount of garlic. [F]

**air** /ɛə/, *n.* **1.** a mixture of oxygen, nitrogen and other gases, which surrounds the earth and forms its atmosphere. **2.** a movement of the atmosphere; a light breeze. **3.** *Obs.* breath. **4.** circulation; publication; publicity: *to give air to one's ideas.* **5.** the general character or complexion of anything; appearance. **6.** the peculiar look, appearance, and bearing of a person. **7.** *(pl.)* affected manner; manifestation of pride or vanity; assumed haughtiness: *to put on airs.* **8.** *Music.* **a.** a tune; a melody. **b.** the soprano or treble part. **c.** an aria. **d.** an Elizabethan song. **9.** *Radio.* the atmosphere through which radio waves are sent. **10. air and exercise,** *Obs. Colloq.* a gaol sentence. **11. clear the air,** to eliminate dissension, ambiguity, or tension from a discussion, situation, etc. **12. give oneself airs,** to behave in a conceited, haughty or high-handed manner. **13. in the air, a.** without foundation or actuality; visionary or uncertain. **b.** in circulation. **c.** undecided or unsettled (oft. prec. by *up*). **14. into thin air,** completely or entirely out of sight or reach. **15. off the air,** no longer being broadcast; not on the air. **16. on the air,** in the act of broadcasting; being broadcast. **17. take the air,** to go out of doors; walk or ride a little distance. **18. walk** (or **tread**) **on air,** to feel very happy or elated. *–v.t.* **19.** to expose to the air; give access to the open air; ventilate. **20.** to expose to warm air; to dry with heated air: *to air sheets.* **21.** to expose ostentatiously; bring into public notice; display: *to air one's opinions or theories.* [ME *ayre, eir,* from OF *air,* from L *āēr,* from Gk: air, mist]

**air alert** /'ɛər əlɜt/, *n. Mil.* **1.** the act of flying while waiting for orders or for enemy aeroplanes to appear. **2.** the signal to take stations for such action.

**air ambulance** /ɛər 'æmbjələns/, *n.* a light aircraft equipped like an ambulance, used to fly patients esp. from outback and country centres to a hospital.

**air base** /'ɛə beɪs/, *n.* **1.** a base for military aircraft. **2.** in photogrammetry, the line joining two air stations or the length of that line.

**air-bed** /'ɛə-bɛd/, *n.* an inflatable mattress.

**air-beef** /ɛə-'bif/, *n.* frozen cattle carcasses transported to markets or export ports by air.

**air-bell** /'ɛə-bɛl/, *n.* **1.** a bubble of air. **2.** *Photog.* a bubble of air which leaves marks on a photograph during processing.

**air-bladder** /'ɛə-blædə/, *n.* **1.** a vesicle or sac containing air. **2.** *Ichthyol.* a symmetrical sac filled with air whose principal function is the regulation of the hydrostatic equilibrium of the body; a swim bladder.

**airborne** /'ɛəbɔn/, *adj.* **1.** borne up, carried, or transported by air. **2.** in the air; (of aircraft) having taken off. **3.** *Mil.* trained for and allotted to air operations: *an airborne division.*

**airborne early warning system,** *n. Mil.* the detection of enemy air or surface units by radar or other equipment carried in an airborne vehicle and the transmitting of a warning to friendly units.

**airborne magnetometer** /ˌɛəbɔn mægnə'tɒmətə/, *n.* →**aerial magnetometer.**

**air-bound** /'ɛə-baʊnd/, *adj.* stopped up or blocked by a volume of air.

**air-brake** /'ɛə-breɪk/, *n.* **1.** *Aeron.* a hinged flap or other extendable device for reducing the speed of an aircraft. **2.** a brake or system of brakes operated by compressed air.

**air breathing** /ɛə 'briðɪŋ/, *n.* (of a jet-engine) requiring an intake of air for the combustion of its fuel.

**airbrick** /'ɛəbrɪk/, *n.* a perforated block let into a wall for ventilation.

**air-brush** /'ɛə-brʌʃ/, *n.* a small pencil-type spray gun used for very fine paint work or stencilling.

**airburst** /'ɛəbɜst/, *n. Mil.* **1.** an explosion of a bomb, shell, etc., in the atmosphere. **2.** an explosion of a nuclear weapon in the air at a height greater than the maximum radius of the fireball.

**airbus** /'ɛəbʌs/, *n.* a passenger aircraft operating over short routes.

**air-cell** /'ɛə-sɛl/, *n.* a small cavity full of air in plant or animal tissue; air-sac; air-bladder.

**air-chamber** /'ɛə-tʃeɪmbə/, *n.* **1.** a chamber containing air, as in a pump or a lifeboat. **2.** a compartment of a hydraulic system containing air which by its elasticity equalises the pressure and flow of liquid within the system.

**air chief marshal,** *n.* **1.** an officer in the Royal Australian Air Force or any of various other airforces, equivalent in rank to a general in the army or admiral in the navy. **2.** the rank.

**air-cock** /'ɛə-kɒk/, *n.* →**air-valve.**

**air commodore** /'ɛə kɒmədɔ/, *n.* **1.** an officer in the Royal Australian Air Force or any of various other airforces, equivalent in rank to a commodore in the navy or brigadier in the army. **2.** the rank.

**air-condenser** /'ɛə-kəndɛnsə/, *n.* **1.** *Radio.* a capacitor in which the dielectric is air. **2.** a machine for condensing air.

**air-condition** /'ɛə-kəndɪʃən/, *v.t.* **1.** to furnish with an air-conditioning system. **2.** to treat (air) with such a system. – **air-conditioned,** *adj.*

**air-conditioner** /'ɛə-kəndɪʃənə/, *n.* an apparatus for air-conditioning a room, house, car, etc.

**air-conditioning** /'ɛə-kəndɪʃənɪŋ/, *n.* **1.** a system of treating air in buildings to assure temperature, humidity, dustlessness, and movement at levels most conducive to personal comfort, manufacturing processes, or preservation of items stored, as books, etc. *–adj.* **2.** denoting or pertaining to such a system.

**air-cool** /'ɛə-kul/, *v.t.* **1.** *Mach.* to remove the heat of combustion, friction, etc., from, as by a stream of air flowing over a finned engine cylinder. **2.** to air-condition. – **aircooled,** *adj.*

**air-corridor** /ɛə-'kɒrədɔ/, *n.* an air-route established by international agreement or government regulation.

**air cover** /'ɛə kʌvə/, *n.* **1.** the protection of ground forces by an air force. **2.** the aircraft so employed.

**aircraft** /'ɛəkraft/, *n., pl.* **-craft.** any machine supported for flight in the air by buoyancy (such as balloons and other lighter-than-air craft) or by dynamic action of air on its surfaces (such as aeroplanes, helicopters, gliders, and other heavier-than-air craft).

**aircraft-carrier** /'ɛəkraft-ˌkæriə/, *n.* a large naval ship, designed to serve as an air base at sea, with a long strip of deck for the taking off and landing of aircraft.

**aircraftman** /'ɛəkraftmən/, *n., pl.* **-men.** one of the lowest rank in the Royal Australian Air Force. Also, **aircraftsman.** – **aircraftwoman, aircraftswoman,** *n. fem.*

**aircrew** /'ɛəkru/, *n.* the crew of an aircraft.

**air-curtain** /'ɛə-kɜtn/, *n.* a stream of compressed air directed, usu. downwards, across a doorway, to form a shield against draughts, etc.

**air-cushion** /'ɛə-kʊʃən/, *n.* **1.** an inflatable airtight cushion. **2.** →**air-chamber** (def. 2). **3.** the cushion of air supporting a hovercraft. *–adj.* **4.** denoting or pertaining to a hovercraft.

**air-cylinder** /'ɛə-sɪləndə/, *n.* a cylinder containing air, esp. (with a piston) as a device for checking the recoil of a gun.

**air-drain** /'ɛə-dreɪn/, *n.* a cavity in the external walls of a building to prevent damp from penetrating.

**air dribble** /'ɛə drɪbəl/, *n. Basketball.* a movement in which a player throws the ball into the air and bats it before it touches the ground.

**air-drive** /'ɛə-draɪv/, *n.* a drive (def. 31) for ventilation, esp. in a tunnel or mine; airshaft.

**airdrome** /'ɛədroʊm/, *n. Chiefly U.S.* →**aerodrome.**

**airdrop** /'ɛədrɒp/, *n.* **1.** delivery of supplies, troops, etc., from the air by parachute. *–adj.* **2.** of or pertaining to such a delivery.

**air-dry** /'ɛə-draɪ/, *v.,* **-dried, -drying,** *adj.* *–v.t.* **1.** to remove moisture from by evaporation in free air. *–adj.* **2.** dry beyond further evaporation.

**air-duct** /'ɛə-dʌkt/, *n.* **1.** a channel or pipe carrying warmed air in a heating system. **2.** a channel, tube, or pipe which forms part of a ventilation system.

**Airedale** /'ɛədeɪl/, *n.* a large heavy kind of terrier with a rough brown or tan coat which is black or grizzled over the back. [from *Airedale* in Yorkshire, England]

Airedale

**airfield** /'ɛəfild/, *n.* a level area, usu. equipped with hardsurfaced runways, buildings, etc., for the operation and maintenance of aircraft.

**airflight** /'ɛəflaɪt/, *n.* a flight by an aircraft.

**airflow** /'ɛəfloʊ/, *n.* air currents caused by a moving aircraft, car, etc.

**airfoil** /'ɛəfɔɪl/, *n. Chiefly U.S.* →**aerofoil.**

**airforce** /'ɛəfɔs/, *n.* **1.** the branch of the armed forces of any country concerned with military aircraft. *–adj.* **2.** of or pertaining to an airforce.

**airframe** /'ɛəfreɪm/, *n.* the whole body of an aeroplane without its engines.

**airfreight** /'ɛəfreɪt/, *n.* **1.** cargo transported by aircraft. **2.** the charge made for this service. *–v.t.* **3.** to despatch by aircraft.

**air-gap** /'ɛə-gæp/, *n.* **1.** an air-insulated gap in a magnetic circuit. **2.** a spark gap in air between two conducting electrodes.

**airglow** /'ɛəgloʊ/, *n.* a faint light emitted as a result of the excitation of atoms and molecules in the earth's upper atmosphere.

**airgun** /'ɛəgʌn/, *n.* a gun operated by compressed air.

**airhead** /'ɛəhɛd/, *n.* an area of hostile or enemy controlled territory secured usu. by paratroops.

**airhole** /'ɛəhoʊl/, *n.* **1.** an opening to admit or discharge air. **2.** a natural opening in the frozen surface of a river or pond. **3.** *Aeron.* →**air-pocket.**

**air hostess** /'ɛə hoʊstɛs/, *n.* a woman employed to attend to the needs of passengers on an airliner.

**airily** /'ɛərəli/, *adv.* **1.** in a gay manner; jauntily. **2.** lightly; delicately. – **airiness** /'ɛərinəs/, *n.*

**airing** /'ɛərɪŋ/, *n.* **1.** an exposure to the air, or to a source of heat as for drying. **2.** a walk, drive, or the like, in the open air.

**air-intake** /'ɛər-ɪnteɪk/, *n.* **1.** an opening in an aircraft for introducing air, mainly for the engines. **2.** the opening through which air enters a carburettor. **3.** a quantity of air taken in.

**air-jacket** /'ɛə-dʒækət/, *n.* **1.** an envelope of enclosed air about part of a machine, as for checking the transmission of heat. **2.** a lifebelt.

**airlane** /'ɛəleɪn/, *n.* a route regularly used by aeroplanes; airway.

**airless** /'ɛələs/, *adj.* **1.** lacking air. **2.** without fresh air; stuffy. **3.** still.

**air letter** /'ɛə lɛtə/, *n.* →**aerogram.**

**airlift** /'ɛəlɪft/, *n.* **1.** a system of transporting people, supplies, equipment, etc., by aircraft when surface routes are blocked, as during a military blockade, or at a time of national emergency. **2.** the act or process of transporting such a load. *–v.t.* **3.** to transport by airlift.

**airline** /'ɛəlaɪn/, *n.* **1.** a system furnishing (usu.) scheduled air transport between specified points. **2.** the aeroplanes, airports, navigational aids, etc., of such a system. **3.** a company that owns or operates such a system. **4.** a scheduled route followed by such a system.

**airliner** /'ɛəlaɪnə/, *n.* a large passenger aircraft operated by an airline.

**airlock** /'ɛəlɒk/, *n.* **1.** *Civ. Eng., etc.* an airtight transition compartment at the entrance of a pressure chamber, as in a spacecraft or a submerged caisson. **2.** *Engineering.* an obstruction to or stoppage of a flow of liquid in a pipe caused by an air bubble. **3.** *Archit.* an area between doors which impedes the flow of air between sections of a building.

**airmail** /'ɛəmeɪl/, *n.* **1.** the system of transmitting mail by aircraft. **2.** mail transmitted by aircraft. *–adj.* **3.** of or sent by airmail.

**airman** /'ɛəmən/, *n., pl.* **-men.** an aviator, esp. a member of an airforce. – **airmanship,** *n.*

**air marshal** /'ɛə maʃəl/, *n.* **1.** an officer in the Royal Australian Air Force or any of various other airforces, equivalent in rank to a lieutenant general in the army or vice-admiral in the navy. **2.** the rank.

**air-mass** /'ɛə-mæs/, *n. Meteorol.* a body of air which approximates horizontal uniformity in its properties.

**air mattress** /'ɛə mætrəs/, *n.* →**air-bed.**

**air mile** /'ɛə maɪl/, *n. Aeron. Obs.* a distance equal to a nautical mile.

**air-minded** /'ɛə-maɪndəd/, *adj.* **1.** interested in aviation or in the aviation aspects of problems. **2.** favouring increased use of aircraft. – **airmindedness,** *n.*

**air picket** /'ɛə pɪkət/, *Mil.* airborne early warning aircraft disposed around a position, area, or formation, primarily to detect, report and track approaching enemy aircraft.

**airplane** /'ɛəpleɪn/, *n. Chiefly U.S.* →**aeroplane.**

**airplay** /'ɛəpleɪ/, *n.* the amount of playing time given to broadcasting a record.

**air-pocket** /'ɛə-pɒkət/, *n.* **1.** *Aeron.* a downward current of air, usu. causing a sudden loss of altitude. **2.** any pocket of air, as in a mine, where gas or water is held back by the air-pressure in the pocket.

**airport** /'ɛəpɔt/, *n.* a large airfield usu. equipped with a control tower, hangars, and accommodation for the receiving and discharging of passengers and cargo.

**air-pressure** /'ɛə-prɛʃə/, *n.* **1.** the pressure of the atmosphere. **2.** the pressure exerted by the air, as inside a tyre.

**airproof** /'ɛəpruf/, *adj.* **1.** impervious to air. *–v.t.* **2.** to make impervious to air.

**airpump** /'ɛəpʌmp/, *n.* an apparatus for drawing in, compressing, and discharging air.

**air-raid** /'ɛə-reɪd/, *n.* **1.** a raid or incursion by hostile aircraft, esp. for dropping bombs or other missiles. *–v.t.* **2.** to attack from the air. *–v.i.* **3.** *Colloq.* to protest volubly; nag; scold. – **air-raider,** *n.*

**air-raid shelter** /'– ʃɛltə/, *n.* a security area or place used as a refuge during an air-raid.

**air-raid warden** /'– wɔdən/, *n.* a person who has temporary police duties during an air-raid alert.

**air-rifle** /'ɛə-raɪfəl/, *n.* an airgun with rifled bore.

**air-route** /'ɛə-rut/, *n.* an established flight path from one place to another, usu. organised into stages with intermediate stopping points, etc.

**air-sac** /'ɛə-sæk/, *n.* **1.** a sac containing air. **2.** any of certain cavities in a bird's body connected with the lungs. **3.** a saclike dilatation of an insect trachea.

**airscrew** /'ɛəskru/, *n.* an aeroplane propeller.

**airshaft** /'ɛəʃaft/, *n.* →**air-drive.**

**airshift** /'ɛəʃɪft/, *n.* in radio, that part of the working hours of a continuity announcer, disc jockey, etc., spent on air in a studio.

**airship** /'ɛəʃɪp/, *n.* a self-propelled, lighter-than-air craft with means of controlling the direction of flight, usu. classed as rigid, semi-rigid, or non-rigid.

**airsick** /'ɛəsɪk/, *adj.* ill as the result of travelling in the air. – **airsickness,** *n.*

**air-slake** /'ɛə-sleɪk/, *v.t.,* **-slaked, -slaking.** to slake by moist air, as lime.

**airsock** /'ɛəsɒk/, *n.* →**windsock.**

**airspace** /'ɛəspeɪs/, *n.* the part or region of the atmosphere above the territory of a nation or other political division which is considered under its jurisdiction.

**airspeed** /'ɛəspid/, *n.* the forward speed of an aircraft relative to the air through which it moves (in contrast to ground speed).

**airspeed indicator** /'– ɪndəkeɪtə/, *n.* a device in an aeroplane to measure its speed relative to the air.

**air-spray** /'ɛə-spreɪ/, *adj.* pertaining to compressed-air spraying devices or to liquids used in them.

**airstream** /'ɛəstrim/, *n.* **1.** an airflow. **2.** a wind, esp. one at a high altitude.

**air strike** /'ɛə straɪk/, *n.* an attack by fighters, bombers or attack aircraft on a specific objective.

**airstrip** /'ɛəstrɪp/, *n.* a runway, esp. a single runway forming a landing ground in a remote place.

**air structure** /'ɛə strʌktʃə/, *n.* the set of routes flown by a particular airline.

**air support** /'– səpɔt/, *n.* assistance given to ground troops by an air force.

**air-switch** /'ɛə-swɪtʃ/, *n.* an electrical switch in which the interruption of the circuit occurs in air.

**air-taxi** /'ɛə-tæksi/, *n.* a light aircraft used for chartered trips.

**air terminal** /'ɛə tɜmənəl/, *n.* a place of assembly for air passengers, not necessarily at an airport, with administrative offices, etc.

**airtight** /'ɛətaɪt/, *adj.* **1.** so tight or close as to be impermeable to air. **2.** having no weak points or openings of which an opponent may take advantage.

**air to air missile,** *n.* a missile, usu. guided, fired from an aircraft at a target above the ground.

**air to surface missile,** *n.* a missile, usu. guided, designed to be fired from an aircraft at a target on the ground. Also, **air to ground missile.**

**air traffic control,** *n.* direction of airborne aircraft movement by ground-based personnel via a radiotelephone link or, in emergencies, by light signals.

**air-trap** /'ɛə-træp/, *n.* a device which uses a water seal to prevent the escape of foul air from sinks, drains, etc.

**air turbine** /'ɛə tɜbaɪn/, *n.* →**turbine** (def. 2).

**air-valve** /'ɛə-vælv/, *n.* **1.** a device for controlling the flow of air through a pipe. **2.** a device for releasing air that has accumulated in a pipeline, as at the top of a hill.

**air vesicle** /'ɛə vɛsɪkəl/, *n.* a large air-filled pocket, present mainly in plants which float on water.

**air vice-marshal** /ˌɛə vaɪs-'maʃəl/, *n.* **1.** an officer in the Royal Australian Air Force or any of various other airforces, equivalent in rank to a major general in the army or rear-admiral in the navy. **2.** the rank.

**airwards** /'ɛəwədz/, *adv.* up in the air; towards the air. Also, **airward.**

**airwaves** /'ɛəweɪvz/, *n. pl.* (in non-technical use) the medium used for transmission of television and radio signals.

**airway** /'ɛəweɪ/, *n.* **1.** an air-route fully equipped with emergency landing fields, beacon lights, radio beams, etc. **2.** any passage in a mine used for purposes of ventilation; an air course. **3.** *Med.* a tube used to achieve unobstructed respiration in general anaesthesia.

**air-well** /'ɛə-wɛl/, *n.* →**air-drive.**

**airwoman** /'ɛəwʊmən/, *n., pl.* **-women.** a woman aviator.

**airworthy** /'ɛəwɜði/, *adj.* (of an aircraft) meeting accepted standards for safe flight; equipped and maintained in condition to fly. – **airworthiness,** *n.*

**airy** /'ɛəri/, *adj.* **airier, airiest. 1.** open to a free current of air; breezy: *airy rooms.* **2.** consisting of or having the character of air; immaterial: *airy phantoms.* **3.** light in appearance; thin: *airy lace.* **4.** light in manner; sprightly; gay; lively: *airy songs.* **5.** light in movement; graceful; delicate: *an airy tread.* **6.** light as air; unsubstantial; unreal; imaginary: *airy dreams.* **7.** visionary; speculative. **8.** performed in the air; aerial. **9.** lofty; high in the air. **10.** casual, off-hand; superficial, flippant.

**airy-fairy** /ˌɛəri-'fɛəri/, *adj. Colloq.* light and delicate, whimsical; fanciful.

**A.I.S.** /eɪ aɪ 'ɛs/, Australian Illawarra Shorthorn.

**aisle** /aɪl/, *n.* **1.** a passageway between seats in a church, hall, etc. **2.** *Archit.* **a.** a lateral division of a church or other building separated from the nave by piers or columns. **b.** a similar division at the side of the choir or a transept. **c.** any of the lateral divisions of a church or hall, as the nave. **3. lay them in the aisles,** *Colloq.* to impress people favourably. [var. of *isle*, translation of late ML *insula* aisle (in L island); replacing ME *ele*, from OF, from L *āla* shoulder, wing; *ai-* of current spelling from F *aile*] – **aisled** /aɪld/, *adj.*

**aitch** /eɪtʃ/; *deprecated* /heɪtʃ/, *n.* the letter H, h.

**aitchbone** /'eɪtʃboʊn/, *n.* **1.** the rump bone, as of beef. **2.** the cut of beef which includes this bone. [ME *nache-bone*; *a nache-bone* became *an aitch-bone* by false division into words; *nache*, from OF, from L *natis* buttock]

**ajar**[1] /ə'dʒa/, *adv.* **1.** neither quite open nor shut; partly opened: *leave the door ajar.* –*adj.* **2.** partly open. [ME *on char* on the turn; *char*, OE *cerr* turn. See A-[1], CHAR[3]]

**ajar**[2] /ə'dʒa/, *adj.* out of harmony; jarring: *ajar with the world.* [for *at jar* at discord. See JAR[2], n.]

**ajax** /'eɪdʒæks/, *v.t. Colloq.* to clean (baths, etc.) using a household cleaning powder. [from the Trademark *Ajax*, name of such a powder]

**ajinomoto** /ədʒɪnə'moʊtoʊ/, *n.* →**monosodium glutamate.**

**A.K.** /eɪ 'keɪ/, Knight of the Order of Australia.

**aka** /'aka/, *n.* any of several species of woody, climbing vines of the genus *Metrosideros*; rata. [Maori]

**akeake** /'akiˌaki/, *n.* **1.** a large tropical hardwooded shrub, *Dodonaea viscosa*, with young twigs compressed or triangular and viscid. **2.** either of two New Zealand trees, *Olearia avicenniaefolia* and *O. traversii.* Also, **ake.** [Maori]

**akela** /a'keɪlə/, *n.* the adult in charge of a pack of cubs in the Scout movement. [named after *Akela*, leader of the wolf pack in the *Jungle Book* of Rudyard Kipling]

**akimbo** /ə'kɪmboʊ/, *adv.* with hand on hip and elbow bent outwards: *to stand with arms akimbo.* [ME *in kene bowe*, apparently, in keen bow, in a sharp bent; but cf. Icel. *kengboginn* bent double, crooked]

**akin** /ə'kɪn/, *adj.* **1.** of kin; related by blood. **2.** allied by nature; partaking of the same properties. [A-[2] + KIN]

**Akkadian** /ə'keɪdiən/, *n.* **1.** the eastern group of Semitic languages, all extinct, including Babylonian and Assyrian. **2.** any member of this group. **3.** one of the Akkadian people. –*adj.* **4.** of or belonging to Akkad. **5.** designating or pertaining to the primitive inhabitants of Babylonia or the non-Semitic language ascribed to them. **6.** designating or pertaining to the (later) Semitic language of Babylonia.

**al-,** variant of **ad-** before *l*, as in *allure.*

**-al**[1], an adjective suffix meaning 'of or pertaining to', 'connected with', 'of the nature of', 'like', 'befitting', etc., occurring in numerous adjectives and in many nouns of adjectival origin, as *annual, choral, equal, regal.* [L: stem of *-ālis* (neut. *-āle*) pertaining to; often replacing ME *-el*, from F]

**-al**[2], a suffix forming nouns of action from verbs, as in *refusal, denial, recital, trial.* [L *-āle* (pl. *-ālia*), neut. of adj. suffix *-ālis*; often replacing ME *-aille*, from OF]

**-al**[3], a suffix indicating that a compound includes an alcohol or aldehyde group, as in *chloral.* [short for AL(COHOL) or AL(DEHYDE)]

**Al,** aluminium.

**AL,** Anglo-Latin. Also **A.L.**

**à la** /'a la/, **1.** according to the: *à la carte, à la mode.* **2.** (short for *à la mode (de)*) after the manner or fashion of: *à la Dame Edna.* [F: at, to, in + the; fem. form used before a word beginning with a consonant]

**ala** /'eɪlə/, *n., pl.* **alae** /'eɪli/. **1.** a wing. **2.** a winglike part, process, or expansion, as of a bone, a shell, a seed, a stem, etc. **3.** one of the two side petals of a papilionaceous flower. [L: wing]

**alabaster** /'æləbæstə/, *n.* **1.** a finely granular variety of gypsum, often white and translucent, used for ornamental objects or work, such as lamp bases, figurines, etc. **2.** a variety of calcite, often with a banded structure, used for similar purposes (**oriental alabaster**). –*adj.* Also, **alabastrine** /ælə'bæstrən/. **3.** made of alabaster: *an alabaster column.* **4.** resembling alabaster; smooth and white as alabaster: *her alabaster throat.* [ME, from L, from Gk *alábastros*, var. of *alábastos* an alabaster box]

**à la carte** /a la 'kat/, according to the menu; with a stated price for each dish: *dinner à la carte.* [F]

**alack** /ə'læk/, *interj. Archaic.* (an exclamation of sorrow, regret, or dismay.) Also, **alackaday** /ə'lækədeɪ/.

**alacrity** /ə'lækrəti/, *n.* **1.** liveliness; briskness; sprightliness. **2.** cheerful readiness or willingness. [L *alacritas*] – **alacritous,** *adj.*

**à la king** /a la 'kɪŋ/, *adj.* (*usu. following the noun*) served in a cream sauce with peppers and mushroom: *chicken à la king.*

**alalia** /ə'leɪliə/, *n.* loss of the power of speech due to impairment of the muscles or sense organs involved in speech. [Gk]

**alameda** /ælə'meɪdə/, *n. Chiefly U.S.* a public walk shaded with poplar or other trees. [Sp., from *alamo* poplar]

**alamo** /'æləmoʊ/, *n., pl.* **-mos.** *U.S.* a cottonwood. [Sp.: POPLAR]

**à la mode** /a la 'moʊd/, *adv.* **1.** in or according to the fashion. –*adj.* **2.** (of beef) larded and braised or stewed with vegetables, herbs, etc., and served with a rich brown gravy. Also, **alamode.** [F]

**alanine** /'ælənin, -naɪn/, *n.* an amino acid, $CH_3CH(NH_2)COOH$, found in many proteins.

**alar** /'eɪlə/, *adj.* **1.** pertaining to or having wings; alary. **2.** winglike; wing-shaped. **3.** *Anat., Bot.* →**axillary.** [L *ālāris*, from *āla* wing]

**alarm** /ə'lam/, *n.* **1.** a sudden fear or painful suspense excited by an apprehension of danger; apprehension; fright. **2.** any sound, outcry, or information intended to give notice of approaching danger: *a false alarm.* **3.** a self-acting contrivance of any kind used to call attention, rouse from sleep, warn of danger, etc. **4.** a warning sound; signal for attention. **5.** a call to arms. **6.** *Fencing.* an appeal or a challenge made by a step or stamp on the ground with the advancing foot. –*v.t.* **7.** to surprise with apprehension of danger; disturb with sudden fear. **8.** to give notice of danger to; rouse to vigilance and exertions for safety. [ME *alarme*, from OF, from It. *allarme* tumult, fright, from *all' arme* to arms] – **alarmed,** *adj.* – **alarmingly,** *adv.*

**alarm bird** /'– bɜd/, *n.* **1.** →**spur-winged plover. 2.** →**kookaburra.**

**alarm clock** /'– klɒk/, *n.* a clock which can be set to sound a bell or the like at a particular time, used to rouse people from sleep.

**alarmist** /ə'lamәst/, *n.* one given to raising alarms, esp. without sufficient reason, as by exaggerating dangers, prophesying calamities, etc. – **alarmism,** *n.*

**alarum** /ə'larәm/, *n.* **1.** *Archaic.* alarm. **2.** *Horol.* **a.** a device designed to ring a warning bell at a certain hour. **b.** the bell itself.

**alary** /'eɪlәri/, *adj.* **1.** of or pertaining to wings. **2.** *Biol.* wing-shaped. [L *ālārius,* from *āla* wing]

**alas** /ə'læs, ə'las/, *interj.* (an exclamation expressing sorrow, grief, pity, concern, or apprehension of evil.) [ME *allas,* from OF *a las, ha las,* from *a, ha* ah + *las* miserable, from L *lassus* weary]

**alaska** /ə'læskə/, *n.* **1. a.** a yarn made of cotton mixed with wool or mohair. **b.** a heavy dress and coat fabric made from cotton and wool. **2.** a baked icecream dessert, usu. made on a sponge cake base, with fruit or other flavouring, the whole enclosed in meringue, as baked alaska, bombe alaska. – **alaskan,** *adj.*

**alastrim** /ə'læstrәm/, *n.* a mild form of smallpox. [Pg]

**alate** /'eɪleɪt/, *adj.* **1.** winged. **2.** having membranous expansions like wings. Also, **alated.** [L *ālātus* winged]

**alb** /ælb/, *n.* a white linen robe with close sleeves, worn by an officiating priest. [ME and OE *albe,* from L *alba* (*vestis*) white (garment)]

alb

**albacore** /'ælbəkɔ/, *n., pl.* **-cores,** (esp. collectively) **-core. 1.** a medium-sized tuna of warm seas, *Thunnus germo,* with dark blue back and silvery belly, and having a characteristically long pectoral fin. **2.** any of various fishes related to or resembling the tuna. [Pg. *albacor(a),* from Ar. *al bakūra*]

**Albania** /æl'beɪniə/, *n.* a republic in southern Europe on the Balkan peninsula. Official name: **People's Republic of Albania.**

**Albanian** /æl'beɪniәn, ɔl-/, *adj.* **1.** pertaining to Albania, its inhabitants, or their language. *–n.* **2.** a native or inhabitant of Albania. **3.** the language of Albania, an Indo-European language.

**Albany doctor** /ælbәni 'dɒktə/, *n. Colloq.* a strong, cool wind blowing after a hot day in Albany, a town in Western Australia.

**albatross** /'ælbәtrɒs/, *n.* **1.** any of various large web-footed seabirds related to the petrels, esp. of the genus *Diomedea,* of the Pacific and southern waters, noted for their powers of flight. **2.** *Golf. Colloq.* a score of three strokes below the par figure for a hole. [var. of *algatross,* from Pg. *alcatraz* seafowl, cormorant; change of *-g-* to *-b-* ? by association with L *alba* white (the bird's colour)]

albatross

**albedo** /æl'bidoʊ/, *n.* **1.** *Astron.* the ratio of the light reflected by a planet or satellite to that received by it. **2.** *Physics.* the ratio of the neutrons reflected (in a neutron reflector) to those absorbed. [L: whiteness]

**albeit** /ɔl'biɪt, æl-/, *conj.* although; notwithstanding that: *to choose a strategic albeit inglorious retreat.* [ME *al be it* although it be]

**albert** /'ælbәt/, *n.* a kind of watch-chain. Also, **Albert Chain.** [named after Prince *Albert,* consort of Queen Victoria]

**alberti bass** /æl,bɜti 'beɪs/, *n.* an eighteenth century style of left-hand piano accompaniment characterised by broken chords.

**Albert lyrebird** /ælbәt 'laɪәbɜd/, *n.* the smaller of the two lyrebird species, *Menura alberti,* duller in colour and having a less elaborate tail than the superb lyrebird.

**alberts** /'ælbәts/, *n. pl. Colloq.* covering for the feet made from sacking, cloth, etc. worn by swagmen, tramps, etc. Also, **Prince Alberts.** [named after Prince *Albert,* because of his alleged poverty before he became Queen Victoria's consort]

**albescent** /æl'bɛsәnt/, *adj.* becoming white; whitish. [L *albescens,* ppr.] – **albescence,** *n.*

**albinism** /'ælbәnɪzәm/, *n.* the state or condition of being an albino. – **albinistic** /ælbə'nɪstɪk/, *adj.*

**albino** /æl'binoʊ/, *n., pl.* **-nos. 1.** a person with a pale, milky skin, light hair, and pink eyes, resulting from a congenital absence of pigmentation. **2.** an animal or plant with a marked deficiency in pigmentation. **3.** *Northern Aust. Colloq.* (usu. derog.) a white woman. *–adj.* **4.** of or pertaining to albinos or albinism. [Pg., from *albo,* from L *albus* white]

**Albion** /'ælbiәn/, *n. Poetic.* Britain. [L, said to be derived from *albus* white]

**albite** /'ælbaɪt/, *n.* a very common mineral of the plagioclase felspar group, sodium aluminium silicate, $NaAlSi_3O_8$, usu. white, occurring in many igneous rocks. [L *albus* white + -ITE[1]]

**album** /'ælbәm/, *n.* **1.** a book consisting of blank leaves for the insertion or preservation of photographs, stamps, autographs, etc. **2.** a book of selections, esp. of music. **3.** a folder containing two or more gramophone records. **4.** long-playing recording on which there is a collection of songs or pieces: *Neil Diamond's latest album.* [L: tablet, properly neut. of *albus* white]

**albumen** /'ælbjәmәn/, *n.* **1.** the white of an egg. **2.** *Bot.* the nutritive matter about the embryo in a seed. **3.** *Biochem.* →**albumin.** [L (def. 1), from *albus* white]

**albumenise** /æl'bjumәnaɪz/, *v.t.,* **-nised, -nising.** to treat with an albuminous solution. Also, **albumenize.**

**albumin** /'ælbjәmәn/, *n.* any of a class of water-soluble proteins occurring in animal and vegetable juices and tissues. In animal plasma albumin is involved in osmotic regulation and transport, as of lipids. [L *albūmen*]

**albuminate** /æl'bjumәneɪt/, *n.* a compound resulting from the action of an alkali or an acid upon albumin.

**albuminoid** /æl'bjumәnɔɪd/, *adj.* resembling albumen or albumin. [L *albūmen* white of egg + -OID] – **albuminoidal,** *adj.*

**albuminous** /æl'bjumәnәs/, *adj.* **1.** of albumin. **2.** containing albumin. **3.** resembling albumin.

**albuminuria** /æl,bjumə'njuriə/, *n.* the presence of albumin in the urine, usu. a symptom of disease of the kidneys but sometimes resulting from other physiological conditions, as pregnancy. [ALBUMIN + -URIA] – **albuminuric,** *adj.*

**alcahest** /'ælkәhɛst/, *n.* →**alkahest.**

**Alcaic** /æl'keɪɪk/, *adj.* **1.** pertaining to certain metres or a form of strophe or stanza used by, or named after, the poet Alcaeus. *–n.* **2.** (*pl.*) Alcaic verses or strophes. [named after *Alcaeus,* a Gk lyric poet of Mytilene, fl. c. 600 B.C.]

**alchemise** /'ælkәmaɪz/, *v.t.,* **-mised, -mising.** to change by alchemy; transmute, as metals. Also, **alchemize.**

**alchemist** /'ælkәmәst/, *n.* one who practises or is versed in alchemy. – **alchemistic** /ælkə'mɪstɪk/, **alchemistical** /ælkə'mɪstɪkәl/, *adj.*

**alchemy** /'ælkәmi/, *n.* **1.** the medieval chemical science which sought in particular to transmute baser metals into gold, and to find a universal solvent and an elixir of life. **2.** any magical power or process of transmuting. [ME *alkamye,* from OF *alcamie,* from ML *alchimia,* from Ar. *al kīmiyā'* (*kīmiyā'* ? from LGk *chýma* molten metal)] – **alchemic** /æl'kɛmɪk/, **alchemical,** *adj.* – **alchemically,** *adv.*

**alcheringa** /ælt∫ə'rɪŋgə/, *n.* →**Dreamtime.** Also, **alchera** /'ælt∫әrə/. [Aboriginal]

**alcidine** /'ælsәdin, -daɪn/, *adj.* pertaining to or resembling the Alcidae, the auk family.

**alcohol** /'ælkәhɒl/, *n.* **1.** a colourless, inflammable liquid (**ethyl alcohol,** $C_2H_5OH$), the intoxicating principle of fermented liquors, formed from certain sugars (esp. glucose) by fermentation, now usu. prepared by treating grain with malt and adding yeast. **2.** any intoxicating liquor containing this spirit. **3.** *Chem.* any of a class of chemical compounds having the general formula ROH, where R represents an alkyl group; derived from the hydrocarbon by replacement of a hydrogen atom by the hydroxyl radical, OH. [ML: orig., fine powder; hence, essence or rectified spirits, from Ar. *al kuhl* the powdered antimony, kohl]

**alcoholic** /ælkə'hɒlɪk/, *adj.* **1.** pertaining to or of the nature of alcohol. **2.** containing or using alcohol. **3.** caused by alcohol. **4.** suffering from alcoholism. **5.** preserved in alcohol. *–n.* **6.** a person suffering from alcoholism. **7.** one addicted to intoxicating drinks.

**alcoholicity** /ˌælkəhɒlˈɪsəti/, *n.* alcoholic quality or strength.

**alcoholic strength** /ælkəˌhɒlɪk ˈstrɛŋθ/, *n.* the quantity of ethyl alcohol in a wine or spirit, expressed as per cent alcohol by volume or per cent proof spirit.

**alcoholise** /ˈælkəhɒlaɪz/, *v.t.*, **-lised, -lising.** **1.** to treat with alcohol. **2.** to make alcoholic. Also, **alcoholize.**

**alcoholism** /ˈælkəhɒlɪzəm/, *n.* a diseased condition due to the excessive use of alcoholic beverages.

**alcoholometer** /ˌælkəhɒlˈɒmətə/, *n.* an instrument for finding the percentage of alcohol in a liquid. – **alcoholometry,** *n.*

**alcotest** /ˈælkəˌtɛst/, *n.* initial test for measuring alcohol content of exhaled breath, administered at roadside to drivers alleged to have committed certain driving offences. [Trademark]

**alcove** /ˈælkoʊv/, *n.* **1.** a recess opening out of a room. **2.** a recess in a room for a bed, for books in a library, or for other similar furnishings. **3.** any recessed space, as in a garden. [F, from Sp. *alcoba*, from Ar. *al qubba* the vaulted space]

**alcyonarian** /ˌælsiənˈɛəriən/, *n.* **1.** any anthozoan of the subclass Alcyonaria, having the body parts in groups of eight. *–adj.* **2.** belonging to the Alcyonaria.

**Ald.,** Alderman. Also, **ald.**

**aldehyde** /ˈældəhaɪd/, *n.* one of a group of organic compounds with the general formula R-CHO, which yield acids when oxidised and alcohols when reduced. [short for NL *al(cohol) dehyd(rogenātum)* alcohol deprived of hydrogen] – **aldehydic** /ældəˈhaɪdɪk/, *adj.*

**al dente** /æl ˈdɛnteɪ/, *adj.* (of spaghetti, etc.) cooked lightly so that it still offers resistance to the teeth. [It.: to the tooth]

**alder** /ˈɔldə/, *n.* **1.** any betulaceous shrub or tree of the genus *Alnus*, growing in moist places in northern temperate or colder regions. **2.** any of various trees or shrubs resembling, or with timber resembling, this genus. [ME; OE *alor, aler*]

**alderfly** /ˈɔldəflaɪ/, *n., pl.* **-flies.** any of several dark neuropterous insects of the family Sialidae, much used as a fishing fly.

**alderman** /ˈɔldəmən/, *n., pl.* **-men.** **1.** a local government representative elected by constituents of a municipality. **2.** a local government officer in any of various other countries, as the U.S., having powers varying according to locality. [ME; OE *aldormann, ealdormann*, from *ealdor* chief, elder + *mann* man] – **aldermanity** /ɔldəˈmænəti/, **aldermanship,** *n.* – **aldermanic** /ɔldəˈmænɪk/, *adj.*

**Alderman Lushington** /– ˈlʌʃɪŋtən/, *n.* →**lushington.**

**Alderney** /ˈɔldəni/, *n.* one of a breed of cattle originally reared in the Channel Islands, as Jersey or Guernsey cattle. [named after *Alderney*, the northernmost of the Channel Islands in the English Channel]

**Aldine** /ˈɔldaɪn/, *adj.* **1.** of or from the press of Aldus Manutius and his family, of Venice (about 1490-1597), chiefly noted for compactly printed editions of the classics. *–n.* **2.** any Aldine or other early edition. **3.** any of certain styles of printing types.

**Aldis lamp** /ˈɔldəs læmp/, *n.* a portable signalling lamp. [Trademark]

**aldol** /ˈældɒl/, *n.* a colourless fluid, $CH_3CHOHCH_2$ CHO, from an acetaldehyde condensation, used medicinally as a sedative and hypnotic. [ALD(EHYDE) + (ALCOH)OL]

**aldolase** /ˈældəleɪz/, *n.* an enzyme of animal tissues and plant cells which plays a part in glycolysis.

**aldose** /ˈældoʊz, -oʊs/, *n.* a monosaccharose sugar containing the aldehyde group.

**aldosterone** /ældəˈstɪəroʊn, ælˈdɒstəroʊn/, *n.* a hormone produced by the adrenal cortex, which controls the metabolism of electrolytes and water.

**Aldrin** /ˈɔldrən/, *n. Chem.* an organochlorine compound highly toxic to animal life and used as a systemic insecticide. [Trademark]

**ale** /eɪl/, *n.* **1.** any of various English types of beer brewed by the top fermentation method. **2.** any beer. **3.** *Obs.* any unhopped beer. [ME; OE *ealu*, c. Icel. *öl*]

**aleatory** /æliˈeɪtəri/, *adj.* **1.** dependent on chance. **2. aleatory contract,** a contract or agreement of which the effects with respect both to the advantages and the losses depend on uncertain events; a wagering contract.

**alec** /ˈælɪk/, *n. Colloq.* →**smart alec.**

**alectryomancy** /əˈlɛktriəˌmænsi/, *n.* a form of divination whereby a bird, usu. a black hen or a white gamecock, is allowed to pick grains of corn from a circle of letters, thus forming words. [Gk *alektruṓn* cock + -MANCY]

**alee** /əˈli/, *adv.* on or towards the leeside of a ship (opposed to *aweather*).

**alembic** /əˈlɛmbɪk/, *n.* **1.** a vessel with a beaked cap or head, formerly used in distilling; an ancient retort. **2.** anything that transforms, purifies, or refines. [ME *alambic*, from ML *alambicus*, from Ar. *al anbīq* the still (*anbīq* from Gk *ámbix* cup)] – **alembicated,** *adj.*

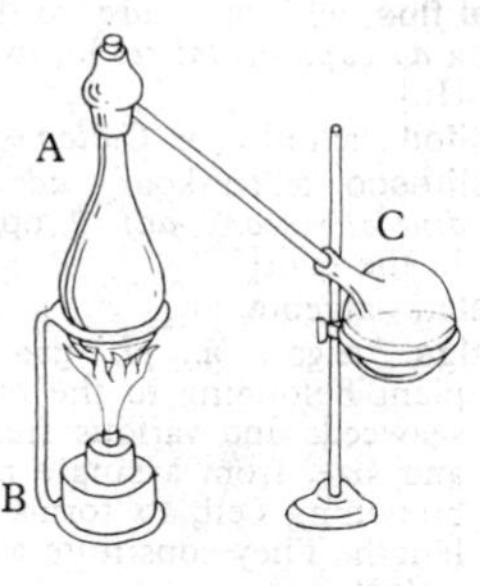

A, alembic; B, lamp; C, receiver

**Alençon lace** /ələnsən ˈleɪs/, *n.* **1.** a delicate needlepoint lace made in Alençon. **2.** a machine reproduction of this lace, with a cordlike outline. [from *Alençon*, a town in NW France]

**aleph** /ˈaləf/, *n.* the first letter in the Hebrew alphabet (א).

**aleph-nought** /aləf-ˈnɔt/, *n. Maths.* the cardinal number of a countable set, such as the set of positive integers. *Symbol*: $\aleph_0$ Also, **aleph-null, aleph-zero.**

**Aleppo gall** /əˈlɛpoʊ gɔl/, *n.* the gall of the oak tree, rich in tannin; nut-gall. [from *Aleppo*, a town in NW Syria]

**alert** /əˈlɜt/, *adj.* **1.** vigilantly attentive: *an alert mind.* **2.** moving with celerity; nimble. *–n.* **3.** an attitude of vigilance, wariness or caution: *on the alert.* **4.** an air-raid warning. **5.** the period during which an air-raid warning is in effect. **6. red alert,** a condition of preparedness, to meet an imminent attack or emergency. *–v.t.* **7.** to prepare (troops, etc.) for action. **8.** to warn of an impending raid or attack. [F *alerte*, from It. *all' erta* on the lookout] – **alerted,** *adj.* – **alertly,** *adv.* – **alertness,** *n.*

**-ales,** a suffix of (Latin) names of botanical orders. [L, pl. of *-ālis*, adj. suffix. See -AL[1]]

**aleuromancy** /əˈlurəmænsi, əˈlju-/, *n.* a form of divination in which fortune cookies are used. [F *aleuromancie*, from Gk *áleuron* flour + -MANCY]

**aleurone** /əˈljurən, -roʊn/, *n.* minute albuminoid granules (protein) found in connection with starch and oily matter, in the endosperm of ripe seeds, and in a special layer of cells in grains of wheat, etc. [Gk *áleuron* flour] – **aleuronic** /æljəˈrɒnɪk/, *adj.*

**alevin** /ˈæləvən/, *n.* a young fish, esp. a salmon. [F]

**alexanders** /æləgˈzændəz/, *n., pl.* **alexanders.** a biennial umbelliferous plant of southern Europe, *Smyrnium olusatrum*, with dense umbels of yellowish flowers and black fruits.

**Alexandrian** /æləgˈzændriən, -ˈzan-/, *adj.* **1.** of Alexandria. **2.** pertaining to the schools of philosophy, literature, and science in ancient Alexandria. **3.** erudite and critical rather than original or creative. **4.** of Alexander the Great. *–n.* **5.** a native or inhabitant of Alexandria.

**Alexandrine** /æləgˈzændrin, -draɪn/, *n.* **1.** *Pros.* **a.** a verse or line of poetry of six iambic feet. **b.** (in French poetry) a verse of alternate couplets of twelve and thirteen syllables. *–adj.* **2.** *Pros.* designating such a verse or line. **3.** of or pertaining to Alexandria. [F *alexandrin*, from poems in this metre on *Alexander* the Great]

**alexandrite** /ˌæləgˈzændraɪt/, *n.* a variety of chrysoberyl, green by daylight and red-violet by artificial light, used as a gem. [named after *Alexander II* of Russia + -ITE[1]]

**alexia** /əˈlɛksiə/, *n.* a cerebral disorder marked by inability to read. [A-[6] + stem of Gk *léxis* a speaking + -IA]

**alexin** /əˈlɛksən/, *n. Immunol.* **1.** any of certain substances in normal blood serum which destroy bacteria, etc. **2.** →**complement** (def. 10). [stem of Gk *aléxein* ward off + -IN[2]] – **alexinic** /ælɛkˈsɪnɪk/, *adj.*

**alexipharmic** /əˌlɛksiˈfamɪk/, *Med. –adj.* **1.** warding off poisoning or infection; antidotal; prophylactic. *–n.* **2.** an alexipharmic agent, esp. an internal antidote. [Gk *alexiphármakon* a remedy against poison; final syll., properly *-ac*, conformed to the suffix -IC]

**alf** /ælf/, *n. Colloq.* **1.** a heterosexual male. **2.** a male whose behaviour shows contempt for cultural pursuits, prejudice towards minority groups, low estimation of women as a class, and a marked preference for male social company. **3.** a dull and ineffectual person.

**alfalfa** /æl'fælfə/, *n. Chiefly U.S.* →**lucerne** (def. 1).

**al fine** /æl 'fini/, *adv.* to the end (a musical direction, as after a *da capo* or *dal segno*, to continue to *fine*, the indicated end). [It.]

**alfoil** /'ælfɔɪl/, *n. Colloq.* →**aluminium foil.** [Trademark]

**alfresco** /æl'frɛskoʊ/, *adv.* **1.** in the open air; out-of-doors: *to dine alfresco.* *–adj.* **2.** open-air: *an alfresco cafe.* [It. *al fresco* in the cool]

**alg.**, algebra.

**alga** /'ælgə/, *n., pl.* **-gae** /-dʒi/. any chlorophyll-containing plant belonging to the phylum Thallophyta, comprising the seaweeds and various freshwater forms and varying in form and size, from a single microscopic or sometimes large and branching cell, to forms with trunklike stems many feet in length. They constitute a subphylum, the Algae. [L: seaweed] – **algal**, *adj.*

**algarroba** /ælgə'roʊbə/, *n.* **1.** any of certain mesquites, esp. *Prosopis juliflora.* **2.** its beanlike pod. **3.** →**carob.** Also, **algaroba, algarrobo.** [Sp., from Ar. *al kharrūba.* See CAROB]

**algebra** /'ældʒəbrə/, *n.* **1.** the mathematical art of reasoning about (quantitative) relations by means of a systematised notation including letters and other symbols; the analysis of equations, combinatorial analysis, theory of fractions, etc. **2.** any special system of notation adapted to the study of a special system of relationships: *algebra of classes.* **3.** *Maths.* **a.** the study of mathematical systems possessing operations analogous to those of addition and multiplication. **b.** the name given to particular systems of the above type: *vector algebra, matrix algebra.* [ML, from Ar. *al jebr, al jabr* bone-setting, reunification (referring to the solving of algebraic equations)]

**algebraic** /ældʒə'breɪɪk/, *adj.* **1.** of or occurring in algebra. **2.** *Maths.* (of a number), satisfying a polynomial equation with integral coefficients: $\sqrt{2}$ *is algebraic as it satisfies the equation* $x^2 - 2 = 0$. Also, **algebraical.** – **algebraically,** *adv.*

**algebraist** /ældʒə'breɪəst/, *n.* an expert in algebra.

**Algeria** /æl'dʒɪəriə/, *n.* a republic in north-western Africa. – **Algerian, Algerine,** *adj., n.*

**-algia,** a noun suffix meaning 'pain', as in *neuralgia.* [NL, from Gk]

**algid** /'ældʒəd/, *adj.* cold or chilly, esp. applied to a cold fit at the onset of fever. [L: stem of *algidus*] – **algidity** /æl'dʒɪdəti/, *n.*

**algin** /'ældʒən/, *n.* any hydrophilic, colloidal substance found in or obtained from various kelps, esp. from *Macrocystis pyrifera.* [ALG(A) + -IN[2]]

**alginate** /'ældʒəneɪt/, *n.* a gelatinous substance, the sodium salt of alginic acid, extracted from various kelps, used in the manufacture of ice-cream, in sizing cloth, in dyes, plastics, and explosives, and for various other industrial purposes. [ALGIN + -ATE[2]]

**alginic acid** /æl,dʒɪnɪk 'æsəd/, *n.* insoluble acid, ($C_6H_8$-$O_6$)n, found in certain seaweeds; used as a thickening agent in foods and for sizing paper.

**algo-**, a word element meaning 'pain', as in *algolagnia.* [combining form representing Gk *álgos*]

**algoid** /'ælgɔɪd/, *adj.* like algae. [ALG(A) + -OID]

**ALGOL** /'ælgɒl/, *n.* an internationally accepted language in which computer programs are written, in algebraic notation following the rules of Boolean algebra. Also, **Algol.** [ALGO(RITHMIC) + L(ANGUAGE)]

**algolagnia** /ælgə'lægniə/, *n.* sexual gratification derived from administering or experiencing pain, including both sadism and masochism. [ALGO- + Gk *lagneía* lust] – **algolagnic,** *adj.* – **algolagnist,** *n.*

**algology** /æl'gɒlədʒi/, *n.* the branch of botany that deals with algae. – **algological** /ælgə'lɒdʒɪkəl/, *adj.* – **algologist,** *n.*

**algometer** /æl'gɒmətə/, *n.* a device for determining sensitiveness to pain due to pressure. – **algometric** /ælgə'mɛtrɪk/, **algometrical** /ælgə'mɛtrɪkəl/, *adj.* – **algometry,** *n.*

**Algonkian** /æl'gɒŋkiən/, *n.* **1.** *Geol.* Proterozoic; late Pre-Cambrian. **2.** →**Algonquian.** [after the rock formations in the Great Lake District, U.S.A., homeland of the Algonquian Indians] – **Algonkian,** *adj.*

**Algonquian** /æl'gɒŋkiən/, *n.* **1.** one of the principal linguistic stocks of North America. **2.** an Algonquian tribe member. *–adj.* **3.** belonging to or constituting this stock. Also, **Algonkian.**

**Algonquian-Mosan** /æl,gɒŋkiən-'moʊsən/, *n.* a great linguistic phylum of North America including Algonquian, Salishan, and Wakashan.

**algophobia** /,ælgə'foʊbiə/, *n.* an abnormal dread of pain.

**algor** /'ælgɔ/, *n.* coldness or chill, esp. at the onset of fever. [L: cold]

**algorism** /'ælgərɪzəm/, *n.* **1.** the Arabic system of arithmetical notation (with the figures 1, 2, 3, etc.). **2.** the art of computation with the Arabic figures, one to nine, plus the zero; arithmetic. **3.** →**algorithm.** [ME *algorisme,* from OF, from ML *algorismus,* from Ar. *al Khwārizmī* the native of *Khwārizm* Khiva (i.e. *Abū Ja'far Mohammed ibn Mūsā,* 9th-century Arab mathematician, author of a famous treatise on algebra translated into ML]

**algorithm** /'ælgərɪðəm/, *n.* an effective procedure for solving a particular mathematical problem in a finite number of steps. Also, **algorism.** [var. of ALGORISM by association with ARITHMETIC] – **algorithmic** /ælgə'rɪðmɪk/, *adj.*

**alhaji** /æl'hædʒi/, *n.* **1.** a Muslim who has made a pilgrimage to Mecca. **2.** (*cap.*) a title of respect accorded to one who has done this. [Ar.]

**alhambresque** /ælhæm'brɛsk/, *adj.* resembling the fanciful style of ornamentation of the Spanish Alhambra, a fourteenth century palace of the Moorish kings at Granada, Spain. [Sp., from Ar. *al hamā'* the red (referring to the colour of the soil)]

**alias** /'eɪliəs/, *adv., n., pl.* **aliases.** *–adv.* **1.** at another time; in another place; in other circumstances; otherwise. 'Simpson alias Smith' means a person calling himself at one time or one place 'Smith', at another 'Simpson'. *–n.* **2.** assumed name; another name. [L: at another time or place]

**alibi** /'æləbaɪ/, *n., pl.* **-bis.** **1.** *Law.* a defence by an accused person that he was elsewhere at the time the offence with which he is charged was committed. **2.** the evidence that proves one was elsewhere. **3.** *Colloq.* an excuse. [L: elsewhere]

**alible** /'æləbəl/, *adj.* →**nutritive.** [L *alibilis*] – **alibility** /ælə'bɪləti/, *n.*

**alicyclic** /ælə'saɪklɪk, -'sɪk-/, *adj.* denoting organic compounds, essentially aliphatic in chemical behaviour, but differing structurally in that the essential carbon atoms are connected as in a ring instead of an open chain.

**alidade** /'ælədeɪd/, *n.* **1.** an instrument or part thereof which is used for the determination of direction and which depends upon a beam, equipped with sights, a telescope, etc., which turns within a circle with a graduated circumference. *–adj.* **2.** of or pertaining to an alidade. [ME, from ML *alhidada,* from Ar. *al 'idāda* the revolving radius of a graduated circle]

**alidade bubble** /'– bʌbəl/, *n.* a device operating like a spirit level to determine the horizontal or vertical plane of reference from which the alidade takes measurement.

**alien** /'eɪliən/, *n.* **1.** one born in or belonging to another country who has not acquired citizenship by naturalisation and is not entitled to the privileges of a citizen. **2.** a foreigner. **3.** one who has been estranged or excluded; an outsider. *–adj.* **4.** residing under another government or in another country than that of one's birth, and not having rights of citizenship in such a place of residence. **5.** belonging or pertaining to aliens: *alien property.* **6.** foreign; strange; not belonging to one: *alien speech.* **7.** opposed; incompatible; repugnant (fol. by *to*): *ideas alien to our way of thinking.* [ME, from L *aliēnus* belonging to another]

**alienable** /'eɪliənəbəl/, *adj. Law.* capable of being sold or transferred. – **alienability** /eɪliənə'bɪləti/, *n.*

**alienage** /'eɪliənɪdʒ/, *n.* the state of being an alien; the legal standing of an alien.

**alienate** /ˈeɪliəneɪt/, *v.t.*, **-nated, -nating.** **1.** to make indifferent or averse; estrange. **2.** to turn away: *to alienate the affections.* **3.** *Law.* to transfer or convey, as title, property, or other right, to another: *to alienate lands.* [L *aliēnātus*, pp., estranged] – **alienator,** *n.*

**alienation** /eɪliənˈeɪʃən/, *n.* **1.** a withdrawal or estrangement, as of feeling or the affections. **2.** *Law.* a transfer of the title to property by one person to another by conveyance or will (as distinguished from *inheritance*). **3.** *Psychol.* mental or psychiatric illness. [ME, from L *aliēnātio* a transferring, also insanity]

**alienee** /eɪliəˈni/, *n. Law.* one to whom property is alienated.

**alienism** /ˈeɪliənɪzəm/, *n.* **1.** alienage. **2.** the study or treatment of mental diseases.

**alienist** /ˈeɪliənəst/, *n. Obs.* a psychiatrist or other specialist in mental diseases. [F *aliéniste*, from L *aliēnus* insane + *-iste* -IST]

**alienor** /ˈeɪliənə, ˌeɪliəˈnɔ/, *n. Law.* one who transfers property.

**aliform** /ˈeɪləfɔm/, *adj.* wing-shaped; winglike; alar. [L *āla* wing + -I- + -FORM]

**alight**[1] /əˈlaɪt/, *v.i.*, **alighted** or **alit** /əˈlɪt/, **alighting.** **1.** to get down from a horse or out of a vehicle; dismount. **2.** to settle or stay after descending: *a bird alights on a tree.* **3.** (of aircraft) to land. **4.** to come accidentally, or without design (fol. by *on* or *upon*). [ME *alighte(n)*, OE *alīhten*, from A-[1] + *līhtan* LIGHT[3], v.]

**alight**[2] /əˈlaɪt/, *adv.*, *adj.* provided with light; lighted up; burning. [ME; orig. pp. of *alight*, *v.*, light up, but now regarded as from A-[1] + LIGHT[1], n. Cf. AFIRE]

**align** /əˈlaɪn/, *v.t.* **1.** to adjust to a line; lay out or regulate by line; form in line. **2.** to bring into line. **3.** *Politics.* to bring into line with a particular tradition, policy, group or power. *–v.i.* **4.** to fall or come into line; be in line. **5.** to join with others in a cause. Also, **aline.** [F *aligner*, from *à* A-[5] + *ligner* (from L *līneāre* line)] – **aligner,** *n.*

**alignment** /əˈlaɪnmənt/, *n.* **1.** an adjustment to a line; arrangement in a line. **2.** the line or lines formed. **3.** a taking of sides; joining a group, party or cause. **4.** the cause, group, or attitude so supported. **5.** →**building line.** **6.** a ground plan of a railway or road. **7.** *Archaeol.* a line or an arrangement of parallel or converging lines of upright stones (menhirs). Also, **alinement.**

**alike** /əˈlaɪk/, *adv.* **1.** in the same manner, form, or degree; in common; equally: *known to treat all customers alike.* *–adj.* **2.** having resemblance or similarity; having or exhibiting no marked or essential difference (used regularly of a plural substantive or idea, and only in the predicate): *he thinks all politicians are alike.* [ME, from Scand.; cf. Icel. *ālīka* similar]

**aliment** /ˈæləmənt/, *n.*; /ˈæləmɛnt/, *v.* *–n.* **1.** that which nourishes; nutriment; food. **2.** that which sustains; support. *–v.t.* **3.** to sustain; support. [L *alimentum* food] – **alimental** /æləˈmɛntl/, *adj.* – **alimentally,** *adv.*

**alimentary** /æləˈmɛntri/, *adj.* **1.** concerned with the function of nutrition. **2.** pertaining to food; nutritious. **3.** providing sustenance or maintenance. **4.** *Law.* protective: *an alimentary trust.*

**alimentary canal** /– kəˈnæl/, *n.* the digestive passage in any animal from mouth to anus. Also, **alimentary tract.**

**alimentation** /æləmɛnˈteɪʃən/, *n.* **1.** nourishment; nutrition. **2.** maintenance; support.

**alimentative** /æləˈmɛntətɪv/, *adj.* →**nutritive.**

**alimony** /ˈæləməni/, *n. U.S.* →**maintenance** (def. 4). [L *alimōnia* sustenance]

**A-line** /ˈeɪ-laɪn/, *adj.* **1.** (of a dress, skirt, etc.) slightly flaring so as to resemble somewhat the letter 'A'. *–n.* **2.** a dress, etc., in this style.

**aline** /əˈlaɪn/, *v.t., v.i.*, **alined, alining.** →**align.** – **alinement,** *n.* – **aliner,** *n.*

**aliped** /ˈæləpɛd/, *adj. Zool.* having the toes connected by a winglike membrane, as the bats. [L *ālipēs* having winged feet]

**aliphatic** /æləˈfætɪk/, *adj.* pertaining to or concerned with those organic compounds which are open chains, as the paraffins or olefines. [Gk *áleiphar* oil, fat + -IC]

**aliquant** /ˈæləkwənt, -kwɒnt/, *adj. Maths. Obs.* contained in a number or quantity, but not dividing it evenly: *5 is an aliquant part of 16.* [L *aliquantus* some]

**aliquot** /ˈæləkwɒt/, *adj. Maths. Obs.* forming an exact proper divisor: *5 is an aliquot part of 15.* [L: some, several]

**aliquot scaling** /ˈ– skeɪlɪŋ/, *n.* a method (used by some pianoforte makers) of producing a fuller tone in the upper strings of a piano by adding a set of sympathetic strings sounding an octave higher.

**alit** /əˈlɪt/, *v.* past tense and past participle of **alight**[1].

**aliunde** /æliˈʊndi/, *adj. Law.* from another place or person: *evidence aliunde* is evidence outside the record. [L: from another place]

**alive** /əˈlaɪv/, *adj.* (*rarely used attributively*) **1.** in life or existence; living. **2.** (by way of emphasis) of all living: *the proudest man alive.* **3.** in a state of action; in force or operation; unextinguished: *keep a memory alive.* **4.** full of life; lively: *alive with excitement.* **5.** filled as with living things; swarming; thronged; teeming. **6.** (of electric circuits or equipment) functioning; connected to a power supply; live. **7. alive and kicking,** *Colloq.* very much alive. **8. alive to,** attentive to; awake or sensitive to. [ME; OE *on līfe* in life] – **aliveness,** *n.*

**alizarin** /əˈlɪzərən/, *n.* one of the earliest known dyes, originally obtained from madder but now made from anthraquinone. [F *alizarine*, from *alizari*, from Ar. *al'usāra* the extract]

**Aljawara** /ælˈjawərə/, *n.* →**Alyawarra.**

**alkahest** /ˈælkəhɛst/, *n.* the universal solvent sought by the alchemists. Also, **alcahest.** [NL, probably coined by Paracelsus, a Swiss–German physician and alchemist, 1493?-1541]

**alkalescent** /ælkəˈlɛsənt/, *adj.* tending to become alkaline; slightly alkaline. – **alkalescence, alkalescency,** *n.*

**alkali** /ˈælkəlaɪ/, *n.*, *pl.* **-lis, -lies.** **1.** *Chem.* **a.** any of various bases, the hydroxides of the alkali metals and of ammonium, which neutralise acids to form salts and turn red litmus paper blue. **b.** any of various other more or less active bases, as calcium hydroxide. **c.** *Obsolesc.* any of various other compounds, as the carbonates of sodium and potassium. **2.** *Agric.* a soluble mineral salt, or a mixture of soluble salts, occurring in soils, etc., usu. to the damage of crops. [ME *alkaly*, from MF *alcali*, from Ar. *al qily*, later *al qalī* the saltwort ashes]

**alkalify** /ˈælkələfaɪ/, *v.*, **-fied, -fying.** *–v.t.* **1.** to alkalise. *–v.i.* **2.** to become alkaline. – **alkalifiable** /ˌælkələˈfaɪəbəl/, *adj.*

**alkali metal** /ˌælkəlaɪ ˈmɛtəl/, *n.* a monovalent metal, one of the first group of the periodic system, including potassium, sodium, lithium, rubidium, caesium, and francium, whose hydroxides are alkalis.

**alkalimeter** /ælkəˈlɪmətə/, *n.* an instrument for determining the concentration of alkalis in solution. – **alkalimetry,** *n.*

**alkaline** /ˈælkəlaɪn/, *adj.* of or like an alkali; having the properties of an alkali.

**alkaline earth** /– ˈɜθ/, *n.* the oxide of an alkaline-earth metal.

**alkaline-earth metal** /ˌælkəlaɪn-ɜθ ˈmɛtl/, *n.* a bivalent metal, one of the second group of the periodic system, including calcium, strontium, barium, and radium. Sometimes beryllium and magnesium are also included.

**alkalinity** /ælkəˈlɪnəti/, *n.* **1.** alkaline condition; the quality which constitutes an alkali. **2.** the extent to which a solution is alkaline. See pH.

**alkalise** /ˈælkəlaɪz/, *v.t.*, **-lised, -lising.** to make alkaline; change into an alkali. Also, **alkalize.** [ALKAL(I) + -ISE[1]] – **alkalisation** /ˌælkəlaɪˈzeɪʃən/, *n.*

**alkali soil** /ˌælkəlaɪ ˈsɔɪl/, *n.* any of various soils in poorly drained or arid regions, containing a large amount of soluble mineral salts (chiefly of sodium) which in dry weather appear on the surface as a (usu. white) crust or powder.

**alkaloid** /ˈælkəlɔɪd/, *n.* **1.** one of a class of basic nitrogenous organic compounds occurring in plants, such as nicotine, atropine, morphine, or quinine. *–adj.* **2.** Also, **alkaloidal** /ælkəˈlɔɪdl/. resembling an alkali; alkaline.

**alkalosis** /ælkəˈlousəs/, *n.* excessively alkaline state of the body tissue and blood. [ALKAL(I) + -OSIS]

**alkane** /ˈælkeɪn/, *n.* any member of the methane series.

**alkanet** /ˈælkənɛt/, *n.* **1.** a European boraginaceous plant, *Alkanna tinctoria*, whose root yields a red dye. **2.** the root. **3.** the dye; anchusin. **4.** any of several similar plants, as the bugloss *Anchusa officinalis*, and the puccoon *Lithospermum.*

[ME, from Sp. *alcaneta*, diminutive of *alcana* henna, from Ar. *al ḥennā'*]

**alkaptonuria** /æl,kæptə'njuriə/, *n.* the excretion of intermediates in phenylalanine and tyrosine breakdown, a congenital biochemical disorder, resulting in severe mental retardation.

**alkene** /'ælkin/, *n.* any member of the ethylene series.

**alkie** /'ælki/, *n. Colloq.* a heavy drinker; an alcoholic. Also, **alky.**

**Alkoran** /ælkə'ran/, *n.* →**Koran.**

**alky** /'ælki/, *Colloq.* –*n.* **1.** an alcoholic. –*adj.* **2.** alcoholic. Also, **alkie.**

**alkyd resin** /ælkəd 'rɛzən/, *n.* →**glyptal resin.**

**alkylation** /ælkə'leɪʃən/, *n.* the replacement of a hydrogen atom in a cyclic organic compound by an alkyl group.

**alkyl group** /'ælkəl grup/, *n.* a univalent group or radical derived from an aliphatic hydrocarbon, by removal of a hydrogen atom, having the general formula $C_nH_{2n+1}$. Also, **alkyl radical.** [ALK(ALI) + -YL]

**alkyl halide** /ælkəl 'hælaɪd/, *n.* an organic compound with the type formula RX, where R is a radical derived from a hydrocarbon of the methane series and X is a halogen, as chloromethane, $CH_3Cl$.

**alkyne** /'ælkaɪn/, *n.* any member of the acetylene series. Also, **alkine.**

**all** /ɔl/, *adj.* **1.** the whole of (with reference to quantity, extent, duration, amount, or degree): *all Australia, all the year round.* **2.** the whole number of (with reference to individuals or particulars, taken collectively): *all women.* **3.** a plurality of; many (chiefly with kinds, sorts, manner). **4.** any; any whatever: *beyond all doubt.* **5.** the greatest possible: *with all speed.* –*pron.* **6.** the whole quantity or amount: *to eat all of something.* **7.** the whole number: *all of us.* **8.** everything: *is that all?* –*n.* **9.** a whole; a totality of things or qualities. **10.** one's whole interest, concern, or property: *to give, or lose one's all.* **11.** Some special noun phrases are:

**above all,** before everything else.

**after all, 1.** after everything has been considered; not withstanding. **2.** in spite of all that was done, said, etc.: *he lost the fight after all.*

**all aboard!, 1.** a warning cry to intending passengers used by transport attendants, conductors, etc. **2.** *N.Z.*, a cry given by shearers, when shearing is about to begin.

**all in all, 1.** (taking) everything together. **2.** one's sole and exclusive concern in life: *he is her all in all.*

**all up,** *Colloq.* **1.** at an end; at the point of defeat or failure. **2.** *Horseracing.* a cumulative bet.

**and all,** as well as everything else; moreover.

**and all that,** and so on; et cetera.

**at all, 1.** in any degree: *not bad at all.* **2.** for any reason: *I was surprised at his coming at all.* **3.** in any way: *no offence at all.*

**for all that,** notwithstanding; in spite of.

**for good and all,** forever; finally.

**in all,** all included: *a hundred people in all.*

**once (and) for all,** for the final time.

–*adv.* **12.** wholly; entirely; quite: *all alone.* **13.** only; exclusively: *he spent his income all on pleasure.* **14.** each; apiece: *the score was one all.* **15.** by so much; to that extent (fol. by *the* and a comparative adjective): *rain made conditions all the worse.* **16.** *Archaic and Poetic.* even; just. **17.** Some special adverbial phrases are:

**all cush,** *Colloq.* okay; all right.

**all piss-'n-wind,** *Colloq.* loquacious; insincere.

**all serene,** *Colloq.* okay; all right.

**all Sir Garnet,** *Colloq.* okay; all right. Also, **all cigarnette (segarnio) (sogarnio).** [probably after *Sir Garnet* Wolseley, 1833-1913, British field marshal noted for his probity] [ME; OE *all, eall,* c. G *all*]

**all-** variant of **allo-** before vowels, as in *allonym.*

**alla breve** /ælə 'briv/, *adv.* **1.** an expression denoting a species of time in which every bar contains a breve, or four minims. **2.** a time value of four crotchets to a bar, but taken with the minim as the unit, i.e. twice as fast. [It.]

**Allah** /'ælə/, *n.* the Muslim name of the Supreme Being. [Ar. *Allāh*, contraction of *al ilāh* the God]

**alla marcia** /ælə 'maʃə/, *adv.* (a musical direction) in march style. [It.]

**allanite** /'ælənaɪt/, *n.* a mineral, a silicate of calcium, cerium, aluminium, and iron, chiefly occurring in brown to black masses or prismatic crystals; orthite. [named after Thomas *Allan*, 1777-1833, English mineralogist. See -ITE[1]]

**allantoic** /ælən'toʊɪk/, *adj.* pertaining to the allantois.

**allantoid** /ə'læntɔɪd/, *adj.* **1.** *Zool.* →**allantoic. 2.** *Bot.* sausage-shaped. –*n.* **3.** →**allantois.** – **allantoidal** /ælən'tɔɪdl/, *adj.*

**allantois** /ə'læntɔɪs, ælən'toʊɪs/, *n.* a foetal appendage of mammals, birds, and reptiles, typically developing as an extension of the urinary bladder. [NL, earlier *allantoïdes*, from Gk *allantoeidḗs* sausage-shaped]

**alla prima** /ælə 'primə/, *adj.* (of a painting) completed by a single application of pigments, as distinguished from painting built up in stages by applying successive layers of pigments; direct painting.

**allargando** /ælə'gændoʊ/, *adv.* (a musical direction) progressively slower and often increasing in power. [It.]

**alla tedesca** /ælə tə'dɛskə/, *adv.* (a musical direction) in German style; implies waltz rhythm with changing tempo. [It.]

**alla turca** /ælə 'tɜkə/, *adv.* (a musical direction) in Turkish style; implies a noisy piece with a harmonically repetitive accompaniment. [It.]

**allay** /ə'leɪ/, *v.,* **-layed, -laying.** –*v.t.* **1.** to put at rest; quiet (tumult, fear, suspicion, etc.); appease (wrath). **2.** to mitigate; relieve or alleviate: *to allay pain.* –*v.i.* **3.** to abate. [ME *aleyen*, OE *ālecgan* put down, suppress, from *ā-* A-[3] + *lecgan* lay; spelt *all-* by false identification of prefix *a-* with L *ad-*] – **allayer,** *n.*

**All Blacks** /'ɔl blæks/, *n. pl.* the New Zealand international Rugby Union football team. [from the colour of the team's uniform]

**all-burnt** /ɔl-'bɜnt/, *n.* the stage in the operation of a rocket motor when the supply of fuel has been exhausted and ceases to provide thrust; burnout.

**all clear** /ɔl 'klɪə/, *n.* **1.** a signal, etc., that an air-raid, or other cause for alarm or activity, is over. **2.** *Aus. Rules.* the signal given to the goal umpire by the field umpire that there has been no infringement of rules immediately before an attempt at a goal or a behind, thus leaving the goal umpire free to signal whether a goal or behind has been scored.

**all-day sucker** /,ɔl-deɪ 'sʌkə/, *n.* a large flat round sweet, often on a stick.

**allegation** /ælə'geɪʃən/, *n.* **1.** a mere assertion made without proof. **2.** a statement offered as a plea, an excuse, or a justification. **3.** the act of alleging; affirmation. **4.** an assertion made by a party in a legal proceeding, which he undertakes to prove. [ME, from L *allēgātio*]

**allege** /ə'lɛdʒ/, *v.t.,* **-leged, -leging. 1.** to assert without proof. **2.** to declare before a court, or elsewhere as if upon oath. **3.** to declare with positiveness; affirm; assert. **4.** to plead in support of; urge as a reason or excuse. **5.** *Archaic.* to cite or quote in confirmation. [ME *allegge(n)*, from AF *alegier* (from L *ex-* EX-[1] + *lītigāre* sue), with sense of L *allēgāre* adduce] – **allegeable,** *adj.* – **alleger,** *n.*

**allegedly** /ə'lɛdʒədli/, *adv.* according to allegation.

**allegiance** /ə'lidʒəns/, *n.* **1.** the obligation of a subject or citizen to his sovereign or government; duty owed to a sovereign or state. **2.** observance of obligation; faithfulness to any person or thing. [ME *alegeaunce* (with *a-* of obscure orig.), from OF *ligeance.* See LIEGE]

**allegiant** /ə'lidʒənt/, *adj.* loyal.

**allegorical** /ælə'gɒrɪkəl/, *adj.* consisting of or pertaining to allegory; of the nature of or containing allegory; figurative: *an allegorical poem, meaning, etc.* Also, **allegoric.** – **allegorically,** *adv.*

**allegorise** /'æləgəraɪz/, *v.,* **-rised, -rising.** –*v.t.* **1.** to turn into allegory; narrate in allegory. **2.** to understand in an allegorical sense; interpret allegorically. –*v.i.* **3.** to use allegory. Also, **allegorize.** –**allegorisation,** /,æləgəraɪ'zeɪʃən/, *n.* –**allegorise,** *n.*

**allegorist** /'æləgərəst/, *n.* one who uses or writes allegory.

**allegoristic** /æləgə'rɪstɪk/, *adj.* relating in the form of allegory, interpreting with allegorical meaning.

**allegory** /'æləgəri, -gri/, *n., pl.* **-ries. 1.** figurative treatment of one subject under the guise of another; a presentation of an abstract or spiritual meaning under concrete or material forms. **2.** a symbolic narrative: *the political allegory of Piers Plowman.* **3.** *Obs.* an emblem. [ME *allegorie*, from L *allēgoria*, from Gk]

**allegretto** /ælə'grɛtoʊ/, *adv., n., pl.* **-tos.** *–adv.* **1.** (a musical direction) in rapid tempo; more rapid than andante, but slower than allegro. *–adj.* **2.** fairly fast. *–n.* **3.** a movement, of a graceful character, played in this tempo. [It., diminutive of *allegro* ALLEGRO]

**allegro** /ə'leɪgroʊ/, *adv. n., pl.* **-gros.** *–adv.* **1.** (a musical direction) in rapid tempo. *–adj.* **2.** very fast; brisk. *n.* **3.** a movement played in this tempo. [It., from L *alacer* brisk]

**allele** /ə'lil/, *n.* →**allelomorph.** [Gk *allḗlōn* (gen.) reciprocally] – **allelic** /ə'lilɪk/, *adj.*

**allelomorph** /ə'liləmɔf, ə'lɛlə-/, *n.* one of two or more alternative, hereditary units or genes at identical loci of homologous chromosomes, giving rise to contrasting Mendelian characters. [*allelo-* (combining form of ALLELE) + -MORPH] – **allelomorphic** /əlilə'mɔfɪk/, *adj.* – **allelomorphism** /əlilə'mɔfɪzəm/, *n.*

**alleluia** /ælə'lujə/, *interj.* **1.** praise to the Lord; hallelujah. *–n.* **2.** a song of praise to God. [L, from Gk *allēloúia*, from Heb. *hallēlūyāh* praise ye Jehovah]

**allemande** /'æləmænd, -mɒnd, -mand/, *n.* **1.** either of two dances of German origin. **2.** a piece of music in moderate common measure, usu. starting with a short up-beat, it often follows the prelude in the classical suite. **3.** a figure performed in a quadrille. [F: lit., German]

**allemande sauce** /'– sɔs/, *n.* a savoury white sauce containing eggs and cream.

**all-embracing** /ɔl-əm'breɪsɪŋ/, *adj.* applying to the whole of a group; covering every eventuality.

**allergen** /'ælədʒən/, *n.* any substance which might induce an allergy. [ALLER(GY) + -GEN]

**allergenic** /ælə'dʒɛnɪk/, *adj.* causing allergic sensitisation.

**allergic** /ə'lɜdʒɪk/, *adj.* **1.** of or pertaining to allergy. **2.** affected with allergy.

**allergy** /'ælədʒi/, *n., pl.* **-gies.** **1.** a state of physical hypersensitivity to certain things, as pollens, food, fruits, etc., which are normally harmless. Hay fever, asthma, and hives are common allergies. **2.** the symptoms produced by reaction to an allergen, as oedema and inflammation. **3.** altered or acquired susceptibility produced by a first inoculation or treatment as exhibited in reaction to a subsequent one of the same nature. See **anaphylaxis.** **4.** *Colloq.* a dislike or antipathy: *an allergy to hard work.* [NL *allergia*, from Gk *állos* other + *-ergia* work]

**alleviate** /ə'livieɪt/, *v.t.,* **-ated, -ating.** to make easier to be endured; lessen; mitigate: *to alleviate sorrow, pain, punishment, etc.* [LL *alleviātus*, pp.] – **alleviator,** *n.*

**alleviation** /əlivi'eɪʃən/, *n.* **1.** the act of alleviating. **2.** something that alleviates.

**alleviative** /ə'liviətɪv/, *adj.* **1.** serving to alleviate. *–n.* **2.** something that alleviates. – **alleviant,** *n., adj.*

**alleviatory** /ə'livi,eɪtəri, ə'livjətri/, *adj.* →**alleviative.**

**alley**[1] /'æli/, *n., pl.* **alleys.** **1.** a narrow enclosed lane. **2.** a narrow backstreet. **3.** a walk, enclosed with hedges or shrubbery, in a garden. **4.** a long narrow enclosure with a smooth wooden floor for bowling, etc. **5.** a two-up school run on organised lines and under strict control. **6.** *Horse-racing Colloq.* position at the barrier (def. 7), drawn by a horse for a race: *from a wide alley he went to the front.* **7. up one's alley,** in the sphere that one knows or likes best. *–v.i.* **8. alley up,** *Colloq.* to pay up (a debt, etc.). [ME *aley*, from OF *alee* a going, passage, from *aler* go]

**alley**[2] /'æli/, *n., pl.* **alleys.** **1.** a large playing marble. **2. toss in the alley,** *Obs. Colloq.* to die. **3. make one's alley good,** *Colloq.* to curry favour. [diminutive abbrev. of ALABASTER]

**alley**[3] /'æli/, *v.i. Colloq.* to go. [? F *allez*, imperative *aller* to go]

**alley clerk** /'– klak/, *n.* a person who arranges bets for a two-up player.

**alley loafer** /'– loʊfə/, *n.* a moneyless two-up player who is never allowed a seat round a ring.

**alleyway** /'æliweɪ/, *n.* **1.** a narrow passageway between buildings. **2.** an alley (def. 1).

**all-fired** /'ɔlfaɪəd/, *adj. U.S. Colloq.* **1.** extreme; excessive.

**all-fives** /ɔl-'faɪvz/, *n.* a variety of the game of dominoes.

**alliaceous** /æli'eɪʃəs/, *adj.* **1.** *Bot.* belonging to the genus *Allium,* which includes the garlic, onion, leek, etc. **2.** having the smell or taste of garlic, onion, etc.

**alliance** /ə'laɪəns/, *n.* **1.** the state of being allied or connected; relation between parties allied or connected. **2.** marriage, or the relation or union brought about between families through marriage. **3.** formal agreement by two or more nations to cooperate for specific purposes. **4.** any joining of efforts or interests by persons, families, states, or organisations: *an alliance between church and state.* **5.** the persons or parties allied. **6.** relationship in qualities; affinity: *the alliance between logic and metaphysics.* **7.** *Bot.* a subclass; a group of related families of plants. [ME *aliaunce*, from OF *aliance.* See ALLY]

**allied** /'ælaɪd/, *adj.* **1.** joined by treaty. **2.** related: *allied species.* **3.** (*cap.*) pertaining to the Allies.

**allied angles** /'– æŋgəlz/, *n. pl. Maths.* a pair of angles formed by the intersection of two parallel lines with a transversal, such that both angles lie on the same side of the transversal and are between the parallel lines; co-interior angles.

**allies** /'ælaɪz/, *n.pl.* **1.** plural of **ally.** **2.** (*cap.*) those countries which fought against Germany and the countries aligned with her in the two World Wars.

**alligator** /'æləgeɪtə/, *n.* **1.** the broad-snouted representative of the crocodile group found in the south-eastern U.S. **2.** a name used erroneously for crocodiles and gavials found in other parts of the world, as the Australian sea-going crocodile *Crocodilus porosus.* **3.** *Metall.* a machine for bringing the balls of iron from a puddling furnace into compact form so that they can be handled. [Sp. *el lagarto* the lizard, from L *lacertus* lizard]

**alligator pear** /'– pɛə/, *n.* →**avocado** (def. 1).

**all-important** /ɔl-ɪm'pɔtnt/, *adj.* essential; important above all things.

**all in** /ɔl 'ɪn/, *adj. Colloq.* exhausted.

**all-in** /'ɔl-ɪn/, *adj.* **1.** with extras included; inclusive: *at the all-in rate.* **2.** without restrictions: *all-in wrestling.*

**all-in bet** /- 'bɛt/, *n.* a bet in which the backer loses his money if the contestant in a race fails to win, whatever the reason, as failure to start.

**all-inclusive** /ɔl-ɪn'klusɪv/, *adj.* covering everything necessary: *an all-inclusive price.*

**all-in-one** /,ɔl-ɪn-'wʌn/, *n.* →**jumpsuit** (def. 2).

**alliterate** /ə'lɪtəreɪt/, *v.,* **-rated, -rating.** *–v.i.* **1.** to show alliteration (*with*): *the 'h' in 'harp' does not alliterate with the 'h' in 'honoured'.* **2.** to use alliteration: *Swinburne often alliterates.* *–v.t.* **3.** to compose or arrange with alliteration: *he alliterates the 'w's' in that line.*

**alliteration** /əlɪtə'reɪʃən/, *n.* **1.** the commencement of two or more stressed syllables of a word group: **a.** with the same consonant sound or sound group (**consonantal alliteration**), as in *from stem to stern.* **b.** with a vowel sound which may differ from syllable to syllable (**vocalic alliteration**), as in *each to all.* **2.** the commencement of two or more words of a word group with the same letter, as in *apt alliteration's artful aid.* [AL- + stem of L *lītera* letter + -ATION]

**alliterative** /ə'lɪtərətɪv/, *adj.* pertaining to or characterised by alliteration: *alliterative verse.* – **alliteratively,** *adv.* – **alliterativeness,** *n.*

**allium** /'æliəm/, *n.* a flower or plant of the amaryllidaceous genus *Allium,* comprising bulbous plants with a peculiar pungent smell, including the onion, leek, shallot, garlic, and chive. [L: garlic]

**all-night** /'ɔl-naɪt/, *adj.* **1.** in operation throughout the night; open all night. **2.** continuing all night. – **all-nighter,** *n.*

**all-night chemist** /– 'kɛməst/, *n.* a chemist shop which stays open all or part of the night, after normal closing time.

**allo-,** a word element indicating difference, alternation, or divergence, as in *allonym, allomerism.* Also, **all-.** [Gk, combining form of *állos* other]

**allocate** /'æləkeɪt/, *v.t.,* **-cated, -cating.** **1.** to set apart for a particular purpose; assign or allot: *to allocate shares.* **2.** to fix the place of; locate. [ML *allocātus*, pp. of *allocāre*, from

L *al-* AL- + *locāre* place]

**allocation** /ælə'keɪʃən/, *n.* **1.** the act of allocating; apportionment. **2.** the share or proportion allocated. **3.** *Accounting.* a system of dividing expenses and incomes among the various branches, etc., of a business.

**allocution** /ælə'kjuʃən/, *n.* an address, esp. a formal, authoritative one. [L *allocūtio*]

**allodial** /ə'loudiəl/, *adj.* free from the tenurial rights of a feudal overlord. Also, **alodial.** [ML *allōdiālis*]

**allodium** /ə'loudiəm/, *n., pl.* **-dia** /-diə/. land owned absolutely, not subject to any rent, service, or other tenurial right of an overlord. Also, **alodium.** [ML, from OLG *allōd* (from *all* ALL + *ōd* property). See -IUM]

**alloerotism** /ælou'ɛrətɪzəm/, *n.* sexual love in relation to another person (opposed to *autoerotism*). Also, **alloeroticism** /ˌælouə'rɒtəsɪzəm/.

**allogamy** /ə'lɒgəmi/, *n.* →**cross-fertilisation.** – **allogamous,** *adj.*

**allomerism** /ə'lɒmərɪzəm/, *n.* variability in chemical constitution without change in crystalline form. [ALLO- + Gk *méros* part + -ISM] – **allomerous,** *adj.*

**allomorph** /'æləmɔf/, *n.* one of several speech forms representing the same morpheme, as in the plural ending in cats /-s/, dogs /-z/, and boxes /-əz/.

**allomorphism** /ælə'mɔfɪzəm/, *n.* variability in crystalline form without change in chemical constitution; a form of allotropy. – **allomorphous,** *adj.*

**allonge** /ə'lɒndʒ/, *n.* a slip of paper attached to a bill of exchange to take further endorsements. [F: lengthening]

**allonym** /'ælənɪm/, *n.* the name of someone else assumed by the author of a work. [ALL(O)- + Gk *ónyma* name]

**allopath** /'æləpæθ/, *n.* one who practises or favours allopathy. Also, **allopathist** /ə'lɒpəθəst/.

**allopathy** /ə'lɒpəθi/, *n.* the method of treating disease by the use of agents producing effects different from those of the disease treated (opposed to *homeopathy*). – **allopathic** /ælə'pæθɪk/, *adj.* – **allopathically** /ælə'pæθɪkli/, *adv.*

**allophane** /'æləfeɪn/, *n.* a mineral, an amorphous hydrous silicate of aluminium, occurring in blue, green, or yellow masses, resinous to earthy. [Gk *allophanés* appearing otherwise (with reference to its change of appearance under the blowpipe)]

**allophone** /'æləfoun/, *n.* one of several phones belonging to the same phoneme.

**alloplasm** /'æləplæzəm/, *n.* that part of protoplasm which is differentiated to perform a special function, as that of the flagellum.

**allopolyploid** /ælə'pɒləplɔɪd/, *adj.* **1.** having more than two haploid sets of chromosomes that are dissimilar and derived from different species. *–n.* **2.** an allopolyploid cell or organism. [ALLO- + POLYPLOID] – **allopolyploidy** /ælə'pɒləˌplɔɪdi/, *n.*

**all-ordinaries index** /ˌɔl-ɔdənəriz 'ɪndɛks/, *n.* a weighted average given by a stock exchange of ordinary share prices of a specified large group of companies expressed in relation to a base period. Also, **all-ords.**

**all-ords** /ɔl-'ɔdz/, *n.* →**all-ordinaries index.**

**allot** /ə'lɒt/, *v.t.*, **-lotted, -lotting. 1.** to divide or distribute as by lot; distribute or parcel out; apportion: *to allot shares.* **2.** to appropriate to a special purpose: *to allot money for a new park.* **3.** to assign as a portion (*to*); set apart; appoint. [MF *aloter*, from *a* to + *loter* divide by lot, from *lot* lot, of Gmc orig.] – **allotter,** *n.*

**allotment** /ə'lɒtmənt/, *n.* **1.** the act of allotting; distribution; apportionment. **2.** a portion, share, or thing allotted. **3.** a block of land: *vacant allotment.* **4.** a small plot of land let out by a public authority to individuals for gardening, esp. vegetable-growing.

**allotrope** /'ælətroup/, *n.* one of two or more existing forms of a chemical element: *charcoal, graphite, and diamond are allotropes of carbon.*

**allotropic** /ælə'trɒpɪk/, *adj.* pertaining to or characterised by allotropy. Also, **allotropical.** – **allotropically,** *adv.* – **allotropicity** /ælətrə'pɪsəti/, *n.*

**allotropy** /ə'lɒtrəpi/, *n.* a property of certain chemical elements, as carbon, sulphur and phosphorus, of existing in two or more distinct forms in the solid, liquid, or gaseous state. Also, **allotropism.** [Gk *allotropía* variety. See ALLO-, -TROPY]

**all' ottava** /æl ə'tavə/, *adv.* a musical direction (8va) placed above or below the stave, to indicate that the passage covered is to be played one octave higher or lower respectively. [It.]

**allottee** /əlɒ'ti/, *n.* one to whom something is allotted.

**all-out** /'ɔl-aʊt/, *adj.* using all one's resources; complete; total: *an all-out effort.*

**all-over** /'ɔl-ouvə/, *adj.* extending or repeated all over, as a decorative pattern on embroidered or lace fabrics.

**all-overish** /ɔl-'ouvərɪʃ/, *adj. Obs. Colloq.* drunk.

**all-over painting** /'ɔl-ouvə ˌpeɪntɪŋ/, *n.* **1.** a method used in action painting whereby the painting surface is covered in a random fashion, with no distinct top or bottom. **2.** a painting which has an overall design of almost identical elements or an almost uniform colour field.

**allow** /ə'laʊ/, *v.t.* **1.** to grant permission to or for; permit: *to allow a student to be absent, no smoking allowed.* **2.** to let have; grant or give as one's share or suited to one's needs; assign as one's right: *to allow a person $100 for expenses, to allow someone so much a year.* **3.** to permit involuntarily, by neglect or oversight: *to allow an error to occur.* **4.** to admit; acknowledge; concede: *to allow a claim.* **5.** to take into account; set apart; abate or deduct: *to allow an hour for changing trains.* **6.** *U.S. Dial.* to say or think. **7.** *Archaic.* to approve; sanction. *–v.i.* **8.** to permit; make possible: *to spend more than one's salary allows.* **9. allow for,** to make concession, allowance, or provision for: *to allow for breakage.* [ME *alowe(n)*, from OF *alouer* assign (from LL *allocāre*)]

**allowable** /ə'laʊəbəl/, *adj.* that may be allowed; legitimate; permissible. – **allowableness,** *n.* – **allowably,** *adv.*

**allowance** /ə'laʊəns/, *n., v.,* **-anced, -ancing.** *–n.* **1.** a definite amount or share allotted; a ration. **2.** a definite sum of money allotted or granted to meet expenses or requirements: *an allowance of pocket-money.* **3.** an addition on account of some extenuating or qualifying circumstance. **4.** a deduction: *allowance for breakages.* **5.** *Horseracing.* **a.** a reduction in weight carried by the horse because the rider is an apprentice or eligible rider. **b.** a reduced handicap on a horse to allow for age, sex, money not won: *weight for age with allowances.* **6.** acceptance; admission: *the allowance of a claim.* **7.** sanction; tolerance. **8.** →**tolerance** (def. 6). **9.** *Mach.* a prescribed variation in dimensions. Cf. **tolerance** (def. 5). *–v.t.* **10.** to put upon an allowance. **11.** to limit (supplies, etc.) to a fixed or regular amount.

**allowedly** /ə'laʊədli/, *adv.* admittedly; in a manner that is allowed.

**alloy** /'ælɔɪ/, *n.;* /ə'lɔɪ, 'ælɔɪ/, *v.* *–n.* **1.** a substance composed of two or more metals (or, sometimes, a metal and a nonmetal) which have been intimately mixed by fusion, electrolytic deposition, or the like. **2.** a less costly metal mixed with a more valuable one. **3.** standard; quality; fineness. **4.** admixture, as of good with evil. **5.** a deleterious element. *–v.t.* **6.** to mix (metals) so as to form an alloy. **7.** to reduce a value by an admixture of a less costly metal. **8.** to debase, impair, or reduce by admixture. [F *aloyer*, OF *aleier*, from L *alligāre* combine]

**all-powerful** /ɔl-'paʊəfəl/, *adj.* having or exercising exclusive and unlimited authority; omnipotent.

**all-purpose** /ɔl-'pɜpəs/, *adj.* for every purpose.

**all right** /ɔl 'raɪt/, *adj.* **1.** safe and sound: *are you all right?* **2.** yes; very well; okay. **3.** satisfactory; acceptable: *his work is all right, but I have seen better employees.* *–adv.* **4.** satisfactorily; acceptably; correctly: *he did the job all right.* **5.** without fail; certainly (often ironically): *all right! you'll be sorry.* **6.** *Colloq.* settled, or agreed on by bribery: *the job is all right.* **7. make it (all) right with,** *Colloq.* to bribe.

**all-round** /'ɔl-raund/, *adj.* **1.** able to do many things. **2.** having general use; not too specialised. **3.** *U.S.* extending all about. Also, *U.S.*, **all-around.**

**all-rounder** /ɔl-'raundə/, *n.* **1.** one able to do many things with equal competence (opposed to *specialist*). **2.** *Sport.* **a.** one skilled in all aspects of a game, as a cricketer who bowls, bats, and fields equally well. **b.** one skilled in many sports.

**allseed** /'ɔlsid/, *n.* any of various many-seeded plants, as *Polycarpon tetraphyllum.*

**allspice** /'ɔlspaɪs/, *n.* **1.** the berry of a tropical American myrtaceous tree, *Pimenta dioica.* **2.** a mildly sharp and fragrant spice made from it; pimento.

**all-star** /'ɔl-sta/, *adj.* (of a theatre production or the like) having all or many of the parts played by stars.

**all-time** /'ɔl-taɪm/, *adj.* (greatest) of all time to date; outstanding: *he's an all-time rogue.*

**allude** /ə'lud/, *v.i.*, **-luded, -luding. 1.** to make an allusion, refer casually or indirectly (fol. by *to*): *he often alluded to his poverty.* **2.** to contain a casual or indirect reference (fol. by *to*): *the letter alludes to something now forgotten.* [L *allūdere* play with]

**all-up** /'ɔl-ʌp/, *adj.* **1.** total, inclusive: *the all-up weight is three tonnes.* *–adv.* **2. bet all-up,** to place the winnings of a previous race on one or more later races.

**allure** /ə'luə, ə'ljuə/, *v.*, **-lured, -luring.** *n.* *–v.t.* **1.** to attract by the offer of some real or apparent good; tempt by something flattering or acceptable. **2.** to fascinate; charm. *–n.* **3.** fascination; charm. [ME *alure(n)*, from OF *alurer*, from *a* to + *lurer* LURE] – **allurer,** *n.*

**allurement** /ə'luəmənt, ə'ljuə-/, *n.* **1.** fascination; charm. **2.** the means of alluring. **3.** the act or process of alluring.

**alluring** /ə'luərɪŋ, ə'ljuə-/, *adj.* **1.** tempting; enticing; seductive. **2.** fascinating; charming. – **alluringly,** *adv.* – **alluringness,** *n.*

**allusion** /ə'luʒən/, *n.* **1.** a passing or casual reference; an incidental mention of something, either directly or by implication: *a classical allusion.* **2.** *Obs.* a metaphor. [L *allūsioa* playing with]

**allusive** /ə'lusɪv/, *adj.* **1.** having reference to something not fully expressed or stated; containing, full of, or characterised by allusions. **2.** *Obs.* metaphorical. – **allusively,** *adv.* – **allusiveness,** *n.*

**alluvial** /ə'luviəl/, *adj.* **1.** of or pertaining to alluvium. **2.** of or pertaining to a mine, claim, diggings, etc. on alluvial soil. *–n.* **3.** alluvial soil. **4.** gold-bearing alluvial ground. [L *alluvium* ALLUVIUM + -AL[1]]

**alluvial fan** /– 'fæn/, *n.* a fan-shaped alluvial deposit formed by a stream where its velocity is abruptly decreased, as at the mouth of a ravine or at the foot of a mountain. Also, **alluvial cone.**

**alluvial ground** /– 'graʊnd/, *n.* an area of auriferous soil made up of sediments deposited by streams.

**alluvial miner** /– 'maɪnə/, *n.* one who seeks for alluvial gold.

**alluvion** /ə'luviən/, *n.* **1.** →**alluvium. 2.** *Law.* land gained gradually on a shore or a river bank through the recent action or recession of water, whether from natural or artificial causes. **3.** overflow; flood. [F, from L *alluvio* inundation]

**alluvium** /ə'luviəm/, *n., pl.* **-via** /-viə/, **-viums. 1.** a deposit of sand, mud, etc., formed by flowing water. **2.** the sedimentary matter deposited thus within recent times, esp. in the valleys of large rivers. [L, neut. of *alluvius* alluvial, washed to]

**all-weather** /'ɔl-wɛðə/, *adj.* of or for any or all types of weather.

**ally** /ə'laɪ/, *v.*, **-lied, lying;** /'ælaɪ/, *n., pl.* **-lies.** *–v.t.* **1.** to unite by marriage, treaty, league, or confederacy; connect by formal agreement (fol. by *to* or *with*). **2.** to bind together; connect by some relation, as by resemblance or friendship; associate. *–v.i.* **3.** to enter into an alliance; join or unite. *–n.* **4.** one united or associated with another, esp. by treaty or league; an allied nation, sovereign, etc. **5.** one who helps another or cooperates with him; supporter; associate. [F *allier*, from L *alligāre* bind to; replacing ME *alie(n)*, from OF *alier*]

**allyl alcohol** /ˌæləl 'ælkəhɒl/, *n.* a colourless liquid, $C_3H_5OH$, whose vapour is very irritating to the eyes; propenol.

**allyl group** /'æləl grup/, *n.* a univalent aliphatic radical, $C_3H_5$, with a double bond. [L *all(ium)* garlic + -YL] – **allylic** /ə'lɪlɪk/, *adj.* Also, **allyl radical.**

**allyl resin** /æləl 'rɛzən/, *n.* any of a class of synthetic resins formed by the polymerisation of compounds containing the allyl group.

**allyl sulphide** /æləl 'sʌlfaɪd/, *n.* a colourless or pale yellow liquid with antiseptic properties, $(C_3H_5)_2S$, found in garlic; oil of garlic.

**allylthiourea** /ˌæləlˌθaɪoʊju'riə/, *n. Chem.* →**thiosinamine.**

**alma** /'ælmə/, *n.* an abominable snowman associated with Russian wastelands. [from *Alma-Ala*, capital of Kazakhstan, a constituent republic of the Soviet Union]

**almacantar** /ælmə'kæntə/, *n.* →**almucantar.**

**almagest** /'ælmədʒɛst/, *n.* any of various medieval works on astrology or alchemy. [after an important Gk treatise on astronomy by Ptolemy: ME *almageste*, from OF, from Ar. *al majistī*, from *al* the + Gk *megístē (sýntaxis)* greatest (composition)]

**almah** /'ælmə/, *n.* (in Egypt) a professional dancing or singing girl. Also, **alma, alme, almeh.** [Ar. *'ālima* (fem.) learned]

**alma mater** /ælmə 'meɪtə, 'matə/, *n.* (*sometimes caps*) one's school, college, or university. [L: fostering mother]

**almanac** /'ɔlmənæk, 'æl-/, *n.* a calendar of the days of the year, in weeks and months, indicating the time of various events or phenomena during the period, as anniversaries, sunrise and sunset, changes of the moon and tides, etc., or giving other pertinent information. Also, **almanack.** [ME *almenak*, from ML *almanac, almanach*, from Sp., ? from Ar. **al manākh*]

**almandine** /'ælməndin, -daɪn/, *n.* a mineral, iron aluminium garnet, $Fe_3Al_2Si_3O_{12}$, used as a gem and abrasive. [ML *almand(īna)* (var. of *alabandīna*, from L *Alabanda*, name of a city in Asia Minor) + -INE[2]]

**alme** /'ælmi/, *n.* →**almah.** Also, **almeh.**

**almery** /'amri/, *n.* →**ambry.**

**almighty** /ɔl'maɪti/, *adj.* **1.** possessing all power; omnipotent: *God Almighty.* **2.** having great might; overpowering: *the almighty power of the press.* **3.** *Colloq.* great; extreme: *he's in an almighty fix.* *–adv.* **4.** (an intensifier); very: *too almighty clever.* *–n.* **5. the Almighty,** God. [ME; OE *ælmihtig, ealmihtig* all mighty] – **almightily,** *adv.* – **almightiness,** *n.*

**almond** /'amənd/, *n.* **1.** the stone (nut) or kernel (sweet or bitter) of the fruit of the almond tree, *Prunus dulcis*, which grows in warm temperate regions. **2.** the tree itself. **3.** a flavour or flavouring of or like almonds. **4.** a delicate pale tan colour. **5.** →**almond green. 6.** anything shaped like an almond. [ME *almonde*, from OF *almande, alemandle*, from L *amygdala*, from Gk *amygdálē*] – **almond-like,** *adj.*

**almond-eyed** /'amənd-aɪd/, *adj.* having eyes with a long or narrow oval shape.

**almond green** /amənd 'grin/, *adj.* the pale clear green colour of the fruit of the almond.

**almond oil** /'– ɔɪl/, *n.* **1.** a colourless, fatty oil expressed from almonds and used in cosmetics, as a lubricant, etc. **2.** Also, **bitter almond oil,** an oil extracted from bitter almonds whose chief constituent is benzaldehyde, used in medicine, for flavouring, etc. **3.** any of various nut oils similar to bitter almond oil. **4.** →**benzaldehyde.**

**almonds** /'aməndz/, *n. Colloq.* socks [rhyming slang, *almond rocks* socks]

**almoner** /'amənə/, *n.* **1.** a social worker with some medical training attached to a hospital. **2.** *Hist.* a dispenser of alms or charity, esp. for a religious house, a princely household, etc. [ME *aumoner*, from OF, from LL *eleēmosynārius* of alms, from LL *eleēmosyna* ALMS]

**almonry** /'amənri/, *n., pl.* **-ries.** the place where an almoner resides, or where alms are distributed.

**almost** /'ɔlmoʊst/, *adv.* very nearly; all but. [ME; OE *eal māst*, var. of *æl mæst* nearly]

**alms** /amz/, *n. sing. or pl.* that which is given to the poor or needy; anything given as charity. [ME *almes*, OE *ælmysse*, from LL *eleēmosyna*, from Gk *eleēmosýnē* compassion, alms]

**almsgiving** /'amzgɪvɪŋ/, *n.* the act or practice of giving alms. – **almsgiver,** *n.*

**almshouse** /'amzhaʊs/, *n.* a house endowed to give free or cheap accommodation to the poor.

**almsman** /'amzmən/, *n., pl.* **-men;** *fem.* **-woman,** *pl.* **-women.** one who lives on alms.

**almucantar** /ælmjə'kæntə/, *n.* **1.** a circle of altitude, parallel to the horizontal plane. **2.** an instrument for measuring altitudes and azimuths. Also, **almacantar.**

**alodium** /ə'loʊdiəm/, *n., pl.* **-dia** /diə/. →**allodium.** – **alodial,** *adj.*

**aloe** /'æloʊ/, *n., pl.* **-oes. 1.** any plant of the liliaceous genus *Aloe*, chiefly African, various species of which yield a drug **(aloes)** and a fibre. **2.** (*oft. pl. construed as sing.*) a bitter purgative drug, the inspissated juice of the leaves of several species of *Aloe.* **3.** American aloe; the century plant. **4.** (*pl. construed as sing.*) a fragrant resin of wood from the heart of an East Indian tree, the eaglewood. [ME (usu. pl.) *aloen*, OE *aluwan*, from L *aloē*, from Gk] – **aloetic** /æloʊ'ɛtɪk/, *adj.*

**aloft** /ə'lɒft/, *adv., adj.* **1.** high up; in or into the air; above the ground. **2.** *Naut.* at or towards the masthead; in the upper rigging. [ME, from Scand.; cf. Icel. *á lopti* in the air]

**alogia** /ə'loʊgiə/, *n.* →**aphasia.**

**alogical** /eɪ'lɒdʒɪkəl, ə-/, *adj.* outside the domain or operation of logic. [A-[6] + LOGICAL] – **alogically,** *adv.*

**aloha** /ə'loʊha, ə'loʊə/, *interj.* a Hawaiian greeting used at meeting and parting.

**aloin** /'æloʊən/, *n.* an intensely bitter, crystalline, purgative substance obtained from aloes.

**alomancy** /'æləmænsi/, *n.* divination by means of salt.

**alone** /ə'loʊn/, *adj.* (*used in the pred. or following the noun*). **1.** apart from another or others: *to be alone.* **2.** to the exclusion of all others or all else: *man shall not live by bread alone.* **3. leave alone, a.** to allow (someone) to be by himself. **b.** *Colloq.* to refrain from bothering or interfering with. **4. let alone, a.** not to mention. **b.** to refrain from bothering or interfering with. **5.** *Obs.* unique. *–adv.* **6.** solitarily. **7.** only; merely. **8. stand alone,** to be unique by virtue of one's talents, ability, etc. [ME *al one* ALL (wholly) ONE] – **aloneness,** *n.*

**along**[1] /ə'lɒŋ/, *prep.* **1.** implying motion or direction through or by the length of; from one end to the other of: *to walk along a road.* **2.** by the length of; parallel to or in a line with the length of: *a row of poppies along the path.* *–adv.* **3.** in a line, or with a progressive motion; onwards. **4.** by the length; lengthways. **5.** in company; together (fol. by *with*): *I'll go along with you.* **6.** as a companion; with one: *he took his sister along.* **7. all along, a.** all the time. **b.** throughout; continously. **c.** from end to end. **d.** at full length. **8. be along,** *Colloq.* to come to a place: *he will soon be along.* **9. get along,** *Colloq.* **a.** to go; depart. **b.** to be on amicable terms. **c.** manage successfully; cope. **10. get along with you,** (an exclamation of dismissal or disbelief). **11. go along with,** agree with. [ME; OE *andlang*]

**along**[2] /ə'lɒŋ/, *adv.* (generally considered to be bad usage) owing to; on account of (fol. by *of*). [ME; OE *gelang*]

**alongshore** /əlɒŋ'ʃɔ/, *adv.* by or along the shore or coast.

**alongside** /əlɒŋ'saɪd/, *adv.* **1.** along or by the side; at or to the side of anything: *we brought the boat alongside.* *–prep.* **2.** beside; by the side of.

**aloof** /ə'luf/, *adv.* **1.** at a distance, but within view; withdrawn: *to stand aloof.* *–adj.* **2.** reserved; unsympathetic; disinterested. [A-[1] + *loof* LUFF, windward] – **aloofly,** *adv.* – **aloofness,** *n.*

**alopecia** /ælə'pifiə/, *n.* **1.** loss of hair; baldness. **2. alopecia areata** /– ɛəri'atə/, a condition in which patches of hair fall out. [L, from Gk *alōpekía* mange of foxes]

**aloud** /ə'laʊd/, *adv.* **1.** with the natural tone of the voice as distinguished from in a whisper or silently: *to read aloud.* **2.** with a loud voice; loudly: *to cry aloud.*

**alp** /ælp/, *n.* **1.** a high mountain. **2.** (*pl.*) a high mountain system, usu. with snowy peaks, as the Australian Alps, the Swiss Alps, etc. [L *Alpēs*, pl., the Alps, the mountain system of southern Europe,? from Celtic]

alpaca

**A.L.P.** /eɪ ɛl 'pi/, Australian Labor Party. Also, **ALP.**

**alpaca** /æl'pækə/, *n.* **1.** a domesticated sheeplike South American ruminant of the genus *Lama* allied to the llama and the guanaco, having long, soft, silky hair or wool. **2.** the hair. **3.** a fabric made of it. **4.** a glossy, wiry, commonly black woollen fabric with cotton warp. **5.** a rayon and alpaca crepe, with a viscose and acetate rayon warp. [Sp., from *paco*, Peruvian animal name (to which the Ar. article, *al*, has been prefixed)]

**alpenglow** /'ælpənglou/, *n.* a reddish glow often seen on the summits of snow covered mountains before sunrise and after sunset. [translation of G *Alpenglühen*]

**alpenhorn** /'ælpənhɔn/, *n.* a long, powerful horn of wood or bark used in the Alps, as by cowherds. Also, **alphorn.** [G]

alpenhorn

**alpenstock** /'ælpənstɒk/, *n.* a strong staff pointed with iron, used by mountain climbers. [G]

**alpha** /'ælfə/, *n.* **1.** the first letter in the Greek alphabet (Α, α), correspondinding to A. **2.** the first; beginning. **3.** the highest mark in an examination. **4.** *Astron.* a star, usu. the brightest of a constellation. **5.** *Chem.* (of a compound) one of the possible positions of substituted atoms or groups.

**alpha-amino acid** /ælfə-əˌminoʊ 'æsəd/, *n.* See **amino acid.**

**alpha-amylase** /ˌælfə-'æməleɪz/, *n.* See **amylase.**

**alpha and omega,** *n.* beginning and end.

**alphabet** /'ælfəbɛt/, *n.* **1.** the letters of a language in their customary order. **2.** any system of characters or signs for representing sounds or ideas. **3.** first elements; simplest rudiments: *the alphabet of radio.* [L *alphabētum*, from Gk *alphábētos*, from *álpha* A + *bêta* B]

**alphabetical** /ælfə'bɛtɪkəl/, *adj.* **1.** in the order of the alphabet: *alphabetical arrangement.* **2.** pertaining to an alphabet; expressed by an alphabet: *alphabetical writing.* Also, **alphabetic.** – **alphabetically,** *adv.*

**alphabetise** /'ælfəbətaɪz/, *v.t.,* **-tised, -tising. 1.** to arrange in order of the alphabet: *to alphabetise a list of names.* **2.** to express by an alphabet. Also, **alphabetize.** – **alphabetisation** /ˌælfəbətaɪ'zeɪʃən/, *n.* – **alphabetiser,** *n.*

**alpha decay** /ælfə də'keɪ/, *n.* a radioactive disintegration in which alpha particles are emitted.

**alpha-eucaine** /ælfə-'jukeɪn/, *n.* →**eucaine** (def. 1).

**alpha-helix** /ælfə-'hilɪks/, *n.* a stabilising structure found in proteins, formed by hydrogen bonding between different peptide bonds within the protein.

**alpha iron** /'ælfər aɪən/, *n.* a form of iron which, when pure, exists up to approximately 900°C; consisting of body-centred cubic crystals.

**alpha-keto acid** /ælfə-kitoʊ 'æsəd/, *n.* See **keto acid.**

**alpha-ketoglutaric acid** /ælfə-ˌkitoʊgluˌtærɪk 'æsəd/, *n.* a dibasic acid, $HOOCCH_2 \cdot CH_2 \cdot COCOOH$, formed from glutamic acid, and one of the intermediates in the citric acid cycle.

**alphanumeric** /ˌælfənju'mɛrɪk/, *adj.* (of a set of characters) conveying information by using both letters and numbers. Also, **alphanumerical.** [b. ALPHA(BET) + NUMERIC(AL)] – **alphanumerically,** *adv.*

**alpha particle** /ælfə 'patɪkəl/, *n.* a positively charged particle composed of two protons and two neutrons (and therefore equivalent to the nucleus of a helium atom) and spontaneously emitted by some radioactive substances.

**alpha radiation** /ˌælfə reɪdi'eɪʃən/, *n.* radiation consisting of streams of alpha particles; alpha rays.

**alpha ray** /'ælfə reɪ/, *n.* a stream of alpha particles.

**alpha wave** /'– weɪv/, *n.* a periodic variation in the electrical potential of the normal cerebral cortex with a frequency about 8 to 12 parts in the resting state. Also, **alpha rhythm.** Cf. **beta wave.**

**alphitomancy** /æl'fɪtəˌmænsi/, *n.* a means of divination using special cakes that are said to have a pleasant taste only for persons with a clear conscience. [Gk *álphiton* barley meal + -MANCY]

**alphorn** /'ælphɔn/, *n.* →**alpenhorn.**

**alphosis** /æl'foʊsəs/, *n.* lack of pigment in the skin, as in albinism. [Gk *alphós* kind of leprosy + -OSIS]

**alpine** /'ælpaɪn/, *adj.* **1.** of or pertaining to any lofty mountain. **2.** very high; elevated. **3.** *Bot.* growing on mountains, above the limit of tree growth. **4.** (*cap.*) *Geol.* of or pertaining to the major mountain-building episode which occurred in Europe and Northern Africa in the Tertiary period. **5.** of or pertaining to rapid downhill skiing, including slalom racing. [L *Alpīnus*, from *Alpēs* the Alps, the mountain system in southern Europe]

**alpinist** /ˈælpənəst/, *n.* a mountain climber. – **alpinism**, *n.*

**already** /ɔlˈrɛdi/, *adv.* **1.** by this (or that) time; previously to or at some specified time. **2.** *U.S.* yet. [ME *al redy* all ready. See ALL, READY]

**alright** /ɔlˈraɪt, ɔˈraɪt/, *adv.* →**all right.**

**Alsatian** /ælˈseɪʃən/, *n.* a highly intelligent wolflike breed of dog much used for police work, or as a guide-dog, etc; German shepherd dog.

**alsike** /ˈælsaɪk, -sɪk, ˈɔl-/, *n.* a European clover, *Trifolium hybridum*, with whitish or pink flowers. Also, **alsike clover.** [named after *Alsike*, in Sweden]

**alsinaceous** /ælsəˈneɪʃəs/, *adj.* **1.** →**caryophyllaceous. 2.** relating to or resembling the chickweed. [Gk *alsín(ē)* + -ACEOUS]

**also** /ˈɔlsoʊ/, *adv.* in addition; too; further. [ME; OE *alswā*, *ealswā* all (wholly or quite) so]

**also-ran** /ˈɔlsoʊ-ˌræn/, *n.* **1.** an unplaced horse in a race. **2.** a nonentity.

**alt** /ælt/, *Music.* –*adj.* **1.** high. –*n.* **2. in alt,** in the first octave above the treble stave. [It. *alto* high]

**alt-**, variant of **alto-** before vowels.

**alt.**, **1.** alternate. **2.** altitude. **3.** alto.

**Altaic** /ælˈteɪɪk/, *n.* **1.** a family of languages consisting of the Turkic, Tungusic, and Mongolian branches or subfamilies. –*adj.* **2.** belonging, or pertaining to these languages.

**altar** /ˈɔltə, ˈɒl-/, *n.* **1.** an elevated place or structure, on which sacrifices are offered or at which religious rites are performed. **2.** (in most Christian churches) the communion table. **3.** *Civ. Eng.* one of the steps in a drydock wall. **4. lead to the altar,** to marry (a woman). [ME *alter*, OE *altar(e)*, from LL. Cf. L *altāria*, pl., high altar]

**altar boy** /ˈ– bɔɪ/, *n.* an altar attendant of minor rank; server; acolyte.

**altarpiece** /ˈɔltəpis, ˈɒl-/, *n.* a work of art or decorative screen behind and above an altar; a reredos.

**altazimuth** /ælˈtæzəməθ/, *n.* a mounting of telescopes or theodolites which provides two axes, one horizontal and one vertical, so that the instrument may be turned in the plane of the horizon and in any vertical plane. Altazimuths are used to determine altitudes and azimuths of heavenly bodies. [ALT(ITUDE) + AZIMUTH]

**alter** /ˈɔltə, ˈɒl-/, *v.t.* **1.** to make different in some particular; modify. **2.** *Colloq.* to castrate or spay. –*v.i.* **3.** to become different in some respect [F *altérer*, from L *alter* other]

**alter.**, alteration.

**alterable** /ˈɔltrəbəl, ˈɒl-/, *adj.* capable of being altered. – **alterability** /ɔltrəˈbɪləti, ɒl-/, **alterableness**, *n.* – **alterably**, *adv.*

**alterant** /ˈɔltərənt, ˈɒl-/, *adj.* **1.** producing alteration. **2.** *Med.* gradually restoring healthy bodily functions. –*n.* **3.** something that causes alteration. **4.** *Med.* an alterant drug or medicine.

**alteration** /ɔltəˈreɪʃən, ɒl-/, *n.* **1.** the act of altering. **2.** the condition of being altered. **3.** a change; modification.

**alterative** /ˈɔltərətɪv, ˈɒl-/, *adj.* **1.** tending to alter. **2.** *Med. Obs.* alterant. –*n.* **3.** *Med. Obs.* an alterant drug or medicine.

**altercate** /ˈɔltəkeɪt, ˈɒl-/, *v.i.*, **-cated, -cating.** to argue with zeal, heat, or anger; wrangle. [L *altercātus*, pp., having wrangled]

**altercation** /ˈɔltəkeɪʃən, ˈɒl-/, *n.* a heated or angry dispute; a noisy wrangle. – **altercative** /ˈɔltəkeɪtɪv, ˈɒl-/, *adj.*

**altered** /ˈɔltəd, ˈɒl-/, *n.* a type of dragster with a short frame, individually constructed with a body put together from separate components of existing standard models of cars.

**altered chord** /– ˈkɔd/, *n. Music.* a chord in which at least one note has been changed from its normal pitch in the key.

**alter ego** /ˌæltər ˈigoʊ, ˈɔl-/, *n.* **1.** a second self. **2.** an inseparable friend. [L: lit., another I]

**alternant** /ɔlˈtɜnənt, ɒl-/, *adj.* alternating. [L *alternans*, ppr.]

**alternate** /ˈɔltəneɪt, ˈɒl-/, *v.*, **-nated, -nating**; /ɔlˈtɜnət, ɒl-/, *adj.*, *n.* –*v.i.* **1.** to follow one another in time or place reciprocally (usu. fol. by *with*): *day and night alternate with each other.* **2.** to change about by turns between points, states, actions, etc.: *he alternates between hope and despair.* **3.** *Elect.* to reverse direction or sign periodically. **4.** *Theat.* to understudy. –*v.t.* **5.** to perform by turns, or one after another. **6.** to interchange successively: *to alternate hot and cold compresses.* –*adj.* **7.** arranged or following each after the other, in succession: *alternate winter and summer.* **8.** every other one of a series: *read only the alternate lines.* **9.** reciprocal. **10.** *Bot.* **a.** (of leaves, etc.) placed singly at different heights on the axis, on each side alternately, or at definite angular distances from one another. **b.** opposite to the intervals between other organs: *petals alternate with sepals.* –*n.* **11.** *U.S.* a person authorised to take the place of and act for another in his absence; substitute. [L *alternātus*, *pp.*] – **alternateness** /ɔlˈtɜnətnəs/, *n.*

alternate leaves

**alternate angles** /– ˈæŋgəlz/, *n. pl. Maths.* a pair of equal angles formed by the intersection of two parallel lines with a transversal, such that one angle lies on each side of the transversal and both lie between the parallel lines.

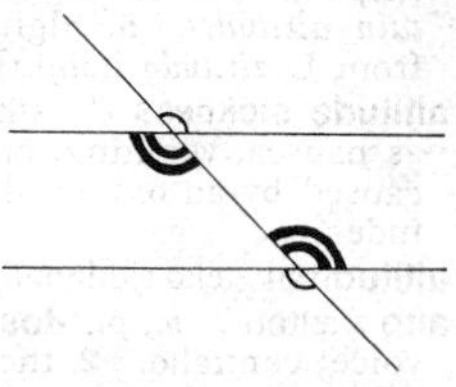
alternate angle: alternate exterior angles shown by single arc; alternate interior angles shown by double arc

**alternately** /ɔlˈtɜnətli, ɒl-/, *adv.* **1.** in alternate order; by turns. **2.** in alternate position.

**alternating current** /ˌɔltəneɪtɪŋ ˈkʌrənt, ˌɒlt-/, *n.* a current that reverses direction in regular cycles. *Abbrev.:* a.c.

**alternation** /ɔltəˈneɪʃən, ɒl-/, *n.* alternate succession; appearance, occurrence, or change by turns.

**alternation of generations**, *n.*, an alternating in a line of reproduction, between generations unlike and generations like a given progenitor, esp. the alternation of asexual with sexual reproduction.

**alternative** /ɔlˈtɜnətɪv, ɒl-/, *n.* **1.** a possibility of one out of two (or, less strictly, more) things: *the alternative of remaining neutral or attacking.* **2.** one of the things thus possible: *they chose the alternative of attacking.* **3.** a remaining course or choice: *we had no alternative but to move.* –*adj.* **4.** affording a choice between two things, or a possibility of one thing out of two. **5.** (of two things) mutually exclusive, so that if one is chosen the other must be rejected: *alternative results of this or that course.* **6.** *Logic.* (of a proposition) asserting two or more alternatives, at least one of which is true. **7.** offering standards and criteria of behaviour of a minority group within and opposed to an established western society: *alternative society, alternative medicine.* See **counter culture.** [ML *alternātīvus*] – **alternatively**, *adv.* – **alternativeness**, *n.*

**alternative technology** /– tɛkˈnɒlədʒi/, *n.* technology which takes into account such matters as conservation of the ecology.

**alternative vote** /– ˈvoʊt/, *n.* the second vote in a preferential voting system.

**alternator** /ˈɔltəneɪtə, ˈɒl-/, *n.* a generator of alternating current.

**althaea** /ælˈθiə/, *n.* **1.** any plant of the genus *Althaea.* **2.** a malvaceous flowering garden shrub, *Hibiscus syriacus.* Also, **althea.** [L, from Gk *althaía* wild mallow]

**althorn** /ˈælthɔn/, *n.* a valved brass instrument, a horn, a fourth or fifth below the ordinary cornet; a tenor saxhorn. Also, **alto horn.**

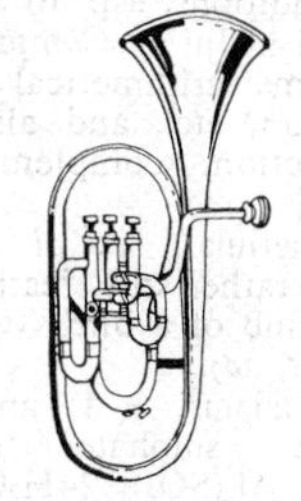
althorn

**although** /ɔlˈðoʊ/, *conj.* even though (practically equivalent to *though*, but often preferred to it in stating fact). Also, **altho'.** [ME, from *al* even + THOUGH. See ALL, adv.]

**alti-**, variant of **alto-**.

**altimeter** /ˈæltəmitə/, *n.* **1.** a sensitive aneroid barometer calibrated and graduated to measure altitudes by the decrease of atmospheric pressure with height, used in aircraft for finding distance above sea-level, terrain, or some other reference point. **2.** any device used for the same purpose which operates by some other means, as by radio waves, etc. [ALTI- + METER[1]] – **altimetry** /æl'tɪmətri/, *n.*

**altissimo** /æl'tɪsɪmoʊ/, *Music.* *–adj.* **1.** very high. *–n.* **2. in altissimo,** in the second octave above the treble stave. [It.]

**altitude** /'æltətʃud/, *n.* **1.** the height above sea-level of any point on the earth's surface or in the atmosphere. **2.** extent or distance upwards. **a.** *Astron.* the angular distance of a star, planet, etc., above the horizon. **b.** *Survey, etc.* the angle of elevation of any point above the horizon. **3.** *Geom.* **a.** the perpendicular distance from the base of a figure to its highest point. **b.** the line through the highest point of a figure perpendicular to the base. **4.** a high point or region: *mountain altitudes.* **5.** high or exalted position, rank, etc. [ME, from L *altitūdo* height]

**altitude sickness** /'– sɪknəs/, *n.* illness with such symptoms as nausea, vomiting, breathlessness, anorexia, and nosebleed, caused by an oxygen deficiency, as encountered at high altitudes.

**altitudinal** /æltə'tjudənəl/, *adj.* relating to height.

**alto** /'æltoʊ/, *n., pl.* **-tos,** *adj.* *–n.* *Music.* **1.** the lowest female voice; contralto. **2.** the highest male voice; countertenor. **3.** a singer with an alto voice. **4.** a musical part for an alto voice. **5.** the viola. **6.** an althorn. *–adj.* **7.** *Music.* of the alto; having the compass of the alto. **8.** high. [It., from L *altus* high]

**alto-,** a word element meaning 'high', as in *altostratus.* Also, **alt-, alti-.** [combining form representing L *altus*]

**alto clef** /'æltoʊ klɛf/, *n.* *Music.* a sign placing middle C on the third line of the stave.

**altocumulus** /ˌæltoʊ'kjumjələs/, *n.* a cloud type consisting of globular masses or patches, more or less in a layer, somewhat darker underneath and larger than cirrocumulus.

**altogether** /ɔltə'gɛðə/, *adv.* **1.** wholly; entirely; completely; quite: *altogether bad.* **2.** in all: *the debt amounted altogether to twenty dollars.* **3.** on the whole: *altogether, I'm glad it's over.* *–n.* **4.** a whole. **5. the altogether,** *Colloq.* the nude. [var. of ME *altogeder,* from *al* ALL, adj. + *togeder* TOGETHER]

**alto horn** /æltoʊ 'hɔn/, *n.* →**althorn.**

**alto-rilievo** /ˌæltoʊ-rə'livoʊ/, *n.,pl.* **-vos.** sculpture in high relief, in which the figures project from the background by at least half their depth (contrasted with *bas-relief*). Also, **alto-relievo.** [It.]

**altostratus** /ˌæltoʊ'stratəs, -'streɪtəs/, *n.* a moderately high, veil-like or sheetlike cloud, without definite configurations, more or less grey or bluish.

**altricial** /æl'trɪʃəl/, *adj.* (of birds) confined to the nesting place for a period after hatching. [NL *altrīciālis,* from L *altrix* nurse]

**altruism** /'æltruˌɪzəm/, *n.* **1.** the principle or practice of seeking the welfare of others (opposed to *egoism*). **2.** self-sacrificing behaviour exhibited by animals. [F *altruisme,* from It. *altrui* of or to others]

**altruist** /'æltruəst/, *n.* a person devoted to the welfare of others (opposed to *egoist*).

**altruistic** /ˌæltru'ɪstɪk/, *adj.* regardful of others; having regard to the well-being or best interests of others (opposed to *egoistic*). – **altruistically,** *adv.*

**alts and adds** /ɔlts ən 'ædz/, *n. pl.* *Bldg. Trades.* alterations and additions, esp. to a house.

**ALU** /ei ɛl 'ju/, *n.* *Computers.* the section of a computer which performs arithmetical processes, as addition, subtraction, negation, etc., and also logical functions, as conjunction, disjunction, complementation, etc. [*A(rithmetic) L(ogic) U(nit)*]

**alula** /'æljulə/, *n., pl.* **-lae** /-li/. the group of three to six small, rather stiff, feathers growing on the first digit, pollex, or thumb of a bird's wing. [NL, diminutive of L *āla* wing] – **alular,** *adj.*

**alum** /'æləm/, *n* **1.** an astringent crystalline substance, a double sulphate of aluminium and potassium, $K_2SO_4 \cdot Al_2(SO_4)_3 \cdot 24H_2O$, or $KAl(SO_4)_2 \cdot 12H_2O$, used in medicine, dyeing, and many technical processes. **2.** one of a class of double sulphates analogous to the potassium alum, having the general formula $R_2SO_4 \cdot X_2(SO_4)_3 \cdot 24H_2O$, or $RX(SO_4)_2 \cdot 12H_2O$, where R is a monovalent alkali metal or ammonium, and X one of a number of trivalent metals. **3.** *Obs.* aluminium sulphate $Al_2(SO_4)_3$. [ME, from OF, from L *alūmen*]

**alumina** /ə'lumənə/, *n.* **1.** *Mineral.* the oxide of aluminium, $Al_2O_3$, occurring widely in nature as corundum (in the ruby and sapphire, emery, etc.). **2.** *Obs.* aluminium. [NL, from L *alūmen* alum]

**aluminate** /ə'lumənеɪt, əl'ju-/, *n.* **1.** *Chem.* a salt or the acid form of aluminium hydroxide. **2.** *Mineral.* a metallic oxide combined with alumina.

**aluminiferous** /əˌlumə'nɪfərəs, əlˌju-/, *adj.* containing or yielding aluminium.

**aluminise** /ə'lumənaɪz, əl'ju-/, *v.t.,* **-nised, -nising.** to treat with aluminium. Also, **aluminize.**

**aluminium** /ˌæljə'mɪniəm/, *n.* **1.** a silver-white metallic element, light in weight, ductile, malleable, and not readily oxidised or tarnished, occurring combined in nature in igneous rocks, shales, clays, and most soils. It is much used in alloys and for lightweight utensils, castings, aeroplane parts, etc. *Symbol:* Al; *at. wt:* 26.9815; *at. no.:* 13; *sp. gr.:* 2.70 at 20°C. *–adj.* **2.** belonging to or containing aluminium. Also, *U.S.,* **aluminum.** [NL, from L *alūmen* alum]

**aluminium foil** /– 'fɔɪl/, *n.* a thin sheet of aluminium used for wrapping food, tobacco, and other domestic articles.

**aluminosilicate** /əˌlumənoʊ'sɪləkət/, *n.* a salt which is both an aluminate and a silicate.

**aluminothermy** /əˌlumənoʊ'θɜmi, -ˌlju-/, *n.* a process of producing high temperatures by causing finely divided aluminium to react with the oxygen from another metallic oxide. Also, **aluminothermics.** [*alumino-* (combining form of ALUMINIUM) + -THERMY]

**aluminous** /ə'lumənəs, -'lju-/, *adj.* of the nature of or containing alum or alumina. [L *alūminōsus*]

**aluminum** /ə'lumənəm/, *n.* *U.S.* →**aluminium.**

**alumna** /ə'lʌmnə/, *n. pl.* *Chiefly U.S.* feminine of **alumnus.**

**alumnus** /ə'lʌmnəs/, *n., pl.* **-ni** /-naɪ/. *Chiefly U.S.* a graduate or former student of a school, college, university, etc. [L: foster child, pupil]

**alumroot** /'æləmrut/, *n.* **1.** any of several plants of the saxifragaceous genus *Heuchera,* with astringent roots, esp. *H. sanguinea.* **2.** the root. Also, **alumstone.**

**alunite** /'æljənaɪt/, *n.* a mineral, a hydrous sulphate of potassium and aluminium, $KAl_3(SO_4)_2(OH)_6$, commonly occurring in fine-grained masses. [F *alun* alum + -ITE[1]]

**Alupent** /'æljupɛnt, 'æljə-/, *n.* a bronchodilator which assists breathing in respiratory diseases without significant effect on the heart rate. [Trademark]

**alveolar** /æl'viələ, ælvi'oʊlə/, *adj.* **1.** *Anat., Zool.* pertaining to an alveolus or to alveoli. **2.** *Phonet.* with the tongue touching or near the alveolar ridge.

**alveolar arch** /– 'atʃ/, *n.* that part of the upper jawbone in which the teeth are set.

**alveolar ridge** /– 'rɪdʒ/, *n.* the ridgelike inward projection of the gums between the hard palate and the upper front teeth; teethridge.

**alveolar theory** /'– θɪəri/, *n.* the theory that protoplasm consists of viscid bubbles or chambers filled with more fluid substances.

**alveolate** /æl'viələt, -ˌleɪt/, *adj.* **1.** having alveoli; deeply pitted, as a honeycomb. **2.** inserted in an alveolus. Also, **alveolated.** – **alveolation** /ælˌviə'leɪʃən/, *n.*

**alveolus** /æl'viələs, ælvi'oʊləs/, *n., pl.* **-li** /-ˌlaɪ/. **1.** a little cavity, pit, or cell, as a cell of a honeycomb. **2.** an air-cell of the lungs, formed by the terminal dilation of tiny air passageways. **3.** one of the terminal secretory units of a racemose gland. **4.** the socket within the jawbone in which the root or roots of a tooth are set. **5.** (*pl.*) alveolar ridge. [L, diminutive of *alveus* a hollow]

**alway** /'ɔlweɪ/, *adv.* *Archaic.* always. [ME; OE *ealneweg,* orig. *ealne weg.* See ALL, WAY]

**always** /'ɔlweɪz, -wəz/, *adv.* **1.** all the time; uninterruptedly. **2.** every time; on every occasion (opposed to *sometimes* or *occasionally*): *he always works on Saturday.* [ME, from ALWAY + adv. gen. suffix *-(e)s*]

**Alyawarra** /æl'jawərə/, *n.* an Australian Aboriginal language, still in tribal use in the Lake Nash area of Central Australia.

Also, **Aljawara.**

**alyssum** /əˈlɪsəm/, *n.* **1.** any of the herbs constituting the cruciferous genus *Alyssum*, characterised by small yellow or white racemose flowers. **2.** →**sweet alyssum.** [NL, from Gk *ályssos* name of a plant, lit., curing (canine) madness]

**am** /æm/, *weak forms* /əm, m/, *v.* 1st person singular present indicative of **be.** [OE *am*, *eam*, var. of *eom*, c. Icel. *em*, Goth. *im*. Cf. Irish *am*, Gk *eimí*]

**a.m.** /eɪ ˈɛm/, **1.** before noon. **2.** the period from 12 midnight to 12 noon. [L *ante merīdiem*]

**AM** /eɪ ˈɛm/, amplitude modulation.

**A.M.** /eɪ ˈɛm/, Member of the Order of Australia.

**A.M.A.** /eɪ ɛm ˈeɪ/, Australian Medical Association. Also, **AMA.**

**amadavat** /æmədəˈvæt/, *n.* a small finchlike Indian bird, *Estrilda amandava*, exported as a cagebird. Also, **avadavat.** [Gujarati; named after *Ahmedabad*, a city in W India]

**amadou** /ˈæmədu/, *n.* a spongy substance prepared from fungi (*Polyporus* [*Fomes*] *fomentarius* and allied species) growing on trees, used as tinder and in surgery. [F]

**amah** /ˈamə, ˈama/, *n.* (used among Europeans in the Far East). **1.** a nurse, esp. a wet nurse. **2.** a maidservant. [Anglo-Indian, from Pg. *ama*]

**amain** /əˈmeɪn/, *adv. Archaic.* **1.** with full force; vigorously; violently. **2.** at full speed. **3.** suddenly; hastily. **4.** exceedingly; greatly. [A-[1] + MAIN[1]]

**amalgam** /əˈmælgəm/, *n.* **1.** a mixture or combination. **2.** an alloy of mercury with another metal or metals. **3.** a rare mineral, an alloy of silver and mercury, occurring as silver-white crystals or grains. [ME, from ML *amalgama*, from L *malagma* poultice, from Gk]

**amalgamate** /əˈmælgəmeɪt/, *v.*, **-mated, -mating.** *–v.t.* **1.** to mix so as to make a combination; blend; unite; combine: *to amalgamate two companies.* **2.** *Metall.* to mix or alloy (a metal) with mercury. *–v.i.* **3.** to combine, unite, or coalesce. **4.** to blend with another metal, as mercury. **– amalgamable,** *adj.* **– amalgamative,** *adj.* **– amalgamator,** *n.*

**amalgamation** /əmælgəˈmeɪʃən/, *n.* **1.** the act of amalgamating. **2.** the resulting state. **3.** *Comm.* a merger of two or more companies. **4.** *Ethnol.* the biological fusion of diverse racial stocks. **5.** *Metall.* the extraction of the precious metals from their ores by treatment with mercury.

**amandine** /ˈamændin, -daɪn/, *adj.* prepared or garnished with almonds: *sauce amandine.* [F *amande* almond]

**amanita** / æməˈnaɪtə, æməˈnitə/, *n.* any fungus of the genus *Amanita*, composed chiefly of poisonous species. [NL, from Gk *amanîtai*, pl., kind of fungi]

**amanuensis** /əmænjuˈɛnsəs/, *n.*, *pl.* **-ses** /-siz/. a person employed to write or type what another dictates or to copy what has been written by another; secretary. [L: secretary, orig. adj., from (*servus*) *ā manū* secretary + *-ensis* belonging to]

**amaranth** /ˈæmərænθ/, *n.* **1.** *Poetic.* a flower that never fades. **2.** any plant of the genus *Amaranthus*, comprising mostly herbs or small shrubs and including species cultivated for their showy flowers, as love-lies-bleeding, or their coloured foliage (green, purple, etc.). **3.** *U.S.* a purplish red azo dye used to colour foods. [var. (by association with Gk *ánthos* flower) of *amarant*, from L *amarantus*, from Gk *amárantos* unfading]

**amaranthaceous** /æmərænˈθeɪʃəs/, *adj.* belonging to the family Amaranthaceae (or Amarantaceae), comprising mostly herbaceous or shrubby plants, as the cockscomb, the amaranth, etc.

**amaranthine** /æməˈrænθaɪn/, *adj.* **1.** of or like the amaranth. **2.** unfading; everlasting. **3.** purplish.

**amarelle** /æməˈrɛl/, *n. U.S.* →**morello.**

**amaryllidaceous** /ˌæmərɪləˈdeɪʃəs/, *adj.* belonging to the Amaryllidaceae family of plants, which includes the amaryllis, narcissus, snowdrop, etc.

**amaryllis** /æməˈrɪləs/, *n.* **1.** a bulbous plant, *Amaryllis belladonna*, the belladonna lily, with large, lily-like, normally rose-coloured flowers. **2.** any of several related plants once referred to the genus *Amaryllis.* [L, from Gk: shepherdess in classical and later pastoral poetry]

**amass** /əˈmæs/, *v.t.* **1.** to gather for oneself; collect as one's own: *to amass a fortune.* **2.** to collect into a mass or pile; bring together. [F *amasser*, from *masse* mass, from L *massa* lump (of dough, etc.)] **– amassable,** *adj.* **– amasser,** *n.* **– amassment,** *n.*

**amateur** /ˈæmətə, ˈæmətʃə/, *n.* **1.** one who cultivates any study or art or other activity for personal pleasure instead of professionally or for gain. **2.** an athlete who has never competed for money. **3.** a superficial or unskilful worker; dabbler. **4.** *Obs.* one who admires. [F, from L *amātor* lover] **– amateurship,** *n.*

**amateurish** /ˈæmətərɪʃ, -tʃərɪʃ/, *adj.* characteristic of an amateur; having the faults or deficiencies of an amateur. **– amateurishly,** *adv.* **– amateurishness,** *n.*

**amateurism** /ˈæmətərɪzəm, -tʃə-/, *n.* the practice or character of an amateur.

**amatol** /ˈæmətɒl/, *n.* an explosive mixture of ammonium nitrate and TNT.

**amatory** /ˈæmətri/, *adj.* pertaining to lovers or lovemaking; expressive of love: *amatory poems, an amatory look.* Also, **amatorial.** [L *amātōrius*]

**amaurosis** /æmɔˈrousəs/, *n.* partial or total loss of sight without obvious disease of the optic nerve or retina. [NL, from Gk, from *amaurós* dim] **– amaurotic** /æmɔˈrɒtɪk/, *adj.*

**amaze** /əˈmeɪz/, *v.*, **amazed, amazing,** *n. –v.t.* **1.** to overwhelm with surprise; astonish greatly. **2.** *Obs.* to bewilder. *–n.* **3.** *Archaic.* amazement. [OE *āmasian* Cf. MAZE] **– amazedly** /əˈmeɪzədli/, *adv.* **– amazedness,** *n.*

**amazement** /əˈmeɪzmənt/, *n.* **1.** overwhelming surprise or astonishment. **2.** *Obs.* stupefaction. **3.** *Obs.* perplexity. **4.** *Obs.* consternation.

**amazing** /əˈmeɪzɪŋ/, *adj.* causing great surprise; wonderful. **– amazingly,** *adv.*

**amazon** /ˈæməzən/, *n.* a tall, powerful aggressive woman. [ME, from L, from Gk, one of a race of female warriors in Gk. legend]

**Amazon ant** /– ˈænt/, *n.* a species of red ant, *Polyergus rufescens*, that steals and enslaves the young of other species.

**amazonian** /æməˈzouniən/, *adj.* characteristic of an amazon; warlike; masculine.

**amazon-stone** /ˈæməzən-stoun/, *n.* a green felspar, a variety of microline, used as an ornamental material. Also, **amazonite** /ˈæməzənaɪt/. [*Amazon* (river) + STONE]

**ambary** /æmˈbari/, *n.* **1.** a plant of India, *Hibiscus cannabinus*, which yields a useful fibre. **2.** the fibre itself. Also **ambari.** [Hind.]

**ambassador** /æmˈbæsədə/, *n.* **1.** a diplomatic agent of the highest rank who represents his or her country's interests in another country. Australian ambassadors may be **resident,** or **non-resident** (i.e., living in a nearby country). British ambassadors may be **ordinary,** or with full powers, **ambassadors plenipotentiary,** or on temporary special service, **ambassadors extraordinary,** equivalent to *U.S.* **ambassadors-at-large. 2.** an authorised messenger or representative. **3.** a person of some personal distinction as a sportsman, actor, etc., who wins goodwill for his or her country in another: *she was a real ambassador for Australia in Sweden.* [ME *ambassadour*, from F *ambassadeur*, from It. *ambasciatore*; probably of Celtic origin] **– ambassadorial** /æmbæsəˈdɔriəl/, *adj.* **– ambassadorship,** *n.*

**ambassadress** /æmˈbæsədrəs/, *n.* **1.** a female ambassador. **2.** an ambassador's wife.

**amber** /ˈæmbə/, *n.* **1.** a pale yellow, sometimes reddish or brownish, fossil resin of vegetable origin, translucent, brittle, and capable of gaining a negative electrical charge by friction. **2.** the yellowish brown colour of resin. **3.** an amber light used as a warning in signalling. *–adj.* **4.** of amber. **5.** resembling amber. **6.** yellowish brown. [ME *ambra*, from ML, from Ar. *ʻanbar* ambergris]

**amber fluid** /– ˈfluəd/, *n. Colloq.* beer. Also, **amber liquid.**

**ambergris** /ˈæmbəgris, -grɪs/, *n.* an opaque, ash-coloured substance, a morbid secretion of the sperm whale, fragrant when heated, usu. found floating on the ocean or cast ashore, used chiefly in perfumery. [late ME *imbergres*, from F *ambre gris* grey amber]

**amberjack** /ˈæmbədʒæk/, *n.* a sportfish, *Seriola purpurascens*, of the Great Barrier Reef, closely related to the yellowtail kingfish.

**amberoid** /'æmbərɔɪd/, *n.* synthetic amber made by compressing pieces of various resins, esp. amber, at a high temperature. Also, **ambroid.**

**amber potch** /æmbə 'pɒtʃ/, *n.* potch containing amber-coloured opal.

**ambi-**, a word element meaning 'both', 'around', 'on both sides', as in *ambidextrous.* [combining form representing L *ambi-* around, or *ambo* both]

**ambidexter** /æmbi'dɛkstə/, *n.* **1.** a person who uses both hands equally well. **2.** *Archaic.* a double-dealer, esp. a deceitful lawyer or juror. *–adj.* **3.** *Archaic.* ambidextrous. [ML, from *ambi-* AMBI- + *dexter* right]

**ambidexterity** /ˌæmbidɛks'tɛrəti/, *n.* **1.** ambidextrous facility. **2.** unusual cleverness. **3.** *Archaic.* duplicity.

**ambidextrous** /æmbi'dɛkstrəs/, *adj.* **1.** able to use both hands equally well. **2.** unusually skilful; facile. **3.** *Archaic.* double-dealing; deceitful. Also, **ambidextral.** – **ambidextrously,** *adv.* – **ambidextrousness,** *n.*

**ambience** /'æmbiəns/, *n.* **1.** environment; surrounding atmosphere. **2.** the mood, character, quality, atmosphere, etc., as of a place or milieu. [F]

**ambient** /'æmbiənt/, *adj.* **1.** completely surrounding: *ambient air.* **2.** circulating. [L *ambiens,* ppr., going around]

**ambient dose** /– 'doʊs/, *n.* in a nuclear explosion, the radiation dose as measured outside shielding material.

**ambiguity** /æmbə'gjuəti/, *n., pl.* **-ties.** **1.** doubtfulness or uncertainty of meaning: *to speak without ambiguity.* **2.** an equivocal or ambiguous word or expression: *the law is free of ambiguities.* [ME *ambiguite,* from L *ambiguitas*]

**ambiguous** /æm'bɪgjuəs/, *adj.* **1.** open to various interpretations; having a double meaning; equivocal: *an ambiguous answer.* **2.** of doubtful or uncertain nature; difficult to comprehend, distinguish, or classify: *a rock of ambiguous character.* **3.** lacking clearness or definiteness; obscure; indistinct. [L *ambiguus* doubtful] – **ambiguously,** *adv.* – **ambiguousness,** *n.*

**ambiplasma** /æmbi'plæzmə/, *n.* a hypothetical mixture of matter and antimatter in the plasma state.

**ambit** /'æmbət/, *n.* **1.** boundary; limits; sphere. **2.** scope; extent. **3.** circumference. [ME, from L *ambitus* compass]

**ambit claim** /'– kleɪm/, *n.* a claim made by employees to a conciliation and arbitration court which anticipates bargaining and compromise with the employer and is therefore extreme in its demands.

**ambitendency** /æmbi'tɛndənsi/, *n. Psychol.* the co-existence of opposite tendencies.

**ambition** /æm'bɪʃən/, *n.* **1.** an eager desire for distinction, preferment, power, or fame. **2.** the object desired or sought after: *the crown was his ambition.* **3.** desire for work or activity; energy. *–v.t.* **4.** *Obs.* to desire strongly; have as an ambition. [ME, from L *ambitio* striving for honours] – **ambitionless,** *adj.*

**ambitious** /æm'bɪʃəs/, *adj.* **1.** having ambition; eagerly desirous of obtaining power, superiority, or distinction. **2.** showing ambition; aiming high: *an ambitious undertaking.* **3.** intended to be, or appearing to be, superior, distinctive, etc.: *an ambitious style.* **4.** strongly desirous; eager: *ambitious of power.* [ME, from L *ambitiōsus*] – **ambitiously,** *adv.* – **ambitiousness,** *n.*

**ambivalence** /æm'bɪvələns/, *n.* **1.** the coexistence in one person of opposite and conflicting feelings towards the same person or object. **2.** uncertainty or ambiguity, esp. due to inability to make up one's mind. – **ambivalent,** *adj.*

**ambiversion** /æmbi'vɜʒən/, *n.* a state or condition intermediate between extrovert and introvert personality types.

**ambivert** /'æmbivɜt/, *n. Psychol.* one who is intermediate between an introvert and an extrovert.

**amble** /'æmbəl/, *v.,* **-bled, -bling,** *n.* *–v.i.* **1.** to move with the gait of a horse, when it lifts first the two legs on one side and then the two on the other. **2.** to go at an easy pace. *–n.* **3.** an ambling gait. **4.** an easy or gentle pace. [ME, from OF *ambler,* from L *ambulāre* walk] – **ambler,** *n.* – **ambling,** *adv.*

**amblygonite** /æm'blɪgənaɪt/, *n.* a rare mineral, lithium aluminium fluorophosphate, $Li(AlF)PO_4$, an ore of lithium found in pegmatites. [G *Amblygonit,* from Gk *amblygōnios* obtuse-angled + *-it* -ITE[1]]

**amblyopia** /æmbli'oʊpiə/, *n.* dimness of sight, without apparent organic defect. [NL, from Gk] – **amblyopic** /æmbli'ɒpɪk/, *adj.*

**ambo**[1] /'æmboʊ/, *n., pl.* **-bos, -bones** /æm'boʊniz/. (in early Christian churches) one of the two raised desks from which gospels and epistles were read or chanted. [ML, from Gk *ámbōn*]

**ambo**[2] /'æmboʊ/, *n. Colloq.* an ambulanceman.

**amboceptor** /'æmboʊˌsɛptə/, *n.* a substance which develops during infection in the blood and which has affinities for both the bacterial cell or red blood cells and the complement. [L *ambo* both + -CEPTOR]

**amboyna** /æm'bɔɪnə/, *n.* the mottled, curled wood of an East Indian tree, *Pterocarpus indicus,* used in making furniture. Also, **amboina.**

**ambroid** /'æmbrɔɪd/, *n.* →**amberoid.**

**ambrosia** /æm'broʊziə/, *n.* **1.** the food of the gods of classical mythology, imparting immortality. **2.** anything imparting the sense of divinity, as poetic inspiration, music, etc. **3.** something especially delicious to taste or smell. **4.** a mild, originally Swedish, cheese with a tangy flavour and smooth, buttery taste. **5.** fungi cultivated for food by ambrosia beetles. **6.** →**bee-bread.** **7.** any plant of the genus *Ambrosia* comprising the American ragweeds. [L, from Gk: food of the gods, from *ámbrotos* immortal]

**ambrosia beetle** /'– bitl/, *n.* a bark-beetle of the family Scolytidae.

**ambrosiaceous** /æmbroʊzi'eɪʃəs/, *adj.* belonging to the Ambrosiaceae, or ragweed family of plants.

**ambrosial** /æm'broʊziəl/, *adj.* **1.** exceptionally pleasing to taste or smell; especially delicious, fragrant, or sweetsmelling. **2.** worthy of the gods; divine. Also, **ambrosian.** – **ambrosially,** *adv.*

**Ambrosian chant** /æmˌbroʊziən 'tʃænt/, *n.* a mode of singing or chanting introduced by St Ambrose, A.D. 340?-397, in Milan.

**ambry** /'æmbri/, *n., pl.* **-bries.** **1.** a cupboard; dresser. **2.** a storeroom; pantry. **3.** a recess for church vessels. Also, **aumbry, almery.** [ME *almarie,* from L *armārium* closet]

**ambs-ace** /'eɪmz-eɪs, 'æmz-/, *n.* **1.** the double ace, the lowest throw at dice. **2.** bad luck; misfortune. **3.** the smallest amount or distance. Also, **ames-ace.** [ME *ambes as,* from OF, from L *ambās as* double ace]

**ambulacrum** /æmbjə'lækrəm/, *n., pl.* **-cra.** one of the radial areas on the underside of an echinoderm bearing the tubular protrusions by which the creature moves. [ L: walk, avenue] – **ambulacral,** *adj.*

**ambulance** /'æmbjələns/, *n.* a vehicle specially equipped for carrying sick or wounded persons. [F, from (*hôpital*) *ambulant* walking (hospital)]

**ambulanceman** /'æmbjələnsmæn/, *n.* the driver of an ambulance, or other trained officer working with him.

**ambulant** /'æmbjələnt/, *adj.* **1.** moving from place to place; shifting. **2.** *Med.* →**ambulatory** (def. 4). [L *ambulans,* ppr., walking]

**ambulate** /'æmbjəleɪt/, *v.i.,* **-lated, -lating.** to walk or move about, or from place to place. [L *ambulātus,* pp., walked] – **ambulation,** *n.*

**ambulatory** /'æmbjələtri/, *adj., n., pl.* **-ries.** *–adj.* **1.** pertaining to or capable of walking. **2.** adapted for walking, as the limbs of many animals. **3.** moving about; not stationary. **4.** *Med.* not confined to bed: *ambulatory patient.* **5.** *Law.* not fixed; alterable or revocable: *ambulatory will.* *–n.* **6.** *Archit.* a place for walking: **a.** the side aisle surrounding the choir or chancel of a church. **b.** the arcaded walk around a cloister.

**ambury** /'æmbəri, -bri/, *n.* →**anbury.**

**ambuscade** /æmbəs'keɪd/, *n., v.,* **-caded, -cading.** *–n.* **1.** an ambush. *–v.i.* **2.** to lie in ambush. *–v.t.* **3.** to attack from a concealed position. [F *embuscade,* from *embusquer,* It. *imboscata* and OF *embûcher.* See AMBUSH] – **ambuscader,** *U.S., n.*

**ambush** /'æmbʊʃ/, *n.* **1.** the act of lying concealed so as to attack by surprise. **2.** the act of attacking unexpectedly from a concealed position. **3.** a secret or concealed position where men lie in wait to attack unawares. **4.** a person or body of men lying in wait. *–v.t.* **5.** to attack from ambush. [ME *enbusshe*, from OF *embusche*, from *bûche* bush, of Gmc orig.] **– ambusher,** *n.*

**A.M.D.G.,** for the greater glory of God. [L: *a(d) m(ajōrem) D(eī) g(lōriam)*]

**ameba** /əˈmibə/, *n., pl.* **-bas, -bae** /-bi/. *U.S.* →**amoeba.** **– amebic,** *adj.*

**ameer** /əˈmɪə/, *n.* →**amir.**

**ameliorate** /əˈmiliəreɪt, əˈmiljəreɪt/, *v.t., v.i.,* **-rated, -rating.** to make or become better; improve; meliorate. [F *améliorer* + -ATE[1]; modelled on earlier MELIORATE] **– ameliorable,** *adj.* **– ameliorant,** *n.* **– ameliorative,** *adj.* **– ameliorator,** *n.*

**amelioration** /əˌmiliəˈreɪʃən, -jəˈreɪʃən/, *n.* **1.** the act of ameliorating. **2.** the resulting state. **3.** something which is improved; an improvement.

**amen** /eɪˈmɛn, a-/, *interj.* **1.** it is so; so be it (used after a prayer, creed, or other formal statement). *–adv.* **2.** verily; truly. *–n.* **3.** an expression of concurrence or assent. **4.** the last word. *–v.t.* **5.** to say amen to. [OE, from LL, from Gk, from Heb.: certainty, truth]

**amenable** /əˈmɛnəbəl, əˈmin-/, *adj.* **1.** disposed or ready to answer, yield, or submit; submissive; tractable. **2.** liable to be called to account; answerable; legally responsible. **3.** liable or exposed (to charge, claim, etc.): *amenable to criticism.* [F *amener* bring to (from *à* to + *mener* bring, from L *minäre* drive) + -ABLE] **– amenability** /əˌmɛnəˈbɪləti/, **amenableness,** *n.* **– amenably,** *adv.*

**amend** /əˈmɛnd/, *v.t.* **1.** to alter (a motion, bill, constitution, etc.) by due formal procedure. **2.** to change for the better; improve: *to amend one's ways.* **3.** to remove or correct faults in; rectify: *an amended spelling.* *–v.i.* **4.** to grow or become better by reforming oneself. [ME *amende(n)*, from OF *amender*, from L *ēmendāre* correct] **– amendable,** *adj.* **– amender,** *n.*

**amendatory** /əˈmɛndətəri, -tri/, *adj. U.S.* serving to amend; corrective.

**amendment** /əˈmɛndmənt/, *n.* **1.** the act of amending; correction; improvement. **2.** the alteration of a motion, bill, constitution, etc. **3.** a change so made, either by way of correction or addition.

**amends** /əˈmɛndz/, *n. sing. or pl.* **1.** reparation or compensation for a loss, damage, or injury of any kind; recompense: *to make amends.* **2.** *Obs.* recovery of health. [ME *amendes*, from OF, pl. of *amende* reparation]

**amenity** /əˈmɛnəti, əˈmin-/, *n., pl.* **-ties.** **1.** (*pl.*) agreeable features, circumstances, ways, etc. **2.** (*pl.*) features, facilities, or services of a house, estate, district, etc., which make for a comfortable and pleasant life. **3.** the quality of being pleasant or agreeable in situation, prospect, disposition, etc.; pleasantness: *the amenity of the climate.* **4.** (*pl.*) public toilets. [late ME, from L *amoenitas*]

**amenorrhoea** /əmɛnəˈrɪə, eɪ-/, *n.* absence of menstruation. Also, *Chiefly U.S.,* **amenorrhea.** [A-[6] + *meno-* (combining form representing Gk *mēn* month) + -(R)RHOEA]

**Amen snorter** /eɪˈmɛn snɔtə/, *n. Colloq.* a clergyman.

**ament** /əˈmɛnt, ˈeɪmənt/, *n.* a mentally deficient person; one suffering from amentia.

**amentaceous** /æmənˈteɪʃəs/, *adj.* **1.** consisting of a catkin. **2.** bearing catkins.

**amentia** /əˈmɛnʃə, eɪˈmɛnʃə/, *n.* permanent mental deficiency, either congenital or because of deficiencies in developmental processes. Cf. **dementia.** [L: lack of reason]

**amentiferous** /æmənˈtɪfərəs/, *adj.* bearing amenta or catkins.

**amentum** /əˈmɛntəm/, *n., pl.* **-ta.** a spike of unisexual apetalous flowers with scaly bracts, usu. deciduous; a catkin. Also, **ament.** [L: strap, thong]

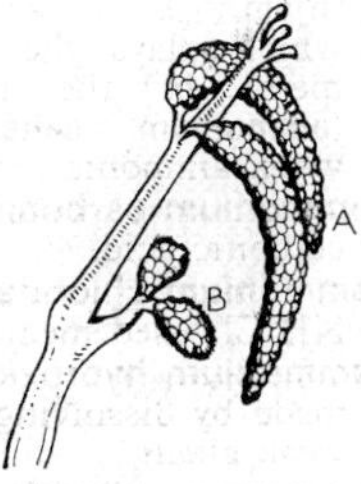

amentum: A, staminate; B, pistillate

**Amer.,** American.

**amerce** /əˈmɜs/, *v.t.,* **amerced, amercing.** **1.** to punish by an arbitrary or discretionary fine, i.e., one not fixed by statute. **2.** to punish by inflicting a discretionary penalty of any kind. [ME *amercy*, from OF phrase (*estre*) *a merci* (to be) at the mercy of] **– amerceable,** *adj.* **– amercement,** *n.* **– amercer,** *n.*

**America** /əˈmɛrɪkə/, *n.* **1.** the United States of America. **2.** North, Central and South America together with the offshore islands. [named after *Amerigo* Vespucci, 1451-1512, Italian merchant and explorer]

**American** /əˈmɛrɪkən/, *adj.* **1.** of or pertaining to the United States of America: *an American citizen.* **2.** of or pertaining to North or South America. **3.** *Ethnol.* denoting or pertaining to the so-called 'red' race, characterised by a reddish or brownish skin, dark eyes, black hair, and prominent cheekbones, and embracing the aborigines of North and South America (sometimes excluding the Eskimos), known as American Indians or Amerindians. *–n.* **4.** a citizen of the United States of America. **5.** a native or an inhabitant of the western hemisphere. **6.** an aborigine of the western hemisphere. **7.** the English language as spoken in the United States.

**Americana** /əmɛrɪˈkanə/, *n.pl.* books, papers, etc., relating to America, esp. to its history and geography. [NL. See -ANA]

**American aloe** /əˌmɛrɪkən ˈæloʊ/, *n.* →**century plant.**

**American buggy** /– ˈbʌgi/, *n.* →**buggy**[1] (def. 2).

**American eagle** /– ˈigəl/, *n.* the bald eagle, esp. as depicted on the coat of arms of the United States of America.

**American football** /– ˈfʊtbɔl/, *n.* a game similar to Rugby football, played by two teams of eleven players, each of which tries to score touchdowns by running or passing the ball to the opponent's goal line, and field goals by kicking the ball over the cross bars of the opponent's goalpost; gridiron.

**American Indian** /– ˈɪndiən/, *n. adj.* →**Amerindian.**

**Americanise** /əˈmɛrɪkənaɪz/, *v.t., v.i.,* **-nised, -nising.** to make or become American in character; assimilate to the customs and institutions of the United States of America. Also, **Americanize.** **– Americanisation** /əˌmɛrɪkənaɪˈzeɪʃən/, *n.*

**Americanism** /əˈmɛrɪkənɪzəm/, *n.* **1.** an English language usage peculiar to the people of the United States of America. **2.** a custom, trait, or thing peculiar to the United States of America or its citizens. **3.** devotion to or preference for the United States of America and its institutions.

**American organ** /əmɛrɪkən ˈɔgən/, *n.* a keyboard instrument similar to the harmonium, but in which the air is sucked through the reeds.

**American sandwich** /– ˈsænwɪtʃ/, *n.* a sandwich with large amounts of filling.

**americium** /æməˈrɪsiəm/, *n.* a radioactive element, one of the products of the bombardment of uranium and plutonium by very energetic helium ions. *Symbol:* Am; *at. no.:* 95. [AMERIC(A) + -IUM]

**Amerindian** /ˌæməˈrɪndiən/, *n.* **1.** Also, **Amerind.** a member of the aboriginal race of America or of any of the aboriginal North and South American stocks, often excepting the Eskimos. **2.** any of the languages of the Amerindians. *–adj.* **3.** denoting, belonging to, or pertaining to the race embracing the aborigines of America. **4.** of or pertaining to any of the Amerindian languages. [b. AMER(ICAN) + INDIAN] **– Amerindic,** *adj.*

**ames-ace** /ˌeɪmz-ˈeɪs, ˌæmz-/, *n.* →**ambs-ace.**

**amethyst** /ˌæməθəst/, *n.* **1.** *Mineral.* a coarsely crystallised purple or violet quartz used in jewellery. **2.** the violet sapphire (**oriental amethyst**). **3.** a purplish tint. [L *amethystus*, from Gk *améthystos* lit., remedy for drunkenness; replacing ME *ametiste*, from OF] **– amethystine** /ˌæməˈθɪstin, -taɪn/, *adj.* **– amethystlike,** *adj.*

**amethystine python** /æməˌθɪstin ˈpaɪθən/, *n.* the largest of Australian pythons, *Liasis amethystinus*, distributed from Queensland to New Guinea; rock python; Schneider python.

**ametropia** /æməˈtroʊpiə/, *n.* an abnormal condition of the eye causing faulty refraction of light rays, as in astigmatism, myopia, etc. [NL, from Gk *ámetros* irregular + *-opia* -OPIA] **– ametropic,** *adj.*

**A.M.F.** /eɪ ɛm ˌɛf/, Australian Military Forces. Also, **AMF.**

**Amharic** /æmˈhærɪk/, *n.* one of the semitic languages of Ethiopia, spoken by the inhabitants of Amhara, a former kingdom in north-western Ethiopia.

**amiable** /ˈeɪmiəbəl/, *adj.* **1.** having or showing agreeable personal qualities, as sweetness of temper, kindheartedness, etc. **2.** friendly; kindly: *an amiable mood.* **3.** *Obs.* lovable, lovely. [ME *amyable*, from OF *amiable*, from L *amīcābilis* friendly] – **amiability** /eɪmiəˈbɪləti/, **amiableness,** *n.* – **amiably,** *adv.*

**amianthus** /æmiˈænθəs/, *n.* a fine variety of asbestos, with delicate, flexible filaments. [var. (with *-th. Cf. amaranth*) of *amiantus*, from L, from Gk *amíantos* (*líthos*) undefiled (stone)]

**amicable** /ˈæmɪkəbəl/, *adj.* characterised by or exhibiting friendliness; friendly; peaceable: *an amicable settlement.* [L *amīcābilis*] – **amicability** /æmɪkəˈbɪləti/, **amicableness,** *n.* – **amicably,** *adv.*

**amice**[1] /ˈæməs/, *n.* an oblong piece of linen worn by the clergy about the neck and shoulders under the alb, or, formerly, on the head. [ME *amyse*, from OF *amis*, from L *amictus* cloak]

**amice**[2] /ˈæməs/, *n.* a furred hood or hooded cape with long ends hanging down in front, formerly worn by the clergy. [late ME *amisse*, from F *aumusse*, from Pr. *almussa*, from Ar. *al* the + G *Mütze* cap]

**amicus curiae** /əˌmikʊs ˈkjurii, -riaɪ/, *n.* a person not a party to the litigation who volunteers or is invited by the court to give advice to the court upon some matter pending before it. [L: friend of the court]

**amid** /əˈmɪd/, *prep.* in the midst of or surrounded by; among; amidst. [ME *amidde*, OE *amiddan*, for *on middan* in the middle. See MID[1]]

**amide** /ˈæmaɪd/, *n. Chem.* **1.** a metallic derivative of ammonia in which the $NH_2$ grouping is retained, as *potassium amide*, $KNH_2$. **2.** an organic compound obtained by replacing the OH group in acids by the $NH_2$ radical. [AM(MONIA) + -IDE] – **amidic** /əˈmɪdɪk/, *adj.*

**amidin** /ˈæmədən/, *n.* the soluble matter of starch. [ML *amidum*, var. of L *amylum* (from Gk *ámylon* fine meal) + -IN[2]]

**amido-** **1.** a prefix denoting the replacement of an OH group by the $NH_2$ radical. **2.** (*sometimes*) →**amino-**. [combining form of AMIDE]

**amidogen** /əˈmidədʒən, əˈmɪd-/, *n.* the $NH_2$ radical. If attached to CO in a compound it is called an **amido group,** without CO, an **amino group.**

**Amidol** /ˈæmədɒl/, *n.* a colourless crystalline phenol derivative, $C_6H_8N_2O \cdot 2HCl$, used as a photographic developer. [Trademark]

**amidships** /əˈmɪdʃɪps/, *adv.* **1.** in or towards the middle of a ship, or the part midway between stem and stern. **2.** lengthways. Also, **amid ship.**

**amidst** /əˈmɪdst/, *prep.* amid. [ME *amiddes*, from *amidde* amid + adv. gen. *-s*; for later *-t*, cf. AGAINST, etc.]

**amigo** /əˈmigoʊ/, *n., pl.* **-gos** /-goʊz, -gɒs/. friend. [Sp]

**amine** /əˈmin, ˈæmin/, *n.* any of a class of compounds prepared from ammonia by replacing one, two, or all hydrogen atoms with organic radicals. [AM(MONIA) + -INE[2]]

**amino-,** a prefix denoting an amino group [combining form of AMINE]

**amino acid** /əˌminoʊ ˈæsəd, ˌæmənoʊ/, *n.* any of a group of organic compounds containing an amino group and a carboxyl group. Up to twenty alpha-amino acids are considered the building blocks from which proteins are formed, while others can be found in some antibiotics.

**amino group** /– ˈgrup/, *n.* the universal basic radical, $NH_2$. Also, **amino radical.**

**aminopeptidase** /əˌminoʊˈpɛptədeɪz/, *n.* a proteolytic enzyme produced in the intestinal mucosa which catalyses the hydrolysis of proteins.

**aminophylline** /əˌminoʊˈfɪlin/, *n.* a mixture of theophylline and ethylene diamine used as a vasodilator and antispasmodic.

**amino resin** /əˌminoʊ ˈrɛzən/, *n.* any of a class of thermosetting resins formed by the interaction of an amine with an aldehyde, used chiefly for coatings for paper and textiles.

**amir** /əˈmɪə/, *n.* **1.** →**emir. 2.** (*cap.*) the former title of the ruler of Afghanistan. **3.** the former title of certain Turkish officials. Also **ameer.** [Ar. *amīr* commander. See EMIR]

**amiss** /əˈmɪs/, *adv.* **1.** out of the proper course or order; in a faulty manner; wrongly: *to speak amiss.* **2. take amiss,** to be offended at; resent. **3. come amiss,** to be unwelcome; be received with ingratitude; be inopportune. *–adj.* **4.** (used only predicatively) wrong; faulty; out of order; improper (sometimes fol. by *with*): *there is something amiss with it.* [ME *amis*, from A-[1] + *mis* wrong. See MISS[1]]

**amitosis** /æməˈtoʊsəs/, *n.* the direct method of cell division characterised by simple cleavage of the nucleus, without the formation of chromosomes. [A-[6] + MITOSIS] – **amitotic** /æməˈtɒtɪk/, *adj.*

**amity** /ˈæməti/, *n., pl.* **-ties.** friendship; harmony; good understanding, esp. between nations. [ME *amytie*, from F *amité* from L *amīcus* friend]

**ammeter** /ˈæmətə/, *n.* an instrument for measuring the strength of electric currents in amperes. [AM(PERE) + -METER[1]]

**ammiaceous** /æmiˈeɪʃəs/, *adj.* →**apiaceous.**

**ammine** /ˈæmin, əˈmin/, *n.* a compound containing one or more ammonia molecules in coordinate linkage. [AMM(ONIA) + -INE[2]]

**ammo** /ˈæmoʊ/, *n. Colloq.* ammunition.

**ammocete** /ˈæməsit/, *n.* the larval stage of a lamprey, used as bait. It resembles the theoretical ancestor of the vertebrates. Also, **ammocoete.** [from NL *ammocoetes* something bedded in sand, from Gk *ámmos* sand + *koítē* bed]

**ammon** /ˈæmən/, *n.* →**argali.**

**ammonal** /ˈæmənəl/, *n.* a high explosive, a mixture of ammonium nitrate and powdered aluminium. [short for *ammon(ium nitrate and) al(uminium)*]

**ammonia** /əˈmoʊniə, -jə/, *n.* **1.** a colourless, pungent, suffocating gas, $NH_3$, a compound of nitrogen and hydrogen, very soluble in water. **2.** Also, **ammonia water** or **aqueous ammonia.** this gas dissolved in water, the common commercial form. [NL; so called as being obtained from *sal ammoniac.* See AMMONIAC]

**ammoniac** /əˈmoʊniæk/, *n.* **1.** →**gum ammoniac.** *–adj.* **2.** ammoniacal. [ME, from L *ammōniacum*, from Gk *ammōniakón*, applied to a salt and a gum said to come from near the shrine of the Egyptian divinity, *Ammon*, in Libya]

**ammoniacal** /æməˈnaɪəkəl/, *adj.* **1.** consisting of, containing, or using ammonia. **2.** like ammonia. Also, **ammoniac.**

**ammoniate** /əˈmoʊnieɪt/, *v.,* **-ated, -ating,** *n.* *–v.t.* **1.** to treat or cause to unite with ammonia. *–n.* **2.** a compound formed with ammonia.

**ammonic** /əˈmoʊnɪk, əˈmɒnɪk/, *adj.* of or pertaining to ammonia or ammonium.

**ammonisation** /ˌæmənaɪˈzeɪʃən/, *n.* the formation of ammonia or its compounds, as in soil, etc., by soil organisms. Also, **ammonization.** [AMMON(IA) + -ISATION]

**ammonise** /ˈæmənaɪz/, *v.,* **-nised, -nising.** *–v.t.* **1.** to convert into ammonia or ammonium compounds. *–v.i.* **2.** to become ammonised; produce ammonisation. Also, **ammonize.**

**ammonite** /ˈæmənaɪt/, *n.* one of the coiled, chambered fossil shells of the extinct cephalopod molluscs, suborder Ammonoidea. [NL *Ammōnītes*, from ML *cornū Ammōnis* horn of Ammon, an Egyptian divinity]

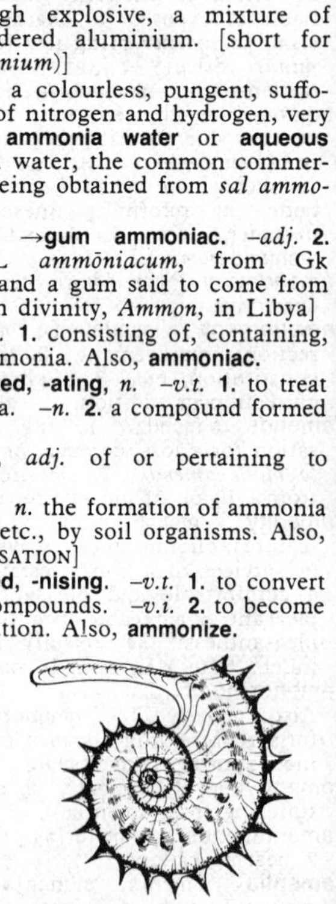

ammonite

**ammonium** /əˈmoʊniəm, -njəm/, *n.* a radical, $NH_4$, which plays the part of a metal in the compounds (**ammonium salts**) formed when ammonia reacts with acids. [AMMON(IA) + -IUM]

**ammonium carbonate** /– ˈkabəneɪt/, *n.* an ammonium salt of carbonic acid.

**ammonium chloride** /– ˈklɔraɪd/, *n.* a white granular powder, $NH_4Cl$, used medicinally and industrially; sal ammoniac.

**ammonium hydroxide** /– haɪˈdrɒksaɪd/, *n.* a basic compound, made by dissolving ammonia in water, used extensively as a weak alkali.

**ammonium nitrate** /– ˈnaɪtreɪt/, *n.* a white, soluble solid, the nitrate of ammonia, $NH_4NO_3$, used in explosives, freezing mixtures, and the preparation of nitrous oxide.

**ammunition** /ˌæmjəˈnɪʃən/, *n.* **1.** all the material used in discharging all types of firearms or any weapon that throws projectiles; powder, shot, shrapnel, bullets, cartridges, and the means of igniting and exploding them, as primers and fuses. Chemicals, bombs, grenades, mines, pyrotechnics are also ammunition. **2.** any material or means used in combat. **3.** *Obs.* military supplies. **4.** *Colloq.* evidence used to support an argument. *–adj.* **5.** supplied from army stores. *–v.t.* **6.** to supply with ammunition. [F (obs.) *amunition* for *munition*, *la munition* being understood as *l'amunition*]

**amnesia** /æm'niʒə, -ziə/, *n.* loss of a large block of interrelated memories. [NL, from Gk: forgetfulness] – **amnesiac** /æm'niziæk/, **amnesic** /æm'nisɪk, -zɪk/, **amnestic** /æm'nɛstɪk/, *adj.*

**amnesty** /'æmnəsti/, *n., pl.* **-ties**, *v.*, **-tied**, **-tying.** *–n.* **1.** a general pardon for offences against a government. **2.** the granting of immunity for past offences against the laws of war. **3.** *Law.* a pardon granted by an act of Parliament originated by the Crown. **4.** *U.S. Law.* protection against punishment granted a witness in order to compel him to testify to incriminating facts. **5.** a forgetting or overlooking of any offence. *–v.t.* **6.** to grant amnesty to; pardon. [L *amnēstia*, from Gk *amnēstía* forgetfulness]

**amniocentesis** /ˌæmnioʊsɛn'tisəs/, *n., pl.* **-ses** /-siz/. removal of some amniotic fluid, esp. to diagnose chromosomal abnormality in a foetus. [AMNIO(N) + *centesis* (from NL, from Gk *kéntēsis* a pricking]

**amnion** /'æmniən/, *n., pl.* **-nia** /-niə/. the innermost of the embryonic or foetal membranes of insects, reptiles, birds, and mammals; the sac containing the amniotic fluid and the embryo. [NL, from Gk] – **amnionic** /ˌæmni'ɒnɪk/, *adj.*

**amniotic** /ˌæmni'ɒtɪk/, *adj.* of or pertaining to the amnion.

**amniotic fluid** /– 'fluəd/, *n.* the watery fluid in the amnion, in which the embryo is suspended.

**amniotic membrane** /– 'mɛmbreɪn/, *n.* →**amnion.**

**amoeba** /ə'mibə/, *n., pl.* **-bae** /-bi/ **-bas.** **1.** a microscopic, one-celled animal consisting of a naked mass of protoplasm constantly changing in shape as it moves and engulfs food. **2.** a protozoan of the genus *Amoeba.* Also, *U.S.*, **ameba.** [NL, from Gk *amoibḗ* change] – **amoeba-like,** *adj.*

**amoebaean** /æmə'biən/, *adj.* alternately responsive, as verses in dialogue. Also, **amoebean.**

**amoebic** /ə'mibɪk/, *adj.* **1.** of, pertaining to, or resembling an amoeba. **2.** characterised by, or due to the presence of, amoebae, as certain diseases. Also, *U.S.*, **amebic.**

**amoebic dysentery** /– 'dɪsəntri/, *n.* a variety of dysentery whose causative agent is a protozoan, *Endamoeba histolytica*, characterised esp. by intestinal ulceration.

**amoebic meningitis** /– mɛnən'dʒaɪtəs/, *n.* meningitis caused by a protozoan, *Endamoeba histolytica*, a very rare complication of an amoebic infection.

**amoeboid** /ə'mibɔɪd/, *adj.* resembling or related to amoebae. Also, *U.S.*, **ameboid.** [AMOEB(A) + -OID]

**amok** /ə'mʌk/, *adv.* →**amuck.**

**amole** /ə'moʊleɪ/, *n.* **1.** the roots of various plants, chiefly of south-western North America, as Mexican species of *Agave*, used as a substitute for soap. **2.** any such plant. [Mex. Sp., from Nahuatl]

**among** /ə'mʌŋ/, *prep.* **1.** in or into the midst of; in association or connection with; surrounded by: *he fell among thieves.* **2.** to each of; by or for distribution to: *divide these among you.* **3.** in the number, class, or group of; of or out of: *that's among the things we must do.* **4.** with or by all or the whole of: *popular among the people.* **5.** by the joint or reciprocal action of: *settle it among yourselves.* **6.** each with the other; mutually: *to quarrel among themselves.* [OE *amang*, for *on (ge)mang* in the crowd, in the midst of]

**amongst** /ə'mʌŋst/, *prep.* among. [ME *amonges*, from AMONG + adv. gen. *-es*; for later *-t* after the gen. *-s*, cf. AGAINST, etc.]

**amontillado** /əmɒntə'ladoʊ/, *n.* a full-bodied, aged flor sherry. [from *Montilla*, a village in Spain]

**amoral** /eɪ'mɒrəl, æ-/, *adj.* without moral quality; neither moral nor immoral. [A-[6] + MORAL] – **amorality** /eɪmə'ræləti, æm-/, *n.* – **amorally,** *adv.*

**amoretto** /æmə'rɛtoʊ/, *n., pl.* **-retti** /-'rɛti/. a little cupid. Also, **amorino** /æmə'rinoʊ/. [It., diminutive of *amore*, from L *amor* love]

**amorist** /'æmərəst/, *n.* **1.** a lover; a gallant. **2.** one who writes about love. **3.** one who seeks sexual experiences. [L *amor* love + -IST] – **amorism,** *n.*

**amoroso** /æmə'roʊsoʊ/, *adv.* **1.** (a musical direction) tenderly. *–adj.* **2.** tender; loving. [It.]

**amorous** /'æmərəs/, *adj.* **1.** inclined or disposed to love: *an amorous disposition.* **2.** in love; enamoured. **3.** showing love: *amorous sighs.* **4.** pertaining to love: *amorous poetry.* [ME, from OF, from L *amōrōsus*, from *amor* love] – **amorously,** *adv.* – **amorousness,** *n.*

**amorphism** /ə'mɔfɪzəm/, *n.* the state or quality of being amorphous.

**amorphous** /ə'mɔfəs/, *adj.* **1.** lacking definite form; having no specific shape. **2.** of no particular kind or character; indeterminate; formless; unorganised: *an amorphous style.* **3.** *Geol.* occurring in a mass, as without stratification or crystalline structure. **4.** *Chem.* non-crystalline. [Gk *ámorphos*] – **amorphously,** *adv.* – **amorphousness,** *n.*

**amorphous semiconductor** /– sɛmikən'dʌktə/, *n. Elect.* a non-crystalline, glassy material with semiconducting properties.

**amortisation** /əmɔtə'zeɪʃən, æmətaɪ'zeɪʃən/, *n.* **1.** the act of amortising a debt. **2.** the money devoted to this purpose. Also, **amortization, amortisement, amortizement** /ə'mɔtəzmənt/.

**amortise** /ə'mɔtaɪz, 'æmətaɪz/, *v.t.*, **-tised, -tising.** **1.** to liquidate or extinguish (an indebtedness or charge) usu. by periodic payments (or by entries) made to a sinking fund, to a creditor, or to an account. **2.** *Old Eng. Law.* to convey to a corporation; alienate in mortmain. Also, **amortize.** [ME *amortise(n)*, from OF *amortiss-*, stem of *amortir* deaden, buy out, from *mort* death. Cf. ML *admortizāre*] – **amortisable,** *adj.*

**amount** /ə'maʊnt/, *n.* **1.** quantity or extent: *the amount of resistance.* **2.** the full effect, value, or import. **3.** the sum total of two or more sums or quantities; the aggregate: *the amount of 7 and 9 is 16.* **4.** the sum of the principal and interest of a loan. *–v.i.* **5.** to reach, extend, or be equal in number, quantity, effect, etc. (fol. by *to*). [ME *amount(en)*, from OF *amonter* mount up to, from *amont* upward, orig. phrase *a mont* to the mountain]

**amount of substance,** *n.* a basic physical quantity that is proportional to the number of specified particles of a substance. The specified particle may be an atom, molecule, ion, radical, electron, etc., or any specified group of such particles. The basic SI unit of amount of substance is the mole. See **mole**[4].

**amour** /ə'mɔ/, *n.* a love affair, esp. a clandestine one. [F, probably from Pr. *amor*, from L *amor* love]

**amour-propre** /ˌamɔ-'proʊprə, əmɔ-'proʊprə/, *n.* self-esteem; self-respect. [F]

**amove** /ə'muv/, *v.t. Law.* to remove; remove from office. [L *āmovēre* move away] – **amotion** /ə'moʊʃən/, *n.*

**amp** /æmp/, *n. Colloq.* an amplifier.

**amp.,** **1.** amperage. **2.** ampere.

**ampelography** /æmpə'lɒgrəfi/, *n.* the scientific study and description of the vine, esp. the grape vine. [F *ampélographie*, from Gk *ámpelos* vine + -GRAPHY] – **ampelographer,** *n.*

**ampelopsis** /æmpə'lɒpsəs/, *n.* any plant of the vitaceous genus *Ampelopsis*, comprising climbing woody vines or shrubs, esp. Virginia creeper. [NL, from Gk *ámpelos* vine + *-opsis* -OPSIS]

**amperage** /'æmpərɪdʒ/, *n.* the strength of an electric current measured in amperes.

**ampere** /'æmpɛə/, *n.* the base SI unit of current, defined as the current which, if maintained in two parallel conductors of infinite length, of negligible cross-section, and separated by one metre in a vacuum, would produce a force of $2 \times 10^{-7}$ newtons per metre. *Symbol:* A [named after A.M. *Ampère*, 1775-1836, French physicist]

**ampere hour** /– 'aʊə/, *n.* a non-SI unit of measurement equal to 3600 coulombs; the quantity of electricity transferred by a current of one ampere in one hour. *Symbol*: A·h

**ampere-turn** /ˌæmpɛə-'tɜn/, *n.* **1.** one complete turn or convolution of a conducting coil, through which one ampere of current passes. **2.** the magnetomotive force produced by one ampere passing through one complete turn or convolution of a coil.

**ampersand** /'æmpəsænd/, *n.* the name of the character *&*,

meaning *and.* [contraction of *and per se and*, that is, *&* by itself (equals) *and*]

**amphetamine** /æm'fɛtəmin, -maɪn/, *n.* a drug which, diluted with water, is used as a spray or inhaled to relieve nasal congestion and is taken internally to stimulate the central nervous system.

**amphi-**, a word element meaning 'on both sides', 'on all sides', 'around', 'round about', as in *amphicoelous.* [Gk, representing *amphí*, prep. and adv.]

**amphiarthrosis** /æmfia'θroʊsəs/, *n., pl.* **-ses** /-siz/. a form of articulation which permits slight motion, as that between the vertebrae. [AMPHI- + Gk *árthrōsis* articulation]

**amphiaster** /'æmfiæstə/, *n. Biol.* the achromatic spindle with two asters that forms during mitosis.

**amphibian** /æm'fɪbiən/, *n.* **1.** any animal of the class Amphibia, that class of vertebrates that comprises the frogs, salamanders, and caecilians (with various extinct types), representing the essential basic characteristics of the ancestral stock of all land vertebrates. Typically they lay eggs that hatch in water and the young go through a fishlike, larval, or tadpole stage, later metamorphosing into lung-breathing quadrupeds. **2.** an amphibious plant. **3.** an aeroplane that can take off from and land on either land or water. **4.** an amphibious vehicle. *–adj.* **5.** belonging to the class Amphibia. **6.** capable of operating on land or water; amphibious. [NL *Amphibia* (neut. pl. of *amphibius*, from Gk *amphíbios* living a double life) + -AN]

**amphibiotic** /,æmfibaɪ'ɒtɪk/, *adj. Zool.* living on land during an adult stage and in water during a larval stage. [AMPHI- + Gk *biōtikós* pertaining to life]

**amphibious** /æm'fɪbiəs/, *adj.* **1.** living both on land and in water; belonging to both land and water. **2.** capable of operating on both land and water: *amphibious plane.* **3.** of a twofold nature. [Gk *amphíbios* living a dual life] **– amphibiously,** *adv.* **– amphibiousness,** *n.*

**amphibole** /'æmfəboʊl/, *n.* any of a complex group of hydrous silicate minerals, containing chiefly calcium, magnesium, sodium, iron, and aluminium, and including hornblende, tremolite, asbestos, etc., and occurring as important constituents of many rocks. [F, from Gk *amphíbolos* ambiguous]

**amphibolic**[1] /æmfə'bɒlɪk/, *adj.* of or pertaining to amphibole. [AMPHIBOL(E) + -IC]

**amphibolic**[2] /æmfə'bɒlɪk/, *adj.* equivocal; uncertain; changing; ambiguous. [AMPHIBOL(Y) + -IC]

**amphibolite** /æm'fɪbəlaɪt/, *n.* a metamorphic rock composed basically of amphibole or hornblende. [AMPHIBOL(E) + -ITE[1]]

**amphibology** /æmfə'bɒlədʒi/, *n., pl.* **-gies.** ambiguity of speech, esp. from uncertainty of the grammatical construction rather than of the meaning of the words. [LL *amphibologia*, replacing L *amphibolia* (see AMPHIBOLY), which was remodelled after *tautologia* and the like] **– amphibological** /æm,fɪbə'lɒdʒɪkəl/, *adj.*

**amphibolous** /æm'fɪbələs/, *adj.* ambiguous; equivocal; susceptible of two meanings. [L *amphibolus*, from Gk *amphíbolos*]

**amphiboly** /æm'fɪbəli/, *n., pl.* **-lies.** →**amphibology.** [L *amphibolia* ambiguity, from Gk]

**amphibrach** /'æmfəbræk/, *n.* (in prosody) a trisyllabic foot in which the syllables come in the following order: short, long, short (quantitative metre), or unstressed, stressed, unstressed (accentual metre). Thus, *together* is an accentual amphibrach. [L *amphibrachys*, from Gk: short on both sides]

**amphichroic** /æmfə'kroʊɪk/, *adj.* giving either of two colours, one with acids and one with alkalis. Also, **amphichromatic** /æmfəkrə'mætɪk/. [AMPHI- + Gk *chróa* colour + -IC]

**amphicoelous** /æmfə'siləs/, *adj.* concave on both sides, as the bodies of the vertebrae of fishes. [Gk *amphíkoilos* hollowed all round]

**amphidiploid** /æmfə'dɪplɔɪd/, *n.* a plant type possessing the sum of the chromosome numbers of two parental species, ordinarily arising from the doubling of the chromosomes of a hybrid of two species.

**amphigory** /æm'fɪgəri, 'æmfəgri/, *n., pl.* **-ries.** a meaningless rigmarole; a nonsensical parody. **– amphigoric** /æmfə'gɒrɪk/, *adj.*

**amphimacer** /æm'fɪməsə/, *n.* (in poetry) a trisyllabic foot in which the syllables come in the following order: long, short, long (quantitative metre), or stressed, unstressed, stressed (accentual metre). Thus, *anodyne* is an accentual amphimacer. [L *amphimacrus*, from Gk *amphímakros* long on both sides]

**amphimixis** /æmfə'mɪksəs/, *n.* **1.** *Biol.* the merging of the germ plasm of two organisms in sexual reproduction. **2.** *Embryol., Genetics.* the combining of paternal and maternal hereditary substances. [AMPHI- + Gk *míxis* a mingling]

**amphioxus** /æmfi'ɒksəs/, *n.* →**lancelet.**

**amphipod** /'æmfipɒd/, *n.* **1.** any of a type of small crustaceans, Amphipoda, including beach fleas, etc. *–adj.* **2.** of or pertaining to the amphipods.

**amphiprostyle** /æm'fɪprəstaɪl, æmfə'proʊstaɪl/, *adj.* having a prostyle porch in front and rear but no columns along the sides. [L *amphiprostȳlos*, from Gk]

**amphiprotic** /æmfə'prɒtɪk/, *adj.* capable of acting either as an acid or a base, i.e., as a proton donor or acceptor, according to the nature of the environment.

**amphisbaena** /æmfəs'binə/, *n.* any of various burrowing wormlike lizards of the family Amphisbaenidae with reduced limbs or no limbs at all, having tiny, concealed eyes and ears and obtuse head and tail, and moving forwards or backwards with equal ease. [L, from Gk *amphísbaina*; in classical mythology, a venemous serpent having a head at each end and able to move in either direction]

**amphitheatre** /'æmfiθɪətə/, *n.* **1.** a level area of oval or circular shape surrounded by rising ground. **2.** any place for public contests or games; an arena. **3.** a building with tiers of seats around an arena or central area, as those used in ancient Rome for gladiatorial contests. **4.** a semi-circular sloping gallery in a modern theatre. Also, *U.S.,* **amphitheater.** [L *amphitheātrum*, from Gk *amphithéātron*]

**amphitheatric** /æmfiθi'ætrɪk/, *adj.* of or pertaining to an amphitheatre. Also, **amphitheatrical. – amphitheatrically,** *adv.*

**amphithecium** /æmfi'θisiəm/, *n., pl.* **-cia** /-siə/. the layer or layers of cells in the capsule of a moss surrounding the spores. [NL *amphi-* AMPHI- + *thēcium* (from Gk *thēkíon*, diminutive of *thḗkē* case)]

**amphitricha** /æm'fɪtrəkə/, *n. pl.* bacteria having the organs of locomotion on both poles. [AMPHI- + *trich-* (stem of Gk *thríx* hair)] **– amphitrichate, amphitrichous,** *adj.*

**amphometer** /æm'fɒmətə/, *n.* a device for estimating the speed with which a vehicle covers a specified distance. [AMPH(I)- + -O- + METER[1]]

**amphora** /'æmfərə/, *n., pl.* **-rae** /-ri/. a two-handled, narrow-necked vessel, commonly big-bellied and narrowed at the base, used by the ancient Greeks and Romans for holding wine, oil, etc. [L, from Gk *amphoreús*, short for *amphiphoreús*] **– amphoral,** *adj.*

amphora

**amphoric** /æm'fɒrɪk/, *adj.* producing or like the sound made by blowing across the top of a bottle: *amphoric breathing.*

**amphoteric** /æmfə'tɛrɪk/, *adj.* functioning as an acid or as a base. [Gk *amphóteros* (comparative of *ámphō* both) + -IC]

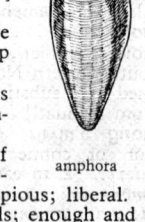

**ample** /'æmpəl/, *adj.,* **-pler, -plest. 1.** of great extent, size, or amount; large; spacious. **2.** in full or abundant measure; copious; liberal. **3.** fully sufficient for the purpose or for needs; enough and to spare. **4.** rather bulky or full in form or figure. [ME, from L *amplus*] **– ampleness,** *n.*

**amplexicaul** /æm'plɛksəkɔl/, *adj.* clasping the stem, as some leaves do at their base. [NL *amplexicaulis*, from L *amplexus* embracing + *caulis* stem]

**amplification** /æmpləfə'keɪʃən/, *n.* **1.** the act of amplifying. **2.** expansion of a statement, narrative, etc., as for rhetorical purposes. **3.** a statement, narrative, etc., so expanded. **4.** an addition made in expanding. **5.** *Elect.* increase in the strength of current, voltage, or power. [L *amplificātio*] **– amplificatory,** *adj.*

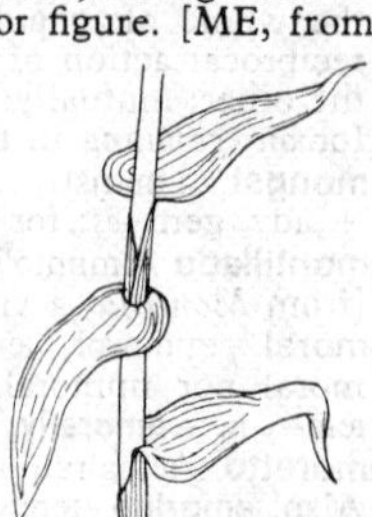
amplexicaul leaves

i = peat ɪ = pit ɛ = pet æ = pat a = part ɒ = pot ʌ = putt ɔ = port ʊ = put u = pool ɜ = pert ə = apart aɪ = buy eɪ = bay ɔɪ = boy aʊ = how
oʊ = hoe ɪə = here ɛə = hair ʊə = tour g = give θ = thin ð = then ʃ = show ʒ = measure tʃ = choke dʒ = joke ŋ = sing j = you õ = Fr. bon

**amplifier** /'æmpləfaɪə/, *n.* **1.** one who amplifies or enlarges. **2.** *Elect.* a device for increasing the amplitudes of electric waves or impulses by means of the control exercised by the input over the power supplied to the output from a local source of energy. Commonly it is a radio valve or transistor, or a device employing them. **3.** such a device used to magnify the sound produced by a radio, record-player, or any of certain musical instruments, as an electric guitar. **4.** *Photog.* an additional lens for expanding the field of vision.

**ampliform** /'æmpləfɔm/, *v.t.* to enlarge and stretch aluminium extrusions into shapes and forms which can be many times stronger than the original.

**amplify** /'æmpləfaɪ/, *v.*, **-fied, -fying.** *–v.t.* **1.** to make larger or greater; enlarge; extend. **2.** to expand in stating or describing, as by details, illustration, etc. **3.** *Elect.* to increase the amplitude of (impulses or waves). **4.** to make louder; magnify (the sound of). **5.** *U.S. Colloq.* to exaggerate. *–v.i.* **6.** to discourse at length; expatiate or dilate (usu. fol. by *on*). [ME *amplify(en)*, from F *amplifier*, from L *amplificāre* enlarge. See -FY]

**amplitude** /'æmplətʃud/, *n.* **1.** extension in space, esp. breadth or width; largeness; extent. **2.** large or full measure; abundance; copiousness. **3.** *Physics.* the distance or range from one extremity of an oscillation to the middle point or neutral value. **4.** *Elect.* the maximum strength of an alternating current during its cycle, as distinguished from the mean or effective strength. **5.** *Astron.* the arc of the horizon from the east or west point to a heavenly body at its rising or setting. [L *amplitūdo*]

**amplitude modulation** /– mɒdʒə'leɪʃən/, *n.* a system of radio transmission in which the carrier wave is modulated by changing its amplitude (distinguished from *frequency modulation*). *Abbrev.*: AM

**amply** /'æmpli/, *adv.* in an ample manner; sufficiently.

**ampoule** /'æmpul/, *n.* a sealed glass bulb used to hold hypodermic solutions. [F, from L *ampulla* bottle]

**ampster** /'æmstə/, *n.* a decoy who works with a sideshow operator, acting as if he were an enthusiastic member of the audience so as to arouse the interest of others; a spruiker's stooge. Also, **amster.** [from *Amsterdam*, rhyming slang for RAM[2]]

**ampulla** /æm'pʊlə/, *n.*, *pl.* **-pullae** /-'pʊli/. **1.** *Anat.* a dilated portion of a canal or duct, esp. of the semicircular canals of the ear. **2.** *Eccles.* **a.** a vessel for the wine and water used at the altar. **b.** a vessel for holding consecrated oil. **3.** a two-handled bottle used by the ancient Romans for oil, etc. **4.** ampoule. [L] – **ampullary,** *adj.*

**ampullaceal** /,æmpʊ'leɪʃəl/, *adj.* like an ampulla; bottle-shaped. Also, **ampullaceous.**

**amputate** /'æmpjəteɪt/, *v.t.*, **-tated, -tating. 1.** to cut off (a limb, arm, etc.) by a surgical operation. **2.** *Obs.* to prune, as branches of trees. [L *amputātus*, pp.] – **amputation** /æmpjə'teɪʃən/, *n.* – **amputator,** *n.*

**amputee** /æmpjə'ti/, *n.* one who has lost an arm, hand, leg, etc., by amputation.

**amrita** /æm'ritə/, *n. Hindu Myth.* **1.** the ambrosial drink of immortality. **2.** the immortality conferred by it. Also, **amreeta.** [Skt *amṛta* immortal; as n., the drink of immortality. Cf. Gk *ám(b)rotos* immortal]

**amster** /'æmstə/, *n.* →**ampster.**

**amt,** amount.

**AMT** /eɪ ɛm 'ti/, audiomagnetotellurics.

**amu** /'æmju/, *n.* atomic mass unit.

**amuck** /ə'mʌk/, *adv. in the phrase* **run amuck, 1.** to rush about in a murderous frenzy. **2.** to rush about wildly. Also, **amok.**

**amulet** /'æmjələt/, *n.* an object superstitiously worn to ward off evil; a protecting charm. [L *amulētum*]

**amulla** /ə'mʌlə/, *n.* a shrub, *Myoporum debile*, with an ovoid, pinkish-red fruit, growing on grassland in warmer parts of Australia.

**amuse** /ə'mjuz/, *v.t.*, **amused, amusing. 1.** to hold the attention of agreeably; entertain; divert. **2.** to excite mirth in. **3.** to cause (time, leisure, etc.) to pass agreeably. **4.** *Archaic.* to keep in expectation by flattery, pretences, etc. **5.** *Obs.* to engross. **6.** *Obs.* to puzzle. [late ME, from MF *amuser* occupy with trifles, divert, from *a* to + *muser* stare. See MUSE[1]] – **amusable,** *adj.* – **amuser,** *n.*

**amused** /ə'mjuzd/, *adj.* **1.** filled with interest; pleasurably occupied. **2.** displaying amusement: *an amused expression.* **3.** aroused to mirth. – **amusedly** /ə'mjuzədli/, *adv.*

**amusement** /ə'mjuzmənt/, *n.* **1.** the state of being amused; enjoyment. **2.** that which amuses; pastime; entertainment. **3.** a mechanical entertainment, as a roundabout at a fair. [F]

**amusement arcade** /'– akeɪd/, *n.* an arcade with various devices for entertainment as pin ball machines, shooting galleries, etc.

**amusement park** /'– pak/, *n.* a commercially run enclosed ground where amusements (def. 3) are permanently situated.

**amusing** /ə'mjuzɪŋ/, *adj.* **1.** pleasantly entertaining or diverting. **2.** exciting moderate mirth; delighting the fancy. – **amusingly,** *adv.* – **amusingness,** *n.*

**amydaloidal** /əmidə'lɔɪdl/, *adj.*, *n.*→**amygdaloidal.** Also, **amydaloid.**

**amygdala** /ə'mɪgdələ/, *n.*, *pl.* **-lae** /-li/. **1.** *Anat.* **a.** an almond-shaped part. **b.** (*pl.*) the tonsils. **c.** a lobe of the cerebellum. **2.** *Obs.* an almond. [L, from Gk *amygdálē* almond. Cf. OE *amygdal*]

**amygdalate** /ə'mɪgdələt, -leɪt/, *adj.* pertaining to, resembling, or made of almonds.

**amygdale** /ə'mɪgdeɪl/, *n.* an almond-shaped cavity in an igneous rock, formed by the expansion of steam and later filled with minerals. Also, **amygdule.**

**amygdalin** /ə'mɪgdələn/, *n.* a crystalline principle, $C_{20}H_{27}O_{11}N \cdot 3H_2O$, existing in bitter almonds, and in the leaves, etc., of species of the genus *Prunus* and of some of its near allies.

**amygdaline** /ə'mɪgdəlin, -laɪn/, *adj.* of or pertaining to the amygdalae. See **amygdala.**

**amygdaloidal** /əmɪgdə'lɔɪdl/, *adj. Geol.* **1.** (of rocks) containing amygdales. *–n.* **2.** *Obs.* amygdaloidal rock. Also, **amydaloidal, amygdaloid.**

**amygdule** /ə'mɪgdjul/, *n.* →**amygdale.**

**amyl** /'æməl/, *n.* a univalent radical $C_5H_{11}$, derived from pentane. Its compounds are found in fusel oil, fruit extracts, etc. [L *amylum* starch (Gk *ámylon*); the *-yl* was identified with -YL]

**amyl-,** a variant of **amylo-,** as in *amyloysis.*

**amylaceous** /æmə'leɪʃəs/, *adj.* of the nature of starch; starchy. [AMYL(O)- + -ACEOUS]

**amyl acetate** /æməl 'æsəteɪt/, *n.* a colourless liquid, $CH_3COOC_5H_{11}$, used as a solvent, in perfumes, and as a flavouring.

**amyl alcohol** /– 'ælkəhɒl/, *n.* a colourless liquid, $C_5H_{11}OH$, consisting of a mixture of two or more isomeric alcohols, derived from the pentanes and serving as a solvent and intermediate for organic syntheses.

**amylase** /'æməleɪz/, *n.* any of several enzymes, occurring in digestive juices, blood, and plants which hydrolyse starches to simple sugars such as glucose and maltose; the main types are alpha-amylase and beta-amylase.

**amylene** /'æməlin/, *n.* any of certain unsaturated isomeric hydrocarbons with the formula $C_5H_{10}$; pentene.

**amyl nitrite** /æməl 'naɪtraɪt/, *n.* a yellowish volatile liquid, $C_5H_{11}NO_2$, with a fragrant odour, used in perfumes and in medicine as a vasodilator in the treatment of such illnesses as angina pectoris.

**amylo-,** a combining form of **amyl** and **amylum,** indicating starch. Also, **amyl-.** [L *amylum* starch]

**amyloid** /'æməlɔɪd/, *n.* a hard, homogeneous, glossy substance deposited in tissues in certain kinds of degeneration. – **amyloidal** /æmə'lɔɪdl/, *adj.*

**amyloidosis** /æməlɔɪ'doʊsəs/, *n.* a disease resulting from the deposit of amyloid in tissue or organs.

**amylolysis** /æməl'ɒləsəs/, *n.* the conversion of starch into sugar. [AMYLO- + -LYSIS] – **amylolytic** /æməloʊ'lɪtɪk/, *adj.*

**amylopectin** /æməloʊ'pɛktən/, *n.* the gel component of starch. It turns red in iodine.

**amylopsin** /æmə'lɒpsən/, *n.* an enzyme of the pancreatic juice, capable of converting starch into sugar; pancreatic amylase. [b. AMYLO(LYSIS) and (PE)PSIN]

**amylose** /ˈæməloʊs/, *n.* the sol or soluble component of starch. It turns intense blue in iodine.

**amylum** /ˈæmələm/, *n.* →**starch** (def. 1). [L, from Gk *ámylon* fine meal, starch]

**amytal** /ˈæmətæl/, *n.* a colourless crystalline substance, $C_{11}H_{18}N_2O_3$, used esp. as a sedative.

**an**[1] /æn/, *weak form* /ən/ *adj. or indefinite article.* the form of **a** before an initial vowel sound. See **a**[1]. [ME; OE *ān.* See ONE]

**an**[2] /æn/; *weak form* /ən/ *conj. Archaic.* if. Also, **an'**. [var. of AND]

**an-**[1], a prefix meaning 'not', 'without', 'lacking', used before vowels and *h*, as in *anarchy.* Also, **a-**[6]. [Gk]

**an-**[2], variant of **ad-**, before *n*, as in *announce.*

**an-**[3], variant of **ana-**, used before vowels, as in *anaptotic.*

**-an**, a suffix meaning: **1.** 'belonging to', 'pertaining or relating to', 'adhering to', and commonly expressing connection with a place, person, reader, class, order, sect, system, doctrine, or the like, serving to form adjectives, many of which are also used as nouns, as *Australian, Christian, Elizabethan, republican*, and hence serving to form other nouns of the same type, as *historian, theologian.* **2.** *Zool.* 'relating to a certain class', as in *mammalian.* [L *-ānus*; replacing ME *-ain, -en*, from OF]

**an.**, in the year. [L *annō*, from *annus* year]

**An**, actinon.

**AN**, Anglo-Norman.

**ana**[1] /ˈanə/, *n.* **1.** a collection of miscellaneous information, esp. in the form of table talk, gossip, etc. **2.** the information so collected. [independent use of -ANA]

**ana**[2] /ˈænə/, *adv.* in equal quantities; of each (used in medical prescriptions, with reference to ingredients, and often written āā). [ML, from Gk. See ANA-]

**ana-**, a prefix meaning 'up', 'throughout', 'again', 'back', occurring originally in words from the Greek, but used also in modern words (English and other) formed on the Greek model, as in *anabatic.* [Gk, representing *aná*, prep.]

**-ana**, a noun suffix denoting a collection of material pertaining to a given subject, as in *Shakespeariana, Australiana.* [L, neut. pl. of *-ānus* -AN]

**anabaena** /ænəˈbinə/, *n., pl.* **-nas.** any of the freshwater algae constituting the genus *Anabaena*, commonly occurring in masses, and often contaminating drinking water, giving it a fishy taste and smell. [NL, from Gk *anabaínein* go up]

**anabantid** /ænəˈbæntəd/, *n.* **1.** any of various small, spiny-finned, freshwater fishes of the family Anabantidae found in southern Asia and tropical Africa. *–adj.* **2.** belonging or pertaining to the Anabantidae. [NL *Anabantidae* (from ANABAS + -IDAE)]

**anabaptise** /ænəbæpˈtaɪz, -ˈbæptaɪz/, *v.t.* to baptise again. Also, **anabaptize.**

**Anabaptist** /ænəˈbæptəst/, *n.* **1.** an adherent of a religious and social movement which arose in Europe shortly after 1520 and was distinguished by its insistence on its members being baptised again, its rejection of infant baptism, and by its attempts to establish a Christian communism. **2.** (*l.c.*) a member of a later sect or religious body holding the same doctrines. **3.** *Archaic.* →**Baptist** (def. 1). – **anabaptism,** *n.*

**anabas** /ˈænəbæs/, *n.* any member of the genus *Anabas* which comprises small, freshwater, perch-like fishes of southern Asia and Africa. [NL, from Gk, aorist participle of *anabaínein* go up]

**anabasis** /əˈnæbəsəs/, *n., pl.* **-ses** /-siz/. a military expedition or march. [from *Anabasis*, the account by the Greek historian, Xenophon, c.434 - c.355 B.C., of the march from the coast into the interior by Cyrus the Younger against Artaxerxes II]

**anabatic** /ænəˈbætɪk/, *adj.* (of winds and air currents) moving upwards or up a slope. [Gk *anabatikós* pertaining to climbing]

**anabiosis** /ænəbaɪˈoʊsəs/, *n.* a bringing back or returning to consciousness; reanimation (after apparent death). [NL, from Gk: revival] – **anabiotic** /ænəbaɪˈɒtɪk/, *adj.*

**anabolic steroid** /ˌænəbɒlɪk ˈstɪərɔɪd/, *n.* any of a group of synthetic androgens which accelerate bone and muscle growth.

**anabolism** /əˈnæbəlɪzəm/, *n.* constructive metabolism (opposed to *catabolism*). [Gk *anabolḗ* a throwing up + -ISM] – **anabolic** /ænəˈbɒlɪk/, *adj.*

**anabranch** /ˈænəbræntʃ/, *n.* a branch of a river which leaves the main stream and either enters it again, dries up, or sinks into the ground. [short for *ana(stomosing) branch*]

**anacardiaceous** /ˌænəkadiˈeɪʃəs/, *adj.* belonging to the Anacardiaceae, a family of trees and shrubs including the cashew, mango, pistachio, sumach, etc. [NL *Anacardiāceae* (*ana-* ANA- + Gk *kardía* heart + *-āceae* -ACEAE) + -OUS]

**anachronism** /əˈnækrənɪzəm/, *n.* **1.** an error assigning a custom, event, person, or thing to an age other, esp. earlier, than the correct one. **2.** something placed or occurring out of its proper time. [Gk *anachronismós*]

**anachronistic** /ənækrəˈnɪstɪk/, *adj.* containing an anachronism. Also, **anachronistical.**

**anachronous** /əˈnækrənəs/, *adj.* →**anachronistic.** – **anachronously,** *adv.*

**anaclisis** /ænəˈklaɪsəs/, *n.* the choice of an object of libidinal attachment on the basis of a resemblance to early childhood protective and parental figures. [Gk *anáklisis* a leaning back]

**anaclitic** /ænəˈklɪtɪk/, *adj.* exhibiting or pertaining to anaclisis.

**anacoluthia** /ænəkəˈluθiə/, *n.* lack of grammatical sequence or coherence, esp. in the same sentence. [L, from Gk *anakolouthía*] – **anacoluthic,** *adj.*

**anacoluthon** /ænəkəˈluθən/, *n., pl.* **-tha** /-θə/. a construction involving a break in grammatical sequence; a case of anacoluthia. [L, from Gk *anakólouthon*, neut. adj., inconsequent]

**anaconda** /ænəˈkɒndə/, *n.* **1.** a large South American snake, *Eunectes murinus*, of the boa family. **2.** any boa constrictor. [orig. unknown: ? from Singhalese]

**Anacreontic** /ənækriˈɒntɪk/, *adj.* **1.** convivial; amatory. **2.** of or in the manner of Anacreon (c. 563 - c. 478 B.C.), Greek lyric poet known for his love poems and drinking songs.

**anacrusis** /ænəˈkrusəs/, *n.* an unstressed syllable or syllable group which begins a line of verse but is not counted as part of the first foot, which properly begins with a stressed syllable. [L, from Gk *anákrousis*, from *anakroúein* strike up]

**anacusis** /ænəˈkjusəs/, *n.* total loss of the ability to perceive sound. Also, **anakusis.** [AN-[1] + Gk *ákousis* hearing]

**anadiplosis** /ænədəˈploʊsəs/, *n.* repetition in the first part of one clause of a prominent word in the latter part of the preceding clause. [Gk: repetition]

**anadromous** /əˈnædrəməs/, *adj.* (of fishes) going from the sea up a river or into coastal waters to spawn (contrasted with *catadromous*). [Gk *anádromos* running up]

**anaemia** /əˈnimiə/, *n.* **1.** a quantitative deficiency of the haemoglobin, often accompanied by a reduced number of red blood cells, and causing pallor, weakness, and breathlessness. **2.** bloodlessness; paleness. Also, *Chiefly U.S.*, **anemia.** [NL, from Gk *anaimía* want of blood]

**anaemic** /əˈnimɪk/, *adj.* **1.** suffering from anaemia. **2.** sickly, colourless; without body or vigour. Also, *Chiefly U.S.*, **anemic.**

**anaerobe** /æˈnɛəroʊb/, *n.* a bacterium or other micro-organism which does not require free oxygen or is not destroyed by its absence (opposed to *aerobe*). [backformation from *anaerobia*, pl. of ANAEROBIUM (NL, from Gk *an-* AN-[1] + *āero-* AERO- + *bíos* life)]

**anaerobic** /ænəˈroʊbɪk/, *adj.* **1.** *Biol., Physiol.* (of organisms or tissues) requiring the absence of free oxygen or not destroyed by its absence. **2.** pertaining to or caused by the absence of oxygen. **3.** affected by or involving the activities of anaerobes. – **anaerobically,** *adv.*

**anaerobiont** /ænəˈroʊbiənt/, *n.* →**anaerobe.**

**anaerobiosis** /ˌænəroʊbaɪˈoʊsəs/, *n.* life in the absence of oxygen. – **anaerobiotic,** *adj.* – **anaerobiotically,** *adv.*

**anaerobium** /ænəˈroʊbiəm/, *n., pl* **-bia** /-biə/. →**anaerobe.**

**anaes.**, **1.** anaesthesia. **2.** anaesthetic.

**anaesthesia** /ænəsˈθiʒə, -ziə/, *n.* **1.** *Med.* general or local insensibility, as to pain and other sensation, induced by certain drugs. **2.** *Pathol.* general loss of the senses of feeling, such as pain, heat, cold, touch, and other less common varieties of sensation. **3.** the science of anaesthetics. Also, *Chiefly U.S.*, **anesthesia.** [NL, from Gk *anaisthēsía* insensibility]

**anaesthesin** /ænəsˈθizən/, *n.* →**benzocaine.**

**anaesthetic** /ænəs'θɛtɪk/, *n.* **1.** a substance such as ether, chloroform, cocaine, etc., that produces anaesthesia. *–adj.* **2.** pertaining to or causing physical insensibility. **3.** insensitive. Also, *Chiefly U.S.*, **anesthetic.**

**anaesthetise** /ə'nisθətaɪz/, *v.t.*, **-tised, -tising.** to render physically insensible, as by an anaesthetic. Also, **anaesthetize,** *Chiefly U.S.*, **anesthetize.** – **anaesthetisation** /əˌnisθətaɪ'zeɪʃən/, *n.*

**anaesthetist** /ə'nisθətəst/, *n.* a person who administers anaesthetics, usu. a specially trained doctor. Also, *Chiefly U.S.*, **anesthetist.**

**anaglyph** /'ænəglɪf/, *n.* **1.** something executed in low relief, as a cameo or an embossed ornament. **2.** *Photog.* a picture composed of two images, one red and one green, which, when viewed through red and green spectacles, appears stereoscopic. [Gk *anáglyphos* wrought in low relief] – **anaglyphic** /ænə'glɪfɪk/, **anaglyptic** /ænə'glɪptɪk/, *adj.*

**anagoge** /'ænəgɒdʒi/, *n.* the spiritual interpretation or application of a word, passage or text, as of Scriptures, esp. the application of the types and allegories of the Old Testament to subjects of the New Testament. [LL, from Gk: a bringing up, elevation] – **anagogic** /ænə'gɒdʒɪk/, **anagogical,** *adj.* – **anagogically,** *adv.*

**anagram** /'ænəgræm/, *n.* **1.** a transposition of the letters of a word or sentence to form a new word or sentence, as *caned* is an anagram of *dance.* *–v.t., v.i.* **2.** to anagrammatise. [NL *anagramma,* backformation from Gk *anagrammatismós* transposition of letters]

**anagrammatic** /ænəgrə'mætɪk/, *adj.* of or pertaining to an anagram. Also, **anagrammatical.** – **anagrammatically,** *adv.*

**anagrammatise** /ænə'græmətaɪz/, *v.*, **-tised, -tising.** *–v.t.* **1.** to transpose into an anagram. *–v.i.* **2.** to make anagrams. Also, **anagrammatize.** – **anagrammatism,** *n.* – **anagrammatist,** *n.*

**anakusis** /ænə'kusəs/, *n.* →**anacusis.**

**anal** /'eɪnəl/, *adj.* of, pertaining to, or near the anus.

**anal.,** **1.** analogous. **2.** analogy. **3.** analysis.

**anal canal** /eɪnəl kə'næl/, *n.* the end part of the rectum leading to the anus.

**analcite** /'ænəlsaɪt, ə'næl-/, *n.* a white or slightly coloured zeolite mineral, generally found in crystalline form. Also, **analcime** /ə'nælsim, -saɪm/. [Gk *analkḗs* weak + -ITE[1]]

**analects** /'ænəlɛkts/, *n.pl.* selected passages from the writings of an author or of different authors. Also, **analecta** /ænə'lɛktə/. [L *analecta,* pl., from Gk *análekta* things gathered] – **analectic** /ænə'lɛktɪk/, *adj.*

**analeptic** /ænə'lɛptɪk/, *adj.* **1.** restoring; invigorating; giving strength after disease. **2.** awakening, esp. from drug stupor. *–n.* **3.** an analeptic remedy. [Gk *analēptikós* restorative]

**anal fin** /eɪnəl 'fɪn/, *n.* (in fishes) the median ventral unpaired fin.

**analgesia** /ænəl'dʒiziə/, *n.* absence of sense of pain. [NL, from Gk]

**analgesic** /ænəl'dʒizɪk, -sɪk/, *n.* **1.** a remedy that relieves or removes pain. *–adj.* **2.** pertaining to or causing analgesia.

**analog** /'ænəlɒg/, *adj.* *Electronics.* pertaining to the use of physical quantities (such as voltages, etc.) as analogues to the variables in a mathematical problem, as in an analog computer. Also, **analogue.**

**analog computer** /– kəm'pjutə/, *n.* a type of calculating machine in which numbers are represented by directly measurable quantities (as voltages, resistances, or rotations). Also, **analogue computer.**

**analogical** /ænə'lɒdʒɪkəl/, *adj.* based on, involving, or expressing an analogy. Also, **analogic.** – **analogically,** *adv.*

**analogise** /ə'nælədʒaɪz/, *v.*, **-gised, -gising.** *–v.t.* **1.** to study or explain by analogy. *–v.i.* **2.** to make use of analogy in reasoning, argument, etc. **3.** to be analogous; exhibit analogy. Also, **analogize.**

**analogist** /ə'nælədʒəst/, *n.* **1.** one who uses or argues from analogy. **2.** one who looks for analogies. – **analogism,** *n.*

**analogous** /ə'næləgəs, -dʒəs/, *adj.* **1.** having analogy; corresponding in some particular. **2.** *Biol.* corresponding in function, but not evolved from corresponding organs, as the wings of a bee and those of a hummingbird. [L *analogus,* from Gk *análogos* proportionate] – **analogously,** *adv.* – **analogousness,** *n.*

**analog-to-digital converter** /ˌænəlɒg-tə-ˌdɪdʒətl kən'vɜtə/, *n.* a device which converts an analog signal to a digital equivalent. Also, **analog-digital converter.**

**analogue** /'ænəlɒg/, *n.* **1.** something having analogy to something else. **2.** *Biol.* an organ or part analogous to another. *–adj.* **3.** →**analog.** [F, from Gk *análogon*]

**analogy** /ə'nælədʒi/, *n., pl.* **-gies.** **1.** an agreement, likeness, or correspondence between the relations of things to one another; a partial similarity in particular circumstances on which a comparison may be based: *the analogy between the heart and a pump.* **2.** agreement; similarity. **3.** *Biol.* an analogous relationship. **4.** (in linguistic change) the tendency of inflections and formations to follow existing models and regular patterns, as when the more common '*-s*' plural *brothers* replaces the older *brethren.* **5.** *Logic.* a form of reasoning in which similarities are inferred from a similarity of two or more things in certain particulars. [L *analogia,* from Gk: orig., equality of ratios, proportion]

**analphabetic** /ˌænælfə'bɛtɪk/, *adj.* **1.** not alphabetical. **2.** unable to read and write; illiterate.

**analyse** /'ænəlaɪz/, *v.t.*, **-lysed, -lysing.** **1.** to resolve into elements or constituent parts; determine the elements or essential features of: *to analyse an argument.* **2.** to examine critically, so as to bring out the essential elements or give the essence of: *to analyse a poem.* **3.** to subject to mathematical, chemical, grammatical, etc., analysis. **4.** →**psychoanalyse.** Also, *U.S.*, **analyze.** [backformation from ANALYSIS] – **analysable,** *adj.*

**analyser** /'ænəlaɪzə/, *n.* **1.** one who or that which analyses. **2.** *Optics.* a component of an optical system which rotates the plane of polarisation of polarised light.

**analysis** /ə'næləsəs/, *n., pl.* **-ses** /-siz/. **1.** separation of a whole, whether a material substance or any matter of thought, into its constituent elements (opposed to *synthesis*). **2.** this process as a method of studying the nature of a thing or of determining its essential features: *the grammatical analysis of a sentence.* **3.** a brief presentation of essential features; an outline or summary, as of a book; a synopsis. **a.** the branch of mathematics dealing with the investigation and properties of limiting processes. **b.** the discussion of a problem by algebra as opposed to geometry. **4.** *Chem.* **a.** intentionally produced decomposition or separation of a substance into its ingredients or elements, to find their kind or quantity. **b.** the ascertainment of the kind or amount of one or more of the constituents of a substance, whether actually obtained in separate form or not. **5.** →**psychoanalysis.** [ML, from Gk: a breaking up]

**analysis of variance,** *n.* a statistical procedure for resolving the total variance of a set of variates into component variances, which are associated with factors affecting the variates.

**analyst** /'ænələst/, *n.* **1.** one who analyses or who is skilled in analysis. **2.** →**psychoanalyst.**

**analytic** /ænə'lɪtɪk/, *adj.* **1.** pertaining to or proceeding by analysis (opposed to *synthetic*). **2.** (of languages) characterised by the use of separate words (**free forms**) rather than of inflectional adjuncts (**bound forms**) to show syntactic relationships, as in English or Chinese (opposed to *synthetic*). **3.** *Logic.* (of a proposition) necessarily true because its denial involves a contradiction, as *all spinsters are unmarried.* Also, **analytical.** [ML *analyticus,* from Gk *analytikós*] – **analytically,** *adv.*

**analytical geometry** /ænəˌlɪtɪkəl dʒi'ɒmətri/, *n.* geometry treated by algebra, the position of any point being determined by numbers which are its coordinates with respect to a system of coordinates; coordinate geometry.

**analytics** /ænə'lɪtɪks/, *n.* mathematical or algebraic analysis. [n. use of ANALYTIC. See -ICS]

**analyze** /'ænəlaɪz/, *v.t.*, **-lyzed, -lyzing.** *Chiefly U.S.* →**analyse.**

**anamnesis** /ænæm'nisəs/, *n.* **1.** the recalling of things past; recollection. **2.** *Med.* a case history. [NL, from Gk: a recalling to mind]

**anamorphoscope** /ænə'mɔfəskoʊp/, *n.* **1.** a camera or viewing device designed to produce an anamorphic image, in the form of radial slits on a rotating disc. **2.** a curved mirror or other device for giving a correct image of a picture or the like distorted by anamorphosis.

**anamorphosis** /ænə'mɔfəsəs/, *n., pl.* **-ses** /-siz/. **1.** a distorted image, esp. a drawing, which appears in natural form under certain conditions, as when viewed at a raking angle or reflected from a curved mirror. **2.** the method of producing such images. [NL, from Gk: a forming anew] – **anamorphic, anamorphous,** *adj.*

**anandrous** /æn'ændrəs/, *adj. Bot.* having no stamens. [Gk *ánandros* without a man]

**ananthous** /æn'ænθəs/, *adj. Bot.* without flowers. [AN-[1] + stem of Gk *ánthos* flower + -OUS]

**anapaest** /'ænəpɛst, -pist/, *n.* a foot of three syllables, two short followed by one long (quantitative metre), or two unstressed followed by one stressed (accentual metre). Thus, *for the nonce* is an accentual anapaest. Also, **anapest.** [L *anapaestus*, from Gk *anápaistos* struck back, reversed (as compared with a dactyl)] – **anapaestic** /ænə'pɛstɪk/, *adj., n.*

**anaphase** /'ænəfeɪz/, *n. Biol.* the stage in mitotic cell division after cleavage of the chromosomes, in which the chromosomes move away from each other to opposite ends of the cell.

**anaphora** /ə'næfərə/, *n.* **1.** *Rhet.* the intentional repetition of a word or phrase at the beginning of several clauses, sentences, or paragraphs. **2.** *Linguistics.* the explication of a word by words appearing previous to it in the text: *Mary died. She was very old.* (*She* is explained by *Mary.*) – **anaphoric** /ænə'fɒrɪk/, *adj.*

**anaphrodisiac** /æn,æfrə'dɪziæk/, *adj.* **1.** capable of diminishing sexual desire. *–n.* **2.** an anaphrodisiac agent. [AN-[1] + APHRODISIAC]

**anaphylaxis** /ænəfə'læksəs/, *n.* increased susceptibility to a foreign protein resulting from previous exposure to it, as in serum treatment. [NL, from Gk *ana-* ANA- + *phýlaxis* a guarding] – **anaphylactic,** *adj.*

**anaplasmosis** /ænəplæz'mousəs/, *n.* a disease of cattle caused by a blood-infecting protozoan parasite, transmitted by bloodsucking flies and ticks.

**anaplastic** /ænə'plæstɪk/, *adj.* **1.** *Surg.* →**plastic** (def. 6). **2.** *Pathol.* **a.** (of cells) having reverted to a more primitive form. **b.** (of tumours) having a high degree of malignancy.

**anaplasty** /'ænəplæsti/, *n.* anaplastic surgery. [Gk *anáplastos* plastic + -Y[3]]

**anaptotic** /ænæp'tɒtɪk/, *adj.* (of languages) tending to become uninflected, in accordance with a theory that languages evolve from uninflected to inflected and back. [AN-[3] + stem of Gk *áptōtos* indeclinable + -IC]

**anarchic** /ə'nakɪk/, *adj.* **1.** of, like, or tending to anarchy. **2.** advocating anarchy. **3.** lawless. Also, **anarchical.** – **anarchically,** *adv.*

**anarchise** /'ænəkaɪz/, *v.t.* to make anarchic. Also **anarchize.**

**anarchism** /'ænəkɪzəm/, *n.* **1.** the doctrine (advocated under various forms) urging the abolition of government and governmental restraint as the indispensable condition of political and social liberty. **2.** the methods or practices of anarchists.

**anarchist** /'ænəkəst/, *n.* **1.** one who advocates anarchy as a political idea; a believer in an anarchic theory of society, esp. an adherent of the social theory of Proudhon, Bakunin, or Kropotkin; or one who seeks to overturn by violence all constituted forms and institutions of society and government, with no purpose of establishing any other system of order in the place of that destroyed. **2.** any person who promotes disorder or excites revolt against an established rule, law, or custom. **3.** *Colloq.* a match (def. 1). [Gk *ánarchos* without a ruler + -IST] – **anarchistic** /ænə'kɪstɪk/, *adj.*

**anarchy** /'ænəki/, *n.* **1.** a state of society without government or law. **2.** political and social disorder due to absence of governmental control. **3.** absence of government or governmental restraint. **4.** a theory which regards the union of order with the absence of all direct or coercive government as the political ideal. **5.** confusion in general; disorder. [Gk *anarchia* lack of a ruler]

**anarthria** /æn'aθriə/, *n.* loss of the ability to articulate speech because of damage to the central nervous system or to the peripheral nerves. [NL, from Gk: want of vigour]

**anarthrous** /æn'aθrəs/, *adj.* **1.** *Zool.* without joints or articulated limbs. **2.** (esp. in Greek grammar) used without the article. [Gk *ánarthros*]

**anasarca** /ænə'sakə/, *n.* a pronounced generalised dropsy. [? Gk phrase *anà sárka* throughout flesh] – **anasarcous,** *adj.*

**anastigmatic** /,ænəstɪg'mætɪk, ə,næstɪg'mætɪk/, *adj.* (of a lens) not astigmatic; forming point images of a point object located off the lens axis.

**anastomose** /ə'næstəmouz/, *v.t., v.i.,* **-mosed, -mosing.** to communicate or connect by anastomosis.

**anastomosis** /ənæstə'mousəs/, *n., pl.* **-ses** /-siz/. **1.** *Physiol.* communication between blood vessels by means of collateral channels. **2.** *Biol.* connection between parts of any branching system. [NL, from Gk: opening] – **anastomotic,** *adj.*

**anastrophe** /ə'næstrəfi/, *n.* inversion of the usual order of words. [L, from Gk: a turning back]

**anat.,** **1.** anatomical. **2.** anatomy.

**anatase** /'ænəteɪz/, *n.* a black to brown mineral, titanium dioxide, $TiO_2$, occurring in octahedral crystals; octahedrite. [F, from Gk *anátasis* extension]

**anathema** /ə'næθəmə/, *n., pl.* **-mas. 1.** a formal ecclesiastical curse involving excommunication. **2.** any imprecation of divine punishment. **3.** a curse; an execration. **4.** a person or thing accursed or consigned to damnation or destruction. **5.** a person or thing detested or loathed. [LL, from Gk: something devoted (to evil)]

**anathematise** /ə'næθəmətaɪz/, *v.,* **-tised, -tising.** *–v.t.* **1.** to pronounce an anathema against; denounce; curse. *–v.i.* **2.** to pronounce anathemas; curse. Also, **anathematize.** – **anathematisation** /ə,næθəmətaɪ'zeɪʃən/, *n.* – **anathematic** /ənæθə'mætɪk/, *adj.*

**anatine** /'ænətin, -taɪn/, *adj.* **1.** of or pertaining to the Anatidae, the duck family. **2.** resembling a duck; ducklike. [L *anatinus*]

**Anatolian** /ænə'touliən/, *adj.* **1.** of Anatolia, an area between the Black Sea and the Mediterranean. **2.** of, or belonging to, a group or family of languages that includes cuneiform Hittite and its nearest congeners.

**anatomical** /ænə'tɒmɪkəl/, *adj.* **1.** pertaining to anatomy. **2.** *Colloq.* bawdy; sexual. Also, **anatomic.** – **anatomically,** *adv.*

**anatomise** /ə'nætəmaɪz/, *v.t.* **-mised, -mising. 1.** to dissect, as a plant or an animal, to show the position, structure, and relation of the parts; display the anatomy of. **2.** to analyse or examine very minutely. Also, **anatomize.** – **anatomisation,** *n.*

**anatomist** /ə'nætəməst/, *n.* an expert in anatomy.

**anatomy** /ə'nætəmi/, *n., pl.* **-mies. 1.** the structure of an animal or plant, or of any of its parts. **2.** the science of the structure of animals and plants. **3.** dissection of animals or plants, or their parts, for study of structure, position, etc. **4.** an anatomical subject or model. **5.** a skeleton. **6.** any analysis or minute examination. **7.** *Colloq.* body; bodily form; figure. [LL *anatomia*, from Gk, var. of *anatomḗ* dissection; replacing ME *anothomia*, from ML]

**anatropous** /ə'nætrəpəs/, *adj.* (of an ovule) inverted at an early stage of growth, so that the micropyle is turned towards the funicle, the chalaza being situated at the opposite end. [NL *anatropus* inverted. See ANA-, -TROPOUS]

**anatto** /ə'nætou/, *n.*→**annatto.**

**anbury** /'ænbəri, -bri/, *n.* **1.** a soft, spongy tumour or wart of horses, oxen, etc. **2.** a disease of cruciferous plants, esp. the turnip, in which the roots become clubbed. Also, **ambury, anberry.** [orig. uncert.; ? from OE *ang-* pain + BERRY. Cf. HANGNAIL]

**anc.,** ancient.

**-ance,** a suffix of nouns denoting action, state, or quality, or something exemplifying one of these, often corresponding to adjectives in *-ant*, as *brilliance, distance,* or formed directly from verbs, as in *assistance, defiance.* Cf. **-ence.** [ME *-ance*, from F, from L *-antia, -entia,* orig. ppr. endings]

**ancestor** /'ænsɛstə/, *n.* **1.** one from whom a person is descended, usually distantly; a forefather; a progenitor. **2.** *Biol.* the actual or hypothetical form or stock of an earlier and presumably lower type, from which any organised being is known or inferred to have developed. **3.** *Law.* one from whom an inheritance is derived (correlative of *heir*). [ME *ancestre*, from OF, from L *antecessor* predecessor] – **ances-**

**tress**, *n. fem.*

**ancestral** /æn'sɛstrəl/, *adj.* pertaining to ancestors; descending or claimed from ancestors: *an ancestral home.* – **ancestrally**, *adv.*

**ancestry** /'ænsəstri, -sɛs-/, *n., pl.* **-tries. 1.** ancestral descent. **2.** honourable descent. **3.** a series of ancestors.

**anchor** /'æŋkə/, *n.* **1.** a device for holding boats, vessels, floating bridges, etc., in place. **2.** any similar device for holding fast or checking motion. **3.** a metallic strap or belt built into masonry to hold facing or other materials. **4.** a means of stability: *hope is his anchor.* **5.** *Mil.* a key defensive position. **6.** (*pl.*) *Colloq.* brakes: *hit the anchors.* **7. at anchor**, held still by an anchor; anchored. **8. cast anchor,** to put down or drop the anchor. **9. weigh anchor,** to take up the anchor. **10. swallow the anchor,** *Colloq.* (of a sailor) to settle down on shore. *–v.t.* **11.** to hold fast by an anchor. **12.** to fix or fasten; affix firmly. *–v.i.* **13.** to drop anchor. **14.** to lie or ride at anchor. **15.** to keep hold or be firmly fixed. **16.** *Colloq.* to take up residence (in a place); settle. [ME *anker, ancre,* OE *ancor*, from L *ancora*, from Gk *ánkȳra*] – **anchorless**, *adj.* – **anchor-like**, *adj.*

**anchorage** /'æŋkərɪdʒ/, *n.* **1.** a place for anchoring. **2.** a charge for anchoring. **3.** the act of anchoring. **4.** the state of being anchored. **5.** that to which anything is fastened. **6.** a means of anchoring or making fast. **7.** a means of support or stability, esp. for the mind.

**anchor buoy,** /'æŋkə bɔɪ/, *n.* a small buoy made fast to an anchor and floating above it, to indicate its position.

**anchoress** /'æŋkərɛs/, *n.* a female anchorite.

**anchoret** /'æŋkərɛt, -rət/, *n.* →**anchorite.** [LL *anachōrēta* (from Gk *anachōrētḗs* a recluse) by association with obs. *anchor* hermit (OE *ancora*)] – **anchoretic** /æŋkə'rɛtɪk/, *adj.*

**anchor-ice** /'æŋkər-aɪs/, *n.* →**ground ice.**

**anchorite** /'æŋkəraɪt/, *n.* one who has retired to a solitary place for a life of religious seclusion; a hermit; a recluse. [ME *ancorite*, from ML *anachōrīta*, var. of LL *anachōrēta*] – **anchoritic** /æŋkə'rɪtɪk/, *adj.*

**anchor light** /'æŋkə laɪt/, *n.* a light carried at the bow or stern of a ship at anchor, visible from any direction for at least three kilometres. Also, **riding light.**

**anchorman** /'æŋkəmæn/, *n.* **1.** a key person; mainstay. **2.** *Sport.* the person who is most heavily relied upon in a team, as the last runner in a relay race, the man holding the end of the rope in a tug-of-war team, etc. **3.** *Radio, T.V.* the compere of a program. **4.** a man who blocks a sewer with his body while repairs, etc., are being done.

**anchor point** /'æŋkə pɔɪnt/, *n.* the position on an archer's face towards which the bowstring is drawn for each shot.

**anchor ring** /'– rɪŋ/, *n. Maths.* →**torus.**

**anchovy** /'æntʃəvi, æn'tʃouvi/, *n., pl.* **-vies. 1.** a small, herring-like, marine fish, *Engraulis australis*, occurring in bays and estuaries of the Australian coastline south of the tropic of Capricorn. **2.** any of a number of fishes of the same family (Engraulidae) found elsewhere, esp. *Engraulis encrasicholus*, abundant in southern Europe, much used pickled and in the form of a salt paste. **3.** *U.S.* →**smelt**[2]. [Sp. and Pg. *anchova*, probably from It. (Genoese) *anciova*, from LL *apiuva*, from Gk *aphýē*]

**anchovy pear** /– 'pɛə/, *n.* **1.** the fruit of a West Indian tree, *Grias cauliflora*, often pickled, and somewhat resembling the mango. **2.** the tree.

**anchusin** /æŋ'kjusən/, *n.* →**alkanet** (def. 3).

**anchylose** /'æŋkəlouz/, *v.t., v.i.,* **-losed, -losing.** →**ankylose.** – **anchylosis** /æŋkə'lousəs/, *n.* – **anchylotic** /æŋkə'lɒtɪk/, *adj.*

**anchylostomiasis** /,æŋkəlɒstə'maɪəsəs/, *n.* →**ankylostomiasis.**

**ancien régime** /,ɒ̃sjɒ̃ reɪ'ʒim/, *n.* a former system of government. [F; the political and social system of France before the Revolution of 1789]

**ancient** /'eɪnʃənt, 'eɪntʃənt/, *adj.* **1.** of or in time long past, esp. before the end of the Western Roman Empire, A.D. 476: *ancient history.* **2.** dating from a remote period; of great age. **3.** very old (applied to persons). **4.** *Archaic.* venerable. **5.** *Law.* having been in existence for a statutory period of time, often 20 years: *in ancient matters the normal requirements of proof are relaxed.* *–n.* **6.** a person who lived in ancient times, esp. one of the ancient Greeks, Romans, Hebrews, etc. **7.** (*usu. pl.*) one of the classical writers of antiquity. **8.** an old man. [ME *auncien*, from OF *ancien*, from LL *antiānus* former, old, from L *ante* before] – **ancientness**, *n.*

**Ancient Greek** /– 'grik/, *n.* Greek as spoken before c. 300 B.C. See **Greek** (def. 5).

**ancient history** /– 'hɪstəri/, *n.* **1.** history before the end of the Western Roman Empire in A.D. 476. **2.** *Colloq.* information or events of the recent past which are common knowledge or are no longer relevant.

**ancient light** /– 'laɪt/, *n.* a window or other opening that has been used 20 or more years without interruption and is therefore protected at common law against obstruction by an adjoining owner.

**anciently** /'eɪnʃəntli, 'eɪntʃəntli/, *adv.* in ancient times; of old.

**ancillary** /æn'sɪləri/, *adj.* accessory; auxiliary. [L *ancillāris* pertaining to a handmaid]

**ancillary relief** /– rə'lif/, *n. Law.* supplementary or incidental relief sought in addition to the main relief as in matrimonial causes, proceedings for maintenance, custody, settlement of property or damages for adultery.

**ancipital** /æn'sɪpətl/, *adj. Bot., Zool.* two-edged: *ancipital stems.* Also, **ancipitous.** [L *anceps* two-headed + -AL[1]]

**ancon** /'æŋkən/, *n., pl.* **ancones** /æŋ'kouniz/. **1.** *Archit.* any projection, as a console, supporting a cornice or the like. **2.** *Anat.* the elbow. [L, from Gk *ankṓn* a bend, the elbow] – **anconeal** /æŋ'kouniəl/, *adj.*

**-ancy,** an equivalent of **-ance,** used chiefly in nouns denoting state or quality, as in *buoyancy.* [L *-antia*]

**ancylostomiasis** /,ænsəlɒstə'maɪəsəs/, *n.* →**ankylostomiasis.**

**and** /ænd/; *weak forms* /ənd, ən, n/, *conj.* **1.** with; along with; together with; besides; also; moreover (used to connect grammatically coordinate words, phrases, or clauses): *pens and pencils.* **2.** as well as: *nice and warm.* **3.** *Colloq.* to (used between verbs): *try and do it.* **4.** *Archaic.* also; then (used to introduce a sentence, implying continuation): *And he said unto Moses.* **5.** *Archaic.* if: *and you please.* *–n.* **6.** the ampersand sign. **7.** (*oft. pl.*) an additional consideration, detail, or the like. [OE; akin to G *und*]

**andalusite** /ændə'lusaɪt/, *n.* a mineral, aluminium silicate, $Al_2SiO_5$, found in schistose rocks. [named after *Andalusia*, a region in S Spain. See -ITE[1]]

**Andamooka matrix** /,ændəmukə 'meɪtrɪks/, *n.* a pale, porous opal matrix (def. 4) which can be processed to give the appearance of a good gem opal. [named after *Andamooka*, opal mining town in S Australia]

**andante** /æn'dænteɪ, -ti/, *adv.* **1.** (a musical direction) moderately slow and even. *–n.* **2.** a movement or piece of music played in this tempo. [It.: lit., walking] – **andante,** *adj.*

**andantino** /,ændæn'tinou/, *adv., n., pl.* **-nos.** *–adv.* **1.** (a musical direction) slightly faster than andante. *–n.* **2.** a movement or piece of music played in this tempo. [It., diminutive of *andante* ANDANTE]

**Andersonian** /ændə'souniən/, *adj.* of or pertaining to the philosophy of John Anderson, Professor of Philosophy at Sydney University (1927-58), relating to ontology and realism in epistemology.

**Anderson shelter** /'ændəsən ʃɛltə/, *n.* a small corrugated steel air-raid shelter. [named after Sir John *Anderson*, 1882-1958, British Home Secretary at the outbreak of World War II]

**andesine** /'ændəzin, -zaɪn/, *n.* a plagioclase mineral occurring as crystals in igneous rocks. [named after the *Andes*, a mountain system in S America + -INE[2]]

**andesite** /'ændəzaɪt/, *n.* a volcanic rock composed essentially of plagioclase felspar together with pyroxene, resembling trachyte in appearance. [named after the *Andes*, a mountain system in S America, + -ITE[1]]

**andiron** /'ændaɪən/, *n.* one of a pair of metallic stands used to support wood in an open fire; a firedog. [ME *andyre,* from OF *andier,* ? from Gallic **andera* young cow (through use of cows' heads as decorations on andirons); *-iron* by association with *iron*]

**Andorra** /æn'dɒrə/, *n.* a small republic in the eastern Pyrenees between France and Spain under the joint suzerainty of France and the Spanish Bishop of Urgel.

**andr-,** variant of **andro-**, used before vowels, as in *androecium.*

**andradite** /'ændrədaɪt/, *n.* a mineral, calcium-iron garnet, $Ca_3Fe_2Si_3O_{12}$, occurring in brown, green, or black crystals. [named after José Bonifacio d'*Andrada* e Silva, 1763-1838, Brazilian mineralogist; see -ITE[1]]

**andrase** /'ændreɪz, -dreɪs/, *n.* an androgenic enzyme or hormone.

**andro-,** a word element meaning 'man', 'male', as contrasted with 'female', as in *androsphinx.* Also, **andr-.** [Gk, combining form of *anḗr* man, male]

**androclinium** /ændrə'klɪniəm/, *n.* →**clinandrium.**

**androecium** /æn'drisiəm/, *n., pl.* **-cia** /-siə/. the stamens of a flower collectively. [NL, from Gk *andr-* ANDR- + *oikíon* house] – **androecial,** *adj.*

**androgen** /'ændrədʒən/, *n.* any steroid which promotes masculine characteristics. – **androgenic** /ændrə'dʒɛnɪk/, *adj.*

**androgynous** /æn'drɒdʒənəs/, *adj.* **1.** *Bot.* having staminate and pistillate flowers in the same inflorescence. **2.** being both male and female; hermaphroditic. [L *androgynus,* from Gk *andrógynos* hermaphrodite] – **androgyny,** *n.*

**androsphinx** /'ændrəsfɪŋks/, *n.* a sphinx with the head of a man.

**androsterone** /æn'drɒstəroun/, *n.* an androgenic sex hormone, $C_{19}H_{30}O_2$, usually present in male urine.

**-androus,** a word element meaning 'male', as in *polyandrous.* [NL *-andrus,* from Gk *-andros* of a man]

**andy mac** /ændi 'mæk/, *n. Obs. Colloq.* a zack. [rhyming slang]

**ane** /eɪn/, *adj., n., pron. Scot.* one.

**-ane,** **1.** a noun suffix used in chemical terms, esp. names of hydrocarbons of the methane or paraffin series, as *decane, pentane, propane.* **2.** an adjective suffix used when a similar form (with a different meaning) exists in **-an,** as *human, humane.* [L *-ānus,* adj. suffix]

**anecdotage**[1] /'ænəkˌdoutɪdʒ/, *n.* anecdotes collectively. [ANECDOT(E) + -AGE]

**anecdotage**[2] /'ænəkˌdoutɪdʒ/, *n. Colloq.* a state of old age in which a person is given to excessive reminiscence. [ANECDOTE + DOTAGE]

**anecdotal** /ænək'doutl/, *adj.* pertaining to, marked by, or consisting of anecdotes.

**anecdote** /'ænəkdout/, *n.* a short narrative of a particular incident or occurrence of an interesting nature. [ML *anecdota,* from Gk *anékdota* things unpublished]

**anecdotic** /ænək'doutɪk/, *adj.* **1.** →**anecdotal.** **2.** given to relating anecdotes. Also, **anecdotical.**

**anecdotist** /'ænəkdoutəst/, *n.* a relater of anecdotes.

**anechoic** /ænɛ'kouɪk/, *adj.* free from echo and reverberation, as an anechoic chamber.

**anechoic chamber** /– 'tʃeɪmbə/, *n.* a room especially built and treated for acoustic measurement and research.

**anemia** /ə'nimiə/, *n. Chiefly U.S.* →**anaemia.** – **anemic,** *adj.*

**anemo-,** a word element meaning 'wind', as in *anemometer.* [Gk, combining form of *ánemos* wind]

**anemogram** /ə'niməgræm/, *n.* an anemographic record.

**anemograph** /ə'niməgræf, -graf/, *n.* an instrument for measuring and recording the velocity, force, or direction of the wind. – **anemographic** /ənimə'græfɪk/, *adj.* – **anemography** /æni'mɒgrəfi/, *n.*

**anemology** /ænə'mɒlədʒi/, *n.* the science of winds.

**anemometer** /ænə'mɒmətə/, *n.* **1.** an instrument for indicating wind velocity. **2.** any instrument for measuring the rate of flow of a fluid. – **anemometric** /ænəmə'mɛtrɪk/, **anemometrical** /ænəmə'mɛtrɪkəl/, *adj.* – **anemometry,** *n.*

**anemone** /ə'nɛməni/, *n.* **1.** any plant of the genus *Anemone,* esp. *A. coronaria,* a native of the Mediterranean area, widely cultivated for its mostly red and blue flowers. **2.** →**sea-anemone.** [L, from Gk: windflower]

**anemone fish** /– fɪʃ/, *n.* any of various damselfishes of the genus *Amphiprion.* See **clownfish.**

**anemophilous** /ænə'mɒfələs/, *adj.* (of seed plants) fertilised by windborne pollen. [ANEMO- + -PHILOUS; lit., wind-loving] – **anemophily,** *n.*

**anemoscope** /ə'niməskoup/, *n.* any device showing the existence and direction of the wind.

**anent** /ə'nɛnt/, *prep.* **1.** *Archaic and Scot.* in regard to; concerning. **2.** *Archaic.* opposite to; over against; close to. [var. (with excrescent *-t*) of ME *anen,* OE *on emn, on efen* on even (ground), with, beside]

**anergy** /'ænədʒi/, *n.* **1.** *Pathol.* deficiency of energy. **2.** *Med.* lack of immunity to an antigen. [NL *anergia,* from Gk: *an* - AN-[1] + *-ergia* work]

**aneroid** /'ænərɔɪd/, *adj.* **1.** using no fluid. –*n.* **2.** →**aneroid barometer.** [A-[6] + Gk *nērós* liquid + -OID]

**aneroid barometer** /– bə'rɒmətə/, *n.* an instrument for measuring atmospheric pressure and, indirectly, altitude, by registering the pressure exerted on the elastic top of a box or chamber exhausted of air.

**anesthesia** /ænəs'θiʒə, -ziə/, *n. Chiefly U.S.,* →**anaesthesia.** – **anesthetic** /ænəs'θɛtɪk/, *adj., n.* – **anesthetist** /ə'nisθətəst/, *n.*

**anesthetize** /ə'nisθətaɪz/, *v.t.,* **-tized, -tizing.** *Chiefly U.S.* →**anaesthetise.** – **anesthetization** /ənisθətaɪ'zeɪʃən/, *n.*

**anethole** /'ænəθoul/, *n.* a compound, $C_{10}H_{12}O$, found in anise and fennel oils, and used in perfumes and as an antiseptic and carminative, etc. [Gk *ánēthon* anise (properly, dill) + -OLE]

**aneuploid** /'ænjəplɔɪd/, *adj.* not having an integral multiple of the haploid set of chromosomes and therefore genetically unbalanced.

**aneurin** /ə'njurən/, *n.* →**vitamin B$_1$.** See **thiamine.**

**aneurism** /'ænjərɪzəm/, *n.* a permanent cardiac or arterial dilatation usually caused by weakening of the vessel wall by diseases such as syphilis or arteriosclerosis. Also, **aneurysm.** [Gk *aneúrysma* dilatation] – **aneurysmal, aneurismal** /ˌænjə'rɪzməl/, *adj.*

**anew** /ə'nju/, *adv.* **1.** over again; once more: *to write a story anew.* **2.** in a new form or manner. [ME *onew,* etc., OE *ofniowe,* replacing OE *edniwe* once more]

**anfractuosity** /ˌænfræktʃu'ɒsəti/, *n., pl.* **-ties.** **1.** the state or quality of being anfractuous. **2.** a channel, crevice, or passage full of windings and turnings.

**anfractuous** /æn'fræktʃuəs/, *adj.* characterised by windings and turnings; sinuous; circuitous: *an anfractuous path.* Also, **anfractuose** /æn'fræktʃuˌous/. [L *anfractuōsus* winding]

**angary** /'æŋgəri/, *n. Internat. Law.* the right of a belligerent state to seize and use the property of neutrals for purposes of warfare, subject to payment of full compensation. [L *angaria* forced service (to a lord), from Gk *angareía*]

**angel** /'eɪndʒəl/, *n.* **1.** *Theol.* one of a class of spiritual beings, attendants of God (in medieval angelology divided, according to their rank, into nine orders, ranging from highest to lowest as follows: seraphim, cherubim, thrones, dominations or dominions, virtues, powers, principalities or princedoms, archangels, angels). **2.** a conventional representation of such a being, in human form, with wings. **3.** a messenger, esp. of God. **4.** a person, esp. a woman, who resembles an angel in beauty, kindliness, etc. **5.** an attendant or guardian spirit. **6.** *Colloq.* a financial backer of a play, campaign, actor, candidate, etc. **7.** an English gold coin, struck between 1470 and 1634, bearing a figure of the archangel Michael overcoming the dragon. **8.** →**angie.** [ME and OE, var. of *engel,* pre-E **angil,* from L *angelus,* from Gk *ángelos,* orig., messenger] – **angelhood,** *n.*

**angelfish** /'eɪndʒəlfɪʃ/, *n., pl.* **-fishes,** (esp. collectively) **-fish.** **1.** any of various small, brilliantly coloured marine fishes of the family Pomacanthidae found in tropical waters. **2.** any shark of the genus *Squatina* of Atlantic and Pacific waters, with a depressed flat body and large, winglike pectoral fins. **3.** Also, **scalare.** any of the South American freshwater ciclids of the genus *Pterophyllum,* commonly kept in aquariums. **4.** a butterfly fish, *Holacanthus nicobariensis,* of the Indian Ocean, having blue and black stripes. **5.** *U.S.* any of several brightly coloured marine fishes of the coasts of North America as *Chaetodipterus faber* and *Angelichthys ciliaris.*

angelfish (def. 3)

**angel food cake,** *n.* a light cake made from egg-whites, sugar, flour and flavouring, usually cooked in a ring tin. Also, **angel**

**cake.**

**angelic** /æn'dʒɛlɪk/, *adj.* **1.** of or belonging to angels. **2.** like an angel; saintly. Also, **angelical.** – **angelically,** *adv.*

**angelica** /æn'dʒɛlɪkə/, *n.* **1.** any plant of the genus *Angelica,* tall umbelliferous plants found in both hemispheres, esp. *A. archangelica,* cultivated in Europe for its aromatic smell and medicinal root and for its stalks, which are preserved as a cake decoration, etc.; archangel. **2.** the preserved stalks. **3.** an essence made from this plant, used as a flavouring, esp. in making liqueurs. [ML: angelic (herb)]

**angelo-,** a combining form of **angel.**

**angelolatry** /eɪndʒə'lɒlətri/, *n.* angel-worship.

**angelology** /eɪndʒə'lɒlədʒi/, *n.* doctrine concerning angels.

**angel-on-horseback** /ˌeɪndʒəl-ɒn-'hɔsbæk/, *n.* **1.** an oyster wrapped in bacon, grilled and sometimes served on toast as an hors d'oeuvre. **2.** a stoned prune, similarly prepared. Also, **devil-on-horseback.**

**angel shark** /'eɪndʒəl ʃak/, *n.* **1.** →**rabbit-fish** (def. 2). **2.** →**angelfish** (def. 2).

**angelskin** /'eɪndʒəlskɪn/, *n.* a fabric, as a crepe or satin, with a dull, waxy finish.

**angelus** /'ændʒələs/, *n. Rom. Cath. Ch.* **1.** *(often cap.)* a devotion in memory of the Annunciation. **2.** the bell (**angelus bell**) tolled in the morning, at noon, and in the evening, to indicate the time when the angelus is to be recited. [LL (the first word of the recitation). See ANGEL]

**angel-water** /'eɪndʒəl-wɔtə/, *n.* a scented water originally made with angelica but later with various other substances, as ambergris or rosewater.

**anger** /'æŋgə/, *n.* **1.** a strongly felt displeasure aroused by real or supposed wrongs, often accompanied by an impulse to retaliate; wrath; ire. **2.** *Obs.* pain or smart, as of a sore. **3.** *Obs.* grief; trouble –*v.t.* **4.** to excite to anger or wrath. **5.** *Obs.* to cause to smart; inflame. [ME, from Scand.; cf. Icel. *angr* grief, sorrow]

**angie** /'ændʒi/, *n. Colloq.* →**cocaine.**

**angina** /æn'dʒaɪnə/, *n.* **1.** any inflammatory affection of the throat or fauces, as quinsy, croup, mumps, etc. **2.** →**angina pectoris.** [L: quinsy, lit., strangling. Cf. Gk *anchónē*] – **anginal,** *adj.*

**angina pectoris** /–'pɛktərəs/, *n.* a syndrome characterised by paroxysmal, constricting pain below the sternum, most easily precipitated by exertion or excitement and caused by ischaemia of the heart muscle, usu. due to a coronary artery disease, such as arteriosclerosis. [NL: angina of the chest]

**angio-,** word element meaning 'vessel', or 'container', as in *angiology.* [NL, from Gk *angeio-,* combining form of *angeîon* vessel]

**angiogram** /'ændʒiəgræm/, *n.* a diagram resulting from angiography.

**angiography** /ændʒi'ɒgrəfi/, *n.* determination of arrangement and character of blood or lymph vessels without dissection, as by radiography after injection of a radiopaque substance. – **angiographer** *n.*

**angiology** /ændʒi'ɒlədʒi/, *n.* the part of the science of anatomy that deals with blood vessels and lymphatics.

**angioma** /ændʒi'oʊmə/, *n., pl.* **-mas, -mata** /-mətə/. a tumour consisting chiefly of dilated or newly formed blood or lymph vessels. [ANGI(O)- + -OMA] – **angiomatous** /ændʒi'ɒmətəs, -'oʊmə-/, *adj.*

**angiosperm** /'ændʒiəˌspɜm/, *n.* a plant having its seeds enclosed in an ovary (opposed to *gymnosperm*). – **angiospermous** /ˌændʒiə'spɜməs/, *adj.*

**angle**[1] /'æŋgəl/, *n., v.,* **-gled, -gling.** –*n.* **1.** *Maths.* **a.** the space within two lines or three planes diverging from a common point, or within two planes diverging from a common line. **b.** the figure so formed. **c.** the amount of rotation needed to bring one line or plane into coincidence with another. **2.** an angular projection; a projecting corner: *the angles of a building.* **3.** an angular recess; a nook, corner. **4.** a point of view; standpoint: *a new angle on the problem.* **5.** an aspect, side; phase: *to consider all angles of the question.* **6.** *Colloq.* a devious, artful scheme, method, etc. **7.** *Engineering.* →**angle iron. 8. at an angle,** slanting; not perpendicular (to). –*v.t.* **9.** to move, direct, bend or present at an angle or in an angular course. **10.** to put a slant or bias on (a question, statement, etc.). **11.** to put into a corner; corner. –*v.i.* **12.** to move or bend in angles. [ME, from F, from L *angulus*]

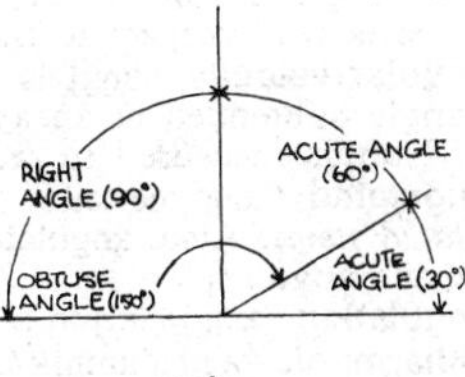

angles

**angle**[2] /'æŋgəl/, *v.,* **-gled, -gling,** *n.* –*v.i.* **1.** to fish with hook and line. **2. angle for,** to try to get something by scheming, using tricks or artful means: *to angle for a compliment.* –*n.* **3.** *Archaic.* a fishhook or fishing tackle. [OE *angel, angul;* akin to ANGLE[1]]

**angle bracket** /'– brækət/, *n.* an L-shaped metal bracket used to support a shelf, etc.

**angled** /'æŋgəld/, *adj.* having an angle or angles.

**angle iron** /'æŋgəl aɪən/, *n.* **1.** a bar of iron in the form of an angle. **2.** a rolled iron or steel bar with an L-shaped cross-section, used mainly in iron constructions. Also, **angle, angle section.**

**angle of attack,** *n.* the acute angle between the chord line of an aerofoil and the direction of its motion relative to the air.

**angle of incidence,** *n.* **1.** the angle that a line, ray of light, etc., meeting a surface, makes with the perpendicular to that surface at the point of meeting. **2.** *Aeron.* the angle between the chord line of an aerofoil and the longitudinal axis of the fuselage. **3. rigging angle of incidence,** the fixed angle between the chord line of the wing or tailplane and the axis of the fuselage.

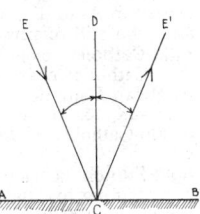

ECD, angle of incidence on surface AB; CD, perpendicular; E[1]CD, angle of reflection

**angle of reflection,** *n.* the angle that a ray of light, or the like, reflected from a surface, makes with a perpendicular to that surface at the point of reflection.

**angle of refraction,** *n.* the angle that a refracted ray of light makes with the perpendicular to the interfacial surface at the point of refraction.

**angle park** /'æŋgəl pak/, *v.t.* to park (a car) at an angle to the kerb, generally at an angle of 45°, usu. with rear to kerb. – **angle parking,** *n.*

**angler** /'æŋglə/, *n.* **1.** one who angles; one who fishes for pleasure. **2.** any of various fishes of the family Lophiidae having a modified dorsal spine above the mouth forming a 'fishing rod' which can be moved to entice smaller fish, as *Lophiomus laticeps* of the Queensland and New South Wales continental shelf, or *Lophius piscatorius* of Europe and America. **3.** any of a number of small Australian fishes with a similar modification, variously coloured and often camouflaged, belonging to the family Antennaridae, as the striped angler, *Phrynelox striatus.* **4.** any of various similar fishes of the order Pediculati.

**anglesite** /'æŋgəlsaɪt/, *n.* a mineral, lead sulphate, $PbSO_4$, found in massive forms or in colourless or variously tinted crystals; a common lead ore. [named after *Anglesey,* an island in NW Wales. See -ITE[1]]

**angleworm** /'æŋgəlwɜm/, *n.* an earthworm used for bait in angling.

**Anglican** /'æŋglɪkən/, *adj. Eccles.* **1.** of or pertaining to the Church of England. **2.** of or pertaining to any church related in origin to, or in commission with the Church of England, as the Anglican Church in Australia. –*n.* **3.** a member of an Anglican church. **4.** (formerly) a High-Churchman or Anglo-Catholic. [ML *Anglicānus*]

**Anglican Church** /– 'tʃɜtʃ/, *n.* the Church of England and the churches in other countries in full accord with it as to doctrine and church order, as the Anglican Church in Australia, the Church of Ireland, the Episcopal Church of Scotland, the Church of Wales, the Protestant Episcopal Church in the U.S., etc.

**Anglicanism** /'æŋglɪkənɪzəm/, *n.* Anglican principles; the Anglican Church system.

**anglicise** /'æŋgləsaɪz/, *v.t., v.i.,* **-cised, -cising.** *(sometimes cap.)* to make or become English in form or character: *to* *anglicise the pronunciation of a Russian name.* Also, **anglicize.** – **anglicisation** /ˌæŋgləsaɪˈzeɪʃən/, *n.*

**Anglicism** /ˈæŋgləsɪzəm/, *n.* an English idiom.

**angling** /ˈæŋglɪŋ/, *n.* **1.** the act or art of fishing with a hook and line, usually attached to a rod. **2.** in surfing, the practice of directing a board across a wave rather than straight towards the beach.

**Anglo-**, a word element meaning 'pertaining to England or the English', as in *Anglo-American.* [combining form representing ML *Anglus* Englishman, *Anglī* (pl.) the English]

**Anglo-American** /æŋgloʊ-əˈmɛrɪkən/, *adj.* **1.** belonging or relating to, or connected with, England and America, esp. the United States, or with the people of both: *Anglo-American commerce.* **2.** pertaining to the English who have settled in America, esp. in the United States, or have become American citizens. *–n.* **3.** a native or descendant of a native of England who has settled in America, esp. in the United States, or has become an American citizen.

**Anglo-Australian** /æŋgloʊ-ɒstˈreɪljən/, *adj.* **1.** belonging or relating to, or connected with England and Australia, or with the people of both. **2.** pertaining to the English who have settled in Australia, or have become Australian citizens. *–n.* **3.** a native or descendant of a native of England who has settled in Australia, or who has become an Australian citizen and who still retains emotional ties with England.

**Anglo-Catholic** /æŋgloʊ-ˈkæθlɪk/, *n.* **1.** one who emphasises the Catholic character of the Anglican Church. **2.** an Anglican Catholic, as opposed to a Roman or Greek Catholic. *–adj.* **3.** of or pertaining to Anglo-Catholicism or Anglo-Catholics. – **Anglo-Catholicism** /ˌæŋgloʊ-kəˈθɒləsɪzəm/, *n.*

**Anglo-French** /æŋgloʊ-ˈfrɛntʃ/, *adj.* **1.** English and French. **2.** pertaining to Anglo-French (def. 3). *–n.* **3.** that dialect of French current in England from the Norman Conquest to the end of the Middle Ages.

**Anglo-Indian** /æŋgloʊ-ˈɪndiən/, *n.* **1.** a person of mixed English and Indian parentage; a Eurasian. **2.** a person of British birth who has lived long in India. *–adj.* **3.** Eurasian. **4.** of, pertaining to, or relating to England and India as politically associated. **5.** of the English language as spoken in India.

**Anglo-Irish** /æŋgloʊ-ˈaɪrɪʃ/, *adj.* **1.** English and Irish. **2.** pertaining to the English who have settled in Ireland. *–n.* **3.** the people of English birth or descent living in Ireland.

**Anglomania** /æŋgləˈmeɪniə/, *n.* an excessive attachment to, respect for, or imitation of English institutions, manners, customs, etc. – **Anglomaniac,** *n.*

**Anglo-Norman** /æŋgloʊ-ˈnɔmən/, *adj.* **1.** pertaining to that period, 1066-1154, when England was ruled by Normans. **2.** pertaining to the Normans who settled in England, or their descendants, or their dialect of French. *–n.* **3.** a Norman who settled in England after 1066, or one of his descendants. **4.** Anglo-French.

**Anglo-Nubian** /æŋgloʊ-ˈnjubiən/, *n.* one of a breed of British goats developed by interbreeding native British breeds with Nubian goats.

**Anglophile** /ˈæŋgləfaɪl/, *n.* one who is friendly to or admires England or English customs, institutions, etc. Also, **Anglophil.**

**Anglophobe** /ˈæŋgləfoʊb/, *n.* one who hates or fears England or the English.

**Anglophobia** /æŋgləˈfoʊbiə/, *n.* an intense hatred or fear of England, or of whatever is English.

**Anglophone** /ˈæŋgləfoʊn/, *adj.* English-speaking.

**Anglo-Saxon** /æŋgloʊ-ˈsæksən/, *n.* **1.** one who belongs to the English-speaking world, irrespective of historical periods, political boundaries, geographical areas, or racial origins. **2.** an Englishman of the period before the Norman conquest. **3.** a person of English stock and traditions; in the U.S., usu. a person of colonial descent and/or British origin. **4.** →**Old English** (def. 1). **5.** the English language. **6.** plain English. **7.** →**pre-English** (def. 1). *–adj.* **8.** of, pertaining to, or characteristic of the Anglo-Saxons. **9.** pertaining to Anglo-Saxon. [ML *Anglo-Saxonēs* the English people; replacing OE *Angulseaxan,* from ML *Anglī Saxonēs,* Latinisations of the OE folk names *Angle* and *Seaxan*]

**Angola** /æŋˈgoʊlə/, *n.* a country in south-western Africa.

**angophora** /æŋˈgɒfərə/, *n.* any of a number of species of *Angophora,* trees of eastern Australia related to *Eucalyptus,* such as *A. costata,* with gnarled pink branches, and *A. hispida,* a small, rough-barked tree with creamy white flowers in summer, both species being common in the Sydney area.

**Angora** /æŋˈgɔrə/, *n.* **1.** an Angora rabbit. **2.** an Angora cat. **3.** (*sometimes l.c.*) **a.** the hair of the Angora goat or rabbit. **b.** a yarn or fabric made from this. **4.** (*l.c.*) **act the angora,** *Colloq.* to behave in a foolish fashion. [from *Angora,* variant of *Ankara,* capital of Turkey]

**Angora cat** /– ˈkæt/, *n.* a long-haired variety of the domestic cat, orig. from Angora.

**Angora goat** /– ˈgoʊt/, *n.* a variety of goat, orig. from Angora, reared for its long, silky hair which is called mohair.

**Angora rabbit** /– ˈræbət/, *n.* a long-haired variety of domestic rabbit.

**angostura bark** /ˌæŋgəstʃurə ˈbak/, *n.* the bitter aromatic bark of a South American tree, *Galipea officinalis,* supposed to be valuable as a tonic. Also, **angostura.** [named after *Angostura,* the former name of Ciudad Bolívar, a town in E Venezuela]

**angostura bitters** /æŋgəˌstʃurə ˈbɪtəz/, *n.* a bitter aromatic tonic prepared in Trinidad from barks, roots, herbs, etc., under a secret formula. [Trademark]

**angry** /ˈæŋgri/, *adj.,* **-grier, -griest. 1.** feeling or showing anger or resentment (*with* or *at* a person, *at* or *about* a thing). **2.** characterised by anger; wrathful: *angry words.* **3.** *Med.* inflamed, as a sore; exhibiting inflammation. **4.** *Colloq.* expressing the attitude of an angry young man. [ME ANGER + -Y[1]] – **angrily,** *adv.* – **angriness,** *n.*

**angry young man,** *n.* a young man, esp. a writer, outspokenly disgusted with the existing social order.

**angst** /æŋst/, *n.* a feeling or outlook of dread, fear, etc. [G *Angst*]

**angstrom** /ˈæŋstrəm/, *n.* a unit of length for measuring very short wavelengths and distances between atoms in molecules, equal to $10^{-10}$ metres. *Symbol:* Å [named after A. J. *Ångström,* 1814-74, Swedish physicist]

**anguilliform** /æŋˈgwɪləfɔm/, *adj.* having the shape or form of an eel. [L *anguilla* eel + -(I)FORM]

**anguine** /ˈæŋgwən/, *adj.* pertaining to or resembling a snake. [L *anguīnus*]

**anguish** /ˈæŋgwɪʃ/, *n.* **1.** excruciating or agonising pain of either body or mind; acute suffering or distress: *the anguish of grief.* *–v.t., v.i.* **2.** to affect with or suffer anguish. [ME, from OF *anguisse, angoisse,* from L *angustia* straitness, pl. straits, distress]

**angular** /ˈæŋgjələ/, *adj.* **1.** having an angle or angles. **2.** consisting of, situated at, or forming an angle. **3.** of, pertaining to, or measured by an angle. **4.** bony; gaunt. **5.** acting or moving awkwardly. **6.** stiff in manner; unbending. [L *angulāris*] – **angulary,** *adv.* – **angularness,** *n.*

**angular acceleration** /– əksɛləˈreɪʃən/, *n.* rate of change of angular velocity.

**angular diameter** /– daɪˈæmətə/, *n.* the angle which the apparent diameter of a celestial body subtends at the observer's eye.

**angular distance** /– ˈdɪstəns/, *n.* the distance between two bodies in terms of the angle subtended by them at the point of observation.

**angular frequency** /– ˈfrikwənsi/, *n.* the frequency of a periodic phenomenon expressed in radians per second, which is equal to $2\pi$ multiplied by the frequency in hertz.

**angularity** /æŋgjəˈlærəti/, *n., pl.* **-ties. 1.** angular quality. **2.** (*pl.*) sharp corners; angular outlines.

**angular momentum** /ˌæŋgjələ moʊˈmɛntəm/, *n.* the product of the angular velocity of a rotating body and its moment of inertia with respect to the same axis.

**angular velocity** /æŋgjələ vəˈlɒsəti/, *n.* rate of change of the angle subtended at an axis by a moving object or point; in SI units, measured in radians per second.

**angulated** /ˈæŋgjəleɪtəd/, *adj.* of angular form; angled: *angulated stems.* Also, **angulate** /ˈæŋgjələt, -leɪt/. [L *angulātus,* pp., made angular]

**angulation** /æŋgjəˈleɪʃən/, *n.* angular formation.

**anharmonic** /ænhaˈmɒnɪk/, *adj.* not harmonic

**anhedral** /ænˈhidrəl/, *adj.* (of an aircraft) having the wings sloping downwards, so that the wingtip is below the wingroot.

See **dihedral.**

**anhinga** /æn'hɪŋgə/, *n.* →**darter** (def. 2).

**anhydride** /æn'haɪdraɪd, -drəd/, *n.* **1.** a compound formed by abstraction of water, an oxide of a non-metal (**acid anhydride**) or a metal (**basic anhydride**) which forms an acid or a base, respectively, when united with water. **2.** a compound from which water has been abstracted. [Gk *ánydros* without water (with etymological *h* inserted) + -IDE]

**anhydrite** /æn'haɪdraɪt/, *n.* a mineral anhydrous calcium sulphate, $CaSO_4$, usually in whitish or slightly coloured masses.

**anhydrous** /æn'haɪdrəs/, *adj.* indicating loss of all water, esp. water of crystallisation. [Gk *ánydros* without water (with *h* from *hydrous*)]

**ani** /'ani/, *n., pl.* **anis.** either of two black cuckoo-like birds of the genus *Crotophaga,* inhabiting the warmer parts of America. [Sp. or Pg., from Tupi]

**anil** /'ænəl/, *n.* **1.** a shrub, *Indigofera suffruticosa,* one of the plants which yield indigo, native to the West Indies. **2.** indigo; deep blue. [F, from Pg., from Ar. *al-nīl,* from *al* the + *nīl* (from Skt *nīlī* indigo)]

**anile** /'eɪnaɪl/, *adj.* of or like a weak old woman: *anile ideas.* [L *anīlis,* from *anus* old woman]

**aniline** /'ænələn/, *n.* **1.** an oily liquid, $C_6H_5NH_2$, obtained first from indigo but now prepared from benzene, and serving as the basis of many brilliant dyes, and in the manufacture of plastics, resins, etc. *–adj.* **2.** pertaining to or derived from aniline: *aniline colours.* [ANIL + -INE[2]]

**aniline dye** /– 'daɪ/, *n.* any organic dye made from a coal-tar base (because the earliest ones were made from aniline).

**anilingus** /eɪni'lɪŋgəs/, *n.* erotic, oral stimulation of the anus. [*ani-,* combining form of ANUS + (CUNNI)LINGUS] – **anilingual,** *adj.*

**anility** /ə'nɪləti/, *n., pl.* **-ties. 1.** an anile state. **2.** an anile notion or procedure.

**anima** /'ænəmə/, *n.* **1.** soul; life. **2.** (in the psychology of C. G. Jung) **a.** the inner personality that is turned towards the unconscious of the individual (constrasted with *persona*). **b.** the feminine principle, esp. as present in men (contrasted with *animus*). [L: breath, soul]

**animadversion** /ænəmæd'vɜʒən/, *n.* **1.** a remark, usually implying censure; a criticism or comment. **2.** the act or fact of criticising. [L *animadversio*]

**animadvert** /ænəmæd'vɜt/, *v.i.* **1.** to comment critically; make remarks by way of criticism or censure (fol. by *on* or *upon*). **2.** *Obs.* to take cognisance or notice. *–v.t.* **3.** to consider. **4.** to remark. [L *animadvertere* regard, notice]

**animal** /'ænəməl/, *n.* **1.** any living thing that is not a plant, generally capable of voluntary motion, sensation, etc. **2.** any animal other than man. **3.** an inhuman person; brutish or beastlike person. *–adj.* **4.** of, pertaining to, or derived from animals: *animal life, animal fats.* **5.** pertaining to the physical or carnal nature of man, rather than his spiritual or intellectual nature: *animal needs.* [L: living being]

**animal black** /– 'blæk/, *n.* any black pigment made from calcined bone or similar animal matter.

**animalcule** /ænə'mælkjul/, *n.* **1.** a minute or microscopic animal, nearly or quite invisible to the naked eye, as an infusorian or rotifer. **2.** *Rare.* a tiny animal, such as a mouse, fly, etc. [NL *animalculum,* diminutive of L *animal* animal] – **animalcular,** *adj.*

**animalculum** /ænə'mælkjələm/, *n., pl.* **-la** /-lə/. →**animalcule.**

**animal husbandry** /ænəməl 'hʌzbəndri/, *n.* the science of breeding, feeding, and care of animals, esp. on a farm.

**animalise** /'ænəməlaɪz/, *v.t.,* **-lised, -lising.** to excite the animal passions of; brutalise; sensualise. Also, **animalize.** – **animalisation** /ˌænəməlaɪ'zeɪʃən/, *n.*

**animalism** /'ænəməlɪzəm/, *n.* **1.** an animal state; state of being actuated by sensual appetites, and not by intellectual or moral forces; sensuality. **2.** the doctrine that human beings are without a spiritual nature.

**animalist** /'ænəmələst/, *n.* **1.** one who believes in the doctrine of animalism. **2.** a painter, sculptor, writer, etc., who portrays animals. – **animalistic** /ænəmə'lɪstɪk/, *adj.*

**animality** /ænə'mæləti/, *n.* **1.** the animal nature in man. **2.** animal life.

**animal kingdom** /ænəməl 'kɪŋdəm/, *n.* the animals of the world collectively (distinguished from *plant kingdom*).

**animally** /'ænəməli/, *adv.* physically.

**animal magnetism** /ænəməl 'mægnətɪzəm/, *n.* **1.** attractive power or charm exerted by one's physical or animal nature, esp. by physical beauty, strength, etc. **2.** *Obs.* **a.** hypnotism. **b.** hypnotic powers.

**animal spirits** /- 'spɪrəts/, *n.* exuberance of health and life; animation and good humour; buoyancy.

**animal starch** /– 'statʃ/, *n.* →**glycogen.**

**animate** /'ænəmeɪt/, *v.,* **-mated, -mating;** /'ænəmət/, *adj.* *–v.t.* **1.** to give life to; make alive. **2.** to make lively, vivacious, or vigorous. **3.** to encourage: *to animate weary troops.* **4.** to move to action; actuate: *animated by religious zeal.* **5.** to cause to appear or move as if alive, as in an animated cartoon. *–adj.* **6.** alive; possessing life: *animate creatures.* **7.** lively. [L *animātus*] – **animater, animator,** *n.* – **animatingly,** *adv.*

**animated** /'ænəmeɪtəd/, *adj.* **1.** full of life, action, or spirit; lively; vigorous: *an animated debate.* **2.** moving or made to move as if alive. – **animatedly,** *adv.*

**animated cartoon** /– ka'tun/, *n.* a film consisting of a series of drawings, each slightly different from the ones before and after it, run through a projector.

**animation** /ænə'meɪʃən/, *n.* **1.** animated quality; liveliness; vivacity; spirit; life. **2.** the act of animating; act of enlivening. **3.** the process of preparing animated cartoons.

**animatism** /'ænəmətɪzəm/, *n.* the attribution of consciousness to inanimate objects.

**animato** /ænə'matoʊ/, *adv.* (a musical direction) animatedly (often taken as indicating a quickening of tempo). – **animato,** *adj.*

**animé** /'ænəmeɪ/, *n.* any of various resins or copals, esp. that from *Hymenaea courbaril,* a tree of tropical America, used in making varnish, scenting pastilles, etc. [Sp., probably from native dialect]

**animism** /'ænəmɪzəm/, *n.* **1.** the belief that all natural objects and the universe itself possess a soul. **2.** the belief that natural objects have souls which may exist apart from their material bodies. **3.** the doctrine that the soul is the principle of life and health. **4.** belief in spiritual beings or agencies. [L *anima* soul + -ISM] – **animist,** *n., adj.* – **animistic** /ænə'mɪstɪk/, *adj.*

**animosity** /ænə'mɒsəti/, *n., pl.* **-ities.** a feeling of ill will or enmity animating the conduct, or tending to display itself in action (fol. by *between* or *towards*). [late ME *animosite,* from L *animōsitas* courage]

**animus** /'ænəməs/, *n.* **1.** hostile spirit; animosity. **2.** purpose; intention; animating spirit. **3.** (in the psychology of C.G. Jung) the masculine principle, esp. as present in women (contrasted with *anima*). **4.** *Law.* intention, as *animus furandi,* intention of stealing; *animus possidendi,* intention of possessing; *animus revertendi,* intention of returning; *animus revocandi,* intention of revoking (a will).

**anion** /'ænaɪən/, *n.* **1.** a negatively charged ion which is attracted to the anode in electrolysis. **2.** any negatively charged atom, radical, or molecule. [Gk: going up (ppr. neut.)]

**anise** /'ænis, 'ænəs/, *n.* **1.** a herbaceous plant, *Pimpinella anisum,* of Mediterranean regions, yielding aniseed. **2.** →**aniseed.** [ME *anys,* from OF *anis,* from L *anīsum,* from Gk *ánīson* dill, anise]

**aniseed** /'ænəsid/, *n.* **1.** the aromatic seed of the anise, used in medicine, in cookery, etc. **2.** a stout aromatic New Zealand herb, *Gingidia montana.*

**aniseikonia** /ænˌaɪsaɪ'koʊniə/, *n.* a condition of the eyes in which one eye sees an image of shape and size different from that seen by the other. [NL, from *anis(o)-* ANISO- + Gk *eikṓn* image + *-ia* -IA]

**anisette** /ænə'zɛt, -'sɛt/, *n.* a cordial or liqueur flavoured with aniseed. [F]

**aniso-,** a word element meaning 'unlike' or 'unequal'. [combining form representing Gk *ánisos* unequal, from *an-* AN-[1] + *ī́sos* equal]

**anisocarpic** /ænˌaɪsoʊ'kapɪk/, *adj.* (of a flower) having fewer carpels than other floral parts.

**anisodactylous** /ænˌaɪsoʊ'dæktələs/, *adj.* **1.** *Zool.* unequal-toed; having the toes unlike. **2.** *Ornith.* having three toes pointing forwards and one backwards.

**anisole** /ˈænəsoʊl/, *n.* a colourless fluid, $C_7H_8O$, used in the perfume industry and for killing lice. [ANISE + -OLE]

**anisomerous** /ænəˈsɒmərəs/, *adj.* unsymmetrical (applied to flowers which do not have the same number of parts in each circle). – **anisomery,** *n.*

**anisometric** /æn,aɪsoʊˈmɛtrɪk/, *adj.* **1.** not isometric; of unequal measurement. **2.** (of crystals) having three dimensionally unequal axial directions.

**anisometropia** /æn,aɪsoʊməˈtroʊpiə/, *n.* inequality in the power of the two eyes to refract light. [NL: *aniso-* ANISO- + Gk *métron* measure + *-opia* -OPIA]

**anisotropic** /æn,aɪsoʊˈtrɒpɪk/, *adj.* **1.** *Physics.* of different properties in different directions. **2.** *Bot.* of different dimensions along the different axes. – **anisotropy** /,ænaɪˈsɒtrəpi/, *n.*

**ankerite** /ˈæŋkəraɪt/, *n.* a mineral, an iron-bearing variety of dolomite containing iron in place of part of the magnesium. [named after Prof. M. J. *Anker,* d. 1843, Austrian mineralogist]

**ankh** /æŋk/, *n.* a tau cross with a loop at the top, used as a symbol of generation or enduring life. [Egypt.: life, soul]

ankh

**ankle** /ˈæŋkəl/, *n.* **1.** the aggregate joint connecting the foot with the leg. **2.** the slender part of the leg above the foot. [ME *ankel,* from Scand. (cf. Dan. *ankel*); replacing OE *anclēow(e)*]

**anklebone** /ˈæŋkəlboʊn/, *n.* →**astragalus.**

**ankle deep** /æŋkəl-ˈdip/, *adj.* high or deep enough to cover the ankles.

**ankle-sock** /ˈæŋkəl-sɒk/, *n.* a sock which reaches just above the ankle.

**anklet** /ˈæŋklət/, *n.* an ornament for the ankle, corresponding to a bracelet for the wrist or forearm.

**ankus** /ˈæŋkəs/, *n.* an elephant goad. [Hind.]

**ankylose** /ˈæŋkəloʊz/, *v.,* **-losed, -losing.** *–v.t.* **1.** to join together or consolidate, as two otherwise freely approximating similar or dissimilar hard tissues, like the bones of a joint or the root of a tooth and its surrounding bone. *–v.i.* **2.** to grow together or become joined by ankylosis. Also, **anchylose.**

**ankylosis** /æŋkəˈloʊsəs/, *n.* **1.** *Pathol.* morbid adhesion of the bones of a joint. **2.** *Anat.* consolidation or union of two similar or dissimilar hard tissues previously freely approximating, as the bones of a joint, or the root of a tooth and its surrounding bone. Also, **anchylosis.** [NL, from Gk: stiffening of the joints] – **ankylotic** /æŋkəˈlɒtɪk/, *adj.*

**ankylostomiasis** /,æŋkəlɒstəˈmaɪəsəs/, *n.* →**hookworm disease.** Also, **anchylostomiasis, ancylostomiasis.** [NL *Ancylostom(a)* genus of hookworms (from Gk *ankýlo(s)* bent, hooked + *stóma* mouth) + -IASIS]

**ANL** /eɪ ɛn ˈɛl/, Australian National Line.

**anlace** /ˈænləs/, *n.* a medieval dagger or short sword, worn in front of the person. [ME, from OF *ale(s)naz,* from *alesne* awl, from Gmc *alisna*]

**anlage** /ˈænlagə/, *n., pl.* **-gen** /-gən/. **1.** →**primordium.** **2.** →**blastema.** [G: set-up, layout]

**ann.,** annual.

**anna** /ˈænə/, *n.* a former unit of currency in India. [Hind. *ānā*]

**annabergite** /ˈænə,bɜgaɪt/, *n.* a mineral, hydrous nickel arsenate, $Ni_3As_2O_8 \, 8H_2O$, occurring in apple-green crystalline masses; nickel bloom. [named after *Annaberg,* town in Saxony. See -ITE[1]]

**annal** /ˈænəl/, *n.* a register or record of the events of a year. See **annals.**

**annalist** /ˈænələst/, *n.* a chronicler of yearly events.

**annalistic** /ænəˈlɪstɪk/, *adj.* of or pertaining to an annalist. – **annalistically,** *adv.*

**annals** /ˈænəlz/, *n.pl.* **1.** history or relation of events recorded year by year. **2.** historical records generally. **3.** a periodical publication containing formal reports of learned societies, etc. [L *annālēs* (*librī* books) yearly records]

**Annamese** /ænəˈmiz/, *adj., n., pl.* **-mese.** *–adj.* **1.** of or pertaining to Annam, its people, or their language. *–n.* **2.** a native of Annam. **3.** (formerly) the Vietnamese language. **4.** the linguistic family to which this belongs, widespread in Tonkin and Annam, and of no certainly known relationships.

**Annamite** /ˈænəmaɪt,/, *n., adj.* →**Annamese.**

**annatto** /əˈnætoʊ/, *n.* **1.** a small tree, *Bixa orellana,* of tropical America. **2.** a yellowish red dye obtained from the pulp enclosing its seeds, used for colouring fabrics, butter, varnish, etc. Also, **anatto, annatta, anatta, arnotto.** [Carib]

**anneal** /əˈniəl/, *v.t.* **1.** to heat (glass, earthenware, metals, etc.) to remove or prevent internal stress. **2.** to free from internal stress by heating and gradually cooling. **3.** to toughen or temper: *to anneal the mind.* [ME *anele(n),* OE *anǣlan,* from *an* on + *ǣlan* burn]

**annelid** /ˈænəlɪd/, *n.* a member of the Annelida, a phylum of worms comprising earthworms, leeches, various marine worms, etc., characterised by their ringed or segmented bodies. [F *annélide,* from L *ānellus* (diminutive of *ānulus* ring) + *-ide* -ID[2]]

**annex** /ˈænɛks, əˈnɛks/, *v.;* /ˈænɛks/, *n.* *–v.t.* **1.** to attach, join, or add, esp. to something larger or more important; unite; append; subjoin. **2.** to take possession of, take to one's own use permanently. **3.** *Colloq.* to take without permission; appropriate. *–n.* **4.** something annexed or added, esp. a supplement to a document: *an annex to a treaty.* **5.** annexe. [ME *a(n)nexe(n),* from ML *annexāre,* from L *annexus,* pp., joined] – **annexable,** *adj.*

**annexation** /ænɛkˈseɪʃən/, *n.* **1.** the act of annexing, esp. new territory. **2.** the fact of being annexed. **3.** something annexed. – **annexationist,** *n.*

**annexe** /ˈænɛks/, *n.* **1.** a subsidiary building or an addition to a building. **2.** something annexed. Also, **annex.** [F]

**annexure** /əˈnɛkʃə/, *n.* →**annex** (def. 4).

**annihilable** /əˈnaɪələbəl/, *adj.* susceptible of annihilation. – **annihilability** /ə,naɪələˈbɪləti/, *n.*

**annihilate** /əˈnaɪəleɪt/, *v.t.,* **-lated, -lating.** **1.** to reduce to nothing; destroy utterly: *the bombing annihilated the city.* **2.** to destroy the form or collective existence of: *to annihilate an army.* **3.** to cancel the effect of; annul: *to annihilate a law.* **4.** *Colloq.* to defeat utterly, as in argument, competition, or the like. [LL *annihilātus,* pp.] – **annihilative** /əˈnaɪələtɪv/, *adj.* – **annihilator,** *n.*

**annihilation** /ənaɪəˈleɪʃən/, *n.* **1.** the act of annihilating. **2.** extinction; destruction. – **annihilationist,** *n.*

**annihilation radiation** /– reɪdiˈeɪʃən/, *n.* the radiation produced when a particle and an antiparticle, such as an electron and a positron, disappear with a resultant release of energy.

**anniv.,** anniversary.

**anniversary** /ænəˈvɜsəri/, *n., pl.* **-ries,** *adj.* *–n.* **1.** the yearly recurrence of the date of a past event. **2.** the celebration of such a date. *–adj.* **3.** returning or recurring each year. **4.** pertaining to an anniversary: *an anniversary gift.* [L *anniversārius*]

**anno aetatis suae** /,ænoʊ aɪtatəs ˈsuaɪ, –itatəs ˈsui/, in the year of his age. [L]

**anno Domini** /,ænoʊ ˈdɒmənaɪ, -ni/, in the year of our Lord. *Abbrev.:* A.D. as A.D. 597. [L]

**annotate** /ˈænəteɪt/, *v.,* **-tated, -tating.** *–v.t.* **1.** to supply with notes; remark upon in notes: *to annotate the works of Bacon.* *–v.i.* **2.** to make annotations or notes. [L *annotātus,* pp.] – **annotator,** *n.*

**annotation** /ænəˈteɪʃən/, *n.* **1.** the act of annotating. **2.** a note commenting upon, explaining, or criticising some passage of a book or other writing.

**announce** /əˈnaʊns/, *v.t.,* **-nounced, -nouncing.** **1.** to make known publicly; give notice of. **2.** to state the approach or presence of: *to announce guests or dinner.* **3.** to make known to the mind or senses. [ME *announce(n),* from OF *anoncier,* from L *annuntiāre*]

**announcement** /əˈnaʊnsmənt/, *n.* **1.** public or formal notice announcing something. **2.** the act of announcing.

**announcer** /əˈnaʊnsə/, *n.* one who announces, esp. on radio or television.

**annoy** /əˈnɔɪ/, *v.t.* **1.** to disturb (a person) in a way that displeases, troubles, or slightly irritates him. **2.** *Mil.* to molest; harm. *–v.i.* **3.** to be disagreeable or troublesome. *–n.* **4.**

*Archaic or Poetic.* something annoying. [ME *anoye,* from OF *enui,* from *en(n)uyer* displease, from LL *inodiāre,* from *in odiō* in hatred] – **annoyer,** *n.*

**annoyance** /ə'nɔɪəns/, *n.* **1.** that which annoys; a nuisance: *some visitors are an annoyance.* **2.** the act of annoying. **3.** the feeling of being annoyed. **4.** *Acoustics.* the (degree of) psychological distress caused by excessive noise.

**annoying** /ə'nɔɪɪŋ/, *adj.* causing annoyance: *annoying habits.* – **annoyingly,** *adv.* – **annoyingness,** *n.*

**annual** /'ænjuəl/, *adj.* **1.** of, for, or pertaining to a year; yearly. **2.** occurring or returning once a year: *an annual celebration.* **3.** *Bot.* living only one growing season, as beans or maize. **4.** performed during a year: *the annual course of the sun.* –*n.* **5.** a plant living only one year or season. **6.** a literary production published annually. **7.** *Colloq.* a bath; ablutions.

**annual ring** /– 'rɪŋ/, *n.* one of the yearly growth rings on a cross-section of a tree.

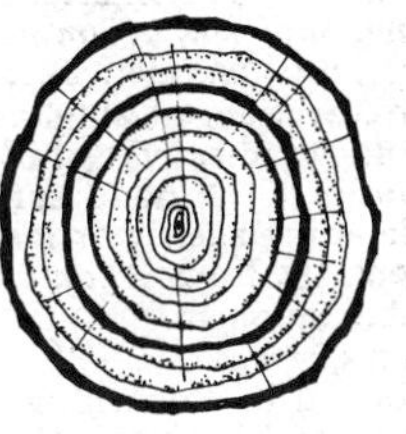

annual ring (cross section)

**annuitant** /ə'njuətənt/, *n.* one who receives an annuity.

**annuity** /ə'njuəti/, *n., pl.* **-ties.** **1.** a specified income payable at stated intervals for a fixed or a contingent period, often for the recipient's life, in consideration of a stipulated premium paid either in prior instalment payments or in a single payment. **2.** the right to receive such an income, or the duty to make such a payment or payments. [ME *annuitee,* from F *annuité,* from L *annuus* yearly]

**annul** /ə'nʌl/, *v.t.,* **annulled, annulling.** **1.** to make void or null; abolish (used esp. of laws or other established rules, usages, and the like): *to annul a marriage.* **2.** to reduce to nothing: obliterate. [ME *anulle(n),* from LL *annullāre*] – **annullable,** *adj.*

**annular** /'ænjələ/, *adj.* **1.** having the form of a ring. **2.** bearing a ring. –*n.* **3.** the ring finger. [L *annulāris*] – **annularity** /ænjə'lærəti/, *n.* – **annularly,** *adv.*

**annular eclipse** /– i'klɪps/, *n.* an eclipse of the sun in which a portion of its surface is visible as a ring surrounding the dark moon (opposed to *total eclipse*).

**annular ligament** /– 'lɪgəmənt/, *n.* the general ligamentous envelope which surrounds the wrist or ankle.

**annulate** /'ænjulət, -leɪt/, *adj.* **1.** formed of ringlike segments, as an annelid worm. **2.** having rings or ringlike bands.

**annulated** /'ænjuleɪtəd/, *adj.* **1.** *Archit.* (of a column) formed of several shafts banded together. **2.** annulate.

**annulation** /ænjə'leɪʃən/, *n.* **1.** formation with or into rings. **2.** a ringlike formation or part.

**annulet** /'ænjələt/, *n.* **1.** a little ring. **2.** *Archit.* an encircling band, moulding, or fillet, as on a Doric capital. **3.** *Her.* a small circle. [L *annulus* ring + -ET]

**annulment** /ə'nʌlmənt/, *n.* **1.** an invalidation, as of a marriage. **2.** act of annulling.

**annulose** /'ænjəlous/, *adj.* furnished with rings; composed of rings: *annulose animals.* [NL *annulōsus,* from L *annulus* ring]

**annulus** /'ænjələs/, *n., pl.* **-li** /-laɪ/, **-luses.** a ring; a ringlike part, band, or space. [L, var. of *ānulus* ring]

**annunciate** /ə'nʌnsieɪt/, *v.t.,* **-ated, -ating.** to announce. [ME *annunciat,* ppl. adj., announced, from ML *annunciātus,* replacing L *annuntiātus,* pp.]

**annunciation** /ənʌnsi'eɪʃən/, *n.* **1.** (*often cap.*) the announcement by the angel Gabriel to the Virgin Mary of the incarnation of Christ. **2.** (*cap.*) the festival (25 March) instituted by the church in memory of this. **3.** *Rare.* the act of announcing; proclamation.

**anoa** /ə'nouə/, *n.* a dwarf buffalo, *Anoa depressicornis,* of Indonesia: the smallest wild representative of the cattle tribe.

**anociassociation** /əˌnousiəˌsousi'eɪʃən/, *n.* a method for preventing shock and other harmful effects resulting from an operation, consisting principally in giving general and local anaesthesia and in avoiding all unnecessary trauma during the operation. Also, **anociation** /ənousi'eɪʃən/. [A-[6] + *noci-* (combining form representing L *nocēre* harm) + ASSOCIATION]

**anodal** /ə'noudəl/, *adj.* →**anodic.**

**anode** /'ænoud/, *n.* **1.** the electrode which gives off positive ions, or towards which negative ions or electrons move or collect in electrolysis, as a voltaic cell, radio valve, etc. **2.** the positive pole of a battery or other source of current. **3.** the plate of a radio valve (opposed to *cathode*). [Gk *ánodos* way up]

**anodic** /ə'noudɪk/, *adj.* pertaining to an anode or the phenomena in its vicinity. Also, **anodal.**

**anodise** /'ænədaɪz/, *v.t.,* **-dised, -dising.** to coat a metal, esp. magnesium or aluminium, with a protective film by chemical or electrolytic means. Also, **anodize.** [ANOD(E) + -ISE[1]]

**anodyne** /'ænədaɪn/, *n.* **1.** a medicine, esp. a drug, that relieves or removes pain. **2.** anything relieving distress. –*adj.* **3.** relieving pain. **4.** soothing to the feelings. [L *anōdynus,* from Gk *anṓdynos* freeing from pain]

**anoestrus** /ə'nistrəs/, *n.* the resting period of the oestrous cycle, when the animal is not on heat. – **anoestrous,** *adj.*

**anoint** /ə'nɔɪnt/, *v.t.* **1.** to put oil on; apply an unguent or oily liquid to. **2.** to smear with any liquid. **3.** to consecrate by applying oil. [ME *anoynte(n),* from OF *enoint,* pp. of *enoindre,* from L *inunguere*] – **anointer,** *n.* – **anointment,** *n.*

**anole** /ə'noul/, *n.* any of numerous American iguanid lizards of the genus *Anolis,* capable of changing the colour of the skin.

**anolyte** /'ænəlaɪt/, *n.* that part of an electrolyte which surrounds the anode in electrolysis. [b. ANODE and ELECTROLYTE]

**anomalism** /ə'nɒməlɪzəm/, *n. Obs.* **1.** anomalous quality. **2.** an anomaly.

**anomalistic** /ənɒmə'lɪstɪk/, *adj.* of or pertaining to an anomaly.

**anomalistic month** /– 'mʌnθ/, *n.* the average interval between consecutive passages of the moon through the perigee.

**anomalistic year** /– 'jɪə/, *n.* the average interval between consecutive passages of the earth through the perihelion.

**anomalous** /ə'nɒmələs/, *adj.* deviating from the common rule, type, or form; abnormal; irregular. [L *anōmalus,* from Gk *anṓmalos* irregular] – **anomalously,** *adv.* – **anomalousness,** *n.*

**anomaly** /ə'nɒməli/, *n., pl.* **-lies.** **1.** deviation from the common rule or analogy. **2.** something anomalous: *the anomalies of human nature.* **3.** *Astron.* **a.** an angular quantity used in defining the position of a point in an orbit. **b. true anomaly,** the angular distance of a planet from the perihelion of its orbit, as observed from the sun. **c. mean anomaly,** a quantity increasing uniformly in a given time and equal to the true anomaly at perihelion and aphelion. **4.** *Geol.* a distinctive local deviation from average values determined in a mineral exploration survey (particularly geophysical or geochemical). [L *anōmalia,* from Gk]

**anomia** /eɪ'noumiə/, *n.* loss of the ability to name objects or to recall names.

**anomie** /'ænəmi/, *n.* **1.** a social vacuum marked by the absence of social norms or values. **2.** the state of alienation experienced as a result of the absence of social norms or values. Also, **anomy.** [F, from Gk *anomía* lawlessness] – **anomic** /ə'nɒmɪk/, *adj.*

**anomuran** /ænə'mjurən/, *adj.* **1.** of or belonging to the Anomura, a division of decapod crustaceans having the abdomen more or less reduced and the tail irregular. –*n.* **2.** an anomuran crustacean, as the hermit crab or the ghost nipper.

**anon** /ə'nɒn/, *adv. Archaic.* **1.** in a short time; soon. **2.** at another time. **3.** at once; immediately. **4. ever and anon,** now and then. [ME; OE *on ān* into one, *on āne* in one, immediately]

**anon.,** anonymous.

**anonym** /'ænənɪm/, *n.* **1.** an assumed or false name. **2.** an anonymous person or publication.

**anonymous** /ə'nɒnəməs/, *adj.* **1.** without any name acknowledged, as that of author, contributor, or the like: *an anonymous pamphlet.* **2.** of unknown name; whose name is withheld: *an anonymous author.* **3.** lacking individuality; without distinguishing features; without identity. [Gk *anṓnymos*] – **anonymity** /ænə'nɪməti/, **anonymousness,** *n.* – **anonymously,** *adv.*

**anopheles** /ə'nɒfəliz/, *n., pl.* **-les.** any mosquito of the genus

*Anopheles,* which, when infested with the organisms causing malaria, may transmit the disease to human beings. [NL, from Gk: useless, hurtful]

**anorak** /ˈænəræk/, *n.* →**parka.** [Eskimo *anorag*]

**anorexia** /ænəˈrɛksiə/, *n.* lack of appetite. Also, **anorexy.** [AN-[1] + Gk *órexis* longing]

**anorexia nervosa** /– nɜˈvoʊsə/, *n.* a mental disorder, most common in adolescent girls, causing an aversion to food, which may lead to serious malnutrition.

**anorthic** /æˈnɔθɪk/, *adj.* →**triclinic.**

**anorthite** /æˈnɔθaɪt/, *n.* a mineral of the plagioclase felspar group, calcium aluminium silicate, $CaAl_2Si_2O_8$, occurring in basic igneous rocks; indianite. [AN-[1] + Gk *orthós* straight + -ITE[1]] – **anorthitic** /ˌænɔˈθɪtɪk/, *adj.*

**anorthosite** /æˈnɔθəsaɪt/, *n.* a granular igneous rock composed largely of labradorite or a more calcic felspar. [AN-[1] + Gk *orthós* straight + -ITE[1]. Cf. F *anorthose* a felspar]

**anosmia** /æˈnɒzmiə/, *n.* loss of the sense of smell. [NL, from Gk *an-* AN-[1] + stem of *osmḗ* smell + *-ia* -IA] – **anosmatic** /ænəzˈmætɪk/, *adj.*

**another** /əˈnʌðə/, *adj.* **1.** a second; a further; an additional: *another piece of cake.* **2.** a different; a distinct; of a different kind: *at another time, another man.* –*pron.* **3.** one more; an additional one: *try another.* **4.** a different one; something different: *going from one house to another.* **5.** one just like. **6. one another,** one the other; each other: *love one another.* [ME; orig. *an other*]

**anotherie** /əˈnʌðəri/, *n. Colloq.* another. Also, **anothery.**

**another place** /– ˈpleɪs/, *n.* **1.** a term used in one chamber of a bicameral parliament to refer to the other chamber. In the House of Representatives it is understood to mean the Senate, and vice versa. Also, **the other place. 2.** a term in general use as a reference to an associated or rival group or enterprise. [orig. from the traditional ill-feeling between the two British houses of parliament]

**anovulation** /ænɒvjəˈleɪʃən/, *n.* failure to ovulate. – **anovulatory,** *adj.*

**anoxia** /əˈnɒksiə/, *n.* **1.** an absence of oxygen. **2.** a pathological deficiency of oxygen, esp. hypoxia. [AN-[1] + OX(YGEN) + -IA]

**ans.,** answer.

**ansate** /ˈænseɪt/, *adj.* having a handle or handle-like part: *an ansate cross* (ankh). [L *ansātus*]

**anserine** /ˈænsərin, -səraɪn/, *adj.* **1.** *Ornith.* of or pertaining to the subfamily Anserinae, the goose family. **2.** resembling a goose; gooselike. **3.** stupid; foolish; silly. [L *anserīnus*]

**answer** /ˈænsə, ˈan-/, *n.* **1.** a spoken or written reply to a question, request, letter, etc. **2.** a reply or response in act: *the answer was a volley of fire.* **3.** a reply to a charge or an accusation. **4.** *Law.* a pleading of facts by a defendant in opposition to those stated in the plaintiff's declaration; defence to a divorce petition. **5.** a solution to a doubt or problem, esp. in mathematics. **6.** a piece of work (written or otherwise) performed as a demonstration of knowledge or ability in a test or examination. **7.** a re-echoing, imitation, or repetition of sounds. **8.** *Music.* the entrance of a fugue subject, usually on the dominant, after its first presentation in the main key. –*v.i.* **9.** to make answer; reply. **10.** to respond by a word or act: *to answer with a nod.* **11.** to respond (to a stimulus, direction, command, etc.); obey; acknowledge (fol. by *to*): *to answer to the whip, to one's name.* **12.** to be or declare oneself responsible or accountable (fol. by *for*): *I will answer for his safety.* **13.** to give assurance of; vouch (fol. by *for*): *he answered for the truth of the statement.* **14.** to act or suffer in consequence of (fol. by *for*): *to answer for one's sins.* **15.** to be satisfactory or serve (fol. by *for*): *to answer for a purpose.* **16.** to correspond; conform (fol. by *to*): *to answer to a description.* **17. answer back,** to make a rude or impertinent reply. –*v.t.* **18.** to make answer to; to reply or respond to: *to answer a person or a question.* **19.** to give as an answer. **20.** to make a defence against (a charge); meet or refute (an argument). **21.** to act in reply or response to: *to answer the bell, answer a summons.* **22.** to respond to (mechanical direction or steering): *the car answered the wheel.* **23.** to serve or suit: *this will answer the purpose.* **24.** to discharge (a responsibility, claim, debt, etc.). **25.** to conform or correspond to; be similar or equivalent to: *to answer a description.* **26.** to atone for; make amends for. [ME; OE *andswaru,* from *and-* against + *swaru,* akin to *swerian* swear] – **answerer,** *n.* – **answerless,** *adj.*

**answerable** /ˈænsərəbəl/, *adj.* **1.** accountable, responsible (*for* a person, act, etc.): *I am answerable for his safety.* **2.** liable to be called to account or asked to defend one's actions (*to* a person): *he is answerable to his employer.* **3.** capable of being answered. **4.** proportionate; correlative (fol. by *to*). **5.** corresponding; suitable (fol. by *to*). – **answerableness,** *n.* – **answerably,** *adv.*

**ant** /ænt/, *n.* **1.** any of certain small hymenopterous insects constituting the family Formicidae, very widely distributed in thousands of species, all of which have some degree of social organisation. **2. have ants in one's pants,** *Colloq.* to be restless or impatient. [ME *amte,* OE *æmete*] – **antlike,** *adj.*

**an't** /ant/, *for defs 1 and 2;* /eɪnt/ *for def. 3;* /ænt/ *for def. 4, v. Archaic.* **1.** contraction of *are not.* **2.** contraction of *am not* (as an interrogative). **3.** *Obs.* contraction of *is not, has not, have not,* or *am not* (as a statement). **4.** *Obs.* contraction of *an it* (**an**[2], def. 2): *an't please you.*

**ant-,** variant of **anti-,** esp. before a vowel or *h,* as in *antacid.*

**-ant,** **1.** adjective suffix, originally participial, as in *ascendant, pleasant.* **2.** noun suffix used in words of participial origin, denoting agency or instrumentality, as in *servant, irritant.* Cf. **-ent.** [F, from L *-ant-,* nom. *-ans,* ppr. ending]

**ant.,** antonym.

**anta** /ˈæntə/, *n., pl.* **-tae** /-ti/. a square pier or pilaster, formed by thickening a wall at its extremity, often having a base and a capital. [L (found only in pl.)]

**antacid** /æntˈæsəd/, *adj.* **1.** neutralising acids; counter-acting acidity, as of the stomach. –*n.* **2.** an antacid agent or remedy. [ANT- + ACID]

**antagonise** /ænˈtægənaɪz/, *v.,* **-nised, -nising.** –*v.t.* **1.** to make hostile; make an antagonist of: *his speech antagonised half the voters.* **2.** *Physiol.* to counteract the action of; act in opposition to. **3.** *U.S.* to oppose. Also, **antagonize.**

**antagonism** /ænˈtægənɪzəm/, *n.* **1.** the activity or the relation of contending parties or conflicting forces; active opposition. **2.** an opposing force, principle, or tendency. [Gk *antagṓnisma*]

**antagonist** /ænˈtægənəst/, *n.* **1.** one who is opposed to or strives with another in any kind of contest; opponent; adversary. **2.** *Physiol.* a muscle which acts in opposition to another (the agonist). [Gk *antagōnistḗs*]

**antagonistic** /ænˌtægəˈnɪstɪk/, *adj.* acting in opposition; mutually opposing. – **antagonistically,** *adv.*

**antalkali** /æntˈælkəlaɪ/, *n., pl.* **-lis, -lies.** something that neutralises alkalis or counteracts alkalinity. – **antalkaline,** *adj., n.*

**antarctic** /æntˈaktɪk/, *adj.* **1.** of, at, or near the South Pole. **2.** extremely cold. –*n.* **3. the Antarctic, a.** the area south of the Antarctic Circle. **b.** →**Antarctica.** [L *antarcticus,* from Gk *antarktikós* opposite the north; replacing ME *antartik,* from OF *antartique*]

**Antarctica** /ænˈtaktɪkə/, *n.* the continent around the South Pole, almost wholly covered by a vast continental icesheet. Also, **Antarctic Continent.**

**Antarctic beech** /ænˌtaktɪk ˈbitʃ/, *n.* any tree of the genus *Nothofagus* of southern temperate regions, as *Nothofagus cunninghamii* of Tasmania, a very tall evergreen of cool moist areas, with small leaves.

**Antarctic Circle** /– ˈsɜkəl/, *n.* the northern boundary of the South Frigid Zone, 23° 28′ from the South Pole.

**ant-bear** /ˈænt-bɛə/, *n.* **1.** a large terrestrial tropical American edentate, the great anteater, *Myrmecophaga jubata,* subsisting on termites, ants, and other insects, and having powerful front claws, a long, tapering snout and extensile tongue, and a shaggy grey coat marked with a conspicuous black band. **2.** →**aardvark.**

ant-bear

**ant bed** /ˈænt bɛd/, *n.* an extensive ants' nest in the ground, sometimes forming a slight mound.

**ante** /'ænti/, *n.*, *v.*, **-ted** or **-teed, -teing.** *–n.* **1.** *Poker.* a stake put into the pool by each player after seeing his hand but before drawing new cards, or, sometimes, before seeing his hand. **2.** the amount paid as one's share. **3.** a payment, usually monetary, extracted as part of a bargain. **a. raise** or **up the ante,** to increase suddenly the price to be paid for goods or services. **b.** to raise the requirements (for a job, etc.) *–v.t.* **4.** *Poker.* to put (one's stake) into the pool. *–v.i.* **5. ante up,** *Colloq.* **a.** to pay one's share as contribution. **b.** to put up the price or amount to be paid or contributed. [Cf. L *ante* before]

**ante-,** a prefix meaning 'before in space or time', as in *antedate, antediluvian, anteroom, antecedent.* [L]

**anteater** /'æntitə/, *n.* **1.** any of the echidnas or spiny anteaters of Australia and New Guinea. **2.** →**numbat.** **3.** any of three edentates of tropical America, feeding chiefly on termites: **a.** the ant-bear or **great anteater. b.** the tamandua or **lesser anteater. c. silky** or **two-toed anteater,** a yellowish, arboreal, prehensile-tailed species, *Cyclopes didactylus,* about the size of a rat. **4.** →**aardvark.** **5.** any of the pangolins or scaly anteaters of Africa and tropical Asia.

anteater

**antebellum** /,ænti'bɛləm/, *adj.* before the war, esp. before the American Civil War. [L: *ante bellum*]

**antecede** /æntə'sid/, *v.t.*, **-ceded, -ceding.** to go before, as in order; precede. [backformation from ANTECEDENT]

**antecedence** /æntə'sidəns/, *n.* **1.** the act of going before; precedence. **2.** the quality or condition of being antecedent. **3.** *Astron.* (of a planet) apparent retrograde motion. Also, **antecedency.**

**antecedent** /æntə'sidənt/, *adj.* **1.** going or being before; preceding; prior (often fol. by *to*): *an antecedent event.* *–n.* **2.** (*pl.*) **a.** ancestry. **b.** one's past history. **3.** a preceding circumstance, event, etc. **4.** *Gram.* the word or phrase, usually a noun or its equivalent, which is replaced by a pronoun or other substitute later (or rarely, earlier) in the sentence or in a subsequent sentence. In *Jack lost a hat and he can't find it, Jack* is the antecedent of *he,* and *hat* is the antecedent of *it.* **5.** *Maths.* the first term of a ratio; the first or third term of a proportion. **6.** *Logic.* the first member of a conditional or hypothetical proposition. [L *antecēdens,* ppr.] – **antecedently,** *adv.*

**antechamber** /'æntitʃeɪmbə/, *n.* a chamber or an apartment through which access is had to a principal apartment. [F *antichambre,* from It. *anticamera,* from *anti-* ANTE- + *camera* chamber (from L *camera* vault)]

**antechapel** /'æntitʃæpəl/, *n.* (in a school or college) an outer part or lobby at the west end of the chapel.

**antechoir** /'æntikwaɪə/, *n.* an enclosed space in front of the choir of a church.

**antedate** /'æntideɪt, ænti'deɪt/, *v.*, **-dated, -dating;** /'æntideɪt/, *n.* *–v.t.* **1.** to be of older date than; precede in time: *the Peruvian empire antedates that of Mexico.* **2.** to affix a date earlier than the true one to (a document, etc.): *to antedate a cheque.* **3.** to assign to an earlier date: *to antedate a historical event.* **4.** to cause to return to an earlier time. **5.** to cause to happen sooner; accelerate. **6.** to take or have in advance; anticipate. *–n.* **7.** a prior date.

**antediluvian** /,æntidə'luviən/, *adj.* **1.** belonging to the period before the Flood, i.e., the universal deluge recorded as having occurred in the days of Noah. **2.** antiquated; primitive: *antediluvian ideas.* **3.** old; outmoded. *–n.* **4.** one who lived before the Flood. **5.** one who is very old or old-fashioned. [ANTE- + L *dīluvi(um)* deluge + -AN]

**antefix** /'æntifɪks/, *n.*, *pl.* **-fixes, -fixa.** *Archit.* **1.** an upright ornament at the eaves of a tiled roof, to conceal the foot of a row of convex tiles which cover the joints of the flat tiles. **2.** an ornament above the top moulding of a cornice. [L *antefixum,* prop. neut. of *antefixus* fixed before] – **antefixal** /ænti'fɪksəl/, *adj.*

**anteflexion** /ænti'flɛkʃən/, *n.* *Pathol.* a bending forwards, esp. of the body of the uterus.

**antelope** /'æntəloʊp/, *n.*, *pl.* **-lopes,** (*esp. collectively*) **-lope.** **1.** a slenderly built, hollow-horned ruminant allied to cattle, sheep, and goats, found chiefly in Africa and Asia. **2.** leather made from its skin. [ME, from OF *antelop,* from ML *antalopus,* from LGk *anthólops*]

**antelope kangaroo** /– kæŋgə'ru/, *n.* a large kangaroo, *Macropus antilopinus,* found in plains and woodland areas from northern Queensland to the Kimberley district of western Australia.

**ante meridiem** /,ænti mə'rɪdiəm/, **1.** before noon. **2.** the time between 12 midnight and 12 noon. *Abbrev.:* A.M. or a.m. [L] – **antemeridian,** *adj.*

**ante-mortem** /ænti-'mɔtəm/, *adj.* before death: *an ante-mortem confession.* [L]

**antemundane** /,æntimʌn'deɪn/, *adj.* before the creation of the world.

**antenatal** /ænti'neɪtl/, *adj.* **1.** before birth; during pregnancy: *an antenatal clinic.* *–n.* **2.** an antenatal examination.

**antenna** /æn'tɛnə/, *n.*, *pl.* **-tennae** /-'tɛni/ *for def. 1;* **-tennas** *for def. 2.* **1.** *Zool.* one of the jointed appendages occurring in pairs on the heads of insects, crustaceans, etc., often called feelers. **2.** a radio or television aerial. [L: a sailyard] – **antennal, antennary,** *adj.*

**antenna mine** /'– maɪn/, *n.* a contact mine fitted with antennae, which, when touched by a steel ship, fire the mine.

**antenniform** /æn'tɛnəfɔm/, *adj.* shaped like an antenna.

**antennule** /æn'tɛnjul/, *n.* a small antenna, specifically one of the anterior pair in crustaceans.

**antependium** /ænti'pɛndiəm/, *n.*, *pl.* **-dia** /-diə/. the decoration of the front of an altar, as a covering of silk, or a painted panel. [ML. See ANTE-, PEND, -IUM]

**antepenult** /æntipə'nʌlt/, *n.* the last syllable but two in a word, as *-syl-* in *monosyllable.* [L: short for *antepaenultima* (*syllaba*)]

**antepenultimate** /,æntipə'nʌltəmət/, *adj.* **1.** last but two. *–n.* **2.** the last but two; the third from the end.

**anterior** /æn'tɪəriə/, *adj.* **1.** placed before; situated more to the front (opposed to *posterior*). **2.** going before in time; preceding; earlier: *an anterior age.* **3.** *Phonet.* pronounced with an air-stream obstruction located at or in front of the alveolar ridge. [L: compar. adj. from *ante* before] – **anteriority,** *n.* – **anteriorly,** *adv.*

**anteroom** /'æntirum/, *n.* **1.** a smaller room through which access is had to a main room. **2.** a waiting room.

**anteversion** /ænti'vɜʃən, -'vɜʒən/, *n.* a tipping forward of the uterus with its fundus directed towards the pubis. [L *anteversio* a putting before]

**antevert** /ænti'vɜt/, *v.t.* to displace (the uterus) by tipping forward. [L *antevertere* precede]

**ant heap** /'ænt hip/, *n.* a pile of dirt thrown up by ants in building a nest.

**anthelion** /ænt'hiliən, æn'θi-/, *n.*, *pl.* **-lia** /-liə/. (esp. in polar regions) a luminous ring seen round the shadow of the observer's head as thrown by the sun on a cloud, fogbank, or moist surface. [Gk, prop. neut. of *anthḗlios* opposite the sun]

**anthelmintic** /ænθəl'mɪntɪk/, *adj.* **1.** destroying or expelling intestinal worms. *–n.* **2.** an anthelmintic remedy. [ANT- + Gk *hélmins* worm + -IC]

**anthem** /'ænθəm/, *n.* **1.** a hymn, as of praise, devotion, or patriotism. **2.** a piece of sacred vocal music, usually with words taken from the Scriptures. **3.** a hymn sung in alternate parts. *–v.t.* **4.** to celebrate with an anthem. [ME *antem,* OE *antemn(e), antefn(e),* from VL *antefna,* from LL *antifona,* var. of *antiphōna,* from Gk. See ANTIPHON]

**anthemion** /æn'θimiən/, *n.*, *pl.* **-mia** /-miə/. an ornament of floral forms in a flat radiating cluster, as in architectural decoration, vase painting, etc. [NL, from Gk: flower]

**anther** /'ænθə/, *n.* the pollen-bearing part of a stamen. [NL *anthēra,* from Gk, fem. of *anthērós* flowery]

**antheridium** /ænθə'rɪdiəm/, *n.*, *pl.* **-ridia** /-'rɪdiə/. a male sex organ in algae, fungi, mosses, and ferns, which contains motile male gametes. [NL, diminutive of *anthēra* ANTHER] – **antheridial,** *adj.*

**antherozoid** /'ænθərəzɔɪd/, *n.* the motile male gamete produced in an antheridium.

**anthesis** /æn'θisəs/, *n.* the period or act of expansion in flowers, esp. the maturing of the stamens. [NL, from Gk: full bloom]

**ant hill** /ˈænt hɪl/, *n.* a mound of earth typically one to two metres high, built up by ants or termites in forming a nest. Also, **anthill.**

ant hill

**antho-,** a word element meaning 'flower', as in *anthocyanin.* [Gk, combining form of *ánthos*]

**anthocyanin** /ænθəˈsaɪənən/, *n.* **1.** any of a class of water-soluble pigments including most of those that give red and blue flowers these colours. **2.** the main colour pigment of red grapes. Also, **anthocyan.**

**anthodium** /ænˈθoʊdiəm/, *n., pl.* **-dia** /-diə/. a flower head or capitulum. [NL, from Gk *anthṓdēs* flower-like + *-ium* -IUM]

**anthol.,** anthology.

**anthologise** /ænˈθɒlədʒaɪz/, *v.,* **-gised, -gising.** *–v.i.* **1.** to make an anthology. *–v.t.* **2.** to include in an anthology. Also, **anthologize.**

**anthology** /ænˈθɒlədʒi/, *n., pl.* **-gies.** **1.** a collection of short, choice poems, especially epigrams, of varied authorship. **2.** any collection of literary pieces of varied authorship. [Gk *anthología,* lit., a flower-gathering] **– anthological** /ænθəˈlɒdʒɪkəl/, *adj.* **– anthologist,** *n.*

**anthophore** /ˈænθəfɔ/, *n.* a form of floral stipe, produced by the elongation of the internode between the calyx and the corolla, and bearing the corolla, stamens, and pistil. [Gk *anthophóros* flower-bearing]

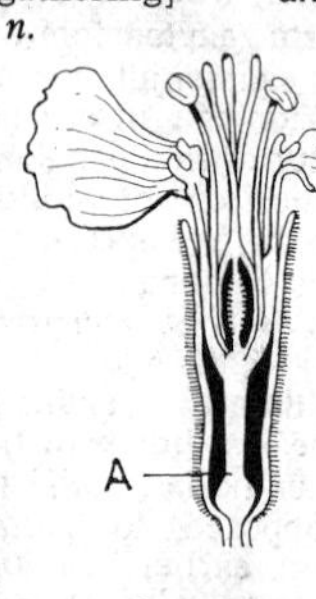

A, anthophore

**anthotaxy** /ˈænθətæksi/, *n.* the arrangement of flowers on the axis of growth; inflorescence.

**ant-house plant** /ˈænt-haʊs ˌplænt/, *n.* any member of the genera *Hydnophytum* and *Myrmecodia* of the family Rubiaceae, comprising epiphytic shrubs which house ants in a hollow tuber-like stock.

**anthozoan** /ænθəˈzoʊən/, *n.* **1.** any animal of the Anthozoa, a class of the phylum Coelenterata, comprising sessile marine animals of the polyp type, single or colonial, having a columnar body with the interior partitioned by septa and an oral disc with one to many circles of tentacles. It includes anemones, corals, sea-pens, etc. *–adj.* **2.** belonging to this class.

**anthracene** /ˈænθrəsin/, *n.* a hydrocarbon $C_6H_4(CH_2)_2C_6H_4$ found in coal tar, important commercially as a source of alizarin. [Gk *ánthrax* coal + -ENE]

**anthracite** /ˈænθrəsaɪt/, *n.* a hard black lustrous coal containing little of the volatile hydrocarbons and burning almost without flame; hard coal. [L *anthracītes,* from Gk *anthrakī́tēs* kind of precious stone (properly coal-like)] **– anthracitic** /ænθrəˈsɪtɪk/, *adj.*

**anthracnose** /ænˈθræknoʊs/, *n.* a necrotic plant disease with restricted lesions, affecting bean plants, cotton plants, berries, grape vines, etc. [Gk *ánthrax* carbuncle, coal + *nósos* disease]

**anthracoid** /ˈænθrəkɔɪd/, *adj.* resembling anthrax.

**anthracosis** /ænθrəˈkoʊsəs/, *n.* a diseased condition of the lungs caused by inhalation of coaldust in mines.

**anthraquinone** /ænθrəkwəˈnoʊn, -ˈkwɪnoʊn/, *n.* a yellow crystalline substance, $C_6H_4(CO)_2C_6H_4$, obtained from anthracene or phthalic anhydride, used in the preparation of alizarin. [ANTHRA(CENE) + QUINONE]

**anthrax** /ˈænθræks/, *n., pl.* **-thraces** /-θrəsiz/. **1.** a malignant infectious disease of cattle, sheep, and other animals and of man, caused by *Bacillus anthracis.* **2.** a malignant carbuncle which is the diagnostic lesion of anthrax disease in man. [L, from Gk: carbuncle, coal] **– anthracic** /ænˈθræsɪk/, *adj.*

**anthrop** /ˈænθrɒp/, *n. Colloq.* an anthropologist.

**anthrop.,** **1.** anthropological. **2.** anthropology.

**anthropo-,** a word element meaning 'man', 'human being', as in *anthropocentric.* Also, **anthrop-.** [Gk, combining form of *ánthrōpos*]

**anthropocentric** /ˌænθrəpəˈsɛntrɪk/, *adj.* **1.** regarding man as the central fact of the universe. **2.** assuming man to be the final aim and end of the universe. **3.** viewing and interpreting everything in terms of human experience and values. **– anthropocentricism** /ˌænθrəpəˈsɛntrəsɪzəm/, *n.*

**anthropogenesis** /ˌænθrəpəˈdʒɛnəsəs/, *n.* the genesis or development of the human race, esp. as a subject of scientific study. Also, **anthropogeny** /ˌænθrəˈpɒdʒəni/. **– anthropogenic,** *adj.*

**anthropogeography** /ˌænθrəpoʊdʒiˈɒgrəfi/, *n.* the study of the geographical distribution of human communities and the relationship between such communities and their natural environment.

**anthropography** /ˌænθrəˈpɒgrəfi/, *n.* the branch of anthropology that describes the varieties of mankind and their geographical distribution.

**anthropoid** /ˈænθrəpɔɪd/, *adj.* Also, **anthropoidal. 1.** resembling man. *–n.* **2.** an anthropoid ape. [Gk *anthrōpoeidḗs*]

**anthropoid ape** /– ˈeɪp/, *n.* any ape of the family Pongida, comprising the gorilla, chimpanzee, orang-utan, and gibbon, without cheek pouches or developed tail.

**anthropologist** /ænθrəˈpɒlədʒəst/, *n.* one who studies or is versed in anthropology.

**anthropology** /ænθrəˈpɒlədʒi/, *n.* **1.** the science that treats of the origin, development (physical, intellectual, moral, etc.), and varieties, and sometimes esp. the cultural development, customs, beliefs, etc., of mankind. **2.** the study of man's agreement with and divergence from other animals. **3.** the science of man and his works. **– anthropological** /ænθrəpəˈlɒdʒɪkəl/, **anthropologic,** *adj.* **– anthropologically,** *adv.*

**anthropomancy** /ˈænθrəpəmænsi/, *n.* divination using human entrails. [ANTHROPO- + -MANCY]

**anthropometrics** /ænθrəpəˈmɛtrɪks/, *n.* the science of anthropometry.

**anthropometry** /ænθrəˈpɒmətri/, *n.* the measurement of the size and proportions of the human body. **– anthropometric** /ˌænθrəpəˈmɛtrɪk/, **anthropometrical,** *adj.*

**anthropomorphic** /ænθrəpəˈmɔfɪk/, *adj.* ascribing human form or attributes to beings or things not human, esp. to a deity.

**anthropomorphise** /ænθrəpəˈmɔfaɪz/, *v.t., v.i.,* **-phised, -phising.** to ascribe human form or attributes (to). Also, **anthropomorphize.**

**anthropomorphism** /ænθrəpəˈmɔfɪzəm/, *n.* anthropomorphic conception or representation, as of a deity. **– anthropomorphist,** *n.*

**anthropomorphosis** /ænθrəpəˈmɔfəsəs/, *n.* transformation into human form.

**anthropomorphous** /ænθrəpəˈmɔfəs/, *adj.* **1.** having or resembling the human form. **2.** anthropomorphic. [Gk *anthrōpómorphos*]

**anthroponomy** /ænθrəˈpɒnəmi/, *n.* the science that treats of the laws regulating the development of the human organism in relation to other organisms and to environment. Also, **anthroponomics** /ænθrəpəˈnɒmɪks/. **– anthroponomical,** *adj.*

**anthropopathy** /ænθrəˈpɒpəθi/, *n.* ascription of human passions or feelings to beings not human, esp. to God. Also, **anthropopathism.** [Gk *anthrōpopátheia* humanity]

**anthropophagi** /ænθrəˈpɒfəgaɪ/, *n. pl., sing.* **-agus** /-əgəs/. man-eaters; cannibals. [L, pl. of *anthrōpophagus,* from Gk *anthrōpophágos*]

**anthropophagite** /ænθrəˈpɒfəgaɪt/, *n.* a man-eater; a cannibal.

**anthropophagy** /ænθrəˈpɒfədʒi/, *n.* the eating of human flesh; cannibalism. **– anthropophagic** /ænθrəpəˈfædʒɪk/, **anthropophagical, anthropophagous** /ænθrəˈpɒfəgəs/, *adj.*

**anthroposophy** /ænθrəˈpɒsəfi/, *n.* **1.** wisdom arising from knowledge of the nature of man. **2.** the spiritualistic system of religion and philosophy taught by the Austrian philosopher, Rudolf Steiner, 1861-1925. [ANTHROPO- + -SOPHY] **– anthroposophist,** *n.*

**anti** /ˈænti/, *n., pl.* **-tis. 1.** one who is opposed to a particular practice, party, policy, action, etc. *–adj.* **2.** against; opposed to; antagonistic (to).

**anti-,** a prefix meaning 'against', 'opposed to', with the following particular meanings: **1.** opposed; in opposition: *anti-British, antislavery.* **2.** rival or spurious; pseudo-: *anti-*

i = peat ɪ = pit ɛ = pet æ = pat a = part ɒ = pot ʌ = putt ɔ = port ʊ = put u = pool ɜ = pert ə = apart aɪ = buy eɪ = bay ɔɪ = boy aʊ = how oʊ = hoe ɪə = here ɛə = hair ʊə = tour g = give θ = thin ð = then ʃ = show ʒ = measure tʃ = choke dʒ = joke ŋ = sing j = you õ = Fr. bon

*bishop, anti-Messiah.* **3.** the opposite or reverse of: *antihero, anticlimax.* **4.** not; un-: *antilogical, antigrammatical.* **5.** placed opposite: *antipole, anti-chorus.* **6.** moving in a reverse or the opposite direction: *anticyclone.* **7.** *Med.* corrective; preventive; curative: *antifat, antipyretic, antistimulant.* Also, **ant-**. [Gk]

**anti-aircraft** /ænti-ˈɛəkraft/, *adj.* designed for or used in defence against enemy aircraft.

**antiar** /ˈæntia/, *n.* **1.** →**upas.** **2.** an arrow poison prepared from the sap of the upas. [Javanese *antjar*]

**antibiosis** /ˌæntibaɪˈoʊsəs/, *n.* an association between organisms which is injurious to one of them. [ANTI- + Gk *bíōsis* act of living]

**antibiotic** /ˌæntibaɪˈɒtɪk/, *n.* **1.** a chemical substance produced by micro-organisms which, in dilute solutions, may inhibit the growth of and even destroy bacteria and other micro-organisms. **2.** such a substance isolated and purified (as penicillin, streptomycin) and used in the treatment of infectious diseases of man, animals, and plants. *–adj.* **3.** of or involving antibiotics. **4.** *Obs.* inimical to life; destroying.

**antibody** /ˈæntibɒdi/, *n., pl.* **-bodies.** any of various substances existing in the blood or developed in immunisation which counteract bacterial or viral poisons or destroy bacteria in the system.

**antic** /ˈæntɪk/, *n., adj. v.,* **-ticked, -ticking.** *–n.* **1.** (*often pl.*) a grotesque, fantastic, or ludicrous gesture or posture; fantastic trick. **2.** *Archaic.* a grotesque pageant; ridiculous interlude. **3.** *Archaic.* an actor playing a grotesque or ludicrous part; buffoon; clown. **4.** *Obs.* a grotesque, caricatured, or distorted artistic representation, esp. in architecture, as a gargoyle. *–adj.* **5.** *Archaic.* fantastic; odd; grotesque: *an antic disposition.* *–v.i.* **6.** *Obs.* to perform antics; to caper. [It. *antico* old (but used as if It. *grottesco* grotesque), from L *antīquus*]

**anticatalyst** /æntiˈkætələst/, *n.* a substance which prevents or slows a chemical reaction (opposed to *catalyst*).

**anticathode** /æntiˈkæθoʊd/, *n.* the plate, often of platinum, on which cathode rays impinge in an X-ray tube, thus producing X-rays.

**anticay** /ˈæntikeɪ/, *n.* a product of calcium sucrose phosphate, which in soluble form, mixes with carbohydrates, to assist in preventing tooth decay. [Trademark]

**antichlor** /ˈæntiklɔ/, *n.* any of various substances, esp. sodium thiosulphate, used for removing excess chlorine from paper pulp, textiles, fibres, etc., after bleaching. [ANTI- + CHLOR(INE)] – **antichloristic** /ˌæntikləˈrɪstɪk/, *adj.*

**anticholinergic** /ˌæntikɒləˈnɜdʒɪk/, *adj.* **1.** antagonistic to acetylcholine. *–n.* **2.** an anticholinergic substance.

**Antichrist** /ˈæntikraɪst/, *n. Theol.* **1.** a particular personage or power (variously identified or explained) conceived as appearing in the world as a mighty antagonist of Christ. **2.** (*sometimes l.c.*) an opponent of Christ; a person or power antagonistic to Christ. [Gk *antíchrīstos;* replacing ME *antecrist,* from OF] – **antichristian** /æntiˈkrɪstʃən/, *adj., n.*

**anticipant** /ænˈtɪsəpənt/, *adj.* **1.** anticipative (fol. by *of*). *–n.* **2.** one who anticipates.

**anticipate** /ænˈtɪsəpeɪt/, *v.,* **-pated, -pating.** *–v.t.* **1.** to realise beforehand; foretaste or foresee: *to anticipate pleasure.* **2.** to expect: *to anticipate an acquittal.* **3.** to perform (an action) before another has had time to act. **4.** to be before (another) in doing something; forestall: *anticipated by his predecessors.* **5.** to consider or mention before the proper time: *to anticipate more difficult questions.* **6.** *Finance.* **a.** to expend (funds) before they are legitimately available for use. **b.** to discharge (an obligation) before it is due. *–v.i.* **7.** to think, speak, act, etc., in advance or prematurely. [L *anticipātus,* pp.] – **anticipator,** *n.* – **anticipatable,** *adj.*

**anticipation** /ænˌtɪsəˈpeɪʃən/, *n.* **1.** the act of anticipating. **2.** realisation in advance; foretaste; expectation; hope. **3.** previous notion; slight previous impression; intuition. **4.** *Law.* the act of expending funds before they are legally due. **5.** *Music.* a note introduced in advance of its harmony so that it sounds against the preceding chord.

anticipation (def. 5): A, semiquaver, is introduced in anticipation of the final chord, D major

**anticipative** /ænˈtɪsəpətɪv, -peɪtɪv/, *adj.* anticipating or tending to anticipate; containing anticipation: *an anticipative action or look.* – **anticipatively,** *adv.*

**anticipatory** /ænˈtɪsəpeɪtəri, -pətri/, *adj.* of, showing, or expressing anticipation. – **anticipatorily,** *adv.*

**anticlastic** /æntiˈklæstɪk/, *adj. Maths.* (of a surface) having principal curvatures of opposite sign at a given point opposed to *synclastic.*

**anticlerical** /æntiˈklɛrɪkəl/, *adj.* opposed to the influence and activities of the clergy in public affairs. – **anticlericalism,** *n.*

**anticlimax** /æntiˈklaɪmæks/, *n.* **1.** a noticeable or ludicrous descent in discourse from lofty ideas or expressions to what is much less impressive. **2.** an abrupt descent in dignity; an inglorious or disappointing conclusion. – **anticlimactic** /ˌæntiklaɪˈmæktɪk/, *adj.*

**anticlinal** /æntiˈklaɪnəl/, *adj.* **1.** inclining in opposite directions from a central axis. **2.** inclining downwards on both sides from a median plane (the axial plane), as an upward fold of rock strata. [ANTI- + *-clinal* adj. combining form indicating slope]

Axis

anticlinal fold (cross-section showing axis)

**anticline** /ˈæntiklaɪn/, *n.* an anticlinal rock structure.

**anticlinorium** /ˌæntiklaɪˈnɔriəm/, *n., pl.* **-oria** /-ɔriə/. a compound anticline, consisting of a series of subordinate anticlines and synclines, the whole having the general contour of an arch.

---

**anti-abortion,** *adj.*
**anti-aesthetic,** *adj.*
**anti-alcoholic,** *adj., n.*
**anti-alcoholism,** *n.*
**antibacterial,** *adj.*
**anticensorship,** *n.*
**anticlassical,** *adj.*
**anticlassically,** *adv.*
**anticlassicism,** *n.*
**anticlassicist,** *n.*
**anticommunism,** *n.*
**anticommunist,** *n., adj.*
**anticonservatism,** *n.*
**anticonservative,** *n., adj.*
**anticonservatively,** *adv.*
**anticorrosive,** *adj.*
**antidemocrat,** *n.*
**antidemocratic,** *adj.*
**antidemocratically,** *adv.*
**antidisestablishmentarian,** *n., adj.*
**antidisestablishmentarianism,** *n.*
**antidiuretic,** *adj., n.*
**anti-dumping,** *adj.*
**anti-enzyme,** *n.*
**antifascism,** *n.*
**antifascist,** *n., adj.*
**anti-female,** *adj.*
**antifeminism,** *n.*
**antifeminist,** *n., adj.*
**antigovernment,** *adj.*
**anti-immigration,** *adj.*
**anti-imperialism,** *n.*
**anti-imperialist,** *adj., n.*
**anti-inflationary,** *adj.*
**anti-intellectual,** *adj., n.*
**anti-intellectualism,** *n.*
**anti-litter,** *adj.*

**anticlockwise** /ænti'klɒkwaɪz/, *adv.* in a direction opposite to that of the rotation of the hands of a clock. – **anticlockwise,** *adj.*

**anticoagulant** /ˌæntikoʊ'ægjələnt/, *adj.* **1.** preventing or reducing coagulation, esp. of blood. *–n.* **2.** an anticoagulant agent.

**anticoincidence** /ˌæntikoʊ'ɪnsədəns/, *adj. Electronics.* pertaining to a device with two input terminals which delivers an output pulse if only one input terminal receives a pulse, but none if both input terminals receive a pulse.

**anti-conscription** /ˌænti-kən'skrɪpʃən/, *adj.* in opposition to conscription of young men into the armed services: *the anti-conscription movement.*

**anti-conservationist** /ˌænti-kɒnsə'veɪʃənəst/, *n.* one who is in opposition to the conservation movement and its assessment of the need for programs to conserve natural and historic resources. – **anti-conservation,** *adj.*

**anticonvulsant** /æntikən'vʌlsənt/, *n.* **1.** a drug used to treat convulsions. *–adj.* **2.** of or pertaining to such a drug or treatment.

**anticrop agent** /ˌæntikrɒp 'eɪdʒənt/, *n.* a living organism or chemical used to cause disease or damage to selected food or industrial crops.

**anticyclone** /ænti'saɪkloʊn/, *n.* an extensive horizontal movement of the atmosphere spirally around and away from a gradually progressing central region of high barometric pressure, the spiral motion being clockwise in the Northern Hemisphere, anticlockwise in the Southern. – **anticyclonic** /ˌæntisaɪ'klɒnɪk/, *adj.*

**antidazzle** /'ænti‚dæzəl/, *n.* →**antiglare.**

**antidepressant** /ˌæntidə'prɛsənt/, *n.* **1.** any of a class of drugs used for raising the spirits in treating mental depression. *–adj.* **2.** of, pertaining to, or denoting, this class of drugs.

**antidiphtheritic** /ˌæntidɪfθə'rɪtɪk/, *adj.* **1.** curing or preventing diphtheria. *–n.* **2.** an antidiphtheritic remedy.

**antidote** /'æntidoʊt/, *n.* **1.** a medicine or other remedy for counteracting the effects of poison, disease, etc. **2.** whatever prevents or counteracts injurious effects. [L *antidotum,* from Gk *antídotos* (verbal adj.) given against] – **antidotal,** *adj.*

**antidromic** /ænti'drɒmɪk/, *adj.* **1.** *Physiol.* conducting nerve impulses in a direction opposite to the usual one. **2.** *Bot.* (of a species of plant) exhibiting both left and right-hand twining. [ANTI- + Gk *drómos* a running + -IC]

**antifebrile** /ænti'fibraɪl/, *adj.* **1.** efficacious against fever; febrifuge; antipyretic. *–n.* **2.** an antifebrile agent.

**antifebrin** /ænti'fibrən/, *n.* →**acetanilide.**

**antifouling** /ænti'faʊlɪŋ/, *adj.* **1.** preventing growth of marine organisms on a ship's bottom. *–n.* **2.** an antifouling agent, usually in the form of a paint.

**antifreeze** /'æntifriz/, *n.* a liquid used in the radiator of an internal-combustion engine to lower the freezing point of the cooling medium.

**antifriction** /ænti'frɪkʃən/, *adj.* **1.** preventing or reducing friction; lubricating. *–n.* **2.** an antifriction agent.

**antigen** /'æntidʒən, 'æntə-/, *n.* any substance which when injected into animal tissues will stimulate the production of antibodies. [ANTI(BODY) + -GEN] – **antigenic** /ænti'dʒɛnɪk/, *adj.*

**antiglare** /'æntiglɛə/, *adj.* designed to reduce the glare of sunlight or headlights on the windscreen of a vehicle. Also, **antidazzle.**

**antihelix** /ænti'hilɪks/, *n., pl.* **-helices** /-'hiləsiz/, **-helixes.** the inner curved ridge of the pinna of the ear.

**antihero** /'ænti‚hɪəroʊ/, *n.* a hero or central character who does not possess the traditional heroic virtues or characteristics. Also, **non-hero.** – **antiheroic** /ˌæntihə'roʊɪk/, *adj.*

**antihistamine** /ænti'hɪstəmin, -maɪn/, *n.* any of certain medicines or drugs which neutralise or inhibit the effect of histamine in the body, used mainly in the treatment of allergic disorders. – **antihistamine, antihistaminic** /ˌæntihɪstə'mɪnɪk/, *adj.*

**antiketogenesis** /ˌæntikitoʊ'dʒɛnəsəs/, *n.* prevention of the excessive formation of acetone bodies in the body, such as occurs in diabetes. [ANTI- + KETO(SIS) + -GENESIS] – **antiketogenic,** *adj.*

**antiknock** /'æntinɒk/, *n.* a material, usu. a lead compound, added to the fuel to eliminate or minimise detonation in an internal-combustion engine.

**antilegomena** /ˌæntilə'gɒmənə/, *n.pl.* a group of books now part of the New Testament which were not at first universally accepted, including the Apocalypse. [Gk: (neut. pl. ppr. pass.) things spoken against]

**antilog** /'æntilɒg/, *n.* antilogarithm.

**antilogarithm** /ænti'lɒgərɪðəm/, *n.* the number corresponding to a logarithm.

**antilogism** /æn'tɪlədʒɪzəm/, *n. Logic.* a group of three inconsistent propositions, two of which are premises of a syllogism that contradicts the third.

**antilogy** /æn'tɪlədʒi/, *n., pl.* **-gies.** a contradiction in terms or ideas. [Gk *antilogía* contradiction] – **antilogous** /æn'tɪləgəs/, *adj.*

**antimacassar** /ˌæntimə'kæsə/, *n.* an ornamental covering for the backs and arms of chairs, sofas, etc., to keep them from being soiled. [ANTI- + *Macassar,* hair oil obtained from Macassar, a seaport in Indonesia]

**antimalarial** /ˌæntimə'lɛəriəl/, *adj.* **1.** preventive of or efficacious against malaria. *–n.* **2.** an antimalarial agent.

**antimasque** /'æntimask/, *n.* a comic or grotesque interlude between the acts of a masque. Also, **antimask.**

**antimatter** /'æntimætə/, *n. Physics.* matter (sometimes hypothetical) consisting of antiparticles; contact between antimatter and matter results in the annihilation of both with the production of gamma radiation.

**antimere** /'æntimɪə/, *n.* →**actinomere.** – **antimeric** /ænti'mɛrɪk/,

---

**antimagnetic,** *adj.*
**antimilitarism,** *n.*
**antimilitarist,** *n., adj.*
**antimilitary,** *adj.*
**antimonarchic,** *adj.*
**antimonarchical,** *adj.*
**antimonarchically,** *adv.*
**antimonarchism,** *n.*
**antimonarchist,** *n., adj.*
**antimonarchy,** *n.*
**antinational,** *adj.*
**antinationalisation,** *n.*
**antipapal,** *adj.*
**antiparliamentary,** *adj.*
**antiparliamentarian,** *n., adj.*
**antiparliamentarianism,** *n.*
**antipatriotic,** *adj.*
**antipoetic,** *adj.*
**anti-pollution,** *adj.*
**antiracial,** *adj.*
**antiracially,** *adv.*
**antiradical,** *n., adj.*
**antiradicalism,** *n.*
**antireform,** *adj.*
**antireforming,** *adj.*
**antireligious,** *adj.*
**antirevisionist,** *adj., n.*
**antiroyalism,** *n.*
**antiroyalist,** *n., adj.*
**antisocialist,** *n., adj.*
**antisocialism,** *n.*
**antistatic,** *adj.*
**antitheism,** *n.*
**antitheist,** *n.*
**anti-union,** *adj.*
**anti-unionist,** *n.*
**anti-vignetting,** *adj.*
**anti-war,** *adj.*

*adj.* – **antimerism** /æn'tɪmərɪzəm/, *n.*

**antimissile** /ænti'mɪsaɪl/, *adj.* **1.** designed or used in defence against guided missiles. *–n.* **2.** a ballistic device with a homing instrument, for defence.

**antimonic** /ænti'mɒnɪk/, *adj.* of or containing antimony, esp. in the pentavalent state.

**antimonite** /'æntɪmənaɪt/, *n.* →**stibnite.**

**antimonous** /æn'tɪmənəs/, *adj.* containing trivalent antimony. Also, **antimonious** /æntə'mouniəs/.

**antimonsoon** /ˌæntimɒn'sun/, *n.* a current of air moving in a direction opposite to that of a given monsoon and lying above it.

**antimony** /'æntəməni/, *n.* a brittle, lustrous, white metallic element occurring in nature free or combined, used chiefly in alloys and (in compounds) in medicine. *Symbol:* Sb; *at. no.:* 51; *at. wt:* 121.75. [late ME, from ML *antimōnium*] – **antimonial** /æntə'mouniəl/, *adj., n.*

**antimony glance** /– 'glæns/, *n.* →**stibnite.**

**antimonyl** /'æntəmənɪl, æn'tɪmə-/, *n.* a radical containing antimony and oxygen (SbO) which forms salts. [ANTIMON(Y) + -YL]

**antineuralgic** /ˌæntinju'rældʒɪk/, *adj.* **1.** preventing or relieving neuralgia or neuralgic pain. *–n.* **2.** an antineuralgic substance.

**antineutrino** /ˌæntinju'trinou/, *n.* the antiparticle of a neutrino.

**antineutron** /ænti'njutrɒn/, *n.* an antiparticle which annihilates a neutron on collision.

**antinode** /'æntinoud/, *n.* a point, line, or region in a vibrating medium at which the amplitude of variation of the disturbance is greatest, situated halfway between two adjacent nodes.

**antinomian** /ænti'noumiən/, *n.* one who maintains that Christians are freed from the moral law by the dispensation of grace set forth in the gospel. – **antinomian,** *adj.* – **antinomianism,** *n.*

**antinomy** /æn'tɪnəmi/, *n., pl.* **-mies. 1.** opposition between laws and principles; contradiction in law. **2.** *Philos.* the mutual contradiction of two principles or correctly drawn inferences, each of which is supported by reason. [L *antinomia,* from Gk]

**antinovel** /'æntinɒvəl/, *n.* a novel in which the traditional approach to such aspects as plot, form, character, etc., is deliberately rejected.

**antinuclear** /ænti'njukliə/, *adj.* opposed to the development of nuclear technology: *an antinuclear scientist, an antinuclear demonstration.*

**anti-oxidant** /ænti-'ɒksədənt/, *n.* **1.** any substance which when added to rubber inhibits its deterioration. **2.** any substance inhibiting oxidation.

**antiparallel** /ænti'pærəlel/, *adj. Physics.* parallel, but in opposite directions.

**antiparticle** /ænti'patɪkəl/, *n. Physics.* a particle, sometimes hypothetical, corresponding to a particular elementary particle with equal mass and opposite electric charge.

**antipasto** /ænti'pæstou/, *n.* an appetiser course of relishes, smoked meat, fish, etc.; hors d'oeuvres. [It.]

**antipathetic** /ˌæntipə'θetɪk/, *adj.* having a natural antipathy, contrariety, or constitutional aversion (oft. fol. by *to*): *he was antipathetic to any change.* – **antipathetically,** *adv.*

**antipathy** /æn'tɪpəθi/, *n., pl.* **-thies. 1.** a natural or settled dislike; repugnance; aversion. **2.** an instinctive contrariety or opposition in feeling. **3.** an object of natural aversion or settled dislike. [L *antipathīa,* from Gk *antipátheia,* from *antipathḗs* having opposite feelings]

**antiperiodic** /ˌæntipɪəri'ɒdɪk/, *adj.* **1.** efficacious against periodic diseases, as intermittent fever. *–n.* **2.** an antiperiodic agent.

**antiperistalsis** /ˌæntiperi'stælsəs/, *n.* inverted peristaltic action of the intestines, by which their contents are carried upwards. – **antiperistaltic,** *adj.*

**antipersonnel** /ˌæntipɜsə'nel/, *adj. Mil.* used against individuals rather than against mechanised vehicles, equipment, defences, etc.: *antipersonnel bombs.*

**antiperspirant** /ænti'pɜspərənt/, *n.* any preparation for decreasing or preventing perspiration.

**antiphlogistic** /ˌæntiflə'dʒɪstɪk/, *adj.* **1.** checking inflammation. *–n.* **2.** an antiphlogistic remedy.

**antiphon** /'æntəfən/, *n.* **1.** a verse sung in response. **2.** *Eccles.* **a.** a psalm, hymn, or prayer sung in alternate parts. **b.** a verse or a series of verses sung as a prelude or conclusion to some part of the service. [ML *antiphōna,* from Gk: (properly neut. pl.) sounding in answer]

**antiphonal** /æn'tɪfənəl/, *adj.* **1.** pertaining to antiphons or antiphony; responsive. *–n.* **2.** →**antiphonary.** – **antiphonally,** *adv.*

**antiphonary** /æn'tɪfənəri/, *n., pl.* **-naries.** a book of antiphons. Also, **antiphoner.**

**antiphony** /æn'tɪfəni/, *n., pl.* **-nies. 1.** alternate or responsive singing by a choir in two divisions. **2.** a psalm, etc., so sung; an antiphon. **3.** a responsive musical utterance. – **antiphonic** /æntə'fɒnɪk/, *adj.*

**antiphrasis** /æn'tɪfrəsəs/, *n.* the use of words in a sense opposite to the proper meaning; irony. [L, from Gk] – **antiphrastic** /ænti'fræstɪk/, *adj.* – **antiphrastically,** *adv.*

**antiplant agent** /ænti'plænt eɪdʒənt/, *n.* a living organism or a chemical used to cause disease or damage to vegetation.

**antipode** /'æntipoud/, *n. Chiefly U.S.* the direct or exact opposite.

**antipodes** /æn'tɪpədiz/, *n.pl.* **1.** points diametrically opposite to each other on the earth or any globe. **2.** those who dwell there. **3.** the part or parts of the world diametrically opposite. **4.** (*sometimes construed as sing.*) the direct or exact opposite. **5. the Antipodes, a.** Australia. **b.** Australasia, as the Antipodes of Britain. [L, from Gk: pl. of *antípous* with feet opposite] – **antipodean** /ænˌtɪpə'diən/, *adj., n.*

**antipope** /'æntipoup/, *n.* one who is elected pope in opposition to another held to be canonically chosen.

**antiproton** /ænti'proutɒn/, *n.* a subatomic particle of unit negative charge with a mass equal to that of a proton. [ANTI- + PROTON]

**antipyretic** /ˌæntipaɪ'retɪk/, *adj.* **1.** checking or preventing fever. *–n.* **2.** an antipyretic agent.

**antipyrine** /ænti'paɪrin, -rən/, *n.* a white powder, $C_{11}H_{12}N_2O$, used as a sedative, antipyretic, antirheumatic, and antineuralgic.

**antiq.,** antiquity.

**antiquarian** /æntə'kweəriən/, *adj.* **1.** pertaining to the study of antiquities or to antiquaries. *–n.* **2.** →**antiquary.** – **antiquarianism,** *n.*

**antiquary** /'æntəkwəri/, *n., pl.* **-quaries.** an expert on ancient things; a student or collector of antiquities. [L *antīquārius* of antiquity]

**antiquate** /'æntəkweɪt/, *v.t.,* **-quated, -quating. 1.** to make old and useless by substituting something newer and better. **2.** to make antique. [L *antīquātus,* pp., made old] – **antiquation** /æntə'kweɪʃən/, *n.*

**antiquated** /'æntəkweɪtəd/, *adj.* **1.** grown old; obsolete or obsolescent. **2.** ill adapted to present use. **3.** aged. – **antiquatedness,** *n.*

**antique** /æn'tik/, *adj., n., v.,* **-tiqued, -tiquing.** *–adj.* **1.** belonging to former times as contrasted with modern. **2.** dating from an early period: *antique furniture.* **3.** *Colloq.* old-fashioned; antiquated: *an antique garment.* **4.** *Archaic.* aged; ancient. *–n.* **5.** an object of art or a furniture piece of a former period. **6.** the antique (usually Greek or Roman) style, esp. in art. **7.** *Print.* a style of boldface type. **8.** *Print.* book paper featuring a rough surface. *–v.t.* **9.** to make appear antique. [L *antīquus* old] – **antiquely,** *adv.* – **antiqueness,** *n.*

**antiquity** /æn'tɪkwəti/, *n., pl.* **-ties. 1.** the quality of being ancient; great age: *a family of great antiquity.* **2.** ancient times; former ages: *the errors of dark antiquity.* **3.** the time before the Middle Ages. **4.** the ancients collectively; the people of ancient times. **5.** (*usu. pl.*) something belonging to or remaining from ancient times.

**antirachitic** /æntirə'kɪtɪk/, *adj.* pertaining to the prevention or cure of rickets.

**antiradiation missile** /ˌæntireɪdi'eɪʃən ˌmɪsaɪl/, *n.* a missile which homes passively on a radiation source.

**antirheumatic** /ˌæntiru'mætɪk/, *adj.* **1.** preventing or relieving rheumatism or rheumatic pain. *–n.* **2.** antirheumatic substance.

**anti-roll bar** /ænti-ˈroʊl ba/, *n.* a torsion bar added to suspension systems in motor vehicles, to prevent roll when cornering. Also, **anti-sway bar.**

**antirrhinum** /æntiˈraɪnəm/, *n.* any plant of the genus *Antirrhinum,* herbs native to the Old World; snapdragon. [NL, from Gk *antirrhīnon* calf's snout]

**antiscorbutic** /ˌæntiskɔˈbjutɪk/, *adj.* **1.** efficacious against scurvy. *–n.* **2.** an antiscorbutic agent.

**anti-Semite** /ænti-ˈsɛmaɪt/, *n.* one hostile to the Jews. – **anti-Semitic** /-səˈmɪtɪk/, *adj.* – **anti-Semitically** /-səˈmɪtɪkli/, *adv.* – **anti-Semitism,** *n.*

**antisepsis** /æntiˈsɛpsəs/, *n.* destruction of the micro-organisms that produce sepsis or septic disease.

**antiseptic** /æntəˈsɛptɪk/, *adj.* **1.** pertaining to or causing antisepsis. *–n.* **2.** an antiseptic agent. – **antiseptically,** *adv.*

**antisepticise** /æntəˈsɛptəsaɪz/, *v.t.,* **-cised, -cising.** to treat with antiseptics. Also, **antisepticize.**

**antiserum** /æntiˈsɪərəm/, *n., pl.* **-serums, -sera** /-ˈsɪərə/. serum containing antibodies, as antitoxins or agglutinins, obtained by inoculation of animals and used for injection into the bloodstream of other animals to provide immunity to a specific disease.

**antislavery** /æntiˈsleɪvəri/, *adj.* opposed to slavery, esp. Negro slavery.

**antisocial** /æntiˈsoʊʃəl/, *adj.* **1.** unwilling or unable to associate normally with one's fellows. **2.** opposed, damaging, or motivated by antagonism to social order, or to the principles on which society is constituted. – **antisocially,** *adv.*

**antispasmodic** /ˌæntispæzˈmɒdɪk/, *adj.* **1.** checking spasms. *–n.* **2.** an antispasmodic agent.

**antistatic** /æntiˈstætɪk/, *adj.* of or pertaining to anything which reduces static energy or resists acquiring it: *an antistatic device, an antistatic fabric.*

**antistrophe** /ænˈtɪstrəfi/, *n.* **1.** the part of an ancient Greek choral ode, answering to a previous strophe, sung by the chorus when returning from left to right. **2.** the second of two metrically corresponding systems in a poem. [L, from Gk: a turning about] – **antistrophic** /æntiˈstrɒfɪk/, *adj.*

**anti-sway bar** /ænti-ˈsweɪ ba/, *n.* →**anti-roll bar.**

**antitank** /æntiˈtæŋk/, *adj.* designed for use against tanks or other armoured vehicles: *antitank gun.*

**antithesis** /ænˈtɪθəsəs/, *n., pl.* **-ses** /-siz/. **1.** opposition; contrast: *the antithesis of theory and fact.* **2.** the direct opposite (fol. by *of* or *to*). **3.** *Rhet.* **a.** the setting of one clause or other member of a sentence against another to which it is opposed. **b.** a clause or member thus set in opposition. [LL, from Gk: opposition]

**antithetic** /æntəˈθɛtɪk/, *adj.* **1.** of the nature of or involving antithesis. **2.** directly opposed or contrasted. Also, **antithetical.** – **antithetically,** *adv.*

**antitoxic** /æntiˈtɒksɪk/, *adj.* **1.** counteracting toxic influences. **2.** of or serving as an antitoxin.

**antitoxin** /æntiˈtɒksən/, *n.* **1.** a substance formed in the body, which counteracts a specific toxin. **2.** the antibody formed in immunisation with a given toxin, used in treating or immunising against certain infectious diseases.

**antitrade** /æntiˈtreɪd/, *n.* **1.** any of the upper tropical winds moving counter to and above the trade winds, but descending beyond the trade wind limits, and becoming the westerly winds of middle latitudes. *–adj.* **2.** denoting such a wind.

**antitragus** /ænˈtɪtrəgəs/, *n., pl.* **-gi** /-dʒi/. a process (def. 5) of the external ear. [NL, from Gk *antitragos*]

**anti-transportationist** /ˌænti-trænspɔˈteɪʃənəst/, *n.* →**abolitionist.**

**antitrust** /æntiˈtrʌst/, *adj.* of or pertaining to trade practices law regulating commercial agreements and practices which restrict or impede competition in a market economy.

**antitype** /æntiˈtaɪp/, *n.* that which is foreshadowed by a type or symbol, as a New Testament event prefigured in the Old Testament. [Gk *antitypos* corresponding as a stamp to the die] – **antitypic** /æntiˈtɪpɪk/, **antitypical,** *adj.*

**antivenene** /ˌæntivəˈnin/, *n.* **1.** an antitoxin produced in the blood by repeated injections of venom, as of snakes. **2.** the antitoxic serum obtained from such blood. Also, **antivenin.**

**antivivisectionist** /ˌæntivɪvəˈsɛkʃənəst/, *n.* one who opposes the practice of vivisection. – **antivivisection,** *adj.* – **antivivisectionism,** *n.*

**antler** /ˈæntlə/, *n.* one of the solid deciduous horns, usually branched, of an animal of the deer family. [ME *auntelere,* from OF *antoillier,* from L *ant(e)* before + *oculus* eye]

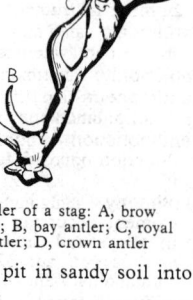

antler of a stag: A, brow antler; B, bay antler; C, royal antler; D, crown antler

**antlered** /ˈæntləd/, *adj.* **1.** having antlers. **2.** decorated with antlers.

**ant-lion** /ˈænt-laɪən/, *n.* the predacious larva of various neuropterous insects, which digs a deep-sided pit in sandy soil into which ants and other small insects fall.

**antonomasia** /æntənəˈmeɪʃə/, *n.* **1.** the identification of a person by an epithet or appellative not his name, as *his lordship.* **2.** the use of a personal name to denote a class of similar persons, as *a Shylock.* [L, from Gk, from *antonomázein* call instead]

**antonym** /ˈæntənɪm/, *n.* a word opposed in meaning to another (opposed to *synonym*): *'good' is the antonym of 'bad'.* [ANT- + Gk *ónyma* name; modelled on SYNONYM] – **antonymic,** *adj.*

**ant orchid** /ˈænt ɔkəd/, *n.* a terrestrial orchid *Chiloglottis formicifera,* found on the central coast of New South Wales and in New Zealand, the flower of which is fancifully thought to resemble an ant.

ant orchid

**antrorse** /ænˈtrɔs/, *adj. Bot., Zool.* bent or directed forwards or upwards. [NL *antrorsus,* from L *antero-* front + *versus,* pp., turned] – **antrorsely,** *adv.*

**antrum** /ˈæntrəm/, *n., pl.* **-tra** /-trə/. a cavity in a bone, esp. that in the maxilla. [L, from Gk *ántron*]

**ants' nest** /ˈænts nɛst/, *n.* a place made by ants, as by tunnelling in the earth, or used by them, for the depositing of their eggs and the shelter of their young.

**ants pants** /ænts ˈpænts/, *n. Colloq.* the ultimate in style, novelty or cleverness.

**A.N.U.** /eɪ ɛn ˈju/, Australian National University. Also, **ANU.**

**anural** /əˈnjurəl/, *adj.* **1.** tailless. **2.** →**anuran.** Also, **anurous.** [AN-[1] + Gk *ourá* tail + -AL[1]]

**anuran** /əˈnjurən, eɪ-/, *adj.* Also, **anural.** **1.** of or pertaining to the Anura, an order of Amphibians, as frogs and toads. *–n.* **2.** a frog or toad.

**anuresis** /ænjuˈrisəs/, *n.* the inability to urinate. Cf. **anuria.** [NL, from *an-* AN-[1] + Gk *oúrēsis* urination]

**anuria** /əˈnjuriə/, *n.* the absence or suppression of urine.

**anus** /ˈeɪnəs/, *n.* the opening at the lower end of the alimentary canal, through which the solid refuse of digestion is excreted. [L]

**anvil** /ˈænvəl/, *n.* **1.** a heavy iron block with a smooth face, frequently of steel, on which metals, usu. red-hot or white-hot, are hammered into desired shapes. **2.** anything on which blows are struck. **3.** *Music.* a percussion instrument consisting of a small steel bar which is struck with a hard mallet. **4.** the fixed jaw in certain measuring instruments. **5.** →**incus.** **6. on the anvil,** unformulated; under discussion; under construction. [ME *anvilt,* OE *anfilt(e),* c. MD *anvilte*]

**anvil bird** /ˈ– bɜd/, *n.* the buff-breasted pitta, *Pitta versicolor,* of eastern Australia which feeds on snails and uses a stone or small stump as an 'anvil' on which to break the shells.

**anxiety** /æŋˈzaɪəti/, *n., pl.* **-ties.** **1.** distress or uneasiness of mind caused by apprehension of danger or misfortune. **2.** solicitous desire; eagerness. **3.** *Psychol.* a state of apprehension and psychic tension found in some forms of mental disorder. [L *anxietas*]

**anxious** /ˈæŋʃəs, ˈæŋk-/, *adj.* **1.** full of anxiety or solicitude; greatly troubled or solicitous: *to be anxious about someone's safety.* **2.** earnestly desirous (fol. by infinitive or *for*): *anxious* *to please.* **3.** attended with or showing solicitude or uneasiness: *anxious forebodings.* **4.** causing anxiety or worry; difficult: *an anxious business, an anxious time.* [L *anxius* troubled] – **anxiously,** *adv.* – **anxiousness,** *n.*

**any** /ˈɛni/, *adj.* **1.** one, a, an, or (with plural noun) some; whatever or whichever it may be: *if you have any witnesses, produce them.* **2.** in whatever quantity or number, great or small: *have you any butter?* **3.** every: *any schoolboy would know that.* **4.** (with a negative) none at all. **5.** a great or unlimited (amount): *any number of things.* **6. any one,** any single or individual (person or thing): *any one part of the town.* *–pron.* **7.** (*construed as sing.*) any person; anybody, or (*construed as pl.*) any persons: *he does better than any before him; unknown to any.* **8.** any single one or any one's; any thing or things; any quantity or number: *I haven't any.* **9. get any,** *Colloq.* to have sexual intercourse. *–adv.* **10.** in any degree; to any extent; at all: *Do you feel any better? Will this route take any longer?* [ME; OE *ǣnig,* from *ān* one]

**anybody** /ˈɛnibɒdi, -bədi/, *pron., n., pl.* **-bodies. 1.** any person. **2.** a person of little importance.

**anyhow** /ˈɛnihaʊ/, *adv.* **1.** in any case; at all events. **2.** in a careless manner. **3.** in any way whatever.

**anyone** /ˈɛniwʌn/, *pron.* any person; anybody.

**anything** /ˈɛniθɪŋ/, *pron.* **1.** any thing whatever; something, no matter what. *–n.* **2.** a thing of any kind. *–adv.* **3.** in any degree; to any extent. **4. like anything,** *Colloq.* greatly; with great energy or emotion.

**any way** /ˈɛni weɪ/, *adv.* **1.** in any way or manner. **2.** carelessly; haphazardly; anyhow.

**anyway** /ˈɛniweɪ/, *adv.* in any case; anyhow.

**anyways** /ˈɛniweɪz/, *adv. Colloq.* **1.** any way. **2.** anyway.

**anywhere** /ˈɛniwɛə/, *adv.* in, at, or to any place.

**anywise** /ˈɛniwaɪz/, *adv.* in any way or respect.

**ANZAAS** /ˈænzəs, -zæs/, Australian and New Zealand Association for the Advancement of Science. Also, **A.N.Z.A.A.S.**

**Anzac** /ˈænzæk/, *n.* **1.** a member of the Australian and New Zealand Army Corps during World War I. **2.** a soldier from Australia or New Zealand. [*A(ustralian and) N(ew) Z(ealand) A(rmy) C(orps)*]

**anzac biscuit** /– ˈbɪskət/, *n.* a biscuit made from wheat flour, rolled oats, dessicated coconut and golden syrup.

**Anzac button** /ˈ– bʌtn/, *n.* a nail used in place of a missing button.

**Anzac Day** /ˈ– deɪ/, *n.* 25 April, the anniversary of the Anzac landing on Gallipoli in 1915.

**ANZUS** /ˈænzəs/, *n.* Australia, New Zealand, and the United States, esp. as associated in the mutual defence treaty (**ANZUS Pact** or **Treaty)** of 1952.

**A/O,** account for. Also, **a/o.**

**A.O.** /eɪ ˈoʊ/, Officer of the Order of Australia.

**A-OK** /eɪ-oʊˈkeɪ/, *adj. U.S.* very good; functioning correctly. Also, **A-okay.**

**A-one** /eɪ-ˈwʌn/, *adj.* →**A-1.**

**aorist** /ˈɛərəst/, *n.* **1.** a tense of the Greek verb expressing action (in the indicative, past action) without further limitation or implication as to completion, continuation, etc. *–adj.* **2.** of or in the aorist. [Gk *aóristos* indefinite]

**aoristic** /ɛəˈrɪstɪk/, *adj.* **1.** *Gram.* pertaining to the aorist. **2.** indefinite; indeterminate.

**aorta** /eɪˈɔtə/, *n., pl.* **-tas, -tae** /-ti/. *Anat.* the main trunk of the arterial system, conveying blood from the left ventricle of the heart to all of the body except the lungs. [NL, from Gk *aortḗ*] – **aortic, aortal,** *adj.*

**AOT** /eɪ oʊ ˈti/, *adv. Colloq.* upside-down; head over heels. [*A(rse) O(ver) T(it)*]

**Aotearoa** /ˌaoʊtiəˈroʊə/, *n.* New Zealand. [Maori *ao tea roa* Land of the Long White Cloud]

**aoudad** /ˈaudæd/, *n.* a wild sheep of northern Africa, *Ammotragus lervia.* [F, from Berber *audad*]

aoudad

**ap-,** variant of **ad-,** before *p* as in *appear.*

**Ap.,** April.

**A.P.** /eɪ ˈpi/, **1.** Associated Press. **2.** Also, **AP.** Australia Party.

**apace** /əˈpeɪs/, *adv.* with speed; quickly; swiftly.

**apache** /əˈpæʃ, əˈpaʃ/, *n.* a Parisian gangster or tough. [F, special use of APACHE]

**Apache** /əˈpætʃi/, *n., pl.* **Apaches, Apache. 1.** one of a group of Indian tribes of Athabascan speech stock in the southwestern U.S. **2.** any of several Athabascan languages of Arizona and the Rio Grande basin.

**apache dance** /əˈpæʃ dæns/, *n.* an energetic dance, originating in Parisian burlesque and vaudeville shows, esp. one for a man and a woman imitating a Parisian gangster and his girl.

**apagoge** /æpəˈgoʊdʒi/, *n.* the technique of indirectly proving something by showing that the alternative is false, impossible, or absurd. [Gk: a leading away] – **apagogic** /æpəˈgɒdʒɪk/, **apagogical,** *adj.* – **apagogically,** *adv.*

**apanage** /ˈæpənɪdʒ/, *n.* →**appanage.**

**apantomancy** /æˈpæntəˌmænsi/, *n.* forecasting from chance meetings with animals, as a black cat.

**apart** /əˈpat/, *adv.* **1.** in pieces, or to pieces: *to take a watch apart.* **2.** separately or aside in motion, place, or position. **3.** to or at one side, with respect to purpose or function: *to set something apart.* **4.** separately or individually in consideration. **5.** aside (used with a gerund or noun): *joking apart, what do you think?* **6. apart from,** aside from: *apart from other considerations.* *–adj.* **7.** separate; independent: *a class apart.* [ME, from OF *a part,* from L *ad partem* to the side]

**apartheid** /əˈpateɪt/, *n.* (esp. in South Africa) racial segregation. [Afrikaans, from *apart* APART + *-heid* -HOOD]

**apartment** /əˈpatmənt/, *n.* **1.** a single room in a building. **2.** (*pl.*) a suite of furnished rooms, among others in a building. **3.** *Chiefly U.S.* a flat. **4.** a home unit. [F *appartement,* from It. *appartemento,* from *appartare* separate. See APART]

**apartment house** /ˈ– haʊs/, *n. U.S.* a building divided into apartments (def. 3).

**apatetic** /æpəˈtɛtɪk/, *adj.* (of animals) assuming colours and forms which effect deceptive camouflage. [Gk *apatētikós* fallacious]

**apathetic** /æpəˈθɛtɪk/, *adj.* **1.** having or exhibiting little or no emotion. **2.** indifferent. Also, **apathetical.** – **apathetically,** *adv.*

**apathy** /ˈæpəθi/, *n., pl.* **-thies. 1.** lack of feeling; absence or suppression of passion, emotion, or excitement. **2.** lack of interest in things which others find moving or exciting. [L *apathía,* from Gk *apátheia* insensibility]

**apatite** /ˈæpətaɪt/, *n.* a common mineral, calcium fluorophosphate, $Ca_5FP_3O_{12}$, occurring crystallised and massive, and varying in colour, used in the manufacture of phosphate fertilisers. [Gk *apátē* deceit + -ITE[1]; so called because often mistaken for other minerals]

**APC** /eɪ pi ˈsi/, *n.* the mixture of acetylsalicyclic acid, phenacetin, and caffeine, formerly used in headache powders.

**ape** /eɪp/, *n., v.,* **aped, aping,** *adv.* *–n.* **1.** a tailless monkey or a monkey with a very short tail. **2.** an anthropoid ape. **3.** an imitator; a mimic. **4.** any monkey. **5.** (formerly) £500. *–v.t.* **6.** to imitate servilely; mimic. *–adv.* **7. go ape,** *Colloq.* to react with excessive and unrestrained pleasure, excitement, etc. (fol. by *over*). [ME, from OE *apa;* c. G *Affe*] – **apelike,** *adj.*

**ape hangers** /ˈeɪp hæŋəz/, *n. pl. Colloq.* bicycle handlebars so curved that the handles are above the level of the rider's shoulders.

**apeman** /ˈeɪpmæn/, *n., pl.* **-men. 1.** loosely applied to any of the various extinct apelike forerunners of man. **2.** (*derog.*) an uncouth, virile man.

**aperient** /əˈpɪəriənt/, *adj.* **1.** purgative; laxative. *–n.* **2.** a medicine or an article of diet that acts as a mild laxative. [L *aperiens,* ppr., opening]

**aperiodic** /ˌeɪpɪəriˈɒdɪk/, *adj.* **1.** not periodic; irregular. [A-[6] + PERIODIC] – **aperiodicity** /ˌeɪpɪəriəˈdɪsəti/, *n.*

**aperitif** /əˈpɛrətif/, *n.* a small alcoholic drink as a cocktail or glass of sherry, often taken as an appetiser. Also, **aperitive** /əˈpɛrətɪv/. [F *apéritif*]

**aperture** /ˈæpətʃə/, *n.* **1.** a hole, slit, crack, gap, or other opening. **2.** *Optics.* an opening that limits the quantity of light that can enter an optical instrument. [L *apertūra*]

**aperture synthesis** /– 'sɪnθəsəs/, *n.* the use of two small aerials in a radio telescope to synthesise a large aperture.

**apery** /'eɪpəri/, *n., pl.* **-eries.** **1.** apish behaviour; mimicry. **2.** a silly trick. [AP(E) + -ERY]

**apetalous** /ə'pɛtələs/, *adj.* having no petals.

**apex** /'eɪpɛks/, *n., pl.* **apexes, apices** /'eɪpəsiz/. **1.** the tip, point, or vertex of anything; the summit. **2.** climax; acme. [L: point, summit]

**Apgar score** /'æpga skɔ/, *n.* the score used to evaluate the fitness of a newborn infant, based on heart rate, respiration, muscle tone, cough reflex and colour.

**aph-**, variant of **ap-, apo-**, used before an aspirate.

**aphaeresis** /ə'fɛrəsəs/, *n.* the omission of a letter, phoneme, or unstressed syllable at the beginning of a word, as in *squire* for *esquire.* Also, *Chiefly U.S.,* **apheresis.** [L, from Gk *aphaíresis* removal] – **aphaeretic** /æfə'rɛtɪk/, *adj.*

**aphagia** /ə'feɪdʒiə/, *n.* the inability to swallow. [NL, from *a-* A-[6] + Gk *-phagía,* from *phageîn* to eat]

**aphanite** /'æfənaɪt/, *n.* any fine-grained igneous rock having such compact texture that the constituent minerals cannot be detected with the naked eye. [Gk *aphanḗs* obscure + -ITE[1]] – **aphanitic** /æfə'nɪtɪk/, *adj.*

**aphasia** /ə'feɪʒə, -ziə/, *n.* loss or impairment of the faculty of symbolic formulation and of speech due to a lesion of the central nervous system. [NL, from Gk: speechlessness]

**aphasiac** /ə'feɪziæk/, *n.* →**aphasic.**

**aphasic** /ə'feɪzɪk/, *adj.* **1.** pertaining to or affected with aphasia. *–n.* **2.** one affected with aphasia.

**aphelion** /ə'filiən/, *n., pl.* **-lia** /-liə/. the point of a planet's, comet's, or artificial satellite's orbit most distant from the sun (opposed to *perihelion*). [Hellenised form of NL *aphēlium.* See APH-, HELIO-]

A, aphelion; P, perihelion; S, sun

**apheliotropic** /əfiliə'trɒpɪk/, *adj.* growing away from the sun, as of plant roots. [see APO-, HELIOTROPIC]

**apheresis** /ə'fɛrəsəs/, *n. Chiefly U.S.* →**aphaeresis.**

**aphesis** /'æfəsəs, ə'fisəs/, *n.* (in historical linguistic process) the gradual disappearance of an unstressed initial vowel or syllable, as in *mend* from *amend.* [Gk: a letting go]

**aphetic** /ə'fɛtɪk/, *adj.* of, pertaining to, or due to aphesis.

**aphid** /'eɪfəd/, *n.* any of the plant-sucking insects of the family Aphididae; greenfly; plant-louse. [NL *aphis*] – **aphidian** /ə'fɪdiən/, *adj., n.*

**aphis** /'eɪfəs/, *n., pl.* **aphides** /'eɪfədiz/. an aphid.

**aphonia** /ə'foʊniə/, *n.* loss of voice, due to an organic or functional disturbance of the vocal organs. [Gk: speechlessness]

**aphonic** /eɪ'fɒnɪk/, *Pathol. –adj.* **1.** affected with aphonia. *–n.* **2.** one affected with aphonia.

**aphorise** /'æfəraɪz/, *v.i.,* **-rised, -rising.** to utter aphorisms; write or speak in aphorisms. Also, **aphorize.**

**aphorism** /'æfərɪzəm/, *n.* a terse saying embodying a general truth. [ML *aphorismus,* from Gk *aphorismós* definition, a short pithy sentence] – **aphorismic, aphorismatic** /æfərɪz'mætɪk/, *adj.*

**aphorist** /'æfərəst/, *n.* a maker of aphorisms.

**aphoristic** /æfə'rɪstɪk/, *adj.* **1.** of, like, or containing aphorisms: *his sermons were always richly aphoristic.* **2.** given to making or quoting aphorisms. – **aphoristically,** *adv.*

**aphotic** /ə'fɒtɪk/, *adj.* **1.** without light. **2.** of or pertaining to a plant growing in the aphotic region. [A-[6] + PHOTIC]

**aphotic region** /'– ridʒən/, *n.* a biogeographical region of deep water characterised by the absence of light, as in the depths of the ocean.

**aphrodisiac** /æfrə'dɪziæk/, *adj.* **1.** arousing sexual desire. *–n.* **2.** a drug or food that arouses sexual desire. [Gk *aphrodīsiakós* venereal]

**aphyllous** /ə'fɪləs/, *adj. Bot.* naturally leafless. [Gk *áphyllos* leafless]

**aphylly** /ə'fɪli/, *n. Bot.* leaflessness.

**apiaceous** /æpi'eɪʃəs/, *adj.* related to the umbelliferous genus *Apium,* including parsley, celery, etc. [L *apium* parsley + -ACEOUS]

**apian** /'eɪpiən/, *adj.* of or pertaining to bees. [L *apiānus*]

**apiarian** /eɪpi'ɛəriən/, *adj.* relating to the breeding and care of bees.

**apiarist** /'eɪpiərəst/, *n.* one who keeps an apiary; a bee-keeper.

**apiary** /'eɪpiəri/, *n., pl.* **-ries.** a place in which bees are kept; a stand or shed containing a number of beehives. [L *apiārium*]

**apical** /'æpɪkəl, 'eɪ-/, *adj.* **1.** of, at, or forming the apex. **2.** *Phonetics.* pertaining to speech sounds formed with the tip of the tongue as articulator, as for example, [t], [s], [n]. [L *apex* summit + -AL[1]] – **apically,** *adv.*

**apices** /'eɪpəsiz/, *n., pl.* of **apex.**

**apiculate** /ə'pɪkjələt, -leɪt/, *adj.* tipped with a short, abrupt point, as a leaf.

**apiculture** /'eɪpikʌltʃə/, *n.* the rearing of bees. [L *api(s)* bee + CULTURE] – **apicultural,** *adj.* – **apiculturist,** *n.*

**apiece** /ə'pis/, *adv.* for each piece, thing, or person; for each one; each: *an orange apiece; costing a dollar apiece.* [orig. two words, *a* to or for each + PIECE]

**apish** /'eɪpɪʃ/, *adj.* **1.** having the qualities, appearance, or ways of an ape. **2.** slavishly imitative. **3.** foolishly affected. – **apishly,** *adv.* – **apishness,** *n.*

**apivorous** /eɪ'pɪvərəs/, *adj.* feeding on bees, as certain birds. [L *api(s)* bee + -VOROUS]

**aplacental** /eɪplə'sɛntl/, *adj.* not placental; having no placenta, as the lowest mammals.

**aplanatic** /æplə'nætɪk/, *adj. Optics.* free from spherical aberration and coma. [Gk *aplánētos* not wandering + -IC] – **aplanatism,** *n.*

**aplasia** /ə'pleɪʒə, -ziə/, *n.* defective development or congenital absence of a bodily tissue or organ. [NL, from *a-* A-[6] + *-plasia* -PLASIA] – **aplastic** /eɪ'plæstɪk/, *adj.*

**aplastic anaemia** /eɪ,plæstɪk ə'nimiə/, *n.* a severe anaemia due to destruction or depressed function of the bone marrow, with no regenerative hyperplasia.

**aplenty** /ə'plɛnti/, *adj.* (*fol. noun*) in abundance: *there's food aplenty for all.* [A[1] + PLENTY]

**aplite** /'æplaɪt/, *n.* a fine-grained granite composed essentially of felspar and quartz. Also, **haplite** /'hæplaɪt/. [Gk *haplóos* single, simple + -ITE[1]] – **aplitic** /ə'plɪtɪk/, *adj.*

**aplomb** /ə'plɒm/, *n.* **1.** imperturbable self-possession, poise, or assurance. **2.** a perpendicular position. [F: *à* according to + *plomb* plummet]

**apnoea** /æp'niə/, *n.* **1.** suspension of respiration. **2.** →**asphyxia.** Also, *U.S.,* **apnea.** [NL, from Gk *ápnoia* lack of wind] – **apnoeal, apnoeic** /æp'niɪk/, *adj.*

**apo-**, a prefix meaning 'from', 'away', 'off', 'asunder', as in *apomorphine, apophyllite.* Also, **ap-, aph-.** [Gk. Cf. AB-[1]]

**Apoc.**, Apocalypse.

**apocalypse** /ə'pɒkəlɪps/, *n.* revelation; discovery; disclosure. [from writings, so named, Jewish and Christian, which appeared from about 200 B.C. to A.D. 350, assuming to make revelation of the ultimate divine purpose; Gk *apokálypsis* revelation]

**apocalyptic** /əpɒkə'lɪptɪk/, *adj.* of or like an apocalypse; affording a revelation. Also, **apocalyptical.** – **apocalyptically,** *adv.*

**apocarp** /'æpəkap/, *n. Bot.* a gynoecium with apocarpous carpels.

**apocarpous** /æpə'kapəs/, *adj. Bot.* having the carpels separate. [APO- + Gk *karpós* fruit + -OUS]

apocarpous flower

**apochromatic** /æpəkrə'mætɪk/, *adj. Optics.* having a high degree of correction for chromatic and spherical aberration and for coma. [modelled on ACHROMATIC. See APO-]

**apocope** /ə'pɒkəpi/, *n.* the cutting off of the last part of a word, as *cinema* from *cinematograph.* [L, from Gk *apokopḗ* a cutting off] – **apocopate,** *v.* – **apocopation,** *n.*

**apocrypha** /ə'pɒkrəfə/, *n. pl.* (*now construed as sing.*) works of doubtful authorship or authenticity. [from Christian reli-

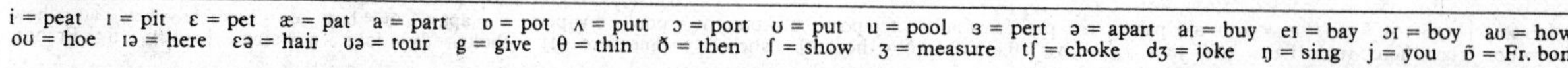

gious writings so named, of uncertain origin, regarded by some as inspired, but rejected by most authorities]

**apocryphal** /ə'pɒkrəfəl/, *adj.* **1.** of doubtful authorship or authenticity. **2.** false; spurious. **3.** fabulous; fictitious; mythical. – **apocryphally,** *adv.* – **apocryphalness,** *n.*

**apocynthion** /æpə'sɪnθiən/, *n.* the point of a satellite's orbit about the moon most distant from the moon. Cf. **pericynthion.** [APO- + *Cynth(ia)* the goddess of the moon + -ION]

**apodal** /'æpədl/, *adj.* **1.** having no distinct feet or footlike members. **2.** belonging to the Apoda or Apodes (various groups of apodal animals). Also, **apod** /'æpɒd/. [Gk *ápous* footless + -AL[1]]

**apodictic** /æpə'dɪktɪk/, *adj.* **1.** incontestable because demonstrated or demonstrable. **2.** *Logic.* descriptive of a proposition (in Aristotelian logic) or a judgment (in Kantian), the truth of which it claims to be necessary. Also, **apodeictic** /æpə'daɪktɪk/, **apodictical.** [Gk *apodeiktikós* demonstrative] – **apodictically,** *adv.*

**apodosis** /ə'pɒdəsəs/, *n., pl.* **-ses** /-siz/. (in a conditional sentence) the clause stating the consequence. Cf. **protasis.** [L, from Gk: return, answering clause]

**apogamy** /ə'pɒgəmi/, *n.* the development of a sporophyte from a cell or cells of the gametophyte other than the egg. [APO- + -GAMY] – **apogamic** /æpə'gæmɪk/, **apogamous,** *adj.*

**apogee** /'æpədʒi/, *n.* **1.** *Astron.* the point in the orbit of a heavenly body or artificial satellite most distant from the earth (opposed to *perigee*). **2.** the highest or most distant point; climax. [F *apogée,* from L *apogēum,* from Gk *apógaion* (*diástēma*) (distance) from the earth] – **apogeal, apogean,** *adj.*

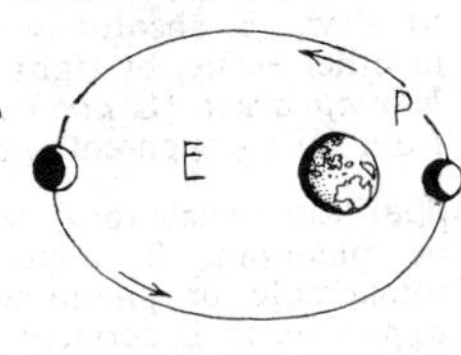

A, apogee; P, perigee; E, earth

**apogeotropism** /æpədʒi'ɒtrəpɪzəm/, *n.* (of a plant) growth or tendency away from the earth; negative geotropism. – **apogeotropic** /æpədʒiə'trɒpɪk/, *adj.*

**apolitical** /eɪpə'lɪtɪkəl/, *adj.* **1.** having no interest in political issues. **2.** not involving obligations to a particular political party: *the vote on this issue is apolitical.*

**Apollo** /ə'pɒloʊ/, *n.* an unusually handsome young man. [from *Apollo,* a Greek and Roman god renowned for his beauty]

**apollonian** /æpə'loʊniən/, *adj.* serene; stately; poised; having the properties of classic beauty. [See APOLLO]

**apologetic** /əpɒlə'dʒɛtɪk/, *adj.* **1.** making apology or excuse for fault, failure, etc. **2.** defending by speech or writing. Also, **apologetical.** [LL *apologēticus,* from Gk *apologētikós*] – **apologetically,** *adv.*

**apologetics** /əpɒlə'dʒɛtɪks/, *n.* **1.** the science or technique of defensive argument. **2.** the branch of theology concerned with the defence of Christianity.

**apologia** /æpə'loʊdʒiə/, *n.* a formal defence or justification in speech or writing, as of a cause or doctrine. [L, from Gk: a speech in defence]

**apologise** /ə'pɒlədʒaɪz/, *v.i.,* **-gised, -gising. 1.** to offer excuses or regrets for some fault, insult, failure, or injury. **2.** to make a formal defence in speech or writing. Also, **apologize.** – **apologiser,** *n.*

**apologist** /ə'pɒlədʒəst/, *n.* **1.** one who makes an apology or defence in speech or writing. **2.** *Eccles.* **a.** a defender of Christianity. **b.** one of the authors of the early Christian apologies.

**apologue** /'æpəlɒg/, *n.* **1.** a didactic narrative; a moral fable. **2.** an allegory. [F, from L *apologus,* from Gk *apólogos* a story, tale]

**apology** /ə'pɒlədʒi/, *n., pl.* **-gies. 1.** an expression of regret offered for some fault, failure, insult, or injury. **2.** an apologia. **3.** a poor specimen or substitute; a makeshift: *a sad apology for a hat.* [L *apologia,* from Gk *apología,* speech in defence]

**apolune** /'æpəlun/, *n.* the highest point in the orbit of a body which is circling the moon, with respect to the moon's centre. [APO- + *lune* (L *lūna* moon), modelled on APOGEE]

**apomict** /'æpəmɪkt/, *n.* an organism produced by apomixis.

**apomixis** /æpə'mɪksəs/, *n., pl.* **-mixes** /-'mɪksiz/. reproduction which replaces or is a substitute for sexual reproduction, so that all progeny so derived have the same genetic constitution. [Gk, from APO- + *míxis* mixing]

**apomorphine** /æpə'mɔfin/, *n.* an artificial crystalline alkaloid prepared from morphine, used in the form of the hydrochloride as an emetic and expectorant. Also, **apomorphin** /æpə'mɔfən/, **apomorphia** /æpə'mɔfiə/.

**aponeurosis** /æpənju'roʊsəs/, *n., pl.* **-ses** /-siz/. a whitish fibrous membrane formed by the expansion of a tendon. [NL, from Gk, from *aponeuroûsthai* become a tendon] – **aponeurotic** /æpənju'rɒtɪk/, *adj.*

**apophasis** /ə'pɒfəsəs/, *n. Rhet.* denial of an intention to speak of something which is at the same time hinted or insinuated. [L, from Gk: denial]

**apophthegm** /'æpəθɛm/, *n.* a short, pithy, instructive saying; a terse remark or aphorism. Also, **apothegm.** [Gk *apóphthegma*] – **apophthegmatic** /æpəθɛg'mætɪk/, **apophthegmatical,** *adj.*

**apophthegmatise** /æpə'θɛgmətaɪz/, *v.i.,* **-tised, -tising.** to speak in apophthegms. Also, **apophthegmatize.** – **apophthegmatist,** *n.*

**apophyge** /ə'pɒfədʒi/, *n.* **1.** the small, hollow outward spread at the bottom of the shaft of a pillar by which it joins the base. **2.** a similar but slighter spread at the top of the shaft. [Gk: lit., an escape]

**apophyllite** /ə'pɒfəlaɪt/, *n.* a mineral, a hydrous potassium and calcium fluorosilicate occurring in white crystals. [APO- + Gk *phýllon* leaf + -ITE[1]; so named because of its tendency to exfoliate]

**apophysis** /ə'pɒfəsəs/, *n., pl.* **-ses** /-siz/. an outgrowth; a process; a projection or protuberance. [NL, from Gk: an offshoot]

**apoplectic** /æpə'plɛktɪk/, *adj.* Also, **apoplectical. 1.** of or pertaining to apoplexy. **2.** having or inclined to apoplexy. **3.** *Colloq.* bad-tempered; choleric. –*n.* **4.** a person having or disposed to apoplexy. – **apoplectically,** *adv.*

**apoplexy** /'æpəplɛksi/, *n.* **1.** marked loss of bodily function due to cerebral haemorrhage. **2.** haemorrhage into the tissue of any organ, esp. the brain. [ME *apoplexie,* from L *apoplēxia,* from Gk, from *apoplḗssein* disable by a stroke]

**aport** /ə'pɔt/, *adv. Naut.* on or towards the port side.

**aposiopesis** /æpəsaɪə'pisəs/, *n. Rhet.* a sudden breaking off in the middle of a sentence, as if from unwillingness to proceed. [L, from Gk, *aposiōpân* be silent] – **aposiopetic** /ˌæpəsaɪə'pɛtɪk/, *adj.*

**apostasy** /ə'pɒstəsi/, *n., pl.* **-sies.** a total desertion of, or departure from, one's religion, principles, party, cause, etc. [ME *apostasie,* from L *apostasia,* from Gk, var. of *apóstasis* defection, revolt]

**apostate** /ə'pɒsteɪt/, *n.* **1.** one who forsakes his church, cause, party, etc. –*adj.* **2.** guilty of apostasy.

**apostatise** /ə'pɒstətaɪz/, *v.i.,* **-tised, -tising.** to commit apostasy. Also, **apostatize.**

**a posteriori** /ˌeɪ pɒsteri'ɔri/, from effect to cause; based upon actual observation or upon experimental data (opposed to *a priori*): *an a posteriori argument.* [L: from the subsequent or latter]

**apostil** /ə'pɒstəl/, *n.* a marginal annotation or note. Also, **apostille.** [F *apostille,* from *apostiller,* from *à* to + *postille* marginal note, probably from ML *postilla,* from *post* after + *illa* those things]

**apostle** /ə'pɒsəl/, *n.* **1.** one of the twelve disciples sent forth by Christ to preach the gospel. **2.** a pioneer of any great moral reform. **3.** a vigorous and zealous upholder (of a principle, cause, etc.). [ME *apostel,* OE *apostol,* from L *apostolus,* from Gk *apóstolos* one sent away. Cf. ME *apostle,* from OF] – **apostleship,** *n.*

**apostle bird** /'– bɜd/, *n.* a greyish-brown, communal nest-building flock bird of the Australian interior, *Struthidea cinerea;* happy family bird; twelve apostle bird.

apostle bird

**apostle spoon** /'– spun/, *n.* a small silver spoon with a figure of an apostle at the end of the handle; formerly a common christening present.

**apostolate** /ə'pɒstələt, -leɪt/, *n.* **1.** the dignity or office of an apostle. **2.** *Rom. Cath. Ch.* the dignity or office of the pope, the holder of the Apostolic See.

**apostolic** /æpə'stɒlɪk/, *adj.* **1.** pertaining to or characteristic of an apostle, esp. of the twelve apostles. **2.** derived from the apostles in regular sequence. **3.** of the pope; papal. Also, **apostolical.** – **apostolically,** *adv.* – **apostolicism,** *n.* – **apostolicity** /əpɒstə'lɪsəti/, *n.*

**apostolic delegate** /– 'dɛləgət/, *n.* an ecclesiastical representative of the Pope in a country which has no diplomatic relations with the Vatican.

**apostolic succession** /– sək'sɛʃən/, *n. Eccles.* the descent of faith and order from Christ's apostles through the consecration of bishops.

**apostrophe**[1] /ə'pɒstrəfi/, *n.* the sign (') used to indicate: **1.** the omission of one or more letters in a word, as in *o'er* for *over, halo'd* for *haloed.* **2.** the possessive case, as in *lion's, lions'.* **3.** certain plurals, as in *several M.D.'s.* [special use of APOSTROPHE[2], by confusion with F *apostrophe,* from L *apostrophus,* from Gk *apóstrophos* turned away, elided] – **apostrophic** /æpə'strɒfɪk/, *adj.*

**apostrophe**[2] /ə'pɒstrəfi/, *n.* a digression from a discourse, esp. in the form of a personal address to someone not present. [L, from Gk: a turning away] – **apostrophic** /æpə'strɒfɪk/, *adj.*

**apostrophise** /ə'pɒstrəfaɪz/, *v.,* **-phised, -phising.** *–v.t.* **1.** to address by apostrophe. *–v.i.* **2.** to utter an apostrophe. Also, **apostrophize.**

**apothecaries' measure** /ə'pɒθəkriz mɛʒə/, *n.* (formerly) a system of units used in compounding and dispensing liquid drugs.

**apothecaries' ounce** /ə'pɒθəkriz aʊns/, *n.* See **ounce**[1] (def. 2).

**apothecaries' weight** /ə'pɒθəkriz weɪt/, *n.* (formerly) a system of weights used in compounding and dispensing drugs.

**apothecary** /ə'pɒθəkri, -kəri/, *n., pl.* **-ries.** *Archaic.* a chemist; a pharmacist. [ME *apothecarie,* from LL *apothēcārius* shopkeeper, from L *apothēca,* from Gk *apothḗkē* storehouse; replacing ME *apotecarie,* from OF *apotecaire.* See -ARY[1]]

**apothecium** /æpə'θisiəm/, *n., pl.* **-cia** /-siə/. the fruit of certain lichens, usually an open, saucer- or cupshaped body, the inner surface of which is covered with a layer which bears asci. [NL, from L *apothēca* (from Gk *apothḗkē* storehouse) + diminutive *-ium*] – **apothecial** /æpə'θisiəl/, *adj.*

**apothegm** /'æpəθɛm/, *n.* →**apophthegm.** – **apothegmatic** /æpəθɪg'mætɪk/, **apothegmatical,** *adj.*

**apothem** /'æpəθɛm/, *n. Maths,* a perpendicular from the centre of a regular polygon to one of its sides. [APO- + Gk *théma,* from *tithénai* to set]

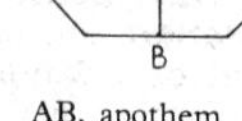

AB, apothem

**apotheosis** /əpɒθi'oʊsəs/, *n., pl.* **-ses** /-siz/. **1.** exaltation to the rank of a god. **2.** the glorification of any person. **3.** a deified or glorified ideal. [L, from Gk: deification]

**apotheosise** /ə'pɒθiəsaɪz/, *v.t.,* **-sised, -sising.** to deify. Also, **apotheosize.**

**app.,** **1.** apparent. **2.** appended. **3.** appendix. **4.** appointed. **5.** approval. **6.** approved. **7.** approximate.

**appal** /ə'pɔl/, *v.t.,* **-palled, -palling.** **1.** to overcome with fear; fill with consternation and horror. **2.** *Colloq.* to shock; dismay. [ME *apalle(n),* from OF *apallir* become or make pale]

**appalling** /ə'pɔlɪŋ/, *adj.* **1.** causing dismay or horror: *an appalling accident.* **2.** *Colloq.* very bad; objectionable. **3.** *Colloq.* noticeable. – **appallingly,** *adv.*

Appaloosa

**Appaloosa** /æpə'lusə/, *n.* a horse of the Palouse pony breed.

**appanage** /'æpənɪdʒ/, *n.* **1.** land or some other source of revenue assigned for the maintenance of a member of the family of a ruling house. **2.** whatever belongs or falls to one's rank or station in life. **3.** a natural or necessary accompaniment. Also, **apanage.** [F, from OF *apaner,* from ML *appānāre* furnish with bread]

**appar.,** **1.** apparent. **2.** apparently.

**apparatchiki** /apə'ratʃiki/, *n. pl.* the agents, especially technical specialists, of politicians or political bodies. [Russ.]

**apparatus** /æpə'ratəs, -'reɪtəs/, *n., pl.* **-tus, -tuses.** **1.** an assemblage of instruments, machinery, appliances, materials, etc., for a particular use. **2.** any complex appliance for a particular purpose. **3.** *Physiol.* a collection of organs, differing in structure, which all minister to the same function. **4.** an organisation or subdivision of an organisation, esp. that part concerned with general administration: *the apparatus of a political party.* [L: preparation]

**apparel** /ə'pærəl/, *n., v.,* **-relled, -relling,** or (*U.S.*) **-reled, -reling.** *–n.* **1.** a person's outer clothing; raiment. **2.** *Archaic.* aspect; guise. **3.** *Naut.* the furnishings or equipment of a ship, as sails, anchors, guns, etc. *–v.t.* **4.** *Archaic.* to dress or clothe; adorn; ornament. [ME *aparaile(n)* from OF *apareiller* clothe, from L *ad-* AD- + diminutive of *par* equal]

**apparent** /ə'pærənt/, *adj.* **1.** capable of being clearly perceived or understood; plain or clear. **2.** seeming; ostensible: *the apparent motion of the sun.* **3.** observed without correction (as opposed to *mean* or *true*). **4.** exposed to the sight; open to view. **5.** absolutely entitled to an inherited throne, title, or other estate, by right of birth (opposed to *presumptive*): *the heir apparent.* [L *appārens* appearing; replacing ME *aparant,* from OF] – **apparently,** *adv.* – **apparentness,** *n.*

**apparition** /æpə'rɪʃən/, *n.* **1.** a ghostly appearance; a spectre or phantom. **2.** anything that appears, esp. something remarkable or phenomenal. **3.** the act of appearing. [LL *appāritio,* in L service] – **apparitional,** *adj.*

**appassionato** /ə,pæʃiə'natoʊ/, *adj.* (a musical direction) impassioned; with passion or strong feeling. [It.]

**appeal** /ə'pil/, *n.* **1.** a call for aid, support, mercy, etc.; an earnest request or entreaty. **2.** a fund-raising enterprise undertaken by or on behalf of a charitable or other needy organisation: *a Red Cross appeal.* **3.** application or reference to some person or authority for corroboration, vindication, decision, etc. **4.** *Sport.* a call from a player to the referee or umpire for his decision on a point of play. **5.** *Law.* **a.** an application or proceeding for review by a higher tribunal. **b.** *Obs.* a formal charge or accusation. **6.** power to attract or to move the feelings: *the game has lost its appeal; sex appeal.* **7.** *Obs.* a summons or challenge. *–v.i.* **8.** to call for aid, mercy, sympathy, or the like; make an earnest entreaty. **9.** *Law.* to apply to a higher tribunal for review of a case or particular issue. **10.** to resort for proof, decision, or settlement: *to appeal to force.* **11.** *Sport.* to appeal to the referee or umpire for his decision. **12.** to offer a peculiar attraction, interest, enjoyment, etc.: *this colour appeals to me.* *–v.t.* **13.** *Law.* **a.** to apply to a higher tribunal for review of (a case). **b.** *Obs.* to charge with a crime before a tribunal. [ME *apele(n),* from OF *apeler,* from L *appellāre* approach, address, summon] – **appealable,** *adj.* – **appealer,** *n.* – **appealingly,** *adv.*

**appear** /ə'pɪə/, *v.i.* **1.** to come into sight; become visible: *a cloud appeared on the horizon.* **2.** to have an appearance; seem; look: *to appear wise.* **3.** to be obvious; be clear or made clear by evidence: *it appears to me that you are right.* **4.** to come or be placed before the public: *his biography appeared last year.* **5.** *Law.* to come formally before a tribunal, authority, etc., as defendant, plaintiff, or counsel. [ME *apere(n),* from OF *aper-,* stem of *aparier,* from L *appārēre*]

**appearance** /ə'pɪərəns/, *n.* **1.** the act or fact of appearing, as to the eye, the mind, or the public. **2.** *Law.* **a.** the formal coming into court of a party to a suit. **b.** formal notice of intent to defend an action. **3.** outward look or aspect; mien: *a man of noble appearance.* **4.** outward show or seeming; semblance: *to avoid the appearance of coveting an honour.* **5.** (*pl.*) outward signs; indications; apparent conditions or circumstances: *don't judge by appearances.* **6.** **keep up appearances,** to maintain a (socially acceptable) outward show (often to conceal inner fault). **7.** **to all appearances,** apparently; so far as can be seen. **8.** an apparition. **9.** *Philos.* the sensory,

or phenomenal, aspect of existence to an observer.
**appearance money** /ˈ– mʌni/, *n.* a sum of money paid to an employee for reporting for work whether or not there is work available on that day. Also, **attendance money.**
**appease** /əˈpiz/, *v.t.,* **-peased, -peasing. 1.** to bring to a state of peace, quiet, ease, or content: *to appease an angry king.* **2.** to satisfy: *to appease one's hunger.* **3.** to accede to the belligerent demands of (a country, government, etc.) by a sacrifice of justice. [ME *apese(n),* from OF *apaisier,* from *a* to + *pais* (from L *pax*) peace] – **appeaseable,** *adj.* – **appeasement, appeaser,** *n.*
**appel** /əˈpɛl/, *n. Fencing.* **1.** a tap or stamp of the foot, formerly serving as a warning of one's intent to attack. **2.** a smart stroke with the blade used for the purpose of procuring an opening. [F]
**appellant** /əˈpɛlənt/, *n.* **1.** one who appeals. **2.** *Law.* one who appeals to a higher tribunal. *–adj.* **3.** appellate. [L *appellans,* ppr., appealing]
**appellate** /əˈpɛlət/, *adj. Law.* **1.** pertaining to appeals. **2.** having power to review and decide appeals. [L *appellātus,* pp., appealed]
**appellation** /æpəˈleɪʃən/, *n.* **1.** a name, title, or designation. **2.** the act of naming. [L *appellātio* name]
**appellative** /əˈpɛlətɪv/, *n.* **1.** a common noun as opposed to a proper name. **2.** a descriptive name; a designation, as *Odd* in *Odd John.* *–adj.* **3.** pertaining to a common noun. **4.** designative; descriptive. – **appellatively,** *adv.*
**appellee** /æpɛlˈi/, *n. Law.* one against whom an accusation or an appeal is lodged. [OF *apele* summoned]
**append** /əˈpɛnd/, *v.t.* **1.** to add, as an accessory; subjoin; annex. **2.** to attach as a pendant. [L *appendere* hang (something) on]
**appendage** /əˈpɛndɪdʒ/, *n.* **1.** a subordinate attached part of anything. **2.** *Biol.* any member of the body diverging from the axial trunk. **3.** *Bot.* any subsidiary part superadded to another part.
**appendant** /əˈpɛndənt/, *adj.* **1.** hanging to; annexed; attached. **2.** associated as an accompaniment or consequence: *the salary appendant to a position.* **3.** *Law.* pertaining to a legal appendant. *–n.* **4.** a person or thing attached or added. **5.** *Law.* an interest (usually in land) connected with or dependent on some other interest. Also, **appendent.** – **appendance, appendence,** *n.*
**appendicectomy** /əpɛndəˈsɛktəmi/, *n., pl.* **-mies.** *Surg.* excision of the vermiform appendix. Also, *Chiefly U.S.,* **appendectomy** /ˌæpɛnˈdɛktəmi/. [L *appendix* APPENDIX + -ECTOMY]
**appendicitis** /əpɛndəˈsaɪtəs/, *n.* inflammation of the vermiform appendix. [NL, from L *appendix* APPENDIX + *-ītis* -ITIS]
**appendicle** /əˈpɛndɪkəl/, *n.* a small appendage. [L *appendicula,* diminutive of *appendix* APPENDIX] – **appendicular** /ˌæpɛnˈdɪkjələ/, **appendiculate** /ˌæpɛnˈdɪkjələt, -leɪt/, *adj.*
**appendix** /əˈpɛndɪks/, *n., pl.* **-dixes, -dices** /-dəsiz/. **1.** matter which supplements the main text of a book, generally explanatory, statistical, or bibliographic material. **2.** *Anat.* **a.** a process or projection. **b.** the vermiform appendix. [L: appendage, addition]
**apperceive** /æpəˈsiv/, *v.t.,* **-ceived, -ceiving. 1.** to be conscious of perceiving; comprehend. **2.** to comprehend by assimilating (a new idea) with the mass of concepts, etc., already in the mind. [from APPERCEPTION, modelled on *perceive, perception*]
**apperception** /æpəˈsɛpʃən/, *n.* **1.** conscious perception. **2.** the act of apperceiving. [F] – **apperceptive,** *adj.*
**appertain** /æpəˈteɪn/, *v.i.* to belong as a part, member, possession, attribute, etc.; pertain (fol. by *to*). [ME *aperteine(n),* from OF *apertenir,* from LL *appertinēre*]
**appestat** /ˈæpəstæt/, *n.* that part of the brain, thought to be the hypothalamus, which is concerned with the control of food intake. [APPE(TITE) + -STAT]
**appetence** /ˈæpətəns/, *n.* **1.** strong natural craving; appetite; intense desire. **2.** instinctive inclination or natural tendency. **3.** material or chemical attraction or affinity. [L *appetentia* seeking after] – **appetent,** *adj.*
**appetency** /ˈæpətənsi/, *n., pl.* **-cies.** →**appetence.**
**appetiser** /ˈæpətaɪzə/, *n.* a food or drink that stimulates the desire for food. Also, **appetizer.**
**appetising** /ˈæpətaɪzɪŋ/, *adj.* exciting or appealing to the appetite. Also, **appetizing.** – **appetisingly,** *adv.*
**appetite** /ˈæpətaɪt/, *n.* **1.** a desire for food or drink: *to work up an appetite.* **2.** a desire to supply any bodily want or craving: *the natural appetites.* **3.** an innate or acquired demand or propensity to satisfy a want: *an appetite for reading.* [ME *appetit,* from OF, from L *appetītus* onset, desire for]
**appetitive** /əˈpɛtətɪv, ˈæpətaɪtɪv/, *adj.* pertaining to appetite.
**applaud** /əˈplɔd/, *v.i.* **1.** to express approval by clapping the hands, shouting, etc. **2.** to give praise; express approval. *–v.t.* **3.** to praise or show approval of by clapping the hands, shouting, etc.: *to applaud an actor.* **4.** to praise in any way; commend; approve: *to applaud one's conduct.* [L *applaudere*] – **applauder,** *n.*
**applause** /əˈplɔz/, *n.* **1.** hand-clapping, shouting, or other demonstration of approval. **2.** any expression of approbation or approval. [L *applausus,* pp.] – **applausive,** *adj.*
**apple** /ˈæpəl/, *n.* **1.** the edible fruit, usu. round and with red, yellow or green skin, of the tree, *Malus pumila.* **2.** the tree, cultivated in most temperate regions. **3.** the fruit of any of certain other species of tree of the same genus. **4.** any of these trees. **5.** any of various other fruits, or fruitlike products or plants, usu. specially designated, as the custard-apple, love apple (tomato), oak-apple. **6.** the forbidden fruit of the tree in the Garden of Eden; temptation. **7.** any of various myrtaceous trees of the genus *Angophora,* of temperate eastern Australia. **8.** a large, spreading Australian tree, *Eucalyptus bridgesiana,* thought to resemble an apple tree; but but. **9. she's apples** or **she'll be apples,** *Colloq.* all is well. [ME; OE *æppel,* c. G *Apfel*]
**apple-berry** /ˈæpəl-bɛri/, *n.* **1.** a slender vine *Billardiera Scandius,* growing in eucalypt forests and having pendulous usu. greenish yellow flowers ripening to a green, yellow or, less commonly, red berry. **2.** the berry of this vine.
**apple caramel** /æpəl ˈkærəməl/, *n.* →**apple crumble.**
**applecart** /ˈæpəlkat/, *n.* **1.** a cart or market barrow for apples. **2. upset the applecart,** to disrupt plans.
**applecatchers** /ˈæpəlkætʃəz/, *n. Colloq.* →**knickerbockers.**
**apple charlotte** /æpəl ˈʃalət/, *n.* →**charlotte.**
**apple crumble** /– ˈkrʌmbəl/, *n.* a baked sweet dish of sliced apple topped with a crumbly pastry of brown sugar, flour and butter.
**apple green** /– ˈgrin/, *n.* a clear, light green. – **apple-green,** *adj.*
**apple gum** /ˈ– gʌm/, *n.* any of certain Australian trees thought to resemble an apple tree, as apple (def. 8). Also, **apple box.**
**Apple Islander** /– ˈaɪləndə/, *n., adj.* →**Tasmanian.**
**Apple Isle** /– ˈaɪl/, *n. Colloq.* the island of Tasmania, one of the States of Australia.
**applejack** /ˈæpəldʒæk/, *n.* a brandy distilled from fermented (i.e. rough) cider.
**apple of discord,** *n.* an object of disputation and envy. [orig. with reference to the apple inscribed 'for the fairest' and thrown into an assembly of the Greek gods]
**apple of Peru,** *n.* an erect, pale blue-flowered herb, *Nicandra physalodes,* native to South America but a weed of cultivation elsewhere.
**apple of Sodom,** *n.* a prickly herbaceous perennial, *Solanum sodomaeum,* native to Mediterranean regions.
**apple of the eye,** *n.* **1.** the pupil of the eye. **2.** something very precious or dear.
**apple pandowdy** /ˌæpəl pænˈdaʊdi/, *n.* a pudding of stewed apple slices topped with a spiced dough and baked.
**apple-pie** /æpəl-ˈpaɪ/, *n.* **1.** a pie made with apples. **2. apple-pie bed,** a bed shortsheeted, or in any way made uncomfortable as a joke. **3. apple-pie order,** perfect order.
**apples** /ˈæpəlz/, *n. pl. Colloq.* stairs. [rhyming slang, *apples and pears*]
**apple sauce**[1] /æpəl ˈsɔs/, *n.* **1.** apples stewed to soft pulp. *–interj. Brit.* **2.** nonsense, rubbish.
**apple sauce**[2] /– ˈsɔs/, *n. Colloq.* a horse [rhyming slang]
**apple strudel** /– ˈstrudl/, *n.* →**strudel.**
**Appleton layers** /ˈæpəltən leɪəz/, *n.pl.* the upper layers of the ionosphere, beyond the Heaviside layer, important in the ref-

lection of radio waves. [named after Sir Edward *Appleton,* 1892-1965, English scientist]

**appliance** /ə'plaɪəns/, *n.* **1.** an instrument, apparatus, or device, esp. one operated by electricity and designed for household use. **2.** the act of applying; application. [APPLY + -ANCE]

**applicable** /ə'plɪkəbəl, 'æp-/, *adj.* capable of being applied; fit; suitable; relevant. – **applicability** /ə,plɪkə'bɪləti/, **applicableness,** *n.* – **applicably,** *adv.*

**applicant** /'æpləkənt/, *n.* one who applies; a candidate: *an applicant for a position.* [L *applicans,* ppr.]

**application** /æplə'keɪʃən/, *n.* **1.** the act of putting to a special use or purpose: *the application of common sense to a problem.* **2.** the quality of being useable for a particular purpose or in a special way; relevance: *this has no application to the case.* **3.** use (of a word, phrase, etc.) with assignation of a particular meaning or reference. **4.** the lesson, point, or bearing (of a fable). **5.** the act of applying: *the application of salve to a wound.* **6.** the thing or remedy applied. **7.** the act of requesting. **8.** a written or spoken request or appeal. **9.** close attention; persistent effort: *application to one's studies.* [L *applicātio* a joining to]

**applicative** /'æpləkətɪv/, *adj.* applying or capable of being applied; applicatory; practical.

**applicator** /'æpləkeɪtə/, *n.* any device used for applying, as a rodlike instrument for applying medication.

**applicatory** /'æpləkeɪtəri/, *adj.* fitted for application or use; practical.

**applied** /ə'plaɪd/, *adj.* **1.** put to practical use, as a science when its laws are concrete phenomena (distinguished from *abstract, theoretical,* or *pure* science). **2.** laid flat against.

**appliqué** /'æpləkeɪ/, *adj., n., v.,* **-quéd, -quéing.** *–adj.* **1.** formed with ornamentation of one material sewn or otherwise applied to another. *–n.* **2.** the ornamentation used to make an appliqué material. **3.** work so formed. *–v.t.* **4.** to apply or form as in appliqué work. [F pp. of *appliquer* put on]

**apply** /ə'plaɪ/, *v.,* **-plied, -plying.** *–v.t.* **1.** to lay on; bring into physical proximity or contact: *to apply a match to powder.* **2.** to bring to bear; put into practical operation, as a principle, law, rule, etc. **3.** to put to use; employ: *they know how to apply their labour.* **4.** to devote to some specific purpose: *to apply a sum of money to pay a debt.* **5.** to use (a word or statement) with reference to some person or thing as applicable or pertinent: *to apply the testimony to the case.* **6.** to give with earnestness or assiduity; employ with attention; set: *to apply one's mind to one's lessons.* **7.** to appliqué. *–v.i.* **8.** to have a bearing or reference; be pertinent: *the argument applies to the case.* **9.** to make application or request; ask: *to apply for a job.* [ME *aplie(n),* from OF *aplier,* from L *applicāre* attach] – **applier,** *n.*

**appoggiatura** /əpɒdʒə'tjurə/, *n. Music.* a note of embellishment (short or long) preceding another note and taking a portion of its time. [It., from *appoggiare,* properly, lean]

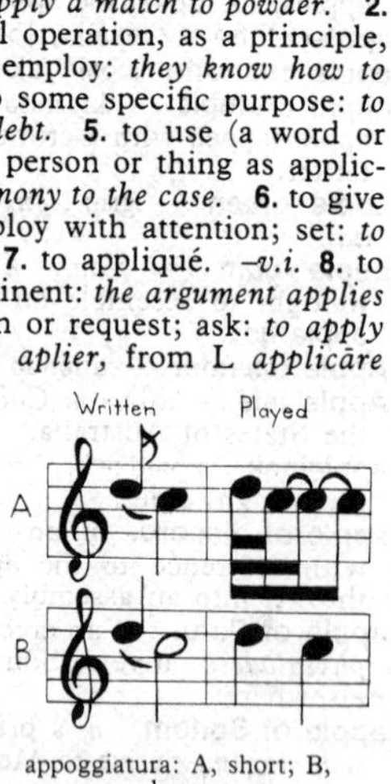

Written Played

A

B

appoggiatura: A, short; B, long

**appoint** /ə'pɔɪnt/, *v.t.* **1.** to nominate or assign to a position, or to perform a function; set apart; designate: *to appoint a new secretary.* **2.** to constitute, ordain, or fix by decree, order, or decision; decree: *laws appointed by God.* **3.** to determine by authority or agreement; fix; settle: *a time appointed for the meeting.* **4.** *Law.* to designate (a person) to take the benefit of an estate created by a deed or will. **5.** to provide with what is requisite; equip. **6.** *Obs.* to point at by way of censure. *–v.i.* **7.** *Obs.* to ordain; resolve; determine. [ME *apoint(en),* from OF *apointer,* from *a-* A-[5] + *pointer* POINT] – **appointer,** *n.*

**appointee** /əpɔɪn'ti/, *n.* **1.** a person appointed. **2.** a beneficiary under a legal appointment.

**appointive** /ə'pɔɪntɪv/, *adj. Chiefly U.S.* pertaining to or dependent on appointment: *an appointive office.*

**appointment** /ə'pɔɪntmənt/, *n.* **1.** the act of appointing, designating, or placing in office: *to fill a vacancy by appointment.* **2.** an office held by a person appointed. **3.** the act of fixing by mutual agreement; engagement: *an appointment to meet at six o'clock.* **4.** (*usu. pl.*) equipment, as for a ship, hotel, etc. **5.** decree; ordinance.

**appointor** /ə'pɔɪntə/, *n. Law.* a donee of a power; a person who nominates another for an office.

**apportion** /ə'pɔʃən/, *v.t.* to divide and assign in just proportion or according to some rule; distribute or allocate proportionally: *to apportion expenses.* [F *apportionner,* from *à* to + *portionner* PORTION, v.] – **apportionable,** *adj.*

**apportionment** /ə'pɔʃənmənt/, *n.* the act of apportioning.

**appose** /æ'poʊz, ə-/, *v.t.,* **-posed, -posing.** **1.** to put or apply (one thing) to or near to another. **2.** to place next, as one thing to another; place side by side, as two things. [F *apposer,* from *à* AD- + *poser* POSE[2], associated with derivatives of L *apponere.* See APPOSITE]

**apposite** /'æpəzət/, *adj.* suitable; well-adapted; pertinent: *an apposite answer.* [L *appositus,* pp., put to] – **appositely,** *adj.* – **appositeness,** *n.*

**apposition** /æpə'zɪʃən/, *n.* **1.** the act of adding to or together; a placing together; juxtaposition. **2.** *Gram.* a syntactic relation between expressions, usu. consecutive, which have the same function and the same relation to other elements in the sentence, the second expression identifying or supplementing the first. For example: *Adam, the first man,* has *the first man* in apposition to *Adam.* – **appositional,** *adj.* – **appositionally,** *adv.*

**appositive** /ə'pɒzətɪv/, *Gram. –adj.* **1.** placed in apposition. *–n.* **2.** a word or phrase placed in apposition. – **appositively,** *adv.*

**appraisal** /ə'preɪzəl/, *n.* **1.** the act of assessing the worth, quality, or condition of anything. **2.** an assessment or statement of worth, quality, or condition. **3.** the act of placing an estimated value on an asset or assets. **4.** valuation; an estimate of value, as for sale.

**appraise** /ə'preɪz/, *v.t.,* **-praised, -praising.** **1.** to estimate generally, as to quality, size, weight, etc. **2.** to value in current money; estimate the value of. [b. *apprize* (from ME *aprise(n),* from OF *apriser,* from phrase *à pris* for sale) and PRAISE] – **appraisable,** *adj.* – **appraiser,** *n.* – **appraisingly,** *adv.*

**appraisement** /ə'preɪzmənt/, *n.* →**appraisal** (defs 3 and 4).

**appreciable** /ə'priʃəbəl/, *adj.* **1.** capable of being perceived or estimated; noticeable. **2.** fairly large. – **appreciably,** *adv.*

**appreciate** /ə'priʃieɪt, ə'prisi-/, *v.,* **-ated, -ating.** *–v.t.* **1.** to place a sufficiently high estimate on: *her great ability was not appreciated.* **2.** to be fully conscious of; be aware of; detect: *to appreciate the dangers of a situation.* **3.** to be sensible of the good qualities (of a person, thing, or action); to be pleased or grateful with. **4.** to raise in value. *–v.i.* **5.** to increase in value. [L *appretiātus,* pp., appraised] – **appreciator,** *n.*

**appreciation** /əpriʃi'eɪʃən, əprisi-/, *n.* **1.** the act of estimating the qualities of things and giving them their due value. **2.** clear perception or recognition, esp. of aesthetic quality. **3.** sensibility to good qualities or good actions; pleasure; gratitude. **4.** increase in value, as of property. **5.** a critical essay, esp. a favourable one.

**appreciative** /ə'priʃətɪv, -ʃiətɪv/, *adj.* capable of appreciating; feeling or manifesting appreciation. – **appreciatively,** *adv.* – **appreciativeness,** *n.*

**appreciatory** /ə'priʃətri/, *adj.* appreciative. – **appreciatorily,** *adv.*

**apprehend** /æprə'hɛnd/, *v.t.* **1.** to take into custody; arrest by legal warrant or authority. **2.** to grasp the meaning of; understand; conceive. **3.** to entertain suspicion or fear of; anticipate: *I apprehend no violence.* *–v.i.* **4.** to understand. **5.** to be apprehensive; fear. [L *apprehendere* seize] – **apprehender,** *n.*

**apprehensible** /æprə'hɛnsəbəl/, *adj.* capable of being understood. – **apprehensibility** /,æprəhɛnsə'bɪləti/, *n.*

**apprehension** /æprə'hɛnʃən/, *n.* **1.** anticipation of adversity; dread or fear of coming evil. **2.** the faculty of apprehending; understanding. **3.** a view, opinion, or idea on any subject. **4.** the act of arresting; seizure. [L *apprehensio*]

**apprehensive** /æprə'hɛnsɪv/, *adj.* **1.** uneasy or fearful about something that may happen: *apprehensive of* (or *for*) *one's safety.* **2.** quick to learn or understand. **3.** perceptive (fol. by *of*). – **apprehensively,** *adv.* – **apprehensiveness,** *n.*

**apprentice** /ə'prɛntəs/, *n., v.,* **-ticed, -ticing.** *–n.* **1.** one who works for another with obligations to learn a trade. **2.** a learner; a novice. **3.** *Horseracing.* a trainee jockey under 21 years of age. *–v.t.* **4.** to bind to or put under the care of an employer for instruction in a trade. [ME *aprentys,* from OF *aprentis,* from *a(p)rendre* teach, learn, APPREHEND] – **apprenticeship,** *n.*

**apprise** /ə'praɪz/, *v.t.,* **-prised, -prising.** to give notice to; inform; advise (oft. fol. by *of*). Also, **apprize.** [F *a(p)pris,* pp. of *a(p)prendre* learn, teach. See APPRENTICE]

**appro** /'æproʊ/, *n. Colloq.* **1.** approval. **2.** approbation. **3. on appro,** for examination, without obligation to buy.

**approach** /ə'proʊtʃ/, *v.t.* **1.** to come nearer or near to: *to approach the city.* **2.** to come near to in quality, character, time, or condition: *approaching Homer as a poet.* **3.** to bring near to something. **4.** to make advances or a proposal to: *to approach the minister with a suggestion.* **5.** to begin work on; set about: *to approach a problem.* *–v.i.* **6.** to come nearer; draw near: *the storm approaches.* **7.** to come near in character, time, amount, etc.; approximate. *–n.* **8.** the act of drawing near: *the approach of a horseman.* **9.** nearness or close approximation: *a fair approach to accuracy.* **10.** any means of access; the area through which one approaches: *the approaches to a city.* **11.** the method used or steps taken in setting about a task, problem, etc. **12.** (*sing. or pl.*) advances made to a person. **13.** (*pl.*) *Mil.* works for protecting forces in an advance against a fortified position. **14.** *Golf.* a stroke after teeing off, by which a player endeavours to get his ball on the putting green. [ME *aproche(n),* from OF *aprochier,* from LL *appropiāre*]

**approachable** /ə'proʊtʃəbəl/, *adj.* **1.** capable of being approached; accessible. **2.** (of a person) easy to approach. – **approachability** /əproʊtʃə'bɪləti/, **approachableness,** *n.*

**approbate** /'æprəbeɪt/, *v.t.,* **-bated, -bating.** **1.** *Scot. Law.* to accept as valid. **2. approbate and reprobate,** *Law.* to accept those parts of a legal instrument which are favourable to one while repudiating the unfavourable parts. **3.** *Chiefly U.S.* to approve officially. [L *approbātus,* pp., favoured]

**approbation** /æprə'beɪʃən/, *n.* **1.** approval; commendation. **2.** sanction. **3.** *Obs.* conclusive proof.

**approbatory** /'æprəbeɪtəri/, *adj.* approving; expressing approbation. Also, **approbative.**

**appropriable** /ə'proʊpriəbəl/, *adj.* capable of being appropriated.

**appropriate** /ə'proʊpriət/, *adj.;* /ə'proʊprieɪt/, *v.,* **-ated, -ating.** *–adj.* **1.** suitable or fitting for a particular purpose, person, occasion, etc. : *an appropriate example.* **2.** belonging or peculiar to one: *each played his appropriate part.* *–v.t.* **3.** to set apart for some specific purpose or use: *parliament appropriated funds for the university.* **4.** to take to or for oneself; take possession of. **5.** to filch; annex; steal. [L *appropriātus,* pp., made one's own] – **appropriately,** *adv.* – **appropriateness,** *n.* – **appropriative** /ə'proʊpriətɪv/, *adj.* – **appropriator** /ə'proʊprieɪtə/, *n.*

**appropriation** /əproʊpri'eɪʃən/, *n.* **1.** anything appropriated for a special purpose, as money. **2.** the act of appropriating. **3.** an act of a legislature authorising money to be paid from the treasury for a special use.

**approval** /ə'pruvəl/, *n.* **1.** the act of approving; approbation. **2.** sanction; official permission. **3. on approval,** for examination, without obligation to buy.

**approve**[1] /ə'pruv/, *v.,* **-proved, -proving.** *–v.t.* **1.** to pronounce or consider good; speak or think favourably of: *to approve the policies of the government.* **2.** to confirm or sanction officially; ratify. **3.** *Obs.* to demonstrate in practice; show. **4.** *Obs.* to make good; attest. **5.** *Obs.* to prove by trial. **6.** *Obs.* to convict. *–v.i.* **7.** to speak or think favourably (usu. fol. by *of*): *to approve of him.* [ME *aprove(n),* from OF *aprover,* from L *approbāre*] – **approvable,** *adj.* – **approver,** *n.* – **approvingly,** *adv.*

**approve**[2] /ə'pruv/, *v.t.,* **-proved, -proving.** *Law.* to improve; increase the value of; turn to one's own profit. [ONF *approer* profit]

**approved** /ə'pruvd/, *n.* **1.** →**approved handicap.** **2.** →**approved horse.**

**approved handicap** /– 'hændikæp/, *n.* a restricted race for horses which are specified as being in the approved class in accordance with the rules operating in each State.

**approved horse** /– 'hɔs/, *n.* a horse eligible to run in an approved handicap. Also, **approved class horse.**

**approvement** /ə'pruvmənt/, *n. Law.* enclosure of part of a stretch of common land.

**approver** /ə'pruvə/, *n. Law.* (formerly) an accomplice in crime who accuses others of the same offence and is admitted as a witness at the discretion of the court to give evidence against his companions. Also, **prover.** [F *approver,* to consent unto]

**approx.** /ə'prɒks/, *adv.* approximately.

**approximal** /ə'prɒksəməl/, *adj. Anat.* near or adjacent, as surfaces of teeth.

**approximant** /ə'prɒksɪmənt/, *n. Phonet.* a sound produced by the approximation of two articulators but without turbulence in the air-stream.

**approximate** /ə'prɒksəmət/, *adj.;* /ə'prɒksəmeɪt/ *v.,* **-mated, -mating.** *–adj.* **1.** nearly exact, equal, or perfect. **2.** inaccurate; rough. **3.** near; close together. **4.** very similar. *–v.t.* **5.** to come near to; approach closely to: *to approximate a solution to a problem.* **6.** to bring near. *–v.i.* **7.** to come near in position, character, amount, etc. [L *approximātus,* pp.] – **approximately,** *adv.*

**approximation** /əprɒksə'meɪʃən/, *n.* **1.** a drawing, moving, or advancing near in space, position, degree, or relation. **2.** a result which is not exact, but is sufficiently so for a given purpose.

**appurtenance** /ə'pɜtənəns/, *n.* **1.** something accessory to another and more important thing; an adjunct. **2.** *Law.* a right, privilege, or improvement belonging to and passing with a principal property. **3.** (*pl.*) apparatus; mechanism. [ME *appurtena(u)nce,* from AF *apurtenance,* from L *appertinēre* belong to]

**appurtenant** /ə'pɜtənənt/, *adj.* **1.** appertaining or belonging; pertaining. *–n.* **2.** an appurtenance.

**Apr.,** April.

**apraxia** /eɪ'præksiə/, *n.* the inability to perform simple purposeful acts, as a result of damage to the nervous system. [NL, from Gk: inaction]

**après-ski** /ˌæpreɪ-'ski/, *adj.* **1.** of or pertaining to (a party, social occasion) held at the end of a day spent skiing. *–n.* **2.** such a party. [F: after ski]

**apricot** /'eɪprikɒt, -prə-/, *n.* **1.** the downy yellow fruit, somewhat resembling a small peach, of the tree *Prunus armeniaca.* **2.** the tree. **3.** a pinkish yellow or yellowish pink. [var. of *apricock,* possibly b. L *praecoqua* apricots (neut. pl. of *praecoquus* early ripe) and F *abricot* apricot, from Pg. *albricoque,* from Sp. *albar(i)coque,* from Ar. *al barqūq,* from LGk *praikókion,* from L (as above)]

**apricot brandy** /– 'brændi/, *n.* a drink with a base of brandy flavoured with apricots.

**April** /'eɪprəl/, *n.* the fourth month of the year, containing 30 days. [L *Aprīlis*]

**April fool** /– 'ful/, *n.* a victim on April Fools' Day.

**April Fools' Day,** *n.* 1 April; the day observed by playing jokes on unsuspecting people.

**a priori** /eɪ pri'ɔri, a praɪ'ɔraɪ/, **1.** from cause to effect; from a general law to a particular instance; valid independently of observation (opposed to *a posteriori*). **2.** claiming to report matters of fact but actually not supported by factual study. [L: from something prior] – **apriority** /eɪpraɪ'ɒrəti/, *n.* – **aprioristic** /eɪpraɪə'rɪstɪk/, *adj.* – **aprioristically,** *adv.*

**apron** /'eɪprən/, *n.* **1.** a piece of clothing made in various ways for covering, and usu. also protecting, the front of the person more or less completely. **2.** a flat continuous conveyor belt. **3.** *Mach.* that part of a lathe carriage containing the clutches and gears that transmit feeder or lead screw motion to the carriage. **4.** *Civ. Eng.* **a.** any device for protecting a surface of earth such as a river bank, from the action of moving water. **b.** a platform to receive the water falling over a dam. **5.** a panel or board below a window, projecting slightly into a room. **6.** *Boxing.* the part of the ring canvas outside the ropes. **7.** a paved or hard-packed area abutting on airfield buildings and hangars. **8.** the part of the stage in front of the proscenium arch. **9.** *Naut.* a timber fixed behind the lower part of the stem above the fore end of the keel. **10.** *Geol.* a deposit of gravel and sand extending forward from a moraine. **11.** the neck fold of a merino ram. *–v.t.* **12.** to put an apron on; furnish with an apron. [ME *napron* (*napron* being later taken as *an apron*), from OF *naperon,* diminutive of *nape,* from L *nappa* napkin, cloth] – **apronlike,** *adj.*

**apron-strings** /'eɪprən-strɪŋz/, *n.pl.* **1.** the ties of an apron. **2. tied to the apron-strings,** emotionally dependent on or bound to a person, as a child is to its mother.

**apropos** /æprə'poʊ/, *adv.* **1.** to the purpose; opportunely. **2.** with reference or regard; in respect (fol. by *of*): *apropos of nothing.* **3.** by the way. *–adj.* **4.** opportune; pertinent: *apropos remarks.* [F *à propos*]

**apse** /æps/, *n.* **1.** *Archit.* a vaulted semicircular or polygonal recess in a building, esp. at the end of the choir of a church. **2.** *Astron.* **a.** →**apsis. b. apse line,** line of apsides. [L *apsis,* from Gk *(h)apsis* loop, circle, bow, arch, apse] – **apsidal** /'æpsədl/, *adj.*

**apsis** /'æpsəs/, *n., pl.* **apsides** /æp'saɪdiz, 'æpsədiz/. **1.** *Astron.* **a.** either of two points in an eccentric orbit, the one (**higher apsis**) farthest from the centre of attraction, and the one (**lower apsis**) nearest to it. **b. line of apsides,** the line coinciding with the major axis of an orbit. **2.** *Archit.* an apse. [L. See APSE]

**apt** /æpt/, *adj.* **1.** inclined; disposed; prone: *too apt to slander others.* **2.** unusually intelligent; quick to learn: *an apt pupil.* **3.** suited to the purpose or occasion: *an apt metaphor.* **4.** *Archaic.* prepared; ready; willing. [ME, from L *aptus* fastened, joined, fitted] – **aptly,** *adv.* – **aptness,** *n.*

**apteral** /'æptərəl/, *adj.* **1.** (esp. of a classical temple) without columns or a porch along the sides. **2.** (of a church) without aisles. [Gk *ápteros* without wings]

**apterous** /'æptərəs/, *adj.* **1.** *Zool.* wingless, as some insects. **2.** *Bot.* without membranous expansions, as a stem. [Gk *ápteros* without wings]

**apterygial** /æptə'rɪdʒiəl/, *adj.* without wings, fins, or limbs, as snakes and eels. [A-[6] + Gk *pterýgion* little wing + -AL[1]]

**apteryx** /'æptərɪks/, *n., pl.* **-teryxes** /-tərɪksəz/. any of several flightless ratite birds of New Zealand, constituting the genus *Apteryx,* allied to the extinct moa; kiwi. [NL, from Gk: *a-* A-[6] + *ptéryx* wing]

apteryx

**aptitude** /'æptətʃud/, *n.* **1.** a natural tendency or acquired inclination; both capacity and propensity for a certain course. **2.** readiness in learning; intelligence; talent. **3.** the state or quality of being apt; special fitness. [ML *aptitūdo,* from L *aptus* fit]

**aptitude test** /'– tɛst/, *n.* a test for special fitness; a test given to find out what sort of work a person has the ability to learn, such as clerical work, mechanical work, etc.

**apyretic** /eɪpaɪ'rɛtɪk/, *adj.* free from fever. [Gk *apýretos* without fever + -IC]

**Aq.,** water. Also, **aq.** [L *aqua*]

**AQ** /eɪ 'kju/, achievement quotient.

**aqua** /'ækwə/, *n., pl.* **aquae** /'ækwi/. **1.** *Chiefly Pharm.* water; a liquid; a solution. **2.** light blue-green or greenish blue. [L: water]

**aqua ammoniae** /– ə'moʊnii/, *n.* →**ammonia** (def. 2). Also, **aqua ammonia.** [NL]

**aqua fortis** /– 'fɔtɪs/, *n.* concentrated nitric acid. [NL: strong water]

**aqualung** /'ækwəlʌŋ/, *n.* a cylinder of compressed air, usu. strapped on to the back, with a tube leading to a special mouthpiece or watertight mask, which enables a swimmer to move about freely at a considerable depth for an extended length of time.

**aquamarine** /ækwəmə'rin/, *n.* **1.** a transparent light-blue or greenish blue variety of beryl, used as a gem. **2.** light blue-green or greenish blue. [L *aqua marīna* sea water; replacing *aigue marine,* from F]

**aquanaut** /'ækwənɔt/, *n.* **1.** a person working and temporarily living in an underwater research installation. **2.** a skindiver. [L *aqua* water + (ASTRO)NAUT]

**aquaphobia** /ækwə'foʊbiə/, *n.* an irrational fear of water, esp. a fear of drowning.

**aquaplane** /'ækwəpleɪn/, *n., v.,* **-planed, -planing.** *–n.* **1.** a single broad water-ski. *–v.i.* **2.** to ride an aquaplane. **3.** (of a motor vehicle, etc.) to ride up at high speed on water on the road surface so that the wheels lose contact with the surface. [L *aqua* water + PLANE[1]; modelled on AEROPLANE]

**aqua regia** /ækwə 'ridʒə/, *n.* a mixture of one part of nitric acid and three parts of hydrochloric acid. [NL: royal water (with allusion to its power to dissolve gold)]

**aquarelle** /ækwə'rɛl/, *n.* a painting in transparent watercolours. [F, from It. *acquarello,* diminutive of *acqua* water] – **aquarellist,** *n.*

**Aquarian** /ə'kwɛəriən/, *n.* **1.** a person born under the sign of Aquarius, and (according to tradition) exhibiting the typical Aquarian personality traits in some degree. **2.** of or pertaining to Aquarius. *–adj.* **3.** of or pertaining to such a person or such a personality trait.

**aquarist** /'ækwərəst/, *n.* **1.** a curator of an aquarium. **2.** a student of marine life.

**aquarium** /ə'kwɛəriəm/, *n., pl.* **aquariums, aquaria** /ə'kwɛəriə/. a pond, tank, or establishment in which living aquatic animals or plants are kept, as for exhibition. [L, properly neut. of *aquārius* pertaining to water]

**Aquarius** /ə'kwɛəriəs/, *n.* **1.** a constellation and sign of the zodiac, represented by the Water-bearer. **2.** →**Aquarian.** [L: water-bearer, properly *adj.,* pertaining to water]

**aquatic** /ə'kwɒtɪk/, *adj.* **1.** of or pertaining to water. **2.** living or growing in water. **3.** practised on or in water: *aquatic sports.* [L *aquāticus* watery]

**aquatics** /ə'kwɒtɪks/, *n. pl.* (*construed as sing.*) sports practised on or in water.

**aquatint** /'ækwətɪnt/, *n.* **1.** a process imitating the broad flat tints of ink or wash drawings by etching a microscopic crackle on the copperplate intended for printing. **2.** an etching made by this process. *–v.t., v.i.* **3.** to etch in aquatint. [F *aquatinte,* from It. *acqua tinta,* from L *aqua tincta* tinted water]

**aquavit** /'ækwəvɪt/, *n.* a clear Scandinavian liquor distilled from potato or grain and usu. flavoured with caraway seeds. [Swed., Dan. and Norw. *akvavit,* from ML *aqua vītae* water of life]

**aqua vitae** /ækwə 'vitaɪ, – 'vaɪti/, *n.* **1.** alcohol. **2.** spirituous drink, as brandy or whisky. [ML: water of life]

**aqueduct** /'ækwədʌkt/, *n.* **1.** *Civ. Eng.* **a.** a conduit or artificial channel for conducting water from a distance, the water usu. flowing by gravity. **b.** a structure which carries a conduit or canal across a valley or over a river. **2.** *Anat.* a canal or passage through which liquids pass. [L *aquae ductus* conveyance of water]

**aqueous** /'ækwiəs, 'eɪkwi-/, *adj.* **1.** of, like, or containing water; watery. **2.** (of rocks) formed of matter deposited in or by water.

**aqueous ammonia** /– ə'moʊniə/, *n.* →**ammonia** (def. 2).

**aqueous humour** /– 'hjumə/, *n.* the limpid watery fluid which fills the space between the cornea and the crystalline lens in the eye.

**aquiculture** /'ækwəkʌltʃə, 'eɪkwɪ-/, *n.* cultivation of the resources of the sea or of inland waters, as opposed to their exploitation. [*aqui-* (combining form representing L *aqua* water) + CULTURE]

**aquifer** /'ækwəfə/, *n.* a layer of rock which holds water and allows water to percolate through it. Also, **aquafer.**

**aquilegia** /ækwə'lidʒiə/, *n.* any plant of the genus *Aquilegia*; columbine. [ML, var. of *aquilēja* columbine]

**aquiline** /'ækwəlaɪn/, *adj.* **1.** of or like the eagle. **2.** (of the nose) curved like an eagle's beak; hooked. [L *aquilīnus*]

**ar-,** variant of **ad-** (by assimilation) before *r,* as in *arrear.*

**-ar**[1], **1.** an adjective suffix meaning 'of or pertaining to', 'of the nature of', 'like', as in *linear, regular.* **2.** a suffix forming adjectives not directly related to nouns, as *similar, singular.* [L *-āris;* replacing ME *-er,* from AF]

**-ar**[2], a noun suffix, as in *vicar, scholar, collar.* [representing

L *-ārius, -āris,* etc.]

**-ar**[3], a noun suffix denoting an agent (replacing regular **-er**[1]), as in *beggar, liar.* [special use of -AR[2]]

**Ar,** (an alternative symbol for) argon.

**Ar.,** **1.** Arabic. **2.** Aramaic.

**Arab** /ˈærəb/, *n.* **1.** a member of the Arabic race (now widely spread in Asia and Africa, and formerly in southern Europe). **2.** a native of Arabia; an Arabian. **3.** a horse of graceful, intelligent breed native to Arabia and adjacent countries. **4.** →**street Arab.** **5.** *Colloq.* a foreigner. *–adj.* **6.** belonging or pertaining to Arabs. **7.** inhabited by Arabs. [ME, from L *Arabs,* from Gk *"Araps,* from Arabic *'arab*]

**Arab.,** **1.** Arabia. **2.** Arabic.

**arabesque** /ærəˈbɛsk/, *n.* **1.** a kind of ornament in which flowers, foliage, fruits, vases, animals, and figures (in strict Muslim use, no animate objects) are represented in a fancifully combined pattern. **2.** a pose in ballet in which one leg is stretched horizontally behind and the body lowered forward from the hips. **3.** *Music.* a short composition with florid decoration. *–adj.* **4.** in the Arabian style, esp. of ornamentation. [F: Arabian from It. *arabesco,* from *Arabo* Arab]

**Arabia** /əˈreɪbiə/, *n.* a peninsula in South-West Asia.

**Arabian** /əˈreɪbiən/, *adj.* **1.** pertaining or belonging to the Arabs. **2.** in Arabia. *–n.* **3.** a native or inhabitant of Arabia. **4.** an Arab (def. 1).

**Arabian camel** /– ˈkæməl/, *n.* →**camel** (def. 1a).

**Arabic** /ˈærəbɪk/, *adj.* **1.** of or pertaining to Arabia or the Arabs. **2.** pertaining to or derived from the languages or culture of Arabia or the Arabs. *–n.* **3.** any of the languages that developed out of the language of the Arabians of the time of Mohammed, now spoken in North Africa, Egypt, Arabia, Jordan, Syria, and Iraq. **4.** the standard literary and classical language as established by the Koran. [L *Arabicus*]

**Arabic numerals** /– ˈnjumərəlz/, *n.pl.* the characters 0, 1, 2, 3, 4, 5, 6, 7, 8, 9, introduced into general Western use since the 12th century. Also, **Arabic figures.**

**arabinose** /əˈræbənouz, -ous, ˈærəbə-/, *n.* the pentose sugar, $C_5H_{10}O_5$, derived from plant gums or made synthetically from glucose. [ARAB(IC) + -IN[2] + -OSE[2]]

**Arabist** /ˈærəbəst/, *n.* an authority on Arabia and the Arabs or on the Arabic language and literature.

**arable** /ˈærəbəl/, *adj.* **1.** capable, without much modification, of producing crops by means of tillage. *–n.* **2.** arable land. [L *arābilis* that can be ploughed; replacing ME (from *ear,* v., plough + -ABLE)] – **arability** /ærəˈbɪləti/, *n.*

**Araby** /ˈærəbi/, *n. Poetic.* Arabia. [ME *Arabye,* from F]

**arachnid** /əˈræknɪd/, *n.* any arthropod of the class Arachnida, which includes the spiders, scorpions, mites, etc. [NL *Arachnida,* from Gk *aráchnē* spider, spider's web + *-ida* -ID[2]] – **arachnidan** /əˈræknɪdən/, *adj., n.*

**arachnoid** /əˈræknɔɪd/, *adj.* **1.** resembling a spider's web. **2.** of or belonging to the arachnids. **3.** *Anat.* pertaining to the serous membrane (between the dura mater and the pia mater) enveloping the brain and spinal cord. **4.** *Bot.* formed of or covered with long, delicate hairs or fibres. *–n.* **5.** →**arachnid.** **6.** the arachnoid membrane. [Gk *arachnoeidēs* like a cobweb]

**aragonite** /əˈrægənaɪt/, *n.* a mineral, calcium carbonate, $CaCO_3$, chemically identical with calcite but differing in crystallisation, and in having a higher specific gravity, less marked cleavage, etc. [*Aragon,* a region in Spain, + -ITE[1]]

**araldite** /ˈærəldaɪt/, *n.* (*also cap.*) an epoxy resin, some grades of which are used as adhesives. [Trademark]

**aralia** /əˈreɪliə/, *n.* any plant of the genus *Aralia,* a group of decorative ivies much grown for indoor ornament.

**araliaceous** /əreɪliˈeɪʃəs/, *adj. Bot.* belonging to the Araliaceae, the ivy family, including the aralias, ginseng, etc.

**Aram.,** Aramaic.

**Aramaean** /ærəˈmiən/, *n.* Also, **Aramean.** **1.** a Semite of the division associated with Aram. **2.** the Aramaic language. *–adj.* **3.** of or pertaining to Aram or Aramaic. [L *Aramaeus* (from Gk *Aramaîos*) pertaining to Aram or Syria + -AN]

**Aramaic** /ærəˈmeɪɪk/, *n.* **1.** any of a group of Semitic languages which became the speech of Syria, Palestine, and Mesopotamia after circa 300 B.C., including Syriac and the language of Christ. *–adj.* **2.** pertaining to Aram, or to the languages spoken there.

**Aranda** /ˈærəndə/, *n.* an Australian Aboriginal language with several dialects, still in extensive use throughout Central Australia, esp. around the Finke River and in the Simpson Desert. Also, **Arunta.**

**arapaima** /ærəˈpaɪmə/, *n.* a large freshwater fish, *Arapaima gigas,* of Brazil and Guiana, said to attain a length of 4.5 metres and a weight of 180 kilograms. [Pg., from Tupi]

**Araucanian** /ærɔˈkeɪniən/, *n.* **1.** one of a tribe of South American Indians in central Chile. **2.** a linguistic stock of Chile and northern Argentina.

**araucaria** /ærəˈkɛəriə/, *n.* any tree of the coniferous genus *Araucaria* of the Southern Hemisphere as hoop pine, klinki pine and monkey puzzle. [NL, from *Arauco,* province of S Chile + *-āria* -ARIA]

**Arawak** /ˈærəwæk/, *n.* one of a numerous and widely scattered Amerindian language stock of northern and north-eastern South America and the West Indies. – **Arawakan** /ærəˈwækən/, *adj.*

**arbalest** /ˈabələst/, *n.* a powerful medieval crossbow. Also, **arbalist.** [OE *arblast,* from OF *arbaleste* kind of catapult, from L *arcuballista.* See ARC, BALLISTA] – **arbalester,** *n.*

**arbiter** /ˈabətə/, *n.* **1.** a person empowered to decide points at issue. **2.** one who has the sole or absolute power of judging or determining. [L: witness, judge]

**arbitrable** /ˈabətrəbəl/, *adj.* capable of arbitration; subject to the decision of an arbiter or arbitrator.

**arbitrage** /ˈabətrɪdʒ/, *n.* the simultaneous purchase and sale of the same securities, commodities, or moneys in different markets to profit from unequal prices. [F from *arbitrer* arbitrate] – **arbitrager,** *n.*

**arbitral** /ˈabətrəl/, *adj.* of or pertaining to arbitration.

**arbitrament** /aˈbɪtrəmənt/, *n.* **1.** →**arbitration.** **2.** the decision or sentence pronounced by an arbiter. **3.** the power of absolute and final decision. [ML *arbitrāmentum;* replacing ME *arbitrement,* from OF]

**arbitrary** /ˈabətrəri, ˈabətri/, *adj., n., pl.* **-ries.** *–adj.* **1.** subject to individual will or judgment; discretionary. **2.** not attributable to any rule or law; accidental. **3.** capricious; uncertain; unreasonable: *an arbitrary interpretation.* **4.** uncontrolled by law; using or abusing unlimited power; despotic; tyrannical: *an arbitrary government.* **5.** selected at random or by convention: *an arbitrary constant.* *–n.* **6.** *Print.* →**special sort.** [L *arbitrārius* of arbitration, uncertain] – **arbitrarily** /ˈabətrərəli/, *adv.* – **arbitrariness,** *n.*

**arbitrate** /ˈabətreɪt/, *v.,* **-trated, -trating.** *–v.t.* **1.** to decide as arbiter or arbitrator; determine. **2.** to submit to arbitration; settle by arbitration: *to arbitrate a dispute.* *–v.i.* **3.** to act as arbiter; decide between opposing parties or sides. **4.** to submit a matter to arbitration. [L *arbitrātus,* pp.] – **arbitrative,** *adj.*

**arbitration** /abəˈtreɪʃən/, *n.* **1.** *Law.* the hearing or determining of a dispute between parties by a person or persons chosen, agreed between them, or appointed by virtue of a statutory obligation. **2.** *Indust. Law.* the presentation of legal argument by parties (for whom conciliation has failed), before a government-appointed arbitrator who is empowered to make a binding decision. **3.** *Internat. Law.* the application of judicial methods to the settlement of international disputes. – **arbitrational,** *adj.*

**arbitration court** /ˈ– kɔt/, *n.* **1.** (in the Australian Federal sphere) the Conciliation and Arbitration Commission, which has powers to conciliate and arbitrate in industrial disputes. **2.** (in the Australian State sphere) a commission, having arbitral and judicial powers in industrial disputes.

**arbitrator** /ˈabətreɪtə/, *n.* a person chosen to decide a dispute, esp. one empowered to examine the facts and to decide an issue. Also, *Obs.,* **arbitrer** /ˈabətrə/.

**arbitress** /ˈabətrəs/, *n.* a female arbiter.

**arbor**[1] /ˈabə/, *n.* →**arbour.**

**arbor**[2] /ˈabə/, *n.* **1.** *Mach.* **a.** a beam, shaft axis, or spindle. **b.** a bar or shaft used to support either the work or the cutting tools during a machining process. **2.** *Foundry.* a reinforcing member of a core or mould. [Latinised var. of earlier *arber,* from F *arbre*]

**arbor**[3] /ˈabɔ/, *n., pl.* **arbores** /ˈabəriz/. a tree (used chiefly in botanical names). [L]

**arbor.**, arboriculture.

**Arbor Day** /ˈabə deɪ/, *n.* the day set aside for the planting of trees and for encouraging public awareness of the value of trees and the need to care for them.

**arboreal** /aˈbɔriəl/, *adj.* **1.** pertaining to trees; treelike. **2.** living in or among trees. **3.** *Zool.* adapted for living and moving about in trees, as the limbs and skeleton of possums, monkeys, and apes.

**arboreous** /aˈbɔriəs/, *adj.* **1.** abounding in trees; wooded. **2.** →**arboreal.** **3.** →**arborescent.** [L *arboreus* pertaining to trees]

**arborescent** /abəˈrɛsənt/, *adj.* treelike in size or form. [L. *arborescens,* ppr., becoming a tree] – **arborescence,** *n.*

**arboretum** /abəˈritəm/, *n., pl.* **-ta** /-tə/. a plot of land where different trees or shrubs are grown for study or popular interest. [L: a plantation of trees]

**arboriculture** /əˈbɒrikʌltʃə/, *n.* the cultivation of trees and shrubs. [*arbori-* (combining form representing L *arbor* tree) + CULTURE] – **arboricultural** /əbɒriˈkʌltʃərəl/, *adj.*

**arborisation** /abəraɪˈzeɪʃən/, *n.* a treelike appearance, as in certain minerals or fossils. Also, **arborization.**

**arborist** /ˈabərəst/, *n.* a specialist in the care and cultivation of trees.

**arborous** /ˈabərəs/, *adj.* of or pertaining to trees.

**arbor vitae** /abə ˈvitaɪ, – ˈvaɪti/, *n.* **1.** an evergreen tree of the coniferous genus *Thuja,* esp. *T. occidentalis,* planted for hedges, etc. See **red cedar** (def. 2). **2.** *N.Z.* the endemic cypress, *Libocedrus plumosa;* kawaka. **3.** *Anat.* a treelike appearance in a vertical section of the cerebellum, due to the arrangement of the white and grey nerve tissues. Also, **arborvitae.** [L: tree of life]

**arbour** /ˈabə/, *n.* **1.** a bower formed by trees, shrubs, or vines, often on a trellis. **2.** *Obs.* a grass plot; lawn; garden; orchard. Also, **arbor.** [ME *(h)erber,* from AF, var. of OF *(h)erbier,* from L *herbārium,* from *herba* plant; influenced by L *arbor* tree]

**arbutus** /aˈbjutəs/, *n.* **1.** any of the evergreen shrubs or trees of the ericaceous genus *Arbutus,* esp. *A. unedo,* of southern Europe, with scarlet berries, cultivated for ornament and food. **2.** a creeping ericaceous plant, *Epigaea repens,* of the U.S., with fragrant white and pink flowers (**trailing arbutus**). [L: strawberry tree]

**arc** /ak/, *n., v.,* **arced** /akt/, **arcing** /ˈakɪŋ/ or **arcked, arcking.** –*n.* **1.** any part of a circle or other curved line. **2.** *Elect.* the luminous bridge formed by the passage of a current across a gap between two conductors or terminals, due to the incandescence of the conducting vapours. **3.** *Astron.* the part of a circle representing the apparent course of a heavenly body. **4.** anything bow-shaped. **5. strike an arc,** in electric welding, to apply a rod to the material to be welded, thereby causing an arc (def. 2). –*v.i.* **6.** to form an electric arc. [ME *ark,* from L *arcus* bow]

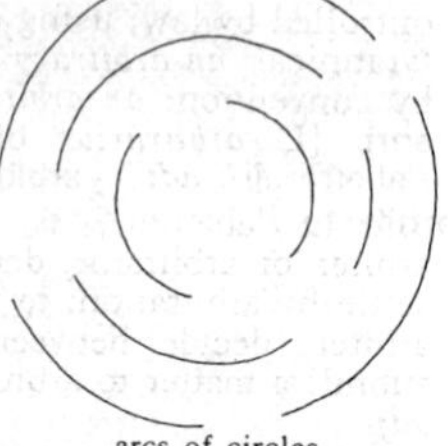

arcs of circles

**arcade** /aˈkeɪd/, *n., v.,* **-caded, -cading.** –*n.* **1.** *Archit.* **a.** a series of arches supported on piers or columns. **b.** an arched, roofed-in gallery. **2.** an arched or covered passageway with shops on either side. **3.** a pedestrian way with shops on one side or both sides. –*v.t.* **4.** to provide with or form as an arcade or arcades. [F, from It. *arcata* arch, from *arco* bow, arch, from L *arcus*]

**Arcadian** /aˈkeɪdiən/, *adj.* **1.** of Arcadia, a mountainous district in ancient Greece, proverbial for the contented pastoral simplicity of its people. **2.** pastoral; rustic; simple; innocent. [L, from Gk *Arkadia*]

**arcane** /aˈkeɪn/, *adj.* mysterious; secret; obscure: *poor writing can make even the most familiar things seem arcane.* [L *arcānus,* from *arcēre* shut up, keep]

**arcanum** /aˈkeɪnəm/, *n., pl.* **-na** /-nə/. **1.** *(oft. pl.)* a secret; a mystery, esp. of tarot cards. **2.** a supposed great secret of nature which the alchemists sought to discover. **3.** a secret and powerful remedy. [L, neut. of *arcānus* secret, hidden.]

**arch**[1] /atʃ/, *n.* **1.** a curved structure resting on supports at both extremities, used to sustain weight, to bridge or roof an open space, etc. **2.** an archway. **3.** something bowed or curved; any bowlike part: *the arch of the foot.* **4.** any curvature in the form of an arch: *the arch of the heavens.* **5.** one of the principal ridge-shapes of a fingerprint, forming a set of simple curves (distinguished from *loop* and *whorl*). –*v.t.* **6.** to cover with a vault, or span with an arch. **7.** to throw or make into the shape of an arch or vault; curve: *a horse arches its neck.* –*v.i.* **8.** to form an arch. [ME, from OF *arche,* a fem. var. of *arc* (from L *arcus* bow), due to confusion with *arche* ark (from L *arca* coffer)]

arch

**arch**[2] /atʃ/, *adj.* **1.** chief; most important; principal: *the arch rebel.* **2.** cunning; sly; roguish: *an arch smile.* –*n.* **3.** *Obs.* a chief. [separate use of ARCH-] – **archly,** *adv.* – **archness,** *n.*

**arch-,** a prefix meaning 'first', 'chief', as in *archbishop, arch-priest.* [ME *arch-,* OE *arce-, erce-,* from L *arch-, arche-, archi-,* from Gk, combining forms of *archós* chief]

**-arch,** a suffix meaning 'chief', as in *monarch.* [see ARCH-]

**arch.**, **1.** archaic. **2.** archaism. **3.** archery. **4.** archipelago. **5.** architect. **6.** architectural. **7.** architecture.

**Arch.**, archbishop.

**Archaean** /aˈkiən/, *Geol.* –*n.* **1.** (formerly) the Pre-Cambrian era or series of rocks. **2.** (formerly) the early Pre-Cambrian era or series of predominantly igneous and metamorphic rocks formed then. –*adj.* **3.** pertaining to a division of early Pre-Cambrian rocks. Also, **Archean.** [ARCHAE(O)- + -AN]

**archaeo-,** a word element meaning 'primeval', 'primitive', 'ancient', as in *archaeology, archaeopteryx.* Also, *(esp. before a vowel)* **archae-, archeo-.** [Gk *archaio-* combining form of *archaîos*]

**archaeol.**, **1.** archaeological. **2.** archaeology.

**archaeological** /ˌakiəˈlɒdʒɪkəl/, *adj.* of or pertaining to archaeology. Also, **archeological, archaeologic.** – **archaeologically,** *adv.*

**archaeology** /akiˈɒlədʒi/, *n.* **1.** the scientific study of any culture, esp. a prehistoric one, by excavation and description of its remains. **2.** *Now Rare.* ancient history; the study of antiquity. Also, **archeology.** [Gk *archaiología* antiquarian lore] – **archaeologist,** *n.*

**archaeomagnetism** /ˌakioʊˈmægnətɪzəm/, *n.* the magnetic properties of archaeological remains.

**archaeopteryx** /akiˈɒptərɪks/, *n.* a fossil bird, the oldest known avian type, with teeth and a long, feathered, vertebrate tail, found in the later Jurassic. [NL, from *archaeo-* ARCHAEO- + Gk *ptéryx* wing, bird]

**Archaeozoic** /ˌakiəˈzoʊɪk/, *adj.* **1.** pertaining to the most ancient period of the earth's history, during which the earliest forms of life presumably appeared. –*n.* **2.** the Archaeozoic era. **3.** *Geol.* the series of rocks preceding the Proterozoic. Also, **Archeozoic.** [ARCHAEO- + Gk *zōḗ* life + -IC]

**archaic** /aˈkeɪɪk/, *adj.* **1.** marked by the characteristics of an earlier period; old-fashioned. **2.** no longer used in ordinary speech or writing; borrowed from older usage (distinguished from *obsolete*). [Gk *archaïkós* antique] – **archaically,** *adv.*

**archaise** /ˈakeɪˌaɪz/, *v.,* **-ised, -ising.** –*v.t.* **1.** to give an archaic appearance or quality to. –*v.i.* **2.** to use archaisms. Also, **archaise.** – **archaiser,** *n.*

**archaism** /ˈakeɪˌɪzəm/, *n.* **1.** something archaic, as a word or expression. **2.** the use of what is archaic, as in literature. **3.** archaic quality or style. [Gk *archaïsmós*] – **archaist,** *n.* – **archaistic** /ˌakeɪˈɪstɪk/, *adj.*

**archangel** /ˈakeɪndʒəl/, *n.* **1.** a chief or principal angel; one of a particular order of angels. **2.** *Bot.* →**angelica** (def. 1). **3.** →**deadnettle.** **4.** a breed of pigeon. [ME, from L *archangelus,* from Gk *archángelos* chief angel] – **archangelic** /ˌakænˈdʒɛlɪk/, *adj.*

**arch bar** /ˈatʃ ba/, *n.* a metal bar which supports bricks above a door or window, etc.

**archbishop** /atʃˈbɪʃəp/, *n.* a bishop of the highest rank. [OE *arcebiscop* (representing *hēahbiscop* high bishop), replacing L *archiepiscopus,* from Gk *archiepískopos.* See ARCH-, BISHOP]

**archbishopric** /atʃ'bɪʃəprɪk/, *n.* the see, diocese, or office of an archbishop.

**Archbp.,** Archbishop.

**archdeacon** /atʃ'dikən/, *n.* **1.** an ecclesiastic who has charge of the temporal and external administration of a diocese, with jurisdiction delegated from the bishop. **2.** *Eccles.* (generally) a title of honour conferred only on a member of a cathedral chapter. [OE *arcediacon,* from L *archidiāconus,* from Gk *archidiákonos*] – **archdeaconate** /atʃ'dikənət/, **archdeaconship,** *n.*

**archdeaconry** /atʃ'dikənri/, *n., pl.* **-ries.** the jurisdiction, residence, or office of an archdeacon.

**archdiocese** /atʃ'daɪəsəs/, *n.* the diocese of an archbishop.

**archducal** /atʃ'djukəl/, *adj.* pertaining to an archduke or an archduchy.

**archduchess** /atʃ'dʌtʃəs/, *n.* **1.** the wife of an archduke. **2.** a princess of the Austrian imperial family.

**archduchy** /atʃ'dʌtʃi/, *n., pl.* **-ies.** the territory of an archduke or an archduchess.

**archduke** /atʃ'djuk/, *n.* a title of the sovereign princes of the former ruling house of Austria. – **archdukedom,** *n.*

**arche-**[1], variant of **archi,** as in *archegonium.*

**arche-**[2], variant of **archae-.**

**Archean** /a'kiən/, *n., adj.* →**Archaean.**

**arched** /atʃt/, *adj.* **1.** made, covered, or spanned with an arch. **2.** having the form of an arch.

**arched dam** /– 'dæm/, *n.* a dam designed in the shape of an arch, in order to resist the pressure of impounded water.

**archegonium** /aki'goʊniəm/, *n., pl.* **-nia** /-niə/. the female reproductive organ in ferns, mosses, etc. [NL, from Gk *archégonos* first of a race + *-ium* -IUM] – **archegonial, archegoniate** /aki'goʊniət, -eɪt/, *adj.*

**archenemy** /atʃ'ɛnəmi/, *n., pl.* **-mies. 1.** a chief enemy. **2.** Satan; the Devil.

**archenteron** /a'kɛntərɒn/, *n. Embryol.* the primitive enteron or digestive cavity of a gastrula. [ARCH- + Gk *énteron* intestine] – **archenteric** /akən'tɛrɪk/, *adj.*

**archeology** /aki'ɒlədʒi/, *n.* →**archaeology.** – **archeological** /ˌakiə'lɒdʒɪkəl/, **archeologic,** *adj.* – **archeologically,** *adv.* – **archeologist,** *n.*

**Archeozoic** /ˌakiə'zoʊɪk/, *adj., n.* →**Archaeozoic.**

**archer** /'atʃə/, *n.* **1.** one who shoots with a bow and arrow; a bowman. **2.** (*cap.*) the zodiacal constellation or sign Sagittarius. [ME, from AF, var. of OF *archier,* from L *arcārius,* from *arcus* bow]

**archerfish** /'atʃəfɪʃ/, *n.* any of several species of small tropical fishes as *Toxotes jaculator* of north-eastern Queensland and South-East Asian waters, which catch insects by stunning them with a jet of water forced through a hole in the mouth.

archerfish

**archery** /'atʃəri/, *n.* **1.** the practice, art, or skill of an archer. **2.** archers collectively. **3.** an archer's bows, arrows, and other weapons.

**archespore** /'akəspɔ/, *n.* the primitive cell, or group of cells, which give rise to the cells from which spores are derived. Also, **archesporium** /akə'spɔriəm/. – **archesporial,** *adj.*

**archetype** /'akitaɪp/, *n.* a model or first form; the original pattern or model after which a thing is made. [L *archetypum,* from Gk *archétypon,* neut. of *archétypos* first-moulded, original] – **archetypal, archetypical** /akə'tɪpɪkəl/, *adj.*

**archi-,** a prefix: **1.** variant of **arch-. 2.** *Biol.* 'original' or 'primitive', as in *archicarp.* [L, from Gk. See ARCH-]

**archicarp** /'akikap/, *n.* the female sex organ in various ascomycetous fungi, commonly a multicellular coiled hypha differentiated into a terminal trichogyne and the ascogonium.

**archidiaconal** /ˌakidaɪ'ækənəl/, *adj.* of or pertaining to an archdeacon or his office. – **archidiaconate,** *n.*

**archiepiscopal** /ˌakiə'pɪskəpəl/, *adj.* of or pertaining to an archbishop or his office. – **archiepiscopate** /ˌakiə'pɪskəpət, -peɪt/, **archiepiscopacy** /ˌakiə'pɪskəpəsi/, *n.*

**archimandrite** /aki'mændraɪt/, *n.* (in the Greek Church) **1.** the head of a monastery; an abbot. **2.** a superior abbot, having charge of several monasteries. **3.** a title given to distinguished celibate priests. [ML *archimandrīta,* from LGk *archimandrítēs*]

**Archimedean** /akə'midiən/, *adj.* of or pertaining to Archimedes, 287?-212 B.C., Greek mathematician, physicist, and inventor.

**Archimedes' Principle** /ˌakəmidiz 'prɪnsəpəl/, *n.* the principle that the apparent loss in weight of a body totally or partially immersed in a liquid is equal to the weight of the liquid displaced.

**Archimedes' screw** /– 'skru/, *n.* a device consisting essentially of a spiral passage within an inclined cylinder for raising water to a height when rotated.

Archimedes' screw

**arching** /'atʃɪŋ/, *n.* arched work or formation.

**archipelago** /akə'pɛləgoʊ/, *n., pl.* **-gos, -goes. 1.** any large body of water with many islands. **2.** the island groups in such a body of water. [It. *arcipelago,* lit., chief sea, from *arci-* ARCHI- + Gk *pélagos* sea] – **archipelagic** /akəpə'lædʒɪk/, *adj.*

**archiphoneme** /'akiˌfoʊnim/, *n.* an abstract linguistic unit postulated as underlying the expression of two phonemes in cases where the differences between these phonemes have been neutralised by contact.

**archiplasm** /'akəplæzəm/, *n.* →**archoplasm.**

**archit.,** architecture.

**architect** /'akətɛkt/, *n.* **1.** one whose profession it is to design buildings and superintend their construction. **2.** the deviser, maker, or creator of anything. [L *architectus,* from Gk *architéktōn* chief builder]

**architectonic** /akətɛk'tɒnɪk/, *adj.* **1.** pertaining to architecture. **2.** pertaining to construction or design of any kind. **3.** resembling architecture in manner or technique of structure. **4.** having the grandeur of monumental architecture. **5.** (of a science or structure) giving the principle of organisation of a system. [L *architectonicus,* from Gk *architektonikós*] – **architectonical,** *adj.* – **architectonically,** *adv.*

**architectonics** /akətɛk'tɒnɪks/, *n.* **1.** the science of architecture. **2.** the (science of the) systematic arrangement of knowledge.

**architectural** /akə'tɛktʃərəl/, *adj.* **1.** of or pertaining to architecture. **2.** conforming to the basic principles of architecture. **3.** having the qualities of architecture. – **architecturally,** *adv.*

**architecture** /'akətɛktʃə/, *n.* **1.** the art or science of building, including plan, design, construction, and decorative treatment. **2.** the style of building. **3.** the action or process of building; construction. **4.** a building. **5.** buildings collectively. [L *architectūra*]

**architrave** /'akətreɪv/, *n. Archit.* **1.** the lowest division of an entablature, resting immediately on the columns. **2.** a band of mouldings or other ornamentation about a rectangular door or other opening or a panel. **3.** a decorative band about openings or panels of any shape. [It. from *archi-* ARCHI- + *trave* (from L *trabs* beam)]

**archival** /a'kaɪvəl/, *adj.* pertaining to archives or valuable records; contained in such archives or records.

**archive** /'akaɪv/, *v.t.* to file in archives.

**archives** /'akaɪvz/, *n.pl.* **1.** a place where public records or other historical documents are kept. **2.** documents or records relating to the activities, rights, claims, treaties, constitutions, etc., of a family, corporation, community, or nation. [F, from L *archīvum,* from Gk *archeîon* public building, pl., records]

**archivist** /'akəvəst/, *n.* a custodian of archives.

**archivolt** /'akəvɒlt/, *n. Archit.* a band of mouldings or other ornamentation about an arched opening. [It.: stem of *archivolto,* from *archi-* ARCH[1] + *volto* turned]

**archlet** /'atʃlət/, *n.* a small arch.

**archlute** /'atʃlut/, *n.* →**theorbo.**

**archon** /ˈakɒn/, *n.* **1.** a higher magistrate in ancient Athens. **2.** any ruler. [Gk *árchōn* ruler, properly ppr. of *árchein* be first, rule] – **archonship,** *n.*

**archoplasm** /ˈakoupləzəm, ˈakə-/, *n.* **1.** protoplasm. **2.** *Cytology.* (in cell division) the substance surrounding the centrosome. Also, **archiplasm.** – **archoplasmic,** *adj.*

**archpriest** /atʃˈprist/, *n.* a priest holding first rank, as among the members of a cathedral chapter or among the clergy of a district outside the episcopal city. – **archpriesthood,** *n.*

**archway** /ˈatʃweɪ/, *n.* **1.** an entrance or passage under an arch. **2.** a covering or enclosing arch.

**archwise** /ˈatʃwaɪz/, *adv.* in the shape of an arch.

**-archy,** a word element meaning 'rule', 'government', as in *monarchy.* [Gk *-archía*]

**arc light** /ˈak laɪt/, *n.* **1.** Also, **arc lamp.** a lamp in which the light source of high intensity is an electric arc, usu. between carbon rods. **2.** the light produced.

**arco** /ˈakou/, *adv.* **1.** (a musical direction) played with the bow, as the violin. *–n.* **2.** a passage so played. [It.: bow] – **arco,** *adj.*

**arcograph** /ˈakougræf, ˈakə-/, *n.* an instrument once used for drawing arcs, having a flexible arc-shaped part adjusted by an extensible straight bar connecting its sides; cyclograph.

**arc sine** /ˈak saɪn/, *n.* the inverse mathematical function to the sine, if y is the sine of θ, then θ is the arc sine of y; inverse sine. Also, **arcsin.**

**arc tangent** /ˈ– tændʒənt/, *n.* the inverse function to the tangent; if y is the tangent of θ, then θ is the arc tangent of y; inverse tangent. Also, **arctan.**

**arctic** /ˈaktɪk/, *adj.* **1.** of, at, or near the North Pole; frigid. **2.** extremely cold. *–n.* **3.** (*cap.*) the region north of the Arctic Circle. [L *arcticus,* from Gk *arktikós* of the Bear (constellation), northern; replacing ME *artik,* from OF *artique*]

**Arctic Circle** /– ˈsɜkəl/, *n.* the southern boundary of the North Frigid Zone, 23°28′ from the North Pole.

**Arctogaea** /aktəˈdʒiə/, *n.* a biogeographical region now considered more realistically divided into five distinct realms: Holarctic, Ethiopian, Madagascan, Oriental, Neotropical.

**arcuate** /ˈakjueɪt, -ət/, *adj.* curved like a bow. Also, **arcuated.** [L *arcuātus,* pp.] – **arcuation** /akjuˈeɪʃən/, *n.*

**arc welder** /ak ˈweldə/, *n.* **1.** a person employed to do arc welding. **2.** the machinery or equipment used in arc welding.

**arc welding** /ak ˈweldɪŋ/, *n.* welding in which the heat is provided by an electric arc.

**-ard,** a noun suffix, originally intensive but now often depreciative or without special force as in *coward, drunkard, wizard.* Also, **-art.** [OF *-ard, -art,* from G *-hart, hard, hardy* c. HARD]

**ardency** /ˈadənsi/, *n.* warmth of feeling; ardour.

**ardent** /ˈadənt/, *adj.* **1.** glowing with feeling, earnestness, or zeal; passionate; fervent: *ardent vows, an ardent patriot.* **2.** glowing; flashing. **3.** burning, fiery, or hot. [L *ardens,* ppr., burning; replacing ME *ardaunt,* from OF *ardant*] – **ardently,** *adv.*

**ardent spirits** /– ˈspɪrəts/, *n.pl.* strong alcoholic drinks made by distillation, as brandy, whisky, or gin.

**ardour** /ˈadə/, *n.* **1.** warmth of feeling; fervour; eagerness; zeal. **2.** burning heat. Also, *U.S.,* **ardor.** [ME, from OF, from L]

**arduous** /ˈadʒuəs/, *adj.* **1.** requiring great exertion; laborious; difficult: *an arduous enterprise.* **2.** energetic; strenuous: *making an arduous effort.* **3.** hard to climb; steep: *an arduous path.* **4.** hard to endure; severe; full of hardships: *an arduous winter.* [L *arduus*] – **arduously,** *adv.* – **arduousness,** *n.*

**are**[1] /a/; *weak form* /ə/, *v.* present indicative pl. of the verb **be.** [dialect OE (Northumbrian) *aron*]

**are**[2] /ɛə/, *n.* a non-SI metric surface measure equal to 100 square metres; a hundredth of a hectare. [F, from L *ārea* AREA]

**area** /ˈɛərɪə/, *n., pl.* **areas, areae** /ˈɛəri,i/. **1.** any particular extent of surface; region; tract: *the settled area.* **2.** extent, range or scope: *the whole area of science.* **3.** a piece of unoccupied ground; an open space. **4.** *Chiefly Brit.* a sunken space leading to a cellar or basement entrance, or in front of basement or cellar windows. **5.** *Maths.* amount of surface (plane or curved); two-dimensional extent; the SI unit of area is the square metre ($m^2$). **6.** *Anat., Physiol.* a zone of the cerebral cortex with a specific function. [L: piece of level ground, open space] – **areal,** *adj.*

**area code** /ˈ– koud/, *n.* a sequence of numbers or letters preceding a telephone subscriber's number, indicating the area or exchange. Also, **S.T.D. code.**

**area navigation** /– nævəˈgeɪʃən/, *n. Aeron.* flying with the required accuracy on any track in a defined air space by processing instrumental data which provide the pilot with continuous positional information.

**area rule** /ˈ– rul/, *n.* a method of design for obtaining minimum drag from the overall configuration of an aircraft.

**area school** /ˈ– skul/, *n.* →**central school.**

**areca** /ˈærɪkə, əˈri-/, *n.* **1.** any palm of the genus *Areca,* of tropical Asia and the Malay Archipelago, esp. *A. catechu,* the betel palm, which bears a nut (the **areca nut**). **2.** the nut itself. **3.** any of various palms formerly referred to the genus *Areca.* Also, **areca palm** for defs 1, 3. [Pg., from Malayalam *ādekka,* from Tamil]

**arena** /əˈrinə/, *n.* **1.** the oval space in a Roman amphitheatre for combats or other performances. **2.** an enclosure for sports contests, shows, etc. **3.** a field of conflict or endeavour: *the arena of politics.* [L: sand, sandy place]

**arenaceous** /ærəˈneɪʃəs/, *adj.* **1.** sandlike; sandy. **2.** of or pertaining to sedimentary rock composed of sand particles and others down to 0.002 mm in diameter. [L *arēnāceus* sandy]

**arenicolous** /ærəˈnɪkələs/, *adj.* inhabiting sand. [L *arēna* sand + -I- + -COLOUS]

**aren't** /ant/, *v.* **1.** contraction of *are not.* **2.** contraction of *am not* (as an interrogative). **3.** (*generally considered bad usage*) contraction of *am not* (as a statement).

**areocentric** /æriouˈsentrɪk/, *adj. Astron.* having the planet Mars as centre. [*areo-* (combining form of Ares, Greek god of war) + CENTRIC]

**areodesy** /æriˈɒdəsi/, *n.* that branch of applied mathematics which determines by observation and measurement, the shape and area of large tracts of the surface of the planet Mars, or the shape and size of the planet. [*areo-* (combining form of *Ares,* the Greek god of war, + *-desy,* modelled on GEODESY] – **areodetic,** *adj.*

**areola** /əˈrɪələ/, *n., pl.* **-lae** /-li/. **1.** a small ring of colour, as around a pustule or the human nipple. **2.** a small interstice, as between the fibres of connective tissue. [L diminutive of *ārea* AREA] – **areolar,** *adj.* – **areolate,** *adj.* – **areolation** /əriəˈleɪʃən/, *n.*

**areole** /ˈɛərioul/, *n. Biol.* an areola. [F, from L *areola,* diminutive of *area* open space]

**arête** /əˈreɪt/, *n.* a sharp ridge of a mountain; the divide between two glaciated valleys. [F, from L *arista* awn, spine]

**arg.,** argentum.

**argal**[1] /ˈagəl/, *n.* →**argol.**

**argal**[2] /ˈagəl/, *n.* →**argali.**

**argali** /ˈagəli/, *n., pl.* **-li.** a wild sheep of Asia, *Ovis ammon,* with long, thick, spirally curved horns; the ammon. Also, **argal.** [Mongolian]

Siberian argali

**Argand diagram** /ˈagænd ˌdaɪəgræm/, *n. Maths.* **1.** a plane geometrical representation of the complex number $z=x+iy$, the point having rectangular coordinates (x,y). **2.** a graph or figure obtained by the above method expressing some given relationship between complex numbers. [named after Jean Robert *Argand,* 1768-1822, French mathematician]

**argent** /ˈadʒənt/, *n.* **1.** *Archaic.* silver. **2.** *Her.* the silver or silvery white used in armorial bearings. **3.** *Obs.* money. *–adj.* **4.** like silver; silvery white. [F, from L *argentum* silver]

**argental** /aˈdʒentl/, *adj.* of, pertaining to, containing, or resembling silver.

**argentic** /aˈdʒentɪk/, *adj.* of or containing silver, with a valency greater than the corresponding argentous compound.

**argentiferous** /adʒən'tɪfərəs/, *adj.* silver-bearing. [L *argentum* silver + -I- + -FEROUS]

**Argentina** /adʒən'tinə/, *n.* a republic in southern South America. Official name: **Argentine Republic.**

**argentine** /'adʒəntaɪn, -tin/, *adj.* **1.** pertaining to or resembling silver. *–n.* **2.** a silvery substance obtained from fish scales, used in making imitation pearls. [L *argentum* silver + -INE[1]]

**Argentine** /'adʒəntaɪn/, *n.* **1.** a native or inhabitant of Argentina, a republic in southern South America. **2. the Argentine,** Argentina. *–adj.* **3.** of or pertaining to Argentina. Also, **Argentinean** /adʒən'tɪniən/.

**Argentine ant** /ˌadʒəntin 'ænt/, *n.* a very destructive small brown ant, *Iridomyrmex humilis,* now spread widely throughout the world from its original centre in South America.

**argentite** /'adʒəntaɪt/, *n.* silver sulphide, $Ag_2S$, a dark lead-grey sectile mineral, crystalline or massive, an important ore of silver; silver glance. [L *argentum* silver + -ITE[1]]

**argentous** /a'dʒɛntəs/, *adj.* containing monovalent silver, as *argentous chloride,* AgCl.

**argentum** /a'dʒɛntəm/, *n. Chem.* silver. [L]

**argie-bargie** /ˌadʒi 'badʒi/, *v.i., n.* →**argy-bargy.**

**argil** /'adʒəl/, *n.* clay, esp. potter's clay. [var. of *argil(l)e,* from L *argilla,* from Gk: white clay]

**argillaceous** /adʒə'leɪʃəs/, *adj.* **1.** of the nature of or resembling clay; clayey. **2.** *Geol.* of or pertaining to sedimentary rock composed of particles less than 0.002 mm in diameter.

**argilliferous** /adʒə'lɪfərəs/, *adj.* containing clayey matter.

**argillite** /'adʒəlaɪt/, *n.* any compact sedimentary rock composed mainly of clay minerals and slightly metamorphosed; claystone. [L *argilla* white clay + -ITE[1]]

**arginine** /'adʒənin, -naɪn/, *n.* an essential amino acid, $NH{=}C(NH_2)\cdot NH\cdot(CH_2)_3\cdot CH(NH_3^+)COO^-$, found in proteins, an intermediate in the urea cycle.

**arginine phosphate** /– 'fɒsfeɪt/, *n.* the phosphate of arginine, present as the phosphagen in tissues of most invertebrates.

**argle-bargle** /agəl-'bagəl/, *v.i., n.* →**argy-bargy.**

**argol** /'agɒl/, *n.* crude tartar; wine stone. Also, **argal.** [ME *argoile,* from AF *argoil*]

**argon** /'agɒn/, *n.* a colourless, odourless, chemically inactive, monatomic, gaseous element. *Symbol:* Ar; *at. no.:* 18; *at. wt:* 39·948. [NL, from Gk, prop. neut. of *argós* idle]

**argonaut** /'agənɔt/, *n.* →**paper nautilus.** [from the *argonauts,* sailors on Jason's ship, the *Argo,* in his quest for the golden fleece (Gk legend)]

**argon laserphotocoagulator** /ˌagɒn ˌleɪzəˌfoutoukou-'ægjəleɪtə/, *n. Med.* an instrument which projects small points of heat onto an opaque surface, used to treat some diseases of the eye, esp. retinal detachment.

**argon welding** /– 'wɛldɪŋ/, *n.* a form of electric welding in which argon is used as a shield around the weld to keep out air and prevent oxidation.

**argosy** /'agəsi/, *n., pl.* **-sies. 1.** a large merchant ship, esp. one with a rich cargo. **2.** a fleet of such ships. [It. *Ragusea* a vessel of Ragusa, a port in Sicily]

**argot** /'agou/, *n.* the peculiar language or jargon of any class or group; cant; originally, that of thieves and vagabonds, devised for purposes of disguise and concealment. [F; orig. unknown] – **argotic** /a'gɒtɪk/, *adj.*

**arguable** /'agjuəbəl/, *adj.* **1.** capable of being maintained; plausible. **2.** open to dispute or argument. **3.** capable of being argued. – **arguably,** *adv.*

**argue** /'agju/, *v.,* **-gued, -guing.** *–v.i.* **1.** to present reasons for or against a thing: *to argue for or against a proposed law.* **2.** to contend in argument; dispute: *to argue with someone about something.* *–v.t.* **3.** to state the reasons for or against: *counsel argued the cause.* **4.** to maintain in reasoning: *to argue that something must be so.* **5.** to argue in favour of; support by argument: *his letter argues restraint.* **6.** to persuade, drive, etc., by reasoning: *to argue one out of a plan.* **7.** to show; prove or imply: *his clothes argue poverty.* **8. argue the toss,** dispute a decision or command. [ME *argue(n),* from OF *arguer,* from L *argūtāre,* frequentative of *arguere* show] – **arguer,** *n.*

**arguendo** /agju'ɛndou/, *adv. Law.* in the course of argument. [L]

**argufy** /'agjəfaɪ/, *v.t., v.i.,* **-fied, -fying.** (*generally considered bad usage*) to argue or wrangle. [ARGU(E) + -FY]

**argument** /'agjəmənt/, *n.* **1.** an argumentation; debate. **2.** a matter of contention. **3.** a process of reasoning; series of reasons. **4.** a statement or fact tending to support a point. **5.** an address or composition intended to convince others of the truth of something. **6.** an abstract or summary of the chief points in a book or sections of a book. **7.** the theme or thesis of a literary composition. **8.** *Maths.* (of a function) an independent variable. **9.** *Computers.* a datum or value used while transferring information from part to part of a program. **10.** *Obs.* evidence or proof. [ME, from L *argūmentum* proof]

**argumentation** /agjəmən'teɪʃən/, *n.* **1.** debate; discussion; reasoning. **2.** the setting forth of reasons together with the conclusion drawn from them; formal or logical reasoning. **3.** the premises and conclusion so set forth.

**argumentative** /agjə'mɛntətɪv/, *adj.* **1.** given to argument; disputatious. **2.** controversial. – **argumentatively,** *adv.* – **argumentativeness,** *n.*

**argumentum** /agjə'mɛntəm/, *n.* argument, as **argumentum ad hominem,** argument designed to appeal to the prejudices of an audience or attack the character of an opponent; or **argumentum ad rem,** argument confined strictly to relevant issues. [L]

**argus** /'agəs/, *n.* **1.** any observant or vigilant person. **2.** (*l.c.*) any pheasant of the Malayan genera *Argusianus* and *Rheinardia,* marked with eyelike spots. [Gk: *Argus,* a giant with a hundred eyes]

**argus-eyed** /'agəs-aɪd/, *adj.* keen-eyed; vigilant.

**argy-bargy** /ˌadʒi-'badʒi/, *n., v.,* **-bargied, -bargying.** *Colloq.* *–n.* **1.** argumentative talk; wrangling; disputation. *–v.i.* **2.** to wrangle; argue tediously; bandy words. Also, **argie-bargie, argle-bargle.**

**argyle** /'agaɪl/, *n.* **1.** a diamond-shaped pattern of two or more colours, used in knitting socks, sweaters, etc. *–adj.* **2.** having such a pattern. [var. of *Argyll,* Scotland; arbitrary designation]

**Argyle apple** /– 'æpəl/, *n.* a medium-sized tree, *Eucalyptus cinerea,* of eastern Australia, often cultivated for its picturesque appearance and blue-grey foliage.

**argyrol** /'adʒərɒl/, *n.* a compound of silver and a protein, applied to mucous membranes as a mild antiseptic. [Gk *árgyros* silver + *-ol* (unexplained)]

**arhat** /'ahət/, *n.* a Buddhist who has attained nirvana.

**arhythmia** /eɪ'rɪðmiə/, *n. Pathol.* →**arrhythmia.**

**aria** /'ariə/, *n.* **1.** an air or melody. **2.** an elaborate melody for a single voice, with accompaniment, in an opera, oratorio, etc., esp. one consisting of a principal and a subordinate section, and a repetition of the first with or without alterations. [It., from L *āēr* air]

**-aria,** *Bot., Zool.* a suffix used in names of genera and groups. [L, neut. pl. n. and adj. termination]

**-arian,** a compound suffix of adjectives and nouns, often referring to pursuits, doctrines, etc., or to age, as in *antiquarian, humanitarian, octogenarian.* [*-ary*[1] + -AN]

**Arian**[1] /'ɛəriən/, *n.* an adherent of the doctrine of Arius (died 336 A.D.) who held that Christ the Son was not consubstantial with God the Father. [L *Ariānus,* from *Arius*] – **Arianism,** *n.*

**Arian**[2] /'ɛəriən/, *adj., n.* →**Aryan.**

**Arian**[3] /'ɛəriən/, *n.* **1.** a person born under the sign of Aries, and (according to tradition) exhibiting the typical Arian personality traits in some degree. *–adj.* **2.** of or pertaining to Aries. **3.** of or pertaining to such a person or such a personality trait.

**arid** /'ærəd/, *adj.* **1.** dry; without moisture; parched with heat. **2.** uninteresting; dull; unrewarding. **3.** barren; unproductive; lacking spiritual or creative life. [L *āridus* dry] – **aridity** /ə'rɪdəti/, **aridness,** *n.* – **aridly,** *adv.*

**ariel** /'ɛəriəl/, *n.* an Arabian gazelle, *Gazella arabica.* Also, **ariel gazelle.** [Ar. *aryal* stag or ibex]

**Aries** /'ɛəriz/, *n.* **1.** the Ram, a constellation and sign of the zodiac. **2.** the point on the celestial equator where the sun passes from south to north declination. **3.** →**Arian**[3].

[L: a ram]

**arietta** /æri'ɛtə/, *n.* a short aria. Also, **ariette** /æri'ɛt/. [It., diminutive of *aria.* See ARIA]

**aright** /ə'raɪt/, *adv.* rightly; correctly; properly.

**aril** /'ærəl/, *n.* an accessory covering or appendage of certain seeds, esp. one arising from the placenta, funicle or hilum. [NL *arillus,* from ML *arillī* dried grapes, from Sp. *arillos*]

**arillate** /'ærəleɪt/, *adj.* having an aril.

**arillode** /'ærəloʊd/, *n.* a false aril; an aril which originates from the micropyle instead of at or below the hilum, as in the nutmeg. [see ARIL, -ODE[1]]

**arioso** /æri'oʊsoʊ, -zoʊ/, *adv.* (a musical direction) in the manner of an air or melody. [It., *aria* ARIA] – **arioso,** *adj.*

**-arious,** an adjective suffix meaning 'connected with', 'having to do with', as in *gregarious.* [L *-ārius*]

**arise** /ə'raɪz/, *v.i.,* **arose, arisen, arising. 1.** to come into being or action; originate; appear: *new questions arise.* **2.** to result or proceed (fol. by *from*). **3.** to move upwards. **4.** to rise; get up from sitting, lying, or kneeling. [ME *arise(n),* OE *ārīsan,* from *ā-* up + *rīsan* rise]

**arista** /ə'rɪstə/, *n., pl.* **-tae** /-ti/. **1.** *Bot.* a bristle-like appendage of grain, etc.; an awn. **2.** *Entomol.* a prominent bristle on the antenna of some dipterous insects. [L. See ARÊTE]

**aristate** /ə'rɪsteɪt/, *adj.* **1.** *Bot.* having aristae; awned. **2.** *Zool.* tipped with a thin spine. [LL *aristātus,* from L *arista* awn]

**aristo-,** a word element meaning 'best', 'superior', as in *aristocratic.* [Gk, combining form of *áristos* best]

**aristocracy** /ærə'stɒkrəsi/, *n., pl.* **-cies. 1.** a government or a state characterised by the rule of a nobility, elite, or privileged upper class. **2.** a body of persons holding exceptional prescriptive rank or privileges; a class of hereditary nobility. **3.** government by the best men in the state. **4.** a governing body composed of the best men in the state. **5.** any class ranking as socially or otherwise superior. [L *aristocratia,* from Gk *aristokratía* rule of the best. See ARISTO-, -CRACY]

**aristocrat** /'ærəstəkræt/, *n.* **1.** one who has the tastes, manners, etc., of the members of a superior group or class. **2.** (one of) the best of its kind. **3.** a member of an aristocracy. **4.** an advocate of an aristocratic form of government. – **aristocratism** /ærəs'tɒkrətɪzəm/, *n.*

**aristocratic** /ærəstə'krætɪk/, *adj.* **1.** befitting an aristocrat; stylish, grand, or exclusive. **2.** like an aristocrat. **3.** belonging to or favouring the aristocracy. **4.** of or pertaining to government by an aristocracy. Also, **aristocratical.** – **aristocratically,** *adv.*

**Aristotelian** /ærɪstə'tiliən/, *adj.* **1.** of or pertaining to Aristotle or to his doctrines. *–n.* **2.** a follower of Aristotle, Greek philosopher (384-322 B.C.). **3.** one who thinks in particulars and scientific deductions as distinct from the metaphysical speculation of Platonism. Also, **Aristotelean.** – **Aristotelianism,** *n.*

**Aristotelian logic** /– 'lɒdʒɪk/, *n.* **1.** the logic of Aristotle esp. in the modified form taught in the Middle Ages. **2.** formal logic, dealing with the logical form, rather than the content, of propositions, and based on the four propositional forms; all S is P; no S is P; some S is P; some S is not P.

**aristotle** /'ærəstɒtl/, *n. Colloq.* a bottle. Also, **aris** /'ærəs/. [rhyming slang]

**arith., 1.** arithmetic. **2.** arithmetical.

**arithmetic** /ə'rɪθmətɪk/, *n.;* /ærəθ'mɛtɪk/, *adj.* *–n.* **1.** the art or skill of computation with figures (the most elementary branch of mathematics). **2.** Also, **theoretical arithmetic.** the theory of numbers; the study of the divisibility of whole numbers, the remainders after division, etc. **3.** a book on this subject. *–adj.* **4.** of or pertaining to arithmetic. [L *arithmētica,* from Gk *arithmētiké,* prop. fem. of *arithmētikós* of or for reckoning; replacing ME *arsmetik,* from OF *arismetique*]

**arithmetical** /ærəθ'mɛtɪkəl/, *adj.* of or pertaining to arithmetic. – **arithmetically,** *adv.*

**arithmetical progression** /– prə'grɛʃən/, *n.* a sequence in which each term is obtained by the addition of a constant number to the preceding term. For example, 1, 4, 7, 10, 13, and 6, 1, –4, –9, –14. Also, **arithmetic series.**

**arithmetician** /'ærəθmətɪʃən, ə'rɪθ-/, *n.* an expert in arithmetic.

**arithmetic mean** /ˌærəθmɛtɪk 'min/, *n. Maths.* the mean obtained by adding several quantities together and dividing the sum by the number of quantities. For example, the arithmetic mean of 1, 5, 2, 8 is 4.

**arithmetic unit** /– 'junət/, *n.* the section of a computer which does arithmetical processes.

**arithmomancy** /ə'rɪθməmænsi/, *n.* an ancient form of numerology.

**a rivederci** /ə rivə'dɜtʃi/, *interj.* →**arrivederci.**

**ark** /ak/, *n.* **1.** the vessel built by Noah for safety during the Flood. Gen. 6-9. **2.** any similar large floating vessel. **3.** Also, **ark of the covenant.** a chest or box of great sanctity representing the presence of the Deity, borne by the Israelites in their desert wandering (Num. 10:35), the most sacred object of the tabernacle and of the temple in Jerusalem, where it was kept in the holy of holies. **4. out of the ark,** *Colloq.* very old. [ME; OE *arc, earc,* from L *arca* a chest, coffer]

**arkose** /'akoʊz, -oʊs/, *n.* a coarse hard sandstone composed of quartz, felspar and other products derived from the disintegration of granite rocks.

**arm**[1] /am/, *n.* **1.** the upper limb of the human body from the shoulder to the hand. **2.** this limb, exclusive of the hand. **3.** the forelimb of any vertebrate. **4.** some part of an organism like or likened to an arm. **5.** any armlike part, as of a lever or of the yard (**yardarm**) of a ship. **6.** a covering for the arm, as the sleeve of a garment. **7.** a branch or subdivision of an organisation. **8.** a projecting support for the forearm at the side of a chair, sofa, etc. **9.** an inlet, creek, or cove: *an arm of the sea.* **10.** power; might; strength; authority: *the arm of the law.* **11. arm in arm,** with arms linked; close together. **12. at arm's length,** at a distance, yet almost within reach. **13. chance one's arm,** *Colloq.* to take a risk. **14. in arms,** carried in the arms, as a child; unready; not yet independent or fully developed. **15. with open arms,** cordially. *–v.t.* **16.** to escort arm in arm. [OE *arm, earm,* c. G *Arm,* L *armus* shoulder, Gk *harmós* joint] – **armless,** *adj.* – **armlike,** *adj.*

**arm**[2] /am/, *n.* **1.** (*usu. pl.*) an offensive or defensive implement for use in war; a weapon. **2.** *Mil.* a fighting branch of the military service, as the infantry, cavalry, field artillery, air corps, etc. *–v.i.* **3.** to enter into a state of hostility or of readiness for war. *–v.t.* **4.** to equip with arms. **5.** to cover or provide with whatever will add strength, force, or security. **6.** to fit or prepare (a thing) for any specific purpose or effective use. [ME *arme(n),* from F *armer,* from L *armāre*]

**armada** /a'madə/, *n.* **1.** a fleet of warships. **2.** a large number of boats or ships. [the *Armada,* a Spanish fleet sent unsuccessfully against England in 1588; from Sp., from L *armāta* armed forces (properly pp. neut. pl. of *armāre* ARM[2], v.). See ARMY]

**armadillo** /amə'dɪloʊ/, *n., pl.* **-los.** any of a great variety of burrowing mammals, having a jointed, protective covering of bony plates. They constitute a suborder, Cingulata, of the edentates, distributed in many species throughout South America and north as far as Texas, and widely used for food. They are omnivorous and mostly nocturnal. The **Texas armadillo,** *Dasypus novemcinctus,* is unique for always producing quadruplets of one sex. [Sp., diminutive of *armado* armed, from L *armātus,* pp.]

armadillo

**Armageddon** /amə'gɛdn/, *n.* **1.** the place where the final cataclysmic battle will be fought between the forces of good and evil, prophesied in the Bible to occur at the end of the world. **2.** any great crucial armed conflict. [LL *Armagedōn,* from G, from Hebrew *har megiddōn,* the mountain region of *Megiddo,* site of several great battles in the Old Testament.]

**Armagnac** /'amənjæk/, *n.* a brandy made in the Armagnac District of France.

**armalite** /'aməlaɪt/, *n.* (*also. cap.*) a light automatic rifle for infantry use. [Trademark]

**armament** /'aməmənt/, *n.* **1.** the weapons with which a military unit, esp. an aeroplane, vehicle, or warship, is equipped. **2.** a land, sea, or air force equipped for war. **3.** the process of equipping or arming for war. [L *armāmenta,* pl., implements, equipment, ship's tackle]

**armature** /ˈamətʃə/, *n.* **1.** armour. **2.** *Biol.* the protective covering of an animal or plant, or any part serving for defence or offence. **3.** *Elect.* **a.** the iron or steel applied across the poles of a permanent magnet to close it, or to the poles of an electromagnet to communicate mechanical force. **b.** the part of an electrical machine which includes the main current-carrying winding (distinguished from the *field*). **c.** a pivoted part of an electrical device as a buzzer or relay, activated by a magnetic field. **4.** a framework upon which a sculptor builds a work in clay, plaster, or other plastic substance. [L *armātūra* armour]

**armband** /ˈambænd/, *n.* a band of material worn round the sleeve to indicate authority, allegiance, etc., or, if black, mourning.

**armchair** /ˈamtʃɛə/, *n.* **1.** a chair with arms to support the forearms or elbows. *–adj.* **2.** stay-at-home; amateur: *an armchair critic, an armchair philosopher.* **3.** seen or enjoyed at home: *the armchair theatre.*

**armchair ride** /– ˈraɪd/, *n.* (usu. in a competitive situation) easy progress, easy success.

**armed** /amd/, *adj.* **1.** bearing arms. **2.** supported or maintained by arms: *armed peace.* **3.** provided with a defence; ready.

**armed bullhead** /– ˈbʊlhɛd/, *n.* →**pogge.**

**armed constabulary** /– kənˈstæbjələri/, *n. N.Z.* (formerly) a militia-style constabulary force formed to protect settlers during the Maori Wars of the mid nineteenth century.

**armed services** /– ˈsɜvəsəz/, *n. pl.* all of the principal naval or military forces of a country or countries including the army, navy, marines, airforce, etc. Also, **armed forces.**

**Armenian** /aˈminiən/, *adj.* **1.** pertaining to Armenia, an ancient country in western Asia, or to its inhabitants. *–n.* **2.** a native of Armenia. **3.** the language of the Armenians, an Indo-European language.

**armful** /ˈamfʊl/, *n., pl.* **-fuls.** as much as the arm, or both arms, can hold.

**armguard** /ˈamgad/, *n.* any contrivance, appliance or attachment designed to protect the arm as, in archery, a bracer.

**armhole** /ˈamhoʊl/, *n.* a hole in a garment for the arm.

**armiger** /ˈamədʒə/, *n.* **1.** one entitled to armorial bearings. **2.** an armour-bearer to a knight; a squire. [ML: squire, L armour-bearer]

**armillary** /aˈmɪləri/, *adj.* consisting of hoops or rings. [L *armilla* armlet, ring + -ARY[1]]

**armillary sphere** /– ˈsfɪə/, *n. Astron.* an arrangement of rings, all circles of a single sphere, showing the relative positions of the principal circles of the celestial sphere.

**arming** /ˈamɪŋ/, *n.* a piece of tallow placed in a cavity at the lower end of a sounding lead to bring up a sample of the sand, mud, etc., of the sea bottom.

**Arminian** /aˈmɪniən/, *adj.* **1.** of or pertaining to Jacobus Arminius (*Jacob Harmensen*), 1560-1609, Dutch protestant theologian who modified certain Calvinistic doctrines, esp. that of predestination, or to his doctrines. *–n.* **2.** an adherent of the Arminian doctrines. – **Arminianism,** *n.*

**armipotent** /aˈmɪpətənt/, *adj.* mighty in arms or war. [ME, from L *armipotens* powerful in arms]

**armistice** /ˈaməstəs/, *n.* a temporary suspension of hostilities by agreement of the parties, as to discuss peace; a truce. [NL *armistitium,* from L: *armi-* (combining form of *arma* arms) + *-stitium* (from *sistere* stop)]

**armlet** /ˈamlət/, *n.* **1.** an ornamental band worn on the arm. **2.** a little arm: *an armlet of the sea.*

**armoire** /aˈmwa/, *n.* a large wardrobe or movable cupboard, with doors and shelves. [F. See AMBRY]

**armor** /ˈamə/, *n. U.S.* →**armour.**

**armorial** /aˈmɔriəl/, *adj.* **1.** belonging to heraldry or to heraldic bearing. *–n.* **2.** a book containing heraldic bearings and devices.

**armorial bearings** /– ˈbɛərɪŋz/, *n. pl.* a coat of arms.

**Armorican** /aˈmɒrɪkən/, *adj.* **1.** pertaining to Armorica, an ancient region in north-western France, corresponding generally to Brittany, or to an Armorican. **2.** *Geol.* of or pertaining to the major mountain-building episode which occurred in Europe in the Upper Carboniferous and Permian periods. *–n.* **3.** a native of Armorica. **4.** the Breton language. Also, **Armoric** for defs 1, 3, and 4.

**armorist** /ˈamərəst/, *n.* one skilled in heraldry or the blazoning of arms.

**armory** /ˈaməri/, *n., pl.* **-ries.** **1.** *Heraldry.* the art of blazoning arms. **2.** *Archaic.* heraldic bearings or arms. **3.** *Chiefly U.S.* an armourer's shop; an arsenal. [var. spelling of ARMOURY]

**armour** /ˈamə/, *n.* **1.** defensive equipment; any covering worn as a protection against offensive weapons. **2.** a metallic sheathing or protective covering, esp. metal plates used on warships, armoured vehicles, aeroplanes, and fortifications. **3.** any protective covering, as the scales of a fish. **4.** that which serves as a protection or safeguard. **5.** the outer wrapping of metal, usu. fine, braided steel wires, on a cable, primarily for the purpose of mechanical protection. *–v.t.* **6.** to cover with armour or armour plate. Also, *U.S.,* **armor.** [ME *armure,* from OF *armeüre,* from L *armātūra*]

suit of armour

**armour-bearer** /ˈamə-bɛərə/, *n.* a retainer bearing the armour or arms of a warrior. Also, *U.S.,* **armorbearer.**

**armoured** /ˈaməd/, *adj.* **1.** protected by armour or armour-plate. **2.** consisting of troops using armoured vehicles: *an armoured division.* Also, *U.S.,* **armored.**

**armoured car** /– ˈka/, *n.* a military vehicle with wheels, light armour, and, usu., machine-guns. Also, *U.S.,* **armored car.**

**armourer** /ˈamərə/, *n.* **1.** a maker or repairer of armour. **2.** a manufacturer of arms. **3.** an official, soldier, or sailor in charge of the upkeep of small arms in a regiment or on a naval vessel. Also, *U.S.,* **armorer.**

**armour-plate** /ˈamə-pleɪt/, *n.* a plate or plating of specially hardened steel used to cover warships, tanks, aircraft, fortifications, etc., to protect them from enemy fire. Also, *U.S.,* **armor plate; armour-plating.** – **armour-plated,** *adj.*

**armoury** /ˈaməri/, *n., pl.* **-ries.** **1.** a storage place for weapons and other war equipment. **2.** a collection of arms or armour. **3.** armour collectively. Also, *U.S.,* **armory.** [ME *armurie.* See ARMOUR, -Y[3]]

**armpit** /ˈampɪt/, *n.* the hollow under the arm at the shoulder; the axilla.

**armrest** /ˈamrɛst/, *n.* a rest or support, as on a chair, for the arm.

**arms** /amz/, *n.pl.* **1.** →**arm**[2] (def. 1). **2.** *Mil.* small arms. **3.** heraldic bearings. **4. bear arms,** to serve as a soldier. **5. take arms,** to resort to fighting; fight. **6. under arms,** armed. **7. (up) in arms, a.** armed and prepared to resist. **b.** angry; in rebellion (against something); violently resentful. [ME *armes,* from OF, from L *arma*]

**arms race** /ˈ– reɪs/, *n.* competition between nations in building up military resources.

**arm-wrestling** /ˈam-rɛslɪŋ/, *n.* a game in which two contestants sit facing each other with their elbows resting on a table and their hands clasped, the aim of the game being to push the opponents arm flat onto the table. Also, **arm-bending.**

**army** /ˈami/, *n., pl.* **-mies.** **1.** (*cap. or l.c.*) the military forces of a nation, exclusive of the naval and, in some countries, the airforces. **2.** (in large military land forces) the second largest unit, consisting of two or more corps. **3.** a large body of men trained and armed for war. **4.** any body of persons organised for any cause: *the Salvation Army.* **5.** a host; a great multitude. [ME *armee,* from OF, from L *armāta* armed forces]

**army ant** /ˈ– ænt/, *n.* any ant of the tropical and subtropical genus *Dorylinae,* characterised by travelling in vast swarms.

**army list** /ˈ– lɪst/, *n.* a list of all commissioned military officers.

**army of occupation,** *n.* an army established in conquered territory to maintain order and to ensure the carrying out of peace or armistice terms.

**army surplus store,** *n.* originally a shop selling discarded military goods as camping equipment, apparel, tools, etc. but now also selling similar goods at low prices. Also, **army disposals store.**

**army worm** /ˈami wɜm/, *n.* **1.** a kind of caterpillar, the larva of a noctuid moth, *Leucania unipuncta,* which often travels in hosts over a region, destroying grass, grain, etc. **2.** some similarly destructive larva.

**arnica** /ˈanɪkə/, *n.* **1.** any plant of the genus *Arnica,* esp. *A. montana.* **2.** a tincture of the flowers of such a plant, applied medicinally to sprains and bruises.

**aroid** /ˈærɔɪd, ˈɛə-/, *Bot. adj.* **1.** belonging to or resembling the Araceae or arum family of plants which includes the arum, taro, etc. *–n.* **2.** an aroid plant. [AR(UM) + -OID]

**aroint thee** /əˈrɔɪnt ði/, *exclam. Archaic.* avaunt! begone!

**aroma** /əˈroʊmə/, *n.* **1.** a smell arising from spices, plants, etc., esp. an agreeable smell; fragrance. **2.** (of wines and spirits) the smell or bouquet. **3.** a characteristic, subtle quality. [L, from Gk: spice, sweet herb]

**aromatic** /ærəˈmætɪk/, *adj.* **1.** having an aroma; fragrant; sweet-scented; spicy. **2.** *Chem.* of or pertaining to aromatic compounds. *–n.* **3.** a plant, drug, or medicine yielding a fragrant smell, as certain spices, oils, etc. – **aromatically,** *adv.* – **aromaticity** /ærəməˈtɪsəti/, *n.*

**aromatic compound** /– ˈkɒmpaʊnd/, *n.* any of a class of organic compounds including benzene, naphthalene, anthracene, and their derivatives, which contain an unsaturated ring of carbon atoms. Many have an agreeable smell.

**aromatisation** /əˌroʊmətaɪˈzeɪʃən/, *n.* the catalytic conversion of aliphatic hydrocarbons to aromatic hydrocarbons. Also, **aromatization.**

**aromatise** /əˈroʊmətaɪz/, *v.t.,* **-tised, -tising.** to make aromatic or fragrant. Also, **aromatize.**

**arose** /əˈroʊz/, *v.* past tense of **arise.**

**around** /əˈraʊnd/, *adv.* **1.** in a circle or sphere; round about; on every side. **2.** here and there; about: *to travel around.* **3.** *Colloq.* somewhere about or near: *to hang around for a person.* *–prep.* **4.** about; on all sides; encircling; encompassing: *a halo around his head.* **5.** *Colloq.* here and there in: *to roam around the country.* **6.** *Colloq.* somewhere in or near: *to stay around the house.* **7.** *Colloq.* approximately; near in time, amount, etc.: *around ten o'clock, around a million.* [A-[1] + ROUND]

**arouse** /əˈraʊz/, *v.,* **aroused, arousing.** *–v.t.* **1.** to excite into action; stir or put in motion; call into being: *aroused to action, arousing suspicion.* **2.** to wake from sleep. *–v.i.* **3.** to become aroused. [ROUSE[1], modelled on ARISE] – **arousal,** *n.* – **arouser,** *n.*

**arpeggio** /aˈpɛdʒioʊ/, *n., pl.* **-os.** **1.** the sounding of the notes of a chord separately and in succession instead of simultaneously. **2.** (esp. on keyboard instruments and the harp) the breaking or spreading of a chord so that the notes are sounded in very rapid succession and finally all sound together. **3.** a chord sounded in either of these ways. [It. *arpeggiare* play on the harp]

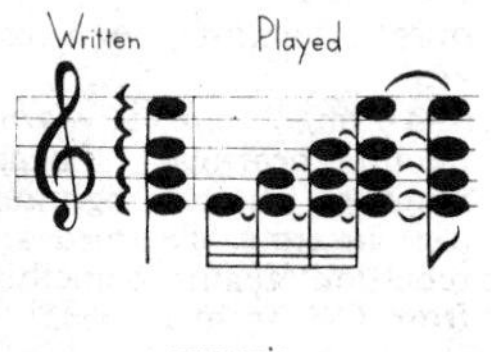

arpeggio

**arquebus** /ˈakwəbəs/, *n.* a light hand gun with matchlock or wheel-lock mechanism. Also, **harquebus.** [F *arquebuse,* from It. (obs.) *arcobuso,* from D *haakbus*]

**arr.,** **1.** arranged. **2.** arrival. **3.** arrive; arrived.

**arrack** /ˈærək, -æk/, *n.* any of various spirits distilled in the East Indies and elsewhere in the East from toddy (def. 2), molasses, or other materials. Also, **arak.** [Ar. *ʻaraq* (fermented) juice]

**arraign** /əˈreɪn/, *v.t.* **1.** *Law.* to call or bring before a court to answer to a charge or accusation. **2.** to accuse or charge in general. *–n.* **3.** *Obs. or Law.* arraignment. [ME *araine(n),* from AF *arainer,* from ML **arratiōnāre* call to account] – **arraigner,** *n.*

**arraignment** /əˈreɪnmənt/, *n.* **1.** *Law.* the act of arraigning. **2.** a calling in question for faults; accusation.

**arrange** /əˈreɪndʒ/, *v.,* **-ranged, -ranging.** *–v.t.* **1.** to place in proper, desired, or convenient order; adjust properly: *to arrange books on a shelf.* **2.** to come to an agreement or understanding regarding: *to arrange a bargain.* **3.** to prepare or plan: *to arrange the details of a meeting.* **4.** *Music.* to adapt (a composition) for a particular mode of rendering by voices or instruments. *–v.i.* **5.** to make a settlement; come to an agreement. **6.** to make preparations. [ME *araynge(n),* from OF *arangier,* from *a-* A-[5] + *rangier* RANGE, v.] – **arranger,** *n.*

**arrangement** /əˈreɪndʒmənt/, *n.* **1.** the act of arranging. **2.** the state of being arranged. **3.** the manner in which things are arranged. **4.** a final settlement; adjustment by agreement. **5.** (*usu. pl.*) preparatory measure; previous plan; preparation. **6.** something arranged in a particular way: *a floral arrangement.* **7.** *Music.* **a.** the adaptation of a composition to voices or instruments, or to a new purpose. **b.** a piece so adapted. [F]

**arrant** /ˈærənt/, *adj.* **1.** downright; thorough: *an arrant fool.* **2.** notorious. **3.** *Obs.* wandering. [var. of ERRANT] – **arrantly,** *adv.*

**arras** /ˈærəs/, *n.* **1.** rich tapestry. **2.** a tapestry weave. **3.** a wall hanging. [named after *Arras,* a town in N France]

**array** /əˈreɪ/, *v.t.* **1.** to place in proper or desired order, as troops for battle. **2.** to clothe with garments, esp. of an ornamental kind; deck. *–n.* **3.** order, as of troops drawn up for battle. **4.** an impressive group of things on exhibition, as a window display. **5.** regular order or arrangement. **6.** attire; dress. **7.** *Computers.* a series of elements or sets of elements arranged in a meaningful pattern, as in the rows and columns forming a matrix. **8.** *Geol., Physics.* an ordered arrangement of geophones, current or potential electrodes used in geophysical prospecting. [ME from AF *arai,* var. of OF *arei,* from *a* to + *rei* order, of Gmc origin]

**arrayal** /əˈreɪəl/, *n.* **1.** the act of arraying; muster; array. **2.** whatever is arrayed.

**arrear** /əˈrɪə/, *n.* **1.** (*usu. pl.*) the state of being behindhand. **2.** (*usu. pl.*) that which is behind in payment; a debt which remains unpaid, though due. **3.** **in arrear** or **in arrears,** behind in payments. **4.** *Archaic.* the rear. [ME *arere,* from OF, from L *ad-* AD- + *retrō* backwards]

**arrearage** /əˈrɪərɪdʒ/, *n.* **1.** the state or condition of being behind in payments due or in arrears. **2.** arrears; amount or amounts overdue. **3.** a thing or part kept in reserve. [ME *arerage,* from OF. See ARREAR, -AGE]

**arrest** /əˈrɛst/, *v.t.* **1.** to seize (a person) by legal authority or warrant. **2.** to capture; seize. **3.** to catch and fix: *to arrest the attention.* **4.** to bring to a standstill; stop; check: *to arrest the current of a river.* **5.** *Med.* to stop the active growth of: *arrested cancer.* *–n.* **6.** taking a person into custody in connection with a legal proceeding. **7.** any seizure or taking by force. **8.** the act of stopping. **9.** the state of being stopped. **10.** *Mach.* any device for arresting motion in a mechanism. [ME *arest(e),* from OF *areste* stoppage, from *arester,* from LL *adrestāre* (L: *ad-* AD- + *restāre* stop)] – **arrester,** *n.*

**arrestee** /ərɛsˈti/, *n. Scot. Law.* one who is under an arrestment (def. 2).

**arresting** /əˈrɛstɪŋ/, *adj.* catching the attention; striking: *an arresting painting.*

**arrestment** /əˈrɛstmənt/, *n.* **1.** *Law.* the state of being under arrest; detention. **2.** *Scot. Law.* the prevention of a debtor (the arrestee) from paying a creditor, until a claim upon that creditor by another person (the arrester) has been met.

**arrhythmia** /eɪˈrɪðmiə/, *n.* any disturbance in the rhythm of the heartbeat. [Gk: want of rhythm] – **arrhythmic,** *adj.*

**arrière-pensée** /ˌæriɛə-ˈpɒnseɪ/, *n.* a mental reservation; hidden motive.

**arris** /ˈærəs/, *n. Archit.* **1.** a sharp ridge, as between adjoining channels of a Doric column. **2.** the line, edge, or hip in which the two straight or curved surfaces of a body, forming an exterior angle, meet. [F *areste,* from L *arista* ear of grain, bone of a fish]

**arrival** /əˈraɪvəl/, *n.* **1.** the act of arriving: *the time of arrival.* **2.** the reaching or attainment of any object or condition: *arrival at a decision.* **3.** the person or thing that arrives, or has arrived.

**arrive** /əˈraɪv/, *v.,* **-rived, -riving.** *–v.i.* **1.** to come to a certain point in the course of travel; reach one's destination. **2.** to reach in any course or process; attain (fol. by *at*): *to arrive at a conclusion.* **3.** to come: *the time has arrived.* **4.** to happen; occur. **5.** to attain a position of success in the world. **6.** *Obs.* to come to shore. *–v.t.* **7.** *Obs.* to reach; come to. **8.** *Obs.* to happen to. [ME *a(r)rive(n),* from OF *a(r)river,* from LL *arrīpāre* come to shore]

**arrivederci** /ərivə'dɜtʃi/, *interj.* until we see each other again; goodbye for the present. [It.]

**arrivisme** /ə'rivɪzəm/, *n.* acting in accordance with unbridled ambition, esp. when social climbing or in the pursuit of a career. [F]

**arriviste** /ærə'vist/, *n.* an ambitious person; social climber or careerist. [F]

**arroba** /ə'roubə/, *n.* **1.** a unit of weight, about 11 kg in some Spanish-speaking countries, about 15 kg in some Portuguese-speaking countries. **2.** a varying unit of liquid measure in Spanish-speaking countries, about 16 litres when used to measure wine. [Sp. and Pg., from Ar. *ar-rub'* the quarter (of a quintal)]

**arrogance** /'ærəgəns/, *n.* the quality of being arrogant; offensive exhibition of assumed or real superiority; overbearing pride. Also, **arrogancy.** [ME, from F, from L *arrogantia*]

**arrogant** /'ærəgənt/, *adj.* **1.** making unwarrantable claims or pretensions to superior importance or rights; overbearingly assuming; insolently proud. **2.** characterised by or proceeding from arrogance: *arrogant claims.* [ME, from L *arrogans,* ppr., assuming] – **arrogantly,** *adv.*

**arrogate** /'ærəgeɪt/, *v.t.,* **-gated, -gating.** **1.** to claim unwarrantably or presumptuously; assume or appropriate to oneself without right. **2.** to attribute or assign to another without just reason. [L *arrogātus,* pp., assumed, asked of] – **arrogation** /ærə'geɪʃən/, *n.*

**arrondissement** /ə'rɒndəsmənt, əˌrɒndɪs'mõ/, *n.* **1.** the largest administrative division of a French department. Each arrondissement is divided into cantons. **2.** a borough of Paris. [F]

**arrow** /'ærou/, *n.* **1.** a slender, straight, generally pointed, missile weapon made to be shot from a bow. The shaft is nearly always made of light wood, fitted with feathers at the neck end to help guide it. **2.** anything resembling an arrow in form, as the inflorescence of a sugarcane. **3.** a figure of an arrow used to indicate direction. **4.** See **broad arrow.** *–v.i.* **5.** *Agric.* to produce an arrow-shaped inflorescence, as sugarcane when ripening. [ME and OE *arwe,* c. Icel. *ör*] – **arrowless,** *adj.* – **arrow-like,** *adj.* – **arrow-shaped,** *adj.*

**arrow-grass** /'ærou-gras/, *n.* any one of the grasslike marsh plants of the genus *Triglochin;* the burst seed capsule resembles an arrowhead.

**arrowhead** /'ærouhɛd/, *n.* **1.** the head of an arrow, usu. wedge-shaped or barbed. **2.** any plant of the genus *Sagittaria,* usu. aquatic, species of which have arrow-shaped leaves. **3.** anything shaped like an arrowhead; a wedge-shaped design or ornament.

**arrow-poison frog** /ˌærou-pɔɪzən 'frɒg/, *n.* →**dendrobates.**

**arrowroot** /'ærərut/, *n.* **1.** a tropical American plant, *Maranta arundinacea,* or related species, whose rhizomes yield a nutritious starch. **2.** the starch itself. **3.** a similar starch from other plants, used in puddings, biscuits, etc.

**arrowroot biscuit** /– 'bɪskət/, *n.* a plain, semi-sweet, dry biscuit, made with arrowroot starch.

**arrowshot** /'ærouʃɒt/, *n.* the range of an arrow.

**arrowworm** /'ærouwɜm/, *n.* a small transparent pelagic animal of elongate form with fins, comprising the class or phylum Chaetognatha.

**arrowy** /'æroui/, *adj.* **1.** like an arrow in shape, speed, effect, etc.; swift or piercing. **2.** consisting of arrows.

**arroyo** /ə'rɔɪjou/, *n.* **1.** a creek or stream. **2.** a steep-sided gully or channel. [Sp. *arroyo,* from L *arrugio* gallery in a mine]

**arse** /as/, *n., v.,* **arsed, arsing.** *Colloq.* *–n.* **1.** rump; bottom; buttocks; posterior. **2.** a despised person. **3.** impudence: *what arse!* **4.** a woman considered as a sex object: *she's a nice bit of arse.* **5.** Some special noun phrases are:

**arse about face,** changed in direction; back to front.

**arse over apex,** fallen heavily and awkwardly, usu. in a forward direction. Also, **arse over kettle, arse over tit, arse over turkey.**

**down on one's arse,** out of luck; destitute.

**give (someone) the arse,** to reject or rebuff (someone).

**smart arse,** →**smart alec.**

**up Cook's arse,** *N.Z.* (an expression of disgust).

*–v.i.* **6. arse about** or **around,** to act like a fool; waste time. **7. arse up,** to spoil; cause to fail. [ME; OE *ears*]

**arse bandit** /'– bændət/, *n. Colloq.* a homosexual who is sexually aggressive.

**arsehole** /'ashoul/, *Colloq.* *–n.* **1.** the anus. **2. a.** a despised place: *this town is the arsehole of the universe.* **b.** a despised person. **3. from arsehole to breakfast time,** completely. *–v.t.* **4.** to remove a person from a place quickly and without ceremony; to throw someone out. **5.** to dismiss, sack. *–v.i.* **6. arsehole about,** to fool around. **7. arsehole off,** to depart quickly or unobtrusively.

**arse holes** /'as houlz/, *interj. Colloq.* (an exclamation of disgust or disbelief).

**arse-licker** /'as-lɪkə/, *n. Colloq.* a sycophant.

**arsenal** /'asənəl/, *n.* **1.** a repository or magazine of arms and military stores of all kinds for land or naval service. **2.** a building having that incidental purpose but used mainly for the training of troops. **3.** a public establishment where military equipment or munitions are manufactured. [It *arsenale* dock (Venetian d. *arzanà*), from Ar. *dar ṣināʻa* workshop]

**arsenate** /'asəneɪt, -nət/, *n.* salt of arsenic acid.

**arsenic** /'asənɪk/, *n.* **1.** a greyish white element having a metallic lustre, volatilising when heated, and forming poisonous compounds. *Symbol:* As; *at. wt:* 74.9216; *at. no. :* 33. **2.** arsenic trioxide or white arsenic, $As_2O_3$, which is used in medicine and painting, and in poison for vermin. **3.** a mineral, the native element, occurring in white or grey masses. *–adj.* **4.** of or containing arsenic, esp. in the pentavalent state. [ME *arsenik,* from L *arsenicum,* from Gk *arsenikón* orpiment]

**arsenic acid** /aˌsɛnɪk 'æsəd/, *n.* a water-soluble, crystalline compound, $H_3AsO_4 \cdot \frac{1}{2}H_2O$, used in the manufacture of arsenates.

**arsenical** /a'sɛnɪkəl/, *adj.* **1.** containing or relating to arsenic. *–n.* **2.** (*pl.*) a group of insecticides, drugs, etc., containing arsenic.

**arsenide** /'asənaɪd/, *n.* a compound containing two elements, of which arsenic is the negative one, as *silver arsenide,* $Ag_3As$.

**arsenite** /'asənaɪt/, *n.* **1.** a salt of any of the hypothetical arsenous acids. **2.** →**arsenic** (def. 2).

**arseniuret** /a'sinjurət, a'sɛn-/, *n.* →**arsenide.** [ARSENI(C) + -URET]

**arseniuretted** /a'sinjurɛtəd, a'sɛn-/, *adj.* combined with arsenic so as to form an arsenide. Also, *U.S.,* **arseniureted.**

**arsenopyrite** /asənou'paɪraɪt, asənə-/, *n.* a common mineral, iron arsenic sulphide, FeAsS, occurring in silver-white to steel-grey crystals or masses, an ore of arsenic; white mundic. [*arseno-* (combining form of ARSENIC) + pyrite]

**arsenous** /'asənəs/, *adj.* containing trivalent arsenic, as *arsenous chloride,* $AsCl_3$.

**arse-up** /as-'ʌp/, *Colloq.* *–adj.* **1.** wrong side up, topsy-turvy. *–adv.* **2.** in a clumsy fashion.

**arsine** /'asin/, *n.* **1.** arseniuretted hydrogen, $AsH_3$, a colourless, inflammable, highly poisonous gas, with a fetid garlic-like smell, used in chemical warfare. **2.** any derivative of this compound, in which one or more hydrogen atoms are replaced by organic radicals. [ARS(ENIC) + -INE[2]]

**arsis** /'asəs/, *n., pl.* **-ses** /-siz/. **1.** *Pros.* **a.** (originally) the unaccented syllable of a foot in verse. **b.** (in later use) the unstressed part of a rhythmical unit (opposed to *thesis*). **2.** *Music.* the anacrusis, or upbeat (opposed to *thesis*). [L, from Gk: a raising (apparently of hand or voice)]

**arson** /'asən/, *n.* the malicious burning of a house or outbuilding belonging to another, or (as fixed by statute) the burning of any building (including one's own). [AF, from LL *arsio* a burning]

**arsphenamine** /as'fɛnəmin, -maɪn/, *n.* a yellow crystalline powder subject to rapid oxidisation, $C_{12}H_{12}N_2O_2As_2 \cdot 2HCl + 2H_2O$, used to treat diseases caused by spirochete organisms, esp. syphilis and trench mouth; first known as '606'. [ARS(ENIC) + PHEN(YL) + AMINE]

**ars poetica** /az pou'ɛtɪkə/, *n.* the art of poetry or poetics. [L]

**arsy** /'asi/, *adj. Colloq.* lucky. Also, **arsey, arsie.**

**arsy-versy** /asi-'vɜsi/, *adj. Colloq.* back to front, topsy turvy.

**art**[1] /at/, *n.* **1.** the production or expression of what is beautiful (esp. visually), appealing, or of more than ordinary significance. **2.** *Journalism.* any illustration in a newspaper or magazine. **3.** a department of skilled performance: *industrial art.* **4.** (*pl.*) a branch of learning or university study. **5.** (*pl.*) liberal arts. **6.** skilled workmanship, execution, or agency (often opposed to *nature*). **7.** a skill or knack; a method of doing a thing, esp. if it is difficult. **8.** craft; cunning: *glib and oily art.* **9.** studied action; artificiality in behaviour. **10.** (*usu. pl.*) an artifice or artful device: *the arts and wiles of politics.* **11.** learning or science. [ME, from OF, from L *ars* skill, art]

**art**[2] /at/, *v. Archaic.* 2nd pers. sing. pres. indic. of **be.** [ME; OE *eart*]

**-art,** variant of **-ard,** as in *braggart.*

**art.,** **1.** article. **2.** artificial.

**art brut** /at ˈbrut/, *n.* the spontaneous pictorial compositions of psychotics, children and amateur painters, sometimes considered to have formal aesthetic value. [F: raw art]

**Art Deco** /at ˈdɛkoʊ, ˈdeɪkoʊ/, *n.* a decorative style, originally of the 1920s and 1930s, characterised by rectilinear and streamlined forms and the innovative use of materials as plastic, glass, etc. Also, **art deco.** [F *Art Déco,* shortened form of *Exposition Internationale des Arts Décoratifs,* Paris, 1925]

**artefact** /ˈatəfækt/, *n.* **1.** any object made by man with a view to subsequent use. **2.** *Biol.* a substance, structure, or the like, not naturally present in tissue, but formed by reagents, death, etc. Also, **artifact.** [L: *arti-* (combining form of *ars* art) + *factus,* pp., made]

**artel** /aˈtɛl/, *n.* (in the Soviet Union) a peasants' or workers' cooperative enterprise. [Russ.]

**arterial** /aˈtɪəriəl/, *adj.* **1.** *Physiol.* pertaining to the blood in the arteries which has been charged with oxygen during its passage through the lungs, and, in the higher animals, is usually bright red. **2.** *Anat.* of, pertaining to, or resembling the arteries. **3.** having a main channel and many branches: *arterial drainage.* **4.** carrying the main flow of traffic between large towns: *an arterial road.* *–n.* **5.** an arterial road.

**arterialise** /aˈtɪəriəlaɪz/, *v.t.,* **-lised, -lising.** to make arterial. Also, **arterialize.** – **arterialisation** /aˌtɪəriəlaɪˈzeɪʃən/, *n.*

**arteriole** /aˈtɪərioʊl/, *n.* a small artery. [NL *arteriola,* diminutive of *artēria* artery]

**arteriosclerosis** /aˌtɪərioʊskləˈroʊsəs/, *n. Pathol.* an arterial disease occurring esp. in the elderly, characterised by inelasticity and thickening of the vessel walls, with lessened blood flow. [NL, from Gk: *artērio-* (combining form of *artēría* artery) + *sklḗrōsis* hardening] – **arteriosclerotic** /aˌtɪərioʊskləˈrɒtɪk/, *adj.*

**arteritis** /atəˈraɪtəs/, *n.* inflammation of an artery. [L *artēria* artery + -ITIS]

**artery** /ˈatəri/, *n., pl.* **-teries. 1.** *Anat.* a blood vessel which conveys blood from the heart to any part of the body. **2.** a main channel in any ramifying system of communications or transport, as in drainage or roads. [ME *arterie,* from L *artēria,* from Gk]

**artesian basin** /aˌtiʒən ˈbeɪsən/, *n.* a geological structural feature or combination of such features in which water is confined under pressure.

**artesian bore** /– ˈbɔ/, *n.* a bore whose shaft penetrates an aquifer and in which the water level rises above ground by hydrostatic pressure. Also, **artesian well.** [F *artésien* pertaining to *Artois,* former province of France where such wells were bored]

artesian bore (cross-section): A, impermeable strata; B, permeable strata; C, artesian boring and well

**artesian water** /– ˈwɔtə/, *n.* water from an artesian bore.

**artful** /ˈatfəl/, *adj.* **1.** crafty; cunning; tricky: *artful schemes.* **2.** skilful in adapting means to ends; ingenious.

**arthralgia** /aˈθrældʒə, -dʒiə/, *n. Pathol.* pain in a joint. – **arthralgic,** *adj.*

**arthritic** /aˈθrɪtɪk/, *adj.* **1.** suffering or tending to suffer from arthritis. **2.** of or of the nature of arthritis. *–n.* **3.** an arthritic person.

**arthritis** /aˈθraɪtəs/, *n. Pathol.* inflammation of a joint, as in gout or rheumatism. [L, from Gk: joint disease]

**arthro-,** *Anat.* a word element meaning joint, as in *arthropod.* Also, **arthr-.** [Gk, combining form of *árthron*]

**arthromere** /ˈaθrəmɪə/, *n.* one of the segments or parts into which the body of articulated animals is divided.

**arthropod** /ˈaθrəpɒd/, *n.* **1.** any of the Arthropoda, the phylum of segmented invertebrates, having jointed legs, as the insects, arachnids, crustaceans, and myriapods. *–adj.* **2.** Also, **arthropodal** /aθrəˈpoʊdl, aˈθrɒpədl/, **arthropodous.** belonging to or pertaining to the Arthropoda.

**arthrospore** /ˈaθrəspɔ/, *n.* **1.** *Bacteriol.* an isolated vegetative cell which has passed into a resting state, occurring in bacteria, and not regarded as a true spore. **2.** *Bot.* one of a number of spores of various low fungi and algae, united in the form of a string of beads, formed by fission.

**Arthurian** /aˈθuriən, aˈθju-, aˈθjʊə-/, *adj.* of or pertaining to Arthur, legendary King in ancient Britain, the leader of the Knights of the Round Table, and the subject of a great body of medieval romantic literature.

**artic** /ˈatɪk/, *n. N.Z. Colloq.* →**semitrailer.** [shortened form of ARTICULATED LORRY]

**artichoke** /ˈatətʃoʊk, ˈatɪtʃoʊk/, *n.* **1.** a herbaceous, thistle-like plant, *Cynara scolymus,* with an edible flower head; globe artichoke. **2.** the edible portion, used as a table vegetable. **3.** →**Jerusalem artichoke.** [It: *articiocco,* from Pr. *arquichaut,* from Ar. *al kharshūf*]

artichoke

**artichoke heart** /ˈ– hat/, *n. Cookery.* the fleshy middle part of the globe artichoke, trimmed and cooked.

**artichoke thistle** /–ˈ θɪsəl/, *n.* a large thistle, *Cynara cardunculus,* native to Mediterranean regions; cardoon.

**article** /ˈatɪkəl/, *n., v.,* **-cled, -cling** *–n.* **1.** a piece of writing on a specific topic, forming an independent part of a book or literary publication, esp. of a newspaper, magazine, review, or other periodical. **2.** an individual piece or thing of a class; an item or particular: *an article of food or dress.* **3.** a thing, indefinitely: *what is that article?* **4.** (in some languages) any word, as the English words *a* or *an* (**indefinite article**) and *the* (**definite article**), whose main function is to precede nouns of a certain class (**common nouns**), esp. when these are not preceded by other limiting modifiers. **5.** a clause, item, point, or particular in a contract, treaty, or other formal agreement; a condition or stipulation in a contract or bargain. **6.** a separate clause or provision of a statute. **7.** (*pl.*) a document drawn up in articles; an agreement or code. **8.** a matter or subject. **9.** *Archaic.* juncture or moment. *–v.t.* **10.** to set forth in articles; charge or accuse specifically. **11.** to bind by articles of covenant or stipulation: *to article an apprentice.* **12.** to bind by articles of agreement. [ME, from F, from L *articulus,* diminutive of *artus* joint]

**articled clerk** /ˌatɪkəld ˈklak/, *n.* a person under articles of agreement to serve a solicitor in return for training.

**articles of association,** *n.pl.* **1.** the regulations and constitution of a registered company. **2.** the document containing these regulations, etc.

**articles of faith,** *n.pl.* (a statement of) the essential points of faith held by a particular Church.

**articular** /aˈtɪkjələ/, *adj.* of or pertaining to the joints. [L *articulāris*]

**articulate** /aˈtɪkjəleɪt/, *v.,* **-lated, -lating;** /aˈtɪkjələt/, *adj., n.* *–v.t.* **1.** to utter articulately. **2.** *Phonet.* to make the movements and adjustments of the speech organs necessary to utter (a speech sound). **3.** to unite by a joint or joints. *–v.i.* **4.** to utter distinct syllables or words: *to articulate distinctly.* **5.** *Phonet.* to articulate a speech sound. **6.** to form a joint. *–adj.* **7.** clear; distinct. **8.** uttered clearly in distinct syllables. **9.** capable of speech; not speechless; eloquent. **10.** Also, **articulated.** having joints or articulations; composed of segments. *–n.* **11.** *Rare.* a segmented invertebrate. [L *articulātus,* pp.] – **articulately,** *adv.* – **articulateness,** *n.* – **articulator,** *n.*

**articulated lorry** /aˌtɪkjəleɪtəd ˈlɒri/, *n. Brit., N.Z.* a semi-trailer, often with the trailer fully enclosed. Also, **articulated truck.**

**articulation** /aˌtɪkjəˈleɪʃən/, *n.* **1.** *Phonet.* **a.** the act or process of articulating speech. **b.** the adjustments and movements of speech organs involved in pronouncing a particular sound, taken as a whole. **c.** any of these adjustments and movements. **d.** any speech sound, esp. a consonant. **2.** clarity of diction; distinctness. **3.** the act of jointing. **4.** a jointed state or formation; a joint. **5.** *Bot.* **a.** a joint or place between two parts where separation may take place spontaneously, as at the point of attachment of a leaf. **b.** a node in a stem, or the space between two nodes. **6.** *Anat., Zool.* a joint, as the joining or juncture of bones or of the movable segments of an arthropod. **7.** the way in which the elements of an architectural design are interrelated through different degrees of emphasis. **8.** *Music.* the manner of performing a passage, as with notes detached, slurred, etc.

**articulatory phonetics** /aˌtɪkjələtri fəˈnɛtɪks/, *n.* the branch of phonetics concerned with how the body produces speech sounds.

**artifact** /ˈatəfækt/, *n.* →**artefact.**

**artifice** /ˈatəfəs/, *n.* **1.** a crafty device or expedient; a clever trick or stratagem. **2.** craft; trickery. **3.** skilful or apt contrivance. **4.** *Obs.* workmanship. [F, from L *artificium*]

**artificer** /aˈtɪfəsə/, *n.* **1.** a skilful or artistic worker; craftsman. **2.** one who is skilful in devising ways of making things; an inventor. **3.** *Mil.* a soldier or sailor mechanic who does repairs, maintains machinery, etc.

**artificial** /atəˈfɪʃəl/, *adj.* **1.** made by human skill and labour (opposed to *natural*). **2.** made in imitation of or as a substitute; not genuine. **3.** feigned; fictitious; assumed. **4.** full of affectation; affected. **5.** *Biol.* based on arbitrary rather than organic criteria. **6.** *Obs.* artful; crafty. [ME, from L *artificiālis*] – **artificially,** *adv.* – **artificialness,** *n.*

**artificial grass** /– ˈgras/, *n.* **1.** imitation grass made from nylon, synthetics, etc. **2.** →**improved pasture.**

**artificial horizon** /– həˈraɪzən/, *n.* **1.** a level reflector, as a surface of mercury, used in determining the altitudes of stars, etc. **2.** the bubble in a sextant or octant for aerial use.

**artificial insemination** /– ɪnˌsɛməˈneɪʃən/, *n.* a method of inducing pregnancy by artificial introduction of viable sperm into the canal of the cervix, widely practised on cattle and horses for the purpose of selective breeding.

**artificial intelligence** /– ɪnˈtɛlədʒəns/, *n.* decision-making computers.

**artificiality** /ˌatəfɪʃiˈæləti/, *n., pl.* **-ties. 1.** artificial quality. **2.** an artificial thing or trait.

**artificial kidney** /ˌatəfɪʃəl ˈkɪdni/, *n.* →**kidney machine.**

**artificial radioactivity** /ˌatəfɪʃəl ˌreɪdioʊækˈtɪvəti/, *n.* →**induced radioactivity.**

**artificial respiration** /– rɛspəˈreɪʃən/, *n.* a method for restarting the breathing of a person who has been half-drowned or otherwise asphyxiated, as by alternately pressing on and releasing the rib cage, or by the kiss of life.

**artificial selection** /– səˈlɛkʃən/, *n.* →**selection** (def. 7).

**artificial silk** /– ˈsɪlk/, *n.* rayon or any other similar synthetic material.

**artillery** /aˈtɪləri/, *n.* **1.** mounted guns, movable or stationary, light or heavy, as distinguished from small arms. **2.** the troops, or the branch of an army, concerned with the service of such guns. **3.** the science which treats of the use of such guns. [ME *artilrie,* from OF *artillerie* implements of war]

**artilleryman** /aˈtɪlərimən/, *n., pl.* **-men.** one who serves a piece of artillery, or is in a regiment of artillery.

**artillery-plant** /aˈtɪləri-plænt/, *n.* a small-leaved succulent plant, *Pilea microphylla,* grown in gardens and a weed in tropical areas.

**artiodactyl** /ˌatioʊˈdæktəl/, *adj.* **1.** *Zool.* having an even number of toes or digits on each foot. *–n.* **2.** any animal of the mammalian order Artiodactylia, which comprises the even-toed quadrupeds, as the swine, the hippopotamuses and the ruminants, cattle, sheep, goats, deer, camels, etc., sometimes classified as a suborder of ungulates. [Gk: *ártio(s)* even + *dáktylos* finger or toe] – **artiodactylous,** *adj.*

**artisan** /ˈatəzən/, *n.* **1.** one skilled in an industrial or applied art; a craftsman. **2.** a member of the urban working classes. **3.** any of certain ratings in the Royal Navy. **4.** *Obs.* an artist. [F, from It. *artigiano,* from *arte* guild]

**artist** /ˈatəst/, *n.* **1.** a person who practises one of the fine arts, esp. a painter or a sculptor. **2.** a member of one of the histrionic professions, as an actor or singer. **3.** one who exhibits art in his work, or makes an art of his employment. **4.** *Obs.* an artisan. **5.** *Colloq.* a person noted or notorious for a reprehensible aspect of his behaviour. [F *artiste,* from It. *artista,* from LL. See ART[1], -IST]

**artiste** /aˈtist/, *n.* **1.** a female artist, esp. an actor, singer, dancer, or other public performer. **2.** (often mockingly, or tongue-in-cheek) a female artist in the more popular theatrical arts, with more pretensions than talent. **3.** a stripper.

**artistic** /aˈtɪstɪk/, *adj.* **1.** conformable to the standards of art; aesthetically excellent or admirable. **2.** of, like, or befitting an artist. **3.** stormy, emotional, and capricious, as temperament or behaviour popularly ascribed to artists. Also, **artistical.** – **artistically,** *adv.*

**artistry** /ˈatəstri/, *n., pl.* **-tries. 1.** artistic workmanship, effect, or quality. **2.** artistic pursuits.

**artist's proof** /atəsts ˈpruf/, *n.* any of the proofs in a limited edition of original prints, usu. numbered and signed by the artist.

**artless** /ˈatləs/, *adj.* **1.** free from deceit, cunning, or craftiness; ingenuous: *an artless mind.* **2.** natural; simple: *artless beauty.* **3.** lacking art, knowledge, or skill. – **artlessly,** *adv.* – **artlessness,** *n.*

**art music** /ˈat mjuzɪk/, *n.* music which has a theoretical foundation and consequently some form of notation, as distinct from folk music.

**Art Nouveau** /– nuˈvoʊ/, *n.* an international style of art, architecture and interior decoration, popular from 1890 to 1914, characterised by a naturalistic depiction of organic and vegetable forms, and by flowing curves and lines. Also, **art nouveau.** [F: lit., new art]

**art paper** /ˈ– peɪpə/, *n. Print.* **1.** coated paper, usu. with a high gloss surface. **2.** heavy paper used for art or craft projects.

**art silk** /– ˈsɪlk/, *n.* →**artificial silk.**

**art union** /– ˈjunjən/, *n.* **1.** a lottery. **2.** *N.Z.* a major lottery, endorsed and taxed by the Government. **3.** (originally) a lottery with works of art as prizes.

**artwork** /ˈatwɜk/, *n.* any piece of specially designed material from which a printer's plate or block, etc., is composed.

**arty** /ˈati/, *adj.,* **-tier, -tiest,** *n. Colloq.* *–adj.* **1.** ostentatious in display of artistic interest. *–n.* **2.** an arty person.

**arty-crafty** /ati-ˈkrafti/, *adj.* affectedly artistic; artistic but useless, pretentious, or trivial.

**arty-farty** /ati-ˈfati/, *adj. Colloq.* pretentious; precious.

**arum** /ˈɛərəm/, *n.* **1.** any plant of the genus *Arum,* having an inflorescence consisting of a spadix enclosed in a large spathe, as the cuckoopint. **2.** any of various allied plants in cultivation, as the arum lily, *Zantedeschia aethiopica.* [L, from Gk *áron*] – **arum-like,** *adj.*

**arundinaceous** /ərʌndəˈneɪʃəs/, *adj.* pertaining to or like a reed or cane; reedlike; reedy. [L *arundinăceus,* from *(h)arundo* reed]

**Arunta** /əˈrʌntə/, *n.* →**Aranda.**

**arvo** /ˈavoʊ/, *n. Colloq.* afternoon. Also, **aftie, afto.** [modified shortened form of AFTERNOON + -O]

**-ary**[1], **1.** an adjective suffix meaning 'pertaining to', attached chiefly to nouns (*honorary*) and to stems appearing in other words (*voluntary*). **2.** a suffix forming nouns from other nouns or adjectives indicating location or repository (*dictionary, granary, apiary*), officers (*functionary, secretary*), or other relations (*adversary*). **3.** a suffix forming collective numeral nouns, esp. in time units (*centenary*). [L *-ārius,* neut. *-ārium*]

**-ary**[2], variant of **-ar**[1], as in *exemplary, military.*

**Aryan** /'ɛəriən/, *n.* **1.** *Ethnol.* a member or descendant of the prehistoric people who spoke Indo-European. **2.** (in Nazi doctrine) a non-Jewish Caucasian, esp. one of Nordic physical type. **3. a.** Indo-European. **b.** the hypothetical parent language of Indo-European. *–adj.* **4.** of or pertaining to an Aryan or the Aryans. **5.** Indo-European. Also, **Arian.** [Skt *Arya,* name by which the Sanskrit-speaking immigrants into India called themselves + -AN]

**Aryanise** /'ɛəriənaɪz/, *v.t.,* **-nised, -nising.** (in Nazi doctrine) to remove all non-Aryan persons from (office, business, etc.). Also, **Aryanize.**

**aryl** /'ærɪl/, *adj.* of or pertaining to any of the organic radicals obtained from the aromatic hydrocarbons by removing a hydrogen atom, as phenyl ($C_6H_5$) from benzene ($C_6H_6$). [AR(OMATIC) + -YL]

**arylamine** /ə'rɪləmin, -maɪn/, *n. Chem.* any of a group of amines in which one or more of the hydrogen atoms of ammonia are replaced with aromatic radicals.

**arytenoid** /'ærətənɔɪd, ə'rɪtənɔɪd, ærə'tinɔɪd/, *Anat. –adj.* **1.** ladle- or cup-shaped (applied to two small cartilages at the top of the larynx, and to some of the muscles connected with them). *–n.* **2.** an arytenoid cartilage. Also, **arytaenoid, arytenoidal** /ærətə'nɔɪdl/. [Gk *arytainoeidḗs* ladle-shaped]

**as** /æz/; *weak form* /əz/, *adv.* **1.** to such a degree or extent: *as good as gold.* **2. as well as,** as much or as truly as; just as; equally as; as also; in addition to: *goodness as well as beauty.* **3. as well, a.** equally; also; too: *beautiful, and good as well.* **b.** as well as not; equally well; better; advisable: *it is as well to avoid trouble.* *–conj.* **4.** the consequent in the correlations *as* (or *so*)...*as, same...as,* etc., denoting degree, extent, manner, etc. (*as good as gold, in the same way as before*), or in the correlations *so as, such as,* denoting purpose or result (fol. by infinitive): *to listen so as to hear.* **5.** (without antecedent) in the degree, manner, etc., of or that: *quick as thought, speak as he does.* **6.** according to what, or the manner in which, or the extent to which: *as I hear, we help as we are able.* **7.** though: *bad as it is, it could be worse.* **8.** as if; as though: *he spoke quietly, as to himself.* **9.** when or while. **10.** since; because. **11.** for instance. **12. as for, as to,** with regard or respect to; for the matter of. **13. as if, as though,** as it would be if. **14. as it were,** in some sort; so to speak. **15. as yet, a.** up to now; even yet. **b.** for the moment; in the near future; just yet. *–rel. pron.* **16.** that; who; which (esp. after *such* and *the same*). **17.** (of) which fact, contingency, etc. (referring to a statement): *I may fail you, as you realize.* *–prep.* **18.** in the role, function, status, or manner of: *to appear as Othello, serve as a warning.* [ME *as, als, alse, also,* OE *alswā, ealswā* all so, quite so, quite as, as. Cf. ALSO]

**as-,** variant of **ad-** before *s,* as in *assert.*

**As,** *Chem.* arsenic.

**AS,** Anglo-Saxon. Also, **A.-S., A.S.**

**asafoetida** /æsəfə'tidə/, *n.* a gum resin having an obnoxious, alliaceous smell, obtained from the roots of several species of the umbelliferous genus *Ferula* and once used in medicine. [ML *asa* (from Pers. *azā* mastic) + L *foetida* fetid]

**asana** /ə'sanə/, *n.* (in yoga) control of the body through the adoption and practice of certain bodily postures. [Skt.]

**a.s.a.p.** /ˌeɪ ɛs eɪ 'pi/, as soon as possible.

**asbestos** /əs'bɛstəs, æs-/, *n.* **1.** *Mineral.* **a.** a fibrous amphibole, used for making incombustible or fireproof articles. **b.** the mineral chrysotile, similarly used. **2.** a fire-resistant fabric woven from asbestos fibres. *–adj.* **3.** Also, **asbestine.** made of or pertaining to this fabric. [L, from Gk: unquenchable; replacing ME *asbeston,* from OF]

**asbestosis** /æsbɛs'toʊsəs/, *n.* inflammation of the lungs caused by the inhalation of asbestos particles.

**ascarid** /'æskərɪd/, *n. Zool.* any of the Ascaridae, a family of nematode worms including the roundworm and pinworm. [NL *ascaridae,* from Gk *askarídes* (pl.) threadworms]

**ascend** /ə'sɛnd/, *v.i.* **1.** to climb or go upwards; mount; rise. **2.** to rise to a higher point or degree; proceed from an inferior to a superior degree or level. **3.** to go towards the source or beginning; go back in time. **4.** *Music.* to rise in pitch; pass from any tone to a higher one. *–v.t.* **5.** to go or move upwards upon or along; climb; mount: *to ascend a hill or ladder.* [ME *ascende(n),* from L *ascendere* climb up] **– ascendible, ascendable,** *adj.*

**ascendancy** /ə'sɛndənsi/, *n.* the state of being in the ascendant; governing or controlling influence; domination. Also, **ascendency, ascendance, ascendence.**

**ascendant** /ə'sɛndənt/, *n.* **1.** a position of dominance or controlling influence; superiority; predominance: *in the ascendant.* **2.** an ancestor (opposed to *descendant*). **3.** *Astrol.* **a.** the point of the ecliptic or the sign of the zodiac rising above the horizon at the time of a birth, etc. **b.** the horoscope. *–adj.* **4.** superior; predominant. **5.** *Bot.* directed or curved upwards. **6.** rising. Also, **ascendent.**

**ascender** /ə'sɛndə/, *n.* **1.** one who or that which ascends. **2.** *Print.* the part of such letters as *b, h, d,* and *f* that rises above the body of most lower-case letters.

**ascending** /ə'sɛndɪŋ/, *adj.* **1.** rising. **2.** *Bot.* growing or directed upwards, esp. obliquely or in a curve from the base.

**ascension** /ə'sɛnʃən/, *n.* the act of ascending; ascent. [ME, from L *ascensio*]

**ascent** /ə'sɛnt/, *n.* **1.** the act of ascending; upward movement; rise. **2.** a rising from a lower to a higher state, degree, or grade; advancement. **3.** the act of climbing or travelling up. **4.** the way or means of ascending; upward slope. **5.** a procedure towards a source or beginning. **6.** gradient. [from ASCEND, modelled on DESCENT]

**ascertain** /æsə'teɪn/, *v.t.* **1.** to find out by trial, examination, or experiment, so as to know as certain; determine. **2.** *Archaic.* to make certain, clear, or definitely known. [ME *ascertain,* from OF *ascertener* make certain, from *a*-A-[5] + *certain* CERTAIN] **– ascertainable,** *adj.* **– ascertainableness,** *n.* **– ascertainably,** *adv.* **– ascertainment,** *n.*

**ascetic** /ə'sɛtɪk/, *n.* **1.** a person who leads an abstemious life. **2.** one who practises religious austerities. **3.** (in the early Christian Church) a monk; hermit. *–adj.* **4.** pertaining to asceticism or ascetics. **5.** rigorously abstinent; austere. **6.** unduly strict in religious exercises or mortifications. [Gk *askētikós* pertaining to a monk or hermit, from *askētḗs* monk, hermit (orig. athlete)]

**ascetical** /ə'sɛtɪkəl/, *adj.* pertaining to ascetic discipline or practice. **– ascetically,** *adv.*

**asceticism** /ə'sɛtəsɪzəm/, *n.* **1.** the life or practice of an ascetic; the principles and historic course of the ascetics. **2.** *Theol.* the theory or systemic exposition of the means (whether negative, as self-denial and abstinence, or positive, as the exercise of natural and Christian virtues) by which a complete conformity with the divine will may be attained. **3.** rigorous self-discipline.

**ascidian** /ə'sɪdiən/, *n.* **1.** a tunicate or seasquirt. *–adj.* **2.** of or belonging to the Ascidia or Tunicata. [ASCIDI(UM) + -AN]

**ascidium** /ə'sɪdiəm/, *n., pl.* **-cidia** /-'sɪdiə/. *Bot.* a baglike or pitcher-shaped part. [NL, from Gk *askídion,* diminutive of *askós* bag]

**ascites** /ə'saɪtiz/, *n.* an abnormal collection of fluid in the peritoneal cavity. [L, from Gk *askítēs* a kind of dropsy, from *askós* bag, belly] **– ascitic** /ə'sɪtɪk/, *adj.*

**asclepiad** /əs'klipiæd/, *n.* a plant belonging to the Asclepiadaceae, or milkweed family of plants. [NL *Asclēpias* the milkweed genus (Gk. *asklēpiás* kind of plant, named after *Asklēpiós* Asclepius, the Gk god of medicine)] **– asclepiadaceous,** *adj.*

**Asclepiadean** /əsˌklipiə'diən/, *Class. Pros. –adj.* **1.** denoting or pertaining to a kind of verse consisting of a spondee, two (or three) choriambi, and an iamb. *–n.* **2.** an Asclepiadean verse. [so called after the Greek poet *Asclepiades*]

**asco-,** a word element meaning 'bag'. [Gk *asko-,* combining form of *askós*]

**ascocarp** /'æskoʊkap/, *n.* (in ascomycetous fungi) the fructification bearing the asci, a general term embracing apothecium, perithecium, etc.

**ascogonium** /æskə'goʊniəm/, *n., pl.* **-nia** /-niə/. (in certain ascomycetous fungi) **1.** the female sexual organ; the archicarp. **2.** the portion of the archicarp which receives the antheridial nuclei and puts out the hyphae bearing the asci. **– ascogonial,** *adj.*

**ascomycete** /ˌæskəmaɪ'sit/, *n.* a fungus of the class Ascomycetes, including the yeasts, mildews, truffles, etc., characterised by bearing the sexual spores in a sac.

**ascorbic acid** /əskɔbɪk 'æsəd/, *n.* the antiscorbutic vitamin, or vitamin C, found in citrus fruits, tomatoes, capsicum, and green vegetables, and also made industrially.

**ascospore** /ˈæskəspɔ/, *n.* a spore formed in an ascus. – **ascosporous, ascosporic** /æskəˈspɔrɪk/, *adj.*

**ascribe** /əˈskraɪb/, *v.t.,* **ascribed, ascribing. 1.** to attribute impute, or refer, as to a cause or source; assign: *the alphabet is usually ascribed to the Phoenicians.* **2.** to consider or allege to belong. [L *ascrībere* add to a writing; replacing ME *ascrive(n),* from OF *ascriv-,* stem of *ascrire*] – **ascribable,** *adj.*

**ascription** /əˈskrɪpʃən/, *n.* **1.** the act of ascribing. **2.** a statement ascribing something, specifically, praise to the Deity. Also, **adscription.**

**ascus** /ˈæskəs/, *n., pl.* **asci** /ˈæski/. the sac in ascomycetes in which the sexual spores are formed. [NL, from Gk *askós* bag, wineskin, bladder]

**asdic** /ˈæzdɪk/, *n.* a device to determine the presence and location of objects under water by measuring the direction and return time of a sound echo. [acronym from *Allied Submarine Detection Investigation Committee*]

**-ase,** a noun suffix used in names of enzymes, as in *lactase, pectase.* [from (DIAST)ASE]

**ASEAN** /ˈæziæn, ˈæs-/, Association of South-East Asian Nations.

**asepsis** /əˈsɛpsəs, eɪ-/, *n.* **1.** absence of the micro-organisms that produce sepsis or septic disease. **2.** *Med.* methods or treatment, as by surgical operation, characterised by the use of instruments, dressings, etc., that are free from such micro-organisms. [A-[6] + SEPSIS]

**aseptic** /eɪˈsɛptɪk/, *adj.* free from the living germs of disease, fermentation, or putrefaction. – **aseptically,** *adv.*

**asexual** /eɪˈsɛkʃuəl/, *adj.* **1.** not sexual. **2.** having no sex or no sexual organs. **3.** independent of sexual processes. – **asexuality** /ˌeɪsɛkʃuˈæləti/, *n.* – **asexually,** *adv.*

**ash**[1] /æʃ/, *n.* **1.** (*usu. pl., used as sing. chiefly in scientific and commercial language*) the powdery residue of matter that remains after burning: *hot ashes, soda ash.* **2.** *Geol.* finely pulverised lava thrown out by a volcano in eruption. See **ashes.** [ME; OE *asce, æsce*]

**ash**[2] /æʃ/, *n.* **1.** any tree of the genus *Fraxinus,* family Oleaceae, of the Northern Hemisphere. **2.** the wood, tough, straight-grained, and elastic, and valued as timber. **3.** any of many Southern Hemisphere trees whose timber or foliage resembles that of the ash, esp. species of the genera *Eucalyptus, Flindersia* and *Elaeocarpus.* [ME *asch,* OE *æsc,* c. G *Esche*]

**ash**[3] /æʃ/, *n.* the name of the old English letter *æ.* See **æ** (def. 2).

**ashamed** /əˈʃeɪmd/, *adj.* **1.** feeling shame; abashed by guilt. **2.** unwilling or restrained through fear of shame: *ashamed to speak.* **3.** loath to acknowledge (fol. by *of*): *ashamed of her husband.* – **ashamedly** /əˈʃeɪmədli/, *adv.* – **ashamedness,** *n.*

**ash-blond** /ˈæʃ-blɒnd/, *adj.;* /æʃ-ˈblɒnd/, *n.* –*adj.* **1.** very light blond in colour. –*n.* **2.** a person with ash-blond hair.

**ash can** /ˈæʃ kæn/, *n. U.S.* →**garbage bin.**

**ashen**[1] /ˈæʃən/, *adj.* **1.** ash-coloured; grey. **2.** consisting of ashes. [ASH[1] + -EN[2]]

**ashen**[2] /ˈæʃən/, *adj.* **1.** pertaining to the ash tree or its timber. **2.** made of wood from the ash tree. [ASH[2] + -EN[2]]

**ashes** /ˈæʃəz/, *n. pl.* **1.** ruins, as from destruction by burning: *the ashes of an ancient empire.* **2.** the remains of the human body after cremation. **3.** a dead body or corpse; mortal remains. **4. the Ashes,** the trophy, a wooden urn containing a cremated cricket stump, kept permanently in England, played for by England and Australia in test cricket.

**ashet** /ˈæʃət/, *n. Chiefly Scot.* a type of platter, esp. for serving meat. [F *assiette,* from MF, seating of guests at a table, course at a meal.]

**ash fall** /ˈæʃ fɔl/, *n.* **1.** a rain of airborne volcanic ash falling from the cloud which follows an eruption. **2.** a deposit of volcanic ash resulting from such a fall and found lying on the ground surface.

**ash flow** /ˈæʃ floʊ/, *n.* **1.** an avalanche of volcanic ash, generally a highly heated mixture of volcanic gases and ash and produced by sudden explosion. **2.** a deposit of volcanic ash and other debris resulting from such a flow and found lying on the ground surface.

**ash-grey** /æʃ-ˈgreɪ/, *n., adj.* pale grey of ashes. Also, **ash colour.**

**Ashkenazim** /æʃkəˈnazəm/, *n. pl., sing.* **-nazi.** central or eastern European Jews (as distinguished from the *Sephardim* or Spanish-Portuguese Jews). [Heb., pl. of *Ashk'naz,* a descendant of Japheth (Gen. 10:3); also, in medieval use, Germany] – **Ashkenazic,** *adj.*

**ashlar** /ˈæʃlə/, *n.* **1.** a squared block of building stone, finished or rough. **2.** such stones collectively. **3.** masonry made of them. **4.** one of the pieces of timber used in ashlaring; a stud. Also, **ashler.** [ME *asheler,* from OF *aisselier,* from L *axis* board]

**ashlaring** /ˈæʃlərɪŋ/, *n.* pieces of timber fixed between the rafters and floor joists of an attic to form a partition wall cutting off the angle where the joists and rafters meet. Also, **ashlar pieces, ashlering.**

**ashlering** /ˈæʃlərɪŋ/, *n.* **1.** →**ashlar** (def. 3). **2.** →**ashlaring.**

**ashore** /əˈʃɔ/, *adv.* **1.** to shore; on or to the land. –*adj.* **2.** on land (opposed to *aboard* or *afloat*).

**ashram** /ˈæʃræm, ˈɒʃrəm/, *n.* a community of people, together for spiritual development, as through yoga, meditation, etc. [Skt *āsʼrama,* from *ā* towards near to + *sʼrama* fatigue, exertion, religious exercise]

**ashtray** /ˈæʃtreɪ/, *n.* a small tray, saucer, or bowl for tobacco ash.

**ashy** /ˈæʃi/, *adj.,* **ashier, ashiest. 1.** ash-coloured; pale. **2.** of ashes. **3.** sprinkled or covered with ashes.

**ASI** /eɪ ɛs ˈaɪ/, air speed indicator.

**Asian** /ˈeɪʒən, ˈeɪʃən/, *adj.* **1.** of or belonging to, or characteristic of the continent of Asia or its inhabitants. –*n.* **2.** a native of Asia. – **Asianic** /eɪʒiˈænɪk/, *adj.*

**Asian flu** /– ˈflu/, *n.* a form of influenza caused by a virus believed to have been carried from Asia. Also, **Asian influenza;** *Chiefly U.S.,* **Asiatic flu, Asiatic influenza.**

**Asiatic** /eɪʒiˈætɪk, -zi-/, *adj., n.* →**Asian.**

**Asiatic cholera** /– ˈkɒlərə/, *n.* an infectious epidemic disease, which is often fatal, originally from Asia. See **cholera** (def. 1b).

**A side** /ˈeɪ saɪd/, *n.* the principal side of a gramophone record.

**aside** /əˈsaɪd/, *adv.* **1.** on or to one side; to or at a short distance; apart; away from some position or direction: *to turn aside.* **2.** away from one's thoughts or consideration: *to put one's cares aside.* –*n.* **3.** *Theat.* a part of an actor's lines not supposed to be heard by others on the stage and intended only for the audience. **4.** words spoken in an undertone, so as not to be heard by some of the people present. **5.** a remark or comment which is incidental to the main subject.

**asinine** /ˈæsənaɪn/, *adj.* stupid; obstinate. [L *asinīnus,* from *asinus* ass] – **asininely,** *adv.* – **asininity** /æsəˈnɪnəti/, *n.*

**ASIO** /ˈeɪzioʊ, ˈæzioʊ/, Australian Security Intelligence Organisation. Also, **A.S.I.O.**

**-asis,** a word element forming names of diseases. [L, from Gk]

**ASIS** /ˈeɪzəs/, Australian Secret Intelligence Service. Also, **A.S.I.S.**

**ask** /ask/, *v.t.* **1.** to put a question to: *ask him.* **2.** to seek to be informed about: *to ask the way;* (or, with a double object) *to ask him the way.* **3.** to seek by words to obtain; request: *to ask advice or a favour.* **4.** to solicit; request of (with a personal object, and with or without *for* before the thing desired): *I ask you a great favour, ask him for advice.* **5.** to demand; expect: *to ask a price for something.* **6.** to call for; require: *the job asks time.* **7.** to invite: *to ask guests.* **8.** *Archaic.* to publish (banns); publish the banns of (person). **9. I ask you,** (an exclamatory phrase indicating surprise, disgust, disdain etc.). **10. if you ask me,** (a rhetorical phrase meaning 'in my opinion'). –*v.i.* **11.** to make inquiry; inquire: *she asked after or about him.* **12.** to request or petition (fol. by *for*): *ask for bread.* **13. ask for it (trouble),** *Colloq.* to behave so as to invite trouble. **14. ask (someone) out,** to ask a member of the opposite sex to a social engagement. [ME *asken,* OE *āscian,* also *ācsian,* c. OHG *eiscōn*] – **asker,** *n.*

**askance** /əsˈkæns/, *adv.* **1.** with suspicion, mistrust, or disapproval: *he looked askance at my offer.* **2.** with a side glance; sideways. Also, **askant** /əsˈkænt/. [orig. uncert.]

**askew** /əs'kju/, *adv.* **1.** to one side; out of line; obliquely; awry. *–adj.* **2.** oblique. [A-[1] + SKEW]

**asking price** /'askɪŋ praɪs/, *n.* the price demanded by a seller, usu. considered as subject to bargaining or discount.

**aslant** /ə'slænt/, *adv.* **1.** at a slant; slantingly; obliquely. *–adj.* **2.** slanting; oblique. *–prep.* **3.** slantingly across; athwart. [ME *on slont, on slent* on slope. Cf. Sw. *slänt* slope]

**asleep** /ə'slip/, *adv.* **1.** in or into a state of sleep. *–adj.* **2.** sleeping. **3.** dormant; inactive. **4.** (of the foot, hand, leg, etc.) numb. **5.** dead.

**aslope** /ə'sloʊp/, *adv.* **1.** at a slope. *–adj.* **2.** sloping.

**asocial** /eɪ'soʊʃəl/, *adj.* **1.** *Psychol., Sociol., etc.* avoiding or withdrawn from the environment; not social. **2.** inconsiderate of others; selfish; not scrupulous.

**asp**[1] /æsp/, *n.* **1.** any of several poisonous snakes, esp. the Egyptian cobra, *Naja naja,* said to have caused Cleopatra's death, and much used by snake-charmers. **2.** the common European viper or adder. **3.** *Archeol.* →**uraeus.** [L *aspis,* from Gk]

**asp**[2] /æsp/, *n., adj. Poetic or Obs.* aspen. [OE *æspe* (see ASPEN)]

**asparagine** /ə'spærədʒin, -dʒaɪn/, *n.* an amino acid, $NH_2^-COCH_2CH(NH_3^+)COO^-$, occurring in proteins; the amide from aspartic acid. [from ASPARAGUS]

**asparagus** /ə'spærəgəs/, *n.* **1.** any plant of the genus *Asparagus,* esp. *A. officinalis,* cultivated for its edible shoots. **2.** the shoots, used as a table vegetable. [L, from Gk *aspáragos*]

**aspartic acid** /əspatɪk 'æsəd/, *n.* an amino acid, $HOO\ CCH_2\ CH(NH_3^+)COO^-$, found esp. in young sugar cane and sugar-beet. [*Aspartic,* from ASPARAGUS, because it is obtained from an amino acid found in asparagus]

**aspect** /'æspɛkt/, *n.* **1.** appearance to the eye or mind; look: *the physical aspect of the country.* **2.** countenance; facial expression. **3.** a way in which a thing may be viewed or regarded: *both aspects of a question.* **4.** view commanded; exposure: *the house has a southern aspect.* **5.** the side or surface facing a given direction: *the dorsal aspect of a fish.* **6.** *Gram.* **a.** (in some languages) a category of verb inflection denoting various relations of the action or state of the verb to the passage of time, as duration, repetition, or completion. Examples: *he ate* (completed action); *he was eating* (incompleted action); *he ate and ate* (durative action). **b.** (in other languages) one of several contrasting constructions with similar meanings: *the durative aspect.* **c.** a set of such categories or constructions in a particular language. **d.** the meaning of, or typical of, such a category or construction. **e.** such categories or constructions, or their meanings collectively. **7.** *Astrol.* the relative position of planets as determining their influence. **8.** *Archaic.* a look; glance. [ME from L *aspectus,* from *aspicere* look at]

**aspect ratio** /– 'reɪʃioʊ/, *n.* **1.** *Aeron, Naut.* the ratio between the dimension at right angles to the motion, and the dimension parallel to the motion; thus for an aerofoil the ratio of the span to the mean chord, for a fore-and-aft sail the ratio of the luff to the foot, etc. **2.** *Television.* the ratio of the width of an image to its height.

**aspectual** /æs'pɛktʃuəl/, *adj. Gram.* **1.** of, pertaining to, or producing a particular aspect or aspects. **2.** used as or like a form inflected for a particular aspect.

**aspen** /'æspən/, *n.* **1.** any of various species of poplar, as *Populus tremula* of Europe, and *P. tremuloides* (**quaking aspen**) or *P. alba* (**white aspen**) in America, with leaves that tremble in the slightest breeze. *–adj.* **2.** of or pertaining to the aspen. **3.** trembling or quivering, like the leaves of the aspen. [ME *aspen,* adj., from *asp* white poplar (OE *æspe*) + -EN[2]]

**aspergillosis** /æs,pɜdʒə'loʊsəs/, *n., pl.* **-ses** /-siz/. disease in an animal caused by aspergilli.

**aspergillum** /æspə'dʒɪləm/, *n., pl.* **-gilla** /-dʒɪlə/, **-gillums.** a brush or instrument for sprinkling holy water; aspersorium. [L *aspergere* sprinkle + *-illum,* diminutive suffix]

**aspergillus** /æspə'dʒɪləs/, *n., pl.* **-gilli** /-dʒɪli/. any fungus of the genus *Aspergillus,* family Aspergillaceae, whose sporophores are distinguished by a bristly, knoblike top. [See ASPERGILLUM]

**asperity** /æs'pɛrəti, əs-/, *n., pl.* **-ties. 1.** roughness or sharpness of temper; severity; acrimony. **2.** hardship; difficulty; rigour. **3.** roughness of surface; unevenness. **4.** something rough or harsh. [L *asperitas* roughness; replacing ME *asprete,* from OF]

**asperse** /ə'spɜs/, *v.t.,* **aspersed, aspersing. 1.** to assail with damaging charges or insinuations; cast reproach upon; slander. **2.** to sprinkle; bespatter. [L *aspersus,* pp., sprinkled] – **asperser,** *n.*

**aspersion** /ə'spɜʒən, -spɜʃən/, *n.* **1.** a damaging imputation; a derogatory criticism: *to cast aspersions on one's character.* **2.** the act of aspersing: *to baptise by aspersion.* **3.** a shower or spray.

**aspersorium** /æspə'sɔriəm/, *n., pl.* **-soria** /-'sɔriə/, **-soriums. 1.** a vessel for holding holy water. **2.** →**aspergillum.** [ML. See ASPERSE, -ORIUM]

**asphalt** /'æʃfɛlt, 'æsfɛlt/, *n.* **1.** any of various dark-coloured, solid bituminous substances, composed mostly of mixtures of hydrocarbons, occurring native in various parts of the earth. **2.** a similar artificial substance, the byproduct of petroleum-cracking operations. **3.** a mixture of such a substance with crushed rock, etc., used for roads, etc. *–v.t.* **4.** to cover or pave with asphalt. Also, **asphaltum.** [LL *asphaltum,* from Gk *ásphalton*] – **asphaltic,** *adj.* – **asphalt-like,** *adj.*

**asphodel** /'æsfədɛl/, *n.* **1.** any of various liliaceous plants of the genera *Asphodelus* and *Asphodeline,* native to southern Europe, with white, pink, or yellow flowers; in Greek mythology, the flower of the dead. **2.** any of various other plants, as the daffodil. [L *asphodelus,* from Gk *asphódelos*]

**asphyxia** /əs'fɪksiə/, *n. Pathol.* the extreme condition caused by lack of oxygen and excess of carbon dioxide in the blood, caused by sufficient interference with respiration, as in choking. [Gk: stopping of the pulse]

**asphyxiant** /əs'fɪksiənt/, *adj.* **1.** asphyxiating or tending to asphyxiate. *–n.* **2.** an asphyxiating agent or substance. **3.** an asphyxiating condition.

**asphyxiate** /əs'fɪksieɪt/, *v.,* **-ated, -ating.** *–v.t.* **1.** to produce asphyxia in. *–v.i.* **2.** to become asphyxiated. – **asphyxiation** /æsfɪksi'eɪʃən/, *n.* – **asphyxiator,** *n.*

**aspic**[1] /'æspɪk/, *n.* **1.** a cold dish of meat, fish, etc., served set in a jellied mould. **2.** the jellied garnish, made from fish or meat stock, sometimes with added gelatine. [F, ? from ASPIC[2] (snake) from the different colours of the jelly, like those of a snake]

**aspic**[2] /'æspɪk/, *n. Poetic.* an asp[1]. [F, from L *aspis*]

**aspic**[3] /'æspɪk/, *n.* the great lavender, *Lavandula latifolia,* yielding an oil used in perfumery. [F, from ML (*lavendula*) *spīca* (lavender) spike]

**aspidistra** /æspə'dɪstrə/, *n.* a smooth, stemless Asian herb, *Aspidistra elatior,* family Liliaceae, bearing large evergreen leaves often striped with white, once widely grown as a house plant; often seen as a symbol of genteel respectability. [NL, from Gk *aspís* shield]

**aspirant** /'æspərənt, ə'spaɪrənt/, *n.* **1.** a person who aspires; one who seeks advancement, honours, a high position, etc. *–adj.* **2.** *Rare.* aspiring.

**aspirate** /'æspəreɪt/, *v.,* **-rated, -rating;** /'æspərət/, *n. adj.* *–v.t.* **1.** *Phonet.* **a.** to release (a stop) in such a way that the breath escapes with audible friction, as in *title* where the first *t* is aspirated, the second is not. **b.** to begin (a word or syllable) with an *h* sound, as in *when* (pronounced *hwen*), *howl,* opposed to *wen, owl.* **2.** *Med.* to remove (fluids) from body cavities by use of an aspirator. **3.** to draw or remove by suction. *–n.* **4.** *Phonet.* a puff of unvoiced air before or after another sound, represented in many languages by *h,* and in Greek by the sign of rough breathing (῾). *–adj.* **5.** *Phonet.* aspirated. [L *aspīrātus,* pp., breathed on]

**aspiration** /æspə'reɪʃən/, *n.* **1.** the act of aspiring; lofty or ambitious desire. **2.** an act of aspirating; a breath. **3.** *Phonet.* **a.** the fricative unstopping or release of a stop consonant, as in *too,* where the breath escapes with audible friction as the *t* is brought to an end by the withdrawal of the tongue from contact with the alveolar ridge. **b.** the use of an aspirate in pronunciation. **4.** *Med.* the act of removing a fluid, as pus or serum, from a cavity of the body, by a hollow needle or trocar connected with a suction syringe.

**aspirator** /'æspəreɪtə/, *n.* **1.** an apparatus or device employing suction. **2.** a jet pump used in laboratories to produce a partial vacuum. **3.** *Med.* an instrument for removing fluids from the body by suction.

**aspiratory** /ə'spɪrətri/, *adj.* pertaining to or suited for aspiration.

**aspire** /ə'spaɪə/, *v.i.*, **-spired, -spiring.** **1.** to long, aim, or seek ambitiously; be eagerly desirous, esp. for something great or lofty (fol. by *to, after,* or an infinitive): *to aspire after immortality, to aspire to be a leader among men.* **2.** *Archaic or Poetic.* to rise up; soar; mount; tower. [ME *aspyre,* from L *aspīrāre* breathe on] – **aspirer,** *n.* – **aspiring,** *adj.*

**aspirin** /'æsprən/, *n.* **1.** a white crystalline derivative of salicylic acid, $C_9H_8O_4$, used to relieve the pain of headache, rheumatism, gout, neuralgia, etc.; acetylsalicylic acid. **2.** a tablet of aspirin. [G (orig. trademark): *A(cetyl)* ACETYL + *Spir(säure)* salicylic (acid) (see SPIRAEA) + -in -IN[2]]

**asprawl** /ə'sprɔl/, *adv.* sprawling; in a sprawl.

**aspro**[1] /'æsproʊ/, *n. Colloq.* Associate Professor. [Abbrev.]

**aspro**[2] /'æsproʊ, 'as-/, *n. Colloq.* a male prostitute. [ARSE + PRO(FESSIONAL); pun on the trademark Aspro, a form of ASPIRIN]

**asquint** /ə'skwɪnt/, *adv.* with an oblique glance. [A-[1] + *squint* (of obscure orig.; cf. D *schuinte* slope)]

**ass** /æs/, *n.* **1.** a long-eared, usu. ash-coloured mammal, *Equus asinus,* related to the horse, serving as a slow, patient, sure-footed beast of burden; the donkey. **2.** any allied wild species, as the **Mongolian wild ass,** *E. hemionus.* **3.** a fool; a blockhead. **4.** *Colloq. U.S.* →**arse.** [ME; OE *assa,* from OWelsh *asyn* ass, from L *asinus*]

ass

**Ass.,** **1.** Assistant. **2.** Association.

**assagai** /'æsəgaɪ/, *n., pl.* **-gais,** *v.t.,* **-gaied, -gaiing.** →**assegai.**

**assai** /ə'saɪ/, *adv.* (a musical direction) very: *allegro assai* (very quick). [It.]

**assail** /ə'seɪl/, *v.t.* **1.** to set upon with violence; assault. **2.** to set upon vigorously with arguments, entreaties, abuse, etc. **3.** to undertake with the purpose of mastering. [ME *asaile(n),* from OF *asalir,* from VL *adsalīre,* from L: *ad-* AD- + *salīre* leap] – **assailable,** *adj.* – **assailer,** *n.* – **assailment,** *n.*

**assailant** /ə'seɪlənt/, *n.* **1.** one who assails. *–adj.* **2.** assailing; attacking.

**assassin** /ə'sæsən/, *n.* one who undertakes to murder, esp. from fanaticism or for a reward. [named after one of an order of Muslim fanatics, active in Persia and Syria from about 1090 to 1272, whose chief object was to assassinate Crusaders; F, from ML *assassīnus,* from Ar. *hashshāshin,* pl., hashish eaters]

**assassinate** /ə'sæsəneɪt/, *v.t.,* **-nated, -nating.** **1.** to kill by sudden or secret, premeditated assault, esp. for political or religious motives. **2.** to blight or destroy treacherously: *to assassinate a person's character.* [ML *assassīnātus,* pp.] – **assassination** /əsæsə'neɪʃən/, *n.* – **assassinator,** *n.*

**assassin bug** /ə'sæsən bʌg/, *n.* any insect of the heteropterous family Reduviidae, most of which are predacious and some of which are blood-sucking parasites of warm-blooded animals.

**assault** /ə'sɒlt, -'sɔlt/, *n.* **1.** the act of assailing; an attack; onslaught. **2.** *Mil.* the stage of close combat in an attack. **3.** *Law.* an unlawful physical attack upon another; an attempt or offer to do violence to another, with or without a battery, as by holding a stone or club in a threatening manner. **4.** →**indecent assault.** *–v.t.* **5.** to make an assault upon; attack; assail. **6.** to rape or attempt to rape. [ME *assaut,* from OF, from *asalir* ASSAIL] – **assaulter,** *n.*

**assault and battery,** *n. Law.* an assault with an actual touching or other violence upon another.

**assay** /ə'seɪ/, *v.*; /ə'seɪ, 'æseɪ/, *n.* *–v.t.* **1.** to examine by trial; put to test or trial: *to assay one's strength.* **2.** *Metall.* **a.** to test ores or minerals by chemical methods. **b.** to determine the proportions of metals in ores by smelting. **3.** *Pharm., etc.* to subject (a drug, etc.) to an analysis for the determination of its potency. **4.** to try in combat. **5.** to attempt; endeavour; essay. **6.** to judge the quality of; evaluate. *–v.i.* **7.** to make an attempt; endeavour; try. **8.** *U.S.* to contain, as shown by analysis, a certain proportion of (usu. precious) metal. *–n.* **9.** *Metall.* an examination of a mineral ore or alloy to determine certain constituents. **10.** *Pharm., etc.* determination of the strength, purity, etc., of a pharmaceutical substance or ingredient. **11.** a substance undergoing analysis or trial. **12.** a listing of the findings in assaying a substance. **13.** examination; trial; attempt; essay. [ME, from OF, from LL *exagium* a weighing. Cf. ESSAY, *n.*] – **assayer,** *n.* – **assayable,** *adj.*

**assegai** /'æsəgaɪ/, *n., pl.* **-gais,** *v.,* **-gaied, -gaing,** or **-gaiing.** *–n.* **1.** the slender throwing spear of the Bantu peoples of southern Africa. **2.** a South African tree, *Curtisia faginea,* from whose wood such spears are made. *–v.t.* **3.** to pierce with an assegai. Also, **assagai.** [Sp. *azagaya,* from Ar. *al* the + (Berber) *zaghāyah* spear]

**assemblage** /ə'sɛmblɪdʒ/, *n.* **1.** a number of persons or things assembled; an assembly. **2.** the act of assembling. **3.** the state of being assembled. **4.** *Art.* **a.** a method of composing a three-dimensional work of art by combining different elements, as found objects and painting and sculpture by the artist, on a hanging surface or independently of the wall. **b.** a construction thus composed. [F]

**assemble** /ə'sɛmbəl/, *v.,* **-bled, -bling.** *–v.t.* **1.** to bring together; gather into one place, company, body or whole. **2.** to put or fit (parts) together; put together the parts of (a mechanism, etc.). *–v.i.* **3.** to come together; gather; meet. [ME *as(s)emble(n),* from OF *as(s)embler,* from LL **assimulāre* compare, imitate]

**assemblé** /asɒm'bleɪ/, *n.* (in ballet) a leap with one leg extended, followed by a landing with the feet crossed. [F]

**assembler** /ə'sɛmblə/, *n.* **1.** one who or that which assembles. **2.** *Computers.* a program which converts symbolic language to machine language on a word for word basis.

**assembly** /ə'sɛmbli/, *n., pl.* **-blies.** **1.** a company of persons gathered together, usu. for the same purpose, whether religious, political, educational, or social. **2.** (*cap.*) *Govt.* a legislative body, sometimes esp. a lower house of a legislature. **3.** the act of assembling. **4.** the state of being assembled. **5.** *Mil.* a signal, as by drum or bugle, for troops to fall into ranks or otherwise assemble. **6.** the putting together of complex machinery, as aeroplanes, from interchangeable parts of standard dimensions. **7.** such parts, before or after assembling. [ME *as(s)emblee,* from OF]

**assembly anchorage** /'– æŋkərɪdʒ/, *n. Mil.* an anchorage or port intended primarily for the assembly and onward routing of ocean-going shipping.

**assembly line** /'– laɪn/, *n.* an arrangement of machines, tools, and workers in which each worker performs a special operation on an incomplete unit, which usually passes down a line of workers until it is finished.

**assent** /ə'sɛnt/, *v.i.* **1.** to agree by expressing acquiescence or admitting truth; express agreement or concurrence (oft. fol. by *to*): *to assent to a statement.* *–n.* **2.** agreement, as to a proposal; acquiescence; concurrence. **3.** Also, **Royal assent.** the formal act of recognition by the sovereign's representative (the Governor-General in Federal Parliament, the Governor in State Parliaments) which transforms a parliamentary bill into an act of parliament. [ME *as(s)ente(n),* from OF *as(s)enter,* from L *assentārī,* frequentative of *assentīrī*] – **assenter,** *n.*

**assert** /ə'sɜt/, *v.t.* **1.** to state as true; affirm; declare: *to assert that one is innocent.* **2.** to maintain or defend (claims, rights, etc.). **3.** to put (oneself) forward boldly and insistently. [L *assertus,* pp., joined to] – **asserter, assertor,** *n.*

**assertion** /ə'sɜʃən/, *n.* **1.** a positive statement; an unsupported declaration. **2.** the act of asserting.

**assertive** /ə'sɜtɪv/, *adj.* given to asserting; positive; dogmatic. – **assertively,** *adv.* – **assertiveness,** *n.*

**assertoric** /æsɜ'tɒrɪk/, *adj. Logic.* (in Kantian logic) descriptive of a proposition or judgment which claims to be true, but is not necessarily true.

**assertory** /ə'sɜtəri/, *adj.* affirming; assertive.

**asses' bridge** /æsəz 'brɪdʒ/, *n. Geom.* →**pons asinorum.**

**assess** /ə'sɛs/, *v.t.* **1.** to estimate officially the value of (property, income, etc.) as a basis for taxation (fol. by *at*): *the property was assessed at two million dollars.* **2.** to fix or determine the amount of (damages, a tax, a fine, etc.). **3.** to impose a tax or other charge on. [ME *assesse(n),* from OF *assesser,* from LL *assessāre* fix a tax, frequentative of L *assidēre* sit at] – **assessable,** *adj.*

**assessment** /ə'sɛsmənt/, *n.* **1.** the act of assessing. **2.** an amount assessed as payable; an official valuation of taxable property, etc., or the value assigned.

**assessor** /ə'sɛsə/, *n.* **1.** one who makes assessments, as of damage for insurance purposes, or of property, etc., for taxation purposes. **2.** an advisory associate or assistant. **3.** one who advises a court on questions which involve technical or scientific knowledge. **4.** one who shares another's position, rank, or dignity. [L: assistant judge, ML assessor of taxes; replacing ME *assessour,* from OF] – **assessorial** /ˌæsɛ'sɔriəl/, *adj.*

**asset** /'æsɛt/, *n.* **1.** a useful thing or quality: *neatness is an asset.* **2.** a single item of property.

**asset backing** /'– bækɪŋ/, *n.* support for a commercial enterprise provided by its assets.

**assets** /'æsɛts/, *n.pl.* **1.** *Comm.* resources of a person or business consisting of such items as real property, machinery, inventories, notes, securities, cash, etc. **2.** property or effects (opposed to *liabilities*). **3.** *Accounting.* the detailed listing of property owned by a firm and money owing to it. **4.** *Law.* **a.** property in the hands of an executor or administrator sufficient to pay the debts or legacies of the testator or intestate. **b.** any property available for paying debts, etc. [ME, from AF, from OF *asetz,* adv., enough, taken as pl. noun, from L *ad-* AD- + *satis* enough]

**asset-stripping** /'æsɛt-strɪpɪŋ/, *n.* the practice of buying up a business with the intention of transferring its assets to one's own company and then discarding it.

**asseverate** /ə'sɛvəreɪt/, *v.t.,* **-rated, -rating.** to declare earnestly or solemnly; affirm positively. [L *asseverātus,* pp.]

**asseveration** /ə'sɛvəreɪʃən/, *n.* **1.** the act of asseverating. **2.** an emphatic assertion.

**assibilate** /ə'sɪbəleɪt/, *v.,* **-lated, -lating.** *Phonet. –v.t.* **1.** to change into or pronounce with the accompaniment of a sibilant sound or sounds. *–v.i.* **2.** to change by assibilation. **3.** to become a sibilant or a sound containing a sibilant. – **assibilation** /əsɪbə'leɪʃən/, *n.*

**assiduity** /æsɪ'djuəti/, *n., pl.* **-ties.** **1.** constant or close application; diligence. **2.** (*pl.*) devoted or solicitous attentions.

**assiduous** /ə'sɪdʒuəs/, *adj.* **1.** constant; unremitting: *assiduous reading.* **2.** constant in application; attentive; devoted. [L *assiduus* sitting down to] – **assiduously,** *adv.* – **assiduousness,** *n.*

**assign** /ə'saɪn/, *v.t.* **1.** to make over or give, as in distribution; allot: *assign rooms at a hotel.* **2.** to appoint, as to a post or duty: *assign to stand guard.* **3.** (formerly) to allocate a convict for employment by an officer or settler. **4.** to designate; specify: *to assign a day.* **5.** to ascribe; attribute; refer: *to assign a reason.* **6.** *Law.* to transfer: *to assign a contract.* **7.** *Mil.* to place permanently on duty with a unit or under a commander. *–v.i.* **8.** *Law.* to transfer property, esp. in trust for the benefit of creditors. *–n.* **9.** (*usu. pl.*) *Law.* a person to whom the property or interest of another is or may be transferred: *my heirs and assigns.* [ME *assigne(n)* from OF *as(s)igner,* from L *assignāre*] – **assigner;** *Chiefly Law,* **assignor** /æsɪ'nɔ/, *n.*

**assignable** /ə'saɪnəbəl/, *adj.* **1.** capable of being specified. **2.** capable of being attributed. **3.** *Law.* capable of being assigned. **4.** (formerly) of a convict, suitable for assignment. – **assignability** /əsaɪnə'bɪləti/, *n.* – **assignably,** *adv.*

**assignation** /æsɪg'neɪʃən/, *n.* **1.** an appointment for a meeting, now esp. an illicit love-meeting. **2.** the act of assigning; assignment.

**assignee** /əsaɪ'ni/, *n.* **1.** *Law.* one to whom some right or interest is transferred, either for his own enjoyment or in trust. **2.** (formerly) a convict assigned as a servant.

**assignment** /ə'saɪnmənt/, *n.* **1.** something assigned, as a particular task or duty. **2.** the act of assigning. **3.** *Law.* **a.** the transference of a right, interest, or title, or the instrument of transfer. **b.** a transference of property to assignees for the benefit of creditors.

**assignment system** /'– sɪstəm/, *n.* (formerly) a system under which convicts in Australia were assigned to settlers as servants and labourers, discontinued in 1841.

**assimilable** /ə'sɪmələbəl/, *adj.* capable of being assimilated. – **assimilability** /əˌsɪmələ'bɪləti/, *n.*

**assimilate** /ə'sɪməleɪt/, *v.,* **-lated, -lating.** *–v.t.* **1.** to take in and incorporate as one's own; absorb (fol. by *to* or *with*). **2.** *Physiol.* to convert (food, etc.) into a substance suitable for absorption into the system. **3.** to make like; cause to resemble (fol. by *to* or *with*). **4.** to compare; liken (fol. by *to* or *with*). **5.** *Phonet.* to articulate more like another sound in the same utterance, as *ant* for earlier *amt.* *–v.i.* **6.** to be or become absorbed. **7.** *Physiol.* (of food, etc.) to be converted into the substance of the body; be absorbed into the system. **8.** to become or be like; resemble (fol. by *to* or *with*). [L *assimilātus,* pp., likened]

**assimilation** /əsɪmə'leɪʃən/, *n.* **1.** the act or process of assimilating. **2.** the state or condition of being assimilated. **3.** *Physiol.* the conversion of absorbed food into the substance of the body. **4.** *Bot.* the total process of plant nutrition, including absorption of external foods and photosynthesis. **5.** *Zool.* the resemblance of an animal to its surroundings, in both shape and colour. **6.** the process whereby individuals or groups of differing ethnic heritage, as migrant groups, or minority groups, acquire the basic attitudes, habits and mode of life of another all-embracing national culture. (distinguished from *acculturation*). **7.** *Phonet.* the changing of a sound to one more like, or the same as, another sound near it.

**assimilative** /ə'sɪmələtɪv/, *adj.* characterised by assimilation; assimilating. Also, **assimilatory** /ə'sɪmələtri/.

**assist** /ə'sɪst/, *v.t.* **1.** to give support, help, or aid to in some undertaking or effort, or in time of distress. **2.** to be associated with as an assistant. *–v.i.* **3.** to give aid or help. **4.** *Obs.* to be present, as at a meeting, ceremony, etc. *–n.* **5.** *Ice Hockey.* a play which helps a team-mate to score, officially scored and credited as such. [F *assister,* from L *assistere* stand by] – **assister;** *Law,* **assistor,** *n.*

**assistance** /ə'sɪstəns/, *n.* the act of assisting; help; aid. [F; replacing ME *assystence,* from ML *assistentia*]

**assistant** /ə'sɪstənt/, *n.* **1.** one who assists a superior in some office or work; helper. *–adj.* **2.** assisting; helpful. **3.** associated with a superior in some office or work: *assistant manager.*

**assize** /ə'saɪz/, *n.* **1.** *Brit.* (*usu. pl.*) (in England and Wales) a trial session, civil or criminal, held periodically in specific locations by a judge (usu. of the High Court) on circuit through the English counties. **2.** (formerly) a legislative enactment. [ME, from OF *as(s)ise* session, from *aseeir,* from L *assidere* sit by]

**assn,** association. Also, **Assn.**

**assoc.,** **1.** associate. **2.** associated. **3.** association.

**associable** /ə'souʃiəbəl, -ʃəbəl/, *adj.* capable of being associated. [F] – **associability** /əˌsouʃiə'bɪləti, -ʃə'bɪləti/, *n.*

**associate** /ə'souʃieɪt, ə'sousieɪt/, *v.,* **-ated, -ating;** /ə'souʃiət, -siət/, *n., adj.* *–v.t.* **1.** to connect by some relation, as in thought. **2.** to join as a companion, partner, or rally. **3.** to unite; combine: *coal associated with shale.* *–v.i.* **4.** to enter into a league or union; unite. **5.** to keep company, as a friend or intimate: *to associate only with wealthy people.* *–n.* **6.** a partner in interest, as in business or in an enterprise or action. **7.** a companion or comrade: *my most intimate associates.* **8.** a confederate; an accomplice; an ally. **9.** anything usu. accompanying or associated with another; an accompaniment or concomitant. **10.** one who is admitted to a subordinate degree of membership in an association or institution: *an associate of an automobile club.* **11.** *Law.* an officer of a superior court who sits below the judge and assists him. *adj.* **12.** associated, esp. as a companion or colleague: *an associate partner.* **13.** having subordinate membership; without full rights and privileges. **14.** allied; concomitant. [orig. adj., ME *associat,* from L *associātus,* pp., joined to]

**Associate Professor** /– prə'fɛsə/, *n.* a university teacher ranking next below a professor. Cf. **reader** (def. 6).

**association** /əsousi'eɪʃən/, *n.* **1.** an organisation of people with a common purpose and having a formal structure. **2.** the act of associating. **3.** the state of being associated. **4.** companionship or intimacy. **5.** connection or combination. **6.** the connection of ideas in thought, or an idea connected with or suggested by a subject of thought. **7.** *Ecol.* a group of plants of one or more species living together under uniform environmental conditions and having a uniform and distinctive aspect. **8.** →**Association Football.** – **associational,** *adj.*

**Association Football** /–'fʊtbɔl/, *n. Brit.* →**soccer.**

**association of ideas,** *n.* the tendency of a sensation, perception, thought, etc., to recall others previously coexisting in consciousness with it or with states similar to it.

**associative** /ə'soʊʃiətɪv, -siət-/, *adj.* **1.** pertaining to or resulting from association. **2.** tending to associate or unite. – **associatively,** *adv.*

**assoil** /ə'sɔɪl/, *v.t. Archaic.* **1.** to absolve; acquit; pardon. **2.** to atone for. [ME, from OF, pres. indic. of *a(s)soldre,* from L *absolvere* loosen]

**assonance** /'æsənəns/, *n.* **1.** resemblance of sounds. **2.** a substitute for rhyme, in which the same vowel sounds, though with different consonants, are used in the terminal words of lines, as *penitent* and *reticence.* **3.** alliteration; use of the same consonant sounds and different vowels, as *cheery* and *chary.* **4.** partial agreement. [F, from *assonant,* from L *assonans,* ppr., sounding to] – **assonant,** *adj., n.* – **assonantal** /æsə'næntl/, *adj.*

**assonate** /'æsəneɪt/, *v.i.,* **-nated, -nating.** **1.** to have corresponding vowel sounds. **2.** to use assonance.

**assort** /ə'sɔt/, *v.t.* **1.** to distribute according to sort or kind; classify. **2.** to furnish with a suitable assortment or variety of goods; make up of articles likely to suit a demand. **3.** to group or classify (*with*). *–v.i.* **4.** to agree in sort or kind; be matched or suited. **5.** *Archaic.* to associate; consort. [late ME, from MF *assorter* distribute, join, from *a-* A-[5] + *sorte* kind, b. with *sort* lot, fate]

**assorted** /ə'sɔtəd/, *adj.* **1.** consisting of selected kinds; arranged in sorts or varieties. **2.** consisting of various kinds; miscellaneous. **3.** matched; suited.

**assortment** /ə'sɔtmənt/, *n.* **1.** the act of assorting; distribution; classification. **2.** an assorted collection.

**ASSR,** Autonomous Soviet Socialist Republic. Also, **A.S.S.R.**

**asst,** assistant.

**assuage** /ə'sweɪdʒ/, *v.t.,* **-suaged, -suaging.** **1.** to make milder or less severe; mitigate; ease: *to assuage grief or wrath.* **2.** to appease; satisfy: *to assuage appetite, thirst, craving, etc.* **3.** to mollify; pacify. [ME *assuage(n),* from OF *a(s)suagier,* from L: *ad-* AD- + derivative of *suāvis* sweet] – **assuagement,** *n.* – **assuager,** *n.*

**assuasive** /ə'sweɪsɪv/, *adj.* soothing; alleviative.

**assume** /ə'sjum/, *v.t.,* **-sumed, -suming.** **1.** to take for granted or without proof; suppose as a fact: *assume a principle in reasoning.* **2.** to take upon oneself; undertake: *to assume office, an obligation,* etc. **3.** to take on or put on oneself: *to assume new habits of life.* **4.** to pretend to have or be; feign: *to assume a false humility.* **5.** to appropriate or arrogate: *to assume a right to oneself.* **6.** *Archaic.* to take into relation or association; adopt. *–v.i.* **7.** to be arrogant; make presumptuous claims. [late ME, from L *assūmere* take up] – **assumable,** *adj.* – **assumer,** *n.*

**assumed** /ə'sjumd/, *adj.* **1.** pretended. **2.** taken for granted. **3.** usurped. – **assumedly** /ə'sjumədli/, *adv.*

**assuming** /ə'sjumɪŋ/, *adj.* arrogant; presuming. – **assumingly,** *adv.*

**assumpsit** /ə'sʌmsət/, *n. Law.* **1.** (formerly) a legal action for breach of a simple contract (a promise not under seal). **2.** an actionable promise. [L: he undertook]

**assumption** /ə'sʌmʃən, ə'sʌmpʃən/, *n.* **1.** the act of taking for granted or supposing. **2.** something taken for granted; a supposition. **3.** the act of taking to or upon oneself. **4.** arrogance; presumption. **5.** *Eccles.* **a.** (*oft. cap.*) the bodily taking up into heaven of the Virgin Mary after her death. **b.** (*cap.*) a feast commemorating it, celebrated on 15 August. **6.** *Logic.* the minor premise of a syllogism.

**assumptive** /ə'sʌmtɪv, ə'sʌmptɪv/, *adj.* **1.** taken for granted. **2.** characterised by assumption. **3.** presumptuous.

**assurance** /ə'ʃɔrəns, -'ʃʊə-/, *n.* **1.** a positive declaration intended to give confidence. **2.** pledge; guarantee; surety. **3.** full confidence or trust; freedom from doubt; certainty. **4.** freedom from timidity; self-reliance; courage. **5.** presumptuous boldness; impudence. **6.** insurance (now usu. restricted to life insurance). **7.** *Law.* the transference and securing of the title to property.

**assure** /ə'ʃɔ/, *v.t.,* **-sured, -suring.** **1.** to declare earnestly to; inform or tell positively. **2.** to make (one) sure or certain; convince, as by a promise or declaration. **3.** to make (a future event) sure; ensure: *this assures the success of our work.* **4.** to secure or confirm; render safe or stable: *to assure a person's position.* **5.** to give confidence to; encourage. **6.** to insure, esp. against death. **7.** *Law.* to transfer or convey (property). [ME *assure(n),* from OF *aseürer,* from LL *assēcūrāre*] – **assurer;** *Law,* **assuror,** *n.*

**assured** /ə'ʃɔd/, *adj.* **1.** made sure; sure; certain. **2.** bold; confident. **3.** boldly presumptuous. *–n.* **4.** *Insurance.* **a.** the beneficiary under a policy. **b.** the person whose life or property is covered by a policy. – **assuredly** /ə'ʃɔrədli/, *adv.* – **assuredness,** *n.*

**assurgent** /ə'sɜdʒənt/, *adj.* **1.** *Bot.* curving upwards, as leaves; ascending. **2.** *Her.* shown rising out of the sea. [L *assurgens,* ppr., rising up] – **assurgency,** *n.*

**Assyrian** /ə'sɪriən/, *adj.* **1.** pertaining to Assyria, an ancient empire in South-West Asia, to the Assyrians, or to their language. *–n.* **2.** a native or an inhabitant of Assyria. **3.** a Semitic language of the Akkadian group, spoken in northern Mesopotamia.

**Assyriology** /əˌsɪri'ɒlədʒi/, *n.* the science of Assyrian antiquities. – **Assyriologist,** *n.*

**astable** /eɪ'steɪbəl/, *adj. Electronics.* of a type of switching circuit, that has no stable states.

**astatic** /eɪ'stætɪk, ə-/, *adj.* unstable; unsteady. [Gk *ástatos* unstable + -IC] – **astatically,** *adv.* – **astaticism** /eɪ'stætəsɪzəm, ə-/, *n.*

**astatic galvanometer** /– gælvə'nɒmətə/, *n.* a moving-magnet galvanometer in which the magnets are so arranged that the earth's magnetic field (or any other uniform field) exerts no controlling torque on the moving system.

**astatine** /'æstətin, -taɪn/, *n. Chem.* a rare element of the halogen family. *Symbol:* At; *at. no.* : 85. [Gk *ástatos* unstable + -INE[2]]

**aster** /'æstə/, *n.* **1.** *Bot.* any plant of the large genus *Aster,* family Compositae, having rays varying from white or pink to blue around a yellow disc. **2.** a plant of some allied genus, as *Stokesia cyanea* (**Stoke's aster**). **3.** *Biol.* either of two star-shaped structures formed in a cell during mitosis. [L, from Gk: star]

**-aster**[1], a suffix used to form nouns denoting something that imperfectly resembles or merely apes the true thing, or an inferior or petty instance of something, as *criticaster, poetaster, oleaster.* [L]

**-aster**[2], *Chiefly Biol.* a suffix meaning 'star'. [representing Gk *astēr*]

**asteria** /æ'stɪəriə/, *n.* a precious stone which shows asterism when cabochon-cut, as the star-sapphire.

**asterisk** /'æstərɪsk/, *n.* **1.** the figure of a star (*), used in writing and printing as a reference mark or to indicate omission, doubtful matter, etc. **2.** something in the shape of a star or asterisk. [LL *asteriscus,* from Gk *asterískos,* diminutive of *astḗr* star]

**asterism** /'æstərɪzəm/, *n.* **1.** *Astron.* **a.** a group of stars. **b.** a constellation. **2.** *Crystall.* a property of some crystallised minerals of showing a starlike luminous figure in transmitted light or, in a cabochon-cut stone, by reflected light. [Gk *asterismós,* from *asterízein* mark with stars] – **asteriated,** *adj.*

**astern** /ə'stɜn/, *adv. Naut.* **1.** to the rear (of); behind; in a backward direction. **2.** in the rear; in a position behind.

**asternal** /eɪ'stɜnəl, ə-/, *adj. Anat., Zool.* not reaching to or connected with the sternum. [A-[6] + STERNAL]

**asteroid** /'æstərɔɪd/, *n.* **1.** *Zool.* any of the Asteroidea, a class of echinoderms characterised by a starlike body with radiating arms or rays, as the starfishes. **2.** *Astron.* one of several hundred planetoids with orbits lying mostly between those of Mars and Jupiter. *–adj.* **3.** starlike. **4.** *Zool.* belonging to or pertaining to the asteroids (def. 1). [Gk *asteroeidḗs* starlike]

**asteroidean** /æstə'rɔɪdiən/, *n., adj.* →**asteroid** (defs 1 and 4).

**asthenia** /əs'θiniə/, *n. Pathol.* lack or loss of strength; debility. [NL, from Gk *asthéneia*]

**asthenic** /əs'θɛnɪk/, *adj.* **1.** of or pertaining to asthenia. **2.**

weak; lacking strength. **3.** *Anat.* of a physical type characterised by a small trunk, slight muscular development, and long limbs. *–n.* **4.** an asthenic person or type.

**asthenosphere** /əs'θinəsfɪə, -'θɛn-/, *n. Geol.* a relatively weak layer of the earth beneath the lithosphere, extending from 80 to 150 kilometres below the earth's surface.

**asthma** /'æsmə/, *n.* a paroxysmal disorder of respiration with laboured breathing, a feeling of constriction in the chest, and coughing. [Gk: panting; replacing ME *asma,* from ML]

**asthma-plant** /'æsmə-plænt/, *n.* a common tropical weed, *Euphorbia pilulifera,* thought to alleviate pulmonary complaints. Also, **asthma-herb.**

**asthmatic** /æs'mætɪk/, *adj.* **1.** suffering from asthma. **2.** pertaining to asthma. *–n.* **3.** one suffering from asthma. – **asthmatically,** *adv.*

**astigmatic** /ˌæstɪg'mætɪk/, *adj.* pertaining to, exhibiting, or correcting astigmatism.

**astigmatism** /ə'stɪgmətɪzəm/, *n.* a defect of the eye or of a lens whereby rays of light from an external point converge unequally in different meridians, thus causing imperfect vision or images. [A-[6] + Gk *stígma* point + -ISM]

**astilbe** /ə'stɪlbi/, *n.* any plant of the saxifragaceous genus *Astilbe,* grown in cool climates for the clusters of small, showy flowers.

**astir** /ə'stɜ/, *adj.* **1.** in a stir; in motion or activity. **2.** up and about; out of bed.

**asti spumante** /ˌæsti spju'mænti/, *n.* a sweet, sparkling, white wine made in the area around Asti in Italy. [It. *spumante* foaming]

**astomatous** /ə'stɒmətəs, ə'stoʊ-/, *adj. Zool., Bot.* having no mouth, stoma, or stomata. [A-[6] + Gk *stóma* mouth + -OUS]

**astonish** /ə'stɒnɪʃ/, *v.t.* to strike with sudden and overpowering wonder; surprise greatly; amaze. [earlier *astony,* ? OE *āstunian,* intensive of *stunian* resound. Cf. ASTOUND, STUN] – **astonisher,** *n.*

**astonishing** /ə'stɒnəʃɪŋ/, *adj.* causing astonishment; amazing. – **astonishingly,** *adv.*

**astonishment** /ə'stɒnɪʃmənt/, *n.* **1.** overpowering wonder or surprise; amazement. **2.** an object or cause of amazement.

**astound** /ə'staʊnd/, *v.t.* **1.** to overwhelm with amazement; astonish greatly. *–adj.* **2.** *Archaic.* astonished. [pp. of obs. *astone, astun.* See ASTONISH, STUN] – **astoundingly,** *adv.*

**astr.,** **1.** astronomer. **2.** astronomical. **3.** astronomy.

**astraddle** /ə'strædl/, *adv.* with one leg on each side; in a straddling position; astride. – **astraddle,** *adj.*

**astragal** /'æstrəgəl/, *n.* **1.** *Archit.* **a.** a small convex moulding cut into the form of a string of beads. **b.** a plain convex moulding. **2.** any similar moulding, as in carpentry or metalwork. **3.** (*pl.*) dice. [L *astragalus.* See ASTRAGALUS]

**astragalus** /æs'trægələs/, *n., pl.* **-li** /-laɪ/. the uppermost bone of the tarsus; anklebone; talus; tibiale. [L, from Gk *astrágalos*] – **astragalar,** *adj.*

**astrakhan** /'æstrəkæn, æstrə'kæn/, *n.* **1.** a kind of fur of young lambs, with lustrous closely curled wool. **2.** Also, **astrakhan cloth.** a fabric with curled pile resembling it. [named after *Astrakhan,* a city in the USSR]

**astral** /'æstrəl/, *adj.* **1.** pertaining to or proceeding from the stars; consisting of or resembling stars; starry; stellar. **2.** *Biol.* relating to or resembling an aster: *starshaped.* **3.** *Theosophy.* pertaining to a supersensible substance supposed to pervade all space and form the substance of a second body belonging to each individual. *–n.* **4.** an astral body or spirit. [L *astrālis,* from *astrum* star, from Gk *ástron*]

**astral spirit** /– 'spɪrət/, *n.* **1.** a celestial intelligence (such as the soul of a dead man, a demon, etc.) **2.** *Theosophy.* a spirit composed of astral substance.

**astral trip** /– 'trɪp/, *n.* an extrasensory experience of travelling out of the tangible world.

**astraphobia** /æstrə'foʊbiə/, *n.* a morbid dread of lightning and thunder. [Gk *astrapḗ* lightning + -PHOBIA]

**astray** /ə'streɪ/, *adv.* out of the right way or away from the right; straying; wandering. – **astray,** *adj.*

**astrict** /ə'strɪkt/, *v.t.* **1.** to bind fast; confine; constrain or restrict. **2.** to bind morally or legally. [L *astrictus,* pp., drawn close] – **astriction,** *n.*

**astride** /ə'straɪd/, *adv.* **1.** in the posture of striding or straddling. *–prep.* **2.** with a leg on each side of.

**astringe** /ə'strɪndʒ/, *v.t.,* **astringed, astringing.** to compress; bind together; constrict. [L *astringere*]

**astringent** /ə'strɪndʒənt/, *adj.* **1.** (as affecting the skin) refreshing, tightening, drying: *an astringent after-shave lotion.* **2.** severe, sharp, austere: *an astringent style.* **3.** (of tastes) unpleasantly dry, hard (in wines, from the presence of tannin). **4.** *Med.* contracting; constrictive; styptic. *–n.* **5.** an astringent agent (esp. cosmetic). **6.** *Med.* a substance which contracts the tissues or canals of the body, thereby diminishing discharges, as of blood. [L: stem of *astringens,* ppr.] – **astringency,** *n.* – **astringently,** *adv.*

**astro-,** a word element meaning 'star', as in *astrology.* [Gk, combining form of *ástron*]

**astrobiology** /ˌæstroʊbaɪ'ɒlədʒi/, *n.* the study of the possibility that life exists outside the earth's immediate environment.

**astrobotany** /ˌæstroʊ'bɒtəni/, *n.* the study of the possibility that plant life exists outside the earth's immediate environment.

**astrocompass** /'æstroʊˌkʌmpəs/, *n.* a compass for indicating direction relative to the stars.

**astrocyte** /'æstroʊsaɪt/, *n.* a star-shaped cell, esp. in neurology. [ASTRO- + -CYTE]

**astrodome** /'æstrədoʊm/, *n.* a transparent dome on the top of the fuselage of an aeroplane, for astronomical observation. [ASTRO- + DOME]

**astrogeology** /ˌæstroʊdʒi'ɒlədʒi/, *n.* the study of the geological structure of planets other than the earth, and of other bodies in the solar system.

**astrograph** /'æstrəgræf, -graf/, *n.* an instrument which portrays star altitude curves on a chart.

**astrol.,** **1.** astrologer. **2.** astrological. **3.** astrology.

**astrolabe** /'æstrəleɪb/, *n.* an astronomical instrument for taking the altitude of the sun or stars and for the solution of other problems in astronomy and navigation. [ML *astrolabium,* from Gk *astrolábon* (*órganon*) armillary sphere replacing ME *astrelabe,* from OF]

**astrology** /əs'trɒlədʒi/, *n.* **1.** a study which assumes, and professes to interpret, the influence of the heavenly bodies on human affairs. **2.** (formerly) practical astronomy, the earliest form of the science. [ME, from L *astrologia,* from Gk. See ASTRO-, -LOGY] – **astrologer,** *n.* – **astrological** /æstrə'lɒdʒɪkəl/, **astrologic,** *adj.* – **astrologically,** *adv.*

**astrometry** /ə'strɒmətri/, *n.* measurement of the positions, motions, and distances of the celestial bodies.

**astron.,** **1.** astronomer. **2.** astronomical. **3.** astronomy.

**astronaut** /'æstrənɔt/, *n.* a person trained as a pilot, navigator, etc., to take part in the flight of a spacecraft; cosmonaut. [backformation from ASTRONAUTICS]

**astronautic** /æstrə'nɔtɪk/, *adj.* of astronautics or astronauts. Also, **astronautical.** [ASTRO- + NAUTIC(AL)] – **astronautically,** *adv.*

**astronautics** /æstrə'nɔtɪks/, *n.* the science and technology of flight outside the atmosphere of the earth. [pl. of ASTRONAUTIC. See -ICS]

**astronavigation** /ˌæstroʊnævə'geɪʃən/, *n.* **1.** the navigation of a spacecraft. **2.** →**celestial navigation.**

**astronomer** /əs'trɒnəmə/, *n.* an expert in astronomy; a scientific observer of the celestial bodies.

**astronomical** /æstrə'nɒmɪkəl/, *adj.* **1.** of, pertaining to, or connected with astronomy. **2.** very large, like the numbers used in astronomical calculations. Also, **astronomic.** – **astronomically,** *adv.*

**astronomical clock** /– 'klɒk/, *n.* an electrically controlled pendulum clock which reads sidereal time.

**astronomical day** /– 'deɪ/, *n.* See **day** (def. 3d).

**astronomical unit** /– 'junət/, *n.* the mean distance between the centre of the earth and the centre of the sun, about 149.6 $\times 10^9$ metres or 92.9 $\times 10^6$ miles, used as a unit of distance within the solar system. *Symbol:* AU Also, **astronomic unit.**

**astronomical year** /– 'jɪə/, *n.* →**year** (def. 5).

**astronomy** /əs'trɒnəmi/, *n.* the science of the celestial bodies, their motions, positions, distances, magnitudes, etc. [ME *astronomie,* from L *astronomia,* from Gk. See ASTRO-, -NOMY]

**astrophotography** /ˌæstroʊfə'tɒgrəfi/, *n.* the photography of stars and other celestial objects.

**astrophysics** /ˌæstroʊˈfɪzɪks/, *n.* astronomical physics, a branch of physics treating of the physical properties and phenomena of the celestial bodies. – **astrophysical,** *adj* – **astrophysicist** /ˌæstroʊˈfɪzəsəst/, *n.*

**astrosphere** /ˈæstrəsfɪə/, *n. Biol.* **1.** the central portion of an aster, in which the centrosome lies. **2.** the whole aster exclusive of the centrosome; attraction sphere.

**astute** /əsˈtjut/, *adj.* of keen penetration or discernment; sagacious; shrewd; cunning. [L *astūtus,* from *astus* adroitness, cunning] – **astutely,** *adv.* – **astuteness,** *n.*

**astylar** /əˈstaɪlə, eɪ-/, *adj. Archit.* without columns. [Gk *ástylos* without columns + -AR[1]]

**asunder** /əˈsʌndə/, *adv.* **1.** into separate parts; in or into pieces: *to tear asunder.* **2.** apart or widely separated: *as wide asunder as the poles.* [ME *asunder, o(n)sunder,* OE *on sundran* apart. See A-[1], SUNDER]

**aswarm** /əˈswɔm/, *adj.* swarming; teeming with.

**asyllabic** /eɪsəˈlæbɪk/, *adj.* not syllabic.

**asylum** /əˈsaɪləm/, *n.* **1.** an institution for the maintenance and care of the insane, the blind, orphans or the like. **2.** an inviolable refuge, as formerly for criminals and debtors; a sanctuary. **3.** *Internat. Law.* a temporary refuge granted political offenders, esp. in a foreign legation: *political asylum.* **4.** any secure retreat. [L, from Gk *ásylon,* neut. of *ásylos* inviolable]

**asymmetric** /eɪsəˈmɛtrɪk/, *adj.* **1.** not symmetrical; without symmetry. **2.** *Logic.* denoting relations which, if they hold between one term and a second, do not hold between the second and the first: *the relation 'being an ancestor of' is asymmetric.* Also, **asymmetrical.** **3.** *Chem.* of or pertaining to a molecule which has no elements of symmetry. – **asymmetrically,** *adv.*

**asymmetry** /eɪˈsɪmətri/, *n.* lack of symmetry or proportion. [Gk *asymmetría*]

**asymptomatic** /eɪˌsɪmptoʊˈmætɪk/, *adj.* neither displaying nor causing symptoms. – **asymptomatically,** *adv.*

**asymptote** /ˈæsəmtoʊt/, *n. Maths.* a straight line which is approached more and more closely by a point moving along a curved line but which is not touched by that point however far it moves. [Gk *asýmptōtos* not close] – **asymptotic** /æsəmˈtɒtɪk/, **asymptotical,** *adj.* – **asymptotically,** *adv.*

AB, asymptote

**asynchronism** /əˈsɪŋkrənɪzəm, əˈsɪn-/, *n.* want of synchronism, or coincidence in time. – **asynchronous,** *adj.*

**asyndeton** /əˈsɪndətən/, *n. Rhet.* the omission of conjunctions. [L, from Gk, neut. of *asýndetos* unjoined] – **asyndetic** /æsɪnˈdɛtɪk/, *adj.* – **asyndetically,** *adv.*

**at,** technical atmosphere

**at** /æt/; *weak form* /ət/ *prep.* a particle specifying a point occupied, attained, sought, or otherwise concerned, as in place, time, order, experience, etc., and hence used in many idiomatic phrases expressing circumstantial or relative position, degree or rate, action, manner: *to stand at the door, to aim at a mark, at home, at hand, at noon, at zero, at work, at ease, at length, at a risk, at cost, at one's best.* Some special phrases are:

**at it again,** acting in a characteristic manner.

**at sea, a.** on the ocean; sailing. **b.** bewildered; confused.

**at someone,** be critical.

**at that,** as things stand: *let it go at that.*

**be at,** *Colloq.* engaged in, occupied: *what are you at these days?* [ME; OE *æt;* c. Icel. *at,* L *ad* AD-]

**at-,** variant of **ad-** before *t,* as in *attend.*

**at.,** atomic.

**a.t.,** ampere turn. Also, **A.T.**

**At,** *Chem.* astatine.

**atabal** /ˈætəbæl/, *n.* a kind of drum used by the Moors, a people of North Africa. Also, **attabal.** [Sp., Ar. *aṭ tabl* the drum]

**atabrine** /ˈætəbrən/, *n.* an antimalarial substance, $C_{23}H_{30}N_3OCl$, a hydrochloride of mepacrine, with properties similar to plasmoquin. Also, **atabrin.**

**atactic** /əˈtæktɪk/, *adj.* **1.** pertaining to or afflicted with ataxia. **2.** *Chem.* of a polymer, having substituent groups or atoms arranged randomly along the backbone of a polymer chain. Also, **ataxic.**

**ataghan** /ˈætəgæn/, *n.* →**yataghan.**

**ataman** /ˈætəmən/, *n., pl.* **-mans.** a chief of Cossacks, elected by the whole group, serving as a chairman in peace and a leader in war; hetman. [Russ.]

**ataractic** /ætəˈræktɪk/, *adj.* **1.** of or pertaining to ataraxia. –*n.* **2.** a drug used to induce a state of tranquillity free from emotional disturbance and anxiety; tranquilliser. Also, **ataraxic.**

**ataraxia** /ætəˈræksiə/, *n.* a state of tranquillity, free from emotional disturbance and anxiety. Also, **ataraxy** /ætəˈræksi/. [NL, from Gk: impassiveness]

**atavism** /ˈætəvɪzəm/, *n.* **1.** *Biol.* the reappearance in an individual of characteristics of some more or less remote ancestor that have been absent in intervening generations. **2.** reversion to an earlier type. [L *atavus* ancestor + -ISM] – **atavist,** *n.* – **atavistic** /ætəˈvɪstɪk/, *adj.*

**ataxia** /əˈtæksiə/, *n.* **1.** loss of coordination of the muscles, esp. of the extremities. **2.** →**locomotor ataxia.** [NL, from Gk: disorder] – **ataxic, atactic,** *adj.*

**ate** /eɪt, ɛt/, *v.* past tense of **eat.**

**-ate**[1], a suffix forming: **1.** adjectives equivalent to **-ed** (in participial and other adjectives), as in *accumulate, separate.* **2.** nouns denoting esp. persons charged with some duty or function, or invested with some dignity, right, or special character, as in *advocate, candidate, curate, legate, prelate.* **3.** nouns denoting some product or result of action, as in *mandate* (lit., a thing commanded). **4.** verbs, originally taken from Latin past participles but now formed from any Latin or other stem, as in *actuate, agitate, calibrate.* [L *-ātus, -āta, -ātum*]

**-ate**[2], a suffix forming nouns denoting a salt formed by action of an acid on a base, esp. where the name of the acid ends in *-ic,* as in *acetate.* [L *-ātum* neut. of *-ātus* -ATE[1]]

**-ate**[3], a suffix forming nouns denoting condition, estate, office, officials, or an official, etc., as in *consulate, senate.* [L *-ātus,* suffix making nouns of 4th declension]

**Atebrin** /ˈætəbrən/, *n.* →**atabrine.** [Trademark]

**atelier** /aˈtɛljeɪ, ə-/, *n.* the workshop or studio of an artist. [F: workplace, originally pile of chips, from OF *astele* chip, from LL *astella,* from L *astula*]

**a tempo** /a ˈtɛmpoʊ/, (a musical direction) resuming the speed which obtained preceding *rit.* or *accel.* [It.]

**Athabascan** /æθəˈbæskən/, *n.* an American Indian linguistic stock.

**athanasia** /æθəˈneɪziə, -ʒə/, *n.* deathlessness; immortality. Also, **athanasy** /əˈθænəsi/. [Gk]

**Athanasian** /æθəˈneɪʒən/, *adj.* **1.** of or pertaining to Saint Athanasius, A.D. 296? - 373, bishop of Alexandria, opponent of Arianism. –*n.* **2.** *Theol.* a follower of Athanasius or a believer in his creed.

**Athanasian Creed** /– ˈkrid/, *Theol.* a (probably) post-Augustinian creed of the Christian faith, of unknown authorship, formerly ascribed to Athanasius.

**Atharva-Veda** /ətavə-ˈveɪdə/, *n.* See **Veda.**

**atheism** /ˈeɪθiˌɪzəm/, *n.* **1.** the doctrine that there is no God. **2.** disbelief in the existence of a God (or gods). **3.** godlessness. [Gk *átheos* without a god + -ISM]

**atheist** /ˈeɪθiəst/, *n.* one who denies or disbelieves the existence of God (or gods).

**atheistic** /ˌeɪθiˈɪstɪk/, *adj.* pertaining to or characteristic of atheists; involving, containing, or tending to atheism. Also, **atheistical.** – **atheistically,** *adv.*

**athel** /ˈæθəl/, *n.* a tree, *Tamarix aphylla,* native to southern Asia and North Africa, cultivated in desert areas as it thrives in poor soil and tolerates extreme temperatures. [Ar. *athl*]

**atheling** /ˈæθəlɪŋ/, *n.* an Anglo-Saxon of royal blood; a prince. [ME; OE *ætheling,* from *æthelu* noble family + *-ing,* suffix of appurtenance]

**athenaeum** /æθəˈniəm/, *n.* **1.** an institution for the promotion of literary or scientific learning. **2.** a library or reading room. Also, **atheneum.** [L, from Gk *Athḗnaion,* temple of Athena at Athens, frequented by poets and men of learning]

**Athenian** /əˈθiniən/, *adj.* **1.** pertaining to Athens, capital of

i = peat ɪ = pit ɛ = pet æ = pat a = part ɒ = pot ʌ = putt ɔ = port ʊ = put u = pool ɜ = pert ə = apart aɪ = buy eɪ = bay ɔɪ = boy aʊ = how
oʊ = hoe ɪə = here ɛə = hair ʊə = tour g = give θ = thin ð = then ʃ = show ʒ = measure tʃ = choke dʒ = joke ŋ = sing j = you õ = Fr. bon

Greece. *–n.* **2.** a native or citizen of Athens.

**athermancy** /ə'θɜmənsi/, *n. Physics.* the power of stopping radiant heat.

**athermanous** /ə'θɜmənəs/, *adj. Physics.* impermeable to or able to stop radiant heat. [A-[6] + Gk *thermaínein* heat + -OUS]

**atheroma** /æθə'roumə/, *n. Pathol.* →**atherosclerosis.** [Gk] – **atheromatous,** *adj.*

**atherosclerosis** /ˌæθərousklə'rousəs/, *n.* a form of the disease arteriosclerosis in which fatty substances deposit in and beneath the intima of the arteries. [NL, from Gk *athḗr* chaff + SCLEROSIS]

**athirst** /ə'θɜst/, *adj.* **1.** having a keen desire; eager (oft. fol. by *for*). **2.** *Archaic.* thirsty.

**athlete** /'æθlit/, *n.* **1.** anyone trained to exercises of physical agility and strength. **2.** one trained for track and field events only. [L *āthlēta,* from Gk *āthlētḗs* contestant in games]

**athlete's foot** /ˌæθlits 'fut/, *n.* a contagious disease, a ringworm of the feet, caused by a fungus that thrives on moist surfaces.

**athletic** /æθ'lɛtɪk/, *adj.* **1.** physically active and strong. **2.** of, like, or befitting an athlete. **3.** of a physical type characterised by long limbs, a large build, and well-developed muscles. **4.** of or pertaining to athletics. – **athletically,** *adv.* – **athleticism,** *n.*

**athletics** /æθ'lɛtɪks/, *n.* **1.** (*usu. construed as pl.*) athletic sports, as running, rowing, boxing, etc. **2.** (*usu. construed as sing.*) track and field events only. **3.** (*usu. construed as sing.*) the practice of athletic exercises; the principles of athletic training.

**athletic support** /æθˌlɛtɪk sə'pɔt/, *n.* →**jockstrap.**

**athodyd** /'æθoudid/, *n. Aeron.* →**ramjet.** [from *a(ero) th(erm)ody(namic) d(uct)*]

**at-home** /ət-'houm/, *n.* a reception in one's home.

**athwart** /ə'θwɔt/, *adv.* **1.** from side to side (often in an oblique direction): transversely. **2.** perversely; awry; wrongly. **3.** *Naut.* at right angles to a ship's keel. *–prep.* **4.** from side to side of; across. **5.** in opposition to; contrary to. **6.** *Naut.* across the line or course of. [A-[1] + THWART, adv.]

**athwartships** /ə'θwɔtʃɪps/, *adv.* **1.** at right angles to the ship's keel.

**atilt** /ə'tɪlt/, *adv.* **1.** at a tilt or inclination; tilted. **2.** in a tilting encounter. – **atilt,** *adj.*

**-ation,** a suffix forming nouns denoting action or process, state or condition, a product or result, or something producing a result, often accompanying verbs or adjectives of Latin origin ending in *-ate,* as in *agitation, decoration, elation, migration, separation,* but also formed in English from any stem, as in *botheration, flirtation, starvation.* See **-ion, -tion.** [L *-ātio* = -ATE[1] + -ION; identical with G *-ation,* etc., all from L]

**-ative,** an adjective suffix expressing tendency, disposition, function, bearing, connection, etc., as in *affirmative, demonstrative, talkative.* See **-ive.** [L *-ātivus* = -ATE[1] + -IVE; representing also F *-atif* (masc.), *-ative* (fem.)]

**Atlantean** /ətlæn'tiən, ət'læntiən/, *adj.* **1.** pertaining to the demigod Atlas, condemned to support the sky on his shoulders. **2.** having the strength of an Atlas. [L. *Atlantēus* pertaining to Atlas + -AN.]

**atlantes** /ət'læntiz/, *n. pl., sing.* **atlas.** *Archit.* figures of men used as supporting or decorative columns. [L, from Gk.]

**atlantic** /ət'læntɪk/, *n. Railways.* a steam locomotive with a particular wheel arrangement consisting of a four wheel front truck, two pairs of driving wheels and one idling wheel.

**atlas** /'ætləs/, *n.* **1.** a bound collection of maps. **2.** a volume of plates or tables illustrating any subject. **3.** *Anat.* the first cervical vertebra, which supports the head. **4.** (*cap.*) one who supports a heavy burden; a mainstay. **5.** sing. of **atlantes. 6.** (formerly) a large size of fine quality drawing or writing paper. [named after the demigod in classical mythology, condemned to support the sky on his shoulders; L, from Gk]

**Atlas moth** /'– mɒθ/, *n.* a very large emperor moth, *Coscinocera hercules,* of Queensland and the island of New Guinea.

**atm,** standard atmosphere.

**atman** /'ætmən/, *n. Hinduism.* **1.** the breath. **2.** the principle of life. **3.** the spiritual self. **4.** the world spiritual self, from which all individual souls derive, and to which they return as the supreme goal of existence. **5.** (*cap.*) Brahma, the Supreme Being. [Skt]

**atmolysis** /ət'mɒləsəs/, *n.* the separation of a mixture of gases through the walls of a porous vessel due to the different diffusion rates of the constituent molecules.

**atmosphere** /'ætməsfɪə/, *n.* **1.** the gaseous fluid surrounding the earth; the air. **2.** this medium at a given place. **3.** *Astron.* the gaseous envelope surrounding any of the heavenly bodies. **4.** *Chem.* any gaseous envelope or medium. **5.** See **standard atmosphere. 6.** See **technical atmosphere. 7.** environing or pervading influence: *an atmosphere of freedom.* **8.** the quality in a work of art which produces a predominant mood or impression. [NL *atmosphaera,* from Gk *atmó(s)* vapour + *sphaîra* SPHERE]

**atmospheric** /ætməs'fɛrɪk/, *adj.* **1.** pertaining to, existing in, or consisting of the atmosphere: *atmospheric vapours.* **2.** caused, produced, or operated on by the atmosphere: *atmospheric pressure.* *–n.* **3.** (*pl.*) *Radio.* →**static** (def. 8). Also, **atmospherical.** – **atmospherically,** *adv.*

**at. no.,** atomic number.

**A to D** /eɪ tə 'di/, *adj.* analog to digital.

**atoll** /'ætɒl/, *n.* a ringlike coral island enclosing a lagoon. [Maldive *atol*]

**atom** /'ætəm/, *n.* **1.** *Physics, Chem.* the smallest unitary constituent of a chemical element, composed of a more or less complex aggregate of protons, neutrons, and electrons, whose number and arrangement determine the element. **2.** (esp. formerly) a hypothetical particle of matter so minute as to admit of no division. **3.** anything extremely small; a minute quantity. [L *atomus,* from Gk *átomos* indivisible]

atoll

**atomic** /ə'tɒmɪk/, *adj.* **1.** pertaining to atoms. **2.** propelled or driven by atomic energy. **3.** using or having developed atomic weapons. **4.** *Chem.* existing as free uncombined atoms. **5.** extremely minute. Also, **atomical.** – **atomically,** *adv.*

**atomic age** /– 'eɪdʒ/, *n.* the period in history initiated by the first use of the atomic bomb and characterised by atomic energy as a military, political, and industrial factor.

**atomic bomb** /– 'bɒm/, *n.* a bomb whose potency is derived from nuclear fission of atoms of fissionable material, with consequent conversion of part of their mass into energy; its explosion is extremely violent and attended by great heat, brilliant light and strong gamma-ray radiation. Also, **atom bomb, A-bomb.** Cf. **hydrogen bomb.**

**atomic clock** /– 'klɒk/, *n.* a highly accurate clock in which an electric oscillator, as a crystal, is regulated by the vibration of an atomic system.

**atomic energy** /– 'ɛnədʒi/, *n.* **1.** the energy obtained from changes within the atomic nucleus, chiefly from nuclear fission, or fusion. *n.* **2.** this energy regarded as a source of power, as for industrial usage.

**atomic heat** /– 'hit/, *n.* the product of the specific heat and the atomic weight of an element; approximately equal to 25 200 joules per kelvin, or to 6 calories per gram per degree for solid elements at normal temperatures.

**atomicity** /ætə'mɪsəti/, *n.* **1.** the number of atoms in the molecule of a gas. **2.** *Obs.* valency.

**atomic mass** /əˌtɒmɪk 'mæs/, *n.* the mass of an isotope of an element measured in atomic mass units.

**atomic mass unit,** *n.* a unit for expressing the mass of an individual isotope, based on the isotope of carbon, ${}^{12}_{6}C$. It is equal to $1.660\ 53 \times 10^{-27}$ kg. *Symbol:* u

**atomic number** /əˌtɒmɪk 'nʌmbə/, *n.* the number of protons in the nucleus of an atom of a given element. *Abbrev.:* at. no.

**atomic philosophy** /– fə'lɒsəfi/, *n.* →**atomism.**

**atomic pile** /– 'paɪl/, *n.* →**pile** (def. 7).

**atomic power** /– 'pauə/, *n.* **1.** energy released in nuclear reactions. **2.** a world power having developed its own atomic

i = peat ɪ = pit ɛ = pet æ = pat a = part ɒ = pot ʌ = putt ɔ = port ʊ = put u = pool ɜ = pert ə = apart aɪ = buy eɪ = bay ɔɪ = boy aʊ = how
oʊ = hoe ɪə = here ɛə = hair ʊə = tour g = give θ = thin ð = then ʃ = show ʒ = measure tʃ = choke dʒ = joke ŋ = sing j = you ɒ̃ = Fr. bon

weapons. Also, **nuclear power.**

**atomics** /ə'tɒmɪks/, *n. Colloq.* the branch of nuclear physics dealing with atomic energy, nuclear fission, etc.

**atomic structure** /əˌtɒmɪk 'strʌktʃə/, *n. Physics.* the theoretically derived concept of an atom composed of a positively charged nucleus surrounded and electrically neutralised by negatively charged electrons, revolving in orbits at varying distances from the nucleus, the constitution of the nucleus and the arrangement of the electrons differing with the different chemical elements.

**atomic theory** /– 'θɪəri/, *n.* **1.** *Physics, Chem.* the modern theory of the atom having a complex internal structure and electrical properties. **2.** *Physics.* the mathematical and geometrical description of the motions of the electrons in the atom about the nucleus. **3.** →**Dalton's atomic theory.** **4.** *Philos.* →**atomism.** Also, **atomic hypothesis.**

**atomic warfare** /– 'wɔfɛə/, *n.* warfare in which atomic weapons are used.

**atomic weapon** /– 'wɛpən/, *n.* any weapon (esp. a bomb, shell, or missile) in which the destructive power is derived from atomic energy.

**atomic weight** /– 'weɪt/, *n.* the average weight of the atoms of a given specimen of an element, measured in atomic mass units. *Abbrev.:* at. wt, a.w.

**atomise** /'ætəmaɪz/, *v.t.*, **-mised, -mising.** **1.** to reduce to atoms. **2.** to reduce to fine particles or spray. Also, **atomize.** – **atomisation** /ˌætəmaɪ'zeɪʃən/, *n.*

**atomiser** /'ætəmaɪzə/, *n.* an apparatus for reducing liquids to a fine spray, as for medicinal application. Also, **atomizer.**

**atomism** /'ætəmɪzəm/, *n.* the theory that minute discrete, finite, unchangeable, and indivisible elements are the ultimate constituents of all matter, and that all observable change is attributable to change in the relation of such elements to one another. – **atomist,** *n.* – **atomistic** /ætə'mɪstɪk/, *adj.*

**atom-smasher** /'ætəm-smæʃə/, *n. Colloq.* any device for disintegrating or splitting atoms, as an accelerator (def. 5).

**atomy**[1] /'ætəmi/, *n., pl.* **-mies.** *Archaic.* **1.** an atom; a mote. **2.** a pygmy. [L *atomī* atoms]

**atomy**[2] /'ætəmi/, *n., pl.* **-mies.** *Obs.* a skeleton. [from ANATOMY, taken as *an atomy*]

**atonal** /ə'toʊnəl, eɪ-/, *adj. Music.* having no key or tonal centre. [A-[6] + TONAL] – **atonalism,** *n.* – **atonalistic** /ˌeɪtoʊnə'lɪstɪk/, *adj.* – **atonally,** *adv.*

**atonality** /ˌeɪtoʊ'næləti/, *n. Music.* **1.** the absence of key or tonal centre. **2.** an atonal principle or style of composition.

**atone** /ə'toʊn/, *v.*, **atoned, atoning.** *–v.i.* **1.** to make amends or reparation, as for an offence or a crime, or for an offender (fol. by *for*). **2.** to make up, as for errors or deficiencies (fol. by *for*). **3.** *Obs.* to agree. *–v.t.* **4.** to make amends for; expiate. **5.** *Rare.* to harmonise; make harmonious. [back-formation from ATONEMENT] – **atoner,** *n.* – **atonable,** *adj.*

**atonement** /ə'toʊnmənt/, *n.* **1.** satisfaction or reparation for a wrong or injury; amends. **2.** *Theol.* the reconciliation of God and man by means of the life, sufferings, and death of Christ. **3.** *Obs.* reconciliation; agreement. [phrase *at one* in accord + -MENT]

**atonic** /ə'tɒnɪk, eɪ-/, *adj.* **1.** *Phonet.* **a.** unaccented. **b.** *Obs.* voiceless (def. 5). **2.** *Pathol.* characterised by atony. *–n.* **3.** *Gram.* an unaccented word, syllable, or sound.

**atony** /'ætəni/, *n. Pathol.* lack of tone or energy; muscular weakness, esp. in a contractile organ. [ML *atonia,* from Gk: languor]

**atop** /ə'tɒp/, *adv.* **1.** on or at the top. *–prep.* **2.** on the top of: *atop the house.*

**ATP** /eɪ ti 'pi/, →**adenosine triphosphate.**

**atrabilious** /ˌætrə'bɪljəs/, *adj.* melancholic or hypochondriac; splenetic. Also, **atrabiliar.** [L *ātrabīli(s)* black bile + -OUS] – **atrabiliousness,** *n.*

**atremble** /ə'trɛmbəl/, *adv.* in a trembling state.

**atrioventricular node** /ætrioʊvenˌtrɪkjələ 'noʊd/, *n.* a mass of specialised conductive tissue in the heart, which transmits electrical impulses to initiate contraction; A-V node.

**atrip** /ə'trɪp/, *adj.* (of an anchor) raised just enough to clear the bottom.

**atrium** /'ætriəm, 'eɪ-/, *n., pl.* **-tria** /-triə/. **1.** *Archit.* **a.** the central main room of an ancient Roman private house. **b.** a courtyard, mostly surrounded by colonnades, in front of an early Christian or medieval church. **2.** *Zool.* an internal cavity or space; applied variously to different cavities in different organisms. **3.** *Anat.* **a.** one of the two chambers of the heart through which blood from the veins passes into the ventricles. **b.** the part of the tympanic cavity of the ear below the head of the malleus. [(def. 1) L; (defs 2 and 3) from NL, special use of L *atrium*] – **atrial** /'eɪtriəl/, *adj.*

**atrocious** /ə'troʊʃəs/, *adj.* **1.** extremely or shockingly wicked or cruel; heinous. **2.** shockingly bad or lacking in taste; execrable. **3.** *Colloq.* very bad. [ATROCI(TY) + -OUS] – **atrociously,** *adv.* – **atrociousness,** *n.*

**atrocity** /ə'trɒsəti/, *n., pl.* **-ties.** **1.** the quality of being atrocious. **2.** an atrocious deed or thing. [L *atrōcitas*]

**atrophied** /'ætrəfid/, *adj.* exhibiting or affected with atrophy; wasted.

**atrophy** /'ætrəfi/, *n., v.*, **-phied, -phying.** *–n.* **1.** *Pathol.* wasting away of the body or of an organ or part, as from defective nutrition or other cause. **2.** degeneration; reduction in size and functional power through lack of use. *–v.t., v.i.* **3.** to affect with or undergo atrophy. [earlier *atrophie,* from L *atrophia,* from Gk: lack of nourishment] – **atrophic** /ə'troʊfɪk/, *adj.*

**atropine** /'ætrəpən, -in/, *n.* a poisonous crystalline alkaloid, $C_{17}H_{23}NO_3$, obtained from belladonna (deadly nightshade) and other solanaceous plants, which prevents the response of various body structures to certain types of nerve stimulation; it is used medicinally as an antispasmodic, to dilate the pupil of the eye, or as an anaesthetic. [NL *Atropa,* the belladonna genus (from Gk *Atropos,* in Gk mythology, one of the Fates who cut off the thread of life) + -INE[2]]

**atropism** /'ætrəpɪzəm/, *n.* the morbid state induced by atropine.

**attabal** /'ætəbæl/, *n.* →**atabal.**

**attaboy** /ætə'bɔɪ/, *Colloq.* (an exclamation of approbation or exhortation).

**attacca** /ə'tækə/, *v.i.* (*usu. imperative*) (a musical direction) to begin (the next movement) without a pause. [It., imperative of *attaccare* ATTACK]

**attach** /ə'tætʃ/, *v.t.* **1.** to fasten to; affix; join; connect: *to attach a cable.* **2.** to join in action or function. **3.** to place on duty with or in assistance to an organisation or working unit temporarily, esp. a military unit. **4.** to connect as an adjunct; associate: *a curse is attached to this treasure.* **5.** to assign or attribute: *to attach significance to a gesture.* **6.** to bind by ties of affection or regard. **7.** *Law.* to arrest (a person) or distrain (property) in payment of a debt by legal authority. **8.** *Obs.* to lay hold of; seize. *–v.i.* **9.** to adhere; pertain; belong (fol. by *to* or *upon*): *no blame attaches to him.* [ME *attache(n),* from OF *atachier,* from *a-* AD- + word akin to TACK[1]] – **attachable,** *adj.*

**attaché** /ə'tæʃeɪ/, *n.* one attached to an official staff, esp. that of an embassy or legation. [F, properly pp. of *attacher* ATTACH]

**attaché case** /'– keɪs/, *n.* a small rectangular case with a hinged lid, for documents, etc.

**attachment** /ə'tætʃmənt/, *n.* **1.** the act of attaching. **2.** the state of being attached. **3.** affection that binds one to another person or to a thing; regard. **4.** that which attaches; a fastening or tie: *the attachments of a pair of skis or of a harness.* **5.** an adjunct or supplementary device: *attachments to a reaping machine.* **6.** *Law.* **a.** arrest of a person, for contempt of court, by legal authority. **b.** the process of ordering someone (the garnishee) who owes money to a judgment debtor, to pay this money to the judgment creditor, in settlement of the judgment.

**attack** /ə'tæk/, *v.t.*, **1.** to set upon with force or weapons; begin hostilities against: *attack the enemy.* **2.** to direct unfavourable criticism, argument, etc. against; blame or abuse violently. **3.** to set about (a task) or go to work on (a thing) vigorously. **4.** (of disease, destructive agencies, etc.) to begin to affect. **5.** *Football, etc.* to threaten the goal of the opposing team. *–v.i.* **6.** to make an attack; begin hostilities. *–n.* **7.** the act of attacking; onslaught; assault. **8.** criticism; abuse; calumny. **9.** an offensive military operation with the aim of overcoming the enemy and destroying his armed forces and will to resist. **10.** *Pathol.* seizure by disease. **11.** the initial (offensive) movement in a contest; onset. **12.** the act or manner of beginning anything; start; approach, as of a musical tone. **13.** vigour, precision, and flair in approach to or execution of anything, esp. in the performance of a musical work. **14.** *Football, etc.* the forwards. **15.** *Cricket.* **a.** the fielding side's bowlers, esp. its top-line bowlers. **b.** the strategic placing of fieldsmen. [F *attaquer,* from It. *attaccare* attack, ATTACH] – **attacker,** *n.*

**attain** /ə'teɪn/, *v.t.* **1.** to reach, achieve, or accomplish by continued effort: *to attain one's ends.* **2.** to come to or arrive at in due course: *to attain the opposite shore.* *–v.i.* **3. attain to,** to arrive at; succeed in reaching or obtaining. [ME *attaine(n),* from OF *ataindre,* from L *attingere* touch upon]

**attainable** /ə'teɪnəbəl/, *adj.* capable of being attained. – **attainability** /əteɪnə'bɪləti/, **attainableness,** *n.*

**attainder** /ə'teɪndə/, *n.* **1.** *Law.* (formerly) the loss of all civil rights following judgment of death or outlawry for treason or felony. **2.** *Obs.* dishonour. [ME, from OF *ataindre* ATTAIN; later associated with F *taindre* stain, from L *tingere.* See ATTAINT]

**attainment** /ə'teɪnmənt/, *n.* **1.** the act of attaining. **2.** something attained; a personal acquirement.

**attainment test** /'– tɛst/, *n.* a test designed to measure the level of knowledge attained by an individual, as opposed to native ability or intelligence; achievement test.

**attaint** /ə'teɪnt/, *v.t.* **1.** *Law.* (formerly) to condemn by a sentence or a bill or act of attainder. **2.** to disgrace. **3.** *Archaic.* to accuse. **4.** *Obs.* to prove the guilt of. *–n.* **5.** attainder. **6.** *Obs.* a stain, disgrace; taint. **7.** *Obs.* a touch or hit, esp. in tilting. [ME *ataynte(n),* from OF *ataint,* pp. of *ataindre* ATTAIN; in part confused with TAINT]

**attar** /'ætə/, *n.* a perfume or essential oil obtained from flowers or petals, esp. of damask roses. [Pers. *'atar,* from Ar. *'itr*]

**attemper** /ə'tɛmpə/, *v.t.* **1.** to qualify, modify, or moderate by mixing or blending (with something different or opposite). **2.** to regulate or modify the temperature of. **3.** to soothe; mollify; mitigate. **4.** to accommodate; adapt (fol. by *to*). [L *attemperāre* fit; replacing ME *atempre(n),* from OF *atemprer*]

**attempt** /ə'tɛmpt, ə'tɛmt/, *v.t.* **1.** to make an effort at; try; undertake; seek: *to attempt a conversation, to attempt to study.* **2.** to attack; make an effort against: *to attempt a person's life.* **3.** *Archaic.* to tempt. *–n.* **4.** effort put forth to accomplish something; a trial or essay. **5.** an attack or assault: *an attempt upon one's life.* [L *attemptāre* try] – **attemptability** /əˌtɛmptə'bɪləti, -tɛmt-/, *n.* – **attemptable,** *adj.* – **attempter,** *n.*

**attend** /ə'tɛnd/, *v.t.* **1.** to be present at: *to attend school or a meeting.* **2.** to go with as a concomitant or result; accompany: *a cold attended with fever.* **3.** to minister to; devote one's services to. **4.** to wait upon or accompany as a servant. **5.** to take charge of; tend. **6.** *Obs.* to wait for; expect. *–v.i.* **7.** to give attention; pay regard or heed. **8.** to apply oneself: *to attend to one's work.* **9.** to take care or charge of: *to attend to a task.* **10.** to be consequent (*on*) **11.** to wait (*on*) with service. **12.** *Obs.* to wait. [ME *atende(n),* from OF *atendre,* from L *attendere* stretch towards]

**attendance** /ə'tɛndəns/, *n.* **1.** the act of attending. **2.** the (number of) persons present. **3.** the number of times (out of a maximum) that a person is present. **4.** *Obs.* attendants collectively.

**attendance money** /'– mʌni/, *n.* →**appearance money.**

**attendance officer** /'– ɒfəsə/, *n.* an officer of a State Child Welfare Department whose duties particularly include checking on children who habitually absent themselves from school; truant officer.

**attendant** /ə'tɛndənt/, *n.* **1.** one who attends another, as for service or company. **2.** one employed to take care or charge of someone or something, esp. when this involves directing or assisting the public: *a cloakroom attendant.* **3.** one who is present, as at a meeting. **4.** that which goes along with or follows as a natural consequence. *–adj.* **5.** being present or in attendance; accompanying. **6.** concomitant; consequent: *attendant evils.*

**attention** /ə'tɛnʃən/; *for def. 6* /ətɛn'ʃʌn/, *n.* **1.** the act or faculty of attending. **2.** *Psychol.* concentration of the mind upon an object; maximal integration of the higher mental processes. **3.** observant care; consideration; notice: *your letter will receive early attention.* **4.** civility or courtesy: *attention to a stranger.* **5.** (*pl.*) acts of courtesy indicating regard, as in courtship. **6.** *Mil.* **a.** a command to take an erect position, with eyes to the front, arms hanging to the sides, heels together, and toes turned outwards at an angle of 45 degrees. **b.** the state of so standing: *at attention.* [ME *attencíoun,* from L *attentio*]

**attentive** /ə'tɛntɪv/, *adj.* **1.** characterised by or giving attention; observant. **2.** assiduous in service or courtesy; polite; courteous. – **attentively,** *adv.* – **attentiveness,** *n.*

**attenuant** /ə'tɛnjuənt/, *adj.* diluting, as a liquid. [L *attenuans,* ppr.]

**attenuate** /ə'tɛnjueɪt/, *v.,* **-ated, -ating;** /ə'tɛnjuət, -eɪt/, *adj.* *–v.t.* **1.** to make thin; make slender or fine; rarefy. **2.** to weaken or reduce in force, intensity, effect, quantity, or value. *–v.i.* **3.** to become thin or fine. **4.** to grow less; weaken. *–adj.* **5.** attenuated; thin. **6.** *Bot.* tapering gradually to a narrow extremity. [L *attenuātus,* pp., made thin]

**attenuation** /ətɛnju'eɪʃən/, *n.* **1.** the act of attenuating. **2.** the resulting state. **3.** *Physics.* the loss of power suffered by radiation when it passes through matter. **4.** *Electronics.* the loss of power suffered by an electrical signal as it passes through a system. **5. attenuation factor,** a measure of attenuation (def. 3).

**attenuator** /ə'tɛnjueɪtə/, *n.* **1.** one who or that which attenuates. **2.** *Electronics.* an electronic network that reduces the amplitude of a signal without distortion.

**attest** /ə'tɛst/, *v.t.* **1.** to bear witness to; certify; declare to be correct, true, or genuine; declare the truth of, in words or writing; esp., affirm in an official capacity: *to attest the truth of a statement.* **2.** to give proof or evidence of; manifest: *his works attest his industry.* *–v.i.* **3.** to certify to the genuineness of a document by signing as witness. *–n.* **4.** *Archaic.* witness; testimony; attestation. [L *attestarí* bear witness] – **attestor, attester,** *n.*

**attestation** /ætɛs'teɪʃən/, *n.* **1.** the act of attesting. **2.** an attesting declaration; testimony; evidence.

**Att. Gen.,** Attorney-General.

**attic** /'ætɪk/, *n.* **1.** that part of a building, esp. a house, directly under a roof; a garret. **2.** a room or rooms in that part, frequently used for storage. **3.** a low storey or decorative wall above an entablature or the main cornice of a building. [F *attique,* from L *Atticus* Attic (orig., as applied to a square column in building)]

**Attic** /'ætɪk/, *adj.* **1.** pertaining to Attica, the region around Athens, Greece. **2.** (*oft. l.c.*) displaying simple elegance, incisive intelligence, and delicate wit. *–n.* **3.** a native or an inhabitant of Attica; an Athenian. **4.** the Ionic dialect of ancient Athens which became the standard of Greek literature (from the 5th century B.C.). **5. Attic order,** *Archit.* a square column of any of the five orders of columns. [L *Atticus,* from Gk *Attikós*]

**Atticism** /'ætəsɪzəm/, *n.* **1.** peculiarity of style or idiom belonging to Attic Greek, the Greek of the region around Athens. **2.** Attic elegance of diction. **3.** concise and elegant expression. Also, **atticism.**

**Attic salt** /ˌætɪk 'sɒlt/, *n.* dry, delicate wit. Also, **Attic wit.**

**attire** /ə'taɪə/, *v.,* **-tired, -tiring,** *n.* *–v.t.* **1.** to dress, array, or adorn, esp. for special occasions, ceremonials, etc. *–n.* **2.** clothes or apparel, esp. rich or splendid garments. **3.** the horns of a deer. [ME *atire(n),* from OF *atirer* put in order, from *a-* AD- + *tire* row]

**attitude** /'ætətjud/, *n.* **1.** position, disposition, or manner with regard to a person or thing: *a menacing attitude.* **2.** position of the body appropriate to an action, emotion, etc. **3.** *Aeron.* the inclination of the three principal axes of an aircraft relative to the wind, to the ground, etc. **4.** a pose in ballet in which the dancer stands on one leg, the other bent behind. [F, from It. *attitudine* aptness, from ML *aptitūdo* APTITUDE] – **attitudinal** /ætə'tjudənəl/, *adj.*

**attitudinarian** /ˌætətjudə'nɛəriən/, *n.* one who studies attitudes.

**attitudinise** /ætə'tjudənaɪz/, *v.i.,* **-nised, -nising.** to assume affected attitudes; pose for effect. Also, **attitudinize.** – **attitudiniser,** *n.*

**atto-** /'ætoʊ-/, a prefix denoting $10^{-18}$ of a given unit, as in *attogram. Symbol:* a [Dan. or Norw. *atter* eighteen, from ON *āttjān*]

**attorn** /ə'tɜn/, *Law. –v.i.* **1.** to acknowledge the relation of tenant to a new landlord. *–v.t.* **2.** to turn over to another; transfer. [ML *attornāre,* from OF *atorner* transfer, from *a-* AD- + *torner* turn] – **attornment,** *n.*

**attorney** /ə'tɜni/, *n., pl.* **-neys. 1.** one duly appointed or empowered by another to transact any business for him (**attorney in fact**). **2. power of attorney.** Also, **letter of attorney, warrant of attorney.** a formal document by which one person authorises another to act for him. **3.** *Now Chiefly U.S.* →**lawyer.** [ME *atorne,* from OF, pp. of *atorner* assign]

**attorney at law,** *n. Law, now Chiefly U.S.* a solicitor; an officer of the court authorised to appear before it as representative of a party to a legal controversy.

**attorney-general** /– 'dʒɛnrəl/, *n., pl.* **attorneys-general, attorney-generals.** the chief law officer of a government and the minister responsible for the administration of justice.

**attract** /ə'trækt/, *v.t.* **1.** to act upon by a physical force causing or tending to cause approach or union (opposed to *repel*). **2.** to draw by other than physical influence; invite or allure; win: *to attract attention or admirers. –v.i.* **3.** to possess or exert the power of attraction. [L *attractus,* pp., drawn to] – **attractable,** *adj.* – **attractor, attracter,** *n.*

**attraction** /ə'trækʃən/, *n.* **1.** the act, power, or property of attracting. **2.** allurement; enticement. **3.** that which allures or entices; a charm. **4.** *Physics.* a force which draws two or more bodies together, or causes them to orbit about a common centre. **5.** an entertainment offered to the public. **6.** *Gram.* the tendency (uncommon in English) for a word to be altered from its correct case, number, or gender to agree with a word near to it, as in *the wages of sin is death,* where *is* agrees with *death* instead of *wages.*

**attraction money** /'– mʌni/, *n.* a component of rates of pay designed to attract people to employment in certain positions.

**attraction sphere** /'– sfɪə/, *n. Biol.* →**astrosphere.**

**attractive** /ə'træktɪv/, *adj.* **1.** appealing to one's liking or admiration; engaging; alluring; pleasing. **2.** having the quality of attracting. – **attractively,** *adv.* – **attractiveness,** *n.*

**attrib., 1.** attribute. **2.** attributive.

**attribute** /ə'trɪbjut/, *v.,* **-uted, -uting;** /'ætrəbjut/, *n. –v.t.* **1.** to consider as belonging; regard as owing, as an effect to a cause (oft. fol. by *to*). *–n.* **2.** something attributed as belonging; a quality, character, characteristic, or property: *wisdom is one of his attributes.* **3.** *Gram.* **a.** a word or phrase grammatically subordinate to another, serving to limit (identify, particularise, describe, or supplement) the meaning of the form to which it is attached. For example: in *the red house, red* limits the meaning of *house;* it is an attribute of *house.* **b.** an attributive word; adjunct. **4.** *Fine Arts.* a symbol of office, character, or personality. **5.** *Logic.* that which is predicated or affirmed of a subject. **6.** *Obs.* reputation. [ME (as adj.), from L *attribūtus,* pp., assigned] – **attributable** /ə'trɪbjətəbəl/, *adj.* – **attributer, attributor,** *n.*

**attribution** /ætrə'bjuʃən/, *n.* **1.** the act of attributing; ascription. **2.** that which is ascribed; an attribute. **3.** authority or function assigned.

**attributive** /ə'trɪbjətɪv/, *adj.* **1.** pertaining to or having the character of attribution or an attribute. **2.** *Gram.* expressing an attribute; in English, applied esp. to adjectives and adverbs preceding the words which they modify (distinguished from *predicate* and *appositive*), as *first* in *the first day. –n.* **3.** a word expressing an attribute; attributive word, phrase, or clause. – **attributively,** *adv.* – **attributiveness,** *n.*

**attrite** /ə'traɪt/, *adj. Obs.* worn by rubbing or attrition. Also, **attrited.** [L *attrītus,* pp.]

**attrition** /ə'trɪʃən/, *n.* **1.** a rubbing against; friction. **2.** a wearing down or away by friction; abrasion. **3.** *Theol.* sorrow for one's sins motivated by fear of punishment rather than love of God. **4.** *Mil.* the reduction of the effectiveness of a force caused by loss of personnel and material. **5.** a natural, gradual reduction in membership or personnel, as by retirement, resignation or death. [L *attrītio*]

**attune** /ə'tjun, ə'tʃun/, *v.t.,* **-tuned, -tuning.** to adjust to tune or harmony; bring into accord. [AT- + TUNE]

**atua** /'ætuə/, *n. N.Z.* a god, supernatural being, or demon. [Maori]

**atwain** /ə'tweɪn/, *adv. Archaic.* in twain; in two; asunder. Also, **atwo** /ə'tu/. [ME; from A-[1] + TWAIN]

**at. wt,** atomic weight.

**atypical** /eɪ'tɪpɪkəl/, *adj.* not typical; not conforming to the type; irregular; abnormal. Also, **atypic.** [A-[6] + TYPICAL] – **atypically,** *adv.*

**Au,** *Chem.* gold. [L *aurum*]

**AU,** astronomical unit.

**aubergine** /'oʊbədʒin/, *n.* **1.** →**eggplant.** *–adj.* **2.** the colour of the dark-fruited eggplant, ranging from reddish-purple to blueish-purple. [F.]

**au bleu** /oʊ 'blɜ/, *adj.* (of fish) cooked in a court-bouillon or stock containing a lot of vinegar, and as a result, turning bluish in colour. [F: *bleu* blue]

**aubrietia** /ɔ'briʃə/, *n.* any of the trailing, purple-flowered plants of the cruciferous genus *Aubrietia,* much grown in rock gardens.

**auburn** /'ɔbən/, *n.* **1.** a reddish brown or golden brown colour. *–adj.* **2.** having auburn colour: *auburn hair.* [ME *auburne,* from OF *auborne,* from L *alburnus* whitish, from *albus* white]

**Aubusson carpet** /ˌoʊbəsɒn 'kapət/, *n.* a fine French carpet with a flat tapestry weave, hand woven in Aubusson, a town in central France.

**AUC** /eɪ ju 'si/, Australian Universities Commission.

**au citron** /oʊ sɪ'trɒn/, *adj.* with lemon juice, peel, etc. [F: with lemon]

**au contraire** /oʊ kɒn'trɛə/, *adj.* **1.** on the contrary. **2.** on the opposite or adverse side. [F]

**au courant** /oʊ ku'rɒ̃/, *adj.* acquainted with what is going on. [F]

**auction** /'ɒkʃən, 'ɔkʃən/, *n.* **1.** a public sale at which property or goods are sold to the highest bidder. **2.** *Cards.* **a.** →**auction bridge. b.** (in bridge or certain other games) the competitive bidding to fix a contract that a player or players undertake to fulfil. *–v.t.* **3.** to sell by auction (sometimes fol. by *off*): *he auctioned off his furniture.* [L *auctio* an increasing]

**auction bridge** /– 'brɪdʒ/, *n.* a variety of bridge in which all tricks won, whether bid or not, score towards game. Cf. **contract.**

**auctioneer** /ɒkʃə'nɪə, ɔk-/, *n.* **1.** one who conducts sales by auction. *–v.t.* **2.** to auction.

**auctioneer bird** /'– bɜd/, *n.* →**chowchilla** (def. 1).

**auctorial** /ɔk'tɔriəl/, *adj.* of or pertaining to an author; authorial. [L *auctor* originator + -IAL]

**audacious** /ɔ'deɪʃəs/, *adj.* **1.** bold or daring; spirited; adventurous: *audacious warrior.* **2.** reckless or bold in wrongdoing; impudent and presumptuous. [AUDACI(TY) + -OUS] – **audaciously,** *adv.* – **audaciousness,** *n.*

**audacity** /ɔ'dæsəti/, *n.* **1.** boldness or daring, esp. reckless boldness. **2.** effrontery or insolence. [L *audācia* daring + -TY[2]]

**audible** /'ɔdəbəl/, *adj.* capable of being heard; actually heard; loud enough to be heard. [ML *audībilis,* from L *audīre* hear] – **audibility** /ɔdə'bɪləti/, **audibleness,** *n.* – **audibly,** *adv.*

**audience** /'ɔdiəns/, *n.* **1.** an assembly of hearers or spectators: *the audience at a film.* **2.** the persons reached by a book, radio broadcast, etc.; public. **3.** liberty or opportunity of being heard or of speaking with or before a person or group. **4.** *Govt.* admission of a diplomatic representative to a sovereign or high officer of government; formal interview. **5.** the act of hearing or attending to words or sounds. [ME, from OF, from L *audientia* attention, hearing]

**audient** /'ɔdiənt/, *adj.* **1.** hearing; listening. *–n.* **2.** a listener. [L *audiens,* ppr.]

**audile** /'ɔdaɪl/, *n.* **1.** *Psychol.* one in whose mind auditory images are especially distinct. *–adj.* **2.** of or pertaining to hearing.

**audio** /'ɔdioʊ/, *adj.* **1.** designating electronic apparatus using audio frequencies: *audio amplifier. –n.* **2.** such apparatus.

**audio-,** a word element meaning 'hear', 'of or for hearing', as in *audiometer.* [combining form representing L *audīre* hear]

**audio frequency** /– 'frikwənsi/, *n.* any frequency at which a sound wave is audible to the human ear, in the range 15 cycles per second to 20 000 cycles per second. *Abbrev.:* A.F.

**audiology** /ɔdi'ɒlədʒi/, *n.* the study of the hearing mechanism, esp. the diagnosis and measurement of impaired function. – **audiological** /ɔdiəˈlɒdʒɪkəl/, *adj.* – **audiologist,** *n.*

**audiomagnetotellurics** /ˌɔdioumægˌnitoutɛlˈjurɪks/, *n.* a geophysical procedure using audio signals to determine the earth's resistivity. *Abbrev.:* AMT.

**audiometer** /ɔdiˈɒmətə/, *n.* an instrument for measuring and recording hearing threshholds for pure tones at normally audible frequencies. – **audiometric** /ɔdiouˈmɛtrɪk/, *adj.*

**audiometry** /ɔdiˈɒmətri/, *n.* the study and practice of the measurement of auditory capability.

**audiophile** /ˈɔdioufaɪl/, *n.* one who interests himself in the high-fidelity reproduction of sound. [AUDIO- + -PHILE]

**audio system** /ˈɔdiou ˌsɪstəm/, *n.* a combination of audio components, as record players, speakers, mixers, amplifiers, tape decks, etc., which comprise a system. Also, **sound system.**

**audiovisual** /ɔdiouˈvɪʒuəl/, *adj.* involving or directed simultaneously at the faculties of seeing and hearing: *an audiovisual aid to teaching.*

**audiphone** /ˈɔdəfoun/, *n.* a kind of diaphragm held against the upper teeth to assist hearing by transmitting sound vibrations to the auditory nerve.

**audit** /ˈɔdət/, *n.* **1.** an official examination and verification of accounts and records, esp. of financial accounts. **2.** an account or a statement of account. **3.** a calling to account. **4.** *Archaic.* a judicial hearing. **5.** *Rare.* audience. *–v.t.* **6.** to make audit of; examine (accounts, etc.) officially. **7.** to attend (lectures, classes, etc.) with official approval, but not for credit and without obligation to do the work of the course. *–v.i.* **8.** to examine and verify an account or accounts by reference to vouchers. [late ME *audite,* from L *audītus* a hearing]

**audition** /ɔˈdɪʃən/, *n.* **1.** the act, sense, or power of hearing. **2.** a hearing given to a musician, speaker, etc., to test voice qualities, performance, etc. **3.** *Rare.* what is heard. *–v.t.,* **4.** to give (someone) an audition. *–v.i.* **5.** to be tested or to perform in an audition. [L *audītio* a hearing]

**auditor** /ˈɔdətə/, *n.* **1.** a hearer; listener. **2.** a person appointed and authorised to examine accounts and accounting records, compare the charges with the vouchers, verify balance sheet and income items, and state the result.

**auditor-general** /ˌɔdətə-ˈdʒɛnrəl/, *n., pl.* **auditors-general, auditor-generals.** an officer whose duty it is to investigate and report to parliament whether any expenditure by government departments is not authorised by Act or regulation.

**auditorium** /ɔdəˈtɔriəm/, *n., pl.* **-toriums, -toria** /-ˈtɔriə/. **1.** the space for the audience in a concert hall, theatre, school, or other building. **2.** a large building or room for meetings, assemblies, theatrical performances, etc. [L]

**auditory** /ˈɔdətri, -təri/, *adj.* pertaining to hearing, to the sense of hearing, or to the organs of hearing: *the auditory nerve.* [L *audītōrius*]

**auditory canal** /– kəˈnæl/, *n.* the tubular passage leading from the projecting outer portion of the ear to the eardrum. Also, **ear canal.**

**au fait** /ou ˈfeɪ/, *adj.* having experience or practical knowledge of a thing; expert; versed. [F]

**au fond** /ou ˈfõ/, *adj.* at bottom or to the bottom; thoroughly; in reality; fundamentally. [F]

**auf Wiedersehen** /auf ˈvidəzeɪn, -zeɪən/, *interj.* until we meet again; goodbye for the present. [G]

**Aug.,** August.

**augend** /ˈɔdʒɛnd/, *n.* a number to which another number, the addend, is added. [L *augendum* the thing to be increased, neut. ger. of *augēre*]

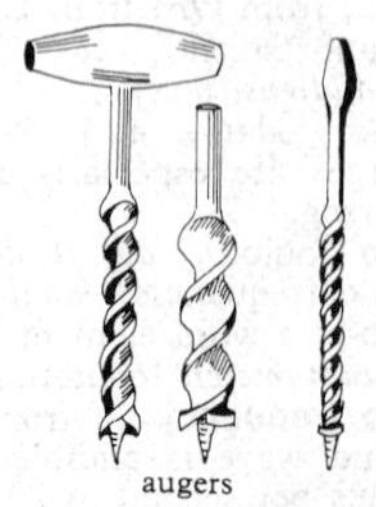
augers

**auger** /ˈɔgə/, *n.* **1.** a carpenter's tool larger than a gimlet, with a spiral groove for boring holes in wood. **2.** a large tool for boring holes deep in the ground. **3.** a tool, often simply the thread of a drill bit, used for extracting a small sample of a mineral deposit from a depth without actual excavation. [ME, var. of *nauger* (*a nauger* being taken as *an auger*), OE *nafogār*]

**aught**[1] /ɔt/, *n.* **1.** anything whatever; any part: *for aught I know.* *–adv.* **2.** *Archaic.* in any degree; at all; in any respect. Also, **ought.** [ME *aught, ought,* OE *āwiht, ōwiht* at all, anything, from *ā, ō* ever + *wiht* thing]

**aught**[2] /ɔt/, *n. Obs.* nought; zero (0). [apparently alteration of NAUGHT; *a naught* being taken as *an aught*]

**augite** /ˈɔdʒaɪt/, *n.* a mineral, a silicate, chiefly of calcium, magnesium, iron, and aluminium, a dark green to black variety of pyroxene, characteristic of basic eruptive rocks like basalt. [L *augītēs* precious stone, from Gk] – **augitic** /ɔˈdʒɪtɪk/, *adj.*

**augment** /ɔgˈmɛnt/, *v.;* /ˈɔgmənt/, *n.* *–v.t.* **1.** to make larger; enlarge in size or extent; increase. **2.** *Gram.* to add an augment to. *–v.i.* **3.** to become larger. *–n.* **4.** *Gram.* (in Greek, Sanskrit, etc.) a prefixed vowel or a lengthened initial vowel, which characterises certain forms in the inflection of verbs. [ME *augment(en),* from L *augmentāre* increase] – **augmentable,** *adj.* – **augmenter,** *n.*

**augmentation** /ɔgmənˈteɪʃən/, *n.* **1.** the act of augmenting. **2.** an augmented state. **3.** that by which anything is augmented. **4.** *Music.* modification of a theme by increasing the time value of all its notes (opposed to *diminution*).

**augmentative** /ɔgˈmɛntətɪv/, *adj.* **1.** serving to augment. **2.** *Gram.* pertaining to or productive of a form denoting increased size or intensity. In Spanish, *-ón* added to a word indicates increased size (*silla,* 'chair'; *sillón,* 'armchair'); hence it is an augmentative suffix. *–n.* **3.** *Gram.* an augmentative element or formation.

**augmented** /ɔgˈmɛntəd/, *adj. Music.* (of an interval) greater by a semitone than the corresponding perfect or major interval.

**augmentor** /ɔgˈmɛntə/, *n.* **1.** *Zool.* any nerve that increases the activity rate of an organ as a gland or muscle. **2.** *Zool.* (in vertebrates) the nerve which increases the heartbeat rate. **3.** *Aerospace.* a device, as an afterburner, which achieves additional thrust from a jet or rocket engine.

**au gratin** /ou ˈgrætn, grəˈtæn/, *adj.* (of food) cooked with a covering of browned breadcrumbs or grated cheese or with both. [F: with a crust]

**augur** /ˈɔgə/, *n.* **1.** one of a body of ancient Roman officials charged with observing and interpreting omens, for guidance in public affairs. **2.** any soothsayer; prophet. *–v.t.* **3.** to divine or predict, as from omens; prognosticate. **4.** to afford an omen of. *–v.i.* **5.** to conjecture from signs or omens; presage. **6.** to be a sign; bode (*well* or *ill*). [L] – **augural** /ˈɔgjərəl/, *adj.* – **augurship,** *n.*

**augury** /ˈɔgjəri/, *n., pl.* **-ries. 1.** the art or practice of an augur; divination. **2.** a rite or observation of an augur. **3.** an omen, token, or indication. [ME, from L *augurium*]

**august** /ɔˈgʌst/, *adj.* **1.** inspiring reverence or admiration; of supreme dignity or grandeur; majestic: *an august spectacle.* **2.** venerable: *your august father.* [L *augustus*] – **augustly,** *adv.* – **augustness,** *n.*

**August** /ˈɔgəst/, *n.* the eighth month of the year, containing 31 days. [named after *Augustus* Caesar, 63 B.C. - A.D. 14, first Roman emperor]

**Augustan** /ɔˈgʌstən/, *adj.* **1.** pertaining to Augustus Caesar, first Roman emperor, 27 B.C. to A.D. 14, or to his reign (the **Augustan Age**). **2.** having some of the characteristics of Augustan literature, as classicism, correctness, brilliance, nobility (in English literature, the 17th-18th century). *–n.* **3.** an author in an Augustan age.

**Augustinian** /ɔgəsˈtɪniən/, *adj.* **1.** pertaining to St Augustine (A.D. 354-430), to his doctrines, or to any religious order following his rule. *–n.* **2.** one who adopts the views or doctrines of St Augustine. – **Augustinianism, Augustinism** /ɔˈgʌstənɪzəm/, *n.*

**au jus** /ou ˈʒus/, *adj.* (meat) served in its own gravy. [F]

**auk** /ɔk/, *n.* **1.** any of certain short-winged, three-toed diving birds of the family Alcidae of northern seas, esp. certain species of this family, as the **razor-billed auk,** *Alca torda,* and the extinct, flightless **great auk,** *Pinguinis impennis.* **2. little auk,** a small, short-billed black and white bird, *Plautus alle,* of Greenland, Novaya Zemlya, etc. [Scand.: cf. Dan. *alke*]

**auklet** /ˈɔklət/, *n.* any of various small members of the auk family found in north Pacific waters, as the **crested auklet,**

*Aethia cristatella,* and its allies.

**au lait** /oʊ 'leɪ/, *adj.* prepared or served with milk. [F]

**auld lang syne** /oʊld læŋ 'zaɪn/, **1.** old times, esp. times fondly remembered. **2.** old or long friendship. **3.** (*caps*) a song traditionally sung to celebrate friendship, as on New Years Eve, the departure of a passenger ship, etc. [Scot. *auld langsyne* old long since]

**aulos** /'ɔləs/, *n., pl.* **-loi** /-lɔɪ/. an ancient Greek double-reed wind instrument.

**aum** /ɔm/, *n.* →**om.**

**aumbry** /'ɔmbri/, *n.* →**ambry.**

**au naturel** /oʊ nætʃə'rɛl/, *adj.* **1.** in the natural state; naked. **2.** cooked plainly. **3.** uncooked. [F]

**aunt** /ant/, *n.* **1.** the sister of one's father or mother. **2.** the wife of one's uncle. **3.** (a term of address used by children to a female friend of the family). **4. my sainted aunt!** (an expression of surprise or disbelief).

**Aunt Sally** /– 'sæli/, *n.* **1.** *Chiefly Brit.* a figure, typically of a woman smoking a pipe, at which objects are thrown at a fair. **2.** a person who is the butt of jibes, insults, etc.

**aunty** /'anti/, *n.* **1.** a familiar or diminutive form of aunt. **2.** *Colloq.* a conservative body or organisation, esp. the Australian Broadcasting Commission. **3.** *Colloq.* an effeminate or homosexual older male. Also, **auntie.**

**aunty's downfall** /antiz 'daʊnfɔl/, *n. Colloq.* (*joc.*) gin; mother's ruin.

**au pair** /oʊ 'pɛə/, *adj.* **1.** by exchange; used **a.** of a system whereby young people living in different countries stay in each other's homes to learn the language. **b.** of young girls, esp. foreigners, who do domestic work for a small payment and their keep. *–n.* **2.** a girl or, occasionally, a boy, who does this. [F]

**au poivre** /oʊ 'pwavr/, *adj.* cooked with ground black pepper. [F: with pepper]

**aura** /'ɔrə/, *n., pl.* **auras, aurae** /'ɔri/. **1.** a distinctive air, atmosphere, character, etc. : *an aura of culture.* **2.** a subtle emanation proceeding from a body and surrounding it as an atmosphere. **3.** *Elect.* the motion of the air at an electrified point. **4.** *Pathol.* a sensation, as of a current of cold air, or other sensory experience, preceding an attack of epilepsy, hysteria, etc. [L, from Gk: breath of air]

**aural**[1] /'ɔrəl/, *adj.* of or pertaining to an aura. [AUR(A) + -AL[1]]

**aural**[2] /'ɔrəl/, *adj.* of, or perceived by, the organs of hearing. [L *auris* ear + -AL[1]] – **aurally,** *adv.*

**aureate** /'ɔrieɪt/, *adj.* **1.** golden. **2.** brilliant; splendid. [ME *aureat,* from L *aureātus* adorned with gold]

**aureole** /'ɒrioʊl, 'ɔ-/, *n.* **1.** a radiance surrounding the head or the whole figure in the representation of a sacred personage. **2.** any encircling ring of light or colour; a halo. **3.** *Astron.* →**corona** (defs 1 and 2). **4.** *Geol.* a zone surrounding an igneous intrusion in which contact metamorphism of the country rock has taken place; contact zone. Also, **aureola** /ɒri'oʊlə, ɔ'riələ/. [L *aureola,* fem. of *aureolus* golden]

**aureomycin** /ˌɔrioʊ'maɪsən/, *n. Med.* an antibiotic effective against diseases of bacterial origin by stopping bacterial protein synthesis. [Trademark]

**au revoir** /oʊ rə'vwa, oʊ 'vwa/, *interj.* until we see each other again; goodbye for the present. [F]

**auric** /'ɔrɪk/, *adj.* of or containing gold, esp. in the trivalent state. [L *aurum* gold + -IC]

**auricle** /'ɔrɪkəl, 'ɒr-/, *n.* **1.** *Anat.* **a.** the projecting outer portion of the ear; the pinna. **b.** →**atrium** (def. 3a). **2.** *Bot., Zool.* a part like or likened to an ear. [L *auricula,* diminutive of *auris* ear] – **auricled,** *adj.*

**auricula** /ə'rɪkjələ/, *n., pl.* **-lae.** any of a wide variety of cultivated plants derived from *Primula auricula,* native to the European Alps.

**auricular** /ɔ'rɪkjələ/, *adj.* **1.** of or pertaining to the organs of hearing. **2.** perceived by or addressed to the ear: *auricular confession.* **3.** dependent on hearing; aural. **4.** shaped like an ear; auriculate. **5.** *Anat.* pertaining to an auricle of the heart. **6.** *Ornith.* denoting certain feathers, usu. of peculiar structure, which overlie and defend the outer opening of a bird's ear. *–n.* **7.** (*usu. pl.*) *Ornith.* an auricular feather.

**auriculate** /ɔ'rɪkjələt, -leɪt/, *adj.* **1.** having auricles, or earlike parts. **2.** shaped like an ear. Also, **auriculated.**

**auriferous** /ɔ'rɪfərəs/, *adj.* yielding or containing gold. [L *aurifer* gold-bearing + -OUS]

**Aurignacian** /ɔrɪg'neɪʃən/, *adj.* of or belonging to a sequence of related Upper Palaeolithic cultures. [named after *Aurignac,* a village in S France where remains were first found]

aurochs

**aurist** /'ɔrəst/, *n.* →**otologist.**

**aurochs** /'ɔrɒks/, *n., pl.* **-rochs.** **1.** a European wild ox, *Bos primigenius,* now extinct; the urus. **2.** →**wisent.** [G, var. of *Auerochs,* MHG *ūr-ochse,* from *ūr* (c. OE *ūr* wild ox) + *Ochse* ox]

**aurora** /ə'rɔrə/, *n.* a display in the skies of moving streamers, bands, curtains, arcs, etc., of light, visible at high latitudes and probably caused by streams of charged particles from the sun, passing into the earth's magnetic field.

**aurora australis** /– ɒs'traləs/, *n.* the aurora of the Southern Hemisphere. [NL]

**aurora borealis** /– bɔri'aləs/, *n.* the aurora of the Northern Hemisphere; northern lights. [NL]

**auroral** /ə'rɔrəl/, *adj.* **1.** of or like the dawn. **2.** pertaining to a polar aurora. – **aurorally,** *adv.*

**aurous** /'ɔrəs/, *adj.* **1.** *Chem.* containing monovalent gold. **2.** of or containing gold. [AUR(UM) + -OUS]

**aurum** /'ɔrəm/, *n. Chem.* gold. *Symbol:* Au

**Aus** /ɒz/, *Colloq. –n.* **1.** an Australian. *–adj.* **2.** Australian. Also, **Aus'.**

**AUS** /eɪ ju 'ɛs/, Australian Union of Students.

**auscultate** /'ɒskəlteɪt/, *v.,* **-tated, -tating.** *–v.t.* **1.** *Med.* to examine (a person) by auscultation. *–v.i.* **2.** to examine by auscultation. – **auscultative** /ɒskəl'teɪtɪv/, /ɒs'kʌltətɪv/, *adj.* – **auscultator,** *n.*

**auscultation** /ɒskəl'teɪʃən/, *n.* **1.** *Med.* the act of listening, either directly or through a stethoscope or other instrument, to sounds within the body, as a method of diagnosis, etc. **2.** the act of listening. [L *auscultātio* a listening]

**auslese** /'aʊsleɪzə, 'ɒzleɪz/, *adj.* (of wine) made from grapes which have been carefully selected. [G *Ausles* choice wine]

**auspicate** /'ɔspəkeɪt/, *v.,* **-cated, -cating.** *Obs. or Rare.* *–v.t.* **1.** to initiate with ceremonies calculated to ensure good luck; inaugurate. *–v.i.* **2.** to augur. [L *auspicātus,* pp.]

**auspice** /'ɔspəs/, *n., pl.* **auspices** /'ɔspəsəz/. **1.** (*usu. pl.*) favouring influence; patronage: *under the auspices of the Australian Red Cross Society.* **2.** a propitious circumstance. **3.** a divination or prognostication, originally, from birds. [F, from L *auspicium*] – **auspicial** /ɔ'spɪʃəl/, *adj.*

**auspicious** /ɔ'spɪʃəs, ə-/, *adj.* **1.** of good omen; betokening success; favourable; an auspicious moment. **2.** favoured by fortune; prosperous; fortunate. [L *auspicium* divination + -OUS] – **auspiciously,** *adv.* – **auspiciousness,** *n.*

**Aus. Rules** /ɒz 'rulz/, *n.* →**Australian Rules.**

**Aussie** /'ɒzi/, *Colloq. –adj.* **1.** Australian. *–n.* **2.** an Australian. **3.** Australia.

**Aussieland** /'ɒzilænd/, *n. Colloq.* Australia. – **Aussielander,** *n.*

**Aussie Rules** /ˌɒzi 'rulz/, *n. pl. Colloq.* →**Australian Rules.**

**Aust.,** **1.** Australia. **2.** Australian.

**austenite** /'ɒstənaɪt/, *n.* a solid solution of one or more elements in face-centred cubic iron; unless otherwise designated (such as nickel austenite) the solute is generally assumed to be carbon. – **austenitic** /ɒstə'nɪtɪk/, *adj.*

**austere** /ɒs'tɪə, ɔs-/, *adj.* **1.** harsh in manner; stern in appearance; forbidding. **2.** severe in disciplining or restraining oneself; morally strict. **3.** grave; sober; serious. **4.** severely simple; without ornament: *austere writing.* **5.** rough to the taste; sour or harsh in flavour. [ME, from L *austērus,* from Gk *austērós*] – **austerely,** *adv.* – **austereness,** *n.*

**austerity** /ɒs'tɛrəti/, *n., pl.* **-ties.** **1.** austere quality; severity of manner, life, etc.; lack of luxury or ornament. **2.** (*usu. pl.*) a severe or ascetic practice. *–adj.* **3.** evincing austerity; adopted for the sake of, or because of, austerity.

**austral** /'ɒstrəl/, *adj.* **1.** southern. **2.** (*cap.*) Australian. *–n.* **3.** *S.A. Obs.* →**fritz.** [L *austrālis*]

**Austral.,** **1.** Australasia. **2.** Australia.

**Australasia** /ˌɒstrəˈleɪʒə, -ʃə/, *n.* Australia, New Zealand, and neighbouring islands of the South Pacific Ocean. – **Australasian,** *adj., n.*

**Australasian breed** /ɒstrəˌleɪʒən ˈbrid/, *n.* one of several breeds of sheep evolved in Australia and New Zealand.

**Australia,** /ɒsˈtreɪljə, əs-/, *n.* **1.** the continent south-east of Asia. **2.** a country consisting of the federated states and territories of the continent of Australia and the island of Tasmania; an independent member of the Commonwealth. Official name: **Commonwealth of Australia.**

**Australia Felix** /ɒstreɪljə ˈfilɪks/, *n.* the former name of the colony of Victoria.

**Australian** /ɒsˈtreɪljən, əs-/, *adj.* **1.** of or pertaining to Australia. *–n.* **2. the great Australian adjective,** (*joc.*) bloody (def. 5). **3.** a person native to or resident in Australia. **4.** the English language as spoken in Australia.

**Australiana** /ɒˌstreɪliˈanə, əs-/, *n. pl.* items, esp. of historical interest, originating in or relating to Australia, as early books, furniture, paintings, etc.

**Australian Antarctic Territory,** *n.* a sector of Antarctica including most of the land between 45° and 160° E longitude; an Australian territory.

**Australian badger** /ɒstreɪljən ˈbædʒə/, *n. Obs.* →**wombat.**

**Australian ballot** /– ˈbælət/, *n. Chiefly U.S. and Brit.* a ballot which ensures secrecy in voting, originally used in South Australia.

**Australian Capital Territory,** *n.* a federal territory in south-eastern Australia, within New South Wales, where Canberra, the national capital, is situated. *Abbrev.:* **ACT, A.C.T.**

**Australian cattle dog,** *n.* a purebred dog with black or red face and ears and dark blue body speckled with lighter blues, developed in Australia for work with cattle by crossing the blue merle Scotch collie with the dingo, then crossing result with the Dalmation and the black-and-tan kelpie; blue heeler. Also, **Australian blue-speckle cattle dog.**

**Australian coot** /ˈ– kut/, *n.* See **coot** (def. 1).

**Australian courser** /– ˈkɔsə/, *n.* a small, long-legged, reddish-brown bird, *Stilitia isabella,* which runs rapidly over the ground and frequents bare open areas in Australia and southern New Guinea; Australian pratincole.

**Australian crawl** /– ˈkrɔl/, *n.* →**crawl**[1] (def. 7).

**Australian edelweiss** /– ˈeɪdlvaɪs/, *n.* a spreading herb, *Ewartia nubigena,* family Compositae, having grey foliage and small flowers, restricted to high altitudes in the Australian Alps, somewhat resembling the European edelweiss.

**Australian English** /– ˈɪŋglɪʃ/, *n.* that dialect of English which is spoken by native-born Australians. It is characterised by particular accent, lexis, and idiom.

**Australian flag** /ˈ– flæg/, *n. Colloq.* the bottom of a man's shirt when it has come out from his trousers.

**Australian Football** /– ˈfʊtbɔl/, *n.* →**Australian Rules.**

**Australian fur seal,** *n.* a small-eared Antarctic and southern Australian seal, *Arctocephalus doriferus.*

**Australian gannet** /– ˈgænət/, *n.* See **gannet.**

**Australian goshawk** /– ˈgɒshɔk/, *n.* a brown goshawk, *Accipiter fasciatus,* common throughout Australia; chicken-hawk.

**Australian ground-thrush** /– ˈgraʊnd-θrʌʃ/, *n.* a shy, sedentary bird, *Zoothera dauma,* bronze-brown above with buff underparts and with distinct rounded black tips to its feathers giving the appearance of scales; found in eastern coastal and tableland areas.

**Australian Illawarra Shorthorn,** *n.* a breed of horned dairy cattle with a thick smooth coat, usu. deep red, free from black or brindle marking.

**Australianise** /ɒsˈtreɪljənaɪz, əs-/, *v.t. Colloq.* to make or become Australian in character; assimilate to the customs and institutions of Australia.

**Australianism** /ɒsˈtreɪljənɪzəm, əs-/, *n.* a word or phrase originating in or peculiar to Australia.

**Australianist** /ɒsˈtreɪljənəst/, *adj.* consciously Australian: *a writer with Australianist tendencies.*

**Australian national flag,** *n.* a flag consisting of five white stars of the Southern Cross and the white Commonwealth star on a blue background with a Union Jack in canton.

**Australian National Football,** *n.* →**Australian Rules.**

**Australianness** /ɒsˈtreɪljənnəs, əs-/, *n.* the quality of being Australian. Also, **Australianity.**

**Australian pipit** /ɒsˌtreɪljən ˈpɪpət/, *n.* a ground-living pipit, *Anthus novaeseelandiae,* creamy brown mottled with dark brown, found in open country all over Australia and throughout New Zealand, New Guinea and much of Africa and Asia; Richard's pipit; groundlark.

**Australian pratincole** /– ˈprætɪŋkoʊl/, *n.* →**Australian courser.**

**Australian realm** /– ˈrɛlm/, *n.* a biogeographical realm comprising Australia, Tasmania, and the islands south-east of Wallace's line, including the islands of New Guinea and the Solomons, but excluding the New Zealand realm.

**Australian Rules** /– ˈrulz/, *n pl.* a code of football which originated in Australia and which is most popular in the southern and western States. It has its origins in Gaelic football. Also, **Australian National Football, Australian Football, Aussie Rules.**

Australian Rules: player taking a mark (def. 22)

**Australian salmon** /– ˈsæmən/, *n.* a large sport fish, *Arripis trutta,* of Australian and New Zealand coastal waters, superficially resembling a salmon but actually a marine perch. Also, **salmon-trout.**

**Australian silky terrier,** *n.* a small, lightly built dog of medium length with erect ears, docked tail and long, silky, blue or grey-blue coat with tan markings. Also, **Sydney silky.**

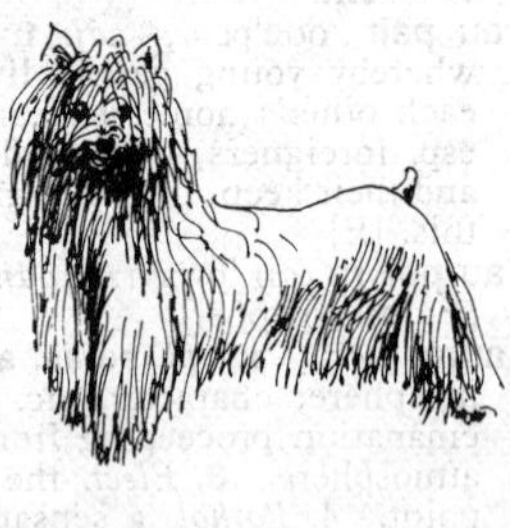

**Australian terrier** /– ˈtɛriə/, *n.* a small, sturdy, low-set and rather elongated dog with erect ears, docked tail, and a short, coarse coat, usu. grey-blue with rich tan markings on face and legs.

**australite** /ˈɒstrəlaɪt/, *n.* tektite found in Australia.

Australian silky terrier

**Australoid** /ˈɒstrəlɔɪd/, *adj.* **1.** of or relating to an ethnic group which includes the Australian Aborigines and certain peoples of Asia and the Pacific islands. *–n.* **2.** a person having the physical characteristics of this group. [AUSTRAL(IAN) + -OID]

**australopithecine** /ˌɒstrəloʊˈpɪθəsin/, *n.* **1.** a primate of the extinct genus *Australopithecus,* of the Pleistocene epoch, found first in southern Africa, having jaws resembling those of man and a skull resembling that of the apes. *–adj.* **2.** belonging or pertaining to the genus *Australopithecus.* [NL *australopithec(us)* (from *australo-,* combining form of *australis* southern + *pithecus,* from Gk *píthēkos* ape) + -INE[1]]

Australian terrier

**Australorp** /ˈɒstrəlɔp/, *n.* one of the Australian breed of Orpington fowl, usu. black in colour and kept chiefly for egg production.

**Austria** /ˈɒstriə/, *n.* a country in central Europe. – **Austrian,** *adj., n.*

**Austro-**[1], a word element, meaning southern, as *Austro-Asian.* [L *auster* the south]

**Austro-**[2], a word element, meaning 'Austria', 'Austrian'.

**austromancy** /ˈɒstrəmænsi/, *n.* divination by a study of the winds.

**Austronesia** /ˌɒstrəˈniʒə/, *n.* islands of the central and south Pacific. [AUSTRO-[1] + Gk *nēsos* island + -IA]

**Austronesian** /ɒstrəˈniʒən, -ʃən/, *adj.* **1.** of or pertaining to Austronesia. *–n.* **2.** a family of languages spoken in the Pacific, consisting of four divisions, Indonesian, Melanesian, Micronesian, and Polynesian; Malayo-Polynesian.

**aut-**, variant of **auto-**[1] before most vowels, as in *autacoid.*
**autacoid** /'ɔtəkɔɪd/, *n.* a substance secreted by one organ into the bloodstream or lymph, and controlling organic processes elsewhere in the body; a hormone. [AUT- + Gk *ákos* remedy + -OID]
**autarchy** /'ɔtaki/, *n., pl.* **-chies. 1.** absolute sovereignty. **2.** self-government. [Gk *autarchía* self-rule] – **autarchic,** *adj.*
**autarky** /'ɔtaki/, *n., pl.* **-kies. 1.** the condition of self sufficiency, esp. economic, as applied to a state. **2.** a national policy of economic independence. [Gk *autárkeia*] – **autarkical** /ɔ'takɪkəl/, *adj.* – **autarkist,** *n., adj.*
**autecism** /'ɔtəsɪzəm/, *n. U.S.* →**autoecism.**
**autecology** /ɔtə'kɒlədʒi/, *n.* that branch of ecology which deals with the individual organism and its environment. Cf. **synecology.**
**auth., 1.** author. **2.** authorised.
**authentic** /ɔ'θɛntɪk/, *adj.* **1.** entitled to acceptance or belief; reliable; trustworthy: *an authentic story.* **2.** of the authorship or origin reputed; of genuine origin: *authentic documents.* **3.** *Law.* executed with all due formalities: *an authentic deed.* **4.** *Music.* (of a church mode) having a range extending from the final to the octave above. Cf. **plagal. 5.** *Obs.* authoritative. Also, **authentical.** [LL *authenticus,* from Gk *authentikós* warranted] – **authentically,** *adv.*
**authenticate** /ɔ'θɛntəkeɪt/, *v.t.,* **-cated, -cating. 1.** to make authoritative or valid. **2.** to establish as genuine. – **authenticable** /ɔ'θɛntɪkəbəl/, *adj.* – **authentication** /ɔˌθɛntə'keɪʃən/, *n.* – **authenticator,** *n.*
**authenticity** /ˌɔθɛn'tɪsəti/, *n.* the quality of being authentic; reliability; genuineness.
**author** /'ɔθə/, *n.* **1.** a person who writes a novel, poem, essay, etc.; the composer of a literary work, as distinguished from a compiler, translator, editor, or copyist. **2.** the originator, beginner, or creator of anything. **3.** the literary productions of a writer: *to find a passage in an author.* –*v.t.* **4.** to be the author of; write. [ME *autor,* from OF, from L *auctor* originator] – **authoress** /'ɔθərəs/, *n. fem.* – **authorial** /ɔ'θɔriəl/, *adj.* – **authorless,** *adj.*
**authorisation** /ˌɔθəraɪ'zeɪʃən/, *n.* the act of authorising; permission from or establishment by an authority. Also, **authorization.**
**authorise** /'ɔθəraɪz/, *v.t.,* **-rised, -rising. 1.** to give authority or legal power to; empower (to do something). **2.** to give authority for; formally sanction (an act or proceeding). **3.** to establish by authority or usage: *authorised by custom.* **4.** to afford a ground for; warrant; justify. Also, **authorize.** – **authoriser,** *n.*
**authorised** /'ɔθəraɪzd/, *adj.* **1.** authoritative; endowed with authority. **2.** legally or duly sanctioned.
**authorised capital** /– 'kæpətəl/, *n.* the amount of a company's capital which directors are able to issue without seeking the shareholders' approval.
**Authorised Version** /– 'vɜʒən/, *n.* an English revision of the Bible prepared under James I and published in 1611.
**authoritarian** /ɔˌθɒrə'tɛəriən, ə-/, *adj.* **1.** favouring the principle of subjection to authority as opposed to that of individual freedom. –*n.* **2.** one who favours authoritarian principles. [AUTHORIT(Y) + -ARIAN] – **authoritarianism,** *n.*
**authoritative** /ɔ'θɒrətətɪv, ə-/, *adj.* **1.** having due authority; having the sanction or weight of authority: *an authoritative opinion.* **2.** having an air of authority; positive; peremptory; dictatorial. – **authoritatively,** *adv.* – **authoritativeness,** *n.*
**authority** /ɔ'θɒrəti, ə-/, *n., pl.* **-ties. 1.** the right to determine, adjudicate, or otherwise settle issues or disputes; the right to control, command, or determine. **2.** a person or body with such rights. **3.** an accepted source of information, advice, etc. **4.** a standard author or his writing; an expert on a subject. **5.** a statute, court rule, or judicial decision which establishes a rule or principle of law; a ruling. **6.** title to respect or acceptance; commanding influence. **7.** a warrant for action; justification. **8.** testimony; witness. [ME *auctorite,* from L *auctōritas*]
**authorship** /'ɔθəʃɪp/, *n.* **1.** the occupation or career of writing books, articles, etc. **2.** origin as to author, composer, or compiler: *the authorship of a book.*
**autism** /'ɔtɪzəm/, *n.* **1.** *Psychol.* fantasy; introverted thought; daydreaming; marked subjectivity of interpretation. **2.** *Psychiatry.* a syndrome of unknown aetiology, chiefly characterised by some degree of inability to comprehend or communicate, failure to relate affectively, and inappropriate or obsessive behaviour. [AUT- + -ISM] – **autistic** /ɔ'tɪstɪk/, *adj.*
**autistic** /ɔ'tɪstɪk/, *adj.* **1.** of or pertaining to autism. –*n.* **2.** one who suffers from autism.
**auto**[1] /'ɔtoʊ/, *n., pl.* **-tos.** *Chiefly U.S.* automobile. [shortened form]
**auto**[2] /'ɔtoʊ/, *n.* **1.** →**automatic control. 2. on auto,** *Colloq.* **a.** (of a machine, as an aeroplane) on automatic control. **b.** (of a person) not giving full attention; not thinking.
**auto-**[1], a word element meaning 'self', 'same', as in *autograph.* Also, **aut-.** [Gk, combining form of *autós*]
**auto-**[2], a combining form of **automobile.**
**auto-analyser** /ˌɔtoʊ-'ænəlaɪzə/, *n. Med.* a machine which estimates the concentrations of constituents of fluid, esp. blood.
**autobahn** /'ɔtoʊban/, *n.* a motorway. [G]
**autobiographical** /ˌɔtəbaɪə'græfɪkəl/, *adj.* dealing with one's life history. Also, **autobiographic.** – **autobiographically,** *adv.*
**autobiography** /ˌɔtəbaɪ'ɒgrəfi/, *n., pl.* **-phies.** an account of a person's life written by himself. – **autobiographer,** *n.*
**autocade** /'ɔtoʊkeɪd, 'ɔtə-/, *n. U.S.* →**motorcade.**
**autocephalous** /ˌɔtoʊ'sɛfələs, ˌɔtə-/, *adj.* **1.** not under the jurisdiction of another. **2.** *Eastern Ch.* (of a church) appointing its own bishop, though still in communion with the ecumenical patriarch. [MGk *autoképhalos* having its own head. See AUTO-[1], -CEPHALOUS] – **autocephaly,** *n.*
**autochthon** /ɔ'tɒkθən/, *n., pl.* **-thons, -thones** /-θəniz/. **1.** an aboriginal inhabitant. **2.** *Ecol.* one of the indigenous animals or plants of a region. **3.** in alpine geology, a succession of beds moved comparatively little from their original site of formation, despite being intensely folded and faulted. [Gk: lit., sprung from the land itself]
**autochthonous** /ɔ'tɒkθənəs/, *adj.* **1.** pertaining to autochthons; aboriginal; indigenous. **2.** *Geol.* (of rocks) having had their dominant constituents formed in situ, as rock salt. Also, **autochthonal, autochthonic** /ˌɔtɒk'θɒnɪk/. – **autochthonism, autochthony,** *n.*
**autoclave** /'ɔtəkleɪv/, *n.* **1.** a heavy vessel in which chemical reactions take place under high pressure. **2.** a pressure cooker. **3.** *Med.* a strong closed vessel in which steam under pressure effects sterilisation. [F: self-regulation, from *auto-* AUTO-[1] + L *clāvis* key]
**autocracy** /ɔ'tɒkrəsi/, *n., pl.* **-cies. 1.** uncontrolled or unlimited authority over others, invested in a single person; the government or power of an absolute monarch. **2.** independent or self-derived power. [Gk *autokrasía*]
**autocrat** /'ɔtəkræt/, *n.* **1.** an absolute ruler; a monarch who holds and exercises the powers of government as by inherent right, not subject to restrictions. **2.** a person invested with, or claiming to exercise, absolute authority. [Gk *autokratḗs* ruling by oneself]
**autocratic** /ɔtə'krætɪk/, *adj.* pertaining to or of the nature of autocracy; absolute; holding independent and unlimited powers of government. Also, **autocratical.** – **autocratically,** *adv.*
**autocue** /'ɔtoʊkju/, *n.* →**teleprompter.** [Trademark]
**auto-da-fé** /ˌɔtoʊ-da-'feɪ/, *n., pl.* **autos-da-fé.** the public declaration of the judgment passed on persons tried in the courts of the Spanish Inquisition, followed by execution of the sentences imposed, including burning (by civil authorities) of heretics at the stake. [Pg.: act of (the) faith]
**autodestruct** /ɔtoʊdə'strʌkt/ *v.i.;* /'ɔtoʊdəstrʌkt/, *n. adj.* →**selfdestruct.**
**autodidact** /ˌɔtə'daɪdækt, ˌɔtoʊ-/, *n.* a person who is self-taught. [AUTO-[1] + Gk *didaktós* taught] – **autodidactic,** *adj.*
**autodigestion** /ˌɔtoʊdaɪ'dʒɛstʃən/, *n.* →**autolysis.** – **autodigestive,** *adj.*
**autoecism** /ɔ'tisɪzəm/, *n.* the development of the entire life cycle of a parasitic fungus on a single host or group of hosts. Also, *U.S.,* **autecism.** [AUT- + Gk *oîkos* house + -ISM] – **autoecious** /ɔ'tiʃəs/, *adj.*
**auto-electrician** /ˌɔtoʊ-ɛlɛk'trɪʃən/, *n.* one who specialises in the repair and servicing of the electrical circuits of motor cars.

**autoerotic** /ˌɔtoʊəˈrɒtɪk/, *adj.* producing sexual emotion without association with another person.

**autoerotism** /ˌɔtoʊˈɛrətɪzəm/, *n.* the arousal and satisfaction of sexual emotion within or by oneself, usu. by masturbation. Also, **autoeroticism** /ˌɔtoʊəˈrɒtəsɪzəm/.

**autofermenter** /ˌɔtoʊfəˈmɛntə/, *n.* a vessel used in wine-making in which the cap (def. 16) remains submerged during fermentation.

**autogamy** /ɔˈtɒgəmi/, *n.* fecundation of the ovules of a flower by its own pollen; self-fertilisation (opposed to *allogamy*). – **autogamous,** *adj.*

**autogenesis** /ɔtəˈdʒɛnəsəs/, *n.* →**abiogenesis.** Also, **autogeny** /ɔˈtɒdʒəni/.

**autogenetic** /ɔtədʒəˈnɛtɪk, ɔtoʊ-/, *adj.* **1.** self-generated. **2.** *Biol.* of autogenesis. – **autogenetically,** *adv.*

**autogenous** /ɔˈtɒdʒənəs/, *adj.* **1.** self-produced; self-generated. **2.** *Physiol.* pertaining to substances generated in the body. [Gk *autogenḗs* self-produced + -OUS] – **autogenously,** *adv.*

**autogiro** /ɔtoʊˈdʒaɪroʊ/, *n.* →**autogyro.**

**autograft** /ˈɔtəgraft/, *n.* living tissue transferred from one part of a patient's body to another.

**autograph** /ˈɔtəgræf, -graf/, *n.* **1.** a person's own signature. **2.** a person's own handwriting. **3.** a manuscript in the author's handwriting. **4.** a machine which produces a stereoscopic effect from a series of aerial survey photographs and simultaneously draws at scale and dimension the topography of the area photographed. –*adj.* **5.** written by a person's own hand: *an autograph letter.* **6.** containing autographs: *an autograph album.* –*v.t.* **7.** to write one's name on or in: *to autograph a book.* **8.** to write with one's own hand. [L *autographum,* from Gk *autógraphon.* See AUTO-[1], -GRAPH] – **autographic** /ˌɔtəˈgræfɪk/, **autographical,** *adj.* – **autographically,** *adv.*

**autography** /ɔˈtɒgrəfi/, *n.* **1.** autograph writing. **2.** exact reproduction of the outline of a drawing or writing; production of a facsimile.

**autogyro** /ɔtəˈdʒaɪroʊ, ɔtoʊ-/, *n.* an aircraft with horizontally rotating blades turned in flight by air forces resulting from its forward motion. [Sp. See AUTO-[1], GYRO-]

**autoharp** /ˈɔtoʊhap/, *n.* a zither played with the fingers or a plectrum, which has a number of button-controlled damper bars designed for the production of common chords, and which is easily learned. [Trademark]

**autohypnosis** /ˌɔtoʊhɪpˈnoʊsəs/, *n.* self-induced hypnosis or hypnotic state. – **autohypnotic** /ˌɔtoʊhɪpˈnɒtɪk/, *adj.*

**autoicous** /ɔˈtɔɪkəs/, *adj.* having antheridia and archegonia on the same plant, synoicous, paroicous, or otherwise. [AUT- + Gk *oîkos* house + -OUS]

**auto-ignition** /ˌɔtoʊ-ɪgˈnɪʃən/, *n.* **1.** the ignition of the fuel and air mixture in an internal-combustion engine due to the heat of the combustion chamber or to compression. **2.** spontaneous combustion.

**auto-immune** /ˌɔtoʊ-ɪmˈjun/, *adj.* caused by, or associated with, auto-immunisation. – **auto-immunity,** *n.*

**auto-immunisation** /ˌɔtoʊ-ɪmjənaɪˈzeɪʃən/, *n. Med.* the sensitisation of a person to a substance elaborated in his own body. Also, **auto-immunization.**

**auto-infection** /ˌɔtoʊ-ɪnˈfɛkʃən/, *n.* infection from within the body.

**auto-inoculation** /ˌɔtoʊ-ɪnɒkjəˈleɪʃən/, *n.* inoculation of a healthy part with an infective agent from a diseased part of the same body.

**auto-intoxication** /ˌɔtoʊ-ɪntɒksəˈkeɪʃən/, *n. Pathol.* poisoning with toxic substances formed within the body, as during intestinal digestion.

**autokinetic** /ˌɔtoʊkəˈnɛtɪk, -kaɪ-/, *adj.* self-moving; automatic. [Gk *autokī́nētos* self-moved + -IC]

**autoland gear** /ˌɔtoʊlænd ˈgɪə/, *n. Aeron.* automatic landing gear.

**autolysin** /ɔˈtɒləsən, ɔtəˈlaɪsən/, *n.* an autolytic agent.

**autolysis** /ɔˈtɒləsəs/, *n.* the breakdown of plant or animal tissue by the action of enzymes contained in the tissue affected; self-digestion. [AUTO-[1] + -LYSIS] – **autolytic** /ɔtəˈlɪtɪk/, *adj.*

**automat** /ˈɔtəmæt/, *n.* an automatic apparatus for serving articles, esp. food, to customers upon the dropping of the proper coins or tokens into a slot. [Gk *autómaton.* See AUTOMATON]

**automata** /ɔˈtɒmətə/, *n.* plural of **automaton.**

**automate** /ˈɔtəmeɪt/, *v.t.,* **-mated, -mating. 1.** to apply the principles of automation to (a mechanical process). **2.** to operate or control by automation. [backformation from AUTOMATION]

**automatic** /ˌɔtəˈmætɪk/, *adj.* **1.** having the power of self-motion; self-moving or self-acting; mechanical. **2.** *Physiol.* occurring independently of volition, as certain muscular actions. **3.** (of a firearm, pistol, etc.) utilising the recoil, or part of the force of the explosive, to eject the spent cartridge shell, introduce a new cartridge, cock the arm, and fire it repeatedly. **4.** done unconsciously or from force of habit; mechanical (opposed to *voluntary*). –*n.* **5.** a machine which operates automatically, as a motor car with automatic gear shift. **6.** →**automatic rifle. 7.** →**automatic pistol.** [Gk *autómatos* self-acting + -IC] – **automatically,** *adv.*

**automatic computer** /– kəmˈpjutə/, *n.* →**digital computer.**

**automatic control** /– kənˈtroʊl/, *n.* the control of a system by a mechanism which is capable of acting to compensate for disturbances in the system without human intervention.

**automatic data processing,** *n.* the use of computers and other information-handling machines to store, organise, and perform calculations on large quantities of numerical data with the minimum of human intervention. *Abbrev.:* ADP

**automatic direction finder,** *n.* a radio navigation aid.

**automatic flight control system,** *n.* a system which includes all equipment to control automatically the flight of an aircraft or missile to a path or altitude described by references internal or external to the aircraft or missile.

**automatic gain control,** *n.* that part of an amplifier which varies the gain inversely with the strength of the input signed, thus maintaining an approximately constant output. Also. **A.G.C.**

**automatic pilot** /– ˈpaɪlət/, *n.* an automatic steering device in an aircraft.

**automatic pistol** /– ˈpɪstəl/, *n.* a pistol which can be fired automatically or semiautomatically.

**automatic rifle** /– ˈraɪfəl/, *n.* a type of rifle which can be fired automatically or semiautomatically.

**automatic transmission** /– trænzˈmɪʃən/, *n.* a transmission system on a motor vehicle in which gear-changing is operated automatically in accordance with car or engine speed rather than manually by the driver; slush box.

**automation** /ɔtəˈmeɪʃən/, *n.* **1.** the science of applying automatic control to industrial processes; the replacement of manpower by sophisticated machinery. **2.** the process or act of automating a mechanical process. **3.** the degree to which a mechanical process is automatically controlled. [b. AUTOM(ATIC) + (OPER)ATION]

**automatism** /ɔˈtɒmətɪzəm/, *n.* **1.** action or condition of being automatic; mechanical or involuntary action. **2.** *Philos.* the doctrine that all activities of animals, including men, are controlled only by physiological causes, consciousness being considered a non-causal by-product; epiphenomenalism. **3.** *Physiol.* the involuntary functioning of an organic process, esp. muscular, without neural stimulation. **4.** *Psychol.* an act performed by an individual without his awareness or will, as sleep-walking. **5.** a technique used by surrealist painters of relaxing or evading conscious thought to release unconscious ideas and feelings for artistic expression. – **automatist,** *n.*

**automaton** /ɔˈtɒmətən/, *n., pl.* **-tons, -ta** /-tə/. **1.** a mechanical figure or contrivance constructed to act as if spontaneously through concealed motive power. **2.** a person who acts in a monotonous routine manner, without active intelligence. **3.** something capable of acting spontaneously or without external impulse. [Gk, properly neut. of *autómatos* self-acting]

**automobile** /ˈɔtəməbil/, *n.* **1.** *Chiefly U.S.* a motor car (or other self-propelled road transport vehicle). –*adj.* **2.** automotive. [F. See AUTO-[1], MOBILE] – **automobilist** /ɔtəˈmoʊbələst, ɔtəməˈbiləst/, *n.*

**automotive** /ɔtəˈmoʊtɪv/, *adj.* **1.** propelled by a self-contained power plant. **2.** of or pertaining to motor vehicles.

**autonomic** /ɔtəˈnɒmɪk/, *adj.* **1.** autonomous. **2.** *Physiol.* pertaining to or designating a system of nerves and ganglia (the **autonomic, involuntary,** or **vegetative nervous system**) leading from the spinal cord and brain to glands, blood vessels, the viscera, and the heart and smooth muscles, constituting their efferent innervation and controlling their involuntary functions (opposed to *cerebrospinal*). **3.** *Bot.* produced by internal forces or causes; spontaneous. **4.** of or pertaining to autonomics. – **autonomically,** *adv.*

**autonomics** /ɔtəˈnɒmɪks/, *n. construed as sing.* the science, study, or practice of developing a number of self-governing systems, as within a large business organisation.

**autonomous** /ɔˈtɒnəməs/, *adj.* **1.** *Govt.* **a.** self-governing; independent; subject to its own laws only. **b.** pertaining to an autonomy. **2.** independent; self-contained; self-sufficient; self-governing. **3.** *Philos.* containing its own guiding principles. **4.** *Biol.* existing as an independent organism and not as a mere form or state of development of an organism. **5.** *Bot.* spontaneous. [Gk *autónomos*] – **autonomously,** *adv.*

**autonomy** /ɔˈtɒnəmi/, *n., pl.* **-mies. 1.** *Govt.* **a.** the condition of being autonomous; self-government, or the right of self-government. **b.** a self-governing community. **2.** independence; self-sufficiency; self-regulation. **3.** *Philos.* the doctrine that the individual human will contains its own principles and laws. [Gk *autonomía*] – **autonomist,** *n.*

**autonym** /ˈɔtənɪm/, *n.* a work published under the author's own name. [AUT- + Gk *ónyma* name]

**autopilot** /ˈɔtoʊˌpaɪlət/, *n.* →**automatic pilot.**

**autoplasty** /ˈɔtəplæsti/, *n.* surgical repair of defects with the tissue from another part of the patient. Also, **autoplastic transplantation.** [Gk *autóplastos* self-formed + -Y[3]]

**autopsy** /ˈɔtɒpsi/, *n., pl.* **-sies. 1.** inspection and dissection of a body after death, as for determination of the cause of death; a post-mortem examination. **2.** personal observation. [Gk *autopsía* seeing with one's own eyes]

**autoradiograph** /ˌɔtoʊˈreɪdiəgræf/, *n.* an image obtained on a photographic plate by placing on it a specimen containing a radioactive isotope. The result shows the distribution of the radioactive element in the specimen. – **autoradiography** /ˌɔtoʊreɪdiˈɒgrəfi/, *n.*

**autorotation** /ˌɔtoʊrəˈteɪʃən/, *n. Aeron.* **1.** the free rotation of rotor blades without engine power. **2.** an uncontrolled rolling of an aircraft, as in a spin.

**autosome** /ˈɔtəsoʊm, -zoʊm/, *n.* any chromosome other than the sex chromosome in species having both types of chromosomes.

**autosuggestion** /ˌɔtəsəˈdʒɛstʃən, ˌɔtoʊ-/, *n. Psychol.* suggestion arising from within a person (as opposed to one from an outside source, esp. another person).

**autotimer** /ˈɔtoʊtaɪmə/, *n.* a device for turning a cooking stove on at a preset time.

**autotomy** /ɔˈtɒtəmi/, *n.* the spontaneous casting off of a damaged or trapped body part, such as tails by lizards, legs by spiders and crabs, etc.

**auto tow** /ˈɔtoʊ ˌtoʊ/, *n.* (of a glider) a tow by an automobile, until the glider reaches sufficient altitude to cast off.

**autotoxaemia** /ˌɔtətɒkˈsimiə, ˌɔtoʊ-/, *n.* →**auto-intoxication.** Also, **autotoxemia.**

**autotoxin** /ɔtəˈtɒksən/, *n.* a toxin or poisonous principle formed within the body and acting against it. – **autotoxic,** *adj.*

**autotrophic** /ɔtəˈtroʊfɪk/, *adj.* (of plants) building their own nutritive substances, esp. by photosynthesis or chemosynthesis.

**autotype** /ˈɔtətaɪp/, *n.* **1.** →**facsimile. 2.** a photographic process for producing permanent prints in a carbon pigment. **3.** a picture so produced. *–v.t.* **4.** to produce by an autotypic process. – **autotypic** /ɔtəˈtɪpɪk/, *adj.* – **autotypy** /ˈɔtətaɪpi/, *n.*

**autoxidation** /ˌɔtɒksəˈdeɪʃən/, *n.* **1.** the oxidation of a compound by its exposure to air. **2.** an oxidation reaction in which another substance must be included for the reaction to be completed.

**autrefois acquit** /ˌɔtəfɔɪz əˈkwɪt, ˌoʊtrəfwa –/, *n.* a plea to a prosecution, that the prisoner has already been tried for the same offence and has been acquitted. [F: formerly acquitted]

**autrefois attaint** /ˌɔtəfɔɪz əˈteɪnt, ˌoʊtrəfwa –/, *n.* (formerly) a plea to a prosecution that a man was attainted of treason or felony, and could thus not be indicted for another treason or felony while the attainder remained in force, because he was considered dead in law. [F: formerly attainted]

**autrefois convict** /ˌɔtəfɔɪz kənˈvɪkt, ˌoʊtrəfwa –/, *n.* a plea to a prosecution, that the prisoner has been already tried and convicted for the same offence. [F: formerly convicted]

**autumn** /ˈɔtəm/, *n.* **1.** the season of the year between summer and winter; in the Southern Hemisphere, March, April and May. **2.** a period of maturity passing into decline. [L *autumnus;* replacing ME *autompne,* from OF]

**autumnal** /ɔˈtʌmnəl/, *adj.* **1.** belonging to or suggestive of autumn; produced or gathered in autumn. **2.** past maturity or middle life. – **autumnally,** *adv.*

**autumnal equinox** /– ˈikwənɒks/, *n.* See **equinox** (def. 1). Also, **autumnal point.**

**autumn crocus,** /ɔtəm ˈkroʊkəs/, *n.* any of several plants of the genus *Colchicum,* family Liliaceae, producing their flowers in autumn, esp. *C. autuminale.*

**autumn leaf** /– ˈlif/, *n.* **1.** a leaf of a deciduous tree which changes colour and falls in the autumn. **2.** *Colloq.* in horse-racing, the name given to a jockey, apprentice, etc., who has often fallen from his mount.

**autunite** /ˈɔtənaɪt/, *n.* a yellow mineral, a hydrous calcium uranium phosphate, $CaU_2P_2O_{12} \cdot 8H_2O$, occurring in crystals as nearly square tablets; a minor ore of uranium. [named after *Autun,* a town in E France. See -ITE[1]]

**au vin** /oʊ ˈvæn/, *adj.* cooked with wine. [F: with wine]

**aux.,** auxiliary. Also, **auxil.**

**auxanometer** /ɔksəˈnɒmətə/, *n.* an instrument which measures the growth of plants. [*auxano-* (from Gk *auxánein* increase) + -METER[1]]

**auxiliary** /ɔgˈzɪljəri, ɒg-/, *adj., n., pl.* **-ries.** *–adj.* **1.** giving support; helping; aiding; assisting. **2.** subsidiary; additional: *auxiliary troops.* **3.** used as a reserve: *an auxiliary engine.* *–n.* **4.** person or thing that gives aid of any kind; helper. **5.** →**auxiliary verb. 6.** a group or organisation which assists or is supplementary to a larger one: *the ladies' auxiliary of the club.* **7.** (*pl.*) foreign troops in the service of a nation at war. **8.** a sailing vessel carrying auxiliary power. [L *auxiliārius,* from *auxilium* aid]

**auxiliary note** /– ˈnoʊt/, *n.* a melody note not part of the harmony, to which a part moves by one step up or down in between two harmony notes.

**auxiliary verb** /– ˈvɜb/, *n.* a verb customarily preceding certain forms of other verbs, used to express distinctions of time, aspect, mood, etc., as *do, am,* etc., as in I *do* think; I *am* going; we *have* spoken; *may* we go?; *can* they see?; we *shall* walk.

**auxin** /ˈɔksən/, *n.* a class of substances which in minute amounts regulate or modify the growth of plants, esp. root formation, bud growth, fruit and leaf drop, etc. [? var. of *auxein,* from Gk *aúxē* increase + -IN[2]]

**auxochrome** /ˈɔksəkroʊm/, *n.* any group of atoms which make a chromogen acidic or basic, giving it the ability to adhere to wool and silk. [*auxo-* (representing Gk *auxánein* increase) + CHROME]

**av.,** **1.** average.

**A.V.,** **1.** Audio-Visual. **2.** Authorised Version.

**avadavat** /ævəˈdeɪvət/, *n.* →**amadavat.**

**avail** /əˈveɪl/, *v.i.* **1.** to have force or efficacy; be of use; serve. **2.** to be of value or profit. *–v.t.* **3.** to be of use or value to; profit; advantage. **4. avail oneself of,** to give oneself the advantage of; make use of. *–n.* **5.** efficacy for a purpose; advantage to an object or end: *of little or no avail.* [ME, from OF: *a-* A-[5] + *vail,* 1st person sing. pres. indic. of *valoir,* from L *valēre* be strong, have effect] – **availingly,** *adv.*

**availability** /əveɪləˈbɪləti/, *n., pl.* **-ties.** the state of being available: *the availability of a candidate.*

**available** /əˈveɪləbəl/, *adj.* **1.** suitable or ready for use; at hand; of use or service: *available resources.* **2.** having sufficient power or efficacy; valid. **3.** *Archaic.* profitable; advantageous. – **availableness,** *n.* – **availably,** *adv.*

**avalanche** /ˈævəlæntʃ, -lanʃ/, *n., v.,* **-lanched, -lanching.** *–n.* **1.** a large mass of snow, ice, etc., detached from a mountain slope and sliding or falling suddenly downwards. **2.** anything like an avalanche in suddenness and destructiveness: *an avalanche of misfortunes.* **3.** *Physics.* a shower of particles resulting from the collision of a high energy particle, such as a cosmic ray, with any other form of matter. *–v.i.* **4.** to come down in, or like, an avalanche. [F: b. d. *avaler* go down (from L *ad-* AD- + *vallis* valley) and F (Swiss) *lavenche* of pre-Latin orig.]

**avant-garde** /ˌævɒnt-ˈgad/, *n.* **1.** the vanguard; the leaders in progress in any field, esp. the arts; the new ideas or thinkers. *–adj.* **2.** of or pertaining to the avant-garde. **3.** modern; experimental; (affectedly) ultra-modern. [F: vanguard]

**avanturine** /əˈvæntʃərin/, *n., adj.* →**aventurine.**

**avarice** /ˈævərəs/, *n.* insatiable greed for riches; inordinate, miserly desire to gain and hoard wealth. [ME, from OF, from L *avāritia* greed]

**avaricious** /ævəˈrɪʃəs/, *adj.* characterised by avarice; greedy; covetous. – **avariciously,** *adv.* – **avariciousness,** *n.*

**avast** /əˈvast/, *interj. Naut.* stop! hold! cease! stay! [probably from D *houd vast* hold fast]

**avatar** /ævəˈta/, *n.* **1.** *Hindu Myth.* the descent of a deity to the earth in an incarnate form or some manifest shape; the incarnation of a god. **2.** a supreme manifestation; embodiment. [Skt *avatāra* descent]

**avaunt** /əˈvɒnt/, *interj. Obs.* go away! [ME, from OF *avant* before, onward, from Rom. *abante,* from L *ab* from + *ante* before]

**ave** /ˈaveɪ/, *interj.* **1.** hail! welcome! *–n.* **2.** the salutation 'ave'. **3.** (*cap.*) Ave Maria. **4.** (*cap.*) the time for the recitation of the Angelus, so called because the Ave Maria is thrice repeated in it. [L, imperative of *avēre* be or fare well]

**Ave.,** avenue. Also, **ave.**

**Ave Maria** /aveɪ məˈriə/, *n.* **1.** the 'Hail, Mary', a prayer in the Roman Catholic Church, based on the salutation of the angel Gabriel to the Virgin Mary and the words of her kinswoman Elizabeth. **2.** the hour for saying the prayer. **3.** a recitation of this prayer. **4.** the bead or beads on a rosary used to count off each prayer as spoken. **5.** any of the numerous musical settings of the Ave Maria, for choirs, orchestra, etc. Also, **Ave Mary** /aveɪ ˈmɛəri/. [L: hail, Mary]

**avenaceous** /ævəˈneɪʃəs/, *adj.* of or like oats; of the oat kind. [L *avēnāceus,* from *avēna* oats]

**avenge** /əˈvɛndʒ/, *v.,* **avenged, avenging.** *–v.t.* **1.** to take vengeance or exact satisfaction for: *to avenge a death.* **2.** to take vengeance on behalf of: *avenge your brother.* *–v.i.* **3.** to take vengeance. [ME *avenge(n),* from OF *avengier,* from *a-* A-[5] + *vengier* revenge, from L *vindicāre* punish] – **avenger,** *n.* – **avengement,** *n.*

**aventurine** /aˈvɛntʃərin, -ən/, *n.* **1.** an opaque, brown glass containing fine, gold-coloured particles; goldstone. **2.** any of several varieties of minerals, esp. quartz or felspar, spangled with bright particles of mica, haematite, or other minerals. *–adj.* **3.** spangled; glittering. Also, **avanturine.** [F, from It. *avventurina,* from *aventura* chance (the mineral being rare and found only by chance)]

**avenue** /ˈævənju/, *n.* **1.** *Brit.* the main way of approach, lined with trees, through grounds to a country house or monumental building. **2.** any double row of trees, whether lining a road or not. **3.** any street so called, esp. one which is wide and lined with trees. **4.** a way or opening for entrance into a place: *the avenue to India.* **5.** means of access or attainment: *avenue of escape, avenues of success.* [F, orig. pp. fem. of *avenir,* from L *advenīre* come to]

**aver** /əˈvɜ/, *v.t.,* **averred, averring.** **1.** to affirm with confidence; declare in a positive or peremptory manner. **2.** *Law.* to allege as a fact. [ME *aver(en),* from OF *averer,* from L *ad-* AD- + *vērus* true]

**average** /ˈævərɪdʒ, -vrɪdʒ/, *n., adj., v.,* **-raged, -raging.** *–n.* **1.** an arithmetical mean. **2.** a quantity intermediate to a set of quantities. **3.** the ordinary, normal, or typical amount, rate, quality, kind, etc.; the common run. **4.** *Comm.* **a.** a small charge paid by the master on account of the ship and cargo, such as pilotage, towage, etc. **b.** an expense, partial loss, or damage to ship or cargo. **c.** the incidence of such an expense or loss on the owners or their insurers. **d.** an equitable apportionment among all the interested parties of such an expense or loss. **5.** the number of sheep a shearer expects to shear in a typical day. *–adj.* **6.** of or pertaining to an average; estimated by average; forming an average. **7.** intermediate, medial, or typical in amount, rate, quality, etc. **8.** *Colloq.* mediocre in quality or performance. *–v.t.* **9.** to find an average value for; reduce to a mean. **10.** to result in, as an arithmetical mean; amount to, as a mean quantity: *the profit averages $5 a week.* *–v.i.* **11.** to have or show an average: *to average as expected.* **12.** **average down,** to purchase more of a security or commodity at a lower price to reduce the average cost of one's holdings. **13.** **average up,** to purchase more of a security or commodity at a higher price to take advantage of a contemplated further rise in prices. **14.** **average out,** *Colloq.* to divide or sort out, more or less evenly. [cf. F *avarie* customs duty, etc., c. It. *avaria,* from Ar. *'awārīya* damages. See -AGE] – **averagely,** *adv.*

**averment** /əˈvɜmənt/, *n.* **1.** the act of averring. **2.** a positive statement. **3.** *Law.* an allegation.

**Averroism** /ˌævəˈroʊɪzəm/, *n.* the philosophy of Averroes 1126? - 1198, Arab philosopher in Spain, consisting chiefly of a pantheistic interpretation of the doctrines of Aristotle. Also, **Averrhoism.** – **Averroist,** *n.* – **Averroistic,** *adj.*

**averse** /əˈvɜs/, *adj.* **1.** disinclined, reluctant, or opposed: *averse to* (formerly *from*) *flattery.* **2.** *Bot.* turned away from the central axis (opposed to *adverse*). [L *āversus,* pp., turned away] – **aversely,** *adv.* – **averseness,** *n.*

**aversion** /əˈvɜʒən, -vɜʃən/, *n.* **1.** an averted state of the mind or feelings; repugnance, antipathy, or rooted dislike (usu. fol. by *to*). **2.** a cause of dislike; an object of repugnance. **3.** *Obs.* a turning away.

**aversion therapy** /ˈ– ˌθɛrəpi/, *n.* a form of behaviour therapy in which punishment or aversive stimulation is used to eliminate undesired responses, as an electric shock administered when an obsessive subject is shown a picture of his obsession.

**aversive** /əˈvɜsɪv/, *adj.* inducing an aversion.

**avert** /əˈvɜt/, *v.t.* **1.** to turn away or aside: *to avert one's eyes.* **2.** to ward off; prevent: *to avert evil.* [ME, from OF *avertir,* from L *āvertere* turn away] – **averter,** *n., adj.* – **avertedly** /əˈvɜtədli/, *adv.*

**Aves** /ˈeɪviz/, *n.pl.* the class of vertebrates comprising the birds, distinguished from all other animals by their feathers, and from their closest relatives, the Reptilia, by their warm-bloodedness, the hard shell of their eggs, and significant anatomical features. [L, pl. of *avis* bird]

**Avesta** /əˈvɛstə/, *n.* the Books of Wisdom; the sacred writings of Zoroastrianism containing the teachings of Zoroaster, the ancient Persian religious teacher.

**Avestan** /əˈvɛstən/, *n.* **1.** the language of the Avesta, closely related to Old Persian. *–adj.* **2.** of or pertaining to the Avesta or its language. [AVESTA + -AN]

**avg.,** average. Also, **avge.**

**avgas** /ˈævgæs/, *n.* aviation fuel.

**avi-,** a word element meaning 'bird'. [L, combining form of *avis* bird]

**avian** /ˈeɪviən/, *adj.* of or pertaining to birds.

**aviary** /ˈeɪvəri, ˈeɪvjəri/, *n., pl.* **-ries.** a large cage or enclosure in which birds are kept. [L *aviārium,* from *avis* bird]

**aviation** /ˌeɪviˈeɪʃən/, *n.* **1.** the act, art, or science of flying by mechanical means, esp. with heavier-than-air craft. **2.** the aircraft (with equipment) of an air force. [F. See AVI-, -ATION]

**aviation medicine** /– ˈmɛdsən/, *n.* the special field of medicine which is related to the biological and psychological problems of flight.

**aviator** /ˈeɪvieɪtə/, *n.* a pilot of an aeroplane or other heavier-than-air craft. – **aviatrix** /ˈeɪviˌeɪtrɪks/, **aviatress** /ˈeɪviˌeɪtrəs/, *n. fem.*

**aviculture** /ˈeɪvəˌkʌltʃə/, *n.* the rearing or keeping of birds. – **aviculturist** /eɪvəˈkʌltʃərəst/, *n.*

**avid** /ˈævəd/, *adj.* **1.** keenly desirous; eager; greedy (oft. fol. by *of* or *for*): *avid of pleasure or power.* **2.** keen: *avid hunger.* [L *avidus* eager] – **avidly,** *adv.*

**avidin** /ˈævədən/, *n.* a protein found in the white of egg which combines with biotin causing a biotin deficiency in the diet of the consumer.

**avidity** /əˈvɪdəti/, *n.* eagerness; greediness.

**avifauna** /eɪvəˈfɔnə/, *n.* the birds of a given region; avian fauna. – **avifaunal,** *adj.*

**avionics** /ˌeɪviˈɒnɪks/, *n.* the study and use of electronic equipment for aircraft. [AVI(ATION) + (ELECTR)ONICS]

**avirulent** /əˈvɪrələnt/, *adj.* (of organisms) having no virulence, as a result of age, heat, etc.

**avitaminosis** /ˌeɪvaɪtəmə'noʊsəs/, *n.* a disease caused by a lack of vitamins. [A-[6] + VITAMIN + -OSIS]

**A-V node** /eɪ-vi 'noʊd/, *n.* →**atrioventricular node.**

**avocado** /ævə'kadoʊ/, *n., pl.* **-dos. 1.** a tropical American fruit, green to black in colour and commonly pear-shaped, borne by the tree *Persea americana,* eaten raw, esp. as a salad fruit; alligator pear. **2.** the tree. Also, **avocado pear.** [Sp. (lit., lawyer), alteration of *oguacate,* from Nahuatl *ahuacatl* lit., testicle]

**avocation** /ævə'keɪʃən/, *n.* **1.** minor or occasional occupations; hobbies. **2.** (*also pl.*) one's regular occupation, calling, or vocation. **3.** diversion or distraction. [L *āvocātio* a calling off]

**avocatory** /ə'vɒkətri/, *adj.* calling away, off, or back.

**avocet** /'ævəsɛt/, *n.* any of several long-legged, web-footed shorebirds constituting the genus *Recurvirostra,* having a long, slender beak curving upwards towards the end, as the **red-necked avocet.** Also, **avoset.** [F *avocette,* from It. *avocetta*]

**Avogadro's hypothesis** /ævəˌgædroʊz haɪ'pɒθəsəs/, *n.* the hypothesis which states that equal volumes of gases under the same conditions of temperature and pressure contain equal numbers of molecules. [named after Count Amadeo *Avogadro,* 1776-1856, Italian physicist and chemist] Cf. **Avogadro's number.**

**Avogadro's number** /– 'nʌmbə/, *n.* the number of atoms or molecules in a mole of substance; $6.0 \times 10^{23}$ per mole. Also, **Avogadro's constant.**

**avoid** /ə'vɔɪd/, *v.t.* **1.** to keep away from; keep clear of; shun; evade: *to avoid a person or a danger.* **2.** *Law.* to make void or of no effect; invalidate. **3.** *Obs.* to empty; eject or expel. *–v.i.* **4.** *Obs.* to go away; leave. [ME *avoide(n),* from AF *avoider,* var. of OF *esvuidier* empty out; from *es-* EX-[1] + *vuidier* (from L *viduāre*) empty. See VOID, *adj.*] – **avoidable,** *adj.* – **avoidably,** *adv.* – **avoider,** *n.*

**avoidance** /ə'vɔɪdəns/, *n.* **1.** the act of keeping away from: *avoidance of scandal.* **2.** *Law.* a making void. **3.** tax avoidance.

**avoirdupois** /ˌævwadju'pwa, ævədə'pɔɪz/, *n.* **1.** →**avoirdupois weight. 2.** weight; heaviness. [ME *avoir de pois,* from OF: goods sold by weight, lit., to have weight]

**avoirdupois weight** /'– weɪt/, *n.* a system of weights formerly used in most English-speaking countries for goods other than gems, precious metals and drugs. $27^{11}/_{32}$ grains = 1 dram; 16 drams = 1 ounce; 16 ounces = 1 pound; 112 pounds or (U.S.) 100 pounds = 1 hundredweight; 20 hundredweight = 1 ton. The pound contained 7000 grains and was equivalent to 0.453 592 37 kg.

**avoset** /'ævəsɛt/, *n.* →**avocet.**

**avouch** /ə'vaʊtʃ/, *v.t. Archaic.* **1.** to make frank affirmation of; declare or assert with positiveness. **2.** to assume responsibility for; guarantee. **3.** to admit; confess. [ME *avouche(n),* from OF *avochier,* from L *advocāre* summon] – **avouchment,** *n.*

**avow** /ə'vaʊ/, *v.t.* **1.** to admit or acknowledge frankly or openly; own; confess. **2.** to state; assert; affirm; declare. [ME *avowe(n),* from OF *avoer,* from L *advocāre* summon] – **avowable,** *adj.* – **avower,** *n.*

**avowal** /ə'vaʊəl/, *n.* **1.** frank acknowledgment or admission. **2.** open declaration; assertion; affirmation.

**avowed** /ə'vaʊd/, *adj.* acknowledged; declared: *an avowed enemy.* – **avowedly** /ə'vaʊədli/, *adv.* – **avowedness,** *n.*

**avulsed** /ə'vʌlst/, *adj. Surg.* (of a wound) having the tissue torn away.

**avulsion** /ə'vʌlʃən/, *n.* **1.** a tearing away. **2.** *Law.* the sudden removal of soil by change in a river's course or by a flood, from the land of one owner to that of another. **3.** a part torn off. [L *āvulsio*]

**avuncular** /ə'vʌŋkjələ/, *adj.* of or pertaining to an uncle; like an uncle: *avuncular affection.* [L *avunculus* uncle (diminutive of *avus* grandfather) + -AR[1]]

**a.w.,** atomic weight.

**awa** /ə'wa, ə'wɔ/, *adv. Scot.* away.

**await** /ə'weɪt/, *v.t.* **1.** to wait for; look for or expect. **2.** to be in store for; be ready for. **3.** *Obs.* to lie in wait for. *–v.i.* **4.** to wait, as in expectation. [ME *awaite(n),* from ONF *awaitier,* from *a-* A-[5] + *waitier* watch. See WAIT]

**awake** /ə'weɪk/, *v.* **awoke** or **awaked, awaking,** *adj. –v.t.* **1.** to rouse from sleep; wake up. **2.** to stir the interest of; excite. **3.** to stir, disturb (the memories, fears, etc.). *–v.i.* **4.** to wake up. **5.** to come to a realisation of the truth; to rouse to action, attention, etc.: *he awoke to the realities of life. –adj.* **6.** waking, not sleeping. **7.** vigilant; alert: *awake to a danger.* **8. awake up,** fully aware: *he's awake up to what's going on.* See **wake-up.** [ME; OE weak v. *awacian* and (for pret. and pp.) OE strong v. *onwæcnan,* later *awæcnan* (pret. *onwōc, awōc,* pp. *onwacen, awacen*)]

**awaken** /ə'weɪkən/, *v.t., v.i.* →**waken.** [ME *awak(e)ne(n),* OE *onwæcnian,* later *awæcnian*] – **awakener,** *n.*

**awakening** /ə'weɪkənɪŋ/, *adj.* **1.** rousing; reanimating; alarming. *–n.* **2.** the act of awaking from sleep. **3.** an arousal or revival of interest or attention; a waking up, as from indifference, ignorance, etc.

**award** /ə'wɔd/, *v.t.* **1.** to adjudge to be due or merited; assign or bestow: *to award prizes.* **2.** to bestow by judicial decree; assign or appoint by deliberate judgment, as in arbitration. *–n.* **3.** something awarded, as a payment or medal. **4.** *Law.* **a.** the decision of arbitrators on points submitted to them. **b.** a decision after consideration; a judicial sentence. [ME *awarde(n),* from AF *awarder,* var. of *esguarder* observe, decide, from L: *ex-* EX-[1] + *guardāre* watch, guard, of Gmc orig.] – **awardable,** *adj.* – **awarder,** *n.*

**award wage** /– 'weɪdʒ/, *n.* a wage arrived at by mutual consent or arbitration and fixed by an industrial court, payable by law to all employees in a particular occupation.

**aware** /ə'wɛə/, *adj.* cognisant or conscious (*of*); informed: *aware of the danger.* [ME; OE *gewær* watchful. See WARE[2], WARY] – **awareness,** *n.*

**awash** /ə'wɒʃ/, *adj.* **1.** *Naut.* just level with the surface of the water, so that the waves break over. **2.** covered with water. **3.** washing about; tossed about by the waves.

**away** /ə'weɪ/, *adv.* **1.** from this or that place; off: *to go away.* **2.** apart; at a distance: *to stand away from the wall.* **3.** aside: *turn your eyes away.* **4.** out of possession, notice, use, or existence: *to give money away.* **5.** continuously; on: *to blaze away.* **6.** without hesitation: *fire away.* **7.** immediately; forthwith: *right away.* **8. away with,** take away: *away with this man.* **9. do** or **make away with,** to put out of existence; get rid of; kill. **10. make away with,** to run off with; steal. *–adj.* **11.** absent: *away from home.* **12.** distant: *six kilometres away.* **13.** *Colloq.* on the move; having started; in full flight. **14.** *Sport.* **a.** (played) on the opponents' ground. **b.** *Racing.* of or pertaining to the outward or first half of the race. *–interj.* **15.** go away! depart! [ME; OE *aweg,* earlier *on weg* on way]

**awe** /ɔ/, *n., v.,* **awed, awing.** *–n.* **1.** respectful or reverential fear, inspired by what is grand or sublime: *in awe of God.* **2.** *Archaic.* power to inspire fear or reverence. **3.** *Obs.* fear or dread. *–v.t.* **4.** to inspire with awe. **5.** to influence or restrain by awe. [ME, from Scand.; cf. Icel. *agi* fear]

**aweather** /ə'wɛðə/, *adv. Naut.* on or to the weather side of a vessel; in the direction of the wind (opposed to *alee*).

**aweigh** /ə'weɪ/, *adj. Naut.* (of an anchor) raised just enough to be clear of the bottom.

**awe-inspiring** /'ɔr-ɪnspaɪrɪŋ/, *adj.* **1.** filling one with awe. **2.** worthy of awe; magnificent. **3.** *Colloq.* amazing; exciting; worthy of amazement, excitement, or admiration: *an awe-inspiring performance.*

**awesome** /'ɔsəm/, *adj.* **1.** inspiring awe. **2.** characterised by awe. – **awesomely,** *adv.* – **awesomeness,** *n.*

**awe-struck** /'ɔ-strʌk/, *adj.* filled with awe. Also, **awe-stricken** /'ɔstrɪkən/.

**awful** /'ɔfəl/, *adj.* **1.** *Colloq.* extremely bad; unpleasant; ugly. **2.** *Colloq.* very; very great. **3.** inspiring fear; dreadful; terrible. **4.** full of awe; reverential. **5.** inspiring reverential awe; solemnly impressive. [ME; from AWE + -FUL, replacing OE *egeful* dreadful] – **awfully,** *adv.* – **awfulness,** *n.*

**awheto** /'awɛtoʊ/, *n. N.Z.* →**vegetable caterpillar.** Also, **aweto, awhato.**

**awhile** /ə'waɪl/, *adv.* for a short time or period.

**awkward** /'ɔkwəd/, *adj.* **1.** lacking dexterity or skill; clumsy; bungling. **2.** ungraceful; ungainly; uncouth: *awkward gestures.* **3.** ill-adapted for use or handling; unhandy: *an awk-*

*ward method.* **4.** requiring caution; somewhat hazardous: *there's an awkward step there.* **5.** difficult to handle; dangerous: *an awkward customer.* **6.** embarrassing or trying: *an awkward predicament.* **7.** deliberately obstructive, difficult, or perverse. **8.** *Obs.* oblique; backward; inverted. **9. the awkward squad,** *Colloq.* one of a number of groups, as sporting teams, marching squads, etc., to which the clumsiest and most awkward people have been assigned. [*auk* backhanded (from Scand.; cf. Icel. *öfugr* turned the wrong way) + -WARD] – **awkwardly,** *adv.* – **awkwardness,** *n.*

**awl** /ɔl/, *n.* a pointed instrument for piercing small holes in leather, wood, etc. [ME *al,* OE *æl,* c. G *Ahle*]

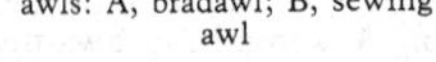

awls: A, bradawl; B, sewing awl

**A.W.L.** /eɪ dʌbəlju 'ɛl/, absent without leave.

**awn** /ɔn/, *n.* **1.** a bristle-like appendage of a plant, esp. on the glumes of grasses. **2.** such appendages collectively, as those forming the beard of wheat, barley, etc. **3.** any similar bristle. [ME, from Scand.; cf. Sw. *agn,* Icel. *ögn* husk] – **awned,** *adj.* – **awnless,** *adj.*

**awning** /'ɔnɪŋ/, *n.* **1.** a rooflike shelter of canvas, etc., before a window or door, over a deck, etc., as for protection from the sun. **2.** →**shop awning. 3.** a shelter.

**awoke** /ə'woʊk/, *v.* past tense of **awake.**

**A.W.O.L.** /eɪ ˌdʌbəlju oʊ 'ɛl, 'eɪwɒl/, *Chiefly U.S. Mil.* absent without leave.

**awry** /ə'raɪ/, *adv.* **1.** with a turn or twist to one side; askew: *to glance or look awry.* **2.** away from reason or the truth. **3.** amiss; wrong: *our plans went awry.* [ME *on wry.* See A-[1], WRY]

**AWU** /eɪ dʌblju 'ju/, Australian Workers' Union. Also, **A.W.U.**

**axe** /æks/, *n., pl.* **axes,** *v.* **axed, axing.** *–n.* **1.** an instrument with a bladed head on a handle or helve, used for hewing, cleaving, chopping, etc. **2.** *Colloq.* a musical instrument, esp. when associated with rock, jazz, etc. **3. have an axe to grind,** to have a private purpose or selfish end to attain. **4. the axe,** *Colloq.* **a.** a drastic cutting down (of expenses). **b.** dismissal from a job, position, or the like; the sack. *–v.t.* **5.** to shape or trim with an axe. **6.** *Colloq.* to cut down; reduce (expenditure, prices, etc.) sharply. **7.** *Colloq.* to dismiss from a position. Also, *Chiefly U.S.,* **ax.** [ME; OE *æx,* akin to G *Axt,* L *ascia,* Gk *axīnē*] – **axelike,** *adj.*

**axe-breaker** /'æks-breɪkə/, *n. Colloq.* any tree whose timber has a hard, close or interlocking grain.

**axel** /'æksəl/, *n.* (in figure skating) a jump executed by a skater who leaps from the forward outer edge of one skate, makes one and a half turns in the air, then lands on the backward outer edge of the other skate. [named after *Axel* Paulsen, d. 1938, Norwegian figure skater]

**axeman** /'æksmən/; *for def. 2* /'æksˌmæn/, *n., pl.* **-men** /-mən/. **1.** one who wields an axe. **2.** *Colloq.* a personnel officer or the like, one of whose duties is to dismiss staff. Also, *Chiefly U.S.,* **axman.**

**axenic** /eɪ'zinɪk/, *adj.* free of foreign organisms; uncontaminated. [A-[6] + XEN(O)- + -IC]

**axes**[1] /'æksiz/, *n.* plural of **axis**[1].

**axes**[2] /'æksəz/, *n.* plural of **axe.**

**axial** /'æksiəl/, *adj.* **1.** of, pertaining to, or forming an axis. **2.** situated in an axis or on the axis. Also, **axile** /'æksəl, 'æksaɪl/.

**axially** /'æksiəli/, *adv.* in the line of the axis.

**axil** /'æksəl/, *n.* the angle between the upper side of a leaf or stem and the supporting stem or branch. [L *axilla* armpit]

A, axil

**axilla** /æk'sɪlə/, *n., pl.* **axillae** /æk'sɪli/. **1.** *Anat.* the armpit. **2.** *Ornith.* the corresponding region on a bird. **3.** *Bot.* an axil. [L]

**axillary** /æk'sɪləri/, *adj., n., pl.* **-aries.** *–adj.* **1.** pertaining to the axilla. **2.** *Bot.* pertaining to or growing from the axil (of plants). *–n.* **3.** *Ornith.* (*usu. pl.*) a feather growing from the axilla (def. 2). Also, **axillar.**

**axiology** /ˌæksi'ɒlədʒi/, *n.* the science of values in general, including ethics, aesthetics, religion, etc. [Gk *áxio(s)* worthy + -LOGY] – **axiological** /ˌæksiə'lɒdʒɪkəl/, *adj.*

**axiom** /'æksiəm/, *n.* **1.** a recognised truth. **2.** an established and universally accepted principle or rule. **3.** *Logic, Maths., etc.* a proposition which is assumed without proof for the sake of studying the consequences that follow from it. [L *axiōma,* from Gk: a requisite]

**axiomatic** /ˌæksiə'mætɪk/, *adj.* **1.** pertaining to or of the nature of an axiom; self-evident. **2.** aphoristic. Also, **axiomatical.** – **axiomatically,** *adv.*

**axis**[1] /'æksəs/, *n., pl.* **axes** /'æksiz/. **1.** the line about which a rotating body, such as the earth, turns. **2.** the central line of any symmetrical, or nearly symmetrical, body: *the axis of a cylinder, of the eye, etc.* **3.** a fixed line adopted for reference, as in plotting a curve on a graph, in crystallography, etc. **4.** *Anat.* **a.** a central or principal structure, about which something turns or is arranged: *the skeletal axis.* **b.** the second cervical vertebra. **5.** *Bot.* the longitudinal support on which organs or parts are arranged; the stem, root; the central line of any body. **6.** *Aeron.* one of three fixed lines of reference defining the lines of an aeroplane, mutually perpendicular and meeting at the centre of gravity. **a. longitudinal axis,** from nose to tail. **b. lateral axis,** from wingtip to wingtip. **c. vertical axis,** from top to bottom. **7.** *Fine Arts.* one or more theoretical central lines around which an artistic form is organised or composed. **8.** an alliance of two or more nations to coordinate their foreign and military policies, and to draw in with them a group of dependent or supporting powers. [L: axle, axis, board. Cf. AXLE]

**axis**[2] /'æksəs/, *n.* any of several species of East Asiatic deer, as *Axis axis* and related forms, having a reddish-brown coat with conspicuous white spots; chital. Also, **axis deer.** [L]

**axis of symmetry,** *n. Maths.* a straight line for which every point on a given curve has corresponding to it another point such that the line connecting the two points is bisected by the given line.

**axle** /'æksəl/, *n.* **1.** *Mach.* the pin, bar, shaft, or the like, on which or with which a wheel or pair of wheels rotate. **2.** either end (spindle) of an axletree or the like. **3.** the whole (fixed) axletree, or a similar bar connecting and turning with two opposite wheels of a vehicle. [OE *eaxl(e)* shoulder, crossbeam (in *eaxle-gespann* crossbeam attachment place). Cf. Icel. *öxl* shoulder, axle]

**axle-grease** /'æksəl-gris/, *n.* **1.** grease for axles. **2.** *Colloq.* butter.

**axletree** /'æksəltri/, *n.* a bar fixed crosswise under a vehicle, with a rounded spindle at each end upon which a wheel rotates. [ME, from AXLE + TREE]

**axman** /'æksmən/, *n., pl.* **-men** /-mən/. *Chiefly U.S.* →**axeman.**

**Axminster carpet** /ˌæksmɪnstə 'kapət/, *n.* a kind of carpet having a stiff jute back and a cut pile of wool. [named after *Axminster,* a town in England]

**axolotl** /æksə'lɒtl, 'æksəlɒtl/, *n.* **1.** any of several Mexican salamanders that breed in the larval stage, in Mexico prized as food. **2.** the larva of any salamander (esp. of the genus *Ambystoma*) that matures sexually in the larval stage. [Nahuatl]

axolotl

**axon** /'æksən/, *n.* the appendage of the neuron which transmits impulses away from the cell. Also, **axone** /'æksoʊn/. [Gk: axis]

**axonometric** /æksənə'mɛtrɪk/, *adj.* (of a projection, drawing, etc.) having all lines in a representation of a three-dimensional object drawn to scale, resulting in the optical distortion of diagonals and curves.

**ay**[1] /aɪ/, *adv., n., pl.* **ayes.** *–adv.* **1.** yes. *–n.* **2.** an affirmative vote or voter: *the ayes have it.* Also, **aye.** [earlier *I,* ? var. of ME *yie,* OE *gī* YEA (with loss of *y* as in IF)]

**ay**[2] /eɪ/, *adv., n.* →**aye**[1].

**ayah** /'aɪə/, *n.* (in India) a native maid or nurse. [Hind. *āya,*

i = peat ɪ = pit ɛ = pet æ = pat a = part ɒ = pot ʌ = putt ɔ = port ʊ = put u = pool ɜ = pert ə = apart aɪ = buy eɪ = bay ɔɪ = boy aʊ = how oʊ = hoe ɪə = here ɛə = hair ʊə = tour g = give θ = thin ð = then ʃ = show ʒ = measure tʃ = choke dʒ = joke ŋ = sing j = you õ = Fr. bon

from Pg. *aia*, fem. of *aio* tutor]

**ayatollah** /aɪə'tɒlə/, *n.* **1.** the title of a high-ranking religious leader in the Shiite sect of Islam, the official religion of Iran. **2.** *Colloq.* any autocratic leader.

**aye**[1] /eɪ/, *adv. Poetic.* ever; always. Also, **ay.** [ME *ei, ai,* from Scand.: cf. Icel. *ei,* c. OE *ā* ever]

**aye**[2] /aɪ/, *adv.* →**ay**[1].

**aye-aye** /'aɪ-aɪ/, *n.* a nocturnal lemur, *Daubentonia madagascariensis,* of Madagascar, about the size of a cat and with rodent-like front teeth. [F, from Malagasy *aiay;* probably imitation of its cry]

aye-aye

**Aylesbury duck** /ˌeɪlzbri 'dʌk/, *n.* one of a breed of white, domestic ducks. [named after *Aylesbury,* a town in England]

**Aymara** /aɪmə'ra/, *n.* an important Indian nationality and speech group in Bolivia and Peru, still existing around Lake Titicaca. – **Aymaran** /aɪmə'ræn/, *adj.*

**Ayrshire** /'ɛəʃə, -ʃɪə/, *n.* one of a hardy breed of dairy cattle, well-muscled, of medium size, and brown and white in colour. [originating in the county of *Ayr,* SW Scotland]

**az-,** variant of **azo-** used before vowels, as in *azole.*

**azalea** /ə'zeɪljə/, *n.* any plant of a particular group (Azalea) of the genus *Rhododendron,* family Ericaceae, comprising species with handsome, variously coloured flowers, some of which are familiar in cultivation. Azalea was once considered a botanical genus but is now a nursery or horticultural classification. [NL, from Gk: (fem. adj.) dry; so named as growing in dry soil]

**azan** /æ'zan/, *n.* (in Muslim countries) the call to prayer, proclaimed by the crier (muezzin) from the minaret of a mosque five times daily. [Ar. *adhān* invitation. See MUEZZIN]

**azedarach** /ə'zɛdəræk/, *n.* →**white cedar.** [F *azédarac,* from Pers. *āzād dirakht* noble tree]

**azeotrope** /ə'ziətroup/, *n.* any solution having constant minimum and maximum boiling points. [A-[6] + *zeo-* (combining form representing Gk *zeîn* boil) + -TROPE]

**azide** /'eɪzaɪd/, *n.* a salt, or other derivative, of hydrazoic acid, many of which are explosive.

**azimuth** /'æzəməθ/, *n.* **1.** *Astron., Navig.* the arc of the horizon from the celestial meridian to the foot of the great circle passing through the zenith, the nadir, and the point of the celestial sphere in question (in astronomy commonly reckoned from the south point of the horizon towards the west point; in navigation reckoned from the north point of the horizon towards the east point). **2.** *Survey., Gunnery, etc.* an angle measured clockwise from the south or north. [ME *azimut,* from OF, from Ar. *assumūt,* from *as* (=*al*) the + *sumūt,* pl. of *samt* way] – **azimuthal** /æzə'mjuθəl/, *adj.* – **azimuthally,** *adv.*

**azimuthal projection** /æzəˌmjuθəl prə'dʒɛkʃən/, *n.* a map projection based on the concept of projecting the earth's surface on to a tangent plane surface; zenithal projection.

**azine** /'æzin, -aɪn/, *n.* any of a group of organic compounds having six atoms, one or more of them nitrogen, arranged in a ring, the number of nitrogen atoms being indicated by a prefix, as in *diazine, triazine, tetrazine.* Also, **azin.** [AZ- + -INE[2]]

**azo-,** a word element meaning nitrogen. [Gk *ázōos* lifeless]

**azobenzene** /ˌæzou'bɛnzin, -bɛn'zin/, *n.* an orange-red crystalline substance, $C_6H_5N = NC_6H_5$, obtained from nitrobenzene in an alkaline solution.

**azo dye** /ˌæzou 'daɪ/, *n.* any of a large group of synthetic colouring substances which contain the **azo group,** –N = N–.

**azoic** /ə'zouɪk/, *adj.* pertaining to geologic time before life appeared. [Gk *ázōos* lifeless + -IC]

**azole** /'æzoul, ə'zoul/, *n.* any of a group of organic compounds having five atoms, one or more of them nitrogen, arranged in a ring; the number of nitrogen atoms is indicated by a prefix, as in *diazole.* [AZ- + -OLE]

**azolla** /æ'zɒlə, ə-/, *n.* any species of the genus *Azolla,* small floating ferns forming a carpet on slow-moving or still water.

**azonal soil** /eɪˌzounəl 'sɔɪl/, *n.* one of a group of immature soils on which climate and vegetation have had little influence.

**azonic** /eɪ'zounɪk/, *adj.* not confined to any particular zone or region; not local.

**azote** /æ'zout, ə'zout/, *n. Obs.* nitrogen. [F, from Gk *ázōtos,* properly, ungirt (mistakenly thought to mean lifeless, the gas being unfit to support life in respiration)] – **azoted** /æ'zoutəd, ə'zoutəd/, *adj.*

**azoth** /'æzɒθ/, *n. Alchemy.* mercury, as the assumed first principle of all metals. [F, var. of *azoch,* from Ar. *az zāwūq* the mercury]

**azotic** /ə'zɒtɪk/, *adj.* of or pertaining to azote; nitric.

**azotise** /'æzətaɪz/, *v.t.,* **-tised, -tising.** to nitrogenise. Also, **azotize.**

**Aztec** /'æztɛk/, *n.* **1.** a member of an Indian people dominant in Central Mexico at the time of the Spanish invasion (1519). **2.** a Uto-Aztecan language of the Nahuatl subgroup, still extensively spoken in Mexico; Nahuatl. – **Aztecan,** *adj.*

**azure** /'eɪʒə/, *adj.* **1.** of a sky blue colour. *–n.* **2.** the blue of an unclouded sky. **3.** a blue pigment, now esp. cobalt blue. **4.** the sky. [ME, from OF *azur,* from Ar. *lāzward,* from Pers. *lajward* lapis lazuli] – **azury,** *adj.*

**azurite** /'æʒjəraɪt/, *n.* **1.** a blue mineral, a hydrous copper carbonate, $Cu_3(CO_3)_2(OH)_2$, an ore of copper. **2.** a gem of moderate value, ground from this mineral.

**azygous** /ə'zɪgəs/, *adj. Zool., Bot.* not being one of a pair; single. [Gk *ázygos*]

Bb Roman ROMANA  Bb Sans Serif FUTURA  Bb Script BRUSH  Bb Decorative ARNOLD BLOCKIN

*Although there are numerous typefaces in the world they can be divided into four main classifications. These are:*

*ROMAN or SERIF. This typeface came into being from the technique of the Roman masons who, working in stone, finished off each letter with a serif or small stroke projecting from the top or bottom. This was done to correct any feeling of unevenness or imbalance they may have created in cutting the characters in stone.*

*SANS SERIF (without serif). This typeface is geometric in design and has straight-edged characters and lines of a regular thickness.*

*SCRIPT. Based on the movement of the hand, this typeface is often italicised or slanted, as if drawn by a brush or quill pen.*

*DECORATIVE. Any typeface that exaggerates the characteristics of any of the other three classifications to a degree that places it outside of them.*

*The dictionary entries in this book use a SAN SERIF typeface called Helvetica (set in a bold face for the head words) and a SERIF typeface Plantin (used throughout the body of the entries).*

**B, b** /bi/, *n., pl.* **B's** or **Bs, b's** or **bs. 1.** the second letter of the English alphabet. **2.** the second in any series: *schedule B.* **3.** the second highest mark for school, college, or university work; beta. **4.** *Music.* **a.** the seventh degree in the scale of C major or the second degree in the relative minor scale (A minor). **b.** a written or printed note representing this tone. **c.** a key, string, or pipe tuned to this note. **d.** (in solmisation) the seventh note of the scale of C, called **te. 5. not to know B from a bull's foot,** *Colloq.* to be stupid and ignorant.

**b,** barn.

**b., 1.** born. **2.** bass. **3.** basso. **4.** blend of; blended. **5.** book. **6.** *Cricket.* bowled. **7.** breadth. **8.** brother. **9.** (euphemistic for) any obscene or colloquial word beginning with b. **10.** bound. **11.** batsman. **12.** bedroom.

**B,** boron.

**B., 1.** bay. **2.** Bible. **3.** British. **4.** Brotherhood.

**B5,** an international standard size of paper, 250 × 176 mm, falling between A4 and A5, used for general publications and periodicals.

**Ba,** *Chem.* barium.

**B.A.** /bi 'eɪ/, Bachelor of Arts. [L *Baccalaureus Artium*]

**baa** /ba/, *v.,* **baaed, baaing,** *n.* *–v.i.* **1.** (of a sheep) to bleat. *–n.* **2.** the bleating of a sheep. [imitative]

**baal** /bal/, *Colloq.* *–adv.* **1.** not. *–interj.* **2.** no. [Aboriginal]

**Baal** /bal/, *n., pl.* **Baalim** /'balɪm/. any false god. [Heb. *ba'al* lord; any of numerous local deities among the ancient Semitic peoples, esp. the chief god of the Phoenicians] **– Baalism,** *n.* **– Baalist, Baalite,** *n.*

**baa-lamb** /'ba-læm/, *n.* (*in children's speech*) a lamb.

**baas** /bas/, *n. S. African.* sir; boss. [Afrikaans. See BOSS[1]]

**bab** /bæb/, *n. Colloq.* →**babbler.**

**baba** /'babə/, *n.* a dessert made from yeast-leavened dough, sometimes mixed with raisins and currants, and flavoured while still hot with a rum or other syrup.

**babbitt** /'bæbət/, *n.* **1.** →**babbitt metal. 2.** a bearing or lining of babbitt metal. *–v.t.* **3.** to line, face or furnish with babbitt metal.

**Babbitt** /'bæbət/, *n.* **1.** a conformist and complacent middle-class businessman, esp. of the American Middle West. **2.** (*also l.c.*) a self-satisfied person who conforms readily to middle-class ideas and ideals. [named after George *Babbitt,* title character of a novel by Sinclair Lewis (1922)]

**babbitt metal** /'bæbət mɛtl/, *n.* **1.** an antifriction metal, an alloy of tin, antimony, lead, and copper, used for bearings, etc. **2.** any of various similar alloys. [named after Isaac *Babbitt,* 1799-1862, U.S. inventor]

**Babbittry** /'bæbətri/, *n., pl.* **-tries.** (*also l.c.*) **1.** the condition or quality of being a Babbitt. **2.** the group of people who manifest the qualities of being a Babbitt.

**babble** /'bæbəl/, *v.,* **-led, -ling,** *n.* *–v.i.* **1.** to utter words imperfectly or indistinctly. **2.** to talk idly, irrationally, or foolishly; chatter. **3.** to make a continuous murmuring sound: *a babbling brook.* *–v.t.* **4.** to utter incoherently or foolishly. **5.** to reveal foolishly or thoughtlessly: *he babbled the whole secret.* *–n.* **6.** inarticulate speech. **7.** idle, irrational or foolish talk; chatter. **8.** a murmuring sound. [ME *babele(n)*; of imitative orig. Cf. Icel. *babla*] **– babbly,** *adj.*

**babbler**[1] /'bæblə/, *n.* **1.** one who or that which babbles. **2.** any of several noisy, gregarious, insectivorous birds of the family Timaliidae, common in scrub and open forest of Australia, as the grey-crowned babbler, *Pomatostomus temporalis.* **3.** any of various other tropical and subtropical birds of the same family.

**babbler**[2] /'bæblə/, *n. Colloq.* →**babbling brook.**

**babbling brook** /bæblɪŋ 'brʊk/, *n. Colloq.* a cook. [rhyming slang]

**babe** /beɪb/, *n.* **1.** a baby. **2.** an innocent or inexperienced person: *babe in the woods.* **3.** *Colloq.* a girl. [ME]

**babe-in-a-cradle** /,beɪb-ɪn-ə-'kreɪdl/, *n.* a terrestrial orchid, *Epiblema grandiflorum,* with a long slender stem and lilac to deep mauve flowers, and having a column supposed to resemble a baby in a cradle; found in wet places in south-west Western Australia.

**babel** /'beɪbəl/, *n.* **1.** a confused mixture of sounds. **2.** a scene of noise and confusion. [Heb. *Bābel* Babylon, an ancient city where, according to the Bible (Gen. 11), a tower to reach heaven was begun and language was confounded]

**babies'-breath** /,beɪbiz-'brɛθ/, *n.* **1.** a tall herb, *Gypsophila paniculata,* of the pink family, bearing numerous small, fragrant, white or pink flowers. **2.** any of certain other plants with small, fragrant flowers, as the grape hyacinth, *Muscari.* Also, **baby's-breath.**

**babiroussa** /bæbə'rusə/, *n.* an East Indian swine, *Babirussa babyrussa.* The male has peculiar curved tusks growing upwards, one pair from each jaw. Also,

babiroussa

**babirussa, babirusa.** [Malay *bābi rūsa* hog-deer]

**Babism** /ˈbeɪbɪzəm/, *n.* the doctrine of a pantheistic Persian sect, founded about 1844, inculcating a high morality, recognising the equality of the sexes, and forbidding polygamy. – **Babist,** *n., adj.*

**baboon** /bæˈbun, bə-/, *n.* any of various large, terrestrial monkeys, with a doglike muzzle, large cheek pouches, and a short tail, which constitute the genus *Papio* of Africa and Arabia. [ME *babewyne,* from OF *babouin* stupid person] – **baboonish,** *adj.*

**baboonery** /bəˈbunəri/, *n.* baboonish behaviour.

**babu** /ˈbabu/, *n.* **1.** (formerly) a title in Bengal corresponding to English *Mr.* **2.** a Hindu gentleman. **3.** an Indian clerk who writes English. **4.** any Indian having a smattering of English culture, esp. with ludicrous results. Also, **baboo.** [Hind.] – **babuism,** *n.*

**babu English** /babu ˈɪŋglɪʃ/, *n.* English as used by babus, full of long and learned words, frequently misapplied, esp. with a ludicrous effect.

**babul** /baˈbul, ˈbabul/, *n.* **1.** any of several trees of the genus *Acacia,* which yield a gum, esp. *A. arabica* of India. **2.** the gum, pods, or bark of such a tree. [Hind.]

**babushka** /bəˈbʊʃkə/, *n.* a woman's headscarf, often triangular, with the ends tied under the chin or at the back of the neck. [Russ.: lit., grandmother]

**baby** /ˈbeɪbi/, *n., pl.* **-bies,** *adj., v.,* **-bied, bying.** *–n.* **1.** an infant; young child of either sex. **2.** a young animal. **3.** the youngest member of a family, group, etc. **4.** a childish person. **5.** *Colloq.* an invention or creation of which one is particularly proud. **6.** *Colloq.* a girl. **7. leave (someone) holding the baby,** *Colloq.* to abandon (someone) with a problem or responsibility not rightly his. **8.** a quarter bottle of wine. *–adj.* **9.** of, like, or suitable for a baby: *baby clothes.* **10.** infantile; babyish: *a baby face.* **11.** small; comparatively little: *a baby grand (piano).* *–v.t.* **12.** to treat like a young child; pamper. [ME *babi, babee,* diminutive of BABE]

**baby boom** /ˈ– bum/, *n.* a sudden and marked increase in the number of babies born in a specified community.

**baby bulge** /ˈ– bʌldʒ/, *n.* a conspicuous increase in the number of babies born in a specified community or a short period of time.

**baby-farm** /ˈbeɪbi-fam/, *n. (derog.)* an establishment providing board and lodging for young children and babies at commercial rates.

**baby health centre,** *n.* a centre, usu. staffed by a nursing sister, where parents can obtain advice on the care of their infants.

**Babylon** /ˈbæbəlɒn/, *n.* any great, rich, and luxurious or wicked city. [from *Babylon,* an ancient city of SW Asia, on the river Euphrates]

**Babylonian** /bæbəˈloʊniən/, *adj.* **1.** pertaining to Babylon or Babylonia, an ancient empire in south-western Asia, in the lower Euphrates valley. **2.** sinful. *–n.* **3.** an inhabitant of ancient Babylonia. **4.** a language of Babylonia, esp. the Semitic language of the Akkadian group.

**baby marrow** /beɪbi ˈmæroʊ/, *n.* →**zucchini.**

**baby's bottle** /ˈbeɪbiz bɒtl/, *n.* →**feeding bottle** (def. 1).

**baby-sit** /ˈbeɪbi-sɪt/, *v.,* **-sat, -sitting.** *–v.i.* **1.** to take charge of a child while the parents are temporarily absent. *–v.t.* **2.** to mind (a child).

**baby-sitter** /ˈbeɪbi-sɪtə/, *n.* a person who minds a child or family while the parents are away, as for an evening, holiday, etc.

**baby snatcher** /ˈbeɪbi snætʃə/, *n.* **1.** a person who kidnaps a small child. **2.** →**cradlesnatcher.**

**baby's tears** /beɪbiz ˈtɪəz/, *n.* →**mind-your-own-business.**

**baby talk** /ˈbeɪbi tɔk/, *n.* **1.** the imperfect language of babies or infants just beginning to speak. **2.** adult speech resembling this.

**baby tooth** /ˈ– tuθ/, *n.* →**milk tooth.**

**baby walker** /ˈ– wɔkə/, *n.* a light frame usu. on four wheels in which a baby is supported while learning to walk.

**baccalaureate** /bækəˈlɔriət/, *n.* **1.** the bachelor's degree. **2.** (in France) the first grade of university examination, taken by high-school pupils. [ML *baccalaureātus,* from *baccalaureus* (as if from L *bacca* berry + *laureus* of laurel), var. of *baccalārius* BACHELOR] – **baccalaurean,** *adj.*

**baccarat** /ˈbækəra, bækəˈra/, *n.* a gambling card game played by a banker and two or more punters. Also, **baccara.** [F; orig. unknown]

**baccate** /ˈbækeɪt/, *adj.* **1.** berry-like. **2.** bearing berries. [L *baccātus* berried]

**bacchanal** /ˈbækənal/, *n.* **1.** a follower of Bacchus, in Roman mythology the god of wine. **2.** a drunken reveller. **3.** an occasion of drunken revelry; an orgy. *–adj.* **4.** pertaining to Bacchus; bacchanalian. [L *bacchānālis*]

**bacchanalia** /bækəˈnaliə, -ˈneɪ-/, *n.pl.* drunken orgies. [L, neut. pl. of *bacchānālis* BACCHANAL, *adj.*] – **bacchanalian,** *adj.* – **bacchanalianism,** *n.*

**bacchant** /bæˈkænt/, *n., pl.* **bacchants, bacchantes** /bəˈkæntiz/. **1.** a priest, priestess or votary of Bacchus; a bacchanal. **2.** a drunken reveller. [L *bacchans,* ppr., celebrating the festival of Bacchus] – **bacchantic** /bəˈkæntɪk/, *adj.*

**bacchante** /bəˈkænti/, *n.* a female bacchant. [F, from L *bacchans* BACCHANT]

**bacchic** /ˈbækɪk/, *adj.* **1.** relating to or in honour of Bacchus; connected with bacchanalian rites or revelries. **2.** jovial; riotously or jovially intoxicated; drunken.

**bacchius** /ˈbækiəs/, *n., pl.* **-chii** /-iˌi/. a metrical foot in classical prosody of three syllables, the first short (or unaccented) and the other two long (or stressed).

**bacci-,** a word element meaning 'berry', as in *bacciform.* [L, combining form of *bacca*]

**bacciferous** /bækˈsɪfərəs/, *adj.* bearing or producing berries. [L *baccifer* + -OUS]

**bacciform** /ˈbæksəfɔm/, *adj.* berry-shaped.

**baccivorous** /bækˈsɪvərəs/, *adj.* feeding on berries.

**baccy** /ˈbæki/, *n. Colloq.* tobacco. Also, **bacco.** [abbrev. of TOBACCO]

**bach** /bætʃ/, *n.* **1.** *Colloq.* a bachelor. **2.** *Chiefly N.Z.* **a.** a weekend cottage or house, usu. at the beach. **b.** any shack. *–v.i.* **3.** Also, **batch.** *Colloq.* to keep house alone or with a companion when neither is accustomed to housekeeping: *she was baching with a friend at North Sydney.* [abbrev. of BACHELOR] – **bacher,** *n.* – **baching,** *n.*

**bach.,** bachelor.

**bachelor** /ˈbætʃələ/, *n.* **1.** an unmarried man of any age. **2.** a person who has taken the first or lowest degree at a university: *Bachelor of Arts.* **3.** a young feudal knight who followed the banner of another. **4.** a young male fur seal kept from the breeding grounds by the older males. [ME *bacheler,* from OF, from ML *baccalāris, baccalārius,* apparently orig. small dairy farmer, ? akin to L *baculum* staff] – **bachelordom** /ˈbætʃələdəm/, *n.* – **bachelorhood,** *n.* – **bachelorism,** *n.* – **bachelorship,** *n.*

**bachelor-at-arms** /ˌbætʃələr-ət-ˈamz/, *n., pl.* **bachelors-at-arms.** →**bachelor** (def. 3).

**bachelor flat** /ˈbætʃələ flæt/, *n.* a small dwelling unit, usu. containing one living area and a bathroom.

**bachelor girl** /ˈbætʃələ gɜl/, *n.* a young unmarried woman, esp. one living away from her family.

**bachelorise** /ˈbætʃələraɪz/, *v.,* **-rised, -rising.** →**bach.** Also, **bachelorize.**

**bachelor's button** /ˌbætʃələz ˈbʌtn/, *n.* **1.** any of various plants of the herbaceous genus *Craspedia,* having round flower heads usu. yellow to deep orange. **2.** any similar plant of the family Compositae. **3.** Also, **globe amaranth.** an annual herb, *Gomphrena globosa,* family Amaranthaceae, of India, now widely cultivated in many horticultural varieties as an ornamental.

**Bach trumpet** /bak ˈtrʌmpət/, *n.* a clarion or clarino.

**bacillary** /bəˈsɪləri/, *adj.* **1.** of or like a bacillus; rod-shaped. **2.** characterised by bacilli. Also, **bacillar** /bəˈsɪlə/.

**bacilliform** /bəˈsɪləfɔm/, *adj.* rod-shaped.

**bacillus** /bəˈsɪləs/, *n., pl.* **-cilli** /-ˈsɪli/. **1.** any of the group of rod-shaped bacteria which produce spores in the presence of free oxygen. **2.** (formerly) any of the rod-shaped or cylindrical bacteria. [LL, diminutive of *baculus* rod]

**bacitracin** /bæsəˈtreɪsən/, *n.* an antibiotic effective against diseases caused by certain bacteria, viruses and rickettsia. [BACI(LLUS) + (Margaret) *Trac(y)* name of American patient in whose tissues such bacteria were first identified + -IN[2]]

**back**[1] /bæk/, *n.* **1.** the hinder part of the human body, extending from the neck to the end of the spine. **2.** the part of the body of animals corresponding to the human back. **3.** the rear portion of any part or organ of the body: *the back of the head.* **4.** the whole body, with reference to clothing: *the clothes on his back.* **5.** the part opposite to or farthest from the face or front; the hinder side; the rear part: *the back of a hall.* **6.** the part covering the back, as of clothing. **7.** the spine: *to break one's back.* **8.** any rear part of an object serving to support, protect, etc.: *the back of a book.* **9.** *Naut.* the keel and keelson of a vessel. **10.** the strength to carry a burden or responsibility. **11.** *Football, etc.* one of the defending players behind the forwards. **12.** *Mining.* (of a level or layer) the side nearest the surface of the ground, including the earth between that level and the next. **13.** *Print.* the inside margin of a page. **14.** Some special noun phrases are:

**behind someone's back,** in secret; deceitfully; in someone's absence.

**be (or get) on someone's back,** *Colloq.* to stand over, to urge constantly to further action: *he's always on my back.*

**break the back of, 1.** to deal with or accomplish the most difficult or arduous part of (a task, etc.) **2.** to overburden or overwhelm.

**get off someone's back,** *Colloq.* to cease to annoy or harrass someone.

**get one's back up,** to become annoyed.

**out the back,** *Colloq.* in the backyard.

**on the back of,** close behind; immediately following in space or time.

**put one's back into,** to do (something) with all one's energy and strength.

**put (someone's) back up,** *Colloq.* to arouse (someone's) resentment.

**see the back of, 1.** to be rid of (a person). **2.** to be finished with (a situation, task, etc.)

**turn one's back on,** to disregard, neglect, or ignore.

*–v.t.* **15.** to support, as with authority, influence, or money (oft. fol. by *up*). **16.** to cause to move backwards; reverse the action of: *to back a car.* **17.** to bet in favour of: *to back a horse in the race.* **18.** *Archaic.* to get upon the back of; mount. **19.** to furnish with a back. **20.** to lie at the back of; form a back or background for: *sandhills back the beach.* **21.** to write on the back of; endorse. *–v.i.* **22.** to go backwards (oft. fol. by *up*). **23.** *Naut.* (of wind) to change direction anticlockwise. *–v.* **24.** Some special verb phrases are:

**back and fill, 1.** *Naut.* to manoeuvre a sailing vessel to and fro in a channel by trimming the sails to be alternately full and then slack. **2.** *Colloq.* to drive a motor vehicle backwards and forwards usu. while parking. **3.** *Colloq.* to vacillate.

**back down, 1.** to retreat from or abandon an argument, opinion, claim. **2.** *Rowing.* to row a boat backwards.

**back off,** to retreat or withdraw (oft. fol. by *from*)

**back out, 1.** to go or cause to move out backwards. **2.** to withdraw; retreat (fol. by *of*). **3.** *Surfing.* to slide off a wave by manoeuvring so that the front of the surfboard lifts.

**back up, 1.** to give support to; encourage. **2.** to go or cause to move backwards. **3.** *Mountaineering.* to climb a chimney or cleft by pressing the feet on one side and the back on the other. **4.** *Cricket.* (of the batsman not playing the ball) to advance down the wicket in readiness to run as the ball is bowled. **5.** *Cricket.* (of a fielder) to cover a player receiving a return of the ball to prevent an overthrow. **6.** to become clogged; cease to move freely.

**back up for,** *Colloq.* to seek more of (something such as money or a further helping of food).

**back water,** *Naut.* to reverse the direction of a vessel.

*–adj.* **25.** lying or being behind: *a back door.* **26.** away from the front position or rank; remote: *back country.* **27.** relating to the past: *back files; back pay.* **28.** coming or going back; backward: *back current.* **29.** *Phonet.* pronounced with the tongue drawn back in the mouth as the vowel /ɔ/ in *bought* /bɔt/ or the palatal consonant /k/ in *cup* /kʌp/. [ME *bak,* OE *bæc,* Icel. c. *bak*]

**back**[2] /bæk/, *adv.* **1.** at, to, or towards the rear; backwards: *to step back.* **2.** towards the past: *to look back on one's youth.* **3.** ago: *a long while back.* **4.** towards the original starting point, place, or condition: *to go back to the old home.* **5.** returned home; in the original starting point, place, or condition again: *back where he started from.* **6.** in reply; in return: *to pay back a loan.* **7.** in reversal of the usual course: *to take back a gift.* **8. back and forth,** from side to side, to and fro. [aphetic var. of ABACK]

**back**[3] /bæk/, *n.* a tub or vat. [D *bak,* from F *bac* tub, trough, ferryboat]

**backache** /ˈbækeɪk/, *n.* an ache in one's back.

**back beat** /ˈbæk bit/, *n.* a drum beat on the second and fourth beats of the bar, characteristic of rock'n'roll music.

**back bench** /bæk ˈbɛntʃ/, *n.* one of the rows of seats behind the front benches in the House of Representatives, the Senate, the British House of Parliament, or a similar legislative chamber, traditionally occupied by members who are not ministers or shadow ministers.

**backbench** /ˈbækbɛntʃ/, *n.* the non-office-holding parliamentary membership of a political party: *the Labor backbench will give him hearty applause.* – **backbench,** *adj.*

**backbencher** /bækˈbɛntʃə/, *n.* a member of a lower house of parliament who is not a minister or shadow minister, and who therefore by tradition sits on one of the benches behind the front bench occupied by ministers, shadow ministers and party leaders.

**backbite** /ˈbækbaɪt/, *v.,* **-bit, -bitten** or (*Colloq.*) **-bit, -biting.** *–v.t.* **1.** to attack the character or reputation of secretly. *–v.i.* **2.** to speak evil of the absent; gossip. – **backbiter,** *n.* – **backbiting,** *n.*

**backblocks** /ˈbækblɒks/, *n. pl.* **1.** remote, sparsely inhabited inland country. **2.** *Colloq.* the outer suburbs of a city. – **backblock,** *adj.* – **backblocker,** *n.*

**backboard** /ˈbækbɔd/, *n.* **1.** a board placed at or forming the back of anything. **2.** a board worn to support or straighten the back. **3.** *Basketball.* the board fixed behind the basket.

**back bond** /ˈbæk bɒnd/, *n.* a bond of indemnity given to a surety.

**backbone** /ˈbækboʊn/, *n.* **1.** the spinal or vertebral column; the spine. **2.** something resembling a backbone in appearance, position, or function. **3.** strength of character; resolution. **4. to the backbone,** *Colloq.* through and through: *loyal to the backbone.* **5. see (one's) backbone,** (formerly) to flog. – **backboned,** *adj.* – **backboneless,** *adj.*

**backbreaker** /ˈbækbreɪkə/, *n.* **1.** a physically exhausting task. **2.** a wrestling hold in which the victim's body is bent backwards over his opponent's knee or shoulder.

**backbreaking** /ˈbækbreɪkɪŋ/, *adj.* extremely arduous; physically exhausting.

**back-burn** /ˈbæk-bɜn/, *v.t.* **1.** to clear (land, grass or scrub) by burning into or against the wind. *–v.i.* **2.** to control a fire by burning off an area in advance of it, often into or against the wind. *–n.* **3.** the action or result of back-burning. – **back-burning,** *n.*

**backchat** /ˈbæktʃæt/, *n.* impertinent talk; answering back.

**backcloth** /ˈbækklɒθ/, *n.* →**backdrop.**

**backcomb** /ˈbækkoʊm/, *v.t.* →**tease** (def. 4).

**back country** /ˈbæk kʌntri/, *n.* **1.** sparsely populated rural regions. **2.** the remoter and less developed parts of a large rural property.

**back-country** /ˈbæk-kʌntri/, *adj.* belonging to or characteristic of back country.

**back-countryman** /bæk-ˈkʌntrimən/, *n., pl.* **-men.** one who lives in back country; bushman.

**back-court** /ˈbæk-kɔt/, *n.* the area of a basketball or netball court between a team's own end line and the centre circle.

**backcross** /ˈbækkrɒs/, *v.t.* **1.** to cross (a hybrid of the first generation) with either of its parents, or a member of the parental stock. *–n.* **2.** an instance of such crossing. **3.** an individual produced by such crossing.

**back cut** /ˈbæk kʌt/, *n. Cricket.* a stroke played by the batsman with his weight on the back foot.

**backdate** /ˈbækdeɪt/, *v.t.* to date (something) earlier; apply retrospectively: *we shall backdate the pay rise.*

**back door** /bæk ˈdɔ/, *n.* **1.** a door at the rear of a building. **2. by** or **through the back door,** secretly; by hidden, obscure or dishonourable means.

**backdoor** /ˈbækdɔ/, *adj.* secret; clandestine.

**backdrop** /ˈbækdrɒp/, *n.* the painted curtain or hanging at the back of a theatrical set; backcloth.

**backed** /bækt/, *adj.* **1.** having a back: *a high-backed chair.* **2.** having backing: *a government-backed measure.*

**back-end** /ˈbæk-ɛnd/, *adj.* of or pertaining to the final stages of a project, plan, etc.

**backer** /ˈbækə/, *n.* **1.** one who backs. **2.** one who has a bet on the outcome of a race, esp. a horse race. **3.** one who provides financial support for a venture, esp. a theatrical production.

**backfall** /ˈbækfɔl/, *n.* **1.** that which falls back. **2.** *Wrestling.* a fall in which a wrestler is thrown on his back.

**backfatter** /ˈbækfætə/, *n.* a pig whose carcase carries a high proportion of fat to lean meat, thus rendering it suitable only for small goods.

**backfill** /ˈbækfɪl/, *n.* **1.** the material used to refill an excavation or support the roof of a worked mine. **2.** sand or earth placed behind timber, steel or concrete linings in mine shafts or tunnels. **3.** *Bldg Trades.* material used to refill an excavation after the drain pipe, conduit, etc. for which it was required has been installed. *–v.t., v.i.* **4.** to fill with backfill.

**backfire** /bækˈfaɪə/, *v.*, **-fired, -firing,** *n.* *–v.i.* **1.** (of an internal-combustion engine) to have a premature explosion in the cylinder or in the admission or exhaust passages. **2.** *Chiefly U.S.* to check a forest or prairie fire by burning off an area in advance of it. **3.** to bring results opposite to those planned: *the plot backfired.* *–n.* **4.** (in an internal-combustion engine) premature ignition of fuel, resulting in loss of power and loud explosive sound in the manifold. **5.** an explosion coming out of the breech of a firearm. **6.** *Chiefly U.S.* a fire deliberately started in front of a forest or prairie fire in order to check it.

**backformation** /ˈbækfɔmeɪʃən/, *n.* **1.** the formation of a new word by morphological shortening, in reverse of the normal process of derivation. **2.** a word formed in this way, as *edit* from *editor, donate* from *donation, laze* from *lazy.*

**backgammon** /ˈbækgæmən, bækˈgæmən/, *n.* **1.** a game played by two persons at a board with pieces or men moved in accordance with throws of dice. **2.** a victory at this game, esp. one resulting in a tripled score. *–v.t.* **3.** to defeat at backgammon, esp. to win a triple score over. [BACK[1], *adj.* + GAMMON[1]; game so called because the pieces often go back and re-enter]

**background** /ˈbækgraʊnd/, *n.* **1.** the ground or parts situated in the rear. **2. a.** the surface or ground against which the parts of a picture are relieved. **b.** the portions of a picture represented as in the distance. **3.** the social, historical and other antecedents which explain an event or condition: *the background of the war.* **4.** a person's origin and education, in relation to present character, status, etc. **5. in the background,** out of sight or notice; in obscurity. **6.** *Physics.* the counting rate of a Geiger counter or other counter tube due to radioactive sources other than the one being measured. **7.** *Computers.* a program tolerant of interrupts, which continues on an extended task unless there is an interrupt task to be performed. *–adj.* **8.** of or pertaining to the background; in the background. **9.** *Computers.* of or pertaining to a program of low priority. *–v.t.* **10.** to provide background information for.

**background count** /– ˈkaʊnt/, *n.* the estimate of radiations resulting from naturally occuring radioactivity and cosmic rays, etc., as opposed to the estimate of radiations from some particular agency being examined.

**background radiation** /ˌ– reɪdiˈeɪʃən/, *n.* the low radiation from cosmic rays and from radioactive substances naturally present in the atmosphere.

**backhand** /ˈbækhænd/, *n.* **1.** the hand turned backwards in making a stroke, as in tennis. **2. a.** a stroke, as in tennis, by a right-handed player from the left of the body (or the reverse for a left-handed player). **b.** *Bowls.* a delivery of a bowl by a right-handed player in a left-hand direction with the bias inwards. **3.** writing which slopes backwards or to the left. *–adj.* **4.** backhanded. **5.** *Surfing.* of or pertaining to a surfing manoeuvre in which one's back is to the wave.

**backhanded** /bækˈhændəd/, *adj.* **1.** performed with the hand turned backwards, crosswise, or in any oblique direction, or with the back of the hand in the direction of the stroke. **2.** sloping to the left: *backhanded writing.* **3.** oblique or opposite in meaning; indirect: *a backhanded compliment.* **4.** (of a rope) twisted in the opposite way from the usual or right-handed method. – **backhandedly,** *adv.* – **backhandedness,** *n.*

**backhander** /ˈbækhændə/, *n.* **1.** a backhanded blow or stroke. **2.** an indirectly insulting remark. **3.** *Colloq.* a bribe: *he slipped the witness a backhander.*

**backhoe** /ˈbækhoʊ/, *n.* a small tractor (usu. with rubber wheels) with a hydraulically operated scoop at the back for digging trenches, etc.

**backhouse** /ˈbækhaʊs/, *n.* *Chiefly U.S.* an outdoor toilet.

**backing** /ˈbækɪŋ/, *n.* **1.** aid or support of any kind. **2.** supporters or backers collectively. **3.** that which forms the back or is placed at or attached to the back of anything to support or strengthen it. **4.** the coating on the base of photographic film as opposed to the emulsion side. **5.** musical background for a singer.

**backing dog** /ˈ– dɒg/, *n.* a sheepdog that will run across the backs of sheep to aid mustering or droving.

**backing store** /ˈ– stɔ/, *n.* an auxiliary memory store attached to a digital computer.

**backlash** /ˈbæklæʃ/, *n.* **1.** any sudden, violent, or unexpected reaction. **2.** an antagonistic political or social reaction, sometimes sudden and violent, to a previous action construed as a threat. **3.** the jarring reaction, or the play, between loosely fitting or worn parts of a machine or mechanical device. **4.** *Angling.* a tangled line on a reel, caused by a faulty cast. **5.** *Canoeing.* a wave rising against the current as against a fixed obstacle.

**backless** /ˈbækləs/, *adj.* **1.** without a back. **2.** (of a dress) cut low at the back.

**back line** /ˈbæk laɪn/, *n.* **1.** in a jazz band, the rhythm players as distinct from the solo players. **2.** *Rugby Football.* the backs, esp. when lined out across the field ready to receive the ball, as at a scrum or line-out.

**back-load** /ˈbæk-loʊd/, *n.* a load which can be transported by a truck back to its base once its main load has been deposited, thereby making the truck's journey more profitable.

**backlog** /ˈbæklɒg/, *n.* **1.** an accumulation (of business resources, stock, etc.) acting as a reserve. **2.** an accumulation (of work, correspondence, etc.) awaiting attention. **3.** a log at the back of a fire.

**back man** /ˈbæk mæn/, *Aus. Rules.* a player in one of the back positions. Also, **back.**

**backmost** /ˈbækmoʊst/, *adj.* farthest to the back.

**back number** /ˈbæk nʌmbə/, *n.* **1.** an out-of-date issue of a serial publication. **2.** anything out of date.

**back of beyond,** *Colloq.* *–n.* **1.** a remote, inaccessible place. **2.** the far outback. *–adv.* **3.** in the outback. **4.** to the outback. Also, **back o' beyond.**

**back of Bourke,** *n.* *Colloq.* any remote outback area. [*Bourke,* town in far west N.S.W.]

**back-pack** /ˈbæk-pæk/, *n.* portable equipment carried on the back, as television or film cameras, or fire-fighting, hiking, camping equipment, etc.

**back paddock** /ˈ– pædək/, *n.* a paddock remote from the station homestead.

**back passage** /ˈ– pæsɪdʒ/, *n.* the anal passage.

**back pay** /ˈ– peɪ/, *n.* payment already earned by an employee and owed to him by his employer.

**back-pedal** /ˈbæk-pɛdl/, *v.i.*, **-alled, -alling,** or (*U.S.*) **-aled, -aling. 1.** to press the pedals of a bicycle backwards, as in slowing down. **2.** to make an effort to slow down, or reverse one's course, as to avoid danger. **3.** to retreat in argument by moderating one's view or tone. **4.** *Boxing.* to retreat while facing one's opponent. **5.** *Tennis.* to go backwards, off balance, without control over the shot being played.

**back play** /ˈ– pleɪ/, *n.* *Cricket.* the style of batting in which the batsman steps back when playing the ball.

**back pocket** /ˈ– pɒkət/, *n.* *Aus. Rules.* either of the two players who defend the areas on either side of the goal front.

**back projection** /ˈ– prədʒɛkʃən/, *n.* the projection of pictures on a screen behind actors who are being filmed to create the illusion that they are moving or are in a place distant from the studio. Also, **background projection.**

**back rest** /ˈ– rɛst/, *n.* a support for the back, as in a vehicle.

**back road** /'– roʊd/, *n.* an unfrequented road, used as a detour to avoid a main route.

**backroom** /'bækrum/, *adj.* **1.** doing or pertaining to important work behind the scenes. **2. backroom boys,** *Colloq.* people operating behind the scenes, usu. in areas which they do not wish to make public.

**back run** /'– rʌn/, *n.* a tract of grazing land towards the back boundary of a property.

**back-run** /'bæk-rʌn/, *n.* (of a periodical, newspaper, etc.) a run of past issues.

**back-saw** /'bæk-sɔ/, *n.* a saw with a thick ridge on the back for stiffness.

**back-scarf** /'bæk-skaf/, *v.t.* to cut a scarf on (a tree) away from the direction of intended fall.

**backscatter** /'bækskætə/, *n.* **1.** Also, **backscattering.** the deflection of waves or alpha particles through angles greater than 90° by an obstacle such as an electromagnetic force. **2.** the waves or particles so deflected. *–v.t.* **3.** (of an obstacle) to deflect (particles or waves) through angles greater than 90°.

**back scratcher** /'bæk skrætʃə/, *n.* **1.** a long-handled implement usu. of plastic or wood, often fashioned so that one end resembles a small hand, and which can be used to scratch one's own back. **2.** *Colloq.* one who provides a service to another in expectation of receiving a similar service in return.

**back-scull** /'bæk-skʌl/, *v.i.* to scull (def. 7) while floating on the back.

**back seat** /bæk 'sit/, *n.* **1.** a seat at the back. **2. take a back seat,** to retire into obscurity, or into an insignificant or subordinate position.

**back-seat driver** /ˌbæk-sit 'draɪvə/, *n.* **1.** a passenger in a car who offers unnecessary advice to the driver, as though trying to drive the car himself. **2.** one who interferes with advice or orders in matters which are not his responsibility.

**backsheesh** /'bækʃiʃ, bæk'ʃiʃ/, *n., v.t., v.i.* →**baksheesh.** Also, **backshish.**

**backside** /bæk'saɪd/, *n.* **1.** the back part. **2.** the buttocks.

**backsight** /'bæksaɪt/, *n. Survey.* **1.** a sight on a previously occupied instrument station. **2.** the reading on a levelling rod that is held on a point of known elevation, used in computing the elevation of the levelling instrument.

**back slang** /'bæk slæŋ/, *n.* a form of slang in which words are pronounced as though spelt backwards.

**backslapping** /'bækslæpɪŋ/, *n.* **1.** hearty fraternisation, esp. between men. *–adj.* **2.** overly jovial and friendly.

**backslide** /'bækslaɪd, bæk'slaɪd/, *v.i.,* **-slid, -slidden** or **-slid, -sliding.** to relapse into error or sin. – **backslider,** *n.*

**backspace** /'bækspeɪs/, *v.i.* (in typing) to move the carriage back one space at a time, by depressing a particular key.

**backspin** /'bækspɪn/, *n.* reverse spinning of a ball causing it to bounce backwards or stop in the shortest possible time, as in golf or tennis.

**backsplash** /'bæksplæʃ/, *n.* the splash caused by the blade of an oar entering the water too slowly.

**backspring** /'bæksprɪŋ/, *n.* a rope leading from a point forward on a ship to a point aft on the quay, or vice versa, to prevent the moored ship surging ahead or astern.

**backstab** /'bækstæb/, *v.,* **-stabbed, -stabbing.** *–v.t.* to do harm to (somebody), esp. somebody defenceless or unsuspecting, as by making a treacherous attack upon his reputation. – **backstabber,** *n.*

**backstage** /bæk'steɪdʒ/, *adv.;* /'bæksteɪdʒ/, *adj.* *–adv.* **1.** out of the view of the audience in a theatre; in the wings or dressing rooms, or behind the curtain on the stage. **2.** towards the rear of the stage; upstage. **3.** *Colloq.* behind the scenes; in private. *–adj.* **4.** situated, occurring, etc., backstage.

**backstairs** /bæk'stɛəz/, *n.;* /'bækstɛəz/, *adj.* *–n.* **1.** a secondary staircase, originally for servants. *–adj.* **2.** Also, **backstair.** indirect; underhand; clandestine: *backstairs gossip.*

**back-station** /'bæk-steɪʃən/, *n.* **1.** a station (def. 8b) in the remote inland. **2.** (formerly) a stockman's hut and run (def. 118) remote from the main station.

**backstay** /'bæksteɪ/, *n.* **1.** *Mach.* a supporting or checking piece in a mechanism. **2.** *Naut.* a stay leading from a mast backwards.

**backstitch** /'bækstɪtʃ/, *n.* **1.** stitching or a stitch in which the thread doubles back each time on the preceding stitch. *–v.i.* **2.** to make such stitches. *–v.t.* **3.** to sew by backstitch.

**backstop** /'bækstɒp/, *n., v.,* **-stopped, -stopping.** *–n.* **1.** *Sport.* a person, screen, or fence placed to prevent a ball going too far. **2.** a person who or a thing which is relied on for assistance when all else fails: *I have $500 as a backstop.* **3.** *Rowing.* a wooden block at the bow end of the seat slide, that prevents the seat running off the runners. **4.** *Cricket.* →**wicket-keeper.** *–v.i.* **5.** to act as a backstop.

**back straight** /bæk 'streɪt/, *n.* the straight part of a racing track circuit on the opposite side to the home straight.

**back-strapped** /'bæk-stræpt/, *adj.* (of a vessel) held powerless by wind or tide in a dangerous or difficult position.

**backstreet** /'bækstrit/, *n.* **1.** a small, unimportant street. *–adj.* **2.** illegal, illicit or improper.

**backstroke** /'bækstroʊk/, *n., v.,* **-stroked, -stroking** *–n.* **1.** a backhanded stroke. **2.** a blow or stroke in return; recoil. **3.** *Swimming.* a stroke in which the swimmer is on his back performing a flutter-kick and rotating his arms alternately backwards. **4.** *Cricket.* a stroke played with the player's weight on the foot nearer the stumps. *–v.i.* **5.** *Swimming.* to perform backstroke.

**back swing** /'bæk swɪŋ/, *n.* a backward and upward movement of a bat, club or racquet, made by a player before hitting the ball.

**backsword** /'bæksɔd/, *n.* **1.** a sword with only one sharp edge; a broadsword. **2.** a cudgel with a basket hilt, used like a foil in fencing. – **backswordsman,** *n.*

**back talk** /'bæk tɔk/, *n.* answering back in a manner considered impertinent.

**back-to-basics** /bæk-tə-'beɪsɪks/, *adj.* advocating or characterised by an endeavour to return to first principles or the origins of a school of thought.

**back-to-front** /ˌbæk-tə-'frʌnt/, *adj.* reversed; disordered.

**backtrack**[1] /'bæktræk/, *v.i.* **1.** to return over the same course or route. **2.** to withdraw from an undertaking, position, etc.; pursue a reverse policy. [BACK[2] + TRACK[1]] – **backtracker,** *n.*

**backtrack**[2] /'bæktræk/, *n.* a minor road in worse condition than the main road and passing through less populated areas. [BACK[1] + TRACK[1]]

**backup** /'bækʌp/, *n.* **1.** support given subsequently; corroboration: *backup to the doctors' warnings.* **2.** a pent-up accumulation, esp. of a liquid: *the backup of flood water.* **3.** a reserve supply or resource; a second means of support. **4.** *Print.* the presswork on the reverse side of a printed sheet. *–adj.* **5.** of or pertaining to support given subsequently or that which so supports: *a backup campaign.* Also, **back-up.**

**back vent** /'bæk vɛnt/, *n. Plumbing.* a pipe with access to the open air, connected to a waste pipe to prevent siphonic action from occurring.

**backward** /'bækwəd/, *adj.* **1.** Also, **backwards.** directed towards the back or past: *a backward glance.* **2.** Also, **backwards.** reversed; returning: *a backward movement.* **3.** behind in time or progress; late; slow: *a backward child.* **4.** reluctant; hesitating; bashful. *–adv.* **5.** →**backwards.** [ME *bakward,* from *bak* BACK[1] + -WARD] – **backwardly,** *adv.* – **backwardness,** *n.*

**backwardation** /bækwə'deɪʃən/, *n. Stock Exchange.* the position in a futures market where the more distantly traded contracts are selling at a discount to the nearer dated contracts.

**backwards** /'bækwədz/, *adv.* **1.** towards the back or rear. **2.** with the back foremost. **3.** in reverse of the usual or right way: *to spell backwards.* **4.** towards the past. **5.** towards a worse or less advanced condition; retrogressively. **6. backwards and forwards,** to and fro. **7. bend** or **lean** or **fall over backwards,** *Colloq.* to go to a great deal of trouble. Also, **backward.** [ME *bakweardes.* See BACKWARD, -WARDS]

**backwash** /'bækwɒʃ/, *n.* **1.** *Naut.* the water thrown back by a motor, oars or paddlewheels. **2.** *Aeron.* the air which flows back from the propellers of an aircraft. **3.** a condition lasting after the event which caused it. **4.** water running down the beach towards the surf after a wave has broken. *–v.t.* **5.** to remove the oil from (combed wool). **6.** to send the water of (a swimming pool) through its filtering system in a reverse direction, so as to clean the filters.

**backwasher** /'bækwɒʃə/, *n.* a machine for washing wool after it has been carded.

**backwater** /ˈbækwɔtə/, *n.* **1.** *Naut.* water held or forced back, as by a dam, flood, tide, or current. **2.** a body of stagnant water connected to a river. **3.** a place or state considered to be stagnant or backward. **4.** a quiet, peaceful place. **5.** →**backwash** (def. 1) –*v.i.* **6.** to move a boat backwards by paddling with the oars.

**backwind** /ˈbækwɪnd/, *n. Naut.* the turbulent air flowing off a sail; dirty wind.

**backwoods** /ˈbækwʊdz/, *n.pl.* **1.** →**back country.** **2.** *Chiefly U.S.* wooded or partially uncleared and unsettled districts. **3.** any unfamiliar or unfrequented area: *the backwoods of English literature.* –*adj.* Also, **backwood. 4.** of or pertaining to the backwoods. **5.** rustically unsophisticated and uncouth.

**backwoodsman** /ˈbækwʊdzmən/, *n., pl.* **-men. 1.** one living in the backwoods. **2.** *Chiefly U.S.* a rustic and unsophisticated person.

**backyard** /bækˈjad/, *n.* **1.** an area, often of some size with gardens and lawn, at the back of a building, usu. a house. –*adj.* **2.** of or pertaining to a tradesman whose small or part-time business is conducted from his place of residence: *a backyard motor mechanic.* **3.** illegal, illicit, improper or unqualified: *backyard abortionist.*

**backyarder** /bækˈjadə/, *n. Colloq.* **1.** an abortionist without recognised medical training. **2.** a person who carries on business in the backyard of his home.

**bacon** /ˈbeɪkən/, *n.* **1.** meat from the back and sides of the pig, salted and dried or smoked. **2. bring home the bacon,** *Colloq.* **a.** to support a family; provide for material needs. **b.** to succeed in a specific task. **3. save (one's) bacon,** *Colloq.* to save from a dangerous or awkward situation. [ME, from OF, from Gmc; cf. OHG *bahho,* MHG *bache* buttock, ham]

**bacon-and-eggs** /beɪkən-ən-ˈɛgz/, *n.* **1.** any of various small shrubs of the family Papilionaceae, having reddish-brown and yellow flowers, as plants from the Australian genera *Daviesia, Dillwynia* and *Pultenea.* **2.** any of various other plants having similarly coloured flowers, as bird's-foot trefoil and toadflax. Also, **eggs-and-bacon.**

**baconer** /ˈbeɪkənə/, *n.* a pig carrying the proportion of lean and fat meat which will render its carcase suitable for curing.

**bact.,** bacteriology.

**bacteraemia** /bæktəˈrimiə/, *n.* the presence (for transient periods) of harmful bacteria in the blood. Also, **bacteremia.** [BACTER- + -AEMIA]

**bacteri-,** a word element meaning 'bacteria' or 'bacterial'. Also, **bacter-, bacterio-, bactero-.** [combining form of BACTERIUM]

**bacteria** /bækˈtɪəriə/, *n., pl. of* **bacterium.** the morphologically simplest group of usu. non-green vegetable organisms, various species of which are concerned in fermentation and putrefaction, the production of disease and the fixing of atmospheric nitrogen; schizomycetes. [NL, from Gk *baktḗrion,* diminutive of *báktron* stick] – **bacterial,** *adj.* – **bacterially,** *adv.*

A B C

bacteria (greatly magnified): A, cocci; B, baccilli; C, spirilla

**bactericide** /bækˈtɪərəsaɪd/, *n.* any agent which can kill bacteria. [BACTERI- + -CIDE] – **bactericidal,** *adj.*

**bacterin** /ˈbæktərən/, *n.* a vaccine prepared from dead or attenuated bacteria.

**bacteriochlorophyll** /bækˌtɪəriouˈklɒrəfɪl/, *n.* a green substance similar to chlorophyll, found in certain photosynthetic bacteria.

**bacteriol.,** bacteriology.

**bacteriology** /bækˌtɪəriˈɒlədʒi/, *n.* the science that deals with bacteria. [BACTERIO- + -LOGY] – **bacteriological,** *adj.* – **bacteriologically,** *adv.* – **bacteriologist,** *n.*

**bacteriolysis** /bækˌtɪəriˈɒləsəs/, *n.* disintegration or dissolution of bacteria. [BACTERIO- + -LYSIS] – **bacteriolytic** /bækˌtɪəriəˈlɪtɪk/, *adj.*

**bacteriophage** /bækˈtɪəriəfeɪdʒ/, *n.* a virus that is specifically parasitic on bacteria, esp. one that destroys bacteria. [BACTERIO- + -PHAGE]

**bacteriostasis** /bækˌtɪəriəˈsteɪsəs/, *n.* the inhibition of the multiplication of bacteria not proceeding to their destruction. [BACTERIO- + STASIS] – **bacteriostatic** /bækˌtɪəriəˈstætɪk/, *adj.*

**bacteriotoxic** /bækˌtɪəriəˈtɒksɪk/, *adj.* **1.** harmful to bacteria. **2.** caused by toxins of bacterial origin. – **bacteriotoxin,** *n.*

**bacterium** /bækˈtɪəriəm/, *n.* **1.** singular of **bacteria. 2.** a group of non-spore-forming, non-motile, rod-shaped bacteria (as distinct from the bacillus and clostridium groups). [NL, from Gk *baktḗrion,* diminutive of *báktron* stick]

**bactero-,** variant of **bacteri-.**

**bacteroid** /ˈbæktərɔɪd/, *n.* **1.** any of various minute rodlike or branched organisms, many of which are bacteria, as in the root nodules of nitrogen-fixing plants. –*adj.* **2.** resembling bacteria.

**Bactrian camel** /bæktriən ˈkæməl/, *n.* the two-humped camel, *Camelus bactrianus.*

Bactrian camel

**baculiform** /bəˈkjuləfɔm, ˈbækjələ-/, *adj.* (of a biological organism) rod-shaped. [L *baculum* rod + -I- + -FORM]

**baculine** /ˈbækjəlin, -laɪn/, *adj.* pertaining to the cane or to its use in punishing. [L *baculum* rod + -INE[1]]

**bad**[1] /bæd/, *adj.,* **worse, worst,** *n., adv.* –*adj.* **1.** not good: *bad conduct, a bad life.* **2.** defective; worthless: *a bad coin, a bad debt.* **3.** unsatisfactory; poor; below standard; inadequate: *bad heating, a bad businessman.* **4.** incorrect; faulty: *a bad shot.* **5.** unskilful; incompetent (fol. by *at*): *bad at tennis.* **6.** not valid; not sound: *a bad claim.* **7.** having an injurious or unfavourable tendency or effect: *bad air, bad for him.* **8.** in ill health; sick: *to feel bad.* **9.** regretful; contrite; sorry; upset: *to feel bad about an error.* **10.** unfavourable; unfortunate: *bad news.* **11.** offensive; disagreeable; painful: *a bad temper.* **12.** severe: *a bad sprain.* **13.** rotten; decayed. **14. go bad,** decay; rot. **15. not bad,** *Colloq.* **a.** fair; not good. **b.** excellent. –*n.* **16.** that which is bad. **17.** a bad condition, character, or quality. **18. go to the bad,** become morally ruined, wicked, or corrupt. **19. in bad with,** *Colloq.* out of favour with. **20. to the bad,** in deficit; out of pocket: *two hundred dollars to the bad.* –*adv.* **21.** badly. [ME *badde;* ? backformation from OE *bǣddel* effeminate person] – **badness,** *n.*

**bad**[2] /bæd/, *v.* past tense of **bid.**

**bad apple** /– ˈæpəl/, *n.* **1.** a morally reprehensible person. **2.** one of a group, worse than the rest.

**bad blood** /– ˈblʌd/, *n.* hate; long-standing enmity; dislike.

**baddie** /ˈbædi/, *n. Colloq.* a bad person, esp. a villain in a story, play or film.

**baddish** /ˈbædɪʃ/, *adj.* fairly bad.

**bade** /bæd/, *v.* past tense of **bid.**

**bad egg** /bæd ˈɛg/, *n. Colloq.* a person of reprehensible character.

**bad form** /bæd ˈfɔm/, *n.* a breach of good manners or the accepted code of behaviour.

**badge** /bædʒ/, *n.* **1.** a mark, token or device worn as a sign of allegiance, membership, authority, achievement. **2.** any emblem, token, or distinctive mark. [ME *bage, bagge;* orig. unknown]

**badger** /ˈbædʒə/, *n.* **1.** any of the various burrowing carnivorous mammals of the Mustelidae, as *Meles meles,* a European species, and *Taxidea taxus,* a similar American species. **2.** the fur of this mammal. **3.** *Obs.* (erroneously) a wombat. **4.** *Obs.* (erroneously) a bandicoot (def. 2). **5.** →**hyrax. 6.** →**ratel. 7.** a brush, esp. a paintbrush, of badger's hair. –*v.t.* **8.** to harass; torment. [earlier *bageard,* ? from BADGE (with allusion to white mark on head) + -ARD]

badger

**badger-box** /ˈbædʒə-bɒks/, *n.* (formerly) a badly built house.

**bad hat** /bæd ˈhæt/, *n. Colloq.* a person of reprehensible character.

**badinage** /ˈbædənaʒ, -adʒ/, *n.* light, playful banter or raillery. [F, from *badiner* jest, from *badin* fool, from Pr., from *badar*

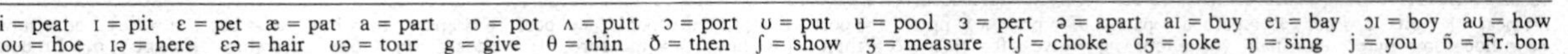

gape, from LL *badāre*]

**badlands** /ˈbædlændz/, *n. pl. U.S.* a barren area in which soft rock strata are eroded into varied, fantastic forms.

**bad lot** /bæd ˈlɒt/, *n. Colloq.* a dishonest, disreputable person, usu. considered a failure in life.

**badly** /ˈbædli/, *adv.* **1.** in a bad manner; ill. **2.** very much: *to need or want badly.*

**badminton** /ˈbædmɪntən/, *n.* a game, similar to lawn tennis, but played with a high net and shuttlecock. [named after *Badminton,* village in Gloucestershire, England]

**badmouth** /ˈbædmaʊθ/, *v.t.* to speak unfavourably of, to criticise with malice.

**bad news** /bæd ˈnjuz/, *n. Colloq.* anything or anyone likely to bring trouble or misfortune: *those kids are bad news.*

**bad penny** /– ˈpɛni/, *n. Colloq.* someone or something unwanted that seems to be constantly returning: *he kept turning up in Darwin like a bad penny.*

**bad shot** /– ˈʃɒt/, *n.* **1.** a badly aimed shot. **2.** an unsuccessful attempt. **3.** a poor marksman.

**bad-tempered** /bæd-ˈtɛmpəd/, *adj.* cross; cantankerous.

**bad trot** /bæd ˈtrɒt/, *n. Colloq.* a period of ill fortune.

**bad turn** /– ˈtɜn/, *n.* →**turn** (def. 82).

**baff** /bæf/, *v.i.* **1.** to strike the ground with a golf club in making a stroke. *–n.* **2.** a baffing stroke, unduly lofting the ball. [? imitative]

**baffle** /ˈbæfəl/, *v.,* **-fled, -fling,** *n.* *–v.t.* **1.** to thwart or frustrate disconcertingly; balk; confuse. **2.** to puzzle or mystify. **3.** *Naut.* (of the wind, current, etc.) to force (a ship, etc.) to take a variable course by being greatly changeable. **4.** *Obs.* to hoodwink; cheat. *–v.i.* **5.** to struggle ineffectually, as a ship in a gale. *–n.* **6.** an artificial obstruction for checking or deflecting the flow of gases (as in a boiler), sounds (as in a radio), etc. **7.** *Obs.* a balk or check; perplexity. [orig. uncert.] – **bafflement,** *n.* – **baffler,** *n.* – **baffling,** *adj.* – **bafflingly,** *adv.*

**baffleboard** /ˈbæfəlbɔd/, *n.* a board on which a loudspeaker is mounted in order to improve the low frequency section of the sound it produces.

**baffle plates** /ˈbæfəl pleɪts/, *n.pl.* →**baffle** (def. 6).

**baffy** /ˈbæfi/, *n., pl.* **baffies.** a short wooden golf club (now little used) having a deeply pitched face, for lofting the ball.

**bag** /bæg/, *n., v.,* **bagged, bagging.** *–n.* **1.** a receptacle of leather, cloth, paper, etc. **2.** a suitcase or other portable receptacle for carrying articles as in travelling. **3.** a handbag. **4.** the contents of a bag. **5.** *Hunting.* a sportsman's take of game, etc. **6.** any of various measures of capacity. **7.** (*pl.*) *Colloq.* a lot; an abundance (of). **8.** something resembling or suggesting a bag. **9.** Also, **old bag.** *Colloq.* a disagreeable and unattractive woman. **10. a.** a sac, as in the body of an animal or insect. **b.** an udder. **11.** a baggy part. **12.** *Baseball, Softball.* a base. **13.** (*pl.*) trousers. **14.** *Colloq.* chosen occupation, hobby, pursuit, etc.: *golfing is his bag.* **15. bag and baggage,** *Colloq.* with all one's possessions; completely. **16. bag of bones,** an animal or person emaciated through want. **17. bag of tricks,** *Colloq.* **a.** a miscellaneous collection of items. **b.** a person never at a loss. **18. bag of wind,** *Colloq.* **a.** a loquacious person. **b.** a football. **19. in the bag,** secured; certain to be accomplished: *the contract is in the bag.* **20. the bag,** *Colloq.* the breathalyser. *–v.i.* **21.** to swell or bulge. **22.** to hang loosely like an empty bag. *–v.t.* **23.** to put into a bag. **24.** to cause to swell or bulge; distend. **25.** to spread mortar from the joints in a thin film over the face of brickwork with a damp hessian or other bag. **26.** to kill or catch, as in hunting. **27.** *Colloq.* to arrest and gaol. **28.** to grab; seize; steal. **29.** *Colloq.* to criticise sarcastically. [ME *bagge,* probably from Scand.; cf. Icel. *baggi* pack, bundle]

**bagasse** /bəˈgæs/, *n.* crushed, juiceless remains of sugar cane after sugar-making, used commercially for the production of wallboard, etc. [F, from Pr. *bagasso*]

**bagatelle** /bægəˈtɛl/, *n.* **1.** something of little value; a trifle. **2.** a game played on a board having at one end holes into which balls are to be struck with a cue. **3.** →**pinball. 4.** a short and light musical composition, usu. for the piano. [F, from It. *bagattella,* diminutive of *baga, baca* berry]

**bagboy** /ˈbægbɔɪ/, *n. Colloq.* a bookmaker's clerk.

**bagel** /ˈbeɪgəl/, *n.* a small ring-shaped, hard roll, made of dough. [Yiddish *beygel*]

**bagful** /ˈbægfʊl/, *n., pl.* **-fuls, bagsful.** as much as a bag will hold.

**baggage** /ˈbægɪdʒ/, *n.* **1.** luggage, esp. as for transportation in bulk. **2.** any luggage. **3.** the portable equipment of an army. **4.** *Colloq.* a pert or impudent young woman.

**bagged** /bægd/, *adj. Colloq.* compelled to undergo a breathalyser test.

**baggies** /ˈbægiz/, *n. pl. Colloq.* trousers, slacks, jeans, etc. with wide legs.

**bagging**[1] /ˈbægɪŋ/, *n.* woven material, as of hemp or jute, for bags.

**bagging**[2] /ˈbægɪŋ/, *n. Colloq.* severe, esp. sarcastic, criticism: *he gave me a bagging this morning over my smelly feet.*

**baggy** /ˈbægi/, *adj.,* **-gier, -giest.** baglike; hanging loosely. – **baggily,** *adv.* – **bagginess,** *n.*

**bagman** /ˈbægmən/, *n., pl.* **-men. 1.** (formerly) a swagman; tramp. **2.** *Colloq.* a bookmaker. **3.** (formerly) a travelling pedlar. **4.** *Colloq.* a person who collects bribes.

**bagman's gazette** /ˌbægmənz gəˈzɛt/, *n. Colloq.* formerly, a fictitious journal said to be the source of rumours.

**bagman's two-up** /ˌbægmənz ˈtu-ʌp/, *n. Colloq.* a swagman's blanket made from two chaff or corn sacks cut open and stitched together.

**bag moth** /ˈbæg mɒθ/, *n.* →**case moth.**

**bagnio** /ˈbænjoʊ/, *n., pl.* **bagnios. 1.** a prison for slaves, as in the Orient. **2.** a brothel. **3.** a bath or bathing house. [It. *bagno,* from L *balneum* bath]

**bag of fruit,** *n. Colloq.* a suit. [rhyming slang]

**bag of mystery,** *n. Colloq.* a saveloy or sausage.

**bagpipes** /ˈbægpaɪps/, *n.* a reed instrument consisting of a melody pipe and one or more accompanying drone pipes protruding from a windbag into which the air is blown by the mouth or a bellows. – **bagpipe,** *adj.* – **bagpiper,** *n.*

bagpipes

**bags** /bægz/, *v.t.* **1.** to claim as one's right. *–interj.* **2.** Also, **I bags.** (an exclamation by which one establishes a right by virtue of making the first claim): *bags I have first ride.*

**bagswinger** /ˈbægswɪŋə/, *n.* **1.** *Colloq.* a streetwalking prostitute. **2.** *Colloq.* a bookmaker.

**bag test** /ˈbæg tɛst/, *n. Colloq.* examination by the breathalyser.

**baguette** /bæˈgɛt/, *n.* **1.** a gem cut in a long, rectangular shape. **2.** this shape. **3.** *Archit.* a small, convex, semicircular moulding. Also, **baguet.** [F: wand, rod, from It. *bacchetta,* diminutive of *bacchio,* from L *baculum*]

**bagworm** /ˈbægwɜm/, *n.* the caterpillar of any moth of the Psychidae which constructs a bag of silk, leaves, etc., in which it lives.

**bah** /ba/, *interj.* (an expression of contempt, frustration, impatience, etc).

**bahadur** /bəˈhadə/, *n.* a title of respect commonly affixed to the names of officers and public figures in India. [Hind. *bahādur* hero]

**Bahai** /ˈbahaɪ, bəˈhaɪ/, *n., pl.* **-hais,** *adj.* *–n.* **1.** an adherent of Bahaism. *–adj.* **2.** of or pertaining to Bahaism or a Bahai. [Pers. *Baha'* (*ullah*) splendour (of God), title of the founder]

**Bahaism** /ˈbahaɪ-ɪzəm, bəˈhaɪ-/, *n.* Babism as accepted by the followers of Mirza Husain Ali, who in 1863 proclaimed himself leader of the Babists under the name Baha'ullah. – **Bahaist,** *n., adj.*

**Bahamas** /bəˈhaməz/, *n.* a country comprising an archipelago of over 700 islands in the West Indies, south-east of Florida. Also, **Bahama Islands.** – **Bahamian,** *adj., n.*

**Bahasa Indonesia** /bəˌhazə ɪndəˈniʒə/, *n.* the official language of the Republic of Indonesia, based mainly on Malay.

**Bahrain** /baˈreɪn/, *n.* a country consisting of a group of islands in the western Persian Gulf.

**bail**[1] /beɪl/, *n.* **1.** property given as surety that a person released from legal custody will return at an appointed time. **2.** the person or persons giving such surety. **3.** the position or the privilege of being bailed. **4.** release from prison on bond. 5. **jump bail,** to forfeit one's bail by absconding or failing to appear in court at the appointed time. 6. **stand** or **go bail for,** to supply bail for (someone). *–v.t.* 7. Also, **bail out.** to grant or to obtain the liberty of (a person under arrest) on security given for his appearance when required, as in court for trial. 8. to deliver possession of (goods, etc.) for storage, hire or other special purpose, without transfer of ownership. 9. **bail up, a.** to bring (a wild pig, etc.) to bay with dogs. **b.** to hold up and rob. **c.** to delay (someone) unnecessarily, as in conversation. *–v.i.* 10. **bail up,** of wild animals, esp. pigs, to halt at bay. [ME *bayle,* from OF *bail* control, *baillier* deliver, from L *bāiulāre* carry]

bail[1] (def. 9b): bail up

**bail**[2] /beɪl/, *n.* 1. the semicircular handle of a kettle or pail. 2. a hooplike support, as for a wagon cover. [ME *beyl,* probably from Scand.; cf. Icel. *beyglast* become bent]

**bail**[3] /beɪl/, *v.t., v.i., n.* →**bale**[3].

**bail**[4] /beɪl/, *n.* 1. *Cricket.* either of the two small bars or sticks laid across the tops of the stumps which form the wicket. 2. a bar for separating horses in a stable. 3. a framework for securing a cow's head during milking. 4. Also, **bail rod** or **paper bail.** (in a typewriter) the rod which holds paper in place. *–v.t.* 5. to secure (the head of a cow) in a bail (fol. by *up*). *–v.i.* 6. **bail up,** (of a cow) to go into a bail. [ME *baile,* from OF: barrier; of obscure origin]

**bailable** /ˈbeɪləbəl/, *adj.* 1. capable of being set free on bail. 2. admitting of bail: *a bailable offence.*

**bailee** /beɪˈli/, *n.* one to whom goods are delivered in bailment.

**bailer** /ˈbeɪlə/, *n.* 1. baler. See **bale**[3]. 2. *Cricket.* a ball which strikes or removes the bails without disturbing the stumps.

**bailer shell** /ˈ– ʃɛl/, *n.* 1. the shell of the volute mollusc *Melo amphora.* 2. any capacious shell.

**bailey** /ˈbeɪli/, *n., pl.* **-leys.** *Archaic.* the wall of defence about the outer court of a feudal castle, or the outer court itself, (still used in some proper names, as in the *Old Bailey,* London). [ME *baily;* var. of BAIL[4]]

**Bailey bridge** /beɪli ˈbrɪdʒ/, *n.* a bridge of prefabricated steel units, used esp. in military operations. [named after Sir Donald *Bailey,* b. 1910, the inventor]

**bail head** /ˈbeɪl hɛd/, *n.* the framework at the front of a crush (def. 15) for securing an animal's head during routine handling.

**bailie** /ˈbeɪli/, *n.* a Scottish municipal officer or magistrate. [ME *bailli,* from OF, var. of *baillif* BAILIFF]

**bailiff** /ˈbeɪləf/, *n.* 1. an officer employed by a sheriff to serve writs, summonses, execute processes, make arrests or court orders, collect payments of judgment debts, etc.; sherriff's officer. 2. (formerly) a person charged with local administration of justice. 3. an overseer of a landed estate. [ME *baillif,* from OF, from *baillir* govern]

**bailiwick** /ˈbeɪliwɪk/, *n.* 1. the office or jurisdiction of a person such as a sheriff. 2. a person's area of skill, work, etc. [BAILIE + *wick* office (ME *wike,* OE *wīce*)]

**bailment** /ˈbeɪlmənt/, *n.* 1. the act of bailing a prisoner or accused person. 2. the act of delivering property, etc. as surety.

**bailor** /ˈbeɪlə, -ˈlɔ/, *n.* one who delivers goods, etc., in bailment.

**bailsman** /ˈbeɪlzmən/, *n., pl.* **-men.** one who gives bail or security.

**bain-marie** /bæn-məˈri/, *n.* 1. a cooking vessel containing hot water into which another vessel is placed to heat its contents gently. 2. *Obs.* a vessel used in chemistry. [F: bath of Mary or Miriam, ref. to Miriam the sister of Moses, in the Middle Ages considered an alchemist]

**bairn** /bɛən/, *n. Chiefly Scot.* a child. [Scot. var. of obsolete E *barn,* OE *bearn*]

**bait** /beɪt/, *n.* 1. food or some substitute used as a lure in fishing, trapping, etc. 2. food containing a harmful additive such as poison or razor blades used to lure and kill animals considered pests. 3. food containing a drug used to dope greyhounds, racehorses, etc. 4. an allurement; enticement. 5. *Archaic.* a halt on a journey. *–v.t.* 6. to prepare (a hook or trap) with bait. 7. to add harmful substances to (food) to kill or drug animals. 8. to lure as with bait; seek to entrap. 9. to set dogs upon (an animal) for sport. 10. to goad to anger; torment (someone) for amusement. 11. *Archaic.* to feed (a beast of burden) during a journey. *–v.i.* 12. *Archaic.* to stop for refreshment during a journey. [ME, from Scand.; cf. Icel. *beita*] – **baiter,** *n.*

**baited** /ˈbeɪtəd/, *adj.* 1. (of a hook or trap) prepared with bait. 2. (of a hook) having had the bait taken. 3. (of meat, etc.) poisoned or drugged.

**baitlayer** /ˈbeɪtleɪə/, *n. Colloq.* a cook.

**baitworm** /ˈbeɪtwɜm/, *n.* a sand-dwelling marine polychaete, *Australonereis ehlersi,* up to 10 cm in length, characterised by a blood vessel running down the middle of its back.

**baize** /beɪz/, *n., v.,* **baized, baizing.** *–n.* 1. a soft, usually green, woollen fabric resembling felt, used chiefly for the tops of billiard and card tables. *–v.t.* 2. to cover or line with baize. [earlier *bays,* from F *baies,* pl., from *bai* bay-coloured, from L *badius*]

**bake** /beɪk/, *v.,* **baked, baking.** *–v.t.* 1. to cook by dry heat in an oven, under coals, or on heated metals or stones. 2. to harden by heat. *–v.i.* 3. to bake bread, etc. 4. to become baked. 5. *Colloq.* to become very hot, esp. by sunbathing. [ME *bake(n),* OE *bacan,* c. G *backen*]

**baked alaska** /beɪkt əˈlæskə/, *n.* →**alaska** (def. 2).

**baked beans** /– ˈbinz/, *n.* kidney beans which have been soaked, boiled and then baked slowly with such ingredients as onion, tomato, bacon and seasoning; available tinned in commercial varieties.

**baked custard** /– ˈkʌstəd/, *n.* a mixture of sugar, eggs and milk gently heated in an oven until it has set.

**bakehouse** /ˈbeɪkhaʊs/, *n.* →**bakery.**

**bakelite** /ˈbeɪkəlaɪt/, *n.* 1. a thermosetting plastic derived by heating phenol or cresol with formaldehyde and ammonia under pressure, used for making radio cabinets, telephone receivers, electric insulators, and moulded plastic ware. *–adj.* 2. of or pertaining to objects made from this plastic. [Trademark; named after its inventor, L.H. *Baekeland* (1863-1944), Belgian-American chemist]

**baker** /ˈbeɪkə/, *n.* 1. one who bakes; one who makes and sells bread, cake, etc. 2. →**floury baker.**

**baker's dozen** /beɪkəz ˈdʌzən/, *n.* thirteen, reckoned as a dozen.

**bakery** /ˈbeɪkəri/, *n., pl.* **-ries.** 1. a building or room to bake in; bakehouse. 2. a baker's shop.

**Bakewell tart** /ˌbeɪkwɛl ˈtat/, *n.* an open tart with a pastry base and a cakelike filling. [named after *Bakewell,* a town in Derbyshire, England]

**baking** /ˈbeɪkɪŋ/, *n.* 1. the act of one who or that which bakes. 2. the quantity baked at one time; a batch. *–adj.* 3. *Colloq.* very hot; sweltering.

**baking powder** /ˈ– paʊdə/, *n.* any of various powders used as a leavening agent in baking, composed of sodium bicarbonate and an acid substance (such as cream of tartar) which together react with moisture to release carbon dioxide.

**baking soda** /ˈ– soʊdə/, *n.* →**sodium bicarbonate.**

**baklava** /bəˈklava, ˈbækləvə/, *n.* a Near-Eastern pastry of very thin dough, nuts, and honey. [Turk.]

**baksheesh** /ˈbækʃiʃ, bækˈʃiʃ/, (used in Middle Eastern countries) *n.* 1. a charitable gift or gratuity. *–v.t.* 2. to give a charitable gift or gratuity (to). Also, **bakshish, backsheesh, backshish.** [Pers. *bakhshīsh,* from *bakhshīdan* give]

**bal** /bæl/, *n.* 1. a mine. 2. a collection of mines. 3. **scatter the bal,** to close down the mines and dispose of the plant. [Cornish]

**bal.,** balance.

**balaclava** /bæləˈklavə/, *n.* a knitted woollen hood that covers the whole head except for the face, originally worn by soldiers in the Crimean War. Also, **balaclava helmet.** [named

i = peat ɪ = pit ɛ = pet æ = pat a = part ɒ = pot ʌ = putt ɔ = port ʊ = put u = pool ɜ = pert ə = apart aɪ = buy eɪ = bay ɔɪ = boy aʊ = how oʊ = hoe ɪə = here ɛə = hair ʊə = tour g = give θ = thin ð = then ʃ = show ʒ = measure tʃ = choke dʒ = joke ŋ = sing j = you õ = Fr. bon

after *Balaklava,* a port on the Black Sea, scene of the charge of the Light Brigade in the Crimean War, 1854]

**balalaika** /bælə'laɪkə/, *n.* a Russian musical instrument with a triangular body and guitar-like neck, and usu. three strings. [Russ.]

balalaika

**balance** /'bæləns/, *n., v.,* **-anced, -ancing.** *–n.* **1.** an instrument for weighing, typically a bar poised or swaying on a central support according to the weights borne in scales (pans) suspended at the ends. **2.** power to decide as by a balance; authoritative control. **3.** a state of equilibrium or equipoise; equal distribution of weight, amount, etc. **4.** mental steadiness; habit of calm behaviour, judgment, etc. **5.** harmonious arrangement or adjustment, esp. in the arts of design. **6.** the relationship of alcohol, acid and tannin distinguishable in the flavour of a wine. **7.** something used to produce equilibrium; a counterpoise. **8.** the act of balancing; comparison as to weight, amount, importance, etc.; estimate. **9.** the remainder or rest. **10.** *Comm.* **a.** equality between the totals of the two sides of an account. **b.** the difference between the debit total and the credit total of an account. **c.** unpaid difference represented by the excess of debits over credits. **11.** an adjustment of accounts. **12.** *Horol.* a wheel which oscillates against the tension of a hairspring for regulating the beats of a watch or clock. **13.** (*cap.*) the zodiacal constellation or sign Libra. **14.** *Dancing.* a balancing movement. *–v.t.* **15.** to weigh in a balance. **16.** to estimate the relative weight or importance of; compare: *balance probabilities.* **17.** to serve as a counterpoise to; counterbalance; offset. **18.** to bring to or hold in equilibrium; poise: *to balance a book on one's head.* **19.** to arrange, adjust, or proportion the parts of symmetrically. **20.** to be equal or proportionate to. **21.** *Comm.* **a.** to add up the two sides of (an account) and determine the difference. **b.** to make the necessary entries in (an account) so that the sums of the two sides will be equal. **c.** to settle by paying what remains due on an account; equalise or adjust. **22.** *Dancing.* to move in rhythm to and from: *to balance one's partner.* *–v.i.* **23.** to have an equality or equivalence in weight, parts, etc.; be in equilibrium: *the account doesn't balance; do these scales balance?* **24.** *Comm.* to reckon or adjust accounts. **25.** to waver, hesitate. **26.** *Dancing.* to move forwards and backwards, or in opposite directions; set. [ME, from OF, from LL *bilanx* having two scales] – **balanceable,** *adj.*

**balance bar** /'– ba/, *n.* any projecting bar which offsets the weight of a hinged gate, as the beam projecting from a lock gate.

**balance of nature,** *n.* that natural, balanced state in which plants, insects, animals, etc., co-exist, feeding on each other without endangering the existence of any species.

**balance of payments,** *n.* the difference between a nation's total payments to foreign countries (debits) and its total receipts from foreign sources (credits).

**balance of power,** *n.* a distribution and an opposition of forces among nations such that no single nation will be strong enough to dominate all the others.

**balance of trade,** *n.* the difference between the value of the exports and imports of a country, said to be favourable or unfavourable as exports are greater or less than imports.

**balancer** /'bælənsə/, *n.* **1.** one who or that which balances. **2.** →**haltere. 3.** an acrobat. **4.** *Colloq.* a fraudulent bookmaker.

**balance sheet** /'bæləns ʃit/, *n.* a statement of the financial position of a business on a specified date, consisting of lists of all assets and liabilities, set out in such a way that the total of each is equal, or in balance.

**balance spring** /'– sprɪŋ/, *n.* →**hairspring.**

**balance wheel** /'– wil/, *n. Horol.* →**balance** (def. 12).

**balanitis** /bælən'aɪtəs/, *n.* inflammation of the glans penis or glans clitoridis.

**balas** /'bæləs, 'ba-/, *n.* a rose red variety of spinel. Also, **balas ruby.** [ME, from OF *balais,* from Ar. *balakhsh* kind of ruby, from Pers. *Badakhshān,* a province where found]

**balata** /bə'latə, 'bælətə/, *n.* **1.** the dried juice or gum (**balata gum**) obtained from the bully tree, *Manilkara bidentata,* used as a substitute for gutta-percha and in making chewing gum. **2.** →**bully tree.** [Amer. Sp.]

**balbriggan** /bæl'brɪgən/, *n.* a kind of unbleached cotton originally made at Balbriggan, in Ireland, used esp. in underwear, etc.

**balcony** /'bælkəni/, *n., pl.* **-nies. 1.** a balustraded or raised and railed platform projecting from the wall of a building. **2.** (in some cinemas and theatres) the highest gallery. [It. *balcone,* from *balco* scaffold, from OHG. See BALK] – **balconied,** *adj.*

**bald** /bɔld/, *adj.* **1.** lacking hair on some part of the scalp: *a bald head; a bald person.* **2.** destitute of some natural growth or covering: *a bald mountain.* **3.** (of pneumatic tyres) having the rubber tread worn off. **4.** bare; plain; unadorned: *a bald prose style.* **5.** open; undisguised: *a bald lie.* **6.** *Zool.* having white on the head: *a bald eagle.* [ME *balled,* from obs. *ball* white spot (cf. Welsh *bali* whiteness) + -ED[3]] – **balding,** *adj.* – **baldish,** *adj.* – **baldly,** *adv.* – **baldness,** *n.*

**baldachin** /'bɔldəkən/, *n.* **1.** *Archit.* a fixed canopy, of metal, wood, or stone, above the isolated high altar of a church or above a tomb. **2.** a portable canopy carried in religious processions. [F *baldaquin,* from It. *baldacchino,* orig., silk from Baghdad, from *Baldacco* Baghdad]

**bald coot** /bɔld 'kut/, *n.* →**swamphen.**

**bald eagle** /bɔld 'igəl/, *n.* a large eagle, *Haliaetus leucocephalus,* of the U.S. and Canada, having a fully feathered head and, when adult, a white head and tail.

bald eagle

**balderdash** /'bɔldədæʃ/, *n.* **1.** idle, ill-informed talk; rubbish. **2.** a senseless jumble of words; nonsense. **3.** *Obs.* a mixture of spirits.

**baldfish** /'bɔldfɪʃ/, *n.* an Australian deep-sea fish, *Rouleina eucla,* lacking scales on the head.

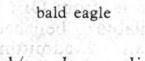

**baldhead** /'bɔldhɛd/, *n. Colloq.* one who has a bald head.

**baldheaded** /'bɔldhɛdəd/ *adj.;* /bɔld'hɛdəd/, *adv.* *–adj.* **1.** having a bald head. *–adv.* **2. go at (something) baldheaded,** to act suddenly with great (and often rash) energy.

**baldmoney** /'bɔldmʌni/, *n.* →**spignel.**

**baldoo** /bɔl'du/, *n.* an annual herb, *Atriplex lindleyi,* family Chenopodiaceae, of drier parts of Australia, where it and other saltbushes provide much of the food for grazing animals.

**baldpate** /'bɔldpeɪt/, *n. Colloq.* one who has a bald head. – **baldpated,** *adj.*

**baldric** /'bɔldrɪk/, *n.* a belt, sometimes richly ornamented, worn diagonally from shoulder to hip, supporting a sword, horn, etc. [ME *bawdrik,* orig. and history obscure; akin to MHG *balderich* girdle; replacing ME *baudry,* from OF, from MHG (as above)]

**baldyhead** /'bɔldihɛd/, *n.* →**white-fronted chat.**

**bale**[1] /beɪl/, *n., v.,* **baled, baling.** *–n.* **1.** a large bundle or package prepared for storage or transportation, esp. one closely compressed and secured by cords, wires, hoops or the like, sometimes with a wrapping: *a bale of wool.* *–v.t.* **2.** to make into bales. [ME, from Flem., from OF *balle,* from Gmc (cf. OHG *balla* BALL[1])] – **baler,** *n.*

**bale**[2] /beɪl/, *n. Archaic.* **1.** evil; harm; misfortune. **2.** woe; misery; sorrow. [ME; OE *balu, bealo*]

**bale**[3] /beɪl/, *v.,* **baled, baling,** *n.* *–v.t.* **1.** to remove (water) esp. from a boat, as with a bucket or a can. **2.** to empty (a boat) of water by dipping (usu. fol. by *out*): *to bale out a boat.* *–v.i.* **3.** to bale water. **4. bale out, a.** to make a parachute jump from a plane. **b.** *Colloq.* to abandon a dangerous position or course. *–n.* **5.** a bucket or other vessel for baling. Also, **bail.** [ME *bayle,* from OF *baille* bucket, from VL *bājula* vessel] – **baler,** *n.*

**baleen** /bə'lin/, *n. Zool.* →**whalebone** (def. 1). [ME *balene,* from OF *baleine,* from L *balaena* whale]

**balefire** /'beɪlfaɪə/, *n. Archaic.* **1.** a bonfire or signal fire. **2.** a funeral pyre. [ME *balefyre,* OE *bǣlfyr,* from *bǣl* bonfire + *fȳr* fire]

**baleful** /'beɪlfəl/, *adj.* **1.** full of menacing or malign influences; pernicious. **2.** *Archaic.* wretched; sorrowful. [ME; OE *bealofull*] – **balefully,** *adv.* – **balefulness,** *n.*

**balisage** /ˈbæləsaʒ/, *n.* the marking of a route by a system of dim beacon lights, enabling vehicles to be driven under blackout conditions at near day-time speeds.

**balk** /bɔk/, *v.i., v.t., n.* →**baulk.**

**Balkanise** /ˈbɔlkənaɪz/, *v.t.,* **-nised, -nising.** to divide into small states hostile to one another. Also, **Balkanize.** – **Balkanisation,** *n.*

**Balkan States** /bɔlkən ˈsteɪts/, *n. pl.* the countries in the Balkan Peninsula: Yugoslavia, Rumania, Bulgaria, Albania, Greece, and the European part of Turkey.

**ball**[1] /bɔl/, *n.* **1.** a spherical or approximately spherical body; a sphere. **2.** a round or roundish body, of different materials and sizes, hollow or solid, for use in various games, as cricket, football, tennis, or golf. **3.** a game played with a ball. **4.** a throw, play, action, movement, etc., of a ball: *a low or high ball, a flighted ball.* **5.** *Baseball, Softball.* a pitch by the pitcher that passes above the batter's shoulder, below his knee or outside his reach, four of which entitle the batter to take a walk. **6.** *Mil.* **a.** a solid projectile, usu. spherical, for a cannon, rifle, pistol, etc. (distinguished from a *shell*). **b.** projectiles, esp. bullets, collectively. **7.** any part of a thing, esp. of the human body that is rounded or protuberant: *the ball of the thumb.* **8.** *Colloq.* a testicle: *she kicked him in the balls.* **9.** *Astron.* a planetary or celestial body, esp. the earth. **10. a ball of muscle (strength) (style),** *Colloq.* a person who is very healthy and in good spirits (very strong) (very stylish). **11. do one's balls on,** *Colloq.* to become infatuated with (someone). **12. have (someone) by the balls,** *Colloq.* to have (someone) in one's power. **13. have the ball at one's feet,** be on the road to success. **14. have the ball in one's court,** *Colloq.* to have the opportunity or obligation to act. **15. keep the ball rolling,** *Colloq.* to keep something going; to keep up the rate of progress or activity. **16. on the ball,** *Colloq.* in touch with a situation, reality, etc.; alert; sharp. **17. play ball,** *Colloq.* to work together (with); cooperate. **18. start the ball rolling,** to start an operation; set an activity in motion. **19. that's the way the ball bounces,** *Chiefly U.S., Colloq.* that's how things are. *–v.t.* **20.** to make into a ball or balls. **21.** *Colloq.* to have intercourse with. **22.** to clog or entangle, as of snow in the shoe of a horse (freq. fol. by *up*). **23. ball up,** *U.S., Brit., Colloq.* to bring to a state of confusion. *–v.i.* **24.** to form or gather into a ball. [ME *bal,* from Scand.; cf. Icel. *böllr*]

**ball**[2] /bɔl/, *n.* **1.** a social gathering (usu. formal) at which people dance. **2.** an enjoyable occasion: *we had a ball; to have oneself a ball.* [F. *bal,* from OF *baler* dance, from LL *ballāre*]

**ballad** /ˈbæləd/, *n.* **1.** a simple narrative poem, often of popular origin, composed in short stanzas, esp. one of romantic character and adapted for singing. **2.** any light, simple song, esp. one of sentimental or romantic character, having two or more stanzas, all sung to the same melody. **3.** the musical setting for a ballad. **4.** a slick and sentimentalised pop song. [ME *balade,* from OF, from Pr. *balada* dance, from *balar* dance, from LL *ballāre*]

**ballade** /bæˈlad/, *n.* **1.** a poem consisting commonly of three stanzas having an identical rhyme scheme, followed by an envoy. The same last line is used for each of the stanzas and envoy. **2.** *Music.* a composition in free style and romantic mood, often for solo piano or for orchestra. [F. See BALLAD]

**balladeer** /bæləˈdɪə/, *n.* a singer of ballads.

**ballad-monger** /ˈbæləd-mʌŋgə/, *n.* **1.** a seller of ballads. **2.** a bad poet.

**ballad opera** /ˈbæləd ˌɒprə/, *n.* a light opera, often humorous or satirical, in which the tunes are taken from popular songs, and the dialogue is spoken.

**balladry** /ˈbælədri/, *n.* **1.** ballad poetry. **2.** the writing or singing of ballads.

**ballad stanza** /ˈbæləd stænzə/, *n.* the metrical form for ballad verse, ordinarily consisting of four lines.

ball-and-socket joint

**ballahoo** /bæləˈhu/, *n.* →**garfish** (def. 1). Also, **balloo.**

**ball and chain,** *n.* **1.** a heavy iron ball fastened by a chain to a prisoner's leg. **2.** any restraint. **3. the old ball and chain,** *Colloq.* the wife.

**ball-and-socket joint** /ˌbɔl-ənd-ˈsɒkət dʒɔɪnt/, *n.* a joint formed by a ball or knob in a socket, admitting a degree of rotary movement in every direction.

**ballarat** /bæləˈræt/, *n. Colloq.* a cat. [rhyming slang; from *Ballarat,* a town in Victoria]

**ballart** /ˈbælat/, *n.* any species of the Australian parasitic shrubs or trees of the genus *Exocarpos,* characterised by an enlarged succulent pedicel, and fruit which is edible in some species. Also, **ballee, ballot.**

**ballast** /ˈbæləst/, *n.* **1.** any heavy material carried by a ship or boat for ensuring proper stability, so as to avoid capsizing and to secure the greatest effectiveness of the propelling power. **2.** something heavy, as bags of sand, placed in the car of a balloon for control of altitude or, less frequently, of attitude. **3.** anything that gives mental, moral, or political stability or steadiness. **4.** gravel, broken stone, slag, etc., placed between and under railway sleepers to give stability, provide drainage, and distribute the load. **5.** a mixture of small stones and sand, used as a building material. *–v.t.* **6.** to furnish with ballast: *to ballast a ship.* **7.** to give steadiness to; keep steady. [MLG: *bal* bad + *last* load; but cf. ODan. *barlast* (from *bar* BARE[1], mere + *last* load)]

**ball-bearing** /bɔl-ˈbɛərɪŋ/, *n.* **1.** a bearing in which the shaft or journal of a machine turns upon a number of steel balls running in an annular track. **2.** any of the steel balls so used.

**ball boy** /ˈbɔl bɔɪ/, *n.* **1.** *Tennis.* a person employed to retrieve balls and return them to the server. **2.** *Rugby Football.* a boy who retrieves the ball when it goes out of play, carries sand on which to place the ball during a kick at goal, etc.

**ball catch** /ˈbɔl kætʃ/, *n.* an automatic door fastening in which a spring-loaded ball projecting slightly from the door engages with a hole in a striking plate on the door frame.

**ballcock** /ˈbɔlkɒk/, *n.* a device for regulating the supply of water in a tank, cistern, or the like, consisting essentially of a valve which opens and shuts with the rise and fall of a hollow floating ball connected to it.

**ballee** /ˈbæli/, *n.* →**ballart.**

**ballerina** /bæləˈrinə/, *n., pl.* **-nas. 1.** the principal female dancer in a ballet company. **2.** any female ballet-dancer. [It.]

**ballet** /ˈbæleɪ/, *n.* **1.** a spectacular entertainment, often designed to tell a story, and rendered by a company of professional dancers. **2.** the style of dancing employed in such a performance, using an elaborate formal technique and characterised by grace and precision of movement. **3.** the music for a ballet. **4.** the choreography of a ballet. **5.** a dance interlude in an operatic or dramatic performance. **6.** a company of dancers. [F, from It. *balletto,* diminutive of *ballo* BALL[2]]

**ballet-dancer** /ˈbæleɪ-ˌdænsə/, *n.* a male or female dancer trained in ballet techniques.

**balletomane** /ˈbælətəmeɪn/, *n.* a ballet enthusiast.

**balletomania** /ˌbælətəˈmeɪniə/, *n.* great or excessive enthusiasm for ballet.

**ballflower** /ˈbɔlflaʊə/, *n.* a medieval architectural ornament resembling a ball placed in a circular flower, the three (or four) petals of which form a cup around it.

**ball-frame** /ˈbɔl-freɪm/, *n.* →**abacus** (def. 1).

**ball game** /ˈbɔl geɪm/, *n.* **1.** a game played with a ball. **2.** *Chiefly U.S.* →**baseball. 3. a (whole) new ball game,** a new set of circumstances calling for a different approach.

**ballista** /bəˈlɪstə/, *n., pl.* **-tae** /-ti/. an ancient military engine for hurling stones or other missiles. [L, from Gk *bállein* throw]

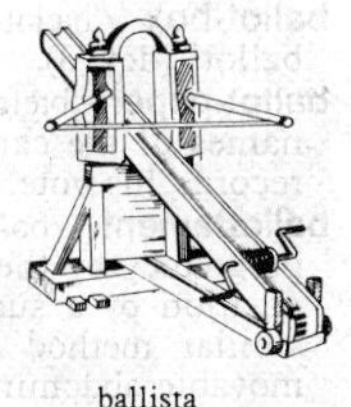

ballista

**ballistic** /bəˈlɪstɪk/, *adj.* **1.** of or pertaining to ballistics. **2.** relating to projectiles. **3.** relating to an instrument, as a ballistic galvanometer, for measuring the effect of a transient source of energy or an impact. **4.** of or pertaining to the motion of projectiles proceeding under no power and acted on only by gravitational force, etc.

**ballistic galvanometer** /– gælvəˈnɒmətə/, *n.* a galvanometer for measuring surges of electric current.

**ballistic missile** /– ˈmɪsaɪl/, *n.* a missile, such as a rocket, which is propelled and guided only in the initial phase of its flight, but reaches its target by a ballistic descent. Cf., **guided missile.**

**ballistic pendulum** /– ˈpɛndʒələm/, *n.* a heavy block of wood suspended on strings so that it can swing in one plane only, used for measuring the momentum of bullets, etc.

**ballistics** /bəˈlɪstɪks/, *n.* the science or study of the motion of projectiles, such as bullets, shells, bombs, rockets, etc., proceeding under no power and acted upon only by gravitational forces and the resistance of the medium through which they pass. – **ballistician** /bæləˈstɪʃən/, *n.*

**ball lightning** /ˈbɔl ˌlaɪtnɪŋ/, *n.* →**fireball** (def. 4).

**ball mill** /ˈbɔl mɪl/, *n.* a machine used for crushing rocks by the agitation of large steel balls.

**ballonet** /bæləˈnɛt/, *n.* an air or gasbag compartment in a balloon, etc., used to control buoyancy and maintain shape. [F *ballonnet,* diminutive of *ballon* balloon]

**balloo** /bæˈlu/, *n.* →**ballahoo.**

**balloon** /bəˈlun/, *n.* **1.** a usu. spherical bag made of some material impermeable to gas and filled with some gas lighter than air, designed to rise and float in the atmosphere, and in the large forms having a car or compartment attached for passengers. **2.** an inflatable rubber bag, usu. brightly coloured, used as a children's toy. **3.** *Chem.* a round-bottomed flask. **4.** →**balloon glass. 5.** (in drawings and cartoons) a balloon-shaped figure enclosing words represented as issuing from the mouth of the speaker. **6.** a kick or stroke which sends a ball high into the air. *–v.i.* **7.** to go up or ride in a balloon. **8.** to swell or puff out like a balloon. *–v.t.* **9.** (of an aeroplane) to rise up in the air, esp. as the result of a hard bounce on landing. *–v.t.* **10.** to fill with air; inflate or distend (something) like a balloon. **11.** to send (a ball) high into the air. *–adj.* **12.** puffed out like a balloon: *balloon sleeves.* [It. *ballone,* augmentative of *balla* ball] – **balloonist,** *n.*

**balloon barrage** /ˈ– bæradʒ/, *n.* a barrage of anchored balloons intended to destroy or deter low-flying hostile aircraft.

**ballooner** /bəˈlunə/, *n. Colloq.* a large, well-rounded headsail or staysail.

**balloo net** /ˌbælu ˈnɛt/, *n.* a net for catching garfish. [Aboriginal]

**balloon glass** /bəˈlun glas/, *n.* a short-stemmed glass having a large bowl tapering towards the rim, used esp. to intensify the aroma of brandy.

**balloon jib** /bəˈlun dʒɪb/, *n.* a large triangular sail of light canvas used by yachts in light winds, instead of the jib.

**balloon tyre** /ˈ– taɪə/, *n.* a large pneumatic tyre in which the pressure is low to prevent the shock of uneven surfaces.

**balloon vine** /ˈ– vaɪn/, *n.* **1.** a climbing plant, *Cardiospermum halicacabum,* of tropical America, much cultivated elsewhere for its large, ornamental bladderlike fruits. **2.** any of various other climbing plants of the genus *Cardiospermum.*

**ballot**[1] /ˈbælət/, *n., v.,* **-loted, -loting.** *–n.* **1.** a ticket or paper used in voting. **2.** the number of votes cast or recorded: *a large ballot.* **3.** Also, **secret ballot.** the system or practice of secret voting by means of printed or written ballots or voting machines. **4.** franchise: *to give the ballot to Aborigines.* **5.** a little ball used in voting or drawing lots, as (formerly) in the Australian conscription system. *–v.i.* **6.** to vote by ballot. **7.** to draw lots: *to ballot for places.* [It. *ballotta* bullet, lot, diminutive of *balla* ball] – **ballotter,** *n.*

**ballot**[2] /ˈbælət/, *n.* →**ballart.**

**ballot-box** /ˈbælət-bɒks/, *n.* **1.** a box to receive ballots. **2.** ballot[1] (def. 3).

**ballot-paper** /ˈbælət-peɪpə/, *n.* a piece of paper which lists the names of the candidates for election, and on which the voter records his vote.

**ballottement** /bəˈlɒtmənt/, *n.* **1.** a method of diagnosing pregnancy by the rebound of a foetal part displaced from its position by a sudden push with the examining finger. **2.** a similar method employed in testing for a floating kidney, movable abdominal tumours, etc. [F: a tossing, from *ballotter* toss as a ball]

**ballpark** /ˈbɔlpak/, *n.* **1.** *U.S.* a park in which games, esp. baseball, are played. **2. off the ballpark,** *Colloq.* unofficially; at a guess. *–adj.* **3.** estimated: *a ballpark figure.*

**ballpein hammer** /ˈbɔlpeɪn ˌhæmə, ˈbɔlpin/, *n.* a hammer having a head with one end shaped like a ball, suitable for beating metal. Also, **ballpeen hammer.**

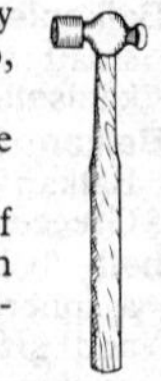

**ballpoint pen** /ˌbɔlpɔɪnt ˈpɛn/, *n.* a pen in which the point is a fine ball-bearing, depositing an extremely thin film of ink, which is stored in a cartridge. Also, **ballpoint.**

ballpein hammer

**ballroom** /ˈbɔlrum/, *n.* a large room in a private residence, hotel, etc., in which dances are held.

**ballroom dancing** /– ˈdænsɪŋ/, *n.* the dancing of certain formal dances as the tango, fox-trot, etc., in conventional formal evening dress, either in competition or for pleasure alone.

**balls** /bɔlz/, *interj.* **1.** (an exclamation of repudiation, ridicule, etc.). *–v.i.* **2. balls around,** to deliberately waste time in inconsequential activity. [pl. from BALL[1] (def. 8)]

**ball sense** /ˈbɔl sɛns/, *n.* an ability to catch and throw a ball well, and to judge how a thrown ball will act.

**balls-up** /ˈbɔlz-ʌp/, *Colloq.* *–n.* **1.** confusion arising from a mistake; a mess. **2.** the mistake itself. *–v.t.* **3.** to bring to a state of hopeless confusion or difficulty. [probably from *ball-up,* BALL[1] (def. 23), by confusion with BALL[1] (def. 8)]

**ball-up** /ˈbɔl-ʌp/, *n.* (in Australian Rules) the bouncing of the ball by the field umpire to restart play after the ball has been smothered in a pack.

**ball valve** /ˈbɔl vælv/, *n.* a valve which allows fluid to pass through it in one direction only and consists of a ball, usu. of metal, which moves against its seating to close off the flow when it is coming from the wrong direction.

**bally** /ˈbæli/, *Colloq.* *–adj.* **1.** confounded (used humorously or for emphasis). *–adv.* **2.** very. [? orig. euph. for BLOODY]

**ballyhoo** /bæliˈhu/, *n., pl.* **-hoos,** *v.,* **-hooed, -hooing.** *–n.* **1.** a clamorous attempt to win customers or advance any cause; blatant advertising or publicity. **2.** clamour or outcry. *–v.t.* **3.** to advertise by sensational methods. [orig. obscure]

**balm** /bam/, *n.* **1.** any of various oily, fragrant, resinous substances, often of medicinal value, exuding from certain plants, esp. tropical trees of the genus *Commiphora.* **2.** a plant or tree yielding such a substance. **3.** any aromatic or fragrant ointment. **4.** aromatic fragrance; sweet smell. **5.** any of various aromatic plants, esp. of the genus *Melissa,* as *M. officinalis,* a lemon-scented perennial herb. **6.** anything which heals, soothes, or mitigates pain. [ME *basme,* from OF, from L *balsamum* BALSAM]

**balmacaan** /bælməˈkan/, *n.* a man's loose, full overcoat originally with raglan sleeves, originally of rough woollen cloth. [named after *Balmacaan,* in Scotland]

**balmaiden** /ˈbælmeɪdən/, *n.* a woman working in a mine, esp. on the surface, dressing ore. [BAL + MAIDEN]

**Balmain bug** /ˌbælmeɪn ˈbʌg/, *n.* an edible, curiously flattened crustacean, *Ibacus incisus,* first discovered in Sydney harbour; closely related to the shovel-nosed lobster. [named after *Balmain,* a suburb of Sydney, N.S.W.]

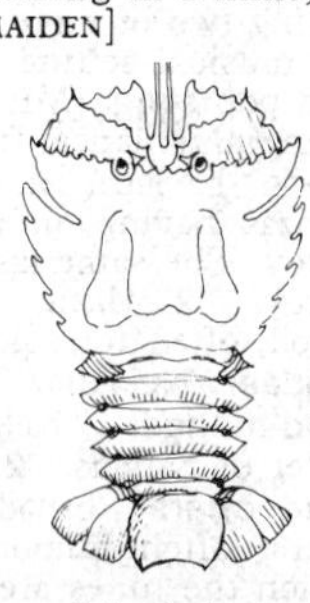

**balm of Gilead,** *n.* **1.** any of several species of the genus *Commiphora,* esp. *C. gileadensis,* which yield a fragrant oleoresin. **2.** the resin itself. **3.** any of various other plants yielding aromatic resins, as the balsam poplar.

Balmain bug

**balmoral** /bælˈmɒrəl/, (*also cap.*) *n.* **1.** a kind of brimless cap of Scottish origin with a flat top projecting all round the head. **2.** a kind of laced shoe. **3.** a coloured woollen petticoat formerly worn under a looped-up skirt.

**balmy** /ˈbami/, *adj.,* **balmier, balmiest. 1.** mild and refreshing; soft; soothing: *balmy weather.* **2.** having the qualities of balm; aromatic; fragrant: *balmy leaves.* **3.** producing balm. **4.** *Colloq.* →**barmy.** – **balmily,** *adv.* – **balminess,** *n.*

**balneal** /ˈbælniəl/, *adj.* of or pertaining to baths or bathing. [L *balneum* bath + -AL[1]]

**balneology** /ˌbælniˈɒlədʒi/, *n.* the science of using baths and bathing in therapeutics. [L *balneum* bath + -O- + -LOGY] – **balneologist,** *n.*

**baloney** /bəˈloʊni/, *n. Colloq.* nonsense; insincere or idle talk; eyewash; waffle. Also, **boloney.**

**balsa** /ˈbɔlsə/, *n.* **1.** a tree, *Ochroma lagopus,* of the family Bombacaceae, of tropical America, with an exceedingly light wood used for life-preservers, rafts, etc. **2.** a raft made of balsa wood. **3.** any raft. [Sp]

**balsam** /ˈbɔlsəm, ˈbɒl-/, *n.* **1.** any of various fragrant exudations from certain trees, esp. of the genus *Commiphora* (see **balm** def. 1), as the balm of Gilead (**balsam of Mecca**). **2.** a similar product (**balsam of Peru** and **balsam of Tolu**) yielded by the trees, *Myroxylon pereirae* and *M. balsamum* of Central and South America. **3.** →**oleoresin** (def. 1). **4.** any of certain transparent turpentines, as Canada balsam. **5.** a plant or tree yielding a balsam. **6.** →**balsam fir. 7.** any of various plants of the genus *Impatiens,* as *I. balsamina,* a common garden annual and *I. sultanii,* a common garden perennial with red, pink or white flowers. **8.** any aromatic ointment, whether for ceremonial or medicinal use. **9.** any healing or soothing agent or agency. [OE, from L *balsamum,* from Gk *bálsamon*] – **balsamaceous** /bɔlsəˈmeɪʃəs, bɒl-/, *adj.*

**balsam fir** /– ˈfɜ/, *n.* **1.** a North American species of fir, *Abies balsamea,* which yields Canada balsam. **2.** the wood of this tree. **3.** any of certain other firs, esp. of North America.

**balsamic** /bɔlˈsæmɪk, bɒl-/, *adj.* of, like, or containing balsam. – **balsamically,** *adv.*

**balsamiferous** /bɔlsəˈmɪfərəs, bɒl-/, *adj.* yielding balsam. [BALSAM + -I- + -FEROUS]

**balsam poplar** /bɔlsəm ˈpɒplə/, *n.* a tree, *Populus balsamifera,* of North America, having broad heart-shaped leaves and buds coated in an aromatic resin, much cultivated as a shade tree.

**balsam spruce** /– ˈsprus/, *n.* either of two North American conifers of the genus *Picea, P. pungens,* the blue spruce and *P. engelmannii.*

**balsawood** /ˈbɔlsəwʊd/, *n.* →**balsa** (def. 1).

**Balt** /bɔlt/, *n.* **1.** a member of any of the Baltic-speaking peoples. **2.** (*l.c.*) *Colloq.* (*offensive*) an immigrant to Australia from any of the countries of Central or Eastern Europe.

**balthazar** /ˈbælθəza/, *n.* a large bottle of wine used mainly for display purposes, and having a capacity of 16 normal bottles. [named after *Balthazar* (Belshazzar), king of Babylonia, C6th BC]

**Baltic** /ˈbɔltɪk/, *adj.* **1.** of or pertaining to the Baltic Sea or the countries on its shores. **2.** of or pertaining to the Baltic States, Lithuania, Latvia and Estonia. **3.** of or pertaining to the Baltic languages. *–n.* **4.** a subgroup of the Indo-European language family, consisting of Lithuanian, Latvian and Old Prussian. [ML *Balticum,* ? from L *balteus* belt]

**Baltic States** /bɔltɪk ˈsteɪts/, *n. pl.* the formerly independent republics of Estonia, Latvia, and Lithuania, sometimes including Finland.

**Balto-Slavic** /bɔltoʊ-ˈslavɪk/, *n.* a grouping of Indo-European languages comprising the Baltic and Slavic groups.

**Baluchi** /bəˈlutʃi/, *n., pl.* **Baluchi, Baluchis. 1.** a member of a Muslim people living in Baluchistan, in southern Asia. **2.** the Iranian language of this people.

**baluster** /ˈbæləstə/, *n.* one of a series of short pillar-like supports (usu. of stone) for a railing or coping, as of a parapet. [F *balustre,* from It. *balaust(r)o,* from L *balaustium,* from Gk *balaústion* pomegranate flower]

A, baluster; B, balustrade

**balustrade** /bæləˈstreɪd/, *n.* a railing or coping with the row of balusters supporting it.

**bambino** /bæmˈbinoʊ/, *n., pl.* **-ni** /-ni/. **1.** a child or baby. **2.** an image of the infant Jesus. [It., diminutive of *bambo* simple]

**bamboo** /bæmˈbu/, *n., pl.* **-boos. 1.** any of the woody or treelike tropical and semitropical grasses of the genus *Bambusa* and allied genera. **2.** the hollow woody stem of such a plant, used for building purposes and for making furniture, poles, etc. [earlier *bambus,* from D *bamboes,* from Malay *mambu*]

**bamboo curtain** /ˌbæmbu ˈkɜtn/, *n.* (*also caps.*) a military, political and ideological barrier between territories under the control of Communist China and non-Communist countries.

**bamboozle** /bæmˈbuzəl/, *v.t.* **-zled, -zling. 1.** to deceive by trickery; impose upon. **2.** to perplex; mystify. [? of cant orig.] – **bamboozlement,** *n.* – **bamboozler,** *n.*

**ban**[1] /bæn/, *v.,* **banned, banning,** *n. –v.t.* **1.** to prohibit; interdict: *to ban a meeting or book.* **2.** *Archaic.* **a.** to pronounce an ecclesiastical curse upon. **b.** to curse; execrate. *–n.* **3.** an authoritative interdiction or condemnation. **4.** informal denunciation or prohibition, as by public opinion. **5.** a prohibition by law or decree. **6.** *Archaic.* a formal ecclesiastical denunciation; excommunication. **7.** a malediction; curse. [ME, from Scand.; cf. Icel. *banna* forbid, curse, c. OE *bannan* summon]

**ban**[2] /bæn/, *n.* **1.** a public proclamation or edict. **2. a.** (in feudal times) the summons of the sovereign's vassals for military service. **b.** the whole body liable to this summons. [OE *gebann*]

**banal** /ˈbeɪnəl, bəˈnal/, *adj.* hackneyed; trite. [F, from OF *ban,* from Gmc: proclamation, c. BAN[2]] – **banality** /bəˈnæləti/, *n.* – **banally,** *adv.*

**banana** /bəˈnanə/, *n.* **1.** a plant of the tropical genus *Musa,* of which various species are cultivated for their nutritious fruit. **2.** the pulpy fruit, esp. that of *M.* × *paradisiaca,* with yellow skin when ripe, growing in clusters. **3.** (*pl.*) **go bananas,** *Colloq.* to become uncontrollably angry. [Pg., Sp., from native name in Guinea]

**bananabender** /bəˈnanəbɛndə/, *n. Colloq.* →**Queenslander.**

**banana-bird** /bəˈnanə-bɜd/, *n.* **1.** →**Lewin honeyeater. 2.** →**southern figbird.**

**banana chair** /bəˈnanə tʃɛə/, *n.* a light folding chair, often of aluminium and plastic, used outdoors, and having back, seat and leg supports which are adjustable to a variety of positions.

**banana kick** /ˈ– kɪk/, *n. Colloq.* (in Australian Rules) a punt kick in which the ball is dropped at a diagonal angle across the boot, and swerves sharply in flight; the banana kick is used mainly in shooting for goal from difficult angles.

**banana oil** /– ˈɔɪl/, →**amyl acetate.**

**banana passionfruit** /– ˈpæʃənfrut/, *n.* a perennial climber, *Tacsonia mollissima,* bearing decorative soft pink flowers and a long, edible fruit.

**banana prawn** /ˈ– prɔn/, *n. Colloq.* a prawn, *Penaeus merguiensis,* of northern Australian tropical waters, fished commercially.

**banana republic** /– rəˈpʌblɪk/, *n.* **1.** any small tropical country, esp. of South or Central America, considered as backward, politically unstable, etc., and dependent on the trade of rich foreign nations. **2.** any backward country or state. **3. the Banana Republic,** *Colloq.* Queensland.

**banana split** /– ˈsplɪt/, *n.* a confection or dessert made from a peeled banana cut in half lengthwise, with any of a number of combinations of ice-cream, whipped cream, flavouring and nuts.

**banbury cake** /ˈbænbəri keɪk/, *n.* a kind of mince pie. [named after *Banbury,* a town in Oxfordshire, England]

**band**[1] /bænd/, *n.* **1. a.** a company of persons associated or acting together; company, party or troop. **b.** a group of animals. **2.** a company of musicians constituted according to the kind of music played, usu. playing for performance or as an accompaniment to dancing. *–v.t.* **3.** to unite in a group, troop, company or confederacy. *–v.i.* **4.** to unite; form a group; confederate (usu. fol. by *together*). [F *bande,* from Gmc]

**band**[2] /bænd/, *n.* **1.** any strip that contrasts with its surroundings in colour, texture or material. **2.** a thin, flat strip of some material for binding, confining, reinforcing, trimming, or some other purpose: *hatband; rubber band.* **3.** a strip, as of colour or decorative work. **4.** *Mining.* a stratum of stone, containing ore or similar valuable material, esp. opal. **5.** the high, falling or flat collar or ruff commonly worn by men and women in the 17th century in western Europe. **6.** (*pl.*) a form of collar from the front of which hang two square-ended strips of white linen, often worn as part of academic, legal or clerical dress. **7.** *Radio.* a range of frequencies lying between any two well-defined limits.

–*v.t.* **8.** to mark or fasten with a band or bands; stripe. [ME *bande,* from F, ultimately c. BAND[3]]

**band**[3] /bænd/, *n.* **1.** (*usu. pl.*) anything which binds the person or the limbs; a shackle, manacle, or fetter. **2.** an obligation; bond: *the nuptial bands.* [ME, from Scand.; cf. Icel. *band*]

**bandage** /'bændɪdʒ/, *n., v.,* **-daged, -daging.** –*n.* **1.** a strip of cloth or other material used to bind up a wound, hold a dressing in place, etc. **2.** anything used as a band or ligature. –*v.t.* **3.** to bind or cover with a bandage. [F, from *bande* band] – **bandager,** *n.*

**bandaid** /'bændeɪd/, *n.* a light adhesive dressing for covering superficial wounds. [Trademark]

**bandaid solution** /– sə'luʃən/, *n. Colloq.* a temporary, expedient and generally unsatisfactory solution to a problem.

**bandanna** /bæn'dænə/, *n.* **1.** a large coloured handkerchief or scarf with spots or figures, usu. white on a red or blue background. **2.** any large handkerchief. Also, **bandana.** [apparently from Hind. *bandhnu,* mode of dyeing in which the cloth is tied so as to prevent parts from receiving the dye]

**bandbox** /'bændbɒks/, *n.* **1.** a light box usu. of cylindrical pasteboard or thin wood, originally for holding a hat, collars, etc. **2. come** or **step out of a bandbox,** to be especially well and smartly dressed.

**bandbrake** /'bændbreɪk/, *n.* a braking device consisting of a band which tightens round a moving wheel or drum.

**b. & b.** **1.** bed and breakfast. **2.** blood and bone.

**b. and d.** /bi ən 'di/, *n. Colloq.* **1.** brandy and dry ginger ale. **2.** bondage and discipline.

**bandeau** /bæn'doʊ/, *n., pl.* **-deaux** /-'doʊz/, a band worn about or on the head; a headband; a fillet. [F, diminutive of *bande* BAND[2]]

**banded** /'bændəd/, *adj.* **1.** striped. **2.** fastened (as with a band). **3.** *Mining.* of or pertaining to a stratum of stone containing valuable material, esp. opal.

**banded anteater** /– 'æntitə/, *n.* →**numbat.**

**banded landrail** /– 'lændreɪl/, *n.* a rail, *Rallus philippensis,* black and brown flecked with white above and barred black and white below with a chestnut band across the chest, found in swamps and wet grasslands where abundant vegetation provides cover.

**banded sea-snake** /– 'sisneɪk/, *n.* a fast-swimming, highly venomous, marine snake, *Laticauda colubrina,* of northern Australian waters, having yellow and brown banding; ringed sea-snake.

**banded tintac** /– 'tɪntæk/, *n.* →**white-fronted chat.**

**banderol** /'bændəroʊl/, *n.* **1.** a small flag or streamer with a forked end borne on a lance, at a masthead, etc. **2.** a narrow scroll, esp. one bearing an inscription. **3.** a sculptured band adapted to receive an inscription. Also, **banderole, bannerol.** [F, from It. *banderola* small banner, from *bandiera* banner]

**bandicoot** /'bændikut/, *n.* **1.** any of various small omnivorous somewhat ratlike Australian marsupials of the family Paramelidae of which there are two main types, the long-eared bandicoot, and the short-eared bandicoot. **2.** any of the very large rats of the genus *Nesokia,* of India and Sri Lanka, as *N. bandicota;* Malabar rat; pig-rat. **3.** *Colloq.* **a. bald as a bandicoot,** remarkably bald. **b. bandy as a bandicoot,** remarkably bandy-legged. **c. barmy as a bandicoot,** mad. **d. like a bandicoot on a burnt ridge,** lonely and forlorn. **e. lousy as a bandicoot,** miserly. **f. miserable** or **poor as a bandicoot,** of wretched character. –*v.t.* **4.** to dig, in the fashion of a bandicoot. **5.** *Colloq.* to dig up (root vegetables, potatoes, etc.) with the fingers, leaving the top of the plant undisturbed. [orig. used of def. 2, from Telugu *pandikokku* pig-rat]

bandicoot

**bandit** /'bændət/, *n., pl.* **-dits, banditti** /bæn'diti/. **1.** a robber, esp. one who robs by violence. **2.** an outlaw. **3.** *Colloq.* →**one-armed bandit.** [It. *bandito,* from *bandire* proscribe]

**banditry** /'bændətri/, *n.* **1.** the work or practice of bandits. **2.** bandits collectively; banditti.

**bandmaster** /'bændmastə/, *n.* the conductor of a band.

**band moll** /'bænd mɒl/, *n. Colloq.* a young female who serves the sexual needs of the members of a rock group.

**bandolier** /bændə'lɪə/, *n.* a broad belt worn over the shoulder by soldiers, and having a number of small loops or pockets, each containing a cartridge or cartridges. Also, **bandoleer.** [F *bandoulière,* from Sp. *bandolera,* from *banda* band, sash, from It., of Gmc orig.]

**bandore** /bæn'dɔ, 'bændɔ/, *n.* an old musical stringed instrument resembling the lute or the guitar. [Sp. *bandurria,* var. of *pandora,* from LL *pandūra,* from Gk *pandoûra,* musical instrument with three strings]

**band-pass filter** /'bænd-pas fɪltə/, *n.* (in electronics) a filter which allows only signals with frequencies between certain values, which may be fixed or variable, to pass. See **high-pass filter, low-pass filter.**

**b. and s.** /bi ən 'ɛs/, *n.* a dance for young people in a country area, often held in a wool-shed. [abbrev. for *bachelors' and spinsters'* dance]

**bandsaw** /'bændsɔ/, *n.* a power saw consisting of an endless toothed steel band coupled to, and driven around the circumferences of, two wheels.

**bandsman** /'bændzmən/, *n., pl.* **-men.** a musician who plays in a band, esp. a brass band.

**band spectrum** /'bænd spɛktrəm/, *n.* an emission or absorption spectrum consisting of a number of bands of lines, as produced by molecules.

**bandstand** /'bændstænd/, *n.* a platform, for band performances, often roofed when outdoors.

**bandstone** /'bændstoʊn/, *n.* ferruginous and siliceous rock found in thin hard layers just above or below workable seams of opal.

**b. & w.,** black and white.

**band wagon** /'bænd wægən/, *n.* **1.** *U.S.* a wagon often elaborately decorated, used to transport musicians, as at the head of a procession or parade. **2.** the successful or winning side or cause. **3. climb** or **jump on the band wagon,** to join the winning side; take advantage of a popular movement or fashion; follow the crowd.

**bandwidth** /'bændwɪdθ/, *n.* the difference between the upper and lower frequencies of a band (**band**[2] def. 7).

**bandy** /'bændi/, *v.,* **-died, -dying,** *adj., n., pl.* **-dies.** –*v.t.* **1.** to pass from one to another, or back and forth; give and take: *to bandy blows or words.* **2.** to throw or strike to and fro, or from side to side, as a ball in tennis. –*adj.* **3.** (of legs) having a bend or crook outward. **4.** →**bandy-legged.** **5. knock someone bandy,** *Colloq.* to get the best of someone; to astonish someone. –*n.* **6.** →**bandy-ball.** **7.** a stick similar to a hockey stick, used in bandy-ball. [orig. obscure. Cf. F *bander* bandy, *se bander* band together, ? from *bande* side]

**bandy-ball** /'bændi-bɔl/, *n. Obs.* an early form of hockey.

**bandy-bandy** /bændi-'bændi/, *n.* a small, nocturnal, venomous snake, *Vermicella annulata,* with distinctive black and white stripes across its back, and widely distributed in New South Wales. [Aboriginal]

**bandy-legged** /'bændi-lɛgəd, -lɛgd/, *adj.* having crooked legs; bowlegged.

**Bandywallop** /bændi'wɒləp/, *n.* an imaginary remote town.

**bane** /beɪn/, *n.* **1.** that which causes death or destroys life. **2.** a deadly poison. **3.** a person or thing that ruins or destroys: *he was the bane of her life.* **4.** ruin; destruction; death. [ME; OE *bana* slayer]

**baneberry** /'beɪnbri/, *n., pl.* **-ries.** **1.** any herb of the ranunculaceous genus *Actaea,* of northern temperate and arctic regions, bearing nauseous, poisonous berries, especially *A. spicata,* herb Christopher. **2.** the berry of any such plant.

**baneful** /'beɪnfəl/, *adj.* destructive; pernicious; poisonous: *a baneful superstition; baneful herbs.* – **banefully,** *adv.*

**bang**[1] /bæŋ/, *n.* **1.** a loud, sudden explosive noise, as the discharge of a gun. **2.** a resounding stroke or blow. **3.** a knock; a bump. **4.** *Colloq.* sexual intercourse. **5.** *U.S. Colloq.* energy; spirit. **6.** *Colloq.* a thrill; excitement. **7. with a bang,** *Colloq.* impressively; successfully: *the party went with a bang.* –*v.t.* **8.** to strike or beat resoundingly: *she banged the desk with her fist.* **9.** to slam: *he always bangs the door.* **10.** to knock or bump: *he banged his head.* **11.** to place or move with a bang: *to bang a plate down.* **12.** *Colloq.* (of a man) to have sexual intercourse with (a woman) (oft. fol. by *up*). –*v.i.* **13.** to strike violently or noisily: *to bang on the door.* **14.** to make a loud noise, as of violent blows: *the guns banged* *away.* **15.** to slam; to slam repeatedly: *the door banged.* **16.** **bang (something) over,** to accomplish (a task) quickly or with little effort: *we'll bang it over in no time.* *–adv.* **17.** exactly; precisely; just: *bang in the middle.* **18.** **bang on,** *Colloq.* dead-centre. *–adj.* **19.** **the whole bang lot,** *Colloq.* everything. [probably from Scand.; cf. Icel. *banga* to hammer, *bang* hammering, bungling]

**bang**[2] /bæŋ/, *n.* **1.** (*oft. pl.*) a fringe of banged hair. *–v.t.* **2.** to cut (the hair) so as to form a fringe over the forehead. **3.** to dock (the tail of a horse, etc.). [short for BANGTAIL]

**bang**[3] /ˈbæŋ/, *n.* →**bhang.**

**bangalay** /bæŋˈæli/, *n.* a tree, *Eucalyptus botryoides,* family Myrtaceae, of New South Wales and eastern Victoria, growing near the coast, and yielding durable red timber.

**bangalow** /ˈbæŋgəloʊ/, *n.* a slender palm tree, *Archontophoenix cunninghamiana,* of New South Wales and Queensland, sometimes growing in clumps in areas near the coast; piccabeen. Also, **bangalow palm.** [Aboriginal]

**bange** /ˈbændʒi/, *v.,* **bangying, bangied,** *n.* *–v.i.* **1.** to rest; relax. *–n.* **2.** a rest. Also, **banje.** [Brit. d. *benge* to lounge around]

**banged up** /bæŋd ˈʌp/, *adj. Colloq.* pregnant.

**banger** /ˈbæŋə/, *n. Colloq.* **1.** →**bunger.** **2.** *Brit.* a sausage.

**Bangladesh** /bæŋgləˈdɛʃ/, *n.* a country bordering on India and Burma.

**bangle** /ˈbæŋgəl/, *n.* **1.** a bracelet in the form of a ring, without a clasp. **2.** an ornamental anklet. [Hind. *bangrī* bracelet of glass]

**bang-on** /ˈbæŋ-ɒn/, *adj. Colloq.* right on the mark; correct. Also, *in predicative use,* **bang on** /bæŋ ˈɒn/.

**Bang's disease** /ˈbæŋz dəziz/, *n. Vet. Sci.* →**brucellosis.**

**bangtail** /ˈbæŋteɪl/, *n.* **1.** a docked tail. **2.** an animal with a docked tail, esp. a horse. *–adj.* **3.** **bangtail muster, a.** a round-up of cattle for counting. **b.** a carnival or sports day in a country town. [*bang* (nasal var. of *bag* cut) + TAIL[1]] – **bangtailed,** *adj.*

**bang-up** /ˈbæŋ-ʌp/, *adj. Colloq.* first-rate; bang-on.

**banian** /ˈbænjən/, *n.* **1.** a loose shirt, jacket, or gown worn in India. **2.** a Hindu trader or merchant of a particular caste which abstains from eating flesh. **3.** →**banyan.** [Pg., probably from Ar. *banyān,* from Gujarati *vāniyo* merchant, from Skt *vanij*]

**banish** /ˈbænɪʃ/, *v.t.* **1.** to condemn to exile; expel from or relegate to a country or place by authoritative decree. **2.** to compel to depart; send, drive, or put away: *to banish sorrow.* [ME *banysshe(n),* from OF *baniss-,* stem of *banir,* from LL *bannīre* ban; of Gmc orig. and akin to BAN[1], *v.*] – **banisher,** *n.* – **banishment,** *n.*

**banister** /ˈbænəstə/, *n.* **1.** one of the supports of a stair rail, either plain or resembling a pillar. **2.** (*oft. pl.*) a stair rail and its supports. Also, **bannister.** [var. of BALUSTER]

**banister brush** /ˈ– brʌʃ/, *n.* a small brush, usu. used in combination with a dustpan.

**banjo** /ˈbændʒoʊ/, *n., pl.* **-jos.** **1.** a musical instrument of the guitar family, having a circular body covered in front with tightly stretched parchment, and played with the fingers or a plectrum. **2.** *Colloq.* a shovel or spade. **3.** *Colloq.* a frying pan. **4.** *Colloq.* a shoulder of mutton. **5.** *Tin Mining.* **a.** a hole in the ground shaped like the musical instrument and lined with a bag, in which tin was cleaned by scooping water over it. **b.** a V-shaped wooden box used for a similar purpose; V-box. [var. of BANDORE] – **banjoist,** *n.*

banjo

**banjoing** /ˈbændʒoʊɪŋ/, *n.* the process of mining by means of a banjo (def. 5).

**banjolele** /ˌbændʒəˈleɪli/, *n.* a small banjo with gut strings. [b. BANJO and (UKU)LELE]

**bank**[1] /bæŋk/, *n.* **1.** a long pile or mass: *bank of earth; bank of snow; bank of clouds.* **2.** a slope or acclivity. **3.** *Phys. Geog.* the slope immediately bordering the course of a river along which the water normally runs. **4.** **bank and bank,** *N.Z.* (of a river) in flood. **5.** *Oceanog.* a broad submarine elevation in the continental shelf lying some distance off the coast, over which the water is relatively shallow. **6.** *Coal Mining.* the surface around the mouth of a shaft. **7.** the lateral inclination of an aeroplane, esp. during a curve. **8.** the lateral inclination of a road at curves. *–v.t.* **9.** to border with or like a bank; embank. **10.** to form into a bank or mass (fol. by *up*): *to bank up the snow.* **11.** to tip or incline (an aeroplane) laterally. **12.** to cover up (a fire) with ashes or fuel and close the dampers, to make it burn long and slowly. *–v.i.* **13.** to rise in or form banks, as clouds or snow. **14.** to tip or incline laterally, as of an aeroplane, a road, a cycle racing track, etc. as an aircraft or a road. [ME *banke,* probably from Scand.]

**bank**[2] /bæŋk/, *n.* **1.** an institution for receiving and lending money (in some cases, issuing notes or holding current accounts that serve as money) and transacting other financial business. **2.** the office or quarters of such an institution. **3.** (in games) **a.** the stock or fund of pieces from which the players draw. **b.** the fund of the manager or the dealer. **4.** any storage place. **5.** any store or reserve: *a blood bank.* *–v.i.* **6.** to exercise the functions of a bank or banker. **7.** to keep money in, or have an account with, a bank. **8.** (in games) to hold the bank. **9.** *Colloq.* to rely or count (fol. by *on* or *upon*). **10.** **bank up,** to accumulate: *the line of cars banked up.* *–v.t.* **11.** to deposit in a bank. [ME *banke,* from F *banque,* from It. *banca,* orig. bench, table; of Gmc. orig. See BANK[1], BENCH]

**bank**[3] /bæŋk/, *n.* **1.** an arrangement of objects in line. **2.** *Music.* a row of keys in an organ. **3.** a bench for rowers in a galley. **4.** a row or tier of oars. **5.** the rowers on one bench or to one oar. [ME *banck,* from OF *banc* bench, from LL *bancus,* from the Gmc source of BENCH]

**bankable** /ˈbæŋkəbəl/, *adj.* receivable by a bank.

**bank acceptance** /ˈbæŋk əkseptəns/, *n.* a draft endorsed or otherwise formally acknowledged by a bank on which it is drawn.

**bank account** /ˈ– əkaʊnt/, *n.* an account with a bank.

**bank bill** /ˈ– bɪl/, *n.* a commercial bill which has been accepted or endorsed by a trading bank.

**bankbook** /ˈbæŋkbʊk/, *n.* a book held by a depositor in which a bank enters a record of his account; a bank passbook or a series of bank statements.

**bank card** /ˈbæŋk kad/, *n.* a credit card issued by several cooperating banks, allowing a credit-worthy customer to purchase goods and services up to a certain value from vendors who have agreed to participate in the scheme. Also, **bankcard.**

**bank charge** /ˈbæŋk tʃadʒ/, *n.* a charge for bank services debited to a customer's account.

**bank cheque** /ˈ– tʃɛk/, *n.* a cheque issued by a bank in its own name.

**bank clerk** /ˈ– klak/, *n.* a clerk employed by a bank.

**bank-draft** /ˈbæŋk-draft/, *n.* a draft drawn by one bank on another, payable on demand or at a specified future date.

**banker**[1] /ˈbæŋkə/, *n.* **1.** one who manages a bank or is in the banking business. **2.** one who holds or supplies money for another. **3.** (in games) the keeper or holder of the bank. **4.** a gambling card game. [BANK[2] + -ER[1]]

**banker**[2] /ˈbæŋkə/, *n.* **1.** a bank-high flood. **2.** **run a banker,** to be flowing up to the top of the banks.

**banker's card** /ˈbæŋkəz kad/, *n. Brit.* a small card issued on request by certain banks to credit-worthy customers, undertaking that the holder's cheques up to a specified amount will be honoured.

**banker's draft** /– ˈdraft/, *n.* →**bank-draft.**

**banker's order** /– ˈɔdə/, *n.* a customer's written order to a bank to make a payment or a series of payments on his behalf.

**bank holiday** /bæŋk ˈhɒlədeɪ/, *n.* a weekday on which banks are closed by law.

**banking**[1] /ˈbæŋkiŋ/, *n.* **1.** the business of a bank or banker. *–adj.* **2.** pertaining to a bank or banking.

**banking**[2] /ˈbæŋkɪŋ/, *n.* →**superelevation.**

**banknote** /ˈbæŋknoʊt/, *n.* a promissory note, payable on demand, issued by a bank and intended to circulate as money.

**bank passbook** /ˌbæŋk ˈpasbʊk/, *n.* a bankbook for a deposit account.

**bank rate** /ˈ– reɪt/, *n.* the rate at which the central bank of a country is prepared to discount bills, as the Reserve Bank.

**bankroll** /ˈbæŋkroʊl/, *n.* **1.** a roll of money notes. *–v.t.* **2.** to provide funds for; act as backer for.

**bankrupt** /ˈbæŋkrʌpt/, *n.* **1.** *Law.* a person who upon his own petition or that of his creditors is adjudged insolvent by a court, and whose property is administered for and divided among his creditors, under a bankruptcy law. **2.** any insolvent debtor; one unable to satisfy any just claims made upon him. **3.** a person completely depleted of some human quality or resource: *a moral bankrupt.* *–adj.* **4.** *Law.* subject to, or under, legal process because of insolvency. **5.** completely depleted of some human quality or resource: *creatively bankrupt; hack politicians bankrupt of ideas and imagination.* **6.** pertaining to bankrupts. *–v.t.* **7.** to make bankrupt. [F *banqueroute* (after L *ruptus* broken) from It. *bancarotta* bankruptcy, from *banca* bank + *rotta,* pp. fem. of *rompere* break, from L *rumpere*]

**bankruptcy** /ˈbæŋkrʌpsi, -rəp-/, *n., pl.* **-cies. 1.** the state of being or becoming bankrupt. **2.** complete depletion of some human quality or resource.

**banksia** /ˈbæŋksiə/, *n.* **1.** any plant of the Australian genus *Banksia* comprising shrubs and trees with leathery leaves and dense cylindrical heads of flowers, sometimes called a bottlebrush. **2.** Also, **Banksia rose, Banksian rose.** a Chinese species of climbing rose, *Rosa banksiae,* having yellow or white flowers. [NL, named after Sir Joseph *Banks* 1743-1820, English naturalist]

banksia

**bank statement** /ˈbæŋk steɪtmənt/, *n.* a printed sheet bearing a complete record of a current account, sent periodically to a customer.

**bank-up** /ˈbæŋk-ʌp/, *n.* an accumulation: *the strike will cause a bank-up of mail.*

**banlon** /ˈbænlɒn/, *n.* a soft, textured synthetic yarn, as used for underclothes. [Trademark, after J. *Bancroft*]

**banner** /ˈbænə/, *n.* **1.** the flag of a country, army, troop, etc. **2.** an ensign or the like bearing some device or motto, as one borne in processions. **3.** a piece of cloth, attached by one side to a pole or staff, formerly used as the standard of a sovereign, lord, or knight. **4.** anything displayed as a profession of principles: *the banner of freedom.* **5.** *Her.* a square flag bearing heraldic devices. **6.** *Journalism.* a headline which extends across the width of the newspaper, usually at the top of the first page. [ME *banere,* from OF, from LL *bandum* standard; of Gmc orig. (cf. Goth. *bandwo* sign)] **– bannered,** *adj.*

**banneret** /ˈbænərət, -ərɛt/, *n.* **1.** a knight who could bring a company of followers into the field under his own banner. **2.** a rank of knighthood; knight banneret. **3.** a bannerette. [ME *baneret,* from OF, from *banere* BANNER]

**bannerette** /ˌbænəˈrɛt/, *n.* a small banner. [OF, diminutive of *banere* BANNER]

**bannerol** /ˈbænəroʊl/, *n.* →**banderol.**

**bannister** /ˈbænəstə/, *n.* →**banister.**

**bannock** /ˈbænək/, *n.* a flat Scottish cake made of oatmeal or barley meal, commonly baked on a griddle. [OE *bannuc* bit, small piece, from OBrit. Cf. OCornish *banna* drop]

**banns** /bænz/, *n.pl. Eccles.* notice of an intended marriage, formerly required by English law to be given three times in the parish church of each of the betrothed. Also, **bans.** [var. of *bans,* pl. of BAN², *n.*]

**banquet** /ˈbæŋkwət/, *n., v.,* **-queted, -queting.** *–n.* **1.** a formal and ceremonious meal, often one given to celebrate an event or to honour a person. *–v.i.* **2.** to partake in a banquet. *–v.t.* **3.** to give (someone) a banquet. [F, from It. *banchetto* table, sumptuous meal, diminutive of *banco* bench, table] **– banqueter,** *n.*

**banquette** /bæŋˈkɛt/, *n.* **1.** *Fort.* a platform inside a parapet or trench, for soldiers to stand on when firing. **2.** a built-in upholstered seat, as in a café. **3.** *Southern U.S.* →**pavement.**

**bans** /bænz/, *n.pl.* →**banns.**

**banshee** /ˈbænʃi, bænˈʃi/, *n.* a supernatural being in Irish and Scottish mythology supposed to give warning by its wails of an approaching death in the family. [Irish *bean sīdhe* woman of the fairies]

**bant** /bænt/, *v.i.* to reduce weight by banting. [backformation from BANTING]

**bantam** /ˈbæntəm/, *n.* **1.** (*oft. cap.*) a domestic fowl of any of certain varieties or breeds characterised by very small size. **2.** a small person, esp. a quarrelsome one. **3.** →**bantamweight.** *–adj.* **4.** (of persons) small, esp. small and quarrelsome.

**bantamweight** /ˈbæntəmweɪt/, *n.* a boxer weighing between 51 and 54 kg (in the amateur ranks) or between 50.80 and 53.521 kg (in the professional ranks).

**banteng** /ˈbæntɛŋ/, *n.* a wild ox, *Bos banteng,* of south-eastern Asia, sometimes domesticated. [Malay]

**banter** /ˈbæntə/, *n.* **1.** playfully teasing language; goodhumoured raillery. *–v.t.* **2.** to address with banter; chaff. *–v.i.* **3.** to use banter. [orig. unknown] **– banterer,** *n.* **– bantering,** *adj.* **– banteringly,** *adv.*

**banting** /ˈbæntɪŋ/, *n.* a method of reducing one's weight, based upon a high protein and low fat and carbohydrate diet. [named after William *Banting,* 1797-1878, English dietitian] **– bantingism,** *n.*

**bantling** /ˈbæntlɪŋ/, *n. Archaic.* a young child; brat. [G *Bänkling* bastard. See BENCH, -LING¹]

**Bantu** /ˈbæntu, bænˈtu/, *n., pl.* **-tu, -tus,** *adj.* *–n.* **1.** a principal linguistic family of Africa, its languages being prevalent from the Equator to South Africa, including Swahili, Tswana, Zulu, Ganda, and Kongo. **2.** any of the negroid peoples who speak these languages. *–adj.* **3.** of or pertaining to the Bantu languages or peoples.

**Bantustan** /ˈbæntustæn, -stan/, *n.* (in the Republic of South Africa) an area set up for black Africans as a self-contained and self-governing settlement.

**banyalla** /bænˈjælə/, *n.* a small tree, *Pittosporum bicolor,* of New South Wales, Tasmania and Victoria, growing in wet forest gullies, and yielding a hard, durable wood; cheesewood, tallowwood.

**banyan** /ˈbænjæn/, *n.* any of various species of *Ficus,* fig, whose branches send out adventitious roots to the ground, sometimes causing the tree to spread over a wide area. Also, **banian.** [orig. a particular tree under which BANIAN traders had built a pagoda]

banyan

**banzai** /bænˈzaɪ/, *interj.* **1.** (a Japanese complimentary salutation or patriotic shout, as in honour of the emperor, meaning): **a.** long life. **b.** forward; attack. *–adj.* **2.** reckless; suicidal. [Jap.: ten thousand years]

**baobab** /ˈbeɪoʊˌbæb/, *n.* a large, exceedingly thick-trunked tree of the genus *Adansonia,* family Bombacaceae, native to tropical Africa and northern Australia; bottle tree; sour gourd. [native African]

baobab

**bap** /bæp/, *n.* (esp. in Scotland) a large soft bread roll. [orig. unknown]

**bap.,** baptised.

**baptise** /bæpˈtaɪz/, *v.,* **-tised, -tising.** *–v.t.* **1.** to immerse in water, or sprinkle or pour water on, in the Christian rite of baptism. **2.** to cleanse spiritually; initiate or dedicate by purifying. **3.** to christen. *–v.i.* **4.** to administer baptism. [ME *baptise(n),* from OF *baptiser,* from LL *baptīzāre,* from Gk *baptízein* immerse] **– baptiser,** *n.*

**baptism** /ˈbæptɪzəm/, *n.* **1.** a ceremonial immersion in water, or application of water, as an initiatory rite or sacrament of the Christian church. **2.** any similar ceremony or action of initiation, dedication, etc. **– baptismal** /bæpˈtɪzməl/, *adj.*

– **baptismally,** *adv.*

**baptism of fire,** *n.* **1.** the first battle a soldier experiences. **2.** any severe ordeal; crucial test.

**Baptist** /ˈbæptəst/, *n.* **1.** *Relig.* a member of a Christian denomination which maintains that baptism (usu. implying immersion) should follow only upon a personal profession of Christian faith. **2.** one who baptises.

**baptistery** /ˈbæptəstri/, *n., pl.* **-ries.** **1.** a building, or a part of a church, in which baptism is administered. **2.** (in Baptist Churches) a tank containing water for baptism by immersion. [L *baptistērium,* from Gk *baptistērion*]

**bar**[1] /ba/, *n., v.,* **barred, barring,** *prep.* *–n.* **1.** a relatively long and evenly shaped piece of some solid substance, esp. one of wood or metal used as a guard or obstruction, or for some mechanical purpose: *the bars of a fence.* **2.** *Athletics.* the cross-piece of wood, metal or plastic which jumpers must clear in the high jump or the pole vault. **3.** an oblong piece of any solid material: *a bar of soap; a bar of toffee.* **4.** the amount of material in a bar. **5.** an ingot, lump, or wedge of gold or silver. **6.** a band or stripe: *a bar of light.* **7.** *Mining.* a band of rock or gravel which traps gold in a stream. **8.** a ridge of sand or gravel in coastal waters, near or slightly above the surface, and extending across the mouth of a bay or river or parallel to the shore. **9.** anything which obstructs, hinders, or impedes; an obstacle; a barrier: *a bar to vice.* **10.** *Music.* **a.** Also, **bar-line.** the vertical line drawn across the stave to mark the metrical accent. **b.** that which is included between two bars. **11.** a counter or a room where alcoholic drinks, etc., are served to customers. **12.** any counter or place specialising in the sale of one particular commodity: *wine bar.* **13.** practising barristers collectively. **14.** the legal profession. **15.** a railing in a courtroom separating the general public from the part of the room occupied by the judges, jury, barristers, solicitors, and other members of the legal profession. **16.** the place in court where prisoners stand or sit: *a prisoner at the bar.* **17.** (in a house of parliament) a bar or line opposite the Speaker's chair, marking the boundary of the house. **18.** *Law.* **a.** an objection which nullifies an action or claim. **b.** a stoppage or defeat of an alleged right of action. **19.** any tribunal: *the bar of public opinion.* **20.** (in lace) a bride (see **bride**[2] def. 1). **21.** *Her.* a wide horizontal band crossing the field. **22.** a strip of silver or some other metal added to a medal below the clasp as a further distinction: *D.S.O. and bar.* **23. go off the bars,** *Prison Colloq.* to commit suicide by hanging. **24. not to have a bar (of),** not to tolerate: *I won't have a bar of it.* *–v.t.* **25.** to provide or fasten with a bar or bars: *to bar the door.* **26.** to shut in or out by or as by bars. **27.** to block (a way, etc.) as with a barrier; prevent or hinder, as access. **28.** to exclude; except. **29.** to forbid; preclude: *no holds barred.* **30.** to mark with bars, stripes, or bands. *–prep.* **31.** except; omitting; but: *bar none.* [ME *barre,* from OF, from LL *barra,* of disputed origin]

bar (def. 10): A, single; B, double

**bar**[2] /ba/, *n.* a unit of pressure equal to 100 000 pascals [Gk *báros* weight]

**bar**[3] /ba/, *adj.* **1.** (*in children's speech*) inviolate: *don't touch me, I'm bar.* *–n.* **2.** in children's games, anything which acts as a sanctuary; a position from which one cannot be assailed. *–interj.* **3.** (an appeal for respite, freedom from assault.) [from BARLEY[2]]

**bar.,** **1.** barometer. **2.** barrister.

**barathea** /bærəˈθiə/, *n.* **1.** a durable worsted fabric in twilled hopsack weave for men's and women's suits. *–adj.* **2.** made of this fabric. [Trademark]

**barb**[1] /bab/, *n.* **1.** a point or pointed part projecting backwards from a main point, as of a fishhook, an arrowhead, or a fence wire. **2.** a sharp or unkind implication in a remark; cutting comment. **3.** *Bot., Zool.* a beardlike growth or part. **4.** *Ornith.* one of the processes attached to the rachis of a feather. **5.** any of a large number of small, Old World cyprinoid fishes of the genera *Barbus* or *Puntius* widely cultivated for home aquariums. **6.** (*usu. pl.*) *Vet. Sci.* a small protuberance under the tongue in horses and cattle, esp. when inflamed and swollen. **7.** a linen covering for the throat and breast, formerly worn by women mourners, and now by nuns. **8.** *Obs.* a beard. *–v.t.* **9.** to furnish with a barb or barbs. [ME *barbe,* from OF, from L *barba* beard] – **barbed,** *adj.*

**barb**[2] /bab/, *n.* **1.** a horse of a breed developed in North Africa, related to the Arab horse. **2.** a breed of domestic pigeon, similar to the carriers or homers, having a short broad bill, originally from Barbary. **3.** a black dog like a kelpie. [F *barbe,* from It. *barbero* of Barbary, a country of N Africa]

**Barbados** /baˈbeɪdɒs, -doʊs/, *n.* a country consisting of the easternmost island in the West Indies.

**barbarian** /baˈbɛəriən/, *n.* **1.** a person belonging to a non-literate culture regarded as uncivilised, esp. any of the ancient European peoples other than the Greeks and Romans. **2.** an ignorant and uncouth person. *–adj.* **3.** belonging to an uncivilised culture. **4.** ignorant and uncouth. [F *barbarien,* from L *barbaria* barbarous country] – **barbarianism,** *n.*

**barbaric** /baˈbærɪk/, *adj.* **1.** pertaining to or characteristic of barbarians; uncivilised, uncouth or cruel. **2.** (of art and culture) crude and vigorous. [ME *barbarik,* from L *barbaricus,* from Gk *barbarikós* foreign, barbaric] – **barbarically,** *adv.*

**barbarise** /ˈbabəraɪz/, *v.,* **-rised, -rising.** *–v.t.* **1.** to make barbarous or crude; to corrupt. *–v.i.* **2.** to become barbarous. Also, **barbarize.** – **barbarisation,** *n.*

**barbarism** /ˈbabərɪzəm/, *n.* **1.** the state or condition of being barbarian or barbarous. **2.** an act or product typical of barbarians. **3.** a linguistic usage considered to be erroneous, ignorant and threatening to the purity of a particular standard or style of language.

**barbarity** /baˈbærəti/, *n., pl.* **-ties.** **1.** the state or condition of being barbarian or barbarous. **2.** a barbarous act or product, esp. an instance of cruelty. **3.** crudity of style, taste, etc.

**barbarous** /ˈbabərəs/, *adj.* **1.** pertaining to or characteristic of barbarians; uncivilised, uncouth or cruel. **2.** stylistically unacceptable. [L *barbarus,* from Gk *bárbaros* foreign, non-Greek]

**Barbary ape** /ˌbabəri ˈeɪp/, *n.* an ape, *Macaca sylvana,* of northern Africa and Gibraltar.

**barbate** /ˈbabeɪt/, *adj.* bearded; tufted or furnished with hairs. [L *barbātus* bearded]

**barbecue** /ˈbabəkju/, *n., v.t.* **-cued, -cuing.** *–n.* **1.** a metal frame for cooking meat, etc., above an open fire of coals, wood, etc. **2.** an often portable fireplace containing this. **3.** the meat cooked in this way. **4.** a rack or spit on which large animals as pig, lamb, etc., are roasted whole. **5.** a social occasion, usu. out of doors, where barbecued food is served. *–v.t.* **6.** to cook on a barbecue. Also, **barbeque, bar-b-q.** [Sp. *barbacoa,* from Haitian *barboka*]

**barbecue sauce** /– ˈsɔs/, *n.* a highly seasoned sauce somewhat similar to tomato sauce, used esp. with barbecued meat, and sometimes used for basting.

**barbed wire** /babd ˈwaɪə, bab ˈwaɪə/, *n.* steel wire to which barbs are attached at short intervals, used largely for fencing in livestock, protecting a defensive military position, etc. Also, **barbwire.**

**barbel** /ˈbabəl/, *n.* **1.** a slender cylindrical tactile process appended to the mouth of certain fishes. **2.** any of various cyprinoid fishes of the genus *Barbus,* esp. *B. barbus,* of Europe. [ME *barbelle,* from OF *barbel,* from LL *barbellus,* diminutive of *barbus*]

**barbell** /ˈbabɛl/, *n.* an apparatus in weight-lifting consisting of a steel bar, about 2 metres long, to the ends of which disc-shaped weights are attached.

**barbellate** /ˈbabəleɪt, -lət/, *adj.* having short, stiff hairs. [NL *barbella* (diminutive of L *barbula* little beard) + -ATE[1]]

**barbeque** /ˈbabəkju/, *n., v.t.* →**barbecue.**

**barber** /ˈbabə/, *n.* **1.** one whose occupation it is to cut and dress the hair of customers and to shave or trim the beard. **2.** *N.Z.* a cold, keen, cutting wind. *–v.i.* **3.** *Prison Colloq.* to steal from residential premises. *–v.t.* **4.** to trim or dress the beard and hair of. [ME *barbour,* from AF, from L *barba* beard]

**barberry** /ˈbabəri/, *n., pl.* **-ries.** **1.** a shrub of the genus *Berberis,* esp. *B. vulgaris* often cultivated as a hedge plant or an ornamental. **2.** its red, elongated, acid fruit. [ME *barbere,* from ML *barbaris, berberis*]

**barber's pole** /ˈbabəz poʊl/, *n.* a pole painted in red and white, or red, white and blue, spirals, displayed outside a barber's shop.

**barber's rash** /– ˈræʃ/, *n.* any of various irritable eruptions of the bearded sections of the head and neck. Also, **barber's itch.**

**barbet** /ˈbabət/, *n.* any of numerous tropical non-passerine birds of the family Capitonidae, most of which are brightly coloured and large-headed, and have bristles at the base of the bill. [F, masc. diminutive of *barbe* beard]

**barbette** /baˈbɛt/, *n.* **1.** a platform or mound of earth within a fortification, from which guns may be fired over the parapet instead of through embrasures. **2.** *Navy.* an armoured cylinder to protect a turret on a warship. [F, fem. diminutive of *barbe* beard]

**barb-grass** /ˈbab-gras/, *n.* either of two species of grass from the Mediterranean region, *Parapholis incurva* and *Monerma cylindrica.*

**barbican** /ˈbabəkən/, *n.* an outwork of a castle or fortified place. [ME, from OF *barcane,* from ML *barbicana;* orig. obscure, ? from Ar. Pers. *bāb khāne* gatehouse, or Pers. *bālā khāne* high house]

**barbicel** /ˈbabəsɛl/, *n. Ornith.* one of the minute processes fringing the barbules of certain feathers. [NL *barbicella,* diminutive of L *barba* beard]

**bar billiards** /ˈba bɪljədz/, *n.* a game resembling billiards, played on a small table with a time limit, after the expiry of which a bar drops, preventing the return of balls for play.

**barbital** /ˈbabətæl/, *n. U.S.* →**barbitone.**

**barbitone** /ˈbabətoʊn/, *n.* a drug, diethylbarbituric acid, used as a sedative; veronal. [See BARBITURIC ACID, -ONE]

**barbiturate** /baˈbɪtʃərət, -eɪt/, *n.* a derivative of barbituric acid, esp. a sedative drug.

**barbituric acid** /babɪˌtʃʊərɪk ˈæsəd/, *n.* an acid, $C_4H_4N_2O_3 \cdot 2H_2O$, a crystalline powder from which several hypnotic and sedative drugs are derived; malonyl urea. [G *Barbitursäure,* perhaps from the name *Barbara* + UR(IC) + *Säure* acid]

**barbule** /ˈbabjul/, *n.* **1.** a little barb. **2.** one of the small processes fringing the barbs of a feather. [L *barbula,* diminutive of *barba* beard]

**barbwire** /babˈwaɪə/, *n.* **1.** →**barbed wire.** *–adj.* **2.** made from barbed wire.

**barbwire grass** /ˈ– gras/, *n.* an erect tufted perennial grass, *Cymbopogon refractus,* native to Australia.

**barby** /ˈbabi/, *n. Colloq.* a barbecue. Also, **barbie.**

**barcarolle** /bakəˈroʊl/, *n.* **1.** a boating song of the Venetian gondoliers. **2.** a piece of music composed in the style of such songs. Also, **barcarole.** [F *barcarolle,* from It. *barcar(u)ola* boatman's song, from *barcar(u)olo* a boatman, from *barca* BARQUE]

**B.Arch.,** Bachelor of Architecture.

**barchan** /ˈbakæn/, *n.* a crescent-shaped sand-dune with the horns pointing downwind, the profile being asymmetric with the gentler slope on the convex side, and the steeper slope on the concave or leeward side. Also, **barchane, barkhan.**

**bar chord** /ˈba kɔd/, *n.* one of the series of chords formed by consistently shortening the strings of a lute or guitar by using the index finger as a bar placed behind a fret, while using the remaining fingers to form chord configurations based on suitable chords in the unbarred position, the advantage being that very few chord configurations have to be learnt.

**Barcoo rot** /ˌbaku ˈrɒt/, *n. Colloq.* chronic streptococcal skin infection. [*Barcoo* River, Queensland]

**Barcoo salute** /– səˈlut/, *n.* →**salute** (def. 8).

**Barcoo spews** /– ˈspjuz/, *n.pl. Colloq.* attacks of heat-induced vomiting.

**bard**[1] /bad/, *n.* **1.** a member of the order of poets in the ancient and medieval Celtic societies. **2.** a member of the revived order of Welsh poets. **3.** *Archaic.* any poet. **4. the Bard,** Shakespeare. [ME, from Celtic (cf. Irish *bard,* Welsh *bardd*), whence also L *bardus,* Gk *bárdos*] – **bardic,** *adj.*

**bard**[2] /bad/, *n.* **1.** *Obs.* any of various pieces of defensive armour for a horse. **2.** a slice of bacon or pork fat placed on meat or game before roasting. *–v.t.* **3.** to caparison with bards (def. 1). **4.** to cover or thread meat with bards (def. 2). [F *barde,* from Ar. *hardha'ah* pack saddle]

**bardolatry** /baˈdɒlətri/, *n.* excessive adulation of Shakespeare. [BARD[1] (def. 4) + -OLATRY]

**bardy** /ˈbadi/, *n., pl.* **-dies. 1.** an edible wood-boring grub, *Bardistus cibarius,* or its larvae. **2. starve the bardies!** (an exclamation of surprise or disgust). Also, **bardi.** [Aboriginal]

**bare**[1] /bɛə/, *adj.* **barer, barest,** *v.,* **bared, baring.** *–adj.* **1.** without covering or clothing; naked or nude: *bare knees.* **2.** with the head uncovered. **3.** without the usual furnishings, contents, etc.: *bare walls.* **4.** open to view; unconcealed; undisguised. **5.** unadorned; bald; plain: *the bare facts.* **6.** napless or threadbare. **7.** scarcely or just sufficient: *bare necessities.* *–v.t.* **8.** to make bare. [ME; OE *bær,* c. G *bar*] – **bareness,** *n.*

**bare**[2] /bɛə/, *v. Archaic.* past tense of **bear**[1].

**bareback** /ˈbɛəbæk/, *adv.* **1.** without a saddle: *we rode bareback.* *–adj.* **2.** Also, **barebacked.** (of a horse) ridden without a saddle.

**barebelly** /ˈbɛəbɛli/, *n.* a sheep with bare belly and legs, as a result of defective wool growth; rosella. Also, **bluebelly.** – **barebellied,** *adj.*

**barefaced** /ˈbɛəfeɪst/, *adj.* **1.** with the face uncovered. **2.** undisguised; boldly open. **3.** shameless; impudent; audacious: *a barefaced lie.* – **barefacedly** /ˈbɛəˌfeɪsədli, -ˌfeɪstli/, *adv.* – **barefacedness,** *n.*

**barefoot** /ˈbɛəfʊt/, *adj.* with the feet bare. Also, **barefooted** /ˈbɛəfʊtəd/.

**barefoot doctor** /– ˈdɒktə/, *n.* a third-world field labourer with some basic knowledge of medicine or first aid, able to treat his fellow workers.

**barehanded** /bɛəˈhændəd/, *adj.* **1.** with hands uncovered. **2.** with hands alone; unaided by tools or weapons.

**bareheaded** /bɛəˈhɛdəd/, *adj.* with the head uncovered.

**barelegged** /bɛəˈlɛgəd, -ˈlɛgd/, *adj.* with bare legs.

**barely** /ˈbɛəli/, *adv.* **1.** only; just; no more than: *she is barely sixteen.* **2.** without disguise or concealment; openly: *a question barely put.*

**Barera** /bəˈrɛərə/, *n.* →**Burera.**

**baresark** /ˈbɛəsak/, *n.* **1.** a berserker. *–adv.* **2.** without armour. [translation var. of *berserk* taken as *bare* + *serk* sark, shirt]

**barf** /baf/, *U.S. Colloq.* *–v.i.* **1.** to vomit. *–n.* **2.** an act or instance of vomiting.

**bar fly** /ˈba flaɪ/, *n. Colloq.* a habitual drinker at bars.

**bargain** /ˈbagən/, *n.* **1.** an agreement between parties settling what each shall give and take, or perform and receive, in a transaction. **2.** such an agreement as affecting one of the parties: *a losing bargain.* **3.** *Stock Exchange.* an agreement to sell or to purchase; a sale or purchase. **4.** that which is acquired by bargaining. **5.** an advantageous purchase. **6. into the bargain,** over and above what is stipulated; moreover; besides. **7. strike a bargain,** to make a bargain; come to terms. *–v.i.* **8.** to discuss the terms of a bargain; haggle over terms. **9.** to come to an agreement; make a bargain. **10. bargain for,** to be prepared for; expect: *he got more than he bargained for.* **11. bargain on,** to count on; rely on. *–v.t.* **12.** to arrange by bargain; stipulate. [ME, from OF *bargaigne*] – **bargainer,** *n.*

**barge** /ˈbadʒ/, *n., v.,* **barged, barging.** *–n.* **1.** a large flat-bottomed vessel, usu. moved by towing, used for transporting freight. **2.** a ceremonial vessel of state. **3.** a naval boat reserved for a flag officer. **4.** *Colloq.* any old or unwieldy boat. **5.** *Colloq.* a cumbersome surfboard. *–v.t.* **6.** to transport by barge. *–v.i.* **7.** to move aggressively or with undue energy often knocking others out of the way: *to barge through a crowd.* **8.** to bump or collide. **9. barge in,** to intrude clumsily as into a conversation. **10. barge into,** to collide clumsily with (someone or something). [ME, from OF, from L *bāris,* from Gk: (Egyptian) boat or barge]

**bargeboard** /ˈbadʒbɔd/, *n.* an overhanging board along the projecting sloping edge of a gable roof.

**barge course** /ˈbadʒ kɔs/, *n.* the part of a gable roof that projects beyond the end wall.

**bargee** /baˈdʒi/, *n.* **1.** one of the crew of a barge. **2.** one who has charge of a barge.

**barge pole** /ˈbadʒ poʊl/, *n.* **1.** a pole used to propel a barge. **2. not to touch with a barge pole,** to have nothing to do with; not to go near.

**baric**[1] /ˈbɛərɪk, ˈbærɪk/, *adj.* of or containing barium. [BAR(IUM) + -IC]

**baric**[2] /ˈbærɪk/, *adj.* of or pertaining to weight, esp. that of the atmosphere. [Gk *báros* weight + -IC]

**barilla** /bəˈrɪlə/, *n.* **1.** either of two European saltworts, *Salsola kali* and esp. *S. soda,* whose ashes yield an impure carbonate of soda. **2.** the alkali obtained from the ashes of these and certain other maritime plants. [Sp. *barrilla*]

**barit.,** baritone.

**barite** /ˈbɛəraɪt/, *n.* →**barytes.**

**baritone** /ˈbærətoʊn/, *n.* **1.** a male voice or voice part intermediate between tenor and bass. **2.** a singer with such a voice. **3.** a large, valved brass instrument, slightly smaller in bore than a euphonium, used chiefly in military bands. *–adj.* **4.** of or pertaining to the baritone; having the compass of the baritone. Also, **barytone.** [Gk *barýtonos* deep sounding]

**barium** /ˈbɛəriəm/, *n.* a whitish, malleable, active, divalent, metallic element occurring in combination chiefly as barytes or as witherite. *Symbol:* Ba; *at. wt:* 137·34; *at. no.:* 56; *sp. gr.:* 3·5 at 20°C. [NL; from BAR(YTES) + -IUM]

**barium enema** /– ˈɛnəmə/, *n.* a preparation of barium sulphate which is ingested before a radiological examination to show up any abnormality in the colon or rectum.

**barium meal** /– ˈmil/, *n.* a preparation of barium sulphate ingested before a radiological examination to show up any abnormality of the stomach or duodenum.

**barium sulphate** /– ˈsʌlfeɪt/, *n.* a fine white powder, $BaSO_4$, used as a filler in textiles and as a radio-opaque medium in X-rays of the human body.

**barium swallow** /– ˈswɒloʊ/, *n.* a preparation of barium sulphate ingested before a radiological examination to show up any abnormality of the oesophagus.

**bark**[1] /bak/, *n.* **1.** the abrupt, explosive cry of a dog. **2.** a similar sound made by another animal or by a person. *–v.i.* **3.** to utter an abrupt, explosive cry or a series of such cries, as a dog. **4.** to make a similar sound: *the big guns barked.* **5.** to speak or cry out sharply or gruffly. **6.** *Colloq.* to advertise a cheap show at its entrance. **7. bark up the wrong tree,** to mistake one's object; assail or pursue the wrong person or purpose. **8.** *Colloq.* to vomit. *–v.t.* **9.** to utter or give forth with a bark: *he barked an order.* [ME *berke(n),* OE *beorcan*]

**bark**[2] /bak/, *n.* **1.** the external covering of the woody stems, branches, and roots of plants, as distinct and separable from the wood itself. **2.** *Tanning.* a mixture of oak and hemlock barks. **3.** →**tanbark.** *–v.t.* **4.** to strip off the bark of; peel. **5.** to remove a circle of bark from; ringbark. **6.** to cover or enclose with bark. **7.** to treat with a bark infusion; tan. **8.** to rub off the skin of: *to bark one's shins.* [ME, from Scand.; cf. Dan. *bark*] – **barker,** *n.*

**bark**[3] /bak/, *n.* →**barque.**

**bark beetle** /ˈbak bitl/, *n.* any beetle of the family Scolytidae, the adults and larvae of which do great damage to living trees, esp. to conifers.

**bark-bound** /ˈbak-baʊnd/, *adj.* (of a plant) having the internal tissues compressed and inhibited by the failure of the bark to grow or split.

**barkeep** /ˈbakip/, *n.* →*U.S.* **barman.** – **barkeeper,** *n.*

**barkentine** /ˈbakəntin/, *n.* →**barquentine.**

**barker** /ˈbakə/, *n.* **1.** an animal or person that barks. **2.** *Colloq.* one who stands before a shop, nightclub, etc., calling passers-by to enter. [BARK[1] + -ER[1]]

**barkhan** /baˈkan/, *n.* →**barchan.**

**barking jackass** /ˌbakɪŋ ˈdʒækæs/, *n.* →**kookaburra** (def. 2).

**bark painting** /ˈbak peɪntɪŋ/, *n.* **1.** the art of painting on bark, extensively practised by Australian Aborigines. **2.** a painting on bark.

bark painting

**barky** /ˈbaki/, *adj.,* **barkier, barkiest.** consisting of or containing bark; covered with or resembling bark.

**barley**[1] /ˈbali/, *n.* **1.** a widely distributed cereal plant of the genus *Hordeum,* whose awned flowers grow in tightly bunched spikes, with three small additional spikes at each node. **2.** the grain of this plant, used as food, and in the making of beer and whisky. [ME *barly,* OE *bærlīc;* cf. BARN[1]]

**barley**[2] /ˈbali/, *Brit. Obs. Colloq. interj.* (an appeal for respite, freedom from assault usu. verbal assault).

**barleycorn** /ˈbalikɔn/, *n.* **1.** barley, or a grain of barley. **2.** *Obs.* a measure equal to one third of an inch. **3. John Barleycorn,** whisky; spirits.

**barley grass** /ˈbali gras/, *n.* **1.** any species of the grass genus *Hordeum,* esp. *H. leporinum,* a winter fodder grass resembling barley. **2.** any of several other similar grass species.

**barley sugar** /ˈbali ʃʊgə/, *n.* a sweet made from boiled sugar, orig. boiled in a decoction of barley.

**barley water** /ˈbali wɔtə/, *n.* a drink made from pearl barley, sugar, lemon rind and water, strained and served cold.

**bar line** /ˈba laɪn/, *n.* the vertical line dividing two bars in a musical score.

**barm** /bam/, *n.* a froth of yeast formed on malt liquors while fermenting. [ME *berme,* OE *beorma,* c. G *Bärme*]

**barmaid** /ˈbameɪd/, *n.* a woman who serves drinks in a bar.

**barmaid's blush** /bameɪdz ˈblʌʃ/, *n.* **1.** a drink made from rum and raspberry. **2.** a drink made from port wine and lemonade.

**barman** /ˈbamən/, *n., pl.* **-men.** a man who serves drinks in a bar; bartender.

**barmecidal** /ˈbaməsaɪdl/, *adj.* of benefits, imagined or illusory. Also, **barmecide.** [from the name of a member of a Persian family who gave a beggar a pretended feast with empty dishes]

**bar mitzvah** /ba ˈmɪtsvə/, *n.* (in Judaism) **1.** a boy at the age of thirteen, when he acquires religious obligations. **2.** the ceremony and feast marking this. Also, **bar mizvah.** [Heb. son of the commandment]

**barmy** /ˈbami/, *adj.* **barmier, barmiest.** *Colloq.* mad; stupid; silly. [orig. full of froth, from BARM]

**barn**[1] /ban/, *n.* **1.** a building for storing hay, grain, etc., and often for stabling livestock. *–v.t.* **2.** to store in a barn. [ME *bern,* OE *berern,* from *bere* barley + *ærn* place, house]

**barn**[2] /ban/, *n.* a unit used in measuring cross-sectional areas of atomic nuclei, equal to $0.1 \times 10^{-27}$ $m^2$. *Symbol:* b [special use of BARN[1], ref. to relatively large size of unit]

**barnacle**[1] /ˈbanəkəl/, *n.* **1.** any of certain crustaceans of the group Cirripedia, as the **goose barnacles,** stalked species which cling to ship bottoms and floating timber, and the **rock barnacles,** species which attach themselves to marine rocks. **2.** a thing or person that clings tenaciously. **3.** →**barnacle goose.** [late ME *bernacle,* of obscure orig. (cf. ML *bernacula,* F *bernicle, barnacle*); replacing ME *bernekke, bernake* (cf. ML *bernaca,* OF *bernaque*)] – **barnacled,** *adj.*

goose barnacle

**barnacle**[2] /ˈbanəkəl/, *n.* (*usu. pl.*) an instrument with two hinged branches for pinching the nose of an unruly horse. [ME *bernacle,* from OF *bernac*]

**barnacle goose** /ˈ– gus/, *n.* a wild goose of northern Europe, allied to the brent. Also, **bernicle goose.**

**Barnardo boy** /bəˈnadoʊ ˌbɔɪ/, *n.* a boy cared for in a house owned by a foundation established by Dr. Thomas Barnardo, 1845-1905, a philanthropist.

**barn-dance** /ˈban-dæns/, *n.* **1.** a social gathering typically held in a barn and featuring country dances, often of American origin. **2.** a country dance similar to a schottische.

**barn-doors** /ˈban-dɔz/, *n. pl. Colloq.* the metal shutter controls on the front of lights used for filming.

**barney** /ˈbani/, *Colloq.* *–n.* **1.** an argument; fight. **2.** humbug; cheating. **3.** an unfair contest or prizefight. **4.** a spree. *–v.i.* **5.** to argue; fight. [Brit. d.]

**barn owl** /ˈban aʊl/, *n.* a predatory, nocturnal bird, *Tyto alba,* having light brown and white plumage, and commonly frequenting barns, where it destroys mice.

barn owl

**barnstorm** /ˈbanstɔm/, *v.i.* **1.** to conduct a vigorous and impressive political campaign in rural regions, making many stops and frequent speeches: *both candidates went barnstorming for the farm vote.* –*v.t.* **2.** to canvass (a region or group) by such a campaign: *the candidate barnstormed New South Wales.* [orig. US theatrical colloq., to take a show through rural districts; lit. to storm the barns] – **barnstormer,** *n.* – **barnstorming,** *adj.*

**barn swallow** /ˈban swɒloʊ/, *n.* →**swallow**[2] (def. 1).

**barnyard** /ˈbanjad/, *n.* **1.** a yard next to a barn. –*adj.* **2.** found in a barnyard. **3.** appropriate to a barnyard: *barnyard behaviour.*

**barnyard grass** /ˈ– gras/, *n.* any species of the genus *Echinochloa,* such as *E. crusgalli,* now widespread as a weed in warmer countries, esp. in areas of rice cultivation.

**baro-,** a word element meaning 'weight', 'pressure', as in *barogram.* [combining form representing Gk *báros* weight]

**bar of the house,** *n.* in a house of parliament, a bar or rail opposite the presiding officer's chair, dividing from the body of the house a space to which non-members may be admitted for business purposes.

**barogram** /ˈbærəgræm/, *n.* a record traced by a barograph or similar instrument.

**barograph** /ˈbærəgræf/, *n.* an automatic recording barometer. – **barographic** /bærəˈgræfɪk/, *adj.*

**barolo** /bəˈroʊloʊ/, *n.* a highly regarded red wine made in the district of Barolo in Italy.

**barometer** /bəˈrɒmətə/, *n.* **1.** an instrument for measuring atmospheric pressure, thus determining height, weather changes, etc. **2.** anything that indicates changes: *the barometer of public opinion.* – **barometric** /bærəˈmɛtrɪk/, *adj.* **barometrical,** *adj.* – **barometrically,** *adv.* – **barometry,** *n.*

**baron** /ˈbærən/, *n.* **1.** a man holding a peerage of the lowest titular rank. **2.** a feudal tenant-in-chief holding lands directly from a king. **3.** a rich and powerful man; magnate: *a squatter baron.* **4.** →**baron of beef.** [ME from OF, from ML *barō* man, free man, vassal]

**baronage** /ˈbærənɪdʒ/, *n.* **1.** the whole body of barons. **2.** →**barony.**

**baroness** /ˈbærənɛs/, *n.* **1.** the wife of a baron. **2.** a lady holding a baronial title in her own right.

**baronet** /ˈbærənət, -nɛt/, *n.* a member of a British hereditary order of honour, ranking below the barons and made up of commoners, designated by *Sir* before the name, and *Baronet,* usually abbreviated *Bart.,* after: *Sir Thomas Mitchell, Bart.*

**baronetage** /ˈbærənətɪdʒ/, *n.* **1.** the order of baronets; baronets collectively. **2.** →**baronetcy.**

**baronetcy** /ˈbærənətsi, -ˈnɛtsi/, *n., pl.* **-cies.** the rank or patent of a baronet.

**barong** /bəˈrɒŋ/, *n.* a large broad-bladed knife or cleaver used by the Moros of the Philippines. [native name probably akin to Malay *Parang*]

**baronial** /bəˈroʊniəl/, *adj.* **1.** pertaining to a baron, a barony, or to the order of barons. **2.** befitting a baron; grand.

**baron of beef,** *n.* a joint of beef consisting of the two sirloins joined at the backbone.

**barony** /ˈbærəni/, *n., pl.* **-nies. 1.** the rank or dignity of a baron. **2.** the domain of a baron. [ME *baronie,* from OF, from *baron* BARON]

**baroque** /bəˈrɒk, bəˈroʊk/, *adj.* **1.** *Art.* of or pertaining to a style developed in Italy in the 16th century, characterised by the use of asymmetry, florid illusionism, direct imagery and lavish ornamentation. **2.** *Music.* of or pertaining to the ornate style of composition of the 17th and early 18th centuries. **3.** extravagantly ornamented. –*n.* **4.** the baroque style or period. **5.** a work in the baroque style. [F, from Pg. *barroco* irregular]

**baroscope** /ˈbærəskoʊp/, *n.* an instrument showing roughly the variations in atmospheric pressure. – **baroscopic** /bærəˈskɒpɪk/, *adj.*

**barostat** /ˈbærəstæt/, *n.* a device for maintaining a constant pressure, esp. in aircraft, to compensate for variation of atmospheric pressure with altitude.

**barotrauma** /bærəˈtrɔmə/, *n. Med.* injury to the eardrum or Eustachian tube caused by difference between atmospheric and intratympanic pressure.

**barouche** /bəˈruʃ/, *n.* a four-wheeled carriage having a seat outside for the driver, seats inside for two couples facing each other and a folding hood. [G *Barutsche,* from It. *biroccio,* from L *birotus* two-wheeled]

barouche

**barque** /bak/, *n.* **1.** *Naut.* a sailing vessel having three or more masts, square-rigged on all but the aftermost mast, which is fore-and-aft rigged. **2.** *Poetic.* any boat or sailing vessel. Also, **bark.** [ME; from LL *barca*]

**barquentine** /ˈbakəntin/, *n. Naut.* a sailing vessel having three or more masts, square-rigged on the foremast and fore-and-aft rigged on the other masts. Also, **barquantine, barkentine.** [BARQUE + (BRIGA)NTINE]

barque

**barra** /ˈbærə/, *n. Colloq.* a barramundi.

**barrack**[1] /ˈbærək/, *n.* (*usu. pl.*) **1.** a building or range of buildings for lodging soldiers, esp. in garrison. **2.** any large, plain building in which many people are lodged. –*v.t.* **3.** to lodge in barracks. [F *baraque,* from It. *baracca;* orig. uncert.]

**barrack**[2] /ˈbærɪk/, *v.i.* to support; shout encouragement and approval (fol. by *for*). [? N. Ireland d. *barrack* to brag, boast of fighting powers] – **barracker,** *n.*

**barrack**[3] /ˈbærɪk/, *v.i.* to jeer, shout derisively at (a player, team, etc.). [Aboriginal *barak* (a negative)] – **barracker,** *n.*

**barracouta** /bærəˈkutə/, *n.* **1.** Also, **couta.** an elongated, cold water, sport and food fish of genus *Leionura,* widespread in southern seas. **2.** *N.Z. Colloq.* a long, raised bread loaf. [from BARRACUDA]

**barracuda** /bærəˈkudə/, *n.* **1.** Also, **sea-pike.** any of various species of elongated, predacious, tropical and sub-tropical marine fishes of the family Sphyraenidae, some of which are used extensively for food. **2.** *N.Z. Colloq.* a long, raised bread loaf. [Sp., from W. Ind.]

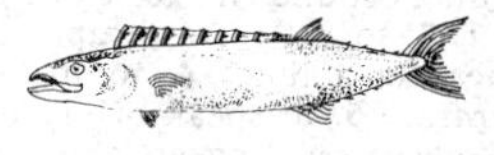

barracuda

**barrage** /ˈbæraʒ, -adʒ/, *n., v.,* **-raged, -raging.** –*n.* **1.** *Mil.* a barrier of artillery fire used to prevent the enemy from advancing, to enable troops behind it to operate with a minimum of casualties, or to cut off the enemy's retreat in one or more directions. **2.** any similar defensive device, as a balloon barrage. **3.** any overwhelming quantity: *a barrage of questions.* **4.** *Civ. Eng.* an artificial obstruction in a watercourse to increase the depth of the water, facilitate irrigation, etc. **5.** *Fencing.* a tie in a bout. –*v.t.* **6.** to cut off by or subject to a barrage. [F, from *barrer,* v., bar. Cf. F phrase *tir de barrage* barrage fire]

**barrage balloon** /ˈ– bəlun/, *n.* a balloon used in a balloon barrage.

**barrage rocket** /ˈ– rɒkət/, *n. Mil.* a combined blast and fragmentation weapon designed for firing from ship to shore in amphibious attack.

**barramundi** /bærəˈmʌndi/, *n.* **1.** →**giant perch. 2.** Also, **saratoda, saratoga.** a primitive freshwater fish of genus *Scleropages.* [Aboriginal]

**barrator** /ˈbærətə/, *n.* one who commits barratry. Also, **barrater.** [ME *baratour,* from OF *barateor* fraudulent dealer, from *barater* exchange, cheat]

**barratry** /ˈbærətri/, *n. Law.* **1.** fraud by a master or crew at the expense of the owners of the ship or its cargo. **2.** the offence of frequently exciting and stirring up suits and quarrels. **3.** the purchase or sale of ecclesiastical preferments or of offices of state. [ME *barratrie,* from OF *barateric.* See BARRATOR] – **barratrous,** *adj.* – **barratrously,** *adv.*

**barred** /bad/, *adj.* **1.** provided with one or more bars: *a barred gate.* **2.** striped; streaked: *barred fabrics.*

**barred bandicoot** /– ˈbændikut/, *n.* a long-nosed bandicoot, *Perameles bougainville,* of arid areas of southern Australia, having faint bars across the hindquarters; marl.

**barrel**[1] /ˈbærəl/, *n.*, *v.*, **-relled, -relling,** or (U.S.) **-reled, -reling.** *–n.* **1.** a wooden cylindrical vessel made of staves hooped together, and having slightly bulging sides and flat parallel ends. **2.** a unit of quantity in the imperial system, equal to $159.11315 \times 10^{-3}$ $m^3$, and in the U.S., to $158.9873 \times 10^{-3}$ $m^3$. **3.** any vessel, case, or part similar in form. **4.** the tube of a gun. **5.** *Bldg Trades.* (*usu. pl.*) that part of a pipe through which the bore and the wall thickness remain uniform. **6.** *Mach.* the chamber of a pump, in which the piston works. **7.** *Horol.* the cylindrical case in a watch or clock within which the mainspring is coiled. **8.** *Ornith.* the hard, horny, hollow part of the stem at the base of a feather; the calamus or quill. **9.** *Naut.* the main portion of a capstan about which the rope winds. **10.** *Colloq.* →**benefit** (def. 3). **11. over a barrel,** at a disadvantage; in difficulty. *–v.t.* **12.** to put or pack in a barrel or barrels. **13.** *Colloq.* to knock over or run into (as in football): *I'll barrel the bloke.* *–v.i.* **14. barrel along,** *Colloq.* to move along swiftly and confidently. [ME *barel,* from OF *baril,* probably from *barre* bar, stave]

**barrel**[2] /ˈbærəl/, *n. Colloq.* a hat. [rhyming slang, *barrel of fat* hat]

**barrel bolt** /ˈ– boʊlt/, *n.* a sliding bolt used for fastening a door, gate or window.

**barrel-chested** /ˈbærəl-tʃɛstəd/, *adj.* having a strong, thick chest.

**barrelful** /ˈbærəlfʊl/, *n., pl.* **-fuls.** as much as a barrel will hold.

**barrel-house** /ˈbærəl-haʊs/, *n.* a style of piano playing which is an early form of jazz, characterised by left-hand riffs and elaborate right-hand improvisation.

**barrel organ** /ˈbærəl ɔgən/, *n.* a musical instrument in which air from a bellows is admitted to a set of pipes by means of pins inserted into a revolving barrel; hand organ.

**barrel vault** /ˈ– vɔlt/, *n. Archit.* a simple hemicylindrical vault.

**barren** /ˈbærən/, *adj.* **1.** incapable of producing, or not producing, offspring; sterile: *a barren woman.* **2.** unproductive; unfruitful: *barren land.* **3.** destitute of interest or attraction. **4.** mentally unproductive; dull; stupid. **5.** not producing results; fruitless: *a barren pen.* **6.** lacking (usu. fol. by *of*): *barren of feeling.* **7.** (*usu. pl.*) *U.S.* relatively infertile, level or slightly rolling land, usu. having sandy soil and few trees. [ME *barein,* from OF *baraine,* of pre-L orig.] **– barrenly,** *adv.* **– barrenness,** *n.*

**barricade** /ˈbærəkeɪd, bærəˈkeɪd/, *n., v.,* **-caded, -cading.** *–n.* **1.** a defensive barrier hastily constructed, as in a street, to stop an enemy. **2.** any barrier or obstruction to passage: *a barricade of rubbish.* *–v.t.* **3.** to obstruct or block with a barricade. **4.** to shut in and defend with or as with a barricade. [F, probably from Pr. *barricada* a barricade, orig. made of casks filled with earth, from *barrica* cask] **– barricader,** *n.*

**barrier** /ˈbæriə/, *n.* **1.** anything built or serving to bar passage, as a stockade or fortress, or a railing. **2.** any natural bar or obstacle: *a mountain barrier.* **3.** anything that restrains or obstructs progress, access, etc.: *a trade barrier.* **4.** a limit or boundary of any kind: *the barriers of caste.* **5.** (*oft. cap.*) *Phys. Geog.* the portion of the polar icecap of Antarctica extending many kilometres out beyond land, and resting in places on the ocean bottom. **6.** *Oceanog.* a bar formed offshore by the action of waves and currents, separated from the mainland by lagoons or marshes. **7.** *Horseracing.* a gate which keeps horses in line before the start of a race. **8.** (*pl.*) the palisades or railing surrounding the ground where tourneys and jousts were carried on. [ME *barrere,* from AF, from *barre* bar]

**barrier cream** /ˈ– krim/, *n.* a cream with a silicon base to protect hands from water and other substances that might damage or soil them.

**barrier reef** /– ˈrif/, *n.* a long narrow ridge of coral close to or above the surface of the sea off the coast of a continent or island.

**barrier stall** /ˈ– stɔl/, *n. Horseracing.* a stall attached to the barrier in which horses are positioned for the start of a race.

**barrier trial** /ˈ– traɪəl/, *n.* a trial horse race started from the barrier stalls and used to educate or condition horses, and to test their racing capacities.

**barring** /ˈbarɪŋ/, *prep.* excepting; except for: *barring accidents, I'll be there.*

**barringtonia** /bærɪŋˈtoʊniə/, *n.* a tree, *Barringtonia asiatica,* of tropical sea beaches in Asia, tropical Australia and the western Pacific. The hard fruit and seeds are often found on eastern Australian beaches.

**barrio** /ˈbærioʊ/, *n., pl.* **-rios. 1.** (in Spain and countries colonised by Spain) one of the divisions into which a town or city, together with the contiguous rural territory is divided. **2.** *U.S.* a Spanish-speaking neighbourhood in a city. [t. Sp.]

**barrister**[1] /ˈbærəstə/, *n.* a lawyer admitted to plead at the bar in any court. [*barri-* (combining form of BAR[1]) + -STER]

**barrister**[2] /ˈbærəstə/, *n.* a tropical climber, *Mezoneurum scortechinii,* of eastern Australia, with strong recurved prickles.

**barrister-at-law** /ˌbærəstər-ət-ˈlɔ/, *n., pl.* **barristers-at-law.** barrister (chiefly as a formal title).

**barrow**[1] /ˈbæroʊ/, *n.* **1.** a pushcart or horsedrawn cart used by street vendors, esp. those selling fruit and vegetables. **2.** →**wheelbarrow. 3.** →**handbarrow** (def. 1). **4. push one's barrow,** *Colloq.* to campaign vigorously in one's own interest. **5. push someone's barrow,** *Colloq.* to take up someone's cause for them. [ME *barewe,* OE *Bearwe;* probably akin to OE *beran* BEAR[1], *v.* ]

**barrow**[2] /ˈbæroʊ/, *n.* **1.** an ancient or prehistoric burial mound; a tumulus. **2.** a hill (now chiefly in placenames). [ME *berwe,* OE *beorg* hill, mound, c. G *Berg* hill, mountain]

**barrow**[3] /ˈbæroʊ/, *n.* a castrated male pig. [ME *barow,* OE *bearg*]

**barrow**[4] /ˈbæroʊ/, *v.i.* (of a shedhand who is learning to become a shearer) to finish shearing a sheep left partly shorn by a shearer at the end of a shearing run. **– barrower,** *n.* **– barrowing,** *n.* **– barrowman,** *n.*

**barrowman** /ˈbæroʊmæn/, *n.* a man who sells fruit and vegetables from a barrow or cart.

**barsac** /baˈsæk/, *n.* a highly regarded sweet white table wine made in the Bordeaux district of France. [named after *Barsac,* a town in the district where this wine is made]

**bar sinister** /ba ˈsɪnəstə/, *n.* **1.** *Her.* (erroneously) a baton or a bend sinister. **2.** the implication or proof of bastard birth.

**bart** /bat/, *n. Colloq. Obs.* a girl. [orig. unknown]

**Bart.,** Baronet.

**bartender** /ˈbatɛndə/, *n.* →**barman.**

**barter** /ˈbatə/, *v.i.* **1.** to trade by exchange of commodities rather than by the use of money. *–v.t.* **2.** to exchange in trade as one commodity for another; trade. **3.** to bargain away unwisely or dishonourably (fol. by *away*). *–n.* **4.** the act of bartering. **5.** the thing bartered. [ME *bartre,* frequentative of obs. *barrat,* v., from OF *barater* exchange, cheat. Cf. BARRATOR] **– barterer,** *n.*

**bartizan** /batəˈzæn, ˈbatəzən/, *n. Archit.* a small overhanging turret on a wall or tower. [alteration of BRATTISHING] **– bartizaned,** *adj.*

bartizan

**Bartlett** /ˈbatlət/, *n.* a large, yellow, juicy variety of pear. Also, **Bartlett pear.** [named by Enoch *Bartlett* (1779-1860), American merchant]

**bar useful** /ba ˈjusfəl/, *n.* an unskilled assistant who works in a hotel, esp. behind the bar. Also, **useful.**

**barycentre** /ˈbærisɛntə/, *n.* →**centre of mass.** [Gk *barýs* heavy + CENTRE]

**barye** /ˈbæri/, *n.* a unit of pressure equal to one dyne per square centimetre.

**baryon** /ˈbæriən/, *n.* one of the group of elementary particles consisting of nucleons and hyperons.

**barysphere** /ˈbærəsfɪə/, *n.* →**centrosphere** (def. 2). [Gk *barýs* heavy + SPHERE]

**baryta** /bəˈraɪtə/, *n.* **1.** barium oxide, BaO. **2.** barium (in phrases): *carbonate of baryta.* [see BARYTES] **– barytic** /bəˈrɪtɪk/, *adj.*

**barytes** /bəˈraɪtiz/, *n.* a common mineral, barium sulphate, $BaSO_4$, the principal ore of barium, occurring in tabular crystals; heavy spar. [Gk: weight]

**barytone**[1] /ˈbærətoʊn/, *n.* **1.** Also, **baryton.** a form of bass viol having sympathetic strings. **2.** →**baritone.** *–adj.* **3.** →**baritone.**

**barytone**[2] /ˈbærətoʊn/, *adj.* **1.** (in classical Greek) having a grave accent on the last syllable. *–n.* **2.** a barytone word. [Gk *barýtonos*]

**basal** /ˈbeɪsəl/, *adj.* **1.** of, at, or forming the base. **2.** fundamental: *basal characteristics.* **3.** *Physiol.* **a.** indicating a standard level of activity of an organism as present during total rest. **b.** of an amount required to maintain this level. **– basally,** *adv.*

**basal metabolic rate** *n.* the rate of oxygen intake and heat discharge in an organism in a basal state.

**basal metabolism** /ˌbeɪsəl məˈtæbəlɪzəm/, *n.* the energy turnover of an organism during total rest.

**basalt** /ˈbæsɔlt/, *n.* the dark, dense igneous rock of a lava flow or minor intrusion, composed essentially of plagioclase and pyroxene, and often displaying a columnar structure. [L *basaltes* a dark, hard marble of Ethiopia] **– basaltic** /bəˈsɔltɪk/, *adj.*

**basaltware** /ˈbæsəltwɛə/, *n.* unglazed stoneware developed by Josiah Wedgwood, usu. black, with a dull gloss.

**bascule** /ˈbæskjul/, *n.* a device operating like a balance or seesaw, esp. an arrangement of a movable bridge (**bascule bridge**) by which the rising floor or section is counterbalanced by a weight. [F: a seesaw, replacing *bacule,* apparently from *ba(ttre)* strike + *cul* the posterior]

**base**[1] /beɪs/, *n., v.t.,* **based, basing.** *–n.* **1.** the bottom of anything, considered as its support; that on which a thing stands or rests. **2.** a fundamental principle or groundwork; foundation; basis. **3.** *Archit.* **a.** the part of a column on which the shaft immediately rests. **b.** the lowest member of a wall or monument. **c.** the lower elements of a complete structure. **4.** *Biol.* **a.** the part of an organ nearest its point of attachment. **b.** the point of attachment. **5.** the principal element or ingredient of anything, considered as its fundamental part. **6.** *Baseball.* one of the four fixed stations to which players run. **7.** a starting point for competitors in a race. **8.** the goal in hockey and some other games. **9.** *Mil.* **a.** a fortified or protected area or place used by any of the armed services. **b.** a supply installation. **10.** *Maths.* **a.** the number which serves as a starting point for a logarithmic or other numerical system. **b.** the side or face of a geometric figure to which an altitude is thought to be drawn. **11.** →**baseline. 12.** *Electronics.* the part of a transistor which controls the current flow. **13.** *Chem.* **a.** any of numerous compounds which react with an acid to form a salt, as metallic oxides and hydroxides, amines, alkaloids and ammonia. **b.** the hydroxide of an electropositive element or radical. **c.** a radical or molecule which takes up or accepts protons. **14.** *Gram.* the form to which affixes are added in the construction of a complex word; root; stem. For example, *want* is the base in *unwanted.* **15.** *Her.* the lower part of a shield. **16.** *Colloq.* the buttocks. **17. not to get to first base,** *Colloq.* to fail to establish any contact or rapport (fol. by *with*). *–adj.* **18.** serving as a base. *–v.t.* **19.** to make or form a base or foundation for. **20.** to establish, as a fact or conclusion (fol. by *on* or *upon*). **21.** to place or establish on a base or basis; ground; found; establish. [ME, from OF, from L *basis,* from Gk: a stepping, a step, pedestal, base]

**base**[2] /beɪs/, *adj.,* **baser, basest,** *n. –adj.* **1.** morally low; without dignity of sentiment; mean-spirited; selfish; cowardly. **2.** characteristic of an inferior person or thing. **3.** of little value: *the base metals.* **4.** debased or counterfeit: *base coin.* **5.** of illegitimate birth. **6.** *Old Eng. law.* (of an estate or tenant) not held or holding by honourable tenure. **7.** not classical or refined: *base language.* **8.** deep or grave in sound; bass: *the base tones of a piano.* **9.** *Archaic.* of humble origin or station. **10.** *Archaic.* of small height. **11.** *Archaic.* low in position or degree. *–n.* **12.** *Music. Obs.* →**bass**[1]. [ME, from OF *bas,* from LL *bassus* low] **– basely,** *adv.* **– baseness,** *n.*

**baseball** /ˈbeɪsbɔl/, *n.* **1.** a game played with a wooden bat and a hard ball, by two opposing teams of nine players, each team batting and fielding alternately, and each batter having to run a course of four bases laid out in a diamond pattern in order to score. **2.** the ball used in playing this game.

**baseboard** /ˈbeɪsbɔd/, *n.* **1.** a board forming the base of anything. **2.** *U.S.* →**skirting board.**

**baseborn** /ˈbeɪsbɔn/, *adj.* **1.** of humble birth. **2.** born out of wedlock. **3.** base-natured; mean.

**base component** /ˈbeɪs kəmpoʊnənt/, *n.* (in transformational grammar) the rule-system which specifies the deep structure.

**base course material,** *n.* material used as a foundation, as for a road, before the finishing or sealing surface is applied.

**base hospital** /ˈbeɪs hɒspətəl/, *n.* a hospital, usu. in a rural area, to which smaller hospitals in the district refer patients for whom their facilities are not adequate.

**baseless** /ˈbeɪsləs/, *adj.* having no base; without foundation; groundless: *a baseless claim.*

**base level** /ˈbeɪs lɛvəl/, *n.* the lowest level to which running water can theoretically erode the land.

**baseline** /ˈbeɪslaɪn/, *n.* **1.** *Survey.* an accurately measured line forming one side of a triangle or system of triangles from which all other sides are computed. **2.** *Tennis.* a line at the end of the court. **3.** *Baseball.* a line joining bases. **4.** a line at the base of anything.

**basement** /ˈbeɪsmənt/, *n.* **1.** a storey of a building partly or wholly underground. **2.** the portion of a structure which supports those portions which come above it. **3.** the substructure of a columnar or arched construction. **4.** *Geol.* **a.** →**basement complex. b.** an underlying complex of rocks that behaves as a unit mass and is not deformed during folding of the overlying material.

**basement complex** /– ˈkɒmplɛks/, *n.* a series of metamorphic and igneous rocks, often of Pre-Cambrian age, underlying dominantly sedimentary rocks. Also, **basement rock.**

**basenji** /bəˈsɛndʒi/, *n.* a small smooth-haired dog of an African breed, having a chestnut or black coat, characterised by its inability to bark. [Lingala (a Bantu language of the Congo): from the bush, from Swahili *washenzi* savage, worthless]

basenji

**base over apex,** *adv. Colloq.* fallen heavily and awkwardly, usu. in a forward direction. Also, **arse over apex.**

**bases**[1] /ˈbeɪsiz/, *n.* plural of **basis.**

**bases**[2] /ˈbeɪsəz/, *n.* plural of **base**[1].

**base wallah** /ˈbeɪs wɒlə/, *n. Colloq.* a member of the armed services employed on a military base. [BASE[1] (def. 9) + WALLAH]

**base walloper** /ˈ– wɒləpə/, *N.Z. Colloq.* a member of the armed services employed on a military base. [b. BASE WALLAH + WALLOPER, pun on *base* arse]

**bash** /bæʃ/, *v.t.* **1.** to strike with a crushing or smashing blow. *–n.* **2.** a crushing blow. **3.** *Colloq.* a drinking spree. **4. bash one's brains out,** *Colloq.* to expend a great deal of effort in intellectual activity. **5. give it a bash,** *Colloq.* **a.** to make an attempt. **b.** to go on a drinking spree. **6. have a bash,** *Colloq.* make an attempt (often fol. by *at*). *–interj.* **7. bash it,** *Colloq.* (an exclamation of contempt, disgust, etc.)

**bashaw** /bəˈʃɔ/, *n.* **1.** →**pasha. 2.** *Obs.* an important personage; bigwig. [Turk: *bāsha,* var. *pāsha* PASHA]

**bashful** /ˈbæʃfəl/, *adj.* **1.** uncomfortably diffident or shy; timid and easily embarrassed. **2.** indicative of, accompanied with, or proceeding from bashfulness. [obs. *bash,* v. (aphetic var. of ABASH) + -FUL] **– bashfully,** *adv.* **– bashfulness,** *n.*

**bash hat** /ˈbæʃ hæt/, *n. Colloq.* a safety helmet; hard hat.

**bashibazouk** /bæʃibəˈzuk/, *n.* one of a class of irregular mounted troops in the 19th century Turkish military service. [Turk. *bashi-bozuq* irregular soldier, lit., wrongheaded]

**basic** /ˈbeɪsɪk/, *Chiefly U.S.* /ˈbæsɪk/ *adj.* **1.** of, pertaining to, or forming a base; fundamental: *a basic principle, ingredient, etc.* **2.** *Chem.* **a.** pertaining to, of the nature of, or containing a base. **b.** not having all of the hydroxyls of the base replaced by the acid radical, or having the metal or its equivalent united partly to the acid radical and partly to oxygen. **c.** alkaline. **3.** *Metall.* denoting, pertaining to, or made by a steelmaking process in which the furnace is lined with a basic or non-siliceous material, principally burnt magnesite and a small amount of ground basic slag, to aid in sintering. **4.** (of rocks) having relatively little silica. **5.** *Mil.* **a.** primary: *basic training.* **b.** *U.S.* receiving basic training: *a basic airman.* *–n.* **6.** something that is basic or essential. **7.** (*pl.*) **back to basics,** back to first principles; back to the origins.

**BASIC** /ˈbeɪsɪk/, *n.* a relatively simple computer language for both numerical and non-numerical applications. Also, **Basic.** [*B*(*eginner's*) *A*(*ll-purpose*) *S*(*ymbolic*) *I*(*nstruction*) *C*(*ode*)]

**basically** /ˈbeɪsɪkli/, *adv.* fundamentally.

**Basic English** /ˌbeɪsɪk ˈɪŋglɪʃ/, *n.* a simplified English with a restricted vocabulary, intended as an international auxiliary language and for use in teaching English.

**basicity** /beɪˈsɪsəti/, *n. Chem.* **1.** the state of being a base. **2.** the power of an acid to react with bases, dependent on the number of replaceable hydrogen atoms of the acid.

**basic slag** /beɪsɪk ˈslæg/, *n.* non-siliceous or base-forming slag used for lining furnaces to remove impurities in pig iron during steelmaking.

**basic wage** /– ˈweɪdʒ/, *n.* **1.** the minimum wage, determined by the Arbitration Commission in some States and varied from time to time, that can be paid to an adult worker employed under an award or agreement. **2.** the specific amount of this wage.

**basidiomycete** /bəˌsɪdioʊmaɪˈsit/, *n.* a basidiomycetous organism. [NL *Basidiomycētes.* See BASIDIUM, -MYCETES]

**basidiomycetous** /bəˌsɪdioʊmaɪˈsitəs/, *adj.* belonging or pertaining to the Basidiomycetes, a large class of fungi which bear the spores on a basidium, including the smuts, rusts, mushrooms, puffballs, etc.

**basidiospore** /bəˈsɪdioʊˌspɔ/, *n.* a spore that is produced by a basidium.

**basidium** /bəˈsɪdiəm/, *n., pl.* **-sidia** /-ˈsɪdiə/. a special form of sporophore, characteristic of basidiomycetous fungi, on which the sexual spores are borne, usually at the tips of slender projections. [BAS(IS) + -IDIUM] – **basidial,** *adj.*

basidia

**basifixed** /ˈbeɪsifɪkst/, *adj.* attached at or by the base, as of anthers.

**basil**[1] /ˈbæzəl/, *n.* any of various herbs of the genus *Ocimum,* family Labiatae, of tropical and subtropical region, having aromatic leaves used in cooking, as **sweet basil,** *O. basilicum,* of tropical Asia. [ME *basile,* from OF, from L: short for *basilicum,* from Gk *basilikón* (neut.) lit., royal]

**basil**[2] /ˈbæzəl/, *n.* the finished dressed leather obtained from sheep skin.

**basilar** /ˈbæsələ/, *adj.* **1.** pertaining to or situated at the base, esp. the base of the skull. **2.** basal. Also, **basilary** /ˈbæsələri/.

**basilic** /bəˈsɪlɪk/, *adj.* **1.** kingly; royal. **2.** of a basilica. Also, **basilican** /bəˈsɪlɪkən/, **basilical.** [F *basilique,* from L *basilicus,* from Gk *basilikós* kingly]

**basilica** /bəˈsɪlɪkə, -ˈzɪ-/, **1.** an oblong building, esp. a church with a nave higher than its aisles. **2.** one of the seven main churches of Rome or another Roman Catholic church accorded certain religious privileges. [L, from Gk *basiliké,* fem. of *basilikós* royal; in ancient Rome, a large oblong building near the Forum, used as a hall of justice and public meeting place]

Christian basilica: A, apse; B, secondary apse; C, high altar; D, transept; E, nave; F, aisle

**basilic vein** /bəˈsɪlɪk veɪn/, *n.* a large vein on the inner side of the arm.

**basilisk** /ˈbæsəlɪsk, ˈbæz-/, *n.* **1.** a tropical American lizard of the genus *Basiliscus,* of the family Iguanidae, with a crest on the back of the head and along the back and tail. **2.** a kind of ancient brass cannon. [L *basiliscus,* from Gk *basilískos,* properly diminutive of *basileús* king]

basilisk

**basin** /ˈbeɪsən/, *n.* **1.** a circular container of greater width than depth, contracting towards the bottom, used chiefly to hold water or other liquid, esp. for washing. **2.** a sink; washbasin. **3.** a small circular container of approximately equal width and depth, used chiefly for mixing, cooking, etc. **4.** any container of similar shape. **5.** the quantity held by such a container. **6.** a natural or artificial hollow place containing water, esp. one in which ships are docked. **7.** *Geol.* an area in which the strata dip from the margins towards a common centre. **8.** *Phys. Geog.* **a.** a hollow or depression in the earth's surface, wholly or partly surrounded by higher land: *ocean basin, lake basin, river basin.* **b.** the tract of country drained by a river and its tributaries. [ME, from OF *bacin,* from LL *bachinus,* from *bacca* water vessel] – **basined,** *adj.* – **basin-like,** *adj.*

**basinet** /ˈbæsənət, -ˌnɛt/, *n.* a steel globe-shaped medieval military cap or helmet. [ME, from OF *bacinet,* diminutive of *bacin* BASIN]

**basinful** /ˈbeɪsənfʊl/, *n.* **1.** as much as a basin contains. **2.** *Colloq.* a superabundance of trouble, distress, etc.

**basipetal** /beɪˈsɪpətl/, *adj.* (of a plant structure) developing towards the base during growth.

**basis** /ˈbeɪsəs/, *n., pl.* **-ses** /-siz/. **1.** the bottom or base of anything, or that on which it stands or rests. **2.** a groundwork or fundamental principle. **3.** the principal constituent; a fundamental ingredient. [L, from Gk. See BASE[1]]

**bask** /bask/, *v.i.* **1.** to lie in or be exposed to a pleasant warmth: *to bask in the sunshine.* **2.** to enjoy a pleasant situation: *he basked in royal favour.* *–v.t.* **3.** *Archaic.* to expose to warmth or heat, etc. [ME *baske(n),* from Scand.: cf. Icel. *badhask,* from *badha* bathe]

**basket** /ˈbaskət/, *n.* **1.** a receptacle made of twigs, rushes, thin strips of wood, or other flexible material, woven together. **2.** a container made of pieces of thin veneer, used for packing berries, vegetables, etc.; punnet. **3.** the contents of a basket. **4.** anything like a basket in shape or use. **5.** *Bldg Trades.* a perforated metal or wire cap over the top end of a downpipe to keep out leaves. **6.** *Basketball, Netball, etc.* **a.** a short open net, suspended before the backboard, through which the ball must pass to score points. **b.** a score, counting one point on a free throw and two for a field goal. **7.** *Econ.* a list of retail goods from which the consumer price index is calculated. **8.** (*euph.*) bastard. [ME; orig. unknown] – **basketful,** *n.* – **basketless,** *adj.* – **basketlike,** *adj.*

**basketball** /ˈbaskətbɔl/, *n.* **1.** a game played by two teams of five men (or six women) each, in which points are scored by throwing the ball through the elevated baskets at the opponent's end of a rectangular court. **2.** the large round inflated ball used in this game.

**basket case** /ˈbaskət keɪs/, *n. Colloq.* a person in an advanced state of nervous tension or mental instability.

**basket chair** /– tʃɛə/, *n.* a chair made of basketwork.

**basket hilt** /ˈ– hɪlt/, *n.* an elaborate basket-like hilt of a sword, serving to cover and protect the hand.

**basketry** /ˈbaskətri/, *n.* **1.** basketwork; baskets. **2.** the art or process of making baskets.

**basket weave** /ˈbaskət wiv/, *n.* a plain weave with two or more yarns woven together, resembling that of a basket.

**basketwork** /ˈbaskətwɜk/, *n.* work of the basket kind or weave; wickerwork; interwoven work; the craft of making baskets.

**basking shark** /ˈbaskɪŋ ʃak/, *n.* a very large shark, *Cetorhinus maximus,* which frequently comes to the surface to bask in the sun.

**baso-,** variant of **basi-.**

**basophil** /ˈbeɪsəfɪl/, *n.* a cell, esp. a white blood cell, having an affinity for basic dyes. Also, **basophile** /ˈbeɪsəfaɪl/. [BAS(IC) + -O- + -PHIL] – **basophilic, basophilous,** *adj.*

**basque** /bask/, *n.* **1.** (*cap.*) one of a people of unknown origin inhabiting the western Pyrenees region of Spain and France. **2.** (*cap.*) their language, historically connected only with Iberian. **3.** a woman's close-fitting bodice, sometimes having an extension over the hips. **4.** this extension or skirt hanging from the waistline of a garment. **5.** a band of tightly knitted ribbing on the lower edge and cuffs of a jumper, cardigan, etc. [F]

**bas-relief** /ba-rəˈlif/, *n.* sculpture in low relief, in which the figures project only slightly from the background. [F, from It. *basso-rilievo* low relief]

**bass**[1] /beɪs/, *adj.* **1.** low in pitch; of the lowest pitch or range: *a bass voice, part, singer, or instrument.* **2.** of or pertaining to the lowest part in harmonised music. *–n.* **3.** the bass part. **4.** a bass voice, singer, or instrument. [var. of BASE[2] (see def. 12)]

**bass**[2] /bæs/, *n.* **1.** an Australian freshwater fish of genus *Percalates.* **2.** elsewhere, any of the spiny-finned sea-fish of the family Serranidae, or similar fish of other families. [var. of d. E *barse,* OE *bærs*]

**bass clef** /beɪs 'klɛf/, *n. Music.* the symbol placed on the fourth line of a stave to indicate that the notes are pitched below middle C; F clef.

**bass drum** /beɪs 'drʌm/, *n.* a musical instrument, the largest of the drum family, having a cylindrical body and two membranes.

**basset**[1] /'bæsət/, *n.* a long-bodied, short-legged dog resembling a dachshund but larger and heavier. Also, **basset hound.** [F, orig. diminutive of *bas* low]

basset

**basset**[2] /'bæsət/, *n., v.,* **-seted, -seting.** *–n.* **1.** an outcrop, as at the edge of a geological stratum. **2.** the shallow or rise side of a working. *–v.i.* **3.** to emerge as an outcrop. [? F: something low. See BASSET[1]]

**basset horn** /– 'hɔn/, *n.* an alto clarinet with a soft tone. [G *Bassett-horn,* from *Bassett* voice (or instrument) pitched between tenor and bass (from It. *bassetto,* diminutive of *basso* low) + *Horn,* pun on name of inventor]

**bass guitar** /beɪs gə'ta/, *n.* **1.** a four-string electric guitar which functions as a bass instrument in a rock group, replacing the doublebass. **2.** the person who plays the bass guitar.

**bass horn** /beɪs 'hɔn/, *n.* **1.** a tuba. **2.** an old wind instrument related to the serpent.

**bassinette** /bæsə'nɛt/, *n.* a basket in which a baby sleeps; Moses basket. Also, **bassinet.** [F, diminutive of *bassin* BASIN]

**bassist** /'beɪsəst/, *n.* a bass player.

**basso** /'bæsoʊ/, *n., pl.* **-sos, -si** /-si/. one who sings bass; a bass. [It., from LL *bassus* low]

**basso continuo** /– kən'tɪnjuoʊ/, *n.* →**continuo** (def. 1). [It.: lit., continuous bass]

**bassoon** /bə'sun/, *n.* **1.** a double reed woodwind instrument, the bass of the oboe class, having a wooden tubular body doubled back on itself and a curved metallic crook and mouthpiece. **2.** a reed stop on the organ having a tone resembling that of the bassoon.

**basso ostinato** /ˌbæsoʊ ɒstə'natoʊ/, *n.* →**ground bass.**

**basso profundo** /ˌbæsoʊ prə'fʊndoʊ/, *n.* **1.** a bass voice of the lowest range. **2.** a singer having such a voice. [It.: deep bass]

**basso-rilievo** /ˌbæsoʊ-rə'livoʊ/, *n., pl.* **-vos.** →**bas-relief.** Also, **basso-relievo.**

bassoon

**bass viol** /beɪs 'vaɪəl/, *n.* →**viola da gamba** (def. 1).

**basswood** /'bæswʊd/, *n.* **1.** any of the Australian species of *Tieghemopanax* and their timber. **2.** a North American linden, esp. *Tilia americana.* **3.** its wood, much used for furniture. [ME; OE *bæst,* c. G *Bast*]

**bast** /bæst/, *n.* **1.** →**phloem. 2.** the inner bark of the lime and other trees, used in making matting, etc. [ME; OE *bæst,* c. G *Bast*]

**bastard** /'bastəd/, *n.* **1.** an illegitimate child. **2.** something irregular, inferior, spurious, or unusual. **3.** *Colloq.* an unpleasant or despicable person. **4.** *Colloq.* any person (without pejorative sense). *–adj.* **5.** illegitimate in birth. **6.** spurious; not genuine; false. **7.** of abnormal or irregular shape or size; of unusual make or proportions. **8.** having the appearance of; resembling in some degree: *bastard box.* **9.** **a bastard of a thing,** *Colloq.* a terrible thing: *that's a bastard of a thing to say.* [ME, from OF: probably from *bast* pack-saddle + *-ard* -ARD, through meaning of mule; for semantic development, cf. MULATTO]

**bastard file** /'– faɪl/, *n.* a file having rough, coarse teeth.

**bastard from the bush,** *n. Colloq.* a person who is ruthlessly overbearing and who cadges shamelessly. [from a poem *The Captain of the Push* attributed to Henry Lawson, 1867-1922, Australian poet and short-story writer]

**bastardise** /'bastədaɪz/, *v.t.,* **-dised, -dising. 1.** *Archaic.* to prove or declare to be a bastard. **2.** to debase; adulterate. **3.** to seek to humiliate, as part of initiation into a regiment, college, etc. Also, **bastardize.** – **bastardisation,** *n.*

**bastardly** /'bastədli/, *adj.* **1.** *Obs.* bastard; baseborn. **2.** *Obs.* worthless; spurious; counterfeit. **3.** *Colloq.* mean; despicable.

**bastard myall** /bastəd 'maɪɔl/, *n.* any of several wattle trees, as the yarran or the raspberry jam tree.

**bastardry** /'bastədri/, *n.* obnoxious and unpleasant behaviour.

**bastard title** /bastəd 'taɪtl/, *n.* →**half-title.**

**bastard wing** /'– wɪŋ/, *n.* →**alula.**

**bastardy** /'bastədi/, *n., pl.* **-dies. 1.** condition of a bastard; illegitimacy. **2.** *Obs.* the act of begetting a bastard.

**baste**[1] /beɪst/, *v.t.,* **basted, basting.** to sew with temporary stitches, as a garment in the first stages of making; tack. [ME, from OF *bastir,* from OG; cf. OHG *bestan* sew with bast, from *bast* BAST]

**baste**[2] /beɪst/, *v.t.,* **basted, basting.** to moisten (meat, etc.) while cooking, with dripping, butter, etc. [? F; cf. OF *basser* soak, moisten]

**baste**[3] /beɪst/, *v.t.,* **basted, basting. 1.** to beat with a stick; thrash; cudgel. **2.** to denounce or scold vigorously. [Scand.; cf. Icel. *beysta* beat, thresh]

**bastille** /bæs'til/, *n.* **1.** a prison, esp. one conducted in a tyrannical way. [orig. with ref. to the *Bastille* in Paris, a fortress-prison destroyed in 1789]. **2.** a tower, as of a castle; a small fortress. [ME, from F, from *bastir* build]

**bastinado** /bæstə'nadoʊ/, *n., pl.* **-does,** *v.,* **-doed, -doing.** *–n.* **1.** a blow or a beating with a stick, etc. **2.** an oriental mode of punishment consisting of blows with a stick on the soles of the feet, or on the buttocks. **3.** a stick or cudgel. *–v.t.* **4.** to beat with a stick, etc., esp. on the soles of the feet or on the buttocks. Also, *Archaic,* **bastinade.** [Sp. *bastonada,* from *baston* stick]

**basting** /'beɪstɪŋ/, *n.* **1.** sewing with loose or temporary stitches. **2.** (*pl.*) the stitches taken, or the threads used. [BASTE[1] + -ING[1]]

**bastion** /'bæstiən/, *n.* **1.** a projecting portion of a rampart or fortification, forming an irregular pentagon attached at the base to the main work. **2.** a fortified place. **3.** any person or object which affords support or defence. [F, from It. *bastione,* from *bastire* build] – **bastioned,** *adj.*

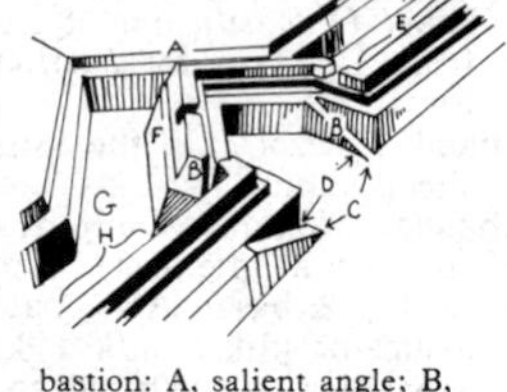
bastion: A, salient angle; B, flank; C, ramp; D, gorge; E, parapet; F, face; G, moat; H, curtain

**bastnasite** /'bæstnəsaɪt/, *n.* a fluorocarbonate of the cerium metals (CeF)$CO_3$. Also, **bastnaesite.**

**bat**[1] /bæt/, *n., v.,* **batted, batting.** *–n.* **1.** *Sport.* **a.** the club used in certain games, as cricket and baseball, to strike the ball. **b.** a racket, esp. one used in table tennis. **2.** the right or turn to bat. **3.** batsman: *he is a good bat.* **4.** a heavy stick, club, or cudgel. **5.** *Colloq.* a blow as with a bat. **6.** any fragment of brick or hardened clay. **7.** →**kip**[2]. **8.** a thin flat piece of wood with a handle used for beating flat or tenderising meat such as cutlets. **9.** *Colloq.* rate of motion: *to go at a fair bat.* **10.** *Colloq.* a spree; binge: *to go on a bat.* **11.** →**batt.** **12. carry one's bat. a.** *Cricket.* to remain at the wicket as a batsman throughout an innings. **b.** *Colloq.* to accomplish any difficult, lengthy, or dangerous task. **13.** a small length of thin wood used as an inner support for a confection: *an ice-cream bat.* **14.** a rectangular-shaped ice-cream on a bat. **15. off one's own bat,** independently; without prompting or assistance. *–v.t.* **16.** to strike or hit with or as with a bat or club. *–v.i.* **17.** *Cricket, etc.* **a.** to strike at the ball with the bat. **b.** to take one's turn as a batsman. **18.** *Colloq.* to rush. [ME *batte,* OE *batt* cudgel]

**bat**[2] /bæt/, *n.* **1.** any of the nocturnal or crepuscular flying mammals constituting the order Chiroptera, characterised by modified forelimbs which serve as wings and are covered with a membranous skin extending to the hind limbs. **2.** *Colloq.* a cranky or silly woman: *she's an old bat.* **3. have bats**

bat[2]

i = peat ɪ = pit ɛ = pet æ = pat a = part ɒ = pot ʌ = putt ɔ = port ʊ = put u = pool ɜ = pert ə = apart aɪ = buy eɪ = bay ɔɪ = boy aʊ = how oʊ = hoe ɪə = here ɛə = hair ʊə = tour g = give θ = thin ð = then ʃ = show ʒ = measure tʃ = choke dʒ = joke ŋ = sing j = you õ = Fr. bon

**in the belfry,** to have mad notions; to be crazy or peculiar. **4. like a bat out of hell,** at speed; quickly. [var. of ME *bakke,* from Scand.; cf. Dan. *-bakke*] – **batlike,** *adj.*

**bat**[3] /bæt/, *v.t.*, **batted, batting. 1.** to wink or flutter (one's eyelids). **2. not bat an eye** or **eyelid,** to show no emotion or surprise.

**batch**[1] /bætʃ/, *n.* **1.** a quantity or a number taken together; a group: *a batch of prisoners.* **2.** the quantity of material prepared or required for one operation or that quantity produced by one operation. *–n.* **3.** the quantity of bread made at one baking. **4.** *Mining.* the quantity of ore sent to the surface by a working party. *–v.t.* **5.** *Computers.* to deal with (programs, data, etc.) by batch processing. [ME *batche,* OE *gebæc* baking, from *bacan* bake]

**batch**[2] /bætʃ/, *v.i.* →**bach.**

**batch costing** /ˈbætʃ kɒstɪŋ/, *n. Comm.* a form of job costing in which a convenient unit or quantity of production is treated as a batch or job.

**batcher** /ˈbætʃə/, *n.* one who prepares batches, esp. of concrete.

**bate** /beɪt/, *v.t.*, **bated, bating. 1.** to moderate or restrain (the breath): *to wait with bated breath.* **2.** to lessen; abate. [aphetic var. of ABATE]

**bateau** /bæˈtoʊ/, *n., pl.* **-teaus** *or* **-teaux** /-ˈtoʊz/. **1.** a light boat, esp. one having a flat bottom and tapering ends. **2.** a pontoon of a floating bridge. [F; in OF *batel.* Cf. ML *batellus,* diminutive of *bat(t)us* boat, probably from OE *bāt*]

**bateleur eagle** /ˌbætələ ˈigəl/, *n.* a large African eagle, *Terathopius ecaudatus,* with white underwings. [*bateleur* from F: lit., puppeteer]

**batfish** /ˈbætfɪʃ/, *n.* **1.** any of various crescent-shaped marine and estuarine fishes of the families Platacidae and Monodactylidae. **2.** any of the flat-bodied marine fishes of the family Ogcocephalidae, as *Ogcocephalus vespertilio,* common along the southern Atlantic coast of the U.S. [BAT[2] + FISH, *n.*]

**batfowl** /ˈbætfaʊl/, *v.i.* to catch birds at night by dazzling them with a light, then taking them in a net. [probably BAT[1] + FOWL, *v.*] – **batfowler,** *n.*

**bath** /baθ/, *n., pl.* /baθs/ *or* (*esp. def. 6*) /baðz/; *v.t.* /baθ/ *–n.* **1.** a washing of the body in, or an exposure of it to the action of, water or other liquid, or vapour, etc., as for cleaning, refreshment, medical treatment, etc. **2.** water or other agent used for this purpose. **3.** a vessel for containing this, as a bathtub. **4.** a room equipped for bathing; bathroom. **5.** (*oft. pl.*) a building containing apartments for washing or bathing, or fitted up for bathing. **6.** (*pl.*) a public swimming pool. **7.** (*usu. pl.*) a town or place resorted to for medical treatment by bathing, etc. **8.** a preparation, as an acid solution, in which something is immersed. **9.** the vessel containing such a preparation. **10.** a heating or cooling apparatus by means of a surrounding medium such as sand, water, or oil. **11.** the state of being covered by a liquid: *he was in a bath of perspiration.* *–v.t.* **12.** to put or wash in a bath. [ME; OE *bæth,* c. G *Bad*] – **bathless,** *adj.*

**bath brick** /ˈ– brɪk/, *n.* a compacted mass of fine siliceous sand, used for scouring metal. [named after *Bath,* England]

**bath bun** /– ˈbʌn/, *n.* a sweet, spiced bun containing dried fruit.

**bathchair** /ˈbaθtʃɛə/, *n.* a type of invalid's wheelchair.

**bath cube** /ˈ– kjub/, *n.* a cube of cosmetic or perfumed crystals designed to dissolve in bath water to make it more pleasant, therapeutic, etc.

**bathe** /beɪð/, *v.*, **bathed, bathing,** *n.* *–v.t.* **1.** to immerse in water or other liquid for cleansing, refreshment, etc. **2.** to wet; wash. **3.** to moisten or suffuse with any liquid. **4.** to apply water or other liquid to, with a sponge, cloth, etc. **5.** to cover or surround with anything like water. *–v.i.* **6.** to take a bath. **7.** to swim for pleasure. **8.** to be covered or surrounded as if with water. *–n.* **9.** the act of bathing, as in the sea. [ME *bathien,* OE *bathian,* from *bæth* bath] – **bather,** *n.*

**bathers** /ˈbeɪðəz/, *n.pl.* →**swimming costume.**

**bathhouse** /ˈbaθhaʊs/, *n.* a house or building for bathing or one containing dressing-rooms for bathers.

**bathing beauty** /ˈbeɪðɪŋ bjuti/, *n.* **1.** an entrant in a beauty competition, esp. one in which the contestants wear swimming costumes. **2.** an especially good-looking woman. Also, **bathing belle.**

**bathing cap** /ˈbeɪðɪŋ kæp/, *n.* a close-fitting waterproof covering for the hair, worn when swimming.

**bathing suit** /ˈbeɪðɪŋ sut/, *n.* →**swimming costume.**

**bathing trunks** /ˈbeɪðɪŋ trʌŋks/, *n.* a man's swimming costume.

**bath mat** /ˈbaθ mæt/, *n.* a mat placed beside a bath or shower to prevent slipping or contact with the floor.

**batho-,** a word element meaning 'deep', as in *batholith.* [combining form representing Gk *báthos* depth]

**batholith** /ˈbæθəlɪθ/, *n.* a large body of igneous rock, bounded by irregular, cross-cutting surfaces or fault planes, and believed to have crystallised at a considerable depth below the earth's surface. Also, **batholite** /ˈbæθəlaɪt/, **bathylith.** – **batholithic, batholitic** /bæθəˈlɪtɪk/, *adj.*

**bathometer** /bəˈθɒmətə/, *n. Oceanog.* a device for ascertaining the depth of water. Also, **bathymeter.** – **bathometric** /bæθəˈmɛtrɪk/, *adj.* – **bathometry,** *n.*

**bathos** /ˈbeɪθɒs/, *n.* **1.** a ludicrous descent from the elevated to the commonplace; anticlimax. **2.** triteness or triviality in style. **3.** insincere pathos; sentimentality. [Gk: depth] – **bathetic** /bəˈθɛtɪk/, *adj.*

**bathplug** /ˈbaθplʌg/, *n.* **1.** a plug, usu. of rubber or plastic, used as a stopper to prevent water from running out of a bath. **2.** *Colloq.* bastard (def. 3).

**bathrobe** /ˈbaθroʊb/, *n.* a loose garment, often long, for wear in going to and from a bath.

**bathroom** /ˈbaθrum/, *n.* **1.** a room fitted with a bath or a shower (or both), and sometimes with a toilet and washbasin. **2. a.** a room fitted with a toilet. **b.** a toilet.

**baths** /baðz/, *n. pl.* (*sometimes construed as singular*) **1.** →**bath** (def. 6). **2.** →**bath** (def. 5).

**bath salts** /ˈbaθ sɒlts/, *n.pl.* a crystalline compound, often coloured, used to perfume or soften bath water.

**bath sheet** /ˈ– ʃit/, *n.* a large bath towel.

**bath towel** /ˈ– taʊəl/, *n.* a large towel for drying the body after a bath or shower.

**bathtub** /ˈbaθtʌb/, *n.* **1.** a tub to wash oneself in, esp. one forming a permanent fixture in a bathroom. **2.** *Colloq.* a bastard (def. 3).

**Bathurst burr** /bæθəst ˈbɜ/, *n.* a composite plant, *Xanthium spinosum,* with numerous hooked burrs; native to South America, but widely naturalised. [from *Bathurst,* a town in central N.S.W.]

Bathurst burr

**bathylith** /ˈbæθəlɪθ/, *n.* →**batholith.**

**bathymeter** /bəˈθɪmətə, ˈbæθəmitə/, *n.* →**bathometer.** – **bathymetric** /ˌbæθəˈmɛtrɪk/, *adj.* – **bathymetry,** *n.*

**bathyscaphe** /ˈbæθəskeɪf/, *n.* a small submarine for deep-sea exploration and research, having a spherical cabin on its underside. Also, **bathyscaph.**

**bathysphere** /ˈbæθəsfɪə/, *n.* a spherical diving apparatus from which to study deep-sea life. Also, **bathyscape** /ˈbæθəskeɪp/, **bathyscope** /ˈbæθəskoʊp/. [Gk *bathý(s)* deep + -SPHERE]

**batik** /ˈbætɪk, ˈbatik/, *n.* **1.** a method of printing cloth using a wax deposit to achieve the desired pattern. **2.** the fabric so decorated. Also, **battik.** [Malay (Javanese)]

**batiste** /bəˈtist/, *n.* a fine, delicate fabric of plain weave. [F *Baptiste,* name of the alleged first maker]

**batman** /ˈbætmən/, *n., pl.* **batmen.** a soldier assigned to an army officer as a servant.

**baton** /ˈbætn/, *n.* **1.** a staff, club, or truncheon, esp. as a mark of office or authority. **2.** *Music.* the wand used by a conductor. **3.** *Her.* a sinister ordinary cut off at each end, borne in England as a mark of bastardy. **4.** *Athletics.* (in relay racing) a metal or wooden tube, handed on by one relay runner to the next. **5.** a staff carried and twirled by a drum-major or drum-majorette. [F, replacing obs. *baston,* from OF, from LL *bastum;* orig. uncert.]

**batrachian** /bəˈtreɪkiən/, *Zool.* *–adj.* **1.** of or pertaining to the Batrachia, a term formerly applied to the Amphibia, though sometimes restricted to the salientians. *–n.* **2.** an amphibian, esp. a salientian. [Gk *bátrachos* frog + -IAN]

**bats** /bæts/, *adj. Colloq.* mad; crazy.

**batsman** /ˈbætsmən/, *n., pl.* **-men.** *Cricket, etc.* one who wields a bat or whose turn it is to bat.

**bats-wing coral-tree** /ˌbæts-wɪŋ ˈkɒrəl-tri/, *n.* a small to medium-sized tree, *Erythrina vespertilio,* found in subtropical and tropical Australia, and having red flowers and leaves resembling bat's wings.

**batt** /bæt/, *n.* a rectangular sheet of matted fibreglass, cottonwool, etc., used for insulating houses, filling quilts, etc. Also, **bat.**

**battalion** /bəˈtæljən/, *n.* **1.** *Mil.* a ground-force unit composed of three or more companies or similar units. **2.** an army in battle array. **3.** (*oft. pl.*) a large number; force. [F *bataillon,* from It. *battaglione*]

**battement** /batˈmɒ̃/, *n.* (in ballet) a movement in which one leg is extended one or more times forwards, backwards or sideways from the body. [F]

**batten**[1] /ˈbætn/, *v.i.* **1.** to become fat. **2.** to live in luxury; prosper at the expense of others (fol. by *on*). [Scand; cf. Icel. *batna* improve, from *bati* change for the better. Cf. OE *bet* better]

**batten**[2] /ˈbætn/, *n.* **1.** a light strip of wood usu. having an oblong cross-section and used to fasten main members of a structure together. **2.** *Naut.* **a.** a thin strip of wood inserted in a sail to keep it flat. **b.** a strip of wood, as one used to secure the edges of a tarpaulin over a hatchway. *–v.t.* **3.** to furnish with battens. **4.** *Naut.* to fasten (as hatches) with battens and tarpaulins (usu. fol. by *down*). [var. of BATON]

**battenburg cake** /ˈbætnbɜg keɪk/, *n.* an oblong sponge cake divided sectionally into four squares in two colours, with jam between the squares and a marzipan outer covering.

**batten holder** /ˈbætn hoʊldə/, *n.* a fixed fitting, as on a wall or ceiling, for an incandescent light bulb.

**batter**[1] /ˈbætə/, *v.t.* **1.** to beat persistently or hard; pound. **2.** to damage by beating or hard usage. *–v.i.* **3.** to deal heavy, repeated blows; pound. *–n.* **4.** *Print.* **a.** a damaged spot on the face of type or a plate. **b.** the resulting defect in print. [ME *batere(n)*; frequentative of BAT[1]]

**batter**[2] /ˈbætə/, *n.* **1.** a mixture of flour, milk or water, eggs, etc., beaten together for use in cookery. *–v.t.* **2.** to coat with batter: *battered oysters.* [late ME *bater,* n. use of BATTER[1], but cf. OF *bature* beating]

**batter**[3] /ˈbætə/, *n.* **1.** one who or that which bats. **2.** *Baseball.* the batsman.

**batter**[4] /ˈbætə/, *v.i.* **1.** (of walls, etc.) to slope backwards from the base. *–n.* **2.** the receding slope, usu. decreasing in thickness. [orig. uncert.]

**battered baby syndrome,** *n.* a syndrome of multiple, often severe injuries to a baby or young child, caused by maltreatment by one or both parents or other caretaker.

**battered sav** /bætəd ˈsæv/, *n.* a saveloy cooked in batter, often sold on a stick with tomato sauce.

**battering ram** /ˈbætərɪŋ ræm/, *n.* an ancient military machine with a heavy horizontal beam for battering down walls, etc.

**battery** /ˈbætəri, -tri/, *n., pl.* **-ries.** **1.** *Elect.* either of two chemical cells or groups of cells: **a.** one which produces electrical energy; primary cell. **b.** one which stores electrical energy; accumulator storage cell. **2.** a set or series of similar machines, parts, or the like, as a group of boilers. **3.** a group of similar items to be used together: *a battery of psychological tests.* **4.** an imposing or impressive group of people: *a battery of experts.* **5.** a large number of cages in which chickens, etc., are reared for intensive productivity. **6.** *Mil.* **a.** a parapet or fortification equipped with artillery. **b.** two or more pieces of artillery used for combined action. **c.** a tactical unit of artillery, usu. consisting of four guns together with the artillerymen, equipment, etc. **d.** the personnel or complement of officers and men attached to it. **7.** *Navy.* a group of guns on, or the whole armament of, a vessel of war. **8.** *Music.* the percussion section of an orchestra. **9.** the act of beating or battering. **10.** *Law.* an unlawful attack upon another by beating or wounding, or by touching in an offensive manner. **11.** the instrument used in battering. [F *batterie,* from *battre* beat]

**battery stick** /ˈ– stɪk/, *n.* a cylinder containing a battery used as a prod to control cattle by giving them a small electric shock.

**battik** /ˈbætɪk/, *n.* →**batik.**

**batting** /ˈbætɪŋ/, *n.* **1.** the act or manner of using a bat in a game of ball. **2.** →**batt.**

**battle** /ˈbætl/, *n., v.* **battled, battling.** *–n.* **1.** a hostile encounter or engagement between opposing forces. **2.** any extended or intense fight, struggle or contest: *the battle between sandminers and conservationists.* **3.** *Archaic.* a battalion. *–v.i.* **4.** to engage in battle. **5.** to struggle; strive: *to battle for freedom.* *–v.t.* **6.** to fight. **7.** to achieve (an advantage or goal) (fol. by *through*): *he battled his way through the surf.*

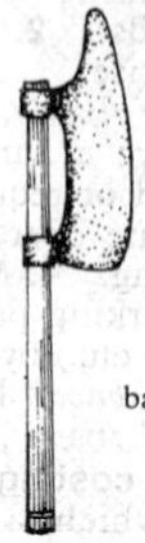

battleaxe

**battleaxe** /ˈbætəlæks/, *n.* **1.** an axe for use as a weapon of war. **2.** *Colloq.* a domineering woman. Also, *U.S.,* **battleax.**

**battleaxe block** /ˈ– blɒk/, *n.* a block or section of land, behind those with street frontages and accessible through a drive or lane. Also, **battleaxe section.**

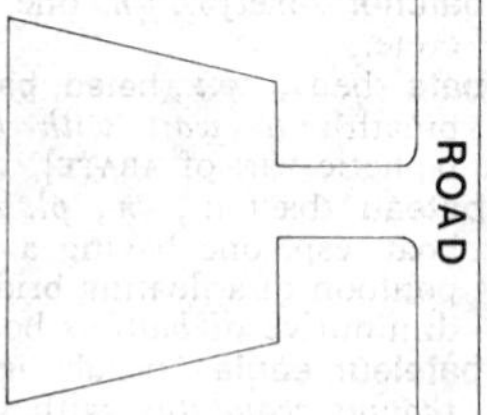

battleaxe block

**battle cruiser** /ˈbætl kruzə/, *n.* a warship of maximum speed and fire power, but with lighter armour than a battleship.

**battle cry** /ˈ– kraɪ/, *n.* **1.** a cry or shout of troops in battle. **2.** the phrase or slogan in any contest or campaign.

**battledore** /ˈbætldɔ/, *n., v.,* **-dored, -doring.** *–n.* **1.** an instrument shaped like a tennis racquet, but smaller, used in striking a shuttlecock in play. **2. battledore and shuttlecock,** the game played with this racquet and a shuttlecock. **3.** a wooden bat-shaped instrument used in washing or smoothing clothes. *–v.t.* **4.** to toss to and fro. *–v.i.* **5.** to toss (a ball) to and fro. [ME *batyldore,* ? from *bater* BATTER[1] + *dore* beetle, with dissimilation]

**battledress** /ˈbætldrɛs/, *n.* a simple, tough uniform without ornamental features, as worn by soldiers in battle.

**battle fatigue** /ˈbætl fətig/, *n.* **1.** a neurosis occurring among soldiers and resulting from the cumulative strain of active service in modern warfare. **2.** (*pl.*) →**battledress.**

**battlefield** /ˈbætlfild/, *n.* the field or ground on which a battle is fought. Also, **battleground** /ˈbætlgraʊnd/.

**battle jacket** /ˈbætl dʒækət/, *n.* **1.** the upper half of battledress. **2.** a similar garment, with front pockets, and a fitted band at the waist, usu. of corduroy or denim.

**battleline** /ˈbætlˌlaɪn/, *n.* **1.** the place where opposing ground forces are engaged in battle: *the battleline was only five kilometres away.* **2.** →**line of battle.**

**battlement** /ˈbætlmənt/, *n.* an indented parapet, having a series of openings, originally for shooting through; a crenellated upper wall. [ME *batelment,* ? from OF *bastiller* fortify] **–battlemented** /ˈbætlmɛntəd/, *adj.*

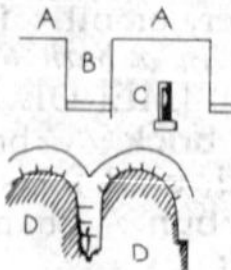

battlement: A, merlon; B, crenel; C, loophole; D, machicolation

**battler** /ˈbætlə/, *n.* **1.** one who struggles continually and persistently against heavy odds. **2.** a conscientious worker, esp. one living at subsistence level. **3.** an itinerant worker reduced to living as a swagman. **4.** *Colloq.* a prostitute.

**battle royal** /bætl ˈrɔɪəl/, *n.* **1.** a fight in which more than two combatants are engaged. **2.** a hard fight or a heated argument; a fight to the finish.

**battle-scarred** /ˈbætl-skad/, *adj.* bearing scars or damages received in battle.

**battleship** /ˈbætlʃɪp/, *n.* one of a class of warships which are the most heavily armoured and equipped with the most powerful batteries.

**battue** /bæˈtu/, *n.* **1.** *Hunting.* **a.** the beating or driving of game from cover, to be killed by sportsmen. **b.** a hunt of this kind. **2.** indiscriminate slaughter of defenceless or unresisting crowds. [F, properly fem. pp. of *battre* beat]

**batty** /ˈbæti/, *adj.*, **-ier, -iest. 1.** *Colloq.* crazy; silly. **2.** of or like a bat. [BAT[2] (def. 2) + -Y[1]]

**bat-wing sleeve** /bæt-wɪŋ ˈsliv/, *n.* a widely flared sleeve.

**bauble** /ˈbɔbl/, *n.* **1.** a cheap piece of ornament; trinket. **2.** a jester's staff. [ME *babel,* from OF: toy, probably from *bel,* from L *bellus* pretty]

**bauera** /ˈbaʊərə/, *n.* a genus of shrubs endemic in Australia often cultivated for its nodding pink flowers.

**Bauhaus** /ˈbaʊhaʊs/, *adj.* of or relating to a school of design, which concentrated on the development of a functional architecture, and which synthesised the fine, applied and industrial arts in its artistic production. [G: building house, coined by Walter Gropius, founder of the Bauhaus school, Weimar, 1919]

**bauhinia** /boʊˈhɪniə/, *n.* any shrub or tree of the genus *Bauhinia,* family Caesalpiniaceae, of tropical regions, now widely cultivated for their variously coloured flowers.

**baulk** /bɔk/, *v.i.* **1.** to stop, as at an obstacle: *he baulked at making the speech.* **2.** (of horses) to stop short and stubbornly refuse to go on. **3.** *Sport.* to make an incomplete or misleading move, esp. an illegal one. *–v.t.* **4.** to place a baulk in the way of; hinder; thwart: *baulked in one's hopes.* **5.** to let slip; fail to use: *to baulk an opportunity.* *–n.* **6.** a check or hindrance; a defeat or disappointment. **7.** a miss, slip, or failure: *to make a baulk.* **8. a.** *Baseball.* an illegal move, esp. a false move by the pitcher to throw the ball when there are runners on the base. **b.** in other sports, an incomplete or misleading motion. **9.** a strip of land left unploughed. **10.** a cross-beam in the roof of a house which unites and supports the rafters. **11.** a roughly squared timber beam. **12.** a rope connecting a line of fishing nets. **13.** *Archaeol.* a strip of earth left standing between the trenches of an excavation so that a sample of the stratigraphy remains available for study until the last possible moment. **14.** *Billiards.* **a.** any of the eight panels or compartments lying between the cushions of the table and the baulk lines. **b. in baulk,** inside any of these spaces. **15.** *Croquet.* a line a short distance in from the base line and parallel to it at the top right hand or bottom left hand end of a croquet lawn, from which play may begin. Also, **balk.** [ME; OE *balca* ridge, c. OHG *balco* beam] **– baulker,** *n.*

**baulk line** /ˈbɔk laɪn/, *n. Billiards.* **1.** a straight line drawn across the table, behind which the cue balls are placed in beginning the game; string line. **2.** any of four lines, each near to and parallel with one side of the cushion, which divide the table into a large central panel or compartment and eight smaller compartments (**baulks**) lying between this. Also, **baulk.**

**Baumé scale** /ˈboʊmeɪ ˌskeɪl/, *n.* **1.** one of two hydrometer scales for measuring the density of liquids, one for liquids lighter than water, the other for liquids heavier than water. **2.** *Winemaking.* a measurement of the sugar content in grapes. [named after Antoine *Baumé* (1728-1804), French pharmacist]

**bauxite** /ˈbɔksaɪt/, *n.* a rock, the principal ore of aluminium, consisting chiefly of aluminium oxide or hydroxide with various impurities. [Les *Baux,* in southern France + -ITE[1]]

**bauxite cement** /ˌbɔksaɪt səˈmɛnt/, *n.* a quick-setting cement consisting principally of calcium aluminate, made from bauxite and lime.

**Baw-Baw berry** /ˈbɔ-bɔ ˌbɛri/, *n.* a plant, *Wittsteinia vacciniacea,* placed with some doubt in the family Epacridaceae, having broad leaves, greenish flowers and whitish fruit, found at high altitudes in Victoria. [Mount *Baw Baw,* a mountain in Victoria]

**bawd** /bɔd/, *n.* **1.** a procuress. **2.** a prostitute. **3.** *Archaic.* a pimp. [ME *bawde,* ? from F *baud* gay, from WGmc; cf. OE *bald* bold]

**bawdry** /ˈbɔdri/, *n.* **1.** promiscuous sexual behaviour. **2.** indecent or lewd talk.

**bawdy** /ˈbɔdi/, *adj.* **-dier, -diest,** *n.* *–adj.* **1.** rollickingly vulgar; lewd. *–n.* **2.** →**bawdry. – bawdily,** *adv.* **– bawdiness,** *n.*

**bawdy house** /ˈbɔdi haʊs/, *n.* →**brothel.**

**bawl** /bɔl/, *v.i.* **1.** to cry loudly and vigorously. **2.** to cry out loudly. *–v.t.* **3.** to utter or proclaim by outcry. **4.** to call (wares) for sale. **5.** *Orig. U.S.* to scold (fol. by *out*). *–n.* **6.** a loud shout; a wail; an outcry. [ME *bawl(en),* probably from ML *baulāre* bark as a dog; but cf. Icel. *baula* low as a cow] **– bawler,** *n.*

**bay**[1] /beɪ/, *n.* **1.** a recess or inlet in the shore of a sea or lake between two capes or headlands, not as large as a gulf but larger than a cove. **2.** a recess of land, partly surrounded by hills or woods. **3.** *U.S.* an arm of a prairie, extending into woods, and partly surrounded by them. [ME *baye,* from OF *baie,* from LL *baia,* of doubtful orig.]

**bay**[2] /beɪ/, *n.* **1. a.** the part of a window included between two mullions. **b.** a recessed space projecting outwards from the line of a wall, as to contain a window. **c.** a bay window. **d.** a space or division of a wall, building, etc., between two vertical architectural features or members. **2.** the aisle between parallel shelvings as in a library. **3. a.** any portion of an aeroplane set apart by two successive bulkheads or other bracing members. **b.** a compartment in an aircraft: *a bomb bay; an engine bay.* **4.** a compartment, as in a barn for storing hay. **5.** a recess or area set back from the general flow of traffic: *parking bay.* **6.** a loading bay. **7.** the forward part of a ship between decks on either side, formerly often used as a hospital. [ME, from OF *baee* an opening, from LL *batāre* gape]

bay[2]: A, window bay

**bay**[3] /beɪ/, *n.* **1.** a deep, prolonged bark, as of a hound or hounds in hunting. **2.** a stand made by a hunted animal to face or repel pursuers, or of a person forced to face a foe or difficulty: *to stand at bay, be brought to bay.* **3.** the position of the pursuers or foe thus kept off. *–v.i.* **4.** to bark, esp. with a deep prolonged sound, as a hound in hunting. *–v.t.* **5.** to beset with deep prolonged barking. **6.** to express by barking. **7.** to bring to or hold at bay. [ME *baye(n),* aphetic var. of *abay,* from OF *abaier*]

**bay**[4] /beɪ/, *n.* **1.** the European laurel, *Laurus nobilis;* sweet bay. **2.** a West Indian tree, *Pimenta racemosa,* whose leaves are used in making bay rum. **3.** any of various laurel-like trees. **4.** any of several magnolias. **5.** an honorary garland or crown bestowed for victory or excellence. [ME, from OF *baie,* from L *bāca, bacca* berry]

**bay**[5] /beɪ/, *n.* **1.** reddish brown. **2.** a bay horse or animal. *–adj.* **3.** (of horses, etc.) of the colour bay. [ME, from OF *bai,* from L *badius*]

**baya** /ˈbiwa/, *n.* a semi-spherical metal hand drum of the tabla set, used in North Indian music and played with the left hand.

**bayberry** /ˈbeɪbɛri/, *n., pl.* **-ries. 1.** any of certain North American shrubs or trees of the genus *Myrica,* as wax-myrtle *M. cerifera.* **2.** the berry of such a plant. **3.** a West Indian tree, *Pimenta racemosa,* whose leaves are used in making bay rum; pimento. [BAY[4] + BERRY]

**bayonet** /ˈbeɪnət/, *n., v.,* **-neted, -neting.** *–n.* **1.** a stabbing or slashing instrument of steel, made to be attached to or at the muzzle of a rifle. *–v.t.* **2.** to kill or wound with the bayonet. [F *baïonette,* from *Bayonne,* in France, where such weapons were first manufactured]

**bayonet cap** /ˈ– kæp/, *n.* the type of head of an electric light bulb or appliance which is held in place by two opposite pins and a spring on the terminal plates.

**bayonet grass** /ˈ– gras/, *n.* →**spaniard plant.**

**bayonet holder** /ˈ– hoʊldə/, a socket designed to receive a bayonet cap.

**bayou** /ˈbaɪju/, *n., pl.* **-yous.** *Southern U.S.* an arm or outlet of a lake, river, etc., esp. one which is stagnant or marshy. [Louisiana F, from Choctaw (Muskhogean) *bayuk* small stream]

**Bayreuth bark** /ˌbaɪrɔɪt ˈbak/, *n.* an unpleasing, declamatory way of singing, at one time associated with the music dramas of Richard Wagner. [from *Bayreuth,* town in Bavaria and scene of the Wagner festivals + BARK[1]]

**bay rum** /beɪ ˈrʌm/, *n.* a fragrant liquid used as a cosmetic, etc., esp. after shaving, prepared by distilling the leaves of the bayberry, *Pimenta racemosa,* with rum, or by mixing oil from them with alcohol, water, and other oils.

**bay salt** /ˈbeɪ sɒlt/, *n.* a coarse-grained salt obtained by the evaporation of sea water.

**bay tree,** /ˈbeɪ tri/, *n.* the European laurel, *Laurus nobilis.*

**bay trout** /beɪ 'traʊt/, *n. Vic.* →**Australian salmon.**

**bay whale** /'beɪ weɪl/, *n.* →**right whale.** [from its habit of entering bays for calving]

**bay whaling** /'beɪ weɪlɪŋ/, *n.* whaling from stations based on land.

**bay window** /beɪ 'wɪndoʊ/, *n.* **1.** a window forming a recess in a room and projecting outwards from the wall of the building. **2.** *Colloq.* a protruberant belly; paunch.

**bazaar** /bə'za/, *n.* **1.** a marketplace or quarter containing shops, particularly in the Orient. **2.** any place where miscellaneous goods are sold. **3.** a sale of miscellaneous articles, as for some charitable purpose. [F *bazar,* from Ar., from Pers.]

**bazooka** /bə'zukə/, *n.* a cylindrical rocket-launcher, an individual infantry weapon that fires a rocket capable of penetrating several centimetres of armour-plate, used to destroy tanks and other armoured military vehicles. [fanciful coinage, orig. applied to an invented musical instrument]

**B.B.A.** /bi bi 'eɪ/, Bachelor of Business Administration.

**B.B.C.** /bi bi 'si/, British Broadcasting Corporation.

**BB gun** /'bi bi gʌn/, *n.* a small airgun with a smooth bore which is designed to use BB shot; daisy gun.

**bbl,** *pl.* **bbls.** barrel.

**b-bows** /'bi-boʊz/, *n. pl.* a type of hand shears with curved handles, used for shearing sheep. Also, **bows.**

**BBQ,** barbecue.

**BB shot** /'bi bi ʃɒt/, *n.* gun shot of a particular size (about the size of a dried pea).

**B.C.** /bi 'si/, before Christ: *from 20 B.C. to A.D. 50 is 70 years.*

**B.C.E.** /bi si 'i/, **1.** Bachelor of Chemical Engineering. **2.** Bachelor of Civil Engineering.

**BCG** /bi si 'dʒi/, *n.* a strain of attenuated bovine tubercle bacilli, used in immunisation against tuberculosis. [*(b)acillus (C)almette (G)uérin*]

**bch,** beach.

**B.Ch.,** Bachelor of Surgery. [L *Baccalaureus Chīrurgiae*]

**B.Ch.D.,** Bachelor of Dental Surgery. [L *Baccalaureus Chīrurgiae Dentālis*]

**B.Ch.E.,** Bachelor of Chemical Engineering.

**B.Com.** /bi 'kɒm/, Bachelor of Commerce. Also, **B.Comm.**

**b.c.w.** /bi si 'dʌbəlju/, *n.* →**bogie cattle wagon.**

**bd,** *pl.* **bds. 1.** board. **2.** bond. **3.** bound.

**b/d,** *Accounting.* brought down.

**B.D.,** Bachelor of Divinity.

**bdellium** /'dɛliəm/, *n.* **1.** a fragrant gum resin obtained from certain plants, as of the genus *Commiphora.* **2.** a plant yielding it. **3.** a substance mentioned in the Bible, variously interpreted to mean gum resin, carbuncle, crystal, or pearl. [L (Vulgate) (Gen. 2:12 and Num. 11:7), from Gk *bdéllion,* translating Heb. *b'dōlakh;* replacing ME *bdelyum* (Wyclif)]

**bdge,** bridge.

**B.D.S.** /bi di 'ɛs/, Bachelor of Dental Surgery.

**B.D.Sc.** /bi di ɛs 'si/, Bachelor of Dental Science.

**be** /bi/, *v., pres. indic. sing.* 1 **am**; 2 **are** or (*Archaic*) **art**; 3 **is**; *pl.* **are**; *pt. indic.* 1 **was**; 2 **were** or (*Archaic*) **wast** or **wert**; 3 **was**; *pl.* **were**; *pres. subj.* **be**; *pt. subj.* 1 **were** 2 **were** or (*Archaic*) **wert**; 3 **were**; *pl.* **were**; *pp.* **been**; *ppr.* **being.** *–substantive.* **1.** to exist; have reality; live; take place; occur; remain as before: *he is no more; it was not to be; think what might have been; the wedding was last week.* *–copula.* **2.** (a link connecting a subject with predicate or qualifying words in assertive, interrogative, and imperative sentences, or serving to form infinitive and participial phrases): *you are late; he is much to blame; is he here? try to be just; the art of being agreeable.* *–auxiliary.* **3.** (used with the present participle of a principal verb to form the progressive tense (*I am waiting*), or with a past participle in passive forms, regularly of transitive verbs (*the date was fixed; it must be done*) and formerly, as still to some extent, of intransitives (*I am done; he is come*). [ME *been,* OE *beon,* from IE base *bheu-* become; now used to make inf., pres. and past participles, and pres. subj.; for pres. ind., see AM, IS, ARE[1] (from IE base *es-* exist); for pret., see WAS, WERE (from IE base *wes-* remain)]

**be-,** a prefix of western Germanic origin, meaning 'about', 'around', 'all over', and hence having an intensive and often disparaging force, much used as an English formative of verbs (and their derivatives), as in *besiege, becloud, bedaub, beplaster, bepraise,* and often serving to form transitive verbs from intransitives or from nouns or adjectives, as in *begrudge, belabour, befriend, belittle.* [OE, unstressed form of *bī* by]

**Be,** *Chem.* beryllium.

**B.E.,** Bachelor of Engineering.

**beach** /bitʃ/, *n.* **1.** the sand or loose water-worn pebbles of the seashore. **2.** that part of the shore of the sea, or of a large river or lake, washed by the tide or waves. **3.** the seaside as a place of recreation. **4. on the beach,** *Colloq.* **a.** without a job. **b.** without money. *–v.t.* **5.** *Naut.* to run or haul up (a ship or boat) on the beach. [? from OE *bece* brook, with sense 'pebbly course of stream', hence 'shingle'] **– beachless,** *adj.*

**beach ball** /'– bɔl/, *n.* a large, often inflated, brightly coloured ball for playing with on a beach.

**beach break** /'– breɪk/, *n.* **1.** surf having waves at regular intervals and breaking close to the beach. **2.** a successful ride on a surfboard.

**beach buggy** /'– bʌgi/, *n.* a light motor vehicle having tyres of wide tread for travelling over sand.

**beach bum** /'– bʌm/, *n.* one who spends most of his or her life lazing about on a beach.

**beach claim** /'– kleɪm/, *n. Mining.* gold claim on a river beach.

**beachcomber** /'bitʃkoʊmə/, *n.* **1.** one who lives by gathering articles along the beaches, as from wreckage. **2.** a vagrant of the beach or coast, esp. a white man in South Pacific regions. **3.** a long wave rolling in from the ocean.

**beacher** /'bitʃə/, *n.* **1.** a wave which carries a surfer to the beach. **2.** *N.Z.* a miner who works the black-iron sands of a beach.

**beach flea** /'bitʃ fli/, *n.* any of various small hopping amphipods (family Orchestidae) found on beaches; a sandhopper.

**beachhead** /'bitʃhɛd/, *n.* the area of lodgment which is the first objective of a military force landing on an enemy shore.

**beach hut** /'bitʃ hʌt/, *n.* **1.** a hut on or near the beach front. **2.** *Brit.* a cabin or cubicle on a seafront used for changing clothes or living in.

**beach inspector** /'bitʃ ɪnspɛktə/, *n.* one employed to police regulations on a beach with regard to costume, behaviour, etc., and also usu. to act as a life-saver; lifeguard.

**Beach-la-mar** /ˌbitʃ-lə-'ma/, *n.* →**Bislama.** Also, **Biche-la-mar.** [corruption of F BÊCHE-DE-MER lit., sea spade, from Pg. *bicho do mar* trepang, so called because this pidgin was orig. used in the trepang trade]

**beach mat** /'bitʃ mæt/, *n.* a mat made from straw, plastic, etc., on which to sit or lie while on the beach.

**beach robe** /'bitʃ roʊb/, *n.* a garment designed to cover a swimsuit, usu. made of towelling.

**beach stone curlew,** *n.* a shy, nocturnal shorebird with a mournful cry, *Burhinus neglectus,* grey-brown in colour with a white belly, a black band through a yellow eye, with white bands above and below, found on beaches in northern Australia.

**beachworm** /'bitʃwɜm/, *n.* **1.** any of various polychaetous annelids of the family Onuphidae, esp. the kingworm and the slimy, that live in sandy beaches, and can be attracted to the surface by the stimulus of food. **2.** →**giant beachworm.**

**beacon** /'bikən/, *n.* **1.** a guiding or warning signal, such as a fire, esp. one on a pole, tower, hill, etc. **2.** a tower or hill used for such purposes. **3.** a lighthouse, signal buoy, etc. on a coast or over dangerous spots at sea to warn and guide vessels. **4.** a radio beacon. **5.** any person, thing, or act that warns or guides. *–v.t.* **6.** to serve as a beacon to; guide: *the kindly light that beacons me on.* **7.** to furnish or mark with beacons. *–v.i.* **8.** to serve or shine as a beacon. [ME *beken,* OE *bēac(e)n*] **– beaconless,** *adj.*

**bead** /bid/, *n.* **1.** a small ball of glass, pearl, wood, etc., with a hole through it, strung with others like it, and used as an ornament or in a rosary. **2.** (*pl.*) a necklace. **3.** (*pl.*) a rosary. **4. say, tell,** or **count one's beads,** to say prayers and count them off by means of the beads on the rosary. **5.** any small globular or cylindrical body. **6.** a bubble rising

i = peat ɪ = pit ɛ = pet æ = pat a = part ɒ = pot ʌ = putt ɔ = port ʊ = put u = pool ɜ = pert ə = apart aɪ = buy eɪ = bay ɔɪ = boy aʊ = how oʊ = hoe ɪə = here ɛə = hair ʊə = tour g = give θ = thin ð = then ʃ = show ʒ = measure tʃ = choke dʒ = joke ŋ = sing j = you õ = Fr. bon

through effervescent liquid. **7.** a mass of such bubbles on the surface of a liquid. **8.** a drop of liquid: *beads of sweat, etc.* **9.** the front sight of a gun. **10.** *U.S.* aim. **11.** *Archit., etc.* **a.** a narrow convex moulding, usu. more or less semicircular in section. **b.** any of various pieces similar in some sections to this type of moulding. **12.** *Chem.* a globule of borax or some other flux, supported on a platinum wire, in which a small amount of some substance is heated in a flame as a test for its constituents, etc. **13.** *Metall.* the rounded mass of refined metal obtained by cupellation. *–v.t.* **14.** to ornament with beads. *–v.i.* **15.** to form beads; form in beads or drops. [ME *bede* prayer, rosary bead, aphetic var. of *ibed,* OE *gebed* prayer] – **beaded,** *adj.* – **beadlike,** *adj.*

**beadhouse** /ˈbidhaʊs/, *n. Brit.* an almshouse whose beneficiaries were required to pray for the founder. Also, **bedehouse.** [BEAD (def. 3) + HOUSE]

**beading** /ˈbidɪŋ/, *n.* **1.** material composed of or adorned with beads. **2.** narrow lacelike trimming. **3.** narrow openwork trimming through which ribbon may be run. **4.** a narrow ornamental strip of wood used on walls, furniture, etc. **5.** bead (def. 11).

**beadle** /ˈbidl/, *for def. 1,* /bəˈdɛl/ *for def. 2. n.* **1.** *Eccles.* a parish officer having various subordinate duties. **2.** Also, **bedel** or **bedell.** in universities, an official bearing a mace on ceremonial occasions, formerly one who marshalled academic processions. [south-eastern ME *bedel,* OE *bydel* apparitor, herald]

**beadledom** /ˈbidldəm/, *n.* a stupid show or exercise of authority, as by subordinate officials.

**beadroll** /ˈbidroʊl/, *n.* **1.** a list formerly used in the Roman Catholic Church of persons to be prayed for. **2.** any list or catalogue.

**beadsman** /ˈbidzmən/, *n., pl.* **-men. 1.** one who prays for another, as a duty, and esp. when paid for it. **2.** an inmate of a poorhouse. Also, **bedesman.** – **beadswoman** /ˈbidzwʊmən/, *n., fem.*

**beadwork** /ˈbidwɜk/, *n.* **1.** ornamental work made of or with beads. **2.** beading.

**beady** /ˈbidi/, *adj.,* **beadier, beadiest. 1.** beadlike; small, globular, and glittering: *beady eyes.* **2.** covered with or full of beads.

**beagle** /ˈbigəl/, *n., v.,* **-gled, -gling.** *–n.* **1.** one of a breed of small hounds with short legs and drooping ears, used esp. in hunting. **2.** a spy; man-hunter. *–v.i.* **3.** to hunt with beagles, on foot not on horseback. [ME *begle;* orig. uncert.]

beagle

**beak**[1] /bik/, *n.* **1.** the horny bill of a bird; the neb. **2.** a similar horny head part in certain animals such as the turtle, platypus, etc. **3.** *Colloq.* a person's nose. **4.** anything beaklike or ending in a point, as the lip of a pitcher or a beaker. **5.** *Bot.* a narrowed or prolonged tip. **6.** *Naut.* a powerful construction of metal, or of timber sheathed with metal forming a part of the bow of many older-type warships, for ramming an enemy's ship. **7.** *Archit.* a little pendent fillet, with a channel behind it forming a drip and preventing water from trickling down the faces of lower architectural members. [ME *beke,* from OF *bec,* from L *beccus,* of Celtic orig.] – **beaked** *adj.* – **beakless,** *adj* – **beaklike,** *adj.* – **beaky,** *adj.*

**beak**[2] /bik/, *n. Colloq.* **1.** a magistrate; judge. **2.** schoolmaster. [orig. unknown]

**beaker** /ˈbikə/, *n.* **1.** a large drinking vessel with a wide mouth. **2.** contents of a beaker. **3.** a flat-bottomed cylindrical vessel usu. having a pouring lip, used in laboratories. [var. (influenced by BEAK[1]) of d. E *bicker,* ME *biker,* from Scand.; cf. Icel. *bikarr* (? from VL **bicārium*)]

beaker

**be-all and end-all,** *n.* **1.** the final and exclusive aim; the ultimate conclusion.

**beam** /bim/, *n.* **1.** a thick, long piece of timber, shaped for structural use. **2.** a similar piece of metal, stone, etc. **3.** *Bldg Trades.* one of the main horizontal supporting members in a building or the like, as for supporting a roof or floor. **4.** *Shipbuilding.* one of the strong transverse pieces of timber or metal stretching across a ship to support the deck, hold the sides in place, etc. **5.** *Naut.* **a.** the side of a vessel, or the direction at right angles to the keel, with reference to the wind, sea, etc. **b.** the greatest breadth of a ship. **6.** the widest part. **7.** *Mach.* **a.** an oscillating lever of a steam engine, transferring the motion from piston rod to crankshaft. **b.** a roller or cylinder in a loom, on which the warp is wound before weaving. **c.** a similar cylinder on which cloth is wound as it is woven. **8.** the transverse bar of a balance from the ends of which the scales or pans are suspended. **9.** a ray, or bundle of parallel rays, of light or other radiation. **10.** the angle at which a microphone or loudspeaker functions best. **11.** the cone-shaped range of effective use of a microphone or loudspeaker. **12.** a gleam; suggestion: *a beam of hope.* **13.** *Radio, Aeron.* a signal transmitted along a narrow course, used to guide pilots through darkness, bad weather, etc. **14. on the beam. a.** on the course indicated by a radio beam. **b.** *Naut.* at right angles with the keel. **c.** *Colloq.* just right; exact; correct; in touch with the situation. **15. fly** or **ride the beam,** *Radio, Aeron.* to be guided by a beam. **16. off (the) beam, a.** not on the course indicated by a radio beam. **b.** *Colloq.* wrong; incorrect; out of touch with the situation. **c.** *Colloq.* crazy. *–v.t.* **17.** to emit in or as in beams or rays. **18.** *Radio.* to transmit (a signal) on a narrow beam. *–v.i.* **19.** to emit beams, as of light. **20.** to look or smile radiantly. [ME *beem,* OE *bēam* tree, piece of wood, ray of light, c. G *Baum* tree] – **beamed,** *adj.* – **beamless,** *adj.* – **beamlike,** *adj.*

**beam-ends** /ˈbim-ɛndz/, *n. pl.* **1.** *Naut.* the ends of a ship's beams. **2. on her beam-ends,** *Naut.* so far inclined on one side that the deck beams are practically vertical. **3. on one's beam ends,** *Colloq.* in acute distress or poverty.

**beamer** /ˈbimə/, *n. Cricket.* a full toss, usu. fast, which goes towards the batsman's head; bean-ball.

**beaming** /ˈbimɪŋ/, *adj.* radiant; bright; cheerful. – **beamingly,** *adj.*

**beam-riding** /ˈbim-raɪdɪŋ/, *n. Radio, Aeron.* the guidance of missiles along the axis of a radio beam. – **beamrider,** *n.*

**beam tube** /ˈbim tjub/, *n.* a valve as a diode in which the stream of electrons flowing to the plate is focused by the action of a set of auxiliary, charged elements.

**beamwidth** /ˈbimwɪdθ/, *n.* a measurement of the area in which a directional transmitting device is effective, commonly taken to be the angle formed by the transmitter and any two points equidistant from it, at which the power received is half the maximum value receivable at that distance.

**beamy** /ˈbimi/, *adj.,* **beamier, beamiest. 1.** emitting beams, as of light; radiant. **2.** broad in the beam, as a ship. **3.** *Zool.* having antlers, as a stag.

**bean** /bin/, *n.* **1.** the edible fruit or seed of various species of the family Papilionaceae esp. of the genus *Phaseolus.* **2.** a plant producing such seeds, used either fresh or dried. **3.** any of various other beanlike seeds or plants, as the coffee bean. **4.** *Colloq.* a coin; anything of the least value: *I haven't a bean.* **5.** *Colloq.* a head. **6. full of beans,** energetic; vivacious. **7. give (someone) beans,** *Colloq.* to berate, attack someone. **8. know how many beans make five,** *Colloq.* to be aware, be well informed. **9. a row of beans,** *Colloq.* anything significant: *it doesn't add up to a row of beans.* **10. spill the beans,** *Colloq.* to divulge information, often unintentionally. [ME *bene,* OE *bēan,* c. G *Bohne*] – **beanlike,** *adj.*

**beanbag** /ˈbinbæg/, *n.* **1.** a small cloth bag filled with beans, used as a toy. **2.** a large triangular cushion used as a chair filled with pellets of synthetic material, as expanded polystyrene, which yields to accommodate the shape of the body.

**bean-ball** /ˈbin-bɔl/, *n.* →**beamer.**

**beancurd** /ˈbinkɜd/, *n.* a jelly or paste made from beans used in Asian cookery.

**beanfeast** /ˈbinfist/, *n. Colloq.* a festivity; celebration; a lavish feast.

**beanie** /ˈbini/, *n. Colloq.* a small close-fitting knitted cap, often having a pompom or other decoration on top.

**beano** /ˈbinoʊ/, *n. Colloq.* →**beanfeast.**

**beanpole** /ˈbinpoʊl/, *n.* **1.** a tall pole for a bean plant to climb on. **2.** *Colloq.* a tall, lanky person.

**bean shoot** /ˈbin ʃut/, *n.* the very young shoot and radicle of any of certain beans, especially the mung bean or the soya bean, used in Chinese and some other Asian cookery.

**beansprout** /ˈbinspraʊt/, *n.* →**bean shoot.**

**beanstalk** /ˈbinstɔk/, *n.* the stem of a bean plant.

**bean tree** /ˈbin tri/, *n.* any of several trees bearing pods resembling those of a bean, as the catalpa and the carob tree.

**bear**[1] /bɛə/, *v.*, **bore** /bɔ/, or (*Archaic*) **bare, borne** or **born, bearing.** *–v.t.* **1.** to hold up; support: *to bear the weight of the roof.* **2.** to carry: *to bear gifts.* **3.** to conduct; guide; take: *they bore him to his quarters.* **4.** to press or push against: *the crowd was borne back by the police.* **5.** to render; afford; give: *to bear witness.* **6.** to transmit or spread (gossip, tales, etc.). **7.** to sustain without yielding or suffering injury (usually negative unless qualified): *I can't bear your scolding.* **8.** to undergo; suffer: *to bear pain.* **9.** to accept or have as an obligation: *to bear responsibility, cost, blame, etc.* **10.** to hold up under; sustain: *his claim doesn't bear close examination.* **11.** to be fit for or worthy of: *the story doesn't bear repeating.* **12.** to have and be entitled to: *to bear title.* **13.** to possess as a quality, characteristic, etc.; have in or on: *bear traces, an inscription, etc.* **14.** to stand in (a relation or ratio): *the relation that price bears to profit.* **15.** to carry in the mind: *to bear love, a grudge, etc.* **16.** to exhibit; show. **17.** to have and use; exercise: *to bear sway.* **18.** to manage (oneself, one's body, head, etc.): *to bear oneself erectly.* **19.** to conduct (oneself). **20.** to give birth to: *to bear quintuplets.* **21.** to produce by natural growth: *plants bear leaves.* **22. bear a hand,** to give assistance. **23. bear arms,** to perform military service. **24. bear out,** to confirm; prove right: *the facts bear me out.* *–v.i.* **25.** to hold, or remain firm, as under pressure (oft. fol. by *up*). **26.** to be patient (fol. by *with*). **27.** to press (fol. by *on, against, down,* etc.). **28.** to have an effect, reference, or bearing (fol. by *on*): *time bears heavily on him.* **29.** to have relevance to: *this remark bears on the subject.* **30.** to tend in course or direction; move; go: *the ship bears due west.* **31.** to be located or situated: *the headland bears due west from us.* **32.** to bring forth young, fruit, etc. **33. bear away,** to alter course away from the wind. **34. bear down, a.** *Med.* (of a woman in labour) to make a voluntary muscular expulsive effort. **b.** of a ship, car, etc., to approach, usu. at speed. **35. bring to bear,** to bring into effective operation; bring about. [ME *bere(n),* OE *beran;* akin to G *gebären* bring forth, L *ferre* bear, Gk *phérein,* Skt *bhar-*]

**bear**[2] /bɛə/, *n., adj., v.,* **beared, bearing.** *–n.* **1.** any of the plantigrade, carnivorous or omnivorous mammals of the family Ursidae, having massive bodies, coarse, heavy fur, relatively short limbs, and almost rudimentary tails. **2.** any of various animals resembling the bear, as the ant-bear. **3.** a gruff, clumsy, or rude person. **4.** (in general business) one who believes that conditions are or will be unfavourable. **5.** *Stock Exchange.* one who sells (often what he does not possess) with the expectation of buying in at a lower price and making a profit of the difference (opposed to a *bull*). **6. like a bear with a sore head,** *Colloq.* intensely irritable; grumpy. *–adj.* **7.** *Stock Exchange.* of, having to do with, or caused by declining prices in stocks, etc.: *a bear market.* *–v.t.* **8.** *Stock Exchange.* to attempt to lower the price of (stocks). *–v.i.* **9.** *Stock Exchange.* to operate in stocks for a decline in price. [ME *bere,* OE *bera,* c. G *Bär*]

bear[2]

**bearable** /ˈbɛərəbəl/, *adj.* capable of being borne or endured. **– bearableness,** *n.* **– bearably,** *adv.*

**bear-baiting** /ˈbɛə-beɪtɪŋ/, *n.* the practice of setting dogs to fight a captive bear as entertainment.

**beard** /bɪəd/, *n.* **1.** the growth of hair on the face of an adult male, sometimes exclusive of the moustache. **2.** *Zool.* a tuft, growth, or part resembling or suggesting a human beard, as the tuft of long hairs on the lower jaw of a goat, or a cluster of fine, hairlike feathers at the base of the beak of certain birds. **3.** *Bot.* a tuft or growth of awns or the like, as in wheat, barley, etc. **4.** a barb or catch on an arrow, fishhook, knitting needle, crochet hook, etc. **5.** *Print.* the part of a type which connects the face with the shoulder of the body; the neck. *–v.t.* **6.** to seize, or pull the beard of. **7.** to oppose boldly; defy. **8.** to supply with a beard. [ME *berd,* OE *beard,* c. G *Bart*] **– bearded,** *adj.* **– beardless,** *adj.* **– beardlike,** *adj.* **– beardlessness,** *n.*

**bearded dragon** /bɪədəd ˈdrægən/, *n.* **1.** →**bearded lizard. 2.** →**frill-necked lizard.**

**bearded lizard** /– ˈlɪzəd/, *n.* an agamid, dragon lizard, *Amphibolurus barbatus,* of Australia, possessing an erectable frill or beard about the neck; frilled lizard; Jew lizard. Also, **bearded dragon.**

**bearded tit** /– ˈtɪt/, *n.* →**reedling.** Also, **bearded titmouse.**

**bearded vulture** /– ˈvʌltʃə/, *n.* →**lammergeyer.**

**beard grass** /ˈbɪəd gras/, *n.* **1.** any of various tufted, hairy grasses of the genus *Chrysopogon,* found in northern central Australia. **2.** a grass with beardlike flowering spikes, *Polypogon monspeliensis,* of marshy areas near the sea.

beard grass

**beard-heath** /bɪəd-ˈhiθ/, *n.* any of a number of shrubs of the Australian genus *Leucopogon* with hairy corolla lobes.

**beardie**[1] /ˈbɪədi/, *n.* a variety of sheepdog with very long hair; bearded collie.

**beardie**[2] /ˈbɪədi/, *n.* →**ling**[1] (def. 1).

**beardy** /ˈbɪədi/, *n.* any plant of the terrestrial orchid genus *Calochilus* of Australia, New Zealand and New Caledonia, with a labellum covered with long, dense, bright red hairs; Father Christmas. Also, **beard orchid.**

beardy

**bearer** /ˈbɛərə/, *n.* **1.** a person or thing that carries, upholds, or brings. **2.** (in India and Africa, formerly) a native servant of a European. **3.** one who presents an order for money or goods. **4.** a tree or plant that yields fruit or flowers. **5.** the holder of rank or office. **6.** →**pallbearer.**

**bear garden** /ˈbɛə gadn/, *n.* **1.** (formerly) a place for keeping or exhibiting bears, as for bear-baiting. **2.** any place of tumult.

**bear hug** /ˈbɛə hʌg/, *n.* **1.** a wrestling hold in which the wrestler squeezes his opponent around the body as hard as possible. **2.** *Colloq.* a warm, powerful embrace.

**bearing** /ˈbɛərɪŋ/, *n.* **1.** the manner in which a person bears or carries himself, including posture, gestures, etc.: *a man of dignified bearing.* **2.** the act, capability, or period of producing or bringing forth: *a tree past bearing.* **3.** that which is produced; a crop. **4.** the act of enduring or capacity to endure. **5.** reference, relation, or relevance (fol. by *on*): *some bearing on the problem.* **6.** *Archit.* **a.** a supporting part, as in a structure. **b.** the contact area between a load-carrying member and its support. **7.** *Mach.* a part in which a journal, pivot, or the like, turns or moves. **8.** (*oft. pl.*) direction or relative position: *the pilot lost his bearings.* **9.** *Geog.* a horizontal angle measured from 0° to 90° fixing the direction of a line with respect to either the north or south direction. **True bearings** are referred to the true north direction, **magnetic bearings** to magnetic north (or south). **10.** *Her.* any single device on a coat of arms; a charge.

**bearing rein** /ˈ– reɪn/, *n.* a short rein attached to the saddle of a harness to prevent a horse from lowering its head.

**bearish** /ˈbɛərɪʃ/, *adj.* **1.** like a bear; rough; burly; morose; rude. **2.** *Stock Exchange.* unfavourable and tending to cause a decline in price. **– bearishly,** *adv.* **– bearishness,** *n.*

**bear market** /ˈbɛə makət/, *n. Stock Exchange.* a gloomy period of trading during and after a decline in share prices when traders consider there is little prospect of immediate recovery.

**bearnaise sauce** /ˌbɛəneɪz ˈsɔs/, *n.* a rich white sauce, made from egg yolks with lemon or vinegar, flavoured with herbs, esp. tarragon, served with meat or fish. Also, **sauce béarnaise.**

**bear's-breech** /ˈbɛəz-britʃ/, *n.* a perennial acanthaceous herb, *Acanthus mollis,* with whitish flowers, of southern Europe. Also, **bear's-breeches** /ˈbɛəz-brɪtʃəz/.

**bearskin** /ˈbɛəskɪn/, *n.* **1.** the skin or pelt of a bear. **2.** a tall black fur cap worn esp. by soldiers. **3.** a coarse, shaggy woollen cloth for overcoats.

**beast** /bist/, *n.* **1.** any animal except man, but esp. a large four-footed one. **2.** a steer or bullock raised for meat production. **3.** the animal nature common to man and non-humans. **4.** a coarse, filthy, or otherwise beastlike human. **5.** (*cap.*) *Bible.* Antichrist. [ME *beste,* from OF, from LL *besta,* var. of L *bestia*] – **beastlike,** *adj.*

**beastings** /ˈbistɪŋs/, *n.pl.* →**beestings.**

**beastly** /ˈbistli/, *adj.* **beastlier, beastliest. 1.** of or like a beast; bestial. **2.** *Colloq.* nasty; disagreeable. – **beastliness,** *n.*

**beast of burden,** *n.* an animal used for carrying loads.

**beat** /bit/, *v.,* **beat, beaten** or **beat, beating,** *n., adj.* –*v.t.* **1.** to strike repeatedly and usu. violently. **2.** to thrash, cane, or flog, as a punishment. **3.** to whisk; stir, as in order to thicken or aerate: *to beat cream, beat egg-white.* **4.** to dash against: *rain beating the trees.* **5.** to assault; cause damage to (usu. fol. by *up*). **6.** to flutter or flap: *a bird beating its wings.* **7.** to sound as on a drum. **8.** to hammer (metal) thin; flatten (usu. fol. by *out*). **9.** to forge or make by repeated blows (usu. fol. by *out*). **10.** to produce or elucidate (an idea, attitude, etc.) (usu. fol. by *out*). **11.** to make (a path) by repeated treading. **12.** *Music.* to mark (time) by strokes, as with the hand or a metronome. **13.** *Hunting.* to scour (forest, grass, bush, etc.) in order to rouse game. **14.** to overcome in a contest; defeat. **15.** to break or destroy (a habit or the like). **16.** to be superior to. **17.** to frustrate or baffle; be too difficult for: *it beats me how he survived the avalanche.* **18.** to take measure to counteract or offset: *leaving early to beat the rush hour.* **19.** to anticipate; reach or achieve (a goal) before someone else: *she beat him to the corner.* **20.** *U.S.* to swindle or cheat: *to beat someone out of five hundred dollars.* –*v.i.* **21.** to strike repeated blows; pound. **22.** to throb or pulsate. **23.** to radiate intense light or heat; glare: *the sun beat down on his head.* **24.** to fall violently: *the rain beat down on the roof.* **25.** to dash (*against, on,* etc.). **26.** to resound under blows, as a drum. **27.** to play, as on a drum. **28.** to scour cover in order to rouse game. **29.** to permit or admit of beating: *this cream won't beat.* **30.** *Physics.* to make a beat or beats. **31.** *Naut.* to make progress to windward by sailing full and by, first on one tack and then on the other. –*v.* **32.** Some special verb phrases are:

**beat about the bush,** to approach a matter in a roundabout way; avoid coming to the point.

**beat a retreat,** to withdraw hurriedly.

**beat down, 1.** to subdue; subject; overcome. **2.** to suppress or override (opposition, etc.). **3.** *Colloq.* to secure a lower price from by haggling.

**beat it,** *Colloq.* to go away; depart.

**beat off,** to repulse; thrust aside.

**beat the bounds, 1.** to define the boundaries (of a parish) by striking the ground with rods, or some other method. **2.** to delimit or define the scope, as of a topic, argument, or the like.

**beat the count,** *Boxing.* to rise from the floor of the ring before the referee has counted ten.

**beat the punch,** *Boxing.* to strike the opponent before he can land a blow.

**beat up,** to assault or damage.

–*n.* **33.** a stroke or blow. **34.** the sound made by it. **35.** a throb or pulsation. **36.** *Horol.* the stroke made by the action of the escapement of a watch or clock. **37.** a beaten path or habitual round, as of a policeman. **38.** the area of land a musterer must clear of sheep or cattle. **39.** *Music.* **a.** the audible, visual, or mental marking of the metrical divisions of music. **b.** a stroke of the hand, baton, etc., marking time division or accent for music during performance. **40.** *Pros.* the accent stress, or ictus, in a foot or rhythmical unit of poetry. **41.** *Physics.* a periodic pulsation caused by simultaneous occurrence of two waves, currents, or sounds of slightly different frequency. **42.** *Fencing.* a firm movement against the opponent's blade, made with the object of deflecting it. **43.** *Hunting.* **a.** the act of scouring for game. **b.** a shoot in which game is raised by beating. **44.** *Colloq.* a beatnik. **45.** *Colloq.* a deadbeat; loafer; sponger. –*adj.* **46.** *Colloq.* exhausted; worn out. **47.** *Colloq.* defeated. **48.** of or pertaining to the beat generation or their culture. **49.** abhorring traditional conventions of dress, behaviour, etc.; cool. [ME *bete(n),* OE *bēatan,* c. Icel. *bauta*]

**beaten** /ˈbitn/, *adj.* **1.** having undergone blows; hammered. **2.** much trodden; commonly used: *the beaten track.* **3.** defeated. **4.** exhausted.

**beater** /ˈbitə/, *n.* **1.** a person or thing that beats. **2.** an implement or device for beating something: *an egg-beater.* **3.** *Hunting.* one who rouses game from cover.

**beat generation** /ˈbit dʒɛnəreɪʃən/, *n.* members of the generation that came of age in the post World War II era, who had lost faith in Western cultural traditions and rejected traditional standards of behaviour, dress, etc., and adopted an attitude of detachment and relaxation. [claimed as coined by Jack Kerouac, 1922-69, U.S. writer]

**beat group** /ˈbit grup/, *n.* a group of performers, usu. youthful, of beat music.

**beatific** /biəˈtɪfɪk/, *adj.* **1.** bestowing blessedness or beatitude: *a beatific gesture.* **2.** blissful: *a beatific vision or smile.* [LL *beātificus*] – **beatifically,** *adv.*

**beatification** /biˌætəfəˈkeɪʃən/, *n.* **1.** the act of beatifying. **2.** the state of being beatified. **3.** *Rom. Cath. Ch.* the official act of the pope whereby a deceased person is declared to be beatified.

**beatify** /biˈætəfaɪ/, *v.t.,* **-fied, -fying. 1.** to make blissfully happy. **2.** *Rom. Cath. Ch.* to declare (a deceased person) to be among the blessed, and thus entitled to specific religious honour. [F *béatifier,* from L *beātificāre* make happy]

**beating** /ˈbitɪŋ/, *n.* **1.** the act of a person or thing that beats. **2.** the same act administered as punishment; whipping. **3.** a defeat. **4.** a pulsation or throb.

**beatitude** /biˈætəˌtjud/, *n.* **1.** supreme blessedness; exalted happiness. **2.** (*oft. cap.*) *Theol.* any one of the declarations of blessedness pronounced by Christ in the Sermon on the Mount, as 'Blessed are the poor'. [L *beātitūdo*]

**beat music** /ˈbit mjuzɪk/, *n.* pop music with a strong, insistent beat, using electronically amplified instruments.

**beatnik** /ˈbitnɪk/, *n. Colloq.* **1.** a member of the beat generation. **2.** one who avoids traditional conventions of behaviour, dress, etc.

**beat-up** /ˈbit-ʌp/, *n. Colloq.* **1.** a media story of small significance which is given spurious importance by an expanded, often sensational treatment. –*adj.* **2.** old; dilapidated: *a beat-up old car.*

**beau** /boʊ/, *n., pl.* **beaus, beaux** /boʊz/. **1.** a lover; sweetheart. **2.** a lady's escort. **3.** a dandy; fop. [ME, from OF, n. use of *beau* (earlier *bel*) handsome, from L *bellus.* See BELLE] – **beauish,** *adj.*

**Beaufort scale** /ˈboʊfət skeɪl/, *n.* a numerical scale for indicating the force or velocity of the wind, ranging from 0 for calm to 12 for hurricane, or velocities above 120 km/h. [named after Sir Francis *Beaufort,* 1774-1857, British admiral who devised it]

**beau geste** /boʊ ˈʒɛst/, *n.* a fine gesture, often only for effect. [F]

**beau ideal** /boʊ aɪˈdil/, *n.* **1.** a conception of perfect beauty. **2.** a model of excellence. [F]

**beaujolais** /boʊʒɒˈleɪ/, *n.* a wine from the region of that name in south-eastern France.

**beau monde** /boʊ ˈmɒnd/, *n.* the fashionable world. [F]

**beaut** /bjut/, *Colloq.* –*adj.* **1.** fine; good: *a beaut car.* –*interj.* **2.** Also, **you beaut!** (an exclamation of approval, delight, enthusiasm, etc.) –*n.* **3.** Also, **beauty. a.** something successful or highly valued. **b.** a pleasant, agreeable, trustworthy person.

**beauteous** /ˈbjutiəs/, *adj.* beautiful. – **beauteously,** *adv.* – **beauteousness,** *n.*

**beautician** /bjuˈtɪʃən/, *n.* a person skilled in cosmetic treatment and beauty aids.

**beautiful** /ˈbjutəfʊl/, *adj.* **1.** having or exhibiting beauty. **2.** very pleasant: *a beautiful meal.* **3.** perfect: *a beautiful example.* –*n.* **4. the beautiful,** an aesthetic or philosophical concept of beauty. – **beautifully,** *adv.*

**beautiful people** /ˈ– pipəl/, *n.* **1.** a fashionable social set of wealthy, well-groomed, usu. young people. **2.** hippies. Also, **Beautiful People.**

**beautify** /ˈbjutəfaɪ/, *v.,* **-fied, -fying.** –*v.t.* **1.** to decorate, adorn or make more beautiful: *a plan to beautify the city.* –*v.i.* **2.** *Archaic.* to become beautiful. [BEAUTY + -FY] – **beautification** /bjutəfəˈkeɪʃən/, *n.* – **beautifier,** *n.*

**beauty** /ˈbjuti/, *n., pl.* **beauties. 1.** that quality or characteristic which excites an admiring pleasure, or delights the eye or the aesthetic sense. **2.** something or someone beautiful: *the tree was a beauty to behold.* **3.** a grace, charm or pleasing excellence. **4.** *Colloq.* an excellent or remarkable example of its kind: *the fish was a beauty.* **5.** a particular advantage: *one of the beauties of this job is that I have so much spare time.* *–interj.* **6.** (an exclamation of approval, delight, etc.) [ME *beute,* from OF *beaute,* from *beau.* See BEAU]

**beauty case** /'- keɪs/, *n.* →**vanity case.**

**beauty salon** /'– sælɒn/, *n.* an establishment where hairdressing, manicuring, facials, etc. are performed. Also, **beauty parlour, beauty shop.**

**beauty sleep** /'– slip/, *n. Colloq.* sleep begun early in the night ostensibly as an aid to beauty.

**beauty spot** /'– spɒt/, *n.* **1.** a patch worn on the face or elsewhere to set off the fairness of the skin. **2.** a mole or other trifling mark on the skin. **3.** a place of scenic beauty. **4.** any spot, place, or feature of especial beauty.

**beaux** /boʊz/, *n.* a plural of **beau.**

**beaver**[1] /'bivə/, *n.* **1.** an amphibious rodent of the genus *Castor,* of Europe, Asia and North America, valued for its fur and formerly for castor, and noted for its ingenuity in damming streams with trees, branches, stones, mud, etc. **2.** its fur. **3.** a flat, round hat made of beaver fur or a similar fabric. **4.** a man's high silk hat. **5.** a heavy woollen cloth. *–v.i.* **6.** to work hard, like a beaver (fol. by *away*) [ME *bever,* OE *beofor,* akin to G *Biber*] – **beaver-like,** *adj.*

beaver[1]

**beaver**[2] /'bivə/, *n.* **1.** a piece of armour protecting the lower part of the face. **2.** →**visor** (def. 1). **3.** a full style of beard. [late ME *baviere,* from MF: orig., bib, from *bave* saliva]

B, beaver[2]

**beaverboard** /'bivəbɔd/, *n. U.S.* a light, stiff sheeting made of wood fibre and used in building, esp. for partitions, temporary structures, etc. [Trademark]

**bebeerine** /bə'bɪərin, -raɪn/, *n.* an alkaloid resembling quinine, obtained from the bark of the greenheart and other plants. [BEBEER(U) + -INE[2]]

**bebeeru** /bə'bɪəru/, *n.* →**greenheart** (def. 1). [native name in Guyana]

**bebop** /'bibɒp/, *n.* a style of jazz composition and performance characterised by dissonant harmony, complex rhythmic devices, and experimental, often bizarre, instrumental effects. Also, **bop, rebop.** [fanciful coinage] – **bebopper,** *n.*

**B.Ec.,** Bachelor of Economics.

**becalm** /bi'kam, bə'kam/, *v.t.* **1.** (*usu. in pp.*) to halt (a ship, etc.) through lack of wind. **2.** to calm.

**became** /bə'keɪm/, *v.* past tense of **become.**

**because** /bi'kɔz, -'kɒz, bə-/, *conj.* **1.** for the reason that; due to the fact that: *the game was abandoned because it rained.* *–adv.* **2.** by reason; on account (fol. by *of*): *the game was abandoned because of rain.* [ME *bi cause* by cause]

**beccafico** /bɛkə'fikoʊ/, *n., pl.* **-cos.** any of several small European birds, esp. the garden warbler, *Sylvia hortensis,* esteemed as a delicacy in Italy. [It: *becca(re)* peck + *fico* fig]

**bechamel sauce** /ˌbɛʃəmɛl 'sɔs/, *n.* a thick white sauce made by stirring hot milk or cream into a mixture of melted butter and flour, sometimes flavoured with bay leaf, nutmeg, etc. Also, **sauce béchamel.** [F., named after the creator, Louis de *Béchamel,* steward of Louis XIV]

**bechance** /bə'tʃæns, -'tʃans/, *v.,* **-chanced, -chancing,** *adv.* *–v.i.* **1.** to happen; chance. *–v.t.* **2.** to befall; happen to. *–adv.* **3.** by chance.

**becharm** /bə'tʃam/, *v.t.* to charm; captivate.

**bêche-de-mer** /bɛʃ-də-'mɛə/, *n.* **1.** an edible sea-cucumber. **2.** →**Bislama.** [See BEACH-LA-MAR]

**B.E.Chem.,** Bachelor of Chemical Engineering.

**beck**[1] /bɛk/, *n.* **1.** a beckoning gesture. **2.** *Scot.* a bow or curtsy of greeting. **3. at one's beck and call,** ready to obey one immediately; subject to one's slightest wish. [short for BECKON]

**beck**[2] /bɛk/, *n. Brit.* a brook. [ME, from Scand.; cf. Icel. *bekkr,* akin to OE *bece*]

**becket** /'bɛkət/, *n. Naut.* **1.** any of various contrivances for holding spars, etc., in position, as a short rope with a knot at one end which can be secured in a loop at the other end. **2.** a loop or ring of rope forming a handle, or the like. **3.** a fitting on a pulley block for securing a rope. [origin unknown]

**Beckmann thermometer** /ˌbɛkmən θə'mɒmətə/, *n.* a type of differential thermometer, used for measuring small changes in temperature. Also, **Bechmann thermometer.**

**beckon** /'bɛkən/, *v.t.* **1.** to signal, summon, or direct by a gesture of the head or hand. **2.** to lure; entice. *–v.i.* **3.** to make a summoning gesture. *–n.* **4.** a beckoning. [ME *bek-nen,* OE *bēcnan,* from *bēacen* sign. Cf. BEACON] – **beckoner,** *n.*

**becloud** /bə'klaʊd, bi-/, *v.t.* **1.** to darken or obscure with clouds. **2.** to make confused: *becloud the argument.*

**become** /bə'kʌm, bi-/, *v.,* **became, become, becoming.** *–v.i.* **1.** to come into being; come or grow to be (as stated): *he became tired.* **2.** to be the fate (of): *what will become of him?* *–v.t.* **3.** to befit; suit: *that dress becomes you.* [ME *become(n),* OE *becuman* come about, happen]

**becoming** /bə'kʌmɪŋ, bi-/, *adj.* **1.** attractive: *a becoming dress.* **2.** suitable; proper: *a becoming sentiment.* *–n.* **3.** any process of change. **4.** *Aristotelian Metaphys.* any change involving realisation of potentialities, as a movement from the lower level of potentiality to the higher level of actuality. – **becomingly,** *adv.* – **becomingness,** *n.*

**B.Econ.,** Bachelor of Economics.

**becquerel** /'bɛkərəl/, *n.* the SI derived unit of the activity of a radionuclide equal to a reciprocal second ($s^{-1}$). *Symbol:* Bq [named after A.H. *Becquerel,* 1852-1908, French physicist]

**bed** /bɛd/, *n., v.,* **bedded, bedding.** *–n.* **1.** a piece of furniture upon which or within which a person sleeps. **2.** the mattress and bedclothes together with the bedstead. **3.** the bedstead alone. **4.** the use of a bed for the night; lodging. **5.** matrimonial rights and duties; the union of man and woman, esp. as father and mother. **6.** any resting place. **7.** something resembling a bed in form or position. **8.** a piece of ground (in a garden) in which plants are grown. **9.** the ground under a body of water: *the bed of a river.* **10.** a piece or part forming a foundation or base. **11.** *Geol.* a sedimentary rock unit with essentially uniform composition, marked by a more or less well-defined divisional plane from its neighbours above and below. **12.** a foundation surface of earth or rock supporting a track or pavement: *a road bed.* **13.** the undersurface of a brick, shingle, slate, or tile in position. **14.** either of the horizontal surfaces of a stone in position. **15.** *Print.* the flat surface in a printing press on which the forme of type is laid. **16.** *Zool.* flesh enveloping the base of a claw. **17. a bed of roses,** an extremely pleasant situation. **18. put to bed, a.** to help (someone) to go to bed. **b.** *Print.* to lock up (formes) in a press before printing. **c.** *Colloq.* to prepare (an edition of a newspaper, etc.) for press, by working on it up to the time of going to press. *–v.t.* **19.** to provide with a bed (fol. by *down*). **20.** to put to bed (fol. by *down*). **21.** to make a bed for (a horse, cattle, etc.) (fol. by *down.*) **22.** *Hort.* to plant in or as in a bed. **23.** to lay flat, or in a bed or layer. **24.** to embed, as in a substance. **25.** to go to bed with, usu. for the purpose of sexual intercourse. *–v.i.* **26.** to go to bed (fol. by *down*). [ME; OE *bedd,* c. D *bed,* G *Bett*]

**B.Ed.,** Bachelor of Education.

**bed and board,** *n.* sleeping accommodation and meals.

**bed and breakfast,** *n.* **1.** (in a motel or the like) the provision of sleeping accommodation and breakfast. *Abbrev.:* b. & b. **2.** *Prison Colloq.* imprisonment for seven days.

**bedaub** /bə'dɔb, bi-/, *v.t.* **1.** to daub all over; besmear; soil. **2.** to ornament gaudily or excessively.

**bedazzle** /bə'dæzəl, bi-/, *v.t.,* **-zled, -zling.** to blind or confuse by dazzling.

**bedbug** /'bɛdbʌg/, *n.* a small flat, wingless, hemipterous, bloodsucking insect, *Cimex lectularius,* that infests houses and esp. beds; cimex.

**bedchamber** /'bɛdtʃeɪmbə/, *n. Archaic.* →**bedroom.**

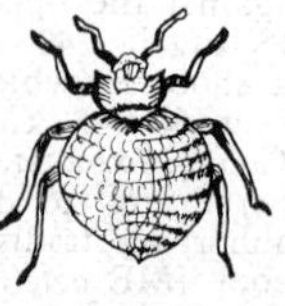
bedbug

**bedclothes** /ˈbɛdkloʊðz/, *n.pl.* coverings for a bed; sheets, blankets, etc.
**beddable** /ˈbɛdəbəl/, *adj. Colloq.* sexually attractive; suitable for taking to bed.
**bedding** /ˈbɛdɪŋ/, *n.* **1.** blankets, sheets, for a bed; bedclothes. **2.** litter; straw, etc., as a bed for animals. **3.** *Bldg Trades.* foundation or bottom layer of any kind. **4.** *Geol.* arrangement of rocks in strata.
**beddy-byes** /ˈbɛdi-baɪz/, *n. in the phrase* **go (to) beddy-byes,** to go to bed.
**bedeck** /bəˈdɛk, bi-/, *v.t.* to deck out; showily adorn.
**bedeguar** /ˈbɛdɪgə/, *n.* a mossy growth on the stems of roses, caused by gall. [F *bédeguar,* from Pers. *bādāwar* brought by the wind]
**bedehouse** /ˈbidhaʊs/, *n.* →**beadhouse.**
**bedel** /bəˈdɛl/, *n.* →**beadle.**
**bedesman** /ˈbidzmən/, *n., pl.* **-men.** →**beadsman.** – **bedeswoman** /ˈbidzwʊmən/, *n. fem.*
**bedevil** /bəˈdɛvəl, bi-/, *v.t.,* **-illed, -illing,** or *(U.S.)* **-iled, -iling. 1.** to treat diabolically; torment maliciously. **2.** to possess as with a devil; bewitch. **3.** to confound; muddle; spoil. – **bedevilment,** *n.*
**bedew** /bəˈdju, bi-/, *v.t.* to wet with or as with dew.
**bedfellow** /ˈbɛdfɛloʊ/, *n.* **1.** a sharer of one's bed. **2.** close companion: *politics makes strange bedfellows.*
**bedford cord** /bɛdfəd ˈkɔd/, *n.* a fabric, esp. wool, woven to give a distinctive lengthwise or diagonal corded effect.
**bedight** /bəˈdaɪt, bi-/, *v.t.,* **-dight, -dight** or **-dighted, -dighting.** *Archaic.* to deck out; array.
**bedim** /bəˈdɪm, bi-/, *v.t.,* **-dimmed, -dimming.** to make dim.
**bedizen** /bəˈdaɪzən, -ˈdɪzən, bi-/, *v.t.* to dress or adorn gaudily. [BE- + obs. *dizen* deck out, dress (a distaff) with flax; akin to *dis-* in DISTAFF] – **bedizenment,** *n.*
**bedjacket** /ˈbɛddʒækət/, *n.* a jacket of wool or warm material worn in bed.
**bedlam** /ˈbɛdləm/, *n.* **1.** a scene of wild uproar and confusion. **2.** any lunatic asylum; a madhouse. [ME *bedlem,* alteration of *Bethlehem,* from the former Royal Bethlehem Hospital, a lunatic asylum in SE London]
**bedlamite** /ˈbɛdləmaɪt/, *n. Archaic.* a lunatic.
**bed linen** /ˈbɛd lɪnən/, *n.* sheets and pillowcases.
**bed moulding** /ˈbɛd moʊldɪŋ/, *n. Archit.* **1.** the moulding, or series of mouldings, between the corona and the frieze of an entablature. **2.** any moulding under a projection.
**bedouin** /ˈbɛduən/, *n.* **1.** an Arab of the desert, in Asia or Africa; nomadic Arab. **2.** a nomad; wanderer. [F, from Ar. *badawīyīn,* pl. of *badawī* desert dweller]
**bedourie** /bəˈdaʊri/, *n.* a bushman's camp oven, the lid of which serves as a frying pan. [from *Bedourie,* town in Qld]
**Bedourie shower** /– ˈʃaʊə/, *n.* a dust storm. [from *Bedourie,* town in Qld]
**bedpan** /ˈbɛdpæn/, *n.* **1.** a shallow toilet pan for use by persons confined to bed. **2.** a warming pan.
**bedplate** /ˈbɛdpleɪt/, *n.* a plate, platform, or frame supporting the lighter parts of a machine.
**bedpost** /ˈbɛdpoʊst/, *n.* one of the upright supports of a bedstead.
**bedraggle** /bəˈdrægəl, bi-/, *v.t.,* **-gled, -gling.** to make limp and soiled as with wet or dirt.
**bedrail** /ˈbɛdreɪl/, *n.* a board connecting the headboard and footboard along the side of a bed.
**bedridden** /ˈbɛdrɪdn/, *adj.* confined to bed. [var. (by confusion with pp.) of *bedrid,* obs., bedridden, from ME *bedrede,* OE *bedreda, -rida* lit., bed-rider]
**bedrock** /ˈbɛdrɒk/, *n.* **1.** *Geol.* unbroken solid rock, overlaid in most places by soil or rock fragments. **2.** any firm foundation. **3. get down to bedrock,** *Colloq.* to come to the essentials.
**bed-roll** /ˈbɛd-roʊl/, *n.* bedding rolled up so as to be easily carried.
**bedroom** /ˈbɛdrum/, *n.* **1.** a room set aside to sleep in. *–adj.* **2.** of or pertaining to sexually explicit scenes in a film, play, etc., usu. taking place in a bedroom.
**bedroom comedy** /– ˈkɒmədi/, *n.* a play, film, etc., in which much play is made of sexually suggestive situations.
**bedroom eyes** /bɛdrum ˈaɪz/, *n. pl.* large eyes expressive of latent sexual passion.
**bedroom mug** /– ˈmʌg/, *n. Colloq.* a chamber-pot.
**bedside** /ˈbɛdsaɪd/, *n.* **1.** the side of a bed, esp. as the place of one in attendance on the sick. *–adj.* **2.** attending a sick person: *a good bedside manner.* **3.** at or for a bedside: *a bedside table.*
**bed-sitter** /bɛdˈsɪtə/, *n. Chiefly Brit.* bed-sitting room.
**bed-sitting room** /bɛd-ˈsɪtɪŋ rum/, *n.* a single-room dwelling place with both a bed and daytime living facilities.
**bedsore** /ˈbɛdsɔ/, *n.* a sore due to prolonged confinement in bed, as in a long illness.
**bedspace** /ˈbɛdspeɪs/, *n.* the accommodation available for bedridden patients in a hospital, nursing home, etc.
**bedspread** /ˈbɛdsprɛd/, *n.* an outer covering, usu. decorative, for a bed.
**bedspring** /ˈbɛdsprɪŋ/, *n.* one of a set of springs for the support of a mattress.
**bedstead** /ˈbɛdstɛd/, *n.* the framework of a bed supporting the springs and a mattress.
**bedstraw** /ˈbɛdstrɔ/, *n.* any plant of the genus *Galium,* family Rubiaceae, so named from the former use of some species as straw for beds.
**bedtime** /ˈbɛdtaɪm/, *n.* time to go to bed.
**bedward** /ˈbɛdwəd/, *adv.* to bed. Also, **bedwards.**
**bed-wetting** /ˈbɛd-wɛtɪŋ/, *n.* →**enuresis.**
**bed-worthy** /ˈbɛd-wɜði/, *adj. Colloq.* sexually attractive. – **bed-worthiness,** *n.*
**bee**[1] /bi/, *n.* **1.** any of various hymenopterous insects of the super-family Apoidea, which includes many social and solitary bees of several families, as the bumblebees, honeybees, etc. **2.** the common honeybee, *Apis mellifera.* **3.** a local gathering for work, entertainment, contests, etc.: *spelling bee, working bee.* **4. bee in one's bonnet, a.** an obsession. **b.** a slightly crazy idea, attitude, fad, etc. **5. the bee's knees,** *Colloq.* someone or something arousing great admiration. [ME; OE *bēo,* c. D *bij,* Icel. *bý*] – **beelike,** *adj.*

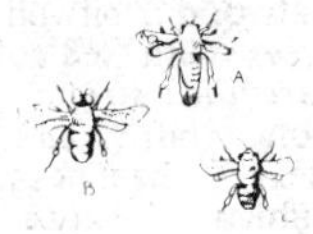
bee[1]: A, queen; B, drone; C, worker

**bee**[2] /bi/, *n. Naut.* a piece of hard wood, bolted to the side of the bowsprit, through which to reeve stays. [ME *beh* ring, OE *bēag, bēah* ring]
**bee-beetle** /ˈbi-bitl/, *n.* a European beetle, *Trichodes apiarius,* which sometimes infests beehives.
**bee-bread** /ˈbi-brɛd/, *n.* a protein food mixture, containing pollen, manufactured and stored up by bees for their young; ambrosia.
**beech** /bitʃ/, *n.* **1.** any tree of the genus *Fagus,* of temperate regions, having a smooth grey bark, and bearing small edible triangular nuts. **2.** the wood of such a tree. **3.** any species of *Nothofagus* of southern temperate regions. **4.** any of certain unrelated species thought to be similar in appearance or timber, as the **white beech.** [ME *beche,* OE *bēce*] – **beechen,** *adj.*
**beech mast** /ˈ– mast/, *n.* the edible nuts of the beech, esp. when lying on the ground.
**beechnut** /ˈbitʃnʌt/, *n.* the small, triangular, edible nut of the beech.
**beech orange** /ˈbitʃ ɒrɪndʒ/, *n.* an edible fungus of the genus *Cyttaria,* parasitic on most species of *Nothofagus.*
**beech orchid** /ˈ– ɔkəd/, *n.* either of two orchids found in beech forests in Australia: **a.** *Dendrobium falcorostrum,* an epiphyte of northern New South Wales and southern Queensland. **b.** *Townsonia viridis,* a terrestrial orchid of Tasmania.
**beechwood** /ˈbitʃwʊd/, *n.* →**beech** (def. 2).
**bee-eater** /ˈbi-itə/, *n.* **1.** →**rainbow bee-eater. 2.** any of various European members of the family Meropidae, insectivorous birds with long slender bills and brilliant plumage.
**beef** /bif/, *n., pl.* **beeves** /bivz/ *for def. 2;* **beefs** *for def. 5; v. –n.* **1.** the flesh of an animal of the genus *Bos,* used for food. **2.** a bull, cow, or steer, esp. if intended for meat. **3.** *Colloq.* brawn; muscular strength. **4.** *Colloq.* weight, as of human flesh. **5.** *Chiefly U.S. Colloq.* a complaint. *–v.i.* **6.** *Chiefly U.S. Colloq.* to complain; grumble. *–v.t.* **7.** *Colloq.*

to increase; enlarge (fol. by *up*): *the airline will beef up the number of flights.* [ME, from OF *boef,* from L *bōs* ox] – **beefless,** *adj.*

**beefalo** /'bifəlou/, *n.* a breed of beef cattle interbred with buffalo.

**beef ant** /'bif ænt/, *n.* →**meat ant.**

**beef bayonet** /– 'beɪənət/, *n.* an erect penis. Also, **beef bugle.**

**beefburger** /'bifbɜgə/, *n.* →**hamburger.**

**beefcake** /'bifkeɪk/, *n. Colloq.* male cheesecake (def. 2).

**beef cattle** /'bif kætl/, *n. pl.* cattle raised for beef.

**beef chain** /'– tʃeɪn/, *n.* a conveyor in a meatworks carrying beef-cattle carcases.

**beefeater** /'bifitə/, *n.* **1.** one who eats beef. **2.** a yeoman of the guard or a warder of the Tower of London. **3.** *U.S. Colloq.* an Englishman.

**beefer** /'bifə/, *n.* an animal bred for beef.

**bee-fly** /'bi-flaɪ/, *n.* any fly of the dipterous family Bombyliidae, members of which more or less resemble bees.

**Beefmaster** /'bifmastə/, *n.* one of a breed of cattle which is a three-way cross of Brahman (Zebu), Hereford and Shorthorn.

**beefroad** /'bifroud/, *n.* a road expressly constructed for road trains carrying beef cattle to market.

**beefsteak** /'bifsteɪk/, *n.* a prime slice of beef for grilling or frying, as fillet, rump, sirloin, etc.

**beef tea** /bif 'ti/, *n.* an extract of beef made by heating chopped beef in water and straining it.

**beef train** /'– treɪn/, *n.* a road train carrying beef cattle.

**beefwood** /'bifwud/, *n.* any of several unrelated Australian trees with red-coloured timber, esp. *Casuarina stricta* and *Grevillea striata.*

**beefy** /'bifi/, *adj.,* **beefier, beefiest.** fleshy; brawny; solid; heavy. – **beefiness,** *n.*

**beehive** /'bihaɪv/, *n.* **1.** a hive or receptacle, traditionally dome-shaped, serving as a habitation for bees. **2.** a crowded, busy place. **3.** a hat, house, or other object shaped like a traditional beehive. *–adj.* **4.** dome-shaped, like a traditional beehive.

**beehive house** /'– haus/, *n.* a prehistoric circular building, found throughout Europe, usu. of stone and having a dome-shaped covering.

**beekeeper** /'bikipə/, *n.* one who keeps bees; an apiarist. Also, **beemaster.**

**bee-killer** /'bi-kɪlə/, *n.* →**robber fly.**

**beeline** /'bilaɪn/, *n.* a direct line, like the course of bees returning to a hive: *the hungry children made a beeline for the food.*

**Beelzebub** /bi'ɛlzibʌb/, *n.* **1.** the devil. **2.** a devil. **3.** (in Milton's *Paradise Lost*) one of the fallen angels, second only to Satan himself. [orig. with ref. to Beelzebub, 'the prince of the devils' Matt. 12:24; from Heb. *Ba'al-zebub* Philistine god, II Kings 1:2 (? meaning 'lord of flies')]

**bee-moth** /'bi-mɒθ/, *n.* a brown moth, *Galleria mellonella,* whose larvae feed on beeswax. Also, **wax-moth.**

**been** /bin/; *weak form* /bən/, *v.* past participle of **be.**

**bee orchid** /'bi ɔkəd/, *n.* any of various orchids with flowers resembling a bee, as *Ophrys apifera, Caleana major, Diuris carinata.*

**beep** /bip/, *n.* **1.** the sound made by a horn on a car or other vehicle. **2.** a short, high-pitched sound often electronically produced. *–v.t.* **3.** to make something emit a beep, as in sounding a horn. *–v.i.* **4.** to emit a beep.

**beeper** /'bipə/, *n. Colloq.* →**pager.**

**beer** /bɪə/, *n.* **1.** an alcoholic beverage made by brewing and fermentation from cereals, usu. malted barley and flavoured with hops, etc., to give a bitter taste. **2.** any of various beverages, whether alcoholic or not, made from roots, molasses, or sugar, yeast, etc.: *root beer, ginger beer.* **3.** a glass, can, etc., of beer: *let's have a beer.* [ME *bere,* OE *bēor,* c. G *Bier*]

**beer and skittles,** *n.* drinks and pleasure; any pleasurable activity.

**beerenauslese** /bɛərən'ɒzleɪz, -aus'leɪzə/, *adj.* (of wine), made from specially selected berries. [G *Beeren* berries + *auslesen* to select]

**beer garden** /'bɪə gadn/, *n.* an outdoor area of a hotel premises, usu. furnished with tables and chairs, where drinks are sold at public bar prices.

**beer gut** /'bɪə gʌt/, *n. Colloq.* a paunch caused by excessive beer drinking.

**beer-hall** /'bɪə-hɔl/, *n. S. African.* **1.** a public hall where beer is sold. **2.** a public hall in South Africa where weak beer is sold to non-whites.

**beer money** /'bɪə mʌni/, *n. Colloq.* **1.** a gratuity. **2.** any money set aside for spending on pleasure, esp. by a husband.

**beer-up** /'bɪər-ʌp/, *n. Colloq.* a drinking party devoted largely to beer-drinking and talk.

**beery** /'bɪəri/, *adj.,* **beerier, beeriest. 1.** of, like, or abounding in beer. **2.** affected by or suggestive of beer. – **beeriness,** *n.*

**beestings** /'bistɪŋz/, *n.pl.* milk secreted by a mammal, esp. a cow, just before and for a short period after giving birth, containing antibodies to protect the offspring against disease; colostrum. Also **beastings, biestings.**

**beeswax** /'bizwæks/, *n.* **1.** the wax secreted by bees, of which they construct their honeycomb; wax (def. 1). *–v.t.* **2.** to rub, polish, or treat with beeswax.

**beeswing** /'bizwɪŋ/, *n.* a thin film formed on port and some other wines after long keeping. – **beeswinged,** *adj.*

**beet** /bit/, *n.* **1.** any of various biennial plants of the genus *Beta,* whose varieties include the red beet, which has a fleshy edible root, and the sugar beet, which yields sugar. **2.** the root of such a plant. **3.** the leaves served as a salad or cooked vegetable. [OE *bēte,* from L *bēta*] – **beetlike,** *adj.*

**beetfly** /'bitflaɪ/, *n.* a dipterous insect, *Pegomya nyoscyami,* var. *betae-curt,* a very common pest of beet and other root crops; mangold fly.

**beetle**[1] /'bitl/, *n., v.,* **-tled, -tling.** *–n.* **1.** any insect of the order Coleoptera, characterised by having forewings modified as hard, horny structures, useless in flight. **2.** any of various insects resembling beetles, as the common cockroach. **3.** *Colloq.* a Volkswagen car of the first type produced, so called because of its shape. **4.** a dice game in which the aim is to assemble or draw a beetle-shaped figure. *–v.i.* **5.** *Colloq.* to move swiftly, esp. in an aeroplane (oft. fol. by *off* or *along*). [ME *bētylle, bityl,* OE *bitula* lit., biter]

**beetle**[2] /'bitl/, *n., v.,* **-tled, -tling.** *–n.* **1.** a heavy hammering or ramming instrument, usu. of wood, used to drive wedges, force down paving stones, consolidate earth, etc. **2.** any of various wooden instruments for beating linen, mashing potatoes, etc. *–v.t.* **3.** to use a beetle on; drive, ram, beat, or crush with a beetle. **4.** to finish (cloth) by means of a beetling machine. [ME and d. OE *bētel,* replacing OE *bīetl,* from *bēatan* beat]

**beetle**[3] /'bitl/, *adj., v.,* **-tled, -tling.** *–adj.* **1.** projecting, overhanging: *beetle brows.* *–v.i.* **2.** to project; jut out; overhang. [backformation from BEETLE-BROWED] – **beetling,** *adj.*

**beetle-browed** /'bitl-braud/, *adj.* **1.** having heavy projecting eyebrows. **2.** scowling; sullen. [ME *bitel-browed,* from *bitel* biting + BROW + -ED[3]. See BEETLE[1]]

**beetroot** /'bitrut/, *n.* the edible root of the red beet.

**beet sugar** /'bit ʃugə/, *n.* sugar from the roots of the sugar beet.

**beeves** /bivz/, *n.* plural of **beef** (def. 1).

**befall** /bə'fɔl, bi-/, *v.,* **-fell, -fallen, -falling.** *–v.i.* **1.** to happen or occur. **2.** *Archaic.* to come (*to*) as by right. *–v.t.* **3.** to happen to. [ME *befallen,* OE *befeallan*]

**befit** /bə'fɪt, bi-/, *v.t.,* **-fitted, -fitting.** to be fitting or appropriate for; be suited to: *his clothes befit the occasion.*

**befitting** /bə'fɪtɪŋ, bi-/, *adj.* fitting; proper. – **befittingly,** *adv.*

**befog** /bə'fɒg, bi-/, *v.t.,* **-fogged, -fogging.** to involve in fog or obscurity; confuse.

**befool** /bə'ful, bi-/, *v.t.* **1.** to fool; deceive; dupe. **2.** to treat as a fool.

**before** /bə'fɔ, bi-/, *adv.* **1.** in front; in advance; ahead. **2.** in time preceding; previously. **3.** earlier or sooner: *begin at noon, not before.* *–prep.* **4.** in front of; ahead of; in advance of: *before the house.* **5.** previously to; earlier than: *before the war.* **6.** ahead of; in the future of; awaiting: *the golden age is before us.* **7.** in preference to; rather than: *they would die before yielding.* **8.** in precedence of, as in order or rank: *we put freedom before fame.* **9.** in the presence or sight of: *before an audience.* **10.** under the jurisdiction or consideration of: *before a magistrate.* **11. before the wind,** *Naut.* blown along by the wind. *–conj.* **12.** previously to the time when: *before we go.* **13.** sooner than; rather than: *I will die before I submit.* [ME *before(n),* OE *beforan,* from *be* by + *foran* before]

**beforehand** /bəˈfɔhænd, bi-/, *adv.* in anticipation; in advance; ahead of time.

**beforetime** /bəˈfɔtaɪm, bi-/, *adv. Archaic.* formerly.

**befoul** /bəˈfaʊl, bi-/, *v.t.* to make foul; defile; sully.

**befriend** /bəˈfrɛnd, bi-/, *v.t.* to act as a friend to; aid.

**befuddle** /bəˈfʌdl, bi-/, *v.t.,* **-dled, -dling. 1.** to make stupidly drunk. **2.** to confuse, as with glib argument.

**beg** /bɛg/, *v.,* **begged, begging.** *–v.t.* **1.** to ask for in charity; ask as alms. **2.** to ask for, or of, with humility or earnestness, or as a favour: *to beg forgiveness, to beg him to forgive me.* **3. beg yours,** *Colloq.* beg your pardon. **4.** to assume or demand permission (to say or do something): *beg to differ, beg to point out an error.* **5.** to take for granted without justification. **6. beg the question, a.** to assume the very point raised in a question. **b.** to evade the point at issue. *–v.i.* **7.** to ask alms or charity; live by asking alms. **8.** to ask humbly or earnestly: *begging for help.* **9. go begging,** to be unwanted; be unclaimed. **10. beg off,** to excuse oneself from: *to beg off going to the pictures.* [ME *beggen,* OE *bedecian*]

**began** /bəˈgæn, bi-/, *v.* past tense of **begin.**

**begat** /bəˈgæt, bi-/, *v. Archaic.* past tense of **beget.**

**beget** /bəˈgɛt, bi-/, *v.t.,* **begot, begotten** or **begot, begetting. 1.** to procreate or generate (used chiefly of the male parent). **2.** to cause; produce as an effect. [ME *begete(n),* from BE- + GET; replacing OE *begitan*] – **begetter,** *n.*

**beggar** /ˈbɛgə/, *n.* **1.** one who begs alms, or lives by begging. **2.** a penniless person. **3.** (in playful use) a wretch or rogue: *a dear little beggar.* **4.** *Colloq.* one who is remarkably keen on or adept at something: *he's a beggar for work; a beggar at chess* **5. beggar for punishment,** a person who consistently exerts himself. *–v.t.* **6.** to reduce to beggary; impoverish. **7.** to exhaust the resources of: *to beggar description.* [ME *beggar,* from BEG + -ER[1] See -AR[3]] – **beggardom** /ˈbɛgədəm/, **beggarhood,** *n.* – **beggarman,** *n.*

**beggarly** /ˈbɛgəli/, *adj.* like or befitting a beggar; wretchedly poor; mean. – **beggarliness,** *n.*

**beggar-my-neighbour** /bɛgə-mə-ˈneɪbə/, *n.* a card game for two players. Also, **beggar-your-neighbour.**

**beggars-on-the-coals** /ˌbɛgəz-ɒn-ðə-ˈkoʊlz/, *n.pl.* small, thin dampers. Also, **beggars-in-the-pan.**

**beggar's tick** /ˈbɛgəz tɪk/, *n.* **1.** any plant of the genus *Bidens* or other similar plant having barbed fruits which adhere to clothing. **2.** the fruits themselves.

**beggary** /ˈbɛgəri/, *n.* **1.** the condition of utter poverty. **2.** beggars collectively.

**begin** /bəˈgɪn/, *v.,* **began, begun, beginning.** *–v.i.* **1.** to enter upon an action; take the first step; commence; start. **2.** to come into existence; arise; originate. **3. to begin with, a.** in the first place; firstly. **b.** as a start. *–v.t.* **4.** to take the first step in; set about; start; commence. **5.** to originate; be the originator of. [ME *beginne(n),* OE *beginnan*] – **beginner,** *n.*

**beginning** /bəˈgɪnɪŋ/, *n.* **1.** the act or fact of entering upon an action or state. **2.** the point of time or space at which anything begins: *the beginning of the Christian era.* **3.** the first part or initial stage of anything: *the beginnings of science.* **4.** origin; source; first cause: *humility is the beginning of wisdom.*

**begird** /bəˈgɜd/, *v.t.,* **-girt** or **-girded, -girding.** to gird about; encompass; surround. [ME *begirden,* OE *begyrdan.* See BE-, GIRD[1]]

**begone** /bəˈgɒn, bi-/, *v.i.* (*usu. imperative*) to go away, depart.

**begonia** /bəˈgoʊniə, -jə/, *n.* any plant of the tropical genus *Begonia,* including species much cultivated for their handsome, succulent, often varicoloured leaves and waxy flowers. [named after Michel *Bégon,* 1638–1710, French patron of science]

**begorrah** /bəˈgɒrə/, *interj. Irish.* (a mild oath). Also, **begorra.** [euph. modification of *by god*]

**begot** /bəˈgɒt, bi-/, *v.* past tense and past participle of **beget.**

**begotten** /bəˈgɒtn, bi-/, *v.* past participle of **beget.**

**beg-pardon** /bɛg-ˈpadn/, *n.* an apology: *there were no beg-pardons as they vied for first place.*

**begrime** /bəˈgraɪm, bi-/, *v.t.,* **-grimed, -griming.** to make grimy.

**begrudge** /bəˈgrʌdʒ, bi-/, *v.t.,* **-grudged, -grudging. 1.** to be discontented at seeing (a person) have (something): *to begrudge a man his good fortune.* **2.** to be reluctant to give, grant, or allow: *to begrudge him the money he earned.*

**beguile** /bəˈgaɪl, bi-/, *v.t.,* **-guiled, -guiling. 1.** to influence by guile; mislead; delude. **2.** to take away from by artful tactics (fol. by *of*). **3.** to charm or divert. **4.** to while away (time) pleasantly. – **beguilement,** *n.* – **beguiler,** *n.*

**beguine** /bəˈgin/, *n.* **1.** a South American dance in bolero rhythm. **2.** a modern social dance based on the beguine. **3.** music for either of these dances. [Creole F: fem. form of *béguin* flirtation]

**begum** /ˈbigəm/, *n.* (in India) **1.** a Muslim woman ruler. **2.** a high-ranking Muslim lady, often a widow. [Hind. *begam*]

**begun** /bəˈgʌn, bi-/, *v.* past participle of **begin.**

**behalf** /bəˈhaf, bi-/, *n.* **1.** side, interest, or aid (prec. by *on*): *on behalf of his country.* **2.** *U.S.* favour or interest (prec. by *in*). [ME *behalve* beside, in OE a phrase, *be healfe* (*him*) by (*his*) side; later used as n. by confusion with ME *on his halve* on his side. See HALF]

**behave** /bəˈheɪv, bi-/, *v.,* **-haved, -having.** *–v.i.* **1.** to conduct oneself or itself; act: *the ship behaves well.* **2.** to act in a socially acceptable manner: *did the child behave?* *–v.t.* **3. behave oneself, a.** to conduct oneself in a specified way. **b.** to conduct oneself properly. [late ME, apparently from BE- + HAVE hold oneself a certain way]

**behaviour** /bəˈheɪvjə, bi-/, *n.* **1.** manner of behaving or acting. **2.** *Psychol.* **a.** the actions or activities of the individual as matters of psychological study. **b.** an activity or a pattern of activities of a particular organism. **3.** the action of any material: *the behaviour of tin under heat.* Also, *U.S.,* **behavior.** – **behavioural;** *U.S.* **behavioral,** *adj.*

**behaviourism** /bəˈheɪvjəˌrɪzəm, bi-/, *n.* the study in men and animals of externally observable behavioural responses as functions or environmental stimuli; mental states are either ignored or redefined in stimulus/response terms. Also, *U.S.* **behaviorism.** – **behaviourist;** *U.S.* **behavorist,** *n., adj.*

**behaviour pattern** /bəˈheɪvjə pætn/, *n.* a recurrent way of acting by an individual or group towards a given object or in a given situation.

**behaviour therapy** /ˈ– θɛrəpi/, *n.* a set of therapeutic procedures based upon behaviourist conditioning principles.

**behead** /bəˈhɛd, bi-/, *v.t.* to cut off the head of; kill or execute by decapitation.

**beheld** /bəˈhɛld, bi-/, *v.* past tense and past participle of **behold.**

**behemoth** /bəˈhiməθ/, *n.* **1.** *Bible.* an animal, perhaps the hippopotamus. **2.** *Colloq.* a huge and powerful man, beast, etc. [Heb. *behēmōth,* pl. (intensive form) of *behēmah* beast]

**behest** /bəˈhɛst, bi-/, *n.* bidding or injunction; mandate or command. [ME; OE *behǣs* promise]

**behind** /bəˈhaɪnd, bi-/, *prep.* **1.** at the back of; at the rear of: *behind the house.* **2.** after; later than: *behind schedule.* **3.** less advanced than; inferior to: *behind his class in mathematics.* **4.** on the farther side of; beyond: *behind the mountain.* **5.** supporting; promoting: *a millionaire is behind the project.* **6.** hidden or unrevealed by: *malice lay behind her smile.* *–adv.* **7.** at or towards the back; in the rear. **8.** in a place, state or stage already passed: *he left his wallet behind.* **9.** remaining; in reserve: *greater support is behind.* **10.** in arrears; behindhand: *behind with the rent.* **11.** slow, as a watch or clock. *–n.* **12.** the buttocks. **13.** *Aus. Rules.* **a.** a score of one point achieved by putting the ball between a goal post and a behind post. **b.** a score of one point achieved by putting the ball between the goal posts as a result of any action other than a kick by a player of the scoring team. **c.** a score of one point achieved by the ball hitting a goal post. [ME *behinden,* OE *behindan* See BE-, HIND[1]]

**behindhand** /bəˈhaɪndhænd, bi-/, *adj.* **1.** late. **2.** behind in progress; backward. **3.** in arrears: *behindhand with payments.*

**behind line** /bəˈhaɪnd laɪn/, *n. Aus. Rules.* the line running between the goal and behind posts.

**behind post** /ˈ– poʊst/, *n. Aus. Rules.* either of two posts standing one on each side of the goal posts, and shorter than them, marking, with the nearer goal post, a space through which the ball may be put to score a behind.

**behold** /bəˈhoʊld, bi-/, *v.*, **-held, -holding,** *interj.* *–v.t.* **1.** to observe; look at; see. *–interj.* **2.** look! see! [ME *beholde(n)*, OE *behaldan* keep] – **beholder,** *n.*

**beholden** /bəˈhoʊldn, bi-/, *adj.* under an obligation; indebted.

**behoof** /biˈhuf/, *n. Archaic.* use; advantage; benefit: *on my behoof.* [ME *behove,* OE *behōf* profit, need, c. G *Behuf*]

**behove** /bəˈhoʊv, bi-/, *v.*, **-hoved, -hoving.** *–v.t.* **1.** to be needful or proper for or incumbent on (now only in impersonal use): *it behoves me to see him.* *–v.i.* **2.** *Archaic.* to be needful, proper, or due (in impersonal use). Also, *Chiefly U.S.,* **behoove** /bəˈhuv/. [ME *behove(n)*, OE *behōfian* need. See BEHOOF]

**beige** /beɪʒ/, *n., adj.* very light brown, as of undyed wool; light grey with brownish tinge. [F]

**beignet** /ˈbeɪnjeɪ/, *n. Cookery.* a fritter. [F]

**being** /ˈbiɪŋ/, *n.* **1.** existence, as opposed to non-existence. **2.** conscious existence; life: *the aim of our being.* **3.** mortal existence; lifetime. **4.** substance or nature: *of such a being as to arouse fear.* **5.** something that exists: *beings on a strange planet.* **6.** a living thing. **7.** a human being; person. **8.** (*cap.*) God. **9.** *Philos.* **a.** that which has actuality either materially or in idea. **b.** absolute existence in a complete or perfect state, lacking no essential characteristic; essence.

**bejesus** /bəˈdʒizəz, -ˈdʒeɪ-/, *Colloq.* *–interj.* **1.** (an exclamation of astonishment, disgust, etc.). *–n.* **2. knock the bejesus out of,** to destroy the self-confidence of or defeat utterly.

**bejewel** /bəˈdʒuəl, bi-/, *v.t.*, **-elled, -elling** or (*U.S.*) **-eled, -eling.** to adorn with or as with jewels.

**bel** /bɛl/, *n.* ten decibels. [named after A. G. BELL, 1847–1922, inventor of the telephone]

**belabour** /bəˈleɪbə, bi-/, *v.t.* **1.** to beat vigorously; ply with heavy blows. **2.** to assail persistently, as with ridicule. **3.** *Obs.* to labour at. Also, *U.S.,* **belabor.**

**belah** /ˈbilə, bəˈla/, *n.* a tree, *Casuarina cristata,* of dry temperate eastern Australia, forming an important part of the vegetation in some inland areas. Also, **belar.** [Aboriginal]

**belated** /bəˈleɪtəd, bi-/, *adj.* coming or being late or too late. – **belatedly,** *adv.* – **belatedness,** *n.*

**belay** /bəˈleɪ, bi-/, *v.*, **-layed, -laying,** *n.* *–v.t.* **1.** *Naut.* to fasten (a rope) by winding around a pin or short rod inserted in a holder so that both ends of the rod are clear. **2.** *Mountaineering.* to secure (a rope or person) by a turn of rope round a rock or piton. *–v.i.* **3.** to stop (used chiefly in the imperative). **4.** to make a rope fast. *–n.* **5.** *Mountaineering.* a knot or turn of rope round a rock or piton by which a climbing-rope is held secure. [ME *belegge(n)*, OE *belecgan* cover. See BE-, LAY[1]]

**belaying pin** /bəˈleɪɪŋ pɪn/, *n. Naut.* a pin for use in securing the ends of ropes.

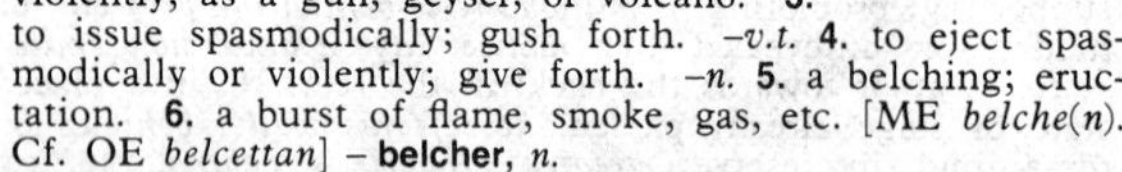
belaying pins

**bel canto** /bɛl ˈkæntoʊ/, *n.* a smooth, cantabile style of singing. [It.]

**belch** /bɛltʃ/, *v.i.* **1.** to eject wind spasmodically and noisily from the stomach through the mouth; eructate. **2.** to emit contents violently, as a gun, geyser, or volcano. **3.** to issue spasmodically; gush forth. *–v.t.* **4.** to eject spasmodically or violently; give forth. *–n.* **5.** a belching; eructation. **6.** a burst of flame, smoke, gas, etc. [ME *belche(n)*. Cf. OE *belcettan*] – **belcher,** *n.*

**beldam** /ˈbɛldæm/, *n. Archaic.* **1.** an old woman, esp. an ugly one; hag. **2.** grandmother. Also, **beldame** /ˈbɛldam/. [ME: grandmother, from *bel-* (from OF: *bel, belle* fair) used like GRAND (def. 12) + *dam* DAME]

**beleaguer** /bəˈligə, bi-/, *v.t.* **1.** to surround with an army. **2.** to surround: *beleaguered with annoyances.* [D *belegeren,* from *be-* about + *leger* camp] – **beleaguered,** *adj.* – **beleaguerer,** *n.*

**belemnite** /ˈbɛləmnaɪt/, *n.* a small conical fossil, consisting of the internal calcareous rod of an extinct animal allied to the cuttlefish; a thunderstone. [Gk *bélemnon* dart + -ITE[1]]

**belfry** /ˈbɛlfri/, *n., pl.* **-fries.** **1.** a belltower, either attached to a church or other building or standing apart. **2.** that part of a steeple or other structure in which a bell is hung. **3.** a frame of timberwork which may sustain a bell. **4.** *Hist.* **a.** a watchtower. **b.** a movable tower for attacking fortifications. **5.** *Colloq.* the head or mind. [ME *belfray,* dissimilated var. of *berfrey,* from OF *berfrei,* from Gmc; cf. MHG *bercfrit* defence shelter]

**Belg.,** **1.** Belgian. **2.** Belgium.

**Belgian** /ˈbɛldʒən/, *n.* **1.** a native or an inhabitant of Belgium. *–adj.* **2.** of or pertaining to Belgium.

**Belgium** /ˈbɛldʒəm/, *n.* a kingdom in western Europe on the North Sea, north of France.

**Belgium sausage** /– ˈsɒsɪdʒ/, *n.* →**devon** (def. 3).

**belial** /ˈbiliəl, bəˈlaɪəl/, *n.* **1.** (in the Bible and rabbinical commentary) worthlessness, wickedness, or destruction. **2.** (in Milton's *Paradise Lost*) the spirit of evil personified; the devil; Satan. [Heb. *belī-ya'al* worthlessness]

**belie** /bəˈlaɪ, bi-/, *v.t.*, **-lied, -lying.** **1.** to misrepresent: *his face belied his thoughts.* **2.** to show to be false: *his trembling belied his calm words.* **3.** to prove false to; fail to justify: *to belie one's faith.* **4.** to lie about; slander. [ME *belye(n)*, OE *belēogan,* from *be-* BE- + *lēogan* LIE[1]] – **belier,** *n.*

**belief** /bəˈlif, bi-/, *n.* **1.** that which is believed; an accepted opinion. **2.** conviction of the truth or reality of a thing, based upon grounds insufficient to afford positive knowledge: *statements unworthy of belief.* **3.** confidence; faith; trust: *a child's belief in his parents.* **4.** a religious tenet or tenets: *the Christian belief.* [ME *bilēve* (with *-ē-* from v.), replacing early ME *bilēafe,* replacing OE *gelēafa,* c. G *Glaube*]

**believe** /bəˈliv, bi-/, *v.*, **-lieved, -lieving.** *–v.i.* **1.** to have confidence (*in*); trust; rely through faith (*on*). **2.** to be persuaded of the truth of anything; accept a doctrine, principle, system, etc. (fol. by *in*): *to believe in public schools.* *–v.t.* **3.** to have belief in; credit; accept as true: *to believe a person or a story.* **4.** to think: *I believe he has left the city.* [ME *bileve(n)*, from *bi-* + *lēven,* d. OE *lēfan;* replacing OE *(ge)līefan,* c. G *glauben*] – **believable,** *adj.* – **believer,** *n.* – **believingly,** *adv.*

**belike** /bəˈlaɪk/, *adv. Archaic.* very likely; perhaps; probably. [BE- + LIKE[1]]

**Belisha beacon** /bəˌliʃə ˈbikən/, *n. Brit.* a yellow globe, usu. mounted on a black-and-white ringed post, and containing an intermittently flashing light, to mark a pedestrian crossing. [named after Leslie Hore-*Belisha,* 1893-1957, British politician, minister of transport 1934-37]

**belittle** /bəˈlɪtl, bi-/, *v.t.*, **-tled, -tling.** to make little or less important; depreciate; disparage.

**bell**[1] /bɛl/, *n.* **1.** a sounding instrument, usu. of metal, cup-shaped with a flaring mouth, rung by the strokes of a clapper, tongue, or hammer suspended within it. **2.** any instrument emitting a ringing signal, esp. an electrical device in which an electromagnet causes a hammer to strike repeatedly a hollow metal hemisphere, producing a continuous ringing sound, as a doorbell. **3.** the stroke, sound, or signal emitted by such an instrument. **4.** *Colloq.* a telephone call: *to give someone a bell.* **5. ring a bell,** *Colloq.* to remind one; jog the memory. **6.** *Naut.* the half-hourly subdivisions of a watch of four hours, each being marked by single or double strokes of a bell. **7.** any object in the shape of a traditional bell (def. 1). **8.** the end of a musical wind instrument, or any tube when its edge has been turned out and enlarged. **9.** a pouch of skin and hair that hangs from the neck of certain deer. **10.** *Zool.* →**umbrella** (def. 2). *–v.t.* **11.** to put a bell on. **12. bell the cat,** to undertake a dangerous enterprise for the common good. **13.** to cause to swell into a bell shape. **14.** *Colloq.* to give (someone) a telephone call. *–v.i.* **15.** to take or have the form of a bell. [ME and OE *belle.* See BELL[2], BELLOW] – **bell-like,** *adj.*

**bell**[2] /bɛl/, *v.i., v.t.* **1.** to bellow like a deer in the rutting season. **2.** *Obs.* to bellow; roar. *–n.* **3.** the cry of a rutting deer. [ME *belle(n)*, OE *bellan* roar, c. G *bellen* bark]

**belladonna** /bɛləˈdɒnə/, *n.* **1.** a poisonous solanaceous plant, *Atropa belladonna;* deadly nightshade. **2.** either of two drugs, atropine and hyoscyamine, obtained from this plant, and used as a cardiac or respiratory stimulant, or an antispasmodic. [It.: lit., fair lady]

**belladonna lily** /– ˈlɪli/, *n.* →**amaryllis** (def. 1).

**bellbird** /ˈbɛlbɜd/, *n.* **1.** Also, **bell-miner.** a yellowish-green honeyeater, *Manorina melanophrys,* with a distinctive, tinkling, bell-like call, found esp. near water in wooded coastal and mountain areas from southern Queensland to Victoria.

2. a New Zealand honeyeater, *Anthornis melanura;* mocker; korimako; makomako.

**bell-bottomed** /ˈbɛl-bɒtəmd/, *adj.* widening into a bell-shape at the lower end.

**bellboy** /ˈbɛlbɔɪ/, *n.* a young employee in a hotel who carries luggage, runs errands, etc.

**bell buoy** /ˈbɛl bɔɪ/, *n.* a buoy containing a bell which is rung by the action of the waves.

**bellcast batten** /ˈbɛlkast ˌbætn/, *n. Bldg Trades.* the batten under the bottom tile in a roof, used to retain the correct pitch of the tiles at the gutter.

**bellcote** /ˈbɛlkoʊt/, *n.* a framework in a roof from which bells are hung.

**belle** /bɛl/, *n.* a woman or girl admired for her beauty; a reigning beauty. [F, fem. of *beau* BEAU]

**belleek** /bəˈlik/, *n.* a fragile, ornamental porcelain with a bright lustre. Also, **Belleek ware.** [named after *Belleek,* in Northern Ireland]

**belles-lettres** /bɛl-ˈlɛtrə/, *n.pl.* the finer or more elegant forms of literature; literature regarded as a fine art. [F] – **belletrist** /bɛlˈlɛtrəst/, *n.* – **belletristic** /bɛlˌlɛtˈrɪstɪk/, *adj.*

**bellflower** /ˈbɛlflaʊə/, *n.* →**campanula.**

**bell-foundry** /ˈbɛl-ˌfaʊndri/, *n.* a place where bells are made. – **bell-founder,** *n.*

**bell-fruit tree** /ˈbɛl-frut ˌtri/, *n.* a small tree, *Codonocarpus cotinifolius,* family Gyrostemonaceae, widespread in inland Australia, having bell-shaped fruit.

**bell glass** /ˈbɛl glas/, *n.* →**bell jar.**

**bell heather** /ˈ– hɛðə/, *n.* a perennial shrub, *Erica cinerea,* of western Europe.

**bellhop** /ˈbɛlhɒp/, *n. U.S.* →**bellboy.**

**bellicose** /ˈbɛləkoʊs/, *adj.* inclined to war; warlike; pugnacious. [L *bellicōsus,* from *bellum* war] – **bellicosely,** *adv.* – **bellicosity** /bɛləˈkɒsəti/, *n.*

**belligerence** /bəˈlɪdʒərəns/, *n.* **1.** warlike nature. **2.** the state or act of carrying on war; warfare. **3.** the state of being actually at war. Also, **belligerency.**

**belligerent** /bəˈlɪdʒərənt/, *adj.* **1.** warlike; given to waging war. **2.** of warlike character: *a belligerent tone.* **3.** waging war; engaged in war: *the belligerent powers.* **4.** pertaining to war, or to those engaged in war: *belligerent rights, etc.* **5.** aggressive; argumentative. *–n.* **6.** a state or nation at war, or a member of the military forces of such a state. [L *belligerans,* ppr.] – **belligerently,** *adv.*

**bell jar** /ˈbɛl dʒa/, *n.* a bell-shaped glass vessel or cover, as for protecting delicate instruments, bric-a-brac, etc., or for holding gases in chemical operations. Also, **bell glass.**

**bell lap** /ˈbɛl læp/, *n.* the final lap in a race, the beginning of which is signalled by the ringing of a bell.

**bell magpie** /– ˈmægpaɪ/, *n.* →**currawong.**

**bellman** /ˈbɛlmən/, *n., pl.* **-men.** *Archaic.* a man who carries or rings a bell, esp. a town crier or watchman.

**bell metal** /ˈbɛl mɛtl/, *n.* a hard alloy of copper and tin of low damping capacity, used for bells.

**bell-miner** /bɛl-ˈmaɪnə/, *n.* →**bellbird** (def. 1).

**bell-mouthed** /ˈbɛl-maʊθt, -maʊðd/, *adj.* having a flaring mouth like that of a bell.

**bellow** /ˈbɛloʊ/, *v.i.* **1.** to make a hollow, loud, animal cry, as a bull or cow. **2.** to roar; bawl: *bellowing with rage.* *–v.t.* **3.** to utter in a loud deep voice: *to bellow forth an answer.* *–n.* **4.** the act or sound of bellowing. [ME *belwe(n),* apparently b. OE *bellan* BELL² and *bylgan* bellow] – **bellower,** *n.*

**bellows** /ˈbɛloʊz/, *n. sing. and pl.* **1.** an instrument or machine for producing a strong current of air, as for a draught for a fire or sounding an organ or other musical instrument, consisting essentially of an air-chamber which can be expanded to draw in air through a valve and contracted to expel the air through a tube or tubes. **2.** anything resembling or suggesting a bellows, as the collapsible part of a camera or enlarger. [ME *belwes,* pl., OE *belg* short for *blǣst-belg* blast-bag. See BELLY]

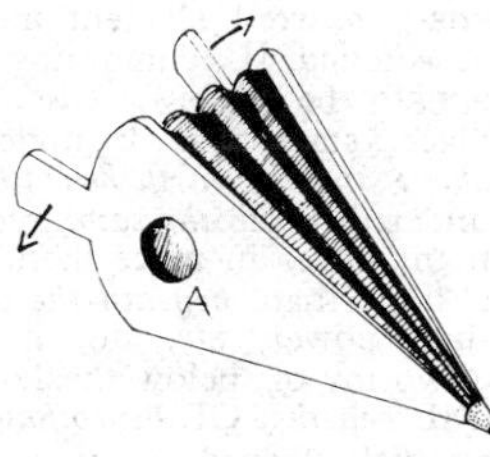

bellows: air enters through valve (A) as bellows is expanded

**bell pepper** /ˈbɛl pɛpə/, *n.* →**sweet pepper.**

**bellpull** /ˈbɛlpʊl/, *n.* a rope or handle for sounding a bell.

**bellpush** /ˈbɛlpʊʃ/, *n.* a button for operating an electric bell.

**bellringer** /ˈbɛlrɪŋə/, *n.* **1.** one who rings church bells. **2.** a performer playing musical handbells. – **bellringing,** *n.*

**bell sheep** /ˈbɛl ʃip/, *n.* the last sheep shorn by any shearer before meal or tea intervals or at the end of the day.

**bells-of-Ireland** /bɛlz-əv-ˈaɪələnd/, *n.* →**Molucca balm.**

**bell tent** /bɛl ˈtɛnt/, *n.* a tent shaped like a traditional bell.

**bell-topper** /bɛl-ˈtɒpə/, *n.* a top hat, usu. of black silk.

**belltower** /ˈbɛltaʊə/, *n.* →**campanile.**

**bell-vine** /ˈbɛl-vaɪn/, *n.* a climbing plant, *Ipomoea plebeia,* found in tropical areas.

**bellwether** /ˈbɛlwɛðə/, *n.* **1.** a wether or other male sheep which leads the flock, usu. bearing a bell. **2.** a person whom others follow blindly.

**belly** /ˈbɛli/, *n., pl.,* **-ies,** *v.,* **-ied, -ying.** *–n.* **1.** the front or underpart of a vertebrate body from the breastbone to the pelvis, containing the abdominal viscera; the abdomen. **2.** the stomach with its adjuncts. **3.** appetite for food; gluttony. **4.** the womb. **5.** the inside or interior of anything: *the belly of a ship.* **6.** a protuberant or bulging surface of anything: *the belly of a flask.* **7.** *Archery.* the curved innerside of the bow. **8.** *Anat.* the fleshy part of a muscle. **9.** the front, inner, or undersurface or part (opposed to *back*). **10.** (*pl.*) belly wool of sheep. **11.** *Music.* the front surface of a violin or similar instrument, bearing the strings. **12.** (*pl.*) wool shorn from the belly of a sheep. *–v.i.* **13.** to swell out. *–v.t.* **14.** to cause to bulge. **15.** to shear the wool from the belly of the sheep, before shearing the main fleece. [ME *bely,* OE *belig* bag, skin, var. of *belg* (whence *bellow(s)*]

**belly-ache** /ˈbɛli-eɪk/, *n. Colloq.* **1.** a pain in the stomach, esp. colic. **2.** a cause of discontent. **3.** a complaint. *–v.t.* **4.** to complain or grumble.

**bellyband** /ˈbɛlibænd/, *n.* a band worn about the belly, as of a harnessed horse.

**bellyboard** /ˈbɛlibɔd/, *n.* the principal board of a billycart.

**bellybuster** /ˈbɛliˌbʌstə/, *n. Colloq.* a badly-judged dive in which one's stomach hits the water first.

**bellybutton** /ˈbɛlibʌtn/, *n. Colloq.* the navel. Also, **belly button.**

**belly dance** /ˈbɛli dæns/, *n.* a solo dance of oriental origin performed by a woman by stressing movements of the abdominal muscles.

**bellyflop** /ˈbɛliflɒp/, *n., v.,* **-flopped, -flopping.** *Colloq.* *–n.* **1.** Also, **bellyflopper.** →**bellybuster.** *–v.i.* **2.** to dive so that one's stomach hits the water first.

**bellyful** /ˈbɛlifʊl/, *n. Colloq.* enough or more than enough.

**bellyland** /ˈbɛlilænd/, *v.i.* to land an aircraft without undercarriage, on the belly of the fuselage. – **bellylanding,** *n.*

**belly laugh** /ˈbɛli laf/, *n.* a deep, loud, and uninhibited laugh.

**belly-wool** /ˈbɛli-wʊl/, *n.* the wool on or from a sheep's belly. Also, **bellies.**

**belong** /bəˈlɒŋ, bi-/, *v.i.* **1.** to have one's rightful place; to bear relation as a member, adherent, inhabitant, etc. (fol. by *to*): *he belongs to Sydney.* **2. belong to, a.** to be the property of: *the book belongs to him.* **b.** to be an appurtenance, adjunct, or part of: *that cover belongs to this jar.* **c.** to be a property, function, or concern of: *attributes which belong to nature.* **3.** to have the proper social qualifications: *he doesn't belong.* **4.** to be proper or due. [ME *belonge(n),* from BE- + *longen* belong, adj., aphetic var. of d. *along,* OE *gelang* belonging to]

**belonging** /bəˈlɒŋɪŋ, bi-/, *n.* **1.** something that belongs. **2.** (*pl.*) possessions; goods; personal effects.

**beloved** /bəˈlʌvəd, -ˈlʌvd, bi-/, *adj.* **1.** greatly loved; dear to the heart. *–n.* **2.** one who is greatly loved.

**below** /bəˈloʊ, bi-/, *adv.* **1.** in or to a lower place; lower down; beneath. **2.** on or to a lower floor; downstairs. **3.** on earth. **4.** in hell or the infernal regions. **5.** at a later point on a page or in writing: *see the statistics below.* **6.** in a lower rank or grade: *he was demoted to the class below.* *–prep.* **7.** lower down than: *below the knee.* **8.** lower in rank, degree, amount, rate, etc., than: *below cost.* **9.** too low or base to be worthy of. **10.** downstream of: *below the bridge.* [ME *bilooghe* by low. See BE-, LOW[1]]

**bel paese** /bɛl 'peɪzə, peɪ'izə/, *n.* a mild Italian table cheese. [Trademark]

**Belsen horror** /bɛlsən 'hɒrə/, *n.* one who is unusually thin, or emaciated. [from *Belsen,* German concentration camp]

**belt** /bɛlt/, *n.* **1.** a band of flexible material, as leather, worn around the waist to support clothing, for decoration, etc. **2.** *Sport.* such a band as a token of honour or achievement. **3.** any encircling or transverse band, strip, or strips. **4.** a large strip of land having distinctive properties or characteristics: *the wheat belt.* **5.** *Mach.* **a.** a flexible band or cord connecting and pulling about each of two or more wheels, pulleys or the like, to transmit or change the direction of motion. **b.** conveyor belt. **6.** *Navy.* a series of armour-plates around a ship. **7.** *Mil.* **a.** a cloth strip with loops, or a series of metal links with grips, for holding cartridges which are fed into an automatic gun. **b.** a band of leather or webbing, worn around the waist and used as a support for weapons, ammunition, etc. **8.** *Boxing.* an imaginary line round the body at the level of the navel below which the boxer must not strike. **9. below the belt,** against the rules; unfairly. *–v.t.* **10.** to gird or furnish with a belt. **11.** to surround or mark as if with a belt. **12.** to fasten on (a sword, etc.) by means of a belt. **13.** to beat with a belt, strap, etc. **14.** *Colloq.* to give a thwack or blow to. **15.** to sing very loudly and often raucously (fol. by *out*). **16.** *Colloq.* to eat or drink quickly (fol. by *into*): *belt that food into you.* *–v.i.* **17.** *Colloq.* to move quickly or expeditiously: *to belt along.* **18. belt into,** to begin with speed and vigour. **19. belt up,** *Colloq.* **a.** be quiet; shut up. **b.** to fasten a safety belt. [ME and OE, ? from L *balteus*]

**belting** /'bɛltɪŋ/, *n.* **1.** material for belts. **2.** belts collectively. **3.** a belt. **4.** *Colloq.* a thrashing or beating.

**beltman** /'bɛltmən/, *n.* the member of a surf-lifesaving team who wears the belt attached to the surf-line and swims to the rescue of a person in difficulties.

**beluga** /bə'lugə/, *n.* **1.** the white whale, a cetacean, *Delphinapterus leucas,* chiefly arctic, having a rounded head, and white in colour. **2.** a white sturgeon, *Acipenser huso,* of the Caspian and the Black Sea, yielding caviar and isinglass. [Russ. *bielukha,* from *bielo-* white]

**belut** /bə'lut/, *n.* the one-gilled eel, *Fluta alba,* found in oriental rice fields but introduced into Australia.

**belvedere** /'bɛlvədɪə/, *n.* **1.** an upper storey or any structure or building designed to afford a fine view. **2.** (*cap.*) the Vatican art gallery in Rome. [It.: beautiful view]

**B.E.M.,** British Empire Medal.

**bema** /'bimə/, *n., pl.* **-mata** /-mətə/. **1.** a rostrum from which ancient Greek orators made speeches. **2.** *Gk Orth. Ch.* the enclosed space surrounding the altar; the sanctuary or chancel. [Gk: step, platform]

**bemaul** /bə'mɔl, bi-/, *v.t.* to maul severely.

**bemean** /bə'min, bi-/, *v.t.* to make mean; debase (oneself).

**bemire** /bə'maɪə, bi-/, *v.t.,* **-mired, -miring. 1.** to soil with mire. **2.** to sink in mire.

**bemoan** /bə'moun, bi-/, *v.t.* **1.** to moan over; bewail; lament. **2.** to express pity for. *–v.i.* **3.** to lament; mourn. [BE- + MOAN; replacing ME *bemene(n),* OE *bemænan*]

**bemused** /bə'mjuzd, bi-/, *adj.* **1.** confused; muddled; stupefied. **2.** lost in thought; preoccupied.

**ben**[1] /bɛn/, *n.* **1.** a tree, *Moringa oleifera,* of Arabia, India, and elsewhere, bearing a winged seed (nut) which yields an oil (**oil of ben**), used in extracting flower perfumes, lubricating delicate machinery, etc. **2.** the seed of such a tree. [Ar. *bān*]

**ben**[2] /bɛn/, *n. Scot.* a mountain peak. [Gael. *beann*]

**benadryl** /'bɛnədrɪl/, *n.* a synthetic drug, diphenhydramine hydrochloride, used esp. to relieve hay fever and hives. [Trademark]

**bench** /bɛntʃ/, *n.* **1.** a long seat with or without a back to accommodate several people. **2.** a seat on which members sit in a house of parliament. **3. a.** the seat on which judges sit in court. **b.** the court itself: *a High Court bench.* **4.** the position or office of a judge: *appointed to the bench.* **5.** the body of persons sitting as judges. **6.** *Brit.* the bishops of the Church of England. **7.** a seat occupied by a person in his or her official capacity. **8.** the persons themselves. **9.** the strong work-table of a carpenter or other mechanic. **10.** a platform on which animals are placed for exhibition, esp. at a dog show. **11.** a dog show. **12.** →**berm** (def. 1). **13.** *Mining.* **a.** a step or working elevation in a mine. **b.** a shelf formed in working an open excavation on more than one level. **14.** *Phys. Geog.* a flat, terrace-like tract of land on a valley slope above the stream bed, or along a coast above the level of sea or lake. *–v.t.* **15.** to furnish with benches. **16.** *to seat on a bench.* **17.** to place in exhibition: *to bench a dog.* [ME; OE *benc.* See BANK[2], BANK[3]] – **benchless,** *adj.*

**bencher** /'bɛntʃə/, *n.* **1.** *Brit.* a senior member of an Inn of Court. **2. frontbencher,** a minister of the Government or an Opposition spokesman. **3. backbencher,** a member of Parliament not holding ministerial office and not appointed Opposition spokesman.

**benchman** /'bɛntʃmən/, *n.* the operator working the sawbench of a mill.

**benchmark** /'bɛntʃmak/, *n.* **1.** *Survey.* a point of known elevation, usu. a mark cut into some durable material, as stone or a concrete post with a bronze plate, to serve as a reference point in running a line of levels for the determination of elevations. **2.** a point of reference from which quality or excellence is measured.

**bench press** /'bɛntʃ prɛs/, *n. Weightlifting.* a competition lift where the competitor lies on a bench and lifts the weights above his chest to arm's length.

**bench warrant** /'– wɒrənt/, *n.* a warrant issued or ordered by a judge or court for the apprehension of an offender.

**bend**[1] /bɛnd/, *v.,* **bent** or (*Archaic*) **bended, bending,** *n.* *–v.t.* **1.** to bring (a bow, etc.) into a state of tension by curving it. **2.** to force into a different or particular, esp. curved, shape, as by pressure. **3.** to cause to submit: *to bend someone to one's will.* **4.** to turn in a particular direction. **5.** to incline mentally (fol. by *to* or *towards*). **6.** to alter the pitch of (a tone) slightly, as in blues music. **7.** *Naut.* to fasten. **8.** *Archaic.* to strain or brace tensely (fol. by *up*). *–v.i.* **9.** to become curved, crooked, or bent. **10.** to assume a bent posture; stoop. **11.** to bow in submission or reverence; yield; submit. **12.** to turn or incline in a particular direction; be directed. **13.** to direct one's energies. **14. bend over backwards,** to exert oneself to the utmost; make a strenuous effort. **15. bend the elbow,** *Colloq.* to drink alcoholic liquor usu. to excess. *–n.* **16.** the act of bending. **17.** the state of being bent. **18.** a bent thing or part; curve; crook. **19.** *Naut.* a knot by which a rope is fastened to another rope or to something else. **20. round the bend,** *Colloq.* mad. **21. the bends,** a sometimes fatal disorder involving the formation of nitrogen bubbles in the blood and caused by a too rapid decrease in the pressure to which the body is subjected; found in divers who have surfaced too quickly, pilots of unpressurised aircraft, workers in compressed air, etc., and characterised by pains in the lungs, the limbs and joints, and the adoption of a bent position; caisson disease. [ME *bende(n),* OE *bendan* bind, bend (a bow)] – **bendable,** *adj.*

**bend**[2] /bɛnd/, *n. Her.* a diagonal band extending from the dexter chief to the sinister base. [OE *bend* band; in ME identified with OF *bende* band]

**bender** /'bɛndə/, *n.* **1.** one who or that which bends. **2.** *Colloq.* a drinking spree. [Brit.]

**bend sinister** /bɛnd 'sɪnəstə/, *n. Her.* a diagonal band extending from the sinister chief to the dexter base (a supposed mark of bastardy).

bend sinister

**bene-,** a word element meaning 'well', as in *benediction.* [L, combining form of *bene,* adv.]

**beneath** /bə'niθ, bi-/, *adv.* **1.** below; in a lower place, state, etc. **2.** underneath: *the heaven above and the earth beneath.* *–prep.* **3.** below; under: *beneath the same roof.* **4.** farther down than; lower in place than. **5.** lower down on a slope than: *beneath the crest of a hill.* **6.** inferior in position, power, etc., to: *a captain is beneath a major.* **7.** unworthy of; below the level or dignity of: *beneath contempt.* [ME *benethe,* OE *beneothan,* from *be* by + *neothan* below]

**benedick** /'bɛnədɪk/, *n.* a newly married man, esp. one who has been long a bachelor. [in Shakespeare's *Much Ado About Nothing,* the confident bachelor who courts and finally marries Beatrice] Also, **benedict.**

**Benedictine** /ˌbɛnəˈdɪktin/, *n.* **1.** *Eccles.* a member of an order of monks founded at Monte Cassino, between Rome and Naples, by St Benedict about A.D. 530, or of various congregations of nuns following his rule. The rules of the order (**benedictine rule**) enjoined silence and useful employment when not in divine service. **2.** (*usu. l.c.*) a French liqueur originally made by Benedictine monks. *–adj.* **3.** pertaining to St Benedict or to an order following his rule. [F *bénédictin*]

**benediction** /bɛnəˈdɪkʃən/, *n. Eccles.* **1.** the act of uttering a blessing. **2.** the form of blessing pronounced by an officiating minister, as at the close of divine service, etc. **3.** a ceremony by which things are set aside for sacred uses, as a church, vestments, bells, etc. **4.** the advantage conferred by blessing; a mercy or benefit. [ME, from L *benedictio*] – **benedictional,** *adj.* – **benedictory** /bɛnəˈdɪktəri/, *adj.*

**Benedict's test** /ˈbɛnədɪkts ˌtɛst/, *n.* a chemical test for detecting the presence of reducing sugars in urine. [named after Stanley R. *Benedict,* 1884-1936, U.S. biochemist]

**Benedictus** /bɛnəˈdɪktəs/, *n. Eccles.* **1.** the short canticle or hymn beginning in Latin 'Benedictus qui venit in nomine Domini', and in English 'Blessed is He that cometh in the name of the Lord'. **2.** the canticle or hymn beginning in Latin 'Benedictus Dominus Deus Israel', and in English 'Blessed be the Lord God of Israel'. **3.** a musical setting of either of these canticles. [L: pp., blessed]

**benefaction** /bɛnəˈfækʃən/, *n.* **1.** the act of conferring a benefit; doing good. **2.** the benefit conferred; charitable donation. [LL *benefactio*]

**benefactor** /ˈbɛnəfæktə, bɛnəˈfæktə/, *n.* **1.** one who confers a benefit; kindly helper. **2.** one who makes a bequest or endowment. [L] – **benefactress** /ˈbɛnəfæktrəs, bɛnəˈfæktrəs/, *n. fem.*

**benefice** /ˈbɛnəfəs/, *n., v.,* **-ficed, -ficing.** *–n.* **1.** an ecclesiastical living. **2.** the revenue itself. *–v.t.* **3.** to invest with a benefice or ecclesiastical living. [ME, from OF, from L *beneficium* benefit, favour]

**beneficence** /bəˈnɛfəsəns/, *n.* **1.** the doing of good; active goodness or kindness; charity. **2.** beneficent act or gift; benefaction. [L *beneficentia*]

**beneficent** /bəˈnɛfəsənt/, *adj.* doing good or causing good to be done; conferring benefits; kindly in action or purpose. – **beneficently,** *adv.*

**beneficial** /bɛnəˈfɪʃəl/, *adj.* **1.** conferring benefit; advantageous; helpful. **2.** *Law.* **a.** helpful in the meeting of needs: *a beneficial association.* **b.** involving the personal enjoyment of proceeds: *a beneficial owner.* – **beneficially,** *adv.*

**beneficiary** /bɛnəˈfɪʃəri/, *n., pl.* **-aries.** **1.** one who receives benefits, profits, or advantages. **2.** *Law.* a person designated as the recipient of funds or other property under a trust, insurance policy, etc. **3.** *Eccles.* the holder of a benefice.

**beneficiation** /ˌbɛnəfɪʃiˈeɪʃən/, *n.* **1.** the dressing or processing of ores to regulate the size of the product, remove unwanted constituents and improve the quality, purity or assay grade. **2.** concentration or other preparation of ore for smelting by drying, flotation, or magnetic separation.

**benefit** /ˈbɛnəfət/, *n., v.,* **-fited, -fiting.** *–n.* **1.** an act of kindness. **2.** anything that is for the good of a person or thing. **3.** a theatrical performance or other public entertainment to raise money for a worthy purpose. **4.** a payment or other assistance given by an insurance company, mutual benefit society, or public agency. *–v.t.* **5.** to do good to; be of service to. *–v.t.* **6.** to gain advantage; make improvement. [partial Latinisation of ME *benfet,* from AF, from L *benefactum,* from *bene* -BENE- + *factum* thing done. See and cf. FACT]

**benefit of clergy,** *n.* **1.** *Colloq.* church rites, as marriage. **2.** an early right of church authorities to try, in an ecclesiastical court, any clergyman accused of serious crime.

**Benelux** /ˈbɛnəlʌks/, *n.* **1.** a customs union (since 1 January, 1948) of Belgium, the Netherlands, and Luxembourg, now part of the Common Market. **2.** these countries collectively.

**benevolence** /bəˈnɛvələns/, *n.* **1.** desire to do good for others; goodwill; charitableness. **2.** an act of kindness; charitable gift. **3.** *Eng. Hist.* a forced contribution to the sovereign.

**benevolent** /bəˈnɛvələnt/, *adj.* **1.** desiring to do good for others. **2.** intended for benefits rather than profit: *a benevolent institution.* [L *benevolens* well-wishing; replacing ME *benyvolent,* from OF *benivolent*] – **benevolently,** *adv.*

**benevolent society** /ˈ– səˌsaɪəti/, *n.* **1.** →**friendly society.** **2.** a charitable organisation. Also, **benevolent association, benevolent fund.**

**B.Eng.,** Bachelor of Engineering.

**Bengali** /bɛnˈgɔli, bɛŋ-/, *n.* **1.** a native or an inhabitant of Bengal. **2.** the language of Bengal, an Indic language. *–adj.* **3.** of or pertaining to Bengal, its inhabitants, or their language. – **Bengalese,** *n., adj.*

**bengaline** /ˈbɛŋgəlin, bɛŋgəˈlin/, *n.* a corded fabric resembling poplin but with heavier cords; it may be silk or rayon with worsted cord. [F]

**Bengal light** /ˌbɛŋgɔl ˈlaɪt/, *n.* a vivid, sustained, blue light used in signalling, fireworks, etc. Also, **Bengal match.**

**benighted** /bəˈnaɪtəd/, *adj.* **1.** intellectually or morally ignorant; unenlightened. **2.** overtaken by darkness or night. [pp. of *benight,* v., from BE- + NIGHT]

**benign** /bəˈnaɪn/, *adj.* **1.** of a kind disposition; kind. **2.** showing or caused by gentleness or kindness: *a benign smile.* **3.** favourable; propitious: *benign planets.* **4.** (of weather) salubrious. **5.** *Pathol.* not malignant: *a benign tumour.* [ME *benigne,* from OF, from L *benignus* kind] – **benignly,** *adv.*

**benignant** /bəˈnɪgnənt/, *adj.* **1.** kind, esp. to inferiors; gracious. **2.** exerting a good influence; beneficial. **3.** *Pathol.* benign. [b. BEN(IGN) and (MAL)IGNANT] – **benignancy** /bəˈnɪgnənsi/, *n.* – **benignantly,** *adv.*

**benignity** /bəˈnɪgnəti/, *n., pl.* **-ties.** **1.** the quality of being benign; propitiousness; kindness. **2.** a good deed.

**Benin** /bəˈnin/, *n.* a kingdom in West Africa.

**benison** /ˈbɛnəsən, -zən/, *n. Archaic.* benediction. [ME *benisoun,* from OF *beneison,* from L *benedictio*]

**benne** /ˈbɛni/, *n.* the sesame, *Sesamum indicum,* from the seeds of which a fixed oil (**oil of benne** or **benne oil**) is expressed. [Malay]

**bennet** /ˈbɛnət/, *n.* →**herb bennet.**

**Bennett's tree-kangaroo** /ˌbɛnəts tri-kæŋgəˈru/, *n.* a stocky, brownish kangaroo, *Dendrolagus bennettianus,* with powerful forelegs and a long, cylindrical, non-prehensile tail, found in mountainous rainforest of north-eastern Queensland; tcharibeena. [named after Dr. George *Bennett,* 1814-93, naturalist]

**Bennett's wallaby** /– ˈwɒləbi/, *n.* →**red wallaby.**

**benny** /ˈbɛni/, *n. Colloq.* a benzedrine pill.

**bent**[1] /bɛnt/, *adj.* **1.** curved; crooked: *a bent stick, bow, etc.* **2.** determined; set; resolved (fol. by *on*). **3.** *Colloq.* stolen: *to sell bent goods.* **4.** *Colloq.* thievish; having little or no regard for the law; dishonest: *a bent cop.* **5.** *Colloq.* diverging from what is considered to be normal or conservative behaviour, as by taking illegal drugs, practising homosexuality, etc. **6.** *Music.* of a tone, slightly altered from the pitch of the diatonic scale, as a bent note. *–n.* **7.** bent state or form. **8.** direction taken; inclination; leaning; bias: *a bent for painting.* **9.** capacity of endurance. **10.** *Civ. Eng.* a transverse frame of a bridge or a building, designed to support either vertical or horizontal loads. **11.** *Colloq.* one who diverges from the orthodox patterns of society as a homosexual, a taker of illegal drugs, etc. [pp. of BEND[1]]

**bent**[2] /ˈbɛnt/, *n.* **1.** →**bent grass.** **2.** a stalk of such grass. **3.** (formerly) any stiff grass or sedge. [ME; OE *beonet,* c. G *Binse* rush]

**bent-arm balance** /bɛnt-am ˈbæləns/, *n. Gymnastics.* a position of the body in which it is balanced vertically above the hands with the arms bent.

**bent cop** /bɛnt ˈkɒp/, *n. Colloq.* a dishonest policeman, esp. one who takes bribes.

**bent grass** /ˈbɛnt gras/, *n.* any of the species of *Agrostis,* esp. browntop, used for fine lawns. Also, **bent.**

**Benthamism** /ˈbɛnθəmɪzəm/, *n.* the variety of utilitarianism put forth by Jeremy Bentham (1748-1832) characterised esp. by the principle of the greatest happiness (good) for the greatest number. – **Benthamite** /ˈbɛnθəmaɪt/, *n., adj.*

**benthos** /ˈbɛnθɒs/, *n.* the animals and plants that are fixed to or crawl upon the sea bottom. Also, **benthon.** [Gk: depth (of the sea)] – **benthic,** *adj.*

**bent note** /ˈbɛnt ˌnoʊt/, *n. Music.* a tone which is slightly altered from the pitch of the diatonic scale by the stretching of strings or by other pitch-altering techniques.

**bentonite** /'bɛntənaɪt/, *n.* a clay formed by the decomposition of volcanic ash, having the ability to absorb large quantities of water and to expand to several times its normal volume; used as a fining agent in wine, and as a drilling mud in oil exploration. Also, **Bentonitic clay.** [named after Fort *Benton,* Montana]

**bentwing swift moth,** *n.* a large hepialid moth, *Zelotypia stacyi,* having large larvae which attack various species of eucalypts.

**bentwood** /'bɛntwʊd/, *n.* **1.** wood steamed and bent for use in furniture. *–adj.* **2.** of or denoting such furniture.

**benumb** /bə'nʌm, bi-/, *v.t.* **1.** to make numb; deprive of sensation: *benumbed by cold.* **2.** to render inactive; stupefy. [ME *benome(n),* OE *benumen,* pp. of *beniman* deprive]

**benz-,** variant of **benzo-,** chiefly used before vowels.

**benzaldehyde** /bɛn'zældəhaɪd/, *n.* an aldehyde, $C_6H_5CHO$, obtained from natural oil of bitter almonds or other oils, or produced artificially, used in dyes, as a flavouring agent, etc.

**benzamine** /'bɛnzəmin/, *n.* →**eucaine** (def. 2).

**benzedrine** /'bɛnzədrən, -drin/, *n. Colloq.* amphetamine, or any stimulant drug. [Trademark]

**benzene** /'bɛnzin, bɛn'zin/, *n.* a colourless, volatile, inflammable, liquid, aromatic hydrocarbon, $C_6H_6$, obtained chiefly from coal tar, and used as a solvent for resins, fats, etc., and in the manufacture of dyes, etc.

**benzene ring** /bɛnzin 'rɪŋ/, *n.* the graphic representation of the structure of benzene as a hexagon with a carbon atom at each of its points. Each carbon atom is united with an atom of hydrogen, one or more of which may be replaced to form benzene derivatives. Also, **benzene nucleus.**

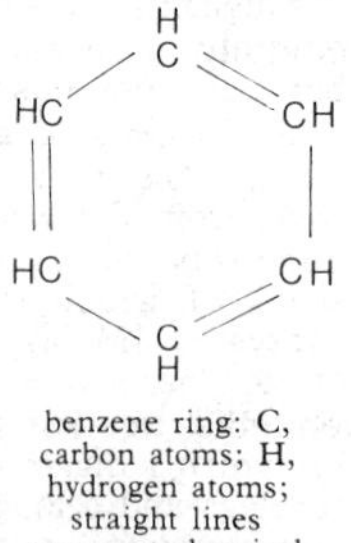

benzene ring: C, carbon atoms; H, hydrogen atoms; straight lines represent chemical bonds

**benzidine** /'bɛnzədin/, *n.* a basic compound, $NH_2C_6H_4C_6H_4HH_2$, occurring as greyish scales or a crystalline powder, used in the manufacture of certain dyes, as Congo red. [BENZ- + -ID³ + -INE²]

**benzine** /'bɛnzin, bɛn'zin/, *n.* **1.** a colourless, volatile, inflammable liquid, a mixture of various hydrocarbons, obtained in the distillation of petroleum, and used in cleaning, dyeing, etc. **2.** *Chiefly U.S.* →**petrol.**

**benzo-,** a combining form meaning 'pertaining to or derived from benzene' or designating the presence of benzoic acid. Also, **benz-.**

**benzoate** /'bɛnzoʊeɪt, -ət/, *n.* a salt or ester of benzoic acid.

**benzocaine** /'bɛnzəkeɪn/, *n.* a water-insoluble crystalline ester, $NH_2C_6H_4COOC_2H_5$ (ethyl p-aminobenzoate), used as a local anaesthetic. Also, **anaesthesin.**

**benzoic acid** /bɛn,zoʊɪk 'æsəd/, *n.* a white, crystalline acid, $C_6H_5COOH$, obtained from benzoin and other balsams or from toluene, used in medicine, aniline dye manufacture, as a food preservative, etc.

**benzoin** /'bɛnzɔɪn, 'bɛnzoʊən/, *n.* **1.** a balsamic resin obtained from species of *Styrax,* esp. S. *benzoin,* a tree of Java, Sumatra, etc., and used in perfumery, medicine, etc. **2.** any plant of the lauraceous genus *Lindera* (also known as *Benzoin*) which includes the spicebush and other aromatic plants. **3.** *Chem.* white or yellowish crystals with slight camphor smell, $C_6H_5CHOHCOC_6H_5$; bitter almond-oil camphor. [earlier *benjoin,* from F, through Sp. or Pg., from Ar. *lubān jāwi* incense of Java (*lu-* apparently taken as 'the')]

**benzol** /'bɛnzɒl/, *n.* crude industrial benzene. Also, **benzole.**

**benzoline** /'bɛnzəlin/, *n.* **1.** →**benzene. 2.** →**benzine.** Also, **benzolin.** [Trademark]

**benzophenone** /,bɛnzoʊfə'noʊn/, *n.* a water-insoluble crystalline ketone, $C_6H_5COC_6H_5$, used in organic synthesis. [BENZO- + PHEN- + -ONE]

**benzoquinone** /,bɛnzoʊkwə'noʊn/, *n.* →**quinone** (def. 1).

**benzoyl** /'bɛnzoʊəl/, *n.* a univalent radical, $C_6H_5CO$, present in benzoic acid and allied compounds.

**benzpyrene** /bɛnz'paɪrin/, *n.* a yellow crystalline polycyclic hydrocarbon, $C_{20}H_{12}$, occurring in minute quantities in coal tar. It is carcinogenic, and thought to be one of the most harmful constituents of tobacco smoke.

**benzyl** /'bɛnzəl/, *n.* a univalent organic radical, $C_6H_5CH_2$, from toluene.

**bequeath** /bə'kwið, '-kwiθ/, *v.t.* **1.** *Law.* to dispose by last will of (personal property, esp. money). **2.** to hand down; pass on. **3.** *Obs.* to commit; entrust. [ME *bequethe(n),* OE *becwethan,* from BE- + *cwethan* say] – **bequeathal** /bə'kwiðəl/, *n.*

**bequest** /bə'kwɛst, bi-/, *n.* **1.** *Law.* a disposition in a will concerning personal property, esp. money. **2.** a legacy. [ME *biqueste,* OE *gequis,* c. Goth. *gakwiss* consent]

**berate** /bə'reɪt/, *v.t.,* **-rated, -rating.** to scold.

**Berber** /'bɜbə/, *n.* **1.** a member of a group of North African tribes living in Barbary and the Sahara. **2.** the Hamitic languages of the Berbers, spoken from Tunisia, west to the Atlantic and in the Sahara, including Kabyle, Tuareg, and other languages. *–adj.* **3.** of or pertaining to the Berbers or their language.

**berberine** /'bɜbərin/, *n.* a widely distributed alkaloid, $C_{20}H_{19}NO_5$, found in a considerable number of plants whose extracts have a yellow colour and a bitter taste.

**berceuse** /bɜ'sɜz/, *n., pl.* **-ceuses** /-'sɜz/. a cradlesong; lullaby. [F]

**bereave** /bə'riv, bi-/, *v.t.,* **-reaved** or **-reft, -reaving. 1.** to deprive (*of*) ruthlessly, esp. of hope, joy, etc.: *bereft of all their lands.* **2.** to make desolate through loss (*of*), esp. by death: *bereaved of their mother.* **3.** *Obs.* to take away by violence. [ME *bereve(n),* OE *berēafian,* from BE- + *rēafian* rob] – **bereavement,** *n.*

**bereft** /bə'rɛft/, *v.* **1.** past participle of **bereave.** *–adj.* **2.** suffering loss; deprived of possession: *bereft of his family.* **3.** lacking: *bereft of meaning.*

**beresk** /bə'rɛsk/, *adj. Colloq.* berserk.

**beret** /'bɛreɪ/, *n.* a soft, round, peakless cap that fits closely. [F, from Béarn dialect *berreto,* from Gallo-Rom. *birretum* cap, from LL *birrum* cloak]

**berg**¹ /bɜg/, *n.* →**iceberg.** [short for ICEBERG]

**berg**² /bɜg/, *n.* (in South Africa) a mountain. [Afrikaans]

**Bergalia tussock** /bə,geɪliə 'tʌsək/, *n.* a tussocky sedge, *Carex longibrachiata,* found in pastures on the south coast of New South Wales; drooping sedge.

**bergamasque** /'bɜgəmask/, *n.* a rustic dance based on a regular sequence of chords, with improvised melodies. Also, **bergamask.** [It., *Bergamesco,* of Bergamo, a town in Italy]

**bergamot** /'bɜgəmɒt/, *n.* **1.** a small tree of the citrus family, *Citrus bergamia,* the rind of whose fruit yields a fragrant essential oil (**essence of bergamot**). **2.** the oil or essence itself. **3.** any of various plants of the mint family, as *Mentha citrata,* yielding an oil resembling essence of bergamot and *Monarda didyma,* cultivated for its scented foliage. **4.** *Hort.* one of a group of globular oblate, evenly and regularly shaped pears. [F *bergamote,* from It. *bergamotta,* apparently from Turk *begarmūdi* prince's pear]

**bergoo** /'bɜgu/, *n. Colloq.* →**burgoo.**

**Bergsonism** /'bɜgsənɪzəm/, *n.* a doctrine of creative evolution put forward by Henri Bergson (1859-1941), emphasising duration as the central fact of experience and an *élan vital* (vital drive) as an original life-force essentially governing all organic processes.

**berhyme** /bə'raɪm/, *v.t.,* **-rhymed, -rhyming.** to celebrate in verse. Also, **berime.**

**beribboned** /bə'rɪbənd/, *adj.* adorned with ribbons.

**beri-beri** /'bɛri-bɛri/, *n.* a disease of the peripheral nerves caused by deficiency in vitamin $B_1$ and marked by pain in and paralysis of the extremities, and severe emaciation or swelling of the body. [Singhalese, reduplication of *beri* weakness]

**berigora** /bɛri'gɔrə/, *n.* a medium-sized, slow-moving brown falcon, *Falco berigora,* found in open country throughout Australia and New Guinea.

**berk** /bɜk/, *n. Colloq.* (*derog.*) an unpleasant or despicable person. Also, **birk, burk, burke.** [rhyming slang, *Berkshire Hunt* cunt]

**Berkeleian** /'bakliən/, *adj.* **1.** pertaining or relating to George Berkeley, (1685-1753, Irish philosopher) or to his philosophy. *–n.* **2.** one who holds Berkeley's system of idealism; one who denies the existence of a material world. – **Berkeleianism,** *n.*

**berkelium** /bə'kiliəm/, *n.* a synthetic, radioactive, metallic element. *Symbol:* Bk; *at, no.:* 97. [*Berkel(ey),* California, where first identified + -IUM]

**berko** /'bɜkoʊ/, *adj. Colloq.* berserk.

**Berkshire** /'bakʃɪə, 'bɜk-, -ʃə/, *n.* one of a breed of black pigs originating in Berkshire (English county) characterised by white markings on feet.

**berley** /'bɜli/, *n.* **1.** any bait, as chopped fish or broken bread or chopped green weed mixed with sand, spread on the water by fishermen to attract fish. **2.** *Colloq.* vomit, resulting from seasickness. **3.** *Colloq.* leg-pulling; good humoured deceit. Also, **burley, birley.** [orig. uncert.]

**berlin** /bɜ'lɪn/, *n.* **1.** large four-wheeled closed carriage hung between two perches, having two interior seats. **2.** berline. **3.** →**berlin wool.** [named after *Berlin,* a city in Germany]

berlin

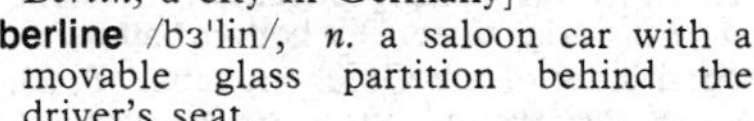

**berline** /bɜ'lin/, *n.* a saloon car with a movable glass partition behind the driver's seat.

**berlin wool** /bɜlɪn 'wʊl/, *n.* a soft woollen yarn for tapestry work, etc.

**berm** /bɜm/, *n.* **1.** Also, **berme.** *Fort.* a narrow terrace between the rampart and moat. **2.** the ledge or shoulder alongside a road. **3.** *Geol.* a nearly horizontal portion of a beach or backshore formed by the deposit of material by wave action. **4.** *Archaeol.* the flat space which separates a mound from its ditch, or a spoil heap from its trench. [F *berme,* from MD]

**berm-type building** /'bɜm-taɪp bɪldɪŋ/, *n.* a building in which the spoil from excavation is piled against the base, coming perhaps a metre or more up the wall to reinforce and strengthen the structure.

**bermuda grass** /bə'mjudə gras/, *n.* →**couch**².

**Bermuda rig** /bə'mjudə rɪg/, *n.* a fore-and-aft rig on a sailing boat in which the sails have a triangular shape, there being no gaff. Also, **Bermudan rig.**

**bermuda shorts** /– 'ʃɔts/, *n.pl.* shorts reaching to the knee, worn by men and women in casual dress.

**bernicle goose** /'bɜnɪkəl gus/, *n.* →**barnacle goose.**

**berretta** /bə'rɛtə/, *n.* →**biretta.**

**berried** /'bɛrid/, *adj.* **1.** covered with berries. **2.** of or like a berry; baccate. **3.** (of lobsters, etc.) having eggs.

**berrigan** /'bɛrɪgən/, *n.* a slender drooping tree of inland Australia, *Pittosporum phylliraeoides.*

**berrin-berrin** /bɛrən-'bɛrən/, *n.* →**rainbow bee-eater.**

**berry** /'bɛri/, *n., pl.* **-ries,** *v.,* **-ried, -rying.** *–n.* **1.** any small, (usu.) stoneless and juicy fruit, irrespective of botanical structure, as the gooseberry, strawberry, holly berry, rose hip, etc. **2.** a dry seed or kernel, as of wheat. **3.** a knob on a swan's bill. **4.** *Bot.* a simple fruit having a pulpy pericarp in which the seeds are embedded, as the grape, gooseberry, currant, tomato, etc. **5.** one of the eggs of the lobster. *–v.i.* **6.** to bear or produce berries. **7.** to gather berries. [ME and OE *berie,* c. G *Beere*] – **berryless,** *adj.* – **berrylike,** *adj.*

**berserk** /bə'zɜk/, *adj.* **1.** violently and destructively frenzied. *–n.* **2.** →**berserker.**

**berserker** /bə'zɜkə/, *n.* (in Scandinavian legend) one of the ancient Norse warriors of great strength and courage, reputed to have fought with frenzied fury in battle; baresark. [Icel. *berserkr* wild warrior; orig. uncert.]

**berth** /bɜθ/, *n.* **1.** a shelf-like space, bunk, or whole room allotted to a traveller on a vessel or a train as a sleeping space. **2.** *Naut.* **a.** room for a vessel to moor at a dock or ride at anchor. **b.** a space allowed for safety or convenience between a vessel and other vessels, rocks, etc. **3.** any place allotted to a person. **4.** *Colloq.* job; position. **5. give a wide berth to,** to avoid; keep away from. *–v.t.* **6.** *Naut.* to assign or allot anchoring ground to; give space to lie in, as a ship in a dock. *–v.i.* **7.** *Naut.* to come to a dock, anchorage, or mooring. [probably from BEAR¹]

**bertha** /'bɜθə/, *n.* a kind of collar or trimming, as of lace, worn about the shoulders by women, as on a low-necked dress. [F *berthe,* from *Berthe* Bertha, mother of Charlemagne, 742-814 A.D. noted for her modesty]

**Bertillon system** /'bɜtələn ˌsɪstəm/, *n.* a system of identifying persons, esp. criminals, by a record of individual physical measurements and peculiarities. [named after the inventor, Alphonse *Bertillon,* 1853-1914, French anthropologist]

**beryl** /'bɛrəl/, *n.* **1.** a mineral, beryllium aluminium silicate, $Be_3Al_2Si_6O_{18}$, usu. green (but also blue, rose, white, and golden) and both opaque and transparent, the latter variety including the gems emerald and aquamarine; the principal ore of beryllium. **2.** pale bluish green; seagreen. [ME, from L *bēryllus,* from Gk *bḗryllos*] – **beryline** /'bɛrəlin, -laɪn/, *adj.*

**beryllium** /bə'rɪliəm/, *n.* a steel grey, divalent, hard, light, metallic element, the salts of which are said to have a sweetish taste (hence it is called glucinum by the French). Its chief use is in copper alloys not subject to fatigue, used for springs and contacts. *Symbol:* Be; *at. wt:* 9.0122; *at. no.:* 4; *sp. gr.:* 1.8 at 20°C. [BERYL + -IUM]

**beseech** /bə'sitʃ, bi-/, *v.t.,* **-sought** or **-seeched, -seeching. 1.** to implore urgently. **2.** to beg eagerly for; solicit. [ME *biseche(n),* from BE- + *sechen,* OE *sēcan* seek] – **beseecher,** *n.* – **beseechingness,** *n.* – **beseeching,** *adj.* – **beseechingly,** *adv.*

**beseem** /bə'sim, bi-/, *v.t.* **1.** to be fit for or worthy of. *–v.i.* **2.** to be seemly or fitting.

**beset** /bə'sɛt, bi-/, *v.t.,* **-set, -setting. 1.** to attack on all sides; assail; harass: *beset by enemies, difficulties, etc.* **2.** to surround; hem in. [ME *besette(n),* OE *besettan,* from BE- + *settan* SET] – **besetment,** *n.*

**besetting** /bə'sɛtɪŋ, bi-/, *adj.* constantly attacking, tempting, etc.: *our besetting sins.*

**beshrew** /bə'ʃru, bi-/, *v.t. Archaic.* to curse; invoke evil upon. [ME *beshrewen,* from BE- + *shrew,* obs. v., curse. See SHREW]

**beside** /bə'saɪd, bi-/, *prep.* **1.** by or at the side of; near: *sit down beside me.* **2.** compared with. **3.** *Rare.* over and above; in addition to; besides. **4.** apart from; not connected with: *beside the point or question.* **5. beside oneself,** out of one's senses through strong emotion. *–adv.* **6.** in addition; besides. [ME; OE *be sīdan* by side]

**besides** /bə'saɪdz, bi-/, *adv.* **1.** moreover. **2.** in addition. **3.** otherwise; else. *–prep.* **4.** over and above; in addition to. **5.** other than; except. [BESIDE + adv. *-s*]

**besiege** /bə'sidʒ, bi-/, *v.t.,* **-sieged, -sieging. 1.** to lay siege to. **2.** to crowd round. **3.** to assail or ply, as with requests, etc. – **besiegement,** *n.* – **besieger,** *n.*

**besmear** /bə'smɪə, bi-/, *v.t.* **1.** to smear over. **2.** to sully; soil. [ME *bismeren,* OE *besmerian.* See BE-, SMEAR]

**besmirch** /bə'smɜtʃ, bi-/, *v.t.* **1.** to soil; stain, as with soot. **2.** to detract from the honour of: *to besmirch one's name.*

**besom** /'bizəm/, *n.* **1.** brush or twigs bound together as a broom. **2.** a broom of any kind. [ME *besum* broom, rod, OE *besema,* c. G *Besen*]

**besot** /bə'sɒt, bi-/, *v.t.,* **-sotted, -sotting. 1.** to infatuate. **2.** to make stupid or foolish. **3.** to stupefy with drink.

**besought** /bə'sɔt, bi-/, *v.* past tense and past participle of **beseech.**

**bespake** /bə'speɪk, bi-/, *v. Archaic.* past tense of **bespeak.**

**bespangle** /bə'spæŋgəl, bi-/, *v.t.,* **-gled, -gling.** to adorn with, or as with, spangles.

**bespatter** /bə'spætə, bi-/, *v.t.* **1.** to soil by spattering; sprinkle with mud, dirty water, etc. **2.** to slander.

**bespeak** /bə'spik, bi-/, *v.,* **-spoke** or (*Archaic*) **-spake, -spoken** or **-spoke, -speaking,** *n.* *–v.t.* **1.** to ask for in advance; stipulate: *to bespeak a calm hearing or the reader's patience.* **2.** to reserve beforehand; engage in advance; make arrangements for: *to bespeak a seat in a theatre.* **3.** *Poetic.* to speak to; address. **4.** to show; indicate: *this bespeaks a kindly heart.* *–n.* **5.** *Obs.* an actor's benefit performance. [ME *bespeken,* OE *besprecan* speak against, speak of, from *be-* BE- + *sprecan* (for loss of *-r-* see SPEAK)]

**bespectacled** /bə'spɛktəkəld, bi-/, *adj.* wearing spectacles.

**bespoke** /bə'spoʊk, bi-/, *adj.* **1.** made to order: *bespoke goods.* **2.** working to order: *a bespoke tailor.* **3.** previously claimed; spoken for.

**bespread** /bə'sprɛd, bi-/, *v.t.,* **-spread, -spreading.** to spread over; cover with.

**besprent** /bə'sprɛnt, bi-/, *adj. Poetic.* besprinkled; bestrewed. [pp. of *bespreng* (obs.), OE *besprengan*]

**besprinkle** /bə'sprɪŋkəl, bi-/, *v.t.,* **-kled, -kling.** to sprinkle over with something; bespatter.

**Bessemer converter** /bɛsəmə kən'vɜtə/, *n.* a huge pear-shaped metal container used in the Bessemer process.

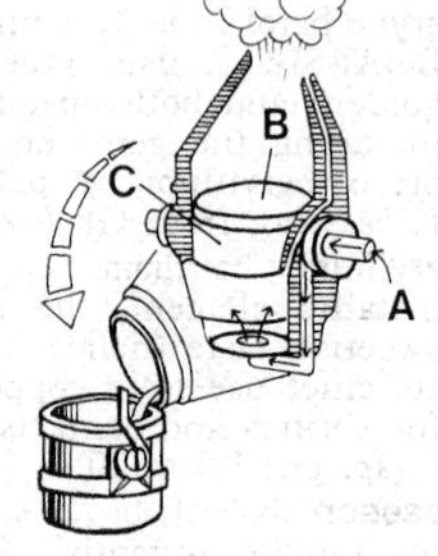

Bessemer converter: A, air; B, slag; C, molten steel

**Bessemer process** /'– ˌprousɛs/, *n.* a process of producing steel, in which impurities are removed by forcing a blast of air through molten iron. [named after Sir Henry *Bessemer,* 1813-98, English engineer]

**besser block** /'bɛsə blɒk/, *n.* a type of building block, moulded in concrete. Also, **besser brick.** [Trademark]

**best** /bɛst/, *adj.* (*superlative of* **good**). **1.** of the highest quality, excellence, or standing: *the best judgment.* **2.** most advantageous, suitable, or desirable: *the best way.* **3.** largest; most: *the best part of a day.* **4.** favourite: *best friend. –adv.* (*superlative of* **well**). **5.** most excellently or suitably; with most advantage or success. **6.** in or to the highest degree; most fully. **7. had best,** would be wiser, safer, etc., to. *–n.* **8.** the best thing, state, or part. **9.** one's finest clothing. **10.** utmost or best quality. **11. all the best,** (an expression of good will, used as a farewell or a toast). **12. at best, a.** in the best circumstances. **b.** in the most favourable view. **13. at one's best,** appearing or performing as well as possible. **14. for the best, a.** having an unexpectedly good result. **b.** with good intentions or motives. **15. get** or **have the best of,** to defeat. **16. give** (**someone** or **something**) **best,** *Colloq.* to admit defeat to (someone or something). **17. make the best of,** to manage as well as one can (in unfavourable or adverse circumstances). *–v.t.* **18.** to defeat; beat. **19.** to outdo; surpass. [ME *beste,* OE *betst,* c. Goth. *batist-*]

**best and fairest,** *n. Football.* an award made to a player for skill and fair play.

**best boy** /'bɛst bɔɪ/, *n. Films, Television.* a gaffer's assistant.

**bestead** /bə'stɛd, bi-/, *v.,* **-steaded, -steaded** or **-stead, -steading,** *adj. –v.t. Archaic.* **1.** to help; assist; serve; avail. *–adj.* **2.** placed; situated. [ME, from BE- + *stead,* v., help, be of use to, from *stead,* n., profit, support]

**best end** /'bɛst ɛnd/, *n.* (in a butchered animal) the end of the neck nearest the ribs. Also, **best end of neck.**

**bester** /'bɛstə/, *n. Colloq.* a fraudulent bookmaker.

**bestial** /'bɛstiəl/, *adj.* **1.** of or belonging to a beast. **2.** brutal; inhuman; irrational. **3.** depravedly sensual; carnal. [ME, from L *bestiālis*] – **bestially,** *adv.*

**bestialise** /'bɛstiəlaɪz/, *v.t.,* **-lised, -lising.** to make bestial. Also, **bestialize.**

**bestiality** /bɛsti'æləti/, *n.* **1.** bestial character or conduct; beastliness. **2.** excessive appetites or indulgence. **3.** sexual relations of a human with an animal; sodomy.

**bestiary** /'bɛstiəri/, *n., pl.* **-ries.** a type of book very popular in the Middle Ages, consisting of a collection of moralised fables about natural history objects, mostly animals, modelled on one attributed to an Alexandrian Greek of the 4th century after Christ. [ML *bestiārium,* properly neut. of L *bestiārius* pertaining to beasts]

**bestir** /bə'stɜ, bi-/, *v.t.* (*generally reflexive*), **-stirred, -stirring.** to stir up; rouse to action. [ME *bestyrie(n),* OE *bestyrian* heap up]

**best man** /bɛst 'mæn/, *n.* the chief attendant of the bridegroom at a wedding.

**best neck**/– 'nɛk/, *n.* See **neck** (def. 2).

**bestow** /bə'stoʊ, bi-/, *v.t.* **1.** to present as a gift; give; confer. **2.** to dispose of; apply to some use. **3.** *Colloq.* to provide quarters for. **4.** to put; stow; deposit; store. – **bestowal, bestowment,** *n.*

**bestraddle** /bə'strædl, bi-/, *v.t.,* **-dled, -dling.** to bestride.

**bestrew** /bə'stru, bi-/, *v.t.,* **-strewed, -strewn** or **-strewed, -strewing.** **1.** to strew or cover (a surface). **2.** to strew or scatter about. **3.** to lie scattered over. [ME *bistrewe(n),* OE *bestrēowian*]

**bestride** /bə'straɪd, bi-/, *v.t.,* **-strode** or **-strid, -stridden** or **-strid, -striding.** **1.** to get or be astride of; spread the legs on both sides of. **2.** to step over or across. [ME *bestride(n),* OE *bestrīdan,* from BE- + *strīdan* stride]

**best-seller** /bɛst-'sɛlə/, *n.* **1.** a book that has a very large sale during a given period. **2.** the author of such a book.

**bestud** /bə'stʌd, bi-/, *v.t.,* **-studded, -studding.** to set with studs distributed over a surface; dot.

**bet.,** between.

**bet** /bɛt/, *v.,* **bet** or **betted, betting,** *n. –v.t.* **1.** to pledge as a forfeit to another who makes a similar pledge in return, in support of an opinion; stake; wager. **2. bet London to a brick,** *Colloq.* to be firmly convinced. *–v.i.* **3.** to lay a wager. **4.** to make a practice of betting. **5. you bet,** *Colloq.* you may be sure; certainly. *–n.* **6.** a pledge of something to be forfeited, in case one is wrong, to another who has the opposite opinion. **7.** that which is pledged. **8.** chance of success. **9.** a thing, person, or eventuality on which to gamble or stake one's hopes: *he's a bad bet.* [orig. uncert.] – **better, bettor,** *n.*

**beta** /'bitə/, *n.* the second letter of the Greek alphabet (Β, β), often used to designate the second in a series, esp. in scientific classification, as: **a.** *Astron.* (of a constellation) the second brightest star: *Rigel is β (or Beta) Orionis.* **b.** *Chem.* (of a compound) one of the possible positions of substituted atoms or groups. **c.** (in examinations, etc.) the second highest mark or grade.

**beta-amylase** /'bitə-æməleɪz/, *n.* See **amylase.**

**beta-blocker** /'bitə-blɒkə/, *n.* a drug used in the management of various conditions, notably angina pectoris and certain heart rhythm disorders, and which prevents the effects of sympathetic nervous stimulation in this organ.

**beta cell** /'bitə sɛl/, *n.* any of certain basophilic secretory cells, as the insulin-secreting cells in the islets of Langerhans.

**beta decay** /'bitə dəˌkeɪ/, *n.* a radioactive transformation in which beta particles are emitted.

**beta-eucaine** /bitə-'jukeɪn/, *n.* →**eucaine** (def. 2). Also, **betacaine** /'bitəkeɪn/.

**beta-glucosidase** /bitə-ˌglukoʊ'saɪdeɪz/, *n.* See **glucosidase.**

**beta-hydroxybutyric acid** /ˌbitə-haɪdrɒksibjuˌtɪrɪk 'æsəd/, *n.* a carboxylic acid, $CH_3$ CHOH $CH_2$ COOH, distributed widely in nature; it is one of the ketone bodies and is an intermediate in fatty acid synthesis and breakdown.

**betaine** /'biteɪn/, *n.* a non-poisonous crystalline substance, $(CH_3)_3{}^+NCH_2COO^-$, a methylated derivative of glycine which is a sweetish-tasting alkaloid found in sugar beets, cottonseed, the sprouts of wheat and barley. [L *bēta* beet + -INE[2]]

**betake** /bə'teɪk, bi-/, *v.t.* (*generally reflexive*), **-took, -taken, -taking.** **1.** to go: *she betook herself to the market.* **2.** to resort to; undertake: *he betook himself to flight.*

**beta-naphthol** /ˌbitə-'næfθɒl, -'næp-/, *n.* a crystalline antiseptic, $C_{10}H_7OH$.

**beta-oxidation** /ˌbitə-ɒksə'deɪʃən/, *n.* the enzymic process whereby fatty acids are broken down to two carbon atoms at a time starting from the carboxyl group; used for energy production.

**beta particle** /bitə 'patɪkəl/, *n.* an electron or positron spontaneously emitted by some radioactive substances, or produced in a particle accelerator such as a betatron.

**beta radiation** /ˌ– reɪdi'eɪʃən/, *n.* radiation consisting of streams of beta particles; beta rays.

**beta ray** /'– reɪ/, *n.* a stream of beta particles.

**beta transformation** /– trænsʃə'meɪʃən/, *n.* →**beta decay.**

**betatron** /'bitətrɒn/, *n.* a device based on the principle of the transformer, which accelerates electrons to high energy.

**beta wave** /'bitə weɪv/, *n.* a periodic variation in the electrical potential of the normal cerebral cortex with a frequency about 18 to 30 hertz in the alert waking state. Also, **beta rhythm.** Cf. **alpha wave.**

**betel nut** /'bitl nʌt/, *n.* the fruit of the betel palm, chewed in New Guinea and many parts of tropical Asia with lime derived from burnt coral or shells, and with any of various hot substances, as the leaves or bark of the betel pepper; areca nut.

betel nut

**betel palm** /'– pam/, *n.* a tall, graceful, Asiatic palm, *Areca catechu,* that bears the areca nut or betel nut, so named from its association in native usage with the betel pepper; areca palm.

**betel pepper** /'– pɛpə/, *n.* an East Indian pepper plant, *Piper betle.* Cf. **betel nut.** [Pg. *betele,* earlier *vitele,* from Malay *vettila,* Tamil *vettilei* + PEPPER]

**bête noire** /bɛt 'nwa/, *n.* something that one especially dislikes or dreads, either a person, task, or object; bugbear. [F: black beast]

**bethel** /'bɛθəl/, *n.* **1.** a hallowed spot. **2.** a dissenters' chapel or meeting house. **3.** *Chiefly U.S.* a church or chapel for seamen, often afloat in a harbour. [Heb. *bēth-ēl* house of God]

**bethink** /bə'θɪŋk, bi-/, *v.,* **-thought, -thinking.** *Archaic –v.t.* (*generally reflexive*) **1.** to remember; recall. **2.** to think; consider. **3.** to determine; resolve. **4.** to bear in mind; remember. *–v.i.* **5.** to consider; meditate. [ME *bethenken,* OE *bethencan,* from BE- + *thencan* consider]

**betide** /bə'taɪd, bi-/, *v.,* **-tided, -tiding.** *Archaic. –v.t.* **1.** to happen; befall; come to: *woe betide the villain! –v.i.* **2.** to come to pass. [ME *betide(n),* from BE- + *tiden,* OE *tīdan* betide]

**betimes** /bə'taɪmz, bi-/, *adv.* **1.** before it is too late; early. **2.** soon. [ME *betymes,* from *betime* by time + adv. *-s*]

**bêtise** /bə'tiz/, *n.* **1.** stupidity. **2.** a stupid or foolish act or remark. **3.** an absurdity; trifle. [F, from *bête* beast]

**betoken** /bə'toʊkən, bi-/, *v.t.* **1.** to give evidence of; indicate. **2.** to be or give a token of; portend.

**betony** /'bɛtəni/, *n.* **1.** a plant, *Stachys* (formerly *Betonica*) *officinalis,* of the mint family, formerly used in medicine and dyeing. **2.** any of various similar plants. [LL *betoni(ca)*; replacing ME *beteine,* from OF; replacing OE *betonice,* from LL (as above)]

**betook** /bə'tʊk, bi-/, *v.* past tense of **betake.**

**betray** /bə'treɪ, bi-/, *v.t.* **1.** to deliver or expose to an enemy by treachery or disloyalty. **2.** to be unfaithful in keeping or upholding: *to betray a trust.* **3.** to be disloyal to; disappoint the hopes or expectations of. **4.** to reveal or disclose in violation of confidence: *to betray a secret.* **5.** to reveal unconsciously (something one would preferably conceal). **6.** to show; exhibit. **7.** to deceive; mislead. **8.** to seduce and desert. **9. betray oneself,** to reveal one's real character, plans, etc. [ME *bitraien,* from *bi-* BE- + *traien,* from OF *traïr,* from L *trādere* give over] **– betrayal,** *n.* **– betrayer,** *n.*

**betroth** /bə'troʊð, -'troʊθ, bi-/, *v.t.* **1.** to promise to marry. **2.** to arrange for the marriage of; affiance. [ME *betrouthen,* var. of *betreuthien,* from BE- + *treuthe,* OE *trēowth* pledge. See TROTH, TRUTH]

**betrothal** /bə'troʊðəl, bi-/, *n.* the act or ceremony of betrothing; engagement. Also, **betrothment.**

**betrothed** /bə'troʊðd, bi-/, *adj.* **1.** engaged to be married. *–n.* **2.** an engaged person.

**better** /'bɛtə/, *adj.* (*comparative of* **good**). **1.** of superior quality or excellence: *a better position.* **2.** of superior value, use, fitness, desirability, acceptableness, etc.: *a better time for action.* **3.** larger; greater: *the better part of a lifetime.* **4.** improved in health; healthier. **5.** completely recovered in health; well. *–adv.* (*comparative of* **well**). **6.** in a more excellent way or manner: *to behave better.* **7.** in a superior degree: *to know a man better.* **8.** more: *better than a kilometre to town.* **9. had better,** would be wiser, safer, etc., to. **10. better off,** in better circumstances. **11. think better of, a.** to reconsider and decide more wisely. **b.** to think more favourably of. *–v.t.* **12.** to make better; improve; increase the good qualities of. **13. better oneself,** to improve one's social standing, education, etc. **14.** to improve upon; surpass; exceed: *they bettered working conditions. –v.i.* **15.** *Colloq.* to become better. *–n.* **16.** that which has superior excellence, etc.: *the better of two choices.* **17.** (*usu. pl.*) one's superior in wisdom, wealth, etc. **18.** superiority: *to get the better of someone.* [ME *bettre,* OE *betera,* c. Goth. *batiza*]

**better half** /bɛtə 'haf/, *n. Colloq.* one's wife.

**betterment** /'bɛtəmənt/, *n.* **1.** improvement. **2.** (*usu. pl.*) *Law.* an improvement of real property, other than mere repairs.

**betting ring** /'bɛtɪŋ ˌrɪŋ/, *n.* **1.** *Horseracing.* the space devoted to betting at a race course. **2.** any area, often circular, used for gambling esp. illegal gambling in the bush.

**betting shop** /'bɛtɪŋ ˌʃɒp/, *n.* a licensed bookmaking establishment that takes off-course bets on horseraces, etc.

**bettong** /bɛ'tɒŋ/, *n.* **1.** a short-nosed rat-kangaroo of genus *Bettongia.* **2.** (formerly) any small kangaroo. [Aboriginal]

**betulaceous** /bɛtju'leɪʃəs/, *adj.* belonging to the Betulaceae, a family of trees and shrubs including the birch, alder, etc. [L *betula* birch + -ACEOUS]

**between** /bə'twin, bi-/, *prep.* **1.** in the space separating (two or more points, objects, etc.). **2.** intermediate to, in time, quantity, or degree: *between 12 and 1 o'clock, between pink and red.* **3.** connecting: *a link between parts.* **4.** involving; concerning; of: *war between nations, choice between things.* **5.** by joint action or possession of: *to own land between them.* **6.** distinguishing one thing from another: *he can't tell the difference between butter and margarine.* **7. between you and me** or **between ourselves,** in confidence. **8. go between,** to act as a mediator. *–adv.* **9.** in the intervening space or time; in an intermediate position or relation: *visits far between.* [ME *betwene,* OE *betwēonan, betwēonum,* from *be* by + *-twēonan, -twēonum,* from *twā* two]

**betweenwhiles** /bə'twinwaɪlz, bi-/, *adv.* in the meantime; in between other activities. Also, **between-time.**

**betwixt** /bə'twɪkst, bi-/, *prep., adv.* **1.** *Archaic.* between. **2. betwixt and between,** neither the one nor the other; in a middle position. [ME *betwix,* OE *betweox;* for final *-t* cf. *against,* etc.]

**betyl** /'bɛtl/, *n. Archaeol.* a sacred stone, often standing, trimmed to a conical shape.

**beurre manié** /bɜ mʌn'jeɪ/, *n.* butter kneaded with flour into small balls, used to thicken soups, etc. [F]

**beurre noire** /bɜ 'nwa/, *n.* →**black butter sauce.** [F: black butter]

**bevatron** /'bɛvətrɒn/, *n.* a synchroton type of particle accelerator, capable of accelerating electrons to very high energies.

bevel

**bevel** /'bɛvəl/, *n., v.,* **-elled, -elling** or (*U.S.*) **-eled, -eling,** *adj. –n.* **1.** the inclination that one line or surface makes with another when not at right angles. **2.** an adjustable instrument used by woodworkers for laying out angles or adjusting the surface of work to a particular inclination. *–v.t., v.i.* **3.** to cut or slant at a bevel. *–adj.* **4.** oblique; sloping; slanted. [orig. obscure] **– beveller,** *n.*

**bevel gear** /'– gɪə/, *n.* a gear in which the axis or shaft of the driver forms an angle with the axis or shaft of the wheel driven.

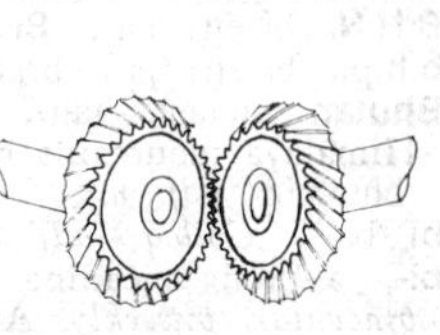

bevel gear

**bevel square** /'– skwɛə/, *n.* →**bevel** (def. 2).

**beverage** /'bɛvrɪdʒ, 'bɛvərɪdʒ/, *n.* a drink of any kind: *intoxicating beverages.* [ME, from OF *bevrage,* from *bevre,* from L *bibere* drink]

**bevery** /'bɛvəri/, *n.* **1.** a place where drinks are served. **2.** →**snack bar.**

**bevy** /'bɛvi/, *n., pl.* **bevies. 1.** a flock of birds, esp. larks or quails. **2.** a group, esp. of girls or women. [ME *bevey;* orig. uncert.]

**bewail** /bə'weɪl, bi-/, *v.t.* **1.** to express deep sorrow for; lament. *–v.i.* **2.** to express grief.

**beware** /bə'wɛə, bi-/, *v.* (*now only used as imperative or infinitive*). *–v.i.* **1.** to be wary, cautious, or careful (fol. by *of* or a clause). *–v.t.* **2.** *Archaic.* be wary of.

**bewdy** /'bjudi/, *Colloq. interj.* →**beauty** (def. 6).

**bewigged** /bə'wɪgd, bi-/, *adj.* wearing a wig.

**bewilder** /bə'wɪldə, bi-/, *v.t.* to confuse or puzzle completely; perplex. [BE- + WILDER] **– bewildered,** *adj.* **– bewildering,** *adj.* **– bewilderingly,** *adv.* **– bewilderedly,** *adv.*

**bewilderment** /bə'wɪldəmənt/, *n.* bewildered state.

**bewitch** /bə'wɪtʃ, bi-/, *v.t.* **1.** to affect by witchcraft or magic; throw a spell over. **2.** to enchant. **– bewitcher,** *n.* **– bewitchment,** *n.* **– bewitchery,** *n.* **– bewitching,** *adj.* **– bewitchingly,** *adv.*

**bey** /beɪ/, *n., pl.* **beys.** **1.** (formerly) the governor of a minor Turkish province. **2.** a Turkish title of respect. **3.** (formerly) the title of the native ruler of Tunis. [Turk. *beg*]

**beygel** /ˈbeɪgəl/, *n.* →**bagel.**

**beyond** /bəˈjɒnd, bi-/, *prep.* **1.** on or to the farther side of: *beyond the house.* **2.** farther on than; more distant than: *beyond the horizon.* **3.** later than: *they stayed beyond the time limit.* **4.** outside the understanding, limits, or reach of; past: *beyond human comprehension.* **5.** superior to; surpassing; above: *wise beyond all others.* **6.** more than; in excess of; over and above. *–adv.* **7.** farther on or away: *as far as the house and beyond.* *–n.* **8.** the life after the present one. [ME *beyonde,* OE *begeondan,* from *be* by + *geondan* beyond]

**bezant** /ˈbɛzənt, bəˈzænt/, *n.* **1.** the solidus, a gold coin of the Byzantine emperors, widely circulated in Europe during the Middle Ages. **2.** *Archit.* an ornament in the form of a flat disc. **3.** *Her.* a small gold circle. [ME, from OF *besant,* from L *Bȳzantius* Byzantine]

**bezel** /ˈbɛzəl/, *n.* **1.** a sloping face or edge of a chisel or other cutting tool. **2.** the upper oblique faces of a brilliant-cut gem. **3.** the grooved ring or rim holding a gem or watch crystal in its setting. [probably from F, from *biais* slant. See BIAS]

**bezique** /bəˈzik/, *n.* a card game for two or more players, played with 64 cards. [F *bésigue*]

**bezoar** /ˈbizɔ/, *n.* **1.** a calculus or concretion found in the stomach or intestines of certain animals, esp. ruminants, formerly reputed to be efficacious against poison. **2.** *Obs.* a counterpoison or antidote. [Ar. *bāzahr,* from Pers. *pādzahr* counterpoison]

**bezonian** /bəˈzoʊniən/, *n. Archaic.* an indigent rascal; scoundrel. [from obs. *besonio,* from It. *bisogno* need, needy fellow]

**b/f,** *Comm.* brought forward.

**b.f.,** /bi ˈɛf/, *n. Colloq.* bloody fool.

**B-grade film** /ˌbi-greɪd ˈfɪlm/, *n.* a small budget film, usu. of modest artistic achievement.

**B-grade western** /ˌbi-greɪd ˈwɛstən/, *n.* an inferior western film in which the emphasis is on the plot rather than on the development of character.

**bhang** /bæŋ/, *n.* **1.** the Indian hemp plant. **2.** a preparation of its leaves and tops used in India as an intoxicant and narcotic. Also, **bang.** [Hind. *bhāng,* from Skt *bhangā* hemp]

**bharal** /ˈbarəl/, *n.* a wild goat, *Pseudois nayaur,* of the Himalayas.

**bheesti** /ˈbisti/, *n.* (in India) a water-carrier. Also, **bheesty, bheestie, bhistee.** [Hind. *bhīstī,* from Pers. *bihishtī* water-carrier, derivative (presumably jocular) of *bihisht* paradise]

**B.H.N.** /bi eɪtʃ ˈɛn/, Brinell Hardness Number.

**b.h.p.,** /bi eɪtʃ ˈpi/, brake horsepower.

**Bhutan** /buˈtæn, -ˈtan/, *n.* a kingdom in central Asia in the Himalaya mountains between India and Tibet. – **Bhutanese** /butəˈniz/, *adj., n.*

**bi** /baɪ/, *Colloq.* *–adj.* **1.** bisexual. *–n.* **2.** a bisexual.

**bi-,** a prefix meaning 'twice, doubly, two', as in *bilateral, binocular, biweekly.* Also, **bin-.** [L, combining form of *bis* twice, doubly]

**b.i.,** built-in.

**Bi,** *Chem.* bismuth.

**bianco** /biˈæŋkoʊ/, *adj.* (of wine) white. [It. *bianco* white]

**biangular** /baɪˈæŋgjələ/, *adj.* having two angles or corners.

**biannual** /baɪˈænjuəl/, *adj.* occurring twice a year. – **biannually,** *adv.*

**biannulate** /baɪˈænjələt, -ˌleɪt/, *adj. Zool.* having two rings or ringlike bands, as of colour.

**bias** /ˈbaɪəs/, *n., adj., adv., v.,* **biased, biasing.** *–n.* **1.** an oblique or diagonal line of direction, esp. across a woven fabric: *to cut cloth on the bias.* **2.** a particular tendency or inclination, esp. one which prevents unprejudiced consideration of a question. **3.** *Bowling.* **a.** bulge or a greater weight on one side of the bowl, causing it to swerve. **b.** the swerved course of a bowl, due to shape or weighting. **4.** *Radio.* the direct voltage placed on the grid of an electronic valve. *–adj.* **5.** cut, set, folded, etc., diagonally. *–adv.* **6.** slantingly; obliquely. *–v.t.* **7.** to influence, usu. unfairly; prejudice; warp. [F *biais* slant, probably from L *biaxius* having two axes]

**bias binding** /– ˈbaɪndɪŋ/, *n.* a binding for cloth, cut on the bias, used esp. in hems.

**biathlon** /baɪˈæθlɒn/, *n.* a cross-country ski contest combined with rifle marksmanship. [BI- + Gk *âthlon* contest]

**biauricular** /ˌbaɪɔˈrɪkjələ/, *adj. Anat.* **1.** having two auricles. **2.** pertaining to the two ears.

**biauriculate** /ˌbaɪɔˈrɪkjələt, -ˌleɪt/, *adj. Biol.* having two auricles or earlike parts.

**biaxial** /baɪˈæksiəl/, *adj.* **1.** having two axes. **2.** (of a crystal) having two directions in which no double refraction occurs. – **biaxially,** *adv.*

**bib** /bɪb/, *n., v.,* **bibbed, bibbing.** *–n.* **1.** an article of clothing worn under the chin by a child, esp. while eating, to protect the dress. **2.** the upper part of an apron. **3.** an edible fish, *Gadus luscus,* of the north-eastern Atlantic. **4. keep one's bib out,** *Colloq.* to refrain from interfering with or inquiring into (the affairs of another). **5. put or stick one's bib in,** *Colloq.* to interfere. *–v.t.* **6.** *Obs.* to tipple. *–v.i.* **7.** *Colloq.* to interfere (fol. by *in*). [ME *bibben;* orig. uncert., ? from L *bibere* drink] – **biblike,** *adj.*

**Bib.,** **1.** Bible. **2.** Biblical.

**bib and tucker,** *n. Colloq.* clothes, esp. one's best: *for the party she put on her best bib and tucker.*

**bibasic** /baɪˈbeɪsɪk/, *adj. Chem.* dibasic.

**bibber** /ˈbɪbə/, *n.* a steady drinker; tippler.

**bib cock** /ˈbɪb kɒk/, *n.* a water tap fed by a horizontal supply pipe, having the nozzle bent downwards.

**bibelot** /ˈbɪbloʊ/, *n.* a small object of curiosity, beauty, or rarity. [F]

**bibful** /ˈbɪbfʊl/, *n. Colloq.* an unexpected and sometimes embarrassing disclosure: *yesterday the Prime Minister spilt a bibful.*

**bi-bivalent** /ˌbaɪ-baɪˈveɪlənt, baɪ-ˈbɪvə-/, *adj.* denoting an electrolytic compound which splits into two ions, each with a valency of two.

**bibl.,** **1.** biblical. **2.** bibliographical.

**Bible** /ˈbaɪbəl/, *n.* **1.** the collection of sacred writings of the Christian religion, comprising the Old and the New Testament. **2.** the Old Testament only. **3.** (*oft. l.c.*) the sacred writings of any religion. **4.** (*l.c.*) any book accepted as authoritative. [ME *bibul,* from ML *biblia,* from Gk: pl. of *biblíon,* diminutive of *bíblos* book]

**bible-basher** /ˈbaɪbəl-bæʃə/, *n.* a person of excessive religious, esp. evangelical, zeal often relying much on narrow biblical interpretations. Also, **bible-banger.**

**Bible Belt** /ˈbaɪbəl bɛlt/, *n.* an area, originally of the southern U.S., noted for its fundamentalist religious beliefs.

**biblical** /ˈbɪblɪkəl/, *adj.* **1.** of or in the Bible. **2.** in accord with the Bible. – **biblically,** *adv.*

**Biblical Latin** /ˈ– lætn/, *n.* the form of Latin used in the translation of the Bible, which became current in Western Europe at the beginning of the Middle Ages.

**biblicist** /ˈbɪbləsəst/, *n.* **1.** an adherent of the letter of the Bible; a fundamentalist. **2.** a biblical scholar. – **biblicism,** *n.*

**biblio-,** a word element meaning: **1.** book, as in *bibliophil.* **2.** Bible, as in *bibliolatry.* [Gk, combining form of *biblíon* book]

**biblio film** /ˈbɪblioʊ ˌfɪlm/, *n.* a microfilm used esp. in libraries for reproducing the pages of valuable or much-used books.

**bibliog.,** **1.** bibliographer. **2.** bibliography.

**bibliographer** /bɪbliˈɒgrəfə/, *n.* one occupied with or expert in bibliography. Also, **bibliograph** /ˈbɪbliəgræf/. [Gk *bibliográphos* book-writer + -ER[1]]

**bibliography** /bɪbliˈɒgrəfi/, *n., pl.* **-phies.** **1.** a complete or selective list of literature on a particular subject. **2.** a list of works by a given author. **3.** a list of source materials used or consulted in the preparation of a work. **4.** the systematic description, history, classification, etc., of books and other written or printed works. – **bibliographic** /ˌbɪbliəˈgræfɪk/, **bibliographical,** *adj.*

**bibliolatry** /bɪbliˈɒlətri/, *n.* excessive reverence for the Bible. – **bibliolater,** *n.* – **bibliolatrous,** *adj.*

**bibliomancy** /ˈbɪbliəmænsi/, *n.* divination by means of a book, as the Bible, opened at random at some verse taken as significant.

**bibliomania** /bɪbliəˈmeɪniə/, *n.* an enthusiasm for collecting books, esp. rare or valuable ones. – **bibliomaniac,** *adj., n.*

– **bibliomaniacal** /ˌbɪbliəmə'naɪəkəl/, *adj.*

**bibliopegy** /bɪbli'ɒpədʒi/, *n.* the art of binding books. [BIBLIO- + Gk *-pēgía,* from *pēgnýnai* fasten]

**bibliophil** /'bɪbliəfɪl/, *n.* a lover of books. Also, **bibliophile** /'bɪbliəfaɪl/, **bibliophilist** /bɪbli'ɒfələst/. [F. See BIBLIO-, -PHIL] – **bibliophilism,** *n.* – **bibliophilistic,** *adj.*

**bibliopole** /'bɪbliəpoʊl/, *n.* a bookseller, esp. a dealer in books unique for their rarity, artistic format, etc. Also, **bibliopolist** /bɪbli'ɒpələst/. [L *bibliopōla,* from Gk *bibliopṓlēs*] – **bibliopolic** /bɪbliə'pɒlɪk/, **bibliopolical,** *adj.* – **bibliopolism** /bɪbli'ɒpəlɪzəm/, **bibliopoly,** *n.*

**bibliotheca** /ˌbɪbliə'θikə/, *n.* **1.** a collection of books; library. **2.** a printed catalogue of books. [L: library, from Gk *bibliothḗkē,* from *biblio-* BIBLIO- + *thḗkē* case]

**Biblist** /'bɪbləst/, *n.* **1.** one who regards the Bible as the only rule of faith. **2.** a biblicist.

**bibulous** /'bɪbjələs/, *adj.* **1.** in the habit of alcoholic drinking. **2.** absorbent; spongy. [L *bibulus* freely drinking] – **bibulously,** *adv.* – **bibulousness,** *n.*

**bicameral** /baɪ'kæmərəl/, *adj.* having two branches, chambers, or houses, as a legislative body.

**bicarb.,** /'baɪkab/, *n.* →**sodium bicarbonate.**

**bicarbonate** /baɪ'kabənət, -neɪt/, *n.* a salt of carbonic acid, containing the $HCO_3$ radical; an acid carbonate, as *sodium bicarbonate,* $NaHCO_3$.

**bicarbonate of soda,** *n.* →**sodium bicarbonate.**

**bice** /baɪs/, *n.* blue or green pigment as of carbonates of copper. [ME *bis,* from OF: dark-coloured, brownish grey]

**bicentenary** /baɪsən'tinəri, -'tɛnəri/, *adj., n., pl.* **-naries.** *–adj.* **1.** of or pertaining to a 200th anniversary. *–n.* **2.** a 200th anniversary. **3.** its celebration.

**bicentennial** /baɪsən'tɛniəl/, *adj.* **1.** consisting of or lasting 200 years: *a bicentennial period.* **2.** recurring every 200 years. *–n.* **3.** *U.S.* a bicentenary.

**bicephalous** /baɪ'sɛfələs/, *adj.* having two heads. [BI- + Gk *kephalḗ* head + -OUS]

**biceps** /'baɪsəps, -sɛps/, *n.* a muscle having two heads of origin, esp. in anatomy: **a. biceps brachii,** the muscle on the front of the upper arm, which bends the forearm. **b. biceps femoris,** the hamstring muscle on the back of the thigh. [L: two-headed]

**Biche-la-mar** /bitʃ-lə-'ma/, *n.* →**Beach-la-mar.**

**bichir** /'bɪʃə/, *n.* a large primitive, bony, freshwater fish, *Polypterus bichir,* found in the upper Nile and in certain neighbouring waters.

**bichloride** /baɪ'klɔraɪd/, *n.* **1.** a compound in which two atoms of chlorine are combined with another element or radical. **2.** →**mercuric chloride.**

**bichloride of mercury,** *n. Chem.* →**corrosive sublimate.**

**bichordal** /baɪ'kɔdl/, *adj.* of a musical instrument for each note of which there are two strings tuned to the same pitch, as the mandolin, lute, etc. Also, **bichord.**

**bichromate** /baɪ'kroʊmeɪt, -mət/, *n. Chem.* **1.** →**dichromate.** **2.** chromate of potassium, $K_2Cr_2O_7$.

**bicipital** /baɪ'sɪpətl/, *adj.* **1.** having two heads. **2.** *Anat.* pertaining to the biceps. [L *biceps* two-headed + -AL[1]]

**bicker** /'bɪkə/, *v.i.* **1.** to engage in petulant argument; wrangle. **2.** to run rapidly; move quickly; rush; hurry. **3.** to quiver; flicker; glitter. *–n.* **4.** an angry dispute; squabble. [ME *biker(en).* Cf. MLG *bicken* prick, thrust] – **bickerer,** *n.*

**bickie** /'bɪki/, *n. Colloq.* **1.** a biscuit. **2. big bickies,** *Colloq.* a lot of money. Also, **bikkie.**

**bicollateral** /baɪkə'lætərəl/, *adj.* (of a vascular bundle) having the xylem lined with phloem on both its inner and outer faces.

**bicolour** /'baɪkʌlə/, *adj.* of two colours: *a bicolour flower.* Also, **bicoloured;** *U.S.,* **bicolor, bicolored.**

**biconcave** /baɪ'kɒnkeɪv, ˌbaɪkɒn'keɪv/, *adj.* concave on both sides, as a lens.

**biconvex** /baɪ'kɒnvɛks, ˌbaɪkɒn'vɛks/, *adj.* convex on both sides, as a lens.

**bicorn** /'baɪkɔn/, *adj.* having two horns or hornlike parts. Also, **bicornuate** /baɪ'kɔnjuət, -ˌeɪt/. [L *bicornis* two-horned]

**bicorporal** /baɪ'kɔpərəl/, *adj.* having two bodies. Also, **bicorporeal** /ˌbaɪkɔ'pɔriəl/.

**bicuspid** /baɪ'kʌspəd/, *adj.* Also, **bicuspidate.** **1.** having two cusps or points, as certain teeth. *–n.* **2.** *Anat.* one of eight such teeth in man, four on each jaw between the cuspid and the first molar teeth. [BI- + L *cuspis* point]

**bicycle** /'baɪsɪkəl/, *n., v.,* **-cled, -cling.** *–n.* **1.** a vehicle with two wheels, one in front of the other, and having a saddle-like seat for the rider. It is steered by handlebars and driven by pedals. *–v.t.* **2.** to ride a bicycle. [F, from *bi-* BI- + Gk *kýklos* circle, wheel] – **bicyclist,** *n.*

**bicycle clip** /'– klɪp/, *n.* one of a pair of clips used by cyclists to keep trousers tight around the ankles and away from the chain.

**bicycle lizard** /'– lɪzəd/, *n.* →**frill-necked lizard** (def. 1).

**bicycle pump** /'– pʌmp/, *n.* a hand-held pump used for inflating the tyres on a bicycle.

**bicyclic** /baɪ'saɪklɪk, -'sɪklɪk/, *adj.* **1.** consisting of or having two circles, cycles, etc. **2.** *Bot.* in two whorls, as the stamens of a flower. Also, **bicyclical.**

**bid** /bɪd/, *v.,* **bade** /bæd/ or **bad** /bæd/ *(for defs 1, 2)* or **bid** *(for defs 3-7),* **bidden** or **bid, bidding,** *n.* *–v.t.* **1.** to command; order; direct: *bid them depart.* **2.** to say as a greeting or benediction: *to bid farewell.* **3.** *Comm.* to offer, as a price at an auction or as terms in a competition to secure a contract. **4.** *Comm.* **a.** to overbid all offers for (property) at an auction in order to retain ownership (fol. by *in*). **b.** to increase (the market price) by increasing bids (fol. by *up*). **5.** *Cards.* to enter a bid of a given quantity or suit; call: *to bid two no-trumps.* *–v.i.* **6.** to make an offer to purchase at a price. **7. bid fair,** to seem likely. *–n.* **8.** the act of one who bids. **9.** an offer, as at an auction. **10.** the price of terms offered. **11.** *Cards.* **a.** the number of points or tricks a player offers to make. **b.** the turn of a person to bid. **12.** an attempt to attain some goal or purpose: *a bid for power.* [ME *bidde(n),* OE *(ge)bidden* beg, ask, pray; sense devel. influenced by ME *bede(n),* OE *bēodan* offer, proclaim, command] – **bidder,** *n.*

**bid-a-bid** /'bɪd-ə-bɪd/, *n.* →**biddy-biddy.**

**bidarka** /baɪ'dakə/, *n.* the sealskin boat of the Alaskan Eskimo. Also, **bidarkee** /baɪ'daki/. [Russ., diminutive of *baidara* coracle]

**biddable** /'bɪdəbəl/, *adj.* **1.** willing to do what is asked; obedient; docile. **2.** *Cards.* adequate to bid upon: *a biddable hand at bridge.*

**bidden** /'bɪdn/, *v.* past participle of **bid.**

**bidding** /'bɪdɪŋ/, *n.* **1.** invitation; command; order. **2.** a bid. **3.** bids collectively.

**biddy** /'bɪdi/, *n., pl.* **-dies.** *Colloq.* old woman. [orig. uncert.]

**biddy-biddy** /'bɪdi-bɪdi/, *n.* any low-growing herb of the genus *Acaena,* family Rosaceae, bearing a clinging burr. Also, **bidi-bidi, biddy-bid, bid-a-bid, biddy, piripiri.** [Maori *piri-piri*]

**bide** /baɪd/, *v.,* **bided** *(for def. 1)* or **bode** *(for def. 2),* **biding.** *–v.t.* **1. bide one's time,** to wait for a favourable opportunity. **2.** *Archaic.* to endure; bear. *–v.i.* **3.** *Archaic.* to dwell; abide; wait; remain; continue. [ME *biden,* OE *bīdan*]

**bidet** /'bideɪ/, *n.* a small low bath, straddled by the user, for washing the genitals. [F]

**Biedermeier** /'bidəmaɪə/, *adj.* **1.** pertaining to a conventional style of interior decoration, furniture, etc., common among the middle classes in German-speaking countries during the 19th century. **2.** conventional in outlook. [named after Gottlieb *Biedermeier,* fictitious philistine contributor to 19th-century German literary periodicals]

**biennial** /baɪ'ɛniəl/, *adj.* **1.** happening every two years: *the biennial Adelaide festival.* **2.** *Bot.* (esp. in cool temperate regions) completing the normal term of life in two years, flowering and fruiting in the second year, as parsnip. *–n.* **3.** any event occurring once in two years. **4.** a biennial plant. [L *biennium* two-year period + -AL[1]] – **biennially,** *adv.*

**bier** /bɪə/, *n.* a frame or stand on which a corpse, or the coffin containing it, is laid before burial. [ME *bere,* OE *bēr, bær,* c. G *Bahre*]

**biestings** /'bistɪŋz/, *n. pl.* →**beestings.**

**bifacial** /baɪ'feɪʃəl/, *adj.* **1.** having two faces or fronts. **2.** having the opposite surfaces alike. **3.** *Bot.* having the opposite surfaces unlike, as a leaf.

**bifcus** /'bɪfkəs/, *n. Colloq.* a black-faced cuckoo-shrike. [from the letters BFCS]

**biff** /bɪf/, *Colloq.* *–n.* **1.** a blow; punch. *–v.t.* **2.** to punch.

**bifid** /ˈbaɪfəd/, *adj.* cleft into two parts or lobes. [L *bifidus*] **– bifidity,** /baɪˈfɪdəti/, *n.* **– bifidly,** *adv.*

**bifilar** /baɪˈfaɪlə/, *adj.* furnished or fitted with two filaments or threads. **– bifilarly,** *adv.*

**biflagellate** /baɪˈflædʒəleɪt, -lət/, *adj. Zool.* having two whip-like appendages or flagella.

**biflex** /ˈbaɪflɛks/, *adj.* bent at two places.

**bifocal** /baɪˈfoʊkəl/, *adj.* **1.** *Chiefly Optics.* having two foci. **2.** (of spectacle lenses) having two portions, one for near and the other for far vision. *–n.* **3.** (*pl.*) spectacles with bifocal lenses.

**bifoliate** /baɪˈfoʊliət, -eɪt/, *adj.* having two leaves or leaflets.

**biform** /ˈbaɪfɔm/, *adj.* having or combining two forms, as a centaur, mermaid, etc. Also, **biformed.** [L *biformis*]

**bifurcate** /ˈbaɪfəkeɪt/, *v.,* **-cated, -cating;** /ˈbaɪfəkət, -keɪt/, *adj.* *–v.t.* **1.** to divide or fork into two branches. *–v.i.* **2.** to separate into two parts. *–adj.* **3.** divided into two branches. [ML *bifurcātus,* from L *bi-* BI- + *furca* fork] **– bifurcation,** *n.*

**big** /bɪg/, *adj.,* **bigger, biggest,** *adv.* *–adj.* **1.** large in size, height, width, amount, etc. **2.** pregnant: *big with child.* **3.** filled; teeming: *eyes big with tears.* **4.** loud: *a big noise.* **5.** large in compass or conception; magnanimous; generous; liberal: *a big heart, big gesture.* **6.** important in influence, standing, wealth, etc.: *big business, a big financier.* **7.** haughty; pompous; boastful: *big words, a big talker.* **8.** *Colloq.* strong; powerful: *Mr. Big.* **9.** (of a wine) full-bodied, fruity. **10.** requiring large amounts of financial backing: *big science.* *–adv.* **11.** *Colloq.* boastfully: *to talk big.* **12.** *Colloq.* on a grand scale; liberally: *to think big.* **13. be in big on,** to be an important confidant or partner in, frequently, a commercial venture. **14. be in big with,** to be highly favoured by (someone). **15. big on,** knowledgeable and enthusiastic about: *big on wine.* [ME; orig. uncert.] **– biggish,** *adj.* **– bigness,** *n.*

**big A** /bɪg ˈeɪ/, *n. Colloq.* **1.** arse. **2. give someone the big A,** to get rid of someone.

**bigamist** /ˈbɪgəməst/, *n.* a person guilty of bigamy.

**bigamous** /ˈbɪgəməs/, *adj.* **1.** having two wives or husbands at the same time; guilty of bigamy. **2.** involving bigamy. [ML *bigamus,* from *bi-* BI- + *-gamus* (from Gk *-gamos* married)] **– bigamously,** *adv.*

**bigamy** /ˈbɪgəmi/, *n.* the crime of marrying while one has a wife or husband still living, from whom no valid divorce has been effected. [ME *bigamie,* from OF, from *bigame* BIGAMOUS]

**big band** /ˈbɪg bænd/, *n.* a large group of musicians playing jazz or dance music.

**big bang theory,** *n.* the cosmological theory that the universe originated with an explosion of a single superdense agglomeration of matter. The observed expansion of the universe is explained as the fragments from this explosion continuing to fly apart. Cf. **steady state theory.**

**Big Brother** /bɪg ˈbrʌðə/, *n.* a dictator, esp. one who tries to control people's private lives and thoughts. [from a character in the novel *'1984',* by George Orwell (1903-1950)]

**big business** /bɪg ˈbɪznəs/, *n.* powerful financial or business resources, esp. considered collectively.

**big dipper** /bɪg ˈdɪpə/, *n.* a turning, sloping railway in an amusement park with open cars, ridden for the thrills of speed and rapid turns; roller-coaster; switchback.

**big end** /bɪg ˈɛnd/, *n. Motor Vehicles.* the larger end of the connecting rod in a reciprocating engine, which bears on the crankshaft. [short for *big end bearing*]

**biggada** /bɪˈgadə/, *n.* →**wallaroo.**

**big game** /bɪg ˈgeɪm/, *n.* **1.** large animals, esp. when hunted for sport. **2.** an important prize or objective.

**biggie** /ˈbɪgi/, *n. Colloq.* (*esp. in children's speech*) a big person or thing.

**big gun** /bɪg ˈgʌn/, *n. Colloq.* a very important person.

**bighead** /ˈbɪghɛd/, *n.* **1.** *Vet. Sci.* an inflammatory swelling of the tissues of the head of sheep. **2.** *Colloq.* a conceited person.

**big-headed** /bɪgˈhɛdəd/, *adj.* conceited; vain.

**big-hearted** /bɪg-ˈhatəd/, *adj.* generous; kind.

**bighorn** /ˈbɪghɔn/, *n., pl.* **-horn, -horns.** a wild sheep of the U.S., *Ovis canadensis,* of the Rocky Mountains, with large, curving horns.

bighorn

**bight** /baɪt/, *n.* **1.** the part of a rope between the ends. **2.** the loop or bent part of a rope, as distinguished from the ends. **3.** a bend or curve in the shore of a sea or a river. **4.** a body of water bounded by such a bend; a bay. *–v.t.* **5.** to fasten with a bight of rope. [ME *byght,* OE *byht* a bend]

**big league** /ˈbɪg lig/, *n.* the top level in any business or pursuit: *he's in (or playing) the big league now.* **– big-league,** *adj.*

**big lunch** /ˈbɪg lʌntʃ/, *n.* (*in children's speech*) **1.** the lunch period in the school day. **2.** the food eaten then. Cf. **play-lunch.**

**big mouth** /ˈbɪg maʊθ/, *n.* **1.** a garrulous person. **2. shut one's big mouth,** *Colloq.* to cease disclosing information.

**big-mouth** /ˈbɪg-maʊθ, -maʊð/, *v.t.* **1.** (*reflexive*) to boast; skite. **2.** to extol the virtues of; praise.

**big noise** /bɪg ˈnɔɪz/, *n. Colloq.* a very important person.

**bignonia** /bɪgˈnoʊniə/, *n.* any plant of the genus *Bignonia,* or related genera, mostly tropical, much cultivated for their showy trumpet-shaped flowers. [NL; named after the Abbé *Bignon,* librarian to Louis XV]

**bignoniaceous** /bɪg,noʊniˈeɪʃəs/, *adj.* belonging or pertaining to the Bignoniaceae, a family of plants including the trumpet flower, catalpa, etc.

**big-note** /ˈbɪg-noʊt/, *v.t. Colloq.* to boast of or promote (oneself): *he big-notes himself at every committee meeting.*

**bigot** /ˈbɪgət/, *n.* a person who is intolerantly convinced of the rightness of a particular creed, practice, etc. [F; orig. uncert.]

**bigoted** /ˈbɪgətəd/, *adj.* of or denoting a bigot or his actions. **– bigotedly,** *adv.*

**bigotry** /ˈbɪgətri/, *n., pl.,* **-ries. 1.** intolerant attachment to a particular creed, opinion, practice, etc. **2.** the actions or beliefs of a bigot.

**big red** /bɪg ˈrɛd/, *n.* the mature male of the red kangaroo, *Megaleia rufa.*

**big shot** /ˈ– ʃɒt/, *n. Colloq.* a very important person.

**big smoke** /ˈ– smoʊk/, *n. Colloq.* the city.

**big spit** /– ˈspɪt/, *n. Colloq.* vomit: *to go for the big spit.*

**big sticks** /ˈbɪg stɪks/, *n. pl. Colloq.* in Australian Rules, the goal posts: *he's dobbed it through the big sticks.*

**big-time** /ˈbɪg-taɪm/, Colloq. *–adj.* **1.** at the top level in any business or pursuit: *big-time boys.* *–n.* **2.** the top level, esp. in business. **3. the big-time,** the social milieu of those who have achieved fame and success: *she has hit the big-time now.*

**big toe** /bɪg ˈtoʊ/, *n.* (in man) the hallux.

**big top** /– ˈtɒp/, *n.* **1.** the main tent in a circus. **2.** the circus.

**bigwig** /ˈbɪgwɪg/, *n. Colloq.* a very important person.

**bihourly** /baɪˈaʊəli/, *adj.* occurring every two hours.

**bijou** /ˈbiʒu/, *n., pl.* **-joux** /-ʒuz/. **1.** a jewel. **2.** something small and choice. *–adj.* **3.** small; choice: *bijou cottage.* [F]

**bijouterie** /biˈʒutəri/, *n.* jewellery. [F]

**bike** /baɪk/, *n. Colloq.* **1.** a bicycle, tricycle, or motorcycle. **2. get off one's bike,** *Colloq.* to get angry; lose control of oneself. **3.** *Colloq.* a woman who will have sexual intercourse with any man who asks her: *the town bike.*

**bikie** /ˈbaɪki/, *n. Colloq.* a member of a gang of motorcycle riders.

**bikini** /bəˈkini/, *n.* a very brief two-piece swimming costume. [probably from *Bikini Atoll* of Marshall Islands, prominent as a site for nuclear bomb tests, 1946]

**bikkie** /ˈbɪki/, *n. Colloq.* →**bickie.**

**bilabial** /baɪˈleɪbiəl/, *Phonet. –adj.* **1.** pronounced with the two lips brought close together or touching. In the English bilabial consonants *p, b,* and *m,* the lips touch; in the bilabial *w,* they do not. *–n.* **2.** a bilabial speech sound.

bilabiate calyx and corolla

**bilabiate** /baɪˈleɪbieɪt, -ət/, *adj. Bot.* two-lipped, as a corolla.

**bilander** /ˈbɪləndə/, *n.* a small merchant vessel with two masts, used on canals and along the coast in Holland, etc. [D *bijlander,* from *bij* by + *land* land + *-er* -ER[1]]

**bilateral** /baɪˈlætrəl/, *adj.* **1.** pertaining to, involving, or affecting two sides or parties. **2.** *Law, etc.* (of a contract) binding the parties to reciprocal obligations. **3.** *Bot., Zool.* pertaining to both sides: *bilateral symmetry.* **4.** disposed on opposite sides of an axis; two-sided. – **bilateralism, bilateralness,** *n.* – **bilaterally,** *adv.*

**bilberry** /ˈbɪlbəri/, *n., pl.* **-ries. 1.** a deciduous shrub, *Vaccinium myrtillus,* of the Old World, bearing black edible fruits; blaeberry; whortleberry. **2.** the fruit of this plant. [*bil* (from Scand.; cf. Dan *bölle* bilberry) + BERRY]

**bilbo**[1] /ˈbɪlboʊ/, *n., pl.* **-boes.** (*usu. pl.*) a long iron bar or bolt with sliding shackles and a lock, formerly used to confine the feet of prisoners. [orig. uncert.]

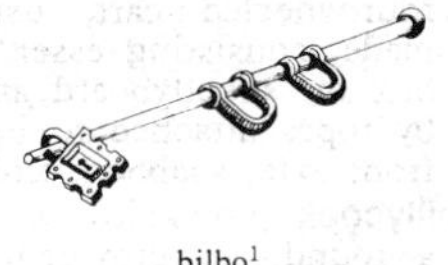
bilbo[1]

**bilbo**[2] /ˈbɪlboʊ/, *n., pl.* **-boes.** *Archaic.* a sword. [short for *Bilbo sword* sword of Bilbao (Spain)]

**bilby** /ˈbɪlbi/, *n.* either of the rabbit-eared bandicoots of genus *Macrotis* of the regions west of the Australian Great Dividing Range; dalgyte. [Aboriginal]

**bile** /baɪl/, *n.* **1.** *Physiol.* a bitter yellow or greenish liquid secreted by the liver and aiding in digestion, principally by emulsifying fats. **2.** ill nature; peevishness. [F, from L *bīlis*]

**bilection** /bəˈlɛkʃən/, *n. Archit.* →**bolection.**

**bile pigment** /ˈbaɪl pɪgmənt/, *n.* a decomposition product of haemoglobin present in bile.

**bile salt** /ˈ– sɒlt/, *n.* a substance (sodium taurocholate and sodium glycocholate) present in bile which aids emulsification of fats in the intestine.

**bilestone** /ˈbaɪlstoʊn/, *n. Pathol.* →**gallstone.**

**bilge** /bɪldʒ/, *n., v.,* **bilged, bilging.** –*n.* **1.** *Naut.* **a.** either of the rounded underportions at either side of a ship's hull. **b.** the lowest portion of a ship's interior. **c.** Also, **bilge water.** foul water that collects in a ship's bilge. **2.** *Colloq.* nonsense; rubbish. **3.** the wider part or belly of a cask. –*v.i.* **4.** *Naut.* to spring a leak in the bilge. **5.** to bulge or swell out. –*v.t.* **6.** *Naut.* to break in the bilge of. [orig. unknown]

**bilge artist** /ˈ– atəst/, *n. Colloq.* a person notorious for speaking or writing specious nonsense.

**bilge keel** /ˈ– kil/, *n.* either of two keel-like projections extending lengthwise along a ship's bilge, one on each side, to retard rolling. Also, **bilge piece.**

**bilgy** /ˈbɪldʒi/, *adj.* smelling like bilge water.

**bilharzia** /bɪlˈhaziə/, *n.* **1.** any parasite blood fluke of the family Schistosomidae; a schistosome. **2.** →**schistosomiasis.** [named after Theodor *Bilharz,* 1829-94, German physician]

**bilharziasis** /bɪlhaˈzaɪəsəs/, *n.* →**schistosomiasis.** Also, **bilharziosis.**

**biliary** /ˈbɪljəri/, *adj.* **1.** *Physiol.* **a.** of bile. **b.** conveying bile: *a biliary duct.* **2.** *Pathol.* bilious: *biliary colic.* [NL *bīliāris,* from L *bīlis* bile]

**bilinear** /baɪˈlɪniə/, *adj. Maths.* (of a function of two variables) linear with respect to each variable.

**bilingual** /baɪˈlɪŋgwəl/, *adj.* **1.** able to speak one's native language and another with approximately equal facility. **2.** expressed or contained in two different languages. –*n.* **3.** a bilingual person. [L *bilinguis* speaking two languages + -AL[1]] – **bilingually,** *adv.*

**bilingualism** /baɪˈlɪŋgwəlɪzəm/, *n.* **1.** habitual use of two languages. **2.** ability in being bilingual.

**bilious** /ˈbɪljəs/, *adj.* **1.** *Physiol., Pathol.* pertaining to bile or to an excess secretion of bile. **2.** *Pathol.* suffering from, caused by, or attended by trouble with the bile or liver. **3.** peevish; testy; cross. **4.** sickly; nauseating: *a bilious colour.* [L *bīliōsus* full of bile] – **biliously,** *adv.* – **biliousness,** *n.*

**bilirubin** /biliˈrubən/, *n.* the major bile pigment, orange in colour, a breakdown product from haemoglobin.

**-bility,** a suffix forming nouns from adjectives in *-ble,* as in *nobility.* [ME *-bilite,* from F, from L *bilitas*]

**biliverdin** /biliˈvɜdən/, *n.* a bile pigment, green in colour, a breakdown product from haemoglobin.

**bilk** /bɪlk/, *v.t.* **1.** to evade payment of (a debt). **2.** to defraud; cheat. **3.** to frustrate. **4.** to escape from; elude. –*n.* **5.** a trick; a fraud. **6.** a cheater; a swindler. [orig. unknown] – **bilker,** *n.*

**bill**[1] /bɪl/, *n.* **1.** an account of money owed for goods or services supplied. **2.** a slip or ticket showing the amount owed for goods consumed or purchased, esp. in a restaurant. **3.** *Govt.* a form or draft of a proposed statute presented to a legislature, but not yet enacted or passed and made law. **4.** a written or printed public notice or advertisement. **5.** any written paper containing a statement of particulars: *a bill of charges or expenditures.* **6.** a bill of exchange. **7.** *U.S.* a piece of paper money; note. **8.** *Law.* a bill of indictment. **9.** a printed theatre program or the like. **10.** program; entertainment: *there is a good bill at the theatre.* **11.** *Obs.* an acknowledgment of debt; a promissory note. –*v.t.* **12.** to announce by bill or public notice: *a new actor was billed for this week.* **13.** to schedule as part of a program. **14.** to render an account of money owed. [ME *bille,* from Anglo-L *billa,* var. of ML *bulla* seal (see BULL[3])]

**bill**[2] /bɪl/, *n.* **1.** that part of the jaws of a bird covered with a horny sheath; a beak. **2.** *Geog.* a beaklike promontory or headland. –*v.i.* **3.** to join bills or beaks, as doves. **4.** *Colloq.* to kiss. **5. bill and coo, a.** (of doves etc.) to join beaks and make soft murmuring sounds. **b.** *Colloq.* to kiss and talk fondly. [ME; OE *bile* beak]

**bill**[3] /bɪl/, *n.* **1.** a medieval shafted weapon with a broad hook-shaped blade and a spike at the back. **2.** a billhook. **3.** *Naut.* the point or extremity of the fluke of an anchor. [OE *bill* sword, c. G *Bille* pickaxe]

**bill**[4] /bɪl/, *n.* the cry of the bittern. [cf. OE *bylgan* bellow, c. Icel. *bylgja* roar]

**billabong** /ˈbɪləbɒŋ/, *n.* **1.** a waterhole in an anabranch, replenished only in flood time. **2.** a waterhole in a river or creek that dries up outside the rainy season. [Aboriginal]

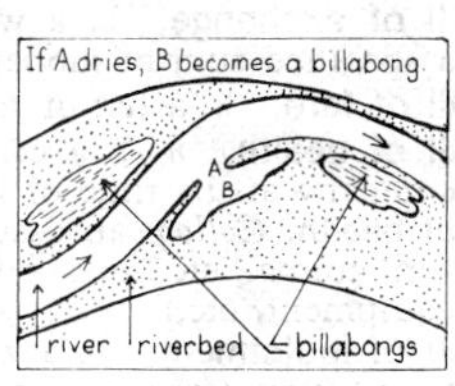

billabong

**billbergia** /bɪlˈbɜdʒə/, *n.* any stemless perennial plant of the genus *Billbergia,* family Bromeliaceae, of South and Central America, many of which, such as *B. nutans,* are popular indoor and garden plants.

**billboard**[1] /ˈbɪlbɔd/, *n.* →**hoarding**[2]. [BILL[1] (def. 4) + BOARD]

**billboard**[2] /ˈbɪlbɔd/, *n.* a projection placed abaft the cathead, for the bill or fluke of an anchor to rest on. [BILL[3] (def. 3) + BOARD]

**billet**[1] /ˈbɪlət/, *n., v.,* **-eted, -eting.** –*n.* **1. a.** lodging for a soldier, esp. lodging in private or non-military public buildings. **b.** private, usu. unpaid, temporary lodgings arranged for members of a group or team. **2.** *Mil.* an official order, written or verbal, directing the person to whom it is addressed to provide such lodging. **3.** a place assigned, as a berth or the like to a member of a ship's crew. **4.** job; appointment, esp. (formerly) that obtained by a convict, often as an indulgence. **5.** a small paper or note in writing. –*v.t.* **6.** *Mil.* to direct (a soldier) by ticket, note, or verbal order, where to lodge. **7.** to provide lodging for; quarter. [ME *billette,* from OF, b. *bille* a writing and *bullette* certificate, from *bulle* BULL[3]]

**billet**[2] /ˈbɪlət/, *n.* **1.** a small thick stick of wood, esp. one cut for fuel. **2.** *Metall.* a bar or slab of iron or steel, esp. when obtained from an ingot by forging, etc. **3.** *Archit.* one of a series of short rods forming part of a moulding. **4.** a short strap used for connecting various straps and portions of a harness. **5.** a pocket or loop into which the end of a strap is inserted after passing through a buckle. [ME *billette,* from OF *billete,* diminutive of *bille* log]

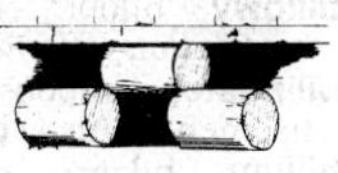
architectural billets

**billet-doux** /bɪleɪ-ˈdu/, *n., pl.* **billets-doux** /bɪleɪ-ˈduz/. a love-letter. [F: lit., sweet note]

**billfish** /ˈbɪlfɪʃ/, *n. pl.* **-fishes,** (*esp. collectively*) **-fish.** any of various large game fish as the marlin, or the sailfish, in which the upper jaw projects in a long spear-like process.

**billfold** /ˈbɪlfoʊld/, *n. U.S.* a wallet or pocket-book.

**billhook** /ˈbɪlhʊk/, *n.* an instrument with a curved, hooked blade for pruning, etc. Also, **bill.**

**billiard** /ˈbɪljəd/, *adj.* of or used in billiards.

**billiards** /ˈbɪljədz/, *n.* a game played by two or more persons on a rectangular table enclosed by an elastic ledger or cushion, with balls (**billiard balls**) of ivory or other hard material, driven by means of cues. [F *billard,* from *bille* log. Cf. BILLET[2]] – **billiardist,** *n.*

**billing** /ˈbɪlɪŋ/, *n.* **1.** the relative position in which a performer or act is listed on handbills, posters, etc. **2.** publicity or advertising, esp. for consumer goods. **3.** the total business of an advertising agency during a given period.

**billingsgate** /ˈbɪlɪŋzgeɪt/, *n.* coarse language or abuse. [orig., the kind of language heard at *Billingsgate,* a fish market in central London]

**billion** /ˈbɪljən/, *n.* **1.** a million times a million, or $10^{12}$. **2.** *U.S.* a thousand times a million, or $10^{9}$. **3.** *Colloq.* a large amount. *–adj.* **4.** amounting to a billion in number. [F: from *bi-* BI- + (*mi*)*llion,* i.e. the second power of one million] – **billionth,** *adj., n.*

**billionaire** /bɪljəˈnɛə/, *n.* the owner of a billion pounds, dollars, francs, etc.

**Bill Masseys** /bɪl ˈmæsiz/, *n.pl. N.Z. Colloq.* boots, esp. military boots. [named after William (*Bill*) F. *Massey,* Prime Minister of New Zealand, 1912-25]

**bill of attainder,** *n.* (formerly) a legal act depriving a person of his property if found guilty of treason or a felony.

**bill of exchange,** *n.* a written authorisation or order to pay a specified sum of money to a specified person.

**bill of fare,** *n.* a list of foods that are served; menu.

**bill of health,** *n.* **1.** a certificate as to the health of a ship's company at the time of her clearing any port. **2. a clean bill of health,** *Colloq.* an assurance of the good health of (a person, animal, etc.) or good condition of (a piece of machinery, equipment, etc.).

**bill of indictment,** *n.* a written accusation of crime delivered to a court (formerly to a grand jury), which becomes an indictment if endorsed by an officer of the court, usu. the attorney general.

**bill of lading,** *n.* a written receipt given by a carrier for goods accepted for transporting.

**bill of quantities,** *n. Bldg Trades.* a document giving all particulars of materials and labour necessary for the erection of a building.

**bill of rights,** *n.* a formal statement of the fundamental rights of the people of a nation.

**bill of sale,** *n.* a document transferring title in personal property from one person to another, either temporarily as security against a loan or debt (**conditional bill of sale**), or permanently (**absolute bill of sale**).

**billon** /ˈbɪlən/, *n.* **1.** an alloy used in coinage, consisting of gold or silver with a preponderating admixture of some base metal. **2.** an alloy of silver with copper or the like, used for coins of small denomination. **3.** any coin struck from such an alloy. [F, from *bille* log]

**billow** /ˈbɪloʊ/, *n.* **1.** a great wave or surge of the sea. **2.** any surging mass: *billows of smoke.* *–v.i.* **3.** to rise or roll in or like billows; surge. [Scand.; cf. Icel. *bylgja*]

**billowy** /ˈbɪloʊi/, *adj.,* **-lowier, -lowiest.** full of billows; surging: *billowy flames.* – **billowiness,** *n.*

**billposter** /ˈbɪlpoʊstə/, *n.* one who pastes up bills and advertisements. Also, **billsticker** /ˈbɪlstɪkə/.

**billum** /ˈbɪləm/, *n.* a large string bag made by the women of Papua New Guinea used for carrying goods or as a type of hammock for a baby.

**billy**[1] /ˈbɪli/, *n., pl.* **billies,** *adj.* *–n.* **1.** a cylindrical container for liquids, sometimes enamelled, usu. having a close-fitting lid. **2.** any container, often makeshift, for boiling water, making tea, etc. **3. boil the billy,** to make tea. *–adj.* **4.** made in a billy, as billy tea, billy bread. [probably from Scot. d. *bally* a milk-pail]

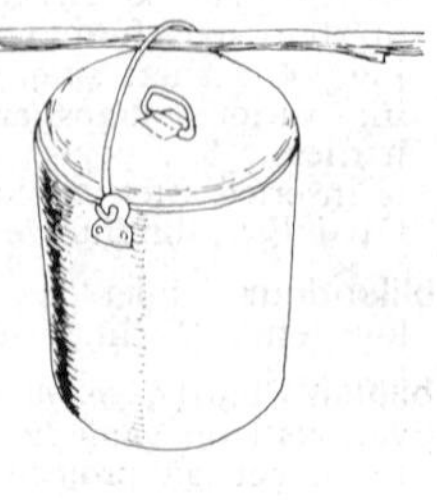

billy[1] (def. 2)

**billy**[2] /ˈbɪli/, *n.* quartzitic rock formed by the silicification of Tertiary sands and gravels by adjacent flows of basalt.

**billy**[3] /ˈbɪli/, *n.* →**billygoat.**

**billy button** /ˈbɪli bʌtn/, *n.* any of certain plants with flowers in rounded heads, esp. species of *Craspedia,* common at high altitudes in Australia.

**billy can** /ˈ– kæn/, *n.* →**billy**[1].

**billycart** /ˈbɪlikat/, *n.* a small four-wheeled cart, usu. home-made, consisting essentially of a box on a bellyboard and steered by ropes attached to its movable front axle; soapbox; trolley.

billycart

**billycock** /ˈbɪlikɒk/, *n. Colloq.* **1.** a round, low-crowned, soft felt hat. **2.** a bowler hat. [var. of *bully-cocked* (*hat*), i.e. hat cocked in the style of a bully]

**billygoat** /ˈbɪligoʊt/, *n.* **1.** a male goat. **2.** *Colloq.* one who is incompetent.

**billygoat rider** /ˈ– raɪdə/, *n. Colloq.* a Freemason. [from the goat used in certain ceremonies of the Freemasons]

**billygoat weed** /ˈ– wid/, *n.* any species of *Ageratum* found as a weed in subtropical and tropical Australia.

**billyo** /ˈbɪlioʊ/, *n. Colloq. in the phrases* **1. like billyo. a.** with gusto: *we laughed like billyo.* **b.** with great speed: *he rode like billyo.* **2. off to billyo, a.** off course; astray; in error. **b.** a long way away. Also, **billyoh.**

**billy tea** /bɪli ˈti/, *n.* tea made in a billy.

**billy tongs** /ˈ– tɒŋz/, *n.pl.* a device for gripping and lifting a hot billy, etc., from a camp fire.

**bilobed** /ˈbaɪloʊbd/, *adj.* having or divided into two lobes. Also, **bilobated.**

**bilocular** /baɪˈlɒkjələ/, *adj.* divided into two compartments, or containing two cells internally. Also, **biloculate** /baɪˈlɒkjələt, -ˌleɪt/.

**biltong** /ˈbɪltɒŋ/, *n.* (in South Africa) strips of lean meat dried in the open air. [Afrikaans]

**bimanous** /ˈbɪmənəs, baɪˈmeɪ-/, *adj. Zool.* two-handed. [NL *bimana* (*animālia*) two-handed (animals) + -OUS]

**bimanual** /baɪˈmænjuəl/, *adj.* involving the use of both hands. – **bimanually,** *adv.*

**bimble box** /ˈbɪmbəl bɒks/, *n.* a tree, *Eucalyptus populnea,* of New South Wales and southern Queensland, growing mostly on the western plains, having a broad dense crown of shiny green leaves, and yielding a durable timber.

**bimbo** /ˈbɪmboʊ/, *n.* a homosexual. [It: a baby boy]

**bimensal** /baɪˈmɛnsəl/, *adj.* occurring once in two months; bimonthly.

**bimestrial** /baɪˈmɛstriəl/, *adj.* **1.** occurring every two months; bimonthly. **2.** lasting two months. [L *bimestri*(*s*) of two months' duration + -AL[1]]

**bimetallic** /baɪməˈtælɪk/, *adj.* **1.** of two metals. **2.** pertaining to bimetallism. [F *bimétallique*]

**bimetallism** /baɪˈmɛtəlɪzəm/, *n.* **1.** the use of two metals, ordinarily gold and silver, at a fixed relative value, as the monetary standard. **2.** the doctrine or policies supporting such a standard. – **bimetallist,** *n.*

**bimonthly** /baɪˈmʌnθli/, *adj., n., pl.* **-lies,** *adv.* *–adj.* **1.** occurring every two months. **2.** occurring twice a month; semi-monthly. *–n.* **3.** a bimonthly publication. *–adv.* **4.** every two months. **5.** twice a month; semi-monthly.

**bimorph** /ˈbaɪmɔf/, *n.* **1.** an electronic device consisting of two layers of piezo-electric crystals, which respond to electric current in different ways, one by expanding, and the other by contracting, creating a bending or twisting movement which converts electrical energy to mechanical energy. **2.** a similar device in hi-fi pickups, etc., which works conversely, mechanical energy from needle vibration being converted to electrical energy. [BI- + -MORPH]

**bin** /bɪn/, *n., v.,* **binned, binning.** *–n.* **1.** a box or enclosed space used for storing grain, wool as it is shorn, coal, refuse, etc. **2.** a partitioned stand used by a winemaker for storing wine in bottles. **3.** (of wine) a particular bottling, usu. of above average quality. **4.** *Colloq.* a pocket in a garment. **5.** *Colloq.* gaol. *–v.t.* **6.** to store in a bin. [ME *binne,* OE *binn(e)* crib]

**bin-,** a form of **bi-**, sometimes used before a vowel, as in *binaural.* [L *bīnī* two apiece]

**binary** /ˈbaɪnəri/, *adj., n., pl.* **-ries.** *–adj.* **1.** consisting of, indicating, or involving two. **2.** using, involving, or expressed in the binary number system. **3.** *Maths.* having two variables. *–n.* **4.** a whole composed of two. **5.** *Astron.* a binary star. [L *bīnārius* consisting of two things]

**binary arithmetic** /– əˈrɪθmətɪk/, *n.* arithmetic using the binary number system.

**binary code** /ˈ– koʊd/, *n.* any means of representing information by a sequence of the digits 1 and 0.

**binary compound** /ˈ– ˌkɒmpaʊnd/, *n. Chem.* a compound containing only two elements or radicals.

**binary digit** /ˈ– ˌdɪdʒət/, *n.* a single digit in a binary number.

**binary fission** /– ˈfɪʃən/, *n.* (of a cell or atomic nucleus) reproduction by division into two approximately equal parts.

**binary form** /ˈ– fɔm/, *n.* a musical form founded on two themes, or on two balancing or answering sections or phrases.

**binary notation** /– noʊˈteɪʃən/, *n.* →**binary number system.**

**binary number** /– ˈnʌmbə/, *n.* a number expressed in the binary number system.

**binary number system,** *n.* a number system which uses only the digits 1 and 0, based on the rules $1+0=1$, $1+1=10$. Also, **binary system.**

**binary scale** /baɪnəri ˈskeɪl/, *n.* →**binary number system.**

**binary star** /ˈ– sta/, *n.* a system of two stars which revolve round their common centre of gravity.

**binate** /ˈbaɪneɪt/, *adj. Bot.* double; produced or borne in pairs. [NL *bīnātus,* from L *bīnī* two at a time] **–binately,** *adv.*

binate leaves

**binaural** /baɪnˈɔrəl/, *adj.* **1.** of, with, or for both ears: *binaural hearing, a binaural stethoscope.* **2.** having two ears.

**binche lace** /ˈbɪnʃ leɪs/, *n.* a bobbin lace featuring a floral pattern on coarse mesh. [named after *Binche,* Belgium, where it was originally made]

**bind** /baɪnd/, *v.,* **bound, binding,** *n. –v.t.* **1.** to make fast with a band or bond. **2.** to encircle with a band or ligature: *bind up one's hair.* **3.** to swathe or bandage (oft. fol. by *up*). **4.** to fasten around; fix in place by girding. **5.** to cause to cohere or harden. **6.** to unite by any legal or moral tie: *bound by duty, debt, etc.* **7.** to hold to a particular state, place, employment, etc. **8.** (*usu. passive*) to place under obligation or compulsion: *all are bound to obey the laws.* **9.** *Law.* to put under legal obligation (fol. by *over*): *to bind a man over to keep the peace.* **10.** to make compulsory or obligatory: *to bind an order with a deposit.* **11.** to indenture as an apprentice (oft. fol. by *out*). **12.** *Pathol.* to hinder or restrain (the bowels) from their natural operations; constipate. **13.** to fasten or secure within a cover, as a book. **14.** to cover the edge of, as for protection or ornament. *–v.i.* **15.** to become compact or solid; cohere. **16.** to be obligatory: *an obligation that binds.* **17.** to tie up anything, esp. sheaves of grain. *–n.* **18.** something that binds. **19.** *Colloq.* a nuisance; bore. **20.** →**bine**[1]. **21.** *Mining.* hardened clay between layers of coal. **22.** *Music.* a tie. **23.** *Fencing.* a thrust which forces the opponent's sword diagonally across the target. [ME *binden,* OE *bindan,* c. G *binden*]

**binder** /ˈbaɪndə/, *n.* **1.** a person or thing that binds. **2.** a detachable cover for loose papers. **3.** one who binds books; a bookbinder. **4.** *Agric.* **a.** an attachment to a harvester or reaper for binding the cut grain. **b.** a machine that both cuts and binds grain. **c.** wool fibres that grow from one staple to another and hold the fleece together. **5.** *Law.* an informal contract, in force while a more formal document is being drawn up. **6.** a tie beam, esp. in a floor. **7.** *Metall.* a substance used: **a.** to hold crushed ore dust together before and during sintering or refining. **b.** to hold metallic powders (mixed sometimes with non-metals) together after compacting and before sintering in powder metallurgy. **8.** *Bldg Trades.* a material, as cement, used to join masonry. **9.** *Colloq.* a solid meal; a feed.

**bindery** /ˈbaɪndəri/, *n.* an establishment for binding books.

**bindi-eye** /ˈbɪndi-aɪ/, *n.* **1.** any of a number of plants with fruit which break into small spiny pieces, esp. *Calotis hispidula,* a composite plant, which has heads of cypselas with fine barbed awns. **2.** →**jo-jo.** Also, **bindii.**

**binding** /ˈbaɪndɪŋ/, *n.* **1.** the act of fastening or uniting. **2.** anything that binds. **3.** the covering within which the leaves of a book are bound. **4.** a strip that protects or adorns the edge of cloth, etc. **5.** *Skiing.* a device which holds the ski to the boot with straps and springs in such a way as to release the boot from the ski in a fall. *–adj.* **6.** having power to bind or oblige; obligatory: *a binding engagement.* **–bindingly,** *adv.* **–bindingness,** *n.*

**binding energy** /ˈ– ˌɛnədʒi/, *n.* the energy required to split an atomic nucleus into its constituent nucleons.

**bindweed** /ˈbaɪndwid/, *n.* any of various twining or vinelike plants, esp. *Convolvulus arvensis.*

**bindy** /ˈbɪndi/, *n., pl.* **-dies.** →**bindi-eye.**

**bindy-eye** /ˈbɪndi-aɪ/, *n.* →**bindi-eye.** Also, **bindy.**

**bine**[1] /baɪn/, *n.* **1.** a twining plant stem, as of the hop. **2.** any bindweed. **3.** →**woodbine** (defs 1, 2). [var. of BIND]

**bine**[2] /baɪn/, *n. W.A. Colloq.* a newly-arrived Englishman. [from their supposed habit of smoking *Woodbines,* a cheap brand of cigarettes originating in England]

**Binet test** /ˈbineɪ tɛst/, *n.* a test for determining the relative development of the intelligence of children and others, consisting of a series of questions and tasks graded with reference to the ability of the normal child to deal with them at successive age levels. Also, **Binet-Simon test** /bineɪ-ˈsaɪmən/. [named after Alfred *Binet,* 1857-1911, French psychologist]

**binge** /bɪndʒ/, *n. Colloq.* a spree; a period of excessive indulgence, as in eating or drinking. [Lincolnshire d. *binge* (v.) to soak]

**binghi** /ˈbɪŋi/, *n.* **1.** *Colloq.* an Aboriginal. **2.** (formerly, esp. in pidgin) brother. [Aboriginal: brother]

**bingie** /ˈbɪndʒi/, *n. Colloq.* the stomach; belly. Also, **bingy, bingey, bingee, binjy.** [Aboriginal]

**bingle** /ˈbɪŋgəl/, *n. Colloq.* **1.** a dent or fracture in a motor vehicle, surfboard, etc. **2.** a minor accident in a motor vehicle, on a surfboard, etc.

**bingo** /ˈbɪŋgoʊ/, *n.* →**housie-housie.**

**binnacle** /ˈbɪnəkəl/, *n.* a special stand of non-magnetic material built in the hull of a ship for housing the compass and fitted with lights by which the compass can be read at night. [earlier *bittacle,* from Pg. *bitacola,* or from Sp. *bitácula,* from L *habitāculum* dwelling place]

**binocular** /bəˈnɒkjələ/, *adj.* **1.** involving (the use of) two eyes: *binocular vision.* *–n.* **2.** (*pl.*) a double telescope used by both eyes at once; field-glasses. **–binocularity** /bənɒkjəˈlærəti/, *n.* **–binocularly,** *adv.*

**binomial** /baɪˈnoʊmiəl/, *n.* **1.** *Maths.* an expression which is a sum or difference of two terms, as $3x + 2y$ and $x^2 - 4x$. **2.** *Zool., Bot.* →**binominal.** *–adj.* **3.** *Maths.* consisting of or pertaining to two terms or a binomial. **4.** *Zool., Bot.* →**binominal.** [LL *binōmius* having two names + -AL[1]] **–binomially,** *adv.*

**binomial distribution** /– dɪstrəˈbjuʃən/, *n. Statistics.* a distribution giving the probability of obtaining a specified number of successes in a set of trials where each trial can end in either a success or a failure.

**binomial theorem** /– ˈθɪərəm/, *n.* a formula giving the power of any binomial without multiplying out all the terms.

**binominal** /baɪˈnɒmənəl/, *n.* **1.** a botanical or zoological name consisting of two terms, denoting respectively genus and species, as *Felis leo,* the lion. *–adj.* **2.** consisting of or characterised by binominals. Also, **binomial.** [BI- + NOMINAL]

**bint** /bɪnt/, *n. Colloq.* a girl. [Ar.]

**binturong** /ˈbɪntjərɒŋ/, *n.* a large, arboreal South-East Asian civet, *Arctictis binturong.*

**binucleate** /baɪˈnjukliˌeɪt, -ət/, *adj.* having two nuclei, as some cells. Also, **binuclear, binucleated.**

**bio** /ˈbaɪoʊ/, *n. Colloq.* a short biography of an important person, as issued by a press secretary, etc. [shortened form of BIOGRAPHY]

**bio-**, a word element meaning 'life', 'living things', as in *biology*. [Gk, combining form of *bíos* life]

**bio-assay** /baɪoʊ-ˈæseɪ/, *n.* determination of the strength of a drug by comparing its effect with that of a standard preparation.

**bioastronautics** /ˌbaɪoʊæstrəˈnɔtɪks/, *n.* the science dealing with the effects of space travel on animals and plants.

**bio-availability** /ˌbaɪoʊ-əveɪləˈbɪləti/, *n.* the ease with which a given drug is absorbed into the body tissues.

**biocatalyst** /baɪoʊˈkætələst/, *n.* a substance, esp. an enzyme, that initiates or accelerates a biochemical process.

**bioccelate** /baɪˈɒsəleɪt, -lət, baɪoʊˈsɛlət/, *adj. Zool., Bot.* marked with two ocelli or eyelike parts.

**biocenology** /ˌbaɪoʊsəˈnɒlədʒi/, *n.* the branch of biology or ecology concerned with interaction and relationships within a natural community. Also, **biocoenology.** [BIO- + CENO-[2] + -LOGY]

**biochem.** /baɪoʊˈkɛm/, biochemistry.

**biochemistry** /baɪoʊˈkɛməstri/, *n.* the chemistry of living matter. *Abbrev.:* biochem. – **biochemical** /baɪoʊˈkɛmɪkəl/, **biochemic,** *adj.* – **biochemically,** *adv.* – **biochemist,** *n.*

**biocide** /ˈbaɪəsaɪd/, *n.* a substance that is capable of killing living organisms.

**bioclimatology** /ˌbaɪoʊklaɪməˈtɒlədʒi/, *n.* the study of the effect of climate on the life and health of animals, esp. humans.

**bioconversion** /ˌbaɪoʊkənˈvɜʒən/, *n.* the conversion of biological waste, etc., into useful products.

**biocycle** /ˈbaɪəsaɪkəl/, *n.* any of the major divisions of the biosphere as fresh water, salt water, or land.

**biodegradable** /ˌbaɪoʊdəˈgreɪdəbəl/, *adj.* capable of being decomposed by the action of living organisms, esp. of bacteria: *a biodegradable detergent.* – **biodegradability,** *n.* – **biodegradation,** *n.*

**biodynamics** /ˌbaɪoʊdaɪˈnæmɪks/, *n.* the branch of biology that treats of energy, or of the activity of living organisms (opposed to *biostatics*). – **biodynamic, biodynamical,** *adj.*

**bio-engineering** /ˌbaɪoʊ-ɛndʒəˈnɪərɪŋ/, *n.* the application of engineering principles to the design and manufacture of such medical aids as artificial limbs.

**bio-feedback** /ˌbaɪoʊ-ˈfidbæk/, *n.* the relaying to a patient by means of visual display, information about pulse rate, blood pressure and other indicators of his body's functioning.

**biog.,** **1.** biographical. **2.** biography.

**biogenesis** /ˌbaɪoʊˈdʒɛnəsəs/, *n.* **1.** the doctrine that living organisms come from other living organisms only. Also, **biogeny** /baɪˈɒdʒəni/. **2.** the development of living organisms from prior living organisms. – **biogenetic** /ˌbaɪoʊdʒəˈnɛtɪk/, *adj.* – **biogenetically,** *adv.*

**biogeographical realm** /baɪoʊdʒiəˌgræfɪkəl ˈrɛlm/, *n.* a region of the world characterised by distinctive flora and fauna. The realms are: Holarctic, Ethiopian, Madagascan, Oriental, Neotropical, Australian, New Zealand, Polynesian.

**biogeography** /ˌbaɪoʊdʒiˈɒgrəfi/, *n.* the study of the geographical distribution of living things. – **biogeographical,** *adj.*

**biograph** /ˈbaɪoʊgræf/, *n. Obs.* →**picture theatre.**

**biographer** /baɪˈɒgrəfə/, *n.* a writer of biography.

**biographical** /ˌbaɪəˈgræfɪkəl/, *adj.* **1.** of or pertaining to a person's life. **2.** pertaining to biography. Also, **biographic.** – **biographically,** *adv.*

**biography** /baɪˈɒgrəfi/, *n., pl.* **-phies. 1.** a written account of a person's life. **2.** such writings collectively. **3.** the study of the lives of individuals. **4.** the art of writing a biography. [Gk *biographia*]

**biol.,** **1.** biological. **2.** biology.

**biological** /baɪəˈlɒdʒɪkəl/, *adj.* Also, **biologic. 1.** pertaining to biology. **2.** of or pertaining to the products and operations of applied biology: *a biological preparation or test.* –*n.* **3.** *Biol., Pharm.* any biochemical product, esp. serums, vaccines, etc., produced from micro-organisms. – **biologically,** *adv.*

**biological clock** /– ˈklɒk/, *n.* a mechanism built into living organisms which controls their biorhythms regardless of external time.

**biological control** /– kənˈtroʊl/, *n.* a method of controlling pests by introducing one of their natural enemies.

**biological shield** /– ˈʃild/, *n.* a thick wall surrounding a nuclear reactor, to protect workers from radiation.

**biological timeclock** /– ˈtaɪmklɒk/, *n.* a timing mechanism in the body which allows it to time itself to a set cycle, as a menstrual cycle, etc.

**biological warfare** /– ˈwɔfɛə/, *n.* warfare which makes use of biologically produced poisons that affect man, domestic animals, or food crops, esp. bacteria or viruses. Also, **B.W.**

**biological weapon** /– ˈwɛpən/, *n.* a weapon used in biological warfare.

**biology** /baɪˈɒlədʒi/, *n.* the science of life or living matter in all its forms and phenomena, esp. with reference to origin, growth, reproduction, structure, etc. – **biologist,** *n.*

**bioluminescence** /ˌbaɪoʊluməˈnɛsəns/, *n.* the production of light by living organisms. – **bioluminescent,** *adj.*

**biolysis** /baɪˈɒləsəs/, *n.* dissolution of a living being; death; the destruction of the phenomena of life, esp. the chemical decomposition of organic matter. – **biolytic** /baɪəˈlɪtɪk/, *adj.*

**biomagnification** /ˌbaɪoʊmægnəfəˈkeɪʃən/, *n.* the increase in toxicity of a chemical as a result of its progress along a food chain.

**biomagnify** /baɪoʊˈmægnəfaɪ/, *v.i.,* **-fied, -fying.** (of a toxic substance) to undergo biomagnification.

**biome** /ˈbaɪoʊm/, *n.* a major regional ecological community of plants and animals extending over large natural areas, as coral reef, tropical rain forest, etc.

**biomedical** /ˌbaɪoʊˈmɛdɪkəl/, *adj.* denoting the biological sciences which relate directly to medicine as histology, embryology.

**biometrics** /baɪəˈmɛtrɪks/, *n.* **1.** *Biol.* the application of mathematical-statistical theory to biology. **2.** biometry. – **biometric, biometrical,** *adj.* – **biometrically,** *adv.*

**biometry** /baɪˈɒmətri/, *n.* the calculation of the probable duration of human life.

**bionic** /baɪˈɒnɪk/, *adj.* **1.** of or pertaining to bionics. **2.** *Colloq.* having body parts or functions replaced or imposed by electronic equipment: *a bionic hand.*

**bionics** /baɪˈɒnɪks/, *n.* the study of biological systems as an aid to the development of such electronic or mechanical equipment as artificial limbs. [BI(O)- + (ELECTR)ONICS]

**bionomics** /baɪəˈnɒmɪks/, *n.* →**ecology** (def. 1). [BIO- + *-nomics,* as in ECONOMICS] – **bionomic, bionomical,** *adj.* – **bionomically,** *adv.* – **bionomist** /baɪˈɒnəməst/, *n.*

**biophysics** /baɪəˈfɪzɪks/, *n.* that branch of biology which deals with biological structures and processes in terms of physics. – **biophysical,** *adj.*

**bioplasm** /ˈbaɪoʊplæzəm/, *n.* →**protoplasm.**

**biopsy** /ˈbaɪɒpsi/, *n. Med.* the excision and diagnostic study of a piece of tissue from a living body.

**biorhythm** /ˈbaɪoʊrɪðəm/, *n.* **1.** a theory that our well-being is affected by three internal cycles, the physiological, emotional, and intellectual. **2.** (*pl.*) the rhythms themselves. **3.** (*pl.*) the cycle of biological processes, as eating, sleeping, etc., that occur in a living organism at specific intervals of time; circadian rhythms.

**bioscope** /ˈbaɪəskoʊp/, *n.* **1.** *Chiefly S. African.* cinema. **2.** an early form of film projector (about 1900). **3.** *Obs.* a film, esp. a newsreel.

**bioscopy** /baɪˈɒskəpi/, *n. Med.* examination of the body to discover whether or not it is alive.

**-biosis,** a word element meaning 'way of life', as in *symbiosis.* [combining form representing Gk *bíōsis*]

**biosphere** /ˈbaɪəsfɪə/, *n.* the part of the earth where living organisms are to be found.

**biostatics** /baɪoʊˈstætɪks/, *n.* the branch of biology that treats of the structure of organisms in relation to their functions (opposed to *biodynamics*). – **biostatic, biostatical,** *adj.*

**biosynthesis** /baɪoʊˈsɪnθəsəs/, *n.* the synthesis of complex substances from simpler compounds by living organisms. – **biosynthetic** /ˌbaɪoʊsɪnˈθɛtɪk/, *adj.*

**biot** /ˈbaɪɒt/, *n.* an electromagnetic unit of current equal to ten amperes.

**biota** /baɪˈoʊtə/, *n.* the total animal and plant life of a region, or sometimes a period, as seen collectively and interdependently. [NL, from Gk *biotḗ* life]

**biotic** /baɪˈɒtɪk/, *adj.* pertaining to life, esp. to the animal and plant life of a region or period. Also, **biotical.**

**biotin** /'baɪətən/, *n.* a crystalline acid, one of the vitamin B complex factors, found in liver, eggs, yeast, and other foods; vitamin H.

**biotite** /'baɪətaɪt/, *n.* a very common mineral of the mica group, occurring in dark brown or green or black sheets and scales, an important constituent of igneous rocks. [named after J. B. *Biot,* 1774-1862, French physicist. See -ITE[1]] – **biotitic** /baɪə'tɪtɪk/, *adj.*

**biotite schist** /– 'ʃɪst/, *n.* a common variety of metamorphic rock.

**biotype** /'baɪətaɪp/, *n.* a group of organisms with the same hereditary characteristics; genotype. – **biotypic** /baɪə'tɪpɪk/, *adj.*

**biparietal** /baɪpə'raɪətl/, *adj.* pertaining to both parietal bones.

**biparous** /'bɪpərəs/, *adj.* **1.** *Zool.* bringing forth offspring in pairs. **2.** *Bot.* bearing two branches or axes.

**bipartisan** /baɪ'patɪzæn, -zən/, *adj.* representing, supported, or characterised by two parties, esp. political parties. – **bipartisanship,** *n.*

**bipartite** /baɪ'pataɪt/, *adj.* **1.** *Law.* **a.** being in two corresponding parts: *a bipartite contract.* **b.** affecting two parties; bilateral. **2.** *Bot.* divided into two parts nearly to the base, as a leaf. [L. *bipartītus,* pp., divided into two parts] – **bipartitely,** *adv.* – **bipartition** /ˌbaɪpa'tɪʃən/, *n.*

**biped** /'baɪpɛd/, *n.* **1.** a two-footed animal. *–adj.* **2.** having two feet. [L *bipēs* two-footed]

**bipedal** /'baɪpɛdl/, *adj.* →**biped.**

**bipetalous** /baɪ'pɛtələs/, *adj.* (of a flower) having two petals.

**biphenyl** /baɪ'fɛnəl, -'finəl/, *n.* a colourless crystalline compound, $C_6H_5C_6H_5$, composed of two phenyl groups, of which the benzidine dyes are derivatives.

**bipinnate** /baɪ'pɪneɪt, -ət/, *adj.* pinnate, as a leaf, with the divisions also pinnate.

bipinnate leaf

**biplane** /'baɪpleɪn/, *n.* an aeroplane or glider with two pairs of wings, one above and usu. slightly forward of the other.

**bipod** /'baɪpɒd/, *n.* a two-legged support, as for a machine-gun. [BI- + -POD. Cf. TRIPOD]

**bipolar** /baɪ'poʊlə/, *adj.* **1.** having two poles. **2.** pertaining to or found at both poles. **3.** *Electronics.* (of transistors) employing both electrons and holes as carriers. – **bipolarity** /baɪpə'lærəti/, *n.*

**bipropellant** /baɪprə'pɛlənt/, *n.* a liquid rocket propellant in the form of two substances, a fuel and an oxidant.

**biquadrate** /baɪ'kwɒdreɪt, -rət/, *n. Maths.* the fourth power.

**biquadratic** /ˌbaɪkwɒd'rætɪk/, *adj. Maths.* involving the fourth, but no higher, power of the unknown or variable.

**biradial symmetry** /baɪˌreɪdiəl 'sɪmətri/, *n.* symmetry manifested both bilaterally and radially in the same creature, as in ctenophores.

**birch** /bɜtʃ/, *n.* **1.** any tree or shrub of the genus *Betula,* comprising species with a smooth, laminated outer bark and close-grained wood. **2.** the wood itself. **3.** other unrelated trees with similar timbers such as *Baloghia lucida* and *Schizomeria ovata.* **4.** *N.Z.* any species of *Nothofagus,* beech. **5.** a birch rod, or a bundle of birch twigs, used as a whip. *–adj.* **6.** of or pertaining to birch. **7.** consisting or made of birch. *–v.t.* **8.** to beat or punish with a birch. [ME *birche,* OE *bierce,* c. G *Birke*]

**birchen** /'bɜtʃən/, *adj. Archaic.* →**birch.**

**bird**[1] /bɜd/, *n.* **1.** any of the Aves, a class of warm-blooded vertebrates having a body more or less completely covered with feathers, and the forelimbs so modified as to form wings by means of which most species fly. **2.** *Sport.* **a.** a game bird. **b.** a clay pigeon. **3.** *Colloq.* a person, esp. one having some peculiarity. **4.** *Colloq.* a sound of derision, esp. hissing: *to give someone the bird.* **5.** *Horseracing Colloq.* a certainty to win, a cert. **6.** *Colloq.* a girl; a girlfriend. **7.** *Colloq.* a secret source of information: *a little bird told me.* **8. birds of a feather,** *Colloq.* people of similar character or like tastes. **9.** *Colloq.* an aeroplane. **10. like a bird,** easily, swiftly. **11. for the birds,** trivial, worthless. **12.** *Archaic.* the young of any fowl. *–v.i.* **13.** to catch or shoot birds. [ME *byrd, bryd,* OE *brid(d)* young bird, chick] – **birdlike,** *adj.*

**bird**[2] /bɜd/, *n. Colloq.* **1.** a prison sentence. **2.** a prison. [rhyming slang, *birdlime* time]

**birdbath** /'bɜdbaθ/, *n.* a small bath, usu. of stone, placed in a garden for wild birds.

**bird brain** /'bɜd breɪn/, *n. Colloq.* a frivolous or scatterbrained person.

**birdcage** /'bɜdkeɪdʒ/, *n.* **1.** a wicker or wire cage for tame birds. **2.** an enclosure on a racecourse where horses are paraded before a race and to which they return after it. **3.** *N.Z. Colloq.* a used-car dealer's display yard, enclosed by a wire fence.

**birdcage boy** /'– bɔɪ/, *n. N.Z. Colloq.* a used-car dealer.

**bird call** /'bɜd kɔl/, *n.* **1.** a sound made by a bird. **2.** a sound imitating that of a bird. **3.** a device used to imitate the sound of a bird.

**bird-cherry** /bɜd-'tʃɛri/, *n.* **1.** an Old World wild cherry, *Prunus padus.* **2.** its fruit.

**bird dog** /'bɜd dɒg/, *n. U.S.* →**gun dog.**

**bird-eating spider** /'bɜd-itɪŋ spaɪdə/, *n.* one of the largest mygalomorph spiders, *Selenocosmia crassipes,* with huge fangs, a body length up to 55 mm and leg span up to 170 mm, which digs a deep burrow and feeds on frogs, beetles and other insects.

bird-eating spider

**birder** /'bɜdə/, *n. Colloq.* →**mutton-birder.**

**bird-fancier** /'bɜd-fænsiə/, *n.* one who rears or sells birds.

**bird flower** /'bɜd flaʊə/, *n.* any of many species of *Crotalaria,* a genus of the family Papilionaceae with a strongly angled keel.

**bird-foot** /'bɜd-fʊt/, *n.* →**bird's-foot.**

**birdie** /'bɜdi/, *n.* **1.** *Colloq.* a bird; small bird. **2.** *Golf.* a score of one stroke under par on a hole.

**birdlime** /'bɜdlaɪm/, *n., v.,* **-limed, -liming.** *–n.* **1.** a sticky material, prepared from holly, mistletoe or other plants and smeared on twigs to catch small birds which light on it. *–v.t.* **2.** to smear or catch with or as with birdlime.

**birdlime tree** /'– tri/, *n.* a rainforest tree, *Pisonia umbellifera,* often found on tropical coasts.

**birdman** /'bɜdmæn, -mən/, *n., pl.* **-men** /-mɛn, -mən/. **1.** →**fowler.** **2.** an ornithologist. **3.** *Colloq.* an aviator.

**bird netting** /'bɜd nɛtɪŋ/, *n.* wire netting of fine gauge to prevent poultry and other birds from escaping, or to afford protection to the birds from predators.

**bird of paradise,** *n.* **1.** any bird of the family Paradiseidae of Australia and New Guinea, noted for magnificent plumage, as *Paradisea apoda.* **2.** a perennial, musaceous plant, *Strelitzia reginae,* with scapes of purple and orange flowers.

bird of paradise

**bird of passage,** *n.* **1.** a bird that migrates seasonally. **2.** a restless person; one who does not stay in one place for long.

**bird of peace,** *n.* a dove.

**bird of prey,** *n.* any of numerous predatory, flesh-eating birds such as the eagles, hawks, kites, vultures, owls, etc., most of which have strong beaks and claws for catching, killing and tearing to pieces the animals on which they feed.

**bird orchid** /'bɜd ɔkəd/, *n.* any of several species of terrestrial orchid belonging to the genus *Chiloglottis,* having flowers which are thought to resemble birds.

**birdseed** /'bɜdsid/, *n.* small seed, esp. that used as food for birds.

**bird's-eye** /'bɜdz-aɪ/, *adj.* **1.** seen from above: *a bird's-eye view of a city.* **2.** general; not detailed: *a bird's eye view of history.* **3.** having spots or markings resembling birds' eyes: *bird's-eye maple.* **4.** a type of weave with small, eye-like figures. **5.** a fabric, either cotton or linen, of such a weave, used esp. for towelling.

**birdseye chilli** /– 'tʃɪli/, *n.* a small, very hot green or red fruit of the bird pepper, *Capsicum frutescens.*

**bird's-foot** /'bɜdz-fʊt/, *n.* any of the slender leguminous herbs of the genus *Ornithopus,* esp. *O. perpusillus,* in which the pods on each stalk are spread out and resemble the claws of a bird's foot.

**bird's-foot delta** /– 'dɛltə/, *n.* a delta formed by the outgrowth of fingers or pairs of natural levees at the mouth of river distributaries making a bird's-foot shape, as typified by the Mississippi delta.

**bird's-foot trefoil** /– 'trɛfɔɪl/, *n.* **1.** a herbaceous plant, *Lotus corniculatus,* having yellow flowers, sometimes with red markings, the legumes of which spread like a crow's foot. **2.** any similar plant of the same genus.

**bird's-nest** /'bɜdz-nɛst/, *v.i.* to search for birds' nests, often in order to steal the eggs.

**bird's-nest fern** /– 'fɜn/, *n.* an epiphytic or terrestrial fern, *Asplenium nidus,* family Polypodiaceae, of Australia, India and Polynesia, having large fronds thought to resemble a bird's nest.

**bird's-nest soup** /– 'sup/, *n.* a Chinese soup prepared from the gelatinous nests of any of several species of Indo-Australian swift of the Collocalia family.

**birdsong** /'bɜdsɒŋ/, *n.* the song of a bird.

**bird-spider** /'bɜd-spaɪdə/, *n.* any of several large bird-eating spiders found in Brazil, of the family Aviculariidae.

**bird-table** /'bɜd-teɪbəl/, *n.* a table in a garden on which scraps, etc., are put for wild birds, esp. in winter.

**birdwatcher** /'bɜdwɒtʃə/, *n.* **1.** one who makes a hobby of observing and identifying birds in their natural habitats. **2.** *Colloq.* (*joc.*) one who displays a keen interest in looking at beautiful young women.

**birdwood grass** /'bɜdwʊd ˌgras/, *n.* a tropical pasture grass, *Cenchrus setigerus,* native to Africa and India, cultivated and naturalised elsewhere esp. in north-western Australia.

**birefringence** /baɪrə'frɪndʒəns/, *n.* double refraction of light, as exhibited by crystalline minerals esp. calcite. [BI- + REFRINGENCE] – **birefringent,** *adj.*

**bireme** /'baɪrim/, *n.* a galley having two banks or tiers of oars. [L *birēmis,* lit., two-oared]

**biretta** /bə'rɛtə/, *n.* a stiff, square cap with three (or four) upright projecting pieces extending from the centre of the top to the edge, worn by Roman Catholic ecclesiastics. Also, **berretta.** [It. *berretta,* from L *birrus* cap]

biretta

**birko** /'bɜkoʊ/, *n.* a container with an electric element sealed into the base, used for heating water, milk, etc. [Trademark]

**birl** /bɜl/, *n., v., Colloq.* →**burl**[2].

**birley** /'bɜli/, *n.* →**berley.**

**biro** /'baɪroʊ/, *n.* a ballpoint pen. [Trademark]

**birth** /bɜθ/, *n.* **1.** the fact of being born: *the day of his birth.* **2.** the act of bearing or bringing forth; parturition. **3.** lineage; extraction; descent: *of Grecian birth.* **4.** high or noble lineage. **5.** supposedly natural heritage: *a musician by birth.* **6.** that which is born. **7.** any coming into existence; origin: *the birth of Protestantism.* [ME *byrth(e)* from Scand.; cf. Icel. *byrdh*]

**birth certificate** /'– səˌtɪfɪkət/, *n.* a certificate issued by a registrar upon the birth of each person, recording sex and parentage.

**birth control** /'– kəntroʊl/, *n.* the regulation of birth through the deliberate control or prevention of conception.

**birthday** /'bɜθdeɪ/, *n.* **1.** (of persons) the day of one's birth. **2.** (of things) origin or beginning. **3.** the anniversary of one's birth or the origin of something. *–adj.* **4.** given on, held on, or connected with a birthday. **5. birthday boy (girl),** *Colloq.* a child or adult in honour of whose birthday a festivity is being held.

**birthday honours** /– 'ɒnəz/, *n.pl.* a list of honours conferred on the official birthday of a ruling monarch.

**birthday suit** /'– sut/, *n. Colloq.* the naked skin; state of nakedness.

**birthmark** /'bɜθmak/, *n.* a congenital mark on the body.

**birthplace** /'bɜθpleɪs/, *n.* place of birth or origin.

**birthrate** /'bɜθreɪt/, *n.* the proportion of the number of births in a place in a given time to the total population.

**birthright** /'bɜθraɪt/, *n.* any right or privilege to which a person is entitled by birth.

**birthstone** /'bɜθstoʊn/, *n.* a precious stone associated with a person's month of birth and worn as a lucky charm.

**birthwort** /'bɜθwɜt/, *n.* **1.** a plant, *Aristolochia clematitis,* a native of Europe, said to ease childbirth. **2.** any of certain other species of the genus *Aristolochia.*

**bis** /bɪs/, *adv.* **1.** twice. **2.** a second time: used (esp. in music) to direct a repetition. [L. See BI-]

**biscuit** /'bɪskət/, *n.* **1. a.** a stiff, sweet mixture of flour, liquid, shortening and other ingredients, shaped into small pieces before baking or sliced after baking. **b.** a savoury, unleavened similar mixture, rolled, sliced and baked crisp. **2.** a pale brown colour. **3.** pottery after the first baking and before glazing. **4.** a layer of hay, a number of which make up a bale. *–adj.* **5.** pale brown. [ME *besquite,* from OF *bescuit,* from *bes* (from L *bis*) twice + *cuit,* pp. of *cuire* cook (from L *coquere*)] – **biscuit-like, biscuity,** adj.

**bisect** /baɪ'sɛkt/, *v.t.* **1.** to cut or divide into two parts. **2.** *Geom.* to cut or divide into two equal parts. *–v.i.* **3.** to split into two, as a road; fork. – **bisection,** *n.* – **bisectional,** *adj.* – **bisectionally,** *adv.*

**bisector** /baɪ'sɛktə/, *n. Geom.* a line or plane bisecting an angle or line segment.

**biserrate** /baɪ'sɛreɪt, -rət/, *adj.* (of a leaf) double serrate; notched like a saw, with the teeth also notched.

**bisexual** /baɪ'sɛkʃuəl/, *adj.* **1.** of both sexes. **2.** combining male and female organs in one individual; hermaphroditic. **3.** exhibiting or pertaining to bisexuality. *–n.* **4.** *Biol.* one who has the reproductive organs of both sexes. **5.** a person sexually attracted to either sex. – **bisexualism,** *n.* – **bisexually,** *adv.*

**bisexuality** /ˌbaɪsɛkʃu'æləti/, *n.* attraction to both males and females as sexual partners.

**bishop** /'bɪʃəp/, *n.* **1.** a clergyman consecrated for the spiritual direction of a diocese, being in the Greek, Roman Catholic, Anglican, and other churches a member of the highest order in the ministry. **2.** a spiritual overseer in the early Christian Church, either of a local church or of a number of churches. **3.** *Chess.* a piece which moves obliquely on squares of the same colour. **4.** a hot drink made of port wine, oranges, cloves, etc. [ME; OE *bisc(e)op,* from VL *(e)biscopus,* var. of L *episcopus,* from Gk *epískopos* overseer]

**Bishop Barker** /bɪʃəp 'bakə/, *n. Colloq.* beer served in a tall glass. [named after Frederick *Barker,* Bishop of Sydney 1845-81, who was unusually tall]

**bishopric** /'bɪʃəprɪk/, *n.* the see, diocese, or office of a bishop. [ME *bisshoprike,* OE *bisceoprice,* from *bisceop* bishop + *rice* dominion]

**bishop sleeve** /bɪʃəp 'sliv/, *n.* a long, wide sleeve gathered at the wrist.

**bishop's weed** /'bɪʃəps wid/, *n.* a tall umbelliferous herb, *Ammi majus,* native to Mediterranean regions but widely naturalised.

**bisk** /bɪsk/, *n.* →**bisque**[1].

**Bislama** /bɪslə'ma/, *n.* the dialect of Neo-Melanesian spoken in Vanuatu; Beach-la-mar. [see BEACH-LA-MAR]

**bismillah** /bɪz'mɪlə, bɪs-/, *interj.* in the name of Allah. [Ar.]

**bismuth** /'bɪzməθ/, *n.* a brittle, metallic element, having compounds used in medicine. *Symbol:* Bi; *at. no.:* 83; *at. wt:* 208.98; *sp. gr.:* 9.8 at 20° C. [G, var. of *Wismut;* orig. uncert.] – **bismuthal,** *adj.*

**bismuthic** /bɪz'mjuθɪk, -'mʌθɪk/, *adj.* of or containing bismuth, esp. in the pentavalent state.

**bismuthinite** /bɪz'mʌθənaɪt/, *n.* a mineral, bismuth sulphide, $Bi_2S_3$, occurring in lead-coloured masses; an ore of bismuth.

**bismuthous** /'bɪzməθəs/, *adj.* containing trivalent bismuth.

**bison** /ˈbaɪsən/, *n., pl.* **-son.** *Zool.* **1.** a large North American bovine ruminant, *Bison bison* (**American bison,** or buffalo), with high, wellhaired shoulders. **2.** →**wisent.** [L, from Gmc; cf. G *Wisent*]

American bison

**bisque**[1] /bɪsk/, *n.* **1.** any smooth, creamy soup. **2.** a thick soup made of shellfish or game stewed long and slowly. Also, **bisk.** [F]

**bisque**[2] /bɪsk/, *n.* a point, extra turn, or the like, allowed to a player as odds in tennis and other games. [F; orig. UNKNOWN]

**bisque**[3] /bɪsk/, *n.* **1.** pottery which has been baked but not glazed; biscuit. **2.** a variety of white unglazed porcelain. [short for BISCUIT]

**bissextile** /bɪˈsɛkstaɪl/, *adj.* **1.** containing or denoting the extra day of leap year. *–n.* **2.** a leap year. [LL *bissextīlis (annus)* leap year]

**bistable** /ˈbaɪsteɪbəl/, *adj. Electronics.* of a type of switching circuit, that switches between two stable states.

**bistort** /ˈbɪstɔt/, *n.* **1.** a European perennial herb, *Polygonum bistorta,* with a twisted root, which is sometimes used as an astringent. **2.** a plant of other allied species, as **Virginia bistort,** *P. virginianum,* and **Alpine bistort,** *P. viviparum.* [L: *bis* twice + *torta,* pp. fem., twisted]

**bistoury** /ˈbɪstəri/, *n., pl.* **-ries.** a small, narrow surgical knife. [F *bistouri*]

**bistre** /ˈbɪstə/, *n.* **1.** a brown pigment extracted from the soot of wood, much used in pen and wash drawings. **2.** a dark brown colour. Also, *U.S.,* **bister.** [F *bistre;* orig. unknown, ? akin to F *bis* dark grey]

**bistro** /ˈbɪstroʊ/, *n.* **1.** a wine bar. **2.** a small unpretentious restaurant.

**bisulphate** /baɪˈsʌlfeɪt/, *n.* a salt of sulphuric acid, containing the radical $-HSO_4$.

**bisulphide** /baɪˈsʌlfaɪd/, *n.* →**disulphide.**

**bisulphite** /baɪˈsʌlfaɪt/, *n.* a salt of sulphurous acid, containing the radical $-HSO_3$.

**bisymmetrical** /ˌbaɪsəˈmɛtrɪkəl/, *adj. Bot.* having two planes of symmetry at right angles to each other. Also, **bisymmetric.** – **bisymmetrically,** *adv.* – **bisymmetry** /baɪˈsɪmətri/, *n.*

**bit**[1] /bɪt/, *n., v.,* **bitted, bitting.** *–n.* **1.** the metal mouthpiece of a bridle, with the adjacent parts to which the reins are fastened. **2.** anything that curbs or restrains. **3.** *Mach.* the cutting or penetrating part of various tools: **a.** the cutting portion of an axe or hatchet or the removable cutter in the plane, brace, etc. **b.** the movable boring or drilling part (in many forms) used in a carpenter's brace, a drilling machine, or the like. **4.** the part of a key which enters the lock and acts on the bolt and tumblers. **5. on the bit,** (of a horse) restrained by pressure on the bit. **6. take the bit between one's teeth, a.** to throw off control; rush headlong. **b.** to take the plunge, rejecting all restraint; throw one's energies into something. *–v.t.* **7.** to put a bit in the mouth of. **8.** to curb; restrain. **9.** to grind a bit on. [ME *byt,* OE *bite* action of biting]

spiral bits (def. 3b)

**bit**[2] /bɪt/, *n.* **1.** a small piece or quantity of anything: *a bit of string, a bit of one's mind.* **2.** a short time: *wait a bit.* **3.** *Obs.* a coin worth more than one unit of currency: *threepenny bit.* **4.** the smallest amount; jot; whit. **5.** share or part of a duty, task, etc: *do one's bit.* **6.** *Colloq.* a girl. **7.** *U.S. Colloq.* twelve and a half cents. **8. bit by bit,** slowly; gradually; in stages. **9. a bit of,** rather: *a bit of a nuisance.* **10. a bit of all right,** something or someone exciting admiration. **11. a bit on the side,** *Colloq.* **a.** something beyond the usual arrangement. **b.** an extra-marital affair. **12. have a bit both ways,** *Colloq.* to attempt to cover oneself against any eventuality. **13. not a bit of it,** not at all; by no means. [ME *bite,* OE *bita* bit, morsel]

**bit**[3] /bɪt/, *n.* a single, basic unit of information, used in connection with computers and communication theory. [short for B(INARY DIG)IT]

**bitartrate** /baɪˈtatreɪt/, *n.* a tartrate in which only one of the acid hydrogens of tartaric acid is replaced by a metal or a positive radical; an acid tartrate.

**bitch** /bɪtʃ/, *n.* **1.** a female dog. **2.** a female of canines generally. **3.** *Colloq.* a woman, esp. a disagreeable or malicious one. **4.** *Colloq.* a complaint. *–v.i.* **5.** *Colloq.* to complain. *–v.t.* **6.** *Colloq.* to spoil; bungle. [ME *biche,* OE *bicce,* c. Icel. *bikkja*] – **bitchiness, bitchery,** *n.* – **bitchily,** *adv.*

**bitchy** /ˈbɪtʃi/, *adj.,* malicious; disagreeable.

**bite** /baɪt/, *v.,* **bit, bitten** or **bit, biting,** *n.* *–v.t.* **1.** to cut into or wound, or cut (*off, out,* etc.) with the teeth. **2.** to grip with the teeth. **3.** to cut or pierce. **4.** to sting, as an insect. **5.** to cause to smart or sting. **6.** to eat into or corrode, as an acid does. **7.** *Colloq.* to trouble; worry; disturb: *what's biting him?* **8.** to cadge off (someone): *I'll bite you for five bucks.* **9.** to beg, borrow (fol. by *off*). **10.** *Etching.* to use acid for eating into such parts of a copper or other surface as are left bare of a protective coating. **11.** to make a great impression on: *bitten by the love of music.* **12.** to close the teeth tightly on. **13.** to take firm hold or act effectively on. **14.** to cheat; deceive. **15.** *Colloq.* to react angrily: *don't tease her, she bites.* **16. bite back, a.** to restrain: *she bit back her angry reply.* **b.** *Colloq.* to reply sharply. **17. bite the dust,** *Colloq.* **a.** to fall dead, esp. in combat. **b.** to fall. *–v.i.* **18.** to press the teeth (*into, on,* etc.); snap. **19.** *Angling.* (of fish) to take the bait. **20.** to accept a deceptive offer or suggestion. **21.** to act effectively; grip; hold. *–n.* **22.** the act of biting. **23.** a wound made by biting. **24.** *Dentistry.* the angle at which the upper and lower teeth meet. **25.** a cutting, stinging, or nipping effect. **26.** pungency; sharpness. **27.** a small piece bitten off. **28.** food: *not a bite to eat.* **29.** a small meal. **30.** *Mach.* **a.** the catch or hold that one object or one part of a mechanical apparatus has on another. **b.** a surface brought into contact to obtain a hold or grip, as in a lathe, chuck, or similar device. **31.** (of a file) the roughness or power of abrasion. **32.** *N.Z. Colloq.* a nagging person. **33.** *Colloq.* a brazen attempt to borrow: *put the bite on, go the bite.* **34.** *Colloq.* a person from whom one anticipates borrowing money: *he'd be a good bite.* **35.** a reaction: *did you get a bite from Robin?* **36. on the bite,** (of fish) taking the bait. **37. put the bite on,** *Colloq.* to cadge. **38. raise a bite,** *Colloq.* to tease someone until one gets a reaction. [ME *biten,* OE *bītan,* c. G *beissen*] – **biter,** *n.*

**bitie** /ˈbaɪti/, *n. Colloq.* (*esp. in children's speech*) anything that bites, or is otherwise dangerous.

**biting** /ˈbaɪtɪŋ/, *adj.* **1.** nipping; keen: *biting cold.* **2.** cutting; sarcastic: *a biting remark.* – **bitingly,** *adv.*

**bitonality** /ˌbaɪtoʊˈnæləti/, *n.* the use in a musical composition, etc., of two keys simultaneously.

**bit part** /ˈbɪt pat/, *n. Theat.* a small or unimportant role.

**bitser** /ˈbɪtsə/, *n. Colloq.* **1.** a mongrel. **2.** *Colloq.* any contrivance the parts of which come from miscellaneous sources. **3.** *Colloq.* an animal or person of mixed stock. Also, **bitzer.**

**bitstock** /ˈbɪtstɒk/, *n.* →*Mach.* **brace.**

**bitt** /bɪt/, *n.* **1.** a strong post of wood or iron projecting (usu. in pairs) above the deck of a ship, and used for securing cables, lines for towing, etc. *–v.t.* **2.** to put (a cable, etc.) round the bitts. [var. of BIT[1]]

**bitten** /ˈbɪtn/, *v.* past participle of **bite.**

**bitter** /ˈbɪtə/, *adj.* **1.** having a harsh, disagreeable taste, like that of quinine. **2.** hard to admit or receive: *a bitter lesson.* **3.** hard to bear; grievous; distressful: *a bitter sorrow.* **4.** causing pain; piercing; stinging: *bitter cold.* **5.** characterised by intense animosity: *bitter hatred.* **6.** harsh; sarcastic; cutting: *bitter words.* *–n.* **7.** that which is bitter; bitterness. **8.** *Chiefly Brit.* a lager or ale type of beer brewed with additional hops for extra bitterness. *–v.t.* **9.** to make bitter. [OE *biter;* akin to BITE] – **bitterish,** *adj.* – **bitterly,** *adv.* – **bitterness,** *n.*

**bitterbark** /ˈbɪtəbak/, *n.* a tree of inland Australia, *Alstonia constricta,* with bark which may be used in a tonic preparation.

**bittercress** /ˈbɪtəkrɛs/, *n.* **1.** any herb of the genus *Cardamine,* cosmopolitan but concentrated in cool and temperate regions, as the hairy bittercress, *C. hirsuta,* probably originally of Europe, now widespread as a weed, and *C. tenuifolia,* a perennial herb of New South Wales, South Australia, Tasmania and Victoria. **2.** →**swinecress.**

**bitter end** /bɪtər ˈɛnd/, *n.* **1.** *Naut.* the extreme tail-end of a cable or rope. The bitter end of an anchor cable is secured to the ship inside the chain locker. **2. to the bitter end,** to the very end (usu. of something difficult or unpleasant): *they fought to the bitter end.* [*bitter* (from BITT + -ER[1]) + END[1]]

**bittern**[1] /'bɪtən/, *n.* any of several small or medium-sized herons as the **brown bittern,** *Botaurus poiciloptilus,* of southern Australia, New Caledonia and New Zealand. [ME *bitter, botor,* from OF *butor;* orig. uncert. Cf. L *būtio* bittern]

**bittern**[2] /'bɪtən/, *n.* a bitter, oily liquid remaining as a by-product of salt-making after the salt has crystallised out of sea water or brine, used as a source of bromine, etc. [d. var. of *bittering,* from BITTER + -ING[1]]

**bitter-pea** /bɪtə-'pi/, *n.* any shrub of the Australian genus *Daviesia,* family Papilionaceae, with red and yellow flowers and somewhat triangular pods.

**bitters** /'bɪtəz/, *n.pl.* **1.** a spirituous or other drink in which bitter herbs or roots are steeped. **2.** *Pharm.* **a.** a liquid, usu. alcoholic, impregnated with a bitter medicine, as gentian, quassia, etc., used as a stomachic, tonic, or the like. **b.** bitter medicinal substances in general, as quinine, gentian, etc.

**bittersweet** /'bɪtəswit/, *n.;* /bɪtə'swit/, *adj.* *–n.* **1.** the woody nightshade, *Solanum dulcamara,* a climbing or trailing solanaceous plant with scarlet berries. **2.** any climbing plant of the genus *Celastrus,* with orange capsules opening to expose red-coated seeds, esp. *Celastrus scandens.* *–adj.* **3.** both bitter and sweet to the taste. **4.** both pleasant and painful.

**bitterwood** /'bɪtəwʊd/, *n.* **1.** any tree of the tropical genus *Picrasma.* **2.** the bitter wood of this tree, from which a substitute for quassia is prepared.

**bitty** /'bɪti/, *adj.* **1.** scrappy; disjointed; not unified. **2.** (of a liquid) containing bits of skin, sediment, etc.: *bitty milk, bitty paint.*

**bitumen** /'bɪtʃəmən/, *n.* **1.** any of various natural substances, as asphalt, maltha, gilsonite, etc. consisting mainly of hydrocarbons. **2.** a brown tar or asphalt-like substance used in painting. **3. the bitumen, a.** a tarred or sealed road. **b.** any bituminised area. [L] – **bituminoid** /bə'tʃumənɔɪd/, *adj.*

**bitumen blonde** /– 'blɒnd/, *n. Colloq.* **1.** a brunette. **2.** an Aboriginal woman.

**bituminise** /bə'tʃumənaɪz, 'bɪtʃə-/, *v.t.,* **-nised, -nising.** to treat with bitumen, esp. of road surfacing. Also, **bituminize.** – **bituminisation,** *n.*

**bituminous** /bə'tʃumənəs/, *adj.* of, like, or containing bitumen: *bituminous shale.*

**bituminous coal** /– 'koʊl/, *n.* a mineral coal which contains volatile hydrocarbons and tarry matter, and burns with a yellow, smoky flame; soft coal.

**biuret** /'baɪjurɛt/, *n.* an organic compound formed by heating urea, $NH_2CONHCONH_2$, which gives, in strongly alkaline solution, a violet colour with copper sulphate (the biuret reaction).

**bivalent** /baɪ'veɪlənt, 'bɪvələnt/, *adj.* **1.** *Chem.* **a.** having a valency of 2. **b.** having two valencies, as mercury, with valencies 1 and 2. **2.** *Biol.* pertaining to composites of two similar or identical chromosomes, or chromosome sets. *–n.* **3.** *Biol.* a bivalent pair or set of chromosomes. – **bivalence, bivalency,** *n.*

**bivalve** /'baɪvælv/, *n.* **1.** *Zool.* a mollusc having two shells hinged together, as the oyster, clam, mussel; a lamellibranch. *–adj.* **2.** *Bot.* having two valves, as a seed case. **3.** *Zool.* having two shells, usu. united by a hinge. – **bivalvular** /baɪ'vælvjulə/, *adj.*

**bivouac** /'bɪvuæk/, *n., v.,* **-acked, -acking.** *–n.* **1.** a temporary camp, esp. a military one, made out in the open with little or no equipment. *–v.i.* **2.** to sleep out; make a bivouac. [F, probably from d. G. *Biwache.* Cf. G *Beiwacht* patrol]

**bivvy** /'bɪvi/, *n., pl.* **-vies,** *v.* **-vied, -vying.** *–n.* **1.** *Colloq.* bivouac. **2.** a small tent. *–v.i.* **3.** to bivouac. [See BIVOUAC]

**biweekly** /baɪ'wikli/, *adj., n., pl.* **-lies,** *adv.* *–adj.* **1.** occurring every two weeks. **2.** occurring twice a week; semiweekly. *–n.* **3.** a periodical issued every other week. *–adv.* **4.** every two weeks. **5.** twice a week.

**biyearly** /baɪ'jɪəli/, *adj.* **1.** →**biennial.** *–adv.* **2.** twice yearly.

**biz** /bɪz/, *n. Colloq.* **1.** business: *big biz; show biz.* **2. what's the biz?** what is the latest news? [short for BUSINESS]

**bizarre** /bə'za/, *adj.* singular in appearance, style, or general character; whimsically strange; odd. [F: odd, from Sp. *bizarro* brave, ? from Basque *bizar* beard] – **bizarrely,** *adv.* – **bizarreness,** *n.*

**bizzo** /'bɪzoʊ/, *n. Colloq.* **1.** worthless or irrelevant ideas, talks, writing, etc.: *politics, and all that bizzo.* **2.** any object or device for which one does not know the correct name. [shortened form of BUSINESS + -O]

**Bjelke blue** /bjɛlki 'blu/, *n.* a type of cheese containing peanuts, made in Queensland. [named after Joh *Bjelke-Petersen,* b. 1911, Premier of Queensland since 1968]

**bk,** **1.** bank. **2.** book.

**bl.,** barrel.

**B.L.,** Bachelor of Law.

**blab** /blæb/, *v.,* **blabbed, blabbing,** *n.* *–v.t.* **1.** to reveal indiscreetly and thoughtlessly. *–v.i.* **2.** to talk or chatter indiscreetly and thoughtlessly. **3.** to let out a secret; tell tales; talk. *–n.* **4.** idle, indiscreet chattering. **5.** a person who blabs. [orig. uncert.; cf. Icel. *blabbra,* OHG *blabbizōn*]

**blabber** /'blæbə/, *n.* **1.** one who blabs. *–v.t., v.i.* **2.** to blab.

**blabbermouth** /'blæbəmaʊθ/, *n., pl.* **-mouths** /-maʊðz/. *Colloq.* one who talks too much or who talks indiscreetly.

**blachan** /'blækan/, *n.* a pink mushy paste made from rotted shrimp. [Malay]

**black** /blæk/, *adj.* **1.** without brightness or colour; absorbing all or nearly all the rays emitted by a light source. **2.** wearing black or dark clothing, armour, etc.: *the black prince.* **3.** *Anthrop.* **a.** pertaining or belonging to an ethnic group characterised by dark skin pigmentation. **b.** pertaining specifically to the 'black races' of Africa, Oceania, and Australia: the Negroes, Negritos, Papuans, Melanesians, and Australian Aborigines. **4.** soiled or stained with dirt. **5.** characterised by absence of light; involved or enveloped in darkness: *a black night.* **6.** gloomy; dismal: *a black outlook.* **7.** boding ill; sudden; forbidding: *black words, black looks.* **8.** without any moral light or goodness; evil; wicked. **9.** caused or marked by ruin or desolation. **10.** indicating censure, disgrace, or liability to punishment: *a black mark on one's record.* **11.** illicit. **12.** prohibited or banned by a trade union. **13.** (of coffee or tea) without milk or cream. *–n.* **14.** a colour without hue at one extreme end of the scale of greys, opposite to white. A black surface absorbs light of all hues equally. **15.** (*sometimes cap.*) a member of a dark-skinned people; a Negro. **16.** a black speck, flake, or spot, as of soot. **17.** black clothing, esp. as a sign of mourning: *to be in black.* **18.** *Chess, Draughts.* the dark-coloured men or pieces. **19.** black pigment: *lampblack.* **20. in the black, a.** financially solvent. **b.** of betting odds, any bet above or including even money. *–v.t.* **21.** to make black; put black on. **22.** to clean and polish (shoes) with blacking. **23.** (of a trade union) to ban or prevent normal industrial working in (a factory, industry, or the like.). **24. black out, a.** to obscure by concealing all light in defence against air-raids. **b.** to jam (a radio). **c.** to suppress (news). *–v.i.* **25.** to become black; take on a black colour. **26.** to lose consciousness (fol. by *out*). [ME *blak,* OE *blæc,* c. OHG *blah-, blach-*] – **blackish,** *adj.* – **blackishly,** *adv.* – **blackness,** *n.*

**blackamoor** /'blækəmɔ/, *n. Archaic.* **1.** a Negro. **2.** any dark-skinned person. [var. of *black Moor*]

**black-and-blue** /blæk-ən-'blu/, *adj.* discoloured, as by bruising. Also (*esp. in predicative use*), **black and blue.**

**black and tan,** *n.* drink made by mixing beer and stout.

**black and white,** *n.* **1.** print or writing. **2.** a drawing or picture done in black and white only. **3. in black and white, a.** in print or in writing. **b.** with oppositions clearly defined.

**black-and-white** /blæk-ən-'waɪt/, *adj.* **1.** of or pertaining to a film, a television program, or photographs which are not in colour. **2.** of or pertaining to a television set which does not receive colour transmissions. **3.** with apparent oppositions and limited range of options. *–n.* **4.** a black-and-white photograph. **5.** a black-and-white television set.

**black-and-white artist** /– 'atəst/, *n.* an artist who specialises in line drawings.

**black art** /blæk 'at/, *n.* witchcraft; magic.

**blackball** /'blækbɔl/, *v.t.* **1.** to ostracise. **2.** to vote against. **3.** to reject (a candidate) by placing a black ball in the ballot box. *–n.* **4.** an adverse vote. **5.** a black ball placed in a ballot box signifying a negative vote. **6.** *N.Z.* a hard, round, black sweet. **7.** →**humbug** (def. 4). – **black-baller,** *n.*

**black ban** /'blæk bæn/, *n.* a refusal by a group interest, as of producers, trade unions, consumers, to supply or purchase goods or services.

**black bass** /– 'bæs/, *n.* any of several American freshwater fish of the genus *Micropterus.*

**black bean** /'– bin/, *n.* a rainforest tree, *Castanospermum australe,* of northern New South Wales and Queensland, having dark green leaves and pea-like flowers of yellow to red; Moreton Bay chestnut.

**black bear** /– 'bɛə/, *n.* a species of American bear, *Euarctos americanus,* with a pale face and dense black fur.

**black beech** /– 'bitʃ/, *n.* a lowland and montane forest tree of New Zealand, *Nothofagus solandri.*

**black beetle** /– 'bitl/, *n.* a large black beetle, *Heteronychus arator,* introduced from South Africa, the larvae of which attack the roots of plants as lawn grass, maize, etc.

**black belt** /'– bɛlt/, *n. Judo.* **1.** a belt worn by an experienced contestant ranking up to eighth Dan. **2.** a contestant entitled to wear this.

**blackberry** /'blækbəri, -bri/, *n., pl.* **-ries.** **1.** the fruit, black or very dark purple when ripe, of *Rubus fruticosus* and other *Rubus* spp. **2.** the plant bearing this fruit; the bramble. [ME *blakeberie,* OE *blace berian* (pl.)] – **blackberry-like,** *adj.*

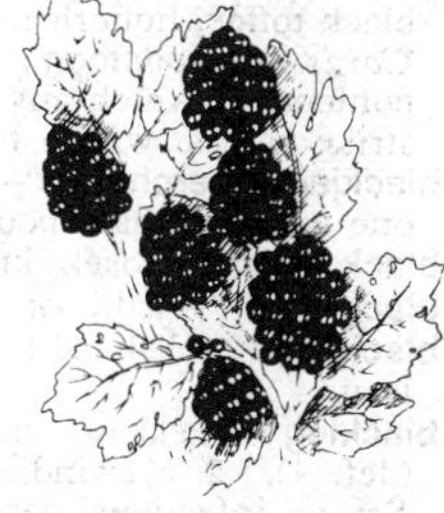
blackberry

**black bindweed** /blæk 'baındwid/, *n.* a slender twining plant, *Polygonum convolvulus,* found widely as a weed.

**blackbird** /'blækbɜd/, *n.* **1.** a European songbird of the thrush family, *Turdus merula,* introduced into Australia. **2.** any of various unrelated birds having black plumage in the male. **3.** *U.S.* any of various American birds of the family Icteridae. **4.** (formerly) a Kanaka kidnapped and transported to Australia as a slave labourer.

**blackbirding** /'blækbɜdıŋ/, *n.* (formerly) trade in kidnapped Kanaka labourers. – **blackbirder,** *n.*

**blackboard** /'blækbɔd/, *n.* a smooth dark board, used in schools, etc., for writing or drawing on with chalk.

**blackboard jungle** /– 'dʒʌŋgəl/, *n.* the school system viewed as anarchic and dealing with uncontrollable and delinquent children.

**black body** /blæk 'bɒdi/, *n. Physics.* **1.** a body which emits thermal radiation when heated, the spectral distribution of which depends only on its temperature. **2.** a theoretical body which, if it existed, would absorb all and reflect none of the radiation falling upon it.

**black book** /'– bʊk/, *n.* **1.** a book of names of people liable to censure or punishment. **2.** a small book containing a private list of names and addresses of associates in business, partners in sex, crime, etc. **3. be in someone's black books,** to be in disfavour.

**black box** /– 'bɒks/, *n.* **1.** a unit, not necessarily coloured black, which contains and protects electronic equipment, esp. equipment which automatically records information about the journey of an aircraft, train, etc., which may be inspected after a crash. **2.** any device, invention, etc., the workings of which are mysterious or kept secret. **3.** *Electronics Colloq.* a device which has input and/or output connections but whose detailed circuit is not given.

**black boy** /'– bɔı/, *n.* **1.** any species of plant belonging to the genera *Xanthorrhoea* and *Kingia* found in temperate Australia and thought to resemble a grass-skirted native figure bearing a spear; grasstree. **2.** a horticultural variety of rose producing large, dark red flowers in spring. Also, **blackboy.**

black boy

**black bread** /'– brɛd/, *n.*→**pumpernickel.**

**black bream** /– 'brım/, *n.* **1.** →**luderick.** **2.** a fine food and sport fish of eastern Australian waters, *Acanthopagrus australis;* usu. dark in colour but may appear silvery in broken water.

**black-breasted buzzard** /blæk-brɛstəd 'bʌzəd/, *n.* a large Australian hawk, *Hamirostra melanosterna,* which frequents open forests and grasslands throughout Australia, feeding on small ground animals and carrion.

**black-browed** /'blæk-braʊd/, *adj.* **1.** having black eye-brows. **2.** having a sullen, brooding, or angry appearance.

**black bryony** /blæk 'braıəni/, *n.* a twining Old World perennial vine with red berries, *Tamus communis.*

**black buck** /– 'bʌk/, *n.* a common Indian antelope, *Antilope cervicapra,* of medium size and blackish brown colour.

**blackbutt** /'blækbʌt/, *n.* any of several Australian species of *Eucalyptus,* esp. *E. pilularis,* with dark bark at the base of their trunks.

**black butter sauce,** *n.* a sauce, esp. one for fish made from butter cooked until dark brown, and seasoned vinegar. [F *beurre noire* black butter]

**black cap** /blæk 'kæp/, *n.* a square cap, part of judicial full dress, worn over the wig by judges on certain solemn or state occasions, as on passing sentence of death.

**blackcap** /'blækkæp/, *n.* **1.** →**white-naped honeyeater.** **2.** →**black-headed honeyeater.** **3.** any of various European birds having the top of the head black, as a black headed warbler, *Sylvia atricapilla.* **4.** *U.S.* a popular name of the plant and fruit of the black raspberry, *Rubus occidentalis.*

**black coal** /'blæk koʊl/, *n.* ordinary coal containing more than 80 per cent of carbon; includes bituminous coal and anthracite; formed from peat or brown coal by increased temperature and pressure.

**black comedy** /– 'kɒmədi/, *n.* a comedy expressing an underlying pessimism or bitterness, or one dealing with a tragic or gruesome subject.

**black cotton soil,** *n.* →**regur.**

**black cuckoo** /blæk 'kʊku/, *n.* →**koel.**

**blackcurrant** /blæk'kʌrənt/, *n.* **1.** the small, black edible fruit of the shrub *Ribes nigrum.* **2.** the shrub itself.

**black cypress pine,** *n.* →**black pine** (def. 1).

**blackdamp** /'blækdæmp/, *n. Mining.* air in which the oxygen has been replaced by carbon dioxide.

**Black Death** /blæk 'dɛθ/, *n.* bubonic plague, which spread over Europe in the 14th century.

**black diamond** /– 'daıəmənd/, *n.* **1.** →**carbonado** (def. 2). **2.** (*pl.*) coal.

**black disease** /'– dəziz/, *n.* an acute, often fatal disease of sheep caused by general toxaemia from *Clostridium novyi,* an anaerobic organism which multiplies in the liver in areas damaged by the common liver fluke.

**black drummer** /– 'drʌmə/, *n.* →**rock blackfish.**

**black duck** /– 'dʌk/, *n.* a duck, *Anas superciliosa,* mottled brown in colour with white stripes above and below the eye and a lead-grey bill, found in great numbers in deepwater swamps throughout Australia.

black duck

**black earth** /'– ɜθ/, *n.* **1.** any of various dark-coloured, fertile, calcareous soils, very good for cereal production, esp. that which covers a large area of southern Russia; chernozem. **2.** →**regur.**

**black elder** /– 'ɛldə/, *n.* →**elder**[2] (def. 1).

**blacken** /'blækən/, *v.,* **-ened, -ening.** *–v.t.* **1.** to make black; darken. **2.** to speak evil of; defame. *–v.i.* **3.** to grow or become black. – **blackener,** *n.*

**black eye** /blæk 'aı/, *n.* bruising round the eye, resulting from a blow, etc.

**black-eyed Susan** /ˌblæk-aıd 'suzən/, *n.* any of many unrelated flowers with dark centres, as species of *Tetratheca,* Australian plants with nodding pink flowers with dark stamens, and *Thunbergia alata,* a twining plant whose orange flowers have a dark throat.

**blackface** /'blækfeıs/, *n.* **1.** *Theat.* **a.** an entertainer who blacks his face, hands, etc., to mimic a Negro. **b.** the make-up for such an entertainer or performer. **2.** *Print.* bold-face type.

**black-faced cuckoo-shrike** /blæk-feıst 'kʊku-ʃraık/, *n.* a bird with light grey plumage and a black face, *Coracina novaehollandia,* widely distributed throughout Australia.

**black-faced kangaroo** /ˌblæk-feɪst kæŋgəˈru/, *n.* →**western grey kangaroo.**

**blackfellow** /ˈblækfɛloʊ, -fɛlə/, *n.* (*esp. in Aboriginal pidgin*) an Aborigine. Also, **blackfella, blackfeller.**

**blackfellow's bread** /ˌblækfɛləz ˈbrɛd/, *n.* the underground sclerotium of the Australian fungus *Polyporus mylittae* found in forests.

**blackfellow's button** /ˌblækfɛləz ˈbʌtn/, *n.* →**australite.**

**blackfellow's hemp** /ˌblækfɛləz ˈhɛmp/, *n.* a tall shrub, *Commersonia fraseri,* which yields long fibres and was used by the Aborigines for making nets.

**blackfellow's yam** /ˌblækfɛləz ˈjæm/, *n.* a herb, *Microseris scapigera,* family Compositae, with a yellow flower and a root used as food by Australian Aboriginals; native dandelion; myrrnong. Also, **yam daisy.**

**blackfish** /ˈblækfɪʃ/, *n.* **1.** any of various dark-coloured Australian fishes as the luderick, the rock blackfish, or the river blackfish. **2.** →**black whale.**

**blackfish-weed** /ˈblækfɪʃ-ˌwid/, *n.* any of several species of the genus *Enteromorpha,* green algae of eastern Australia, used as bait.

**black flag** /blæk ˈflæg/, *n.* the pirate flag, usu. of black cloth with the white skull and crossbones on it.

**black fly** /ˈ– flaɪ/, *n.* any of the minute, black-bodied gnats of the dipterous family Simuliidae; the larvae are aquatic.

**black Friday** /– ˈfraɪdeɪ/, *n.* any Friday which falls on the 13th of the month, thought to be generally unlucky.

**black frost** /– ˈfrɒst/, *n.* a cold so intense as to blacken vegetation, without a white frost.

**black gin** /ˈ– dʒɪn/, *n.* a tall woody-stemmed perennial herb, *Kingia australis,* family Liliaceae, of western Australia, having a tuft of grasslike leaves and a group of small flowering spikes at the top.

**black gold** /– ˈgoʊld/, *n.* **1.** coal. **2.** oil. **3.** rutile, the main titanium ore.

**black gram** /ˈ– græm/, *n.* **1.** an annual herb, *Phaseolus mungo,* family Papilionaceae, of India, cultivated there and elsewhere in Asia as a food crop. **2.** any of certain similar plants cultivated in parts of Asia for food or fodder.

**black grouse** /– ˈgraʊs/, *n.* a large grouse, *Lyrurus tetrix,* found in the northern parts of Europe and western Asia. The male is black, the female mottled grey and brown.

**blackguard** /ˈblægad/, *n.* **1.** a coarse, despicable person; a scoundrel. *–v.t.* **2.** to revile in scurrilous language. *–v.i.* **3.** to behave like a blackguard. [BLACK + GUARD] – **blackguardism,** *n.*

**blackguardly** /ˈblægadli/, *adj.* **1.** of, like, or befitting a blackguard. *–adv.* **2.** in the manner of a blackguard.

**black gum** /ˈblæk gʌm/, *n.* certain eucalypts with an overall darkish appearance.

**black hat** /ˈblæk hæt/, *n.* (formerly) an immigrant; new chum, i.e. one still wearing city clothes.

**blackhead** /ˈblækhɛd/, *n.* **1.** a small black-tipped, fatty mass in a follicle of the face. **2.** any of several birds having a black head, as the scaup duck. **3.** *Vet. Sci.* a malignant, infectious, protozoan disease of turkeys, chickens, and many wild birds, attacking esp. the intestines and liver.

**black-headed honeyeater** /ˌblæk-hɛdəd ˈhʌniitə/, *n.* a honeyeater, *Melithreptus affinis,* olive-brown in colour with white neck, grey underparts, and black head, found in dry sclerophyll forests in Tasmania and adjacent islands; blackcap.

**black-headed python** /ˌblæk-hɛdəd ˈpaɪθən/, *n.* a nonvenomous snake of Queensland, *Aspidites melanocephalus,* remarkable in being a keen devourer of other snakes; snake-eater; tarpot.

**blackheart** /ˈblækhat/, *n.* **1.** a plant disease, as of apricot trees, in which internal plant tissues blacken. **2.** a kind of cherry bearing a large, sweet, somewhat heartshaped fruit with a nearly black skin.

**black-hearted** /ˈblæk-ˌhatəd/, *adj.* evil.

**black hole**[1] /blæk ˈhoʊl/, *n.* **1.** a military cell or lock-up. **2.** *Colloq.* any small, overcrowded room. [from *Black Hole of Calcutta,* a small cell in Fort William, Calcutta, into which, in 1756, 146 Europeans were thrust for a night, only 23 of whom were alive in the morning]

**black hole**[2] /blæk ˈhoʊl/, *n.* a region postulated as arising from the collapse of a star under its own gravitational forces and from which no radiation or matter can escape.

**black house spider,** *n.* an Australian spider, *Ixeuticus robustus,* often found indoors in undisturbed areas where it builds a web with a central funnel. Its bite is painful and causes nausea.

**blacking** /ˈblækɪŋ/, *n.* any preparation for producing a black coating or finish, as on shoes, stoves, etc.

**blackjack** /ˈblækdʒæk/, *n.* **1.** *Hist.* a large drinking cup or jug for beer, ale, etc., originally one made of leather coated externally with tar. **2.** the black flag of a pirate. **3.** *Colloq.* a thick black bituminous waterproofing compound. **4.** a short club, usu. leather covered, consisting of a heavy head and a flexible shaft or strap. **5.** *Mineral.* a dark, iron-rich variety of sphalerite; blende. **6.** caramel, burnt sugar, treacle, black toffee, liquorice, or any other dark sweet substance. **7.** *Cards.* **a.** →**pontoon**[2]. **b.** the ace of spades. **c.** a variety of pontoon in which any player may become dealer. *–v.t.* **8.** to strike or beat with a blackjack. **9.** to compel by threat.

**blackjack merchant** /ˈ– mɜtʃənt/, *n. Colloq.* a bad plumber; one who disguises poor work under much blackjack (def. 3).

**black kingfish** /blæk ˈkɪŋfɪʃ/, *n.* →**cobia.**

**black lead** /ˈ– lɛd/, *n.* graphite; plumbago.

**black-lead** /ˈblæk-lɛd/, *v.t.* to blacken or polish with black lead.

**blackleg** /ˈblæklɛg/, *n., v.,* **-legged, -legging.** *–n.* **1.** →**scab** (def. 4). **2.** a swindler esp. in racing or gambling. **3.** *Vet. Sci.* an infectious, generally fatal disease of cattle and sheep characterised by painful, gaseous swellings in the muscles, usu. of the upper parts of the legs. **4.** *Hort.* a plant disease, as of cabbage and potato, in which the lower stems turn black and decay. *–v.i.* **5.** to scab.

**black-letter** /ˈblæk-lɛtə/, *Print. –n.* **1.** a heavy-faced type in gothic style like that in early English printed books. *–adj.* **2.** of, pertaining to, set in, or resembling black-letter.

**black-letter day** /blæk-ˈlɛtə deɪ/, *n.* an unlucky day.

**black light** /blæk ˈlaɪt/, *n.* ultraviolet light.

**black lightning** /blæk ˈlaɪtnɪŋ/, *n.* an Aboriginal cooking fire, signal smoke fire, ceremonial fire, etc., regarded as the cause of a bush-fire.

**black list** /ˈ– lɪst/, *n.* a list of persons under suspicion, disfavour, censure, etc., or a list of fraudulent or unreliable customers or firms.

**black-list** /ˈblæk-lɪst/, *v.t.* to put on a black list.

**black locust** /blæk ˈloʊkəst/, *n.* the durable wood of the American tree *Robinia pseudoacacia.*

**blackly** /ˈblækli/, *adv.* darkly; gloomily; wickedly.

**black magic** /blæk ˈmædʒɪk/, *n.* magic used for evil purposes.

**blackmail** /ˈblækmeɪl/, *n.* **1.** *Law.* **a.** any payment extorted by intimidation, as by threats of injurious revelations or accusations. **b.** the extortion of such payment. **2.** *Brit. Hist.* a tribute exacted in the north of England and in Scotland by freebooting chiefs for protection from pillage. *–v.t.* **3.** to extort blackmail from. [BLACK + *mail* coin, rent (ME *maille,* from OF)] – **blackmailer,** *n.*

**blackman's potatoes** /ˌblækmænz pəˈteɪtoʊz/, *n.pl.* →**early Nancy.**

**black maria** /blæk məˈraɪə/, *n. Colloq.* a closed vehicle used for conveying prisoners to and from gaol. Also, **Black Maria.**

**black mark** /– ˈmak/, *n.* a mark of failure or censure.

**black market** /– ˈmakət/, *n.* an illegal market violating price controls, rationing, etc.

**black marketeer** /– makəˈtɪə/, *n.* a dealer on a black market.

**black mass** /– ˈmæs/, *n.* a travesty of the mass, as performed by devil-worshippers.

**black measles** /– ˈmizəlz/, *n.* a severe form of measles characterised by a haemorrhagic rash.

**Black Muslim** /– ˈmʊzləm/, *n.* a member of a Negro organisation in the U.S. advocating modified teachings of Islam and racial segregation.

**black nightshade** /– ˈnaɪtʃeɪd/, *n.* a common weed, *Solanum nigrum,* with white flowers and black berries.

**black oak** /ˈ– oʊk/, *n.* →**belah.**

**black oat** /ˈ– oʊt/, *n.* →**wild oat** (def. 1).

**black opal** /– ˈoʊpəl/, *n.* a rare variety of opal, dark, but flashing many colours when catching the light.

**blackout** /ˈblækaʊt/, *n.* **1.** the extinguishing of all visible lights in a city, etc., as a wartime protection. **2.** the extinguishing or failure of light as in a power failure. **3.** *Theat.* the extinguishing of all stage lights. **4.** temporary loss of consciousness or vision, esp. in aviation due to high acceleration. **5.** loss of memory. **6.** fade-out of radio signals. – **blackout,** *adj.*

**black pepper** /blæk ˈpɛpə/, *n.* a hot, sharp condiment prepared from the dried berries of a tropical vine, *Piper nigrum.*

**black perch** /– ˈpɜtʃ/, *n. Colloq.* →**morwong.**

**black peter** /– ˈpitə/, *n.* a punishment cell in a prison, usu. without light, where a prisoner is put in solitary confinement.

**black pine** /– ˈpaɪn/, *n.* **1.** the small coniferous tree of eastern Australia, *Callitris endlicheri.* **2.** the New Zealand conifer, *Podocarpus spicatus;* matai. **3.** the timber of either.

**black plate** /– ˈpleɪt/, *n.* sheet steel or iron which has not been coated with a covering of tin.

**blackpoll** /ˈblækpoʊl/, *n.* a North American warbler, *Dendroica striata,* the adult male of which has the top of the head black.

**black power** /blæk ˈpaʊə/, *n.* **1.** a movement originating in the U.S. advocating the advancement of blacks (in Australia esp. of the Aborigines) through violence or political means. **2.** a similar movement elsewhere.

**black prince** /– ˈprɪns/, *n. Colloq.* a large slim-bodied cicada, *Cyclochila australasiae,* basically black with some olive green markings on its back; a colour variant of the greengrocer.

**black pudding** /– ˈpʊdɪŋ/, *n.* a dark sausage made of blood, suet, and other ingredients.

**black rhinoceros** /– raɪˈnɒsərəs/, *n.* a two-horned rhinoceros, *Rhinoceros bicornis,* of Africa, characterised by a pointed upper lip.

**black rot** /ˈ– rɒt/, *n.* any of various diseases of vegetables caused by bacteria, or fungi, producing black discoloration and decay.

**black rust** /– ˈrʌst/, *n.* an obligate fungal parasite of cereals and grasses in which black masses of spores appear on leaves and stems.

**black sand** /ˈ– sænd/, *n. N.Z.* black iron sands on some west coast beaches, occasionally auriferous.

**black-sander** /blæk-ˈsændə/, *n. N.Z.* one who works black sands for gold. – **blacksanding,** *n.*

**black sauce** /blæk ˈsɔs/, *n. Colloq.* →**Worcestershire sauce.**

**black scum** /– ˈskʌm/, *n.* a covering of algae on areas of turf which have poor drainage. Also, **green scum.**

**black sheep** /– ˈʃip/, *n.* a person regarded as worthless despite a good background.

**black skink** /– ˈskɪŋk/, *n.* →**land mullet.**

**blacksmith** /ˈblæksmɪθ/, *n.* **1.** a person who makes horseshoes and shoes horses. **2.** an artisan who works in iron. [BLACK (in ref. to iron or black metal) + SMITH. Cf. WHITESMITH]

**black snake** /ˈblæk sneɪk/, *n.* **1.** →**red-bellied black snake.** **2.** a large, aggressive, highly venomous snake, the **Papuan black snake,** *Pseudechis papuanus,* usu. glossy black in colour and growing to two metres or more in length.

**black soil** /ˈ– sɔɪl/, *n.* fine fertile black clay soils rich in humus and lime, and in natural conditions grass covered; common in the north-western plains of New South Wales and in the central west of Queensland.

**black spot** /ˈ– spɒt/, *n.* **1.** *Brit.* a place on a road where accidents frequently occur. **2.** any of various fungal infections causing black spots on plant foliage.

**black spruce** /– ˈsprus/, *n.* **1.** a conifer of North America, *Picea mariana,* noted for its extremely dark green needles. **2.** an easily worked light wood from this tree.

**black swan** /– ˈswɒn/, *n.* a large, stately swimming bird, *Cygnus atratus,* with black plumage and a red bill, found throughout Australia but particularly in the south-east and south-west and introduced in New Zealand.

black swan

**black-tailed wallaby** /ˌblæk-teɪld ˈwɒləbi/, *n.* →**swamp wallaby.**

**black tea** /blæk ˈti/, *n.* **1.** a tea which has been allowed to wither and ferment in the air for some time before being subjected to a heating process. **2.** tea drunk without milk.

**black thistle** /blæk ˈθɪsəl/, *n.* →**spear thistle.**

**blackthorn** /ˈblækθɔn/, *n.* **1.** a much-branched thorny shrub, *Bursaria spinosa,* bearing white flowers. **2.** a similar shrub, *Prunus spinosa;* sloe. **3.** its wood.

**black tie** /blæk ˈtaɪ/, *n.* **1.** a black bow tie for men, worn with a formal style of evening dress. **2.** a formal style of evening dress for men, of which the characteristic garments are a black bow tie and a dinner jacket (distinguished from *white tie*).

**blacktop** /ˈblæktɒp/, *n., adj., v.,* **-topped, -topping.** *–n.* **1.** a bituminous substance, as asphalt, used for surfacing roads, specifically as a top dressing for concrete roads. **2.** a road surfaced with blacktop. *–adj.* **3.** of or surfaced with blacktop. *–v.t.* **4.** to surface a road or path with blacktop.

**blacktracker** /ˈblæktrækə/, *n.* an Aborigine tracker employed by police.

**black velvet** /blæk ˈvɛlvət/, *n. Colloq.* **1.** a drink made from a mixture of stout and champagne. **2.** a black girl or woman, considered as a sex object. Cf. **yellow satin.**

**black vomit** /– ˈvɒmət/, *n.* **1.** a dark-coloured substance, consisting chiefly of altered blood, vomited in some cases of yellow fever, usu. presaging a fatal issue of the disease. **2.** the act of throwing up this matter. **3.** the disease itself.

**black wallaby** /– ˈwɒləbi/, *n.* →**swamp wallaby.**

**black walnut** /– ˈwɔlnʌt/, *n.* **1.** a tree, *Juglans nigra,* of North America, which yields a valuable timber. **2.** the nut thereof. **3.** the wood of this tree.

**blackwater fever** /ˌblækwɔtə ˈfivə/, *n.* a severe form of malaria found chiefly in the tropics but occasionally in the southern U.S.

**black wattle** /blæk ˈwɒtl/, *n.* **1.** a small tree, *Acacia mearnsii,* of eastern Australia with creamy-yellow flowers and a bark which yields tannin. **2.** a tall shrub, *Callicoma serratifolia,* found in shady gullies of coastal New South Wales.

**black whale** /– ˈweɪl/, *n.* a dolphin-like cetacean of the genus *Globicephalus;* a blackfish.

**black widow** /– ˈwɪdoʊ/, *n.* a poisonous female spider, *Latrodectus mactans,* that eats its mate; common in the U.S.

**black witch** /ˈ– wɪtʃ/, *n.* a witch who uses her power to do evil deeds. Cf. **white witch.**

**blackwood** /ˈblækwʊd/, *n.* a tall dense-foliaged wattle, *Acacia melanoxylon,* found in eastern Australia, esp. in Tasmania where it is a valuable timber tree; mudgerabah.

**bladder** /ˈblædə/, *n.* **1.** *Anat., Zool.* **a.** a distensible pelvic sac with membranous and muscular walls, for storage and expulsion of urine by the kidneys. **b.** any similar sac or receptacle. **2.** *Bot.* a sac or the like containing air, as in certain seaweeds. **3.** any inflatable or distensible bag, as the inner bag of a football, or the bellows of bagpipes. **4.** anything inflated, empty, or unsound. **5. have a weak bladder,** *Colloq.* to suffer from frequency (def. 7). [ME; OE *blædre* bladder, blister, akin to BLOW², *v.,* BLAST] – **bladderless,** *adj.* – **bladder-like,** *adj.* – **bladdery,** *adj.*

**bladder campion** /– ˈkæmpiən/, *n.* a herb *Silene cucubalus,* native to Europe and Asia, characterised by an inflated greenish-white calyx.

**bladder fern** /ˈ– fɜn/, *n.* any fern of the rhizomatous genus *Cystopteris,* esp. the **brittle bladder fern,** *C. fragilis.*

**bladdernose** /ˈblædənoʊz/, *n.* a large seal, *Cystophora cristata,* of the northern Atlantic, the male of which has a large, distensible, hoodlike sac upon the head; the hooded seal.

**bladder worm** /ˈblædə wɜm/, *n.* the bladder-like encysted larva of a tapeworm; a cysticercus, coenurus, or hydatid.

**bladderwort** /ˈblædəwɜt/, *n.* any of various carnivorous herbs of the genera *Utricularia* and *Polypompholyx,* family Lentibulariaceae, which trap insects in small bladders.

**bladderwrack** /ˈblædəræk/, *n.* a branched brown seaweed of the northern hemisphere, *Fucus vesiculosus,* bearing airbladders; found attached to rocks in the intertidal zone.

**blade** /bleɪd/, *n.* **1.** the flat cutting part of sword, knife, etc. **2.** a sword. **3.** (*pl.*) hand-held shears for shearing sheep. **4.**

the leaf of a plant, esp. of a grass or cereal. **5.** *Bot.* the broad part of a leaf, as distinguished from the stalk or petiole. **6.** a cut of beef adjacent to the shoulder blade. **7.** a thin, flat part of something, as of a bone, an oar, a propeller, a bat, etc. **8.** a dashing, swaggering, or rakish young fellow. **9.** *Anat.* the scapula or shoulder-blade. **10.** *Phonet.* the upper surface and edges of the tongue for a short distance back from the tip. [ME; OE *blæd,* c. G *Blatt*] – **bladed,** *adj.* – **bladeless,** *adj.* – **bladelike,** *adj.*

**bladebone** /ˈbleɪdboʊn/, *n.* →**blade** (def. 6).

**bladeshearer** /ˈbleɪdʃɪərə/, *n.* one who shears sheep with blades.

**blady grass** /ˈbleɪdi gras/, *n.* a coarse leafy species of grass, *Imperata cylindrica,* found in coastal areas of eastern and northern Australia and extending to Polynesia and Asia where it is used for thatching.

**blaeberry** /ˈbleɪbəri/, *n., pl.* **-ries.** →**bilberry.** [ME *blaberie;* from OE *blæ-* blue (c. ON *blār*) + BERRY]

**blah** /bla/, *n. Colloq.* high-sounding empty talk; eloquent rubbish.

**blain** /bleɪn/, *n.* an inflammatory swelling or sore. [ME *bleine,* OE *blegen*]

**blamable** /ˈbleɪməbəl/, *adj.* deserving blame; censurable. Also, **blameable.** – **blamableness,** *n.* – **blamably,** *adv.*

**blame** /bleɪm/, *v.,* **blamed, blaming,** *n.* –*v.t.* **1.** to lay the responsibility of (a fault, error, etc.) on a person: *I blame the accident on him.* **2.** to find fault with; censure: *I blame you for that.* **3.** *U.S. Colloq.* (*as a humorous imperative or optative*) to blast: *blame my hide if I go.* **4. to blame,** responsible for a fault or error; blamable; culpable: *he is to blame.* –*n.* **5.** imputation of fault; censure. **6.** responsibility for a fault, error, etc. [ME *blamen,* from OF *blasmer,* from LL *blasphēmāre* BLASPHEME]

**blamed** /bleɪmd/, *U.S. Colloq.* –*adj.* **1.** confounded. –*adv.* **2.** confoundedly; excessively.

**blameful** /ˈbleɪmfəl/, *adj.* deserving blame. – **blamefully,** *adv.* – **blamefulness,** *n.*

**blameless** /ˈbleɪmləs/, *adj.* free from blame; guiltless. – **blamelessly,** *adv.* – **blamelessness,** *n.*

**blameworthy** /ˈbleɪmwɜði/, *adj.* deserving rebuke or censure. – **blameworthiness,** *n.*

**blanc fixe** /blɒŋk ˈfɪks/, *n.* barium sulphate, used in paints as an extender. [F: lit., fixed white]

**blanch** /blænʃ, blanʃ/, *v.t.* **1.** to whiten by removing colour. **2.** *Hort.* to whiten or prevent from becoming green by excluding the light (a process applied to the stems or leaves of plants, such as celery, lettuce, etc.). **3.** to remove the skin from (nuts, fruits, etc.) by immersion in boiling water, then in cold. **4.** to separate (the grains or strands of rice, macaroni, etc.) by immersing in boiling water, then in cold. **5.** to scald (meat, etc.). **6.** *Metall.* to give a white lustre to (metals), as by means of acids. **7.** to make pale, as with sickness or fear. –*v.i.* **8.** to become white; turn pale. [ME *blaunche(n),* from OF *blanchir,* from *blanc* white. See BLANK] – **blancher,** *n.*

**blancmange** /bləˈmɒnʒ, -ˈmɒndʒ/, *n.* a jelly-like preparation of milk thickened with cornflour, gelatine, or the like, and flavoured. [ME *blancmanger,* from OF: lit., white food]

**bland** /blænd/, *adj.* **1.** (of a person's manner) suave; deliberately agreeable or pleasant but often without real feeling. **2.** soothing or balmy, as air. **3.** mild, as food or medicines: *a bland diet.* **4.** non-stimulating, as medicines. [L *blandus*] – **blandly,** *adv.* – **blandness,** *n.*

**blandish** /ˈblændɪʃ/, *v.t.* to treat flatteringly; coax; cajole. [ME *blaundysh(en),* from OF *blandiss-,* stem of *blandir,* from L *blandīre* flatter] – **blandisher,** *n.*

**blandishment** /ˈblændɪʃmənt/, *n.* (*oft. pl.*) flattering action or speech.

**blank** /blæŋk/, *adj.* **1.** (of paper, etc.) free from marks; not written or printed on. **2.** not filled in: *a blank cheque.* **3.** unrelieved or unbroken by ornament or opening: *a blank wall.* **4.** lacking some usual or completing feature; empty. **5.** void of interest, results, etc. **6.** showing no attention, interest, or emotion: *a blank face.* **7.** disconcerted; nonplussed: *a blank look.* **8.** complete, utter, or unmitigated: *blank stupidity.* **9.** white or pale. **10.** *Colloq.* (euphemistic for any vulgar or taboo epithet). –*n.* **11.** a place where something is lacking: *a blank in one's memory.* **12.** a void; emptiness. **13.** a space left (to be filled in) in written or printed matter. **14.** a printed form containing such spaces. **15.** a dash put in place of an omitted letter or word, esp. profanity or obscenity. **16.** *Mach.* a piece of metal prepared to be stamped or cut into a finished object, such as a coin or key. **17.** *Archery.* the white mark in the centre of a butt or target at which an arrow is aimed. **18.** a blank cartridge. **19.** a domino unmarked on one or both of its halves. **20.** a lottery ticket which does not win. **21. draw (a) blank,** to get no results; be unsuccessful; fail. **22. in blank,** (of a document) with spaces left to be filled in. –*v.t.* **23.** to make blank or void (fol. by *out*): *to blank out an entry.* **24.** *Mach.* to stamp or punch out of flat stock as with a die. [ME, from OF *blanc* white, from Gmc; cf. G *blank* bright, shining] – **blankness,** *n.*

**blank cartridge** /– ˈkatrɪdʒ/, *n.* a cartridge containing powder only, without a bullet.

**blank cheque** /– ˈtʃɛk/, *n.* **1.** a cheque bearing a signature but no stated amount. **2.** a free hand; carte blanche.

**blank endorsement** /– ənˈdɔsmənt/, *n.* an endorsement on a cheque or note naming no payee, and payable to bearer.

**blanket** /ˈblæŋkət/, *n.* **1.** a large rectangular piece of soft, loosely woven fabric, usu. wool, used esp. as a bed covering. **2.** a covering for a horse, etc. **3.** *North America.* the chief garment worn by some Indians. **4.** any heavy concealing layer or covering: *a blanket of clouds.* –*v.t.* **5.** to cover with or as with a blanket. **6.** to obscure by increasing prominence of the background (oft. fol. by *out*). **7.** to toss in a blanket, as for punishment. **8.** *Naut.* to take the wind out of the sails of (a vessel) by passing to windward of it. –*adj.* **9.** covering or intended to cover a group or class of things, conditions, etc.: *a blanket indictment.* [ME, from OF *blancquete,* diminutive of *blanc* white] – **blanketless,** *adj.*

**blanket bush** /ˈblænkət bʊʃ/, *n.* →**cottonwood** (def. 1).

**blanketing** /ˈblæŋkətɪŋ/, *n.* **1.** *Radio.* the effect of a signal from a powerful transmitter which interferes with or prevents the reception of other signals. **2.** cloth for making blankets. **3.** a tossing in a blanket.

**blanket-leaf** /ˈblæŋkət-lif/, *n.* a small tree of mountain forests, *Bedfordia salicina,* family Compositae, found in south-eastern Australia.

**blanket party** /ˈblæŋkət pati/, *n.* →**pyjama party.**

**blanket stitch** /ˈ– stɪtʃ/, *n.* the loop stitch used to bind the edges of blankets, etc.

**blanket table** /ˈ– teɪbəl/, *n. Mining.* an incline table, covered with a blanket or thick cloth used to catch fine gold as a water, sand and gold mixture is poured on it.

**blankly** /ˈblæŋkli/, *adv.* **1.** without expression or understanding. **2.** flatly; directly; point-blank.

**blank verse** /blæŋk ˈvɜs/, *n.* **1.** unrhymed verse. **2.** the unrhymed iambic pentameter verse most frequently used in English dramatic, epic, and reflective poems.

**blanquette** /blɒŋˈkɛt/, *n.* a white meat stew, usu. of veal or chicken, with a white sauce thickened with cream or egg-yolks. [F, from *blanc* white]

**Blanquette** /blɒŋˈkɛt/, *n.* a grape variety grown mainly in the Hunter River district of New South Wales to produce a dry white table wine.

**blare** /blɛə/, *v.,* **blared, blaring,** *n.* –*v.i.* **1.** to emit a loud raucous sound. –*v.t.* **2.** to sound loudly; proclaim noisily. –*n.* **3.** a loud raucous noise. **4.** glaring intensity of colour. [ME *blaren,* from MD]

**blarney** /ˈblani/, *n., v.,* **-neyed, -neying.** –*n.* **1.** flattering or wheedling talk; cajolery. –*v.t.* **2.** to ply or beguile with blarney; use blarney; wheedle. [from the *Blarney* stone, a stone in Blarney Castle near Cork, Ireland, said to confer skill in flattery to anyone who kisses it]

**blasé** /blaˈzeɪ, ˈblazeɪ/, *adj.* indifferent to and bored by pleasures of life. [F, pp. of *blaser* exhaust, satiate, ? from D *blasen* blow]

**blaspheme** /blæsˈfim/, *v.,* **-phemed, -pheming.** –*v.t.* **1.** to speak impiously or irreverently of (God or sacred things). **2.** to speak evil of; abuse. –*v.i.* **3.** to utter impious words. [LL *blasphēmāre,* from Gk *blasphēmeîn* speak ill; replacing ME *blasfeme(n),* from OF *blasfemer*] – **blasphemer,** *n.*

**blasphemous** /ˈblæsfəməs/, *adj.* uttering, containing, or exhibiting blasphemy. – **blasphemously,** *adv.* – **blasphemousness,** *n.*

**blasphemy** /ˈblæsfəmi/, *n., pl.* **-mies.** **1.** impious utterance or action concerning God or sacred things. **2.** *Judaism.* **a.** (in Talmudic law) cursing and reviling the 'ineffable name' of the Lord. **b.** (in later Hebrew history) the violation of religious law by pronouncing one of the four-letter symbols for God rather than using one of the substitute words. **3.** *Theol.* the crime of assuming to oneself the rights or qualities of God. **4.** irreverent behaviour towards anything held sacred. [LL *blasphēmia,* from Gk: slander; replacing ME *blasfemie,* from OF]

**blast** /blast/, *n.* **1.** a sudden blowing or gust of wind. **2.** the blowing of a trumpet, whistle, etc. **3.** the sound produced by this. **4.** a forcible stream of air from the mouth, from bellows, or the like. **5.** *Metall.* air under pressure directed into a blast furnace, cupola, etc., to support combustion. **6.** a jet of exhaust steam directed into a chimney to augment the draught, as in a locomotive. **7.** a draught thus increased. **8.** *Mining, Civ. Eng., etc.* the charge of dynamite or other explosive used at one firing in blasting operations. **9.** the act of exploding; explosion. **10.** the forcible movement of air, or the shock wave, caused by an explosion. **11.** severe criticism, esp. noisy or choleric. **12.** any pernicious or destructive influence, esp. on animals or plants; a blight. **13. full blast,** *Colloq.* very actively; very successfully. *–v.t.* **14.** to blow (a trumpet, etc.). **15.** to cause to shrivel or wither; blight. **16.** to affect with any pernicious influence; ruin; destroy: *to blast one's hopes.* **17.** to tear (rock, etc.) to pieces with an explosive. **18.** to criticise someone abusively. *–v.i.* **19.** to wither; be blighted. *–interj.* **20.** (an exclamation of anger or irritation). [ME; OE *blǣst*] – **blaster,** *n.*

**-blast,** a combining form meaning 'embryo', 'sprout', 'germ', as in *ectoblast.* [Gk *blastós*]

**blast area** /ˈblast ɛəriə/, *n.* the area within which casualties and damage are to be expected due to the force of an explosion.

**blasted** /ˈblastəd/, *adj.* **1.** withered; shrivelled; blighted. **2.** (intensifier expressing anger, annoyance, disgust, etc.) **3.** *Colloq.* intoxicated.

**blast effect** /ˈblast əˌfɛkt/, *n. Mil.* destruction of or damage to structures and personnel by the blast of an explosion on or above the surface of the ground (opposed to *cratering* and *ground-shock effect*).

**blastema** /blæsˈtimə/, *n., pl.* **-mata** /-mətə/. an aggregation of embryonic cells, capable of differentiation into primordia and organs. [NL, from Gk: sprout] – **blastemic** /blæsˈtɛmɪk, -ˈtimɪk/, *adj.*

**blaster** /ˈblastə/, *n. Golf.* →**sand wedge.**

**blast furnace** /ˈblast fɜnəs/, *n.* a vertical, steel cylindrical furnace using a forced blast to produce molten iron which may be converted into steel or formed into pig-iron.

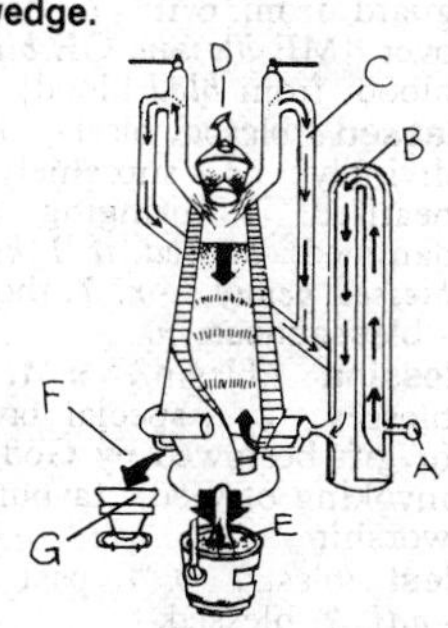

blast furnace: A, cold air; B, hot air; C, hot gases; D, raw materials; E, molten iron; F, slag runner; G, slag ladle

**blasto-,** a word element meaning 'embryo' or 'germ', as in *blastocyst.* Also, before vowels, **blast-.** [Gk, combining form of *blastós*]

**blastocoel** /ˈblæstəsil/, *n.* the cavity of a blastula, arising in the course of cleavage. Also, **blastocoele.**

**blastocyst** /ˈblæstəsɪst/, *n.* **1.** the germinal vesicle. **2.** the vesicular stage in early mammalian development, following cleavage.

**blastoderm** /ˈblæstədɜm/, *n.* **1.** the primitive membrane or layer of cells which results from the segmentation of the ovum. **2.** the membrane forming the wall of the blastula, and in most vertebrates enclosing a cavity or a yolk mass. – **blastodermic,** *adj.*

**blastodisc** /ˈblæstədɪsk/, *n.* the small disc of protoplasm, containing the egg nucleus, which appears on the surface of the yolk mass in very heavily yolked eggs, as of birds and reptiles.

**blast-off** /ˈblast-ɒf/, *n.* **1.** *Aerospace.* →**lift-off.** **2.** a rapid departure. *–v.i.* **3.** to depart immediately.

**blastogenesis** /ˌblæstouˈdʒɛnəsəs/, *n.* **1.** reproduction by gemmation or budding. **2.** the theory of the transmission of hereditary characters by germ plasm.

**blastomere** /ˈblæstəmɪə/, *n.* any cell produced during the early stages of cleavage. – **blastomeric** /ˌblæstəˈmɛrɪk/, *adj.*

**blastopore** /ˈblæstəpɔ/, *n.* the orifice of an archenteron. – **blastoporic** /ˌblæstəˈpɒrɪk/, *adj.*

**blastosphere** /ˈblæstəsfɪə/, *n.* **1.** →**blastula.** **2.** →**blastocyst** (def. 2).

**blastula** /ˈblæstjələ/, *n., pl.* **-lae** /-ˌli/. an early developmental stage of a metazoan, consisting in typical cases of a hollow sphere formed by a single layer of cells. [NL, diminutive of Gk *blastós* sprout, germ] – **blastular,** *adj.*

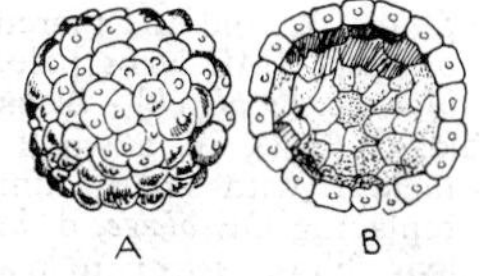

blastula: A, exterior view; B, cross-section

**blast weapon** /ˈblast wɛpən/, *n.* a weapon which relies on the force of an explosion, as a bomb.

**blatant** /ˈbleɪtnt/, *adj.* **1.** (of actions, etc.) flagrantly obvious or undisguised: *a blatant error, a blatant lie.* **2.** (of persons) offensively conspicuous in or unconcerned by (bad) behaviour; brazen; barefaced. **3.** *Obs.* bleating: *blatant herds.* [coined by Spenser. Cf. L *blatīre* babble] – **blatancy,** *n.* – **blatantly,** *adv.*

**blather** /ˈblæðə/, *n.* **1.** foolish talk. *–v.i., v.t.* **2.** to talk or utter foolishly. Also, **blether.** [ME, from Scand.; cf. Icel. *bladhra* talk nonsense]

**blatherskite** /ˈblæðəskaɪt/, *n.* one given to voluble, empty talk. Also, **blatherskate, bletherskate.** [BLATHER + *skite* SKATE[3]]

**blatt** /blæt/, *n.* **1.** a printed sheet as a daily communiqué, a set of instructions, etc. **2. the daily blatts,** *Colloq.* the daily newspapers. [G *Blatt* leaf]

**blaze**[1] /bleɪz/, *n., v.,* **blazed, blazing.** *–n.* **1.** a bright flame or fire. **2.** a bright, hot gleam or glow: *the blaze of day.* **3.** a sparkling brightness: *a blaze of jewels.* **4.** a sudden, intense outburst, as of fire, passion, fury. *–v.i.* **5.** to burn brightly. **6.** to shine like flame. **7.** (of guns) to fire continuously. **8.** *Poetic.* to be meritoriously conspicuous. *–v.t.* **9.** to exhibit vividly. [ME and OE *blase* torch, flame]

**blaze**[2] /bleɪz/, *n., v.,* **blazed, blazing.** *–n.* **1.** a spot or mark made on a tree, as by removing a piece of the bark, to indicate a boundary or a path in a forest. **2.** a white spot on the face of a horse, cow, etc. *–v.t.* **3.** to mark with blazes. **4. blaze a trail, a.** to mark out a trail with blazes. **b.** to break new ground; pioneer. [LG *bläse* white mark on head of horse or steer, c. Icel. *blesa*]

**blaze**[3] /bleɪz/, *v.t.,* **blazed, blazing.** **1.** to make known; proclaim; publish. **2.** *Obs.* to blow, as from a trumpet. [ME *blase(n),* from MD, c. Icel. *blāsa* blow]

**blazer** /ˈbleɪzə/, *n.* **1.** one who or that which blazes. **2.** *Colloq.* anything intensely bright or hot. **3.** a lightweight jacket, often brightly coloured, as worn by sportsmen. **4.** a jacket, usu. bearing some badge or crest, as worn by schoolchildren.

**blazes** /ˈbleɪzəz/, *n.pl.* **1.** hell. **2. go to blazes,** (an exclamation of dismissal, contempt, anger, etc.). **3. the blazes,** (an intensive): *what the blazes is going on here?*

**blazing** /ˈbleɪzɪŋ/, *adj.* **1.** burning fiercely. **2.** very hot; scorching. **3.** bright; dazzling. **4.** violently angry. **5.** noticeable as an outstanding example of its kind: *a blazing indiscretion.*

**blazon** /ˈbleɪzən/, *v.t.* **1.** to set forth conspicuously or publicly; display; proclaim. **2.** to describe in heraldic terminology. **3.** to depict (heraldic arms, etc.) in proper form and colour. *–n.* **4.** a heraldic shield; armorial bearings. **5.** the heraldic description of armorial bearings. [ME *blason,* from OF: shield, later armorial bearings] – **blazoner,** *n.*

**blazonry** /ˈbleɪzənri/, *n.* **1.** *Her.* **a.** armorial bearings. **b.** a description of heraldic devices. **2.** brilliant decoration or display.

**bldg,** building.

**-ble,** variant of **-able,** as in *noble;* occurring first in words of Latin origin which came into English through French, later in words taken directly from Latin. Also, after consonant stems, **-ible.** [OF, from L *-bilis,* suffix forming verbal adjectives]

**bleach** /blitʃ/, *v.t.* **1.** to make white, pale, or colourless. *–v.i.* **2.** to become white, pale or colourless. *–n.* a bleaching agent. **3.** degree of paleness achieved in bleaching. **4.** the act of bleaching. [ME *blechen,* OE *blǣcean*] – **bleacher,** *n.*

**bleacher** /ˈblitʃə/, *n.* **1.** one who or that which bleaches. **2.** a vessel used in bleaching. **3.** (*usu. pl.*) an uncovered seat or stand for spectators at games.

**bleaching powder** /ˈblitʃɪŋ paʊdə/, *n.* a powder used for bleaching, esp. chloride of lime.

**bleak**[1] /blik/, *adj.* **1.** bare, desolate, and windswept: *a bleak plain.* **2.** cold and piercing: *a bleak wind.* **3.** dreary: *a bleak prospect.* [ME *bleke* pale, b. *bleche* (OE *blǣc*) and *blake* (OE *blāc*), c. G *bleich*] – **bleakly,** *adv.* – **bleakness,** *n.*

**bleak**[2] /blik/, *n.* a small freshwater European fish, *Alburnus lucidus,* with small, shiny scales. [Scand. (cf. Icel. *bleikja*); replacing OE *blǣge,* d. *blay*]

**blear** /blɪə/, *v.t.* **1.** to make (the eyes or sight) dim, as with tears or inflammation. *–adj.* **2.** bleary. **3.** a blur; a bleared state. [ME *blere(n)* (orig. adj.); orig. uncert.]

**bleary** /ˈblɪəri/, *adj.,* **blearier, bleariest. 1.** (of the eyes) dim from a watery discharge, or from tiredness. **2.** →**bleary-eyed. 3.** misty; dim; indistinct. [BLEAR + -Y[1]] – **blearily,** *adv.* – **bleariness,** *n.*

**bleary-eyed** /ˈblɪəri-aɪd/, *adj.* **1.** having bleared eyes. **2.** dull of perception. Also, **blear-eyed.**

**bleat** /blit/, *v.i.* **1.** to cry as a sheep, goat, or calf. **2.** to speak with a bleating sound. **3.** to complain; moan. *–v.t.* **4.** to give forth with a bleat. *–n.* **5.** the cry of a sheep, goat, or calf. **6.** any similar sound. **7.** a feeble protest or complaint. [ME *blete(n),* OE *blǣtan*] – **bleater,** *n.* – **bleatingly,** *adv.*

**bleb** /blɛb/, *n. Rare.* **1.** a blister or pustule. **2.** a bubble. – **blebby,** *adj.*

**bleed** /blid/, *v.,* **bled** /blɛd/, **bleeding,** *n. –v.i.* **1.** to lose blood, from the body or internally from the vascular system. **2.** to be severely wounded or die, as in battle: *bled for the cause.* **3.** to cause blood to flow, esp. surgically. **4.** (of blood, etc.) to flow out. **5.** to exude sap, juice, etc. **6.** (of colour in dyeing) to run. **7.** to feel pity, sorrow, or anguish: *a nation bleeds for its dead heroes.* **8.** *Print.* to run off the edges of a printed page, either by design or through mutilation caused by too close trimming. *–v.t.* **9.** to cause to lose blood, esp. surgically. **10.** to lose or emit, as blood or dye, etc. **11.** to drain, draw sap, liquid, etc., from. **12.** *Colloq.* to obtain, as in excessive amount, or extort money from. **13.** *Print.* **a.** to permit (printed illustrations or ornamentation) to run off the page or sheet. **b.** to trim the margin of (a book or sheet) so closely as to mutilate the text or illustration. *–n.* **14.** *Print.* a sheet or page margin trimmed in this way. **15.** a part thus trimmed off. [ME *blede(n),* OE *blēdan,* from *blōd* blood]

**bleeder** /ˈblidə/, *n.* **1.** a person predisposed to bleeding; haemophiliac. **2.** *Chiefly Brit. Colloq.* **a.** (a term of abuse.) **b.** a person; fellow. **3.** a beast which, having been immunised against tick fever, is used as a blood reservoir for innoculating other cattle in tick-infested areas. **4.** a racehorse that bleeds or tends to bleed from the nose when galloped, and is therefore by various regulations forbidden to race. **5.** a resistor which presents an alternative path to an electric current.

**bleeding** /ˈblidɪŋ/, *n.* **1.** loss of blood. **2.** letting of blood. **3.** exuding of sap from a cut. *–adj.* **4.** emanating pity. **5.** *Brit. Colloq.* bloody.

**bleeding-heart** /blidɪŋ-ˈhat/, *n.* **1.** any of various plants of the genus *Dicentra,* esp. *D. spectabilis,* a common garden plant with racemes of red, heart-shaped flowers. **2.** any of certain other species such as *Omalanthus populifolius* with red heart-shaped leaves.

**bleep** /blip/, *v.i.* **1.** to emit a high-pitched broken sound, or a radio signal. *–n.* **2.** a single short high-pitched sound. [imitative]

**B.Leg.S.** /bi lɛg ˈɛs/, Bachelor of Legal Studies.

**blemish** /ˈblɛmɪʃ/, *v.t.* **1.** to destroy the perfection of. *–n.* **2.** a defect; a disfigurement; stain. [ME *blemissh(en),* from OF *blemiss-,* stem of *ble(s)mir* make livid] – **blemisher,** *n.*

**blench**[1] /blɛntʃ/, *v.i.* to shrink; flinch; quail. [ME *blenchen,* OE *blencan* deceive] – **blencher,** *n.*

**blench**[2] /blɛntʃ/, *v.i.* **1.** to become pale or white; blanch. *–v.t.* **2.** to make pale or white. [var. of BLANCH]

**blend** /blɛnd/, *v.,* **blended, blending,** *n. –v.t.* **1.** to mix smoothly and inseparably together. **2.** to mix (various sorts or grades) in order to obtain a particular kind or quality. **3.** to prepare by such mixture. **4.** to prepare (food) using a blender. *–v.i.* **5.** to mix or intermingle smoothly and inseparably. **6.** to have no perceptible separation: *sea and sky seemed to blend.* *–n.* **7.** the act or manner of blending: *tea of our own blend.* **8.** a mixture or kind produced by blending. **9.** *Linguistics.* a word made by putting together parts of other words, as *dandle,* a blend of *dance* and *handle.* [ME *blenden,* OE *blendan, blandan,* c. Icel. *blanda*]

**blende** /blɛnd/, *n.* **1.** sphalerite; zinc sulphide. **2.** any of certain other sulphides. [G, from *blenden* blind, deceive]

**blended** /ˈblɛndəd/, *adj.* (of a whisky) consisting of either two or more whiskies, or of whiskies and neutral spirits.

**blender** /ˈblɛndə/, *n.* **1.** one who or that which blends. **2.** an electric device, usu. with very rapidly rotating sharp blades in the base of a cylindrical container, used for chopping or pulverising dry ingredients, and for combining and mixing dry and liquid food ingredients; vitamiser.

**blennioid** /ˈblɛniɔɪd/, *adj.* **1.** resembling a blenny. **2.** pertaining to the blennies.

**blennorrhagia** /blɛnəˈreɪdʒiə/, *n. Pathol.* →**blennorrhoea** (def. 2). [Gk *blénnos* slime + -RHAGIA]

**blennorrhoea** /blɛnəˈriə/, *n. Pathol.* **1.** a discharge of mucus. **2.** a discharge of mucus from the genital organs, due to gonorrhoea. **3. acute blennorrhoea,** purulent conjunctivitis caused by gonorrhoea. Also, *Chiefly U.S.,* **blennorrhea.** [Gk *blénnos* slime + *rhoía* -(R)RHOEA modelled on GONORRHOEA]

**blenny** /ˈblɛni/, *n., pl.* **-ies.** any of various fishes of Blenniidae and related families, with an elongated tapering body and small pelvic fins inserted farther forward than the pectoral fins. [L *blennius,* from Gk *blénnos* blenny, orig. slime]

**blephar-,** a word element meaning 'eyelid', as in *blepharitis.* Also, **blepharo-.** [combining form representing Gk *blépharon* eyelid]

**blepharitis** /blɛfəˈraɪtəs/, *n.* inflammation of the eyelids. [BLEPHAR- + -ITIS]

**bless** /blɛs/, *v.t.,* **blessed** or **blest, blessing. 1.** to consecrate by a religious rite; make or pronounce holy. **2.** to request of God the bestowal of divine favour on. **3.** to bestow good of any kind upon: *a nation blessed with peace.* **4.** to feel thankful or grateful for (something) or grateful to (someone). **5.** to extol as holy; glorify. **6.** to protect or guard from evil. **7.** *Eccles.* to make the sign of the cross over. [ME *blessen,* OE *blētsian, blēdsian* consecrate, orig. with blood, from *blōd* blood]

**blessed** /ˈblɛsəd, blɛst/, *adj.* **1.** consecrated; sacred; holy. **2.** divinely or supremely favoured; fortunate; happy. **3.** beatifed. **4.** bringing happiness; pleasurable. **5.** (*euph.*) dammed: *blessed if I know.* **6.** (used for emphasis): *every blessed penny.* *–n.* **7.** those who are blessed. – **blessedly,** *adv.* – **blessedness,** *n.*

**blessing** /ˈblɛsɪŋ/, *n.* **1.** the act or words of one who blesses. **2.** a special favour, mercy, or benefit. **3.** a favour or gift bestowed by God, thereby bringing happiness. **4.** the invoking of God's favour upon a person. **5.** praise; devotion; worship.

**blest** /blɛst/, *v.* **1.** past tense and past participle of **bless.** *–adj.* **2.** blessed.

**blether** /ˈblɛðə/, *v.i., v.t., n. Brit.* →**blather.**

**bletherskate** /ˈblɛðəskeɪt/, *n. Brit.* →**blatherskite.** Also, **bletherskite.**

**blew** /blu/, *n.* past tense of **blow.**

**blewits** /ˈbiuəts/, *n.* any of several edible fungi of the genus *Lepista.*

**blight** /blaɪt/, *n.* **1.** a widespread and destructive plant disease, such as **pome fruit blight** or **tomato blight. 2.** any cause of destruction, ruin, or frustration. **3.** →**sandy blight.** *–v.t.* **4.** to cause to wither or decay; blast. **5.** to destroy; ruin; frustrate. *–v.i.* **6.** to suffer blight. [orig. unknown]

**blightbird** /ˈblaɪtbɜd/, *n.* any of various silver-eyes of the genus *Zosterops* which feed largely on insects and sometimes damage ripening fruit, esp. the grey-breasted silver-eye, *Z. lateralis.*

**blighter** /ˈblaɪtə/, *n. Colloq.* **1.** a person; fellow. **2.** a despicable person; cad.

**Blighty** /ˈblaɪti/, *n. Brit. Mil. Colloq.* **1.** England. **2.** (chiefly in World War I) a wound serious enough to get one sent back to England. Also, **blighty.** [Hind *bilāyatī* foreign, European]

**blimey** /ˈblaɪmi/, *interj. Colloq.* (an exclamation expressing surprise or amazement). Also, **blimy.** [See GORBLIMEY]

**blimp**[1] /blɪmp/, *n.* **1.** (formerly) a small, non-rigid airship or dirigible, used chiefly for observation. **2.** *Colloq.* any dirigible. **3.** a soundproof cover enclosing a movie camera to obliterate the sound of the mechanism during shooting. [orig. uncert.]

**blimp**[2] /blɪmp/, *n. Brit.* an elderly person, usu. military, with reactionary views. [from Colonel *Blimp,* cartoon character created by David Low, 1891-1963, British cartoonist, born in New Zealand]

**blind** /blaɪnd/, *adj.* **1.** lacking the sense of sight. **2.** unwilling or unable to try to understand: *blind to all arguments.* **3.** not controlled by reason: *blind tenacity.* **4.** not possessing or proceeding from intelligence. **5.** lacking all awareness: *a blind stupor.* **6.** drunk. **7.** hard to see or understand: *blind reasoning.* **8.** hidden from view: *a blind corner.* **9.** having no outlets. **10.** closed at one end: *a blind street.* **11.** done without seeing: *blind flying.* **12.** made without knowledge in advance: *a blind date.* **13.** of or pertaining to blind persons. *–v.t.* **14.** to make blind, as by injuring, dazzling, or bandaging the eyes. **15.** to make obscure or dark. **16.** to deprive of discernment or judgment. **17.** to outshine; eclipse. *–n.* **18.** something that obstructs vision or keeps out light. **19.** a shade for a window, as a strip of cloth on a roller, or a venetian blind. **20.** a lightly built structure of brush or other growths, esp. one in which hunters conceal themselves; a hide. **21.** a cover for masking action or purpose; decoy. **22.** *Colloq.* a bout of excessive drinking; drinking spree. **23. the blind,** sightless people. *–adv.* **24.** without being able to see one's way: *to fly blind.* **25.** without assessment or prior consideration: *to enter into a deal blind.* [OE, c. G *blind*] **– blinding,** *adj.* **– blindingly,** *adv.* **– blindly,** *adv.* **– blindness,** *n.*

**blindage** /ˈblaɪndɪdʒ/, *n.* a screen or other structure as for protecting soldiers in a trench. [F, from *blinder* to armour, from G *blinden* blind]

**blind alley** /ˌblaɪnd ˈæli/, *n.* **1.** a road, street, etc., closed at one end. **2.** a position or situation offering no hope of progress or improvement.

**blind copy** /– ˈkɒpi/, *n.* a copy of a letter, etc., sent to someone other than the person addressed, no mention of this being made on the addressee's copy.

**blinder** /ˈblaɪndə/, *n.* **1.** a person or thing that blinds. **2.** *Colloq.* a dazzling display of skill, esp. at sport. **3.** a bout of excessive drinking; a drinking spree.

**blindfish** /ˈblaɪndfɪʃ/, *n.* any of various small fishes, as of the genus *Amblyopsis,* having rudimentary functionless eyes; found in subterranean streams.

**blindfold** /ˈblaɪndfoʊld/, *v.t.* **1.** to prevent sight by covering (the eyes); cover the eyes of. **2.** to impair the clear thinking of. *–n.* **3.** a bandage over the eyes. *–adj.* **4.** with eyes covered: *a blindfold test.* **5.** rash; unthinking. [BLIND + FOLD[1] wrap up, replacing *blindfell,* lit., a blind-fall. Cf. OE *(ge)blindfellian* make blind]

**blind Freddy** /ˌblaɪnd ˈfrɛdi/, *n. in the phrase* **even blind Freddy could see that,** (an expression used to indicate that something needs no explanation).

**blind hole** /– ˈhoʊl/, *n. Golf.* a hole played by a player who cannot see the next green and flag from the tee.

**blindman's buff** /ˌblaɪndmænz ˈbʌf/, *n.* a game in which a blindfolded player tries to catch and identify one of the others. [see BUFF[2]]

**blind side** /ˈblaɪnd saɪd/, *n. Rugby Football.* the side of the scrum away from the half back who puts the ball into the scrum.

**blind snake** /ˈ– sneɪk/, *n.* a small, subterranean, nonvenomous snake, *Rhamphotyphlops nigrescens,* of eastern Australia; worm snake; slow-worm.

**blind spot** /ˈ– spɒt/, *n.* **1.** *Anat.* a small area on the retina, insensitive to light, at which the optic nerve leaves the eye. **2.** a matter about which one is ignorant, unintelligent, or prejudiced, despite knowledge of related things. **3.** *Radio, T.V., etc.* an area in which signals are weak and their reception poor. **4.** (in a motor car) a line of sight obscured by a window column or other obstruction.

**blind-stab** /blaɪnd-ˈstæb/, *v.i. Prison Colloq.* to break and enter without ascertaining beforehand whether valuable goods are present.

**blind staggers** /blaɪnd ˈstægəz/, *n.* any of various forms of cerebral and spinal disease in horses, cattle and other animals, characterised by blindness, a staggering gait, sudden falling, etc; megrims. Also, **staggers.**

**blindstorey** /ˈblaɪndstɔri/, *n., pl.* **-ries.** *Archit.* →**triforium.**

**blind stroke** /blaɪnd ˈstroʊk/, *n. Golf.* a stroke made by a player who cannot see the next green and flag.

**blindworm** /ˈblaɪndwɜm/, *n.* →**slow-worm** (def. 2).

**blind-your-eyes** /ˈblaɪnd-jər-aɪz/, *n.* any of various trees with blistering milky sap, esp. *Excoecaria* species of the eastern hemisphere tropics.

**blink** /blɪŋk/, *v.i.* **1.** to wink, esp. rapidly and repeatedly. **2.** to look with winking or half-shut eyes. **3.** to cast a glance; take a peep. **4.** to look evasively or with indifference; ignore (oft. fol. by *at*). **5.** to shine unsteadily or dimly; twinkle. *–v.t.* **6.** to cause to blink. **7.** to shut the eyes to; evade, shirk. *–n.* **8.** a blinking. **9.** a glance or glimpse. **10.** a gleam; glimmer. **11.** *Meteorol.* →**iceblink. 12. on the blink,** *Colloq.* not working properly. [ME *blinken,* var. of *blenken* blench. Cf. G *blinken*]

**blinker** /ˈblɪŋkə/, *n.* **1.** a device for flashing light signals; indicator. **2.** either of two flaps on a bridle, to prevent a horse from seeing sideways or backwards.

**blinking** /ˈblɪŋkɪŋ/, *adj. Colloq.* confounded; blasted. **– blinkingly,** *adv.*

**blinks** /blɪŋks/, *n.* a small herb, *Montia fontana,* of the family Portulacaceae.

**blip** /blɪp/, *n.* a spot of light on a radar screen indicating the position of an aeroplane, submarine, or other object.

**bliss** /blɪs/, *n.* **1.** lightness of heart; blitheness; gladness. **2.** supreme happiness or delight. **3.** *Theol.* the joy of heaven. **4.** a cause of great joy or happiness. [ME *blisse,* OE *bliss, blīths,* from *blīthe* BLITHE]

**blissful** /ˈblɪsfəl/, *adj.* full of, abounding in, enjoying, or conferring bliss; supremely joyful. **– blissfully,** *adv.* **– blissfulness,** *n.*

**blister**[1] /ˈblɪstə/, *n.* **1.** a thin vesicle on the skin, containing watery matter or serum, as from a burn or other injury. **2.** any similar swelling, as an air bubble in a casting or a paint blister. **3.** (formerly) a transparent bulge on the fuselage of an aeroplane, usu. for mounting a gun. **4.** a blister plaster. **5.** *Brit. Colloq.* an unpleasant person. **6.** *Colloq.* a summons (def. 3). **7.** *Colloq.* a summary demand for payment of a debt. **8.** *Colloq.* a scathing communication: *the boss sent me a blister.* *–v.t.* **9.** to raise a blister or blisters on. **10.** to apply a blister plaster to. **11.** to subject to burning scorn, sarcasm, or criticism. *–v.i.* **12.** to rise in blisters; become blistered. [ME *blister, blester,* ? from OF *blestre* clod, lump (probably of Gmc orig.)] **– blistery,** *adj.*

**blister**[2] /ˈblɪstə/, *n. Colloq.* sister. [rhyming slang]

**blister beetle** /ˈ– bitl/, *n.* any of various beetles of the family Meloidae, many of which produce a secretion capable of blistering the skin, as the Spanish fly. Also, **blister fly.**

**blister copper** /ˈ– kɒpə/, *n.* an impure intermediate product in the refining of copper, produced by blowing copper matter into a converter. Large blisters form on the cast surface during the liberation of $SO_2$ and other gases.

**blister gas** /ˈ– gæs/, *n. Chem. Warfare.* a poison gas that burns or blisters the tissues of the body.

**blister pack** /ˈ– pæk/, *n.* **1.** a method of packaging medicines, toys, etc. where the object is placed on cardboard or foil and sealed over with clear plastic. *–v.t.* **2.** to package in this way. **– blister-packed,** *adj.*

**blister plaster** /ˈ– ˌplastə/, *n. Med.* (formerly) a plaster (often bearing blister beetles) applied to the skin to raise blisters.

**B.Lit.** /bi ˈlɪt/, Bachelor of Literature.

**blithe** /blaɪð/, *adj.* joyous, merry, or gay in disposition; glad; cheerful. [ME; OE *blīthe* kind, pleasant, joyous] – **blithely,** *adv.*

**blither** /ˈblɪðə/, *v.i.* →**blather.**

**blithering** /ˈblɪðərɪŋ/, *adj.* **1.** nonsensical; jabbering. **2.** blinking.

**blithesome** /ˈblaɪðsəm/, *adj.* lighthearted; merry; cheerful: *a blithesome nature.* – **blithesomely,** *adv.* – **blithesomeness,** *n.*

**B.Litt.** /bi ˈlɪt/, Bachelor of Letters.

**blitz** /blɪts/, *n.* **1.** *Mil.* war waged by surprise, swiftly and violently, as by the use of aircraft. **2. the Blitz,** night air-raids by German bombers in World War II on London and elsewhere, esp. in the period 1940-41. **3.** any swift, vigorous attack: *a blitz on litterbugs.* –*v.t.* **4.** to attack with a blitz. Also, **blitzkrieg** /ˈblɪtskrig/. [G: lightning (war)]

**blitz buggy** /ˈ– bʌgi/, *n.* a large, four-wheel drive truck, esp. of World War II.

**blizzard** /ˈblɪzəd/, *n.* **1.** a violent windstorm with dry, driving snow and intense cold. **2.** a widespread and heavy snowstorm. [var. of d. *blizzer* blaze, flash, blinding flash of lightning; sense widened from lightning to storm. Cf. OE *blysa, blyse* torch, and *blysian* burn]

**bloat** /bloʊt/, *v.t.* **1.** to make distended, as with air, water, etc.; cause to swell. **2.** to puff up; make vain or conceited. **3.** to cure (fishes) as bloaters. –*v.i.* **4.** to become swollen; be puffed out or dilated. –*n.* **5.** *Vet. Sci.* Also, **bloating.** (in cattle, sheep, horses and other ruminants) a distension of the rumen or paunch or of the large colon by gases of fermentation, caused by ravenous eating of green forage, esp. legumes. [*bloat,* adj., swollen, from ME *blout* puffy, from Scand.; cf. Icel. *blautr* soft]

**bloater** /ˈbloʊtə/, *n. Chiefly Brit.* **1.** a herring cured by being salted and briefly smoked and dried. **2.** a mackerel similarly cured.

**blob** /blɒb/, *n.* **1.** a small globe of liquid; a bubble. **2.** a small lump, drop, splotch, or daub. **3.** *Colloq.* (in cricket) nought; no runs: *out for a blob.* **4.** *Colloq.* a fool. [? imitative]

**bloc** /blɒk/, *n.* **1.** a group of states or territories united by some common factor. **2.** *Politics.* a coalition of factions or parties for a particular measure or purpose. [F. See BLOCK]

**block** /blɒk/, *n.* **1.** a solid mass of wood, stone, etc., usu. with one or more plane or approximately plane faces. **2.** a child's building brick. **3.** a mould or piece on which something is shaped or kept in shape, as a hat block. **4.** *Qld.* one of the wooden supports by which a house is elevated above the ground. **5.** a piece of wood prepared for cutting, or as cut, for wood engraving. **6.** *Print.* a letter-press printing plate mounted on a base to make it type-high. **7.** a (wooden) bench or board for chipping or cutting on. **8.** the support on which a person about to be beheaded lays his head. **9.** a platform from which an auctioneer sells. **10.** *Mech.* **a.** a device consisting of one or more grooved pulleys mounted in a casing or shell, to which a hook or the like is attached, used for transmitting power, changing direction of motion, etc. **b.** the casing or shell holding the pulley. **11.** an obstacle or hindrance. **12.** a blocking or obstructing, or blocked or obstructed state or condition. **13.** *Pathol.* an obstruction, as of a nerve. **14.** a dull, stolid, or insensitive person. **15.** *Colloq.* the head. **16.** *Sport.* a hindering of an opponent's actions. **17.** *Cricket.* a mark made by the batsman on the crease when taking guard. **18.** a quantity, portion, or section taken as a unit or dealt with at one time: *block of tickets.* **19.** *Computers.* a set of data or instructions. **20. a.** a fairly large area of land, esp. for settlement, mining, farming, etc. **b.** a section of land, frequently suburban, as for building a house, etc.: *a block of land, a building block.* **21.** *N.Z.* the area of land, esp. Crown or State forest, over which a trapper or hunter is licensed to operate. **22.** a row of contiguous buildings, or one large building, divided into separate houses, flats, shops, etc. **23. a.** a portion of a city, town, etc., enclosed by (usu. four) neighbouring and intersecting streets. **b.** the length of one side of this; distance between one intersection and the next. **24.** a block section. **25.** a stage direction added to a script. **26.** a large number of shares taken together, as on the stock exchange. **27.** a writing or sketching pad. **28.** *Philately.* a group of four or more unseparated stamps, not in a strip. **29.** *Athletics.* a starting block. **30.** *Bowls.* a bowl which blocks the opponent's logical course to the jack. **31.** a blocked shoe. **32.** a wristwatch. **33. do the block,** to promenade the fashionable area of town. **34.** *Colloq.* **lose** or **do one's block,** to become very angry. **35. off one's block,** insane. –*v.t.* **36.** to fit with blocks; mount on a block. **37.** to shape or prepare on or with a block. **38.** to cut into blocks. **39.** to sketch or outline roughly or in a general plan, without details (fol. by *out* or *in*). **40.** to write in stage directions on (a script). **41.** to obstruct (a space, progress, etc.); check or hinder (a person, etc.) by placing obstacles in the way. **42.** to obscure from view (fol. by *out*): *the smoke blocked out the sun.* **43.** to prevent penetration by: *this cream blocks out radiation.* **44.** to restrict the use of (a currency, etc.) **45.** to determine the three dimensional character of an ore body, usu. by diamond drilling (fol. by *out*). **46.** *Pathol., Physiol.* to stop the passage of impulses in (a nerve, etc.). –*v.i.* **47.** to act so as to obstruct an opponent (as in football, boxing, etc.). **48.** *Cricket.* to stop the ball with the bat; to bat defensively. [ME *blok,* apparently from OF *bloc* block, mass, from Gmc (cf. G *Block*)]

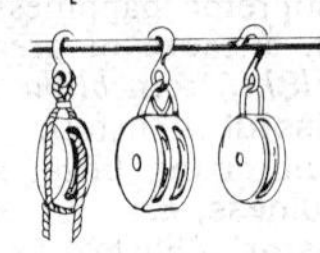

single and double blocks (def. 10)

**blockade** /blɒˈkeɪd/, *n., v.,* **-kaded, -kading.** –*n.* **1.** *Navy, Mil.* the shutting up of a place, esp. a port, harbour, or part of a coast by hostile ships or troops to prevent entrance or exit. **2.** any obstruction of passage or progress. –*v.t.* **3.** to subject to a blockade. – **blockader,** *n.*

**blockage** /ˈblɒkɪdʒ/, *n.* an obstruction.

**block and tackle,** *n.* the pulley blocks and ropes used for hoisting.

**blockbuster** /ˈblɒkbʌstə/, *n.* **1.** an aerial bomb containing high explosives and usu. weighing several tonnes, used in World War II as a large-scale demolition bomb. **2.** *Colloq.* anything large and spectacular, as a lavish theatrical production, impressive political campaign, etc.

**block coefficient** /blɒk koʊəˈfɪʃənt/, *n.* the ratio of the volume of the displacement of a ship to the volume of a rectangular block having the same length, breadth, and draught.

**block diagram** /ˈ– ˌdaɪəgræm/, *n.* **1.** *Electronics, Engineering.* a diagram which shows the interconnections between the parts of a system. **2.** *Geol.* a drawing in three dimensions to show the structural relationships between rocks below the surface.

**blocked** /blɒkt/, *adj. Colloq.* dazed, stupefied as a result of drugs.

**blocked shoe** /– ˈʃu/, *n.* a dance shoe with a stiffened toe, worn by a ballerina to enable her to dance on the tip of her toes. Also, **point shoe.**

**blocker** /ˈblɒkə/, *n.* **1.** one who or that which blocks. **2.** the occupier of an irrigation block. **3.** *S.A.* the owner of a vineyard.

**blockfield** /ˈblɒkfild/, *n.* an area of large, angular blocks of stone produced by glacial mass movement.

**block-graze** /blɒk-ˈgreɪz/, *v.t.* to graze (cattle, etc.) in enclosed sections of the available land, ensuring that the pasture on each section is eaten before allowing them into the next.

**blockhead** /ˈblɒkhɛd/, *n.* a stupid fellow; a dolt.

**blockhouse** /ˈblɒkhaʊs/, *n.* **1.** *Mil.* a fortified structure with ports or loopholes for gunfire, used against bombs, artillery, and small-arms fire. **2.** (formerly) a building, usu. of hewn timber and with a projecting upper storey, having loopholes for musketry. **3.** a house built on squared logs.

**blockie** /ˈblɒki/, *n.* a small farmer.

**blocking** /ˈblɒkɪŋ/, *n. Print.* the embossed lettering or ornamentation on the cover of a book.

**blockish** /ˈblɒkɪʃ/, *adj.* like a block; dull; stupid. – **blockishly,** *adv.* – **blockishness,** *n.*

**block lava** /ˈblɒk lavə/, *n.* lava flows composed of rough angular blocks.

**block letter** /– ˈlɛtə/, *n.* **1.** Also, **block capital.** a plain typelike capital letter. **2.** *Print.* a typeface or letter designed without serifs.

**block-out cream** /ˈblɒk-aʊt krim/, *n.* a cream applied to exposed parts of the body, which gives protection against damaging ultra-violet radiation from the sun.

**block plane** /'– pleɪn/, *n.* a small plane used for cutting across the grain of the wood.

**block print** /'– prɪnt/, *n. Fine Arts.* a design printed by means of blocks of wood or metal.

**block system** /'– sɪstəm/, *n.* any system of controlling train movements by allowing only one train at a time into a section of the railway.

**block type** /– 'taɪp/, *n.* →**block letter** (def. 2).

**blocky** /'blɒki/, *adj.* (of stock, esp. cattle) solid, with good lines; square as opposed to rangy.

**bloke** /bloʊk/, *n. Colloq.* man; fellow; guy. [Shelta]

**blond** /blɒnd/, *adj.* **1.** light-coloured. **2.** (of a person) having light-coloured hair and skin. *–n.* **3.** a blond person. [F, from ML *blondus* yellow. Cf. OE *blondenfeax* grey-haired] – **blondness,** *n.*

**blonde** /blɒnd/, *n.* **1.** a female with light-coloured hair. *–adj.* **2.** (of a female) having light-coloured hair and skin. **3.** (of a female's hair) light; fair. – **blondeness,** *n.*

**Blonde d'Aquitaine** /,blɒnd 'dækwətein/, *n.* one of a breed of beef cattle of European origin with a large frame and lean body, suited for the white veal trade.

**blood** /blʌd/, *n.* **1.** the fluid that circulates in the arteries and veins or principal vascular system of animals, in man being of a red colour and consisting of a pale yellow plasma containing semisolid corpuscles. **2.** body fluids spilling or spilled out; gore. **3.** the vital principle; life. **4.** bloodshed; slaughter; murder. **5.** the juice or sap of plants. **6.** temper or state of mind: *a person of hot blood.* **7.** man's fleshly nature: *the frailty of men's blood.* **8.** a man of fire or spirit. **9.** a profligate or dissolute man, esp. one in fashionable society. **10.** physical and cultural extraction. **11.** royal extraction. **12.** descent from a common ancestor: *related by blood.* **13.** *Stock Breeding.* recorded and respected ancestry; pure-bred breeding. **14. in cold blood,** calmly, coolly, and deliberately. **15. one's blood is up,** one's anger or belligerence is aroused. **16. one's blood is worth bottling,** *Colloq.* one is exceptionally meritorious or praiseworthy. *–v.t.* **17.** to cause to bleed. **18.** *Hunting.* **a.** to give (hounds, etc.) a first taste or sight of blood. **b.** to smear with blood, as after a hunt. **19.** to initiate. [ME; OE *blōd,* c. G. *Blut*] – **bloodlike,** *adj.*

**blood alcohol level,** *n.* the concentration of alcohol in the blood.

**blood and bone,** *n.* fertiliser made by treating animal residues from abattoirs and reducing them to powder.

**blood and thunder,** *n.* violence; sensationalism; bombast; extravagant anger.

**blood-and-thunder** /,blʌd-ən-'θʌndə/, *adj.* (of films, plays, etc.) characterised by violence and bombast.

**blood bank** /'blʌd bæŋk/, *n.* a place where blood is stored for later use.

**bloodbath** /'blʌdbaθ/, *n.* **1.** a massacre. **2.** a bath in blood.

**blood blister** /'blʌd blɪstə/, *n.* a blister containing a bloody fluid.

**blood brother** /'– brʌðə/, *n.* one who has sworn lifelong brotherhood to, and mingled his blood with, another.

**blood count** /'– kaʊnt/, *n.* the count of the number of red or white blood cells in a specific volume of blood.

**bloodcurdling** /'blʌd,kɜdlɪŋ/, *adj.* frightening; terrifyingly horrible.

**blood donor** /'blʌd doʊnə/, *n.* **1.** one who gives blood for a blood bank or transfusion. **2.** *Colloq.* →**make-up** (def. 8).

**blooded** /'blʌdəd/, *adj.* **1.** having blood: *warm-blooded animals.* **2.** (of horses, etc.) derived from ancestors of good blood; having a good pedigree. **3.** having been through battle: *blooded troops.* **4.** initiated.

**blood feud** /'blʌd fjud/, *n.* →**vendetta.**

**blood group** /'– grup/, *n.* one of several classifications into which the blood may be grouped according to its clotting reactions. Also, **blood type.**

**blood guilt** /'– gɪlt/, *n.* guilt of murder or bloodshed. – **blood-guilty,** *adj.* – **blood-guiltiness,** *n.*

**blood heat** /'– hit/, *n.* the normal temperature (about 98.4°F or 37°C) of human blood.

**bloodhound** /'blʌdhaʊnd/, *n.* **1.** one of a breed of large, powerful dogs with a very acute sense of smell, used for tracking game, human fugitives, etc. **2.** *Colloq.* a detective; sleuth.

bloodhound

**bloodhouse** /'blʌdhaʊs/, *n. Colloq.* a particularly rough hotel, uncomfortable and disorderly.

**bloodless** /'blʌdləs/, *adj.* **1.** without blood; pale. **2.** free from bloodshed: *a bloodless victory.* **3.** spiritless; without energy. **4.** cold-hearted: *bloodless charity.* – **bloodlessly,** *adv.*

**blood-letting** /'blʌd-lɛtɪŋ/, *n.* **1.** the act of letting blood by opening a vein. **2.** →**bloodshed.**

**bloodmobile** /'blʌdməbil/, *n.* a vehicle containing medical equipment for receiving blood donations.

**blood money** /'blʌd mʌni/, *n.* **1.** a fee paid to a hired murderer. **2.** compensation paid to the survivors of a slain man. **3.** small remuneration earned by great effort.

**blood oath** /– 'oʊθ/, *interj.* (an exclamation usu. expressing agreement, affirmation, etc.) Also, **bloody oath!, my bloody oath!**

**blood orange** /'– ɒrɪndʒ/, *n.* a variety of orange with blood-red flesh and skin when ripe.

**blood plasma** /'– plæzmə/, *n.* the liquid part of human blood, often stored in hospitals, etc., for transfusions.

**blood-poisoning** /'blʌd-pɔɪznɪŋ/, *n.* a morbid condition of the blood due to the presence of toxic matter or micro-organisms; toxaemia; septicaemia; pyaemia.

**blood pressure** /'blʌd prɛʃə/, *n.* the pressure of the blood against the inner walls of the blood vessels, varying in different parts of the body, during different phases of contraction of the heart, and under different conditions of health, exertion, etc.

**blood pudding** /blʌd 'pʊdɪŋ/, *n.* →**black pudding.**

**blood rain** /'blʌd reɪn/, *n.* rain coloured red by small particles of dust, as in the desert.

**blood-red** /blʌd-'rɛd, 'blʌd-rɛd/, *adj.* **1.** of the deep red colour of blood. **2.** red with blood.

**blood relation** /'blʌd rəleɪʃən/, *n.* one related by birth. Also, **blood relative.**

**bloodroot** /'blʌdrut/, *n.* **1.** a species of the Australian genus *Haemodorum* which has a red exudation from the rootstock. **2.** →**tormentil.** **3.** a North American plant, *Sanguinaria canadensis,* with red root and root sap.

**blood serum** /'blʌd sɪərəm/, *n.* →**serum** (def. 1).

**bloodshed** /'blʌdʃɛd/, *n.* destruction of life; slaughter.

**bloodshot** /'blʌdʃɒt/, *adj.* (of the eyes) red from dilated blood vessels. [var. of *blood-shotten,* from BLOOD + *shot(ten),* pp. of SHOOT]

**blood sports** /'blʌd spɔts/, *n.pl.* sports involving bloodshed, as hunting.

**bloodstain** /'blʌdsteɪn/, *n.* a spot or trace of blood.

**bloodstained** /'blʌdsteɪnd/, *adj.* **1.** stained with blood. **2.** guilty of bloodshed.

**bloodstock** /'blʌdstɒk/, *n.* thoroughbred stock, esp. stud horses.

**bloodstone** /'blʌdstoʊn/, *n.* a greenish variety of chalcedony with small bloodlike spots of red jasper scattered through it; heliotrope.

**bloodstream** /'blʌdstrim/, *n.* the blood flowing through a circulatory system.

**bloodsucker** /'blʌdsʌkə/, *n.* **1.** any animal that sucks blood. esp. a leech. **2.** →**jacky lizard.** **3.** →**waratah anemone.** **4.** *Colloq.* an extortioner. **5.** *Colloq.* a person who sponges on others.

**blood test** /'blʌd tɛst/, *n.* a test of a sample of blood to determine blood type, presence of infection, parentage, etc.

**bloodthirsty** /'blʌdθɜsti/, *adj.* eager to shed blood; murderous. – **bloodthirstily,** *adv.* – **bloodthirstiness,** *n.*

**blood transfusion** /'blʌd træns,fjuʒən/, *n.* the injection of blood from one person or animal into the bloodstream of another.

**blood vessel** /ˈblʌd vɛsəl/, *n.* any of the vessels (arteries, veins, capillaries) through which the blood circulates.

**bloodwood** /ˈblʌdwʊd/, *n.* any tree of a number of species of *Eucalyptus* with characteristic bark of short fibres and transverse cracks, widespread in warmer parts of Australia, many species of which tend to have an exudation of a reddish colour.

**bloodworm** /ˈblʌdwɜm/, *n.* **1.** any of various freshwater insect larvae of the genus *Chironomus,* which live in the muddy sediment of a river bottom, and which are more or less bright red, according to the degree of oxygenation of their environment, to which is related the amount of haemaglobin in them. **2.** →**baitworm.**

**bloody** /ˈblʌdi/, *adj.*, **bloodier, bloodiest,** *v.*, **bloodied, bloodying,** *adv.* *–adj.* **1.** stained with blood. **2.** attended with bloodshed: *a bloody battle.* **3.** inclined to bloodshed. **4.** of the nature of, or pertaining to blood; containing or composed of blood. **5.** *Colloq.* (an intensive signifying approval, as in *bloody beauty,* or disapproval, as in *bloody bastard*). **6.** *Colloq.* **a.** (of people) difficult; obstinate; cruel. **b.** (of events) cruel; unjust; unbearable. *–v.t.* **7.** to stain with blood. *–adv.* **8.** *Colloq.* very; extremely. [ME *blody,* OE *blōdig*] – **bloodily,** *adv.* – **bloodiness,** *n.*

**bloody mary** /– ˈmɛəri/, *n.* a cocktail consisting chiefly of tomato juice and vodka. Also, **bloody Mary.**

**bloody-minded** /blʌdi-ˈmaɪndəd/, *adj. Colloq.* **1.** obstructive; unhelpful; difficult. **2.** deliberately cruel or unpleasant. – **bloody-mindedness,** *n.*

**bloom**[1] /blum/, *n.* **1.** the flower of a plant. **2.** flowers collectively. **3.** the state of having the buds opened. **4.** a flourishing, healthy condition: *the bloom of youth.* **5.** prime; state of full development; perfection. **6.** a glow or flush on the cheek indicative of youth and health. **7.** *Bot.* a whitish powdery deposit or coating consisting of minute particles of oxidised pigment, wild yeasts, etc., as on the surface of certain fruits and leaves. **8.** any similar surface coating or appearance. **9.** any of certain minerals occurring as a pulverulent encrustation. **10.** a discoloration of water given by the development of certain algae. *–v.i.* **11.** to produce or yield blossoms. **12.** to flourish. **13.** to be in a state of healthy beauty and vigour. **14.** to glow with a warm colour. [ME *blom(e),* from Scand.; cf. Icel. *blōm* flower, *blōmi* prosperity] – **bloomless,** *adj.*

**bloom**[2] /blum/, *n.* a semi-finished steel ingot rolled to reduced size. [OE *blōma* lump of metal]

**bloomer** /ˈblumə/, *n.* **1.** a plant which blooms. **2.** *Colloq.* an embarrassingly foolish mistake; laughable blunder. [BLOOM[1] + -ER[1]]

**bloomers** /ˈbluməz/, *n.* **1.** loose trousers gathered at the knee, formerly much worn by women as part of gymnasium, riding, or other like dress. **2.** a woman's undergarment so designed. [named after a Mrs. Amelia *Bloomer* of New York, about 1850]

bloomers

**blooming** /ˈblumɪŋ/, *adj.* **1.** in bloom; blossoming; in flower. **2.** glowing as with youthful freshness and vigour. **3.** flourishing; prospering. **4.** *Colloq.* (*euph.*) bloody.

**bloomy** /ˈblumi/, *adj.* **1.** covered with blossoms; in full flower. **2.** having a bloom (def. 7), as fruit.

**blooper** /ˈblupə/, *n.* a slip of the tongue, esp. of a broadcaster, resulting in a humorous or indecorous misreading.

**blossom** /ˈblɒsəm/, *n. Bot.* **1.** the flower of a plant, esp. of one producing an edible fruit. **2.** the flowers of a fruit tree, collectively: *apple blossom.* **3.** the state of flowering: *the apple tree is in blossom.* *–v.i.* **4.** *Bot.* to produce or yield blossoms. **5.** to flourish; develop (oft. fol. by *out*). [ME *blosme, blossem,* OE *blōs(t)m(a)* flower] – **blossomless,** *adj.* – **blossomy,** *adj.*

**blot** /blɒt/, *n., v.,* **blotted, blotting.** *–n.* **1.** a spot or stain, esp. of ink on paper. **2.** a blemish or reproach on character or reputation. **3.** an erasure or obliteration, as in a writing. **4.** the anus. *–v.t.* **5.** to spot, stain, or bespatter. **6.** to darken; make dim; obscure or eclipse. **7.** to make indistinguishable

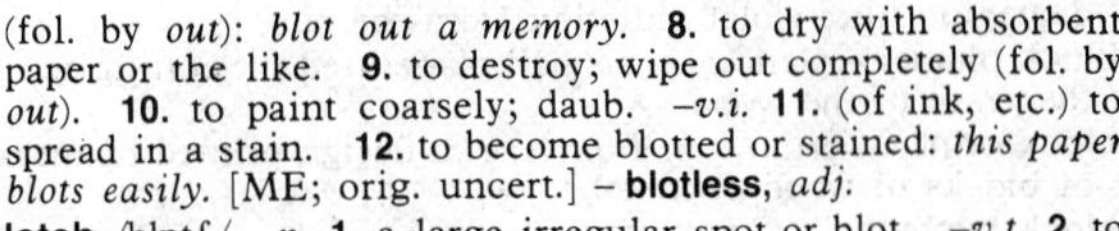

(fol. by *out*): *blot out a memory.* **8.** to dry with absorbent paper or the like. **9.** to destroy; wipe out completely (fol. by *out*). **10.** to paint coarsely; daub. *–v.i.* **11.** (of ink, etc.) to spread in a stain. **12.** to become blotted or stained: *this paper blots easily.* [ME; orig. uncert.] – **blotless,** *adj.*

**blotch** /blɒtʃ/, *n.* **1.** a large irregular spot or blot. *–v.t.* **2.** to mark with blotches; blot, spot, or blur. [b. BLOT and BOTCH] – **blotchy,** *adj.*

**blot drawing** /ˈblɒt drɔ-ɪŋ/, *n.* a technique of using any fortuitous blot made on paper as a basis for imaginative pictorial composition.

**blotter** /ˈblɒtə/, *n.* **1.** anything used to absorb excess ink. **2.** a piece, book, or pad of blotting paper.

**blotting paper** /ˈblɒtɪŋ ˌpeɪpə/, *n.* **1.** a soft, absorbent, unsized paper, used esp. for drying ink. **2.** *Colloq.* food taken while drinking alcoholic beverages, to mitigate the effects of the alcohol.

**blotto** /ˈblɒtoʊ/, *adj. Colloq.* under the influence of drink.

**blouse** /blaʊz/, *n.* **1.** a light, loosely fitting bodice or shirt, esp. one that is gathered or held in at the waist. **2.** a jockey's silk jacket. **3.** a loose upper garment, reaching about to the knees, worn esp. by peasants; a smock frock. *–v.i.* **4.** to hang loose and full. **5.** to fill with air (oft. fol. by *out*). *–v.t.* **6.** to drape loosely. [F, ? from Pr (*lano*) *blouso* short (wool)] – **blouselike,** *adj.*

**bloused** /blaʊzd/, *adj.* (of women's clothes) having fullness above the waistline or belt, esp. at the back; blouse-like. [BLOUS(E) + -ED[3]]

**blow**[1] /bloʊ/, *n.* **1.** a sudden stroke with hand, fist, or weapon. **2.** a sudden shock, or a calamity or reverse. **3.** a sudden attack or drastic action. **4.** the first and longest stroke made in shearing a sheep. **5. at one blow,** with a single act. **6. come to blows,** to start to fight. **7. strike a blow,** to begin or resume work. [northern ME *blaw;* orig. uncert.]

**blow**[2] /bloʊ/, *v.,* **blew** /blu/, **blown, blowing,** *n.* *–v.i.* **1.** (of the wind or air) to be in motion. **2.** to move along, carried by or as by the wind: *the dust was blowing.* **3.** to produce or emit a current of air, as with the mouth, a bellows, etc.: *blow on your hands.* **4.** *Music.* **a.** (of horn, trumpet, etc.) to give out sound. **b.** *Colloq.* to play on any musical instrument, or sing, usu. with other musicians. **5.** to make a blowing sound; whistle. **6.** to breathe hard or quickly; pant. **7.** *Colloq.* to boast; brag. **8.** *Colloq.* to depart. **9.** *Zool.* (of a whale) to spout. **10.** *Colloq.* to ejaculate; experience orgasm. **11.** (of a fuse, gasket, light bulb, radio valve, tyre, etc.) to burn out or perish; become unusable (oft. fol. by *out*). **12.** to be extinguished, as by the wind (fol. by *out*). **13.** *Horseracing Colloq.* (of odds on a horse offered by bookmakers) to lengthen (oft. fol. by *out*). **14. blow in,** *Colloq.* to make an unexpected visit; drop in; call. **15. blow over, a.** to cease; subside. **b.** to be forgotten. **16. blow through,** *Colloq.* **a.** to depart. **b.** to evade a responsibility. **17. blow up, a.** to come into being: *a storm blew up.* **b.** to explode: *the ship blew up.* **c.** *Colloq.* to lose one's temper. **d.** *N.Z. Sport.* to halt play for an infringement by blowing on a whistle. *–v.t.* **18.** to drive by means of a current of air. **19.** to spread by report. **20.** to divulge (a secret). **21.** to extinguish (a flame, etc.) with a puff of air (fol. by *out*). **22.** to drive a current of air upon. **23.** to clear or empty by forcing air through. **24.** to shape (glass, etc.) with a current of air. **25.** to cause to sound, esp. by a current of air. **26.** to cause to explode (fol. by *up, to bits,* etc.). **27.** *Photog.* to reproduce by enlargement (fol. by *up*). **28.** to expel noisily (fol. by *off*). **29.** to put (a horse) out of breath by fatigue. **30.** (pp. **blowed**), *Colloq.* (*euph.*) to damn. **31.** waste; squander: *to blow one's money.* **32.** to fail in something: *to blow an exam.* **33. blow (someone) up,** *Colloq.* to scold or abuse (someone). **34. blow one's mind,** *Colloq.* to achieve a state of euphoria, as with drugs. **35. blow the whistle on,** *Colloq.* to inform upon; report to authority. *–n.* **36. a.** a storm with a high wind. **b.** a high wind. **37. a.** the act of producing a blast of air, as in playing a wind instrument. **b.** a musical performance, usu. with other musicians, and often improvised; gig; jam. **38.** *Colloq.* a walk in the fresh air; airing. **39.** *Colloq.* boasting or bragging. **40.** *Metall.* **a.** the blast of air used in making steel in a converter. **b.** the time during which, or that part of a process in which, it is used. **41.** an outcrop of discoloured quartz-rich rock; sometimes thought to indicate mineral deposits below. **42.** *Colloq.* a rest: *we'll have a blow now.* [ME *blowe(n)*, OE *blāwan*]

**blow**[3] /bloʊ/, *v.*, **blew** /blu/, **blown, blowing,** *n.* *–v.i., v.t.* **1.** to blossom; bloom; flower. *–n.* **2.** a yield or display of blossoms. **3.** the state of blossoming. [ME *blowen*, OE *blōwan*]

**blow-drier** /ˈbloʊ-draɪə/, *n.* a hand-held machine which blows out warm air and is used to dry the hair.

**blow-dry** /ˈbloʊ-draɪ/, *v.*, **-dried, -drying,** *n.*, *pl.* **-dries.** *–v.t.* **1.** to style hair by brushing it into shape while drying it with a blow-drier. *–n.* **2.** an instance of blow-drying: *I'd like a wash and blow-dry please.*

**blower** /ˈbloʊə/, *n.* **1.** a person or thing that blows. **2. a.** a machine for forcing air through a furnace, building, mine, etc. **b.** *Colloq.* →**supercharger. 3.** a whale. **4.** *Colloq.* a telephone or speaking tube.

**blowfish** /ˈbloʊfɪʃ/, *n.* →**toado.**

**blowfly** /ˈbloʊflaɪ/, *n.*, *pl.* **-flies.** any of various true flies, of the order Diptera, which deposit their eggs or larvae on carcasses or meat, or in sores, wounds, etc., esp. the **blue blowfly,** *Lucilia cuprina.*

**blowfly grass** /ˈbloʊflaɪ ˌgras/, *n.* the Mediterranean grass *Briza maxima;* quaking grass.

**blowfly strike** /ˈbloʊflaɪ ˌstraɪk/, *n.* →**sheep strike.**

**blowgun** /ˈbloʊgʌn/, *n.* →**blowpipe** (def. 1).

**blowhole** /ˈbloʊhoʊl/, *n.* **1.** an air or gas vent. **2.** either of two nostrils or spiracles, or a single one at the top of the head in whales and other cetaceans, through which they breathe. **3.** a hole in the ice to which whales or seals come to breathe. **4.** *Metall.* a defect in a casting caused by trapped steam or gas. **5.** a hole in a coastal rock formation through which sea water is forced violently up by tide or wave.

**blowie** /ˈbloʊi/, *n.* *Colloq.* a blowfly.

**blow-in** /ˈbloʊ-ɪn/, *n.* *Colloq.* a newcomer.

**blowing** /ˈbloʊɪŋ/, *n.* **1.** the sound of any vapour or gas issuing from a vent under pressure. **2.** *Metall.* a disturbance caused by gas or steam blowing through molten metal. **3.** *Textiles.* the process of blowing dry steam through a cloth, to settle the fabric and take the curliness from the yarn.

**blow job** /ˈbloʊ dʒɒb/, *n.* *Colloq.* →**fellatio.**

**blowlamp** /ˈbloʊlæmp/, *n.* a small portable apparatus which gives a hot flame by forcing kerosene under pressure through a small nozzle and burning it in air.

**blown**[1] /bloʊn/, *adj.* **1.** inflated; distended. **2.** out of breath; fatigued; exhausted. **3.** flyblown. **4.** formed by blowing: *blown glass.* **5.** (of a car, etc., or its internal combustion engine) supercharged (opposed to *unblown*). [see BLOW[2]]

**blown**[2] /bloʊn/, *adj.* fully expanded or opened, as a flower. [see BLOW[3]]

**blown grass** /ˈbloʊn gras/, *n.* any of many species of the widespread grass genus, *Agrostis.*

**blown oil** /ˈ– ɔɪl/, *n.* vegetable oil which has been thickened by having air blown through it at an elevated temperature.

**blow-out** /ˈbloʊ-aʊt/, *n.* **1.** a rupture of a motor-car tyre. **2.** the blowing of a fuse. **3.** a sudden or violent escape of air, steam, crude oil or gas from a well, or the like. **4.** *Colloq.* a big meal or lavish entertainment; spree.

**blowpipe** /ˈbloʊpaɪp/, *n.* **1.** a pipe or tube through which missiles are blown by the breath. **2.** a tube through which a stream of air or gas is forced into a flame to concentrate and increase its heating action. **3.** *Glass-blowing.* a long iron pipe used to gather and blow the viscous glass. **4.** *Med.* an instrument used to observe or clean a cavity.

**blowtorch** /ˈbloʊtɔtʃ/, *n.* a portable apparatus which gives an extremely hot flame by forcing oxyacetylene under pressure through a small nozzle and burning it in air; used in welding, etc.

**blow-up** /ˈbloʊ-ʌp/, *n.* **1.** an explosion or other drastic trouble. **2.** a violent outburst of temper or scolding. **3.** *Photog.* an enlargement.

**blow-wave** /ˈbloʊ-weɪv/, *n.* **1.** a non-permanent wave produced by styling wet hair with a blow-waver. *–adj.* **2.** of such a hair style.

**blow-waver** /ˈbloʊ-weɪvə/, *n.* a hand hair-drier with styling attachments such as brush or comb.

**blowy** /ˈbloʊi/, *adj.* windy.

**blowzy** /ˈblaʊzi/, *adj.*, **blowzier, blowziest. 1.** dishevelled; unkempt: *blowzy hair.* **2.** red-faced. Also, **blowzed** /blaʊzd/. [from *blowze* wench, of unknown origin]

**blub** /blʌb/, *v.i.*, **blubbed, blubbing.** *Colloq.* to weep; cry noisily. [short for BLUBBER]

**blubber** /ˈblʌbə/, *n.* **1.** *Zool.* the fat found between the skin and muscle of whales and other cetaceans, from which oil is made. **2.** the act of blubbering. *–v.i.* **3.** to weep, usu. noisily and with contorted face. *–v.t.* **4.** to say while weeping. **5.** to disfigure with weeping. *–adj.* **6.** swollen. [ME *bluber*, n. *blubren;* v.; apparently imitative, Cf. G *blubbern* bubble] – **blubberer,** *n.* – **blubberingly,** *adv.*

**blubbery** /ˈblʌbəri/, *adj.* **1.** abounding in or resembling blubber. **2.** (of a cetacean) fat. **3.** blubbered; disfigured; swollen.

**blucher** /ˈblutʃə/, *n.* **1.** a kind of strong leather half-boot. **2.** a shoe with the vamp continued up beneath the top, which laps over it from the sides. [named after Field Marshal von *Blücher*]

**bludge** /blʌdʒ/, *v.*, **bludged, bludging,** *n.* *Colloq.* *–v.i.* **1.** to evade responsibilities. **2.** to impose on others (fol. by *on*). **3.** →**pimp** (def. 4). *–v.t.* **4.** to cadge. *–n.* **5.** a job which entails next to no work. **6. on the bludge,** imposing on others. [short for BLUDGEON] – **bludger,** *n.*

**bludgeon** /ˈblʌdʒən/, *n.* **1.** a short, heavy club with one end loaded, or thicker and heavier than the other. *–v.t.* **2.** to strike or fell with a bludgeon. **3.** to force (someone) into something; bully. [orig. unknown] – **bludgeoner,** *n.*

**blue** /blu/, *n. adj.*, **bluer, bluest,** *v.*, **blued, blueing** or **bluing.** *–n.* **1.** the pure hue of clear sky; deep azure (between green and violet in the spectrum). **2. the blue, a.** the sky. **b.** the sea. **c.** the unknown; the dim distance; nowhere: *out of the blue.* **3.** Also, **washing blue.** a substance, an indigo, used to whiten clothes in laundering them. **4.** a blue thing. **5.** a person who wears blue, or is a member of a group characterised by a blue symbol. **6. a.** a sportsman who represents or has represented his university in a contest with another. **b.** the honour awarded for this. **c.** the colours awarded for this. **7.** (*pl.*) blue clothes. **8.** a bluestocking. **9.** (*pl.*) →**blues. 10.** *Colloq.* a fight; dispute. **11.** *Colloq.* a summons in law. **12.** *Colloq.* a mistake. **13.** *Colloq.* (a nickname for a red-headed person). **14. cop the blue,** *Colloq.* to take the blame. *–adj.* **15.** of the colour blue. **16.** tinged with blue. **17.** (of the skin) discoloured by cold, contusion, fear, rage, or vascular collapse. **18.** depressed in spirits. **19.** dismal: *I'm feeling blue.* **20.** out of tune: *a blue note.* **21.** obscene, or pertaining to obscenity. **22. once in a blue moon,** rarely and exceptionally. **23. scream blue murder, a.** (of a child) to scream loudly. **b.** to protest vociferously. **24. true blue,** loyal; faithful; genuine. *–v.t.* **25.** to make blue; dye a blue colour. **26.** to treat (laundry) with blue (def. 3). **27.** *Colloq.* to spend wastefully; squander. *–v.i.* **28.** *Colloq.* to fight. [ME *blew,* from OF *bleu,* from Gmc (cf. G *blau*)] – **bluely,** *adv.* – **blueness,** *n.*

**blue ant** /ˈ– ænt/, *n.* the wingless female of a large Australian thynnid wasp, *Diamma bicolor,* having a metallic blue-green body, red legs and a very painful sting.

**blue-arsed fly** /blu-ast ˈflaɪ/, *n.* **1.** *Colloq.* the fly which causes sheep strike, the blue blowfly, *Lucilia cuprina.* **2. like a blue-arsed fly,** *Colloq.* in an erratic and frenzied fashion.

**blue asbestos** /blu æsˈbɛstəs/, *n.* →**crocidolite.**

**blue baby** /ˈ– beɪbi/, *n.* an infant with congenital cyanosis.

**blue-bag** /ˈblu-bæg/, *n.* a sachet of blue (def. 3) used in laundering.

**blue balloon** /blu bəˈlun/, *n.* *Colloq.* →**breathalyser.**

**Bluebeard** /ˈblubɪəd/, *n.* any man with a reputation as a lover. [a nickname of the chevalier Raoul, whose seventh wife found in a forbidden room the bodies of the other six]

**bluebell** /ˈblubɛl/, *n.* **1.** any Australian or New Zealand herb of the genus *Wahlenbergia,* family Campanulaceae, chiefly of southern temperate regions,

bluebell (def. 1)

having blue bell-shaped flowers, as Australian bluebell, *W. trichogyna,* of temperate mainland Australia. **2.** any herb of the genus *Campanula,* family Campanulaceae, of northern temperate regions and tropical mountains, having similar flowers, as the harebell, *C. rotundifolia,* of northern temperate regions; campanula. **3.** any of various plants having blue, more or less bell-shaped flowers, esp. the wood hyacinth, *Scilla nonscripta,* family Liliaceae, of Europe; scilla.

**blue-bellied black snake,** *n.* a medium to large, elapid, Australian snake, *Pseudechis guttatus,* distributed mainly in Queensland and New South Wales. Also, **spotted black snake.**

**bluebelly** /ˈblubɛli/, *n.* →**barebelly.**

**blueberry** /ˈblubəri/, *n., pl.* **-ries. 1.** the edible berry, usu. bluish, of any of various shrubs of the genus *Vaccinium.* **2.** any of these shrubs. **3.** any of various unrelated species with blue fruit.

**blueberry ash** /– ˈæʃ/, *n.* a graceful tree of eastern Australia, *Eleaocarpus reticulatus,* with fringed bell-like flowers and blue berries.

**bluebird** /ˈblubɜd/, *n.* **1.** any bird of the genus *Sialia,* comprising small North American passerine songbirds whose prevailing colour is blue, esp. the well-known eastern bluebird, *S. sialis,* which appears early in the spring. **2.** any of various other birds of which the predominant colour is blue.

**blue-black** /blu-ˈblæk/, *n., adj.* black tinged with blue, or with a blue sheen.

**blue blood** /ˈblu blʌd/, *n.* **1.** aristocratic descent. **2.** a member of the aristocracy. – **blue-blooded,** *adj.*

**blue-bonnet** /ˈblu-bɒnət/, *n.* **1.** a broad, flat bonnet of blue wool, formerly much worn in Scotland. **2.** a Scottish soldier who wore such a bonnet. **3.** any Scot. Also, **bluecap.**

**blue borage** /blu ˈbɒrɪdʒ/, *n.* →**viper's bugloss.**

**bluebottle** /ˈblubɒtl/, *n.* **1.** a hydrozoan of genus *Physalia* found in warm seas and having an elongated, deep blue, gas-filled bladder typically up to 13 centimetres long, from which trail numerous tentacles, possibly many metres in length and capable of inflicting a painful sting. It is actually a group of individual organisms specialised for particular purposes such as feeding, inflating the bladder, reproduction, etc. **2.** any of several large, metallic blue and green flies of the dipterous family Calliphoridae; the larvae of some are parasites of domestic animals.

bluebottle

**bluebush** /ˈblubʊʃ/, *n.* any of a number of herbaceous shrubs of the genus *Kochia* with blue-grey appearance, found on dry and often saline inland plains of Australia.

**bluecap** /ˈblukæp/, *n.* **1.** a year-old salmon, with blue markings on its head. **2.** the blue titmouse. **3.** →**blue-bonnet.**

**blue cattle dog,** *n.* →**Australian cattle dog.**

**blue cheese** /ˈblu tʃiz/, *n.* →**blue vein.**

**blue chip** /ˈblu tʃɪp/, *n.* **1.** a blue-coloured poker chip, usu. of high value. **2.** *Stock Exchange.* a stock in which investment is secure, though less secure than in gilt-edged. **3.** a valuable asset.

**blue-chip** /ˈblu-tʃɪp/, *adj.* **1.** pertaining to or constituting a blue chip. **2.** having an outstanding quality among items in a particular group.

**blue chord** /ˈblu kɔd/, *n.* a dominant seventh chord with a bent minor tenth.

**blue-collar** /ˈblu-kɒlə/, *adj.* belonging or pertaining to workers other than white-collar, as factory, production line workers, etc.

**blue comb** /blu ˈkoʊm/, *n.* enteritis in turkeys.

**blue couch** /– ˈkutʃ/, *n.* **1.** any of several species of couch which are blue-green in colour, esp. *Cynodon incompletus,* which can infest pasture and which is poisonous to stock. **2.** →**Queensland blue couch.**

**blue crane** /– ˈkreɪn/, *n.* →**white-faced heron.**

**blued** /blud/, *adj. Colloq.* drunk.

**blue devil** /blu ˈdɛvəl/, *n.* a blue-tinged spiny plant, *Eryngium rostratum,* common on tableland areas of New South Wales.

**blue devils** /– ˈdɛvəlz/, *n.pl.* **1.** low spirits. **2.** →**delirium tremens.**

**blue duck** /– ˈdʌk/, *n. N.Z.* **1.** a native mountain duck, *Hymenolaimus malacorhyncus.* **2.** *Chiefly Mil.* a baseless rumour; a failure.

**blue ensign** /– ˈɛnsən/, *n.* a blue flag with a Union Jack in canton and an insignia usu. denoting a government agency.

**blue-eye** /ˈblu-aɪ/, *n.* **1.** any of a number of tiny Australian brackish to freshwater fish of genus, *Pseudomugil,* usu. yellow and having vivid blue eyes. **2.** →**blue-faced honeyeater.**

**blue-eyed** /ˈblu-aɪd/, *adj.* **1.** having blue eyes. **2.** *Colloq.* darling; favourite. **3.** *Colloq.* ingenuous; innocent.

**blue-faced honeyeater** /blu-feɪst ˈhʌniitə/, *n.* a honeyeater, *Entomyzon cyanotis,* which is olive-green with white underparts and which has a distinctive large blue eye-patch of bare skin; found in northern and eastern Australia; blue-eye.

**blue fanny** /blu ˈfæni/, *n.* →**blue triangle.**

**blue fining** /– ˈfaɪnɪŋ/, *n.* a chemical fining of potassium ferrocyanide which reacts upon the metallic ingredients of wine. See **fining** (def. 2).

**bluefin tuna** /blufɪn ˈtjunə/, *n.* **1.** either of two species of tuna occurring off the east coast of Australia. The southern species, *Thunnus maccoyii,* is an important commercial fish. **2.** a very large tuna, *Thunnus thynnus,* widely distributed in temperate seas.

**bluefish** /ˈblufɪʃ/, *n.* **1.** an Australian and New Zealand marine fish, *Girella cyanea,* of violet-blue colouring. **2.** a predacious marine food fish, *Pomatomus saltatrix,* bluish or greenish in colour, of the Atlantic coast of the Americas. **3.** any of many diverse kinds of fishes, usu. of a bluish colour.

**blue flier** /blu ˈflaɪə/, *n.* the mature female of the red kangaroo, *Megaleia rufa.*

**blue fox** /blu ˈfɒks/, *n.* **1.** a variety of the small arctic fox, *Alopex lagopus,* having a year-round bluish pelt. **2.** any fox of this species while having a bluish fur in the summer season. **3.** the blue fur. **4.** any white fox fur dyed blue.

**blue funk** /– ˈfʌŋk/, *n. Colloq.* a state of extreme fear.

**bluegill** /ˈblugɪl/, *n.* a freshwater sunfish, *Lepomis macrochirus,* of the Mississippi and its tributaries, much used for food and important among the smaller game fishes.

**blue grass** /ˈblu gras/, *n.* **1.** any of various grasses of the genus *Poa,* as the Kentucky blue grass, *P. pratensis,* etc. **2.** any of various grasses of other unrelated genera, esp. *Bothriochloa* and *Dichanthium.* **3. the Blue grass,** a region in the U.S., in central Kentucky, famous for its luxuriant crops of blue grass. **4.** music of the south-eastern U.S. characterised by instruments such as pedal steel guitar, banjo and fiddle. Also, **bluegrass.**

**blue-green** /blu-ˈgrin/, *n., adj.* (of) a colour about midway between blue and green in the spectrum.

**blue-green algae** /– ˈældʒi/, *n.* unicellular or filamentous, asexual algae belonging to the class Myxophyceae (Cyanophyceae), usu. bluish green as the result of blue pigments added to their chlorophyll.

**blue-grey** /blu-ˈgreɪ/, *n., adj.* (of) a colour between blue and grey.

**blue ground** /ˈblu graʊnd/, *n.* a blue-grey decomposed agglomerate which contains diamonds, found in the diamond pipes of South Africa and Brazil.

**blue gum** /ˈ– gʌm/, *n.* any of several species of *Eucalyptus* with smooth and often bluish-coloured bark.

**blue heeler** /– ˈhilə/, *n.* one of a pure breed of cattle dog established in Australia in 1897. Also, **Queensland blue heeler, Australian blue speckle cattle dog.**

**blueing** /ˈbluɪŋ/, *n.* **1.** the process of colouring or tingeing something blue. **2.** the production of a film of blue oxide on polished steel. **3.** treatment of clothes with blue to increase their whiteness. Also, **bluing.**

**blueish** /ˈbluɪʃ/, *adj.* →**bluish.**

**bluejacket** /ˈbludʒækət/, *n.* **1.** a naval rating. **2.** any sailor.

**blue jay** /ˈblu dzeɪ/, *n.* →**black-faced cuckoo-shrike.**

**blue lupin** /– ˈlupən/, *n.* a sweet lupin, *Lupinus digitatus,* grown for fodder mainly in the temperate coastal area of western Australia.

**blue manna** /– ˈmænə/, *n.* →**blue swimmer.**

**blue metal** /ˈ– mɛtl/, *n.* crushed dark igneous rock used in construction work; road metal.

**blue movie** /– ˈmuvi/, *n. Colloq.* a pornographic film.

**bluenose** /ˈblunoʊz/, *n.* a kind of wrasse, *Pseudolabrus tetricus,* common in southern Australian and Tasmanian waters, which grows to a length of 50 cm. The colour varies with growth, adults having two broad bands across the body, bright yellow fins, and chin and throat of deep blue. Also, **blue-throated parrot fish.**

**blue-pencil** /blu-ˈpɛnsəl/, *v.t.,* **-cilled, -cilling,** or (*U.S.*) **-ciled, -ciling.** to alter, abridge, or cancel with or as with, a pencil that makes a blue mark, as in editing manuscript, or in censoring.

**blue peter** /blu ˈpitə/, *n.* a blue flag with a white square in the centre, symbol of the letter P in the International Code of Signals, hoisted by a ship as a signal that it is ready to leave port. [BLUE + *peter,* orig. REPEATER]

**blue pointer** /– ˈpɔɪntə/, *n.* **1.** →**mako. 2.** →**blue shark.**

**blueprint** /ˈbluprɪnt/, *n.* **1.** a process of photographic printing, based on ferric salts, in which the prints are white on a blue ground; cyanotype. It is used chiefly in making copies of tracings. **2.** a copy made using this process. **3.** a detailed outline or plan. *–v.t.* **4.** to make a blueprint of.

blue peter

**blue riband** /blu ˈrɪbənd/, *n.* **1.** any high distinction. **2.** a distinction awarded for the fastest crossing of the Atlantic by a liner.

**blue ribbon** /blu ˈrɪbən/, *n.* **1.** →**blue riband. 2.** a high distinction esp. a prize in an exhibition or show: *her cake won a blue ribbon.*

**blue-ribbon** /ˈblu-rɪbən/, *adj.* **1.** an electorate, sure to be held by a particular party or candidate; safe; certain: *a blue-ribbon seat for Labor.* **2.** of or pertaining to a prize-winner: *a blue-ribbon stallion.*

**blue-ringed octopus** /ˌblu-rɪŋd ˈɒktəpəs/, *n.* a small octopus, *Octopus maculosus,* of eastern Australia, distinctively marked by blue to purple banding on the tentacles and having a highly venomous bite.

**blue-rinse** /ˈblu-rɪns/, *adj.* (*derog.*) of or pertaining to well-off, middle-aged women of conservative and trivial outlook: *the blue-rinse set.*

**blue ruin** /ˌblu ˈruən/, *n. Brit. Colloq.* →**gin**[1].

**blues** /bluz/, *n. pl.* **1.** despondency; melancholy. **2.** *Jazz.* a type of song, of American Negro origin, predominantly melancholy in character and usu. performed in slow tempo. [short for BLUE DEVILS]

**blue shark** /ˈblu ʃak/, *n.* a large, voracious shark, *Prionace glauca,* of most tropical and temperate seas.

**blue shift** /ˈ– ʃɪft/, *n.* a shift of spectral lines toward the blue end of the visible spectrum of the light emitted by an approaching celestial body; thought to be a consequence of the Doppler effect of red shift.

**blue skin** /ˈ– skɪn/, *n.* a tree, *Acacia irrorata,* common in New South Wales.

**blue spruce** /– ˈsprus/, *n.* →**balsam spruce.**

**bluestocking** /ˈblustɒkɪŋ/, *n.* **1.** a woman who devotes herself to intellectual pursuits to the exclusion of other interests as fashion, social life, etc. **2.** a member of the mid-18th century London literary circle. *–adj.* **3.** of or pertaining to literary or intellectual women. [so called because members of this group (def. 2) wore blue woollen instead of formal black silk stockings]

**bluestone** /ˈblustoʊn/, *n.* **1.** →**blue vitriol. 2.** a bluish argillaceous sandstone used for building purposes, flagging, etc. **3.** →**basalt.**

**blue streak** /blu ˈstrik/, *n. Colloq.* something moving very fast.

**blue swimmer** /– ˈswɪmə/, *n.* an edible Australian crab, *Portunus pelagicus,* of blue-green colour and capable of powerful sustained swimming; sandcrab. Also, **blue swimmer crab, blue manna.**

**bluesy** /ˈbluzi/, *adj.* of or pertaining to music in a blues style.

**blue thistle** /– ˈθɪsəl/, *n.* any of several species of *Eryngium,* family Umbelliferae, rigid spiny plants resembling thistles.

**blue-throated parrot fish,** *n.* →**bluenose.**

**bluetit** /ˈblutɪt/, *n.* a species of titmouse with a blue patch on the head and blue wingtips.

**blue-tongue** /ˈblu-tʌŋ/, *n.* **1.** Also, **blue-tongue lizard.** any of several large, stout-bodied Australian skinks of the genus *Tiliqua,* as the common *T. scincoides,* which are harmless but display their broad blue tongues in a threatening manner when disturbed. **2.** →**rouseabout.**

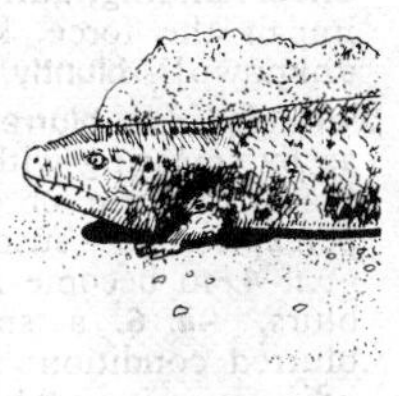
blue-tongue lizard

**blue top** /ˈblu tɒp/, *n.* **1.** →**purple top. 2.** *Chiefly Qld.* →**billygoat weed.**

**blue triangle** /ˌblu ˈtraɪæŋgəl/, *n.* a common, beautiful, swallowtail butterfly, *Graphium sarpedon,* found in eastern Australia and in various parts of Asia. Also, **blue fanny.**

**blue vein** /ˈ– veɪn/, *n.* a type of semi-soft ripened cheese with blue-green veins of *Penicillium* mould culture throughout the ripened curd.

**blue vitriol** /– ˈvɪtriəl/, *n.* sulphate of copper, $CuSo_4 \cdot 5H_2O$, a compound occurring in large, transparent, deep blue triclinic crystals, used in calico printing, medicine, etc. Also, **bluestone.**

**blue water sailing,** *n.* ocean sailing as opposed to sailing in enclosed or sheltered waters.

**blue weed** /ˈ– wid/, *n.* **1.** →**viper's bugloss. 2.** a perennial plant, *Helianthus ciliaris,* of south-western United States which has become a weed of wheatfields in Australia.

**blue whale** /– ˈweɪl/, *n.* a rorqual, *Sibbaldus musculus,* of northern and southern oceans, with yellowish underparts, the largest mammal that has ever lived; sulphur-bottom.

**blue-winged teal** /ˌblu-wɪŋd ˈtil/, *n.* a small pond and river duck, *Anas discors,* of North America, with greyish blue patches on the wings.

**blue wren** /ˈblu rɛn/, *n.* See **wren** (def. 1).

**bluey** /ˈblui/, *adj.* **1.** somewhat blue; bluish. *–n.* **2.** →**swag**[2] (def. 1). **3.** *Colloq.* (a nickname for a red-headed person). **4.** *Colloq.* a summons in law. **5.** →**blue swimmer. 6.** *Qld.* →**rainbow lorikeet. 7.** a slimy, so called because of the bluish-black spots on the anterior parapodia which emerge first as the worm comes out of the sand.

**bluff**[1] /blʌf/, *adj.* **1.** somewhat abrupt and unconventional in manner; hearty; frank. **2.** presenting a bold and nearly perpendicular front, as a coastline. **3.** *Naut.* (of a ship) presenting a broad, flattened front. *–n.* **4.** a cliff, headland, or hill with a broad, steep face. [probably from LG *blaf* flat] – **bluffly,** *adv.* – **bluffness,** *n.*

**bluff**[2] /blʌf/, *v.t.,* **1.** to mislead by presenting a bold front. **2.** to gain by bluffing: *he bluffed his way.* **3.** *Poker.* to deceive by a show of confidence in the strength of one's cards. **4.** **call one's bluff,** to challenge or expose someone's bluff. *–v.i.* **5.** to mislead someone by presenting a bold front. *–n.* **6.** an act of bluffing. **7.** one who bluffs. [orig. uncert.] – **bluffer,** *n.*

**bluing** /ˈbluɪŋ/, *n.* **1.** *Chiefly U.S.* →**blue** (def. 3). **2.** →**blueing.**

**bluish** /ˈbluɪʃ/, *adj.* somewhat blue. Also, **blueish.** – **bluishness,** *n.*

**blunder** /ˈblʌndə/, *n.* **1.** a gross or stupid mistake. *–v.i.* **2.** to move or act blindly, stupidly, or without direction or steady guidance. **3.** to make a gross or stupid mistake, esp. through mental confusion. **4.** *Horseracing.* (of a horse) to lose the rhythm of galloping. *–v.t.* **5.** to bungle; botch. **6.** to utter thoughtlessly; blurt out. [ME *blondren,* from Scand.; cf. OSw. *blundra*] – **blunderer,** *n.* – **blunderingly,** *adv.*

**blunderbuss** /ˈblʌndəbʌs/, *n.* **1.** a short musket of wide bore with expanded muzzle to scatter shot, bullets, or slugs at close range. **2.** a stupid blundering person. [alteration of D *donderbus,* from *donder* thunder + *buss* gun, orig. box]

**blunge** /blʌndʒ/, *v.t.,* **blunged, blunging.** *Pottery.* to mix (clay or the like) with water, forming a liquid suspension. [b. BLEND and PLUNGE]

**blunger** /ˈblʌndʒə/, *n.* **1.** one who or that which blunges. **2.** a piece of machinery designed for blunging.

blunderbuss

**blunt** /blʌnt/, *adj.* **1.** having an obtuse, thick, or dull edge or tip; rounded; not sharp. **2.** abrupt in address or manner; forthright; plain-spoken. **3.** slow in perception or understanding; dull. *–v.t.* **4.** to make blunt. **5.** to weaken or impair the force, keenness, or susceptibility of. [ME; orig. unknown] – **bluntly,** *adv.* – **bluntness,** *n.*

**blur** /blɜ/, *v.,* **blurred, blurring,** *n.* *–v.t.* **1.** to obscure or sully as by smearing with ink, etc. **2.** to obscure by making confused in form or outline; make indistinct. **3.** to dim the perception or susceptibility of; make dull or insensible. *–v.i.* **4.** to become indistinct: *the vision blurred.* **5.** to make blurs. *–n.* **6.** a smudge or smear which obscures. **7.** a blurred condition; indistinctness. [? akin to BLEAR] – **blurry,** *adj.*

**blurb** /blɜb/, *n.* an announcement or advertisement, usu. an effusively laudatory one, esp. on the jacket flap of a book or the cover of a record. [coined by Gelett Burgess, 1866-1951, American humorist and illustrator]

**blurt** /blɜt/, *v.t.* **1.** to utter suddenly or inadvertently; divulge unadvisedly (usu. fol. by *out*). *–n.* **2.** an abrupt utterance. [? imitative]

**blurter** /ˈblɜtə/, *n. Colloq.* the anus.

**blush** /blʌʃ/, *v.i.* **1.** to redden as from embarrassment, shame, or modesty. **2.** to feel shame (*at, for,* etc.). **3.** (of the sky, flowers, etc.) to become rosy. *–v.t.* **4.** to make red; flush. **5.** to make known by a blush. *–n.* **6.** a reddening, as of the face. **7.** a rosy or pinkish tinge. **8. at the first blush,** at first sight. *–adj.* **9.** pale pink. [ME *blusche(n),* OE *blyscan* redden] – **blusher,** *n.* – **blushful,** *adj.* – **blushless,** *adj.* – **blushingly,** *adv.*

**blusher** /ˈblʌʃə/, *n.* a brush-on rouge.

**bluster** /ˈblʌstə/, *v.i.* **1.** to roar and be tumultuous, as wind. **2.** to be loud, noisy, or swaggering; utter loud, empty menaces or protests. *–v.t.* **3.** to force or accomplish by blustering. *–n.* **4.** boisterous noise and violence. **5.** noisy, empty menaces or protests; inflated talk. [cf. Icel. *blāstr* blowing] – **blusterer,** *n.* – **blusteringly,** *adv.* – **blustery, blusterous,** *adj.*

**Blvd,** boulevard.

**B.M.E.,** **1.** Also, **B.Mech.E.** Bachelor of Mechanical Engineering. **2.** Bachelor of Mining Engineering.

**B.Mus.** /bi ˈmʌs/, Bachelor of Music.

**bn,** battalion.

**BO** /bi ˈoʊ/, *n. Colloq.* body odour, esp. due to excessive perspiration.

**boa** /ˈboʊə/, *n., pl.* **boas.** **1.** any of various non-venomous snakes of the family Boidae, notable for their vestiges of hind limbs, as the boa constrictor of the American tropics. **2.** a long, snake-shaped wrap of silk, feathers, or other material, worn about the neck by women. [L]

**boab** /ˈboʊæb/, *n.* →**baobab.**

**boa constrictor** /boʊə kənˈstrɪktə/, *n.* **1.** a boa, *Constrictor constrictor,* of Central and South America, noted for its size and crushing power. **2.** any large python or other snake of the boa family.

**boar** /bɔ/, *n.* **1.** an uncastrated male pig. **2.** a wild boar. [ME *boor,* OE *bār*]

**board** /bɔd/, *n.* **1.** a piece of timber sawn thin, and of considerable length and breadth compared with the thickness. **2.** (*pl.*) *Theat.* the stage. **3.** Also, **shearing board. a.** the floor of a woolshed. **b.** the shearers employed in a woolshed. **4.** the killing floor of a meatworks. **5.** a flat slab of wood for some specific purpose: *an ironing-board, jigger board.* **6.** *Squash.* a band of wood, tin or other resonating material 60 cm high across the base of the front wall. **7.** a sheet of wood, paper, etc., with or without markings, for some special use: *a chess-board.* **8.** a blackboard. **9.** stiff cardboard covered with paper, cloth, or the like, to form the binding for a book. **10.** a table, esp. to serve food on. **11.** daily meals, esp. as provided for pay. **12.** an official body of persons who direct or supervise some activity: *a board of directors, board of trade.* **13.** the border or edge of anything, as in *seaboard.* **14.** *Naut.* **a.** the side of a ship. **b.** one leg, or tack, of the course of a ship beating to windward. **15. across the board,** in a comprehensive fashion. **16. by the board,** over the ship's side. **17. go by the board,** to be discarded, neglected or destroyed. **18. on board,** on or in a ship, aeroplane, or vehicle. **19. sweep the board,** (of gambling, esp. cards) to win all. *–v.t.* **20.** to cover or close with boards. **21.** to furnish with food, or with food and lodging, esp. for pay. **22.** to arrange for the furnishing of meals and lodging to (sometimes fol. by *out*). **23.** to go on board of or enter (a ship, train, etc.). **24.** to come up alongside of (a ship), as to attack or to go on board. **25.** to approach; accost. *–v.i.* **26.** to take one's meals, or be supplied with food and lodging at a fixed price. **27. board out,** *Mil.* to discharge or retire a (serviceman) on medical grounds. [OE *bord* board, table, shield.]

**board boy** /ˈbɔd bɔɪ/, *n.* a shedhand.

**boarder** /ˈbɔdə/, *n.* **1.** one who is supplied with meals and lodging. **2.** a pupil at a boarding school. **3.** a person chosen to board an enemy ship.

**board foot** /ˈbɔd fʊt/, *n.* →**superficial foot.**

**boardie** /ˈbɔdi/, *n.* an enthusiast for the sport of surfboard riding.

**boarding** /ˈbɔdɪŋ/, *n.* **1.** wooden boards collectively. **2.** a structure of boards, as in a fence or a floor.

**boarding house** /ˈ– haʊs/, *n.* a place, usu. a home, at which board is furnished, often with lodging.

**boarding school** /ˈ– skul/, *n.* a school at which board and lodging are furnished for the pupils.

**board lump** /ˈbɔd lʌmp/, *n.* a lump on the leg which a surfer may develop from continued board riding. Also, **board bump.**

**board of reference,** *n.* a committee appointed to deal with industrial disputes arising from a particular award.

**boardroom** /ˈbɔdrum/, *n.* a room in which a board (def. 12) meets to carry out a business.

**board rule** /ˈbɔd rul/, *n.* a measuring device having scales for finding the cubic contents of a board without calculation.

**board shorts** /ˈ– ʃɔts/, *n. pl.* shorts with an extended leg, originally designed to protect surfers against waxed surfboards.

**boarfish** /ˈbɔfɪʃ/, *n.* any of various fishes of different genera which have a projecting snout, as *Pentaceropsis recurvirostris,* found in deep waters around Australia.

**boarhound** /ˈbɔhaʊnd/, *n.* any of various large dogs used originally for hunting wild boars, esp. a dog of a German breed (**German boarhound**) or a Great Dane.

**boarish** /ˈbɔrɪʃ/, *adj.* swinish; sensual; cruel.

**boast**[1] /boʊst/, *v.i.* **1.** to speak exaggeratedly and objectionably, esp. about oneself. **2.** to speak with pride (fol. by *of*). *–v.t.* **3.** to speak of with excessive pride, vanity, or exultation. **4.** to be proud in the possession of: *the town boasts a new school.* **5.** *Squash.* to cause the ball to bounce off a side wall on its way to the front court wall. *–n.* **6.** a thing boasted of. **7.** exaggerated or objectionable speech; bragging. [ME *bosten;* orig. unknown] – **boaster,** *n.* – **boastingly,** *adv.*

**boast**[2] /boʊst/, *v.t.* to dress or shape (stone, etc.) roughly. [orig. uncert.]

**boaster** /ˈboʊstə/, *n.* a steel chisel with a 50mm cutting edge for boasting.

**boastful** /ˈboʊstfəl/, *adj.* given to or characterised by boasting. – **boastfully,** *adv.* – **boastfulness,** *n.*

**boat** /boʊt/, *n.* **1.** a vessel for transport by water, constructed to provide buoyancy by excluding water and shaped to give stability and permit propulsion. **2.** a small ship, generally for specialised use. **3.** a small vessel carried for use by a large one. **4.** *Colloq.* a ship. **5.** an open dish resembling a boat: *a gravy boat.* **6. in the same boat,** faced with the same circumstances, esp. unfortunate ones. **7. burn one's boats,** to commit oneself; make an irrevocable decision. *–v.i.* **8.** to go in a boat. *–v.t.* **9.** to transport in a boat. [ME *boot,* OE *bāt,* c. Icel. *beit*]

**boatbill** /ˈboʊtbɪl/, *n.* a bird of the genus *Cochlearius,* of the heron family, containing the single species *C. cochlearius,* of tropical America.

**boat-deck** /ˈboʊt-dɛk/, *n.* the top deck of a ship where the small boats are carried.

**boat drill** /ˈboʊt drɪl/, *n.* a practising of procedures for entering life-boats undertaken by the crew and passengers of a ship.

**boatel** /boʊˈtɛl/, *n.* a motel near navigable water which provides accommodation for boats as well as their owners' motor vehicles.

**boater** /ˈboʊtə/, *n.* **1.** one who is boating. **2.** a straw hat with a flat hard brim.

**boatful** /ˈboʊtfʊl/, *n.* as much as a boat will hold.

**boathook** /ˈboʊthʊk/, *n.* a metal hook fixed to a pole, for pulling or pushing a boat.

**boathouse** /ˈboʊthaʊs/, *n.* a house or shed for sheltering boats. Also, **boatshed.**

**boatie** /ˈboʊti/, *n.* a person who owns and runs a small craft.

**boating** /ˈboʊtɪŋ/, *n.* the use of boats, esp. for pleasure.

**boatload** /ˈboʊtloʊd/, *n.* **1.** the cargo that a vessel carries. **2.** the cargo that a vessel is capable of carrying.

**boatman** /ˈboʊtmən/, *n., pl.* **-men.** a person skilled in the use of small craft. – **boatmanship,** *n.*

**boat people** /ˈboʊt pipəl/, *n.* refugees from South-East Asia, setting out for Malaysia, Hong Kong or Australia by boat.

**boatrace** /ˈboʊtreɪs/, *n.* **1.** a race between rowing boats. **2.** *Colloq.* a competition between teams of beer drinkers to see which team can drink its beer the fastest; a drinking competition. **3.** *Horseracing.* a race in which the result is predetermined or rigged. **4.** *Colloq.* any situation in which the outcome has been secretly secured. Also, **boat race.**

**boatswain** /ˈboʊsən/, *n.* a warrant officer on a warship, or a petty officer on a merchant vessel, in charge of rigging, anchors, cables, etc. Also, **bo's'n, bosun.** [OE *bātswegen* boatman]

**boatswain's chair** /boʊsənz ˈtʃɛə/, *n. Naut.* →**cradle** (def. 5). Also, **bosun's chair.**

**boattail** /ˈboʊtteɪl/, *n.* the conical section of a ballistic body that progressively decreases in diameter towards the tail to reduce overall aerodynamic drag.

**boat-train** /ˈboʊt-treɪn/, *n.* a train making connection with a ship.

**bob**[1] /bɒb/, *n., v.,* **bobbed, bobbing.** *–n.* **1.** a short jerky motion: *a bob of the head.* **2.** a quick curtsy. **3.** *Mining.* the beam of a pumping engine. *–v.t.* **4.** to move quickly down and up: *to bob the head.* **5.** to indicate with such a motion: *to bob a greeting.* *–v.i.* **6.** to make a jerky motion with head or body. **7.** to curtsy. **8.** to move up and down with a bouncing motion, as a boat. **9.** to rise to the surface or into view suddenly or jerkily (fol. by *up*). **10.** to arrive, happen (fol. by *up*): *look who's bobbed up now!* **11.** to move about with jerky motions. [ME: orig. uncert.]

**bob**[2] /bɒb/, *n., v.,* **bobbed, bobbing.** *–n.* **1.** a style of short haircut for women and children. **2.** a horse's tail cut short. **3.** a small dangling or terminal object, as the weight on a pendulum or a plumbline. **4.** *Poetry.* **a.** a short line either at the end of a stanza or followed by a wheel (see **bob and wheel**). **b.** a short-lined refrain or burden. **5.** *Angling.* **a.** a knot of worms, rags, etc., on a string. **b.** a float for a fishing line. **6.** *Colloq.* a bunch; a cluster. **7.** a bobsleigh or one of its runners. *–v.t.* **8.** to cut short; dock. *–v.i.* **9.** *Angling.* to fish with a bob. [ME *bobbe* bunch, cluster, knob; orig. obscure]

**bob**[3] /bɒb/, *n., v.,* **bobbed, bobbing.** *–n.* **1.** a tap; light blow. *–v.t.* **2.** to tap; strike lightly. [ME *bobben*; ? imitative.]

**bob**[4] /bɒb/, *n. Colloq.* **1.** (formerly) a shilling. **2.** *Convict Obs. Colloq.* a flogging of fifty lashes. See **tester**[3], **bull**[2], **canary**[2]. [orig. uncert.]

**bob**[5] /bɒb/, *n. Bellringing.* a name given to a set of changes rung on six (**bob minor**), eight (**bob major**), ten (**bob royal**), or twelve (**bob maximus**) bells.

**bob and wheel,** *n. Poetry.* a short line (the bob) followed by a group of longer lines (the wheel) usu. at the end of a stanza.

**bobber** /ˈbɒbə/, *n.* **1.** one who or that which bobs. **2.** a fishing bob.

**bobberie** /ˈbɒbəri/, *n. Colloq.* commotion; fuss.

**bobbin** /ˈbɒbən/, *n.* a reel, cylinder, or spool upon which yarn or thread is wound, as used in spinning, machine sewing, etc. [F *bobine,* from *bobiner* to wind up]

**bobbinet** /bɒbəˈnɛt/, *n.* lacelike fabric of hexagonal mesh, made on a lace machine. [var. of *bobbin-net,* from BOBBIN + NET[1]]

**bobbin lace** /ˈbɒbən ˌleɪs/, *n.* lace made by hand with bobbins of thread, the threads being twisted round pins stuck into a pattern placed on a pillow.

**bobble** /ˈbɒbəl/, *n.* **1.** a small pendant ball, usu. of wool, for trimming scarves or other garments. **2.** any small ball which dangles or bobs.

**bobby**[1] /ˈbɒbi/, *n., pl.* **-ies.** *Colloq.* a policeman. [special use of *Bobby,* for Sir *Robert* Peel]

**bobby**[2] /ˈbɒbi/, *n. Chiefly W.A. Colloq.* **1.** a small beer glass. **2.** the contents of such a glass. [Brit. d. *bobby* small]

**bobby calf** /ˈ– kaf/, *n.* a young calf for slaughter as veal. [BOBBY[2] + CALF]

**bobby-dazzler** /bɒbi-ˈdæzlə/, *n. Colloq.* an excellent thing or person: *you little bobby-dazzler.* Also, **ruby-dazzler.**

**bobby lizard** /ˈ– ˌlɪzəd/, *n.* →**stump-tailed skink.**

**bobby pin** /ˈ– pɪn/, *n.* a metal hairpin with two slender prongs which clamp together in order to hold the hair; hairgrip.

**bobbysocks** /ˈbɒbisɒks/, *n.pl. Chiefly U.S. Colloq.* ankle-socks, esp. as worn by young girls.

**bobbysoxer** /ˈbɒbisɒksə/, *n. Chiefly U.S. Colloq.* an adolescent or teenage girl.

**bobby veal** /ˈbɒbi vil/, *n.* →**stirk veal.**

**bobcat** /ˈbɒbkæt/, *n.* **1.** an American wildcat, esp. the species *Lynx rufus,* which is widespread in the U.S. **2.** a small, rubber-tyred, four-wheeled loader used in underground and trench work.

**Bob Hope** /bɒb ˈhoʊp/, *n. Colloq.* **1.** soap. **2.** dope. [rhyming slang]

**Bob Munro** /ˌbɒb mənˈroʊ/, *n. in the phrase* **in you go says Bob Munro,** *N.Z. Colloq.* (an expression of encouragement addressed to someone entering upon some enterprise; a toast).

**bobolink** /ˈbɒbəlɪŋk/, *n.* a common North American passerine songbird, *Dolichonyx oryzivorus,* which winters in South America. [short for *Bob o' Lincoln,* supposed to be the bird's call]

bobolink

**bobsled** /ˈbɒbslɛd/, *n., v.,* **-sledded, -sledding.** →**bobsleigh.**

**bobsleigh** /ˈbɒbsleɪ/, *n.* **1.** a racing sledge carrying two or more people, having two sets of runners, one at the back and one at the front. **2.** (formerly) a sleigh formed of two short sledges coupled one behind the other. **3.** either of these two short sledges. *–v.i.* **4.** to ride on a bobsleigh. [BOB[2] + SLEIGH]

**bobstay** /ˈbɒbsteɪ/, *n. Naut.* a rope, chain, or rod from the outer end of the bowsprit to the cutwater, holding the bowsprit in.

**bobsy-die** /ˌbɒbzɪ-ˈdaɪ/, *n. Colloq.* **1.** a fuss; panic. **2.** boisterous merriment: *kick up bobsy-die.* [Brit. d. *bobs-a-dying*]

**bob's your uncle,** *interj.* **1.** (also as a response in conversation expressing compliance) it's all right; there you are. **2.** (as a response to a statement which proves nothing) so what?

**bobtail** /ˈbɒbteɪl/, *n.* **1.** a short or docked tail. **2.** a bobtailed animal. *–adj.* **3.** bobtailed; cut short. *–v.t.* **4.** to cut short the tail of; dock.

**bobtail lizard** /– ˈlɪzəd/, *n.* →**stump-tailed skink.**

**bobuck** /ˈboʊbʌk/, *n.* a species of eastern Australian phalanger, *Trichosurus caninus,* inhabiting high country and closely related to the common brush-tailed possum, *T. vulpecula;* mountain possum.

**bobwig** /ˈbɒbwɪg/, *n.* a short curled wig.

**bocce** /ˈbɒtʃeɪ/, *n.* an Italian form of the game of bowls, played out of doors.

**boche** /bɒʃ/, *n. Colloq.* (*offensive*) a German. Also, **Boche.** [F, ? alteration of F *caboche* head, pate, noodle, from d. stem *cab-,* from L *caput* head]

**bock beer** /ˈbɒk bɪə/, *n.* a strong, dark German beer. Also, **bock.** [G *Bockbier,* for *Eimbocker Bier* beer of Eimbock, or Einbeck, in Lower Saxony]

**bocking** /ˈbɒkɪŋ/, *n.* a coarse woollen fabric, resembling baize, formerly used as a floor-covering. [named after *Bocking,* a village in England]

**boco**[1] /ˈboʊkoʊ/, *n. Colloq.* →**boko**[1].

**boco**[2] /ˈboʊkoʊ/, *n.* →**boko**[2].

**bod** /bɒd/, *n. Colloq.* a person: *an odd bod.* [short for BODY]

**bode**[1] /boʊd/, *v.,* **boded, boding.** *–v.t.* **1.** to be an omen of; portend. **2.** *Archaic.* to announce beforehand; predict. *–v.i.* **3.** to portend. [ME *boden,* OE *bodian* announce, foretell, from *boda* messenger] – **bodement,** *n.*

**bode**[2] /boʊd/, *v.* past tense and past participle of **bide** (def. 2).

**bodega** /bəˈdeɪgə, -ˈdigə/, *n.* **1.** a storehouse for wine, esp. one which is above ground. **2.** a wineshop, esp. one which also sells groceries. **3.** a wine bar. [Sp, from L *apothēca,* from Gk *apothḗkē* storehouse]

**bodgie**[1] /ˈbɒdʒi/, *adj., n., v.,* **bodgied, bodgying,** *Colloq.* –*adj.* **1.** inferior; worthless. **2.** (of names) false; assumed. –*n.* **3.** a worthless person. **4.** a person who has assumed an alias or who is in some way acting under false pretences. **5.** an alias. –*v.t.* **6.** to repair superficially; to remove temporarily any obvious defects (fol. by *up*). Also, **bodger.** [Obs. Brit. *bodge* to patch or mend clumsily]

**bodgie**[2] /ˈbɒdʒi/, *n. Colloq.* esp. in the 1950s, one of a group of young men usu. dressed in an extreme fashion and given to wild or exuberant behaviour.

**bodhisattva** /bɒdəˈsætvə/, *n. Buddhism.* an enlightened being who delays entry into nirvana in order to help others to attain enlightenment. [Skt: enlightened being]

**bodice** /ˈbɒdəs/, *n.* **1.** the fitted upper part of or body of a woman's dress. **2.** an undergarment covering the upper part of the body, usu. of a warm material, worn by very young girls. **3.** a woman's laced outer garment covering the waist and bust, common in peasant dress. **4.** *Obs.* stays or a corset. [var. of *bodies,* pl. of BODY]

**bodiless** /ˈbɒdiləs/, *adj.* having no body or material form; incorporeal.

**bodily** /ˈbɒdəli/, *adj.* **1.** of or pertaining to the body. **2.** corporeal or material, in contrast with spiritual or mental. –*adv.* **3.** as a whole; without taking apart.

**boding** /ˈboʊdɪŋ/, *n.* **1.** a foreboding; omen. –*adj.* **2.** foreboding; ominous. – **bodingly,** *adv.*

**bodkin** /ˈbɒdkən/, *n.* **1.** a small pointed instrument for making holes in cloth, etc. **2.** a blunt needle-like instrument for drawing tape, cord, etc., through a loop, hem, or the like. **3.** a long pin-shaped instrument used by women to fasten up the hair. **4.** *Obs.* a small dagger; a stiletto. [ME *boydekin* dagger; orig. unknown]

**Bodoni** /bəˈdoʊni/, *n. Print.* a style of type. [named after Giambattista *Bodoni,* 1740-1813, Italian printer, who originally designed it]

**body** /ˈbɒdi/, *n., pl.* **bodies,** *v.,* **bodied, bodying,** *adj.* –*n.* **1.** the physical structure of an animal (and sometimes, of a plant) living or dead. **2.** a corpse; carcass. **3.** the trunk or main mass of a thing. **4.** *Zool.* the physical structure of an animal minus limbs and head. **5.** *Archit.* the central structure of a building, esp. the nave of a church; the major mass of a building. **6.** a vehicle minus wheels and other appendages. **7.** *Naut.* the hull of a ship. **8.** *Aeron.* the fuselage of an aeroplane. **9.** *Print.* the shank of a type, supporting the face. **10.** *Geom.* a figure having the dimensions, length, breadth, and thickness; a solid. **11.** *Physics.* anything having inertia; a mass. **12.** any of the larger visible spherical objects in space, as a sun, moon, or planet: *heavenly bodies.* **13.** the major portion of an army, population, etc. **14.** the central part of a speech or document, minus introduction, conclusion, indexes, etc. **15.** *Colloq.* a person. **16.** *Law.* the physical person of an individual. **17.** a collective group, or an artificial person: *body politic, body corporate.* **18.** a number of things or people taken together. **19.** consistency or density; substance; strength as opposed to thinness: *wine of a good body.* **20.** matter or physical substance (as opposed to *spirit* or *soul*). **21.** that part of a dress which covers the trunk, or the trunk above the waist. **22.** *Agric.* the quality possessed by wool when the staple appears full and bulky. **23. keep body and soul together,** to remain alive. –*v.t.* **24.** to invest with or as with a body. **25.** to represent in bodily form (usu. fol. by *forth*). –*adj.* **26.** *Print.* (of printed matter) used mainly for the text, generally less than 14 point (as distinguished from *display matter*). [ME; OE *bodig,* c. MHG *potih*] – **bodied,** *adj.*

**body blow** /ˈ– bloʊ/, *n.* **1.** *Boxing.* a blow to an opponent's body between the breastbone and the waistline. **2.** a serious (but not decisive) setback or defect.

**body building** /ˈ– bɪldɪŋ/, *n.* the performance of regular exercises designed to increase the power and size of the body's muscles.

**body carpet** /ˈ– kapət/, *n.* wall-to-wall carpet.

**body cavity** /ˈ– kævəti/, *n. Zool., Anat., etc.* the general or common cavity of the body, as distinguished from special cavities or those of particular organs.

**body-centred** /ˈbɒdi-ˌsɛntəd/, *adj.* (of a crystal structure) having atomic or ionic centres at the midpoint of each cubic cell, as at the corners. Cf. **face-centred.**

**bodycheck** /ˈbɒditʃɛk/, *n.* **1.** *Lacrosse, Ice Hockey, etc.* the act of placing oneself between an opponent and his objective. **2.** *Wrestling.* the act of striking or stopping a moving opponent with the whole body. –*v.i.* **3.** to perform a bodycheck. –*v.t.* **4.** to obstruct.

**body colour** /ˈbɒdi kʌlə/, *n.* →**gouache.**

**body corporate** /– ˈkɔpərət/, *n.* **1.** *Law.* a person, association or group of persons legally incorporated in a corporation. **2.** the governing body of a block of home units consisting of the home unit owners or their representatives.

**bodyguard** /ˈbɒdigad/, *n.* **1.** a personal or private guard, as for a high official. **2.** a retinue; escort.

**body language** /ˈbɒdi læŋgwɪdʒ/, *n.* →**paralinguistics.**

**bodyline bowling** /ˌbɒdilaɪn ˈboʊlɪŋ/, *n.* a style of fast bowling pitched consistently at the leg side of the batsman so as to appear to be aimed at the body. [coined by J. Worrell, cricketer-turned-writer, to describe English bowling attack in 1932-33 Test]

**body matter** /ˈbɒdi ˌmætə/, *n. Print.* text matter as distinct from decorative matter.

**body politic** /– ˈpɒlətɪk/, *n.* a people as forming a political body under an organised government.

**body scissors** /ˈ– sɪzəz/, *n Wrestling.* a hold in which a wrestler falls to the canvas and holds both legs around his opponent's body and squeezes.

**body-search** /ˈbɒdi-sɜtʃ/, *n.* a searching of the body, as at airports, seaports, etc., for concealed weapons or other forbidden matter.

**body-servant** /ˈbɒdi-ˌsɜvənt/, *n.* →**valet.**

**body shirt** /ˈbɒdi ʃɜt/, *n.* a shirt shaped to fit the body closely.

**body-shoot** /ˈbɒdi-ʃut/, *v.t.* to shoot (a wave) without the assistance of a surf-board, float, etc.

**body shop** /ˈ– ʃɒp/, *n. Colloq.* an agency for computer programmers.

**body size** /ˈ– saɪz/, *n. Print.* the depth of print as distinct from its type face.

**body-snatching** /ˈbɒdi-ˌsnætʃɪŋ/, *n.* the act of robbing a grave to obtain a body for dissection. – **body-snatcher,** *n.*

**bodystocking** /ˈbɒdistɒkɪŋ/, *n.* a one-piece undergarment for women completely covering the torso. Also, **bodysuit.**

**body-surf** /ˈbɒdi-sɜf/, *v.i.* to engage in body-surfing.

**body-surfing** /ˈbɒdi-ˌsɜfɪŋ/, *n.* →**surfing** (def. 2).

**bodywork** /ˈbɒdiwɜk/, *n.* the outer shell of the body of a vehicle, or its construction.

**Boehm system** /ˈbɜm ˌsɪstəm/, *n.* a system of fingering now widely used for the flute and occasionally the oboe, and also adapted to the clarinet. [invented by Theobald *Boehm,* ? 1793-1881, German flautist and musician]

**Boer** /bɔ/, *n.* **1.** a South African of Dutch extraction. –*adj.* **2.** of or pertaining to the Boers. [D: peasant, countryman. See BOOR]

**boffin** /ˈbɒfən/, *n. Colloq.* a person who is enthusiastic for and knowledgeable in any pursuit, activity, study, etc., esp. a research scientist.

**Bofors gun** /ˈboʊfəz gʌn/, *n.* an automatic anti-aircraft gun. [named after *Bofors,* town in S Sweden, where it was first made]

**bog** /bɒg/, *n., v.,* **bogged, bogging.** –*n.* **1.** wet, spongy ground, with soil composed mainly of decayed vegetable matter. **2.** an area or stretch of such ground. **3.** *Colloq.* defecation. **4.** a lavatory or latrine. –*v.t., v.i.* **5.** to sink in or as in a bog (oft. fol. by *down*). **6.** to defecate. **7. bog in,** *Colloq.* to eat voraciously. [Irish or Gaelic: soft] – **boggish,** *adj.* – **boggy,** *adj.*

**bogan flea** /boʊgən ˈfli/, *n.* the small barbed fruit of the daisy *Calotis hispidula.*

**Bogan gate** /boʊgən ˈgeɪt/, *n.* a gate roughly constructed from droppers and fencing wire.

**bogey**[1] /ˈboʊgi/, *n., pl.* **bogies.** *Golf.* **1.** the number of strokes a good player may be reckoned to need to play a certain hole; a score of one over par. *–v.t.* **2.** to score a bogey. [from *The Bogey Man,* a popular song c. 1908, thought of as a feared and invincible opponent]

**bogey**[2] /ˈboʊgi/, *n.* →**bogie**[2].

**bog-eye** /ˈbɒg-aɪ/, *n.* →**bogghi.**

**bogeyhole** /ˈboʊgiˌhoʊl/, *n.,* →**bogie**[2] (def. 2).

**boggabri** /ˈbɒgəbraɪ/, *n.* any of several rather weedy herbs of inland Australia, as fat-hen.

**bogghi** /ˈbɒgaɪ/, *n.* **1.** (formerly) the handpiece of clippers used in shearing sheep. **2.** the shears themselves. Also, **boggi, bog-eye.**

**boggi** /ˈbɒgaɪ/, *n.* →**bogghi.**

**boggle**[1] /ˈbɒgəl/, *v.,* **-gled, -gling,** *n.* *–v.i.* **1.** to take alarm; start with fright. **2.** to hesitate, as if afraid to proceed; waver; shrink. **3.** to dissemble; equivocate. **4.** to be awkward; bungle. *–n.* **5.** the act of shying or taking alarm. **6.** *Colloq.* bungle; botch. [? special use of BOGGLE[2]] – **boggler,** *n.*

**boggle**[2] /ˈbɒgəl/, *n.* →**bogle.**

**boghouse** /ˈbɒghaʊs/, *n. Colloq.* a toilet, esp. an outside toilet.

**bogie**[1] /ˈboʊgi/, *n.* **1.** a low truck or trolley. **2.** one of a pair of pivoted trucks supporting a railway locomotive, carriage, tram, etc. [? var. of BOGY]

**bogie**[2] /ˈboʊgi/, *n., Colloq.* **1.** a swim or bath. **2.** a swimming hole. Also, **bogey.** [Aboriginal]

**bogie**[3] /ˈboʊgi/, *n. Colloq.* →**snot** (def. 1). Also, **bogey.**

**bogie cattle wagon,** *n.* a railway van used to carry cattle, horses, camels. *Abbrev:* b.c.w.

**bogie sheep van,** *n.* a railway van used to carry sheep. *Abbrev:* b.s.v.

**bog-Irish** /bɒg-ˈaɪrɪʃ/, *n. Colloq.* an uneducated, ignorant Irishman.

**bogle** /ˈboʊgəl, ˈbɒgəl/, *n.* a bogy; a spectre. Also, **boggle.** [from obs. *bog,* var. of BUG bugbear]

**bog moss** /ˈbɒg mɒs/, *n.* →**sphagnum.**

**bog myrtle** /– ˈmɜtl/, *n.* an aromatic marsh shrub, *Myrica gale;* sweet gale.

**bog oak** /– ˈoʊk/, *n.* oak (or other wood) preserved in peat bogs.

**bogong** /ˈboʊgɒŋ/, *n.* an Australian noctuid moth, *Agrostis infusa.* Also, **bugong.** [Aboriginal]

**bog-rush** /ˈbɒg-rʌʃ/, *n.* any of several plants of the genus *Schoenus,* found in damp places.

**bog spavin** /ˈbɒg spævən/, *n.* a swelling on the hock joint of a horse. See **spavin.**

**bogtrotter** /ˈbɒgtrɒtə/, *n.* **1.** one who lives among bogs. **2.** *Colloq.* (*derog.*) a rural Irishman. **3.** *Colloq.* an itinerant labourer.

**bogus** /ˈboʊgəs/, *adj.* counterfeit; spurious; sham. [orig. uncert.]

**bogy** /ˈboʊgi/, *n., pl.* **bogies. 1.** a hobgoblin; evil spirit. **2.** anything that haunts, frightens or annoys one. **3.** *Mil. Colloq.* an unidentified aircraft. Also, **bogey, bogie.** [from obs. *bog.* See BOGLE]

**bogyman** /ˈboʊgimæn, ˈbugimæn/, *n.* →**bogy** (defs 1 and 2).

**bohemia** /boʊˈhimiə/, *n.* a social milieu in which a bohemian atmosphere is prevalent. [from *Bohemia,* a province of Czechoslovakia, regarded as the home of the gipsies]

**bohemian** /boʊˈhimiən/, *n.* **1.** (*cap.*) a native or inhabitant of Bohemia (a region in western Czechoslovakia). **2.** (*cap.*) the Czech language. **3.** a person with artistic or intellectual tendencies or pretensions who lives and acts without regard for conventional rules of behaviour. **4.** a gipsy. *–adj.* **5.** (*cap.*) pertaining to Bohemia, its people, or their language. **6.** pertaining to or characteristic of bohemians (def. 3). – **bohemianism,** *n.*

**Bohr theory** /ˈbɔ ˌθɪəri/, *n.* a theory of atomic structure in which the electrons are described as moving in individual orbits about a central nucleus. [named after Niels *Bohr,* 1885-1962, Danish physicist]

**bohunk** /ˈboʊhʌŋk/, *n. U.S. Colloq.* (*derog.*) an unskilled or semiskilled foreign-born labourer, specifically, a Bohemian, Magyar, Slovak, or Croatian. Cf. **hunky**[2].

**boil**[1] /bɔɪl/, *v.i.* **1.** to change from liquid to gaseous state, producing bubbles of gas that rise to the surface of the liquid, agitating it as they rise. **2.** to be in a similarly agitated state: *the sea was boiling.* **3.** to be agitated by angry feeling. **4.** to contain, or be contained in, a liquid that boils: *the pot is boiling, the meat is boiling.* **5.** *Colloq.* to feel very hot. **6. boil down,** to be in essence: *it all boils down to this.* **7. boil over, a.** to overflow while boiling. **b.** to be unable to suppress excitement, anger, etc. **8. boil up,** to make tea. *–v.t.* **9.** to cause to boil. **10.** to cook by boiling. **11.** to separate (sugar, salt, etc.) from something containing it by heat. **12. boil down, a.** to reduce by boiling. **b.** to shorten; abridge. **13. boil the billy,** make tea; have a break. *–n.* **14.** the act of boiling. **15.** the state or condition of boiling. **16.** the agitated flow of silt, etc., into an excavation due to the pressure of water in the surrounding earth. [ME *boile(n),* from OF *boillir,* from L *bullire*]

**boil**[2] /bɔɪl/, *n.* a painful, suppurating, inflammatory sore forming a central core, caused by microbic infection, *Staphylococcus aureus;* a furuncle. [ME *bule,* OE *bȳl,* c. G *Beule*]

**boil-down** /ˈbɔɪl-daʊn/, *n.* the process of boiling to liberate oil, etc.

**boiled shirt** /ˈbɔɪld ʃɜt/, *n. Colloq.* **1.** a white or dress shirt. **2.** a pompous person.

**boiler** /ˈbɔɪlə/, *n.* **1.** a closed vessel together with its furnace, in which steam or other vapour is generated for heating or for driving engines. **2.** a stove or kitchen fire for heating water, or the stove and water tank. **3.** a tank for storing hot water. **4.** a vessel for boiling or heating, esp. a copper one. **5.** a fowl which is or appears to be fit to be eaten only when boiled. **6.** *Colloq.* an old woman.

**boilermaker** /ˈbɔɪləmeɪkə/, *n.* **1.** a tradesman who marks out, develops and fabricates boilers or metal cylinders. **2.** *Colloq.* whisky followed by a beer chaser.

**boilersuit** /ˈbɔɪləsut/, *n.* a one-piece garment of some cheap tough material for rough work.

**boiling-down works** /bɔɪlɪŋ-ˈdaʊn ˌwɜks/, *n.* **1.** a place where old or useless livestock are processed into products as soap, animal food, fertiliser, etc. or where whales, seals, etc., are boiled down to recover their oil. **2.** the equipment for this process.

**boiling point** /ˈbɔɪlɪŋ pɔɪnt/, *n.* **1.** the equilibrium temperature of the liquid and vapour phases of the substance, usu. at a pressure of 101 325 pascals. **2.** the peak of excitement or emotion.

**boiling-water reactor** /bɔɪlɪŋ-ˈwɔtə riˌæktə/, *n.* a type of nuclear reactor in which water is used both as coolant and moderator.

**boilover** /ˈbɔɪloʊvə/, *n.* **1.** a sudden conflict between persons. **2.** *Horseracing. Colloq.* a race won by an outsider.

**boil-up** /ˈbɔɪl-ʌp/, *n. Colloq.* **1.** Also, **brew-up.** a break for tea. **2.** a sudden excitement or conflict.

**boisterous** /ˈbɔɪstrəs/, *adj.* **1.** rough and noisy; clamorous; unrestrained. **2.** (of waves, weather, wind, etc.) rough and stormy. **3.** *Obs.* rough and massive. [ME *boistrous,* earlier *boistous;* orig. unknown] – **boisterously,** *adv.* – **boisterousness,** *n.*

**Bokhara clover** /bəkarə ˈkloʊvə/, *n.* a perennial papilionaceous herb, *Melilotus alba,* native to Europe and western Asia but widely cultivated and naturalised elsewhere.

**Bokmål** /ˈbukmoʊl/, *n.* a literary and urban language of Norway, based on Danish; Dano-Norwegian. Cf. **Nynorsk.**

**boko**[1] /ˈboʊkoʊ/, *n. Colloq.* the nose. Also, **boco.**

**boko**[2] /ˈboʊkoʊ/, *n.* an animal which has lost one eye. Also, **boco.**

**bola** /ˈboʊlə/, *n.* a weapon used by the Indians and Gauchos of southern South America, consisting of two or more heavy balls secured to the ends of one or more strong cords, which entangle the victim at which it is thrown. Also, **bolas.** [Sp.: a ball, from L *bulla* bubble, round object]

**bolar** /ˈboʊlə/, *adj.* of or pertaining to bole or clay.

**bolar blade** /– ˈbleɪd/, *n.* a cut of beef from the blade, usu. used for roasting.

**bold** /boʊld/, *adj.* **1.** not hesitating in the face of actual or possible danger or rebuff. **2.** not hesitating to breach the rules of propriety; forward. **3.** calling for daring, unhesitating action. **4.** overstepping usual bounds or conventions. **5.**

conspicuous to the eye: *bold handwriting.* **6.** steep; abrupt: *a bold promontory.* **7.** a term applied to well-grown wool of good character. **8.** *Print.* (of type, etc.) with heavy lines; in bold face. **9.** *Obs.* trusting; assured. **10. make bold to,** to venture to. [ME; OE *b(e)ald,* c. G *bald*] – **boldly,** *adv.* – **boldness,** *n.*

**bold face** /'– feɪs/, *n. Print.* type that has thick, heavy lines, used for emphasis, etc. – **bold-face,** *adj.*

**bold-faced** /'bouldˌfeɪst/, *adj.* **1.** impudent; brazen. **2.** *Print.* (of type) having thick lines.

**bole**[1] /boʊl/, *n.* the stem or trunk of a tree. [ME, from Scand.; cf. Icel. *bolr*]

**bole**[2] /boʊl/, *n.* **1.** any of several varieties of friable earthy clay usually coloured red by iron oxide and consisting essentially of hydrous silicates of aluminium and less often of magnesium. **2.** a bright red, waxy soil formed by the decomposition of basaltic rocks. [LL *bōlus,* from Gk *bôlos* clod, limp]

**bolection** /boʊ'lɛkʃən/, *n. Archit.* a moulding which projects beyond the surface of the work it decorates. Also, **bilection.** [orig. uncert.]

**bolero** /bə'lɛəroʊ, bə'lɪəroʊ/, *n., pl.* **-ros. 1.** a lively Spanish dance in three-four time. **2.** the music for it. **3.** a short jacket ending above or at the waistline. [Sp.]

**boletus** /boʊ'litəs, bə-/, *n.* any species of the genus *Boletus,* a group of umbrella-shaped mushrooms in which the stratum of tubes on the underside of the cap is easily separable. [L, from Gk *bōlītēs* kind of mushroom]

**bolide** /'boʊlaɪd, -ləd/, *n.* a large, brilliant meteor, esp. one that explodes; a fireball. [F, from L *bolis* large meteor, from Gk: missile]

**Bolivia** /bə'lɪviə/, *n.* a republic in South America. – **Bolivian,** *adj., n.*

**boll** /boʊl/, *n.* a rounded seed vessel or pod of a plant, as of flax or cotton. [var. of BOWL[1]]

**bollard** /'bɒlad/, *n.* **1.** a strong post on a kerb or traffic island used as a protection or to prevent vehicles from mounting pavements. **2.** *Naut.* a vertical post on which hawsers are made fast. **3.** *Mountaineering.* a pillar of snow or ice, used as an anchor. **4.** *Bldg Trades.* a vertical post, often used as an anchor for ropes, chains, etc. [? BOLE[1] + -ARD]

**bollocks** /'bɒləks/, *n.pl. Colloq.* rubbish; nonsense. See **ball**[1] (def. 8). Also, **bollicks.**

**bollocky** /'bɒləki/, *adj. Colloq.* **1.** naked: *stark bollocky.* –*n.* **2. in the bollocky,** naked. Also, **bollicky, bols.**

**boll weevil** /boʊl 'wivəl/, *n.* a beetle of the southern U.S., *Anthonomus grandis,* that attacks the bolls of cotton.

boll weevil: A, larva; B, adult; C, pupa

**bollworm** /'boʊlwɜm/, *n.* any of various moth larvae which attack cotton bolls, as the **pink bollworm,** the larva of a Queensland moth, *Pectinophora scutigera.*

**bolly gum** /'bɒli gʌm/, *n.* **1.** a tall rainforest tree, *Litsea reticulata,* of north-eastern Australia, with useful timber. **2.** any species with similar timber. Also, **bolly wood.**

**bolognaise sauce** /ˌbɒləneɪz 'sɔs/, *n.* a sauce for spaghetti, made with minced meat, onions, garlic, tomato paste and seasonings. Also, **bolognese sauce.** [F *Bolognaise;* pertaining to Bologna in Italy]

**bologna sausage** /bəˌloʊnjə 'sɒsɪdʒ/, *n.* a large-sized variety of sausage containing a mixture of meats; devon. Also, **bologna.**

**bolograph** /'boʊləgræf, -graf/, *n. Physics.* a record made by a bolometer. [Gk *bolḗ* ray + -O- + -GRAPH] – **bolographic** /boʊlə'græfɪk/, *adj.*

**bolometer** /boʊ'lɒmətə/, *n. Physics.* an electrical resistance element for measuring minute amounts of radiant energy. [Gk *bolḗ* ray + -O- + -METER[1]] – **bolometric** /boʊlə'mɛtrɪk/, *adj.*

**boloney** /bə'loʊni/, *n.* **1.** *Colloq.* →**bologna sausage. 2.** →**baloney.**

**bolo punch** /'boʊloʊ pʌntʃ/, *n. Boxing.* a type of uppercut beginning with a backward arc of the arm before thrusting forward to the body.

**bols** /bɒlz/, *adj. Colloq.* →**bollocky.**

**Bolshevik** /'bɒlʃəvɪk/, *n., pl.* **Bolsheviks. 1.** (in any country) a member of a Communist Party. **2.** (*derog.*) any radical or progressive. Also, **bolshevik.** [Russ., from *bolshe* greater, more, with allusion to the majority (Russ. *bolshinstvo*) of the Russian Social Democratic Party at the 1903 congress, advocating abrupt and forceful seizure of power by the proletariat]

**bolshevise** /'bɒlʃəvaɪz/, *v.,* **-vised, -vising.** –*v.t.* **1.** to bring under the influence or domination of bolshevists; render Bolshevik or bolshevistic. –*v.i.* **2.** to become Bolshevik or bolshevistic; act like a Bolshevik. Also, **bolshevize.** – **bolshevisation** /ˌbɒlʃəvaɪ'zeɪʃən/, *n.*

**bolshevism** /'bɒlʃəvɪzəm/, *n.* **1.** the doctrines, methods, or procedure of the Bolsheviks. **2.** the principles or practices of ultraradical socialists or political ultraradicals generally.

**bolshevist** /'bɒlʃəvəst/, *n.* **1.** a follower or advocate of the doctrines or methods of the Bolsheviks. **2.** an ultraradical socialist; any political ultraradical. –*adj.* **3.** bolshevistic.

**bolshevistic** /bɒlʃə'vɪstɪk/, *adj.* pertaining to or characteristic or suggestive of bolshevists or bolshevism.

**bolshie** /'bɒlʃi/, *Colloq.* –*n.* **1.** (*sometimes cap.*) Bolshevik. –*adj.* **2.** bolshevistic. **3.** obstinate; difficult; tiresome. Also, **bolshy.**

**bolson** /'boʊlsən/, *n.* a broad and nearly flat mountain-rimmed desert basin with interior drainage. [Sp.: large purse. See BURSE]

**bolster** /'boʊlstə/, *n.* **1.** a long ornamental pillow for a bed, sofa, etc. **2.** something resembling this in form or use. **3.** a pillow, cushion, or pad. **4.** a support, as one for a bridge truss. **5.** a chisel with a 110 mm cutting face. –*v.t.* **6.** to support with or as with a pillow. **7.** to prop, support, or uphold (something weak, unworthy, etc.) (oft. fol. by *up*). [ME *bolstre,* OE *bolster,* c. G *Bolster*] – **bolsterer,** *n.*

**bolt**[1] /boʊlt/, *n.* **1.** a movable bar which when slid into a socket fastens a door, gate, etc. **2.** the part of a lock which is protruded from and drawn back into the case, as by the action of the key. **3.** a strong metal pin, often with a head at one end and with a screw thread at the other to receive a nut. **4. a.** a woven length of cloth. **b.** a roll of wallpaper. **5.** the uncut edge of a sheet folded to make a book. **6.** a sudden swift motion or escape. **7.** any sudden dash, run, flight, etc. **8.** a jet of any liquid, esp. molten glass. **9.** an arrow, esp. one for a crossbow. **10.** a rod or bar which closes the breech of a rifle. **11.** a shaft of lightning; a thunderbolt. **12. bolt out of (from) the blue,** a sudden and entirely unexpected occurrence. **13. have shot one's bolt,** to have reached the limit of one's endurance or effort. –*v.t.* **14.** to fasten with or as with bolts. **15.** to shoot; discharge (a missile). **16.** to blurt; utter hastily. **17.** to swallow (one's food) hurriedly or without chewing. **18.** to make (cloth, wallpaper, etc.) into bolts. –*v.i.* **19.** to run away in alarm and uncontrollably, esp. of horses and rabbits. **20.** *U.S.* to desert a political party, etc. –*adv.* **21.** suddenly; with sudden meeting or collision. **22. bolt upright,** stiffly upright. [ME and OE, c. G *Bolzen*] – **bolter,** *n.* – **boltless,** *adj.* – **boltlike,** *adj.*

**bolt**[2] /boʊlt/, *v.t.* **1.** to sift through a cloth or sieve. **2.** to examine or search into, as if by sifting. Also, **boult.** [ME *bult(en),* from OF *bulter* sift, from MD *buitelen*] – **bolter,** *n.*

**bolter** /'boʊltə/, *n.* **1.** *Horseracing Colloq.* a horse which wins a race unexpectedly, or by an unexpectedly large margin. **2.** (formerly) an escaped convict.

**bolthead** /'boʊlthɛd/, *n.* **1.** the head of a bolt. **2.** *Chem.* (formerly) a matrass.

**bolthole** /'boʊlthoʊl/, *n.* any refuge; place or means of escape.

**boltrope** /'boʊltroʊp/, *n.* **1.** *Naut.* a rope or the cordage sewn on the edges of a sail or the like to strengthen it. **2.** a superior grade of rope.

**Boltzmann's constant** /ˌbɒltsmənz 'kɒnstənt/, *n. Physics.* a fundamental constant relating macroscopic and microscopic thermodynamics, equal to the ratio of the gas constant to Avogadro's number or $1.380\,622 \times 10^{-23}$ joule per kelvin. *Symbol:* k [named after Ludwig *Boltzmann,* 1844-1906, Austrian physicist]

**bolus** /'boʊləs/, *n. Med.* **1.** a round mass of medicine, larger than an ordinary pill, forming a dose. **2.** a lump of masticated food which enters the oesophagus at one swallow. [LL, from Gk *bôlos* lump]

i = peat ɪ = pit ɛ = pet æ = pat a = part ɒ = pot ʌ = putt ɔ = port ʊ = put u = pool ɜ = pert ə = apart aɪ = buy eɪ = bay ɔɪ = boy aʊ = how oʊ = hoe ɪə = here ɛə = hair ʊə = tour g = give θ = thin ð = then ʃ = show ʒ = measure tʃ = choke dʒ = joke ŋ = sing j = you õ = Fr. bon

**bolwarra** /bɒl'wɒrə/, *n.* a shrub or small tree, *Eupomatia laurina,* found in forests of eastern Australia.

**bomb** /bɒm/, *n.* **1.** a hollow projectile filled with an explosive charge. **2.** any similar missile or explosive device. **3.** *Geol.* a rough spherical or ellipsoidal mass of lava ejected from a volcano. **4.** *Colloq.* an old car. **5.** *Colloq.* a failure, as in an examination. **6.** a jump into water, made in a crouched position. **7. go like a bomb,** *Colloq.* **a.** to go successfully. **b.** (of a motor vehicle, etc.) to go rapidly. **8.** *Rugby League.* an up-and-under directed near or over the opponents' goal-line. **9.** *Colloq.* a drug. *–v.t.* **10.** to hurl bombs at; drop bombs upon, as from an aeroplane; bombard. **11.** to jump onto (someone) in water. **12.** to fail; perform badly at: *he bombed the exam.* *–v.i.* **13.** to explode a bomb or bombs. **14.** to hurl or drop bombs. **15.** to jump into water, as from the side of a swimming pool, river bank, etc. **16.** to err; to fail (oft. fol. by *out*): *he bombed out.* **17.** to be heavily under the influence of drugs (oft. fol. by *out*). [F *bombe,* from It. *bomba,* from L *bombus* a booming sound, from Gk *bómbos*]

**bombard** /bɒm'bad/, *v.;* /'bɒmbad/, *n.* *–v.t.* **1.** to attack or batter with artillery. **2.** to attack with bombs. **3.** *Physics.* to direct a constant stream of high-speed particles towards. **4.** to assail vigorously: *bombard someone with questions.* *–n.* **5.** the earliest kind of cannon, originally throwing stone balls. [ME *bombarde,* from OF: cannon, from L *bombus* loud noise. See BOMB] – **bombardment,** *n.*

**bombardier** /bɒmbə'dɪə/, *n.* **1.** *Mil.* the lowest rank of NCO in an artillery regiment. **2.** *Mil.* the member of a bomber crew who operates the bomb release mechanism. **3.** *Hist.* an artilleryman. [F]

**bombardier beetle** /– 'bitl/, *n.* an Australian ground beetle, *Pherosophus verticalis,* which when disturbed emits a cloud of vapour making an explosive sound.

**bombardon** /'bɒmbədən, bɒm'badn/, *n.* *Music.* **1.** a bass reedstop of the organ. **2.** a large, deep-toned, valved brass instrument not unlike a tuba. [It. *bombardone;* akin to BOMBARD]

**bombasine** /'bɒmbəzin, bɒmbə'zin/, *n.* a fine-twilled fabric with a silk warp and worsted weft, formerly much used (in black) for mourning. Also, **bombazine.** [F *bombasin,* from LL *bombasīnum,* from *bombax.* See BOMBAST]

**bombast** /'bɒmbæst/, *n.* **1.** high-sounding and often insincere words; verbiage. **2.** *Obs.* cotton or other material used to stuff garments; padding. *–adj.* **3.** *Obs.* bombastic. [earlier *bombace,* from F, from LL *bombax* cotton, for L *bombyx* silkworm, silk, from Gk]

**bombastic** /bɒm'bæstɪk/, *adj.* (of speech, etc.) high-sounding; high-flown; inflated; turgid. Also, **bombastical.** – **bombastically,** *adv.*

**Bombay** /bɒm'beɪ/, *adj.* **1.** of or pertaining to a mild to hot Indian dish using a mixture of foods, esp. vegetables and seafoods. *–n.* **2.** such a dish. [from *Bombay,* India, where the dish originated]

**Bombay bloomers** /– 'bluməz/, *n.pl.* *Colloq.* loose-fitting shorts for summer or physical education wear.

**Bombay duck** /– 'dʌk/, *n.* a dried fish (the bummalo), eaten as a savoury with curries.

**bomb bay** /'bɒm beɪ/, *n.* the compartment of an aeroplane in which bombs are carried.

**bombe** /bɒm/, *n.* **1.** a sweet usu. made in a round mould, with an outer layer of plain ice-cream and a filling of a softer iced mixture of different flavour often with other ingredients, such as fruit, nuts, liqueur, etc. **2.** the circular mould or dish for containing such a sweet.

**bombe Alaska** /– ə'læskə/, *n.* an alaska in a bombe shape.

**bombed** /bɒmd/, *adj.* heavily under the influence of drugs. Also, **bombed out.**

**bomber** /'bɒmə/, *n.* **1.** one who throws or places bombs. **2.** an aeroplane employed to carry and drop bombs.

**bombload** /'bɒmloud/, *n.* the load of bombs carried by an aeroplane.

**bombo** /'bɒmbou/, *n.* *Colloq.* cheap wine.

**bombora** /bɒm'bɒrə/, *n.* **1.** a submerged reef of rocks. **2.** a dangerous current over a reef. [Aboriginal]

**bombproof** /'bɒmpruf/, *adj.* strong enough to resist the impact and explosive force of bombs or shells.

**bomb rack** /'bɒm ræk/, *n.* a device for carrying bombs in an aircraft.

**bombshell** /'bɒmʃɛl/, *n.* **1.** a bomb. **2.** a sudden or devastating action or effect: *his resignation was a bombshell.* **3.** a woman who is physically well-endowed.

**bombsight** /'bɒmsaɪt/, *n.* an aiming instrument used to tell when to drop a bomb from an aircraft so that it will hit a specified target.

**bombsite** /'bɒmsaɪt/, *n.* the remains of a building which has been destroyed by a bomb.

**bombycid** /'bɒmbəsɪd/, *n.* any of the Bombycidae, the family of moths that includes the silkworm moths. [L *bombyx* silkworm (from Gk) + -ID[2]]

**bona fide** /ˌbounə 'faɪdi/, *adj.* **1.** Also, **bona-fide.** good faith; without fraud. *–n.* **2. bona fides,** evidence of good faith. [L]

**bonanza** /bə'nænzə/, *n.* **1. a.** a mine of wealth; good luck. **b.** any fortunate and profitable occasion. **2.** *U.S.* a rich mass of ore, as found in mining. [Sp.: fair weather, prosperity, from L *bonus* good]

**bon appétit** /bɒn æpə'ti/, *interj.* (an expression used indicating the speaker's wish for someone to have a satisfying meal). [F]

**bonbon** /'bɒnbɒn/, *n.* **1.** a fondant, fruit, or nut centre dipped in fondant or chocolate. **2.** a piece of confectionery. **3.** a small firework made from a paper roll twisted at each end and containing a gift, joke, motto, etc., which makes a loud report when pulled sharply at both ends. Also, **bon bon, bon-bon.** [F]

**bonbonnière** /ˌbɒnbɒni'ɛə/, *n.* **1.** a box of chocolates. **2.** a small ornate dish for serving chocolates, etc. [F]

**bond** /bɒnd/, *n.* **1.** something that binds, fastens, confines, or holds together. **2.** a cord; rope; band; ligament. **3.** something that unites individual people into a group. **4.** something that constrains a person to a certain line of behaviour. **5.** a bondsman or security. **6.** a sealed document under which a person or corporation guarantees to pay a stated sum of money on or before a specified day. **7.** any written obligation under seal. **8.** a written undertaking to work for a specified period, or to pay back an agreed sum of money in default, as a condition for accepting certain scholarships, awards or privileges from an employer: *he is under bond to the Education Department.* **9.** *Law.* **a.** a written acknowledgment of a debt. **b.** such an acknowledgment dependent upon the condition that one party shall do or refrain from doing a certain action. **10.** the state of dutiable goods on which the duties are unpaid (esp. in phrase *in bond*). **11.** *Finance.* a certificate of ownership of a specified portion of a debt due by government or other corporation to individual holders, and usually bearing a fixed rate of interest. **12.** *Insurance.* **a.** a surety agreement. **b.** the money deposited, or the promissory arrangement entered into, under any such agreement. **13.** →**bond money.** **14.** a substance that causes particles to adhere; a binder. **15.** *Chem.* any linkage between atoms in a compound. **16.** bond paper. **17.** *Bldg Trades.* the connection of the stones or bricks in a wall, etc., made by overlapping them in order to bind the whole into a compact mass. *–v.t.* **18.** to put (goods, an employee, official, etc.) in or under bond. **19.** *Finance.* to place a bonded debt on; mortgage. **20.** *Bldg Trades.* to cause (bricks or other building materials) to hold together firmly by laying them in some overlapping pattern. *–v.i.* **21.** to hold together by being bonded, as bricks in a wall. [ME, var. of BAND[3]] – **bonder,** *n.*

**bondage** /'bɒndɪdʒ/, *n.* **1.** slavery or involuntary servitude; serfdom. **2.** the state of being bound by or subjected to external control. **3.** a form of sexual play in which one partner submits to being bound by the other. **4.** *Old Eng. Law.* tenure of land by villeinage.

**Bondaian** /bɒn'daɪən/, *n.* **1.** a cultural period of Aboriginal development recognised in eastern Australia and reaching a climax about 1600 years B.P. (it follows the Capertian but overlaps to some extent). *–adj.* **2.** of, or pertaining to, the period. [from *Bondi,* a suburb of Sydney]

**bonded** /'bɒndəd/, *adj.* **1.** secured by or consisting of bonds: *bonded debt.* **2.** placed in bond: *bonded goods.* **3.** (of textiles) bound by a continuous wad or layer of fibres onto a prepared backing fabric.

**bonded warehouse** /– 'wɛəhaus/, *n.* →**bond store.**

**bond energy** /ˈbɒnd ɛnədʒi/, *n.* the energy required to separate two atoms joined by a bond.

**bondholder** /ˈbɒndhouldə/, *n.* a holder of bonds issued by a government or corporation. – **bondholding,** *adj., n.*

**Bondi** /ˈbɒndaɪ/, *n. in the phrases* **1. give someone Bondi,** *Obs. Colloq.* to give someone a thrashing. **2. shoot through like a Bondi tram,** to depart in haste. [from *Bondi,* a suburb of Sydney]

Bondi tram

**bonding process** /ˈbɒndɪŋ prousɛs/, *n.* the process, occurring in the first hours and days after birth, which establishes through physical contact the instinctive relationship between parent, esp. mother, and child.

**Bondi point** /ˌbɒndaɪ ˈpɔɪnt/, *n. Archaeol.* a sharpened stone flake characteristic of the Bondaian period of Aboriginal development. Also, **Bondai point.**

Bondi point

**bond length** /ˈbɒnd lɛŋθ/, *n.* the distance between nuclei of atoms joined by a bond.

**bondmaid** /ˈbɒndmeɪd/, *n.* **1.** a female slave. **2.** a female bound to service without wages.

**bondman** /ˈbɒndmən/, *n., pl.* **-men. 1.** a male slave. **2.** a man bound to service without wages. **3.** *Old Eng. Law.* a villein or other unfree tenant. Also, **bondsman.**

**bond money** /ˈbɒnd mʌni/, *n.* money additional to any rent which a new tenant pays as surety against damages to the premises rented.

**bond paper** /ˈbɒnd peɪpə/, *n.* a superior variety of white paper.

**bond rate** /ˈ– reɪt/, *n.* the interest yield to maturity on Commonwealth bonds, either maturing within five years (short-term) or beyond fifteen years (long-term).

**bondservant** /ˈbɒndsɜvənt/, *n.* **1.** one who serves in bondage; a slave. **2.** (formerly) an assigned servant bonded to a free settler.

**bondsman** /ˈbɒndzmən/, *n., pl.* **-men. 1.** *Law.* one who is bound or who by bond becomes surety for another. **2.** →**bondman.**

**bond store** /ˈbɒnd stɔ/, *n.* a warehouse licensed under the Customs Act for the storage of goods on which duty has not yet been paid.

**bondwoman** /ˈbɒndwʊmən/, *n., pl.* **-women** /-wɪmən/. a female slave. Also, **bondswoman.**

**bone** /boun/, *n., v.,* **boned, boning.** *–n.* **1.** *Anat., Zool.* **a.** any of the separate pieces of which the skeleton of a vertebrate is composed. **b.** the hard tissue which composes the skeleton. **2.** a bone or piece of a bone with the meat adhering to it, as an article of food. **3.** (*pl.*) the skeleton. **4.** (*pl.*) a body. **5.** any of various similar substances, such as ivory, whalebone, etc. **6.** something made of bone, or of a substance resembling bone. **7.** a strip of whalebone used to stiffen corsets, etc. **8.** (*pl.*) →**dice** (def. 1). **9.** (*pl.*) *Theat.* **a.** noisemakers of bone or wood used by a minstrel endman. **b.** an endman. **10. the bone of contention,** a matter which causes disagreement. **11.** →**hambone. 12.** a point of dispute; a matter for complaint: *I have a bone to pick with you.* **13. feel in one's bones,** to understand intuitively. **14. make no bones,** to be absolutely frank (fol. by *about*). **15. point the bone at, a.** *Colloq.* to bring or wish bad luck upon. **b.** *Colloq.* to indicate (a guilty person). **c.** *Anthropol.* (among tribal Aborigines) to induce the death of (an allegedly guilty person) by pointing a bone at him. *–v.t.* **16.** to take out the bones of: *to bone a fish.* **17.** to put whalebone into (clothing). **18.** *Agric.* to put ground bone into, as fertiliser. **19.** *Colloq.* to steal. *–v.i.* **20. bone up,** *Colloq.* to study hard; acquire information (fol. by *on*). [ME *boon,* OE *bān,* c. G. *Bein* leg] – **boned,** *adj.* – **boneless,** *adj.* – **bonelike,** *adj.*

**bone ash** /ˈ– æʃ/, *n.* the remains of bones calcined in the air. Also, **bone earth.**

**bone bed** /ˈ– bɛd/, *n.* a layer of rock containing bone remains.

**boneblack** /ˈbounblæk/, *n.* a black carbonaceous substance obtained by calcining bones in closed vessels.

**bone china** /boun ˈtʃaɪnə/, *n.* a kind of china in which bone ash is used.

**bonecrusher** /ˈbounkrʌʃə/, *n. Rugby Football Colloq.* a heavy tackle.

**bone-dry** /boun-ˈdraɪ/, *adj. Colloq.* dry as a bone; very dry.

**bone earth** /ˈboun ɜθ/, *n.* →**bone ash.**

**bonefish** /ˈbounfɪʃ/, *n.* a marine fish, *Albula vulpes,* of shallow Australian waters.

**bonehead** /ˈbounhɛd/, *n. Colloq.* a stupid, obstinate person; a blockhead. – **boneheaded,** *adj.*

**bone-idle** /boun-ˈaɪdl/, *adj. Colloq.* extremely lazy.

**bone-in** /boun-ˈɪn/, *adj.* (of meat) with bone intact: *blade steak, bone-in.*

**bonemeal** /ˈbounmil/, *n.* bones ground to a coarse powder, used as a fertiliser or animal feed.

**bone oil** /ˈboun ɔɪl/, *n.* a fetid, tarry liquid obtained in the dry distillation of bone.

**bone-pointer** /ˈboun-pɔɪntə/, *n. Colloq.* an elder in an Aboriginal tribe, who is believed to have magical powers, as the power to sing an enemy to death.

**boner** /ˈbounə/, *n.* **1.** one who, in a slaughterhouse, takes the bones from a carcass. **2.** *Colloq.* a mistake: *he made a boner that time.*

**boneseed** /ˈbounsid/, *n.* a yellow-flowered shrub, *Chrysanthemoides monilifera,* native to South Africa but naturalised elsewhere and often a troublesome weed.

**bonesetter** /ˈbounsɛtə/, *n.* a medical practitioner who treats broken bones and similar disorders without the formal qualifications of a surgeon; an osteopath.

**boneshaker** /ˈbounʃeɪkə/, *n.* **1.** an early type of bicycle with solid tyres and no springs. **2.** *Colloq.* any ancient and rickety bicycle or other vehicle.

**boneyard** /ˈbounjad/, *n. Colloq.* →**cemetery.**

**bonfire** /ˈbɒnfaɪə/, *n.* **1.** a large fire in an open place, for entertainment, celebration, or as a signal. **2.** any fire built in the open. [earlier *bonefire;* heaps of wood and bones were burned at certain old festivals]

**bonfire night** /ˈ– naɪt/, *n.* →**cracker night.**

**bong**[1] /bɒŋ/, *v.t.* **1.** *Colloq.* to hit, esp. on the head. *–n.* **2.** *Colloq.* a blow.

**bong**[2] /ˈbɒŋ/, *n.* a type of waterpipe, used for smoking hashish.

**bongo**[1] /ˈbɒŋgou/, *n., pl.* **-gos.** a large forest-dwelling antelope, *Taurotragus eurycerus,* of tropical Africa, of a chestnut colour striped with white, with spiralling horns.

**bongo**[2] /ˈbɒŋgou/, *n., pl.* **-gos, -goes.** one of a pair of small drums, played by beating with the fingers. [Amer. Sp.]

**bonhomie** /bɒnˈɒmi/, *n.* frank and simple good-heartedness; a good-natured manner. Also, **bonhommie.** [F *bonhomme* good man]

**bonito** /bəˈnitou/, *n., pl.* **-tos, -toes. 1.** any of several fishes belonging to the tuna family, as *Sarda chiliensis australis* found along the eastern Australian coast. **2.** any of various other fishes of the genus *Sarda* as *S. sarda* of the Atlantic. [Sp.]

**bonjour** /bɒnˈʒɔ/, *interj.* **1.** good day; hello. *–n.* **2.** such a greeting. [F]

**bonkers** /ˈbɒŋkəz/, *adj. Colloq.* crazy.

**bonk wagon** /ˈbɒŋk ˌwægən/, *n. Cycling Colloq.* a vehicle which accompanies cyclists taking part in road races and carries spare parts, spare clothing and food supplies. Also, **sag wagon.**

**bon mot** /bɒn ˈmou/, *n. pl.* **bons mots** /-ˈmou/. a particularly appropriate word or expression; a clever saying; witticism. [F: lit., good word]

**bonne femme** /bɒn ˈfʌm/, *adj.* cooked in a simple home style, with a garnish of herbs and, often, mushrooms. [F]

**bonnet** /ˈbɒnət/, *n.* **1.** a woman's or child's outdoor head covering, commonly fitting down over the hair, and often tied under the chin. **2.** *Chiefly Scot.* a man's or boy's cap. **3.** any of various hoods, covers, or protective devices. **4.** a cowl for a chimney to

bonnet

stabilise the draught. **5.** a hinged cover over the engine (in some makes over the luggage section) at the front of a motor vehicle. **6.** *Naut.* an additional piece of canvas laced to the foot (formerly the top) of a jib or other sail. *–v.t.* **7.** to put a bonnet on. **8.** (formerly) to jeer at; abuse, often by pelting (someone) with mud. [ME *bonet,* from OF: cap (orig. its material); ? of Gmc orig.] – **bonnet-like,** *adj.*

**bonny** /'bɒni/, *adj.,* **-ier, -iest.** **1.** radiant with health; handsome; pretty. **2.** *Scot.* fine (often used ironically). Also, **bonnie.** [ME *bonie.* See BOON[2]] – **bonnily,** *adv.* – **bonniness,** *n.*

**bonnyclabber** /'bɒniklæbə/, *n.* sour, thick milk. [Irish *bainne clabair,* lit., milk of the clabber (i.e. ? the churn-dasher)]

**bonsai** /'bɒnsaɪ/, *n.* **1.** the practice, originally Japanese, of growing very small examples of trees and shrubs in ornamental pots, by skilful pruning of roots and branches. **2.** a tree or shrub so grown. [Jap.: pot plant, from *bon* bowl, pot + *sai* to plant]

**bonsoir** /bɒn'swa/, *interj.* good evening; good night. [F] – **bonsoir,** *n.*

**bon ton** /bɔ̃ 'tɔ̃/, *n.* good or elegant form or style; good breeding; fashionable society. [F: good tone]

**bonus** /'boʊnəs/, *n.* **1.** something given or paid over and above what is due. **2.** a sum of money paid to a shareholder, partner, employee, or agent of a company, a returned soldier, etc., over and above his regular dividend or pay. **3.** *Stock Exchange.* →**bonus issue.** **4.** something free added in a corporate sale of securities. **5.** *Insurance.* **a.** dividend. **b.** free additions to the sum assured. See **reversionary bonus, terminal bonus.** **6.** a premium paid for a loan, contract, etc. **7.** *Colloq.* a bribe. **8.** any unsolicited or unexpected gift. *–adj.* **9.** of or pertaining to something given as a bonus. [L: (adj.) good]

**bonus issue** /'– ɪʃu/, *n.* a free issue of shares to shareholders of a company. Also, **bonus.**

**bonus work** /'– wɜk/, *n.* the carrying out of more than a specified amount of work, as the production of more than a specified number of items in a given work period, in order to earn extra payment. Also, **task work.**

**bon vivant** /bɔ̃ vi'vɔ̃/, *n., pl.* **bons vivants** /bɔ̃ vi'vɔ̃/. **1.** a person who lives luxuriously, self-indulgently, etc. **2.** a jovial companion. [F]

**bon viveur** /bɔ̃ vi'vɜ/, *n.* a bon vivant. [F]

**bon voyage** /bɔ̃ vwa'jaʒ, vɔɪ'jaʒ/, *interj.* pleasant trip. [F]

**bony** /'boʊni/, *adj.,* **bonier, boniest.** **1.** of or like bone. **2.** full of bones. **3.** having prominent bones; big-boned. – **boniness,** *n.*

**bony bream** /– 'brɪm/, *n.* an Australian freshwater clupeid fish, *Fluvialosa richardsoni.*

**bonze** /bɒnz/, *n.* a Buddhist monk, esp. of Japan or China. [F, from Pg. *bonzo,* from Jap. *bonzô,* from Chinese *fan sung* ordinary (member) of the assembly]

**bonzer** /'bɒnzə/, *adj. Colloq.* excellent, attractive, pleasing. Also, **bonza, boshter.**

**boo** /bu/, *interj., n., pl.* **boos,** *v.,* **booed, booing.** *–interj.* **1.** (an exclamation used to express contempt, disapprobation, etc., or to frighten.) *–n.* **2.** this exclamation. *–v.i.* **3.** to cry 'boo'. *–v.t.* **4.** to cry 'boo' at; show disapproval of by booing.

**booay** /'bueɪ/, *n. Colloq.* **1.** a remote country district. **2. up the booay, a.** in the backblocks. **b.** in difficulties; in a predicament. **c.** completely wrong. Also, **boo-eye, boo-ai, boohai.** [Maori *puhoi*]

**boob**[1] /bub/, *n. Colloq.* **1.** a fool; a dunce. **2.** a foolish mistake. **3.** *Colloq.* a woman's breast. *–v.i.* **4.** to blunder; make a mistake. [See BOOBY]

**boob**[2] /bub/, *n. Colloq.* prison. [shortened form of prison colloq. *booby-hutch* police station, gaol]

**boob happy** /'– hæpi/, *adj. Prison Colloq.* suffering from a form of neurosis brought about by the strain of gaol routine.

**boobhead** /'bubhɛd/, *n. Prison Colloq.* a recidivist.

**boobialla** /bubi'ælə/, *n.* any of several species of *Myoporum,* especially *M. insulare* which is often grown as a hedge. [Aboriginal]

**boo-boo** /'bu-bu/, *n.* **1.** *Colloq.* an error, usu. of judgment: *he made a classic boo-boo.* *–v.i.* **2.** to make an error.

**boobook** /'bubʊk/, *n.* a small owl or mopoke, *Ninox novaeseelandiae,* brownish, with white-spotted back and wings and large dark patches behind the eyes; widely distributed in Australia, New Zealand and adjacent islands.

boobook owl

**boob tube** /'bub tjub/, *n. Colloq.* a television set.

**booby** /'bubi/, *n., pl.* **-bies.** **1.** a stupid person; a dunce. **2.** the worst student, player, etc., of a group. **3.** a large, robust, seabird with long wings and a wedge-shaped tail as the **brown booby,** *Sula leucogaster,* of tropical seas and northerly parts of the Australian coastline. [probably from Sp. *bobo* fool, also the bird booby, from L *balbus* stammering] – **boobyish,** *adj.*

**booby hatch** /'– hætʃ/, *n.* **1.** *Naut.* a wooden hood over a hatch. **2.** *U.S. Colloq.* a lunatic asylum. **3.** *U.S. Colloq.* gaol.

**booby prize** /'– praɪz/, *n.* a prize given in consolation or good-natured ridicule to the worst player in a game or contest.

**booby trap** /'– træp/, *n.* **1.** an object so placed as to fall on or trip up an unsuspecting person. **2.** *Mil.* a hidden or disguised bomb or mine so placed that it will be set off by an unsuspecting person. *–v.t.* **3.** to set with a booby trap.

**boodie rat** /'budi ræt/, *n.* a burrowing species of bettong or rat-kangaroo, *Bettongia lesueur.* Also, **Lesueur's rat-kangaroo, tungo, tungoo.**

**boodle**[1] /'budəl/, *n., v.,* **-dled, -dling.** *Chiefly U.S. Colloq.* *–n.* **1.** (*oft. derog.*) the lot, pack, or crowd: *the whole boodle.* **2.** a bribe or other illicit gain in politics. **3.** →**loot** (def. 2). *–v.i.* **4.** to obtain money dishonestly, as by corrupt bargains. [D *boedel, boel* stock, lot] – **boodler,** *n.*

**boodle**[2] /'budəl/, *n., v.,* **boodled, boodling.** *–n.* **1.** broken-up soil, stones or waste material of any kind, to be cleared from a trench, building site, railway line, etc. *–v.i.* **2.** to clear away boodle, usu. with a shovel. – **boodler,** *n.*

**boofhead** /'bʊfhɛd/, *n. Colloq.* a fool.

**boogaloo** /'bugəlu, bugə'lu/, *n.* a dance similar to the twist.

**boogie bass** /bugi 'beɪs/, *n.* a bass part consisting of a repetitive rhythmic pattern, as in boogie-woogie.

**boogieman** /'bugimæn/, *n.* →**bogy** (defs 1 and 2).

**boogie-woogie** /ˌbʊgi-'wʊgi, ˌbugi-'wugi/, *n.* a form of instrumental blues using melodic variations over a constantly repeated bass figure. Also, **boogie.**

**boohai** /'buhaɪ/, *n.* →**booay.**

**boohoo** /bu'hu/, *v.,* **-hooed, -hooing,** *n., pl.* **-hoos.** *–v.i.* **1.** to weep noisily; blubber. *–n.* **2.** the sound of noisy weeping. [imitative]

**book** /bʊk/, *n.* **1.** a written or printed work of some length, as a treatise or other literary composition, esp. on consecutive sheets fastened or bound together. **2.** a number of sheets of writing paper bound together and used for making entries, as of commercial transactions. **3. the books,** a record of commercial transactions. **4.** a division of a literary work, esp. one of the larger divisions. **5. the Book,** the Bible. **6.** *Music.* the text of an opera, operetta, etc. **7.** a record of bets, as on a horserace. **8.** *Cards.* the number of tricks or cards which must be taken before any trick counts in the score. **9.** a set of tickets, cheques, stamps, etc., bound together like a book. **10.** a pile or package of leaves, as of tobacco. **11.** a number of mares, bitches, etc., to be mated with the one sire. **12.** anything that serves for the recording of facts or events: *the book of Nature.* **13.** *Colloq.* one's intentions, plans or arrangements: *it doesn't suit my book.* **14. bring to book,** to bring to account. **15. by (the) book, a.** formally. **b.** authoritatively; correctly. **16. clean the books up,** *Prison Colloq.* to confess to numerous unsolved crimes. **17. closed book, a.** something which is incomprehensible: *maths is a closed book to me.* **b.** a matter which is to be discussed no further. **18. a. in someone's good books,** in favour. **b. in someone's bad books,** out of favour. **19. make a book,** *Horseracing.* to lay and receive bets at such odds that whichever horse wins, a profit is made. **20. on the books,** entered on the list of members. **21. open book, a.** anyone whose feelings, motives, etc., can be clearly interpreted. **b.** anything which can be clearly understood or interpreted. **22. take a leaf out of someone's book,** to emulate. **23. throw the**

**book at,** *Colloq.* **a.** to bring all possible charges against (an offender). **b.** sentence (an offender) to the maximum penalties. **c.** punish severely. **24. without book, a.** by memory. **b.** without authority. *–v.t.* **25.** to enter in a book or list; record; register. **26.** to engage (a place, passage, etc.) beforehand. **27.** to put (somebody, something) down for a place, passage, etc. **28.** to engage (a person or company) for a performance or performances. **29.** to record the name of, with a view to possible prosecution for a minor offence: *the police booked him for speeding.* *–v.i.* **30.** to register one's name (fol. by *in*). **31.** to engage a place, services, etc. [ME; OE *bōc,* c. G *Buch*] – **bookless,** *adj.*

**bookbinder** /ˈbʊkbaɪndə/, *n.* one whose business or work is the binding of books. – **bookbinding,** *n.*

**bookcase** /ˈbʊkkeɪs/, *n.* a set of shelves for books.

**book club** /ˈbʊk klʌb/, *n.* **1.** a club which lends or sells (usu. at a discount) books to its members. **2.** a club organised for the discussion and reviewing of books.

**book debt** /ˈ– dɛt/, *n.* an amount showing in a trader's accounts as due to him.

**book editor** /ˈ– ɛdətə/, *n.* an editor in a book publishing house.

**bookend** /ˈbʊkɛnd/, *n.* a support placed at the end of a row of books to hold them upright.

**book figure** /ˈbʊk fɪgə/, *n.* →**book value.**

**bookie** /ˈbʊki/, *n.* *Colloq.* →**bookmaker.**

**bookie's runner** /ˌbʊkiz ˈrʌnə/, *n.* *Horseracing Colloq.* a bookmaker's assistant engaged in collecting prices and laying off bets with other bookmakers, etc.

**booking** /ˈbʊkɪŋ/, *n.* **1.** advance engagement of a place or passage. **2.** an engagement to perform.

**booking clerk** /ˈ– klak/, *n.* an official who sells tickets, as for a railway journey.

**booking office** /ˈ– ɒfəs/, *n.* a place where tickets are sold, as at a railway station.

**bookish** /ˈbʊkɪʃ/, *adj.* **1.** given to reading or study. **2.** more acquainted with books than with real life. **3.** of or pertaining to books; literary. **4.** stilted; pedantic. – **bookishly,** *adv.* – **bookishness,** *n.*

**bookkeeping** /ˈbʊkkipɪŋ/, *n.* the work or skill of keeping account books or systematic records of money transactions. – **bookkeeper,** *n.*

**book-learning** /ˈbʊk-lɜnɪŋ/, *n.* knowledge gained by reading books, as distinguished from that obtained through observation and experience. Also, **book knowledge, booklore** /ˈbʊklɔ/. – **book-learned** /ˈbʊk-lɜnəd/, *adj.*

**booklet** /ˈbʊklət/, *n.* a little book, esp. one with paper covers; pamphlet.

**booklouse** /ˈbʊklaʊs/, *n., pl.* **-lice** /-laɪs/. any insect of the order Corrodentia, which damages books by eating away the glue, and is injurious to other products in houses, granaries, etc.

**bookmaker** /ˈbʊkmeɪkə/, *n.* a professional betting man, who accepts the bets of others, as on horses in racing. – **bookmaking,** *n.*

**bookman** /ˈbʊkmən/, *n., pl.* **-men. 1.** a studious or learned man; a scholar. **2.** *Colloq.* a person whose occupation is selling or publishing books.

**bookmark** /ˈbʊkmak/, *n.* **1.** a ribbon or the like placed between the pages of a book to mark a place. **2.** →**bookplate.** Also, **bookmarker.**

**bookmobile** /ˈbʊkməbil/, *n.* a truck or trailer equipped to serve as a mobile lending library.

**book of prime entry,** *n.* a book of account in which transactions are initially recorded before being transferred to the ledger, as a cashbook or daybook. Also, **book of original entry, book of originating entry;** *U.S.,* **book of account.**

**bookplate** /ˈbʊkpleɪt/, *n.* a label, bearing the owner's name, a design, etc., for pasting in a book.

**book post** /ˈbʊk poʊst/, *n.* *Chiefly Brit.* an arrangement for the conveyance of books at cheaper rates than other parcels.

**bookrack** /ˈbʊkræk/, *n.* **1.** a rack for supporting an open book. **2.** a rack for holding books.

**books closing date,** *n.* the date on which a company closes its books to determine those shareholders registered for a dividend, new issue, etc. See **ex date.**

**book scorpion** /ˈbʊk skɔpiən/, *n.* any of the minute arachnids, superficially resembling a tailless scorpion, which constitute the order Chelonethi (Pseudoscorpionida), as *Chelifer cancroides,* found in old books, etc.

**bookseller** /ˈbʊksɛlə/, *n.* a person whose occupation or business is selling books.

**bookshelf** /ˈbʊkʃɛlf/, *n.* a shelf for holding books.

**bookshop** /ˈbʊkʃɒp/, *n.* a shop where books are sold.

**bookstall** /ˈbʊkstɔl/, *n.* **1.** a stall, esp. at a station or airport, where newspapers, magazines, and books are sold. **2.** a stall at which books (usu. secondhand) are sold.

**bookstand** /ˈbʊkstænd/, *n.* **1.** →**bookrack. 2.** →**bookstall.**

**book-token** /ˈbʊk-toʊkən/, *n.* a gift token for books to a stated value.

**book trade** /ˈbʊk treɪd/, *n.* publishers, printers and booksellers together; all those engaged in the manufacture and selling of books.

**book value** /ˈ– vælju/, *n.* *Econ.* the amount which a trader shows in his accounts as the value of an item. Also, **book figure.**

**bookworm** /ˈbʊkwɜm/, *n.* **1.** any of various insects that feed on books. **2.** a person closely addicted to reading or study.

**Boolean algebra** /ˌbuliən ˈældʒəbrə/, *n.* a mathematical means of representing statements in logic. [named after George *Boole,* 1815-65, English mathematician]

**boom**[1] /bum/, *v.i.* **1.** to make a deep, prolonged, resonant sound; make a rumbling, humming, or droning noise. **2.** to move with a resounding rush or great impetus. **3.** to progress or flourish vigorously, as a business, a city, etc. *–v.t.* **4.** to give forth with a booming sound (usu. fol. by *out*): *the clock boomed out twelve.* **5.** to promote (a cause, a new product, etc.) vigorously (oft. fol. by *up*). *–n.* **6.** a deep, hollow, continued sound. **7.** a roaring, rumbling, or reverberation, as of waves or distant guns. **8.** the cry of the bittern. **9.** a rapid increase in prices, business activity, etc. **10. a.** a rise in popularity, as of a political candidate. **b.** efforts to bring this about. *–adj.* **11.** caused by a boom: *boom prices.* **12. boom galloper,** *Horseracing Colloq.* a horse whose previous performance has been outstanding and which thus is tipped to win his next races easily. [imit. Cf. ZOOM]

**boom**[2] /bum/, *n.* **1.** *Naut.* a long pole or spar used to extend the foot of certain sails. **2.** a chain or cable or a series of connected floating timbers, etc., serving to obstruct navigation, to confine floating timber, etc. **3.** the area thus shut off. **4.** *Mach.* a spar or beam projecting from the mast of a derrick, supporting or guiding the weights to be lifted. **5.** (in a television or film studio) a movable arm supporting a microphone or floodlight above the actors, or an aerial camera. [D: tree, beam. See BEAM]

B, boom; G, gaff

**boom alley** /– ˈæli/, *n.* *Aeron.* *Colloq.* a flight path for supersonic aircraft.

**boomer** /ˈbumə/, *n.* **1.** *Colloq.* something large, as a surfing wave. **2.** *Colloq.* something successful or popular as a party or song; bottler. **3.** the mature male great grey or forester kangaroo, *Macropus gigantus.* **4.** any large male kangaroo. **5.** the brown bittern, *Botaurus poiciloptilus.* [Warwickshire d.]

**boomerang** /ˈbumərætŋ/, *n.* **1.** a bent or curved piece of hard wood used as a missile by Aborigines, one form of which can be thrown so as to return to the thrower. **2.** a scheme, plan, argument, etc., which recoils upon the user. **3.** *Colloq.* that which is expected to be returned by a borrower. **4.** *Colloq.* a dishonoured cheque. *–v.i.* **5.** to return to, or recoil upon, the originator: *the argument boomeranged; the cheque boomeranged.* *–adj.* **6.** returning; rebounding: *a boomerang decision.* [Aboriginal]

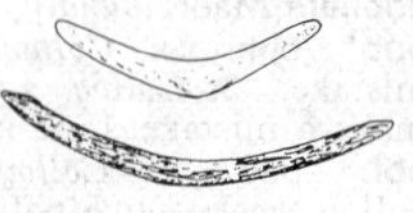
boomerang

**boomerang bender** /ˈbumərætŋ bɛndə/, *n.* *Colloq.* a teller of tall stories.

**boom gate** /ˈbum geɪt/, *n.* **1.** a barrier to traffic, usu. consisting of a long beam pivoted at one end and raised or lowered as required. **2.** a gate in a boom (def. 2).

**boom spray** /'- spreɪ/, *n. Agric.* a long pipe with several nozzles through which water or chemicals are pumped to cover a large area.
**boomster** /'bumstə/, *n.* a person who initiates or fosters a mining boom.
**boom town** /'bum taʊn/, *n.* a town that has grown rapidly or is enjoying a spell of prosperity. Also, **boomtown.**
**boom vang** /'bum væŋ/, *n.* →**vang.**
**boon**[1] /bun/, *n.* **1.** a benefit enjoyed; a thing to be thankful for; a blessing. **2.** *Archaic.* that which is asked; a favour sought. [ME, from Scand.; cf. Icel. *bōn* request, petition]
**boon**[2] /bun/, *adj.* jolly; jovial; convivial: *boon companion.* [ME, from OF *bon,* from L *bonus* good]
**boonaree** /bunə'ri/, *n.* →**boonery.**
**boondocks** /'bundɒks/, *n. Chiefly U.S. Colloq.* **1.** an uninhabited and densely overgrown area, as a swamp, forest, etc. **2.** a remote suburb or rural area: *the firm moved to the boondocks.*
**boondoggle** /'bundɒgəl/, *v.,* **-doggled, -doggling,** *n.* *–v.i.* **1.** to fritter away one's time on work that is unnecessary. *–n.* **2.** pointless and time-wasting activities. [orig. the plaited leather cord worn around the neck by Boy Scouts; considered to be a pointless handicraft; coined in 1925 by R.H. Link, an American scoutmaster]
**boondy** /'bʊndi/, *n. W.A.* a stone or pebble.
**boonery** /'bunəri/, *n., pl.* **-ries.** a small, native fodder tree, *Heterodendrum oleifolium,* of inland Australia. Also, **boonaree.** [orig. uncert; probably Aboriginal]
**boong** /bʊŋ/, *n. Colloq. (derog.)* **1.** an Aborigine. **2.** a black man.
**boongary** /bun'gɛəri/, *n.* →**Lumholtz's tree-kangaroo.**
**boor** /bɔ, bʊə/, *n.* **1.** a rude or unmannerly person. **2.** a peasant; a rustic. **3.** an illiterate or clownish peasant. **4.** a Dutch or German peasant. **5.** any foreign peasant. **6.** *(cap.)* Boer. [D *boer* peasant, or from LG *būr* peasant]
**boorish** /'bɔrɪʃ, 'bʊərɪʃ/, *adj.* of or like a boor; rustic; rude. **– boorishly,** *adv.* **– boorishness,** *n.*
**boost** /bust/, *v.t.* **1.** to lift or raise by pushing from behind or below. **2.** to advance or aid by speaking well of. **3.** to increase; push up: *to boost prices.* **4.** *Aeron., Motor Vehicles.* to supercharge. *–n.* **5.** an upward shove or push. **6.** an aid that helps one to rise in the world. **7.** *Aeron., Motor Vehicles.* the difference between the induction pressure in a supercharged internal-combustion engine and the atmospheric pressure. [b. BOOM[1] and HOIST]
**booster** /'bustə/, *n.* **1.** one who or that which boosts. **2.** *Elect.* a device connected in series with a current for increasing or decreasing the nominal circuit voltage. **3.** *Aeron., Motor Vehicles.* a supercharger in an internal-combustion engine. **4.** *Astronautics.* **a.** a rocket engine used as the main supply of thrust in a missile flight. **b.** the stage of a missile containing this engine, usu. detached at all-burnt. **5.** *Mil.* a high-explosive element sufficiently sensitive to be activated by small explosive elements in a fuse or primer and powerful enough to cause detonation of the main explosive filling. **6.** *Pharm.* a substance, usu. injected, for prolonging a person's immunity to a specific infection.
**booster pump** /'- pʌmp/, *n.* a pump for circulating water through a central heating system.
**boot**[1] /but/, *n.* **1.** a heavy shoe, esp. one reaching above the ankle. **2.** a covering, usu. of leather, rubber or a similar synthetic material, for the foot and leg, reaching up to and sometimes beyond the knee. **3.** *Hist.* an instrument of torture for the leg. **4.** a protective covering for the foot and part of the leg of a horse. **5.** place for baggage, usu. at the rear of a vehicle. **6.** *Agric.* the stage in the development of inflorescence of a plant, as wheat. **7.** a kick. **8.** *Colloq.* an electric shock. **9. bet your boots,** to be certain. **10. boots and all,** completely; with all one's strength or resources: *go in boots and all.* **11. the boot's on the other foot,** the true position is the reverse. **12. get the boot,** to be discharged. **13. heart in one's boots,** extreme despondency; loss of morale. **14. put in the boot, put the boot into (someone),** *Colloq.* **a.** to assault by kicking as in a street brawl. **b.** to make a malicious verbal attack on (someone). *–v.t.* **15.** to put boots on. **16.** *Hist.* to torture with the boot. **17.** *Colloq.* to kick; drive by kicking. **18.** *Colloq.* to dismiss; discharge. **19. boot home,** *Colloq.* **a.** *Horseracing.* to ride to win, kicking the horse to greater speed. **b.** to emphasise strongly. **c.** to push into position forcibly. [ME *bote,* from OF; of Gmc orig. See SABOT]
**boot**[2] /but/, *n.* **1. to boot,** into the bargain; in addition. **2.** *Obs.* remedy. *–v.i.* **3.** *Obs. or Poetic.* to be of profit, advantage, or avail: *it boots not to complain.* [ME *bote,* OE *bōt* advantage]
**boot**[3] /but/, *v.t.* to initiate a bootstrap program on (a computer system, etc.). [See BOOTSTRAP (def. 2)]
**bootblack** /'butblæk/, *n.* a person whose occupation it is to shine shoes, boots, etc.
**booted** /'butəd/, *adj.* **1.** equipped with boots. **2.** *Ornith.* (of the tarsus of certain birds) covered with a continuous horny, bootlike sheath.
**bootee** /'buti/, *n.* a baby's knitted shoe.
**booth** /buð, buθ/, *n.* **1.** a temporary structure of boughs, canvas, boards, etc., as for shelter. **2.** a stall or light structure for the sale of goods or for display purposes, as at a market or fair. **3.** a small compartment for a telephone, film projector, etc. **4.** →**polling booth.** [ME *bōthe,* from Scand.; cf. Dan. *bod*]
**bootjack** /'butdʒæk/, *n.* a device used to hold a boot while the foot is drawn out of it.
**bootlace** /'butleɪs/, *n.* **1.** a string or lace for fastening a boot. **2.** *(usu. pl.)* strips of skin cut off from sheep by rough shearers. **3.** a shoelace.
**bootlace bush** /'- ˌbʊʃ/, *n.* a soft-wooded shrub, *Pimelea axiflora,* family Thymeleaceae, found in south-eastern Australia.
**bootleg** /'butlɛg/, *n., v.,* **-legged, -legging,** *adj. Chiefly U.S.* *–n.* **1.** alcoholic drink secretly and unlawfully made, sold, or transported. **2.** that part of a boot which covers the leg. *–v.t.* **3.** to deal in (spirits or other goods) illicitly. *–v.i.* **4.** to carry goods, as spirits, about secretly for illicit sale. *–adj.* **5.** made, sold, or transported unlawfully. **6.** unlawful; clandestine. **7.** of or pertaining to bootlegging. [def. 2 orig. meaning; others arose from the practice of concealing illegal spirits in the bootleg] **– bootlegger,** *n.*
**bootless** /'butləs/, *adj.* without advantage; unavailing; useless. [OE *bōtlēas* unpardonable, from *bōt* BOOT[2] + *-lēas* -LESS] **– bootlessly,** *adv.* **– bootlessness,** *n.*
**bootlicker** /'butlɪkə/, *n. Colloq.* one who curries favour; a flatterer.
**boots** /buts/, *n., pl.* **boots.** *Brit.* a servant, as at a hotel, who cleans shoes, carries luggage, etc.
**boots-and-all** /buts-ən-'ɔl/, *adj. Colloq.* wholehearted: *a boots-and-all capitalist.*
**boots and saddles,** *n. U.S.* a cavalry bugle call for mounted formation.
**bootstrap** /'butstræp/, *n.* **1.** a loop sewn on the side of a boot to assist in pulling it on. **2.** *Computers.* a program or procedure by which a computer can be made to translate progressively more complex programs. **3. pull oneself up by the bootstraps,** to advance to success solely by one's own efforts.
**boot tree** /'but tri/, *n.* →*U.S.* **shoetree.**
**booty** /'buti/, *n., pl.* **-ties.** **1.** spoil taken from an enemy in war; plunder; pillage. **2.** that which is seized by violence and robbery. **3.** a prize or gain, without reference to use of force. [late ME *boyte;* cf. G *Beute*]
**booze** /buz/, *n., v.,* **boozed, boozing.** *Colloq.* *–n.* **1.** alcoholic drink. **2.** a drinking bout; spree. **3. on the booze,** drinking immoderately. *–v.i., v.t.* **4.** to drink immoderately. [ME *bouse,* from MD *būsen*]
**booze artist** /'- atəst/, *n. Colloq.* a person noted for being a heavy drinker.
**booze hound** /'- haʊnd/, *n. Colloq.* a heavy drinker.
**boozer** /'buzə/, *n. Colloq.* **1.** one who drinks immoderately. **2.** a hotel.
**boozeroo** /buzə'ru/, *n. N.Z. Colloq.* **1.** a drinking spree. **2.** a public house.
**booze-up** /'buz-ʌp/, *n.* a drinking party, bout or spree.
**boozington** /'buzɪŋtən/, *n. Colloq.* a drunkard.
**boozy** /'buzi/, *adj.* **boozier, booziest.** *Colloq.* **1.** drunken. **2.** addicted to alcohol. **– booziness,** *n.*

**bop** /bɒp/, *n., v.,* **bopped, bopping.** –*n.* **1.** →**bebop.** **2. have a bop,** to dance to pop or rock music. –*v.i.* **3.** to dance or move rhythmically to pop or rock music (oft. fol. by *along*).

**bo-peep** /boʊ-'pip/, *n. Colloq.* a peep, view: *have a bo-peep at that!*

**bopple nut** /'bɒpəl nʌt/, *n.* →**macadamia nut.**

**bora**[1] /'bɔrə/, *n.* a violent, dry, cold wind on the coasts of the Adriatic, blowing from the north or north-east. [d. It., from L *Boreas* north wind]

**bora**[2] /'bɔrə/, *n.* **1.** a sacred piece of ground where certain initiation ceremonies are performed by the Aborigines. **2.** a special Aboriginal initiation rite. [Aboriginal]

**boracic** /bə'ræsɪk/, *adj. Chem.* →**boric.**

**boracite** /'bɔrəsaɪt/, *n.* a mineral, a borate and chloride of magnesium, $Mg_6Cl_2B_{14}O_{26}$, occurring in white or colourless crystals or fine-grained masses, strongly pyroelectric. [*borac-*, stem of ML *borax* BORAX + -ITE[1]]

**borage** /'bɒrɪdʒ, 'bɔ-/, *n.* **1.** a plant, *Borago officinalis,* native to southern Europe, with hairy leaves and stems, used in salads and medicinally. **2.** any of various allied or similar plants. [ME, from AF *burage,* var. of OF *bourrace,* from *bourrer* stuff, from ML *burra* wool]

**boraginaceous** /bərædʒə'neɪʃəs/, *adj.* belonging to the Boraginaceae, or borage family of plants, including borage, bugloss, heliotrope, forget-me-not, etc.

**borak** /'bɔræk/, *n. Colloq.* ridicule: *to poke borak at someone.* Also, **borac, borack, borax.** [Aboriginal]

**borane** /'bɔreɪn/, *n.* a hydride of boron, used industrially as a high-energy fuel.

**borate** /'bɔreɪt/, *n., v.,* **-rated, -rating.** *n.* **1.** a salt of orthoboric acid. **2.** (loosely) a salt of any boric acid. –*v.t.* **3.** to treat with borate, boric acid, or borax.

**borax** /'bɔræks/, *n.* a white, crystalline sodium borate, $Na_2B_4O_7 \cdot 10H_2O$, occurring naturally or prepared artificially and used as a flux, cleansing agent, in the manufacture of glass, etc. [ML, from Ar. *būraq,* from Pers. *bōrah* (OPers. *bōrak*); replacing ME *boras,* from OF]

**borazon** /'bɔrəzɒn, -zən/, *n.* a very hard substance compounded industrially of boron and nitrogen.

**Bordeaux** /bɔ'doʊ/, *n.* **1.** wine produced in the region surrounding Bordeaux, a seaport in south-western France. **2.** →**Bordeaux mixture.** [F]

**Bordeaux mixture** /'– ˌmɪkstʃə/, *n.* a fungicide consisting of a mixture of copper sulphate, lime, and water.

**bordelaise** /bɔdə'leɪz/, *n.* a brown sauce flavoured with red wine. [F]

**bordelais espalier** /bɔdəleɪ ɛ'spæliə/, *n.* a method of grapevine pruning leaving both rod and spur on the vine. [F *bordelais* of Bordeaux + ESPALIER]

**bordello** /bɔ'dɛloʊ/, *n.* a brothel. [It.]

**border** /'bɔdə/, *n.* **1.** a side, edge, or margin. **2.** the line that separates one country, state, or province from another; frontier line. **3.** the district or region that lies along the boundary line of a country. **4.** brink; verge. **5.** an ornamental strip or design around the edge of a printed page, a drawing, etc. **6.** a piece of ornamental trimming around the edge of a garment, cap, etc. **7.** *Hort.* a narrow strip of ground in a garden, enclosing a portion of it. –*v.t.* **8.** to make a border about; adorn with a border. **9.** to form a border or boundary to. **10.** to lie on the border of; adjoin. –*v.i.* **11. border on** or **upon, a.** to touch or abut at the border. **b.** to approach closely in character; verge. [ME *bordure,* from OF, from *bord* side, edge; of Gmc orig. See BOARD] – **bordered,** *adj.* – **borderless,** *adj.*

**border collie** /– 'kɒli/, *n.* a medium-sized dog, originating in the English-Scottish borderlands, with white markings on the chest, feet and tail, recognised as a breed in Australia.

**borderer** /'bɔdərə/, *n.* one who dwells on or near the border of a country, region, etc., esp. that between England and Scotland.

**borderland** /'bɔdəlænd/, *n.* **1.** land forming a border or frontier. **2.** an uncertain intermediate district, space, or condition.

**Border Leicester** /bɔdə 'lɛstə/, *n.* a popular British long wool sheep highly sought after in Australia for cross breeding with the Merino.

**borderline** /'bɔdəlaɪn/, *adj.* **1.** on or near a border or boundary. **2.** uncertain; indeterminate. **3.** (in examinations, etc.) qualifying or failing to qualify by a narrow margin. **4.** not quite average, standard, or normal. **5.** verging on indecent or obscene. **6.** verging on insanity. –*n.* **7.** a line that determines or marks a border. **8.** an indefinite line between two qualities or conditions.

**bordure** /'bɔdjuə/, *n. Her.* the outer fifth of the shield. [ME, from OF. See BORDER]

**bore**[1] /bɔ/, *v.,* **bored, boring,** *n.* –*v.t.* **1.** to pierce (a solid substance) or make (a round hole, etc.) with an auger, drill, or other rotated instrument. **2.** to force by persistent forward thrusting. **3.** *Horseracing.* to push aside persistently; crowd out. **4. bore up (someone),** to upbraid; rebuke vehemently. **5. bore it up (you),** *Colloq.* (an offensive retort expressing contempt, dismissal). **6.** to make a hole, as with an auger or drill. **7.** to admit of being pierced with an auger or the like, as a substance. –*n.* **8.** a hole made by boring, or as if by boring. **9.** a deep hole of small diameter bored to the aquifer of an artesian basin, through which water rises under hydrostatic pressure. **10.** the inside diameter of a hollow cylindrical object or device, such as a bush or bearing, or the barrel of a gun. [ME *boren,* OE *borian,* c. G *bohren;* akin to L *forāre* pierce]

**bore**[2] /bɔ/, *v.,* **bored, boring,** *n.* –*v.t.* **1.** to weary by tedious repetition, dullness, unwelcome attentions, etc. –*n.* **2.** a dull, tiresome, or uncongenial person. **3.** a cause of ennui or annoyance. [orig. unknown]

**bore**[3] /bɔ/, *n.* an often dangerous wave which rises in front of a flood tide in a narrowing estuary; eagre. [ME, from Scand.; cf. Icel. *bāra* wave]

**bore**[4] /bɔ/, *v.* past tense of **bear**[1].

**boreal** /'bɔriəl/, *adj.* **1.** pertaining to the north wind. **2.** northern. **3.** pertaining to Boreas. [L *boreālis,* from *Boreas* north wind]

**boredom** /'bɔdəm/, *n.* the state or an instance of being bored; tedium; ennui.

**boree** /bɔ'ri/, *n.* any of several wattle trees as the weeping myall, the bastard myall and the *Acacia cana* of central and northern Queensland. [Aboriginal *booreah* fire]

**borehole** /'bɔhoʊl/, *n.* a hole bored into the surface of the earth, as for extracting oil.

**borer** /'bɔrə/, *n.* **1.** one who or that which bores or pierces. **2.** *Mach.* a tool used for boring; an auger. **3.** *Entomol.* any insect that burrows in trees, fruits, etc., esp. any beetle of certain groups. **4.** *Zool.* any of various molluscs, etc., that bore into wood, etc. **5.** a marsipobranch fish, as a hagfish, that bores into other fish to feed on their flesh.

**boresafe fuse** /ˌbɔseɪf 'fjuz/, *n.* a type of fuse having an interrupter in the explosive train that prevents a projectile from exploding until after it has cleared the muzzle of a weapon.

**bore sinker** /'bɔ sɪŋkə/, *n.* one who drills artesian bores.

**bore water** /'– wɔtə/, *n.* water from an artesian bore.

**boric** /'bɔrɪk/, *adj.* of or containing boron. Also, **boracic.**

**boric acid** /– 'æsəd/, *n.* any of a group of acids derived from boron trioxide with varying amounts of water esp. orthoboric acid, $B_2O_3 \cdot 3H_2O$ (or $H_3BO_3$), used as an antiseptic, preservative, and in fireproofing compounds, cosmetics, cements and enamel, but also metaboric acid, $B_2O_3 \cdot H_2O$ (or $HBO_2$), pyroboric acid, $2B_2O_3 \cdot 3H_2O$ (or $H_6B_4O_6$), or tetraboric acid, $2B_2O_3 \cdot H_2O$ (or $H_2B_4O_7$).

**boride** /'bɔraɪd/, *n.* any hard, heat-resistant compound, usu. containing two elements only, of which boron is the more electropositive.

**boring**[1] /'bɔrɪŋ/, *n.* **1.** the act or process of piercing or perforating. **2.** the hole so made. **3.** (*pl.*) the chips, fragments, or dust produced in boring.

**boring**[2] /'bɔrɪŋ/, *adj.* dull; tedious; uninteresting.

**born** /bɔn/, *adj.* **1.** brought forth by birth. **2.** possessing from birth the quality or character stated: *a born fool.* **3. born with a silver spoon in one's mouth,** born wealthy. **4. not born yesterday,** not easily deceived. –*v.* **5.** a past participle of **bear,** now normally replaced in all senses by borne. [properly pp. of BEAR[1]; ME and OE *boren*]

**born-again** /bɔn-ə'gɛn/, *adj.* **1.** evangelical; revivalistic. –*n.*

**2.** a member of an evangelical sect, esp. one converted through a personal religious experience.

**borne** /bɔn/, *v.* past participle of **bear.**

**borneol** /ˈbɔniɒl/, *n.* terpene alcohol, $C_{10}H_{17}OH$, closely resembling common camphor, found in concrete masses in the trunk of *Dryobalanops aromatica,* a large tree of Borneo, Sumatra, etc. [*Borneo,* an island in the Malay Archipelago, + -OL[1]]

**bornite** /ˈbɔnaɪt/, *n.* a common mineral, copper iron sulphide, $Cu_5FeS_4$, characterised by reddish colour on fresh fractures tarnishing to iridescent purple; an important ore of copper. [after I. von *Born,* 1742-91, Austrian mineralogist. See -ITE[1]]

**boron** /ˈbɔrɒn/, *n.* a non-metallic element present in borax, etc., and obtained in either an amorphous or a crystalline form when reduced from its compound.

**boron carbide** /– ˈkabaɪd/, *n.* a black crystalline solid, $B_4C$, which is the hardest known substance after diamond, and which is used as an abrasive and to form control rods in nuclear reactions.

**boronia** /bəˈroʊniə/, *n.* any of a number of Australian shrubs of the genus *Boronia,* as *B. megastigma,* with brown flowers and a strong perfume, and *B. heterophylla,* with rose-pink flowers. [after It. botanist Francesco *Borone,* 1769-94]

boronia

**boron trifluoride** /ˌbɔrɒn traɪˈfluraɪd/, *n.* a pungent colourless gas, $BF_3$, which fumes in moist air, formed by the action of fluorine on boron trioxide.

**boron trioxide** /ˌbɔrɒn traɪˈɒksaɪd/, *n.* a colourless crystalline solid, $B_2O_3$, which forms boric acid on hydration. Also, **boron oxide.**

**borosilicate** /ˌbɔroʊˈsɪləkət, -keɪt/, *n.* a salt of boric and silicic acids.

**borosilicic acids** /ˌbɔroʊsəˌlɪsɪk ˈæsədz/, *n. pl.* hypothetical acids yielding borosilicate.

**borough** /ˈbʌrə/, *n.* **1.** *Vic.* an area of land corresponding to a municipality in the other States of Australia. **2.** *Brit.* **a.** an urban community incorporated by royal charter. **b.** an urban electoral constituency, usu. subdivided. **3.** *Brit.* (formerly) a fortified town, or a town possessing municipal organisation. **4.** *U.S.* **a.** one of the five administrative divisions of New York City. **b.** (in certain states) a municipality smaller than a city. [ME *burgh* town, OE *burg* stronghold, c. G *Burg*]

**borrow** /ˈbɒroʊ/, *v.t.* **1.** to take or obtain (a thing) on the promise to return it or its equivalent; obtain the temporary use of. **2.** to get from another or from a foreign source; appropriate or adopt: *borrowed words.* **3.** *Arith.* (in subtraction) to take from one denomination to add to the next lower. *–v.i.* **4.** to borrow something. **5.** *Golf.* to play a ball up a hill or a slope, instead of straight across the green, so that the slope will cause the ball to return towards the hole. *–n.* **6.** *Golf.* the allowance made by the golfer for undulations in the putting green. [ME *borowe(n),* OE *borgian,* from *borg* a pledge] – **borrower,** *n.*

**borsch** /bɔʃ/, *n.* a Russian stock soup containing beetroot, served hot or chilled. Also **borsh, borscht, borshch, bortsch.** [Russ. *borshch*]

**borstal** /ˈbɔstl/, *n. Brit.* **1.** a reformatory for young offenders between the ages of 16 and 21. *–adj.* **2.** coming from or having to do with a borstal. [named after *Borstal,* village in Kent, where the first such reformatory is situated]

**bort** /bɔt/, *n.* flawed, low quality diamonds, and diamond fragments, valuable only for crushing to diamond dust. [cf. OF *bort* bastard] – **borty,** *adj.*

**borzoi** /ˈbɔzɔɪ/, *n., pl.* **-zois.** a large swift dog with a soft coat and long, pointed nose, originally bred in Russia; Russian wolfhound. [Russ.: lit., swift]

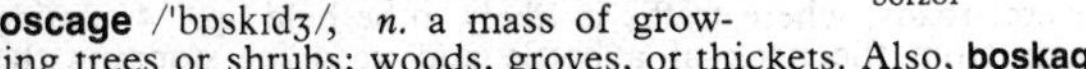

borzoi

**boscage** /ˈbɒskɪdʒ/, *n.* a mass of growing trees or shrubs; woods, groves, or thickets. Also, **boskage.** [ME, from OF, from *bosc,* from Gmc. See BOSKY]

**Bose-Einstein statistics** /boʊs-ˌaɪnstaɪn stəˈtɪstɪks/, *n.* a system of statistical mechanics applicable to elementary particles which do not obey the exclusion principle. [named after S. N. *Bose,* b. 1894, Indian physicist and A. *Einstein,* 1879-1955, German-U.S. physicist.]

**bosh**[1] /bɒʃ/, *n. Colloq.* complete nonsense; absurd or foolish talk or opinions. [Turk.: empty, vain]

**bosh**[2] /bɒʃ/, *n.* the lower portion of a blast furnace, extending from the widest part to the hearth. [cf. G *Böschung* slope]

**bosie** /ˈboʊzi/, *n. Cricket Colloq.* →**googly.** [named after the inventor of the googly, B.J.T. *Bosanquet,* 1877-1936, English cricketer] – Also, **bosey.**

**bosker** /ˈbɒskə/, *adj. Colloq.* excellent; delightful. Also, **boshter.**

**bosket** /ˈbɒskət/, *n.* a grove; a thicket. Also, **bosquet.** [F *bosquet,* from It. *boschetto,* diminutive of *bosco* wood. See BUSH[1]]

**bosky** /ˈbɒski/, *adj.* **1.** woody; covered with bushes. **2.** shady. [ME *bosk* (var. of *busk,* var. of BUSH[1]) + -Y[1]]

**bo's'n** /ˈboʊsən/, *n. Naut.* →**boatswain.**

**bosom** /ˈbʊzəm/, *n.* **1.** the breast of a human being, esp. a woman. **2.** that part of a garment which covers the breast. **3.** the breast, conceived of as the seat of thought or emotion. **4.** the enclosure formed by the breast and the arms; affectionate embrace. **5.** something likened to the human bosom: *the bosom of the earth.* *–adj.* **6.** of or pertaining to the bosom. **7.** intimate or confidential: *a bosom friend.* *–v.t.* **8.** to take to the bosom; embrace; cherish. **9.** to hide from view; conceal. [ME; OE *bōsm,* c. G *Busen*]

**bosomy** /ˈbʊzəmi/, *adj.* (of a woman) having large or prominent breasts.

**boson** /ˈboʊzɒn/, *n. Physics.* any elementary particle which conforms to Bose-Einstein statistics, such as a photon or meson.

**bosquet** /ˈbɒskət/, *n.* →**bosket.**

**boss**[1] /bɒs/, *n. Colloq.* **1.** one who employs or superintends workmen; a foreman or manager. **2.** anyone who asserts mastery, esp. one who controls a political or other body. **3.** headmaster or headmistress of a school. **4.** *Colloq.* an informal mode of address, not necessarily implying difference in status. *–v.t.* **5.** to be master of or over; manage; direct; control. *–v.i.* **6.** to be boss. **7.** to be domineering. *–adj.* **8.** chief; master: *boss cook.* [D *baas* master. See BAAS]

**boss**[2] /bɒs/, *n.* **1.** *Bot. Zool.* a protuberance or roundish excrescence on the body or on some organ of an animal or plant. **2.** *Geol.* **a.** a knoblike mass of rock, esp. such an outcrop of eruptive rock. **b.** a small mass of intrusive rock having a circular, elliptical or irregular ground plan and descending into the earth with steep sides; stock. **3.** an ornamental protuberance of metal, ivory, etc. **4.** *Archit.* a knoblike projection of ornamental character, as at the intersection of ribs or groins. **5.** *Mach.* the enlarged part of a shaft. *–v.t.* **6.** to ornament with bosses. **7.** →**emboss.** [ME *bos,* from OF *boce.* See BOTCH]

**bossa nova** /ˌbɒsə ˈnoʊvə/, *n.* **1.** jazz-influenced music of Brazilian origin, rhythmically related to the samba. **2.** a dance performed to this music. Also, **bossa.**

**bossboy** /ˈbɒsbɔɪ/, *n.* the supervisor of a labour force, as in South Africa, Papua New Guinea.

**boss cocky** /bɒs ˈkɒki/, *n. Colloq.* **1.** a farmer who employs labour. **2.** a boss.

**bosset** /ˈbɒsət/, *n.* the rudimentary stub of a horn or antler on a young deer. [BOSS[2] + -ET]

**boss-eyed** /ˈbɒs-aɪd/, *adj.* **1.** having a squint. **2.** *Colloq.* lacking in perception; based on false perception: *a boss-eyed attempt.*

**bossiaea** /ˈbɒsiə/, *n.* any of the small shrubs of the genus *Bossiaea,* family Papilionaceae, of Australia, with yellow pea-like flowers often suffused with red.

**boss of the board,** *n.* **1.** *Shearing.* the owner-manager or contractor who hires shearers. **2.** a boss. Also, **boss over the board.**

**boss-shot** /ˈbɒs-ʃɒt/, *n.* a wild error or blunder.

**bossy**[1] /ˈbɒsi/, *adj.,* **bossier, bossiest.** *Colloq.* given to acting like a boss; domineering. [BOSS[1] + -Y[1]]

**bossy**[2] /ˈbɒsi/, *adj.* studded with ornamental bosses; projecting as decorative work. [BOSS[2] + -Y[1]]

**Boston terrier** /bɒstən ˈtɛriə/, *n.* any of a breed of small, smooth-coated dogs with short hair and brindle or dark brown coat with white markings, originated in the U.S. by crossing the English bulldog and the bull-terrier. Also, **Boston bull.**

Boston terrier

**bosun** /ˈboʊsən/, *n.* →**boatswain.**

**bosun's chair** /boʊsənz ˈtʃɛə/, *n.* →**boatswain's chair.**

**bot** /bɒt/, *n., v.,* **botted, botting.** *Colloq.* –*n.* **1.** a person who cadges persistently. **2. on the bot,** cadging. **3.** an insect larva infecting the skin, sinuses, nose, eye, stomach, or other parts of animals or man. **4. the bot,** tuberculosis, or other chest complaint. **5.** *N.Z.* a minor ailment as, a bad cold; the wog. **6. how're the bots biting,** *N.Z.* (a humorous greeting). **7.** bottom; the buttocks. –*v.t., v.i.* **8.** to cadge. [orig. uncert.]

**bot.,** **1.** botanical. **2.** botanist. **3.** botany.

**botanical** /bəˈtænɪkəl/, *adj.* **1.** pertaining to plants or the study of plants. –*n.* **2.** a crude drug made from part of a plant, as the bark, roots, etc. Also, **botanic.** [ML *botanicus* (Gk *botanikós*) + -AL[1]] – **botanically,** *adv.*

**botanical garden** /– ˈgadn/, *n.* (*oft. pl.*) a large garden usu. open to the public where trees, shrubs and plants typically from many lands, are grown and studied.

**botanise** /ˈbɒtənaɪz/, *v.,* **-nised, -nising.** –*v.i.* **1.** to study plants. **2.** to collect specimens for botanical study. –*v.t.* **3.** to explore (an area) seeking knowledge of its plant life. Also, **botanize.** – **botaniser,** *n.*

**botanist** /ˈbɒtənəst/, *n.* one who is skilled in botany.

**botanomancy** /ˈbɒtənəˌmænsi/, *n.* a method of divination entailing the burning of tree branches and leaves.

**botany** /ˈbɒtəni/, *n., pl.* **-nies.** **1.** the science of plants; the branch of biology that deals with plant life. **2.** the plant life of an area: *the botany of the Simpson Desert.* **3.** the biology of a plant or plant group: *the botany of deciduous trees.* **4.** a botanical system or treatise: *outlined in 19th century botanies.* [*botan(ic)* (see BOTANICAL) + -Y[3]]

**Botany Bay** /bɒtəni ˈbeɪ/, *adj.* (formerly) of or pertaining to New South Wales.

**Botany Bay dozen,** *n. Convict Obs. Colloq.* a punishment consisting of twenty-five lashes. [from *Botany Bay,* N.S.W., formerly a place of detention and punishment]

**botany wool** /ˈbɒtəni wʊl/, *n.* a fine wool obtained from merino sheep. Also, **botany.** [from *Botany* Bay, N.S.W.]

**botch** /bɒtʃ/, *v.t.* **1.** to spoil by poor work; bungle. **2.** to do or say in a bungling manner. **3.** to mend or patch in a clumsy manner (oft. fol. by *up*). –*n.* **4.** Also, **botch-up.** a clumsy or poor piece of work; a bungle: *his carpentry was a complete botch.* **5.** a clumsily added part or patch. [ME *bocchen;* orig. uncert.] – **botcher,** *n.* – **botchery,** *n.*

**botchy** /ˈbɒtʃi/, *adj.,* **botchier, botchiest.** poorly made or done; bungled.

**botfly** /ˈbɒtflaɪ/, *n., pl.* **-flies.** any of a number of dipterous insects of the families Oestridae and Gastrophilidae, the larvae of which are parasitic in the skin or other parts of animals or man. [see BOT]

**both** /boʊθ/, *adj., pron.* **1.** the one and the other; the two together: *give both dates, both had been there.* –*conj., adv.* **2.** alike; equally: *both men and women, he is both ready and willing.* [ME *bothe, bathe,* from Scand.; cf. Icel. *bādhir,* c. G *beide*]

**bother** /ˈbɒðə/, *v.t.* **1.** to give trouble to; annoy; pester; worry. **2.** to bewilder; confuse. –*v.i.* **3.** to trouble oneself. **4.** to cause annoyance or trouble. –*n.* **5.** something bothersome. **6.** an annoying disturbance. **7.** worried or perplexed state. **8.** someone who bothers. –*interj.* **9.** (a mild exclamation.) [orig. unknown]

**botheration** /bɒðəˈreɪʃən/, *interj.* (a mild exclamation indicating vexation or annoyance.)

**bothersome** /ˈbɒðəsəm/, *adj.* troublesome.

**bothy** /ˈbɒθi/, *n., pl.* **bothies.** *Scot.* a hut or small cottage, esp. for lodging farmhands or workmen. [? from BOOTH]

**bo tree** /ˈboʊ tri/, *n.* the pipal or sacred fig tree, *Ficus religiosa,* of India, under which the founder of Buddhism is reputed to have attained the enlightenment which constituted him the Buddha. [*bo,* from Singhalese, from Pali *bodhi-(taru)* perfect knowledge (tree)]

**botryoidal** /ˌbɒtriˈɔɪdl/, *adj.* having the form of a bunch of grapes. Also, **botryoid.** [Gk *botryoeidḗs* + -AL[1]] – **botryoidally,** *adv.*

**botryomycosis** /ˌbɒtrioʊmaɪˈkoʊsəs/, *n.* a disease of horses, usu. following castration, in which there is tumefaction of the stump of the spermatic cord.

**botryose** /ˈbɒtrioʊs/, *adj.* **1.** →**botryoidal.** **2.** →**racemose.**

**botrytis cinerea** /bəˌtraɪtəs səˈnɪəriə/, *n.* a fungus which attacks grapes, resulting in a concentration of the sugars; noble rot. [Gk *bótrus* + bunch of grapes + -ITIS; L *cinerea* ash-coloured]

**bots** /bɒts/, *n.* (*construed as pl.*) a disease caused by the attachment of the larvae of botflies to the stomach of a horse.

**Botswana** /bɒtˈswanə/, *n.* a republic in southern Africa.

**bott** /bɒt/, *n.* →**bot.**

**botte** /bɒt/, *n. Fencing.* a thrust or hit. [F]

**bottle** /ˈbɒtl/, *n., v.,* **-tled, -tling.** –*n.* **1.** a portable vessel with a neck or mouth, now commonly made of glass, used for holding liquids. **2.** the contents of a bottle; as much as a bottle contains: *a bottle of wine.* **3.** a bottle with a rubber nipple from which a baby sucks milk, etc. **4.** (in hospitals, etc.) a portable container with a wide tilted neck into which bed-ridden males urinate. **5.** *Colloq.* a compressed air cylinder. **6. be on the bottle,** *Colloq.* to be on a drinking bout; be intoxicated. **7. hit the bottle,** *Colloq.* to drink heavily; become an alcoholic. **8. the bottle, a.** intoxicating drink. **b.** bottled milk for babies (opposed to *the breast*): *raised on the bottle.* –*v.t.* **9.** to put into or seal in a bottle; to preserve (fruit or vegetables) in bottles. **10. bottle up,** to shut in or restrain closely: *to bottle up one's feelings.* **11.** *Colloq.* to knock over people as though they were bottles: *bottle 'im!* [ME *botel,* from OF *botele,* from LL *butticula,* diminutive of *buttis* BUTT[4]] – **bottlelike,** *adj.* – **bottler,** *n.*

**bottle age** /ˈ– eɪdʒ/, *n.* the character of a wine, obtained by long storage in the bottle.

**bottle baby** /ˈ– beɪbi/, *n.* a baby fed by bottle from birth instead of being breast-fed.

**bottlebrush** /ˈbɒtlbrʌʃ/, *n.* **1.** a brush for cleaning bottles. **2.** any species of the Australian genus *Callistemon* whose flower spikes resemble a cylindrical brush. **3.** a member of other related, and occasionally unrelated, species with similar flowers.

bottlebrush (def. 2)

**bottle department** /ˈbɒtl dəpatmənt/, *n.* a section of a hotel which sells bottles and cans of drink for customers to take away and consume off the premises. Also, **bottle shop.**

**bottled gas** /bɒtld ˈgæs/, *n.* →**liquefied petroleum gas.**

**bottle-drive** /ˈbɒtl-draɪv/, *n.* the collection of saleable empty bottles to raise money for a particular cause.

**bottle-feed** /ˈbɒtl-fid/, *v.,* **-fed, -feeding.** *v.t.* **1.** to feed (a baby or young animal) with prepared milk from a bottle (opposed to *breast-feed*). –*v.i.* **2.** to feed in this manner.

**bottle-glass** /ˈbɒtl-glas/, *n.* a kind of thick, dark green glass used for making bottles.

**bottle green** /bɒtl ˈgrin/, *adj.* deep green.

**bottle-holder** /ˈbɒtl-hoʊldə/, *n. Colloq.* **1.** a boxer's or wrestler's second. **2.** any supporter or assistant.

**bottleneck** /ˈbɒtlnɛk/, *n.* **1.** a narrow entrance or passage way. **2.** a place, or stage in a process, where progress is retarded. **3. a.** a narrow part of a road between two wide stretches. **b.** a congested junction, road, town, etc., fed by several roads, where traffic is likely to be held up. **4.** a slide made from the neck of a bottle and used for stopping the strings of a steel guitar. *–adj.* **5.** of or pertaining to the type of guitar played with such a slide, or the type of music associated with it.

**bottleneck playing** /'– pleɪɪŋ/, *n.* →**slide guitar.** [so called because negro blues players used the neck of a bottle to produce a glissando effect on the guitar]

**bottle nose** /'bɒtl noʊz/, *n.* a swollen red or purple pimply nose, popularly believed to be caused by alcoholic drink. – **bottle-nosed** /'bɒtl-noʊzd/, *adj.*

**bottlenose** /'bɒtlnoʊz/, *n.* any of various dolphins, whales, etc., with a bottle-shaped nose.

**bottle-o** /'bɒtl-oʊ/, *n. Colloq.* one who collects empty bottles for sale or re-use. Also, **bottle-oh.**

**bottle party** /'bɒtl pati/, *n.* a party to which each guest brings a bottle of some alcoholic drink.

**bottler** /'bɒtlə/, *n.* **1.** someone who puts something in bottles. **2.** a marble (def. 7) composed of glass. **3.** *Colloq.* something exciting admiration or approval: *you little bottler.*

**bottle shop** /'bɒtl ʃɒp/, *n.* **1.** →**bottle department. 2.** →**liquor store.**

**bottle sickness** /'– sɪknəs/, *n.* a temporary deterioration of some table wines, occurring shortly after bottling.

**bottle tree** /'– tri/, *n.* **1.** any of various tree species with bottle-shaped trunks, esp. some Australian species of *Brachychiton,* but also *Adansonia gregorii* of Australia and *Cavanillesia arborea* of Brazil. **2.** →**baobab.**

bottle tree

**bottle-washer** /'bɒtl-wɒʃə/, *n.* **1.** one whose occupation is washing bottles. **2. chief cook and bottle-washer,** *Colloq.* a person who, as well as being responsible for some enterprise, also does much of the work, esp. manual work, for it.

**bottley** /'bɒtli/, *n. Colloq.* a clear-glass marble, originally the stopper in an obsolete type of aerated-water bottle.

**bottling** /'bɒtlɪŋ/, *n.* the act, process, or business of preserving fruit, etc., in bottles or jars.

**bottom** /'bɒtəm/, *n.* **1.** the lowest or deepest part of anything, as distinguished from the top: *the bottom of a hill, of a page, etc.* **2.** the place of least honour, dignity, or achievement: *the bottom of the class, of the table, etc.* **3.** the lowest gear of a motor; first gear. **4.** the underside: *the bottom of a flat-iron.* **5.** the ground under any body of water: *the bottom of the sea.* **6.** *Phys. Geog.* low-lying alluvial land adjacent to a river. **7.** *Naut.* **a.** the part of a ship below the wales. **b.** a ship. **8.** the seat of a chair. **9.** the buttocks. **10.** the fundamental part; basic aspect: *from the bottom of my heart.* **11.** the inmost part or inner end of a recess, bay, lane, etc. **12. at bottom,** in reality; fundamentally. **13. bottoms up!** (an exclamation used as an encouragement to finish a drink). *–v.t.* **14.** to furnish with a bottom. **15.** to base or found (fol. by *on* or *upon*). **16.** to reach mineral (gold, etc.) at depth (fol. by *on*). **17.** to get to the bottom of; fathom. *–v.i.* **18.** to be based; rest. **19.** to strike against the bottom or end; reach the bottom. **20. a.** (of car springs or shock absorbers), to be forced into an extreme position of compression: *the springs bottomed as the car hit the cattle-grid.* **b.** (of the undercarriage of a motor vehicle) to make contact with the ground. **21.** *Mining.* to reach bedrock or a point in a mine beyond which further mining is useless. **22. bottom out,** to reach a lowest level of economic activity thought likely: *the recession in the economy has bottomed out.* *–adj.* **23.** lowest; undermost. **24.** fundamental: *the bottom cause.* [ME; OE *botm,* c. G *Boden*]]

**bottom board** /'– bɔd/, *n.* **1.** one of several removable planks inside a boat at the bottom to protect the outer planking. **2.** the base of a beehive.

**bottom drawer** /– 'drɔ/, *n.* →**glory box.**

**bottom fermentation** /– fɜmɛn'teɪʃən/, *n.* a brewing method using a strain of yeast that sinks to the bottom of the vessel at the completion of fermentation, producing new beer or lager. Cf. **top fermentation.**

**bottomless** /'bɒtəmləs/, *adj.* **1.** without a bottom. **2.** immeasurably deep. **3. the bottomless pit,** hell.

**bottommost** /'bɒtəmmoʊst/, *adj.* lowest; at the very bottom.

**bottomry** /'bɒtəmri/, *n. Marine Law.* a contract, of the nature of a mortgage, by which the owner of a ship borrows money to make a voyage, pledging the ship as security. [modelled on D *bodemerij,* from *boden* keel of a ship]

**bottom turn** /'bɒtəm tɜn/, *n.* in surf riding, a change of direction or turn at the base of a wave.

**botulin** /'bɒtʃələn/, *n.* the toxin causing botulism.

**botulinus** /bɒtʃə'linəs/, *n.* the bacterium *Clostridium botulinum,* which forms botulin.

**botulism** /'bɒtʃəlɪzəm/, *n.* a disease of the nervous system caused by botulin developed in spoiled sausage, preserved and other foods eaten by animals and man, often fatal. [L *botulus* sausage + -ISM]

**bouclé** /'bukleɪ/, *n.* yarn with loops, which produces a woven or knitted fabric with rough appearance. [F]

**boudoir** /'budwa/, *n.* a lady's bedroom or private room. [F *bouder* pout, sulk]

**bouffant** /'bufõ/, *adj.* puffed out; full, as sleeves, hairstyle, or draperies. [F]

**bougainvillea** /boʊgən'vɪliə/, *n.* any shrub or spiny climber of the tropical American genus *Bougainvillea* with brightly coloured bracts, widely cultivated in tropical and subtropical Australia. [named after Louis Antoine de *Bougainville,* 1729-1811, French explorer of the Pacific]

**bough** /baʊ/, *n.* **1.** a branch of a tree, esp. one of the larger of the main branches. **2.** *Archaic.* the gallows. [ME; OE *bōg, bōh* shoulder, bough, c. D *boeg,* LG *bug,* Icel. *bōgr* shoulder, bow of a ship] – **boughless,** *adj.*

**bought** /bɔt/, *v.* past tense and past participle of **buy.**

**bougie** /'buʒi/, *n.* **1.** *Med.* **a.** a slender flexible instrument for introduction into passages of the body for dilating or opening, etc. **b.** a suppository. **2.** a wax candle. [F, name of *Bougie,* Algerian town, centre of wax trade]

**bouillabaisse** /'bujəbeɪs/, *n.* a stew or thick soup made of several kinds of fish and shellfish cooked in water or white wine, with oil and tomatoes, flavoured with garlic, saffron and other herbs. [F, from Pr. *bouiabaisso,* from *boui* boil + *abaisso* (go) down]

**bouillon** /'bujɒn/, *n.* a plain unclarified stock or broth made by boiling beef, veal or chicken in water, with herbs. [F, *bouillier* boil]

**boulder** /'boʊldə/, *n.* a detached and rounded or worn rock, esp. a large one. [short for *boulder stone,* ME *bulder-,* from Scand.; cf. d. Sw. *buldersten* big stone (in a stream)]

**boulder clay** /'– kleɪ/, *n.* a layer of clay containing boulders and stones, deposited by ancient glaciers.

**boulevard** /'buləvad/, *n.* **1.** a broad avenue of a city, often having trees and used as a promenade. **2.** a street. [F, from MLG *boleverk.* See BULWARK]

**boulevardier** /bul'vadieɪ/, *n.* one who frequents boulevards; a pleasure seeker. [F]

**bouleversement** /bʊl'vɜsmənt/, *n.* an overturning; upsetting; confusion; turmoil. [F]

**boulter** /'boʊltə/, *n.* a long, stout fishing line with several hooks attached.

**bounce** /baʊns/, *v.,* **bounced, bouncing,** *n., adv.* *–v.i.* **1.** to move with a bound, and rebound, as a ball: *a ball bounces back from the wall.* **2.** to burst ebulliently (*into* or *out of*): *to bounce into and out of a room.* **3.** to boast; show off. **4.** *Colloq.* (of cheques) to be dishonoured; to be returned unpaid. *–v.t.* **5.** to cause to bound or rebound: *to bounce a ball, to bounce a child up and down.* **6.** *Colloq.* to eject or discharge summarily. **7.** to persuade (someone) by bluff. **8.** *Colloq.* to arrest. *–n.* **9.** a rebound or bound: *catch the ball on the first bounce.* **10.** a sudden spring or leap. **11.** impudence; bluster; swagger. **12.** ability to bounce; resilience. **13.** *Aus. Rules.* →**ball-up. 14. the bounce,** *Aus. Rules.* the start of the game. **15.** *U.S. Colloq.* expulsion; discharge; dismissal. [ME *bunsen* thump, from LG, *bums!* thump! Cf. D *bonzen* thwack, etc.]

**bouncer** /'baʊnsə/, *n.* **1.** one who or that which bounces. **2.** Also, **baby bouncer.** a spring seat or harness in which a baby may bounce up and down. **3.** *Colloq.* one employed in a place of public resort to eject disorderly persons. **4.** something large of its kind. **5.** an impudent, brash person. **6.** *Cricket.* a bumper.

**bounce up** /ˈbaʊns ʌp/, *n. Soccer.* the bouncing of the ball by the referee to restart the game after a stoppage for any reason other than an infringement.

**bouncinette** /baʊnsəˈnɛt/, *n.* a metal frame with netting stretched over it and gently sloped so that a baby may recline or bounce on it. [Trademark]

**bouncing** /ˈbaʊnsɪŋ/, *adj.* **1.** stout, strong, or vigorous: *a bouncing baby.* **2.** exaggerated; big; hearty; noisy: *a bouncing lie.*

**bouncing Bett** /– ˈbɛt/, *n.* the common soapwort. Also, **bouncing Bess** /– ˈbɛs/, **bouncing Bet.**

**bouncy** /ˈbaʊnsi/, *adj.* **1.** of or pertaining to that which bounces, as a ball, a woman's hair, etc. **2.** of or pertaining to that which is suitable to bounce on, as a bed, a chair, etc. **3.** of a personality which is cheerful and enthusiastic.

**bound**[1] /baʊnd/, *adj.* **1.** tied; in bonds: *a bound prisoner.* **2.** made fast as by a band or bond: *bound by one's word.* **3.** secured within a cover, as a book. **4.** under obligation, legally or morally: *in duty bound to help.* **5.** destined or sure: *it is bound to happen.* **6.** determined or resolved: *he is bound to go.* **7.** constipated; costive. **8. bound up in** or **with, a.** inseparably connected with. **b.** having the affections centred in: *his life is bound up in his children.* [pp. of BIND]

**bound**[2] /baʊnd/, *v.i.* **1.** to move by leaps; leap; jump; spring. **2.** to rebound, as a ball. *–v.t.* **3.** to cause to bound. *–n.* **4.** a leap onwards or upwards; a jump. **5.** a rebound. [F *bondir* leap, orig., resound, ? from L *bombitāre* hum]

**bound**[3] /baʊnd/, *n.* **1.** (*usu. pl.*) a limiting line, or boundary: *the bounds of space and time.* **2.** that which limits, confines, or restrains. **3.** (*pl.*) territory on or near a boundary. **4.** (*pl.*) an area included within boundary lines: *within the bounds of his estate, within the bounds of reason.* **5. out of bounds,** forbidden of access to certain persons or to the general public. *–v.t.* **6.** to limit as by bounds. **7.** to form the boundary or limit of. **8.** to name the boundaries of. *–v.i.* **9.** to have boundaries (*on*); abut. [ME *bounde, boune,* from OF *bodne,* from LL *butina*]

**bound**[4] /baʊnd/, *adj.* **1.** going or intending to go; on the way (*to*); destined (*for*): *the train is bound for Bathurst.* **2.** *Archaic.* prepared; ready. [ME *boun,* from Scand.; cf. Icel. *būinn,* pp. of *būa* get ready]

**boundary** /ˈbaʊndri/, *n., pl.* **-ries,** *adj.* *–n.* **1.** something that indicates bounds or limits; a limiting or bounding line. **2.** *Agric.* a fence which serves to indicate the limits of a property. **3.** *Cricket.* **a.** the marked limits of the field within which the game is played. **b.** a stroke which drives the ball beyond those limits. **c.** the four, or, if the ball reaches the boundary without touching the ground, six runs scored by such a stroke. *–adj.* **4.** *Physics.* surrounding the exterior of a solid or liquid body. **5.** denoting a boundary.

**boundary conditions** /– kənˈdɪʃənz/, *n.pl. Maths.* mathematical expressions which describe the behaviour of a mathematical function usu. at extreme values of the variable.

**boundary layer** /ˈ– leɪə/, *n. Physics, Aeron., etc.* the thin layer of fluid next to the surface of a moving body in which there is a transition between the velocity of the body on one side, and the velocity of the fluid on the other.

**boundary rider** /ˈ– raɪdə/, *n.* a station hand who keeps fences in good repair and prevents stock from straying. – **boundary riding,** *n.*

**boundary umpire** /ˈ– ˌʌmpaɪə/, *n. Aus. Rules.* one of two umpires on the boundary line who decides when the ball is out of bounds, and who restarts play following the ball's going out of bounds; linesman.

**bounden** /ˈbaʊndən/, *adj.* morally obligatory (only in phrase *bounden duty*). [var. of BOUND[1]; orig. pp. of BIND]

**bounder** /ˈbaʊndə/, *n. Colloq.* an obtrusive, ill-bred person; a vulgar upstart.

**bound form** /ˈbaʊnd fɔm/, *n.* a linguistic form which never occurs by itself but always as part of some larger construction, as *-ed* in *seated.*

**boundless** /ˈbaʊndləs/, *adj.* without bounds; unlimited: *his boundless energy amazed them.* – **boundlessly,** *adv.* – **boundlessness,** *n.*

**bounteous** /ˈbaʊntiəs/, *adj.* **1.** giving or disposed to give freely; generously liberal. **2.** freely bestowed; plentiful; abundant. [*bounte* (earlier var. of BOUNTY) + -OUS; replacing ME *bontyvous,* from OF *bontif* benevolent] – **bounteously,** *adv.* – **bounteousness,** *n.*

**bountiful** /ˈbaʊntəfəl/, *adj.* **1.** liberal in bestowing gifts, favours, or bounties; munificent; generous. **2.** abundant; ample: *a bountiful supply.* – **bountifully,** *adv.* – **bountifulness,** *n.*

**bounty** /ˈbaʊnti/, *n., pl.* **-ties. 1.** generosity in giving. **2.** whatever is given bounteously; a benevolent, generous gift. **3.** a premium or reward, esp. one offered by a government. **4.** a sum paid for the killing of an animal declared a pest: *dingo bounty.* [ME *bounte,* from OF *bonte(t),* from L *bonitas* goodness]

**bounty hunter** /ˈ– hʌntə/, *n. Chiefly U.S.* one who hunts predatory animals, criminals, etc., for the reward or bounty offered for capturing or killing them.

**bounty system** /ˈ– sɪstəm/, *n.* a system in which money was granted as a bounty by the governor of a colony to a settler who assisted in the immigration of a skilled person to the colony.

**bouquet** /buˈkeɪ, boʊˈkeɪ/, *n.* **1.** a bunch of flowers; a nosegay. **2.** the characteristic aroma of wine, liqueurs, etc. **3.** an offensive smell. **4.** approval, applause: *to get no bouquets.* **5. throw a bouquet,** to compliment; flatter. [F: bunch, clump of trees, from OF *bosquet* little wood, diminutive of *bosc* wood. See BUSH[1]]

**bouquet garni** /– gaˈni/, *n.* a bunch of herbs, usu. including a bayleaf, thyme and parsley, and used to give flavour to sauces, stews, etc. tied together so that it can be removed later.

**bourbon** /ˈbɜbən/, *n.* a kind of whisky distilled from a mash containing 51 per cent or more maize. Also, **bourbon whisky.** [orig. the whisky produced in *Bourbon* County, Kentucky]

**bourdon** /ˈbɔdn/, *n.* **1.** the drone of a bagpipe, or of a monotonous and repetitious ground melody. **2.** a low-pitched tone; a bass. **3.** an organ stop producing such a tone. [F]

**Bourdon gauge** /ˈbɔdn geɪdʒ/, *n.* a pressure gauge for steam boilers. [named after Eugène *Bourdon,* 1808-84, French hydraulic engineer]

**bourgeois**[1] /ˈbʊəʒwa, ˈbu-/, *n., pl.* **-geois,** *adj.* *–n.* **1.** a member of the middle class. **2.** a shopkeeper or other trader. **3.** one whose outlook is said to be determined by a concern for property values; a capitalist, as opposed to a member of the wage-earning class. *–adj.* **4.** belonging to or consisting of the middle class. **5.** lacking in refinement or elegance; conventional. **6.** dominated or characterised by a concern for property values or by materialistic pursuits. [F; c. BURGESS]

**bourgeois**[2] /bɜˈdʒɔɪs/, *n.* a printing type (9 point) of a size between brevier and long primer. [? proper name]

**bourgeoisie** /bʊəʒwaˈzi/, *n.* **1.** the bourgeois class. **2.** (in Marxist ideology) the class opposed to the proletariat or wage-earning class. [F]

**bourgeon** /ˈbɜdʒən/, *n., v.* →**burgeon.**

**bourguignon** /ˈbʊəginjɒn/, *adj.* (of meat, eggs, fish or poultry) served with a sauce of red wine, mushrooms and onions. [F, from *Bourgogne,* Burgundy]

**Bourke parrot** /bɜk ˈpærət/, *n.* the small parrot, *Neophema bourkii,* predominantly brown with blue wings and pink throat and breast, with semi-nocturnal habits.

**bourn** /bɔn/, *n.* **1.** a bound; limit. **2.** destination; goal. **3.** realm; domain. Also, **bourne.** [F *borne*]

**bournonite** /ˈbɔnənaɪt/, *n.* a mineral sulphide of lead, copper, and antimony; occurring in wheel-shaped twins; wheel ore.

**bourrée** /ˈbʊreɪ/, *n.* **1.** an old French and Spanish dance, resembling a gavotte. **2.** the music for it.

**Bourse** /bʊəs/, *n.* a stock exchange, esp. that of Paris. [F: orig., purse, from LL *bursa,* from Gk *býrsa* hide]

**bouse**[1] /baʊz/, *v.t.* **boused, bousing.** →**bowse.**

**bouse**[2] /buz/, *n., v.,* **boused, bousing.** →**booze.**

**boustrophedon** /bustrəˈfidn, baʊ-/, *n.* an ancient method of writing in which the lines run alternately from right to left and from left to right. [Gk: adv., with turning like that of oxen in ploughing]

**bousy** /ˈbuzi/, *adj.* →**boozy.**

**bout** /baʊt/, *n.* **1.** a contest esp. a boxing or wrestling match; a trial of strength. **2.** a turn at work or any action. **3.** period; spell: *a bout of illness.* [var. of obs. *bought* bend, turn, from BOW[1]]

**boutade** /bu'tad/, *n.* a sally; witticism.

**boutique** /bu'tik/, *n.* a small shop selling fashionable or luxury articles esp. for women. [F]

**boutonniere** /bu,tɒni'ɛə/, *n.* a buttonhole bouquet or flower. [F: buttonhole]

**bouzouki** /bə'zuki/, *n.* a stringed instrument from Greece, related to a mandolin, played by plucking. [Modern Gk *mpouzouki*]

**bovid** /'boʊvɪd/, *adj.* of or pertaining to the Bovidae, or ox family, comprising the hollow-horned ruminants, as oxen, sheep, and goats.

**bovine** /'boʊvaɪn/, *adj.* **1.** of the ox family (Bovidae). **2.** oxlike. **3.** stolid; dull. *–n.* **4.** a bovine animal. [LL *bovīnus,* from L *bōs* ox]

**bow**[1] /baʊ/, *v.i.* **1.** to bend or curve downwards; stoop: *the pines bowed low.* **2.** to yield; submit: *to bow to the inevitable.* **3.** to bend the body or head in worship, reverence, respect, or submission. **4.** to incline the head or body, or both, in salutation, etc. **5. bow and scrape,** to be servile. **6. bow out,** to retire; leave the scene. *–v.t.* **7.** to bend or incline in worship, submission, respect, civility, or agreement: *to bow one's head.* **8.** to cause to submit; subdue; crush. **9.** to cause to stoop: *age had bowed his head.* **10.** to express by a bow, or by bowing: *to bow one's thanks.* **11.** to usher (*in, out,* etc.) with a bow. **12.** to cause to bend; make curved or crooked. *–n.* **13.** an inclination of the head or body in salutation, assent, thanks, reverence, respect, or submission. [ME *bowe(n),* OE *būgan,* c. G *biegen* bend] **– bowed** /baʊd/, *adj.*

**bow**[2] /boʊ/, *n.* **1.** a strip of flexible wood or other material bent by a string stretched between its ends, used for shooting arrows. **2.** a bend or curve. **3.** something curved or arc-shaped. **4.** a looped knot, as of ribbon, composed of one or two loops and two ends. **5.** (pl.) →**b-bows.** **6.** *Music.* **a.** an implement, originally curved, but now almost always straight, with horsehairs stretched upon it, designed for playing any stringed instrument. **b.** a single stroke of such an implement. **7.** the arched front part of a saddle. **8.** a U-shaped piece under an animal's neck to hold a yoke. **9.** a rainbow. *–adj.* **10.** curved; bent like a bow: *bow legs.* *–v.t.* **11.** to bend into the form of a bow; curve. **12.** *Music.* **a.** to perform by means of a bow upon a stringed instrument. **b.** to make a single downward or upward stroke of the bow. *–v.i.* **13.** to bend into a curve or bow. **14.** to play a stringed instrument with a bow. [ME *bowe,* OE *boga,* c. G *Bogen*] **– bowless,** *adj.* **– bowlike,** *adj.* **– bower,** *n.*

**bow**[3] /baʊ/, *n.* **1.** (*sometimes pl.*) the front or forward part or end of a ship, boat, airship, etc. **2.** the foremost oar used in rowing a boat. **3.** the person who pulls that oar; the bow oar; bowman. **4. on the port** (or **starboard**) **bow,** within 45° to port (or starboard) of the direction in which the stem of the ship is pointing. [LG *boog,* or D *boeg.* Cf. Dan. *bov,* c. BOUGH]

**bow compass** /'boʊ kʌmpəs/, *n. Tech. Drawing.* one of a set of compasses whose legs are joined by a bow-shaped piece.

**bowdlerise** /'baʊdləraɪz/, *v.t.,* **-rised, -rising.** to expurgate prudishly. Also, **bowdlerize.** [from Thomas *Bowdler,* who in 1818 published an expurgated edition of Shakespeare] **– bowdlerism,** *n.* **– bowdlerisation** /ˌbaʊdləraɪ'zeɪʃən/, *n.* **– bowdleriser,** *n.*

**bowel** /'baʊəl/, *n., v.,* **-elled, -elling,** or (*U.S.*) **-eled, -eling.** *–n.* **1.** *Anat.* **a.** an intestine. **b.** (*usu. pl.*) the parts of the alimentary canal below the stomach; the intestines or entrails. **2.** the inward or interior parts: *the bowels of the ship.* **3.** (*pl.*) *Archaic.* feelings of pity or compassion. **4. one's bowels turn to water,** one loses courage. *–v.t.* **5.** to disembowel. [ME bouel, from OF *boel,* from L *botellus,* diminutive of *botulus* sausage]

**bower**[1] /'baʊə/, *n.* **1.** a leafy shelter or recess; an arbour. **2.** *Archaic.* a rustic dwelling; a cottage. **3.** *Poetic.* a chamber; a boudoir. *–v.t.* **4.** to enclose in or as in a bower; embower. [ME *bour,* OE *būr* a dwelling, cottage, akin to *būan* dwell] **– bowerlike,** *adj.*

**bower**[2] /'baʊə/, *n.* an anchor carried at a ship's bow. Also, **bower anchor.** [BOW[3] + -ER[2]]

**bower**[3] /'baʊə/, *n.* (in euchre and other card games) the knave of trumps (**right bower**) or the other knave of the same colour (**left bower**); the highest cards in the game, unless the joker (often called the **best bower**) is used. [G *Bauer* peasant, jack (in cards)]

**bower**[4] /'baʊə/, *n.* one who or that which bows or bends. [BOW[1] + -ER[1]]

**bowerbird** /'baʊəbɜd/, *n.* **1.** any of various oscine birds of Australia and New Guinea, related to birds of paradise, as *Ptilonorhynchus violaceus,* which build bowerlike structures, used, not as nests, but as places of resort to attract the females. **2.** one who collects useless objects.

satin bowerbird

**bowery** /'baʊəri/, *adj.* bowerlike; containing bowers; shady: *a bowery maze.*

**bowfin** /'boʊfɪn/, *n.* a North American freshwater ganoid fish, *Amia calva.*

**bow-fronted** /boʊ-'frʌntəd/, *adj.* of or pertaining to furniture, etc., which is curved in front.

**bow hand** /'boʊ hænd/, **1.** *Archery.* the hand that holds the bow, usu. the left hand. **2.** *Music.* the hand that draws the bow, usu. the right hand.

**bowhand** /'baʊhænd/, *n.* a paddler who kneels or sits in the forward position of a canoe.

**bowhead** /'boʊhɛd/, *n.* a whale, *Balaena mysticetus,* of arctic seas.

**bowie knife** /'boʊi naɪf/, *n.* a heavy sheath-knife having a long, single-edged blade. [named after James *Bowie,* 1796-1836, American pioneer]

bowie knife

**bowing** /'boʊɪŋ/, *n. Music.* the style in which the bow is used in playing a particular passage.

**bowl**[1] /boʊl/, *n.* **1.** a rather deep, round dish or basin, used chiefly for holding liquids, food, etc. **2.** the contents of a bowl. **3.** a rounded, hollow part: *the bowl of a pipe.* **4.** a large drinking cup; a goblet. **5.** festive drinking; conviviality. **6.** any bowl-shaped depression or formation. **7.** an edifice with a bowl-like interior, as for athletic contests, etc. [ME *bolle,* OE *bolla,* c. Icel. *bolli.* See BOLL] **– bowl-like,** *adj.*

**bowl**[2] /boʊl/, *n.* **1.** one of the biased or weighted balls used in the game of bowls. **2.** one of the balls, having little or no bias, used in playing ninepins or tenpin bowling. **3.** a cast or delivery of the ball in bowling. **4.** a bowling alley. **5.** *Mach.* a rotating cylindrical part in a machine, as one to reduce friction. *–v.i.* **6.** to play with bowls, or at bowling. **7.** to roll a bowl, as in the game of bowls. **8.** to move along smoothly and rapidly. **9.** *Cricket.* to deliver the ball with a straight arm in such a way that it bounces once before reaching the batsman. *–v.t.* **10.** to roll or trundle, as a ball, hoop, etc. **11.** to knock or strike, as by the ball in bowling (fol. by *over* or *down*). **12.** to disconcert; upset (fol. by *over*). **13.** to carry or convey as in a wheeled vehicle. **14.** *Cricket.* to dismiss (a batsman) by delivering a ball which breaks the batsman's wicket. [ME *boule,* from OF: ball, from L *bulla* bubble]

**bowleg** /'boʊlɛg/, *n.* **1.** outward curvature of the legs causing a separation of the knees when the ankles are close or in contact. **2.** a leg so curved. **– bow-legged** /boʊ 'lɛgəd, 'boʊlɛgd/, *adj.*

**bowler**[1] /'boʊlə/, *n.* a hard felt hat with a rounded crown and narrow brim. [BOWL[1] + -ER[2]]

**bowler**[2] /'boʊlə/, *n.* **1.** one who bowls (a ball). **2.** *Cricket.* a member of a team who specialises in bowling. [BOWL[2] + -ER[1]]

**bowler hat** /– 'hæt/, *n.* →**bowler**[1]. **– bowler-hatted** /boʊlə-'hætəd/, *adj.*

**bowline** /'boʊlaɪn, 'boʊlən/, *n.* **1.** Also, **bowline knot.** a knot which forms a non-slipping loop. **2.** *Naut.* **a.** a rope leading forward and fastened to the leech of a square sail, used to steady the weather leech of the sail and keep it forward. **b. on a bowline,** sailing close

bowline (def. 1)

to the wind.

**bowling** /ˈboʊlɪŋ/, *n.* **1.** the act of playing with or at bowls. **2.** the game of bowls. **3.** *Cricket.* the act of delivering the ball to the batsman. **4.** →**tenpin bowling.**

**bowling alley** /ˈ– æli/, *n.* **1.** a long enclosure for playing bowls, etc. **2.** a covered place with a long, narrow, planked enclosure, for tenpin bowling.

**bowling club** /ˈ– klʌb/, *n.* **1.** a group of people who pursue the sport of bowls. **2.** the clubhouse of such a group adjacent to the green, providing refreshment and facilities for the members.

**bowling crease** /ˈ– kris/, *n.* →**crease**[1] (def. 3a).

**bowling green** /ˈ– grin/, *n.* a level plot of turf for bowls.

**bowls** /boʊlz/, *n.* **1.** →**lawn bowls.** **2.** →**carpet bowls.** **3.** skittles, ninepins, or tenpin bowling.

**bowman**[1] /ˈboʊmən/, *n., pl.* **-men.** **1.** an archer. **2.** (in medieval warfare) a soldier armed with a bow. [BOW[2] + MAN]

**bowman**[2] /ˈbaʊmən/, *n., pl.* **-men.** →**bow**[3] (def. 3). [BOW[3] + MAN]

**bow oar** /ˈbaʊ ɔ/, *n.* →**bow**[3] (def. 3).

**bow pen** /ˈboʊ pɛn/, *n.* a bow compass with a pen at the end of one leg.

**bow rudder** /ˈbaʊ rʌdə/, *n. Canoeing.* a stroke made with the paddle to move the bow towards the bow-hand's paddling side.

**bowsaw** /ˈboʊsɔ/, *n.* a saw with a thin blade held taut in a bowlike frame, used esp. for cutting curves.

**bowse** /baʊz/, *v.t.* **bowsed, bowsing.** *Naut.* **1.** to tighten up; secure. **2.** to haul with tackle.

**bowser** /ˈbaʊzə/, *n.* **1.** a petrol pump. **2.** a petrol tanker used for refuelling aircraft, etc. [Trademark]

**bowshot** /ˈboʊʃɒt/, *n.* the distance a bow sends an arrow.

**bowside** /ˈbaʊsaɪd/, *n. Rowing.* the starboard side of the boat.

**bowsprit** /ˈboʊsprɪt/, *n.* a large spar projecting forward from the stem of a ship or other vessel. [ME *bouspret,* from *bou* bow of a ship + *spret* (OE *sprēot* pole)]

A, bowsprit; B, jib boom; C, bobstay

**bowstring** /ˈboʊstrɪŋ/, *n., v.,* **-stringed** or **-strung, -stringing.** *–n.* **1.** the string of a bow. **2.** a string used, as by the Turks, for execution by strangling. *–v.t.* **3.** to strangle with a bowstring or any string or band.

**bowstring hemp** /– ˈhɛmp/, *n.* any of various fibrous plants esp. of the genera *Sansevieria* and *Calotropis* of Asia and Africa.

**bow thruster** /ˈbaʊ θrʌstə/, *n.* a propellor near the bow of a ship, usu. in a tube running athwart, which permits the bow to be pushed sideways when the ship is mooring.

**bow tie** /boʊ ˈtaɪ/, *n.* a small, bow-shaped tie.

**bow window** /boʊ ˈwɪndoʊ/, *n.* **1.** a rounded bay window. **2.** *Colloq.* a protuberant belly.

**bow-wow** /ˈbaʊ-waʊ/, *n.* **1.** the bark of a dog. **2.** an imitation of this. **3.** (*in children's speech*) a dog.

**bowyang** /ˈboʊjæŋ/, *n. Colloq.* a string or strap round the trouser leg to prevent the turn-up from dragging and to allow freedom of movement when crouching or bending. [Brit d. *bowy-yanks* leather leggings]

bowyang

**bowyer** /ˈboʊjə/, *n.* a maker or seller of bows.

**box**[1] /bɒks/, *n.* **1.** a case or receptacle, usu. rectangular, of wood, metal, cardboard, etc., with a lid or removable cover. **2.** *Music.* **a.** a speaker box. **b.** any amplifier or electronic device. **3.** the quantity contained in a box. **4.** a packet or case containing presents. **5.** the present or gift itself, esp. as given to tradesmen at Christmas; Christmas box. **6.** a collection of money for a charitable purpose, etc. **7.** a compartment or place shut or railed off for the accommodation of a small number of people in a public place, esp. in theatres, opera houses, ballrooms, etc. **8.** (in a court of law) a stand or pew reserved for witnesses, the accused or the jury. **9.** a small shelter: *a watchman's box.* **10.** *Brit.* a small house, as for use while following some sport: *a shooting box.* **11.** the driver's seat on a horse-drawn carriage. **12.** a loosebox. **13.** part of a page of a periodical set off by lines, border, or white space. **14.** *Mach.* an enclosing, protecting, or hollow part; a casing; a chamber; a bush; a socket. **15.** *Cricket, etc.* a lightweight padded shield worn to protect the genitals. **16.** *Baseball.* the space where the batter stands (or, less often, the pitcher or coach). **17.** *Squash.* the square marked on the court floor from which a player serves. **18.** a mixing up of separate flocks of sheep. **19.** *Agric.* a bowl or pit cut in the side of a tree for collecting sap. **20. be a box of birds,** be happy and in good health. **21.** *Colloq.* the vagina. **22. make a box of,** to muddle. **23. nothing out of the box,** *Colloq.* not remarkable; mediocre. **24. one out of the box,** an outstanding person or thing. **25. the box,** *Colloq.* a television set. **26. the whole box and dice,** the whole; the lot. *–v.t.* **27.** to put into a box. **28.** to enclose or confine as in a box (oft. fol. by *up* or *in*). **29.** to furnish with a box. **30.** to form into a box or the shape of a box. **31.** *Naut.* a boxhaul (oft. fol. by *off*). **32.** to make a hole or cut in (a tree) for the sap to collect. **33.** to mix (separate mobs of sheep) (fol. by *up*). **34.** to mix (paint). **35. box in, a.** to build a box around. **b.** to surround, hem in: *to be boxed in by traffic.* **c.** *Athletics, Racing, etc.* to join with other competitors in preventing (a rival) from forging ahead by hemming him in. **36. box on, a.** to argue; fight. **b.** to show no sign of giving in. **37. box up,** to bring about a state of confusion as a result of mismanagement. **38. box the compass,** *Naut.* to name the compass points in order. [special use of BOX[3]] **– boxful,** *n.* **– boxlike,** *adj.*

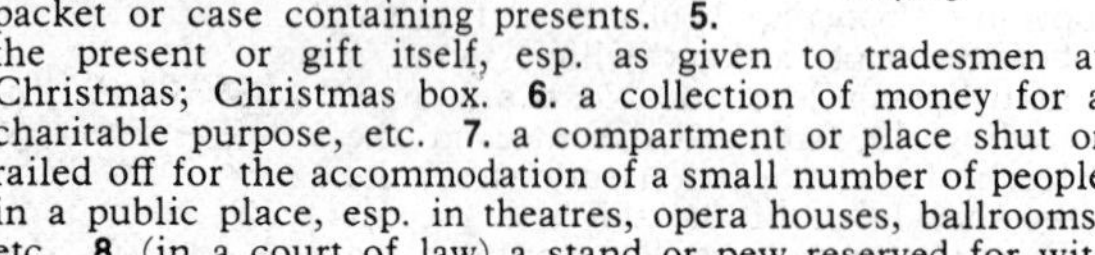

**box**[2] /bɒks/, *n.* **1.** a blow as with the hand or fist. *–v.t.* **2.** to strike with the hand or fist, esp. on the ear. **3.** to fight in a boxing match. *–v.i.* **4.** to fight with the fists; spar. [ME; orig. unknown]

**box**[3] /bɒks/, *n.* **1.** an evergreen shrub or small tree of the genus *Buxus,* esp. *B. sempervirens,* much used for ornamental borders, hedges, etc., and yielding a hard, durable wood. **2.** the wood itself. See **boxwood.** **3.** any tree of a group of species in the genus *Eucalyptus* with a characteristic close, short-fibred bark. **4.** any of various other species of shrubs or trees. [ME and OE, from L *buxus,* from Gk *pýxos*]

**box bed** /ˈ– bɛd/, **1.** a bed the base of which is completely enclosed so as to resemble a box, and which may have drawers. **2.** a bed that folds up in the form of a box.

**boxboard** /ˈbɒksbɔd/, *n.* a thin, tough board made from wood and wastepaper pulp.

**box brownie** /bɒks ˈbraʊni/, *n.* a simple and inexpensive box camera. [Trademark]

**box calf** /ˈ– kaf/, *n.* a chrome-tanned calfskin with square markings produced by graining.

**box camera** /ˈ– kæmərə/, *n.* a boxlike camera, without bellows.

**boxcar** /ˈbɒkska/, *n. U.S. Railways.* a large, enclosed and covered freight van.

**boxcloth** /ˈbɒksklɒθ/, *n.* a heavy cloth, usu. light brown, used in making warm coats.

**box coat** /ˈbɒks koʊt/, *n.* **1.** an outer coat with a straight, unfitted back. **2.** (formerly) a heavy overcoat worn by coachmen.

**boxed** /bɒkst/, *adj.* confused; muddled.

**box elder** /bɒks ˈɛldə/, *n.* a fast-growing North American maple, *Acer negundo,* cultivated for shade.

**boxer** /ˈbɒksə/, *n.* **1.** one who boxes; a pugilist. **2.** a man who looks after the bets in a two-up game. **3.** a smooth-coated, brown dog of medium size, related to the bulldog and terrier. **4.** →**bowler hat.** **5.** one who runs a two-up school and receives a set proportion, usu. twenty per cent, of the spinner's earnings; ringie.

boxer (def. 3)

**boxer shorts** /ˈ– ʃɔts/, *n.pl.* **1.** loose-fitting shorts, with an elasticised waist. **2.** men's underpants in a similar style.

**box fish** /ˈbɒks fɪʃ/, *n.* **1.** any of various species of the families Acaranidae and Ostracionidae having a bony carapace and poisonous flesh. **2.** →**cowfish** (def. 1).

**box-frame** /ˈbɒks-freɪm/, *n. Bldg Trades.* a rigid frame, usu. of steel, used as a basis for certain structures.

**box girder** /ˈbɒks gɜdə/, *n.* a hollow girder which is square or rectangular in cross-section.

**box-girder bridge** /ˈbɒks-gɜdə brɪdʒ/, *n.* a bridge constructed with box girders.

**boxhaul** /ˈbɒkshɔl/, *v.t.* to veer (a ship) round on her heel by bracing the head yards aback, etc.

**boxing**[1] /ˈbɒksɪŋ/, *n.* **1.** the material used to make boxes or casings. **2.** a boxlike enclosure. **3.** the act of putting into or furnishing with a box. [BOX[1] + -ING[1]]

**boxing**[2] /ˈbɒksɪŋ/, *n.* the act or art of fighting with the fists, with or without boxing gloves. [BOX[2] + -ING[1]]

**Boxing Day** /ˈbɒksɪŋ deɪ/, *n.* the day after Christmas Day, observed as a holiday. [traditionally the day on which Christmas boxes or presents were given to employees]

**boxing glove** /ˈ– glʌv/, *n.* a padded mitten worn in boxing.

**boxing match** /ˈ– mætʃ/, *n.* an organised fight following strict rules, between two pugilists.

**box iron** /ˈbɒks aɪən/, *n.* a smoothing iron which is heated by placing a hot iron in its boxlike holder.

**box jellyfish** /– ˈdʒɛlifɪʃ/, *n.* a type of jellyfish, Cubomedusa, found in tropical seas, in which the more usual umbrella shape is replaced by a cuboidal mass with tentacles hanging from each of the lower corners. The common Australian species *Chironex fleckeri* is highly venomous; sea wasp. Also, **box jelly.**

**box junction** /ˈ– dʒʌŋkʃən/, *n.* **1.** *Elect.* a box of some non-magnetic material as cast-iron, containing a cable joint or joints. **2.** *Brit.* a road junction marked with crossed yellow lines on the road surface, which traffic may not enter unless an exit is clear.

**box kite** /ˈ– kaɪt/, *n.* a kite consisting of a light, box-shaped frame, covered except on the ends and a space along the middle.

box kite

**box number** /ˈ– nʌmbə/, *n.* **1.** a number of a box at a post office, used as an address. **2.** a number given in a newspaper advertisement as an address to which replies may be directed, care of the newspaper office.

**box office** /ˈ– ɒfəs/, *n.* **1.** the office in which tickets are sold at a theatre or other place of public entertainment. **2.** receipts from a play or other entertainment. **3.** the ability of an entertainment or performer to draw an audience: *this show will be good box office.* *–adj.* **4.** pertaining to the size of the audience: *a box office success.*

**box-on** /ˈbɒks-ɒn/, *n. Colloq.* a dispute; fight.

**box pleat** /ˈbɒks plit/, *n.* a double pleat, with the material folded under at each side. – **box-pleated,** *adj.*

**box poison** /– ˈpɔɪzən/, *n.* a shrub, *Oxylobium parviflorum,* family Papilionaceae, native to western Australia, which is extremely poisonous to stock.

**boxroom** /ˈbɒksrum/, *n.* a storage room for pieces of furniture, etc.

**box seat** /bɒks ˈsit/, *n.* **1.** a seat in a theatre box, etc. **2.** *Colloq.* any position of vantage. **3.** *Horseracing.* in trotting races, a position just behind the leader. **4.** the driving seat of a horse-drawn coach. **5. be in the box seat,** to have reached a peak of success; be in the most favourable position.

**box sluicing** /ˈ– slusɪŋ/, *n. Mining.* sluicing auriferous earth in specially constructed frames or boxes.

**box spanner** /ˈ– spænə/, *n.* a hollow tube shaped at one or both ends to fit a nut, and turned by a bar inserted through the diameter.

**boxthorn** /ˈbɒksθɔn/, *n.* any of several plant species of the genus *Lycium,* of the family Solanaceae.

**box-trailer** /bɒks-ˈtreɪlə/, *n.* a trailer designed to be attached to a car, with a box-shaped tray.

**boxwood** /ˈbɒkswʊd/, *n.* **1.** the hard, fine-grained, compact wood of species of *Buxus,* esp. *B. sempervirens,* much used for wood engravers' blocks, musical and mathematical instruments, etc. **2.** the tree or shrub itself. **3.** any of several trees of the families Celastraceae, Pittosporaceae and others with timber similar to that of box[3], *Buxus sempervirens.*

**boy** /bɔɪ/, *n.* **1.** a male child, from birth to full growth, but esp. to the beginning of youth. **2.** a young man who lacks maturity, vigour, judgment, etc. **3.** a grown man. **4.** a boyfriend. **5.** a young servant; a page. **6.** (in India, Africa, China, Japan, etc.) a native male servant, working as a butler, waiter, houseboy, etc. *–interj.* **7.** (an exclamation of surprise, delight, etc.) [ME; orig. uncert.]

**boyar** /ˈbɔɪə, boʊˈja/, *n.* **1.** *Russian Hist.* a member of the old nobility of Russia, before Peter the Great made rank depend on state service. **2.** (formerly) one of a privileged class in Rumania. Also, **boyard** /ˈbɔɪəd, boʊˈjad/. [Russ. *boyarin* lord]

**boycott** /ˈbɔɪkɒt/, *v.t.* **1.** to combine in abstaining from, or preventing dealings with, as a means of intimidation or coercion: *to boycott a person, foreign goods, etc.* **2.** to abstain from buying or using: *to boycott a commercial product.* *–n.* **3.** the practice of boycotting. **4.** an instance of boycotting. [from Captain Charles C. *Boycott,* 1832-97, land agent for the Earl of Erne, County Mayo, Ireland, ostracised by the tenants]

**boyfriend** /ˈbɔɪfrɛnd/, *n.* **1.** a man by whom a girl or woman is courted. **2.** any young male friend.

**boyhood** /ˈbɔɪhʊd/, *n.* the state or period of being a boy.

**boyish** /ˈbɔɪɪʃ/, *adj.* of, like, or befitting a boy; high-spirited. – **boyishly,** *adv.* – **boyishness,** *n.*

**Boyle's law** /ˈbɔɪlz lɔ/, *n.* the principle that at a constant temperature the volume occupied by a given quantity of an ideal gas is inversely proportional to the pressure upon the gas. See **gas laws.** [named after Robert *Boyle,* 1627-91, English chemist and physicist]

**boyo** /ˈbɔɪoʊ/, *n.* **1.** a disorderly or rowdy young man, esp. from the country. **2.** *Chiefly Irish.* (a term of address used for a male friend or companion).

**boy scout** /bɔɪ ˈskaʊt/, *n.* **1.** a member of an organisation of boys (the Boy Scouts), founded in England in 1908 by Lt. Gen. Sir Robert S. S. Baden-Powell, with the intention of developing in its members a manly character, self-reliance, and usefulness to others. **2.** a member of any similar society elsewhere. **3.** *Colloq.* an earnest, serious-minded person.

**boysenberry** /ˈbɔɪzənbɛri, -bri/, *n., pl.* **-ries.** a blackberry-like fruit with a flavour similar to that of raspberries, developed by crossing various species of *Rubus.* [named after R. *Boysen,* 20th C U.S. botanist]

**bp,** bishop.

**B.P.** /bi ˈpi/, before 1950, being the accepted radiocarbon dating reference year: *the Bondaian period reached a climax about 1600 years B.P.* [abbrev. (B)efore (P)resent]

**B.Pharm.** /bi ˈfam/, Bachelor of Pharmacy.

**B.Phil.** /bi ˈfɪl/, Bachelor of Philosophy.

**Bq.,** becquerel.

**br.,** bridge.

**b.r.,** bedroom.

**Br,** *Chem.* bromine.

**Br.,** **1.** Britain. **2.** British.

**bra** /bra/, *n.* →**brassiere.**

**braccate** /ˈbrækeɪt/, *adj. Ornith.* having legs covered by feathers. [L *brac(c)atus* having breeches]

**brace** /breɪs/, *n., v.,* **braced, bracing.** *–n.* **1.** something that holds parts together or in place, as a clasp or clamp. **2.** anything that imparts rigidity or steadiness. **3.** *Mach.* a device for holding and turning tools for boring or drilling. **4.** *Bldg Trades.* a piece of timber, metal, etc., used to support or position another piece or portion of a framework. **5.** *Naut.* (on a square-rigged ship) a rope by which a yard is swung about and secured horizontally. **6.** *Music.* leather loops sliding upon the tightening cords of a drum to change their tension and therewith the pitch. **7.** *Archery.* to string a bow. **8.** *Canoeing.* a steadying stroke made with the paddle to prevent capsizing. **9.** (*oft. pl.*) *Dentistry.* a round or flat metal wire placed against surfaces of the teeth, and used to straighten irregularly arranged teeth. **10.** *Med.* an appliance for supporting a weak joint or joints. **11.** (*pl.*) straps or bands worn over the shoulders for holding up the trousers. **12.** a pair; a couple. **13. a.** one of two characters ,{ or }, for connecting written or printed lines. **b.** (*pl.*) Also, **curly brackets.** *Maths.* →**bracket** (def. 6a). **14.** *Music.* connected staves. **15.** a defence or protection for the arm, esp. one used in archery. **16. in a brace of shakes,** *Colloq.* immediately. *–v.t.* **17.** to furnish, fasten, or strengthen with or as with a brace. **18.** to fix firmly; make steady. **19.** to make tight; increase the tension of. **20.** to act as a stimulant to. **21.** *Naut.* to swing or turn round (the yards of a ship) by means of the braces. *–v.i.* **22. brace up,** *Colloq.* to rouse one's strength or vigour. [ME *brase(n)* from OF *bracier* embrace, from *brace* the two arms (Cf. def. 10), from L *brāchia*]

**brace and bit,** *n.* a boring tool consisting of a bit and a handle for rotating it.

brace and bit

**bracelet** /ˈbreɪslət/, *n.* **1.** an ornamental band or circlet for the wrist or arm. **2.** *Colloq.* a handcuff. [ME, from OF, diminutive of *bracel,* from L *brāc(c)hium* arm]

**bracer**[1] /ˈbreɪsə/, *n.* **1.** one who or that which braces, binds, or makes firm. **2.** *Colloq.* a stimulating drink; tonic. [BRACE + -ER[1]]

**bracer**[2] /ˈbreɪsə/, *n.* *Archery.* a guard for the left wrist and lower arm worn as a protection against the friction or the catching of the bow-string. [ME *braser,* from OF *brasseüre,* from *bras* arm, from L *brāchium*]

**brach** /brætʃ/, *n.* *Obs.* a bitch of the hound kind. Also, **brachet** /ˈbrætʃət/. [ME *braches,* pl., from OF, pl. of *brachet,* diminutive of *brac,* from OHG *bracco* a hound hunting by scent]

**brachial** /ˈbreɪkiəl, ˈbræk-/, *adj.* **1.** belonging to the arm, foreleg, wing, pectoral fin, or other forelimb of a vertebrate. **2.** belonging to the upper part of such member, from the shoulder to the elbow. **3.** armlike, as an appendage. [L *brāchiālis*]

**brachialgia** /breɪkiˈældʒə, bræk-/, *n.* pain in the nerves of the upper arm.

**brachiate** /ˈbreɪkieɪt, -ət, ˈbræk-/, *adj.* **1.** *Bot.* having widely spreading branches in alternate pairs. *–v.i.* **2.** to swing by the arms from branch to branch, as some apes.

**brachio-,** a word element meaning 'arm', as in *brachiopod.* Also (before a vowel), **brachi-.** [NL, combining form representing L *brāchium,* or its source, Gk *brachī́ōn*]

**brachiopod** /ˈbreɪkiəpɒd, ˈbræk-/, *n.* any of the Brachiopoda, a largely extinct phylum of mollusc-like animals, the lampshells, having dorsal and ventral shells.

**brachiosaur** /ˈbrækiəsɔ/, *n.* one of the *Brachiosaurus,* a genus of large dinosaurs of the Upper Jurassic period.

**brachium** /ˈbreɪkiəm, ˈbræk-/, *n., pl.* **brachia** /ˈbreɪkiə, ˈbræk-/. **1.** the arm as a whole. **2.** the upper arm, from the shoulder to the elbow. **3.** the part of any limb, as in the wing of a bird, corresponding to the upper arm. **4.** an armlike part or process. [L: arm]

**brachy-,** a word element meaning 'short', as in *brachycephalic.* [Gk, combining form of *brachý́s*]

**brachycephalic** /ˌbrækisəˈfælɪk/, *adj.* short-headed (opposed to *dolichocephalic*); having a breadth of head at least four-fifths the length from front to back. Also, **brachycephalous** / brækiˈsɛfələs/. – **brachycephaly** / brækiˈsɛfəli/, *n.*

**brachycome** /brækiˈkoʊmi/, *n.* any daisy of the large, mostly Australian genus *Brachycome,* family Compositae, as *B. iberidifolia,* Swan River daisy, which has flowers of blue to purple, and is cultivated as a garden plant.

**brachycranic** /brækiˈkreɪnɪk/, *adj.* short-skulled (opposed to *dolichocranic*).

**brachylogy** /bræˈkɪlədʒi/, *n., pl.* **-gies.** brevity of diction; a concise or abridged form of expression. [Gk *brachylogía.* See BRACHY-, -LOGY]

**brachypterous** /bræˈkɪptərəs/, *adj.* *Ornith.* short-winged. [BRACHY- + -PTEROUS]

**brachyuran** /brækiˈjurən/, *adj.* **1.** belonging or pertaining to the Brachyura, a group of stalk-eyed decapod crustaceans with short tails, the common crabs. *–n.* **2.** a brachyuran crustacean.

**brachyurous** /brækiˈjurəs/, *adj.* *Zool.* short-tailed, as the crabs (opposed to *macrurous*).

**bracing** /ˈbreɪsɪŋ/, *adj.* **1.** strengthening; invigorating. *–n.* **2.** a brace. **3.** braces collectively. – **bracingly,** *adv.*

**bracken** /ˈbrækən/, *n.* **1.** a large, coarse fern, esp. *Pteridium esculentum,* a perennial native which is widespread throughout the higher rainfall areas of Australia. **2.** a clump of ferns. [ME *braken,* from Scand.; cf. Sw. *bräken* fern]

bracken

**bracket** /ˈbrækət/, *n.* **1.** a wooden, metal, etc., support of triangular outline placed under a shelf or the like. **2.** a shelf or shelves supported by a bracket. **3.** *Archit.* an ornamental projection from the face of a wall intended to support a statue, pier, etc.; a corbel. **4.** a projecting fixture for gas or electricity. **5.** one of two marks, [ or ], used in writing or printing to enclose parenthetical matter, interpolations, etc. **6.** *Maths.* **a.** (*pl.*) parentheses of various forms indicating that the enclosed quantity is to be treated as a unit. **b.** →**vinculum** (def. 2). **7.** a grouping of persons, esp. as based on the amount of their taxable income: *low income bracket.* **8.** a small group of musical items: *a bracket of songs.* **9.** *Colloq.* the nose. **10.** *Gunnery.* a range or elevation producing both shorts and overs on a target. *–v.t.* **11.** to furnish with or support by a bracket or brackets. **12.** to place within brackets; couple with a brace. **13.** to associate or mention together, implying equality of some kind. **14.** *Gunnery.* to place (shots) both beyond and short of a target. [earlier *bragget,* from F *braguette,* from Pr., or Sp., diminutive of *bragga,* from L *brācae,* pl., breeches, of Celtic orig.]

**bracketing** /ˈbrækətɪŋ/, *n.* the series of wooden supports, often of fanciful jigsaw form, nailed to the ceiling, joists, and battening to support cornices.

**brackish** /ˈbrækɪʃ/, *adj.* **1.** slightly salt; having a salty or briny flavour. **2.** distasteful. [*brack* brackish (from D *brak*) + -ISH[1]] – **brackishness,** *n.*

**bract** /brækt/, *n.* a specialised leaf or leaflike part, usu. situated at the base of a flower or inflorescence. [L *bractea* thin plate of metal] – **bracteal** /ˈbræktiəl/, *adj.* – **bractless,** *adj.*

**bracteate** /ˈbræktiət/, *n.* **1.** *Archeol.* a thin ornamental plate of gold or silver. *–adj.* **2.** *Bot.* having bracts.

**bracteolate** /ˈbræktiələt, -eɪt/, *adj.* having bracteoles.

**bracteole** /ˈbræktioʊl/, *n.* a small or secondary bract, as on a pedicel. Also, **bractlet** /ˈbræktlət/.

A, bract of marigold

**brad** /bræd/, *n.* **1.** a small wire nail with a head projecting on only one side, or not projecting at all. *–v.t.* **2.** to turn down (the end of a nail which projects a short way through the work). [ME *brad,* var. of *brod,* from Scand.; cf. Icel. *broddr* spike]

**bradawl** /ˈbrædɔl/, *n.* *Carp.* an awl for making small holes in wood for brads, etc.

**bradycardia** /brædəˈkadiə/, *n.* abnormal slowness of the pulse, usu. below 60 beats per minute. [Gk, combining form of *bradý́s* slow + *kardía* heart]

**brae** /breɪ/, *n.* *Scot.* a slope; a declivity; a hillside. [ME *bra,* from Scand.; cf. Icel. *brā* eyelash, c. OE *brĕaw* eyebrow, eyelid; G *Braue* eyebrow]

**Braford** /ˈbrafəd/, *n.* one of a breed of cattle which is a cross between Brahman (Zebu) and Hereford.

**brag** /bræg/, *v.,* **bragged, bragging,** *n.* *–v.i.* **1.** to use boastful language; boast. *–n.* **2.** a boast or vaunt; bragging. **3.** a boaster. [Scand.; cf. Icel. *bragga sig* take heart, *braggasi* thrive] – **bragger,** *n.*

**braggadocio** /brægəˈdoʊtʃioʊ/, *n., pl.* **-os. 1.** empty boasting; brag. **2.** a boasting person; a braggart. [from *Braggadochio,* name of a boastful character in Spenser's '*Faerie Queen*']

**braggart** /ˈbrægat/, *n.* **1.** one given to bragging. *–adj.* **2.** bragging; boastful. [BRAG + *-art,* from -ARD; cf. F (obs.) *bragard* boastful] – **braggartism,** *n.*

**Bragg reflection** /bræg rəˈflɛkʃən/, *n.* the diffraction of X-rays by a crystal lattice which for certain angles of incidence resembles a reflection. [named after Sir William Henry *Bragg,*

1862-1942, and his son Sir William Lawrence *Bragg*, 1890-1971, British physicists]

**brahma** /ˈbramə/, *n.* a breed of large domestic fowls, of Asiatic origin, with feathered legs and small wings and tail. [named after and short for *Brahmaputra,* a river in India]

**Brahma** /ˈbramə/, *n.* **1.** (in philosophic Hinduism) the impersonal Supreme Being, the primal Source and the ultimate Goal of all being; Atman, the World Soul. **2.** (in later Hinduism) a trinity of the personal Creator together with Vishnu the Preserver and Siva the Destroyer. [Skt *bráhma,* neut., worship, prayer, the impersonal divinity (see def. 1); from *brahmá* masc., worshipper, priest, the divinity as personified (see def. 2)]

**Brahman** /ˈbramən/, *n., pl.* **-mans. 1.** a member of the highest, or priestly, caste among the Hindus. **2.** (*oft. l.c.*) a person of great culture and intellect. **3.** (*oft. l.c.*) a snobbish or aloof intellectual. **4.** an animal of a breed of cattle originating in India, derived from the Zebu, and used widely in Australia for crossbreeding. Also, **Brahmin.** [Skt *brāhmana*] – **Brahmanic** /braˈmænɪk/, **Brahmanical** /braˈmænɪkəl/, *adj.*

Brahman (def. 4)

**Brahmanism** /ˈbramənɪzəm/, *n.* the religious and social system of the Brahmans and orthodox Hindus, characterised by the caste system and diversified pantheism. – **Brahmanist,** *n.*

**Brahmin** /ˈbramən/, *n., pl.* **Brahmin.** →**Brahman.**

**braid** /breɪd/, *v.t.* **1.** to weave together strips or strands of; plait. **2.** to form by such weaving. **3.** to bind or confine (the hair) with a band, ribbon, etc. **4.** to trim (garments) with braid. *–n.* **5.** a braided length, or plait, of hair, etc. **6.** a narrow band or tape, formed by plaiting or weaving together several strands of silk, cotton, wool, or other material, often with gold or silver wire, used as trimming for garments, etc. **7.** a band, ribbon, etc., for binding or confining the hair. [ME *braide(n),* OE *bregdan* move quickly, move to and fro, weave, c. Icel. *bregdha*] – **braider,** *n.*

**braiding** /ˈbreɪdɪŋ/, *n.* **1.** braids collectively. **2.** braided work.

**brail** /breɪl/, *n.* **1.** *Naut.* one of certain ropes made fast to the after leech of a sail, to assist in taking in the sail. *–v.t.* **2.** to gather or haul in (a sail) by means of brails (usu. fol. by *up*). [ME *brayle,* from OF *braiel* cincture, from L *brācāle* belt, from *brācae* breeches]

B, brail

**braille** /breɪl/, *n.* a system of writing or printing for the blind, in which combinations of tangible points are used to represent letters, etc. [named after Louis *Braille,* 1809-52, the inventor]

**brain** /breɪn/, *n.* **1.** (*sometimes pl.*) the soft convoluted mass of greyish and whitish nerve substance which fills the cranium of man and other vertebrates; centre of sensation, body coordination, thought, emotion, etc. **2.** *Zool.* (in many invertebrates) a part of the nervous system more or less corresponding to the brain of vertebrates. **3.** (*usu. pl.*) understanding; intellectual power; intelligence. **4.** *Colloq.* a highly intelligent or well-informed person. **5. have something on the brain,** to have an obsession; be preoccupied with. **6. go off (one's) brain,** to become frenzied with worry, anger, etc. **7. pick someone's brains,** to use another person's work or ideas to one's own advantage. *–v.t.* **8.** to dash out the brains of. [ME; OE *bregen,* c. MLG *bregen*]

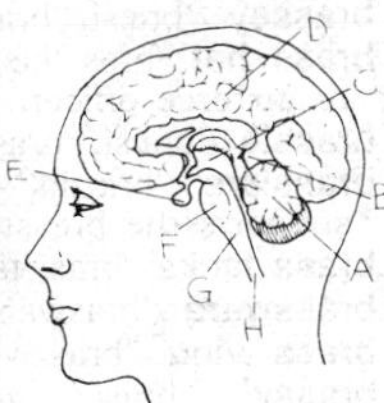

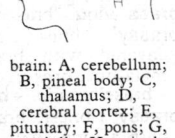

brain: A, cerebellum; B, pineal body; C, thalamus; D, cerebral cortex; E, pituitary; F, pons; G, medulla; H, spinal cord

**brain cell** /ˈbreɪn sɛl/, *n.* a neurone in the brain.

**brainchild** /ˈbreɪntʃaɪld/, *n., pl.* **-children.** a product of one's creative work or thought.

**brain death** /ˈbreɪn dɛθ/, *n.* the failure of the brain to maintain its control over respiration, commonly accepted as a criterion of death.

**brain drain** /ˈ– dreɪn/, *n. Colloq.* the steady flow of young scientists, artists, etc., emigrating to work in countries other than the country of their birth.

**brain fever** /ˈ– fivə/, *n.* →**cerebrospinal meningitis.**

**brain-fever bird,** /ˈbreɪn-fivə ˌbɜd/, *n.* **1.** →**pallid cuckoo. 2.** an Indian cuckoo, *Cuculus varius,* having a loud repetitive cry.

**brainless** /ˈbreɪnləs/, *adj.* mentally weak; witless; stupid. – **brainlessness,** *n.*

**brainpan** /ˈbreɪnpæn/, *n.* the skull or cranium.

**brainsick** /ˈbreɪnsɪk/, *adj.* crazy; mad. – **brainsickly,** *adv.* – **brainsickness,** *n.*

**brainstorm** /ˈbreɪnstɔm/, *n.* **1.** a sudden, violent attack of mental disturbance. **2.** *Colloq.* a sudden inspiration, idea, etc.

**brainstorming** /ˈbreɪnstɔmɪŋ/, *n.* a technique in which a group meets in order to stimulate creative thinking, develop new ideas, etc.

**brains trust** /ˈbreɪnz trʌst/, *n.* **1.** a group of informed persons who discuss topics for public entertainment. **2.** Also, **brain trust.** a group of experts who give counsel, help shape policy, etc.

**brainwash** /ˈbreɪnwɒʃ/, *v.t.* to indoctrinate by brainwashing. [backformation from *brainwashing*] – **brainwasher,** *n.*

**brainwashing** /ˈbreɪnwɒʃɪŋ/, *n.* systematic indoctrination that changes or undermines one's convictions, esp. political.

**brainwave** /ˈbreɪnweɪv/, *n.* **1.** *Colloq.* a sudden idea or inspiration. **2.** (*pl.*) *Med.* →**electroencephalogram.**

**brainy** /ˈbreɪni/, *adj.,* **brainier, brainiest.** having brains; intelligent; clever. – **braininess,** *n.*

**braise** /breɪz/, *v.t.,* **braised, braising.** to cook (meat or vegetables) by sautéing in fat and then cooking slowly in very little moisture. [F *braiser,* from *braise* hot charcoal, live coals; of Gmc orig.]

**brake**[1] /breɪk/, *n., v.,* **braked, braking.** *–n.* **1.** any mechanical device for arresting the motion of a wheel, a motor, or a vehicle, chiefly by means of friction or pressure. **2.** (*pl.*) the drums, shoes, tubes, levers, etc., making up the brake system. **3.** a tool or machine for breaking up flax or hemp, to separate the fibre. **4.** a heavy kind of harrow. **5.** Also, **break.** →**shooting brake. 6.** a brake van. *–v.t.* **7.** to slow or stop the motion of (a wheel, motor vehicle, etc.) as by a brake. **8.** to furnish with brakes. **9.** to process (flax or hemp) by crushing it in a brake. *–v.i.* **10.** to use or apply a brake. **11.** to run a hoisting machine. **12.** to slow down. [ME, from MLG and/or MD; akin to BREAK] – **brakeless,** *adj.*

**brake**[2] /breɪk/, *n.* a place overgrown with bushes, shrubs, brambles, or cane; a thicket. [cf. MLG *brake*]

**brake**[3] /breɪk/, *n.* any large or coarse fern, esp. *Pteridium aquilinum* or some allied species. [ME, var. of BRACKEN]

**brake**[4] /breɪk/, *v. Archaic.* past tense of **break.**

**brakeage** /ˈbreɪkɪdʒ/, *n.* **1.** the action of a brake or set of brakes, as in stopping a vehicle. **2.** brakes collectively.

**brake band** /ˈbreɪk bænd/, *n.* a part of brake mechanism consisting of a flexible band which grips a drum when tightened.

**brake block** /ˈ– blɒk/, *n.* (on railway vehicles, bicycles, etc.) the brake shoe.

**brake drum** /ˈ– drʌm/, *n.* the steel or cast-iron drum attached to the wheel hub or propeller shaft of a motor vehicle, etc., against which the brake lining is forcefully applied to arrest its turning when the brake is operated.

**brake fluid** /ˈ– fluəd/, *n.* a liquid used in a hydraulic brake system to transmit pressure.

**brake horsepower** /– ˈhɔspaʊə/, *n.* the useful horsepower developed by an engine or motor as measured by the resistance offered by a brake. *Abbrev.:* b.h.p.

**brakelight** /ˈbreɪklaɪt/, *n.* a tail-light linked to the brakes of a vehicle so that it shows when they are applied; stoplight.

**brake lining** /ˈbreɪk laɪnɪŋ/, *n.* a material, usu. asbestos combined with other materials, used as the friction-producing element of a brake; brake shoe.

**brake pad** /'– pæd/, *n.* →**brake shoe.**

**brake parachute** /– 'pærəʃut/, *n.* a parachute attached to the tail of an aeroplane which may be opened to assist as a brake when landing.

**brake shoe** /'– ʃu/, *n.* the part of a brake which presses against the brake drum or wheel to slow it.

**brake van** /'– væn/, *n.* the coach on a train from which a braking system may be applied; the guard's van.

**bramble** /'bræmbəl/, *n., v.,* **-bled, -bling.** *–n.* **1.** the common blackberry, *Rubus fruticosus.* **2.** any plant of the genus *Rubus.* **3.** any rough prickly shrub. *–v.i.* **4.** to gather blackberries. [OE *bræmbel, brembel,* var. of *bræmel, brēmel,* from *brōm* broom] – **brambly,** *adj.*

**brambling** /'bræmblɪŋ/, *n.* an Old World finch, *Fringilla montifringilla,* closely related to the chaffinch. [earlier *brambling,* from BROOM + -LING[1]]

**bran** /bræn/, *n.* **1.** the ground husk of wheat or other grain, separated from flour or meal by bolting. **2.** by-products or grain processing used as feed. [ME, from OF]

**branch** /bræntʃ/, *n.* **1.** *Bot.* a division or subdivision of the stem or axis of a tree, shrub, or other plant (the ultimate or smaller ramifications being called branchlets, twigs, or shoots). **2.** a limb, offshoot, or ramification: *the branches of a deer's horns.* **3.** any member or part of a body or system; a section or subdivision: *the various branches of learning.* **4.** a local operating division of a company, chain-store, library, or the like. **5.** a line of family descent, in distinction from some other line or lines from the same stock. **6.** (in the classification of languages) a subdivision of a family; a group. **7.** *Geog.* **a.** a tributary stream. **b.** any stream that is not a large river or a creek. *–v.i.* **8.** to put forth branches; spread in branches. **9.** to divide into separate parts or subdivisions; diverge. **10. branch out,** to expand in a new direction. *–v.t.* **11.** to divide as into branches. **12.** to adorn with needlework; decorate with embroidery, as in textile fabrics. [ME, from OF *branche,* from LL *branca* paw, claw] – **branchless,** *adj.* – **branchlike,** *adj.* – **branchy,** *adj.*

**branchia** /'bræŋkiə/, *n.pl.* →**branchiae.** [L (sing.), from Gk *bránchia* (neut. pl.) gills] – **branchial,** *adj.*

**branchiae** /'bræŋkii/, *n.pl.* the respiratory organs or gills of fishes, etc.

**branchiate** /'bræŋkiət, -eɪt/, *adj.* having branchiae.

**branchiopod** /'bræŋkiəpɒd/, *n.* any of the Branchiopoda, a group of crustaceans having branchiae or gills on the feet. [Gk *bránchia* gills + -(O)POD]

**branch line** /'bræntʃ laɪn/, *n.* a minor railway line, often connected to the main line at one end only.

**brand** /brænd/, *n.* **1.** a trademark or trade name to identify a product, as that of a distributor, or a manufacturer or other producer. **2.** kind, grade, or make, as indicated by a brand, stamp, trademark, or the like. **3.** a mark made by burning or otherwise, to indicate kind, grade, make, ownership, etc. **4.** a mark formerly put upon criminals with a hot iron. **5.** any mark of infamy; a stigma. **6.** an iron for branding. **7.** a burning or partly burnt piece of wood. **8.** *Archaic or Poetic.* a torch. **9.** *Archaic or Poetic.* a sword. *–v.t.* **10.** to mark with a brand. **11.** to mark with infamy; stigmatise. [ME and OE; akin to BURN[1]] – **brander,** *n.*

**brandied** /'brændid/, *adj.* flavoured with brandy.

**brandings** /'brændɪŋz/, *n.pl.* a children's game in which a ball, as a tennis ball, etc., is thrown at a child with such force that a red mark appears on the skin, after which a scramble for the ball determines who next shall throw. Also, **branders.**

**brandish** /'brændɪʃ/, *v.t.* **1.** to shake or wave, as a weapon; flourish. *–n.* **2.** a wave or flourish, as of a weapon. [ME *braundish(en),* from OF *brandiss-,* stem of *brandir,* from *brand* sword; of Gmc orig. See BRAND] – **brandisher,** *n.*

**brandling** /'brændlɪŋ/, *n.* a small, reddish brown earthworm, *Helodrilus foetidus,* with yellow markings, found chiefly in manure heaps, used as a bait in fishing. [BRAND + -LING[1]]

**brand-new** /brænd-'nju, bræn-'nju/, *adj.* completely new. [BRAND + NEW]

**brandy** /'brændi/, *n., pl.* **-dies,** *v.,* **-died, -dying.** *–n.* **1.** the spirit distilled from the fermented juice of grapes or, sometimes, of apples, peaches, plums, etc. *–v.t.* **2.** to mix, flavour, or preserve with brandy. [short for *brandywine,* from D *brandewijn* burnt (i.e. distilled) wine]

**brandy alexander** /– æləg'zændə/, *n.* a drink made from brandy, crème de cacao, fresh cream and nutmeg. Also, **brandy Alexander.**

**brandyball** /'brændibɔl/, *n.* a small, round, brandycoloured sweet.

**brandy balloon** /'brændi bəlun/, *n.* a balloon glass, usu. large, for brandy.

**brandysnap** /'brændisnæp/, *n.* a thin, sticky ginger biscuit flavoured with brandy.

**Brangus** /'bræŋgəs/, *n.* one of a breed of cattle which is about one third Brahman and two thirds Aberdeen Angus.

**branks** /bræŋks/, *n.pl.* a bridle formerly used to punish a scold. [orig. uncert]

**branle** /'brænəl/, *n.* an early French country dance performed by dancers linked in a circle. [OF *branber* to shake]

**branny** /'bræni/, *adj.* of, containing, or like bran.

**brant goose** /brænt 'gus/, *n. Chiefly U.S.* →**brent.**

**brasco** /'bræskoʊ/, *n. Prison. Colloq.* a toilet.

**brash** /bræʃ/, *adj.* **1.** impertinent; impudent; forward. **2.** headlong; hasty; rash. *–n.* **3.** loose fragments of rock. **4.** *Naut.* small fragments of crushed ice collected by winds or currents near the shore. [orig. obscure]

**brashy** /'bræʃi/, *adj.* **1.** loosely fragmented; rubbishy. **2.** brittle; liable to break into fragments.

**brasier** /'breɪziə/, *n.* →**brazier.**

**brasilin** /'bræzələn/, *n. Chem.* →**brazilin.**

**brass** /bras/, *n.* **1.** a durable, malleable, and ductile yellow alloy, consisting essentially of copper and zinc. **2.** a utensil, ornament, or other article made of brass. **3.** *Mach.* a bearing, bush, or the like. **4.** a collective term for musical instruments of the trumpet and horn families (brass instruments), usu. made of brass and having a funnel-shaped mouthpiece without a reed. **5.** a memorial tablet incised with an effigy, coat of arms or the like. **6.** metallic yellow; lemon, amber, or reddish yellow. **7.** Also, **top brass.** *Colloq.* **a.** high-ranking military officers. **b.** the people in the most senior positions in an organisation. **8.** *Colloq.* excessive assurance; impudence; effrontery. **9.** *Colloq.* money. *–adj.* **10.** of brass. **11.** using musical instruments of the horn and trumpet family. **12. part brass rags,** *Mil. Colloq.* to have an argument (fol. by *with*). *–v.i.* **13.** to welsh. *–v.t.* **14.** *Colloq.* to cheat or defraud. [ME *brass,* OE *bræs*] – **brasslike,** *adj.*

**brassage** /'brasɪdʒ/, *n.* a charge to cover costs of coining money. [F, from *brasser* stir (welded metal), from L *brace* white corn, of Celtic orig.]

**brassard** /'bræsad/, *n.* **1.** a badge worn round the upper arm. **2.** *Armour.* Also, **brassart** /'bræsət/. a piece of armour for the arm. [F, from *bras* arm]

**brass band** /bras 'bænd/, *n.* a band made up chiefly or exclusively of instruments of the horn and trumpet families.

**brassed** /brast/, *Colloq. adj.* **1.** cheated: defrauded. **2. brassed off,** bad-tempered; disenchanted; disillusioned.

**brasserie** /'bræsəri/, *n.* an establishment where drinks, esp. beer, and food are served to the public. [F: brewery]

**brassey** /'bræsi, 'brasi/, *n.* →**brassy**[2]

**brass hat** /bras 'hæt/, *n. Colloq.* a high-ranking army, navy, or airforce officer.

**brassie** /'bræsi, 'brasi/, →**brassy**[2]

**brassiere** /'bræziə, -siə/, *n.* a woman's undergarment which supports the breasts. [F: little camisole, from *bras* arm]

**brass tacks** /bras 'tæks/, *n.pl. Colloq.* basic facts; realities.

**brassware** /'braswɛə/, *n.* articles of brass.

**brass wind** /'bras wɪnd/, *n. Music.* →**brass** (def. 4).

**brassy**[1] /'brasi/, *adj.,* **brassier, brassiest. 1.** made of or covered with brass. **2.** resembling brass. **3.** harsh and metallic: *brassy tones.* **4.** *Colloq.* brazen. [BRASS + -Y[1]] – **brassily,** *adv.* – **brassiness,** *n.*

**brassy**[2] /'bræsi, 'brasi/, *n., pl.* **-ies.** *Golf.* a club (No. 2 wood) with a long shaft and a wooden head. Also, **brassey, brassie.**

**brat** /bræt/, *n.* a child (used usu. in contempt or irritation). [cf. d. *brat* rag, trash, OE *bratt* cloak]

**brattice** /'brætəs/, *n., v.,* **-ticed, -ticing.** *–n.* **1.** a partition or lining, as of planks or cloth to confine the air and force it into the working faces of a mine. *–v.t.* **2.** to provide with a brattice; line with planks or cloth. [ME *bretage,* from OF *bretesche* parapet, ? from OE *brittisc* British, i.e. foreign or Celtic (fortification)]

**brattishing** /'brætəʃɪŋ/, *n.* ornamental work along the cornice or coping of a building. Also, **bratticing.** [alteration of BRATTICE + -ING[1]]

**brattle** /'brætl/, *n., v.,* **-tled, -tling.** *–n.* **1.** a clattering noise. *–v.i.* **2.** to scamper noisily.

**braunite** /'braʊnaɪt/, *n.* a mineral, manganese oxide and silicate, $Mn_7SiO_{12}$, an ore of manganese. [named after A.E. *Braun,* 1809-56, German archaeologist]

**bravado** /brə'vadoʊ/, *n., pl.* **-does, -dos.** boasting; swaggering pretence. [Sp. *bravada.* See BRAVE]

**brave** /breɪv/, *adj.,* **braver, bravest,** *n., v.,* **braved, braving.** *–adj.* **1.** possessing or exhibiting courage or courageous endurance. **2.** making a fine appearance. **3.** *Archaic.* excellent; fine; admirable. *–n.* **4. the brave,** brave people collectively. **5.** a North American Indian or other savage warrior. **6.** *Obs.* a bully. **7.** *Archaic.* a boast; a challenge; a defiance. *–v.t.* **8.** to meet or face courageously: *to brave misfortunes.* **9.** to defy; challenge; dare. **10.** *Obs.* to make splendid. **11. brave it out,** to ignore or defy suspicion, blame or impudent gossip. *–v.i.* **12.** *Obs.* to boast; brag. [F, from It. *bravo* brave, bold, fine, from Sp.: vicious (first applied to bulls)] – **bravely,** *adv.* – **braveness,** *n.*

**bravery** /'breɪvəri/, *n., pl.* **-ries. 1.** brave spirit or conduct; courage; valour. **2.** *Archaic.* showiness; splendour; magnificence.

**bravo**[1] /bra'voʊ/, *interj., n., pl.* **-vos.** *–interj.* **1.** well done! good! *–n.* **2.** a shout of 'bravo!' [It., properly adj. See BRAVE]

**bravo**[2] /'bravoʊ/, *n., pl.* **-voes, -vos.** a daring bandit or assassin or murderer. [It. See BRAVE]

**bravura** /brə'vurə, -'vju-/, *n.* **1.** *Music.* a florid passage or piece, requiring great skill and spirit in the performer. **2.** a display of daring; brilliant performance. *–adj.* **3.** *Music.* spirited; florid; brilliant. [It.: bravery, spirit]

**braw** /brɔ, bra/, *adj. Scot.* fine or finelooking; excellent. [var. of BRAVE]

**brawl**[1] /brɔl/, *n.* **1.** a noisy quarrel; a squabble. **2.** a bubbling or roaring noise; a clamour. *–v.i.* **3.** to quarrel angrily, noisily; wrangle. **4.** to make a bubbling or roaring noise, as water flowing over a rocky bed. [ME *brall(en),* from *brawl* brawler, var. of *broll* brat, contraction of *brothel* good-for-nothing, from OE *brēothan* go to ruin] – **brawler,** *n.*

**brawl**[2] /brɔl/, *n.* an old folk dance of French origin. [orig. unknown]

**brawn** /brɔn/, *n.* **1.** well-developed muscles. **2.** muscular strength. **3.** meat, esp. pork, boiled, pickled, and pressed into a mould. [ME *brawne,* from OF *braon,* from Gmc; cf. G *braten* roast]

**brawny** /'brɔni/, *adj.,* **brawnier, brawniest.** muscular; strong. – **brawniness,** *n.*

**braxy** /'bræksi/, *n.* **1.** an acute bacterial disease of sheep involving inflammation of the bowels, usu. fatal. *–adj.* **2.** affected with braxy. [probably n. use of adj., OE *bræcsēoc* ill with falling sickness, from *bræc* rheum + *sēoc* sick]

**bray**[1] /breɪ/, *n.* **1.** a harsh, breathy cry, as of the donkey. **2.** any similar loud, harsh sound. **3.** a harsh, noisy human utterance, as a protest or laugh. *–v.i.* **4.** to utter a loud, harsh cry as the donkey. **5.** to make a loud, harsh, disagreeable sound, as a trumpet. **6.** to utter a harsh, noisy sound, as a protest or laugh. *–v.t.* **7.** to utter with a loud, harsh sound, like the donkey. [ME *braye(n),* from OF *braire*] – **brayer,** *n.*

**bray**[2] /breɪ/, *v.t.* to pound or crush fine, as in a mortar. [ME *braye(n),* from OF *breier*]

**brayer** /'breɪə/, *n.* **1.** an instrument for crushing; a pestle. **2.** *Print.* a small roller for inking type or plates by hand (usu. for making a proof). [BRAY[2] + -ER[1]]

**braze**[1] /breɪz/, *v.t.,* **brazed, brazing. 1.** to make of brass. **2.** to cover or ornament with brass, or as if with brass. **3.** to make brasslike. [OE *bræsian,* from *bræs* brass]

**braze**[2] /breɪz/, *v.t.,* **brazed, brazing.** to unite (pieces of brass, steel, etc.) by intensely heating the parts to be joined and applying any one of a number of high melting solders which range in melting point from alloys rich in silver to pure copper. [? F *braser,* from *braise* live coals. See BRAISE]

**brazen** /'breɪzən/, *adj.* **1.** made of brass. **2.** like brass, as in sound, colour, strength, etc. **3.** shameless or impudent: *brazen effrontery.* *–v.t.* **4.** to face with boldness and effrontery (fol. by *out*). **5.** to make brazen or bold. [ME *brasen,* OE *bræsen,* from *bræs* brass] – **brazenly,** *adv.* – **brazenness,** *n.*

**brazen-faced** /'breɪzən-feɪst/, *adj.* openly shameless; impudent.

**brazier**[1] /'breɪziə/, *n.* a person who works in brass. Also, **brasier.** [ME *brasiere;* from BRAZE[1], *v.* + -IER]

**brazier**[2] /'breɪziə/, *n.* a metal receptacle for holding burning charcoal or other fuel, as for heating a room. Also, **brasier.** [F *brasier,* from *braise* live coals. See BRAISE, -ER[2]]

**brazil** /brə'zɪl/, *n.* **1.** a wood from various tropical American trees of the genus *Caesalpinia* (esp. *C. echinata*) and allied genera, yielding red and purple dyes. **2.** the red dye extracted from it. **3.** (originally) a hard East Indian wood yielding a red colour, from the tree *Caesalpinia sappan.* **4.** a brazil nut. [ME *brasile,* from Sp. or Pg. *brasil,* from OF *brésil* reddish-tinted wood, from *brèze, braise* glowing coals; Brazil was named after the tree]

**Brazil** /brə'zɪl/, *n.* a republic in South America. Official name: **United States of Brazil.** – **Brazilian,** *adj., n.*

**brazilin** /'bræzələn/, *n.* a yellow substance, $C_{16}H_{14}O_5$, from brazil, used as a dye and indicator. Also, **brasilin.**

**brazil nut** /brə'zɪl nʌt/, *n.* the triangular edible seed (nut) of the tree *Bertholletia excelsa* and related species, of Brazil and elsewhere.

brazil nut: open pod

**brazilwood** /brə'zɪlwʊd/, *n.* →**brazil.**

**breach** /britʃ/, *n.* **1.** the act or result of breaking; a break or rupture. **2.** a gap made in a wall, dyke, fortification, etc.; rift; fissure. **3.** an infraction or violation, as of law, trust, faith, promise, etc. **4.** a severance of friendly relations. **5.** the springing of a whale from the water. **6.** *Obs.* a wound. *–v.t.* **7.** to make a breach or opening in. [ME *breche,* from OF, from Gmc (cf. OHG *brecha*); replacing ME *bruche,* OE *bryce,* akin to BREAK]

**breach of contract,** *n.* the breaking, by action or omission, of an obligation imposed by a contract.

**breach of privilege,** *n.* an abuse of any of the privileges accorded to members of parliament.

**breach of promise,** *n.* a violation of one's promise to marry.

**breach of the peace,** *n.* a violation of the public peace, by a riot, disturbance, etc.

**breach of trust,** *n.* **1.** *Law.* a violation of duty by a trustee. **2.** *Colloq.* a violation of duty by any fiduciary.

**bread** /brɛd/, *n.* **1.** a food made of flour or meal, milk or water, etc., made into a dough or batter, with or without yeast or the like, and baked. **2.** food or sustenance; livelihood: *to earn one's bread.* **3.** *Eccles.* the wafer or bread used in the Eucharist. **4.** *Colloq.* money; earnings. **5. break bread, a.** to partake of or share food. **b.** *Eccles.* to administer or join in Communion. *–v.t.* **6.** *Cookery.* to cover or dress with breadcrumbs or meal. [ME *breed,* OE *brēad,* c. G *Brot*] – **breadless,** *adj.*

**bread and butter,** *n.* **1.** bread spread with butter. **2.** *Colloq.* means of living; livelihood.

**bread-and-butter** /ˌbrɛd-ən-'bʌtə/, *adj.* **1.** seeking the means of living; mercenary. **2.** *Colloq.* matter-of-fact. **3.** expressing thanks for hospitality, as a letter.

**bread and butter pudding,** *n.* a baked pudding made with bread and custard filling.

**breadbasket** /'brɛdbaskət/, *n.* **1.** a basket for containing bread. **2.** *Colloq.* the stomach.

**breadbin** /'brɛdbɪn/, *n.* a bin for containing bread.

**breadboard** /'brɛdbɔd/, *n.* a wooden board on which bread is sliced.

**breadcrumb** /'brɛdkrʌm/, *n., v.,* **-crumbed** /-krʌmd/, **-crumbing.** *–n.* **1.** (*usu. pl.*) a small fragment of bread. **2.** the soft, spongy inner part of a loaf. *–v.t.* **3.** to dress (food) with breadcrumbs.

**breadfruit** ['brɛdfrut/, *n.* **1.** a large, round, starchy fruit yielded by the tree, *Artocarpus altilis,* of the Pacific islands, etc., much used, baked or roasted, for food. **2.** the tree bearing this fruit.

**breadknife** /ˈbrɛdnaɪf/, *n.* a knife, usu. with a serrated edge, for cutting bread.

**breadline** /ˈbrɛdlaɪn/, *n.* **1.** a line of needy persons assembled to receive food given as charity. **2. on the breadline,** living at subsistence level, sustained by public assistance or charity.

**breadmould** /ˈbrɛdmoʊld/, *n.* a black fungus, *Rhizopus nigricans,* often seen on bread.

**bread sauce** /brɛd ˈsɔs/, *n.* a sauce made of milk infused with onion, bay leaf and pepper, and strained over breadcrumbs.

**bread stick** /ˈ– stɪk/, *n.* **1.** a pencil-shaped roll of bread dough baked until hard and crisp; grissini. **2.** *Colloq.* French bread.

**breadth** /brɛdθ/, *n.* **1.** *Maths.* the measure of the second principal diameter of a surface or solid, the first being length, and the third (in the case of a solid) thickness; width. **2.** an extent or piece of something as measured by its width, or of definite or full width: *a breadth of cloth.* **3.** freedom from narrowness or restraint; liberality: *breadth of understanding.* **4.** size in general; extent. **5.** *Art.* broad or general effect due to subordination of details or non-essentials. [earlier *breade* (OE *brǣdu*) + -TH[1]; modelled on LENGTH]

**breadthways** /ˈbrɛdθweɪz/, *adv.* in the direction of the breadth. Also, *esp. U.S.,* **breadthwise** /ˈbrɛdθwaɪz/.

**breadwinner** /ˈbrɛdwɪnə/, *n.* one who earns a livelihood for a family or household.

**break** /breɪk/, *v.,* **broke** or (*Archaic*) **brake; broken,** or (*Archaic*) **broke; breaking,** *n.* *–v.t.* **1.** to divide into parts violently; reduce to pieces or fragments. **2.** to violate: *to break a law or promise.* **3.** to dissolve or annul (oft. fol. by *off*). **4.** to fracture a bone of. **5.** to lacerate; wound: *to break the skin.* **6.** to discontinue abruptly; interrupt; suspend: *to break the silence.* **7.** to destroy the regularity of. **8.** to put an end to; overcome. **9.** to interrupt the uniformity or sameness of: *to break the monotony.* **10.** to destroy the unity, continuity, or arrangement of. **11.** to exchange for a smaller amount or smaller units. **12.** to make one's way through; penetrate. **13.** *Law.* to open or force one's way into (a dwelling, store, etc.): *to break and enter.* **14.** to make one's way out of: *to break gaol.* **15.** to surpass; outdo: *to break a record.* **16.** to disclose or divulge, with caution or delicacy. **17.** to disable or destroy by or as by shattering or crushing. **18.** to open the breech of (a gun) either for safety or for unloading. **19.** to ruin financially, or make bankrupt. **20.** to reduce in rank. **21.** to impair or weaken in strength, spirit, force, or effect. **22.** to publish (a news item). **23.** to defeat the purpose of (a strike). **24.** to train to obedience; tame (oft. fol. by *in*): *to break in a horse.* **25.** to cultivate virgin land (oft. fol. by *in*): *to break in a new paddock.* **26.** to train away from a habit or practice (fol. by *of*). **27.** *Cricket.* **a.** to strike so as to dislodge the bails from (a wicket). **b. break one's duck,** (of a batsman) to score his first run in an innings. **28.** *Golf.* to bend the wrists on the back swing. **29.** *Elect.* to render (a circuit) incomplete; stop the flow of (a current). **30.** *Music.* to arpeggiate. **31.** to void or expel: *to break wind.* *–v.i.* **32.** to become broken; separate into parts or fragments, esp. suddenly and violently. **33.** to become suddenly discontinuous or interrupted; leave off abruptly (fol. by *off,* etc.) **34.** to happen, come about to one's advantage: *it broke his way.* **35.** to become detached (fol. by *off, from,* etc.). **36.** to make a pause (oft. fol. by *off*). **37.** to dissolve and separate (fol. by *up*). **38.** to sever relations (fol. by *up* or *with*). **39.** (of a ball) to change direction on bouncing. **40.** (of a wave) to topple forward after developing a crest through the opposing pull of an undertow in shallow water. **41.** to free oneself or escape suddenly, as from restraint (oft. fol. by *away*). **42.** (of a news item) to appear in print. **43.** (of sheep) to run away from a mob. **44.** to force a way (fol. by *in, through, out,* etc.). **45.** to burst (fol. by *in, forth, from,* etc.). **46.** to come suddenly, as into notice. **47.** to change state or activity (fol. by *into*). **48.** to dawn, as the day. **49.** (of a fish) to come to the surface. **50.** to give way or fail as under strain (oft. fol. by *down*). **51.** (of the heart) to be crushed or overwhelmed, esp. by grief. **52.** (of stock-exchange prices) to drop quickly and considerably. **53.** (of the voice) to vary between two registers, esp. in emotion or during adolescence. **54.** *Music.* to change or go from one register to another, as a musical instrument. **55.** *Linguistics.* to undergo breaking. **56.** *Billiards.* to make a break (def. 81). **57.** *Boxing.* to discontinue a clinch. **58.** *Rugby.* to disband, as a scrummage, to outdistance suddenly the rest of the field. **59.** (in a race) to start before the signal to do so has been given. *–v.* **60.** Some special verb phrases are:

**break away, 1.** (in racing) to start prematurely. **2.** *Football.* to elude defending players and run towards the opposing goal. **3.** to remove oneself with effort from contact with or the influence of another person (fol. by *from*). **4.** to secede.

**break bulk, 1.** to open a ship's hatch and discharge the first sling of cargo. **2.** to open a fully enclosed container and unload the first part of the load.

**break camp,** to pack up tents and equipment and resume a march.

**break down, 1.** to take down or destroy by breaking. **2.** to overcome. **3.** to analyse. **4.** to collapse. **5.** to cease to function. **6.** *Timber Industry.* to cut logs into flitches; to make the first cuts in heavy logs. **7.** to add water to spirits, etc., to reduce the alcoholic strength.

**break even or square,** to have one's credits or profits equal one's debits or losses.

**break in, 1.** to interrupt. **2.** to adapt to one's convenience by use: *break in a new pair of shoes.* **3.** to accustom a horse to harness and use. **4.** to enter (a house or the like) forcibly, as a burglar.

**break into, 1.** to interrupt. **2.** to enter (a house or the like) forcibly.

**break it down,** *interj.* **a.** stop it. **b.** calm down; be reasonable.

**break new ground,** to venture into a new area of activity.

**break off, 1.** to sever by breaking. **2.** to put a sudden stop to; discontinue. **3.** to cease suddenly.

**break out, 1.** to issue forth; arise. **2.** *Pathol.* (of certain diseases) to appear in eruptions. **3.** to have a sudden appearance of various eruptions on the skin.

**break service,** *Tennis.* to win a game when receiving the service.

**break step,** *Mil.* to cease marching in step.

**break up, 1.** to separate; disband (esp. of a school at end of term). **2.** to put an end to; discontinue. **3.** to cut up (fowl, etc.). **4.** *Colloq.* to collapse with laughter.

*–n.* **61.** a forcible disruption or separation of parts; a breaking; a fracture, rupture, or shattering. **62.** an opening made by breaking; a gap. **63.** a rush away from a place; an attempt to escape: *a break for freedom.* **64.** an interruption of continuity; suspension, stoppage. **65.** an abrupt or marked change, as in sound or direction. **66.** (of sheep) a stampede. **67.** *Wool.* a distinct weakness in one part of the wool staple caused by a temporary interference with the growth of the staple. **68.** *Colloq.* an opportunity; chance. **69.** *Colloq.* a social error or slip; an unfortunate remark. **70.** a small amount; portion. **71.** a brief rest, as from work, esp. a mid-morning pause, usu. of fifteen minutes, between school classes. **72.** a short holiday: *a three day break.* **73.** *Pros.* a pause or caesura. **74.** *Jazz.* an instrumental solo usu. over a twelve-bar pattern, during which the accompanying band rests. **75.** *Music.* the point in the scale where the quality of voice of one register changes to that of another, as from chest to head. **76.** *Stock Exchange.* a sudden drop in prices. **77.** *Elect.* an opening or discontinuity in a circuit. **78.** *Print.* a wordbreak. **79. a.** a series of successful shots, strokes, or the like, in a game. **b.** *Billiards.* the score made in such a series. **80.** any continuous run, esp. of good fortune. **81.** *Billiards.* **a.** the shot that breaks or scatters the balls at the beginning of the game. **b.** the right to the first shot. **82.** a premature start in racing. **83.** *Cricket, etc.* change in direction of a ball when it bounces, usu. caused by a spinning motion imparted by the bowler. **84.** *Tenpin Bowling.* a failure to knock down all ten pins after bowling twice. **85.** *Horseracing.* a change in the pace of a horse, from a trot to a gallop: *he pulled the horse into a break.* **86.** shooting brake. **87.** *C.B. Radio.* access to a radio channel. **88. give (someone) a break,** *Colloq.* to give (someone) a fair chance. **89. those are the breaks,** *Colloq.* that is how life is. [ME *breke(n),* OE *brecan,* c. G *brechen,* Goth. *brikan*] – **breakable,** *adj.*

**breakable** /ˈbreɪkəbəl/, *adj.* **1.** capable of being broken. *–n.* **2.** an item, esp. of china, which can be easily broken.

**breakage** /ˈbreɪkɪdʒ/, *n.* **1.** an act of breaking; a break. **2.** the amount or quantity of things broken. **3.** an allowance or compensation for loss or damage of articles broken in transit or in use.

**breakaway** /ˈbreɪkəweɪ/, *n.* **1.** the act of breaking away, becoming separate. **2.** the formation of a splinter group in a political party, or similar group: *there was a breakaway in the Victorian Labor party.* **3.** Also, *Brit., N.Z.,* **flanker, wing forward.** *Rugby Union.* either of two players who pack down on either side of the back row in a scrum. **4.** *Chiefly U.S.* a premature start in racing; break. **5.** a panic rush of or among a mob of cattle, horses, etc. **6.** an animal which breaks away from a flock or herd. **7.** a gully formed by erosion. **8.** →**frangible.** *–adj.* **9.** of or pertaining to that which has broken away or seeks to break away. **10.** →**frangible** (def. 2).

**breakbone fever** /ˌbreɪkboʊn ˈfivə/, *n.* →**dengue.**

**break-bulk** /ˈbreɪk-bʌlk/, *adj.* of or pertaining to a quantity of cargo stowed loosely in a compartment or a container.

**breakdown** /ˈbreɪkdaʊn/, *n.* **1.** a ceasing to function, as of a machine. **2.** a collapse of physical or mental health. **3.** *Chem.* →**decomposition.** **4.** statistical or other analysis. **5.** *Elect.* the sudden formation of a conducting path, as when an insulator fails to withstand the application of a high voltage. **6.** *U.S.* a noisy, lively folk dance.

**breakdown product** /ˈ– ˌprɒdʌkt/, *n.* that which is produced by the disintegration or decomposition of a substance.

**breakdown saw** /– ˈsɔ/, *n.* *Timber Industry.* a saw used for breaking down logs.

**breaker**[1] /ˈbreɪkə/, *n.* **1.** one who or that which breaks. **2.** a wave that breaks or dashes into foam. **3.** *Elect.* →**circuit-breaker.** **4.** *C.B. Radio.* a radio operator requesting access to a channel. *–interj.* **5. breaker, breaker!** *C.B. Radio.* (a call used by an operator to request access to a channel). [BREAK + -ER[1]]

**breaker**[2] /ˈbreɪkə/, *n.* *Naut.* a small water cask for use in a boat. [Sp.: alteration of *barrica* cask]

**breaker-down** /ˈbreɪkə-daʊn/, *n.* *Timber Industry.* a man operating a breakdown saw.

**break even** /breɪk ˈivən/, *v.i.* to neither win nor lose on a transaction.

**break-even** /ˌbreɪk-ˈivən/, *n.* the point at which one is neither gaining nor losing.

**breakfast** /ˈbrɛkfəst/, *n.* **1.** the first meal of the day; a morning meal. **2.** the food eaten at the first meal. **3.** a meal or food in general. *–v.i.* **4.** to take breakfast. *–v.t.* **5.** to supply with breakfast. [ME *brekfast,* from *brek* break + *fast* FAST[2]] – **breakfaster,** *n.*

**breakfast room** /ˈ– rum/, *n.* →**morning room.**

**breakfast-time** /ˈbrɛkfəs-taɪm/, *n.* **1.** the time in the morning when breakfast is eaten. *–adj.* **2.** denoting, pertaining to, or taking place at this time.

**break-in** /ˈbreɪk-ɪn/, *n.* **1.** a breaking and entering. **2.** →**interrupt** (def. 5).

**breaking** /ˈbreɪkɪŋ/, *n.* (in the history of English and of some other languages) the change of a vowel to diphthong under the influence of a following consonant or combination of consonants; e.g., in Old English, the change of *-a-* to *-ea-* and of *-e-* to *-eo-* before preconsonantal *-r-* or *-l-* and before *-h-*, as in *earm* (arm) developed from *arm* and *eorthe* (earth) from *erthe.*

**breaking and entering,** *n.* forcible entry into the dwelling house of another with intent to commit a felony.

**breaking point** /ˈbreɪkɪŋ pɔɪnt/, *n.* the point at which a given material, person, etc., gives way under stress.

**breakneck** /ˈbreɪknɛk/, *adj.* dangerous; hazardous.

**break of day,** *n.* dawn; daybreak.

**break-of-gauge** /ˈbreɪk-əv-geɪdʒ/, *n.* the occurrence of adjoining lengths of railway track of different widths.

**break-out** /ˈbreɪk-aʊt/, *n.* an escape, as from prison.

**break pin** /ˈbreɪk pɪn/, *n.* →**shear pin.**

**breakpoint** /ˈbreɪkpɔɪnt/, *n.* **1.** an instruction inserted by a debug program. **2.** the point in a program at which such an instruction operates.

**breakthrough** /ˈbreɪkθru/, *n.* **1.** *Mil.* a movement or advance all the way through and beyond a defensive system into the unorganised areas in the rear. **2.** any development, as in science, technology, or diplomacy, which removes a barrier to progress.

**break-up** /ˈbreɪk-ʌp/, *n.* **1.** disintegration; disruption; dispersal. **2.** an itemisation: *to give a break-up of an inventory.* **3.** the closing of a school for its term holidays.

**breakwater** /ˈbreɪkwɔtə/, *n.* a barrier which breaks the force of waves, as before a harbour.

**breakweather** /ˈbreɪkwɛðə/, *n.* →**windbreak.**

**breakwind** /ˈbreɪkwɪnd/, *n.* →**windbreak.**

**bream** /brɪm/, *n.* **1.** in Australia, any of various marine sparid fishes of the genera *Mylio* and *Acanthopagrus,* highly prized as food and for sport, as the **black bream,** *A. australis* of eastern Australian waters. **2.** elsewhere, **a.** any of various freshwater cyprinoid fishes of the genus *Abramis,* as *A. brama* of Europe, with a compressed, deep body. **b.** any of various related and similar species, as the **white bream,** *Blicca bjoerkna.* [ME *breme,* from OF *bresme,* of Gmc orig.; ? related to OHG *brehan* glitter]

**breast** /brɛst/, *n.* **1.** *Anat., Zool.* the outer front part of the thorax, or the front part of the body from neck to belly; the chest. **2.** *Zool.* the corresponding part in lower animals. **3.** a standard cut of meat from this area. **4.** *Anat., Zool.* a mammary or milk gland, esp. of a woman, or of female animals whose milk glands are similarly formed. **5.** that part of a garment which covers the chest. **6.** the bosom regarded as the seat of thoughts and feelings. **7.** thoughts; feelings; mind. **8.** any surface or part resembling or likened to the human breast. **9.** *Mining.* the face or heading at which the working is going on. **10.** in coal mines, a chamber driven in the seam from the gangway for the extraction of coal. **11. make a clean breast of,** to make a full confession of. **12. a.** to meet or oppose with the breast, as in racing: *to breast the (finishing) tape.* **b.** to bring up to the breast, as in card playing: *to breast the card.* **13.** to face; meet boldly or advance against: *the ship breasted the waves.* [ME *brest,* OE *brēost,* akin to G *Brust*]

**breastbone** /ˈbrɛstboʊn/, *n.* →**sternum.**

**breastfeed** /ˈbrɛstfid/, *v.,* **-fed, -feeding.** *–v.t.* **1.** to give suck to (a child) with the breast (opposed to *bottle-feed*). *–v.i.* **2.** to feed a child in this manner.

**breastpin** /ˈbrɛstpɪn/, *n.* a pin worn on the breast or at the throat; a brooch.

**breastplate** /ˈbrɛstpleɪt/, *n.* **1.** armour for the front of the torso. **2.** part of the harness that runs across a saddle-horse's breast. **3.** a square ornament worn on the breast by the Jewish high priest.

breastplate (def. 1)

**breast stroke** /ˈbrɛst stroʊk/, *n.* *Swimming.* a stroke made in the prone position in which both hands move simultaneously forwards, outwards and rearwards from in front of the chest, and the legs move in a frog-like manner. – **breast-stroke,** *v.*

**breastwork** /ˈbrɛstwɜk/, *n.* *Fort.* a defensive work, usu. breast high, hastily thrown up.

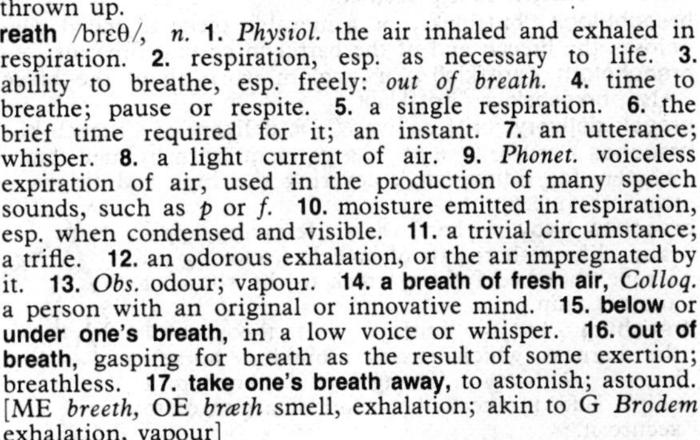

**breath** /brɛθ/, *n.* **1.** *Physiol.* the air inhaled and exhaled in respiration. **2.** respiration, esp. as necessary to life. **3.** ability to breathe, esp. freely: *out of breath.* **4.** time to breathe; pause or respite. **5.** a single respiration. **6.** the brief time required for it; an instant. **7.** an utterance; whisper. **8.** a light current of air. **9.** *Phonet.* voiceless expiration of air, used in the production of many speech sounds, such as *p* or *f.* **10.** moisture emitted in respiration, esp. when condensed and visible. **11.** a trivial circumstance; a trifle. **12.** an odorous exhalation, or the air impregnated by it. **13.** *Obs.* odour; vapour. **14. a breath of fresh air,** *Colloq.* a person with an original or innovative mind. **15. below** or **under one's breath,** in a low voice or whisper. **16. out of breath,** gasping for breath as the result of some exertion; breathless. **17. take one's breath away,** to astonish; astound. [ME *breeth,* OE *brǣth* smell, exhalation; akin to G *Brodem* exhalation, vapour]

**breathalyser** /ˈbrɛθəlaɪzə/, *n.* **1.** →**alcotest.** **2.** the Breath Analysis Machine Test; a test to determine the exact amount of alcohol in exhaled breath, administered at a police station to a driver with a positive reading on an alcotest. Also, **breath-test.** [b. BREATH and ANALYSER]

**breathe** /brið/, *v.*, **breathed** /briðd/, **breathing.** *–v.i.* **1.** to inhale and exhale air; respire. **2.** (in speech) to control the outgoing breath in producing voice and speech sounds. **3.** to pause, as for breath; take rest (only in infinitive): *give me a chance to breathe.* **4.** to blow lightly, as air. **5.** to live; exist. **6.** to exhale an odour. **7.** to be redolent (*of*). **8.** (of a film) to undergo an intermittent loss of sharp focus as a result of the film not being held flat in the gate of the projector. *–v.t.* **9.** to inhale and exhale in respiration. **10.** to allow to rest or recover breath. **11.** to put out of breath; tire or exhaust. **12.** to give utterance to; whisper. **13.** to express; manifest. **14.** to exhale: *dragons breathing fire.* **15.** to inject by breathing; infuse. **16.** to exercise briskly. – **breathable,** *adj.*

**breathed** /briðd/ *for def. 1;* /brɛθt/ *for def. 2, adj.* **1.** *Phonet.* without use of the vocal chords; voiceless. **2.** having a breath, as in *sweet-breathed.*

**breather** /ˈbriðə/, *n.* **1.** a pause for rest. **2.** one who breathes.

**breathing** /ˈbriðɪŋ/, *n.* **1.** the act of one that breathes; respiration. **2.** a single breath. **3.** utterance or words. **4.** aspiration or longing. **5.** gentle blowing, as of wind. **6.** *Gram.* **a.** aspiration; pronunciation with reference to the use or omission of an *h*-sound. **b.** a sign to indicate this, as in Greek, where ʽ (**rough breathing**) indicates aspiration and ʼ (**smooth breathing**) indicates non-aspiration. **7.** *Motor Vehicles.* the passage of air through an internal combustion engine during its operation.

**breathing space** /ˈbriðɪŋ speɪs/, *n.* opportunity to breathe easily; pause to rest.

**breathless** /ˈbrɛθləs/, *adj.* **1.** out of breath: *the blow left him breathless.* **2.** with the breath held, as in suspense: *breathless listeners.* **3.** that takes away the breath: *a breathless ride.* **4.** *Archaic.* dead. **5.** motionless, as the air. – **breathlessly,** *adv.* – **breathlessness,** *n.*

**breathtaking** /ˈbrɛθteɪkɪŋ/, *adj.* causing extreme excitement: *a breathtaking performance.*

**breath-test** /ˈbrɛθ-tɛst/, *n.* →**breathalyser** (def. 2).

**breathy** /ˈbrɛθi/, *adj.* (of the voice) characterised by excessive emission of breath.

**breccia** /ˈbrɛtʃiə/, *n.* **1.** rock composed of angular fragments of older rocks embedded in a matrix. *–v.t.* **2.** to form into breccia. [It.] – **brecciate,** *v.t.*

**bred** /brɛd/, *v.* past tense and past participle of **breed.**

**breech** /britʃ/, *n.* **1.** the lower part of the trunk of the body behind; the posterior or buttocks. **2.** the hinder or lower part of anything. **3.** *Ordn.* the mass of metal behind the bore of a cannon, or the part of a small arm behind the barrel. **4.** *Mach.* the lowest part of a pulley. *–v.t.* **5.** *Ordn.* to fit or furnish (a gun) with a breech. **6.** to clothe with breeches. **7.** *Archaic.* to flog on the buttocks. [ME *breeche,* OE *brēc,* pl., c. Icel. *brækr,* pl. of *brōk.* Cf. L *brācae,* pl., breeches, of Celtic orig.]

**breech birth** /ˈ– bɜθ/, *n.* a birth in which the baby's posterior, not its head, is first presented.

**breechblock** /ˈbritʃblɒk/, *n.* a movable piece of metal which closes the breech end of the barrel in certain firearms.

**breechcloth** /ˈbritʃklɒθ/, *n.* a cloth worn about the breech. Also, **breechclout** /ˈbritʃklaʊt/.

**breech delivery** /britʃ dəˈlɪvəri/, *n.* delivery of a breech birth.

**breeches** /ˈbrɪtʃəz/, *n.pl.* **1.** a garment worn by men (and by women for riding, etc.), covering the hips and thighs. **2.** trousers. [BREECH + -ES]

**breeches buoy** /ˈ– bɔɪ/, *n.* a life-saving apparatus, like a short pair of breeches, moving on a rope stretched from a wreck to the shore or another ship.

breeches buoy

**breeching** /ˈbrɪtʃɪŋ, ˈbritʃɪŋ/, *n.* **1.** the part of the harness which passes around a horse's breech. **2.** *Navy.* a strong rope fastened to a ship's side, to check the recoil of a gun or to secure it.

**breech-loader** /ˈbritʃ-loʊdə/, *n.* a firearm, as a rifle, loaded at the breech.

**breech-loading** /ˈbritʃ-loʊdɪŋ/, *adj.* of a firearm, loaded at the breech.

**breed** /brid/, *v.*, **bred, breeding,** *n.* *–v.t.* **1.** to produce (offspring). **2.** to procure by the mating of parents; propagate. **3.** *Hort.* **a.** to cause to reproduce by controlled pollination. **b.** to improve by controlled pollination and selection. **4.** to raise (livestock, etc.). **5.** to procreate; engender. **6.** to cause; occasion; produce: *dirt breeds disease.* **7.** to be the native place or the source of: *stagnant water breeds mosquitoes.* **8.** to produce by training. *–v.i.* **9.** to produce offspring. **10.** to be engendered or produced; grow; develop. **11.** to procure the birth of young, as in raising stock. *–n.* **12.** *Genetics.* a relatively homogeneous group of animals within a species, developed and maintained by man. **13.** race; lineage; strain. **14.** sort; kind. [ME *brede(n),* OE *brēdan* nourish, from *brōd* brood] – **breeder,** *n.*

**breeder** /ˈbridə/, *n.* **1.** one who or that which breeds. **2.** a female animal old enough to be used for breeding. **3.** Also, **breeder reactor.** *Physics.* a nuclear reactor in which fissile material is used as a source of neutrons to produce more fissile nuclei than are consumed.

**breeding** /ˈbridɪŋ/, *n.* **1.** the act of one who or that which breeds. **2.** the rearing of livestock to improve their quality or merit. **3.** *Hort.* the production of new forms by selection, crossing, and hybridising. **4.** nurture; training. **5.** the results of training as shown in behaviour and manners; good manners. **6.** *Physics.* the production of more fissile material than is consumed in a breeder reactor.

**breeze**[1] /briz/, *n., v.*, **breezed, breezing.** *–n.* **1.** a wind or current of air, esp. a light or moderate one. **2.** *Meteorol.* any wind of Beaufort scale numbers 2 to 6 inclusive, comprising velocities from 4 to 27 knots, i.e. 6 to 49 km/h. **3.** *Colloq.* an easy task: *it's a breeze.* **4. bat the breeze,** *Colloq.* to engage in idle conversation. **5. have the breeze up,** *Colloq.* to be afraid. **6. put the breeze up,** *Colloq.* to make afraid. *–v.i.* **7.** *Colloq.* to move or proceed in a casual, quick, gay manner (often fol. by *along, in*). **8. breeze through,** *Colloq.* to perform without effort. [Sp. (and Pg.) *briza*]

**breeze**[2] /briz/, *n.* →**gadfly.** [ME *brese,* OE *briosa*]

**breezeblock** /ˈbrizblɒk/, *n.* *Bldg Trades.* a light brick compounded of coke cinders and concrete.

**breezeway** /ˈbrizweɪ/, *n.* a passageway, usu. running through a house, such that air may blow through it to cool the building.

**breezy** /ˈbrizi/, *adj.* **breezier, breeziest.** **1.** abounding in breezes; windy. **2.** fresh; sprightly; cheerful. – **breezily,** *adv.* – **breeziness,** *n.*

**bregma** /ˈbrɛgmə/, *n., pl.* **-mata** /-mətə/. the point of junction of the sagittal and coronal sutures of the skull. [Gk: front of the head] – **bregmatic** /brɛgˈmætɪk/, *adj.*

**brekkie** /ˈbrɛki/, *n.* *Colloq.* breakfast.

**bremsstrahlung** /ˈbrɛmstralʊŋ/, *n.* electromagnetic radiation emitted when a charged particle is undergoing acceleration. [G: braking radiation]

**Bren gun** /ˈbrɛn gʌn/, a kind of light machine-gun. [named after *Br(no),* in Czechoslovakia, where it was first manufactured + *En(field),* in England, where construction was perfected]

**brent** /brɛnt/, *n., pl.* **brents,** (*esp. collectively*) **brent.** any of several species of small, dark-coloured geese of the genus *Branta,* esp. *B. bernicla,* which breed in high northern latitudes and migrate south in autumn. Also, *Chiefly U.S.,* **brant.** [cf. Icel. *brandgās*]

**brer** /brɛə, brɜ/, *n.* *Southern U.S. Colloq.* brother. Also, **br'er.**

**brethren** /ˈbrɛðrən/, *n.* **1.** *Archaic.* plural of **brother.** **2.** fellow members.

**Breton** /ˈbrɛtən/, *n.* **1.** a native of Brittany. *–adj.* **2.** the Celtic language of Brittany. **3.** pertaining to Brittany, the Bretons, or their language. [F. See BRITON]

**breve** /briv/, *n.* **1.** a mark (˘) placed over a vowel to show that it is pronounced short, as in ŭ. **2.** *Law.* **a.** an initial writ. **b.** a writ, as one issued by a court of law. **3.** a letter of authority, esp. one from a sovereign or the pope. **4.** *Music.* the longest modern note, now seldom used, equivalent to two semibreves. [It., from L *brevis* short]

**brevet** /ˈbrɛvət/, *n., v.*, **-vetted, -vetting** or **-veted, -veting.** *–n.* **1.** a commission promoting a military officer to a higher rank without increase of pay and with limited exercise of the higher rank. *–v.t.* **2.** to appoint or promote by brevet. [ME, from F, diminutive of *bref* letter. See BRIEF]

**brevi-,** a word element meaning 'short', as in *brevirostrate.* [L, combining form of *brevis*]

**breviary** /ˈbrɛvjəri, ˈbri-, -vəri/, *n., pl.* **-ries. 1.** *Rom. Cath. Ch.* a book of daily prayers and readings to be read by those in major orders. **2.** *Eccles.* a similar book in some other churches. [L *breviārium* abridgment, properly neut. of *breviārius* abridged]

**brevier** /brəˈvɪə/, *n.* a printing type (8 point) of a size between minion and bourgeois. [so called from use in printing breviaries; said to be from G: breviary, from F *bréviaire,* from L *breviārium*]

**brevirostrate** /ˌbrɛvəˈrɒstreɪt/, *adj.* of birds, having a short beak or bill.

**brevity** /ˈbrɛvəti/, *n., pl.* **-ties. 1.** shortness of time or duration; briefness: *the brevity of human life.* **2.** condensation in speech; conciseness. [L *brevitas,* from *brevis* short]

**brew** /bru/, *–v.t.* **1.** to make (beer, ale, etc.) from malt, etc., by steeping, boiling, and fermentation. **2.** to prepare (a beverage) by or as by brewing. **3.** to make (tea) (oft. fol. by *up*). **4.** to concoct or contrive; bring about: *to brew mischief.* *–v.i.* **5.** to brew beer, ale, etc. **6.** (of tea, etc.) to be in preparation. **7.** to be in preparation; be forming or gathering (oft. fol. by *up*): *trouble was brewing.* *–n.* **8.** a quantity brewed in a single process. **9.** a particular brewing or variety of malt liquor. **10.** a beverage prepared by or as by brewing: *let's have a brew (of tea).* **11.** the process of brewing (esp. tea) as a social occasion. [ME *brewen;* OE *brēowan.* Cf. BROTH] – **brewer,** *n.*

**brewage** /ˈbruɪdʒ/, *n.* a fermented liquor brewed from malt, etc.

**brewer's droop** /bruəz ˈdrup/, *n. Colloq.* alcoholically induced sexual impotence.

**brewer's yeast** /– ˈjist/, *n.* a yeast, *Saccharomyces cerevisiae,* used in brewing.

**brewery** /ˈbruəri/, *n., pl.* **-ries.** an establishment for brewing beer, ale, etc.

**brewing** /ˈbruɪŋ/, *n.* **1.** the act of one who brews. **2.** a quantity brewed at once.

**briar** /ˈbraɪə/, *n.* **1.** the white heath, *Erica arborea,* of France and Corsica, whose woody root is used for making tobacco pipes. **2.** a pipe made of this or similar wood. **3.** a prickly shrub or plant, esp. the sweetbriar, *Rosa rubiginosa.* Also, **brier.** [F *bruyère* heath, from LL derivative of Gallic *brūcus* heather] – **briary,** *adj.*

**briar-root** /ˈbraɪə-rut/, *n.* **1.** the rootwood of the briar. **2.** certain other woods from which tobacco pipes are made. **3.** a pipe made of briar-root. Also, **brier-root.**

**briarwood** /ˈbraɪəwʊd/, *n.* →**briar-root.** Also, **brierwood.**

**bribe** /braɪb/, *n., v.,* **bribed, bribing.** *–n.* **1.** any valuable consideration given or promised for corrupt behaviour in the performance of official or public duty. **2.** anything given or serving to persuade or induce. **3.** *Textiles.* a length of damaged woollen fabric removed from a piece of cloth. *–v.t.* **4.** to give or promise a bribe to. **5.** to influence or corrupt by a bribe. *–v.i.* **6.** to give bribes; practise bribery. [ME; cf. OF *bribe* piece of bread given to a beggar, *briber* beg, c. Sp. *bribar*] – **bribable,** *adj.* – **bribability** /ˌbraɪbəˈbɪləti/, *n.* – **briber,** *n.*

**bribery** /ˈbraɪbəri/, *n., pl.* **-ries.** the act or practice of giving or accepting bribes.

**bric-a-brac** /ˈbrɪk-ə-bræk/, *n.* miscellaneous ornamental articles of antiquarian, decorative, or other interest. Also, **bric-à-brac.** [F]

**brick** /brɪk/, *n.* **1.** a block of clay, usu. rectangular, hardened by drying in the sun or burning in a kiln, and used for building, paving, etc. **2.** such blocks collectively. **3.** the material. **4.** any similar block, esp. a small one of painted wood, used as a child's toy. **5.** *Colloq.* a good fellow. **6.** *Colloq.* a social blunder or solecism: *to drop a brick.* **7.** *Colloq.* **a.** (formerly) the sum of £10. **b.** the sum of $10. **8.** *Music Colloq.* an amplifier. **9.** *Prison Colloq.* prison sentence of ten years' duration. **10. a brick short (of a load),** *Colloq.* simple-minded. **11. built like a brick,** *Colloq.* (of a person) well-built; stocky. *–v.t.* **12.** to lay, line, wall, build, or enclose with brick (oft. fol. by *up*). [ME *brik,* from MD *bricke;* akin to BREAK] – **bricklike,** *adj.*

**brickbat** /ˈbrɪkbæt/, *n.* **1.** a piece of broken brick, esp. one used as a missile. **2.** any rocklike missile. **3.** *Colloq.* an unkind remark; caustic criticism.

**brick clay** /ˈbrɪk kleɪ/, *n.* clay suitable for making bricks.

**brickfield** /ˈbrɪkfild/, *n.* →**brickyard.**

**brickfielder** /ˈbrɪkfildə/, *n. Colloq.* **1.** a dry, dusty wind. **2.** (in Sydney) a southerly buster. [from *Brickfield* Hill in Sydney from which winds blew dust]

**brickie** /ˈbrɪki/, *n. Colloq.* a bricklayer.

**brick-kiln** /ˈbrɪk-kɪln/, *n.* a kiln or furnace in which bricks are baked or burned.

**bricklaying** /ˈbrɪkleɪɪŋ/, *n.* the art or occupation of laying bricks in construction. – **bricklayer,** *n.*

**brick red** /brɪk ˈrɛd/, *adj.* yellowish or brownish red.

**brick veneer** /– vəˈnɪə/, *n.* **1.** a veneer of bricks. **2.** a building whose external walls each consist of a timber framework faced with a single skin of bricks, the brickwork being non-structural. – **brick-veneer,** *adj.*

**brickwork** /ˈbrɪkwɜk/, *n.* brick construction (as contrasted with that of other materials).

**brickyard** /ˈbrɪkjad/, *n.* a place where bricks are made, stored, etc.

**bricole** /brɪˈkoʊl, ˈbrɪkəl/, *n.* **1.** *Billiards.* a shot in which the cue ball strikes the cushion first. **2.** *Royal Tennis.* a stroke rebounding from the side wall of the court. **3.** an indirect action or unexpected stroke. [F, from Pr. *bricola* catapult]

**bridal** /ˈbraɪdl/, *adj.* **1.** of or pertaining to a bride or a wedding. *–n.* **2.** a wedding. **3.** *Archaic.* a wedding feast. [ME *bridale,* OE *brȳdealo* bride ale, from *brȳd* bride + *ealo* ale, feast, associated with adj. suffix -AL[1]]

**bride**[1] /braɪd/, *n.* a woman newly married, or about to be married. [ME; OE *brȳd,* c. G *Braut*]

**bride**[2] /braɪd/, *n.* **1.** (in needlework, lacemaking, etc.) a bar, link, or tie between patterns. **2.** an ornamental bonnet string. [F: bridle, string, tie, from Gmc. See BRIDLE]

**bridegroom** /ˈbraɪdgrum/, *n.* a man newly married, or about to be married. [var. of ME *bridegome,* OE *brȳdguma,* from *brȳd* bride + *guma* man (c. L *homo*)]

**bridesmaid** /ˈbraɪdzmeɪd/, *n.* a young unmarried woman who attends the bride at a wedding.

**bridge**[1] /brɪdʒ/, *n., v.,* **bridged, bridging.** *–n.* **1.** a structure spanning a river, chasm, road, or the like, and affording passage. **2.** *Naut.* a raised platform from side to side of a ship above the rail, for the officer in charge. **3.** *Anat.* the ridge or upper line of the nose. **4.** *Dentistry.* an artificial replacement of a missing tooth or teeth, supported by natural teeth adjacent to the space, which may be fixed or removable. **5.** *Music.* a thin support across which the strings of a stringed instrument are stretched above the sounding-board. **6.** (on spectacles) the part which joins the two lenses and rests on the bridge or sides of the nose. **7.** *Elect.* an instrument for measuring electrical impedance. **8.** *U.S. Railways.* a signal gantry. **9.** *Metall.* a ridge or wall-like projection of firebrick or the like, at either end of the hearth in a metallurgical furnace. **10.** *Billiards.* a notched piece of wood with a long handle, used to support a cue when the distance is otherwise too great to reach; rest. *–v.t.* **11.** to make a bridge over; span. **12.** to make (a way) by a bridge. [ME *brigge,* OE *brycg,* c. G *Brücke*] – **bridgeable,** *adj.* – **bridgeless,** *adj.*

**bridge**[2] /brɪdʒ/, *n. Cards.* a game for four players, derived from whist, in which one partnership plays to fulfil a certain declaration against opponents acting as defenders. See **contract bridge** and **auction bridge.** [orig. uncert.]

**bridge deck** /ˈ– dɛk/, *n.* **1.** the deck of a ship on which the bridge is located. **2.** a small transverse deck on a pleasure boat.

**bridgehead** /ˈbrɪdʒhɛd/, *n.* **1.** a position held on the enemy side of a river or defile, to cover the crossing of friendly troops. **2.** any fortified position established in enemy territory, as by parachute troops. **3.** a defensive work covering or protecting the end of a bridge towards the enemy.

**bridgehouse** /ˈbrɪdʒhaʊs/, *n.* a house built at one end of a bridge, as for the purpose of defending it, collecting tolls, etc.

**bridgework** /ˈbrɪdʒwɜk/, *n.* **1.** *Dentistry.* **a.** dental bridges collectively. **b.** any of several different types of dental bridges. **2.** the building of bridges.

**bridging** /ˈbrɪdʒɪŋ/, *n. Bldg Trades.* a piece or an arrangement of pieces fixed between floor or roof joists to keep them in place.

**bridging finance** /ˈ– ˌfaɪnæns/, *n.* a temporary loan at high interest, usu. to one who has disposed of one asset, as a house, but who has not yet been paid for it, and who is obliged to pay for another.

**bridle** /ˈbraɪdl/, *n., v.,* **-dled, -dling.** *–n.* **1.** the part of the harness of a horse, etc., about the head, consisting usu. of headstall, bit, and reins, and used to restrain and guide the animal. **2.** anything that restrains or curbs. **3.** *Mach.* a link, flange, or other attachment for limiting the movement of any part of a machine. **4.** *Naut.* a short chain or rope span, both ends of which are made fast. **5.** a bridling, or drawing up of the head, as in disdain. *–v.t.* **6.** to put a bridle on. **7.** to control as with a bridle; restrain; curb. *–v.i.* **8.** to draw up the head and draw in the chin, as in disdain or resentment; to be resentful or annoyed (oft. fol. by *at*). [ME; OE *brīdel,* earlier *brigdils*] – **bridler,** *n.*

**bridlepath** /ˈbraɪdlpaθ/, *n.* a path suitable for use by horseback riders or walkers.

**bridle-track** /ˈbraɪdl-træk/, *n.* →**bridlepath.**

**brie** /bri/, *n.* a kind of salted, white, soft cheese, ripened through bacterial action, waxy to semiliquid, as made in Brie, a district in northern France.

**brief** /brif/, *adj.* **1.** of little duration. **2.** using few words; concise; succinct. **3.** abrupt or curt. **4.** close-fitting and short in length or extent: *brief underpants.* *–n.* **5.** a short and concise writing or statement. **6.** an outline, the form of which is determined by set rules, of all the possible arguments and information on one side of a controversy: *a debater's brief.* **7.** *Law.* a writ summoning one to answer to any action. **8.** *Law.* a memorandum of points of fact or of law, etc., for use in conducting a case. **9. hold a brief for,** to espouse. **10.** a briefing. **11.** *Rom. Cath. Ch.* a papal letter less formal than a bull, sealed with the pope's signet ring or stamped with the device borne on this ring. **12.** *Obs.* a letter. **13. in brief,** in few words; in short. *–v.t.* **14.** to instruct by a brief or briefing. **15.** *Law.* to retain as advocate in a suit. [F, from L *brevis*] – **briefly,** *adv.* – **briefness,** *n.*

**briefcase** /ˈbrifkeɪs/, *n.* a flat, rectangular leather case used for carrying documents, books, manuscripts, etc. Also, **dispatch case.**

**briefing** /ˈbrifɪŋ/, *n.* a short, accurate summary of the details of a plan or operation as one given to a military unit, crew of an aeroplane, etc., before it undertakes the operation.

**briefs** /brifs/, *n.* close-fitting, legless underpants.

**brier** /ˈbraɪə/, *n.* →**sweetbriar.**

**brig** /brɪg/, *n. Naut.* **1.** a two-masted vessel square-rigged on both masts. **2.** the compartment of a ship where prisoners are confined. [shortened form of BRIGANTINE]

brig[1]

**Brig.,** *Mil.* **1.** Brigade. **2.** Brigadier.

**brigade** /brəˈgeɪd/, *n., v.,* **-gaded, -gading.** *–n.* **1.** a unit consisting of several regiments, squadrons, groups, or battalions. **2.** a large body of troops. **3.** a body of individuals organised for a special purpose: *a fire brigade.* *–v.t.* **4.** to form into a brigade. **5.** to group together. [F, from It. *brigata* troop, from *brigare* strive, contend]

**brigade major** /– ˈmeɪdʒə/, *n.* the chief staff officer of a brigade.

**brigadier** /brɪgəˈdɪə/, *n. Mil.* **1.** a rank between colonel and major general in the Australian Army. **2.** an equivalent rank in any other army. **3.** an officer of either of these ranks. [F, from *brigade* BRIGADE. See -IER]

**brigadier general** /– ˈdʒɛnrəl/, *n., pl.* **brigadier generals. 1.** (formerly) a brigadier in the British Army. **2.** *U.S. Army.* **a.** an officer between colonel and major general. **b.** this rank.

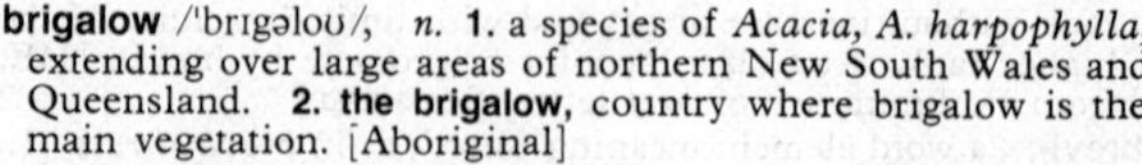

**brigalow** /ˈbrɪgəloʊ/, *n.* **1.** a species of *Acacia, A. harpophylla,* extending over large areas of northern New South Wales and Queensland. **2. the brigalow,** country where brigalow is the main vegetation. [Aboriginal]

**brigalow itch** /– ˈɪtʃ/, *n.* an irritation of the skin from contact with brigalow.

**brigand** /ˈbrɪgənd/, *n.* a bandit; one of a gang of robbers in mountain or forest regions. [ME *brigant,* from OF, from It. *brigante,* from *brigare.* See BRIGADE] – **brigandish,** *adj.*

**brigandage** /ˈbrɪgəndɪdʒ/, *n.* the practice of being a brigand; plundering. Also, **brigandry.**

**brigandine** /ˈbrɪgəndin, -ən/, *n.* a flexible body armour of overlapping steel plates riveted to the exterior covering of linen, velvet, leather, etc. [late ME *brigandyne,* from OF *brigandine*]

**brigantine** /ˈbrɪgəntin/, *n.* a two-masted vessel in which the foremast is square-rigged and the mainmast bears a fore-and-aft mainsail and square topsails. [F *brigantin,* from It. *brigantino,* from *brigante* BRIGAND]

brigantine

**bright** /braɪt/, *adj.* **1.** radiating or reflecting light; luminous; shining. **2.** filled with light. **3.** vivid or brilliant, as colour. **4.** clear or translucent, as liquids. **5.** radiant or splendid. **6.** illustrious or glorious, as a period. **7.** quick-witted or intelligent. **8.** clever or witty, as a remark. **9.** animated; lively; cheerful, as a person. **10.** characterised by happiness or gladness. **11.** favourable or auspicious: *bright prospects.* *–n.* **12.** *Archaic.* brightness; splendour. *–adv.* **13.** in a bright manner; brightly. [ME; OE *brhyt, beorht,* c. OHG *beraht,* Icel. *bjartr,* Goth. *bairhts*] – **brightly,** *adv.*

**brighten** /ˈbraɪtn/, *v.i., v.t.* to become or make bright or brighter. – **brightener,** *n.*

**brightness** /ˈbraɪtnəs/, *n.* **1.** bright quality. **2.** luminosity apart from hue; value. Pure white is of maximum brightness and pure black is of zero brightness. **3.** *Physics.* the luminous intensity per unit area of an extended source of light, measured in candelas per square metre. **4.** *Wool.* the white colour and light-reflecting power associated with the finer types of wool.

**Bright's disease** /ˈbraɪts dəziz/, *n.* a disease of the kidneys characterised by albuminuria and heightened blood pressure. [named after Richard *Bright,* 1789-1858, English physician, who described it]

**brill** /brɪl/, *n., pl.* **brill** or **brills.** a European flatfish, *Scophthalmus rhombus,* closely allied to the turbot.

**brillante** /briˈlanteɪ/, *adv.* (a musical direction) brilliantly. – **brillante,** *adj.*

**brilliance** /ˈbrɪljəns/, *n.* **1.** great brightness; splendour; lustre. **2.** remarkable excellence or distinction; conspicuous mental ability. **3.** brightness (def. 2). **4.** *Music.* **a.** (of tone) abundance in high harmonies. **b.** (of style in playing) vivacity; liveliness. Also, **brilliancy.**

**brilliant** /ˈbrɪljənt/, *adj.* **1.** shining brightly; sparkling; glittering; lustrous. **2.** distinguished; illustrious: *a brilliant achievement.* **3.** having or showing great intelligence or mental ability. **4.** *Music.* **a.** (of tone) characterised by the presence of a number of high harmonies. **b.** (of style in playing) lively; vivacious. **5.** (of wine) displaying good colour and clarity. *–n.* **6.** a diamond (or other gem) of a particular cut, typically round in outline and shaped like two pyramids united at their bases, the top one cut off near the base and the bottom one close to the apex, with many facets on the slopes. **7.** this form. **8.** a printing type (about 3 point). [F *brilliant,* ppr. of *briller,* corresponding to It. *brillare* shine, sparkle, ? from LL *brillāre,* from L *bēryllus* BERYL] – **brilliantly,** *adv.* – **brilliantness,** *n.*

**brilliantine** /ˈbrɪljəntin/, *n.* **1.** a toilet preparation for the hair; hairdressing. **2.** *U.S.* a dress fabric resembling alpaca. [F]

**brim** /brɪm/, *n., v.,* **brimmed, brimming.** *–n.* **1.** the upper edge of anything hollow; rim: *the brim of a cup.* **2.** a projecting edge: *the brim of a hat.* **3.** *Archaic.* edge or margin. *–v.i.* **4.** to be full to the brim; to be full to overflowing: *a brimming glass.* *–v.t.* **5.** to fill to the brim. [ME *brimme* shore, OE *brim* sea. Cf. Icel. *brim* surf]

**brimful** /brɪm'fʊl/, *adj.* full to the brim; completely full. Also, **brimfull.**

**brimstone** /'brɪmstoʊn/, *n.* **1.** →**sulphur. 2.** a common yellow butterfly, *Gonepteryx rhamni,* of the family Pieridae. [ME *brinston,* etc., from *brinn(en)* burn + *ston* stone] – **brimstony,** *adj.*

**brindabella** /brɪndə'bɛlə/, *n.* a shearer's drink made by mixing rum and beer.

**brindisi** /brɪn'dizi/, *n.* a drinking song in an opera.

**brindle** /'brɪndl/, *n.* **1.** a brindled colouring. **2.** a brindled animal. [backformation from BRINDLED]

**brindled** /'brɪndld/, *adj.* grey or tawny with darker streaks or spots. Also, **brinded** /'brɪndəd/. [cf. Icel. *bröndöttr;* ? akin to BRAND]

**brindled bandicoot** /– 'bændikut/, *n.* a short-nosed bandicoot, *Isoodon macrourus,* found in the area from western New South Wales to the Kimberly district of Western Australia.

**brine** /braɪn/, *n., v.,* **brined, brining.** *–n.* **1.** water saturated or strongly impregnated with salt. **2.** water strongly salted for pickling. **3.** the sea or ocean. **4.** the water of the sea. *–v.t.* **5.** to treat with or steep in brine. [ME; OE *brȳne,* c. D *brijn*] – **brinish,** *adj.*

**Brinell machine** /brə'nɛl məʃin/, *n.* an instrument for calculating the hardness (**Brinell hardness**) of metal, esp. heat-treated steels, by forcing a hard steel or tungsten carbide ball of standard dimensions into the material being tested, under a fixed pressure. [named after J. A. *Brinell,* 1849-1925, Swedish engineer]

**Brinell number** /'– nʌmbə/, *n.* a numerical expression of Brinell hardness, found by determining the diameter of a dent made by the Brinell machine.

**bring** /brɪŋ/, *v.t.,* **brought** /brɔt/, **bringing. 1.** to cause to come with oneself; take along to the place or person sought; conduct or convey. **2.** to cause to come, as to a recipient or possessor, to the mind or knowledge, into a particular position or state, to a particular opinion or decision, or into existence, view, action, or effect. **3.** to lead or induce: *he couldn't bring himself to do it.* **4.** *Law.* to put forward before a tribunal; declare in or as if in court. *–v.* **5.** Some special verb phrases are:

**bring about, 1.** to cause; accomplish. **2.** *Naut.* to turn (a ship) on to the opposite tack.

**bring back,** to recall to the mind; remind one of.

**bring down, 1.** to shoot down or cause to fall (a plane, animal, footballer, etc.) **2.** to reduce (a price); lower in price. **3.** to humble or subdue. **4.** introduce proposed legislation: *to bring down a bill.*

**bring forth, 1.** to produce. **2.** to give rise to; cause.

**bring forward, 1.** to produce to view. **2.** to adduce. **3.** *Accounting.* to transfer (a figure) to the top of the next column.

**bring in, 1.** to introduce. **2.** to pronounce (a verdict). **3.** to produce; yield (an income, cash, etc.). **4.** *N.Z.* to bring (land) into cultivation.

**bring off, 1.** to bring to a successful conclusion; achieve. **2.** to bring away (from a ship, etc.). **3.** to induce an orgasm in.

**bring on, 1.** to induce; cause. **2.** cause to advance. **3.** to excite sexually, so as to induce orgasm.

**bring out, 1.** to expose; show; reveal. **2.** to encourage (a timid or diffident person) **3.** to publish. **4.** to formally introduce (a girl) into society. **5.** to induce (workers, etc.) to leave work and go on strike.

**bring over,** to convince; convert.

**bring round, 1.** to convince of an opinion. **2.** to restore to consciousness, as after a faint.

**bring to, 1.** to bring back to consciousness. **2.** *Naut.* to head a ship close to or into the wind and kill her headway by manipulating helm and sails.

**bring under,** to subdue.

**bring up, 1.** to care for during childhood; rear. **2.** to introduce to notice or consideration. **3.** to cause to advance, as troops. **4.** to vomit. **5.** *Naut.* to stop (a ship); make fast to a buoy or quay, etc.

**bring up with a jolt,** to cause to stop suddenly, esp. for re-appraisal. [ME *bringen,* OE *bringan,* c. G *bringen*]

**bringing-up** /brɪŋɪŋ-'ʌp/, *n.* **1.** →**upbringing. 2.** child training or care.

**brinjal** /'brɪndʒəl/, *n.* →**eggplant.** [Skt]

**brink** /brɪŋk/, *n.* **1.** the edge or margin of a steep place or of land bordering water. **2.** any extreme edge; verge. [ME, from Scand.; cf. Dan. *brink*]

**brinkman** /'brɪŋkmən/, *n. Colloq.* one who practises brinkmanship.

**brinkmanship** /'brɪŋkmənʃɪp/, *n. Colloq.* the practice of courting disaster, esp. nuclear war, to gain one's ends.

**brinnie** /'brɪni/, *n. Colloq.* a small stone. Also, **brinny.**

**briny** /'braɪni/, *adj.,* **brinier, briniest. 1.** of or like brine; salty. *–n.* **2.** *Colloq.* the sea. – **brininess,** *n.*

**bri-nylon** /braɪ-'naɪlɒn/, *n.* nylon originally manufactured in Britain. [Trademark]

**brio** /'brioʊ/, *n.* liveliness; spirit; vivacity. [It.]

**brioche** /'briɒʃ, -oʊʃ/, *n.* a kind of light, sweet bun or roll, raised with eggs and yeast. [F, from *brier,* d. form of *broyer* knead]

**briolette** /briə'lɛt/, *n.* a pear-shaped gem having its entire surface cut with triangular facets. [F]

**briquette** /brɪ'kɛt/, *n.* a moulded block of compacted coal dust for fuel. Also, **briquet.** [F]

**brisance** /'brizəns/, *n.* the shattering power of high explosives. [F]

**Brisb.,** Brisbane.

**Brisbanite** /'brɪzbənaɪt/, *n.* **1.** one who was born in Brisbane, the capital city of Queensland, or who has come to regard it as his home town. *–adj.* **2.** of or pertaining to the city of Brisbane.

**brise-soleil** /ˌbriz-sɒ'leɪ/, *n.* a structure, usu. of horizontal or vertical strips of concrete, etc., used in hot climates to shade a window from the sun; a sunbreak. [F *brise* (verbal n. of *briser* to break) + *soleil* sun]

**brisk** /brɪsk/, *adj.* **1.** quick and active; lively: *a brisk breeze, a brisk walk.* **2.** sharp and stimulating: *brisk weather.* **3.** (of alcoholic drinks) effervescing vigorously: *brisk cider.* *–v.t.* **4.** to make brisk. (fol. by *up*). [? akin to BRUSQUE] – **briskish,** *adj.* – **briskly,** *adv.* – **briskness,** *n.*

**brisket** /'brɪskət/, *n.* **1.** the breast of an animal, or the part of the breast lying next to the ribs. **2.** *Colloq.* the human chest. [ME *brusket,* apparently from OF *bruschet,* from Gmc; cf. LG *bröske,* Icel. *brjōsk* cartilage]

**brisling** /'brɪzlɪŋ/, *n.* →**sprat.**

**bristle** /'brɪsəl/, *n., v.,* **-tled, -tling.** *–n.* **1.** one of the short, stiff, coarse hairs of certain animals, esp. swine, used extensively in making brushes, etc. **2.** any short, stiff hair or hairlike appendage (often used facetiously of human hair). *–v.i.* **3.** to stand or rise stiffly, like bristles. **4.** to erect the bristles, as an irritated animal: *the dog bristled.* **5.** to be thickly set with something suggestive of bristles: *the plain bristled with bayonets, the enterprise bristled with difficulties.* **6.** to be visibly roused to anger, hostility, or resistance. *–v.t.* **7.** to erect like bristles. **8.** to furnish with a bristle or bristles. **9.** to make bristly. [ME *bristel,* from *brist* (OE *byrst*) + *-el,* diminutive suffix] – **bristly,** *adj.*

**bristlebird** /'brɪsəlbɜd/, *n.* any of three species of red-brown medium-sized, ground-dwelling birds of the genus *Dasyornis,* which run fast but have feeble powers of flight and which have strongly developed sensory bristles around the nostrils.

**bristlegrass** /'brɪsəlgras/, *n.* any grass of the widespread genus *Setaria,* and other similar grasses.

**bristletail** /'brɪsəlteɪl/, *n.* any of various wingless insects of the order Thysanura, having long bristle-like caudal appendages.

**Bristol blue** /brɪstəl 'blu/, *n.* the colour of some rich dark-blue glass, made in England in the late 18th century, in the manufacture of which smalt, imported from Saxony into the port of Bristol (England), was an important constituent.

**Bristol board** /'– bɔd/, *n.* a fine, smooth kind of pasteboard, sometimes glazed.

**Bristol fashion,** /'– fæʃən/, *adj.* all in order; shipshape; with perfect efficiency and neatness.

**Bristols** /'brɪstlz/, *n.pl. Colloq.* breasts. [rhyming slang, *Bristol cities* titties, breasts]

**brit** /brɪt/, *n.* the young of herring and sprat. [Cornish; akin to Welsh *brith* speckled]

**Brit** /brɪt/, *n. Colloq. (oft. pejor.)* an Englishman.

**Brit.** **1.** Britain. **2.** British.

**Britain** /ˈbrɪtn/, *n.* **1.** Great Britain. **2.** Britannia (def. 1a). [ME *Bretayne,* from OF *Bretaigne,* from L *Britannia.* See BRITISH]

**Britannia** /brəˈtænjə/, *n.* **1.** *Chiefly Poetic.* England, Scotland, and Ireland. **2.** the feminine personification of Great Britain or the British Empire. **3.** →**britannia metal.** [L]

**britannia metal** /brəˈtænjə mɛtl/, *n.* a white alloy of tin, copper, and antimony, usu. with small amounts of zinc, etc., used for tableware.

**Britannic** /brəˈtænɪk/, *adj.* **1.** British: *Her Britannic Majesty.* **2.** →**Brythonic.** [L *Britannicus*]

**britches** /ˈbrɪtʃəz/, *n.pl. Colloq.* **1.** trousers. **2. too big for one's britches,** conceited. [var. of BREECHES]

**Briticise** /ˈbrɪtəsaɪz/, *v.t.,* **-cised, -cising.** *Chiefly U.S.* to assimilate to British culture or usage. Also, **Briticize.**

**Briticism** /ˈbrɪtəsɪzəm/, *n.* an English usage peculiar to, or predominantly used by, those living in the British Isles.

**British** /ˈbrɪtɪʃ/, *adj.* **1.** of or pertaining to Britain and its inhabitants. **2.** of or pertaining to the Commonwealth of Nations, the former British Empire, or their inhabitants. **3.** of or pertaining to the variety of English spoken in Britain, esp. the standard English language as spoken in southern England. **4.** of or pertaining to the ancient Britons. **5.** used loosely of mannerisms thought to be English: *a frightfully British accent.* **6. best of British** (**luck**), (an expression of goodwill sometimes implying that the recipient has little chance of success or lucky outcome). *–n.* **7.** the British people, taken collectively. **8.** the language of the ancient Britons and the languages which have developed from it, namely Welsh, Cornish (no longer spoken), and Breton. [ME *Brytysshe,* OE *Bryttisc,* from *Bryttas, Brettas* Britons, from Celtic] – **Britisher,** *n.* – **Britishism,** *n.*

**British Empire** /– ˈɛmpaɪə/, *n.* **1.** (formerly) the dominions, colonies, protectorates, dependencies, trusteeships, etc., collectively, under the control of the British Crown. **2. Order of the,** a military and civil order of knighthood.

**British Isles** /– ˈaɪlz/, *n.pl.* a group of islands in western Europe, comprising Britain, Ireland, the Isle of Man and adjacent islands.

**British thermal unit,** *n.* a unit of measurement in the imperial system equal to the amount of heat required to raise the temperature of 1lb of water by 1° F; 1055.055 852 62 joules. *Symbol:* Btu

**Briton** /ˈbrɪtn/, *n.* **1.** a native or inhabitant of Britain, or (sometimes) of the Commonwealth. **2.** one of the Celtic people who in early times occupied the southern part of the island of Britain. [ML *Brito;* replacing ME *Breton,* from OF, from L *Bretto*]

**britska** /ˈbrɪtskə/, *n.* →**britzka.**

**brittle** /ˈbrɪtl/, *adj.* **1.** breaking readily with a comparatively smooth fracture, as glass. **2.** tense; irritable. **3.** strained; insincere. *–n.* **4.** a sweet made with treacle and nuts: *peanut brittle.* [ME *britel,* from OE *brēotan* break] – **brittleness,** *n.*

**brittle-star** /ˈbrɪtl-sta/, *n.* a starfish of the class Ophiuroidea, having slender arms sharply marked off from the central disc.

**britzka** /ˈbrɪtskə/, *n.* an open carriage with a calash top. Also, **britska, britzska.** [Pol. *bryczka,* diminutive of *bryka* wagon]

**Brizzie** /ˈbrɪzi/, *n. Colloq.* Brisbane.

**bro.,** pl. **bros.** brother. Also, **Bro.**

**broach** /broʊtʃ/, *n.* **1.** *Mach.* an elongated and tapered tool with serrations which enlarges a given hole as the tool is pulled through the hole, which may be round, square, etc. **2.** (in a lock) the pin about which the barrel of the key fits. **3.** *Archit.* the projecting corner of the tower of a broach spire. **4.** a spit for roasting meat. **5.** a gimlet for tapping casks. **6.** →**brooch.** *–v.t.* **7.** to enlarge and finish with a broach. **8.** to tap or pierce. **9.** to draw as by tapping: *to broach liquor.* **10.** to mention or suggest for the first time: *to broach a subject.* *–v.i.* **11.** *Naut.* (of a ship) to veer to windward, esp. so as to be broadside to the wind (fol. by *to*). [ME *broche,* from OF, from L *brocc(h)us* projecting] – **broacher,** *n.*

**broach spire** /ˈ– spaɪə/, *n.* an octagonal spire rising from a square tower.

**broad**[1] /brɔd/, *adj.* **1.** of great breadth: *a broad river or street.* **2.** of great extent; large: *the broad expanse of ocean.* **3.** widely diffused; open; full: *broad daylight.* **4.** not limited or narrow; liberal: *broad experience.* **5.** of extensive range or scope: *broad sympathies.* **6.** main or general: *the broad outlines of a subject.* **7.** plain or clear: *a broad hint.* **8.** bold; plain-spoken. **9.** indelicate; indecent: *a broad joke.* **10.** (of conversation) rough; coarse; countrified. **11.** unconfined; free; unrestrained: *broad mirth.* **12.** (of pronunciation) strongly dialectal: *broad Scots.* **13. broad a,** the sound of 'a' in 'father', contrasted with the **flat a,** the sound of 'a' in 'fat'. Some words may be pronounced with either the broad or flat 'a', as dance, chance, etc. **14.** *Phonet.* (of a transcription) **a.** phonemic. **b.** representing some phonemes by the same symbol, their difference being indicated by diacritics. Cf. **narrow. 15.** of wools which are strong for their quality number, or for their type. *–adv.* **16.** fully: *broad awake.* *–n.* **17.** the broad part of anything. **18.** *Colloq.* a woman. [ME *brood,* OE *brād,* c. G *breit*] – **broadish,** *adj.* – **broadly,** *adv.*

**broad**[2] /brɔd/, *n. Brit.* a shallow lake, esp. one in East Anglia.

**broad arrow** /– ˈæroʊ/, *n.* **1.** a mark of the shape of a broad arrow-head, placed upon British governmental stores, and formerly on prison clothing or convict. **2.** *Archery.* an arrow having an expanded head.

**Broad Australian** /– ɒsˈtreɪljən/, *n.* that pronunciation of Australian English which is least acceptable as a prestige form and in which the characteristics of Australian pronunciation are at their most extreme. See **Spectrum of Australian English.**

**broadaxe** /ˈbrɔdæks/, *n.* **1.** an axe for hewing timber. **2.** a battleaxe. Also, *U.S.,* **broadax.**

**broad bean** /brɔd ˈbin/, *n.* an erect annual herb, *Vicia faba,* of the family Papilionaceae, often cultivated for its large edible seeds.

**broadbill** /ˈbrɔdbɪl/, *n.* **1.** any of various birds with a broad bill, as the scaup duck, shoveler, and spoonbill. **2.** →**swordfish.**

**broad-billed roller** /brɔd-bɪld ˈroʊlə/, *n.* →**dollar bird.**

**broadbrim** /ˈbrɔdbrɪm/, *n.* **1.** a hat with a broad brim, as that worn by Quakers. **2.** (*cap*) *U.S. Colloq.* a Friend or Quaker. – **broadbrim,** *adj.*

**broadcast** /ˈbrɔdkast/, *v.,* **-cast** or **-casted, -casting,** *n. adj., adv.* *–v.t.* **1.** to send (messages, speeches, music, etc.) by radio. **2.** to cast or scatter abroad over an area, as seed in sowing. **3.** to spread or disseminate widely: *to broadcast gossip.* *–v.i.* **4.** to send radio messages, speeches, etc. **5.** to scatter or disseminate something widely. *–n.* **6.** that which is broadcast. **7.** *Radio.* **a.** the broadcasting of radio messages, speeches, etc. **b.** a radio program. **c.** a single period of broadcasting. **8.** a method of sowing by scattering seed. *–adj.* **9.** sent out by broadcasting, as radio messages, speeches, music, etc. **10.** of or pertaining to broadcasting. **11.** cast abroad or all over an area, as seed sown thus. **12.** widely spread or disseminated: *broadcast discontent.* *–adv.* **13.** so as to reach an indefinite number of radio receiving stations or instruments. **14.** so as to be cast abroad over an area: *seed sown broadcast.* – **broadcaster,** *n.*

**Broad Church** /brɔd ˈtʃɜtʃ/, *n.* those members of the Anglican communion who favour a liberal interpretation of doctrine and ritual, and such conditions of membership as will promote wide Christian inclusiveness. – **Broad-Church,** *adj.* – **Broad-Churchman,** *n.*

**broadcloth** /ˈbrɔdklɒθ/, *n.* **1. cotton broadcloth,** cotton shirting or dress material, usu. mercerised, resembling fine poplin. **2. rayon broadcloth,** spun rayon fabric similar to cotton broadcloth. **3. woollen broadcloth,** woollen dress goods with nap laid parallel with selvage.

**broaden** /ˈbrɔdn/, *v.i.* **1.** to become broad; widen. *–v.t.* **2.** to make broad.

**broad gauge** /brɔd ˈgeɪdʒ/, *n.* →**gauge** (def. 13). Also, **broad gage.** – **broad-gauged, broad-gaged,** *adj.*

**broad-headed snake** /ˌbrɔd-hɛdəd ˈsneɪk/, *n.* a small, venomous, nocturnal snake, *Hoplocephalus bungaroides,* of pugnacious habits, found on the east coast of Australia; night tiger; fierce snake.

**broadie** /ˈbrɔdi/, *n. Colloq.* →**U-ie.**

**broad jump** /ˈbrɔd dʒʌmp/, *n.* →**long jump.**

**broadleaf** /ˈbrɔdlif/, *n.* **1.** any of several cigar tobaccos which have broad leaves. **2.** *N.Z.* any of various broad-leaved trees or large shrubs of the genus *Griselinia,* esp. *G. littoralis.* *–adj.* **3.** having broad leaves.

**broadloom carpet** /ˌbrɔdlum 'kapət/, *n.* any kind of carpet woven on a broad loom to avoid the need for seams.

**broad-minded** /brɔd-'maɪndəd/, *adj.* free from prejudice or bigotry; liberal; tolerant. **– broad-mindedly,** *adv.* **– broad-mindedness,** *n.*

**broad seal** /'brɔd sil/, *n.* the official seal of a country or state.

**broadsheet** /'brɔdʃit/, *n.* **1.** a sheet of paper, esp. of large size, printed on one side only, as for distribution or posting. **2.** a ballad, song, tract, etc., printed or originally printed on a broadsheet. **3.** a newspaper printed on the standard sheet size of paper, usu. giving greater depth of reporting. *–adj.* **4.** (of a ballad) printed or originally printed on a broadsheet. **5.** pertaining to or as in a broadsheet.

**broadside** /'brɔdsaɪd/, *n.* **1.** *Naut.* the whole side of a ship above the waterline, from the bow to the quarter. **2.** *Navy.* **a.** all the guns that can be fired to one side of a ship. **b.** a simultaneous discharge of all the guns on one side of a vessel of war. **3.** any comprehensive attack, as of criticism. **4.** →**broadsheet** (def. 1). **5.** any broad surface or side, as of a house. *–adv.* **6.** broadways.

**broad spectrum** /brɔd 'spɛktrəm/, *n.* a general view rather than a specific one; an overview.

**broad-spectrum** /'brɔd-spɛktrəm/, *adj.* of or pertaining to drugs which can deal with a wide range of diseases.

**broadsword** /'brɔdsɔd/, *n.* a straight, broad, flat sword, usu. with a basket hilt.

**broadtail** /'brɔdteɪl/, *n. Textiles.* the fur or skin of a very young, often prematurely born karakul lamb, having a flat and wavy appearance resembling moiré silk.

**broad-toothed rat** /ˌbrɔd-tuθt 'ræt/, *n.* a primitive Australian rodent, *Mastacomys fuscus,* once widespread in southern and south-eastern Australia but now found only as isolated communities in cold, moist regions.

**broadways** /'brɔdweɪz/, *adv.* breadthways; along or across the breadth; laterally (oft. fol. by *on*). Also, *esp. U.S.,* **broadwise** /'brɔdwaɪz/.

**brocade** /brə'keɪd/, *n., v.,* **-caded, -cading.** *–n.* **1.** fabric woven with an elaborate design from any yarn. The right side has a raised effect. *–v.t.* **2.** to weave with a design or figure. [Sp. *brocado,* c. It. *broccato,* from *broccare* interweave with gold or silver, from L *brocc(h)us.* See BROACH] **– brocaded,** *adj.*

**brocatelle** /brɒkə'tɛl/, *n.* **1.** a kind of brocade, in which the design is in high relief. **2.** an ornamental marble with variegated colouring, esp. from Italy and Spain. Also, *U.S.,* **brocatel.** [F, from It. *broccatello*]

**broccoli** /'brɒkəli, -laɪ/, *n.* **1.** a plant, *Brassica oleracea* var. *botrytis,* of the mustard family, resembling the cauliflower. **2.** a form of this plant which does not produce a head, the green saps and the stalk of which are a common vegetable. Also, **broccoli sprouts.** [It., pl. of *broccolo* sprout, from L *brocchus* projecting]

**broché** /'brouʃeɪ/, *adj.* woven with a pattern; brocaded. [F, pp. of *brocher* BROCADE, *v.*]

**brochette** /brɒ'ʃɛt/, *n.* **1.** a skewer, for use in cookery. **2. en brochette** /õ brɒ'ʃɛt/, on a small spit. [F, diminutive of *broché* spit. See BROACH]

**brochure** /'brouʃə, brə'ʃuə/, *n.* →**pamphlet.** [F, from *brocher* stitch]

**brock** /brɒk/, *n.* a badger. [OE *brocc,* from Gaelic *broc*]

**Brocken spectre** /brɒkən 'spɛktə/, *n.* a phenomenon sometimes observed in mountain regions during fog or mist when the sun is behind the observer. The observer's shadow will appear to be surrounded by rainbow colours; glory. [named after *Brocken,* the highest elevation of the Harz Mountains in W East Germany]

**brocket** /'brɒkət/, *n.* **1.** the male red deer in the second year, with the first growth of straight horns. **2.** a small swamp deer, genus *Mazama,* of tropical America.

**broderie anglaise** /ˌbroudəri 'ɒŋgleɪz/, *n.* white embroidery on white material with eyelet and cutwork designs. [F: English embroidery]

**brogan** /'brougən/, *n.* a coarse, stout shoe. [Irish]

**brogue**[1] /broug/, *n.* a broad accent, esp. Irish, in the pronunciation of English. [special use of BROGUE[2]]

**brogue**[2] /broug/, *n.* a strongly made, comfortable type of ordinary shoe, often with decorative perforations on the vamp and upper. [Irish, Gaelic *brōg* shoe]

**broider** /'brɔɪdə/, *v.t. Archaic.* to embroider. [ME *broudre(n),* from OF *bro(u)der, brosder,* of Gmc orig.] **– broidery,** *n.*

**broil**[1] /brɔɪl/, *v.t.* **1.** to cook by direct radiant heat, as on a gridiron or griller, or under an electric coil, gas grill or the like; grill; pan fry. **2.** to scorch; make very hot. *–v.i.* **3.** to be subjected to great heat. **4.** to burn with impatience, etc. *–n.* **5.** something broiled. [ME *brule(n),* ? from OF *bruiller* burn, from LL verb, probably b. Gmc *brand* a burning and L *ustulāre* burn a little (from *ūrere* burn)]

**broil**[2] /brɔɪl/, *n.* **1.** an angry quarrel or struggle; a disturbance; a tumult. *–v.i.* **2.** to quarrel; brawl. [ME, from OF *brouiller* disorder, probably from *bro(u)* broth, from OHG *brod*]

**broiler** /'brɔɪlə/, *n.* **1.** any device for broiling meats or fish; a grate or pan for broiling. **2.** a young chicken, twelve to fourteen weeks old.

**brokage** /'broukɪdʒ/, *n.* →**brokerage.**

**broke** /brouk/, *v.* **1.** past tense of **break.** **2.** *Archaic or Colloq.* past participle of **break.** **3.** Also, **broke to the wide.** *Colloq.* out of money; bankrupt. **4. flat broke,** *Colloq.* completely out of money.

**broken** /'broukən/, *v.* **1.** past participle of break. *–adj.* **2.** reduced to fragments. **3.** ruptured; torn; fractured. **4.** fragmentary or incomplete: *a broken set.* **5.** infringed or violated. **6.** interrupted or disconnected: *broken sleep;* (of employment) *broken time.* **7.** uneven; (of ground) rough; (of water) with a disturbed surface as choppy water, surf, etc.; (of weather) patchy, unsettled. **8.** weakened in strength, spirit, etc. **9.** reduced to submission; tamed: *the horse was not yet broken to the saddle.* **10.** imperfectly spoken, as language. **11.** ruined; bankrupt. **12.** *Phonet.* (of a vowel) diphthongised. **13.** *Wool.* of or pertaining to the best wool of the skirtings, having the characteristics of fleece wool. *–n.* **14.** (*pl.*) *Wool.* broken wool. **– brokenly,** *adv.* **– brokenness,** *n.*

**broken chord** /– 'kɔd/, *n. Music.* a chord whose tones are played consecutively rather than simultaneously.

**broken-down** /'broukən-daun/, *adj.* **1.** shattered or collapsed. **2.** having given way to despair. **3.** unserviceable (of machinery, electronic equipment, etc.).

**broken-hearted** /broukən-'hatəd/, *adj.* crushed by grief.

**broken-mouthed** /'broukən-mauðd/, *adj.* of or pertaining to a sheep some of the incisor teeth of which have fallen out or become badly worn and irregular because of old age or hard grazing. Also, *esp. in predicative use,* **broken mouthed.**

**broken up** /– 'ʌp/, *adj.* (of a person) distressed; dismayed.

**broken white** /– 'waɪt/, *adj.* an off-white colour in which the whiteness has been slightly yellowed or browned.

**broken wind** /– 'wɪnd/, *n.* →**heaves.** **– broken-winded,** *adj.*

**broken wool** /'– wul/, *n.* the best wool of the skirtings, having the characteristics of fleece wool.

**broker** /'broukə/, *n.* **1.** an agent who buys or sells for a principal on a commission basis without having title to the property. **2.** a middleman or agent. [ME *brocor,* from AF *brocour,* orig., broacher (of casks), tapster (hence retailer); akin to BROACH]

**brokerage** /'broukərɪdʒ/, *n.* **1.** the business of a broker. **2.** the commission of a broker.

**broking** /'broukɪŋ/, *adj.* of or pertaining to brokerage.

**brolga** /'brɒlgə/, *n.* a large, silvery-grey crane, *Grus rubicunda,* of northern and eastern Australia which performs an elaborate dance, perhaps as part of a courtship display; native companion. [Aboriginal]

brolga

**brolly** /'brɒli/, *n.* **1.** *Colloq.* an umbrella. **2.** *Brit. Mil. Colloq.* a parachute.

**bromal** /'brouməl/, *n.* a colourless, oily liquid, $CBr_3CHO$, used in medicine as an anodyne and hypnotic. [BROM(INE) + AL(COHOL)]

**bromate** /ˈbroumeɪt/, *n., v.,* **-mated, -mating.** *–n.* **1.** a salt of bromic acid. *–v.t.* **2.** to combine with bromine.

**brome** /ˈbroum/, *n.* any grass of the genus *Bromus,* widely distributed in about 40 species, esp. *B. inermis,* a perennial used for pasture. Also, **brome grass.** [*brome,* from L *bromus,* from Gk *brómos* kind of oats]

**bromeliaceous** /brouˌmiliˈeɪʃəs/, *adj. Bot.* belonging to the Bromeliaceae, a large family of herbaceous plants, mostly of the tropical Americas, and including the pineapple and many ornamentals. [NL *Bromelia* (named after Olaf *Bromel,* 1639-1705, Swedish botanist) + -ACEOUS]

**bromeliaed** /brouˈmiliæd/, *n.* any bromeliaceous plant.

**bromic** /ˈbroumɪk/, *adj.* containing pentavalent bromine ($Br^{+5}$).

**bromic acid** /– ˈæsəd/, *n.* an acid, $HBrO_3$, containing bromine and oxygen, used as an oxidising agent.

**bromide** /ˈbroumaɪd/, *n.* **1.** *Chem.* a compound usu. containing two elements only, one of which is bromine. **2.** silver bromide, esp. in photography. **3.** *Colloq.* a sedative. **4.** *Colloq.* a person who is platitudinous and boring. **5.** *Colloq.* a tiresome platitude. **6.** light-sensitive paper used in phototypesetting. **7.** typeset material produced by means of a phototypesetter on light-sensitive paper.

**brominate** /ˈbroumənelt/, *v.t.,* **-nated, -nating.** *Chem.* to treat or combine with bromine. – **bromination,** /brouməˈneɪʃən/, *n.*

**bromine** /ˈbroumin, -aɪn/, *n.* an element, a dark-reddish fuming liquid, resembling chlorine and iodine in chemical properties. *Symbol:* Br; *at. wt:* 79.909; *at. no.:* 35; *sp. gr. (liquid):* 3.119 at 20°C. [Gk *brômos* stench + -INE[2]]

**bromism** /ˈbroumɪzəm/, *n.* poisoning by bromides, characterised by psychosis, skin rashes, muscle tremors, etc.

**bromureide** /brouˈmjuriaɪd/, *n.* any of a group of organic bromine compounds used as sedatives.

**bronchi** /ˈbrɒŋki/, *n.* plural of **bronchus.**

**bronchia** /ˈbrɒŋkiə/, *n.pl.* the ramifications of the bronchi or tubes. [LL, from Gk, from *brónchos* windpipe]

**bronchial** /ˈbrɒŋkiəl/, *adj.* pertaining to the bronchia or bronchi.

**bronchial tubes** /– tjubz/, *n.pl.* the bronchi, or the bronchi and their ramifications.

**bronchiole** /ˈbrɒŋkioul/, *n.* one of the small subdivisions of a bronchus. [NL *bronchiolum,* from *bronchi(a)* BRONCHIA + *-olum* diminutive suffix]

**bronchitis** /brɒŋˈkaɪtəs/, *n.* a inflammation of the membrane lining of the bronchial tubes. [NL; from BRONCH(O)- + -ITIS] – **bronchitic** /brɒŋˈkɪtɪk/, *adj.*

**broncho** /ˈbrɒŋkou/, *n., pl.* **-chos.** →**bronco.**

**broncho-,** a word element meaning 'bronchial'. Also, **bronch-.** [Gk, combining form of *brónchos* windpipe]

**bronchodilator** /ˌbrɒŋkoudaɪˈleɪtə/, *n.* a drug which causes relaxation of the bronchial muscle, resulting in expansion of the air passages of the bronchi.

**bronchopneumonia** /ˌbrɒŋkounjəˈmouniə/, *n.* inflammation of the bronchia and lungs; a form of pneumonia.

**bronchoscope** /ˈbrɒŋkəskoup/, *n.* a tubular instrument for examining bronchi and for the removal of foreign bodies therefrom.

**bronchus** /ˈbrɒŋkəs/, *n., pl.* **-chi** /-kaɪ/. either of the two main branches of the trachea. [NL, from Gk *brónchos* windpipe]

**bronco** /ˈbrɒŋkou/, *n., pl.* **-cos.** *Orig. U.S.* a pony or mustang esp. one that is not broken, or is only imperfectly broken in. Also, **broncho, bronc, bronk.** [Sp.: rough, rude]

**bronco-buster** /ˈbrɒŋkou-ˌbʌstə/, *n.* one who breaks in broncos. Also, **broncobuster.**

**brontosaurus** /brɒntəˈsɔrəs/, *n.* a large amphibious herbivorous dinosaur of the American Jurassic. [*bronto-,* combining form from Gk *brontḗ* thunder + -SAURUS]

brontosaurus

**bronze** /brɒnz/, *n., v.,* **bronzed, bronzing.** *–n.* **1.** *Metall.* **a.** a durable brown alloy, consisting essentially of copper and tin. **b.** any of various other copper base alloys, such as aluminium bronze, manganese bronze, silicon bronze, etc. The term implies a product superior in some way to brass. **2.** a metallic brownish colour. **3.** a work of art, as a statue, statuette, bust, or medal, composed of bronze, whether cast or wrought. **4.** Also, **bronzo.** *Colloq.* the anus. *–adj.* **5.** the colour of bronze. *–v.t.* **6.** to give the appearance or colour of bronze to. **7.** to make brown, as by exposure to the sun. *–v.i.* **8.** to turn a bronze colour; become sunburnt. [F, from It. *bronzo*] – **bronzy,** *adj.*

**Bronze Age** /– eɪdʒ/, *n.* the age in the history of mankind (between the Stone and Iron Ages) marked by the use of bronze implements.

**bronze medal** /– ˈmɛdl/, *n.* a prize awarded for third place in a race or other competition, esp. the Olympics. See **gold medal, silver medal.**

**bronzer** /ˈbrɒnzə/, *n. Colloq.* a male homosexual.

**bronze whaler** /brɒnz ˈweɪlə/, *n.* a shark, *Galeolamma ahenea,* of eastern Australia, having a bronze colouring of its dorsal surface.

**bronze-wing** /ˈbrɒnz-wɪŋ/, *n.* **1.** any of various Australian birds whose wings display a golden metallic sheen, as the **bronze-wing pigeon, bronze-wing cuckoo. 2.** *N.T., W.A.* a half-caste Aboriginal.

common bronze-wing

**brooch** /broutʃ/, *n.* a clasp or ornament for the dress, having a pin at the back for passing through the clothing and a catch for securing the pin. [var. of BROACH, *n.*]

**brood** /brud/, *n.* **1.** a number of young creatures produced or hatched at one time; a family of offspring or young. **2.** breed or kind. *–v.t.* **3.** to sit as a bird over (eggs or young); incubate. **4.** to dwell persistently or moodily in thought on; ponder. *–v.i.* **5.** to sit as a bird over eggs to be hatched. **6.** to rest fixedly. **7.** to meditate with morbid persistence. *–adj.* **8.** kept for breeding purposes: *a brood mare.* [ME; OE *brōd,* c. G *Brut.* Cf. BREED]

**broodbitch** /ˈbrudbɪtʃ/, *n.* a bitch kept for breeding purposes.

**brooder** /ˈbrudə/, *n.* **1.** a device or structure for the artificial rearing of young chickens or other birds. **2.** one who or that which broods.

**brooder pneumonia** /– njuˈmounjə/, *n.* an acute pulmonary disease, caused by *Aspergillus fumigatus* bacteria and resulting in high mortality among poultry, esp. turkeys; aspergillosis.

**broody** /ˈbrudi/, *adj.,* **broodier, broodiest. 1.** moody. **2.** inclined to brood or sit on eggs: *a broody hen.*

**brook**[1] /bruk/, *n.* a small, natural stream of fresh water; creek. [ME; OE *brōc* stream, c. G *Bruch* marsh]

**brook**[2] /bruk/, *v.t.* to bear; suffer; tolerate (usu. in a negative sentence). [ME *brouke(n),* OE *brūcan,* c. G *brauchen* use; akin to L *fruī* enjoy]

**brooklet** /ˈbruklət/, *n.* a little brook.

**brooklime** /ˈbruklaɪm/, *n.* a kind of speedwell, *Veronica beccabunga,* common in wet places.

**brookweed** /ˈbrukwid/, *n.* either of two primulaceous plants, the water-pimpernel, *Samolus valerandi,* of Europe, and *S. floribundus,* of North America, both bearing small white flowers.

**broom** /brum/, *n.* **1.** a sweeping implement consisting of a flat brush of bristles, nylon, etc., on a long handle. **2.** a sweeping implement consisting of a bunch of twigs or plant stems on a handle; besom. **3.** any of the shrubby plants of the genus *Cytisus,* esp. *C. scoparius,* common in western Europe, which grows on uncultivated ground and has long, slender branches bearing yellow flowers. **4.** any of several shrubs of the genus *Genista.* **5.** any of certain similar plants of other genera of the Papilionaceae esp. species with leafless stems and yellow flowers. *–v.t.* **6.** to sweep. [ME *brōme,* OE *brōm,* c. OHG *brāmo* Cf. BRAMBLE] – **broomy,** *adj.*

**broomcorn** /ˈbrumkɔn/, *n.* →**broom millet.**

**broom finish** /ˈbrum ˌfɪnɪʃ/, *n. Bldg Trades.* (of concrete) a finish produced by dragging a stiff bristle broom over freshly poured concrete. Also, **broomed finish.**

**broomie** /ˈbrumi/, *n.* one who uses a broom, esp. in a shearing shed.

**broom millet** /brum ˈmɪlət/, *n.* a tall variety of *Sorghum dochna,* with long seed-heads which, after removal of the seed, was used for broom-making.

**broomrape** /ˈbrumreɪp/, *n.* any of various parasitic plants, esp. of the genus *Orobanche,* living on the roots of broom and other plants.

**broomstick** /ˈbrumstɪk/, *n.* the long stick forming the handle of a broom.

**bros,** brothers. Also, **Bros.**

**brose** /broʊz/, *n. Scot.* a dish made by stirring boiling liquid into oatmeal or other meal. [Scot. var. of d. *brewis,* from ME *browes,* from OF *broez,* from OHG *brod* BROTH]

**broth** /brɒθ/, *n.* **1.** thin soup of concentrated meat or fish stock. **2.** a decoction of water in which meat or fish has been boiled, with vegetables or barley added. [ME and OE, c. OHG *brod.* Cf. BREW]

**brothel** /ˈbrɒθəl/, *n.* **1.** a house of prostitution. **2.** *Colloq.* any room in a disorderly state.

**brothel boots** /ˈbrɒθəl buts/, *n.pl. Colloq.* soft-soled footwear. Also, **brothel creepers.**

**brother** /ˈbrʌðə/, *n., pl.* **brothers, brethren,** *v.* *–n.* **1.** a male child of the same parents, as another, (**full brother** or **brother-german**). **2.** a male child of only one of one's parents (**half-brother**). **3.** a male member of the same kinship group, nationality, profession, etc.; an associate; a fellow countryman, fellow man, etc. **4.** *Eccles.* **a.** a male lay member of a religious organisation which has a priesthood. **b.** a man who devotes himself to the duties of a religious order without taking holy orders, or while preparing for holy orders. **5.** (*pl.*) all members of a particular race, or of the human race in general. *–v.t.* **6.** to treat or address as a brother. [ME; OE *brōthor,* c. G *Bruder*]

**brother-brother** /ˈbrʌðə-brʌðə/, *n.* a shrub, *Oxylobium tetragonophyllum,* family Papilionaceae, native to western Australia, and extremely poisonous to stock.

**brotherhood** /ˈbrʌðəhʊd/, *n.* **1.** condition or quality of being a brother or brothers. **2.** quality of being brotherly. **3.** a fraternal or trade organisation. **4.** all those engaged in a particular trade or profession.

**brother-in-law** /ˈbrʌðər-ɪn-lɔ/, *n., pl.* **brothers-in-law. 1.** one's husband's or wife's brother. **2.** one's sister's husband. **3.** the husband of one's wife's or husband's sister.

**brotherly** /ˈbrʌðəli/, *adj.* **1.** of, like, or befitting a brother; fraternal. *–adv.* **2.** as a brother, fraternally. – **brotherliness,** *n.*

**brougham** /brum, ˈbruəm, ˈbroʊəm/, *n.* **1.** a four-wheeled, boxlike, closed carriage for two or four persons, with the driver's perch outside. **2.** an early type of motor car, often battery driven. [named after Lord *Brougham,* 1778-1868, British statesman]

**brought** /brɔt/, *v.* past tense and past participle of **bring.**

**Broughton pea** /brɔtn ˈpi/, *n.* a species of *Swainsona, S. procumbens,* with purple pea-shaped flowers, widespread in inland areas of eastern Australia.

**brouhaha** /ˈbruhaha/, *n.* an uproar; turmoil. [F, probably onomatopoeic]

**brow** /braʊ/, *n.* **1.** the ridge over the eye. **2.** the hair growing on that ridge; eyebrow. **3.** (*sing. or pl.*) the forehead: *to knit one's brows.* **4.** the countenance. **5.** the edge of a steep place. **6.** *Mining.* the top of the shaft; pithead. **7.** *Naut.* a narrow gangway. [ME *browe,* OE *brū*]

**browbeat** /ˈbraʊbit/, *v.t.,* **-beat, -beaten, -beating.** to intimidate by overbearing looks or words; bully.

**brown** /braʊn/, *n.* **1.** a dark shade with yellowish or reddish hue. **2.** *Colloq. Obs.* a copper coin, esp. a penny. *–adj.* **3.** of the colour brown. **4.** having skin of that colour. **5.** sunburned or tanned. *–v.t.* **6.** to make brown. *–v.i.* **7.** to become brown. [ME; OE *brūn,* c. G *braun*] – **brownish,** *adj.* – **brownness,** *n.*

**brown ale** /– ˈeɪl/, *n.* a sweet dark ale, heavily malted.

**brown algae** /– ˈældʒi/, *n.* algae belonging to the class Phaeophyceae, usu. brown as a result of brown pigments added to their chlorophyll.

**brown-banded mullet** /braʊn-bændəd ˈmʌlət/, *n.* →**flat-tail mullet.**

**brown bandicoot** /braʊn ˈbændikut/, *n.* →**quenda.**

**brown barrel** /– ˈbærəl/, *n.* a large tree, *Eucalyptus fastigata,* found in eastern Australia.

**brown bear** /– ˈbɛə/, *n.* **1.** a variety of the black bear of Europe and America, *Ursus arctos,* inhabiting northern regions. **2.** a variety of the common black bear, *Ursus americanus,* having a brownish coat.

**brown betty** /– ˈbɛti/, *n.* a baked pudding made of sliced apples, raisins, spices, breadcrumbs, butter and sugar.

**brown bomber** /– ˈbɒmə/, *n. Colloq.* an officer employed to enforce parking and other associated traffic regulations.

**brown bread** /– ˈbrɛd/, *n.* any bread made of flour darker in colour than bolted wheat flour.

**brown brother** /– ˈbrʌðə/, *n.* (formerly) a native inhabitant of Papua New Guinea.

**brown coal** /– ˈkoʊl/, *n.* →**lignite.**

**browned off** /braʊnd ˈɒf/, *adj. Colloq.* bored; discontented; fed up. Also (*esp. in attributive positions*), **browned-off**

**brown fieldlark** /braʊn ˈfildlak/, *n.* →**singing bushlark.**

**brown forest soil,** *n.* a soil rich in humus derived from leaves, characteristic of temperate areas where the natural vegetation is or was deciduous forest. Also, **brown earth.**

**Brownian motion** /ˌbraʊniən ˈmoʊʃən/, *n.* erratic random movements, as of microscopic particles suspended in a liquid, smoke particles in air, etc. Also, **Brownian movement.** [first noticed (in 1827) by Robert *Brown,* 1773-1858, Scottish botanist]

**brownie** /ˈbraʊni/, *n.* **1.** (in folklore) a little brown goblin, esp. one who helps secretly in household work. **2.** (*cap.*) a member of the junior division of the Girl Guides. **3.** a loaf baked in a camp oven from a flour, fat, sugar and water dough with currants and raisins added to it; bush plum cake. **4.** a cake-like biscuit made of flour, butter, eggs, cocoa and walnuts. **5.** *Colloq.* a bottle of beer.

**browning** /ˈbraʊnɪŋ/, *n.* **1.** the process of turning something brown. **2.** a substance or preparation used to turn something brown, esp. gravy.

**brownout** /ˈbraʊnaʊt/, *n.* a partial blackout.

**brown owl** /ˈbraʊn aʊl/ *for def. 1;* /braʊn ˈaʊl/ *for def. 2,* *n.* **1.** the tawny owl. **2.** the woman in charge of a group of Brownies (def. 2).

**brown paper** /– ˈpeɪpə/, *n.* a type of strong, coarse, brown-coloured paper, used mainly for wrapping.

**brown patch** /ˈ– pætʃ/, *n.* a disease of turf grasses, caused mainly by a soil-inhabiting fungus.

**brown pine** /– ˈpaɪn/, *n.* a coniferous tree, *Podocarpus elatus,* of eastern Australia, the seeds of which are borne on a large blue-black fleshy receptacle; plum pine.

**brown rice** /– ˈraɪs/, *n.* rice from which the bran layers and germs have not been removed by polishing.

**brown rot** /– ˈrɒt/, *n.* a disease, as of apples, peaches, plums, etc., caused by fungi of the genus *Sclerotinia.*

**Brown's dock** /braunz ˈdɒk/, *n.* a native perennial, *Rumex brownii,* with a long, narrow seed head and small red hooked fruits, found in the higher rainfall areas of Australia, esp. as a weed in lawns. Also, **swamp dock.**

**brown snake** /ˈbraʊn sneɪk/, *n.* any of certain venomous Australian snakes of the genus *Pseudonaja* brownish or olive in colour, as the **common brown snake,** or the gwardar.

**brown spider** /– ˈspaɪdə/, *n.* any spider of the genus *Loxosceles,* originally native to the Mediterranean area but now spread widely through the temperate regions of the world, characterised by long thin legs, a straw-brown coloured body, and a venomous bite; fiddleback spider.

**brownstone** /ˈbraʊnstoʊn/, *n. U.S.* **1.** a reddish brown sandstone, extensively used by the prosperous classes as a building material. *–adj.* **2.** belonging or pertaining to the well-to-do class.

**brown study** /braʊn ˈstʌdi/, *n.* deep, serious absorption in thought.

**brown sugar** /– ˈʃʊgə/, *n.* unrefined or partially refined sugar.

**browntop** /ˈbraʊntɒp/, *n.* a fine turf grass, *Agrostis tenuis,* native to temperate areas of Europe and Asia, and used for sporting greens; extensively grown in New Zealand as pasture and for the seed; bent grass.

**brown trout** /braʊn 'traʊt/, *n.* the common river-trout of northern Europe, *Salmo trutta fario.*

**browse** /braʊz/, *v.,* **browsed, browsing,** *n.* *–v.t.* **1.** (of cattle, deer, etc.) to nibble at; eat from. **2.** (of cattle, deer, etc.) to feed on; pasture on; graze. *–v.i.* **3.** (of cattle, etc.) to graze. **4.** to glance at random through a book or books. *–n.* **5.** tender shoots or twigs of shrubs and trees as food for cattle, deer, etc. [apparently from MF *broust* young sprout, from Gmc; cf. OS *brustian* to sprout] – **browser,** *n.*

**brucellosis** /brusə'loʊsəs/, *n.* infection with bacteria of the *Brucella* group, frequently causing abortions in animals and undulant fever in man. [NL from *Brucella* genus name (named after Sir David *Bruce,* 1855-1931, Australian physician, + *-ella* diminutive suffix) + *-osis* -OSIS]

**brucine** /'brusin, -saɪn/, *n.* a bitter, poisonous alkaloid, $C_{23}H_{26}N_3O_4$, obtained from the nux vomica tree, *Strychnos nux vomica,* and from other species of the same genus, resembling strychnine in action but less powerful. [James *Bruce,* 1730-94, Scottish explorer of Africa, + -INE[2]]

**bruin** /'bruən/, *n.* a bear. [MD: lit., brown, the name of the bear in the medieval fable, *Reynard the Fox*]

**bruise** /bruz/, *v.,* **bruised, bruising.** *n.* *–v.t.* **1.** to injure by striking or pressing, without breaking the skin or drawing blood. **2.** to injure or hurt superficially: *to bruise a person's feelings.* **3.** to crush (drugs or food) by beating or pounding. **4.** to scratch or mark the surface of (leather or rock), usu. for decoration. *–v.i.* **5.** to develop a discoloured spot on the skin as the result of a blow, fall, etc. **6.** to be injured superficially: *his feelings bruise easily.* *–n.* **7.** an injury due to bruising; a contusion. **8.** a mark or scratch made on a surface, as of leather or rock. [ME *bruse(n), brise(n),* coalescence of OE *brȳsan* crush, bruise and OF *br(u)isier* break, from Gallic *bris-, brus-* beat]

**bruiser** /'bruzə/, *n.* **1.** a boxer. **2.** *Colloq.* a tough fellow; bully.

**bruit** /brut/, *v.t.* **1.** to noise abroad; rumour (mainly in the passive): *the report was bruited about.* *–n.* **2.** *Archaic.* rumour. **3.** *Archaic.* a din. [ME, from OF, from *bruire* make a noise]

**brum** /brʌm/, *adj., n.* →**brummy.**

**brumal** /'bruməl/, *adj.* wintry. [L *brūmālis*]

**brumby** /'brʌmbi/, *n.* a wild horse, esp. one descended from runaway stock. [Aboriginal]

**brume** /brum/, *n.* mist; fog. [F: fog, from Pr. *bruma,* from L *brūma* winter, winter solstice, lit., shortest day] – **brumous** /brumәs/, *adj.*

**brummy** /'brʌmi/, *Colloq.* *–adj.* **1.** shoddy; cheap. *–n.* **2.** anything shoddy or cheap. Also, **brum.** [from *Brummagem,* alter. *Birmingham;* orig. with ref. to the counterfeit groats made there c. 1680, more recently to the cheap articles manufactured there]

**brunch** /brʌntʃ/, *n.* a midmorning meal that serves as both breakfast and lunch. [b. BR(EAKFAST and L)UNCH]

**brunch coat** /'– koʊt/, *n.* a short, light-weight dressing gown, worn by women. Also, **brunchie**/'brʌntʃi/.

**brunet** /bru'nɛt/, *adj.* **1.** brunette. *–n.* **2.** *Obs.* a man or boy with dark hair, skin, and eyes. [F, diminutive of *brun,* fem. *brune* brown; of Gmc orig. Cf. BROWN]

**brunette** /bru'nɛt/, *adj.* **1.** (of skin, eyes, or hair) dark; brown. **2.** (of a person) having dark or brown hair, eyes, or skin. *–n.* **3.** a woman or girl with dark hair, skin, and eyes.

**brunoise** /brun'waz/, *adj.* **1.** (of vegetables, etc.) cut into very small dice before cooking. *–n.* **2.** a rich dark beef consommé garnished with vegetables cut in this way. [F, from *brun* brown]

**Brunswick black** /brʌnzwɪk 'blæk/, *n.* a dark, glossy opaque varnish consisting of gilsonite or petroleum pitch dissolved in white spirit or aromatic hydrocarbons.

**Brunswick blue** /– 'blu/, *n.* a pigment consisting of an iron blue mixed with a large quantity of barium sulphate.

**Brunswick green** /– 'grin/, *n. Chem.* cupric oxychloride or copper (11) oxidechloride, a green pigment used as a pesticide.

**brunt** /brʌnt/, *n.* **1.** the shock or force of an attack, etc.; the main stress, force, or violence: *to bear the brunt of their criticism.* **2.** *Archaic.* a violent attack. [ME; orig. uncert.]

**brush**[1] /brʌʃ/, *n.* **1.** an instrument consisting of bristles, hair, or the like, set in or attached to a handle, used for painting, cleaning, polishing, rubbing, etc. **2.** an act of brushing; an application of a brush. **3.** the bushy tail of an animal, esp. of a fox. **4.** *Colloq.* **a.** the female pubic area. **b.** a girl. **5.** the art or skill of a painter of pictures. **6.** a painter. **7.** a slight skimming touch or contact. **8.** a brief hostile encounter; argument; skirmish. **9.** *Elect.* **a.** a conductor serving to maintain electric contact between stationary and moving parts of a machine or other apparatus. **b.** →**corona** (def. 7). *–v.t.* **10.** to sweep, rub, clean, polish, etc., with a brush. **11.** to touch lightly in passing; pass lightly over. **12.** to remove by brushing or by lightly passing over (usu. fol. by *aside*). **13. brush up, a.** to polish up; smarten. **b.** to revise and renew or improve one's skill in. *–v.i.* **14.** to move or skim with a slight contact. [ME *brusshe,* from OF *broisse,* from Gmc; cf. MHG *büriste* brush] – **brushy,** *adj.*

**brush**[2] /brʌʃ/, *n.* **1.** a dense growth of bushes, shrubs, etc.; scrub; a thicket. **2.** a sparsely settled region covered with scrub. **3.** tall dense rainforest. [ME *brusche,* from OF *broce.* See BRUSH[1]] – **brushy,** *adj.*

**brush bloodwood** /– 'blʌdwʊd/, *n.* a tree, *Baloghia lucida,* family Euphorbiaceae, found in forests of eastern Australia, the sap of which is blood-red.

**brush box** /– 'bɒks/, a tall evergreen forest tree, *Tristania conferta,* of eastern Australia, commonly grown as an ornamental and street tree.

**brush discharge** /– dɪs'tʃadʒ/, *n. Elect.* →**corona** (def. 7).

**brush kangaroo** /– kæŋgə'ru/, *n.* →**red wallaby.**

**brush-off** /'brʌʃ-ɒf/, *n. Colloq.* an abrupt or final dismissal or refusal.

**brushstroke** /'brʌʃstroʊk/, *n.* the stroke of a brush, as in painting.

**brush-tailed bettong** /,brʌʃ-teɪld 'bɛtɒŋ/, *n.* →**woylie.**

**brush turkey** /brʌʃ 'tɜki/, *n.* a large mound-building bird, *Alectura lathami,* of the wooded regions of eastern Australia. Also, **scrub turkey.**

brush turkey

**brushwood** /'brʌʃwʊd/, *n.* **1.** branches of trees cut or broken off. **2.** densely growing small trees and shrubs. **3.** the branches of various shrubs, especially of *Melaleuca uncinata,* family Myrtaceae, of drier parts of southern Australia, bound with wire and used to make fences. [BRUSH[2] + WOOD[1]]

**brushwork** /'brʌʃwɜk/, *n.* **1.** the skill, style, or manner in which a painter uses his brush. **2.** painting or other work done with a brush.

**brusque** /brʌsk, brʊsk/, *adj.* abrupt in manner; blunt; rough: *a brusque welcome.* [F, from It. *brusco* rude, sharp, from L *bruscum,* b. L *ruscum* butcher's broom and *brūcum* broom] – **brusquely,** *adv.* – **brusqueness,** *n.*

**brusquerie** /'brʊskəri/, *n.* brusqueness. [F]

**brussels carpet** /brʌsəlz 'kapət/, *n.* a kind of worsted carpet woven on a Jacquard loom, in which uncut loops form a heavy pile. [from *Brussels,* the capital of Belgium]

**brussels lace** /– 'leɪs/, *n.* handmade lace from Brussels, the capital of Belgium.

**brussels sprout** /– 'spraʊt/, *n.* **1.** a plant, *Brassica oleracea* var. *gemmifera,* having small edible heads or sprouts along the stalk, which resemble miniature cabbage heads. **2.** one of the heads or sprouts themselves. Also, **brussel sprout, sprout.**

**brut** /brut/, *adj.* (of wines, usu. champagne) very dry. [F: raw]

**brutal** /'brutl/, *adj.* **1.** savage; cruel; inhuman. **2.** crude; coarse; harsh. **3.** irrational; unreasoning. **4.** of or pertaining to lower animals. – **brutally,** *adv.*

**brutalise** /'brutəlaɪz/, *v.* **-lised, -lising.** *–v.t.* **1.** to make brutal. *–v.i.* **2.** to become brutal. Also, **brutalize.** – **brutalisation** /,brutəlaɪ'zeɪʃən/, *n.*

**brutalism** /'brutəlɪzəm/, *n.* a modern architectural style expressing structure and using materials with machine-like directness.

**brutality** /bru'tæləti/, *n., pl.* **-ties.** **1.** quality of being brutal. **2.** a brutal act.

**brute** /brut/, *n.* **1.** a non-human animal; beast. **2.** a brutal person. **3.** *Colloq.* a selfish or unsympathetic person. **4.** the animal qualities, desires, etc., of man. *–adj.* **5.** wanting reason; animal; not human. **6.** not characterised by intelligence; irrational. **7.** characteristic of animals; of brutal character or quality. **8.** savage; cruel. **9.** sensual; carnal. [F *brut,* from L *brūtus* dull]

**brutify** /'brutəfaɪ/, *v.t., v.i.,* **-fied, -fying.** to brutalise.

**brutish** /'brutɪʃ/, *adj.* **1.** brutal. **2.** gross; carnal; bestial. **3.** uncivilised; like an animal. – **brutishly,** *adv.* – **brutishness,** *n.*

**bryology** /braɪ'ɒlədʒi/, *n.* the part of botany that treats of bryophytes. [Gk *brýo(n)* moss + -LOGY] – **bryological** /braɪə'lɒdʒɪkəl/, *adj.* – **bryologist,** *n.*

**bryony** /'braɪəni/, *n., pl.* **-nies.** **1.** any plant of the genus *Bryonia* or related genera of the family Cucurbitaceae, comprising vines or climbers with acrid juice and emetic and purgative properties, as white bryony, *Bryonia dioica.* **2.** →**black bryony.** [L *bryōnia,* from Gk]

**bryophyte** /'braɪəfaɪt/, *n.* any of the Bryophyta, a primary division or group of plants comprising the true mosses and liverworts. [NL *Bryophyta,* pl., from Gk *brýo(n)* moss + *-phyta* (see -PHYTE)]

**bryozoan** /braɪə'zouən/, *adj.* **1.** of or pertaining to the Bryozoa, a phylum of marine and freshwater animals, of sessile habits, forming branching, encrusting, or gelatinous colonies of many small polyps, each having a circular or horseshoe-shaped ridge bearing ciliated tentacles. Branching marine types are termed sea-moss and are used as ornaments. *–n.* **2.** any of the Bryozoa. Also, **polyzoan.** [Gk *brýo(n)* moss + -ZO(A) + -AN]

**Brython** /'brɪθən/, *n.* **1.** a Celt in Britain using the Brythonic form of the Celtic language, which was confined mainly to the western part of southern Britain after the English conquest. **2.** a Briton. [Welsh]

**Brythonic** /brə'θɒnɪk/, *adj.* **1.** pertaining to the Celtic dialects used in north-western and south-western England, Wales and Brittany. *–n.* **2.** the British subgroup of Celtic (distinguished from *Goidelic*).

**B.S.** /bi 'ɛs/, Bachelor of Surgery.

**B.Sc.,** /bi ɛs 'si/, Bachelor of Science.

**B side** /'bi saɪd/, *n.* the secondary side of a gramophone recording.

**B.Soc.Wk.,** Bachelor of Social Work.

**b.s.v.** /bi ɛs 'vi/, *n.* →**bogie sheep van.**

**Bt,** Baronet.

**btu,** /bi ti 'ju/, British thermal unit. Also, **B.Th.U.**

**bty,** battery.

**bub** /bʌb/, *n. Colloq.* **1.** Also, **bubba.** a baby. **2.** one of the breasts of a woman.

**bubal** /'bjubəl/, *n.* a large antelope, one of the hartebeests, *Alcelaphus boselaphus,* of northern Africa. Also, **bubalis** /'bjubələs/. [L *būbalus* an oxlike antelope, from Gk *boúbalos*]

**bubaline** /'bjubəlaɪn, -lin/, *adj.* **1.** (of antelopes), resembling or like the bubal, as the hartebeests, etc. **2.** pertaining to or resembling the true buffaloes.

**bubble** /'bʌbəl/, *n., v.,* **-bled, -bling.** *–n.* **1.** a small globule of gas in or rising through a liquid. **2.** a small globule of gas in a thin liquid envelope. **3.** a globule of air or gas, or a globular vacuum, in a solid substance. **4.** anything that lacks firmness, substance, or permanence; a delusion; a worthless, deceptive matter. **5.** an inflated speculation, esp. if fraudulent. **6.** the act or sound of bubbling. *–v.i.* **7.** to send up bubbles; effervesce. **8.** to flow or run with a gurgling noise; gurgle. *–v.t.* **9.** to cause to bubble; make (bubbles) in. **10.** *Archaic.* to cheat; deceive; swindle. [ME *bobel,* c. D *bobbelen,* Swed. *bubla.* Cf. BURBLE]

**bubble-and-squeak** /bʌbəl-ən-'skwik/, *n.* **1.** left-over potato and cabbage fried together. **2.** left-over meat and vegetables fried together.

**bubble bath** /'bʌbəl baθ/, *n.* a bath in which the water has been made to foam by the addition of perfumed chemicals.

**bubble car** /'- ka/, *n.* a small motor car with a bubble-shaped body.

**bubble chamber** /'- tʃeɪmbə/, *n.* an apparatus for determining the movements of charged particles by producing visible tracks of bubbles in their paths as they traverse a transparent medium.

**bubblegum** /'bʌbəlgʌm/, *n.* a type of chewing gum which can be blown into bubbles.

**bubblegum music** /'- ˌmjuzɪk/, *n. Colloq.* pop music designed to appeal to pre-teenagers; cradle rock.

**bubbler** /'bʌblə/, *n.* →**drinking fountain.**

**bubbly** /'bʌbli/, *adj.* **1.** containing bubbles; bubbling. **2.** of or like bubbles. *–n.* **3.** *Colloq.* champagne.

**bubbly Jock** /- 'dʒɒk/, *n.* →**wompoo pigeon.** Also, **bubbly Mary.**

**bubo** /'bjubou/, *n., pl.* **-boes.** an inflammatory swelling of a lymphatic gland, esp. in the groin or armpit. [LL, from Gk *boubṓn,* lit., groin]

**bubonic** /bju'bɒnɪk/, *adj.* **1.** of or pertaining to a bubo. **2.** accompanied by or affected with buboes.

**bubonic plague** /- 'pleɪg/, *n.* a contagious epidemic disease in which the victims suffer chills, fevers, and buboes, and are prostrate, and which often has rat-fleas as its carrier.

**bubonocele** /bju'bɒnəsil/, *n.* an inguinal hernia, esp. one in which the protrusion of the intestine is limited to the region of the groin.

**buccal** /'bʌkəl/, *adj.* **1.** of or pertaining to the cheek. **2.** pertaining to the sides of the mouth or to the mouth; oral. **3.** pertaining to the mouth as a whole. [L *bucca* cheek, mouth + -AL[1]]

**buccaneer** /bʌkə'nɪə/, *n.* **1.** a pirate. **2.** one of the piratical adventurers who raided Spanish colonies and shipping in America. *–v.i.* **3.** to act like, or lead the life of, a buccaneer. [F *boucanier,* from *boucan* frame for curing meat, from Tupi; alteration of *mukém*] – **buccaneering,** *n., adj.*

**bucchero** /'bukərou/, *n.* an ancient fine grey pottery with a black or, less commonly, grey shiny surface.

**buccinator** /'bʌksəneɪtə/, *n.* a thin flat muscle lining the cheek, assisting in mastication, blowing wind instruments, etc. [L: trumpeter, from *buccināre* blow a trumpet] – **buccinatory,** *adj.*

**Buchmanism** /'bʌkmənɪzəm/, *n.* the Moral Rearmament movement. [named after Frank *Buchman,* 1878-1961, who founded it] – **Buchmanite** /'bʌkmənaɪt/, *n.*

**buck**[1] /bʌk/, *n.* **1.** the male of certain animals, as the deer, antelope, rabbit, or hare. **2.** a young man viewed as a sexual animal; a fop; dandy. **3.** *U.S. Colloq.* (*derog.*) a male Indian or Negro. *–adj.* **4.** (*derog.*) male: *a buck nigger.* [ME *bukke,* coalescence of IE *bucca* he-goat and *bucc* male deer, c. G *Bock*]

**buck**[2] /bʌk/, *v.i.* **1.** (of a saddle or pack animal) to leap with arched back and come down with head low and forelegs stiff, in order to dislodge rider or pack. **2.** *Colloq.* to resist obstinately; object strongly: *to buck at improvements.* **3.** *Colloq.* to hurry (fol. by *up*) **4.** *Colloq.* to become more cheerful, vigorous, etc. (fol. by *up*). *–v.t.* **5.** to throw or attempt to throw (a rider) by bucking. **6.** *Colloq.* to resist obstinately; object strongly to: *to buck the system.* **7.** *Colloq.* to force or urge (someone) to hurry (fol. by *up*). **8.** *Colloq.* to make more cheerful, vigorous, etc. (fol. by *up*). *–n.* **9.** an act of bucking. **10. give it a buck,** *Colloq.* to make an attempt; chance. **11. have a buck at,** to try; make an attempt. [special use of BUCK[1]]

**buck**[3] /bʌk/, *n.* **1.** *Poker.* any object in the kitty which reminds the winner that he has some privilege or duty when his turn to deal next comes. **2. pass the buck,** *Colloq.* to shift the responsibility or blame to another person. [orig. uncert.]

**buck**[4] /bʌk/, *n. Orig. U.S. Colloq.* **1.** a dollar. **2. a fast buck,** money earned with little effort, often by dishonest means. [shortened form of BUCKSKIN, an accepted form of exchange in the U.S. frontier.]

**buckaroo** /bʌkə'ru/, *n., pl.* **-roos.** a cowboy. Also, **buckayro.** [Sp.]

**buckboard** /'bʌkbɔd/, *n.* **1.** *U.S.* a light four-wheeled carriage in which a long elastic board or lattice frame is used in place of body and springs. **2.** *Colloq.* a utility.

buckboard

**buckeen** /bʌ'kin/, *n.* (in Ireland) a young man of the middle class or lower aristocracy who copies the habits of wealthier people.

**bucker** /'bʌkə/, *n.* a horse that bucks.

**bucket** /'bʌkət/, *n., v.,* **-eted, -eting.** *–n.* **1.** a vessel, usu. round with flat bottom and a semicircular handle, for carrying water, sand, etc. **2.** anything resembling or suggesting this. **3.** one of the scoops attached to or forming the endless chain in certain types of conveyers or elevators. **4.** a cupped vane of a water wheel, turbine, etc. **5.** a bucketful. **6.** a small carton of ice-cream; dixie. **7.** →**bucket seat. 8. kick the bucket,** *Colloq.* to die. *–v.t.* **9.** to lift, carry, or handle in a bucket (oft. fol. by *up* or *out*). **10.** to shake or toss jerkily (fol. by *about*). **11.** Also, **empty (tip) the bucket on.** to make scandalous accusations or revelations about (someone); criticise strongly. *–v.i.* **12.** to be shaken or tossed jerkily (fol. by *about.*). **13.** *Rowing.* to row unrhythmically. **14.** of rain, to pour down heavily (fol. by *down*). [ME *bocket,* apparently from OF *bucket* pail, tub, probably from some cognate of OE *buc* pitcher] – **bucketful** /'bʌkətfʊl/, *n.*

**bucket-of-water-wood** /,bʌkət-əv-'wɔtə-,wʊd/, *n.* →**kotukutuku.**

**bucket seat** /'bʌkət sit/, *n.* (in a car, etc.) a seat with a rounded or moulded back, to hold one person. Also, **bucket.**

**buckeye** /'bʌkaɪ/, *n.* any of various trees or shrubs of the U.S. genus *Aesculus,* allied to the true horse chestnut, as *A. glabra* (**Ohio buckeye**), a large tree with an ill-smelling bark. [BUCK[1] stag + EYE, in allusion to the appearance of the seed]

**buckhorn** /'bʌkhɔn/, *n.* the hard material of which a buck's horn consists, used to manufacture knife handles, etc. Also, **buck's-horn.**

**buckhound** /'bʌkhaʊnd/, *n.* a hound for hunting bucks, etc., similar to the staghound, but smaller.

**buckish** /'bʌkɪʃ/, *adj.* **1.** (of a horse) inclined to buck. **2.** *Colloq.* (of a person) in fine form; fit and lively. **3.** foppish; dapper. – **buckishly,** *adv.* – **buckishness,** *n.*

**buckjump** /'bʌkdʒʌmp/, *v.i.* (of a horse) to buck. [BUCK[2] + JUMP] – **buckjumping,** *n.*

**buckjumper** /'bʌkdʒʌmpə/, *n.* **1.** a horse which bucks. **2.** a rider of such a horse. **3.** a small damper or scone. **4.** *Colloq.* a tram.

**buckle** /'bʌkl/, *n., v.,* **-led, -ling.** *–n.* **1.** a clasp consisting of a rectangular or curved rim with one or more movable tongues, used for fastening together two loose ends, as of a belt or strap. **2.** any similar contrivance used for such a purpose. **3.** an ornament of metal, beads, etc., of similar appearance. **4.** a bend, bulge, or kink, as in a saw blade. *–v.t.* **5.** to fasten with a buckle or buckles. **6.** to bend and shrivel, by applying heat or pressure; warp; curl. **7.** to prepare (oneself) for action; apply (oneself) vigorously to something. **8.** take from; extract (fol. by *for*): *the tax people buckled us for a lot of money.* *–v.i.* **9.** to set to work with vigour (fol. by *to* or *down to*). **10.** to bend, warp, or give way suddenly, as with heat or pressure. **11.** to grapple; contend. **12. buckle under, a.** to yield; give way (fol. by *to*). **b.** to give up; despair. **13. get buckled,** *Prison Colloq.* to be arrested. [ME *bocle,* from F *boucle* buckle, boss of a shield, from L *buccula,* diminutive of *bucca* cheek, mouth]

**buckler** /'bʌklə/, *n.* **1.** a round shield, with grip for holding, and sometimes with straps through which the arm is passed. **2.** any means of defence; a protection. [ME *bokeler,* from OF *boucler* shield, orig., one with a boss, from *boucle* boss. See BUCKLE, n.]

**Buckley's chance** /'bʌkliz tʃæns/, *n.* Also, **Buckley's, Buckley's hope. 1.** a very slim chance; forlorn hope. **2. Buckley's and none,** (*joc.*) two chances amounting to next to no chance. [probably pun on *Buckley and Nun,* an expensive Melbourne store]

**buckling** /'bʌklɪŋ/, *n.* →**bloater.** [G *bückling* bloater]

**bucko** /'bʌkoʊ/, *n. Colloq.* **1.** a young man. **2.** a blustering bully.

**buck-passing** /'bʌk-pasɪŋ/, *n.* avoiding responsibility by passing it on to another. – **buck-passer,** *n.*

**buckra** /'bʌkrə/, *n.* a white man (used among the Negroes of the African coast, the West Indies, and the southern U.S.) [? from W African (Calabar) *mbākara* demon, powerful being, white man]

**buck rake** /'bʌk reɪk/, *n.* a rake with long straight horizontal teeth used to gather hay and transport it to a stack.

**buckram** /'bʌkrəm/, *n., v.,* **-ramed, -raming.** *–n.* **1.** stiff cotton fabric for interlining, binding books, etc. **2.** stiffness of manner; extreme preciseness or formality. *–v.t.* **3.** to strengthen with buckram. **4.** to give (a person, etc.) a false appearance of importance or strength. [ME *bokeram.* Cf. OF *boquerant,* It. *bucherame,* ? from *Bukhara* a city in W Asia, whence the cloth was exported]

**buck rarebit** /bʌk 'rɛəbət/, *n.* a dish consisting of Welsh rarebit topped by a poached egg. Also, **buck rabbit.**

**bucksaw** /'bʌksɔ/, *n.* a saw consisting of a blade set across an upright frame or bow, one bar of which is extended to form a handle, used with both hands in cutting wood.

bucksaw

**buckshee** /bʌk'ʃi/, *adj. Colloq.* free of charge. [var. of BAKSHEESH]

**buck's-horn** /'bʌks-hɔn/, *n.* →**buckhorn.**

**buckshot** /'bʌkʃɒt/, *n.* a large size of lead shot used on big game.

**buckskin** /'bʌkskɪn/, *n.* **1.** the skin of a buck or deer. **2.** a strong, soft, yellowish or greyish leather, originally prepared from deerskin, now usu. from sheepskin. **3.** (*pl.*) *U.S.* breeches made of buckskin.

**bucks party** /'bʌks pati/, *n.* a party held on the eve of a wedding for the bridegroom by his male friends. Also, **bucks' party.**

**buckthorn** /'bʌkθɔn/, *n.* **1.** any of several trees or shrubs (sometimes thorny) belonging to the genus *Rhamnus,* as *R. cathartica,* a shrub whose berries were formerly much used in medicine as a purgative, and *R. frangula,* yielding the **buckthorn bark** used in medicine. **2.** a tree or shrub of the sapotaceous genus *Bumelia,* esp. *B. lycioides,* a tree common in the southern U.S.

**bucktooth** /bʌk'tuθ/, *n., pl.* **-teeth** /-'tiθ/. a projecting tooth.

**buckwheat** /'bʌkwit/, *n.* **1.** a herbaceous plant, *Fagopyrum esculentum,* cultivated for its triangular seeds, which are used as a food for animals, and in the U.S. made into a flour for cakes, etc. **2.** the seeds of the buckwheat. **3.** buckwheat flour. [*buck* (OE *bōc* beech) + WHEAT. Cf. D *boekweit,* G *Buchweizen* buckwheat, lit., beech wheat; so called from its beechnut-shaped seed]

**bucolic** /bju'kɒlɪk/, *adj.* Also, **bucolical. 1.** of or pertaining to shepherds; pastoral. **2.** rustic; rural; agricultural: *bucolic isolation.* *–n.* **3.** a farmer; a shepherd; a rustic. **4.** a pastoral poem. [L *būcolicus,* from Gk *boukolikós* rustic] – **bucolically,** *adv.*

**bud**[1] /bʌd/, *n., v.,* **budded, budding.** *–n.* **1.** *Bot.* **a.** a small axillary or terminal protuberance on a plant, containing rudimentary foliage (**leaf bud**), the rudimentary inflorescence (**flower bud**), or both (**mixed bud**). **b.** an undeveloped or rudimentary stem or branch of a plant. **2.** *Zool.* (in certain animals of low organisation) a prominence which develops into a new individual, sometimes permanently attached to the parent and sometimes becoming detached; a gemma. **3.** *Anat.* any small rounded part, as a tactile bud or a gustatory bud. **4.** an immature or undeveloped person or thing. **5. nip in the bud,** to stop (something) before it gets under way. *–v.i.* **6.** to put forth or produce buds, as a plant. **7.** to begin to grow and develop. **8.** to be in an early stage of development. *–v.t.* **9.** to cause to bud. **10.** *Hort.* to graft by inserting a single bud into the stock. [ME *budde;* orig. uncert.]

leaf buds

**bud**[2] /bʌd/, *n. U.S. Colloq.* **1.** brother. **2.** man or boy (as a term of address). [alteration of BROTHER]

**budburst** /'bʌdbɜst/, *n.* (of grape vines, etc.) the time in spring when the vine leafs out.

**budda** /'bʌdə/, *n.* a small tree, *Eremophila mitchellii,* of drier inland areas of New South Wales and Queensland.

**Buddhism** /'bʊdɪzəm/, *n.* the cult, founded by the religious teacher Buddha, (fl. India, sixth century B.C.), which teaches that life is intrinsically full of suffering and that the supreme felicity (Nirvana) is achieved by destroying greed, hatred, and delusion. – **Buddhist,** *n., adj.* – **Buddhistic** /bʊˈdɪstɪk/, *adj.*

**buddle** /ˈbʌdl/, *Mining.* –*n.* **1.** circular device in which finely-divided ore, in water, is delivered from a central point and flows gently to the perimeter; the heaviest and coarsest particles bed down, while the lightest overflow. –*v.t.* **2.** to separate ore by means of a buddle. [? G *butteln* to shake]

**buddleia** /ˈbʌdliə/, *n.* any shrub of the genus *Buddleia,* mainly tropical ornamental perennials of the family Loganiaceae, having a two-celled, many-seeded fruit. [NL; after Adam *Buddle,* d. 1715, English botanist]

**buddy** /ˈbʌdi/, *n., pl.* **-dies.** *Colloq.* comrade; mate. [see BUD[2]]

**buddy-buddy** /ˈbʌdi-ˌbʌdi/, (*oft. derog.*) *n.* **1.** a close friend or associate, esp. one in a relationship based on a common interest or ambition. –*adj.* **2.** sycophantic: *buddy-buddy tactics.* –*v.t.* **3.** to behave in a sycophantic manner: *to buddy-buddy an official.*

**buddy system** /ˈbʌdi sɪstəm/, *n.* a system of diving in pairs, sharing one oxygen outlet from a back tank.

**budge** /bʌdʒ/, *v.* **budged, budging.** –*v.i.* **1.** to move slightly; give way (usu. with negative). –*v.t.* **2.** to cause to budge (usu. with negative). [F *bouger,* from L *bullīre* BOIL[1]]

**budgeree** /ˈbʌdʒəri, bʌdʒəˈri/, *adj. Obs. Colloq.* good; fine. [Aboriginal]

**budgerigar** /ˈbʌdʒəriˌga/, *n.* a small yellow and green parakeet, *Melopsittacus undulatus,* of inland regions of Australia, that has been widely domesticated and bred in many coloured varieties. Also, **budgerygah.** [Aboriginal: early forms include *betcherrygah* and *gijoriga;* the popular but erroneous translation 'good parrot' derives from an imagined association with BUDGEREE]

budgerigar

**budget** /ˈbʌdʒət/, *n., v.,* **-eted, -eting.** –*n.* **1.** an estimate, often itemised, of expected income and expenditure, or operating results, for a given period in the future. **2.** specifically, estimates of government income and expenditure. **3.** a plan of operations based on such an estimate. **4.** an itemised allotment of funds for a given period. **5.** a stock; a collection. **6.** *Obs.* a small bag; a pouch. –*v.t.* **7.** to plan allotment of (funds, time, etc.). **8.** to deal with (specific funds) in a budget. [late ME *bougette,* from F, diminutive of *bouge* bag, from L *bulga*] – **budgetary** /ˈbʌdʒətri/, *adj.*

**budget account** /ˈ– əkaʊnt/, *n.* an account with a department store, etc., enabling a customer to obtain goods of a specified value, and pay for them over a specified period.

**budgie** /ˈbʌdʒi/, *n. Colloq.* a budgerigar.

**buff**[1] /bʌf/, *n.* **1.** a kind of thick leather, originally and properly made of buffalo skin but later also of other skins, light yellow with napped surface, used for making belts, pouches, etc. **2.** a thick coat of buff leather, worn esp. by soldiers. **3.** yellowish brown; medium or light tan. **4.** a buffwheel. **5.** *Colloq.* the bare skin. **6.** *Colloq.* an enthusiast; an expert (sometimes self-proclaimed): *a wine buff.* [from the buff uniforms worn by New York volunteer firemen in the 1820s] –*adj.* **7.** made of buff (leather). **8.** having the colour of buff. –*v.t.* **9.** to polish (metal) or to give a grainless finish of high lustre to (plated surfaces). **10.** to dye or stain in a buff colour. [apparently from earlier *buffle,* from F: buffalo, from It. *bufalo.* See BUFFALO]

**buff**[2] /bʌf/, *v.t.* **1.** to reduce or deaden the force of, as a buffer. –*n.* **2.** a blow; a slap; a buffet. [late ME *buffe,* ? from OF; or backformation from BUFFET[1]. But cf. LG *buff* blow]

**buffalo** /ˈbʌfəloʊ/, *n., pl.* **-loes, -los,** (*esp. collectively*) **-lo,** *v.* –*n.* **1.** any of several mammals of the ox kind, as **a.** *Bos bubalus* or *Bubalus buffelus,* an Old World species, originally from India, valued as a draught animal. **b.** *Bos caffer* or *Bubalus caffer* (**Cape buffalo**), a southern African species. **c.** *Bison bison* (the **American buffalo** or bison). –*v.t.* **2.** to confuse; bewilder; over-awe. [It. *bufalo,* from d. L *būfalus,* var. of *būbalus* BUBAL]

buffalo

**buffalo burr** /– ˈbɜ/, *n.* a poisonous weed *Solanum rostratum,* native to Mexico.

**buffalo grass** /ˈ– gras/, *n.* **1.** a lawn grass, *Stenotaphrum secundatum,* coarse and springy with a dense growth of runners, grown in warm districts. **2.** a short grass, *Buchloe dactyloides,* very prevalent on the dry plains of midwestern U.S. **3.** any of many species of short grasses.

**buff-breasted pitta** /ˌbʌf-brɛstəd ˈpɪtə/, *n.* a small, brilliantly coloured, eastern Australian bird, *Pitta versicolor,* which feeds on snails and uses a stone or stump as an 'anvil' on which to break the shells; anvil bird.

**buffel grass** /ˈbʌfəl gras/, *n.* a tropical pasture grass, *Cenchrus ciliaris,* native to Africa and India, cultivated and naturalised in northern Australia.

**buffer**[1] /ˈbʌfə/, *n.* **1.** an apparatus, such as one of the two at each end of a railway carriage, for absorbing the concussion between a moving body and something against which it strikes. **2.** anything serving to neutralise the shock of opposing forces. **3.** *Electronics.* a circuit which links two electronic systems which cannot be joined directly together. –*v.t.* **4.** *Chem.* to oppose a change of composition, esp. of acidity or alkalinity. [BUFF[2], *v.* + -ER[1]]

**buffer**[2] /ˈbʌfə/, *n.* **1.** a device for polishing; buffwheel or buffstick. **2.** one who uses such a device. [BUFF[1] + -ER[1]]

**buffer**[3] /ˈbʌfə/, *n.* a foolish man, esp. one who is elderly and pompous. [ME, ? alteration of BUFFOON]

**buffer distance** /ˈ– ˌdɪstəns/, *n. Mil.* the minimum distance which when added to the radius of safety of a nuclear explosion implies no more than a specified risk from fallout.

**buffer solution** /ˈ– səˌluʃən/, *n.* a solution whose acidity or alkalinity remains almost unchanged by dilution or by the addition of acid or alkali.

**buffer state** /ˈ– steɪt/, *n.* a smaller state or zone lying between potentially hostile larger states. Also, **buffer zone.**

**buffet**[1] /ˈbʌfət/, *n., v.,* **-feted, -feting.** –*n.* **1.** a blow, as with the hand or fist. –*v.t.* **2.** to strike, as with the hand or fist. **3.** to contend against; battle. –*v.i.* **4.** to struggle with blows of hand or fist. **5.** to force one's way by a fight, struggle, etc. [ME, from OF, diminutive of *buffe* a blow] – **buffeter,** *n.*

**buffet**[2] /ˈbʌfeɪ, ˈbʊfeɪ/, *n.* **1.** a counter, bar, or the like, for lunch or refreshments. **2.** a restaurant containing such a counter or bar. **3.** a meal so served. **4.** a sideboard or cabinet for holding china, plate, etc. –*adj.* **5.** (of a meal) spread on tables or buffets from which the guests serve themselves. [F: orig., chair, table]

**buffet car** /ˈ– ka/, *n.* a restaurant car on a train in which drinks and light meals are served.

**buffeting** /ˈbʌfətɪŋ/, *n.* **1.** a pushing or jostling, as by wind. **2.** a series of physical or mental blows. **3.** *Aeron.* the vibration of all or part of an aircraft, induced by its own aerodynamic wake.

**buffing wheel** /ˈbʌfɪŋ wil/, *n.* →**buffwheel.**

**bufflehead** /ˈbʌfəlhɛd/, *n.* a small North American duck, *Glaucionetta albeola,* the male of which has fluffy head plumage; butterball. [obs. *buffle* buffalo + HEAD]

**buffo** /ˈbʊfoʊ/, *n., pl.* **-fi** /-fi/. (in opera) a comedy part, usu. bass. [It.: ridiculous, from *buffare* blow with puffed cheeks]

**buffoon** /bəˈfun/, *n.* **1.** one who amuses others by tricks, odd gestures and postures, jokes, etc. **2.** one given to coarse or undignified joking. [F *bouffon,* from It. *buffone* jester, from *buffa* a jest] – **buffoonery** /bəˈfunəri/, *n.*

**buffstick** /ˈbʌfstɪk/, *n.* a small stick covered with leather or the like, used in polishing.

**buffwheel** /ˈbʌfwil/, *n.* a wheel for polishing metal, etc., usu. covered with leather bearing a polishing powder.

**bufo** /ˈbufoʊ/, *n.* **1.** in Australia, the introduced toad *Bufo marinus,* now widespread and abundant in Queensland; cane toad. **2.** a

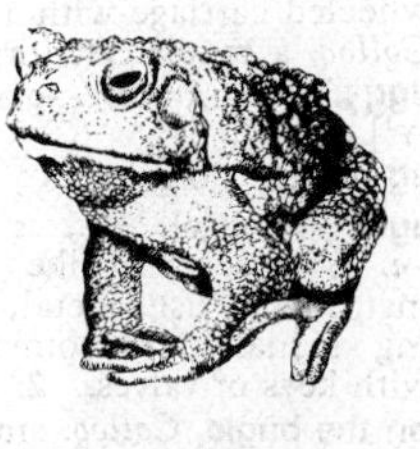
bufo

large genus of the family Bufonidae, represented in all continents other than Australia. **3.** any toad of the genus *Bufo.*

**bug** /bʌg/, *n., v.t.,* **bugged, bugging.** *–n.* **1.** loosely, any insect, esp. one of the suborder Heteroptera (order Hemiptera), characterised by having the forewings thickened at base and membranous at tip, and the hindwings membranous. Sucking mouth parts enable the majority to suck plant juices and others to feed on animals, including man. **2.** →**bedbug. 3.** *Colloq.* a malady, esp. a virus infection. **4.** (*oft. pl.*) *Colloq.* defect or difficulty: *eliminating the bugs in television.* **5.** *Computers.* an error in a program or the machine itself, often undetected by the most stringent tests. **6.** *Colloq.* an idea or belief with which one is obsessed. **7.** *Colloq.* a microphone hidden in a room to tap conversation. **8.** a small electronic device implanted for telemetering some physiological process in a person or animal. **9.** →**contact microphone. 10.** a bogy; hobgoblin. *–v.t.* **11.** *Colloq.* to install a bug in (a room, etc.). **12.** *Colloq.* to cause annoyance or distress to (a person). **13.** *Colloq.* to equip a building with burglar alarms. **14.** to put a sudden end to (a plan, etc.) **15.** to fit with a contact microphone. [ME *bugge.* Cf. Welsh *bug* bogy, ghost]

**bugaboo** /ˈbʌgəbu/, *n., pl.* **-boos.** some imaginary thing that causes fear or worry; a bugbear; a bogy. [BUG (def. 9) + BOO (def. 1); for the *-a-*, cf. BLACKAMOOR]

**bugaku** /bugaˈku/, *n.* a Japanese court dance for which there is music similar to gagaku.

**bugbear** /ˈbʌgbɛə/, *n.* **1.** any source, real or imaginary, of needless fright or fear. **2.** *Obs.* a goblin thought to eat up naughty children. [BUG (def. 10) + BEAR[2]]

**bugger** /ˈbʌgə/, *n.* **1.** one who practises bestiality or sodomy. **2.** *Colloq.* (*joc.*) person; child: *come on, you old bugger.* **3.** *Colloq.* a foul, contemptible person. **4. bugger all,** *Colloq.* nothing. **5.** *Colloq.* a nuisance, a difficulty; unpleasant or nasty: *that recipe is a real bugger; it's a bugger of a day.* **6. play silly buggers,** *Colloq.* to engage in time-wasting activities and frivolous behaviour. *–v.t.* **7.** to practise bestiality or sodomy on. **8.** *Colloq.* to cause damage, frustration or inconvenience to (fol. by *up*). **9.** to incapacitate; render incapable of (fol. by *for*): *exercise buggers me for anything else.* **10.** *Colloq.* to damn or curse, as an indication of contempt or dismissal: *bugger him, I'm going home; bugger it.* **11.** *Colloq.* to cause inconvenience to someone; delay. *–v.i.* **12. bugger about** or **around,** *Colloq.* to mess about; fiddle around. **13. bugger off,** *Colloq.* to remove oneself; depart. *–interj.* **14.** (a strong exclamation of annoyance, disgust, etc.): *Oh, bugger!* [F *bougre,* from ML *Bulgarus* a Bulgarian, a heretic; certain Bulgarian heretics being charged with this activity] – **buggery,** *n.*

**bugger-all** /bʌgər-ˈɔl/, *n. Colloq.* very little; nothing: *he's done bugger-all all day.*

**buggered** /ˈbʌgəd/, *adj. Colloq.* **1.** tired out; exhausted. **2.** broken; wrecked. **3.** damned: *I'm buggered if I'll do that.*

**buggerise** /ˈbʌgəraɪz/, *v. Colloq. –v.t.* **1.** to convert a person to buggery. *–v.i.* **2. buggerise about** or **around,** to behave aimlessly or ineffectually.

**buggerlugs** /ˈbʌgəlʌgz/, *n. Colloq.* (a mock abusive term, used affectionately).

**buggery** /ˈbʌgəri/, *n.* **1.** the practice of bestiality or sodomy. **2. like buggery,** considerably: *it hurts like buggery. –interj.* **3. go to buggery!,** go away; leave me alone. **4. off to buggery, a.** greatly off course; in error; astray. **b.** a long way away.

**buggy**[1] /ˈbʌgi/, *n., pl.* **-gies. 1.** a two-wheeled horse-drawn carriage with or without a hood. **2.** *U.S.* A light four-wheeled carriage with a single seat on a transverse spring. **3.** *Colloq.* a motor car. [orig. uncert.]

**buggy**[2] /ˈbʌgi/, *adj.,* **-gier, -giest.** infested with bugs. [BUG + -Y[1]]

**bug-hunter** /ˈbʌg-hʌntə/, *n. Colloq.* a collecting entomologist.

**bugle**[1] /ˈbjugəl/, *n., v.,* **-gled, -gling.** *–n.* **1.** a cornet-like military wind instrument, usu. metal, used for sounding signals and sometimes furnished with keys or valves. **2.** *Colloq.* nose. **3. on the bugle,** *Colloq.* smelly. *–v.i.* **4.** to sound a bugle. **5.** to make a noise similar to the sound produced by a bugle. [ME, from OF, from L *būculus,* diminutive of *bōs* ox] – **bugler,** *n.*

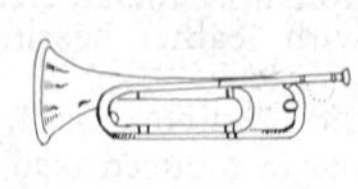
bugle

**bugle**[2] /ˈbjugəl/, *n.* any plant of the genus *Ajuga,* esp. *A. reptans* a low, blue-flowered herb. [F, from LL *bugula* kind of plant]

**bugle bead** /ˈ– bid/, *n.* a small decorative bead which is sewn, usu. in clusters or designs, onto fabrics, woollens, etc.

**bugloss** /ˈbjuglɒs/, *n.* any of various plants of the family Boraginaceae, esp. of the genera *Echium, Anchusa* and *Lycopsis.* [F *buglosse,* from L *būglossa,* from Gk *boúglōssos* ox-tongue]

**bugong** /ˈbjugɒŋ/, *n.* →**bogong.**

**bug rake** /ˈbʌg reɪk/, *n. Colloq.* a comb.

**buhl** /bul/, *n.* elaborate inlaid work of woods, metals, tortoiseshell, ivory, etc. Also, **buhlwork** /ˈbulwɜk/. [apparently Germanised sp. of F *boulle* or *boule,* named after A. C. *Boulle* or *Boule,* 1642-1732, French cabinet-maker]

**buhrstone** /ˈbɜstoun/, *n.* →**burstone.**

**build** /bɪld/, *v.,* **built** or (*Archaic*) **builded, building,** *n. –v.t.* **1.** to construct (something relatively complex) by assembling and combining parts: *build a house or an empire.* **2.** to establish, increase, and strengthen (oft. fol. by *up*): *build up a business.* **3.** to base; form; construct: *to build one's hopes on promises.* **4.** to fill in with houses (usu. fol. by *up*). **5.** *Games.* **a.** to make (words) from letters. **b.** to add (cards) to each other according to number, suit, etc. **6.** to claim public attention for (a person or product) by means of an advertising campaign (fol. by *up*). **7.** to obstruct the view from (a building) by erecting another building close to it (fol. by *out*). *–v.i.* **8.** to engage in the art or business of building. **9.** to form or construct a plan, system of thought, etc. (fol. by *on* or *upon*). **10.** to add a room or rooms to a house (fol. by *on*). *–n.* **11.** manner or form of construction: *a person's build.* [ME *bilden, bulde(n),* OE *byldan,* from *bold* dwelling, house]

**builder** /ˈbɪldə/, *n.* **1.** a person who builds. **2.** a person who contracts for the construction of buildings and supervises the workmen who build them.

**building** /ˈbɪldɪŋ/, *n.* **1.** anything built or constructed. **2.** the act, business, or art of constructing houses, etc.

**building alignment** /ˈ– əˌlaɪnmənt/, *n.* →**building line.**

**building block** /ˈ– blɒk/, *n.* →**block** (def. 20b).

**building covenant** /ˈ– ˌkʌvənənt/, *n.* a restriction imposed on the form, position or appearance of a building by the local authority or the vendor of the site.

**building line** /ˈ– laɪn/, *n.* a boundary set on either side of a street by a planning authority, beyond which buildings may not project. Also, **building alignment.**

**building society** /ˈ– səˌsaɪəti/, *n.* a business organisation that advances money to enable people to buy or build a house.

**build-up** /ˈbɪld-ʌp/, *n.* **1.** any progressive increase. **2.** *Mil.* a concentration of troops, etc., for an offensive. **3.** a publicity campaign on behalf of a person or a product.

**built** /bɪlt/, *v.* **1.** past tense and past participle of **build. 2.** *Orig. U.S. Colloq.* of a woman, well-developed.

**built-in** /ˈbɪlt-ɪn/, *adj.* **1.** built so as to be an integral, permanent part of a larger unit, esp. of the fitting of a house. **2.** included as an integral part; intended; inherent: *built-in obsolescence. –n.* **3.** a piece of built-in furniture.

**built-up area** /ˌbɪlt-ʌp ˈɛəriə/, *n.* an area of dense habitation within which speed-limits apply to traffic.

**bulb** /bʌlb/, *n.* **1.** *Bot.* **a.** a bud, having fleshy leaves and usu. subterranean, in which the stem is reduced to a flat disc, rooting from the underside, as in the onion, lily, etc. **b.** a plant growing from a bulb. **2.** any round, enlarged part, esp. one at the end of a long, slender body: *the bulb of a thermometer.* **3.** *Elect.* **a.** the glass housing, which contains the filament of an incandescent electric lamp. **b.** an incandescent electric lamp. **4.** a valve (def. 7). **5.** *Anat.* **a. bulb of the spinal cord** or **brain,** the medulla oblongata. **b. bulb of the urethra,** the rounded mass of erectile tissue that surrounds the urethra at the posterior end of the penis, just in front of the anus. [L *bulbus,* from Gk *bolbós*] – **bulbar** /ˈbʌlbə/, *adj.* – **bulblike,** *adj.*

**bulbaceous** /bʌlˈbeɪʃəs/, *adj.* →**bulbous.**

**bulbiferous** /bʌlˈbɪfərəs/, *adj.* producing bulbs.

**bulbil** /ˈbʌlbɪl/, *n.* **1.** a little bulb. **2.** a small aerial bulb growing in the axils of leaves, as in the tiger lily, or replacing flower buds, as in the common onion. [NL *bulbillus,* diminutive of L *bulbus* BULB]

**bulbous** /ˈbʌlbəs/, *adj.* **1.** bulb-shaped; bulging. **2.** having, or growing from, bulbs. Also, **bulbaceous** /bʌlˈbeɪʃəs/.

**bulbul** /ˈbʊlbʊl/, *n.* **1.** a small crested Asian bird, *Pycnonotus jocosus,* introduced into Australia during the 1880s. **2.** any bird of the tropical oriental family Pycnonotidae, much referred to in Persian poetry, and noted as songsters. [Pers.]

**Bulgar** /ˈbʌlga, ˈbʊlga/, *n.* →**Bulgarian.**

**Bulgaria** /bʌlˈgɛəriə/, *n.* a republic in south-eastern Europe.

**Bulgarian** /bʌlˈgɛəriən, bʊl-/, *n.* **1.** a native or inhabitant of Bulgaria. **2.** a Slavic language, the language of Bulgaria. *–adj.* **3.** of or pertaining to Bulgaria, its people, or their language.

**bulge** /bʌldʒ/, *n., v.,* **bulged, bulging.** *–n.* **1.** a rounded projecting or protruding part; protuberance; hump. **2.** *Obs. Naut.* the bilge, or bottom of a ship's hull. *–v.i.* **3.** to swell out; be protuberant. *–v.t.* **4.** to make protuberant. [ME, from OF *boulge,* from L *bulga* bag, of Celtic orig.] – **bulgy,** *adj.*

**bulger** /ˈbʌldʒə/, *n. Golf.* a club with a convex face.

**bulimia** /bjuˈlɪmiə/, *n.* morbidly voracious appetite; a disease marked by constant hunger. Also, **bulimy** /ˈbjuləmi/. [NL, from Gk *boulimía* great hunger] – **bulimic,** *adj.*

**bulk** /bʌlk/, *n.* **1.** magnitude in three dimensions: *a ship of great bulk.* **2.** the greater part; the main mass or body: *the bulk of a debt.* **3.** goods or cargo not in packages, boxes, bags, etc. **4.** the thickness of a printed work or paper relative to its weight. **5. in bulk, a.** unpackaged. **b.** in large quantities. **6.** *Rare.* the body of any large living creature. *–v.i.* **7.** to be of bulk, size, weight, or importance. *–adj.* **8.** packaged to be bought in large quantities at wholesale prices. [ME *bolke* heap, from Scand.; cf. Icel. *būlki* heap, cargo]

**bulkbill** /bʌlkˈbɪl/, *v.i.* (of a doctor) to make a consolidated claim on a central agency, such as Medibank, for payment for services given to many patients. – **bulkbilling,** *n.*

**bulk carrier** /bʌlk ˈkæriə/, *n.* a ship designed for the carriage of cargo in bulk.

**bulk classing** /– ˈklasɪŋ/, *n.* the bulking together and rebaling into larger lines under another brand, of different brands and descriptions of fleece wools of similar type and yield.

**bulkhead** /ˈbʌlkhɛd/, *n.* **1.** *Naut.* one of the upright partitions dividing a ship into compartments. **2.** a partition built to withstand pressure, as between the airlock and the cabin of a submarine or spacecraft. **3.** *Civ. Eng.* a partition built in a subterranean passage to prevent the passage of air, water, or mud. **4.** *Bldg Trades.* **a.** a horizontal or inclined outside door over a stairway leading to a cellar. **b.** a boxlike structure on a roof, etc., covering the head of a staircase or other opening.

**bulk modulus** /bʌlk ˈmɒdʒələs/, *n. Physics.* elastic modulus as applied to a body having uniform stress distributed over the whole of its surface.

**bulk wine** /– ˈwaɪn/, *n.* wine bought in bulk.

**bulky** /ˈbʌlki/, *adj.* **bulkier, bulkiest. 1.** of great and cumbersome bulk or size. **2.** of or pertaining to a well-nourished wool of substance, length and density. – **bulkily,** *adv.* – **bulkiness,** *n.*

**bull**[1] /bʊl/, *n.* **1.** the male of a bovine animal, esp. of the genus *Bos,* with sexual organs intact and capable of reproduction. **2.** the male of certain other animals: *a bull elephant.* **3.** a violent or powerful, bull-like person. **4.** (in general business) one who believes that conditions are or will be favourable. **5.** *Stock Exchange.* one who buys in the hope of selling later at a profit due to a rise in prices (opposed to *bear*). **6.** (*cap.*) the zodiacal constellation or sign Taurus. **7.** *Mil. Colloq.* the polishing and cleaning of equipment. **8.** *Colloq.* a police officer. **9. bull at a gate,** an impatient and headstrong person. **10. bull in a china shop,** an inept or clumsy person in a situation requiring care or tact. *–adj.* **11.** male. **12.** bull-like; large. **13.** (in the stock exchange, etc.) pertaining to the bulls; marked by a rise in price. **14.** *Naut.* (of a hull form) of high block coefficient, with blunt bow and stern (opposed to *fine*). *–v.t.* **15.** *Colloq.* to have intercourse with (a woman). **16.** (in the stock exchange, etc.) to endeavour to raise the price of (stocks, etc.). **17.** to operate in, for a rise in price. [ME *bule,* OE *bula;* also ME *bulle,* OE *bull-* in *bulluc* bull calf. Cf. Icel. *boli*]

**bull**[2] /bʊl/, *n. Convict Obs. Colloq.* a flogging of seventy-five lashes. [from obs. Brit. slang *bull* a crown piece or five shillings. See TESTER[3], BOB[4], CANARY[2]]

**bull**[3] /bʊl/, *n.* **1.** a bulla or seal. **2.** *Rom. Cath. Ch.* a formal papal document having a bulla attached. [ME *bulle,* from ML *bulla* seal, document, from L: bubble, knob]

**bull**[4] /bʊl/, *n.* **1.** →**bullseye** (def. 1). **2.** →**bullseye** (def. 2). **3.** the score-value of a bull's-eye: *he scored a bull.*

**bull**[5] /bʊl/, *Colloq. –n.* **1.** nonsense. **2.** trivial or boastful talk. *–v.t.* **3.** to deceive; dupe. *–v.i.* **4.** to boast; exaggerate. *–interj.* **5.** Also, **bulls.** (an exclamation implying that what has been said is nonsensical or wrong.) [shortened form of BULLSHIT]

**bull.,** bulletin.

**bulla** /ˈbʊlə, ˈbʌlə/, *n., pl.* **bullae** /ˈbʊli, ˈbʌli/. **1.** a seal attached to an official document, as a papal bull. **2.** *Pathol.* **a.** a large vesicle. **b.** a blister-like or bubble-like part of a bone. [ML. See BULL[3]]

**bull-a-bull** /ˈbʊl-ə-bʊl/, *n.* →**poroporo.**

**Bullamakanka** /bʊləməˈkæŋkə/, *n.* an imaginary remote town.

**bull ant** /ˈbʊl ænt/, *n.* any of the large, aggressive, primitive ants of the genus *Myrmecia* having powerful jaws and a most painful sting. Also, **bulldog ant.**

bull ant

**bull artist** /ˈ– atəst/, *n. Colloq.* one notorious for his excessive talk which is usu. boastful, exaggerated and unreliable. Also, **bullshit artist.**

**bullate** /ˈbʊleɪt, -ət, ˈbʌl-/, *adj.* **1.** *Bot., Zool.* having the surface covered with irregular and slight elevations, giving a blistered appearance. **2.** *Anat.* inflated; vaulted. [L *bullātus* having bubbles]

**bull-bar** /ˈbʊl-ba/, *n.* a metal grid placed in front of a car to prevent damage to the vehicle in case of collision, esp. with kangaroos, stray cattle, etc., on outback roads.

bull-bar

**bullbat** /ˈbʊlbæt/, *n.* →**nighthawk** (def. 2).

**bull burn** /ˈbʊl bɜn/, *n.* (of cattle) coital exanthema.

**bull car** /ˈbʊl ka/, *n. Colloq.* a police car.

**bulldog** /ˈbʊldɒg/, *n.* **1.** a large-headed, short-haired, heavily built variety of dog, of comparatively small size but very muscular and vigorous. **2.** a short-barrelled revolver of large calibre. **3.** in certain universities, an assistant to the proctor in his disciplinary duties. **4.** *Colloq.* an invigilator.

bulldog

**bulldog ant** /ˈ– ænt/, *n.* →**bull ant.**

**bulldog clip** /ˈ– klɪp/, *n.* a type of spring-operated clip, originally having teeth-like serrations to hold papers, etc.

**bulldogging** /ˈbʊldɒgɪŋ/, *n.* the throwing of a steer by hanging onto its horns and twisting its neck until the steer collapses. – **bulldogger,** *n.* – **bulldogging,** *adj.*

**bulldoze** /ˈbʊldoʊz/, *v.t.,* **-dozed, -dozing. 1.** to use a bulldozer on. **2.** *Colloq.* to put pressure on; to coerce or intimidate, often with violence or threats. **3.** *Colloq.* to push legislation, a motion, etc., through the process of a parliament, meeting, etc., with undue haste. [BULL[1] + *doze* (southern U.S. d. var. of DOSE), i.e., give a dose fit for a bull]

**bulldozer** /ˈbʊldoʊzə/, *n.* **1.** a powerful caterpillar tractor having a vertical blade at the front end for moving earth, tree stumps, rocks, etc. **2.** *Colloq.* a person who intimidates.

**bulldust** /ˈbʊldʌst/, *n. Colloq.* **1.** fine dust on outback roads. **2.** →**bullshit** (def. 2). *–v.i.* **3.** to boast, to exaggerate.

**bullet** /ˈbʊlət/, *n.* **1.** a small metal projectile, part of a cartridge, for firing from small arms. **2.** a small ball. **3.** *Colloq.* a recording which is moving rapidly up the popularity chart. **4.** *Colloq.* the symbol placed beside the name of such a recording on the charts. **5.** *Colloq.* dismissal from employment: *to get the bullet.* **6. bite the bullet,** *Colloq.* to face up bravely; resign oneself to an unavoidable ordeal. [F *boulet(ti)*, diminutive of *boule* ball]

**bullet-head** /'bʊlət-hɛd/, *n.* **1.** a round head. **2.** a person having such a head. **3.** an obstinate or stupid person. – **bullet-headed,** *adj.*

**bulletin** /'bʊlətən/, *n.* **1.** a brief account or statement, as of news or events, issued for the information of the public. **2.** a periodical publication, as of a learned society. *–v.t.* **3.** to make known by a bulletin. [F, from It. *bullettino,* diminutive of *bulletta,* diminutive of *bulla* edict. See BULL[3], BULLA]

**bulletin board** /'– bɔd/, *n. U.S.* →**noticeboard.**

**bulletproof** /'bʊlətpruf/, *adj.* capable of resisting the impact of a bullet.

**bull fiddle** /bʊl 'fɪdl/, *n. Colloq.* a double-bass or a bass-viol.

**bullfight** /'bʊlfaɪt/, *n.* a combat between men and a bull or bulls in an enclosed arena. – **bullfighter,** *n.* – **bullfighting,** *n.*

**bullfinch** /'bʊlfɪntʃ/, *n.* **1.** a rosy-breasted European fringilline bird, *Pyrrhula pyrrhula,* with a short, stout bill, valued as a cagebird. **2.** any of various allied or similar birds. [BULL[1] + FINCH]

**bullfrog** /'bʊlfrɒg/, *n.* any of various large, loud-voiced frogs, as the Australian marsh frog, *Limnodynastes dorsalis,* or the American *Rana catesbeiana.*

**bullhead** /'bʊlhɛd/, *n.* **1.** a small freshwater fish, *Cottus gobio,* having a number of strong spines, but devoid of scales. **2.** an obstinate or stupid person.

**bull-headed** /bʊl-'hɛdəd/, *adj.* **1.** obstinate; blunderingly stubborn; stupid. *–adv.* **2.** obstinately. **3. go bull-headed at,** to act aggressively, blunderingly.

**bullhorn** /'bʊlhɔn/, *n.* →**loudhailer.**

**bullion** /'bʊljən/, *n.* **1.** gold or silver in the mass. **2.** gold or silver in the form of bars or ingots. **3.** a cordlike trimming made of twisted gold or silver wire, or a trimming of cord covered with gold or silver thread (**bullion fringe**), used to ornament uniforms, etc. [ME *bullioun,* from AF *bullion* mint, from *bouillir* boil, from L *bullīre;* in part confused with OF *billon* debased metal]

**bullish** /'bʊlɪʃ/, *adj.* **1.** like a bull. **2.** obstinate or stupid. **3.** (in the stock exchange, etc.) tending to cause a rise in price. **4.** optimistic.

**bull Joe** /'bʊl dʒoʊ/, *n. Colloq.* →**bull ant.**

**bull market** /'bʊl makət/, *n. Stock Exchange.* a buoyant period of trading during and immediately after a rise in share prices when traders consider that there are strong prospects of further price rises.

**bull-mastiff** /bʊl-'mæstɪf/, *n.* one of a breed of dogs produced by crossing the mastiff with the bulldog.

**bull-necked** /'bʊl-nɛkt/, *adj.* thick-necked.

**bull nose** /'bʊl noʊz/, *n.* **1.** *Vet. Sci.* a disease of pigs caused by bacterial infection of the tissues of the snout causing gross malformation of the part and frequently serious blocking of the nasal passages. **2.** a brick having one corner rounded off.

**bullo** /'bʊloʊ/, *n. Colloq.* nonsense; rubbish. [BULL[5] + -O]

**bull oak** /'bʊl oʊk/, *n.* a tree of inland areas of eastern Australia, *Casuarina luehmannii.*

**bullock** /'bʊlək/, *n.* **1.** a castrated male of a bovine animal, not having been used for reproduction; ox; steer. *–v.t.* **2.** to force: *to bullock one's way through.* *–v.i.* **3.** to work strenuously. [ME *bullok,* OE *bulluc.* See BULL[1], -OCK]

**bullock dray** /'– dreɪ/, *n.* a dray formerly used for the transport of heavy loads, as wool, mining machinery, etc., and drawn by a team of bullocks. Also, **bullock wagon.**

bullock team

**bullocker** /'bʊləkə/, *n.* the driver of a bullock team.

**bullock-puncher** /'bʊlək-pʌntʃə/, *n.* the driver of a bullock team. Also, **bull-puncher.**

**bullocky** /'bʊləki/, *n.* **1.** the driver of a bullock team. **2.** violent language. *–adj.* **3.** squat, built like a bullock.

**bullocky's joy** /,bʊləkiz 'dʒɔɪ/, *n. Colloq.* golden syrup; treacle. Also, **cocky's joy.**

**bullpen** /'bʊlpɛn/, *n.* **1.** a pen for a bull or bulls. **2.** *U.S. Colloq.* a place for the temporary confinement of prisoners or suspects.

**bull-puncher** /'bʊl-pʌntʃə/, *n.* →**bullock-puncher.**

**bullring** /'bʊlrɪŋ/, *n.* an arena for a bullfight.

**bullroarer** /'bʊlrɔrə/, *n.* a long, thin, narrow piece of wood attached to a string, by which it is whirled in the air, making a roaring sound, used for religious rites by certain primitive tribes, as Australian Aborigines, American Indians, etc., and as a children's toy; thunder stick; churinga.

**bullrout** /'bʊlraʊt/, *n.* an Australian heavy-bodied scorpaenid fish, *Notesthes robusta,* having poison spines in front of the gill covers.

**bullseye** /'bʊlzaɪ/, *n.* **1.** the central spot, usu. black, of a target. **2.** a shot that strikes the bullseye. **3.** a small circular opening or window. **4.** a thick disc or lenslike piece of glass inserted in a deck or the like to admit light. **5.** the central boss in a sheet of blown glass. **6.** *Naut.* an oval or circular wooden block having a groove around it and a hole in the centre through which to reeve a rope. **7.** a big, round, hard sweet, often of peppermint. **8.** a reddish-pink, large-eyed, marine fish of the family Priacanthidae common along the eastern coast of Australia.

**bullsh** /bʊlʃ/, *n.* →**bullshit** (def. 2). Also, **bulsh.**

**bullshit** /'bʊlʃɪt/, *n.* **1.** the excrement of bulls. **2.** *Colloq.* nonsense. *–v.t.* **3.** *Colloq.* to deceive; outwit. *–v.i.* **4.** *Colloq.* to deceive. *–interj.* **5.** *Colloq.* (an expression of disgust, disbelief, etc.).

**bullshit artist** /'– ,atəst/, *n. Colloq.* →**bull artist.**

**bullswool** /'bʊlzwʊl/, *n.* **1.** the fibrous inner bark of certain stringybark trees. **2.** *Colloq.* nonsense. *–interj.* **3.** (an exclamation of disbelief, disgust etc.).

**bull-terrier** /bʊl-'tɛriə/, *n.* one of a breed of dogs produced by crossing the bulldog and the terrier.

bull-terrier

**bull-trout** /'bʊl-traʊt/, *n.* **1.** the sea-trout. **2.** any large trout. **3.** the salmon.

**bully**[1] /'bʊli/, *n., pl.* **-lies,** *v.,* **-lied, -lying,** *adj., interj.* *–n.* **1.** a blustering, quarrelsome, overbearing person who brow-beats smaller or weaker people. **2.** *Archaic.* a man hired to do violence. **3.** *Obs.* a pimp; procurer. **4.** *Obs.* good friend; good fellow. **5.** *Obs.* sweetheart; darling. *–v.t.* **6.** to act the bully towards. *–v.i.* **7.** to be loudly arrogant and overbearing. *–adj.* **8.** *Colloq.* fine; excellent; very good. **9.** dashing; jovial; high-spirited. *–interj.* **10.** *Colloq.* good! well done! [D *boele* lover]

**bully**[2] /'bʊli/, *n.* bully beef. [? F *bouilli* boiled beef, properly pp. of *bouillir* boil]

**bully**[3] /'bʊli/, *n. Hockey.* **1.** the procedure by which play is started or restarted. Two opposing players with the ball between them strike the ground and the opponent's stick alternately three times, and then try to strike the ball first. *–v.i.* **2.** Also, **bully off.** to start play in this way.

**bully beef** /'bʊli bif/, *n. Colloq.* corned beef.

**bully mullet** /'– mʌlət/, *n.* a mature mullet, more than 20 cm in length; sea mullet.

**bullyrag** /'bʊliræg/, *v.t.,* **-ragged, -ragging.** to bully; badger; abuse; tease. Also, **ballyrag.**

**bully tree** /'bʊli tri/, *n.* any of various sapotaceous trees of tropical America, as *Manilkara bidentata* of Guiana, which yields the gum balata. [*bully,* said to be from BALATA]

**buln-buln** /'bʊln-bʊln/, *n.* **1.** →**ringneck parrot. 2.** →**lyre-bird.** Also, **bullen-bullen.** [Aboriginal, probably imitative]

**bulrush** /'bʊlrʌʃ/, *n.* **1.** →**cumbungi. 2.** (in biblical use) the papyrus, *Cyperus papyrus.* **3.** any of various large rushes or rushlike plants of the genus *Scirpus,* as *S. lacustris,* a tall perennial from which mats, bottoms of chairs, etc. are made.

Also, **bull-rush.** [*bull* large (cf. BULL-TROUT) + RUSH[2]]

**bulwark** /'bʊlwək/, *n.* **1.** *Fort.* a defensive mound of earth or other material situated round a place; a rampart. **2.** any protection against annoyance or injury from outside. **3.** (*usu. pl.*) *Naut.* a solid part of a ship's side extending like a fence above the level of the deck. *–v.t.* **4.** to fortify with a bulwark or rampart; secure by a fortification; protect. [ME *bulwerk.* Cf. G *Bollwerk,* apparently orig. bole (tree trunk) work. Cf. BOULEVARD]

**bum** /bʌm/, *n. v.,* **bummed, bumming.** *–n.* **1.** the rump; buttocks. **2.** a shiftless or dissolute person. **3.** a habitual loafer and tramp. **4. (go) bite your bum,** *Colloq.* (an impolite dismissal indicating the speaker's wish to end the conversation). *–v.t.* **5.** *Colloq.* to get for nothing; borrow without expectation of returning: *to bum a cigarette.* **6. bum a ride,** to appeal successfully for a free ride in a car, plane, etc. *–v.i.* **7.** *Colloq.* to sponge on others for a living; lead an idle or dissolute life. *–adj.* **8.** *Colloq.* of poor, wretched, or miserable quality; bad. **9.** (of a musical note) out of tune; badly executed. [akin to BUMP]

**bumbailiff** /bʌm'beɪlɪf/, *n. Archaic.* (derog.) a bailiff or underbailiff employed in serving writs, making arrests, etc.

**bumble** /'bʌmbəl/, *v.,* **bumbled, bumbling.** *Colloq.* *–v.i.* **1.** to proceed clumsily or inefficiently: *to bumble along.* *–v.t.* **2.** to mismanage: *the government bumbled its way through crisis after crisis.*

**bumblebee** /'bʌmbəlbi/, *n.* **1.** any of various large, hairy social bees of the family Bombidae. Also, **humblebee. 2.** an Australian gobiid fish, *Lindemanella iota.* [*bumble* BUZZ + BEE[1]]

bumblebee: worker

**bumbledom** /'bʌmbəldəm/, *n.* a petty officiousness in a minor office. [after *Bumble* in Dickens's *Oliver Twist*]

**bumble foot** /'bʌmbəl fʊt/, *n.* a swelling on the feet of turkeys and fowls where the infection *Staphylococcus aureus* enters through an abrasion.

**bumble footed** /– 'fʊtəd/, *adj.* clumsy; inept.

**bumble puppy** /'– pʌpi/, *n.* **1.** a bat with ball attached, usu. by elastic so that when the ball is hit, it returns to the bat. **2.** a game in which a ball attached by elastic to a pole is hit from either side of the pole by two players so that the ball winds up or down the pole; tether tennis.

**bumboat** /'bʌmboʊt/, *n. Naut.* a boat used in peddling provisions and small wares among vessels lying in port or offshore. – **bumboatman** /'bʌmboʊtmən/, *n.*

**bumboy** /'bʌmbɔɪ/, *n. Colloq.* (*derog.*) a follower or employee who is obsequious and servile.

**bumf** /bʌmf/, *n.* →**bum fodder** (def. 2). Also, **bumph.**

**bumfluff** /'bʌmflʌf/, *n. Colloq.* light hair growing on the face of an adolescent male.

**bum fodder** /'bʌm fɒdə/, *n. Colloq.* **1.** toilet paper. **2.** (*derog.*) written or printed matter judged suitable only for toilet paper.

**bumfreezer** /'bʌmfrizə/, *n. Chiefly Brit. Colloq.* a short coat.

**bumkin** /'bʌmkən/, *n. Naut.* →**bumpkin**[2].

**bummalo** /'bʌməloʊ/, *n.* →**Bombay duck.** [Marathi *bombīla*]

**bummer** /'bʌmə/, *n. Colloq.* **1.** a fiasco; failure; disappointment. **2.** a sodomite.

**bump** /bʌmp/, *v.t.* **1.** to come more or less heavily in contact with; strike; collide with. **2.** to cause to strike or collide: *to bump one's head against the wall.* **3.** *Colloq.* to increase (in extent, etc.) (fol. by *up*). **4.** *Brit. Rowing.* to beat in a race by making a successful bump on. **5.** *Cricket.* to bowl (the ball) in such a way that it bounces high on pitching. **6.** *Aus. Rules.* to use the hip or shoulder to harass the player in possession of the ball. **7. bump off,** *Colloq.* to kill. *–v.i.* **8. a.** to come in contact with; collide (oft. fol by *against, into*). **b.** to meet by chance (fol. by *into*). **9.** to jolt in the course of movement (oft. fol. by *about*). **10.** *Brit. Rowing.* to make a successful bump. **11.** *Cricket.* (of the ball) to bounce high on pitching when bowled. *–n.* **12.** the act of bumping; a blow. **13.** a dull thud; the noise of collision. **14.** the shock of a blow or collision. **15.** a swelling or contusion from a blow. **16.** a small area raised above the level of the surrounding surface, as on the skull or on a road. **17.** *Aeron.* a rapidly rising current of air which gives an aeroplane a dangerous jolt or upward thrust. [imitative]

**bump ball** /– 'bɔl/, *n. Cricket.* a ball which strikes the ground immediately after being struck by the batsman, and which therefore does not put him out if it is caught.

**bump cap** /'– kæp/, *n. Colloq.* →**safety helmet.**

**bumper** /'bʌmpə/, *n.* **1.** a person or thing that bumps. **2.** →**bumper bar. 3.** a cup or glass filled to the brim, esp. when drunk as a toast. **4.** *Colloq.* something unusually large or full. **5.** *Colloq.* a cigarette end; a discarded cigarette, partly smoked. **6.** *Colloq.* a pickpocket's accomplice. **7.** *Bowls.* a bowl which is bounced on to the green by a player who fails to bend low enough over the mat. **8. not worth a bumper,** worthless. *–adj.* **9.** unusually abundant: *bumper crops.* **10.** *Cricket.* a ball which is so bowled that it bounces high when it pitches; bouncer. *–v.t.* **11.** to fill to the brim. **12.** to drink a bumper as a toast to. *–v.i.* **13.** to drink toasts.

**bumper bar** /'– ba/, *n.* a horizontal bar affixed to the front or rear of a vehicle to give some protection in collisions.

**bumper sticker** /'– stɪkə/, *n.* a long, thin sticker (def. 2) designed to be affixed to a bumper bar.

**bumper-to-bumper** /,bʌmpə-tə-'bʌmpə/, *adj. Colloq.* (of traffic) dense, and moving slowly. – **bumper-to-bumper,** *adv.*

**bumping race** /'bʌmpɪŋ reɪs/, *n. Brit.* a boatrace in which the object is to catch up and bump the boat in front.

**bumpkin**[1] /'bʌmpkən/, *n.* an awkward, clumsy yokel. [MD *bommekyn* little barrel]

**bumpkin**[2] /'bʌmpkən/, *n. Naut.* a beam or spar projecting outwards from the bow, side, or stern of a ship to extend a sail, secure blocks, or the like. Also, **bumkin.** [MD *boomken* little tree]

**bumpology** /bʌmp'ɒlədʒi/, *n. Colloq.* →**phrenology.**

**bumptious** /'bʌmpʃəs/, *adj.* offensively self-assertive: *he's a bumptious young upstart.* [BUMP + *-tious,* modelled on FRACTIOUS, etc.] – **bumptiously,** *adv.* – **bumptiousness,** *n.*

**bumpy** /'bʌmpi/, *adj.* **bumpier, bumpiest. 1.** of uneven surface: *a bumpy road.* **2.** full of jolts: *a bumpy ride.* **3.** giving rise to jolts: *bumpy air.* – **bumpily,** *adv.* – **bumpiness,** *n.*

**bum's rush** /bʌmz 'rʌʃ/, *n.* **1.** the peremptory dismissal or bodily removal of an unwanted person. **2.** the peremptory rejection of an idea or proposal.

**bum steer** /bʌm 'stɪə/, *n.* incorrect information or advice.

**bun** /bʌn/, *n.* **1.** a kind of bread roll, usu. slightly sweetened and round-shaped, and sometimes containing spice, dried currants, citron, etc. **2.** hair arranged at the back of the head in a bun shape. **3. do one's bun,** *N.Z. Colloq.* to lose one's temper. **4. have a bun in the oven,** *Colloq.* to be pregnant. [ME *bunne*; orig. uncert.]

**buna** /'bunə, 'bjunə/, *n.* **1.** any synthetic rubber made by copolymerising butadiene with other material. **2.** (originally) a synthetic rubber made by polymerising butadiene by means of styrene. [BU(TADIENE) + NA (the symbol for sodium)]

**bunce** /bʌns/, *n. Colloq.* **1.** profit, esp. unexpected. **2.** a share or commission. [orig. obscure]

**bunch** /bʌntʃ/, *n.* **1.** a connected group; cluster: *a bunch of bananas.* **2.** a group of things; lot: *a bunch of papers.* **3.** *Colloq.* a group of human beings: *a fine bunch of boys.* **4.** a knob; lump; protuberance. *–v.t.* **5.** to group together; make a bunch of. *–v.i.* **6.** to gather into a cluster or protuberance; gather together. [ME *bunche;* orig. uncert.]

**buncher resonator** /bʌntʃə 'rɛzəneɪtə/, *n.* →**klystron.**

**bunches** /'bʌntʃəz/, *n.pl.* a woman's hairstyle in which the hair is divided into two sections, is tied tight to the scalp, and falls loose below the ties.

**bunch of fives,** *n. Colloq.* the fist.

**bunchy** /'bʌntʃi/, *adj.,* **bunchier, bunchiest. 1.** having bunches. **2.** bulging or protuberant.

**buncombe** /'bʌŋkəm/, *n. U.S.* →**bunkum.**

**bund** /bʌnd/, *n.* (in India, China, Japan, etc.) an embankment; an embanked quay. [Hind. *band*]

**Bundaberg honey** /,bʌndəbɜg 'hʌni/, *n. Colloq.* →**golden syrup.**

**bundle** /'bʌndl/, *n., v.,* **-dled, -dling.** *–n.* **1.** a group loosely held together: *a bundle of hay.* **2.** something wrapped for carrying; package. **3.** a number of things considered together. **4.** *Biol.* an aggregation of strands of specialised conductive and mechanical tissue. **5.** *Brit. Textiles.* a measure of cloth, equal to 60 000 yards of linen yarn, or 20 hanks of cotton cloth. **6. drop a bundle,** *Colloq.* to give birth. **7. drop one's bundle,** *Colloq.* to give up, esp. out of a sense of despair or inadequacy. *–v.t.* **8.** to dress snugly (fol. by *up*). **9.** to send away hurriedly or unceremoniously (fol. by *off, out,* etc.). **10.** to tie or wrap in a bundle. *–v.i.* **11.** to leave hurriedly or unceremoniously (fol. by *off, out,* etc.) **12.** to dress warmly (fol. by *up*). **13.** to sleep or lie in the same bed without undressing, esp. of sweethearts, as formerly in Wales, New England (U.S.), and elsewhere. [ME *bundel,* from MD, c. G *Bündel;* akin to OE *byndele* binding together] – **bundler,** *n.*

**bundy**[1] /ˈbʌndi/, *n. Colloq.* **1.** a clock which marks the time on a card inserted in it, used to record arrival and departure times of employees; time clock. **2.** a clock used to regulate the punctuality of bus services, etc. **3. punch the bundy,** *Colloq.* to begin work. [Trademark]

**bundy**[2] /ˈbʌndi/, *n.* any of several species of *Eucalyptus.*

**bunfight** /ˈbʌnfaɪt/, *n. Colloq.* any noisy or disorganised gathering of people, as at a crowded party. Also, **bun fight.**

**bung** /bʌŋ/, *n.* **1.** a stopper, as for the hole of a cask. **2.** a bunghole. **3.** *Colloq.* a memo to an employee, esp. of a government department, calling him to account for a break of regulations on his part. *–v.t.* **4.** to close with or as a bung (oft. fol. by *up*). **5.** *Colloq.* to put: *bung it in the cupboard.* **6.** *Colloq.* to toss to another person; throw. **7. bung on,** *Colloq.* **a.** stage; put on: *bung on airs and graces.* **b.** to prepare or arrange, esp. at short notice: *we'll bung on a party.* **8. bung it on,** to behave temperamentally. *–adj.* **9.** *Colloq.* not in good working order; impaired; injured. **10. go bung,** *Colloq.* **a.** to break down; cease to function. **b.** to fail; become bankrupt. [ME *bunge,* from MD *bonghe*]

**bungalow** /ˈbʌŋgəloʊ/, *n.* **1.** a house or cottage of one storey. **2.** (in India) a house, usu. surrounded by a verandah. [Hind. *banglā,* lit., of Bengal]

**bunger** /ˈbʌŋə/, *n.* **1.** a firework which produces a loud bang. **2.** *N.Z.* →**ponga.**

**bunghole** /ˈbʌŋhoʊl/, *n.* **1.** a hole or orifice in a cask through which it is filled. **2.** *Colloq.* cheese.

**bungie** /ˈbʌŋi/, *n. N.Z.* →**ponga.**

**bungle** /ˈbʌŋgəl/, *v.,* **-gled, -gling,** *n. –v.i.* **1.** to do something awkwardly and clumsily. *–v.t.* **2.** to do clumsily and awkwardly; botch. *–n.* **3.** a bungling performance. **4.** a bungled job. [? imitative] – **bungler,** *n.* – **bunglingly,** *adv.*

**bungum worm** /ˈbʌŋəm wɜm/, *n. S.A. Colloq.* →**slimy.**

**bungy** /ˈbʌŋgi/, *v.t.* to launch a glider by catapult from the top of a hill; bungy launch. Also, **bungee.**

**bungy launch** /ˈ– lɔntʃ/, *n. Gliding.* a method of launching a glider by catapult from the top of a hill. Also, **bungee launch.**

**bun hat** /ˈbʌn hæt/, *n. N.Z. Colloq.* a bowler hat.

**bunion** /ˈbʌnjən/, *n.* a swelling on the foot caused by the inflammation of a synovial bursa, esp. of the great toe. [orig. obscure]

**bunk**[1] /bʌŋk/, *n.* **1.** a built-in platform bed, as on a ship. **2.** *Colloq.* any bed. *–v.i.* **3.** *Colloq.* to occupy a bunk; sleep, esp. in rough quarters. [orig. unknown]

**bunk**[2] /bʌŋk/, *n. Colloq.* humbug; nonsense. [short for BUNKUM]

**bunk**[3] /bʌŋk/, *n. in the phrase* **do a bunk,** to run away; take flight.

**bunker**[1] /ˈbʌŋkə/, *n.* **1.** a chest or box; a large bin or receptacle: *a coal bunker.* **2.** *Golf.* a shallow excavation, usu. at the side of a green, which has been nearly filled with sand and which serves as a hazard. *–v.t.* **3.** *Golf.* **a.** to drive (a ball) into a bunker. **b.** to impede or trap (as in a sand trap). **4.** to obtain fuel for (a ship). *–v.i.* **5.** (of a ship) to refuel. [orig. uncert.]

**bunker**[2] /ˈbʌŋkə/, *n.* a bombproof shelter, often underground. [G]

**bunkering** /ˈbʌŋkərɪŋ/, *n.* refuelling, as of vessels or vehicles, esp. with heavy fuels.

**bunkhouse** /ˈbʌŋkhaʊs/, *n.* a rough building used for sleeping quarters.

**bunkum** /ˈbʌŋkəm/, *n.* **1.** insincere talk; claptrap; humbug. **2.** *Chiefly U.S.* insincere speechmaking intended merely to please political constituents. Also, *U.S.,* **buncombe.** [alteration of *Buncombe,* a county in the U.S., in North Carolina, from its Congressional representative's phrase, 'talking for Buncombe']

**bunny** /ˈbʌni/, *n., pl.* **-nies.** *Colloq.* **1.** a rabbit. **2.** a fool. **3.** one who accepts the responsibility for a situation, sometimes willingly: *to be the bunny.* **4.** →**bunny girl.** **5.** *U.S.* a squirrel.

**bunny club** /ˈ– klʌb/, *n.* a night club in which the hostesses wear a costume with simulated rabbit's ears and tail.

**bunny girl** /ˈ– gɜl/, *n.* a hostess in a bunny club.

**bunny-rug** /ˈbʌni-rʌg/, *n.* a baby's blanket.

**bun rush** /ˈbʌn rʌʃ/, *n.* the movement of a disorganised crowd of people, all attempting to do something at the same time.

**Bunsen burner** /bʌnsən ˈbɜnə/, *n.* a type of gas burner with which a very hot, practically non-luminous flame is obtained by allowing air to enter at the base and mix with the gas. [named after R. W. *Bunsen,* 1811-99, German chemist]

**bunt**[1] /bʌnt/, *v.t.* **1.** to push (something) with the horns or head. **2.** *Baseball.* to bat a ball with a half swing so that the ball rolls slowly in front of the infielders. *–v.i.* **3.** (of a goat or calf) to push with the horns or head. **4.** *Baseball.* to bunt a ball. *–n.* **5.** a push with the head or horns; butt. **6.** *Baseball.* **a.** the act of bunting. **b.** a bunted ball. [nasalised var. of BUTT[3]]

**bunt**[2] /bʌnt/, *n.* **1.** *Naut.* the middle part of a square sail. **2.** the bagging part of a fishing net or the like. [orig. unknown]

**bunt**[3] /bʌnt/, *n.* a disease of wheat in which the kernels are replaced by black fungus spores. [orig. unknown]

**bunting**[1] /ˈbʌntɪŋ/, *n.* **1.** a coarse open fabric of worsted or cotton used for flags, signals. **2.** flags, esp. a vessel's flags, collectively. **3.** festive decorations made from bunting, paper etc., usu. in the form of draperies, wide streamers, etc. [cf. G *bunt* particoloured]

**bunting**[2] /ˈbʌntɪŋ/, *n.* any of numerous small fringilline birds of the genera *Emberiza, Passerina,* and *Plectrophenax* as, respectively, the **reed bunting** (*E. shoeniclus*) of Europe, the **indigo bunting** (*P. cyanea*) of the U.S. and Canada, and the **snow bunting** (*P. nivalis*) of arctic regions. [ME *bountyng;* orig. uncert.]

**buntline** /ˈbʌntlən, -laɪn/, *n. Naut.* one of the ropes attached to the foot of a square sail to haul it up to the yard for furling. [BUNT[2] + LINE[1]]

**bun wagon** /ˈbʌn wægən/, *n. Colloq.* →**black maria.**

**bunya-bunya** /ˈbʌnjə-bʌnjə/, *n.* a tall, dome-shaped coniferous tree of Australia, *Araucaria bidwilli,* bearing edible seeds. [Aboriginal]

**bunyip** /ˈbʌnjəp/, *n.* **1.** an imaginary creature of Aboriginal legend, said to haunt rushy swamps and billabongs. **2.** an imposter. [Aboriginal]

**bunyip aristocracy** /– ærəsˈtɒkrəsi/, *n.* (*derog.*) Australians who consider themselves to be aristocrats. [orig. derogatory title for suggested Australian peerage]

**buoy** /bɔɪ/, *n. Naut.* **1.** a distinctively marked and shaped anchored float, sometimes carrying a light, whistle, or bell, marking a channel or obstruction. **2.** →**life-buoy.** *–v.t.* **3.** to support by or as by a buoy; keep afloat in a fluid. **4.** *Naut.* to furnish or mark with a buoy or buoys: *to buoy or buoy off a channel.* **5.** to bear up or sustain, as hope or courage does. *–v.i.* **6.** to float; rise by reason of lightness. [ME *boye,* from MD *boeie* buoy, from L *boia* fetter]

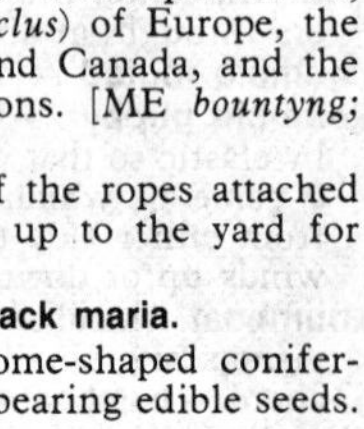


buoys (def. 1): A, light buoy; B, spar buoy; C, mooring buoy

**buoyage** /ˈbɔɪɪdʒ/, *n. Naut.* **1.** a system of buoys. **2.** buoys collectively. **3.** the providing of buoys.

**buoyancy** /ˈbɔɪənsi/, *n.* **1.** the power to float or rise in a fluid; relative lightness. **2.** the power of supporting a body so that it floats; upward pressure exerted by the fluid in which a body is immersed. **3.** elasticity of spirit; cheerfulness.

**buoyant** /ˈbɔɪənt/, *adj.* **1.** tending to float or rise in a fluid. **2.** capable of keeping a body afloat, as a liquid. **3.** not easily depressed; cheerful. **4.** cheering or invigorating. **5.** (of production levels, prices, etc.) having the capacity of recovering from a reverse. – **buoyantly,** *adv.*

i = peat ɪ = pit ɛ = pet æ = pat a = part ɒ = pot ʌ = putt ɔ = port ʊ = put u = pool ɜ = pert ə = apart aɪ = buy eɪ = bay ɔɪ = boy aʊ = how oʊ = hoe ɪə = here ɛə = hair ʊə = tour g = give θ = thin ð = then ʃ = show ʒ = measure tʃ = choke dʒ = joke ŋ = sing j = you õ = Fr. bon

**buprestid** /bju'prɛstəd/, *n.* any beetle of the family Buprestidae, rising the metallic wood-borers, noted for their brilliant colouration. [L *būprestis,* from Gk *boúprēstis,* lit., ox-sweller + -ID[2]]

**bur** /bɜ/, *n., v.,* **burred, burring.** →**burr**[1].

**buran** /bu'ran/, *n.* a violent storm of wind on the steppes of Russia and Siberia, esp. one accompanied by driving snow and intense cold. [Turk.]

**burberry** /'bɜbəri/, *n.* a waterproof gaberdine raincoat. [Trademark]

**burble** /'bɜbəl/, *v.,* **-bled, -bling,** *n.* *–v.t.* **1.** to make a bubbling sound; bubble. **2.** to speak with a burble. *–n.* **3.** a bubbling or gentle gush. **4.** a bubbling flow of speech. **5.** *Aeron.* the breakdown of smooth airflow around a wing at a high angle of incidence. [probably imitative]

**burbot** /'bɜbət/, *n., pl.* **-bots,** (*esp. collectively*) **-bot.** a freshwater fish of the cod family, *Lota lota,* of Europe, Asia, and North America, with an elongated body and a barbel on the lower jaw. [ME *borbot,* from F *borbote* (apparently from L *barba* beard, b. with *borbe* slime)]

**Burdekin plum** /bɜdəkən 'plʌm/, *n.* a tree, *Pleiogynium cerasiferum,* common in tropical Queensland and bearing purplish acid stone fruit.

**burden**[1] /'bɜdn/, *n.* **1.** that which is carried; a load. **2.** that which is borne with difficulty: *burden of responsibilities.* **3.** *Comm.* the duty to discharge an obligation or responsibility: *the burden of a contract.* **4.** that part of the cost of manufacture which is not directly productive; oncost. **5.** *Naut.* **a.** the weight of a ship's cargo. **b.** the carrying capacity of a ship: *a ship of a hundred tonnes burden.* *–v.t.* **6.** to load heavily. **7.** to load oppressively; oppress. Also, *Archaic,* **burthen.** [var. of BURTHEN, OE *byrthen;* akin to BEAR[1]]

**burden**[2] /'bɜdn/, *n.* **1.** something often repeated or much dwelt upon; the principal idea. **2.** *Music.* **a.** the refrain or recurring chorus of a song. **b.** bourdon. [ME *burdoun,* from OF *bourdon* a humming, the drone of a bagpipe, from L *burda* pipe; later associated with BURDEN[1]]

**burden of proof,** *n. Chiefly Law.* **1.** the obligation incumbent in the first place upon the prosecution, to offer evidence which the court or jury could reasonably believe, in support of a contention, failing which the party will lose its case. **2.** the obligation to establish an alleged fact by convincing the tribunal of its probable truth (**the burden of persuasion**).

**burdensome** /'bɜdnsəm/, *adj.* oppressively heavy. Also, *Archaic,* **burthensome.** – **burdensomely,** *adv.* – **burdensomeness,** *n.*

**burdock** /'bɜdɒk/, *n.* a plant of the genus *Arctium* of the family Compositae, esp. *A. lappa,* a coarse, broad-leaved weed with prickly heads or burrs which stick to clothing. [BUR(R)[1] + DOCK[4]]

**bure** /'bʊreɪ/, *n.* **1.** a Fijian native thatched cottage. **2.** a tourist hotel unit designed to resemble a native cottage.

**bureau** /'bjuroʊ, bju'roʊ/, *n., pl.* **-eaus, -eaux** /-oʊz/. **1.** a desk or writing table with drawers for papers. **2.** a division of a government department or independent administrative unit. **3.** an office for giving out information, etc.: *travel bureau.* **4.** a chest of drawers. [F: desk, office, OF *burel* cloth-covered table, kind of woollen cloth, from L *būra,* var. of *burra* long-haired woollen cloth]

**bureaucracy** /bju'rɒkrəsi/, *n., pl.* **-cies.** **1.** government by officials against whom there is inadequate public right of redress. **2.** the body of officials administering bureaus. **3.** excessive multiplication of, and concentration of power in, administrative bureaus; a system characterised by power without responsibility. **4.** excessive governmental red tape and routine. [F *bureaucratie.* See BUREAU, -CRACY]

**bureaucrat** /'bjurəkræt/, *n.* **1.** an official of a bureaucracy. **2.** an official who works by fixed routine without exercising intelligent judgment. – **bureaucratic** /bjurə'krætɪk/, *adj.* – **bureaucratically,** *adv.*

**Burera** /bə'rɛərə/, *n.* an Australian Aboriginal language of the Blyth River, Northern Territory, with about 400 speakers, mostly at Maningrida. Also, **Barera.**

**burette** /bju'rɛt/, *n.* a graduated glass tube, commonly having a stopcock at the bottom, used for accurately measuring, or measuring out, small quantities of liquid. [F: cruet, diminutive of *buire* vessel for wine, etc. Cf. BUCKET]

**burg** /bɜg/, *n.* **1.** *Hist.* a fortified town. **2.** *U.S. Colloq.* a city or town. [var. of BURGH]

**burgee** /'bɜdʒi/, *n. Naut.* **1.** a swallow-tailed flag or pennant, in the merchant service generally bearing the ship's name. **2.** a small flag bearing a particular club's pattern, flown at the masthead of a yacht. [orig. uncert.; ? from *burge* burgeon]

**burgeon** /'bɜdʒən/, *v.i.* **1.** to begin to grow, as a bud; to put forth buds, shoots, as a plant (oft. fol. by *out, forth*). *–v.t.* **2.** to put forth as buds. *–n.* **3.** a bud; a sprout. Also, **bourgeon.** [ME *burjon,* from OF, ? from Gmc]

**burger** /'bɜgə/, *n.* →**hamburger.**

**burgess** /'bɜdʒəs/, *n.* **1.** an inhabitant, esp. a citizen or freeman, of an English borough. **2.** *Hist.* a representative of a borough, corporate town, or university in Parliament. **3.** *U.S. Hist.* a representative in the popular branch of the colonial legislature of Virginia or Maryland. [ME *burgeis,* from OF, from LL *burgēnsis* a citizen. Cf. BOURGEOIS[1]]

**burgh** /'bʌrə/, *n.* a borough (esp. as applied to chartered towns in Scotland). [var. of BOROUGH] – **burghal** /'bɜgəl/, *adj.*

**burgher** /'bɜgə/, *n.* an inhabitant of a borough; a citizen.

**burglar** /'bɜglə/, *n.* one who commits burglary. [cf. Anglo-L *burglātor,* var. of *burgātor,* Latinisation of AF *burgur* burglar, from *burgier* pillage]

**burglar alarm** /'bɜglər əˌlam/, *n.* an electric device which sounds a loud alarm if a building is forcibly entered.

**burglarious** /bɜg'lɛəriəs/, *adj.* pertaining to or involving burglary. – **burglariously,** *adv.*

**burglarise** /'bɜgləraɪz/, *v.t.,* **-rised, -rising.** *U.S.* →**burgle.**

**burglary** /'bɜgləri/, *n., pl.* **-ries.** the felony of breaking into and entering the house of another with intent to commit a felony therein.

**burgle** /'bɜgəl/, *v.,* **-gled, -gling.** *v.t.* **1.** to commit burglary in. *–v.i.* **2.** to commit burglary. [backformation from BURGLAR]

**burgomaster** /'bɜgəˌmastə/, *n.* the chief magistrate of a municipal town in Holland, Flanders, Germany, or Austria. [D *burgemeester,* lit., town master]

**burgonet** /'bɜgəˌnɛt/, *n.* an open helmet usu. with pivoted peak and hinged cheek-pieces. [F *bourguignotte,* from *Bourgogne* Burgundy]

**burgoo** /'bɜgu, bɜ'gu/, *n., pl.* **-goos.** **1.** a thick oatmeal gruel, esp. as eaten by seamen. **2.** *Colloq.* any similar porridge-like food, as prison hominy. Also, **bergoo.** [? Ar. *burghul,* from Pers. *burghul* bruised grain]

**burgrave** /'bɜgreɪv/, *n. German Hist.* **1.** the appointed head of a fortress. **2.** hereditary governor of a castle or town. [G *Burggraf,* from *Burg* castle + *Graf* count]

**burgundy** /'bɜgəndi/, *n., pl.* **-dies.** **1.** wine of many varieties, red and white, mostly still, full, and dry, produced in the Burgundy region of France. **2.** a similar wine made elsewhere. **3.** dull reddish blue (colour).

**burial** /'bɛriəl/, *n.* the act of burying. [BURY + -AL[2] (cf. FUNERAL); replacing ME *buriel,* OE *byrgels* burying place, from pre-E* *burgh-* + *-ils* (var. of *-isl*) suffix; for dropping of *-s* (mistaken for plural sign), cf. RIDDLE, CHERRY]

**burial ground** /'– graʊnd/, *n.* a tract of land for burial of the dead.

**burial mound** /'– maʊnd/, *n.* →**barrow**[2].

**burial society** /'– səsaɪəti/, *n.* an insurance society providing for funeral expenses.

**burier** /'bɛriə/, *n.* one who or that which buries.

**burin** /'bjurən/, *n.* **1.** a tempered steel rod, with a lozenge-shaped point and a rounded handle, used for engraving furrows in metal. **2.** a similar tool used by marble-workers. **3.** an engraver's individual style. **4.** a specialised stone tool used formerly by the Aborigines of eastern New South Wales. [F, probably of Gmc orig.; cf. OHG *bora* gimlet. See BORE[1]] – **burinist,** *n.*

**burke** /bɜk/, *v.t.,* **burked, burking.** **1.** to murder, as by suffocation, so as to leave no or few marks of violence. **2.** to get rid of by some indirect manoeuvre. **3.** to silence or suppress. [from W. *Burke,* hanged at Edinburgh in 1829 for murders of this kind]

**Burkitt's lymphoma** /bɜkəts lɪm'foʊmə/, *n.* a tumour of lymphoid tissue, caused by a virus, and mainly found in children in specific areas of central Africa.

**burl**[1] /bɜl/, *n.* **1.** a small knot or lump in wool, thread, or cloth. **2.** a dome-shaped growth on the trunk of a tree; a wartlike structure sometimes 60 cm across and 30 cm or more in height, sliced to make burlwood veneer. *–v.t.* **3.** to remove burls from (cloth) in finishing. [ME *burle,* from OF *bourle,* from LL *burra* flock of wool] – **burled,** *adj.*

**burl**[2] /bɜl/, *n. Colloq.* **1.** an attempt: *give it a burl.* **2.** a gamble as in two-up: *have a burl.* *–v.i. Colloq.* **3.** to move quickly: *to burl along.* *–v.t.* **4.** *Colloq.* to cause (a coin, etc.) to spin. **5.** *Colloq.* to taunt and jeer at: *to burl the science master.* **6.** *U.S. Timber Industry.* to cause a floating log to rotate rapidly by treading on it. Also, **birl.** [northern Brit. d. *birl* to spin]

**burlap** /ˈbɜlæp/, *n.* hessian; gunny.

**burlesque** /bɜˈlɛsk/, *n., adj., v.,* **-lesqued, -lesquing.** *–n.* **1.** an artistic composition, esp. literary or dramatic, which, for the sake of laughter, vulgarises lofty material or treats ordinary material with mock dignity. **2.** any ludicrous take-off or debasing caricature. **3.** a theatrical or cabaret entertainment featuring coarse, crude, often vulgar comedy and dancing. *–adj.* **4.** involving ludicrous or debasing treatment of a serious subject. **5.** of or pertaining to risqué burlesque. *–v.t.* **6.** to make ridiculous by mocking representation. *–v.i.* **7.** to use caricature. [F, from It. *burlesco,* from *burla* jest, mockery] – **burlesquer,** *n.*

**burley** /ˈbɜli/, *n.* →**berley.**

**burlwood veneer** /ˌbɜlwʊd vəˈnɪə/, *n.* a veneer made from layers sliced from a burl[1] (def. 2).

**burly** /ˈbɜli/, *adj.,* **-lier, -liest.** **1.** great in bodily size; stout; sturdy. **2.** bluff; brusque. [ME *borli, burlich, burli; orig.* uncert.] – **burlily,** *adv.* – **burliness,** *n.*

**Burma** /ˈbɜmə/, *n.* a republic in south-eastern Asia.

**Burmese cat** /bɜmiz ˈkæt/, *n.* one of a breed of cats resembling the Siamese but having deep-brown fur and orange eyes.

**burn**[1] /bɜn/, *v.,* **burnt** or **burned, burning,** *n.* *–v.i.* **1.** to be on fire: *the fuel burns.* **2.** (of a furnace, etc.) to contain fire. **3.** to feel heat or a physiologically identical sensation: *his face burned in the wind.* **4.** to give light: *the lights in the house burn all night.* **5.** to glow like fire. **6.** (in games) to be extremely close to finding a concealed object or guessing an answer. **7.** to feel strong passion: *he was burning with anger.* **8.** *Chem.* to undergo combustion; oxidise. **9.** to become discoloured, tanned, or charred through heat. **10.** *U.S. Colloq.* to be electrocuted in an electric chair. **11. burn ahead,** (of bush fires) to intensify and travel in a manner difficult or impossible to control: *the fire's burning ahead on a wide front.* **12. burn out,** to die out for want of fuel. *–v.t.* **13.** to consume, partly or wholly, with fire. **14.** to put to death by burning: *they were burnt at the stake.* **15.** to cause to feel the sensation of heat. **16.** to injure, discolour, char, or treat with heat. **17.** to produce with fire: *to burn charcoal.* **18.** *Chem.* to cause to undergo combustion; oxidise. **19.** to calcine (earth, etc.) so as to obtain a pigment: *burnt sienna, burnt umber.* **20.** to pass through or over quickly and easily (fol. by *up*): *to burn up the kilometres in a car.* **21.** to clear or improve land by burning the cover (oft. fol. by *off*). **22.** *Colloq.* to race, on a motorcycle or in a car (oft. fol. by *off*). **23. burn one's fingers,** to suffer through rash interference or imprudence. *–n.* **24.** *Pathol.* an injury produced by heat or by abnormal cold, chemicals, poison gas, electricity, or lightning. A **first-degree burn** is characterised by reddening; a **second-degree burn** by blistering; a **third-degree burn** by charring. **25.** the operation of burning or baking, as in brickmaking. **26.** *Colloq.* **a.** an unofficial speed trial, on a motor cycle or in a car. **b.** a fast run. **27.** Also, **burn-off. a.** the action or result of clearing land by fire. **b.** the area of land so burnt. [coalescence in later ME of OE *beornan,* v.i. (c. Goth. *brinnan*) and OE *bærnan,* v.t. (c. Goth. *brannjan*) with (weak) inflection of *bærnan* and phonetic form of *beornan*]

**burn**[2] /bɜn/, *n. Scot.* a brook or rivulet. [ME *burne, bourne,* OE *burna, burne;* akin to G *Born, Brunnen* spring]

**burn-back** /ˈbɜn-bæk/, *n.* **1.** the deliberate burning of undergrowth, etc., esp. as a measure to prevent bush fires. **2.** →**back-burn.**

**burner** /ˈbɜnə/, *n.* **1.** one who or that which burns. **2.** an incinerator. **3.** that part of a gas stove, lamp, etc. from which flame issues or in which it is produced.

**burnet** /ˈbɜnɛt/, *n.* **1.** a plant of the genus *Sanguisorba,* esp. *S. minor,* an erect herb whose leaves are used for salad. **2.** one of several similar or related plants. **3.** →**burnet moth.** [ME, from OF *brunette,* diminutive of *brun* brown]

**burnet moth** /ˈbɜnɛt mɒθ/, *n.* **1.** any moth of the genus *Zygaena,* with bright red hindwings, and spots of the same colour in the dark green forewing. **2.** any of several other moths having a dark green colouring, as *Anthrocera filipendula.*

**burning** /ˈbɜnɪŋ/, *adj.* **1.** intense; serious; much-discussed: *a burning question.* *–n.* **2.** the final heat treatment used to develop hardness and other properties in ceramic products. – **burningly,** *adv.*

**burning bush** /ˌbɜnɪŋ ˈbʊʃ/, *n.* any of various plants which yield a volatile and inflammable oil. [from the burning bush in Exodus 3:2-4]

**burning-glass** /ˈbɜnɪŋ-glas/, *n.* a convex lens used to produce heat or ignite substances by focusing the sun's rays.

**burnish** /ˈbɜnɪʃ/, *v.t.* **1.** to polish (a surface) by friction. **2.** to make smooth and bright. *–n.* **3.** gloss; brightness; lustre. [ME *burnissh(en),* from OF *burniss-,* stem of *burnir* make brown, polish, from *brun* brown, from Gmc; see BROWN]

**burnisher** /ˈbɜnɪʃə/, *n.* a tool, usu. with a smooth, slightly convex head, used for polishing, as in dentistry, etc.

**burnous** /bɜˈnus, -ˈnuz/, *n.* a hooded mantle or cloak, such as that worn by Arabs, etc. Also, **burnouse** /bɜˈnuz/. [F, from Ar. *burnus*]

**burnout** /ˈbɜnaʊt/, *n.* the point in time or in the trajectory of a missile or rocket when combustion of fuels in the rocket engine is terminated by other than programmed cutoff.

**burnout velocity** /ˈbɜnaʊt vəˌlɒsəti/, *n.* the velocity attained by a rocket missile at the point of burnout.

**burnsides** /ˈbɜnsaɪdz/, *n.pl. U.S.* a style of beard consisting of side-whiskers and a moustache, the chin being clean-shaven. [named after A. E. *Burnside,* 1824-81, a general in the American Civil War]

burnous

**burnt** /bɜnt/, *v.* a past tense and past participle of **burn.**

**burnt offering** /bɜnt ˈɒfərɪŋ/, *n.* **1.** an offering burnt upon an altar in sacrifice to a deity. **2.** *Colloq.* over-cooked food.

**burnt sienna** /– siˈɛnə/, *n.* See **sienna.**

**burp** /bɜp/, *n. Colloq.* **1.** →**belch** (def. 5). *–v.i.* **2.** →**belch** (def. 1). *–v.t.* **3.** cause (a baby) to belch, esp. to relieve flatulence after feeding. [imitative]

**burr**[1] /bɜ/, *n., v.,* **burred, burring.** *–n.* **1.** *Bot.* the rough, prickly case around the seeds of certain plants, as of the chestnut and burdock. **2.** any burr-bearing plant. **3.** something or someone that adheres like a burr. **4.** any of various knots, knobs, lumps, or excrescences. Also, **bur.** [ME *burre,* from Scand.; cf. Dan. *borre*]

**burr**[2] /bɜ/, *n.* **1.** any of various tools and appliances for cutting or drilling. **2.** a rough protuberance, ridge, or area left on metal after cutting, drilling, or ploughing with an engraver's tool, etc. **3.** to form a rough point or edge on. Also, **bur.** [var. of BURR[1]]

**burr**[3] /bɜ/, *n.* **1.** a washer placed at the head of a rivet. **2.** the blank punched out of a piece of sheet metal. Also, **bur.** [ME *burwhe* circle, from Scand.; cf. Icel. *borg* wall]

**burr**[4] /bɜ/, *n.* **1.** a retracted pronunciation of the letter *r* (as in certain Northern English dialects). **2.** any rough or dialectal pronunciation. **3.** a whirring noise or sound. *–v.i.* **4.** to speak with a burr. **5.** to speak roughly, indistinctly, or inarticulately. **6.** to make a whirring noise or sound. *–v.t.* **7.** to pronounce with a burr. Also, **bur.** [apparently imitative; ? associated with idea of roughness in BURR[1]]

**burr**[5] /bɜ/, *n.* **1.** burstone. **2.** a mass of harder siliceous rock in soft rock. Also, **bur.** [orig. uncert.; ? akin to BURR[1]]

**burramys** /ˈbʌrəmɪs/, *n.* the mountain pigmy possum, *Burramys parvus,* known only in fossil form until mid 1960s, very rare and restricted in habitat to Mount Hotham, Victoria.

**burrawang** /ˈbʌrəwæŋ/, *n.* any native, palm-like plant of the genus *Macrozamia,* esp. *M. spiralis,* having nuts which were once a part of Aboriginal diet; zamia. [Aboriginal]

**burr-daisy** /bɜ-ˈdeɪzi/, *n.* any plant of the genus *Calotis,* which bears heads of fruit with barbed awns. Also, **daisy-burr.**

**burren** /ˈbʌrən/, *n. Archaeol.* a tula-adze flake worn away on both margins.

**burr grass** /ˈbɜ gras/, *n.* **1.** any grass of the genus *Cenchrus,* characterised by having burrs. **2.** any other grass with burr-like seeds, as small burr grass.

**burrino** /bəˈrinoʊ/, *n.* a cheese related to mozzarella, with a knob of butter moulded into the centre of the curd. [It. *burro* butter]

**burr-marigold** /bɜ-ˈmærəgoʊld/, *n.* a weed, *Bidens tripartita,* whose barbed fruits adhere to clothing.

**burr medic** /bɜ ˈmɛdɪk/, *n.* any of several species of pasture herbs of the genus *Medicago,* as *M. minima* and *M. polymorpha,* with coiled pods bearing small hooks. Also, **burr medick.**

**burro** /ˈbʌroʊ, ˈbʊroʊ/, *n., pl.* **-ros.** **1.** a pack donkey. **2.** any donkey. [Sp., from *burrico* small horse, from L *burricus*]

**burrow** /ˈbʌroʊ/, *n.* **1.** a hole in the ground made by a rabbit, fox, or similar small animal, for refuge and habitation. **2.** a similar place of retreat, shelter, or refuge. *–v.i.* **3.** to make a hole or passage (*in, into,* or *under* something). **4.** to lodge in a burrow. **5.** to hide. *–v.t.* **6.** to put a burrow or burrows into (a hill, etc.). [ME *borow.* Cf. OE *beorg* burial place, *gebeorg* refuge, *burgen* grave] – **burrower,** *n.*

**burrowing owl** /ˈbʌroʊɪŋ ˌaʊl/, *n.* a long-legged, terrestrial owl, *Speotyto cunicularia,* of North and South America, which digs its nesting burrow in open prairie land; ground owl.

**burrowing rat-kangaroo** /ˌbʌroʊɪŋ ˈræt-kæŋgəru/, *n.* →**boodie rat.**

**burrstone** /ˈbɜstoʊn/, *n.* →**burstone.**

**burry**[1] /ˈbɜri/, *adj.* full of burs; burr-like; prickly.

**burry**[2] /ˈbʊri/, *n. Colloq.* (*usu. derog.*) an Aborigine.

**bursa** /ˈbɜsə/, *n., pl.* **-sae** /-si/, **-sas.** a pouch, sac, or vesicle, esp. a sac containing synovia, to facilitate motion, as between a tendon and a bone. [ML: bag, purse, from Gk *býrsa* hide] – **bursal,** *adj.*

**bursar** /ˈbɜsə/, *n.* **1.** a treasurer or business officer, esp. of a college or university. **2.** a student holding a bursary. [ML *bursārius,* from *bursa* purse] – **bursarship,** *n.*

**bursarial** /bɜˈsɛəriəl/, *adj.* of, pertaining to, or paid to or by a bursar, or a bursary.

**bursary** /ˈbɜsəri/, *n., pl.* **-ries.** **1.** the treasury of a monastery or other institution. **2.** a scholarship. [ML *bursāria*]

**burse** /bɜs/, *n.* **1.** a pouch or case for some special purpose. **2.** *Eccles.* a case or receptacle for the corporal. [F *bourse* wallet, from L *bursa,* from Gk *býrsa* hide]

**bursiform** /ˈbɜsəfɔm/, *adj.* pouch-shaped; saccate. [ML *bursa* bag, purse + -(I)FORM]

**bursitis** /bɜˈsaɪtəs/, *n.* inflammation of a bursa. [NL. See BURSA, -ITIS]

**burst** /bɜst/, *v.,* **burst, bursting,** *n. –v.i.* **1.** to fly apart or break open with sudden violence; explode. **2.** to issue forth suddenly and forcibly from or as from confinement. **3.** to break or give way from violent pain or emotion: *to burst into speech or tears.* **4.** to be extremely full, as if ready to break open. **5.** to become visible, audible, evident, etc., suddenly and clearly. *–v.t.* **6.** to cause to burst; break suddenly and violently. **7.** to cause or suffer the rupture of. *–n.* **8.** the act of bursting. **9.** a sudden display of activity or energy: *a burst of applause or speed.* **10.** a sudden expression or manifestation of emotion, etc. **11.** a sudden and violent issuing forth. **12.** *Mil.* **a.** the explosion of a projectile, esp. in a specified place. **b.** a series of shots fired by one pressure on the trigger of an automatic weapon. **13.** the result of bursting: *a burst in the dyke.* **14.** a sudden opening to sight or view. [ME *berst(en), burst(en),* etc., OE *berstan;* from *burst* orig. past only; c. G *bersten,* Icel. *bresta*] – **burster,** *n.*

**burstone** /ˈbɜstoʊn/, *n.* **1.** *Geol.* any of various siliceous rocks used for millstones. **2.** a millstone of such material. Also, **buhr, buhrstone, burrstone.** [BUR(R)[4] + STONE]

**burthen** /ˈbɜðən/, *n., v.t. Archaic.* →**burden**[1]. – **burthensome,** *adj.*

**burton** /ˈbɜtn/, *n. Naut.* **1.** any of various kinds of tackle used for setting up rigging, raising sails, etc. **2.** any of various small tackles, esp. one having a two-sheave and a one-sheave block. **3. go for a burton,** to be killed or destroyed; to disappear. [? var. of BRETON]

**Burton's legless lizard,** *n.* a lizard, *Lialis burtonis,* with vestigial hind limbs and an elongated snout, widely distributed in Australia; lance-head lizard.

**Burundi** /bəˈrʊndi/, *n.* a kingdom in central Africa, east of the Congo.

**bury** /ˈbɛri/, *v.t.,* **buried, burying.** **1.** to put in the ground and cover with earth. **2.** to put (a corpse) in the ground or a vault, or into the sea, often with ceremony. **3.** to cause to sink in: *to bury a dagger in one's heart.* **4.** to cover in order to conceal from sight. **5.** to occupy (oneself) completely: *he buried himself in his work.* **6.** to put out of one's mind: *to bury an injury.* **7. bury the hatchet,** to be reconciled after hostilities. **8. bury the bishop,** *Colloq.* of a man, to have sexual intercourse. [ME *berien, buryen,* OE *byrgan;* akin to OE *beorg* burial place] – **burier,** *n.*

**burying beetle** /ˈbɛriɪŋ ˌbitl/, *n.* any beetle of the genus *Necrophorus,* esp. *N. vestigator,* that buries small creatures as food for its larvae.

**bus** /bʌs/, *n., pl.* **buses** or **busses,** *v.,* **bussed, bussing** or **bused, busing.** *–n.* **1.** a vehicle with a long body equipped with seats or benches for passengers, usu. operating as part of a scheduled service; an omnibus. **2.** *Colloq.* a motor car or aeroplane. **3.** *Computers.* a circuit or group of circuits which provide a communication path between two or more devices, as between a central processor, a memory bank, and peripherals. **4. miss the bus,** to miss an opportunity; be too late. *–v.i.* **5.** to travel by bus. [short for OMNIBUS]

**bus.,** **1.** bushel. **2.** business

**busbar** /ˈbʌsba/, *n.* a metal bar which supplies power to several electrical units.

**bus boy** /ˈbʌs bɔɪ/, *n. U.S.* a waiter's helper in a restaurant or other public dining room, for the more menial tasks.

**busby** /ˈbʌzbi/, *n., pl.* **-bies.** **1.** a tall fur hat with a bag hanging from the top over the right side, worn by hussars, etc., in the British Army. **2.** →**bearskin** (def. 2). [? akin to obs. *buzz wig*]

busby

**bush**[1] /bʊʃ/, *n.* **1.** a woody plant, esp. a low one, with many branches which usu. arise from or near the ground. **2.** *Bot.* a small cluster of shrubs appearing as a single plant. **3.** something resembling or suggesting this, as a thick, shaggy head of hair. **4.** a fox's tail. **5.** *Geog.* a stretch of land covered with bushy vegetation or trees. **6.** the countryside in general, as opposed to the towns. **7.** *Hist.* a bunch of ivy, etc., hung as a sign before a tavern or vintner's shop. **8. beat about the bush,** to fail to come to the point, prevaricate. **9. go bush, a.** to turn one's back on civilisation; adopt a way of life close to nature. **b.** Also, **take to the bush.** to disappear suddenly from one's normal surroundings or circle of friends. **10. in the bush,** *Surfing.* beyond the line of the breakers. *–v.i.* **11.** to be or become bushy; branch or spread as or like a bush. *–v.t.* **12.** to cover with bushes; protect with bushes set round about; support with bushes. **13.** *Agric.* to clear the ground, chiefly under citrus trees. *–adj.* **14.** uncivilised; rough; makeshift. **15.** *Colloq.* imprecisely estimated, usu. underestimated or unrealistic: *it takes five days to get there, two days by bush reckoning.* [ME; unexplained var. of *busk,* from Scand.; cf. Dan. *busk*]

**bush**[2] /bʊʃ/, *Mach. –n.* **1.** a lining of metal or the like let into an orifice to guard against wearing by friction, erosion, etc. **2.** a metal lining, usu. detachable, used as a bearing. *–v.t.* **3.** to furnish with a bush; line with metal. [MD *busse,* n.]

**bush.,** bushel; bushels.

**bushbaby** /ˈbʊʃbeɪbi/, *n.* any of the small lemurs of the loris family, of the genus *Galago,* esp. *G. grassicaudatus,* of eastern Africa, with nocturnal habits.

**bush ballad** /ˈbʊʃ bæləd/, *n.* a poem in a ballad metre dealing with aspects of life in the Australian bush.

**bush band** /ˈ– bænd/, *n.* a band which performs Australian folk music, usu. with such instruments as the accordion, tea-chest bass, guitar, etc.

**bush Baptist** /– ˈbæptəst/, *n. Colloq.* person of vague but strong religious beliefs, not necessarily associated with a particular denomination.

**bush bashing** /'– bæʃɪŋ/, *n.* **1.** clearing virgin bush. **2.** (in bushwalking) making a path through virgin bush.

**bush boss** /'– bɒs/, *n. N.Z. Timber Industry.* an overseer of logging in the bush.

**bush breakfast** /– 'brɛkfəst/, *n.* a rough, improvised breakfast partaken of while camping in the bush.

**bush brother** /'– brʌðə/, *n.* a priest belonging to one of the Church of England brotherhoods which minister to people in outback areas.

**bush-burn** /'bʊʃ-bɜn/, *n. N.Z.* **1.** the clearing of bush by fire. **2.** the area of land so cleared.

**bush canary** /bʊʃ kə'nɛəri/, *n.* **1.** →**white-throated warbler.** **2.** a small olive brown and bright yellow bird, *Mohoua ochrocephala,* of the New Zealand rainforest.

**bush carpenter** /– 'kapəntə/, *n.* a rough amateur carpenter.

**bush champagne** /– ʃæm'peɪn/, *n. Colloq.* a drink made from a saline and methylated spirits.

**bush-country** /'bʊʃ-kʌntri/, *n.* →**bush**[1] (def. 6).

**bushcraft** /'bʊʃkraft/, *n.* the ability to live in and travel through the bush with a minimum of equipment and assistance.

**bush cure** /'bʊʃ kjuə/, *n.* a household remedy; traditional medicine, esp. as practiced in bush communities.

**bushed** /bʊʃt/, *adj.* **1.** lost. **2.** exhausted. **3.** confused.

**bushel** /'bʊʃəl/, *n.* **1.** a unit of dry measure in the imperial system equal to 36.368 72 × $10^{-3}$m$^{3}$ (8 gal). **2.** *U.S.* equal to 35.239 070 × $10^{-3}$m$^{3}$) (Winchester bushels). **3.** before the introduction of SI units, the bushel of wheat was prescribed as 60lb of wheat, of oats as 40lb and so on, in effect prescribing the mass of specified materials which could be deemed equal to one bushel. **4. hide one's light under a bushel,** to conceal one's abilities or good qualities. [ME *boyschel,* from OF *boissiel,* diminutive of *boisse,* from Gallic word meaning hollow of the hand]

**busher** /'bʊʃə/, *n.* one who clears away undergrowth, fallen timber, etc.

**bush-faller** /'bʊʃ-fɔlə/, *n. N.Z.* one who fells trees for a living. Also, **bush-feller**. – **bush-falling,** *n.*

**bush farm** /'bʊʃ fam/, *n. N.Z.* farm cleared from forest. – **bush-farmer,** *n.* – **bush-farming,** *n.*

**bushfire** /'bʊʃfaɪə/, *n.* a fire in forest or scrub country.

**bushfire blonde** /– 'blɒnd/, *n. Colloq.* →**strawberry blonde.**

**bush fly** /'bʊʃ flaɪ/, *n.* any of the small, troublesome, black flies, esp. *Musca vetustissima,* that swarm about humans and animals in the bush.

**bush-hen** /'bʊʃ-hɛn/, *n.* a medium-sized, brownish rail, *Amaurornis olivaceus,* inhabiting thickly vegetated, swampy areas of north-eastern Australia, New Guinea and islands further north.

**bush house** /'bʊʃ haʊs/, *n.* **1.** a rough dwelling in the bush. **2.** a small garden shelter in which plants being cultivated are protected from wind and weather, usu. with roof and sides thatched with dead native foliage.

**bushido** /bʊ'ʃidoʊ/, *n.* **1.** a code of behaviour attributed to the warriors of feudal Japan, actually a development at the end of the feudal period, tinged with Confucian influences. **2.** (in modern usage) fanatical disregard of life in the service of the Japanese emperor. [Jap.: lit. the way of the warrior]

**bushie** /'bʊʃi/, *n.* a person, usu. unsophisticated and uncultivated, who lives in the bush. Cf. **townie.**

**bushiness** /'bʊʃinəs/, *n.* bushy state or form.

**bushing**[1] /'bʊʃɪŋ/, *n. Elect.* a lining for a hole through which conductors pass, intended to insulate them or protect them from abrasion. [BUSH[2] + -ING[1]]

**bushing**[2] /'bʊʃɪŋ/, *n.* the pruning of citrus trees so that they remain relatively low growing. [BUSH[1] + -ING[1]]

**bushlark** /'bʊʃlak/, *n.* →**singing bushlark.**

**bush-lawyer** /bʊʃ-'lɔɪjə/, *n.* **1.** any of several Australian and New Zealand prickly trailing plants, of the genus *Rubus.* **2.** *Colloq.* a person who pretends to a knowledge of the law. Also, **bush lawyer.**

**bush-line** /'bʊʃ-laɪn/, *n.* →**timber line** (def. 1).

**bushman** /'bʊʃmən/, *n.* **1.** a pioneer; dweller in the bush. **2.** one skilled in bushcraft. **3.** *N.Z.* →**bush-faller.** **4.** (*cap.*) a member of a racially distinct southern African people.

**bushman's clock** /bʊʃmənz 'klɒk/, *n.* →**kookaburra.**

**bushmanship** /'bʊʃmənʃɪp/, *n.* the ability to fend for oneself in rough country.

**bushman's saw** /bʊʃmənz 'sɔ/, *n.* a bow-shaped steel hand saw with coarse teeth used to trim trees.

**bushmaster** /'bʊʃmastə/, *n.* a large venomous snake, *Lachesis mutus,* of tropical America.

**bushoo** /bʌ'ʃu/, *n.* a rich pocket of ore.

**bush oyster** /bʊʃ 'ɔɪstə/, *n. Colloq.* (*joc.*) a testicle, usu. of a sheep.

**bush-pea** /bʊʃ-'pi/, *n.* any of the numerous species of shrub belonging to the Australian genus *Pultenaea,* family Papilionaceae, common in temperate regions of the continent.

**bush-pilot** /bʊʃ-'paɪlət/, *n.* a pilot of a small aeroplane carrying passengers or cargo in the outback.

**bush plum cake,** *n.* →**brownie** (def. 3).

**bushranger** /'bʊʃreɪndʒə/, *n.* **1.** (formerly) a bandit or criminal who hid in the bush and led a predatory life. **2.** (formerly) one able to fend for himself in rough country; a bushman. **3.** →**conman.** **4.** *N.Z.* (formerly) a European volunteer for bush-warfare against the Maoris in the 19th century. **5.** (*derog.*) any man seen as unprincipled and extorting. – **bushranging,** *n.*

bushranger: Ned Kelly

**bush rat** /'bʊʃ ræt/, *n.* any of a number of species of indigenous rodents of genus *Rattus* in Australia, some of which are regarded as 'Old Endemics'.

**bush refrigerator** /ˌ– rə'frɪdʒəreɪtə/, *n. Colloq.* →**cool safe.**

**bush robin** /– 'rɒbən/, *n. N.Z.* a robin-like forest bird, *Miro australis.*

**bush shower** /– 'ʃaʊə/, *n.* an apparatus for showering consisting of a canvas bag to hold water, fitted with a shower nozzle, and a rope for attaching it to a tree, etc.,

**bush-sick** /'bʊʃ-sɪk/, *adj.* **1.** of or pertaining to cows, sheep, etc., suffering bush sickness. **2.** of or pertaining to the land itself.

**bush sickness** /'bʊʃ sɪknəs/, *n.* a loss of vigour and weight ultimately leading to death in sheep, cattle and goats, due to mineral deficiency in pastures growing in soil deficient in certain trace elements.

**bush stone curlew,** *n.* a greyish-brown bird marked with black, with yellow eyes a black bill and long dark green legs, *Burhinus magnirostris,* found in grassy woodland throughout most of Australia and distinguished by its mournful cry.

**bush tea** /– 'ti/, *n.* **1.** tea brewed in a billy on an open fire. **2.** (formerly) tea made from any of various tea substitutes, as the leaves of the tea-tree.

**bush telegram** /– 'tɛləgræm/, *n. Colloq.* an unofficial communication, as by word of mouth. Also, **bush wire.**

**bush telegraph** /– 'tɛləgræf, -graf/, *n.* **1.** a system of communication over wide distances among primitive peoples, by drumbeats or other means. **2.** *Colloq.* an unofficial chain of communication by which information is conveyed and rumour spread, as by word of mouth. Also, **bush wireless.**

**bushtit** /'bʊʃtɪt/, *n.* any of several small chickadee-like birds of the North American genus *Psaltiparus,* known for their pendent nests.

**bush track** /bʊʃ 'træk/, *n.* **1.** an unsealed road in a remote district. **2.** a racecourse in the country.

**bush tucker** /– 'tʌkə/, *n.* simple fare, as eaten by one living in or off the bush.

**bushwalk** /'bʊʃwɔk/, *v.i.* to hike through the bush for pleasure. – **bushwalker,** *n.*

**bushwalking** /'bʊʃwɔkɪŋ/, *n.* the sport of making one's way on foot through the bush, often on tracks designed for this but sometimes for longer periods through virgin terrain.

**bush week** /'bʊʃ wik/, *n. Colloq.* **1.** a fictitious festive week when country people come to town. **2.** circumstances in

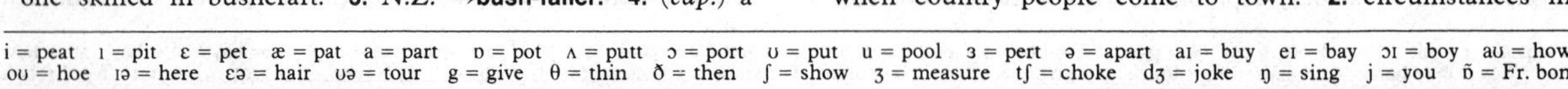
i = peat ɪ = pit ɛ = pet æ = pat a = part ɒ = pot ʌ = putt ɔ = port ʊ = put u = pool ɜ = pert ə = apart aɪ = buy eɪ = bay ɔɪ = boy aʊ = how
oʊ = hoe ɪə = here ɛə = hair ʊə = tour g = give θ = thin ð = then ʃ = show ʒ = measure tʃ = choke dʒ = joke ŋ = sing j = you õ = Fr. bon

which unsuspecting people are imposed upon: *what do you think this is – bush week?* **3.** a week of student festivities at the Australian National University. Also, **bushweek.**

**bushwhack** /ˈbʊʃwæk/, *Colloq. –v.i.* **1.** to live as a bushwhacker. **2.** to ambush. Also, **bushwack. 3.** *N.Z.* to clear land of timber. [backformation from BUSHWHACKER] – **bushwhacking,** *n.*

**bushwhacked** /ˈbʊʃwækt/, *adj. Colloq.* **1.** extremely fatigued; beaten; exhausted. **2.** astonished; annoyed. Also, **bushwacked.**

**bushwhacker** /ˈbʊʃwækə/, *n.* **1.** *Colloq.* one who lives in the bush; a bushie. **2.** *Colloq.* a native person. **3.** *N.Z. Colloq.* one who clears the land of bush, esp. an axeman engaged in cutting timber. **4.** *U.S.* one who lives in a remote wooded area. Also, **bushwacker.** [BUSH[1] + WHACKER]

**bush wire** /ˈbʊʃ waɪə/, *n. Colloq.* →**bush telegram.**

**bush wren** /ˈ– rɛn/, *n. N.Z.* a wren-like forest bird, *Xenicus longpipes.*

**bushy** /ˈbʊʃi/, *adj.,* **bushier, bushiest. 1.** resembling a bush. **2.** full of or overgrown with bushes.

**bushytailed** /ˈbʊʃiteɪld/, *adj.* **1.** having a bushy tail, as a possum, squirrel, etc. **2. bright-eyed and bushytailed,** *Colloq.* full of health and good spirits.

**busily** /ˈbɪzəli/, *adv.* **1.** in a busy manner; actively. **2.** with an unnecessary flurry of activity; officiously.

**business** /ˈbɪznəs/, *n.* **1.** one's occupation, profession, or trade. **2.** *Econ.* the purchase and sale of goods in an attempt to make a profit. **3.** *Comm.* a person, partnership, or corporation engaged in this; an established or going enterprise or concern: *to be in business.* **4.** volume of trade; patronage. **5.** one's place of work. **6.** that with which one is principally and seriously concerned. **7.** that with which one is rightfully concerned. **8.** affair; matter. **9.** *Theat.* any movement or gesture by an actor used for dramatic expression (generally not applied to actions like exits, etc.) **10.** *Colloq.* defecation. **11.** *Colloq.* prostitution. **12. business as usual,** proceeding normally. **13. mean business,** to be in earnest. [ME *busines,* OE (North) *bisignes.* See BUSY, -NESS]

**business college** /ˈ– ˌkɒlɪdʒ/, *n.* a private institution where subjects of use commercially, as shorthand, typing, bookkeeping etc., are taught.

**businesslike** /ˈbɪznəslaɪk/, *adj.* conforming to the methods of business or trade; methodical; systematic.

**businessman** /ˈbɪznəsmən/, *n., pl.* **-men** /-mən/. a man who engages in business or commerce. – **businesswoman** /ˈbɪznəswʊmən/, *n. fem.*

**business name** /ˈbɪznəs neɪm/, *n.* the name other than a surname under which a person carries on a business or profession, such name being necessarily registered.

**busk**[1] /bʌsk/, *n.* **1.** a strip of wood, steel, whalebone, or other stiffening material placed in the front of a corset to keep it in shape. **2.** the whole corset. [F *busc,* from It. *busco* stick]

**busk**[2] /bʌsk/, *v.i.* **1.** to perform as a busker. **2.** *Jazz.* to improvise freely within the framework of a given tune.

**busker** /ˈbʌskə/, *n.* an entertainer who gives impromptu performances in streets, parks, markets, etc.

**buskin** /ˈbʌskən/, *n.* **1.** a half-boot, or outer covering for the foot and leg reaching to the calf or higher. **2.** the high shoe or cothurnus of ancient Greek and Roman tragic actors. **3.** tragedy; tragic drama. [orig. uncert. Cf. F (obs.) *brousequin,* D *broosken,* Sp. *borceguí,* It. *borzacchino*]

buskins (def. 1)

**buskined** /ˈbʌskənd/, *adj.* **1.** wearing buskins. **2.** pertaining to tragedy.

**busman** /ˈbʌsmən/, *n., pl.* **-men** /-mən/. the driver or conductor of a bus.

**busman's holiday** /bʌsmənz ˈhɒlədeɪ/, *n.* a holiday on which one does one's regular work or some similar activity.

**buss** /bʌs/, *n., v.t., v.i.* kiss. [cf. d. G *Buss*]

**bus-shelter** /ˈbʌs-ʃɛltə/, *n.* a rain-shelter beside a bus-stop.

**bus-stop** /ˈbʌs-stɒp/, *n.* a place at the roadside, usu. marked by a standard sign, where buses stop for people to board and alight.

**bust**[1] /bʌst/, *n.* **1.** the head and shoulders of a person done in sculpture, either in the round or in relief. **2.** the chest or breast; the bosom. [F *buste,* from It. *busto,* of unknown orig.]

**bust**[2] /bʌst/, *Colloq. –v.i.* **1.** to burst. **2.** to go bankrupt (oft. fol. by *up*). **3.** to part finally; quarrel and part (fol. by *up*). *–v.t.* **4.** to burst (oft. fol. by *in*). **5.** to smash (fol. by *up*). **6.** to bankrupt; ruin (oft. fol. by *up*). **7.** to interrupt violently a political meeting or other gathering (fol. by *up*). **8.** to reduce in rank or grade; demote. **9.** to subdue; break the spirits of (a brumby, etc.). **10.** *Colloq.* to break and enter with intent to steal. **11. bust a gut** or **one's boiler,** to overdo anything: *don't bust a gut over that job.* *–n.* **12.** a complete failure; bankruptcy. **13.** a drunken party or spree; brawl. **14.** *Colloq.* the act of breaking and entering. **15.** *Colloq.* a police raid. *–adj.* **16.** Also, **busted.** broken; ruined. **17.** bankrupt. [d. or colloq. var. of BURST]

**bustard** /ˈbʌstəd/, *n.* **1.** Also, **plain turkey.** a large, heavy bird of the family Otididae, *Eupodotis australis,* inhabiting grassy plains and open scrub country of Australia. **2.** any of several other large birds of the same family found in Europe and Africa. [ME, from OF, b. *bistarde* (from It. *bistarda*) and *oustarde,* both from L *avis tarda* slow bird]

**bustard quail** /ˈ– ˌkweɪl/, *n.* any of various birds of the family Turnicidae resembling quails but distinguished by the absence of the hind toe, as the **little quail,** *Turnix velox,* found throughout continental Australia except in northern and eastern coastal areas.

bustard

**busted** /ˈbʌstəd/, *adj.* **1.** raided by the police. **2.** out of a cardgame because one has a card which raises one's score higher than that of the bank.

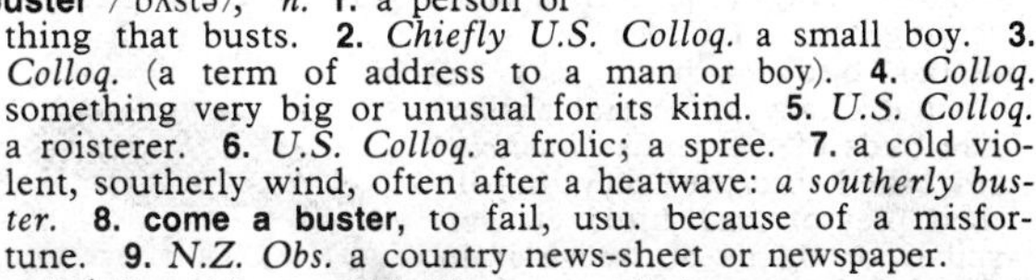

**buster** /ˈbʌstə/, *n.* **1.** a person or thing that busts. **2.** *Chiefly U.S. Colloq.* a small boy. **3.** *Colloq.* (a term of address to a man or boy). **4.** *Colloq.* something very big or unusual for its kind. **5.** *U.S. Colloq.* a roisterer. **6.** *U.S. Colloq.* a frolic; a spree. **7.** a cold violent, southerly wind, often after a heatwave: *a southerly buster.* **8. come a buster,** to fail, usu. because of a misfortune. **9.** *N.Z. Obs.* a country news-sheet or newspaper.

**bustle**[1] /ˈbʌsəl/, *v.,* **-tled, -tling,** *n.* *–v.i.* **1.** to move or act with a great show of energy (oft. fol. by *about*). *–v.t.* **2.** to cause to bustle. *–n.* **3.** activity with great show of energy; stir, commotion. [? var. of obs. *buskle*] – **bustlingly,** *adv.*

**bustle**[2] /ˈbʌsəl/, *n.* (formerly) a pad, cushion, or wire framework worn by women on the back part of the body below the waist, to expand and support the skirt. [? from BUSTLE[1]]

bustle[2], 19th century French dress with bustle

**bust-up** /ˈbʌst-ʌp/, *n. Colloq.* **1.** a disruption; disturbance or commotion, as one which brings a meeting to a sudden end. **2.** a final parting, often with ill-feeling. **3.** a financial or commercial failure. **4.** *Colloq.* a riotous party.

**busty** /ˈbʌsti/, *adj.* bosomy.

**busy** /ˈbɪzi/, *adj.,* **busier, busiest,** *v.,* **busied, busying.** *–adj.* **1.** actively and attentively engaged: *busy with his work.* **2.** not at leisure; otherwise engaged. **3.** full of or characterised by activity. **4.** officious; meddlesome; prying. [ME *busi, bisi,* OE *bysig,* c. D *bezig,* LG *besig*] *–v.t.* **5.** to keep occupied; make or keep busy: *to busy oneself keeping the lawn in order.* **6.** *Chiefly U.S.* →**engaged** (defs 7, 8, 9). [ME *bisien,* OE *bysgian,* from *bysig* BUSY, *adj.*] – **busyness,** *n.*

**busybody** /ˈbɪzibɒdi/, *n., pl.* **-bodies.** a person who pries into and meddles in the affairs of others.

**but** /bʌt/; *weak form* /bət/, *conj.* **1.** on the contrary; yet: *they all went, but I didn't.* **2.** except, rather than, or save: *anywhere but here.* **3.** except that (fol. by a clause, oft. with *that* expressed): *nothing would do but, or but that, I should come in.* **4.** without the circumstance that, or that not: *it never rains but it pours.* **5.** otherwise than: *I can do nothing but go.* **6.** that (esp. after *doubt, deny,* etc., with a negative): *I*

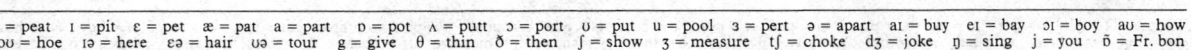

i = peat ɪ = pit ɛ = pet æ = pat a = part ɒ = pot ʌ = putt ɔ = port ʊ = put u = pool ɜ = pert ə = apart aɪ = buy eɪ = bay ɔɪ = boy aʊ = how oʊ = hoe ɪə = here ɛə = hair ʊə = tour g = give θ = thin ð = then ʃ = show ʒ = measure tʃ = choke dʒ = joke ŋ = sing j = you õ = Fr. bon

*don't doubt but he will do it.* **7.** that not (after a negative or question); *the children never played but that a quarrel followed.* **8.** who or which not: *no leader worthy of the name ever existed but was an optimist* (who was not an optimist). **9. but for,** except for; had it not been for; were it not for. *–prep.* **10.** with the exception of; except; save: *no one replied but me.* *-adv.* **11.** only; just: *there is but one God.* **12.** (a mildly adversative addition with the force of 'however' or 'though', used in standard speech at the beginning of a sentence and, in substandard speech, often at the end of a sentence). **13. all but,** almost: *all but dead.* *–n.* **14.** a restriction or objection: *no buts about it.* [ME; OE *b(e)ūta(n)* on the outside, without, from *be-* by + *ūt* out + *-an* adv. suffix]

**butadiene** /ˌbjutəˈdaɪin, -daɪˈin/, *n.* an inflammable, colourless, hydrocarbon gas, $H_2C = CH\text{-}CH = CH_2$, used in making synthetic rubber. [BUTA(NE) + DI-[1] + -ENE]

**butane** /ˈbjuteɪn, bjuˈteɪn/, *n.* a saturated aliphatic hydrocarbon, $C_4H_{10}$, existing in two isomeric forms and used as a fuel and a chemical intermediate. [BUT(YL) + -ANE]

**butanol** /ˈbjutənɒl/, *n.* butyl alcohol, usu. the *n*-isomer.

**butanone** /ˈbjutənoun/, *n.* an inflammable ketone, $C_4H_8O$, used as a solvent and in making plastics.

**but but** /ˈbʌt bʌt/, *n.* →**apple** (def. 8).

**butch** /butʃ/, *n. Colloq.* **1.** a lesbian, homosexual, or woman exhibiting extravagantly masculine characteristics. **2.** a man, esp. one of notable physical strength. *–adj.* **3.** of a man or woman, exhibiting masculine characteristics. [? from BUTCHER]

**butcher**[1] /ˈbutʃə/, *n.* **1.** a retail dealer in meat. **2.** one who slaughters certain domesticated animals, or dresses their flesh, for food or for market. **3.** a person guilty of cruel or indiscriminate slaughter. *–v.t.* **4.** to kill or slaughter for food or for market. **5.** to murder indiscriminately or brutally. **6.** to bungle; botch: *to butcher a job.* [ME *bocher,* from OF, from *boc* he-goat, from Gmc. See BUCK[1]]

**butcher**[2] /ˈbutʃə/, *n. S.A.* a small glass, used primarily for serving beer. [G *Becher*]

**butcher bird** /ˈ– bɜd/, *n.* **1.** in Australia, any of several shrike-like birds of the genus *Cracticus,* so called because they impale their prey of small birds, etc., on spikes or thorns or wedge it in the forks of trees, as the **grey butcherbird,** *Cracticus torquatus.* **2.** elsewhere, a shrike of the genus *Lanius,* as the common European species *L. excubitor.*

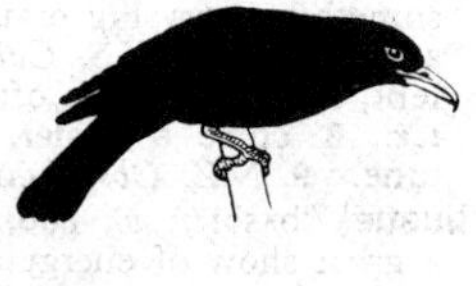
butcher bird

**butcherly** /ˈbutʃəli/, *adj.* like a butcher; cruel.

**butchers**[1] /ˈbutʃəz/, *adj. Colloq.* **1.** ill. **2. go butchers (hook) at,** to become angry with. [rhyming slang, *butcher's hook* crook]

**butchers**[2] /ˈbutʃəz/, *n. Colloq.* a look. [rhyming slang, *butcher's hook*]

**butchery** /ˈbutʃəri/, *n., pl.* **-eries. 1.** the trade or business of a butcher. **2.** brutal slaughter of human beings; carnage.

**butene** /ˈbjutin/, *n. Chem.* →**butylene.**

**butler** /ˈbʌtlə/, *n.* **1.** the head male servant of a household. **2.** the male servant having charge of the wines, plate, etc. [ME *buteler,* from AF *butuiller,* from *bouteille* bottle] – **butlership,** *n.*

**butler's pantry** /bʌtləz ˈpæntri/, *n.* a room between a kitchen and a dining room arranged for the storage of china and silverware and containing a sink.

**butlery** /ˈbʌtləri/, *n., pl.* **-leries.** a butler's room or pantry; a buttery. [BUTLER + -Y[3]; replacing ME *botelerye,* from OF *bouteillerie* storeroom for wine]

**butt**[1] /bʌt/, *n.* **1.** the end or extremity of anything, esp. the thicker, larger, or blunt end, as of a rifle, fishing rod, whip handle, arrow, log, etc. **2.** an end which is not used up: *a cigarette butt.* **3.** buttock. **4. a.** (of beef) a hind leg of beef on the bone, below the rump, including topside, round and silverside. **b.** *Orig. U.S.* (of pork) the body end of a shoulder of pork. *–v.t.* **5.** to extinguish: *to butt a cigarette.* [ME *bott* buttock; apparently short for BUTTOCK]

**butt**[2] /bʌt/, *n.* **1.** a person or thing that is an object of wit, ridicule, sarcasm, etc., or contempt. **2.** (in rifle or archery practice) **a.** a wall of earth behind the targets of a target range, which prevents bullets or arrows from scattering over a wide area. **b.** (*pl.*) a wall in front of the targets of a target range, behind which men can safely lower, score, and raise targets during firing. **3.** the target for archery practice. **4.** (*pl.*) a range for rifle or archery practice. **5.** a low wall or bank from behind which sportsmen shoot game birds. **6.** a hinge for a door or the like, secured to the butting surfaces or ends instead of the adjacent sides. **7.** *Obs.* a goal; limit. *–v.i.* **8.** to have an end or projection (*on*); be adjacent (*to*). *–v.t.* **9.** to join an end of (something); join the ends of (two things) together. [late ME, from OF *bout* end, extremity, of Gmc orig.]

**butt**[3] /bʌt/, *v.t.* **1.** to strike with the head or horns. *–v.i.* **2.** to strike something or at something with the head or horns. **3.** to project. **4.** *Colloq.* to interrupt; interfere; intrude (fol. by *in*). *–n.* **5.** a push with head or horns. [ME *butt(en),* from OF *bouter* strike, thrust, abut, touch, from *bout* end, of Gmc orig.]

**butt**[4] /bʌt/, *n.* **1.** a large cask for wine, beer, or ale. **2.** any cask or barrel. **3.** a unit of capacity, equal to two hogsheads. **4.** *Wool.* a package of greasy wool in a standard wool pack weighing less than 102 kg or in the case of lambs wool, less than 91 kg. [late ME; cf. OF *botte, bote,* c. It. *botte,* from LL *butta, buttis* vessel, cask]

**butte** /bjut/, *n. U.S. and Canada.* an isolated hill or mountain rising abruptly above the surrounding land. [F: hill, properly, mound for target]

**butter** /ˈbʌtə/, *n.* **1.** the fatty portion of milk, separating as a soft whitish or yellowish solid when milk or cream is agitated or churned. **2.** this substance, processed for cooking and table use. **3.** any of various other spreads of similar consistency: *butter icing, peanut butter.* **4.** any of various substances of butter-like consistency, as various metallic chlorides, and certain vegetable oils solid at ordinary temperatures. *–v.t.* **5.** to put butter on or in. **6.** *Colloq.* to flatter grossly (oft. fol. by *up*). [ME; OE *butere,* from L *būtyrum,* from Gk *boútyron*] – **butter-like,** *adj.*

**butterball** /ˈbʌtəbɔl/, *n.* **1.** the bufflehead. **2.** *Colloq.* a fat, round person. **3.** a small round butterscotch lolly.

**butterbean** /ˈbʌtəbin/, *n.* a variety of small-seeded lima beans, *Phaseolus lunatus.*

**butter cake** /ˈbʌtə keɪk/, *n.* a basic plain cake made with butter, sugar, eggs and flour.

**buttercup** /ˈbʌtəkʌp/, *n.* any plant of the genus *Ranunculus,* with yellow or white, usu. cup-shaped flowers.

**butterdish** /ˈbʌtədɪʃ/, *n.* a small container in which butter is placed on the table.

**butterfat** /ˈbʌtəfæt/, *n.* butter; milk fat; a mixture of glycerides, mainly butyrin, olein, and palmitin.

**butter-fingers** /ˈbʌtə-fɪŋgəz/, *n.* a person who fails to catch or drops things easily.

**butterfish** /ˈbʌtəfɪʃ/, *n.* **1.** any of various Australian fishes of genera *Selenotoca* and *Scatophagus,* often silvery or butter-coloured and variously banded or spotted and having strong, often venomous dorsal spines. **2.** *N.Z.* a reef fish, *Coridodax pullus,* often found browsing on kelp; greenbone. **3.** an elongated blenny, *Pholis gunnellus,* of the coastal waters of the North Atlantic. **4.** a small, flattened, marine food fish, *Poronotus triacanthus,* of the Atlantic coast of the U.S., having very small scales and smooth skin. **5.** *S.A.* →**jewfish.**

**butterfly** /ˈbʌtəflaɪ/, *n., pl.* **-flies. 1.** any of a group of lepidopterous insects characterised by clubbed antennae, large, broad wings, often conspicuously coloured and marked, and diurnal habits. **2.** Also, **social butterfly.** a person who flits gaily but aimlessly from one diversion to another. **3.** *Colloq.* →**floater** (def. 6). **4.** (*pl.*) nervousness: *butterflies in the stomach.* **5.** →**butterfly stroke.** [OE *buttorflēoge,* ? orig. used of a butter-coloured (yellow) species]

**butterfly cake** /ˈ– keɪk/, *n.* a cup cake with two small pieces cut from the top, joined back to it with cream, fancifully like butterfly wings.

**butterfly clip** /ˈ– klɪp/, *n.* a clip (clip[2], def. 1), usu. for holding hair in position, the finger grips of which are fancifully thought to resemble butterflies.

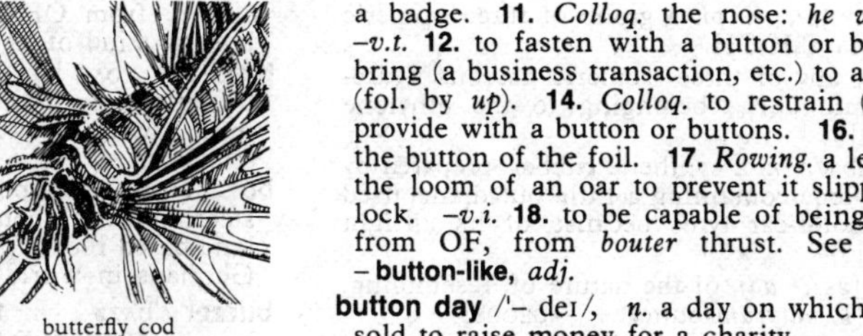
butterfly cod

**butterfly cod** /ˈ– kɒd/, *n.* a graceful, brilliantly coloured scorpaenid fish, *Pterois volitans,* common in Great Barrier Reef waters.

**butterfly fish** /ˈ– fɪʃ/, *n.* any of the tropical marine fishes of the family Chaetodontidae which are suggestive in shape or colouring of the butterfly; coralfish.

**butterfly net** /ˈ– nɛt/, *n.* a fine net on a hoop attached to a pole, used for catching butterflies.

**butterfly nut** /ˈ– nʌt/, *n.* →**wing nut.**

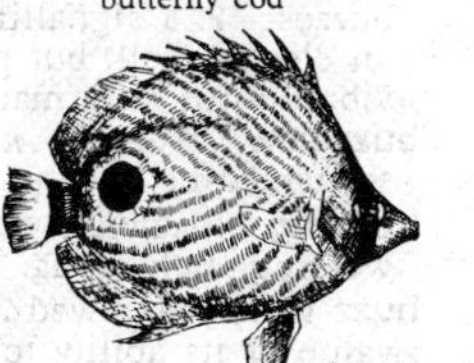
butterfly fish

**butterfly pea** /ˈ– pi/, *n.* a leguminous tropical plant, *Clitoria ternatea,* with blue flowers.

**butterfly steak** /ˈ– steɪk/, *n.* a standard cut of pork, being a trimmed, boneless mid-loin steak, after the fillet has been removed.

**butterfly stroke** /ˈ– stroʊk/, *n.* a stroke made in the prone position in which both arms are lifted simultaneously out of the water and flung forward, usu. done in combination with the dolphin kick.

**butterfly table** /ˈ– teɪbəl/, *n.* a small, occasional table with drop leaves having butterfly-shaped supports.

**butterfly valve** /ˈ– vælv/, *n.* **1.** a double clackvalve (as in a lift-pump piston) which consists of two semicircular clappers hinged to a cross rib. **2.** a damper or throttle valve in a pipe which consists of a disc turning on a diametral axis.

**butterknife** /ˈbʌtənaɪf/, *n.* a blunt-edged, flat-bladed utensil for cutting and serving butter at table.

**buttermilk** /ˈbʌtəmɪlk/, *n.* the more or less acidulous liquid remaining after the butter has been separated from milk or cream.

**butternut** /ˈbʌtənʌt/, *n.* **1.** the edible oily nut of an American tree, *Juglans cinerea,* of the walnut family. **2.** the tree itself. **3.** →**souari nut. 4.** dark brown. **5.** →**butternut pumpkin.**

**butternut pumpkin** /– ˈpʌmpkən/, *n.* a variety of gramma, widely used as a cooked vegetable.

**butterscotch** /ˈbʌtəskɒtʃ/, *n.* **1.** a kind of toffee made with butter. **2.** a flavour produced in puddings, icing, ice-cream, etc., by a combination of brown sugar, vanilla extract, and butter, with other ingredients.

**buttery**[1] /ˈbʌtəri/, *adj.* **1.** like, containing, or spread with, butter. **2.** *Colloq.* grossly flattering. [BUTTER + -Y[1]]

**buttery**[2] /ˈbʌtəri/, *n., pl.* **-ries. 1.** a room in which the wines, liquors, and provisions of a household are kept; a pantry. **2.** a room, as esp. in universities, from which certain articles of food and drink are supplied to the students. [ME *boterie,* from OF, from *bot(t)e* cask]

**buttinski** /bʌˈtɪnski/, *n. Colloq.* a stickybeak; an interfering person.

**butt joint** /ˈbʌt dʒɔɪnt/, *n. Bldg Trades.* a joint formed by two pieces of wood or metal united end to end without overlapping.

**buttock** /ˈbʌtək/, *n.* **1.** *Anat.* **a.** either of the two protuberances which form the rump. **b.** (*pl.*) the rump. **2.** Also, **buttock line.** in the lines plan of a vessel, a line indicating the intersection of fore-and-aft vertical planes with the hull surface. **3.** *Wrestling.* any of various moves which involve the use of the buttocks as a fulcrum to throw the opponent. *–v.t.* **4.** *Wrestling.* to throw, using the buttocks as a fulcrum. [ME *buttok,* OE *buttuc*]

**button** /ˈbʌtn/, *n.* **1.** a disc or knob on a piece of cloth which, when passed through a slit or loop either in the same piece or another, serves as a fastening. **2.** anything resembling a button. **3.** an object of little value: *not worth a button.* **4.** *Bot.* a bud or other protuberant part of a plant. **5.** a young or undeveloped mushroom. **6.** a disc pressed to close an electric circuit, as in ringing a bell; push-button. **7.** (*pl*). *Colloq.* a page or bellboy. **8.** *Metall.* a globule or mass of metal lying at the bottom of a crucible after fusion. **9.** *Fencing.* the protective knob fixed to the point of a foil. **10.** a badge. **11.** *Colloq.* the nose: *he was hit on the button.* *–v.t.* **12.** to fasten with a button or buttons. **13.** *Colloq.* to bring (a business transaction, etc.) to a successful conclusion (fol. by *up*). **14.** *Colloq.* to restrain (fol. by *down*). **15.** to provide with a button or buttons. **16.** *Fencing.* to touch with the button of the foil. **17.** *Rowing.* a leather projection round the loom of an oar to prevent it slipping through the rowlock. *–v.i.* **18.** to be capable of being buttoned. [ME *boton,* from OF, from *bouter* thrust. See BUTT[2]] **– buttoner,** *n.* **– button-like,** *adj.*

**button day** /ˈ– deɪ/, *n.* a day on which buttons or badges are sold to raise money for a charity.

**button grass** /ˈ– gras/, *n.* **1.** an annual fodder grass of the genus *Dactyloctenium,* esp. the Australian native *Dactyloctenium radulans,* with seeds in a cluster resembling a button. **2.** a Tasmanian sedge, *Gymnoschoenus sphaerocephalus.*

**buttonhole** /ˈbʌtnhoʊl/, *n., v.,* **-holed, -holing.** *–n.* **1.** the hole, slit, or loop through which a button is passed. **2.** a small flower or nosegay worn in the buttonhole in the lapel of a jacket. *–v.t.* **3.** to sew with buttonhole stitch. **4.** to make buttonholes in. **5.** to seize by or as by the buttonhole in the lapel of the jacket and detain in conversation. **– buttonholer,** *n.*

**buttonhole stitch** /ˈ– stɪtʃ/, *n.* a looped stitch used to strengthen the edge of material, as in a buttonhole.

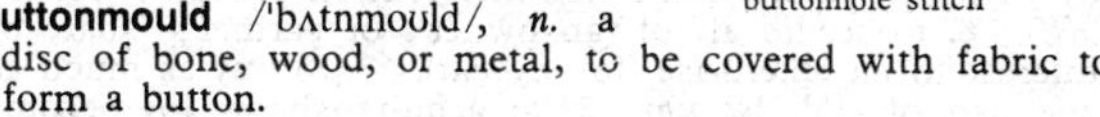
buttonhole stitch

**buttonhook** /ˈbʌtnhʊk/, *n.* a small metal or other stiff hook used for buttoning shoes, gloves, etc.

**buttonmould** /ˈbʌtnmoʊld/, *n.* a disc of bone, wood, or metal, to be covered with fabric to form a button.

**button mushroom** /bʌtn ˈmʌʃrum/, *n.* a small champignon.

**button quail** /ˈ– kweɪl/, *n.* →**bustard quail.**

**buttons** /ˈbʌtnz/, *n.pl.* any of a number of plant species, esp. of the family Compositae, with button-like flower heads as, **billy buttons** of the genus *Craspedia,* and **water buttons,** *Cotula coronopifolia.*

**button tree** /ˈbʌtn tri/, *n.* **1.** a tropical tree or shrub, *Conocarpus erectus,* with heavy, hard, compact wood and button-like fruits. **2.** →**buttonwood.**

**buttonwood** /ˈbʌtnwʊd/, *n.* a tall, North American plane tree, *Platanus occidentalis,* yielding a useful timber (so called from its small pendulous fruit). Also, **button tree.**

**buttony** /ˈbʌtəni/, *adj.* **1.** like a button. **2.** having many buttons.

A, buttress; B, flying buttress

**buttress** /ˈbʌtrəs/, *n.* **1.** *Archit.* a structure built against a wall or building for the purpose of giving it stability. **2.** any prop or support. **3.** a thing shaped like a buttress, as a rock-wall projecting from a mountainside. *–v.t.* **4.** *Archit.* to support by a buttress. **5.** to prop up; support. [ME *boterace,* from OF *bouterez,* pl., from *bouter* thrust, abut]

**buttress root** /ˈ– rut/, *n.* a flattened, plank-like expansion formed from root and trunk of certain often shallow-rooted trees, esp. of the rain forest.

buttress root

**butt weld** /ˈbʌt wɛld/, *n. Bldg Trades.* a weld formed by joining the flattened ends of two pieces of iron at a white heat.

**butty** /ˈbʌti/, *n. Brit. Colloq.* **1.** a workmate, esp. in a colliery. **2.** a thick slice of buttered bread. [BUTT(ER) + -Y]

**butyl** /ˈbjutəl/, *n.* a univalent radical, $C_4H_9$, from butane. [BUT(YRIC) + -YL]

**butyl alcohols** /– 'ælkəhɒlz/, *n. pl.* a group of three isomeric alcohols of the formula $C_4H_9OH$.

**butylene** /'bjutəlin/, *n.* any of three isomeric gaseous hydrocarbons of the formula $C_4H_8$, belonging to the ethylene series. [BUTYL + -ENE]

**butyl rubber** /bjutəl 'rʌbə/, *n.* a synthetic rubber, prepared by polymerisation of butylene containing a little butadiene, used for inner tubes of motor-car tyres because of its airtight qualities. [Trademark]

**butyraceous** /ˌbjutə'reɪʃəs/, *adj.* of the nature of, resembling, or containing butter. [L *būtyrum* butter + -ACEOUS]

**butyrate** /'bjutəreɪt/, *n.* a salt or ester of butyric acid.

**butyric** /bju'tɪrɪk/, *adj.* pertaining to or derived from butyric acid. [L *būtyrum* butter + -IC]

**butyric acid** /– 'æsəd/, *n.* either of two isomeric acids $C_3H_7$-COOH, esp. the one, a rancid liquid, present in spoiled butter, etc., as an ester and sometimes free.

**butyrin** /'bjutərən/, *n.* a colourless liquid fat or ester present in butter, and formed from glycerine and butyric acid. [L *būtyrum* butter + -IN[2]]

**buxom** /'bʌksəm/, *adj.* **1.** (of a woman) full-bosomed, plump, and attractive because of radiant health. **2.** (usu. of a woman) healthy, attractive, cheerful, and lively. [ME; early ME *buhsum* pliant, from OE *būgan* bend, bow. See -SOME[1]] – **buxomly,** *adv.* – **buxomness,** *n.*

**buy** /baɪ/, *v.,* **bought, buying,** *n.* –*v.t.* **1.** to acquire the possession of, or the right to, by paying an equivalent, esp. in money. **2.** to acquire by giving any kind of recompense: *to buy favour with flattery.* **3.** to hire; bribe. **4.** *Chiefly Theol.* to redeem; ransom. **5.** to get rid of (a claim, opposition, etc.) by payment; purchase the non-intervention of; bribe (fol. by *off.*). **6.** to secure all of (an owner's or partner's) share or interest in an enterprise (fol. by *out*). **7.** to buy as much as one can of (fol. by *up*). **8.** to acquire shares in; become involved in (fol. by *in, into*). **9.** *Colloq.* to accept: *do you think he'll buy the idea?* **10. buy it,** *Colloq.* to die: *he bought it at Bathurst.* –*v.i.* **11.** to be or become a purchaser. **12. buy in, a.** *Stock Exchange.* (of a broker) to obtain a share scrip from another broker to cover his position after a third broker fails to deliver shares. **b.** to join in; become involved. **13. buy into,** to choose to become involved in: *buy into an argument.* **14. buy into trouble,** to undertake a course of action against the better judgment of oneself or others. –*n.* **15.** *Colloq.* a bargain: *a good buy.* [ME *b(u)yen* etc., OE *byg-,* stem of *bycgan,* c. OS *buggian,* Goth. *bugjan*] – **buyable,** *adj.*

**buy-back market** /'baɪ-bæk ˌmakət/, *n.* that section of the money market in which a lender buys securities from the borrower who agrees to buy back those securities at an agreed price and time.

**buyer** /'baɪə/, *n.* **1.** one who buys; a purchaser. **2.** a purchasing agent, as for a chain-store.

**buyers' market** /baɪəz 'makət/, *n.* a market in which the buyer is at an advantage because of oversupply.

**Buys Ballot's Law** /bis bə'lɒts lɔ, bɔɪs/, *n.* the principle that in the Northern Hemisphere atmospheric pressure is higher on the left when facing into the wind; in the Southern Hemisphere it is higher on the right. [named after C. H. D. *Buys Ballot,* 1817-90, Danish meteorologist]

**buzz** /bʌz/, *n.* **1.** a low, vibrating, humming sound, as of bees. **2.** a rumour or report. **3.** *Colloq.* a telephone call. **4.** *Colloq.* a feeling of exhilaration or pleasure, esp. as induced by drugs. –*v.i.* **5.** to make a low, vibrating, humming sound. **6.** to speak or whisper with such a sound. **7.** to move busily from place to place (usu. fol. by *about*). **8.** *Colloq.* to go; leave (usu. fol. by *off* or *along*). –*v.t.* **9.** to make a buzzing sound with: *the fly buzzed its wings.* **10.** to spread (a rumour) secretively. **11.** to communicate with buzzes, as in signalling. **12.** *Colloq.* to make a telephone call to. **13.** *Aeron. Colloq.* **a.** to fly an aeroplane very low over: *to buzz a field.* **b.** to signal or greet (someone) by flying an aeroplane low and slowing the motor spasmodically. [imitative]

**buzzard** /'bʌzəd/, *n.* **1.** →**black-breasted buzzard. 2.** →**red goshawk. 3.** any of various more or less heavily built hawks of the genus *Buteo* and allied genera, as *B. vulgaris,* a rather sluggish European species. **4.** any of various carrion-eating birds, as the honey buzzard and the turkey buzzard. [ME *busard,* from OF, from *buse* buzzard, from L *būteo* kind of hawk]

turkey buzzard

**buzz bar** /'bʌz ba/, *n.* **1.** *Music.* a cadential formula in rock music. **2.** *Electronics.* a bar in a circuit to which all earth leads are attached.

**buzzbomb** /'bʌzbɒm/, *n.* a type of self-steering aerial bomb, launched from large land-based rocket platforms, and used by the Germans in World War II over England.

**buzzer** /'bʌzə/, *n.* **1.** one who or that which buzzes. **2.** a signalling apparatus similar to an electric bell, but producing sound by the vibration of an armature.

**buzz-saw** /'bʌz-sɔ/, *n.* a small circular saw, so named because of the noise it makes.

**buzzwig** /'bʌzwɪg/, *n.* **1.** a large, bushy wig. **2.** a person wearing such a wig. **3.** a person of consequence; bigwig.

**buzz word** /'bʌz wɜd/, *n. Colloq.* a word used for its emotive value or its ability to impress the listener.

**BV,** brick veneer, Also, **bv.**

**B.V.** /bi 'vi/, Blessed Virgin. [L *Beāta Virgo*]

**B.Vet.Sci.** /bi vɛt 'saɪ/, Bachelor of Veterinary Science.

**B.V.M.** /bi vi 'ɛm/, Blessed Virgin Mary. [L *Beāta Virgo Maria*]

**B.V.Sc.** /ˌbi vi ɛs 'si/, Bachelor of Veterinary Science.

**B/W,** black and white.

**bwana** /'bwanə/, *n.* sir; master. [Swahili]

**by** /baɪ/, *prep.* **1.** near to: *a house by the river.* **2.** using as a route: *he came by the main road.* **3.** through or on as a means of conveyance: *he journeyed by water.* **4.** to and past a point near: *he went by the church.* **5.** within the compass or period of: *by day, by night.* **6.** not later than: *by two o'clock.* **7.** to the extent of: *longer by a metre.* **8.** through evidence or authority of: *by his own account.* **9.** with the participation of: *regretted by all.* **10.** in conformity with: *by any standards this is a good book.* **11.** before; in the presence of: *to swear by all that is sacred.* **12.** through the agency or efficacy of: *founded by Napoleon, done by force.* **13.** after; in serial order: *piece by piece.* **14.** combined with in multiplication or relative dimension: *five metres by six metres.* **15.** involving as unit of measure: *beef by the kilogram.* –*adv.* **16.** near to something: *it's close by.* **17.** to and past a point near something: *the car drove by.* **18.** aside: *put it by for the moment.* **19.** over; past: *in times gone by.* **20. by and by,** at some time in the future; before long; presently. **21. by and large,** in general; on the whole. –*adj.* **22.** situated to one side. **23.** secondary, incidental. –*n.* **24.** bye. [ME; OE *bī,* stressed form answering to unstressed *be-,* c. G *bei* by, near]

**by-,** a prefix meaning: **1.** secondary; incidental, as in *by-product.* **2.** out of the way; removed, as in *byway.* **3.** near, as in *bystander.* Also, **bye-.**

**by-blow** /'baɪ-bloʊ/, *n.* →**bastard** (def. 1).

**bye** /baɪ/, *n.* Also, **by. 1.** *Sport.* the state of having no competitor in a contest where several competitors are engaged in pairs, conferring the right to compete in the next round in an eliminatory competition. **2.** *Golf.* the holes of a stipulated course still unplayed after the match is decided. **3.** *Cricket.* a run made on a ball not struck by the batsman. **4.** something subsidiary, secondary, or out of the way. **5. by the bye.** Also, **by the by,** incidentally; by the way. –*adj.* **6.** by. [var. spelling of BY, *prep.,* in noun use]

**bye-,** variant of **by-.**

**bye-bye** *interj.* /baɪ-'baɪ/; *n.* /'baɪ-baɪ/, *pl.* **bye-byes.** *Colloq.* –*interj.* **1.** goodbye. –*n.* **2.** (*pl.*) (*in children's speech*) sleep: *go to bye-byes.*

**by-election** /'baɪ-əlɛkʃən/, *n.* a parliamentary election held between general elections, to fill a vacancy. Also, **bye-election.**

**Byelorussian Soviet Socialist Republic,** *n.* a country west of the Soviet Union. Also, **Byelorussia.**

**bygone** /'baɪgɒn/, *adj.* **1.** past; gone by; out of date: *bygone days.* –*n.* **2.** that which is past.

**by-law** /'baɪ-lɔ/, *n.* **1.** an ordinance of an authority having legal effect only within the boundaries of that authority's jurisdiction. **2.** a subsidiary law. **3.** a standing rule, as of a company or society, not in its constitution. Also, **bye-law.**

[BY- + LAW; replacing ME *bilawe,* from *by* town (from Scand.; cf. Dan. *by*) + *lawe* law]

**by-line** /'baɪ-laɪn/, *n.* **1.** *Journalism.* a line under the heading of a newspaper or magazine article giving the writer's name. **2.** Also, **goal line.** *Soccer.* a white line marking the limits of the playing area of a soccer pitch.

**byname** /'baɪneɪm/, *n.* **1.** a secondary name; cognomen; surname. **2.** a nickname.

**B.Y.O.** /bi waɪ 'oʊ/, *adj.* **1.** of a party, dinner, etc. to which one brings one's own supply of liquor. *–n.* **2.** an unlicensed restaurant which allows clients to bring liquor in. [short for *(b)ring (y)our (o)wn*] Also, **B.Y.O.G.**

**B.Y.O.G.** /ˌbi waɪ oʊ 'dʒi/, *adj., n.* →**B.Y.O.** [short for *(b)ring (y)our (o)wn (g)rog*]

**bypass** /'baɪpas/, *n.* **1.** a road enabling motorists to avoid towns and other heavy traffic points or any obstruction to easy travel on a main road. **2.** a secondary pipe or other channel connected with a main passage as for conducting a liquid or gas around a fixture, pipe or appliance. **3.** *Elect.* →**shunt** (def. 8). *–v.t.* **4.** to avoid (obstructions, etc.) by following a bypass. **5.** to cause (fluid, traffic, etc.) to follow such a channel. **6.** to go over the head of (one's immediate supervisor, etc.).

**bypass operation** /'– ɒpəˌreɪʃən/, *n. Med. Colloq.* a surgical operation to divert the passage of food to avoid normal digestion and absorption, used in the treatment of obesity.

**bypath** /'baɪpaθ/, *n.* an indirect course or means; byway.

**byplay** /'baɪpleɪ/, *n.* action or speech carried on aside while the main action proceeds, esp. on the stage.

**by-product** /'baɪ-prɒdʌkt/, *n.* a secondary or incidental product, as in a process of manufacture.

**byre** /'baɪə/, *n.* a cowhouse or shed; a cattlepen. [OE *bȳre,* from OE *būr* hut. Cf. BOWER[1]]

**byrnie** /'bɜni/, *n.* a shirt of mail; a hauberk. [var. of ME *brynie,* from Scand.; cf. Icel. *brynja,* c. OE *byrne* coat of mail]

**byroad** /'baɪroʊd/, *n.* a side road.

**byronic** /baɪ'rɒnɪk/, *adj.* darkly world-weary; melodramatically melancholy. [from Lord *Byron,* 1788-1824, whose personality, esp. as reflected in his poetry, was of this nature] – **byronically,** *adv.* – **byronism,** *n.*

**byssus** /'bɪsəs/, *n., pl.* **byssuses, byssi** /'bɪsaɪ/. **1.** *Zool.* a collection of silky filaments by which certain molluscs attach themselves to rocks. **2.** (among the ancients) **a.** (originally) a fine yellowish flax, or the linen made from it, as the Egyptian mummy-cloth. **b.** (later) cotton or silk. [L, from Gk *býssos,* of oriental orig.] – **byssaceous** /bə'seɪʃəs/, *adj.*

**bystander** /'baɪstændə/, *n.* a person present but not involved; a chance looker-on.

**bystreet** /'baɪstrit/, *n.* a separate, private, or obscure street; a side street; a byway.

**byte** /baɪt/, *n.* a unit of information, usu. eight bits, stored by a computer. Cf **bit**[3].

**by-the-wind sailor** /ˌbaɪ-ðə-wɪnd 'seɪlə/, *n.* →**velella.**

**byway** /'baɪweɪ/, *n.* **1.** a secluded, or obscure road. **2.** a subsidiary or obscure field of research, endeavour, etc.

**byword** /'baɪwɜd/, *n.* **1.** the name of a quality or concept which characterises some person or group; the epitome (of): *his name is a byword for courage.* **2.** a word or phrase used proverbially; a common saying; a proverb. **3.** an object of general reproach, derision, scorn, etc. **4.** an epithet, often of scorn. [OE *bīword*]

**by-your-leave** /baɪ-jə-'liv/, *n.* a request for permission, or an apology.

**Byzantine** /'bɪzəntin, -taɪn, bə'zæntaɪn -tən/, *adj.* **1.** of or pertaining to Byzantium. **2.** of or pertaining to the Byzantine Empire, the Eastern Roman Empire after the fall of the Western Empire in A.D. 476, having Constantinople as its capital. **3.** of, pertaining to, or resembling Byzantine architecture. *–n.* **4.** a native or inhabitant of Byzantium. [L *Bȳzantīnus*]

**Byzantine architecture** /– 'akətɛktʃə/, *n.* a style of architecture developed in Byzantium and its provinces during the 5th and 6th centuries A.D., characterised by centralised plans, vaulting, and rich use of light, shade, colourful mosaics, paintings, and decoration.

**Byzantine Empire** /– 'ɛmpaɪə/, *n.* the Eastern Roman Empire after the fall of the Western Empire in A.D. 476, having Constantinople as its capital.

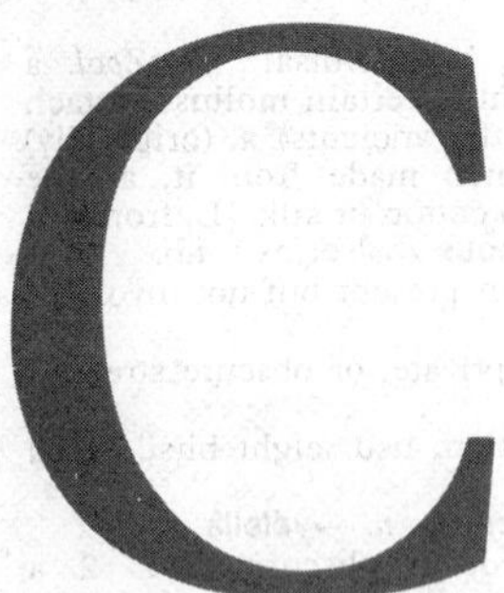

Cc Roman GARAMOND   Cc Sans Serif UNIVERS   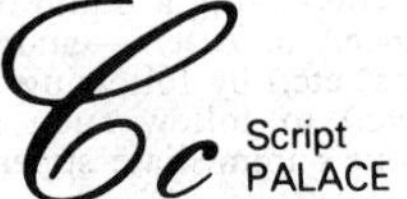 Script PALACE   Cc Decorative CAMPANILE

*Although there are numerous typefaces in the world they can be divided into four main classifications. These are:*

*ROMAN or SERIF. This typeface came into being from the technique of the Roman masons who, working in stone, finished off each letter with a serif or small stroke projecting from the top or bottom. This was done to correct any feeling of unevenness or imbalance they may have created in cutting the characters in stone.*

*SANS SERIF (without serif). This typeface is geometric in design and has straight-edged characters and lines of a regular thickness.*

*SCRIPT. Based on the movement of the hand, this typeface is often italicised or slanted, as if drawn by a brush or quill pen.*

*DECORATIVE. Any typeface that exaggerates the characteristics of any of the other three classifications to a degree that places it outside of them.*

*The dictionary entries in this book use a SAN SERIF typeface called Helvetica (set in a bold face for the head words) and a SERIF typeface Plantin (used throughout the body of the entries).*

**C, c** *n., pl.* **C's** or **Cs, c's** or **cs. 1.** a consonant, the third letter of the English alphabet. **2.** *Music.* **a.** the first or key-note, of the C major scale, the third degree of the relative minor scale (A minor). **b.** a written or printed note representing this tone. **c.** a key, string, or pipe tuned to this note. **d.** (in solmisation) the first note of the scale of C, called **do. e.** middle C.

**c., 1.** *Elect.* capacity. **2.** *Cricket.* caught. **3.** cent; cents. **4.** centigrade. **5.** centime. **6.** centimetre. **7.** century. **8.** chapter. **9.** Also, **c** about. [L *circa, circiter, circum*] **10.** cognate with. **11.** cubic. **12.** *Physics.* the velocity of light in a vacuum. **13.** cycle.

**C, 1.** *Elect.* capacitance. **2.** *Chem.* carbon. **3.** 100. [L *centum*] See **Roman numerals. 4.** centigrade. **5.** celsius. **6.** century: *19thC.* **7.** *Music.* (as a time signature) common time. **8.** coulomb. **9.** *U.S. Colloq.* a hundred-dollar bill.

**C., 1.** Cape. **2.** centigrade.

**C/-,** care of.

**ca,** about: *ca A.D.* 476. [L *circa*]

**ca.,** centiare.

**Ca,** *Chem.* calcium.

**cab** /kæb/, *n.* **1.** →**taxicab. 2.** (formerly) any of various one-horse vehicles for public hire, as the hansom or the brougham. **3.** the covered part of a locomotive or truck where the driver sits. **4. first cab off the rank,** *Colloq.* the first person to do something. [short for CABRIOLET]

**cabal** /kəˈbal, kəˈbæl/, *n., v.,* **-balled, -balling.** *–n.* **1.** the secret schemes of a small group of plotters; an intrigue. **2.** a small group of secret plotters. **3.** (*oft. cap.*) *Eng. Hist.* a group of five ministers of Charles II in 1672. *–v.i.* **4.** to form a cabal; intrigue; conspire; plot. [var. of *cabbal,* from ML *cabbāla.* See CABBALA. Def. 3 from the names of the ministers: C(*lifford*), A(*rlington*), B(*uckingham*), A(*shley*), L(*auderdale*)]

**cabala** /kəˈbalə/, *n.* →**cabbala. – cabalism,** *n.* **– cabalist,** *n.*

**cabaletta** /kæbəˈlɛtə/, *n.* in Italian opera of the late 18th and earlier 19th century, the short and often showy fast section which followed the recitative and aria.

**caballero** /kæbəˈljɛəroʊ/, *n., pl.* **-ros.** a Spanish gentleman. [Sp., from L *caballārius* horseman. See CAVALIER]

**cabana** /kəˈbanə/, *n. Chiefly U.S.* **1.** a cabin; cottage; hut. **2.** a bathhouse near the water's edge. [Sp.]

**cabane** /kəˈbæn/, *n. Mountaineering.* a hut at a high altitude, used for overnight stays.

**cabanossi** /kæbəˈnɒsi/, *n.* a thin, pre-cooked, seasoned beef sausage. Also, **kabanossi.** [Slavic, from Turkic Ta-tar *kaban* boar]

**cabaret** /ˈkæbəreɪ/, *n.* **1.** a form of musical, variety, or other entertainment at a restaurant, nightclub, etc., often late into the night; a floor show. **2.** a club, etc., that provides such entertainment. **3.** *Qld.* a dance (def. 11) at which alcoholic drink is available. [F: cellar, orig. uncert.]

**cabbage** /ˈkæbɪdʒ/, *n., v.,* **-baged, -baging.** *–n.* **1.** any of various cultivated varieties of *Brassica oleracea,* var. *capitata,* with short stem and leaves formed into a compact, edible head. **2.** any of various plants resembling a cabbage. **3.** the head of the ordinary cabbage. **4.** *Colloq.* paper money. **5. the cabbage garden, land** or **patch,** *Colloq.* Victoria. *–v.i.* **6.** to form a head like a cabbage. [ME *caboche,* from F, probably from Pr. *caboso,* from *cap* head, from L *caput*]

**cabbage butterfly** /– ˈbʌtəflaɪ/, *n.* a large, white butterfly of the Old World, *Pieris rapae,* introduced into Australia, the larvae of which feed on cabbage. Also, **cabbage white butterfly.**

**cabbage fly** /ˈ– flaɪ/, *n.* a small dipterous fly, *Erioischia brassicae,* the grubs of which feed on the roots of cabbage.

**cabbage-gardener** /ˈkæbɪdʒ-gadənə/, *n.* **1.** someone who obtains a living from growing vegetables. **2.** Also, **cabbage-patcher, cabbage-lander.** *Colloq.* →**Victorian** (def. 6).

**cabbage gum** /ˈkæbɪdʒ gʌm/, *n.* a smooth-barked tree, *Eucalyptus amplifolia,* common on swampy ground in coastal New South Wales.

**cabbage moth** /ˈ– mɒθ/, *n.* any of a number of moths, esp. of the genera *Plutella* and *Plusia,* the larvae of which feed on cabbage and other cruciferous plants.

**cabbage palm** /ˈ– pam/, *n.* any of several palm trees with large terminal leaf buds which are eaten like cabbage, as *Roystonea oleracea* of the West Indies. Also, **cabbage tree.**

cabbage palm

**cabbage roll** /ˈ– roʊl/, *n.* a blanched cabbage leaf filled with a mixture of minced cooked meat or other filling, rolled up and braised.

**cabbage tree** /'– tri/, *n.* **1.** a tall palm with large leaves, *Livistona australis,* of the coastal areas of eastern Australia. **2.** *N.Z.* the small tufted tree *Cordyline australis* of New Zealand, frequently cultivated as an ornamental; ti. **3.** →**cabbage palm. 4.** →**cabbage tree hat.**

cabbage tree hat

**cabbage tree hat,** *n.* a wide-brimmed hat made from the leaves of the local cabbage tree, a common form of hat in the early days of the colony and later regarded as a symbol of Australian nationalistic feeling.

**cabbage white butterfly** /'– waɪt/, *n.* →**cabbage butterfly.** Also, **cabbage white.**

**cabbage worm** /'– wɜm/, *n.* the larva of the cabbage butterfly.

**cabbala** /kə'balə/, *n.* **1.** (among certain Jewish rabbis and medieval Christians) a system of esoteric theosophy, based on a mystical interpretation of the Scriptures. **2.** any occult or secret doctrine or science. Also, **cabala, kabala, kabbala.** [ML, from Heb. *qabbālāh* tradition] – **cabbalism,** *n.* – **cabbalist,** *n.*

**cabbalistic** /kæbə'lɪstɪk/, *adj.* **1.** pertaining to the cabbala. **2.** mystic; occult. Also, **cabbalistical.**

**cabbie** /'kæbi/, *n. Colloq.* a cab driver. Also, **cabby.**

**caber** /'keɪbə/, *n.* a pole or beam, esp. one thrown as a trial of strength in the Scottish Highland game of **tossing the caber.** [Gaelic *cabar* pole]

**Cabernet Sauvignon** /,kæbəneɪ 'soʊvɪnjɒ̃/, *n.* a highly regarded grape variety widely used in the making of claret-style wines. [F]

**cabin** /'kæbən/, *n.* **1.** a small house; hut, esp. a temporary structure, as on a building site. **2.** an apartment or room in a ship, as for passengers. **3.** (in a passenger ship) a room used for the accommodation of higher-fare passengers or officers. **4.** *Naval* **a.** (in a warship) the apartment used by the commanding officer or flag officer. **b.** the quarters of any officer in a shore establishment. **5.** *Aeron.* the enclosed place in an aircraft for the pilot, passengers, or cargo. *–v.i.* **6.** to live in a cabin. *–v.t.* **7.** to confine; enclose tightly; cramp. [ME *cabane,* from F, from Pr. *cabana,* from LL *capanna,* of uncert. orig.]

**cabin boy** /'– bɔɪ/, *n.* a boy employed to wait on the officers and passengers of a ship.

**cabin class** /'– klas/, *n.* a class of accommodation on a passenger ship superior to tourist class but inferior to first class.

**cabin crew** /'– kru/, *n.* the crew of flight attendants who attend to passengers on an aeroplane.

**cabin cruiser** /'– kruzə/, *n.* a motor boat with a cabin and berths.

**cabinet** /'kæbənət, 'kæbnət/, *n.* **1.** (*also cap.*) a council advising a sovereign or chief executive; the group of ministers responsible for the government of a nation. See **shadow cabinet. 2.** a piece of furniture with shelves, drawers, etc., for holding or displaying valuable objects, dishes, etc. **3.** a piece of furniture holding a record-player, radio, television, or the like. **4.** a case with compartments for precious objects, etc. **5.** a private room. **6.** *Archaic.* a small room. **7.** *Obs.* a small cabin. **8.** a standard size for a sheet of paper or for a photographic print. *–adj.* **9.** pertaining to a political cabinet: *a cabinet meeting.* **10.** pertaining to a private room. **11.** private; confidential; secret. **12.** of suitable value, beauty, or size for a private room, small case, etc.: *a cabinet edition of Milton.* **13.** (of a projection, drawing, etc.) having all vertical and horizontal lines in a representation of a three-dimensional object drawn to exact scale, with oblique lines reduced to about half scale so as to offset the appearance of distortion. [F, from It. *gabinetto,* ? from *gabbia* cage, from L *cavea;* in some senses, diminutive of CABIN]

**cabinet booth** /'– buð/, *n.* an enclosure so arranged and equipped as to protect a spray painter and others in the vicinity from fumes.

**cabinet government** /– 'gʌvənmənt/, *n.* a system of government in which the head of state acts on the advice of a committee of ministers in charge of the various executive departments of state.

**cabinet-maker** /'kæbənət-meɪkə/, *n.* a workman who uses tools, woodworking machines, and wood to build items for storage and household equipment.

**cabinet minister** /'kæbənət mɪnəstə/, *n.* a minister who is a member of the cabinet.

**cabinet pudding** /– 'pʊdɪŋ/, *n.* a steamed pudding made from bread, butter, and raisins.

**cabinet wood** /'– wʊd/, *n.* timber used in the making of furniture and veneers, usu. of a high grade or attractive grain.

**cabinetwork** /'kæbnətwɜk/, *n.* **1.** the making of fine furniture, etc. **2.** the product made.

**cable** /'keɪbəl/, *n., v.,* **-bled, -bling.** *–n.* **1.** a thick, strong rope, often one of several wires twisted together. **2.** *Naut.* **a.** the rope or chain used to hold a vessel at anchor. **b.** cable's length. **3.** *Elect.* a stranded conductor, or a combination of conductors insulated from one another. **4.** a telegram sent abroad, esp. by submarine cable. *–v.t.* **5.** to send (a message) by submarine cable. **6.** to send a cable to. **7.** to fasten with a cable. **8.** to furnish with a cable or cables. *–v.i.* **9.** to send a message by submarine cable. [ME *cable, cabel,* c. D, MLG, MHG, G *Kabel,* all from Rom.; cf. F *cable* (from Pr.), Sp. *cable,* all from LL *capulum* halter]

**cable car** /'– ka/, *n.* **1.** a carriage of a cable tram. **2.** a car on a funicular railway.

**cablegram** /'keɪbəlgræm/, *n.* →**cable** (def. 4).

**cable-laid** /keɪbəl-'leɪd/, *adj.* (of a rope) made by laying three plain-laid ropes together with a left-handed twist.

**cable length** /'keɪbəl lɛŋθ/, *n.* a unit of length, one tenth of a nautical mile. Also, **cable's length.**

**cable lift** /'– lɪft/, *n.* →**ski-lift.**

**cable moulding** /– 'moʊldɪŋ/, *n. Archit.* a style of moulding carved to resemble thick rope.

**cable railway** /– 'reɪlweɪ/, *n.* **1.** a funicular railway. **2.** a railway on which the cars are hauled by a moving cable.

**cable release** /– rə'lis/, *n.* a cable by which the shutter of a camera may be operated without risk of shaking the camera.

**cablese** /keɪbə'liz/, *n.* the language used in cables, characterised by shortened forms, abbreviated syntax, blends, etc.

**cable stitch** /'keɪbəl stɪtʃ/, *n.* a knitting pattern whereby one set of stitches is crossed over another so that a ropelike effect is produced.

**cablet** /'keɪblət/, *n.* a small cable (def. 1). [CABLE + -ET]

**cable television** /keɪbəl 'tɛləvɪʒən/, *n.* television conveyed from the television station to the home by cable instead of being transmitted through the air.

**cable tram** /'– træm/, *n.* a cable-hauled tram.

**cable tramway** /– 'træmweɪ/, *n.* a tramway on which the cars are pulled by a moving cable under the roadway.

**cable transfer** /'– trænsfɜ/, *n. U.S.* →**telegraphic transfer.**

**cableway** /'keɪbəlweɪ/, *n.* a construction for transporting goods or passengers in which the car hangs from a cable and is pulled by another, between two terminal towers; teleferic.

**cabling** /'keɪblɪŋ/, *n.* **1.** *Engineering.* a collection of electrical and wire-rope cables. **2.** *Textiles.* two tightly twisted yarns which are subsequently twisted loosely together. **3.** →**cable moulding.**

**cabob** /kə'bɒb/, *n.* →**kebab.**

**cabochon** /'kæbəʃɒn/, *n.* a precious stone of convex hemispherical form, which has been polished but not cut into facets. [F, from *caboche* head]

**caboodle** /kə'budl/, *n. Colloq.* the (whole) lot, pack, or crowd. [unexplained var. of BOODLE[1] (def. 1)]

**caboose** /kə'bus/, *n.* **1.** a kitchen on the deck of a ship; galley. **2.** *U.S.* a wagon (usu. the last) on a goods train, used by the crew; guard's van. **3. a.** a small dwelling; a hut. **b.** gaol. [LG *kabūse*]

**cabotage** /'kæbətaʒ/, *n.* **1.** trade or navigation in coastal waters. **2.** the legal arrangement by which the right to engage in air transportation within a country's borders is restricted to domestic carriers. [F *caboter* to coast]

**cab rank** /'kæb ræŋk/, *n.* →**taxi rank.**

**cabriole** /'kæbrioʊl/, *n.* **1.** *Furnit.* a leg, curved and tapering, often ending in the form of an animal's paw, used esp. by Chippendale. **2.** *Ballet.* a leap in which one leg is raised in the air and the other is brought up to beat against it. [F. See CAPRIOLE]

cabriole (def. 1): 17th century

**cabriolet** /ˈkæbrioʊˌleɪ/, *n. Obs.* **1.** a type of motor car resembling a coupé, with a folding top; a convertible coupé. **2.** a light, hooded one-horse carriage with two seats. [F, from *cabriole* a leap. See CAPRIOLE]

**cac-**, variant of **caco-**.

**cacao** /kəˈkeɪoʊ, -ˈkaoʊ/, *n., pl.* **-caos. 1.** a small evergreen sterculiaceous tree, *Theobroma cacao,* native to tropical America, cultivated for its seeds, the source of cocoa, chocolate, etc. **2.** the fruit and seeds of this tree. [Sp., from Nahuatl *caca-uatl*]

cacao: open seed pod

**cacao bean** /ˈ– bin/, *n.* →**cocoa bean.**

**cacao butter** /ˈ– bʌtə/, *n.* →**cocoa butter.**

**cacciatore** /kætʃəˈtɔri/, *adj.* (of fowl or game dishes) braised in a sauce of onions, tomatoes, wine, etc. [It. *cacciatore* hunter]

**cachalot** /ˈkæʃəlɒt/, *n.* →**sperm whale.** [F, from Pg. *cachalote,* from L *caccabus* pot]

**cache** /kæʃ/, *n., v.,* **cached, caching.** *–n.* **1.** a hiding place, esp. one in the ground, for provisions, treasure, etc. **2.** the store of provisions, etc., so hidden. **3.** a store of food collected by some animals for the winter. *–v.t.* **4.** to put in a cache; conceal; hide. [F, from *cacher* hide]

**cachet** /ˈkæʃeɪ, kæˈʃeɪ/, *n.* **1.** a seal as on a letter. **2.** a distinguishing mark or characteristic. **3.** kudos; prestige. **4.** *Pharm.* a hollow wafer for enclosing an ill-tasting medicine. **5.** *Philately.* a slogan, design, etc., stamped or printed on mail. [F, from *cacher* hide]

**cachexia** /kəˈkɛksiə/, *n.* general ill health, with emaciation, due to a chronic disease, as cancer. Also, **cachexy.** [NL, from Gk: bad condition] – **cachectic,** *adj.*

**cachinnate** /ˈkækəneɪt/, *v.i.,* **-nated, -nating.** to laugh loudly or immoderately. [L *cachinnātus,* pp.] – **cachinnation** /kækəˈneɪʃən/, *n.*

**cachou** /ˈkæʃu/, *n.* **1.** →**catechu. 2.** a pill or pastille for sweetening the breath. **3.** small spherical confections, usu. silver in colour and used for cake decoration. [F, from Pg. *cachu,* from Malay *kāchu* CATECHU]

**cachucha** /kəˈtʃutʃə/, *n.* **1.** a lively dance. **2.** the music for it.

**cacio cavallo** /ˌkætʃoʊ kəˈvæloʊ/, *n.* a cheese, similar to provolone, rectangular in shape, often allowed to mature, and used for grating. [It.: horse cheese, perhaps from the region of Monte *Cavallo,* Italy]

**cacique** /kəˈsik/, *n.* **1.** (in Mexico and the West Indies) a chief of an Indian clan or tribe. **2.** (in Spain and Spanish America) a local political boss. **3.** any of a genus of American oscinine passerine birds of the family Icteridae, including numerous species from Mexico and Central and South America, typical forms having a large bill somewhat swollen at the base. [Sp., from Arawak]

**cack** /kæk/, *n.Colloq.* **1.** muck; filth **2.** faeces. *–v.i.* **3.** to defecate. *–v.t.* **4.** to eliminate as excrement. **5.** to soil with excrement: *he cacked his corduroys.* [ME *kakken* defecate; c. Icel. *kuka* defecate, L *cacāre,* Gk *kakós* bad]

**cack-handed** /ˈkæk-hændəd/, *adj. Colloq.* **1.** clumsy with the hands; maladroit. **2.** →**left-handed.** Also, **cacky-handed.** [? CACK + HANDED]

**cackle** /ˈkækəl/, *v.,* **-led, -ling,** *n. –v.i.* **1.** to utter a shrill, broken sound or cry, as a hen after laying an egg. **2.** to laugh brokenly. **3.** to chatter noisily. *–v.t.* **4.** to utter with cackles; express by cackling. *–n.* **5.** the act or sound of cackling. **6.** idle talk. **7. cut the cackle,** *Colloq.* to be quiet. [ME *cackelen;* imitative. Cf. D *kakelen,* LG *kâkeln,* Swed. *kackla*] – **cackler,** *n.*

**cackle berry** /ˈ– bɛri/, *n. Colloq.* an egg. Also, **cackle fruit.**

**cacky** /ˈkæki/, *adj.* **1.** dirty; mucky. **2.** faecal. [CACK + -Y[1]]

**cacky-handed** /ˌkæki-ˈhændəd/, *adj.* →**cack-handed.**

**caco-,** a word element meaning 'bad', 'deformed', or 'unpleasant', often used in forming medical terms. Also, **cac-.** [Gk *kako-,* combining form of *kakós* bad]

**cacodemon** /kækəˈdimən/, *n.* an evil spirit; a devil. Also, **cacodaemon.** [Gk *kakodaímōn*]

**cacodyl** /ˈkækədɪl/, *n.* **1.** any compound containing the $(CH_3)_2As$ radical. **2.** a poisonous, ill-smelling liquid, $As_2(CH_3)_4$. [Gk *kakṓdēs* ill-smelling + -YL] – **cacodylic,** *adj.*

**cacoethes** /kækoʊˈiθiz/, *n.* an irresistible urge; mania. [L, from Gk *kakóēthes* bad habit (properly neut. of *kakoḗthēs* malignant)]

**cacogenics** /kækoʊˈdʒɛnɪks/, *n.* →**dysgenics.** [CACO- + (EU)GENICS] – **cacogenic,** *adj.*

**cacography** /kæˈkɒgrəfi/, *n.* **1.** bad handwriting (opposed to *calligraphy*). **2.** incorrect spelling (opposed to *orthography*). – **cacographer,** *n.* – **cacographic** /kækəˈgræfɪk/, **cacographical** /kækəˈgræfɪkəl/, *adj.*

**cacomistle** /ˈkækəmɪsəl/, *n.* a carnivorous animal, *Bassariscus astutus,* of Mexico and the south-western U.S., related to the raccoon but smaller, with a sharper snout and longer tail. Also, **cacomixle** /ˈkækəmɪsəl, -mɪksəl/. [Sp. *cacomixtle,* from Nahuatl *tlacomiztli,* from *tlaco* middle-sized + *miztli* lion]

**cacoon** /kəˈkun/, *n.* the shiny flattened seed of the tropical climbing plant, *Entada scandens.*

**cacophonous** /kæˈkɒfənəs/, *adj.* having a harsh sound; discordant.

**cacophony** /kəˈkɒfəni/, *n., pl.* **-nies. 1.** the quality of having a harsh sound; dissonance. **2.** *Music.* frequent use of discords of a harshness and relationship difficult to understand. [NL *cacophonia,* from Gk *kakophōnía*]

**cacto** /ˈkæktoʊ/, *n. Colloq.* →**cactoblastis.**

**cactoblastis** /kæktəˈblæstəs/, *n.* a small moth, *Cactoblastis cactorum,* the larvae of which feed on the prickly-pear.

**cactus** /ˈkæktəs/, *n., pl.* **-ti** /-ti, -taɪ/, **-tuses,** *adj. –n.* **1.** any of various fleshy-stemmed plants of the family Cactaceae, usu. leafless and spiny, often producing showy flowers, chiefly native to the hot, dry regions of America. **2.** *Colloq.* the backblocks. **3. in the cactus,** *Colloq.* in difficulties, in trouble. *–adj.* **4.** *Colloq.* ruined; useless. [L, from Gk *káktos* kind of prickly plant]

**cacuminal** /kæˈkjumənəl/, *Phonet. –adj.* **1.** →**retroflex.** *–n.* **2.** a retroflex consonant. [L *cacūmen* top + -AL[1]]

**cad** /kæd/, *n.* a contemptible, ill-bred person; one who does not behave like a gentleman. [short for CADDIE[1] (def. 2)]

**CAD** /si eɪ ˈdi/, *n.* a computer program for calculations involved in design work, as in engineering, aeronautical design, etc. [*C*(*omputer*) *A*(*ided*) *D*(*esign*)]

**cadagi** /kəˈdadʒi/, *n.* a tropical and sub-tropical tree, *Eucalyptus torelliana,* with large roundish leaves and smooth green trunk. Also, **cadaga** /kəˈdagə/.

**cadastral** /kəˈdæstrəl/, *adj.* of or pertaining to the records of a cadastre; concerned with keeping a cadastre.

**cadastral map** /– ˈmæp/, *n.* a map showing boundaries and ownership of land.

**cadastral survey** /– ˈsɜveɪ/, *n.* a survey relating to boundaries and subdivision of land.

**cadastre** /kəˈdæstə/, *n.* an official register of property, with details of boundaries, ownership, etc. [F, from It. *catastro,* var. of *catastico,* from LGk *katástichon* register, from the phrase *katà stíchon* line by line]

**cadaver** /kəˈdævə, -ˈdavə/, *n.* a dead body, esp. of a human being; a corpse. [L] – **cadaveric,** *adj.*

**cadaverine** /kəˈdævərin/, *n.* a colourless ptomaine, $NH_2(CH_2)_5NH_2$, produced by protein hydrolysis and decomposition of lysine.

**cadaverous** /kəˈdævərəs/, *adj.* **1.** of or like a corpse. **2.** pale, wan; ghastly. **3.** haggard and thin. – **cadaverously,** *adv.* – **cadaverousness,** *n.*

**caddie**[1] /ˈkædi/, *n., v.,* **-died, -dying.** *–n.* **1.** *Golf.* an attendant, hired to carry the player's clubs, find the ball, etc. **2.** a person who runs errands, does odd jobs, etc. *–v.i.* **3.** to work as a caddie. Also, **caddy.** [F *cadet* CADET]

**caddie**[2] /ˈkeɪdi/, *n.* →**cady.** Also, **caddy.**

**caddis fly** /ˈkædəs flaɪ/, *n.* any of various adult insects of the order Trichoptera, characterised by four membranous, more or less hairy wings. Also, **caddice fly.** [orig. uncert.]

**caddish** /ˈkædɪʃ/, *adj.* ill-bred; ungentlemanly: *caddish behaviour.* – **caddishly,** *adv.* – **caddishness,** *n.*

**caddis worm** /ˈkædəs wɜm/, *n.* the larva of the caddis fly, used as fish bait. Also, **caddis, caddice.**

**Caddoan** /kæˈdoʊən/, *n.* a family of North American Indian languages.

**caddy**[1] /ˈkædi/, *n., pl.* **-ies.** a small box, tin, or chest, esp.

one for holding tea. [var. of CATTY[2] from Malay *katī* a unit of weight]

**caddy**[2] /ˈkædi/, *n., pl.* **-dies**, *v.i.*, **-died, -dying.** →**caddie**[1].

**cade**[1] /keɪd/, *n.* a species of juniper, *Juniperus oxycedrus,* of the Mediterranean area, whose wood on destructive distillation yields an oily liquid (**oil of cade**) used in treating skin affections. [F, from Pr.]

**cade**[2] /keɪd/, *adj.* (of the young of animals) left by the mother and raised by hand: *a cade lamb.* [orig. uncert.]

**cadelle** /kəˈdɛl/, *n.* a small blackish beetle, *Tenebrioides mauritanicus,* all stages of which are commonly destructive to cereals. [F, from Pr. *cadello,* from L *catellus, catella* little animal]

**cadence** /ˈkeɪdəns/, *n.* **1.** rhythmic flow, as of verses; rhythm. **2.** the beat of any rhythmical movement. **3.** a fall in pitch of the voice, as in speaking. **4.** the general modulation of the voice. **5.** *Music.* a sequence of notes or chords which indicates the momentary or complete end of a composition, section, phrase, etc. **6.** *Mil.* the rate of stepping in marching: *a cadence of 120 steps per minute.* Also, **cadency.** [ME, from F, from It. *cadenza,* from LL *cadentia,* from L *cadens,* ppr., falling] – **cadenced,** *adj.*

**cadent** /ˈkeɪdənt/, *adj.* **1.** having cadence. **2.** *Archaic.* falling. [L *cadens,* ppr., falling]

**cadenza** /kəˈdɛnzə/, *n.* an elaborate showy passage, frequently unaccompanied, for a singer usu. near the end of an aria or for an instrumentalist usu. near the end of a movement of a concerto. [It. See CADENCE]

**cadet** /kəˈdɛt/, *n.* **1.** a person undergoing training in the armed services, police, public service, at sea, etc. **2.** a member of a military training unit in a secondary school. **3.** *N.Z.* a young man in apprenticeship to farming. **4.** a younger son or brother. *–adj.* **5.** pertaining to or traced through a younger son: *the cadet branch of a family.* [F, from d. (Gascon) *capdet* chief, from L *caput* head] – **cadetting,** n.

**cadetship** /kəˈdɛtʃɪp/, *n.* **1.** the position or status of being a cadet. **2.** a training position in a large organisation.

**cadge** /kædʒ/, *v.,* **cadged, cadging.** *–v.t.* **1.** to obtain by imposing on another's generosity or friendship. **2.** to borrow without intent to repay. **3.** to beg or obtain by begging. *–v.i.* **4.** to obtain things from others with no intention of repayment. **5.** to beg. [orig. unknown] – **cadger,** *n.*

**cadi** /ˈkædi, ˈka-/, *n., pl.* **-dis.** a judge in a Muslim community, whose decisions are based on Islamic religious law. Also, **kadi.** [Ar. *qādī* judge]

**cadmium** /ˈkædmiəm/, *n.* a white, ductile, divalent metallic element like tin in appearance, used in plating and in making certain alloys. As it is a good absorber of neutrons it is also used in the control rods of nuclear reactors. *Symbol:* Cd; *at. wt:* 112.410; *at. no.:* 48; *sp. gr.:* 8.6 at 20°C. [NL, from L *cadmia,* from Gk *kadmeía (gê)* Cadmean (earth), i.e. calamine (with which cadmium is usu. associated)] – **cadmic,** *adj.*

**cadmium cell** /ˈ– sɛl/, *n. Physics.* →**Weston cell.**

**cadmium orange** /– ˈɒrɪndʒ/, *adj.* a yellow colour approaching orange.

**cadmium yellow** /– ˈjɛloʊ/, *adj.* a bright, or lemon, yellow colour.

**cadre** /ˈkadə/, *n.* **1.** *Mil.* the key group of officers and other ranks necessary to establish and train a new military unit. **2.** a unit within an organisational framework, esp. personnel. [F: frame, from It. *quadro,* from L *quadrum* a square]

**caduceus** /kəˈdjusiəs/, *n., pl.* **-cei** /-sii/. **1.** the staff carried by Hermes, or Mercury, as herald or messenger of the gods. **2.** a similar staff used as an emblem of the medical profession and as the insignia of the Medical Corps of the armed services. [L, from d. Gk *kārýkeion* herald's staff] – **caducean,** *adj.*

caduceus

**caducity** /kəˈdjusəti/, *n.* **1.** the infirmity of old age; senility. **2.** frailty; transitoriness. [F *caducité.* See CADUCOUS]

**caducous** /kəˈdjukəs/, *adj.* **1.** *Bot.* **a.** tending to fall. **b.** deciduous; dropping off very early, as leaves. **2.** *Zool.* subject to shedding. **3.** transitory. [L *cadūcus* falling]

**cady** /ˈkeɪdi/, *n. Colloq.* **1.** a hard straw hat formerly worn by men, esp. on recreational outings; boater. **2.** a man's hat, of any style or material. Also, **caddie.** [orig. unknown]

**CAE** /si eɪ ˈi/, College of Advanced Education.

**caecilian** /səˈsɪljən/, *n.* any of the limbless and elongate burrowing amphibians of the order Apoda. [L *caecilia* lizard + -AN]

**caeco-,** a word element meaning 'the caecum'. Also, before vowels, **caec-.**

**caecum** /ˈsikəm/, *n., pl.* **-ca** /-kə/. a cul-de-sac, esp. the one at the beginning of the human large intestine, bearing the vermiform appendix. Also, **coecum,** *U.S.,* **cecum.** [L, neut. of *caecus* blind] – **caecal,** *adj.*

**caeno-,** variant of **caino-.**

**caeoma** /siˈoʊmə/, *n.* (in fungi) an aecium in which the spores are formed in chains and not enclosed in a peridium. [Gk *kaíein* smelt + -OMA]

**Caerphilly** /kɛəˈfɪli, ka-/, *n.* a creamy white, quick-maturing cheese with a mild, delicate flavour.

**caerulean** /səˈruliən/, *adj., n.* →**cerulean.**

**caesalpiniaceous** /sɛzˌælpəˈneɪʃəs, sɛs-/, *adj.* belonging to the Caesalpiniaceae, a family of leguminous plants including the cassia, royal poinciana, and numerous tropical genera. [NL *Caesalpinia,* the typical genus (named after Andrea *Caesalpino,* 1519-1603, Italian botanist) + -ACEOUS]

**Caesar** /ˈsizə/, *n.* **1.** a title of the Roman emperors from Augustus to Hadrian, and later of the heir presumptive. **2.** any emperor. **3.** a tyrant; dictator. **4.** (*l.c.*) *Colloq.* a caesarean section. [from Gaius Julius *Caesar,* c.100-44 B.C., Roman general, statesman and historian]

**Caesarean** /səˈzɛəriən/, *n.* **1.** (*l.c.*) a caesarean section. *–adj.* **2.** pertaining to Caesar or the Caesars: *a Caesarean conquest.* Also, **Caesarian, Cesarean, Cesarian.**

**caesarean section** /– ˈsɛkʃən/, *n.* the operation by which a foetus is taken from the womb by cutting through the walls of the abdomen and womb (supposedly performed at the birth of Julius Caesar).

**Caesarism** /ˈsizərɪzəm/, *n.* absolute government; imperialism. – **Caesarist,** *n.*

**caesar salad** /ˌsizə ˈsæləd/, *n.* an American salad containing lettuce, bread croutons, parmesan cheese and sometimes anchovies, seasoned and dressed with egg, oil and vinegar.

**caesium** /ˈsiziəm/, *n.* a rare, extremely active, soft, monovalent metallic element showing blue lines in the spectrum. *Symbol:* Cs; *at. wt:* 132.91; *at. no.:* 55; *sp. gr.* 1.9 at 20°C; melts at 28.5°C. The radioactive isotope, **caesium-137,** is obtained from nuclear reactors and is used in radiotherapy and for sterilising foodstuffs. Also, **cesium.** [NL, special use of *caesium* (neut.) bluish grey]

**caesium clock** /– ˈklɒk/, *n.* a very accurate type of clock based on the frequency of a particular line in the spectrum of caesium.

**caespitose** /ˈsɛspətoʊs/, *adj. Bot.* matted together; growing in dense tufts. Also, *U.S.,* **cespitose.** [L *caespes* turf + -OSE[1]] – **caespitosely,** *adv.*

**caesura** /səˈʒurə/, *n., pl.* **-ras, -rae** /-ri/. **1.** *Eng. Pros.* a break, esp. a sense pause, usu. near the middle of a verse, and marked in scansion by a double vertical line, as in *know then thyself ‖ presume not God to scan.* **2.** *Gk and Latin Pros.* a division made by the ending of a word within a foot (or sometimes at the end of a foot), esp. in certain recognised places near the middle of a verse. Also, **cesura.** [L: a cutting] – **caesural,** *adj.*

**caf** /kæf/, *n. Colloq.* →**cafeteria.**

**cafe** /ˈkæfeɪ/; (*joc.*) /keɪf/, *n.* **1.** a room or building where coffee and light refreshments are served. **2.** (in continental Europe and other countries) a similar room or building where alcoholic and other refreshments are served. **3.** a restaurant, usu. low-priced. Also, **café.** [F. See COFFEE]

**café au lait** /ˌkæfeɪ oʊ ˈleɪ/, *n.* **1.** hot coffee with scalded milk. **2.** a light brown colour. *–adj.* **3.** of a light brown colour or complexion, esp. as applied to a light-skinned negro or one of mixed blood.

**cafe curtain** /ˈkæfeɪ kɜtən/, *n.* a straight hanging curtain, usu. hung in pairs on a rod by rings or loops and used to cover the lower part of a window.

**cafeteria** /kæfəˈtɪəriə/, *n.* an inexpensive restaurant or snack-bar, usu. self-service. [Amer. Sp.: coffee shop]

**caff** /kæf/, *n. Colloq.* →**cafeteria.**

**caffeine** /ˈkæfin/, *n.* a bitter crystalline alkaloid, $C_8H_{10}N_4O_2 \cdot H_2O$, obtained from coffee, tea, etc., used in medicine as a stimulant, diuretic, etc., [F *caféine*, from *café* coffee. See -INE[2] (def. 3)]

**caftan** /ˈkæftæn/, *n.* **1.** a long garment having long sleeves and tied at the waist by a girdle, worn under a coat in the Near East. **2.** a loose garment, either short or floor length, with long, bell-shaped sleeves, in imitation of this garment. Also, **kaftan.** [Turk., Pers. *qaftān*] – **caftaned,** *adj.*

**cage** /keɪdʒ/, *n., v.,* **caged, caging.** –*n.* **1.** a box-shaped receptacle or enclosure for confining birds or other animals, made with openwork of wires, bars, etc. **2.** anything that confines or imprisons; prison. **3.** something like a cage in structure or purpose. **4.** the enclosed platform of a lift, esp. one in a coal mine. **5.** any skeleton framework. **6.** *Hockey.* the structure forming the goal. –*v.t.* **7.** to put or confine in or as in a cage. [ME, from OF, from L *cavea* enclosure]

**cagebird** /ˈkeɪdʒbɜd/, *n.* a bird kept in a cage.

**cageling** /ˈkeɪdʒlɪŋ/, *n.* →**cagebird.**

**cagey** /ˈkeɪdʒi/, *adj.,* **cagier, cagiest.** *Colloq.* cautious; secretive. Also, **cagy.** – **cagily** *adv.* – **caginess,** *n.*

**cahier** /ˈkajeɪ/, *n.* **1.** a number of sheets of paper or leaves of a book placed together, as for binding. **2.** a report of the proceedings of any body. [F, from LL word meaning fourth, group of four sheets. See QUIRE[1]]

**cahoot** /kəˈhut/, *n. in the phrase* **in cahoot** or **cahoots,** in partnership; in league. [? F *cahute* hut, cabin]

**CAI** /si eɪ ˈaɪ/, *n.* a computer program for instructional purposes, as in language teaching, mathematical instruction, etc. [*C(omputer) A(ided) I(nstruction)*]

**caiman** /ˈkeɪmən/, *n., pl.* **-mans.** any of several tropical American crocodilians of the genus *Caiman* and related genera resembling and related to the alligators but having overlapping ventral scutes. Also, **cayman.** [Sp., Pg. from Carib]

**Cain** /keɪn/, *n.* **1.** a murderer. **2. raise Cain, a.** to make a commotion. **b.** to complain or remonstrate vociferously. [from *Cain*, first son of Adam and Eve, who murdered his brother Abel (Gen. 4)]

**caino-,** a word element meaning 'new', 'recent', as in *Cainozoic.* Also, **ceno-, caeno-.** [See -CENE]

**cainogenesis** /ˌkaɪnoʊˈdʒɛnəsəs/, *n.* development of an individual which does not repeat the phylogeny of its race, stock, or group (opposed to *palingenesis*). Also, **kainogenesis;** *Chiefly U.S.,* **cenogenesis.** [CAINO- + GENESIS] – **cainogenetic** /ˌkaɪnoʊdʒəˈnɛtɪk/, *adj.*

**Cainozoic** /ˌkaɪnoʊˈzoʊɪk, ˌkeɪ-/, *adj.* **1.** pertaining to the geological era of rocks of most recent age, extending to the present. –*n.* **2.** the era or rocks representing the most recent major division of earth history. Also, **Cenozoic, Kainozoic.** [CAINO- + ZO(O)- + -IC]

**caique** /kaɪˈik/, *n.* a long, narrow skiff or rowing boat as used on the Bosporus. [F, from It. *caicco,* from Turk. *kayik*]

**cairn** /kɛən/, *n.* a heap of stones set up as a landmark, monument, tombstone, etc. [Scot., from Gaelic *carn* pile of stones] – **cairned,** *adj.*

**cairngorm** /ˈkɛəngɔm/, *n.* a yellow or brown ornamental quartz. [so called from the *Cairngorms,* a range of mountains in Scotland]

**cairn terrier** /kɛən ˈtɛriə/, *n.* a short-legged, long-bodied terrier with silver-grey wiry hair.

**caisson** /ˈkeɪsən/, *n.* **1.** a structure in which men can work on river beds, etc., consisting essentially of an airtight box or chamber with an open bottom, the water being kept out by the high air pressure maintained within. **2.** a boatlike structure used as a gate for a dock or the like. **3.** →**pontoon**[1] (def. 3). **4.** a wooden chest containing bombs or explosives, used as a mine; an ammunition chest. **5.** an ammunition wagon. **6.** *Bldg Trades.* a deeply recessed panel in a ceiling, archway, or the like. [F: b. *caisse* chest and earlier *casson* (from It. *cassone,* augmentative of *cassa,* from L *capsa* box). See CASE[2]]

**caisson disease** /ˈ– dəˌziz/, *n.* the bends. See **bend**[1] (def. 21).

**caitiff** /ˈkeɪtɪf/, *Archaic, Poetic.* –*n.* **1.** a base, despicable person. –*adj.* **2.** base; despicable. [ME *caitif,* from ONF, from LL **cactīvus,* assimilatory var. of L *captīvus* (see CAPTIVE)]

**cajole** /kəˈdʒoʊl/, *v.,* **-joled, -joling.** to persuade by flattery or promises; wheedle; coax. [F *cajoler,* ? b. *caresser* caress and *enjôler* capture] – **cajolement,** *n.* – **cajoler,** *n.*

**cajolery** /kəˈdʒoʊləri/, *n., pl.* **-ries.** persuasion by flattery or promises; wheedling; coaxing.

**Cajun** /ˈkeɪjən/, *n.* (in Louisiana, U.S.) a descendant of the exiles from Acadia; Acadian. Also, **Cajian.** [var. of ACADIAN. Cf. *Injun* for *Indian*]

**cajuput** /ˈkædʒəpʊt/, *n.* **1.** a small tree, *Melaleuca cajuputi,* found from south-eastern Asia to northern Australia. **2.** a green oil having a distinctive smell, distilled from the leaves of this tree, used as a stimulant, antispasmodic, and diaphoretic. **3.** a tree, *Umbellularia californica,* whose aromatic leaves are used medicinally. Also, **cajeput.** [D *kajoepoetih,* from Malay, from *kāyu* wood + *pūtih* white]

**cake** /keɪk/, *n., v.,* **caked, caking.** –*n.* **1.** a sweet baked food in loaf or layer form, made with or without shortening, usu. with flour, sugar, eggs, flavouring, usu. with baking powder or soda, and a liquid. **2.** a flat, thin mass of bread, esp. unleavened bread. **3.** a shaped or moulded mass of other food. **4.** a shaped or compressed mass: *a cake of soap, ice, etc.* **5. cakes and ale,** the good things and pleasures of life. **6. piece of cake,** *Colloq.* something easily accomplished or obtained. **7. take the cake, a.** to win the prize. **b.** to surpass all others; excel. –*v.t.* **8.** to form into a cake or compact mass. –*v.i.* **9.** to become formed into a cake or compact mass: *mud caked on his shoes.* [ME, from Scand.; cf. Icel. *kaka;* akin to D *koek,* G *Kuchen*]

**cakehole** /ˈkeɪkhoʊl/, *n. Colloq.* mouth.

**cakewalk** /ˈkeɪkwɔk/, *n.* **1.** a promenade or march, of American Negro origin, in which the couples with the most intricate or eccentric steps receive cakes as prizes. **2.** a dance based on this promenade. **3.** music for this dance. –*v.i.* **4.** to walk or dance in or as in a cakewalk. – **cakewalker,** *n.*

**cal,** calorie (def. 1a).

**cal.,** **1.** *Music.* calando. **2.** calibre.

**Cal,** calorie (def. 1b).

**Calabar bean** /ˌkæləba ˈbin/, *n.* the poisonous seed of an African climbing plant, *Physostigma venenosum,* the active principle of which is physostigmine.

**calabash** /ˈkæləbæʃ/, *n.* **1.** any of various gourds, esp. the fruit of the bottle gourd, *Lagenaria siceraria.* **2.** any of the plants bearing them. **3.** the fruit of a bignoniaceous tree, *Crescentia cujete,* of tropical America. **4.** Also, **calabash tree.** the tree itself. **5.** the dried hollow shell of the calabash (either def. 1 or 3) used as a vessel or otherwise. **6.** a bottle, kettle, tobacco-pipe bowl, etc., made from it. **7.** (formerly) a promissory note; an I.O.U. **8.** a gourd used as a rattle, drum, etc., esp. by American Indians. [F *calebasse,* from Sp. *calabaza* gourd, ? from Pers. *kharbuz* melon]

**calabash nutmeg** /– ˈnʌtmɛg/, *n.* **1.** the fruit of a tropical shrub, *Monodora myristica,* containing many aromatic oily seeds with the flavour of nutmegs. **2.** the shrub itself.

**calaboose** /ˈkæləbus, kæləˈbus/, *n. U.S. Colloq.* prison cell; gaol. [Creole F, from Sp. *calabozo* dungeon, orig. uncert.]

**caladenia** /kæləˈdiniə/, *n.* any of the numerous species of the orchid genus *Caladenia* widespread in temperate Australia.

**caladium** /kəˈleɪdiəm/, *n.* a plant of the genus *Caladium,* mostly herbs of the American tropics, cultivated for its variegated, colourful leaves. [NL, from Malay *kaladi*]

**calamanco** /kæləˈmæŋkoʊ/, *n., pl.* **-cos.** a glossy woollen fabric checked or brocaded in the warp so that the pattern shows on one side only, much used in the 18th century. [orig. uncert.; ? from ML *calamancus* kind of cap]

**calamander** /kæləˈmændə/, *n.* the hard wood of a tree, *Diospyros quaesita,* of Ceylon and India, used for cabinetwork. [metathetic var. of *Coromandel* Coast, in SE India]

**calamari** /kæləˈmari/, *n.* →**squid.** [It.]

**calamine** /ˈkæləmaɪn/, *n.* **1.** Also, **calamine lotion.** a liquid soothing to the skin, prepared from zinc oxide with $\frac{1}{2}$ per cent ferric oxide. **2.** →**smithsonite. 3.** *U.S.* →**hemimorphite.** [F, from ML *calamīna,* apparently alteration of L *cadmia.* See CADMIUM]

**calamite** /ˈkæləmaɪt/, *n.* any of a group of extinct sporebearing trees which flourished in the Carboniferous period. [NL *Calamītes,* from Gk *kalamítēs* reedlike]

**calamitous** /kəˈlæmətəs/, *adj.* causing or involving calamity; disastrous: *a calamitous defeat.* [L *calamitōsus*] – **calamitously,** *adv.* – **calamitousness,** *n.*

**calamity** /kəˈlæməti/, *n., pl.* **-ties. 1.** grievous affliction; adversity; misery. **2.** a great misfortune; a disaster. [late ME *calamyte,* from L *calamitas*]

**calamus** /ˈkæləməs/, *n., pl.* **-mi** /-mi/. **1.** the sweet flag, *Acorus calamus.* **2.** its aromatic root. **3.** any palm of the genus *Calamus,* yielding rattan, canes, etc. **4.** the hollow base of a feather; a quill. [L, from Gk *kálamos* reed]

**calando** /kəˈlændoʊ/, *adj., n., pl.* **-dos.** *Music.* –*adj.* **1.** gradually diminishing in loudness and tempo. –*n.* **2.** a calando passage. [It.]

**calash** /kəˈlæʃ/, *n.* **1.** a light, low-wheeled carriage, either with or without a folding top. **2.** the folding top (**calash top**) of such a vehicle. **3.** a kind of hood formerly worn by women. [F *calèche,* from G *Kalesche,* from Slavic; cf. Czech *kolésa*]

calash

**calaverite** /kəˈlævəraɪt/, *n.* a mineral, gold telluride, $AuTe_2$, which occurs in long striated crystals from which gold is recovered. [named after *Calaveras,* county in California, U.S.]

**calcaneum** /kælˈkeɪniəm/, *n., pl.* **-nea** /-niə/. →**calcaneus.**

**calcaneus** /kælˈkeɪniəs/, *n., pl.* **-nei** /-nii/. **1.** *Anat.* (in man) the largest tarsal bone, forming the prominence of the heel. **2.** *Zool.* the corresponding bone in other vertebrates. Also, **calcaneum.** [L: heel]

**calcar** /ˈkælka/, *n., pl.* **calcaria** /kælˈkɛəriə/. *Biol.* a spur, or spurlike process. [L: a spur]

**calcarate** /ˈkælkəreɪt/, *adj. Biol.* furnished with a calcar or calcaria; spurred. Also **calcarated.**

**calcareous** /kælˈkɛəriəs/, *adj.* of, coated with, containing, or like calcium carbonate; chalky: *calcareous earth.* [var. of *calcarious,* from L *calcārius* pertaining to lime]

**calcariferous** /kælkəˈrɪfərəs/, *adj. Biol.* bearing a spur or spurs. [CALCAR + -(I)FEROUS]

**calceiform** /ˈkælsiəfɔm/, *adj.* →**calceolate.** [L *calceus* a shoe + -(I)FORM]

**calceolaria** /ˌkælsiəˈlɛəriə/, *n.* any plant of the genus *Calceolaria,* often cultivated for its slipper-like flowers. [NL, from L *calceolus* slipper (diminutive of *calceus* shoe) + *-āria* -ARIA]

calcarate foot of pheasant

**calceolate** /ˈkælsiəleɪt/, *adj.* having the form of a shoe or slipper, as the labellum of certain orchids.

**calces** /ˈkælsiz/, *n.* plural of **calx.**

**calcic** /ˈkælsɪk/, *adj.* pertaining to or containing lime or calcium. [L *calx* lime + -IC]

**calciferol** /kælˈsɪfərɒl/, *n.* vitamin $D_2$; a fat-soluble, crystalline alcohol, found in milk and fish-liver oils and produced by the activation of ergosterol by ultraviolet irradiation.

**calciferous** /kælˈsɪfərəs/, *adj.* **1.** forming salts of calcium, esp. calcium carbonate. **2.** containing calcium carbonate. [L *calx* lime + -(I)FEROUS]

**calcific** /kælˈsɪfɪk/, *adj.* making or converting into salt of lime or chalk.

**calcification** /kælsəfəˈkeɪʃən/, *n.* **1.** a changing into lime. **2.** *Physiol.* the deposition of lime or insoluble salts of calcium, as in a tissue. **3.** *Anat., Geol.* a calcified formation. **4.** a soil process in which the surface soil is supplied with calcium in such a way that the soil colloids are always close to saturation.

**calcifuge** /ˈkælsəfjudʒ/, *n.* a plant that does not thrive in lime-rich soil, as daphne, rhododendron, azalea.

**calcify** /ˈkælsəfaɪ/, *v.,* **-fied, -fying.** *Physiol.* –*v.i.* **1.** to become calcareous or bony; harden by the deposit of calcium salts. –*v.t.* **2.** to make calcareous. [L *calx* lime + -(I)FY]

**calcimine** /ˈkælsəmaɪn/, *n., v.,* **-mined, -mining.** →**kalsomine.**

**calcination** /kælsəˈneɪʃən/, *n.* **1.** the act or process of calcining. **2.** the calcined state.

**calcine** /ˈkælsaɪn, -sən/, *v.,* **-cined, -cining,** *n.* –*v.t.,* **1.** to convert into calx by heat. **2.** to burn to a friable substance; roast. **3.** to oxidise by heating. **4.** to frit. –*v.i.* **5.** to undergo calcination. –*n.* **6.** ore after it has been oxidised. [F *calciner,* from L *calx* lime] – **calcinatory** /kælˈsɪnətəri, ˈkæl-, -tri/, *adj., n.*

**calcite** /ˈkælsaɪt/, *n.* one of the commonest minerals, calcium carbonate, $CaCO_3$, occurring in a great variety of crystalline forms; calcspar. Limestone, marble, and chalk consist largely of calcite. [L *calx* lime + -ITE[1]]

**calcium** /ˈkælsiəm/, *n.* a silver-white divalent metal, occurring combined in limestone, chalk, gypsum, etc. *Symbol:* Ca; *at. wt:* 40.08; *at. no.:* 20; *sp. gr.:* 1.55 at 20°C. [NL, from L *calx* lime + -IUM]

**calcium carbide** /– ˈkabaɪd/, *n.* a crystalline compound of calcium and carbon, $CaC_2$, which reacts with water to form acetylene.

**calcium carbonate** /– ˈkabəneɪt/, *n.* a crystalline compound, $CaCO_3$, occurring in nature as calcite, etc.

**calcium chloride** /– ˈklɔraɪd/, *n.* a white, deliquescent powder, $CaCl_2$, used as a drying agent, preservative, etc.

**calcium hydroxide** /– haɪˈdrɒksaɪd/, *n.* slaked lime, $Ca(OH)_2$.

**calcium light** /– ˈlaɪt/, *n.* a brilliant white light produced by heating lime to incandescence in an oxyhydrogen or other hot flame.

**calcium phosphate** /– ˈfɒsfeɪt/, *n.* any of several phosphates of calcium occurring naturally in some rocks and in animal bones, and used in medicine, industry, etc.

**calcium proprionate** /– ˈproʊpriəneɪt/, *n.* a white, water-soluble powder, $Ca(CH_3CH_2COO)_2$, used in battery products to inhibit the growth of fungi.

**calcrete** /ˈkælkrit/, *n.* a hard soil composed of gravel, sand or desert debris cemented by porous calcium carbonate; caliche.

**calc-sinter** /ˈkælk-sɪntə/, *n.* →**travertine.** [G *Kalksinter* lime slag]

**calcspar** /ˈkælkspa/, *n.* →**calcite.**

**calc-tufa** /ˈkælk-tufə/, *n.* calcareous tufa. See **tufa.** Also, **calc-tuff** /ˈkælk-tʌf/.

**calculable** /ˈkælkjələbəl/, *adj.* **1.** that can be calculated. **2.** that can be counted on; reliable; dependable.

**calculate** /ˈkælkjəleɪt/, *v.,* **-lated, -lating.** –*v.t.* **1.** to ascertain by mathematical methods; compute: *to calculate the velocity of light.* **2.** to make suitable, adapt, or fit for a purpose: *calculated to inspire confidence.* **3.** to do deliberately or cold-bloodedly: *a calculated insult.* **4.** to estimate the possibility of failure before undertaking (a course of action): *a calculated risk.* **5.** *U.S. Colloq.* **a.** to think; suppose. **b.** to intend; plan. –*v.i.* **6.** to make a computation; form an estimate. **7.** to count or rely (fol. by *on* or *upon*). [L *calculātus,* pp., counted. See CALCULUS]

**calculating** /ˈkælkjəleɪtɪŋ/, *adj.* **1.** that performs calculations: *a calculating machine.* **2.** shrewd; cautious. **3.** selfishly scheming.

**calculation** /kælkjəˈleɪʃən/, *n.* **1.** the act or process of calculating; computation. **2.** result or product of calculating. **3.** an estimate based on the various facts in a case; a forecast. **4.** forethought; prior or careful planning. – **calculative** /ˈkælkjələtɪv/ *adj.*

**calculator** /ˈkælkjəleɪtə/, *n.* **1.** one who calculates or computes. **2.** a machine that performs mathematical operations mechanically, electro-mechanically or electronically. **3.** a set of tables that facilitates calculation. [L]

**calculous** /ˈkælkjələs/, *adj. Pathol.* characterised by the presence of calculus or stone.

**calculus** /ˈkælkjələs/, *n., pl.* **-luses** (*def. 1*) **-li** /-laɪ/ (*def. 2*). **1. a.** a method of calculation, esp. a highly systematic method of treating problems by a special system of algebraic notation. **b.** *Maths.* the differential and integral calculus. **2.** *Pathol.* a stone or concretion found in the gall bladder, kidneys, or other parts of the body. [L: stone used in counting, diminutive of *calx* small stone, lime]

**Calcutta** /kælˈkʌtə/, *n.* a type of sweep in which the names of the contestants in the race are not allocated for a fixed price to the participants in the sweep but are auctioned off to the highest bidder.

**caldarium** /kæl'dɛəriəm/, *n., pl.* **-daria** /-'dɛəriə/. (in Roman baths) a room with hot water. [L]

**caldera** /kæl'dɛərə/, *n.* a large crater formed by the explosion or subsidence of the cone of a volcano. [Sp.: lit., cauldron]

**caldron** /'kɔldrən/, *n.* →**cauldron.**

**Caledonia** /kælə'doʊniə/, *n. Chiefly Poetic.* Scotland.

**Caledonian** /kælə'doʊniən/, *adj.* **1.** *Chiefly Poetic.* Scottish. **2.** *Geol.* of or pertaining to the major mountain-building episode, which occurred in Europe, reaching its height at the end of the Silurian period. *–n.* **3.** a Scotsman.

**calefacient** /kælə'feɪʃənt/, *n.* **1.** *Med.* a substance which produces a sensation of heat when applied to the body, as mustard. *–adj.* **2.** heating; warming. [L *calefaciens,* ppr., making hot]

**calefaction** /kælə'fækʃən/, *n.* **1.** the act of heating. **2.** a heated state. [L *calefactio*] – **calefactive,** *adj.*

**calefactory** /kælə'fæktəri, -tri/, *adj., n., pl.* **-ries.** *–adj.* **1.** serving to heat. *–n.* **2.** a heated sitting room in a monastery. [L *calefactōrius* having heating power]

**calendar** /'kæləndə/, *n.* **1.** any of various systems of reckoning time, esp. with reference to the beginning, length, and divisions of the year: *the Gregorian calendar.* **2.** a tabular arrangement of the days of each month and week in a year. **3.** a list, index, or register, esp. one arranged chronologically, as a list of the cases to be tried in a court. **4.** *Obs.* a guide or example. *–v.t.* **5.** to enter in a calendar; register. [L *calendārium* account book, from *calendae* CALENDS; replacing ME *calender,* from AF]

**calendar day** /– 'deɪ/, *n.* the period from one midnight to the following one.

**calendar month** /– 'mʌnθ/, *n.* →**month** (def. 2).

**calendar week** / – 'wik/, *n.* the period from midnight on one Sunday to midnight on the following Sunday.

**calendar year** /– 'jɪə/, *n.* →**year** (def. 1).

**calender** /'kæləndə/, *n.* **1.** a machine in which cloth, paper, or the like is smoothed, glazed, etc., by pressing between revolving cylinders. **2.** *Print.* paper glazed by such a machine. *–v.t.* **3.** to press in a calender. [F *calandre,* probably from Pr. *calandra,* from L *cylindrus* CYLINDER] – **calenderer,** *n.*

**Calender** /'kæləndə/, *n.* (*oft. l.c.*) (in Muslim countries) one of an order of mendicant dervishes founded in the 14th century. [Pers. *qalandar*]

**calends** /'kæləndz/, *n.pl.* (in the Roman calendar) the first day of the month. Also, **kalends.** [ME *kalendes* (rarely sing.), OE *cālend* (beginning of) a month, from L *calendae* (usu. *kalendae*)]

**calendula** /kə'lɛndʒələ/, *n.* **1.** any plant of the genus *Calendula,* esp. *C. officinalis,* the marigold. **2.** the dried florets of this plant, used in medicine as a vulnerary, etc. [NL, diminutive of L *calendae* CALENDS; so called as flowering almost every month of the year]

**calenture** /'kæləntʃʊə/, *n.* a violent fever with delirium, affecting persons in the tropics. [F, from Sp. *calentura* heat, from L *calēre* be hot]

**calescent** /kə'lɛsənt/, *adj.* growing warm; increasing in heat. [L *calescens,* ppr., growing hot] – **calescence,** *n.*

**calf**[1] /kaf/, *n., pl.* **calves. 1.** the young of the cow or of other bovine mammals (in cattle usu. under one year of age). **2.** the young of certain other animals, as the elephant, seal, and whale. **3.** calfskin leather. **4.** *Colloq.* an awkward, silly boy or man. **5.** a mass of ice detached from a glacier, iceberg, or floe. **6. kill the fatted calf,** to prepare an elaborate welcome. [ME and d. OE, replacing OE *cealf,* c. G *Kalb*] – **calf-like,** *adj.*

**calf**[2] /kaf/, *n., pl.* **calves.** the fleshy part of the back of the human leg below the knee. [ME, from Scand.; cf. Icel. *kālfi*]

**calfdozer** /'kafdoʊzə/, *n.* a small bulldozer.

**calf love** /'kaf lʌv/, *n.* →**puppy love.**

**calfskin** /'kafskɪn/, *n.* **1.** the skin or hide of a calf. **2.** leather made from it. *–adj.* **3.** of, or made of, calfskin.

**calf starter** /'kaf statə/, *n.* feed used to replace milk for young calves and given during weaning as a supplement to the diet.

**calibrate** /'kæləbreɪt/, *v.t.,* **-brated, -brating. 1.** to determine the calibre of. **2.** to determine, check, or rectify the graduation or accuracy of (any instrument, machine, or gun). – **calibrator,** *n.*

**calibration** /kælə'breɪʃən/, *n.* **1.** the act or process of calibrating. **2.** *Ordn.* the assessment of a gun for accuracy.

**calibre** /'kæləbə/, *n.* **1.** the diameter of something of circular section, as a bullet, or esp. that of the inside of a tube, as the bore of a gun. **2.** *Ordn.* the diameter of the bore of a gun taken as a unit in stating its length. **3.** *Horol.* the arrangement of the components of a watch or clock. **4.** degree of capacity or ability; personal character. **5.** degree of merit, or importance; quality. Also, *U.S.,* **caliber.** [F, from It. *calibro,* from Ar. *qālib* mould]

**calices** /'kæləsiz/, *n.* plural of **calix.**

**caliche** /kæ'litʃi/, *n.* **1.** a surface deposit consisting of sand or clay impregnated with crystalline salts, such as sodium nitrate or sodium chloride. **2.** a horizon of calcium or mixed carbonates in soils of semi-arid regions. [Sp., from *cal* lime, from L *calx*]

**calicle** /'kælɪkəl/, *n.* a cuplike depression or formation, as in corals. [L *caliculus,* diminutive of *calix* cup]

**calico** /'kælɪkoʊ/, *n., pl.* **-coes, -cos,** *adj. –n.* **1.** white cotton cloth. **2.** *U.S.* a printed cotton cloth, superior to percale. **3.** (originally) cotton cloth imported from India. *–adj.* **4.** made of calico. **5.** *Chiefly U.S.* resembling printed calico; spotted; piebald. [named after *Calicut,* a city on the coast of Malabar, India]

**calif** /'keɪləf/, *n.* →**caliph.**

**califate** /'kæləfeɪt, -fət/, *n.* →**caliphate.**

**califont** /'kæləfɒnt/, *n. N.Z.* a gas-fired water heater. [Trademark]

**Californian poppy** /kælə,fɔniən 'pɒpi/, *n.* a pale green herb with showy yellow flowers, *Eschscholtzia californica.*

**californium** /kælə'fɔniəm/, *n.* a synthetic, radio-active, metallic element. *Symbol:* Cf; *at. no.:* 98. [(University of) *Californ(ia),* where first identified, + -IUM]

**caliginous** /kə'lɪdʒənəs/, *adj. Rare.* misty; dim; dark. [L *cālīginōsus* misty] – **caliginosity** /kəlɪdʒə'nɒsəti/ *n.*

**calipash** /'kæləpæʃ/, *n.* that part of a turtle next to the upper shield, a greenish gelatinous substance. Also, **callipash.** [orig. uncert.]

**calipee** /'kæləpi/, *n.* that part of a turtle next to the lower shield, consisting of a yellowish gelatinous substance. [cf. CALIPASH]

**caliper** /'kæləpə/, *n., v.t. Chiefly U.S.* →**calliper.**

**caliph** /'keɪləf/, *n.* successor (usu. of Mohammed); a title for the head of a Muslim state. Also, **calif, kaliph, khalif, khalifa.** [ME *califfe,* from OF *calife,* from ML *calipha,* from Ar. *khalīfa* successor, vicar]

**caliphate** /'kæləfeɪt, -fət/, *n.* the rank, jurisdiction or government of a caliph. Also, **califate.**

**calisaya** /kælə'seɪə/, *n.* the bark of trees of the genus *Cinchona,* often used medicinally. [S Amer. Sp., probably from Quechua]

**calisthenics** /kæləs'θɛnɪks/, *n.* →**callisthenics.** – **calisthenic,** *adj.*

**calix** /'keɪlɪks, 'kælɪks/, *n., pl.* **calices** /'kæləsiz/. *Rom. Cath. Ch.* →**chalice** (def. 1). [L: cup]

**calk**[1] /kɔk/, *v.t.* →**caulk.** – **calker,** *n.*

**calk**[2] /kɔk/, *n.* **1.** Also, **calkin.** a projection on a horseshoe to prevent slipping. **2.** *Chiefly U.S.* a similar device on the heel or sole of a shoe. *–v.t.* **3.** to provide with calks. **4.** to injure with a calk. [L *calx* heel, or *calcar* spur]

**calk**[3] /kɔk/, *v.t.* to transfer (an outline or design) from a sheet backed with an unstable colouring material on to another sheet placed underneath by exerting pressure along the design with a blunt point. Also, **calque.** [L *calcāre* to tread, from *calx* heel. See CALK[2]]

**call** /kɔl/, *v.t.* **1.** to cry out in a loud voice. **2.** (of a bird or other animal) to utter (its characteristic cry). **3.** to announce; proclaim: *call a halt.* **4.** to read over (a roll or list) in a loud voice. **5.** to attract the attention of by loudly uttering something. **6.** to attract (someone's attention) to something: *he called the policeman's attention to the disturbance.* **7.** to rouse from sleep as by a call: *call me at 8 o'clock.* **8.** to command or request to come; summon: *the boy was called by his mother; call a cab; call a witness.* **9.** to summon to an office, duty, etc.: *call someone to the ministry.* **10.** to summon to the degree of barrister-at-law: *to call to the bar.* **11.** to convoke or convene, as a meeting or assembly: *call a committee meeting.* **12.** to bring under consideration or discussion: *call a case.* **13.** to telephone to (oft. fol. by *up*). **14.** to attract or lure (wild birds, etc.) by a particular cry or sound. **15.** *U.S.* to demand payment or fulfilment of (a loan, etc.). **16.** *U.S.* to demand (bonds, etc.) for payment. **17.** *Econ.* to ask for payment of all or part of the unpaid part of a company's share capital. **18.** to give a name to; name: *his parents named him James but the boys call him Jim.* **19.** to designate as something specified: *he called me a liar.* **20.** to reckon; consider; estimate: *to call a thing a success.* **21.** *Cricket.* **a.** to announce the end of (an over). **b.** to announce that (a bowler) has bowled a no-ball. **c.** (of a batsman) to cry out to his partner as a signal to attempt or not attempt a run. **22.** *Billiards.* to request (the player) to state his intended shot. **23.** *Poker.* to require (a player) to show his hand, after equalling his bet. **24.** *Cards.* to bid. **25.** *Two-up.* to nominate heads or tails to win the toss. **26.** to describe (a race) on radio or television, or over the course broadcasting system. **27. call attention (to oneself),** to behave in such a manner that people will take notice. *–v.i.* **28.** to speak loudly, as to attract attention; shout; cry: *who calls so loudly?* **29.** (of a bird or animal) to utter its characteristic cry. **30.** to make a short visit; stop at a place on some errand or business: *to call at a house or place for a person or thing, or upon a person.* **31.** to telephone a person. **32.** *Poker.* to demand a showing of hands. *–v.* **33.** Some special verb phrases are:

**call after,** to hail; recall.

**call back, 1.** to recall; summon or bring back. **2.** to revoke; retract: *call back one's words.*

**call down, 1.** to invoke from above; cause to descend. **2.** to reprimand; scold.

**call for, 1.** to go and get. **2.** to require; demand; need: *the occasion calls for a cool head.*

**call forth,** to bring or summon into action.

**call in, 1.** to collect: *call in debts.* **2.** to withdraw from circulation: *call in gold, notes.* **3.** to invite; summon to or as to one's assistance.

**call into being,** to create.

**call into play,** to activate.

**call in(to) question,** to throw doubt upon.

**call it a day,** to bring an activity to a close whether temporarily or permanently.

**call off, 1.** to order to desist. **2.** to cancel or postpone. **3.** to terminate an activity.

**call on, 1.** to appeal to: *call on a person for a song.* **2.** to make a short visit to: *to call on friends.*

**call out, 1.** to utter in a loud voice. **2.** to summon into service: *call out the militia.* **3.** to bring into play; elicit. **4.** *Obs.* to challenge to a duel.

**call over,** *Law.* to mention (a case) in court so that the solicitor concerned may inform the court whether he is ready to proceed or not.

**call up, 1.** to bring into action, discussion, etc. **2.** to require payment of. **3.** to summon for military service. **4.** to recollect: *to call up my sorrows afresh.*

*–n.* **34.** a cry or shout. **35.** the cry of a bird or other animal. **36.** an instrument for imitating this cry and attracting or luring the animal. **37.** a summons or signal sounded by a bugle, bell, etc. **38.** a note blown on a horn to encourage hounds. **39.** a short visit: *to make a call on someone.* **40.** a telephone conversation. **41.** a summons; invitation; bidding. **42.** *Theat.* a notice of rehearsal posted by the stage manager. **43.** a sense of divine appointment to a vocation or service. **44.** a request or invitation to take up a post, as a priest, or a professor in a university, etc. **45.** the summons (to the bar) to receive the degree of barrister-at-law. **46.** a need or occasion: *he had no call to say such things.* **47.** a demand or claim: *to make a call on a person's time.* **48.** a roll call. **49.** Also, **the call of the Senate.** a rollcall of senators to ensure their attendance for discussion of an important bill. **50.** the verbal description of a race by a race commentator on radio or television, or over the course broadcasting system. **51.** *Poker.* a demand for the showing of hands. **52.** *Cricket.* a signal from one batsman to his partner to attempt or not attempt a run. **53.** a contract which permits its purchaser to buy a certain amount of stock, etc., at a specified price for a limited period of time. **54.** *Cards.* a bid. **55.** a demand for payment of an obligation, esp. where payment is at the option of the creditor. **56.** *Stock Exchange.* the option of claiming stock at or before a given date. **57. call for margin,** *Stock Exchange.* a demand for payment upon the balance owed a stockbroker because of the shrinking value of the security. **58. on call, a.** *Comm.* payable or subject to return without advance notice. **b.** (of doctors, etc.) available for duty at short notice. **59. the call, a.** permission from the chair to speak at a meeting: *the minister was given the call.* **b.** *Two-up.* the right to call. *–adj.* **60.** *Comm.* repayable on demand: *call money, a call loan.* [ME *calle(n)* (cf. OE *calla* herald), replacing OE *ceallian,* c. Icel. *kalla*]

**calla** /ˈkælə/, *n.* **1.** a plant of the genus *Zantedeschia* (or *Richardia*), native to Africa, esp. the arum lily, *Z. aethiopicum,* which has a large white spathe enclosing a yellow spadix, and is familiar in cultivation. **2.** an araceous plant, *Calla palustris,* of cold marshes of Europe and North America, with heart-shaped leaves. [NL, ? special use of L *calla* plant name]

**callable** /ˈkɔləbəl/, *adj.* **1.** that may be called. **2.** subject to redemption upon notice, as a bond. **3.** subject to payment on demand, as money loaned.

**callbox** /ˈkɔlbɒks/, *n. Brit.* →**telephone box.**

**callboy** /ˈkɔlbɔɪ/, *n.* **1.** a boy who summons actors just before they go on the stage. **2.** →**pageboy. 3.** a member of a railway staff who calls locomotive crews for duty.

**call-button** /ˈkɔl-bʌtn/, *n.* the button of a signalling system whereby servants, stewards, nurses, etc., may be summoned when required.

**caller** /ˈkɔlə/, *n.* **1.** one that calls. **2.** one who makes a short visit. **3.** →**race caller.** [CALL + -ER[1]]

**callgirl** /ˈkɔlgɜl/, *n.* a prostitute who makes herself available for appointments by telephone.

**calli-,** a word element meaning 'beauty'. [Gk *kalli-,* combining form of *kállos*]

**calligraphy** /kəˈlɪgrəfi/, *n.* **1.** beautiful handwriting. **2.** handwriting; penmanship. **3.** *Painting.* free and rhythmic brushwork, which displays the variety and flexibility of fine penmanship. [Gk *kalligraphía*] – **calligrapher, calligraphist,** *n.* – **calligraphic** /kæləˈgræfɪk/, *adj.*

**calling** /ˈkɔlɪŋ/, *n.* **1.** the act of one that calls. **2.** a vocation, profession, or trade. **3.** a summons. **4.** an invitation. **5.** a convocation. **6.** *Cards.* a bidding.

**calling card** /ˈ– kad/, *n.* →**visiting card.**

**calliope** /kəˈlaɪəpi/, *n.* a harsh musical instrument consisting of a set of steam whistles, played from a keyboard. [orig. with ref. to *Calliope* the Muse of heroic poetry; L, from Gk *kalliópē,* lit. beautiful-voiced]

**calliopsis** /kæliˈɒpsəs/, *n.* →**coreopsis.**

**callipash** /ˈkæləpæʃ/, *n.* →**calipash.**

**calliper** /ˈkæləpə/, *n.* **1.** (*usu. pl.*) a tool in its simplest form having two legs and resembling a draughtsman's compass, used for obtaining inside and outside measurements, esp. across curved surfaces. **2.** Also, **calliper brake.** a brake on bicycles, etc., consisting of two brake blocks which are drawn towards each other through a central pivot and which grip the rim of the wheel. **3.** *Med.* an appliance used on limbs to provide external support or correct deformities. *–v.t.* **4.** to measure with callipers. Also, **caliper.** [var. of CALIBRE]

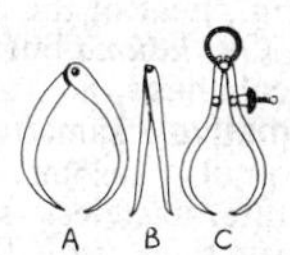

callipers: A, outside callipers; B, inside callipers; C, spring adjusting callipers

**calliper rule** /ˈ– rul/, *n.* a calliper with one jaw fixed to, or integral with, a graduated straight bar on which the other jaw slides.

**callipygian** /kæləˈpɪdʒən/, *adj.* having well-shaped buttocks. Also, **callipygous** /kæləˈpɪdʒəs/. [Gk *kallipýgos*]

**callistemon** /kəˈlɪstəmən/, *n.* →**bottlebrush** (def. 2).

**callisthenics** /kæləsˈθɛnɪks/, *n.* **1.** (*construed as sing.*) the practice or art of callisthenic exercises; exercising the muscles for the purpose of gaining health, strength, and grace of form and movement; eurhythmics. **2.** (*construed as pl.*) light gymnastic exercises designed to develop grace as well as organic vigour and health. Also, **calisthenics.** [CALLI- + Gk *sthénos* strength + -ICS] – **callisthenic,** *adj.*

**Callithumpian** /kælə'θʌmpiən/, *n.* a person of vague religious beliefs, not necessarily associated with a particular denomination. [? Brit. d.; from *Gallithumpians,* a society of social reformers]

**call number** /'kɔl nʌmbə/, *n.* the number given to a library book to facilitate sorting and correct shelf placement.

**callop** /'kæləp/, *n.* →**golden perch.** [Aboriginal]

**call option** /'kɔl ɒpʃən/, *n. Stock Exchange.* the right to buy a specified parcel of shares at an agreed price within a specified period of time.

**callosity** /kæ'lɒsəti/, *n., pl.* **-ties. 1.** a callous condition. **2.** *Bot.* a hardened or thickened part of a plant. **3.** →**callus** (def. 1a).

**callous** /'kæləs/, *adj.* **1.** hardened. **2.** hardened in mind, feelings, etc. **3.** having a callus; indurated, as parts of the skin exposed to friction. [L *callōsus* hard-skinned] – **callously,** *adv.* – **callousness,** *n.*

**call-over** /'kɔl-oʊvə/, *n.* the reading out in court of cases yet to be dealt with so that the solicitor concerned may inform the court whether he is ready to proceed or not.

**call-over list** /'– lɪst/, *n.* a list of cases to be read in a call-over.

**call-over notice** /'– noʊtəs/, *n.* a notice of a call-over, appearing in the law lists of a newspaper.

**callow** /'kæloʊ/, *adj.* **1.** immature or inexperienced: *a callow youth.* **2.** (of a young bird) featherless; unfledged. *–n.* **3.** an underburnt brick, softer than common or clinker brick. [ME and OE *calu, calw-,* c. G *kahl*] – **callowness,** *n.*

**call sign** /'kɔl saɪn/, *n.* **1.** a preliminary morse signal, as by a ship, to attract attention. **2.** the preliminary call of a radio station or transmitter which serves to identify it.

**call-up** /'kɔl-ʌp/, *n.* a summons to military service.

**callus** /'kæləs/, *n., pl.* **-luses,** *v.* *–n.* **1.** *Pathol., Physiol.* **a.** a hardened or thickened part of the skin; a callosity. **b.** a new growth of osseous matter at the ends of a fractured bone, serving to unite them. **2.** *Bot.* **a.** the tissue which forms over the wounds of plants, protecting the inner tissues and causing healing. **b.** a deposit on the perforated area of a sieve tube. **c.** the hard projection at the base of the floret or spikelet of some grasses. *–v.i.* **3.** to make a callus. [L: hardened skin]

**calm** /kam/, *adj.* **1.** without rough motion; still: *a calm sea.* **2.** not windy; of Beaufort scale force nil. **3.** free from excitement or passion; tranquil: *a calm face, voice, manner, etc.* *–n.* **4.** freedom from motion or disturbance; stillness. **5.** absence of wind. **6.** freedom from agitation, excitement, or passion; tranquillity; serenity. *–v.t.* **7.** to make calm: *calm fears, calm an excited dog, etc.* *–v.i.* **8.** to become calm (usu. fol. by *down*). [ME *calme,* from OF, from It. *calma* (as if orig., heat of the day, hence, time for resting, quiet), from LL b. Gk. *kaûma* burning heat and L *calēre* be hot] – **calmly,** *adv.* – **calmness,** *n.*

**calmative** /'kamətɪv/, *adj., n. Med.* →**sedative.**

**calomel** /'kæləmɛl, -məl/, *n.* mercurous chloride, $Hg_2Cl_2$, a white, tasteless solid, used in medicine as a mercurial, a purgative, etc. [F, short for *calomélas,* from Gk *kalós* beautiful + *mélās* black]

**calorescence** /kælə'rɛsəns/, *n.* the absorption of radiation of one wavelength by a body and the subsequent emission of radiation of a different wavelength, esp. of a shorter wavelength.

**caloric** /kə'lɒrɪk, keɪ-/, *n.* **1.** heat. **2.** *Old Physics.* a hypothetical imponderable fluid whose presence in matter determined its thermal state. *–adj.* **3.** pertaining or relating to heat. **4.** (of engines) driven by heated air. [F *calorique,* from L *calor* heat. Cf. CALORIE] – **caloricity** /kælə'rɪsəti, keɪ-/, *n.*

**calorie** /'kæləri/, *n.* **1. a.** Also, **gram calorie** or **small calorie.** a non-SI unit of measurement for quantity of heat, originally defined as the quantity of heat required to raise the temperature of one gram of water by one degree centigrade. Several calories exist, the original definition and hence the energy content of which vary. **b. kilogram calorie** or **large calorie,** (*usu. cap.*) a quantity of heat equal to 1000 gram calories. **2.** a non-SI unit equal to the large calorie, used to express the heat output of an organism or the energy value of a food. The recommended SI unit is the kilojoule; 1 calorie is equivalent to 4.1868 kJ. [F, from L *calor* heat]

**calorific** /kælə'rɪfɪk, keɪ-/, *adj.* pertaining to conversion into heat. [L *calōrificus* heat-producing]

**calorific value** /– 'vælju/, *n.* the amount of heat produced by the complete combustion of a given quantity of a substance, esp. a fuel.

**calorimeter** /kælə'rɪmətə, keɪ-/, *n.* an apparatus for measuring quantities of heat. [L *calor* heat + -I- + -METER[1]]

**calorimetry** /kælə'rɪmətri, keɪ-/, *n.* the measurement of heat. – **calorimetric** /kælərə'mɛtrɪk, keɪ-/, **calorimetrical** /kælərə'mɛtrɪkəl, keɪ-/, *adj.* – **calorimetrically** /kælərə'mɛtrɪkli, keɪ-/, *adv.*

**calotte** /kə'lɒt/, *n.* **1.** a plain skullcap, as that worn by Catholic ecclesiastics. **2.** *Archit.* a small dome in a low ceiling. [F, diminutive of *cale* cap. Cf. CAUL]

**caloyer** /'kælɔɪə, kæ'lɔɪə/, *n.* a monk of the Greek Orthodox Church. [F, from It. *caloiero,* from LGk *kalógēros* venerable, monk]

**calpac** /'kælpæk/, *n.* →**kalpak.**

**calque**[1] /kɔk/, *v.t.,* **calqued, calquing.** →**calk**[3]. [F]

**calque**[2] /kælk/, *n. Linguistics.* **1.** an expression translated literally from a foreign expression, esp. loan translation, as, for example, *blue blood* which is a translation of Spanish *sangre azue* applied to Castilian families who claimed never to have intermarried with other (esp. Moorish) non-Castilian people. *–v.t.* **2.** to borrow (an expression) by this means.

**cal-sil** /kæl-'sɪl/, *adj.* denoting certain white bricks of which calcium silicate is an important ingredient.

**caltrop** /'kæltrəp/, *n.* **1.** *Bot.* **a.** any of various plants having spiny heads or fruit, esp. of the genera *Tribulus* and *Kallstroemia.* **b.** →**star thistle. c.** Also, **caltrops.** an Old World plant, *Tribulus terrestris,* which is an annual, summer growing, creeping vine. **d.** →**water-chestnut. 2.** *Mil.* an iron ball with four projecting spikes so disposed that when the ball is on the ground one of them always points upwards, used to obstruct the passage of cavalry, etc. Also, **caltrap.** [ME *calketrappe,* OE *col(te)træppe, calcatrippe* spiny plant, apparently from L *calx* heel + ML *trappa* trap]

caltrop (def. 2)

**calumet** /'kæljəmɛt/, *n.* a long, ornamented tobacco pipe used by North American Indians on ceremonial occasions, esp. in token of peace. [F, from diminutive of L *calamus* reed]

**calumniate** /kə'lʌmnieɪt/, *v.t.,* **-ated, -ating.** to make false and malicious statements about; slander. [L *calumniātus,* pp.] – **calumniator,** *n.*

**calumniation** /kə͵lʌmni'eɪʃən/, *n.* **1.** the act of calumniating; slander. **2.** a calumny.

calumet

**calumnious** /kə'lʌmniəs/, *adj.* of, involving, or using calumny; slanderous; defamatory. Also, **calumniatory** /kə'lʌmniətəri, -tri/. – **calumniously,** *adv.*

**calumny** /'kæləmni/, *n., pl.* **-nies. 1.** a false and malicious statement designed to injure someone's reputation. **2.** slander. [L *calumnia*]

**calvados** /'kælvədɒs/, *n.* a liqueur made from apple juice; apple brandy. [from *Calvados,* a department in Normandy, NW France]

**calvaria** /kæl'vɛəriə/, *n.* the dome of the skull. [L. See CALVARY]

**Calvary** /'kælvəri/, *n., pl.* **-ries** (*def. 2*). **1.** Golgotha, the place where Jesus was crucified. **2.** (*l.c.*) a sculptured representation of the Crucifixion, usu. erected in the open air. [L *calvāria* skull, used to render Aram. *goghaltā,* from Heb. *gulgolĕth* skull]

**calve** /kav/, *v.,* **calved, calving.** *–v.i.* **1.** to give birth to a calf. **2.** (of a glacier, iceberg, etc.) to give off a detached piece. *–v.t.* **3.** to give birth to (a calf). **4.** to give off (a detached piece). [ME *calve(n),* from *calf* calf; replacing OE *cealfian,* from *cealf* calf]

**calves** /kavz/, *n.* plural of **calf.**

**Calvinism** /'kælvənɪzəm/, *n.* **1.** *Theol.* **a.** the doctrines and church practices taught by John Calvin, 1509-64, French religious reformer, leader of Protestant Reformation in Geneva, Switzerland. Calvin emphasised the sovereignty of God, predestination, the authority of Scriptures, presbyterian polity, and strict church discipline. **b.** the doctrines of later theologians who accepted Calvin's teachings with various modifications. **2.** adherence to these doctrines. – **Calvinist,** *n., adj.*

**Calvinistic** /kælvən'ɪstɪk/, *adj.* strict; austere. Also, **Calvinistical.**

**calvities** /kæl'vɪʃiˌiz, -'vɪʃiz/, *n. Chiefly Med.* baldness. [L]

**calx** /kælks/, *n., pl.* **calces** /'kælsiz/, **calxes. 1.** the oxide or ashy substance which remains after metals, minerals, etc., have been thoroughly roasted or burnt. **2.** lime. [L: small stone, lime]

**calyces** /'kæləsiz, 'keɪ-/, *n.* a plural of **calyx.**

**calycle** /'kæləkəl/, *n.* a set of bracts resembling an outer calyx. [L *calyculus,* diminutive of *calyx* calyx]

**calypso** /kə'lɪpsoʊ/, *n., pl.* **-sos. 1.** a song, based on a musical pattern of West Indian origin, with topical, usu. improvised lyrics. **2.** a terrestrial orchid of the genus *Calypso* (*Cytherea*), widespread in the Northern Hemisphere, having a single variegated purple, yellow, and white flower. *–adj.* **3.** pertaining to a calypso (def. 1).

calyces: A, gamosepalous calyx; B, bilabiate calyx

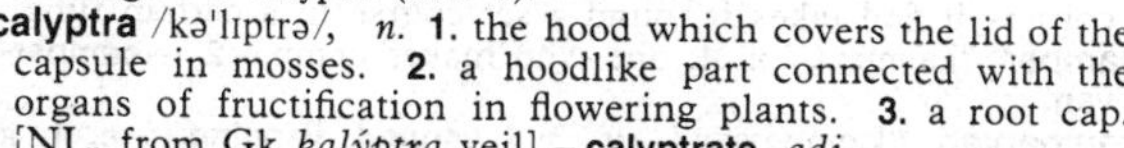

**calyptra** /kə'lɪptrə/, *n.* **1.** the hood which covers the lid of the capsule in mosses. **2.** a hoodlike part connected with the organs of fructification in flowering plants. **3.** a root cap. [NL, from Gk *kalýptra* veil] – **calyptrate,** *adj.*

**calyptrogen** /kə'lɪptrədʒən/, *n.* the histogen layer which develops into the root cap of a plant.

**calyx** /'keɪlɪks, 'kæl-/, *n., pl.* **calyces** /'kæləsiz, 'kei-/, **calyxes. 1.** *Bot.* the outermost group of floral parts, usu. green; the sepals. **2.** *Anat., Zool.* a cuplike part. [L, from Gk *kályx* covering, husk, calyx]

**cam** /kæm/, *n.* a device for converting regular rotary motion into irregular rotary or reciprocating motion, etc., commonly consisting of an oval-, needle-, or heart-shaped, or other specially shaped flat piece, an eccentric wheel or the like, fastened on and revolving with a shaft, and engaging with other mechanism. [D or LG *kam, kamm* cog. See COMB[1]]

cams: A, heart cam; B, elliptical cam; C, cam wheel

**camaraderie** /kæmə'radəri/, *n.* comradeship; close friendship. [F]

**camarilla** /kæmə'rɪlə/, *n.* a group of private advisers; a cabal; a clique. [Sp., diminutive of *cámara* CHAMBER]

**camass** /'kæmæs/, *n.* any of various plants of the lily family (genus *Camassia*), esp. *C. quamash,* a species in western North America, with sweet, edible bulbs. Also, **camas.** [N Amer. Ind.]

**camber** /'kæmbə/, *v.t., v.i.* **1.** to arch slightly; bend or curve upwards in the middle. *–n.* **2.** a slight arching or convexity above, as of a ship's deck or a road surface. **3.** a slightly arching piece of timber. **4.** *Aeron.* the curvature of the upper or lower surface of an aerofoil with respect to its chord. **5.** *Naut.* **a.** a small dock. **b.** a slipway for hauling ships on land. **c.** the fullness of a sail created by a sailmaker. **6.** a setting of the front wheels of a motor vehicle such that they are closer together at the bottom than at the top. [F *cambre,* adj., bent, from L *camur*]

**camber angle** /'kæmbər æŋgəl/, *n.* the angle between the cambered front wheel of a motor vehicle and the vertical.

**Camberwell beauty** /ˌkæmbəwɛl 'bjuti/, *n.* →**mourning cloak.**

**cambist** /'kæmbəst/, *n.* **1.** a dealer in bills of exchange. **2.** an expert in the science of monetary exchange. **3.** a manual giving the moneys, weights, and measures of different countries, with their equivalents. [F *cambiste,* from It. *cambista,* from *cambiare* CHANGE]

**cambium** /'kæmbiəm/, *n.* a cylindrical layer of meristematic cells which give rise to secondary tissues towards the inside and outside, thus causing increase in girth of a stem or root. [LL: exchange]

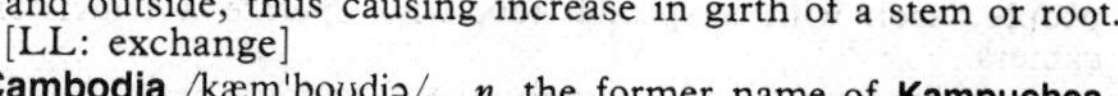

**Cambodia** /kæm'boʊdiə/, *n.* the former name of **Kampuchea.**

**cambogia** /kæm'boʊdʒiə/, *n. Pharm.* →**gamboge** (def. 1).

**cambrel** /'kæmbrəl/, *n.* →**gambrel.**

**Cambria** /'kæmbriə/, *n.* medieval Latin name of Wales. [Latinisation of Welsh *Cymry*]

**Cambrian** /'kæmbriən/, *adj.* **1.** *Geol.* pertaining to the oldest geological period or a system of rocks characterised by the presence of numerous well-preserved fossils. **2.** pertaining to Cambria (Wales). *–n.* **3.** *Geol.* the period or system comprising the first main division of the Palaeozoic era **4.** a Welshman.

**cambric** /'keɪmbrɪk/, *n.* a cotton or linen fabric of fine close weave, usu. white. [Flem. *Kameryk* Cambrai, a city in N france]

**came**[1] /keɪm/, *v.* past tense of **come.**

**came**[2] /keɪm/, *n.* a slender grooved bar of lead for holding together the pieces of glass in windows of latticework or stained glass. [apparently var. of *calm* mould for casting metallic objects]

**camel** /'kæməl/, *n.* **1.** either of two large Old World ruminant quadrupeds of the genus *Camelus,* used as beasts of burden: **a.** the **Arabian camel,** or dromedary, with one hump (*C. dromedarius*). **b.** the **Bactrian camel,** with two humps (*C. bactrianus*). **2.** a brown colour somewhat lighter than fawn. **3.** *Civ. Eng., Naut.* →**pontoon**[1] (def. 2). [ME and OE, from L *camēlus,* from Gk *kámēlos;* of Semitic orig.] – **camelish, camel-like,** *adj.*

**cameleer** /kæmə'lɪə/, *n.* **1.** a camel driver. **2.** a soldier on a camel.

**camelhair** /'kæməlhɛə/, *n.* **1.** the hair of the camel, used for cloth, certain oriental rugs, etc. **2.** cloth made of this hair, or of a substitute, usu. tan in colour. *–adj.* **3.** made of camel's hair. **4.** (of a painter's brush) made from the tail hairs of squirrels.

**camellia** /kə'miljə/, *n.* one of several species of the genus *Camellia,* shrubs or trees, native to Asia, with glossy evergreen leaves and white, pink, red, or variegated waxy roselike flowers, familiar in cultivation. [named after G. J. *Kamel,* 1661-1706, Moravian Jesuit missionary]

**camelopard** /kə'mɛləpad, 'kæmələpad/, *n. Obs.* a giraffe. [LL *camēlopardus,* L *camēlopardālis,* from Gk *kamēlopárdalis* giraffe]

**camel's-thorn** /'kæməlz-θɔn/, *n.* a thorny plant of the genus *Alhagi,* family Papilionaceae, found in the Mediterranean region and western Asia and naturalised elsewhere. Also, **camel-thorn.**

**camembert** /'kæməmbɛə/, *n.* a rich, cream-coloured variety of soft, ripened cheese, usu. made in small, flat, round loaves, covered with a thin greyish-white rind. [named after *Camembert,* a town in Normandy, France]

**cameo** /'kæmioʊ/, *n., pl.* **-os. 1.** an engraving in relief upon a gem, stone, etc., with differently coloured layers of the stone often utilised to produce a background of one hue and a design of another. **2.** a gem, stone, etc., so engraved. **3.** a short piece of ornate, highly polished writing. [It. *cammeo;* probably of oriental orig.]

**cameo part** /'– pat/, *n.* a minor theatrical role with attractive acting possibilities.

**cameo ware** /'– wɛə/, *n.* pottery with figures moulded in relief on a different-coloured background.

**camera** /'kæmrə, 'kæmərə/, *n., pl.* **-eras** *for defs 1 and 2,* **-erae** /-əri/ *for def. 3.* **1.** a photographic apparatus in which sensitive plates or film are exposed, the image being formed by means of a lens. **2.** (in a television transmitting apparatus) the device in which the picture to be televised is formed before it is changed into electrical impulses. **3.** a judge's private room. **4. in camera, a.** *Law.* in the privacy of a judge's chambers. **b.** privately. [L: arch, vault, ML chamber, treasury. Cf. CHAMBER]

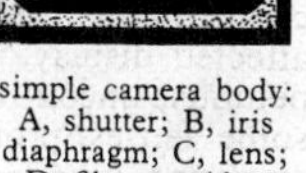

simple camera body: A, shutter; B, iris diaphragm; C, lens; D, film cartridge

**camera crew** /'– kru/, *n.* the group of

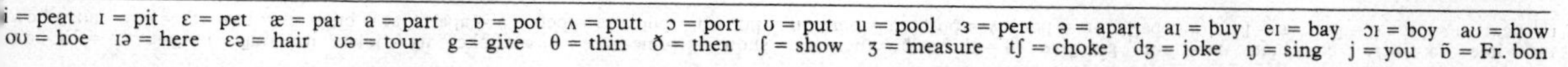

people, each with a specific job, who operate a television camera.

**cameral** /'kæmərəl/, *adj.* pertaining to a camera (esp. defs 3, 4).

**camera lucida** /kæmrə 'lusədə/, *n.* an optical instrument by which the image of an external object is projected on a sheet of paper, etc., upon which it may be traced. [LL: light chamber]

**cameraman** /'kæmrəmæn/, *n., pl.* **-men.** a man who operates a camera, esp. a cinema or television camera.

**camera obscura** /kæmrə ɒbs'kjurə/, *n.* **1.** a darkened box-like device in which images of external objects, received through an aperture, as with a convex lens, are exhibited in their natural colours on a surface arranged to receive them; used for sketching, exhibition purposes, etc. **2.** →**camera** (def. 1). [LL: dark chamber]

**camera-ready copy** /ˌkæmrə-rɛdi 'kɒpi/, *n.* matter to be printed in a final form which can be photographed for plate-making.

**camera-shy** /'kæmrə-ʃaɪ/, *adj.* unwilling to be photographed.

**Cameroon** /kæmə'run/, *n.* a country in central Africa, with a coastline on the bight of Biafra.

**camion** /'kæmiən/, *n.* a strongly built lorry or cart for carrying heavy loads. [F; orig. uncert.]

**camisole** /'kæməsoʊl/, *n.* **1.** an ornamental underbodice, worn under a thin outer bodice. **2.** a woman's dressing jacket. **3.** a sleeved jacket or jersey once worn by men. **4.** a type of straitjacket. [F, from Sp. *camisola,* diminutive of *camisa* shirt]

**camlet** /'kæmlət/, *n.* **1.** a durable waterproof cloth used for cloaks, etc. **2.** apparel made of this material. **3.** (formerly) a rich fabric, apparently originally made of camel's or goat's hair. [var. of *camelot,* from F; replacing late ME *chamelot,* from OF, probably from Ar. *khamla,* from *khaml* nap]

**Cammeraygal** /'kæməreɪˌgʌl/, *n.* →**Kameraigal.**

**camomile** /'kæməmaɪl/, *n.* →**chamomile.**

**camorra** /kə'mɒrə/, *n.* a society or group associated with blackmail, robbery, etc. [from a Neapolitan secret society, about 1820; It., from Sp.: dispute, quarrel] – **camorrism,** *n.* – **camorrist,** *n.*

**camouflage** /'kæməflaʒ, -fladʒ/, *n., v.,* **-flaged, -flaging.** *–n.* **1.** *Mil.* act, art, means, or result of disguising things to deceive the enemy, as by painting or screening objects so that they are lost to view in the background, or by making up objects which, from a distance, have the appearance of fortifications, guns, roads, etc. **2.** the means by which any object or creature renders itself indistinguishable from its background, as by assuming the colour, shape, or texture of objects in that background. **3.** disguise; deception; false pretence. *–v.t.* **4.** to disguise, hide, or deceive by means of camouflage: *camouflaged ships.* [F, from *camoufler* disguise]

**camp**[1] /kæmp/, *n.* **1.** a group of tents, caravans, or other temporary shelters in one place. **2.** the persons sojourning in such shelters. **3.** the place where the shelters are situated; a camping ground. **4.** a sleep; rest. **5.** an (overnight) resting place for livestock. **6.** a place where flying foxes settle for the night. **7.** a site where soldiers are housed, in structures originally intended to be temporary. **8.** army life. **9.** a group of people favouring the same ideals, doctrines, etc.: *the socialist camp.* **10.** any position in which ideals, doctrines, etc., are strongly entrenched. *–v.i.* **11.** to establish or pitch a camp. **12.** to live temporarily in a tent (oft. fol. by *out*). **13.** of livestock, to assemble or rest at a favoured place. **14.** *Colloq.* to sleep: *you take that bed, I'll camp here.* *–v.t.* **15.** to put or station (troops, etc.) in a camp shelter. [F, from It. *campo* field, from L *campus*]

**camp**[2] /kæmp/, *adj.* **1.** exaggerated and often amusing or effeminate in style. **2.** effeminate; given to acting and speaking with exaggerated mannerisms. **3.** homosexual. *–n.* **4.** an exaggerated, often amusing or effeminate style, mannerism, or the like. **5.** a person or his work displaying this quality. *–v.i.* **6.** to act in a camp manner. **7.** to be a homosexual. **8.** to perform or imbue (something) with a camp quality. **9. camp it up, a.** to make an ostentatious or affected display. **b.** to flaunt homosexuality. [? d. *camp* impetuous, uncouth person, hence objectionable, effeminate; in some senses, probably special use of CAMP[1] brothel]

**campagna** /kæm'panjə/, *n.* a flat, open plain; champaign. [It., a low plain surrounding the city of Rome, from L *campānia* level plain]

**campaign** /kæm'peɪn/, *n.* **1.** the military operations of an army in the field during one season or enterprise. **2.** any course of aggressive activities for some special purpose: *a sales campaign.* **3.** the competition by rival political candidates and organisations for public office. *–v.i.* **4.** to serve in, or go on, a campaign. [F *campagne,* from L *campus* plain] – **campaigner,** *n.*

**campanile** /kæmpə'nili/, *n., pl.* **-niles, -nili** /-'nili/. a bell tower (often a detached structure). [It., from *campana* bell, from L]

**campanology** /kæmpə'nɒlədʒi/, *n.* **1.** the study of bells. **2.** the principles of bellringing, bell-founding, etc. [NL *campanologia,* from LL *campāna* bell + -O- + -LOGY] – **campanologist, campanologer,** *n.*

**campanula** /kəm'pænjələ/, *n.* any plant of the genus *Campanula,* as the bluebell or the Canterbury bell; a bellflower. [NL, diminutive of LL *campāna* bell]

**campanulate** /kəm'pænjələt, -leɪt/, *adj.* bell-shaped, as a corolla.

**camp bed** /'kæmp bɛd/, *n.* a light folding bed, usu. of canvas stretched over a collapsible metal frame.

**camp chair** /'– tʃɛə/, *n.* a light folding chair.

**camp-dog** /'kæmp-dɒg/, *n.* a dog, often a dingo cross, which lives in an Aboriginal camp.

**camp draft** /'kæmp draft/, *n.* a competition in which a mounted horseman selects a steer from a group in a corral, corners it and takes it round a set course in a certain time.

**camper** /'kæmpə/, *n.* **1.** one who makes camp. **2.** →**campervan.**

**campervan** /'kæmpəvæn/, *n., v.,* **-vanned, vanning.** *–n.* **1.** a motor van in which people may live, usu. temporarily, furnished with beds, stove, sink, etc. *–v.i.* **2.** to live, as for a holiday, in a campervan. – **campervanner,** *n.*

**camp fire** /'kæmp faɪə/, *n.* a fire in a camp for warmth, cooking, or protection.

**camp follower** /– 'fɒloʊə/, *n.* **1.** a person who follows an army moving from camp to camp, without official connection, as a washerwoman, prostitute, etc. **2.** any unofficial or insignificant hanger-on, as of a political movement, a well-known personality, etc.

**camphane** /'kæmfeɪn, kæm'feɪn/, *n.* a white crystalline saturated hydrocarbon, $C_{10}H_{18}$, from which the camphor group is derived.

**camphene** /'kæmfin, kæm'fin/, *n.* a white, feathery, unsaturated hydrocarbon, $C_{10}H_{16}$, present in certain essential oils.

**camphol** /'kæmfəl, -fɒl/, *n. Chem.* →**borneol.**

**camphor** /'kæmfə/, *n.* **1.** a whitish, translucent, crystalline, pleasant-smelling terpene ketone, $C_{10}H_{16}O$, obtained chiefly from the camphor laurel and used in medicine, the manufacture of celluloid, etc. **2.** any of various similar substances, for household use as an insect deterrent. [ML *camphora,* from Ar. *kāpūr,* from Malay *kāpūr;* replacing ME *caumfre,* from AF] – **camphoric** /kæm'fɒrɪk/, *adj.*

**camphorate** /'kæmfəreɪt/, *v.t.,* **-rated, -rating.** to impregnate with camphor.

**camphor ball** /'kæmfə bɔl/, *n.* a mothball, usu. consisting of naphthalene, and sometimes of camphor, etc.

**camphor ice** /'kæmfər aɪs/, *n.* a preparation made chiefly of camphor, white wax, spermaceti, and castor oil, used esp. for skin infections.

**camphor laurel** /kæmfə 'lɒrəl/, *n.* a tree, *Cinnamomum camphora,* family Lauraceae, of Japan, Taiwan, China, etc., now growing wild in parts of Australia, yielding camphor.

**camphorwood** /'kæmfəwʊd/, *n.* **1.** →**camphor laurel. 2.** the fragrant wood of the camphor laurel. **3.** any of several cypress pines with a fragrant wood.

**camping body** /'kæmpɪŋ bɒdi/, *n.* the body of a car, or motor vehicle, equipped with seats which fold down to make room for a sleeping compartment.

**camping ground** /'– graʊnd/, *n.* a supervised site on which tents may be erected and caravans parked for holiday occupation. Also, **camping site.**

**campion** /'kæmpiən/, *n.* any of certain plants of the pink family, genera *Silene* or *Lychnis,* as the **rose campion,** *L. coronaria.* [probably from L *campus* field]

**campo** /ˈkæmpoʊ/, *n., pl.* **-pos.** (in South America) an extensive, nearly level, grassy plain. [Pg., Sp., from L *campus* field, plain]

**camp oven** /kæmp ˈʌvən/, *n.* a cast-iron pot with three short legs and a lid shaped for holding hot ashes, used for cooking in a camp fire.

**camp pie** /– ˈpaɪ/, *n.* a type of ready cooked tinned food, usu. made from meat and cereal.

**camp site** /ˈ– saɪt/, *n.* **1.** an area where a camp has been established or where it would be suitable to establish one. **2.** an area, often provided with amenities, where it is permitted to set up a camp.

**camp stool** /ˈ– stul/, *n.* a light folding seat.

**camp stretcher** /– ˈstretʃə/, *n.* →**stretcher** (def. 1).

**campus** /ˈkæmpəs/, *n.* **1.** the grounds of a university or other institute of higher education. **2.** such a university, etc. [L: field]

**campylotropous** /kæmpəˈlɒtrəpəs/, *adj.* of an ovule which is curved so that its axis is at right angles to the funicle.

**camshaft** /ˈkæmʃaft/, *n.* a shaft with cams.

**camwheel** /ˈkæmwil/, *n.* →**cam.**

**camwood** /ˈkæmwʊd/, *n.* the hard red wood of the West African tree *Baphia nitida,* formerly used for making dye, etc. [orig. uncert.]

**can**[1] /kæn/; *weak forms* /kən, kn/ or (if followed by k or g) /kŋ/ *v., pres. sing.* 1 **can;** 2 **can** or (*Archaic*) **canst;** 3 **can;** *pt.* **could.** *–aux.* **1.** to know how to; be able to; have the ability, power, right, qualifications, or means to: *you can lift the box.* **2.** *Colloq.* may; have permission: *can I speak to you a moment?* **3. can do!** (an exclamation indicating acquiescence to a request). *–v.t., v.i.* **4.** *Obs.* to know. [ME and OE *cann, can,* 1st and 3rd pers. sing. pres. ind. (pret. *cūthe*) of *cunnan,* c. G *können.* Cf. KEN and KNOW]

**can**[2] /kæn/, *n., v.,* **canned, canning.** *–n.* **1.** a container, sometimes sealed, usu. for a liquid and made of sheet iron coated with tin or other metal. **2.** the contents of a can. **3.** a tin (def. 4). **4.** a drinking vessel. **5.** a dustbin; wastebin. **6.** *Colloq.* the blame for something: *to carry the can.* **7.** (*pl.*) *Colloq.* a set of earphones. **8.** *U.S. Colloq.* dismissal. **9.** *U.S. Colloq.* the toilet or bathroom. **10.** *U.S. Colloq.* the buttocks. **11.** *Navy.* a depth charge. **12. can of worms,** a situation, problem, etc., bristling with difficulties. **13. in the can, a.** (of a film) ready for distribution; filmed, developed, and edited. **b.** completed; made final. **14. the can,** *Colloq.* gaol. *–v.t.* **15. a.** to put in a container, usu. sealed for preservation. **b.** to withhold or put aside (a report, film, etc.). **16.** *U.S. Colloq.* to dismiss; fire. **17. can it,** *Colloq.* to be or become silent. [ME and OE *canne,* c. G *Kanne* can, pot, mug]

**Canaan** /ˈkeɪnən/, *n.* land of promise; heaven. [from the ancient region, included in modern Palestine (now Israel and Jordan), lying between the river Jordan, the Dead Sea, and the Mediterranean Sea (Gen. 12); from Heb. *Kanaan*]

**Canada** /ˈkænədə/, *n.* a country in the northern half of North America.

**Canada balsam** /– ˈbɔlsəm/, *n.* a transparent turpentine obtained from the balsam fir, *Abies balsamea,* used for mounting objects for the microscope.

**Canada goose** /– ˈgus/, *n.* the common wild goose, *Branta canadensis,* of North America.

**Canadian** /kəˈneɪdiən/, *adj.* **1.** of Canada or its people. *–n.* **2.** a native or inhabitant of Canada.

**Canadian pondweed** /– ˈpɒndwid/, *n.* a submerged aquatic herb, *Elodea canadensis,* native to North America but naturalised and widespread elsewhere, a troublesome weed in irrigation systems.

**canaille** /kæˈnaɪ/, *n.* riffraff; the rabble. [F, from It. *canaglia,* from *cane* dog, from L *canis*]

**canal** /kəˈnæl/, *n., v.,* **-nalled, -nalling.** *–n.* **1.** an artificial waterway for navigation, drainage, irrigation, etc. **2.** a long, narrow arm of the sea penetrating far inland. **3.** a tubular passage or cavity for food, air, etc., esp. in an animal or plant; a duct. **4.** *Astron.* one of the long, narrow, dark lines on the surface of the planet Mars. **5.** *Obs.* a channel or watercourse. *–v.t.* **6.** to make a canal through. **7.** to furnish with canals. [late ME, from L *canālis* pipe, groove, channel]

**canal boat** /ˈ– boʊt/, *n.* a craft built to fit canal locks.

**canaliculus** /kænəˈlɪkjələs/, *n., pl.* **-li** /-li/. a small canal or tubular passage, as in bone. [L, diminutive of *canālis* channel. See CANAL] **– canalicular, canaliculate, canaliculated,** *adj.*

**canalise** /ˈkænəlaɪz/, *v.t.,* **-lised, -lising. 1.** to make a canal or canals through. **2.** to convert into a canal. **3.** to divert into certain channels; give a certain direction to or provide a certain outlet for. Also, **canalize. – canalisation** /ˌkænəlaɪˈzeɪʃən/, *n.*

**canal rays** /kəˈnæl reɪz/, *n. pl.* the rays (consisting of positively charged ions) which pass through a hole in the cathode, in a direction away from the anode, when an electric discharge takes place in a vacuum tube.

**canapé** /ˈkænəpeɪ/, *n.* **1.** a thin piece of bread, toast, etc., spread or topped with cheese, caviar, anchovies, or other appetising foods. **2.** any of various types of 18th-century French sofas. [F. See CANOPY]

**canard** /kæˈnad/, *n.* **1.** a false story, report, or rumour; a hoax. **2.** *Aeron.* a very early kind of aeroplane, having a pusher engine with the rudder and elevator assembly in front of the wings. [F: lit., duck]

**canary**[1] /kəˈnɛəri/, *n., pl.* **-ries. 1.** Also, **canary bird.** a well-known cagebird, a kind of finch, *Serinus canarius,* native to the Canary Islands, and originally of a brownish or greenish colour, but through modification in the domesticated state now usu. a bright, clear yellow. **2.** Also, **canary yellow.** a bright, clear yellow colour. **3.** a sweet white wine of the Canary Islands, resembling sherry. **4.** Also, **canary bird.** (formerly) a convict (after his black and yellow prisoner's clothing). **5.** *Obs.* a lively French and English dance, similar to the jig. *–adj.* **6.** canary-coloured; bright yellow. [named after the *Canary* Islands, in the Atlantic]

**canary**[2] /kəˈnɛəri/, *n. Convict Obs. Colloq.* a flogging of one hundred lashes. [shortened form of *canary*-bird, obs. Brit. thieves' slang for guinea. See TESTER[3], BOB[4], BULL[2]]

canary[1] (def. 4)

**canary creeper** /– ˈkripə/, *n.* a climbing plant native to Peru, *Tropaeolum peregrinum,* with yellow flowers.

**canary grass** /ˈ– gras/, *n.* any of various grasses of the genus *Phalaris,* as *P. canariensis,* native to the Canary Islands, which yields a seed used as food for cagebirds, or Toowoomba canary grass, *Phalaris tuberosa,* a valuable fodder species in Australia.

**canary pudding** /– ˈpʊdɪŋ/, *n.* a steamed sponge pudding which has flavouring or fruit put in the bottom of the basin before the pudding mixture is poured in.

**canary sassafras** /– ˈsæsəfræs/, *n.* a rain forest tree of the Australian east coast, *Doryphora sassafras,* the bark of which was used by early settlers as a tea substitute and tonic. Also, **yellow sassafras.**

**canary seed** /ˈ– sid/, *n.* →**birdseed.**

**canasta** /kəˈnæstə/, *n.* a card game of the rummy family in which the main object is to meld sets of seven or more cards. [Sp.: ? *canasta* kind of basket. Cf. CANISTER]

**Canberra** /ˈkænbərə, ˈkænbrə/, *n.* the Australian government in relation to other national governments or to the State governments. [from *Canberra,* the capital city of Australia]

**canc., 1.** cancelled. **2.** cancellation.

**cancan** /ˈkænkæn/, *n.* a form of quadrille marked by extravagant leaping and kicking, which came into vogue about 1830 in Paris. [F]

**cancel** /ˈkænsəl/, *v.,* **-celled, -celling** or (*U.S.*) **-celed, -celing,** *n.* *–v.t.* **1.** to cross out (writing, etc.) by drawing a line or lines over. **2.** to make void; annul. **3.** to mark or perforate (a postage stamp, bus ticket, etc.) to render it invalid for re-use. **4.** to neutralise; counterbalance; compensate for. **5.** *Maths.* to eliminate by striking out (a factor common to both terms of a fraction, equivalent quantities on opposite sides of an equation, etc.). **6.** *Print.* to omit. *–n.* **7.** the act of cancelling. **8.** *Print.* omission. **9.** *Print., Bookbinding.* an omitted part, or the replacement for it. **10.** a piston for shutting off a group of stops on an organ. [late ME, from L *cancellāre* to make like a lattice, to strike out a writing] **– canceller,** *n.*

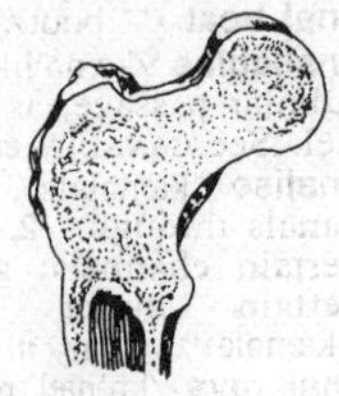
cancellate bone structure

**cancellate** /'kænsəleɪt/, *adj.* of spongy or porous structure, as bone. Also, **cancellous.** [L *cancellātus,* pp., latticed. See CANCEL]

**cancellation** /kænsə'leɪʃən/, *n.* **1.** the act of cancelling. **2.** the marks or perforations made in cancelling. **3.** something cancelled.

**cancer** /'kænsə/, *n.* **1.** *Pathol.* a malignant and invasive growth or tumour, esp. one originating in epithelium, tending to recur after excision and to metastasise to other sites. **2.** any evil condition or thing that spreads destructively. **3.** (*cap.*) a constellation and sign of the zodiac, represented by a crab. **4.** →**Cancerian. 5. Tropic of.** See **tropic** (defs 1a and 2a). [L: crab, tumour] – **cancerous,** *adj.*

**Cancerian** /kæn'sɪəriən/, *n.* **1.** a person born under the sign of Cancer, and (according to tradition) exhibiting the typical Cancerian personality traits in some degree. *–adj.* **2.** of or pertaining to Cancer. **3.** of or pertaining to such a person or such a personality trait.

**cancerophobia** /kænsərə'foubiə/, *n.* a morbid fear of cancer.

**cancer smear** /'kænsə smɪə/, *n.* →**Pap smear.**

**cancer stick** /'– stɪk/, *n. Colloq.* a cigarette.

**cancroid** /'kæŋkrɔɪd/, *adj.* **1.** *Pathol.* resembling a cancer, as certain tumours. **2.** *Zool.* resembling a crab. *–n.* **3.** *Pathol.* a form of cancer of the skin.

**c. & b.,** *Cricket.* caught and bowled.

**candela** /kæn'dilə, -'deɪlə/, *n.* the SI base unit of luminous intensity; the luminous intensity in the perpendicular direction of a surface of 1/600 000 of one square metre of a black body radiator at the temperature of solidification of platinum under a pressure of 101 325 pascals. *Symbol:* cd [L: candle]

**candelabra** /kændə'labrə/, *n.* **1.** a plural of **candelabrum. 2.** (*pl. but taken as sing. with pl.* **-bras**) →**candelabrum.**

**candelabrum** /kændə'labrəm/, *n., pl.* **-bra** /-brə/. an ornamental branched candlestick. [L, from *candēla* candle]

candelabrum

**candela per square metre,** *n.* the SI unit of measurement of luminance.

**candent** /'kændənt/, *adj.* glowing with heat; at a white heat. [L *candens,* ppr., shining]

**candescent** /kæn'dɛsənt/, *adj.* glowing; incandescent. [L *candescens,* ppr., beginning to glow] – **candescence,** *n.* – **candescently,** *adv.*

**c. & f.,** cost and freight.

**candid** /'kændəd/, *adj.* **1.** frank; outspoken; open and sincere: *candid account.* **2.** honest; impartial: *candid mind.* **3.** *Obs.* white. **4.** clear; pure. *–n.* **5.** a photograph having an unposed or informal subject. [L *candidus* white, sincere] – **candidly,** *adv.* – **candidness,** *n.*

**candidate** /'kændədeɪt, -dət/, *n.* **1.** one who seeks an office, an honour, etc. **2.** one who is selected by others as a contestant for an office, etc. **3.** one who seeks an academic qualification or the like, usu. by examination. **4.** *Colloq.* a suitable subject: *that idea is a candidate for the wastepaper basket.* [L *candidātus* clad in white, as a Roman candidate for office] – **candidacy** /'kændədəsi/, **candidature** /'kændədətʃə/, **candidateship,** *n.*

**candid-camera** /kændəd-'kæmrə/, *adj.* of or pertaining to a television program, etc., in which people are filmed without their knowledge in contrived situations designed to make them look foolish.

**candidiasis** /kændədi'eɪsəs/, *n.* →**monilia** (def. 2).

**candied** /'kændid/, *adj.* **1.** impregnated or encrusted with or as with sugar. **2.** crystallised, as sugar. **3.** honeyed or sweet; flattering.

**candle** /'kændl/, *n., v.,* **-dled, -dling.** *–n.* **1.** a long, usu. slender, piece of tallow, wax, etc., with an embedded wick, burnt to give light. **2.** something like this in appearance or use. **3. international candle,** a unit of luminous intensity established by international agreement, defined in terms of specially constructed electric lamps, now replaced by the **candela. 4. burn the candle at both ends,** to lead a too strenuous existence; attempt to do too much, as by making an excessive demand on one's available energy, rising early and retiring late, etc. **5. can't hold a candle to,** *Colloq.* to be totally inferior to. **6. not worth the candle,** not worth the effort or expense. *–v.i.* **7.** to examine (esp. eggs for freshness) by holding between the eye and a light. [OE *candel,* from L *candēla*]

**candle bark** /'– bak/, *n.* **1.** the ribbon-like bark which peels and hangs in strips from some species of *Eucalyptus.* **2.** a species of *Eucalyptus, E. rubida,* with smooth and often red-suffused bark, found in highlands of eastern Australia.

**candleberry** /'kændlbɛri/, *n., pl.* **-ries. 1.** →**wax-myrtle. 2.** its berry. **3.** →**candlenut.**

**candlefish** /'kændlfɪʃ/, *n.* a small edible fish, *Thaleichthys pacificus,* of the north-western coast of America, of the smelt family, with flesh so oily that when the fish is dried it may be used as a candle.

**candlelight** /'kændl,laɪt/, *n.* **1.** the light of a candle. **2.** artificial light. **3.** twilight; dusk.

**Candlemas** /'kændlmæs/, *n.* an ecclesiastical festival, 2 February, in honour of the presentation of the infant Jesus in the Temple and the purification of the Virgin Mary. Candles are blessed on this day. [ME *candelmasse,* OE *candelmæsse.* See CANDLE, -MAS]

**candlenut** /'kændlnʌt/, *n.* **1.** the oily fruit or nut of a tree, *Aleurites moluccana,* of the South Sea Islands, etc., the kernels of which, when strung together, are used as candles by the natives. **2.** the tree itself. Also, **candleberry.**

**candlepin** /'kændlpɪn/, *n.* **1.** a slender, candle-shaped pin used in ninepin or tenpin bowling. **2.** (*pl.*) a game using such pins.

**candlepower** /'kændlpauə/, *n. Photom.* **1.** the illuminating capacity or luminous intensity of a candela. **2.** luminous intensity (of a light) or illuminating capacity (of a lamp or other device), measured in candelas.

**candlestick** /'kændlstɪk/, *n.* a holder for a candle.

**candletree** /'kændltri/, *n.* **1.** →**wax-myrtle. 2.** →**candlenut** (def. 2).

**candlewick** /'kændlwɪk/, *n.* **1.** the wick of a candle. *–adj.* **2.** (of a fabric) usu. unbleached cotton, into which small, short bunches of wicking have been hooked to form a design, used for bedspreads, etc.; chenille.

**candlewood** /'kændlwʊd/, *n.* **1.** any resinous wood used for torches or as a substitute for candles. **2.** any of various trees or shrubs yielding such wood.

**candour** /'kændə/, *n.* **1.** frankness, as of speech; sincerity; honesty. **2.** freedom from bias; fairness; impartiality. **3.** *Obs.* kindliness. **4.** *Obs.* purity. Also, *U.S.,* **candor.** [L *candor* radiance, purity, candour]

**C & W** /si ən 'dʌbəlju/, country and western music.

**candy** /'kændi/, *n., pl.* **-dies,** *v.,* **-died, -dying.** *–n.* **1.** a sweet made of sugar crystallised by boiling. **2.** *U.S.* any of a variety of confections made with sugar, syrup, etc., combined with other ingredients. **3.** *U.S.* a single piece of such a confection. *–v.t.* **4.** to cook in heavy syrup until transparent, as fruit, fruit peel, or ginger. **5.** *U.S.* to cook in sugar or syrup, as yams. **6.** to reduce (sugar, etc.) to a crystalline form, usu. by boiling down. **7.** to cover with sugar-like crystals, as of ice. **8.** to make sweet, palatable, or agreeable. *–v.i.* **9.** to become covered with sugar. **10.** to crystallise. [short for *sugar candy,* from F *sucre candi* candied sugar (*candi* from Ar. *qand* sugar, from Pers., apparently c. Skt *khanda* piece)]

**candy floss** /'– flɒs/, *n.* →**fairy floss.**

**candy stripe** /'– straɪp/, *n.* candy-striped fabric.

**candy-striped** /'kændi-straɪpt/, *adj.* having a colour pattern made up of narrow stripes of colour on a white or lighter-coloured base, esp. red on pink in the manner of certain lollies. [see CANDY (def. 2)]

**candytuft** /'kænditʌft/, *n.* a plant of the genus *Iberis,* esp. *I. umbellata* and *I. amara,* cultivated annuals with tufted flowers, originally from Candia (Crete). [from *Candy* (for *Candia* Crete) + TUFT]

**cane** /keɪn/, *n., v.,* **caned, caning.** *–n.* **1.** a long, hollow or pithy, jointed woody stem, as that of bamboo, rattan, sugar cane, certain palms, etc. **2.** a plant having such a stem. **3.**

such stems as a material. **4.** any of various tall, woody, bamboo-like grasses. **5.** the stem of the raspberry or blackberry. **6.** sugar cane. **7.** the stem of a bamboo, etc., used as a rod for punishing school children. **8.** a walking stick. **9.** a slender piece of sealing wax, etc. *–v.t.* **10.** to beat with a cane. **11.** to furnish or make with cane: *to cane chairs.* [ME, from OF, from Pr. or It., from L *canna,* from Gk *kánna* reed. Cf. Heb. *qāneh*] **– caner,** *n.*

**cane-beetle** /ˈkeɪn-bitl/, *n.* a large beetle, *Dermolepida albohirtum,* the larvae of which are a serious pest of sugar cane.

**cane bin** /ˈkeɪn bɪn/, *n.* a large bin which as part of a cane train is used for hauling sugar cane.

**canebrake** /ˈkeɪnbreɪk/, *n. U.S.* a thicket of canes.

**cane chair** /ˈkeɪn tʃɛə/, *n.* a chair made of interwoven rattan cane.

**cane-cocky** /ˈkeɪn-kɒki/, *n.* a farmer growing sugar cane on a small scale of operation.

**canecutter** /ˈkeɪnkʌtə/, *n.* **1.** one employed in cutting sugar cane. **2.** a machine which cuts sugar cane.

**cane grass** /ˈkeɪn gras/, *n.* a tall rigid perennial grass, *Eragrostis australasica,* of inland swamps and lagoons of northern Australia.

**canegrower** /ˈkeɪngroʊə/, *n.* one who grows sugar cane. Also, **canefarmer.**

**cane-ite** /ˈkeɪn-aɪt/, *n.* an extremely soft building board used for room lining, etc., and made from the fibres of the sugar cane. [Trademark]

**canella** /kəˈnɛlə/, *n.* the cinnamon-like bark of a West Indian tree, *Canella winterana,* used as a condiment and in medicine. [ML: cinnamon, diminutive of L *canna* CANE]

**canephor** /ˈkænəfɔ/, *n. Archit.* a caryatid having a basket-like cushion upon the head. Also, **canephora** /kəˈnɛfərə/, *pl.* **-rae** /-ri/. [L *canēphoros,* from Gk *kanēphóros* basket-bearer]

**cane rat** /ˈkeɪn ræt/, *n.* a large nocturnal rodent, *Thryonomys swinderenianus,* of Africa, resembling a rat.

**canescent** /kəˈnɛsənt/, *adj.* **1.** *Biol.* white or grey because of the presence of short white hairs. **2.** becoming white. [L *cānescens,* ppr.]

**cane sugar** /ˈ– ʃʊgə/, *n.* sugar obtained from sugar cane.

**cane toad** /ˈ– toʊd/, *n.* →**bufo.**

**cane train** /ˈ– treɪn/, *n.* a train comprising a small locomotive and a number of cane bins for transporting harvested sugar cane from a plantation to the sugar mill.

**canfield** /ˈkænfild/, *n.* a game of patience often adapted for gambling purposes. [from R.A. *Canfield,* d. 1914, American gambling house proprietor]

**cangue** /kæŋ/, *n.* (in China, formerly) a kind of portable pillory worn about the neck by criminals. [F, probably from Pg. *canga* yoke, from Annamite *gong*]

**canine** /ˈkeɪnaɪn/, *adj.* **1.** of or like a dog; pertaining to or characteristic of dogs. **2.** *Anat., Zool.* of or pertaining to the four pointed teeth, esp. prominent in dogs, situated one on each side of each jaw, next to the incisors. *–n.* **3.** *Zool.* any animal of the dog family, the Canidae, including the wolves, jackals, hyenas, coyotes, and foxes. **4.** a dog. **5.** a canine tooth. [L *canīnus* pertaining to a dog]

**canis** /ˈkænəs/, *n.* the canine genus that includes the domestic dog, *Canis familiaris,* the wild dogs, the wolves, and the jackals, all having 42 teeth. [L: dog]

**canister** /ˈkænəstə/, *n.* **1.** a small box, usu. of metal, for holding tea, coffee, etc. **2.** case shot (**canister shot**). [L *canistrum,* from Gk *kánastron* wicker basket]

**canker** /ˈkæŋkə/, *n.* **1.** *Pathol.* a gangrenous or ulcerous sore, esp. in the mouth. **2.** *Vet. Sci.* a disease affecting horses' feet, usu. the soles, characterised by a foul-smelling exudate. **3.** *Vet. Sci.* eczema in dogs' ears. **4.** *Vet. Sci.* an abscess or ulcer in birds. **5.** *Plant Pathol.* a stem disease in which a dead area is surrounded by living tissues. **6.** anything that corrodes, corrupts, destroys, or irritates. **7.** *Obs.* dogrose. *–v.t.* **8.** to infect with canker. **9.** to corrupt; destroy slowly. *–v.i.* **10.** to become infected with or as with canker. [ME; OE *cancer,* from L *cancer* gangrene]

**cankerous** /ˈkæŋkərəs/, *adj.* **1.** of the nature of or resembling canker. **2.** causing canker.

**cankerworm** /ˈkæŋkəwɜm/, *n.* a striped green caterpillar injurious to fruit trees and other plants. It is the larva of any of several geometrid moths.

**canna** /ˈkænə/, *n.* any plant of the tropical genus *Canna* (family Cannaceae), various species of which are cultivated for their large handsome leaves and showy flowers; Indian shot. [L: reed. See CANE]

**cannabidiol** /kænəˈbɪdiɒl/, *n.* a component of marijuana.

**cannabin** /ˈkænəbən/, *n.* a poisonous resin extracted from Indian hemp. [CANNAB(IS) + -IN²]

**cannabinol** /kænəˈbinɒl/, *n.* a component of marijuana.

**cannabis** /ˈkænəbəs/, *n.* hashish; the dried pistillate parts of Indian hemp. [L: hemp]

**canned** /kænd/, *adj. Orig. U.S.* **1.** preserved in a can, tin, or jar. **2.** *Colloq.* recorded: *canned laughter.* **3.** *Colloq.* prepared in advance. **4.** *Colloq.* drunk.

**cannel** /ˈkænəl/, *n.* a compact coal containing much volatile matter which burns readily and brightly. Also, **cannel coal.** [apparently for *candle coal*]

**cannelloni** /kænəˈloʊni/, *n.pl.* tubular or rolled pieces of pasta usu. filled with a mixture of meat or cheese and served with a tomato or cream sauce. [It.]

**cannelure** /ˈkænəljʊə/, *n.* **1.** a groove or channel in a surface. **2.** *Ballistics.* a groove in a bullet which has been fired. [F *canneler* to groove, channel]

**canner** /ˈkænə/, *n.* **1.** one who cans meat, fruit, etc., for preservation. **2.** Also, **tinner.** *Agric.* low-grade or aged meat, so classified for marketing.

**cannery** /ˈkænəri/, *n., pl.* **-ries.** a place where meat, fish, fruit, etc., are canned.

**cannibal** /ˈkænəbəl/, *n.* **1.** a human being who eats human flesh. **2.** any animal that eats its own kind. *–adj.* **3.** pertaining to or characteristic of cannibals. **4.** given to cannibalism. [Sp. *Canîbal,* for *Carîbal,* from *Caribe* Carib]

**cannibalise** /ˈkænəbəlaɪz/, *v.t.,* **-lised, -lising.** to repair (damaged motor vehicles, etc.) by the use of parts of other assembled vehicles, etc., instead of using spare parts. Also, **cannibalize. – cannibalisation** /ˌkænəbəlaɪˈzeɪʃən/, *n.*

**cannibalism** /ˈkænəbəlɪzəm/, *n.* **1.** the practice of eating one's own kind. **2.** savage cruelty; barbarism. **– cannibalistic** /kænəbəˈlɪstɪk/, *adj.* **– cannibalistically** /kænəbəˈlɪstɪkli/, *adv.*

**cannikin** /ˈkænəkən/, *n.* a little can; a cup. [MFlem. or D *cannekin* little can]

**canning** /ˈkænɪŋ/, *n.* the act, process, or business of preserving meat, fruits, etc., in sealed cans or tins.

**Canning's little dog,** *n.* →**crest-tailed marsupial mouse.** [named after Alfred *Canning,* 1861-1936, surveyor and explorer]

**cannon** /ˈkænən/, *n., pl,* **-nons,** (*esp. collectively*) **-non,** *v.* *–n.* **1.** a large ancient gun for firing heavy projectiles, mounted on a carriage. **2.** a powerful automatic gun for firing explosive shells. **3.** *Colloq.* a revolver. **4.** *Mach.* a hollow cylinder fitted over a shaft and capable of revolving independently. **5.** a smooth round bit. **6.** Also, **cannon bit, canon bit.** the part of a bit that is in the horse's mouth. **7.** the metal loop of a bell by which it is hung. **8.** *Zool.* **a.** the cannon bone. **b.** the part of the leg in which it is situated; instep. **9.** *Armour.* a cylindrical or semicylindrical plate covering the forearm or upper arm; rerebrace or vambrace. **10.** *Croquet.* a stroke in which a croqueted ball runs into three or four others already in contact. **11.** *Billiards.* a shot in which the ball struck with the cue is made to hit two balls in succession. **12.** any strike and rebound, as a ball striking a wall and glancing off. *–v.i.* **13.** to discharge cannon. **14.** to make a cannon in billiards. **15.** to come into collision with; crash (fol. by *into*). [F *canon,* from It. *cannone,* augmentative of *canna* tube, from L *canna.* See CANE]

**cannonade** /kænəˈneɪd/, *n., v.,* **-naded, -nading.** *–n.* **1.** a continued discharge of guns of any sort, esp. during an attack. *–v.t.* **2.** to attack with cannon. *–v.i.* **3.** to discharge cannon. [F *canonnade*]

**cannonball** /ˈkænənbɔl/, *n.* (formerly) a missile, usu. round and made of iron or steel, designed to be fired from a cannon.

**cannon bit** /ˈkænən bɪt/, *n.* →**cannon** (def. 6).

**cannon bone** /ˈ– boʊn/, *n.* the greatly developed middle metacarpal or metatarsal bone of hoofed quadrupeds, extending from wrist or ankle to the first joint of the digit. [from CANNON (as being tube-shaped) + BONE]

**cannon fodder** /'– fɒdə/, *n.* soldiers treated as expendable victims of military technology.

**cannonry** /'kænənri/, *n., pl.* **-ries.** **1.** a discharge of artillery. **2.** →**artillery** (def. 1).

**cannon shot** /'kænən ʃɒt/, *n.* **1.** a ball or shot for a cannon. **2.** the shooting of a cannon. **3.** the range of a cannon.

**cannot** /'kænɒt, kæ'nɒt/, *v.* a form of **can not.**

**cannula** /'kænjələ/, *n.* a metal tube for insertion into the body, used to keep a passage open, to draw off fluid, or to introduce medication. [L, diminutive of *canna.* See CANE]

**cannular** /'kænjələ/, *adj.* tubular. Also, **cannulate** /'kænjəleɪt, -ət/.

**canny** /'kæni/, *adj.,* **-nier, -niest,** *adv.* *–adj.* **1.** careful; cautious; wary. **2.** knowing; sagacious; shrewd; astute. **3.** *Archaic.* having supernatural powers. *–adv.* **4.** in a canny manner. [apparently from CAN[1]] – **canniness,** *n.*

**canoe** /kə'nu/, *n., v.,* **-noed, -noeing.** *–n.* **1.** any light and narrow boat, often canvas-covered, that is propelled by paddles in place of oars. **2.** any native boat of very light construction, as the Algonquian birchbark canoe. **3. paddle one's own canoe,** to be independent; manage on one's own. *–v.i.* **4.** to paddle a canoe. **5.** to go in a canoe. *–v.t.* **6.** to transport by canoe. [earlier *canow,* var. of *canoa,* from Sp., from Carib *kanoa*] – **canoeing,** *n.* – **canoeist,** *n.*

**canoe stern** /'– stɜn/, *n.* usu. of fishing or other work boats, a rounded rising stern. Cf. **transom stern.**

**canon**[1] /'kænən/, *n.* **1.** an ecclesiastical rule or law enacted by a council or other competent authority, and (in the Roman Catholic Church) approved by the pope. **2.** the body of ecclesiastical law. **3.** any rule or law. **4.** a fundamental principle. **5.** a standard; criterion. **6.** the books of the Bible recognised by the Christian Church as genuine and inspired. **7.** any officially recognised set of sacred books. **8.** the body of works of a writer generally accepted as genuine. **9.** a catalogue or list, as of the saints acknowledged by the Church. **10.** *Liturgy.* that part of the mass between the Sanctus and the communion. **11.** *Music.* a kind of composition in which the same melody is played or sung through by two or more voice parts at the same or at a different pitch overlapping each other. **12.** a large size of printing type. [ME and OE, from L: rule, canon, from Gk *kanṓn* straight rod, rule, standard]

**canon**[2] /'kænən/, *n.* **1.** one of a body of dignitaries or prebendaries attached to a cathedral or a collegiate church; a member of the chapter of a cathedral or a collegiate church. **2.** *Rom. Cath. Ch.* one of the members (**canons regular**) of certain religious orders. [ME *canoun,* from ONF *canon,* from ML. See CANON[1]]

**canon bit** /'– bɪt/, *n.* →**cannon** (def. 6).

**canoness** /'kænənɛs/, *n.* one of a community of women living under a rule, but not under a vow.

**canonical** /kə'nɒnɪkəl/, *adj.* **1.** conforming to canon law. **2.** included in the canon of the Bible. **3.** authorised; recognised by canon law; accepted: *canonical criticism.* *–n.* **4.** (*pl.*) the dress prescribed by canon for the clergy when officiating. [ML *canonicālis,* from L *canonicus,* from Gk *kanonikós.* See CANON[1]] – **canonically,** *adv.*

**canonical hours** /– 'aʊəz/, *n. pl.* **1.** *Eccles.* any of certain periods of the day set apart for prayer and devotion, namely, matins (with lauds), prime, tierce, sext, nones, vespers, and complin; now replaceable by the offices of *The Prayer of the Church.* **2.** *Brit.* any hour between 8 a.m. and 6 p.m., during which marriage may be legally performed in parish churches.

**canonicate** /kə'nɒnəkeɪt, -kət/, *n.* the office or dignity of a canon; a canonry.

**canonicity** /kænə'nɪsəti/, *n.* canonical character.

**canonise** /'kænənaɪz/, *v.t.,* **-nised, -nising.** **1.** *Eccles.* to place in the canon of saints. **2.** to glorify. **3.** to make canonical: *canonised books.* Also, **canonize.** – **canonisation** /kænənaɪ'zeɪʃən/, *n.*

**canonist** /'kænənəst/, *n.* one versed in canon law.

**canon law** /kænən 'lɔ/, *n.* the body of ecclesiastical law.

**canonry** /'kænənri/, *n., pl.* **-ries.** **1.** the office or benefice of a canon. **2.** the body or group of canons.

**canonship** /'kænənʃɪp/, *n.* the position or office of canon; canonry.

**canoodle** /kə'nudl/, *v.,* **-dled, -dling.** *Colloq.* *–v.i.* **1.** to indulge in fondling and petting. *–v.t.* **2.** to fondle and pet.

**can-opener** /'kæn-oʊpnə/, *n.* →**tin-opener.**

**Canopic** /kə'noʊpɪk/, *adj.* denoting a vase used to hold the ashes of the dead. [L *Canōpicus,* from *Canōpus,* an ancient city of Egypt]

Canopic vase

**canopy** /'kænəpi/, *n., pl.* **-pies,** *v.,* **-pied, -pying.** *–n.* **1.** a covering suspended or supported over a throne, bed, etc., or held over a person, sacred object, etc. **2.** an overhanging protection or shelter. **3.** *Archit.* an ornamental roof-like projection or covering. **4.** the sky. **5.** the transparent, opening cover to the cockpit of some aircraft. **6.** fabric body of a parachute. *–v.t.* **7.** to cover with or as with a canopy: *clouds canopy the sky.* [ME *canape,* from ML *canapēum,* alteration of L *cōnōpēum* net curtains, from Gk *kōnōpeîon* mosquito net]

**canopy booth** /'– buð/, *n.* an arrangement of walls and ceiling forming a canopy or hood which encloses an article being spray-painted and protects the operator.

**canorous** /kə'nɒrəs/, *adj.* melodious; musical. [L *canōrus*] – **canorously,** *adv.* – **canorousness,** *n.*

**canst** /kænst/, *v. Archaic or Poetic.* 2nd person singular present of **can.**

**cant**[1] /kænt/, *n.* **1.** insincere statements, esp. conventional pretence of enthusiasm for high ideals; insincere expressions of goodness or piety. **2.** the special secret language or jargon spoken by thieves, gipsies, etc.; argot. **3.** the words, phrases, etc., peculiar to a particular class, party, profession, etc. **4.** whining or singsong speech, esp. of beggars. *–v.i.* **5.** to make religious remarks insincerely or hypocritically; pretend goodness or piety. **6.** to speak in the whining or singsong tone of a beggar; beg. **7.** to use the secret language of thieves, gipsies, etc. [cf. OE *cantere* singer, from L *cantor*] – **canter,** *n.*

**cant**[2] /kænt/, *n.* **1.** a salient angle. **2.** a sudden movement that tilts or overturns a thing. **3.** a slanting or tilted position. **4.** superelevation. **5.** an oblique line or surface, as one formed by cutting off the corner of a square or cube. **6.** an oblique or slanting face of anything. **7.** a sudden pitch or toss. *–v.t.* **8.** *Mech.* to bevel. **9.** to put in an oblique position; tilt; tip. **10.** to throw with a sudden jerk. *–v.i.* **11.** to take or have an inclined position; tilt; turn. *–adj.* **12.** tilted; at an angle. **13.** having flat surfaces and no curves: *a cant moulding.* [MD, or MLG *kant,* both probably from ONF *cant,* from L *canthus* corner, side]

**can't** /kant/, *v.* contraction of *cannot.*

**Cantab.,** of Cambridge. [ML *Cantabrigiensis*]

**cantabile** /kæn'tabəleɪ/, *adj.* **1.** (a musical direction) with a singing tone; flowing in style. *–n.* **2.** a cantabile style, passage, or piece. [It., from LL *cantābilis* that may be sung]

**Cantabrigian** /kæntə'brɪdʒiən/, *adj.* **1.** of Cambridge or Cambridge University. *–n.* **2.** a native or inhabitant of Cambridge. **3.** a student or graduate of Cambridge University. [from *Cantabrigia* Latin form of the name Cambridge + -AN]

**cantaloupe** /'kæntəlup/, *n.* →**rockmelon.** Also, **cantaloup.** [F *cantaloup,* from It. *Cantalupo,* a former estate of the Pope near Rome, where it was first grown in Europe]

**cantando** /kæn'tændoʊ/, *adv.* (a musical direction) in a singing style. [It.]

**cantankerous** /kæn'tæŋkərəs/, *adj.* ill-natured; quarrelsome; perverse or contrary, as in disposition: *a cantankerous old maid.* [? from ME *contek* contention] – **cantankerously,** *adv.* – **cantankerousness,** *n.*

**cantata** /kæn'tatə/, *n.* **1.** a choral composition, either sacred and resembling a short oratorio, or secular, as a lyric drama set to music but not to be acted. **2.** (originally) a metrical narrative set to recitative, or alternate recitative and air, usu. for a single voice, accompanied by one or more instruments. [It., from *cantare* sing, from L]

**cantatrice** /kɒntə'tris/, *n.* a female singer. [F]

**cant dog** /'kænt dɒg/, *n.* a wooden lever with a movable iron hook near the lower end, used for grasping and canting or turning over logs, etc. Also, **cant hook.**

**canteen** /kæn'tin/, *n.* **1.** a restaurant or cafeteria attached to a factory, office, etc. **2.** a school tuckshop. **3.** a place where refreshment and sometimes entertainment, are provided for military personnel. **4.** a temporary food supply set up during an emergency. **5.** the drinking and eating utensils of a soldier. **6.** a box containing a set of plate or cutlery. **7.** the cutlery itself. **8.** a small container used by soldiers and others for carrying water or other liquids. [F *cantine,* from It. *cantina* cellar, wine cellar, from *canto* side, from L *canthus*]

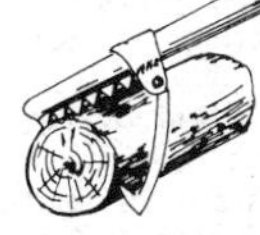
cant dog

**canter** /'kæntə/, *n.* **1.** an easy gallop. *–v.i.* **2.** to go or ride at a canter. *–v.t.* **3.** to make (a horse) go at a canter. **4. win at a canter,** to win easily. [short for *Canterbury gallop* (as of pilgrims to Canterbury, England)]

**canterbury** /'kæntəbri/, *n.* a piece of furniture with partitions in which music, magazines, etc. may be stored.

**Canterbury bell** /ˌkæntəbri 'bɛl/, *n.* a plant, *Campanula medium,* having bell-shaped flowers of various colours ranging from violet-blue, to pink, to white.

**Canterbury lamb** /– 'læm/, *n.* certain grades of lamb or mutton exported from New Zealand to Britain. [Trademark]

**cantharid** /'kænθərɪd/, *adj.* of or pertaining to the Cantharidae, a family of elongated, soft-bodied beetles, often brightly coloured, as the soldier beetle, *Chauliognathus pulchellus.*

**cantharides** /kæn'θærədiz/, *n.pl., sing.* **cantharis** /'kænθərəs/. **1.** a preparation of powdered blister beetles, esp. the Spanish fly, *Lytta vesicatoria,* used medicinally as a skin irritant, diuretic, and aphrodisiac. **2.** (*sing.*) the beetle itself. [L, from Gk: pl., blister flies]

**cant hook** /'kænt hʊk/, *n.* →**cant dog.**

**canthus** /'kænθəs/, *n., pl.* **-thi** /-θi/. the angle or corner on each side of the eye, formed by the junction of the upper and lower lids. [NL, from Gk *kanthós* corner of the eye]

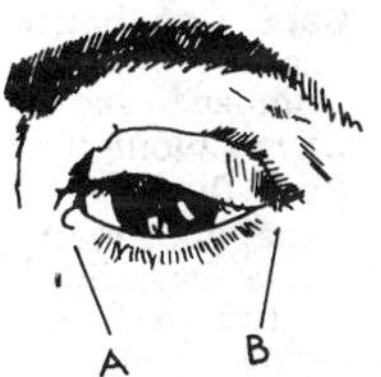

A, inner canthus; B, outer canthus

**canticle** /'kæntɪkəl/, *n.* **1.** one of the non-metrical hymns or chants used in church services. **2.** a little song; a song. **3.** (*cap., pl.*) a book of the Old Testament, also known as the *Song of Solomon.* [ME, from L *canticulum,* diminutive of *canticum* song]

**cantilena** /kæntə'linə, -'leɪnə/, *n.* **1.** a little song. **2.** that section of a larger composition which has the nature of a little song. [It.]

**cantilever** /'kæntəlivə/, *n.* **1.** *Mach.* a free part of any horizontal member projecting beyond a support. **2.** *Civ. Eng.* either of two bracket-like arms projecting towards each other from opposite banks or piers, serving to form the span of a bridge (**cantilever bridge**) when united. **3.** *Aeron.* a form of wing construction in which no external bracing is employed (**cantilever wing**). **4.** *Archit.* an extended bracket for supporting a balcony, cornice, or the like. [orig. uncert.]

**cantle** /'kæntl/, *n.* **1.** the hind part of a saddle, usu. curved upwards. **2.** a corner; piece; portion. [ME *cantel,* from ONF, diminutive of *cant* corner, CANT[2]]

**canto** /'kæntoʊ/, *n., pl.* **-tos.** **1.** one of the main or larger divisions of a long poem, as in Dante's *Inferno.* **2.** *Music.* **a.** a song or melody. **b.** the part in a polyphonic composition which carries the melody, usu. the soprano. [It., from L *cantus* song]

**canto fermo** /– 'fɜmoʊ/, *n.* →**cantus firmus.**

**canton** /'kæntɒn, kæn'tɒn/ *for defs 1, 2 and 4;* /'kæntən/ *for def. 3;* /kæn'tɒn/ *for defs 5 and 6;* /kən'tun/ *for def. 7,* *n.* **1.** a small territorial district, esp. one of the states of the Swiss confederation. **2.** a subdivision of a French arrondissement. **3.** *Her.* a square division in the upper dexter corner of an escutcheon, etc. **4.** a division, part, or portion of anything. *–v.t.* **5.** to divide into parts or portions. **6.** to divide into cantons or territorial districts. **7.** to allot quarters to (soldiers, etc.). [F: corner, from L *canthus* corner, CANT[2]] **– cantonal** /'kæntənəl/, *adj.*

**Canton crepe** /kæntɒn 'kreɪp/, *n.* a thin, light silk or rayon crepe with a finely wrinkled surface, heavier in texture than crepe de chine. [named after *Canton,* China]

**Cantonese** /kæntə'niz/, *n., pl.* **-nese,** *adj.* *–n.* **1.** a Chinese language of southern China. **2.** a native or inhabitant of Canton. *–adj.* **3.** pertaining to Canton, its inhabitants, or their language.

**Canton flannel** /kæntɒn 'flænəl/, *n.* →**cotton flannel.**

**cantonment** /kən'tunmənt/, *n.* **1.** a camp (usu. of large size) where men are trained for military service. **2.** military quarters. **3.** the quarters, esp. winter quarters, of an army in the field. [F *cantonnement*]

**cantor** /'kæntə/, *n.* **1.** an officer whose duty is to lead the singing in a cathedral or in a collegiate or parish church; a precentor. **2.** the Jewish religious official singing the liturgy. [L: singer]

**cantoris** /kæn'tɔrəs/, *n.* the part of a cathedral choir on the north or precentor's side.

**cantus** /'kæntəs/, *n., pl.* **-tus.** **1.** a song; melody. **2.** an ecclesiastical style of music. [L. See CHANT]

**cantus firmus** /– 'fɜməs/, *n.* **1.** *Eccles.* the ancient traditional vocal music of the Christian Church, having its form settled and its use prescribed by ecclesiastical authority. **2.** *Music.* a fixed melody to which other melodic parts are added. Also, **canto fermo.** [ML]

**Canuck** /kə'nʌk/, *n. Colloq.* a Canadian, esp. a French Canadian.

**canvas** /'kænvəs/, *n.* **1.** a closely woven, heavy cloth of hemp, flax, or cotton, used for tents, sails, etc. **2.** a piece of this material on which an oil painting is made. **3.** an oil painting on canvas. **4.** a tent, or tents collectively: *campers living under canvas.* **5.** sailcloth. **6.** sails collectively: *a ship under full canvas.* **7.** *Rowing.* the (originally canvas-covered) narrowing part of a racing eight between the bow oarsman and the actual bow of the boat, or between the cox and the stern. **8.** *Rowing.* the corresponding part of any other racing boat. **9.** *Rowing.* this part considered as a unit of length: *to win by a canvas.* **10.** *Boxing, Wrestling.* the floor of the ring: *he fell to the canvas.* **11.** any fabric, of linen, cotton, etc., of a coarse loose weave, used as a foundation for embroidery stitches, for interlining, etc. [ME *canevas,* from ONF, from L *cannabis* hemp]

**canvasback** /'kænvəsbæk/, *n.* a North American wild duck, *Aythya valisineria,* with a whitish back, prized for the delicacy of its flesh.

**canvass** /'kænvəs/, *v.t.* **1.** to solicit votes, subscriptions, opinions, etc., from (a district, group of people, etc.). **2.** to engage in a political campaign. **3.** to examine carefully; investigate by inquiry; discuss; debate. **4.** *Obs.* to criticise severely. *–v.i.* **5.** to solicit votes, opinions, etc. **6.** *U.S.* to review election returns. **7.** to engage in discussion or debate. *–n.* **8.** examination; close inspection; scrutiny. **9.** a soliciting of votes, orders, etc. **10.** *Chiefly U.S.* a campaign for election to government office. [var. of CANVAS *n.*; orig. meaning to toss (someone) in a canvas sheet (cf. def. 4)] **– canvasser,** *n.*

**canyon** /'kænjən/, *n.* a deep valley with steep sides, often with a stream flowing through it. [Sp. *cañón* tube, from *caña,* from L *canna* reed]

**canzone** /kæn'tsoʊneɪ/, *n., pl.* **-zoni** /-'tsoʊni/. **1.** a variety of lyric poetry in the Italian style, of Provençal origin, which closely resembles the madrigal. **2.** a Provençal troubadour song. **3.** a musical form in 16th-and 17th-century Italian secular music, either vocal or instrumental. [It., from L *cantio* song]

**canzonet** /kænzə'nɛt/, *n.* a short song, esp. a light and gay one.

**caoutchouc** /'kaʊtʃʊk/, *n.* **1.** the gummy coagulated juice of certain tropical plants; indiarubber. **2.** pure rubber. [F, from Sp. *cauchú,* of S Amer. orig.]

**cap**[1] /kæp/, *n., v.,* **capped, capping.** *–n.* **1.** a covering for the head, esp. one fitting closely and made of softer material than a hat, and having little or no brim, but often having a peak, as worn by schoolboys. **2.** the flat, peaked headdress worn by soldiers and others. **3.** a special headdress denoting rank, occupation, etc.: *a cardinal's cap, nurse's cap.* **4.** →**mortarboard.** **5. a.** a headdress denoting that the wearer has been selected for a special team, as one representing his country, in certain sports, as cricket. **b.** membership of such a team. **6.** a close-fitting waterproof headdress worn when swimming, etc. **7.** a covering of lace, etc., for a woman's head, usu. worn indoors. **8.** the detachable protective top of a fountain pen, jar, etc. **9.** anything resembling or suggestive of a covering for the head in shape, use, or position. **10.** the acme. **11.** the top or upper surface, as of a wave, etc. **12.** *Bot.* the pileus of a mushroom. **13.** →**percussion cap. 14.** a noisemaking device for toy pistols, made of a small quantity of explosive wrapped in paper or other thin material. **15.** →**diaphragm** (def. 4). **16.** (in wine-making) the skins and seeds forming the head in a fermentation tank. **17. cap and bells,** the traditional dress of a jester. **18. cap and gown,** academic dress. **19. cap in hand,** humbly, submissively; as a suppliant. **20. if the cap fits, wear it,** *Colloq.* if the judgment applies, accept it. **21. set one's cap at,** to try to capture admiration and attention; ogle. *–v.t.* **22.** to provide or cover with or as with a cap. **23.** to select as a member of a representative team in football, cricket, etc. **24.** *N.Z.* to confer a degree on. **25.** to complete. **26.** to surpass; follow up with something as good or better. [ME *cappe,* OE *cæpe,* from LL *cappa, cāpa* cap, hooded cloak, cape, apparently from *caput* head]

**cap**[2] /kæp/, *n. Colloq.* a capsule.

**cap**[3] /kæp/, *n. Colloq.* a caption.

**cap.,** **1.** capital. **2.** capitalise. **3.** capitalised. **4.** (*pl.* **caps**) capital letter.

**Cap.,** Captain.

**capability** /keɪpə'bɪləti/, *n., pl.* **-ties. 1.** quality of being capable; capacity; ability. **2.** quality of admitting of certain treatment. **3.** (*usu. pl.*) a quality, ability, etc., that can be developed or used.

**capable** /'keɪpəbəl/, *adj.* **1.** having much intelligence or ability; competent; efficient; able: *a capable instructor.* **2. capable of, a.** having the ability, strength, etc., to; qualified or fitted for: *a man capable of judging art.* **b.** susceptible to; open to the influence or effect of: *a situation capable of improvement.* **c.** predisposed to; inclined to: *capable of murder.* [LL *capābilis*] **–capableness,** *n.* **–capably,** *adv.*

**capacious** /kə'peɪʃəs/, *adj.* capable of holding much. [CAPACI(TY) + -OUS] **–capaciously,** *adv.* **–capaciousness,** *n.*

**capacitance** /kə'pæsətəns/, *n.* **1. a.** the property of a system which enables it to store electrical charge. **b.** the extent of this, usu. measured in farads; electrical capacity. **2.** the ratio of a change in quantity of electricity (in a conductor) to the corresponding change in potential; electrical capacity. **3.** a capacitor. [CAPACIT(Y) + -ANCE]

**capacitate** /kə'pæsəteɪt/, *v.t.,* **-tated, -tating. 1.** to make capable; enable. **2.** to furnish with legal powers. **–capacitation** /kəpæsə'teɪʃən/, *n.*

**capacitive** /kə'pæsətɪv/, *adj.* pertaining to capacitance or capacity.

**capacitor** /kə'pæsətə/, *n.* a device for accumulating and holding an electric charge, consisting of two conducting surfaces separated by an insulator or dielectric; a condenser.

**capacity** /kə'pæsəti/, *n., pl.* **-ties. 1.** the power of receiving or containing. **2.** cubic contents; volume. **3.** power of receiving impressions, knowledge, etc.; mental ability: *the capacity of a scholar.* **4.** power, ability, or possibility of doing something (fol. by *of, for,* or infinitive): *capacity for self-protection.* **5.** quality of being susceptible to certain treatment. **6.** position; function; relation: *in the capacity of legal adviser.* **7.** legal qualification or legal rights. **8.** *Elect.* **a.** capacitance. **b.** a measure of output performance. [late ME *capacyte,* from L *capācitas*]

**cap-a-pie** /kæp-ə-'pi/, *adv.* from head to foot. Also, **cap-à-pie.** [F (obs.)]

**caparison** /kə'pærəsən/, *n.* **1.** a covering, usu. ornamental, laid over the saddle or harness of a horse, etc. **2.** dress; equipment; outfit. *–v.t.* **3.** to cover with a caparison. **4.** to dress finely; deck. [MF *caparasson,* from Sp. *caparazón,* from Pr. *caparaso,* from *capa* CAPE[1]]

**cape**[1] /keɪp/, *n.* a sleeveless garment fastened round the neck and falling loosely over the shoulders, worn separately or attached to a coat, etc. [F, from Sp. *capa,* from LL *cāpa.* See CAP[1]]

**cape**[2] /keɪp/, *n.* **1.** a piece of land jutting into the sea or some other body of water. **2.** (*cap.*) **run via the Cape,** *Horseracing Colloq.* to race wide (from the long sea route to England, via the Cape of Good Hope). [ME, from F *cap,* from Pr., from L *caput* head]

**Cape** /keɪp/, *adj.* **1.** pertaining to a mid-Palaeozoic period or system in southern Africa, roughly equivalent to the Upper Silurian to Lower Carboniferous.

**Cape ash** /– 'æʃ/, *n.* a timber tree, *Ekebergia capensis,* family Meliaceae, of southern Africa.

**Cape Barren goose** *n.* a rare Australian anatine bird, *Cereopsis novae-hollandiae,* greyish in colour with pink legs and a black bill with prominent greenish cere. [named after *Cape Barren,* an island in Bass Strait, where the geese were first found]

Cape Barren goose

**Cape buffalo** /keɪp 'bʌfəloʊ/, *n.* a large buffalo, *Syncerus caffer,* of southern Africa, having massive curved horns.

**Cape chestnut** /– 'tʃɛsnʌt/, *n.* a large tree, *Calodendrum capense,* family Rutaceae, native to southern Africa, widely planted for its clusters of flesh-coloured flowers.

**Cape cobra** /– 'kɒbrə/, *n.* a large, common poisonous snake of southern Africa, *Naja nivea,* yellow or brown in colour; geelslang.

**cape-cod** /keɪp-'kɒd/, *v.t.,* **-codded, -codding.** to extend (a single storey house) by adding a second storey with a steeply pitched roof and rooms under the roof.

**Cape Cod house,** *n.* a house with two storeys usu. with dormer windows and rooms under a steeply pitched roof, similar to the style of houses in Cape Cod, U.S.

**Cape Coloured** /keɪp 'kʌləd/, *n.* →**coloured** (def. 7).

**Cape Dutch** /– 'dʌtʃ/, *n.* →**Afrikaans.**

**Cape gooseberry** /– 'gʊzbəri/, *n.* **1.** a tropical solanaceous herb, *Physalis peruviana,* cultivated for its yellow edible berry, native to South America, and naturalised in high rainfall areas of southern Africa, the east coast of Australia, and other areas of similar climate. **2.** its fruit.

**Cape ivy** /– 'aɪvi/, *n.* a climbing plant, *Senecio mikanioides,* of southern Africa, having ivy-shaped leaves.

**capelin** /'kæpələn/, *n.* either of two small fishes of the smelt family, of the North American coasts of the Atlantic (*Mallotus villosus*) and Pacific (*M. catervarius*). [F *caplan, capelan,* probably from Pr. See CHAPLAIN]

**capellmeister** /'kæpəl,maɪstə/, *n.* →**kapellmeister.**

**Cape pondweed** /keɪp 'pɒndwid/, *n.* a perennial aquatic herb with floating leaves, *Aponogeton distachyos,* native to southern Africa often planted and naturalised elsewhere.

**caper**[1] /'keɪpə/, *v.i.* **1.** to leap or skip about in a sprightly manner; prance. *–n.* **2.** a playful leap or skip. **3.** a prank; capricious action; harebrained escapade. **4.** *Colloq.* a trick; dodge. [fig. use of L *caper* he-goat] **–caperer,** *n.*

**caper**[2] /'keɪpə/, *n.* **1.** a shrub, *Capparis spinosa,* of Mediterranean regions. **2.** its flower bud, which is pickled and used for garnish or seasoning. [ME *caperis,* from L *capparis,* from Gk *kápparis*]

**capercailzie** /kæpə'keɪlji, -'keɪlzi/, *n.* the woodgrouse, *Tetrao urogallus,* a very large gallinaceous bird of northern Europe. Also, **capercaillie** /kæpə'keɪlji/. [Gaelic *capullcoille,* lit., horse of the wood, with *r* for *l* by dissimilation]

**caper sauce** /keɪpə 'sɔs/, *n.* a sauce, usu. white sauce, to which capers have been added.

**Capertian** /kæpə'tiən/, *n.* **1.** a cultural period of Aboriginal development recognised in eastern Australia, beginning about 6 000 years B.P. and ending about 2 000 years B.P. *–adj.* **2.** of, or pertaining to the period. [named after *Capertee,* N.S.W.]

**Cape Sparrow** /keɪp 'spæroʊ/, *n.* →**mossie**[1].

**Cape teak** /– 'tik/, *n.* a large African tree, *Pterocarpus angolensis,* with durable wood resembling teak.

**Cape tulip** /– 'tjuləp/, *n.* either of two perennial iridaceous herbs, of the genus *Homeria,* of southern Africa, originally cultivated in Australia for their flowers, but now growing wild and regarded as troublesome, poisonous weeds.

**Cape Verde** /– 'vɜd/, *n.* a country comprising a group of islands in the Atlantic Ocean, west of Senegal. Also, **Cape Verde Islands.**

**capeweed** /'keɪpwid/, *n.* a low-growing, spreading, herbaceous weed, *Arctotheca calendula,* native to Africa, with yellow flowers and hairy seeds which can form hair balls in an animal's stomach.

**Cape wren-warbler** /keɪp 'rɛn-wɔblə/, *n.* →**tinktinkie.**

**capful** /'kæpfʊl/, *n., pl.* **-fuls.** as much as a cap will hold.

**capias** /'keɪpiəs/, *n.* a writ commanding an officer to take a specified person into custody. [L: take thou]

**capias ad satisfaciendum** /ˌkeɪpiəs æd sætəsfæki'ɛndəm/, *n. Law.* a writ for the arrest of the defendant in a civil action when judgment has been recovered against him for a sum of money and has not been satisfied. *Abbrev.:* ca. sa.

**capillaceous** /kæpə'leɪʃəs/, *adj.* hairlike; capillary. [L *capillāceus* hairy]

**capillarity** /kæpə'lærəti/, *n.* **1.** the state of being capillary. **2.** *Physics.* →**capillary** (def. 2b).

**capillary** /kə'pɪləri/, *adj., n., pl.* **-laries.** *–adj.* **1.** pertaining to or occurring in or as in a tube of fine bore. **2.** *Physics.* **a.** pertaining to the property of surface tension. **b. capillary action,** the elevation or depression of liquids in fine tubes, etc., due to intermolecular forces, such as surface tension, and those forces between the molecules of the liquid and the tube, etc. **c. capillary attraction** or **repulsion,** the apparent attraction or repulsion between a liquid and a tube, etc., observed in such phenomena. **3.** *Bot.* resembling hair in the manner of growth or in shape. **4.** *Anat.* pertaining to a capillary or capillaries. *–n.* **5.** *Anat.* one of the minute blood vessels between the terminations of the arteries and the beginnings of the veins. **6.** Also, **capillary tube.** a tube with a small bore. [L *capillāris* pertaining to the hair]

**capillary fitting** /'– fɪtɪŋ/, *n.* any of various joints between two tubes or pipes held by solder, esp. as in domestic plumbing.

**capita** /'kæpətə/, *n.* plural of **caput.**

**capital**[1] /'kæpətl/, *n.* **1.** the city or town which is the official seat of government in a country, state, etc. **2.** a capital letter. **3.** the wealth, whether in money or property, owned or employed in business by an individual, firm, etc. **4.** an accumulated stock of such wealth. **5.** any form of wealth employed or capable of being employed in the production of more wealth. **6.** *Accounting.* the ownership interest in a business. **7.** any source of profit, advantage, power, etc. **8.** capitalists as a group or class. **9.** resources. *–adj.* **10.** pertaining to capital: *capital stock.* **11.** principal; highly important. **12.** chief, esp. as being the official seat of government of a country, state, etc. **13.** excellent or first-rate. **14.** (of letters) of the large size used at the beginning of a sentence or as the first letter of a proper name. **15.** involving the loss of the head or life, usu. as punishment; punishable by death. **16.** fatal; serious: *a capital error.* **17.** of the largest, most heavily armed, etc., type: *a capital ship.* [ME, from L *capitālis* pertaining to the head or to life, chief (ML *capitāle,* n., wealth)]

**capital**[2] /'kæpətl/, *n. Archit.* the head, or uppermost part, of a column, pillar, etc. [ME *capital(e),* from L *capitellum,* diminutive of *caput* head; influenced by CAPITAL[1], *adj.*]

A B C

capital[2]: A, Doric; B, Ionic; C, Corinthian

**capital account** /– ə'kaʊnt/, *n.* **1.** a business account stating the owner's or shareholder's interest in the assets. **2.** (*pl.*) *Accounting.* accounts showing the net worth, as in a business enterprise, as assets minus liabilities.

**capital appreciation** /– əprisi'eɪʃən/, *n.* an increase in the value of an asset over a period of time.

**capital assets** /– 'æsets/, *n. pl.* →**fixed assets.**

**capital distribution** /– dɪstrə'bjuʃən/, *n.* the issue of bonus shares to shareholders in a company.

**capital expenditure** /– ək'spɛndɪtʃə/, *n.* an addition to the value of a fixed asset, as by the purchase of a new building.

**capital gains** /– 'geɪnz/, *n. pl.* profits from the sale of capital assets, such as bonds, real property, etc.

**capital gains tax,** *n.* a tax paid on the increased value of capital invested.

**capital goods** /kæpətl 'gʊdz/, *n. pl.* goods used in the production of other goods.

**capital-intensive** /'kæpətl-ɪnˌtɛnsɪv/, *adj.* of or pertaining to an industry which, while requiring relatively little labour, requires a high capital investment in plant, etc. (opposed to *labour-intensive*).

**capitalisation** /kæpətəlaɪ'zeɪʃən/, *n.* **1.** the act of capitalising. **2.** the authorised and paid up shares or stock of a company. **3.** *Accounting.* **a.** the total investment of the owner or owners in a business enterprise. **b.** the total corporate liability. **c.** the total arrived at after addition of liabilities. **4.** conversion into stocks or bonds. **5.** the act of computing the present value of future periodical payments. Also, **capitalization.**

**capitalise** /'kæpətəlaɪz/, *v.t.,* **-lised, -lising. 1.** to write or print in capital letters, or with an initial capital. **2.** to authorise a certain amount of stocks and bonds in the corporate charter: *to capitalise a company.* **3.** to convert (floating debt) into stock or shares. **4.** *Accounting.* to set up (expenditures) as business assets in the books of account instead of treating as expense. **5.** to supply with capital. **6.** to estimate the value of (a stock or an enterprise). **7.** to take advantage of; turn to one's advantage (oft. fol. by *on*): *capitalise on one's opportunities.* Also, **capitalize.**

**capitalism** /'kæpətəlɪzəm/, *n.* **1.** a system under which the means of production, distribution, and exchange are in large measure privately owned and directed. **2.** the concentration of capital in the hands of a few, or the resulting power or influence. **3.** a system favouring such concentration of wealth.

**capital issue** /kæpətl 'ɪʃu/, *n.* →**capital distribution.**

**capitalist** /'kæpətələst/, *n.* **1.** one who has capital, esp. extensive capital employed in business enterprises. *–adj.* **2.** pertaining to capital or capitalists; founded on or believing in capitalism. – **capitalistic** /kæpətə'lɪstɪk/, *adj.* – **capitalistically** /kæpətə'lɪstɪkli/, *adv.*

**capitalist roader** /– 'roʊdə/, *n.* (*derog.*) a revisionist; from a Marxist socialist viewpoint, one who is in sympathy with capitalist theories and practices.

**capital levy** /kæpətl 'lɛvi/, *n.* a tax based on total assets.

**capitally** /'kæpətəli/, *adv.* **1.** in a capital manner; excellently; very well. **2.** by capital punishment.

**capital ship** /kæpətl 'ʃɪp/, *n.* one of a class of the largest warships; a battleship, battle cruiser, or aircraft-carrier.

**capital stock** /– 'stɒk/, *n.* **1.** the total shares issued by a company. **2.** the book value of all the shares of a company, including unissued shares and those not completely paid in.

**capital sum** /– 'sʌm/, *n.* the sum stated to be payable on the happening of some event against which insurance has been effected.

**capital surplus** /– 'sɜpləs/, *n.* the surplus of a business, exclusive of its earned surplus.

**capital transfer tax,** *n.* →**gift tax.**

**capitate**[1] /'kæpəteɪt/, *adj.* having a globular head; collected in a head. [L *capitātus* having a head]

**capitate**[2] /'kæpəteɪt/, *n.* a small bone forming part of the carpus of the hand. [NL *capitātum,* adj., in *os capitātum* capitate bone]

**capitation** /kæpə'teɪʃən/, *n.* **1.** a numbering or assessing by the head. **2.** a poll tax. **3.** a fee or payment of a uniform amount for each person. [LL *capitātio* poll tax]

**capitular** /kə'pɪtʃələ/, *n.* **1.** a member of an ecclesiastical chapter. **2.** (*pl.*) the laws or statutes of a chapter or of an ecclesiastical council. *–adj.* **3.** *Bot.* capitate. **4.** pertaining to an ecclesiastical or other chapter: *a capitular cathedral.* [ML *capitulāris,* from L *capitulum* CAPITULUM]

**capitulary** /kə'pɪtʃələri/, *adj., n., pl.* **-ries.** *–adj.* **1.** pertaining to a chapter, esp. an ecclesiastical one. *–n.* **2.** a member of a chapter, esp. an ecclesiastical one. **3.** (*pl.*) the ordinances or laws of a Frankish sovereign.

**capitulate** /kə'pɪtʃəleɪt/, *v.i.,* **-lated, -lating.** to surrender unconditionally or on stipulated terms. [ML *capitulātus,* pp. of *capitulāre* arrange in chapters, from L *capitulum* CAPITULUM]

**capitulation** /kəpɪtʃə'leɪʃən/, *n.* **1.** a surrender unconditionally or upon certain terms. **2.** the instrument containing a surrender. **3.** a statement of the heads of a subject; a summary or enumeration. **4.** (*pl.*) any of the treaties of the sultans of Turkey which granted to foreigners residing there rights of personalty of law, extraterritoriality, etc. **5.** a treaty by which Christian states obtained the right to establish courts for their nationals in non-Christian states.

**capitulum** /kə'pɪtʃələm/, *n., pl.* **-la** /-lə/. **1.** *Bot.* a close head of sessile flowers; a flower head. **2.** *Anat.* the head of a bone. [L: small head, capital of column, chapter, diminutive of *caput* head]

**Cap'n** /'kæpn, 'kæpm/, *n.* Captain.

**capnomancy** /'kæpnəmænsi/, *n.* the study of smoke rising from a fire for divination.

**capo**[1] /'keɪpoʊ/, *n.* a device which holds a bar across the fingerboard of a guitar, raising the pitch of all the strings so that difficult keys can be played more easily. [It. *capo tasto* head stop]

**capo**[2] /'kapoʊ/, *n.* a leader in the Mafia organisation. [It.: head]

**capon** /'keɪpən/, *n.* a cock castrated to improve the flesh for use as food. [OE *capun,* from L *cāpo*]

**caporal** /kæpə'ral/, *n.* a kind of tobacco. [F, from It. *caporale* superior. See CORPORAL[2]]

**capote** /kə'poʊt/, *n.* **1.** a long cloak with a hood. **2.** a close, caplike bonnet worn by women and children. [F, diminutive of *cape* hood]

**capped** /kæpt/, *adj.* of bales of wool from which the cap has been removed, according to regulations, to facilitate close inspection on the show floor.

**capped hock** /– 'hɒk/, *n.* any swelling, inflammatory or otherwise, on the point of the hock of horses.

**capper** /'kæpə/, *n.* **1.** one who or that which caps. **2. put the capper on,** *N.Z. Colloq.* finish; give the final touches to.

**capping ceremony** /'kæpɪŋ ˌserəməni/, *n. N.Z.* a ceremony at which university degrees are conferred.

**capping day** /'– deɪ/, *n. N.Z.* the day of student festivities on which a capping ceremony is performed.

**cappuccino** /kæpə'tʃinoʊ/, *n.* coffee made on an espresso machine, topped with hot milk which has been frothed up by passing steam through it. [It. *cappuccio* hood]

**capreolate** /'kæpriəˌleɪt, kə'pri-/, *adj.* **1.** *Bot.* having tendrils. **2.** *Anat.* resembling tendrils. [L *capreolus* tendril + -ATE[1]]

**capriccio** /kə'prɪtʃioʊ/, *n., pl.* **-cios, -ci** /-tʃi/. **1.** a caper; a prank. **2.** a caprice. **3.** *Music.* a lively composition in a free, irregular style. [It., from *capro* goat, from L *caper*]

**capriccioso** /kəprɪtʃi'oʊsoʊ/, *adj.* (a musical direction) capricious; fantastic in style. [It.]

**caprice** /kə'pris/, *n.* **1.** a sudden change of mind without apparent or adequate motive; whim. **2.** a tendency to change one's mind without apparent or adequate motive; whimsicality; capriciousness. **3.** *Music.* →**capriccio** (def. 3). [F, from It. *capriccio* CAPRICCIO]

**capricious** /kə'prɪʃəs/, *adj.* **1.** subject to, led by, or indicative of caprice or whim. **2.** *Obs.* fanciful or witty. – **capriciously,** *adv.* – **capriciousness,** *n.*

**Capricorn** /'kæprəkɔn/, *n.* **1.** Also, **Capricornus.** a constellation and sign of the zodiac, represented by a goat. **2.** →**Capricornian. 3. Tropic of.** See **tropic** (defs 1a and 2a). [L *Capricornus,* lit., goat-horned]

**Capricornian** /kæprə'kɔniən/, *n.* **1.** a person born under the sign of Capricorn, and (according to tradition) exhibiting the typical Capricornian personality traits in some degree. *–adj.* **2.** of or pertaining to Capricorn. **3.** of or pertaining to such a person or such a personality trait.

**caprifoliaceous** /ˌkæprəfoʊli'eɪʃəs/, *adj.* belonging to the Caprifoliaceae, a family of plants including the honeysuckle, elder, viburnum, snowberry, etc. [ML *caprifolium* honeysuckle + -ACEOUS]

**capriole** /'kæprioʊl/, *n.* **1.** a caper or leap. **2.** an upward spring made by a horse with all four feet and without advancing. *–v.i.* **3.** to execute a capriole. [F, from It. *capriola* caper, from *capro* goat, from L *caper*]

**cap rock** /'kæp rɒk/, *n.* a layer of relatively hard or impervious rock which lies over some valuable deposit, as coal or an oil-bearing rock. Also, **caprock.**

**caproic acid** /kəˌproʊɪk 'æsəd/, *n.* an organic acid, $CH_3(CH_2)_4COOH$, found in fatty animal tissue and in coconut oil, used to make artificial flavouring agents. [*capro-* (combining form representing L *caper* goat) + -IC; so called from its smell]

**caps,** capital letters.

**capsaicin** /kæp'seɪəsən/, *n.* a bitter irritant principle from paprika; colourless crystalline amide, $C_{18}H_{27}NO_3$, related to guaiacol. [L *capsa* box + -IC + -IN[2]]

**cap screw** /'kæp skru/, *n.* a bolt with a cylindrical head which is turned by a wrench designed to fit into the hexagonal recess in the head.

**capsicum** /'kæpsəkəm/, *n.* **1.** any plant of the genus *Capsicum,* as *C. frutescens,* the common pepper of the garden, in many varieties, with mild to hot, pungent seeds enclosed in a podded or bell-shaped pericarp which also ranges from mild to extremely hot. **2.** the fruit of these plants, or some preparation of it, used as a condiment and once widely used internally and externally as a local irritant. [NL, from L *capsa* box + *-icum,* neut. of *-icus* -IC]

**capsize** /kæp'saɪz/, *v.,* **-sized, -sizing.** *–v.i.* **1.** to overturn: *the boat capsized.* *–v.t.* **2.** to upset: *they capsized the boat.* [orig. unknown]

**cap spinning** /kæp 'spɪnɪŋ/, *n.* a method of wool spinning in which each spindle has a metal cap to guide the yarn onto the bobbin.

**capstan** /'kæpstən/, *n.* a device resembling a windlass but with a vertical axis, commonly turned by a bar or lever, and winding a cable, for raising weights (as an anchor) or drawing things closer (as a ship to its jetty). [ME, from Pr. *cabestan,* earlier *cabestran,* from *cabestre,* from L *capistrum* halter]

capstan: A, capstan head; B, barrel; C, toothed rim and pawls; D, capstan bar

**capstan bar** /'– ba/, *n.* one of the levers, by which a capstan is turned.

**capstan lathe** /'– leɪð/, *n.* a lathe having the cutting tools mounted on a capstan-like holder.

**capstone** /'kæpstoʊn/, *n.* **1.** →**coping. 2.** *Geol.* →**calcrete.**

**capsular** /'kæpʃələ/, *adj.* of, in, or resembling a capsule.

**capsulate** /'kæpʃəleɪt, -lət/, *adj.* enclosed in or formed into a capsule. Also, **capsulated.**

**capsule** /'kæpʃul, -ʃəl/, *n.* **1.** a small case, envelope, or covering. **2.** a gelatinous case enclosing a dose of medicine; the dose itself. **3.** *Bot.* **a.** a dry dehiscent fruit composed of two or more carpels. **b.** the spore case of various cryptogamic plants. **4.** *Anat., Zool.* **a.** a membranous sac or integument. **b.** either of two strata of white matter in the cerebrum. **5.** the compartment of a spacecraft containing the crew or instruments. **6.** that part of a spacecraft or aircraft which is detachable. **7.** anything short or condensed, as a story or news item. [earlier *capsul,* from L *capsula,* diminutive of *capsa* box]

capsules (def. 3a) after dehiscence: A, asphodel; B, prickly poppy; C, violet

**capt.,** caption.

**Capt.,** Captain.

**captain** /'kæptn/, *n.* **1.** one who is at the head of or in authority over others; a chief; leader. **2.** an officer in the Australian army, ranking above a lieutenant and below a major. **3.** an officer of corresponding rank in any other army. **4.** the commander or master of a merchant ship or other vessel. **5.** an officer in the navy ranking above a commander and below a rear admiral, usu. in command of a warship. **6.** the officer responsible for an aircraft while it is in flight, usu. the senior pilot. **7.** the rank of a captain (defs 2 or 5). **8.** the leader of a team, club, or side in any sport or game. **9.** the head student of a school or division of a school. **10.** the manager of a mine. [orig. Cornish d.] *–v.t.* **11.** to lead or command as a captain. *–v.i.* **12.** *Colloq.*

(of women) to accept drinks from a stranger in a hotel, in return for the promise of sexual intercourse. [ME *capitain,* from OF, from LL *capitāneus* chief, from L *caput* head] – **captaincy,** *n.* – **captainship,** *n.*

**captain ball** /'– bɔl/, *n.* a competitive ballgame in which the captains of each team throw the ball as quickly as possible to each of the other team members in turn; each person in the team takes it in turn to act as captain.

**Captain Cook** /kæptn 'kʊk/, *n. Colloq.* a look. Also, **Captain, captain.** [rhyming slang; from *Captain* James *Cook,* 1728-79, English navigator and explorer]

**Captain Cooker** /– 'kʊkə/, *n. N.Z.* **1.** a wild boar. **2.** any pig, esp. a poor, mangy specimen.

**caption** /'kæpʃən/, *n.* **1.** a heading or title, as of a chapter, article, or page. **2.** *Print.* a legend for a picture or illustration. **3.** *Films.* the title of a scene, the text of a speech, etc., shown on the screen. **4.** *Law.* that part of a legal document which states on what authority it is made. *–v.t.* **5.** to provide with a caption. [L *captio*]

**captious** /'kæpʃəs/, *adj.* **1.** apt to make much of trivial faults or defects; fault-finding; difficult to please. **2.** proceeding from a fault-finding or cavilling disposition: *captious remarks.* **3.** apt or designed to ensnare or perplex, esp. in argument: *captious questions.* [L *captiōsus* sophistical] – **captiously,** *adv.* – **captiousness,** *n.*

**captivate** /'kæptəveɪt/, *v.t.,* **-vated, -vating.** to enthral by beauty or excellence; enchant; charm. [LL *captīvātus,* pp., taken captive] – **captivation** /kæptə'veɪʃən/, *n.* – **captivator,** *n.*

**captive** /'kæptɪv/, *n.* **1.** a prisoner. **2.** one who is enslaved by love, beauty, etc. *–adj.* **3.** made or held prisoner, esp. in war. **4.** kept in confinement or restraint. **5.** enslaved by love, beauty, etc.; captivated. **6.** of or pertaining to a captive. [L *captīvus*]

**captive audience** /– 'ɔdiəns/, *n.* people who have entered into a situation for a particular purpose, as at a restaurant, and are subjected to advertisements, propaganda, solicitations, etc., without their consent.

**captive balloon** /– bə'lun/, *n.* a balloon held in a particular place by means of a rope or cable, as for military observation purposes.

**captivity** /kæp'tɪvəti/, *n., pl.* **-ties.** the state or period of being captive.

**captor** /'kæptə/, *n.* a person who captures.

**capture** /'kæptʃə/, *v.,* **-tured, -turing,** *n.* *–v.t.* **1.** to take by force or stratagem; take prisoner; seize: *the chief was captured.* *–n.* **2.** the act of taking by force or stratagem. **3.** the thing or person captured. **4.** *Physics.* the process by which an atomic or nuclear system acquires an additional particle. **5.** *Geog.* the process by which one river acquires the tributaries of another, usu. smaller and slower river. [F, from L *captūra*] – **capturer,** *n.*

**capuche** /kə'puʃ/, *n.* a hood or cowl, esp. the long, pointed cowl of the Capuchins, an order of Franciscan Friars. [F, from It. *cappuccio*]

**capuchin** /'kæpjətʃən, -ʃən/, *n.* **1.** a prehensile-tailed monkey of Central and South America, *Cebus capucinus,* whose head hair presents a cowl-like appearance. **2.** any monkey of the genus *Cebus.* **3.** a hooded cloak for women. [F, from It. *cappuccino,* from *cappuccio* hood]

capuchin monkey

**caput** /'kæpət, 'keɪpət/, *n., pl.* **capita** /'kæpətə/. *Anat.* any head or headlike expansion on a structure, as on a bone. [L: the head]

**capybara** /kæpi'barə/, *n.* the largest living rodent, *Hydrochoerus hydrochaeris,* about one metre long, living along the banks of South American rivers, sand-coloured and virtually tailless. [Pg. *capibara,* from Tupi *kapigwara* grass-eater]

capybara

**car** /ka/, *n.* **1.** a motor car. **2.** *Poetic.* a chariot, as of war or triumph. **3.** a vehicle of various kinds running on rails, as a restaurant car, tramcar, etc. **4.** a railway carriage or wagon. **5.** the part of a balloon, lift, etc., in which the passengers, etc., are carried. [ME *carre,* from ONF, from L *carrus,* of Celtic orig.]

**car.,** carat.

**carabin** /'kærəbən/, *n.* **1.** →**carbine. 2.** *Hist.* a mounted soldier armed with a carbine. Also, **carabine** /'kærəbaɪn/. [F; probably alteration of ONF *escarrabin* corpse-bearer, from *scarabée* dung-beetle, from L *scarabaeus* SCARAB]

**carabineer** /kærəbə'nɪə/, *n.* (formerly) a soldier armed with a carbine. Also, **carbineer, carabinier.**

car: Holden

**caracal** /'kærəkæl/, *n.* a large cat, *Felis caracal,* of Africa and parts of Asia, having reddish brown fur and tufted ears. [F or Sp., from Turk., equivalent to *kara* black + *kulak* ear]

**caracara** /karə'karə/, *n.* any of certain vulture-like birds of the subfamily Polyborinae of the warmer parts of America. [Sp., Pg., from Tupi; imitative of its cry]

**caracol** /'kærəkɒl/, *n., v.i.,* **-colled, -colling.** →**caracole.**

**caracole** /'kærəkoʊl/, *n., v.,* **-coled, -coling.** *–n.* **1.** a half-turn executed by a horseman in riding. *–v.i.* **2.** to execute caracoles; wheel. [F, from Sp. *caracol* snail, wheeling movement]

**caracul** /'kærəkəl/, *n.* **1.** the skin of the very young offspring of certain Asiatic or Russian sheep, karakul, dressed as a fur, resembling astrakhan, but with flatter, looser curl. **2.** →**karakul** (sheep). Also, **karakul.** [named after *Kara Kul* (Turk.: Black Lake), in Uzbekistan, where the breed comes from]

**carafe** /kə'raf, -'ræf, 'kærəf/, *n.* **1.** a glass bottle for water, wine, etc. **2.** the contents of such a bottle. [F, from It. *caraffa,* probably from Sp. *garrafa,* from Ar. *gharrâf* drinking vessel]

**caramel** /'kærəməl/, *n.* **1.** burnt sugar, used for colouring and flavouring food, etc. **2.** a kind of sweet, commonly in small blocks, made from sugar, butter, milk, etc. **3.** the light brown colour of caramel. *–adj.* **4.** of the colour of caramel. [F, from Sp. *caramelo*]

**caramelise** /'kærəməlaɪz/, *v.t.,* **-lised, -lising. 1.** to melt (sugar) in a pan to the point where it is a clear, light brown syrup. **2.** to add such sugar to.

**carangid** /kə'ræŋgəd, -'rændʒəd/, *adj.* **1.** of or pertaining to the Carangidae, a family of marine fishes as the trevally, horse mackerel, etc., having the body tapering sharply towards a forked or lunate tail and strongly spined dorsal and ventral fins. **2.** of or descriptive of the characteristic body movement of such fish and others in locomotion. *–n.* **3.** a carangid fish. Also, **carangoid** /kə'ræŋgɔɪd/. [NL *Caranx,* the typical genus (cf. Sp. *carangue* a West Indian flatfish) + -ID[2]]

**carapace** /'kærəpeɪs/, *n.* a shield, test, or shell covering some or all of the dorsal part of an animal. [F, from Sp. *carapacho*]

**carat** /'kærət/, *n.* **1.** Also, **metric carat.** a unit of weight in gem stones, 0.2 × $10^{-3}$ kg. *Abbrev.:* CM **2.** a twenty-fourth part (used in expressing the fineness of gold, pure gold being 24 carats fine). [F, from It. *carato,* from Ar. *qīrat* light weight, from Gk *kerátion* carob bean, carat, diminutive of *kéras* horn]

**caravan** /'kærəvæn/, *n., v.* **-vanned, -vanning.** *–n.* **1.** a vehicle in which people may live, whether temporarily or permanently, usu. having two wheels and designed to be drawn by a motor car. **2.** such a vehicle having four cartwheels and horse-drawn, traditionally inhabited by gipsies and circus folk, etc. **3.** a group of merchants or others travelling together, as for safety, esp. over deserts, etc., in Asia or Africa. *–v.i.* **4.** to live, as for a holiday, in a caravan. [F *caravane,* from Pers. *kārwān*]

**caravan park** /'– pak/, *n.* a supervised area where caravans may park or may be hired.

**caravanserai** /kærə'vænsəraɪ, -reɪ/, *n., pl.* **-rais.** (in the Near East) a kind of inn for the accommodation of caravans (def. 3), usu. a large building surrounding a spacious court. Also, **caravansary** /kærə'vænsəri/. [Pers. *karwansarāī,* from *kārwān* caravan + *sarāī* inn]

**caravel** /ˈkærəvɛl/, *n.* (formerly) a kind of small three-masted ship used esp. by the Spaniards and Portuguese. Also, **carvel.** [F *caravelle,* from It. *caravella.* Cf. LL *carabus,* Gk *kárabos* kind of light ship]

caravel

**caraway** /ˈkærəweɪ/, *n.* **1.** an umbelliferous condimental herb, *Carum carvi,* bearing aromatic seedlike fruit (**caraway seeds**) used in cookery and medicine. **2.** the fruit or seeds. [late ME, from ML *carui,* from Ar. *karawyā.* Cf. L *careum,* Gk *káron*]

**carb-,** variant of **carbo-** before vowels, as in *carbazole.*

**carbamate** /ˈkabəmeɪt/, *n.* a salt or ester of carbamic acid.

**carbamic acid** /kaˌbæmɪk ˈæsəd/, *n.* a hypothetical compound, $NH_2COOH$, known only in the form of its salts and esters. [CARB- + AM(IDE) + -IC]

**carbamide** /ˈkabəmaɪd/, *n. Chem.* →**urea.**

**carbanion** /kaˈbænaɪən/, *n.* a carbon compound bearing a negative charge concentrated on the carbon; an unstable intermediate in reactions.

**car-basket** /ˈka-baskət/, *n.* **1.** Also, **carry-cot.** a light, portable container, often of cane, in which a baby is carried. **2.** →**carry basket.**

**carbazole** /ˈkabəzoʊl/, *n.* a weakly acidic, crystalline compound, $C_{12}H_9N$, found with anthracene in coal tar. Many dyes are derived from it. [CARB- + AZ- + -OLE]

**carbide** /ˈkabaɪd/, *n.* **1.** a compound of carbon with a more electropositive element or radical. **2.** →**calcium carbide.** [CARB- + -IDE]

**carbide lamp** /ˈ– læmp/, *n.* a lamp burning acetylene gas formed by dripping water onto calcium carbide.

**carbie** /ˈkabi/, *n. Colloq.* →**carburettor.**

**carbine** /ˈkabaɪn, ˈkabən/, *n.* **1.** (formerly) a short rifle for cavalry use. **2.** a light semi-automatic or fully automatic rifle of a carbine type, as an armalite, useful in circumstances that restrict movement or in difficult terrain. [F *carabine,* orig. a small arquebus, from *carabin* CARABIN]

**carbineer** /kabəˈnɪə/, *n.* →**carabineer.**

**carbinol** /ˈkabənɒl/, *n.* **1.** →**methyl alcohol. 2.** an alcohol derived from it. [CARBON + -OL[1]]

**carbo-,** a word element meaning 'carbon', as in *carborundum.* Also, **carb-.** [combining form of CARBON]

**carbocyclic compounds** /ˌkaboʊsaɪklɪk ˈkɒmpaʊndz, -sɪklɪk/, *n. pl.* a group of organic compounds in which all the atoms composing the ring are carbon atoms, as naphthalene.

**carboholic** /kabəˈhɒlɪk/, *n.* a person addicted to foods high in carbohydrates, as sweets, biscuits, etc. [b. CARBO(HYDRATE) + (ALCO)HOLIC]

**carbohydrase** /kaboʊˈhaɪdreɪz/, *n.* any enzyme that acts upon carbohydrates, as alpha-amylase.

**carbohydrate** /kabəˈhaɪdreɪt/, *n.* any of a class of organic compounds which are polyhydroxy aldehydes or polyhydroxy ketones, or change to such substances on simple chemical transformations, such as hydrolysis, oxidation, or reduction. Including sugars, starch, and cellulose, they form the supporting tissues of plants and are important food for animals.

**carbolated** /ˈkabəleɪtəd/, *adj.* containing carbolic acid.

**carbolic acid** /kaˌbɒlɪk ˈæsəd/, *n.* →**phenol** (def. 1). [CARB- + -OL[2] + -IC]

**carbon** /ˈkabən/, *n.* **1.** *Chem.* a widely distributed element which forms organic compounds in combination with hydrogen, oxygen, etc., and which occurs in a pure state as charcoal. *Symbol:* C; *at. wt;* 12.011; *at. no.:* 6; *sp. gr.:* (of diamond) 3.51 at 20°C; (of graphite) 2.26 at 20°C. **2.** *Elect.* **a.** the carbon rod through which the current is conducted between the electrode-holder and the arc in carbon arc lighting or welding. **b.** the rod or plate, composed in part of carbon, used in batteries. **3.** a sheet of carbon paper. **4.** a carbon copy. **5.** the isotope carbon 14; radiocarbon. [F *carbone,* from L *carbo* coal, charcoal]

**carbonaceous** /kabəˈneɪʃəs/, *adj.* of, like, or containing carbon.

**carbonade** /ˈkabəneɪd/, *n.* thin slices of meat braised in beer. Also, **carbonnade.**

**carbonado** /kabəˈneɪdoʊ/, *n., pl.* **-does, -dos,** *v.,* **-doed, -doing.** –*n.* **1.** a piece of meat, fish, etc., scored and broiled. **2.** an opaque, dark-coloured, massive form of diamond, found chiefly in Brazil, and used for drills; black diamond. –*v.t.* **3.** to score and broil. **4.** to slash; hack. [Sp. *carbonada,* from *carbón,* from L *carbo* coal]

**carbon arc** /ˈkabən ak/, *n.* an electric arc produced between two carbon electrodes as in an arc light, or between one carbon electrode and metal, as in certain arc welders.

**carbonate** /ˈkabəneɪt, -nət/ *n.*; /ˈkabəneɪt/, *v.,* **-nated, -nating.** –*n.* **1.** *Chem.* a salt of carbonic acid, as *calcium carbonate,* $CaCO_3$. –*v.t.* **2.** to form into a carbonate. **3.** to charge or impregnate with carbon dioxide. [NL *carbonātum* (something) carbonated]

**carbonation** /kabəˈneɪʃən/, *n.* **1.** saturation with carbon dioxide, as in making soda-water. **2.** reaction with carbon dioxide to remove lime, as in sugar refining. **3.** carbonisation. – **carbonator,** *n.*

**carbon black** /ˈkabən blæk/, *n.* the finely divided carbon produced by burning hydrocarbons, used in manufacturing ink, rubber products, etc.

**carbon copy** /– ˈkɒpi/, *n.* a duplicate copy made by using carbon paper.

**carbon cycle** /ˈ– saɪkəl/, *n.* **1.** *Biol.* the circulation on earth of carbon atoms, from the atmosphere through plants and animals back into the atmosphere. **2.** *Astrophysics.* a cycle of nuclear transformations, with the release of atomic energy, in the interiors of the stars, by means of which hydrogen is gradually converted into helium.

**carbon dating** /ˈ– deɪtɪŋ/, *n.* →**radiocarbon dating.**

**carbon dioxide** /– daɪˈɒksaɪd/, *n.* a colourless, odourless, incombustible gas, $CO_2$, used extensively in industry as dry ice, and in fizzy drinks, fire-extinguishers, etc. It is present in the atmosphere and is formed during respiration.

**carbon dioxide snow,** *n.* carbon dioxide, $CO_2$, solidified under great pressure; dry ice. It is used as a refrigerant because it passes directly from a solid to a gas, absorbing a great amount of heat.

**carbon disulphide** /ˌkabən daɪˈsʌlfaɪd/, *n.* a colourless inflammable liquid, $CS_2$, used as a solvent in the rubber and plastic industries.

**carbon fibre** /ˈ– faɪbə/, *n.* a thread of pure carbon used for reinforcing heat-stressed ceramics, metals, turbine blades, etc.

**carbonic** /kaˈbɒnɪk/, *adj.* containing tetravalent carbon, as carbonic acid, $H_2CO_3$.

**carbonic acid** /– ˈæsəd/, *n.* the acid, $H_2CO_3$, formed when carbon dioxide dissolves in water, known in the form of its salts and esters, the carbonates.

**carbonic acid gas,** *n.* →**carbon dioxide.**

**carbonic anhydrase** /kaˌbɒnɪk ænˈhaɪdreɪz/, *n.* an enzyme which catalyses the formation of carbonic acid from water and carbon dioxide; important in carbon dioxide transport and pH control of urine in mammals.

**Carboniferous** /kabəˈnɪfərəs/, *adj.* **1.** pertaining to a geological period or a system of rocks preceding the Permian, and following the Devonian; divided into **Upper Carboniferous, Lower Carboniferous,** and sometimes **Middle Carboniferous. 2.** (*l.c.*) producing coal. –*n.* **3.** a late Palaeozoic period or system next following the Devonian. [CARBON + -I- + -FEROUS]

**carbonisation** /kabənaɪˈzeɪʃən/, *n.* **1.** *Chem.* formation of carbon from organic matter. **2.** coal distillation, as in coke ovens. **3.** treatment of wool or wool fabric to remove vegetable matter. Also, **carbonization.**

**carbonise** /ˈkabənaɪz/, *v.t.,* **-nised, -nising. 1.** to char, forming carbon. **2.** to coat or enrich with carbon. **3.** to treat (wool or wool fabric) chemically to remove vegetable matter, as burrs, seeds, etc. Also, **carbonize.**

**carbonium ion** /kaˈboʊniəm ˌaɪən/, *n.* a positively charged organic ion such as $H_3C^+$,$R_2C^+$=O, having one less electron than the corresponding free radical; a reactive intermediate in many organic reactions.

**carbon microphone** /kabən ˈmaɪkrəfoʊn/, *n.* an early type of microphone in which variations in air pressure caused by sound were transmitted to granules of carbon, the electrical resistance of which varied with the pressure.

**carbon monoxide** /kabən mɒ'nɒksaɪd/, *n.* a colourless, odourless, poisonous gas, CO, burning with a pale blue flame, formed when carbon burns with an insufficient supply of air.

**carbon paper** /'– peɪpə/, *n.* **1.** paper faced with a preparation of carbon or other material, used between two sheets of plain paper in order to reproduce upon the lower sheet that which is written or typed on the upper. **2.** a paper for making photographs by the carbon process.

**carbon process** /'– prousɛs/, *n.* a method of making photographic prints by the use of a pigment, such as carbon, contained in sensitised gelatine.

**carbon silicide** /– 'sɪləsaɪd/, *n.* →**silicon carbide.**

**carbon steel** /'– stil/, *n.* steel whose hardness and other properties are determined by the quantity of carbon in it.

**carbon tetrachloride** /ˌ– tɛtrə'klɔraɪd/, *n.* a non-inflammable, colourless liquid, $CCl_4$, used in medicine, and as a fire-extinguisher, cleaning fluid, solvent, etc.

**carbonyl** /'kabənəl/, *n.* **1.** the divalent radical = CO occurring in acids, ketones, aldehydes, and their derivatives. **2.** a compound containing metal combined with carbon monoxide, as *nickel carbonyl,* $Ni(CO)_4$. [CARBON + -YL] – **carbonylic,** *adj.*

**carbora** /ka'bɔrə/, *n. Obs.* a water worm that bores into timber in tidal rivers. [Aboriginal]

**carborundum** /kabə'rʌndəm/, *n.* **1.** *Chem.* silicon carbide, SiC, an important abrasive produced in the electric furnace. **2.** a block of this or a similar material for sharpening knives, etc. [CARBO- + (CO)RUNDUM]

**carbo type** /'kabou taɪp/, *n.* very burry wool, usu. short, from which the vegetable matter cannot be removed economically by mechanical methods. [CARBONISE (def. 3)]

**carboxyl group** /ka'bɒksəl grup/, *n.* a univalent radical, –COOH, present in and characteristic of the formulae of all organic acids. Also, **carboxyl radical.** [CARB- + OX(YGEN) + -YL]

**carboxylic acid** /kabɒkˌsɪlɪk 'æsəd/, *n.* an organic acid (as acetic acid, benzoic acid), characterised by the presence of one or more carboxyl groups.

**carboxypeptidase** /kabɒksi'pɛptədeɪz/, *n.* a proteolytic enzyme produced in the stomach.

**carboy** /'kabɔɪ/, *n.* a large glass bottle, esp. one protected by basketwork or a wooden box, as for containing acids. [Pers. *qarābah* large flagon]

**carbuncle** /'kabʌŋkəl/, *n.* **1.** a painful circumscribed inflammation of the subcutaneous tissue, resulting in suppuration and sloughing, and having a tendency to spread (somewhat like a boil, but more serious in its effects). **2.** a garnet cut in a convex rounded form without facets. **3.** *Obs.* a rounded red gem, as a ruby or garnet. **4.** deep red. **5.** brownish red. [ME, from ONF, from L *carbunculus,* diminutive of *carbo* (live) coal] – **carbuncled,** *adj.* – **carbuncular** /ka'bʌŋkjələ/, *adj.*

**carburant** /'kabjərənt/, *n.* the fuel used in carburation.

**carburation** /kabjə'reɪʃən/, *n.* the process of mixing air and fuel in the proper proportions for combustion before feeding it into an internal-combustion engine. Also, **carburetion.**

**carburet** /'kabjərɛt/, *v.t.,* **-retted, -retting** or (*U.S.*) **-reted, -reting.** to combine or mix with carbon or hydrocarbons. [CARB- + -URET]

**carburettor** /'kabjərɛtə, kabjə'rɛtə/, *n.* **1.** a device in an internal-combustion engine for mixing a volatile fuel with the correct proportion of air in order to form an explosive gas. **2.** an apparatus for adding hydrocarbons to non-luminous or poor gases, for the purpose of producing an illuminating or explosive gas. Also, **carburetter;** *U.S.,* **carburetor.**

**carburise** /'kabjəraɪz/, *v.t.,* **-rised, -rising. 1.** to cause to unite with carbon. **2.** *Metall.* to introduce carbon into the surface of steel by heating it while it is in contact with a suitable source of carbon, as a form of case-hardening. **3.** to carburet. Also, **carburize.** – **carburisation** /kabjəraɪ'zeɪʃən/, *n.* – **carburiser,** *n.*

**carbylamine** /kabələ'min, -'æmin/, *n.* an organic compound containing the group –NC.

**carcajou** /'kakədʒu, -ʒu/, *n.* the American glutton, *Gulo gulo;* wolverine. [Canadian F, from Amer. Ind. (Algonquian)]

**carcase** /'kakəs/, *n.* **1.** the body of a slaughtered animal after removal of the offal, etc. **2.** →**carcass.**

**carcass** /'kakəs/, *n.* **1.** the dead body of an animal or (now only in contempt) of a human being. **2.** (*joc.*) a living body. **3.** →**carcase. 4.** anything from which life and power are gone. **5.** an unfinished framework or skeleton, as of a house or ship. **6. move (shift) one's carcass,** *Colloq.* to move away; get out of the way. Also, **carcase.** [F *carcasse,* from It. *carcassa;* replacing ME *carkeis,* from AF]

**carcinogen** /ka'sɪnədʒən/, *n.* any substance which tends to produce a cancer in a body. – **carcinogenic** /kasənə'dʒɛnɪk/, *adj.*

**carcinogenesis** /kasənə'dʒɛnəsəs/, *n.* the inception or production and growth of cancer.

**carcinoma** /kasə'noumə/, *n., pl.* **-mata** /-mətə/, **-mas.** a malignant and invasive epithelial tumour that spreads by metastasis and often recurs after excision; a cancer. [L, from Gk *karkínōma* a cancer]

**carcinomatosis** /ˌkasənoumə'tousəs/, *n.* a condition marked by the production of an overwhelming number of carcinomata throughout the body. – **carcinomatous** /kasə'nɒmətəs, -'noumə-/, *adj.*

**card**[1] /kad/, *n.* **1.** a piece of stiff paper or thin pasteboard, usu. rectangular, for various uses: *a business card.* **2.** →**postcard. 3.** a piece of cardboard with more or less elaborate ornamentation, bearing a complimentary greeting: *a Christmas card.* **4.** one of a set of small pieces of cardboard with spots or figures, used in playing various games, in prognostication, etc. **5.** (*pl.*) a game or games played with such a set. **6.** *Colloq.* a resource, plan, idea, approach to a problem or proposition, etc.: *that's his best card, to have a card up one's sleeve.* **7.** a program of events, as at horse-races. **8. pick the card,** *Horseracing Colloq.* to choose the winners in every race on the program. **9.** the circular piece of paper or other material on which the 32 points indicating direction are marked in a compass. **10.** *Textiles.* a perforated strip of cardboard, etc., used to control the pattern in weaving. **11.** *Colloq.* a person of some indicated characteristic: *a queer card.* **12.** *Colloq.* a likeable, amusing, or facetious person. **13. house of cards, a.** a structure, as made by children, of cards placed vertically and horizontally on top of each other. **b.** any flimsy structure of hopes or plans without foundation. **14. on the cards,** likely to happen. **15. put one's cards on the table,** to speak plainly, candidly; disclose all information in one's possession. *–v.t.* **16.** to place (data) on cards for reference, as for a card index. **17.** *Golf.* to score. [ME, from F *carte,* from L *charta* (see CHART)]

**card**[2] /kad/, *n.* **1.** an implement used in disentangling and combing out fibres of wool, flax, etc., preparatory to spinning. **2.** a similar implement for raising the nap on cloth. *–v.t.* **3.** to dress (wool, etc.) with a card. [late ME *carde,* from OF, from LL *cardus,* L *carduus* thistle] – **carder,** *n.*

**cardamom** /'kadəməm/, *n.* **1.** the aromatic seed capsule of various plants of the genera *Amomum* and *Elettaria,* native to tropical Asia, used as a spice or condiment and in medicine. **2.** any of these plants. Also, **cardamon, cardamum.** [L *cardamōmum,* from Gk *kardámōmon*]

**cardan** /'kadn/, *adj. Mach.* capable of transmitting rotary movement from a different angle than that of the final drive, as the wheels of a vehicle: *cardan joint, cardan shaft.* [named after G. *Cardano,* 1501-76, Italian mathematician]

**cardboard** /'kadbɔd/, *n.* **1.** thin, stiff pasteboard. *–adj.* **2.** made of cardboard. **3.** resembling cardboard in appearance, texture, etc. **4.** existing or performing a function in appearance only; insubstantial: *a cardboard prime minister, a cardboard empire.*

**card-carrying** /'kad-kæriɪŋ/, *adj.* possessing full membership, as of a trade union or political party.

**cardcase** /'kadkeɪs/, *n.* a small pocket case for visiting cards, etc.

**card catalogue** /'kad kætəlɒg/, *n.* a definite arrangement of cards of uniform size (**catalogue cards**) in drawers, each card usu. identifying a single publication in a library.

**card file** /'– faɪl/, *n.* →**card index.**

**cardi-,** variant of **cardio-** before vowels, as in *cardialgia.*

**cardiac** /'kadiæk/, *adj.* **1.** pertaining to the heart. **2.** pertaining to the oesophageal portion of the stomach. [L *car-*

*diacus* of the heart, from Gk *kardiakós*]

**cardiac arrest** /ˌ– əˈrɛst/, *n.* a serious arrhythmia in which the heart stops pumping blood through the circulatory system, commonly caused by coronary occlusion, electric shock, drowning or asphyxia.

**cardiac glycoside** /– ˈglaɪkəsaɪd/, *n.* one of a group of drugs used to stimulate the heart in cases of heart failure, obtained from a number of plants, as the foxglove, squill, or yellow oleander. Also, **cardiac glucoside.**

**cardialgia** /kadiˈældʒə/, *n.* pain in the region of the heart; heartburn (def. 1). [CARDI- + -ALGIA]

**cardie** /ˈkadi/, *n. Colloq.* →**cardigan**[1].

**cardigan**[1] /ˈkadɪgən/, *n.* a knitted jacket made from wool, synthetics, etc. [named after the 7th Earl of *Cardigan,* 1797-1868]

**cardigan**[2] /ˈkadɪgən/, *n.* a variety of the Welsh corgi breed of dogs. See **Welsh corgi.** [named after *Cardigan,* a town in Wales]

**cardinal** /ˈkadənəl/, *adj.* **1.** of prime importance; chief; principal; fundamental: *of cardinal significance.* **2.** deep rich red. *–n.* **3.** one of the seventy members of the Sacred College of the Roman Catholic Church, ranking next to the pope. **4.** Also, **cardinal bird, cardinal grosbeak.** a crested North American finch, *Richmondina cardinalis,* notable for its song. The male is brilliant red, the female brown. **5.** any of various similar birds. **6.** a deep rich red colour. **7.** a cardinal number. [ME, from L *cardinālis* pertaining to a hinge, chief] – **cardinally,** *adv.* – **cardinalship,** *n.*

**cardinalate** /ˈkadənəleɪt/, *n. Rom. Cath. Ch.* **1.** the body of cardinals. **2.** the office, rank, dignity, or incumbency of a cardinal.

**cardinal flower** /ˈkadənəl flaʊə/, *n.* any of several North American species of the genus of plants *Lobelia,* as *L. cardinalis,* having red, pink, or white flowers.

**cardinal number** /– ˈnʌmbə/, *n. Maths.* a number such as *one, two, three,* etc., which indicates how many things are in a given set, and not the order in which those things occur (the latter is indicated by the ordinal numbers, *first, second, third,* etc.).

**cardinal points** /– ˈpɔɪnts/, *n. pl.* **1.** the four chief directions of the compass; the north, south, east, and west points. **2.** *Optics.* (of a lens) the two principal foci, the two nodal points, and the two principal points.

**cardinal sins** /– ˈsɪnz/, *n.pl.* →**deadly sins.**

**cardinal virtues** /– ˈvɜtʃuz/, *n.pl.* **1.** the most important elements of good character. **2.** *Ancient Philos.* justice, prudence, temperance, and fortitude.

**cardinal vowel** /– ˈvaʊəl/, *n.* one in a set of vowels evenly spaced auditorily around the outside of the possible vowel area and designed to act as fixed reference points for phoneticians.

**card index** /ˈkad ˌɪndɛks/, *n.* **1.** a case or file containing uniform cards arranged in a definite order, each bearing an item of information. **2.** the cards. **3.** the information.

**carding** /ˈkadɪŋ/, *n.* **1.** the process of preparing fibres as wool, cotton, etc., for spinning. **2.** the placing of data on cards for reference.

**cardio-,** a word element meaning 'heart'. Also, **cardi-.** [Gk *kardio-,* combining form of *kardía*]

**cardiogenic shock** /kadioʊˌdʒɛnɪk ˈʃɒk/, *n.* the physical manifestations of sudden inadequacy of the circulation, due to cardiac malfunction, as after a myocardial infarction.

**cardiogram** /ˈkadiəgræm/, *n.* →**electrocardiogram.**

**cardiograph** /ˈkadiəgræf/, *n.* →**electrocardiograph.** [CARDIO- + -GRAPH] – **cardiographic** /kadiəˈgræfɪk/, *adj.* – **cardiography** /kadiˈɒgrəfi/, *n.*

**cardioid** /ˈkadiɔɪd/, *n. Maths.* a somewhat heart-shaped curve, being the path of a point on a circle which rolls externally, without slipping on another equal circle. [Gk *kardioeidḗs* heart-shaped. See CARDIO-, -OID]

cardioid

**cardiology** /kadiˈɒlədʒi/, *n.* the study of the heart and its functions. – **cardiologist,** *n.*

**cardiovascular** /ˌkadioʊˈvæskjələ/, *adj.* relating to the heart and blood vessels.

**cardioversion** /ˌkadioʊˈvɜʒən/, *n.* the restoration of normal heart rhythm using an electric shock.

**carditis** /kaˈdaɪtəs/, *n.* inflammation of the pericardium, myocardium, or endocardium, separately or in combination. [CARD(IO)- + -ITIS]

**cardoon** /kaˈdun/, *n.* a perennial edible plant, *Cynara cardunculus,* native to Mediterranean regions, related to the artichoke. [F *cardon,* from Pr., from L *carduus* thistle]

**cardpunch** /ˈkadpʌntʃ/, *n.* →**key punch.**

**card-reader** /ˈkad-ridə/, *n. Computers.* a machine which senses the holes in a punched card and transmits the information obtained to other equipment.

**cardsharper** /ˈkadʃapə/, *n.* a person, esp. a professional gambler, who cheats at card games. Also, **cardsharp.** – **cardsharping,** *n.*

**card-vote** /ˈkad-voʊt/, *n.* (at trade-union conferences, etc.) a vote in which each delegate carries a number of votes according to the number of card-carrying members he represents.

**care** /kɛə/, *n., v.,* **cared, caring.** *–n.* **1.** worry; anxiety; concern: *care had aged him.* **2.** a cause of worry, anxiety, distress, etc.: *to be free from care.* **3.** serious attention; solicitude; heed; caution: *devote great care to work.* **4.** protection; charge: *under the care of a doctor.* **5.** an object of concern or attention. **6. care of.** Also, **c/o.** at the address of. *–v.i.* **7.** to be troubled; to be affected emotionally. **8.** to be concerned or solicitous; have thought or regard. **9.** to have a liking or taste (fol. by *for;* usu. with a negative): *I don't care for cabbage.* **10.** to have a fondness or affection (fol. by *for*): *he cares greatly for her.* **11.** to look after; make provision (fol. by *for*): *the welfare state must care for the needy.* **12.** to be inclined: *I don't care to do it today.* **13. (someone) couldn't care less,** *Colloq.* (someone) doesn't care at all. [ME; OE *caru* (*cearu*), c. Goth. *kara*]

**careen** /kəˈrin/, *v.t.* **1.** to cause (a ship) to heel over or lie wholly or partly on its side, as for repairing or the like. **2.** to clean or repair (a ship in such a position). *–v.i.* **3.** to lean, sway, or tip to one side, as a ship. **4.** to careen a ship. *–n.* **5.** a careening. **6.** the position of a careened ship. [F *carine,* from L *carīna* keel] – **careenage,** *n.* – **careener,** *n.*

**career** /kəˈrɪə/, *n.* **1.** general course of action or progress of a person through life, as in some profession, in some moral or intellectual action, etc. **2.** an occupation, profession, etc., followed as one's lifework: *a career in law.* **3.** speed; full speed. **4.** *Obs.* a charge at full speed. *–v.i.* **5.** to run or move rapidly along. [F *carrière,* from It. *carriera,* from *carro,* from L *carrus.* See CAR]

**career girl** /ˈ– gɜl/, *n.* a girl or woman who puts considerations of her career before those of her private life. Also, **career woman.**

**career industry** /kərɪər ˈɪndəstri/, *n.* an industry in which employees advance progressively to positions of greater responsibility over considerably long periods and in which rates of pay are therefore awarded by a scale increasing with years of service.

**careerist** /kəˈrɪərəst/, *n.* one intent on self-advancement.

**careers adviser** /kəˈrɪəz ədvaɪzə/, *n.* a teacher in a secondary school who advises students about careers, and about courses in tertiary institutions suited to their needs.

**carefree** /ˈkɛəfri/, *adj.* without anxiety or worry.

**careful** /ˈkɛəfəl/, *adj.* **1.** cautious in one's actions. **2.** taking pains in one's work; exact; thorough. **3.** (of things) done or performed with accuracy or caution. **4.** solicitously mindful (fol. by *of, about, in*). **5.** *Colloq.* mean; parsimonious. **6.** *Archaic.* troubled. **7.** *Archaic.* attended with anxiety. – **carefully,** *adv.* – **carefulness,** *n.*

**careless** /ˈkɛələs/, *adj.* **1.** not paying enough attention to what one does. **2.** not exact or thorough: *careless work.* **3.** done or said heedlessly or negligently; unconsidered: *a careless remark.* **4.** not caring or troubling; having no care or concern; unconcerned (fol. by *of, about, in*): *careless of his health, about his person, in speech.* **5.** *Archaic.* free from anxiety. – **carelessly,** *adv.* – **carelessness,** *n.*

**caress** /kəˈrɛs/, *n.* **1.** an act or gesture expressing affection, as an embrace, pat, kiss, etc. *–v.t.* **2.** to touch or pat gently to show affection. **3.** to touch, etc., as if in affection. [F *caresse,* from It. *carezza,* from L *cārus* dear] – **caresser,** *n.* – **caressingly,** *adv.*

**caret** /'kærət/, *n.* a mark (‸) made in written or printed matter to show the place where something is to be inserted. [L: there is lacking]

**caretaker** /'kɛəteɪkə/, *n.* **1.** a person who takes care of a thing or place, esp. one whose job is to maintain and protect a building or group of buildings. *–adj.* **2.** holding office temporarily until a new appointment, election, etc., can be made, as an administration.

**careworn** /'kɛəwɔn/, *adj.* showing signs of care; tired and troubled with worries: *a careworn mother.*

**car ferry** /'ka fɛri/, *n.* a ferry for transporting motor vehicles over a river, channel, etc.

**car fridge** /'– frɪdʒ/, *n.* →**esky.**

**cargo** /'kagoʊ/, *n., pl.* **-goes. 1.** the lading or freight of a ship. **2.** load. [Sp., from *cargar* load]

**cargo cult** /'– kʌlt/, *n.* any of various cults practised by primitive tribes, particularly in the Papua New Guinea region, the devotees of which believe that by proper acts, desired objects such as food, consumer goods, etc., will be received, usu. by sea or air; originally inspired by the arrival of military supplies during World War II.

**cargo deadweight mass,** *n.* the mass of the cargo on a ship.

**Carib** /'kærɪb/, *n.* **1.** a member of an Indian people of north-eastern South America, formerly dominant through the Lesser Antilles. **2.** an extensive linguistic stock of the West Indies and of north-eastern South America. [Sp. *Caribe.* See CANNIBAL] – **Cariban,** *adj.*

**caribou** /'kærəbu/, *n., pl.* **-bou.** any of several North American species or varieties of reindeer, esp. *Rangifer caribou* and *R. tarandus.* [Canadian F, from Algonquian *xalibu* pawer, scratcher]

caribou

**caricature** /'kærəkətʃʊə/, *n., v.,* **-tured, -turing.** *–n.* **1.** a picture, description, etc., ludicrously exaggerating the peculiarities or defects of persons or things. **2.** the art or process of making such pictures, etc. **3.** any imitation or copy so inferior as to be ludicrous. *–v.t.* **4.** to make a caricature of; represent in caricature. [F, from It. *caricatura,* from *caricare* (over)load, exaggerate. See CHARGE, *v.*] – **caricaturist,** *n.*

**caries** /'kɛəriz/, *n.* decay, as of bone or teeth, or of plant tissue. [L]

**carillon** /kə'rɪljən/, *n., v.,* **-lonned, -lonning.** *–n.* **1.** a set of stationary bells hung in a tower and sounded by manual or pedal action, or by machinery. **2.** a melody played on such bells. **3.** an organ stop which imitates the peal of bells. **4.** a set of horizontal metal plates, struck by hammers, used in the modern orchestra. *–v.i.* **5.** to play a carillon. [F: chime of (orig. four) bells, alteration of OF *carignon,* from L *quattuor* four]

**carillonist** /kə'rɪljənəst/, *n.* one who plays a carillon.

**carillonneur** /kərɪljə'nɜ/, *n.* →**carillonist.** [F]

**carina** /kə'rinə/, *n., pl.* **-nae** /-ni/. *Bot., Zool.* a keel-like part or ridge. [L: keel] – **carinal,** *adj.*

**carinate** /'kærəneɪt/, *adj. Bot., Zool.* formed with a carina; keel-like. Also, **carinated.** [L *carinātus,* pp., keel-shaped] – **carination** /kærə'neɪʃən/, *n.*

**carioca** /kæri'oʊkə/, *n.* **1.** a Brazilian dance. **2.** a piece of music to which it may be danced. [Pg., from Tupi *cari* white + *oca* house; the Pg. word meant first an inhabitant of Rio de Janeiro and then the dance which originated there]

**cariogenic** /ˌkɛərioʊ'dʒɛnɪk/, *adj.* causing caries.

**cariole** /'kærioʊl/, *n.* **1.** a small, open, two-wheeled vehicle. **2.** a covered cart. Also, **carriole.** [F *carriole,* from It. *carriuola,* from L *carrus*]

**carious** /'kɛəriəs/, *adj.* having caries, as teeth; decayed. [L *cariōsus*] – **cariosity** /kɛəri'ɒsəti/, **cariousness,** *n.*

**cark** /kak/, *Colloq. –v.i.* **1.** to collapse; die. *–v.t.* **2. cark it,** **a.** to collapse; die. **b.** (of a machine) to fail; break down. [? shortened form of CARCASS]

**carking** /'kakɪŋ/, *adj. Archaic.* anxious; burdensome. [ME, ppr. of *cark(en),* from ONF *carkier,* from LL *carcāre* burden, CHARGE]

**carl** /kal/, *n.* **1.** *Archaic.* a churl. **2.** *Archaic.* a farmer. **3.** *Obs.* a bondman. Also, **carle.** [ME and OE, from Scand.; cf. Icel. *karl* man, c. *Charles* proper name. Cf. CHURL]

**carline**[1] /'kalaɪn/, *n.* a biennial Old World composite plant, *Carlina vulgaris.* Also, **carline thistle.** [ML *carlina,* ? fem. *Carolus* Charles, ult. orig. uncert.]

**carline**[2] /'kalən/, *n. Chiefly Scot.* **1.** an old woman. **2.** a hag; witch. [northern ME *kerling,* from Scand.; cf. Icel. *kerling* old woman. See CARL]

**carling** /'kalɪŋ/, *n.* one of the fore-and-aft timbers in a ship which form part of the deck framework. [var. of CARLINE[2]]

**carlisle** /'kalaɪl/, *n.* a fishhook with a long shank to which several other hooks can be attached.

**Carlovingian** /kalə'vɪndʒiən/, *adj.* →**Carolingian.**

**carmagnole** /kamən'joʊl/, *n.* a dance and song popular during the French Revolution. [F, ? from *Carmagnola,* town in NW Italy]

**carminative** /'kamənətɪv/, *n.* **1.** a drug causing expulsion of gas from the stomach or bowel. *–adj.* **2.** expelling gas from the body; relieving flatulence. [L *carminātus,* pp., carded + -IVE]

**carmine** /'kamaɪn/, *n.* **1.** a crimson or purplish red colour. **2.** a crimson pigment obtained from cochineal. *–adj.* **3.** crimson or purplish red. [ML *carmīnus,* contraction of *carmesīnus,* from Sp. *carmesí* CRIMSON]

**carn** /kan/, *interj. Colloq.* (a sporting barracker's cry) come on!: *carn the Blues!*

**carnage** /'kanɪdʒ/, *n.* **1.** the slaughter of a great number, as in battle; butchery; massacre. **2.** *Archaic.* dead bodies, as of men slain in battle. [F, from It. *carnaggio,* from *carne* meat, from L *caro* flesh]

**carnal** /'kanəl/, *adj.* **1.** not spiritual; merely human; temporal; worldly. **2.** pertaining to the flesh or the body, its passions and appetites; sensual. **3.** sexual. [ME, from L *carnālis,* from *caro* flesh] – **carnality** /ka'næləti/, *n.* – **carnally,** *adv.*

**carnal car** /'– ka/, *n. Colloq.* →**shaggin' wagon.**

**carnal knowledge** /– 'nɒlɪdʒ/, *n.* **1.** sexual intercourse esp. with one under the age of consent. **2.** *Law.* the penetration, however slight, of the female organ by the male organ.

**carnallite** /'kanəlaɪt/, *n.* a mineral, a hydrous potassium magnesium chloride, $KMgCl_3 \cdot 6H_2O$, a valuable source of potassium. [named after R. von *Carnall,* 1804-74, Prussian mining official. See -ITE[1]]

**carnassial** /ka'næsiəl/, *adj.* **1.** (of teeth) adapted for shearing flesh, as certain of the upper and lower cheek teeth of cats, dogs, etc. *–n.* **2.** a carnassial tooth, esp. the last upper premolar or the first lower molar tooth of certain carnivores. [F *carnassier* flesh-eating (from Pr. *carnasier,* from L *caro* flesh) + -AL[1]]

**carnation** /ka'neɪʃən/, *n.* **1.** any of numerous cultivated varieties of clove pink, *Dianthus caryophyllus,* with fragrant flowers of various colours. **2.** pink; light red. **3.** the colours of flesh as represented in painting. *–adj.* **4.** coloured a light red. [L *carnātio* fleshiness, NL representation of flesh in painting]

**carnauba** /ka'noʊbə/, *n.* **1.** the Brazilian wax-palm, *Copernicia cerifera.* **2.** a yellowish or greenish wax derived from the young leaves of this tree, used as a polish. [Brazilian Pg.]

**carnelian** /ka'niliən/, *n.* a red or reddish variety of chalcedony, used in jewellery, etc. Also, **cornelian.** [ME *corneline,* from OF, of uncert. orig. Cf. ML *cornelius*]

**carnet** /'kaneɪ/, *n.* a customs licence for the temporary importation of a motor vehicle.

**carney** /'kani/, *n.* **1.** a smooth talker, a flatterer. *–adj.* **2.** devious, sly. *–v.t.* **3.** to flatter.

**carnie**[1] /'kani/, *n. Colloq.* nubile girl under the age for legal sexual intercourse. [*carn(al),* in legal phrase, unlawful carnal knowledge + -IE]

**carnie**[2] /'kani/, *n. Colloq.* **1.** a person who works in a carnival. *–adj.* **2.** in the style of or suitable for a carnival. [CARN(IVAL) + -IE]

**carnival** /ˈkanəvəl/, *n.* **1.** revelry and merrymaking, usu. riotous and noisy, and accompanied by processions, etc. **2.** a festive procession. **3.** a fair or amusement show, esp. one erected temporarily for a period of organised merrymaking. **4.** a series of sporting events as a racing carnival, a surfing carnival, etc. **5.** a period set aside for riotous merrymaking, esp. the season immediately preceding Lent. [It. *carnevale,* alteration of *carnesciale,* from *carnescialare, carnelasciare* leave off (eating) meat]

**carnivore** /ˈkanəvɔ/, *n.* **1.** *Zool.* one of the Carnivora, the order of mammals, chiefly flesh-eating, that includes the cats, dogs, bears, seals, etc. **2.** *Bot.* a flesh-eating plant. [see CARNIVOROUS]

**carnivorous** /kaˈnɪvərəs/, *adj.* flesh-eating. [L *carnivorus*] – **carnivorously,** *adv.* – **carnivorousness,** *n.*

**Carnot cycle** /ˈkanoʊ saɪkəl/, *n. Physics.* an ideal reversible cycle of operations for the working substance of a heat engine which gives the maximum obtainable efficiency for an engine working between two temperatures.

**carnotite** /ˈkanətaɪt/, *n.* a mineral, a yellow, earthy, hydrous potassium uranium vanadate; an ore of uranium. [named after A. *Carnot,* d. 1920, French inspector general of mines. See -ITE[1]]

**Carnot principle** /ˈkanoʊ ˌprɪnsəpəl/, *n.* the law which states that the efficiency of any reversible heat engine depends only on the range of temperature through which it works, and not on any of the properties of the materials used. [named after N.L.S. *Carnot,* 1796-1832, French physicist]

**carob** /ˈkærəb/, *n.* **1.** the fruit of a tree, *Ceratonia siliqua,* of the Mediterranean regions, being a long, dry pod containing hard seeds in a sweet pulp, used for feeding animals and eaten by man. **2.** the tree. [F *carobe,* from Ar. *kharrūba*]

carob pod

**caroche** /kəˈrɒʃ/, *n.* an old form of stately coach or carriage. [F (obs.) *carroche,* from It. *carroccio,* augmentative of *carro* chariot, from L *carrus;* akin to CAR]

**carol** /ˈkærəl/, *n., v.,* **-rolled, -rolling** or (*U.S.*) **-roled, -roling.** *–n.* **1.** a song, esp. of joy. **2.** a Christmas song or hymn. **3.** *Obs.* a kind of circular dance. *–v.i.* **4.** to sing, esp. in a lively, joyous manner; warble. *–v.t.* **5.** to sing joyously. **6.** to praise or celebrate in song. [ME, from OF *carole;* probably from Celtic root *cor-* circle, b. with L *choraula* minstrel, chorus leader, from Gk *choraúlēs*] – **caroller,** *n.*

**Carolean** /kærəˈliən/, *adj.* →**Caroline.**

**Carolina jasmine** /kærəˌlaɪnə ˈdʒæzmən/, *n.* a twining plant, *Gelsemium sempervirens,* with dark green leaves and yellow flowers with a funnel-shaped corolla; yellow jasmine.

**Caroline** /ˈkærəlaɪn/, *adj.* **1.** of or pertaining to the time of Charles I or Charles II, kings of England: *Caroline drama.* **2.** of or pertaining to any other Charles, Charlemagne, etc.

**Carolingian** /kærəˈlɪndʒiən/, *adj.* belonging to the Frankish dynasty which reigned in France from A.D. 751 until A.D. 987 and in Germany until A.D. 911. Also, **Carlovingian.** [ML *Carolingī* (Latinised pl. of OG *Karling* descendant of *Karl*) + -IAN]

**Carolinian** /kærəˈlɪniən/, *adj.* **1.** →**Carolingian.** **2.** →**Caroline.**

**carolus** /ˈkærələs/, *n., pl.* **-luses, -li** /-li/. any of various coins issued under monarchs named Charles, esp. an English gold coin struck in the reign of Charles I, originally worth 20 and later 23 shillings. [ML: Charles]

**carom** /ˈkærəm/, *n.* **1.** →**cannon** (defs 11 and 12). *–v.i.* **2.** →**cannon** (defs 14 and 15). Also, **carrom.** [earlier *carambole,* from F, from Sp. *carambola;* special use of *carambola* a fruit]

**Caro's acid** /ˌkæroʊz ˈæsəd, ˌka-/, *n.* →**persulphuric acid** (def. 1). [named after N. *Caro,* 1871-1935, German chemist]

**carotene** /ˈkærətin/, *n.* any of three isomeric red hydrocarbons, $C_{40}H_{56}$, found in many plants, esp. carrots, and transformed to vitamin A in the liver. Also, **carotin** /ˈkærətən/. [L *carota* CARROT + -ENE]

**carotenoid** /kəˈrɒtənɔɪd/, *n.* **1.** any of a group of red and yellow pigments, chemically similar to carotene, contained in animal fat and some plants. *–adj.* **2.** similar to carotene. **3.** pertaining to carotenoids. Also, **carotinoid.** [CAROTENE + -OID]

**carotid** /kəˈrɒtəd/, *n.* **1.** either of the two great arteries, one on each side of the neck, which carry blood to the head. *–adj.* **2.** pertaining to the carotids. [Gk *karōtídes,* pl., from *káros* stupor (thought to be caused by compression of these arteries)] – **carotidal,** *adj.*

**carousal** /kəˈraʊzəl/, *n.* a noisy or drunken feast or other social gathering; jovial revelry. [CAROUSE, *v.* + -AL[2]]

**carouse** /kəˈraʊz/, *n., v.,* **-roused, -rousing.** *–n.* **1.** a noisy or drunken feast; jovial revelry. *–v.i.* **2.** to engage in a carouse; drink deeply. [n. and v. uses of obs. adv., from G *gar aus* (drink a cup) wholly out]

**carousel** /kærəˈsɛl/, *n.* **1.** →**merry-go-round** (def. 1). **2.** a tournament in which horsemen execute various movements in formation. **3.** a revolving device by which luggage is returned to travellers after a journey by plane, ship, bus, etc. **4.** a circular magazine for holding photographic slides. Also, **carrousel.** [F, from It. *carosello,* from *carro,* from L *carrus* cart]

**carp**[1] /kap/, *v.i.* to find fault; cavil; complain unreasonably: *to carp at minor errors.* [ME *carpe(n),* from Scand.; cf. Icel. *karpa* wrangle, dispute] – **carper,** *n.* – **carpingly,** *adv.*

**carp**[2] /kap/, *n., pl.* **carp.** **1.** a large, coarse freshwater food fish, *Cyprinus carpio* (family Cyprinidae), commonly bred in ponds and introduced into Australia. **2.** any of various other fishes of the same family. [ME *carpe,* from OF, from Pr. *carpa,* from LL *carpa;* of Gmc orig.]

**-carp,** a noun termination meaning 'fruit', used in botanical terms, as *endocarp.* [combining form representing Gk *karpós*]

**carp.,** carpentry.

**carpal** /ˈkapəl/, *adj.* **1.** pertaining to the carpus: *the carpal joint.* *–n.* **2.** →**carpale.** [NL *carpālis,* from L *carpus* wrist]

**carpale** /kaˈpeɪli/, *n., pl.* **-lia** /-liə/. any of the bones of the wrist. Also, **carpal.** [NL, neut. of *carpālis* CARPAL]

**car park** /ˈka pak/, *n.* a place, usu. in the open air, where cars may be parked.

**carpe diem** /kapə ˈdiəm/, enjoy the present day (trusting as little as possible to the future). [L]

**carpel** /ˈkapəl/, *n.* a simple pistil, or a single member of a compound pistil, regarded as a modified leaf. [NL *carpellum,* from Gk *karpós* fruit]

A B

carpels: A, flower with simple pistils; B, tricarpellary fruit

**carpellary** /ˈkapələri/, *adj.* forming part of or arising from a carpel.

**carpellate** /ˈkapəleɪt/, *adj.* (of a flower) having carpels (opposed to *staminate*).

**carpenter** /ˈkapəntə/, *n.* **1.** a workman who erects and fixes the wooden parts, etc., in the building of houses and other structures. **2.** *U.S.* →**joiner.** *–v.i.* **3.** to do carpenter's work. *–v.t.* **4.** to make by carpentry. [ME, from ONF *carpentier,* from LL *carpentārius* wagon-maker, from L *carpentum* wagon] – **carpentry,** *n.*

**carpenter bee** /ˈ– bi/, *n.* any of various solitary bees of the family Xylocopidae that make their nests in wood, boring tunnels in which to deposit their eggs.

**carpet** /ˈkapət/, *n.* **1.** a heavy fabric, commonly of wool, for covering floors. **2.** a covering of this material. **3.** any covering like a carpet: *they walked on the grassy carpet.* **4.** **on the carpet, a.** under consideration or discussion. **b.** before an authority for a reprimand. *–v.t.* **5.** to cover or furnish with, or as with, a carpet. **6.** *Colloq.* to reprimand. [ME *carpete,* from ML *carpeta,* from L *carpere* card (wool)]

**carpetbag** /ˈkapətbæg/, *n.* a bag for travelling, esp. one made of carpeting.

**carpetbagger** /ˈkapətbægə/, *n.* **1.** a person who takes up residence in a place, with no more property than he brings in a carpetbag, to seek special advantages for himself. **2.** (in U.S. history) (*derog.*) a Northerner who went to the South after the Civil War to seek political or other advantages made possible by the disorganised condition of political affairs.

**carpetbag steak** /ˌkapətbæg ˈsteɪk/, *n.* a thick piece of tender steak with a pocket cut in it, stuffed with raw oysters, and then pan fried or grilled.

**carpet bedding** /ˈkapət ˌbɛdɪŋ/, *n.* a system of planting flowers so that they produce a carpet-like pattern.

**carpet beetle** /ˈ– bitl/, *n.* a small beetle, *Anthrenus scrophulariae,* whose larvae are destructive to carpets and other woollen fabrics.
**carpet bowls** /ˈ– boʊlz/, *n.* a game similar to bowls but played indoors.
**carpet grass** /ˈ– gras/, *n.* a summer-growing perennial, *Axonopus affinis,* native to the West Indies, which grows readily on poor soil and which can infest pasture, esp. paspalum.
**carpeting** /ˈkapətɪŋ/, *n.* **1.** material for carpets. **2.** carpets in general.
**carpet page** /ˈkapət peɪdʒ/, *n.* in an illuminated manuscript of the Middle Ages, the page which has no text and is one large design.
**carpet shark** /ˈ– ʃak/, *n.* →**wobbegong.**
**carpet slipper** /ˈ– slɪpə/, *n.* one of a pair of soft slippers, usu. with woollen uppers.
**carpet snake** /ˈ– sneɪk/, *n.* a large, non-venomous Australian python, *Morelia spilotes variegata,* with a particoloured pattern on its skin, often used in silos and barns to control rodent pests.
**carpet-sweeper** /ˈkapət-swipə/, *n.* a device for sweeping carpets, with a revolving brush, etc.
**carpet tile** /ˈkapət taɪl/, *n.* a small square of carpet usu. laid on the floor, with others, to form a wall-to-wall carpet.
**carpet wool** /ˈ– wʊl/, *n.* very strong or coarse wool generally hairy or medullated, employed mainly in the manufacture of carpets.
**carphology** /kaˈfɒlədʒi/, *n.* →**floccillation.**
**carpi** /ˈkapi/, *n.* plural of **carpus.**
**-carpic,** a word element related to **-carp,** as in *endocarpic.* [-CARP + -IC]
**carpo-,** a word element meaning 'fruit' as in *carpology.* [Gk *karpo-,* combining form of *karpós*]
**carpogonium** /kapəˈgoʊniəm/, *n., pl.* **-nia** /-niə/. the one-celled female sex organ of the red algae (Rhodophyceae) which, when fertilised, gives rise to the carpospores. [NL; see CARPO-, -GONIUM] – **carpogonial,** *adj.*
**carpology** /kaˈpɒlədʒi/, *n.* the branch of botany that relates to fruits. – **carpological** /kapəˈlɒdʒɪkəl/, *adj.* – **carpologist,** *n.*
**carpophagous** /kaˈpɒfəgəs/, *adj.* fruit-eating.
**carpophore** /ˈkapəfɔ/, *n.* **1.** a slender prolongation of the floral axis, bearing the carpels of some compound fruits, as in the geranium and in many umbelliferous plants. **2.** the fruit body of the higher fungi.

A, carpophore; B, carpels

**carport** /ˈkapɔt/, *n.* a roofed wall-less shed often projecting from the side of a building, used as a shelter for a motor vehicle.
**carpospore** /ˈkapəspɔ/, *n.* a non-motile spore of the red algae.
**-carpous,** a combining form related to **-carp,** as in *apocarpous.* [-CARP + -OUS]
**carpus** /ˈkapəs/, *n., pl.* **-pi** /-pi/. the wrist, or the eight bones comprising it: the scaphoid, lunate, triquetral, pisiform, trapezoid, capitate, and hamate bones.

carpus

**carr.,** carriage.
**carrack** /ˈkærək/, *n. Archaic.* a galleon. [ME *caracke,* from OF *carraque,* from Sp., Pg. *carraca,* from Ar. *qarāgīr,* pl. of *qurqūr* merchant vessel; or from *harraqa* boat]
**carrageen** /ˈkærəgin, kærəˈgin/, *n.* →**Irish moss** (def. 1). Also, **carragheen.** [named after *Carragheen,* in S Ireland]
**carrel** /kəˈrɛl, ˈkærəl/, *n.* (in a library) a small area or cubicle used by students and others for individual study; a stall. [OF *carole,* from ML *carola*]
**carriage** /ˈkærɪdʒ/, *n.* **1.** a wheeled vehicle for conveying persons, usu. drawn by horses, esp. one designed for comfort and elegance. **2.** *Railways.* a passenger-carrying vehicle unit. **3.** a wheeled support, as for a cannon. **4.** a part, as of a machine, designed for carrying something. **5.** manner of

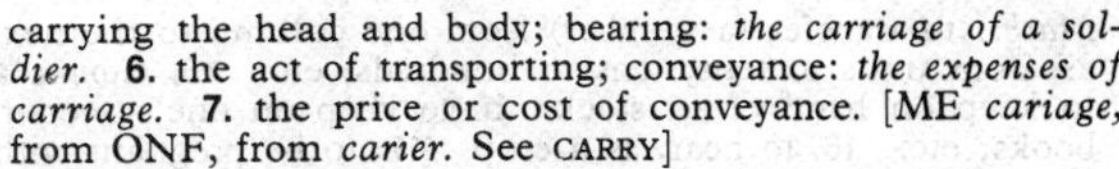

carrying the head and body; bearing: *the carriage of a soldier.* **6.** the act of transporting; conveyance: *the expenses of carriage.* **7.** the price or cost of conveyance. [ME *cariage,* from ONF, from *carier.* See CARRY]
**carriageway** /ˈkærɪdʒweɪ/, *n.* that part of a road which carries vehicles.
**carrick bend** /ˈkærɪk bɛnd/, *n. Naut.* a kind of knot for joining cables or hawsers. [*carrick* ? var. of CARRACK]
**carrick bitt** /ˈ– bɪt/, *n. Naut.* one of the bitts which support the windlass.
**carrier** /ˈkæriə/, *n.* **1.** a person or thing that carries. **2.** a person, company, etc., that undertakes to convey goods or persons. **3.** a small platform on a bicycle used for carrying luggage. **4.** *Mach.* a mechanism by which something is carried or moved. **5.** *Med.* an individual harbouring specific organisms, who, though often immune to the agent harboured, may transmit the disease to others. **6.** *Chem.* a catalytic agent which brings about a transfer of an element or group of atoms from one compound to another. **7.** *Radio.* **a.** Also, **carrier wave.** a wave whose amplitude, frequency phase is varied or modulated in order to transmit a signal. **b.** the mobile electrons or holes which constitute the current in a semiconductor. **8.** *Physics, Biol.* an element which is added to radioactive isotopes of the same, or an analogous, element in order to provide sufficient material for a full-scale chemical or biological process to be followed. **9.** →**aircraft-carrier.** **10.** →**carrier pigeon.**
**carrier bag** /ˈ– bæg/, *n.* →**carry bag.**
**carrier pigeon** /ˈ– pɪdʒən/, *n.* **1.** a pigeon trained to fly home from great distances and thus transport written messages; a homing pigeon. **2.** one of a breed of domestic pigeons characterised by a huge wattle at the base of the beak.
**carriole** /ˈkærioʊl/, *n.* →**cariole.**
**carrion** /ˈkæriən/, *n.* **1.** dead and putrefying flesh. **2.** rottenness; anything vile. *–adj.* **3.** feeding on carrion. **4.** of or like carrion. [ME *carion, caroine,* from ONF, var. of central OF *charoigne,* from L *caro* flesh]
**carrion crow** /ˈ– kroʊ/, *n.* **1.** any of various crows, as the common European crow, *Corvus corone.* **2.** a black vulture, *Coragypo atratus,* of the southern U.S., etc.
**carrion flower** /ˈ– flaʊə/, *n.* any plant with fetid-smelling flowers which attract carrion flies, esp. members of the genera *Amorphophallus* and *Stapelia.*
**carrom** /ˈkærəm/, *n., v.i.* →**carom.**
**carromata** /kærəˈmatə/, *n.* (in the Philippines) a light, two-wheeled covered vehicle, usu. drawn by one horse. [Sp. *carromato,* from *carro* cart, from L *carrus*]
**carronade** /kærəˈneɪd/, *n.* a short piece of muzzle-loading ordnance, formerly in use, esp. in ships. [from *Carron* (Scotland), site of a cannon foundry]
**carron oil** /ˈkærən ɔɪl/, *n.* a liniment containing limewater and oil, formerly used for burns.
**carrot** /ˈkærət/, *n.* **1.** a plant of the umbelliferous genus *Daucus,* esp. D. *carota,* in its wild form a widespread, familiar weed, and in cultivation valued for its reddish edible root. **2.** the root of this plant. **3.** *Colloq.* an incentive: *to dangle a carrot.* **4.** *Colloq.* a migrant. [F *carotte,* from L *carōta,* from Gk *karōtón*]
**carroty** /ˈkærəti/, *adj.* **1.** like a carrot root in colour; yellowish red. **2.** having red hair.
**carrousel** /kærəˈsɛl/, *n.* →**carousel.**
**carry** /ˈkæri/, *v.,* **-ried, -rying,** *n., pl.* **-ries.** *–v.t.* **1.** to convey from one place to another in a vehicle, ship, pocket, hand, etc. **2.** to transmit or transfer in any manner; take or bring: *the wind carries sounds, he carries his audience with him.* **3.** to bear the weight, burden, etc., of; sustain. **4.** to take a (leading or guiding part) in acting or singing; bear or sustain (a part or melody). **5.** to hold (the body, head, etc.) in a certain manner. **6.** to behave or comport (oneself). **7.** to take, esp. by force; capture; win. **8.** to secure the election of (a candidate) or the adoption of (a motion or bill). **9.** to print or publish in a newspaper or magazine. **10.** to extend or continue in a given direction or to a certain point: *to carry the war into enemy territory.* **11.** to lead or impel; conduct. **12.** to have as an attribute, property, consequence, etc.: *his opinion carries great weight.* **13.** to support or give validity to (a related claim, etc.): *one decision carries another.* **14.**

i = peat ɪ = pit ɛ = pet æ = pat a = part ɒ = pot ʌ = putt ɔ = port ʊ = put u = pool ɜ = pert ə = apart aɪ = buy eɪ = bay ɔɪ = boy aʊ = how oʊ = hoe ɪə = here ɛə = hair ʊə = tour g = give θ = thin ð = then ʃ = show ʒ = measure tʃ = choke dʒ = joke ŋ = sing j = you õ = Fr. bon

*Maths.* to transfer (a number) from one column to the next, as from units to tens, tens to hundreds, etc. **15.** *Comm.* **a.** to keep on hand or in stock. **b.** to keep on one's account books, etc. **16.** to bear, as a crop. **17.** to be pregnant with: *she is carrying her third child.* **18.** to support (livestock): *our grain supply will carry the cattle through the winter.* **19.** *Golf.* to advance beyond or go by (an object or expanse) with one stroke. **20.** *Hunting.* to retain and pursue (a scent). **21.** *Ice Hockey.* to move (the puck) along the ice; dribble. *–v.i.* **22.** to act as a bearer or conductor. **23.** to have or exert propelling force: *the rifle carries a long way.* **24.** to be transmitted, propelled, or sustained: *my voice carries farther than his.* **25.** to bear the head in a particular manner, as a horse. **26.** *Soccer.* of the goalkeeper, to infringe the rules by taking more than four steps before putting the ball back into play. *–v.* **27.** Some special verb phrases are:

**carry away, 1.** to influence greatly or beyond reason. **2.** *Naut.* of a mast, sail, etc., to break or tear away from its fastenings.

**carry forward, 1.** to make progress with. **2.** *Bookkeeping.* to transfer (an amount, etc.) to the next column, page, etc.

**carry off, 1.** to win (the prize, honour, etc.). **2.** to face consequences boldly: *he carried it off well.* **3.** to cause the death of.

**carry on, 1.** to manage; conduct. **2.** to behave in an excited, foolish, or improper manner; flirt. **3.** to continue; keep up without stopping.

**carry one's bat,** *Cricket.* of a batsman, to remain not out at the end of the team's innings.

**carry out,** to accomplish or complete (a plan, scheme, etc.): *we carried out the details of his plan.*

**carry over, 1.** to postpone; hold off until later. **2.** *Stock Exchange.* to defer completion of (a contract) so that it falls under a different account. **3.** of vegetables, etc., not sold in a day's trading, to retain for later sale.

**carry the can,** *Colloq.* do the dirty work; bear the responsibility.

**carry the day,** to succeed; triumph.

**carry the fight,** *Boxing.* to attack persistently.

**carry through, 1.** to accomplish; complete. **2.** to support or help (in a difficult situation, etc.)

*–n.* **28.** range, as of a gun. **29.** *Golf.* the distance traversed by a ball before it alights. **30.** land separating navigable waters, over which a canoe or boat must be carried; a portage. **31.** the last manoeuvre of a sheep dog trial in which the dog must take sheep through a gate. **32.** a carrying. [ME *carie(n),* from ONF *carier,* from LL *carricāre* convey by wagon, from L *carrus.* See CAR]

**carryall** /'kæriɔl/, *n.* →**holdall.** [CARRY + ALL]

**carry bag** /'kæri bæg/, *n.* a bag made of strong paper or plastic material, with string, paper or plastic handles. Also, **carrier bag.**

**carry basket** /'– baskət/, *n.* a bassinette with large handles designed to be carried.

**carrying capacity** /'kæriɪŋ kəpæsəti/, *n.* the capacity of land or pasture to support livestock.

**carryings-on** /ˌkæriɪŋz-'ɒn/, *n.pl.* foolish or unconventional behaviour or events. Also, **carry-on.**

**carryover** /'kærioʊvə/, *n.* **1.** the part left over to a later period, account, etc. **2.** *Bookkeeping.* the total of one page on an account carried forward to the next. **3.** *Stock Exchange.* the practice of deferring completion of a contract from one account to another. **4.** a contract carried over.

**carry-over lamb** /'kæri-oʊvə læm/, *n.* a lamb which has not matured sufficiently for sale and which is carried over until the next season.

**car seat** /'ka sit/, *n.* **1.** a seat in a car. **2.** a small seat specially adapted for a baby or small child which attaches to the full-sized car seat.

**carsick** /'kasɪk/, *adj.* nauseated by the motion of a motor vehicle.

**car sticker** /'ka stɪkə/, *n.* a sticker (def. 2) designed to be affixed to a car window.

**cart** /kat/, *n.* **1.** (formerly) a heavy horse-drawn vehicle, usu. with solid tyres and made chiefly of wood, without springs, for the conveyance of heavy goods. **2.** a light two-wheeled vehicle with springs, used for business or pleasure. **3.** any small vehicle moved by hand. **4. in the cart,** *Colloq.* in an awkward or unpleasant predicament. **5. put the cart before the horse, a.** to reverse the natural order. **b.** to confuse cause and effect. *–v.t.* **6.** to convey in or as in a cart. [metathetic var. of OE *cræt,* c. Icel *kartr*]

**cartage** /'katɪdʒ/, *n.* the act or cost of carting.

**carte**[1] /kat/, *n. Fencing.* →**quarte.** [F *quarte,* from It.]

**carte**[2] /kat/, *n.* **1.** menu. Cf. **à la carte. 2.** *Rare or Obs.* a playing card. **3.** *Obs.* a map or chart. [F. See CARD[1]]

**carte blanche** /– 'blɒntʃ/, *n., pl.* **cartes blanches** /kats 'blɒntʃ/. **1.** a signed paper left blank for the person to whom it is given to fill in his own conditions. **2.** unconditional authority; full power.

**cartel** /ka'tɛl/, *n.* **1.** an international syndicate, combine, or trust generally formed to regulate prices and output in some field of business. **2.** a written agreement between belligerents, esp. for the exchange of prisoners. **3.** *Hist.* a challenge to single combat. [F, from It. *cartello,* diminutive of *carta,* from L *charta* paper. See CHART]

**cartelise** /'katəlaɪz/, *v.* **-lised, -lising.** *–v.t.* **1.** to organise into a cartel (def. 1). *–v.i.* **2.** to cause to form into a cartel. Also, **cartelize.** – **cartelisation** /katəlaɪ'zeɪʃən/, *n.*

**carter** /'katə/, *n.* one who carts, esp. one who drives a lorry van, etc. for the delivery of bread, bricks, etc.

**Cartesian** /ka'tiʒən/, *adj.* **1.** pertaining to Descartes, to his mathematical methods, or to his dualistic philosophy which began with the famous phrase *Cogito, ergo sum* (I think, therefore I am), which viewed physical nature mechanically, and which in science emphasised rationalism and logic. *–n.* **2.** a believer in the philosophy of Descartes. [NL *Cartesiānus,* from *Cartesius,* Latinised form of the name of René Descartes, 1596-1650, French philosopher and mathematician] – **Cartesianism,** *n.*

**cartesian coordinates** /kaˌtiʒən koʊ'ɔdənəts/, *n. pl. Maths.* the coordinates of a point in a plane (or in a space) defined by the perpendicular distances of the point from two (or three) intersecting axes which are at right angles to each other.

**carthorse** /'kathɔs/, *n.* a horse that draws a cart; draughthorse.

**car tidy** /'ka taɪdi/, *n.* a small rubbish receptacle used inside a motor vehicle.

**cartilage** /'katəlɪdʒ, 'katlɪdʒ/, *n. Anat., Zool.* **1.** a firm, elastic, flexible substance of a translucent whitish or yellowish colour, consisting of a connective tissue; gristle. **2.** a part or structure composed of cartilage. [F, from L *cartilāgo* gristle]

**cartilage bone** /'– boʊn/, *n.* a bone that is developed from cartilage (distinguished from *membrane bone*).

**cartilaginous** /katə'lædʒənəs/, *adj.* **1.** of or resembling cartilage. **2.** *Zool.* having the skeleton composed mostly of cartilage, as sharks and rays.

**cartload** /'katloʊd/, *n.* **1.** the amount a cart can hold. **2.** *Bldg Trades Obs.* any amount between $\frac{1}{4}$ and $\frac{1}{2}$ a cubic yard.

**cartog.,** cartography.

**cartogram** /'katəgræm/, *n.* a diagrammatic presentation in highly abstracted or simplified form, commonly of statistical data, on a map base or distorted map base. [F *cartogramme.* See CARD[1], -GRAM[1]]

**cartography** /ka'tɒgrəfi/, *n.* the production of maps, including construction of projections, design, compilation, drafting, and reproduction. Also, **chartography.** [*carto-* (combining form of ML *carta* chart, map) + -GRAPHY] – **cartographer,** *n.* – **cartographic** /katə'græfɪk/, **cartographical** /katə'græfɪkəl/, *adj.* – **cartographically** /katə'græfɪkli/, *adv.*

**cartomancy** /'katəmænsi/, *n.* divination by cards, whether a standard pack or a special one such as the tarot pack.

**carton** /'katən/, *n.* **1.** a cardboard box, esp one in which food such as eggs, milk, etc., is packaged and sold. **2.** *Archery, Shooting.* the white disc at the centre of a target. **3.** *Archery, Shooting.* a shot which strikes the carton. [F. See CARTOON]

**cartoon** /ka'tun/, *n.* **1.** a sketch or drawing as in a newspaper or periodical, symbolising or caricaturing some subject or person of current interest, in an exaggerated way. **2.** *Art.* a drawing, of the same size as a proposed decoration or pattern in fresco, mosaic, tapestry, etc., for which it serves as a model to be transferred or copied. **3.** a comic strip. **4.** an animated cartoon. *–v.t.* **5.** to represent by a cartoon. [F *carton,* from It. *cartone* pasteboard, cartoon, augmentative of *carta,* from L *charta* paper. See CHART] – **cartoonist,** *n.*

**cartouche** /ka'tuʃ/, *n.* **1.** *Archit.* a French Renaissance motif, usu. an oval tablet with ornamental scrollwork. **2.** an oval or oblong figure, as on ancient Egyptian monuments, enclosing characters which express royal names. **3.** the case containing the inflammable materials in certain fireworks. **4.** cartridge (def. 1). **5.** a box for cartridges. Also, **cartouch.** [F, from It. *cartoccio,* augmentative of *carta,* from L *charta* paper. See CHART]

**cartridge** /'katrɪdʒ/, *n.* **1.** Also, **cartridge case.** a cylindrical case of pasteboard, metal, or the like, for holding a complete charge of powder, and often also the bullet or the shot, for a rifle, machine-gun, or other small arm. **2.** the case, charge, and bullet or shot; a round (def. 32). **3.** a case containing any explosive charge, as for blasting. **4.** anything resembling a cartridge, as the disposable container of ink for some types of fountain pen. **5.** →**pick-up** (def. 6). **6. a.** (in a tape recorder) a plastic container enclosing recording tape usu. in the form of an endless loop. **b.** (in video recorders, computers, etc.) a device of similar principle, or more loosely of the cassette principle, with wider tape. [from CARTOUCHE]

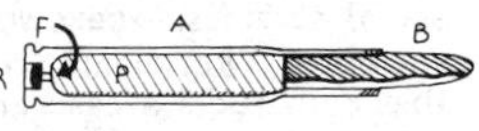

cartridge: A, metallic case of copper or brass; B, bullet; R, primer; F, fulminate; P, powder

**cartridge belt** /'– bɛlt/, *n.* a belt (def. 7b) for ammunition with loops for cartridges or pockets for clips of cartridges.

**cartridge clip** /'– klɪp/, *n.* a metal frame or container holding cartridges for a magazine rifle or automatic pistol; clip.

**cartridge paper** /'– peɪpə/, *n.* an uncoated type of drawing or printing paper, normally made from a bleached sulphate woodpulp, often with a percentage addition of esparto grass.

**cart track** /'kat træk/, *n.* an undeveloped country road, often showing two separated tracks in grass, dirt, etc., caused by the wheels of the vehicles which use it.

**cartulary** /'katʃələri/, *n., pl.* **-ries.** a register of charters, title deeds, etc. Also, **chartulary.** [ML *c(h)artulārium,* from L *c(h)artula.* See CHARTER]

**cartwheel** /'katwil/, *n.* **1.** the wheel of a cart, usu. large, wooden, with spokes and metal tyres. **2.** a somersault, performed sideways, with legs and arms outstretched.

**cartwright** /'katraɪt/, *n.* a maker of carts, etc.

**caruncle** /'kærəŋkəl, kə'rʌŋkəl/, *n.* **1.** *Bot.* a protuberance at or surrounding the hilum of a seed. **2.** *Zool.* a fleshy excrescence, as on the head of a bird; a fowl's comb. [L *caruncula,* diminutive of *caro* flesh] – **caruncular** /kə'rʌŋkjələ/, **carunculous** /kə'rʌŋkjələs/, *adj.*

**carunculate** /kə'rʌŋkjələt, -leɪt/, *adj.* having a caruncle or caruncles. Also, **carunculated.**

**carve** /kav/, *v.,* **carved, carving.** *–v.t.* **1.** to fashion by cutting: *to carve a block of stone into a statue.* **2.** to produce by cutting: *to carve a design in wood.* **3.** to cut into slices or pieces, as meat. **4.** to make or establish for oneself by one's own efforts (oft. fol. by *out*). **5.** *Colloq.* to slash (a person) with a knife or razor (fol. by *up*). *–v.i.* **6.** to decorate by cutting figures, designs, etc. **7.** *Colloq.* to distribute profits, a legacy, illegal gain, an estate, etc. (fol. by *up*). [ME *kerve(n),* OE *ceorfan* cut, c. G *Kerben* notch; akin to Gk *gráphein* mark, write] – **carver,** *n.*

**carvel** /'kavəl/, *n.* →**caravel.**

**carvel-built** /'kavəl-bɪlt/, *adj.* (of a ship) built with the planks flush, not overlapping. Cf. **clinker**[3].

**carven** /'kavən/, *adj. Poetic.* carved.

**carver** /'kavə/, *n.* **1.** a dining chair, with arms. **2. pair of carvers,** a carving set consisting of a carving knife and a matching fork.

**carve-up** /'kav-ʌp/, *n.* a distribution of profits, illegal gain, an estate, etc.

**carving** /'kavɪŋ/, *n.* **1.** the act of fashioning or producing by cutting. **2.** carved work; a carved design.

**carving knife** /'– naɪf/, *n.* a large sharp knife for carving meat, etc.

**carving rest** /'– rɛst/, *n.* a small rest, usu. silver, for a carving knife or fork.

**car wash** /'ka wɒʃ/, *n.* an area or structure with facilities for washing a car mechanically.

**caryard** /'kajad/, *n.* an establishment for the buying and selling of motor cars which has an open-air area in which cars for sale are displayed.

**caryatid** /kæri'ætəd/, *n., pl.* **-ids, -ides** /-ədiz/. *Archit.* a figure of a woman used as a supporting column. [L *Caryātides,* pl., from Gk *Karyátides,* lit., women of Caryae (site of a temple to Artemis)] – **caryatidal,** *adj.*

caryatids

**caryophyllaceous** /,kærioʊfə'leɪʃəs/, *adj.* **1.** belonging to the Caryophyllaceae or pink family of plants. **2.** resembling the pink. [Gk *karyóphyllon* clove tree + -ACEOUS]

**caryopsis** /kæri'ɒpsəs/, *n., pl.* **-opses** /-'ɒpsiz/, **-opsides** /-'ɒpsədiz/. a small, one-celled, one-seeded, dry, indehiscent fruit with the pericarp adherent to the seedcoat, as in wheat. [Gk *káryon* nut + -OPSIS]

**cas** /kæz/, *n. Colloq.* casualty ward.

**cas.,** casual.

**casaba** /kə'sabə/, *n.* a kind of winter muskmelon, having a yellow rind and sweet, juicy flesh. Also, **casaba melon, cassaba.** [named after *Kassaba,* town near Smyrna, Asia Minor]

**casanova** /kæsə'noʊvə, 'kæzə-/, *n.* any man notable for his amorous adventures. [from Giovanni Jacopo *Casanova,* 1725-98, Italian adventurer and writer]

**casbah** /'kæzba/, *n.* →**kasbah.**

**cascade** /kæs'keɪd/, *n., v.,* **-caded, -cading.** *–n.* **1.** a waterfall over steep rocks, or a series of small waterfalls. **2.** an arrangement of lace, etc., in folds falling one over another in a zigzag fashion. **3.** a type of firework resembling a waterfall in effect. **4.** *Chem.* **a.** a series of vessels, from each of which a liquid successively overflows to the next, thus presenting a large absorbing surface, as to a gas. **b.** any process involving a number of repeated stages, each stage effecting an increase in the concentration of the desired end product. **5.** *Elect.* an arrangement of component devices, each of which feeds into the next in succession. *–v.i.* **6.** to fall in or like a cascade. [F, from It. *cascata,* from *cascare,* from L *cadere* fall]

**cascade shower** /– 'ʃaʊə/, *n.* a fast-moving number of electrons, positrons, or photons which appear almost simultaneously from one high-energy particle as a result of pair production or radioactive collisions; soft shower.

**Cascadian** /kæs'keɪdiən/, *adj. Geol.* of or pertaining to the mountain-building episode in North America which reached its height at the end of the Tertiary period.

**cascara** /kæs'karə/, *n.* a species of buckthorn, *Rhamnus purshiana,* of the Pacific coast of the U.S., yielding cascara sagrada. Also, **cascara buckthorn.** [Sp.: bark, from *casca* bark, skin]

**cascara sagrada** /– sə'gradə/, *n.* the bark of the cascara, used as a cathartic or laxative. [Sp.: sacred bark]

**cascarilla** /kæskə'rɪlə/, *n.* **1.** Also, **cascarilla bark.** the bitter aromatic bark of any West Indian shrub of the genus *Croton,* as *C. eluteria;* used as a tonic. **2.** the shrub itself. **3.** any species of *Croton.* [Sp., diminutive of *cáscara* bark]

**case**[1] /keɪs/, *n.* **1.** an instance of the occurrence, existence, etc., of something. **2.** the actual state of things: *that is not the case.* **3.** a question or problem of moral conduct: *a case of conscience.* **4.** situation; condition; plight. **5.** a state of things involving a question for discussion or decision. **6.** a statement of facts, reasons, etc.: *a strong case for the proposed law.* **7.** an instance of disease, etc., requiring medical or surgical treatment or attention. **8.** a medical or surgical patient. **9.** a person, family, or other social unit receiving any kind of professional social assistance. **10.** *Law.* **a.** a suit or action at law; a cause. **b.** the statement of facts as presented to a court. **11.** *Gram.* **a.** a category in the inflection of nouns, pronouns, and adjectives, denoting the syntactic relation of these words to other words in the sentence, indicated by the form or the position of the words. **b.** a set of such categories in a particular language. **c.** the meaning of, or typical of, such a category. **d.** such categories or their meanings collectively. **12.** *Colloq.* a peculiar or unusual person: *he's a case.* **13. in any case,** under any circumstances; anyhow. **14. in case,** if; if it should happen that. **15. in case of,** in the event of. [ME, from OF *cas,* from L *cāsus* a falling, occurrence]

**case**[2] /keɪs/, *n., v.,* **cased, casing.** *–n.* **1.** a thing for containing or enclosing something; a receptacle. **2.** a sheath or outer covering: *a knife case.* **3.** a box with its contents. **4.** the amount contained in a box or other container. **5.** a cased frame. **6.** *Metall.* the case-hardened surface of a piece of steel. **7.** *Bookbinding.* a completed book cover ready to be fitted to form the binding of a book. **8.** *Print.* a tray, of wood or metal, divided into compartments for holding types for the use of a compositor and usu. arranged in a set of two, the **upper case** for capitals, etc., and the **lower case** for small letters, etc. *–v.t.* **9.** to put or enclose in a case; cover with a case. **10.** *Colloq.* to examine or survey (a house, bank, etc.) in planning a crime. [ME *casse,* from ONF, from L *capsa* box, receptacle]

**caseate** /ˈkeɪsieɪt/, *v.i.,* **-ated, -ating.** *Pathol.* to undergo caseous degeneration; become like cheese in consistency and appearance. [L *cāseus* cheese + -ATE[1]]

**caseation** /keɪsiˈeɪʃən/, *n. Pathol.* transformation into a soft cheeselike mass, as of tissue in tuberculosis.

**casebook** /ˈkeɪsbʊk/, *n.* a book in which record is kept by doctors, social workers, etc., of their cases.

**casebound** /ˈkeɪsbaʊnd/, *n., adj.* (of books) hardback.

**cased frame** /keɪst ˈfreɪm/, *n.* a framework, as of a door or window.

**case-harden** /keɪs-ˈhadn/, *v.t.* **1.** *Metall.* to make hard the outside surface of alloys having an iron base, leaving the interior tough and ductile by carburising, cyanide hardening, or nitriding and suitable heat treatment. **2.** to harden in spirit so as to render insensible to external impressions or influences, as a judge.

**case history** /keɪs ˈhɪstri/, *n.* all the relevant information or material gathered about an individual, family, group, etc., for use by a caseworker, doctor, student, or the like, used esp. in social work, sociology, psychiatry, and medicine.

**casein** /ˈkeɪsiən, -sin/, *n.* the major group of proteins in milk, which can be precipitated by rennet, and which forms the basis of cheese and certain plastics. [L *cāseus* cheese + -IN[2]]

**caseinogen** /keɪsiˈɪnədʒən, -ˈsinə-/, *n.* the principal protein of milk, which in the presence of rennet is converted into casein.

**case-knife** /ˈkeɪs-naɪf/, *n.* **1.** a knife carried or kept in a case. **2.** a table knife.

**case law** /ˈkeɪs lɔ/, *n.* law established by judicial decisions in particular cases, instead of by legislation.

**casemate** /ˈkeɪsmeɪt/, *n.* **1.** an armoured enclosure for guns in a warship. **2.** a vault or chamber, esp. in a rampart, with embrasures for artillery. [F, from It. *casamatta,* perhaps from Gk *chásmata,* pl. of *chásma* opening (as military term)] – **casemated,** *adj.*

**casement** /ˈkeɪsmənt/, *n.* **1.** a window sash opening on hinges which are generally attached to the upright side of its frame. **2.** a window with such sashes. **3.** *Poetic.* any window. **4.** a casing or covering. [CASE[2] + -MENT] – **casemented,** *adj.*

casement

**case moth** /ˈkeɪs mɒθ/, *n.* a moth of the Psychoidae, the caterpillar of which constructs a bag of silk, leaves, etc. Also, **bag moth.**

**caseous** /ˈkeɪsiəs/, *adj.* of or like cheese. [L *cāseus* cheese + -OUS]

**caser** /ˈkeɪsə/, *n. Obs. Colloq.* (formerly) a five shilling piece; a crown.

**case record** /keɪs ˈrɛkɔd/, *n.* a file of papers containing a case history.

**casern** /kəˈzɜn/, *n.* (formerly) a lodging for soldiers in a garrison town; a barrack. Also, **caserne.** [F *caserne,* orig., small room for soldiers, from Pr. *cazerna,* from LL var. of *quaterna* group of four]

**case shot** /ˈkeɪs ʃɒt/, *n.* a collection of small projectiles in a case, to be fired from a cannon.

**case stated** /– ˈsteɪtəd/, *n. Law.* form of appeal on a point of law, which consists of a written statement of the facts of the case and the grounds of the decision, submitted to a higher court to obtain its opinion or judgment.

**case study** /ˈ– stʌdi/, *n.* a psychological study of a particular person, family or situation, which serves to illustrate or prove a theory and may be used in management training, social work study, etc.

**casework** /ˈkeɪswɜk/, *n.* practical professional activity in the social services. – **caseworker,** *n.*

**caseworm** /ˈkeɪswɜm/, *n.* a caddis worm or other caterpillar that constructs a case around its body.

**cash** /kæʃ/, *n.* **1.** money, esp. money on hand, as opposed to a money equivalent (as a cheque). **2.** money paid at the time of making a purchase, or sometimes an equivalent (as a cheque), as opposed to credit. *–v.t.* **3.** to give or obtain cash for (a cheque, etc.). **4. cash in one's chips, a.** (in poker, etc.) to hand in one's counters, etc., and get cash for them. **b.** *Colloq.* to die. *–v.i.* **5. cash in, a.** to obtain an advantage. **b.** *U.S. Colloq.* to die. **6. cash in on,** *Colloq.* **a.** to gain a return from. **b.** to turn to one's advantage. **7. cash up, a.** (of shopkeepers, etc.) to add up the takings. **b.** *Obs. Colloq.* to pay in settlement of a debt or fine: *he had to cash up a fiver.* [F *caisse,* from Pr. *caissa,* from L *capsa* box]

**cash account** /ˈ– əkaʊnt/, *n.* **1.** current account. **2.** *Bookkeeping.* a record kept of cash transactions.

**cash and carry,** *n.* **1.** (formerly) a grocer's store which does not deliver goods to the customer's home. **2.** an early form of supermarket.

**cashbook** /ˈkæʃbʊk/, *n.* a book in which to record money received and paid out.

**cash crop** /ˈkæʃ krɒp/, *n.* a crop which, when harvested, offers a quick return of money.

**cash desk** /ˈ– dɛsk/, *n.* a desk in a shop, restaurant, or the like, where money is received from customers.

**cash discount** /– ˈdɪskaʊnt/, *n.* **1.** a term of sale by which the seller deducts a percentage from the bill if the purchaser pays within a stipulated period. **2.** the amount deducted.

**cashed-up** /ˈkæʃt-ʌp/, *adj. Colloq.* (esp. of seasonal workers) recently paid and therefore with ready money: *the cashed-up shearers spent their cheques in the Menindee pubs.*

**cashew** /ˈkæʃu/, *n.* **1.** a tree, *Anacardium occidentale,* native to tropical America, whose bark yields a medicinal gum. **2.** its fruit, a small, edible, kidney-shaped nut (cashew nut). [F, alteration of *acajou,* from Brazilian Pg. *acajú,* from Tupi]

cashew nut

**cash flow** /ˈkæʃ floʊ/, *n.* (of a company) amount of cash generated by a company in a given period. It equals the net profit after tax, less dividends paid out, plus depreciation in that period.

**cashier** /kæˈʃɪə/, *n.* one who has charge of cash or money, esp. one who superintends monetary transactions, as in a bank; bank clerk. [F *caissier,* from *caisse* cash box. See CASH]

**cashmere** /ˈkæʃmɪə/, *n.* **1.** the fine downy wool at the roots of the hair of Kashmir goats of India. **2.** a shawl made of this hair. **3.** a wool fabric of twill weave.

**cash register** /ˈkæʃ rɛdʒəstə/, *n.* a till with a mechanism for indicating amounts of sales, etc.

**casinett** /kæsəˈnɛt/, *n.* a light twill cloth, usu. with wool filling and cotton warp. Also, **casinet, cassinette.**

**casing** /ˈkeɪsɪŋ/, *n.* **1.** a case or covering. **2.** material for a case or covering. **3.** the framework around a door, window or staircase, etc. **4.** the outermost covering of a motor-vehicle tyre. **5.** any frame or framework. **6.** an iron pipe or tubing, esp. as used in oil and gas wells.

**casing shoe** /ˈ– ʃu/, *n.* a steel sleeve fitted to the bottom end of a casing (def. 6) put into a borehole.

**casino** /kəˈsinoʊ/, *n., pl.* **-nos. 1.** a building or large room for meetings, amusements, gambling, etc. **2.** →**cassino. 3.** a small lodge or pavilion. [It., diminutive of *casa* house, from L *casa* cottage]

**cask** /kask/, *n.* **1.** a barrel-like container, usu. wooden, and of varying size, for holding liquids, etc., often one larger and stronger than an ordinary barrel. **2.** the quantity such a container holds. **3.** a lightweight container, usu. cardboard with a plastic lining and small tap, used for holding and serving wine for domestic use. [F *casque,* from Sp. *casco* skull, helmet, cask (for wine, etc.), from *cascar* break, from LL *quassicāre,* from *quassāre* break, shake]

**casket** /'kaskət/, *n.* **1.** a small chest or box, as for jewels. **2.** a coffin. **3. the (Golden) Casket,** a lottery in Queensland. *–v.t.* **4.** *Obs.* to put or enclose in a casket. [orig. uncert.]

**Casparian strip** /kæs'pɛəriən strɪp/, *n. Bot.* an impervious thickened strip in the radial walls of some endodermal cells.

**casque** /kæsk/, *n. Chiefly Poetic.* →**helmet** (def. 1, esp. 1b). [F, from Sp. *casco* helmet. See CASK] – **casqued** /kæskt/, *adj.*

**cassaba** /kə'sabə/, *n.* →**casaba.**

**Cassandra** /kə'sændrə/, *n.* anyone who warns in vain of coming evil. [*Cassandra,* a prophetess of ancient Troy, fated never to be believed]

**cassareep** /'kæsərip/, *n.* the inspissated juice of the root of the bitter cassava, used chiefly in West Indian cookery, as a condiment. [Carib]

**cassata** /kə'satə/, *n.* a gelato containing chopped nuts or mixed dried fruit, etc. [It.]

**cassation**[1] /kæ'seɪʃən/, *n.* annulment; cancellation; reversal. [LL *cassātio,* from *cassāre* annul]

**cassation**[2] /kæ'seɪʃən/, *n.* an 18th century instrumental composition similar to the serenade, often performed out of doors. [G *Kassation,* from *Gasse* street]

**cassava** /kə'savə/, *n.* **1.** any of several tropical plants of the genus *Manihot* of the family Euphorbiaceae, as *M. esculenta* (bitter cassava) and *M. dulcis* (sweet cassava), cultivated for their tuberous roots, which yield important food products. **2.** a nutritious starch from the roots, the source of tapioca. Also, **manioc.** [earlier *casavi,* from Sp. *cazabe,* from Haitian (Taino) *caçábi, cazábbi*]

**casse** /kæs/, *n.* clouding of wine caused by the formation of colloidal complexes of metals. [F]

**Cassegrainian telescope** /kæsə,greɪniən 'tɛləskoʊp/, *n.* a reflecting telescope in which the primary mirror is perforated so that the light may pass through it to the eyepiece or photographic plate. Also, **Cassegrain telescope** /,kæsəgreɪn/. [named after N. *Cassegrain,* 17thC French scientist; see -IAN]

**casserole** /'kæsəroʊl/, *n., v.,* **-roled, -roling.** *–n.* **1.** a baking dish of glass, pottery, etc., usu. with a cover. **2.** any food, usu. a mixture, baked in such a dish. **3.** a small dish with a handle, used in chemical laboratories. *–v.t.* **4.** to bake in a casserole. [F, from *casse* pan, ladle, from LL *cattia,* from Gk *kyáthion* little cup, diminutive of *kýathos*]

**cassette** /kə'sɛt, kæ'sɛt/, *n.* **1.** *Photog.* the film-holder in certain types of camera; magazine. **2. a.** (in a tape recorder) a plastic container enclosing both a recording tape and two hubs about which it winds. **b.** (in a video recorder, computer, etc.) a device of similar principle with wider tape. **3.** a tape recorder designed to use such a device. *–adj.* **4.** (of a tape recorder) designed for playing cassettes.

**cassia** /'kæsiə/, *n.* **1.** a variety of cinnamon (**cassia bark**) from the tree *Cinnamomum cassia,* of southern China. **2.** the tree itself. **3.** any of the herbs, shrubs, and trees constituting the genus *Cassia,* as *C. fistula,* an ornamental tropical tree with clusters of bright yellow flowers, and long pods (**cassia pods**) whose pulp (**cassia pulp**) is a mild laxative, and *C. acutifolia* and *C. angustifolia,* which yield senna. **4.** a cassia pod. **5.** cassia pulp. [OE, from L, from Gk *kasía,* from Heb. *qətsī'āh*]

**cassie-flower** /'kæsi-flaʊə/, *n.* the flower of *Acacia farnesiana* used in perfumery.

**cassimere** /'kæsəmɪə/, *n.* a plain or twilled woollen cloth. [var. of CASHMERE]

**cassino** /kə'sinoʊ/, *n.* a game in which faced cards on the table are taken with eligible cards in the hand. Also, **casino.** [var. of CASINO]

**cassiopeium** /kæsi'oʊpiəm/, *n. Chem.* →**lutetium.**

**cassiterite** /kə'sɪtəraɪt/, *n.* a common mineral, tin dioxide, $SnO_2$, the principal ore of tin. [Gk *kassíteros* tin + -ITE[1]]

**cassock** /'kæsək/, *n.* **1.** a long, close-fitting garment worn by ecclesiastics and others engaged in church functions. **2.** a shorter, light, double-breasted coat or jacket, usu. of black silk, worn under the Geneva gown. [F *casaque,* from It. *casacca,* root *cas-* (cf. F *chasuble*), ? identical with L *casa* house]

**cassowary** /'kæsəwəri/, *n., pl.* **-ries.** any of several large, three-toed, flightless, ratite birds constituting the genus *Casuarius,* of Australasian regions, superficially resembling the ostrich but smaller. [Malay *kasuāri*]

cassowary

**cast** /kast/, *v.,* **cast, casting,** *n.* *–v.t.* **1.** to throw; fling; hurl (oft. fol. by *away, off, out,* etc.) **2.** to throw off or away. **3.** to direct (the eye, a glance, etc.) **4.** to cause (light, etc.) to fall upon something or in a certain direction. **5.** to throw out (a fishing line, anchor, etc.). **6.** to throw down; throw (an animal) on its back or side. **7.** to part with; lose. **8.** to shed or drop (hair, fruit, etc.), esp. prematurely. **9.** to bring forth (young), esp. abortively. **10.** to send off (a swarm), as bees do. **11.** to throw or set aside; discard or reject; dismiss or disband. **12.** to throw forth, as from within; emit or eject; vomit. **13.** to throw up (earth, etc.), as with a shovel. **14.** to put or place, esp. hastily or forcibly. **15.** to deposit (a vote, etc.) **16.** *Theat.* to allow parts of (a play) to actors; select (actors) for a play. **17.** *Metall.* to form (molten metal, etc.) into a particular shape by pouring into a mould; to produce (an object or article) by such a process. **18.** to compute or calculate; add, as a column of figures. **19.** to compute or calculate astrologically, as a horoscope; forecast. **20.** to ponder or consider; contrive, devise, or plan. **21.** to turn or twist; warp. **22.** *Naut.* to bring (a boat) round. **23.** *Naut.* to let go or let loose, as a vessel from a mooring (fol. by *loose, off,* etc.). **24. cast a vote,** to vote (def. 10). *–v.i.* **25.** to throw a fishing line or the like (oft. fol. by *out*). **26.** to calculate or add. **27.** *Obs.* to conjecture; forecast. **28.** to consider; plan or scheme (oft. fol. by *about*). **29.** to search this way and that, as for the scent in hunting (oft. fol. by *about*). **30.** to warp, as timber. **31.** *Naut.* to turn, esp. to get the boat's head away from the wind; tack. **32.** of a sheepdog, to make a wide sweep to get around sheep without disturbing them. *–v.* **33.** Some special verb phrases are:

**cast about,** (fol. by *for* or an infinitive) **1.** to search mentally, as for an excuse. **2.** to scheme.

**cast away, 1.** to reject. **2.** to shipwreck.

**cast back, 1.** to refer to something past. **2.** to show resemblance to a remote ancestor.

**cast down,** to depress; discourage.

**cast off, 1.** to discard or reject. **2.** to let go. **3.** *Print.* to estimate the amount of space necessary for a piece of copy when printed. **4.** *Knitting.* to make the final row of stitches.

**cast on,** *Knitting.* to make the initial row of stitches.

**cast up, 1.** to compute; calculate. **2.** to eject; vomit. **3.** to turn up.

*–n.* **34.** the act of casting or throwing. **35.** *Archery.* the distance a bow can shoot. **36.** the distance to which a thing may be cast or thrown. **37.** *Games.* **a.** a throw of dice. **b.** the number rolled. **38.** *Angling.* **a.** the act of throwing the line or net on the water. **b.** a line so thrown. **c.** the leader, with flies attached. **39.** *Hunting.* a dispersal of the hounds in all directions to recapture a scent. **40.** a secondary swarm of bees, etc. **41.** the sweep a sheepdog makes when rounding up sheep, the first stage of a sheepdog trial. **42.** a stroke of fortune; fortune or lot. **43.** the form in which something is made or written; arrangement. **44.** *Theat.* the actors to whom the parts in a play are assigned. **45.** *Metall.* **a.** the act of casting or founding. **b.** the quantity of metal cast at one time. **46.** something shaped in a mould while in a fluid or plastic state; a casting. **47.** any impression or mould made from an object. **48.** *Med.* rigid surgical dressing usu. made of plaster-of-Paris bandage. **49.** a reproduction or copy, as a plaster model, made in a mould. **50.** outward form; appearance. **51.** sort; kind; style. **52.** tendency; inclination. **53.** a permanent twist or turn, esp. a squint: *to have a cast in one's eye.* **54.** a warp. **55.** a slight tinge of some colour; hue; shade. **56.** a dash or trace; a small amount. **57.** computation; calculation; addition. **58.** a conjecture; forecast. **59.** *Zool.* one of the wormlike coils of sand passed by the lugworm or other worms. **60.** *Geol.* a fossil showing only sur-

face features of an organism. **61.** *Ornith.* a mass of feathers, furs, bones, or other indigestible matters ejected from the stomach by a hawk or other birds. **62.** *Pathol.* effused plastic matter produced in the hollow parts of various diseased organs. **63.** *Naut.* a sounding. *–adj.* **64.** discarded; lost: *the cast shoe of a horse.* **65.** (of a sheep) fallen, and unable to rise. **66.** moulded; having a certain shape. **67.** *Theat.* (of a production) having all actors selected. **68.** *N.Z. Colloq.* drunk. **69. cast for age,** (of sheep, etc.) culled from the flock or herd because of poor condition due to age. [ME *casten,* from Scand.; cf. Icel. *kasta* throw]

**castanet** /kæstəˈnɛt/, *n.* a pair or one of a pair of shells of ivory or hard wood held in the palm of the hand and struck together as an accompaniment to music and dancing. [Sp. *castañeta,* diminutive of *castaña,* from L *castanea* chestnut]

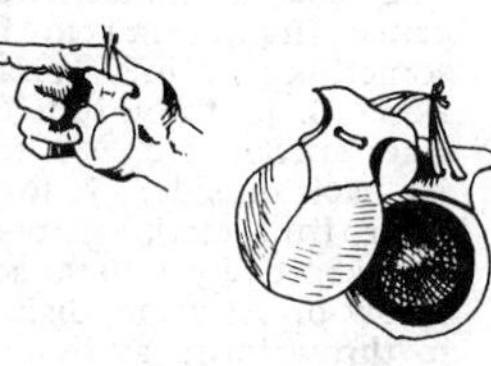
castanets

**castaway** /ˈkastəweɪ/, *n.* **1.** a ship-wrecked person. **2.** an outcast. *–adj.* **3.** cast adrift.

**caste** /kast/, *n.* **1.** *Sociol.* an endogamous and hereditary social group limited to persons in a given occupation or trade, having mores distinguishing it from other such groups. **2. a.** one of the artificial divisions or social classes into which the Hindus are rigidly separated and of which the privileges or disabilities are transmitted by inheritance. **b.** the system or basis of this division. **3.** any rigid system of social distinctions. **4.** the position or rank conferred by the Hindu social system or any similar system: *to lose caste.* [Sp., Pg. *casta* breed, race, from L *castus* pure, CHASTE]

**castellan** /ˈkæstələn/, *n.* the governor of a castle. [L *castellānus* (from *castellum;* see CASTLE); replacing ME *castelain,* from ONF]

**castellany** /ˈkæstəleɪni/, *n., pl.* **-nies.** **1.** the office of a castellan. **2.** the land belonging to a castle.

**castellated** /ˈkæstəleɪtəd/, *adj.* **1.** *Archit.* built like a castle, esp. with turrets and battlements. **2.** having very many castles. – **castellation** /kæstəˈleɪʃən/, *n.*

**castellated nut** /– ˈnʌt/, *n.* a nut having radial slits for the acceptance of a cotter pin; used as a locknut with a bolt having a corresponding hole.

**caster** /ˈkastə/, *n.* **1.** one who or that which casts. **2.** →**castor**².

**caster sugar** /ˈ– ˌʃʊgə/, *n.* finely ground white sugar. Also, **castor sugar.**

**castigate** /ˈkæstəgeɪt/, *v.t.,* **-gated, -gating.** to punish in order to correct; criticise severely. [L *castīgātus,* pp.] – **castigation** /kæstəˈgeɪʃən/, *n.* – **castigator,** *n.*

**Castilian** /kæsˈtɪljən/, *n.* **1.** the accepted standard form of the Spanish language as spoken in Spain. **2.** the dialect of Castile, a former kingdom comprising most of Spain. **3.** a native or inhabitant of Castile. *–adj.* **4.** of or pertaining to Castile.

**casting** /ˈkastɪŋ/, *n.* **1.** the act or process of one that casts. **2.** that which is cast; any article which has been cast in a mould. **3.** the selection of actors for a play, film, etc.

**casting couch** /ˈ– kaʊtʃ/, *n. Colloq.* the couch in a film or stage director's office, supposedly for the seduction of those auditioning; to succeed by means of the casting couch is to gain success in return for sexual favours.

**casting vote** /– ˈvoʊt/, *n.* the deciding vote of the presiding officer when votes are equally divided.

**cast iron** /kast ˈaɪən/, *n.* an alloy of iron, carbon, and other elements, cast as a soft and strong, or as a hard and brittle iron, depending on the mixture and methods of moulding.

**cast-iron** /ˈkast-aɪən/, *adj.* **1.** made of cast iron. **2.** strong; hardy. **3.** inflexible; rigid; unyielding. **4.** incontrovertible: *a cast-iron alibi.*

**castle** /ˈkasəl, ˈkæsəl/, *n., v.,* **-tled, -tling.** *–n.* **1.** a fortified residence, as of a prince or noble in feudal times. **2.** the chief and strongest part of the fortifications of a medieval town. **3.** a strongly fortified, permanently garrisoned stronghold. **4.** a large and stately residence, esp. one which imitates the forms of a medieval castle. **5.** *Chess.* the rook. *–v.t.* **6.** to place or enclose in or as in a castle. **7.** *Chess.* to move (the king) in castling. *–v.i.* **8.** *Chess.* **a.** to move the king sideways two squares and bring the castle to the first square the king passed over. **b.** (of the king) to be moved in this manner. [ME *castel,* from ONF, from L *castellum* fortress, diminutive of *castrum* fortified place; replacing OE *castel* village, from L (Vulgate) *castellum*] – **castled,** *adj.*

**castle in the air,** *n.* a visionary project; a daydream. Also, **castle in Spain.**

**cast-off** /ˈkast-ɒf/, *adj.* **1.** thrown away; rejected; discarded: *cast-off clothing.* *–n.* **2.** a person or thing that has been cast off, esp. an article of clothing. **3.** *Print.* an estimate of the amount of space that a length of copy will occupy when printed.

**castor**[1] /ˈkastə/, *n.* **1.** Also, **castoreum** /kasˈtɔriəm/. a brownish unctuous substance with a strong, penetrating smell, secreted by certain glands in the groin of the beaver, used in medicine and perfumery. **2.** a beaver (hat). **3.** some similar hat. **4.** a beaver. [L, from Gk *kástōr* beaver]

**castor**[2] /ˈkastə/, *n.* **1.** a small wheel on a swivel, set under a piece of furniture, etc., to facilitate moving it. **2.** a bottle or cruet with a perforated top, for holding a condiment. **3.** a stand containing a set of such bottles. **4.** the forward and downward inclination of the kingpin as a means of stabilising the front wheels of a motor car. Also, **caster.** [var. of CASTER]

**castor bean** /– ˈbin/, *n. U.S.* →**castor seed.**

**castor oil** /kastər ˈɔɪl/, *n.* a viscid oil obtained from castor seeds, used as a cathartic, lubricant, etc.

**castor-oil plant** /kastər-ˈɔɪl plænt/, *n.* a tall plant, *Ricinus communis,* native to India but widely naturalised, yielding castor seeds.

**castor seed** /ˈkastə sid/, *n.* the seed of the castor-oil plant.

**castor sugar,** *n.* →**caster sugar.**

**castrate** /ˈkæstreɪt, ˈkas-/, *v.t.,* **-trated, -trating.** **1.** to deprive of the testicles; emasculate. **2.** to deprive of the ovaries. **3.** to mutilate (a book, etc.) by removing parts; expurgate. **4.** (of a woman) to deprive a man of his vigour and self-esteem. [L *castrātus,* pp.] – **castration** /kæsˈtreɪʃən, kas-/, *n.*

**castration complex** /kæsˈtreɪʃən ˌkɒmplɛks/, *n.* in males, the infantile fear of damage to or loss of the genital organs; in females, the fantasy that the penis was once possessed but lost by castration.

**castrato** /kæsˈtratoʊ/, *n., pl.* **-ti** /-ti/, **-tos.** **1.** (in 17th and 18th century opera) a male singer castrated in boyhood to preserve his voice in the upper registers. **2.** the voice of or part sung by such a singer.

**cast steel** /kast ˈstil/, *n.* steel rendered homogeneous by being melted in crucibles or pots.

**casual** /ˈkæʒjuəl/, *adj.* **1.** happening by chance: *a casual meeting.* **2.** unpremeditated; offhand; without any definite intention: *a casual remark, etc.* **3.** careless; tending to leave things to chance; negligent; unconcerned: *a casual air.* **4.** irregular; occasional: *a casual observer.* **5.** informal: *casual clothes.* **6.** accidental: *a casual fire.* **7.** employed only irregularly. **8.** *Obs.* pertaining to persons receiving charity from a district in which they do not permanently live. **9.** *Obs.* uncertain. *–n.* **10.** a worker employed only irregularly. **11.** (*pl.*) relaxed, informal clothes, shoes, etc. [LL *cāsuālis* by chance; replacing ME *casuel,* from OF] – **casually,** *adv.* – **casualness,** *n.*

**casualty** /ˈkæʒjuəlti/, *n., pl.* **-ties.** **1.** an unfortunate accident, esp. one involving bodily injury or death; a mishap. **2.** *Mil.* **a.** a soldier who is missing in action, or who has been killed, wounded, or captured as a result of enemy action. **b.** (*pl.*) loss in numerical strength through any cause, as death, wounds, sickness, capture, or desertion. **3.** one who is injured or killed in an accident. **4.** any person injured accidentally. **5.** Also, **casualty ward.** the section of a hospital to which accident or emergency cases are taken.

**casuarina** /kæʒjəˈrinə/, *n.* any member of the genus *Casuarina,* a group of trees and shrubs with

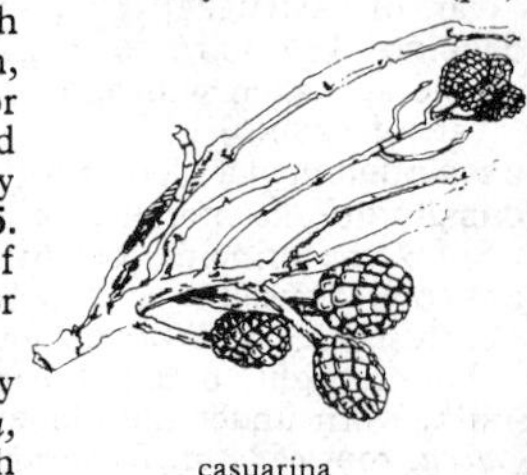
casuarina

few species outside Australia, characterised by jointed stems with leaves reduced to whorls of teeth at the joints; she-oak.

**casuist** /ˈkæʒjuəst/, *n.* **1.** one who studies and resolves cases of conscience or conduct. **2.** an oversubtle or disingenuous reasoner upon such matters. [F *casuiste,* from L *cāsus* CASE[1]]

**casuistic** /kæʒjuˈɪstɪk/, *adj.* **1.** pertaining to casuists or casuistry. **2.** oversubtle; intellectually dishonest; sophistical: *casuistic distinctions.* Also, **casuistical.** – **casuistically,** *adv.*

**casuistry** /ˈkæʒjuəstri/, *n., pl.* **-tries.** the application, or, from an outside point of view, misapplication, of general ethical principles to particular cases of conscience or conduct.

**casus belli** /ˌkasʊs ˈbɛli/, *n.* **1.** an event or political occurrence which brings about a declaration of war. **2.** any event which sparks off a quarrel. [L]

**cat**[1] /kæt/, *n., v.,* **catted, catting.** –*n.* **1.** a domesticated carnivore, *Felis domestica* (or *F. catus*), widely distributed in a number of breeds. **2.** any digitate carnivore of the family Felidae, as the lion, tiger, leopard, jaguar, etc., of the genus *Felis,* and the short-tailed species that constitute the genus *Lynx,* and esp. any of the smaller species of either genus. **3.** a spiteful and gossipy woman. **4.** →**cat-o'-nine-tails. 5.** →**catboat. 6.** →**catfish. 7.** *Naut.* a tackle used in hoisting an anchor to the cathead. **8.** *Colloq.* a person, esp. a young jazz musician or devotee of jazz. **9.** →**tipcat. 10.** *Colloq.* a homosexual who plays a passive role. **11. let the cat out of the bag,** to disclose information, usu. unintentionally. **12. rain cats and dogs,** to rain heavily. **13. the cat's pyjamas (whiskers),** *Colloq.* an excellent person, proposal, etc. –*v.t.* **14.** to flog with a cat-o'-nine-tails. **15.** to hoist (an anchor) to the cathead. [ME; OE *catt, catte,* c. G *Katze,* F *chat;* orig. unknown] – **catlike,** *adj.*

**cat**[2] /kæt/, *n.* a catamaran.

**cat.,** catalogue.

**CAT,** computerised axial tomography.

**cata-,** a prefix meaning 'down', 'against', 'back', occurring originally in words from the Greek, but used also in modern words (English and other) formed after the Greek type, as in *catabolism, catalogue, catalysis, catastrophe.* Also (before a vowel), **cat-;** (before an aspirate), **cath-.** Also, **kata-.** [Gk *kata-,* also (before a vowel) *kat-,* (before an aspirate) *kath-,* representing *katá,* prep., down, through, against, according to]

**catabolism** /kəˈtæbəlɪzəm/, *n. Physiol., Biol.* a breaking down process; destructive metabolism (opposed to *anabolism*). Also, **katabolism.** [Gk *katabolḗ* a throwing down + -ISM] – **catabolic** /kætəˈbɒlɪk/, *adj.* – **catabolically** /kætəˈbɒlɪkli/, *adv.*

**catabolite** /kəˈtæbəlaɪt/, *n. Physiol., Biol.* a product of catabolic action.

**catacaustic** /kætəˈkɒstɪk/, *adj. Optics.* denoting a caustic surface or curve formed by a reflection of light. See **diacaustic.**

**catachresis** /kætəˈkrisəs/, *n., pl.* **-ses** /-siz/. **1.** misuse or strained use of words. **2.** the employment of a word under a false form through misapprehension in regard to its origin: *causeway* and *crawfish* or *crayfish* have their forms by catachresis. [L, from Gk *katáchrēsis* misuse] – **catachrestic** /kætəˈkrɛstɪk/, **catachrestical** /kætəˈkrɛstɪkəl/, *adj.* – **catachrestically** /kætəˈkrɛstɪkli/, *adv.*

**cataclinal** /kætəˈklaɪnəl/, *adj. Geog.* descending with the dip, as a valley. [CATA- + *-clinal* adj. combining form indicating a slope]

**cataclysm** /ˈkætəklɪzəm/, *n.* **1.** any violent upheaval, esp. one of a social or political nature. **2.** *Geog.* a sudden and violent physical action producing changes in the earth's surface. **3.** an extensive flood. [L *cataclysmos,* from Gk *kataklysmós* deluge]

**cataclysmic** /kætəˈklɪzmɪk/, *adj.* **1.** of, pertaining to or resulting from a cataclysm. **2.** of the nature of, or having the effect of, a cataclysm: *cataclysmic changes.* Also, **cataclysmal.**

**catacomb** /ˈkætəkoʊm, -kum/, *n.* **1.** (*usu. pl.*) an underground cemetery, esp. one consisting of tunnels and rooms with recesses dug out for coffins and tombs. **2.** any series of underground tunnels and caves. [ME *catacombe,* OE *catacumbe,* from LL *catacumbas*]

**catadromous** /kəˈtædrəməs/, *adj.* (of fishes) going down a river to the sea to spawn. Cf. **anadromous.**

**catafalque** /ˈkætəfælk/, *n.* a raised structure on which the body of a deceased personage lies or is carried in state. [F, from It. *catafalco,* from LL *cata-* CATA- + *fala* tower + *-icum* -IC; akin to SCAFFOLD]

**Catalan** /ˈkætəlæn, -lən/, *adj.* **1.** pertaining to Catalonia (a region in north-eastern Spain, formerly a province), its inhabitants, or their language. –*n.* **2.** a native or inhabitant of Catalonia. **3.** a Romance language spoken in Catalonia, closely related to Provençal. [Sp.]

**catalane** /kætəˈlani/, *adj.* (of large cuts of meat) garnished with coarsely diced aubergine, sauteed in oil, and served with rice. Also, **à la catalane.** [Sp.]

**catalase** /ˈkætəleɪz/, *n.* an enzyme which catalyses the decomposition of hydrogen peroxide to water and oxygen. [CATAL(YSIS) + -ASE]

**catalectic** /kætəˈlɛktɪk/, *adj.* (of a line of poetry) lacking part of the last foot. Thus the italicised second line is catalectic:

One more unfortunate,
*Weary of breath.*

[LL *catalēcticus,* from Gk *katalēktikós* incomplete]

**catalepsy** /ˈkætəlɛpsi/, *n. Pathol., Psychol.* a morbid bodily condition marked by suspension of sensation, muscular rigidity, fixity of posture, and often by loss of contact with environment. [LL *catalēpsis,* from Gk *katálēpsis* seizure] – **cataleptic** /kætəˈlɛptɪk/, *adj., n.*

**catalo** /ˈkætəloʊ/, *n., pl.* **-loes, -los.** a hybrid resulting from crossing the American bison (buffalo) with cattle of the domestic breeds. Also, **cattalo.** [b. CAT(TLE) and (BUFF)ALO]

**catalogue** /ˈkætəlɒg/, *n., v.,* **-logued, -loguing.** –*n.* **1.** a list, usu. in alphabetical order, with brief notes on the names, articles, etc., listed. **2.** a record of the books and other resources of a library or a collection, indicated on cards, or, occasionally, in book form. **3.** any list or register. –*v.t.* **4.** to make a catalogue of; enter in a catalogue. **5.** to describe the bibliographical and technical features of (a publication and the subject matter it treats). Also, *U.S.,* **catalog.** [F, from LL *catalogus,* from Gk *katálogos* a list] – **cataloguer, cataloguist,** *n.*

**catalpa** /kəˈtælpə/, *n.* any tree of the genus *Catalpa,* of America and Asia, as *C. speciosa,* of the U.S., having large cordate leaves and bell-shaped white flowers; bean tree. [NL, from N Amer. Ind. (Creek) *kutuhlpa* winged head]

**catalyse** /ˈkætəlaɪz/, *v.t.,* **-lysed, -lysing.** *Chem.* to act upon by catalysis. Also, *U.S.,* **catalyze.** – **catalyser,** *n.*

**catalysis** /kəˈtæləsəs/, *n., pl.* **-ses** /-siz/. *Chem.* the causing or accelerating of a chemical change by the addition of a substance (**catalyst**) which is not permanently affected by the reaction. [NL, from Gk *katálysis* dissolution] – **catalytic** /kætəˈlɪtɪk/, *adj., n.* – **catalytically** /kætəˈlɪtɪkli/, *adv.*

**catalyst** /ˈkætələst/, *n.* **1.** *Chem.* a substance that causes catalysis. **2.** the manipulating agent of any event, unaffected by the completion of the event or by its consequences.

**catalytic cracker** /kætəlɪtɪk ˈkrækə/, *n.* a unit (def. 8) for catalytic cracking. Also, **cat cracker, cracker unit.**

**catalytic cracking** /– ˈkrækɪŋ/, *n. Chem.* the cracking of mineral oils of high boiling point by use of a catalyst.

**catamaran** /ˈkætəmərӕn/, *n.* **1.** *Naut.* **a.** a float or raft, usu. of several logs or pieces of wood lashed together. **b.** any craft with twin parallel hulls. **2.** *N.Z.* a bushman's kauri-timber sledge, resembling a catamaran craft. Also, **cat.** [Tamil *katta-maram* tied tree or wood]

catamaran

**catamenia** /kætəˈminiə/, *n.pl. Physiol.* →**menses.** [NL, from Gk *katamḗnia,* neut. pl. of *katamḗnios* monthly] – **catamenial,** *adj.*

**catamite** /ˈkætəmaɪt/, *n.* a boy or youth kept for or participating in homosexual activities. [L *catamītus;* alteration of *Ganymedes.* See GANYMEDE]

**catamount** /ˈkætəmaʊnt/, *n.* →**catamountain.**

**catamountain** /kætəˈmaʊntən/, *n.* any wild animal of the cat family, as the European wildcat, or the leopard or panther. Also, **cat-o'-mountain.**

**cat-and-dog** /kæt-n-ˈdɒg/, *adj.* characterised by constant hostility and frequent quarrels: *they lead a cat-and-dog life together.*

**cataphoresis** /kætəfə'risəs/, *n.* **1.** *Med.* the causing of medicinal substances to pass through or into living tissues in the direction of flow of a positive electric current. **2.** *Phys. Chem.* →**electrophoresis.** [NL, from Gk *kata-* CATA- + *phórēsis* a carrying] – **cataphoretic** /kætəfə'rɛtɪk/, *adj.*

**cataphyll** /'kætəfɪl/, *n. Bot.* a simplified leaf form, as a bud scale or a scale on a cotyledon or rhizome.

**cataplexy** /'kætəplɛksi/, *n. Zool.* a state of complete motionlessness; shamming death. [G *Kataplexie,* from Gk *katáplēxis* amazement]

**catapult** /'kætəpʌlt/, *n.* **1.** a Y-shaped stick with an elastic strip between the prongs for propelling stones, etc. **2.** an ancient military engine for throwing darts, stones, etc. **3.** a device for launching an aeroplane from the deck of a ship, esp. a ship not equipped with a flight deck. *–v.t.* **4.** to hurl as from a catapult. **5.** to hit (an object) by means of a catapult. [L *catapulta,* from Gk *katapéltēs*]

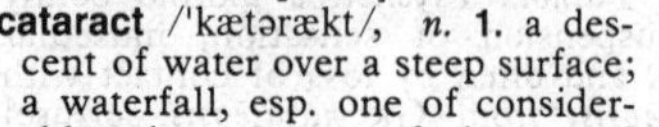

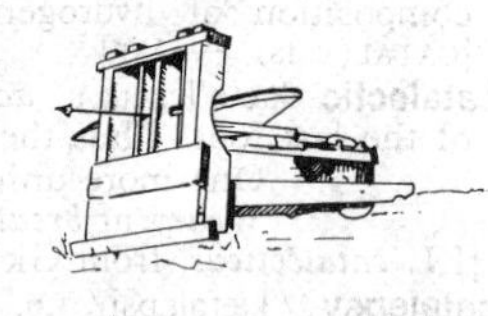

catapult (def. 2)

**cataract** /'kætərækt/, *n.* **1.** a descent of water over a steep surface; a waterfall, esp. one of considerable size. **2.** any furious rush or downpour of water; deluge. **3.** an abnormality of the eye, characterised by opacity of the lens. [ME *cataracte,* from L *cataracta* waterfall, from Gk *kataráktēs* down rushing]

**catarrh** /kə'ta/, *n.* inflammation of a mucous membrane, esp. of the respiratory tract, accompanied by excessive secretions. [L *catarrhus,* from Gk *katárrhous* running down] – **catarrhal,** *adj.*

**catarrhine** /'kætəraɪn/, *adj.* of or relating to a group of primates including the Old World monkeys, higher apes and man, characterised by nostrils which are set close together and directed downward. Cf. **platyrrhine.** [Gk *kata-* CATA- + *rhī́s* nose]

**catastasis** /kə'tæstəsəs/, *n., pl.* **-ses** /-siz/. the part of a drama, preceding the catastrophe, in which the action is at its height. [NL, from Gk *katástasis* appointment, settlement, condition]

**catastrophe** /kə'tæstrəfi/, *n.* **1.** a sudden and widespread disaster. **2.** a final event or conclusion, usu. an unfortunate one; a disastrous end. **3.** (in a drama) the point at which the circumstances overcome the central motive, introducing the close or conclusion; the denouement. **4.** a sudden violent disturbance, esp. of the earth's surface; a cataclysm. [Gk *katastrophḗ* overturning] – **catastrophic** /kætəs'trɒfɪk/, *adj.*

**catastrophism** /kə'tæstrəfɪzəm/, *n. Geol.* the doctrine that certain vast geological changes in the earth's history were caused by catastrophes rather than gradual evolutionary processes. – **catastrophist,** *n.*

**catatonia** /kætə'touniə/, *n.* **1.** *Psychol.* motor behaviour showing abnormal inhibition of movement and negativism. **2.** *Psychiatry.* a form of schizophrenia characterised by extreme negativism, mutism, the assumption of postures, withdrawal, and sometimes excitement. [CATA- + Gk *-tonía,* from *tónos* tension] – **catatonic** /kætə'tɒnɪk/, *adj., n.*

**catbird** /'kætbɜd/, *n.* **1.** a rainforest bird of the family Ptilonorhynchidae, having a call which resembles the mewing of a cat, as the green catbird. **2.** →**white-browed babbler. 3.** a slate-coloured North American songbird, *Dumetella carolinensis.*

**catboat** /'kætbout/, *n.* a boat with one mast, which is set well forward, and a single sail extended by gaff and boom.

**cat-burglar** /'kæt-bɜglə/, *n.* a burglar who enters by climbing.

**catcall** /'kætkɔl/, *n.* **1.** a cry like that of a cat, or an instrument for producing a similar sound, used to express disapproval, at a theatre, meeting, etc. *–v.i.* **2.** to sound catcalls. *–v.t.* **3.** to express disapproval of by catcalls.

**catch** /kætʃ/, *v.,* **caught, catching,** *n., adj. –v.t.* **1.** to capture, esp. after pursuit; take captive. **2.** to ensnare, entrap, or deceive. **3.** to be in time to reach (a train, boat, etc.). **4.** to come upon suddenly; surprise or detect, as in some action: *I caught him doing it.* **5.** to strike; hit: *the blow caught him on the head.* **6.** to intercept and seize (a ball, etc.). **7.** *Cricket.* to dismiss (a batsman) by intercepting and holding the ball after it has been struck by the bat and before it touches the ground. **8.** to check (one's breath, etc.). **9.** to get, receive, incur, or contract (often used figuratively): *to catch a cold, I caught the spirit of the occasion.* **10.** to lay hold of; grasp, seize, or snatch; grip or entangle: *a nail caught his sleeve.* **11.** to allow to be caught; be entangled with: *to catch one's finger in a door, catch one's coat on a nail.* **12.** to fasten with or as with a catch. **13.** to get by attraction or impression: *to catch the eye, the attention, etc.* **14.** to hear or see (a radio or television program): *did you catch that program on the Great Barrier Reef?* **15.** to captivate; charm. **16.** to understand by the senses or intellect: *to catch a speaker's word.* *–v.i.* **17.** to become fastened or entangled: *the kite caught in the trees.* **18.** to take hold: *the door lock catches.* **19.** to become lit, take fire, ignite: *the wood caught instantly.* **20.** to spread or be communicated, as a disease. *–v.* **21.** Some special verb phrases are:

**catch at, 1.** to grasp or snatch. **2.** to be glad to get: *he caught at the chance.*

**catch it,** *Colloq.* to get a scolding or a beating.

**catch on,** *Colloq.* **1.** to become popular. **2.** to grasp mentally, understand.

**catch out, 1.** to trap somebody, as into revealing a secret or displaying ignorance. **2.** to surprise.

**catch up, 1.** to seize quickly: *he caught up the child in his arms.* **2.** to become embroiled or entangled in: *they were caught up in the crowd.* **3.** Also, **catch up with, catch up to.** to follow and reach, become level with, or overtake: *he caught her up by running; he caught up with the rest of the class by hard work.*

**catch up on,** to make up a deficiency: *she caught up on her sleep.*

*–n.* **22.** the act of catching. **23.** anything that catches, esp. a device for checking motion. **24.** that which is caught, as a quantity of fish. **25.** anything worth getting. **26.** *Colloq.* a person of either sex regarded as a desirable matrimonial prospect. **27.** a fragment: *catches of a song.* **28.** *Music.* a round, esp. one in which the words are so arranged as to produce ludicrous effects. **29.** *Cricket.* **a.** the catching and holding of the ball after it has been struck and before it touches the ground. **b.** the wicket so gained. **30.** *Rowing.* the beginning of a stroke. **31.** a difficulty, usu. unseen: *what's the catch?* **32.** →**bell sheep.** *–adj.* **33.** →**catchy** (def. 2). *–v.i.* **34.** to be successful in catching: *this bait catches well.* [ME *cache(n), cacche(n),* from ONF *cachier,* from LL *captiāre,* from L *capere* take]

**catch-as-catch-can** /ˌkætʃ-əz-ˌkætʃ-'kæn/, *n.* a style of wrestling in which any hold is allowed.

**catch-basin** /'kætʃ-beɪsən/, *n.* a receptacle at an opening into a sewer to retain matter that would not pass readily through the sewer. Also, **catchpit.**

**catch-crop** /'kætʃ-krɒp/, *n.* a quick-growing crop grown between the rows of another crop, and harvested first.

**catchcry** /'kætʃkraɪ/, *n.* an ear-catching expression or group of words, voicing a popular sentiment.

**catcher** /'kætʃə/, *n.* **1.** one who or that which catches. **2.** *Baseball.* the player who stands behind the bat or home base to catch the pitched ball.

**catcher resonator** /– 'rɛzəneɪtə/, *n.* →**klystron.**

**catchfly** /'kætʃflaɪ/, *n.* any of various plants, esp. of the genus *Silene,* having a viscid secretion on stem and calyx in which small insects are sometimes caught.

**catching** /'kætʃɪŋ/, *adj.* **1.** infectious. **2.** attractive; fascinating; captivating; alluring.

**catching pen** /'– pɛn/, *n.* **1.** a pen in a woolshed from which a shearer takes sheep to be shorn. **2.** an area of a racetrack for greyhounds which may be enclosed by booms lowered at each end of it, to confine the dogs at the end of their race.

**catching pole** /'– poul/, *n.* long pole used in stockyards to drop a noosed rope over the heads and horns of cattle. Also, **roping pole.**

**catchline** /'kætʃlaɪn/, *n. Print.* headline used for identification purposes as on galley proofs.

**catchment area** /'kætʃmənt ˌɛəriə/, *n.* **1.** Also, **catchment basin.** *Geog.* a drainage area, esp. of a reservoir or river. **2.** *Sociol.* the area from which persons may come to a central institution, as a school or hospital.

**catchpenny** /ˈkætʃpɛni/, *adj., n., pl.* **-ies.** *–adj.* **1.** made to sell readily at a low price, regardless of value or use. *–n.* **2.** anything of little value or use, made merely for quick sale.

**catchphrase** /ˈkætʃfreɪz/, *n.* a phrase caught up and repeated, often meaninglessly, during a vogue.

**catchpit** /ˈkætʃpɪt/, *n.* →**catch-basin.**

**catchpoints** /ˈkætʃpɔɪnts/, *n.pl. Railways.* a break in the rails on an up-gradient designed to catch and derail or divert any trucks accidentally descending against the flow of traffic.

**catchpole** /ˈkætʃpoʊl/, *n. Hist.* a petty officer of justice, esp. one who makes arrests for debt. Also, **catchpoll.** [ME *cachepol,* OE *kæcepol,* from ML *cacepollus* chase-fowl. See CATCH, PULLET]

**catch 22** /ˌkætʃ twɛnti-ˈtu/, *n.* a rule or condition which prevents the completion of a sequence of operations and which may establish a futile self-perpetuating cycle. [from *Catch 22* (1961), by J. Heller, American novelist]

**catch-up** /ˈkætʃ-ʌp/, *adj.* of or pertaining to a price-rise, award increases, etc., which is an attempt to compensate for related increases elsewhere in the economy.

**catchup** /ˈkætʃəp, ˈkɛtʃ-/, *n. Chiefly U.S.* →**ketchup.** Also, **catsup.**

**catchweight** /ˈkætʃweɪt/, *n. Sport.* the chance or optional weight of a contestant, as contrasted with a weight fixed by agreement, etc.

**catchword** /ˈkætʃwɜd/, *n.* **1.** a word or phrase caught up and repeated for effect, as by a political party. **2.** a word printed at the top of a page in a dictionary or other reference book to indicate the first or last article on that page. **3.** a device, used esp. in old books, to assist the reader by inserting at the foot of the page the first word of the following page. **4.** an actor's cue.

**catchy** /ˈkætʃi/, *adj.,* **catchier, catchiest. 1.** pleasing and easily remembered: *a catchy tune.* **2.** tricky; deceptive: *a catchy question.* **3.** occurring in snatches; fitful: *a catchy wind.*

**cat cracker** /ˈkæt krækə/, *n.* →**catalytic cracker.**

**cat-cracking** /ˈkæt-krækɪŋ/, *n. Colloq.* →**catalytic cracking.**

**cate** /keɪt/, *n.* (*usu. pl.*) *Archaic.* a choice food; a delicacy; a dainty. [aphetic var. of ME *acate,* from ONF *acat,* from *acater* buy, from LL *accaptāre* acquire]

**catechesis** /kætəˈkisəs/, *n., pl.* **-ses** /-siz/. oral religious instruction, formerly esp. before baptism or confirmation. [L, from Gk *katēchesis* oral instruction]

**catechetical** /kætəˈkɛtɪkəl/, *adj.* pertaining to teaching by question and answer. Also, **catechetic.**

**catechise** /ˈkætəkaɪz/, *v.t.,* **-chised, -chising. 1.** to instruct orally by means of questions and answers, esp. in Christian doctrine. **2.** to question with reference to belief. **3.** to question closely or excessively. Also, **catechize.** [LL *catēchizāre,* from Gk *katēchízein* teach orally] – **catechisation** /kætəkaɪˈzeɪʃən/, *n.* – **catechiser,** *n.*

**catechism** /ˈkætəkɪzəm/, *n.* **1.** *Eccles.* **a.** an elementary book containing a summary of the principles of the Christian religion, esp. as maintained by a particular church, in the form of questions and answers. **b.** the contents of such a book. **2.** a similar book of instruction in other subjects. **3.** a series of formal questions designed to bring out a person's views. **4.** *Obs.* catechetical instruction. [LL *catēchismus.* See CATECHISE]

**catechist** /ˈkætəkəst/, *n.* **1.** one who catechises. **2.** *Eccles.* one appointed to instruct catechumens in the principles of religion as a preparation for baptism, confirmation, etc. **3.** a student at a theological college, who is appointed part-time to a parish to gain experience. – **catechistic** /kætəˈkɪstɪk/, **catechistical** /kætəˈkɪstɪkəl/, *adj.*

**catechol** /ˈkætətʃɒl, -kɒl/, *n.* a white crystalline benzene derivative, $C_6H_4(OH)_2$, used in photography; pyrocatechol; pyrocatechin. [CATECH(U) + -OL[2]]

**catecholamine** /kætəˈkouləmin/, *n.* any of a group of compounds, as adrenalin, which have important physiological effects on the central nervous system.

**catechu** /ˈkætətʃu/, *n.* any of several astringent substances obtained from various tropical plants, esp. from the wood of two East Indian species of acacia, *Acacia catechu,* used in medicine, dyeing, tanning, etc. Also, **cutch.** [NL, from Malay *kachu*] – **catechuic** /kætəˈtʃuɪk/, *adj.*

**catechumen** /kætəˈkjumən/, *n.* **1.** *Eccles.* one under instruction in the rudiments of Christianity, as in the early Church; a neophyte. **2.** a person being taught the elementary facts, principles, etc., of any subject. [LL *catēchūmenus,* from Gk *katēchoúmenos,* ppr. pass. of *katēcheîn.* See CATECHISE] – **catechumenal,** *adj.*

**categorical** /kætəˈgɒrɪkəl/, *adj.* **1.** not involving a condition, qualification, etc.; explicit; direct: *a categorical answer.* **2.** *Logic.* (of a proposition) unconditional, straightforwardly true or false. **3.** of, pertaining to, or in a category. – **categorically,** *adv.* – **categoricalness,** *n.*

**categorical imperative** /– ɪmˈpɛrətɪv/, *n.* **1.** *Ethics.* the rule of Immanuel Kant, 1724-1804, German philosopher, that one must do only what he can will that all others should do under similar circumstances. **2.** the unconditional command of conscience.

**categorise** /ˈkætəgəraɪz/, *v.t.,* **-rised, -rising.** to class in a category. Also, **categorize.** – **categorist,** *n.*

**category** /ˈkætəgəri, -təgri/, *n., pl.* **-ries. 1.** a classificatory division in any field of knowledge, as a phylum or any of its subdivisions in biology. **2.** any general or comprehensive division; a class. **3.** *Logic, Metaphys.* **a.** a basic mode or phase of existence, as space, quantity, quality. **b.** a basic form or organising principle of reason, as the principle of causality. [L *catēgoria,* from Gk *katēgoría* assertion]

**catena** /kəˈtinə/, *n., pl.* **-nae** /-ni/. a chain or connected series, esp. of extracts from the writings of the fathers of the Church. [L: chain]

**catenary** /kəˈtinəri/, *n., pl.* **-ries,** *adj.* *–n.* **1.** the curve assumed approximately by a heavy uniform cord or chain hanging freely from two points not in the same vertical line. **2.** a system of overhead conductor-wires on an electric railway in which the running wire is suspended from a slack wire strung between supports on either side of the line. *–adj.* **3.** Also, **catenarian** /kætəˈnɛəriən/. pertaining to a catenary. [L *catēnārius* relating to a chain]

**catenate** /ˈkætəneɪt/, *v.,* **-nated, -nating,** *adj. Biol.* *–v.t.* **1.** to link together; form into a connected series. *–adj.* **2.** →**catenulate.** [L *catēnātus* chained] – **catenation** /kætəˈneɪʃən/, *n.*

**catenulate** /kəˈtɛnjələɪt, -lət/, *adj. Biol.* formed of a row or chain of cells or spores.

**cater** /ˈkeɪtə/, *v.i.* **1.** to provide food and service, means of amusement, or the like at functions (fol. by *for*). **2.** to provide that which is desired: *to cater for popular demand, all tastes.* **3.** to go out of one's way to placate or provide for; accommodate (fol. by *to*). [v. use of obs. *cater,* ME *catour,* aphetic var. of *acatour* buyer of provisions, from OF *acateor* buyer. See CATE]

**cater-cornered** /ˈkeɪtə-kɔnəd/, *adj.* **1.** diagonal. *–adv.* **2.** diagonally. [*cater,* adv., diagonally (from F *quatre* four) + *cornered*]

**cater-cousin** /ˈkeɪtə-kʌzən/, *n. Archaic.* **1.** one related by or as by cousinship. **2.** an intimate friend.

**caterer** /ˈkeɪtərə/, *n.* a purveyor of food or provisions, as for entertainments, etc.; one who caters. – **cateress** /ˈkeɪtərɛs/, *n. fem.*

**caterpillar** /ˈkætəpɪlə/, *n.* **1.** the wormlike larva of a butterfly or a moth. **2.** Also, **caterpillar tractor.** a tractor having the driving wheels moving inside endless tracks on either side, thus being capable of hauling heavy loads over rough or soft ground. **3.** the endless tracks themselves. **4.** any device, as a tank or steam-shovel, moving on endless belt (caterpillar) treads; a track-laying vehicle. **5.** *Obs.* one who preys on others; extortioner. [late ME *catyrpel(er),* of uncert. orig. Cf. OF *chatepelose,* lit., hairy cat]

**caterpillar-eater** /ˈkætəpɪlər-itə/, *n.* →**white-winged triller.**

**caterpillar-flower** /ˈkætəpɪlə-flauə/, *n.* a herb of the arum family, *Gymnostachys anceps,* with long narrow leaves and small flowers, which yields a coarse fibre; settler's twine.

**caterpillar weed** /ˈkætəpɪlə wid/, *n.* See **heliotrope** (def. 1).

**caterwaul** /ˈkætəwɔl/, *v.i.* **1.** to cry as cats on heat. **2.** to utter a similar sound; howl or screech. **3.** to quarrel like cats. *–n.* Also, **caterwauling. 4.** the cry of a cat on heat. **5.** any similar sound. [ME *caterw(r)awen,* from *cater* (cf. G *Kater* tomcat) + *wrawen* howl]

**catfall** /ˈkætfɔl/, *n. Naut.* the rope or tackle for hoisting an anchor to the cathead.

**catfight** /ˈkætfaɪt/, *n.* a fight between two women, esp. two prostitutes.

**catfish** /ˈkætfɪʃ/, *n., pl.* **-fishes,** (*esp. collectively*) **-fish. 1.** in Australia, any of various species of fresh water and marine fishes of the families Ariidae (**fork-tail catfish**) or Plotosidae (**eel-tailed catfish**). **2.** elsewhere: **a.** any of numerous fishes having some fancied resemblance to a cat, such as one of the fishes characterised by long barbels, of the North American freshwater family Ameiuridae, many of which are used for food. **b.** any fish of the order Nematognathi, as a bullhead.

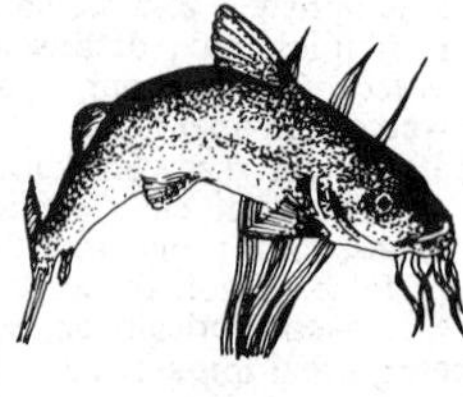
catfish

**catgut** /ˈkætgʌt/, *n.* the intestines of sheep or other animals, dried and twisted, used in surgery as ligatures, as strings for musical instruments, etc.

**cath-,** variant of **cata-** before an aspirate, as in *cathode.*

**Cath.,** Catholic.

**catharsis** /kəˈθasəs/, *n.* **1.** *Aesthetics.* the effect of art in purifying the emotions (applied by Aristotle to the relief or purgation of the emotions of the audience or performers effected through pity and terror by tragedy and certain kinds of music). **2.** *Psychol.* an effective discharge with symptomatic relief but not necessarily a cure of the underlying pathology. **3.** *Psychiatry.* psychotherapy which encourages and permits discharge of pent-up and socially unacceptable effects. **4.** *Med.* purgation. [NL, from Gk *kátharsis* a cleansing]

**cathartic** /kəˈθatɪk/, *adj.* **1.** Also, **cathartical.** inducing catharsis. **2.** evacuating the bowels; purgative. *–n.* **3.** a purgative. [L *catharticus,* from Gk *kathartikós* fit for cleansing, purgative]

**Cathay** /kæˈθeɪ/, *n. Archaic or Poetic.* China. [ML *Cat(h)aya;* cf. Russ. *Kitai,* said to be of Tatar orig.]

**cathead** /ˈkæthɛd/, *n. Naut.* a projecting timber or beam near the bow, to which the anchor is hoisted.

**cathedra** /kəˈθidrə/, *n., pl.* **-drae** /-dri/. **1.** the seat or throne of a bishop in the principal church of his diocese. **2.** an official chair, as of a professor in a university. See **ex cathedra.** [L, from Gk *kathédra* chair]

**cathedral** /kəˈθidrəl/, *n.* **1.** the principal church of a diocese, containing the bishop's throne. *–adj.* **2.** pertaining to or containing a bishop's throne. **3.** pertaining to or emanating from a chair of office or authority.

**catherine-wheel** /ˈkæθrən-wil/, *n.* **1.** a firework which rotates as it burns. **2.** *Archit.* →**rose window.**

**catheter** /ˈkæθətə/, *n. Med.* a flexible or rigid hollow tube employed to drain fluids from body cavities or to distend body passages, esp. one for passing into the bladder through the urethra to draw off urine. [LL, from Gk *kathetḗr,* from *kathiénai* let down]

**catheterise** /ˈkæθətəraɪz/, *v.t.,* **-rised, -rising.** to introduce a catheter into. Also, **catheterize.**

**cathetometer** /kæθəˈtɒmətə/, *n. Physics.* a small telescope so mounted on a graduated vertical pillar that it can move up and down it; used to measure small vertical lengths at a short distance.

**cathexis** /kəˈθɛksəs/, *n. Psychol.* **1.** the investment of emotional significance in an activity, object, or idea. **2.** the charge of mental energy so invested. [Gk *káthexis* holding, retention; rendering G *Besetzung* ]

**cathode** /ˈkæθoʊd/, *n.* **1.** the electrode which emits electrons or gives off negative ions and towards which positive ions move or collect in electrolysis, a radio valve, semiconductor diode, etc. **2.** the negative pole of a battery or other source of current (opposed to *anode*). Also, **kathode.** [Gk *káthodos* way down] – **cathodic** /kəˈθɒdɪk/, *adj.*

**cathode ray** /– ˈreɪ/, *n.* a stream of electrons generated at the cathode during an electric discharge in an evacuated tube.

**cathode-ray oscilloscope** /ˌkæθoʊd-ˌreɪ əˈsɪləskoʊp/, *n. Physics.* an instrument which displays the shape of a voltage or current wave on a cathode-ray tube. Also, **cathode-ray oscillograph.** *Abbrev.:* CRO

**cathode-ray tube** /– ˈtjub/, *n. Electronics.* a vacuum tube that generates a focused beam of electrons which can be deflected by electric and/or magnetic fields. The terminus of the beam is visible as a spot or line of luminescence caused by its impinging on a sensitised screen at one end of the tube. Cathode-ray tubes are used to study the shapes of electric waves, to reproduce pictures in television receivers, as an indicator in radar sets, etc.

**catholic** /ˈkæθlɪk, -əlɪk/, *adj.* **1.** pertaining to the whole Christian body or Church. **2.** universal in extent; involving all; of interest to all. **3.** having sympathies with all; broad-minded; liberal: *to be catholic in one's tastes, interests, etc.* [L *catholicus,* from Gk *katholikós* (def. 2)] – **catholically** /kəˈθɒlɪkli/, *adv.*

**Catholic** /ˈkæθlɪk, -əlɪk/, *adj.* **1.** *Theol.* **a.** (among Roman Catholics) claiming to possess exclusively the characteristics of the one, only, true, and universal Church i.e., unity, visibility, indefectibility, apostolic succession, universality, and sanctity (used in this sense, with these qualifications, only by the Church of Rome, as applicable only to itself and its adherents, and to their faith and organisation; often qualified, esp. by those not acknowledging these claims, by prefixing the word *Roman*). **b.** (among Anglicans) denoting or pertaining to the conception of the Church as the body representing the ancient undivided Christian witness, comprising all the orthodox churches which have kept the apostolic succession of bishops, and including the Anglican Church, the Roman Catholic Church, the Eastern Orthodox Church, Church of Sweden, the Old Catholic Church (in the Netherlands and elsewhere), etc. **2.** pertaining to the Western Church. *–n.* **3.** a member of a Catholic Church, esp. of the Church of Rome.

**Catholic Church** /– ˈtʃɜtʃ/, *n.* a visible society of baptised, professing the same faith under the authority of the invisible head (Christ) and the authority of the visible head (the pope and the bishops in communion with him).

**catholicise** /kəˈθɒləsaɪz/, *v.t., v.i.,* **-cised, -cising.** to make or become catholic or (*cap.*) Catholic. Also, **catholicize.**

**Catholicism** /kəˈθɒləsɪzəm/, *n.* **1.** the faith, system, and practice of the Catholic Church, esp. the Roman Catholic Church. **2.** (*l.c.*) →**catholicity** (def. 1).

**catholicity** /kæθəˈlɪsəti/, *n.* **1.** the quality of being catholic; universality; broad-mindedness. **2.** (*cap.*) the Roman Catholic Church, or its doctrines and usages.

**catholicon** /kəˈθɒləkən/, *n.* a universal remedy; a panacea. [Gk *katholikón*]

**cathouse** /ˈkæthaʊs/, *n. Colloq.* a brothel.

**catiline** /ˈkætəlaɪn/, *n.* any base political conspirator. [named after Lucius Sergius *Catilina,* 108?-62 B.C., Roman politician and conspirator]

**cation** /ˈkætaɪən/, *n. Phys. Chem.* **1.** a positively charged ion which is attracted to the cathode in electrolysis. **2.** any positively charged ion, radical, or molecule. Also, **kation.** [Gk *katión,* ppr. neut., going down]

**catkin** /ˈkætkən/, *n. Bot.* an amentum, as of the willow or birch. [D *katteken* little cat]

**catmint** /ˈkætmɪnt/, *n.* a plant, *Nepeta cataria,* of the mint family, with strongly scented leaves, of which cats are fond. Also, **catnip.** [CAT[1] + MINT[1]]

**catnap** /ˈkætnæp/, *n.* **1.** a short, light nap or doze. *–v.i.* **2.** to take a short, light nap; doze.

**catnip** /ˈkætnɪp/, *n.* →**catmint.** [CAT[1] + *nip,* var. of *nep* catnip, var. of *nept,* from ML *nepta,* L *nepeta*]

**cat-o'-mountain** /kæt-ə-ˈmaʊntən/, *n.* →**catamountain.**

**cat-o'-nine-tails** /ˌkæt-ə-ˈnaɪn-ˌteɪlz/, *n., pl.* **-tails.** a whip, usu. having nine knotted lines or cords fastened to a handle, used to flog offenders.

**catoptrics** /kəˈtɒptrɪks/, *n.* that branch of optics dealing with the formation of images by mirrors. [Gk *katoptrikós* of or in a mirror. See -ICS] – **catoptric, catoptrical,** *adj.*

**cat-rigged** /ˈkæt-rɪgd/, *adj. Naut.* rigged with a single (main) sail and with no headsail.

**CAT scan** /ˈkæt skæn/, *n.* **1.** a series of pictures taken by a CAT scanner. **2.** a medical investigation using this technique.

**CAT scanner** /ˈ– skænə/, *n.* a machine which produces a

series of X-rays by the process of computerised axial tomography.

**cat's cradle** /'kæts kreɪdl/, *n.* **1.** a child's game in which two players alternately stretch a looped string over their fingers in such a way as to produce different designs; sometimes also played by one person alone. **2.** the pattern of string produced in such a game.

**cat's-ear** /'kæts-ɪə/, *n.* any of several species of herb of the genus *Hypochoeris,* as *H. radicata,* a yellow-flowered weed, common on disturbed ground; flat weed. Also, **catsear.**

**cat's-eye** /'kæts-aɪ/, *n.* **1.** any of certain gems exhibiting a chatoyant lustre, but esp. a variety of chrysoberyl (the **oriental** or **precious cat's-eye**). **2.** one of a number of small reflectors marking the centre or side of a road. **3.** the often brightly coloured operculum of certain shellfishes, or the shellfish itself; in New Zealand, commonly, *Lunella smaragda.*

**cat's head** /'kæts hɛd/, *n.* a hardy annual, *Emex australis,* native to southern Africa, having many angular, spiny seeds at ground level, and found as a weed in pasture land; spiny emex.

**cat's-paw** /'kæts-pɔ/, *n.* **1.** a person used by another to serve his purpose; a tool. **2.** *Naut.* a kind of hitch in the bight of a rope, made to hook a tackle on. **3.** *Naut.* a light breeze which ruffles the surface of the water over a comparatively small area. Also, **catspaw.**

**cat's-tail** /'kæts-teɪl/, *n.* **1.** any of the tall marsh plants of the genus *Typha.* **2.** any of certain species of the grass *Koeleria.* Also, **bulrush** (defs 2 and 3).

**catsup** /'kætsəp/, *n.* →**ketchup.**

**cat's whisker** /kæts 'wɪskə/, *n.* **1.** *Radio.* (formerly) the wire forming one contact of the crystal in a crystal detector. **2.** (*pl.*) **the cat's whiskers,** *Colloq.* an excellent proposal, person, etc.: *he thinks he's the cat's whiskers.* **3.** *Colloq.* a small amount, often of distance: *he won the race by a cat's whisker.*

**cattalo** /'kætəloʊ/, *n., pl.* **-loes, -los.** →**catalo.**

**cattery** /'kætəri/, *n.* a place where cats are housed and cared for under appropriate conditions.

**cattish** /'kætɪʃ/, *adj.* **1.** catlike; feline. **2.** spiteful. – **cattishly,** *adv.* – **cattishness,** *n.*

**cattle** /'kætl/, *n.* **1.** ruminants of the bovine kind, of any age, breed, or sex. **2.** such animals together with horses and other domesticated animals. **3.** human beings considered contemptuously or in a mass. [ME *catel,* from ONF, from L *capitāle* wealth, stock. See CAPITAL[1], *n.*]

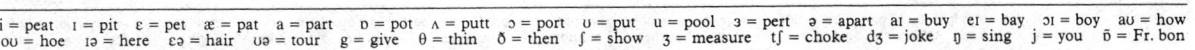

**cattle-bush** /'kætl-bʊʃ/, *n.* any of various Australian trees or shrubs on which cattle may feed in drought periods.

**cattle dog** /'kætl dɒg/, *n.* one of several breeds of dog bred and trained to watch and tend cattle.

cattle dog

**cattleduffer** /'kætldʌfə/, *n.* one who steals cattle, usu. altering the brand. [CATTLE + DUFFER[1]] – **cattleduffing,** *n.*

**cattlegrid** /'kætlgrɪd/, *n.* a pit covered by a grid set in a roadway, designed to prevent the passage of animals, at the same time allowing the passage of wheeled traffic. Also, **cattleramp, cattlepit, cattlestop.**

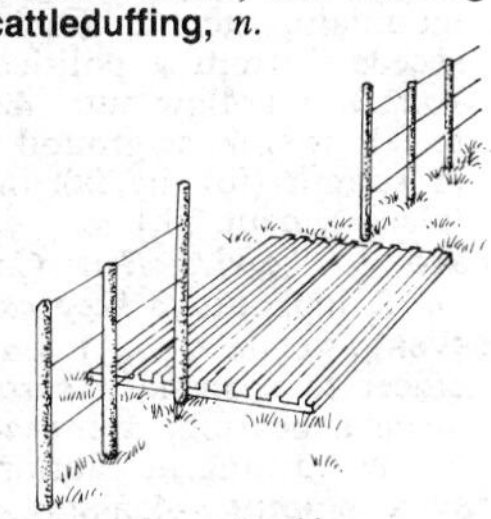

cattlegrid

**cattleman** /'kætlmæn/, *n., pl.* **-men.** the owner or manager of a cattle station.

**cattle prod** /'kætl prɒd/, *n.* →**battery stick.**

**cattle ramp** /'– ræmp/, *n.* →**cattlegrid.**

**cattle-run** /'kætl-rʌn/, *n.* a property on which cattle are grazed for meat production. Also, **cattle station.**

**cattle sickness** /'kætl sɪknəs/, *n.* →**bush sickness.**

**cattlestop** /'kætlstɒp/, *n. N.Z.* →**cattlegrid.**

**cattle tick** /'kætl tɪk/, *n.* any of several ticks which attack cattle.

**cattle trespass** /'– ˌtrɛspəs/, *n. Law.* action brought against the possessor of cattle for damage suffered, irrespective of negligence, if an animal strays from his land onto another's land and thereby causes damage.

**cattle truck** /'– trʌk/, *n.* a truck used for transporting cattle.

**catty**[1] /'kæti/, *adj.,* **-ier, -iest. 1.** catlike. **2.** quietly or slyly malicious; spiteful: *a catty gossip.* [CAT[1] + -Y[1]] – **cattily,** *adv.* – **cattiness,** *n.*

**catty**[2] /'kæti/, *n., pl.* **-ies.** (in China and elsewhere in the East) a weight equal to approx. 0.67 kg. [Malay *katī*]

**catwalk** /'kætwɔk/, *n.* **1.** Also, **manway.** any narrow walking space, as on a bridge, above the stage of a theatre, or in an aircraft. **2.** a long narrow platform on which fashion models parade clothes.

**cat whisker** /'kæt wɪskə/, *n.* →**cat's whisker** (def. 1).

**Caucasia** /kɔ'keɪʒə/, *n.* a region in the Soviet Union between the Black Sea and the Caspian. Also, **Caucasus.**

**Caucasian** /kɔ'keɪʒən/, *adj.* **1.** pertaining to the so-called 'white race', embracing the chief peoples of Europe, south-western Asia, and northern Africa, so named because the native peoples of the Caucasus were considered typical. **2.** of or pertaining to the Caucasus mountain range, in the southern Soviet Union. *–n.* **3.** a member of the Caucasian race. **4.** a native of the Caucasus.

**Caucasic** /kɔ'keɪzɪk/, *adj.* Caucasian.

**Caucasoid** /'kɔkəzɔɪd/, *adj.* Caucasian.

**caucus** /'kɔkəs/, *n.* **1.** a meeting of the parliamentary members of a political party to determine tactics. **2.** *U.S.* a meeting of the local members of a political party to nominate candidates, elect delegates, etc. **3.** *Brit.* (*oft. derog.*) a local committee of a political party exercising a certain control over its actions. [Amer. Ind. (Algonquian) *caucauasa,* adviser]

**caudad** /'kɔdæd/, *adv. Anat., Zool.* towards the tail or posterior end of the body (opposed to *cephalad*). [L *cauda* tail + *ad* to]

**caudal** /'kɔdl/, *adj. Zool.* **1.** of, at, or near the tail. **2.** tail-like: *caudal appendages.* [NL *caudālis,* from L *cauda* tail] – **caudally,** *adv.*

**caudate** /'kɔdeɪt/, *adj. Zool.* having a tail or tail-like appendage. Also, **caudated.** [NL *caudātus,* from L *cauda* tail]

**caudex** /'kɔdɛks/, *n., pl.* **-dices** /-dəsiz/, **-dexes.** *Bot.* **1.** the axis of a plant, including both stem and root. **2.** the woody or thickened persistent base of a herbaceous perennial. [L: tree trunk. See CODEX]

**caudillo** /kɔ'diljoʊ/, *n., pl.* **-los** /-ljoʊz/. the head of the state in some Spanish-speaking countries; leader.

**caudle** /'kɔdl/, *n. Obs.* a warm drink for the sick, as of wine or ale mixed with eggs, bread, sugar, spices, etc. [ME *caudel,* from ONF, diminutive of *caud,* from L *calidus* warm]

**caught** /kɔt/, *v.* past tense and past participle of **catch.**

**caul** /kɔl/, *n.* **1.** a part of the amnion sometimes covering the head of a child at birth, superstitiously supposed to bring good luck and to be an infallible preservative against drowning. **2.** a thin membrane covering the lower intestines of various animals, formerly used to make sausage skins. **3.** *Carp.* a sheet of thin plywood or aluminium used to protect veneers in passing. [ME *calle,* from F *cale* kind of cap]

**cauldron** /'kɔldrən/, *n.* a large kettle or boiler, usu. spherical, with a lid and handle. Also, **caldron.** [ME *cauderon,* from ONF *caudron,* from L *caldāria,* from *cal(i)dus* hot]

**caulescent** /kɔ'lɛsənt/, *adj. Bot.* having an obvious stem rising above the ground. [L *caulis* stalk + -ESCENT]

**caulicle** /'kɔlɪkəl/, *n. Bot.* a small or rudimentary stem. [L *cauliculus,* diminutive of *caulis* stalk]

**caulie** /'kɒli/, *n. Colloq.* a cauliflower.

**cauliflower** /'kɒliflaʊə/, *n.* **1.** a cultivated plant, *Brassica oleracea* var. *botrytis,* whose inflorescence forms a compact, fleshy head. **2.** the head, used as a vegetable. [half adoption, half translation of NL *cauliflōra,* lit., cabbage-flower]

**cauliflower cheese** /– 'tʃiz/, *n.* hot cooked cauliflower served with a cheese sauce.

**cauliflower ear** /– 'ɪə/, *n.* an ear that has been deformed permanently, esp. by blows in boxing.

**cauline** /'kɔlaɪn, -lin/, *adj. Bot.* of or pertaining to a stem, esp. pertaining to or arising from the upper part of a stem. [L *caulis* stalk + -INE[1]]

**caulis** /ˈkɔləs/, *n., pl.* **-les** /-liz/. *Bot.* the main stalk or stem of a plant, esp. of a herbaceous plant. [L]

**caulk** /kɔk/, *v.t.* **1.** to fill or close (a seam, joint, etc.), as in a boat. **2.** to make (a vessel) watertight by filling the seams between its planks with oakum or other materials driven snug. **3.** to drive the edges of (plating) together to prevent leakage. **4.** to fill or close seams or crevices of (a tank, window, etc.) in order to make watertight, airtight, etc. Also, **calk.** [ME *caulke(n)*, from ONF *cauquer,* from L *calcāre* tread, press]

**caulker** /ˈkɔkə/, *n.* **1.** one who caulks. **2.** a caulking tool or device. Also, **calker.** [CAULK + -ER[1]]

**caunter** /ˈkauntə/, *n.* →**counter**[4].

**causal** /ˈkɔzəl/, *adj.* **1.** of, constituting, or implying a cause. **2.** *Gram.* expressing a cause, as a conjunction. – **causally,** *adv.*

**causalgia** /kɔˈzældʒə/, *n.* a neuralgia distinguished by a burning pain along certain nerves, usu. of the upper extremities. [Gk *kaûsis* burning heat + -ALGIA]

**causality** /kɔˈzæləti/, *n., pl.* **-ties. 1.** the relation of cause and effect. **2.** causal quality or agency.

**causation** /kɔˈzeɪʃən/, *n.* **1.** the action of causing or producing. **2.** the relation of cause to effect. **3.** anything that produces an effect; a cause.

**causative** /ˈkɔzətɪv/, *n.* **1.** *Gram.* a word (usu. a verb) denoting causation, as *made* in *he made me eat the apple.* –*adj.* **2.** *Gram.* **a.** pertaining to an affix or other form by which causatives are derived from an underlying word. For example: Gothic *-jan* is a causative affix in *fulljan* (cause to be full, fill). **b.** pertaining to a word or words so derived, esp. one formed from an underlying word that lacks this meaning: *'to fell' is the causative of 'to fall'.* **3.** acting as a cause; productive (fol. by *of*). – **causatively,** *adv.* – **causativeness,** *n.*

**cause** /kɔz/, *n., v.,* **caused, causing.** –*n.* **1.** that which produces an effect; the thing, person, etc., from which something results. **2.** the ground of any action or result; reason; motive. **3.** good or sufficient reason: *to complain without cause.* **4.** *Law.* **a.** a ground of legal action; the matter over which a person goes to law. **b.** a case for judicial decision. **5.** any subject of discussion or debate. **6.** that side of a question which a person or party supports; the aim, purpose, etc., of a group. **7.** *Philos.* the end or purpose for which a thing is done or produced (now only in *final causes*). –*v.t.* **8.** to be the cause of; bring about. [ME, from L *causa*] – **causable,** *adj.* – **causeless,** *adj.* – **causer,** *n.*

**cause célèbre** /– səˈlɛbrə/, *n.* **1.** an issue arousing public debate and partisanship. **2.** *Colloq.* by extension, a cause espoused. [F: a celebrated legal case]

**causerie** /ˈkouzəri/, *n.* **1.** a talk or chat. **2.** a short, informal essay, article, etc. [F, from *causer* talk, from L *causārī* plead]

**causeway** /ˈkɔzweɪ/, *n.* **1.** a raised road or path, as across low or wet ground. **2.** a cobbled or paved way. –*v.t.* **3.** to pave, as a road or street, with cobbles or pebbles. **4.** to provide with a causeway. [var. of *causey way.* See CAUSEY]

**causey** /ˈkɔzi/, *n., pl.* **-seys.** →**causeway.** [ME *cauce,* from ONF *caucie,* earlier *cauciee* (cf. F *chaussée*), from LL *calciāta* paved road]

**causinomancy** /ˈkɔzənou,mænsi/, *n.* divination from objects placed in a fire.

**causse** /kous/, *n. Geog.* a limestone plateau. [F]

**caustic** /ˈkɒstɪk/, *adj.* **1.** capable of burning, corroding, or destroying living tissue: *caustic soda.* **2.** severely critical or sarcastic: *a caustic remark.* **3.** *Maths, Optics.* **a.** denoting a surface to which all the light rays emanating from a single point and reflected by a curved surface (as a concave mirror) are tangent. **b.** denoting a curve formed by a plane section of such a surface. **c.** denoting an analogous surface or curve resulting from refraction. –*n.* **4.** a caustic substance: *lunar caustic.* **5.** *Maths, Optics.* a caustic surface or curve. [L *causticus,* from Gk *kaustikós* capable of burning] – **caustically,** *adv.* – **causticity** /kɒsˈtɪsəti/, *n.*

**caustic potash** /– ˈpɒtæʃ/, *n.* potassium hydroxide, KOH, used in the manufacture of soap, and glass.

**caustic soda** /– ˈsoudə/, *n.* sodium hydroxide, NaOH, used in metallurgy and photography.

**caustic weed** /ˈ– wid/, *n.* a rather succulent prostrate herb, *Euphorbia drummondii,* often poisonous to stock.

**cauter** /ˈkɔtə/, *n.* →**cautery.**

**cauterise** /ˈkɔtəraɪz/, *v.t.,* **-rised, -rising.** to burn with a hot iron, or with fire or a caustic, esp. for curative purposes; treat with a cautery. Also, **cauterize.** – **cauterisation** /,kɔtəraɪˈzeɪʃən/, *n.*

**cautery** /ˈkɔtəri/, *n., pl.* **-ries. 1.** an escharotic substance or a hot iron used to destroy tissue. **2.** the process of destroying tissue with a cautery. [L *cautērium,* from Gk *kautḗrion,* diminutive of *kautḗr* branding iron]

**caution** /ˈkɔʃən/, *n.* **1.** prudence in regard to danger or evil; carefulness; wariness: *proceed with caution.* **2.** a warning. **3.** *Law.* a warning to a person that his words may be used in evidence. **4.** *Mil.* (in drill) a preliminary utterance by an instructor, etc., before a word of command; a precautionary word of command. **5.** *Colloq.* a person or thing that is unusual, odd, amazing, etc. –*v.t.* **6.** to give warning to; advise or urge to take heed. **7.** *Law.* to warn (a person) that his words may be used in evidence. [L *cautio;* replacing ME *caucion* security, from OF]

**cautionary** /ˈkɔʃənri, -əri/, *adj.* of the nature of or containing a warning: *cautionary advice.*

**cautious** /ˈkɔʃəs/, *adj.* having or showing caution or prudence to avoid danger or evil; very careful. – **cautiously,** *adv.* – **cautiousness,** *n.*

**cavalcade** /kævəlˈkeɪd/, *n., v.,* **-caded, -cading.** –*n.* **1.** a procession of persons on horseback or in horse-drawn carriages. **2.** any procession. –*v.i.* **3.** to ride in procession. [F, from It. *cavalcata,* from *cavalcare,* from LL *caballicāre* ride on horseback]

**cavalier** /kævəˈlɪə/, *n.* **1.** a horseman, esp. a mounted soldier; a knight. **2.** one having the spirit or bearing of a knight; a courtly gentleman; a gallant. –*adj.* **3.** haughty, disdainful, or supercilious. **4.** offhand; casual. **5.** unceremonious. –*v.i.* **6.** to play the cavalier. **7.** to be haughty or domineering. [F, from It. *cavalliere,* from *cavallo* horse, from L *caballus*]

**cavalierly** /kævəˈlɪəli/, *adv.* **1.** in a cavalier manner. –*adj.* **2.** characteristic of a cavalier; arrogant.

**cavalla** /kəˈvælə/, *n., pl.* **-la, -las.** →**cavally.**

**cavally** /kəˈvæli/, *n., pl.* **-ly, -lies. 1.** any of various chiefly tropical marine fishes of *Caranx* or related genera. **2.** →**cero.** Also, **cavalla.** [Pg. *cavalla,* Sp. *caballa* horse-mackerel, from L *caballa* mare]

**cavalry** /ˈkævəlri/, *n., pl.* **-ries. 1.** *Mil.* a unit, or units collectively, of an army, which in the past were mounted on horseback, and are now equipped with armoured vehicles in either an armoured or a reconnaissance role. **2.** horsemen, horses, etc., collectively. **3.** *Obs.* horsemanship, esp. of a knight. [F *cavalerie,* from It. *cavalleria* knighthood, from *cavalliere.* See CAVALIER] – **cavalryman** /ˈkævəlrimən/, *n.*

**cavatina** /kævəˈtinə/, *n., pl.* **-ne** /-ni/. a simple song or melody, properly one without a second part and a repeat; an air. [It.]

**cave**[1] /keɪv/, *n., v.,* **caved, caving.** –*n.* **1.** a hollow in the earth, esp. one opening more or less horizontally into a hill, mountain, etc. **2.** *Eng. Hist.* a secession, or a group of seceders, from a political party on some special question. –*v.t.* **3.** to hollow out. **4.** to cause to fall (fol. by *in*). –*v.i.* **5.** to fall or sink, as ground (fol. by *in*). **6.** *Colloq.* to give, yield, or submit (fol. by *in*). [ME, from OF, from L *cava* hollow (places), neut. pl.]

**cave**[2] /ˈkeɪvi/, *Brit. Colloq.* –*v.i., imperative.* **1.** beware. –*n.* **2.** lookout: *to keep cave.* [L]

**caveat** /ˈkeɪviət/, *n.* **1.** *Law.* a legal notice to a court or public officer to suspend a certain proceeding until the notifier is given a hearing: *a caveat filed against the probate of a will.* **2.** any warning or caution. [L: let him beware]

**caveat emptor** /– ˈɛmptɔ/, let the buyer beware (since he buys without recourse). [L]

**caveator** /ˈkeɪvi,eɪtɔ/, *n.* one who enters a caveat.

**cave-dweller** /ˈkeɪv-dwɛlə/, *n.* →**caveman.**

**cave-in** /ˈkeɪv-ɪn/, *n.* a collapse, as of a mine, etc.

**caveman** /ˈkeɪvmæn/, *n.* **1.** a cave-dweller; a man of the Palaeolithic era. **2.** *Colloq.* a man who behaves in a rough, primitive manner, esp. towards women.

**cavendish** /ˈkævəndɪʃ/, *n.* tobacco softened, sweetened, and pressed into cakes.

**cavern** /ˈkævən/, *n.* a cave, esp. a large cave. [ME *caverne,* from F, from L *caverna* cave]

**cavernous** /ˈkævənəs/, *adj.* **1.** containing caverns. **2.** deep-set: *cavernous eyes.* **3.** hollow and deep-sounding: *a cavernous voice.* **4.** full of small cavities; porous. **5.** of a cavern: *cavernous darkness.* – **cavernously,** *adj.*

**cavesson** /kəˈvɛsən/, *n.* the decorative noseband of a bridle or a halter. [It. *cavezzone*]

**cavetto** /kəˈvɛtoʊ/, *n., pl.* **-ti** /-ti/, **-tos.** *Archit.* a concave moulding, as in a cornice, with the curve usu. a quarter circle. [It., diminutive of *cavo,* from L *cavum* hollow (place)]

**caviar** /ˈkævia, kæviˈa/, *n.* **1.** the roe of sturgeon and other large fish, pressed and salted, considered a great delicacy. **2. caviar to the general,** something beyond appeal to the popular taste. Also, **caviare.** [F, from It. *caviaro,* from Turk. *khāviār;* replacing *cavialy,* from It. *caviale,* var. of *caviaro*]

**cavicorn** /ˈkævəkɔn/, *adj. Zool.* hollow-horned, as the ruminants with true horns, as distinguished from bony antlers. [L: *cavi-* (combining form of *cavus* hollow) + stem of *-cornis* horned]

**cavil** /ˈkævəl/, *v.,* **-illed, -illing** or (*U.S.*) **-iled, -iling,** *n.* *–v.i.* **1.** to raise irritating and trivial objections; find fault unnecessarily. *–n.* **2.** a trivial and annoying objection. **3.** the raising of such objections. [F *caviller,* from L *cavillāri,* from *cavilla* a jeering] – **caviller;** *U.S.,* **caviler,** *n.*

**cavitation** /kævəˈteɪʃən/, *n. Engineering.* rapid formation and collapse of vapour pockets in a flowing liquid in regions of very low pressure, a frequent cause of serious structural damage to propellers, pumps, etc.

**cavity** /ˈkævəti/, *n., pl.* **-ties.** **1.** any hollow place; a hollow: *a cavity in the earth.* **2.** *Anat.* a hollow space within the body, an organ, a bone, etc. **3.** *Dentistry.* the loss of tooth structure, most commonly produced by caries; a cavity may be artificially made to support dental restorations. [F *cavité,* from LL *cavitas* hollowness]

**cavity block** /ˈ– blɒk/, *n. Bldg Trades.* a block used for cavity walls.

**cavity-brick wall** /kævəti-brɪk ˈwɔl/, *n.* a brick wall made to a thickness of at least two bricks, with a vertical space left within the wall.

**cavity resonator** /kævəti ˈrɛzəneɪtə/, *n.* →**resonator** (def. 4a).

**cavity wall** /ˈ– wɔl/, *n. Bldg Trades.* a type of double wall designed to retain heat in a building, and prevent the penetration of moisture, having a gap, usu. of 50 mm, between its leaves.

**cavort** /kəˈvɔt/, *v.i. Colloq.* to prance or caper about. [orig. unknown]

**cavy** /ˈkeɪvi/, *n., pl.* **-vies.** any of various short-tailed South American rodents of the family Caviidae, esp. those of the genus *Cavia* which includes the domestic guineapig. [NL *Cavia,* from Galibi *cabiai*]

**caw** /kɔ/, *n.* **1.** the cry of the crow, raven, etc. *–v.i.* **2.** to utter this cry or a similar sound. [imitative]

**cay** /keɪ, ki/, *n.* a small island; key. [Sp. *cayo;* akin to QUAY]

**cayenne** /keɪˈɛn/, *n.* a hot, biting condiment composed of the ground pods and seeds of any of several varieties of *Capsicum;* red pepper. Also, **cayenne pepper.** [named after *Cayenne,* in French Guiana]

**cayman** /ˈkeɪmən/, *n., pl.* **-mans.** →**caiman.**

**Cazaly** /kəˈzeɪli/, *n. in the phrase* **up there Cazaly,** (a cry of encouragement). Also, **up there Cazzer.** [from Roy *Cazaly,* 1893-1963, an Australian Rules footballer]

Up there, Cazaly!

**c.b.,** confined to barracks.

**Cb,** *Chem.* columbium.

**C.B.** /si ˈbi/, **1.** Companion of the (Order of the) Bath. **2.** Also, **CB.** citizen's BAND.

**CBD,** Central Business District.

**C.B.E.** /si bi ˈi/, Commander of the (Order of the) British Empire.

**CBer** /siˈbiə/, *n.* an operator on or owner of a citizen band radio.

**CB radio** /si bi ˈreɪdioʊ/, *n.* a citizen band radio. Also, **CB.**

**CBU,** completely built up.

**cc.,** **1.** cubic capacity. **2.** cubic centimetre or centimetres. **3.** carbon copy. Also, **c.c.**

**C clef** /si ˈklɛf/, *n. Music.* a sign indicating the position of middle C on the stave.

C clef: A, soprano clef; B, alto clef; C, tenor clef

**cd.,** candela.

**Cd,** *Chem.* cadmium.

**C.D.,** **1.** corps diplomatique. **2.** Certificate of Deposit. **3.** Civil Defence.

**Cdo,** commando.

**Cdt,** cadet.

**Ce,** *Chem.* cerium.

**cease** /sis/, *v.,* **ceased, ceasing,** *n.* *–v.i.* **1.** to stop (moving, speaking, etc.): *she ceased to cry.* **2.** to come to an end. **3.** *Obs.* to die. *–v.t.* **4.** to put a stop or end to; discontinue: *to cease work.* *–n.* **5.** *Obs.* cessation. **6. without cease,** endlessly. [ME *cess(en),* from OF *cesser,* from L *cessāre,* frequentative of *cēdere* go, yield]

**cease-fire** /sis-ˈfaɪə/, *n.* **1.** an order to cease firing. **2.** a cessation of active hostilities; truce.

**ceaseless** /ˈsisləs/, *adj.* without stop or pause; unending; incessant. – **ceaselessly,** *adv.*

**cecum** /ˈsikəm/, *n. U.S.* →**caecum**

**cedar** /ˈsidə/, *n.* **1.** any of the Old World coniferous trees constituting the genus *Cedrus,* as *C. libani* (**cedar of Lebanon**), a stately tree native to Asia Minor, etc. **2.** any of various junipers, as *Juniperus virginiana* (**red cedar**), an American tree with a fragrant reddish wood used for making lead pencils, etc. **3.** any of various other coniferous trees as *Libocedrus decurrens,* the **incense cedar** of the south-western U.S. **4.** any of various non-coniferous trees, as *Toona australis* or the New Zealand kohekohe. **5.** the wood of any of these trees. [ME *cedir,* etc., OE *ceder,* from L *cedrus,* from Gk *kédros;* replacing ME *cedre,* from OF]

**cedar-getter** /ˈsidə-gɛtə/, *n.* (formerly) a man employed to cut and haul the cedar trees which were much prized for their timber.

**cedarn** /ˈsidən/, *adj. Poetic.* **1.** of cedar trees. **2.** made of cedar wood.

**cedar wattle** /ˈsidə wɒtl/, *n.* a tree of shady mountain gullies of eastern Australia, *Acacia elata,* with creamy flowers. Also, **mountain cedar wattle.**

**cede** /sid/, *v.t.,* **ceded, ceding.** to yield or formally resign and surrender to another; make over, as by treaty: *to cede territory.* [L *cēdere* go, withdraw, yield, grant]

**cedilla** /səˈdɪlə/, *n.* a mark placed under *c* before *a, o,* or *u,* as in *façade,* to show that it has the sound of *s.* [Sp. *cedilla,* now *zedilla,* the mark (orig. a *z* written after *c*), from diminutive of L *zēta,* from Gk: name of letter *z*]

**cee-spring** /ˈsi-sprɪŋ/, *n.* a spring, shaped like the letter C, which supports the body of a vehicle. Also, **C-spring.**

**ceil** /sil/, *v.t.* **1.** to overlay (the interior upper surface of a building or room) with wood, plaster, etc.; to provide with a ceiling. **2.** to provide (a ship) with interior planking surfaces. [late ME. Cf. F *ciel* sky, heaven, canopy, from L *caelum* sky, heaven]

**ceiling** /ˈsilɪŋ/, *n.* **1.** the overhead interior lining of a room; the surface of a room opposite the floor. **2.** top limit: *a price ceiling on rent.* **3.** *Naut.* the flooring, usu. wooden, covering the double bottom tanks, at the bottom of a ship's hold. **4.** *Aeron.* **a.** the maximum altitude to which a particular aircraft can rise under specified conditions. **b.** the maximum altitude from which the earth can be seen on a particular day, usu. equal to the distance between the earth and the base of the lowest cloudbank. **5.** *Obs.* the act of one who ceils. *–adj.* **6.** *Colloq.* maximum. [from CEIL]

**ceiling dog** /ˈ– dɒg/, *n.* a large nail bent twice at right angles in different planes, so that the points at each end are at right angles to each other in plane, and used to hold cross members of a roof together. Also, **dog nail.**

**ceilometer** /siˈlɒmətə/, *n. Meteorol.* a device for measuring and recording the height of clouds, based on the reflection of a beam of light from a cloud base. [CEIL(ING) + -O- + -METER[1]]

**celadon** /ˈsɛlədɒn/, *n.* **1.** a pale green colour. **2.** pottery or porcelain, esp. from China, with a delicate pale green glaze. *–adj.* **3.** pale green. [F]

**celandine** /ˈsɛləndaɪn/, *n.* **1.** a plant, of Europe and western Asia, *Chelidonium majus* **(greater celandine),** family Papaveraceae, with yellow flowers in loose few-flowered umbels. **2.** a European buttercup, *Ranunculus ficaria* (**lesser celandine**), with bright yellow flowers. [ME *celidoine,* from OF, from L *chelīdonia,* from Gk *chelidónion, chelidṓn* swallow]

**celanese** /sɛləˈniz/, *n.* **1.** an acetate rayon yarn or fabric. **2.** (*cap.*) a trademark for this yarn or fabric.

**celastraceous** /sɛləˈstreɪʃəs/, *adj.* belonging to the plant family Celastraceae.

**-cele**[1], a word element meaning 'tumour', as in *varicocele.* [combining form representing Gk *kḗlē*]

**-cele**[2], variant of **-coele.**

**celebrant** /ˈsɛləbrənt/, *n.* **1. a.** the priest who officiates at the performance of a religious rite. **b.** the secular official who conducts a civil marriage; marriage celebrant. **2.** a participant in a public religious rite. **3.** a participant in any celebration.

**celebrate** /ˈsɛləbreɪt/, *v.*, **-brated, -brating.** *–v.t.* **1.** to observe (a day) or commemorate (an event) with ceremonies or festivities. **2.** to make known publicly; proclaim. **3.** to sound the praises of; extol. **4.** to perform with appropriate rites and ceremonies; solemnise. *–v.i.* **5.** to observe a day or commemorate an event with ceremonies or festivities. **6.** to perform a religious ceremony, esp. mass. **7.** *Colloq.* to engage in a festive activity; have a party. [L *celebrātus,* pp.] – **celebrator,** *n.*

**celebrated** /ˈsɛləbreɪtəd/, *adj.* famous; renowned; well-known.

**celebration** /sɛləˈbreɪʃən/, *n.* **1.** the act of celebrating. **2.** that which is done to celebrate anything.

**celebrity** /səˈlɛbrəti/, *n., pl.* **-ties.** **1.** a famous or wellknown person. **2.** fame; renown.

**celeriac** /səˈlɛriæk/, *n.* a variety of celery having a large bulbous root which is cooked as a vegetable.

**celerity** /səˈlɛrəti/, *n.* swiftness; speed. [ME *celerite,* from L *celeritas*]

**celery** /ˈsɛləri/, *n.* **1.** a plant, *Apium graveolens,* of the parsley family, whose leafstalks are used raw for salad, and cooked as a vegetable. **2.** any of a number of other related or similar plants as *Apium leptophyllum,* **slender celery,** and *Aciphylla glacialis,* **mountain celery.** [F *céleri,* from d. It. *selleri* (pl.), from LL *selīnon,* from Gk: parsley]

**celery cabbage** /– ˈkæbɪdʒ/, *n.* →**Chinese cabbage.**

**celery pine** /– ˈpaɪn/, *n.* →**celery-top pine.**

**celery-top pine** /ˌsɛləri-tɒp ˈpaɪn/, *n.* any tree of the genus *Phyllocladus,* with distinctive deeply cut, fern-like foliage, as the useful softwood timber tree, *P. aspleniifolius* of Tasmania.

**celerywood** /ˈsɛləriwʊd/, *n.* an ornamental tree, *Polyscias elegans,* which emits the smell of celery when the bark is stripped back.

**celesta** /səˈlɛstə/, *n.* a musical instrument consisting essentially of steel plates struck by hammers, and having a keyboard. Also, **celeste** /səˈlɛst/. [F *céleste,* lit., heavenly]

**celestial**[1] /səˈlɛstiəl/, *adj.* **1.** pertaining to the spiritual or invisible heaven; heavenly; divine: *celestial bliss.* **2.** pertaining to the sky or visible heaven. *–n.* **3.** an inhabitant of heaven. [ME, from OF, from *celesti-* (from L *caelestis* heavenly) + *-al* -AL[1]] – **celestially,** *adv.*

**celestial**[2] /səˈlɛstiəl/, *Colloq.* *–n.* **1.** a Chinese; one of Chinese origin. *–adj.* **2.** Chinese. [from *Celestial* Empire, translation of Chinese name for China]

**celestial equator** /– əˈkweɪtə/, *n. Astron., Navig.* a great circle of the celestial sphere, the plane of which is perpendicular to the axis of the earth.

**celestial globe** /– ˈgloʊb/, *n. Astron.* a model of the celestial sphere, on which the relative positions of the stars may be indicated without distortion.

**celestial guidance** /– ˈgaɪdns/, *n.* a system of steering missiles or spacecraft which uses the positions of celestial bodies as points of reference.

**celestial latitude** /– ˈlætətʃud/, *n.* →**latitude** (def. 3a).

**celestial longitude** /– ˈlɒŋgətʃud/, *n.* →**longitude** (def. 2a).

**celestial navigation** /– nævəˈgeɪʃən/, *n.* navigation based on the positions of celestial bodies. Also, **astronavigation.**

**celestial pole** /– ˈpoʊl/, *n.* →**pole**[2] (def. 2).

**celestial sphere** /– ˈsfɪə/, *n. Astron.* the imaginary spherical shell formed by the sky, usu. represented as an infinite sphere of which the observer's position is the centre.

**celestite** /ˈsɛləstaɪt/, *n.* a white to delicate blue mineral, strontium sulphate, $SrSO_4$, occurring in tabular crystals, and the principal ore of strontium. Also, **celestine** /ˈsɛləstən, -əstaɪn/. [L *caelestis* heavenly (in allusion to the delicate blue of some specimens) + -ITE[1]]

**celiac** /ˈsiliæk/, *adj. Anat.* →**coeliac.**

**celibacy** /ˈsɛləbəsi/, *n., pl.* **-cies.** **1.** the unmarried state. **2.** (of priests, etc.) abstention by vow from marriage. **3.** abstension from sexual intercourse; chastity.

**celibate** /ˈsɛləbət/, *n.* **1.** one who remains unmarried, esp. for religious reasons. *–adj.* **2.** unmarried. **3.** chaste. [L *caelibātus,* from *caelebs* unmarried]

**cell** /sɛl/, *n.* **1.** a small room in a convent, prison, etc. **2.** any small compartment, bounded area, receptacle, case, etc. **3.** a small group acting as a unit within a larger organisation. **4.** *Biol.* **a.** a plant or animal structure, usu. microscopic, containing nuclear and cytoplasmic material, enclosed by a semi-permeable membrane (animal) or cell wall (plant); the structural unit of plant and animal life. **b.** a minute cavity or interstice, as in animal or plant tissue. **5.** *Entomol.* one of the areas into which an insect's wing is divided by the veins. **6.** *Bot.* the pollen sac of an anther. **7.** *Elect.* a device which generates electricity and which forms the whole, or a part of, a voltaic battery, consisting in one of its simplest forms of two plates, each of a different metal, placed in a jar containing a dilute acid or other electrolyte (**voltaic cell**). **8.** *Phys. Chem.* a device for producing electrolysis, consisting essentially of the electrolyte, its container, and the electrodes (**electrolytic cell**). **9.** *Aeron.* **a.** the part of the wing structure of a biplane on either side of the fuselage. **b.** the gas-container of a balloon. **10.** *Archit.* one of the compartments of a groin or rib vault; web. **11.** *Eccles.* a monastery or nunnery, usu. small, dependent on a larger religious house. [ME *celle,* OE *cell,* from L *cella* room]

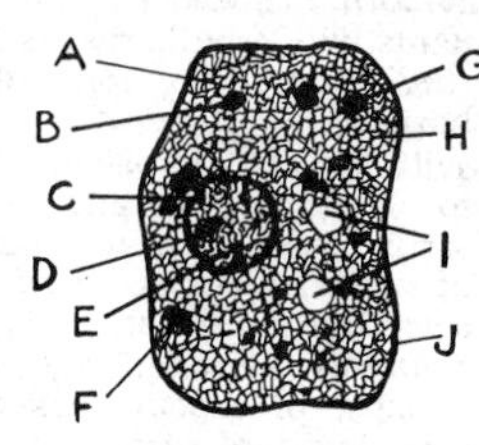


diagram of an organic cell (def. 4a): A, centrosphere; B, centrosome; C, nucleus; D, nucleolus; E, chromatin network; F, karyosome; G, plastid; H, cytoplasm; I, vacuole; J, cell wall

**cella** /ˈsɛlə/, *n., pl.* **cellae** /ˈsɛli/. *Archit.* (in ancient Greek or Roman temples) an enclosed inner room, the sanctuary containing the statue of the divinity. [L]

**cellar** /ˈsɛlə/, *n.* **1.** a room or set of rooms for the storage of foodstuffs, etc., now always either wholly or partly underground, and usu. beneath a building. **2.** an underground room or store; basement. **3.** a wine cellar. **4.** a supply or stock of wines. **5.** (*pl.*) a liquor store. **6.** →**saltcellar.** *–v.t.* **7.** to place or store in a cellar. [L *cellārium* pantry; replacing ME *celer,* from AF, var. of OF *celier,* from L *cellārium*]

**cellarage** /ˈsɛlərɪdʒ/, *n.* **1.** cellar space. **2.** charges for storing in a cellar.

**cellarer** /ˈsɛlərə/, *n.* the steward of a monastery.

**cellaret** /sɛləˈrɛt/, *n.* a cabinet for wine bottles, etc.

**cellarman** /ˈsɛləmən/, *n.* a man in charge of a cellar, esp. that of a hotel or club.

**cellarmaster** /ˈsɛləmastə/, *n.* **1.** the person responsible for the choice, buying and storage of wines in a club, etc. **2.** the person in charge of the wine at a function.

**cell-division** /ˈsɛl-dəvɪʒən/, *n. Biol.* the division of a cell in reproduction or growth.

**cellist** /ˈtʃɛləst/, *n.* a player on the cello. Also, **'cellist, violoncellist.**

**cello** /ˈtʃɛloʊ/, *n., pl.* **-los, -li.** a four-stringed instrument of the violin family, with a pitch between that of the viola and the double bass which is rested vertically on the floor between the player's knees. Also, **'cello, violoncello.** [short form of VIOLONCELLO]

**cellophane** /'sɛləfeɪn/, *n.* a transparent, paper-like product of viscose, impervious to moisture, germs, etc., used to wrap sweets, tobacco, etc. [Trademark; CELL(ULOSE) + -O- + -PHANE]

**cell-sap** /'sɛl-sæp/, *n.* the aqueous solution filling the vacuole of a plant cell.

**cellular** /'sɛljələ/, *adj.* **1.** pertaining to or characterised by cellules or cells, esp. minute compartments or cavities. **2.** *Textiles.* loosely woven, with open airholes. [NL *cellulāris,* from L *cellula* little room]

cello

**cellulase** /'sɛljəleɪz/, *n. Biochem.* an enzyme which hydrolyses cellulose, and is found in bacteria, fungi and lower animals.

**cellule** /'sɛljul/, *n.* a little cell. [L *cellula*]

**cellulite** /'sɛljəlaɪt/, *n.* fatty deposits, resulting in a dimply appearance of the skin, which cannot be removed by dieting or exercise.

**cellulitis** /sɛljə'laɪtəs/, *n. Pathol.* inflammation of cellular tissue. [NL, from L *cellula* little cell + *-ītis* -ITIS]

**celluloid** /'sɛljəlɔɪd/, *n.* **1.** *Chem.* a plastic consisting essentially of a solid solution of soluble guncotton (cellulose nitrate) and camphor, usu. highly flammable, used for toys, toilet articles, photographic film and as a substitute for amber ivory, vulcanite, etc. **2.** films; the cinema. *–adj.* **3.** of or pertaining to films; appearing in a film: *the celluloid hero of my dreams.* **4.** unreal; synthetic. [Trademark; CELLUL(OSE) + -OID]

**cellulose** /'sɛljəlous/, *n.* **1.** *Chem.* an inert substance, a carbohydrate, the chief constituent of the cell walls of plants, and forming an essential part of wood, cotton, hemp, paper, etc. *–v.t.* **2.** to apply a cellulose lacquer to (a motor car, etc.). [L *cellula* little cell + -OSE[2]]

**cellulose acetate** /– 'æsəteɪt/, *n.* an acetic ester of cellulose used to make textiles, artificial leathers, yarns, etc.

**cellulose lacquer** /– 'lækə/, *n.* a quick-drying lacquer consisting of cellulose nitrate or of cellulose acetate, with suitable pigments and plasticisers dissolved in a volatile solvent.

**cellulose nitrate** /– 'naɪtreɪt/, *n.* a nitric ester of cellulose used in the manufacture of lacquers and explosives.

**cellulous** /'sɛljələs/, *adj.* full or consisting of cells.

**cell wall** /'sɛl wɔl/, *n.* the definite boundary or wall which is usu. part of the structure of a biological cell, esp. a plant cell. See **cell** (def. 4a).

**celom** /'siləm/, *n. Zool.* →**coelom.**

**celosia** /sə'louziə/, *n.* any of a number of plant species of the genus *Celosia,* erect herbs native to warmer regions of Asia, Africa and America, some of which, as *C. argentea* var. *cristata,* **cockscomb,** are grown for their large gold or crimson inflorescences.

**Celsius** /'sɛlsiəs/, *adj.* **1.** denoting or pertaining to a scale of temperature on which the temperature in degrees Celsius (°C) is numerically equal to the temperature in kelvins (k) reduced by 273.15. On this scale the triple point of water is 0.01°C and the boiling point of water under a pressure of 101.325 kPa is approximately 100°C. The degree Celsius is the unit of temperature equal to the kelvin. *–n.* **2.** the Celsius scale. *Symbol:* C [named after A. *Celsius,* 1701-44, Swedish astronomer]

**celt** /sɛlt/, *n. Archaeol.* an axe of stone or metal without perforation or groove for hafting. [LL *celtis* chisel]

**Celt** /kɛlt, sɛlt/, *n.* a member of an Indo-European people now represented chiefly by the Irish, Gaels, Welsh, and Bretons. Also, **Kelt.** [L *Celtae,* pl., from Gk *Keltoí*]

**Celt.,** Celtic.

**Celtic** /'kɛltɪk, 'sɛltɪk/, *n.* **1.** a group of Indo-European languages including Irish, Scottish, Gaelic, Welsh, Breton, etc., surviving now in Ireland, the Scottish Highlands, Wales, and Brittany. *–adj.* **2.** of the Celts or their language. Also, **Keltic.** **– Celticism** /'kɛltəsɪzəm, 'sɛl-/, *n.*

**Celtic cross** /– 'krɒs/, *n.* a cross resembling a Latin cross, but having a circle around the upper members centred on their point of intersection.

**Celto-,** a word element meaning 'Celtic'.

**cembalo** /'tʃɛmbəlou/, *n. Music.* **1.** →**dulcimer** (def. 1). **2.** →**harpsichord.** [It.] **– cembalist,** *n.*

**cement** /sə'mɛnt/, *n.* **1.** any of various substances which are soft when first prepared but later become hard or stonelike, used for joining stones, making floors, etc. **2.** a material of this kind (the ordinary variety, often called **Portland cement**) commonly made by burning a mixture of clay and limestone, used for making concrete for foundations or the like, covering floors, etc. **3.** *Geol.* the compact groundmass surrounding and binding together the fragments of clastic rocks. **4.** anything that binds or unites. **5.** *Dentistry.* an adhesive plastic substance used to fill teeth or to pack fillings or inlays into teeth. **6.** *Dentistry.* →**cementum.** **7.** *Metall.* the powder utilised during cementation. *–n.* **8.** a cellulose solvent used for joining cinematograph film. **9.** *Colloq.* →**concrete.** *–v.t.* **10.** to unite by, or as by, cement: *a friendship cemented by time.* **11.** to coat or cover with cement. *–v.i.* **12.** to become cemented; join together or unite; cohere. [L *caementum* rough stone; replacing ME *siment,* from OF] **– cementer,** *n.*

**cementation** /simən'teɪʃən/, *n.* **1.** the act, process, or result of cementing. **2.** *Metall.* the heating of two substances in contact in order to effect some change in one of them; esp., the formation of steel by heating iron in powdered charcoal.

**cementite** /sə'mɛntaɪt/, *n.* a carbide of iron, $Fe_3C$, used in steel to add strength and hardness.

**cement-mixer** /sə'mɛnt-mɪksə/, *n.* a machine which prepares concrete from cement, sand, ballast, and water by mixing them in a revolving drum.

**cement render** /səmɛnt 'rɛndə/, *n.* **1.** a process of plastering brick walls with cement. **2.** the finished plaster.

**cement-render** /səmɛnt-'rɛndə/, *v.t.* to plaster (a brick wall) with cement.

**cementum** /sə'mɛntəm/, *n.* a hard tissue which forms the outer surfaces of the root of a tooth.

**cemetery** /'sɛmətri/, *n., pl.* **-teries.** a burial ground, esp. one not attached to a church; graveyard. [late ME *cymytery,* from LL *coemētērium,* from Gk *koimētḗrion*]

cenotaph

**cenacle** /'sɛnəkəl/, *n.* **1.** a small dining room, usu. on an upper floor. **2.** (*cap.*) the room in which the Last Supper took place. [ME, from OF, from LL *cēnāculum* dining room, from L *cēna* dinner]

**-cene,** a word element meaning 'recent', 'new', as in *Pleistocene.* [combining form representing Gk *kainós*]

**cenesthesia** /sinəs'θiʒə/, *n.* →**coenaesthesia.** Also, **cenesthesis.**

**ceno-**[1], variant of **caino-.**

**ceno-**[2], variant of **coeno-.** Also, before vowels, **cen-.**

**cenobite** /'sinəbaɪt/, *n. Chiefly U.S.* →**coenobite.** **– cenobitic** /sinə'bɪtɪk/, **cenobitical** /sinə'bɪtɪkəl/, *adj.* **– cenobitism** /'sinəbaɪtɪzəm/, *n.*

**cenogenesis** /sinə'dʒɛnəsəs/, *n. Chiefly U.S. Biol.* →**cainogenesis.** **– cenogenetic** /sinədʒə'nɛtɪk/, *adj.*

**cenospecies** /'sinou,spisiz/, *n.pl.* species which can interbreed. [CENO-[2] + SPECIES]

**cenotaph** /'sɛnətaf/, *n.* **1.** a sepulchral monument in memory of a deceased person whose body is elsewhere. **2.** a municipal, civic or national memorial to those killed in war. [L *cenotaphium,* from Gk *kenotáphion* an empty tomb] **– cenotaphic,** *adj.*

**Cenozoic** /sinə'zouɪk/, *adj. Chiefly U.S.* →**Cainozoic.**

**cense** /sɛns/, *v.t.,* **censed, censing.** to burn incense near or in front of; perfume with incense. [aphetic var. of INCENSE[1]]

**censer** /'sɛnsə/, *n.* a container in which incense is burned. [ME *censere,* from OF *encensier.* See INCENSE[1]]

**censor** /'sɛnsə/, *n.* **1.** an official who examines books, plays, news reports,

censer

films, radio programs, etc., for the purpose of suppressing parts deemed objectionable on moral, political, military, or other grounds. **2.** any person who supervises the manners or morality of others. **3.** an adverse critic; a faultfinder. **4.** a member of the board of two officials of republican Rome who kept the register contracts, and supervised manners and morals. **5.** *Psychol.* (in early Freudian theory of dreams) the psychological force which represses ideas, impulses, and feelings, and prevents them from entering consciousness in their original form. *–v.t.* **6.** to examine and act upon as a censor does. **7.** to delete (words, etc.) in censorship. [L] – **censorial** /sɛn'sɔriəl/, *adj.*

**censorious** /sɛn'sɔriəs/, *adj.* severely critical; fault-finding; carping. – **censoriously,** *adv.* – **censoriousness,** *n.*

**censorship** /'sɛnsəʃɪp/, *n.* **1.** the act of censoring. **2.** the office or power of a censor. **3.** the time during which a censor holds office. **4.** *Psychol.* →**censor** (def. 5).

**censurable** /'sɛnʃərəbəl/, *adj.* deserving censure. – **censurableness, censurability** /sɛnʃərə'bɪləti/, *n.* – **censurably,** *adv.*

**censure** /'sɛnʃə/, *n., v.,* **-sured, -suring.** *–n.* **1.** an expression of disapproval; adverse or hostile criticism; blaming. *–v.t.* **2.** to criticise adversely; disapprove; find fault with; condemn. *–v.i.* **3.** to give censure, adverse criticism, or blame. [ME, from L *censūra* censorship, judgment. Cf. CENSOR] – **censurer,** *n.*

**censure motion** /'– moʊʃən/, *n. Parl. Proc.* a challenge by the opposition in any of the houses of parliament expressing lack of confidence in the government or one of its members.

**census** /'sɛnsəs/, *n.* **1.** an official enumeration of inhabitants, with details as to age, sex, pursuits, etc. **2.** (in ancient Rome) the registration of citizens and their property, for purposes of taxation. [L] – **censual,** *adj.*

**cent** /sɛnt/, *n.* **1.** the hundredth part of the dollar. **2.** a coin of this value. **3.** the hundredth part of monetary units elsewhere. [L: short for *centēsimus* hundredth]

**cent-** /sɛnt-/, →**centi-**.

**cent.,** **1.** centigrade. **2.** central. **3.** centum (in *per cent*). **4.** century.

**cental** /'sɛntəl/, *n.* a unit of mass, equal to 100 pounds (approx. 45.36 kg).

**centaur** /'sɛntɔ/, *n. Gk Legend.* one of a race of monsters having the head, trunk, and arms of a man, and the body and legs of a horse. [ME, from L *centaurus,* from Gk *kéntauros*]

**centaury** /'sɛntɔri/, *n., pl.* **-ries.** any of the herbs belonging to the genus *Centaurium,* as the common centaury, *C. erythraea,* and *C. umbellatum,* with medicinal properties. [ME *centaurie,* from ML *centauria,* replacing L *centaurēum,* from Gk *kentaúreion,* from *kéntauros* centaur (here the centaur Chiron, reputed discoverer of the plant's medicinal virtues)]

**centenarian** /sɛntə'nɛəriən/, *adj.* **1.** pertaining to or having lived 100 years. *–n.* **2.** one who has reached the age of a hundred.

**centenary** /sɛn'tinəri, -'tɛn-/, *adj., n., pl.* **-ries.** *–adj.* **1.** of or pertaining to a 100th anniversary. *–n.* **2.** a 100th anniversary. **3.** its celebration. **4.** a period of 100 years; a century. [L *centēnārius* of or containing 100]

**centennial** /sɛn'tɛniəl/, *adj.* **1.** consisting of, or marking the completion of, 100 years. **2.** lasting 100 years. **3.** recurring every 100 years. **4.** 100 years old. *–n.* **5.** *U.S. N.Z.* →**centenary.** [L *centennium* 100 years + -AL[1]; modelled on BIENNIAL] – **centennially,** *adv.*

**center** /'sɛntə/, *n., v. U.S.* →**centre.**

**centering** /'sɛntərɪŋ/, *n.*→**centring.**

**centesimal** /sɛn'tɛsəməl/, *adj.* hundredth; pertaining to division into hundredths. [L *centēsimus* hundredth + -AL[1]] – **centesimally,** *adv.*

**centi-** /'sɛnti-/, a prefix denoting $10^{-2}$ of a given unit, as in **centigram.** Also, before vowels, **cent-.** *Symbol:* c [L, combining form of *centum*]

**Centigrade** /'sɛntəgreɪd/, *n.* **1.** (*l.c.*) non-SI unit of plane angle, equal to $\frac{1}{100}$ of a grade (def. 4) or $10^{-4}$ of a right angle. **2.** the Centigrade scale. *–adj.* **3.** *Obs.* Celsius, as in degree Celsius (°C) or Celsius temperature scale. *Symbol:* C [F. See CENTI-, -GRADE]

**centimetre-gram-second system** /ˌsɛntəmitə-græm-'sɛkənd sɪstəm/, *n.* a system of units based on the centimetre, gram and second as the primary units of length, mass, and time, and now superseded for scientific purposes by the International System of Units (SI). Also, *U.S.,* **centimeter-gram-second system.** *Abbrev.:* c.g.s. (system).

**centipede** /'sɛntəpid/, *n.* any member of the class Chilopoda, active, predacious, and mostly nocturnal arthropods having an elongated flattened body of numerous segments each with a single pair of legs, the first pair of which is modified into poison fangs. Few are dangerous to man. [L *centipeda* hundred-footed insect]

centipede

**centipoise** /'sɛntəpɔɪz/, *n.* a non-SI unit of viscosity equal to 1 millipascal second (1mPa·s, $10^{-3}$ Pa·s).

**centistokes** /'sɛntəstoʊks/, *n.* a non-SI unit of kinematic viscosity equal to 1 square millimetre per second (1 $mm^2/s$, $10^{-6} m^2/s$).

**cento** /'sɛntoʊ/, *n., pl.* **-tos.** **1.** a poem composed wholly of quotations from other authors. **2.** *Archaic.* a patchwork. [L]

**centr-,** variant of **centro-** before vowels.

**centra** /'sɛntrə/, *n.* plural of **centrum.**

**central** /'sɛntrəl/, *adj.* **1.** of or forming the centre. **2.** in, at, or near the centre. **3.** constituting that from which other related things proceed or upon which they depend. **4.** principal; chief; dominant: *the central idea, the central character in a novel.* **5.** *Anat., Physiol.* **a.** pertaining to the brain and spinal cord of the nervous system (as distinguished from *peripheral*). **b.** of or relating to the centrum or body of a vertebra. **6.** *Phonet.* pronounced with the tongue in a neutral position, as for example, the final vowel in *sofa* or *idea.* *–n.* **7.** *U.S.* the office of a telephone system, in which connections are made between different lines. [L *centrālis.* See CENTRE] – **centrally,** *adv.*

**Central African Empire,** *n.* a country in central Africa. Formerly, **Ubangi-Shari.**

**Central America** /sɛntrəl ə'mɛrɪkə/, *n.* continental North America, south of Mexico, comprising the six republics of Guatemala, Honduras, El Salvador, Nicaragua, Costa Rica, Panama and the colony British Honduras. – **Central American,** *adj., n.*

**central bank** /sɛntrəl 'bæŋk/, *n.* →**reserve bank.**

**central cylinder** /– 'sɪləndə/, *n. Bot.* →**stele** (def. 4).

**central heating** /– 'hitɪŋ/, *n.* **1.** a method of heating a building from a central system by circulating hot water, steam or air through pipes. **2.** any method of heating several rooms in a building simultaneously.

**Centralia** /sɛn'treɪljə/, *n. Colloq.* the inland region of continental Australia. – **Centralian,** *adj., n.*

**centralisation** /ˌsɛntrəlaɪ'zeɪʃən/, *n.* **1.** the act of centralising. **2.** the fact of being centralised. **3.** the concentration of administrative power in a central government. **4.** *Sociol.* a process whereby social groups and institutions become increasingly dependent on a central group or institution. Also, **centralization.**

**centralise** /'sɛntrəlaɪz/, *v.,* **-lised, -lising.** *–v.t.* **1.** to draw to or towards a centre. **2.** to bring under one control, esp. in government. *–v.i.* **3.** to come together at a centre. Also, **centralize.** – **centraliser,** *n.*

**centralism** /'sɛntrəlɪzəm/, *n.* **1.** centralisation, or a centralising system. **2.** the principle of centralisation, esp. in government. **3.** the policy of redistributing legislative power so that the States have less and the Commonwealth government has more. – **centralist,** *n., adj.*

**centrality** /sɛn'trælәti/, *n.* central position or state.

**central nervous system,** *n.* the brain and spinal cord considered together. See **central** (def. 5).

**central processor unit,** *n.* →**CPU.**

**central school** /'sɛntrəl skul/, *n.* (in New South Wales and metropolitan Victoria) a government school, sometimes formed by the consolidation of a number of smaller schools in the area, which provides both primary and secondary education. In rural Victoria called a **consolidated school,** in rural South Australia an **area school,** and in Tasmania a **district school.**

**Central Standard Time,** *n.* a time zone lying on the 142nd meridian including South Australia and Northern Territory, nine and a half hours ahead of **Greenwich Mean Time,** a half hour behind **Eastern Standard Time** and one and a half hours ahead of **Western Standard Time.**

**central umpire** /sɛntrəl 'ʌmpaɪə/, *n. Aus. Rules.* →**field umpire.**

**centre** /'sɛntə/, *n., v.* **-tred, -tring.** *–n.* **1.** *Geom.* the middle point, as the point within a circle or sphere equidistant from all points of the circumference or surface, or the point within a regular polygon equidistant from the vertices. **2.** a point, pivot, axis, etc., round which anything rotates or revolves. **3.** a place or collection of buildings forming a central place in a town, city, etc., often set aside as an area for a particular activity: *shopping centre, business centre.* **4.** a person, thing, group, etc., occupying the middle position, esp. troops. **5.** (*usu. cap.*) (in continental Europe) **a.** that part of a legislative assembly which sits in the centre of the chamber, a position customarily assigned to representatives holding views intermediate between those of the conservatives or right and the progressives or left. **b.** a party holding such views. **6.** *Basketball, etc.* the middle player in the attacking or forward line; centre-forward. **7.** *Rugby Football.* →**centre three-quarter. 8.** *Aus. Rules.* **a.** the centre of the playing area, esp. the centre circle. **b.** →**centre-man. 9.** *Colloq.* the one who holds all bets in a game of two-up made by the spinner. **10.** *Physiol.* a cluster of nerve cells governing a specific organic process: *the vasomotor centre.* **11.** *Mach.* **a.** a pointed rod mounted in the headstock spindle (**live centre**) or the tailstock spindle (**dead centre**) of a lathe, upon which the work to be turned is placed. **b.** one of two similar points on some other machine, as a planing machine, enabling an object to be turned on its axis. **c.** a tapered indentation in a piece to be turned on a lathe into which the centre is fitted. **12. the (red) centre,** the remote interior of Australia. *–v.t.* **13.** to place in or on a centre. **14.** to collect at a centre. **15.** to determine or mark the centre of. **16.** to adjust, shape, or modify (an object, part, etc.) so that its axis or the like is in a central or normal position. **17.** *Soccer, Hockey, etc.* to pass (the ball) from the wing to the midfield. *–v.i.* **18.** to be at or come to a centre. **19.** *Soccer, Hockey, etc.* to centre the ball. Also, *U.S.,* **center.** [ME *centre,* from OF, from L *centrum,* from Gk *kéntron* sharp point, centre]

**centre-bit** /'sɛntə-bɪt/, *n.* a carpenter's bit with a sharp, projecting centre point, used for boring holes.

**centreboard** /'sɛntəbɔd/, *n.* a movable fin keel in a boat, esp. a sailing dinghy, that can be drawn up in shallow water into a housing or well; dogger plate. Also, **centreplate.**

**centre circle** /sɛntə 'sɜkəl/, *n.* **1.** *Aus. Rules.* Also, **centre ring.** a circle in mid-field in which the field umpire bounces the ball to start the game and restart it after a goal. **2.** *Soccer.* the similar circle on a soccer field.

**centre-fire** /'sɛntə-faɪə/, *adj.* **1.** of or pertaining to a cartridge which is fired by the action of a hammer or firing pin striking a cap at the centre of the base. **2.** of or pertaining to a rifle designed to fire such cartridges.

**centrefold** /'sɛntəfoʊld/, *n.* the folded pages in the centre of a magazine, designed to be lifted out and unfolded, so as to display a large photograph sometimes of a nude male or female, a pop group, etc.

**centre-forward** /sɛntə-'fɔwəd/, *n.* **1.** *Soccer, Hockey, etc.* the middle player in the forward line. **2.** *Rugby Football.* →**hooker**[1].

**centre-half** /sɛntə-'haf/, *n. Soccer, Hockey, etc.* the middle player in the half-back line.

**centre half-back** /sɛntə 'haf-bæk/, *n. Aus. Rules.* **1.** the centre position on the half-back line, between the two flanks. **2.** one who plays in this position.

**centre half-forward** /– haf-'fɔwəd/, *n. Aus. Rules.* **1.** the centre position on the half-forward line, between the two flanks. **2.** one who plays in this position.

**centre-line** /'sɛntə-laɪn/, *n.* **1.** any line passing through a centre. **2.** *Aus. Rules.* the line of three players comprising the two wingmen and the centre-man. **3.** *Tennis.* a line down the centre of the court, connecting the two service lines.

**centre-man** /'sɛntə-mæn/, *n.* **1.** *Aus. Rules.* the player occupying the centre of the playing area. **2.** Also, **centre man.** →**boxer** (def. 2).

**centre mark** /'sɛntə mak/, *n. Tennis.* a small line bisecting the baselines of a tennis court.

**centre of attraction,** *n.* **1.** the point towards which bodies tend by force of gravity or some other force. **2.** a person, place, etc., of greater interest than the surrounding people or places.

**centre of buoyancy,** *n.* the point in a floating body through which the buoyancy forces act; this is the same as the centre of gravity of the displaced fluid.

**centre of curvature,** *n.* **1.** *Maths.* (of a curve, at a point on it), the centre of that circle (called the **osculating circle**) whose arc best approximates the curve in the vicinity of the point. **2.** *Optics.* (of a lens or mirror) the centre of the sphere of which the surface of the lens or mirror forms a part.

**centre of gravity,** *n.* that point of a body (or system of bodies) from which it could be suspended or on which it could be supported and be in equilibrium in any position in a uniform gravitational field.

**centre of inertia,** *n.* →**centre of mass.**

**centre of mass,** *n.* that point of a body (or system of bodies) at which its entire mass could be concentrated without changing its linear inertia in any direction. For ordinary bodies near the earth, this point is identical with the centre of gravity.

**centre of symmetry,** *n.* a point within a crystal so situated that it bisects any line which joins opposite faces or edges of the crystal.

**centrepiece** /'sɛntəpis/, *n.* **1.** an ornamental object used in a central position, esp. on the centre of a dining table. **2.** the most important or conspicuous item in an exhibition, or in a collection.

**centreplate** /'sɛntəpleɪt/, *n.* →**centreboard.**

**centre-punch** /'sɛntə-pʌntʃ/, *n.* **1.** a tool used to mark the centre of holes to be drilled, consisting of a punch with a conical point. *–v.t.* **2.** to mark with this tool.

**centre spot** /'sɛntə spɒt/, *n. Soccer.* the centre of the centre circle, at which play is started.

**centrespread** /'sɛntəsprɛd/, *n.* a photograph or article covering the double centre page in a publication.

**centre three-quarter** /sɛntə θri-'kwɔtə/, *n. Rugby Football.* one of two middle players in the three-quarter line. Also, **centre.**

**centre turn** /sɛntə 'tɜn/, *n.* →**U-turn.**

**centrewheel** /'sɛntəwil/, *n.* the wheel which drives the minute and hour hands of a clock or watch.

**centri-,** variant of **centro-,** as in *centrifugal.*

**centric** /'sɛntrɪk/, *adj.* pertaining to or situated at the centre; central. Also, **centrical.** **– centrically,** *adv.* **– centricity** /sɛn'trɪsəti/, *n.*

**centrifugal** /sɛn'trɪfjəgəl, sɛntrə'fjugəl/, *adj.* **1.** moving or directed outwards from the centre. **2.** pertaining to or operated by centrifugal force: *a centrifugal pump.* **3.** *Physiol.* →**efferent.** *–n.* **4.** a solid or perforated cylinder rotated rapidly to separate solids from liquid. [NL *centrifugus* centre-fleeing + -AL[1]] **– centrifugally,** *adv.*

**centrifugal force** /– 'fɔs/, *n.* the force exerted outwards by a body moving in a curved path; the reaction of centripetal force. Also, **centrifugal action.**

**centrifugalise** /sɛntrə'fjugəlaɪz/, *v.t.* →**centrifuge** (def. 2). Also, **centrifugalize.**

**centrifuge** /'sɛntrəfjudʒ, -fjuʒ/, *n., v.,* **-fuged, -fuging.** *–n.* **1.** a machine consisting of a rotating container, in which substances of different densities, as cream and milk, may be separated by centrifugal force or in which animals, humans, and instruments are subjected to prolonged accelerations. *–v.t.* **2.** to subject to the action of a centrifuge. [F: centrifugal] **– centrifugation** /sɛn,trɪfjə'geɪʃən/, *n.*

**centring** /'sɛntərɪŋ/, *n.* →**centering.**

**centripetal** /sɛn'trɪpətl/, *adj.* **1.** proceeding or directed towards the centre. **2.** operating by centripetal force. **3.** *Physiol.* →**afferent.** [NL *centripetus* centre-seeking + -AL[1]] **– centripetally,** *adv.*

**centripetal force** /– 'fɔs/, *n.* a force acting on a body, which is directed towards the centre of a circle or curve, which causes it to move in the circle or curve. Also, **centripetal action.**

**centrist** /'sɛntrəst/, *n.* (in continental Europe) a member of a political party of the Centre. See **centre** (def. 5a). [F *centriste,* from *centre* centre]

**centro-**, a word element meaning 'centre'. Also, **centr-**, **centri-**. [combining form representing L *centrum* and Gk *kéntron*]

**centrobaric** /sɛntrəˈbærɪk/, *adj.* pertaining to the centre of gravity. [CENTRO- + Gk *báros* weight + -IC]

**centroclinal** /sɛntrəˈklaɪnəl/, *adj. Geol.* sloping down towards a central point from all directions.

**centroid** /ˈsɛntrɔɪd/, *n. Maths, Mech., etc.* (of a curve, surface, body, etc.) that point whose coordinates are the mean values of the coordinates of all points in the given object. For objects composed of matter of uniform density, the centre of mass coincides with the centroid.

**centromere** /ˈsɛntrəmɪə/, *n.* the part of a chromosome to which the spindle is attached during mitosis. [CENTRO- + -MERE] – **centromeric** /sɛntrəˈmɛrɪk/, *adj.*

**centrosome** /ˈsɛntrəsoʊm/, *n. Biol.* a minute protoplasmic body regarded by some as the active centre of cell division in mitosis. [CENTRO- + -SOME[3]] – **centrosomic** /sɛntrəˈsɒmɪk/, *adj.*

**centrosphere** /ˈsɛntrəsfɪə/, *n.* **1.** *Biol.* the protoplasm around a centrosome; the central portion of an aster, containing the centrosome. **2.** *Geol.* the central or interior portion of the earth; barysphere.

**centrum** /ˈsɛntrəm/, *n., pl.* **-trums, -tra** /-trə/. **1.** a centre. **2.** *Zool.* the body of a vertebra. [L. See CENTRE]

**centum** /ˈkɛntəm/, *adj.* pertaining to those Indo-European languages which retained the velar [k] from primitive Indo-European, in contrast to those which changed the [k] to [s]. Cf. **satem.** [from L *centum* hundred (an example of this retention, the initial *c* representing Indo-European *k*)]

**centuple** /ˈsɛntʃəpəl/, *adj., v.,* **-pled, -pling.** *–adj.* **1.** a hundred times as great; hundredfold. *–v.t.* **2.** to increase a hundred times. [F, from LL *centuplus* hundredfold]

**centuplicate** /sɛnˈtjupləkeɪt/, *v.,* **-cated, -cating;** /sɛnˈtjupləkət/, *adj., n.* *–v.t.* **1.** to increase a hundred times; centuple. *–adj.* **2.** hundredfold. *–n.* **3.** a number or quantity increased a hundredfold. – **centuplication** /sɛnˌtjupləˈkeɪʃən/, *n.*

**centurial** /sɛnˈtjuriəl/, *adj.* pertaining to a century. [L *centuriālis*]

**centurion** /sɛnˈtjuriən/, *n.* (in the Roman Army) the commander of a century (def. 4). [ME, from L *centurio,* from *centuria.* See CENTURY]

**century** /ˈsɛntʃəri/, *n., pl.* **-ries.** **1.** a period of one hundred years. **2.** one of the successive periods of 100 years reckoned forwards or backwards from a recognised chronological epoch, esp. from the assumed date of the birth of Jesus. **3.** any group or collection of 100, as 100 runs in cricket. **4.** (in the Roman Army) a company, consisting of approximately one hundred men. **5.** one of the voting divisions of the Roman people, each division having one vote. **6.** (*cap.*) *Print.* a style of type. [L *centuria* a division of a hundred things]

**century plant** /ˈ– plænt/, *n.* a Mexican species of agave, *Agave americana,* cultivated for ornament, and popularly supposed not to blossom until a century old.

**ceorl** /tʃɛəl/, *n. Old Eng. Hist.* a freeman of the lowest rank, neither a noble nor a slave. [OE. See CHURL] – **ceorlish,** *adj.*

**cephal-**, variant of **cephalo-**, before vowels, as in *cephalad.*

**cephalad** /ˈsɛfəlæd/, *adv. Anat., Zool.* towards the head (opposed to *caudad*). [CEPHAL- + L *ad* to]

**cephalic** /səˈfælɪk/, *adj.* **1.** of or pertaining to the head. **2.** situated or directed towards the head. **3.** of the nature of a head. [L *cephalicus,* from Gk *kephalikós* of the head]

**-cephalic,** a word element meaning 'head', as in *brachycephalic* (related to **cephalo-**).

**cephalic index** /səˌfælɪk ˈɪndɛks/, *n. Anat., Anthrop.* the ratio of the greatest breadth of head to its greatest length from front to back, multiplied by 100.

**cephalin** /ˈkɛfələn, ˈsɛf-/, *n. Biochem.* any of a group of closely related phosphatides occurring mainly in the brain. Also, **kephalin.**

**cephalisation** /sɛfəlaɪˈzeɪʃən/, *n.* a tendency in the development of animals to localisation of important organs or parts in or near the head. Also, **cephalization.**

**cephalo-**, a word element denoting the 'head', as in *cephalopod.* Also, **cephal-**. [Gk *kephalo-*, combining form of *kephalḗ*]

**cephalochordate** /sɛfələˈkɔdeɪt/, *adj.* **1.** denoting or pertaining to the Cephalochordata. *–n.* **2.** a member of the Cephalochordata, a chordate subphylum including the lancelets, having fishlike characters but lacking a vertebral column. [CEPHALO- + CHORDATE]

**cephalom.**, cephalometry.

**cephalomancy** /ˈsɛfələˌmænsi/, *n.* divination by study of the skull or head of a donkey or goat.

**cephalometer** /sɛfəˈlɒmətə/, *n.* an instrument for measuring the head or skull; a craniometer.

**cephalometry** /sɛfəˈlɒmətri/, *n.* the science of the measurement of heads. [CEPHALO- + -METRY]

**cephalopod** /ˈsɛfələpɒd/, *n.* a member of the class Cephalopoda, the most highly organised class of molluscs, including the cuttlefish, squid, octopus, etc., the members of which have tentacles attached to the head. [CEPHALO- + -POD] – **cephalopodan** /sɛfəˈlɒpədən/, *adj., n.*

**cephalothorax** /ˌsɛfəloʊˈθɔræks/, *n.* the anterior part of the body in certain arachnids and crustaceans, consisting of the coalesced head and thorax.

**cephalous** /ˈsɛfələs/, *adj.* having a head. [CEPHAL- + -OUS]

**-cephalous,** a word element related to **cephalo-**. [CEPHAL- + -OUS]

**Cepheid variable** /ˌsifiəd ˈvɛəriəbəl/, *n.* a variable star in which changes in brightness are due to bodily pulsations.

**-ceptor,** a word element meaning 'taker', 'receiver', as in *preceptor.* [L]

**cer-**, variant of **cero-**, used before vowels, as in *ceraceous.*

**Cer.**, Ceramics.

**ceraceous** /səˈreɪʃəs/, *adj.* waxlike; waxy.

**ceramal** /səˈreɪməl/, *n.* →**cermet.** [CERAM(IC) + AL(LOY)]

**ceramet** /ˈsɛrəmɛt/, *n.* →**cermet.**

**ceramic** /səˈræmɪk/, *adj.* pertaining to products made from clay and similar materials, such as pottery, brick, etc., or to their manufacture: *ceramic art.* Also, **keramic.** [Gk *keramikós* of or for potters' clay, pottery]

**ceramics** /səˈræmɪks/, *n.* **1.** (*construed as sing.*) the art and technology of making clay products and similar ware. **2.** (*construed as pl.*) articles of earthenware, porcelain, etc. Also, **keramics.** [pl. of CERAMIC. See -ICS] – **ceramist** /səˈræməst/, **ceramicist,** *n.*

**cerargyrite** /səˈrædʒəraɪt/, *n.* a mineral, silver chloride, an important silver ore in some places; chlorargyrite; horn silver. [Gk *kér(as)* horn + Gk *árgyros* silver + -ITE[1]]

**cerate** /ˈsɪərət, -reɪt/, *n.* an unctuous (often medicated) preparation for external application, consisting of lard or oil mixed with wax, or the like, esp. one which has a firmer consistency than a typical ointment and does not melt when in contact with the skin. [L *cērātum,* neut. pp., covered with wax]

**ceratin** /ˈsɛrətən, ˈkɛr-/, *n. Zool.* →**keratin.** [CERAT(O)- + -IN[2]]

**cerato-**, a word element meaning **1.** *Zool.* horn, horny, or hornlike. **2.** *Anat.* the cornea. Also (before a vowel), **cerat-**. [Gk *kerāto-*, combining form of *kéras* horn]

**ceratodus** /səˈrætədəs, sɛrəˈtoudəs/, *n.* a fish with hornlike ridge on the teeth, being either of the extinct lungfish genus *Ceratodus,* or of the closely related existent genus *Neoceratodus,* as *N. forsteri,* the Queensland lungfish. [NL, from *cerat-* CERATO- + Gk *odoús* tooth]

**ceratoid** /ˈsɛrətɔɪd/, *adj.* hornlike; horny. [Gk *kerātoeidḗs* hornlike]

**ceraunoscopy** /sərɔˈnɒskəpi/, *n.* the drawing of omens from the study of thunder and lightning.

**Cerberus** /ˈsɜbərəs/, *n.* a watchful and formidable or surly keeper or guard. [*Cerberus,* a dog, represented in classical mythology as having three heads, and guarding the entrance to the infernal regions] – **Cerberian** /sɜˈbɪəriən/, *adj.*

**cercaria** /sɜˈkɛəriə/, *n., pl.* **-cariae** /-kɛərii/. *Zool.* a larval stage of flukes, Trematoda, characterised by a body usu. bearing a tail-like appendage, but sometimes enclosed in the tail. [NL, from *cerc-* (combining form representing Gk *kérkos* tail) + *-āria* -ARIA] – **cercarial,** *adj.* – **cercarian,** *adj., n.*

**cercus** /ˈsɜkəs/, *n., pl.* **-ci** /-si/. one of a pair of tail-like appendages in some insects and other arthropods, serving as tactile organs. [NL, from Gk *kérkos* tail] – **cercal** /ˈsɜkəl/, *adj.*

**cere**[1] /sɪə/, *n.* a membrane of waxy appearance at the base of the upper mandible of certain birds, esp. birds of prey and parrots, in which the nostrils open. [late ME *sere,* from ML *cēra,* in L wax, c. Gk *kērós*]

**cere**[2] /sɪə/, *v.t.,* **cered, cering. 1.** *Poetic.* to wrap in or as in a cerecloth, esp. a corpse. **2.** *Obs.* to wax. [ME, from L *cērāre* to wax]

**cereal** /'sɪəriəl/, *n.* **1.** any gramineous plant yielding an edible farinaceous grain, as wheat, rye, oats, rice, maize, etc. **2.** the grain itself. **3.** some edible preparation of it, esp. a breakfast food made from some grain. *–adj.* **4.** of or pertaining to grain or the plants producing it. [L *Cereālis* pertaining to Ceres, ancient Italian goddess of tillage and corn]

**cerebellum** /sɛrə'bɛləm/, *n., pl.* **-bella** /-'bɛlə/. a large expansion of the hindbrain, concerned with the coordination of voluntary movements, posture, and equilibration. In man it lies at the back of and below the cerebrum and consists of two lateral lobes and a central lobe. [L, diminutive of *cerebrum* brain] – **cerebellar,** *adj.*

**cerebral** /'sɛrəbrəl/, *adj.* **1.** of or pertaining to the cerebrum or the brain. **2.** thoughtful; intellectual. **3.** *Phonet.* →**retroflex.** *–n.* **4.** *Phonet.* a cerebral consonant. [NL *cerebrālis,* from L *cerebrum* brain]

**cerebral palsy** /– 'pɔlzi/, *n.* a form of paralysis caused by injury to the brain, most marked in certain motor areas. It is characterised by involuntary motions and difficulty in control of the voluntary muscles; sufferers are called spastics.

**cerebrate** /'sɛrəbreɪt/, *v.i.,* **-brated, -brating. 1.** to use the cerebrum or brain; experience brain action. **2.** *Colloq.* to think.

**cerebration** /sɛrə'breɪʃən/, *n.* **1.** the action of the cerebrum or brain. **2.** thinking; thought.

**cerebric** /'sɛrəbrɪk/, *adj.* pertaining to or derived from the brain.

**cerebro-,** a word element meaning 'cerebrum'. Also (before a vowel), **cerebr-.**

**cerebroside** /sə'ribrəsaɪd, 'sɛrəbroʊˌsaɪd/, *n. Biochem.* any of a group of closely related lipids occurring in the brain.

**cerebrospinal** /ˌsɛrəbroʊ'spaɪnəl/, *adj.* **1.** pertaining to or affecting both the brain and the spinal cord. **2.** pertaining to the central nervous system (distinguished from *autonomic*).

**cerebrospinal meningitis** /– mɛnən'dʒaɪtəs/, *n.* an acute inflammation of the meninges of the brain and spinal cord caused by a specific organism, and accompanied by fever and occasionally red spots on the skin; brain fever. Also, **cerebrospinal fever.**

**cerebrum** /'sɛrəbrəm/, *n., pl.* **-bra** /-brə/. **1.** the anterior and upper part of the brain, consisting of two hemispheres, partially separated by a deep fissure but connected by a broad band of fibres, and concerned with voluntary and conscious processes. **2.** these two hemispheres together with other adjacent parts; the prosencephalon, diencephalon, and mesencephalon together. [L: brain]

**cerecloth** /'sɪəklɒθ/, *n.* **1.** a waxed cloth, used esp. for wrapping the dead. **2.** a piece of such cloth. [earlier *cered cloth.* See CERE[2], *v.*]

**cerement** /'sɪəmənt/, *n.* (*usu. pl.*) **1.** →**cerecloth. 2.** any grave-clothes. [CERE[2] + -MENT. Cf. F *cirement*]

**ceremonial** /sɛrə'moʊniəl/, *adj.* **1.** pertaining to, used for, marked by, or of the nature of ceremonies or ceremony; ritual; formal. *–n.* **2.** a system of ceremonies, rites, or formalities prescribed for or observed on any particular occasion; a rite or ceremony. **3.** *Rom. Cath. Ch.* **a.** the order for rites and ceremonies. **b.** a book containing it. **4.** formality, esp. of etiquette; the observance of ceremony. – **ceremonialism,** *n.* – **ceremonialist,** *n.* – **ceremonially,** *adv.*

**ceremonious** /sɛrə'moʊniəs/, *adj.* **1.** carefully observant of ceremony; formally or elaborately polite. **2.** pertaining to, marked by, or consisting of ceremony; formal. – **ceremoniously,** *adv.* – **ceremoniousness,** *n.*

**ceremony** /'sɛrəməni/, *n., pl.* **-monies. 1.** the formalities observed on some solemn or important public or state occasion. **2.** a formal religious or sacred observance; a solemn rite. **3.** any formal act or observance, esp. a meaningless one. **4.** a gesture or act of politeness or civility. **5.** formal observances or gestures collectively; ceremonial observances. **6.** strict adherence to conventional forms; formality: *to leave a room without ceremony.* **7. stand on ceremony,** to be excessively formal or polite. [ML *cēremōnia,* L *caerimōnia* sacred rite; replacing ME *serimonie,* from OF]

**Cerenkov radiation** /tʃəˌrɛŋkɒf reɪdi'eɪʃən/, *n.* visible radiation emitted by charged particles when they travel through a transparent medium at a velocity greater than the velocity of light in that medium. Also, **Cherenkov radiation.** [named after Pavel Alekseevich *Cherenkov,* b. 1904, Soviet physicist]

**cereous** /'sɪəriəs/, *adj.* waxlike; waxy. [L *cereus*]

**ceresin** /'sɛrəsən/, *n.* a hard and brittle paraffin wax used as a substitute for beeswax in paints and polishes.

**cereus** /'sɪəriəs/, *n.* any member of the genus *Cereus,* family Cactaceae, of tropical America, as *C. jamacaru,* of northern Brazil, which grows to about 13 metres. [L: wax candle]

**ceria** /'sɪəriə/, *n.* cerium oxide, $CeO_2$, used in small amounts in gas mantles.

**cerik** /'sɪərɪk/, *adj.* containing cerium, esp. in the tetravalent state.

**ceriman** /'sɛrəmən/, *n.* →**monstera deliciosa.**

**cerise** /sə'ris, -riz/, *adj., n.* mauve-tinged cherry red.

**cerium** /'sɪəriəm/, *n.* a steel grey, ductile metallic element of the rare-earth group found only in combination. *Symbol:* Ce; *at. wt:* 140.12; *at. no.:* 58. [NL, named after the asteroid *Ceres*]

**cerium metals** /– 'mɛtlz/, *n.pl. Chem.* See **rare-earth elements.**

**cermet** /'sɜmət/, *n.* a substance consisting of a sintered metal compacted with a ceramic material in order to modify the conductivity or heat resistance of the pure metal, used in high-temperature or high-strength applications. Also, **ceramet, ceramal.** [CER(AMIC) + MET(AL)]

**cernuous** /'sɜnjuəs/, *adj.* drooping or bowing down, as a flower. [L *cernuus* stooping]

**cero** /'sɪəroʊ, 'sɪroʊ/, *n., pl.* **-ros. 1.** a large tropical Atlantic mackerel-like fish, *Scomberomorus regalis,* important for food and game. **2.** any related species. [Sp. *sierra* saw, sawfish]

**cero-,** a word element meaning 'wax', as in *cerotype.* Also, **cer-.** [Gk *kēro-,* combining form of *kērós*]

**cerograph** /'sɪərəgræf/, *n.* an engraving on wax. [CERO- + -GRAPH] – **cerographic** /sɪərə'græfɪk/, **cerographical** /sɪərə'græfɪkəl/, *adj.* – **cerographist** /sɪə'rɒgrəfəst/, *n.*

**cerography** /sɪə'rɒgrəfi/, *n.* the art of engraving on wax.

**ceroplastic** /sɪəroʊ'plæstɪk/, *adj.* **1.** pertaining to modelling in wax. **2.** modelled in wax.

**ceroplastics** /sɪəroʊ'plæstɪks/, *n.* **1.** the art of modelling in wax. **2.** waxworks.

**ceroscopy** /sɪə'rɒskəpi/, *n.* a form of divination in which melted wax is poured into cold water, forming bubbles which are then interpreted.

**cerotic acid** /sərɒtɪk 'æsəd/, *n.* the monobasic fatty acid, $C_{26}H_{53}COOH$, of beeswax. [Gk *kērōtón* waxed + -IC]

**cerotype** /'sɪərətaɪp/, *n.* a process of engraving in which the design or the like is cut on a wax-coated metal plate, from which a printing surface is subsequently produced by stereotyping or by electrotyping.

**cerous** /'sɪərəs/, *adj. Chem.* containing trivalent cerium. [CER(IUM) + -OUS]

**cert** /sɜt/, *n. Colloq.* a certainty.

**cert., 1.** certificate. **2.** certified. **3.** certain.

**certain** /'sɜtn/, *adj.* **1.** having no doubt; confident; assured (oft. fol. by *of* before a noun, gerund, or pronoun): *I am certain of being able to finish it by tomorrow.* **2.** sure; inevitable; bound to come (fol. by an infinitive): *it is certain to happen.* **3.** established as true or sure; unquestionable; indisputable: *it is certain that he tried.* **4.** fixed; agreed upon: *on a certain day.* **5.** definite or particular, but not named or specified: *certain persons.* **6.** that may be depended on; trustworthy; unfailing; reliable: *his aim was certain.* **7.** some though not much: *a certain reluctance.* **8.** *Obs.* steadfast. **9. for certain,** without any doubt; surely. [ME, from OF, from L *certus* fixed, certain, orig. pp.]

**certainly** /'sɜtnli/, *adv.* **1.** with certainty; without doubt; assuredly. *–interj.* **2.** yes! of course!

**certainty** /'sɜtnti/, *n., pl.* **-ties. 1.** the state of being certain. **2.** something certain; an assured fact. **3.** *Colloq.* something regarded as certain to happen, to achieve a desired result as winning a race, etc.: *that horse is an absolute certainty.* **4. for a certainty,** without any doubt; surely.

**certes** /'sɜtiz/, *adv. Archaic.* certainly; verily. [ME, from OF, from LL *certas*, adv., from L *certus* CERTAIN]

**certifiable** /'sɜtəfaɪəbəl/, *adj.* **1.** capable of being certified. **2.** committable to a mental institution. – **certifiably,** *adv.*

**certificate** /sə'tɪfəkət/, *n.;* /sə'tɪfəkeɪt/, *v.,* **-cated, -cating.** –*n.* **1.** a writing on paper certifying to the truth of something or to status, qualifications, privileges, etc. **2.** a document issued to a person passing a particular examination. **3.** *Law.* a statement, written and signed, which is by law made evidence of the truth of the facts stated, for all or for certain purposes. **4.** a share certificate. **5.** a trading certificate. **6.** a land certificate. **7.** the certificate held by the master of a ship. –*v.t.* **8.** to attest by a certificate. **9.** to furnish with or authorise by a certificate. [late ME, from ML *certificātum,* neut. pp. of *certificāre.* See CERTIFY]

**certificate of deposit,** *n. Econ.* a short-term, negotiable, interest-bearing note acknowledging indebtedness, issued mainly by trading banks and merchant banks.

**certificate of exemption,** *n.* a certificate issued by the Industrial Registrar to a person who, he is convinced, holds a genuine belief preventing him from belonging to an industrial union of employees and who has paid to the Registrar an amount equivalent to the membership fee of the union covering his calling.

**certificate of origin,** *n.* a shipping document having consular certification that names a boat's origin and type of goods aboard, often required before importation.

**certification** /sɜtəfə'keɪʃən/, *n.* **1.** the act of certifying. **2.** the state of being certified. **3.** a certified statement. **4.** the writing on the face of a cheque by which it is certified. **5.** *Law.* a certificate attesting the truth of some statement or event.

**certified** /'sɜtəfaɪd/, *adj.* **1.** having, or proved by, a certificate. **2.** guaranteed; reliably endorsed. **3.** committed to a mental institution.

**certified cheque** /– 'tʃɛk/, *n.* a cheque bearing a guarantee of payment by the bank on which it is drawn.

**certified mail** /– 'meɪl/, *n.* a pre-paid postal service by which a letter or parcel is delivered only after signature of a receipt by the addressee, the customer thus having proof of mailing date and guarantee of compensation if the article is lost in the post.

**certify** /'sɜtəfaɪ/, *v.,* **-fied, -fying.** –*v.t.* **1.** to guarantee as certain; give reliable information of. **2.** to testify to or vouch for in writing. **3.** to declare insane. **4.** to assure or inform with certainty. **5.** to guarantee; endorse reliably. **6.** *Chiefly U.S.* (of a bank, or one of its officials) to state in writing upon (a cheque) that the bank on which it is drawn has funds of the drawer sufficient to meet it. –*v.i.* **7.** to give assurance; testify (fol. by *to*); vouch (fol. by *for*). [ME *certifie(n),* from F *certifier,* from ML *certificāre*] – **certifier,** *n.*

**certiorari** /ˌsɜtiə'rɛəraɪ/, *n. Law.* a writ issued from a superior court removing a case from a lower court or calling up the record of a proceeding in a lower court for review. [L: to be informed (lit., made more certain)]

**certitude** /'sɜtətʃud/, *n.* sense of absolute conviction; certainty. [late ME, from LL *certitūdo*]

**cerulean** /sə'ruliən/, *adj., n.* sky blue; azure. Also, **caerulean.** [L *caeruleus* dark blue + -AN]

**cerumen** /sə'rumən/, *n.* a yellowish waxlike secretion from certain glands in the external auditory canal, acting as a lubricant and arresting the entrance of dust, insects, etc.; earwax. [NL, from L *cēra* wax]

**ceruse** /sə'rus/, *n.* white lead; a mixture or compound of hydrate and carbonate of lead, much used in painting. [ME, from OF, from L *cērussa*]

**cerussite** /'sɪərəsaɪt/, *n. Chem.* a mineral, lead carbonate, $PbCO_3$, in white crystals or massive; an important ore of lead. [L *cērussa* white lead + -ITE[1]]

**cervic-,** a combining form of **cervical.** Also, **cervico-.**

**cervical** /'sɜvɪkəl, sɜ'vaɪkəl/, *adj.* pertaining to the cervix or neck. [L *cervix* neck + -AL[1]]

**cervical smear** /– 'smɪə/, *n.* →**Pap smear.**

**cervicitis** /sɜvə'saɪtəs/, *n.* inflammation of the cervix (of the uterus).

**cervico-,** variant of **cervic-** used before consonants.

**cervine** /'sɜvaɪn/, *adj.* **1.** deerlike. **2.** of deer or the deer family, the Cervidae. **3.** of a deep tawny colour. [L *cervīnus* pertaining to deer]

**cervix** /'sɜvɪks/, *n., pl.* **cervixes, cervices** /sə'vaɪsiz/. *Anat.* **1.** the neck. **2.** the neck of the uterus, which dilates just before parturition. **3.** any necklike part. [L]

**Cesarean** /sə'zɛəriən/, *adj., n.* →**Caesarean.** Also, **Cesarian.**

**cesium** /'siziəm/, *n. Chem.* →**caesium.**

**cespitose** /'sɛspətoʊz/, *adj. U.S.* →**caespitose.**

**cess**[1] /sɛs/, *n.* (in parts of Britain) **1.** a tax or levy. –*v.t.* **2.** to assess for taxation. [aphetic var. of obs. n. use of ASSESS, *v.*]

**cess**[2] /sɛs/, *n. Irish.* luck: *bad cess to you!* [? aphetic var. of SUCCESS]

**cess**[3] /sɛs/, *n.* **1.** a cesspit or cesspool. **2.** a box at the end of a roof gutter above a drainpipe. **3.** a drain at the foot of a bank, as in a railway cutting. [It. *cesso* privy, ? from L *secessum* a place apart, neut. pp. of *secēdere* to go apart]

**cessation** /sɛ'seɪʃən/, *n.* a ceasing; discontinuance; pause: *a cessation of hostilities.* [L *cessātio*]

**cesser** /'sɛsə/, *n. Law.* the coming to an end, of, or as of the period of duration of a mortgage.

**cession** /'sɛʃən/, *n.* **1.** the act of ceding, as by treaty. **2.** something, as territory, ceded. **3.** the voluntary surrender by a debtor of his effects to his creditors. [L *cessio*]

**cessionary** /'sɛʃənəri/, *n., pl.* **-ries. 1.** a transferee. **2.** →**assignee. 3.** →**grantee.**

**cesspit** /'sɛspɪt/, *n.* a pit containing a cesspool.

**cesspool** /'sɛspul/, *n.* **1.** a cistern, well, or pit for retaining the sediment of a drain or for receiving the filth of a water closet, etc. **2.** any filthy receptacle or place: *a cesspool of iniquity.*

**c'est-à-dire** /seɪt-a-'dɪə/, that is to say. [F]

**c'est la guerre** /seɪ la 'gɛə/, that's war. [F]

**c'est la vie** /seɪ la 'vi/, that's life. [F]

**cestode** /'sɛstoʊd/, *n.* any member of the Cestoda, a class of internally parasitic platyhelminths or flatworms, including the tapeworms characterised by the long ribbon-like body divided into joints. Also, **cestoidean** /sɛs'tɔɪdiən/. [NL *cestōdēs.* See CESTUS[1], -ODE[1]]

**cestoid** /'sɛstɔɪd/, *adj.* (of worms) ribbon-like.

**cestrum** /'sɛstrəm/, *n.* any shrub of the large genus *Cestrum,* family Solanaceae, many of which are cultivated for their tubular flowers, or, as *C. nocturnum,* for their night fragrance.

**cestui que trust** /ˌsɛtə ki 'trʌst/, *n. Law.* beneficiary of a trust. [OF]

**cestui que vie** /ˌsɛtə ki 'vi/, *n. Law.* a person whose property may be held by another during his lifetime. [OF]

**cestus**[1] /'sɛstəs/, *n.* a belt or girdle. [L, from Gk *kestós* girdle, lit., stitched]

**cestus**[2] /'sɛstəs/, *n. Rom. Antiq.* a hand-covering made of leather strips often loaded with metal, worn by boxers. [L *caestus,* prob. var. sp. of *cestus* CESTUS[1]]

**cesura** /sə'ʒurə/, *n.* →**caesura.** – **cesural,** *adj.*

**cet-,** a word element meaning 'whale'. [combining form representing L *cētus* and Gk *kētos* whale]

**cetacean** /sə'teɪʃən/, *adj.* **1.** belonging to the Cetacea, an order of aquatic, chiefly marine, mammals, including the whales, dolphins, porpoises, etc. –*n.* **2.** a cetacean mammal. [NL *Cetācea,* pl. (see CET-, -ACEA) + -AN] – **cetaceous,** *adj.*

**cetane** /'siteɪn/, *n.* a colourless, liquid, paraffin hydrocarbon, $C_{16}H_{34}$, found in petroleum; hexadecane.

**cetane number** /– nʌmbə/, *n.* a measure of the ignition quality of diesel-engine fuels. The fuel is compared with mixtures of the alpha form of methylnaphthalene (value = 0) and cetane (value = 100). Also, **cetane rating.**

**ceteris paribus** /ˌkɛtərɪs 'parəbus/, *n.* the others (other things) being equal. *Abbrev.:* cet. par. [L]

**cetin** /'sitən/, *n.* $C_{32}H_{64}O_2$, the chief constituent of spermaceti.

**cet. par.,** ceteris paribus.

**cevadilla** /sɛvə'dɪlə/, *n.* →**sabadilla.**

**Ceylon** /sə'lɒn/, *n.* the former name of Sri Lanka. – **Ceylonese** /silə'niz/, *adj.*

**Ceylon moss** /– 'mɒs/, *n.* a red seaweed, *Gracilaria lichenoides,* of the East Indies, one of the algae from which agar-agar is obtained.

**cf.,** compare. [L *confer*]

**c/f.** (in accounting) carry forward; carried forward.

**cg,** centigram; centigrams.

**c.g.,** centre of gravity.

**C.G.** /si 'dʒi/, consul general.

**c.g.s.** /si dʒi 'ɛs/, *n.* centimetre-gram-second (system). Also, **cgs.**

**C.G.S.** Chief of General Staff.

**ch,** chain (def. 9).

**ch.,** **1.** chapter. **2.** *Chess.* check. **3.** children. **4.** church. **5.** (in crochet) chain. **6.** chief.

**C.H.** /si 'eɪtʃ/, Companion of Honour.

**chabazite** /'kæbəzaɪt/, *n.* a zeolite mineral, essentially a hydrated sodium calcium aluminium silicate, occurring commonly in red to colourless crystals that are nearly cubes. [earlier *chabazie,* from F, misspelling of Gk *chalázie* (voc.), from *chálaza* hailstone. See -ITE[1]]

**chablis** /'ʃæbli, 'ʃabli/, *n.* **1.** a very dry white table wine from the Burgundy wine region in France. **2.** a similar wine made elsewhere. [*Chablis,* town in N central France]

**Chaburah** /kə'burə/, *n. Judaism.* a devout meal with religious significance eaten on Friday night. [Heb.: a company or group]

**cha-cha-cha** /ˌtʃa-tʃa-'tʃa/, *n.* a dance of Latin American origin, similar to the mambo. Also, **cha-cha** /'tʃa-tʃa/.

**chacma** /'tʃækmə/, *n.* a large baboon, *Papio ursinus,* of southern Africa, about the size of a mastiff. [Hottentot]

chacma

**chaconne** /ʃə'kɒn/, *n.* **1.** an ancient dance, probably of Spanish origin. **2.** the music for it. **3.** a musical form of variations based on a reiterated harmonic pattern. Cf. **passacaglia.** [F, from Sp. *chacona,* from Basque *chacun* pretty]

**chacun à son goût** /ʃaˌkɜn a sõ 'gu/, everyone to his own taste. [F]

**Chad** /tʃæd/, *n.* a country in north-central Africa. Official name: **Republic of Chad.**

**chaddar** /'tʃʌdə/, *n.* →**chuddar.**

**chador** /'tʃadə/, *n.* a dark voluminous mantle which envelops the body and conceals the face below the eyes, worn by Moslem women as an outer garment. Also, **chadur.** [Pers. *chaddar,* from Hind. *chadar* square piece of cloth]

**chaeta** /'kitə/, *n., pl.* **-tae** /-ti/. a bristle or seta, esp. of a chaetopod. [NL, from Gk *chaítē* hair]

**chaeto-,** a word element meaning 'hair', as in *chaetopod.* Also, before vowels, **chaet-.** [combining form representing Gk *chaítē*]

**chaetophorous** /kə'tɒfərəs/, *adj.* bearing bristles; setigerous or setiferous.

**chaetopod** /'kitəpɒd/, *n.* any of the Chaetopoda, a class or group of annelids having the body made up of more or less similar segments provided with muscular processes bearing setae.

**chafe** /tʃeɪf/, *v.,* **chafed, chafing,** *n.* *–v.t.* **1.** to warm by rubbing. **2.** to wear or abrade by rubbing. **3.** to make sore by rubbing. **4.** to irritate; annoy. **5.** *Obs.* to heat; make warm. *–v.i.* **6.** to rub; press with friction. **7.** to become worn or sore by rubbing. **8.** to be irritated or annoyed. **9.** to become impatient; fret. *–n.* **10.** irritation; annoyance. **11.** heat, wear or soreness caused by rubbing. [ME *chaufe(n),* from OF *chaufer,* from LL contraction of L *calefacere* make hot]

**chafer** /'tʃeɪfə/, *n.* any scarabaeid beetle. [ME *cheaffer, chaver,* OE *ceafor.* Cf. G *Käfer*]

**chaff**[1] /tʃaf/, *n.* **1.** the husks of grains and grasses separated from the seed. **2.** straw cut small for fodder. **3.** *Mil.* strips of metal foil of various lengths and frequency responses released in the atmosphere to inhibit radar. **4.** worthless matter; refuse; rubbish. **5.** *Colloq.* money. [ME *chaf,* OE *ceaf,* c. D *kaf*] **– chafflike,** *adj.* **– chaffy,** *adj.*

**chaff**[2] /tʃaf/, *v.t.* **1.** to ridicule or tease goodnaturedly. *–v.i.* **2.** to engage in good-natured teasing; banter. *–n.* **3.** good-natured ridicule or teasing; raillery. [? special use of CHAFF[1]] **– chaffer,** *n.*

**chaff-and-grain store** /tʃaf-ən-'greɪn stɔ/, *n.* →**produce store.**

**chaffcutter** /'tʃafkʌtə/, *n. Colloq.* a motor vehicle, aeroplane, etc., which has a very noisy engine, esp. an air-cooled engine, as in an early model Volkswagen.

**chaffer** /'tʃæfə/, *n.* **1.** bargaining; haggling. *–v.i.* **2.** to bargain; haggle. **3.** to bandy (words). *–v.t.* **4.** *Obs.* trade or deal in; barter. **5.** to bandy (words). [ME *chaffare,* earlier *chapfare* trading journey, from OE *cēap* trade + *faru* a going] **– chafferer,** *n.*

**chaffinch** /'tʃæfɪntʃ/, *n.* a common European finch, *Fringilla coelebs,* with a pleasant short song, and often kept as a cagebird. [OE *ceaffinc.* See CHAFF[1], FINCH]

**chafing dish** /'tʃeɪfɪŋ dɪʃ/, *n.* a dish placed over a flame for cooking or keeping food warm at the table.

**chagrin** /'ʃægrən, ʃə'grin/, *n.* **1.** a feeling of vexation and disappointment or humiliation. *–v.t.* **2.** to vex by disappointment or humiliation. [F. See SHAGREEN]

**chai** /tʃaɪ/, *n. Colloq.* tea. [Hindi *chā,* from Peking Chinese *ch'a*]

**chain** /tʃeɪn/, *n.* **1.** a connected series of metal or other links for connecting, drawing, confining, restraining, etc., or for ornament. **2.** something that binds or restrains. **3.** (*pl.*) bonds or fetters. **4.** (*pl.*) bondage. **5.** a series of things connected or following in succession. **6.** a range of mountains. **7.** a number of similar establishments, as banks, theatres, hotels, etc., under one ownership and management. **8.** *Chem.* a linkage of atoms of the same element, as carbon to carbon. **9.** *Survey.* (formerly) **a.** a measuring instrument consisting of 100 wire rods or links, each 7.92 inches long (**surveyor's** or **Gunter's chain**), or one foot long (**engineer's chain**). **b.** the length of a surveyor's chain (66 feet or 20.1168 metres) or engineer's chain (100 feet or 30.48 metres), a unit of measurement in the imperial system. **10.** *Aeron.* a number of radio stations cooperating for the purpose of providing a navigational system. **11. drag the chain,** *Colloq.* to shirk or fall behind in one's share of work or responsibility. **12. the chain, a.** the overhead moving chain in a meatworks, on which carcases are passed to various specialist hands for dressing and processing. **b.** the specialist hands who work on such a chain, regarded as a group or gang. *–v.t.* **13.** to fasten or secure with a chain. **14.** to fetter; confine: *chained to his desk.* **15.** *Survey.* to measure (a distance on the ground) with a chain or tape. [ME *chayne,* from OF *chaeine,* from L *catēna*] **– chainless,** *adj.*

**chainage** /'tʃeɪnɪdʒ/, *n. Survey.* a length as measured by a surveyor's chain or tape.

**chain-belt** /'tʃeɪn-bɛlt/, *n.* →**chain-drive.**

**chain-bridge** /'tʃeɪn-brɪdʒ/, *n.* a suspension bridge.

**chain cable** /tʃeɪn 'keɪbəl/, *n.* a chain connecting an anchor to a ship.

**chain-drive** /'tʃeɪn-draɪv/, *n.* **1.** transmission of power by means of an endless chain moving between sprocket-wheels. **2.** the endless chain itself.

**chain-driven** /'tʃeɪn-drɪvən/, *adj.* driven by chain-drive.

**chain-gang** /'tʃeɪn-gæŋ/, *n.* a group of convicts chained together, usu. while at work.

**chain-gear** /'tʃeɪn-gɪə/, *n.* a gear in which motion is transmitted between sprockets, etc., by chain-drive.

**chain-grate** /'tʃeɪn-greɪt/, *n.* a form of mechanical boiler stoker in which the grate consists of an endless chain; as the chain slowly rotates fresh fuel is fed into the boiler.

**chain-harrow** /'tʃeɪn-hæroʊ/, *n.* a harrow composed of a number of chains attached to a bar dragged behind a tractor.

**chaining-off** /tʃeɪnɪŋ-'ɒf/, *n. Timber Industry.* the removal of timber or scrub using a chain stretched between two vehicles to drag the timber into a pile.

**chain letter** /'tʃeɪn lɛtə/, *n.* a letter sent to a number of people, each of whom makes and sends copies to a number of other people who do likewise, the object being to spread a message or to raise money.

**chain lightning** /– 'laɪtnɪŋ/, *n.* →**forked lightning.**

**chain locker** /'– lɒkə/, *n.* a steel box-like structure below the forecastle of a ship, in which the anchor chain cable is stowed.

**chain mail** /'– meɪl/, *n.* →**mail**[2] (def. 1).

**chainman** /'tʃeɪnmən/, *n., pl.* **-men.** **1.** a man who holds the chain in making surveying measurements; a surveyor's assistant. **2.** *N.Z.* (in meatworks) one who works on a chain (def. 12).

**chain-measure** /'tʃeɪn-mɛʒə/, *n.* →**chain** (def. 9).

**chain mesh** /tʃeɪn 'mɛʃ/, *n.* →**chain wire.** Also, **chainmesh.**

**chain migration** /– maɪ'greɪʃən/, *n.* group migration which occurs when one person settles in a new country and, once he is well established, brings out other members of his family.

**chain-moulding** /'tʃeɪn-mouldɪŋ/, *n. Archit.* moulding in the pattern of a chain.

**chain-passing** /'tʃeɪn-pasɪŋ/, *n. Rugby Football.* a rapid passing of the ball by a number of players from one to the other.

**chainplate** /'tʃeɪnpleɪt/, *n.* one of a group of horizontal iron plates on the sides of a sailing ship, to which the lower rigging was secured.

**chainpump** /'tʃeɪnpʌmp/, *n.* a mechanism for raising water, etc., in buckets or the like attached to an endless moving chain.

**chain-react** /tʃeɪn-ri'ækt/, *v.i.* to undergo a chain-reaction.

**chain-reacting** /'tʃeɪn-riæktɪŋ/, *adj.* (of a substance) undergoing or capable of undergoing a chain-reaction.

**chain-reaction** /tʃeɪn-ri'ækʃən/, *n.* **1.** *Physics.* a nuclear reaction which produces enough neutrons to sustain itself. **2.** *Chem.* a reaction which results in a product necessary for the continuance of the reaction. **3.** *Colloq.* a series of reactions provoked by one event: *a pay-increase for railwaymen would provoke a chain-reaction of wage claims.*

**chainsaw** /'tʃeɪnsɔ/, *n.* **1.** a power-driven crosscut saw with teeth mounted on an endless chain. **2.** a similar saw used for cutting building stone.

**chain-shot** /'tʃeɪn-ʃɒt/, *n. Ordn.* (formerly) a shot consisting of two balls or half balls connected by a short chain.

**chain-smoke** /'tʃeɪn-smouk/, *v.*, **-smoked, -smoking.** *–v.i.* **1.** to smoke continually, as by lighting one cigarette from the preceding one. *–v.t.* **2.** to smoke (cigarettes) in this manner. – **chain-smoker,** *n.*

**chain-stitch** /'tʃeɪn-stɪtʃ/, *n.* **1.** a kind of ornamental stitching in which each stitch forms a loop through the forward end of which the next stitch is taken. *–v.t.* **2.** to sew with a chain-stitch.

**chain stopper** /'tʃeɪn stɒpə/, *n. Naut.* a chain used to hold temporarily a wire rope before it is permanently secured.

**chain-store** /'tʃeɪn-stɔ/, *n.* one of a group of retail stores under the same ownership and management and stocked from a common supply point or points.

**chain wire** /'tʃeɪn waɪə/, *n.* a wire netting suitable for fencing. Also, **chainwire.**

**chainwork** /'tʃeɪnwɜk/, *n.* decorative work esp. when looped or woven together as in the links of a chain.

**chair** /tʃɛə/, *n.* **1.** a seat with a back and legs or other support, often with arms, usu. for one person. **2.** any thing resembling a chair in appearance or use. **3.** a seat of office or authority. **4.** the position of a judge, chairman, presiding officer, etc. **5.** the person occupying the seat or office, esp. the chairman of a meeting. **6.** a professorship. **7.** →**electric chair. 8.** →**sedan chair. 9.** *Railways.* a metal block to support and secure a rail. **10. take the chair, a.** to assume the chairmanship of a meeting; begin or open a meeting. **b.** to preside at a meeting. **11. be in the chair,** *Colloq.* be the person in a group of drinkers whose turn it is to buy drinks. *–v.t.* **12.** to place or seat in a chair. **13.** to install in office or authority. **14.** to conduct as chairman; preside over. **15.** to place in a chair and carry aloft, esp. in triumph. [ME *chaiere,* from OF, from L *cathedra* seat, from Gk *kathédra*]

**chairborne** /'tʃɛəbɔn/, *adj. Colloq.* having a desk or office job (opposed to a more active one). [b. CHAIR and (AIR)BORNE]

**chairlift** /'tʃɛəlɪft/, *n.* a series of chairs suspended from an endless cable driven by a motor, for conveying people up or down mountains.

**chairman** /'tʃɛəmən/, *n., pl.* **-men. 1.** Also, **chairperson.** the presiding officer of a meeting, committee, board, etc. **2.** someone employed to carry or wheel a person in a chair. – **chairmanship,** *n.*

**chairperson** /'tʃɛəpɜsən/, *n.* →**chairman.**

**chair rail** /'tʃɛə reɪl/, *n.* a moulding on an interior made to protect it from damage by the backs of chairs.

**chairwoman** /'tʃɛəwʊmən/, *n., pl.* **-women.** →**chairman.** (def. 1).

**chaise** /ʃeɪz/, *n.* **1.** a light, open carriage, usu. with a hood, esp. a one-horse, two-wheeled carriage for two persons. **2.** a postchaise. [F: chair, chaise, var. of *chaire.* See CHAIR]

chaise

**chaise longue** /– 'lɒŋ/, *n.* a kind of couch or reclining chair with seat prolonged to form a full-length leg rest. [F: long chair]

**chalaza** /kə'leɪzə/, *n., pl.* **-zae** /-zi/, **-zas. 1.** *Zool.* one of the two albuminous twisted cords which fasten an egg yolk to the shell membrane. **2.** *Bot.* the part of an ovule to which the extremity of the funicle is attached. [NL, from Gk: hail, lump] – **chalazal,** *adj.*

**chalcanthite** /kæl'kænθaɪt/, *n.* →**blue vitriol.**

**chalcedony** /kæl'sɛdəni/, *n., pl.* **-nies.** a microcrystalline translucent variety of quartz, often milky or greyish. [ME, from L (Vulgate) *chalcēdonius,* from Gk *chalkēdṓn* in Rev. 21:19] – **chalcedonic** /kælsə'dɒnɪk/, *adj.*

**chalcid fly** /'kælsəd flaɪ/, *n.* any of the Chalcidoidea, a super family of small hymenopterous insects, often of bright metallic colours, whose larvae are mostly parasitic on various stages of other insects. Also, **chalcid.** [NL *Chalcis,* from Gk *chalkós* copper (with allusion to the metallic coloration) + -ID[2]]

**chalco-,** a word element meaning 'copper' or 'brass'. Also, before vowels, **chalc-.** [Gk *chalko-,* combining form of *chalkós*]

**chalcocite** /'kælkəsaɪt/, *n.* a common mineral, cuprous sulphide, $Cu_2S$, an important ore of copper.

**chalcography** /kæl'kɒgrəfi/, *n.* the art of engraving on copper or brass. – **chalcographer,** *n.* – **chalcographic** /kælkə'græfɪk/, **chalcographical** /kælkə'græfɪkəl/, *adj.*

**chalcopyrite** /kælkə'paɪraɪt/, *n.* a very common mineral, copper iron sulphur, $CuFeS_2$, occurring in brass-yellow crystals or masses, an important ore of copper; copper pyrites.

**Chaldaic** /kæl'deɪɪk/, *n.* →**Chaldean** (defs 3, 4, and 5). – **Chaldean,** *adj.*

**Chaldean** /kæl'diən/, *n.* **1.** one of an ancient Semitic people that formed the dominant element in Babylonia. **2.** an astrologer, soothsayer, or enchanter. **3.** biblical Aramaic. *–adj.* **4.** of or belonging to ancient Chaldea. **5.** pertaining to astrology, occult learning, etc. Also, **Chaldee** /kæl'di/. [L *Chaldaeus* (from Gk *Chaldaîos*) + -AN]

**chalet** /'ʃæleɪ/, *n.* **1.** (originally) a herdsman's hut in the Swiss mountains. **2.** a kind of cottage, low and with wide eaves, common in alpine regions. **3.** any cottage or villa built in this style. **4.** a dwelling for holiday use, as at the seaside. **5.** *Tas.* a self-contained flat detached from a house. [F (Swiss)]

**chalice** /'tʃæləs/, *n.* **1.** *Eccles.* **a.** a cup for the wine of the eucharist or mass. **b.** the wine contained in it. **2.** *Poetic.* a drinking cup. **3.** a cuplike blossom. [ME, from OF, from L *calix* cup; replacing ME *caliz, calc,* OE *calic,* from L *calix*] – **chaliced** /'tʃæləst/, *adj.*

chalice

**chalk** /tʃɔk/, *n.* **1.** *Geol.* a soft, white, pure limestone consisting of calcareous fossil skeletal fragments of microscopic algae. **2.** a prepared piece of chalk or chalk-like substance, esp. calcium sulphate, for marking. **3.** a mark made with chalk. **4. chalk and cheese,** *Colloq.* complete opposites. **5. by a long chalk,** by far; by a considerable extent or degree. *–v.t.* **6.** to mark or write with chalk. **7.** to rub over or whiten with chalk. **8.** to treat or mix with chalk. **9.** to make pale; blanch. **10. chalk out,** to outline (a plan, etc.) **11. chalk up, a.** to score: *they chalked up 360 runs in the first innings.* **b.** to ascribe to: *it may be chalked up to experience.* *–v.i.* **12.** to score, as in darts. [ME *chalke,* OE *cealc,* from L *calx* lime] – **chalklike,** *adj.* – **chalky,** *adj.* – **chalkiness,** *n.*

**chalk and talk,** *n.* that traditional method of teaching in which a teacher talks and writes on a blackboard instead of using more recently developed teaching aids and techniques.

**chalkboard** /ˈtʃɔkbɔd/, *n.* →**blackboard.**

**chalkface** /ˈtʃɔkfeɪs/, *n. in the phrase,* **work at the chalkface,** *Colloq. (joc.)* (of teachers) to be actively engaged in teaching in the classroom. [var. of *work at the coalface.* See COALFACE (def. 2)]

**chalkie** /ˈtʃɔki/, *n. Colloq.* **1.** a schoolteacher. **2.** *Stock Exchange.* the person who records transactions on the board.

**chalk-line** /ˈtʃɔk-laɪn/, *n.* a length of cord dusted with chalk used by bricklayers, etc., to mark levels for new work.

**chalkpit** /ˈtʃɔkpɪt/, *n.* a quarry for chalk.

**challenge** /ˈtʃæləndʒ/, *n., v.,* **-lenged, -lenging.** –*n.* **1.** a call to engage in a contest of skill, strength, etc. **2.** a call to fight, as a duel, etc. **3.** something that makes demands upon one's abilities, endurance, etc.: *this job is a challenge.* **4. a.** a calling to account or into question (as of qualifications, rights to participate, be present at etc.). **b.** *Mil.* the demand of a sentry for identification or the password. **c.** *Law.* a formal objection to the qualifications of a juror or to the legality of an entire jury. **d.** *U.S.* the assertion that a vote is invalid or that a voter is not legally qualified. –*v.t.* **5.** to summon to a contest of skill, strength, etc. **6.** to demand as of right; lay claim to; have a claim to. **7.** to make demands, esp. stimulating demands, upon: *this job will challenge your abilities.* **8.** to take exception to; call in question: *to challenge the wisdom of a procedure.* **9.** *Mil.* to halt and demand identification or password from. **10.** *Law.* to take formal exception to (a juror or jury). **11.** *U.S.* to assert that (a vote) is invalid or (a voter) is not qualified to vote. –*v.i.* **12.** to make or issue a challenge. **13.** *Hunting.* (of hounds) to cry or give tongue on picking up the scent. [ME *chalange,* from OF *chalenge,* from L *calumnia* CALUMNY] – **challengeable,** *adj.*

**challenger** /ˈtʃæləndʒə/, *n.* **1.** one who or that which challenges. **2.** *Sport.* a contestant or member of a team that claims a championship or similar honour from the opponent.

**challenging** /ˈtʃæləndʒɪŋ/, *adj.* **1.** stimulating; thought-provoking: *a challenging idea.* **2.** demanding; difficult but interesting: *a challenging job.* **3.** intriguing; enigmatic: *a challenging smile.*

**challis** /ˈʃæli, ˈʃæləs/, *n.* a printed fabric of plain weave in wool, cotton, or rayon. [orig. uncert.]

**chalone** /ˈkæloʊn/, *n.* an endocrine secretion which reduces physiological activity. [Gk *chalôn,* ppr., slackening]

**chalumeau** /ˈʃæljəmoʊ/, *n. Music.* **1.** early reed pipe instruments collectively. **2.** the low register of the clarinet. [F, in OF *chalemel* a musical instrument, from L *calamellus,* diminutive of *calamus* reed]

**chalybeate** /kəˈlɪbiət, -eɪt/, *adj.* **1.** containing or impregnated with salts of iron, as a mineral spring, medicine, etc. –*n.* **2.** a chalybeate water, medicine, or the like. [apparently from NL *chalybēātus,* from L *chalybēius* of steel, from *chalybs,* from Gk *chálybs* iron]

**chalybite** /ˈkæləbaɪt/, *n.* →**siderite.** [Gk *chálybs* iron + -ITE[1]]

**cham** /kæm/, *n. Archaic.* →**khan.**

**chamber** /ˈtʃeɪmbə/, *n.* **1.** a room or apartment, usu. a private room, and esp. a bedroom. **2.** a room in a palace or official residence. **3.** the meeting hall of a legislative or other assembly. **4.** (*pl.*) a place where a judge hears matters not requiring action in court. **5.** (*pl.*) a suite of rooms of barristers and others. **6.** *Obs.* the place where the moneys due to a government, etc., are received and kept; a treasury or chamberlain's office. **7.** a legislative, judicial, or other like body: *the upper or the lower chamber of a legislature.* **8.** a compartment or enclosed space; a cavity: *a chamber of the heart.* **9.** the space between the upper and lower gates of a lock on a navigable waterway. **10.** a receptacle for one or more cartridges in a firearm, or for a shell in a gun or other cannon. **11.** that part of the barrel of a gun which receives the charge. **12.** →**chamber-pot.** –*v.t.* **13.** to put or enclose in, or as in, a chamber. **14.** to provide with a chamber. **15.** to make or modify a chamber in a firearm to take a particular type of cartridge, shell etc.: *chambered for long rifle cartridges.* [ME, from OF *chambre,* from L *camera*] *adj.*

**chamber concert** /ˈ– kɒnsət/, *n.* a concert of chamber music.

**chamberlain** /ˈtʃeɪmbələn/, *n.* **1.** an official charged with the management of a sovereign's or nobleman's living quarters. **2.** the high steward or factor of a nobleman. **3.** a high official of a royal court. [ME *chamberleyn,* from OF *chamberlenc,* from OG; cf. OHG *chamarlinc*]

**chamber magistrate** /tʃeɪmbə ˈmædʒəstrət/, *n.* a qualified solicitor employed in a Court of Petty Sessions, who gives free legal advice.

**chambermaid** /ˈtʃeɪmbəmeɪd/, *n.* a female servant who takes care of bedrooms.

**chamber music** /ˈtʃeɪmbə mjuzɪk/, *n.* music suited for performance in a room or a small concert hall, esp. for two or more (but usu. less than ten) solo instruments.

**chamber of commerce,** *n.* an association, primarily of businessmen, to protect and promote the business activities of a city, etc.

**chamber of horrors,** *n.* **1.** a place, as at a waxworks, where gruesome or horrible objects are exhibited. **2.** the objects collectively. **3.** any collection of things or ideas that might inspire horror.

**chamber orchestra** /ˈtʃeɪmbə ɔkəstrə/, *n.* a small orchestra of perhaps twenty to thirty players.

**chamber-pot** /ˈtʃeɪmbə-pɒt/, *n.* a portable vessel used chiefly in bedrooms as a toilet; thunder-mug.

**chambray** /ˈʃæmbreɪ/, *n.* a fine variety of gingham, commonly plain, but with the warp and weft of different colours. [var. of CAMBRIC]

**chameleon** /kəˈmiliən, ʃə-/, *n.* **1.** any of a group of lizards, Chamaeleontidae, esp. of the genus *Chamaeleon,* found mainly in Africa and Madagascar, characterised by the greatly developed power of changing the colour of the skin, very slow locomotion, and a projectile tongue. **2.** an inconstant person. [ME *camelion,* from L *chamaeleon,* from Gk *chamailéōn,* lit., ground lion] – **chameleonic** /kəmiliˈɒnɪk, ʃə-/, *adj.* – **chameleon-like,** *adj.*

African chameleon

**chamfer** /ˈtʃæmfə/, *n.* **1.** an oblique surface cut on the edge or corner of a solid, usu. a board, made by removing the arris and usually sloping at 45°. –*v.t.* **2.** to cut so as to form a chamfer. **3.** to cut channels or flutes in (a column). **4.** (fol. by *up*) to improve the appearance of; smarten. [apparently from F *chamfrain,* from *chanfraindre,* from *chant* side + *fraindre* (from L *frangere* break)]

**chamferboard** /ˈtʃæmfəbɔd/, *n.* →**weatherboard** (def. 1).

**chamfrain** /ˈtʃæmfrən/, *n.* armour made for a horse's head. Also, **chamfron, chanfron.** [OF *chanfrain;* orig. uncert.]

**chamois** /ˈʃæmwa/ *for def. 1;* /ˈʃæmi/ *for def. 2., n., pl.* **-ois. 1.** an agile goatlike antelope, *Rupicapra rupicapra,* of high mountains of Europe and south-western Russia. **2.** Also, **chammy.** a soft, pliable leather made from various skins dressed with oil (esp. fish oil), originally prepared from the skin of the chamois; shammy. [F, from LL *camox*]

chamois (def. 1)

**chamomile** /ˈkæməmaɪl/, *n.* **1.** any plant of the genus *Anthemis,* a herb with strongly scented foliage and flowers which are used medicinally. **2.** any of various allied plants, esp. of the genus *Matricaria.* Also, **camomile.** [LL *chamomilla,* var. of *chamaemēlon,* from Gk *chamaímēlon* earth apple]

**champ**[1] /tʃæmp/, *v.t.* **1.** to bite upon, esp. impatiently: *horses champing the bit.* **2.** to crush with the teeth and chew vigorously or noisily; munch. –*v.i.* **3.** to make vigorous chewing or biting movements with the jaws and teeth. **4. to champ at the bit,** to be anxious to begin. –*n.* **5.** the act of champing. [? nasalised var. (cf. BUNT[1]) of *chop* bite at, from *chap, chop* jaw]

**champ**[2] /tʃæmp/, *n. Colloq.* a champion.

**champagne** /ʃæmˈpeɪn/, *n.* **1.** a sparkling white wine produced in the wine region of Champagne, France. **2.** a similar wine produced elsewhere. **3.** the non-sparkling (still) dry white table wine produced in the region of Champagne. **4.** a very pale yellow or cream colour. *–adj.* **5.** having the colour of champagne.

**champagne taste** /– 'teɪst/, *n. Colloq.* extravagant desires usu. beyond the means of one who has them: *a champagne taste and a beer income.*

**champaign** /ʃæm'peɪn/, *n.* **1.** level, open country; plain. *–adj.* **2.** level and open. [ME *champaigne,* from OF, from L *campānia.* See CAMPAIGN]

**champak** /'tʃæmpæk, 'tʃʌmpʌk/, *n.* an East Indian tree, *Michelia champaca,* of the magnolia family, with fragrant golden flowers and a handsome wood used for making images, furniture, etc. Also, **champac.** [Hind.]

**champers** /'ʃæmpəz/, *n. Colloq.* champagne.

**champerty** /'ʃæmpəti/, *n. Law.* an illegal sharing in the proceeds of litigation by one who promotes it. [ME *champartie,* from OF *champart* share of the produce of land, from L *campī pars* part of the field] – **champertous,** *adj.*

**champignon** /'ʃæmpɪnjɔ̃/, *n.* a mushroom (defs 2 and 3), picked for market when very small, that is, before the gills are showing. [F, from L *campānia* flat land, from *campus* field]

**champion** /'tʃæmpiən/, *n.* **1.** one who holds first place in any sport, etc., having defeated all opponents. **2.** anything that takes first place in competition. **3.** one who fights for or defends any person or cause: *a champion of the oppressed.* **4.** a fighter or warrior. *–v.t.* **5.** to act as champion of; defend; support. **6.** *Obs.* to defy. *–adj.* **7.** first among all contestants or competitors. **8.** *Colloq.* first-rate. *–adv.* **9.** *Colloq.* in a first-rate manner. [ME, from OF, from LL *campio,* from L *campus* field (of battle)] – **championess** /'tʃæmpiənɛs/, *n. fem.*

**championship** /'tʃæmpiənʃɪp/, *n.* **1.** the position of being a champion. **2.** the honour of being a champion in competition. **3.** a contest held to decide who shall be champion. **4.** advocacy or defence.

**champlevé** /ʃæmplə'vi/, *adj., n., pl.* **-vés** /-'viz/. *–adj.* **1.** of or pertaining to an enamel piece or enamelling technique in which enamel is fused on to the incised or hollowed areas of a metal base. *–n.* **2.** a champlevé enamel piece. **3.** the champlevé method. [F: lit. lifted field (i.e. the hollowed areas of the metal base)]

**chance** /tʃæns, tʃans/, *n., v.,* **chanced, chancing,** *adj. –n.* **1.** the absence of any known reason why an event should turn out one way rather than another, spoken of as if it were a real agency: *chance governs all.* **2.** fortune; fate; luck. **3.** a possibility or probability of anything happening: *the chances are two to one against us.* **4.** an opportunity: *now is your chance.* **5.** a risk or hazard: *take a chance.* **6.** *Archaic.* an unfortunate event; a mishap. **7. by chance,** accidentally. **8. half a chance,** any opportunity at all. **9. the main chance,** the opportunity to further one's own interests: *he had a constant eye to the main chance.* *–v.i.* **10.** to happen or occur by chance. **11.** to come by chance (fol. by *on* or *upon*). *–v.t.* **12.** *Colloq.* to take the chances or risks of; risk (usu. fol. by impersonal *it*). **13. chance one's arm,** to make an attempt, often in spite of a strong possibility of failure. *–adj.* **14.** due to chance: *a chance occurrence.* [ME *chea(u)nce,* from OF *cheance,* from LL *cadentia* a falling out, from *cadens,* ppr., falling] – **chanceful,** *adj.* – **chanceless,** *adj.*

**chancel** /'tʃænsəl, 'tʃansəl/, *n.* the space about the altar of a church, usu. enclosed, for the clergy, choir, etc. [ME, from OF, from LL *cancellus,* from L *cancellī* (pl.) bars, lattice (which enclosed the chancel)]

**chancellery** /'tʃænsəlri, 'tʃans-/, *n., pl.* **-ries.** **1.** the position of a chancellor. **2.** the office or department of a chancellor. **3.** the office attached to an embassy, etc. **4.** the building or room occupied by a chancellor's department. Also, **chancellory, chancelry.** [ME *chancelerie,* from OF, from *chancelier* CHANCELLOR]

**chancellor** /'tʃænsələ, 'tʃansələ/, *n.* **1.** the title of various important judges and other high officials. **2.** the chief minister of state in any of various German-speaking countries, as present-day West Germany. **3.** a secretary, as of a king, nobleman, or embassy. **4.** the titular, honorary head of a university. **5.** *U.S.* the chief administrator in certain American universities. [ME *chanceler,* from AF, var. of OF *chancelier,* from LL *cancellārius,* orig. officer stationed at a tribunal. See CHANCEL] – **chancellorship,** *n.*

**chance-medley** /'tʃæns-mɛdli, tʃans-/, *n. Law.* a sudden quarrel with violence, in the course of which one party kills or wounds another in self-defence or in the heat of passion. [AF *chance medlée* mixed chance]

**chancery** /'tʃænsəri/, *n., pl.* **-ceries.** **1.** the office or department of a chancellor. **2.** (*cap.*) *Brit.* the Lord Chancellor's court, now a division of the High Court of Justice. **3.** Also, **court of chancery.** *Brit. Law.* a court having jurisdiction in equity. **4. in chancery, a.** *Brit. Law.* in litigation in a court of chancery. **b.** *Wrestling, Boxing.* (of a contestant's head) held under his opponent's arm. **c.** in a helpless or embarrassing position. [ME, var. of CHANCELLERY]

**chancre** /'ʃæŋkə/, *n. Pathol.* the initial lesion of syphilis, commonly a more or less distinct ulcer or sore with a hard base. [F, from L *cancer* crab, cancer] – **chancrous,** *adj.*

**chancroid** /'ʃæŋkrɔɪd/, *Pathol. –n.* **1.** a soft, non-syphilitic venereal sore. **2.** the causative organism, *Haemophilus ducreyi.* *–adj.* **3.** of, pertaining to, or resembling a chancroid or chancre.

**chancy** /'tʃænsi, 'tʃansi/, *adj.,* **chancier, chanciest.** *Colloq.* uncertain; risky. Also, **chancey.** – **chanciness,** *n.*

**chandelier** /ʃændə'lɪə/, *n.* a branched support for a number of lights, esp. one suspended from a ceiling. [F, from *chandel* candle + suffix *-ier*]

**chandelle** /ʃæn'dɛl/, *n. Aeron.* an abrupt climbing turn approximating to a stall, in which momentum is used to obtain a higher rate of climb. [F]

**chandler** /'tʃændlə/, *n.* **1.** a dealer or trader: *a ship's chandler.* **2.** one who makes or sells candles. **3.** *Obs.* a retailer of groceries, etc. [ME *cha(u)ndeler,* from AF, var. of OF *chandelier* candle-seller, from OF *chandelle* CANDLE]

**chandlery** /'tʃændləri/, *n., pl.* **-ries.** **1.** a storeroom for candles. **2.** the warehouse, wares, or business of a chandler.

**chanfron** /'tʃænfrən/, *n.* →**chamfrain.**

**change** /tʃeɪndʒ/, *v.,* **changed, changing,** *n. –v.t.* **1.** to make different; alter in condition, appearance, etc.; turn (oft. fol. by *into*): *change one's habits.* **2.** to substitute another or others for; exchange for something else: *to change one's job.* **3.** to give or get smaller money in exchange for: *to change a dollar note.* **4.** to give or get different currency in exchange for: *to change dollars into francs.* **5.** to give and take reciprocally; interchange: *to change places with someone.* **6.** to remove and replace the coverings of: *to change a baby.* **7.** to select a higher or lower (gear of a motor vehicle). **8. change front,** *Mil.* to shift a military force in another direction. **9. change hands,** to pass from one hand or possessor to another. **10. change one's mind,** to alter one's intentions or opinion. **11. change one's tune,** to assume a different, usu. humbler, attitude. *–v.i.* **12.** to become different; alter (sometimes fol. by *to* or *into*). **13.** to make a change or an exchange. **14.** to change trains or other conveyances. **15.** to change one's clothes. **16.** to change gear (fol. by *up* or *down*). *–n.* **17.** variation; alteration; modification; deviation; transformation. **18.** the substitution of one thing for another. **19.** variety or novelty. **20.** the passing from one place, state, form, or phase to another: *change of the moon.* **21.** the supplanting of one thing by another. **22.** that which is or may be substituted for another. **23.** a fresh set of clothing. **24.** information of advantage: *get no change out of someone.* **25.** a balance of money that is returned when the sum tendered is larger than the sum due. **26.** coins of low denomination. **27.** (*oft. cap.*) *Comm.* a place where merchants meet for business transactions; an exchange. **28.** any of the various sequences in which a peal of bells may be rung. **29.** *Music.* a harmonic progression. **30. ring the changes, a.** to ring a peal of bells according to one of the sequences of changes. **b.** to execute a number of manoeuvres or variations; to try all the possibilities. [ME *change(n),* from OF *changier,* from LL *cambiāre,* L *cambīre*]

**changeable** /'tʃeɪndʒəbəl/, *adj.* **1.** liable to change or to be changed; variable. **2.** *Archaic.* of changing colour or appearance: *changeable silk.* – **changeability** /tʃeɪndʒə'bɪləti/, **changeableness,** *n.* – **changeably,** *adv.*

**changeful** /'tʃeɪndʒfəl/, *adj.* changing; variable; inconstant. – **changefully,** *adv.* – **changefulness,** *n.*

**changeless** /ˈtʃeɪndʒləs/, *adj.* unchanging. – **changelessly,** *adv.* – **changelessness,** *n.*

**changeling** /ˈtʃeɪndʒlɪŋ/, *n.* **1.** a child supposedly substituted secretly for another, esp. by fairies; an elfchild. **2.** *Archaic.* an inconstant person. **3.** *Archaic.* an idiot.

**change of life,** *n.* →**menopause.**

**change of state,** *n. Physics, Chem.* the conversion of a substance from one of the physical states of matter (solid, liquid, or gas) into another.

**change of venue,** *n.* **1.** a change of place. **2.** *Law.* the removal of trial to another jurisdiction.

**changeover** /ˈtʃeɪndʒoʊvə/, *n.* **1.** the transition from one system of working to another. **2.** a reversal of opinion, situation, etc. **3.** *Sport.* the movement of one team to positions at the other end of the field, as at half-time.

**changer** /ˈtʃeɪndʒə/, *n.* **1.** one who or that which changes. **2.** →**record-changer.**

**change-ringing** /ˈtʃeɪndʒ-rɪŋɪŋ/, *n.* **1.** the act of ringing the changes on a peal of bells. **2.** variations on a subject.

**change room** /ˈtʃeɪndʒ rum/, *n.* a room for use when changing clothes, esp. in a gymnasium, squash-court, etc.

**channel**[1] /ˈtʃænəl/, *n., v.,* **-nelled, -nelling** or (*U.S.*) **-neled, -neling.** –*n.* **1.** the bed of a stream or waterway. **2.** the deeper part of a waterway. **3.** a wide strait, as between a continent and an island. **4.** *Naut.* a navigable route between two bodies of water. **5.** (*cap.*) the English Channel. **6.** a means of access. **7.** a course into which something may be directed. **8.** a route through which anything passes or progresses: *channels of communication.* **9.** a frequency band wide enough for one-way communication, the exact width of a channel depending upon the type of transmission involved (as telegraph, telephone, radio, television, etc.). **10.** a tubular passage for liquids or fluids. **11.** a groove or furrow. –*v.t.* **12.** to convey through a channel. **13.** to direct towards or into some particular course: *to channel one's interests.* **14.** to excavate as a channel. **15.** to form a channel in; groove. **16.** to shear (a sheep) below the vulva to prevent wetting by urine. [ME *chanel,* from OF, from L *canālis* CANAL]

**channel**[2] /ˈtʃænəl/, *n.* one of the horizontal planks or ledges attached outside a ship to give more spread to the lower shrouds. [var. of *chain-wale* (see WALE)]

**channel-billed cuckoo** /ˌtʃænəl-bɪld ˈkʊku/, *n.* a large, greyish, migratory bird, *Scythrops novaehollandiae,* with a large bill and a loud, raucous voice, found in northern and eastern Australia, New Guinea and islands to the north; rainbird.

**channel iron** /ˈtʃænəl aɪən/, *n.* a rolled iron, steel or aluminium bar whose section is shaped like three sides of a rectangle.

**chanson** /ʃænˈsɒn, ʃɔ̃ˈsɔ̃/, *n.* a song, esp. a French song. [F, from L *cantio*]

**chanson de geste** /ʃɔ̃ˌsɔ̃ də ˈʒɛst/, *n.* one of a class of old French epic poems, celebrating the deeds of heroic or historic figures. [F: song of heroic deeds]

**chant** /tʃænt, tʃant/, *n.* **1.** a song; singing. **2.** a short, simple melody, specifically one characterised by single notes to which an indefinite number of syllables are intoned, used in singing the psalms, canticles, etc., in the church service. **3.** a psalm, canticle, or the like, chanted or for chanting. **4.** the singing or intoning of all or portions of the spoken parts of a church service. **5.** any monotonous song. **6.** a monotonous intonation of the voice in speaking. –*v.t.* **7.** to sing. **8.** to celebrate in song. **9.** to sing to a chant, or in the manner of a chant, esp. in the church service. –*v.i.* **10.** to sing. **11.** to sing a chant. [ME *chaunte(n),* from OF *chanter,* from L *cantāre,* frequentative of *canere* sing]

**chanter** /ˈtʃæntə, ˈtʃantə/, *n.* **1.** one who chants; a singer. **2.** a chorister; a precentor. **3.** the chief singer or priest of a chantry. **4.** the pipe of a bagpipe, provided with finger holes for playing the melody.

**chanterelle** /tʃæntəˈrɛl, ʃæn-/, *n.* the yellowish fungus, *Cantharellus cibarius,* a popular edible species in Europe. [F, from NL *cantharella,* diminutive of L *cantharus* drinking vessel, from Gk *kántharos*]

**chanteuse** /ʃɒnˈtɜz/, *n.* a woman singer, esp. a nightclub singer. [F]

**chanticleer** /tʃæntəˈklɪə, ʃɒntə-/, *n.* a name for the cock, originally in the medieval fable *Reynard the Fox.* [ME *chauntecler,* from OF *Chantecler,* lit., clear singer, from *chante* (impv. of *chanter* sing) + *cler* clear]

**Chantilly** /ʃænˈtɪli/, *n.* **1.** a fine silk or linen bobbin lace. **2.** (*l.c.*) sweetened whipped cream, sometimes with whipped egg whites folded in. [*Chantilly,* a town in France]

**chantry** /ˈtʃæntri/, *n., pl.* **-tries.** *Eccles.* **1.** an endowment for the singing or saying of mass for the souls of the founders or of persons named by them. **2.** a chapel or the like so endowed. **3.** the priests of a chantry endowment. [ME *chanterie,* from F: singing]

**chaos** /ˈkeɪɒs/, *n.* **1.** utter confusion or disorder, wholly without organisation or order. **2.** (*usu. cap.*) the infinity of space or formless matter supposed to have preceded the existence of the ordered universe. **3.** *Obs.* a chasm or abyss. [L, from Gk]

**chaotic** /keɪˈɒtɪk/, *adj.* in utter confusion or disorder. – **chaotically,** *adv.*

**chap**[1] /tʃæp/, *v.,* **chapped, chapping,** *n.* –*v.t.* **1.** to cause to open in small slits or cracks. **2.** (of cold or exposure) to crack, roughen, and redden (the skin). –*v.i.* **3.** to become chapped. –*n.* **4.** a fissure or crack, esp. in the skin. [ME *chapp(en)*; orig. uncert.]

**chap**[2] /tʃæp/, *n.* **1.** *Colloq.* a fellow; man or boy. **2.** *Obs.* a customer. [short for CHAPMAN]

**chap**[3] /tʃæp/, *n.* **1.** the jaw or the fleshy covering of the jaw (of an animal). **2.** the forepart of the face. **3.** one of the cheeks or jaws of a clamping tool, or vice. Also, **chop**[3].

**chap.,** **1.** chaplain. **2.** chapter. Also, **Chap.**

**chaparral** /ʃæpəˈræl/, *n. U.S.* **1.** a close growth of low evergreen oaks. **2.** any dense thicket. [Sp., from *chaparro* evergreen oak, ? from Basque]

**chaparral cock** /– ˈkɒk/, *n.* a terrestrial cuckoo of the southwestern U.S., *Geococcyx californianus;* the roadrunner.

chaparral cock

**chapatti** /ˈtʃʌpəti, tʃəˈpati/, *n.* a flat Indian unleavened bread made from wholewheat flour and cooked on a griddle. Also, **chapati, chupatti.** [Hindi *chapātī*]

**chapbook** /ˈtʃæpbʊk/, *n.* one of a type of small books or pamphlets of popular tales, ballads, etc., such as were formerly hawked about by chapmen.

**chape** /tʃeɪp/, *n.* the metal mounting or trimming of a scabbard, esp. at the point. [ME, from F. See CAP[1]]

**chapeau** /ʃæˈpoʊ/, *n., pl.* **-peaux, -peaus** /-ˈpoʊz/. a hat. [F, from L *capellus,* diminutive of *capa, cappa.* See CAP[1]]

**chapel** /ˈtʃæpəl/, *n.* **1.** a private or subordinate place of prayer or worship; an oratory. **2.** a separately dedicated part of a church, or a small independent churchlike edifice, devoted to special services. **3.** a room or building for worship in a college or school, country house or royal court, etc. **4.** *Brit.* a place of worship of a religious body outside the established Church. **5.** *Brit.* a separate place of public worship dependent on the church of a parish. **6.** a religious service in a chapel. **7.** a choir or orchestra of a chapel, court, etc. **8.** *Obs.* a printing office. **9.** **a.** the body of members of a trade union in a printing or publishing house. **b.** a meeting of this body. [ME *chapele,* from OF, from LL *cappella* sanctuary for relics (such as the cape of St Martin), diminutive of *capa, cappa.* See CAP[1]]

**chaperone** /ˈʃæpəroʊn/, *n.* **1.** an older person, usu. a matron, who, for propriety, attends a young unmarried woman in public or accompanies a party of young unmarried men and women. –*v.t.* **2.** to attend or accompany as chaperone. Also, **chaperon.** [F: hood, from *chape* CAPE[1]] – **chaperonage** /ʃæpəˈroʊnɪdʒ/, *n.*

**chapfallen** /ˈtʃæpfɔlən/, *adj.* dispirited; chagrined; dejected. Also, **chopfallen.**

**chapiter** /ˈtʃæpətə/, *n. Archit.* →**capital**[2]. [F. See CHAPTER]

**chaplain** /ˈtʃæplən/, *n.* **1.** an ecclesiastic attached to the chapel of a royal court, or, formerly, a noble family, or to a college, school, etc., or to a military unit. **2.** one who says the prayer, invocation, etc., for an organisation or at an assembly or gathering. [ME *chapelayn,* from OF *chapelain,* from LL *capellānus,* from *capella* CHAPEL; replacing OE *capellān,* from LL (as above)] – **chaplaincy, chaplainry, chaplainship,** *n.*

**chaplet** /'tʃæplət/, *n.* **1.** a wreath or garland for the head. **2.** a string of beads. **3.** *Rom. Cath. Ch.* **a.** a string of beads for counting prayers, one third the length of a rosary. **b.** the prayers so counted thereon. **4.** *Archit.* a small moulding carved in the shape of beads or the like. **5.** *Foundry.* a metal piece supporting the core in casting a cylindrical pipe. [ME *chapelet,* from OF, diminutive of *chapel* headdress. See CHAPEAU] – **chapleted,** *adj.*

**Chaplinesque** /tʃæplə'nɛsk/, *adj.* comic, in the manner of Charlie Chaplin. [Charles Spencer *Chaplin,* 1889-1977, comedian, film actor and director]

**chapman** /'tʃæpmən/, *n., pl.* **-men. 1.** *Brit.* a hawker or pedlar. **2.** *Archaic.* a merchant. [ME; OE *cēapman,* from *cēap* trade + *man* man]

**chappie** /'tʃæpi/, *n. Colloq.* →**chap**[2]. Also, **chappy.**

**chaps** /tʃæps, ʃæps/, *n.pl.* strong leather riding breeches or overalls with no seat worn over ordinary trousers to protect the legs. [short for *chaparagjos,* Mex. Sp. var. of *chaparreras,* from *chaparro* bramble bush]

**chapter** /'tʃæptə/, *n.* **1.** a main division, usu. numbered, of a book, treatise, or the like. **2.** a branch, usu. localised, of a society or fraternity. **3.** *Eccles.* **a.** an assembly of the monks in a monastery, or of those in a province, or of the entire order. **b.** a general assembly of the canons of a church. **c.** a meeting of the elected representatives of the provinces or houses of a religious community. **d.** the body of such canons or representatives collectively. **4.** a division of the acts of Parliament passed in a session. **5.** *Horol.* any one of the Roman figures used on clocks and watches to mark the time of day. **6.** *Liturgy.* a short scriptural quotation read at various parts of the office, as after the last psalm in the service of lauds, prime, tierce, etc. **7. chapter and verse,** an exact reference. **8. chapter of accidents,** a series of closely following misfortunes. **9.** →**chapterhouse.** *–v.t.* **10.** to divide into or arrange in chapters. [ME *chapitre,* from OF, var. of *chapitle,* from L *capitulum* small head, capital of column, chapter, diminutive of *caput* head]

**chapterhouse** /'tʃæptəhaʊs/, *n.* **1.** *Eccles.* a building attached to a cathedral or monastery in which the chapter meets. **2.** the building of a chapter of a society, etc.

**char**[1] /tʃa/, *v.,* **charred, charring,** *n.* *–v.t.* **1.** to burn or reduce to charcoal. **2.** to burn slightly; scorch. *–v.i.* **3.** to become charred. *–n.* **4.** a charred substance. **5.** →**charcoal. 6.** *Chem.* dried lignite; used for pollution prevention purposes as desulphurisation. [? short for CHARCOAL] – **charry,** *adj.*

**char**[2] /tʃa/, *n., pl.* **chars,** (*esp. collectively*) **char.** any of several fishes of the genus *Salvelinus,* related to the salmon and trout; often found in deep, cold lakes. Also, **charr.** [cf. Gaelic *ceara* red]

**char**[3] /tʃa/, *n., v.,* **charred, charring.** *Colloq.* *–n.* **1.** →**charwoman.** *–v.i.* **2.** to do housework by the hour or day for money. [ME *cherre,* OE *cerr, cyrr* turn, time, occasion, affair]

**char**[4] /tʃa/, *n.* tea. [Hind. *chā* ]

**char.,** character.

**charabanc** /'ʃærəbæŋk/, *n., pl.* **-bancs** /-bæŋks/. *Brit.* a motor coach, esp. an open one formerly much used in sightseeing. Also, **char-à-banc.** [F *char à bancs* car with benches]

**characin** /'kærəsɪn/, *n.* any of various freshwater fishes of the family Characinidae native to Africa and South America. [NL *Characinus* typical genus, from Gk *chárax* a sea-fish] – **characinoid** /kə'ræsɪnɔɪd/, *adj.*

**character** /'kærəktə/, *n.* **1.** the aggregate of qualities that distinguishes one person or thing from others. **2.** moral constitution, as of a person or people. **3.** good moral constitution or status. **4.** reputation. **5.** good repute. **6.** an account of the qualities or peculiarities of a person or thing. **7.** a formal statement from an employer concerning the qualities and habits of a former servant or employee. **8.** status or capacity. **9.** a person: *a strange character.* **10.** *Colloq.* an odd or interesting person. **11.** a person represented in a drama, story, etc. **12.** *Theat.* a part or role. **13.** *Genetics.* any trait, function, structure, or substance of an organism resulting from the development of a gene interacting with the environment and the remainder of the gene complex; a hereditary characteristic. **14.** a significant visual mark or symbol. **15.** a symbol as used in a writing system, as a letter of the alphabet. **16.** the symbols of a writing system collectively. **17.** *Computers.* a group of bits representing such a symbol or a numeral. **18.** a style of writing or printing. **19.** *Obs.* a cipher or cipher message. **20. in character,** consistent with what is known of previous character, behaviour, etc. **21. out of character,** inconsistent with what is known of previous character, behaviour, etc. *–v.t.* **22.** to portray; describe. **23.** *Archaic.* to engrave or inscribe. [L, from Gk *charaktḗr* instrument for marking, mark; replacing ME *caractere,* from F] – **characterless,** *adj.*

**character actor** /'– æktə/, *n.* an actor who portrays striking or eccentric characters.

**characterisation** /ˌkærəktəraɪ'zeɪʃən/, *n.* **1.** portrayal; description. **2.** the act of characterising. **3.** the creation of fictitious characters. Also, **characterization.**

**characterise** /'kærəktəraɪz/, *v.t.,* **-rised, -rising. 1.** to mark or distinguish as a characteristic; be a characteristic of. **2.** to describe the characteristic or peculiar quality of. **3.** to give character to. Also, **characterize.** – **characteriser,** *n.*

**characteristic** /kærəktə'rɪstɪk/, *adj.* **1.** pertaining to, constituting, or indicating the character or peculiar quality; typical; distinctive. *–n.* **2.** a distinguishing feature or quality. **3.** *Maths.* the integral part of a logarithm.

**characteristically** /kærəktə'rɪstɪkli/, *adv.* in a characteristic manner; typically.

**characteristic velocity** /ˌkærəktərɪstɪk və'lɒsəti/, *n.* *Astronautics.* the speed a rocket would attain with the complete consumption of its propellants if unaffected by external forces.

**character piece** /'kærəktə pis/, *n. Music.* a short 19th-century piano or instrumental composition designed to capture a specific mood.

**character reference** /'– rɛfrəns/, *n.* a reference (def. 9) describing the qualities, disposition, etc., of a person.

**character sketch** /'– skɛtʃ/, *n.* **1.** a short description of someone's character. **2.** a monologue or a short scene in which the character of a person is made clear.

**charactery** /'kærəktəri/, *n., pl.* **-ries. 1.** the use of characters or symbols for the expression of meaning. **2.** characters or symbols collectively.

**charade** /ʃə'rad/, *n.* **1.** a game in which a player or players act out in pantomime a word or phrase which the others try to guess. **2.** a ridiculous or pointless act or series of acts. [F, from Pr. *charrado* entertainment, from *charra* chat]

**Charbray** /'ʃabreɪ/, *n.* one of a breed of cattle which are one eighth to one quarter Brahman, the main strain being Charolais.

**charcoal** /'tʃakoʊl/, *n.* **1.** the carbonaceous material obtained by the imperfect combustion of wood or other organic substances. **2.** a drawing pencil of charcoal. **3.** a drawing made with charcoal. *–v.t.* **4.** to blacken, write or draw with charcoal. [ME *charcole;* orig. uncert.]

**charcoal-burner** /'tʃakoʊl-bɜnə/, *n.* **1.** a person who makes charcoal, esp. (formerly) for a livelihood. **2.** a stove, etc., burning charcoal.

**charcoal-grey** /tʃakoʊl-'greɪ/, *n.* a dark grey colour.

**charcuterie** /ʃa'kutəri/, *n.* **1.** cold cooked meats, esp. pork, ham, sausages, etc. **2.** a shop which sells such products. [F *chair cuite* cooked flesh, *charcuitier* pork butcher]

**chard** /tʃad/, *n.* **1.** the blanched summer shoots of the globe artichoke, *Cynara scolymus.* **2.** the spring flowering shoots of salsify, *Tragopogon porrifolius.* **3.** a form of the common beet, *Beta vulgaris* var. *cicla,* with thick leafstalks (**Swiss chard**). [F *charde,* from L *carduus* thistle, artichoke]

**Chardonnay** /'ʃadɒneɪ/, *n.* a grape variety used in making white burgundy and champagne-style wines.

**charge** /tʃadʒ/, *v.,* **charged, charging,** *n.* *–v.t.* **1.** to put a load or burden on or in. **2.** to fill or furnish (a thing) with the appropriate quantity of that which it is designed to receive. **3.** to supply with a quantity of electricity or electrical energy: *to charge a battery.* **4.** to fill (air, water, etc.) with other matter in a state of diffusion or solution. **5.** to load or burden (the mind, heart, etc.). **6.** to lay a command or injunction upon. **7.** to instruct authoritatively, as a judge does a jury. **8.** to impute as a fault: *charge him with carelessness.* **9.** to lay blame upon; blame; accuse (usu. fol. by *with*): *to charge someone with negligence.* **10.** to hold liable for payment; enter a debit against. **11.** to list or record as a debt or obligation; enter as a debit. **12.** to postpone payment on (a service or purchase) by having it recorded on one's charge account. **13.** to impose or ask as a price. **14.** to attack by rushing violently against. **15.** *Her.* to place a bearing on (a shield, etc.). *–v.i.* **16.** to make an onset; rush, as to an attack. *–n.* **17.** a load or burden. **18.** the quantity of anything which an apparatus is fitted to hold, or holds, at one time. **19.** *Elect.* an electric charge. **20.** a quantity of explosive to be set off at one time. **21.** a duty or responsibility laid upon or entrusted to one. **22.** care, custody, or superintendence: *to have charge of a thing.* **23.** anything or anybody committed to one's care or management. **24.** *Eccles.* a parish or congregation committed to the spiritual care of a minister or priest. **25.** a command or injunction; exhortation. **26.** *Law.* an address by a judge to a jury at the close of a trial, instructing them as to the legal points, the weight of evidence, etc., affecting their verdict in the case. **27.** an accusation or imputation of guilt: *he was arrested on a charge of murder.* **28.** expense or cost: *improvements made at a tenant's own charge.* **29.** a sum or price charged: *a charge of $2 for admission.* **30.** a pecuniary burden, encumbrance, tax, or lien; cost; expense; liability to pay. **31.** an entry in an account of something due. **32.** a charge account. **33.** an impetuous onset or attack, as of soldiers. **34.** a signal by bugle, drum, etc. for a military charge. **35.** the quantity of energy stored in a capacitor or electrical storage battery. **36.** *Her.* →**bearing** (def.10). **37.** *Colloq.* an alcoholic drink. **38.** *Colloq.* a thrill; a kick. **39. in charge,** in command; having supervisory powers. **40. in charge of, a.** having the care or supervision of: *in charge of the class.* **b.** *U.S.* under the care or supervision of: *in charge of the teacher.* **41. in the charge of,** in the care of; under the supervision of. **42. give in charge,** to deliver to the police. **43. charge like a wounded bull,** *Colloq.* to fix prices that are excessive. [ME *charge(n)*, from OF *charg(i)er*, from LL *carricāre* load. See CAR]

**chargeable** /ˈtʃadʒəbəl/, *adj.* **1.** that may or should be charged. **2.** liable to be accused or held responsible; indictable. **3.** liable to become a charge on the public.

**charge account** /ˈtʃadʒ əkaʊnt/, *n.* a credit arrangement with a department store, service station, etc., whereby the purchase of goods is charged to the customer's account.

**charge card** /ˈ– kad/, *n.* →**credit card.**

**charge-coupled device** /ˌtʃadʒ-kʌpəld dəˈvaɪs/, *n.* a form of integrated circuit used for storing electric charges.

**chargé d'affaires** /ˌʃaʒeɪ dəˈfɛə/, *n., pl.* **chargés d'affaires. 1.** (in full: **chargé d'affaires ad interim**) an official placed in charge of diplomatic business during the temporary absence of the ambassador or minister. **2.** an envoy to a state to which a diplomat of higher grade is not sent. Also, **chargé.** [F: lit., entrusted with affairs]

**charge hand** /ˈtʃadʒ hænd/, *n.* the grade of workman below a foreman, and above a leading hand.

**charger**[1] /ˈtʃadʒə/, *n.* **1.** one who or that which charges. **2.** a horse intended, or suitable, to be ridden in battle. **3.** *Elect.* an apparatus which charges storage batteries. [CHARGE, *v.* + -ER[1]]

**charger**[2] /ˈtʃadʒə/, *n.* **1.** a platter. **2.** a large, shallow dish for liquids. [ME *chargeour;* akin to CHARGE]

**charge sheet** /ˈtʃadʒ ʃit/, *n.* a list of people awaiting a hearing in a magistrates' court, together with the charges made against them.

**charging order** /ˈtʃadʒɪŋ ɔdə/, *n. Law.* an order preventing the transfer of the stock, shares, funds or annuities held by one whom the court judges to be a debtor.

**charily** /ˈtʃɛərəli/, *adv.* **1.** carefully; warily. **2.** sparingly.

**chariness** /ˈtʃɛərinəs/, *n.* **1.** chary quality; caution; sparingness. **2.** *Obs.* scrupulous integrity.

**chariot** /ˈtʃæriət/, *n.* **1.** a two-wheeled vehicle used by the ancients in war, racing, processions, etc. **2.** (in the 18th century) a light four-wheeled pleasure carriage. **3.** any more or less stately carriage. *–v.t.* **4.** to convey in a chariot. *–v.i.* **5.** to drive a chariot; ride in a chariot. [ME, from OF, augmentative of *char.* See CAR]

**charioteer** /tʃæriəˈtɪə/, *n.* a chariot driver.

chariot

**charisma** /kəˈrɪzmə/, *n., pl.* **-mata** /-mətə/. **1.** Also, **charism** /ˈkærɪzəm/. a gift or power (such as healing) conferred by the Holy Spirit on a Christian for the good of the church. **2.** those special personal qualities that give an individual influence or authority over large numbers of people. **3.** ability to influence or impress people, esp. when visible in politicians or public figures; personality. [Gk: *chárisma* gift] – **charismatic** /kærəzˈmætɪk/, *adj., n.*

**charitable** /ˈtʃærətəbəl/, *adj.* **1.** generous in gifts to relieve the needs of others. **2.** kindly or lenient in judging others. **3.** pertaining to or concerned with charity: *a charitable institution.* [ME, from OF, from *charite* CHARITY] – **charitableness,** *n.* – **charitably,** *adv.*

**charitable trust** /– ˈtrʌst/, *n.* a trust for the relief of poverty, the advancement of education, religion, or for other purposes beneficial to the community.

**charity** /ˈtʃærəti/, *n., pl.* **-ties. 1.** almsgiving; the private or public relief of unfortunate or needy persons; benevolence. **2.** something given to a person or persons in need; alms. **3.** a charitable act or work. **4.** a charitable fund, foundation, or institution. **5.** benevolent feeling, esp. towards those in need. **6.** Christian love. *–adj.* **7.** of or pertaining to organisations, fund-raising activities, etc., of a charitable nature. [ME *charite,* from OF, from L *cāritas* dearness]

**charity school** /ˈ– skul/, *n. Brit.* a day school for poor children in the 18th and 19th centuries; usu. run by the Church of England.

**charivari** /ʃarəˈvari/, *n., pl.* **-ris.** a mock serenade of discordant noises made with pans, horns, etc., after a wedding. [F]

**charka** /ˈtʃakə/, *n.* (in India and the East Indies) a cotton gin or spinning wheel. Also, **charkha.** [Hind.]

**charlady** /ˈtʃaleɪdi/, *n., pl.* **-dies.** →**charwoman.**

**charlatan** /ˈʃalətən/, *n.* one who pretends to more knowledge or skill than he possesses; a quack. [F, from It. *ciarlatano* from *ciarlare* chatter] – **charlatanic** /ʃaləˈtænɪk/, *adj.*

**charlatanism** /ˈʃalətənɪzəm/, *n.* the practices of a charlatan. Also, **charlatanry** /ˈʃalətənri/.

**Charles's law** /ˈtʃalzəz lɔ/, *n. Physics.* the law which states that, for an ideal gas at constant pressure, a rise in temperature of 1°C will cause the gas to expand by $\frac{1}{273}$ of its volume. See **gas laws.** [named after J. A. C. *Charles,* 1746-1823, French physicist]

**charleston** /ˈtʃalstən/, *n.* a kind of foxtrot, of Negro origin, popular in the 1920s. [from *Charleston,* a seaport in the U.S., in South Carolina]

**charley horse** /ˈtʃali hɔs/, *n. U.S. Colloq.* stiffness in the leg; a sprain.

**charlie**[1] /ˈtʃali/, *n. Colloq.* **1.** a fool; a silly person: *a right charlie.* **2.** (*pl.*) a woman's breasts. Also, **charley.**

**charlie**[2] /ˈtʃali/, *n. Colloq.* a girl. [rhyming slang, *Charlie Wheeler* sheila]

**Charlie** /ˈtʃali/, *n. Mil. Colloq.* an enemy Asian soldier, esp. a Vietnamese soldier. Also, **Charley.** [from mil. signals code *Victor Charlie* for Viet Cong]

**charlock** /ˈtʃalɒk/, *n.* any of several weeds of the family Cruciferae, esp. *Sinapis arvensis.* [ME *carlok,* OE *cerlic*]

**charlotte** /ˈʃalət/, *n.* a hot pudding with a framework of thinly sliced and buttered bread filled with apples or other fruit. [F, orig., woman's name]

**charlotte russe** /– ˈrus/, *n.* a mould of sponge fingers filled with a cream mousse mixture. [F: Russian charlotte]

**charm**[1] /tʃam/, *n.* **1.** a power to please and attract; fascination. **2.** some quality or feature exerting a fascinating influence: *feminine charms.* **3.** something which possesses this power. **4.** a trinket to be worn on a chain, bracelet, etc. **5.** something worn for its supposed magical effect; an amulet. **6.** any action supposed to have magical power. **7.** the chanting or recitation of a magic verse or formula. **8.** a verse or formula credited with magical power. **9. like a**

charm, successfully; perfectly. *–v.t.* **10.** to attract powerfully by beauty, etc.; please greatly. **11.** to act upon with or as with a charm; enchant. **12.** to endow with or protect by supernatural powers. **13.** to calm, soothe, etc. *–v.i.* **14.** to be fascinating or pleasing. **15.** to use charms. **16.** to act as a charm. [ME *charme,* from OF, from L *carmen* song, incantation] – **charmer,** *n.*

**charm**[2] /tʃam/, *n.* blended singing of birds, children, etc. [ME *cherm(e),* OE *cerm, ceorm,* var. of *cierm* outcry. Cf. CHIRM]

**Charmat process** /ˈʃamæt ˌprousɛs/, *n.* a process for making sparkling wines in bulk. [named after Eugene *Charmat,* the French scientist who developed it]

**charmer** /ˈtʃamə/, *n.* **1.** one who is so personally attractive that he or she has unusual power to charm. **2.** a sorcerer.

**charming** /ˈtʃamɪŋ/, *adj.* **1.** pleasing; delightful. **2.** exercising magic power. – **charmingly,** *adv.*

**charnel** /ˈtʃanəl/, *n.* a repository for dead bodies. [ME, from OF, from LL *carnāle,* properly neut. adj. See CARNAL]

**charnel-house** /ˈtʃanəl-haus/, *n.* **1.** a house or place in which the bodies or bones of the dead are deposited. **2.** a hotel, esp. one with a reputation for drunken and disorderly behaviour.

**Charolais** /ˈʃærəleɪ/, *n.* one of a breed of cattle of French origin, with a large frame and white in colour, used in commercial beef production.

**charpoy** /ˈtʃapɔɪ/, *n.* the common light bedstead of India. [Hind. *chārpāī,* lit., four-footed, from Pers. *chahār-pāī*]

**charqui** /ˈtʃaki/, *n.* meat cut into strips and dried; jerked meat, esp. beef. [Sp., from Quechua (Peruvian) *echarqui*]

**charr** /tʃa/, *n., pl.* **charrs,** (*esp. collectively*) **charr.** →**char**[2].

**chart** /tʃat/, *n.* **1.** a sheet exhibiting information in tabulated or methodical form. **2.** a graphic representation, as by curves, of a dependent variable such as temperature, price, etc. **3.** a map, esp. a hydrographic or marine map. **4.** an outline map showing special conditions or facts: *a weather chart.* **5.** (*usu. pl.*) a regularly issued list of the best-selling pop records. **6.** *Music.* a part (def. 11b), sometimes abbreviated or simplified as in the case of giving chord progressions for a song or piece. **7.** *Music. Colloq.* (*pl.*) printed music. *–v.t.* **8.** to make a chart of. **9.** to plan: *to chart a course of action.* [F *charte,* from L *c(h)arta* paper, from Gk *chártēs* leaf of paper] – **chartless,** *adj.*

**chartbound** /ˈtʃatbaund/, *adj. Colloq.* (of a pop-music record) likely to achieve a place in the charts of best-selling records each week.

**charter** /ˈtʃatə/, *n.* **1.** a written instrument or contract, esp. relating to land transfers. **2. a.** a written document, granted by a sovereign or legislature giving privileges, rights, the benefit of a new invention, a peerage, etc. **b.** a written grant by a sovereign power creating or incorporating a borough, university, company or a corporation, as the royal charters granted to establish British colonies in America. **3.** Also, **charter party.** a contract by which part or all of a ship is leased for a voyage or a stated time, and safe delivery of the cargo is agreed. **4.** special privilege or immunity. **5.** *U.S.* the articles or certificate of incorporation taken in connection with the law under which a corporation is organised. *–v.t.* **6.** to establish by charter. **7.** to lease or hire by charter party. **8.** to hire a vehicle, etc. *–adj.* **9.** done or held in accordance with a charter. **10.** founded, granted, or protected by a charter. **11.** hired for a particular purpose or journey: *a charter plane.* **12. go by charter,** to travel on a charter plane. [ME *chartre,* from OF, from L *chartula,* diminutive of *charta*]

**chartered accountant** /tʃatəd əˈkauntənt/, *n.* an accountant in private practice who is a member of one of the institutes of accountants granted a royal charter which have branches in Australia.

**charter flight** /ˈtʃatə flaɪt/, *n.* a flight of or on a charter plane.

**charter member** /ˈ– mɛmbə/, *n.* one of the original members.

**charter plane** /ˈ– pleɪn/, *n.* **1.** an aircraft, usu. small, leased or hired for a particular purpose. **2.** a large aircraft used for cut-price international travel.

**charthouse** /ˈtʃathaus/, *n.* →**chartroom.**

**Chartism** /ˈtʃatɪzəm/, *n.* the principles or movement of a party of political reformers, chiefly working-men, active in England from 1838 to 1848 (so called from the **People's Charter,** the document which contained their principles and demands). [L *charta* charter + -ISM; pronunciation influenced by *charter*]

**chartist** /ˈtʃatəst/, *n. Econ.* **1.** share market analyst who plots the price trends of shares on charts. **2.** one who interprets these price patterns. **3.** (*cap.*) an adherent of Chartism. *–adj.* **4.** of or pertaining to Chartism.

**chartography** /kaˈtɒgrəfi/, *n.* →**cartography.**

**chartreuse** /ʃaˈtrɜz/, *n.* **1.** one of two aromatic liqueurs made by the Carthusian monks, at Grenoble, France, and (1901-46) in Tarragona, Spain. **2.** (*cap.*) a trademark for these liqueurs. **3.** a clear, light green with a yellowish tinge. **4.** a Carthusian monastery. *–adj.* **5.** of the colour chartreuse. [F]

**chartroom** /ˈtʃatrum/, *n.* the room in a ship where charts are kept. Also, **charthouse.**

**chartulary** /ˈtʃatʃələri/, *n., pl.* **-ries.** →**cartulary.**

**charwoman** /ˈtʃawʊmən/, *n., pl.* **-women.** a woman hired to do odd jobs of household work, or to do such work by the hour or day. [CHAR[3] + WOMAN]

**chary** /ˈtʃɛəri/, *adj.,* **charier, chariest. 1.** careful; wary. **2.** shy. **3.** fastidious; choosy. **4.** sparing (oft. fol. by *of*): *chary of his praise.* [ME *chari,* OE *cearig* sorrowful, from *caru* CARE]

**chase**[1] /tʃeɪs/, *v.,* **chased, chasing,** *n. –v.t.* **1.** to pursue in order to seize, overtake, etc. **2.** to pursue with intent to capture or kill, as game; hunt. **3.** to drive by pursuing. **4.** to put to flight. *–v.i.* **5.** to follow in pursuit: *to chase after someone.* **6.** *Colloq.* to run or hasten. *–n.* **7.** the act of chasing; pursuit. **8.** an object of pursuit; a thing chased. **9.** the occupation or sport of hunting. **10.** *Brit.* an unenclosed tract of privately owned land reserved for animals to be hunted. **11.** a flora and fauna reserve. **12.** the right of keeping game or of hunting on the land of others. **13.** a steeplechase. [ME *chace(n),* from OF *chacier,* from L *captiāre* seize. See CATCH]

**chase**[2] /tʃeɪs/, *n., v.,* **chased, chasing.** *–n.* **1.** a rectangular iron frame in which composed type, etc., is secured or locked, for printing or plate-making. **2.** Also, **chasing.** a groove, furrow, or trench; a lengthened hollow. **3.** *Ordn.* **a.** the part of a gun in front of the trunnions. **b.** the part containing the bore. *–v.t.* **4.** to groove or indent, so as to make into a screw. **5.** to cut in making a screw thread. [F *châsse,* from L *capsa* box]

**chase**[3] /tʃeɪs/, *v.t.,* **chased, chasing.** to ornament (metal) by engraving or embossing. [aphetic var. of ENCHASE]

**chaser**[1] /ˈtʃeɪsə/, *n.* **1.** one who or that which chases or pursues. **2.** *Colloq.* a drink of water, beer, or other mild beverage taken after a drink of spirits. **3.** Also, **chase-gun.** a gun on a vessel esp. for use when in chase or being chased. **4.** a hunter. **5.** a second-rate film. **6.** a clerk employed on a building site. [CHASE[1] + -ER[1]]

**chaser**[2] /ˈtʃeɪsə/, *n.* a multiple-toothed tool used in cutting screw threads. [CHASE[2] + -ER[1]]

**chaser**[3] /ˈtʃeɪsə/, *n.* a person who engraves metal. [CHASE[3] + -ER[1]]

**chasings** /ˈtʃeɪsɪŋz/, *n.pl.* (*construed as sing.*) a children's game in which one player chases the others till he touches one of them, who then takes his place as pursuer.

**chasm** /ˈkæzəm/, *n.* **1.** a yawning fissure or deep cleft in the earth's surface; a gorge. **2.** a breach or wide fissure in a wall or other structure. **3.** a marked interruption of continuity; gap. **4.** a sundering breach in relations: *the chasm of death.* **5.** a wide difference of feeling, interest, etc., between persons, groups, nations. [L *chasma,* from Gk] – **chasmal** /ˈkæzməl/, *adj.*

**chassé** /ˈʃæseɪ/, *n., v.,* **chasséd, chasséing.** *Dancing –n.* **1.** a kind of gliding step in which one foot is kept in advance of the other. *–v.i.* **2.** to execute a chassé. [F lit., chased]

**chassepot** /ʃæsˈpoʊ/, *n.* a breech-loading rifle, closed with a sliding bolt, introduced into the French army after the war between Austria and Prussia in 1866. [named after A. A. *Chassepot,* 1833-1905, the (French) inventor]

**chasseur** /ʃæˈsɜ/, *n.* **1.** (in the French army) one of a body of troops (cavalry or infantry) equipped and trained for rapid movement. **2.** a uniformed footman or attendant; a liveried servant. **3.** a huntsman. *–adj.* **4.** Also, **à la chasseur.** garnished with mushrooms cooked with shallots and white wine. [F: lit., chaser]

**chassis** /ˈʃæzi/, *n., pl.* **chassis** /ˈʃæziz/. **1.** the frame, wheels, and machinery of a motor vehicle, on which the body is supported. **2.** *Ordn.* the frame or rails on which a gun carriage moves backwards and forwards. **3.** the main landing gear of an aircraft; that portion of the landing gear that supports an aircraft. **4.** *Radio.* the foundation on which the sections of a television or radio set are mounted. [F: frame; akin to CHASE[2]]

**chaste** /tʃeɪst/, *adj.* **1.** not having had sexual intercourse; virgin, esp. when considered as being virtuous. **2.** free from obscenity; decent. **3.** undefiled or stainless. **4.** pure in style; subdued; simple. **5.** *Obs.* unmarried. [ME from OF, from L *castus* pure] – **chastely,** *adv.* – **chasteness,** *n.*

**chasten** /ˈtʃeɪsən/, *v.t.* **1.** to inflict suffering upon for purposes of moral improvement; chastise. **2.** to restrain; subdue. **3.** to make chaste in style. [obs. *chaste,* v., chasten (from OF *chastier,* from L *castigāre*) + -EN[1]] – **chastener,** *n.*

**chastise** /tʃæsˈtaɪz/, *v.t.,* **-tised, -tising. 1.** to inflict corporal punishment upon. **2.** *Archaic.* to restrain; chasten. **3.** *Archaic.* to refine; purify. [ME; from obs. *chaste* CHASTEN + -ISE[1]] – **chastisement** /ˈtʃæstəzmənt, -ˈtaɪzmənt/, *n.* – **chastiser,** *n.*

**chastity** /ˈtʃæstəti/, *n.* the quality of being chaste. [ME *chastete,* from OF, from *chaste* CHASTE + *-te* -TY[2]]

**chastity belt** /ˈ– bɛlt/, *n.* a belt, from which is supported a padlocked device to prevent a woman having sexual intercourse, used in the Middle Ages.

**chasuble** /ˈtʃæzjəbəl/, *n. Eccles.* a sleeveless outer vestment worn by the celebrant at mass. [F (replacing ME *chesible,* from OF), from LL *casubula,* for L *casula* cloak, diminutive of *casa* house]

chasuble

**chat** /tʃæt/, *v.,* **chatted, chatting,** *n.* –*v.i.* **1.** to converse in a familiar or informal manner. –*v.t.* **2.** *Colloq.* to talk persuasively to or flirt with (fol. by *up*): *to chat up a girl.* **3.** to reprove. –*n.* **4.** informal conversation. **5.** (in Australia) any of several small, ground-feeding, insectivorous birds of the family Epthianuridae, some of which have metallic call notes, as the white-fronted chat, *Epthianura albifrons.* **6.** (elsewhere) any of several birds of the sub-family Turdinae, esp. of the genus *Saxicola,* known for their harsh chattering cries. **7.** *Colloq.* a louse; similar vermin. **8.** *Colloq.* a dirty or slovenly person. [short for CHATTER]

**chateau** /ʃæˈtoʊ/, *n., pl.* **-teaus, -teaux** /-ˈtoʊz/. **1.** a French castle. **2.** a stately residence in imitation of a French castle. **3.** a country estate, esp. a fine French one. Also, **château.** [F, from L *castellum*]

**chateaubriand** /ˌʃætoʊbriˈɒnd/, *n.* a fillet of beef cut thickly and grilled, or sautéed, served with a variety of sauces or garnishes.

**chateau wine** /ˈʃætoʊ ˌwaɪn/, *n.* the wine produced from grapes grown at a given vineyard or chateau originally in the Bordeaux wine region of France.

**chatelaine** /ˈʃætəleɪn/, *n.* **1.** the mistress of a castle. **2.** the mistress of an elegant or fashionable household. **3.** a device for suspending keys, trinkets, etc., worn at the waist by women. Also, **châtelaine.** [F. See CASTELLAN]

**Chatham Island lily,** *n.* a blue-flowered perennial, *Myosotidium hortensia,* family Boraginaceae, endemic to the Chatham Islands.

**chatoyant** /ʃəˈtɔɪənt/, *adj.* **1.** changing in lustre or colour. **2.** *Jewellery.* reflecting a single streak of light when cut in a cabochon. [F, ppr. of *chatoyer* change lustre like a cat's eye, from *chat* cat]

**chat show** /tʃæt ʃoʊ/, *n.* →**talk show.**

**chattel** /ˈtʃætl/, *n.* **1.** a movable article of property. **2.** *Law.* **a. chattel personal,** articles of property both movable and intangible, including debts, patents, copyrights, etc. **b. chattel real,** a leasehold interest in land. **3.** a slave. [ME *chatel,* from OF. See CATTLE]

**chatter** /ˈtʃætə/, *v.i.* **1.** to utter a succession of quick, inarticulate, speechlike sounds: *a chattering monkey.* **2.** to talk rapidly and to little purpose; jabber. **3.** to make a rapid clicking noise by striking together, as the teeth from cold. **4.** *Mach.* to vibrate in cutting, so as to form a series of nicks or notches. –*v.t.* **5.** to utter rapidly or idly. **6.** to cause to chatter. –*n.* **7.** idle or foolish talk. **8.** the act or sound of chattering. [ME; imitative]

**chatterbox** /ˈtʃætəbɒks/, *n.* a very talkative person.

**chatterer** /ˈtʃætərə/, *n.* **1.** one who chatters. **2.** any of several noisy, gregarious babblers of the genus *Pomatostomus,* as the **grey-crowned babbler,** *P. temporalis,* which frequent scrub and open forest in various parts of Australia. **3.** *U.S.* any bird of the genus *Bombycilla;* the waxwing. **4.** *U.S.* any member of the tropical American bird family Cotingidae, fruit-eating birds of diverse colouration.

**chatter marks** /ˈtʃætə maks/, *n.pl.* **1.** marks left by a tool that has been chattering. **2.** →**stria** (def. 2).

**chatty**[1] /ˈtʃæti/, *adj.,* **-tier, -tiest.** given to or full of chat or familiar talk; conversational: *a chatty letter or person.* – **chattily,** *adv.* – **chattiness,** *n.*

**chatty**[2] /ˈtʃæti/, *adj.* **-tier, -tiest.** dirty; lousy. [CHAT + *-t-* + -Y[1]]

**Chaucerian** /tʃɔˈsɪəriən/, *adj.* **1.** of, pertaining to, or characteristic of the writings of Geoffrey Chaucer, 1340?-1400, English poet. –*n.* **2.** a scholar devoted to the study of Chaucer. **3.** an imitator or follower of Chaucer.

**chaud froid sauce** /ˌʃoʊ frwa ˈsɔs/, *n.* a thick cooked sauce applied as a glossy coating to cold choice meats, fish, game, etc., usu. decorated and given a final coating of aspic.

**chauffer** /ˈʃɔfə/, *n.* **1.** a metal basket for holding fire. **2.** a small, portable stove. [F *chauffoir* heater]

**chauffeur** /ˈʃoʊfə, ʃoʊˈfɜ/, *n.* a person, esp. male, employed to drive a private motor car. [F: stoker, from *chauffer* heat. See CHAFE]

**chauffeuse** /ʃoʊˈfɜz/, *n.* a female chauffeur.

**chaulmoogra** /tʃɔlˈmugrə/, *n.* an East Indian tree of the genus *Taraktogenos* (or *Hydnocarpus*), the seeds of which yield a fixed oil used in the treatment of leprosy and skin diseases. [Bengali]

**chausses** /ʃoʊs/, *n.pl. Hist.* medieval armour of mail for the legs and feet. [F, from L *calceus* shoe]

**chauvinism** /ˈʃoʊvənɪzəm/, *n.* **1.** blind enthusiasm for military glory. **2.** zealous and belligerent patriotism or devotion to any cause, as male chauvinism. [F *chauvinisme;* from Nicolas *Chauvin,* an old soldier and overenthusiastic admirer of Napoleon I] – **chauvinist,** *n., adj.* – **chauvinistic** /ʃoʊvəˈnɪstɪk/, *adj.* – **chauvinistically** /ʃoʊvəˈnɪstɪkli/, *adv.*

**chavoo** /tʃəˈvu/, *n.* →**shivoo**

**chaw** /tʃɔ/, *v.t., v.i., n.* →**chew.**

**chayote** /tʃaɪˈoʊti/, *n.* →**choko.**

**chazzan** /kəˈzan, ˈkazən/, *n.* a Jewish cantor.

**Ch.B.,** Bachelor of Surgery.

**Ch.D.,** **1.** Doctor of Chemistry. **2.** Doctor of Surgery.

**cheap** /tʃip/, *adj.* **1.** of a relatively low price; at a bargain. **2.** costing little labour or trouble. **3.** charging low prices: *a very cheap store.* **4.** of poor quality: *that material is cheap and nasty.* **5.** of little account; of small value: *hold his affection cheap.* **6.** base; mean: *cheap conduct.* **7.** *Colloq.* embarrassed; sheepish: *feeling cheap about his mistake.* **8.** obtainable at a low rate of interest: *when money is cheap.* **9.** of decreased value or purchasing power, as currency depreciated due to inflation. –*adv.* **10.** at a low price; at small cost. –*n.* **11. on the cheap.** *Colloq.* at a low price [ME *cheep* (in phrases as *greet cheep* cheap, lit., great bargain), OE *cēap,* c. G. *Kauf* bargain] – **cheaply,** *adv.* – **cheapness,** *n.*

**cheap drunk** /– ˈdrʌŋk/, *n.* one who becomes intoxicated after taking only a little alcoholic liquor.

**cheapen** /ˈtʃipən/, *v.t.* **1.** to make cheap or cheaper. **2.** to belittle; bring into contempt. **3.** *Archaic.* to bargain for. –*v.i.* **4.** to become cheap or cheaper. – **cheapener,** *n.*

**cheapie** /ˈtʃipi/, *n. Colloq.* a cheap product.

**cheapjack** /ˈtʃipdʒæk/, *n.* **1.** a travelling hawker, selling cheap goods. –*adj.* **2.** shoddy; of poor quality.

**cheapskate** /ˈtʃipskeɪt/, *n.* a term of contempt for a stingy person.

**cheat** /tʃit/, *n.* **1.** a fraud; swindle; deception. **2.** a person who cheats or defrauds. **3.** *Law.* the fraudulent obtaining of another's property by a false pretence or trick. **4.** an imposter. –*v.t.* **5.** to defraud; swindle. **6.** to deceive; impose upon. **7.** to beguile; elude. **8.** *Film, T.V.* to move (an object) for the purpose of picture composition, continuity, etc.: *cheat the lamp to the left a bit.* **9. cheat on,** *Colloq.* **a.** to deceive. **b.** to be sexually unfaithful to (one's spouse or lover). **10.** to practise fraud. [ME *chet(e)*, aphetic form of *achet,* var. of ESCHEAT] **– cheatable,** *adj.* **– cheater,** *n.* **– cheatingly,** *adv.*

**cheat sheet** /ˈ– ʃit/, *n. Colloq.* →**time sheet.**

**check** /tʃɛk/, *v.t.* **1.** to stop or arrest the motion of suddenly or forcibly. **2.** to restrain; hold in restraint or control. **3.** to investigate or verify as to correctness. **4.** *U.S.* to tick (oft. fol. by *off*) **5.** to leave in temporary custody (fol. by *in*): *check in your coat and hat.* **6.** to accept for temporary custody: *small parcels checked here.* **7.** *U.S.* to send luggage, etc., through to a final destination, but allowing the accompanying passenger to break the journey: *we checked two trunks through to New York.* **8.** *U.S.* to accept for conveyance, and to convey to a final destination: *check this trunk to New York.* **9.** to mark in a pattern of checks or squares: *a checked dress.* **10.** *U.S. Agric.* to mark the ground in order to plant in checkrows. **11.** *Chess.* to place (an opponent's king) under direct attack. **12.** *Naut.* to ease off; slacken: *to check a brace.* **13.** *Aus. Rules.* to keep close watch on one's opposite number, depriving him of the ball by bumping or shepherding. *–v.i.* **14.** to prove to be right; to correspond accurately: *the reprint checks with the original item for item.* **15.** to make an inquiry or investigation for verification, etc. (usu. fol. by *up* or *on*): *I'll check up on the matter.* **16.** to make a stop; pause. **17.** *Hunting.* (of dogs) to stop on losing the scent or to verify it. **18.** *Falconry.* (of a hawk) to forsake the proper prey and follow baser game (fol. by *at*). **19. check in,** to register one's arrival, as at a hotel, at work, etc. **20. check out,** to leave, as one's quarters at a hotel, etc. *–n.* **21.** a person or thing that checks or restrains. **22.** a sudden arrest or stoppage; repulse; rebuff. **23.** control with a view to ascertaining performance or preventing error. **24.** *Angling.* a rachet device in a reel which controls the free running of the line. **25.** a controlled and carefully observed operation or test procedure to determine actual and potential performance. **26.** a means or standard to insure against error, fraud, etc. **27.** *U.S.* a tick. **28.** *U.S.* a cheque. **29.** *U.S.* →**bill**[1] (def. 2). **30.** *U.S.* →**ticket** (def. 1). **31.** *Music.* the mechanism that holds a piano hammer after striking. **32.** a pattern formed of squares, as on a draughtboard. **33.** a fabric having a check pattern. **34.** *Chess.* the exposure of the king to direct attack. **35.** *U.S.* a counter used in card games; the chip in poker. **36.** *Masonry.* a rabbet-shaped cutting on the edge of a stone, by which it is fitted to another stone. **37. in check, a.** under restraint. **b.** *Chess.* (of a player) having a king which is exposed to direct attack, or (of the king) being exposed to direct attack. *–adj.* **38.** serving to check, control, verify, etc. **39.** ornamented with a checked pattern; chequered. *–interj.* **40.** *Chess.* (an optional call to inform one's opponent that his king is exposed to direct attack.) [ME *chek,* from OF *eschec,* b. OF *eschac* check (from Pers.; see CHECKMATE) and OF *eschiec* booty (from Gmc; cf. OHG *scāh*)] **– checkable,** *adj.* **– checker,** *n.*

**checkbook** /ˈtʃɛkbʊk/, *n. U.S.* →**chequebook.**

**checked** /tʃɛkt/, *adj.* **1.** having a pattern or squares; chequered.

**checker** /ˈtʃɛkə/, *n.* **1.** *U.S.* a draughtsman. **2.** a chequered pattern. *–v.t.* **3.** *U.S.* →**chequer.**

**checkerboard** /ˈtʃɛkəbɔd/, *n.* a draughtboard; a chessboard.

**checkered** /ˈtʃɛkəd/, *adj. U.S.* chequered.

**checkers** /ˈtʃɛkəz/, *n. U.S.* draughts.

**check-in** /ˈtʃɛk-ɪn/, *n.* **1.** the act of registering one's arrival, as at work, at a hotel, etc. **2.** the place where arrival is registered.

**check list** /ˈtʃɛk lɪst/, *n.* items listed together for convenience of comparison or other checking purposes.

**checkmate** /ˈtʃɛkmeɪt/, *n., v.,* **-mated, -mating,** *interj. –n.* **1.** *Chess.* **a.** the act of putting the opponent's king into an inextricable check, thus bringing the game to a close. **b.** the position of the pieces when a king is checkmated. **2.** defeat; overthrow. *–v.t.* **3.** *Chess.* to put (an opponent's king) into inextricable check. **4.** to check completely; defeat. *–interj.* **5.** *Chess.* (the announcing by a player that he has put his opponent's king into inextricable check.) [ME *chek mat,* from Ar. *shāh māt* the king is dead]

**checkout** /ˈtʃɛkaʊt/, *n.* **1.** the cash desk in a supermarket. *–adj.* **2.** of or pertaining to the people, equipment or procedure operating at a checkout.

**checkpoint** /ˈtʃɛkpɔɪnt/, *n.* **1.** a place where traffic is halted for inspection. **2.** a landmark used in flying. **3.** *Mil.* a gunnery target used to test the accuracy of range and direction adjustments.

**checkrail** /ˈtʃɛkreɪl/, *n. Railways.* an extra rail placed alongside the inner rail on curves, points, etc., to prevent derailment; guardrail.

**check rein** /ˈtʃɛk reɪn/, *n.* **1.** a short rein joining the bit of one of a span of horses to the driving rein of the other. **2.** →**bearing rein.**

**checkroom** /ˈtʃɛkrum/, *n. U.S.* **1.** a left-luggage office. **2.** a cloakroom.

**checkrow** /ˈtʃɛkroʊ/, *U.S. Agric. –n.* **1.** one of a number of rows of trees or plants, esp. maize, in which the distance between adjacent trees or plants is equal to that between adjacent rows. *–v.t.* **2.** to plant in checkrows.

**checkup** /ˈtʃɛkʌp/, *n.* **1.** an examination or close scrutiny for purposes of verification as to accuracy, comparison, etc. **2.** a comprehensive physical examination. **3.** an overhaul.

**check valve** /ˈtʃɛk vælv/, *n.* a valve which ensures one-way flow in a pipe.

**cheddar** /ˈtʃɛdə/, *n.* **1.** a smooth white or yellow cheese, with a firm texture, sometimes cracked, the flavour of which depends on the age of the cheese. **2. hard** or **stiff cheddar,** *Colloq.* →**cheese** (def. 5). *–v.t.* **3.** (in cheese making) to turn the curd of (a cheese) in the vat at regular intervals to allow the whey to drain off. [*Cheddar,* a town in Somersetshire, England]

**cheddite** /ˈtʃɛdaɪt, ˈʃɛdaɪt/, *n.* an explosive used for blasting made up of a chlorate or perchlorate mixture with a fatty substance, such as castor oil. [F *Chedde* place name (of Savoy) + *-ite* -ITE[1]]

**cheedam** /ˈtʃidəm/, *n.* a cheese combining the characteristics in flavour and texture of cheddar and edam, developed by the C.S.I.R.O.

**cheek** /tʃik/, *n.* **1.** either side of the face below eye level. **2.** the side wall of the mouth between the upper and lower jaws. **3.** something resembling the human cheek in form or position, as either of two parts forming corresponding sides of a thing. **4.** a buttock. **5.** one side of the head of a hammer. **6.** *Mach.* either of the sides of a pulley or block. **7.** *Print.* one of the sides of a block (def. 6). **8.** *Colloq.* impudence or effrontery. **9. cheek by jowl,** close together; adjacent; in close intimacy. **10. turn the other cheek,** to accept provocation pacifistically. **11. with one's tongue in one's cheek,** mockingly; insincerely. *–v.t.* **12.** *Colloq.* to address saucily; to be impudent. [ME *cheke,* OE *cēace,* c. D *kaak*]

**cheekbone** /ˈtʃikboʊn/, *n.* the bone or bony prominence below the outer angle of the eye.

**cheek pouch** /ˈtʃik paʊtʃ/, *n.* a bag in the cheek of certain animals, as squirrels, for carrying food.

**cheektooth** /ˈtʃiktuθ/, *n., pl.* **-teeth.** a molar or grinder.

**cheeky** /ˈtʃiki/, *adj.,* **cheekier, cheekiest.** *Colloq.* impudent; insolent: *a cheeky fellow, cheeky behaviour.* **– cheekily,** *adv.* **– cheekiness,** *n.*

**cheep** /tʃip/, *v.i.* **1.** to chirp; peep. *–v.t.* **2.** to express by cheeps. *–n.* **3.** a chirp. [imitative]

**cheer** /tʃɪə/, *n.* **1.** a shout of encouragement, approval, congratulation, etc. **2.** that which gives joy or gladness; encouragement; comfort. **3.** state of feeling or spirits: *what cheer?* **4.** gladness, gaiety, or animation: *to make cheer.* **5.** food; provisions. **6. three cheers,** three shouts of hurray, given as a token of approval for someone. **7.** *Archaic.* expression of countenance. *–v.t.* **8.** to salute with shouts of approval, congratulation, etc. **9.** to inspire with cheer; gladden (oft. fol. by *up*). **10.** to encourage or incite (fol. by *on*). *–v.i.* **11.** to utter cheers of approval, etc. **12.** to become cheerful (oft. fol. by *up*). **13.** *Obs.* to be in a particular state of spirits. *–interj.* **14.** (*pl.*) *Colloq.* to your health. [ME *chere,* from OF: face, from LL *cara*] **– cheerer,** *n.* **– cheeringly,** *adv.*

**cheerful** /ˈtʃɪəfəl/, *adj.* **1.** full of cheer; in good spirits: *a cheerful person.* **2.** promoting cheer; pleasant; bright: *cheerful surroundings.* **3.** arising from good spirits or cheerfulness: *cheerful song.* **4.** hearty or ungrudging: *cheerful giving.* – **cheerfully,** *adv.* – **cheerfulness,** *n.*

**cheerio**[1] /tʃɪəri'oʊ/, *interj., n., pl.* **-os.** *Colloq.* goodbye.

**cheerio**[2] /tʃɪəri'oʊ/, *n.* a small frankfurt sausage; a cocktail frankfurt.

**cheerio call** /'– kɔl/, *n.* a greeting sent to one person by another via a radio or television compere as part of a show.

**cheerleader** /'tʃɪəlidə/, *n. Chiefly U.S.* a person who leads cheering, esp. at sports matches.

**cheerless** /'tʃɪələs/, *adj.* without cheer; joyless; gloomy. – **cheerlessly,** *adv.* – **cheerlessness,** *n.*

**cheery** /'tʃɪəri/, *adj.,* **-rier, -riest. 1.** in good spirits; blithe; gay. **2.** too obviously cheerful; over-hearty. **3.** promoting cheer; enlivening. – **cheerily,** *adv.* – **cheeriness,** *n.*

**cheese** /tʃiz/, *n.* **1.** the curd of milk separated from the whey and prepared in many ways as a food. **2.** a cake or definite mass of this substance. **3.** something of similar shape or consistency, as a mass of pomace in cider-making. **4.** a conserve of fruit of the consistency of cream cheese. **5. hard** or **stiff cheese,** *Colloq.* **a.** bad luck. **b.** (an off-hand expression of sympathy). **c.** (a rebuff to an appeal for sympathy). **6.** *Obs.* a low curtsy. [ME *chese,* OE *cēse,* c. G. *Käse,* from *cāseus*]

**cheese board** /'– bɔd/, *n.* a board, usu. of pleasing appearance, on which cheese may be served at a meal.

**cheeseburger** /'tʃizbɜgə/, *n.* a hamburger in which the filling is topped with a slice of cheese.

**cheesecake** /'tʃizkeɪk/, *n.* **1.** a kind of cake or open pie filled with a custard-like preparation containing cheese. **2.** *Colloq.* photographs of pretty girls in newspapers, magazines, etc., posed to display their bodies, and emphasising their sex appeal. **3.** (*usu. derog.*) sex appeal.

**cheesecloth** /'tʃizklɒθ/, *n.* a coarse cotton fabric of open texture, originally used in cheese-making, now also for costumes, etc.

**cheese-cutter** /'tʃiz-kʌtə/, *n.* **1.** that which cuts cheese, specifically a board and attached wire, the wire being drawn downwards through the cheese. **2.** *Naut.* a type of keel, fitted in a boat; lowered through the bottom when in use.

**cheesed-off** /tʃizd-'ɒf/, *adj. Colloq.* bored; fed up. Also (esp. in predicative use), **cheesed off, cheesed.**

**cheese mite** /'tʃiz maɪt/, *n.* a small arachnid, *Tyroglyphus longior,* that breeds in cheese and infests bran, flour, and hay.

**cheeseparing** /'tʃizpɛərɪŋ/, *adj.* **1.** meanly economical; parsimonious. *–n.* **2.** something of little or no value. **3.** niggardly economy. **4.** the remaining rind after the cheese has been pared off.

**cheese straw** /tʃiz 'strɔ/, *n.* a short strip of baked cheese pastry.

**cheese-tree** /'tʃiz-tri/, *n.* a small tree, *Glochidion ferdinandii,* family Euphorbiaceae, common in gullies in coastal areas of New South Wales.

**cheesewood** /'tʃizwʊd/, *n.* →**banyalla.**

**cheesy**[1] /'tʃizi/, *adj.,* **-sier, -siest. 1.** like cheese: *cheesy taste or consistency.* **2.** *Colloq.* smelly. – **cheesiness,** *n.*

**cheesy**[2] /'tʃizi/, *adj.* artificial: *a cheesy grin.* [from CHEESE, spoken to induce a smile while being photographed]

**cheetah** /'tʃitə/, *n.* an animal of the cat family, *Acinonyx jubatus,* of south-western Asia and Africa, resembling the leopard but having certain doglike characteristics, often trained for hunting deer, etc.; fastest four-legged animal. Also, **chetah.** [Hind. *chītā*]

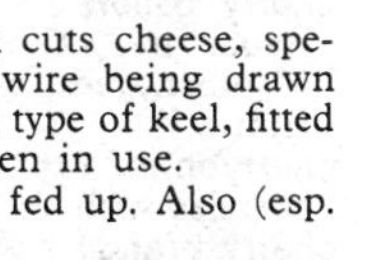

cheetah

**chef** /ʃɛf/, *n.* a cook, esp. a head cook. [F. See CHIEF]

**chef-d'oeuvre** /ʃɛf-'dɜvrə/, *n., pl.* **chefs-d'oeuvre** /ʃɛf-'dɜvrə/. a masterpiece, esp. of an author, painter, etc.

**cheiro-,** variant of **chiro-.**

**chela**[1] /'kilə/, *n., pl.* **-lae** /-li/. the nipper-like organ or claw terminating certain limbs of some arthropods. [NL, from Gk *chēlḗ* claw]

**chela**[2] /'tʃeɪlə/, *n.* (in India) a disciple of a religious teacher. [Hind.: slave, disciple]

**chelate** /'kileɪt/, *n.* **1.** *Chem.* a molecular structure in which a central polyvalent metal ion is combined into a ring of organic compounds or radicals. *–adj.* **2.** *Zool.* having a chela.

**chelating agent** /kə'leɪtɪŋ ˌeɪdʒənt/, *n. Chem.* an organic chemical which is capable of removing unwanted metal ions by chelation, used in industry and research.

chela of lobster

**chelation** /kə'leɪʃən/, *n. Chem.* formation of a heterocyclic ring containing a metal ion, the metal being attached by co-ordinate links to two or more non-metal atoms in the same molecule.

**chelation therapy** /'– θɛrəpi/, *n.* treatment of poisoning by lead or other heavy metals with chelating agents.

**cheli-,** a word element meaning 'claws', as in *cheliferous.* [Gk: combining form of *chēlḗ* CHELA[1]]

**chelicera** /kə'lɪsərə/, *n., pl.* **-rae** /-ri/. one of the pre-oral appendages found in some spiders, scorpions and other arachnids.

**cheliferous** /kə'lɪfərəs/, *adj.* bearing chelae.

**cheliform** /'kiləfɔm/, *adj.* nipper-like.

**Chellean** /'ʃɛliən/, *adj.* →**Abbevillian.** [named after *Chelles,* Seine-et-Marne, France]

**cheloid** /'kilɔɪd/, *n. Pathol.* →**keloid.**

**chelonian** /kə'loʊniən/, *adj.* **1.** of or belonging to the Chelonia, an order or group of reptiles comprising the tortoises and turtles. *–n.* **2.** a tortoise or a turtle. [NL *Chelōnia,* pl. (cf. Gk. *chelṓnē* tortoise) + -AN]

**chelsea bun** /ˌtʃɛlsi 'bʌn/, *n.* a round coiled yeast bun, containing currants, and decorated with sugar.

**chem-,** a word element representing chemic or chemical used before vowels. Also (*esp. before a consonant*), **chemo-.**

**chem.,** **1.** chemical. **2.** chemist. **3.** chemistry.

**chemic** /'kɛmɪk/, *adj. Archaic.* **1.** alchemic. **2.** chemical. [short for ALCHEMIC]

**chemical** /'kɛmɪkəl/, *adj.* **1.** of or concerned with the science or the operations or processes of chemistry. *–n.* **2.** a substance produced by or used in a chemical process. – **chemically,** *adv.*

**chemical affinity** /– ə'fɪnəti/, *n.* **1.** chemical attraction; the force binding atoms together. **2.** the free energy change during a chemical reaction.

**chemical agent** /– 'eɪdʒənt/, *n. Mil.* a solid, liquid, or gas which through its chemical properties produces lethal or damaging effects on man, animals, plants, or material, or produces a screening or signalling smoke.

**chemical bond** /'– bɒnd/, *n.* the linkage between two atoms. See **covalent bond, electrovalent bond, dative bond.**

**chemical engineer** /– ɛndʒə'nɪə/, *n.* one who practises chemical engineering.

**chemical engineering** /– ˌɛndʒə'nɪərɪŋ/, *n.* the science or profession concerned with the design, manufacture, and operation of plant or machinery used in industrial chemical processes.

**chemical equation** /– ə'kweɪʒən/, *n.* a representation of a chemical reaction in symbols.

**chemical kinetics** /– kə'nɛtɪks/, *n.* the study of the rate at which chemical reactions proceed.

**chemical reaction** /– ri'ækʃən/, *n.* a process involving two or more substances in which their molecular constitution is altered.

**chemical warfare** /– 'wɔfɛə/, *n.* warfare with asphyxiating, poisonous, and corrosive gases, oil flames, etc.

**chemiluminescence** /ˌkɛmiluːmə'nɛsəns/, *n.* (in chemical reactions) the production of light at low temperatures.

**chemin de fer** /ʃəmæn də 'fɜ/, *n.* a variation of baccarat. [F: railway]

**chemise** /ʃə'miz/, *n.* **1.** a woman's loose-fitting shirt-like undergarment. **2.** (in women's fashions) a dress, suit, etc., designed to fit loosely at the waist and more tightly at the hips. **3.** a revetment for an earth embankment. [F, from LL *camisia* shirt (prob. from Celtic); replacing ME *kemes,* OE *cemes,* from LL *camisia*]

**chemisette** /ʃɛmə'zɛt/, *n.* a woman's garment of linen, lace, etc., worn with a low-cut or open bodice to cover the neck and breast. [F, diminutive of *chemise*]

**chemisorb** /ˈkɛmisɔb/, *v.t.* to adsorb by chemisorption.

**chemisorption** /kɛmiˈsɔpʃən/, *n. Chem.* adsorption in which a chemical link is formed between the adsorbing and adsorbed substances.

**chemist** /ˈkɛməst/, *n.* **1.** one versed in chemistry or professionally engaged in chemical investigations. **2.** a retailer of medicinal drugs and toilet preparations. **3.** *Obs.* alchemist. [var. of ALCHEMIST]

**chemistry** /ˈkɛməstri/, *n., pl.* **-tries.** **1.** the science concerned with the composition of substances, the various elementary forms of matter, and the interactions between them. **2.** chemical properties, reactions, etc.: *the chemistry of carbon.* [CHEMIST + -RY]

**chemmy** /ˈʃɛmi/, *n. Colloq.* →**chemin de fer.**

**chemo-**, variant of **chem-** used esp. before a consonant.

**chemosphere** /ˈkɛməsfɪə/, *n.* →**mesosphere** (def. 2).

**chemosynthesis** /kɛmoʊˈsɪnθəsəs/, *n. Bot.* production by plants of nutritive substances from carbon dioxide and water with energy derived from other chemical reactions. – **chemosynthetic** /kɛmoʊsɪnˈθɛtɪk/, *adj.* – **chemosynthetically** /kɛmoʊsɪnˈθɛtɪkli/, *adv.*

**chemotaxis** /kɛmoʊˈtæksəs/, *n.* the property in a cell or organism, exhibiting attraction or repulsion to chemical substances. – **chemotactic,** *adj.*

**chemotherapeutics** /ˌkɛmoʊθɛrəˈpjutɪks/, *n. Med.* →**chemotherapy.** – **chemotherapeutic,** *adj.*

**chemotherapy** /kɛmoʊˈθɛrəpi/, *n.* treatment of disease by means of chemicals which have a specific toxic effect upon the disease-producing micro-organisms. – **chemotherapist,** *n.*

**chemotropism** /kəˈmɒtrəˌpɪzəm/, *n.* the property in plants and other organisms of turning or bending (towards or away), as by unequal growth, in response to the presence of chemical substances. – **chemotropic** /kɛmoʊˈtrɒpɪk/, *adj.* – **chemotropically** /kɛmoʊˈtrɒpɪkli/, *adv.*

**chemurgy** /ˈkɛmɜdʒi/, *n.* a division of applied chemistry concerned with the industrial use of organic substances, esp. farm products. – **chemurgic** /kɛmˈɜdʒɪk/, **chemurgical** /kɛmˈɜdʒɪkəl/, *adj.*

**chenanigan** /ʃəˈnænəgən/, *n.* →**shenanigan.**

**chenille** /ʃəˈnil/, *n.* **1.** a velvety cord of silk or worsted, used in embroidery, fringe, etc. **2.** fabric made with a fringed silken thread used as the weft in combination with wool or cotton. **3.** usu. unbleached cotton, into which short bunches of wicking have been hooked to form a design, used for bedspreads, etc.; candlewick.

**chenopod** /ˈkinəpɒd, ˈkɛnə-/, *n.* any plant of the genus *Chenopodium* or the family Chenopodiaceae. [*cheno-* (combining form representing Gk *chḗn* goose) + -POD]

**chenopodiaceous** /ˌkinəpoʊdiˈeɪʃəs, ˌkɛnə-/, *adj.* belonging to the Chenopodiaceae, or goosefoot family of plants, which includes the beet and mangel-wurzel, spinach, and orach. [NL *Chenopodium* (see CHENOPOD) + -ACEOUS]

**cheongsam** /tʃɒŋˈsæm/, *n.* a dress, often of silk, originally worn by Chinese women, which is cut very straight and has a slit up one side of the skirt. [Chinese (Cantonese), var. of Mandarin *ch'ang shan* long jacket]

**cheque** /tʃɛk/, *n.* **1.** *Banking.* a written order, usu. on a standard printed form directing a bank to pay a specified sum of money to, or to the order of, some particular person or the bearer, either *crossed* (payable only through a bank account), or *uncrossed* (payable on demand). **2.** wages, pay. Also, *U.S.,* **check.** [altered spelling of CHECK]

**cheque account** /ˈ– əkaʊnt/, *n.* a bank account from which money may be withdrawn by cheque at any time by the customer.

**chequebook** /ˈtʃɛkbʊk/, *n.* a book of printed forms for drawing cheques or orders on a bank. Also, *U.S.,* **checkbook.**

**chequebook journalism** /ˈ– dʒɜnəlɪzəm/, *n.* a style of journalism which focuses on personal, often scandalous accounts, for which exclusive rights are obtained by the newspaper.

**chequer** /ˈtʃɛkə/, *n.* **1.** a pattern of squares. **2.** a marble or similar token used in Chinese chequers. *–v.t.* **3.** to diversify in colour, variegate. **4.** to diversify in character; subject to alterations. Also, *U.S.,* **checker.** [ME *cheker,* from AF *escheker* chessboard, from *eschec* CHECK]

**chequerboard** /ˈtʃɛkəbɔd/, *n.* →**draughtboard.** Also, *U.S.,* **checkerboard.**

**chequered** /ˈtʃɛkəd/, *n.* **1.** marked by wide or frequent alteration; diversified: *a chequered career.* **2.** marked in squares. **3.** diversified in colour. Also, *U.S.,* **checkered.**

**chequers** /ˈtʃɛkəz/, *n.* →**draughts.**

**cherchez la femme** /ˌʃɛəʃeɪ la ˈfʌm/, look for the cause of the trouble. [F: search for the woman]

**Cherenkov radiation** /tʃəˈrɛnkɒf reɪdiˌeɪʃən/, *n.* →**Cerenkov radiation.**

**chérie** /ʃɛˈri/, *n.* darling. [F (fem. adj.)]

**cherimoya** /tʃɛrəˈmɔɪə/, *n.* a widely cultivated tropical American fruit, *Annona cherimolia.*

**cherish** /ˈtʃɛrɪʃ/, *v.t.* **1.** to hold or treat as dear. **2.** to care for tenderly; nurture. **3.** to cling fondly to (ideas, etc.): *cherishing no resentment.* [ME *cherische(n),* from F *chériss-,* stem of *chérir,* from *cher* dear, from L *cārus*] – **cherisher, cherishment,** *n.* – **cherishingly,** *adv.*

**chernozem** /ˈtʃɜnoʊzɛm/, *n.* →**black earth.**

**cheroot** /ʃəˈrut/, *n.* a cigar having open, unpointed ends. [F *chéroute,* from Tamil *shuruttu* a roll]

**cherry** /ˈtʃɛri/, *n., pl.* **-ries,** *adj.* *–n.* **1.** the fruit of any of various trees of the genus *Prunus,* consisting of a pulpy, globular drupe enclosing a one-seeded smooth stone. **2.** the tree itself. **3.** its wood. **4.** any of various fruits or plants resembling the cherry. **5.** a bright red. **6.** *Cricket Colloq.* a cricket ball, esp. a new one. **7.** *Colloq.* virginity. **8.** a virgin woman. **9. two bites of (at) the cherry,** *Colloq.* two attempts. *–adj.* **10.** bright red. **11.** made of the wood of the cherry tree. [ME *chery, chiri,* backformation from OE *ciris* (the *-s* being taken for plural sign), from VL **ceresia,* from L *cerasus* cherry tree, from Gk *kerasós.* Cf. F *cerise,* ONF *cherise,* etc., from VL (as above)]

**cherry ballart** /– ˈbælat/, *n.* an attractive small eastern Australian tree, *Exocarpos cupressiformis,* parasitic on the roots of other trees, with a swollen cherry-like pedicel below the fruit.

**cherrybobs** /ˈtʃɛribɒbz/, *n.* a children's game using two cherries with the stalks united.

**cherry brandy** /– ˈbrændi/, *n.* a red cherry-flavoured liqueur.

**cherry laurel** /tʃɛri ˈlɒrəl/, *n.* an evergreen ornamental shrub, *Prunus laurocerasus.*

**cherry nose** /ˈ– noʊz/, *n.* a dark, thickset cicada, *Macrotristria angularis,* having a bright red nose; whisky drinker.

**cherry picker** /ˈ– pɪkə/, *n. Colloq.* **1.** an extension arm with a hydraulic movable platform which is used instead of a camera boom. **2.** a crane, esp. one mounted on a truck, with an enclosed platform on the end, designed to lift people to a height where they can perform a function, as changing streetlights, checking stores, etc.

**cherry-pie** /tʃɛri-ˈpaɪ/, *n.* **1.** a pie made with cherries. **2.** the common heliotrope, *Heliotropium arborescens.*

**cherry-plum** /ˈtʃɛri-plʌm/, *n.* **1.** the red or yellow edible fruit of *Prunus cerasifera.* **2.** the tree itself.

**cherry-stone** /ˈtʃɛri-stoʊn/, *n.* **1.** the endocarp of the cherry. **2.** *U.S.* a medium-sized clam.

**chersonese** /ˈkɜsənis/, *n.* **1.** a peninsula. **2. the Chersonese,** Gallipoli Peninsula. [L *chersonēsus,* from Gk *chersónēsos*]

**chert** /tʃɜt/, *n.* a compact rock consisting essentially of cryptocrystalline quartz. [orig. d.; ult. orig. unknown] – **cherty,** *adj.*

**cherub** /ˈtʃɛrəb/, *n., pl.* **cherubs** *for defs 3 and 4;* **cherubim** /ˈtʃɛrəbɪm, kɛ-/ *for defs 1 and 2.* **1.** *Bible.* a kind of celestial being. **2.** *Theol.* a member of the second order of angels, distinguished by knowledge, often represented as a beautiful winged child or as a winged head of a child. **3.** a beautiful or innocent person, esp. a child. **4.** a person with a chubby, innocent face. [ME and OE *cherubin,* pl., ult. from Heb. *kerūb* sing., *karūbīm,* pl.] – **cherubic** /tʃəˈrubɪk/, *adj.* – **cherubically,** *adv.*

**chervil** /ˈtʃɜvəl/, *n.* **1.** a herbaceous plant, *Anthriscus cerefolium,* of the parsley family, with aromatic leaves used to flavour soups, salads, etc. **2.** any of various plants of the same genus or allied genera. [ME *chervelle,* OE *cerfille,* from L *caerephylla,* pl. of *caerephyllum,* from Gk *chairéphyllon*]

**Cheshire cat** /tʃɛʃɪə 'kæt/, *n.* a constantly grinning cat, in *Alice in Wonderland,* named from the old simile 'to grin like a Cheshire cat'.

**cheshire cheese** /tʃɛʃɪə 'tʃiz/, *n.* a pale yellow or whitish cheese often with a flaky texture, and a salty flavour, frequently used for melting or toasting. [orig. made in *Cheshire,* in NW England]

**chess**[1] /tʃɛs/, *n.* a game played by two persons, each with sixteen pieces, on a chequered board. [ME, from OF: aphetic modification of *esches, eschecs,* pl. See CHECK]

**chess**[2] /tʃɛs/, *n., pl.* **chess, chesses.** one of the planks forming the roadway of a pontoon bridge. [orig. uncert.]

**chessboard** /'tʃɛsbɔd/, *n.* the board, identical with a draughtboard, used for playing chess.

**chessman** /'tʃɛsmæn, -mən/, *n., pl.* **-men** /-mɛn, -mən/. one of the pieces used in the game of chess. [earlier *chessemeyne,* lit., chess-company]

**chessylite** /'tʃɛsəlaɪt/, *n.* →**azurite.**

**chest** /tʃɛst/, *n.* **1.** the trunk of the body from the neck to the belly; the thorax. **2.** a box, usu. a large, strong one, for the safekeeping of valuables. **3.** the place where the funds of a public institution, etc., are kept. **4.** a box in which certain goods, as tea, are packed for transit. **5.** the quantity contained in such a box. **6. get (something) off one's chest,** to bring into the open (a pressing worry). [ME; OE *cest, cist,* from L *cista,* from Gk *kístē* box]

**chesterfield** /'tʃɛstəfild/, *n.* a sofa or divan with padded back and arms.

**chest-mark** /'tʃɛst-mak/, *v.t. Aus. Rules.* to take a mark on the chest.

**chest note** /'tʃɛst noʊt/, *n. Music.* a note sung in the chest register.

**chestnut** /'tʃɛsnʌt/, *n.* **1.** the edible nut of trees of the genus *Castanea,* of the beech family. **2.** any of the trees, as *C. sativa* (**Spanish chestnut**), *C. dentata* (**American chestnut**), or *C. crenata* (**Japanese chestnut**). **3.** the wood. **4.** any of various fruits or trees resembling the chestnut, esp. the horse chestnut. **5.** reddish brown. **6.** a horse. **7.** *Colloq.* an old or stale joke, anecdote, etc. **8.** the callosity of the inner side of a horse's leg. *–adj.* **9.** reddish brown. **10.** (esp. of horses) sorrel. [obs. *chesten* chestnut (ME; OE *cisten-,* var. of **cesten,* from WGmc **kastinia,* from L *castanea,* from Gk *kastanéa*) + NUT; replacing ME *chasteine,* from OF]

**chestnut soil** /– 'sɔɪl/, *n.* a crumbly, dark brown soil overlaying a lighter calcareous layer, found in the drier steppes south of the black earth.

**chest of drawers,** *n.* a piece of furniture consisting of a set of drawers fitted into a frame, used for clothing, etc.

**chest of viols,** *n. Music.* a set of viols, for playing in consort.

**chest register** /'tʃɛst rɛdʒəstə/, *n.* the lower register of the voice; thought of as striking sympathetic vibrations in the chest.

**chest tone** /'– toʊn/, *n. Music.* →**chest note.**

**chesty** /'tʃɛsti/, *adj.,* **-tier, -tiest. 1.** *Colloq.* inclined to, or symptomatic of a chest disease. **2.** *Colloq.* bosomy.

**chetah** /'tʃitə/, *n.* →**cheetah.**

**cheval-de-frise** /ʃəvæl-də-'friz/, *n., pl.* **chevaux-de-frise** /ʃəvoʊ-də-'friz/. (*usu. pl.*) *Mil.* an obstacle of projecting spikes or barbed wire used to close a gap to the enemy. [F: lit., horse of Friesland]

**cheval glass** /ʃəvæl 'glas/, *n.* a full-length mirror mounted so as to swing in a frame. [*cheval,* from F: support, horse]

**chevalier** /ʃɛvə'lɪə, ʃə'væljeɪ/, *n.* **1.** a member of certain orders of honour or merit: *a chevalier of the Legion of Honour.* **2.** a knight. **3.** *French Hist.* **a.** the lowest title of rank in the old nobility. **b.** a cadet of the old nobility. **4.** a chivalrous man. **5.** an adventurer: *a chevalier of industry.* [ME *chevalere,* from OF *chevalier,* from *cheval* horse, from L *caballus.* See CAVALIER]

**Cheviot** /'ʃɛviət/, *n.* **1.** one of a breed of sheep valued for their thick wool (named after the Cheviots, range of hills on the boundary of England and Scotland). **2.** (*l.c.*) a worsted fabric in a coarse twill weave and used for coats, suits, etc.

**chevon** /'ʃɛvɒn/, *n.* the meat of the goat used as food. [F *chèvre* goat]

**chevoo** /ʃə'vu/, *n. Colloq.* →**shivoo.**

**chevron** /'ʃɛvrən/, *n.* **1.** a badge consisting of stripes meeting at an angle, worn on the sleeve (by non-commissioned officers, policemen, etc.) as an indication of rank, of service, etc. **2.** *Her.* the lower half of a bend and a bend sinister meeting at the centre of the shield, like an inverted V. **3.** a similar decoration, as in an architectural moulding; a dancette. [F: rafter, chevron, from F *chèvre* goat, from L *caper*]

chevrons

**chevrotain** /'ʃɛvrəteɪn, -tən/, *n.* any of the very small deerlike ruminants, family Tragulidae, of the genera *Tragulus* of Asia, and *Hyemoschus* of Africa. [F, diminutive of OF *chevrot* kid, diminutive of *chèvre* she-goat]

**chevy** /'tʃɛvi/, *v.t., n.* →**chivvy.**

**chew** /tʃu/, *v.t.* **1.** to crush or grind with the teeth; masticate. **2.** to damage or destroy by or as if by chewing (fol. by *up*): *this machine has chewed up the carpet.* **3.** to meditate on; consider deliberately (fol. by *over*). **4. chew the fat** or **rag,** *Colloq.* to gossip. **5. chew someone's ear,** *Colloq.* to talk to someone insistently and at length. *–v.i.* **6.** to perform the act of crushing or grinding with the teeth. *–n.* **7.** the act of chewing. **8.** that which is chewed; a portion, as of tobacco, for chewing. **9.** *N.Z.* (*in children's speech*), a sweet, a lolly. [ME *chewen,* OE *cēowan,* akin to G *kauen*] – **chewer,** *n.*

**chewie**[1] /'tʃui/, *n. Colloq.* **1.** chewing gum. **2. chewie on your boot!** (an exclamation of contempt for the tardiness of another contestant in a race).

**chewie**[2] /'tʃui/, *n.* →**chewy.**

**chewing gum** /'tʃuɪŋ ˌgʌm/, *n.* a preparation for chewing, usu. made of sweetened and flavoured chicle.

**Chewings fescue** /tʃuɪŋz 'fɛskju/, *n.* a variety of red fescue, *Festuca rubra commutata,* of European origin and used extensively for lawns. [named after Charles *Chewings,* 1859-1937 who distributed the seed from New Zealand]

**chew-'n'-spew** /tʃu-ən-'spju/, *n.* **1.** *Prison Colloq.* prison stew. **2.** *Colloq.* any ready cooked snack or meal, such as hamburgers, fish and chips, etc.

**chewy** /'tʃui/, *adj.* requiring chewing; tough: *this steak is too chewy.*

**chez** /ʃeɪ/, *prep.* at the home of. [F]

**chg.,** *Accounting.* charge.

**chi** /kaɪ/, *n.* the twenty-second letter (Χ, χ, = English ch or kh) of the Greek alphabet.

**chiack** /'tʃaɪæk/, *Colloq.* *–v.t.* **1.** to jeer; taunt; deride; tease. *–n.* **2.** jeering; cheek. Also, **chyack.** [Brit. *chi-hike,* a salute, exclamation] – **chiacking,** *n.*

**chian** /'kaɪən/, *n.* a rich, red wine from Chios, a Greek island in the Aegean, celebrated in classical times.

**chianti** /ki'ænti/, *n.* a medium to dry, red or white, full-bodied table wine, usu. bottled in a colourful straw-covered bottle. [named after *Chianti* Mountains in Tuscany]

**chiaroscuro** /kiarə'skjuroʊ/, *n., pl.* **-ros. 1.** the treatment or general distribution of light and shade in a picture. **2.** pictorial art employing only light and shade. **3.** a sketch in light and shade. [It. *chiaro-oscuro* bright-dark] – **chiaroscurist,** *n.* – **chiaroscurism,** *n.*

**chiasm** /'kaɪæzəm/, *n. Anat.* a crossing or decussation, esp. that of the optic nerves at the base of the brain.

**chiasma** /kaɪ'æzmə/, *n., pl.* **-mata** /-mətə/. *Biol.* a crossing point in conjugating chromosomes. [NL from Gk: arrangement in the form of the Greek letter *chi* (Χ)] – **chiasmal, chiasmic,** *adj.*

**chiasmus** /kaɪ'æzməs/, *n.* the reversal of the order in which two grammatical elements occur in a pair of parallel phrases: *I cannot dig, to beg I am ashamed* is an example of chiasmus. [NL, from Gk: *chiasmós.* See CHIASMA] – **chiastic** /kaɪ'æstɪk/, *adj.*

**chiastolite** /kaɪ'æstəlaɪt/, *n.* a variety of andalusite, a section of which often exhibits the form of a cross.

**chibouk** /tʃə'buk/, *n.* a Turkish tobacco pipe with a long, stiff stem (up to 1.5 metres long). Also, **chibouque, chibuk.** [Turk. *chibūq*]

**chic** /ʃik/, *adj.* **1.** cleverly stylish. *–n.* **2.** style; cleverly attractive style, esp. in dress. [F, ? from *chicane* CHICANE]

**chicane** /ʃə'keɪn/, *n., v.,* **-caned, -caning.** *–n.* **1.** chicanery. **2.** *Bridge.* a hand without trumps. **3.** *Motor Racing.* an artificial bend or series of bends, inserted in a straight stretch of a racetrack, in order to make the course more difficult. *–v.i.* **4.** to use chicanery. *–v.t.* **5.** to trick by chicanery. **6.** to quibble over; cavil at. [F, from *chicaner* quibble, ?from MLG *schikken* arrange] – **chicaner,** *n.*

**chicanery** /ʃə'keɪnəri/, *n., pl.* **-ries. 1.** legal trickery, quibbling, or sophistry. **2.** a quibble or subterfuge.

**chicha** /'tʃitʃə/, *n.* a beer of South and Central America, made from fermented maize. [Amer. Sp., from Haitian native name]

**chichi** /'ʃiʃi/, *adj.* pretentiously elegant or stylish.

**chick** /tʃɪk/, *n.* **1.** a young chicken or other bird. **2.** a child. **3.** *Colloq.* a young girl. **4. pull a chick,** *Colloq.* to seduce a girl or woman.

**chickadee** /'tʃɪkədi/, *n.* any of several North American birds of the family Paridae. [imitative of cry]

**chickaree** /'tʃɪkəri/, *n.* the red squirrel, *Sciurus hudsonicus,* of North America. [imitative of cry]

**chicken** /'tʃɪkən/, *n.* **1.** the young of the domestic fowl (or of certain other birds). **2.** a domestic fowl of any age, or its flesh. **3.** any of certain other birds as **Mother Carey's chicken** (the stormy petrel) or the **prairie chicken** (the prairie hen). **4.** *Colloq.* a young person, esp. a young girl. **5.** *Colloq.* a coward. **6. play chicken, a.** to perform a dangerous dare. **b.** (of a person) to stand in the path of an approaching vehicle daring the driver to run him down. **c.** (of the drivers of two vehicles) to proceed along a collision course, as a test of courage. **7. count one's chickens before they are hatched,** *Colloq.* to act on an expectation which has not yet been fulfilled. *–adj.* **8.** *Colloq.* cowardly. *–v.i.* **9. chicken out,** to withdraw because of cowardice, tiredness, etc. [ME *chicken,* OE *cicen, ciken.* Cf. D *kieken*]

**chicken à la king,** *n.* a dish of diced cooked chicken served in a white sauce with mushrooms and cream.

**chicken breast** /'tʃɪkən brɛst/, *n. U.S. Pathol.* →**pigeon breast.**

**chickenfeed** /'tʃɪkənfid/, *n.* **1.** poultry food. **2.** *Colloq.* a meagre or insignificant sum of money. **3.** *Colloq.* anything or anybody insignificant.

**chicken-hawk** /'tʃɪkən-hɔk/, *n.* →**Australian goshawk.**

**chicken-hearted** /tʃɪkən-'hatəd/, *adj.* timid; cowardly.

**chickenpox** /'tʃɪkənpɒks/, *n.* a mild, contagious eruptive disease, commonly of children, caused by a virus; varicella.

**chicken sexer** /'tʃɪkən sɛksə/, *n.* one who determines the sex of newly-hatched chickens.

**chicken wire** /'– waɪə/, *n.* a light-gauge wire netting suitable for enclosing chickens and for a number of other uses, as protecting vegetable gardens, etc. Also, **chicken mesh.**

**chickpea** /'tʃɪkpi/, *n.* **1.** a leguminous plant, *Cicer arietinum,* bearing edible pealike seeds, much used for food in southern Europe, Asia, and Africa. **2.** its seed. [earlier *chich (pease),* from F *(pois) chiche,* from L *cicer* vetch]

chickpea

**chickweed** /'tʃɪkwid/, *n.* **1.** any of various herbs of the genus *Stellaria,* esp. *S. media.* **2.** any of various allied plants, as *Cerastium glomeratum,* mouse-ear chickweed.

**chicle** /'tʃɪkəl/, *n.* a gumlike substance obtained from certain tropical American trees, as the sapodilla, used in the manufacture of chewing gum, etc. Also, **chicle gum.** [Amer. Sp., from Nahuatl *chictli*]

**chicory** /'tʃɪkəri/, *n., pl.* **-ries. 1.** a perennial herb, *Cichorium intybus,* with blue flowers, native to Europe and western Asia; the blanched shoots are used in salads, and the roasted, powdered roots added to coffee. **2.** *U.S.* endive or Belgian endive. [F *chicorée,* from L *cichorēum,* from Gk *kichóreion*]

chickory

**chide** /tʃaɪd/, *v.,* **chided** or **chid; chided, chid** or **chidden; chiding.** *–v.i.* **1.** to scold; find fault. *–v.t.* **2.** to drive, impel, etc., by chiding. **3.** to express disapproval of. [ME *chiden,* OE *cīdan*] – **chider,** *n.* – **chidingly,** *adv.*

**chief** /tʃif/, *n.* **1.** the head or leader of a body of men; the person highest in authority. **2.** the head or ruler of a clan, tribe, or military or youth organisation, etc. **3.** *Colloq.* boss. **4.** *Her.* the upper third of an escutcheon. **5. in chief, a.** *Her.* borne in the upper part of the shield. **b.** especially, most of all. **c.** (of a command) held directly from the sovereign, or legislative power. *–adj.* **6.** highest in rank or authority. **7.** most important: *his chief merit, the chief difficulty.* **8.** standing at the head. *–adv.* **9.** *Archaic.* chiefly; principally. [ME, from OF, from L *caput* head]

**chief commissioner** /– kə'mɪʃənə/, *n.* the permanent head in certain government departments.

**chief constable** /– 'kʌnstəbl/, *n. Brit.* **1.** a police officer who is the head of a county or other police force, responsible ultimately to the Home Secretary. **2.** the rank.

**Chief Justice** /tʃif 'dʒʌstəs/, *n.* the senior justice of any court who presides over that court.

**chiefly** /'tʃifli/, *adv.* **1.** principally; above all. **2.** mainly; mostly.

**chief of staff,** *n.* **1.** *Mil.* the principal staff officer, usu. of the rank of major general, of a higher military formation, as a corps, who on behalf of his commander controls the staff in his headquarters. **2.** any similar officer in any other army. **3.** *U.S.* the senior officer of the army, navy, or airforce.

**chief petty officer,** *n.* the highest naval rank below commissioned officer and warrant officer.

**Chief Rabbi** /tʃif 'ræbaɪ/, *n.* the senior rabbi of a particular Jewish community.

**chief superintendent** /ˌtfɪʃ supərɪn'tɛndənt/, *n.* **1.** a police officer ranking above superintendent. **2.** the rank.

**chieftain** /'tʃiftən/, *n.* **1.** a leader of a group, band, etc. **2.** the chief of a clan or a tribe. [ME *chieftayne,* var. of *chevetaine,* from OF, from LL *capitānus.* See CAPTAIN] – **chieftaincy, chieftainship,** *n.*

**chiffchaff** /'tʃɪftʃæf/, *n.* a common, plain-coloured European warbler, *Phylloscopus collybita.* [imitative]

**chiffon** /ʃə'fɒn, 'ʃɪfɒn/, *n.* **1.** sheer fabric of silk, nylon, or rayon in plain weave. **2.** any bit of feminine finery, as of ribbon or lace. *–adj.* **3.** of food, having a light, fluffy consistency. [F, from *chiffe* rag]

**chiffonier** /ʃɪfə'nɪə/, *n.* **1.** a high chest of drawers. **2.** a low cupboard with shelves for books. Also, **chifonnier.** [F *chiffonnier,* from *chiffon* rag]

**chiffonière** /ʃɪfə'nɪə/, *n.* a small table with a single drawer.

**chiffonnade** /ʃɪfə'neɪd/, *adj.* with a garnish of leafy vegetables, usu. lettuce, cut into fine strips and cooked in butter. [F]

**chigger** /'tʃɪgə/, *n.* **1.** the parasitic larva of certain kinds of mites, which causes severe itching when attached to the skin; the young of the harvest mite. **2.** →**chigoe.** [alteration of CHIGOE]

**chignon** /'ʃinjɒn/, *n.* a large rolled arrangement of the hair, worn at the back of the head by women. [F from L *catēna* chain]

**chigoe** /'tʃɪgoʊ/, *n.* a flea, *Tunga penetrans,* of the West Indies, South America, Africa, etc., the female of which buries itself in the skin of men and animals; chigger; jigger. [Carib. Cf. F *chique*]

**chihuahua** /tʃə'wawə, ʃə'wawa/, *n.* one of the smallest breeds of dog, originating in Mexico.

**chil-,** variant of **chilo-,** used before vowels.

**chilblain** /'tʃɪlbleɪn/, *n.* (*usu. pl.*) *Pathol.* an inflammation on the hands and feet caused by exposure to cold and moisture. [CHIL(L) + BLAIN] – **chilblained,** *adj.*

**child** /tʃaɪld/, *n., pl.* **children. 1.** a baby or infant. **2.** a boy or girl. **3.** *Law.* a young person within a certain age determined by statute. For some purposes a young person less than seventeen years is a child; for others, under eighteen or twenty-one; in legal instruments it is construed to mean a legitimate as opposed to an illegitimate child. **4.** a childish person. **5.** a son or daughter. **6.** any descendant. **7.** any person or thing regarded as the product or result of particular agencies, influences, etc.: *Satan's followers are the children of darkness.* **8.** a disciple or follower. **9. with child,** pregnant. [ME *child,* pl. *childre(n),* OE *cild,* pl. *cild(ru)*] – **childless,** *adj.* – **childlessness,** *n.*

**child allowance** /'– əlaʊəns/, *n.* →**child endowment.**

**child bashing** /'– bæʃɪŋ/, *n.* physical maltreatment of a child usu. by its parents.

**child-bearing** /'tʃaɪld-bɛərɪŋ/, *n.* producing or bringing forth children.

**childbed** /'tʃaɪldbɛd/, *n.* the condition of a woman giving birth to a child; parturition.

**childbed fever** /– 'fivə/, *n.* →**puerperal fever.**

**childbirth** /'tʃaɪldbɜθ/, *n.* →**parturition.**

**child-care** /'tʃaɪld-kɛə/, *n.* **1.** professional superintendence of children. *–adj.* **2.** of or pertaining to such superintendence: *child-care centres.*

**childe** /tʃaɪld/, *n. Archaic.* a youth of noble birth. Also, **child.** [variant spelling of CHILD]

**child endowment** /tʃaɪld ən'daʊmənt/, *n.* a government payment made to parents to assist them in the rearing of their children.

**childermas** /'tʃɪldəmæs/, *n.* Holy Innocents' Day, Dec. 28. [OE *cylda-mæsse* children's mass]

**child guidance** /tʃaɪld 'gaɪdns/, *n.* the readjustment, with psychiatric help, of difficult, retarded, etc., children.

**childhood** /'tʃaɪldhʊd/, *n.* **1.** the state or time of being a child. **2. second childhood,** dotage; childishness in extreme old age.

**childish** /'tʃaɪldɪʃ/, *adj.* **1.** of, like, or befitting a child. **2.** puerile; weak; silly. [ME *childisch,* OE *cildisc*] – **childishly,** *adv.* – **childishness,** *n.*

**child labour** /tʃaɪld 'leɪbə/, *n.* the employment in full-time occupations of children below the minimum legal age. In most countries, the minimum age is the school-leaving age.

**childlike** /'tʃaɪldlaɪk/, *adj.* like or befitting a child, as in innocence, frankness, etc. – **childlikeness,** *n.*

**childminder** /'tʃaɪldmaɪndə/, *n.* one who looks after children, but who has little or no formal training.

**childproof** /'tʃaɪldpruf/, *adj.* so designed that it cannot be opened or damaged by children.

**children** /'tʃɪldrən/, *n.* plural of **child.**

**child restraint** /'tʃaɪld rəstreɪnt/, *n.* a seat belt designed to fit children.

**child's play** /'tʃaɪldz pleɪ/, *n.* something very easy or simple.

**Chile** /'tʃɪli/, *n.* a republic in south-western South America. – **Chilean,** *adj., n.*

**Chile saltpetre** /– 'sɒltpitə/, *n.* sodium nitrate, $NaNO_3$, a crystalline compound used as a fertiliser. Also, **Chile saltpeter, chile nitre.**

**chili**[1] /'tʃɪli/, *n., pl.* **-ies.** →**chilli.**

**chili**[2] /'tʃɪli/, *n., pl.* **-ies.** the hot, dry sirocco wind of North Africa. [ult. from Berber]

**chiliad** /'kɪliæd/, *n.* **1.** a thousand. **2.** a thousand years. [Gk *chīliás,* from *chī́lioi* thousand]

**chiliasm** /'kɪliæzəm/, *n. Theol.* **1.** the doctrine of the expected reign of Christ on earth for a thousand years. **2.** the reign. [Gk *chīliasmós,* from *chīliás.* See CHILIAD] – **chiliast** /'kɪliæst/, *n.* – **chiliastic** /kɪli'æstɪk/, *adj.*

**chill** /tʃɪl/, *n.* **1.** coldness, esp. a moderate but penetrating coldness. **2.** a sensation of cold, usu. with shivering. **3.** a cold stage, as a first symptom of illness. **4.** a depressing influence or sensation. **5.** a metal mould for making chilled castings. **6.** a piece of metal which connects the base of a bed to the bedhead. **7.** *Metall.* **a.** a metal insert embedded in the surface of a sand mould or core, or placed in a mould cavity to increase the cooling rate at that point. **b.** white iron occurring on a grey iron casting. **8.** a coldness of manner, lack of friendliness. *–adj.* **9.** cold; tending to cause shivering. **10.** shivering with cold. **11.** depressing or discouraging. **12.** not warm or hearty: *a chill reception.* *–v.i.* **13.** to become cold. **14.** to be seized with a chill. **15.** *Metall.* to become hard, esp. on the surface, by sudden cooling, as a metal mould. *–v.t.* **16.** to affect with cold; make chilly. **17.** to make cool, but not freeze: *to chill wines.* *–v.t.* **18.** to harden by sudden cooling. **19.** to depress; discourage: *chill his hopes.* **20.** *Metall.* to harden (cast-iron or steel) on the surface by casting in a metal mould. [ME *chile,* OE *ciele, cile* coolness; akin to COOL, COLD] – **chiller,** *n.* – **chillness,** *n.* – **chillingly,** *adv.* – **chilled,** *adj.*

**chilled weight** /tʃɪld 'weɪt/, *n. Meat Industry.* the weight of a dressed carcase after chilling when some excess moisture has been lost in evaporation.

**chilli** /'tʃɪli/, *n., pl.* **-ies. 1.** the pungent fruit of some species of capsicum, usu. small but hot to the taste. **2.** a capsicum bearing such a fruit, sometimes grown as an ornamental plant. Also, **chile, chili, chilli pepper.** [Amer. Sp. *chile,* from Nahuatl *chili*]

**chilli con carne** /ˌtʃɪli kɒn 'kani/, *n.* a popular Mexican dish made from meat and finely chopped red pepper, served with beans. Also, **chili con carne.** [Sp.: chilli with meat]

**chilli sauce** /ˌtʃɪli 'sɔs/, *n.* a highly flavoured sauce made of tomatoes cooked with chilli, spices, and other seasonings.

**chillum** /'tʃɪləm/, *n. Colloq.* a smoking apparatus for hashish or marihuana.

**chilly** /'tʃɪli/, *adj.,* **-ier, -iest,** *adv.* *–adj.* **1.** producing a sensation of cold; causing shivering. **2.** feeling cold; sensitive to cold. **3.** without warmth of feeling: *a chilly reception.* *–adv.* **4.** in a chill manner. – **chillily,** *adv.* – **chilliness,** *n.*

**chillybin** /'tʃɪlibɪn/, *n. Colloq.* a portable icebox; an esky. Also, **chillibin.**

**chilo-,** a word element meaning 'lip', 'labial'. [Gk *cheilo-,* combining form of *cheîlos* lip]

**chiloplasty** /'kaɪləplæsti/, *n.* plastic surgery of the lip.

**chilopod** /'kaɪləpɒd/, *n.* →**centipede.**

**chimaera** /kaɪ'mɪərə, kə-/, *n.* **1.** any of the fishes of the family Chimaeridae, as the rabbit-fish. The male has a spiny clasping organ over the mouth. **2.** any similar fish of the group Holocephali, which includes this family. **3.** chimera. [L. See CHIMERA]

**chimar** /'tʃɪmə/, *n.* →**chimer**[2]

**chimb** /tʃɪm/, *n.* →**chime**[2].

**chime**[1] /tʃaɪm/, *n., v.,* **chimed, chiming.** *–n.* **1.** an arrangement for striking a bell or bells so as to produce a musical sound: *a door chime, the chimes of Big Ben.* **2.** a set of vertical metal tubes struck with a hammer, as used in the modern orchestra. **3.** →**carillon** (defs 1 and 3). **4.** (*oft. pl.*) →**carillon** (def. 2). **5.** harmonious sound in general; music; melody. **6.** harmonious relation; accord. **7.** the rhythm of music, or the beat of verses of poetry. *–v.i.* **8.** to sound harmoniously or in chimes, as a set of bells. **9.** to produce a musical sound by striking a bell, etc.; ring chimes. **10.** to harmonise; agree. **11. chime in, a.** to break suddenly into a conversation, esp. to express agreement. **b.** to join in harmoniously (in music). *–v.t.* **12.** to give forth (music, etc.), as a bell or bells. **13.** to strike (a bell, etc.), so as to produce musical sound. **14.** to put, bring, indicate, etc., by chiming. **15.** to utter or repeat in cadence or singsong. [ME *chimbe,* apparently backformation from OE *cimbal,* from L *cymbalum* cymbal]

**chime**[2] /tʃaɪm/, *n.* the edge or brim of a cask or the like, formed by the ends of the staves beyond the head or bottom. Also, **chimb, chine.** [ME *chimb(e),* OE *cimb* (in compounds and derivatives), c. G *Kimme* edge]

**chimer**[1] /'tʃaɪmə/, *n.* one who or that which chimes.

**chimer**[2] /'tʃɪmə, 'ʃɪmə/, *n.* a loose upper robe, esp. of a bishop, to which the lawn sleeves are usu. attached. Also, **chimar, chimere** /tʃə'mɪə, ʃə-/. [ME *chemer,* ? from Anglo-L *chimēra*]

**chimera** /kɪ'mɪərə, kə-/, *n., pl.* **-ras. 1.** (*oft. cap.*) a mythological fire-breathing monster, commonly represented with a lion's head, a goat's body, and a serpent's tail. **2.** a grotesque monster, as in decorative art. **3.** a horrible or unreal creature of the imagination; a vain or idle fancy. **4.** *Genetics.* an organism composed of two or more genetically distinct tissues, as **a.** an organism which is partly male and partly female. **b.** an artifically produced creature having tissues of several species. Also, **chimaera.** [L *chimaera,* from Gk *chímaira* lit., she-goat; replacing ME *chimere,* from F]

**chimerical** /kaɪ'mɛrɪkəl, kə-/, *adj.* **1.** unreal; imaginary; visionary. **2.** wildly fanciful. Also, **chimeric.** – **chimerically,** *adv.*

**chimney** /'tʃɪmni/, *n., pl.* **-neys. 1.** a structure, usu. vertical, containing a passage or flue by which the smoke, gases, etc., of a fire or furnace are carried off and by means of which a draught is created. **2.** that part of such a structure which rises above a roof. **3.** the smokestack or funnel of a locomotive, steamship, etc. **4.** a tube, commonly of glass, surrounding the flame of a lamp to promote combustion and keep the flame steady. **5.** anything resembling a chimney, such as the vent of a volcano. **6.** *Mountaineering.* a narrow cleft or opening in a rock face. **7.** fireplace. [ME *chiminee,* from OF, from LL *camīnāta,* from L *camīnus* furnace, from Gk *kámīnos*] – **chimneyless,** *adj.*

**chimneybreast** /ˈtʃɪmnibrɛst/, *n.* the projecting wall in a room which contains the fireplace and flues.

**chimney corner** /ˈtʃɪmni ˌkɔnə/, *n.* **1.** the corner or side of a fireplace. **2.** a place near the fire. **3.** fireside.

**chimneypiece** /ˈtʃɪmnipis/, *n.* **1.** mantelpiece. **2.** *Obs.* a decoration over a fireplace.

**chimneypot** /ˈtʃɪmnipɒt/, *n.* **1.** a cylindrical or other pipe, as of earthenware or sheet metal, fitted on the top of a chimney to increase draught, and carry off smoke. **2.** *Colloq.* a top hat.

**chimneystack** /ˈtʃɪmnistæk/, *n.* a group of flues, bricked together.

**chimney swallow** /ˈtʃɪmni ˌswɒloʊ/, *n.* **1.** the common swallow, *Hirundo rustica,* which sometimes nests in barns or chimneys. **2.** the chimney swift, *Chaetura pelagica,* which often builds its nest in a disused chimney.

**chimneysweep** /ˈtʃɪmniswip/, *n.* one whose business it is to clean out chimneys. Also, **chimneysweeper.**

**chimney swift** /ˈtʃɪmni ˌswɪft/, *n.* →**chimney swallow** (def. 2).

**chimp** /tʃɪmp/, *n. Colloq.* a chimpanzee.

**chimpanzee** /tʃɪmpænˈzi/, *n.* a highly intelligent anthropoid ape, *Pan troglodytes,* of equatorial Africa, smaller, with larger ears, and more arboreal than the gorilla. [a Bantu language in Angola, W. Africa; cf. Kongo *kimphenzi* chimpanzee, gorilla]

chimpanzee

**chin** /tʃɪn/, *n., v.,* **chinned, chinning.** *–n.* **1.** the lower extremity of the face, below the mouth. **2.** the point of the lower jaw. **3. keep one's chin up,** to remain cheerful, esp. under stress. **4. take it on the chin,** to take suffering or punishment stalwartly. *–v.t.* **5.** to bring one's chin up to (a horizontal bar, from which one is hanging), by bending the elbows; bring (oneself) to this position. *–v.i.* **6.** to chin oneself. **7.** *Colloq.* to talk. [ME; OE *cin,* c. G *Kinn*]

**Chin.,** Chinese.

**china**[1] /ˈtʃaɪnə/, *n.* **1.** a vitreous, translucent earthenware, originally produced in China. **2.** any porcelain ware. **3.** plates, cups, etc., collectively. **4.** figurines of porcelain, esp. a collection. *–adj.* **5.** made of china.

**china**[2] /ˈtʃaɪnə/, *n. Colloq.* a mate; friend. [rhyming slang, *china plate* mate]

**China** /ˈtʃaɪnə/, *n.* a country in eastern Asia. Official name: **People's Republic of China.**

**china bark** /ˈkaɪnə bak, ˈkinə, ˈtʃaɪnə/, *n.* →**cinchona** (def. 2).

**china clay** /ˈtʃaɪnə kleɪ/, *n.* a natural form of hydrated aluminium silicate, used for making porcelain; kaolin; porcelain clay.

**chinaman** /ˈtʃaɪnəmən/, *n., pl.* **-men.** **1.** (*cap.*) a native or a descendant of a native of China; a Chinese. **2.** *Cricket.* a left-handed bowler's googly, spinning as a leg break to a right-handed batsman. **3.** *Mining.* →**chute**[1] (def. 1). **4.** a cutting, bank or ramp so designed that a vehicle may be driven under it and loaded from above. **5.** *Mining.* a large stone found in gold-bearing gravels. **6.** *Shearing.* an unshorn lock (like a pigtail) on a sheep's rump. **7. kill a Chinaman, a.** to put a jinx on oneself, as by killing a Chinaman. **b.** to commit a peccadillo.

**Chinaman's luck** /tʃaɪnəmənz ˈlʌk/, *n.* infallible good luck.

**China rose** /tʃaɪnə ˈroʊz/, *n.* any of several species of the genus *Rosa,* as *R. chinensis* and *R. indica* with red or white flowers, or *R. semperflorens* with red flowers.

**China stone** /ˈ– stoʊn/, *n.* partly decomposed granite, used in porcelain manufacture.

**China syndrome** /ˈ– sɪndroʊm/, *n. Colloq.* the melting-down point of a nuclear reactor. [from the notion that the meltdown is so powerful that the reactor goes right through the ground to China]

**Chinatown** /ˈtʃaɪnətaʊn/, *n.* the Chinese quarter of a city.

**chinaware** /ˈtʃaɪnəwɛə/, *n.* dishes, etc., of china.

**China watcher** /ˈtʃaɪnə wɒtʃə/, *n.* one who studies political and social developments in China.

**chincapin** /ˈtʃɪŋkəpɪn/, *n.* →**chinquapin.**

**chinch bug** /ˈtʃɪntʃ bʌg/, *n.* any of numerous small hemipterous insects of the family Lygaeidae, some of which are very destructive of fruit, vegetables, gasses and grain crops as the Rutherglen bug. [*chinch* from Sp. *cinche,* from L *cimex* bedbug]

**chincherinchee** /tʃɪntʃəˈrɪntʃi/, *n.* a bulbous plant of southern Africa, *Ornithogalum thyrsoides,* with showy, long-lasting flowers.

**chinchilla** /tʃɪnˈtʃɪlə/, *n.* **1.** a small South American rodent of the genus *Chinchilla,* whose valuable skin is dressed as a fur. **2.** the fur itself. **3.** a thick, napped, woollen fabric for coats, esp. children's coats. **4.** one of a variety of any of certain animals, as a cat or rabbit, with long, soft, grey fur. [Sp., diminutive of *chinche* bug]

chinchilla

**chin-chin** /tʃɪn-ˈtʃɪn/, *n. Colloq.* **1.** good-bye. **2.** (a toast, as in drinking to someone's health).

**chine**[1] /tʃaɪn/, *n.* a ravine or large fissure in a cliff, formed largely by the action of running water particularly in southern England. [ME, n. use of *chine,* v., crack, OE *cīnan,* akin to OE *cime, cine* chink, fissure]

**chine**[2] /tʃaɪn/, *n., v.,* **chined, chining.** *–n.* **1.** the backbone or spine. **2.** the whole or a piece of the backbone of an animal with adjoining parts, cut for cooking. **3.** a ridge or crest, as of land. **4.** the intersecting line between the side and bottom of a flat-bottom or V-bottom boat. *–v.t.* **5.** to cut along or across the backbone. [ME *chyne,* from OF *eschine,* from Gmc. See SHIN]

**chine**[3] /tʃaɪn/, *n.* →**chime**[2].

**chiné** /ˈʃineɪ/, *Textiles.* *–n.* **1.** material that is mottled, with the pattern printed on the warp. *–adj.* **2.** mottled, with the pattern printed on the warp.

**Chinee** /tʃaɪˈni/, *n. Colloq.* a Chinese.

**Chinese** /tʃaɪˈniz/, *n., pl.* **-nese,** *adj.* *–n.* **1.** the standard language of China, based on the speech of Peking; Mandarin. **2.** a group of languages of the Sino-Tibetan family including standard Chinese and most of the other languages of China. **3.** any of the Chinese languages, which vary among themselves to the point of mutual unintelligibility. **4.** a native of or a descendant of a native of China. *–adj.* **5.** of China, its inhabitants, or their language. **6.** of or pertaining to the written characters of the Chinese language.

**Chinese block** /– ˈblɒk/, *n.* a percussion instrument consisting of a resonant hollow block of wood which is struck with a drumstick.

**Chinese burn** /– ˈbɜn/, *n.* the wringing of the skin on the wrist or forearm to cause pain.

**Chinese cabbage** /– ˈkæbɪdʒ/, *n.* a tall, yellow-white, closely-leaved vegetable, *Brassica chinensis,* resembling a head of celery but more tightly packed; celery cabbage.

**Chinese chequers** /– ˈtʃɛkəz/, *n.* a game played by two or more persons with pegs or marbles, on a board with hollows or holes.

**Chinese elm** /– ˈɛlm/, *n.* →**elm.**

**Chinese gooseberry** /– ˈguzbəri/, *n.* **1.** a vine, *Actinidia chinensis,* climbing to 6 metres, with leaves densely tomentose on the lower surface and with cylindrical to subglobose hairy fruit about 7 cm long with a somewhat gooseberry-like flavour; Kiwi fruit. **2.** the fruit.

**Chinese lantern** /– ˈlæntən/, *n.* **1.** a collapsible lantern of thin, coloured paper, often used for decorative lighting. **2.** any of several species of *Abutilon* often cultivated for their lantern-shaped flowers.

**Chinese puzzle** /– ˈpʌzəl/, *n.* **1.** a very complicated puzzle; esp. a series of boxes in boxes. **2.** anything very complicated.

**Chinese red** /– ˈrɛd/, *adj.* **1.** scarlet; orange-red; red chrome. **2.** a pigment consisting of basic lead chromate. Also, **chrome red.**

**Chinese salt** /– 'sɒlt/, *n.* →**monosodium glutamate.**

**Chinese water torture,** *n.* **1.** a form of torture aimed to drive the victim insane by dripping water on his forehead. **2.** a form of torture in which water drops onto a piece of cloth covering the victim's face, making it progressively more difficult to breathe as the cloth becomes saturated with water.

**Chinese white** /– 'waɪt/, *n.* a pigment consisting of zinc oxide ground in water or oil.

**chink**[1] /tʃɪŋk/, *n.* **1.** a crack, cleft, or fissure. **2.** a narrow opening. *–v.t.* **3.** *U.S.* to fill up chinks in. [apparently from OE *cinu, cine* crack, fissure + *-k,* suffix. See -OCK]

**chink**[2] /tʃɪŋk/, *v.i.* **1.** to make a short, sharp, ringing sound, as of coins or glasses striking together. *–v.t.* **2.** to cause (something) to make this sound. *–n.* **3.** a chinking sound. [imitative]

**Chink** /tʃɪŋk/, *n.* (*sometimes l.c.*) *Colloq.* (*derog.*) a Chinese. Also, **Chinkie.**

**chinkapin** /'tʃɪŋkəpɪn/, *n.* →**chinquapin.**

**chinless** /'tʃɪnləs/, *adj.* **1.** with a receding chin; lacking a firm chin. **2.** lacking courage or firmness of purpose; vacillating; of weak character. **3. chinless wonder,** *Colloq.* a foolish man, usu. of good family.

**chino** /'tʃinoʊ/, *n. U.S.* a tough, twilled cotton cloth used for uniforms, sports clothes, etc.

**Chino-,** a combining form meaning 'Chinese'.

**Chinoiserie** /ʃinˌwazə'ri, ʃɪn'wazəri/, *n.* a style of European art, current esp. in the 18th century, based on imitations of motifs in Chinese art.

**chinquapin** /'tʃɪŋkəpɪn/, *n.* **1.** the dwarf chestnut, *Castanea pumila,* a shrub or small tree of the U.S., bearing a small, edible nut, solitary in the burr. **2.** a tree of the Pacific coast, *Castanopsis chrysophylla.* **3.** the nut of either of these trees. Also, **chincapin, chinkapin.** [N Amer. Ind. (Algonquian)]

**chinrest** /'tʃɪnrɛst/, *n.* a device attached to a viola or a violin for controlling its position under the chin.

**chinse** /tʃɪns/, *v.t.,* **chinsed, chinsing.** *Naut.* to caulk, esp. temporarily. [alteration of d. *chinch,* var. of CHINK[1]]

**chinstrap** /'tʃɪnstræp/, *n.* a strap under a chin for holding on a helmet.

**chintz** /tʃɪnts/, *n., pl.* **chintzes. 1.** a printed cotton fabric, glazed or unglazed, used esp. for draperies. **2.** (originally) painted or stained calico from India. [var. of *chints,* pl. of *chint,* from Hind. *chīnt*] – **chintzy,** *adj.*

**chinwag** /'tʃɪnwæg/, *n. Colloq.* a chat; a conversation.

**chip**[1] /tʃɪp/, *n., v.,* **chipped, chipping.** *–n.* **1.** a small piece, as of wood, separated by chopping, cutting, or breaking. **2.** a very thin slice or piece of food, etc.: *chocolate chips.* **3. a.** a deep-fried finger of potato. **b.** →**crisp** (def. 11). **4.** a mark made by chipping. **5.** *Games.* a counter, as of ivory or bone, used in certain card games, etc. **6.** *Electronics.* a minute square of semi-conducting material, processed in various ways to have certain electrical characteristics; esp. such a square before being made into an integrated circuit. **7.** *Colloq.* a small (cut) piece of diamond, etc. **8.** *U.S.* anything trivial or worthless, or dried up or without flavour. **9.** *U.S.* a piece of dried dung. **10.** wood, straw, etc., in thin strips for weaving into hats, baskets, etc. **11.** →**punnet. 12.** *N.Z.* →**chip basket. 13.** *Golf.* →**chip shot. 14.** *Colloq.* a reprimand. **15.** (pl.) *Colloq.* money. **16. cash in one's chips,** *Colloq.* to die. **17. have had one's chips,** *Colloq.* to have lost one's opportunity. **18. chip off the old block,** *Colloq.* a person inheriting marked family characteristics. **19. chip on the shoulder,** *Colloq.* a grudge. **20. the chips are down,** *Colloq.* (the moment of decision has been reached). *–v.t.* **21.** to hew or cut with an axe, chisel, etc. **22.** *Agric.* to use a hoe or similar implement to clear weed growth without disturbing the soil surface. **23.** to cut or break off (bits or fragments). **24.** to disfigure by breaking off fragments. **25.** to cut potatoes into chips. **26.** to shape or produce by cutting away pieces. **27.** *Games.* to bet by means of chips, as in poker (oft. fol. by *in*). **28.** to reduce trees, logs, etc., to small pieces for wood pulp. **29.** to taunt, chaff, poke fun at; to reprimand. *–v.i.* **30.** to break off in small pieces; to become chipped. **31.** *Golf.* to make a chip shot. **32. chip in, a.** *Colloq.* to contribute money, help, etc. **b.** *Colloq.* to interrupt; enter uninvited into a debate or argument being conducted by others. **c.** to turn seed in (with a harrow, etc.). [ME *chippen,* OE *cippian.* Cf. MLG, MD *kippen* chip eggs, hatch]

**chip**[2] /tʃɪp/, *n. Wrestling.* a tricky or special method by which an opponent can be thrown. [from *chip,* v., trip. Cf. Icel. *kippa* scratch, pull]

**chip basket** /'– baskət/, *n.* **1.** a basket of thin interwoven strips of wood used for packing fruit, etc. **2.** a wire basket in which potato chips are placed when frying.

**chipboard** /'tʃɪpbɔd/, *n.* **1.** a resin-bonded artificial wood made from waste wood, sawdust, etc., used in sheets for light structural work. **2.** a board, usu. made of wastepaper, used in box-making, etc. Also, **particle board.**

**chip heater** /'tʃɪp hitə/, *n.* a water heater fired by wood chips.

**chip log** /'– lɒg/, *n.* →**log** (def. 3b).

**chip-mill** /'tʃɪp-mɪl/, *n.* a mill for producing wood pulp.

**chipmunk** /'tʃɪpmʌŋk/, *n.* any of various small striped terrestrial squirrels of the North American genus *Tamias,* and the Asiatic and American genus *Eutamias,* esp. *T. striatus* of eastern North America. [N Amer. Ind. *ačitamo* squirrel]

**chipolata** /tʃɪpə'latə/, *n.* a very small sausage usu. served as a garnish for meat or poultry dishes or as a cocktail snack.

**chippendale** /'tʃɪpəndeɪl/, *adj.* of, or in the style of, Thomas Chippendale, 1718?-79, English cabinet-maker and furniture designer.

chipmunk

**chipper**[1] /'tʃɪpə/, *adj. Colloq.* lively; cheerful. [cf. Brit. d. *kipper* frisky]

**chipper**[2] /'tʃɪpə/, *n.* one who or that which chips or cuts. [CHIP[1] + -ER[1]]

**chippie** /'tʃɪpi/, *n.* **1.** *Colloq.* a carpenter. **2.** →**chip**[1] (def. 3).

**chipping** /'tʃɪpɪŋ/, *n.* a fragment of stone, as used in surfacing roads.

**chipping sparrow** /'– ˌspæroʊ/, *n.* any of several small North American sparrows of the genus *Spizella,* as *S. passerina,* commonly found about houses.

**chip shot** /'tʃɪp ʃɒt/, *n.* **1.** *Golf.* a short shot using a wrist motion, made in approaching the green. **2.** *Tennis.* →**chop stroke.**

**chirality** /kaɪ'rælətі/, *n.* the ability of an asymmetric or dissymetric molecule to turn the plane of plane polarised light. [Gk *cheír* hand] – **chiral,** *adj.*

**chirm** /tʃɜm/, *v.i.* **1.** to chirp, as a bird; sing; warble. *–n.* **2.** the chirping of birds, etc.; charm. [ME; OE *cierm*]

**chiro-,** a word element meaning 'hand', as in *chiropractic.* [Gk *cheiro-,* combining form of *cheír*]

**chirognomy** /kaɪ'rɒgnəmi/, *n.* the art of estimating a person's character by the appearance of the hand; palmistry.

**chirography** /kaɪ'rɒgrəfi/, *n.* →**handwriting.** – **chirographer,** *n.* – **chirographic** /kaɪrə'græfɪk/, **chirographical** /kaɪrə'græfɪkəl/, *adj.*

**chiromancy** /'kaɪrəˌmænsi/, *n.* the art of telling a person's fortune and character by the hand. – **chiromancer,** *n.*

**chironomid** /kaɪ'rɒnəməd/, *n.* one of a genus of midges, *Chironomus,* with aquatic larvae.

**chiropody** /kə'rɒpədi/, *n.* the treatment of minor foot ailments, such as corns, bunions, etc. [CHIRO- + Gk *-podia,* from *poús* foot] – **chiropodist,** *n.*

**chiropractic** /kaɪrə'præktɪk/, *n.* **1.** a therapeutic system based upon the premise that disease is caused by interference with nerve function, the method being to restore normal condition by adjusting the segments of the spinal column. **2.** a chiropractor. [CHIRO- + Gk *praktikós* practical]

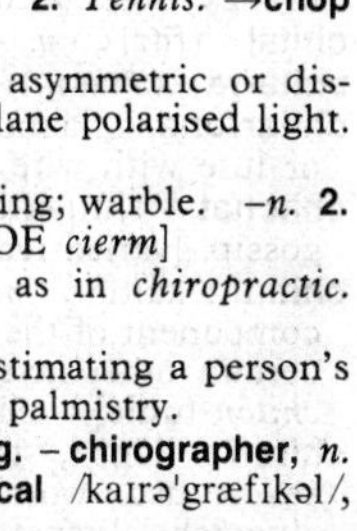
chiromancy

**chiropractor** /'kaɪrəpræktə/, *n.* one who practises chiropractic.

**chiropter** /kaɪ'rɒptə/, *n.* any of the Chiroptera, the order of mammals that comprises the bats. [NL *chiroptera,* pl., from *chiro-* CHIRO- + Gk *pterá* wings]

**chiropteran** /kaɪ'rɒptərən/, *n.* **1.** →**chiropter.** –*adj.* **2.** of or pertaining to a chiropter.

**chirp** /tʃɜp/, *v.i.* **1.** to make a short, sharp sound, as small birds and certain insects. **2.** to make any similar sound. –*v.t.* **3.** to sound or utter in a chirping manner. –*n.* **4.** a chirping sound. – **chirper,** *n.*

**chirpy** /'tʃɜpi/, *adj. Colloq.* cheerful; lively; gay. – **chirpily,** *adv.*

**chirr** /tʃɜ/, *v.i.* **1.** to make a shrill trilling sound, as a grasshopper. **2.** to make a similar sound. –*n.* **3.** the sound of chirring. Also, **chirre, churr.** [apparently backformation from CHIRRUP]

**chirrup** /'tʃɪrəp/, *v.,* **-ruped, -ruping,** *n.* –*v.i.* **1.** to chirp. **2.** to make a chirping sound, as to a cagebird or a horse. –*v.t.* **3.** to utter with chirps. –*n.* **4.** the act or sound of chirruping. [var. of CHIRP] – **chirruper,** *n.*

**chirrupy** /'tʃɪrəpi/, *adj.* →**chirpy.**

**chirurgeon** /kaɪ'rɜdʒən/, *n. Archaic.* →**surgeon.** [b. L *chīrūrgus* surgeon (from Gk *cheirourgós*) and SURGEON; replacing ME *cirurgien,* from OF]

**chirurgery** /kaɪ'rɜdʒəri/, *n. Archaic.* →**surgery.** – **chirurgic, chirurgical,** *adj.*

**chisel** /'tʃɪzəl/, *n., v.,* **-elled, -elling** or (*U.S.*) **-eled, -eling.** –*n.* **1.** a tool, as of steel, with a cutting edge at the extremity, usu. transverse to the axis, for cutting or shaping wood, stone, etc. –*v.t.* **2.** to cut, shape, etc., with a chisel. **3.** *Colloq.* **a.** to cheat; swindle. **b.** to get by cheating or trickery. –*v.i.* **4.** to work with a chisel. **5.** *Colloq.* to use trickery; cheat. [ME, from ONF, from L *caesus,* pp., cut] – **chiseller;** *U.S.* **chiseler,** *n.*

**chiselled** /'tʃɪzəld/, *adj.* **1.** cut, shaped, etc., with a chisel. **2.** clear-cut. Also, *U.S.,* **chiseled.**

**chisel-plough** /'tʃɪzəl-plaʊ/, *n.* **1.** a cultivator with spring tines which can be used for heavy tillage to about 30 cm in depth; it has a ripping action and does not turn a furrow. –*v.t.* **2.** to use a chisel plough to cultivate the soil.

**chi-square test** /'kaɪ-skwɛə ˌtɛst/, *n. Statistics.* a test devised for testing the mathematical goodness of fit of a frequency curve to an observed frequency distribution.

**chit**[1] /tʃɪt/, *n.* **1.** a voucher of money owed for food, drink, etc. **2.** a note; a short memorandum. [short for CHITTY, from Hind. *chitthī*]

**chit**[2] /tʃɪt/, *n.* a young person, esp. a pert girl. [? akin to KITTEN; associated with obs. *chit* sprout]

**chital** /'tʃitəl/, *n.* →**axis**[2].

**chitarra** /kə'tarə, tʃə-/, *n.* an Italian guitar with wire strings.

**chitarrone** /kɪtə'roʊni, tʃɪt-/, *n.* a large double-necked theorbo or lute with wire strings.

**chitchat** /'tʃɪttʃæt/, *n.* **1.** light conversation; small talk. **2.** gossip. [varied reduplication of CHAT]

**chitin** /'kaɪtɪn/, *n.* a horny organic substance which is a component of the cuticula of arthropods and is found also in certain other invertebrates and in fungi. [F *chitine,* from Gk *chitṓn* tunic] – **chitinous,** *adj.*

**chiton** /'kaɪtən, -tɒn/, *n.* **1.** *Gk Antiq.* a garment for both sexes, usu. worn next to the skin. **2.** any of a group of sluggish, limpet-like molluscs which adhere to rocks. [Gk]

chiton (def. 2)

**chitterling** /'tʃɪtəlɪŋ/, *n.* **1.** (*usu. pl.*) a part of the small intestine of pigs, etc., esp. as cooked for food. **2.** *Obs.* a frill or ruff. [cf. G *Kutteln* entrails]

**chitty** /'tʃɪti/, *n.* →**chit**[1].

**chivalric** /'ʃɪvəlrɪk/, *adj.* **1.** pertaining to chivalry. **2.** chivalrous.

**chivalrous** /'ʃɪvəlrəs/, *adj.* **1.** having the high qualities characteristic of chivalry, such as courage, courtesy, generosity, loyalty, etc. **2.** chivalric. **3.** having good and polished manners, and a consideration of others. [ME, from OF *chevalerous,* from *chevalier* CHEVALIER] – **chivalrously,** *adv.* – **chivalrousness,** *n.*

**chivalry** /'ʃɪvəlri/, *n.* **1.** the ideal qualifications of a knight, such as courtesy, generosity, valour, dexterity in arms, etc. **2.** the rules and customs of medieval knighthood. **3.** the medieval system or institution of knighthood. **4.** a group of knights. **5.** gallant warriors or gentlemen. **6.** good manners; consideration of others. **7.** *Obs.* the position or rank of a knight. [ME, from OF *chevalerie,* from *chevalier* CHEVALIER]

**chive** /tʃaɪv/, *n.* a small bulbous plant, *Allium schoenoprasum,* related to the leek and onion, with long, slender leaves which are used as a seasoning in cookery. Also, **chive garlic.** [ME, from ONF, from L *caepa* onion]

**chivvy** /'tʃɪvi/, *v.,* **-ied, -ying,** *n.* –*v.t.* **1.** to harass; worry; nag. **2.** *Brit.* to chase; run after. –*v.i.* **3.** to scamper; race. –*n.* **4.** *Brit.* a hunting cry. **5.** *Brit.* a hunt chase. Also, **chevvy, chevy.** [? short for chevy chase]

**chizz** /tʃɪz/, *n. Brit. Colloq.* a swindle; an unfair or unlucky event.

**chlamydate** /'klæmədeɪt/, *adj. Zool.* having a mantle or pallium, as a mollusc. [Gk *chlamýs* mantle + -ATE[1]]

**chlamydeous** /klə'mɪdiəs/, *adj. Bot.* pertaining to or having a floral envelope. [NL *chlamydeae,* pl., (from Gk *chlamýs* mantle) + -OUS]

**chloanthite** /kloʊ'ænθaɪt/, *n.* a mineral arsenide of nickel which is used as an ore of nickel; white nickel. [Gk *chloanthḗs* pale (from *chlóē* green vegetation + *anthēs* flower) + -ITE[1]]

**chloasma** /kloʊ'æzmə/, *n.* hyperpigmentation of the facial skin in women, caused by increased deposits of melanin as a result of endocrine factors. [Gk: greenness]

**chloe** /'kloʊi/, *n. in the phrase* **drunk as Chloe,** *Colloq.* very drunk.

**chlor-**[1], a word element meaning 'green', as in *chlorine.* Also, **chloro-**[1]. [Gk, combining form of *chlōrós*]

**chlor-**[2], a combining form denoting 'chlorine', as in *chloral.* Also, **chloro-**[2].

**chloracetic acid** /klɔrəˌsitɪk 'æsəd/, *n. Chem.* →**chloroacetic acid.**

**chloral** /'klɔrəl/, *n. Chem., Pharm.* **1.** a colourless, mobile liquid, $CCl_3CHO$, first prepared from chlorine and alcohol and used as a hypnotic. **2.** a white, crystalline substance, $CCl_3CH(OH)_2$ (**chloral hydrate**), formed by combining liquid chloral with water, and used as a hypnotic. [CHLOR-[2] + AL(COHOL)]

**chloramine** /'klɔrəmin/, *n.* **1.** one of a group of compounds obtained by the action of hypochlorite solutions on compounds containing NH or $NH_2$ groups; used as an antiseptic. **2.** an unstable, colourless liquid, $NH_2CL$, with a pungent smell, derived from ammonia.

**chloramphenicol** /klɔrəm'fɛnəkɒl/, *n.* an antibiotic which counters diseases of bacterial origin such as typhoid fever and typhus, by stopping bacterial protein synthesis. Also, **chloromycetin.**

**chloranthy** /klɔ'rænθi, 'klɔrənθi/, *n.* an abnormal condition of a flower where all parts change into leafy structures.

**chlorargyrite** /klɔ'radʒəraɪt/, *n.* →**cerargyrite.**

**chlorate** /'klɔreɪt/, *n.* a salt of chloric acid.

**chlordane** /'klɔdeɪn/, *n.* an organochlorine compound highly toxic to animal life and used as a systemic insecticide. [Trademark]

**chlordiazepoxide** /ˌklɔdaɪˌeɪzə'pɒksaɪd/, *n.* →**librium.**

**chlorella** /klɔ'rɛlə, klə-/, *n.* a genus of microscopic unicellular green algae.

**chlorenchyma** /klə'rɛŋkəmə/, *n.* parenchyma tissue containing chlorophyll.

**chloric** /'klɔrɪk/, *adj.* of or containing chlorine in the pentavalent state. [CHLOR-[2] + -IC]

**chloric acid** /– 'æsəd/, *n.* an acid, $HClO_3$, which exists only in solution and as salts.

**chloride** /'klɔraɪd/, *n.* **1.** a compound usu. of two elements only, one of which is chlorine. **2.** a salt of hydrochloric acid.

**chloride of lime,** *n.* a white powder used in bleaching and disinfecting, made by treating slaked lime with chlorine, and regarded (when dry) as calcium oxychloride, $CaOCl_2$.

**chlorinate** /'klɔrəneɪt, 'klɔ-/, *v.t.,* **-nated, -nating.** **1.** *Chem.* to combine or treat with chlorine. **2.** to disinfect (water) by means of chlorine. **3.** *Metall.* **a.** to remove dissolved gases and entrapped oxides by passing chlorine gas through molten metal (such as aluminium and magnesium). **b.** to expose pulverised ore to chlorine. – **chlorination** /klɒrə'neɪʃən, klɔ-/, *n.* – **chlorinator,** *n.*

**chlorine** /'klɔrin/, *n.* a greenish yellow gaseous element (occurring combined in common salt, etc.), incombustible, and highly irritating to the organs of respiration. It is used as a powerful bleaching agent and in various industrial processes. *Symbol:* Cl; *at. wt:* 35.453; *at. no.:* 17. [CHLOR-[1] + -INE[2]]

**chlorite**[1] /'klɔraɪt/, *n.* a group of minerals consisting of hydrous silicates of aluminium, ferrous iron, and magnesium, occurring in green platelike crystals or scales, and common in some metamorphic rocks. [Gk *chlōrîtis* kind of green stone]

**chlorite**[2] /'klɔraɪt/, *n.* a salt of chlorous acid, as **potassium chlorite,** $KClO$. [CHLOR-[2] + -ITE[1]]

**chloro-**[1], variant of **chlor-**[1], used before consonants, as in *chlorophyll.*

**chloro-**[2], variant of **chlor-**[2], used before consonants, as in *chloroform.*

**chloroacetic acid** /ˌklɔroʊəsitɪk 'æsəd/, *n.* any of three acetic acids: *monochloroacetic acid,* $CH_2Cl \cdot COOH$, which forms rhombic crystals; *dichloroacetic acid,* $CHCl_2 \cdot COOH$, which is a colourless liquid; and *trichloroacetic acid,* $CCl_3 \cdot COOH$, which forms deliquescent rhombic crystals. All forms are used as wart-removers and in the manufacture of dyes. Also, **chloracetic acid.**

**chloroform** /'klɒrəfɔm/, *n.* **1.** a colourless volatile liquid, $CHCl_3$, used as an anaesthetic and solvent. *–v.t.* **2.** to administer chloroform to. **3.** to put chloroform on (a cloth, etc.). [CHLORO-[2] + FORM(YL)]

**chlorohydrin** /klɔroʊ'haɪdrən/, *n.* any of a class of organic compounds containing a chlorine atom and a hydroxyl group, usu. on adjacent carbon atoms.

**chloromethane** /klɔroʊ'miθeɪn/, *n.* a colourless gas, $CH_3Cl$, used as a refrigerant and in organic synthesis; methyl chloride.

**chloromycetin** /klɔrəmaɪ'sitən/, *n. Biochem.* →**chloramphenicol.** [Trademark]

**chlorophyll** /'klɒrəfɪl/, *n.* the green colouring substances of leaves and plants, having two forms: bluish black **chlorophyll a,** $C_{55}H_{72}MgN_4O_5$, and yellowish green **chlorophyll b,** $C_{55}H_{70}MgN_4O_6$. It is associated with the production of carbohydrates by photosynthesis in plants and is used as a dye for cosmetics and oils. Also, *U.S.,* **chlorophyl.** [CHLORO-[1] + -PHYLL]

**chlorophyllous** /klɔroʊ'fɪləs/, *adj.* of or containing chlorophyll. Also, **chlorophyllose** /klɔroʊ'fɪloʊs/.

**chloropicrin** /klɔroʊ'pɪkrən, -'paɪkrən/, *n.* a colourless liquid, $CCl_3NO_2$, used as an insecticide and as a chemical agent in warfare; nitrochloroform; trichloronitromethane. Also, **chlorpicrin.** [CHLORO-[2] + PICR(IC ACID) + -IN[2]]

**chloroplast** /'klɔrəplæst/, *n.* a plastid containing chlorophyll, the site of photosynthesis.

**chloroprene** /'klɔroʊprin/, *n.* a colourless liquid, $CH_2{=}CClCH{=}CH_2$, made by treating vinylacetylene with cold hydrochloric acid and cuprous chloride, and which polymerises readily to neoprene rubber.

**chloroquine** /'klɔroʊkwin/, *n.* a synthetic antimalarial drug, $C_{18}H_{26}ClN_3$.

**chlorosis** /klɔ'roʊsəs/, *n.* **1.** abnormal yellow colour of a plant, as from lack of iron in the soil. **2.** a benign type of iron-deficiency anaemia in adolescent girls, marked by a pale yellow-green complexion. [NL; see CHLOR-[1], -OSIS] – **chlorotic,** *adj.*

**chlorous** /'klɔrəs/, *adj.* containing trivalent chlorine, as **chlorous acid,** $HClO_2$, which occurs only in solution or as its salts, the chlorites. [CHLOR-[2] + -OUS]

**chlorpromazine** /klɔ'proʊməzin/, *n.* a drug which depresses the central nervous system and which is also antispasmodic, antihistaminic, and anticholinergic.

**Ch.M.,** Master of Surgery. [L *Chirugiae Magister*]

**Chnl,** Channel.

**choc.,** chocolate.

**choc-ice** /'tʃɒk-aɪs/, *n.* a chocolate flavoured iceblock on a stick.

**chock** /tʃɒk/, *n.* **1.** a block or wedge of wood, etc., for filling in a space, esp. for preventing movement, as of a wheel or a cask. **2.** *Naut.* **a.** a metal or wooden fitting through which a mooring line, anchor cable, towline, or similar rope passes, usu. on or in the rail. **b.** a shaped standard on which a boat, barrel, or other object rests. *–v.t.* **3.** to furnish with or secure by a chock or chocks. **4.** *Naut.* to place (a boat) upon chocks. *–adv.* **5.** as close or tight as possible; quite: *chock against the edge.* [probably from ONF *choque* log or block of wood. Cf. It. *ciocco* burning log]

**chock-a-block** /tʃɒk-ə-'blɒk/, *adj.* **1.** →*Naut.* **two-blocks. 2.** full; overcrowded. *–adv.* **3.** in a jammed or crowded condition.

**chockalott** /'tʃɒkəlɒt/, *n.* →**Major Mitchell.**

**chock-and-log** /tʃɒk-ən-'lɒg/, *n.* **1.** a rough, wooden fence of logs laid on supporting blocks. *–adj.* **2.** of or pertaining to a fence made in this fashion.

chock-and-log fence

**chocker** /'tʃɒkə/, *adj. Colloq.* **1.** full; replete. **2.** intoxicated. Also, **chockers.** [short for CHOCK-A-BLOCK]

**chock-full** /tʃɒk-'fʊl/, *adj.* full to the utmost; crammed. Also, **chuck-full, choke-full, chocked-full.**

**chockie** /'tʃɒki/, *n. Colloq.* chocolate. Also, **choc, chokkie.**

**chock-stone** /'tʃɒk-stoʊn/, *n. Mountaineering.* a stone jammed in a crack or cleft, intentionally or naturally, providing an anchor.

**choco** /'tʃɒkoʊ/, *n. Colloq.* a member of the Australian militia or a conscripted soldier in World War II. Also, **chocko.** [abbrev. CHOCOLATE SOLDIER]

**chocolate** /'tʃɒklət, 'tʃɒkələt/, *n.* **1.** a preparation of the seeds of cacao, roasted, husked, and ground (without removing any of the fat), often sweetened and flavoured, as with vanilla. **2.** a beverage or confection made from this. **3.** dark brown. *–adj.* **4.** made or flavoured with chocolate. **5.** having the colour of chocolate. [Sp., from Nahuatl *chocolatl* bitter water]

**chocolate-box** /'tʃɒklət-bɒks/, *adj.* gaudily pretty.

**chocolate crackle** /– 'krækəl/, *n.* an uncooked biscuit made by mixing rice bubbles in a chocolate icing made from copha, icing sugar and cocoa, and served in a paper patty pan.

**chocolate drop** /'– drɒp/, *n. Brit. Colloq.* a negro.

**chocolate frog** /– 'frɒg/, *n. Prison Colloq.* an informer. [rhyming slang, *chocolate frog* dog (def. 11)]

**chocolate soldier** /– 'soʊldʒə/, *n.* **1.** a sweet made from chocolate in the form of a soldier. **2.** a reluctant, unheroic soldier. **3.** →**choco.** [def. 2 from the operetta, *The Chocolate Soldier* by Oscar Strauss]

**chocolate wheel** /'– wil/, *n.* a wheel with numbers around the rim which when spun stops at a particular number, used as a fund-raising game of chance at fêtes, etc.

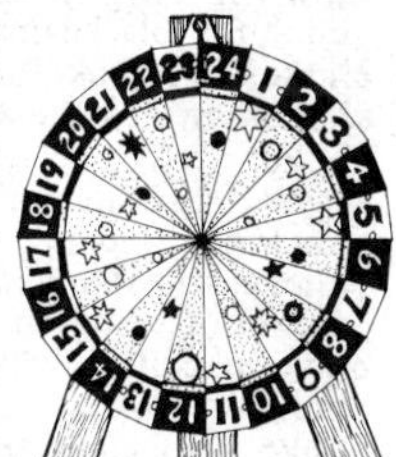

chocolate wheel

**choice** /tʃɔɪs/, *n., adj.,* **choicer, choicest.** *–n.* **1.** the act of choosing; selection. **2.** power of choosing; option. **3.** the person or thing chosen: *this book is my choice.* **4.** an abundance and variety from which to choose: *a wide choice of candidates.* **5.** that which is preferred or preferable to others; the best part of anything. **6.** an alternative. **7.** a well-chosen supply. *–adj.* **8.** worthy of being chosen; excellent; superior. **9.** carefully selected: *delivered in choice words.* **10. choice language,** *Colloq.* colourfully vulgar language. [ME *chois,* from OF, from *choisir* choose, of Gmc orig. and akin to CHOOSE] – **choicely,** *adv.* – **choiceness,** *n.*

**choir** /'kwaɪə/, *n.* **1.** a company of singers, esp. an organised group employed in church service. **2.** any company or band, or a division of one: *string choir.* **3.** *Archit.* **a.** that part of a church used by the singers. **b.** (in a medieval cruciform church) the body of the church which extends from the crossing to the east, or altar, end. **c.** (in cathedrals, etc.) the area between the nave and the main altar. **4.** *Theol.* any of the nine orders of the celestial hierarchy. *–v.t.* **5.** to perform (a piece of music) in chorus. *–v.i.* **6.** to sing in chorus. [ME *quer,* from OF *cuer,* from L *chorus.* See CHORUS]

**choirboy** /'kwaɪəbɔɪ/, *n.* a boy who sings in a choir.

**choir loft** /'kwaɪə lɒft/, *n.* a gallery in which the choir is stationed.

**choirmaster** /'kwaɪəmastə/, *n.* the leader or director of a choir.

**choir organ** /'kwaɪər ɔgən/, *n.* **1.** a small organ for accompanying a choir. **2.** a division of an organ controlled by a separate manual.

**choir school** /'kwaɪə skul/, *n.* a school for choirboys attached to a cathedral, etc.

**choir screen** /'– skrin/, *n.* a screen separating the choir (def. 3b) from the nave of a church.

**choke** /tʃoʊk/, *v.*, **choked, choking,** *n.* *–v.t.* **1.** to stop the breath of, by squeezing or obstructing the windpipe; strangle; stifle; suffocate. **2.** to stop, as the breath or utterance, by or as by strangling or stifling. **3.** to check or stop the growth, progress, or action of: *to choke off discussion.* **4.** to stop by filling; obstruct; clog; congest. **5.** to suppress, as a feeling or emotion. **6.** to fill chock-full. **7.** (in internal-combustion engines) to enrich the fuel mixture by diminishing the air supply to the carburettor, as when starting a motor. **8. choke down,** to bring down a wild horse, steer, etc., by roping it around the neck. *–v.i.* **9.** to suffer strangling or suffocation. **10.** to be obstructed or clogged. **11.** to be temporarily overcome, as with emotion. *–n.* **12.** the act or sound of choking. **13.** (in internal-combustion engines) the mechanism by which the air supply to a carburettor is diminished or stopped. **14.** *Mach.* any such mechanism which, by blocking a passage, regulates the flow of air, etc. **15.** *Elect.* a coil or inductor which allows direct currents to pass freely through but impedes the passage of alternating currents by an amount which increases with the frequency of the alternating current. **16.** a narrowed part, as in a chokebore. **17.** the filamentous, inedible centre of the head of an artichoke. [ME *choke(n)*, *cheke(n)*, aphetic variants of ME *achoke(n)*, *acheke(n)*, OE *acēocian*]

**chokeberry** /'tʃoʊkbɛri/, *n., pl.* **-ries.** **1.** the berry-like fruit of shrubs of the North American genus *Aronia,* esp. *A. arbutifolia.* **2.** the plant bearing it.

**chokebore** /'tʃoʊkbɔ/, *n.* **1.** (in a shotgun) a bore which narrows towards the muzzle to prevent shot from scattering too widely. **2.** a shotgun with such a bore.

**chokecherry** /'tʃoʊktʃɛri/, *n., pl.* **-ries.** **1.** any of several species of cherry, esp. *Prunus virginiana* of North America, which bears an astringent fruit. **2.** the fruit.

**chokedamp** /'tʃoʊkdæmp/, *n. Mining.* mine atmosphere so low in oxygen and high in carbon dioxide as to cause choking; blackdamp.

**choke-full** /tʃoʊk-'fʊl/, *adj.* →**chock-full.**

**chokeman** /'tʃoʊkmæn/, *n. Prison Colloq.* a thug.

**choker** /'tʃoʊkə/, *n.* **1.** a necklace worn tightly round the neck. **2.** *Colloq.* a cravat or high collar.

**choking** /'tʃoʊkɪŋ/, *adj.* **1.** so full of emotion one almost chokes: *to speak in a choking voice.* **2.** that causes the sensation of being choked. – **chokingly,** *adv.*

**choking coil** /'– kɔɪl/, *n. Elect.* →**choke** (def. 15).

**chokkie** /'tʃɒki/, *n. Colloq.* →**chockie.**

**choko** /'tʃoʊkoʊ/, *n.* a perennial vine, *Sechium edule,* bearing pear-shaped green fruit used as a vegetable. Also, **chayote.**

**choky** /'tʃoʊki/, *n., adj.,* **-kier, -kiest.** *–n.* **1.** *Colloq.* prison. *–adj.* **2.** tending to choke or suffocate one. **3.** feeling choked or suffocated. Also, **chokey.**

**chol-,** a word element meaning 'gall' or 'bile'. Also, **chole-, cholo-.** [Gk, combining form of *cholḗ* bile]

**cholecystectomy** /kɒləsɪs'tɛktəmi/, *n., pl.* **-mies.** removal of the gall bladder.

**cholecystostomy** /kɒləsɪs'tɒstəmi/, *n., pl.* **-mies.** a draining of the gall bladder with the organ left in place, usu. done to remove stones.

**choler** /'kɒlə/, *n.* **1.** irascibility; anger; wrath; irritability. **2.** bile (that one of the four humours supposed when predominant to cause irascibility and anger). **3.** *Obs.* biliousness. [LL *cholera* bile, from Gk: name of the disease; replacing ME *colere,* from OF]

**cholera** /'kɒlərə/, *n.* **1.** *Pathol.* **a.** an acute, infectious disease, due to a specific micro-organism, endemic in India, etc., and epidemic generally, marked by profuse diarrhoea, vomiting, cramp, etc., and often fatal. **b.** an acute disorder of the digestive tract, marked by diarrhoea, vomiting, cramp, etc. (**sporadic cholera, bilious cholera,** or **cholera morbus**). **2.** *Vet. Sci.* any disease characterised by violent diarrhoea. See **swine fever** and **fowl cholera.** [L, from Gk] – **choleraic** /kɒlə'reɪɪk/, *adj.*

**cholera infantum** /– ɪn'fæntəm/, *n. Obs. Pathol.* a non-specific diarrhoea in infants and children.

**cholera morbus** /– 'mɔbəs/, *n. Obs. Pathol.* any inflammatory enteritis causing pain and diarrhoea. Also, **cholera nostras** /kɒlərə 'nɒstrəs/. [L: cholera disease]

**choleric** /'kɒlərɪk/, *adj.* **1.** irascible; angry. **2.** *Obs.* bilious. **3.** *Obs.* causing biliousness.

**cholesterol** /kə'lɛstərɒl/, *n.* a sterol, $C_{27}H_{45}OH$, widely distributed in higher organisms, found in bile and gallstones, and in the blood and brain, the yolk of eggs, etc. Also, **cholesterin** /kɒ'lɛstərən/. [CHOL(E)- + Gk *ster(eós)* solid + -OL[2]]

**cholic acid** /koʊlɪk 'æsəd/, *n.* a bile acid, $C_{23}H_{39}O_3 \cdot COOH$, derived from cholesterol. [*cholic* from Gk *cholikós* of bile]

**choline** /'koʊlin/, *n.* a viscous organic base, $(CH_3)_3N^+CH_2CH_2OH$, found in combined form in lecithin, acetylcholine, etc., which prevents the accumulation of fat in the liver and is often included in the vitamin B complex.

**cholo-,** variant of **chol-** before consonants.

**chondriosome** /'kɒndriəsoʊm/, *n.* →**mitochondrion.** [Gk *chondríο(n)*, diminutive of *chóndros* cartilage + -SOME[3]]

**chondroma** /kɒn'droʊmə/, *n., pl.* **-mas, -mata** /-mətə/. a cartilaginous tumour or growth. [Gk *chóndros* cartilage + -OMA]

**choof** /tʃʊf/, *n., v.i.* →**chuff**[1].

**chook** /tʃʊk/, *n.* **1.** Also, **chookie, chooky.** a domestic fowl. **2.** *Colloq.* a woman: *silly old chook.* **3.** a silly person. [Brit. d., imitative]

**choom** /tʃʊm/, *n.* an Englishman. [imitative of Brit. d. pronunciation of *chum*]

**choose** /tʃuz/, *v.,* **chose, chosen** or (*Obs.*) **chose, choosing.** *–v.t.* **1.** to select from a number, or in preference to another or other things or persons. **2.** to prefer and decide (to do something): *he chose to stand for election.* **3.** to want; desire. *–v.i.* **4.** to make a choice. **5. cannot choose but,** cannot do otherwise than: *he cannot choose but hear.* [ME *chose(n)*, OE *ceōsan;* var. of ME *chēse(n)*, OE *cēosan,* c. G *kiesen,* Goth. *kiusan;* akin to L *gustāre* taste] – **chooser,** *n.*

**choosy** /tʃuzi/, *adj. Colloq.* hard to please, particular, fastidious, esp. in making a choice: *choosy about food.* Also, **choosey.**

**chop**[1] /tʃɒp/, *v.,* **chopped, chopping,** *n.* *–v.t.* **1.** to cut with a quick, heavy blow or series of blows, using an axe, etc. **2.** to make by so cutting. **3.** to cut in pieces. **4.** *Tennis, Cricket, etc.* to hit (a ball) with a chop stroke. **5.** *Colloq.* to dismiss; give the sack to; fire. **6.** *Colloq.* to criticise. **7. chop off,** *Colloq.* to finish suddenly. *–v.i.* **8.** to make a quick heavy stroke or a series of strokes, as with an axe. **9.** to go, come, or move suddenly or violently. *–n.* **10.** the act of chopping. **11.** a cutting blow. **12.** a short, downward cutting blow. **13.** →**chop stroke.** **14.** *Colloq.* share, cut (def. 50): *in for one's chop.* **15.** a piece chopped off. **16.** *Colloq.* an accented strum on a guitar. **17.** →**woodchop.** **18.** a slice of mutton, lamb, veal, pork, etc. containing some bone. **19.** a short, irregular, broken motion of waves. **20.** a stretch of water characterised by this wave formation. **21.** *Colloq.* one's deathblow: *he got the chop.* **22.** *Colloq.* the sack; dismissal. **23.** *Obs.* a chap; crack; cleft. [var. of CHAP[1]]

**chop**[2] /tʃɒp/, *v.,* **chopped, chopping.** *–v.i.* **1.** to turn, shift, or change suddenly, as the wind. **2.** *Obs.* to barter. **3.** *Obs.* to bandy words; argue. *–v.t.* **4. chop logic,** to reason or dispute argumentatively; argue. [var. of obs. *chap* barter, ME *chapien,* OE *cēapian.* Cf. CHEAP]

**chop**[3] /tʃɒp/, *n.* **1.** (*pl.*) the jaw. **2. in the chops,** *Colloq.* in the mouth. Also, **chap.** [? special use of CHOP[1]]

**chop**[4] /tʃɒp/, *n.* **1.** (in India, China, etc.) **a.** an official stamp or seal, or a permit or clearance. **b.** a design, corresponding to a brand or trademark, stamped on goods to indicate their special identity. **2.** *Colloq.* quality. **3. not much chop,** *Colloq.* no good. [Hind. *chhāp* impression, stamp]

**chop chop!** /tʃɒp 'tʃɒp/, *interj.* bring it quickly. [Pidgin English *chop* quick]

**chopfallen** /ˈtʃɒpfɔlən/, *adj.* →**chapfallen.**

**chophouse**[1] /ˈtʃɒphaʊs/, *n.* **1.** *Brit., U.S.* →**steakhouse.** **2.** *Brit.* any cheap eating house. [CHOP[1] + HOUSE]

**chophouse**[2] /ˈtʃɒphaʊs/, *n.* (in China, formerly) a customs house. [CHOP[4] + HOUSE]

**chopper**[1] /ˈtʃɒpə/, *n.* **1.** one who or that which chops. **2.** a short axe with a large blade used for cutting up meat, etc.; a butcher's cleaver. **3.** (*pl.*) *Colloq.* teeth. **4.** *Tennis Colloq.* a type of handgrip on a racket used when serving a ball with a spin. **5.** *Colloq.* a helicopter. **6.** a bike with wide, high handle bars.

**chopper**[2] /ˈtʃɒpə/, *n.* a Roman Catholic. [from *rock chopper,* play on abbrev. R.C., Roman Catholic]

**chopping** /ˈtʃɒpɪŋ/, *adj.* →**choppy** (def. 1).

**choppy** /ˈtʃɒpi/, *adj.,* **-pier, -piest. 1.** (of the sea, etc.) forming short, irregular, broken waves. **2.** (of the wind) shifting or changing suddenly or irregularly; variable. [CHOP[2] + -Y[1]]

**chopstick** /ˈtʃɒpstɪk/, *n.* one of a pair of thin sticks, as of wood or ivory, used by Chinese, etc., to raise food to the mouth. [Pidgin English *chop* quick + STICK[1]]

**chop stroke** /ˈtʃɒp stroʊk/, *n. Tennis, Cricket, etc.* a downward stroke made with the racket or bat at an angle.

**chop suey** /– ˈsui/, *n.* a dish consisting of small pieces of meat or chicken cooked with bean sprouts or other vegetables, served in Chinese restaurants in Western countries. [Chinese: mixed bits]

**chop-up** /ˈtʃɒp-ʌp/, *n. Colloq.* a dividing of goods.

**choragus** /kɔˈreɪgəs/, *n., pl.* **-gi** /-dʒaɪ/. **1.** the leader and sponsor of an ancient Greek chorus. **2.** any conductor of an entertainment or festival. [L, from Gk *chorāgós, chorēgós* leader of the chorus] – **choragic** /kɔˈrædʒɪk, -ˈreɪdʒɪk/, *adj.*

**choral** /ˈkɒrəl/, *adj.* **1.** of a chorus or a choir. **2.** sung by or adapted for a chorus or a choir. *–n.* **3.** a chorale. [ML *chorālis,* from L *chorus.* See CHORUS] – **chorally,** *adv.*

**chorale** /kɒˈral/, *n.* **1.** a simple hymnlike tune in slow tempo usually sung by choir and congregation together. **2.** *U.S.* a choir or choral group.

**chord**[1] /kɔd/, *n.* **1.** a string of a musical instrument. **2.** a feeling or emotion. **3.** *Geom.* that part of a straight line between two of its intersections with a curve. **4.** *Civ. Eng.* one of the main members which lie along the top or bottom edge of a truss framework. **5.** *Aeron.* a straight line joining the centres of curvature of the leading and trailing edges of an aerofoil section. **6.** *Anat.* →**cord** (def. 4). [L *chorda* cord, string, from Gk *chordḗ* gut, string of a musical instrument. Cf. CORD] – **chordal, chorded,** *adj.*

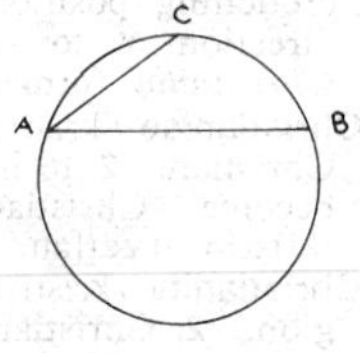

geometrical chords: AB, AC chords, subtending arcs ACB, AC

**chord**[2] /kɔd/, *n. Music.* a combination of three or more tones, mostly in harmonic relation, sounded either simultaneously or in quick succession. [var. spelling (influenced by CHORD[1]) of *cord,* aphetic var. of ACCORD, *n.*]

**chordate** /ˈkɔdeɪt/, *adj.* **1.** belonging or pertaining to the Chordata, the phylum that includes the true vertebrates and those animals (protochordates) that have a notochord, such as the lancelets and the tunicates. *–n.* **2.** a chordate animal. [NL *chordātus* having a chord. See CHORD[1]]

**chord chart** /ˈkɔd tʃat/, *n.* a listing of the chord progressions which are to accompany a particular melody, esp. in jazz, rock or pop music, as distinct from a fully written out accompaniment.

**chording** /ˈkɔdɪŋ/, *n. Music.* **1.** the distribution of notes within a chord. **2.** the intonation of a chord by instrumentalists or vocalists.

**chord of the sixth,** *n.* →**sixth chord.**

**chordophone** /ˈkɔdəfoʊn/, *n.* a musical instrument with stretched strings which are either plucked, bowed or struck; includes zithers, lutes, lyres and harps.

**chore** /tʃɔ/, *n.* **1.** a small or odd job; a piece of minor domestic work. **2.** (*pl.*) routine work around a house or farm. **3.** a hard or unpleasant task. [ME *churre,* OE *cyrr,* var. of *cierr, cerr.* See CHAR[3]]

**chorea** /kɔˈriə/, *n.* **1. Huntington's chorea,** a hereditary disease, characterised by involuntary movements and progressive mental deterioration. **2. Sydenham's chorea,** an acute disease esp. common among children, characterised by irregular, involuntary and uncontrollable movements in the face or extremities; St Vitus's dance.

**choreograph** /ˈkɒriəgræf, -graf/, *v.t.* to provide the choreography for: *Helpmann choreographed The Display.*

**choreographer** /kɒriˈɒgrəfə/, *n.* a person who creates ballet and other dance compositions.

**choreography** /kɒriˈɒgrəfi/, *n.* **1.** the art of composing ballets, etc., and arranging separate dances. **2.** the art of representing the various movements in dancing by a system of notation. **3.** the art of dancing. Also, **choregraphy** /kəˈrɛgrəfi/. [*choreo-* (combining form representing Gk *choreía* dance) + -GRAPHY] – **choreographic** /kɒriəˈgræfɪk/, *adj.*

**choreology** /kɒriˈɒlədʒi/, *n.* the written notation by which the sequences of movements which make up a ballet are recorded. – **choreologist** *n.*

**choriamb** /ˈkɒriˌæmb/, *n. Pros.* a foot of four syllables, two short between two long.

**choriambus** /kɒriˈæmbəs/, *n., pl.* **-bi** /-bi/, **-buses.** →**choriamb.** [L, from Gk *choríambos*]

**choric** /ˈkɒrɪk/, *adj.* of or for a chorus.

**chorioid** /ˈkɔriɔɪd/, *adj., n. Anat.* →**choroid.**

**chorion** /ˈkɔriən/, *n.* the outermost of the extra embryonic membranes of land vertebrates, contributing to the placenta in the placental mammals and next to the shell (or the shell membrane) in egg-laying types. [NL, from Gk] – **chorionic** /kɔriˈɒnɪk/, *adj.*

**chorionic gonadotrophin** /kɔriˌɒnɪk gɒnəˈdɒtrəfən/, *n.* a hormone secreted by the placenta of pregnant women and found in large amounts in the urine, used to stimulate ovulation.

**chorisis** /ˈkɔrəsəs, kəˈraɪsəs/, *n.* an increase in the number of parts of a flower due to the branching of its primary members. [Gk: separation]

**chorister** /ˈkɒrəstə/, *n.* **1.** a singer in a choir. **2.** a male singer in a church choir; a choirboy. [ML *chorista* chorister + -ER[1]; replacing ME *queristre,* from AF, from *quer* CHOIR]

**chorizema** /kɒrəˈzimə/, *n.* any small shrub of the Australian, mostly western Australian, genus *Chorizema,* family Papilionaceae, several species of which are grown for their attractive orange and red pea-like flowers.

**chorizo** /tʃɒˈritzoʊ/, *n.* a Spanish sausage, smoked and heavily spiced. [Sp.]

**chorography** /kəˈrɒgrəfi/, *n. Geog.* the systematic description and analysis of regions or of a region. [L *chōrographia,* from Gk] – **chorographer,** *n.* – **chorographic** /kɒrəˈgræfɪk/, **chorographical** /kɒrəˈgræfɪkəl/, *adj.* – **chorographically** /kɒrəˈgræfɪkli/, *adv.,*

**choroid** /ˈkɔrɔɪd/, *adj.* **1.** like the chorion; membranous (applied esp. to a delicate, highly vascular membrane or coat of the eyeball between the sclerotic coat and the retina). *–n.* **2.** the choroid coat of the eye. Also, **chorioid.** [Gk *choroeidḗs,* properly *chorioeidḗs* like a membrane]

**chorology** /kəˈrɒlədʒi/, *n. Geog.* the systematic description and analysis of geographical distribution in regions. [*choro-* (combining form of Gk *chôros* place) + -O- + -LOGY] – **chorologist,** *n.* – **chorological** /kɒrəˈlɒdʒɪkəl/, *adj.*

**chortle** /ˈtʃɔtl/, *v.,* **-tled, -tling,** *n.* *–v.i.* **1.** to chuckle with glee. *–n.* **2.** a gleeful chuckle. [b. CHUCKLE and SNORT; coined by Lewis Carroll in *Through the Looking-Glass* (1871)] – **chortler,** *n.*

**chorus** /ˈkɔrəs/, *n., pl.* **-ruses,** *v.,* **-rused, -rusing.** *–n.* **1. a.** a group of persons singing in concert. **b.** (in an opera, oratorio, etc.) such a company singing in connection with soloists or individual singers. **c.** a piece of music for singing in concert. **d.** a part of a song in which others join the principal singer or singers. **e.** any recurring refrain. **2.** simultaneous utterance in singing, speaking, etc. **3.** the sounds uttered. **4.** (in musical shows) **a.** the company of dancers and singers. **b.** the singing or song of such a company. **5.** (in ancient Greek use) **a.** a dance performed by a company of persons and accompanied with song or narration, originally as a religious rite. **b.** a company of singers, dancers, or narrators supplementing the performance of the main actors. **6.** (in later use) **a.** a company of persons, or a single person, having a similar function in a play, esp. in the

Elizabethan drama. **b.** a part of a drama rendered by such a company or person. *–v.i.* **7.** to sing or speak in chorus. *–v.t.* **8.** to perform in chorus. [L, from Gk *chorós* dance, band of dancers, chorus]

**chorus girl** /ˈ– gɜl/, *n.* a female member of the chorus (of a musical comedy or the like). – **chorus boy,** *n.*

**chose**[1] /tʃoʊz/, *v.* past tense and obsolete past participle of **choose.**

**chose**[2] /ʃoʊz/, *n. Law.* a thing; an article of personal property. [F: thing, from L *causa* CAUSE]

**chose in action,** *n. Law.* **1.** an intangible form of property as a debt, patent, share, etc., recoverable by an action. **2.** a right which can be protected only by legal action.

**chosen** /ˈtʃoʊzən/, *v.* **1.** past participle of **choose.** *–adj.* **2.** selected from a number; preferred. **3.** →**elect.**

**chosen people** /– ˈpipəl/, *n.pl.* the Israelites.

**chough** /tʃʌf/, *n.* **1.** a European crow, *Pyrrhocorax pyrrhocorax,* of a glossy black colour, with red feet and beak. **2.** **white-winged chough,** a sooty black bird with white wing patches, *Corcorax melanorhamphus,* of eastern Australia. [ME *choghe.* Cf. OE *cēo*]

**chou moellier** /tʃaʊ ˈmɒliə/, *n.* a species of the cruciferous genus *Brassica,* grown in cool temperate regions, sometimes as a stock-feed. Also, **chou mollier.** [F]

**choux pastry** /ʃu ˈpeɪstri/, *n.* a very light pastry made with eggs, water, flour, and butter, used in making éclairs, etc.; cream puff pastry.

**chow**[1] /tʃaʊ/, *n.* **1.** Also, **chow-chow.** one of a Chinese breed of dogs of medium size, with a thick, even coat of brown or black hair and a black tongue. **2.** *Colloq.* food.

**chow**[2] /tʃaʊ/, *n. N.Z. Colloq.* →**chou moellier.**

**Chow** /tʃaʊ/, *n. Colloq.* (*derog.*) a Chinaman. [Pidgin English *chow-chow;* orig. uncert.]

chow

**chowchilla** /tʃaʊˈtʃɪlə/, *n.* either of two birds: **1. northern chowchilla,** a ground-dwelling bird, *Orthonyx spaldingii,* with a resonant call, which inhabits rainforests in north-eastern Queensland. **2. southern chowchilla,** a ground-dwelling bird, *Orthonyx temminckii,* chestnut in colour mottled with black and white, which inhabits temperate and subtropical rainforests in New South Wales. [imitative]

**chow-chow** /ˈtʃaʊ-tʃaʊ/, *n.* **1.** a Chinese mixed fruit preserve. **2.** a mixed pickle in mustard (orig. East Indian). **3.** →**chow**[1] (def. 1). [Pidgin English]

**chowder** /ˈtʃaʊdə/, *n.* a kind of soup or stew made of clams, fish, or vegetables, with potatoes, onions, other ingredients and seasoning. [probably from F *chaudière* cauldron, from LL *caldāria,* from *caldus, calidus* hot]

**chow mein** /tʃaʊ ˈmɪn/, *n.* a dish of noodles mixed with shredded vegetables such as carrots, cabbage, mushrooms, etc., and with small quantities of meat and/or poultry. [Chinese: fried flour]

**chq.,** cheque.

**chrematistic** /krimәˈtɪstɪk/, *adj.* of or pertaining to the acquisition of wealth. [Gk *chrēmatistikós*] – **chrematistics,** *n.*

**chrestomathy** /krɛsˈtɒməθi/, *n., pl.* **-thies.** a collection of selected passages, esp. from a foreign language. –**chrestomathic** /ˌkrɛstoʊˈmæθɪk/, *adj.* [Gk *chrēstomátheia,* lit., useful learning]

**chrism** /ˈkrɪzəm/, *n.* **1.** a consecrated oil used by certain churches in the rites of baptism, confirmation, etc. **2.** consecrated oil generally. **3.** a sacramental anointing; the rite of confirmation, esp. in the Greek Church. Also, **chrisom.** [learned respelling of ME *crisme,* OE *crisma,* from L *chrīsma,* from Gk: unguent, unction] – **chrismal,** *adj.*

**chrismatory** /ˈkrɪzmətri, -mətəri/, *n., pl.* **-ries.** a receptacle for the chrism. [ML *chrīsmatōrium*]

**chrisom** /ˈkrɪzəm/, *n.* **1.** →**chrism.** **2.** *Obs.* a white cloth or robe formerly put on a child at baptism, and also at burial if the child died soon after baptism. [var. of CHRISM]

**Chrissie** /ˈkrɪsi/, *n. Colloq.* Christmas.

**Christ** /kraɪst/, *n.* **1.** the Anointed; the Messiah expected by the Jews. **2.** Jesus of Nazareth, as fulfilling this expectation. [learned respelling of ME and OE *Crist,* from L *Christus,* from Gk *Christós* anointed, trans. of Heb. *māshīah* anointed, MESSIAH]

**christcross** /ˈkrɪskrɒs/, *n. Archaic.* the figure or mark of a cross. Also, **crisscross.** [lit., Christ's cross]

**christen** /ˈkrɪsən/, *v.t.* **1.** to receive into the Christian Church by baptism; baptise. **2.** to give a name to at baptism. **3.** to name and dedicate; give a name to; name. **4.** *Colloq.* to make use of for the first time. [ME *cristene(n),* OE *cristnian* make Christian (by baptism), from *cristen* Christian, from L *Christiānus*]

**Christendom** /ˈkrɪsəndəm/, *n.* **1.** Christians collectively. **2.** the Christian world. [ME and OE *cristendōm,* from *cristen* Christian + -DOM]

**christening** /ˈkrɪsənɪŋ, ˈkrɪsnɪŋ/, *n.* the ceremony of baptism, esp. as accompanied by the giving of the name to the infant baptised.

**Christhood** /ˈkraɪsthʊd/, *n.* the condition of being the Christ.

**Christian** /ˈkrɪstʃən/, *adj.* **1.** pertaining to or derived from Jesus Christ, born c. 4 B.C., crucified c. A.D. 29, or his teachings. **2.** believing in or belonging to the religion of Jesus Christ. **3.** pertaining to Christianity or Christians. **4.** exhibiting a spirit proper to a follower of Jesus Christ; Christlike. **5.** *Colloq.* decent or respectable. **6.** *Colloq.* humane; not brutal. *–n.* **7.** one who believes in the sanctity of Jesus Christ; an adherent of Christianity. **8.** one who exemplifies in his life the teachings of Christ. **9.** *Colloq.* a decent or presentable person. **10.** *Colloq.* a human being as distinguished from an animal. [L *Christiānus*]

**christiana** /krɪstiˈanə/, *n.* →**christiania.**

**Christian Era** /ˈkrɪstʃən ɪərə/, *n.* the period since the assumed date of the birth of Jesus, adopted in Christian countries.

**christiania** /krɪstiˈaniə/, *n. Skiing.* a type of turn originating in Norway in which the body is swung around from a crouching position, in order to turn the skis into a new direction or to stop quickly. Also, **christiania turn.** [from *Christiania,* former name of Oslo, capital of Norway]

**Christianise** /ˈkrɪstʃənaɪz/, *v.,* **-nised, -nising.** *–v.t.* **1.** to make Christian. **2.** to imbue with Christian principles. *–v.i.* **3.** to become Christian. Also, **Christianize.** – **Christianisation** /krɪstʃənaɪˈzeɪʃən/, *n.* – **Christianiser,** *n.*

**Christianity** /krɪstiˈænəti/, *n., pl.* **-ties.** **1.** the Christian religion. **2.** Christian beliefs or practices; Christian quality or character. **3.** a particular Christian religious system. **4.** the state of being a Christian.

**Christian-like** /ˈkrɪstʃən-laɪk/, *adj.* like or befitting a Christian.

**Christianly** /ˈkrɪstʃənli/, *adj.* **1.** Christian-like. *–adv.* **2.** in a Christian manner.

**Christian name** /ˈkrɪstʃən neɪm/, *n.* the name given one at baptism, as distinguished from the family name; the personal name; forename.

**Christian Science** /– ˈsaɪəns/, *n.* a system of religious teaching, based on the Scriptures, the most notable application of which is the treatment of disease by mental and spiritual means, founded in America about 1866 by Mrs Mary Baker Eddy. – **Christian Scientist,** *n.*

**christie** /ˈkrɪsti/, *n.* →**christiania.**

**Christless** /ˈkraɪstləs/, *adj.* without Christ or the spirit of Christ. – **Christlessness,** *n.*

**Christlike** /ˈkraɪstlaɪk/, *adj.* like Christ; showing the spirit of Christ. – **Christlikeness,** *n.*

**Christly** /ˈkraɪstli/, *adj.* **1.** of or like Christ. **2.** Christlike. – **Christliness,** *n.*

**Christmas** /ˈkrɪsməs/, *n.* **1.** the annual festival of the Christian Church commemorating the birth of Jesus, celebrated on 25 December. **2.** 25 December (**Christmas Day**), now generally observed as an occasion for gifts, greetings, etc. **3.** the season when this occurs. **4.** (*pl.*) **have all one's Christmases come at once,** *Colloq.* to have extreme good fortune. **5. think one is Christmas,** *Colloq.* to be pleased with oneself; be elated. *–adj.* **6.** given on, held on, or connected with Christmas. [ME *cristmasse,* OE *Cristes mæsse* mass of Christ. See -MAS]

**Christmas beetle** /ˈ– bitl/, *n.* any of the larger iridescent scarab beetles of genus *Anoplognathus,* generally appearing around mid-summer in Australia.

**Christmas bell** /'– bɛl/, *n.* any species of *Blandfordia,* a plant genus endemic in eastern Australia, bearing pendulous wax-like red and yellow tubular flowers.

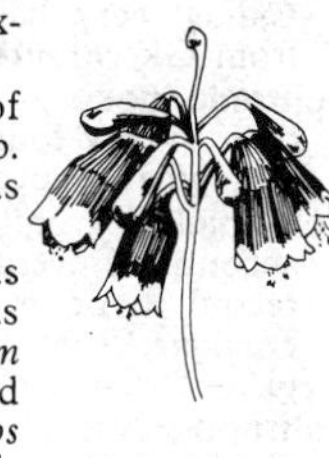
Christmas bell

**Christmas box** /'– bɒks/, *n.* **1.** *Brit.* a gift of money, traditionally given to tradesmen, esp. dustmen, milkmen, etc. **2.** a Christmas present.

**Christmas bush** /'– bʊʃ/, *n.* any of various shrubs or small trees flowering at Christmas and used for decoration, esp. *Ceratopetalum gummiferum* of New South Wales with red fruiting calyces and *Prostanthera lasianthos* of Victoria with white, somewhat bell-shaped flowers.

**Christmas cake** /'– keɪk/, *n.* a rich fruit cake traditionally eaten at Christmas time.

**Christmas Eve** /– 'iv/, *n.* the day preceding Christmas Day.

**Christmas eye** /– 'aɪ/, *n. Med. Colloq.* corneal ulceration occurring in specific geographical areas during summer, thought to be caused by a small insect.

**Christmas hold** /'– hoʊld/, *n.* a hold in which one grabs the opponent's testicles. [from *nuts* (colloq.) testicles; a Christmas hold is a handful of nuts]

**Christmas Island** /– 'aɪlənd/, *n.* an Australian island territory situated in the Indian Ocean north west of Australia.

**Christmas pudding** /– 'pʊdɪŋ/, *n.* a rich steamed or boiled pudding containing raisins, currants, lemon rind, spices, etc., traditionally eaten at Christmas; plum pudding.

**Christmas rose** /– 'roʊz/, *n.* one of a variety of perennial, evergreen, ranunculaceous plants of southern Europe and western Asia, *Helleborus niger,* which produces large white or pinkish flowers in January and February.

**Christmas stocking** /– 'stɒkɪŋ/, *n.* **1.** a fabric container, traditionally a woollen stocking, often a pillow case, put out by children on Christmas Eve for small presents as sweets, toys, etc. **2.** a commercial package of toys, sweets, etc., sold in the form of a red stocking, usu. of cardboard and plastic mesh, for use as a Christmas present, or, if larger and filled with expensive presents, as a prize in Christmas charity raffles, etc.

**Christmassy** /'krɪsməsi/, *adj.* decorative; suitable for the Christmas season.

**Christmastide** /'krɪsməstaɪd/, *n.* the season of Christmas. [CHRISTMAS + TIDE time]

**Christmas tree** /'krɪsməs tri/, *n.* **1.** a tree, usu. pine or fir, hung with decorations at Christmas. **2.** a tree of the mistletoe family, *Nuytsia floribunda,* native to western Australia. **3.** *N.Z.* →**pohutukawa.**

**Christology** /krɪs'tɒlədʒi, kraɪs-/, *n.* a branch of theology concerned with definitions of the nature of Christ.

**Christopher medal** /'krɪstəfə mɛdəl/, *n.* a medal, depicting a man bearing a child (Jesus of Nazareth), carried by travellers as a protective charm. Also, **St Christopher's medal.** [orig. with ref. to St Christopher (d. A.D. 250 ?), Christian martyr, protector of travellers]

**Christ's-thorn** /'kraɪsts-θɔn/, *n.* either of two Old World rhamnaceous spring shrubs, *Paliurus aculeatus* or *Zizyphus spina-christi,* supposed to have been used for Christ's crown of thorns.

**christy** /'krɪsti/, *n.* →**christiania.**

**-chroic,** an adjectival word element indicating colour (of skin, plants, etc.). Cf. **-chroous.** [Gk *chrōikós* coloured]

**chrom-,** **1.** a word element referring to colour, as in *chromic, chromite.* **2.** **a.** a word element referring to chromium, as in *chromic, bichromate.* **b.** a combining form in chemistry used to distinguish a coloured compound from its colourless form. Also, **chromo-.** [def. 1, see -CHROME; def. 2, see CHROMIUM]

**-chrom-,** a word element synonymous with **chrom-,** as in *polychromatic.*

**chroma** /'kroʊmə/, *n.* **1.** purity of a colour, or its freedom from white or grey. **2.** intensity of distinctive hue; saturation of a colour. [Gk: colour]

**chromat-,** variant of **chromato-** before vowels.

**chromate** /'kroʊmeɪt, -mət/, *n.* a salt of chromic acid which contains the divalent radical $CrO_4$.

**chromatic** /krə'mætɪk/, *adj.* **1.** pertaining to colour or colours. **2.** *Music.* **a.** involving a modification of the diatonic scale by the use of accidentals. **b.** progressing by semitone to a note having the same letter name, as from C to C sharp. [L *chrōmaticus,* from Gk *chrōmatikós* relating to colour (chiefly in musical sense)] – **chromatically,** *adv.*

**chromatic aberration** /– æbə'reɪʃən/, *n. Optics.* (of a lens system) the variation of either the focal length or the magnification, with different wavelengths of light, characterised by prismatic colouring at the edges of, and colour distortion within, the optical image.

**chromaticism** /krə'mætəsɪzəm/, *n. Music.* the extending of the diatonic style of composition to include all the semitones of the scale.

**chromatic notes** /krə,mætɪk 'noʊts/, *n.pl. Music.* notes outside the normal diatonic scale in which the piece or passage is written.

**chromatics** /krə'mætɪks/, *n.* the science of colours. Also, **chromatology** /kroʊmə'tɒlədʒi/. – **chromatist** /'kroʊmətəst/, *n.*

**chromatic scale** /krə,mætɪk 'skeɪl/, *n. Music.* a scale progressing entirely by semitones.

**chromatid** /'kroʊmətɪd/, *n.* one of two identical chromosomal strands into which a chromosome splits longitudinally preparatory to cell division.

**chromatin** /'kroʊmətɪn/, *n.* that portion of the animal or plant cell nucleus which readily takes on stains. [CHROMAT- + -IN[2]]

**chromato-,** **1.** a word element referring to colour. **2.** a word element meaning 'chromatin'. [Gk, combining form of *chrôma* colour]

**chromatogram** /'kroʊmətəgræm, kroʊ'mætə-/, *n. Chem.* **1.** the column or paper strip on which some or all the constituents of a mixture have been absorbed in column or paper chromatography. **2.** a graphical representation of the detector response, either against time or volume of carrier gas, in gas chromatography.

**chromatography** /kroʊmə'tɒgrəfi/, *n. Chem.* **1.** the separation of mixtures into their constituents by preferential absorption by a solid such as a column of silica (**column chromatography**), or a thin film of silica (**thin layer chromatography**). **2.** →**gas chromatography.** **3.** →**paper chromatography.** [CHROMATO- + -GRAPHY] – **chromatographic** /,kroʊmətə'græfɪk/, *adj.*

**chromatolysis** /kroʊmə'tɒləsəs/, *n.* the dissolution and disintegration of chromatin.

**chromatophore** /'kroʊmətəfɔ/, *n.* **1.** *Zool.* **a.** a pigmented body or cell, as one of those which through contraction and expansion produce a temporary colour in cuttlefishes, etc. **b.** a coloured mass of protoplasm. **2.** *Bot.* one of the plastids in plant cells. – **chromatophoric** /,kroʊmətə'fɔrɪk, -'fɒrɪk/, *adj.*

**chromatoplasm** /'kroʊmətəplæzəm/, *n. Biol.* the coloured part of protoplasm. Also, **chromoplasm.**

**chrome** /kroʊm/, *n., v.,* **chromed, chroming.** *–n.* **1.** chromium, esp. as a source of various pigments, as chrome yellow and chrome green. **2.** *Dyeing.* the dichromate of potassium or sodium. *–v.t.* **3.** *Dyeing.* to subject to a bath of dichromate of potassium or sodium. [F, from Gk *chrôma* colour]

**-chrome,** a word element meaning 'colour', as in *polychrome.* [Gk *chrôma*]

**chrome alum** /kroʊm 'æləm/, *n.* a dark violet double sulphate of chromium and potassium, $KCr(SO_4)_2 \cdot 12H_2O$, crystallising like common alum, and used in dyeing.

**chrome green** /– 'grin/, *n.* the permanent green colour made from chromic oxide, or any similar pigment made largely from chromic oxide, employed in printing textiles, etc.; Guignet's green.

**chrome red** /– 'rɛd/, *n.* a bright red pigment, $PbO \cdot PbCrO_4$, consisting of the basic chromate of lead.

**chrome steel** /– 'stil/, *n.* steel of great hardness and strength, containing chromium, carbon, and other elements. Also, **chromium steel.**

**chrome tanning** /– 'tænɪŋ/, *n.* a tanning process using chemical rather than vegetable dyes.

**chrome yellow** /– 'jɛloʊ/, *n.* a yellow or orange pigment, $PbCrO_4$, consisting of lead chromate.

**chromic** /ˈkroʊmɪk/, *adj.* of or containing chromium, esp. in the trivalent state.

**chromic acid** /– ˈæsəd/, *n.* a hypothetical acid, $H_2CrO_4$, which exists only in solution and forms chromates.

**chrominance** /ˈkroʊmɪnəns/, *n.* (in colour television) the difference between a colour and a chosen reference colour of particular quality but the same luminous intensity. [b. CHROM- + (LUM)INANCE]

**chromite** /ˈkroʊmaɪt/, *n.* **1.** *Chem.* a salt of chromous acid. **2.** a common mineral, $FeCr_2O_4$, iron magnesium chromite, which is the principal ore of chromium. Also, **chrome iron ore.**

**chromium** /ˈkroʊmiəm/, *n.* a lustrous, hard, brittle metallic element occurring in compounds, which are used for making pigments in photography, to harden gelatine, as a mordant, etc.; also used in corrosion-resisting chromium plating. *Symbol:* Cr; *at. wt:* 51.996; *at. no.:* 24; *sp. gr.:* 7.1. [Gk *chrôm(a)* colour + -IUM]

**chromium plating** /– ˈpleɪtɪŋ/, *n.* a thin film of chromium deposited by electrolysis on other metals to give them corrosion resistance.

**chromium steel** /– ˈstil/, *n.* →**chrome steel.**

**chromo**[1] /ˈkroʊmoʊ/, *n., pl.* **-mos,** *adj.* →**chromolithograph.**

**chromo**[2] /ˈkroʊmoʊ/, *n., pl.* **-mos.** *Colloq.* a prostitute.

**chromo-,** variant of **chrom-,** used before consonants, as in **chromogen.**

**chromogen** /ˈkroʊmədʒən/, *n.* **1.** *Chem.* any substance found in organic fluids which forms coloured compounds when oxidised. **2.** *Dyeing.* a coloured compound which, though not a dye itself, can be converted into a dye.

**chromogenic** /kroʊməˈdʒɛnɪk/, *adj.* **1.** producing colour. **2.** pertaining to chromogen or a chromogen. **3.** (of bacteria) forming some characteristic colour or pigment, usu. valuable in identification.

**chromolithograph** /ˌkroʊmoʊˈlɪθəgræf/, *v.t.* **1.** to produce by chromolithography. *–n.* **2.** a print produced by chromolithography.

**chromolithography** /ˌkroʊmoʊləˈθɒgrəfi/, *n.* the process of lithographing in colours. – **chromolithographer,** *n.* – **chromolithographic** /ˌkroʊmoʊlɪθəˈgræfɪk/, *adj.*

**chromomere** /ˈkroʊməmɪə/, *n.* one of the chromatin granules of a chromosome. – **chromomeric** /kroʊməˈmɛrɪk/, *adj.*

**chromophore** /ˈkroʊməfɔ/, *n.* **1.** any chemical group which produces colour in a compound, as the azo group –N = N–. **2.** the structural layout of atoms which is found in many coloured organic compounds.

**chromoplasm** /ˈkroʊməplæzəm/, *n.* →**chromatoplasm.**

**chromoplast** /ˈkroʊməplæst/, *n.* a plastid, or specialised mass of protoplasm, containing colouring matter other than chlorophyll.

**chromoprotein** /ˌkroʊmoʊˈproʊtin/, *n.* any coloured protein, as haemoglobin, chlorophyll, etc.

**chromosome** /ˈkroʊməsoʊm/, *n.* any of several threadlike, rodlike, or beadlike bodies which contain the chromatin during the meiotic and the mitotic processes. [CHROMO- + -SOME[3]] – **chromosomal** /kroʊməˈsoʊməl/, *adj.*

**chromosome number** /ˈ– nʌmbə/, *n.* the characteristic number of chromosomes for each biological species. In sex cells this number is haploid; in fertilised eggs it is diploid, one half coming from the egg, one half from the sperm. Cf. **polyploid.**

**chromosphere** /ˈkroʊməsfɪə/, *n. Astron.* **1.** a gaseous envelope surrounding the sun outside the photosphere, from which enormous masses of hydrogen and other gases are erupted. **2.** a gaseous envelope surrounding a star. – **chromospheric** /kroʊməˈsfɛrɪk/, *adj.*

**chromous** /ˈkroʊməs/, *adj.* containing divalent chromium.

**chromyl** /ˈkroʊməl/, *adj.* containing the divalent radical $CrO_2$.

**chron-,** a word element meaning 'time', as in *chronaxie.* Also, **chrono-.** [Gk, combining form of *chrónos*]

**chron., 1.** chronological. **2.** chronology. **3.** chronometry.

**Chron.,** *Bible.* Chronicles.

**chronaxie** /ˈkroʊnæksi/, *n. Physiol.* the minimum time that a current of twice the threshold strength (that value below which no excitation occurs) must flow in order to excite a tissue. Also, **chronaxy.** [CHRON- + Gk *axía* value]

**chronic** /ˈkrɒnɪk/, *adj.* **1.** inveterate; constant: *a chronic smoker.* **2.** continuing a long time: *chronic civil war.* **3.** having long had a disease, habit, or the like: *a chronic invalid.* **4.** (of disease) long continued (opposed to *acute*). **5.** *Colloq.* very bad; deplorable. Also, **chronical.** [L *chronicus,* from Gk *chronikós* concerning time] – **chronically,** *adv.*

**chronic dose** /– ˈdoʊs/, *n.* a radiation dose absorbed more than twenty four hours after a nuclear explosion from which biological recovery may be possible.

**chronicle** /ˈkrɒnɪkəl/, *n., v.,* **-cled, -cling.** *–n.* **1.** a record or account of events in the order of time; a history. *–v.t.* **2.** to record in or as in a chronicle. [ME, from AF, var. of OF *cronique,* from ML *chronica,* from Gk *chroniká* annals, neut. pl.] – **chronicler,** *n.*

**chrono-,** variant of **chron-,** used before consonants, as in *chronogram.*

**chronogram** /ˈkrɒnəgræm/, *n.* **1.** an inscription or the like in which certain letters, usu. distinguished from the others, express by their values as Roman numerals a date or epoch. **2.** a record made by a chronograph. – **chronogrammatic** /krɒnəgrəˈmætɪk/, *adj.*

**chronograph** /ˈkrɒnəgræf/, *n.* a clock-driven instrument for recording the exact instant of occurrences, or for measuring small intervals of time. – **chronographic** /krɒnəˈgræfɪk/, *adj.*

**chronological** /krɒnəˈlɒdʒɪkəl/, *adj.* **1.** arranged in the order of time: *chronological tables.* **2.** pertaining to or in accordance with chronology: *chronological character.* Also, **chronologic.** – **chronologically,** *adv.*

**chronologist** /krəˈnɒlədʒəst/, *n.* one versed in chronology. Also, **chronologer.**

**chronology** /krəˈnɒlədʒi/, *n., pl.* **-gies. 1.** a particular statement of the supposed or accepted order of past events. **2.** the science of arranging time in periods and ascertaining the dates and historical order of past events.

**chronometer** /krəˈnɒmətə/, *n.* a timekeeper with special mechanism for ensuring accuracy, for use in determining longitude at sea or for any purpose where very exact measurement of time is required. – **chronometric** /krɒnəˈmɛtrɪk/, **chronometrical** /krɒnəˈmɛtrɪkəl/, *adj.* – **chronometrically** /krɒnəˈmɛtrɪkli/, *adv.*

**chronometry** /krəˈnɒmətri/, *n.* **1.** the art of measuring time accurately. **2.** the measuring of time by periods or divisions.

**chronopher** /ˈkrɒnəfə/, *n. Radio.* an electrical apparatus for broadcasting time signals.

**chronoscope** /ˈkrɒnəskoʊp/, *n.* an instrument for measuring accurately very small intervals of time, as in determining the velocity of projectiles.

**chronotron** /ˈkrɒnətrɒn/, *n. Physics.* an electronic device for measuring the time interval between two events.

**-chroous,** →**-chroic.** [suffix formed from the stem of Gk *chróa* surface, colour + -OUS]

**chrysalid** /ˈkrɪsəlɪd/, *n.* **1.** a chrysalis. *–adj.* **2.** of a chrysalis.

**chrysalis** /ˈkrɪsələs/, *n., pl.* **chrysalises, chrysalids, chrysalides** /krəˈsælədiz/. the hard-shelled pupa of a moth or butterfly; an obtected pupa. [L *chrȳsallis,* from Gk: gold-coloured sheath of butterflies]

chrysalis

**chrysanthemum** /krəˈsænθəməm, krəˈzænθ-/, *n.* **1.** any of the perennial plants constituting the genus *Chrysanthemum,* as *C. leucanthemum,* the oxeye daisy. **2.** any of many cultivated varieties of *C. morifolium,* native to China, and of other species of *Chrysanthemum,* notable for the diversity of colour and size of their autumnal flowers. **3.** the flower of any such plant. [L, from Gk *chrȳsánthemon,* lit., golden flower]

**chryselephantine** /krɪsɛləˈfæntaɪn/, *adj.* overlaid with gold and ivory (used in describing objects of ancient Greece). [Gk *chrȳselephántinos*]

**chrysene** /ˈkraɪsin/, *n.* a hydrocarbon, $C_{18}H_{12}$, which occurs in coal tar.

**chrysie** /ˈkrɪsi/, *n. Colloq.* a chrysanthemum.

**chrysoberyl** /ˈkrɪsəbɛrəl/, *n.* a mineral, beryllium aluminate, $BeAl_2O_4$, occurring in green or yellow crystals, sometimes used as a gem. [L *chrȳsobēryllus,* from Gk *chrȳsobḗryllos*]

**chrysolite** /ˈkrɪsəlaɪt/, *n.* **1.** →**olivine. 2.** *Colloq.* yellow chrysoberyl. [ME *crisolite,* from ML *crīsolitus,* for L *chrysolithos,* from Gk: a bright yellow stone (probably topaz)]

**chrysoprase** /ˈkrɪsəpreɪz/, *n.* a nickel-stained, apple-green chalcedony, much used in jewellery. [L *chrȳsoprasus,* from Gk *chrȳsóprasos,* lit., gold leek; replacing ME *crisopace,* from OF]

**chrysotile** /ˈkrɪsətəl/, *n.* a fibrous variety of serpentine.

**chthonian** /ˈθoʊniən/, *adj. Chiefly Gk Myth.* dwelling in the earth; pertaining to the deities or spirits of the underworld. [Gk *chthónios* in the earth + -AN]

**C.H.U.,** centigrade heat unit.

**chub** /tʃʌb/, *n., pl.* **chubs,** (*esp. collectively*) **chub. 1.** a common freshwater fish, *Leuciscus cephalus,* of Europe, with a thick fusiform body. **2.** any of several allied fishes, as the *Semotilus atromaculatus* of America. **3.** any of several unrelated American fishes, esp. the tautog of the Atlantic and the deep-water whitefishes (Coregonidae) of the Great Lakes. [ME *chubbe*]

**chubby** /ˈtʃʌbi/, *adj.,* **-bier, -biest.** round and plump: *a chubby face, chubby cheeks.*

**chuck**[1] /tʃʌk/, *v.t.* **1.** to pat or tap lightly, as under the chin. **2.** to throw with a quick motion, usu. a short distance. **3.** *Colloq.* to eject (fol. by *out*): *they chucked him out of the nightclub.* **4.** *Colloq.* to resign from (oft. fol. by *in*): *he's chucked his job.* **5.** *Colloq.* to vomit. **6.** *Colloq.* to do; perform, usu. with some flamboyance: *chuck a U-ie, chuck a mental.* **7.** to contribute (fol. by *in*): *I'll chuck ten dollars in.* **8. chuck it (in),** to desist; give up (something begun) without finishing. **9. chuck one's hand in,** to give up; refuse to go on. **10. chuck one's weight about,** to be overbearing; interfere forcefully and unwelcomely. *–v.i.* **11.** *Colloq.* to vomit (sometimes fol. by *up*). **12. chuck off,** *Colloq.* to speak sarcastically or critically about (fol. by *at*). *–n.* **13.** a light pat or tap, as under the chin. **14.** a toss; a short throw. **15. the chuck,** *Colloq.* dismissal. [probably imitative, but cf. F *choquer* knock]

**chuck**[2] /tʃʌk/, *n.* **1.** Also, **chuck steak.** the cut of beef between the neck and the shoulder-blade. **2.** a block or log used as a chock. **3.** a mechanical device for holding tools or work in a machine: *lathe chuck.* [var. of CHOCK]

**chuck**[3] /tʃʌk/, *v.i.* **1.** to cluck. *–n.* **2.** a clucking sound. **3.** *Archaic.* a term of endearment. [imitative]

chuck[2] (def. 3)

**chucker-out** /tʃʌkər-ˈaʊt/, *n. Colloq.* one employed at a place of public entertainment to eject undesirable persons; bouncer. Also, **chucker-outer.**

**chuck-full** /tʃʌk-ˈfʊl/, *adj.* →**chock-full.**

**chuckle** /ˈtʃʌkəl/, *v.,* **chuckled, chuckling,** *n. –v.i.* **1.** to laugh in a soft, amused manner, usu. with satisfaction. **2.** to laugh to oneself. **3.** to cluck, as a fowl. *–n.* **4.** a soft, amused laugh, usu. with satisfaction. **5.** *Obs.* the call of a hen to her young; a cluck. [frequentative of CHUCK[3]] **– chuckler,** *n.*

**chucklehead** /ˈtʃʌkəlhɛd/, *n. Colloq.* a blockhead; fool. **– chuckleheaded,** *adj.* **– chuckleheadedness,** *n.*

**chuck steak** /tʃʌk ˈsteɪk/, *n.* →**chuck**[2] (def. 1).

**chuck wagon** /ˈ– wægən/, *n. U.S.* a wagon carrying provisions, stoves, etc., for cowboys, harvest hands, etc.

**chuckwalla** /ˈtʃʌkwɒlə/, *n.* a fat-bodied iguanid lizard, *Sauromalus obesus,* found commonly in the south-western deserts of the U.S. [Mex. Sp. *chacahuala*]

**chucky chucky** /ˈtʃʌki tʃʌki/, *n.* the edible but bitter fruit of the snowberry (def. 2). [Aboriginal]

**chuddar** /ˈtʃʌdə/, *n.* →**chador.** Also, **chaddar, chuddah, chudder.** [Hind.]

**chuddy** /ˈtʃʌdi/, *n. Colloq.* →**chewing gum.** Also, **chuttie.**

**chufa** /ˈtʃufə/, *n.* a perennial plant, *Cyperus esculentus,* grown in warm regions for its edible tubers. [Sp.]

**chuff**[1] /tʃʌf, tʃʊf/, *n.* **1.** a small puff of exhaust gas, steam, etc., escaping from a relatively slow running engine. **2.** the sound thus produced. *–v.i.* **3.** to move while emitting chuffs (oft. fol. by *along*): *the train chuffed along.* **4. chuff off,** *Colloq.* to go away. Also **choof.** [? b. CHUG + PUFF]

**chuff**[2] /tʃʌf/, *n. Colloq.* buttocks: *get off your chuff, mate.*

**chuff-chuff** /ˈtʃʌf-tʃʌf, ˈtʃʊf-tʃʊf/, *n.* (*in children's speech*) a steam locomotive.

**chuffed** /tʃʌft/, *adj. Colloq.* pleased; delighted.

**chuffer** /ˈtʃʌfə, ˈtʃʊfə/, *n.* any engine which chuffs or any device driven by one as a river boat, but esp. a steam locomotive.

**chug** /tʃʌg/, *n., v.,* **chugged, chugging.** *–n.* **1.** a short, dull explosive sound: *the steady chug of an engine.* *–v.i.* **2.** to make this sound. **3.** to move while making this sound: *the train chugged along.* [imitative]

**chug-a-lug** /tʃʌg-ə-ˈlʌg/, *v.,* **-lugged, -lugging.** *–v.i.* **1.** *Colloq.* to down a drink quickly without pause. *–n.* **2. a.** one long drink swallowed without pause, often at a special social occasion. **b.** a drinking bout. **3.** (a term used as an encouragement to drink in such a manner).

**chukka** /ˈtʃʌkə/, *n.* (in polo) one of the periods of play. Also, **chukker.** [Hind. *chakar*]

**chum**[1] /tʃʌm/, *n., v.,* **chummed, chumming.** *–n.* **1.** an intimate friend or companion: *boyhood chums.* **2.** a companion, one who has shared the same experience. **3.** Also, **choom.** an Englishman. *–v.i.* **4. chum up with,** to become friendly with. **5. chum up to,** to behave obsequiously towards. [orig. uncert.]

**chum**[2] /tʃʌm/, *n.* **1.** refuse from fish, esp. that remaining after expressing oil. **2.** chopped fish, lobsters, etc. thrown overboard to attract fish, as in deep sea fishing. *–v.i.* **3.** to fish with chum. *–v.t.* **4.** to bait (the water) with chum. [orig. uncert.]

**chummy** /ˈtʃʌmi/, *adj.,* **-mier, -miest.** intimate; sociable. **– chummily,** *adv.*

**chump** /tʃʌmp/, *n.* **1.** *Colloq.* a blockhead or dolt. **2.** a short thick piece of wood. **3.** the thick blunt end of anything. **4.** *Colloq.* the head. **5.** *Meat Industry.* a section of lamb, hogget or mutton, between the leg and the loin, each chump containing approximately four chops.

**chump chop** /– ˈtʃɒp/, *n.* a slice of chump (def. 5).

**chunder** /ˈtʃʌndə/, *v.i., v.t. Colloq.* **1.** to vomit. *–n.* **2.** the act of vomiting. **3.** the substance vomited. [orig. uncert.] **– chundering,** *n.* **– chunderer,** *n.*

**chunderous** /ˈtʃʌndrəs/, *adj. Colloq.* revolting, unpleasant.

**chunk** /tʃʌŋk/, *n.* a thick mass or lump of anything: *a chunk of bread.* [nasalised var. of CHUCK[2], *n.*]

**chunky** /ˈtʃʌŋki/, *adj.,* **-kier, -kiest. 1.** thick or stout; thickset; stocky. **2.** in a chunk or chunks. **3.** knitted in very thick wool: *a chunky sweater.* **– chunkiness,** *n.*

**chupardy** /tʃəˈpadi/, *n.* →**chapatti.** [Aboriginal adaptation of word introduced in the Northern Territory by Indian traders]

**chupatti** /tʃəˈpæti/, *n.* →**chapatti.**

**church** /tʃɜtʃ/, *n.* **1.** an edifice for public Christian worship. **2.** public worship of God in a church; church service. **3.** (*cap.*) the whole body of Christian believers. **4.** (*cap.*) any division of this body professing the same creed and acknowledging the same ecclesiastical authority; a Christian denomination: *the Methodist Church.* **5.** (*cap.*) that part of the whole Christian body, or of a particular denomination, belonging to the same city, country, nation, etc. **6.** a body of Christians worshipping in a particular building or constituting one congregation. **7.** the ecclesiastical organisation or power as distinguished from the state. **8.** the clerical profession. **9.** a place of public worship of a non-Christian religion. **10.** (*sometimes cap.*) any non-Christian religious society, organisation, or congregation: *the Jewish Church.* *–v.t.* **11.** to conduct or bring to church, esp. for special services. **12.** to perform a church service of thanksgiving for (a woman after childbirth). [ME *churche, chirche,* OE *cir(i)ce, cyrice* (c. G *Kirche*), from Gk *kȳriakón* (*dôma*) Lord's (house)]

**church commissioner** /– kəˈmɪʃənə/, *n.* a member of a body of trustees charged with the care of the finances of the Church of England, and the administration of its investments and properties.

**churchgoer** /ˈtʃɜtʃgoʊə/, *n.* one who attends church services. **– churchgoing,** *n., adj.*

**churchless** /ˈtʃɜtʃləs/, *adj.* **1.** without a church. **2.** not belonging to or attending any church.

**churchlike** /ˈtʃɜtʃlaɪk/, *adj.* resembling, or appropriate to, a church: *churchlike silence.*

**churchly** /ˈtʃɜtʃli/, *adj.* of or appropriate for the church or a church; ecclesiastical. [OE *ciriclīc;* CHURCH + -LY]

**churchman** /ˈtʃɜtʃmən/, *n., pl.* **-men. 1.** an ecclesiastic; a clergyman. **2.** an adherent or active supporter of a church. **3.** a member of the established church. – **churchmanly,** *adj.* – **churchmanship,** *n.*

**Church of England,** *n.* the established Church in England, Catholic in faith and order but incorporating Protestant features, having the monarch as head and governed under Parliament by chambers of representatives drawn from the clergy and from the laity.

**Church of Rome,** *n.* Roman Catholic Church.

**church parade** /ˈtʃɜtʃ pəreɪd/, *n.* a parade of servicemen or scouts, guides, etc., before a church service.

**church text** /ˈ– tɛkst/, *n. Print.* →**Old English** (def. 2).

**churchwarden** /tʃɜtʃˈwɔdn/, *n.* **1.** *C. of E.* a lay officer who looks after the secular affairs of the church. **2.** a clay tobacco pipe with a very long stem.

**churchwoman** /ˈtʃɜtʃwʊmən/, *n., pl.* **-women.** a female member of a church, esp. of an Anglican church.

**churchy** /ˈtʃɜtʃi/, *adj.* obtrusively religious.

**churchyard** /ˈtʃɜtʃjad/, *n.* the yard or ground adjoining a church, often used as a graveyard.

**churinga** /tʃəˈrɪŋgə/, *n.* a sacred representation of an aboriginal totemic object usu. made of wood or stone; bullroarer. Also, **tchurunga, tjuringa, turinga.** [Aboriginal]

**churl** /tʃɜl/, *n.* **1.** a peasant; a rustic. **2.** a rude, boorish, or surly person. **3.** a niggard; miser. **4.** *Eng. Hist.* a freeman of the lowest rank. [ME; OE *ceorl* freeman of the lowest rank, c. G *Kerl.* Cf. CARL]

**churlish** /ˈtʃɜlɪʃ/, *adj.* **1.** of a churl or churls. **2.** like a churl; boorish; rude; surly. **3.** niggardly; sordid. **4.** difficult to work or deal with, as soil. – **churlishly,** *adv.* – **churlishness,** *n.*

**churn** /tʃɜn/, *n.* **1.** a vessel or machine in which cream or milk is agitated to make butter. **2.** any of various similar vessels or machines. **3.** a large metal container for milk. *–v.t.* **4.** to stir or agitate in order to make into butter: *to churn cream.* **5.** to make by the agitation of cream: *to churn butter.* **6.** to shake or agitate with violence or continued motion. *–v.i.* **7.** to operate a churn. **8.** to move in agitation, as a liquid or any loose matter: *leaves churning.* [ME *chyrne,* OE *cyrin,* c. Icel. *kirna* tub, pail] – **churner,** *n.*

**churned up** /tʃɜnd ˈʌp/, *adj. Colloq.* upset; agitated.

**churning** /ˈtʃɜnɪŋ/, *n.* **1.** the act of one that churns. **2.** the butter made at any one time.

**churr** /tʃɜ/, *v.i., n.* →**chirr.** [? var. of CHIRR]

**chute**[1] /ʃut/, *n.* **1.** a channel, trough, tube, shaft, etc., for conveying water, grain, coal, etc., to a lower level; a shoot. **2.** a waterfall; a steep descent, as in a river; a rapid. **3.** an inclined board, with sides, down which a swimmer may slide into the water. **4.** a parachute. **5.** *Agric.* a narrow passage through which animals are moved for branding, drenching or loading, often having a very steep incline. **6.** a narrow inclined exit for shorn sheep from a woolshed. **7.** *Horse-racing.* a straight stretch of track leading onto the main racecourse track, from which races are sometimes started. Also, **shoot.** [b. F *chute* a fall (b. OF *cheue* and OE *cheoite,* both from OF *cheior* fall, from L *cadere*) and E SHOOT]

**chute**[2] /ʃut/, *n.* a steep slope, as for tobogganing. [Frenchified spelling of d. E *shoot, shute,* ME *shote* steep slope, akin to SHOOT, *v.*]

**chutney** /ˈtʃʌtni/, *n., pl.* **-neys.** a relish of Indian origin which consists of fruit or vegetable cooked with sugar, spices, and vinegar or lime juice. Also, **chutnee.** [Hind. *chatnī*]

**chutney barrel** /ˈ– bærəl/, *n. Colloq.* a toilet, esp. a sanitary can.

**chuttie** /ˈtʃʌti/, *n. Colloq.* →**chewing gum.** Also, **chutty.**

**chutzpah** /ˈtʃʌtspa/, *n. Colloq.* impudence; gall. [Yiddish]

**chyack** /ˈtʃaɪæk/, *v.t.* →**chiack.**

**chylaceous** /kaɪˈleɪʃəs/, *adj.* of or resembling chyle.

**chyle** /kaɪl/, *n.* a milky fluid containing emulsified fat and other products of digestion, formed from the chyme in the small intestine and conveyed by the lacteals and the thoracic duct to the veins. [NL *chȳlus,* from Gk *chȳlós* juice, chyle] – **chylous,** *adj.*

**chyme** /kaɪm/, *n.* the pulpy matter into which food is converted by gastric digestion. [L *chȳmus,* from Gk *chȳmós* juice] – **chymous,** *adj.*

**chymotrypsin** /kaɪmoʊˈtrɪpsən/, *n.* a proteolytic enzyme produced by the pancreas.

**chymotrypsinogen** /ˌkaɪmoʊtrɪpˈsɪnədʒən/, *n.* the inactive precursor of chymotrypsin.

**Ci,** curie.

**C.I.A.** /si aɪ ˈeɪ/, (in U.S.) Central Intelligence Agency.

**ciao** /tʃaʊ/, *interj. Colloq.* **1.** goodbye. **2.** hello. [It., alteration of *schiavo* at your service]

**C.I.B.** /si aɪ ˈbi/, **1.** Criminal Investigation Branch. **2.** *Brit.* Criminal Investigation Bureau.

**ciborium** /səˈbɔriəm/, *n., pl.* **-boria** /-ˈbɔriə/. **1.** a permanent canopy placed over an altar; baldachin. **2.** any vessel designed to contain the consecrated bread or sacred wafers for the Eucharist. [ML: canopy, in L drinking cup, from Gk *kibṓrion* cup, seed vessel of the Egyptian bean]

ciborium (def. 2)

**cicada** /səˈkadə/, *n., pl.* **-dae** /-di/, **-das.** any insect of the family Cicadidae, which comprises large homopterous insects noted for the shrill sound produced by the male by means of vibrating membranes or drums on the underside of the abdomen. [L]

**cicada bird** /ˈ– bɜd/, *n.* a shy bird, *Coracina tenuirostris,* the male being predominantly blue-grey in colour, the female predominantly brown, whose call is thought to resemble the sound of a cicada; found mostly in rainforests and mangroves along the northern and eastern coast of Australia.

cicada

**cicada hunter** /ˈ– hʌntə/, *n.* a large Australian wasp, *Exeirus lateritius,* which preys on cicadas to obtain food for its larva.

**cicatricle** /ˈsɪkətrɪkəl/, *n.* **1.** *Embryol.* the small blastodisc on the yolk of an unincubated bird's egg. **2.** →**cicatrix.** [L *cicātrīcula* a small scar]

**cicatrise** /ˈsɪkətraɪz/, *v.,* **-trised, -trising.** *–v.t.* **1.** to heal by inducing the formation of a cicatrix. *–v.i.* **2.** to become healed by the formation of a cicatrix. Also, **cicatrize.** – **cicatrisation** /sɪkətraɪˈzeɪʃən/, *n.* – **cicatriser,** *n.*

**cicatrix** /ˈsɪkətrɪks/, *n., pl.* **cicatrices** /sɪkəˈtraɪsiz/, **cicatrixes.** **1.** the new tissue which forms over a wound or the like, and later contracts into a scar. **2.** *Bot.* the scar left by a fallen leaf, seed, etc. Also, **cicatrice** /ˈsɪkətrəs/. [L] – **cicatricial** /sɪkəˈtrɪʃəl/, *adj.* – **cicatricose** /ˈsɪkətrəkoʊs/, *adj.*

**cicely** /ˈsɪsəli/, *n., pl.* **-lies.** a plant of the parsley family, *Myrrhis odorata* (the **sweet cicely**), grown for its pleasing smell and sometimes used as a potherb. [? L *seselis,* from Gk: kind of plant]

**cicero** /ˈsɪsəroʊ/, *n. Print.* a European unit of measurement for type, slightly larger than the pica. [used initially in an edition (1458) of the works of *Cicero,* Marcus Tullius, 106-43 B.C., Roman statesman, orator, and writer]

**cicerone** /sɪsəˈroʊni, tʃɪtʃə-/, *n., pl.* **-ni** /-ni/. a guide who shows and explains the antiquities, curiosities, etc., of a place. [It., from L: abl. sing. of *Cicero,* Marcus Tullius, 106-43 B.C., Roman statesman, orator, and writer]

**cichlid** /ˈsɪklɪd/, *n.* any of the Cichlidae, a family of spiny-rayed, freshwater fishes of South America, Africa, and southern Asia; often kept in home aquariums. [NL *Cichlidae,* pl., from Gk *kíchlē* kind of sea fish] – **cichloid** /ˈsɪklɔɪd/, *n., adj.*

**cicisbeo** /tʃɪtʃəzˈbeɪoʊ/, *n., pl.* **-bei** /-ˈbeɪi/. a professed lover of a married woman. [It.]

**C.I.D.** /si aɪ ˈdi/, Criminal Investigation Department.

**-cidal,** adjective form of **-cide.** [-CIDE + -AL[1]]

**-cide,** a word element meaning 'killer' or 'act of killing'. [L: *-cīda* -killer and *-cīdium* act of killing; from *caedere* to kill]

**cider** /ˈsaɪdə/, *n.* the expressed juice of apples (or formerly of some other fruit), used for drinking, either before fermentation (**sweet cider**) or after fermentation (**rough cider**), or for making applejack, vinegar, etc. Also, **cyder.** [ME *sidre,* from OF, from LL *sīcera,* from Gk *síkera,* representing Heb. *shēkār* strong drink]

**cider-cup** /'saɪdə-kʌp/, *n.* a beverage made from sweetened cider and various flavourings.

**cider-press** /'saɪdə-prɛs/, *n.* a press for crushing apples for cider.

**C.I.F.** /si aɪ 'ɛf/, cost, insurance, and freight (included in the price quoted). Also, **c.i.f., c.f.i.**

**cigar** /sə'ga/, *n.* a small, shaped roll of tobacco leaves prepared for smoking. [Sp. *cigarro,* ? from *cigarra* grasshopper, from L *cicāla,* var. of *cicāda* CICADA]

**cigar-cutter** /sə'ga-kʌtə/, *n.* an instrument for cutting the tips off cigars.

**cigarette** /sɪgə'rɛt/, *n.* a roll of finely cut tobacco for smoking, usu. enclosed in thin paper. [F, diminutive of *cigare* CIGAR]

**cigarette-holder** /sɪgə'rɛt-hoʊldə/, *n.* a tubular mouth-piece, often having an ornate pattern, through which the smoke of a cigarette is drawn.

**cigarette paper** /sɪgə'rɛt peɪpə/, *n.* piece of thin paper in which tobacco is rolled to make a cigarette.

**cigarette swag** /'– swæg/, *n.* a swag rolled into a long, thin shape like a cigarette.

**cigarillo** /sɪgə'rɪloʊ/, *n.* a small cigar.

**ciggie** /'sɪgi/, *n. Colloq.* a cigarette.

**cilia** /'sɪliə/, *n.pl., sing.* **cilium** /'sɪliəm/. **1.** the eyelashes. **2.** *Zool.* minute hair-like processes of cells which by their movement produce locomotion of the cell or a current that passes through the cell. **3.** *Bot.* minute, hairlike processes. [L, pl. of *cilium* eyelid, eyelash]

flower with cilia

**ciliary** /'sɪljəri/, *adj.* **1.** denoting or pertaining to a delicate ring of tissue in the eye from which the lens is suspended by means of fine ligaments. **2.** pertaining to cilia.

**ciliate** /'sɪliət, -eɪt/, *n.* **1.** one of the Ciliata, a class of protozoans distinguished by the cilia on part or all of the body, among the most common of microscopic animals. *–adj.* **2.** Also, **ciliated.** having cilia; fringed or surrounded with hairs.

**cilice** /'sɪləs/, *n.* **1.** a garment of haircloth; a hairshirt. **2.** haircloth. [F, from L *cilicium,* from Gk *kilíkion* coarse cloth made of goat's hair, orig. from Cilicia, ancient country and Roman province in Asia Minor; replacing OE *cilic,* from L (as above)]

**ciliolate** /'sɪliələt, -leɪt/, *adj.* furnished with minute cilia.

**cimbalom** /'tʃɪmbələm/, *n.* a Magyar dulcimer.

**cimex** /'saɪmɛks/, *n., pl.* **cimices** /'saɪməsiz/. an insect of the genus *Cimex,* esp. the bedbug.

**cimmerian** /sə'mɪəriən/, *adj.* **1.** pertaining to or suggestive of a mythical western people said by Homer to dwell in perpetual darkness. **2.** very dark; gloomy. [L *Cimmerius* (from Gk *Kimmérios* (*Odyssey* XI 14) + -AN]

**C.-in-C.,** commander-in-chief.

**cinch**[1] /sɪntʃ/, *n.* **1.** a strong girth for a saddle or pack. **2.** *Colloq.* something certain or easy. *–v.t.* **3.** to gird with a cinch; gird or bind firmly. *–v.i.* **4.** to fix the saddle girth; tighten the cinch. [Sp. *cincha,* from L *cincta* girdle, from *cingere* gird] – **cinchy,** *adj.*

**cinch**[2] /sɪntʃ/, *n. Cards.* a variety of all fours. [? Sp. *cinco* five]

**cinchona** /sɪŋ'koʊnə/, *n.* **1.** any of the trees or shrubs constituting the genus *Cinchona,* native to the Andes, cultivated there and in Java and India for their bark, which yields quinine and other alkaloids. **2.** the medicinal bark of such trees or shrubs; Peruvian bark. **3.** the drug prepared from this bark. [NL, named after the Countess of *Chinchón,* 1576-1639, wife of a Spanish viceroy of Peru] – **cinchonic,** *adj.*

**cinchonine** /'sɪŋkənin/, *n.* a colourless, crystalline alkaloid, $C_{19}H_{22}ON_2$, obtained from various species of the cinchona bark, used as an antipyretic and quinine substitute.

**cinchonism** /'sɪŋkənɪzəm/, *n.* poisoning from cinchona or its alkaloids.

**cincinnus** /sɪn'sɪnəs/, *n.* a cymose inflorescence with short alternating internodes forming a coiled axis, as in forget-me-not or comfrey.

**cincture** /'sɪŋktʃə/, *n., v.,* **-tured, -turing.** *–n.* **1.** a belt or girdle. **2.** something surrounding or encompassing like a girdle; a surrounding border. **3.** the act of girding or encompassing. *–v.t.* **4.** to gird with or as with a cincture; encircle; encompass. [L *cinctūra* girdle]

**cinder** /'sɪndə/, *n.* **1.** a burnt-out or partially burnt piece of coal, wood, etc. **2.** (*pl.*) any residue of combustion; ashes. **3.** (*pl.*) *Geol.* coarse scoriae thrown out of volcanoes. *–v.t.* **4.** to reduce to cinders: *cindering flame.* [ME *cyndir, sindir,* OE *sinder* cinder, slag, c. G *Sinter*] – **cindery,** *adj.*

**cinderella** /sɪndə'rɛlə/, *n.* **1.** a neglected, ignored or despised person. **2.** a neglected or ignored section, branch, department or the like: *research is the cinderella in this university.* [from *Cinderella,* heroine of a well-known fairy-tale]

**cinder track** /'sɪndə træk/, *n.* a path covered with small cinders, used in running races.

**cine-,** a word element meaning 'motion', used of films, etc., as in *cinecamera.* [combining form from Gk *kīneîn* move]

**cineaste** /'sɪniæst/, *n.* a devotee of the cinema. [F *cinéaste*]

**cinecamera** /'sɪnikæmrə/, *n.* a camera used for taking moving films.

**cinefilm** /'sɪnifɪlm/, *n.* **1.** a type of film, usu. 8 mm, used in a cinecamera, on which moving pictures are taken. **2.** the pictures so taken.

**cinema** /'sɪnəmə/, *n.* **1.** a theatre where films are shown; picture theatre. **2. the cinema,** films collectively. [short for CINEMATOGRAPH] – **cinematic** /sɪnə'mætɪk/, *adj.* – **cinematically** /sɪnə'mætɪkli/, *adv.*

**cinemagoer** /'sɪnəməgoʊə/, *n.* one who visits the cinema regularly. [modelled on THEATREGOER]

**cinemascope** /'sɪnəməskoʊp/, *n.* a film process using a single-lens camera or projector, an extra-wide screen, and a stereophonic arrangement of loudspeakers. [Trademark]

**cinematise** /'sɪnəmətaɪz/, *v.t., v.i.,* **-tised, -tising.** →**cinematograph** (def. 3). Also, **cinematize.**

**cinematograph** /sɪnə'mætəgræf/, *n.* **1.** a film projector. **2.** a film camera. *–v.t., v.i.* **3.** to take films (of). Also, **kinematograph.** [*cinemato-* (combining form representing Gk *kī́nēma* motion) + -GRAPH] – **cinematographer** /sɪnəmə'tɒgrəfə/, *n.* – **cinematographic,** *adj.* – **cinematography** /sɪnəmə'tɒgrəfi/, *n.*

**cinéma-vérité** /ˌsɪnəmə-'vɛrəteɪ/, *n.* a type of documentary film using lightweight camera equipment, avoiding artificially contrived situations and achieving a directness of impact through selective filming and editing.

**cineol** /'sɪniɒl/, *n.* a colourless liquid, $C_{10}H_{18}O$, a terpene ether found in eucalyptus and other essential oils and used in medicine; eucalyptol. Also, **cineole** /'sɪnioʊl/. [NL *oleum cinae* (reversed), oil of wormwood]

**cine-projector** /'sɪni-prədʒɛktə/, *n.* a projector for cine-films.

**cineradiography** /ˌsɪnireɪdi'ɒgrəfi/, *n.* the process of making X-rays of a moving object in rapid sequence so that a film can be made from them. – **cineradiographic** /ˌsɪnireɪdiə'græfɪk/, *adj.*

**cinerama** /sɪnə'ramə/, *n.* a film process designed to produce a three-dimensional effect by using three cameras, set at different angles, to photograph separate overlapping images of each scene and project them on a large concave screen in conjunction with stereophonic sound. [Trademark]

**cineraria** /sɪnə'rɛəriə/, *n.* any of various horticultural varieties of the plant *Senecio cruentus,* native to the Canary Islands, with heart-shaped leaves and clusters of flowers with white, blue, purple, red, or variegated rays. [NL, properly fem. of L *cinerārius* pertaining to ashes (with reference to the soft white down on the leaves)]

**cinerarium** /sɪnə'rɛəriəm/, *n., pl.* **-raria** /-'rɛəriə/. a place for depositing the ashes of the dead after cremation. [L] – **cinerary** /'sɪnərəri/, *adj.*

**cinereous** /sə'nɪəriəs/, *adj.* **1.** in the state of ashes: *cinereous bodies.* **2.** resembling ashes. **3.** ashen; ash-coloured; greyish: *cinerous crow.* Also, **cineritious** /sɪnə'rɪʃəs/. [L *cinereus* ash-coloured]

**cingulum** /'sɪŋgjələm/, *n., pl.* **-la** /-lə/. *Anat., Zool.* a belt, zone, or girdle-like part. [L: girdle] – **cingulate, cingulated,** *adj.*

**cinnabar** /'sɪnəba/, *n.* **1.** a mineral, mercuric sulphide, HgS, often vermilion coloured, the principal ore of mercury. **2.** red mercuric sulphide, used as a pigment. **3.** bright red; vermilion. **4.** a large red European moth, *Callimorpha jacobaeae,* of the tiger moth (Arctiidae) family. [L *cinnabaris,* from Gk *kinnábari,* of oriental orig.; replacing ME *cynoper,* from ML]

**cinnamic** /sə'næmɪk/, *adj.* of or obtained from cinnamon.

**cinnamic acid** /– 'æsəd/, *n.* an unsaturated acid, $C_6H_5CH{:}CHCOOH$ or $C_6H_5CH{=}CHCOOH$, derived from cinnamon, balsams, etc.

**cinnamon** /'sɪnəmən/, *n.* **1.** the aromatic inner bark of any of several trees of the genus *Cinnamomum* of the East Indies, etc., esp. **Ceylon cinnamon,** *C. verum,* much used as a spice, and **Saigon cinnamon,** *C. loureiri,* used in medicine as a cordial and carminative. **2.** a tree yielding cinnamon. **3.** any of various allied or similar trees. **4.** →**cassia** (def. 1). **5.** yellowish or reddish brown. [LL, from Gk *kínnamon;* replacing ME *cynamome,* from F *cinnamome,* of Semitic orig.; cf. Heb. *qinnāmōn*]

**cinnamon bear** /'– bɛə/, *n.* the cinnamon-coloured variety of the black bear of North America, *Euarctos americanus.*

**cinnamon stone** /'– stoun/, *n.* a light brown grossularite garnet.

**cinque** /sɪŋk/, *n.* the five at dice, cards, etc. [F; replacing ME *cink,* from OF, from L *quinque* five]

**cinquecentist** /ˌtʃɪŋkwə'tʃɛntəst/, *n.* an Italian writer or artist of the 16th century.

**cinquecento** /ˌtʃɪŋkwə'tʃɛntou/, *n.* the 16th century, with reference to Italy, esp. to the Italian art or literature of that period. [It.: five hundred, short for *mille cinquecento* one thousand five hundred]

**cinquefoil** /'sɪŋkfɔɪl/, *n.* **1.** any species of the herbaceous genus *Potentilla,* as *P. recta,* a widespread weed. **2.** a decorative design or feature resembling the leaf of cinquefoil, as an architectural ornament or opening of a generally circular or rounded form divided into five lobes by cusps. **3.** *Her.* a five-leafed clover, used as a bearing. [ME *synkefoile,* through OF (unrecorded), from L *quinquefolium,* from *quinque* five + *folium* leaf]

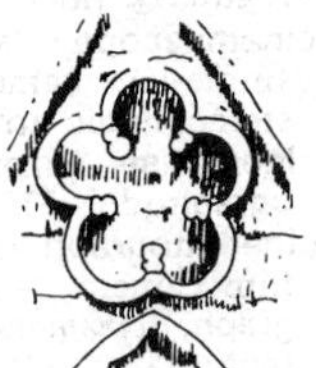
cinquefoil (def. 2)

**-cion,** a suffix having the same function as **-tion,** as in *suspicion.* [L *-cio,* from *-c* in verb stem, + *-io,* n. suffix. Cf. -SION, -TION]

**cipher** /'saɪfə/, *n.* **1.** an arithmetical symbol (0) which denotes nought, or no quantity or magnitude. **2.** any of the Arabic numerals or figures. **3.** Arabic numerical notation collectively. **4.** something of no value or importance. **5.** a person of no influence; a nonentity. **6.** a secret method of writing, as by a specially formed code of symbols. **7.** writing done by such a method. **8.** the key to a secret method of writing. **9.** a combination of letters, as the initials of a name, in one design; a monogram. **10.** the mechanical failure of an organ pipe, causing continuous sounding. *–v.i.* **11.** to use figures or numerals arithmetically. **12.** (of an organ note) to sound continuously without being played. *–v.t.* **13.** to calculate numerically; figure. **14.** to write in, or as in, cipher. Also, **cypher.** [ME *siphre,* from ML *ciphra,* from Ar. *ṣifr,* lit., empty. Cf. ZERO]

**cipolin** /'sɪpələn/, *n.* a variety of marble with alternate white and greenish zones and a laminated structure. Also, **cipollino.** [F, from It. *cipollino* (so called from its layered structure), diminutive of *cipolla* onion, from L *cēpa*]

**cir.,** about. Also, **circ.** [L *circa, circiter, circum*]

**circa** /'sɜkə, 'sɜsə/, *prep., adv.* about (used esp. in approximate dates). *Abbrev.: c., c,* or *ca.* [L]

**circadian** /sɜ'keɪdiən/, *adj.* designating physiological activity which occurs approximately every twenty-four hours, or the rhythm of such activity. [L *circa,* from *circum,* round about]

**Circassian** /sɜ'kæsiən/, *n.* **1.** a native or inhabitant of Circassia, a region on the Black Sea, north west of the Caucasus Mountains in the southern Soviet Union. **2.** a North Caucasian language. **3.** a light fabric originally made of mohair, now often of rayon.

**Circe** /'sɜsi/, *n.* a dangerously or irresistibly fascinating woman. [from the Gk legend of *Circe,* an enchantress supposed to have turned the companions of Odysseus into swine by a magic drink] – **Circean** /'sɜsiən/, *adj.*

**circinate** /'sɜsəneɪt/, *adj.* **1.** made round; ring-shaped. **2.** *Bot.* rolled up on the axis at the apex, as a leaf, etc. [L *circinātus,* pp.] – **circinately,** *adv.*

circinate fronds

**circle** /'sɜkəl/, *n., v.,* **-cled, -cling.** *–n.* **1.** a closed plane curve which is at all points equidistant from a fixed point within it, called the centre. **2.** the portion of a plane bounded by such a curve. **3.** any circular object, formation, or arrangement. **4.** (*usu. pl.*) a dark circular mask around or beneath the eyes, noticeable esp. in sick persons, or in persons who have slept badly. **5.** a ring; a circlet; crown. **6.** the ring of a circus. **7.** an upper section of seats in a theatre: *dress circle.* **8.** *Archaeol.* a ring of widely spaced stones, usu. standing, forming a ritual monument probably of Bronze age; in prehistoric Europe confined to the British Isles and Brittany. **9.** the area within which something acts, exerts influence, etc. **10.** *Hockey.* the semicircle in front of each goal into which the attacking player must have entered before shooting a goal; striking circle. **11.** a series ending where it began, and perpetually repeated: *the circle of the year.* **12.** *Logic.* an inconclusive form of reasoning in which unproved statements, or their equivalents, are used to prove each other; vicious circle. **13.** a complete series forming a connected whole; cycle: *the circle of the sciences.* **14.** a number of persons bound by a common tie; a coterie. **15.** an administrative division, esp. of a province. **16.** *Geog.* a parallel of latitude. **17.** *Astron.* **a.** the orbit of a heavenly body. **b.** an instrument for observing the transit of stars across the meridian of the observer. **18.** a sphere or orb. **19.** a ring of light in the sky; halo. **20.** a circular road. **21.** a punishment section of a prison where small yards adjoining each other comprise a circle; prisoners under solitary confinement are taken from their cells for daily exercise in these separate compartments. *–v.t.* **22.** to enclose in a circle; surround: *the enemy circled the hill.* **23.** to move in a circle or circuit round: *he circled the house cautiously.* *–v.i.* **24.** to move in a circle. [L *circulus,* diminutive of *circus* circle, ring; replacing ME *cercle,* from OF] – **circler,** *n.*

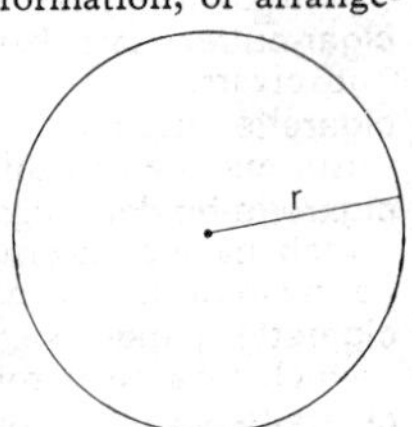

circle: diameter = $2r$; area = $\pi r^2$ ($\pi$ = 3.14), circumference = $2\pi r$

**circlet** /'sɜklət/, *n.* **1.** a small circle. **2.** a ring. **3.** a ring-shaped ornament, esp. for the head.

**circling disease** /'sɜklɪŋ dəˌziz/, *n.* a fatal infectious bacterial disease of cattle and sheep which damages the nervous system and often causes the afflicted animal to walk in circles.

**circs** /sɜks/, *n. pl. Colloq.* circumstances.

**circuit** /'sɜkət/, *n.* **1.** the act of going or moving round. **2.** any circular or roundabout journey; a round. **3.** any racing track which leads back to its starting place so that contestants may move around it continuously. **4.** a periodical journey from place to place, to perform certain duties, as of judges to hold court or ministers to preach. **5.** the route followed, places visited, or district covered by such a journey. **6.** a street which is circular or roughly so. **7.** a number of races in a season or series. **8.** the line going round or bounding any area or object; the distance about an area or object. **9.** the space within a bounding line. **10.** a number of theatres, cinemas, etc., under common control or visited in turn by the same actors, etc. **11.** *Elect.* **a.** the complete path of an electric current, including the generating apparatus or other source, or a distinct segment of the complete path. **b.** a more or less elaborately contrived arrangement of conductors, waveguides, electronic tubes, and other devices, for the investigation or utilisation of electrical phenomena. **c.** the diagram of the connections of such apparatus. *–v.t.* **12.** to go or move round; make the circuit of. *–v.i.* **13.** to go or move in a circuit. [ME, from L *circuitus*]

**circuit-breaker** /'sɜkət-breɪkə/, *n.* a device for interrupting an electric circuit between separable contacts under normal or abnormal conditions.

**circuitous** /sə'kjuətəs/, *adj.* roundabout; not direct: *they took a circuitous route to the house.* – **circuitously,** *adv.* – **circuitousness,** *n.*

**circuitry** /'sɜkətri/, *n.* any system of electrical circuits.

**circuity** /sə'kjuəti/, *n.* circuitous quality; roundabout character: *circuity of language or of a path.*

**circular** /'sɜkjələ/, *adj.* **1.** of or pertaining to a circle. **2.** having the form of a circle; round. **3.** moving in or forming a circle or a circuit. **4.** moving or occurring in a cycle or round. **5.** circuitous; roundabout; indirect. **6.** (of a letter, etc.) addressed to a number of persons or intended for general circulation. **7.** (of a velocity) required to maintain a body in a given circular orbit. *–n.* **8.** a letter, notice, advertisement, or statement for circulation among the general public for business or other purposes. [L *circulāris,* from *circulus* circle; replacing ME *circuler,* from AF] – **circularity** /sɜkjə'lærəti/, *n.*

**circularise** /'sɜkjələraɪz/, *v.t.,* **-rised, -rising. 1.** to send circulars to. **2.** to circulate (a letter, pamphlet, or the like). **3.** to make circular. Also, **circularize.** – **circularisation** /sɜkjələraɪ'zeɪʃən/, *n.* – **circulariser,** *n.*

**circular measure** /sɜkjələ 'mɛʒə/, *n.* the measurement of an angle in radians: 360 degrees = 2 π radians; 1 radian = 57 degrees 17.7 minutes.

**circular mil** /– 'mɪl/, *n.* a unit used principally for measuring the cross-sectional area of wires, being the area of a circle having the diameter of one mil.

**circular saw** /– 'sɔ/, *n.* a saw consisting of a circular plate or disc with a toothed edge, which is rotated at high speed in machines for sawing logs, cutting timber, etc.

**circular store** /– 'stɔ/, *n.* a mode of using the finite memory of a computer in which the memory is continuously sensed as though it were on the circumference of a turning wheel; the continual redefinition of its start makes the memory capable of retaining always the last data of a potentially infinite number of entries.

**circular triangle** /– 'traɪæŋgəl/, *n.* a triangle in which the sides are arcs of circles.

**circulate** /'sɜkjəleɪt/, *v.,* **-lated, -lating.** *–v.i.* **1.** to move in a circle or circuit; move or pass through a circuit back to the starting point, as the blood in the body. **2.** to pass from place to place, from person to person, etc.; be disseminated or distributed. **3.** *Maths. Obs.* (of a decimal) to recur. **4.** *Colloq.* to move amongst the guests at a social function. *–v.t.* **5.** to cause to pass from place to place, person to person, etc.: *to circulate a rumour.* [L *circulātus,* pp., made circular, gathered into a circle] – **circulative,** *adj.* – **circulator,** *n.* – **circulatory** /sɜkjə'leɪtəri/, *adj.*

**circulating capital** /ˌsɜkjəleɪtɪŋ 'kæpətl/, *n. Finance.* capital which has been used to acquire assets intended to be sold or resold at a profit (opposed to *fixed capital*).

**circulating decimal** /– 'dɛsəməl/, *n. Maths. Obs.* a recurring decimal.

**circulating library** /– 'laɪbri/, *n.* →**subscription library.**

**circulating medium** /– 'midiəm/, *n.* **1.** any coin or note passing, without endorsement, as a medium of exchange. **2.** such coins or notes collectively.

**circulation** /sɜkjə'leɪʃən/, *n.* **1.** the act of circulating or moving in a circle or circuit. **2.** the recurrent movement of the blood through the various vessels of the body. **3.** any similar circuit or passage, as of the sap in plants. **4.** the transmission or passage of anything from place to place, person to person, etc. **5.** the distribution of copies of a publication among readers. **6.** the number of copies of each issue of a newspaper, magazine, etc., distributed. **7.** coin, notes, bills, etc., in use as currency; currency. **8.** *Colloq.* (of a person) **a. in circulation,** socially active. **b. out of circulation,** socially inactive.

**circum-,** a prefix referring to movement round or about motion on all sides, as in *circumvent, circumnavigate, circumference.* [L, prefix use of *circum,* adv. and prep., orig. acc. of *circus* circle, ring. See CIRCUS]

**circumambient** /sɜkəm'æmbiənt/, *adj.* surrounding; encompassing: *circumambient gloom.* – **circumambience, circumambiency,** *n.*

**circumambulate** /sɜkəm'æmbjəleɪt/, *v.t., v.i.,* **-lated, -lating.** to walk or go about; wander aimlessly. – **circumambulation** /ˌsɜkəmæmbjə'leɪʃən/, *n.*

**circumcise** /'sɜkəmsaɪz/, *v.t.* **-cised, -cising. 1.** to remove the foreskin of (males) sometimes as a religious rite. **2.** to perform an analogous operation on (females). **3.** to purify spiritually. [ME *circumcise(n),* from L *circumcīsus,* pp., cut around] – **circumciser,** *n.*

**circumcision** /sɜkəm'sɪʒən/, *n.* **1.** the act or rite of circumcising. **2.** spiritual purification. **3.** (*cap.*) a church festival in honour of the circumcision of Jesus, observed on 1 January. [ME *circumcisi(o)un,* from L *circumcīsio*]

**circumdenudation** /sɜkəmˌdinju'deɪʃən/, *n.* a process of erosion which leaves a hard rocky core exposed in the form of a mountain, etc.

**circumference** /sə'kʌmfərəns/, *n.* **1.** the outer boundary, esp. of a circular area. **2.** the length of such a boundary. **3.** the space within a bounding line. [L *circumferentia*] – **circumferential** /səkʌmfə'rɛnʃəl/, *adj.*

**circumflex** /'sɜkəmflɛks/, *n.* **1.** a mark used over a vowel in certain languages or in phonetic keys to indicate quality of pronunciation. **2.** bending or winding round. *–adj.* **3.** marked with a circumflex. *–v.t.* **4.** to bend around. **5.** to mark with a circumflex. [L *circumflexus,* pp., bent round] – **circumflexion** /sɜkəm'flɛkʃən/, *n.*

**circumfluent** /sə'kʌmfluənt/, *adj.* flowing round; encompassing: *two circumfluent rivers.* – **circumfluence,** *n.*

**circumfluous** /sə'kʌmfluəs/, *adj.* **1.** flowing round; encompassing: *circumfluous tides.* **2.** surrounded by water. [L *circumfluus* flowing round]

**circumfuse** /sɜkəm'fjuz/, *v.t.,* **-fused, -fusing. 1.** to pour round; diffuse. **2.** to surround as with a fluid; suffuse. [L *circumfūsus,* pp., poured around] – **circumfusion,** *n.*

**circumjacent** /sɜkəm'dʒeɪsənt/, *adj.* lying round; surrounding: *the circumjacent parishes.*

**circumlittoral** /sɜkəm'lɪtərəl/, *adj.* adjacent to the shoreline.

**circumlocution** /sɜkəmlə'kjuʃən/, *n.* **1.** a roundabout way of speaking; the use of too many words. **2.** a roundabout expression. [L *circumlocūtio*] – **circumlocutory** /sɜkəm'lɒkjətəri, -tri/, *adj.*

**circumlunar** /sɜkəm'lunə/, *adj.* around the moon: *circumlunar orbit.*

**circumnavigate** /sɜkəm'nævəgeɪt/, *v.t.,* **-gated, -gating.** to sail round; make the circuit of by navigation: *he circumnavigated the world.* – **circumnavigation** /ˌsɜkəmnævə'geɪʃən/, *n.* – **circumnavigator,** *n.*

**circumnutate** /sɜkəm'njuteɪt/, *v.i.,* **-tated, -tating.** (of the apex of a stem or other growing part of a plant) to bend or move round in an irregular circular or elliptical path. – **circumnutation** /sɜkəmnju'teɪʃən/, *n.*

**circumpolar** /sɜkəm'poʊlə/, *adj.* around one of the poles of the earth or of the heavens.

**circumrotate** /ˌsɜkəmroʊ'teɪt/, *v.i.,* **-tated, -tating.** to rotate like a wheel.

**circumscissile** /sɜkəm'sɪsaɪl/, *adj. Bot.* opening along a transverse circular line, as a seed vessel.

circumscissile pod

**circumscribe** /'sɜkəmskraɪb, sɜkəm'skraɪb/, *v.t.,* **-scribed, -scribing. 1.** to draw a line round; encircle; surround. **2.** to enclose within bounds; limit or confine, esp. narrowly. **3.** to mark off; define. **4.** *Geom.* **a.** to draw (a figure) round another figure so as to touch as many points as possible. **b.** (of a figure) to enclose (another figure) in this manner. [L *circumscrībere* draw a line round, limit] – **circumscriber,** *n.*

**circumscription** /sɜkəm'skrɪpʃən/, *n.* **1.** the act of circumscribing. **2.** circumscribed state; limitation. **3.** anything that circumscribes, surrounds, or encloses. **4.** periphery; outline. **5.** a circumscribed space. **6.** a circular inscription on a coin, seal, etc. **7.** *Archaic.* limitation of a meaning; definition. – **circumscriptive,** *adj.*

**circumsolar** /sɜkəm'soʊlə/, *adj.* round the sun.

**circumspect** /'sɜkəmspɛkt/, *adj.* **1.** watchful on all sides;

cautious; prudent: *circumspect in behaviour.* **2.** well-considered: *circumspect ambition.* [late ME, from L *circumspectus,* pp., considerate, wary] – **circumspectly,** *adv.* – **circumspectness,** *n.*

**circumspection** /sɜkəm'spɛkʃən/, *n.* circumspect observation or action; caution; prudence.

**circumspective** /sɜkəm'spɛktɪv/, *adj.* given to or marked by circumspection; watchful; cautious: *a circumspective approach.*

**circumstance** /'sɜkəmstæns/, *n., v.,* **-stanced, -stancing.** *–n.* **1.** a condition, with respect to time, place, manner, agent, etc., which accompanies, determines, or modifies a fact or event. **2.** (*usu. pl.*) the existing condition or state of affairs surrounding and affecting an agent: *forced by circumstances to do a thing.* **3.** an unessential accompaniment of any fact or event; a secondary or accessory matter; a minor detail. **4.** (*pl.*) the condition or state of a person with respect to material welfare: *a family in reduced circumstances.* **5.** an incident or occurrence: *his arrival was a fortunate circumstance.* **6.** detailed or circuitous narration; specification of particulars. **7.** ceremonious accompaniment or display: *pomp and circumstance.* **8. in** or **under no circumstances,** never; regardless of events. **9. in** or **under the circumstances,** because of the conditions; such being the case. *–v.t.* **10.** to place in particular circumstances or relations. **11.** *Obs.* to furnish with details. **12.** *Obs.* to control or guide by circumstances. [ME, from L *circumstantia,* pl., surrounding conditions] – **circumstanced,** *adj.*

**circumstantial** /sɜkəm'stænʃəl/, *adj.* **1.** of, pertaining to, or derived from circumstances: *circumstantial evidence.* **2.** of the nature of a circumstance or unessential accompaniment; secondary; incidental. **3.** dealing with or giving circumstances or details; detailed; particular. **4.** pertaining to conditions of material welfare: *circumstantial prosperity.* – **circumstantially,** *adv.*

**circumstantial evidence** /– 'ɛvədəns/, *n.* proof of facts offered as evidence from which other facts are to be inferred (contrasted with *direct evidence*); indirect evidence.

**circumstantiality** /ˌsɜkəmˌstænʃi'ælәti/, *n., pl.* **-ties. 1.** the quality of being circumstantial; minuteness; fullness of detail. **2.** a circumstance; a particular detail.

**circumstantiate** /sɜkəm'stænʃieɪt/, *v.t.,* **-ated, -ating. 1.** to set forth or support with circumstances or particulars. **2.** to describe fully or minutely. – **circumstantiation** /ˌsɜkəmstænʃi'eɪʃən/, *n.*

**circumvallate** /sɜkəm'væleɪt/, *adj., v.,* **-lated, -lating.** *–adj.* **1.** surrounded by, or as by, a rampart, etc. *–v.t.* **2.** to surround with, or as with, a rampart, etc. **3.** *Zool.* (of protozoa) to engulf (food) by surrounding it. [L *circumvallātus,* pp., surrounded with a rampart] – **circumvallation** /sɜkəmvə'leɪʃən/, *n.*

**circumvent** /sɜkəm'vɛnt/, *v.t.* **1.** to surround or encompass as by strategem; entrap. **2.** to gain advantage over by artfulness or deception; outwit; overreach. **3.** to go round: *circumvent the bridge.* [L *circumventus,* pp., surrounded] – **circumventer, circumventor,** *n.* – **circumvention,** *n.* – **circumventive,** *adj.*

**circumvolution** /sɜkəmvə'luʃən/, *n.* **1.** the act of rolling or turning round. **2.** a single complete turn. **3.** a winding or folding about something. **4.** a fold so wound. **5.** a winding in a sinuous course; a sinuosity. **6.** roundabout course or procedure.

**circumvolve** /sɜkəm'vɒlv/, *v.t., v.i.,* **-volved, -volving.** →**revolve.** [L *circumvolvere* roll round]

**circus** /'sɜkəs/, *n.* **1.** a company of performers, animals, etc., esp. a travelling company. **2.** the performance itself. **3.** a circular arena surrounded by tiers of seats, for the exhibition of wild animals, acrobatic feats, etc. **4.** (in ancient Rome) a large, usu. oblong, or oval, roofless enclosure, surrounded by tiers of seats rising one above another, for chariot races, public games, etc. **5.** anything like the Roman circus, as a natural amphitheatre, a circular range of houses as those built in the 18th century, etc. **6.** a flying circus. **7.** a place, originally circular, where several streets converge: *Piccadilly Circus.* **8.** uproar; a display of rowdy sport and behaviour. **9.** an entertaining or humorous person: *he's a real circus.* **10.** *Obs.* a circlet or ring. [L, from Gk *kírkos* ring]

**ciré** /'sɪreɪ/, *n.* **1.** a highly glazed surface produced on fabrics by subjecting them to certain heat treatments. **2.** a fabric having such a surface. [F: waxed]

**cire perdue** /sɪə pə'dju/, *n.* →**lost wax process.** [F: lost wax]

**cirque** /sɜk/, *n.* **1.** a circular space, esp. a natural amphitheatre in mountains formed by glacial action. **2.** *Poetic.* a circle or ring of any kind. **3.** a circus. [F, from L *circus*]

**cirrate** /'sɪreɪt/, *adj.* having cirri. [L *cirrātus* curled, from *cirrus* curl]

**cirrhosis** /sɪ'roʊsəs, sə-/, *n.* a disease of the liver characterised by increase of connective tissue and alteration in gross and microscopic make-up. [NL, from Gk *kirrhós* tawny + *-osis* -OSIS] – **cirrhotic** /sɪ'rɒtɪk/, *adj.*

**cirri** /'sɪraɪ/, *n.* plural of **cirrus.**

**cirriped** /'sɪrəpɛd/, *n.* **1.** any of the Cirripedia, an order or group of barnacle crustaceans, typically having slender legs bearing bristles used in gathering food. *–adj.* **2.** having legs like cirri. **3.** pertaining to the Cirripedia. Also, **cirripede.** [NL *Cirripedia,* pl.; from *cirri-* CIRRO- + *-pedia* footed]

**cirro-,** a combining form of **cirrus.**

**cirrocumulus** /ˌsɪroʊ'kjumjələs/, *n.* a cloud of high altitude, consisting of small fleecy balls or flakes, often in rows or ripples.

**cirrose** /'sɪroʊs, sɪ'roʊs/, *adj.* **1.** having a cirrus or cirri. **2.** of the nature of cirrus clouds. Also, **cirrous** /'sɪrəs/.

**cirrostratus** /ˌsɪroʊ'stratəs/, *n.* a high veil-like cloud or sheet of haze, often giving rise to haloes round the sun and moon, sometimes very thin and only slightly whitening the blue of the sky. – **cirrostrative,** *adj.*

**cirrus** /'sɪrəs/, *n., pl.* **cirri** /'sɪri/. **1.** *Bot.* a tendril. **2.** *Zool.* a filament or slender appendage serving as a barbel, tentacle, foot, arm, etc. **3.** *Meteorol.* a variety of cloud having a thin, fleecy or filamentous appearance, normally occurring at great altitudes and consisting of minute ice crystals. [L: curl, tuft, fringe]

**cirsoid** /'sɜsɔɪd/, *adj.* varix-like; varicose. [Gk *kirsoeidḗs*]

**cis-,** **1.** a prefix denoting relative nearness (this side of), applied to time as well as space, as in *cisalpine.* Cf. **citra-. 2.** *Chem.* See **cis-trans isomerism.** [L, prefix use of *cis,* prep.]

**cis-aconitic acid** /ˌsɪs-ˌækənɪtɪk 'æsəd/, *n.* a tricarboxylic acid, $HOOC \cdot CH_2 \cdot C(COOH){=}CH \cdot COOH$, formed from citrate, an intermediate in the citric acid cycle.

**cisalpine** /sɪs'ælpaɪn/, *adj.* on this (the Roman or south) side of the Alps.

**cisco** /'sɪskoʊ/, *n., pl.* **-coes, -cos.** any of several North American species of whitefish of the genus *Leucichthys.* [N Amer. Ind.]

**cismontane** /sɪs'mɒnteɪn/, *adj.* on this side of the mountains.

**cissoid** /'sɪsɔɪd/, *Geom. –n.* **1.** a curve having a cusp at the origin and a point of inflection at infinity. *–adj.* **2.** included between the concave sides of two intersecting curves (opposed to *sistroid*): *a cissoid angle.* [Gk *kissoeidḗs* ivy-like]

**cissy** /'sɪsi/, *n. Colloq.* →**sissy.** Also, **cissie.**

**cissy bar** /'– ba/, *n.* →**sissy bar.**

**cist**[1] /sɪst/, *n. Class. Antiq.* a box or chest, esp. for sacred utensils. [L *cista,* from Gk *kístē* CHEST]

**cist**[2] /sɪst/, *n.* a prehistoric sepulchral stone tomb or casket. [Welsh, from L *cista.* See CIST[1]]

**cistern** /'sɪstən/, *n.* **1.** a reservoir, tank, or vessel for holding water or other liquid. **2.** *Anat.* a reservoir or receptacle of some natural fluid of the body. [ME, from L *cisterna,* from *cista* box]

**cis-trans isomerism** /ˌsɪs-trænz aɪ'sɒmərɪzəm/, *n.* a form of isomerism occurring in chemical compounds which contain a double bond. Like groups on the same side of the plan of the double bond are called the *cis*-form, like groups on opposite sides are called the *trans*-form. Also, **geometric isomerism.**

**cit.,** **1.** citation. **2.** cited.

**citadel** /'sɪtədɛl/, *n.* **1.** a fortress in or near a city, intended to keep the inhabitants in subjection, or, in a siege, to form a final point of defence. **2.** any strongly fortified place; a stronghold. **3.** a heavily armoured structure on a warship. [F *citadelle,* from It. *cittadella,* from *città* CITY]

**citation** /saɪ'teɪʃən/, *n.* **1.** the act of citing or quoting. **2.** the quoting of a passage, book, author, etc.; a reference to an authority or a precedent. **3.** a passage cited; a quotation. **4.** mention or enumeration. **5.** call or summons, esp. to appear in court. **6.** a document containing such a summons. **7.** *Mil.* mention of a soldier or unit, in orders, usu. for gallantry. [ME *citacion,* from L *citātio*] – **citatory,** *adj.*

**cite** /saɪt/, *v.t.,* **cited, citing.** **1.** to quote (a passage, book, author, etc.), esp. as an authority. **2.** to mention in support, proof, or confirmation; refer to as an example. **3.** to summon officially or authoritatively to appear in court. **4.** to summon or call; rouse to action: *cited to the field of battle.* **5.** to call to mind; mention: *citing my own praise.* **6.** *Mil.* to mention (a soldier, unit, etc.) in orders, as for gallantry. [late ME, from L *citāre,* frequentative of *ciēre, cīre,* move, excite, call] – **citable, citeable,** *adj.*

**cithara** /ˈsɪθərə/, *n.* →**kithara.** [L form of KITHARA]

**cither** /ˈsɪθə/, *n.* →**cittern.** Also, **cithern** /ˈsɪθən/. [L *cithara* KITHARA]

**citied** /ˈsɪtid/, *adj.* **1.** occupied by a city or cities. **2.** formed into or like a city.

**citified** /ˈsɪtifaɪd/, *adj.* having city habits, fashions, etc.

**citizen** /ˈsɪtəzən/, *n.* **1.** a member, native or naturalised, of a state or nation (as distinguished from *alien*). **2.** a person owing allegiance to a government and entitled to its protection. **3.** an inhabitant of a city or town, esp. one entitled to its privileges or franchises. **4.** an inhabitant or denizen. **5.** a civilian (as distinguished from a soldier, police officer, etc.). **6.** **citizen of the world,** a person who is concerned about all nations, not just his own. [ME *citisein,* from AF, var. of OF *citeain,* from *cite* CITY]

**citizen band radio,** *n.* point-to-point broadcasting on an assigned frequency band, with transmitters and receivers appropriate to individual use, as by truck drivers, etc.

**citizenry** /ˈsɪtəzənri/, *n., pl.* **-ries.** citizens collectively.

**citizenship** /ˈsɪtəzənʃɪp/, *n.* the status of a citizen, with its rights and duties.

**citole** /ˈsɪtoʊl, sɪˈtoʊl/, *n.* **1.** →**cittern.** **2.** →**kithara.**

**citra-,** a prefix synonymous with **cis-**. [L, representing *citrā,* adv. and prep., akin to *cis.* See CIS-]

**citral** /ˈsɪtrəl/, *n.* a liquid aldehyde, $C_9H_{15}CHO$, with a strong lemon-like smell, obtained from the oils of lemon, orange, etc., used in perfumery. [CITR(US) + AL(DEHYDE)]

**citrate** /ˈsɪtreɪt, ˈsaɪ-/, *n.;* /sɪˈtreɪt, saɪˈtreɪt/, *v.,* **-trated, -trating.** *–n.* **1.** a salt or ester of citric acid. *–v.t.* **2.** to treat with a citrate, esp. with sodium citrate.

**citreous** /ˈsɪtriəs/, *adj.* lemon yellow; greenish yellow. [L *citreus* of the citron tree]

**citric acid** /sɪtrɪk ˈæsəd/, *n.* an organic acid containing three carboxyl groups, $C_6H_8O_7$, occurring in small amounts in almost all living cells as a component of the citric acid cycle, and in greater amounts in many fruits, esp. in limes and lemons.

**citric acid cycle,** *n.* a cyclic system of reactions, occurring in almost all living cells, whereby pyruvic acid is metabolised to carbon dioxide, and the energy thereby liberated is trapped as chemical energy for use in biosynthesis, etc.; tricarboxylic acid cycle; Krebs cycle.

**citrine** /ˈsɪtrən/, *adj.* **1.** pale yellow; lemon-coloured. *–n.* **2.** a pale yellow colour. **3.** a pellucid yellow variety of quartz. [ME, from F *citrin,* from L *citrus* citron tree]

**citron** /ˈsɪtrən/, *n.* **1.** a pale yellow fruit resembling the lemon but larger and with thicker rind, borne by a small tree or large bush, *Citrus medica,* allied to the lemon and lime. **2.** the tree itself. **3.** the rind of the fruit, candied or preserved. *–adj.* **4.** pale yellow: *a citron dress.* [F, from It. *citrone,* from L *citrus* citron tree]

**citronella** /sɪtrəˈnɛlə/, *n.* a fragrant grass, *Cymbopogon nardus,* of southern Asia, cultivated as the source of an oil (**citronella oil**) used in making liniment, perfume, and soap. [NL, named from its citron-like smell]

**citronellal** /sɪtrəˈnɛləl/, *n.* a colourless, liquid aldehyde, $C_9H_{17}CHO$, found in essential oils, and used as a flavouring agent and in the perfume industry.

**citron wood** /ˈsɪtrən wʊd/, *n.* **1.** the wood of the citron. **2.** the wood of the sandarac.

**citrus** /ˈsɪtrəs/, *n.* **1.** any tree or shrub of the genus *Citrus,* which includes the citron, lemon, lime, orange, grapefruit, etc. *–adj.* **2.** Also, **citrous.** of or pertaining to such trees or shrubs: *citrus fruit.* [L]

**cittern** /ˈsɪtən/, *n.* **1.** an old musical instrument, related to the guitar, having a flat pear-shaped soundbox and wire strings. **2.** →**zither.** Also, **cither, cithern, gittern, zittern.** [b. L *cithara* KITHARA and GITTERN]

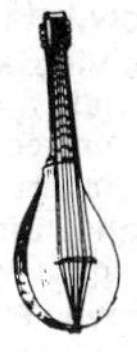

cittern

**city** /ˈsɪti/, *n., pl.* **cities.** **1. a.** a large or important town; a town so nominated. **b.** an area within a large and extended city which has been nominated as a city even though it is essentially suburban as the City of Parramatta within Greater Sydney or the City of Nunawading within Greater Melbourne. **c.** the central business area of a city. **2.** an urban area the extent of which is subject at all times to redefinition but which **a.** (in the cases of Adelaide, Melbourne, Sydney and Perth between 1839 and 1842) was originally so nominated by royal charter **b.** in New South Wales, South Australia, Tasmania (by special Act), and Western Australia, was originally so nominated by a Colonial or subsequently a State Government on the basis of its population, its annual revenue, the presence of a cathedral, etc. **3.** *Brit.* **a.** a borough on which the title of city has been conferred by the crown. **b.** a town which has, or has had a cathedral. **c.** **the city,** the part of London in which commercial and financial interests are chiefly centred. **4.** *U.S.* an incorporated municipality, usu. governed by a mayor and a board of aldermen or councillors. **5.** *Canada.* a municipality of high rank, usu. based on population. **6.** a city-state. **7.** the inhabitants of a city collectively. [ME *cite,* from OF, from L *cīvitas* citizenship, the state, a city]

**city desk** /ˈ– dɛsk/, *n.* **1.** *Brit.* the section of a newspaper handling financial news. **2.** *U.S.* the section of a newspaper handling local news.

**city father** /– ˈfaðə/, *n.* one of the officials and prominent citizens of a city.

**city hall** /– ˈhɔl/, *n.* (in some cities) a building housing the administrative offices of a city; town hall.

**city slicker** /ˈ– slɪkə/, *n.* an often flashily dressed and superficially knowing person who shows considerable adroitness in dealing with a city environment.

**city-state** /sɪti-ˈsteɪt/, *n.* a sovereign state consisting of an autonomous city with its dependencies.

**civet** /ˈsɪvət/, *n.* **1.** a yellowish, unctuous substance with a strong musklike smell, obtained from a pouch in the genital region of civets and used in perfumery. **2.** any of the catlike, carnivorous mammals of southern Asia and Africa (family Viverridae) having glands in the genital region that secrete civet. Also, **civet cat** (for defs 2 and 3). [F *civette,* from It. *zibetto,* from Ar. *zabād*]

African civet

**civic** /ˈsɪvɪk/, *adj.* **1.** of or pertaining to a city; municipal: *civic problems.* **2.** of or pertaining to citizenship; civil: *civic duties.* **3.** of citizens: *civic pride.* [L *cīvicus,* from *cīvis* citizen]

**civic centre** /ˈ– sɛntə/, *n.* the part of a town or city where municipal or civic authorities and public amenities are grouped.

**civic-minded** /sɪvɪk-ˈmaɪndəd/, *adj.* interested in civic affairs; public-spirited.

**civics** /ˈsɪvɪks/, *n.* **1.** the science of civic affairs. **2.** a school subject giving training in good citizenship.

**civil** /ˈsɪvəl/, *adj.* **1.** of or consisting of citizens: *civil life, civil society.* **2.** of the commonwealth or state: *civil affairs.* **3.** of citizens in their ordinary capacity, or the ordinary life and affairs of citizens (distinguished from *military, ecclesiastical, etc.*). **4.** of the citizen as an individual: *civil liberty.* **5.** befitting a citizen: *a civil duty.* **6.** of, or in a condition of, social order or organised government; civilised. **7.** polite; courteous. **8.** not rude or discourteous; polite but without warmth. **9.** (of divisions of time) legally recognised in the ordinary affairs of life: *the civil year.* **10.** *Law.* **a.** of or in agreement with Roman civil law. **b.** of the civil law, as the medieval and modern law derived from the Roman system. **c.** pertaining to the private rights of individuals and to legal proceedings connected with these (distinguished from *criminal, military,* or *political*). [ME *civile,* from L *cīvīlis* pertaining to citizens]

**civil day** /'– deɪ/, *n.* See **day** (def. 3d).

**civil defence** /– də'fɛns/, *n.* the emergency measures to be taken by an organised body of civilian volunteers for the protection of life and property in the case of a natural disaster or an attack or invasion by an enemy.

**civil disobedience** /– dɪsə'bidiəns/, *n.* a refusal, usu. on political grounds, to obey laws, pay taxes, etc.

**civil engineer** /– ɛndʒə'nɪə/, *n.* one versed in the design, construction, and maintenance of public works, such as roads, bridges, dams, canals, aqueducts, harbours, large buildings, etc.

**civil engineering** /– ɛndʒə'nɪərɪŋ/, *n.* the action, work, or profession of a civil engineer.

**civilian** /sə'vɪljən/, *n.* **1.** one engaged in civil pursuits (distinguished from a soldier, etc.) *–adj.* **2.** relating to non-military life and activities.

**civilianise** /sə'vɪljənaɪz/, *v.t.,* **-nised, -nising.** to remove from army control, esp. by replacing army personnel with civilians. – **civilianisation** /səvɪljənaɪ'zeɪʃən/, *n.*

**civilisation** /sɪvəlaɪ'zeɪʃən/, *n.* **1.** an advanced state of human society, in which a high level of art, science, religion, and government has been reached. **2.** those people or nations that have reached such a state. **3.** the type of culture, society, etc., of a specific group: *Greek civilisation.* **4.** the act or process of civilising. Also, **civilization.**

**civilise** /'sɪvəlaɪz/, *v.t.,* **-lised, -lising.** to make civil; bring out of a savage state; elevate in social and individual life; enlighten; refine. Also, **civilize.** [ML *cīvīlizāre.* See CIVIL, -ISE[1]] – **civilisable,** *adj.* – **civiliser,** *n.*

**civilised** /'sɪvəlaɪzd/, *adj.* **1.** having an advanced culture, society, etc. **2.** polite; well-bred; refined. **3.** of or pertaining to civilised people. Also, **civilized.**

**civility** /sə'vɪləti/, *n., pl.* **-ties. 1.** courtesy; politeness. **2.** a polite attention or expression. **3.** (*usu. pl.*) polite conversation. **4.** *Archaic.* civilisation; culture; good breeding.

**civil law** /sɪvəl 'lɔ/, *n.* **1.** the laws of a state or nation regulating ordinary private matters (distinguished from criminal, military, or political matters). **2.** the body of law proper to the city or state of Rome. **3.** the systems of law derived from Roman law (distinguished from *common law, canon law*). **4.** the law of a state (distinguished from other kinds of law, as *international law*).

**civil liberty** /– 'lɪbəti/, *n.* complete liberty of opinion, etc., restrained only as much as necessary for the public good.

**civil list** /'– lɪst/, *n. Brit.* the provision of money by Parliament for the monarch and his household.

**civilly** /'sɪvəli/, *adv.* **1.** politely; considerately; gently. **2.** in accordance with civil law.

**civil marriage** /sɪvəl 'mærɪdʒ/, *n.* a marriage performed by a government official rather than a clergyman.

**civil rights** /– 'raɪts/, *n. pl.* **1.** the personal rights of the individual in society. **2.** *U.S.* rights to personal liberty established by the 13th and 14th Amendments to the Constitution and other Congressional acts.

**civil servant** /– 'sɜvənt/, *n.* →**public servant.**

**civil service** /– 'sɜvəs/, *n.* →**public service.**

**civil war** /– 'wɔ/, *n.* a war between parties, regions, etc., within their own country.

**civvies** /'sɪviz/, *n.pl. Colloq.* civilian clothes (opposed to *military dress*).

**civvy** /'sɪvi/, *n. Colloq.* civilian.

**civvy street** /'– strit/, *n. Colloq.* civilian life.

**C.J.,** chief justice.

**Ck.,** Creek.

**CKD** /si keɪ 'di/, *adj.* of or pertaining to a car which is imported in parts and then assembled. [abbrev. (*C*)*ompletely* (*K*)*nocked* (*D*)*own*]

**cl.,** **1.** centilitre. **2.** council.

**clabber** /'klæbə/, *n.* **1.** →**bonnyclabber.** *–v.i.* **2.** (of milk) to become thick in souring. [Irish *clabar,* short for *bainne clabair* bonnyclabber, curds]

**clachan** /'klakən/, *n.* a small village or hamlet. [Gaelic, from *clach* stone]

**clack** /klæk/, *v.i.* **1.** to make a quick, sharp sound, or a succession of such sounds, as by striking or cracking. **2.** to talk rapidly and continuously, or with sharpness and abruptness; chatter. **3.** to cluck or cackle. *–v.t.* **4.** to utter by clacking. **5.** to cause to clack. *–n.* **6.** a clacking sound. **7.** something that clacks, as a rattle. **8.** rapid, continuous talk; chatter. [ME *clacke(n)*; imitative] – **clacker,** *n.*

**clackbox** /'klækbɒks/, *n.* a box which contains a clackvalve.

**clackers** /'klækəz/, *n.pl. Colloq.* false teeth.

**clackvalve** /'klækvælv/, *n.* a simple non-return valve, as in a locomotive.

**Clactonian** /klæk'toʊniən/, *adj.* of, pertaining to, or characteristic of a Lower Palaeolithic culture in England marked by the production of tools made from stone flakes. [named after *Clacton(-on-sea),* a town in England, where the tools were first unearthed + -IAN]

**clad** /klæd/, *v.* a past tense and past participle of **clothe.**

**cladding** /'klædɪŋ/, *n.* **1.** a covering of any kind, esp. one attached to a building structure, a lock-gate, or the like. **2.** *Physics.* the process of covering a fuel element in a nuclear reactor with a thin layer of another metal, in order to prevent corrosion and the escape of fission products. **3.** *Obs.* clothing.

**clado-,** a word element meaning 'sprout', 'branch'. Also, before vowels, **clad-.** [combining form representing Gk *kládos* sprout]

**cladode** /'klædoʊd/, *n.* a leaf-like flattened branch or stem. Also, **cladophyll** /'klædəfɪl/.

cladode

**clag** /klæg/, *n.* **1.** glue. **2.** anything which is gelatinous or thick in texture, esp. heavy, indigestible food. **3.** *Aeronautics Colloq.* clouds. [Trademark for a brand of glue; from Brit. d., from ME *claggen* to daub with mud] – **claggy,** *adj.*

**claim** /kleɪm/, *v.t.* **1.** to demand by or as by virtue of a right; demand as a right or as due. **2.** to assert, and demand the recognition of (a right, title, possession, etc.); assert one's right to. **3.** to assert or maintain as a fact. **4.** to require as due or fitting. **5.** to need, esp. to need deservingly. *–n.* **6.** a demand for something as due; an assertion of a right or alleged right. **7.** an assertion of something as a fact. **8.** a right to claim or demand; a just title to something. **9.** that which is claimed; a piece of public land to which formal claim is made for mining or other purposes. **10.** a payment demanded in accordance with an insurance policy, etc. [ME *claime(n),* from OF *claimer, clamer,* from L *clāmāre* call] – **claimable,** *adj.* – **claimer,** *n.*

**claimant** /'kleɪmənt/, *n.* one who makes a claim.

**claimholder** /'kleɪmhoʊldə/, *n.* the holder of a mining claim.

**clairaudience** /klɛər'ɔdiəns/, *n.* the alleged power of hearing voices of spirits, etc., not audible to normal ears. – **clairaudient,** *n., adj.*

**clairsentience** /klɛə'sɛntiəns/, *n.* the alleged power of receiving messages from spirits, etc., by touching particular objects. – **clairsentient** *n., adj.*

**clairvoyance** /klɛə'vɔɪəns/, *n.* **1.** the alleged power of seeing objects or actions beyond the natural range of the senses. **2.** quick intuitive knowledge of things; perception. [F]

**clairvoyant** /klɛə'vɔɪənt/, *adj.* **1.** having the power of seeing objects or actions beyond the natural range of the senses. *–n.* **2.** a clairvoyant person. [F, from *clair* clear + *voyant,* ppr. of *voir* see, from L *vidēre*]

**clam**[1] /klæm/, *n., v.,* **clammed, clamming.** *–n.* **1.** any of various bivalve molluscs, as the giant clams of the family Tridacnidae of tropical waters, or certain smaller edible species, as the quahog. **2.** *Colloq.* a secretive or silent person. *–v.i.* **3.** *U.S.* to gather or dig clams. **4. clam up,** *Colloq.* to be silent. **5. clam up on,** *Colloq.* to refuse to talk to (someone). [special use of CLAM[2], with reference to the shell]

clam[1]

**clam**[2] /klæm/, *n.* **1.** →**clamp**[1] (def. 1). **2.** (*pl.*) →**pincers** (def. 1). [ME; OE *clamm* band, bond]

**clamant** /'kleɪmənt/, *adj.* **1.** clamorous. **2.** urgent. [L *clāmans,* ppr., crying out]

**clamatorial** /klæmə'tɔriəl/, *adj.* of or pertaining to the Clamatores, a large group of passerine birds with relatively simple vocal organs and little power of song, as the flycatchers. [NL *Clāmātores* (pl. of L *clāmātor* one who cries out) + -IAL]

**clambake** /'klæmbeɪk/, *n. U.S.* **1.** a picnic by the sea, at which the baking of clams (usu. on hot stones under seaweed) is a main feature. **2.** *Colloq.* any social gathering, esp. a very gay one. **3.** *Colloq.* a bungled or unsuccessful performance or rehearsal.

**clamber** /'klæmbə/, *v.i., v.t.* **1.** to climb, using both feet and hands; climb with effort or difficulty. *–n.* **2.** a clambering. [ME *clambren, clameren,* irregularly formed frequentative of CLIMB; cf. *clamb,* obs. pt. of CLIMB] – **clamberer,** *n.*

**clammy** /'klæmi/, *adj.,* **-mier, -miest.** covered with a cold, sticky moisture; cold and damp. [? Flem. *klammig* sticky; akin to OE *clǣman* anoint, smear] – **clamminess,** *n.*

**clamorous** /'klæmərəs/, *adj.* **1.** full of, marked by, or of the nature of clamour; vociferous; noisy. **2.** vigorous in demands or complaints. – **clamorously,** *adv.* – **clamorousness,** *n.*

**clamour** /'klæmə/, *n.* **1.** a loud outcry. **2.** a vehement expression of desire or dissatisfaction. **3.** popular outcry. **4.** any loud and continued noise. *–v.i.* **5.** to make a clamour; raise an outcry. *–v.t.* **6.** to drive, force, put, etc., by clamouring. **7.** to utter noisily. **8.** *Obs.* to disturb with clamour. Also, *U.S.,* **clamor.** [ME, from OF, from L *clāmor* a cry, shout] – **clamourer,** *n.*

**clamp**[1] /klæmp/, *n.* **1.** a device, usu. of some rigid material, for strengthening or supporting objects or fastening them together. **2.** an appliance with opposite sides or parts that may be screwed or otherwise brought together to hold or compress something. **3.** one of a pair of movable pieces, made of lead or other soft material, for covering the jaws of a vice and enabling it to grasp without bruising. **4.** *Naut.* **a.** a device to secure a spar in a clutch. **b.** a heavy timber acting as a bearer for a deckbeam in a wooden ship. *–v.t.* **5.** to fasten with or fix in a clamp. **6.** to press firmly. *–v.i.* **7. clamp down,** *Colloq.* to become more strict. [MD *klampe* clamp, cleat]

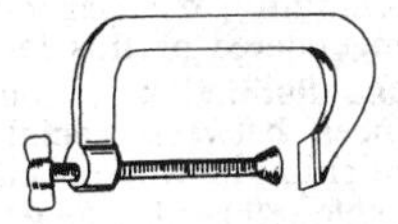

clamp (def. 2)

**clamp**[2] /klæmp/, *v.i.* **1.** to tread heavily; clump. *–n.* **2.** a heavy tread. [imitative]

**clamp**[3] /klæmp/, *n.* **1.** (*Brit.*) a stack of root vegetables, esp. potatoes, stored under earth. **2.** a pile of bricks for burning in the open air. *–v.t.* **3.** to stack (potatoes, etc.). [MD *klamp;* akin to CLUMP]

**clampdown** /'klæmpdaʊn/, *n.* a sudden enforcement, restriction, or stoppage: *a clampdown on the sale of drugs.*

**clamper** /'klæmpə/, *n.* an iron frame with sharp prongs, fastened to the sole of the shoe to prevent slipping on ice.

**clamshell** /'klæmʃɛl/, *n.* **1.** the shell of a clam. **2.** a dredging bucket made of two similar pieces hinged together at one end. **3.** →**eyelid** (def. 2).

**clan** /klæn/, *n.* **1.** a group of families or households, as among the Scots, the heads of which claim descent from a common ancestor. **2.** a group of people of common descent. **3.** a clique, set, society, or party. **4.** *Anthrop.* an association of lineages which have certain interests in common, as the regulation of marriage, common territory, rituals, etc. [Gaelic *clann* family, stock]

**clancy** /'klænsi/, *n. Colloq.* (in the petrol industry) an overflow or spillage of petrol, as when filling a tanker. [from the poem *Clancy of the Overflow,* by Australian poet A.B. (Banjo) Paterson, 1864-1941]

**clandestine** /klæn'dɛstən/, *adj.* secret; private; concealed (generally implying craft or deception): *a clandestine marriage.* [L *clandestīnus*] – **clandestinely,** *adv.* – **clandestineness,** *n.*

**clang** /klæŋ/, *v.i.* **1.** to give out a loud, resonant sound, as metal when struck; ring loudly or harshly. **2.** to emit a harsh cry, as geese. *–v.t.* **3.** to cause to resound or ring loudly. *–n.* **4.** a clanging sound. **5.** the harsh cry of some birds, esp. geese. [imitative. Cf. L *clangere*]

**clanger** /'klæŋə/, *n. Colloq.* a glaring error or mistake, as an embarrassing remark: *to drop a clanger.*

**clangour** /'klæŋə, 'klæŋgə/, *n.* **1.** a loud, resonant sound, as of pieces of metal struck together or of a trumpet; a clang. **2.** clamorous noise. *–v.i.* **3.** to make a clangour; clang. Also, **clangor.** [L] – **clangourous,** *adj.* – **clangourously,** *adv.*

**clank** /klæŋk/, *n.* **1.** a sharp, hard, metallic sound: *the clank of chains.* *–v.i.* **2.** to make such a sound. **3.** to move with such sounds. *–v.t.* **4.** to cause to resound sharply, as metal in collision. [D *klank*]

**clannish** /'klænɪʃ/, *adj.* **1.** of, pertaining to, or characteristic of a clan. **2.** disposed to adhere closely, as the members of a clan. **3.** imbued with or influenced by the sentiments, prejudices, etc., peculiar to clans. – **clannishly,** *adv.* – **clannishness,** *n.*

**clanship** /'klænʃɪp/, *n.* **1.** the system of clans; the association of families under a chieftain. **2.** a feeling of loyalty to a clan.

**clansman** /'klænzmən/, *n., pl.* **-men.** a member of a clan. – **clanswoman** /'klænzwʊmən/, *n. fem.*

**clap**[1] /klæp/, *v.,* **clapped, clapping.** *n. –v.t.* **1.** to strike with a quick, smart blow, producing an abrupt, sharp sound; slap; pat. **2.** to strike together resoundingly, as the hands to express applause. **3.** to applaud in this manner. **4.** to flap (the wings). **5.** to put, place, apply, etc., promptly and effectively. **6. clap eyes on,** *Colloq.* to catch sight of. **7. clap on,** *Colloq.* to increase: *to clap on speed.* *–v.i.* **8.** to make an abrupt, sharp sound, as of bodies in collision. **9.** to move or strike with such a sound. **10.** to clap the hands, as in applause. **11.** to sit down abruptly, crouch suddenly. **12. clap out,** *Colloq.* to break down; cease to function: *the car has clapped out.* *–n.* **13.** the act or sound of clapping. **14.** a resounding blow; a slap. **15.** a loud and abrupt or explosive noise, as of thunder. **16.** a sudden stroke, blow, or act. **17.** an applauding; applause. **18.** →**clapper. 19.** *Obs.* a sudden mishap. [ME *clappen,* OE *clæppan,* c. D and LG *klappen*]

**clap**[2] /klæp/, *n. Colloq.* gonorrhoea, or any other venereal disease (usu. prec. by *the*). [MF *clapier* brothel]

**clapboard** /'klæpbɔd/, *n.* **1.** weatherboard. *–adj.* **2.** of or pertaining to clapboard. *–v.t.* **3.** to cover with clapboards. [MD *klapholt,* with BOARD for *-holt* wood]

**clapmatch** /'klæpmætʃ/, *n.* **1.** the female hair seal or sea lion *Neophoca cinerea.* **2.** any female seal.

**clapnet** /'klæpnɛt/, *n.* a net, as used by entomologists, which closes quickly when a string is pulled.

**clapped-out** /'klæpt-aʊt/, *adj.* **1.** exhausted; weary. **2.** broken; in a state of disrepair.

**clapper** /'klæpə/, *n.* **1.** one who or that which claps. **2.** the tongue of a bell. **3.** *Colloq.* the tongue. **4.** any clapping contrivance. **5.** (*pl.*) clapper board.

**clapperboard** /'klæpəbɔd/, *n.* (in film-making) a board showing details of a scene and having a clapper to mark the soundtrack audibly, shot at the beginning of a take for the editor's guidance.

**clapper bridge** /'klæpə brɪdʒ/, *n.* an ancient type of bridge made of large slabs of stone, some piled to make rough piers and longer ones laid across them to make a roadway.

**clapper loader** /'– loʊdə/, *n.* (in film-making) an assistant responsible for operating the clapperboard and for keeping record of film footage. Also, **clapper preparer.**

**clapping sticks** /'klæpɪŋ stɪks/, *n.pl. Music.* →**claves.**

**claptrap** /'klæptræp/, *n.* **1.** pretentious but insincere or empty language. **2.** nonsense; rubbish.

**claque** /klæk/, *n.* **1.** a set of hired applauders in a theatre. **2.** any group of persons ready to applaud from interested motives. [F, from *claquer* clap]

**clar.,** clarinet.

**clarabella** /klærə'bɛlə/, *n.* an organ stop which gives soft, sweet tones. [L *clāra* (fem. of *clārus* clear) + *bella* (fem. of *bellus* beautiful)]

**clarendon** /'klærəndən/, *n.* a condensed form of printing type, like roman in outline but with thicker lines.

**Clare Riesling** /klɛə 'rizlɪŋ/, *n.* a white wine grape variety grown extensively in the Clare District of South Australia.

**claret** /'klærət/, *n.* **1.** the red (originally the light red or yellowish) table wine of Bordeaux, France. **2.** a similar wine made elsewhere. **3.** Also, **claret red.** a deep purplish red. **4.**

*Colloq.* blood. *–adj.* **5.** deep purplish red. [ME, from OF: somewhat clear, light-coloured, diminutive of *cler,* from L *clārus* clear]

**claret cup** /ˈ– kʌp/, *n.* an iced beverage made of claret with lemon juice, brandy (or other spirits), fruit, sugar, etc.

**clarify** /ˈklærəfaɪ/, *v.t., v.i.,* **-fied, -fying. 1.** to make or become clear, pure, or intelligible. **2.** to make a liquid clear by removing sediment, often by heating gently: *clarified butter.* [ME *clarifie(n),* from OF *clarifier,* from LL *clārificāre*] – **clarification** /klærəfəˈkeɪʃən/, *n.* **-clarifier,** *n.*

**clarinet** /klærəˈnɛt/, *n.* a wind instrument in the form of a cylindrical tube with a single reed attached to its mouthpiece. Also, **clarionet** /klæriəˈnɛt/. [F *clarinette,* diminutive of *clarine* clarion] – **clarinettist,** *n.*

**clarino** /klæˈrinoʊ/, *n.* **1.** the high register of the trumpet. **2.** a clarion. **3.** an organ stop, giving a trumpet-like tone.

**clarion** /ˈklæriən/, *adj.* **1.** clear and shrill. **2.** inspiring; rousing. *–n.* **3.** an old kind of small-bore trumpet used for high-sounding passages; Bach trumpet; clarino. **4.** *Poetic.* the sound of this instrument. **5.** any similar sound. **6.** a rousing call. [ME, from ML *clārio,* from L *clārus* clear]

clarinet

**clarity** /ˈklærəti/, *n.* clearness: *clarity of thinking.* [L *clāritas;* replacing ME *clarte,* from OF]

**Clark cell** /klak ˈsɛl/, *n.* (in physics) a standard primary cell producing 1.4328 volts at 15°C which consists of a mercury cathode and a zinc amalgam anode both dipping into a saturated solution of zinc sulphate.

**clarkia** /ˈklakiə/, *n.* any of the annual plants belonging to the genus *Clarkia,* native to North America, but many, as *C. elegans,* commonly cultivated for their showy flowers. [named after Captain William *Clark,* 1770-1838, U.S. explorer]

**claro** /ˈklaroʊ/, *adj., n., pl.* **-ros.** *–adj.* **1.** (of cigars) light-coloured and, usu., mild. *–n.* **2.** such a cigar. [Sp., from L *clārus* clear]

**clart** /klat/, *v.t. Scot.* to smear or spot with something sticky or dirty. [orig. obscure] – **clarty,** *adj.*

**clary** /ˈklɛəri/, *n., pl.* **claries.** any of several ornamental species of herbaceous plants of the labiate genus *Salvia,* as **meadow clary,** *S. pratensis.* [late ME *sclarreye,* replacing OE *slarie.* Cf. OF *sclaree,* ML *sclarea*]

**clash** /klæʃ/, *v.i.* **1.** to make a loud, harsh noise. **2.** to collide, esp. noisily. **3.** to conflict; disagree, as of temperaments, colours, etc. **4.** to coincide unfortunately (esp. of events). *–v.t.* **5.** to strike with a resounding or violent collision. **6.** to produce (sound, etc.) by, or as by, collision. *–n.* **7.** the noise of, or as of, a collision. **8.** a collision, esp. a noisy one. **9.** a conflict; opposition, esp. of views or interests. [b. CLAP[1] and DASH[1]]

**clasp** /klæsp, klasp/, *n.* **1.** a device, usu. of metal, for fastening things or parts together; any fastening or connection; anything that clasps. **2.** a grasp; an embrace. **3.** a military decoration consisting of a small design of metal fixed on the ribbon which represents a medal that the bearer has been awarded, the clasp usually indicating an additional award. *–v.t.* **4.** to fasten with, or as with, a clasp. **5.** to furnish with a clasp. **6.** to take hold of with an enfolding grasp: *clasping hands.* [ME *claspe(n), clapse(n);* orig. uncert.]

**clasper** /ˈklæspə, klaspə/, *n.* **1.** one who or that which clasps. **2.** *Zool.* a tube-like modification of the pelvic fin of male sharks and rays by which sperm are introduced into the female.

**clasp-knife** /ˈklæsp-naɪf, ˈklasp-/, *n.* a knife with a blade (or blades) folding into the handle.

**clasp-nail** /ˈklæsp-neɪl, ˈklasp-/, *n.* a flat-headed nail that clasps the wood.

**class** /klas/, *n.* **1.** a number of persons, things, animals, etc., regarded as forming one group through the possession of similar qualities; a kind; sort. **2.** any division of persons or things according to rank or grade. **3.** (in universities) a division of candidates into groups, according to merit on the basis of final examinations for degrees. **4. a.** a group of pupils taught together. **b.** a period during which they are taught. **c.** *U.S.* a number of students in a school or university, pursuing the same course or graduated in the same year. **5.** a social stratum sharing essential economic, political or cultural characteristics, and having the same social position. **6.** the system of dividing society; caste. **7.** social rank, esp. high rank. **8.** *Colloq.* acceptable style in dress or manner: *a person of class.* **9.** a grade of accommodation in railway carriages, ships, aeroplanes, etc.: *first class.* **10.** drafted or conscripted soldiers, or men available for draft or conscription, all of whom were born in the same year. **11.** *Zool., Bot.* the usual major subdivision of a phylum or subphylum, commonly comprising a plurality of orders, as the gastropods, the mammals, the angiosperms. **12.** *Gram.* a form class. **13.** (in early Methodism) one of several small companies, each composed of about twelve members under a leader, into which each society or congregation was divided. *–v.t.* **14.** to arrange, place, or rate as to class: *to class justice with wisdom.* **15.** *Agric.* **a.** to grade wool into even lines according to type, yield, and commercial value: *wool classing.* **b.** to cull and select a flock of sheep: *sheep classing.* **c.** to grade rams according to sale value. **d.** to divide a flock of stud ewes into various groups prior to mating. *–v.i.* **16.** to take or have a place in a particular class: *those who class as believers.* *–adj.* **17.** pertaining to a class, or class. **18.** *Colloq.* of high class. [earlier *classe,* from F, from L *classis* class (of people, etc.), army, fleet] – **classable,** *adj.* – **classer,** *n.*

**class.,** **1.** classic. **2.** classical. **3.** classification. **4.** classified.

**class action** /klas ˈækʃən/, *n.* a legal proceeding brought on by a group of people all with the same grievance or claim.

**class boat** /ˈ– boʊt/, *n.* a boat built to a particular set of rules or a particular design.

**class-conscious** /klas-ˈkɒnʃəs/, *adj.* **1.** acutely aware of belonging to a particular social class. **2.** showing hostility engendered by this feeling. – **class-consciousness,** *n.*

**class-distinction** /klas-dəsˈtɪŋkʃən/, *n.* **1.** awareness of differences between social classes. **2.** criteria used in distinguishing between social classes.

**classic** /ˈklæsɪk/, *adj.* **1.** of the first or highest class or rank. **2.** serving as a standard, model, or guide. **3.** of or characteristic of Greek and Roman antiquity, esp. with reference to literature and art. **4.** in the style of the ancient Greek and Roman literature or art; classical. **5.** of, or adhering to, an established set of artistic or scientific standards and methods. **6.** of literary or historical renown. **7.** balanced, simple, austere; pertaining to classicism. **8.** of or pertaining to a garment of simple and conventional cut, whose popularity is largely unaffected by changing fashion. *–n.* **9.** an author or a literary production of the first rank, esp. in Greek or Latin. **10.** (*pl.*) the literature of ancient Greece and Rome; the Greek and Latin languages. **11.** an artistic production of the highest class. **12.** one versed in the classics. **13.** one, as a painter or sculptor, who adheres to classical rules and models. **14.** one whose behaviour exactly conforms to a stereotype. **15.** something considered to be a perfect example of its type. **16.** a traditional race of special importance. **17. a.** *Horseracing.* a race in which only horses included in the Australian Stud Book are eligible to run. **b.** *Brit. Horseracing.* any of the five chief annual flat races for three-year-old horses, the Derby, the Oaks, the St Leger, the 1000-Guineas or the 2000-Guineas. [L *classicus* pertaining to a class, of the first or highest class]

**classical** /ˈklæsɪkəl/, *adj.* **1.** classic. **2.** (*sometimes cap.*) in accordance with ancient Greek and Roman models in literature or art, or with later systems of principles modelled upon them. **3.** pertaining to or versed in the ancient classics. **4.** restrained and simple; affected by classicism. **5.** conforming to established taste or critical standards; adhering to traditional forms. **6.** (of music) deemed to be serious or of intrinsic worth, often taking one of several traditional forms, as a sonata, symphony, etc., and distinguished from simpler and more widely popular music, as pop, folk, rock, etc., thought to be inferior, ephemeral and frivolous. **7.** (of music) following strict stylistic and rhythmic rules, esp. that composed before 1800 (opposed to *romantic*). **8.** (of music) of established value and fame: *classical jazz.* **9.** (of ballet) emphasising form, line and technique rather than dramatic or emotional content. **10.** teaching, or relating to, academic branches of knowledge (the humanities, general sciences, etc.), distinguished from technical subjects. – **classicality** /klæsə'kæləti/, *n.* – **classically,** *adv.*

**classical architecture** /– 'akətɛktʃə/, *n.* **1.** any architectural style distinguished by clarity and balance of design and plan, expressive of poise and dignity, and as a rule by the use of a Greek or Roman vocabulary. **2.** the architecture of Greek and Roman antiquity. **3.** the architectural style popular from 1770-1840, esp. in Europe, which sought to revive Greek and Roman architecture.

**classical economics** /– ɛkə'nɒmɪks/, *n.* a system of thought developed by Adam Smith and David Ricardo, according to which the wealth of nations is promoted by free competition with a minimum of government intervention and by division of labour (labour being the source of wealth).

**classical physics** /– 'fɪzɪks/, *n.* physics either before the quantum theory, or before the theory of relativity, or before both.

**classicise** /'klæsəsaɪz/, *v.,* **-cised, -cising.** *–v.t.* **1.** to make classic. *–v.i.* **2.** to conform to the classic style. Also, **classicize.**

**classicism** /'klæsəsɪzəm/, *n.* **1.** the principles of classical literature or art, or adherence to them. **2.** the classical style in literature or art, characterised esp. by attention to form with the general effect of regularity, simplicity, balance, proportion, and controlled emotion (contrasted with *romanticism*). **3.** a classical idiom or form. **4.** classical scholarship or learning. Also, **classicalism** /'klæsɪkə,lɪzəm/.

**classicist** /'klæsəsəst/, *n.* **1.** one who advocates the study of the ancient classics. **2.** an adherent of classicism in literature or art. **3.** an authority on Greek and Roman studies. Also, **classicalist** /'klæsɪkələst/.

**classification** /klæsəfə'keɪʃən/, *n.* **1.** the act or the result of classifying. **2.** the assignment of plants and animals to groups within a system of categories distinguished by structure, origin, etc. The usual series of categories is phylum (in zoology) or division (in botany), class, order, family, genus, species, and variety. **3.** one of the several degrees (restricted, confidential, secret, top secret, etc.) of security protection for government documents, papers, etc. **4.** (in libraries, etc.) a system for arranging publications according to broad fields of knowledge and specific subjects within each field. – **classificatory** /klæsəfə'keɪtəri/, *adj.*

**classified** /'klæsəfaɪd/, *adj.* **1.** arranged or distributed in classes; placed according to class. **2.** (of military and other government information) placed in categories in relation to security risk. *–n.pl.* **3.** classified ads. **4.** (of roads) having a classification number and receiving government financial assistance.

**classified ad** /– 'æd/, *n. Colloq.* a small newspaper advertisement, usu. single-column, esp. one advertising a vacancy, an object for sale, etc.

**classifier** /'klæsəfaɪə/, *n.* **1.** one who or that which classifies. **2.** in mineral dressing, a device which takes the ball-mill discharge and separates it into two portions, the finished product (which is ground as fine as desired) and oversize material.

**classify** /'klæsəfaɪ/, *v.t.,* **-fied, -fying. 1.** to arrange or distribute in classes; place according to class. **2.** to mark or otherwise declare (a document, paper, etc.) of value to an enemy, and limit and safeguard its handling and use. [L *classi(s)* CLASS + -FY] – **classifiable,** *adj.*

**class inclusion** /klas ɪn'kluʒən/, *n.* the logical relation between one class and a second when every object that belongs to the first class also belongs to the second. For example, the class of *men* is included in the class of *animals.*

**classis** /'klæsəs/, *n., pl.* **classes** /'klæsiz/. **1.** (in certain Reformed churches) the group of pastors and elders which governs a group of churches. **2.** the group of churches so governed. [L. See CLASS]

**classmate** /'klasmeɪt/, *n.* a member of the same class, as at school.

**class meaning** /klas 'minɪŋ/, *n.* **1.** the meaning of a grammatical category or a form class, common to all forms showing the category or to all members of the form class, as in the meaning of possession common to all English nouns in the possessive case. **2.** that part of the meaning of a linguistic form which it has by virtue of membership in a particular form class, as the past tense meaning of *ate* (opposed to *lexical meaning*).

**class resolution** /– rɛzə'luʃən/, *n.* a resolution passed by a specified class of shareholders.

**classroom** /'klasrum/, *n.* a room in a school, etc., in which classes meet.

**class war** /'klas wɔ/, *n.* **1.** conflict between different classes in the community. **2.** (in Marxist thought) the struggle for political and economic power carried on between capitalists and workers.

**classy** /klasi/, *adj. Colloq.* of high class, rank, or grade; stylish; fine.

**clastic** /'klæstɪk/, *adj.* **1.** *Biol.* breaking up into fragments or separate portions; dividing into parts; causing or undergoing disruption or dissolution: *clastic action, the clastic pole of an ovum.* **2.** pertaining to an anatomical model made up of detachable pieces. **3.** denoting or pertaining to rock or rocks composed of fragments of older rocks; fragmental. [Gk *klastós* broken + -IC]

**clathrate** /'klæθreɪt/, *adj.* resembling a lattice; divided or marked like latticework. [L *clāthrātus, pp.,* having a lattice]

**clathrate compound** /– 'kɒmpaʊnd/, *n.* an inclusion complex in which molecules of one substance are completely enclosed within the crystal lattice of the other, as argon within hydroquinone crystals.

**clatter** /'klætə/, *v.i.* **1.** to make a rattling sound, as of hard bodies striking rapidly together. **2.** to move rapidly with such a sound. **3.** to talk fast and noisily; chatter. *–v.t.* **4.** to cause to clatter. *–n.* **5.** a clattering noise; disturbance. **6.** noisy talk; din of voices. **7.** idle talk; gossip. [ME *clatren,* OE *clatrian,* of imitative orig. Cf. D *klateren* rattle]

**claudication** /klɔdə'keɪʃən/, *n.* a limp. [L *claudicātio,* from *claudus* lame]

**clause** /klɔz/, *n.* **1.** *Gram.* a group of words containing a subject and a predicate, forming part of a compound or complex sentence, or coextensive with a simple sentence. **2.** part of a written composition containing complete sense in itself, as a sentence or paragraph (in modern use commonly limited to such parts of legal documents, as of statutes, contracts, wills, etc.). [ME *claus,* from ML *clausa* in sense of L *clausula* clause] – **clausal,** *adj.*

**claustral** /'klɒstrəl/, *adj.* cloistral; cloister-like. [LL *claustrālis,* from *claustrum* enclosure, CLOISTER]

**claustrophobia** /klɒstrə'foʊbiə, klɔs-/, *n.* a morbid dread of confined places. [NL, from *claustro-* (combining form representing L *claustrum* enclosure) + *-phobia* -PHOBIA] – **claustrophobic,** *adj.*

**clavate** /'kleɪveɪt, -vət/, *adj.* club-shaped. [L *clāvātus,* pp., studded with nails; sense influenced by association with L *clāva* club]

**clavecina** /klævə'sinə/, *n.* →**harpsichord.**

**claver** /'klævə/, *Scot. –n.* **1.** idle talk. *–v.i.* **2.** to talk idly; gossip.

**claves** /kleɪvz/, *n. pl.* a musical instrument consisting of two resonant wooden sticks which are struck together; music sticks; clapping sticks; rhythm sticks.

**clavicembalo** /klævə'tʃɛmbəloʊ/, *n.* →**harpsichord.** [It.]

**clavichord** /'klævəkɔd/, *n.* an ancient keyboard instrument, in which the strings were softly struck with metal blades vertically projecting from the rear ends of the keys. [ML *clāvichordium,* from L *clāvi(s)* key + *chord(a)* string (see CHORD[1]) + *-ium* -IUM]

**clavicle** /'klævɪkəl/, *n.* **1.** a bone of the pectoral arch. **2.** (in man) either of two slender bones each articulating with the sternum and a scapula and forming the anterior part of a shoulder; the collarbone. [L *clāvicula,* diminutive of *clāvis* key] – **clavicular** /klə'vɪkjələ/, *adj.*



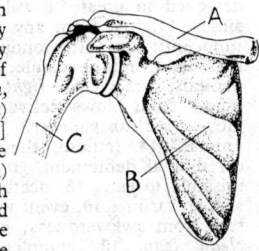

A, clavicle; B, scapula; C, humerus

**clavicorn** /'klævəkɔn/, *adj.* **1.** having club-shaped antennae, as many beetles of the group Clavicornia. **2.** belonging to this group. *–n.* **3.** a clavicorn beetle. [NL *clāvicornis,* from *clāvi-* (combining form representing *clāva* club) + *-cornis* horned] – **clavicornate** /klævə'kɔneɪt/, *adj.*

**clavier** /'klæviə, klə'vɪə/, *n.* **1.** the keyboard of a musical instrument. **2.** any musical instrument with a keyboard, as a harpsichord, clavichord, piano, or organ. [G, from F *clavier* keyboard, from L *clāvis* key]

**claviform** /'klævəfɔm/, *adj.* club-shaped; clavate.

**clavinet** /klævə'nɛt/, *n.* an electronic instrument similar in concept to a harpsichord. [Trademark]

**claw** /klɔ/, *n.* **1.** a sharp, usu. curved, nail on the foot of an animal. **2.** the foot of an animal armed with such nails. **3.** any part or thing resembling a claw, as the cleft end of the head of a hammer. **4.** the pincers of some shellfish and insects. **5.** *Bot.* the narrow basal region of a petal or sepal found in some types of flowers. *–v.t.* **6.** to tear, scratch, seize, pull, etc., with or as with claws. **7.** to scratch fiercely, as to relieve itching. **8.** to make, bring, etc., by clawing: *claw a hole.* **9.** *Naut.* (of or in a sailing ship) to beat to windward to get away from a danger, a lee shore, etc. (oft. fol. by *off*). **10.** to tear or scratch (fol. by *at*). [ME *clawen,* OE *clawian,* from *clawu,* n., c. G *Klaue*]

**claw-foot** /'klɔ-fʊt/, *n.* **1.** a condition in which the arch of the foot is abnormally high due to deformity of the metatarsal bones. **2.** a foot with such a deformity.

**claw hammer** /'klɔ hæmə/, *n.* a hammer having a head with one end curved and cleft for drawing out nails.

**claw-hammer coat** /ˌklɔ-hæmə 'koʊt/, *n. Colloq.* →**tail coat.**

**clay** /kleɪ/, *n.* **1.** a natural earthy material which is plastic when wet, consisting essentially of hydrated silicates of aluminium, and used for making bricks, pottery, etc. **2.** earth; mud. **3.** earth as the material from which the human body was originally formed. **4.** the human body. *–v.t.* **5.** to cover, mix or treat with clay. [ME; OE *clǣg,* c. D *klei* and G *Klei*] – **clayey** /'kleɪi/, *adj.* – **clayish,** *adj.*

**claymore** /'kleɪmɔ/, *n.* **1.** a heavy two-edged sword formerly used by the Scottish Highlanders. **2.** a basket-hilted broadsword, often singled-edged, formerly used by Highlanders.

**claypan** /'kleɪpæn/, *n.* a depression in the ground which retains water.

**clay pigeon** /kleɪ 'pɪdʒən/, *n.* a disc of baked clay or other material hurled into the air as a target to be shot at.

**clay pipe** /– 'paɪp/, *n.* a tobacco pipe made of clay.

**claystone** /'kleɪstoʊn/, *n.* →**argillite.**

**claytonia** /kleɪ'toʊniə/, *n.* any of the low, succulent herbs constituting the genus *Claytonia.* [named after Dr J. *Clayton,* 1685?-1773, American botanist]

**cld,** could.

**-cle,** variant of **-cule.** [L *-culus, -cula, -culum;* in some words, from F]

**clean** /klin/, *adj.* **1.** free from dirt or filth; unsoiled; unstained. **2. a.** free from foreign or extraneous matter. **b.** free of radioactivity. **3.** free from defect or blemish. **4.** free from disease: *a clean bill of health.* **5.** unadulterated; pure. **6.** entirely (or almost) without correction; easily readable: *clean printer's proofs.* **7.** free from encumbrances or obstructions: *a clean harbour.* **8.** (of a ship) **a.** having its bottom free of marine growth, etc. **b.** having a clean bill of health. **9.** (of timber) free from knots. **10.** *Aerodynamics.* designed to create a wake of as little turbulence as possible. **11.** free from any form of defilement; morally pure; innocent; upright; honourable. **12. a.** free of behaviour regarded as reprehensible, such as eye-gouging, attacks to the genitals, etc.: *a clean fight.* **b.** *Boxing.* of a boxer who scores points from blows delivered by the knuckle section of the gloves: *a clean puncher.* **13.** free from dirty habits, as of an animal. **14.** (among the Jews) **a.** (of persons) free from ceremonial defilement. **b.** (of animals, fowl, and fish) permissible to eat. **15.** neatly or evenly made or proportioned; shapely; trim. **16.** even; with a smooth edge or surface. **17.** free from awkwardness; not bungling; dexterous; adroit: *a clean leap.* **18.** complete; perfect: *a clean sweep.* **19.** *Weightlifting.* (of a lift) without touching the barbell against the body. *–adv.* **20.** in a clean manner; cleanly. **21.** wholly; completely; quite. **22.** *Cricket.* (bowled) by a ball, which breaks the wicket without touching the batsman or his bat. **23. come clean,** to make a full confession. *–v.t.* **24.** to make clean. **25. clean out, a.** to rid of dirt, etc. **b.** to use up; exhaust. **c.** to drive out by force. **d.** to empty or rid (a place) of contents, etc.: *clean out the pantry.* **e.** *Colloq.* to take all money from, esp. illegally: *to clean out the bank.* **26. clean up, a.** to rid of dirt, etc. **b.** to put in order; tidy up. **c.** to finish up; reach the end of. **d.** *Colloq.* to make (money, or the like) as profit, gain, etc. **e.** *Sport, etc.* to defeat crushingly: *Carlton cleaned up Richmond last Saturday.* *–v.i.* **27.** to perform or to undergo a process of cleaning. **28.** to get rid of dirt, etc. (fol. by *up*): *to clean up for dinner.* **29.** to make money or the like, as profit or gain. (fol. by *up*). [ME *clene,* OE *clǣne* pure, clear, c. D and G *klein* small] – **cleanable,** *adj.* – **cleanness,** *n.*

**clean bomb** /– 'bɒm/, *n.* →**neutron bomb.**

**clean-bowl** /klin-'boʊl/, *v.t.* (in cricket) to break the wicket without touching the batsman or his bat.

**clean cultivation** /ˌklin kʌltə'veɪʃən/, *n.* intensive cultivation of a paddock or orchard to remove all weed growth.

**clean-cut** /'klin-kʌt/, *adj.* **1.** distinctly outlined. **2.** well-shaped. **3.** definite. **4.** neatly dressed, wholesome: *a clean-cut gentleman.*

**cleaner** /'klinə/, *n.* **1.** one who or that which cleans. **2.** an apparatus or preparation for cleaning. **3. take (someone) to the cleaners,** to strip (someone) of all assets, money, etc., usu. in gambling.

**cleaner upper** /klinər 'ʌpə/, *n. Colloq.* (*joc.*) the person responsible for cleaning or tidying up.

**clean float** /'klin floʊt/, *n.* a shift in the currency value of a country in direct response to changes in the international money market.

**clean hands** /– 'hændz/, *n.pl.* **1.** a clear conscience. **2.** *Law.* the requirement that a plaintiff seeking relief should, in terms of his past conduct, be worthy of it. – **clean-handed,** *adj.*

**cleaning lady** /'klinɪŋ leɪdi/, *n.* →**domestic help.**

**cleanly** /'klinli, 'klɛnli/, *adj.,* **-lier, -liest,** *adv.* *–adj.* **1.** personally neat; careful to keep or make clean. **2.** habitually clean. **3.** *Obs.* cleansing; making clean. *–adv.* **4.** in a clean manner. – **cleanlily** /'klɛnləli/, *adv.* – **cleanliness** /'klɛnlinəs/, *n.*

**clean potato** /klin pə'teɪtoʊ/, *n. Colloq.* **1.** (formerly) a convict set free. **2.** a law-abiding person.

**cleanse** /klɛnz/, *v.t.,* **cleansed, cleansing.** **1.** to make clean. **2.** to remove by, or as by, cleaning: *his leprosy was cleansed.* [ME *clense(n),* OE *clǣnsian,* from *clǣne* clean] – **cleanser,** *n.*

**clean-shaven** /'klin-ʃeɪvən/, *adj.* **1.** having all the hairs shaved off. **2.** having facial hair shaved off.

**cleanskin** /'klinskɪn/, *n.* **1.** an unbranded animal. **2.** one who is free from blame, or has no record of police conviction. **3.** →**cleanskin nobby.**

**cleanskin nobby** /– 'nɒbi/, *n.* an opal found in an abandoned mine, which has been overlooked by previous miners.

**clean-up** /'klin-ʌp/, *n.* **1.** the act or process of cleaning and tidying. **2.** the act or process of cleaning up, esp. of gambling, vice, graft, etc. **3.** *Colloq.* a very large profit.

**clean weapon** /klin 'wɛpən/, *n.* a military weapon in which measures have been taken to reduce the amount of residual radioactivity relative to a normal weapon of the same energy yield.

**clear** /klɪə/, *adj.* **1.** free from darkness, obscurity, or cloudiness; light. **2.** bright; shining. **3.** transparent; pellucid: *good, clear wine.* **4.** of a pure, even colour: *a clear complexion.* **5.** distinctly perceptible to the eye, ear, or mind; easily seen, heard or understood. **6.** distinct; evident; plain. **7.** free from confusion, uncertainty, or doubt. **8.** perceiving or discerning distinctly: *a clear thinker.* **9.** convinced; certain. **10.** free from guilt or blame; innocent. **11.** serene; calm; untroubled. **12.** free from obstructions or obstacles; open: *a clear space.* **13.** unentangled or disengaged; free; quit or rid (fol. by *of*). **14.** not in code; in plain language. **15.** having no parts that protrude, are rough, etc. **16.** freed or emptied of contents, cargo, etc. **17.** without limitation or qualification: *a clear victory.* **18.** without obligation or liability; free from debt. **19.** without deduction or diminution: *a clear $100.* **20.** (of vowel sounds) light; resembling a front vowel in quality. **21. clear as mud,** *Colloq.* not clear; confused. *–adv.* **22.** in a clear manner; clearly; distinctly; entirely. *–v.t.* **23.** to make clear; free from darkness, cloudiness, muddiness, indistinctness, confusion, uncertainty, obstruction, contents, entanglement, obligation, liability, etc. **24.** to free from imputation, esp. of guilt; prove or declare to be innocent. **25.** to pass or get over without entanglement or collision. **26.** to pay (a debt) in full. **27.** to pass (cheques, etc.) through a clearing house. **28.** to free (a person, etc.) from debt. **29.** to gain as clear profit: *to clear $1000 in a transaction.* **30.** *Colloq.* to have approved for further action: *he cleared the letter with his boss.* **31.** to free (a ship, cargo, etc.) from legal detention at a port by satisfying the customs and other required conditions. **32.** *Football, etc.* to get (the ball) away from the area of one's own goal. **33.** to decode. **34.** to approve or authorise, or to obtain approval or authorisation for, a thing or person. **35.** *Mil.* **a.** to unload (a gun) making sure no ammunition remains. **b.** to free (a gun) of stoppages. **36.** to remove trees, undergrowth, etc., from (an area of land). *–v.i.* **37.** to become clear. **38.** (of a ship) **a.** to comply with the customs and other conditions legally imposed upon leaving or entering a port. **b.** to leave port after having complied with such conditions. *–v.* **39.** Some special verb phrases are:

**clear away, off,** etc. **1.** to remove so as to leave something clear. **2.** to disappear; vanish.

**clear out, 1.** to empty, remove, in order to make clear. **2.** to go away.

**clear the air, 1.** to relieve tension. **2.** to remove misunderstanding.

**clear up, 1.** to make clear. **2.** to solve; explain. **3.** to put in order; tidy up. **4.** to become brighter, lighter, etc.

**clear with,** to obtain approval: *to clear with the boss.*

*–n.* **40.** plain language; not code: *the orders were radioed in clear.* **41. in the clear,** free from the imputation of blame, censure, or the like. **42.** (*pl.*) *N.Z.* barren peat-land. [ME *cler,* from OF, from L *clārus*] – **clearable,** *adj.* – **clearer,** *n.*

**clearage** /ˈklɪərɪdʒ/, *n.* **1.** the act of clearing. **2.** a cleared space.

**clearance** /ˈklɪərəns/, *n.* **1.** the act of clearing. **2.** a clear space; a clearing. **3.** an intervening space, as between machine parts for free play. **4.** distance or extent of an object to be passed over or under. **5.** *Football, etc.* the act of getting the ball away from one's own goal area. **6.** *Naut.* **a.** the clearing of a ship at a port. **b.** the official certificate or papers (**clearance papers**) indicating this. **7.** *Rowing.* the distance between the bow end of one puddle, and the stern end of the next. **8.** *Football.* permission granted to a player by one club, to transfer to another club.

**clearance capacity** /ˈ– kəˌpæsəti/, *n.* the ability of an inland communications system to transport supplies from a point of military disembarkation.

**clearance sale** /ˈ– seɪl/, *n.* a sale to obtain money quickly; also, to clear shop-soiled or out-of-date goods or to make more space available in premises.

**clearcole** /ˈklɪəkoʊl/, *n.* a size, or glue, containing whiting.

**clear-cut** /ˈklɪə-kʌt/, *adj.* **1.** cut or formed with clearly defined outlines; distinctly defined. *–v.t.* **2.** →**clear-fell.**

**clear-eyed** /ˈklɪər-aɪd/, *adj.* **1.** having clear, bright eyes; clear-sighted. **2.** mentally acute or discerning.

**clear-fell** /ˈklɪə-fɛl/, *v.t.* to cut down and remove every tree in (a given area). Also, **clear-cut.** – **clear-felling,** *n.* – **clear-felled,** *adj.*

**clear-headed** /ˈklɪə-hɛdəd/, *adj.* having or showing a clear head or understanding. – **clear-headedness,** *n.*

**clearing** /ˈklɪərɪŋ/, *n.* **1.** the act of one who or that which clears. **2.** a tract of cleared land, as in a forest. **3.** the mutual exchange between banks of cheques and drafts, and the settlement of the differences. **4.** (*pl.*) the total of claims settled at a clearing house.

**clearing house** /ˈ– haʊs/, *n.* **1.** a place or institution where mutual claims and accounts are settled, as between banks. **2.** a central office for receiving and distributing information.

**clearing station** /ˈ– steɪʃən/, *n.* a military field hospital where first aid is given, before casualties are sent back to base hospitals. Also, **clearing hospital.**

**clearly** /ˈklɪəli/, *adv.* **1.** in a clear manner. **2.** undoubtedly.

**clearness** /ˈklɪənəs/, *n.* the state or quality of being clear; distinctness; plainness.

**clear-sighted** /ˈklɪə-saɪtəd/, *adj.* having clear sight; having keen mental perception; discerning; perspicacious: *clear-sighted businessman, reason, etc.* – **clear-sightedly,** *adv.* – **clear-sightedness,** *n.*

**clearskin** /ˈklɪəskɪn/, *n.* →**cleanskin.**

**clear-starch** /ˈklɪə-statʃ/, *v.t.* to stiffen and dress (linen, etc.) with clear or transparent (boiled) starch. – **clear-starcher,** *n.*

**clearstory** /ˈklɪəstəri/, *n., pl.* **-ries.** →**clerestory.**

**clearway** /ˈklɪəweɪ/, *n.* a stretch of road, esp. in a built-up area, on which, between stated times, motorists may stop only in emergencies.

**clearwing** /ˈklɪəwɪŋ/, *n.* any of various moths of the family Aegeriidae, having wings which are largely scaleless and transparent.

**cleat** /klit/, *n.* **1.** a small wedge-shaped block, as one fastened to a spar or the like as a support, etc. **2.** *Naut.* **a.** a piece of wood nailed down to secure something from slipping. **b.** a piece of wood or iron consisting of a bar with arms, to which ropes are belayed. **3.** a piece of wood or iron fastened across anything for support, security, etc. **4.** a piece of iron fastened under a shoe to preserve the sole. **5.** *Mining.* in coal, a vertical plane of breakage. The planes of easier breakage are *'face cleats',* lesser planes at right angles are *'butt cleats.'* *–v.t.* **6.** to supply or strengthen with cleats; fasten to or with a cleat. [ME *clete* wedge, c. D *kloot* ball. Cf. CLOT]

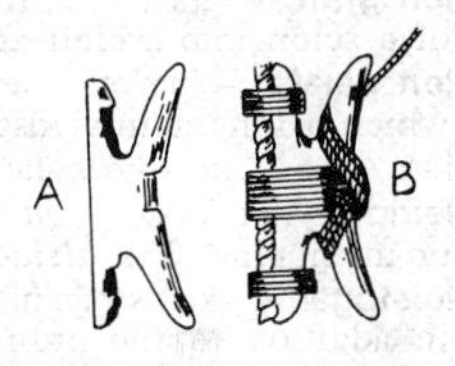

A, cleat; B, cleat lashed to a stay on to which a rope is belayed

**cleavable** /ˈklivəbəl/, *adj.* that may be cleft or split.

**cleavage** /ˈklivɪdʒ/, *n.* **1.** the act of cleaving. **2.** (in rocks) a tendency to split in certain directions. **3.** the state of being cleft or split; division. **4.** *Biol.* the total or partial division of the egg into smaller cells or blastomeres. **5.** *Crystall.* the tendency of many minerals to break in certain definite directions determined by the crystal structure giving more or less smooth surfaces. **6.** *Geol.* a tendency for some metamorphic rocks to split along definite, parallel closely-spaced planes. The property of splitting is developed largely by pressure. **7.** *Chem.* the breaking down of a molecule or compound into simpler molecules or compounds. **8.** *Colloq.* the cleft between a woman's breasts. **9.** *Colloq.* that which is revealed by a woman's low-cut dress.

**cleave**[1] /kliv/, *v.i.,* **cleaved** or (*Archaic*) **clave, cleaved, cleaving.** **1.** to stick or adhere; cling or hold fast (fol. by *to*). **2.** to be attached or faithful (fol. by *to*). [ME *cleve(n),* OE *cleofian,* c. G *kleben*]

**cleave**[2] /kliv/, *v.,* **cleft** or **cleaved** or **clove, cleft** or **cleaved** or **cloven, cleaving.** *–v.t.* **1.** to part by, or as by, a cutting blow, esp. along the grain or any other natural line of division. **2.** to split; rend apart; rive. **3.** to penetrate or pass through (air, water, etc.). **4.** to make by or as by cutting: *to cleave a path through the wilderness.* **5.** to separate or sever by, or as by, splitting. *–v.i.* **6.** to part or split, esp. along a natural line of division. **7.** to penetrate or pass (fol. by *through*). [ME *cleven,* OE *clēofan,* c. G *klieben.* Cf. Gk *glýphein* carve]

**cleaver** /ˈklivə/, *n.* **1.** one who or that which cleaves. **2.** a heavy knife or long-bladed hatchet used by butchers for cutting up carcasses.

cleaver

**cleavers** /ˈklivəz/, *n. sing. and pl.* **1.** a plant, *Galium aparine,* with short hooked bristles by means of which it adheres to clothing, etc.; goosegrass. **2.** any of certain related species. [ME *clivre* (from CLEAVE[1]), replacing OE *clife*]

**cleek** /klik/, *n.* a golf club having an iron head with a long, narrow face. [akin to CLUTCH[1]]

**clef** /klɛf/, *n.* a symbol in music notation placed upon a stave to indicate the name and pitch of the notes corresponding to its lines and spaces. The **G clef** (or **treble clef**) indicates that the second line of the stave corresponds to the G next above middle C. The **F clef** (or **bass clef**) indicates that the fourth line of the stave corresponds to the F next below middle C.

The **C clef** (or **alto clef**) indicates middle C on the third line of the stave. [F, from L *clāvis* key]

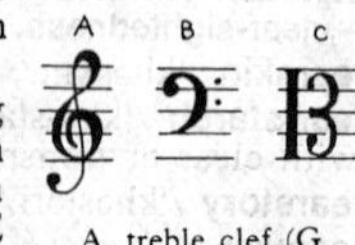

A, treble clef (G clef); B, bass clef (F clef); C, alto clef (C clef)

**cleft**[1] /klɛft/, *n.* **1.** a space or opening made by cleavage; a split. **2.** a division formed by cleaving. **3.** (in horses) a crack on the bend of the pastern. [ME *clift,* OE *geclyft* split, crack, fissure]

**cleft**[2] /klɛft/, *v.* **1.** a past tense and past participle of **cleave**[2]. *–adj.* **2.** cloven; split; divided. **3.** (of a leaf) having divisions formed by incisions or narrow sinuses which extend halfway, or more than halfway, to the midrib or the base.

**cleft graft** /– 'graft/, *n.* the insertion of the wedge-shaped base of a scion into a cleft at the top of a stock.

**cleft palate** /– 'pælət/, *n.* a congenital defect of the palate in which a longitudinal fissure exists in the roof of the mouth.

**cleg** /klɛg/, *n.* →**horsefly.** [ME, from Scand.; cf. Icel. *kleggi*]

**cleidoic** /klaɪ'douɪk/, *adj.* closed-up; totally encased in a shell or membrane. [Gk *kleidó(ein)* lock up + -IC]

**cleistogamy** /klaɪ'stɒgəmi/, *n.* the condition of having (usu. in addition to the ordinary, fully developed flowers) small, inconspicuous flowers which do not open, but are pollinated from their own anthers, as in the case of some violets. [Gk *kleistó(s)* closed + -GAMY] – **cleistogamous, cleistogamic** /klaɪstə'gæmɪk/, *adj.*

**clematis** /klə'meɪtəs, 'klɛmətəs/, *n.* any of the flowering vines or erect shrubs constituting the genus *Clematis,* as *C. glycinoides,* traveller's joy of eastern Australia, and *C. vitalba,* the traveller's joy of Europe and western Asia. [L, from Gk *klēmatís,* diminutive of *klêma* vine branch]

**clemency** /'klɛmənsi/, *n.* **1.** mercy or kind forbearance, esp. as shown towards an enemy: *as an act of clemency he released the wife.* **2.** mildness of personal disposition. **3.** mildness of weather. [late ME, from L *clēmentia*]

**clement** /'klɛmənt/, *adj.* **1.** mild or merciful in disposition; lenient; compassionate. **2.** (of the weather, etc.) mild or pleasant. [late ME, from L *clēmens*] – **clemently,** *adv.*

**clementine** /'klɛməntaɪn/, *n.* a hybrid of a tangerine and the wild orange of North Africa; almost seedless.

**clench** /klɛntʃ/, *v.t.* **1.** to close (the hands, teeth, etc.) tightly. **2.** to grasp firmly; grip. **3.** to settle decisively; clinch. **4.** *Naut.* to clinch. *–n.* **5.** the act of clenching. **6.** a tight hold; grip. **7.** that which holds fast or clenches. **8.** *Naut.* a clinch. [ME *clench(en),* OE *-clencan* (in *beclencan* hold fast)]

**cleome** /kli'oumi/, *n.* any of the numerous herbaceous or shrubby plants constituting the genus *Cleome,* mostly native to tropical regions, and often bearing showy flowers. [NL, from L plant name]

**clepe** /klip/, *v.t.,* **cleped** or **clept** (also **ycleped** or **yclept**), **cleping.** *Archaic.* to call; name (now chiefly in the past participle as *ycleped* or *yclept*). [ME *clepien,* OE *cleopian*]

**clepsydra** /'klɛpsədrə/, *n., pl.* **-dras, -drae** /-dri/. a device for measuring time by the regulated flow of water or mercury through a small aperture. [L, from Gk *klepsýdra*]

**cleptomania** /klɛptə'meɪniə/, *n.* →**kleptomania.** – **cleptomaniac,** *n.*

**cler.,** clerical.

**clerestory** /'klɪəstəri/, *n., pl.* **-ries. 1.** the upper part of the nave, transepts, and choir of a building, esp. a church, perforated with a series of windows above the aisle roofs, and forming the chief source of light for the building. **2.** a similar raised construction in any other structure. Also, **clearstory.** [*cler-* CLEAR (def. 1) + F *estoré* built]

**clergy** /'klɜdʒi/, *n., pl.* **-gies.** the body of men ordained for ministering in the Christian Church, as distinct from the laity. [ME *clergie,* from OF, from LL *clēricus* CLERIC]

**clergyman** /'klɜdʒimən/, *n., pl.* **-men. 1.** a member of the clergy. **2.** an ordained Christian minister.

**cleric** /'klɛrɪk/, *n.* **1.** a member of the clergy. **2.** a member of a clerical party. *–adj.* **3.** pertaining to the clergy; clerical. [LL *clēricus,* from Gk *klērikós,* from *klêros* clergy, orig., lot, allotment]

**clerical** /'klɛrɪkəl/, *adj.* **1.** pertaining to a clerk or to clerks: *a clerical error.* **2.** of, pertaining to, or characteristic of the clergy or a clergyman. **3.** upholding the power or influence of the clergy in politics. *–n.* **4.** a cleric. **5.** (*pl.*) *Colloq.* clerical garments. **6.** a person or a party trying to extend the power of the church in government. [LL *clēricālis,* from *clēricus* clergyman] – **clerically,** *adv.*

**clerical collar** /'– kɒlə/, *n.* a stiff, narrow, white collar, fastened at the back of the neck, worn by certain clergymen or priests.

**clericalism** /'klɛrɪkəlɪzəm/, *n.* **1.** clerical principles. **2.** clerical power or influence in politics. **3.** support of such power or influence. – **clericalist,** *n.*

**clerihew** /'klɛrəhju/, *n.* a four-line jingle epitomising a notable character. [named after E. *Clerihew* Bentley, 1875-1956, English journalist]

**clerisy** /'klɛrəsi/, *n.* learned men as a whole; the literati. [ML *clēricia*]

**clerk** /klak/, *n.* **1.** one employed in an office, shop, etc., to keep records or accounts, attend to correspondence, etc. **2.** *U.S.* an assistant in business, esp. a retail salesman or saleswoman. **3.** one who keeps the records and performs the routine business of a court, legislature, board, etc. **4.** the administrative officer, and chief executive of a town or borough council. **5.** a builder's representative, responsible for the quality of the work on a building site: *clerk of the works.* **6.** *Chiefly Legal.* a clergyman; ecclesiastic. **7.** a layman charged with various minor ecclesiastical duties. **8.** *Archaic.* a person able to read, or to read and write. **9.** *Archaic.* a scholar. *–v.i.* **10.** to act or serve as a clerk. [ME; OE *clerc, cleric,* from LL *clēricus* CLERIC] – **clerkship,** *n.*

**clerkly** /'klakli/, *adj.,* **-lier, -liest,** *adv. –adj.* **1.** of a clerk or clerks. **2.** *Archaic.* scholarly. *–adv.* **3.** in the manner of a clerk. – **clerkliness,** *n.*

**clerk of the course,** *n.* at a horse racing event, one who is in charge of the course.

**clerk of the peace,** *n.* an officer of a court who acts both as a clerk (def. 3) and as the attorney of the crown.

**clerk of works,** *n.* the representative of the owner of the building during day to day supervision of construction works.

**cleveite** /'klivaɪt/, *n.* a crystallised variety of uraninite. [named after P. T. *Cleve,* 1840-1905, Swedish chemist]

**clever** /'klɛvə/, *adj.* **1.** bright mentally; having quick intelligence; able. **2.** dexterous or nimble with the hands or body. **3.** showing adroitness or ingenuity: *a clever remark, a clever device.* **4.** *Colloq.* superficially smart or bright; facile. **5.** *Colloq.* sly; cunning. [ME *cliver;* orig. uncert.] – **cleverish,** *adj.* – **cleverly,** *adv.* – **cleverness,** *n.*

**clever dick** /'– dɪk/, *n. Colloq.* a conceited, smug person, who displays his prowess at the expense of others.

**clevis** /'klɛvəs/, *n.* a piece of metal, usu. U-shaped, with a pin or bolt passing through holes at the two ends, as for attaching an implement to a drawbar for pulling. [akin to CLEAVE[2]]

C, clevis

**clew** /klu/, *n.* **1.** a ball or skein of thread, yarn, etc. **2.** a clue. **3.** (*pl. or sing.*) the rigging for a hammock. **4.** *Naut.* either lower corner of a square sail or the after lower corner of a fore-and-aft sail. *–v.t.* **5.** to coil into a ball. **6.** *Naut.* to haul (the lower corners of a sail) up to the yard by means of the clew lines (fol. by *up*). [ME *clewe,* OE *cleowen,* c. D *kluwen*]

**clew iron** /'– aɪən/, *n.* a ring in the corner of a sail to which the clew lines are secured.

**clew line** /'– laɪn/, *n.* a rope by which a clew of a square sail above the courses is hauled to the yard.

**clianthus** /kli'ænθəs/, *n.* any plant of the small genus *Clianthus,* family Papilionaceae, esp. kaka beak, *C. punicens,* of New Zealand, and Sturt's desert pea *C. formosus,* of inland Australia.

**cliché** /'kliʃeɪ/, *n., pl.* **-chés** /-eɪz/. **1.** a trite, stereotyped expression, idea, practice, etc., as *trials and tribulations.* **2.** *Tarot.* a perceptual image of surrounding conditions. [F, pp. of *clicher* to stereotype. Cf. G *Klitsch* doughy mass]

**clichéd** /'kliʃeɪd/, *adj.* done in a trite, stereotyped fashion, dull, pedestrian.

**click** /klɪk/, *n.* **1.** a slight, sharp sound: *the click of a latch.*

2. some clicking mechanism, as a detent or a pawl. 3. *Phonet.* a speech sound produced by allowing air to flow suddenly into a partial vacuum in the mouth or in part of the mouth. 4. a. the audible movement from one graduation to another in the rear sight of a firearm. b. such a graduation in sight. –*v.i.* 5. to emit or make a slight sharp sound, or series of such sounds, as by the cocking of a pistol. 6. *Colloq.* to make a success; make a hit. 7. to fall into place or be understood: *his story suddenly clicked.* 8. *Colloq.* to establish an immediate affinity, usu. with a member of the opposite sex. –*v.t.* 9. to cut the basic design into (leather). 10. to cause to click; strike with a click. [imitative. Cf. D *klikken*]

**click beetle** /'–bitl/, *n.* an elaterid beetle that makes a clicking sound in springing up, as after having been laid on its back; snapping beetle.

**clicker** /'klɪkə/, *n.* 1. one who or that which clicks. 2. *Colloq.* a foreman in a printing works. 3. *Colloq.* a foreman shoemaker. 4. →**turning-indicator.**

**clicking knife** /'klɪkɪŋ naɪf/, *n.* a knife used to cut the master shape of a shoe.

**clicking press** /'– prɛs/, *n.* a mechanised series of clicking knives used to press leather down into end-grain hard wood.

**clidomancy** /'klɪdoʊ,mænsi/, *n.* divination by means of a dangling key that supposedly answers questions.

**client** /'klaɪənt/, *n.* 1. one who applies to a solicitor for advice or commits his cause or legal interests to a solicitor's management. 2. one who employs or seeks advice from a professional adviser. 3. a customer. 4. (in ancient Rome) a. (originally) a hereditary dependant of one of the nobility. b. a plebeian who lived under the patronage of a patrician. 5. anyone under the patronage of another; a dependant. 6. a recipient of a social welfare payment. [ME, from L *cliens* retainer] – **cliental** /klaɪ'ɛntl/, *adj.*

**clientele** /kliən'tɛl/, *n.* 1. the customers, clients, etc. (of a solicitor, businessman, etc.) as a whole. 2. dependants or followers. Also, **clientage** /'klaɪəntɪdʒ/. [L *clientēla* a body of retainers]

**cliff** /klɪf/, *n.* the high, steep face of a rocky mass; precipice. Also, *Archaic,* **clift** /klɪft/. [ME and OE *clif,* c. Icel. *klif*]

**cliff-hanger** /'klɪf-hæŋə/, *n.* 1. a play, novel, serial, etc., characterised by suspense. 2. a contest, election, etc. so closely matched that the outcome is uncertain until the end. – **cliff-hanging,** *adj.*

**cliff swallow** /'klɪf swɒloʊ/, *n.* a colonial bird, *Petrochelidon pyrrhonota,* of North America, so called because it attaches its bottle-shaped nests of mud to cliffs and walls.

**cliffy** /'klɪfi/, *adj.* having, or formed by, cliffs; craggy.

**climacteric** /klaɪ'mæktərɪk, klaɪmək'tɛrɪk/, *adj.* 1. pertaining to a critical period; crucial. –*n.* 2. a year in which important changes in health, fortune, etc., are said to occur: *the grand climacteric (the sixty-third year).* 3. *Physiol.* a period of decrease of reproductive activity in men and women, culminating, in women, in the menopause. 4. any critical period. Also, **climacterical** /klaɪmək'tɛrɪkəl/. [L *clīmactēricus,* from Gk *klīmaktērikós* of the nature of a critical period]

**climactic** /klaɪ'mæktɪk/, *adj.* pertaining to or forming a climax: *climactic arrangement.* Also, **climactical.**

**climate** /'klaɪmət/, *n.* 1. the composite or generalisation of weather conditions of a region, as temperature, pressure, humidity, precipitation, sunshine, cloudiness, and winds, throughout the year, averaged over a series of years. 2. an area of a particular kind of climate. 3. the general attitude and prevailing opinions of a group of people. [ME *climat,* from LL *clima,* from Gk *klíma* clime, zone, lit., slope (of the earth from equator to pole)] – **climatic** /klaɪ'mætɪk/, *adj.* – **climatically** /klaɪ'mætɪkli/, *adv.*

**climatic allowance** /klaɪ'mætɪk ə,laʊəns/, *n.* a special rate paid to certain employees to compensate them for working in areas where extreme climatic conditions are experienced.

**climatology** /klaɪmə'tɒlədʒi/, *n.* the science that deals with climates or climatic conditions. – **climatologic** /klaɪmətə'lɒdʒɪk/, **climatological** /klaɪmətə'lɒdʒɪkəl/, *adj.* – **climatologist,** *n.*

**climax** /'klaɪmæks/, *n.* 1. the highest point of anything; the culmination. 2. that point in the drama in which it is clear that the central motive will or will not be successful. 3. *Rhet.* a. a figure consisting in a series of related ideas so arranged that each surpasses the preceding in force or intensity. b. (popularly) the last term or member of this figure. 4. *Ecol.* that stage in the ecological succession or evolution of a plant-animal community, which is stable and self-perpetuating. 5. an orgasm. –*v.i.* 6. to reach the climax. –*v.t.* 7. to bring to the climax. [L, from Gk *klímax* ladder, staircase, climax]

**climax community** /– kə'mjunəti/, *n.* a stable community of plants composed of the most mesophytic vegetation that the climate can support, and not replaceable by other communities so long as the climate remains unchanged.

**climb** /klaɪm/, *v.i.* 1. to mount or ascend, esp. by using both hands and feet. 2. to rise slowly by, or as by, continued effort. 3. to slope upward. 4. to ascend by twining or by means of tendrils, adhesive tissues, etc., as a plant. 5. to rise, or attempt to rise, in social position. 6. **climb down,** a. to descend, esp. by using both hands and feet. b. *Colloq.* to withdraw from an untenable position; retract an indefensible argument. –*v.t.* 7. to ascend, go up, or get to the top of, esp. by the use of hands and feet. 8. to descend (a ladder, pole, etc.), esp. by using both hands and feet (fol. by *down*). –*n.* 9. a climbing; an ascent by climbing. 10. a place to be climbed. [ME *climben,* OE *climban,* c. D and G *klimmen*] – **climbable,** *adj.*

**climber** /'klaɪmə/, *n.* 1. one who or that which climbs. 2. a person who strives to associate with social superiors. 3. a climbing plant. 4. a spike attached to a shoe to assist in climbing telegraph poles, etc.

**climbing irons** /'klaɪmɪŋ aɪənz/, *n.pl.* iron frames with spikes attached, worn on the feet or legs to help in climbing trees, etc.

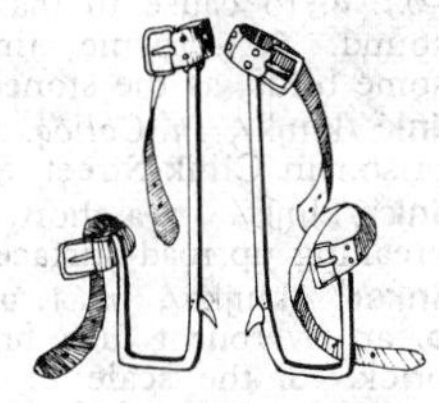
climbing irons

**climbing perch** /– 'pɜtʃ/, *n.* a freshwater fish, *Anabas testudineus,* of southern Asia, able to move over the ground with the aid of its pectoral fins and spiny gill covers and formerly reputed to climb trees.

**clime** /klaɪm/, *n. Poetic.* 1. a tract or region of the earth. 2. climate. [LL *clima* CLIMATE]

**clin.,** 1. clinic. 2. clinical.

**clinah** /'klaɪnə/, *n. Obs. Colloq.* girl friend. Also, **cliner.** [G *kleine* little]

**clinandrium** /klɪ'nændriəm/, *n., pl.* **-dria.** a cavity in the apex of the column in orchids, in which the anthers rest; androclinium. [NL, from Gk *klīnē* bed + Gk *anḗr* man + *-ium* -IUM]

**clinch** /klɪntʃ/, *v.t.* 1. to secure (a driven nail, etc.) by beating down the point. 2. to fasten (work) together thus. 3. to settle (a matter) decisively. 4. *Naut.* to secure overlapping plates on the side of a ship with a fastening. –*v.i.* 5. *Boxing, etc.* to engage in a clinch. 6. to beat down the point of a nail, etc., in order to fasten something. –*n.* 7. the act of clinching. 8. *Boxing, etc.* the act or an instance of one or both contestants holding the other in such a way as to hinder his punches. 9. *Colloq.* an embrace or passionate kiss. 10. a clinched nail or fastening; rivet. 11. the clinched part of a nail, etc. 12. *Naut.* a kind of half-hitch in which the end of the rope is fastened back by seizing or lashing to its main part. [later var. of CLENCH]

**clincher** /'klɪntʃə/, *n.* 1. one who or that which clinches. 2. something decisive.

**cline** /klaɪn/, *n.* a continuous, graded variation in members of a species across a wide geographical or ecological range.

**cliner** /'klaɪnə/, *n.* →**clinah.**

**cling** /klɪŋ/, *v.i.,* **clung, clinging.** 1. to adhere closely; stick. 2. to hold fast, as by grasping or embracing; cleave. 3. to be or remain close. 4. to remain attached (to an idea, hope, memory, etc.). [ME *clingen,* OE *clingan* stick or draw together, shrivel] – **clinger,** *n.* – **clingingly,** *adv.*

**clingfish** /'klɪŋfɪʃ/, *n., pl.* **-fishes,** (*esp. collectively*) **fish.** any fish of the family Gobiesocidae, all of which have a ventral sucking disc constructed from the pectoral as well as the pelvic fins. They use this disc to adhere tightly to rocks.

**cling peach** /klɪŋ 'pitʃ/, *n.* →**clingstone.**

**clingstone** /ˈklɪŋstoʊn/, *adj.* **1.** having a stone to which the pulp adheres closely, as certain peaches. *–n.* **2.** a clingstone peach.

**clingy** /ˈklɪŋi/, *adj.* apt to cling; adhesive or tenacious.

**clinic** /ˈklɪnɪk/, *n.* **1.** a class of medical students which takes place in a hospital ward, where practical instruction in examining and treating patients is given. **2.** one of a number of out-patient sections of a hospital for the specialised treatment of particular conditions and diseases. **3.** any medical centre used for such treatments as X-rays, child care, vaccinations, etc. **4.** a hospital for private patients. [LL *clīnicus* pertaining to a bed, from Gk *klīnikós*]

**clinical** /ˈklɪnɪkəl/, *adj.* **1.** pertaining to a clinic. **2.** pertaining to or used in a sickroom. **3.** pertaining to medical training carried out in a hospital. **4.** concerned with observation and treatment of disease in the patient (as distinguished from an artificial experiment). **5.** scientific; involving professional knowledge and not affected by the emotions: *he has a clinical attitude to even the most distressing cases.* **6.** administered on a sickbed or deathbed: *clinical conversion or baptism.* – **clinically,** *adv.*

**clinical picture** /– ˈpɪktʃə/, *n.* →**picture** (def. 14).

**clinical thermometer** /– θəˈmɒmətə/, *n.* an instrument used to determine the body temperature.

**clinician** /klɪˈnɪʃən/, *n.* a physician who studies diseases at the bedside or is skilled in clinical methods.

**clink**[1] /klɪŋk/, *v.i.* **1.** to make a light, sharp, ringing sound. **2.** to rhyme or jingle. **3.** to move with a clinking sound. *–v.t.* **4.** to cause to make such a sound. *–n.* **5.** a clinking sound. **6.** a rhyme; jingle. **7.** the rather piercing cry of some birds, as the stonechat. [ME *clynk(e).* Cf. D *klinken*]

**clink**[2] /klɪŋk/, *n. Colloq.* a prison; gaol. [apparently from *Clink* prison in Clink Street, Southwark, London]

**clink**[3] /klɪŋk/, *n.* a short, square, pointed steel bar, as used for breaking up road surfaces. [special use of CLINK[1]]

**clinker**[1] /ˈklɪŋkə/, *n.* **1. a.** a hard brick, used for paving, etc. **b.** an overburnt face brick. **2.** a partially vitrified mass of brick. **3.** the scale of oxide formed on iron during forging. **4.** a mass of incombustible matter fused together, as in the burning of coal. *–v.i.* **5.** to form clinkers in burning, as coal. [D *klinker* kind of brick]

**clinker**[2] /ˈklɪŋkə/, *n.* **1.** one who or that which clinks. **2.** *Colloq.* something first-rate or worthy of admiration. **3.** *Mountaineering.* a soft iron edge-nail for climbing-boots.

**clinker**[3] /ˈklɪŋkə/, *adj.* made of pieces, as boards or plates of metal, which overlap one another. Also, **clinker-built** /ˈklɪŋkə-bɪlt/.

**clinker beech** /– ˈbitʃ/, *n.* a New Zealand timber tree of lowland and montane forests, *Nothofagus truncata.* Also, **hard beech.**

**clinkstone** /ˈklɪŋkstoʊn/, *n.* any of several varieties of phonolite which give out a ringing sound when struck.

**clinometer** /klaɪˈnɒmətə, klə-/, *n.* an instrument used to determine inclination or slope. [*clino-* (combining form representing L *-clīnāre* incline) + -METER[1]]

**clinometric** /klaɪnəˈmɛtrɪk/, *adj.* **1.** (of crystals) having oblique angles between one or all axes. **2.** pertaining to or determined by a clinometer. Also, **clinometrical.**

**clinostat** /ˈklaɪnoʊstæt/, *n.* an apparatus for slowly rotating a plant so that all its sides are equally subjected to a unilateral stimulus, as light or gravity.

**clinquant** /ˈklɪŋkənt/, *adj.* **1.** glittering, esp. with tinsel; decked with garish finery. *–n.* **2.** imitation gold leaf; tinsel. **3.** *Obs.* false glitter. [F, ppr. of obs. *clinquer* clink, tinkle, glitter, from D *klinken*]

**clint** /klɪnt/, *n.* a flat-topped ridge between furrows or grikes, caused by solution in a horizontal limestone surface.

**clip**[1] /klɪp/, *v.,* **clipped, clipping,** *n. –v.t.* **1.** to cut, or cut off or out, as with shears; trim by cutting. **2.** to cut or trim the hair or fleece of; shear. **3.** to pare the edge of (a coin). **4.** to punch a hole in (a ticket). **5.** to cut short; curtail. **6.** to omit sounds of (a word) in pronouncing. **7.** *Colloq.* to hit with a quick, sharp blow. **8.** *Colloq.* to defraud. *–v.i.* **9.** to clip or cut something; make the motion of clipping something. **10.** to move swiftly. **11.** *Archaic.* to fly rapidly. *–n.* **12.** the act of clipping. **13.** anything clipped off. **14.** →**woolclip. 15.** (*pl.*) shears. **16.** an excerpt from a film. **17.** *Colloq.* a quick, sharp blow or punch. **18.** *Colloq.* rate; pace: *at a rapid clip.* **19.** *Colloq.* general appearance; looks. [ME *clippen,* from Scand.; cf. Icel. *klippa*]

**clip**[2] /klɪp/, *n., v.,* **clipped, clipping.** *–n.* **1.** a device for gripping and holding tightly; a metal clasp, esp. one for papers, letters, etc. **2.** a flange on the upper surface of a horseshoe. **3.** a holder for ammunition ready for insertion into the magazine of certain weapons. **4.** *Archaic.* an embrace. *–v.t.* **5.** to grip tightly; hold together by pressure. **6.** to encircle; encompass. **7.** *Archaic.* to embrace or hug. [ME *clippe(n),* OE *clyppan* embrace]

**clipboard** /ˈklɪpbɔd/, *n.* a small backing board with a strong clip at the top to hold sheets of paper together, as for notes made while away from a desk, or as a temporary file of related papers as invoices.

**clip-clop** /klɪp-ˈklɒp/, *n., v.i.,* **-clopped, -clopping.** →**clop.**

**clipjoint** /ˈklɪpdʒɔɪnt/, *n. Colloq.* a nightclub or restaurant, etc., where prices are exorbitant and customers are swindled.

**clipper** /ˈklɪpə/, *n.* **1.** one who or that which clips or cuts. **2.** (*oft. pl.*) a cutting tool, esp. shears. **3.** (*oft. pl.*) a tool with rotating or reciprocating knives for cutting hair. **4.** one that clips, or moves swiftly, as a horse. **5.** a sailing vessel built and rigged for speed. **6.** *Colloq.* a first-rate person or thing.

**clipper-built** /ˈklɪpə-bɪlt/, *adj. Naut.* built on sharp, rakish lines conducive to fast sailing.

**clippie** /ˈklɪpi/, *n. Chiefly Brit. Colloq.* one whose job involves clipping tickets, as a tram conductress, a railway employee at a platform barrier, etc.

**clipping** /ˈklɪpɪŋ/, *n.* **1.** the act of one who or that which clips. **2.** a piece clipped off or out. **3.** →**cutting. 4.** (*pl.*) grass from a mown lawn. *–adj.* **5.** that clips. **6.** *Colloq.* swift: *a clipping pace.*

**clipping service** /ˈ– sɜvəs/, *n.* an organisation which collects or forwards clippings to individuals or organisations that require them.

**clique** /klik/, *n., v.,* **cliqued, cliquing.** *–n.* **1.** a small set or coterie, esp. one that is snobbishly exclusive. *–v.i.* **2.** *Colloq.* to form, or associate in, a clique. [F, from OF *cliquer* make a sharp sound. Cf. CLAQUE]

**cliquey** /ˈkliki/, *adj. Colloq.* cliquish. Also, **cliquy.**

**cliquish** /ˈklikɪʃ/, *adj.* of, pertaining to, or savouring of a clique: *a cliquish fashion.* – **cliquishly,** *adv.* – **cliquishness,** *n.*

**clitellum** /kləˈtɛləm/, *n., pl.* **-tella** /-ˈtɛlə/. the glandular part of the epidermis which, in some oligochaete annelid worms, secretes the cocoon within which the eggs are deposited. [NL, from L *clitellae,* pl., pack-saddle]

**clitoridectomy** /klɪtərəˈdɛktəmi, klaɪ-/, *n.* excision of the clitoris.

**clitoris** /ˈklɪtərəs, ˈklaɪ-/, *n.* the erectile organ of the vulva, homologous to the penis of the male. [NL, from Gk *kleitorís,* from *kleíein* shut]

**clivia** /ˈklaɪviə/, *n.* any bulbous plant of the small genus *Clivia,* of southern Africa, often cultivated in gardens for their large heads of orange tubular flowers.

**cloaca** /kloʊˈeɪkə/, *n., pl.* **-cae** /-ki/. **1.** a sewer. **2.** a privy. **3.** a place or receptacle of moral filth. **4.** *Zool.* **a.** the common cavity into which the intestinal, urinary, and generative canals open in birds, reptiles, amphibians, many fishes, and certain mammals (*monotremes*). **b.** a similar cavity in invertebrates. [L, probably from *cluere* cleanse] – **cloacal,** *adj.*

**cloak** /kloʊk/, *n.* **1.** a loose outer garment. **2.** that which covers or conceals; disguise; pretext. *–v.t.* **3.** to cover with, or as with a cloak. **4.** to hide; conceal. [ME *cloke,* from OF, from ML *cloc(c)a* cloak, orig. bell; ? of Celtic orig. See CLOCK[1]]

**cloak-and-dagger** /kloʊk-ən-ˈdægə/, *adj.* melodramatic; concerned with espionage, intrigue, etc.

**cloakroom** /ˈkloʊkrum/, *n.* **1.** a room where cloaks, overcoats, etc., may be left temporarily. **2.** a toilet.

**cloanthite** /kloʊˈænθaɪt/, *n.* →**chloanthite.**

**clobber**[1] /ˈklɒbə/, *v.t. Colloq.* to batter severely; maul. [? b. CLUB and SLOBBER]

**clobber**[2] /ˈklɒbə/, *n. Colloq.* clothes or gear. [alteration of CLOTHES]

**clobber**[3] /ˈklɒbə/, *n.* **1.** a paste used to cover cracks in leather. *–v.t.* **2.** to paint over existing decorations on (a ceramic piece). **3.** *Obs.* to mend. [Scot. Gaelic *clābar* mud]

**cloche** /klɒʃ/, *n.* **1.** a bell-shaped or tunnel-like cover, as used to cover and protect young plants, usu. made of glass. **2.** a woman's bell-shaped, close-fitting hat. [F: lit., bell. See CLOCK[1]]

**clock**[1] /klɒk/, *n.* **1.** an instrument for measuring and indicating time, having pointers which move round on a dial to mark the hour, etc. **2.** such a timepiece not carried on the person (distinguished from a *watch*). **3.** *Colloq.* a piece of measuring equipment having a dial, as an odometer, taximeter, etc. **4.** the dial itself. **5.** *Electronics.* a circuit producing regular pulses which control the speed of operation of a system. **6.** *Prison Colloq.* a prison sentence of twelve months' duration. **7. against the clock, a.** in haste, as to meet a deadline. **b.** (in a competitive sport) in an attempt to beat a record time rather than another contestant. *–v.t.* **8.** to time, test, or ascertain by the clock, esp. of races by athletes, horses, cars, etc. *–v.i.* **9. clock in** or **on,** to register the time of arrival at a place of work. **10. clock out** or **clock off,** to register the time of departure from a place of work. [ME *clokke,* from MD *klocke* instrument for measuring time; cf. OE *clugge* bell, ONF *cloke*]

**clock**[2] /klɒk/, *n.* an embroidered or woven ornament on each side of a stocking, extending from the ankle upwards. [orig. uncert.] – **clocked,** *adj.*

**clock**[3] /klɒk/, *n.* **1.** a punch. *–v.t.* **2.** *Colloq.* to hit; strike. Also, **clonk.** [? echoic]

**clocker** /ˈklɒkə/, *n. Horseracing* →**timekeeper.**

**clock-golf** /ˈklɒk-gɒlf/, *n.* a putting game in which one or more of the players seek to hole a ball from twelve marked clock figures.

**clockmaker** /ˈklɒkmeɪkə/, *n.* a person who makes or repairs clocks.

**clock-pulse** /ˈklɒk-pʌls/, *n.* a regular electric pulse which controls the speed of operation of an electronic system.

**clock-watcher** /ˈklɒk-wɒtʃə/, *n.* an employee who spends much of the time longing for the end of the working day. – **clockwatching,** *n., adj.*

**clockweed** /ˈklɒkwid/, *n.* any of several species of annual or perennial herbs belonging to the North American genus *Gaura,* family Oenotheraceae.

**clockwise** /ˈklɒkwaɪz/, *adv.* in the direction of rotation of the hands of a clock. – **clockwise,** *adj.*

**clockwork** /ˈklɒkwɜk/, *n.* **1.** the mechanism of a clock. **2.** any mechanism similar to that of a clock. **3. like clockwork,** with perfect regularity or precision.

**clod** /klɒd/, *n.* **1.** a lump or mass, esp. of earth or clay. **2.** earth; soil. **3.** anything earthy or base, as the body in comparison with the soul: *this corporeal clod.* **4.** a stupid person; blockhead; dolt. **5.** a part of the shoulder of beef, boned, lying outside the blade. [ME *clodde,* OE *clodd* (in *clodhamer* fieldfare). Cf. CLOUD] – **cloddish,** *adj.* – **cloddy,** *adj* – **cloddishness,** *n.*

**clodhopper** /ˈklɒdhɒpə/, *n.* **1.** a clumsy boor; rustic; bumpkin. **2.** (*pl.*) strong, heavy shoes.

**clodhopping** /ˈklɒdhɒpɪŋ/, *adj.* loutish; boorish.

**clodpoll** /ˈklɒdpoʊl/, *n. Brit.* a blockhead; a stupid person. Also, **clodpole, clodpate** /ˈklɒdpeɪt/.

**clog** /klɒg/, *v.,* **clogged, clogging,** *n. –v.t.* **1.** to encumber; hamper; hinder. **2.** to hinder or obstruct, esp. by sticky matter; choke up. *–v.i.* **3.** to become clogged, encumbered, or choked up. **4.** to stick; stick together. *–n.* **5.** anything that impedes motion or action; an encumbrance; a hindrance. **6.** a heavy block, as of wood, fastened to a man or beast to impede movement. **7.** a kind of shoe with a thick sole usu. of wood. **8.** a similar but lighter shoe worn in the clog dance. **9.** a thick piece of wood. **10.** *Law.* in equity of redemption, any provision in a mortgage which prevents or obstructs the mortgagor's right to redeem his property on payment of the debt; such a provision is void. [ME *clog, clogge;* orig. uncert.] – **cloggy,** *adj.*

**clog dance** /ˈ– dæns/, *n.* a dance performed with clogs to beat time to the music. – **clogdancer,** *n.* – **clogdancing,** *n.*

**cloisonné** /klwʌˈzɒneɪ/, *n.* **1.** enamel-work in which colour areas are separated by thin, metal bands fixed edgeways to the ground. *–adj.* **2.** of, pertaining to, or resembling cloisonné. [F, from *cloison* partition]

**cloister** /ˈklɔɪstə/, *n.* **1.** a covered walk, esp. one adjoining a building, as a church, commonly running round an open court (garth) and opening on to it with an open arcade or colonnade. **2.** a place of religious seclusion; a monastery or nunnery; a convent. **3.** any quiet, secluded place. **4.** life in a monastery or nunnery. *–v.t.* **5.** to confine in a cloister or convent. **6.** to confine in retirement; seclude. **7.** to furnish with a cloister or covered walk. **8.** to convert into a cloister or convent. [ME *cloistre,* from OF, b. *cloison* partition (cf. CLOISONNÉ) and L *claustrum* enclosed place] – **cloister-like,** *adj.*

**cloistered** /ˈklɔɪstəd/, *adj.* solitary; retired from the world: *cloistered seclusion.*

**cloister-garth** /ˈklɔɪstə-gaθ/, *n.* →**garth** (def. 1).

**cloistral** /ˈklɔɪstrəl/, *adj.* **1.** of, pertaining to, or living in a cloister. **2.** cloister-like: *a cloistral house.*

**clomiphene** /ˈkloʊməfin/, *n.* a fertility drug which stimulates the pituitary gland to release gonadotrophins which may cause ovulation, often multiple.

**clone** /kloʊn/, *v.,* **cloned, cloning,** *n. –v.t.* **1.** to bring about the asexual reproduction of (an individual), as by implanting a body cell from a donor individual into an egg cell from which the nucleus has been removed, and allowing the egg cell to develop, the resulting individual being identical with the donor but having no cells in common with the female providing or harbouring the egg cell. *–n.* **2.** an asexually produced descendant. **3.** *Hort.* a group of plants originating as parts of the same individual, from buds or cuttings. Also, **clon** /klɒn, kloʊn/. [Gk *klōn* slip, twig]

**clonk** /ˈklɒŋk/, *v.t.* **1.** to hit, punch. *–v.i.* **2.** to make a clonking sound. *–n.* **3.** a hit, a punch. **4.** a sudden, heavy sound, often metallic. [? echoic]

**clonus** /ˈkloʊnəs/, *n.* a rapid succession of contraction and relaxation of a group of muscles usu. signifying an affection of the brain or spinal cord. [NL, from Gk *klónos* commotion, turmoil] – **clonic** /ˈklɒnɪk/, *adj.* – **clonicity** /klɒˈnɪsəti/, *n.*

**clop** /klɒp/, *n., v.,* **clopped, clopping.** *–n.* **1.** the sound made by a horse's hoofs. *–v.i.* **2.** to move with such a sound. [imitative]

**close** /kloʊz/, *v.,* **closed, closing;** /kloʊs/, *adj.,* **closer, closest,** *adv;* /kloʊz/ *for defs 48-51;* /kloʊs/ *for defs 52-55, n. –v.t.* **1.** to stop or obstruct (a gap, entrance, aperture, etc.). **2.** to stop or obstruct the entrances, apertures, or gaps in. **3.** to shut in or surround on all sides; enclose; cover in. **4.** to refuse access to or passage across: *lifesavers closed the beach because of heavy seas.* **5.** to bring together the parts of; join; unite: *to close the ranks of troops.* **6.** to bring to an end; to shut down, either temporarily or permanently: *to close a debate, to close a shop.* **7. close up,** *Print.* to remove or reduce spacing between (set type). *–v.i.* **8.** to become closed; shut. **9.** to come together; unite. **10.** to come close. **11.** *Naut.* to come close to (fol. by *with*). **12.** to grapple; engage in close encounter (fol. by *with*). **13.** to come to terms (fol. by *with*). **14.** to agree (fol. by *on, upon*). **15.** to come to an end; terminate. **16.** *Stock Exchange.* to be worth at the end of a trading period. **17. close in,** to surround and approach (a place) gradually, as in making a capture. **18. close out,** to nullify one's position in the stock exchange futures market either by selling (from a bought position) or by buying (from a sold position). [ME *close(n),* from OF *clos-,* stem of *clore,* from L *claudere* shut; replacing OE *clȳsan*] *–adj.* **19.** shut; shut tight; not open. **20.** shut in; enclosed. **21.** completely enclosing. **22.** without opening; with all openings covered or closed. **23.** confined; narrow: *close quarters.* **24.** lacking fresh or freely circulating air: *a close room.* **25.** heavy; oppressive: *a spell of close weather.* **26.** narrowly confined, as a prisoner. **27.** practising secrecy; secretive; reticent. **28.** parsimonious; stingy. **29.** scarce, as money. **30.** not open to public or general admission, competition, etc. **31.** under prohibition as to hunting or fishing: *a close season.* **32.** having the parts near together: *a close texture.* **33.** compact; condensed. **34.** near, or near together, in space, time, or relation: *in close contact.* **35.** *Ball Games.* characterised by short passes and cautious tactics: *they played a close game.* **36.** intimate; confidential: *close friendship.* **37.** based upon a strong uniting feeling of love, honour, etc.: *a close union of* *nations.* **38.** fitting tightly, as a cap. **39.** short; near the surface. **40.** not deviating from the subject under consideration: *close attention.* **41.** strict; searching; minute: *close investigation.* **42.** not deviating from a model or original: *a close translation.* **43.** nearly even or equal: *a close contest.* **44.** strictly logical: *close reasoning.* **45.** *Phonet.* pronounced with a relatively small opening above the tongue. *Beet* and *boot* have the closest English vowels. **46.** *Rare.* viscous; not volatile. *–adv.* **47.** in a close manner; closely. [ME *clos,* from F, from L *clausus,* pp., shut] *–n.* **48.** the act of closing. **49.** the end or conclusion. **50.** *Music.* →**cadence**. **51.** a junction; union. **52.** a close encounter; a grapple. **53.** an enclosed place; an enclosure; any piece of land held as private property. **54.** an enclosure about or beside a building, cathedral, etc. **55.** a narrow entry or alley, or a courtyard to which it leads; a cul-de-sac. [(defs 48-51) n. use of v.; (defs 52-55) ME *clos,* from F, from L *clausum* enclosed place] **–closely** /ˈklousli/, *adv.* **–closeness** /ˈklousnəs/, *n.* **–closer** /ˈklouzə/, *n.*

**close call** /klous ˈkɔl/, *n. Colloq.* a narrow escape.

**closed** /klouzd/, *adj.* **1.** restricted or exclusive in any of various ways. **2.** *Phonet.* (of syllables) ending with a consonant.

**closed book** /– ˈbʊk/, *n. Colloq.* **1.** a subject about which one knows nothing. **2.** a matter which has been completely finished.

**closed chain** /– ˈtʃeɪn/, *n.* a linking of atoms in an organic molecule which may be represented by a structural formula which forms a ring or cycle.

**closed circuit** /– ˈsɜkət/, *n.* a path along which electricity can flow.

**closed-circuit television** /ˌklouzd-sɜkət ˈtɛləvɪʒən/, *n.* a system of televising by wire to designated viewing sets, as within a factory for monitoring production operations, etc.

**closed court** /klouzd ˈkɔt/, *n.* a court hearing which is not open to the public.

**close-down** /ˈklouz-daʊn/, *n.* **1.** a general stoppage of work. **2.** the end of a period of broadcasting.

**closed shop** /klouzd ˈʃɒp/, *n.* **1.** a workshop, factory, or the like, in which the employer must call on a particular trade union to furnish employees. *–adj.* **2.** inflexible: *closed shop mentality.*

**closed side** /ˈklouzd saɪd/, *n.* (in ice skating) that side of a skater's body which is on the inside of the curve being skated.

**close field** /ˈklous fild/, *n.* (in cricket) a set of fielding positions close to the batsmen.

**close-fisted** /ˈklous-fɪstəd/, *adj.* stingy; miserly.

**close-grained** /ˈklous-greɪnd/, *adj.* (of wood) having the grain close or fine in texture.

**close harmony** /klous ˈhaməni/, *n.* a style of part-singing, chiefly heard in jazz, in which all the voices except the bass sing in octaves or tenths.

**close-hauled** /klous-ˈhɔld/, *adj.* sailing as close to the wind as a vessel will sail, with sails trimmed as flat as possible.

**close-jammed** /klous-ˈdʒæmd/, *adj.* (of a sailing vessel) sailing too close to the wind and thereby losing some of its driving force. Also, **jammed up.**

**close-knit** /ˈklous-nɪt/, *adj.* united in feeling, as of a family or social sub-set.

**close-lipped** /ˈklous-lɪpt/, *adj.* not talking or revealing much.

**close-order** /ˈklous-ɔdə/, *adj.* (of military drill) carried out with two paces between ranks, as in ceremonial duties.

**close-out** /ˈklouz-aʊt/, *n.* (in surfing) a wave which breaks over a long distance but offers no crest on which to ride.

**close position** /klous pəˈzɪʃən/, *n.* (in music) arrangement of a chord so that the parts are as close together as possible.

**close quarters** /– ˈkwɔtəz/, *n. pl.* **1.** a small, cramped place or position. **2.** direct and close contact in a fight.

**close shave** /– ˈʃeɪv/, *n. Colloq.* a narrow escape.

**closet** /ˈklɒzət/, *n.* **1.** a small room, enclosed recess, or cabinet for clothing, food, utensils, etc. **2.** a small private room, esp. one for prayer, thought, etc. **3.** a water closet; toilet. *–adj.* **4. a.** suited for use or enjoyment in privacy: *a closet drama.* **b.** secret: *a closet drinker; a closet queen.* *–v.t.* **5.** to shut up in a private room for a conference, interview, etc. [ME, from OF, diminutive of *clos,* from L *clausum* enclosed place]

**closet drama** /ˈ– dramə/, *n.* drama written to be read but not to be performed on the stage.

**close thing** /klous ˈθɪŋ/, *n. Colloq.* a narrow escape.

**close-up** /ˈklous-ʌp/, *n.* **1.** a picture taken at close range or with a long focal length lens, on a relatively large scale. **2.** an intimate view or presentation of anything.

**closing order** /ˈklouzɪŋ ɔdə/, *n.* an order, made by a local authority, to close down a condemned property.

**closing time** /ˈ– taɪm/, *n.* the end of the period in which alcoholic drinks may legally be sold in a public house.

**clostridium** /klɒsˈtrɪdiəm/, *n.* any of the group of spore-forming, anaerobic bacteria.

**closure** /ˈklouʒə/, *n., v.,* **-sured, -suring.** *–n.* **1.** the act of closing or shutting. **2.** the state of being closed. **3.** a bringing to an end; conclusion. **4.** a metal or plastic cap for a bottle. **5.** *Obs.* that which closes or shuts. **6.** *Obs.* that which encloses or shuts in; enclosure. **7.** *Phonet.* an articulation which keeps the breath from moving outwards by closing the vocal tract at some point. **8.** Also, **closure motion.** *Parl. Proc.* a method of closing a debate and causing an immediate vote to be taken on the question under discussion, as by moving the previous question. *–v.t.* **9.** *Parl. Proc.* to end (a debate, etc.) by closure. [ME, from OF, from LL *clausura,* from L *clausus,* pp., shut]

**clot** /klɒt/, *n., v.,* **clotted, clotting.** *–n.* **1.** a mass or lump. **2.** a semisolid mass, as of coagulated blood. **3.** *Colloq.* a stupid person. *–v.i.* **4.** to form into clots; coagulate. *–v.t.* **5.** to cause to clot; cover with clots. [ME; OE *clott* lump, c. G *Klotz* block, log]

**cloth** /klɒθ/, *n., pl.* **cloths** /klɒθs/, *adj.* *–n.* **1.** a fabric formed by weaving, felting, etc., from wool, hair, silk, flax, cotton, or other fibre, used for garments, upholstery, and many other purposes. **2.** a piece of such a fabric for a particular purpose: *a tray cloth.* **3.** in theatre, a painted fabric used as a curtain or as scenery. **4.** a particular profession, esp. that of a clergyman. **5. the cloth,** the clergy. **6.** *Naut.* one of several lengths of canvas which are stitched together to make a sail. **7.** *Obs.* a garment; clothing. **8.** *Obs.* a livery or customary garb, as of a trade or profession. *–adj.* **9.** made of, covered with, or pertaining to cloth. [ME; OE *clāth,* c. G *Kleid* garment]

**clothe** /klouð/, *v.t.,* **clothed** or **clad, clothing.** **1.** to dress; attire. **2.** to provide with clothing. **3.** to cover with, or as with, clothing. **4.** to endow; invest (as with meaning). **5.** to conceal. [ME *clothen,* OE *clāthian*]

**clothes** /klouðz/, *n.pl.* **1.** garments for the body; articles of dress; wearing apparel. **2.** bedclothes. [orig., pl. of CLOTH]

**clothes basket** /ˈ– baskət/, *n.* **1.** a basket in which soiled clothes are stored before washing. **2.** a basket in which clothes are sent to and from the wash.

**clothes drier** /ˈ– draɪə/, *n.* **1.** a clothes horse. **2.** a heated cabinet or machine for drying clothes.

**clothes hanger** /ˈ– hæŋə/, *n.* a support for clothes, usu. bow-shaped with a hook.

**clothes hoist** /ˈ– hɔɪst/, *n.* a device consisting of a square, rotating frame, which may be raised or lowered, supporting wires on which clothes may be hung to dry.

**clothes horse** /ˈ– hɔs/, *n.* **1.** a frame on which to hang clothes, etc., esp. for drying. **2.** *Colloq.* a person who pays particular attention to dress and who wears clothes well, esp. a model or mannequin.

**clothes line** /ˈ– laɪn/, *n.* **1.** a rope or wire on which clothes, etc. may be hung to dry. **2.** a device, as a clothes hoist, on which to hang clothes to dry.

**clothes moth** /ˈ– mɒθ/, *n* any of certain small moths whose larvae feed on wool, fur, etc.

**clothes peg** /ˈ– pɛg/, *n.* a forked piece of wood or other device for hanging clothes on a line.

**clothes press** /ˈ– prɛs/, *n.* **1.** a receptacle for clothes, as a chest, wardrobe, or cupboard. **2.** a device for pressing clothes.

**clothes prop** /ˈ– prɒp/, *n.* a pole that holds up a clothes line.

**clothier** /ˈklouðiə/, *n.* a maker or seller of cloth or clothes.

**clothing** /ˈklouðɪŋ/, *n.* **1.** garments collectively; clothes; raiment; apparel. **2.** a covering.

**clothing wool** /'– wʊl/, *n.* short dense wool with good felting properties.

**cloth of gold,** *n.* a tissue of threads of gold and silk or wool.

**clotted cream** /klɒtəd 'krim/, *n.* cream, skimmed off the top of very rich milk after it has been let stand, then gently heated. Also, **Devonshire cream.**

**clottish** /'klɒtɪʃ/, *adj. Colloq.* foolish; silly.

**clotty** /'klɒti/, *adj.* **1.** full of clots. **2.** tending to clot.

**cloud** /klaʊd/, *n.* **1.** a visible collection of particles of water or ice suspended in the air, usu. at an elevation above the earth's surface. **2.** any similar mass, esp. of smoke or dust. **3.** a dim or obscure area in something otherwise clear or transparent. **4.** *Obs.* a patch or spot, differing in colour from the surrounding surface. **5.** anything that obscures, darkens, or causes gloom, trouble, suspicion, disgrace, etc. **6.** a great number of insects, birds, etc., flying together: *a cloud of locusts.* **7.** a multitude; a crowd. **8. have one's head in the clouds,** to be divorced from reality; be in a dreamlike state. **9. in the clouds, a.** imaginary; unreal. **b.** impractical. *–v.t.* **10.** to overspread or cover with, or as with, a cloud or clouds. **11.** to overshadow; obscure; darken. **12.** to make gloomy. **13.** to place under suspicion, disgrace, etc. **14.** to variegate with patches of another colour. *–v.i.* **15.** to grow cloudy; become clouded. [ME *cloud(e)* rock, clod, cloud, OE *clūd* rock, hill; akin to CLOD]

**cloudbank** /'klaʊdbæŋk/, *n.* a thick mass of low cloud.

**cloudburst** /'klaʊdbɜst/, *n.* a sudden and very heavy rainfall.

**cloud-capped** /'klaʊd-kæpt/, *adj.* (of mountains, etc.) having the summit surrounded by clouds. Also, **cloud-capt.**

**cloud chamber** /'klaʊd tʃeɪmbə/, *n. Physics.* an instrument for making the tracks of ionising particles visible as a row of droplets which condense from a saturated vapour.

**cloud-cuckoo-land** /,klaʊd-'kʊku-lænd/, *n.* a fanciful place of unrealistic notions.

**cloudland** /'klaʊdlænd/, *n.* a region of unreality, imagination, etc.; dreamland.

**cloudless** /'klaʊdləs/, *adj.* without clouds; clear. **– cloudlessly,** *adv.* **– cloudlessness,** *n.*

**cloudlet** /'klaʊdlət/, *n.* a little cloud.

**cloud nine** /klaʊd 'naɪn/, *n. Colloq.* a state of bliss.

**cloud-topped** /'klaʊd-tɒpt/, *adj.* having the top covered with clouds.

**cloudy** /'klaʊdi/, *adj.,* **cloudier, cloudiest. 1.** full of or overcast with clouds: *a cloudy sky.* **2.** of or like a cloud or clouds; pertaining to clouds. **3.** having cloud-like markings: *cloudy marble.* **4.** not clear or transparent: *a cloudy liquid.* **5.** obscure; indistinct: *cloudy notions.* **6.** darkened by gloom, trouble, etc.: *cloudy looks.* **7.** under suspicion, disgrace, etc.: *a cloudy reputation.* **– cloudily,** *adv.* **– cloudiness,** *n.*

**clout** /klaʊt/, *n.* **1.** *Colloq.* a blow, esp. with the hand; a cuff. **2.** the mark shot at in archery. **3.** a shot that hits the mark. **4.** effectiveness; force: *the committee has no political clout.* **5.** *Archaic.* a patch, or piece of cloth or other material used to mend something. **6.** *Archaic.* any worthless piece of cloth; a rag. *–v.t.* **7.** *Colloq.* to strike, esp. with the hand; cuff. *–v.i.* **8.** *Colloq.* to steal, or take without permission (fol. by *on*). **9.** *Colloq.* to cheat by evading payment, esp. of a gambling debt; to welsh (fol. by *on*). **10. clout down,** *Colloq.* to clamp down (fol. by *on*). [ME; OE *clūt* piece of cloth or metal. Cf. CLOT]

**clout nail** /'– neɪl/, *n.* a nail with a large flat head used to stud or clout a surface.

**clove**[1] /kloʊv/, *n.* **1.** the dried flower bud of a tropical tree, *Syzygium aromaticum,* used whole or ground as a spice. **2.** the tree. [ME *clowe,* from OF *clou* (from L *clāvus*), in *clou de girofle* nail of clove (see GILLYFLOWER), so called from the shape]

**clove**[2] /kloʊv/, *n.* one of the small bulbs formed in the axils of the scales of a mother bulb, as in garlic. [ME; OE *clufu* clove, bulb, tuber, c. D *kloof* cleft]

**clove**[3] /kloʊv/, *v.* past tense of **cleave**[2].

**clove hitch** /'– hɪtʃ/, *n.* a form of hitch for fastening a rope about a spar, etc., in which two rounds of rope are crossed about the spar, with the ends of the rope issuing in opposite directions between the crossed parts.

**cloven** /'kloʊvən/, *v.* **1.** past participle of **cleave**[2]. *–adj.* **2.** cleft; split; divided: *cloven feet or hoofs.* **3.** cleaved.

**cloven-footed** /kloʊvən-'fʊtəd/, *adj.* **1.** having cloven feet. **2.** devilish; satanic.

**cloven hoof** /kloʊvən 'hʊf/, *n.* the figurative indication of Satan or evil temptation. Also, **cloven foot.**

**cloven-hoofed** /kloʊvən-'hʊft/, *adj.* **1.** having split hoofs, once assumed to represent the halves of a single undivided hoof, as in cattle. **2.** devilish; satanic.

**clove pink** /kloʊv 'pɪŋk/, *n.* a pink, *Dianthus caryophyllus,* with a spicy scent like that of cloves; a carnation.

**clover** /'kloʊvə/, *n.* **1.** any of various herbs of the fabaceous genus *Trifolium,* with trifoliolate leaves and dense flower heads, many species of which, as *T. pratense* (the common **red clover**), are cultivated as forage plants or as a pasture improvement plant, as subterranean clover. **2. in clover,** in comfort or luxury. [ME *clovere,* OE *clāfre,* c. D *klaver*]

**cloverleaf** /'kloʊvəlif/, *n., pl.* **-leaves. 1.** the leaf of a clover. **2.** a road junction consisting of flyovers, underpasses, etc., forming the pattern of a four-leaf clover.

**clown** /klaʊn/, *n.* **1.** a jester or buffoon in a circus, pantomime, etc. **2.** *Colloq.* a fool; idiot. **3.** a peasant; a rustic. **4.** a coarse, ill-bred person; a boor. *–v.i.* **5.** to act like a clown. [orig. uncert. Cf. Icel. *klunni* clumsy fellow] **– clownish,** *adj.* **– clownishly,** *adv.* **– clownishness,** *n.*

**clownery** /'klaʊnəri/, *n., pl.* **-eries. 1.** clownish behaviour. **2.** a clown's performance.

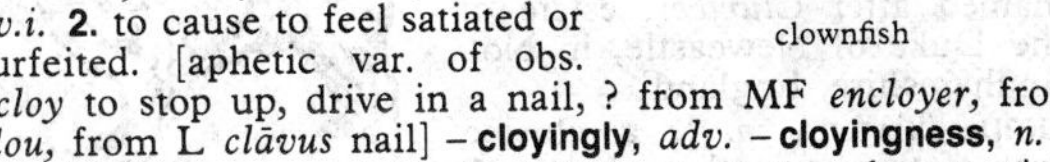

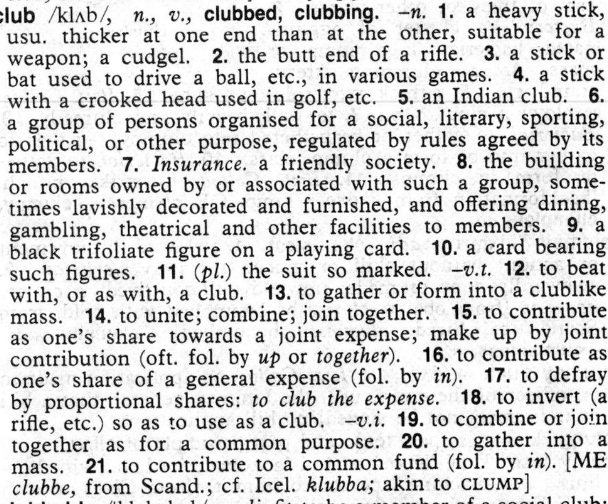

clownfish

**clownfish** /'klaʊnfɪʃ/, *n.* any of various small particoloured fishes of the genera *Actinicola, Amphiprion* and *Premnas,* which live among the stinging tentacles of some large sea-anemones, as the anemone fish.

**cloy** /klɔɪ/, *v.t.* **1.** to weary by an excess of food, sweetness, pleasure, etc.; surfeit; satiate. *–v.i.* **2.** to cause to feel satiated or surfeited. [aphetic var. of obs. *acloy* to stop up, drive in a nail, ? from MF *encloyer,* from *clou,* from L *clāvus* nail] **– cloyingly,** *adv.* **– cloyingness,** *n.*

**club** /klʌb/, *n., v.,* **clubbed, clubbing.** *–n.* **1.** a heavy stick, usu. thicker at one end than at the other, suitable for a weapon; a cudgel. **2.** the butt end of a rifle. **3.** a stick or bat used to drive a ball, etc., in various games. **4.** a stick with a crooked head used in golf, etc. **5.** an Indian club. **6.** a group of persons organised for a social, literary, sporting, political, or other purpose, regulated by rules agreed by its members. **7.** *Insurance.* a friendly society. **8.** the building or rooms owned by or associated with such a group, sometimes lavishly decorated and furnished, and offering dining, gambling, theatrical and other facilities to members. **9.** a black trifoliate figure on a playing card. **10.** a card bearing such figures. **11.** (*pl.*) the suit so marked. *–v.t.* **12.** to beat with, or as with, a club. **13.** to gather or form into a clublike mass. **14.** to unite; combine; join together. **15.** to contribute as one's share towards a joint expense; make up by joint contribution (oft. fol. by *up* or *together*). **16.** to contribute as one's share of a general expense (fol. by *in*). **17.** to defray by proportional shares: *to club the expense.* **18.** to invert (a rifle, etc.) so as to use as a club. *–v.i.* **19.** to combine or join together as for a common purpose. **20.** to gather into a mass. **21.** to contribute to a common fund (fol. by *in*). [ME *clubbe,* from Scand.; cf. Icel. *klubba;* akin to CLUMP]

**clubbable** /'klʌbəbəl/, *adj.* fit to be a member of a social club; sociable. Also, **clubable.**

**clubbie** /'klʌbi/, *n.* a member of an organised surfboard riding club.

**club foot** /klʌb 'fʊt/, *n.* **1.** a deformed or distorted foot. **2.** the condition of such a foot; talipes. **– clubfooted,** *adj.*

**club hammer** /'– hæmə/, *n.* a double-headed hammer.

**club hand** /– 'hænd/, *n.* **1.** a deformed or distorted hand, similar in nature and causation to a club foot. **2.** the condition of such a hand.

**clubhaul** /'klʌbhɔl/, *v.t.* to cause (a ship), in an emergency, to go on the other tack by letting go the lee anchor, and pulling on a hawser leading from the anchor to the lee quarter, the hawser being cut when the ship gathers way on the new tack.

**clubhouse** /ˈklʌbhaʊs/, *n.* a building in which a club meets, designed to cater for the special needs of the members and in close proximity to the place where the club's activities are carried out.

**clubman** /ˈklʌbmən/, *n., pl.* **-men.** a member esp. an active member, of a fashionable club. – **clubwoman,** *n.*

**club moss** /klʌb ˈmɒs/, *n.* any plant of the genus *Lycopodium.*

**clubroom** /ˈklʌbrum/, *n.* a room used by a club.

**club rush** /ˈklʌb rʌʃ/, *n.* any of several species of plant of the genus *Scirpus* of the family Cyperaceae.

**club sandwich** /– ˈsænwɪtʃ/, *n.* a sandwich of toast (usu. three slices) with a filling of cold chicken, salad, etc.

**club steak** /ˈ– steɪk/, *n.* →**delmonico steak.**

**cluck** /klʌk/, *v.i.* **1.** to utter the cry of a hen brooding or calling her chicks. **2.** to make a similar sound. *–v.t.* **3.** to call or utter by clucking: *clucking her sympathy.* *–n.* **4.** the sound uttered by a hen when brooding, or in calling her chicks. **5.** any clucking sound. [var. of *clock* (now Scot. and d.), OE *cloccian*]

**clucky** /ˈklʌki/, *adj.* **1.** (of a hen) broody. **2.** *Colloq.* feeling disposed to have children. **3.** *Colloq.* fussy and over-protective of children.

**clue** /klu/, *n., v.,* **clued, cluing.** *–n.* **1.** anything that serves to guide or direct in the solution of a problem, mystery, etc. **2.** →**clew.** *–v.t.* **3. clue (someone) up,** to give (someone the facts). **4.** →**clew.** [var. of CLEW]

**clued-up** /klud-ˈʌp/, *adj. Colloq.* well informed.

**clueless** /ˈkluləs/, *adj. Colloq.* helpless; stupid; ignorant.

**cluey** /ˈklui/, *adj. Colloq.* **1.** well-informed. **2.** showing good sense and keen awareness.

**clumber** /ˈklʌmbə/, *n.* one of a breed of spaniels with short legs and long, heavy body, valued as retrievers. Also, **clumber spaniel.** [named after *Clumber,* estate of the Duke of Newcastle, in Nottinghamshire, England]

clumber

**clump** /klʌmp/, *n.* **1.** a cluster, esp. of trees, or other plants. **2.** *Bacteriol.* a cluster of agglutinated bacteria. **3.** a lump or mass. **4.** a clumping tread, sound, etc. **5.** a thick extra sole on a shoe. **6.** *Brit. Colloq.* a blow; a clout. *–v.i.* **7.** to walk heavily and clumsily. **8.** *Bacteriol.* to gather or be gathered into clumps. *–v.t.* **9.** to gather into or form a clump; mass. **10.** *Bacteriol.* to gather or form in clumps. **11.** *Brit. Colloq.* to strike; punch. [backformation from *clumper* lump, OE *clympre*] – **clumpy, clumpish,** *adj.*

**clumsy** /ˈklʌmzi/, *adj.,* **-sier, -siest. 1.** awkward in movement or action; without skill or grace: *a clumsy workman.* **2.** awkwardly done or made; unwieldy; ill-contrived: *a clumsy apology.* [from obs. v. *clumse* be benumbed with cold, from Scand.; cf. Swed. *klummsen* benumbed] – **clumsily,** *adv.* – **clumsiness,** *n.*

**clumsy duck** /– ˈdʌk/, *n. Law Colloq.* an application made to an officer of the court, usu. the attorney general, that a bill of indictment not be signed; no bill application.

**clung** /klʌŋ/, *v.* past tense and past participle of **cling.**

**cluny lace** /kluni ˈleɪs/, *n.* **1.** a lace made by hand with bobbins. **2.** a machine lace copied from it. [from *Cluny,* a town in E France where it was originally made]

**clupeid** /ˈklupiɪd/, *n.* **1.** any of the Clupeidae, a family of (chiefly) marine, teleostean fishes, including the herrings, sardines, menhaden, and shad. *–adj.* **2.** relating to the family Clupeidae. [NL *Clupeidae,* pl., from *Clupea* the herring genus (L *clupea* kind of small river fish) + *-idae* (see -ID²)]

**clupeoid** /ˈklupiɔɪd/, *adj.* **1.** herring-like. *–n.* **2.** any member of the Isospondyli, an order of fishes including the clupeids, salmon, smelts, etc.

**cluse** /kluz/, *n.* a narrow gorge cutting through a mountain ridge. [F, from ML *clusa,* L *cl(a)usa,* properly pp. fem., closed]

**cluster** /ˈklʌstə/, *n.* **1.** a number of things of the same kind, growing or held together; a bunch: *a cluster of grapes.* **2.** a group of things or persons near together: *a cluster of bombs.* **3.** *Astron.* a group of stars which move together. **4.** *U.S. Army.* a small metal design placed on the ribbon representing an awarded medal, which indicates that the same medal has been awarded again (equivalent to British *bar*): *oak-leaf cluster.* *–v.t.* **5.** to gather into a cluster. **6.** to furnish or cover with clusters. *–v.i.* **7.** to form a cluster or clusters. [ME and OE, var. of *clyster* bunch] – **clustery,** *adj.*

**clustered column** /klʌstəd ˈkɒləm/, *n.* a group of several pillars attached to each other to form a single unit.

**cluster pack** /ˈklʌstə pæk/, *n.* a plastic packaging which binds together a certain number of bottles or cans into a unit.

**cluster pine** /– ˈpaɪn/, *n.* a tree, *Pinus pinaster,* of the northern Mediterranean region often cultivated for its resinous products and for stabilising sandy soil.

**clutch**¹ /klʌtʃ/, *v.t.* **1.** to seize with, or as with, the hands or claws; snatch. **2.** to grip or hold tightly or firmly. *–v.i.* **3.** to try to seize or grasp (fol. by *at*). *–n.* **4.** the hand, claw, paw, etc., when grasping. **5.** (*usu. pl.*) power of disposal or control; mastery: *in the clutches of an enemy.* **6.** the act of clutching; a snatch; a grasp. **7.** a tight grip or hold. **8.** a device for gripping something. **9.** a coupling or appliance by which working parts of machinery (as a pulley and a shaft) may be made to engage or disengage at will; esp. in a motor vehicle, the device which engages and disengages the engine from the transmission, or the pedal, etc. which operates the device. [ME *clucche(n),* var. of *clycche(n),* OE *clyccan* crook or bend, close (the hand), clench]

**clutch**² /klʌtʃ/, *n.* **1.** a hatch of eggs; the number of eggs produced or incubated at one time. **2.** a brood of chickens. **3.** *Colloq.* a group; a bunch. *–v.t.* **4.** to hatch (chickens). [var. of d. *cletch,* akin to *cleck* hatch, from Scand.; cf. Swed. *kläcka*]

**clutch-start** /ˈklʌtʃ-stat/, *v.t.* **1.** to start (the engine of a motor vehicle) by having it in gear with the clutch disengaged while it is rolled forward, and then suddenly engaging the clutch. **2.** to begin a motor race with the vehicles revving in gear on the starting grid and then suddenly engaging their clutches when the starting signal is given. *–n.* **3.** the result of such a procedure.

**clutter** /ˈklʌtə/, *v.t.* **1.** to heap, litter, or strew in a disorderly manner. *–v.i.* **2.** to run in disorder; move with bustle and confusion. **3.** to make a clatter. **4.** to speak so rapidly and inexactly that distortions of sound and phrasing result. *–n.* **5.** a disorderly heap or assemblage; litter. **6.** confusion; disorder. **7.** confused noise; clatter. **8.** *Radio.* a jumble of unwanted radar signals. [var. of *clotter,* from CLOT; associated with CLUSTER]

**Clydesdale** /ˈklaɪdzdeɪl/, *n.* one of a breed of active, strong and hardy draught horses originally raised in Clydesdale, Scotland.

Clydesdale

**Clydesdale terrier** /– ˈtɛriə/, *n.* a variety of Skye terrier bred for smallness.

**clypeate** /ˈklɪpieɪt, -iət/, *adj.* shaped like a round shield or buckler. [L *clypeātus,* pp., furnished with a shield]

**clypeus** /ˈklɪpiəs/, *n., pl.* **clypei** /ˈklɪpiaɪ/. the shield-shaped area of the facial wall of an insect's head. [L: properly, *clipeus* round shield] – **clypeal,** *adj.*

**clyster** /ˈklɪstə/, *n. Med. Obs.* an enema. [ME *clister,* from L *clyster,* from Gk *klystḗr* syringe]

**cm,** centimetre; centimetres.

**CM,** metric carat.

**cmd,** command. Also, **cmnd.**

**cmdg,** commanding.

**cmdr,** commander.

**cmdt,** commandant.

**C.M.F.** /si ɛm ˈɛf/, Citizens' Military Forces.

**C.M.G.** /si ɛm ˈdʒi/, Companion of the Order of St Michael and St George.

**cnidarian** /naɪˈdɛəriən, knaɪ-/, *n.* **1.** a member of the Cnidaria, a phylum of invertebrate animals belonging to the coelenterates and comprising the jellyfish, sea-anemones, and corals. *–adj.* **2.** belonging to the Cnidaria.

**cnr,** corner.

**co-,** **1.** a prefix signifying association and accompanying action, occurring mainly before vowels and *h* and *gn,* as in *coadjutor, cohabit, cognate.* **2.** a prefix signifying partnership, joint responsibility or ownership, as in *co-producer, co-writer.* **3.** *Maths, Astron.* a prefix meaning 'complement of', as in *cosine, codeclination.* [L, var. of *com-* COM-]

**c/o.,** **1.** care of. **2.** carried over. Also, **c.o.**

**Co,** *Chem.* cobalt.

**Co.,** **1.** company. **2.** county. Also, **co.**

**C.O.** /si 'oʊ/, **1.** commanding officer. **2.** conscientious objector.

**coach** /koʊtʃ/, *n.* **1.** a large, enclosed, four-wheeled carriage used esp. on state occasions. **2.** a stagecoach. **3.** a bus, esp. a single-decker, used for long distances or for sightseeing. **4.** a railway carriage. **5.** a person who trains athletes for games, a contest, etc. **6.** a private tutor who prepares a student for an examination. **7.** Also, **coacher.** a tame beast used to decoy wild cattle. *–v.t.* **8.** to give instruction or advice to in the capacity of a coach. *–v.i.* **9.** to act as a coach. **10.** to study with or be instructed by a coach. [F *coche,* from Hung. *kocsi*]

**coach-and-four** /koʊtʃ-ən-'fɔ/, *n.* a coach drawn by four horses.

**coachbox** /'koʊtʃbɒks/, *n.* the driver's seat on a horse-drawn coach.

**coachbuilder** /'koʊtʃbɪldə/, *n.* one who makes the bodies of motor vehicles, railway carriages, etc.

**coach-built** /'koʊtʃ-bɪlt/, *adj.* (of a vehicle, etc.) with body-work specially built; custom-made.

**coachdog** /'koʊtʃdɒg/, *n.* →**Dalmatian** (def. 4).

**coacher** /'koʊtʃə/, *n.* **1.** one who coaches; a coach. **2.** a coach-horse. **3.** →**coach** (def. 7).

**coach-horn** /'koʊtʃ-hɔn/, *n.* →**post-horn.**

**coach-horse** /'koʊtʃ-hɔs/, *n.* a horse used or fitted to draw a coach.

**coach-house** /'koʊtʃ-haʊs/, *n.* **1.** an outhouse originally for carriages. **2.** *Naut.* a small low deckhouse on a boat.

**coachman** /'koʊtʃmən/, *n., pl.* **-men. 1.** a man employed to drive a coach or carriage. **2.** Also, **coachman's whipbird.** →**whipbird.**

**coach-whip bird** /'koʊtʃ-wɪp ˌbɜd/, *n.* →**whipbird.**

**coachwood** /'koʊtʃwʊd/, *n.* a tree, *Ceratopetalum apetalum,* with light, easily worked timber, found in gullies in eastern Australia.

**coachwork** /'koʊtʃwɜk/, *n.* the body of a motor car (as distinguished from the *chassis,* the *engine,* and the *upholstery*).

**coaction** /koʊ'ækʃən/, *n.* force or compulsion, either in restraining or in impelling. [F, from L *coactio*]

**coactive** /koʊ'æktɪv/, *adj.* compulsory; coercive. – **coactively,** *adj.*

**coadjutor** /koʊ'ædʒətə/, *n.* **1.** an assistant. **2.** an assistant to a bishop or other ecclesiastic. **3.** a bishop who assists another bishop and who may have right of succession to him. [LL: from *co-* CO- + *adjūtor* helper; replacing ME *coadiutoure,* from OF]

**coadjutress** /koʊ'ædʒətrəs/, *n.* a female coadjutor or assistant.

**coadjutrix** /koʊ'ædʒətrɪks/, *n., pl.* **coadjutrices** /koʊə'dʒutrəsiz/. →**coadjutress.**

**coadunate** /koʊ'ædʒənət/, *adj.* united by growth; closely joined. [L *coadūnātus,* pp., joined together] – **coadunation** /koʊˌædʒə'neɪʃən/, *n.*

**coagulable** /koʊ'ægjələbəl/, *adj.* capable of being coagulated: *this substance is highly coagulable.* – **coagulability** /koʊˌægjələ'bɪləti/, *n.*

**coagulant** /koʊ'ægjələnt/, *n.* a substance that produces coagulation. [L *coāgulans,* ppr., curdling]

**coagulate** /koʊ'ægjəleɪt/, *v.,* **-lated, -lating;** /koʊ'ægjələt, -leɪt/, *adj.* *–v.t., v.i.* **1.** to change from a fluid into a thickened mass; curdle; congeal. *–adj.* **2.** *Obs.* coagulated. [L *coāgulātus,* pp., curdled] – **coagulation** /koʊˌægjə'leɪʃən/, *n.* – **coagulative** /koʊ'ægjələtɪv/, *adj.* – **coagulator,** *n.*

**coagulum** /koʊ'ægjələm/, *n., pl.* **-la** /-lə/. a clump, clot, curd, precipitate, or gel. [L: rennet]

**coal** /koʊl/, *n.* **1.** a black or brown coloured compact and earthy organic rock formed by the accumulation and decomposition of plant material and used as a fuel: **hard coal** (anthracite), **soft coal** (bituminous coal), **brown coal** (lignite). **2.** *Obs.* a piece of wood or other combustible substance either glowing, charred or burned out. **3.** *Obs.* charcoal. **4. coals of fire, a.** good actions or the like in return for bad, giving rise to feelings of remorse. **b.** reproaches. **5. coals to Newcastle,** anything supplied unnecessarily. **6. take, haul, rake, etc., over the coals,** to scold; reprimand. **7. add coals to the fire,** to make a bad situation, dissension, etc., worse. *–v.t.* **8.** to burn to coal or charcoal. **9.** to provide with coal. *–v.i.* **10.** to take in coal for fuel. [ME *cole,* OE *col* live coal, c. G. *Kohle*]

**coal black** /– 'blæk/, *adj.* absolutely black; very black.

**coalbunker** /'koʊlbʌŋkə/, *n.* **1.** a structure, usu. of concrete, for storing coal. **2.** a space in a ship, etc., for storing coal.

**coal cellar** /'koʊl sɛlə/, *n.* a shed or cellar for storing coal.

**coaldust** /'koʊldʌst/, *n.* finely powdered coal.

**coaler** /'koʊlə/, *n.* a railway, ship, etc., used mainly to haul or supply coal.

**coalesce** /koʊə'lɛs/, *v.i.,* **-lesced, -lescing. 1.** to grow together or into one body. **2.** to unite so as to form one mass, community, etc. [L *coalescere*] – **coalescence,** *n.* – **coalescent,** *adj.*

**coalface** /'koʊlfeɪs/, *n.* **1.** the part of the coal seam from which coal is cut. **2. work at the coalface,** *Colloq.* to play an active rather than an administrative part in a project, organisation, etc.

**coalfield** /'koʊlfild/, *n.* an area containing coal deposits.

**coalfish** /'koʊlfɪʃ/, *n.* the saithe, a North Atlantic gadoid food fish, *Pollachius virens,* a species of pollack. [named from the colour of its back]

**coal gas** /'koʊl gæs/, *n.* **1.** the gas formed by burning coal. **2.** a gas used for illuminating and heating, produced by distilling bituminous coal, and consisting chiefly of hydrogen, methane and carbon monoxide.

**coal-heaver** /'koʊl-hivə/, *n.* one who carries or shovels coal.

**coalhole** /'koʊlhoʊl/, *n.* **1.** a hole in a pavement through which coal is shot into a cellar. **2.** a small coal cellar.

**coaling station** /'koʊlɪŋ ˌsteɪʃən/, *n.* a place at which coal is supplied to ships, locomotives, etc.

**coalition** /koʊə'lɪʃən/, *n.* **1.** union into one body or mass; fusion. **2.** a combination or alliance, esp., a temporary one between persons, political parties, states, etc. *–adj.* **3.** deriving from such a union. **4. coalition government,** a government formed by more than one political party. [ML *coalitio,* from L *coalescere* coalesce] – **coalitionist,** *n.*

**coalman** /'koʊlmən/, *n.* a man who delivers coal.

**coal measures** /'koʊl mɛʒəz/, *n.pl. Geol.* **1.** coal-bearing strata. **2.** (*caps*) a portion of the carboniferous system in Europe or North America, characterised by coal deposits. **3.** (*caps*) a portion of the Permian system in the Southern hemisphere and India characterised by coal deposits.

**coalmine** /'koʊlmaɪn/, *n.* a mine or pit from which coal is obtained. – **coalminer,** *n.* – **coalmining,** *n., adj.*

**coal pit** /'koʊl pɪt/, *n.* **1.** a pit where coal is dug. **2.** *U.S.* a place where charcoal is made.

**coalscuttle** /'koʊlskʌtl/, *n.* a bucket in which coal is carried into, and kept in, a room.

**coal tar** /'koʊl ta/, *n.* a thick, black, viscid liquid formed during the distillation of coal in the manufacture of coal gas and which upon further distillation yields benzene, anthracene, phenol, etc. (from which are derived a large number of dyes and synthetic compounds), and a final residuum (**coal-tar pitch**) which is used in making pavements, etc.

**coal-tar creosote** /ˌkoʊl-ta 'kriəsoʊt/, *n.* impure phenol or carbolic acid, distinct from the creosote of wood tar.

**coaltit** /'koʊltɪt/, *n.* a European black-headed tit, *Parus ater,* with a white patch on the nape of the neck.

coarctate pupa

**coaly** /'koʊli/, *adj.* of, like, or containing coal.

**coaming** /'koʊmɪŋ/, *n.* **1.** a raised border round an opening in a deck, roof, or floor, designed to prevent water from running below. **2.** *Naut.* one of the pieces, esp. of the fore-and-aft pieces, of such a border.

**coarctate** /koʊ'akteɪt/, *adj.* **1.** *Entomol.* denoting an insect pupa enclosed in the hardened cuticula (puparium) of a preceding larval instar. **2.**

compressed; constricted. [L *coarctātus,* pp., pressed together; replacing ME *coartate,* from L *coartātus,* var. of *coarctātus*]

**coarse** /kɔs/, *adj.,* **coarser, coarsest. 1.** of inferior or faulty quality; not pure or choice; common; base: *coarse manners, a coarse lad.* **2.** composed of relatively large parts or particles: *coarse sand.* **3.** lacking in fineness or delicacy of texture, structure, etc. **4.** harsh. **5.** lacking delicacy of feeling, manner, etc.; not refined. **6.** (of screws) having the threads widely spaced. **7.** (of metals) unrefined. [adjectival var. of COURSE, *n.,* with the sense of ordinary] – **coarsely,** *adv.* – **coarseness,** *n.*

**coarse-grained** /ˈkɔs-greɪnd/, *adj.* **1.** having a coarse texture or grain. **2.** indelicate; crude; gross.

**coarsen** /ˈkɔsən/, *v.t.* **1.** to make coarse. *–v.i.* **2.** to become coarse.

**coast** /koʊst/, *n.* **1.** the land next to the sea; the seashore. **2.** the region adjoining it. **3. the coast,** the seaside. **4.** *Obs.* the boundary or border of a country. **5.** a slide or ride down a hill, etc. **6. the coast is clear,** the danger has gone. *–v.i.* **7.** to move along after effort has ceased; keep going on acquired momentum. **8.** to descend a hill, etc., as on a bicycle, without using pedals, or in a motor vehicle with the engine switched off. **9.** *Colloq.* (formerly) to loaf; move about the country as a tramp. **10.** to proceed or sail along, or sail from port to port of, a coast. **11.** to slide on a sledge down a snowy or icy hillside or incline. **12.** to drift along without aim or effort. **13. coast along,** to act or perform with minimal effort. *–v.t.* **14.** *Archaic.* to proceed along the coast of. **15.** to go along or near to (a coast). [ME *coste,* from OF, from L *costa* rib, side]

**coastal** /ˈkoʊstl/, *adj.* of or at a coast: *coastal defence.*

**coastal plain** /– ˈpleɪn/, *n.* **1.** the broad low plain between a mountain range and the sea. **2.** a lowland bordering a sea coast possibly an exposed sea floor resulting from sea level change, or an area of deposition by rivers.

**coastal saltbush** /–ˈsɒltbʊʃ/, *n.* **1.** a low shrub, *Rhagodia baccata,* family Chenopodiaceae, of drier coastal and some inland areas of Australia, introduced as sheep fodder in America and southern Africa. **2.** Also, **grey saltbush.** a low shrub, *Atriplex cinerea,* family Chenopodiaceae, of Australian sea coasts and some salt lake margins, having grey to nearly white leaves.

**coast disease** /ˈkoʊst dəziz/, *n.* a disease of sheep and cattle brought about by a deficiency of certain minerals in the diet. Also, **coast sickness.**

**coaster** /ˈkoʊstə/, *n.* **1.** one who or that which coasts. **2.** a vessel engaged in trading from port to port along a coast, usu. of the same country. **3.** a bicycle incorporating into its freewheel a form of braking mechanism operating by backpedalling. **4.** the brake itself. **5.** *Colloq.* a lazy person; loafer. **6.** *Obs. Colloq.* a sundowner. **7.** *U.S.* a type of sledge for sliding down icy slopes, etc. **8.** *U.S.* a roller-coaster. **9.** a tray, sometimes on wheels, for holding a decanter to be passed round a dining table. **10.** a small dish or mat placed under glasses, etc., to protect a table from moisture or heat. **11.** *N.Z. Colloq.* a person from the west coast.

**coastguard** /ˈkoʊstgad/, *n.* **1.** a coastal police force responsible for preventing smuggling, watching for ships in distress or danger, etc. **2.** a member of such an organisation.

**coastline** /ˈkoʊstlaɪn/, *n.* the outline or contour of a coast.

**coast rosemary** /koʊst ˈroʊzməri/, *n.* a compact grey-green shrub with white flowers, *Westringia fruticosa,* found on sea cliffs in New South Wales and commonly planted as an ornamental.

**coast sickness** /ˈ– sɪknəs/, *n.* →**coast disease.**

**coast-watcher** /ˈkoʊst-wɒtʃə/, *n.* one who acted during World War II as an observer of enemy shipping usu. living hidden on the coasts of islands north of Australia where such shipping passed.

**coastwise** /ˈkoʊstwaɪz/, *adv.* **1.** Also, **coastways** /ˈkoʊstweɪz/. along the coast. *–adj.* **2.** following the coast: *coastwise drift.*

**coasty** /ˈkoʊsti/, *adj.* **1.** suffering from coast sickness. **2.** sluggish; lethargic. **3.** of or pertaining to country where coast sickness is prevalent.

**coat** /koʊt/, *n.* **1.** an outer garment with sleeves; an overcoat, dress coat, etc. **2.** a natural integument or covering, as the hair, fur, or wool of an animal, the bark of a tree, or the skin of a fruit. **3.** anything that covers or conceals: *a coat of paint.* **4. on the coat,** *Prison Colloq.* ostracised. *–v.t.* **5.** to cover or provide with a coat. **6.** to cover with a layer or coating; cover as a layer or coating does. [ME *cote,* from OF, from Gmc; cf. OS *cott* woollen coat, ML *cotta* kind of tunic] – **coatless,** *adj.*

**coat-armour** /ˈkoʊt-amə/, *n.* a coat of arms.

**coat-card** /ˈkoʊt-kad/, *n. Obs.* →**court card.**

**coated** /ˈkoʊtəd/, *adj.* **1.** (of paper) having a highly polished coating applied to provide a smooth surface for printing. **2.** (of a fabric) having a plastic, paint, or pyroxylin coating, making it impervious to moisture. **3.** having a coat.

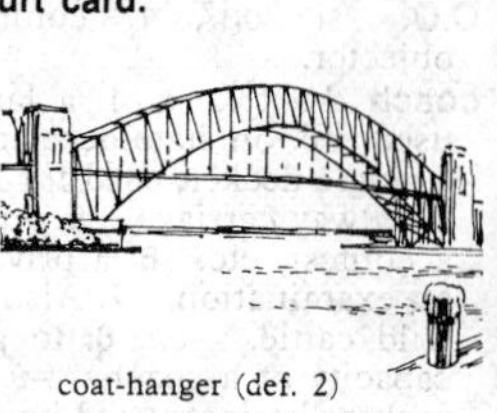
coat-hanger (def. 2)

**coat-hanger** /ˈkoʊt-hæŋə/, *n.* **1.** a curved piece of wood, plastic, etc., with a hook attached, on which clothes are hung. **2. the Coat-hanger,** *Colloq.* the Sydney Harbour Bridge.

**coati** /koʊˈati/, *n., pl.* **-tis.** any of the tropical American plantigrade carnivores constituting the genus *Nasua,* closely related to the raccoon, and having an elongated body, a long, ringed tail, and an attenuated, flexible snout. Also, **coati-mondi, coati-mundi** /koʊ,ati-ˈmʌndi/. [Tupi]

coati

**coating** /ˈkoʊtɪŋ/, *n.* **1.** a layer of any substance spread over a surface. **2.** material for coats.

**coat of arms,** *n.* **1.** a surcoat or tabard embroidered with heraldic devices, worn by medieval knights over their armour. **2.** the heraldic bearings of a person; a hatchment; an escutcheon. [translation of F *cotte d'armes*]

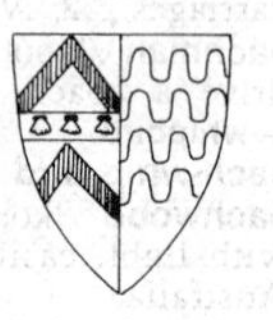
coat of arms (def. 2)

**coat of mail,** *n., pl.* **coats of mail.** a hauberk; a defensive garment made of interlinked metal rings, overlapping metal plates, etc.

**coat-tails** /ˈkoʊt-teɪlz/, *n.pl.* the divided, tapering skirts, or tails of a man's tail coat.

**coat-trailing** /ˈkoʊt-treɪlɪŋ/, *n.* the practice of trailing a coat. See **trail** (def. 9).

**co-author** /koʊ-ˈɔθə/, *n.* **1.** a joint author. *–v.t.* **2.** to write (a book) in partnership with someone else.

**coax** /koʊks/, *v.t.* **1.** to influence by gentle persuasion, flattery, etc. **2.** to get or win by coaxing. **3.** *Obs.* to fondle. **4.** *Obs.* to befool. *–v.i.* **5.** to use gentle persuasion, etc. [from obs. *cokes,* n., fool; of doubtful orig. Cf. COCKNEY] – **coaxer,** *n.* – **coaxingly,** *adv.*

**coaxial** /koʊˈæksiəl/, *adj.* **1.** having a common axis or coincident axes. **2.** (of a cable) composed of an insulated central conductor with tubular stranded conductors laid over it concentrically and separated by layers of insulation. Also, **coaxal** /koʊˈæksəl/.

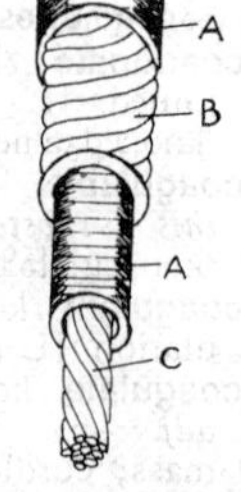

coaxial cable: A, insulation; B, outer conductor; C, inner conductor

**cob**[1] /kɒb/, *n., v.,* **cobbed, cobbing.** *–n.* **1.** a corncob. **2.** a cobnut. **3.** a male swan. **4.** a short-legged, thickset horse. **5.** a horse with an unnaturally high gait. **6.** a small lump of coal, ore, etc. **7.** a roundish mass, lump, or heap. **8.** a mixture of clay and straw, used as a building material. *–v.t.* **9.** to beat; strike. [ME; orig. obscure]

**cob**[2] /kɒb/, *n.* a gull, esp. the great black-backed gull, *Larus marinus.* Also, **cobb.** [orig. unknown. Cf. D *kob*]

**cob**[3] /kɒb/, *n. N.Z.* temper.

**cobalamin** /kəˈbæləmən/, *n.* vitamin $B_{12}$, occurring naturally in liver, eggs, meats, milk and fish, and used to treat pernicious anaemia.

**cobalt** /ˈkoʊbɔlt, -bɒlt/, *n.* **1.** *Chem.* a silver-white metallic element with a faint pinkish tinge, occurring in compounds the silicates of which afford important blue colouring substances for ceramics; also used in alloys, particularly in cobalt steel. *Symbol:* Co; *at. wt:* 58.9332; *at. no.:* 27; *sp. gr.:* 8.9 at 20°C. **2.** a blue pigment containing cobalt. **3.** the isotope, cobalt 60; used in the treatment of cancer. [G *Kobalt*, var. of *Kobold* goblin]

**cobalt bloom** /– ˈblum/, *n.* the mineral erythrite, hydrated cobalt arsenate, $CO_3(AsO_4)_2 \cdot 8H_2O$, usu. of a peach-red colour, and often occurring as a pulverulent encrustation; used for colouring glass and ceramics.

**cobalt blue** /– ˈblu/, *n.* any of a number of pigments containing an oxide of cobalt.

**cobaltic** /koʊˈbɔltɪk/, *adj.* of or containing cobalt, esp. in the trivalent state.

**cobaltite** /koʊˈbɔltaɪt, ˈkoʊbəltaɪt/, *n.* an ore of cobalt, cobalt arsenic sulphide, CoAsS, silver-white with reddish tinge. Also, **cobaltine; cobalt glance.**

**cobaltous** /koʊˈbɔltəs/, *adj.* containing divalent cobalt.

**cobar** /ˈkoʊba/, *n. Colloq.* copper coinage. [named after *Cobar*, a copper-mining town in western N.S.W.]

**Cobar shower** /koʊba ˈʃaʊə/, *n.* a dust storm. [see COBAR]

**cobb**[1] /kɒb/, *n.* (formerly) a type of stagecoach, through-braced rather than sprung. [from *Cobb* & Co., the name of an Australian coaching company]

**cobb**[2] /kɒb/, *n.* →**cob**[2].

**cobber** /ˈkɒbə/, *Colloq.* –*n.* **1.** mate; friend. –*v.i.* **2. cobber up with,** *N.Z.* to make friends with. [orig. uncert., probably related to Brit. d. *cob* to form a friendship with; but cf. Yiddish *chaber* comrade]

**cobble** /ˈkɒbəl/, *n., v.,* **-bled, -bling.** –*n.* **1.** a cobblestone. **2.** (*pl.*) cob coal. **3.** a clumsily completed job of sewing, mending, etc. **4.** *Geol.* a rock fragment between 64 and 256 mm in diameter, rounded by erosion. –*v.t.* **5.** to pave with cobblestones. **6.** to mend (shoes, etc.); patch. **7.** to put together roughly or clumsily. [? COB[1], def. 7]

**cobbler**[1] /ˈkɒblə/, *n.* **1.** one who mends shoes. **2.** a clumsy workman. **3.** an iced drink made of wine, fruit, sugar, etc. **4.** a fruit pie with a biscuit dough topping, usu. made in a deep dish. **5.** one of the Australian eel-tailed catfishes, *Tandanus bostocki.*

**cobbler**[2] /ˈkɒblə/, *n.* a wrinkled sheep that is difficult to shear, often shorn last in the day; snob. Also, **sandy cobbler.** [? pun on *cobbler's last*]

**cobblers** /ˈkɒbləz/, *n.pl. Colloq.* **1.** balls, testicles. **2.** nonsense; rubbish. **3. a load of old cobblers,** a lot of nonsense. [rhyming slang, *cobbler's (awls)* balls]

**cobbler's awl** /kɒbləz ˈɔl/, *n.* **1.** →**eastern spinebill. 2.** →**avocet.**

**cobbler's pegs** /– ˈpɛgz/, *n.* an annual weed of roadsides, *Bidens pilosa,* with barbed awns which stick to clothing. Also, **beggar's tick.**

**cobbler's punch** /– ˈpʌntʃ/, *n.* a hot punch made of beer, spices, etc.

**cobblestone** /ˈkɒbəlstoʊn/, *n.* a naturally rounded stone, large enough for use in paving.

**cobbra** /ˈkɒbrə/, *n. Obs.* the head or skull. [Aboriginal]

**cobelligerent** /koʊbəˈlɪdʒərənt/, *n.* **1.** a nation, state, or individual that cooperates with, but is not bound by a formal alliance to, another in carrying on war. –*adj.* **2.** relating to such cooperation.

**cobia** /ˈkoʊbiə/, *n.* an eastern Australian sport fish, *Rachycentron pondicerianum,* dark-brown to blackish above, striped when young; black kingfish; sergeant fish.

**coble** /ˈkoʊbəl, ˈkɒ-/, *n.* a kind of flat-bottomed rowing or fishing boat. [ME; cf. OE *cuopl*, Welsh *ceubal*, ML *caupulus*]

**cobloaf** /ˈkɒbloʊf/, *n.* a rounded loaf, not baked in a tin.

**cobnut** /ˈkɒbnʌt/, *n.* →**hazelnut.**

**COBOL** /ˈkoʊbɒl/, *n.* a language for writing computer programs of a business nature. Also, **Cobol.** [*Co(mmon) B(usiness) O(riented) L(anguage)*]

**cobra** /ˈkɒbrə, ˈkoʊbrə/, *n.* any snake of the genus *Naja,* exceedingly venomous and characterised by the ability to dilate its neck so that it assumes a hoodlike form. [short for Pg. *cobra* (from L *colubra* serpent) *de capello* hood snake]

**cobweb** /ˈkɒbwɛb/, *n.* **1.** a web or net spun by a spider to catch its prey. **2.** a single thread spun by a spider. **3.** anything fine-spun, flimsy, or unsubstantial. **4.** a network of plot or intrigue; an insidious snare. **5.** anything obscure or confused: *the cobwebs of early medieval scholarship.* [ME *coppeweb,* from *coppe* spider (OE *-coppe* in *ātorcoppe* spider) + WEB] –**cobwebbed,** *adj.* –**cobwebby,** *adj.*

**coca** /ˈkoʊkə/, *n.* **1.** either of two shrubs, *Erythroxylum coca* and *Erythroxylum truxillense,* native to the Andes and cultivated in Java and elsewhere. **2.** their dried leaves, which are chewed for their stimulant properties and which yield cocaine and other alkaloids. [Quechua *cuca*]

**cocaine** /koʊˈkeɪn/, *n.* a bitter crystalline alkaloid, $C_{17}H_{21}NO_4$, obtained from coca leaves, used as a local anaesthetic. Also, **cocain.** [COCA + -INE[2]]

**cocainism** /koʊˈkeɪnɪzəm, kəˈkeɪn-/, *n.* a morbid condition due to excessive or habitual use of cocaine.

**coccid** /ˈkɒksɪd/, *n.* any insect of the homopterous superfamily Coccoidea, including the scale insects, etc.

**coccidia** /kɒkˈsɪdiə/, *n.pl.* microscopic epithelial protozoan parasites of the digestive tract of animals. –**coccidial,** *adj.* –**coccidian,** *adj.*

**coccidioidomycosis** /kɒkˌsɪdiɔɪdoʊmaɪˈkoʊsəs/, *n.* a fungus infection characterised by infective granulomas formed in the viscera and the skin.

**coccidiosis** /kɒkˌsɪdiˈoʊsəs/, *n.* any one of a series of specific infectious diseases caused by epithelial protozoan parasites, which usu. affect the intestines. The disease is known in birds, cattle, swine, sheep, and dogs; it rarely occurs in man.

**coccus** /ˈkɒkəs/, *n., pl.* **-ci** /-saɪ/. **1.** *Bacteriol.* a spherical organism when free, slightly flattened when two or more form in apposition, as in the *Neisseria gonorrhoeae* or *N. meningitidis.* **2.** *Bot.* one of the carpels of a schizocarp. **3.** *Pharm.* cochineal. [NL, from Gk *kókkos* grain, seed] –**coccoid** /ˈkɒkɔɪd/, *adj.*

A B

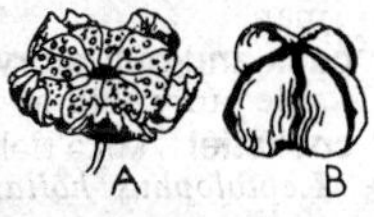

coccus (def. 2): A, fruit composed of ten cocci; B, fruit composed of four cocci

**coccyx** /ˈkɒksɪks, ˈkɒkɪks/, *n., pl.* **coccyges** /kɒkˈsaɪdʒiz/. **1.** a small triangular bone forming the lower extremity of the spinal column in man, consisting of four ankylosed rudimentary vertebrae. **2.** a corresponding part in certain other animals. [L, from Gk *kókkyx* coccyx, orig., cuckoo] –**coccygeal** /kɒksəˈdʒiəl, kɒkˈsɪdʒiəl/, *adj.*

**cochin** /ˈkoʊtʃɪn, ˈkɒtʃɪn/, *n.* (*sometimes cap.*) a breed of large domestic fowls, of Asiatic origin, resembling the brahma but slightly smaller. [named after *Cochin*-China, a region of Vietnam]

cochin (male)

**cochineal** /kɒtʃəˈnil, ˈkɒtʃənil/, *n.* **1.** a red dye prepared from the dried bodies of the females of a scale insect, *Dactylopius coccus,* which lives on cacti of Mexico and other warm regions of Central America. **2.** the insect itself. **3.** the crimson colour of this dye. [F *cochenille,* from Sp. *cochinilla,* orig. woodlouse, from *cochino* pig]

**cochlea** /ˈkɒkliə/, *n., pl.* **-leae** /-lii/. a division, spiral in form, of the internal ear, in man and most other mammals. [L, from Gk *kochlíās* snail, something spiral] –**cochlear,** *adj.*

**cochleate** /ˈkɒkliˌeɪt, -liət/, *adj.* shaped like a snail shell; spiral. Also, **cochleated.** [L *cochleātus*]

**cock**[1] /kɒk/, *n.* **1.** a male chicken. **2.** the male of any bird, esp. of the gallinaceous kind. **3.** the crowing of the cock. **4.** a weathercock. **5.** a leader; chief person; ruling spirit. **6.** a device for permitting or arresting the flow of a liquid or gas from a receptacle or through a pipe; a tap or stop valve. **7.** (in a firearm) **a.** that part of the lock which by its fall or action causes the discharge; the hammer. **b.** the position into which the cock or hammer is brought by being drawn partly or completely back, preparatory to firing. **8.** the pointer or needle of a balance. **9.** *Curling.* the mark aimed at. **10.** *Colloq.* a mate, friend or fellow. **11.** *Colloq.* the penis. **12. cock and bull,** nonsense; an incredible story. **13. cock of the walk,** one who asserts himself domineeringly, as the leader of a gang. **14. hot cock,** *Colloq.* nonsense. *–v.t.* **15.** to pull back and set the cock or hammer of (a firearm) preparatory to firing. **16. cock a snook** or **snoot,** *Colloq.* to put a thumb to the nose, in a contemptuous gesture. *–v.i.* **17.** to cock the firing mechanism of a gun. [ME *cok,* OE *cocc,* c. Icel. *kokkr*]

**cock**[2] /kɒk/, *v.t.* **1.** to set or turn up or to one side, often in an assertive, jaunty, or significant manner. **2. cock up,** to make a mess of; ruin: *you really cocked that up.* *–v.i.* **3.** to stand or stick up conspicuously. **4.** *Obs.* to strut; swagger; put on airs of importance. *–n.* **5.** the act of turning the head, a hat, etc., up or to one side in a jaunty or significant way. **6.** the position of anything thus placed. **7.** the angle to the wrist at which something is held: *the cock of the racquet.* [probably special use of COCK[1]]

**cock**[3] /kɒk/, *n.* **1.** a conical pile of hay, etc. *–v.t.* **2.** to put (hay, etc.) in such piles. [ME. Cf. Norw. *kok* heap]

**cock**[4] /kɒk/, *n. Colloq.* nonsense. [short for POPPYCOCK]

**cockabully** /kɒkə'bʊli/, *n. N.Z.* (*esp. in children's speech*) any of several kinds of small freshwater fish. [? Maori *kokopu*]

**cockade** /kɒ'keɪd/, *n.* a knot of ribbon, rosette, etc., worn on the hat as a badge or a part of a uniform. [alteration of *cockard,* from F *cocarde,* from *coq* cock] – **cockaded,** *adj.*

**cock-a-doodle-doo** /ˌkɒk-ə-dudl-'du/, *n., pl.* **-doos,** *v.* **-dooed, -dooing.** *–n.* **1.** the sound of the crowing of a cock. *–v.i.* **2.** to crow.

**cock-a-hoop** /kɒk-ə-'hup/, *adj.* in a state of unrestrained joy or exultation.

**cock-a-leekie** /kɒk-ə-'liki/, *n.* a soup made from a fowl boiled with leeks, etc. Also, **cocky-leeky, cocka-leekie.** [Scot.]

**cockalorum** /kɒkə'lɔrəm/, *n. Colloq.* a self-important little man.

**cock-and-bull story** /ˌkɒk-ən-'bʊl stɔri/, *n.* an absurd improbable story told as true.

**cockatiel** /kɒkə'tɪəl/, *n.* a small, crested, long-tailed parrot, *Leptolophus hollandicus,* common in inland areas of Australia; quarrion; cockatoo-parrot. [D *kaketielje.* Cf COCKATOO]

**cockatoo** /kɒkə'tu/, *n.* **1.** any of the crested parrots constituting the genera *Cacatua, Callocephalon,* or *Calyptorhynchus,* forming the subfamily Kakatoeinae, of the East Indies, Australia, etc., often white, or white and yellow, pink, or red. **2.** a farmer, esp. one who farms in a small way. **3.** *Colloq.* one who keeps watch during a two-up game, or other illegal activity. [D *kaketoe,* from Malay *kakatūa*]

cockatoo

**cockatoo apple** /– 'æpəl/, *n.* a small tree, *Planchonia careya,* common in northern Australia, with bark used as a fish poison. Also, **cocky apple.**

**cockatoo fence** /– 'fɛns/, *n.* a rough fence made of logs and branches.

**Cockatoo Islander** /kɒkətu 'aɪləndə/, *n.* (formerly) a convict on Cockatoo Island in Sydney Harbour.

**cockatoo-parrot** /ˌkɒkətu-'pærət/, *n.* →**cockatiel.**

**cockatrice** /'kɒkətrəs, -traɪs/, *n.* **1.** a mythical serpent with deadly glance, reputed to be hatched by a serpent from a cock's egg, and commonly represented with the head, legs, and wings of a cock and the body and tail of a serpent. **2.** a basilisk. **3.** *Bible.* an unidentified species of venomous serpent. [ME *cocatris,* from OF, from L *calcāre* tread; used to render Gk *ichneúmōn* ICHNEUMON; associated with COCK[1]]

**cockboat** /'kɒkbout/, *n.* a small boat, esp. one used as a tender.

**cockchafer** /'kɒktʃeɪfə/, *n.* any of certain scarabaeid beetles, esp. the European species, *Melolontha melolontha,* which is very destructive to forest trees. [COCK[1] (def. 5, with reference to size) + CHAFER]

**cockcrow** /'kɒkkrou/, *n.* the time at which cocks crow; dawn. Also, **cockcrowing.**

**cocked hat** /kɒkt 'hæt/, *n.* **1.** a hat having the brim turned up on two or three sides, common in the 18th century. **2. knock into a cocked hat,** *Colloq.* to damage or destroy completely; outdo, overcome, or defeat utterly.

**cocker** /'kɒkə/, *n.* **1.** a cocker spaniel. **2.** one who promotes or patronises cockfighting. [COCK[1], *v.* + -ER[1]]

cocker spaniel

**cockerel** /'kɒkərəl, 'kɒkrəl/, *n.* a young domestic cock. [diminutive of COCK[1]. See -REL]

**cocker spaniel** /kɒkə 'spænjəl/, *n.* one of a breed of small spaniels trained for use in hunting or kept as pets.

**cockeye** /'kɒkaɪ/, *n.* an eye that squints, or is affected with strabismus. [COCK[2], *v.* + EYE]

**cockeye bob** /– 'bɒb/, *n. Colloq.* a sudden storm or squall. Also, **cockeyed bob.**

**cockeyed** /'kɒkaɪd/, *adj.* **1.** having a squinting eye; cross-eyed. **2.** *Colloq.* twisted or slanted to one side. **3.** *Colloq.* foolish; absurd. **4.** *Colloq.* drunk.

**cockfight** /'kɒkfaɪt/, *n.* **1.** a fight between gamecocks, usu. armed with spurs. **2.** a game, often in water, in which contestants on piggyback try to unseat one another by grappling, etc. *–v.i.* **3.** to take part in a cockfight. *–v.t.* **4.** to fight someone in this manner. – **cockfighting,** *n.*

**cockhorse** /kɒk'hɔs/, *n.* **1.** a child's rocking horse or hobby-horse. **2. ride a cockhorse,** to be jubilant.

**cockish** /'kɒkɪʃ/, *adj. Colloq.* cocklike; cocky. – **cockishly,** *adv.* – **cockishness,** *n.*

**cockle** /'kɒkəl/, *n., v.,* **-led, -ling.** *–n.* **1.** any of the bivalve molluscs with somewhat heart-shaped, radially ribbed valves which constitute the genus *Cardium,* esp. *C. edule,* the common edible species of Europe. **2.** any of various allied or similar molluscs. **3.** cockleshell. **4.** a wrinkle; pucker. **5. cockles of the heart,** the inmost parts of the heart; the depths of one's emotions or feelings. **6.** a small shallow or light boat. **7.** a furnace; a stove. *–v.i.* **8.** to contract into wrinkles; pucker. **9.** to rise into short, irregular waves. *–v.t.* **10.** to cause to wrinkle or pucker: *a book cockled by water.* [ME *cockille,* from F *coquille,* b. *coque* shell and L *conchylium,* from Gk *konchýlion,* diminutive of *kónchē* mussel or cockle, CONCH[1]]

**cockleboat** /'kɒkəlbout/, *n.* →**cockboat.**

**cocklerina** /kɒklə'rinə/, *n.* →**Major Mitchell.**

**cockleshell** /'kɒkəlʃɛl/, *n.* **1.** a shell of the cockle. **2.** a shell of some other mollusc, as the scallop. **3.** a small, light boat. **4.** *Hist.* the badge of a pilgrim.

**cockloft** /'kɒklɒft/, *n.* a small upper loft; a small garret.

**cockney** /'kɒkni/, *n., pl.* **-neys,** *adj.* *–n.* (*oft. cap.*) **1.** a native of London, esp. of the East End (often with reference to one who has marked peculiarities of pronunciation and dialect). **2.** this pronunciation or dialect. *–adj.* **3.** of cockneys or their dialect. [ME *cockeney* cock's egg (i.e. malformed egg), from *coken,* gen. pl. of *cok* cock + *ey,* OE *ǣg* egg] – **cockneyish,** *adj.*

**cockney bream** /– 'brɪm/, *n.* →**snapper** (def. 1).

**cockneydom** /'kɒknidəm/, *n.* **1.** the region of cockneys. **2.** cockneys collectively.

**cockneyfy** /'kɒknəfaɪ/, *v.t.,* **-fied, -fying.** to give a cockney character to. Also, **cocknify.**

**cockneyism** /'kɒkniɪzəm/, *n.* **1.** cockney quality or usage. **2.** a cockney peculiarity, as of speech.

**cock-of-the-rock** /kɒk-əv-ðə-'rɒk/, *n.* a brilliant orange-red bird of the genus *Rupicola* with the bill hidden by the frontal plumes, found in northern South America.

**cockpit** /'kɒkpɪt/, *n.* **1.** (in some aeroplanes) an enclosed space containing seats for the pilot and copilot. **2.** the driver's seat in a racing car. **3.** a recess aft, in the deck of a yacht or other boat, which provides a small amount of deck space at a lower level. **4.** *Hist.* a space below the waterline, in warships, used as quarters for certain officers and as a dressing station for the wounded. **5.** a pit or enclosed space for cockfights. **6.** a place where a contest is fought, or which has been the scene of many contests or battles: *Belgium, the cockpit of Europe.*

**cock-rag** /ˈkɒk-ræg/, *n. Colloq.* →**loincloth.**

**cockroach** /ˈkɒkroʊtʃ/, *n.* any of various orthopterous insects of the family Blattidae, usu. nocturnal, and having a flattened body, esp. the dark brown or black oriental roach (black beetle, *Blatta orientalis*). [popular rendition of Sp. *cucaracha.* Cf. popular *sparrow grass* for *asparagus*, etc.]

**cockscomb** /ˈkɒkskoʊm/, *n.* **1.** the comb or caruncle of a cock. **2.** the cap of a professional fool, resembling a cock's comb. **3.** a garden plant, *Celosia argentea* var. *cristata,* with flowers, commonly crimson or gold, in a broad spike somewhat resembling the comb of a cock. **4.** any of several other species of *Celosia.* **5.** →**coxcomb.**

**cocksfoot** /ˈkɒksfʊt/, *n.* a perennial grass, *Dactylis glomerata,* with inflorescences resembling a cock's foot, common in temperate regions.

**cocksfooting** /ˈkɒksfʊtɪŋ/, *n. N.Z.* the gathering of cocksfoot seed for sale. – **cocksfooter,** *n.*

**cockshy** /ˈkɒkʃaɪ/, *n., pl.* **-shies. 1.** the act or sport of throwing missiles at a target. **2.** an object of attack.

**cock sparrow** /ˈkɒk spæroʊ/, *n.* **1.** a male sparrow. **2.** *Colloq.* a conceited little man.

**cockspur** /ˈkɒkspɜ/, *n.* **1.** an annual grass, *Echinochloa crus-galli,* widespread in warm temperate regions. **2.** any of various species of *Centaurea,* esp. *Centaurea melitensis,* Maltese cockspur.

**cocksure** /ˈkɒkʃɔ/, *adj.* **1.** perfectly certain; completely confident in one's own mind. **2.** too certain; overconfident. **3.** *Obs.* perfectly secure or safe. – **cocksureness,** *n.*

**cockswain** /ˈkɒksən, -sweɪn/, *n.* →**coxswain.**

**cocktail** /ˈkɒkteɪl/, *n.* **1.** any of various short mixed drinks, consisting typically of gin, whisky, or brandy, mixed with vermouth, fruit juices, etc. often shaken, usu. chilled and frequently sweetened. **2.** →**seafood cocktail. 3.** a small piece of chicken, fish, etc., served as a savoury. **4.** an appetiser of fruit or tomato juice. **5.** a horse with a docked tail. **6.** a horse which is not thoroughbred. **7.** an ill-bred person passing as a gentleman. *–v.i.* **8.** to attend a cocktail party. [orig. unknown]

**cocktail bar** /ˈ– ba/, *n.* **1.** (in a club, restaurant, etc.) a counter at which drinks are served as cocktails. **2.** Also, **cocktail lounge.** the room in which such a counter stands and which usu. provides comfortable seating accommodation. **3.** (in a private house) a small counter with its ancillary shelves, etc., at which drinks are mixed and dispensed for guests and family.

**cocktail cabinet** /ˈ– kæbənət/, *n.* a piece of furniture often mirror-lined and elaborate, in which bottles of spirits, glasses, etc., are stored and from which drinks are served.

**cocktail frankfurt** /ˈ– fræŋkfət/, *n.* a small frankfurt; cheerio.

**cocktail lounge** /ˈ– laʊndʒ/, *n.* →**cocktail bar** (def. 2).

**cocktail onion** /ˈ– ʌnjən/, *n.* a small, pickled onion, frequently coloured artificially.

**cocktail sauce** /– ˈsɔs/, *n.* a sauce composed of cream or mayonnaise and a number of spiced ingredients as ketchup, chilli sauce, horseradish, etc., served with seafood cocktails, etc.

**cockteaser** /ˈkɒktizə/, *n.* →**prickteaser.**

**cock-up** /ˈkɒk-ʌp/, *n.* **1.** *Print.* a letter rising above other letters; ascender. **2.** *Colloq.* a mess; a tangle.

**cocky**[1] /ˈkɒki/, *adj.,* **cockier, cockiest.** *Colloq.* arrogantly smart; pertly self-assertive; conceited: *a cocky fellow, air, answer.* – **cockily,** *adv.* – **cockiness,** *n.*

**cocky**[2] /ˈkɒki/, *Colloq.* *–n.* **1.** a cockatoo, or other parrot. **2.** a farmer, esp. one who farms in a small way. *–v.i.* **3.** to follow the occupation of a farmer. [abbrev. COCKATOO]

cocky²: cocky farmer

**cocky-leeky** /kɒki-ˈliki/, *n.* →**cock-a-leekie.**

**cockylora** /kɒkiˈlɔrə/, *n.* **1.** a children's game in which a group of children run repeatedly through an area guarded by other children, those who are caught each time joining forces with their catchers until only one child remains uncaught and is the victor. **2.** any of a number of children's games esp. those involving a cockfight (def. 2). Also, **cockylorum** /kɒkiˈlɔrəm/.

**cocky's joy** /kɒkiˈz ˈdʒɔɪ/, *n. Colloq.* golden syrup; treacle. Also, **bullocky's joy.**

**coco** /ˈkoʊkoʊ/, *n., pl.* **-cos. 1.** a tall, slender tropical palm, *Cocos nucifera,* which produces the coconut; coconut palm. **2.** the coconut fruit or seed. [Sp., Pg.: grinning face]

**cocoa** /ˈkoʊkoʊ/, *n.* **1.** the roasted, husked, and ground seeds of the cacao, *Theobroma cacao,* from which much of the fat has been removed. **2.** a beverage made from cocoa powder. **3.** brown; reddish brown. *–adj.* **4.** of or pertaining to cocoa. **5.** of the colour of cocoa. [var. of CACAO]

**cocoa bean** /ˈ– bin/, *n.* the seed of the cacao tree.

**cocoa butter** /ˈ– bʌtə/, *n.* a fatty substance obtained from the seeds of the cacao, used in making soaps, cosmetics, etc. Also, **cacao butter.**

**coconsciousness** /koʊˈkɒnʃəsnəs/, *n.* mental processes dissociated from the main stream of thought or from the dominant personality integration. – **coconscious,** *adj.* – **coconsciously,** *adv.*

**coconut** /ˈkoʊkənʌt/, *n.* **1.** the seed of the coconut palm, large, hard-shelled, lined with a white edible meat, and containing a milky liquid. **2.** *N.Z. Colloq.* (*derog.*) a Pacific Islander.

**coconut butter** /ˈ– bʌtə/, *n.* →**copha.**

**coconut crab** /ˈ– kræb/, *n.* →**robber crab.**

**coconut ice** /– ˈaɪs/, *n.* a confection, usu. pink or white, made from sugar, desiccated coconut, etc.

**coconut matting** /– ˈmætɪŋ/, *n.* matting made from the tough outer fibres of the coconut husks.

**coconut milk** /ˈ– mɪlk/, *n.* **1.** the liquid contained in a coconut. **2.** a drink made by compounding coconut flesh (sometimes desiccated) with water.

**coconut oil** /ˈ– ɔɪl/, *n.* an oil obtained from the dried coconut flesh used in foods, making soap, etc.

**coconut palm** /ˈ– pam/, *n.* →**coco** (def. 1). Also, **coconut tree.**

**coconut-shy** /ˈkoʊkənʌt-ʃaɪ/, *n.* a cockshy with coconuts as targets and prizes.

**cocoon** /kəˈkun/, *n.* **1.** the silky envelope spun by the larvae of many insects, as silkworms, serving as a covering while they are in the chrysalis or pupal state. **2.** any of various similar protective coverings, as the silky case in which certain spiders enclose their eggs. *–v.t.* **3.** to enclose within a protective covering. [F *cocon,* from *coque* shell]

**cocoplum** /ˈkoʊkoʊˌplʌm/, *n.* a small shrub of the Caribbean, *Chrysobalanus icaco,* with an edible fruit.

**Cocos Islands** /ˌkoʊkəs ˈaɪləndz/, *n.pl.* a group of 20 coral islands in the Indian Ocean north west of Australia, a territory of Australia. Also, **Keeling Islands.**

**cocotte** /koʊˈkɒt/, *n.* **1.** a courtesan; immoral woman. **2.** an ovenproof casserole. **3. en cocotte,** cooked and served in a casserole. [F: hen, from *coq* rooster]

**cod**[1] /kɒd/, *n.* **1.** any of a number of often unrelated fishes both freshwater and marine, as the Murray cod, *Maccullochella macquariensis,* butterfly cod, *Pterois volitans,* black rock cod, *Epinephelus damelii,* etc., belonging to several different families and widely distributed in Australian waters. **2.** any of a number of marine species of southern Australia belonging or related to the European cod family, Gadidae, esp. the rock cod and the ling. **3.** one of the most important North Atlantic food fishes, *Gadus callarias.* **4.** *U.S.* any of several other gadoid fishes, as the Pacific cod, *Gadus macrocephalus.* [ME; orig. uncert.]

**cod**[2] /kɒd/, *n.* **1.** a bag or sack. **2.** a pod. **3.** *Colloq.* (*sometimes pl.*) the scrotum. [ME; OE *codd*]

**cod., 1.** codex. **2.** codicil. **3.** codification.

**C.O.D.** /si oʊ ˈdi/, **1.** cash on delivery. **2.** *U.S.* collect on delivery. Also, **c.o.d.**

**coda** /ˈkoʊdə/, *n.* a more or less independent passage, at the end of a musical composition, introduced to bring it to a satisfactory close. [It., from L *cauda* tail]

**coddle** /ˈkɒdl/, *v.t.,* **-dled, -dling. 1.** to cook (eggs, fruit, etc.) slowly in water just below boiling point. **2.** to treat tenderly; nurse or tend indulgently; pamper. [var. of and v. use of *caudle* kind of gruel, from ONF *caudel,* from ML *caldellum,* diminutive of *cal(i)dum* hot drink, neut. of L *calidus* hot]

**code** /koud/, *n., v.,* **coded, coding.** *–n.* **1.** any systematic collection or digest of the existing laws of a country, or of those relating to a particular subject: *the Civil Code of France.* **2.** any system or collection of rules and regulations. **3.** a system of symbols for use in communication by telegraph, heliograph, etc., as morse code. **4.** a symbol (made up of signs, numbers, letters, sounds, etc.) in such a system. **5.** a set of words, pictures or other readily recognised symbols used for conveying messages briefly, as road signs. **6.** a system of arbitrarily chosen symbols, words etc. used for secrecy. **7.** a system of symbols for conveying information or instructions to an electronic computer. *–v.t.* **8.** to arrange in a code; enter in a code. **9.** to translate into a code. [ME, from F, from L *cōdex.* See CODEX]

**codeclination** /ˌkoudɛkləˈneɪʃən/, *n.* (in astronomy) the complement of the declination.

**codefendant** /koudəˈfɛndənt/, *n.* a joint defendant.

**codeine** /ˈkoudin/, *n.* a white, crystalline, slightly bitter alkaloid, $C_{18}H_{21}NO_3H_2O$, obtained from opium, used in medicine as an analgesic, sedative, and hypnotic. Also, **codein, codeia** /kouˈdiə/. [Gk *kṓdeia* head, poppyhead + -INE[2]]

**codetta** /kouˈdɛtə/, *n.* a short coda.

**codex** /ˈkoudɛks/, *n., pl.* **codices** /ˈkoudəsiz, ˈkɒdə-/. a manuscript volume of an ancient classic, the Scriptures, etc. [L, earlier *caudex* tree trunk, book]

**codfish** /ˈkɒdfɪʃ/, *n., pl.* **-fishes,** *(esp. collectively)* **-fish.** →**cod**[1].

**codger** /ˈkɒdʒə/, *n. Colloq.* **1.** a mean, miserly person. **2.** an odd or peculiar (old) person: *a lovable old codger.* **3.** a fellow; a chap. [? var. of CADGER]

**codicil** /ˈkɒdəsɪl/, *n.* **1.** a supplement to a will, containing an addition, explanation, modification, etc., of something in the will. **2.** some similar supplement. [L *cōdicillus,* diminutive of *cōdex.* See CODEX]

**codicillary** /kɒdəˈsɪləri/, *adj.* of the nature of a codicil.

**codification** /koudəfəˈkeɪʃən, kɒdə-/, *n.* **1.** the act or result of arranging in a code. **2.** *Law.* the collection of all the principles of any system of Law into one body after the manner of the Codex Justinianius and other codes.

**codify** /ˈkoudəfaɪ, ˈkɒdə-/, *v.t.,* **-fied, -fying. 1.** to reduce (laws, etc.) to a code. **2.** to digest; arrange in a systematic collection. [COD(E) + -IFY. Cf. F *codifier*] – **codifier,** *n.*

**codling**[1] /ˈkɒdlɪŋ/, *n.* **1.** any of several varieties of elongated apples, used for cooking purposes. **2.** the tree which bears codlings. **3.** an unripe, half-grown apple. Also, **codlin** /ˈkɒdlən/. [ME *querdling,* from *querd* (orig. unknown) + -LING[1]]

**codling**[2] /ˈkɒdlɪŋ/, *n.* the young of the cod. [ME; from COD[1] + -LING[1]]

**codling moth** /ˈ– mɒθ/, *n.* a small moth, *Carpocapsa pomonella,* whose caterpillar (larva) feeds on the pulp around the core of apples and other fruit. Also, **codlin moth.**

**cod-liver oil** /ˌkɒd-lɪvər ˈɔɪl/, *n.* a fixed oil, extracted from the liver of the common cod or of allied species, extensively used in medicine as a source of vitamins A and D.

**codon** /ˈkoudɒn/, *n.* any sequence of three adjacent nucleotides or messenger RNA that specifies the insertion of an amino acid in a particular structural position in a protein being synthesised. [COD(E) + ON]

**codpiece** /ˈkɒdpis/, *n.* (in 15th- and 16th- century male costume) a bagged appendage to the front of tight-fitting hose or breeches, covering the genitals. [COD[2] + PIECE]

**codswallop** /ˈkɒdzwɒləp/, *n. Colloq.* rubbish or nonsense.

**coecum** /sikəm/, *n.* →**caecum.**

**co-ed** /ˈkou-ɛd/, *Colloq. –adj.* **1.** coeducational. *–n.* **2.** *U.S.* a female student in a coeducational institution, esp. in a college or university. Also, *Chiefly U.S.,* **coed.** [short for COEDUCATIONAL]

**coedit** /kouˈɛdət/, *v.t.* to edit jointly.

**coedition** /kouəˈdɪʃən/, *n.* a book published simultaneously by two or more publishers in different countries.

**coeditor** /kouˈɛdətə/, *n.* a joint editor.

**coeducation** /ˌkouɛdʒəˈkeɪʃən/, *n.* joint education, esp. of both sexes in the same institution and classes. – **coeducational,** *adj.*

**coeff.,** coefficient.

**coefficient** /kouəˈfɪʃənt/, *n.* **1.** that which acts together with another thing to produce a result. **2.** *Maths.* a number or quantity placed (generally) before and multiplying another quantity: *3 is the coefficient of x in 3x.* **3.** *Physics.* a quantity, constant for a given substance, body, or process under certain specified conditions, that serves as a measure of some one of its properties: *coefficient of friction.* *–adj.* **4.** cooperating.

**coehorn** /ˈkouhɔn/, *n.* a small mortar for throwing grenades, used in the 18th century.

**coelacanth** /ˈsiləkænθ/, *n.* one of a group of fishes belonging to the suborder Actinistia, which, until a living specimen was caught in southern African waters in 1938, were believed to have been extinct for 70 million years. [*coel-* (combining form representing Gk *koîlos* hollow) + *-acanth* (see ACANTHO-)]

coelacanth

**-coele,** a word element referring to some small cavity of the body. Also, **-cele, -coel.** [combining form representing Gk *koilía* belly and *koîlos* hollow]

**coelenterate** /səˈlɛntəreɪt, -tərət/, *n.* **1.** a member of the Coelenterata, a phylum of invertebrate animals that includes the hydras, jellyfishes, sea-anemones, corals, etc., and is characterised by a single internal cavity serving for digestion, excretion, and other functions. *–adj.* **2.** belonging to the Coelenterata. [COELENTER(ON) + -ATE[1]]

**coelenteron** /səˈlɛntərɒn/, *n., pl.* **-tera** /-tərə/. the body cavity of a coelenterate. [*coel-* (combining form representing Gk *koîlos* hollow) + Gk *énteron* intestine]

**coeliac** /ˈsiliæk/, *adj.* pertaining to the cavity of the abdomen. Also, **celiac.** [L *coeliacus,* from Gk *koiliakós* of the belly]

**coeliac disease** /ˈ– dəziz/, *n.* a congenital disorder characterised by diarrhoea due to intolerance of the bowels to gluten.

**coelom** /ˈsiləm/, *n.* the body cavity of a metazoan, as distinguished from the intestinal cavity. Also, **coelome, celom.** [Gk *koílōma* a hollow]

**coemption** /kouˈɛmpʃən, -ˈɛmʃən/, *n.* the buying up of the whole of a particular commodity, esp. in order to acquire a monopoly. [L *coemptio,* from *coemere* buy up]

**coenaesthesia** /sinəsˈθiʒə/, *n.* the general sense of life, the bodily consciousness, or the total impression from all contemporaneous organic sensations, as distinct from special and well-defined sensations, such as those of touch or sight. Also, **coenesthesia, cenesthesia, coenaesthesis** /sinəsˈθisəs/, **coenesthesis, cenesthesis.** [COEN(O)- + AESTHESIA. Cf. ANAESTHESIA]

**coeno-,** a word element meaning 'common'. Also, **ceno-,** (before a vowel) **coen-.** [Gk *koino-,* combining form of *koinós*]

**coenobite** /ˈsinəbaɪt/, *n.* one of a religious order living in a convent or community. Also, **cenobite.** [LL *coenobīta,* from *coenobium,* from Gk *koinóbion* convent, neut. of *koinóbios* living in a community] – **coenobitic** /sinəˈbɪtɪk/, **coenobitical** /sinəˈbɪtɪkəl/, *adj.* – **coenobitism** /ˈsinəbaɪtɪzəm/, *n.*

**coenobium** /siˈnoubiəm/, *n.* a colony of unicellular organisms.

**coenocyte** /ˈsinəsaɪt/, *n.* an organism made up of many protoplasmic units enclosed by one cell wall, as in some algae and fungi.

**coenosarc** /ˈsinousak/, *n.* the common living tissue uniting the polyps of a compound zoophyte.

**coenurus** /siˈnjuərəs/, *n.* the larva of a tapeworm of the genus *Multiceps,* in which a number of heads (**scoleces**) form in the bladder. One species causes gid in sheep. [NL, from *coen-* COEN- + Gk *ourá* tail]

**coenzyme** /kouˈɛnzaɪm/, *n. Biochem.* →**cofactor.**

**coenzyme A** /– ˈeɪ/, *n.* a coenzyme containing a thiol group which activates carboxylic acids.

**coenzyme Q** /– ˈkju/, *n. Biochem.* →**ubiquinone.**

**coequal** /kouˈikwəl/, *adj.* **1.** equal in rank, ability, etc. *–n.* **2.** a person or thing coequal with another. – **coequality** /ˌkouiˈkwɒləti/, *n.* – **coequally,** *adv.*

**coerce** /kouˈɜs/, *v.t.,* **-erced, -ercing. 1.** to restrain or constrain by force, law, or authority; force or compel, as to do something. **2.** to compel by forcible action: *coerce obedience.* [L *coercēre* hold together] – **coercer,** *n.* – **coercible,** *adj.*

**coercion** /koʊ'ɜʃən, -ʒən/, *n.* **1.** the act or power of coercing; forcible constraint. **2.** government by force.

**coercive** /koʊ'ɜsɪv/, *adj.* serving or tending to coerce. – **coercively,** *adv.* – **coerciveness,** *n.*

**coercive force** /– 'fɔs/, *n.* the strength of the magnetic field required to annul the residual magnetism in a ferromagnetic substance. Also, **coercivity** /koʊɜ'sɪvəti/.

**coessential** /koʊə'sɛnʃəl/, *adj.* united in essence; having the same essence or nature. – **coessentiality** /ˌkoʊəsɛnʃi'æləti/, **coessentialness,** *n.* – **coessentially,** *adv.*

**coetaneous** /koʊə'teɪniəs/, *adj.* of the same age or duration. [LL *coaetāneus* of the same age]

**coeternal** /koʊi'tɜnəl/, *adj.* equally eternal; existing with another eternally. – **coeternally,** *adv.*

**coeternity** /koʊi'tɜnəti/, *n.* coexistence from eternity with another eternal being.

**coeval** /koʊ'ivəl/, *adj.* **1.** of the same age, date, or duration; equally old. **2.** contemporary; coincident. –*n.* **3.** a contemporary. **4.** one of the same age. [L *coaevus* of the same age + -AL[1]] – **coevally,** *adv.*

**coevolution** /ˌkoʊivə'luʃən/, *n.* the contemporaneous evolution of two different plants or animals from a common ancestor.

**coevolve** /koʊi'vɒlv/, *v.i.* **-evolved, -evolving.** to evolve contemporaneously.

**coexecutor** /koʊəg'zɛkjətə/, *n.* a joint executor.

**coexecutrix** /koʊəg'zɛkjətrɪks/, *n., pl.* **-executrices** /-əgzɛkjə'traɪsiz/. a female coexecutor.

**coexist** /koʊəg'zɪst/, *v.i.* to exist together or at the same time. – **coexistence,** *n.* – **coexistent,** *adj.*

**coextend** /koʊək'stɛnd/, *v.t.* **1.** to cause to extend equally through the same space or duration. –*v.i.* **2.** to reach the same limit in space or duration. – **coextension,** *n.*

**coextensive** /koʊək'stɛnsɪv/, *adj.* having equal or coincident extension. – **coextensively,** *adv.*

**cofactor** /'koʊfæktə/, *n.* **1.** an accompanying factor. **2.** *Biochem.* an essential component necessary for many enzymic reactions.

**C. of E.** /si əv 'i/, Church of England.

**coffee** /'kɒfi/, *n.* **1.** a beverage, consisting of a decoction or infusion of the roasted and ground or crushed seeds (**coffee beans**) of the two-seeded fruit (**coffee berry**) of *Coffea arabica* and other species of *Coffea,* trees and shrubs of tropical regions. **2.** the berry or seed of such plants. **3.** the tree or shrub itself. **4.** light brown. [Turk. *qahveh,* from Ar. *qahwa*]

coffee: A, berry; B, open berry showing beans

**coffee bar** /'– ba/, *n.* an establishment where coffee and other refreshments are served.

**coffee break** /'– breɪk/, *n.* a pause from work, usu. in the middle of the morning for coffee, etc.

**coffee bush** /'– bʊʃ/, *n.* any of various species of the genus *Coprosma,* native to New Zealand, esp. *C. lucida.*

**coffee cake** /'– keɪk/, *n.* **1.** a cake flavoured with coffee. **2.** a cake often made esp. to be served with coffee, as a plain spiced cake or petit fours.

**coffee crystals** /'– ˌkrɪstəlz/, *n.pl.* largish brown-coloured sugar crystals.

**coffee cup** /'– kʌp/, *n.* a cup designed expressly to have coffee drunk from it and usu. smaller than a tea cup.

**coffee grinder** /'– graɪndə/, *n.* **1.** a small, electrically or hand-operated apparatus used to crush coffee beans. **2.** →**coffee-grinder winch.**

**coffee-grinder winch** /'kɒfi-graɪndə ˌwɪntʃ/, *n.* on a yacht, a two-man, fast-action winch with the operating handles mounted on a pedestal remote from the winch drum.

**coffee house** /'kɒfi haʊs/, *n.* a public room where coffee and other refreshments are supplied.

**coffeepot** /'kɒfipɒt/, *n.* a container, with a spout or pouring lip, in which coffee is made or served.

**coffee royal** /kɒfi 'rɔɪəl/, *n.* coffee laced with rum.

**coffee shop** /'– ʃɒp/, *n.* **1.** a shop which sells and or serves coffee, tea, etc. **2.** a public room, as in a hotel, where coffee and food are served.

**coffee table** /'– teɪbəl/, *n.* a small, low table, on which coffee may be served, magazines and ornaments arranged, etc.

**coffee-table** /'kɒfi-teɪbəl/, *adj.* of books, magazines, etc., usu. large in format and of general interest in subject-matter, and designed for display as on a coffee table.

**coffee tree** /'kɒfi tri/, *n.* any tree, as *Coffea arabica,* yielding coffee beans.

**coffer** /'kɒfə/, *n.* **1.** a box or chest, esp. one for valuables. **2.** (*pl.*) a treasury; funds. **3.** any of various boxlike enclosures, as a cofferdam. **4.** a canal lock chamber. **5.** a caisson, or watertight box. **6.** an ornamental sunken panel in a ceiling or soffit. –*v.t.* **7.** to deposit or lay up in or as in a coffer or chest. **8.** to ornament with coffers or sunken panels: *a coffered ceiling.* [ME *cofre,* from OF: chest, from L *cophinus* basket. See COFFIN]

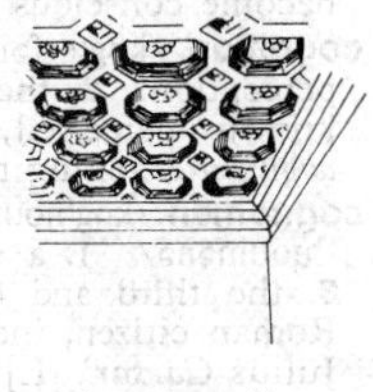

coffers of a ceiling (def. 6)

**cofferdam** /'kɒfədæm/, *n.* a watertight enclosure constructed in rivers, etc., and then pumped dry so that bridge foundations, etc., may be constructed in the open. Also, **coffer.**

**coffin** /'kɒfən/, *n.* **1.** the box or case in which a corpse is placed for burial. **2.** the part of a horse's foot containing the coffin bone. –*v.t.* **3.** to put or enclose in or as in a coffin. [ME *cofin,* from OF: small basket, coffin, from L *cophinus,* from Gk *kóphinos* basket]

**coffin bone** /'– boʊn/, *n.* the terminal phalanx in the foot of the horse and allied animals, enclosed in the hoof.

**coffin nail** /'– neɪl/, *n. Colloq.* a cigarette.

**coffle** /'kɒfəl/, *n.* a train of men or beasts, esp. of slaves, fastened together. [Ar. *qāfila* caravan]

**C. of S.,** chief of staff. Also, **C.O.S.**

**cog**[1] /kɒg/, *n.* **1.** a tooth or projection (usu. one of a series) on a wheel, etc., for transmitting motion to, or receiving motion from, a corresponding tooth or part with which it engages. **2.** a cogwheel. **3.** a person of little importance, in a large organisation. **4.** *Carp.* a rectangular piece of wood let into notches in two adjacent timbers to prevent sliding. [ME *cogge,* akin to CUDGEL]

**cog**[2] /kɒg/, *v.,* **cogged, cogging.** –*v.t.* **1.** to manipulate or load (dice) unfairly. –*v.i.* **2.** to cheat, esp. at dice. [orig. obscure]

**cog.,** cognate.

**cogency** /'koʊdʒənsi/, *n.* power of proving or producing belief; convincing force.

**cogener** /koʊ'dʒinə/, *n.* →**congener.**

**cogent** /'koʊdʒənt/, *adj.* compelling assent or belief; convincing; forcible: *a cogent reason.* [L *cōgens,* ppr., forcing, collecting] – **cogently,** *adv.*

**cogitate** /'kɒdʒəteɪt/, *v.,* **-tated, -tating.** –*v.i.* **1.** to think hard; ponder; meditate. –*v.t.* **2.** to think about; devise. [L *cōgitātus,* pp.] – **cogitator,** *n.*

**cogitation** /kɒdʒə'teɪʃən/, *n.* **1.** meditation. **2.** the faculty of thinking. **3.** a thought; a design or plan.

**cogitative** /'kɒdʒətətɪv/, *adj.* **1.** meditating. **2.** given to meditation; thoughtful: *cogitative pause.* – **cogitatively,** *adv.*

**cognac** /'kɒnjæk/, *n.* **1.** (*oft. cap.*) the brandy distilled in and shipped from the legally delimited area surrounding the town of Cognac, France. **2.** any brandy, esp. one made in France.

**cognate** /'kɒgneɪt/, *adj.* **1.** related by birth; of the same parentage, descent, etc. **2.** related in origin: *cognate languages, words, etc.* **3.** allied in nature or quality. –*n.* **4.** a person or thing cognate with another. [L *cognātus*]

**cognation** /kɒg'neɪʃən/, *n.* cognate relationship.

**cognisable** /'kɒgnəzəbəl, 'kɒnə-/, *adj.* **1.** capable of being perceived or known. **2.** within the jurisdiction of a court. Also, **cognizable.** – **cognisably,** *adv.*

**cognisance** /'kɒgnəzəns, 'kɒnə-/, *n.* **1.** knowledge; notice; perception: *to have or take cognisance of a fact, remark, etc.* **2.** *Law.* **a.** judicial notice as taken by a court in dealing with a cause. **b.** the right of taking judicial notice, as possessed by a court. **c.** acknowledgment; admission, as a plea admitting the fact alleged in the declaration. **d.** knowledge by which a judge is bound to act without having it proved by evidence. **3.** the range or scope of knowledge, observation, etc. **4.** *Her.* a distinctive badge, etc., worn by retainers. Also, **cognizance.** [ME *conisance,* from OF *conoissance,* from *conoistre,* from L *cognoscere* come to know]

**cognisant** /'kɒgnəzənt, 'kɒnə-/, *adj.* **1.** having cognisance; aware (fol. by *of*). **2.** competent to take judicial notice, as of causes. Also, **cognizant.**

**cognise** /'kɒgnaɪz, kɒg'naɪz/, *v.t.,* **-nised, -nising.** to perceive; become conscious of; know. Also, **cognize.**

**cognition** /kɒg'nɪʃən/, *n.* **1.** the act or process of knowing; perception. **2.** the product of such a process; thing thus known, perceived, etc. **3.** *Obs.* knowledge. [ME, from L *cognitio* a getting to know] – **cognitive** /'kɒgnətɪv/, *adj.*

**cognomen** /kɒg'noʊmən/, *n., pl.* **-nomens, -nomina** /-'nɒmənə, -'noʊmənə/. **1.** a surname. **2.** any name, esp. a nickname. **3.** the third and commonly the last name (in order) of a Roman citizen, indicating his house or family, as in 'Caius Julius *Caesar*'. [L] – **cognominal** /kɒg'nɒmənəl, -'noʊmə-/, *adj.*

**cognoscente** /kɒnjə'ʃɛnti, kɒnə-/, *n., pl.* **-ti** /-ti/. a person having a superior knowledge or critical appreciation in a particular branch of the arts; a connoisseur. [It., var. of *conoscente,* ppr. of *conoscere,* from L *cognoscere* know]

**cognoscible** /kɒg'nɒsəbəl/, *adj.* capable of being known. – **cognoscibility** /kɒgˌnɒsə'bɪləti/, *n.*

**cognovit** /'kɒgnəvɪt/, *n. Law.* (formerly) an acknowledgment or confession by a defendant that the plaintiff's cause, or a part of it, is just, wherefore the defendant, to save expense, suffers judgment to be entered without trial. [L: he acknowledged]

**cogon** /'koʊgoʊn/, *n.* a tall, coarse grass, *Imperata cylindrica,* of the tropics and subtropics, furnishing an excellent material for thatching. [Sp., from Tagalog]

**cog railway** /kɒg 'reɪlweɪ/, *n. Chiefly U.S.* →**rack-railway.**

**cogwheel** /'kɒgwil/, *n.* a wheel with cogs, for transmitting or receiving motion. [late ME]

**cohabit** /koʊ'hæbət/, *v.i.* **1.** to live together in a sexual relationship. **2.** *Archaic.* to dwell or reside in company or in the same place. [LL *cohabitāre* dwell with] – **cohabitant, cohabiter,** *n.* – **cohabitation** /ˌkoʊhæbə'teɪʃən/, *n.*

**coheir** /koʊ'ɛə/, *n.* a joint heir. – **coheiress,** *n. fem.* – **coheirship,** *n.*

**cohere** /koʊ'hɪə/, *v.i.,* **-hered, -hering. 1.** to stick together; be united; hold fast, as parts of the same mass. **2.** to be naturally or logically connected. **3.** to agree; be congruous. [L *cohaerēre* stick together]

**coherence** /koʊ'hɪərəns/, *n.* **1.** the act or state of cohering; cohesion. **2.** natural or logical connection. **3.** congruity; consistency. Also, **coherency.**

**coherent** /koʊ'hɪərənt/, *adj.* **1.** cohering; sticking together. **2.** having a natural or due agreement of parts; connected. **3.** consistent; logical. **4.** *Physics.* of electromagnetic radiation, esp. light having its waves in phase. – **coherently,** *adv.*

**coherer** /koʊ'hɪərə/, *n.* an obsolete device for detecting radio waves, usu. a tube filled with a conducting substance in granular form, whose electrical resistance decreases when radio waves pass through it.

**cohesion** /koʊ'hiʒən/, *n.* **1.** the act or state of cohering, uniting, or sticking together. **2.** *Physics.* the state or process by which the particles of a body or substance are bound together, esp. the attraction between the molecules of a liquid. **3.** *Bot.* the congenital union of one part with another.

**cohesive** /koʊ'hisɪv/, *adj.* **1.** characterised by or causing cohesion. **2.** cohering; tending to cohere. – **cohesively,** *adv.* – **cohesiveness,** *n.*

**cohobate** /'koʊhoʊbeɪt/, *v.t.,* **-bated, -bating.** to distil again from the same or a similar substance, as a distilled liquid poured back upon the matter remaining in the vessel, or upon another mass of similar matter. [ML *cohobātus,* pp. of *cohobāre,* from obs. med. term *cohob,* of uncert. orig.]

**cohort** /'koʊhɔt/, *n.* **1.** one of the ten divisions in an ancient Roman legion, numbering from 300 to 600 men. **2.** any group of warriors. **3.** any group or company. [L *cohors* (orig. enclosure; see COURT)]

**cohune** /koʊ'hun/, *n.* a pinnate-leaved palm, *Orbignya cohune,* native to Central America, bearing large nuts whose meat yields an oil resembling that of the coconut. Also, **cohune palm.**

**coif** /kɔɪf/, *n.* **1.** a hood-shaped cap worn under a veil, as by nuns. **2.** a close-fitting cap of various kinds, as one worn by European peasant women. **3.** a cap like the skullcap, retained until the common introduction of the wig, esp. as the headdress of barristers. *–v.t.* **4.** to cover or dress with, or as with, a coif. [ME, from OF *coife,* from LL *cofea* cap; apparently of Gmc orig. (cf. MHG *kupfe* cap)]

**coiffeur** /kwʌ'fɜ/, *n.* a hairdresser. [F, from *coiffer.* See COIFFURE]

**coiffure** /kwʌ'fjʊə/, *n.* **1.** a style of arranging or combing the hair. **2.** a head covering; headdress. [F, from *coiffer,* lit., furnish with a coif]

**coign** /kɔɪn/, *n.* →**quoin.** Also, **coigne.** [var. of COIN (def. 5)]

**coil**[1] /kɔɪl/, *v.t.* **1.** to wind into rings one above another; twist or wind spirally: *to coil a rope.* *–v.i.* **2.** to form rings, spirals, etc.; wind. **3.** to move in winding course. *–n.* **4.** a connected series of spirals or rings into which a rope or the like is wound. **5.** a single such ring. **6.** an arrangement of pipes, coiled or in a series, as in a radiator. **7.** *Elect.* **a.** a conductor, as a copper wire, wound up in a spiral or other form. **b.** a device composed essentially of such a conductor. **8.** *Med.* a spiral device introduced into the uterus to prevent conception. **9.** *Philately.* **a.** a stamp issued in a roll, usu. of 1,000 stamps, and usu. perforated vertically or horizontally only. **b.** a roll of such stamps. [F *cueillir* gather, from a LL form replacing L *colligere.* See COLLECT[1]]

**coil**[2] /kɔɪl/, *n.* **1.** disturbance; tumult; bustle: *this mortal coil.* **2.** trouble. [orig. unknown]

**coil ignition** /– ɪg'nɪʃən/, *n.* a system for supplying the sparking plugs of an internal-combustion engine with a high voltage from an induction coil rather than a magneto.

**coil spring** /'– sprɪŋ/, *n.* a spring coiled helically.

**coin** /kɔɪn/, *n.* **1.** a piece of metal stamped and issued by the authority of the government for use as money. **2.** such pieces collectively. **3. pay (someone) in his own coin,** to treat (someone) as he has treated others. **4. the other side of the coin,** the other side of the argument, the opposing point of view. **5.** *Archit.* →**quoin.** *–v.t.* **6.** to make (money) by stamping metal. **7.** to convert (metal) into money. **8.** *Colloq.* to make or gain (money) rapidly. **9.** to make; invent; fabricate: *to coin words.* **10. coin it,** *Colloq.* to make a lot of money. *–v.i.* **11.** to counterfeit money, etc. [ME, from F: wedge, corner, die, from L *cuneus* wedge] – **coinable,** *adj.* – **coiner,** *n.*

**coinage** /'kɔɪnɪdʒ/, *n.* **1.** the act, process, or right of making coins. **2.** that which is coined. **3.** coins collectively; the currency. **4.** the forming of new words. **5.** anything made, invented, or fabricated.

**coincide** /koʊən'saɪd/, *v.i.,* **-cided, -ciding. 1.** to occupy the same place in space, the same point or period in time, or the same relative position. **2.** to correspond exactly (in nature, character, etc.). **3.** to agree or concur (in opinion, etc.). [ML *coincidere,* from L *co-* CO- + *incidere* fall on]

**coincidence** /koʊ'ɪnsədəns/, *n.* **1.** the condition or fact of coinciding. **2.** a striking occurrence of two or more events at one time apparently by mere chance. **3.** exact agreement in nature, character, etc.

**coincidence circuit** /'– sɜkət/, *n.* an electronic circuit which is so arranged that it will produce an output only if two or more input signals arrive simultaneously (or within a specified interval). Also, **coincidence gate.**

**coincident** /koʊ'ɪnsədənt/, *adj.* **1.** coinciding; occupying the same place or position. **2.** happening at the same time. **3.** exactly corresponding. **4.** in exact agreement (fol. by *with*). – **coincidently,** *adv.*

**coincidental** /koʊɪnsə'dɛntl/, *adj.* showing or involving coincidence. – **coincidentally,** *adv.*

**coinheritance** /koʊɪn'hɛrətəns/, *n.* joint inheritance. – **coinheritor,** *n.*

**coinstantaneous** /ˌkoʊɪnstən'teɪniəs/, *adj.* happening at the same time.

**coinsurance** /koʊɪn'ʃɔrəns/, *n.* **1.** insurance jointly with another or others. **2.** a form of fire and various other forms of property insurance in which a person taking out insurance on property for less than its full value is regarded as a joint insurer and becomes jointly and proportionately responsible for losses. **3.** the method of distributing liability, in case of loss, among several insurers whose policies attach to the same risk.

**coinsure** /koʊɪn'ʃɔ/, *v.t., v.i.,* **-sured, -suring.** to insure jointly with another or others; insure on the basis of coinsurance. – **coinsurer,** *n.*

**co-interior angles** /koʊ-ɪnˌtɪəriər 'æŋgəlz/, *n.pl. Maths.* →**allied angles.**

**coir** /'kɔɪə/, *n.* the prepared fibre of the husk of the coconut fruit, used in making rope, matting, etc. [Malayalam *kāyar* cord]

**coit** /kɔɪt/, *n. Colloq.* →**quoit** (defs 3 and 4).

**coital exanthema** /ˌkoʊətl ɛksən'θimə/, *n.* a virus disease affecting horses and cattle characterised by the appearance of vesicles which later become pustules on the mucous membranes of the genital organs and neighbouring skin. It is transmitted either during mating or by artificial insemination using infected semen.

**coitus** /'koʊətəs/, *n.* sexual intercourse. Also, **coition** /koʊ'ɪʃən/. [L from *coīre* go together, meet]

**coitus interruptus** /– ɪntə'rʌptəs/, *n.* (in sexual intercourse) withdrawal of the penis before orgasm, to avoid conception.

**coke**[1] /koʊk/, *n., v.,* **coked, coking.** –*n.* **1.** the solid product resulting from the distillation of coal in an oven or closed chamber, or by imperfect combustion, used as a fuel, in metallurgy, etc. It contains about 80 per cent carbon. –*v.t.* **2.** to convert into coke. –*v.i.* **3.** to become coke. [? var. of *colk* core]

**coke**[2] /koʊk/, *n. Colloq.* cocaine. [short for COCAINE]

**coke**[3] /koʊk/, *n. Colloq.* →**coca cola.**

**coking coal** /'koʊkɪŋ koʊl/, *n.* black coal which when heated in the absence of air produces a hard coke suitable for steel making.

**col** /kɒl/, *n.* **1.** *Phys. Geog.* a saddle or pass between two higher-standing parts of a mountain range or ridge. **2.** *Meteorol.* the region of relatively low pressure between two anticyclones. [F, from L *collum* neck]

**col-**[1], variant of **com-**, by assimilation before *l,* as in *collateral.*

**col-**[2], variant of **colo-** before vowels, as in *colectomy.*

**col.,** **1.** colour. **2.** coloured. **3.** column.

**Col.,** **1.** Colonel. **2.** *Bible.* Colossians.

**cola**[1] /'koʊlə/, *n.* **1.** the cola nut. **2.** an extract prepared from it. **3.** a carbonated soft drink containing such an extract. **4.** the tree producing it. Also, **kola.** [Latinisation of *Kola, Kolla, Goora,* in Negro languages of W Africa]

**cola**[2] /'koʊlə/, *n.* plural of **colon.**

**colander** /'kʌləndə, 'kɒl-/, *n.* a strainer for draining off liquids, esp. in cookery. Also, **cullender.** [cf. ML *cōlātōrium,* from *cōlāre* strain]

colander

**colane** /kɒ'leɪn/, *n.* a tree, *Owenia acidula,* of the western plains of New South Wales and Queensland which bears edible subacid fruit; gruie.

**cola nut** /'koʊlə nʌt/, *n.* a brownish seed, about the size of a chestnut produced by a tree of western tropical Africa, the West Indies, and Brazil, *Cola acuminata,* and containing both caffeine and theobromine; used as a stimulant in soft drinks. Also, **kola nut.**

**colatitude** /koʊ'lætətʃud/, *n.* the complement of the latitude; the difference between a given latitude and 90°.

**colby** /'kɒlbi/, *n.* a cheese with some similarity in type and manufacture to cheddar, but with a softer body and more open texture, containing more moisture.

**colcannon** /kəl'kænən, 'kɒlkæn-/, *n.* an Irish dish made of cabbage (or greens) and potatoes boiled and mashed together. [COLE + *-cannon* (of uncert. orig. and meaning)]

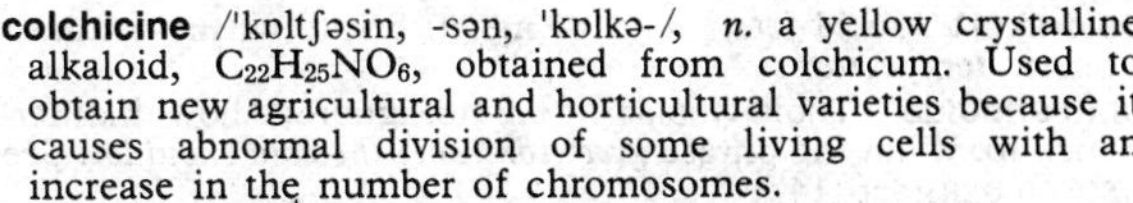

**colchicine** /'kɒltʃəsin, -sən, 'kɒlkə-/, *n.* a yellow crystalline alkaloid, $C_{22}H_{25}NO_6$, obtained from colchicum. Used to obtain new agricultural and horticultural varieties because it causes abnormal division of some living cells with an increase in the number of chromosomes.

**colchicum** /'kɒltʃɪkəm, 'kɒlkɪ-/, *n.* **1.** any plant of the Old World liliaceous genus *Colchicum,* esp. *C. autumnale,* a crocus-like plant. **2.** the dried seeds or corms of this plant. **3.** a medicine or drug prepared from them, used esp. for gout. [L, from Gk *kolchikón;* apparently named after *Colchis,* the legendary land of Medea and the Golden Fleece]

**colcothar** /'kɒlkəθa/, *n.* the red oxide of iron, $Fe_2O_3$, which remains after heating ferrous sulphate, and is used as a pigment and polishing agent; rouge. [ML, from Ar. *qolqotār*]

**cold** /koʊld/, *adj.* **1.** having a temperature lower than the normal temperature of the body: *cold hands.* **2.** having a relatively low temperature; having little or no warmth: *a cold day.* **3.** producing or feeling, esp. in a high degree, a lack of warmth: *I am cold.* **4.** dead. **5.** *Colloq.* unconscious because of a severe blow, shock, etc. **6.** deficient in passion, emotion, enthusiasm, ardour, etc.: *cold reason.* **7.** not affectionate, cordial, or friendly; unresponsive: *a cold reply.* **8.** lacking sensual desire; frigid. **9.** failing to excite feeling or interest. **10.** imperturbable. **11.** depressing; dispiriting: *cold misgivings.* **12.** faint; weak: *a cold scent.* **13.** distant from the object of search. **14.** (of colours) blue in effect, or inclined towards blue in tone: *a picture cold in tone.* **15.** slow to absorb heat, as a soil containing a large amount of clay and hence retentive of moisture. **16.** *Prison Colloq.* innocent of a charge laid against one. **17. cold comfort,** almost no consolation; negligible comfort. **18. cold feet,** loss of courage or confidence for carrying out some undertaking. **19. cold sweat,** perspiration and coldness caused by fear, nervousness, etc. **20. in cold blood,** calmly; coolly and deliberately. **21. leave one cold,** to fail to affect one, as with enthusiasm, sympathy, etc.: *her ravings left him cold.* **22. throw cold water on,** to dampen enthusiasm of (a person), or for (a thing); discourage. –*n.* **23.** the relative absence of heat. **24.** the sensation produced by loss of heat from the body, as by contact with anything having a lower temperature than that of the body. **25.** Also, **the common cold.** an indisposition caused by a virus, characterised by catarrh, hoarseness, coughing, etc. **26. catch** or **take cold,** to suffer from such a cold. **27. the cold,** cold weather. **28. in the cold,** neglected; ignored. [ME; d. OE *cald,* replacing OE *ceald,* c. G *kalt.* Cf. L *gelidus* icy] – **coldish,** *adj.* – **coldly,** *adv.* – **coldness,** *n.*

**cold-blooded** /'koʊld-blʌdəd/, *adj.* **1.** without feeling; unsympathetic; cruel: *a cold-blooded murder.* **2.** sensitive to cold. **3.** designating or pertaining to animals, as fishes and reptiles, whose blood temperature ranges from the freezing point upwards, in accordance with the temperature of the surrounding medium. – **cold-bloodedly,** *adv.* – **cold-bloodedness,** *n.*

**cold chisel** /'koʊld tʃɪzəl/, *n.* a strong steel chisel used on cold metal.

**cold cream** /'– krim/, *n.* an emollient of oily heavy consistency, used to soothe and cleanse the skin, esp. of the face and neck.

**cold frame** /'– freɪm/, *n.* a small glass-covered structure, and the bed of earth which it covers, used to protect plants.

**cold front** /'– frʌnt/, *n.* **1.** the contact surface between two air-masses where the cooler mass is advancing against and under the warmer mass. **2.** the line of intersection of this surface with the surface of the earth.

**cold-hearted** /'koʊld-hatəd/, *adj.* lacking sympathy or feeling; indifferent; unkind.

**coldie** /'koʊldi/, *n. Colloq.* a bottle or can of cold beer.

**cold pack** /'koʊld pæk/, *n.* a cold towel, icebag, etc., applied to the body to reduce swelling, relieve pain, etc.

**cold place** /'– pleɪs/, *n.* a place of work (as a refrigeration plant) where conditions are unpleasant because of the lowness of temperature and where employees are paid a special rate in compensation.

**cold-rolled** /'koʊld-roʊld/, *adj.* (of metal) rolled at a temperature close to atmospheric, producing a smooth surface finish.

**cold saw** /'koʊld sɔ/, *n.* a metal-cutting saw.

**cold-short** /'kould-ʃɔt/, *adj.* (of metal) brittle when at atmospheric temperature.

**cold-shoulder** /kould-'ʃouldə/, *v.t.* to ignore; show indifference to. [from the phrase *give (someone) the cold shoulder.* See SHOULDER (def. 14)]

**cold shut** /'kould ʃʌt/, *n.* an imperfectly fused junction of two streams of metal in a mould.

**cold snap** /– 'snæp/, *n.* a sudden period of cold weather.

**cold sore** /'– sɔ/, *n.* a vesicular eruption on the face often accompanying a cold or a febrile condition; herpes simplex.

**cold steel** /– 'stil/, *n.* a sword, bayonet, etc.

**cold storage** /– 'stɔrɪdʒ/, *n.* **1.** the storage of food, furs, etc., in an artificially cooled place. **2.** abeyance; indefinite postponement.

**cold-turkey** /kould-'tɜki/, *Colloq.* *–n.* **1.** unrelieved, blunt, matter-of-fact statement or procedure. **2.** the sudden and complete withdrawal of narcotics as a treatment of drug addiction. *–v.t.* **3.** to treat (an addict) in this manner.

**cold war** /kould 'wɔ/, *n.* intense economic and political rivalry just short of military conflict.

**cold warrior** /– 'wɒriə/, *n.* an advocate of a cold war.

**coldwater man** /kould'wɔtə mæn/, *n. Obs. Colloq.* a teetotaller.

**cold wave** /'kould weɪv/, *n.* **1.** *Meteorol.* a rapid and considerable fall in temperature, usu. affecting a large area. **2.** a permanent wave in the hair set by chemicals.

**cold-work** /'kould-wɜk/, *v.t.* to work (a metal, etc.) when it is in a solid or cold condition.

**cole** /koul/, *n.* any of various plants of the genus *Brassica,* esp. rape, *Brassica napus.* [ME *col(e),* OE *cāl,* var. of *cāw(e)l,* from L *caulis* stalk, cabbage]

**colectomy** /kə'lɛktəmi/, *n., pl.* **-mies.** the surgical removal of all or part of the colon or large intenstine.

**colemanite** /'koulmənaɪt/, *n.* a mineral, hydrated calcium borate, $Ca_2B_6O_{11}.5H_2O$, occurring in colourless or milky white crystals. [named after W. T. *Coleman* of San Francisco, in whose mine it was found]

**coleopteron** /ˌkɒli'ɒptərɒn/, *n.* a coleopterous insect; a beetle. Also, **coleopteran.** [NL, from Gk *koleópteron,* adj. (neut.), sheath-winged]

**coleopterous** /ˌkɒli'ɒptərəs/, *adj.* belonging or pertaining to the order Coleoptera, the beetles. [Gk *koleópteros* sheath-winged]

**coleoptile** /kɒli'ɒptaɪl/, *n.* (in grasses) the first leaf above the ground, forming a sheath round the stem tip. [NL *coleoptilum,* from Gk *koleón* sheath + *ptílon* soft feathers, down]

**coleorhiza** /kɒliə'raɪzə/, *n., pl.* **-zae** /-zi/. the sheath which envelops the radicle in certain plants, and which is penetrated by the root in germination. [NL, from Gk *koleó(s)* sheath + *rhíza* root]

**coleslaw** /'koulslɔ/, *n.* a dressed salad of finely sliced white cabbage. Also, **slaw.** [D *koolsla,* from *kool* cabbage + *sla,* reduced form of *salade* salad]

**coleus** /'kouliəs/, *n.* any plant of the genus *Coleus,* of tropical Asia and Africa, species of which are cultivated for their showy, coloured foliage. [NL, from Gk *koleós* sheath (so called from the union of the filaments about the style)]

**colic** /'kɒlɪk/, *n.* **1.** paroxysmal pain in the abdomen or bowels. *–adj.* **2.** pertaining to or affecting the colon or the bowels. [ME *colyke,* from L *cōlicus,* from Gk *kōlikós* pertaining to the colon] – **colicky** /'kɒlɪki/, *adj.*

**-coline,** →**-colous.** [L *colere* inhabit + -INE[1]]

**coliseum** /kɒlə'siəm/, *n.* →**colosseum.**

**colitis** /kɒ'laɪtəs, kə-/, *n.* inflammation of the mucous membrane of the colon. [NL; see COL(ON)[2], -ITIS]

**coll.,** **1.** collateral. **2.** collection. **3.** collective. **4.** collector. **5.** college. **6.** colloquial.

**collaborate** /kə'læbəreɪt/, *v.i.,* **-rated, -rating.** **1.** to work, one with another; cooperate, as in literary work. **2.** to cooperate treacherously: *collaborating with the Nazis.* [LL *collabōrātus,* pp.] – **collaboration** /kəlæbə'reɪʃən/, *n.* – **collaborator, collaborationist** /kəlæbə'reɪʃənəst/, *n.*

**collage** /kə'laʒ/, *n.* a pictorial composition made from any or a combination of various materials, as newspaper, cloth, etc., affixed in juxtaposition to a surface, and often combined with colour and lines from the artist's own hand.

**collagen** /'kɒlədʒən/, *n.* the protein contained in connective tissue and bones which yields gelatine on boiling. [F *collagène,* from Gk *kólla* glue + *-gène* -GEN]

**collapse** /kə'læps/, *v.,* **-lapsed, -lapsing,** *n.* *–v.i.* **1.** to fall or cave in; crumble suddenly: *the roof collapsed.* **2.** to be made so that parts can be folded, placed, etc., together: *this card table collapses.* **3.** to break down; come to nothing; fail: *the project collapsed.* **4.** to lose strength, courage, etc., suddenly. **5. a.** to sink into extreme weakness. **b.** (of lungs) to come into an airless state. *–v.t.* **6.** to cause to collapse. *–n.* **7.** a falling in or together. **8.** a sudden, complete failure; a breakdown. [L *collapsus,* pp., fallen together]

**collapsible** /kə'læpsəbəl/, *adj.* **1.** designed to fold into a more compact or manageable size, as a pram, bicycle, etc. **2.** designed to collapse or give way under pressure or in an emergency, as a steering column in a motor vehicle. Also, **collapsable.** – **collapsibility** /kəlæpsə'bɪləti/, *n.*

**collar** /'kɒlə/, *n.* **1.** anything worn or placed round the neck. **2.** the part of a shirt, blouse, coat, etc., round the neck, usu. folded over. **3.** a close-fitting necklace or ornamental band of linen, velvet, or the like, worn by women round the neck. **4.** an ornamental necklace worn as insignia of an order of knighthood. **5.** a leather or metal band put round an animal's neck to restrain or identify it. **6.** part of a harness round the horse's neck that bears some of the weight of the load drawn. **7.** *Bot.* the point of junction of the plumule and the radical. **8.** *Zool.* any of various markings, or structures, about the neck, suggesting a collar. **9.** a cut of bacon taken from the fore end. **10.** →**head** (def. 24). **11.** *Mach.* an enlargement encircling a rod or shaft, and serving usu. as a holding or bearing piece. *–v.t.* **12.** to put a collar on; furnish with a collar. **13.** to seize by the collar or neck. **14.** *Colloq.* **a.** to lay hold of, seize, or take. **b.** to get the better of, as in cricket: *to collar the bowling.* **15.** *Colloq.* to gain a monopoly over: *to collar the market in wool.* **16.** to cook (meat) by first rolling and binding with tape then boiling or roasting. [L *collāre* neckband, neck chain, collar, from *collum* neck; replacing ME *coler,* from AF] – **collarless,** *adj.*

**collar-and-elbow** /kɒlər-ən-'ɛlbou/, *n.* a style of wrestling in which the opponents grip each other by the collar and elbow, the first to relinquish his hold being deemed the loser.

**collarbone** /'kɒləboun/, *n.* →**clavicle.**

**collard** /'kɒləd/, *n.* a kind of cabbage, *Brassica oleracea,* var. *acephala,* cut before the hearts become hard.

**collaret** /kɒlə'rɛt/, *n.* a woman's small collar or neckpiece of lace, embroidery, chiffon, fur, or other material. Also, **collarette.** [COLLAR + -ET, replacing *colleret,* from F *collerette,* diminutive of *collier* collar]

**collar-proud** /'kɒlə-praud/, *adj.* **1.** of draught horses, chafed at the neck from being put in harness after a spell. **2.** unwilling to settle down to work after a holiday.

**collar stud** /'kɒlə stʌd/, *n.* a stud for fastening a collar to a shirt.

**collar tie** /'– taɪ/, *n.* →**tie beam** (def. 2).

**collate** /kə'leɪt, kɒ-/, *v.t.,* **-lated, -lating.** **1.** to compare (texts, statements, etc.) in order to note points of agreement or disagreement. **2.** *Bookbinding.* to verify the arrangement of, as the sheets of a book after they have been gathered. **3.** *Bibliog.* to verify the number and order of the sheets of (a volume) as a means of determining its completeness. **4.** to put together (a document) by sorting its pages into the correct order. **5.** *Eccles.* to present by collation, as to a benefice. [L *collātus,* pp., brought together]

**collateral** /kə'lætərəl/, *adj.* **1.** situated at the side. **2.** running side by side. **3.** *Bot.* standing side by side. **4.** accompanying; attendant; auxiliary. **5.** additional; confirming: *collateral security.* **6.** secured by collateral: *a collateral loan.* **7.** aside from the main subject, course, etc.; secondary; indirect. **8.** descended from the same stock, but in a different line; not lineal. **9.** pertaining to those so descended. *–n.* **10.** security pledged for the payment of a loan. **11.** a collateral kinsman. [ME, from ML *collaterālis.* See COL-[1], LATERAL] – **collaterally,** *adv.*

**collateral agreement** /– ə'grimənt/, *n. Law.* an independent agreement, additional but not subordinate to the main agreement on the same matter.

**collation** /kə'leɪʃən/, *n.* **1.** the act of collating. **2.** description of the technical features of a book; volumes, size, pages,

i = peat ɪ = pit ɛ = pet æ = pat a = part ɒ = pot ʌ = putt ɔ = port ʊ = put u = pool ɜ = pert ə = apart aɪ = buy eɪ = bay ɔɪ = boy aʊ = how oʊ = hoe ɪə = here ɛə = hair ʊə = tour g = give θ = thin ð = then ʃ = show ʒ = measure tʃ = choke dʒ = joke ŋ = sing j = you õ = Fr. bon

illustrations, etc. **3.** the presentation of a clergyman to a benefice, esp. by a bishop who is himself the patron or has acquired the patron's rights. **4.** a light meal which may be permitted on days of general fast. **5.** a light meal. **6.** the act of reading and conversing on the lives of the saints, or the Scriptures (a practice instituted in monasteries by St Benedict). [ME *collacion,* from L *collātio* a bringing together]

**collative** /kəˈleɪtɪv, ˈkɒlə-/, *adj.* **1.** collating. **2.** *Eccles.* presented by collation: *collative benefices.*

**collator** /kəˈleɪtə/, *n.* **1.** one who or that which collates. **2.** *Computers.* a machine which interleaves two packs of punched cards so that those with the same control information are brought together.

**colleague** /ˈkɒlig/, *n.* an associate in office, professional work, etc. [F *collègue,* from L *collēga* one chosen with another] – **colleagueship,** *n.*

**collect**[1] /kəˈlɛkt/, *v.t.* **1.** to gather together; assemble. **2.** to accumulate; make a collection of. **3.** to gather money for contributions or debts, for charity, etc. **4.** to regain control of (one's thoughts, faculties, etc., or oneself). **5.** to fetch; call for and remove. **6.** to run into or collide with, esp. in a motor vehicle. **7.** *Rare.* to infer. *–v.i.* **8.** to gather together; assemble. **9.** to accumulate: *rainwater collecting in the drainpipe.* **10.** to gather or bring together books, stamps, coins, etc., usu. as a hobby. **11.** to win on a race, gamble, etc. *–adj., adv.* **12.** to be paid for by the receiver: *to send a telegram collect.* *–n.* **13.** *Colloq.* a winning bet. [L *collectus,* pp., gathered together] – **collectable, collectible,** *adj.*

**collect**[2] /ˈkɒlɛkt/, *n.* any of certain brief prayers used in Western churches as before the epistle in the communion service, and in Anglican churches, also in morning and evening prayers. [ME *collecte,* from ML *collecta* short prayer, orig., a gathering together. See COLLECT[1]]

**collectanea** /ˌkɒlɛkˈteɪniə/, *n.pl.* collected passages; a miscellany; anthology. [L, neut. pl. of *collectāneus* collected]

**collected** /kəˈlɛktəd/, *adj.* having control of one's faculties; self-possessed. – **collectedly,** *adv.* – **collectedness,** *n.*

**collecting ring** /kəˈlɛktɪŋ ˌrɪŋ/, *n.* an assembly area for horses and riders at an equestrian event.

**collection** /kəˈlɛkʃən/, *n.* **1.** the act of collecting. **2.** the clearing of letter-boxes by a paid official. **3.** that which is collected; a set of objects, specimens, writings, etc., gathered together. **4.** a sum of money collected, esp. for charity or church use. **5.** the gathering of such money. [ME, from L *collectio*]

**collective** /kəˈlɛktɪv/, *adj.* **1.** formed by collection. **2.** forming a collection or aggregate; aggregate; combined. **3.** pertaining to a group of individuals taken together. **4.** (of a fruit) formed by the coalescence of the pistils of several flowers, as the mulberry or the pineapple. *–n.* **5.** a collective noun. **6.** a collective body; aggregate. **7.** *Govt.* a unit of organisation or the organisation in a collectivist system. **8.** a communal enterprise or system, working towards the common good, as opposed to one admitting competition between individuals. – **collectively,** *adv.*

**collective agreement** /– əˈgrimənt/, *n.* the contract, written or oral, made after negotiations following a dispute between an employer or employers and a union or unions on behalf of all the employees represented by the union or unions.

**collective bargaining** /– ˈbagənɪŋ/, *n.* a non-institutionalised system of reaching agreement on a matter of industrial disputation between employers and employees through discussions held by their representatives.

**collective behaviour** /– bəˈheɪvjə/, *n.* the concerted behaviour of individuals acting under the influence of one another.

**collective farm** /– ˈfam/, *n.* (in communist countries) a farm formed of pooled smallholdings worked as a single unit.

**collective noun** /– ˈnaʊn/, *n.* a noun that under the singular form expresses a grouping of individual objects or persons, as *herd, jury,* and *clergy.* The singular verb is used when the noun is thought of as naming a single unit, acting as one, as *family* in *his family is descended from Edward III.* The plural verb is used when the noun is thought of as composed of individuals who retain their separateness, as *my family are all at home.*

**collective security** /– səˈkjurəti/, *n.* a policy or principle in international relations, designed to preserve world peace, according to which all countries collectively guarantee the security of individual countries, as by sanctions or multilateral alliances against an aggressor.

**collective unconscious** /– ʌnˈkɒnʃəs/, *n.* (in psychology, esp. Jungian psychology) those elements in the individual's unconscious derived from the experiences of the race.

**collectivise** /kəˈlɛktəvaɪz/, *v.t.,* **-vised, -vising.** to organise (a people, industry, economy, etc.) according to the principles of collectivism. Also, **collectivize.** – **collectivisation** /kəlɛktəvaɪˈzeɪʃən/, *n.*

**collectivism** /kəˈlɛktəvɪzəm/, *n.* the socialist principle of control by the people collectively, or the state, of all means of production or economic activities. – **collectivist,** *n., adj.* – **collectivistic** /kəlɛktəˈvɪstɪk/, *adj.*

**collectivity** /kɒlɛkˈtɪvəti/, *n., pl.* **-ties.** **1.** collective character. **2.** a collective whole. **3.** the people collectively.

**collector** /kəˈlɛktə/, *n.* **1.** one who or that which collects. **2.** a person employed to collect debts, tickets, taxes, etc. **3.** one who collects, books, paintings, stamps, shells, etc., as a hobby. **4.** *Elect.* **a.** any device for collecting current from contact inductors. **b.** an electrode in a radio valve for collecting unwanted electrons or ions. **c.** an electrode in a transistor. [ME, from LL] – **collectorship,** *n.*

**collector's item** /kəˈlɛktəz aɪtəm/, *n.* an item worthy of having in a collection, because of its rarity, excellence or value.

**colleen** /ˈkɒlin, kɒˈlin/, *n.* a girl. [Irish *cailín*]

**college** /ˈkɒlɪdʒ/, *n.* **1.** a (usu.) post-secondary, diploma-awarding, technical or professional school, as *Teachers' College, Technical College.* **2.** an institution for special or professional instruction, as in medicine, pharmacy, agriculture, music, etc., often part of a university, as the *Royal Australian College of Surgeons.* **3.** an endowed, self-governing association of scholars incorporated within a university, as the church colleges within the University of Sydney. **4.** a similar foundation outside a university. **5.** any of certain large private schools, or sometimes public schools. **6.** *Brit.* a constituent unit of certain universities, sometimes residential, divided into faculties or the like, providing courses of instruction usu. leading to the degree of bachelor. **7.** the building or buildings occupied by any of these educational institutions. **8.** *U.S.* an institution of higher learning. esp. one not divided (like a university) into distinct schools and faculties, and affording a general or liberal education rather than technical or professional training. **9.** (in French use) an institute for secondary education. **10.** an organised association of persons having certain powers and rights, and performing certain duties or engaged in a particular pursuit: *an electoral college.* **11.** a company; assembly. **12.** *Hist.* a body of clergy living together on a foundation for religious service, etc. **13.** *Colloq.* a prison. [ME, from OF, from L *collēgium* association, a society]

**college of advanced education,** *n.* a tertiary institution conducting courses in diverse vocational studies, as accountancy, business management, engineering, librarianship, teacher training, etc.

**college pudding** /kɒlɪdʒ ˈpʊdɪŋ/, *n.* a baked or steamed suet or sponge pudding containing dried fruit.

**collegial** /kəˈlidʒiəl/, *adj.* belonging or pertaining to a college.

**collegian** /kəˈlidʒiən, -dʒən/, *n.* a member of a college.

**collegiate** /kəˈlidʒiət, -dʒət/, *adj.* **1.** of or pertaining to a college. **2.** of the nature of or constituted as a college. **3.** of a town containing a college.

**collegiate church** /– ˈtʃɜtʃ/, *n.* **1.** a church which is endowed for a chapter of canons (usu. with a dean), but which has no bishop's see. **2.** (loosely) a chapel connected with a college.

**col legno** /kɒl ˈleɪnjoʊ/, *adv.* (a musical direction) with the wood (of sound produced by players striking the strings of a bowed instrument with the wooden back of the bow). [It.]

**collembolan** /kəˈlɛmbələn/, *n.* **1.** a member of the Collembola, an order of small wingless insects; springtail. *–adj.* **2.** belonging to the Collembola.

**collenchyma** /kəˈlɛŋkəmə/, *n.* a layer of modified parenchyma consisting of cells which are thickened at the angles and commonly elongated. [NL, from Gk *kólla* glue + *énchyma* infusion]

**collet** /ˈkɒlət/, *n., v.,* **-leted, -leting.** *–n.* **1.** a collar or enclosing band. **2.** the enclosing rim within which a jewel is set. **3.** *Horol.* the tiny collar which supports the inner terminal of the hairspring. *–v.t.* **4.** to set in a collet: *colleted in gold.* [F, diminutive of *col* neck, from L *collum*]

**collide** /kə'laɪd/, *v.i.*, **-lided, -liding. 1.** to come together with force; come into violent contact; crash: *the two cars collided.* **2.** to clash; conflict. [L *collīdere*]

**collie** /'kɒli/, *n.* a dog of any of certain intelligent varieties much used for tending sheep, esp. one of Scottish breed, usu. with a heavy coat of long hair and a bushy tail. Also, **colly.**

collie

**collier** /'kɒliə/, *n.* **1.** a ship for carrying coal. **2.** a sailor in such a ship. **3.** a coal-miner. **4.** *Obs.* one who carries or sells coal.

**colliery** /'kɒljəri/, *n., pl.* **-ries.** a coal mine, including all buildings and equipment.

**colligate** /'kɒləgeɪt/, *v.t.*, **-gated, -gating. 1.** to bind or fasten together. **2.** *Logic.* to bind (facts) together by a general description or by a hypothesis which applies to them all. [L *colligātus,* pp., bound together] – **colligation** /kɒlə'geɪʃən/, *n.*

**colligative properties** /kə,lɪgətɪv 'prɒpətiz/, *n. pl.* the properties of a solution which depend only on the concentration of dissolved particles (molecules or ions) and not on their nature, as osmotic pressure.

**collimate** /'kɒləmeɪt/, *v.t.*, **-mated, -mating. 1.** to bring into line; make parallel. **2.** to adjust accurately the line of sight of (a telescope). **3.** to limit a beam of radiation or a stream of elementary particles to required dimensions. [L *collīmātus,* pp., var. (by false reading) of *collīneātus,* pp., brought into line with] – **collimation** /kɒlə'meɪʃən/, *n.*

**collimator** /'kɒləmeɪtə/, *n.* **1.** a small fixed telescope for use in collimating other instruments. **2. a.** a device for obtaining a parallel beam of light, consisting of a tube containing a convex lens at one end and an adjustable slit at the other; chiefly used in spectroscopes. **b.** the convex lens itself. **3.** (in radiology) an arrangement of absorbers for limiting a beam of radiation to the required dimensions.

**collinear** /kɒ'lɪniə/, *adj.* lying in the same straight line. [COL-[1] + LINEAR] – **collinearly,** *adv.*

**Collins Street cocky,** *n.* one who owns a country property, often for tax loss purposes, but who lives and works in Melbourne. Also, **Collins Street grazier, Collins Street farmer.** Cf. **Pitt Street farmer, Queen Street bushie.** [name of a street in central Melbourne]

**collision** /kə'lɪʒən/, *n.* **1.** the act of colliding; a coming violently into contact; crash. **2.** a clash; conflict. [late ME, from LL *collīsio,* from L *collīdere* COLLIDE]

**collision course** /'– kɔs/, *n.* a course or path of a vehicle which, if unchanged, will cause a collision.

**collocate** /'kɒləkeɪt/, *v.t.*, **-cated, -cating. 1.** to set or place together. **2.** to arrange in proper order: *collocated events.* [L *collocātus,* pp., set in a place]

**collocation** /kɒlə'keɪʃən/, *n.* **1.** the act of collocating. **2.** the state or manner of being collocated. **3.** *Linguistics.* a habitual arrangement or conjoining of particular words, as *green as grass, pass the buck.*

**collocutor** /kə'lɒkjətə/, *n.* one who talks to another; one who takes part in a colloquy.

**collodion** /kə'loʊdiən/, *n.* soluble guncotton dissolved in a mixture of ether and alcohol, used to form a coating or film on wounds, photographic plates, etc. [Gk *kollṓdēs* gluelike + *-ion,* suffix]

**colloid** /'kɒlɔɪd/, *n.* **1.** *Chem.* a substance present in solution in the colloidal state. **2.** *Med.* a homogeneous gelatinous substance occurring in some diseased states. [Gk *kólla* glue + -OID]

**colloidal** /kə'lɔɪdəl/, *adj.* pertaining to, or of the nature of a colloid: *colloidal gold, silver, etc.*

**colloidal graphite** /– 'græfaɪt/, *n.* finely ground graphite which when added to oil reduces its surface tension but not its viscosity.

**colloidal solution** /– sə'luʃən/, *n.* a solution in which the solute is in the colloidal state; a sol.

**colloidal state** /– 'steɪt/, *n.* a system of particles in a dispersion medium in which the particle diameters are between $10^{-5}$ and $10^{-7}$ cm, i.e. between a true molecular solution and a coarse suspension.

**colloid mill** /,kɒlɔɪd 'mɪl/, *n.* a high-speed mill capable of reducing a substance to a particle size of about $10^{-5}$cm.

**collophane** /'kɒləfeɪn/, *n.* →**apatite.**

**colloq., 1.** colloquial. **2.** colloquialism. **3.** colloquially.

**colloquial** /kə'loʊkwiəl/, *adj.* **1.** appropriate to or characteristic of conversational speech or writing in which the speaker or writer is under no particular constraint to choose standard, formal, conservative, deferential, polite, or grammatically unchallengeable words, but feels free to choose words as appropriate from the informal, slang, vulgar, or taboo elements of the lexicon. **2.** conversational. – **colloquially,** *adv.*

**colloquialism** /kə'loʊkwiə,lɪzəm/, *n.* **1.** a colloquial expression. **2.** colloquial style or usage.

**colloquium** /kə'loʊkwiəm/, *n.* an informal conference or group discussion.

**colloquy** /'kɒləkwi/, *n., pl.* **-quies. 1.** a speaking together; a conversation. **2.** a conference. **3.** (in certain Reformed Churches) a governing body corresponding to a presbytery. **4.** a literary composition in dialogue form. [L *colloquium* conversation] – **colloquist,** *n.*

**collotype** /'kɒlətaɪp/, *n.* **1.** *Print.* a process of high-quality printing from a gelatine coating on a glass plate. **2.** the plate. **3.** a print made from it. [*collo-* (combining form representing Gk *kólla* glue) + -TYPE]

**collude** /kə'lud/, *v.i.*, **-luded, -luding. 1.** to act together through a secret understanding. **2.** to conspire in a fraud. [L *collūdere* play with] – **colluder,** *n.*

**collunarium** /kɒljə'nɛəriəm/, *n.* a solution for application to the nose; nose drops. [NL, from L *colluere* wash + *nārēs* nostrils + *-ium* -IUM]

**collusion** /kə'luʒən/, *n.* **1.** secret agreement for a fraudulent purpose; conspiracy. **2.** *Law.* an arrangement between persons apparently in conflict or having conflicting interests, to do some act in order to injure a third person or deceive the court as: *collusion of a husband and wife to obtain a divorce.* [ME, from L *collūsio* a playing together]

**collusive** /kə'luzɪv/, *adj.* involving collusion; fraudulently concerted: *a collusive treaty.* – **collusively,** *adv.* – **collusiveness,** *n.*

**colluvium** /kɒ'luviəm/, *n.* loose and incoherent deposits, usu. at the foot of a slope or cliff line and brought by gravity.

**collyrium** /kɒ'lɪəriəm/, *n., pl.* **-lyria** /-'lɪəriə/, **-lyriums.** a solution for application to the eye; an eyewash. [L, from Gk *kollýrion* poultice, eye salve]

**collywobbles** /'kɒliwɒbəlz/, *n. Colloq.* **1.** stomach-ache. **2.** diarrhoea. [COLIC + WOBBLE(S)]

**colo-,** a combining form of **colon**[2].

**colocynth** /'kɒləsɪnθ/, *n.* **1.** a cucurbitaceous plant, *Citrullus colocynthis,* of the warmer parts of Asia, the Mediterranean region, etc., bearing a fruit with a bitter pulp which yields a purgative drug. **2.** the fruit. **3.** the drug. [L *colocynthis,* from Gk *kolokynthís*]

**cologne** /kə'loʊn/, *n.* a perfumed toilet water; eau de Cologne. Also, **Cologne water.** [for *Cologne water* (made at *Cologne,* Germany, since 1709)]

**Colombia** /kə'lʌmbiə/, *n.* a republic in north-western South America. – **Colombian,** *adj., n.*

**colon**[1] /'koʊlən/, *n., pl.* **-lons** *for def. 1,* **-la** /-lə/ *for def. 2.* **1.** a point of punctuation (:) marking off a main portion of a sentence (intermediate in force between the semicolon and the period). **2.** *Class. Pros.* one of the members or sections of a rhythmical period, consisting of a sequence of from two to six feet united under a principal ictus or beat. [L, from Gk *kôlon* limb, member, clause]

**colon**[2] /'koʊlən/, *n., pl.* **-lons, -la** /-lə/. that portion of the large intestine which extends from the caecum to the rectum. [ME, from L, from Gk *kólon* food, colon]

**colonel** /'kɜnəl/, *n.* **1.** an officer ranking in the Australian Army between lieutenant colonel and brigadier. **2.** an equivalent rank in any other army. [earlier *coronel,* from F *coronnel,* var. of *colonnel,* from It. *colonnello,* diminutive of

i = peat ɪ = pit ɛ = pet æ = pat a = part ɒ = pot ʌ = putt ɔ = port ʊ = put u = pool ɜ = pert ə = apart aɪ = buy eɪ = bay ɔɪ = boy aʊ = how oʊ = hoe ɪə = here ɛə = hair ʊə = tour g = give θ = thin ð = then ʃ = show ʒ = measure tʃ = choke dʒ = joke ŋ = sing j = you õ = Fr. bon

*colonna* COLUMN] – **colonelcy, colonelship,** *n.*

**colonel-in-chief** /kɜnəl-ɪn-'tʃif/, *n.* an honorary colonel.

**colonial** /kə'loʊniəl/, *adj.* **1.** of or pertaining to a colony or colonies. **2.** of or pertaining to a colonist: *paternalism is something demanded by the colonial outlook.* **3. a.** pertaining to the six British colonies in Australia before they federated in 1901, or to their period. **b.** pertaining to the thirteen British colonies which became the United States of America, or to their period. **4.** *Ecol.* forming a colony. **5.** (*cap.*) *Archit.* of or pertaining to the architecture of a colonial period, in Australia esp. the earlier colonial period in which the principal influences were from English Georgian and the wide-verandaed Indian bungalow; in the U.S., a simplification often of contemporary English styles, as the Queen Anne, and their translation into new materials (brick, wood, etc.). **6. my colonial oath,** (*euph.*) my bloody oath. –*n.* **7.** an inhabitant of a colony, esp. one who upholds the values formed in the colony rather than the values of the mother country. – **colonially,** *adv.*

**colonial animals** /– 'ænəməlz/, *n.pl.* **1.** animals that live in a group. **2.** single-celled animals that live together as a single unit.

**colonial dollar** /– 'dɒlə/, *n.* →**holey dollar.**

**colonial experience** /– ək'spɪəriəns/, *n. Colloq.* (formerly) any of the several abilities or skills gained by living in the British colonies, as in Australia and New Zealand. – **colonial experiencer,** *n.*

**colonial goose** /– 'gus/, *n.* a shoulder or leg of mutton, boned, stuffed with seasoned breadcrumbs, and roasted. Also, **colonial duck.**

**colonialism** /kə'loʊniəˌlɪzəm/, *n.* the policy of a nation seeking to extend or retain its authority over other peoples or territories.

**colonial oven** /kəˌloʊniəl 'ʌvən/, *n.* an iron oven, usu. bricked in, and heated from above and below; two-fire stove.

**colonial Robert** /– 'rɒbət/, *n. N.Z. Obs.* a shilling piece.

**colonic** /kə'lɒnɪk/, *adj.* of or affecting the colon.

**colonise** /'kɒlənaɪz/, *v.*, **-nised, -nising.** –*v.t.* **1.** to plant or establish a colony in; form into a colony; settle: *England colonised Australia.* –*v.i.* **2.** to form a colony. **3.** to settle in a colony. Also, **colonize.** – **colonisation** /kɒlənaɪ'zeɪʃən/, *n.* – **coloniser,** *n.*

**colonist** /'kɒlənəst/, *n.* **1.** an inhabitant of a colony. **2.** a member of a colonising expedition.

**colonnade** /'kɒləneɪd, kɒlə'neɪd/, *n.* **1.** a series of columns set at regular intervals, and usu. supporting an entablature, a roof, or a series of arches. **2.** a long row of trees. [F, from It. *colonnato,* from *colonna,* from L *columna* COLUMN] – **colonnaded,** *adj.*

**colony** /'kɒləni/, *n., pl.* **-nies. 1.** a group of people who leave their native country to form in a new land a settlement subject to, or connected with, the parent state. **2.** the country or district settled or colonised. **3.** any people or territory separated from but subject to a ruling power. **4.** any of the several settlements in Australia before their achievement of responsible government, as New South Wales, Van Diemen's Land, etc. **5.** a number of foreigners from a particular country living in a city or country, esp. in one locality: *the American colony in Paris.* **6.** any group of individuals of similar occupation, etc., usu. living in a community of their own: *a colony of artists.* **7.** the district or quarter inhabited by such a group. **8.** an aggregation of bacteria growing together as the descendants of a single cell. **9.** *Ecol.* a group of animals or plants, of the same kind, coexisting in close association. [ME *colonie,* from L *colōnia*]

**colophon** /'kɒləfɒn, -fən/, *n.* **1.** an inscription at the close of a book, used esp. in the 15th and 16th centuries, giving the title, author, and other publication facts. **2.** a publisher's distinctive emblem. [LL, from Gk *kolophṓn* summit, finishing touch]

**colophony** /kɒ'lɒfəni/, *n.* →**rosin.** [L *Colophōnia* (*resina*) (resin) of *Colophon* (Ionian city in Asia Minor)]

**color** /'kʌlə/, *n. U.S.* →**colour.** – **colored,** *adj.* – **colorer,** *n.* – **colorful,** *adj.* – **colored,** *n.* – **colorist,** *n.* – **colorless,** *adj.*

**colorable** /'kʌlərəbəl/, *adj. U.S.* →**colourable.** – **colorability** /kʌlərə'bɪləti/, **colorableness,** *n.*

**colorado** /kɒlə'radoʊ/, *adj.* (of cigars) of medium colour and strength. [Sp.: coloured, red]

**Colorado beetle** /kɒləradoʊ 'bitl/, *n.* a black and yellow beetle, *Leptinotarsa decemlineata,* which is a potato pest.

**colorant** /'kʌlərənt/, *n.* a colouring matter such as dye or pigment.

**coloratura** /kɒlərə'tjurə/, *n.* **1.** runs, trills, and other florid decorations in vocal music. **2.** music marked by this. **3.** a lyric soprano of high range who specialises in such music. Also, **colorature** /'kɒlərətʃʊə/. [It., from *colorare* to colour, from L *colōrāre*]

**color guard** /'kʌlə gad/, *n. U.S.* →**colour party.**

**colorific** /kʌlə'rɪfɪk/, *adj.* **1.** producing or imparting colour. **2.** pertaining to colour. [COLO(U)R + -I- + -FIC]

**colorimeter** /kʌlə'rɪmətə/, *n.* an instrument for analysing colours into their components, as by measuring a given colour in terms of a standard colour, of a scale of colours, or of certain primary colours. [COLO(U)R + -I- + -METER[1]] – **colorimetric** /kʌlərə'mɛtrɪk/, **colorimetrical** /kʌlərə'mɛtrɪkəl/, *adj.* – **colorimetry,** *n.*

**colossal** /kə'lɒsəl/, *adj.* **1.** gigantic; huge; vast. **2.** like a colossus. – **colossally,** *adv.*

**colosseum** /kɒlə'siəm/, *n.* an amphitheatre, stadium, large theatre, etc., for public meetings and entertainment, esp. the Colosseum in Rome, inaugurated A.D. 80. Also, **coliseum.** [L, properly neut. of *colosseus* colossal. Cf. COLOSSUS]

**colossus** /kə'lɒsəs/, *n., pl.* **-lossi** /-'lɒsaɪ/, **-lossuses. 1.** (*cap.*) the legendary bronze statue of Apollo at Rhodes. **2.** any statue of gigantic size. **3.** anything colossal or gigantic. [ME, from L, from Gk *kolossós*]

**colostomy** /kə'lɒstəmi/, *n.* the surgical formation of an artificial anus from an opening in the colon fixed onto the abdominal wall.

**colostrum** /kə'lɒstrəm/, *n.* →**beestings.** [L]

**colour** /'kʌlə/, *n.* **1.** the evaluation by the visual sense of that quality of light (reflected or transmitted by a substance) which is basically determined by its spectral composition; that quality of a visual sensation distinct from form. Any colour may be expressed in terms of three factors: hue, chroma (purity or saturation), and brightness (or value). Generally the most obvious or striking feature of a colour is its hue, which gives it its name. The colour is qualified if necessary as pale, dark, dull, light, etc. **2.** complexion. **3.** a ruddy complexion. **4.** racial complexion other than white, esp. Negro. **5.** a blush. **6.** vivid or distinctive quality, as of literary work. **7.** details in description, customs, speech, habits, etc., of a place or period, included for the sake of realism: *a novel about the Rum Rebellion with much local colour.* **8.** that which is used for colouring; pigment; paint; dye. **9.** the general effect of all the hues entering into the composition of a picture. **10.** in printing, the amount and quality of ink used. **11.** (*pl.*) any distinctive colour, symbol, badge, etc., of identification: *the colours of a school, jockey, etc.* **12.** (*pl.*) an award made to outstanding members of a school team: *cricket colours.* **13.** (*pl.*) a flag, ensign, etc., as of a military body or ship. **14.** outward appearance or aspect; guise or show. **15.** a pretext. **16.** kind; sort; variety; general character. **17.** timbre of sound. **18.** an apparent or prima-facie right or ground (esp. in legal sense): *to hold possession under colour of title.* **19. a.** a trace or particle of valuable mineral, esp. gold, as shown by washing auriferous gravel, etc. **b.** (*oft. pl.*) traces or particles of opal in the potch. **20.** heraldic tincture. **21. change colour,** to turn pale or red. **22. flying colours,** eclat. **23. give** or **lend colour,** to make probable or realistic. **24. join the colours,** to enlist in the army. **25. lose colour,** to turn pale. **26. nail one's colours to the mast,** to commit oneself to a party, action, etc. **27. off colour,** not well; indisposed. **28. show one's true colours,** to reveal one's true nature, opinions, etc. –*v.t.* **29.** to give or apply colour to; tinge; paint; dye. **30.** to cause to appear different from the reality. **31.** to give a special character or distinguishing quality to: *an account coloured by personal feelings.* –*v.i.* **32.** to take on or change colour. **33.** to flush; blush. Also, *U.S.,* **color.** [ME, from OF, from L *color*] – **colourer,** *n.*

**colourable** /'kʌlərəbəl/, *adj.* **1.** capable of being coloured. **2.** specious; plausible. **3.** pretended; deceptive. Also, *U.S.,* **colorable.** – **colourability** /kʌlərə'bɪləti/, **colourableness,** *n.* – **colourably,** *adv.*

**colouration** /kʌlə'reɪʃən/, *n.* colouring; appearance as to colour. Also, **coloration.**

**colour-bar** /'kʌlə-ba/, *n.* an economic, political, or social barrier separating peoples of different colour, esp. one separating non-whites from whites.

**colour-blindness** /'kʌlə-blaɪndnəs/, *n.* defective colour perception, independent of the capacity for distinguishing light and shade, and form. Also, *U.S.*, **color-blindness.** – **colour-blind,** *adj.*

**colourcast** /'kʌləkast/, *n., v.,* **-cast, -casting.** –*n.* **1.** a television program broadcast in colour. –*v.t.* **2.** to broadcast (television) in colour. –*v.i.* **3.** to televise in colour. Also, *U.S.*, **colorcast.**

**colour company** /'kʌlə kʌmpəni/, *n.* a company carrying the flag of a battalion.

**coloured** /'kʌləd/, *adj.* **1.** having colour. **2.** belonging wholly or in part to, or pertaining to, some other race than the white, esp. to the Negro race. **3.** specious; deceptive: *a coloured statement.* **4.** influenced or biased. **5.** *Bot.* of leaves of some hue other than green. –*n.* **6.** any person of a race other than the white, esp. a Negro. **7.** Also, **Cape Coloured.** (in South Africa) a person of mixed blood. Also, *U.S.*, **colored.**

**colour fast** /'kʌlə fast/, *n.* **1.** of fabric dyes, one which is lasting. **2.** of materials, one which can be washed without the colours running or fading.

**colour-filter** /'kʌlə-fɪltə/, *n.* (in photography, etc.) a filter for modifying the reproduction of colours. Also, *U.S.*, **color-filter.**

**colourful** /'kʌləfəl/, *adj.* **1.** abounding in colour. **2.** richly picturesque: *a colourful historical period.* **3.** presenting or suggesting vivid or striking scenes. Also, *U.S.*, **colorful.** – **colourfully,** *adv.* – **colourfulness,** *n.*

**colouring** /'kʌlərɪŋ/, *n.* **1.** the act or method of applying colour. **2.** appearance as to colour. **3.** characteristic aspect or tone. **4.** specious appearance; show. **5.** a substance used to colour something. Also, *U.S.*, **coloring.**

**colourist** /'kʌlərəst/, *n.* **1.** a user of colour, as in painting. **2.** a painter who devotes himself specially to effects of colour. Also, *U.S.*, **colorist.** – **colouristic** /kʌlə'rɪstɪk/, *adj.*

**colourless** /'kʌləlәs/, *adj.* **1.** without colour. **2.** pallid; dull in colour. **3.** without vividness or distinctive character: *a colourless description of the parade.* **4.** unbiased; neutral. Also, *U.S.*, **colorless.** – **colourlessly,** *adv.* – **colourlessness,** *n.*

**colour party** /'kʌlə pati/, *n.* a party of officers and N.C.O.s who carry and escort the colours.

**colour-scheme** /'kʌlə-skim/, *n.* the overall colour conception in a design, plan, etc. Also, *U.S.*, **color-scheme.**

**colour sergeant** /'kʌlə sadʒənt/, *n.* **1.** (formerly) a sergeant who has charge of battalion or regimental colours. Also, *U.S.*, **color sergeant.** **2.** →**quartermaster-sergeant.**

**colour television** /– 'tɛləvɪʒən/, *n.* television in colour, rather than in black and white.

**colourwash** /'kʌləwɒʃ/, *n.* coloured distemper. Also, *U.S.*, **colorwash.**

**-colous,** a word element indicating habitat. [L *colere* inhabit + -OUS]

**colpitis** /kɒl'paɪtəs/, *n. Pathol.* →**vaginitis.** [Gk *kólpos* bosom, womb + -ITIS]

**colportage** /'kɒlpɔtɪdʒ/, *n.* the work of a colporteur. [F, from *colporter* hawk, lit., carry on the neck, from *col* neck + *porter* carry]

**colporteur** /'kɒlpɔtə/, *n.* **1.** a hawker of books, etc. **2.** one employed to travel about distributing Bibles, religious tracts, etc., gratuitously or at a low price. [F. See COLPORTAGE]

**colt** /koʊlt/, *n.* **1.** a male horse not past its fourth birthday. **2.** a young or inexperienced man. **3.** *Naut.* a rope's end used in chastising. [ME and OE; cf. d. Swed. *kult* pig] – **coltish,** *adj.* – **coltishly,** *adv.* – **coltishness,** *n.*

**Colt** /koʊlt/, *n.* a type of revolver. [named after Samuel *Colt*, 1814-62, U.S. inventor]

**Co. Ltd.,** limited company.

**colter** /'koʊltə/, *n.* →**coulter.**

**coltsfoot** /'koʊltsfʊt/, *n., pl.* **-foots.** a perennial, *Tussilago farfara*, native to Europe but widespread as a weed, formerly used in medicine.

**colubrine** /'kɒljəbraɪn, -brən/, *adj.* **1.** of or resembling a snake; snake-like. **2.** of or pertaining to the snake family Colubridae, in which the species are either non-venomous or have the poison fangs located at the rear of the mouth. [L *colubrīnus* like a serpent]

**colugo** /kə'lugoʊ/, *n., pl.* **-gos.** the flying lemur.

**columbarium** /kɒləm'bɛəriəm/, *n., pl.* **-baria** /-'bɛəriə/. **1.** a sepulchral vault or other structure with recesses in the walls to receive the ashes of the dead. **2.** one of the recesses. **3.** a dovecot. **4.** a hole in a wall, left for the insertion of the end of a beam. [L, orig., dovecot, from *columba* dove]

**columbic** /kə'lʌmbɪk/, *adj. Chem.* →**niobic.**

**columbine**[1] /'kɒləmbaɪn/, *n.* any plant of the genus *Aquilegia*, comprising erect branching herbs with handsome flowers. [ME, from LL *columbīna*, properly fem. of L *columbīnus* dovelike; from the resemblance of the inverted flower to a cluster of doves]

**columbine**[2] /'kɒləmbaɪn/, *adj.* **1.** of a dove. **2.** dovelike; dove-coloured. [ME *columbyn*, from L *columbīnus*]

**Columbine** /'kɒləmbaɪn/, *n.* a female character in comedy (originally the early Italian) and pantomime, the sweetheart of Harlequin. [It. *Colombina*, from *colomba* dove, from L *columba*]

**columbite** /kə'lʌmbaɪt/, *n.* a black, crystalline mineral, $FeNb_2O_6$, often containing manganese and tantalum; it is the principal ore of niobium. [COLUMB(IUM) + -ITE[1]]

**columbium** /kə'lʌmbiəm/, *n.* former name for **niobium.** [NL, named after *Columbia* personification of the U.S. (from Christopher *Columbus*)]

**columbous** /kə'lʌmbəs/, *adj. Chem.* →**niobous.**

**columella** /kɒljə'mɛlə/, *n., pl.* **-mellae** /-'mɛli/. a small column-like part; an axis. [L, diminutive of *columna* COLUMN] – **columellar,** *adj.*

**columelliform** /kɒljə'mɛləfɔm/, *adj.* like a columella.

**column** /'kɒləm/, *n.* **1.** *Archit.* **a.** an upright shaft or body of greater length than thickness, usu. serving as a support; a pillar. **b.** a vertical architectural member consisting typically of an approximately cylindrical shaft with a base and a capital. **2.** any column-like object, mass, or formation: *a column of smoke.* **3.** *Bot.* the upright cylindrical structure, formed by the union of stamens in an orchid. **4.** *Geol.* geological sequence deposited through the various periods of geological time. **5.** *Geol.* a cylindrical dripstone formation formed by the union of a stalactite and a stalagmite. **6.** one of the two or more vertical rows of lines of type or printed matter of a page: *there are two columns on this page.* **7.** a perpendicular row of figures. **8.** a regular contribution to a newspaper, usu. signed, and consisting of comment, news, etc. **9.** a journalistic department devoted to short articles, etc., of an entertaining or esp. readable kind furnished by a particular editor or writer with or without the aid of contributors. **10.** a line of ships following one after the other. **11.** a formation of troops, narrow laterally and extended from front to rear. [ME *columpne*, from OF, from L *columna* pillar, post] – **columned** /'kɒləmd/, *adj.*

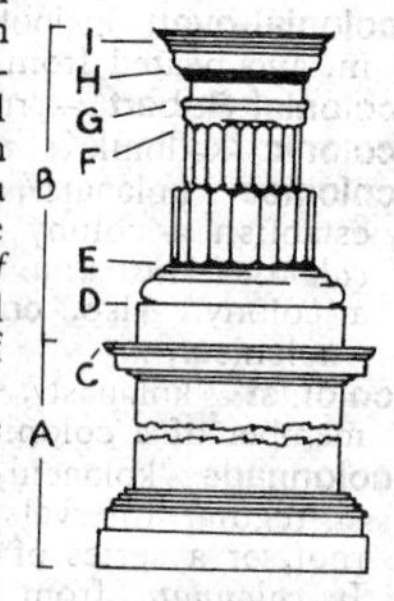

architectural column: A, pedestal; B, column (C-D base, E-F shaft, G-I capital); C, plinth; D, torus; E, apophyge; F, astragal; G, neck; H, echinus; I, abacus

**columnar** /kə'lʌmnə/, *adj.* **1.** shaped like a column. **2.** printed, arranged, etc., in columns.

**columnar jointing** /– 'dʒɔɪntɪŋ/, *n.* that variety of jointing which breaks the rock into columns, esp. of basaltic rock in which the joints form a hexagonal pattern by shrinkage during cooling.

**columnar section** /– 'sɛkʃən/, *n.* a graphic expression of the sequence and stratigraphic relations of rock units in a region.

**columniation** /kəlʌmni'eɪʃən/, *n.* **1.** the use of columns in a structure. **2.** *U.S.* the system of columns used in a structure.

**columnist** /'kɒləməst, 'kɒləmnəst/, *n.* the editor, writer, or organiser of a special column in a newspaper.

**column shift** /'kɒləm ʃɪft/, *n.* a gear lever mounted on the steering column of a motor vehicle.

**colure** /kəl'jʊə/, *n.* either of two great circles of the celestial sphere intersecting each other at the poles, one passing through the equinoctial and the other through the solstitial points of the ecliptic. [L *colūrus,* from Gk *kólouros* dock-tailed (the colures being cut off by the horizon)]

**coly** /'kouli/, *n.* any of the small birds of the African family Coliidae, having soft plumage, prominent crest, and pointed tail; mousebird.

**colza** /'kɒlzə/, *n.* →**rapeseed.** [F, from D *koolzaad* coleseed]

**colza oil** /'kɒlzər ɔil/, *n.* →**rapeseed oil.**

**com** /kɒm/, *n. Colloq.* →**communist.**

**com-,** a prefix meaning 'with', 'jointly', 'in combination' and (with intensive force) 'completely', occurring in this form before *p* and *b,* as in *compare,* and (by assimilation) before *m,* as in *commingle.* Cf. **co-** (def. 1). Also, **con-, col-, cor-.** [L: combining form of *cum* with]

**Com.,** **1.** commander. **2.** commodore.

**coma**[1] /'koumə/, *n., pl.* **-mas.** a state of prolonged unconsciousness from which it is difficult or impossible to rouse a person, due to disease, injury, poison, etc.; stupor. [Gk *kôma* deep sleep]

**coma**[2] /'koumə/, *n., pl.* **-mae** /-mi/. **1.** *Astron.* the nebulous envelope round the nucleus of a comet. **2.** *Optics.* that aberration of optical systems by which rays of an oblique pencil cannot be brought to a sharp focus. **3.** *Bot.* a tuft of silky hairs at the end of a seed. **4.** the leafy branches forming the head of a tree. [L, from Gk *kómē* hair]

**comate**[1] /kou'meɪt/, *n.* a mate or companion. [CO- + MATE[1]]

**comate**[2] /'koumeɪt/, *adj.* **1.** *Bot.* having a coma. **2.** hairy; tufted. [L *comātus* having long hair]

**comatose** /'koumətous/, *adj.* affected with coma; lethargic; unconscious. [*comat-* (combining form representing Gk *kôma* COMA[1]) + -OSE[1]] – **comatosely,** *adv.*

**comatulid** /kə'mætʃəlɪd/, *n.* any of the free-swimming, stalkless crinoids of the genus *Comatula* or a related genus. [NL Comatulidae, the family containing the *Comatula* (NL, properly fem. of L *comātulus,* diminutive of *comātus* COMATE[2])]

**comb**[1] /koum/, *n.* **1.** a toothed piece of bone, metal, etc., for arranging or cleaning the hair, or for keeping it in place. **2.** →**currycomb. 3.** any comblike instrument, object, or formation. **4.** a card for dressing wool, etc. **5.** the fleshy, more or less serrated excrescence or growth on the head of the domestic fowl. **6.** something resembling or suggesting this, as the crest of a wave. **7.** a honeycomb, or any similar group of cells. *–v.t.* **8.** to dress (the hair, etc.) with, or as with, a comb. **9.** to card (wool). **10.** to scrape as with a comb. **11.** to search everywhere and with great thoroughness: *she combed the files for the missing letter.* *–v.i.* **12.** to roll over or break at the crest, as a wave. [OE *comb,* var. of *camb,* c. G *Kamm*]

**comb**[2] /kum/, *n.* →**coomb.**

**comb.,** combined.

**combat** /'kɒmbæt, kəm'bæt/, *v.,* **-bated, -bating;** /'kɒmbæt/, *n.* *–v.t.* **1.** to fight or contend against; oppose vigorously. *–v.i.* **2.** to fight; battle; contend (fol. by *with* or *against*). *–n.* **3.** a fight between two men, armies, etc. [F, from *combattre,* v., from L *com-* COM- + *batt(u)ere* beat] – **combatable** /kəm'bætəbəl/, *adj.* – **combater,** *n.*

**combatant** /'kɒmbətənt/, *n.* **1.** a person or group that fights. *–adj.* **2.** combating; fighting. **3.** disposed to combat.

**combat fatigue** /'kɒmbæt fə,tig/, *n.* →**battle fatigue.**

**combative** /'kɒmbətɪv/, *adj.* ready or inclined to fight; pugnacious. – **combatively,** *adv.* – **combativeness,** *n.*

**combe** /kum/, *n.* →**coomb.**

**combed yarn** /koumd 'jan/, *n.* cotton or worsted yarn made of fibres laid parallel.

**comber** /'koumə/, *n.* **1.** one who or that which combs. **2.** a long curling wave.

**combi** /'kɒmbi/, *n.* →**kombi.**

**combination** /kɒmbə'neɪʃən/, *n.* **1.** the act of combining. **2.** the state of being combined. **3.** a number of things combined. **4.** something formed by combining. **5.** a motorcycle with sidecar attached. **6.** an alliance of persons or parties. **7.** the set or series of numbers or letters used in setting the mechanism of a certain type of lock (**combination lock**) used on safes, etc. **8.** the parts of the mechanism operated by this. **9.** *Boxing.* a cluster of blows delivered in quick succession to break through an opponent's guard. **10.** (*pl.*) a one-piece undergarment combining vest and pants, esp. with long legs and sleeves. **11.** *Maths.* a selection of a specified number of different objects from a given larger number of different objects. The number of combinations of $n$ objects taken $r$ at a time is denoted by ${}^nC_r$ or $\binom{n}{r}$. **12.** *Chem.* chemical union in which a new compound is formed. [LL *combīnātio*] – **combinational,** *adj.*

**combination pill** /'– pɪl/, *n.* an oral contraceptive which contains oestrogen and progesterone.

**combination tone** /'– toun/, *n.* a faint musical tone which results acoustically from the simultaneous sounding of two related tones.

**combinative** /'kɒmbə,neɪtɪv, 'kɒmbənətɪv/, *adj.* **1.** tending or serving to combine. **2.** pertaining to combination.

**combinatorial analysis** /kɒmbɪnə,tɔriəl ə'næləsəs/, *n.* the branch of mathematics which studies the existence and number of configurations satisfying certain given conditions.

**combine** /kəm'baɪn/, *v.,* **-bined, -bining;** /'kɒmbaɪn/, *n.* *–v.t.* **1.** to bring or join into a close union or whole; unite; associate; coalesce. **2.** to possess or exhibit in union. *–v.i.* **3.** to unite; coalesce. **4.** to unite for a common purpose; join forces. **5.** to enter into chemical union. *–n.* **6.** a combination. **7.** a combination of persons or groups for the furtherance of their political, commercial, or other interests. **8.** →**combine harvester. 9.** a work of art created by combine painting. [late ME *combyne(n),* from LL *combīnāre* join together] – **combinable,** *adj.* – **combiner,** *n.*

**combined operations** /kəm,baɪnd ɒpə'reɪʃənz/, *n.pl.* war operations carried out by cooperation of land, sea, and air forces.

**combine harvester** /,kɒmbaɪn 'havəstə/, *n.* a machine that simultaneously combines the operations of reaping, threshing, and winnowing corn.

**combine painting** /– 'peɪntɪŋ/, *n.* a form of artistic composition developed from collage, whereby an arrangement is made of any flat or three-dimensional materials, usu. including painting from the artist's hand, and usu. displayed on a hanging surface.

**combing** /'koumɪŋ/, *n.* an intermediate process in the preparation of worsted yarn, which renders the longer fibres parallel and removes as noil, short fibres, broken ends, tangled neps and larger vegetable particles.

**combings** /'koumɪŋz/, *n.pl.* hairs removed with a comb.

**combing wool** /'koumɪŋ ,wʊl/, *n.* long-stapled wool, suitable for combing.

**combining form** /kəm'baɪnɪŋ fɔm/, *n.* a special form of a word used only in compounds, as *Anglo-* in *Anglophil* and *Anglo-French.*

**comb jelly** /koum 'dʒeli/, *n.* any member of the Ctenophora, lowly marine organisms in which the body is largely a delicate globular mass of translucent jelly with adhesive but non-stinging tentacles, as a sea-gooseberry; ctenophore.

**combo**[1] /'kɒmbou/, *n.* any small band of musicians.

**combo**[2] /'kɒmbou/, *n. Colloq.* **1.** *Northern Aust.* a white man who lives with an Aboriginal woman. **2. go combo,** to begin such a relationship. Also, **wambo, wombo.**

**combust** /kəm'bʌst/, *adj.* (of a star or planet) so near the sun as to be obscured by it. [ME, from L *combūstus,* pp., burned up]

**combustible** /kəm'bʌstəbəl/, *adj.* **1.** capable of catching fire and burning; inflammable. **2.** easily excited. *–n.* **3.** a combustible substance. [LL *combūstibilis,* from L *combūstus,* pp. See COMBUST] – **combustibility** /kəmbʌstə'bɪləti/, **combustibleness,** *n.*

**combustion** /kəm'bʌstʃən/, *n.* **1.** the act or process of burning. **2.** *Chem.* **a.** rapid oxidation accompanied by heat and usu. light. **b.** chemical combination attended by heat and light. **c.** slow oxidation not accompanied by high temperature and light. **3.** violent excitement; tumult. – **combustive,** *adj.*

**combustion chamber** /'– tʃeɪmbə/, *n.* the chamber in an engine where the fuel and oxidant are burnt.

**combustion tube** /'– tjub/, *n.* a tube of hard glass in which a substance may be burnt in a current of air or oxygen (usu. used in a furnace).

**combustor** /kəm'bʌstə/, *n.* the combustion chamber, fuel injection system, and igniter in a jet engine or ramjet.

**come** /kʌm/, *v.*, **came, come, coming,** *n.* *–v.i.* **1.** to move towards the speaker or towards a particular place; approach. **2.** to arrive by movement or in course of progress; approach or arrive in time, succession, etc.: *when Christmas comes.* **3.** to move into view; appear: *the light comes and goes.* **4.** to extend; reach: *the dress comes to her knees.* **5.** to take place; occur; happen. **6.** to occur at a certain point, position, etc. **7.** to be available, produced, offered, etc.: *toothpaste comes in a tube.* **8.** to occur to the mind. **9.** to befall a person. **10.** to issue; emanate; be derived. **11.** to be born in or live in (fol. by *from*). **12.** to arrive or appear as a result: *this comes of carelessness.* **13.** to enter or be brought into a specified state or condition: *to come into use.* **14.** to enter into being or existence; be born. **15.** to become: *to come untied.* **16.** to turn out to be: *his dream came true.* **17.** (in the imperative, used to call attention, express remonstrance, etc.): *come, that will do.* **18.** to germinate, as grain. **19.** *Colloq.* to have an orgasm. *–v.t.* **20.** *Colloq.* to produce; cause: *don't come that rubbish.* **21.** *Colloq.* to play the part of. **22.** Some special verb phrases are:

**come about, 1.** to arrive in due course; come to pass. **2.** to tack (in a boat).

**come across, 1.** to meet with, esp. by chance. **2.** *Colloq.* to pay or give. **3.** to communicate successfully; to be understood. **4.** *Colloq.* (of a woman) to give sexual favours.

**come again, 1.** to return. **2.** *Colloq.* to repeat.

**come along,** to make haste; hurry.

**come at, 1.** to reach. **2.** to rush at; attack. **3.** *Colloq.* to undertake: *he won't come at that.*

**come back, 1.** to return, esp. in memory. **2.** to return to a former position or state.

**come by, 1.** to obtain; acquire. **2.** to stop for a brief visit.

**come clean,** *Colloq.* confess.

**come down, 1.** to lose wealth, rank, etc. **2.** to be handed down by tradition or inheritance. **3.** *Brit.* to leave a university. **4.** to travel, esp. from a town.

**come down on,** to scold; blame.

**come down with,** to become afflicted, esp. with a disease.

**come forward,** to offer one's services, etc.; volunteer.

**come good,** *Colloq.* to improve after an unpromising beginning.

**come in, 1.** to enter. **2.** to arrive. **3.** to become useful, fashionable, etc. **4.** to finish in a race or competition. **5.** (of odds on a horse, dog, etc.) to become lower. **6.** (of cows) to come into milk; to calve

**come in handy,** to be useful.

**come in, spinner!** *Colloq.* (in two-up) toss the coins!

**come into, 1.** to get. **2.** to inherit.

**come nothing,** *Prison Colloq.* to make no admissions.

**come off, 1.** to happen; occur. **2.** to end. **3.** to reach the end; acquit oneself: *to come off with honours.* **4.** to become detached or unfastened.

**come off it,** *Colloq.* to stop; lay aside (a pretentious attitude, etc.).

**come on, 1.** to meet unexpectedly. **2.** to make progress; develop. **3.** to appear onstage. **4.** to begin; start. **5.** to hurry. **6.** →**come** (def. 17).

**come one's guts,** *Prison Colloq.* to confess.

**come out, 1.** to appear; be published. **2.** to be revealed; show itself. **3.** to make a debut in society, on the stage, etc. **4.** to emerge; reach the end. **5.** to admit openly one's homosexuality. **6.** *Obs.* to leave Europe or America to make a home in Australia.

**come out on,** to declare support for: *to come out on abortion.*

**come out with, 1.** to tell; say. **2.** to bring out; publish. **3.** to blurt out.

**come over,** to happen to; affect: *what's come over him?*

**come round, 1.** to relent. **2.** to recover consciousness; revive. **3.** to change (an opinion, direction, etc.).

**come that,** *Colloq.* to attempt to hoodwink (someone) with an argument, device, etc., which is blatantly a deception (fol. by *on*): *don't come that on me.*

**come the raw prawn,** *Colloq.* to try to deceive (fol. by *with*).

**come through, 1.** to succeed; reach an end. **2.** to do as expected or hoped. **3.** to pass through.

**come to, 1.** to recover consciousness. **2.** to amount to; equal. **3.** to take the way off a vessel, as by bringing her head into the wind, anchoring, etc.

**come to light,** to be found after a lapse of time.

**come to light with,** to produce; supply.

**come undone,** or **unstuck,** *Colloq.* to break down; collapse.

**come up, 1.** to arise; present itself. **2.** *Brit.* to come into residence at a school or university. **3.** to be presented for discussion or consideration. **4.** to arrive; travel, esp. to a town.

**come up against,** to meet difficulties or opposition.

**come upon,** to meet unexpectedly.

**come up to, 1.** to equal. **2.** to approach; near.

**come up with, 1.** to produce; supply. **2.** to present; propose. **3.** to come level with another boat.

*–n.* **23.** *Colloq.* semen. [ME *comen,* OE *cuman,* c. G *kommen*]

**comeallyers** /kʌˈmɔljəz/, *n.pl. Colloq.* songs suitable to sing around a campfire. [from the opening words of many such songs *Come all ye*]

**come-at-able** /kʌm-ˈæt-əbəl/, *adj. Colloq.* accessible.

**comeback** /ˈkʌmbæk/, *n.* **1.** *Colloq.* a return to a former position, prosperity, etc., as after a period of retirement. **2.** *Colloq.* a retort; repartee. **3.** *Colloq.* a ground for complaint. **4. a.** a sheep bred to be suitable for wool or mutton by breeding a half-breed sheep that has one merino parent and one parent of a meat-producing breed, to a sheep of one of the parent breeds. **b.** wool from such a sheep. **5.** a type of rust-resistant wheat.

**comedian** /kəˈmidiən/, *n.* **1.** an actor in comedy. **2.** a writer of comedy. **3.** a very amusing person. [COMEDY + -AN. Cf. F *comédien*]

**comedienne** /kəmidiˈɛn/, *n.* **1.** an actress in comedy. **2.** a professional female comic. [F, fem. of *comédien* comedian]

**comedo** /ˈkɒmədoʊ/, *n., pl.* **comedos, comedones** /kɒməˈdoʊniz/. →**blackhead** (def. 1). [L: glutton]

**comedown** /ˈkʌmdaʊn/, *n.* **1.** an unexpected or humiliating descent from dignity, importance, or prosperity. **2.** a letdown; disappointment.

**comedy** /ˈkɒmədi/, *n., pl.* **-dies. 1.** a play, film, etc., of light and humorous character, typically with a happy or cheerful ending; a drama in which the central motive of the play triumphs over circumstances and is therefore successful. **2.** that branch of the drama which concerns itself with this form of composition. **3.** the comic element of drama, of literature generally, or of life. **4.** any literary composition dealing with a theme suitable for comedy, or employing the methods of comedy. **5.** any comic or humorous incident or series of incidents. **6. comedy of errors,** a series of mistakes, with a comic effect. [ME *comedye,* from ML *cōmēdia,* L *cōmoedia,* from Gk *kōmōidía,* from *kōmōidós* comedian, from *kômos* mirth + *ōidós* singer]

**come-hither** /kʌm-ˈhɪðə/, *adj.* deliberately alluring. Also, **come-hitherish.**

**comely** /kʌmli/, *adj.,* **-lier, -liest. 1.** pleasing in appearance; fair. **2.** proper; seemly; becoming. [ME; OE *cȳmlic,* from *cȳme* comely + *līc.* See -LY] – **comeliness,** *n.*

**come-on** /ˈkʌm-ɒn/, *n. Colloq.* inducement; lure.

**comer** /ˈkʌmə/, *n.* **1.** one who or that which comes or has lately come. **2.** *Colloq.* one who or something that is coming on or promising well.

**comestible** /kəˈmɛstəbəl/, *adj.* **1.** edible; eatable. *–n.* **2.** something edible; an article of food. [late ME, from LL *comestibilis,* from L *comestus,* var. of *comēsus,* pp., eaten up]

**comet** /ˈkɒmət/, *n.* a celestial body moving about the sun in an elongated orbit, usu. consisting of a central mass (the *nucleus*) surrounded by a misty envelope (the *coma*) which extends into a stream (the *tail*) in the direction away from the sun. [ME, from L *comēta,* from Gk *komḗtēs,* lit., long-haired] – **cometary** /ˈkɒmətəri/, *adj.* – **cometic** /kɒˈmɛtɪk/, *adj.*

**comet-finder** /ˈkɒmət-faɪndə/, *n.* a telescope of low power but with a wide field, used to search for comets. Also, **comet-seeker.**

**comeuppance** /kʌmˈʌpəns/, *n. Colloq.* a well-deserved punishment or retribution; one's just deserts. Also, **comeupance.**

**comfit** /ˈkʌmfət, ˈkɒm-/, *n. Obs.* a sugar-coated sweet. [ME, from OF *confit,* pp. of *confire* preserve, prepare, from L *conficere*]

**comfiture** /ˈkʌmfətʃʊə/, *n. Obs.* a confection; a preserve, as of fruit. Also, **confiture.** [ME, from F, from *confit* COMFIT]

**comfort** /'kʌmfət/, *v.t.* **1.** to soothe when in grief; console; cheer. **2.** to make physically comfortable. **3.** *Obs.* to aid; encourage. *–n.* **4.** relief in affliction; consolation; solace. **5.** the feeling of relief or consolation. **6.** a person or thing that affords consolation. **7.** a cause or matter of relief or satisfaction. **8.** a state of ease, with freedom from pain and anxiety, and satisfaction of bodily wants. **9.** that which promotes such a state. **10.** *U.S.* a comforter; bedspread. **11.** *Obs.* strengthening aid; assistance. [ME *conforte(n)*, from OF *conforter,* from L *confortāre* strengthen] – **comfortingly,** *adv.* – **comfortless,** *adj.* – **comfortlessly,** *adv.* – **comfortlessness,** *n.*

**comfortable** /'kʌmftəbəl, 'kʌmfətəbəl/, *adj.* **1.** giving comfort, support, or consolation. **2.** producing or attended with comfort or ease of mind or body. **3.** being in a state of comfort or ease; easy and undisturbed. **4.** adequate. **5.** *Obs.* cheerful. *–n.* **6.** *U.S.* a quilted bedcover. – **comfortableness,** *n.* – **comfortably,** *adv.*

**comforter** /'kʌmfətə/, *n.* **1.** one who or that which comforts. **2.** (*cap.*) the Holy Spirit. **3.** a woollen scarf for wrapping round the neck in cold weather. **4.** *U.S.* a quilted bedcover. **5.** *Chiefly U.S.* a baby's dummy. **6. Job's comforter,** one who professes to give comfort but who achieves the opposite result.

**comfort station** /'kʌmfət steɪʃən/, *n.* a rest room with washing facilities, toilets, etc. as provided for road travellers.

**comfort stop** /'– stɒp/, *n.* **1.** a call by a coach or car at a comfort station. **2.** a break in a journey by road in order to relieve oneself (def. 9).

**comfrey** /'kʌmfri/, *n., pl.* **-freys.** any plant of the genus *Symphytum,* of Europe and Asia, as *S. officinale,* formerly used as a vulnerary. [ME *cumfirie,* from ML *cumfiria,* apparently var. of L *conferva*]

**comfy** /'kʌmfi/, *adj. Colloq.* comfortable.

**comic** /'kɒmɪk/, *adj.* **1.** of, pertaining to, or of the nature of comedy, as distinct from tragedy. **2.** acting in or composing comedy. **3.** provoking laughter; humorous; funny; laughable. *–n.* **4.** *Colloq.* a comic actor. **5.** a magazine containing one or more stories in comic strip form. **6.** (*pl.*) *Colloq.* comic strips. **7.** the amusing element in art, life, etc. [L *cōmicus,* from Gk *kōmikós*]

**comical** /'kɒmɪkəl/, *adj.* **1.** provoking laughter, or amusing; funny. **2.** *Obs.* pertaining to or of the nature of comedy. **3.** *Colloq.* queer; odd; strange. – **comicality** /kɒmə'kæləti/, **comicalness,** *n.* – **comically,** *adv.*

**comic cuts** /'kɒmɪk ˌkʌts/, *n.pl. Colloq.* guts. [rhyming slang]

**comic opera** /– 'ɒprə/, *n.* a diverting opera with spoken dialogue and a happy ending.

**comic strip** /'– ˌstrɪp/, *n.* a series of cartoon drawings, in colour or black and white, relating a comic incident, an adventure story, etc.

**coming** /'kʌmɪŋ/, *n.* **1.** approach; arrival; advent. *–adj.* **2.** that comes; approaching. **3.** on the way to fame or success: *up and coming.*

**comitia** /kə'mɪʃiə/, *n. Rom. Hist.* an assembly of the people convened to pass laws, nominate magistrates, etc. [L, pl. of *comitium* place of assembly] – **comitial** /kə'mɪʃəl/, *adj.*

**comity** /'kɒməti/, *n., pl.* **-ties.** **1.** courtesy; civility. **2.** *Internat. Law.* courtesy between nations, as in the respect shown by one country for the laws, judicial decisions, and institutions of another but not binding as rules of international law. [L *cōmitas* courtesy]

**comm** /kɒm/, *n., adj. Colloq.* →**communist.**

**Comm.,** commerce.

**comma** /'kɒmə/, *n.* **1.** a mark of punctuation (,) used to indicate the smallest interruptions in continuity of thought or grammatical construction. **2.** *Class. Pros.* a fragment or smaller section of a colon. **3.** →**comma butterfly.** [L, from Gk *kómma* short clause]

**comma bacillus** /– bə'sɪləs/, *n.* a slightly curved bacterium, *Vibrio cholerae,* which causes Asiatic cholera, is contracted by eating or drinking contaminated food, and which causes a violent form of dysentery.

**comma butterfly** /– 'bʌtəflaɪ/, *n.* a North American nymphalid butterfly, *Polygonia album,* having a white, comma-shaped mark on the underside of the hind wings.

**command** /kə'mænd, -'mand/, *v.t.* **1.** to order or direct with authority. **2.** to require with authority; demand: *he commanded silence.* **3.** to have or exercise authority over; be in control over; be master of; have at one's bidding or disposal. **4.** to dominate by reason of location; overlook: *a hill commanding the sea.* **5.** to deserve and get (respect, sympathy, etc.). **6.** to have charge of and authority over (a military or naval unit or station). *–v.i.* **7.** to issue commands. **8.** to occupy a dominating position; look down upon or over a region, etc. *–n.* **9.** the act of commanding or ordering. **10.** an order given by a commander. **11.** *Mil.* **a.** an order given by an officer or N.C.O. to a military subordinate. **b.** a military formation exercising command over a specific geographical area, or function. **c.** a body of troops, etc., or an area, station, etc., under a commander. **12.** the possession or exercise of controlling authority. **13.** control; mastery; disposal. **14.** a royal invitation. **15.** *Computers.* an expression in part of a program that defines an operation, or results in the performance of an operation. **16.** power of dominating a region by reason of location; extent of view or outlook. [ME *comande(n),* from OF *comander,* from LL *commandāre,* from L *com-* COM- + *mandāre* enjoin] – **commandingly,** *adv.*

**commandant** /'kɒməndænt, -dant/, *n.* the commanding officer of a place, group, etc.; a commander. [F, orig. ppr. of *commander* COMMAND]

**commandeer** /kɒmən'dɪə/, *v.t.* **1.** to order or force into active military service. **2.** to seize (private property) for military or other public use. **3.** *Colloq.* to seize arbitrarily. [Afrikaans *commandeeren,* from F *commander* command]

**commander** /kə'mændə, -'mand-/, *n.* **1.** one who commands. **2.** one who exercises authority; a leader; a chief officer. **3.** the chief commissioned officer (irrespective of rank) of a military unit. **4.** a naval officer ranking below a captain. **5.** a rank in certain modern orders of knighthood. – **commandership,** *n.*

**commander-in-chief** /kəˌmændər-ɪn-'tʃif/, *n., pl.* **commanders-in-chief.** **1.** an officer in supreme command of an army or armed forces. **2.** an officer in command of a particular part of an army or navy.

**commander's concept** /kəˌmændəz 'kɒnsɛpt/, *n.* →**concept of operations.**

**command guidance** /kə'mænd gaɪdəns/, *n.* a system of missile guidance in which computed information transmitted to a missile causes it to follow a planned course.

**commanding officer** /kəmændɪŋ 'ɒfəsə/, *n.* an officer in command.

**commandment** /kə'mændmənt, kə'mand-/, *n.* **1.** a command or edict. **2.** any one of the precepts (the **Ten Commandments**) spoken by God to Israel or delivered to Moses on Mount Sinai. **3.** *Obs.* the act, fact, or power of commanding.

**command module** /kə'mænd mɒdʒul/, *n.* the section of a spacecraft in which the crew live and operate its controls.

**commando** /kə'mændoʊ, -'man-/, *n., pl.* **-dos, -does.** **1.** a small specially trained fighting force used for making quick, destructive raids against enemy held areas. **2.** a member of such a force. **3.** *S. African.* an armed force raised by the Boers for service during the Boer War, 1899-1902. [Afrikaans, from Pg.]

**command performance** /kəmænd pə'fɔməns/, *n.* a performance of a play, etc., by royal command.

**command post** /'– poʊst/, *n. Mil.* the headquarters of a unit and the centre of its operations in the field.

**commeasurable** /kə'mɛʒərəbəl/, *adj.* having the same measure; commensurate.

**commeasure** /kə'mɛʒə/, *v.t.,* **-ured, -uring.** to equal in measure; be coextensive with.

**commedia dell'arte** /kɒˌmeɪdiə dɛl'ateɪ/, *n.* a stylised form of popular comedy developed in Italy in the 16th and 17th centuries, employing improvisations on traditional situations and characters, as Punch (Punchinello, Pierrot), Pantaloon, Columbine, and Harlequin. Cf. **harlequinade, pierrot, Punch and Judy.** [It.]

**comme il faut** /kɒm il 'foʊ/, *adv.* as it should be; proper; properly. [F]

**commem.,** commemorative.

**commemorate** /kə'mɛməreɪt/, *v.t.* **-rated, -rating.** **1.** to serve as a memento of. **2.** to honour the memory of by some solemnity or celebration. **3.** to make honourable mention of. [L *commemorātus,* pp., brought to remembrance] – **commemorator,** *n.*

**commemoration** /kəmɛmə'reɪʃən/, *n.* **1.** the act of commemorating. **2.** a service, celebration, etc., in memory of some person or event. **3.** a memorial. – **commemorational,** *adj.*

**commemorative** /kə'mɛmərətɪv/, *adj.* **1.** serving to commemorate. **2.** (of stamps, coins, etc.) issued to celebrate a particular historical event, in honour of a famous personage, etc. –*n.* **3.** anything that commemorates. – **commemoratively,** *adv.*

**commemoratory** /kə'mɛmərətəri/, *adj.* →**commemorative** (def. 1).

**commence** /kə'mɛns/, *v.* **-menced, -mencing.** –*v.t.* **1.** to begin; start. –*v.i.* **2.** to have a beginning; come into being. [ME *comence(n),* from OF *comencer,* from LL *cominitiāre,* from *com-* COM- + *initiāre* begin] – **commencer,** *n.*

**commencement** /kə'mɛnsmənt/, *n.* **1.** the act or fact of commencing; beginning. **2.** *U.S.* (in universities, colleges, etc.) the ceremony of conferring degrees or granting diplomas at the end of the academic year. **3.** *U.S.* the day on which this takes place.

**commend** /kə'mɛnd/, *v.t.* **1.** to present or mention as worthy of confidence, notice, kindness, etc.; recommend. **2.** to entrust; give in charge; deliver with confidence: *into Thy hands I commend my spirit.* **3.** *Archaic.* to recommend (a person) to the kind remembrance of another. [ME *commend(en),* from L *commendāre* commit. Cf. COMMAND] – **commendable,** *adj.* – **commendableness,** *n.* – **commendably,** *adv.*

**commendam** /kə'mɛndəm/, *n. Eccles.* **1.** the tenure of a benefice to be held until the appointment of a regular incumbent, the benefice being said to be held *in commendam.* **2.** a benefice so held. [ML, acc. sing. of *commenda,* as in *dāre in commendam* give in trust]

**commendation** /kɒmən'deɪʃən/, *n.* **1.** the act of commending; recommendation; praise. **2.** something that commends. **3.** (*pl.*) complimentary greeting.

**commendatory** /kə'mɛndətəri, -dətri/, *adj.* **1.** serving to commend; approving; praising. **2.** holding a benefice in commendam. **3.** held in commendam.

**commensal** /kə'mɛnsəl/, *adj.* **1.** eating together at the same table. **2.** (of an animal or plant) living with, on, or in another, but neither one at the expense of the other (distinguished from *parasite*). –*n.* **3.** a companion at table. **4.** a commensal animal or plant. [ML *commensālis,* from L: *com-* COM- + *mensālis* belonging to the table] – **commensalism,** *n.* – **commensality** /kɒmən'sæləti/, *n.* – **commensally,** *adv.*

**commensurable** /kə'mɛnʃərəbəl/, *adj.* **1.** having a common measure or divisor. **2.** suitable in measure; proportionate. [LL *commensūrābilis* having a common measure] – **commensurability** /kəmɛnʃərə'bɪləti/, *n.* – **commensurably,** *adv.*

**commensurate** /kə'mɛnʃərət/, *adj.* **1.** having the same measure; of equal extent or duration. **2.** corresponding in amount, magnitude, or degree. **3.** proportionate. **4.** having a common measure; commensurable. [LL *commensūrātus,* from L: *com-* COM- + *mensūrātus,* pp., measured] – **commensurately,** *adv.* – **commensuration** /kəmɛnʃə'reɪʃən/, *n.*

**comment** /'kɒmɛnt/, *n.* **1.** a note in explanation, expansion, or criticism of a passage in a writing, book, etc.; an annotation. **2.** explanatory or critical matter added to a text. **3.** a remark, observation, or criticism. –*v.i.* **4.** to write explanatory or critical notes upon a text. **5.** to make remarks. –*v.t.* **6.** to make comments or remarks on; furnish with comments. [ME, from LL *commentum* exposition, L contrivance, invention, properly pp. neut.] – **commenter,** *n.*

**commentary** /'kɒməntəri, -tri/, *n., pl.* **-taries. 1.** a series of comments or annotations. **2.** an explanatory essay or treatise: *a commentary on the Bible.* **3.** anything serving to illustrate a point; comment. **4.** (*usu. pl.*) a record of facts or events: *the Commentaries of Caesar.* **5.** a description of a public event as a cricket match, official opening of parliament broadcast or televised as it happens. **6.** a description accompanying a documentary film. – **commentarial** /kɒmən'tɛəriəl/, *adj.*

**commentate** /'kɒmənteɪt/, *v.i.,* **-tated, -tating.** to act as a commentator.

**commentator** /'kɒmənteɪtə/, *n.* a writer or broadcaster who makes critical or explanatory remarks about news, events, or describes sporting events etc.: *sports commentator.*

**commerce** /'kɒmɜs/, *n.* **1.** interchange of goods or commodities, esp. on a large scale between different countries (**foreign commerce**) or between different parts of the same country (**domestic** or **internal commerce**); trade; business. **2.** social relations. **3.** sexual intercourse. **4.** *Obs.* intellectual interchange. [F, from L *commercium* trade]

**commercial** /kə'mɜʃəl/, *adj.* **1.** of, or of the nature of, commerce. **2.** engaged in commerce. **3.** capable of being sold in great numbers: *is the invention commercial?* **4.** setting possible commercial return above artistic considerations. **5.** preoccupied with profits or immediate gains. **6.** not entirely or chemically pure: *commercial soda.* **7.** (of a vehicle) used primarily for carrying goods for trade, or paying passengers. **8.** *Radio, T.V.* financially dependent on revenue from advertising. **9.** *Music.* created specifically to appeal to the widest market. –*n.* **10.** *Radio, T.V.* an advertisement. – **commerciality** /kəmɜʃi'æləti/, *n.* – **commercially,** *adv.*

**commercial art** /– 'at/, *n.* graphic art created specifically for commercial uses, esp. for advertising, illustrations in magazines or books, etc. – **commercial artist,** *n.*

**commercial bill** /– 'bɪl/, *n.* a security acknowledging a debt, signed by both the borrower (the drawer) and the lender (the acceptor) and stating the date on which repayment is due.

**commercial bill market,** *n.* the market in which commercial bills are sold or discounted.

**commercial cause** /kəmɜʃəl 'kɔz/, *n.* a legal action relating to the ordinary transactions of merchants and traders; heard in a special branch of the Supreme Court.

**commercial college** /'– ˌkɒlɪdʒ/, *n.* →**business college.**

**commercialese** /kəmɜʃə'liz/, *n.* the jargon used by those engaged in commercial activities.

**commercial flag** /'– flæg/, *n.* →**red ensign** (def. 1).

**commercialise** /kə'mɜʃəlaɪz/, *v.t.,* **-lised, -lising.** to make commercial in character, methods, or spirit; make a matter of profit. Also, **commercialize.** – **commercialisation** /kəmɜʃəlaɪ'zeɪʃən/, *n.*

**commercialism** /kə'mɜʃəlɪzəm/, *n.* **1.** the principles, methods, and practices of commerce. **2.** commercial spirit. **3.** a commercial custom or expression. **4.** (*oft. derog.*) preoccupation with profits or immediate gains. – **commercialist,** *n.* – **commercialistic** /kəmɜʃə'lɪstɪk/, *adj.*

**commercial law** /kəmɜʃəl 'lɔ/, *n.* the principles and rules drawn chiefly from custom, determining the rights and obligations of commercial transactions; law merchant.

**commercial music** /– 'mjuzɪk/, *n.* light or sentimental music written for immediate popular appeal.

**commercial traveller** /– 'trævələ/, *n.* a travelling agent, esp. for a wholesale business house, who solicits orders for goods.

**commercial vehicle** /– 'viɪkəl/, *n.* a vehicle able to carry goods or passengers, and designated for use by businesses, as a panel van, utility truck, etc.

**commie** /'kɒmi/, *n. Colloq.* a communist.

**commination** /kɒmə'neɪʃən/, *n.* **1.** a threat of punishment or vengeance. **2.** a denunciation. **3.** (in the Church of England) a penitential office read on Ash Wednesday proclaiming God's anger and judgments against sinners. [late ME, from L *comminātio* a threatening] – **comminatory** /'kɒmənətəri, -tri/, *adj.*

**commingle** /kə'mɪŋgəl/, *v.* **-gled, -gling.** –*v.i.* **1.** to mingle together; blend. –*v.t.* **2.** to mix together; combine.

**comminute** /'kɒmənjut/, *v.t.,* **-nuted, -nuting.** to pulverise; triturate. [L *comminūtus,* pp., made smaller] – **comminution** /kɒmə'njuʃən/, *n.*

**commiserate** /kə'mɪzəreɪt/, *v.,* **-rated, -rating.** –*v.i.* **1.** to sympathise (fol. by *with*) –*v.t.* **2.** to feel or express sorrow or sympathy for; pity. [L *commiserātus,* pp.] – **commiseration** /kəmɪzə'reɪʃən/, *n.* – **commiserative** /kə'mɪzərətɪv/, *adj.* – **commiseratively,** *adv.*

**commissar** /'kɒməsa/, *n.* head of a government department (commissariat) in any republic of the Soviet Union. [Russ. *kommisar,* from F *commissaire*]

**commissariat** /kɒmə'sɛəriət, -riæt/, *n.* **1.** the department of an army charged with supplying provisions, etc. **2.** the organised method or manner by which food, equipment, transport, etc., is delivered to the armies. **3.** any of the governmental divisions of the Soviet Union. [F, from *commissaire.* See COMMISSARY]

**commissary** /ˈkɒməsəri/, *n., pl.* **-saries.** **1.** *Mil.* an officer of the commissariat. **2.** *U.S.* a store that supplies food and equipment, esp. in an army, mining or lumber camp. **3.** one to whom some charge is committed by a superior power; a deputy. **4.** *Eccles.* an officer who, by delegation from the bishop, exercises spiritual jurisdiction in remote parts of a diocese, or is entrusted with the performance of duties of the bishop in his absence. **5.** (in the Soviet Union) a commissar. **6.** (in France) a police official, usu. just below the police chief and mayor. [ME, from ML *commissārius,* from L *commissus,* pp., committed] – **commissarial** /kɒməˈsɛəriəl/, *adj.*

**commission** /kəˈmɪʃən/, *n.* **1.** the act of committing or giving in charge. **2.** an authoritative order, charge, or direction. **3.** authority granted for a particular action or function. **4.** a document or warrant granting authority to act in a given capacity or conferring a particular rank. **5.** a body of persons authoritatively charged with particular functions. **6.** the condition of being placed under special authoritative charge. **7.** the condition of anything in active service or use: *to be in or out of commission.* **8.** a task or matter committed to one's charge. **9.** authority to act as agent for another or others in commercial transactions. **10.** the committing or perpetrating of a crime, error, etc. **11.** that which is committed. **12.** a sum or percentage allowed to an agent, salesman, etc., for his services. **13.** the amount or percentage charged for exchanging money, collecting a bill, or the like. **14.** the position or rank of an officer in the army or navy: *to hold or resign a commission.* **15.** *Navy.* **a.** the condition of a ship ordered to active service, and supplied with a captain and crew. **b. put in** or **into commission,** to transfer (a ship) to active service. *–v.t.* **16.** to give a commission to. **17.** to authorise; send on a mission. **18.** to put (a ship, etc.) in commission. **19.** to give a commission or order for. [ME, from L *commissio* a committing]

**commission agent** /ˈ– eɪdʒənt/, *n.* **1.** Also, **commission merchant.** an agent who receives goods for sale on a commission basis, or who buys on this basis and has the goods delivered to a principal. **2.** *Brit.* a bookmaker.

**commissionaire** /kəmɪʃəˈnɛə/, *n.* a uniformed messenger or doorkeeper at a hotel, office, theatre, etc.

**commissioned officer** /kəmɪʃənd ˈɒfəsə/, *n.* an army, naval, or airforce officer holding rank by commission.

**commissioner** /kəˈmɪʃənə/, *n.* **1.** one commissioned to act officially; a member of a commission. **2.** a government official in charge of a department. – **commissionership,** *n.*

**commissioner for oaths,** *n.* a solicitor or other person appointed to administer oaths or take affidavits.

**commissioning editor** /kəˈmɪʃənɪŋ ˌɛdətə/, *n.* a book editor who commissions authors to provide manuscripts.

**commissure** /ˈkɒməʃʊə/, *n.* **1.** a joint; seam; suture. **2.** *Bot.* the joint or face by which one carpel coheres with another. **3.** *Anat., Zool.* a connecting band of nerve tissue, etc. [late ME, from L *commissūra* joining] – **commissural** /kəˈmɪʃərəl, kɒməˈsjʊərəl/, *adj.*

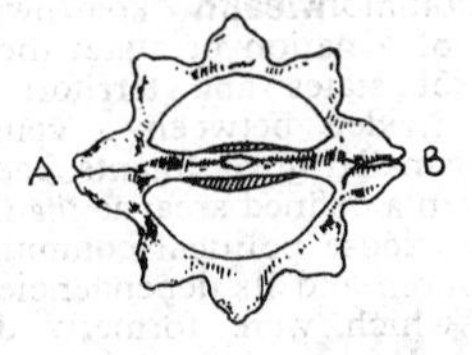

botanical commissure: AB, line of commissural faces of the two carpels

**commit** /kəˈmɪt/, *v.t.,* **-mitted, -mitting.** **1.** to give in trust or charge; entrust; consign. **2.** to consign for preservation: *to commit to writing, memory, etc.* **3.** to consign to custody in an institution, as a gaol, mental hospital, etc. **4.** (of a magistrate) to send (an accused) to trial by jury: *to commit for trial.* **5.** to send troops into battle. **6.** to consign, esp. for safe-keeping; commend: *to commit one's soul to God.* **7.** to hand over for treatment, disposal, etc.: *to commit a manuscript to the flames.* **8.** *Parl. Proc.* to refer (a bill, etc.) to a committee for consideration. **9.** to do; perform; perpetrate: *to commit murder, an error, etc.* **10.** to bind by pledge or assurance; pledge. [ME *committe(n),* from L *committere* bring together, join, entrust] – **committable,** *adj.*

**commitment** /kəˈmɪtmənt/, *n.* **1.** the act of committing. **2.** the state of being committed. **3.** that to which one has committed oneself; a pledge. **4.** *Parl. Proc.* the act of referring or entrusting to a committee for consideration. **5.** consignment, as to prison. **6.** *Law.* a written order of a court directing that someone be confined to prison (formerly more often termed a *mittimus*). **7.** perpetration or commission, as of a crime. **8.** the act of committing, pledging, or engaging oneself. **9.** →**bargain** (def. 3). Also, **committal** for defs 1, 4, 5, 7, 8.

**committal** /kəˈmɪtl/, *n.* **1.** the action of committing. **2.** the consignment of a body to the grave.

**committee**[1] /kəˈmɪti/, *n.* **1.** a person or a group of persons elected or appointed from a larger body to investigate, report, or act in special cases. **2. standing committee,** a permanent committee, as of a legislature, society, etc., intended to consider all matters pertaining to a designated subject. [AF, orig. pp., committed]

**committee**[2] /kɒməˈti/, *n. Law.* one to whom the care of a person (as a lunatic) or an estate was formerly entrusted. [AF orig. pp., committed]

**committeeman** /kəˈmɪtiˌmæn/, *n., pl.* **-men.** **1.** a member of a committee. **2.** (*derog.*) one obsessed with administrative procedures. – **committeewoman** /kəˈmɪtiwʊmən/, *n. fem.*

**Committee of the Whole House,** *n. Parl. Proc.* a committee consisting of all the members of a house of parliament for the purpose of discussing and voting upon details of a proposal before the house. See **committee stage.** Also, **Committee of the Whole.**

**committee stage** /kəˈmɪti steɪdʒ/, *n. Parl. Proc.* a procedure adopted after the second reading of a bill in which each part of it is considered by a committee, usu. of the whole membership of the house.

**committee system** /ˈ– sɪstəm/, *n. Parl. Proc.* the practice of setting up small groups of parliamentarians (from either or both houses) to study, report upon, and make recommendations concerning specific legislation and governmental activity.

**commix** /kɒˈmɪks/, *v.t.* **1.** to mix together. *–v.i.* **2.** to blend; mix.

**commixture** /kɒˈmɪkstʃə/, *n.* a mixing together; the product of mixing; mixture. [L *commixtūra*]

**commo** /ˈkɒmoʊ/, *n. Colloq.* a communist.

**commode** /kəˈmoʊd/, *n.* **1.** a piece of furniture containing drawers or shelves. **2.** a stand or cupboard containing a chamber-pot or washbasin. **3.** a large, high headdress worn by women in the 18th century. [F, from L *commodus* fit, convenient, useful]

**commodious** /kəˈmoʊdiəs/, *adj.* **1.** convenient and roomy; spacious: *a commodious harbour.* **2.** convenient or satisfactory for the purpose. [late ME, from ML *commodiōsus.* See COMMODE] – **commodiously,** *adv.* – **commodiousness,** *n.*

**commodity** /kəˈmɒdəti/, *n., pl.* **-ties.** **1.** a thing that is of use or advantage. **2.** an article of trade or commerce. **3.** *Obs.* a quantity of goods.

**commodore** /ˈkɒmədɔ/, *n.* **1.** *Navy.* a naval officer next in rank below a rear admiral, usu. in temporary command of a squadron. **2.** *Navy.* the senior captain when three or more ships of war are cruising in company. **3.** the senior captain of a line of merchant vessels. **4.** the president or head of a yacht club or boat club. **5.** the ship of a commodore. [earlier *commandore,* possibly from D *kommandeur,* from F *commandeur,* from *commander* command]

**common** /ˈkɒmən/, *adj.* **1.** belonging equally to, or shared alike by, two or more or all in question: *common property.* **2.** joint; united: *to make common cause against the enemy.* **3.** pertaining or belonging to the whole community; public: *common council.* **4.** of or pertaining to any church service or prayer which is shared by others rather than individually undertaken. **5.** generally or publicly known; notorious: *a common thief.* **6.** widespread; general; ordinary: *common knowledge.* **7.** of frequent occurrence; familiar; usual: *a common event, common salt.* **8.** hackneyed; trite. **9.** of mediocre or inferior quality; mean; low. **10.** coarse; vulgar: *common manners.* **11.** ordinary; having no rank, etc.: *common soldier, the common people.* **12.** *Anat.* denoting a trunk from which two or more arteries, veins, or nerves are given off: *the* *common carotid arteries.* **13.** *Pros.* (of a syllable) either long or short. *–n.* **14.** *Chiefly Brit.* a tract of land owned or used in common, esp. by all the members of a community. **15. in common,** in joint possession, use, etc.; jointly. **16.** *Law.* the power, shared with other persons to enter on the land or waters of another, and to remove something therefrom, as by pasturing cattle, catching fish, etc. **17.** (*sometimes cap.*) *Eccles.* an office or form of service used on a festival of a particular kind. **18.** *Obs.* the community or public. **19.** *Obs.* the common people. [ME *comun,* from OF, from L *commūnis* common, general] – **commonness,** *n.*

**commonable** /'kɒmənəbəl/, *adj.* **1.** held in common, or subject to general use, as lands. **2.** that may be pastured on common land.

**commonage** /'kɒmənɪdʒ/, *n.* **1.** the use of anything in common, esp. of a pasture. **2.** the right to such use. **3.** the state of being held in common. **4.** that which is so held, as land. **5.** →**commonalty.**

**commonalty** /'kɒmənəlti/, *n., pl.* **-ties. 1.** the common people as distinguished from the nobility, etc. **2.** the members of an incorporated body.

**common brick** /kɒmən 'brɪk/, *n.* the cheapest brick available from a kiln. Cf. **face brick, clinker**[1].

**common brown snake,** *n.* a medium-sized, venomous snake, *Demansia textilis,* found mainly in dry areas of Australia. Also, **brown snake, mallee snake.**

**common carrier** /kɒmən 'kæriə/, *n.* an individual or company, such as a railway or steamship line, which transports the public or goods for a fee.

**common chord** /– 'kɔd/, *n.* (in music) a major triad.

**common denominator** /– də'nɒməneɪtə/, *n.* **1.** *Maths.* an integer, usu. the least, divisible by all the denominators of a set of fractions. **2.** an interest, belief, etc. shared by a group of people.

**commoner** /'kɒmənə/, *n.* **1.** one of the common people; a member of the commonalty. **2.** one who has a joint right in common land.

**common factor** /kɒmən 'fæktə/, *n. Maths.* an integer which is an exact divisor of two or more given integers. The **highest common factor** (or **greatest common divisor**) is the largest factor of a set of integers.

**common fee** /– 'fi/, *n.* →**most common fee.**

**commonfolk** /'kɒmənfoʊk/, *n.* the average members of a community, viewed collectively. Also, **commonfolks.**

**common fraction** /kɒmən 'frækʃən/, *n. Maths.* a fraction having the numerator above and the denominator below a horizontal or diagonal line (as opposed to a *decimal fraction*).

**common gender** /– 'dʒɛndə/, *n.* the gender of a noun or pronoun which may be either masculine or feminine: for example, *child, person, they.*

**common ground** /– 'graʊnd/, *n.* that part of the matter under discussion to which all parties to a dispute can agree.

**common knowledge** /– 'nɒlɪdʒ/, *n.* information which is known by most people.

**common law** /– 'lɔ/, *n.* **1.** the system of law originating in England as distinct from the civil or Roman law and the canon or ecclesiastical law. **2.** the unwritten law, esp. of England, based on custom or court decision, as distinct from statute law. **3.** the law administered through the system of writs, as distinct from equity, admiralty, etc. – **common-law,** *adj.*

**common logarithm** /– 'lɒgərɪðəm/, *n. Maths.* a logarithm using 10 as the base.

**commonly** /'kɒmənli/, *adv.* **1.** usually; generally; ordinarily. **2.** in a common manner.

**common market** /kɒmən 'makət/, *n.* **1.** a group of countries which agree to trade with one another without tariffs, and to impose common tariffs as countries outside the group. **2.** (*caps*) the European Economic Community.

**common measure** /– 'mɛʒə/, *n.* →**common time.**

**common multiple** /– 'mʌltəpəl/, *n. Maths.* an integer divisible by two or more given integers. The **least** (or **lowest**) **common multiple** is the smallest common multiple of a set of integers.

**common name** /– 'neɪm/, *n.* **1.** a common noun. **2.** the vernacular name of a plant, animal, etc., as opposed to the name used in scientific classification.

**common noun** /– 'naʊn/, *n. Gram.* (in English and some other languages) a noun that can be preceded by an article or other limiting modifier, in meaning applicable to any one or all the members of a class, as *man, men, city, cities,* in contrast to *Shakespeare, Hobart.* Cf. **proper noun.**

**common-or-garden** /ˌkɒmən-ɔ-'gadən/, *adj. Colloq.* ordinary.

**commonplace** /'kɒmənpleɪs/, *adj.* **1.** ordinary; uninteresting; without individuality: *a commonplace person.* **2.** trite; hackneyed: *a commonplace remark.* *–n.* **3.** a well-known, customary, or obvious remark; a trite or uninteresting saying. **4.** anything common, ordinary, or uninteresting. **5.** a place or passage in a book or writing noted as important for reference or quotation. [translation of L *locus commūnis,* Gk (*koinós*) *topós* a stereotyped topic, argument, or passage in literature] – **commonplaceness,** *n.*

**commonplace book** /'– bʊk/, *n.* a book in which noteworthy passages, poems, comments, etc., are written.

**common pleas** /kɒmən 'pliz/, *n. Brit.* the chief common-law court of civil jurisdiction.

**common prayer** /– 'prɛə/, *n.* the liturgy or public form of prayer prescribed by the Anglican Church to be used in all churches and chapels in public worship.

**common room** /'– rum/, *n.* (in schools, universities, etc.) a sitting room for the use of the teaching staff, or, in some cases, of the students.

**common rule** /– 'rul/, *n.* a provision of an award of an industrial tribunal which has general application throughout the whole of the industry in which the award is operative.

**commons** /'kɒmənz/, *n.pl.* **1.** the common people as distinguished from their rulers or a ruling class; the commonalty. **2.** the body of people not of noble birth or ennobled, as represented in England by the House of Commons. **3.** (*cap.*) the representatives of this body. **4.** (*cap.*) the elective house of the parliament of Britain and Northern Ireland, Canada, and some of the other Commonwealth countries. **5.** *Brit.* food provided at a common table as in colleges. **6.** *Brit.* food or provisions in general.

**common sallow** /kɒmən 'sæloʊ/, *n.* →**sallow**[2].

**common seal** /– 'sil/, *n.* the official seal used by a corporation.

**commonsense** /kɒmən'sɛns/, *n.* sound, practical perception or understanding. – **commonsense,** *adj.*

**commonsensical** /kɒmən'sɛnsɪkəl/, *adj.* having or demonstrating the qualities of commonsense. – **commonsensicality** /ˌkɒmənsɛnsə'kæləti/, *n.*

**common shares** /kɒmən 'ʃɛəz/, *n.pl.* stock which ordinarily has no preference in the matter of dividends or assets and represents the residual ownership of a corporate business. Also, *U.S.,* **common stock.**

**common time** /'– taɪm/, *n. Music.* duple and quadruple rhythm. Also, **common measure.**

**commonweal** /'kɒmənwil/, *n.* **1.** the common welfare; the public good. **2.** *Archaic.* the body politic; a commonwealth.

**commonwealth** /'kɒmənwɛlθ/, *n.* **1.** the whole body of people of a nation or state; the body politic. **2.** (*cap.*) a federation of states and territories with powers and responsibilities divided between a central government and a number of smaller governments, each controlling certain responsibilities in a defined area, as *the Commonwealth of Australia.* **3.** (*cap.*) a loose political community consisting of the United Kingdom and its dependencies, and certain self-governing nations which were formerly dominions or colonies. **4.** (*cap.*) a self-governing territory associated with the U.S.; the official name of Puerto Rico. **5.** any body of persons united by some common interest. **6.** *Obs.* the public welfare. [COMMON + WEALTH]

**Commonwealth star** /kɒmənwɛlθ 'sta/, *n.* the large seven-pointed star on the flag of the Commonwealth of Australia, approved in 1908.

**commotion** /kə'moʊʃən/, *n.* **1.** violent or tumultuous motion; agitation. **2.** political or social disturbance; sedition; insurrection.

**commove** /kɒ'muv/, *v.t.,* **-moved, -moving.** to move violently; agitate; excite. [L *commovēre;* replacing ME *commoeve(n),* from F *commouvoir*]

**communal** /kə'mjunəl, 'kɒmjənəl/, *adj.* **1.** pertaining to a commune or a community. **2.** of or belonging to the people of a community: *communal land.* – **communally** /kəˈmjunəli, ˈkɒmjənəli/, *adv.*

**communalise** /kəˈmjunəlaɪz, ˈkɒmjən-/, *v.t.*, **-lised, -lising.** to make communal; convert into municipal property. Also, **communalize.** – **communalisation** /kəmjunəlaɪˈzeɪʃən/, *n.* – **communaliser,** *n.*

**communalism** /kəˈmjunəlɪzəm, ˈkɒmjən-/, *n.* a theory or system of government according to which each commune is virtually an independent state, and the nation merely a federation of such states. – **communalist,** *n.* – **communalistic** /kəmjunəˈlɪstɪk/, *adj.*

**communality** /kɒmjuˈnæləti/, *n.* the communal state, condition, or solidarity. [COMMUNAL + -ITY]

**commune**[1] /kəˈmjun/, *v.*, **-muned, -muning;** /ˈkɒmjun/, *n.* *–v.i.* **1.** to converse; talk together; interchange thoughts or feelings. *–n.* **2.** interchange of ideas or sentiments; friendly conversation. [ME *com(m)une(n),* from OF *comuner* share, from *comun* common]

**commune**[2] /ˈkɒmjun/, *n.* **1.** the smallest administrative division in France, Italy, Switzerland, etc., governed by a mayor assisted by a municipal council. **2.** a similar division in some other country. **3.** any community organised for the protection and promotion of local interests, and subordinate to the state. **4.** any community of like-minded people choosing to live independently of the state, often cherishing ideals differing from those held in the state: *hippy commune.* **5.** the government or citizens of a commune. **6.** *Ethnol.* a representative group in primitive society. [F, fem. of *commun* common]

**communicable** /kəˈmjunɪkəbəl/, *adj.* **1.** capable of being communicated. **2.** communicative. [ML *commūnicābilis*] – **communicability** /kəˌmjunɪkəˈbɪləti/, **communicableness,** *n.* – **communicably,** *adv.*

**communicant** /kəˈmjunɪkənt/, *n.* **1.** one who partakes, or is entitled to partake, of the Eucharist; a member of a church. **2.** one who communicates. *–adj.* **3.** communicating; imparting.

**communicate** /kəˈmjunəkeɪt/, *v.*, **-cated, -cating.** *–v.t.* **1.** to give to another as a partaker; impart; transmit. **2.** to impart knowledge of; make known. **3.** (in writing, painting, etc.) to convey one's feelings, thoughts, etc., successfully to others. **4.** to administer the Eucharist to. **5.** *Archaic.* to share in or partake of. *–v.i.* **6.** to have interchange of thoughts. **7.** to have or form a connecting passage. **8.** to partake of the Eucharist. **9.** *Obs.* to take part or participate. [L *commūnicātus,* pp., shared] – **communicator,** *n.*

**communication** /kəmjunəˈkeɪʃən/, *n.* **1.** the act or fact of communicating; transmission. **2.** the imparting or interchange of thoughts, opinions, or information by speech, writing, or signs. **3.** that which is communicated or imparted. **4.** a document or message imparting views, information, etc. **5.** passage, opportunity of passage, or a means of passage between places. **6.** the science or process of conveying information esp. by electronic or mechanical means. **7.** (*pl.*) **a.** the means of transmitting information by telephone, telegraph, radio, television, etc. **b.** any means of sending military messages, orders, etc. **c.** routes and transportation for moving troops and supplies overseas, or in a theatre of operations.

**communication cord** /ˈ– kɔd/, *n.* a cord or chain running the length of a railway carriage by which a passenger may apply the brakes of the train in case of an emergency.

**communication gap** /ˈ– ˌgæp/, *n.* a failure of two or more parties to understand one another, esp. in an industrial or political confrontation.

**communication satellite** /– ˈsætəlaɪt/, *n.* an artificial earth satellite used for relaying radio and television signals around the curved surface of the earth. Also, **communications satellite.**

**communications protocol** /kəˌmjunəkeɪʃənz ˈproʊtəkɒl/, *n.* a set of signals and responses which comprise an operating procedure on a computerised device.

**communication theory** /kəmjunəˈkeɪʃən θɪəri/, *n.* the study of the methods and principles by which information is conveyed; information theory. Also, **communications theory.**

**communicative** /kəˈmjunəkətɪv/, *adj.* **1.** inclined to communicate or impart. **2.** talkative; not reserved. **3.** of or pertaining to communication. – **communicatively,** *adv.* – **communicativeness,** *n.*

**communicatory** /kəˈmjunəkətri, kəmjunəˈkeɪtəri/, *adj.* of or pertaining to communication.

**communion** /kəˈmjunjən/, *n.* **1.** the act of sharing, or holding in common; participation. **2.** the state of things so held. **3.** association; fellowship. **4.** interchange of thoughts or interests; communication; intimate talk. **5.** *Eccles.* **a.** a body of persons having one common religious faith; a religious denomination. **b.** reception of the Eucharist. **c.** the celebration of the Lord's Supper; the Eucharist. [ME, from L *commūnio* fellowship]

**communiqué** /kəˈmjunəkeɪ/, *n.* an official bulletin or communication as of war news, events at a conference etc., usu. to the press or public. [F]

**communise** /ˈkɒmjənaɪz/, *v.t.*, **-nised, -nising.** **1.** to make the property of the community. **2.** to make communist. Also, **communize.** – **communisation** /kɒmjənaɪˈzeɪʃən/, *n.*

**communism** /ˈkɒmjənɪzəm/, *n.* **1.** a theory or system of social organisation based on the holding of all property in common, actual ownership being ascribed to the community as a whole or to the state. **2.** a system of social organisation in which all economic activity is conducted by a totalitarian state dominated by a single and self-perpetuating political party. **3.** →**communalism.** [F *communisme,* from *commun.* See COMMON]

**communist** /ˈkɒmjənəst/, *n.* **1.** an advocate of communism. **2.** (*oft. cap.*) a person who belongs to the Communist Party, esp. the party in the Soviet Union. **3.** (*derog.*) one who espouses left-wing policies or who disagrees with a ruling right-wing elite. *–adj.* **4.** pertaining to communists or communism.

**communistic** /kɒmjəˈnɪstɪk/, *adj.* **1.** communist. **2.** tending towards or sympathising with communism. – **communistically,** *adv.*

**Communist Party** /ˈkɒmjənəst pati/, *n.* a political party professing the principles of communism.

**communitarian** /kəˌmjunəˈtɛəriən/, *n.* **1.** a member of a communistic community. **2.** an advocate of such a community.

**community** /kəˈmjunəti/, *n., pl.* **-ties.** **1.** a social group of any size whose members reside in a specific locality, share government, and have a cultural and historical heritage. **2.** **the community,** the public. **3.** *Eccles.* a group of men or women leading a common life according to a rule. **4.** a group of organisms, both plant and animal, living together in an ecologically related fashion in a definite region: *an oak forest community.* **5.** joint possession, enjoyment, liability, etc.: *community of property.* **6.** similar character; agreement; identity: *community of interests.* *–adj.* **7.** of or pertaining to radio or television which is owned by the community which uses it. [L *commūnitas;* replacing ME *comunete,* from OF]

**community centre** /ˈ– sɛntə/, *n.* a building in which members of a community meet for social or other purposes.

**community chest** /ˈ– tʃɛst/, *n. Chiefly U.S. and Canada.* a fund for local welfare activities, raised by voluntary contributions.

**community hall** /ˈ– hɔl/, *n.* a hall provided by a community or local government authority for community use.

**community hospital** /– ˈhɒspətl/, *n.* a hospital receiving at least part of its running costs from a municipal authority.

**community justice centre,** *n.* a centre offering a free and confidential mediation service as an alternative to normal legal channels in disputes between parties who have an ongoing relationship, as members of a family, neighbours, etc.

**community singing** /– ˈsɪŋɪŋ/, *n.* organised singing at a public gathering.

**commutable** /kəˈmjutəbəl/, *adj.* that may be commuted; exchangeable. – **commutability** /kəmjutəˈbɪləti/, *n.*

**commutate** /ˈkɒmjuteɪt/, *v.t.*, **-tated, -tating.** *Elect.* **1.** to reverse the direction of (a current or currents), as by a commutator. **2.** to convert (alternating current) into direct current by use of a commutator.

**commutation** /kɒmjuˈteɪʃən/, *n.* **1.** the act of substituting one thing for another; substitution; exchange. **2.** the substitution of one kind of payment for another. **3.** *U.S.* regular travel between home (usu. distant) and work, generally using a season ticket. **4.** the changing of a penalty, etc., for another less severe. **5.** *Elect.* **a.** the act of reversing the direction of the current. **b.** the act of converting an alternating current into a direct current.

**commutative** /kəˈmjutətɪv, ˈkɒmjuˌteɪtɪv/, *adj.* of or pertaining to commutation, exchange, substitution, or interchange.

**commutative law** /ˈ– lɔ/, *n. Maths, Logic.* a law asserting that the order in which certain logical operations are performed is indifferent; in mathematics the two commutative laws are stated symbolically as: $a + b = b + a$ and $ab = ba$. For example: *Smith is ill or out of town* is equipollent with *Smith is out of town or ill.*

**commutator** /ˈkɒmjuteɪtə/, *n.* a device for reversing the direction of an electric current esp. in a dynamo or motor.

**commute** /kəˈmjut/, *v.,* **-muted, -muting.** *–v.t.* **1.** to exchange for another or something else; give and take reciprocally; interchange. **2.** to change (one kind of payment) into or for another, as by substitution. **3.** to change (a penalty, etc.) for one less burdensome or severe. *–v.i.* **4.** to make substitution. **5.** to serve as a substitute. **6.** *Maths, Logic.* to obey the commutative law. **7.** to make a collective payment, esp. of a reduced amount, as an equivalent for a number of payments. **8.** to travel regularly between home (usu. distant) and work, generally using a season ticket. [L *commūtāre* change wholly]

**commuter** /kəˈmjutə/, *n.* one who regularly travels some considerable distance to work from his home, esp. by public transport.

**commuter belt** /ˈ– bɛlt/, *n.* the area around a city from which workers commute.

**comose** /ˈkoʊmoʊs, koʊˈmoʊs/, *adj.* hairy; comate. [L *comōsus* covered with hair]

**comp.,** **1.** comparative. **2.** compare. **3.** compilation. **4.** compiled. **5.** composer. **6.** composition. **7.** compositor. **8.** compound. **9.** compensation.

**compact**[1] /kɒmˈpækt, ˈkɒmpækt/, *adj.;* /kɒmˈpækt/, *v.;* /ˈkɒmpækt/, *n.* *–adj.* **1.** joined or packed together; closely and firmly united; dense; solid. **2.** arranged within a relatively small space. **3.** expressed concisely; pithy; terse; not diffuse. **4.** composed or made (fol. by *of*). *–v.t.* **5.** to join or pack closely together; consolidate; condense. **6.** to make firm or stable. **7.** to form or make by close union or conjunction; make up or compose. **8.** *Metall.* to press (metallic and other powders) in a die. *–n.* **9.** a small case containing a mirror, face powder, a puff, and (sometimes) rouge. **10.** *Metal.* an object produced by the compression of metal powder, generally while confined in a die, with the inclusion of non-metallic constituents. [L *compactus,* pp., joined together] **– compactness,** *n.*

**compact**[2] /ˈkɒmpækt/, *n.* an agreement between parties; a covenant; a contract. [L *compactum,* properly pp. neut., having agreed with]

compact (def. 9)

**compaction** /kəmˈpækʃən/, *n.* the density of material in a backfilled excavation.

**compactus** /kəmˈpæktəs/, *n.* mobile shelving units, usu. electrically operated, which stack against each other or stand free according to need, and are used for bulk storage of material.

**companion**[1] /kəmˈpænjən/, *n.* **1.** one who accompanies or associates with another. **2.** a person, usu. a woman, employed to accompany or assist another. **3.** a mate or match for a thing. **4.** a handbook; guide. **5.** a member of the lowest rank in an order of knighthood, or of a grade in an order. **6.** *Obs.* a fellow (used in contempt). *–v.t.* **7.** to be a companion to; accompany. [LL *compānio* messmate, from L *com-* COM- + *pānis* bread; replacing ME *compainoun,* from OF *compaignon*] **– companionless,** *adj.*

**companion**[2] /kəmˈpænjən/, *n.* **1.** a covering or hood over the top of a companionway. **2.** →**companionway.** [D *kampanje* quarterdeck. Cf. It. *camera della campagna* storeroom]

**companionable** /kəmˈpænjənəbəl/, *adj.* fitted to be a companion; sociable. **– companionableness,** *n.* **– companionably,** *adv.*

**companionate** /kəmˈpænjənət/, *adj.* of, by, or like companions.

**companionate marriage** /– ˈmærɪdʒ/, *n.* a suggested form of marriage in which the partners do not recognise any legal responsibilities towards the other and may divorce by mutual consent.

**companion cell** /kəmˌpænjən ˈsɛl/, *n. Bot.* a cell associated with a sieve tube and, collectively, forming one of the elements of phloem.

**companion plant** /ˈ– plænt/, *n.* a plant grown in proximity to another plant for the benefit which its presence gives, as in repelling insect pests and diseases: *the onion is a companion plant to the rose.*

**companion planting** /ˈ– plæntɪŋ/, *n.* the practice of growing plants in proximity to their companion plants.

**companionship** /kəmˈpænjənʃɪp/, *n.* association as companions; fellowship.

**companionway** /kəmˈpænjənˌweɪ/, *n. Naut.* **1.** the space or shaft occupied by the steps leading down from the deck to a cabin. **2.** the steps themselves.

**company** /ˈkʌmpəni/, *n., pl.* **-nies,** *v.,* **-nied, -nying.** *–n.* **1.** a number of individuals assembled or associated together; a group of people. **2.** an assemblage of persons for social purposes. **3.** companionship; fellowship; association. **4.** a guest or guests. **5.** society collectively. **6.** a number of persons united or incorporated for joint action, esp. for business: *a publishing company.* **7.** the member or members of a firm not specifically named in the firm's title: *John Jones and Company.* **8.** a number of persons associated for the purpose of presenting theatrical productions, etc. **9.** a medieval trade guild. **10.** *Mil.* **a.** a subdivision of a regiment or battalion. **b.** any relatively small group of soldiers. **11.** *Naut.* a ship's crew, including the officers. **12. bear** or **keep company,** to associate or go with. **13. part company, a.** to cease association or friendship with. **b.** to leave or separate from (each other). *–v.i.* **14.** *Archaic.* to associate. *–v.t.* **15.** *Archaic.* to accompany. [ME *compaignie,* from OF. See COMPANION[1]]

**company car** /ˈ– ka/, *n.* a car owned by an employer but given over to the private use of an employee.

**company man** /ˈ– mæn/, *n.* an employee unusually devoted to and supportive of the policies of his employers.

**company tax** /ˈ– tæks/, *n.* a tax imposed on the profits of limited companies, intended to separate the taxation of companies from that of individuals.

**company title** /ˈ– taɪtl/, *n. Law.* a form of interest in property, particularly multi-storey buildings, where the whole of the building is owned by a company, shares in which are held by tenants.

**company town** /ˈ– taʊn/, *n.* a town set up by or dominated by the activities of a particular company, often a mining company.

**compar.,** comparative.

**comparable** /ˈkɒmprəbəl, -pərəbəl/, *adj.* **1.** capable of being compared. **2.** worthy of comparison. **– comparableness,** *n.* **– comparably,** *adv.*

**comparative** /kəmˈpærətɪv/, *adj.* **1.** of or pertaining to comparison. **2.** proceeding by or founded on comparison: *comparative anatomy.* **3.** estimated by comparison; not positive or absolute; relative. **4.** *Gram.* **a.** denoting the intermediate degree of the comparison of adjectives and adverbs. **b.** denoting the form of an adjective or adverb inflected to show this degree. **c.** having or pertaining to the function or meaning of this degree of comparison. *–n.* **5.** *Gram.* **a.** the comparative degree. **b.** a form in it, as English *lower* in contrast to *low* and *lowest, more gracious* in contrast to *gracious* and *most gracious.* **– comparatively,** *adv.*

**comparative linguistics** /– lɪŋˈgwɪstɪks/, *n.* the study of languages concentrating on correspondences between related languages or between different periods of the one language.

**comparator** /kəmˈpærətə/, *n.* **1.** any of various instruments for making comparisons with a standard, as of lengths or distances, tints of colours, etc. **2.** *Computers.* a logical device which gives a result, true if the numbers examined are equal, false if they are not.

**compare** /kəmˈpɛə/, *v.,* **-pared, -paring,** *n.* *–v.t.* **1.** to represent as similar or analogous; liken (fol. by *to*). **2.** to note the similarities and differences of (fol. by *with*). **3.** to bring together for the purpose of noting points of likeness and difference: *to compare two pieces of cloth.* **4.** *Gram.* to form or display the degrees of comparison of (an adjective or adverb). **5. compare notes,** to exchange views, ideas, impressions, etc. *–v.i.* **6.** to bear comparison; be held equal. **7.** to vie. *–n.* **8.** comparison: *joy beyond compare.* [ME, from F *comparer,* from L *comparāre,* lit., bring together] **– comparer,** *n.*

**comparison** /kəm'pærəsən/, *n.* **1.** the act of comparing. **2.** the state of being compared. **3.** a likening; an illustration by similitude; a comparative estimate or statement. **4.** *Rhet.* the considering of two things with regard to some characteristic which is common to both, as the likening of a hero to a lion in courage. **5.** the capability of being compared or likened. **6.** *Gram.* **a.** that function of an adverb or adjective used to indicate degrees of superiority or inferiority in quality, quantity, or intensity. **b.** the patterns of formation involved therein. **c.** the degrees of a particular word, displayed in a fixed order, as *mild, milder, mildest, less mild, least mild.* [ME, from OF *comparaison,* from L *comparātio,* from *comparāre.* See COMPARE]

**compartment** /kəm'patmənt/, *n.* **1.** a part or space marked or partitioned off. **2.** a separate room, section, etc.: *the compartment of a railway carriage, a watertight compartment in a ship.* **3.** *Archit., Art.* an ornamental division of a larger design. *–v.t.* **4.** to divide into compartments. [F *compartiment,* from It. *compartimento,* from LL *compartīrī* divide] **– compartmental,** *adj.*

**compartmentalise** /ˌkɒmpat'mɛntəlaɪz/, *v.t.,* **-ised, -ising.** to divide into compartments or sections. **– compartmentalisation** /ˌkɒmpatˌmɛntəlaɪ'zeɪʃən/, *n.*

**compass** /'kʌmpəs/, *n.* **1.** an instrument for determining directions, consisting essentially of a freely moving magnetised needle indicating magnetic north and south. **2.** the enclosing line or limits of any area; measurement round. **3.** space within limits; area; extent; range; scope. **4.** the total range of notes of a voice or of a musical instrument. **5.** due or proper limits; moderate bounds. **6.** a passing round; a circuit; a detour. **7.** (*usu. pl.*) an instrument for describing circles, measuring distances, etc., consisting generally of two movable legs hinged at one end. **8.** *Obs.* a circle. *–v.t.* **9.** to go or move round; make the circuit of. **10.** to extend or stretch around; hem in; encircle. **11.** to attain or achieve; accomplish; obtain. **12.** to contrive; scheme. **13.** to make curved or circular. **14.** to grasp with the mind. [ME *compas,* from OF, from *compasser* divide exactly, from L *compassus* equal step] **– compassable,** *adj.*

compass

**compass card** /'– kad/, *n.* a circular card attached to the needle of a mariner's compass, on which the degrees or points indicating direction are marked.

**compassion** /kəm'pæʃən/, *n.* **1.** a feeling of sorrow or pity for the sufferings or misfortunes of another; sympathy. *–v.t.* **2.** to have compassion for. [ME, from LL *compassio* sympathy]

**compassionate** /kəm'pæʃənət/, *adj.;* /kəm'pæʃəneɪt/, *v.,* **-nated, -nating.** *–adj.* **1.** having or showing compassion. **2.** on the grounds of compassion: *compassionate leave.* **3.** *Obs.* pitiable. *–v.t.* **4.** to have compassion for; pity. **– compassionately,** *adv.* **– compassionateness,** *n.*

**compass plane** /'kʌmpəs pleɪn/, *n.* a plane, usu. of metal, capable of adjustment to convex or concave curves and used for smoothing curved timbers.

**compass plant** /'– plænt/, *n.* any of various plants whose leaves tend to lie in a plane at right angles to the strongest light, hence usu. north and south, esp. *Lactuca serriola.*

**compass rose** /– 'roʊz/, *n.* the pattern on a map which functions to show the direction of true north and perhaps magnetic north and which is sometimes elaborated into a complicated and artistic design.

**compass saw** /'– sɔ/, *n.* a narrow tapered handsaw used for cutting curves.

**compatible** /kəm'pætəbəl/, *adj.* **1.** capable of existing together in harmony. **2.** capable of orderly, efficient integration with other elements in a system. **3.** (of a drug) capable of tolerating another drug without undesirable chemical reaction or effect. [ML *compatibilis,* from LL *compatī* suffer with] **– compatibility** /kəmpætə'bɪləti/, **compatibleness,** *n.* **– compatibly,** *adv.*

**compatriot** /kəm'peɪtriət/, *n.* **1.** a fellow countryman or fellow countrywoman. *–adj.* **2.** of the same country. [L *compatriōta*] **– compatriotism,** *n.*

**compeer** /'kɒmpɪə/, *n.* **1.** an equal or peer; a comrade; an associate. *–v.t.* **2.** *Archaic.* to be the equal of; match. [ME *comper,* from OF. See COM-, PEER[1]]

**compel** /kəm'pɛl/, *v.t.,* **-pelled, -pelling.** **1.** to force or drive, esp. to a course of action. **2.** to secure or bring about by force. **3.** to force to submit; subdue. **4.** to overpower. **5.** to drive together; unite by force; herd. [ME *compelle(n),* from L *compellere*] **– compellable,** *adj.* **– compeller,** *n.*

**compellability** /kɒmpɛlə'bɪləti/, *n.* *Law.* the readiness with which a person can be compelled to perform a given act, esp. to give evidence.

**compellation** /kɒmpə'leɪʃən/, *n.* **1.** the act or manner of addressing a person. **2.** form of address or designation; appellation. [L *compellātio*]

**compelling** /kəm'pɛlɪŋ/, *adj.* (of a person, writer, actor, etc.) demanding attention, respect.

**compendious** /kəm'pɛndiəs/, *adj.* containing the substance of a subject in a brief form; concise. [L *compendiōsus* abridged] **– compendiously,** *adv.* **– compendiousness,** *n.*

**compendium** /kəm'pɛndiəm/, *n., pl.* **-diums, -dia** /-diə/. **1.** a comprehensive summary of a subject; a concise treatise; an epitome. **2.** a boxed packet of stationery for letter writing. Also, **compend** /'kɒmpɛnd/. [L: a saving, a short way]

**compensate** /'kɒmpənseɪt/, *v.,* **-sated, -sating.** *–v.t.* **1.** to counterbalance; offset; make up for. **2.** to make up for something to (a person); recompense. **3.** *Mech.* to counterbalance (a force or the like); adjust or construct so as to offset or counterbalance variations or produce equilibrium. *–v.i.* **4.** to provide or be an equivalent. **5.** make up; make amends (fol. by *for*). [L *compensātus,* pp., counterbalanced] **– compensator,** *n.*

**compensation** /kɒmpən'seɪʃən/, *n.* **1.** the act of compensating. **2.** something given or received as an equivalent for services, debt, loss, suffering, etc.; indemnity. **3.** *Biol.* the improvement of any defect by the excessive development or action of another structure or organ of the same structure. **4.** *Psychol.* behaviour which compensates for some personal trait, as a weakness or inferiority. **– compensational,** *adj.*

**compensatory** /'kɒmpənseɪtəri/, *adj.* serving to compensate. Also, **compensative** /kɒmpən'seɪtɪv/.

**compere** /'kɒmpɛə/, *n., v.,* **-pered, -pering.** *–n.* **1.** one who introduces and links the acts in an entertainment. *–v.i.* **2.** to act as a compere in (a show, etc.). *–v.t.* **3.** to introduce and link together the acts of an entertainment. [F *compère*]

**compete** /kəm'pit/, *v.i.,* **-peted, -peting.** to contend with another for a prize, profit, etc.; engage in a contest; vie: *to compete in a race, in business, etc.* [L *competere* contend for, (earlier) come together]

**competence** /'kɒmpətəns/, *n.* **1.** the quality of being competent; adequacy; due qualification or capacity. **2.** sufficiency; a sufficient quantity. **3.** an income sufficient to furnish the necessities of life, without great luxuries. **4.** *Law.* the quality or position of being legally competent; legal capacity or qualification (which presupposes the meeting of certain minimum requirements of age, soundness of mind, citizenship, or the like). **5.** *Embryol.* the sum total of possible reactions of any group of blastemic cells under varied external conditions. **6.** *Linguistics.* the ability which all native speakers have to produce sentences which they have never heard before.

**competency** /'kɒmpətənsi/, *n.* **1.** →**competence** (defs 1-4). **2.** *Law.* (of a witness) eligibility to be sworn and testify (presupposing the meeting of requirements of ability to observe, remember, and recount).

**competent** /'kɒmpətənt/, *adj.* **1.** properly qualified, capable. **2.** fitting, suitable, or sufficient for the purpose; adequate. **3.** rightfully belonging; permissible (fol. by *to*). **4.** *Law.* (of a witness, a party to a contract, etc.) having legal capacity or qualification. [L *competens,* ppr., being fit] – **competently,** *adv.*

**competition** /kɒmpə'tɪʃən/, *n.* **1.** the act of competing; rivalry. **2.** a contest for some prize or advantage. **3.** the rivalry between two or more business enterprises to secure the patronage of prospective buyers. **4.** a competitor or competitors. **5.** *Sociol.* rivalry for the purpose of obtaining some advantage over some other person or group, but not involving the destruction of that person or group. **6.** *Ecol.* the struggle among organisms, both of the same and of different species, for food, space, and other factors of existence. [L *competītio*]

**competitive** /kəm'pɛtətɪv/, *adj.* of, pertaining to, involving, or decided by competition: *competitive examination.* Also, **competitory.** – **competitively,** *adv.* – **competitiveness,** *n.*

**competitor** /kəm'pɛtətə/, *n.* one who competes; a rival.

**compilation** /kɒmpə'leɪʃən/, *n.* **1.** the act of compiling: *the compilation of an index to a book.* **2.** something compiled, as a book.

**compile** /kəm'paɪl/, *v.t.,* **-piled, -piling.** **1.** to put together (literary materials) in one book or work. **2.** to make (a book, etc.) of materials from various sources. [ME *compile(n),* from OF *compiler,* from L *compīlāre* snatch together and carry off]

**compiler** /kəm'paɪlə/, *n.* **1.** one who compiles. **2.** *Computers.* a computer program which translates programming languages such as FORTRAN and ALGOL, into the basic commands which activate the computer.

**compl.,** **1.** complement. **2.** complimentary.

**complacency** /kəm'pleɪsənsi/, *n., pl.* **-cies.** **1.** a feeling of quiet pleasure; satisfaction; gratification; self-satisfaction. **2.** that which gives satisfaction; a cause of pleasure or joy; a comfort. **3.** *Obs.* friendly civility. **4.** *Obs.* a civil act. Also, **complacence.**

**complacent** /kəm'pleɪsənt/, *adj.* **1.** pleased, esp. with oneself or one's own merits, advantages, etc.; self-satisfied. **2.** pleasant; complaisant. [L *complacens,* ppr., pleasing] – **complacently,** *adv.*

**complain** /kəm'pleɪn/, *v.i.* **1.** to express grief, pain, uneasiness, censure, resentment, or dissatisfaction; find fault. **2.** to tell of one's pains, ailments, etc. **3.** to state a grievance; make a formal accusation. [ME *complayn(en),* from OF *complaindre,* from LL *complangere* lament] – **complainer,** *n.* – **complainingly,** *adv.*

**complainant** /kəm'pleɪnənt/, *n.* one who makes a complaint, as in a legal action.

**complaint** /kəm'pleɪnt/, *n.* **1.** an expression of grief, regret, pain, censure, resentment, or discontent; lament; faultfinding. **2.** a cause of grief, discontent, lamentation, etc. **3.** a cause of bodily pain or ailment; a malady. **4.** *Law.* the first pleading of the plaintiff in a civil action, stating his cause of action. **5.** *Law.* (in sexual offences) complaints by the victim of the offence to another person directly after the commission of the offence; admissible as evidence of the consistency of the complainant's story. [ME, from OF *complainte,* from *complaindre.* See COMPLAIN]

**complaisance** /kəm'pleɪsəns, -zəns/, *n.* **1.** the quality of being complaisant. **2.** a complaisant act. [F]

**complaisant** /kəm'pleɪsənt, -zənt/, *adj.* disposed to please; obliging; agreeable; gracious; compliant. [F, ppr. of *complaire* please, from L *complacēre*] – **complaisantly,** *adv.*

**compleat** /kɒm'plit/, *adj. Archaic.* complete.

**complement** /'kɒmpləmənt/, *n.;* /'kɒmplə,mɛnt/, *v.* –*n.* **1.** that which completes or makes perfect. **2.** the quantity or amount that completes anything. **3.** either of two parts or things needed to complete the whole. **4.** full quantity or amount; complete allowance. **5.** the full number of officers and crew required to man a ship. **6.** a word or words used to complete a grammatical construction, esp. in the predicate, as an object (*man* in *he saw the man*), predicate adjective (*tall* in *the tree is tall*), or predicate noun (*John* in *his name is John*). **7.** *Geom.* the angular amount needed to bring a given angle to a right angle. **8.** *Logic, Maths.* all the members of any set, class or space of elements, that are not in a given subset. **9.** *Music.* the interval which added to a given interval completes an octave. **10.** *Immunol.* a thermolabile substance which is normally present in all sera. –*v.t.* **11.** to complete; form a complement to. [ME, from L *complēmentum* that which fills up, (later) fulfilment]

**complemental** /kɒmplə'mɛntl/, *adj.* →**complementary.** – **complementally,** *adv.*

**complementarity** /,kɒmpləmɛn'tærəti/, *n. Physics.* a concept which acknowledges that different pieces of evidence relating to atomic systems, obtained under different conditions, cannot necessarily be understood by a single model, thus the concept of complementarity is necessary in order to accept the wave and particle models of an electron.

**complementary** /kɒmplə'mɛntəri, -tri/, *adj.* **1.** forming a complement; completing. **2.** complementing each other.

**complementary angle** /– 'æŋgəl/, *n.* the complement of the given angle.

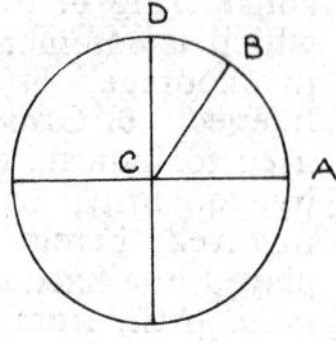


complementary angle: angle BCD, complement of angle ACB; arc BD, complement of arc AB

**complementary cells** /– 'sɛls/, *n.pl. Bot.* cells fitting loosely together in the lenticel.

**complementary colour** /– 'kʌlə/, *n.* **1.** one of a pair of colours which, with its partners, can produce white light when mixed, as yellow with blue. **2.** one of a pair of hues which lie directly opposite each other when all known hues are arranged in their natural order around the circumference of a circle.

**complete** /kəm'plit/, *adj., v.,* **-pleted, -pleting.** –*adj.* **1.** having all its parts or elements; whole; entire; full. **2.** finished; ended; concluded. **3.** thorough; consummate; perfect in kind or quality. **4.** *Archaic.* (of persons) accomplished; skilled; expert. –*v.t.* **5.** to make complete; make whole or entire. **6.** to make perfect. **7.** to bring to an end; finish; fulfil. [ME *compleet,* from L *complētus,* pp., filled up, completed] – **completely,** *adv.* – **completeness,** *n.* – **completer,** *n.* – **completive,** *adj.*

**completely built-up** /kəm,plitli bɪlt-'ʌp/, *adj.* denoting a car, etc., which is imported fully assembled.

**completely knocked-down** /kəm,plitli nɒkt-'daʊn/, *adj.* →**CKD.**

**completion** /kəm'pliʃən/, *n.* **1.** the act of completing. **2.** state of being completed. **3.** conclusion; fulfilment.

**complex** /'kɒmplɛks, kəm'plɛks/, *adj.;* /'kɒmplɛks/, *n.* –*adj.* **1.** composed of interconnected parts; compound; composite. **2.** characterised by an involved combination of parts. **3.** complicated; intricate. **4.** *Gram.* (of a word) consisting of two parts, at least one of which is a bound form, as *boyish* (consisting of the word *boy* and the bound form *-ish*). –*n.* **5.** a complex whole or system; a complicated assembly of particulars: *a shopping complex, a complex of ideas.* **6.** *Psychol.* a group of related ideas, feelings, memories, and impulses which operate together and may be repressed or inhibited together. **7.** *Colloq.* a fixed idea; an obsessing notion. [L *complexus,* pp., having embraced] – **complexly,** *adv.* – **complexness,** *n.*

**complex fraction** /– 'frækʃən/, *n.* a fraction expressing a ratio between fractions or mixed numbers, or between a fraction or mixed number and a whole number.

**complexion** /kəm'plɛkʃən/, *n.* **1.** the natural colour and appearance of the skin, esp. of the face. **2.** appearance; aspect; character. **3.** viewpoint; outlook. **4.** *Old Physiol.* constitution or nature of body and mind, regarded as the result of certain combined qualities. **5.** *Obs.* nature; disposition; temperament. [ME, from LL *complexio* constitution, L combination] – **complexional,** *adj.*

**complexity** /kəm'plɛksəti/, *n., pl.* **-ties.** **1.** the state or quality of being complex; intricacy. **2.** something complex.

**complex number** /,kɒmplɛks 'nʌmbə/, *n. Maths.* a number of the form $z = x + iy$, where $x$ and $y$ are real numbers and $i = \sqrt{-1}$.

**complex sentence** /– 'sɛntəns/, *n.* a sentence containing one or more dependent clauses in addition to the main clause. For example: *When the clock strikes* (dependent clause), *it will be three o'clock* (main clause).

**complex sound** /– 'saʊnd/, *n.* a sound made up of a number of simple sounds.

**compliable** /kəm'plaɪəbəl/, *adj.* →**compliant.** – **compliableness,** *n.* – **compliably,** *adv.*

**compliance** /kəm'plaɪəns/, *n.* **1.** the act of complying; an acquiescing or yielding. **2.** *Obs.* a disposition to yield to others. **3.** base subservience. **4. in compliance with,** in keeping or accordance with. Also, **compliancy** for defs 1-3.

**compliance plate** /'– pleɪt/, *n.* a small metal plate attached to the firewall in the engine compartment of motor vehicles, which certifies that the vehicle complies with certain design rules.

**compliant** /kəm'plaɪənt/, *adj.* complying; yielding; obliging: *they were uncomfortably compliant.* [COMPLY + -ANT] – **compliantly,** *adv.*

**complicacy** /'kɒmpləkəsi/, *n., pl.* **-cies. 1.** a complicated state. **2.** a complication.

**complicate** /'kɒmpləkeɪt/, *v.,* **-cated, -cating;** /'kɒmpləkət/, *adj.* *–v.t.* **1.** to make complex, intricate, or involved. **2.** to fold or twine together; combine intricately (fol. by *with*). *–adj.* **3.** complex; involved. **4.** *Bot.* folded upon itself: *a complicate embryo.* **5.** *Zool.* (of insects' wings) folded longitudinally one or more times. [L *complicātus,* pp., folded together]

**complicated** /'kɒmpləkeɪtəd/, *adj.* **1.** composed of interconnected parts; not simple; complex. **2.** consisting of many parts not easily separable; difficult to analyse, understand, explain, etc. – **complicatedly,** *adv.* – **complicatedness,** *n.*

**complication** /kɒmplə'keɪʃən/, *n.* **1.** the act of complicating. **2.** a complicated or involved state or condition. **3.** a complex combination of elements or things. **4.** a complicating element. **5.** *Pathol.* a concurrent disease or a fortuitous condition which aggravates the original disease.

**complicity** /kəm'plɪsəti/, *n., pl.* **-ties. 1.** the state of being an accomplice; partnership in wrongdoing. **2.** →**complexity.**

**complier** /kəm'plaɪə/, *n.* one who complies.

**compliment** /'kɒmpləmənt/ *n.;* /'kɒmplə,mɛnt/, *v.* *–n.* **1.** an expression of praise, commendation, or admiration: *he paid you a great compliment.* **2.** a formal act or expression of civility, respect, or regard: *the compliments of the season.* **3.** polite, esp. insincere, praise or commendation; flattery. **4.** a present; gift. **5. under a compliment to (someone),** under an obligation to (someone). *–v.t.* **6.** to pay a compliment to: *to compliment a woman on her new hat.* **7.** to show kindness or regard for by a gift or other favour: *he complimented us with tickets for the exhibition.* **8.** to congratulate; felicitate: *to compliment a prince on the birth of a son.* [F, from It. *complimento,* from Sp. *cumplimiento,* from *cumplir* fulfil, from L *complēre*]

**complimentary** /kɒmplə'mɛntri/, *adj.* **1.** of the nature of, conveying, or addressing a compliment. **2.** politely flattering. **3.** free: *a complimentary ticket.* – **complimentarily,** *adv.*

**complin** /'kɒmplən/, *n. Eccles.* **1.** the last of the seven canonical hours, or the service for it, occurring originally after the evening meal but more recently after vespers. **2.** the final service for the day in *The Prayer of the Church.* Also, **compline** /'kɒmplən, -plaɪn/. [ME *compelin,* var. of *cumplie,* from OF, from L *complēta* (*hōra*) completed (hour)]

**complot** /'kɒmplɒt/, *n.;* /kəm'plɒt/, *v.* **-plotted, -plotting.** *–n.* **1.** a joint plot; a conspiracy. *–v.i.* **2.** to plot or scheme together. *–v.t.* **3.** to plot (something) with another. [F: plot, OF concerted plan, also crowd, struggle; orig. uncert.] – **complotter,** *n.*

**comply** /kəm'plaɪ/, *v.i.,* **-plied, -plying. 1.** to act in accordance with wishes, requests, commands, requirements, conditions, etc. (fol. by *with*). **2.** *Obs.* to be courteous or conciliatory. [apparently from It. *complire* fulfil, complete, from Sp. *cumplir,* from L *complēre* COMPLETE]

**compo**[1] /'kɒmpoʊ/, *n. Colloq.* **1.** compensation for injury at or in connection with a person's work; workers' compensation. **2. on compo,** in receipt of such payment. Also, **comp.** [COMPENSATION]

**compo**[2] /'kɒmpoʊ/, *n. Colloq.* any of various combined substances such as plaster or mortar, made by mixing ingredients. [COMPOSITION]

**component** /kəm'poʊnənt/, *adj.* **1.** composing; constituent. *–n.* **2.** a constituent part. **3.** *Physics.* (of a vector quantity such as a force, velocity, etc.) one of the parts which when combined together make up the vector, or into which a vector may be resolved. **4.** *Electronics.* one of the devices which may be used to make up an electronic circuit, as a resistor, capacitor, inductor, semiconductor device or vacuum tube, etc. [L *compōnens,* ppr., composing]

**compony** /kəm'poʊni/, *adj. Her.* composed of a single row of squares, metal and colour alternating. Also, **componé** /kəm'poʊneɪ/. [ME; from AF: pp., composed]

**compo rations** /'kɒmpoʊ ræʃənz/, *n.pl. Mil.* highly concentrated compact food supplies given to soldiers in the field for emergency use; iron rations.

**comport** /kəm'pɔt/, *v.t.* **1.** to bear or conduct (oneself); behave. *–v.i.* **2.** to agree or accord; suit (fol. by *with*). [F *comporter* bear, behave, from L *comportāre* carry together]

**comportment** /kəm'pɔtmənt/, *n.* bearing; demeanour; behaviour.

**compose** /kəm'poʊz/, *v.,* **-posed, -posing.** *–v.t.* **1.** to make or form by uniting parts or elements. **2.** to be the parts or elements of. **3.** to make up; constitute. **4.** to put or dispose in proper form or order. **5.** to arrange the parts or elements of (a picture, etc.). **6.** to devise and make (a literary or musical production). **7.** to arrange or settle, as a quarrel, etc. **8.** to bring (the body or mind) to a condition of repose, calmness, etc.; calm; quiet. **9.** *Print.* **a.** to set (type). **b.** to set the types for (an article, etc.). *–v.i.* **10.** to practise composition. **11.** to enter into composition. [late ME *compose(n),* from OF *composer* (see COM-, POSE[1]), but associated with derivatives of L *compōnere.* See COMPOSITE]

**composed** /kəm'poʊzd/, *adj.* calm; tranquil; serene. – **composedly** /kəm'poʊzədli/, *adv.* – **composedness,** *n.*

**composer** /kəm'poʊzə/, *n.* **1.** one who or that which composes. **2.** a writer of music. **3.** an author.

**composing room** /kəm'poʊzɪŋ rum/, *n.* the room in which compositors work in a printing establishment.

**composing stick** /'– stɪk/, *n. Print.* a small (usu.) metal tray of adjustable width, in which type is set.

**composite** /'kɒmpəzət/, *adj.* **1.** made up of various parts or elements; compound. **2.** (*cap.*) *Archit.* denoting or pertaining to a classical order in which capital and entablature combine features of the Corinthian and Ionic orders. *–n.* **3.** something composite; a compound. **4.** *Bot.* a member of the Compositae, a family of plants, including the daisy, dandelion, aster, etc., in which the florets are borne in a close head surrounded by a common involucre of bracts. [L *compositus,* pp. of *compōnere* put together, compound, compose] – **compositely,** *adv.* – **compositeness,** *n.*

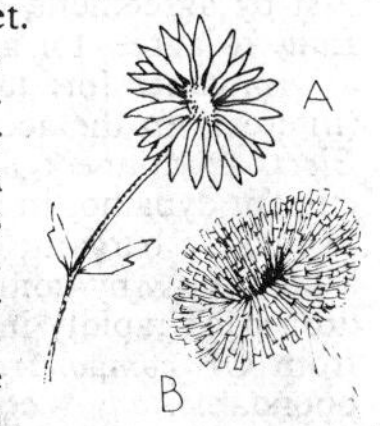

flowers of composite plants: A, daisy; B, dandelion

**composite number** /– 'nʌmbə/, *n. Maths.* an integer greater than 1 which is exactly divisible by some integer other than itself and 1.

**composite photograph** /– 'foʊtəgræf/, *n.* a photograph obtained by combining two or more separate photographs.

**composite rating** /– 'reɪtɪŋ/, *n.* a property rating system based on both unimproved capital value and the commercial value.

**composition** /kɒmpə'zɪʃən/, *n.* **1.** the act of combining parts or elements to form a whole. **2.** the manner in which such parts are combined. **3.** the resulting state or product. **4.** make-up; constitution. **5.** a compound or composite substance. **6.** *Fine Arts.* organisation or grouping of the different parts of a work of art so as to achieve a unified whole. **7.** the art of putting words and sentences together in accordance with the rules of grammar and rhetoric: *Greek prose composition.* **8.** the act of producing a literary work. **9.** the art of composing music. **10.** the resulting production or work. **11.** a short essay written as a school exercise. **12.** *Gram.* the formation of compounds: *the composition of 'bootblack' from 'boot' and 'black'.* **13.** a settlement by mutual agreement. **14.** an agreement or compromise, esp. one by which a creditor (or group of creditors) accepts partial payment from a debtor. **15.** a sum of money so paid. **16.** *Print.* the setting up of type for printing.

**composition of forces,** *n.* the union or combination of two or more forces, velocities, or the like (called *components*) acting in the same or in different directions, into a single equivalent force, velocity, or the like (called the *resultant*).

**compositor** /kəm'pɒzətə/, *n. Print.* a person who assembles the type for a printed page.

**compos mentis** /kɒmpəs 'mɛntəs/, *adj.* sane. [L]

**compost** /'kɒmpɒst/, *n.* **1.** a composition; compound. **2.** a mixture of various kinds of organic matter, as dung, dead leaves, etc., undergoing decay, used for fertilising land. *–v.t.* **3.** to fertilise with compost. **4.** to change (vegetable matter) to compost. [ME, from OF, from L *compositus,* pp., compounded]

**composure** /kəm'poʊʒə/, *n.* serene state of mind; calmness; tranquillity.

**compotation** /kɒmpə'teɪʃən/, *n.* a drinking or tippling together. [L *compōtātio* drinking together] – **compotator** /'kɒmpəteɪtə/, *n.*

**compote** /'kɒmpɒt/, *n.* a preparation or dish of fruit stewed in a syrup. [F, in OF *composte,* from L *compos(i)ta,* fem. of *compositus.* See COMPOSITE]

**compound**[1] /'kɒmpaʊnd/, *adj., n.;* /kəm'paʊnd/, *v.* *–adj.* **1.** composed of two or more parts, elements, or ingredients, or involving two or more actions, functions, etc.; composite. **2.** *Gram.* (of a word) consisting of two or more parts which are also words, but distinguished from a phrase by special phonetic features, in English often consisting of reduction of stress on one constituent, as in *housetop, blackberry,* historically also *cupboard, breakfast.* **3.** *Zool.* (of an animal) composed of a number of distinct individuals which are connected to form a united whole or colony. *–n.* **4.** something formed by compounding or combining parts, elements, etc. **5.** *Chem.* a pure substance composed of two or more elements whose composition is constant. **6.** *Gram.* a compound word. *–v.t.* **7.** to put together into a whole; combine. **8.** to make or form by combining parts, elements, etc.; construct. **9.** to make up or constitute. **10.** to settle or adjust by agreement, esp. for a reduced amount, as a debt. **11.** *Law.* to agree, for a consideration, not to prosecute or punish a wrongdoer for: *to compound a crime or felony.* **12.** to pay (interest) on the accrued interest as well as the principal. **13.** *Elect.* to connect a portion of the field turns of (a direct-current dynamo) in series with the armature circuit. *–v.i.* **14.** to make a bargain; come to terms; compromise. **15.** to settle a debt, etc., by compromise. **16.** *Horseracing.* (of a horse) to drop back rapidly in the field during a race. [ME *compoune(n),* from OF *compondre,* from L *compōnere* put together] – **compoundable,** *adj.* – **compounder,** *n.*

**compound**[2] /'kɒmpaʊnd/, *n.* **1.** (in Africa, India, and elsewhere) an enclosure containing a residence or other establishment of Europeans. **2.** (in South Africa and elsewhere) an enclosure in which African and other non-European labourers are housed during the term of their employment. **3.** any similar enclosure for native workmen. **4.** an enclosure in which prisoners of war are held. **5.** an enclosure in which animals are held. [cf. Malay *kampong* enclosure]

**compound eye** /– 'aɪ/, *n.* an arthropod eye subdivided into many individual light-receptive elements, each including a lens, a transmitting apparatus, and retinal cells.

**compound fraction** /– 'frækʃən/, *n. Maths.* a complex fraction or a fraction of a fraction.

**compound fracture** /– 'fræktʃə/, *n.* a break in a bone such that the fracture line communicates with an open wound.

**compound interest** /– 'ɪntrəst/, *n.* interest paid, not only on the principal, but on the interest after it has periodically come due and, remaining unpaid, been added to the principal.

**compound leaf** /– 'lif/, *n.* a leaf composed of a number of leaflets on a common stalk. It may be either digitately or pinnately compound, and the leaflets may be themselves compound.

pinnately compound leaf

**compound number** /– 'nʌmbə/, *n.* a quantity expressed in more than one denomination or unit, as the amount 4 dollars 50 cents.

**compound sentence** /– 'sɛntəns/, *n.* a sentence having two or more coordinate independent clauses, usu. joined by one or more conjuctions. For example: *the lightning flashed* (independent clause) *and* (conjunction) *the rain fell* (independent clause).

**compound-wound** /'kɒmpaʊnd – waʊnd/, *adj.* (of an electric commutator) having the main magnetic field provided by a combination of two field windings, one in shunt with the armature, the other in series with it.

**comprador** /kɒmprə'dɔ/, *n.* (in China, etc.) a native agent or factotum, as of a foreign business house. Also, **compradore.** [Pg.: a buyer, purveyor]

**comprehend** /kɒmprə'hɛnd/, *v.t.* **1.** to understand the meaning or nature of; conceive; know. **2.** to take in or embrace; include; comprise. [ME, from L *comprehendere* seize] – **comprehendible,** *adj.* – **comprehendingly,** *adv.*

**comprehensible** /kɒmprə'hɛnsəbəl/, *adj.* capable of being comprehended; intelligible. – **comprehensibility** /kɒmprə,hɛnsə'bɪləti/, **comprehensibleness,** *n.* – **comprehensibly,** *adv.*

**comprehension** /kɒmprə'hɛnʃən/, *n.* **1.** the act or fact of comprehending. **2.** inclusion; comprehensiveness; perception or understanding. **3.** capacity of the mind to understand; power to grasp ideas, ability to know. **4.** (in schools) a formal exercise in reading and understanding, usu. tested with a series of short questions. **5.** *Logic.* the sum of all those attributes which make up the content of a given conception (distinguished from *extension or extent*). For example: *rational, sensible, moral, etc.,* form the comprehension of the conception *man.* [L *comprehensio*]

**comprehensive** /kɒmprə'hɛnsɪv/, *adj.* **1.** comprehending; inclusive; comprehending much; of large scope. **2.** comprehending mentally; having a wide mental grasp. – **comprehensively,** *adv.* – **comprehensiveness,** *n.*

**comprehensive insurance** /– ɪn'ʃɔrəns/, *n.* a form of insurance covering all instances in which the insured asset or property may be lost or damaged.

**comprehensive school** /'– ,skul/, *n.* a large secondary school providing a wide range of courses for children of all levels of ability.

**compress** /kəm'prɛs/, *v.;* /'kɒmprɛs/, *n.* *–v.t.* **1.** to press together; force into less space. *–n.* **2.** *Med.* a soft pad of lint, linen, or the like, held in place by a bandage, used as a means of pressure or to supply moisture, cold, heat, or medication. **3.** an apparatus or establishment for compressing cotton bales, etc. [ME *compresse(n),* from L *compressāre*] – **compressible,** *adj.* – **compressibility** /kəmprɛsə'bɪləti/, *n.*

**compressed** /kəm'prɛst/, *adj.* **1.** pressed into less space; condensed. **2.** pressed together. **3.** flattened. **4.** *Bot.* flattened laterally or along the length. **5.** *Zool.* narrow from side to side, and therefore of greater height than width.

**compressed air** /– 'ɛə/, *n.* air, under a higher than atmospheric pressure, the expansive force of which is used to operate drills, brakes, etc.

**compression** /kəm'prɛʃən/, *n.* **1.** the act of compressing. **2.** compressed state. **3.** (in some internal-combustion engines) the reduction in volume and increase of pressure of the air or combustible mixture in the cylinder prior to ignition, produced by the motion of the piston towards the cylinder head after intake. Also, **compressure** /kəm'prɛʃə/ for defs 1 and 2.

**compression ratio** /– 'reɪʃioʊ/, *n.* the ratio of the total volume enclosed in the cylinder of an internal-combustion engine, to the volume at the end of the compression stroke.

**compressive** /kəm'prɛsɪv/, *adj.* compressing; tending to compress. – **compressively,** *adv.*

**compressor** /kəm'prɛsə/, *n.* **1.** one who or that which compresses. **2.** *Anat.* a muscle that compresses some part of the body. **3.** *Surg.* an instrument for compressing a part of the body. **4.** any machine, as a pump, in which a gas is compressed so that its expansion may be utilised as a source of power. In refrigeration the compressor is used to compress the gas so that it can be condensed with water or air at prevailing temperatures. **5.** *Naut.* any of various devices for gripping and stopping an anchor cable. [L]

**comprise** /kəm'praɪz/, *v.t.,* **-prised, -prising.** **1.** to comprehend; include; contain. **2.** to consist of; be composed of. [ME *comprise(n),* from F *compris,* pp. of *comprendre,* from L *compre(he)ndere* seize] – **comprisable,** *adj.* – **comprisal,** *n.*

**compromise** /'kɒmprəmaɪz/, *n., v.,* **-mised, -mising.** *–n.* **1.** a settlement of differences by mutual concessions; an adjustment of conflicting claims, principles, etc., by yielding a part of each; arbitration. **2.** anything resulting from compromise. **3.** something intermediate between different things. **4.** an endangering, esp. of reputation; exposure to danger, suspicion, etc. *–v.t.* **5.** to settle by a compromise. **6.** to make liable to danger, suspicion, scandal, etc.; endanger the reputation. **7.** *Mil.* to subject (classified material) to the risk of passing to an unauthorised person. **8.** to involve unfavourably; commit. **9.** *Obs.* to bind by bargain or agreement. **10.** *Obs.* to bring to terms. *–v.i.* **11.** to make a compromise. [ME, from F *compromis,* from L *comprōmissum* a mutual promise to abide by a decision, properly pp. neut.] – **compromiser,** *n.*

**comptometer** /kɒmp'tɒmətə/, *n.* a high-speed adding and calculating machine. [Trademark]

**Compton effect** /'kɒmptən əfɛkt/, *n. Physics.* the reduction in frequency of a photon when it loses energy in an interaction with a free or loosely bound electron. [named after A.H. *Compton,* 1892-1962, U.S. physicist]

**comptroller** /kən'troʊlə, kɒmp-/, *n.* **1.** →**controller** (def. 1). **2.** the financial officer and controller of a household, esp. of a royal household. [variant spelling of CONTROLLER] – **comptrollership,** *n.*

**compulsion** /kəm'pʌlʃən/, *n.* **1.** the act of compelling; constraint; coercion. **2.** the state of being compelled. **3.** *Psychol.* **a.** a strong irrational impulse to carry out a given act. **b.** the act. [late ME, from LL *compulsio*]

**compulsive** /kəm'pʌlsɪv/, *adj.* **1.** →**compulsory. 2.** *Chiefly Psychol.* pertaining to compulsion.. **3.** addicted. **4.** compelling one to continue, esp. of pleasurable and repetitive activities: *these chips are compulsive.* – **compulsively,** *adv.*

**compulsory** /kəm'pʌlsəri/, *adj.* **1.** using compulsion; compelling; constraining: *compulsory measures.* **2.** compelled; forced; obligatory. – **compulsorily,** *adv.* – **compulsoriness,** *n.*

**compulsory conference** /– 'kɒnfrəns/, *n.* a meeting to which parties to an industrial dispute and, on occasion, other interested parties, are summoned by an industrial tribunal.

**compulsory unionism** /– 'junjənɪzəm/, *n.* the requirement that people become and remain financial members of the union covering their calling as a pre-condition of employment.

**compulsory voting** /– 'voʊtɪŋ/, *n.* a system of voting in which everyone entitled to vote is required to register as a voter and, at elections, to have his name marked off the electoral roll as having received and returned a ballot paper.

**compunction** /kəm'pʌŋkʃən, -'pʌŋʃən/, *n.* uneasiness of conscience or feelings; regret for wrongdoing or giving pain to another; contrition; remorse. [ME, from LL *compunctio* remorse]

**compunctious** /kəm'pʌŋkʃəs, -'pʌŋʃəs/, *adj.* causing compunction; causing misgiving, regret, or remorse.

**compurgation** /,kɒmpз'geɪʃən/, *n.* an early commonlaw method of trial (abolished 1833) in which the defendant was acquitted if a specified number of friends or neighbours would swear to his innocence or veracity. [LL *compurgātio,* from L *compurgāre* purify completely]

**compurgator** /'kɒmpз,geɪtə/, *n.* one who testifies to another's innocence or veracity.

**computation** /,kɒmpju'teɪʃən/, *n.* **1.** the act, process, or method of computing; calculation. **2.** a result of computing; the amount computed.

**computational linguistics** /kɒmpju,teɪʃənəl lɪŋ'gwɪstɪks/, *n.* **1.** the application of computational procedures to the study of languages, esp. formal languages. **2.** the study of the machine translation of languages.

**compute** /kəm'pjut/, *v.,* **-puted, -puting,** *n.* *–v.t.* **1.** to determine by calculation; reckon; calculate: *to compute the distance of the moon from the earth.* *–v.i.* **2.** to reckon; calculate. *–n.* **3.** computation; reckoning. [L *computāre* reckon. Cf. COUNT[1]] – **computability** /kəmpjutə'bɪləti/, *n.*

**computer** /kəm'pjutə/, *n.* **1.** one who computes. **2.** an apparatus for performing mathematical computations electronically according to a series of stored instructions called a program; an **analog computer** represents information in the form of continuously varying voltages; a **digital computer** represents information by patterns of on-off states of voltages.

**computer aided design,** *n.* →**CAD.**

**computer aided instruction,** *n.* →**CAI.**

**computer animation** /kəm,pjutər ænə'meɪʃən/, *n.* the computer controlled animation of images, as diagrams or cartoons.

**computer art** /kəm'pjutər at/, *n.* sculpture, graphics, music, poetry, etc., produced by computer. Also, **programmed art.**

**computer graphics** /– 'græfɪks/, *n.* the technique of using computer-stored information to create diagrams, pictures, etc., sometimes moving and often displayed on a video screen.

**computer graphic terminal,** *n. Computers.* a television-like display screen on which the results of a computer's operation are displayed, often with keyboard or light-pen attached to allow interactive editing or drawing.

**computerise** /kəm'pjutəraɪz/, *v.t.,* **-ised, -ising. 1.** to process or store (data) in a computer. **2.** to furnish or provide with a computer system. Also, **computerize.** – **computerisation** /kəm,pjutəraɪ'zeɪʃən/, *n.*

**computerised axial tomography,** *n.* computerised tomography with the resultant image in the axial plane.

**computerised tomography** /kəm,pjutəraɪzd tə'mɒgrəfi/, *n.* a method of tomography using a reconstruction technique aided by a computer.

**computer program** /kəm'pjutə ,proʊgræm/, *n.* a sequence of commands in a machine language which will cause a computer to perform a desired calculation. Also, **computer programme.**

**computer terminal** /'– tɜmənəl/, *n.* an input or output device connected to a computer but at a distance from it.

**computer typesetting** /– 'taɪpsetɪŋ/, *n.* a system for the high-speed setting of type which depends upon a computer directing the process, either directly or by magnetic or punched tape, which the computer has generated.

**comrade** /'kɒmreɪd, 'kɒmrəd/, *n.* **1.** an associate in occupation or friendship; a close companion; a fellow; a mate. **2.** a fellow member of a political party (esp. the Communist Party), fraternal group, etc. [earlier *camerade,* from F *camarade,* from Sp. *camarada,* lit., group living in one room, from *cámara* room, from L *camera* CHAMBER] – **comradeship,** *n.*

**comsat** /'kɒmsæt/, *n.* →**communication satellite.**

**comstockery** /kɒm'stɒkəri/, *n. Chiefly U.S.* overzealous censorship of the fine arts and literature, often mistaking outspokenly honest works for salacious ones. [named after Anthony *Comstock,* 1844-1915, U.S. moralist]

**con**[1] /'kɒn/, *adv.* **1.** against a proposition, opinion, etc.; not pro (for). *–n.* **2.** the argument, arguer, or voter against (something). [short for L *contrā,* as adv., in opposition, as prep., against]

**con**[2] /kɒn/, *v.t.,* **conned, conning.** to learn; study; commit to memory; peruse or examine carefully. Also, **con up.** [var. of CAN[1], OE *can, con,* a finite form of *cunnan* know]

**con**[3] /kɒn/, *v.,* **conned, conning,** *n. Naut.* *–v.t.* **1.** to direct the steering of (a ship). *–n.* **2.** the station or post of the person who cons. **3.** the act or process of conning. Also, **conn.** [var. of obs. *cond,* short for *condue,* from OF *conduire* CONDUCT]

**con**[4] /kɒn/, *adj., n., v.,* **conned, conning.** *–adj.* **1.** confidence: *con game, con man.* *–n.* **2.** a confidence trick; swindle. *–v.t.* **3.** to swindle; defraud. **4.** to deceive with intent to gain some advantage. [short for CONFIDENCE TRICK or MAN]

**con**[5] /kɒn/, *prep. Music.* with. [It.]

**con**[6] /kɒn/, *n. Colloq.* →**conservatorium.**

**con**[7] /kɒn/, *n. Colloq.* →**convict.**

**con-,** variant of **com-,** before consonants except *b, h, l, p, r, w,* as in *convene, condone,* and, by assimilation, before *n,* as in *connection.* Cf. **co-** (def. 1).

**Con., 1.** Conservatorium. **2.** Consolidated.

**con amore** /kɒn ə'moreɪ/, *adv.* **1.** with love, tender enthusiasm, or zeal. **2.** (a musical direction) tenderly and lovingly. [It.]

**con anima** /– 'ænəmə/, *adv.* (a musical direction) with feeling. [It.]

**conation** /koʊ'neɪʃən/, *n. Psychol.* that portion of mental life having to do with striving, embracing desire and volition. [L *cōnātio* an endeavouring, effort]

**conative** /'koʊnətɪv, 'kɒnətɪv/, *adj.* **1.** *Psychol.* pertaining to or of the nature of conation. **2.** *Gram.* expressing endeavour or effort: *a conative verb.*

**conatus** /koʊ'neɪtəs/, *n., pl.* **-tus. 1.** an effort or striving. **2.** a force or tendency simulating a human effort. [L: effort, endeavour]

**con brio** /kɒn 'brioʊ/, *adv.* (a musical direction) with vigour;

vivaciously. [It.]

**conc.**, **1.** concentrated. **2.** concentration.

**concatenate** /kɒn'kætəneɪt/, *v.*, **-nated, -nating,** *adj.* *–v.t.* **1.** to link together; unite in a series or chain. *–adj.* **2.** linked together as in a chain. [L *concatēnātus*, pp.]

**concatenation** /ˌkɒnkætən'eɪʃən/, *n.* **1.** the act of concatenating. **2.** the state of being concatenated; connection, as in a chain. **3.** a series of interconnected or interdependent things or events.

**concave** /kɒn'keɪv/, *adj.*, *n.*, *v.*, **-caved, -caving.** *–adj.* **1.** curved like the interior of a circle or hollow sphere; hollow and curved, esp. of optical lenses and mirrors. **2.** *Obs.* hollow. *–n.* **3.** a concave surface, part, line, etc. *–v.t.* **4.** to make concave. [L *concavus*] **– concavely,** *adv.* **– concaveness,** *n.*

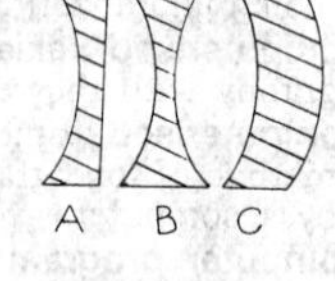

A, concave or plano-concave lens; B, biconcave lens; C, concavo-convex lens

**concavity** /kɒn'kævəti/, *n.*, *pl.* **-ties.** **1.** the state of being concave. **2.** a concave surface or thing; a hollow; cavity.

**concavo-concave** /kɒnˌkeɪvoʊ-kɒn'keɪv/, *adj.* →**biconcave.**

**concavo-convex** /kɒnˌkeɪvoʊ-kɒn'vɛks/, *adj.* **1.** concave on one side and convex on the other. **2.** denoting or pertaining to a lens in which the concave face has a greater degree of curvature than the convex face, the lens being thinnest in the middle.

**conceal** /kən'sil/, *v.t.* **1.** to hide; withdraw or remove from observation; cover or keep from sight. **2.** to forbear to disclose or divulge. [ME *concele(n)*, from OF *conceler*, from L *concēlāre* hide] **– concealable,** *adj.* **– concealer,** *n.*

**concealed lighting** /kənsild 'laɪtɪŋ/, *n.* indirect lighting (in a room) where the light fittings are hidden from view.

**concealment** /kən'silmənt/, *n.* **1.** the act of concealing. **2.** concealed state. **3.** a means or place of hiding.

**concede** /kən'sid/, *v.*, **-ceded, -ceding.** *–v.t.* **1.** to admit as true, just, or proper; admit. **2.** to grant as a right or privilege; yield. **3.** to admit defeat in an election. *–v.i.* **4.** to make concession; yield; admit. [L *concēdere*] **– concededly,** *adv.* **– conceder,** *n.*

**conceit** /kən'sit/, *n.* **1.** an exaggerated estimate of one's own ability, importance, wit, etc. **2.** that which is conceived in the mind; a thought; an idea. **3.** imagination; fancy. **4.** a fancy; whim; a fanciful notion. **5.** a fanciful thought, idea, or expression, esp. of a strained or far-fetched nature. **6.** the use of such thoughts, ideas, etc., as a literary characteristic. **7.** *Archaic.* **a.** favourable opinion; esteem. **b.** personal opinion or estimation. **8.** *Obs.* the faculty of conceiving; apprehension. **9.** *Obs.* a fancy article. *–v.t.* **10.** *Obs.* to flatter (esp. oneself). **11.** *Obs.* to conceive mentally; apprehend. **12.** *Obs.* to imagine. **13.** *Archaic.* to take a fancy to; have a good opinion of. [ME *conceyte;* from CONCEIVE, modelled on DECEIT]

**conceited** /kən'sitəd/, *adj.* **1.** having an exaggerated opinion of one's abilities, importance, etc. **2.** *Obs.* intelligent; clever. **– conceitedly,** *adv.* **– conceitedness,** *n.*

**conceivable** /kən'sivəbəl/, *adj.* capable of being conceived; imaginable. **– conceivability** /kənsivə'bɪləti/, **conceivableness,** *n.* **– conceivably,** *adv.*

**conceive** /kən'siv/, *v.*, **-ceived, -ceiving.** *–v.t.* **1.** to form (a notion, opinion, purpose, etc.). **2.** to form a notion or idea of; imagine. **3.** to apprehend in the mind; understand. **4.** to hold as an opinion; think; believe. **5.** to experience or entertain (a feeling). **6.** to express, as in words. **7.** to become pregnant with. *–v.i.* **8.** to form an idea; think (fol. by *of*). **9.** to become pregnant. [ME *conceive(n)*, from OF *conceveir*, from L *concipere* take in] **– conceiver,** *n.*

**concentrate** /'kɒnsəntreɪt/, *v.*, **-trated, -trating,** *n.*, *adj.* *–v.t.* **1.** to bring or draw to a common centre or point of union; cause to come close together; bring to bear on one point; direct towards one object; focus. **2.** to intensify the action of; make more intense, stronger, or purer by removing or reducing the proportion of what is foreign or inessential. **3.** *Chem.* to increase the strength of a solution, usu. by evaporation. **4.** *Mining.* to separate (meal or ore) from rock, sand, etc., so as to improve the quality of the valuable portion. *–v.i.* **5.** to converge to a centre. **6.** to become more intense, stronger, or purer. **7.** to direct one's thoughts or actions towards one subject. *–n.* **8.** a concentrated form of something; a product of concentration. **9.** *Agric.* condensed feed for stock which usu. has a low fibre and a high starch and/or protein content. **10.** *Mining.* separated metal or ore obtained by removing rock, sand, etc. *–adj.* **11.** concentrated. [CON- + L *centrum* centre + -ATE[1]] **– concentrative** /'kɒnsənˌtreɪtɪv/, *adj.* **– concentrator,** *n.*

**concentration** /kɒnsən'treɪʃən/, *n.* **1.** the act of concentrating. **2.** concentrated state. **3.** exclusive attention to one object; close mental application. **4.** *Mil.* **a.** the assembling of military or naval forces in a particular area in preparation for further operations. **b.** a specified intensity and duration of artillery fire placed on a small area. **5.** something concentrated. **6.** *Chem.* the amount of a given substance in a stated unit of a mixture, solution, or ore; expressed as per cent by weight or by volume, weight per unit volume, normality, molality, etc.

**concentration camp** /'– kæmp/, *n.* a guarded enclosure for the detention or imprisonment of political prisoners, racial minority groups, refugees, etc., esp. any of the camps established by the Nazis before and during World War II for the confinement, persecution, and mass execution of prisoners.

**concentre** /kɒn'sɛntə/, *v.*, **-tred, -tring.** *–v.t.* **1.** to bring or direct towards a common centre. *–v.i.* **2.** to converge or come together at a common centre. Also, *U.S.*, **concenter.**

**concentric** /kən'sɛntrɪk/, *adj.* having a common centre, as circles or spheres. Also, **concentrical. – concentrically,** *adv.* **– concentricity** /kɒnsən'trɪsəti/, *n.*

**concept** /'kɒnsɛpt/, *n.* **1.** a thought, idea, or notion, often one deriving from a generalising mental operation. **2.** a theoretical construct: *the concept of the solar system.* **3.** an idea that includes all that is associated with a word or other symbol. **4.** a pattern or procedure: *a new concept in roof maintenance.* [L *conceptus* a conceiving]

**conceptacle** /kən'sɛptɪkəl/, *n.* *Biol.* an organ or cavity enclosing reproductive bodies. [L *conceptāculum* receptacle]

**concept album** /'kɒnsɛpt ælbəm/, *n.* a gramophone record on which all the various tracks are linked, as by a repeated musical idea, to make a single artistic concept.

**conception** /kən'sɛpʃən/, *n.* **1.** the act of conceiving. **2.** the state of being conceived. **3.** fertilisation; inception of pregnancy. **4.** that which is conceived. **5.** beginning; origination. **6.** the act or power of forming notions, ideas, or concepts. **7.** a notion; idea; concept. **8.** a design; plan. **– conceptional,** *adj.* **– conceptive,** *adj.*

**concept of operations,** *n.* *Mil.* a verbal or written statement outlining in broad detail the purpose and pattern of a military operation. Also, **commander's concept.**

**conceptual** /kən'sɛptʃuəl/, *adj.* pertaining to the forming of concepts or to concepts. [ML *conceptuālis*] **– conceptually,** *adv.*

**conceptual art** /– 'at/, *n.* art in the mind of the artist which may be expressed merely by a written statement, but which does not normally take material form.

**conceptualise** /kən'sɛptʃuəlaɪz/, *v.*, **-lised, -lising.** *–v.t.* **1.** to form concepts or a concept of. *–v.i.* **2.** to form concepts, theories or ideas. Also, **conceptualize.**

**conceptualism** /kən'sɛptʃuəlɪzəm/, *n.* the philosophical doctrine, midway between nominalism and realism, that concepts enable the mind to grasp objective reality. It is often ambiguous as to the existence and status of universals. **– conceptualist,** *n.* **– conceptualistic** /kənˌsɛptʃuə'lɪstɪk/, *adj.*

**concern** /kən'sɜn/, *v.t.* **1.** to relate to; be connected with; be of interest or importance to; affect: *the problem concerns us all.* **2.** to interest, engage, or involve (used reflexively or in the passive, oft. fol. by *with* or *in*): *to concern oneself with a matter, to be concerned in a plot.* **3.** to disquiet or trouble (used in the passive): *to be concerned about a person's health.* *–n.* **4.** that which relates or pertains to one; business; affair. **5.** a matter that engages one's attention, interest, or care, or that affects one's welfare or happiness: *it's no concern of mine.* **6.** solicitude or anxiety. **7.** important relation or bearing. **8.** a commercial or manufacturing firm or establishment. **9.** *Colloq.* any material object or contrivance: *fed up with the whole concern.* [ML *concernere* relate to, LL mix, from L *con-* CON- + *cernere* separate, have respect to]

**concerned** /kən'sɜnd/, *adj.* **1.** interested. **2.** involved. **3.** troubled or anxious: *a concerned look.*

**concerning** /kən'sɜnɪŋ/, *prep.* relating to; regarding; about.

**concernment** /kən'sɜnmənt/, *n.* **1.** importance or moment. **2.** interest or participation. **3.** relation or bearing. **4.** anxiety or solicitude. **5.** a concern or affair. **6.** *Archaic.* a thing in which one is concerned.

**concert** /'kɒnsət/ *for def. 1,* /'kɒnsɜt/ *for def. 2, n.;* /kən'sɜt/, *v.* *–n.* **1. a.** a public performance, usu. by two or more musicians. **b.** a solo recital. **c.** a series of individual items not necessarily all musical, as in a school concert. **2.** agreement of two or more in a design or plan; combined action; accord or harmony. *–v.t.* **3.** to contrive or arrange by agreement. **4.** to plan; devise. *–v.i.* **5.** to plan or act together. [F *concerter,* from It. *concertare* be in accord, from L *concertāre* contend; influenced in meaning by *consertus,* pp., joined]

**concert A** /kɒnsət 'eɪ/, *n.* the note to which concert performers tune their instruments. See **concert pitch.**

**concertante** /kɒntʃə'tænti/, *n. Music.* an 18th-century composition for one or more soloists with an orchestra. [It.]

**concert aria** /kɒnsət 'ariə/, *n. Music.* an aria in the manner of Grand Opera intended to be sung at a concert, i.e., without costume and actions.

**concerted** /kən'sɜtəd/, *adj.* **1.** contrived or arranged by agreement; prearranged; planned or devised: *concerted action.* **2.** *Music.* arranged in parts for several voices or instruments. **– concertedly,** *adv.*

**concert-goer** /'kɒnsət-gouə/, *n.* one who attends concerts on a regular basis. **– concert-going,** *n.*

**concert grand piano,** *n.* See **piano**[1] (def. 2).

**concert-hall** /'kɒnsət-hɔl/, *n.* a building, or a hall within a building, specially designed for the giving of concerts.

**concertina** /kɒnsə'tinə/, *n., v.,* **-naed, -naing.** *–n.* **1.** a small hexagonal accordion. **2.** *Colloq.* a sheep with a very wrinkled skin. **3.** *Colloq.* a side of lamb. *–v.i.* **4.** to fold up or collapse like a concertina. [CONCERT + *-ina,* diminutive suffix]

concertina

**concertina crash** /'– kræʃ/, *n.* a series of motor car accidents usu. in which one vehicle crashes into the back of another, pushing it into a third, and so on.

**concertina wire** /'– waɪə/, *n. Mil. Colloq.* coiled wire used for impeding the progress of intruders by entanglement. Also, **concertina.**

**concertino** /kɒnsə'tinou/, *n., pl.* **-ni** /-ni/. *Music.* **1.** a short concerto. **2.** the group of soloists in the Baroque concerto grosso. [It., diminutive of *concerto*]

**concertmaster** /'kɒnsətmastə/, *n.* →**leader** (def. 3b).

**concerto** /kən'ʃɜtou, kən'tʃɜtou/, *n., pl.* **-tos, -ti** /-ti/. *Music.* a composition for one or more principal instruments, with orchestral accompaniment, now usu. in symphonic form. [It.]

**concerto grosso** /– 'grɒsou, -ˌtʃɜt-/, *n., pl.* **-ti grossi** /-ti 'grɒsi/. *Music.* a composition of the Baroque period for a small group of musicians accompanied by a string orchestra. [It.: a big concerto]

**concert-overture** /'kɒnsət-ouvətʃuə/, *n.* a short piece of music, similar in form to an overture, but intended for independent performance at a concert.

**concert pitch** /'kɒnsət pɪtʃ/, *n.* **1.** the standard pitch to which all instruments are tuned, where the frequency of A above middle C is 440 hertz, at 18°C. **2.** *Colloq.* a state of complete readiness for an event.

**concession** /kən'sɛʃən/, *n.* **1.** the act of conceding or yielding, as a right or privilege, or as a point or fact in an argument. **2.** the thing or point yielded. **3.** something conceded by a government or a controlling authority, as a grant of land, a privilege, or a franchise. [L *concessio,* from *concēdere.* See CONCEDE]

**concessionaire** /kənsɛʃə'nɛə/, *n.* one to whom a concession has been granted, as by a government. [F *concessionnaire*]

**concessionary** /kən'sɛʃənri/, *adj., n., pl.* **-ries.** *–adj.* **1.** pertaining to concession; of the nature of a concession. *–n.* **2.** a concessionaire.

**concessive** /kən'sɛsɪv/, *adj.* **1.** tending or serving to concede. **2.** *Gram.* expressing concession, as the English conjunction *though.* [L *concessīvus*]

**conch**[1] /kɒntʃ, kɒŋk/, *n., pl.* **conchs** /kɒŋks/, **conches,** /'kɒntʃəz/. **1.** the spiral shell of a gastropod, often used as a trumpet. **2.** any of several marine gastropods, esp. *Strombus gigas.* **3.** the fabled shell trumpet of the Tritons. **4.** *Archit.* **a.** the concave surface of a dome or half-dome. **b.** apse. [L *concha,* from Gk *kónchē* mussel or cockle, shell-like part or thing, external ear]

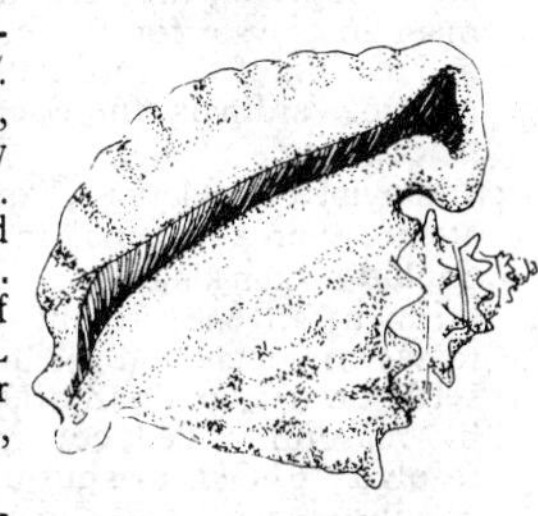

conch

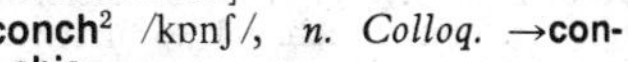

**conch**[2] /kɒnʃ/, *n. Colloq.* →**conchie.**

**conch.,** conchology.

**concha** /'kɒŋkə/, *n., pl.* **-chae** /-ki/. **1.** *Anat.* a shell-like structure, esp. the external ear. **2.** *Archit.* a conch. [see CONCH[1]]

**conchie** /'kɒnʃi/, *Colloq.* *–n.* **1.** a conscientious objector. **2.** one who is overconscientious. *–adj.* **3.** overconscientious. Also, **conchy, conshie, conshy.** [short for CONSCIENTIOUS]

**conchiferous** /kɒŋ'kɪfərəs/, *adj.* shell-bearing.

**conchoid** /'kɒŋkɔɪd, 'kɒn-/, *n.* a plane curve such that if a straight line be drawn from a certain fixed point, called the pole of the curve, to the curve, the part of the line intersected between the curve and its asymptote is always equal to a fixed distance. [see CONCHOIDAL]

**conchoidal** /kɒn'kɔɪdl, kɒŋ-/, *adj.* **1.** pertaining to a conchoid. **2.** *Mineral.* having a shell-like surface produced by the fracture of a brittle substance. [Gk *konchoeidḗs* shell-like + -AL[1]]

**conchology** /kɒn'kɒlədʒi, kɒŋ-/, *n.* the branch of zoology dealing with molluscs. [*concho-* (from Gk *koncho-,* combining form of *kónchē* mussel) + -LOGY] **– conchological** /kɒŋkə'lɒdʒɪkl/, *adj.* **– conchologist,** *n.*

**conchy** /'kɒnʃi/, *n. Colloq.* →**conchie.**

**concierge** /kɒnsi'ɛəʒ/, *n.* **1.** (in France, etc.) one who has charge of the entrance of a building; a janitor or doorkeeper. **2.** *Obs.* a custodian or warden. [F]

**conciliate** /kən'sɪliˌeɪt/, *v.t.,* **-ated, -ating.** **1.** to overcome the distrust or hostility of, by soothing or pacifying means; placate; win over. **2.** to win or gain (regard or favour). **3.** to render compatible; reconcile. [L *conciliātus,* pp., brought together] **– conciliator,** *n.*

**conciliation** /kənsɪli'eɪʃən/, *n.* **1.** the act of conciliating. **2.** a procedure for the resolution of a dispute. **3.** a system of resolving industrial disputes between employees and employers by official talks in the presence of a government-appointed third party. See **arbitration** (def. 2).

**conciliation and arbitration system,** *n.* an established, institutionalised system of resolving industrial disputes by conciliation (def. 3) and arbitration (def. 2). Cf. **collective bargaining.**

**conciliation committee** /kənsɪli'eɪʃən kəˌmɪti/, *n.* a committee consisting of an equal number of representatives of the employers and unions engaged in the calling or industry which the committee is to regulate. It is chaired by a Conciliation Commissioner and has power to award, on application, rates of pay and conditions of employment in the appropriate areas.

**conciliatory** /kən'sɪljətri/, *adj.* tending to conciliate: *a conciliatory manner.* Also, **conciliative.** **– conciliatorily,** *adv.* **– conciliatoriness,** *n.*

**concinnity** /kən'sɪnəti/, *n., pl.* **-ties.** **1.** *Rhet.* **a.** a close harmony of tone as well as logic among the elements of a discourse. **b.** an instance of this effect. **2.** any harmonious adaptation of parts. [L *concinnitas,* from *concinnus* well put together]

**concise** /kən'saɪs/, *adj.* expressing much in few words; brief and comprehensive; succinct; terse: *a concise account.* [L *concisus,* pp., cut up or off] – **concisely,** *adv.*

**conciseness** /kən'saɪsnəs/, *n.* the quality of being concise.

**concision** /kən'sɪʒən/, *n.* **1.** concise quality; brevity; terseness. **2.** a cutting up or off; mutilation.

**conclave** /'kɒnkleɪv, 'kɒŋ-/, *n.* **1.** any private meeting. **2.** the place in which the cardinals of the Roman Catholic Church meet in private for the election of a pope. **3.** the assembly or meeting of the cardinals for the election of a pope. **4.** the body of cardinals; the Sacred College. [ME, from L: lockable place]

**conclavist** /'kɒnkleɪvəst, 'kɒŋ-/, *n.* either of two persons who attend upon a cardinal in conclave.

**conclude** /kən'klud, kəŋ-/, *v.,* **-cluded, -cluding.** *–v.t.* **1.** to bring to an end; finish; terminate: *to conclude a speech.* **2.** to say in conclusion. **3.** to bring to a decision or settlement; settle or arrange finally: *to conclude a treaty.* **4.** to determine by reasoning; deduce; infer. **5.** to decide, determine, or resolve. **6.** *Obs.* to shut up or enclose. **7.** *Obs.* to restrict or confine. *–v.i.* **8.** to come to an end; finish. **9.** to arrive at an opinion or judgment; come to a decision; decide. [ME *conclude(n),* from L *conclūdere* shut up] – **concluder,** *n.*

**conclusion** /kən'kluʒən, kəŋ-/, *n.* **1.** the end or close; the final part. **2.** the last main division of a discourse, containing a summing up of the points. **3.** a result, issue, or outcome: *a foregone conclusion.* **4.** final settlement or arrangement. **5.** final decision. **6.** a deduction or inference: *to jump to a conclusion.* **7.** *Logic.* a proposition concluded or inferred from the premises of an argument. **8.** *Law.* **a.** the effect of an act by which he who did it is bound not to do anything inconsistent therewith; an estoppel. **b.** the end of a pleading or conveyance. **9.** *Gram.* →**apodosis.** **10. in conclusion,** finally. **11. try conclusions with,** to engage (a person) in a contest or struggle for victory or mastery. [ME, from L *conclūsio*]

**conclusive** /kən'klusɪv, kəŋ-/, *adj.* serving to settle or decide a question; decisive; convincing: *conclusive evidence.* – **conclusively,** *adv.* – **conclusiveness,** *n.*

**concoct** /kən'kɒkt, kəŋ-/, *v.t.* **1.** to make by combining ingredients, as in cookery: *to concoct a soup or a dinner.* **2.** to prepare; make up; contrive: *to concoct a story.* [L *concoctus,* pp., cooked together, digested] – **concocter, concoctor,** *n.* – **concoctive,** *adj.*

**concoction** /kən'kɒkʃən, kəŋ-/, *n.* **1.** the act or process of concocting. **2.** something concocted. [L *concoctio*]

**concomitant** /kən'kɒmətənt, kəŋ-/, *adj.* **1.** accompanying; concurrent; attending. *–n.* **2.** a concomitant quality, circumstance, person, or thing. [LL *concomitans,* ppr., accompanying] – **concomitance, concomitancy,** *n.* – **concomitantly,** *adv.*

**concord** /'kɒnkɔd, 'kɒŋ-/, *n.* **1.** agreement between persons; concurrence in opinions, sentiments, etc.; unanimity; accord. **2.** peace. **3.** a compact or treaty. **4.** agreement between things; mutual fitness; harmony. **5.** *Gram.* agreement. **6.** *Music.* consonance. [ME *concorde,* from F, from L *concordia* agreement]

**concordance** /kən'kɔdns, kəŋ-/, *n.* **1.** the state of being concordant; agreement; harmony. **2.** an alphabetical index of the principal words of a book, as of the Bible, with a reference to the passage in which each occurs and usu. some part of the context. **3.** *U.S.* an alphabetical index of subjects or topics.

**concordant** /kən'kɔdnt, kəŋ-/, *adj.* agreeing; harmonious. – **concordantly,** *adv.*

**concordat** /kɒn'kɔdæt, kɒŋ-/, *n.* **1.** an agreement; a compact. **2.** an agreement between the pope and a secular government regarding the regulation of ecclesiastical matters. [F, from ML *concordātum,* properly pp. neut. of L *concordāre* agree]

**concourse** /'kɒnkɔs, 'kɒŋ-/, *n.* **1.** a flocking together of people; a throng so drawn together; an assembly. **2.** an open space or main hall in a public building, esp. a railway station. **3.** grounds for racing, athletic sports, etc. **4.** a running or coming together; confluence. **5.** a building in which airline passengers assemble, often designed with bays and projections so that aeroplanes may be docked adjacent to it. [ME *concours,* from OF, from L *concursus* running together]

**concr.,** concrete.

**concrescence** /kən'krɛsəns, kəŋ-/, *n.* **1.** a growing together, as of parts, cells, etc.; coalescence. **2.** *Embryol.* the moving together and growing together of embryonic parts which give origin to the left and right halves of an embryo or of an organ. **3.** the fusion together of the roots of the upper second and third molar teeth by secondary cementum; false or pathological germination. [L *concrescentia*]

**concrete** /'kɒnkrit, 'kɒŋ-/, *adj., n., v.,* **-creted, -creting.** *–adj.* **1.** constituting an actual thing or instance; real: *a concrete example.* **2.** pertaining to or concerned with realities or actual instances rather than abstractions; particular as opposed to general: *concrete ideas.* **3.** representing or applied to an actual substance or thing as opposed to an abstract quality: *a concrete noun.* **4.** made of concrete: *a concrete pavement.* **5.** formed by coalescence of separate particles into a mass; united in a coagulated, condensed, or solid state. *–n.* **6.** a concrete idea or term; a concrete object or thing. **7.** a mass formed by coalescence or concretion of particles of matter. **8.** an artificial stone-like material used for foundations, etc., made by mixing cement, sand, and broken stones, etc., with water, and allowing the mixture to harden. **9.** this material strengthened by a system of embedded iron or steel bars, netting, or the like, used for building: *reinforced concrete.* *–v.t.* **10.** to treat or lay with concrete. **11.** to form into a mass by coalescence of particles; render solid. *–v.i.* **12.** to coalesce into a mass; become solid; harden. **13.** to use or apply concrete. [L *concrētus,* pp., grown together, hardened] – **concretely,** *adv.* – **concreteness,** *n.* – **concretive,** *adv.* – **concretively,** *adv.* – **concreter,** *n.*

**concrete art** /– 'at/, *n.* abstract art based on simple, precise, purely visual forms, including geometric and non-geometric elements, which represent things which otherwise do not exist in a visible form.

**concrete-mixer** /'kɒnkrit-ˌmɪksə/, *n.* a machine, usu. with a rotating drum, in which aggregates, cement, and water are mixed to make concrete.

concrete-mixer

**concrete music** /ˌkɒnkrit 'mjuzɪk/, *n.* a form of music constructed from recordings of natural sounds and noises. Also, **musique concrète.** [F *musique concrète*]

**concrete poetry** /– 'poʊətri/, *n.* poetry in which the visual appearance is part of the meaning.

**concretion** /kən'kriʃən, kəŋ-/, *n.* **1.** the act or process of concreting. **2.** *Obs.* the state of being concreted. **3.** a solid mass formed by or as by coalescence or cohesion. **4.** a calculus. **5.** a hard solid mass of foreign material in a cavity in the body or within an organism. **6.** the act of becoming solid or calcified. **7.** an adhesion of two parts. **8.** *Geol.* a rounded mass of mineral matter occurring in sandstone, clay, etc., often in concentric layers about a nucleus.

**concretionary** /kən'kriʃənri, kəŋ-/, *adj.* formed by concretion; consisting of concreted matter or masses.

**concubinage** /kɒn'kjubɪnɪdʒ, kən-/, *n.* **1.** cohabitation without legal marriage. **2.** the condition of a concubine.

**concubinary** /kɒn'kjubənri, kən-/, *adj.* **1.** of a concubine. **2.** living in concubinage.

**concubine** /'kɒŋkjubaɪn/, *n.* **1.** (among polygamous peoples) a secondary wife. **2.** a woman who cohabits with a man without being married to him. [ME, from L *concubīna*]

**concupiscence** /kɒn'kjupəsəns/, *n.* **1.** sensual appetite; lust. **2.** eager or illicit desire.

**concupiscent** /kɒn'kjupəsənt/, *adj.* **1.** eagerly desirous. **2.** lustful; sensual. [L *concupiscens,* ppr.]

**concur** /kən'kɜ/, *v.i.,* **-curred, -curring.** **1.** to accord in opinion; agree. **2.** to cooperate; combine; be associated. **3.** to coincide. **4.** to come together, as lines; unite. **5.** *Obs.* to run together. [late ME, from L *concurrere* run together]

**concurrence** /kən'kʌrəns/, *n.* **1.** the act of concurring. **2.** accordance in opinion; agreement. **3.** cooperation, as of agents or causes. **4.** simultaneous occurrence; coincidence. **5.** competition. Also, **concurrency** for defs 1-4.

**concurrent** /kən'kʌrənt/, *adj.* **1.** occurring or existing together or side by side. **2.** acting in conjunction; cooperating. **3.** having equal authority or jurisdiction. **4.** accordant or agreeing. **5.** *Geom.* passing through the same points: *four concurrent lines.* *–n.* **6.** something joint or contributory. **7.** *Rare.* a rival or competitor. – **concurrently,** *adv.*

**concuss** /kənˈkʌs, kəŋ-/, *v.t.* **1.** to injure the brain by concussion; to knock out. **2.** to strike or shake violently. **3.** to overawe; threaten.

**concussion** /kənˈkʌʃən, kəŋ-/, *n.* **1.** the act of shaking or shocking, as by a blow. **2.** shock occasioned by a blow or collision. **3.** *Pathol.* jarring of the brain, spinal cord, etc., from a blow, fall, etc. [L *concussio* shock] – **concussive,** *adj.*

**concyclic** /kənˈsɪklɪk/, *adj.* lying on the circumference of the same circle. – **concyclically,** *adv.*

**cond.,** **1.** condition. **2.** conductor.

**condé** /kɒnˈdeɪ/, *n.* a creamed dessert made with rice, fruit and jam.

**condemn** /kənˈdɛm/, *v.t.* **1.** to pronounce adverse judgment on; express strong disapproval of; censure. **2.** to afford occasion for convicting: *his very looks condemn him.* **3.** to pronounce to be guilty; sentence to punishment; doom. **4.** to judge or pronounce to be unfit for use or service: *the old ship was condemned.* **5.** to declare incurable. **6.** to compel or force into a certain state or action: *the injury to his leg condemned him to a life of inactivity.* [ME *condem(p)ne,* from OF *condem(p)ner,* from L *condem(p)nāre*] – **condemnable,** *adj.* – **condemner,** *n.* – **condemningly,** *adv.*

**condemnation** /ˌkɒndɛmˈneɪʃən/, *n.* **1.** the act of condemning. **2.** strong censure; disapprobation; reproof. **3.** the state of being condemned. **4.** the cause or reason for condemning.

**condemnatory** /kənˈdɛmnətri, ˌkɒndɛmˈneɪtəri/, *adj.* serving to condemn.

**condemned cell** /kənˈdɛmd sɛl/, *n.* a cell for prisoners sentenced to death.

**condensable** /kənˈdɛnsəbəl/, *adj.* capable of being condensed. – **condensability** /kəndɛnsəˈbɪləti/, *n.*

**condensate** /kənˈdɛnseɪt/, *n.* something formed by condensation.

**condensation** /ˌkɒndɛnˈseɪʃən/, *n.* **1.** the act of condensing. **2.** condensed state or form. **3.** a condensed mass. **4.** *Chem.* a reaction between two or more like or unlike organic molecules, leading to the formation of a larger molecule and the splitting out of a simple molecule such as water or alcohol. **5.** the act of reducing a gas or vapour to a liquid or solid form. **6.** *Psychoanal.* the representation of two or more ideas, memories, feelings, or impulses by one word or image, as in wit, slips, allegories, and dreams.

**condensation pump** /ˈ– pʌmp/, *n.* →**diffusion pump.**

**condensation trail** /ˈ– treɪl/, *n.* →**vapour trail.**

**condense** /kənˈdɛns/, *v.,* **-densed, -densing.** *–v.t.* **1.** to make more dense or compact; reduce the volume or compass of. **2.** to reduce to another and denser form, as a gas or vapour to a liquid or solid state. **3.** to compress into fewer words; abridge. **4.** *Optics.* to concentrate light; focus a ray on to a smaller space. *–v.i.* **5.** to become liquid or solid, as a gas or vapour. [late ME, from L *condensāre* make thick]

**condensed milk** /kɒndɛnst ˈmɪlk/, *n.* milk reduced by evaporation to a thick consistency with sugar added.

**condensed type** /– ˈtaɪp/, *n.* a kind of printing type narrow in proportion to its height.

**condenser** /kənˈdɛnsə/, *n.* **1.** one who or that which condenses. **2.** an apparatus for condensing. **3.** *Chem.* any device for reducing gases or vapours to liquid or solid form. **4.** *Optics.* a lens or combination of lenses, used to gather and concentrate the rays of light and direct them upon the object. **5.** *Elect.* →**capacitor.**

**condescend** /kɒndəˈsɛnd/, *v.i.* **1.** to stoop or deign (to do something). **2.** to waive ceremony voluntarily and assume equality with an inferior. **3.** to behave as if one is conscious of descending from a superior position, rank, or dignity. **4.** *Obs.* to yield. **5.** *Obs.* to assent. [ME *condescende(n),* from F *condescendre,* from LL *condēscendere* stoop] – **condescendence,** *n.*

**condescending** /kɒndəˈsɛndɪŋ/, *adj.* showing or implying a gracious descent from dignity; patronising. – **condescendingly,** *adv.*

**condescension** /kɒndəˈsɛnʃən/, *n.* the act of condescending; gracious or patronising complaisance.

**condign** /kənˈdaɪn/, *adj.* (chiefly of punishment, etc.) well-deserved; fitting; adequate. [ME *condigne,* from F, from L *condignus* wholly worthy] – **condignly,** *adv.*

**condiment** /ˈkɒndəmənt/, *n.* something used to give a special or additional flavour to food, as a sauce or seasoning. [L *condīmentum* spice] – **condimental** /kɒndəˈmɛntl/, *adj.*

**condition** /kənˈdɪʃən/, *n.* **1.** particular mode of being of a person or thing; situation with respect to circumstances; existing state or case. **2.** state of health. **3.** fit or requisite state. **4.** *Agric.* **a.** the degree of fatness of a beast or carcase. **b.** the amount of yolk (def. 4) and other impurities present in raw wool. **c.** the amount of moisture present in scoured wool expressed as a percentage of clean dry weight. **5.** social position. **6.** a restricting, limiting, or modifying circumstance. **7.** a circumstance indispensable to some result; a prerequisite; that on which something else is contingent. **8.** something demanded as an essential part of an agreement. **9.** *Law.* **a.** a stipulation in a contract making some liability contingent on the happening of a future uncertain event; a **condition precedent** is one which delays the vesting of the right until the event happens; a **condition subsequent** is where the event is to destroy or divest an existing right. **b.** the event. **10.** *Gram.* →**protasis.** **11.** *Logic.* antecedent. **12.** **on condition that,** if; provided that. *–v.t.* **13.** to put in fit or proper state. **14.** to form or be a condition of; determine, limit, or restrict as a condition. **15.** to subject to something as a condition; make conditional (fol. by *on* or *upon*). **16.** to subject to particular conditions or circumstances. **17.** to test (a commodity) to ascertain its condition. **18.** to make it a condition; stipulate. **19.** *Psychol.* to cause a conditioned response in. *–v.i.* **20.** to make conditions. [ME *condicion,* from L *condicio* (erroneously *conditio*) agreement, stipulation, circumstances] – **conditioner,** *n.*

**conditional** /kənˈdɪʃənəl/, *adj.* **1.** imposing, containing, or depending on a condition or conditions; not absolute; made or granted on certain terms: *a conditional agreement, sale, etc.* **2.** *Gram.* (of a sentence, clause, or mood) involving or expressing a condition. For example: *If the suit is expensive* (conditional clause), *don't buy it.* **3.** *Logic.* **a.** (of a proposition) asserting that one state of affairs is or will be realised if some other state of affairs is realised, as in *if Smith is 18 years old, he is eligible to vote.* **b.** (of a syllogism) containing a conditional proposition as a premise. *–n.* **4.** (in certain languages) a mood, tense, or other category used in expressing conditions, often corresponding to an English verb preceded by *if: Spanish 'comería'* (*he would eat*) *is in the conditional.* **5.** *Computers.* an instruction which is acted upon only when a certain condition pertains; an example of a conditional is: *transfer control to X if A equals zero.* – **conditionality** /kəndɪʃənˈæləti/, *n.* – **conditionally,** *adv.*

**conditional fee** /– ˈfi/, *n. Law.* any fee simple granted with the provision for its ending on the happening or non-happening of some event.

**conditional pardon** /ˈ– padn/, *n.* **1.** a pardon with some conditions. **2.** (formerly) a pardon granted to a convict, who was then called an emancipist, but who could not leave the penal colony to which he had been transported until his original sentence had expired.

**conditional probability** /– prɒbəˈbɪləti/, *n.* the statistical probability of the occurrence of an event under the condition that only a portion of the cases or alternatives are to be considered.

**conditioned** /kənˈdɪʃənd/, *adj.* **1.** existing under or subject to conditions. **2.** trained by people exerting influence, as teachers, parents, etc., or by circumstances, to respond in certain ways.

**conditioned response** /– rəˈspɒns/, *n. Psychol.* an acquired response elicited by a stimulus, object or situation (conditioned stimulus) other than the stimulus to which it is the natural or normal response (unconditioned stimulus). Also, **conditioned reflex.**

**conditioned stimulus** /– ˈstɪmjuləs/, *n.* a stimulus originally ineffective in eliciting a specified response but made effective through having been presented paired with an effective stimulus; a buzzer sounding whenever food is shown to a dog, eventually elicits by itself salivation in the dog.

**conditioner** /kənˈdɪʃənə/, *n.* **1.** a person or thing that conditions: *an air conditioner.* **2.** a substance added to something to improve its quality or useability: *hair conditioner.*

**conditions of sale,** *n.pl. Law.* written terms (usu. standard sets) for the sale of property by auction.

**condole** /kən'doʊl/, *v.,* **-doled, -doling.** *–v.i.* **1.** to express sympathy with one in affliction; grieve (fol. by *with*). *–v.t.* **2.** *Obs.* to grieve with. [LL *condolēre* suffer greatly] – **condolatory,** *adj.* – **condoler,** *n.* – **condolingly,** *adv.*

**condolence** /kən'doʊləns/, *n.* expression of sympathy with a person in affliction. Also, **condolement.**

**condom** /'kɒndɒm/, *n.* a contraceptive device worn over the penis during intercourse; contraceptive sheath. [? named after *Condom,* 18th-cent. English physician said to have devised it]

**condominium** /kɒndə'mɪniəm/, *n.* **1.** joint or concurrent dominion. **2.** *Internat. Law.* joint sovereignty over a territory by several foreign states. **3.** → **home unit.** [NL, from L: *con-* CON- + *dominium* lordship]

**condonation** /kɒndə'neɪʃən/, *n.* the act of condoning.

**condone** /kən'doʊn/, *v.t.,* **-doned, -doning.** **1.** to pardon or overlook (an offence). **2.** to cause the condonation of. **3.** to atone for; make up for. **4.** *Law.* to forgive, or act so as to imply forgiveness of (a violation of the marriage vow). [L *condōnāre* give up] – **condoner,** *n.*

**condor** /'kɒndɔ/, *n.* a large vulture of the New World, as the **Andean condor** (*Sarcorhamphus gryphus*) and **California condor** (*Gymnogyps californianus*). [Sp., from Quechua *cuntur*]

Andean condor

**condottiere** /kɒndɒti'ɛəreɪ/, *n., pl.* **-ri** /-ri/. (in Europe, esp. in the 14th and 15th centuries) a professional military commander or leader of mercenaries, in the service of states at war. [It.: leader, from *condotto* mercenary (soldier), from L *conductus,* pp., led together, hired]

**conduce** /kən'djus/, *v.i.,* **-duced, -ducing.** to lead or contribute to a result (fol. by *to*). [late ME, from L *condūcere* lead together, hire]

**conducive** /kən'djusɪv/, *adj.* conducting; contributive; helpful (fol. by *to*). – **conduciveness,** *n.*

**conduct** /'kɒndʌkt/, *n.;* /kən'dʌkt/, *v.* *–n.* **1.** personal behaviour; way of acting; deportment: *good conduct.* **2.** direction or management; execution: *the conduct of a business.* **3.** the act of conducting; guidance; escort. **4.** *Obs.* a guide; an escort. *–v.t.* **5.** to behave (oneself). **6.** to direct in action or course; manage; carry on: *to conduct a campaign.* **7.** to direct as leader: *to conduct an orchestra.* **8.** to lead or guide; escort. **9.** to serve as a channel or medium for (heat, electricity, sound, etc.). *–v.i.* **10.** to lead. **11.** to act as conductor. [LL *conductus,* n., escort, from L *condūcere* bring together; replacing ME *conduyt,* from OF *conduit*] – **conductible,** *adj.* – **conductibility** /kəndʌktə'bɪləti/, *n.*

**conductance** /kən'dʌktəns/, *n.* the conducting power of a conductor being the reciprocal of resistance for direct current and the resistance divided by the square of impedance for alternating currents; the derived SI unit of conductance is the siemens. *Symbol:* S

**conduct conducing** /,kɒndʌkt kən'djusɪŋ/, *n.* wilful neglect or misconduct on the part of a petitioner in a suit for divorce or legal separation which is judged to have condoned the alleged offence of the respondent.

**conduction** /kən'dʌkʃən/, *n.* **1.** a conducting, as of water through a pipe. **2.** *Physics.* **a.** a conducting, as of heat, electricity or sound through a medium. **b.** →**conductivity.** **3.** *Physiol.* the carrying of an impulse by a nerve or other tissue.

**conductive** /kən'dʌktɪv/, *adj.* having the property of conducting.

**conductivity** /,kɒndʌk'tɪvəti/, *n., pl.* **-ties.** the property or power of conducting heat, electricity, or sound.

**conductor** /kən'dʌktə/, *n.* **1.** one who conducts; a leader, guide, director, or manager. **2.** the person on a public transport vehicle, who collects fares, issues tickets, etc. **3.** *U.S.* →**guard** (def. 16). **4.** the director of an orchestra or chorus, who communicates to the performers by motions of a baton, etc., his interpretation of the music. **5.** that which conducts. **6.** a substance, body, or device that readily conducts heat, electricity, sound, etc. **7.** a lightning conductor. – **conductorship,** *n.* – **conductress,** *n. fem.*

**conductor rail** /'– reɪl/, *n.* **1.** a rail made of abrasive low-resistance steel, usu. laid alongside the running rails in places where a track is prone to wear. **2.** *Brit.* an exposed rail, usu. laid alongside the running rails, for conducting the current to an electric train.

**conduct sheet** /'kɒndʌkt ,ʃit/, *n.* one of a soldier's personal documents which lists his offences against military law and the punishments awarded.

**conduit** /'kɒndɪt, 'kɒndʒuət/, *n.* **1.** a pipe, tube, or the like, for conveying water or other fluid. **2.** some similar natural passage. **3.** *Elect.* a pipe that encases electrical wires or cables to protect them from damage. **4.** (formerly on tramways) an underground trough containing positive and negative conductor rails, from which current is collected by a plough (attached to the underside of the tram) which passes through a slot in the road surface. **5.** *Archaic.* a fountain. [ME *condit,* from OF *conduit,* from LL *conductus.* See CONDUCT]

**conduplicate** /kɒn'djuplɪkət/, *adj.* (of a leaf in the bud) folded lengthways with the upper face of the blade within.

**condyle** /'kɒndəl/, *n.* a rounded protuberance on a bone, serving to form an articulation with another bone. [F, from L *condylus,* from Gk *kóndylos* knuckle, bony knob] – **condylar,** *adj.*

**condyloid** /'kɒndəlɔɪd/, *adj.* of or like a condyle.

**condyloma** /kɒndə'loʊmə/, *n., pl.* **-mata** /-mətə/. a wartlike excrescence on the skin, usu. in the region of the anus or genitals. [L, from Gk *kondýlōma,* from *kóndylos* CONDYLE] – **condylomatous** /kɒndə'lɒmətəs, -'loʊmə-/, *adj.*

**Condy's crystals** /,kɒndiz 'krɪstəlz/, *n.pl.* potassium permanganate, $KMnO_4$, a powerful oxidant, formerly used in the treatment of snake bite, as a disinfectant, etc. [named after Henry Bollman *Condy,* 19thC English physician]

**cone** /koʊn/, *n., v.,* **coned, coning.** *–n.* **1.** *Geom.* a solid whose surface is generated by the straight lines joining a fixed point to the points of a plane curve whose plane does not contain the fixed point. When the plane curve is a circle and the fixed point lies on the perpendicular to the plane of the circle through its centre, the cone is a **right circular cone.** When the plane curve is a circle and the fixed point is not so situated, the cone is an **oblique circular cone.** **2.** *Mach.* a mechanical part having the shape of a cone or conoid. **3.** *Bot.* **a.** the more or less conical multiple fruit of the pine, fir, etc., consisting of imbricated or valvate scales bearing naked ovules or seeds; a strobilus. **b.** a similar fruit, as in cycads, club mosses, etc. **4.** *Zool.* a light-sensitive nerve-cell present in the retina of most invertebrates. **5.** anything cone-shaped. **6.** the conical peak built up with the ejected material from a volcano. **7.** a cone-shaped vessel hoisted as a warning of bad weather. **8.** a conical container of wafer for a portion of ice-cream. *–v.t.* **9.** to shape like a cone or the segment of a cone. [L *cōnus,* from Gk *kônos*]

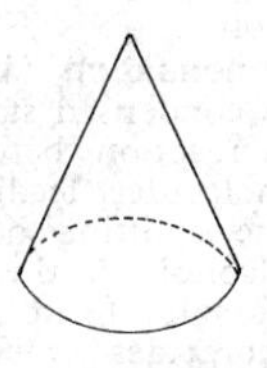
cone

**conebush** /'koʊnbʊʃ/, *n.* any shrub of the Australian genus *Isopogon,* family Proteaceae.

**cone crusher** /'koʊn krʌʃə/, *n.* a machine for reducing the size of materials by means of a truncated cone revolving on its vertical axis within an outer chamber, the annular space between the outer chamber and cone being tapered; gyratory crusher.

**coneflower** /'koʊnflaʊə/, *n.* **1.** →**rudbeckia.** **2.** any of various allied plants.

**cone of silence,** *n.* an inverted cone-shaped space directly over the aerial towers of some forms of radio beacons in which signals are unheard or greatly reduced in volume.

**cone shell** /'koʊn ʃɛl/, *n.* any of numerous chiefly tropical marine gastropods of the genus *Conus,* with a smooth conical shell, many of which are equipped with a poison gland and an injecting mechanism and are highly dangerous to handle.

**con esp.,** *adv.* with expression. [It. *con espressione*]

**coney** /'koʊni/, *n., pl.* **-neys.** →**cony.**

**confab** /'kɒnfæb/, *n., v.,* **-fabbed, -fabbing.** *Colloq.* *–n.* **1.**

confabulation. *–v.i.* **2.** →**confabulate.**

**confabulate** /kən'fæbjuleɪt/, *v.i.*, **-lated, -lating.** to talk together; converse. [L *confābulātus,* pp.] – **confabulation** /kənfæbju'leɪʃən/ *n.*

**confect** /kən'fɛkt/, *v.;* /'kɒnfɛkt/, *n.* *–v.t.* **1.** *Obs.* to make up, compound, or prepare from ingredients or materials. *–n.* **2.** a preserved, crystallised, or other sweet confection; a comfit. [L *confectus,* pp., put together]

**confection** /kən'fɛkʃən/, *n.* **1.** the process of compounding, preparing, or making. **2.** a sweet preparation (liquid or dry) of fruit or the like, as a preserve or sweetmeat. **3.** a sweet or bonbon. **4.** a medicinal preparation, now one made with the aid of sugar, honey, or syrup. *–v.t.* **5.** *Obs.* to prepare as a confection. [ME, from L *confectio* a making ready]

**confectionary** /kən'fɛkʃənəri/, *n., pl.* **-aries,** *adj.* *–n.* **1.** a place where confections are kept or made. **2.** a confection or sweet. **3.** *Obs.* a confectioner. *–adj.* **4.** pertaining to or of the nature of confections or their making.

**confectioner** /kən'fɛkʃənə/, *n.* one who makes or sells sweets, and sometimes ice-cream, cakes, etc.

**confectioners' sugar** /kən'fɛkʃənəz ʃʊgə/, *n.* *U.S.* →**icing sugar.**

**confectionery** /kən'fɛkʃənri/, *n., pl.* **-eries.** **1.** confections or sweets collectively. **2.** the work or business of a confectioner. **3.** a confectioner's shop.

**confederacy** /kən'fɛdərəsi, -'fɛdrəsi/, *n., pl.* **-cies.** **1.** an alliance of persons, parties, or states for some common purpose. **2.** a group of persons, parties, etc., united by such an alliance. **3.** a combination for unlawful purposes; a conspiracy.

**confederate** /kən'fɛdərət/, *adj., n.;* /kən'fɛdəreɪt/, *v.,* **-rated, -rating.** *–adj.* **1.** united in a league or alliance, or a conspiracy. **2.** (*cap.*) denoting or pertaining to the Confederate States of America (the eleven states which seceded from the American Union in 1860-61): *the Confederate army.* *–n.* **3.** one united with others in a confederacy; an ally. **4.** an accomplice. **5.** (*cap.*) an adherent of the Confederate States of America. *–v.t.* **6.** to form into a confederacy. *–v.i.* **7.** to unite in a league or alliance, or a conspiracy. [ME, from LL *confoederātus,* pp., united in a league]

**confederation** /kənfɛdə'reɪʃən/, *n.* **1.** the act of confederating. **2.** the state of being confederated. **3.** a league or alliance. **4.** a body of confederates, esp. of states more or less permanently united for common purposes.

**confederative** /kən'fɛdərətɪv/, *adj.* pertaining to a confederation.

**confer** /kən'fɜ/, *v.,* **-ferred, -ferring.** *–v.t.* **1.** to bestow as a gift, favour, honour, etc. (fol. by *on* or *upon*). **2.** *Obs.* to compare. *–v.i.* **3.** consult together; compare opinions; carry on a discussion or deliberation. [L *conferre* bring together] – **conferment,** *n.* – **conferrable,** *adj.* – **conferrer,** *n.*

**conferee** /ˌkɒnfɜ'ri/, *n.* **1.** one on whom something is conferred. **2.** *U.S.* one who is conferred with or takes part in a conference. Also, **conferree.**

**conference** /'kɒnfərəns/, *n.* **1.** a meeting for consultation or discussion. **2.** the act of conferring or consulting together; consultation, esp. on an important or serious matter. **3.** *Eccles.* **a.** an official assembly of clergy, or of clergy and laymen, customary in many Christian denominations. **b.** a group of churches the representatives of which regularly meet in such an assembly. **4.** a cartel (def. 1) of shipping interests. **5.** an act of conferring; a bestowal. **6.** *U.S. Sport.* an organisation of teams.-**conferential** /kɒnfə'rɛnʃəl/, *adj.*

**confess** /kən'fɛs/, *v.t.* **1.** to acknowledge or avow: *to confess a secret, fault, crime, debt, etc.* **2.** to own or admit; admit the truth or validity of: *I must confess that I haven't read it.* **3.** to acknowledge one's belief in; declare adherence to. **4.** to declare (one's sins) or declare the sins of (oneself), esp. to a priest, for the obtaining of absolution. **5.** (of a priest) to hear the confession of. **6.** *Archaic.* to reveal by circumstances. *–v.i.* **7.** to make confession; plead guilty; own (fol. by *to*). **8.** to make confession of sins, esp. to a priest. [ME *confesse(n),* from LL *confessāre,* from L *confessus,* pp.]

**confessedly** /kən'fɛsədli/, *adv.* by confession or acknowledgment; admittedly.

**confession** /kən'fɛʃən/, *n.* **1.** acknowledgment or avowal; admission or concession: *a confession of guilt.* **2.** acknowledgment of sin or sinfulness. **3.** a disclosing of sins to a priest to obtain forgiveness. **4.** that which is confessed. **5.** Also, **confession of faith.** a formal profession of belief and acceptance of church doctrines, as before being admitted to church membership. **6.** the tomb of a martyr or confessor, or the altar or shrine connected with it. [ME, from L *confessio*]

**confessional** /kən'fɛʃənəl/, *adj.* **1.** of, or of the nature of, confession. *–n.* **2.** the place set apart for the hearing of confessions by a priest. **3.** the practice or institution of confession.

**confessionary** /kən'fɛʃənri/, *adj.* of or pertaining to confession, esp. auricular confession of sins.

**confessor** /kən'fɛsə/, *n.* **1.** Also, **confesser.** one who confesses. **2.** a priest authorised to hear confessions. **3.** one who confesses and adheres to the Christian religion, esp. in spite of persecution and torture.

**confetti** /kən'fɛti/, *n.pl., sing.* **-fetto** /-'fɛtoʊ/. **1.** small bits of coloured paper, thrown at carnivals, weddings, etc. **2.** confections; bonbons. [It., pl. of *confetto* comfit]

**confid.,** confidential.

**confidant** /kɒnfə'dænt, 'kɒnfədənt/, *n.* one to whom secrets are confided or with whom intimate problems are discussed. [F, from It. *confidente,* from L *confīdens,* ppr., trusting] – **confidante,** *n. fem.*

**confide** /kən'faɪd/, *v.,* **-fided, -fiding.** *–v.i.* **1.** to show trust by imparting secrets (fol. by *in*). **2.** to have full trust: *confiding in that parting promise.* *–v.t.* **3.** to tell in assurance of secrecy. **4.** to entrust; commit to the charge, knowledge, or good faith of another. [late ME, from L *confīdere* trust altogether] – **confider,** *n.*

**confidence** /'kɒnfədəns/, *n.* **1.** full trust; belief in the trustworthiness or reliability of a person or thing. **2.** *Politics.* the wish to retain the incumbent government in office, as shown by a vote on a particular issue: *the future of the government rests on a vote of confidence.* **3.** self-reliance, assurance, or boldness. **4.** presumption. **5.** certitude or assured expectation. **6.** a confidential communication; a secret. **7.** *Archaic.* a ground of trust. **8. in confidence,** as a secret or private matter, not to be divulged to others: *I told him in confidence.*

**confidence limits** /'– lɪməts/, *n.pl.* a pair of numbers used to estimate a characteristic of a population from a sample, which are such that it can be stated with a specified probability that the pair of numbers calculated from a sample will include the value of the population characteristic between them.

**confidence man** /'– mæn/, *n.* one who swindles by a confidence trick.

**confidence trick** /'– trɪk/, *n.* a swindle in which the victim's confidence is gained and he is then induced to part with money or property. Also, *U.S.,* **confidence game.** – **confidence trickster,** *n.*

**confident** /'kɒnfədənt/, *adj.* **1.** having strong belief or full assurance; sure: *confident of victory.* **2.** sure of oneself; bold: *a confident bearing.* **3.** overbold. **4.** *Obs.* trustful or confiding. *–n.* **5.** a confidant. – **confidently,** *adv.*

**confidential** /kɒnfə'dɛnʃəl/, *adj.* **1.** spoken or written in confidence; secret: *a confidential document.* **2.** betokening confidence or intimacy; imparting private matters: *a confidential tone.* **3.** enjoying another's confidence; entrusted with secrets or private affairs: *a confidential secretary.* – **confidentiality** /ˌkɒnfədɛnʃi'æləti/, **confidentialness,** *n.* – **confidentially,** *adv.*

**confiding** /kən'faɪdɪŋ/, *adj.* trustful; credulous or unsuspicious. – **confidingly,** *adv.* – **confidingness,** *n.*

**configuration** /kənfɪgə'reɪʃən, -fɪgju-/, *n.* **1.** the relative disposition of the parts or elements of a thing. **2.** external form, as resulting from this; conformation. **3.** *Astron.* the relative position or aspect of heavenly bodies. **4.** *Physics, Chem.* the relative position in space of the atoms in a molecule. **5.** *Geog.* the form of a part of the earth's surface with respect to both its horizontal outline and its elevation. **6.** the relative position of all electrodes as they are placed in electrical (geophysical) prospecting. [LL *configūrātio,* from L *configūrāre* shape after some pattern] – **configurational, configurative** /kən'fɪgərətɪv/, *adj.*

**confine** /kən'faɪn/, *v.,* **-fined, -fining;** /'kɒnfaɪn/, *n.* *–v.t.* **1.** to enclose within bounds; limit or restrict. **2.** to shut or keep in; imprison. **3.** to be in childbed, or be delivered of a child (used in the passive). *–n.* **4.** (*usu. pl.*) a boundary or bound; a border or frontier. [F *confiner,* from It. *confinare,* from *confino* bordering, from L *confīnis*] – **confiner,** *n.*

**confined aquifer** /kənfaɪnd 'ækwəfə/, *n.* an aquifer in which water is confined under pressure by overlying and underlying impermeable strata.

**confined space** /– 'speɪs/, *n.* a work place, the dimensions of which necessitate an employee working in a stooped or otherwise cramped position or without proper ventilation, and as compensation for which employees are paid a special rate.

**confinement** /kən'faɪnmənt/, *n.* **1.** the act of confining; imprisonment. **2.** the state of being confined, esp. of a woman in childbirth.

**confirm** /kən'fɜm/, *v.t.* **1.** to make certain or sure; corroborate; verify: *this confirmed my suspicions.* **2.** to make valid or binding by some formal or legal act; sanction; ratify: *to confirm an agreement, appointment, etc.* **3.** to make firm or more firm; add strength to; settle or establish firmly: *the news confirmed my resolution.* **4.** to strengthen (a person) in habit, resolution, opinion, etc. **5.** *Eccles.* to administer the rite of confirmation to. [L *confirmāre* make firm; replacing ME *conferme(n),* from OF *confermer*] – **confirmable,** *adj.* – **confirmer;** *Law,* **confirmor,** *n.*

**confirmation** /kɒnfə'meɪʃən/, *n.* **1.** the act of confirming. **2.** that which confirms, as a corroborative statement. **3.** *Eccles.* a rite administered to baptised persons, in some Churches as a sacrament for confirming and strengthening the recipient in the Christain faith, in others as a rite without sacramental character by which the recipient is admitted to full communion with the Church.

**confirmatory** /kɒnfə'meɪtəri, kən'fɜmətri/, *adj.* serving to confirm; corroborative. Also, **confirmative.**

**confirmed** /kən'fɜmd/, *adj.* **1.** made firm; settled; ratified. **2.** made certain as regards truth or accuracy; corroborated. **3.** firmly established in a habit or condition; inveterate: *a confirmed drunkard.* **4.** made more resolute or more determined; strengthened. **5.** (of a disease) chronic. **6.** having received the sacrament of confirmation (def. 3).

**confiscable** /kən'fɪskəbəl/, *adj.* liable to be confiscated.

**confiscate** /'kɒnfəskeɪt/, *v.,* **-cated, -cating,** *adj.* *–v.t.* **1.** to seize as forfeited to the public treasury; appropriate, by way of penalty, to public use. **2.** to seize as if by authority; appropriate summarily. *–adj.* **3.** confiscated. [L *confiscātus,* pp., put away in a chest] – **confiscation** /kɒnfəs'keɪʃən/, *n.* – **confiscator,** *n.*

**confiscatory** /kən'fɪskətəri, -tri/, *adj.* characterised by or effecting confiscation.

**confiteor** /kɒn'fitiɔ/, *n.* (in the Roman Catholic Church) a form of prayer beginning with 'Confiteor', in which a general confession of sinfulness is made, used at the beginning of the mass and on other occasions. [L: I confess]

**conflagrate** /'kɒnfləgreɪt/, *v.t., v.i.,* **-grated, -grating.** burn. [L *conflagrātus,* pp., burnt. See CONFLAGRATION] – **conflagrant** /kən'fleɪgrənt/, *adj.*

**conflagration** /kɒnflə'greɪʃən/, *n.* a large and destructive fire. [L *conflagrātio*]

**conflation** /kən'fleɪʃən/, *n. Bibliog.* **1.** the combination of two variant texts into a new one. **2.** the result. [LL *conflātio,* from L *conflāre* blow together]

**conflict** /kən'flɪkt/, *v.;* /'kɒnflɪkt/, *n.* *–v.i.* **1.** to come into collision; clash, or be in opposition or at variance; disagree. **2.** to contend; do battle. *–n.* **3.** a battle or struggle, esp. a prolonged struggle; strife. **4.** controversy; a quarrel: *conflicts between church and state.* **5.** discord of action, feeling, or effect; antagonism, as of interests or principles: *a conflict of ideas.* **6.** a striking together; collision. [L *conflictus,* pp., struck together] – **confliction,** *n.* – **conflictive,** *adj.*

**confluence** /'kɒnfluəns/, *n.* **1.** a flowing together of two or more streams. **2.** the place of junction. **3.** the body of water so formed. **4.** a coming together of people or things. **5.** a throng; an assemblage. Also, **conflux** /'kɒnflʌks/.

**confluent** /'kɒnfluənt/, *adj.* **1.** flowing or running together; blending into one. **2.** *Pathol.* **a.** running together: *confluent efflorescences.* **b.** characterised by confluent efflorescences: *confluent smallpox.* *–n.* **3.** one of two or more confluent streams. **4.** a tributary stream. [L *confluens,* ppr., flowing together]

**confocal** /kɒn'foʊkəl/, *adj.* having the same focus or foci.

**conform** /kən'fɔm/, *v.i.* **1.** to act in accord or harmony; comply (fol. by *to*). **2.** to become similar in form or character. **3.** to comply with the usages of the Church of England. *–v.t.* **4.** to make similar in form or character. **5.** to bring into correspondence or harmony. [ME *conforme(n),* from F *conformer,* from L *conformāre* fashion, shape after] – **conformer,** *n.*

**conformable** /kən'fɔməbəl/, *adj.* **1.** corresponding in form or character; similar. **2.** exhibiting agreement or harmony (usu. fol. by *to*). **3.** compliant, acquiescent, or submissive. **4.** *Geol.* (of strata or beds) having the same dip and strike as a result of successive depositions uninterrupted by crustal movement. – **conformability** /kənfɔmə'bɪləti/, **conformableness,** *n.* – **conformably,** *adv.*

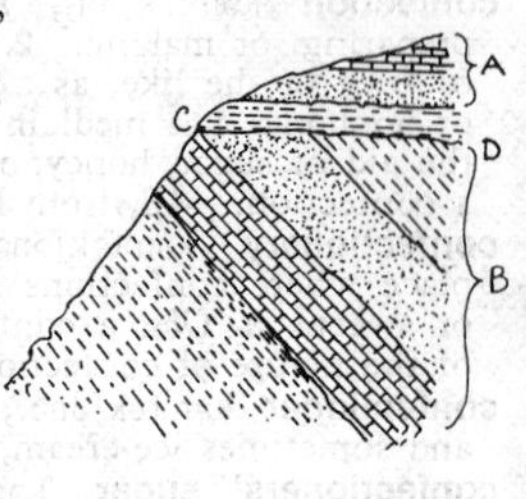


conformable and unconformable strata: A and B, two sets of unconformable strata; CD, line of junction of A and B

**conformance** /kən'fɔməns/, *n.* the act of conforming; conformity.

**conformation** /kɒnfə'meɪʃən/, *n.* **1.** the manner of formation; structure; form. **2.** symmetrical disposition or arrangement of parts. **3.** the act of conforming; adaptation; adjustment. **4.** the state of being conformed. **5.** *Chem.* the spatial arrangement which can normally be obtained by rotation about single (electron-pair) bonds. **6.** the form, outline or shape, esp. of an animal or dressed carcase.

**conformational analysis** /kɒnfəˌmeɪʃənəl ə'næləsəs/, *n.* an analysis of molecular conformation from observed physical and chemical properties.

**conformist** /kən'fɔməst/, *n.* **1.** one who conforms to a usage or practice. **2.** one who conforms to the usages of the Church of England.

**conformity** /kən'fɔməti/, *n., pl.* **-ties. 1.** correspondence in form or character; agreement, congruity, or accordance. **2.** compliance or acquiescence. **3.** compliance with the usages of the Church of England.

**con forza** /kɒn 'fɔtsə/, *adv.* (a musical direction) with force. [It.]

**confound** /kən'faʊnd/, *v.t.* **1.** to mingle so that the elements cannot be distinguished or separated. **2.** to treat or regard erroneously as identical; mix or associate by mistake. **3.** to throw into confusion or disorder: *confusion worse confounded.* **4.** to perplex, as with sudden disturbance or surprise. **5.** to refute in argument; contradict. **6.** *Archaic.* to put to shame; abash. **7.** *Archaic.* to defeat or overthrow; bring to ruin or naught. **8.** (in mild imprecations) to damn: *confound it!* **9.** *Obs.* to spend uselessly, or waste. [ME *confounde(n),* from OF *confondre,* from L *confundere* pour together, mix, confuse] – **confounder,** *n.*

**confounded** /kən'faʊndəd/, *adj.* **1.** discomfited; astonished. **2.** *Colloq.* damned: *a confounded lie.* – **confoundedly,** *adv.*

**confraternity** /kɒnfrə'tɜnəti/, *n., pl.* **-ties. 1.** a lay brotherhood devoted to some particular religious or charitable service. **2.** a society or body of men united for some purpose or in some profession. [late ME *confraternite,* from ML *confrāternitas* brotherhood, from *confrāter.* See CONFRÈRE]

**confrère** /'kɒnfrɛə/, *n.* a fellow member of a profession, association, etc.; a colleague. [ME, from F, translation of ML *confrāter* colleague]

**confront** /kən'frʌnt/, *v.t.* **1.** to stand or come in front of; stand or meet facing; stand in the way of. **2.** to face in hostility or defiance; oppose. **3.** to set face to face. **4.** to bring together for examination or comparison. [F *confronter,* from ML *confrontārī,* from L *con-* CON- + *frons* forehead + *-ārī,* inf. ending] – **confrontation** /ˌkɒnfrən'teɪʃən/, **confrontment,** *n.* – **confronter,** *n.*

**con fuoco** /kɒn 'fwoʊkoʊ/, *adv.* (a musical direction) with fire. [It.]

**confuse** /kən'fjuz/, *v.t.,* **-fused, -fusing. 1.** to combine without order or clearness; jumble; render indistinct. **2.** to throw into disorder. **3.** to fail to distinguish between; associate by mistake; confound: *to confuse dates.* **4.** to perplex or bewilder. **5.** to disconcert or abash. **6.** *Obs.* to bring to ruin or naught. [backformation from *confused,* from ME *confus* (from F, from L *confūsus,* pp., confounded) + -ED[2]] – **confusedly** /kən'fjuzədli/, *adv.* – **confusingly,** *adv.* – **confusedness,** *n.*

**confusion** /kən'fjuʒən/, *n.* **1.** the state of being confused. **2.** disorder. **3.** lack of clearness or distinctness. **4.** embarrassment or abashment. **5.** perplexity; bewilderment. **6.** *Psychol.* a disturbed mental state; a clouding of consciousness; disorientation. **7.** *Archaic.* the act of confusing. **8.** *Obs.* overthrow; defeat. [ME, from L *confūsio*]

**confutation** /kɒnfju'teɪʃən/, *n.* **1.** the act of confuting. **2.** that which confutes. **3.** *Rhet.* the fourth section (of a speech), given over to direct refutation. – **confutative** /kən'fjutətɪv/, *adj.*

**confute** /kən'fjut/, *v.t.,* **-futed, -futing. 1.** to prove to be false or defective; disprove: *to confute an argument.* **2.** to prove to be wrong; convict of error by argument or proof: *to confute one's opponent.* **3.** to confound or bring to naught. [L *confūtāre*] – **confuter,** *n.*

**cong.,** congress.

**conga** /'kɒŋgə/, *n.* **1.** a Latin-American dance consisting of three steps forwards followed by a kick and usu. performed by a group following a leader in a single column, each dancer clasping the waist of the person in front. **2.** a large cylindrical drum of Afro-American origin.

**congé** /'kɒndʒeɪ/, *n.* **1.** leave to depart, or dismissal; leave or permission; leave-taking. **2.** a bow or obeisance. **3.** *Archit.* a type of concave moulding. [F. See CONGEE]

**congeal** /kən'dʒil/, *v.i.* **1.** to change from a fluid or soft to a solid or rigid state, as by freezing or cooling. **2.** to stiffen or coagulate, as blood. **3.** *U.S.* to become fixed, as sentiments, principles, etc. *–v.t.* **4.** to cause to solidify or coagulate. [ME *congele(n),* from L *congelāre* cause to freeze together] – **congealable,** *adj.* – **congealer,** *n.* – **congealment,** *n.*

**congee** /'kɒndʒi/, *n., v.,* **-geed, -geeing.** *Obs. –n.* **1.** →**congé.** *–v.i.* **2.** to take one's leave. **3.** to bow. [ME *congye,* from OF *congie* (F *congé*), from L *commeātus* a going to and fro, leave of absence]

**congelation** /kɒndʒə'leɪʃən/, *n.* **1.** the act or process of congealing. **2.** the state of being congealed. **3.** the product of congealing; a concretion; a coagulation. **4.** formation of stalactites; crystallisation.

**congener** /'kɒndʒənə, kən'dʒinə/, *n.* **1.** one of the same kind or class. **2.** a fellow member of a genus, as of plants or animals. Also, **cogener.** [L: of the same kind]

**congeneric** /kɒndʒə'nɛrɪk/, *adj.* of the same kind or genus. Also, **congenerous** /kən'dʒɛnərəs/.

**congenial** /kən'dʒiniəl/, *adj.* **1.** suited or adapted in spirit, feeling, temper, etc.: *congenial companions.* **2.** agreeable or pleasing; agreeing or suited in nature or character: *a congenial task.* [CON- + L *genius* spirit + -AL[1]] – **congeniality** /kəndʒini'æləti/, *n.* – **congenially,** *adv.*

**congenital** /kən'dʒɛnətl/, *adj.* existing at or from one's birth: *a congenital defect.* [L *congenitus* born together with + -AL[1]] – **congenitally,** *adv.*

**conger** /'kɒŋgə/, *n.* **1.** any of various stout-bodied, scaleless, marine eels of the family Congridae found in tropical and temperate oceans and often reaching a great size. **2.** the very large species, *Conger conger,* an important European food fish. **3.** any other species of the family Congridae. Also, **conger eel.** [ME *congre,* from OF, from L *conger, congrus,* from Gk *góngros*]

**congeries** /kɒn'dʒɪəriz/, *n. sing. and pl.* a collection of several particles or bodies in one mass; an assembly. [L: pile, mass]

**congest** /kən'dʒɛst/, *v.t.* **1.** to fill to excess; overcrowd. **2.** *Pathol.* to cause an unnatural accumulation of blood in the vessels of (an organ or part). **3.** *Obs.* to heap together. *–v.i.* **4.** to become congested. [L *congestus,* pp., brought together] – **congestible,** *adj.* – **congestive,** *adj.* – **congestion,** *n.*

**conglobate** /'kɒŋgləbeɪt, 'kɒŋ-/, *adj., v.,* **-bated, -bating.** *–adj.* **1.** formed into a ball. *–v.i.* **2.** to collect into a ball or rounded mass. *–v.t.* **3.** to form into a ball. [L *conglobātus,* pp.] – **conglobation** /kɒnglə'beɪʃən, kɒŋ-/, *n.*

**conglobe** /kɒn'gloub/, *v.t., v.i.,* **-globed, -globing.** →**conglobate.**

**conglomerate** /kən'glɒmərət, 'kəŋ-/, *n., adj.;* /kən'glɒmәreɪt/, *v.,* **-rated, -rating.** *–n.* **1.** anything composed of heterogeneous materials or elements. **2.** *Geol.* a rock consisting of rounded and waterworn pebbles, etc., embedded in a finer cementing material; consolidated gravel. **3.** a company which controls or undertakes a widely diversified range of activities. *–adj.* **4.** gathered into a rounded mass; consisting of parts so gathered; clustered. **5.** *Geol.* of the nature of a conglomerate. *–v.t.* **6.** to bring together into a cohering mass. **7.** to gather into a ball or rounded mass. *–v.i.* **8.** to collect or cluster together. [L *conglomerātus,* pp., rolled together] – **conglomeratic** /kənglɒmə'rætɪk, kəŋ-/, **conglomeritic** /-'rɪtɪk/, *adj.*

**conglomeration** /kənglɒmə'reɪʃən, kəŋ-/, *n.* **1.** the act of conglomerating. **2.** the state of being conglomerated. **3.** a cohering mass; a cluster. **4.** a heterogeneous combination.

**conglutinate** /kən'glutəneɪt/, *v.,* **-nated, -nating,** *adj. –v.t.* **1.** to join as with glue. *–v.i.* **2.** to become joined. *–adj.* **3.** conglutinated. [L *conglūtinātus,* pp., glued together] – **conglutination,** /kənglutə'neɪʃən/, *n.* – **conglutinative** /kən'glutənətɪv/, *adj.*

**Congo** /'kɒŋgoʊ/, *n.* **1.** a republic in central Africa. Official name: **Republic of Congo. 2.** →**Kongo.** – **Congolese,** *adj., n.*

**Congo colours** /– 'kʌləz/, *n.pl.* a group of azo dyes derived from benzidine which will dye cotton and other vegetable fibres without the aid of a mordant. Also, **Congodyes.**

**congolli** /kəŋ'goʊli/, *n.* a small marine and freshwater fish, *Pseudaphritis urvilli,* entering southern and eastern Australian rivers; tupong; marble fish; freshwater flathead; sand trout. [Aboriginal]

**Congo red** /kɒŋgoʊ 'rɛd/, *n.* one of the Congo colours, used esp. to dye cotton, etc., red. Since it is not acid-fast or light-fast, it is often used as a chemical indicator.

**congo snake** /'kɒŋgoʊ sneɪk/, *n.* either of two primitive, eel-like amphibians of the genus *Amphiuma* of the south-eastern U.S. having two pairs of very short limbs. Also, **congo eel.**

**congou** /'kɒŋgu/, *n.* a kind of black tea from China. Also, **congo** /'kɒŋgoʊ/. [Chinese *kung-fu* labour]

**congratulant** /kən'grætʃələnt, kəŋ-/, *adj.* **1.** congratulating. *–n.* **2.** one who congratulates.

**congratulate** /kən'grætʃəleɪt, kəŋ-/, *v.t.,* **-lated, -lating. 1.** to express sympathetic joy to (a person), as on a happy occasion; compliment with expressions of sympathetic pleasure; felicitate. **2.** to consider (oneself) happy or fortunate. **3.** *Obs.* **a.** to express sympathetic joy or satisfaction at (an event, etc.). **b.** to salute. [L *congrātulātus,* pp.] – **congratulator,** *n.*

**congratulation** /kəngrætʃə'leɪʃən, kəŋ-/, *n.* **1.** the act of congratulating. *–interj.* **2.** (*usu. pl.*) (a congratulatory exclamation).

**congratulatory** /kən'grætʃələtri, kəngrætʃə'leɪtəri, kəŋ-/, *adj.* **1.** conveying congratulations. **2.** inclined to congratulate.

**con grazia** /kɒn 'gratsiə/, *adv.* (a musical direction) with grace. [It.]

**congregate** /'kɒŋgrəgeɪt/, *v.,* **-gated, -gating,** *adj. –v.i.* **1.** to come together; assemble, esp. in large numbers. *–v.t.* **2.** to bring together in a crowd, body, or mass; assemble; collect. *–adj.* **3.** congregated; assembled. **4.** collective. [ME, from L *congregātus,* pp., collected into a flock] – **congregative,** *adj.* – **congregativeness,** *n.* – **congregator,** *n.*

**congregation** /kɒŋgrə'geɪʃən/, *n.* **1.** the act of congregating. **2.** a congregated body; an assemblage. **3.** an assembly of persons met for common religious worship. **4.** an organisation formed for the purpose of providing for worship of God, religious education, and other church activities; a local church society. **5.** (in the Old Testament) the whole body of the Hebrews. **6.** (in the New Testament) the Christian Church in general. **7.** *Rom. Cath. Ch.* **a.** a committee of cardinals or other ecclesiastics. **b.** a community of men or women who observe the simple vows of poverty, chastity, and obedience: *Congregation of the Holy Cross.*

**congregational** /kɒŋgrə'geɪʃənəl/, *adj.* **1.** of or pertaining to a congregation: *congregational singing.* **2.** (*cap.*) pertaining or adhering to a form of church government in which each congregation or local church acts as an independent, self-governing body, while maintaining fellowship with other like congregations.

**congregationalism** /kɒŋgrə'geɪʃənəlɪzəm/, *n.* **1.** the type of church government in which each local religious society is independent and self-governing. **2.** (*cap.*) the system of government and doctrine of Congregational churches. – **congregationalist,** *n., adj.*

**congress** /ˈkɒŋgrɛs/, *n.* **1.** a formal meeting or assembly of representatives, as envoys of independent states, for the discussion, arrangements, or promotion of some matter of common interest. **2.** the act of coming together; an encounter. **3.** (*cap.*) the national legislative body of some nations, as the United States of America. **4.** social relations; converse. **5.** sexual intercourse. *–v.i.* **6.** *Rare.* to meet in congress. [L *congressus* a meeting]

**congressional** /kəŋˈgrɛʃənəl/, *adj.* of a congress, esp. (*cap.*) the Congress of the United States of America.

**congressman** /ˈkɒŋgrəsmən/, *n., pl.* **-men.** (*oft. cap.*) a member of the U.S. Congress, esp. of the House of Representatives. – **congresswoman,** *n. fem.*

**congress tart** /ˌkɒŋgrɛs ˈtat/, *n.* a pastry case filled with jam and almond paste, topped with pastry strips.

**congruence** /ˈkɒŋgruəns/, *n.* **1.** the fact or condition of agreeing; agreement. **2.** *Geom.* the state of being congruent (def. 2). **3.** *Maths.* the property of being congruent (def. 3). Also, **congruency.**

**congruent** /ˈkɒŋgruənt/, *adj.* **1.** agreeing; corresponding; congruous. **2.** *Geom.* coinciding exactly when superposed, as of triangles. **3.** *Maths.* of or pertaining to two or more integers which have the same remainder when divided by a given integer called the modulus: *5 and 12 are congruent to the modulus 7.*

**congruity** /kənˈgruəti, kəŋ-/, *n., pl.* **-ties.** **1.** the state or quality of being congruous; agreement; harmony; appropriateness. **2.** (*usu. pl.*) a point of agreement.

**congruous** /ˈkɒŋgruəs/, *adj.* **1.** agreeing or harmonious in character; accordant; consonant; consistent (fol. by *with* or *to*). **2.** exhibiting harmony of parts. **3.** appropriate or fitting. [L *congruus* fit] – **congruously,** *adv.* – **congruousness,** *n.*

**conic** /ˈkɒnɪk/, *adj.* **1.** Also, **conical.** having the form of, resembling, or pertaining to a cone. *–n.* **2.** *Maths.* a conic section. [Gk *kōnikós* cone-shaped] – **conically,** *adv.*

**conical projection** /ˌkɒnɪkəl prəˈdʒɛkʃən/, *n.* a map projection based on the concept of projecting the earth's surface on a conical surface, which is then unrolled to a plane surface. Also, **conic projection.**

**conics** /ˈkɒnɪks/, *n.* the branch of mathematics dealing with conic sections.

**conic section** /kɒnɪk ˈsɛkʃən/, *n.* **1.** *Maths.* any curve formed by the intersection of a plane with a right circular cone; an ellipse, a parabola, or a hyperbola. **2.** (*pl.*) the branch of mathematics dealing with these curves.

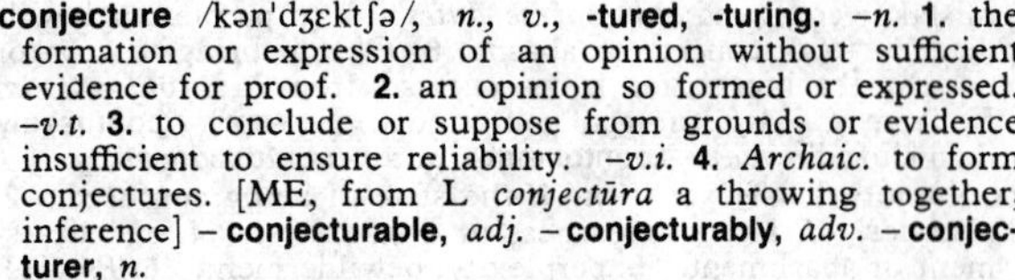

conic section

**conidiophore** /koʊˈnɪdiəfɔ/, *n.* (in fungi) a special stalk or branch of the mycelium, bearing conidia. [*conidio-* (combining form of CONIDIUM) + -PHORE]

**conidium** /koʊˈnɪdiəm/, *n., pl.* **-nidia** /-ˈnɪdiə/. (in fungi) an asexual spore formed by abstriction at the top of a hyphal branch, usu. thin-walled and windborne. [NL, from Gk *kónis* dust + diminutive *-ium*] – **conidial, conidian,** *adj.*

**conifer** /ˈkɒnəfə, ˈkoʊ-/, *n.* any of the (mostly evergreen) trees and shrubs producing naked seeds, usu. on cones, such as pine, spruce, and fir, constituting the gymnospermous order or group Coniferales or Coniferae. [L: cone-bearing]

**coniferous** /kəˈnɪfərəs, kɒ-/, *adj.* belonging or pertaining to the conifers.

**coniform** /ˈkoʊnəfɔm/, *adj.* cone-shaped.

**coniine** /ˈkoʊniin, -ən, -nin/, *n.* a highly poisonous volatile alkaloid, $C_3H_7C_5H_9NH$, constituting the active principle of the poison hemlock. Also, **conin** /ˈkoʊnən/, **conine** /ˈkoʊnin, -nən/. [CONI(UM) + -INE[2]]

**conium** /ˈkoʊniəm/, *n.* **1.** a plant of the umbelliferous genus *Conium*, esp. the poison hemlock, *Conium maculatum.* **2.** its extract as a drug. [L, from Gk *kṓneion* hemlock]

**conj.,** **1.** conjugation. **2.** conjunction. **3.** conjunctive.

**conjectural** /kənˈdʒɛktʃərəl/, *adj.* **1.** of, of the nature of, or involving conjecture; problematical. **2.** given to making conjectures. – **conjecturally,** *adv.*

**conjecture** /kənˈdʒɛktʃə/, *n., v.,* **-tured, -turing.** *–n.* **1.** the formation or expression of an opinion without sufficient evidence for proof. **2.** an opinion so formed or expressed. *–v.t.* **3.** to conclude or suppose from grounds or evidence insufficient to ensure reliability. *–v.i.* **4.** *Archaic.* to form conjectures. [ME, from L *conjectūra* a throwing together, inference] – **conjecturable,** *adj.* – **conjecturably,** *adv.* – **conjecturer,** *n.*

**conjoin** /kənˈdʒɔɪn/, *v.t.* **1.** to join together; unite; combine; associate. *–v.i.* **2.** to become joined or united. [ME *conjoigne(n)*, from F *conjoign-*, stem of *conjoindre,* from L *conjungere* join together] – **conjoiner,** *n.*

**conjoint** /kənˈdʒɔɪnt/, *adj.* **1.** joined together; united; combined; associated. **2.** pertaining to or formed by two or more in combination; joint. [F, pp. of *conjoindre,* from L *conjungere* join together] – **conjointly,** *adv.*

**conjug.,** conjugation.

**conjugal** /ˈkɒndʒəgəl, -dʒu-/, *adj.* concerning husband and wife; marital. [L *conjugālis,* from *conjunx* husband or wife] – **conjugality** /kɒndʒəˈgæləti, -dʒu-/, *n.* – **conjugally,** *adv.*

**conjugate** /ˈkɒndʒəgeɪt/, *v.,* **-gated, -gating;** /ˈkɒndʒəgət, -geɪt/, *adj., n.* *–v.t.* **1.** *Gram.* **a.** to inflect (a verb). **b.** to recite or display all, or some subset of, the inflected forms of (a verb), in a fixed order: *conjugate the present tense verb 'be' as I am, you are, he is, we are, you are, they are.* **2.** *Obs.* to join together, esp. in marriage. *–v.i.* **3.** *Biol.* to unite temporarily. **4.** *Gram.* to be characterised by conjugation: *the Latin verb 'esse' does not conjugate in the passive voice.* *–adj.* **5.** joined together, esp. in a pair or pairs; coupled. **6.** (of words) having a common derivation. **7.** *U.S.* (of two leaves in a book) forming one sheet. **8.** *Maths.* (of two points, lines, etc.) so related as to be interchangeable in the enunciation of certain properties. **9.** *Optics.* (of two points on either side of a lens) so placed that an object placed at either will produce an image at the other. *–n.* **10.** one of a group of conjugate words. **11.** a conjugate number or axis. [L *conjugātus,* pp., joined together, yoked] – **conjugative,** *adj.*

**conjugated bonds** /ˌkɒndʒəgeɪtəd ˈbɒndz/, *n.pl.* a system of chemical bonding where two or more multiple bonds are separated by a single bond, as in butadiene, $CH_2{=}CH{-}CH{=}CH_2$.

**conjugation** /kɒndʒəˈgeɪʃən/, *n.* **1.** *Gram.* **a.** the inflection of verbs. **b.** the whole set of inflected forms of a verb, or the recital or display thereof in a fixed order: *the conjugation of the Latin verb 'amo' begins amō, amas, amat.* **c.** a class of verbs having similar sets of inflected forms, as the Latin *second conjugation.* **2.** the act of joining. **3.** the state of being joined together; union; conjunction. **4.** *Biol.* **a.** the sexual process in ciliate protozoans in which two animals adhere and exchange nuclear material through a temporary area of fusion. **b.** the temporary union or fusion of two cells or individuals, as in certain plants. **5.** *Chem.* alternation of single and multiple bonds in molecules, as $CH_2{=}CH{-}CH{=}CH_2$, which leads to electron delocalisation in the molecule. – **conjugational,** *adj.* – **conjugationally,** *adv.*

**conjunct** /kənˈdʒʌŋkt, ˈkɒndʒʌŋkt/, *adj.* **1.** conjoined; associate. **2.** formed by conjunction. **3.** *Gram.* **a.** occurring only in combination with an immediately preceding or following form of a particular class, and constituting with this form a single phonetic unit, as *'ll* in English *he'll,* and *n't* in *isn't.* **b.** (of a pronoun) having enclitic or proclitic form and occurring with a verb, as French *me, le, se.* **c.** pertaining to a word so characterised. [late ME, from L *conjunctus,* pp., joined together] – **conjunctly,** *adv.*

**conjunction** /kənˈdʒʌŋkʃən/, *n.* **1.** the act of conjoining; combination. **2.** the state of being conjoined; union; association. **3.** a combination of events or circumstances. **4.** *Gram.* **a.** (in some languages) one of the major form classes, or 'parts of speech', comprising words used to link together words, phrases, clauses, or sentences. **b.** such a word, as English *and* or *but.* **c.** any form of similar function or meaning. **5.** *Astron.* **a.** the meeting of heavenly bodies in the same longitude or right ascension. **b.** the situation of two or more heavenly bodies when their longitudes are the same. – **conjunctional,** *adj.* – **conjunctionally,** *adv.*

**conjunctiva** /ˌkɒndʒʌŋkˈtaɪvə/, *n., pl.* **-vas, -vae** /-vi/. the mucous membrane which lines the inner surface of the eyelids and is reflected over the forepart of the sclera and the cornea. [NL, short for *membrāna conjunctīva* membrane serving to connect] – **conjunctival,** *adj.*

**conjunctive** /kənˈdʒʌŋktɪv/, *adj.* **1.** connective. **2.** conjoined; joint. **3.** *Gram.* **a.** (of a pronoun) conjunctive. **b.** of the nature of a conjunction. *–n.* **4.** *Gram.* a conjunctive word; a conjunction. – **conjunctively,** *adv.*

**conjunctivitis** /kəndʒʌŋktəˈvaɪtəs/, *n.* inflammation of the conjunctiva. [NL. See CONJUNCTIVA, -ITIS]

**conjuncture** /kənˈdʒʌŋktʃə/, *n.* **1.** a combination of circumstances or affairs; a particular state of affairs. **2.** a critical state of affairs; a crisis. **3.** *Obs.* conjunction; meeting. [CON- + JUNCTURE]

**conjuration** /kɒndʒəˈreɪʃən/, *n.* **1.** the act of calling on or invoking by a sacred name. **2.** an incantation; a spell or charm. **3.** supernatural accomplishment by invocation or spell. **4.** the practice of legerdemain. **5.** *Archaic.* supplication; solemn entreaty. **6.** *Obs.* a conspiracy.

**conjure** /ˈkʌndʒə/ *for defs 1-3, 6-9, 11;* /kənˈdʒʊə/ *for defs 4, 5, 10,* *v.,* **-jured, -juring.** *–v.t.* **1.** to call upon or command (a devil or spirit) by invocation or spell. **2.** to affect or influence by, or as by, invocation or spell. **3.** to effect, produce, bring, etc., by, or as by, magic. **4.** to appeal to solemnly or earnestly. **5.** to charge solemnly. **6. conjure up, a.** to call, raise up, or bring into existence by magic. **b.** to bring to mind or recall. *–v.i.* **7.** to call upon or command a devil or spirit by invocation or spell. **8.** to practise magic. **9.** to practise legerdemain. **10.** *Obs.* to conspire. **11. to conjure with,** likely to be influential if quoted; effective: *a name to conjure with.* [ME *conjure(n),* from OF *conjurer,* from L *conjūrāre* swear together]

**conjurer** /ˈkʌndʒərə/ *for defs 1 and 2;* /kənˈdʒʊərə/ *for defs 3 and 4,* *n.* **1.** one who conjures spirits or practises magic; magician. **2.** one who practises legerdemain; juggler. **3.** one who solemnly charges or entreats. **4.** one who is bound with others by oath. Also, **conjuror.**

**conk** /kɒŋk/, *n. Colloq.* **1.** a nose. **2.** a blow; a violent stroke. *–v.t.* **3.** *Colloq.* to hit or strike, esp. on the head. *–v.i.* **4. conk out, a.** *Colloq.* (of an engine) to break down. **b.** *Colloq.* to faint; collapse. **c.** *Colloq.* to die. [probably alteration of CONCH[1]]

**conker** /ˈkɒŋkə/, *n. Brit.* **1.** *Colloq.* a horse chestnut. **2.** (*pl.*) a children's game in which one child swings a conker, which has been threaded on a string, in an attempt to break his opponent's conker. [Brit. d.: snail shell (with which the game was originally played)]

**con man** /ˈkɒn mæn/, *n. Colloq.* →**confidence man.**

**con moto** /kɒn ˈmoʊtoʊ/, *adv.* (a musical direction) with movement. [It.]

**conn** /kɒn/, *v.t., n.* →**con**[3].

**connate** /ˈkɒneɪt/, *adj.* **1.** existing in a person or thing from birth or origin; inborn; congenital. **2.** associated in birth or origin. **3.** allied or agreeing in nature; cognate. **4.** *Biol.* congenitally or firmly united into one body. [LL *connātus,* pp., born at the same time] – **connately,** *adv.* – **connation** /kɒˈneɪʃən/, *n.*

**connate water** /– ˈwɔtə/, *n.* water trapped in the interstices of a sedimentary rock at the time the sediment was deposited.

**connatural** /kəˈnætʃərəl/, *adj.* **1.** belonging to a person or thing by nature or from birth or origin. **2.** of the same or like nature. [ML *connātūrālis*] – **connaturally,** *adv.*

**connect** /kəˈnɛkt/, *v.t.* **1.** to bind or fasten together; join or unite; link. **2.** to establish communication between; put in communication (fol. by *with*). **3.** to associate or attach: *the pleasures connected with music.* **4.** to associate mentally. *–v.i.* **5.** to become connected; join or unite. **6.** (of trains, buses, etc.) to run so as to make connections (*with*). **7.** *Baseball, Tennis, etc., Colloq.* to make contact with or hit the ball. [L *connectere,* var. of *cōnectere* join, tie] – **connectedly,** *adv.* – **connecter, connector,** *n.*

**connecting rod** /kəˈnɛktɪŋ rɒd/, *n.* **1.** any rod or bar connecting moveable parts. **2.** the rod connecting the crosshead to the crank in a steam-engine. **3.** the rod connecting the piston to the crankshaft in an internal-combustion engine.

**connection** /kəˈnɛkʃən/, *n.* **1.** the act of connecting. **2.** the state of being connected. **3.** anything that connects; a connecting part. **4.** a joint between two electrical conductors. **5.** association; relationship. **6.** a circle of friends or associates, or a member of such a circle. **7.** union in due order or sequence of words or ideas. **8.** contextual relation. **9.** the meeting of means of transport for transfer of passengers without delay. **10.** a person related to another or others, esp. by marriage or distant consanguinity. **11.** a body of persons connected as by political or religious ties. **12.** a religious denomination. **13.** a channel of communication. **14.** sexual intercourse. **15.** (*usu. pl.*) influential friends, associates, relatives, etc. **16.** (*pl.*) *Horseracing, etc.* the owners of a horse or dog, or the people closely associated with it as the trainer, jockey, etc. Also, **connexion.** [L *connexio*] – **connectional,** *adj.*

**connective** /kəˈnɛktɪv/, *adj.* **1.** serving or tending to connect. *–n.* **2.** that which connects. **3.** *Gram.* a word used to connect words, phrases, clauses, and sentences, as a conjunction. **4.** *Bot.* the tissue joining the two cells of the anther. – **connectively,** *adv.* – **connectivity** /ˌkɒnɛkˈtɪvəti/, *n.*

**connective tissue** /– ˈtɪʃu/, *n.* a tissue, usu. of mesoblastic origin, which connects, supports, or surrounds other tissues, organs, etc., and occurs in various forms throughout the body.

**connie** /ˈkɒni/, *n. Colloq.* **1.** a conductress, usu. on trams. **2.** a type of marble (def. 7).

**conning tower** /ˈkɒnɪŋ taʊə/, *n.* **1.** the superstructure on a submarine which acts as observation tower and main entrance to the interior. **2.** the low, dome-shaped, armoured pilot house of a warship, used esp. during battle.

**conniption** /kəˈnɪpʃən/, *n.* (*oft. pl.*) *Colloq.* a fit of hysteria or anger.

**connivance** /kəˈnaɪvəns/, *n.* **1.** the act of conniving. **2.** *Law.* intentional acquiescence by the petitioner in the adultery of the respondent. Also, **connivence.**

**connive** /kəˈnaɪv/, *v.i.* **-nived, -niving.** **1.** to avoid noticing that which one should oppose or condemn but secretly approves; give aid to wrongdoing, etc., by forbearing to act or speak; be secretly accessory (fol. by *at*): *conniving at their escape.* **2.** to cooperate secretly (fol. by *with*). [L *connīvēre,* var. of *cōnīvēre* shut the eyes] – **conniver,** *n.*

**connivent** /kəˈnaɪvənt/, *adj. Bot., Zool.* lying or standing side by side but not fused. [L *connīvens* winking at]

**connoisseur** /kɒnəˈsɜ/, *n.* one competent to pass critical judgments in an art, esp. one of the fine arts, or in matters of taste. [F (now *connaisseur*), from *connaître,* older *connoître,* from L *cognoscere* come to know]

**connotation** /kɒnəˈteɪʃən/, *n.* **1.** the act or fact of connoting. **2.** that which is connoted; secondary implied or associated meanings (as distinguished from *denotation*): *the word 'bum' has connotations of vulgarity.* **3.** *Logic.* the set of attributes constituting the meaning of a term, and thus determining the range of objects to which that term may be applied; comprehension; intension. – **connotative** /ˈkɒnəteɪtɪv/, *adj.* – **connotatively** /ˈkɒnəteɪtɪvli/, *adv.*

**connote** /kəˈnoʊt/, *v.t.,* **-noted, -noting.** **1.** to denote secondarily; signify in addition to the primary meaning; imply. **2.** to involve as a condition or accompaniment. [ML *connotāre* mark with, from L *con-* CON- + *notāre* mark. See NOTE, *v.*]

**connubial** /kəˈnjubiəl/, *adj.* of marriage or wedlock; matrimonial; conjugal. [L *connūbiālis,* from *connūbium* marriage] – **connubiality** /kənjubiˈæləti/, *n.* – **connubially,** *adv.*

**conoid** /ˈkoʊnɔɪd/, *adj.* **1.** Also, **conoidal.** resembling or approaching a cone in shape. *–n.* **2.** a geometrical solid formed by the revolution of a conic section about one of its axes. [Gk *kōnoeidḗs* cone-shaped]

**conquer** /ˈkɒŋkə/, *v.t.* **1.** to acquire by force of arms; win in war: *to conquer territories.* **2.** to overcome by force; subdue: *to conquer an enemy.* **3.** to gain or obtain by effort. **4.** to gain the victory over; surmount. *–v.i.* **5.** to make conquests; gain the victory. [ME *conquere(n),* from OF *conquerre,* from L *conquaerere, conquīrere* seek for] – **conquerable,** *adj.* – **conqueringly,** *adv.*

**conqueror** /ˈkɒŋkərə/, *n.* one who conquers.

**conquest** /ˈkɒnkwɛst, ˈkɒŋ-/, *n.* **1.** the act of conquering. **2.** captivation, as of favour or affections. **3.** the condition of being conquered; vanquishment. **4.** territory acquired by conquering. **5.** a person whose favour or affections have been captivated. [ME, from OF *conqueste,* fem. collective of *conquest,* pp. of *conquerre* conquer]

**conquian** /ˈkɒŋkiən/, *n.* a card game of the rummy family for two players. [orig. uncert.]

**conquistador** /kɒn'kwɪstədɔ, kɒŋ-/, *n., pl.* **-dors.** one of the Spanish conquerors of Mexico and Peru in the 16th century. [Sp.]

**con rod** /'kɒn rɒd/, *n.* →**connecting rod.**

**cons.,** **1.** consonant. **2.** consulting.

**consanguineous** /kɒnsæŋ'gwɪniəs/, *adj.* related by birth; akin. Also, **consanguine** /kɒn'sæŋgwən/. [L *consanguineus*] – **consanguineously,** *adv.*

**consanguinity** /kɒnsæŋ'gwɪnəti/, *n.* **1.** relationship by blood; kinship. **2.** relationship or affinity.

**conscience** /'kɒnʃəns/, *n.* **1.** the internal recognition of right and wrong as regards one's actions and motives; the faculty which decides upon the moral quality of one's actions and motives, enjoining one to conformity with the moral law. **2.** conscientiousness. **3.** *Obs.* consciousness. **4.** *Obs.* inmost thought. **5. in (all) conscience, a.** in (all) reason and fairness; in truth. **b.** most certainly; assuredly. [ME, from OF, from L *conscientia* joint knowledge] – **conscienceless,** *adj.*

**conscience clause** /'– klɔz/, *n.* a clause or article in an act or law or the like, which relieves persons whose conscientious or religious scruples forbid their compliance with it.

**conscience money** /'– mʌni/, *n.* money paid to relieve the conscience, as for obligations previously evaded.

**conscience-stricken** /'kɒnʃəns-strɪkən/, *adj.* remorseful; disturbed by the knowledge of having acted wrongfully. Also, **conscience-smitten.**

**conscience vote** /'kɒnʃəns voʊt/, *n.* →**free vote.**

**conscientious** /kɒnʃi'ɛnʃəs/, *adj.* controlled by or done according to conscience; scrupulous: *a conscientious judge, conscientious conduct.* – **conscientiously,** *adv.* – **conscientiousness,** *n.*

**conscientious objector** /– əb'dʒɛktə/, *n.* one who on moral or religious grounds, refuses to take part in military service.

**conscionable** /'kɒnʃənəbəl/, *adj.* conformable to conscience; just. – **conscionably,** *adv.*

**conscious** /'kɒnʃəs/, *adj.* **1.** aware of one's own existence, sensations, cognitions, etc.; endowed with consciousness. **2.** inwardly sensible or awake to something: *conscious of one's own faults.* **3.** having the mental faculties awake. **4.** present to consciousness; known to oneself; felt: *conscious guilt.* **5.** aware of what one is doing: *a conscious liar.* **6.** aware of oneself; self-conscious. **7.** deliberate or intentional. **8.** *Obs.* inwardly sensible of wrongdoing. [L *conscius* knowing] – **consciously,** *adv.*

**consciousness** /'kɒnʃəsnəs/, *n.* **1.** the state of being conscious. **2.** inward sensibility of something; knowledge of one's own existence, sensations, cognitions, etc. **3.** the thoughts and feelings, collectively, of an individual, or of an aggregate of people: *the moral consciousness of a nation.* **4.** activity of mental faculties: *to regain consciousness after fainting.* **5. raise one's consciousness,** to raise the level of one's understanding and sensitivity to cultural and social issues.

**consciousness-raising** /'kɒnʃəsnəs-reɪzɪŋ/, *adj.* intended to raise one's consciousness.

**conscribe** /kən'skraɪb/, *v.t.,* **-scribed, -scribing. 1.** to enlist by conscription. **2.** to limit; circumscribe.

**conscript** /'kɒnskrɪpt/, *adj., n.;* /kən'skrɪpt/, *v.* *–adj.* **1.** enrolled or formed by conscription: *a conscript soldier or army.* *–n.* **2.** a recruit obtained by conscription. *–v.t.* **3.** to enrol compulsorily for service in the armed forces. [L *conscriptus,* pp., enrolled]

**conscription** /kən'skrɪpʃən/, *n.* compulsory enrolment of men for service in the armed forces.

**consecrate** /'kɒnsəkreɪt/, *v.,* **-crated, -crating,** *adj.* *–v.t.* **1.** to make or declare sacred; set apart or dedicated to the service of a deity. **2. a.** to induct (a person) into high office by means of a religious rite. **b.** to ordain (bishops, etc.). **3.** to devote or dedicate to some purpose: *a life consecrated to science.* **4.** to make an object of veneration: *a custom consecrated by time.* *–adj.* **5.** *Archaic.* consecrated; sacred. [ME, from L *consēcrātus,* pp., dedicated] – **consecrator,** *n.* – **consecratory** /'kɒnsəˌkreɪtəri/, *adj.*

**consecration** /kɒnsə'kreɪʃən/, *n.* **1.** the act of consecrating; dedication to the service and worship of a deity. **2.** the act of giving the sacramental character to the Eucharistic elements of bread and wine. **3.** ordination to a sacred office.

**consecution** /kɒnsə'kjuʃən/, *n.* **1.** succession; sequence. **2.** logical sequence; inference. [L *consecūtio,* from *consequī* follow after]

**consecutive** /kən'sɛkjətɪv/, *adj.* **1.** following one another in uninterrupted succession; uninterrupted in course or succession; successive. **2.** marked by logical sequence. **3.** *Gram.* expressing consequence or result: *a consecutive clause.* **4.** *Music.* of or pertaining to a succession of similar harmonic intervals. *–n.* **5.** (*pl.*) *Music.* a succession of similar harmonic intervals. [F *consécutif,* from L *consecūtus,* pp., having followed after] – **consecutively,** *adv.* – **consecutiveness,** *n.*

**consensual** /kən'sɛnʃuəl/, *adj.* **1.** formed or existing by mere consent: *a consensual contract.* **2.** *Physiol.* (of an action) involuntarily correlative with a voluntary action, as the contraction of the iris when the eye is opened. [L *consensu(s)* agreement + -AL[1]] – **consensually,** *adv.*

**consensus** /kən'sɛnsəs/, *n.* **1.** general agreement or concord. **2.** majority of opinion. [L: agreement]

**consent** /kən'sɛnt/, *v.i.* **1.** to give assent; agree; comply or yield (fol. by *to* or infinitive). **2.** *Obs.* to agree in sentiment, opinion, etc.; be in harmony. *–n.* **3.** assent; acquiescence; permission; compliance. **4.** agreement in sentiment, opinion, a course of action, etc.: *by common consent.* **5.** *Archaic.* accord; concord; harmony. **6. age of consent,** the age at which consent to certain acts, esp. sexual intercourse and marriage, is valid in law. [ME *consente(n),* from OF from L *consentīre* feel together] – **consenter,** *n.* – **consentingly,** *adv.*

**consent agreement** /'– əgrimənt/, *n.* an arrangement between employers and employees mutually agreed upon and ratified by an arbitration commission.

**consentaneous** /kɒnsɛn'teɪniəs/, *adj.* **1.** agreeing or accordant. **2.** done by common consent; unanimous. [L *consentāneus* agreeing, fit] – **consentaneously,** *adv.* – **consentaneity** /kɒnsɛntə'niəti/, **consentaneousness,** *n.*

**consent award** /kən'sɛnt əwɔd/, *n.* an award of an industrial tribunal which results from agreement of the parties to the award rather than the findings of the tribunal.

**consentient** /kən'sɛnʃənt/, *adj.* **1.** agreeing; accordant. **2.** acting in agreement or harmony. **3.** unanimous, as an opinion. – **consentience,** *n.*

**consequence** /'kɒnsəkwəns/, *n.* **1.** the act or fact of following as an effect or result upon something antecedent. **2.** that which so follows; an effect or result. **3. in consequence,** as a result. **4.** the conclusion of an argument or inference. **5.** importance or significance: *a matter of no consequence.* **6.** importance in rank or position; distinction.

**consequences** /'kɒnsəkwənsəz/, *n.pl., usu. construed as sing.* a parlour game in which each participant contributes to a written story without knowing the rest of it, the object being to produce the utmost absurdity.

**consequent** /'kɒnsəkwənt/, *adj.* **1.** following as an effect or result; resulting. **2.** following as a logical conclusion. **3.** logically consistent. **4.** *Geol.* (of a river) having a course or direction dependent on, or controlled by, the geological structure or by the form and slope of the surface. *–n.* **5.** anything that follows upon something else, with or without implication of causal relation. **6.** *Logic.* the second member of a conditional or hypothetical proposition, as the proposition expressed by the second clause in *If Jones is ill, he will remain indoors.* **7.** *Arith.* the second term of a ratio. [L *consequens,* ppr.]

**consequential** /kɒnsə'kwɛnʃəl/, *adj.* **1.** of the nature of a consequence; following as an effect or result, or as a logical conclusion or inference; consequent; resultant. **2.** self-important; pompous. **3.** logically consistent. **4.** of consequence or importance. – **consequentiality** /ˌkɒnsəkwɛnʃi'æləti/, **consequentialness,** *n.* – **consequentially,** *adv.*

**consequential loss insurance,** *n.* an insurance policy indemnifying against contingent results of accident, esp. the cost of the hire of a car to replace one under repair or the cost of alternative accommodation after a fire.

**consequently** /'kɒnsəkwəntli/, *adv.* by way of consequence; in consequence of something; therefore.

**conservable** /kən'sɜvəbəl/, *adj.* capable of being conserved; preservable.

**conservancy** /kən'sɜvənsi/, *n., pl.* **-cies. 1.** conservation of natural resources. **2.** *Brit.* a court or board with authority to preserve the fisheries, banks, etc., of a river.

**conservation** /kɒnsə'veɪʃən/, *n.* **1.** the act of conserving; preservation, esp. of natural resources. **2.** official supervision of rivers, forests, etc. [L *conservātio*] – **conservational,** *adj.*

**conservationist** /kɒnsə'veɪʃənəst/, *n.* one who advocates or promotes conservation, esp. of the natural resources of a country.

**conservation of physical quantity,** *n. Physics.* the principle that the physical quantity remains constant during a process, as conservation of change, conservation of mass and energy, conservation of momentum.

**conservatism** /kɒn'sɜvətɪzəm/, *n.* **1.** the disposition to preserve what is established; opposition to innovation or change. **2.** the principles and practices of political conservatives of right-wing parties.

**conservative** /kən'sɜvətɪv/, *adj.* **1.** disposed to preserve existing conditions, institutions, etc. **2.** cautious or moderate: *a conservative estimate.* **3.** traditional in style or manner. **4.** having the power or tendency to conserve; preservative. *–n.* **5.** a person of conservative principles. **6.** *Physics.* of or pertaining to a force which acts on a system of particles and which can be derived from a potential energy. – **conservatively,** *adv.* – **conservativeness,** *n.*

**conservatoire** /kən'sɜvətwa/, *n.* →**conservatorium.**

**conservator** /'kɒnsəveɪtə, kən'sɜvətə/, *n.* **1.** one who conserves or preserves; a preserver. **2.** *Law.* a guardian; a custodian. **3.** one who has duties in conservancy (def. 2).

**conservatorium** /kənsɜvə'tɔriəm/, *n.* a place for instruction in music and theatrical arts; a school of music. Also, **con, conservatoire.**

**conservatory** /kən'sɜvətri/, *n., pl.* **-tries,** *adj. –n.* **1.** a glass-covered house or room into which plants in bloom are brought from the greenhouse. **2.** *U.S.* →**conservatorium. 3.** *Obs.* a place where things are preserved. *–adj.* **4.** serving or adapted to conserve; preservative.

**conserve** /kən'sɜv/, *v.,* **served, -serving;** /'kɒnsɜv, kən'sɜv/, *n. –v.t.* **1.** to keep in a safe or sound state; preserve from loss, decay, waste, or injury; keep unimpaired. **2.** *Obs.* to preserve, as fruit, with sugar, etc. *–n.* **3.** (*oft. pl.*) a mixture of several fruits, cooked, with sugar, to a jamlike consistency. [ME, from L *conservāre* preserve] – **conserver,** *n.*

**consgt.,** consignment.

**conshie** /'kɒnʃi/, *adj., n. Colloq.* →**conchie.** Also, **conshy.**

**consider** /kən'sɪdə/, *v.t.* **1.** to contemplate mentally; meditate or reflect on. **2.** to regard as or deem to be: *I consider the examination is justified.* **3.** to think; suppose. **4.** to make allowance for. **5.** to pay attention to; regard: *he never considers others.* **6.** to regard with consideration or respect; hold in honour; respect. **7.** to think about (a position, purchase, etc.) with a view to accepting or buying. **8.** to view attentively, or scrutinise. *–v.i.* **9.** to think deliberately or carefully; reflect. [ME *considere(n),* from L *consīderāre* examine closely]

**considerable** /kən'sɪdrəbəl/, *adj.* **1.** worthy of consideration; important; of distinction. **2.** (of an amount, extent, etc.) worthy of consideration; fairly large or great. – **considerably,** *adv.*

**considerate** /kən'sɪdərət/, *adj.* **1.** showing consideration or regard for another's circumstances, feelings, etc. **2.** marked by consideration or reflection; deliberate. **3.** *Archaic.* given to consideration or reflection; prudent. – **considerately,** *adv.* – **considerateness,** *n.*

**consideration** /kənsɪdə'reɪʃən/, *n.* **1.** the act of considering; meditation or deliberation. **2.** regard or account; something taken, or to be taken, into account. **3.** a thought or reflection. **4.** a recompense for service rendered, etc.; a compensation. **5.** *Law.* in a contract, or other legal transaction, the promise by which some right or benefit accrues to one party, in return for which the party who receives the benefit promises or conveys something to the other. **6.** thoughtful or sympathetic regard or respect; thoughtfulness for others. **7.** importance or consequence. **8.** estimation; esteem. **9. in consideration of, a.** in view of. **b.** in return for. **10. take into consideration,** to consider; take into account. **11. under consideration,** being considered.

**considering** /kən'sɪdərɪŋ/, *prep.* **1.** taking into account; in view of. *–adv.* **2.** with all things considered (used after the statement it modifies). *–conj.* **3.** taking into consideration that: *considering he is so young, he has achieved a great deal.*

**consigliore** /kɒnsɪl'jɔreɪ/, *n.* a legal adviser to a Mafia family. [It.]

**consign** /kən'saɪn/, *v.t.* **1.** to hand over or deliver formally; commit (fol. by *to*). **2.** to transfer to another's custody or charge; entrust. **3.** to set apart, as to a purpose or use; assign. **4. a.** to transmit, as by public carrier, esp. for sale or custody. **b.** to address for such transmission. **5.** *Obs.* to mark with a sign or seal; sign. [F *consigner,* from L *consignāre* furnish or mark with a seal] – **consignable,** *adj.* – **consignation** /kɒnsə'neɪʃən/, *n.*

**consignee** /kɒnsaɪ'ni/, *n.* the person or party to whom merchandise is consigned.

**consignment** /kɒn'saɪnmənt/, *n.* **1.** the act of consigning. **2.** that which is consigned. **3. a.** property sent to an agent for sale, storage, or shipment. **b. on consignment,** (of goods) sent to an agent for sale, title being held by the consignor until they are sold.

**consignor** /kən'saɪnə, ˌkɒnsaɪ'nɔ/, *n.* one who consigns goods, etc. Also, **consigner.**

**consist** /kən'sɪst/, *v.;* /'kɒnsɪst/, *n. –v.i.* **1.** to be made up or composed (fol. by *of*). **2.** to be comprised or contained (fol. by *in*). **3.** to be compatible, consistent, or harmonious (fol. by *with*). *–n.* **4.** *Railways.* the set of wagons in a freight train: *a six car consist.* [L *consistere* place oneself]

**consistency** /kən'sɪstənsi/, *n., pl.* **-cies. 1.** agreement, harmony, or compatibility; agreement among themselves of the parts of a complex thing. **2.** material coherence with retention of form; solidity or firmness. **3.** degree of density or viscosity: *the consistency of cream.* **4.** constant adherence to the same principles, course, etc. Also, **consistence.**

**consistent** /kən'sɪstənt/, *adj.* **1.** agreeing or accordant; compatible; not self-opposed or self-contradictory. **2.** constantly adhering to the same principles, course, etc. **3.** *Obs.* holding firmly together; cohering. **4.** *Obs.* fixed; firm; solid. – **consistently,** *adv.*

**consistory** /kən'sɪstəri/, *n., pl.* **-ries. 1.** any of various ecclesiastical councils or tribunals. **2.** the place where it meets. **3.** the meeting of any such body. [ME *consistorie,* from ONF, from L *consistōrium* place of assembly] – **consistorial** /ˌkɒnsɪs'tɔriəl/, **consistorian,** *adj.*

**consociate** /kən'souʃiət, -ʃət/, *adj., n.;* /kən'souʃieɪt/, *v.i.* **-ated, -ating.** →**associate.** [L *consociātus,* pp.]

**consociation** /kənsousi'eɪʃən/, *n.* **1.** the act or fact of associating together. **2.** fellowship; companionship. **3.** a confederation of churches or religious societies.

**consol** /'kɒnsɒl/, *n.* a long-range radio aid to navigation, the emissions of which, by means of their radio frequency modulation characteristics, enable bearings to be determined.

**consol.,** consolidated.

**consolation** /kɒnsə'leɪʃən/, *n.* **1.** the act of consoling. **2.** the state of being consoled. **3.** one who or that which consoles. [ME, from L *consōlātio*]

**consolation prize** /'– praɪz/, *n.* a prize, usu. of little value, given to the loser, or runner-up, in a contest, etc.

**consolatory** /kən'sɒlətəri, -tri/, *adj.* affording consolation; consoling.

**console**[1] /kən'soul/, *v.t.,* **-soled, -soling.** to alleviate the grief or sorrow of; comfort; solace; cheer. [L *consōlāri* comfort] – **consolable,** *adj.* – **consoler,** *n.* – **consolingly,** *adv.*

**console**[2] /'kɒnsoul/, *n.* **1.** a desk-like structure containing the keyboards, pedals, etc., of an organ, from which the organ is played. **2.** a desk on which are mounted the controls of an electrical or electronic system. **3.** a floor-model radio, television, or radiogram cabinet. **4.** *Computers.* a computer operator's control panel or terminal. **5.** →**console table. 6.** *Archit.* an ornamental corbel or projection, as for supporting a cornice, bust, etc. [F; orig. uncert.]

**console table** /'– teɪbəl/, *n.* **1.** a table supported by consoles or brackets fixed to a wall. **2.** a table, often with bracket-like legs, designed to fit against a wall.

**consolidate** /kən'sɒlədeɪt/, *v.,* **-dated, -dating,** *adj. –v.t.* **1.** to make solid or firm; solidify; strengthen: *to consolidate gains.* **2.** to strengthen by rearranging the position of ground combat troops after a successful attack. **3.** to bring together compactly in one mass or connected whole; unite; combine: *to consolidate two companies.* *–v.i.* **4.** to unite or combine. **5.** to become solid or firm. *–adj.* **6.** *Archaic.* consolidated. [L *consolidātus,* pp., made solid] – **consolidator,** *n.*

**consolidated fund** /kɒnˌsɒlədeɪtəd 'fʌnd/, *n. Brit.* a fund made up by consolidating the yield of various taxes and other sources of public revenue, from which are paid the interest on the national debt, grants to the royal family, etc.

**consolidated revenue** /– 'rɛvənju/, *n.* the funds which a government treasury receives by way of taxes, duties, etc.

**consolidated school** /'– skul/, *n.* →**central school.**

**consolidation** /kənsɒlə'deɪʃən/, *n.* **1.** the act of consolidating; unification. **2.** the state of being consolidated; combination. **3.** a consolidated whole. **4.** *Law.* a statutory combination of two or more previous enactments.

**consols** /'kɒnsɒlz, kən'sɒlz/, *n.pl.* the funded government securities of Britain, which originated in the consolidation in 1751 of various public securities, chiefly in the form of annuities, into a single debt issue without maturity. [short for *consolidated annuities*]

**consomme** /'kɒnsəmeɪ, kən'sɒmeɪ/, *n.* a clear soup made from a concentrated clarified meat or vegetable stock. Also, **consommé.** [F, properly pp. of *consommer,* from L *consummāre* finish]

**consonance** /'kɒnsənəns/, *n.* **1.** accord or agreement. **2.** correspondence of sounds; harmony of sounds. **3.** *Music.* a simultaneous combination of notes conventionally accepted as being in a state of repose (opposite of *dissonance*). Also, **consonancy.**

**consonant** /'kɒnsənənt/, *n.* **1.** *Phonet.* **a.** (as a member of a syllable) a sound subordinated to another sound that has greater sonority; *w* and *g* in *wig* are subordinate to *i,* the sound of greatest sonority in the syllable, and by virtue of this subordination they are called consonants. **b.** (as a member of an articulation class) a sound made with more or less obstruction of the breath stream in its passage outwards, as the *l, s,* and *t* of *list,* each an example of a consonantal subclass: *l* is a *sonorant* (relatively slight obstruction), *s* a *fricative* (relatively great obstruction), and *t* a *stop* (complete obstruction). **2.** a letter which usu. represents a consonant sound. *–adj.* **3.** in agreement; agreeable or accordant; consistent (fol. by *to* or *with*). **4.** corresponding in sound, as words. **5.** harmonious, as sounds. **6.** *Music.* constituting a consonance. **7.** →**consonantal.** [ME, from L *consonans* sounding together] – **consonantly,** *adv.*

**consonantal** /kɒnsə'næntl/, *adj.* **1.** of, or of the nature of, a consonant. **2.** marked by consonant sounds.

**consort** /'kɒnsɔt/, *n.;* /kən'sɔt/, *v.* *–n.* **1.** a husband or wife; a spouse, esp. of a reigning monarch. **2.** one vessel or ship accompanying another. **3.** a group of instruments or voices in harmony. **4.** *Obs.* a companion or partner. **5.** *Obs.* company or association. *–v.i.* **6.** to associate; keep company. **7.** to agree or harmonise. *–v.t.* **8.** to associate. **9.** *Obs.* to accompany; espouse. **10.** *Obs.* to sound in harmony. [late ME, from F: mate, from L *consors* partner, sharer, orig. adj., sharing]

**consorting squad** /kən'sɔtɪŋ skwɒd/, *n.* the section of a police force dealing with known offenders.

**consortium** /kən'sɔtiəm, -ʃiəm/, *n., pl.* **-tia** /-tiə, -ʃə/. **1.** a combination of financial institutions, capitalists, etc., for carrying into effect some financial operation requiring large resources of capital. **2.** an association or union. **3.** *Law.* right of one spouse to the comfort, services and society of the other. [L: partnership]

**conspectus** /kən'spɛktəs/, *n.* **1.** a general or comprehensive view. **2.** a digest; a résumé. [L: survey]

**conspicuous** /kən'spɪkjuəs/, *adj.* **1.** easy to be seen. **2.** readily attracting the attention. [L *conspicuus* visible, striking] – **conspicuously,** *adv.* – **conspicuousness,** *n.*

**conspiracy** /kən'spɪrəsi/, *n., pl.* **-cies. 1.** the act of conspiring. **2.** a combination of persons for an evil or unlawful purpose; a plot. **3.** *Law.* an agreement by two or more persons to commit a crime, fraud, or other wrongful act. **4.** any concurrence in action; combination in bringing about a given result. [CONSPIR(E) + -ACY] – **conspirator,** *n.* – **conspiratress,** *n. fem.*

**conspire** /kən'spaɪə/, *v.,* **-spired, -spiring.** *–v.i.* **1.** to agree together, esp. secretly, to do something reprehensible or illegal; combine for an evil or unlawful purpose. **2.** to act in combination; contribute jointly to a result. *–v.t.* **3.** to plot (something evil or unlawful). [ME *conspire(n),* from L *conspīrāre,* lit., breathe together] – **conspirer,** *n.* – **conspiringly,** *adv.*

**con spirito** /kɒn 'spɪrətoʊ/, *adv.* (a musical direction) with spirit. [It.]

**const.,** constant.

**constable** /'kʌnstəbəl/, *n.* **1.** a police officer ranking below sergeant, the lowest in rank in a police force. **2.** the rank. **3.** an officer of high rank in medieval monarchies, usu. the commander of all armed forces, particularly in the absence of the ruler. **4.** the keeper or governor of a royal fortress or castle. [ME *conestable,* from OF, from LL *comes stabulī* count of the stable, master of the horse] – **constableship,** *n.*

**constabulary** /kən'stæbjələri/, *n., pl.* **-ries,** *adj.* *–n.* **1.** the body of constables of a district or locality. **2.** a body of officers of the peace organised on a military basis. **3.** *Colloq.* the police. *–adj.* **4.** pertaining to constables or their duties. [ML *constabulāria*]

**constancy** /'kɒnstənsi/, *n.* **1.** the quality of being constant; firmness or fortitude; faithfulness to a person or cause. **2.** invariability, uniformity, or regularity. [L *constantia* firmness]

**constant** /'kɒnstənt/, *adj.* **1.** invariable; uniform; always present. **2.** continuing without intermission. **3.** regularly recurrent; continual; persistent. **4.** steadfast, as in attachment; faithful. **5.** standing firm in mind or purpose; resolute. **6.** *Obs.* certain or confident. *–n.* **7.** something constant, invariable, or unchanging. **8.** *Physics.* **a.** a numerical quantity expressing a relation or value that remains unchanged under certain conditions. **b.** →**fundamental constant. 9.** *Maths.* a quantity assumed to be unchanged throughout a given discussion. [ME, from L *constans,* ppr., standing firm] – **constantly,** *adv.*

**constantan** /kɒn'stæntən/, *n. Metall.* a group of copper-nickel alloys, 45 to 60 per cent copper with minor amounts of iron and manganese, and characterised by relatively constant electrical resistivity irrespective of temperature; used in resistors and thermocouples. [CONSTANT + -AN]

**constellate** /'kɒnstəleɪt/, *v.,* **-lated, -lating.** *–v.i.* **1.** to cluster together as stars in a constellation. *–v.t.* **2.** to cause to form into a constellation.

**constellation** /kɒnstə'leɪʃən/, *n.* **1.** *Astron.* **a.** any of various groups of stars to which definite names have been given, as the Southern Cross. **b.** a division of the heavens occupied by such a group. **2.** *Astrol.* **a.** the grouping or relative position of the stars as supposed to influence events, esp. at a person's birth. **b.** *Obs.* character as supposed to be determined by the stars. **3.** any brilliant assemblage. **4.** *Psychol.* a group of emotionally coloured ideas, mostly repressed. [ME, from LL *constellātio* group of stars]

**consternate** /'kɒnstəneɪt/, *v.t.,* **-nated, -nating.** to dismay; terrify (usu. used in the passive).

**consternation** /kɒnstə'neɪʃən/, *n.* amazement and dread tending to confound the faculties. [L *consternātio*]

**constipate** /'kɒnstəpeɪt/, *v.t.,* **-pated, -pating. 1.** to cause constipation in; make costive. **2.** *Obs.* to crowd or pack closely together. [L *constīpātus,* pp., pressed together] – **constipated,** *adj.*

**constipation** /kɒnstə'peɪʃən/, *n.* **1.** a condition of the bowels marked by defective or difficult evacuation. **2.** *Obs.* the act of crowding anything into a smaller compass; condensation.

**constituency** /kɒn'stɪtʃuənsi/, *n., pl.* **-cies. 1.** *Brit.* →**electorate** (defs 1 and 2). **2.** any body of supporters; a clientele.

**constituent** /kɒn'stɪtʃuənt/, *adj.* **1.** serving to make up a thing; component; elementary: *constituent parts.* **2.** having power to frame or alter a political constitution or fundamental law (as distinguished from law-making power): *a constituent assembly.* *–n.* **3.** a constituent element, material, etc.; a component. **4.** a voter, or (loosely) a resident, in a district represented by an elected official. **5.** a person who appoints, by power of attorney, another to act for him. **6.** *Gram.* an element that forms part of a construction. The

**immediate constituents** are the largest parts (usu. two) into which a construction is divisible, any or all of them sometimes further divisible into constituents of their own; the **ultimate constituents** are all the parts of a construction which are not further divisible. The sentence *John's hat looked slightly stained* has the immediate constituents *John's hat* (subject) and *looked slightly stained* (predicate), and the ultimate constituents *John, -'s, hat, look, -ed, slight, -ly, stain* and *ed.* [L *constituens,* ppr., setting up]

**constitute** /ˈkɒnstətjut/, *v.t.*, **-tuted, -tuting. 1.** (of elements, etc.) to compose; form. **2.** to appoint to an office or function; make or create. **3.** to set up or found (an institution, etc.). **4.** to give legal form to (an assembly, court, etc.). **5.** *Obs.* to set up or establish (laws, etc.). **6.** to make up or form elements, material, etc. **7.** *Obs.* to set or place. [L *constitūtus,* pp., set up, established] – **constituter, constitutor,** *n.*

**constitution** /kɒnstəˈtjuʃən/, *n.* **1.** the way in which anything is constituted; make-up or composition: *the physical constitution of the sun.* **2.** the physical character of the body as to strength, health, etc.: *a strong constitution.* **3.** character or condition of mind; disposition; temperament. **4.** the act of constituting; establishment. **5.** the state of being constituted; formation. **6.** any established arrangement or custom. **7.** the system of fundamental principles according to which a nation, state or body politic is governed: *the Australian constitution.* **8.** (*cap.*) a document embodying those principles. [ME, from L *constitūtio*]

**constitutional** /kɒnstəˈtjuʃənəl/, *adj.* **1.** belonging to or inherent in a person's constitution of body or mind: *a constitutional weakness.* **2.** beneficial to, or designed to benefit, the bodily constitution: *a constitutional walk.* **3.** pertaining to the constitution or composition of a thing; essential. **4.** pertaining to, in accordance with, or subject to the constitution of a state, etc.: *a constitutional monarchy.* **5.** having the power of, or existing by virtue of and subject to, a constitution or fundamental organic law: *a constitutional government.* **6.** forming a part of, or authorised by, the constitution or fundamental organic law of a nation or state. –*n.* **7.** a walk or other exercise taken for the benefit of the health. – **constitutionally,** *adv.*

**constitutionalism** /kɒnstəˈtjuʃənəlɪzəm/, *n.* **1.** the principles of constitutional government, or adherence to them. **2.** constitutional rule or authority.

**constitutionalist** /kɒnstəˈtjuʃənələst/, *n.* **1.** an adherent or advocate of constitutionalism, or of an existing constitution. **2.** a student of or writer on a political constitution.

**constitutionality** /ˌkɒnstətjuʃəˈnæləti/, *n.* **1.** the quality of being constitutional. **2.** accordance with the constitution of a state, etc. (as a measure or norm of law-making power).

**constitutive** /ˈkɒnstətʃutɪv/, *adj.* **1.** constituent; making a thing what it is; essential. **2.** having power to establish or appoint to an office. – **constitutively,** *adv.*

**constr.,** **1.** constructed. **2.** construction.

**constrain** /kənˈstreɪn/, *v.t.* **1.** to force, compel, or oblige; bring about by compulsion: *to constrain obedience.* **2.** to confine forcibly, as by bonds. **3.** to repress or restrain. [ME *constreign(en),* from OF *constreindre,* from L *constringere* draw together] – **constrainable,** *adj.* – **constrainer,** *n.*

**constrained** /kənˈstreɪnd/, *adj.* forced; cramped; restrained; stiff or unnatural: *a constrained smile or manner.* – **constrainedly** /kənˈstreɪnədli/, *adv.*

**constraint** /kənˈstreɪnt/, *n.* **1.** confinement or restriction. **2.** repression of natural feelings and impulses. **3.** unnatural restraint in manner, etc.; embarrassment. **4.** something that constrains. **5.** the act of constraining. **6.** the condition of being constrained. [ME *constreinte,* from OF, properly pp. fem. of *constreindre* CONSTRAIN]

**constrict** /kənˈstrɪkt/, *v.t.* **1.** to draw together; compress; cause to contract or shrink. **2.** to restrict, or inhibit. [L *constrictus,* pp., drawn together]

**constriction** /kənˈstrɪkʃən/, *n.* **1.** the act of constricting. **2.** the state of being constricted. **3.** a constricted part. **4.** something that constricts.

**constrictive** /kənˈstrɪktɪv/, *adj.* **1.** constricting, or tending to constrict. **2.** pertaining to constriction.

**constrictor** /kənˈstrɪktə/, *n.* **1.** a snake that crushes its prey in its coils. **2.** *Anat.* a muscle that constricts a hollow part of the body, as the pharynx. **3.** one who or that which constricts. [NL]

**constringe** /kənˈstrɪndʒ/, *v.*, **-stringed, -stringing.** –*v.t.* **1.** to constrict; compress; cause to contract. –*v.i.* **2.** to become close or dense. [L *constringere.* Cf. CONSTRAIN]

**constringent** /kənˈstrɪndʒənt/, *adj.* **1.** constringing. **2.** causing constriction. – **constringency,** *n.*

**construct** /kənˈstrʌkt/, *v.*; /ˈkɒnstrʌkt/, *n.* –*v.t.* **1.** to form by putting together parts; build; frame; devise. **2.** *Gram.* to put together words in syntactical arrangement. **3.** *Geom., etc.* to draw, as a figure, so as to fulfil given conditions. –*n.* **4.** something constructed. **5.** a complex image or idea resulting from a synthesis by the mind. [L *constructus,* pp., constructed, piled or put together] – **constructor, constructer,** *n.*

**construction** /kənˈstrʌkʃən/, *n.* **1.** the act or art of constructing. **2.** the way in which a thing is constructed; structure: *objects of similar construction.* **3.** that which is constructed; a structure. **4.** *Geom.* **a.** the process of drawing a figure so as to fulfil given conditions. **b.** additional parts added to a figure to demonstrate a proof. **5.** *Gram.* **a.** the arrangement of two or more forms in a grammatical unit. Cf. **bound form, free form. b.** a word or phrase consisting of two or more forms arranged in a particular way. **6.** explanation or interpretation, as of a law or a text, or of conduct or the like. **7.** *Law.* the process of ascertaining the meaning of a written document. – **constructional,** *adj.*

**construction area** /ˈ– ˌɛəriə/, *n.* an area in which building, demolition blasting, etc., is under way.

**constructionist** /kənˈstrʌkʃənəst/, *n.* one who construes or interprets, esp. laws or the like.

**constructive** /kənˈstrʌktɪv/, *adj.* **1.** constructing, or tending to construct: *constructive (as opposed to destructive) criticism.* **2.** of, pertaining to, or of the nature of construction; structural. **3.** deduced by construction or interpretation; inferential: *constructive permission.* **4.** *Law.* **a.** not actually existing, but having the same legal effects as one that does: *a constructive possession.* **b.** pertaining to a right, liability or status created by or recognised by the law without regard to intentions of the parties: *constructive notice.* – **constructively,** *adv.* – **constructiveness,** *n.*

**constructivism** /kənˈstrʌktəvɪzəm/, *n.* an art movement originating in Moscow in 1920, whose adherents were concerned with the movement of objects in space, and sought expression by means of mechanical devices and abstract constructions, usu. made from industrial materials.

**construe** /kənˈstru/, *v.*, **-strued, -struing.** –*v.t.* **1.** to show the meaning or intention of; explain; interpret; put a particular interpretation on. **2.** to deduce by construction or interpretation; infer. **3.** to translate, esp. literally. **4.** to explain the syntax of: *in construing the sentence 'He caught a fish' one says 'he' is the subject, 'caught a fish' is the predicate, '(a) fish' is the direct object of the verb 'caught', etc.* **5.** to arrange or combine (words, etc.) syntactically. –*v.i.* **6.** to admit of grammatical analysis or interpretation. –*n.* **7.** the act of construing. [ME *construe(n),* from L *construere* build up, pile together] – **construable,** *adj.* – **construability,** *n.* – **construer,** *n.*

**consubstantial** /kɒnsəbˈstænʃəl/, *adj.* of one and the same substance, essence, or nature. [LL *consubstantiālis,* from L *con-* CON- + *substantia* substance + *-ālis* -AL[1]] – **consubstantiality** /ˌkɒnsəbstænʃiˈæləti/, *n.* – **consubstantially,** *adv.*

**consubstantiate** /kɒnsəbˈstænʃieɪt/, *v.*, **-ated, -ating.** –*v.i.* **1.** to profess the doctrine of consubstantiation. **2.** to become united in one common substance or nature. –*v.t.* **3.** to unite in one common substance or nature. **4.** to regard as so united. [ML *consubstantiātus,* pp., identified in substance]

**consubstantiation** /ˌkɒnsəbstænʃiˈeɪʃən/, *n.* the doctrine that the substance of the body and blood of Christ coexist in and with the substance of bread and wine of the Eucharist, generally accepted in the Lutheran Church.

**consuetude** /ˈkɒnswɪtʃud/, *n.* custom, esp. as having legal force. [ME, from L *consuētūdo* custom]

**consuetudinary** /ˌkɒnswɪˈtjudənri/, *adj.* customary.

**consul** /ˈkɒnsəl/, *n.* **1.** an agent appointed by an independent state to reside in a foreign state and discharge certain administrative duties. **2.** either of the two chief magistrates of the ancient Roman republic. – **consular** /ˈkɒnsjələ/, *adj.* – **consulship,** *n.*

**consular agent** /kɒnsjələr 'eɪdʒənt/, *n.* **1.** a consular officer of one of the lower ranks. **2.** any consular officer.

**consulate** /'kɒnsjələt/, *n.* **1.** the premises officially occupied by a consul. **2.** consulship. **3.** (*oft. cap.*) a government by consuls, as in France from 1799 to 1804. [L *consulātus*]

**consul general** /kɒnsəl 'dʒɛnrəl/, *n.* a consular officer of the highest rank, as one stationed at a place of considerable commercial importance.

**consult** /kən'sʌlt/, *v.t.* **1.** to seek counsel from; ask advice of. **2.** to refer to for information. **3.** to have regard for (a person's interest, convenience, etc.) in making plans. *–v.i.* **4.** to consider or deliberate; take counsel; confer (fol. by *with*). [L *consultāre,* frequentative of *consulere* deliberate, take counsel. Cf. COUNSEL, *n.*, CONSUL] – **consultable,** *adj.* – **consulter,** *n.*

**consultant** /kən'sʌltənt/, *n.* **1.** one who consults. **2.** one who gives professional or expert advice. **3.** *Med.* a medical or surgical specialist.

**consultation** /ˌkɒnsəl'teɪʃən/, *n.* **1.** the act of consulting; conference. **2.** a meeting for deliberation. **3.** an application for advice to one engaged in a profession, esp. to a medical practitioner, etc. **4.** *Colloq.* (*euph.*) a lottery, esp. if held in another State.

**consultative** /kən'sʌltətɪv/, *adj.* of consultation; advisory. Also, **consultatory.**

**consulting** /kən'sʌltɪŋ/, *adj.* employed in giving professional advice, either to the public or to those practising the profession: *a consulting physician.*

**consulting room** /'– rum/, *n.* a room where a doctor interviews and examines patients.

**consume** /kən'sjum/, *v.*, **-sumed, -suming.** *–v.t.* **1.** to destroy or expend by use; use up. **2.** to eat or drink up; devour. **3.** to destroy, as by decomposition or burning. **4.** to spend (money, time, etc.) wastefully. **5.** to absorb; engross. *–v.i.* **6.** to be consumed; suffer destruction; waste away. [ME *consume(n),* from L *consūmere* take up completely] – **consumable,** *adj., n.*

**consumedly** /kən'sjumədli/, *adv.* excessively; extremely.

**consumer** /kən'sjumə/, *n.* **1.** one who or that which consumes. **2.** one who uses a commodity or service (opposed to *producer*).

**consumer durables** /– 'djurəbəlz/, *n. pl.* consumer goods of a permanent nature.

**consumer goods** /'– gʊdz/, *n. pl.* goods ready for consumption in satisfaction of human wants, as clothing, food, etc., and which are not utilised in any further production.

**consumerism** /kən'sjumərɪzəm/, *n.* **1.** a movement which aims at educating consumers to an awareness of their rights and at protecting their interests, as from illegal or dishonest trading practices such as false advertising, misleading packaging, etc. **2.** a theory that the economy of a western capitalist society requires an ever increasing consumption of goods.

**consumer price index,** *n.* the weighted average cost of a standard basket of retail goods expressed in relation to a base period.

**consumer protection** /– prə'tɛkʃən/, *n.* the combined laws relating to the protection of purchasers of goods and services from excessively high prices, faulty design, injurious side-effects, etc.

**consumer society** /'– səsaɪəti/, *n.* a society, as most Western ones, which is oriented towards the production and consumption of goods on a vast scale.

**consummate** /'kɒnsjumeɪt/, *v.*, **-mated, -mating;** /'kɒnsjumət, 'kɒnsəmət/, *adj.* *–v.t.* **1.** to bring to completion or perfection. **2.** to fulfil (a marriage) through sexual intercourse. *–adj.* **3.** complete or perfect; supremely qualified; of the highest quality. [late ME, from L *consummātus,* pp., brought to the highest degree] – **consummately,** *adv.* – **consummative,** *adj.* – **consummator,** *n.*

**consummation** /kɒnsə'meɪʃən/, *n.* the act of consummating, or the state of being consummated; completion; perfection; fulfilment.

**consumption** /kən'sʌmpʃən/, *n.* **1.** the act of consuming; destruction or decay. **2.** destruction by use. **3.** the amount consumed. **4.** *Econ.* the using up of goods and services having an exchangeable value. **5.** *Pathol.* **a.** a wasting disease, esp. tuberculosis of the lungs. **b.** progressive wasting of the body. [ME, from L *consumptio* a wasting]

**consumptive** /kən'sʌmptɪv/, *adj.* **1.** tending to consume; destructive; wasteful. **2.** pertaining to consumption by use. **3.** *Pathol.* **a.** pertaining to or of the nature of consumption. **b.** disposed to or affected with consumption. *–n.* **4.** one who suffers from the disease of consumption. – **consumptively,** *adv.* – **consumptiveness,** *n.*

**cont.,** continued.

**contact** /'kɒntækt/, *n.;* /'kɒntækt, kən'tækt/, *v.;* /'kɒntækt/, *adj.* *–n.* **1.** the state or fact of touching; a touching or meeting of bodies. **2.** immediate proximity or association. **3.** *Elect.* the moving part of a switch or relay which completes and breaks the circuit. **4.** *Maths.* a meeting of two curves or surfaces so that they have a common tangent at the point where they meet. **5.** a person through whom contact is established, often a business acquaintance. **6.** *Med.* **a.** one who has lately been exposed to an infected person. **b.** inflammation of the skin due to contact with an irritating agent. **7.** *Sociol.* **a.** a condition in which two or more individuals or groups are placed in communication with one another. **b. categoric contact,** acting towards one on the basis of the type or group of people he represents rather than on the basis of his personal make-up. **c. primary contact,** a contact characterised by intimacy and personal familiarity. **d. secondary contact,** a contact characterised by impersonal and detached interest on the part of the participants, such as between strangers. **e. sympathetic contact,** acting towards an individual on the basis of his personal or individual make-up instead of on the basis of his group membership. **8. make contact,** to contact. *–v.t.* **9.** to put or bring into contact. **10.** to get in touch with (a person). *–v.i.* **11.** to enter into or be in contact. *–adj.* **12.** establishing or coming into contact. **13.** resulting from or involving contact. [L *contactus* a touching]

**contact aureole** /– 'ɔrioʊl/, *n.* →**aureole** (def. 4).

**contact-breaker** /'kɒntækt-ˌbreɪkə/, *n.* any device for repeatedly making and breaking an electric circuit.

**contact cement** /'– səmɛnt/, *n.* an adhesive which is applied to surfaces which then adhere on contact. Also, **contact glue.**

**contact flight** /'– flaɪt/, *n.* **1.** a flight in which the pilot always sees land or water over which he passes. **2.** navigation by ground observations only.

**contact lenses** /'– lɛnzəz/, *n.pl.* devices to aid defective vision inconspicuously, consisting of small lenses, usu. of plastic, which cover the irises and are held in place by eye fluid.

**contact man** /'– mæn/, *n.* →**contact** (def. 5).

**contact microphone** /– 'maɪkrəfoʊn/, *n.* a small microphone placed in contact with a source of sound, esp. a musical instrument.

**contact mine** /'– maɪn/, *n.* a mine which is exploded by physical contact between a target and the mine case or its appendages.

**contactor** /'kɒntæktə/, *n. Elect.* →**contact-breaker.**

**contact paper** /'kɒntækt peɪpə/, *n.* (in photography) sensitised paper on which a contact print is made.

**contact print** /'– prɪnt/, *n.* a photographic print made by placing a negative upon sensitised paper, and exposing to light.

**contact zone** /'– zoʊn/, *n.* →**aureole** (def. 4)

**contagion** /kən'teɪdʒən/, *n.* **1.** the communication of disease by direct or indirect contact. **2.** a disease so communicated. **3.** the medium by which a contagious disease is transmitted. **4.** pestilential influence; hurtful contact or influence. **5.** the communication of any influence, as enthusiasm, from one to another. [ME, from L *contāgio* a contact]

**contagious** /kən'teɪdʒəs/, *adj.* **1.** communicable to other individuals, as a disease. **2.** carrying or spreading a disease. **3.** tending to spread from one to another: *panic is contagious.* [ME, from LL *contāgiōsus*] – **contagiously,** *adv.* – **contagiousness,** *n.*

**contain** /kən'teɪn/, *v.t.* **1.** to have within itself; hold within fixed limits. **2.** *Geom.* to form the boundary of. **3.** to be capable of holding; have capacity for. **4.** to have as contents or constituent parts; comprise; include. **5.** to keep within proper bounds; restrain: *to contain oneself or one's feelings.* **6.** (of an enemy force, hostile power, disease, etc.) to keep in check, confine within certain limits. **7.** be equal to: *a centilitre contains ten millilitres.* [ME *conteine(n)*, from OF *contenir*, from L *continēre* hold together, hold back] – **containable,** *adj.*

**container** /kən'teɪnə/, *n.* **1.** anything that contains or can contain, as a carton, box, crate, tin, etc. **2.** a box-shaped unit for carrying goods; its standardised size facilitates easy transference from one form of transport to another.

**containerise** /kən'teɪnəraɪz/, *v.t.*, **-rised, -rising. 1.** to send (goods) in containers. **2.** to convert (a goods-carrying system) to the use of containers. Also, **containerize.** – **containerisation,** *n.*

**container ship** /kən'teɪnə ʃɪp/, *n.* a ship designed to carry cargo in containers.

**container terminal** /'– tɜmənəl/, *n.* a shipping terminal designed to load and unload containerised cargo.

**container train** /'– treɪn/, *n.* **1.** a fast railway goods service using containers. **2.** a train carrying such containers.

**container wharf** /'– wɔf/, *n.* a wharf specially designed to facilitate the loading and unloading of containers from ships.

**containment** /kən'teɪnmənt/, *n.* **1.** the act or policy of preventing the expansion beyond certain limits of a hostile power, etc. **2.** *Physics.* the process of preventing the plasma in a controlled thermonuclear reaction from coming into contact with the walls of the containing vessel.

**contaminate** /kən'tæməneɪt/, *v.*, **-nated, -nating;** /kən'tæmənət, -neɪt/, *adj.* –*v.t.* **1.** to render impure by contact or mixture. **2.** to render harmful or unusable by adding radioactive material to. **3.** *Bibliog.* (of variant versions of a text) to influence and cause corruption. [L *contāminātus*, pp.] – **contaminative,** *adj.* – **contaminator,** *n.*

**contamination** /kəntæmə'neɪʃən/, *n.* **1.** the act of contaminating. **2.** the state of being contaminated. **3.** something that contaminates. **4.** *Bibliog.* the corruption of a text by the influence of variant versions. **5.** the exposure of structures, areas, personnel, or objects to radioactive material or agents of biological or chemical warfare.

**contango** /kən'tæŋgoʊ/, *n.* the position in a futures market where the more distantly traded contracts are selling at a premium over the nearer dated contracts.

**contd,** continued.

**contemn** /kən'tɛm/, *v.t. Archaic.* to treat disdainfully or scornfully; view with contempt. [L *contemnere* despise] – **contemner, contemnor** /kən'tɛmnə, kən'tɛmə/, *n.*

**contemp.,** contemporary.

**contemplate** /'kɒntəmpleɪt/, *v.*, **-plated, -plating.** –*v.t.* **1.** to look at or view with continued attention; observe thoughtfully. **2.** to consider attentively; reflect upon. **3.** to have as a purpose; intend. **4.** to have in view as a future event. **5.** **contemplate one's navel,** to indulge in introspection; daydream. –*v.i.* **6.** to think studiously; meditate; consider deliberately. [L *contemplātus*, pp., having surveyed] – **contemplator,** *n.*

**contemplation** /kɒntəm'pleɪʃən/, *n.* **1.** the act of contemplating; thoughtful observation or consideration; reflection. **2.** religious meditation. **3.** purpose or intention. **4.** prospect or expectation.

**contemplative** /'kɒntəm,pleɪtɪv, kən'tɛmplətɪv/, *adj.* **1.** given to or characterised by contemplation. –*n.* **2.** a person devoted to religious contemplation. – **contemplatively,** *adv.* – **contemplativeness,** *n.*

**contemporaneous** /kəntɛmpə'reɪniəs/, *adj.* contemporary. [L *contemporāneus*] – **contemporaneously,** *adv.* – **contemporaneousness,** *n.*

**contemporary** /kən'tɛmpəri, -pri/, *adj., n., pl.* **-raries.** –*adj.* **1.** belonging to the same time; existing or occurring at the same time. **2.** of the same age or date. **3.** of the present time. **4.** *Colloq.* in the most modern style; up-to-date. –*n.* **5.** one belonging to the same time or period with another or others. **6.** a person of the same age as another. [CON- + TEMPORARY]

**contemporise** /kən'tɛmpəraɪz/, *v.*, **-rised, -rising.** –*v.t.* to place in, or regard as belonging to, the same age or time. Also, **contemporize.**

**contempt** /kən'tɛmpt/, *n.* **1.** the act of scorning or despising. **2.** the feeling with which one regards anything considered mean, vile, or worthless. **3.** the state of being despised; dishonour; disgrace. **4.** *Law.* **a.** disobedience to, or open disrespect of, the rules or orders of a court or legislature, or conduct likely to prejudice the fair trial of a litigant or an accused person. **b.** an act showing this disrespect. [ME, from L *contemptus* scorn]

**contemptible** /kən'tɛmptəbəl/, *adj.* deserving of or held in contempt; despicable. – **contemptibility, contemptibleness,** *n.* – **contemptibly,** *adv.*

**contemptuous** /kən'tɛmptʃuəs/, *adj.* manifesting or expressing contempt or disdain; scornful. [L *contemptu(s)* scorn + -OUS] – **contemptuously,** *adv.* – **contemptuousness,** *n.*

**contend** /kən'tɛnd/, *v.i.* **1.** to struggle in opposition. **2.** to strive in rivalry; compete; vie. **3.** to strive in debate; dispute earnestly. –*v.t.* **4.** to assert or maintain earnestly. [L *contendere* stretch out] – **contender,** *n.*

**content**[1] /'kɒntɛnt/, *n.* **1.** (*usu. pl.*) that which is contained: *the contents of a cask, room, or book.* **2.** (*usu. pl.*) the chapters or chief topics of a book or document; a list of such chapters or topics. **3.** substance or purport, as of a document. **4.** the sum of the attributes or notions composing a given conception; the substance or matter of cognition, etc. **5.** power of containing; capacity; volume. **6.** area; extent; size. **7.** the amount contained. [ML *contentum* that which is contained, properly pp. neut.]

**content**[2] /kən'tɛnt/, *adj.* **1.** having the desires limited to what one has; satisfied. **2.** easy in mind. **3.** willing or resigned; assenting. –*v.t.* **4.** to make content. –*n.* **5.** the state or feeling of being contented; contentment. [ME, from L *contentus* satisfied, properly pp.]

**contented** /kən'tɛntəd/, *adj.* satisfied, as with what one has or with something mentioned; content. – **contentedly,** *adv.* – **contentedness,** *n.*

**contention** /kən'tɛnʃən/, *n.* **1.** a struggling together in opposition; strife. **2.** a striving in rivalry; competition; a contest. **3.** strife in debate; a dispute; a controversy. **4.** a point contended for or affirmed in controversy. [ME, from L *contentio* strife]

**contentious** /kən'tɛnʃəs/, *adj.* **1.** given to contention: *a contentious crew.* **2.** characterised by contention: *contentious issues.* **3.** *Law.* pertaining to causes between contending parties. [L *contentiōsus*] – **contentiously,** *adv.* – **contentiousness,** *n.*

**contentment** /kən'tɛntmənt/, *n.* **1.** the state of being contented; satisfaction; ease of mind.

**content word** /'kɒntɛnt wɜd/, *n.* a word like *cat* or *excitement* which refers the mind to some particular entity or aspect of human experience. Cf. **function word.**

**conterminous** /kɒn'tɜmənəs/, *adj.* **1.** having a common boundary; bordering; contiguous. **2.** meeting at their ends. **3.** having the same boundaries or limits; coextensive. Also, **conterminal.** [L *conterminus*] – **conterminously,** *adv.*

**contest** /'kɒntɛst/, *n.;* /kən'tɛst/, *v.* –*n.* **1.** struggle for victory or superiority. **2.** conflict between competitors; a competition. **3.** strife in argument; dispute; controversy. –*v.t.* **4.** to struggle or fight for, as in battle. **5.** to argue against; dispute. **6.** to call in question. **7.** to contend for in rivalry. –*v.i.* **8.** to dispute; contend; compete. [F *contester*, from L *contestārī* call to witness, bring a legal action] – **contestable,** *adj.* – **contester,** *n.*

**contestant** /kən'tɛstənt/, *n.* one who takes part in a contest or competition. [F, ppr. of *contester* contest, used as n.]

**contestation** /,kɒntɛs'teɪʃən/, *n.* **1.** the act of contesting. **2.** an assertion contended for.

**context** /'kɒntɛkst/, *n.* **1.** the parts of a discourse or writing which precede or follow, and are directly connected with, a given passage or word. **2.** the circumstances or facts that surround a particular situation, event, etc. [late ME, from L *contextus* connection]

**contextual** /kən'tɛkstʃuəl/, *adj.* of or pertaining to the context; depending on the context. [L *contextu(s)* connection + -AL[1]] – **contextually,** *adv.*

**contexture** /kən'tɛkstʃə/, *n.* **1.** the disposition and union of the constituent parts of anything; constitution; structure. **2.** an interwoven structure; a fabric. **3.** the act of weaving together. **4.** the fact or manner of being woven together. [F, from L *contexere* weave together. See CON-, TEXTURE]

**contiguity** /kɒntəˈgjuəti/, *n., pl.* **-ties.** the state of being contiguous.

**contiguous** /kənˈtɪgjuəs/, *adj.* **1.** touching; in contact. **2.** in close proximity without actually touching; near. [L *contiguus* touching] – **contiguously,** *adv.* – **contiguousness,** *n.*

**continence** /ˈkɒntənəns/, *n.* **1.** self-restraint, esp. in regard to sexual activity; moderation; chastity. **2.** ability to exercise voluntary control over natural functions, esp. urinating and defecating. Also, **continency.** [ME, from L *continentia*]

**continent** /ˈkɒntənənt/, *n.* **1.** one of the main land masses of the globe, usu. reckoned as seven in number (Europe, Asia, Africa, North America, South America, Australia and Antarctica). **2.** the mainland (as distinguished from islands or peninsulas). **3. the Continent,** the mainland of Europe (as distinguished from the British Isles). **4.** a continuous tract or extent, as of land. *–adj.* **5.** exercising restraint in relation to the desires or passions; temperate. **6.** characterised by the ability to exercise control over natural impulses or functions; chaste. [ME, from L *continens,* pp., lit., holding together]

**continental**[1] /ˌkɒntəˈnɛntl/, *adj.* **1.** of, or of the nature of, a continent. **2.** (*usu. cap.*) of or pertaining to the mainland of Europe. *–n.* **3.** an inhabitant of a continent, esp. (*usu. cap.*) of the mainland of Europe.

**continental**[2] /kɒntəˈnɛntl/, *n.* the least bit; a damn: *I don't give a continental.* [from *continental,* a piece of paper money issued by the Continental Congress during the War of American Independence]

**continental breakfast** /– ˈbrɛkfəst/, *n.* a light breakfast, of European style, of coffee, bread rolls and jam.

**continental climate** /– ˈklaɪmət/, *n.* a type of climate associated with continental interiors and characterised by extremely hot, sunny summers, bitterly cold winters, and little rainfall occurring mainly in early summer.

**continental divide** /– dəˈvaɪd/, *n.* a watershed between river systems that flow into opposite sides of a continent as, in eastern Australia, the Great Dividing Range.

**continental drift** /– ˈdrɪft/, *n.* the supposed movement of the continents away from an original single land mass to their present position.

**continental frankfurt** /– ˈfræŋkfət/, *n.* a variety of frankfurt.

**continental quilt** /– ˈkwɪlt/, *n.* a quilted bedcover, filled with down, or synthetic padding, and often used instead of top sheets and blankets.

**continental shelf** /– ˈʃɛlf/, *n.* that portion of a continent submerged under relatively shallow sea, in contrast with the deep ocean basins from which it is separated by the relatively steep **continental slope.**

**continently** /ˈkɒntənəntli/, *adv.* in a continent manner.

**contingence** /kənˈtɪndʒəns/, *n.* contact or tangency.

**contingency** /kənˈtɪndʒənsi/, *n., pl.* **-cies.** **1.** a contingent event; a chance, accident, or possibility, conditional on something uncertain. **2.** fortuitousness; uncertainty; dependence on chance or on the fulfilment of a condition. **3.** something incidental to a thing.

**contingency table** /ˈ– teɪbəl/, *n.* the frequency distribution for a two-way statistical classification.

**contingent** /kənˈtɪndʒənt/, *adj.* **1.** dependent for existence, occurrence, character, etc., on something not yet certain; conditional (oft. fol. by *on* or *upon*). **2.** liable to happen or not; uncertain; possible. **3.** happening by chance or without known cause; fortuitous; accidental. **4.** *Logic.* (of a proposition) not involving any self-contradiction if denied, so that its truth or falsity can be established only by sensory observation (as opposed to *analytic* or *necessary* propositions). *–n.* **5.** the proportion that falls to one as a share to be contributed or furnished. **6.** a quota of troops furnished. **7.** any one of the representative groups composing an assemblage. **8.** something contingent; a contingency. [ME, from L *contingens,* ppr., touching, bordering on, reaching, befalling] – **contingently,** *adv.*

**contingent remainder** /– rəˈmeɪndə/, *n. Law.* a future interest in property which comes into possession only on the happening of a contingency, as attaining the age of twenty-one years.

**continual** /kənˈtɪnjuəl/, *adj.* **1.** proceeding without interruption or cessation; continuous in time. **2.** of regular or frequent recurrence; often repeated; very frequent. [ML *continuālis;* replacing ME *continuel,* from OF]

**continually** /kənˈtɪnjuəli, -jəli/, *adv.* **1.** without cessation or intermission; unceasingly. **2.** very often; at regular or frequent intervals; habitually.

**continuance** /kənˈtɪnjuəns/, *n.* **1.** the act or fact of continuing; continuation. **2.** the remaining in the same place, condition, etc. **3.** *Law.* adjournment of a step in a proceeding to a future day. [ME, from OF, from *continuer* CONTINUE]

**continuant** /kənˈtɪnjuənt/, *n.* a consonant, such as *f* or *m,* which may be prolonged without change of quality. [L *continuans,* ppr., continuing]

**continuation** /kəntɪnjuˈeɪʃən/, *n.* **1.** the act or fact of continuing or prolonging. **2.** the state of being continued. **3.** extension or carrying on to a further point: *the continuation of a road.* **4.** that by which anything is continued; a sequel, as to a story.

**continuative** /kənˈtɪnjuətiv/, *adj.* **1.** tending or serving to continue, or to cause continuation or prolongation. **2.** expressing continuance of thought. *–n.* **3.** something continuative. **4.** a continuative word or expression. **5.** a mood or aspect of a verb expressing that the action is viewed as a continuous development. **6.** a conjunction which connects a subordinate clause to a main clause. – **continuatively,** *adv.* – **continuativeness,** *n.*

**continuator** /kənˈtɪnjueɪtə/, *n.* one who or that which continues: *the continuator of a story.*

**continue** /kənˈtɪnju/, *v.,* **-ued, -uing.** *–v.i.* **1.** to go forwards or onwards in any course or action; keep on. **2.** to go on after suspension or interruption. **3.** to last or endure. **4.** to remain in a place; abide; stay. **5.** to remain in a particular state or capacity. *–v.t.* **6.** to go on with or persist in: *to continue an action.* **7.** to extend from one point to another in space; prolong. **8.** to carry on from the point of suspension or interruption: *to continue a narrative.* **9.** to say in continuation. **10.** to cause to last or endure; maintain or retain, as in a position. **11.** to carry over, postpone, or adjourn; keep pending, as a legal proceeding. [ME *continue(n),* from L *continuāre* make continuous] – **continuable,** *adj.* – **continuer,** *n.*

**continued fraction** /kənˌtɪnjud ˈfrækʃən/, *n. Maths.* a fraction whose denominator contains a fraction whose denominator contains a fraction, and so on, as

$$\cfrac{2}{7+\cfrac{1}{9+\cfrac{3}{4+\ldots}}}$$

Also, **recurring fraction.**

**continuing education** /kənˌtɪnjuɪŋ ɛdʒəˈkeɪʃən/, *n.* education, usu. part-time, for persons beyond the school leaving age; further education; adult education.

**continuity** /kɒntəˈnjuəti/, *n., pl.* **-ties.** **1.** the state or quality of being continuous. **2.** a continuous or connected whole. **3.** a film scenario giving the complete action, scenes, etc., in detail and in the order in which they are to be shown on the screen. **4.** the full version of a broadcast script, including spoken parts, linking comments, sound effects, etc.

**continuity girl** /ˈ– gɜl/, *n.* a woman or girl employed to ensure complete consistency in a film. – **continuity man,** *n. masc.*

**continuo** /kənˈtɪnjuoʊ/, *n.* **1.** a bass part, usu. for the keyboard accompaniment in a baroque piece of music, in which the harmony is implied by the given bass line, but which is sometimes numbered to indicate chord progressions; figured bass. **2.** a full scoring of a part originally so written. **3.** the instrument or instruments playing such a part, typically a keyboard instrument suported by a mellow instrument as a cello or bassoon. *–adj.* **4.** of such a part or instruments which play it. [It.]

**continuous** /kənˈtɪnjuəs/, *adj.* **1.** having the parts in immediate connection, unbroken. **2.** uninterrupted in time; without cessation. **3.** *Gram.* denoting a verb aspect, or other verb category, which indicates action or state going on at a temporal point of reference: *the progressive form of 'is doing' in 'he is doing it'.* *–n.* **4.** *Maths.* (of a function) having a continuous graph. [L *continuus* hanging together] – **continuously,** *adv.* – **continuousness,** *n.*

**continuous creation** /– kri'eɪʃən/, *n.* the cosmological theory that matter is being continuously created throughout the universe to compensate for its expansion, thus maintaining the universe in a steady state.

**continuous stationery** /'– steɪʃənri/, *n.* stationery, esp. for computer and machine printouts, which is not cut into separate pages but into great lengths equivalent to many pages. See **roll stationery, fanfold.**

**continuous strip camera,** *n.* a camera in an aeroplane in which the film moves continuously past a slit producing a photograph of the terrain flown over in one unbroken length.

**continuous waves** /– 'weɪvz/, *n.pl. Radio.* radiation which is not intermittent or broken up into damped wave-trains. *Abbrev.:* cw

**continuum** /kən'tɪnjuəm/, *n., pl.* **-tinuums, -tinua** /-'tɪnjuə/. **1.** a continuous extent, series, or whole. **2.** *Maths.* the continuum, the set of all real numbers. **3. four-dimensional continuum,** *Physics.* (in the theory of relativity) the three dimensions of space and the dimension of time considered together.

**contort** /kən'tɔt/, *v.t.* to twist; bend or draw out of shape; distort. [L *contortus,* pp., twisted] – **contortion,** *n.*

**contortionist** /kən'tɔʃənəst/, *n.* **1.** one who performs gymnastic feats involving contorted postures. **2.** one who practices contortion: *a verbal contortionist.*

**contour** /'kɒntɔ, -tʊə/, *n.* **1.** the outline of a figure or body; the line that defines or bounds anything. **2.** →**contour line.** *–v.t.* **3.** to mark with contour lines. **4.** to make or form the contour or outline of. **5.** to build (a road, etc.) in conformity to a contour. [F, from It. *contorno,* from *contornare,* from L *con-* CON- + *tornāre* turn]

**contour feathers** /'– fɛðəz/, *n. pl.* any of the feathers which form the surface plumage of a bird, apart from wings, tail, and specialised types, as filoplumes.

**contour interval** /– 'ɪntəvəl/, *n.* the difference in elevation represented by each contour line on a map.

**contour line** /'– laɪn/, *n.* **1.** a line joining points of equal elevation on a surface. **2.** the representation of such a line on a map.

**contour map** /'– mæp/, *n.* a map on which irregularities of land surface are shown by contour lines, the relative spacing of the lines indicating the relative slope of the surface.

contour map: A, contours; B, elevation; C, contour interval

**contour ploughing** /– 'plaʊɪŋ/, *n.* a system of ploughing along the contour lines of the terrain to minimise erosion of topsoil by rain.

**contra-,** a prefix meaning 'against', 'opposite', or 'opposing'. [L, prefix use of *contrā,* adv. and prep.]

**contraband** /'kɒntrəbænd/, *n.* **1.** anything prohibited by law from being imported or exported. **2.** goods imported or exported illegally. **3.** illegal or prohibited traffic; smuggling. **4.** *Internat. Law.* goods which neutrals cannot supply to one belligerent except at the risk of seizure and confiscation by the other (**contraband of war**). *–adj.* **5.** prohibited from export or import. [Sp. *contrabando;* replacing *counterband,* from F *contrebande,* from It. *contrabando,* from *contra* against (from L *contrā*) + *bando* proclamation (from LL *bandum* BAN[2], *n.*)]

**contrabandist** /'kɒntrəbændəst/, *n.* a smuggler.

**contrabass** /kɒntrə'beɪs/, *n.* **1.** (in any family of musical instruments) the member below the bass. **2.** (in the violin family) the double bass. *–adj.* **3.** denoting such instruments: *a contrabass trombone.* – **contrabassist,** *n.*

**contrabassoon** /kɒntrəbə'sun/, *n.* a bassoon larger in size and an octave lower in pitch than the ordinary bassoon; a double bassoon.

**contraception** /kɒntrə'sɛpʃən/, *n.* the prevention of conception by deliberate measures; birth control. [CONTRA- + (CON)-CEPTION]

**contraceptive** /kɒntrə'sɛptɪv/, *adj.* **1.** tending or serving to prevent conception or impregnation. **2.** pertaining to contraception. *–n.* **3.** a contraceptive agent or device.

**contraceptive sheath** /– 'ʃiθ/, *n.* a thin covering, usu. of rubber, worn over the penis during sexual intercourse to prevent conception or venereal infection; condom.

**contraclockwise** /kɒntrə'klɒkwaɪz/, *adj., adv. U.S.* →**anticlockwise.**

**contract** /'kɒntrækt/, *n.;* /'kɒntrækt, kən'trækt/, *v.* *–n.* **1.** an agreement between two or more parties for the doing or not doing of some definite thing. **2.** an agreement enforceable by law. **3.** the writing containing such an agreement. **4.** the division of law dealing with contracts. **5.** the formal agreement of marriage; betrothal. **6.** an agreement to kill a nominated person or persons: *there is a contract out on Slippery Sam.* **7.** Also, **contract bridge.** a modification of auction bridge in which the side which wins the bid can earn towards game only that number of tricks bid, all additional points being credited above the score line. **8.** (in auction or contract bridge) **a.** the highest bid. **b.** the number of tricks so bid. *–v.t.* **9.** to draw together or into smaller compass; draw the parts of together: *to contract a muscle.* **10.** to wrinkle: *to contract the brows.* **11.** to shorten (a word, etc.) by combining or omitting some of its elements. **12.** to acquire, as by habit or contagion; incur, as a liability or obligation: *to contract a disease; to contract debts.* **13.** to settle or establish by agreement: *to contract an alliance.* **14.** to enter into (friendship, acquaintance, etc.). **15.** to betroth. *–v.i.* **16.** to be drawn together or reduced in compass; become smaller; shrink. **17.** to enter into an agreement. **18.** *Law.* to deprive oneself of the benefit of a statute by contracting with others. [ME, from LL *contractus* agreement] – **contractible,** *adj.* – **contractibility, contractibleness,** *n.*

**contracted** /kən'træktəd/, *adj.* **1.** drawn together; shrunken. **2.** abridged; (of a word) shortened by the elision of part of it. – **contractedly,** *adv.* – **contractedness,** *n.*

**contractile** /kən'træktaɪl/, *adj.* capable of undergoing or of producing contraction. – **contractility** /ˌkɒntræk'tɪləti/, *n.*

**contraction** /kən'trækʃən/, *n.* **1.** the act of contracting. **2.** the state of being contracted. **3.** a shortened form of a word, etc., as *e'er* for *ever, can't* for *cannot.* **4.** the change in a muscle by which it becomes thickened and shortened. [L *contractio* a drawing together]

**contractive** /kən'træktɪv/, *adj.* serving or tending to contract. – **contractively,** *adv.* – **contractiveness,** *n.*

**contract note** /'kɒntrækt noʊt/, *n. Stock Exchange.* a note issued by a broker to his client following his carrying out of the client's instructions, giving details of a purchase or sale of shares.

**contractor** /'kɒntræktə, kən'træktə/, *n.* **1.** one who contracts to furnish supplies or perform work at a certain price or rate. **2.** one who or that which contracts. [LL]

**contract sum** /'kɒntrækt ˌsʌm/, *n.* the total sum of money for which a builder (or contractor) undertakes to complete a contract.

**contractual** /kən'træktʃuəl/, *adj.* of, or of the nature of, a contract. [L *contractu(s)* contract + -AL[1]]

**contradance** /'kɒntrədæns/, *n.* →**contredanse.**

**contradict** /kɒntrə'dɪkt/, *v.t.* **1.** to assert the contrary or opposite of; deny directly and categorically. **2.** to deny the words or assertion of (a person). **3.** (of a statement, action, etc.) to be directly contrary to. *v.i.* **4.** to utter a contrary statement. [L *contrādictus,* pp., said against] – **contradictable,** *adj.* – **contradictor,** *n.*

**contradiction** /kɒntrə'dɪkʃən/, *n.* **1.** the act of contradicting; gainsaying or opposition. **2.** assertion of the contrary or opposite; denial. **3.** a statement or proposition that contradicts or denies another or itself. **4.** direct opposition between things compared; inconsistency. **5.** a contradictory act, fact, etc. **6.** →**law of contradiction.** – **contradictious, contradictive,** *adj.*

**contradictory** /kɒntrə'dɪktəri/, *adj., n., pl.* **-ries.** *–adj.* **1.** of the nature of a contradiction; asserting the contrary or opposite; contradicting each other; inconsistent. **2.** given to contradiction. *–n.* **3.** *Logic.* a proposition so related to a second that it is impossible for both to be true or both to be false. – **contradictorily,** *adv.* – **contradictoriness,** *n.*

**contradistinction** /kɒntrədəs'tɪŋkʃən/, *n.* distinction by opposition or contrast: *plants and animals in contradistinction*

i = peat ɪ = pit ɛ = pet æ = pat a = part ɒ = pot ʌ = putt ɔ = port ʊ = put u = pool ɜ = pert ə = apart aɪ = buy eɪ = bay ɔɪ = boy aʊ = how oʊ = hoe ɪə = here ɛə = hair ʊə = tour g = give θ = thin ð = then ʃ = show ʒ = measure tʃ = choke dʒ = joke ŋ = sing j = you õ = Fr. bon

*to man.* – **contradistinctive,** *adj.* – **contradistinctively,** *adv.*

**contradistinguish** /kɒntrədəs'tɪŋgwɪʃ/, *v.t.* to distinguish by contrasting opposite qualities.

**contrail** /'kɒntreɪl/, *n.* →**vapour trail.** [b. CON(DENSATION) + TRAIL]

**contraindicate** /kɒntrə'ɪndəkeɪt/, *v.t.,* **-cated, -cating.** (of a symptom or condition) to give indication against the advisability of (a particular or usual remedy or treatment). – **contraindicant,** *n.* – **contraindication,** *n.*

**contralto** /kən'træltoʊ, -'tral-/, *n., pl.* **-ti,** *adj. Music.* –*n.* **1.** the lowest female voice or voice part, intermediate between soprano and tenor. **2.** the alto, or highest male voice or voice part. **3.** a singer with a contralto voice. –*adj.* **4.** pertaining to the contralto or its compass. [It., from *contra* against, counter to + *alto* high]

**contraposition** /kɒntrəpə'zɪʃən/, *n.* **1.** placing opposite or against. **2.** opposition, antithesis, contrast. **3.** *Logic.* an immediate inference drawn from a given proposition by negating its terms and changing their order. – **contrapositive** /kɒntrə'pɒzətɪv/, *adj.*

**contrapposto** /ˌkɒntrə'pɒstoʊ/, *n. Art.* the posing of the human body so that the parts are twisted in counterpoise around a vertical axis, as a figure with the legs and hips turned one way and the chest and shoulders twisted in the opposite direction. [It.: contraposition]

**contraption** /kən'træpʃən/, *n.* a contrivance; a device.

**contrapuntal** /kɒntrə'pʌntl/, *adj.* **1.** of or pertaining to counterpoint. **2.** composed of two or more relatively independent melodies sounded together. [It. *contrappunto* counterpoint + -AL[1]] – **contrapuntally,** *adv.*

**contrapuntist** /kɒntrə'pʊntəst/, *n.* one skilled in the practice of counterpoint.

**contrariety** /kɒntrə'raɪəti/, *n., pl.* **-ties.** **1.** the state or quality of being contrary. **2.** something contrary or of opposite character; a contrary fact or statement. [LL *contrārietas*]

**contrariwise** /'kɒntrəriwaɪz/ *for defs 1, 2;* /kən'treəriwaɪz/ *for def. 3. adv.* **1.** in the opposite way. **2.** on the contrary. **3.** perversely.

**contrary** /'kɒntrəri/; *for def. 5 also* /kən'treəri/ *adj., n., pl.* **-ries,** *adv.* –*adj.* **1.** opposite in nature or character; diametrically opposed; mutually opposed: *contrary to fact, contrary propositions.* **2.** opposite in direction or position. **3.** being the opposite one of two. **4.** untoward or unfavourable: *contrary winds.* **5.** perverse; self-willed. **6.** *Bot.* at right angles. –*n.* **7.** that which is contrary or opposite: *to prove the contrary of a statement.* **8.** either of two contrary things. **9.** *Logic.* a proposition so related to a second that it is impossible for both to be true, though both may be false. For example: *all judges are male* is the contrary of *no judges are male.* **10. by contraries, a.** by way of opposition. **b.** contrary to expectation. **11. on the contrary,** in opposition to what has been stated. **12. to the contrary,** to the opposite or a different effect. –*adv.* **13.** contrarily; contrariwise. [ME *contrarie,* from AF, from L *contrārius* opposite, hostile] – **contrarily,** *adv.* – **contrariness,** *n.*

**contrary motion** /– 'moʊʃən/, *n.* melodic motion in which one part rises in pitch while the other descends, and vice versa.

**contrast** /kən'trast/, *v.;* /'kɒntrast/, *n.* –*v.t.* **1.** to set in opposition in order to show unlikeness; compare by observing differences. **2.** to afford or form a contrast to; set off. –*v.i.* **3.** to exhibit unlikeness on comparison; form a contrast. –*n.* **4.** the act of contrasting. **5.** the state of being contrasted. **6.** a striking exhibition of unlikeness. **7.** something strikingly unlike. **8.** opposition or juxtaposition of different forms, lines, or colours in a work of art to intensify each other's properties and produce a more dynamic expression. **9.** the variation between light and dark areas of a photographic print or negative. [F *contraster,* from It. *contrastare,* from LL: withstand, oppose] – **contrastable,** *adj.*

**contrastive** /kən'trastɪv/, *adj.* producing or forming a contrast.

**contrastive linguistics** /'– lɪŋgwɪstɪks/, *n.* a study of languages which concentrates on similarities and differences between two or more languages with the aim of finding principles which can be applied to practical problems in language teaching.

**contrasty** /kən'trasti, 'kɒn-/, *adj.* in photography having coarse or sharp gradations of tone, esp. between dark and light areas (opposed to *soft*).

**contrasuggestible** /kɒntrəsə'dʒɛstəbəl/, *adj.* inclined to do or believe the opposite of what is proposed. – **contrasuggestion,** *n.* – **contrasuggestive,** *adj.*

**contravallation** /kɒntrəvə'leɪʃən/, *n.* a chain of redoubts and breastworks raised by besiegers about the place invested. [F *contrevallation,* from *contre-* CONTRA- + LL *vallātio* entrenchment]

**contravene** /kɒntrə'vin/, *v.t.,* **-vened, -vening.** **1.** to come or be in conflict with; go or act counter to; oppose. **2.** to violate, infringe, or transgress: *to contravene the law.* [L *contrāvenīre* oppose] – **contravener,** *n.*

**contravention** /kɒntrə'vɛnʃən/, *n.* the act of contravening; action counter to something; violation.

**contrayerva** /kɒntrə'jɜvə/, *n.* the root of certain plants of the tropical American genus *Dorstenia,* esp. *D. brasiliensis,* used as a stimulant, tonic, and diaphoretic. [Sp: counterherb, antidote, from L *contra-* CONTRA- + Sp. *yerva* herb]

**contredanse** /kɒntrə'dɒns/, *n.* **1.** a variation of the quadrille, in which the dancers face each other. **2.** a piece of music suitable for such a dance. Also, **contradance.** [F, mistranslation of COUNTRY DANCE]

**contretemps** /'kɒntrətɒ̃/, *n., pl.* **-temps** /-tɒ̃/. **1.** an inopportune occurrence; an embarrassing mischance. **2.** *Fencing.* a feint made with the intention of producing a stop from the opponent. [F, respelling of *contretant,* from OF *contrestant* opposing, ppr. of *contrester* oppose, from L *contrāstāre*]

**contrib.,** contributing (share).

**contribute** /kən'trɪbjut/, *v.,* **-uted, -uting.** –*v.t.* **1.** to give in common with others; give to a common stock or for a common purpose: *to contribute money, time, help.* **2.** to furnish to a magazine or journal. –*v.i.* **3.** to make contribution; furnish a contribution. [L *contribūtus,* pp., brought together] – **contributable,** *adj.* – **contributive,** *adj.* – **contributively,** *adv.* – **contributiveness,** *n.*

**contributing share** /kən'trɪbjətɪŋ ʃɛə/, *n. Stock Exchange.* an ordinary share which has some part of its capital unpaid.

**contribution** /kɒntrə'bjuʃən/, *n.* **1.** the act of contributing. **2.** something contributed. **3.** an article contributed to a magazine or the like. **4.** an impost or levy. **5.** *Law.* the right of one or some of several joint tortfeasors who have discharged the joint liability, to seek a contribution from the other tortfeasors. [ME, from L *contribūtio*]

**contributor** /kən'trɪbjutə/, *n.* **1.** one who or that which contributes. **2.** one who contributes articles to a newspaper, magazine, or other joint literary work.

**contributory** /kən'trɪbjutəri, -tri/, *adj., n., pl.* **-ries.** –*adj.* **1.** pertaining to or of the nature of contribution; contributing. **2.** furnishing something towards a result: *contributory negligence.* **3.** subject to contribution or levy. –*n.* **4.** one who or that which contributes. **5.** a person liable to contribute to the assets of a company in the event of its being wound up.

**contrite** /'kɒntraɪt, kən'traɪt/, *adj.* **1.** broken in spirit by a sense of guilt; penitent: *a contrite sinner.* **2.** proceeding from contrition: *contrite tears.* [ME *contrit,* from L *contrītus,* pp., ground, worn down] – **contritely,** *adv.* – **contriteness,** *n.*

**contrition** /kən'trɪʃən/, *n.* **1.** sincere penitence. **2.** *Theol.* sorrow for and detestation of sin with a true purpose of amendment, arising from a love of God for His own perfections (**perfect contrition**), or from some inferior motive, as fear of divine punishment (**imperfect contrition**). [ME, from L *contrītio*]

**contrivance** /kən'traɪvəns/, *n.* **1.** something contrived; a device, esp. a mechanical one. **2.** the act or manner of contriving; the faculty or power of contriving. **3.** a plan or scheme; an expedient.

**contrive** /kən'traɪv/, *v.,* **-trived, -triving.** –*v.t.* **1.** to plan with ingenuity; devise; invent. **2.** to plot (evil, etc.). **3.** to bring about or effect by a device, stratagem, plan, or scheme; manage (to do something). –*v.i.* **4.** to form schemes or designs; plan. **5.** to plot. [ME *contreve(n), controve(n),* from OF *controver,* from *con-* CON- + *trover* find. See TROVER] – **contrivable,** *adj.* – **contriver,** *n.*

**control** /kən'troʊl/, *v.,* **-trolled, -trolling,** *n.* –*v.t.* **1.** to exercise restraint or direction over; dominate; command. **2.** to hold in check; curb. **3.** to test or verify (a scientific experiment) by a parallel experiment or other standard of comparison. *–n.* **4.** the act or power of controlling; regulation; domination or command. **5.** check or restraint. **6.** something that serves to control; a check; a standard of comparison in scientific experimentation. **7.** a person who acts as a check; a controller. **8.** (*pl.*) a coordinated arrangement of devices for regulating and guiding a machine, as a motor, aeroplane, etc. **9.** *Motor Racing, etc.* an appointed place at or from which officials time contestants, check conformity and required conditions, and in general, regulate a race. **10.** (in spiritualism) an agency believed to assist the medium at a seance. **11.** *Philately.* an authenticating letter or number printed on the selvage of a sheet of stamps to indicate the plate or cylinder from which the stamps were printed, or the series to which they belong. [F *contrôler,* in OF *contreroller,* from *contrerolle* register. See COUNTER-, ROLL] – **controllable,** *adj.* – **controllability,** *n.* – **controlment,** *n.*

**control chart** /'– tʃat/, *n.* a statistical chart on which observations are plotted as ordinates in the order in which they are obtained, and on which **control lines** are constructed to indicate whether the population from which the observations are being drawn is remaining the same (used particularly in industrial quality control work).

**control column** /'– kɒləm/, *n.* a control stick usu. in a large plane.

**control computer** /'– kəmpjutə/, *n.* a computer, usu. of small memory but considerable logical complexity, which controls some industrial or other process as controlling the size of ingots in a steel mill.

**control experiment** /'– əkspɛrəmənt/, *n.* an experiment in which the variables are controlled so that the effects of varying one factor at a time may be observed.

**control group** /'– grup/, *n.* a group which acts as a control (def. 6) in an experiment where the results are analysed statistically, as in the testing of drugs.

**controller** /kən'troʊlə/, *n.* **1.** one employed to check expenditures, etc.; a comptroller. **2.** one who regulates, directs, or restrains. **3.** a regulating mechanism. – **controllership,** *n.*

**control rod** /kən'troʊl rɒd/, *n.* **1.** *Physics.* a rod or tube, capable of moving up and down on its axis, which controls the rate of reaction in a nuclear reactor; made from a material containing a strong neutron absorber such as boron or cadmium. **2.** *Radio.* the electrode in a radio valve, lying between the cathode and the anode, which controls the flow of current through the valve.

**control room** /'– rum/, *n.* a room, housing control equipment, as in a recording studio.

**control stick** /'– stɪk/, *n.* a lever by which the pilot controls the ailerons and elevator of an aeroplane; joystick. Also, **control column.**

**control surface** /'– sɜfəs/, *n.* any of various hinged, movable airfoils at the rear of the fixed airfoils, forming the primary controls of an aircraft.

**control tower** /'– taʊə/, *n.* an airport building, usu. tower-shaped, from which landing and take-off instructions are given.

**control unit** /'– junət/, *n.* the part of a digital computer which causes it to perform its program in the correct sequence.

**controversial** /kɒntrə'vɜʃəl/, *adj.* **1.** of, or of the nature of, controversy; polemical. **2.** subject to controversy; debatable. **3.** given to controversy; disputatious. – **controversialist,** *n.* – **controversially,** *adv.*

**controversy** /'kɒntrəvɜsi, kən'trɒvəsi/, *n., pl.* **-sies.** **1.** dispute, debate, or contention; disputation concerning a matter of opinion. **2.** a dispute or contention. [L *contrōversia* debate, contention]

**controvert** /'kɒntrəvɜt, kɒntrə'vɜt/, *v.t.* **1.** to contend against in discussion; dispute; deny; oppose. **2.** to contend about in discussion; debate; discuss. – **controverter,** *n.* – **controvertible,** *adj.* – **controvertibly,** *adv.*

**contumacious** /kɒntʃu'meɪʃəs/, *adj.* stubbornly perverse or rebellious; wilfully and obstinately disobedient to authority. [CONTUMACY + -OUS] – **contumaciously,** *adv.* – **contumaciousness,** *n.*

**contumacy** /'kɒntʃuməsi/, *n., pl.* **-cies.** **1.** stubborn perverseness or rebelliousness; wilful and obstinate resistance or disobedience to authority. **2.** *Law.* wilful refusal to obey an order of a court. [ME *contumacie,* from L *contumācia,* from *contumax* stubborn]

**contumely** /'kɒntʃuməli, kən'tjuməli/, *n., pl.* **-lies.** **1.** insulting manifestation of contempt in words or actions; contemptuous or humiliating treatment. **2.** a humiliating insult. [ME *contumelie,* from L *contumēlia*] – **contumelious** /kɒntʃu'miliəs/, *adj.* – **contumeliously** /kɒntʃu'miliəsli/, *adv.* – **contumeliousness** /kɒntʃu'miliəsnəs/, *n.*

**contuse** /kən'tjuz/, *v.t.,* **-tused, -tusing.** to injure as by a blow with a blunt instrument, without breaking the skin; bruise. [L *contūsus,* pp., beaten together] – **contusive** /kən'tjusɪv/, *adj.*

**contusion** /kən'tjuʒən/, *n.* an injury as from a blow with a blunt instrument, without breaking of the skin; a bruise.

**conundrum** /kə'nʌndrəm/, *n.* **1.** a riddle the answer to which involves a pun or play on words. **2.** anything that puzzles. [orig. unknown]

**conurbation** /ˌkɒnɜ'beɪʃən/, *n.* a large urban agglomeration formed by the growth and gradual merging of formerly separate towns. [CON- + L *urbs* city + -ATION]

**conure** /'kɒnjuə/, *n.* any of several brightly-coloured tropical American parrots of *Aratinga* and related genera. [NL *Conurus* genus name, from Gk *kônos* cone + *ourás* tail]

**convalesce** /kɒnvə'lɛs/, *v.i.,* **-lesced, -lescing.** to grow stronger after illness; make progress towards recovery of health. [L *convalescere* grow strong]

**convalescence** /kɒnvə'lɛsəns/, *n.* **1.** the gradual recovery of health and strength after illness. **2.** the period during which one is convalescing.

**convalescent** /kɒnvə'lɛsənt/, *adj.* **1.** convalescing. **2.** of or pertaining to convalescence or convalescents. *–n.* **3.** a convalescent person.

**convalescent home** /'– hoʊm/, *n.* →**nursing home.**

**convection** /kən'vɛkʃən/, *n.* **1.** *Physics.* the transference of heat by the circulation or movement of the heated parts of a liquid or gas. **2.** *Meteorol.* a mechanical process thermally produced involving the upward or downward transfer of a limited portion of the atmosphere. Convection is essential to the formation of many types of clouds. [LL *convectio,* from L *convehere* carry together] – **convectional,** *adj.* – **convective,** *adj.* – **convectively,** *adv.*

**convectional rain** /kənvɛkʃənəl 'reɪn/, *n.* rain formed from evaporated earth liquids on a hot day.

**convector** /kən'vɛktə/, *n.* a heating device, esp. a room-heater, distributing heat by convection.

**convene** /kən'vin/, *v.,* **-vened, -vening.** *–v.i.* **1.** to come together; assemble, usu. for some public purpose. *–v.t.* **2.** to cause to assemble; convoke. **3.** to summon to appear, as before a judicial officer. [late ME, from L *convenīre* come together] – **convener,** *n.*

**convenience** /kən'viniəns/, *n.* **1.** the quality of being convenient; suitability. **2.** a situation of affairs or a time convenient for one: *to await one's convenience.* **3.** advantage, as from something convenient: *a shelter for the convenience of travellers.* **4.** anything convenient; an advantage; an accommodation; a convenient appliance, utensil, or the like. **5.** (*euph.*) a water closet or urinal; lavatory.

**convenience food** /'– fud/, *n.* any food, as pre-cooked or frozen food, which needs little reheating or other preparation.

**convenient** /kən'viniənt/, *adj.* **1.** agreeable to the needs or purpose; well-suited with respect to facility or ease in use; favourable, easy, or comfortable for use. **2.** at hand; easily accessible. [ME, from L *conveniens,* ppr., agreeing, suiting] – **conveniently,** *adv.*

**convent** /'kɒnvənt/, *n.* **1.** a community of persons, esp. nuns, devoted to religious life under a superior. **2.** the building or buildings occupied by such a community. **3.** a nunnery. **4.** a Roman Catholic or other school where children are taught by nuns. [L *conventus* meeting, assembly, company, in ML convent; replacing ME *covent,* from AF]

**conventicle** /kən'vɛntɪkəl/, *n.* **1.** a secret or unauthorised meeting, esp. for religious worship, as those held by Protestant dissenters in England when they were prohibited by law. **2.** a place of meeting or assembly, esp. a Nonconformist meeting house. [ME, from L *conventiculum,* diminutive of *conventus* meeting] – **conventicler,** *n.*

**convention** /kən'vɛnʃən/, *n.* **1.** a meeting or assembly, esp. a formal assembly, as of representatives or delegates, for action on particular matters. **2.** an agreement, compact, or contract. **3.** an international agreement, esp. one dealing with a specific matter, as postal service, copyright, arbitration, etc. **4.** general agreement or consent; accepted usage, esp. as a standard of procedure. **5.** conventionalism. **6.** a rule, method, or practice established by general consent or usage. **7.** *Bridge.* **a.** a bid or lead, which, if interpreted according to an agreed system and not taken at face value, yields information about the hand. **b.** the system. [L *conventio* a meeting]

**conventional** /kən'vɛnʃənəl/, *adj.* **1.** conforming or adhering to accepted standards, as of conduct or taste. **2.** pertaining to convention or general agreement; established by general consent or accepted usage; arbitrarily determined: *conventional symbols.* **3.** formal, rather than spontaneous or original: *conventional phraseology.* **4.** *Law.* resting on consent, express or implied. **5.** (of weapons, warfare, etc.) not nuclear. – **conventionalist,** *n.* – **conventionally,** *adv.*

**conventionalise** /kən'vɛnʃənəlaɪz/, *v.t.,* **-lised, -lising.** to make conventional. Also, **conventionalize.** – **conventionalisation,** *n.*

**conventionalism** /kən'vɛnʃənəlɪzəm/, *n.* **1.** adherence or the tendency to adhere to that which is conventional. **2.** something conventional.

**conventionality** /kənvɛnʃə'næləti/, *n., pl.* **-ties. 1.** conventional quality or character. **2.** adherence to convention. **3.** a conventional practice, principle, form, etc. **4. the conventionalities,** the conventional rules of propriety.

**convention centre** /kən'vɛnʃən sɛntə/, *n.* a building or group of buildings providing facilities for conventions and usu. accommodation for those who attend.

**conventual** /kən'vɛntʃuəl/, *adj.* **1.** of, belonging to, or characteristic of a convent. *–n.* **2.** an inmate of a convent. [late ME, from ML *conventuālis,* from *conventus* CONVENT]

**converge** /kən'vɜdʒ/, *v.,* **-verged, -verging.** *–v.i.* **1.** to tend to meet in a point or line; incline towards each other, as lines which are not parallel. **2.** to tend to a common result, conclusion, etc. **3.** *Maths.* (of an infinite sequence of numbers) to approach a single number, called the limit of a sequence. *–v.t.* **4.** to cause to converge. [LL *convergere* incline together]

**convergence** /kən'vɜdʒəns/, *n.* **1.** the act or fact of converging. **2.** convergent state or quality. **3.** degree of convergence, or point of convergence. **4.** *Physiol.* a turning of the eyes inwards to bear upon a near point. **5.** *Meteorol.* a condition brought about by a net flow of air into a given region. **6.** *Biol.* similarity of form or structure caused by environment rather than heredity. Also, **convergency** for defs 1-3. – **convergent,** *adj.*

**convergent evolution** /kən,vɜdʒənt ɛvə'luʃən/, *n.* the appearance of apparently similar structures in organisms of different lines of descent.

**conversable** /kən'vɜsəbəl/, *adj.* **1.** that may be conversed with, esp. easily and agreeably. **2.** able or disposed to converse. **3.** pertaining to or proper for conversation. – **conversableness,** *n.* – **conversably,** *adv.*

**conversant** /kən'vɜsənt, 'kɒnvəsənt/, *adj.* familiar by use or study (fol. by *with*): *conversant with a subject.* [ME, from L *conversans,* ppr., associating with] – **conversance, conversancy,** *n.* – **conversantly,** *adv.*

**conversation** /kɒnvə'seɪʃən/, *n.* **1.** informal interchange of thoughts by spoken words; a talk or colloquy. **2.** an instance of this. **3.** association or social intercourse; intimate acquaintance. **4.** *Archaic.* behaviour, or manner of living. [ME, from OF, from L *conversātio* frequent use, intercourse]

**conversational** /kɒnvə'seɪʃənəl/, *adj.* **1.** of, pertaining to, or characteristic of, conversation. **2.** able, or ready to converse; given to conversation. – **conversationally,** *adv.*

**conversationalist** /kɒnvə'seɪʃənələst/, *n.* one given to or excelling in conversation.

**conversation lolly** /kɒnvə'seɪʃən ,lɒli/, *n.* a small confection on which is stamped a short phrase. Also, **conversation sweet.**

**conversation piece** /'– pis/, *n.* **1.** an object that arouses comment because of some striking or unusual quality. **2.** a play emphasising dialogue.

**conversazione** /,kɒnvəsatsi'ouni/, *n., pl.* **-ziones** /-si'ouniz/. **1.** a social gathering for conversation, etc., esp. on literary or scholarly subjects. **2.** a soiree given by a learned society, for demonstrations, exhibition of specimens, etc.

**converse**[1] /kən'vɜs/, *v.,* **-versed, -versing;** /'kɒnvɜs/, n. *–v.i.* **1.** to talk informally with another; interchange thought by speech. **2.** to hold inward communion (fol. by *with*). *–n.* **3.** familiar discourse or talk; conversation. **4.** inward communion. [ME *converse(n),* from OF *converser,* from L *conversārī* dwell or associate with] – **converser,** *n.*

**converse**[2] /'kɒnvɜs/, *adj.* **1.** turned about; opposite or contrary in direction or action. *–n.* **2.** a thing which is the opposite or contrary of another. **3.** *Logic.* **a.** a proposition obtained from another proposition by conversion. **b.** the relation between one term and a second when the second term is related in a certain manner to the first. For example: the relation *descendant of* is the converse of *ancestor of.* [L *conversus,* pp., turned about] – **conversely** /kɒn'vɜsli, 'kɒn-/, *adv.*

**conversion** /kən'vɜʒən, -vɜʃən/, *n.* **1.** the act of converting. **2.** the state of being converted. **3.** change in character, form, or function. **4.** spiritual change from sinfulness to righteousness. **5.** change from one religion, party, etc., to another. **6.** *Maths.* a change in the form or units of an expression. **7.** *Logic.* the transposition of the subject and the predicate of a proposition, in accordance with rules of syllogistic logic, so as to form a new proposition. For example: *no good man is unhappy* becomes by conversion *no unhappy man is good.* **8.** *Law.* **a.** unauthorised assumption and exercise of rights of ownership over personal property belonging to another. **b.** change from realty into personalty, or vice versa, as in sale or purchase of land, minerals, etc. **9.** *Rugby Football.* **a.** the act of converting a try. **b.** the try so converted. **10.** *Psychol.* the process by which a repressed psychic event, idea, feeling, memory, or impulse is represented by a bodily change or symptom, thus simulating physical illnesses or their symptoms. **11.** *Physics.* the process of converting fertile material into fissile material in a nuclear reactor. – **conversicnal, conversionary,** *adj.*

**convert** /kən'vɜt/, *v.;* /'kɒnvɜt/, *n.* *–v.t.* **1.** to change into something of different form or properties; transmute; transform. **2.** *Chem.* to cause (a substance) to undergo a chemical change: *to convert sugar into alcohol.* **3.** to cause to adopt a different religion, party, opinion, etc., esp. one regarded as better. **4.** to change in character; cause to turn from an evil life to a righteous one. **5.** to turn to another or a particular use or purpose; divert from the proper or intended use. **6.** to appropriate wrongfully to one's own use. **7.** *Law.* to assume unlawful rights of ownership of (personal property). **8.** *Rugby Football.* to add a goal to a (try) by kicking the ball over the crossbar of the goalposts, scoring 5 points in all. **9.** *Logic.* to transpose the subject and predicate of (a proposition) by conversion. **10.** to exchange for an equivalent: *to convert banknotes into gold.* **11.** to change stocks or debentures into others of a different type. **12.** *Obs.* to invert or transpose. *–v.i.* **13.** *Rugby Football.* to score a goal from a try. *–n.* **14.** one who has been converted, as to a religion or an opinion. [ME *converte(n),* from L *convertere* turn about, change]

**converter** /kən'vɜtə/, *n.* **1.** one who or that which converts. **2.** *Elect.* **a.** a device which changes alternating current to direct current or vice versa. **b.** a device which alters the frequency of signals. **3.** *Electronics.* a translator from one electrical representation to another as an analog-to-digital converter. **4.** *Metall.* a furnace in which air is blown through a bath of molten metal or matte, oxidising the impurities and maintaining the temperature through the heat produced by the oxidation reaction. **5.** Also, **converter reactor.** *Physics.* a nuclear reactor which produces fissile material from fertile material. Also, **convertor.**

**convertible** /kən'vɜtəbəl/, *adj.* **1.** capable of being converted. **2.** (of a motor car) having a removable top. **3.** (of currency) capable of being exchanged at a fixed price. **4.** (of paper currency) capable of being exchanged for gold on demand to its full value at the issuing bank. *–n.* **5.** *Colloq.* a convertible motor car. – **convertibility** /kənvɜtə'bɪləti/, **convertibleness,** *n.* – **convertibly,** *adv.*

**convertible note** /– 'noʊt/, *n. Stock Exchange.* fixed interest security issued by a borrower which can be converted into ordinary share capital of the borrower at a predetermined rate, usu. within a specified time period, ten years being the absolute minimum.

**convertiplane** /kən'vɜtəpleɪn/, *n.* an aircraft capable of both vertical flight (like a helicopter) and level forward flight as a conventional fixed-wing aircraft.

**convex** /'kɒnvɛks/, *adj.* **1.** (esp. of optical lenses and mirrors) curved like a circle or sphere when viewed from without; bulging and curved. *–n.* **2.** a convex surface, part, or thing. [L *convexus* vaulted, arched; apparently earlier var. of *convectus,* pp., carried together] – **convexly,** *adv.*

A B C

A, convex or plano-convex lens; B, convexo-concave lens; C, biconvex lens

**convexity** /kən'vɛksəti/, *n., pl.* **-ties. 1.** the state of being convex. **2.** a convex surface or thing.

**convexo-concave** /kən,vɛksoʊ-kɒn'keɪv/, *adj.* convex on one side and concave on the other.

**convexo-convex** /kən,vɛksoʊ-kɒn'vɛks/, *adj.* →**biconvex.**

**convexo-plane** /kən,vɛksoʊ-'pleɪn/, *adj.* →**plano-convex.**

**convey** /kən'veɪ/, *v.t.* **1.** to carry or transport from one place to another. **2.** to lead or conduct as a channel or medium; transmit. **3.** to communicate; impart; make known. **4.** *Law.* to transfer; pass the title to. **5.** *Obs.* to take away secretly. **6.** *Obs.* to steal. [ME *conveye(n),* from OF *conveier,* from *con-* CON- + *veier,* from *veie,* from L *via* way, journey] – **conveyable,** *adj.*

**conveyance** /kən'veɪəns/, *n.* **1.** the act of conveying; transmission; communication. **2.** a means of conveyance, esp. a vehicle; a carriage, motor car, etc. **3.** *Law.* **a.** the transfer of property from one person to another. **b.** the instrument or document by which this is effected.

**conveyancer** /kən'veɪənsə/, *n.* a person engaged in conveyancing.

**conveyancing** /kən'veɪənsɪŋ/, *n.* that branch of legal practice consisting of examining titles, giving opinions as to their validity, and preparing of deeds, etc., for the conveyance of property from one person to another.

**conveyor** /kən'veɪə/, *n.* **1.** one who or that which conveys. **2.** a contrivance for transporting material, as from one part of a building to another. Also, **conveyer.**

**conveyor belt** /'– bɛlt/, *n.* a flexible band passing about two or more wheels, etc., used to transport objects from one place to another, esp. in a factory.

**convict** /kən'vɪkt/, *v.;* /'kɒnvɪkt/, *n.* *–v.t.* **1.** to prove or declare guilty of an offence, esp. after a legal trial: *to convict the prisoner of a felony.* **2.** to impress with the sense of guilt. *–n.* **3.** a person proved or declared guilty of an offence. **4.** a person serving a prison sentence. **5.** (formerly) a person transported to the British colonies to serve out a prison sentence. [ME, from L *convictus,* pp., overcome, convicted] – **convictive,** *adj.*

**convict constable** /– 'kʌnstəbəl/, *n.* (formerly) a convict given authority to supervise a working party. Also, **prisoner constable.**

**conviction** /kən'vɪkʃən/, *n.* **1.** the act of convicting. **2.** the fact or state of being convicted. **3.** the act of convincing. **4.** the state of being convinced. **5.** a fixed or firm belief. – **convictional,** *adj.*

**convictism** /'kɒnvɪktɪzəm/, *n.* (formerly) the system of imprisoning convicts in a penal colony, esp. in a penal labour settlement, or as assigned servants to free settlers.

**convince** /kən'vɪns/, *v.t.,* **-vinced, -vincing. 1.** to persuade by argument or proof; cause to believe in the truth of what is alleged (oft. fol. by *of*): *to convince a man of his errors.* [L *convincere* overcome by argument or proof, convict of error or crime, prove] – **convincement,** *n.* – **convincer,** *n.* – **convincible,** *adj.* – **convincingly,** *adv.* – **convincingness,** *n.*

**convivial** /kən'vɪviəl/, *adj.* **1.** fond of feasting, drinking, and merry company; jovial. **2.** of or befitting a feast; festive. **3.** agreeable; sociable; merry. [L *convīviālis* pertaining to a feast] – **convivialist,** *n.* – **conviviality** /kənvɪvi'æləti/, *n.* – **convivially,** *adv.*

**convocation** /kɒnvə'keɪʃən/, *n.* **1.** the act of convoking. **2.** the fact or state of being convoked. **3.** a group of persons met in answer to a summons; an assembly. **4.** (*sometimes cap.*) an assembly of the graduates and friends of a university. [ME, from L *convocātio*] – **convocational,** *adj.*

**convoke** /kən'voʊk/, *v.t.,* **-voked, -voking.** to call together; summon to meet; assemble by summons. [L *convocāre* call together] – **convoker,** *n.*

**convolute** /'kɒnvəlut/, *v.,* **-luted, -luting,** *adj.* *–v.t.* **1.** to coil up; form into a twisted shape. *–adj.* **2.** rolled up together, or one part over another. **3.** *Bot.* coiled up longitudinally, so that one margin is within the coil and the other without, as the petals of cotton. [L *convolūtus,* pp., rolled together] – **convolutely,** *adv.*

**convolution** /kɒnvə'luʃən/, *n.* **1.** a rolled up or coiled condition. **2.** a rolling or coiling together. **3.** a turn of anything coiled; whorl; sinuosity. **4.** *Anat.* one of the sinuous folds or ridges of the surface of the brain.

**convolve** /kən'vɒlv/, *v.,* **-volved, -volving.** *–v.t.* **1.** to roll or wind together; coil; twist. *–v.i.* **2.** to form convolutions. [L *convolvere* roll together]

**convolvulus** /kən'vɒlvjələs/, *n., pl.* **-luses, -li** /-li/. any plant of the genus *Convolvulus,* mostly of temperate regions, comprising erect, twining or prostrate herbs with trumpet-shaped flowers; bindweed; morning glory.

**convoy** /'kɒnvɔɪ/, *v.t.* **1.** to accompany or escort, now usu. for protection: *a merchant ship convoyed by a destroyer.* *–n.* **2.** the act of convoying. **3.** the protection afforded by an escort. **4.** an armed force, warship, etc., that escorts, esp. for protection. **5.** a formation of ships, a train of vehicles, etc., usually accompanied by a protecting escort. **6.** any group of military vehicles travelling together under the same orders. [ME, from F *convoyer,* earlier *conveier* CONVEY]

**convulsant** /kən'vʌlsənt/, *adj.* **1.** causing convulsions. **2.** of or pertaining to a convulsant. *–n.* **3.** a drug that causes convulsions. [F, from *convulser* CONVULSE]

**convulse** /kən'vʌls/, *v.t.,* **-vulsed, -vulsing. 1.** to shake violently; agitate. **2.** to cause to laugh violently. **3.** to cause to suffer violent muscular spasms; distort (the features) as by strong emotion. [L *convulsus,* pp., shattered]

**convulsion** /kən'vʌlʃən/, *n.* **1.** *Pathol.* contortion of the body caused by violent muscular contractions of the extremities, trunk, and head. **2.** violent agitation or disturbance; commotion. **3.** a violent fit of laughter.

**convulsionary** /kən'vʌlʃənəri/, *adj., n., pl.* **-ries.** *–adj.* **1.** pertaining to, of the nature of, or affected with convulsion. *–n.* **2.** one who is subject to convulsions.

**convulsive** /kən'vʌlsɪv/, *adj.* **1.** of the nature of or characterised by convulsions or spasms. **2.** producing or attended by convulsion: *convulsive rage.* – **convulsively,** *adv.* – **convulsiveness,** *n.*

**cony** /'koʊni/, *n., pl.* **-nies. 1.** the fur of a rabbit, esp. when dyed to simulate more expensive furs. **2.** the daman or some other animal of the same genus. **3.** →**pika. 4.** a rabbit. Also, **coney.** [ME *cunin,* from OF *conil,* from L *cunīculus* rabbit]

**coo** /ku/, *v.,* **cooed, cooing,** *n.* *–v.i.* **1.** to utter the soft, murmuring sound characteristic of pigeons or doves, or a similar sound. **2.** murmur or talk fondly or amorously. *–v.t.* **3.** to utter by cooing. *–n.* **4.** a cooing sound. *–interj.* **5.** *Brit. Colloq.* (an exclamation of surprise or amazement.). [imitative] – **cooer,** *n.* – **cooingly,** *adv.*

**cooba** /'kubə/, *n.* any of several species of the genus *Acacia,* native to Australia, esp. *A. salicina,* a pendulous and mainly riparian species; native willow; willow wattle. Also, **coobah, couba.**

**cooee** /'kui, ku'i/, *n., v.,* **-cooeed, -cooeeing.** *–n.* **1.** a prolonged clear call, the second syllable of which rises rapidly in pitch, used most frequently in the bush as a signal to attract attention. **2. within cooee,** within calling distance. **3. not within cooee,** far from achieving a given goal. *–v.i.* **4.** to utter the call 'cooee'. Also, **cooey.** [Aboriginal]

**cooee bird** /'– bɜd/, *n.* →**koel** (def. 1).

**cooey** /'kui, ku'i/, *n., pl.* **cooeys,** *v.,* **cooeyed, cooeying.** →**cooee.**

**coogans** /'kugənz/, *n.pl.* a child's overalls. [popularised by Jackie *Coogan,* an American child film star]

**cook**[1] /kʊk/, *v.t.* **1.** to prepare (food) by the action of heat, as by boiling, baking, roasting, etc. **2.** to subject (anything) to the action of heat. 3. *Colloq.* to concoct; invent falsely; falsify (oft. fol. by *up*): *cook the books.* 4. *Colloq.* to ruin; spoil. 5. **cook one's goose,** to frustrate or spoil one's plans. *–v.i.* 6. to prepare food by the action of heat. 7. (of food) to undergo cooking. *–n.* 8. one who cooks. 9. one whose occupation is the preparation of food for the table. [ME; OE *cōc,* from LL *cocus,* L *coquus*]

**cook**[2] /kʊk/, *n. Colloq.* a look. [rhyming slang, *Captain Cook* a look]

**cookbook** /ˈkʊkbʊk/, *n.* a book containing recipes and instructions for cooking. Also, **cookery book.**

**cooker**[1] /ˈkʊkə/, *n. Brit.* an apparatus, portable or fixed, and in many forms, for cooking, commonly using coal, oil, gas, or electricity.

**cooker**[2] /ˈkʊkə/, *n. N.Z.* →**Captain Cooker.**

**cookery** /ˈkʊkəri/, *n., pl.* **-eries.** 1. the art or practice of cooking.

**cookery book** /ˈ– bʊk/, *n.* →**cookbook.**

**cookhouse** /ˈkʊkhaʊs/, *n.* a kitchen standing alone or detached from the main building, as in gaols, army camps, early farm houses.

**cookie**[1] /ˈkʊki/, *n., pl.* **cookies.** 1. *Chiefly U.S.* a biscuit. 2. *Colloq.* a person: *a smart cookie.* 3. **that's the way the cookie crumbles,** *Colloq.* that's how things are. Also, **cooky.** [D *koekie,* colloq. var. of *koekje,* diminutive of *koek* cake]

**cookie**[2] /ˈkʊki/, *n.* a sheet of opaque material with irregular holes cut in it behind which a light is fixed to create shadows in the area being filmed. [shortened form of *Cukalorise,* the name of the designer]

**cooking** /ˈkʊkɪŋ/, *n.* 1. →**cookery.** *–ppr. Colloq.* 2. **be cooking,** in full swing: *that band is really cooking now.* 3. **be cooking with oil** or **gas,** to be in control of the situation; to begin to achieve some results or understanding. 4. **what's cooking?,** what is happening?

**cooking chocolate** /ˈ– tʃɒklət/, *n.* chocolate that has been made with little or no milk.

**Cook Islands** /kʊk ˈaɪləndz/, *n.pl.* a group of islands in the South Pacific, an internally self-governing state in free association with New Zealand.

**cookout** /ˈkʊkaʊt/, *n. U.S.* 1. a barbecue party. 2. a meal cooked at a barbecue.

**cook-shop** /ˈkʊk-ʃɒp/, *n. N.Z.* a sheep station cookhouse.

**Cooktown orchid** /ˌkʊktaʊn ˈɔkəd/, *n.* an attractive, purple orchid, *Dendrobium bigibbum,* found on rocks and trees in far northern Queensland; the floral emblem of Queensland.

**cookware** /ˈkʊkwɛə/, *n.* utensils for cooking.

**cooky** /ˈkʊki/, *n., pl.* **cookies.** →**cookie**[1].

**cool** /kul/, *adj.* 1. moderately cold; neither warm nor very cold. 2. imparting or permitting a sensation of moderate coldness: *a cool dress.* 3. not excited; calm; unmoved; not hasty; deliberate; aloof. 4. deficient in ardour or enthusiasm. 5. lacking in cordiality: *a cool reception.* 6. calmly audacious or impudent. 7. *Colloq.* (of a number or sum) without exaggeration or qualification: *a cool thousand.* 8. (of colours) with green, blue, or violet predominating. 9. (of jazz) controlled, subtle, and relaxed. 10. *Colloq.* smart; up-to-date; fashionable. 11. *Colloq.* attractive; excellent. *–n.* 12. that which is cool; the cool part, place, time, etc. 13. coolness. 14. *Colloq.* detachment; rejection of involvement. 15. **lose** or **blow one's cool,** to become angry. *–v.i.* 16. to become cool. 17. to become less ardent, cordial, etc.; become more moderate. *–v.t.* 18. to make cool; impart a sensation of coolness to. 19. to lessen the ardour or intensity of; allay; calm; moderate. 20. **cool one's heels,** to be kept waiting. *–v.i.* 21. **cool off** or **down,** *Colloq.* to become calmer; to become more reasonable. [ME, OE *cōl;* akin to COLD, CHILL] – **coolly,** *adv.* – **coolness,** *n.*

coolabah tree

**coolabah** /ˈkuləba/, *n.* a species of eucalypt, *Eucalyptus microtheca,* common in the Australian inland and usu. associated with areas subject to occasional inundation. Also, **coolibah.** [Aboriginal]

**coolamon** /ˈkuləmɒn/, *n.* a basin-shaped wooden dish made and used by the Aborigines. [Aboriginal]

**coolant** /ˈkulənt/, *n.* 1. a substance, usu. a liquid or gas, used to reduce the temperature of a system below a specified value by conducting away the heat evolved in the operation of the system, as the liquid in a motor-car cooling system. The coolant may be used to transfer heat to a power generator, as in a nuclear reactor. 2. a lubricant which serves to dissipate the heat caused by friction. [COOL + -ANT]

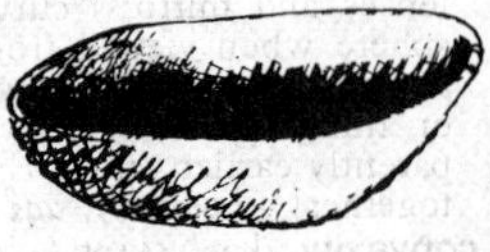

**cooler** /ˈkulə/, *n.* 1. a container or apparatus for cooling or keeping cool: *a water-cooler.* 2. anything that cools or makes cool; refrigerant. 3. *Colloq.* prison.

coolamon

**Coolgardie safe** /kulˌgadi ˈseɪf/, *n.* →**cool safe.** Also, **Coolgardie cooler.** [from *Coolgardie,* town in WA]

**cool-headed** /kul-ˈhɛdəd/, *adj.* not easily excited; calm.

**coolibah** /ˈkuləba/, *n.* →**coolabah.**

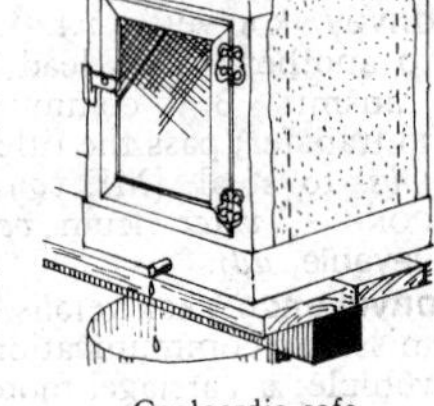
Coolgardie safe

**coolie** /ˈkuli/, *n.* 1. (in India, China, etc.) an unskilled native labourer. 2. (elsewhere) such a labourer employed for cheap service. [probably var. of *kōlī,* name of tribe of Gujarat, but cf. Tamil *kūli* hire, wages]

**cooling tower** /ˈkulɪŋ taʊə/, *n.* a concrete or wooden structure used in industrial processes to cool water after it has passed through a condenser; so arranged that the maximum surface area of water is exposed to the atmosphere.

**coolish** /ˈkulɪʃ/, *adj.* somewhat cool.

**cool safe** /ˈkul seɪf/, *n.* a cabinet, for the storage of perishable foodstuffs, which allows a breeze to blow through wet fabric, such as hessian, thus reducing the temperature inside.

**cooly** /ˈkuli/, *n., pl.* **-lies.** →**coolie.**

**coomb** /kum/, *n.* a narrow valley or deep hollow, esp. one enclosed on all sides but one. Also, **combe, comb.** [OE *cumb* valley, c. d. G *Kumme* trough; but cf. Welsh *cwm* valley]

**coon** /kun/, *n.* 1. (*derog.*) a dark-skinned person. 2. a raccoon.

**coon bug** /ˈ– bʌg/, *n.* either of two native Australian bugs, *Oxycarenus luctuosus* (also known as the **cotton-feed bug**) and *O. arctatus.* The coon bug is small, coloured black and white, feeds chiefly on malvaceous plants but also on vegetables and orchard trees, is widely dispersed throughout Australia, and is classified as a minor pest.

**cooncan** /ˈkunkæn/, *n.* a card game of the rummy family for two players.

**coontie** /ˈkunti/, *n.* 1. an arrowroot plant, *Zamia floridana* of Florida. 2. the flour produced from its starch. [N. Amer. Ind. (Seminole) *kunti* the flour]

**co-op** /ˈkoʊ-ɒp/, *n.* a cooperative shop, store, or society.

**coop** /kup/, *n.* 1. an enclosure, cage, or pen, usu. with bars or wires on one side or more, in which fowls, etc., are confined for fattening, transportation, etc. 2. a wicker basket used for catching fish. 3. any small or narrow place. 4. *Colloq.* a prison. 5. **fly the coop,** *Colloq.* to escape from a prison, etc. *–v.t.* 6. to place in, or as in, a coop; confine narrowly (oft. fol. by *up* or *in*). [ME *coupe, cupe,* OE *cӯpe* basket, c. LG *küpe*]

**cooper** /ˈkupə/, *n.* 1. one who makes or repairs vessels formed of staves and hoops, as casks, barrels, tubs, etc. *–v.t.* 2. to make or repair (casks, barrels, etc.). *–v.i.* 3. to work as a cooper. [ME *couper,* from MD or MLG *kuper,* from VL *cūpārius,* from L *cūpa* cask]

**cooperage** /ˈkupərɪdʒ/, *n.* 1. the work or business of a cooper. 2. the place where it is carried on. 3. the price paid for coopers' work.

**cooperate** /koʊˈɒpəreɪt/, *v.i.,* **-rated, -rating.** 1. to work or act together or jointly; unite in producing an effect. 2. to practise economic cooperation. [LL *cooperātus,* pp., having worked together] – **cooperator,** *n.*

**cooperation** /koʊɒpəˈreɪʃən/, *n.* **1.** the act or fact of cooperating; joint operation or action. **2.** *Ecol.* the conscious or unconscious behaviour of organisms living together and producing a result which has survival value for them. – **cooperationist,** *n.*

**cooperative** /koʊˈɒpərətɪv, -ˈɒprətɪv/, *adj.* **1.** cooperating. **2.** showing a willingness to cooperate; helpful. **3.** pertaining to economic cooperation: *a cooperative farm.* –*n.* **4.** a cooperative society or shop. **5.** a cooperative farm. – **cooperatively,** *adv.* – **cooperativeness,** *n.*

**cooperative farm** /– ˈfam/, *n.* **1.** a farm which shares with others the use of marketing facilities, machinery, labour, etc. **2.** a farm owned by a cooperative society or one run on cooperative principles. **3.** a farm run on a communal basis, as a kibbutz. **4.** →**collective farm.**

**cooperative society** /ˈ– səsaɪəti/, *n.* a business undertaking owned and controlled by its members, and formed to provide them with work or with goods at advantageous prices; a **consumers' cooperative** is owned by its customers, and **producers' cooperative** by its workers.

**cooper's flag** /kupəz ˈflæg/, *n. N.Z.* →**raupo.**

**coopery** /ˈkupəri/, *n., pl.* **-ries.** **1.** the work of a cooper. **2.** a cooper's shop. **3.** articles made by a cooper.

**coopt** /koʊˈɒpt/, *v.t.* to elect into a body by the votes of the existing members. [L *cooptāre*] – **cooption** /koʊˈɒpʃən/, **cooptation,** *n.* – **cooptative,** *adj.*

**coor** /kɔ/, *n. Mining.* a working party or gang of miners on a given shift. [F *corps* group]

**co-ord.,** **1.** coordinate. **2.** coordination.

**coordinal** /koʊˈɔdənəl/, *adj. Bot., Zool.* belonging to the same order.

**coordinate** /koʊˈɔdənət, -neɪt/, *adj., n.;* /koʊˈɔdəneɪt/, *v.,* **-nated, -nating.** –*adj.* **1.** of the same order or degree; equal in rank or importance. **2.** involving coordination. **3.** *Maths.* using or pertaining to systems of coordinates. –*n.* **4.** one who or that which is equal in rank or importance; an equal. **5.** *Maths.* any of the magnitudes which define the position of a point, line, or the like, by reference to a fixed figure, system of lines, etc. –*v.t.* **6.** to place or class in the same order, rank, division, etc. **7.** to place or arrange in due order or proper relative position. **8.** to combine in harmonious relation or action. –*v.i.* **9.** to become coordinate. **10.** to assume proper order or relation. **11.** to act in harmonious combination. [CO- + ORDINATE] – **coordinately,** *adv.* – **coordinateness,** *n.* – **coordinative,** *adj.* – **coordinator,** *n.*

**coordinate bond** /ˈ– bɒnd/, *n.* →**dative bond.**

**coordinate clause** /ˈ– klɒz/, *n.* one of two or more clauses of the same type, which are linked by coordinating conjunctions. See **subordinate clause.**

**coordinate covalent bond,** *n. Chem.* →**semipolar bond.**

**coordinated water** /koʊˌɔdəneɪtəd ˈwɔtə/, that portion of the water of hydration which is retained more tenaciously than the rest, as the molecule of water in $CuSO_4 \cdot 5H_2O$, which remains after the four molecules have been driven off at 100°C.

**coordinate geometry** /koʊˌɔdənət dʒiˈɒmətri/, *n.* →**analytical geometry.**

**coordinating conjunction** /koʊˌɔdəneɪtɪŋ kənˈdʒʌŋkʃən/, *n.* a conjunction such as *and, or* and *but* which links coordinate clauses.

**coordination** /koʊˌɔdəˈneɪʃən/, *n.* **1.** the act of coordinating. **2.** the state of being coordinated. **3.** due ordering or proper relation. **4.** harmonious combination.

**coordination compound** /– ˈkɒmpaʊnd/, *n.* a class of compounds consisting of a central atom or ion surrounded by a set (2 to 9) of other atoms, ions or small molecules called ligands.

**coordination number** /ˈ– nʌmbə/, *n.* **1.** the number of outer, or ligand, atoms bounded to the central atom in a co-ordination compound. **2.** the number of atoms or ions surrounding a central atom or ion in a crystal. Also, **ligancy.**

**coori** /ˈkuri/, *n., adj.* →**koori.**

**coorongite** /ˈkurɒŋgaɪt/, *n.* a boghead coal in the peat stage. [named after the locality where it was first found in 1865 on the shore of the *Coorong* river, S.A.]

**coot** /kut/, *n.* **1.** any of the aquatic birds of the genus *Fulica* characterised by lobate toes and short wings and tail, as the Australian coot, *Fulica atra,* a large black bird with a white frontal shield and bill. **2.** Also, **bald coot.** →**swamphen.** **3.** any of various other swimming and diving birds, as the scoter. **4.** *Colloq.* a fool; simpleton. **5.** *Colloq.* a man. [cf. D *koet*]

coot

**Cootamundra wattle** /ˌkutəmʌndrə ˈwɒtl/, *n.* an attractive small tree, *Acacia baileyana,* with silver-grey leaves and clusters of yellow blossom, native to a small area of New South Wales but widely cultivated elsewhere. [from *Cootamundra,* a town in southern N.S.W.]

**cootie** /ˈkuti/, *n.* the head louse, *Pediculus humanus.*

**cop**[1] /kɒp/, *n., v.,* **copped copping.** –*n.* **1.** *Colloq.* a policeman. **2.** *Colloq.* →**silent cop.** **3.** *Colloq.* an arrest; a state of being caught. **4.** *Colloq.* payment. **5.** *Colloq.* something advantageous, or profitable, as in the phrases:
**a sweet cop,** an easy job.
**a sure cop,** something certain.
**not much cop,** not worthwhile.
–*v.t.* **6.** *Colloq.* to steal. **7.** *Colloq.* to receive in payment. **8.** *Colloq.* to accept resignedly; put up with: *would you cop a deal like that?* **9.** *Colloq.* to be allotted, receive: *he copped more than his fair share.* **10. cop a load,** *Colloq.* to contract venereal disease. **11. cop it,** *Colloq.* to be punished. **12. cop it sweet,** *Colloq.* to have a lucky break. **13. cop the lot,** *Colloq.* to bear the brunt of some misfortune. **14. cop this!** *Colloq.* look at this! –*v.i.* **15. cop out,** *Colloq.* **a.** to opt out of (something). **b.** to fail completely. [OE *coppian* lop, steal]

**cop**[2] /kɒp/, *n.* **1.** a conical mass of thread, etc., wound on a spindle. **2.** *Obs.* the top or crest, esp. of a hill. [OE *cop, copp* top, summit. Cf. G *Kopf* head]

**copaiba** /kɒˈpaɪbə/, *n.* an oleoresin obtained from various tropical (chiefly South American) trees of the genus *Copaiba,* used esp. as a stimulant and diuretic. Also, **copaiva.** [Sp., from Tupi *kupaiba*]

**copal** /ˈkoʊpəl, -pæl/, *n.* a hard, lustrous resin yielded by various tropical trees, used chiefly in making varnishes. [Sp., from Nahuatl *kopalli* resin]

**coparcenary** /koʊˈpasənri/, *n.* (formerly) a special kind of joint ownership by several coheirs of the land of one who had died intestate. It might arise under common law among several daughters or under gavelkind among several sons.

**coparcener** /koʊˈpasənə/, *n.* a member of a coparcenary. [CO- + PARCENER]

**copartner** /koʊˈpatnə/, *n.* a partner; an associate. – **copartnership,** *n.*

**copasetic** /koʊpəˈsitɪk/, *adj. U.S. Colloq.* fine; splendid: *everything is copasetic.* Also, **copacetic.** [orig. unknown]

**cope**[1] /koʊp/, *v.,* **coped, coping.** –*v.i.* **1.** to struggle or contend, esp. on fairly even terms or with a degree of success (fol. by *with*). **2.** *Archaic.* to have to do (fol. by *with*). –*v.t.* **3.** *Colloq.* to cope with. [ME *coupe(n),* from F *couper* strike, from *coup* stroke, blow. See COUP, *n.*]

**cope**[2] /koʊp/, *n., v.,* **coped, coping.** –*n.* **1.** a long mantle of silk or other material worn by ecclesiastics over the alb or surplice in processions and on other occasions. **2.** any cloak-like or canopy-like covering. **3.** the vault of heaven; the sky. **4.** *Archit.* a coping. –*v.t.* **5.** to furnish with or as with a cope or coping. [ME; OE *cāp* (in *cantelcāp* cope), from ML *cāpa* cope]

A, cope[2] (def. 1)

**copeck** /ˈkoʊpɛk/, *n.* →**kopeck.**

**Copenhagen blue** /ˌkoʊpənheɪgən ˈblu/, *n.* grey-blue.

**copepod** /ˈkoʊpəpɒd/, *n.* **1.** any of the Copepoda, a large order of (mostly) minute freshwater and marine crustaceans. –*adj.* **2.** pertaining to the Copepoda. [Gk *kṓpē* handle, oar + -POD]

**coper** /ˈkoʊpə/, *n.* a horse-dealer.

**Copernican** /kə'pɜnɪkən/, *adj.* **1.** relating to the astronomic system of Copernicus, in which the sun is taken as the centre of the planets. **2.** of radical or major importance or degree: *a Copernican step in education.* [named after Nicolaus *Copernicus,* 1473-1543, Polish astronomer]

**copestone** /'koʊpstoʊn/, *n.* →**coping stone.**

**copha** /'koʊfə/, *n.* a white waxy solid derived from coconut flesh, a form of purified coconut oil, used as a shortening agent esp. in refrigerator biscuits; coconut butter. Also, **copha butter.** [Trademark]

**copier** /'kɒpiə/, *n.* **1.** one who copies; a copyist. **2.** →**photocopier.**

**copilot** /'koʊpaɪlət/, *n.* the assistant or second pilot in an aircraft.

**coping** /'koʊpɪŋ/, *n.* the uppermost course of a wall or the like, usu. made sloping so as to carry off water.

**coping saw** /'– sɔ/, *n.* a saw with a short, narrow blade held at both ends in a deeply recessed handle, for cutting curved shapes.

**coping stone** /'– stoʊn/, *n.* **1.** the top stone of a building or the like. **2.** a stone used for or in coping. **3.** the crown or completion. Also, **copestone.**

**copious** /'koʊpiəs/, *adj.* **1.** large in quantity or number; abundant. **2.** having or yielding an abundant supply. **3.** exhibiting abundance or fullness, as of thoughts or words. [ME, from L *cōpiōsus* plentiful] – **copiously,** *adv.* – **copiousness,** *n.*

**coplanar** /koʊ'pleɪnə/, *adj.* lying in the same plane.

**copolymer** /koʊ'pɒləmə/, *n.* a compound made by polymerising different compounds together.

**copolymerise** /koʊpə'lɪməraɪz, koʊ'pɒləməraɪz/, *v.,* **-rised, -rising.** *–v.t.* **1.** to subject to a change analogous to polymerisation, but with a union of unlike molecules. *–v.i.* **2.** to undergo such a change. Also, **copolymerize.** – **copolymerisation** /koʊpəˌlɪməraɪ'zeɪʃən, koʊˌpɒləməraɪ'zeɪʃən/, *n.*

**cop-out** /'kɒp-aʊt/, *n. Colloq.* a way out of a situation of embarrassment or responsibility.

**copper**[1] /'kɒpə/, *n.* **1.** *Chem.* a malleable, ductile metallic element having a characteristic reddish brown colour. *Symbol:* Cu; *at. wt:* 63.54; *at. no.:* 29; *sp. gr.:* 8.92 at 20°C. **2.** a copper coin, as the English penny or half-penny or the U.S. cent. **3.** a container made of copper. **4.** a large vessel (formerly of copper) for boiling clothes. **5.** a metallic reddish brown. *–v.t.* **6.** to cover, coat, or sheathe with copper. *–adj.* **7.** made of copper. **8.** copper-coloured. **9.** pertaining to copper. [ME *coper,* OE *coper, copor* (c. G *Kupfer*), from LL *cuprum,* for L *aes Cyprium* Cyprian metal. See CYPRUS]

**copper**[2] /'kɒpə/, *n. Colloq.* a policeman. [see COP[1]]

**copper 7** /- 'sɛvən/, *n.* a small intra-uterine device made of copper and shaped like a 7.

**copperas** /'kɒpərəs/, *n.* →**ferrous sulphate.** [ME *coperose.* Cf. OF *couperose,* from ML (*aqua*) *cuprōsa,* from LL *cuprum.* See COPPER[1]]

**copper beech** /kɒpə 'bitʃ/, *n.* a variety of the beech, *Fagus sylvatica,* with reddish brown leaves.

**copper-bottomed** /'kɒpə-bɒtəmd/, *adj.* **1.** with bottom covered with copper. **2.** sound, esp. financially sound.

**copperhead** /'kɒpəhɛd/, *n.* **1.** a bulky, marsh-dwelling venomous Australian snake, *Denisonia superba,* brown to black above with a coppery red band behind the head, and reaching about two metres in length. **2.** a venomous snake, *Ancistrodon contortrix,* of the U.S., having a copper-coloured head and reaching a length of about one metre. **3.** (*cap.*) *U.S.* a Northern sympathiser with the South during the American Civil War.

**copperplate** /'kɒpəpleɪt/, *n.* **1.** a plate of polished copper on which a writing, picture, or design is made by engraving or etching. **2.** a print or an impression from such a plate. **3.** engraving or printing of this kind. **4.** an ornate, rounded style of handwriting, formerly much used in engravings. *–adj.* **5.** (of handwriting) ornate, rounded, and formal; in the style of copperplate. **6.** *Colloq.* polished; without blemish; neat; clear.

**copper pyrites** /kɒpə paɪ'raɪtiz/, *n.* →**chalcopyrite.**

**coppersmith** /'kɒpəsmɪθ/, *n.* a worker in copper; one who manufactures copper utensils.

**copper's nark** /kɒpəz 'nak/, *n. Colloq.* a police informer.

**copper stick** /'kɒpə stɪk/, *n.* a long wooden stick used to stir the copper when boiling clothes.

**copper sulphate** /– 'sʌlfeɪt/, *n.* →**blue vitriol.**

**coppertail** /'kɒpəteɪl/, *n.* a working class person (as opposed to a *silvertail*).

**coppertop** /'kɒpətɒp/, *n. Colloq.* a red-headed person. Also, **coppernob.**

**copper uranite** /kɒpə 'jurənaɪt/, *n.* →**torbernite.** Also, **cupro-uranite.**

**copperware** /'kɒpəwɛə/, *n.* articles made of copper.

**coppery** /'kɒpəri/, *adj.* of, like, or containing copper.

**coppice** /'kɒpəs/, *n.* **1.** Also, **copse.** a wood, thicket, or plantation of small trees or bushes. *–v.t.* **2.** to cut, as of *Eucalyptus* trees, to encourage numerous slender trunks to regenerate from the root-stock. [OF *copeiz,* from *couper* cut + *-eiz* (from L *-āticium*)]

**copra** /'kɒprə/, *n.* the dried kernel or meat of the coconut, from which coconut oil is pressed. [Pg., from Malayalam *koppara,* c. Hind. *khoprā* coconut]

**copraemia** /kɒ'primiə/, *n.* blood-poisoning due to absorption of faecal matter. Also, *Chiefly U.S.,* **copremia.** [*copr(o)-* (see COPROLITE) + -AEMIA]

**copro-**, a prefix meaning 'dung' or 'excrement', as in *coprophobia.* [combining form of Gk *kópros* dung]

**coprolite** /'kɒprəlaɪt/, *n.* a roundish, stony mass consisting of petrified faecal matter of animals. [COPRO- + -LITE]

**coprology** /kɒp'rɒlədʒi/, *n.* →**scatology** (def. 3).

**coprophagous** /kɒp'rɒfəgəs/, *adj.* feeding on dung, as certain beetles. [COPRO- + -PHAGOUS]

**coprophilia** /kɒprə'fɪliə/, *n.* a morbid pleasure or interest in faeces, obscenity, or filth.

**coprophilous** /kə'prɒfələs/, *adj.* (of bacteria, insects, etc.) fed by dung. [COPRO- + -PHILOUS]

**coprophobia** /kɒprə'foʊbiə/, *n.* a morbid fear of faeces.

**coprosma** /kə'prɒzmə/, *n.* any member of the very large genus *Coprosma* of South-East Asia and the Pacific, esp. *C. lucida,* native to New Zealand, often grown as a hedge plant for its glossy leaves.

**copse** /kɒps/, *n.* →**coppice** (def. 1).

**cop shop** /'kɒp ʃɒp/, *n. Colloq.* a police station.

**Copt** /kɒpt/, *n.* **1.** one of the natives of Egypt descended from the ancient Egyptians. **2.** an Egyptian Christian of the sect of the Monophysites. [Ar. *qibt, qubt* the Copts, from Coptic *gyptios,* aphetic var. of Gk *Aigýptios* Egyptian]

**copter** /'kɒptə/, *n. Colloq.* a helicopter.

**Coptic** /'kɒptɪk/, *n.* **1.** the extinct language of Egypt which developed from ancient Egyptian, used liturgically by Egyptian Christians. *–adj.* **2.** of the Copts.

**Coptic Church** /– 'tʃɜtʃ/, *n.* the native Christian church in Egypt.

**copula** /'kɒpjələ/, *n., pl.* **-lae** /-li/. **1.** something that connects or links together. **2.** *Gram., Logic.* a word or set of words, as the English verbs *be, seem, appear,* etc., which acts as a connecting link between the subject and the predicate. [L: a band, bond] – **copular,** *adj.*

**copulate** /'kɒpjuleɪt/, *v.,* **-lated, -lating;** /'kɒpjulət/, *adj.* *–v.i.* **1.** to unite in sexual intercourse. *–adj.* **2.** *Obs.* joined. [L *copulātus,* pp., coupled]

**copulation** /kɒpju'leɪʃən/, *n.* **1.** sexual union or intercourse. **2.** a joining together or coupling.

**copulative** /'kɒpjulətɪv/, *adj.* **1.** serving to unite or couple. **2.** involving or consisting of connected words or clauses. **3.** of the nature of a copula: *a copulative verb.* **4.** of or pertaining to copulation. *–n.* **5.** a copulative word. – **copulatively,** *adv.*

**copy** /'kɒpi/, *n., pl.* **copies,** *v.,* **copied, copying.** *–n.* **1.** a transcript, reproduction, or imitation of an original. **2.** that which is to be transcribed, reproduced, or imitated. **3.** written, typed, or printed matter, or artwork, intended to be reproduced in print. **4.** paper, specially prepared for the writing of advertisements, etc., having guide lines to indicate margins and the number of spaces per line. **5.** one of the various examples or specimens of the same book, engraving, or the like. **6.** *Archaic.* an example of penmanship to be copied by a pupil. *–v.t.* **7.** to make a copy of; transcribe; reproduce: *to copy a set of figures.* **8.** to follow as a pattern or model; imitate. **9.** to provide a copy for: *write a letter and copy the staff.* *–v.i.* **10.** to make a copy or copies. **11.** to make or do something in imitation of something else. **12.** to reproduce or make use of unfairly another's written work, as a fellow pupil's. [ME *copie,* from F, from L *cōpia* plenty, ML transcript]

**copybook** /ˈkɒpibʊk/, *n.* **1.** a book in which copies are written or printed for learners to imitate. **2.** *U.S.* a book for or containing copies, as of documents. **3. blot one's copybook,** to spoil, damage or destroy one's reputation or record. *–adj.* **4.** (in some sports) according to the rules; excellent; conforming to established principles.

**copycat** /ˈkɒpikæt/, *n., v.,* **-catted, -catting.** *–n.* **1.** a child who copies another's work. **2.** a slavish imitator. *–v.i.* **3.** to imitate slavishly; copy.

**copy desk** /ˈkɒpi dɛsk/, *n.* the desk in a newspaper office at which news stories, etc., are edited and prepared for printing.

**copyedit** /ˈkɒpiˌɛdət/, *v.t.* to correct, style and mark up copy (def. 3) to make it ready for printing.

**copyeditor** /ˈkɒpiˌɛdətə/, *n.* a book editor who specialises in copyediting.

**copyhold** /ˈkɒpihoʊld/, *n.* **1.** (formerly) a type of ownership of land in England, evidenced by a copy of the manorial court roll establishing the title. **2.** (formerly) land held in this way.

**copyholder** /ˈkɒpihoʊldə/, *n.* **1.** one who or that which holds copy. **2.** a device for holding copy in its place, as on a printer's frame or on a typewriter. **3.** a proofreader's assistant who reads copy aloud, or follows it while proof is read, for the detection of deviations from it in proof. **4.** *Law.* one who holds an estate in copyhold.

**copyist** /ˈkɒpiəst/, *n.* **1.** a transcriber, esp. of documents. **2.** *Music.* one who notates the individual orchestral parts by reference to the full orchestral score; a part copyist. **3.** an imitator.

**copyright** /ˈkɒpiraɪt/, *n.* **1.** the exclusive right, granted by law for a certain term of years, to make and dispose of copies of, and otherwise to control, a literary, musical, dramatic, or artistic work. *–adj.* **2.** protected by copyright. *–v.t.* **3.** to secure a copyright on. – **copyrightable,** *adj.* – **copyrighter,** *n.*

**copytaker** /ˈkɒpiteɪkə/, *n.* a person employed by a newspaper to take copy over the phone from reporters in the field.

**copy typist** /ˈkɒpi taɪpəst/, *n.* a typist who works from written or typed pages, rather than from dictation.

**copywriter** /ˈkɒpiraɪtə/, *n.* a writer of copy for advertisements or publicity releases.

**coq au vin** /kɒk oʊ ˈvæn/, *n.* a chicken cooked in red wine with mushrooms and herbs. [F: chicken in wine]

**coquet** /koʊˈkɛt, kɒˈkɛt/, *v.,* **-quetted, -quetting,** *adj.* *–v.i.* **1.** to trifle in love; flirt; play the coquette. **2.** to act without seriousness; trifle; dally. *–adj.* **3.** coquettish. [F, diminutive of *coq* cock]

**coquetry** /ˈkoʊkətri, ˈkɒk-/, *n., pl.* **-tries.** **1.** the behaviour or arts of a coquette; flirtation. **2.** trifling.

**coquette** /koʊˈkɛt, kɒˈkɛt/, *n.* a woman who tries to gain the admiration and affections of men for mere self-gratification; a flirt. [F. See COQUET] – **coquettish,** *adj.* – **coquettishly,** *adv.* – **coquettishness,** *n.*

**coquilla nut** /kɒˈkiljə nʌt/, *n.* the elongated oval fruit or nut of a South American palm, *Attalea funifera,* having a very hard brown shell. [*coquilla,* from Pg. *coquilho,* diminutive of *coco* coconut]

**coquille** /kɒˈkijə/ *for def. 1;* /kɒˈki/ *for def. 2.* *n.* **1.** a scallop shell, or scallop-shaped dish, in which various seafoods are served, usu. in a white sauce and browned under a griller. **2.** *Fencing.* a saucer-shaped guard on a foil to protect the hand; guard. [F, from L *conchylium,* from Gk *konchýlion* mussel, diminutive of *kónchē* CONCH[1]]

**coquina** /kɒˈkinə/, *n.* a soft, whitish rock made up of fragments of marine shells and coral, used to some extent as a building material. [Sp.: shellfish, cockle]

**coquito** /kɒˈkitoʊ/, *n., pl.* **-tos.** a palm, *Jubaea chilensis,* of Chile, bearing small edible nuts, which yield a sweet syrup. Also, **coquito palm.** [Sp., diminutive of *coco* coconut]

**cor** /kɔ/, *interj. Colloq.* (an exclamation of surprise.)

**cor-,** variant of **com-** before *r,* as in *corrupt.*

**Cor.,** **1.** *Bible.* Corinthians. **2.** coroner.

**coraciiform** /kɒrəˈsaɪəfɔm/, *adj.* belonging or pertaining to the Coraciiformes, the order of birds that includes the kingfishers, motmots, rollers, bee-eaters, and hornbills. [NL *Coracia* genus of birds (from Gk *kórax* raven) + -I- + -FORM]

**coracle** /ˈkɒrəkəl/, *n.* (in Wales and western England) a small boat, nearly or quite as broad as long, made like a basket. [Welsh *corwgl, cwrwgl,* from *corwg, cwrwg* carcass, boat]

**coracoid** /ˈkɒrəkɔɪd/, *adj.* **1.** pertaining to a bony process extending from the scapula towards the sternum in many vertebrates. *–n.* **2.** a coracoid bone. [Gk *korakoeidḗs* raven-like]

**coral** /ˈkɒrəl/, *n.* **1.** the hard, calcareous (red, white, black, etc.) skeleton of any of various, mostly compound, marine coelenterate animals, the individual polyps of which come forth by budding. **2.** such skeletons collectively, as forming reefs, islands, etc. **3.** an animal of this kind. **4.** something made of coral, as an ornament, child's toy, etc. **5.** a reddish yellow; light yellowish red; pinkish yellow. **6.** the unimpregnated roe or eggs of the lobster, which when boiled assume the colour of red coral. *–adj.* **7.** made of coral: *a coral reef, coral ornament.* **8.** making coral: *a coral polyp.* **9.** resembling coral, esp. in colour. [ME, from OF, from L *corallum, coralium,* from Gk *korállion* red coral]

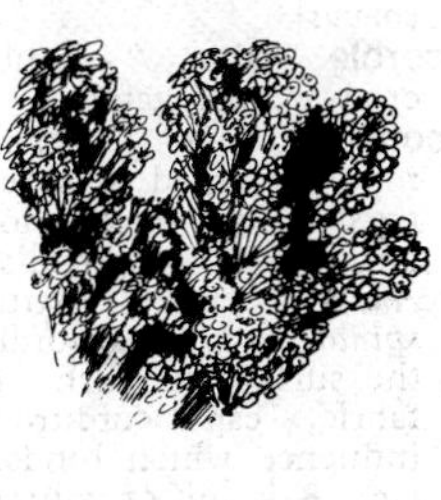
coral

**coralfish** /ˈkɒrəlfɪʃ/, *n.* any of various small, brightly coloured marine fish of coral reefs, as members of the Chaetodontidae family.

**coral fungus** /kɒrəl ˈfʌŋgəs/, *n.* any of the variously tinted fungi of the family Clavariaceae.

**coral island** /– ˈaɪlənd/, *n.* an island made from a coral reef.

**coralliferous** /ˌkɒrəˈlɪfərəs/, *adj.* containing or bearing coral; producing coral.

**coralline** /ˈkɒrəlaɪn/, *adj.* **1.** consisting of or containing deposits of calcium carbonate. **2.** coral-like. **3.** coral-coloured; reddish yellow; light yellowish red; pinkish yellow. *–n.* **4.** any alga having a red colour and impregnated with lime. **5.** any of various coral-like animals, or calcareous algae.

**corallite** /ˈkɒrəlaɪt/, *n.* **1.** skeleton of an individual coral animal. **2.** skeleton of an individual coral in a colony.

**coralloid** /ˈkɒrəlɔɪd/, *adj.* having the form or appearance of coral. Also, **coralloidal.**

**coral-pea** /kɒrəl-ˈpi/, *n.* any red-flowered trailing plant of the genus *Kennedia,* family Papilionaceae, as *K. rubicunda,* of eastern Australia.

**coral reef** /kɒrəl ˈrif/, *n.* a reef or bank formed by the growth and deposit of coral polyps.

**Coral Sea Islands,** *n. pl.* a group of reefs lying off the coast of Queensland; an Australian territory.

**coral snake** /ˈkɒrəl sneɪk/, *n.* **1.** a small, venomous but unaggressive snake, *Brachyurophis australis,* of eastern Australia, red with distinctive black and yellow banding. **2.** any of the brilliantly coloured venomous snakes of the genus *Micrurus,* often with alternating black, yellow, and red rings, including forms found in the southern U.S. and tropical South America. **3.** any snake of the genus *Callophis* of India, reddish in colour and variously patterned. **4.** any of the brightly coloured snakes of the genus *Aspidelaps* of Africa.

**coral tree** /ˈ– tri/, *n.* any of several species of *Erythrina,* tropical trees of the family Papilionaceae, cultivated for their showy red or orange flowers.

**coral trout** /ˈ– traʊt/, *n.* an important commercial food fish of the Great Barrier Reef, *Plectropomus maculatus.*

**cor anglais** /kɔr ˈɒŋgleɪ/, *n.* the alto of the

cor anglais

oboe family, richer in tone and a fifth lower than the oboe; English horn.

**corbel** /ˈkɔbəl/, *n., v.,* **-belled, -belling,** or (*U.S.*) **-beled, -beling.** *Archit.* –*n.* **1.** a supporting projection of stone, wood, etc., on the face of a wall. –*v.t.* **2.** to furnish with or support by a corbel or corbels. [ME, from OF, from LL *corvellus,* diminutive of L *corvus* raven]

**corbelling** /ˈkɔbəlɪŋ/, *n. Archit.* **1.** the construction of corbels. **2.** an overlapping arrangement of stones, etc., supported by corbels. Also, *U.S.,* **corbeling.**

**corbie** /ˈkɔbi/, *n. Scot.* a raven or crow. [ME *corbin,* from OF, diminutive of *corb* raven, from L *corvus*]

corbel

**corbie gable** /ˈ– geɪbəl/, *n.* a crow-stepped gable.

**cord** /kɔd/, *n.* **1.** a string or small rope composed of several strands twisted or woven together. **2.** flex. **3.** a hangman's rope. **4.** *Anat.* a cordlike structure: *the spinal cord.* **5.** a cordlike rib on the surface of cloth. **6.** a ribbed fabric, esp. corduroy. **7.** any influence which binds, restrains, etc. **8.** a unit of volume in the imperial system, used for the measurement of firewood, approximately equal to 3.625 m³. –*v.t.* **9.** to furnish with a cord. **10.** to bind or fasten with cords. **11.** to pile or stack up (wood) in cords. [ME *corde,* from OF, from L *chorda,* from Gk *chordḗ* gut. Cf. CHORD[1]]

**cordage** /ˈkɔdɪdʒ/, *n.* **1.** cords or ropes collectively, esp. in a ship's rigging. **2.** a quantity of wood measured in cords.

**cordate** /ˈkɔdeɪt/, *adj.* **1.** heart-shaped, as a shell. **2.** (of leaves) heart-shaped with the attachment at the notched end. [NL *cordātus,* from L *cor* heart] – **cordately,** *adv.*

**corded** /ˈkɔdəd/, *adj.* **1.** furnished with, made of, having, or in the form of cords. **2.** ribbed, as a fabric. **3.** bound with cords. **4.** (of wood) stacked up in cords.

cordate leaf

**cordelier** /kɔdəˈlɪə/, *n. Her.* a knotted cord. [ME *cordilere,* from F *cordelier,* from *corde* CORD]

**cord grass** /ˈkɔd gras/, *n.* any of various species of grasses of the genus *Spartina,* common on tidal mudflats in many temperate regions.

**cordial** /ˈkɔdiəl/, *adj.* **1.** hearty; warmly friendly. **2.** invigorating the heart; stimulating. **3.** *Obs.* of the heart. –*n.* **4.** anything that invigorates or exhilarates. **5.** a sweet, flavoured, concentrated syrup to be mixed with water as a drink. **6.** *Tas., Qld.* →**soft drink. 7.** *U.S.* →**liqueur. 8.** (formerly) a stimulating medicine. [ME, from ML *cordialis,* from L *cor* heart] – **cordially,** *adv.* – **cordialness,** *n.*

**cordiality** /ˌkɔdiˈælәti/, *n., pl.* **-ties. 1.** cordial quality or feeling. **2.** an instance or expression of cordial feeling.

**cordierite** /ˈkɔdiəraɪt/, *n.* a blue mineral, a silicate of magnesium, aluminium, and iron; a common mineral of metamorphic rocks.

**cordiform** /ˈkɔdəfɔm/, *adj.* heart-shaped. [L *cor* heart + -I- + -FORM]

**cordillera** /kɔdɪlˈjɛərə/, *n.* **1.** a connected mountain chain. **2.** a series of more or less parallel ranges of mountains together with the intervening plateaux and basins. [Sp: mountain chain, from L *chorda* rope] – **cordilleran,** *adj.*

**cordite** /ˈkɔdaɪt/, *n.* a smokeless explosive composed of 30-58 per cent nitroglycerine, 65-37 per cent nitrocellulose and 5-6 per cent mineral jelly. [CORD + -ITE[1]; so named from its cordlike or cylindrical form]

**cordless** /ˈkɔdləs/, *adj.* **1.** without cords. **2.** (of an electrical appliance) run from batteries, which are rechargeable.

**cordon** /ˈkɔdn/, *n.* **1.** a cord or braid worn for ornament or as a fastening. **2.** a ribbon worn, usu. diagonally across the breast, as a badge of a knightly or honorary order. **3.** a line of sentinels, military posts, or the like, enclosing or guarding a particular area. **4.** *Fort.* a projecting course of stone at the base of a parapet. **5.** *Archit.* →**string-course. 6.** a fruit tree, with one branch or opposing branches trained to grow parallel with the ground. –*v.t.* **7.** to enclose or cut off with a cordon. [F, from *corde* CORD]

**cordon bleu** /ˌkɔdɒn ˈblɜ/, *n.* **1.** the sky-blue ribbon worn as a badge by knights of the highest order of French knighthood under the Bourbons. **2.** some similar high distinction, esp. in cookery. **3.** one entitled to wear the cordon bleu. **4.** any person of great distinction in his field, esp. a chef. –*adj.* **5.** (of cooking, esp. in the French tradition) excellent.

**cordovan** /ˈkɔdəvən/, *adj.* **1.** designating or made of a leather made originally at Cordoba, Spain, first of goatskin tanned and dressed, but later also of split horsehide, etc. **2.** cordovan leather.

**cords** /kɔdz/, *n.pl. Colloq.* corduroy trousers.

**corduroy** /ˈkɔdʒərɔɪ, ˈkɔdərɔɪ/, *n.* **1.** a cotton pile fabric with lengthwise cords or ridges. **2.** (*pl.*) trousers made of this. –*adj.* **3.** of or like corduroy. **4.** constructed of logs laid together transversely, as a road across swampy ground. –*v.t.* **5.** to form, as a road, by laying logs together transversely. **6.** to make a corduroy road over. [cf. obs. *duroy,* a kind of coarse woollen fabric]

**core** /kɔ/, *n., v.,* **cored, coring.** –*n.* **1.** the central part of a fleshy fruit, containing the seeds. **2.** the central, innermost, or most essential part of anything: *the core of a curriculum.* **3.** *Elect.* **a.** the piece of iron, bundle of iron wires, or the like, forming the central or inner portion of an electromagnet, induction coil, or the like. **b.** the armature core of a dynamo machine, consisting of the assembled armature laminations without the slot insulation or windings. **c.** a small ferrite ring used to store a binary digit of information by induced magnetism. **d.** →**core store. 4.** *Foundry.* a body of sand, usu. dry, placed in a mould to form openings to give shape to a casting. **5.** a cylinder of rock, soil, etc., cut out by boring. **6.** the inside wood of a tree. **7.** the base to which veneer woods are attached, usu. of a soft or inexpensive wood. **8.** *Physics.* the inner part of a nuclear reactor consisting of the fuel and the moderator. **9.** *Geol.* the central mass of the earth, which is surrounded by the mantle, and is generally thought to consist of nickel iron; the outer portion of the core is probably liquid, the inner portion solid. **10.** Also, **core hole.** *Bldg Trades.* a hole left in masonry or concrete for other elements such as pipes. –*v.t.* **11.** to remove the core of (fruit). **12.** to cut from the central part. **13.** *Bldg Trades.* to leave holes (in masonry or concrete) for other elements such as pipes (fol. by *out*). [ME; orig. unknown] – **coreless,** *adj.*

**core cycle** /ˈ– saɪkəl/, *n.* the time taken to access and restore the contents of a memory location in a computer.

**coregent** /koʊˈridʒənt/, *n.* a joint regent.

**coreligionist** /ˌkoʊrəˈlɪdʒənəst/, *n.* an adherent of the same religion as another.

**corella** /kəˈrɛlə/, *n.* either of two large Australian parrots, the **little corella,** *Cacatua sanguinea,* and the **long-billed corella,** *C. tenuirostris,* having predominantly white plumage tinged with pink or red and, in the latter, more definite orange-red markings. [Latinised form of Aboriginal *carall*]

**core memory** /kɔ ˈmɛməri/, *n.* a read-write random access memory in a computer which retains data in storage on cores.

**coreopsis** /kɒriˈɒpsəs/, *n.* any plant of the genus *Coreopsis,* including familar garden species with yellow, brownish, or particoloured (yellow and red) flowers. [NL, from Gk *kóris* bug + *-opsis* -OPSIS; so called from the form of the seed]

**corer** /ˈkɔrə/, *n.* **1.** a knife for coring apples, etc. **2.** a hollow drill for extracting cores of rock, for samples, etc.

**co-respondent** /koʊ-rəˈspɒndənt/, *n.* the person alleged to have committed adultery with the respondent in a suit for divorce (no longer legally relevant in Australia).

**core store** /ˈkɔ stɔ/, *n.* a randomly addressable moderate speed memory unit in a computer consisting of an array of ferrite cores wired so that any desired core may be switched by an electrical impulse to one of two magnetic states, the pattern of magnetic states defining the data in core.

**core testing** /ˈkɔ tɛstɪŋ/, *n.* the testing for yield and fibre diameter of a known quantity of wool, extracted from a bale of greasy wool, by means of a core or tube.

**core time** /ˈ– taɪm/, *n.* that part of the working day during which one must be at one's place of work. See **flexitime.**

**corf** /kɔf/, *n., pl.*, **corves** /kɔvz/. a small wagon (formerly a wicker basket) for carrying ore, coal, etc., in mines. [MD, from L *corbis* basket]

**corgi** /ˈkɔgi/, *n.* a dog of either of two ancient Welsh breeds, having short legs, squat body, and erect ears, the **Cardigan** variety having a long tail and the **Pembroke** a short tail. Also, **Welsh corgi.**

Welsh corgi

**coriaceous** /kɒriˈeɪʃəs/, *adj.* of or like leather. [LL *coriāceus* leathern]

**coriander** /kɒriˈændə/, *n.* **1.** a herbaceous plant, *Coriandrum sativum*, with aromatic seedlike fruit (**coriander seeds**) used in cookery and medicine. **2.** the fruit or seeds. [ME *coriandre,* from F, from L *coriandrum,* from Gk *koríandron,* var. of *koríannon*]

**Corinthian** /kəˈrɪnθiən/, *adj.* **1.** of Corinth, a city in Greece, noted in ancient times for its artistic adornment, luxury, and licentiousness. **2.** luxurious; licentious. **3.** ornate, as literary style. **4.** *Archit.* designating or pertaining to one of the three Greek orders (def. 33) distinguished by a bell-shaped capital with rows of acanthus leaves and a continuous frieze. *–n.* **5.** a native or inhabitant of Corinth. **6.** a man about town; a profligate. **7.** an amateur sportsman or yachtsman.

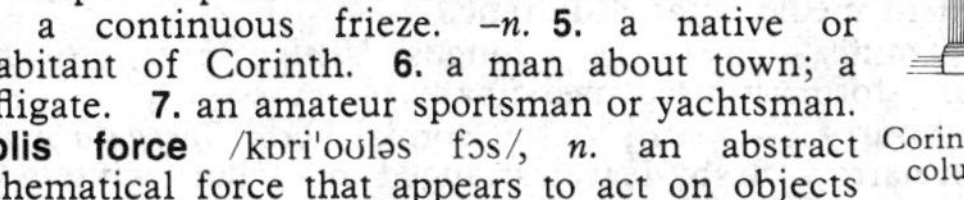
Corinthian column

**Coriolis force** /kɒriˈoʊləs fɔs/, *n.* an abstract mathematical force that appears to act on objects moving relative to the rotating earth, and is responsible for the lateral direction of the trade winds and for the deflection of projectiles.

**corium** /ˈkɔriəm/, *n., pl.* **coria** /ˈkɔriə/. the sensitive vascular layer of the skin, beneath the epidermis; the derma. [L: skin, hide, leather]

**cork** /kɔk/, *n.* **1.** the outer bark of the cork oak, used for making stoppers of bottles, floats, etc. **2.** something made of cork. **3.** a piece of cork, or other material (as rubber), used as a stopper for a bottle, etc. **4.** a small float to buoy up a fishing line or to indicate when a fish bites. **5.** *Bot.* an outer tissue of bark produced by and exterior to the phellogen. **6.** **cork leg** or **knee,** *Colloq.* a leg or knee which has become numb and useless, usu. after a blow, as in a football match. **7.** **put a cork in it,** *Colloq.* to be quiet; cease to talk. *–v.t.* **8.** to provide or fit with cork or a cork. **9.** to stop with, or as with, a cork (oft. fol. by *up*). **10.** to blacken with burnt cork. [Sp. *alcorque* shoe with cork, from Ar. *al qorq,* from L *quercus* oak] – **corklike,** *adj.* – **corky,** *adj.*

**corkage** /ˈkɔkɪdʒ/, *n.* a charge made by a restaurant, etc., for serving liquor not supplied by the house, but brought in by the customers.

**corkboard** /ˈkɔkbɔd/, *n.* **1.** thin sheeting made of compressed and treated cork, used as a finish, for insulation, etc. **2.** a type of noticeboard, made of this material.

**cork cambium** /kɔk ˈkæmbiəm/, *n. Bot.* →**phellogen.**

**corked** /kɔkt/, *adj.* **1.** stopped with a cork. **2.** Also, **corky.** (of wine) tasting of the cork; having the flavour spoilt by poor corking. **3.** blackened with burnt cork. **4.** *Colloq.* drunk. **5.** *Colloq.* (of a muscle or limb) having a deep bruise caused by a direct injury.

**corker** /ˈkɔkə/, *n.* **1.** one who or that which corks. **2.** *Colloq.* something striking or astonishing. **3.** *Colloq.* something very good of its kind.

**corking** /ˈkɔkɪŋ/, *adj. Colloq.* excellent; fine.

**cork oak** /ˈkɔk oʊk/, *n.* a species of oak tree, *Quercus suber,* found in Mediterranean countries, the bark of which yields cork.

**corkscrew** /ˈkɔkskru/, *n.* **1.** an instrument consisting of a metal spiral with a sharp point and a transverse handle, used to draw corks from bottles. *–adj.* **2.** resembling a corkscrew; helical; spiral. *–v.t.* **3.** to cause to move in a spiral or zigzag course. *–v.i.* **4.** to move in such a course.

**corkscrew grass** /ˈ– gras/, *n.* any of the many species of *Stipa,* found in Australian grasslands, bearing long, spirally twisted awns; spear grass.

**cork-tipped** /ˈkɔk-tɪpt/, *adj.* (of cigarettes) having a filter tip made of, or resembling, cork.

**corkwood** /ˈkɔkwʊd/, *n.* any of various trees with light and porous wood or corky bark, esp. *Erythrina vespertilio* and species of the genus *Duboisia.*

**corm** /kɔm/, *n.* a short, swollen upright stem-base in which food is stored, as in the gladiolus. [NL *cormus,* from Gk *kormós* tree trunk with boughs lopped off]

corm

**cormophyte** /ˈkɔməfaɪt/, *n.* any of the Cormophyta, an old primary division or group of plants having an axis differentiated into stem and root, and including all phanerogams and the higher cryptogams. [*cormo-* (combining form of CORM) + -PHYTE] – **cormophytic** /kɔməˈfɪtɪk/, *adj.*

**cormorant** /ˈkɔmərənt/, *n.* **1.** any bird of the family Phalacrocoracidae, comprising large, voracious, totipalmate waterbirds with a long neck and a pouch under the beak in which captured fish are held, as *Phalacrocorax carbo,* a common species of America, Europe, and Asia. **2.** a greedy or rapacious person. *–adj.* **3.** greedy; rapacious; insatiable. [ME *cormoraunte,* from OF *cormoran, cormaran,* from *corp* raven + *marenc* marine (from *mer* sea)]

cormorant

**corn**[1] /kɔn/, *n.* **1.** collectively, any edible grain, esp. wheat in England, oats in Scotland and Ireland, and maize in North America and Australia. **2.** the cereal plants still growing and containing the grain. **3.** a single seed of certain plants, esp. of cereal plants, as wheat, rye, barley, and maize. **4.** *U.S.* maize; Indian corn. **5.** a grain or hard particle, as of salt or sand. **6.** *U.S.* whisky made from Indian corn. **7.** *Colloq.* a trite or sentimental writing or style. *–v.t.* **8.** to granulate, as gunpowder. **9.** to preserve and season with salt in grains. **10.** to lay down in brine, as meat. **11.** to plant (land) with corn. **12.** to feed with corn. [ME and OE; c. G *Korn,* akin to L *grānum* GRAIN]

**corn**[2] /kɔn/, *n.* **1.** a horny induration or callosity of the epidermis, usu. with a central core, caused by undue pressure or friction, esp. on the toes or feet. **2.** **tread on someone's corns,** to hurt someone's feelings. [OF: horn, from L *cornū*]

**cornbrash** /ˈkɔnbræʃ/, *n.* thin limestone of the Oolite and Upper Jurassic, often with clay or sand admixture.

**corncob** /ˈkɔnkɒb/, *n.* **1.** the elongated woody core in which the grains of an ear of maize are embedded. **2.** a tobacco pipe with a bowl made of this.

**corncockle** /ˈkɔnkɒkəl/, *n.* a common weed of cereal crops, *Agrostemma githago.*

**corn colour** /ˈkɔn kʌlə/, *n.* light yellow-gold. – **corn-coloured,** *adj.*

**corncrake** /ˈkɔnkreɪk/, *n.* the land rail, *Crex crex,* of grasslands and grainfields, which breeds in the northern hemisphere and migrates southwards.

**cornea** /ˈkɔniə/, *n., pl.* **-neas** /-niəz/; **-neae** /-nii/. the transparent anterior part of the external coat of the eye, covering the iris and the pupil, and continuous with the sclera. [L, fem. sing. of *corneus* horny] – **corneal,** *adj.*

**corn earworm** /kɔn ˈɪəwɜm/, *n. U.S.* the larva of a noctuid moth, *Heliothis armigera,* destructive to maize, cotton and other plants; bollworm.

**corned** /kɔnd/, *adj.* **1.** preserved or cured with salt. **2.** preserved in brine: *corned beef.*

**cornel** /ˈkɔnəl/, *n.* any of the trees or perennials constituting the genus *Cornus,* as *C. sanguinea,* the European dogwood. [G, from ML *cornolius* cornel tree, from L *cornus*]

**cornelian** /kɔˈniliən/, *n.* →**carnelian.**

**cornemuse** /ˈkɔnəmjuz/, *n.* an ancient instrument resembling the bagpipe. [ME, from OF, backformation from *cornemuser,* v., equivalent to *corne* HORN + *muser,* from VL *musa* pipe]

**corneous** /ˈkɔniəs/, *adj.* consisting of a horny substance; horny. [L *corneus* horny]

**corner** /ˈkɔnə/, *n.* **1.** the meeting place of two converging lines or surfaces. **2.** the space between two converging lines

i = peat ɪ = pit ɛ = pet æ = pat a = part ɒ = pot ʌ = putt ɔ = port ʊ = put u = pool ɜ = pert ə = apart aɪ = buy eɪ = bay ɔɪ = boy aʊ = how oʊ = hoe ɪə = here ɛə = hair ʊə = tour g = give θ = thin ð = then ʃ = show ʒ = measure tʃ = choke dʒ = joke ŋ = sing j = you õ = Fr. bon

or surfaces near their intersection; angle. **3.** a projecting angle. **4.** the place where two streets meet. **5.** an end; margin; edge. **6.** any narrow, secluded, or secret place. **7.** an awkward or embarrassing position, esp. one from which escape is impossible. **8.** any part, even the least or the most remote. **9.** *Finance.* a monopolising or a monopoly of the available supply of a stock or commodity, to a point permitting control of price. **10.** a region; quarter: *all the corners of the earth.* **11.** a piece to protect the corner of anything. **12.** *Soccer, Hockey, etc.* a free kick or hit from the corner of the field taken by the attacking side when the ball has crossed the goal line after last being touched by a member of the defending side. **13.** *Boxing.* the space between the junction of two of the ropes, where the contestants rest between rounds. **14. cut corners, a.** to take short cuts habitually. **b.** to bypass an official procedure, or the like. **15. cut off a corner,** to take a short cut. **16. get one's corner,** *Colloq.* to obtain one's share. **17. the Corner.** Also, **Corner country.** the land where the borders of Queensland, South Australia and New South Wales meet. **18. turn the corner,** to begin to get well; improve. **19. round the corner,** very close; within walking distance. *–v.t.* **20.** to furnish with corners. **21.** to place in or drive into a corner. **22.** to force into an awkward or difficult position, or one from which escape is impossible. **23.** to form a corner in (a stock, etc.). **24. corner a wave,** *Surfing.* to stay on the shoulder of the wave. *–v.i.* **25.** to form a corner in a stock or commodity. **26.** in a motor vehicle, to turn a corner, esp. at speed. *–adj.* **27.** situated at a junction of two roads. **28.** made to be fitted or used in a corner. [ME, from AF, var. of OF *cornere,* from L *cornū* horn, corner]

**corner area** /ˈ– ɛəriə/, *n.* one of the quarter circles drawn in each corner of a soccer field from which corners (def. 12) are taken.

**cornerstone** /ˈkɔnəstoun/, *n.* **1.** a stone which lies at the corner of two walls, and serves to unite them. **2.** a stone built into a corner of the foundation of an important edifice as the actual or nominal starting point in building, usu. laid with formal ceremonies, and often hollowed out and made the repository of documents, etc. **3.** something or someone of prime or fundamental importance.

**corner store** /kɔnə ˈstɔ/, *n.* a small local shop, usu. situated on a corner, selling a wide range of goods for domestic consumption. Also, **corner shop.**

**cornerwise** /ˈkɔnəwaɪz/, *adv.* **1.** with the corner in front. **2.** so as to form a corner. **3.** from corner to corner; diagonally. Also, **cornerways** /ˈkɔnəweɪz/.

**cornet** /ˈkɔnət/, *n.* **1.** a wind instrument of the trumpet class, with valves or pistons. **2.** a player of a cornet in an orchestra. **3.** an organ stop. **4.** a little cone of paper twisted at the end, used for enclosing sweets, groceries, etc. **5.** a cone, as for ice-cream. **6.** a headdress worn by women from the 12th to the 15th centuries. **7.** (formerly) an officer in a troop of cavalry, who carried the colours. [ME *cornette,* from OF *cornet,* from L *cornū* horn]

**cornfield** /ˈkɔnfild/, *n.* a field in which corn is growing, or grows.

**cornflakes** /ˈkɔnfleɪks/, *n.pl.* a breakfast cereal consisting of small toasted flakes made from maize and served with milk, sugar, etc.

**cornflour** /ˈkɔnflauə/, *n.* a starch, or a starchy flour made from maize, rice, or other grain, used as a thickening agent in cooking.

**cornflower** /ˈkɔnflauə/, *n.* a tall herb, *Centaurea cyanus,* a weed of cereal crops in Europe, commonly cultivated for its blue, occasionally pink or white, flowers.

**cornice** /ˈkɔnəs/, *n., v.,* **-niced, -nicing.** *–n.* **1.** *Archit.* **a.** a horizontal moulded projection which crowns or finishes a wall, building, etc. **b.** the uppermost division of an entablature, resting on the frieze. **2.** an overhanging crest of snow. **3.** the moulding or mouldings between the walls and ceiling of a room. **4.** any of the various other ornamental horizontal mouldings or bands, as for concealing hooks or rods from which curtains are hung or for supporting picture hooks. *–v.t.* **5.** to furnish or finish with, or as with, a cornice. [F, from It., from MGk *korōnís* summit, Gk anything curved or bent]

**corniculate** /kɔˈnɪkjələɪt, -lət/, *adj.* resembling a small horn in appearance. [L *corniculus* little horn + -ATE[1]]

**Cornish** /ˈkɔnɪʃ/, *adj.* **1.** of Cornwall, its inhabitants, or the language formerly spoken by them. *–n.* **2.** the old Celtic language of Cornwall. **3.** the dialect of English now spoken in Cornwall. **– Cornishman** /ˈkɔnɪʃmən/, *n.*

A, cornice; B, entablature

**Cornish pasty** /– ˈpæsti/, *n.* →**pasty**[2].

**corn meal** /ˈkɔn mil/, *n.* **1.** →**oatmeal. 2.** *U.S.* meal made of maize or grain; Indian meal.

**cornopean** /kɔˈnoupiən/, *n.* an organ stop for a trumpet-like sound.

**corn plaster** /ˈkɔn plastə/, *n.* a resin plaster, containing salicylic acid, used to cure corns.

**corn poppy** /ˈ– pɒpi/, *n.* the common poppy, *Papaver rhoeas,* bearing bright red flowers, since World War I the symbol of fallen soldiers. Also, **Flanders poppy.**

**cornsack** /ˈkɔnsæk/, *n.* a large bag, made of jute, for carrying grain.

**corn shock** /ˈkɔn ʃɒk/, *n.* a stack of upright cornstalks.

**corn silk** /ˈ– sɪlk/, *n.* the fresh styles and stigmas of *Zea mays,* used in medicine as a diuretic.

**corn smut** /ˈ– smʌt/, *n.* a fungus, *Ustilago zeae,* growing on maize, formerly used medicinally.

**corn spurry** /ˈ– spʌri/, *n.* an annual herb, *Spergula arvensis,* with narrow, fleshy leaves arranged in a whorl, white flowers, and slightly flattened black seeds; a troublesome weed among crops.

**cornstalk** /ˈkɔnstɔk/, *n.* **1.** the stalk or stem of corn. **2.** a person native to or resident in New South Wales. **3.** *Colloq.* a tall, thin person. **4.** *Obs. Colloq.* a native-born Australian, being generally taller and thinner than the immigrant.

**cornstarch** /ˈkɔnstatʃ/, *n. U.S.* →**cornflour.**

**corn syrup** /kɔn ˈsɪrəp/, *n. U.S.* syrup prepared from maize.

**cornu** /ˈkɔnju/, *n., pl.* **-nua** /-njuə/. a horn, esp. a process of bone resembling a horn. [L. See HORN]

**cornucopia** /ˌkɔnjəˈkoupiə/, *n.* **1.** the mythical horn of the goat Amalthaea, which suckled Zeus, represented as overflowing with flowers, fruit, etc., and symbolising plenty. **2.** an overflowing supply. **3.** a horn-shaped or conical receptacle or ornament. [LL, for *cornū cōpiae* horn of plenty] **– cornucopian,** *adj.*

**cornuted** /kɔˈnjutəd/, *adj.* having horns.

**corny**[1] /ˈkɔni/, *adj.,* **-nier, -niest. 1.** *Colloq.* old-fashioned; lacking subtlety. **2.** *Colloq.* sentimental; mawkish and of poor quality. **3.** of or abounding in corn.

**corny**[2] /ˈkɔni/, *adj.* having corns (on the feet).

**coroll.,** corollary.

**corolla** /kəˈrɒlə/, *n.* the internal envelope or floral leaves of a flower, usu. of delicate texture and of some colour other than green; the petals considered collectively. [L: garland, diminutive of *corōna* crown]

**corollaceous** /kɒrəˈleɪʃəs/, *adj.* having or resembling a corolla.

**corollary** /kəˈrɒləri/, *n., pl.* **-ries. 1.** an immediate or easily drawn consequence. **2.** a natural consequence or result. [ME *corolarie,* from LL *corollārium* corollary, L gift, orig. garland, from L *corolla* garland]

corollas: A, unguiculate; B, papilionaceous

**corona** /kəˈrounə/, *n., pl.* **-nas, -nae** /-ni/. **1.** a white or coloured circle of light seen round a luminous body, esp. the sun or moon (in meteorology, restricted to those circles due to the diffraction produced by thin clouds or mist). **2.** *Astron.* a faintly luminous envelope outside the sun's chromosphere, the inner part consisting of highly ionised elements. **3.** *Archit.* that part of a cornice supported by and projecting beyond the bed moulding. **4.** a type of circular chandelier, suspended from the roof of a church. **5.** *Anat.* the upper portion or crown of a part, as of the head. **6.** *Bot.* a crownlike appendage, esp. one on the inner side of a corolla, as in the narcissus. **7.** *Elect.* a discharge, frequently lumi-

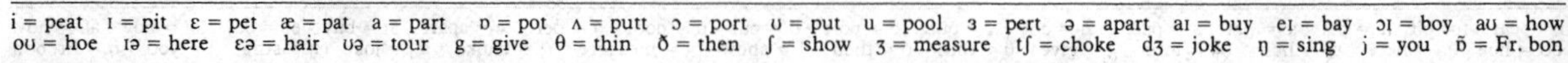
i = peat ɪ = pit ɛ = pet æ = pat a = part ɒ = pot ʌ = putt ɔ = port ʊ = put u = pool ɜ = pert ə = apart aɪ = buy eɪ = bay ɔɪ = boy aʊ = how
oʊ = hoe ɪə = here ɛə = hair ʊə = tour g = give θ = thin ð = then ʃ = show ʒ = measure tʃ = choke dʒ = joke ŋ = sing j = you õ = Fr. bon

nous, at the surface of a conductor, or between two conductors of the same transmission line, accompanied by ionisation of the surrounding atmosphere and power loss; brush discharge. [L: garland, CROWN]

**coronach** /ˈkɒrənək/, *n.* (in Scotland and Ireland) a song or lamentation for the dead; a dirge. [Gaelic *corranach* outcry, dirge]

**coronal** /ˈkɒrənəl/ *for defs 1, 2, 3 and 5;* /kəˈroʊnəl/ *for def. 4, n.* **1.** *Anat.* the coronal suture. **2.** a crown; coronet. **3.** a garland. *–adj.* **4.** of or pertaining to a coronal. **5.** *Phonetics.* with the tip or blade of the tongue raised towards the alveolar ridge. [LL *corōnālis*]

**coronal suture** /– ˈsutʃə/, *n.* a suture extending across the skull between the frontal bone and the parietal bones.

**coronary** /ˈkɒrənri/, *adj.* **1.** of or like a crown. **2.** *Anat.* **a.** encircling like a crown, as certain blood vessels. **b.** pertaining to the arteries which supply the heart tissues and which originate in the root of the aorta. *–n.* **3.** →**coronary thrombosis.** [L *corōnārius*]

**coronary artery** /– ˈatəri/, *n.* an artery supplying heart muscle.

**coronary occlusion** /– əˈkluʒən/, *n.* →**coronary thrombosis.**

**coronary thrombosis** /– θrɒmˈboʊsəs/, *n.* the occlusion of a coronary arterial branch by a blood clot within the vessel, usu. at a site narrowed by arteriosclerosis.

**coronate** /ˈkɒrəneɪt/, *adj.* having or wearing a crown, coronet, or the like.

**coronation** /kɒrəˈneɪʃən/, *n.* the act or ceremony of investing a king, etc., with a crown.

**coroner** /ˈkɒrənə/, *n.* an officer, as of a county or municipality, whose chief function is to investigate by inquest (often before a **coroner's jury**) any death not clearly due to natural causes. [ME, from AF *corouner* officer of the crown, from *coroune.* See CROWN] – **coronership,** *n.*

**coronet** /ˈkɒrənət/, *n.* **1.** a small or inferior crown. **2.** an insignia for the head, worn by peers or members of nobility. **3.** a crownlike ornament or decoration for the head, as of gold or jewels. **4.** the lowest part of the pastern of a horse, just above the hoof. [OF *coronete,* diminutive of *corone* CROWN]

**coroneted** /ˈkɒrənətəd/, *adj.* wearing, or entitled to wear, a coronet. Also, **coronetted.**

**coronial** /kəˈroʊniəl/, *adj.* of or pertaining to a coroner: *coronial court.*

**coronoid** /ˈkɒrənɔɪd/, *adj.* **1.** shaped like a crown; like a corona. **2.** *Anat.* shaped like a crown. [Gk *korṓnē* crow + *eîdos* form]

**coronoid process** /– ˈproʊsɛs/, *n.* **1.** a projection from the ulna which articulates in the coronoid fossa of the humerus. **2.** a process of the mandible.

**coronus** /kəˈroʊnəs/, *n.* crushed coral, used as a road-building material in the Pacific Islands and Papua New Guinea.

**Corp.,** **1.** corporal. **2.** corporation. Also, **corp.**

**corpora** /ˈkɔpərə/, *n.* plural of **corpus.**

**corporal**[1] /ˈkɔpərəl/, *adj.* **1.** of the human body; bodily; physical: *corporal pleasure.* **2.** personal: *corporal possession.* **3.** *Zool.* of the body proper (as distinguished from the head and limbs). **4.** *Obs.* corporeal. [ME, from L *corporālis*] – **corporality,** *n.* – **corporally,** *adv.*

**corporal**[2] /ˈkɔpərəl, -prəl/, *n.* **1.** (in the army and airforce) a non-commissioned officer ranking below sergeant. **2.** *Naval.* a petty officer whose duty is to assist the master-at-arms. [F, obs. var. of *caporal,* from It. *caporale,* from *capo* (from L *caput*) head] – **corporalship,** *n.*

**corporal**[3] /ˈkɔpərəl/, *n.* a fine cloth, usu. of linen, on which the consecrated elements are placed during the celebration of the Eucharist. [ME, from ML *corporālis, corporāle,* from L *corpus* body]

**corporal punishment** /– ˈpʌnɪʃmənt/, *n.* physical injury, esp. by flogging, inflicted on the body of one found guilty of a crime or misdeed.

**corporate** /ˈkɔpərət, -prət/, *adj.* **1.** forming a corporation. **2.** of a corporation. **3.** united in one body. **4.** pertaining to a united body, as of persons. [L *corporātus* pp., formed into a body] – **corporately,** *adv.*

**corporation** /kɔpəˈreɪʃən/, *n.* **1.** an association of individuals, created by law or under authority of law, having a continuous existence irrespective of that of its members, and powers and liabilities distinct from those of its members. **2.** (*cap.*) *Brit.* the principal officials of a borough, etc. **3.** any group of persons united, or regarded as united, in one body. **4.** *Colloq.* the abdomen, esp. when large and prominent in an overweight person.

**corporative** /ˈkɔpərətɪv, -prətɪv/, *adj.* of or pertaining to a corporation.

**corporeal** /kɔˈpɔriəl/, *adj.* **1.** of the nature of the physical body; bodily. **2.** of the nature of matter; material; tangible: *corporeal property.* [L *corporeus* of the nature of body + -AL[1]] – **corporeality, corporealness,** *n.* – **corporeally,** *adv.*

**corporeity** /kɔpəˈriəti/, *n.* material or physical nature or quality; materiality.

**corposant** /ˈkɔpəzænt/, *n.* a light, due to atmospheric electricity, sometimes seen on the mastheads, yardarms, etc., of ships and on church towers, treetops, etc. [Pg. *corpo santo* holy body (L *corpus sanctum*)]

**corps** /kɔ/, *n., pl.* **corps** /kɔz/. **1.** a military unit of ground combat forces consisting of two or more divisions and other troops. **2.** a group so organised for a particular operation. **3.** a group of persons associated or acting together. **4.** *Obs.* corpse. [F. See CORPSE]

**corps-à-corps** /kɔr-ə-ˈkɔ/, *n.* (in fencing) any position in which two fencers are engaged in such a way that neither can use his weapon. [F: body to body]

**corps area** /ˈkɔr ɛəriə/, *n.* the geographical area within which a corps commander exercises military responsibility.

**corps de ballet** /ˌkɔ də ˈbæleɪ/, *n.* the dancers in a ballet company who perform as a group and have no solo parts.

**corps diplomatique** /ˌkɔ dɪploʊməˈtik/, *n.* the whole body of ambassadors and their staffs accredited to a state.

**corpse** /ˈkɔps/, *n.* **1.** a dead body, usu. of a human being. **2.** *Obs.* a living body. *–v.i. Colloq.* **3.** to collapse or fall asleep from exhaustion, alcohol, drugs, etc.

**corpulence** /ˈkɔpjələns/, *n.* bulkiness or largeness of body; fatness; fleshiness; portliness. Also, **corpulency.** [late ME, from F, from L *corpulentia*]

**corpulent** /ˈkɔpjələnt/, *adj.* large or bulky of body; portly; stout; fat. [ME, from L *corpulentus,* from *corpus* body] – **corpulently,** *adv.*

**corpus** /ˈkɔpəs/, *n., pl.* **-pora** /-pərə/. **1.** the body of a man or animal. **2.** *Anat.* any of various bodies, masses, or parts of special character or function. **3.** a large or complete collection of writings, laws, etc. **4.** a principal or capital sum, as opposed to interest or income. **5.** the main part; the bulk. [L]

**corpus allatum** /ˌkɔpəs əˈleɪtəm/, *n., pl.* **corpora allata** /kɔpərə əˈleɪtə/. one of a pair of small, ductless, hormone-secreting glands in the head of an insect behind the brain. [NL: added body]

**corpus callosum** /ˌkɔpəs kəˈloʊsəm/, *n., pl.* **corpora callosa** /kɔpərə kəˈloʊsə/. a great band of deeply situated transverse white fibres uniting the two halves of the cerebrum, peculiar to Mammalia. [NL: hard body]

**corpus cardiacum** /ˌkɔpəs kaˈdaɪəkəm/, *n., pl.* **corpora cardiaca** /ˌkɔpərə kaˈdaɪəkə/. one of a pair of small cellular bodies associated with the corpora allata in the back of an insect's head, generally attached to the aorta, probably organs of hormone secretion.

**corpuscle** /ˈkɔpəsəl/, *n.* **1.** *Physiol.* one of the minute bodies which form a constituent of the blood (**blood corpuscles,** both red and white), the lymph (**lymph corpuscles,** white only), etc. **2.** a minute body forming a more or less distinct part of an organism. **3.** *Physics, Chem., Obs.* a minute or elementary particle of matter, as an electron, proton, or atom. **4.** a minute particle. Also, **corpuscule** /kɔˈpʌskjul/. [L *corpusculum,* diminutive of *corpus* body] – **corpuscular** /kɔˈpʌskjələ/, *adj.*

**corpus delicti** /ˌkɔpəs dəˈlɪktaɪ/, *n.* **1.** the body of essential facts constituting a criminal offence. **2.** *Colloq.* (*joc.*) a shapely young woman. [L: body of the transgression]

**corpus juris** /ˌkɔpəs ˈdʒʊərəs/, *n.* a compilation of law or the collected law of a nation or state. [L]

**corpus luteum** /ˌkɔpəs ˈlutiəm/, *n., pl.* **corpora lutea** /ˌkɔpərə ˈlutiə/. a ductless gland developed within the ovary by the reorganisation of a Graafian follicle following ovulation. [NL: yellow body]

**corpus striatum** /ˌkɔpəs straɪˈeɪtəm/, *n., pl.* **corpora striata** /ˌkɔpərə straɪˈeɪtə/. a mass of grey matter beneath the cortex and in front of the thalamus in each cerebral hemisphere. [NL: striped body]

**corr.,** **1.** correction. **2.** corruption.

**corral** /kɒˈral/, *n., v.,* **-ralled, -ralling.** *–n.* **1.** a pen or enclosure for horses, cattle, etc. **2.** an enclosure formed of wagons during an encampment, for defence against attack. *–v.t.* **3.** to confine in, or as in, a corral. **4.** to form (wagons) into a corral. [Sp.: enclosed yard, from *corro* a ring]

**corrasion** /kəˈreɪʒən/, *n.* erosion caused by loose material during its transportation, as windborne sand or riverborne pebbles.

**correa** /ˈkɒriə/, *n.* any shrub of the genus *Correa,* with large, showy, green-to-white flowers.

**correct** /kəˈrɛkt/, *v.t.* **1.** to set right; remove the errors or faults of. **2.** to point out or mark the errors in. **3.** to admonish or rebuke in order to improve. **4.** to counteract the operation or effect of (something hurtful). **5.** *Physics.* to alter or adjust so as to bring into accordance with a standard or with some required condition. *–adj.* **6.** conforming to fact or truth; free from error, accurate: *a correct statement.* **7.** in accordance with an acknowledged or accepted standard; proper. [ME *correcte(n),* from L *correctus,* pp., made straight, directed] – **correctly,** *adv.* – **correctness,** *n.* – **corrector,** *n.*

**correction** /kəˈrɛkʃən/, *n.* **1.** the act of correcting. **2.** that which is substituted or proposed for what is wrong; an emendation. **3.** punishment; chastisement; discipline; reproof. **4.** *Physics.* a subordinate quantity that has to be applied in order to ensure accuracy, as in the use of an instrument or the solution of a problem. – **correctional,** *adj.*

**correction fluid** /kəˈrɛkʃən fluəd/, *n.* **1.** a white substance in an organic solvent, used to obliterate a typing error; white-out. **2.** a liquid used to obliterate a mistake in a gestetner stencil.

**correctitude** /kəˈrɛktətʃud/, *n.* correctness, esp. of manners and conduct. [CORRECT, *v.* + *-itude,* modelled on RECTITUDE]

**corrective** /kəˈrɛktɪv/, *adj.* **1.** tending to correct; having the quality of correcting. *–n.* **2.** a corrective agent. – **correctively,** *adv.*

**correlate** /ˈkɒrəleɪt/, *v.,* **-lated, -lating,** *adj., n.* *–v.t.* **1.** to place in or bring into mutual or reciprocal relation; establish in orderly connection. *–v.i.* **2.** to have a mutual or reciprocal relation; stand in correlation. *–adj.* **3.** *Rare.* mutually or reciprocally related; correlated. *–n.* **4.** either of two related things, esp. when one implies the other. [COR- + RELATE]

**correlation** /kɒrəˈleɪʃən/, *n.* **1.** mutual relation of two or more things, parts, etc. **2.** the act of correlating. **3.** the state of being correlated. **4.** *Statistics.* the degree of relationship of two attributes or measurements on the same group of elements. **5.** *Physiol.* the interdependence or reciprocal relations of organs or functions.

**correlation coefficient** /– koʊəˈfɪʃənt/, *n.* the statistical measure of correlation, called *r,* having the value +1 for perfect positive linear correlation, −1 for perfect negative linear correlation, and a value of 0 for a complete lack of correlation.

**correlation ratio** /– ˈreɪʃioʊ/, *n.* a mathematical measure of the correlation between two sets of values not linearly correlated.

**correlative** /kɒˈrɛlətɪv/, *adj.* **1.** so related that each implies or complements the other. **2.** being in correlation; mutually related. **3.** having a mutual relation; answering to or complementing one another, as *either* and *or, where* and *there.* **4.** *Biol.* (of a typical structure of an organism) found in correlation with another. *–n.* **5.** either of two things, as two terms, which are correlative. **6.** a correlative expression. – **correlatively,** *adv.* – **correlativeness, correlativity** /kɒrələˈtɪvəti/, *n.*

**correspond** /kɒrəˈspɒnd/, *v.i.* **1.** to be in agreement or conformity (oft. fol. by *with* or *to*): *his words and actions do not correspond.* **2.** to be similar or analogous; be equivalent in function, position, amount, etc. (fol. by *to*). **3.** to communicate by exchange of letters. [ML *corrēspondēre,* from L *cor-* COR- + *rēspondēre* answer] – **correspondingly,** *adv.*

**correspondence** /kɒrəˈspɒndəns/, *n.* **1.** Also, **correspondency.** the act or fact of corresponding. **2.** relation or similarity or analogy. **3.** agreement; conformity. **4.** communication by exchange of letters. **5.** letters that pass between correspondents.

**correspondence chess** /ˈ– tʃɛs/, *n.* a game of chess in which a description of each move is sent by mail to one's opponent.

**correspondence course** /ˈ– kɔs/, *n.* a course of instruction conducted by a correspondence school.

**correspondence school** /ˈ– skul/, *n.* **1.** a system of both primary, secondary and sometimes tertiary education carried out by correspondence between teacher and pupil for students who, for various reasons, as distance between home and the nearest ordinary school, or illness, etc. cannot attend a normal school. **2.** the building where teachers employed in this system work.

**correspondent** /kɒrəˈspɒndənt/, *n.* **1.** one who communicates by letters. **2.** one employed to contribute news, etc., regularly from a distant place. **3.** one who contributes letters to a newspaper. **4.** one who has regular business relations with another, esp. at a distance. **5.** a thing that corresponds to something else. *–adj.* **6.** corresponding; having a relation of correspondence. – **correspondently,** *adv.*

**corresponding angles** /ˌkɒrəspɒndɪŋ ˈæŋgəlz/, *n.pl.* a pair of equal angles formed by the intersection of two parallel lines with a transversal, such that both angles lie on the same side of the transversal and are similarly placed with respect to the parallel lines.

**corresponsive** /kɒrəˈspɒnsɪv/, *adj.* responsive to effort or impulse; answering; corresponding.

**corridor** /ˈkɒrədɔ/, *n.* **1.** a gallery or passage connecting parts of a building. **2.** a passage into which several rooms or apartments open. **3.** a passageway on one side of a railway carriage into which the compartments open. **4.** a narrow tract of land forming a passageway, as one belonging to an inland country and affording an outlet to the sea: *the Polish Corridor.* *–adj.* **5.** (of a building) designed with a series of rooms opening off a central passage way, as a corridor school. [F: long passageway, from It. *corridore* covered way, from Sp. *corredor,* from *correr* run, from L *currere*]

**corrie** /ˈkɒri/, *n.* a circular hollow in the side of a hill or mountain, often containing a small lake, formed by glacial action; cirque. [Gaelic *coire* cauldron]

**Corriedale** /ˈkɒrədeɪl/, *n.* a white-faced breed of sheep, orig. developed in New Zealand from Leicester, Lincoln, Merino and Romney breeds to produce high-quality wool and meat. [from *Corriedale,* the property where it was developed]

**corrigendum** /kɒrəˈdʒɛndəm/, *n., pl.* **-da** /-də/. **1.** an error to be corrected, esp. an error in print. **2.** (*pl.*) a list of corrections of errors in a book, etc. [L *corrigere* correct]

**corrigible** /ˈkɒrədʒəbəl/, *adj.* **1.** capable of being corrected. **2.** submissive to correction. [LL *corrigibilis,* from L *corrigere* correct] – **corrigibility,** *n.* – **corrigibly,** *adv.*

**corroborant** /kəˈrɒbərənt/, *adj.* **1.** corroborating; confirming. **2.** strengthening, invigorating. *–n.* **3.** something that corroborates or strengthens.

**corroborate** /kəˈrɒbəreɪt/, *v.,* **-rated -rating;** /kəˈrɒbərət/, *adj.* *–v.t.* **1.** to make more certain; confirm. *–adj.* **2.** *Archaic.* corroborated. [L *corrōborātus,* pp., strengthened] – **corroborative** /kəˈrɒbərətɪv/, **corroboratory** /kəˈrɒbərətri/, *adj.* – **corroboratively,** *adv.* – **corroborator,** *n.*

**corroboration** /kərɒbəˈreɪʃən/, *n.* **1.** the act of corroborating. **2.** a corroboratory fact, statement, etc. **3.** *Law.* independent evidence which implicates a person accused of a crime, by connecting him with it.

**corroboree** /kəˈrɒbəri/, *n.* **1.** an Aboriginal assembly of sacred, festive, or warlike character. **2.** any large or noisy gathering. **3.** a disturbance; an uproar. [Aboriginal]

**corrode** /kəˈroʊd/, *v.,* **-roded, -roding.** *–v.t.* **1.** to eat away gradually as if by gnawing. **2.** *Chem.* to eat away the surface of a solid, esp. of metals, by chemical action. **3.** to impair; deteriorate: *jealousy corroded his whole being.* *–v.i.* **4.** to become corroded. [L *corrōdere* gnaw away] – **corrodible,** *adj.*

**corrosion** /kəˈroʊʒən/, *n.* **1.** the act or process of corroding. **2.** corroded condition. **3.** a product of corroding, as rust. [L *corrōsio*]

**corrosion fatigue** /'– fətig/, *n.* the failure of a metal under stress when it is exposed to corrosive attack.

**corrosive** /kə'roʊsɪv/, *adj.* **1.** having the quality of corroding, eating away, or consuming. *–n.* **2.** something corrosive, as an acid, drug, etc. – **corrosively,** *adv.* – **corrosiveness,** *n.*

**corrosive sublimate** /– 'sʌbləmət/, *n. Chem.* →**mercuric chloride.**

**corrugate** /'kɒrəgeɪt/, *v.,* **-gated, -gating;** /'kɒrəgeɪt, -ət/, *adj.* *–v.t.* **1.** to draw or bend into folds or alternate furrows and ridges. *–v.i.* **2.** to wrinkle, as the skin, etc. *–adj.* **3.** corrugated; wrinkled; furrowed. [L *corrūgātus,* pp., wrinkled]

**corrugated iron** /ˌkɒrəgeɪtəd 'aɪən/, *n.* a type of sheet iron or steel strengthened for use in construction by being formed into a series of alternating grooves and ridges and usu. galvanised for weather resistance.

**corrugated paper** /– 'peɪpə/, *n.* heavy paper with alternating ridges and grooves, used for protecting packages, etc. Also, **corrugated cardboard.**

**corrugation** /kɒrə'geɪʃən/, *n.* **1.** the act of corrugating. **2.** the state of being corrugated. **3.** a wrinkle; fold; furrow; ridge.

**corrupt** /kə'rʌpt/, *adj.* **1.** dishonest; without integrity; guilty of dishonesty, esp. involving bribery: *a corrupt judge.* **2.** debased in character; depraved; perverted; wicked; evil. **3.** putrid. **4.** infected; tainted. **5.** made bad by errors or alterations, as a text. *–v.t.* **6.** to destroy the integrity of; cause to be dishonest, disloyal, etc., esp. by bribery. **7.** to lower morally; pervert; deprave. **8.** to infect; taint. **9.** to make putrid or putrescent. **10.** to alter (a language, text, etc.) for the worse; debase. **11.** *Archaic.* to mar; spoil. *–v.i.* **12.** to become corrupt. [ME, from L *corruptus,* pp., broken in pieces, destroyed] – **corrupter,** *n.* **corruptness,** *n.* – **corruptive,** *adj.* – **corruptly,** *adv.*

**corruptible** /kə'rʌptəbəl/, *adj.* that may be corrupted. – **corruptibility** /kərʌptə'bɪləti/, **corruptibleness,** *n.* – **corruptibly,** *adv.*

**corruption** /kə'rʌpʃən/, *n.* **1.** the act of corrupting. **2.** the state of being corrupt. **3.** moral perversion; depravity. **4.** perversion of integrity. **5.** corrupt or dishonest proceedings. **6.** bribery. **7.** debasement, as of a language. **8.** a debased form of a word. **9.** putrefactive decay. **10.** any corrupting influence or agency.

**corsage** /kɔ'saʒ/, *n.* **1.** the body or waist of a dress; bodice. **2.** a small bouquet worn by a woman at the waist, on the shoulder, etc. [F, from *cors* body. See CORSE]

**corsair** /'kɔsɛə/, *n.* **1.** a privateer, esp. one of the Barbary Coast. **2.** a pirate. **3.** a fast vessel used for piracy. [F *corsaire,* from It. *corsaro,* runner, from LL *cursārius,* from *cursus* COURSE]

**corse** /kɔs/, *n. Archaic.* →**corpse.** [ME *cors,* from OF, from L *corpus* body]

**corselet** /'kɔslət/, *n.* **1.** a supporting undergarment with very few or no bones, worn by women. **2.** →**corslet.** [F, diminutive of OF *cors.* See CORSE]

**corset** /'kɔsət/, *n.* **1.** (*oft. pl.*) a shaped, close-fitting inner garment stiffened with whalebone or the like and capable of being tightened by lacing, enclosing the trunk and extending for a distance above and below the waistline, worn (chiefly by women) to give shape and support to the body; stays. **2.** *Obs.* a close-fitting outer body garment. [ME, from F, diminutive of OF *cors.* See CORSE]

**corsetiere** /kɔsə'tɪə/, *n.* an expert trained in the fitting and selecting of corsets.

**corsetry** /'kɔsətri/, *n.* **1.** the art of making corsets. **2.** corsets considered collectively.

**corslet** /'kɔslət/, *n.* armour for the body, esp. the breastplate and back piece together. Also, **corselet.**

**cortege** /kɔ'tɛəʒ, -'teɪʒ/, *n.* **1.** a train of attendants; retinue. **2.** a procession. Also, **cortège.** [F, from It. *corteggio,* from *corte* COURT]

**cortex** /'kɔtɛks/, *n., pl.* **-tices** /-təsiz/. **1.** *Bot.* that portion of the stem between the epidermis and the vascular tissue; bark. **2.** *Anat., Zool.* **a.** the rind of an organ, such as the outer wall of the kidney. **b.** the layer of grey matter which invests the surface of the cerebral hemispheres and the cerebellum. [L: bark, rind, shell]

**cortical** /'kɔtɪkəl/, *adj.* **1.** *Anat.* of, or of the nature of, cortex. **2.** *Physiol., Pathol.* due to the function or condition of the cerebral cortex. **3.** *Bot.* of the cortex. [NL *corticālis.* See CORTEX] – **cortically,** *adv.*

**corticate** /'kɔtəkət, -keɪt/, *adj.* having a cortex. Also, **corticated.** [L *corticātus* having bark]

**corticosteroid** /kɔtəkoʊ'stɪərɔɪd/, *n.* any of the steroid hormones secreted by the adrenal cortex.

**cortile** /kɔ'tili/, *n.* an enclosed courtyard, within or attached to a building, usu. roofless. [It.]

**cortisone** /'kɔtəzoʊn/, *n.* a hormone from the adrenal cortex originally obtained by extraction from animal glands, now prepared synthetically from *Strophanthus* or other plants; used in the treatment of arthritic ailments and many other diseases.

**corundum** /kə'rʌndəm/, *n.* a common mineral, aluminium oxide, $Al_2O_3$, notable for its hardness (9 on the Mohs scale). Transparent varieties, including the ruby and sapphire, are prized gems; translucent varieties are used as abrasives. [Tamil *kurundam,* from Skt *kuruvinda* ruby]

**coruscate** /'kɒrəskeɪt/, *v.i.,* **-cated, -cating.** to emit vivid flashes of light; sparkle; gleam. [L *coruscātus,* pp., moved quickly, flashed]

**coruscation** /kɒrə'skeɪʃən/, *n.* **1.** the act of coruscating. **2.** a flashing or a flash of light.

**corvée** /'kɔveɪ/, *n.* **1.** labour, as on the repair of roads, exacted by a feudal lord. **2.** an obligation imposed on inhabitants of a district to perform services, as repair of roads, etc., for little or no remuneration. [F, from L *corrogāre* bring together by entreaty]

**corves** /kɔvz/, *n.* plural of **corf.**

**corvette** /kɔ'vɛt/, *n.* **1.** a warship of the old sailing class, having a flush deck and usually only one tier of guns. **2.** a small, lightly armed, fast vessel, used mostly for convoy escort, ranging between a destroyer and a gunboat in size. [F, from L *corbīta* ship of burden]

corvette

**corvine** /'kɔvaɪn/, *adj.* **1.** pertaining to or resembling a crow. **2.** belonging or pertaining to the Corvidae, a family of birds including the crows, ravens, jays, etc. [L *corvinus,* from *corvus* raven]

**corydalis** /kə'rɪdələs/, *n.* any plant of the genus *Corydalis,* comprising erect or climbing herbs with divided leaves, tuberous or fibrous roots, and very irregular spurred flowers. [NL, from Gk *korydallís* crested lark]

**corymb** /'kɒrɪmb, -rɪm/, *n.* a form of inflorescence resembling a raceme but having a relatively shorter rachis and longer lower pedicles, so that the flowers form a flat-topped or convex cluster, the outermost flowers being the first to expand. [L *corymbus,* from Gk *kórymbos* top, cluster of fruit or flowers] – **corymb-like,** *adj.*

corymb

**corymbose** /kə'rɪmboʊs/, *adj.* characterised by or growing in corymbs; corymb-like. – **corymbosely,** *adv.*

**coryphaeus** /kɒrə'fiəs/, *n., pl.* **-phaei** /-fiі/. **1.** the leader of the chorus in the ancient Greek drama. **2.** (in modern use) the leader of an operatic chorus, or of any band of singers. [L, from Gk *koryphaîos* leader, head man]

**coryphée** /kɒrɪ'feɪ/, *n.* (in ballet) a leading dancer other than one of the soloists. [F, from L *coryphaeus* CORYPHAEUS]

**coryza** /kə'raɪzə/, *n.* **1.** *Pathol.* acute inflammation of the mucous membrane of the nasal cavities; cold in the head. **2.** *Vet. Sci.* a contagious disease of birds, esp. poultry, characterised by the secretion of a thick mucus in the mouth and throat. [LL, from Gk *kóryza* catarrh]

**cos**[1] /kɒs/, *n.* a kind of lettuce, with erect oblong heads and generally crisp leaves. Also, **cos lettuce.** [named after *Cos,* one of the Dodecanese Islands, in the Aegean, whence it orig. came]

**cos**[2] /kɒs/, *n. Maths.* →**cosine.**

**C.O.S.** /si oʊ 'ɛs/, chief of staff.

**cosec** /'koʊsɛk/, *n. Maths.* →**cosecant.**

**cosecant** /koʊ'sikənt/, *n.* the secant of the complement, and hence the reciprocal of the sine, of a given angle. *Abbrev.:* cosec

**cosech** /'koʊsɛʃ/, *n. Maths.* hyperbolic cosecant. See **hyperbolic functions.**

cosecant: ACB being the angle, the ratio of LC to DC or AC is the cosecant; or, DC being equal to unity, it is the line LC

**coseismal** /koʊ'saɪzməl/, *adj.* of, pertaining to, or being in a line, curve, etc., connecting or comprising points on the earth's surface at which an earthquake wave arrives simultaneously. Also, **coseismic.**

**coset** /'koʊsɛt/, *n.* (in mathematics) a set which with another set produces a specified larger set.

**cosh**[1] /kɒʃ, kɒz'eɪtʃ/, *n. Maths.* hyperbolic cosine. See **hyperbolic functions.**

**cosh**[2] /kɒʃ/, *n.* **1.** any instrument, usu. flexible, used as a bludgeon. *–v.t.* **2.** to hit with a cosh.

**cosher** /'kɒʃə, 'koʊʃə/, *n. adj.* →**kosher.**

**cosignatory** /koʊ'sɪgnətəri, -tri/, *adj., n., pl.* **-eries.** *–adj.* **1.** signing jointly with another or others. *–n.* **2.** one who signs a document jointly with another or others.

**cosinage** /'kʌzənɪdʒ/, *n. Law.* kindredship; cousinship; consanguinity. Also, **cosenage.**

**cosine** /'koʊsaɪn/, *n.* the sine of the complement of a given angle. *Abbrev.:* cos

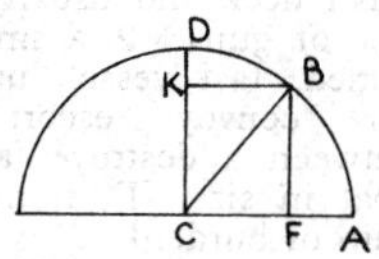


cosine: ACB being the angle, the ratio of FC to BC or that of BK to CD, is the cosine; or, CD being equal to unity, it is the line BK

**cos lettuce** /kɒs 'lɛtəs/, *n.* →**cos**[1].

**cosm-,** variant of **cosmo-,** before vowels.

**cosmetic** /kɒz'mɛtɪk/, *n.* **1.** a preparation for beautifying the complexion, skin, etc. *–adj.* **2.** serving to beautify; imparting or improving beauty, esp. of the complexion. [Gk *kosmētikós* relating to adornment] **– cosmetically,** *adv.*

**cosmetician** /kɒzmə'tɪʃən/, *n.* an expert in making, selling, or applying cosmetics.

**cosmetic surgery** /kɒz,mɛtɪk 'sɜdʒəri/, *n.* plastic surgery undertaken to improve the appearance, as a facelift.

**cosmetology** /kɒzmə'tɒlədʒi/, *n.* the study of cosmetics.

**cosmic** /'kɒzmɪk/, *adj.* **1.** of or pertaining to the cosmos: *cosmic philosophy.* **2.** characteristic of the cosmos or its phenomena; immeasurably extended in time and space; vast. **3.** forming a part of the material universe, esp. outside of the earth. **4.** orderly or harmonious. [Gk *kosmikós* of the world] **– cosmically,** *adv.*

**cosmic dust** /– 'dʌst/, *n.* matter in fine particles collected by the earth from space, like meteorites.

**cosmic rays** /– 'reɪz/, *n. pl.* radiation of extremely high penetrating power originating outside the earth's atmosphere, consisting principally of charged particles moving at nearly the velocity of light. The source of this radiation is not known, but some of it appears to emanate from the sun. Also, **cosmic radiation.**

**cosmism** /'kɒzmɪzəm/, *n.* the philosophy of cosmic evolution. **– cosmist,** *n.*

**cosmo-,** a word element representing **cosmos.**

**cosmodrome** /'kɒzmədroʊm/, *n.* a space-vehicle launching site (used esp. of a Soviet one).

**cosmogony** /kɒz'mɒgəni/, *n., pl.* **-nies.** a theory or story of the genesis or origination of the universe. [Gk *kosmogonía* creation of the world. See COSMO-, -GONY] **– cosmogonic** /kɒzmə'gɒnɪk/, **cosmogonical,** *adj.* **– cosmogonist,** *n.*

**cosmography** /kɒz'mɒgrəfi/, *n., pl.* **-phies. 1.** the science which describes and maps the main features of the heavens and the earth, embracing astronomy, geography, and geology. **2.** a description or representation of the universe in its main features. [Gk *kosmographía* description of the world. See COSMO-, -GRAPHY] **– cosmographer,** *n.* **– cosmographic** /kɒzmə'græfɪk/, **cosmographical,** *adj.*

**cosmology** /kɒz'mɒlədʒi/, *n.* the branch of philosophy that concerns itself with the origin and general structure of the universe, its parts, elements, and laws, esp. with such characteristics as space, time, causality. **– cosmological** /kɒzmə'lɒdʒɪkəl/, **cosmologic,** *adj.* **– cosmologist,** *n.*

**cosmonaut** /'kɒzmənɔt/, *n.* →**astronaut.** [COSMO- + Gk *naútēs* sailor]

**cosmonautic** /kɒzm'nɔtɪk/, *adj.* →**astronautic.** Also, **cosmonautical. – cosmonautically,** *adv.*

**cosmonautics** /kɒzmə'nɔtɪks/, *n.* →**astronautics.**

**cosmopolitan** /kɒzmə'pɒlətn/, *adj.* **1.** belonging to all parts of the world; not limited to one part of the social, political, commercial, or intellectual world. **2.** *Bot., Zool.* widely distributed over the globe. **3.** free from local, provincial, or national ideas, prejudices, or attachments; at home all over the world. **4.** of or characteristic of a cosmopolite. *–n.* **5.** one who is free from provincial or national prejudices. [COSMOPOLITE + -AN] **– cosmopolitanism,** *n.*

**cosmopolite** /kɒz'mɒpəlaɪt/, *n.* **1.** a citizen of the world; one who is cosmopolitan in his ideas or life. **2.** an animal or plant of worldwide distribution. [Gk *kosmopolítēs* citizen of the world] **– cosmopolitism,** *n.*

**cosmorama** /kɒzmə'ramə/, *n.* an exhibition of pictures of different parts of the world. [COSM- + Gk *hórāma* view] **– cosmoramic** /kɒzmə'ræmɪk/, *adj.*

**cosmos** /'kɒzmɒs/, *n.* **1.** the physical universe. **2.** the world or universe as an embodiment of order and harmony (as distinguished from *chaos*). **3.** a complete and harmonious system. **4.** order; harmony. **5.** any plant of genus *Cosmos,* of tropical America, some species of which, as *C. bipinnatus* and *C. sulphureus,* are cultivated for their showy flowers. [NL, from Gk *kósmos* order, form, the world or universe as an ordered whole, ornament]

**cosmosphere** /'kɒzməsfɪə/, *n.* a model for indicating the position of the earth with respect to the fixed stars at any given time, consisting of a hollow glass globe representing the celestial sphere containing within it a small sphere representing the earth.

**cosmotron** /'kɒzmətrɒn/, *n.* a type of proton accelerator used in nuclear physics.

**Cossack** /'kɒsæk/, *n.* one of a people of the southern Soviet Union in Europe and adjoining parts of Asia, noted as horsemen or light cavalry. [Russ. *kazak,* from Turk. *quzzāq* adventurer, freebooter]

**Cossack hat** /'– hæt/, *n.* a fur hat with no brim, commonly worn in Russia.

**cosset** /'kɒsət/, *v.t.* **1.** to treat as a pet; pamper; coddle. *–n.* **2.** a lamb brought up by hand; a pet lamb. **3.** a pet of any kind. [cf. OE *cossetung* kissing]

**cossid** /'kɒsəd/, *adj.* of or pertaining to the Cossidae, a family of heavy-bodied, narrow-winged moths which lay eggs in trees and whose larvae characteristically tunnel into the timber.

**cossie** /'kɒzi/, *n. Colloq.* →**swimming costume.** Also, **cozzie.** [abbrev. COSTUME + -IE]

**cost** /kɒst/, *n., v.,* **cost** or (defs 9, 10) **costed, costing.** *–n.* **1.** the price paid to acquire, produce, accomplish, or maintain anything. **2.** a sacrifice, loss, or penalty: *to work at the cost of one's health.* **3.** outlay or expenditure of money, time, labour, trouble, etc. **4.** (*pl.*) *Law.* the sums which the successful party is usu. entitled to recover for reimbursement of particular expenses incurred in the litigation. **5.** (*pl.*) *Law.* the charges which a solicitor is entitled to make and recover from the client or person employing him as his remuneration for professional services. **6. at all costs,** or **at any cost,** regardless of the cost. *–v.t.* **7.** to require the expenditure of money, time, labour, etc., in exchange, purchase, or payment; be of the price of; be acquired in return for: *it cost 50 cents.* **8.** to result in a particular sacrifice, loss, or penalty: *it may cost him his life.* **9.** to estimate or determine the cost of. *–v.i.* **10.** to estimate or determine costs. [ME, from OF, from *coster,* from L *constāre* stand together] **– costless,** *adj.*

**costa** /'kɒstə/, *n., pl.* **-tae** /-ti/. **1.** a rib or riblike part. **2.** *Entomol.* **a.** a vein in the anterior part of the wing of certain insects. **b.** the anterior edge or border of the wing of such insects. **3.** the midrib of a leaf in mosses or of a pinna. **4.** a ridge. [L: rib, side]

**cost accounting** /ˈkɒst əˌkaʊntɪŋ/, *n.* **1.** an accounting system indicating the cost items involved in production. **2.** the operation of such an accounting system. – **cost accountant,** *n.*

**costal** /ˈkɒstl/, *adj.* pertaining to the ribs or the side of the body: *costal nerves.* [LL *costālis*]

**co-star** /ˈkoʊ-sta/, *v.,* **-starred, -starring,** *n.* –*v.i.* **1.** to share star billing with another actor in a play or film. –*n.* **2.** a star who does this.

**Costa Rica** /kɒstə ˈrikə/, *n.* a republic in Central America between Panama and Nicaragua. – **Costa Rican,** *adj., n.*

**costate** /ˈkɒsteɪt/, *adj.* **1.** bearing ribs. **2.** having a midrib or costa.

**cost-benefit analysis** /kɒst-ˌbɛnəfət əˈnæləsəs/, *n.* the study of whether or not a project would be financially viable by comparing its cost with the expected returns.

**costean** /kɒsˈtin/, *n. Mining.* **1.** a trench or pit cut across the conjectured line of outcrop of a seam or ore body to expose the full width. –*v.i.* **2.** to dig such a trench. Also, **costeen.** [Cornish d., from *coid* wood + *stean* tin]

**cost-effective** /ˈkɒst-əˌfɛktɪv/, *adj.* offering profits deemed to be satisfactory in view of the costs involved.

**costermonger** /ˈkɒstəmʌŋgə/, *n.* a hawker of fruit, vegetables, fish, etc. Also, **coster.** [earlier *costardmonger,* from *costard* type of apple + MONGER]

**costive** /ˈkɒstɪv/, *adj.* **1.** suffering from constipation; constipated. **2.** slow in action or in expressing ideas, opinions, etc. [OF, from L *constipātus,* pp. See CONSTIPATE] – **costively,** *adv.* – **costiveness,** *n.*

**costly** /ˈkɒstli/, *adj.,* **-lier, -liest. 1.** costing much; of great price or value. **2.** *Archaic.* lavish; extravagant. – **costliness,** *n.*

**costmary** /ˈkɒstmɛəri/, *n., pl.* **-maries.** a perennial plant, *Chrysanthemum balsamita,* with fragrant leaves, used in salads, to flavour ale, etc. [OE *cost* (from L *costus,* from Gk *kóstos* kind of aromatic plant) + *Mary* the Virgin Mary]

**costo-,** a word element meaning 'rib', as in *costoscapular.* [combining form representing L *costa*]

**costoclavicular** /ˌkɒstoʊkləˈvɪkjələ/, *adj.* referring to both the ribs and the collarbone.

**cost of living,** *n.* the average retail prices of food, clothing, and other necessities paid by a person, family, etc., in order to live at their usual standard.

**cost-of-living bonus** /kɒst-əv-ˈlɪvɪŋ ˌboʊnəs/, *n.* a bonus, paid to some workers, the sum of which depends on the rise in the cost of living as shown in the cost-of-living index.

**cost-of-living index** /kɒst-əv-ˈlɪvɪŋ ˌɪndɛks/, *n.* an index compiled from official statistics which represents the monthly rise or fall in the cost of living in terms of points as compared with a selected earlier year.

**costoscapular** /kɒstoʊˈskæpjələ/, *adj.* pertaining to ribs and to the scapula.

**cost-plus** /kɒst-ˈplʌs/, *n.* the cost of production plus an agreed rate of profit (often used as a basis of payment in government contracts).

**cost price** /ˈkɒst praɪs/, *n.* **1.** the price at which a merchant buys goods for resale. **2.** the cost of production.

**cost-push inflation** /ˌkɒst-pʊʃ ɪnˈfleɪʃən/, *n.* an economic situation in which prices are forced higher as a result of higher costs, such as wage rises or tax increases. See **demand-pull inflation.**

**costrel** /ˈkɒstrəl/, *n.* a bottle of leather, earthenware, or wood, often of flattened form and commonly having an ear or ears to suspend it by, as from the waist. [ME, from OF *costerel,* apparently originally a flask hung at the side, from *coste* rib, side, from L *costa.* See -REL]

**costume** /ˈkɒstʃum/, *n., v.,* **-tumed, -tuming.** –*n.* **1.** the style of dress, including ornaments and the way of wearing the hair, esp. that peculiar to a nation, class, or period. **2.** dress or garb belonging to another period, place, etc., as worn on the stage, at balls, etc. **3.** a set of garments, esp. a woman's two-piece suit or dress and jacket. **4.** fashion of dress appropriate to a particular occasion or season: *winter costume, swimming costume.* –*v.t.* **5.** to dress; furnish with a costume; provide appropriate dress for: *to costume a play.* [F, from It.: habit, fashion, from L *consuētūdo* custom]

**costume drama** /ˈ– dramə/, *n.* a play in which the characters wear costumes from a former age. Also, **costume piece.**

**costume jewellery** /ˈ– dʒuəlri/, *n.* decorative jewellery of little monetary value.

**costume piece** /ˈ– pis/, *n.* →**costume drama.**

**costumier** /kɒsˈtjumiə/, *n.* one who makes or deals in costumes. Also, **costumer.**

**cost unit** /ˈkɒst junət/, *n.* the basis of computing of costs; a unit of product, a unit of process, or the like.

**cosy** /ˈkoʊzi/, *adj.,* **-sier, -siest,** *n., pl.* **-sies.** –*adj.* **1.** snug; comfortable. –*n.* **2.** a padded covering for a teapot, boiled egg, etc., to retain the heat. [orig. Scot.; probably from Scand.; cf. Norw. *koselig*] – **cosily,** *adv.* – **cosiness,** *n.*

**cot**[1] /kɒt/, *n.* **1.** a child's bed with enclosed sides. **2.** a light, usu. portable, bed, esp. one of canvas stretched on a frame. **3.** *Naut.* a swinging bed made of canvas for officers, sick persons, etc. **4. hit the cot,** *Colloq.* to go to bed. [Anglo-Ind., from Hind. *khāt*]

**cot**[2] /kɒt/, *n.* **1.** a small house; cottage; hut. **2.** a small place of shelter or protection. [ME and OE; orig. unknown]

**cot**[3] /kɒt/, *n. Maths.* →**cotangent.**

**cotan** /ˈkoʊtæn/, *n. Maths.* →**cotangent.**

**cotangent** /koʊˈtændʒənt/, *n.* the tangent of the complement, and hence the reciprocal of the tangent, of a given angle. *Abbrev.:* cot or cotan – **cotangential** /ˌkoʊtænˈdʒɛnʃəl/, *adj.*

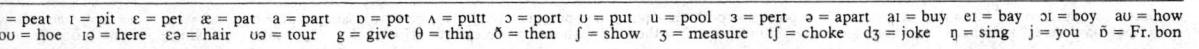

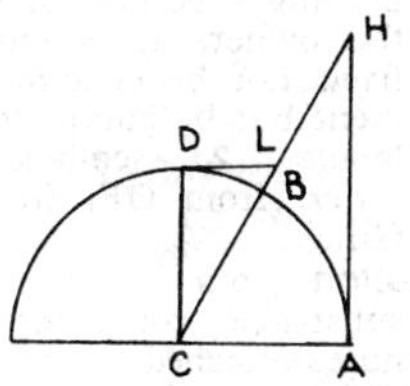

cotangent: ACB being the angle, the ratio of AC to AH, is the cotangent; or, DC being taken as unity, it is the line DL

**cotanh** /ˈkoʊθæn, ˈkoʊtænʃ/, *n.* hyperbolic cotangent. See **hyperbolic functions.**

**cot case** /ˈkɒt keɪs/, *n. Colloq.* (*joc.*) someone who is exhausted, drunk, or in some way incapacitated, and fit only for bed.

**cot death** /ˈkɒt dɛθ/, *n.* the sudden, unexplained death in bed of an apparently healthy infant.

**cote** /koʊt/, *n.* a shelter for doves, sheep, etc. [OE. See COT[2]]

**cotemporaneous** /koʊˌtɛmpəˈreɪniəs/, *adj.* →**contemporaneous.**

**cotemporary** /koʊˈtɛmpərəri/, *adj., n., pl.* **-raries.** →**contemporary.**

**cotenant** /koʊˈtɛnənt/, *n.* one of two or more persons who holds property, esp. a lessee. – **cotenancy,** *n.*

**coterie** /ˈkoʊtəri/, *n.* **1.** a group of persons who associate closely, esp. for social purposes. **2.** a clique. [F: set, association of people; earlier, cottars' tenure, from OF *cotier* cottar. See COTTAR]

**coterminous** /koʊˈtɜmənəs/, *adj.* →**conterminous.**

**coth** /kɒθ/, *n.* hyperbolic cotangent. See **hyperbolic functions.**

**cotidal** /koʊˈtaɪdl/, *adj.* **1.** pertaining to a coincidence of tides. **2.** denoting a line connecting points where it is high tide at the same time.

**cotillion** /kəˈtɪljən/, *n.* a lively French social dance of the 18th century. Also, **cotillon** /kəˈtɪljən/. [F *cotillon,* orig., petticoat, diminutive of *cotte* coat]

**cotinga** /kəˈtɪŋgə/, *n.* any of several chiefly tropical passerine birds of the family Cotingidae of North, Central, and South America. [NL, from F, from Tupi]

**cotise** /ˈkɒtɪs, ˈkoʊtɪs/, *n., v.,* **-ised, -ising.** *Her.* –*n.* **1.** a narrow diminutive of a bend. –*v.t.* **2.** to border with cotises. [NF *co(s)tice,* from L *costa* rib]

**cotoneaster** /kəˌtoʊniˈæstə/, *n.* any plant of the genus *Cotoneaster,* many of which are cultivated for their usually red berries. [NL, from L *cotōnium* quince + *-aster* -ASTER[2]]

**cotta** /ˈkɒtə/, *n.* **1.** →**surplice. 2.** a short surplice, with short sleeves or sleeveless, worn esp. by choristers. [ML. See COAT]

**cottage** /ˈkɒtɪdʒ/, *n.* **1.** a small bungalow. **2.** *Brit.* a small country house.

**cottage cheese** /– ˈtʃiz/, *n.* a kind of soft unripened white cheese made of skimmed milk curds without rennet.

**cottage hospital** /– ˈhɒspətl/, *n.* a small, usu. single-storeyed hospital.

**cottage industry** /– ˈɪndəstri/, *n.* an industry, as knitting, pottery, or weaving, carried out in the home of the worker.

**cottage loaf** /ˈ– loʊf/, *n.* a loaf made by placing a small round lump of dough on top of a larger round lump.

**cottage piano** /ˈ– piænoʊ/, *n.* a small upright piano.

**cottage pie** /– ˈpaɪ/, *n.* →**shepherd's pie.**

**cottage pudding** /– ˈpʊdɪŋ/, *n.* a baked pudding made from a cake dough with raisins.

**cottager** /ˈkɒtɪdʒə/, *n.* **1.** one who lives in a cottage. **2.** a labourer in a village or on a farm.

**cottar** /ˈkɒtə/, *n.* **1.** *Scot.* a person occupying a plot of land under a system similar to cottier tenure. **2.** *Irish.* cottier. **3.** a cottager. Also, **cotter.** [ML *cotārius,* from *cota,* Latinised form of COT[2]]

**cotted** /ˈkɒtəd/, *adj.* of or pertaining to wool which has become partially felted or matted whilst on the sheep's back.

**cotter** /ˈkɒtə/, *n.* **1.** a pin, wedge, key, or the like, fitted or driven into an opening in order to secure something or hold parts together. **2.** →**cotter pin.** [orig. uncert.]

**cotter pin** /ˈ– pɪn/, *n.* a cotter having a split end which is spread after being pushed through a hole, to prevent the cotter from working loose.

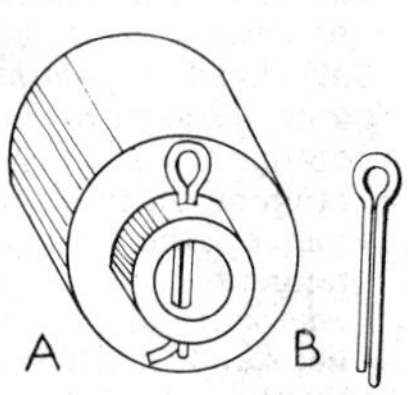

cotter pin: A, cotter pin holding one shaft within another; B, split cotter pin before use

**cottier** /ˈkɒtiə/, *n.* **1.** an Irish peasant holding a portion of land directly from the owner, the amount of rent being fixed not by custom or private agreement but by public competition (**cottier tenure**). **2.** →**cottager** (def. 1). [ME *cotier,* from OF, from *cote* cot, from Gmc]

**cotton** /ˈkɒtn/, *n.* **1.** a soft, white, downy substance, consisting of the hairs of fibres attached to the seeds of plants of the genus *Gossypium,* used in making fabrics, thread, wadding, guncotton, etc. **2.** a plant yielding cotton, as *G. hirsutum* (**upland cotton**) or *G. peruvianum* (**sea-island cotton**). **3.** such plants collectively, as a cultivated crop. **4.** cloth, thread, etc., made of cotton. **5.** any soft, downy substance resembling cotton but growing on some other plant. *–v.i.* **6.** *Colloq.* to make friends. **7.** *Colloq.* to become attached or friendly (fol. by *to* or *with*). **8.** *Colloq.* to get on together; agree. **9.** *Colloq.* to understand; perceive meaning or purpose (oft. fol. by *on*). **10.** *Obs.* to prosper or succeed. [ME *coton,* from OF, from It. *cotone,* from Ar. *quṭn*]

**cottonade** /kɒtnˈeɪd/, *n.* an inferior cotton cloth, often used for making cheap pyjamas, etc.

**cotton belt** /ˈkɒtn bɛlt/, *n.* that part of the southern U.S. where cotton is grown.

**cotton bud** /ˈ– bʌd/, *n.* a small thin stick, the ends of which are wound with cotton wool, suitable for applying cleansing or other lotions to the nostril, ear, etc. [Trademark]

**cottonbush** /ˈkɒtnbʊʃ/, *n.* any of several unrelated plants bearing cotton-like hairs, as **a.** *Kochia aphylla,* a perennial shrub valuable as a fodder plant. **b.** *Asclepias fruticosa,* a slender, erect shrub which is poisonous to stock; milkweed.

**cotton cake** /ˈkɒtn keɪk/, *n.* a mass of compressed cottonseed after the oil has been extracted, used to feed cattle, etc.

**cotton-feed bug** /ˈkɒtən-fid bʌg/, *n.* See **coon bug.**

**cotton flannel** /– ˈflænəl/, *n.* a warm, napped fabric woven of cotton. Also, **Canton flannel.**

**cotton gin** /ˈ– dʒɪn/, *n.* a machine for separating the fibres of cotton from the seeds.

**cottonmouth** /ˈkɒtnmaʊθ/, *n.* the water-moccasin, a venomous snake of the southern U.S.

**cotton-picker** /ˈkɒtn-pɪkə/, *n.* a machine for removing ripe cotton fibre from the standing plant.

**cotton-picking** /ˈkɒtn-pɪkɪŋ/, *adj.* *Orig. U.S. Colloq.* unworthy; simple: *out of one's cotton-picking mind.*

**cotton plant** /ˈkɒtn plænt/, *n.* a sub-alpine New Zealand daisy, *Celmisia spectabilis,* with a soft felted tomentum.

**cotton print** /– ˈprɪnt/, *n.* cotton cloth with a printed design or pattern.

**cottonseed** /ˈkɒtnsid/, *n., pl.* **-seeds,** (*esp. collectively*) **-seed.** the seed of the cotton plant, yielding an oil.

**cottonseed meal** /– ˈmil/, *n.* →**cotton cake.**

**cottonseed oil** /– ˈɔɪl/, *n.* a brown-yellow viscid oil, with a nutlike smell, obtained from the seed of the cotton plant, used in pharmacology and as an oil for salad dressing.

**cottontail** /ˈkɒtnteɪl/, *n.* any of several small North American rabbits of the genus *Sylvilagus* having the underside of the tail white.

**cottontree** /ˈkɒtntri/, *n.* a yellow flowered tree of tropical coasts, *Hibiscus tiliaceus,* with bark fibre useful for cordage.

**cotton waste** /kɒtn ˈweɪst/, *n.* the refuse from manufacturing cotton, as used for cleaning machinery.

**cottonwood** /ˈkɒtnwʊd/, *n.* **1.** a shrub of eastern Australia, *Bedfordia salicina,* with downy leaves; blanket bush. **2.** Also, **tauhinu, tawine.** the New Zealand heath-like shrub, *Cassinia leptophylla,* which has a white tomentum on the undersurface of leaves and branches. **3.** any of several American species of poplar, as *Populus deltoides,* with cotton-like tufts on the seeds.

**cottonwool** /kɒtnˈwʊl/, *n.* **1.** raw cotton for surgical dressings and toilet purposes which has had its natural wax chemically removed. **2.** cotton in its raw state, as on the boll or gathered for use. **3.** *Colloq.* a protected and comfortable state or existence. *–adj.* **4.** made of cottonwool. **5.** *Colloq.* protected and comfortable.

**cottony** /ˈkɒtəni/, *adj.* **1.** of or like cotton; soft. **2.** covered with a down or nap resembling cotton.

**cottony-cushion scale** /ˌkɒtəni-ˈkʊʃən ˌskeɪl/, *n.* a sap-sucking scale insect which infects citrus plants.

**cotyledon** /kɒtəˈlidn/, *n.* **1.** *Bot.* the primary or rudimentary leaf of the embryo of seed plants. **2.** *Zool.* a tuft or patch of villi on the placenta of most ruminants. [L: navelwort (a plant), from Gk *kotylēdṓn* any cup-shaped hollow] – **cotyledonal,** *adj.* – **cotyledonary,** *adj.*

**cotyloid** /ˈkɒtəlɔɪd/, *adj.* *Anat.* shaped like a cup. Also, **cotyloidal** /kɒtəˈlɔɪdl/. [Gk *kotuloeidḗs* cup-shaped]

**couba** /ˈkubə/, *n.* →**cooba.** Also, **coubah.**

**coucal** /ˈkukæl, ˈkukəl/, *n.* **1.** →**pheasant coucal. 2.** any of various long-tailed cuckoos, esp. of the genus *Centropus,* of Africa and southern Asia. [F]

**couch**[1] /kaʊtʃ/, *n.* **1.** a piece of furniture, for seating two to four people, with a back and sometimes armrests. **2.** a similar piece of upholstered furniture, without a back but with a headrest, as used by doctors for their patients. **3.** a bed or other place of rest; any place used for repose. **4.** the lair of a wild beast. **5.** the frame on which barley is spread to be malted. **6.** a coat of paint, etc. *–v.t.* **7.** to arrange or frame (words, a sentence, etc.); put into words; express. **8.** to express indirectly. **9.** to lower or bend down, as the head. **10.** *Archaic.* to lower (a spear, etc.) to a horizontal position, as for attack. **11.** to lay or put down; cause to lie down; lay or spread flat. **12.** to overlay; embroider with thread laid flat on a surface and caught down at intervals. **13.** *Obs.* to place or lodge; conceal. **14.** *Surg.* **a.** to remove (a cataract) by inserting a needle and pushing the opaque crystalline lens downwards in the vitreous humour below the axis of vision. **b.** to remove a cataract from (a person) in this manner. *–v.i.* **15.** to lie at rest; repose; recline. **16.** to crouch; bend; stoop. **17.** to lie in ambush; lurk. **18.** to lie in a heap for decomposition or fermentation, as leaves. [ME *couche(n),* from OF *coucher,* from L *collocāre* lay in its place]

**couch**[2] /kutʃ/, *n.* **1.** any of various grasses of the genus *Cynodon,* esp. *C. dactylon,* characterised by creeping rootstocks, by means of which it multiplies rapidly; popular as lawn grass. **2.** →**twitch**[2]. Also, **couch grass.** [var. *quitch,* from OE *cwice,* c. D *kweck,* Norw. *kvike;* akin to QUICK, *adj.*]

**couch.,** couchant.

**couchant** /ˈkuʃənt/, *adj.* **1.** lying down; crouching. **2.** *Her.* lying down, as of a lion. [F, ppr. of *coucher* lie]

**couchette** /kuˈʃɛt/, *n.* **1.** (in a railway carriage) a bunk for passengers to sleep on. **2.** a railway sleeping-car. [F]

**couching** /ˈkaʊtʃɪŋ/, *n.* **1.** the act of one who or that which couches. **2.** a method of embroidering in which a thread, often heavy, laid upon the surface of the material, is caught down at intervals by stitches taken with another thread through the material. **3.** work so made.

**cougar** /ˈkugə/, *n.* →**puma.** [F *couguar,* from NL *cuguacuara,* representing Tupi *cuacu ara,* Guarani *guacu ara*]

**cough** /kɒf/, *v.i.* **1.** to expel the air from the lungs suddenly and with a characteristic noise. *–v.t.* **2.** to expel by coughing (fol. by *up* or *out*). **3. cough up,** *Colloq.* to give; hand over. *–n.* **4.** the act or sound of coughing. **5.** an illness characterised by frequent coughing. [ME *coghen,* backformation from OE *cohhetan* cough. Cf. G *keuchen* wheeze] – **cougher,** *n.*

**cough drop** /'– drɒp/, *n. Brit.* **1.** →**cough lolly. 2.** *Colloq.* a fool, simpleton.

**cough lolly** /'– lɒli/, *n.* a small medicinal lozenge for relieving a cough, sore throat, etc.

**cough mixture** /'– mɪkstʃə/, *n.* a liquid medicine for the relief of coughing and congestion. Also, **cough medicine.**

**could** /kʊd/, *v. weak form* past tense of **can**[1]. [ME *coude,* OE *cūthe;* modification of *l* improperly inserted, after *would* and *should*]

**couldn't** /'kʊdnt/, *v.* contraction of *could not.*

**couldst** /kʊdst/, *v. Archaic or Poetic.* 2nd pers. sing. of **could.**

**coulee** /'kuleɪ, -li/, *n.* **1.** a stream of lava. **2.** *North America.* a deep ravine or gulch, usu. dry, which has been worn by running water. [F *couler* flow, slide, from L *cōlāre* strain]

**coulisse** /ku'lis/, *n., pl.* **-lisses** /-'lisəz/. **1.** a timber grooved for a frame to slide in it. **2.** (*pl.*) the wings in a theatre.

**couloir** /'kulwa/, *n.* a steep gorge or gully on the side of a mountain. [F *couler.* See COULEE]

**coulomb** /'kulɒm/, *n.* the derived SI unit of electric charge, defined as the quantity of electricity transferred by 1 ampere in 1 second. *Symbol:* C [named after C. A. de *Coulomb,* 1736-1806, French physicist]

**coulomb force** /'– fɔs/, *n.* the force between two electrically charged bodies. If the charges are of the same polarity the force is repulsive; if they are of opposite polarity the force is attractive.

**Coulomb's Law** /'kulɒmz ˌlɔ/, *n.* (in physics) the principle that the attractive or repulsive force between two electrically charged bodies, or magnetic poles, is proportional to the product of the charges, or pole strengths, and inversely proportional to the square of the distance between them.

**coulometer** /ku'lɒmətə/, *n.* →**voltameter.** Also, **coulombmeter.**

**coulter** /'koʊltə/, *n.* a sharp blade or wheel attached to the beam of a plough, used to cut the ground in advance of the ploughshare. Also, *Chiefly U.S.,* **colter.** [ME and OE *culter,* from L: knife]

**coumarin** /'kumərən/, *n.* a toxic white crystalline substance, with a vanilla-like smell, $C_9H_6O_2$, obtained from the tonka bean and certain other plants, or prepared synthetically, and used for flavouring and in perfumery. [F *coumarine,* from *coumarou,* representing Tupi *kumarū* tonka-bean tree]

**coumarone** /'kumərəʊn/, *n.* (in chemistry) a stable inert bicyclic ring compound found in coal tar, $C_6H_4OC_2H_2$; polymerises with indene into coumarone–indene resins which are used for varnishes, printing inks, adhesives, etc.

**council** /'kaʊnsəl/, *n.* **1.** an assembly of persons summoned or convened for consultation, deliberation, or advice. **2.** an ecclesiastical assembly for deciding matters of doctrine or discipline. **3.** a body of persons specially designated or selected to act in an advisory, administrative, or legislative capacity. **4.** (in many of the British crown colonies) a body assisting the governor in either an executive or a legislative capacity, or in both. **5.** the local administrative body of a city, municipality, or shire. [ME *counceil,* from OF *concile,* from L *concilium* assembly, union, but with sense affected by L *consilium* COUNSEL]

**council chamber** /'– tʃeɪmbə/, *n.* **1.** the room where a council meets. **2.** (*pl.*) a building in which the council offices are located.

**council estate** /'– əˌsteɪt/, *n. Brit.* a group of council houses and other amenities within a clearly defined area.

**council house** /'– haʊs/, *n. Brit.* a dwelling house built and let at a subsidised rent, by the local governing authority (county council, urban district council, or rural district council).

**councillor** /'kaʊnsələ/, *n.* a member of a council. Also, *U.S.,* **councilor.** – **councillorship,** *n.*

**council of war,** *n.* **1.** a conference of high-ranking military or naval officers, usu. to discuss major war problems and plans. **2.** any conference to make important plans.

**counsel** /'kaʊnsəl/, *n., v.,* **-selled, -selling** or (*U.S.*) **-seled, -seling.** *–n.* **1.** advice; opinion or instruction given in directing the judgment or conduct of another. **2.** interchange of opinions as to future procedure; consultation; deliberation: *to take counsel with one's partners.* **3.** *Archaic.* wisdom; prudence. **4.** deliberate purpose; plan; design. **5.** a private or secret opinion or purpose: *to keep one's own counsel.* **6.** the barrister or barristers engaged in the direction of a cause in court; a legal adviser. **7.** *Theol.* one of the advisory declarations of Christ, considered as not universally binding but as given for aid in attaining greater moral perfection. **8. keep one's own counsel,** to keep secret one's opinion or plans. **9. counsel of perfection,** excellent but impracticable advice. *–v.t.* **10.** to give counsel to; advise. **11.** to urge the doing or adoption of; recommend (a plan, etc.). *–v.i.* **12.** to give counsel or advice. **13.** *Obs.* to take counsel. [ME *counseil,* from OF, from L *consilium* consultation, plan. Cf. COUNCIL]

**counsellor** /'kaʊnsələ/, *n.* **1.** one who counsels; an adviser. **2.** *U.S. Law.* a lawyer, esp. a trial lawyer. **3.** an adviser, esp. a legal adviser, in an embassy or legation. **4.** a professional psychologist employed by a state education department to advise students on both personal and educational problems. Also, *U.S.,* **counselor.** – **counsellorship,** *n.*

**count**[1] /kaʊnt/, *v.t.* **1.** to check over one by one (the individuals of a collection) in order to ascertain their total number; enumerate. **2.** to reckon up; calculate; compute. **3.** to list or name the numerals up to. **4.** to include in a reckoning; take into account. **5.** to reckon to the credit of another; ascribe; impute. **6.** to esteem; consider. **7. count in,** to include. **8. count out, a.** to exclude: *count me out.* **b.** *Boxing.* to proclaim (one) the loser because of his inability to stand up before the referee has counted ten seconds. **c.** *Brit. Parl. Proc.* to adjourn (a sitting of the House of Commons) because of the lack of a quorum. *–v.i.* **9.** to count the items of a collection one by one in order to know the total. **10.** to list or name the numerals in order. **11.** to reckon numerically. **12.** to depend or rely (fol. by *on* or *upon*). **13.** to have a numerical value (as specified). **14.** to be accounted or worth: *a book which counts as a masterpiece.* **15.** to enter into consideration: *every effort counts.* **16.** to be worth; amount (fol. by *for*). **17.** to divide into groups by calling off numbers in order (fol. by *off*). **18.** *Obs.* to take account (fol. by *of*). *–n.* **19.** the act of counting; enumeration; reckoning; calculation. **20.** the number representing the result of a process of counting; the total number. **21.** an accounting. **22.** *Law.* a distinct charge or cause of action in a declaration or indictment. **23.** *Textiles.* **a.** the number of hanks of a length of cotton or yarn in a specified weight. **b.** the number used to indicate fineness of raw wool. **24.** *Boxing.* the calling aloud by the referee of ten seconds, while a boxer is unable to stand up, after which he is declared to have lost by a knockout. **25.** regard; notice; awareness. **26. on all counts,** in every respect. **27. out for the count,** *Colloq.* **a.** completely exhausted. **b.** unable to continue an activity. [ME *counte(n),* from OF *conter,* from L *computāre* calculate, reckon]

**count**[2] /kaʊnt/, *n.* (in some European countries) a nobleman corresponding in rank to the English earl. [AF *counte,* from L *comes* companion]

**countable** /'kaʊntəbəl/, *adj.* **1.** able to be counted. **2.** *Maths.* of or pertaining to a set whose elements can be arranged in an infinite sequence so that each element occurs exactly once: *the set of positive integers is a countable set.*

**countdown** /'kaʊntdaʊn/, *n.* **1.** the final check prior to the firing of a missile, detonation of an explosive, etc. With the precise moment of firing or detonation designated as zero, the days, hours, minutes, and seconds are counted backwards from the initiation of a project. **2.** the period of time preceding such an event or the procedure carried out in that time. **3.** the final check or period of time preceding any large-scale project.

**countenance** /'kaʊntənəns/, *n., v.,* **-nanced, -nancing.** *–n.* **1.** aspect; appearance, esp. the look or expression of the face. **2.** the face; visage. **3.** composed expression of face. **4.** appearance of favour; encouragement; moral support. **5.** *Obs.* bearing; behaviour. **6. in countenance,** unabashed. **7. out of**

**countenance,** visibly disconcerted, or abashed. *–v.t.* **8.** to give countenance or show favour to; encourage; support. **9.** to tolerate; permit. [ME, from OF *contenance* bearing, from ML *continentia* demeanour, L restraint] – **countenancer,** *n.*

**counter**[1] /ˈkaʊntə/, *n.* **1.** a table or board on which money is counted, business is transacted, or goods are laid for examination. **2.** (in a cafe, restaurant or hotel) a long, narrow table, shelf, bar, etc., at which customers eat. **3. under the counter, a.** clandestine or reserved for favoured customers. **b.** in a manner other than that of an open and honest business transaction; clandestinely and often illegally. **4.** anything used in keeping account, as in games, esp. a round or otherwise shaped piece of metal, ivory, wood, or other material. **5.** an imitation coin or token. [ME, from AF *counteour* counting house, counting table, from OF *conter* COUNT[1]]

**counter**[2] /ˈkaʊntə/, *n.* **1.** one who counts. **2.** an apparatus for counting revolutions or other movements. **3. a.** *Electronics.* a circuit for counting electrical impulses. **b.** Also, **counter tube.** *Physics.* a device for counting ionising events, such as a Geiger counter. **4.** *Computers.* a device, as a register, which is used to record the number of events.

**counter**[3] /ˈkaʊntə/, *adv.* **1.** in the wrong way; contrary to the right course; in the reverse direction. **2.** contrary; in opposition (chiefly with *run* or *go*): *to run counter to the rules.* *–adj.* **3.** opposite; opposed; contrary. *–n.* **4.** that which is opposite or contrary to something else. **5.** a blow delivered in receiving or parrying another blow, as in boxing. **6.** *Fencing.* a circular parry. **7.** that portion of the stern of a boat or vessel extending from the waterline to the full outward swell. **8.** the piece of stiff leather forming the back of a shoe or boot round the heel. **9.** that part of a horse's breast which lies between the shoulders and under the neck. **10.** *Print.* any part of the face that is less than type-high and is therefore not inked. *–v.t.* **11.** to go counter to; oppose; controvert. **12.** to meet or answer (a move, blow, etc.) by another in return. *–v.i.* **13.** to make a counter or opposing move. **14.** to give a blow while receiving or parrying one, as in boxing. [F *contre*, from L *contrā*, adv. and prep., in opposition, against. Cf. COUNTER-]

**counter**[4] /ˈkaʊntə/, *n. Mining.* **1.** a cross vein or lode running across the main lode. **2.** a gangway driven obliquely upwards on a coal seam from the main gangway until it cuts off the faces of the workings and then continues parallel with the main gangway. Also, **caunter.** [Corn. d. *caunter* a cross-handed blow]

**counter-,** **1.** a combining form of **counter**[3], as in *counteract.* **2.** *Her.* a word element signifying opposition to the second element, as in contrary directions (*counter-rampant*), on two opposite sides (*counter-indented*), or having the tinctures reversed (*counter-ermine*). [see COUNTER[3]]

**counteract** /kaʊntərˈækt/, *v.t.* to act in opposition to; frustrate by contrary action. – **counteraction,** *n.* – **counteractive,** *adj.* – **counteractively,** *adv.*

**counterattack** /ˈkaʊntərətæk/, *n.*; /kaʊntərəˈtæk/, *v.* *–n.* **1.** an attack designed to counteract another attack; a responsive attack. **2.** an attack to regain an objective taken by an enemy. *–v.i.* **3.** to deliver a counterattack (to). *–v.t.* **4.** to make a counterattack against (someone).

**counterattraction** /kaʊntərəˈtrækʃən/, *n.* a rival or opposite attraction. – **counterattractive,** *adj.*

**counterbalance** /ˈkaʊntəbæləns/, *n.*; /kaʊntəˈbæləns/, *v.*, **-anced, -ancing.** *–n.* **1.** a weight balancing another weight; an equal weight, power, or influence acting in opposition; counterpoise. *–v.t.* **2.** to weight or act against with an equal weight or force.

**counterblast** /ˈkaʊntəblast/, *n.* **1.** an opposing blast. **2.** an unrestrained and vigorously powerful response to an attacking statement; a denunciation.

**counterbrace** /kaʊntəˈbreɪs, ˈkaʊntəbreɪs/, *v.t.*, **-braced, -bracing.** to brace the fore and main yards on opposite tacks to reduce the headway of a ship.

**counterchange** /kaʊntəˈtʃeɪndʒ, ˈkaʊntətʃeɪndʒ/, *v.t.*, **-changed, -changing.** **1.** to cause to change places, qualities, etc.; interchange. **2.** to diversify; chequer.

**countercharge** /ˈkaʊntətʃadʒ/, *n.*, *v.*, **-charged, -charging.** *–n.* **1.** a charge by an accused person against his accuser. *–v.t.* **2.** to make an accusation against (one's accuser).

**countercheck** /ˈkaʊntətʃɛk/, *n.*; /kaʊntəˈtʃɛk/, *v.* *–n.* **1.** a check that opposes or restrains. **2.** a check controlling or confirming another check. *–v.t.* **3.** to oppose or restrain (some obstacle, etc.) by contrary action. **4.** to control or confirm by a second check.

**counter cheque** /ˈkaʊntə tʃɛk/, *n.* a cheque available in a bank for the use of a customer in making a withdrawal from that bank.

**counterclaim** /ˈkaʊntəkleɪm/, *n.* **1.** a claim set up against another claim. *–v.i.* **2.** to set up a counterclaim. – **counterclaimant** /kaʊntəˈkleɪmənt/, *n.*

**counterclockwise** /ˌkaʊntəˈklɒkwaɪz/, *adj., adv. U.S.* →**anticlockwise.**

**counter culture** /ˈkaʊntə kʌltʃə/, *n.* a minority group within a western capitalised society which is opposed to that society's ethos and lifestyle.

**countercurrent** /ˈkaʊntəkʌrənt/, *n.* a current flowing in an opposite direction.

**counterespionage** /ˌkaʊntərˈɛspiənaʒ, -nadʒ/, *n.* the detection of enemy espionage.

**counterfactual** /kaʊntəˈfæktʃuəl/, *n.* (in logic) a conditional statement, the first clause of which expresses something contrary to fact, as: *if I had known.*

**counterfeit** /ˈkaʊntəfət, -fit/, *adj.* **1.** made to imitate, and pass for, something else; not genuine: *counterfeit coin.* **2.** pretended: *counterfeit grief.* *–n.* **3.** an imitation designed to pass as an original; a forgery. **4.** *Archaic.* a copy. **5.** *Obs.* a likeness; portrait. *–v.t.* **6.** to make a counterfeit of; imitate fraudulently; forge. **7.** to resemble. **8.** to simulate. *–v.i.* **9.** to make counterfeits, as of money. **10.** to feign; dissemble. [ME *countrefet*, from OF *contrefait*, pp. of *contrefaire* imitate, from *contre* CONTRA- + *faire* do (from L *facere*)] – **counterfeiter,** *n.*

**counterfoil** /ˈkaʊntəfɔɪl/, *n.* a complementary part of a bank cheque, etc., which is retained by the issuer, and on which particulars are noted.

**counterindemnity** /ˌkaʊntərɪnˈdɛmnəti/, *n.* a document intended to secure against loss, given in exchange for an indemnity bond or guarantee.

**counterinsurgency** /ˌkaʊntərɪnˈsɜdʒənsi/, *n.* action taken to oppose an insurgency. – **counterinsurgent,** *adj.*

---

**counteraccusation,** *n.*
**counteragent,** *n.*
**counterapproach,** *n.*
**counterargument,** *n.*
**counterblow,** *n.*
**counterbluff,** *n., v.i.*
**countercharm,** *n.*
**counterdemonstration,** *n.*
**counterdrain,** *n.*
**counterevidence,** *n.*
**counterforce,** *n.*
**countergauge,** *n.*
**counterguard,** *n.*
**counterinfluence,** *n.*
**counterinsurgency,** *n.*
**counterinsurgent,** *n., adj.*
**countermeasure,** *n.*
**countermotion,** *n.*
**countermove,** *n., v.i.*
**countermovement,** *n.*
**counteroffer,** *n.*
**counteropening,** *n.*
**counterpace,** *n.*
**counterpale,** *n.*
**counterparole,** *n.*
**counterplea,** *n.*
**counterplead,** *v.i., v.t.*
**counterpressure,** *n.*
**counterproof,** *n.*
**counterpropaganda,** *n.*
**counterproposal,** *n.*
**counterproposition,** *n.*
**counterpunch,** *n., v.t.*
**counterseal,** *n., v.t.*
**countersecurity,** *n.*
**countersense,** *n.*
**countersignal,** *n.*
**counterstatement,** *n.*
**counterstroke,** *n.*
**countertendency,** *n.*
**counterthrust,** *n., v.t.*
**counterturn,** *n., v.t.*
**countertype,** *n., v.t.*
**counterview,** *n.*
**countervote,** *n.*

---

**counterintelligence** /kaʊntərɪn'tɛlədʒəns/, *n.* **1.** the use of various devices, as codes, censorship, etc., to prevent an enemy obtaining information. **2.** the organisation set up to carry this out.

**counterirritant** /kaʊntər'ɪrətənt/, *n.* an agent for producing irritation in one part of the body to counteract irritation or relieve pain or inflammation elsewhere. – **counterirritation,** *n.*

**counterjumper** /'kaʊntədʒʌmpə/, *n. Colloq.* a salesman at a counter.

**counter lunch** /'kaʊntə lʌntʃ/, *n.* lunch served at a counter[1] (def. 2) or bar. Also, **pub lunch.**

**countermand** /ˌkaʊntə'mænd, -'mand/, *v.t.* **1.** to revoke (a command, order, etc.). **2.** to recall or stop by a contrary order. *–n.* **3.** a command, order, etc., revoking a previous one. [ME *countermaund(en),* from OF *contremander,* from *contre* CONTRA- + *mander* command, from L *mandāre* enjoin]

**countermarch** /'kaʊntəmatʃ/, *n.* **1.** a march back again. **2.** a complete reversal of conduct or measures. *–v.i.* **3.** to turn about and march back along the same route; execute a countermarch. *–v.t.* **4.** to cause to countermarch.

**countermark** /'kaʊntəmak/, *n.* **1.** a device stamped on a coin after minting. **2.** an additional mark put on a bale of goods belonging to several merchants so that it shall not be opened except in the presence of all of them. *–v.t.* **3.** to mark with a countermark.

**countermine** /'kaʊntəmaɪn/, *n.;* /kaʊntə'maɪn/, *v.* **-mined, -mining.** *–n.* **1.** *Mil.* a mine intended to intercept or destroy an enemy's mine. **2.** a counterplot. *–v.t.* **3.** to oppose by a countermine. *–v.i.* **4.** to make a countermine. **5.** *Mil.* to destroy enemy mines.

**counteroffensive** /'kaʊntərəˌfɛnsɪv/, *n.* an attack by an army against an enemy force which has been and may still be attacking.

**counterpane** /'kaʊntəpeɪn/, *n.* a quilt or coverlet for a bed; a bedspread. [var. of obs. *counterpoint* cover, from OF]

**counterpart** /'kaʊntəpat/, *n.* **1.** a copy; duplicate. **2.** a part that answers to another, as each part of a document executed in duplicate. **3.** one of two parts which fit each other; a thing that complements something else. **4.** a person or thing closely resembling another.

**counterplot** /'kaʊntəplɒt/, *n., v.,* **-plotted, -plotting.** *–n.* **1.** a plot directed against another plot. **2.** a secondary theme in a play, or other literary work, usually as a contrast to or variation of the main theme. *–v.i.* **3.** to devise a counterplot; plot in opposition. *–v.t.* **4.** to plot against (a plot or plotter); frustrate by a counterplot.

**counterpoint** /'kaʊntəpɔɪnt/, *n. Music.* **1.** the art of combining melodies. **2.** the texture resulting from the combining of individual melodic lines. **3.** a melody composed to be combined with another melody. [F *contrepoint,* from ML (*cantus*) *contrā punctus* (song) pointed against]

**counterpoise** /'kaʊntəpɔɪz/, *n., v.,* **-poised, -poising.** *–n.* **1.** a counterbalancing weight. **2.** any equal and opposing power or force. **3.** the state of being in equilibrium. **4.** an artificial earth plane used to increase the sensitivity of an aerial. *–v.t.* **5.** to balance by an opposing weight; counteract by an opposing force. **6.** to bring into equilibrium. **7.** *Archaic.* to weigh (one thing) against another. [ME *countrepeis,* from OF, var. of *contrepois,* from *contre* CONTRA- + *pois* weight (from L *pensum*)]

**counterpoison** /'kaʊntəpɔɪzən/, *n.* **1.** an agent for counteracting a poison; an antidote. **2.** an opposite poison.

**counterproductive** /kaʊntəprə'dʌktɪv/, *adj.* of or pertaining to activity which reduces the success or efficiency of the task in hand.

**counter-reformation** /ˌkaʊntə-rɛfə'meɪʃən/, *n.* a reformation opposed to or counteracting a previous reformation.

**counter-revolution** /ˌkaʊntə-rɛvə'luʃən/, *n.* **1.** a revolution against a government recently established by revolution. **2.** a political movement that resists revolutionary tendencies.

**counter-revolutionary** /ˌkaʊntə-rɛvə'luʃənri/, *n., pl.* **-aries,** *adj.* *–n.* **1.** Also, **counter-revolutionist.** one who advocates or engages in a counter-revolution. *–adj.* **2.** characteristic of or resulting from a counter-revolution. **3.** opposing a revolution or revolutionary government.

**counterscarp** /'kaʊntəskap/, *n. Fort.* **1.** the exterior slope or wall of the ditch of a fort, supporting the covered way. **2.** this slope with the covered way and glacis. [F *contrescarpe,* from It. *contrascarpa,* from *contra-* COUNTER- + *scarpa* slope of a wall]

**countershading** /kaʊntə'ʃeɪdɪŋ/, *n.* the development (on an animal) of dark colours on parts usually exposed to the sun and of light colours on parts usually shaded, esp. as serving for protection or concealment.

**countershaft** /'kaʊntəʃaft/, *n.* in machines, an intermediate shaft driven from a main shaft.

**countersign** /'kaʊntəsaɪn/, *n.;* /'kaʊntəsaɪn, kaʊntə'saɪn/, *v.* *–n.* **1.** a password given by authorised persons in passing through a guard. **2.** a sign used in reply to another sign. *–v.t.* **3.** to sign (a document) in addition to another signature, esp. in confirmation or authentication. [OF *contresigne,* from It. *contrasegno*]

**countersignature** /kaʊntə'sɪgnətʃə/, *n.* a signature added by way of countersigning.

**countersink** /'kaʊntəsɪŋk/, *v.,* **-sunk, -sinking,** *n.* *–v.t.* **1.** to enlarge the upper part of (a hole or cavity), esp. by chamfering, to receive the cone-shaped head of a screw, bolt, etc. **2.** to cause (the head of a screw, bolt, etc.) to sink into a depression made for it, so as to be flush with or below the surface. *–n.* **3.** a tool for countersinking a hole. **4.** a countersunk hole.

**counterspy** /'kaʊntəspaɪ/, *n.* a spy engaged in counterespionage.

**counterstain** /'kaʊntəsteɪn/, *n.;* /kaʊntə'steɪn/, *v.* *–n.* **1.** a stain applied to a microscopic specimen to distinguish even further parts not retaining a previous stain. *–v.t.* **2.** to treat (a specimen) with a counterstain. *–v.i.* **3.** to become counterstained; take a counterstain.

**counter stern** /'kaʊntə stɜn/, *n.* a ship's stern in which the shape extends out and aft to the after deck; elliptical stern.

**countersubject** /'kaʊntəˌsʌbdʒɛkt/, *n.* (in music) the formal accompaniment to the answer in a fugue.

**countertenor** /kaʊntə'tɛnə/, *n.* **1.** an adult male voice or voice part higher than the tenor. **2.** a singer with such a voice; a high tenor.

**counter-terrorism** /kaʊntə-'tɛrərɪzəm/, *n.* an act of reprisal by a government, etc., against terrorism.

**counter tube** /'kaʊntə tʃub/, *n.* →**counter**[2] (def. 3b).

**countervail** /kaʊntə'veɪl, 'kaʊntəveɪl/, *v.t.* **1.** to act or avail against with equal power, force, or effect; counteract. **2.** to furnish an equivalent of or a compensation for; offset. *–v.i.* **3.** to be of equal force in opposition; avail. [ME *countrevaile(n),* from AF *countrevaloir,* from *countre* against + *valoir* be strong, from L *valēre*]

**countervailing duty** /ˌkaʊntəveɪlɪŋ 'djuti/, *n. Law.* a duty to prevent the dumping of goods by imposing a duty on the importer equal to the exporter's government subsidy.

**counterweigh** /kaʊntə'weɪ/, *v.t.* to counterbalance.

**counterweight** /'kaʊntəweɪt/, *n.* a counterbalancing weight; a counterpoise. – **counterweighted,** *adj.*

**counterword** /'kaʊntəwɜd/, *n.* a word that has come to be used with a meaning less specific than it had originally, as *awful, terrific,* etc.

**counterwork** /'kaʊntəwɜk/, *n.;* /kaʊntə'wɜk/, *v.* *–n.* **1.** opposing work or action; a work in opposition to another work. *–v.i.* **2.** to work in opposition. *–v.t.* **3.** to work in opposition to; hinder. – **counterworker,** *n.*

**countess** /'kaʊntɛs/, *n.* **1.** the wife or widow of a count in the nobility of continental Europe, or of an earl in the British peerage. **2.** a woman having the rank of a count or earl in her own right. [ME *contesse,* from OF, from LL *comitissa,* fem. of L *comes.* See COUNT[2]]

**count-fish** /'kaʊnt-fɪʃ/, *n.* a full-grown snapper.

**counting house** /'kaʊntɪŋ haʊs/, *n.* **1.** (formerly) a building or room in a noble or merchant's household set aside for the transaction of business. **2.** an accounts office.

**counting-out pen** /ˌkaʊntɪŋ-'aʊt pɛn/, *n.* a pen to hold sheep already shorn so that they may be counted, and the tally credited to the shearer.

**counting room** /'kaʊntɪŋ rum/, *n.* a room used as a counting house.

**countless** /'kaʊntləs/, *adj.* incapable of being counted;

innumerable: *the countless stars of the unbounded heavens.*

**count-muster** /'kaʊnt-mʌstə/, *n.* the gathering of cattle together for the purpose of counting them.

**count noun** /'kaʊnt naʊn/, *n.* a noun referring to an object which is being thought of as existing in numbers so that groups of such objects can be counted, as *apples, jugs.* Cf. **mass noun.**

**count palatine** /ˌkaʊnt 'pælətin/, *n., pl.* **counts palatine. 1.** a count of the Holy Roman Empire having independent judicial authority within his own domain. **2.** a count granted certain royal or imperial powers under the German emperors. **3.** an earl palatine.

**countrified** /'kʌntrifaɪd/, *adj.* rustic or rural in appearance, conduct, etc. Also, **countryfied.**

**country** /'kʌntri/, *n., pl.* **-tries,** *adj.* *–n.* **1.** a tract of land considered apart from geographical or political limits; region; district. **2.** any considerable territory demarcated by geographical conditions or by a distinctive population. **3.** the territory of a nation. **4.** a state. **5.** the people of a district, state, or nation. **6.** the public. **7.** the land of one's birth or citizenship. **8.** the rural districts (as opposed to towns or cities). **9.** land, esp. with reference to its character, quality, or use: *good grazing country.* **10.** *Sport Colloq.* any part of the ground on which a sporting event takes place which is far from the main area of activity, as the outfield in cricket, or the part of the course away from the stands in horse-racing. **11. go to the country,** to call an election. *–adj.* **12.** of the country; rural. **13.** rude; unpolished: *country manners.* **14.** of a country or one's own country. [ME *contree,* from OF, from LL *contrāta,* lit., what lies opposite, from L *contrā* opposite to]

**country and western,** *n.* **1.** Also, **country music.** a type of music orginating in the Southern and Western United States, consisting mainly of rural songs accompanied by a stringed instrument such as the guitar or fiddle. *–adj.* **2.** of or pertaining to this type of music.

**country bumpkin** /kʌntri 'bʌmpkən/, *n.* →**bumpkin**[1].

**country club** /'– klʌb/, *n.* a club in the country with a house, grounds, and facilities for outdoor sports, etc.

**country cousin** /– 'kʌzən/, *n.* a relative from the country to whom the sights and activities of a large city are novel and bewildering.

**country dance** /'– dæns/, *n.* a dance of rural (or native) origin, as one in which partners in a group start by facing each other in two lines.

**countryfied** /'kʌntrifaɪd/, *adj.* →**countrified.**

**country house** /'kʌntri haʊs/, *n.* a large house in the country, esp. one part of an estate.

**countryman** /'kʌntrimən/, *n., pl.* **-men. 1.** a man of one's own country. **2.** a native or inhabitant of a particular region. **3.** a man who lives in the country. **– countrywoman** /'kʌntriwʊmən/, *n. fem.*

**country music** /'kʌntri mjuzɪk/, *n.* →**country and western.**

**country quota** /'– kwoʊtə/, *n. N.Z.* (formerly) a statutory extra weighting given to votes in rural constituencies.

**country rock**[1] /'– rɒk/, *n.* (in geology) the rock which surrounds and is penetrated by mineral veins or igneous intrusions.

**country rock**[2] /kʌntri 'rɒk/, *n.* music which combines the characteristics of country and western and of rock 'n' roll, usu. electrically amplified.

**country seat** /– 'sit/, *n.* **1.** a rural estate, esp. a fine one, often one used for only part of the year. **2.** a rural electorate.

**country service** /– 'sɜvəs/, *n.* the period which an employee, as a teacher, bank clerk, etc., may be obliged to spend working in a rural area.

**countryside** /'kʌntrisaɪd/, *n.* **1.** a particular section of a country, esp. rural. **2.** its inhabitants.

**country town** /kʌntri 'taʊn/, *n.* a small town in a rural district.

**country-wide** /'kʌntri-waɪd/, *adj.* throughout the country.

**county** /'kaʊnti/, *n.* **1.** *Brit.* one of the chief administrative divisions of Great Britain and Ireland. **2.** *N.S.W.* **a.** one of 19 areas of land delineated by analogy with the British counties but for which no matching overall public administration was ever set up, as the County of Cumberland in the Sydney region, the County of Northumberland in the Newcastle region, and to which efforts were once made to limit settlement. **b.** one of 40 or more areas of land delineated for administrative convenience or some specific purpose such as development planning or the supply of electricity, but which rarely correspond to the original 19 counties. **3.** *U.S.* the political unit next below the state. **4.** one of the larger divisions, as for purposes of local administration, in Canada, New Zealand, etc. **5.** *Brit.* the inhabitants of a county. **6.** *Brit.* the landed gentry of a county. **7.** *Obs. or Hist.* the domain of a count or an earl. *–adj.* **8.** of or pertaining to a county. **9.** *Brit. Colloq.* belonging or pertaining to the county or landed gentry; upper-class. [ME *counte,* from AF, var. of OF *conte,* from *conte* COUNT[2]]

**county council** /– 'kaʊnsəl/, *n.* **1.** (in N.S.W.) a body elected or appointed to administer some particular activity or activities relating to a specific county (def. 2) as the Richmond River County Council, charged with the eradication of water hyacinth, the Mackeller County Council, charged with the supplying of electricity, etc. **2.** *Brit.* a body elected to administer the public affairs of a county (def. 1.)

**County Court** /– 'kɔt/, *n.* →**District Court.**

**coup** /ku/, *n., pl.* **coups** /kuz/. an unexpected and successfully executed strategem; masterstroke. [F, in OF *colp,* from LL *colpus* blow, for L *colaphus,* from Gk *kólaphos*]

**coup de grâce** /– də 'gras/, *n.* **1.** a death-blow, as a bullet in the head, to make sure an executed person is dead. **2.** a finishing stroke. [F: grace-stroke]

**coup d'état** /– deɪ'ta/, *n.* a sudden and decisive measure in politics, esp. one effecting a change of government illegally or by force. [F: lit., stroke of state]

**coupe** /ku'peɪ, 'kupeɪ, kup/, *n.* **1.** a chilled dessert consisting of fruit and ice-cream. **2. a.** a stemmed glass in which such a dessert may be served. **b.** a shallow, bowl-shaped dish. [ME, from OF, from LL *cuppa* cup]

**coupé** /'kupeɪ/, *n.* **1. a.** an enclosed two-door motor car with only one seat or set of seats. **b.** →**fastback. 2.** a short four-wheeled closed carriage with (usu.) a single cross-seat for two persons and with an outside seat for the driver. [F, properly pp. of *couper* cut]

coupé (def. 2)

**couped** /kupt/, *adj.* in heraldry, cut off, as of a cross cut off so as not to touch the edge of the shield, or an animal, cut off at its chest.

**couple** /'kʌpəl/, *n., v.,* **-led, -ling.** *–n.* **1.** a combination of two; a pair. **2.** two of the same sort connected or considered together. **3.** a man and a woman united by marriage or betrothal, associated as partners in a dance, etc. **4.** *Mech.* a pair of equal, parallel forces acting in opposite directions and tending to produce rotation. **5.** a leash for holding two hounds together. **6.** one of a pair of rafters or beams that meet at the top and are fixed at the bottom by a tie. *–v.t.* **7.** to fasten, link, or associate together in a pair or pairs. **8.** to join; connect. **9.** *Colloq.* to unite in matrimony. **10.** *Radio.* to join or associate by means of a coupler. **11.** to provide an electrical or magnetic link between (two or more wave circuits). *–v.i.* **12.** to join in a pair; unite. **13.** to copulate. [ME, from OF *cople,* from L *copula* band, bond]

**coupler** /'kʌplə/, *n.* **1.** one who or that which couples, or links together. **2.** a device in an organ for connecting keys, manuals, or a manual and pedals, so that they are played together when one is played. **3.** *Radio.* a device for transferring electrical energy from one circuit to another, as a transformer which joins parts of a radio apparatus together by induction.

**couplet** /'kʌplət/, *n.* **1.** a pair of successive lines of verse, esp. such as rhyme together and are of the same length. **2.** a pair; couple. [F, diminutive of *couple* COUPLE]

**coupling** /'kʌplɪŋ/, *n.* **1.** the act of one who or that which couples. **2.** any mechanical device for uniting or connecting parts or things. **3.** a device used in joining railway carriages, etc. **4.** *Elect.* **a.** the association of two circuits or systems in such a way that power may be transferred from one to the other. **b.** a device or expedient to ensure coupling. **5.** the part of the body between the tops of the shoulder-blades and the tops of the hip joints in a dog or horse.

**coupon** /ˈkupɒn/, *n.* **1.** a separable part of a certificate, ticket, advertisement, etc., entitling the holder to something. **2.** one of a number of such parts calling for periodical payments on a bond. **3.** a separate ticket or the like, for a similar purpose. **4.** a printed entry form for football pools, newspaper competitions, etc. **5.** a detachable printed certificate, issued as a means of rationing commodities and goods to ensure fair distribution of short supplies. [F, from *couper* cut]

**courage** /ˈkʌrɪdʒ/, *n.* **1.** the quality of mind that enables one to encounter difficulties and danger with firmness or without fear; bravery. **2.** *Obs.* heart; mind; disposition. **3. have the courage of one's convictions,** to act consistently with one's opinions. [ME *corage,* from OF, from *cuer* heart, from L *cor*]

**courageous** /kəˈreɪdʒəs/, *adj.* possessing or characterised by courage; brave; valiant. – **courageously,** *adv.* – **courageousness,** *n.*

**courante** /kuˈrɒnt/, *n.* **1.** an old-fashioned dance dating back to the 17th century characterised by a running or gliding step. **2.** a piece of music for or suited to this dance. **3.** *Music.* a movement in the classical suite, following the allemande. Also, **courant.** [F, properly fem. of *courant,* ppr. of *courir* run]

**courgette** /kɔˈʒɛt/, *n.* →**zucchini.**

**courier** /ˈkʊriə/, *n.* **1.** a messenger sent in haste. **2.** a state messenger who carries government or embassy papers. **3.** a person employed to take charge of the arrangements of a journey. **4.** a person who works for a courier service. [F, from It. *corriere* runner, from *corre* run, from L *currere;* replacing ME *corour,* from OF *coreor,* from LL *curritor* runner]

**courier service** /ˈ– sɜvəs/, *n.* a private company which provides a letter or parcel delivery service, esp. one which guarantees speed or safety.

**course** /kɔs/, *n., v.,* **coursed, coursing.** –*n.* **1.** advance in a particular direction; onward movement. **2.** the path, route or channel along which anything moves: *the course of a stream, ship, etc.* **3.** the ground, water, etc., on which a race is run, sailed, etc. **4.** the continuous passage or progress through time or a succession of stages: *in the course of a year, a battle, etc.* **5.** customary manner of procedure; regular or natural order of events: *the course of a disease, argument, etc., a matter of course.* **6.** a mode of conduct; behaviour. **7.** a particular manner of proceeding: *try another course with him.* **8.** a systematised or prescribed series: *a course of studies, lectures, medical treatments, etc.* **9.** any one of the studies in such a series: *the first course in algebra.* **10.** a part of a meal served at one time: *the main course was steak.* **11.** *Naut.* **a.** the point of the compass towards which a ship sails. **b.** the lowest square sail on any mast of a square-rigged ship, identified as **fore course, main course,** etc. **12.** a continuous horizontal (or inclined) range of stones, bricks, or the like, in a wall, the face of a building, etc. **13.** *Textiles.* the row of stitches going across from side to side. **14.** (*oft. pl.*) the menses. **15.** a charge, as in tilting. **16.** pursuit of game with dogs. **17.** *Archaic.* a race. **18. in due course,** in the proper or natural order; at the right time. **19. of course, a.** certainly; obviously. **b.** in the natural order. –*v.t.* **20.** to run through or over. **21.** to chase; pursue. **22.** to hunt (game) with hounds, esp. by sight and not by scent. **23.** to cause (dogs) to pursue game. –*v.i.* **24.** to race greyhounds. **25.** to follow a course; direct one's course. **26.** to run; move swiftly; race. **27.** to engage in coursing, in a hunt, a tilting match, etc. [F; replacing ME *cors,* from OF, from L *cursus* a running]

**courser**[1] /ˈkɔsə/, *n.* **1.** one who or that which courses. **2.** a dog for coursing. [COURSE, *v.* + -ER[1]]

**courser**[2] /ˈkɔsə/, *n. Chiefly Poetic.* a swift horse. [ME, from F *coursier,* from *cours* COURSE]

**courser**[3] /ˈkɔsə/, *n.* **1.** →**Australian courser. 2.** any of certain swift-footed, plover-like birds constituting the genus *Cursorius,* of the desert regions of Africa and Asia, as *C. cursor,* occasionally found also in Europe. [L *cursōrius* fitted for running]

**coursing** /ˈkɔsɪŋ/, *n.* **1.** the act of one who or that which courses. **2.** the sport of pursuing hares, etc., with hounds that follow by sight rather than by scent.

**court** /kɔt/, *n.* **1.** an open space wholly or partly enclosed by a wall, buildings, etc. **2.** a large building within such a space. **3.** a stately dwelling; manor house. **4.** a short street. **5.** a smooth, level area on which to play tennis, netball, etc. **6.** one of the divisions of such an area. **7.** the residence of a sovereign or other high dignitary; palace. **8.** the collective body of persons forming his retinue. **9.** a sovereign and his councillors as the political rulers of a state. **10.** a formal assembly held by a sovereign. **11.** homage paid, as to a sovereign. **12.** assiduous attention directed to gain favour, affection, etc.: *to pay court to a pretty woman.* **13.** *Law.* **a.** a place where justice is administered. **b.** a judicial tribunal duly constituted for the hearing and determination of cases. **c.** the judge or judges who sit in a court. **14.** the body of qualified members of a corporation, council, board, etc. **15.** a branch or lodge of a friendly society. **16. out of court, a.** without a hearing; privately. **b.** *Colloq.* out of the question; not to be considered. –*v.t.* **17.** to endeavour to win the favour of. **18.** to seek the affections of; woo. **19.** to attempt to gain (applause, favour, a decision, etc.). **20.** to hold out inducements to; invite. **21.** to provoke or risk provoking as a consequence of one's actions: *to court disaster.* –*v.i.* **22.** to seek another's love; woo. [ME, from OF *cort,* from L *co(ho)rs* enclosure, also division of troops (see COHORT)]

**court bouillon** /– ˈbujɒn/, *n.* a stock, usu. a vegetable stock, used for poaching fish.

**court card** /ˈ– kad/, *n.* a king, queen, or knave in a pack of playing cards.

**court dress** /ˈ- drɛs/, *n.* the formal costume worn on state or ceremonial occasions; for men it includes silk knee breeches and stockings.

**courteous** /ˈkɜtiəs/, *adj.* having or showing good manners; polite. [ME *curteis,* from OF, from *cort* COURT] – **courteously,** *adv.* – **courteousness,** *n.*

**courtesan** /ˈkɔtəzæn/, *n.* **1.** a court mistress. **2.** any prostitute. Also, **courtezan.** [F *courtisane,* from It. *cortigiana* woman of the court, from *corte* COURT]

**courtesy** /ˈkɜtəsi/, *n., pl.* **-sies. 1.** excellence of manners or behaviour; politeness. **2.** a courteous act or expression. **3.** acquiescence; indulgence; consent: *a title by courtesy rather than by right.* [ME *cortesie,* from OF, from *corteis* COURTEOUS]

**courtesy car** /ˈ– ka/, *n.* a car supplied to a customer by a dealer when the customer's car is being serviced or repaired.

**courtesy ensign** /ˈ– ɛnsən/, *n.* the national flag of the country which a foreign ship is visiting flown as a courtesy from the forward yardarm.

**courtesy light** /ˈ– laɪt/, *n.* **1.** an interior light in a motor vehicle, which is automatically switched on when a door is opened. **2.** →**porch light.**

**courtesy title** /ˈ– taɪtl/, *n. Brit.* a title allowed by custom, as to the children of dukes.

**court hand** /ˈkɔt hænd/, *n.* a style of handwriting formerly used in the English law courts.

**courthouse** /ˈkɔthaʊs/, *n.* a building in which courts of law are held.

**courtier** /ˈkɔtiə/, *n.* **1.** one in attendance at the court of a sovereign. **2.** one who seeks favour by obsequiousness.

**court leet** /ˈkɔt lit/, *n.* →**leet.**

**courtly** /ˈkɔtli/, *adj.,* **-lier, -liest,** *adv.* –*adj.* **1.** polite; elegant; refined. **2.** flattering; obsequious. **3.** of the court of a sovereign. –*adv.* **4.** in the manner of courts; elegantly; flatteringly. – **courtliness,** *n.*

**courtly love** /– ˈlʌv/, *n.* a medieval concept originating in the courts of southern France, which idealised illicit love, prescribed a highly conventionalised code of conduct for lovers, and gave rise to an extensive literature on the subject.

**court martial** /ˈkɔt maʃəl/, *n., pl.* **court martials, courts martial.** a court consisting of naval, army, or airforce officers appointed by a commander to try charges of offence against martial law.

**court-martial** /ˈkɔt-maʃəl/, *v.t.,* **-tialled, -tialling** or (*U.S.*) **-tialed, -tialing.** to arraign and try by court martial.

**Court of Appeal,** *n.* **1.** a State Supreme Court which determines appeals from single Justices and lower courts in both criminal and civil matters. **2.** *Brit.* the upper of the two divisions of the Supreme Court of Judicature.

**Court of Common Pleas,** *n. Brit.* a common-law court, established in the thirteenth century, in which are heard chiefly actions by one subject against another.

**Court of Disputed Returns,** *n.* a court assembled expressly for the purpose of hearing and determining electoral disputes, with authority to invalidate parliamentary elections and order re-elections.

**Court of Exchequer,** *n. Brit.* →**exchequer** (def. 2c).

**court of inquiry,** *n.* a body of people appointed to ascertain facts or causes concerning a particular event, esp. a major accident.

**Court of Petty Sessions,** *n.* court of summary jurisdiction of two or more justices of the peace, or more usu. a stipendiary magistrate, to try less serious criminal offences summarily, or, to hear certain civil matters.

**Court of Quarter Sessions,** *n.* a District Court sitting in its criminal jurisdiction.

**court of record,** *n.* a court whose records are automatically matters of judicial notice and appear in law reports; more usu. higher than lower courts.

**court plaster** /ˈkɔt plastə/, *n.* **1.** (formerly) a black patch worn as adornment on the face by court ladies. **2.** cotton or other fabric coated on one side with an adhesive preparation, as of isinglass and glycerine, used for covering slight cuts, etc., on the skin.

**court roll** /ˈ– roʊl/, *n.* (formerly) a book in which an account of all the proceedings of a manorial court was entered by an authorised person.

**courtroom** /ˈkɔtrum/, *n.* a room in which the sessions of a law court are held.

**courtship** /ˈkɔtʃɪp/, *n.* **1.** the wooing of a woman. **2.** solicitation, esp. of favours.

**court shoe** /ˈkɔt ʃu/, *n.* a simply cut heeled shoe, without fastenings, for women. Also, **court.**

**court tennis** /– ˈtɛnəs/, *n. U.S.* →**royal tennis.**

**courtyard** /ˈkɔtjad/, *n.* a space enclosed by walls, next to or within a castle, large house, etc.

**couscous** /ˈkuskus/, *n.* a Tunisian dish, made of steamed flour, etc., served with semolina, stewed lamb, and vegetables. [F, from Ar. *kuskus,* from *kaskasa* to beat, pulverise]

**cousin** /ˈkʌzən/, *n.* **1.** the son or daughter of an uncle or aunt. **2.** one related by descent in a diverging line from a known common ancestor. The children of brothers and sisters are called **cousins, cousins-german, first cousins,** or **full cousins;** children of **first cousins** are called **second cousins,** etc. Often, however, the term **second cousin** is loosely applied to the son or daughter of a **cousin-german,** more properly called **a first cousin once removed.** **3.** a kinsman or kinswoman. **4.** a person or thing related to another by similar natures, languages, etc.: *our Canadian cousins.* **5.** a term of address from one sovereign to another or to a great noble. [F, from L *consobrīnus* mother's sister's child; replacing ME *cosin,* from OF] – **cousinhood, cousinship,** *n.*

**cousin-german** /kʌzən-ˈdʒɛmən/, *n., pl.* **cousins-german.** a first cousin. See **cousin** (def. 2). [F *cousin-germain.* See GERMAN, *adj.*]

**Cousin Jack** /kʌzən ˈdʒæk/, *n.* **1.** a Cornishman. **2.** (formerly) a Cornish miner in South Australia.

**cousinly** /ˈkʌzənli/, *adj.* **1.** like or befitting a cousin. –*adv.* **2.** in the manner of a cousin; as a cousin.

**couta** /ˈkutə/, *n. Colloq.* →**barracouta.**

**couth** /kuθ/, *adj. Colloq.* civilised, well-mannered. [back-formation from UNCOUTH]

**coutil** /kuˈti/, *n.* a strong herringbone twill, used in the manufacture of surgical corsets.

**couture** /kuˈtjʊə/, *n.* the occupation of a couturier; dress-making and designing considered together.

**couturier** /kuˈturiə/, *n.* a person who designs, makes, and sells fashionable clothes for women. [F *couture* sewing] – **couturière** /kuˌturiˈɛə/, *n.fem.*

**couvade** /kuˈvad/, *n.* a practice among some primitive peoples by which, at the birth of a child, the father takes to bed and performs other acts natural rather to the mother. [F *couver* brood, incubate. See COVEY]

**covalency** /koʊˈveɪlənsi/, *n.* the number of electron pairs that an atom can share with those which surround it. Also, *Chiefly U.S.,* **covalence** /koʊˈveɪləns/. – **covalent,** *adj.* – **covalently,** *adv.*

**covalent bond** /koʊveɪlənt ˈbɒnd/, *n.* a chemical bond formed by the sharing of electrons between two atoms each of which donates an equal number of electrons. The conventional single covalent bond involves the sharing of two electrons, the double, the sharing of four electrons and the triple, the sharing of six electrons.

**cove**[1] /koʊv/, *n., v.,* **coved, coving.** –*n.* **1.** a small indentation or recess in the shoreline of a sea, lake, or river. **2.** a sheltered nook. **3.** a hollow or recess in a mountain; cave; cavern. **4.** a recess with precipitous sides in the steep flank of a mountain. **5.** a sheltered area between woods or hills. **6.** *Archit.* a concavity; a concave moulding or member. –*v.t.* **7.** to form into a cove. [ME; OE *cofa* chamber, c. Icel. *kofi* hut]

**cove**[2] /koʊv/, *n.* **1.** *Colloq.* a man: *a rum sort of cove.* **2.** a boss (def. 1), esp. the manager of a sheep station. **3.** (formerly) master of a house or shop. **4.** (formerly) a convict overseer. [said to be from Romany *kova* creature]

**covellite** /ˈkɒvəlaɪt/, *n.* a common indigo-blue secondary mineral; an ore of copper.

**coven** /ˈkʌvən/, *n.* **1.** a gathering of witches. **2.** a company of thirteen witches. [var. of CONVENT]

**covenant** /ˈkʌvənənt/, *n.* **1.** an agreement between two or more persons to do or refrain from doing some act; a compact; a contract. **2.** an incidental clause of agreement in such an agreement. **3.** (in biblical usage) the agreement or engagement of God with man as set forth in the Old and New Testaments. **4.** *Law.* **a.** a formal agreement of legal validity, esp. one under seal. **b.** an early English form of action in suits involving sealed agreements. –*v.i.* **5.** to enter into a covenant. –*v.t.* **6.** to agree to by covenant; stipulate. [ME, from OF, from *covenir,* from L *convenire* agree]

**covenanter** /ˈkʌvənəntə/, *n.* one who enters into a covenant.

**covenantor** /kʌvənənˈtɔ/, *n. Law.* the party who is to perform the obligation expressed in a covenant.

**covenant theology** /kʌvənənt θiˈɒlədʒi/, *n.* →**federal theology.**

**Coventry** /ˈkʌvəntri/, *n. in the phrase* **send to Coventry,** to refuse to associate or speak with. [from the sending of Royalist prisoners to *Coventry* during the English Civil War]

**cover** /ˈkʌvə/, *v.t.* **1.** to put something over or upon as for protection or concealment. **2.** to be or serve as a covering for; extend over; occupy the surface of. **3.** to put a cover or covering on; clothe. **4.** to put one's hat on (one's head). **5.** to bring upon or invest (oneself): *he covered himself with glory.* **6.** to shelter; protect; serve as a defence to. **7.** *Mil.* **a.** to be in line with by occupying a position directly before or behind. **b.** to protect (a soldier, force, or military position) during an expected period of combat by taking a position from which any hostile troops can be fired upon who might shoot at the soldier, force, or position. **8.** *Naut.* **a.** to maintain a position between the next mark of a set course and an opponent. **b.** to maintain a position which interferes with the windflow on the sails of an opposing boat. **9.** to take charge or responsibility for: *an assistant covered his post while he was ill.* **10.** to hide from view; screen. **11.** *Naut.* (of a yacht in the lead in a race) to duplicate, tack for tack, the manoeuvres of a following yacht. **12.** to spread thickly the surface of. **13.** to aim directly at, as with a pistol. **14.** to have within range, as a fortress does certain territory. **15.** to include; comprise; provide for; take in: *this book covers all common English words.* **16.** to suffice to defray or meet (a charge, expense, etc.); offset (an outlay, loss, liability, etc.). **17.** to deposit the equivalent of (money deposited), as in wagering; accept the conditions of (a bet, etc.). **18.** to act as reporter of (occurrences, performances, etc.), as for a newspaper, etc. **19.** to pass or travel over. **20.** (of a male animal) to copulate with. **21.** *Obs.* to brood or sit on eggs. –*v.i.* **22.** to serve as substitute for one who is absent: *she covered for the telephonist during lunch hour.* **23. a.** to play a card, laying it over a card previously played. **b.** to play a card higher than any previously played in the round. **24.** to lay a table for a meal. **25. cover up, a.** to cover completely; enfold. **b.** to attempt to conceal. **c.** *Boxing.* to position the arms so that the opponent's attack can hardly penetrate. **d.** *Fencing.* to position the sword and sword arm so as to prevent the opponent making a direct thrust. *–n.* **26.** that which covers, as the lid of a vessel, the binding of a book, etc. **27.** protection; shelter; concealment. **28.** adequate insurance against risk as loss, damage, etc. **29.** woods, underbrush, etc., serving to shelter and conceal wild animals or game; a covert. **30.** vegetation which serves to protect or conceal animals, such as birds, from excessive sunlight or drying, as predators. **31.** something which veils, screens, or shuts from sight. **32.** a set of articles (plate, knife, fork, etc.) laid at table for one person. **33.** *Finance.* funds to cover liability or secure against risk of loss. **34.** *Philat.* an envelope or outer wrapping for mail, complete with stamp and post mark. **35.** *Cricket.* Also, **the covers.** coverpoint or extra cover. **36. break cover,** to emerge, esp. suddenly, from a place of concealment. **37. take cover,** to seek shelter or safety. **38. under cover, a.** secret. **b.** secretly. **c.** within an envelope. **39.** →**cover version.** [ME *cover(en),* from OF *covrir,* from L *cooperīre*] – **coverer,** *n.* – **coverless,** *adj.*

**coverage** /ˈkʌvərɪdʒ/, *n.* **1.** the extent to which something is covered. **2.** *Insurance.* the total extent of risk, or the total number of risks, as fire, accident, etc., covered in a policy of insurance. **3.** *Finance.* the value of funds held to back up or meet liabilities. **4.** the reporting of an event or series of events in journals or other media. **5.** the members of the public considered together who may be reached through a specified means of communication.

**coverall** /ˈkʌvərɔl/, *n.* an outer protective garment of strong material, usu. a one piece combination of trousers and shirt.

**cover charge** /ˈkʌvə tʃadʒ/, *n.* a fixed amount added to the bill by a restaurant, nightclub, etc., for service or entertainment.

**cover crop** /ˈ– krɒp/, *n.* a crop, preferably leguminous, planted to keep nutrients from leaching, soil from eroding, and land from weeding over, as during the winter.

**cover defence** /– dəˈfɛns/, *n.* (in rugby football) the movement of certain players diagonally across the field behind the play in anticipation of being able to prevent the ball moving deeper into their half.

**cover drive** /ˈ– draɪv/, *n.* (in cricket) a drive which sends the ball towards or past cover-point.

**covered court** /kʌvəd ˈkɔt/, *n.* (in tennis) an indoor court.

**covered wagon** /– ˈwægən/, *n. Chiefly U.S.* a large wagon with a canvas top.

**covered way** /– ˈweɪ/, *n.* **1.** a roofed passage, with open sides, as between buildings. **2.** Also, **covert way.** *Fort.* a protective passage on a counterscarp.

**cover girl** /ˈ– gɜl/, *n.* a girl pictured on the cover of a magazine.

**cover glass** /ˈ– glas/, *n.* a thin piece of glass used to cover an object mounted on a slide for microscopic observation.

**covering** /ˈkʌvərɪŋ/, *n.* **1.** something laid over or wrapped about a thing, esp. for concealment, protection, or warmth. **2.** *Comm.* the operation of buying securities, etc., that one has sold short, in order to return them to the person from whom they were borrowed.

**covering letter** /– ˈlɛtə/, *n.* a letter which explains or commends an accompanying parcel, person, etc.

**coverlet** /ˈkʌvələt/, *n.* **1.** the outer covering of a bed; a bedspread. **2.** any covering or cover. Also, **coverlid.** [ME *coverlite,* from AF *covrelit,* from OF *covre* COVER + *lit* bed]

**cover note** /ˈkʌvə noʊt/, *n.* a document given by an insurance company or agent to the insured to provide temporary coverage until a policy is issued.

**cover-point** /ˈkʌvə-pɔɪnt/, *n.* **1.** *Cricket.* a fielding position between point and mid-off. **2.** *Lacrosse.* a position situated in front of point. **3.** a player in these positions.

**covert** /ˈkʌvət, ˈkoʊvɜt/, *adj.* **1.** covered; sheltered. **2.** concealed; secret; disguised. **3.** *Law.* under cover or protection of a husband. *–n.* **4.** a covering; cover. **5.** shelter; concealment; disguise; a hiding place. **6.** *Hunting.* a thicket giving shelter to wild animals or game. **7.** *(pl.) Ornith.* the smaller feathers that cover the bases of the large feathers of the wing and tail. **8.** covert cloth. [ME, from OF, pp. of *covrir* COVER] – **covertly,** *adv.* – **covertness,** *n.*

**covert cloth** /ˈ– klɒθ/, *n.* a cotton or worsted fabric or twill weave. The warp is of ply yarns, one of which is light-coloured.

**coverture** /ˈkʌvətʃə/, *n.* **1.** a cover or covering; shelter; concealment. **2.** *Law.* the status of a married woman considered as under the protection and authority of her husband. [ME, from OF]

**cover-up** /ˈkʌvər-ʌp/, *n.* **1.** an attempt at concealment. **2.** a fabrication; an excuse. **3.** a garment designed to go over the top of a swimsuit, usu. made of the same material.

**cover version** /ˈkʌvə ˌvɜʒən/, *n.* an additional recording of a song, etc., which has already been released by another performer.

**covet** /ˈkʌvət/, *v.t.* **1.** to desire inordinately, or without due regard to the rights of others; desire wrongfully. **2.** to wish for, esp. eagerly. *–v.i.* **3.** to have an inordinate or wrongful desire. [ME *coveiten,* from OF *cuveitier,* from L *cupiditas* desire] – **covetable,** *adj.* – **coveter,** *n.*

**covetous** /ˈkʌvətəs/, *adj.* **1.** inordinately or wrongly desirous. **2.** eagerly desirous. [ME, from OF *coveitos,* from L *cupiditas* desire] – **covetously,** *adv.* – **covetousness,** *n.*

**covey** /ˈkʌvi/, *n., pl.* **-eys.** a brood or small flock of partridges or similar birds. [ME, from OF *covee,* from *cover* incubate, from L *cubāre* lie]

**coving** /ˈkoʊvɪŋ/, *n.* **1.** an arched or vaulted piece of building. **2.** the arching of a coved ceiling.

**cow**[1] /kaʊ/, *n., pl.* **cows,** *(Archaic)* **kine. 1.** the female of a bovine animal, esp. of the genus *Bos,* that has produced a calf and is usually over three years of age. **2.** the female of various other large animals, as the elephant, whale, etc. **3.** *Colloq.* an ugly or bad-tempered woman. **4.** *Colloq.* (a term of abuse): *you miserable cow.* **5. a cow of a (something** or **someone),** *Colloq.* a difficult, unpleasant, disagreeable (thing or person). **6. a fair cow,** *Colloq.* anything regarded as disagreeable or difficult. **7. poor cow,** *Colloq.* (expressing sympathy) unfortunate person. **8. till the cows come home,** for a long time; for ever. [ME; OE *cu,* c. G *Kuh*]

**cow**[2] /kaʊ/, *v.t.* to frighten with threats, etc.; intimidate. [Scand.: cf. Icel. *kūga* cow, tyrannise over]

**cowage** /ˈkaʊɪdʒ/, *n.* **1.** the hairs on the pods of a tropical leguminous plant, *Stizolobium* (or *Mucuna*) *pruriens,* which causes intense itching; sometimes used as a vermifuge. **2.** the pods. **3.** the plants. Also, **cow-itch.** [Hindi *kawāch*]

**cowan** /ˈkaʊən/, *n.* a person who builds stone walls without mortar. [orig. unknown]

**coward** /ˈkaʊəd/, *n.* **1.** one who lacks courage to meet danger or difficulty; one who is basely timid. *–adj.* **2.** lacking courage; timid. **3.** proceeding from or expressive of fear or timidity: *a coward cry.* [ME, from OF *coart,* from *coe* tail, from L *cauda,* through comparison with an animal with its tail between its legs]

**cowardice** /ˈkaʊədəs/, *n.* lack of courage to face danger, difficulty, opposition, etc.

**cowardly** /ˈkaʊədli/, *adj.* **1.** lacking courage; basely timid. **2.** characteristic of or befitting a coward. *–adv.* **3.** like a coward. – **cowardliness,** *n.*

**cowards' castle** /kaʊədz ˈkasəl/, *n. Colloq.* parliament when used as an arena in which to vilify and abuse others while under parliamentary privilege.

**cowardy custard** /kaʊədi ˈkʌstəd/, *n. (in children's speech)* a coward: *cowardy, cowardy custard.*

**cowbane** /ˈkaʊbeɪn/, *n.* any of several umbelliferous plants supposed to be poisonous to cattle, as the European water-hemlock, *Cicuta virosa.*

**cowbang** /ˈkaʊbæŋ/, *v.i. Colloq.* to run a dairy farm. Also, **cow spank.**

**cowbanger** /ˈkaʊbæŋə/, *n. Colloq.* a dairy farmer; cow cocky. Also, **cowspanker.**

**cowbell** /ˈkaʊbɛl/, *n.* a bell hung round a cow's neck, to indicate her whereabouts.

**cowbird** /ˈkaʊbɜd/, *n.* any of the American blackbirds of the genus *Molothrus,* esp. *M. ater* of North America (so called because they accompany cattle). Also, **cow blackbird, cow bunting.**

**cowboy** /ˈkaʊbɔɪ/, *n.* **1.** a boy in charge of cows. **2.** a man employed in the care of cattle; a stockman.

**cow cake** /ˈkaʊ keɪk/, *n.* →**cow pat.**

**cowcatcher** /ˈkaʊkætʃə/, *n.* **1.** an iron grille or frame at the front of a locomotive or tram to clear the track of obstructions. **2.** a stabilising device similarly placed on the front of a high-speed motor car to keep the car down on the road.

**cow-cocky** /ˈkaʊ-kɒki/, *n. Colloq.* a dairy farmer.

**cow-cockying** /ˈkaʊ-kɒkiɪŋ/, *n.* dairy farming.

**cower** /ˈkaʊə/, *v.i.* **1.** to crouch in fear or shame. **2.** to bend with the knees and back; stand or squat in a bent position. [ME *couren,* from Scand.; cf. Icel. *kūra* sit moping, doze, c. G *kauern* cower, crouch]

**cowfish** /ˈkaʊfɪʃ/, *n., pl.* **-fishes,** (*esp. collectively*) **-fish. 1.** any of various marine fishes with hornlike projections over the eyes, as *Lactophrys tricornis,* found along the southern Atlantic coast of the U.S. to Panama, Brazil, etc.; trunkfish; box fish. **2.** a sirenian, as the manatee. **3.** any of various small cetaceans, as a porpoise or dolphin or the grampus, *Grampus griseus.*

**cowgirl** /ˈkaʊgɜl/, *n.* a girl who assists in herding cattle.

**cow hand** /ˈkaʊ hænd/, *n.* one employed as a stockman; a cowboy.

**cow heel** /ˈ– hil/, *n.* a dish consisting of a cow's or ox's hoof stewed to make an edible jelly.

**cowherd** /ˈkaʊhɜd/, *n.* one whose occupation is the tending of cows.

**cowhide** /ˈkaʊhaɪd/, *n., v.,* **-hided, -hiding.** *–n.* **1.** the hide of a cow. **2.** the leather made from it. **3.** *U.S* a strong, flexible whip made of rawhide or of braided leather. *–v.t.* **4.** *U.S* to whip with a cowhide.

**cow hock** /ˈkaʊ hɒk/, *n.* the hock of a sheep or goat which inclines inwards.

**cowhouse** /ˈkaʊhaʊs/, *n.* a building in which cows are stalled; a byre.

**cow-itch** /ˈkaʊ-ɪtʃ/, *n.* →**cowage.**

**cow-itch tree** /ˈ– tri/, *n.* →**Norfolk Island hibiscus.**

**cowl** /kaʊl/, *n.* **1.** a hooded garment worn by monks. **2.** the hood of this garment. **3.** a hood-shaped covering for a chimney or ventilating shaft, to increase the draught. **4.** the forward part of the motor-car body supporting the rear of the bonnet and the windscreen, and housing the pedals and dashboard. **5.** a cowling. **6.** a wire netting fastened to the top of the chimney of a steam locomotive, to prevent large sparks from being discharged. *–v.t.* **7.** to put a monk's cowl on. **8.** to make a monk of. **9.** to cover with, or as with, a cowl. [ME *couel,* OE *cūle, cug(e)le,* from LL *cuculla* cowl, var. of L *cucullus* hood]

**cowled** /kaʊld/, *adj.* **1.** wearing a cowl. **2.** shaped like a cowl; cucullate.

**cowlick** /ˈkaʊlɪk/, *n.* a tuft of hair turned up, usu. over the forehead.

**cowling** /ˈkaʊlɪŋ/, *n.* a streamlined housing for an aircraft engine, usu. forming a continuous line with the fuselage or wing.

**cowman** /ˈkaʊmən/, *n., pl.* **-men. 1.** a farm labourer who takes care of cows. **2.** an owner of cattle.

**coworker** /koʊˈwɜkə/, *n.* fellow worker. Also, **co-worker.**

**cow-parsley** /ˈkaʊ-pasli/, *n.* a biennial umbelliferous herb with white flowers, *Anthriscus sylvestris,* widespread in hedgerows.

**cow-parsnip** /ˈkaʊ-pasnɪp/, *n.* any plant of the umbelliferous genus *Heracleum,* as *H. spondylium,* of Europe, or *H. lanatum,* of North America.

**cow pat** /ˈkaʊ pæt/, *n. Colloq.* cow dung, congealed in a more or less circular shape where it has fallen in a paddock, etc.; meadow cake. Also, **cow cake.**

**cowpea** /ˈkaʊpi/, *n.* **1.** an annual plant, *Vigna sinensis,* extensively cultivated for forage, soil improvement, etc., the seeds sometimes being used for human food. **2.** the seed.

**Cowper's glands** /kaʊpəz ˈglændz, ku-/, *n.pl.* a pair of accessory prostate or urethral glands in males, which during sexual excitement pour a mucous secretion into the urethra. [named after Wm. *Cowper,* 1666-1709, English anatomist who discovered them]

**cowpox** /ˈkaʊpɒks/, *n.* an eruptive disease appearing on the teats and udders of cows in which small pustules form which contain a virus used in the vaccination of man against smallpox.

**cowpuncher** /ˈkaʊpʌntʃə/, *n. U.S. Colloq.* →**cowboy.**

**cowry** /ˈkaʊri/, *n., pl.* **-ries. 1.** the shell of any of the marine gastropods constituting the genus *Cypraea,* as that of *C. moneta,* a small shell with a fine gloss, used as money in certain parts of Asia, Africa, and the Pacific Islands, or that of *C. tigris,* a large, handsome shell often used as a mantel ornament. **2.** the animal itself. Also, **cowrie.** [Hind. *kauri*]

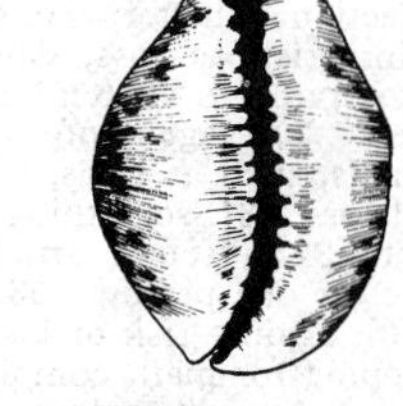

cowry shell

**cowshed** /ˈkaʊʃɛd/, *n.* a shed in which cows are milked; a cowhouse; a byre.

**cow shot** /ˈkaʊ ʃɒt/, *n. Colloq.* (in cricket) a stroke made without style or discrimination.

**cowskin** /ˈkaʊskɪn/, *n.* **1.** the skin of a cow. **2.** the leather made from it.

**cowslip** /ˈkaʊslɪp/, *n.* **1.** an English primrose, *Primula veris,* bearing yellow flowers. **2.** *U.S.* →**kingcup.** [OE *cūslyppe* cowslime, var. of *cū-sloppe* (ME *couslop*) cow-slobber. Cf. OXLIP]

**cowslip orchid** /ˈ- ɔkəd/, *n.* a terrestrial orchid, *Caladenia flava,* with large yellow flowers, widespread in south-western Western Australia.

**cowspank** /ˈkaʊspæŋk/, *v.i. Colloq.* →**cowbang.**

**cowspanker** /ˈkaʊspæŋkə/, *n. Colloq.* →**cowbanger.**

**cow-tail** /ˈkaʊ-teɪl/, *n.* coarse, hairy tipped wool, usu. from stronger crossbred sheep.

**cow-wheat** /ˈkaʊwit/, *n.* any of the species of semiparasitic herbs of the genus *Melampyrum* as the common cow-wheat, *M. pratense,* of Europe and Asia.

**cowyard confetti** /ˌkaʊjad kənˈfɛti/, *n.* nonsense; rubbish. Also, **farmyard confetti, Flemington confetti.**

**cox** /kɒks/, *n.* **1.** the steersman of a boat, esp. in rowing; a coxswain. *–v.i.* **2.** to act as cox. *–v.t.* **3.** to serve as cox for (a boat). – **coxless,** *adj.*

**coxa** /ˈkɒksə/, *n., pl.* **coxae** /ˈkɒksi/. **1.** *Anat.* **a.** the innominate bone. **b.** the joint of the hip. **2.** *Zool.* the first or proximal segment of the leg of insects and other arthropods. [L: hip] – **coxal,** *adj.*

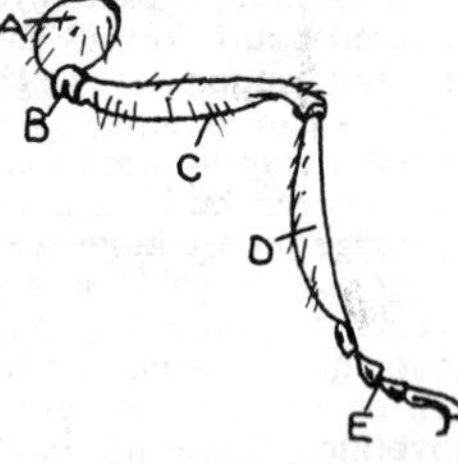


leg of beetle: A, coxa; B, trochanter; C, femur; D, tibia; E, tarsus

**coxalgia** /kɒkˈsældʒə/, *n.* pain in the hip. [NL; from COX(A) + -ALGIA] – **coxalgic,** *adj.*

**coxcomb** /ˈkɒkskoʊm/, *n.* **1.** a conceited dandy. **2.** *Bot.* →**cockscomb. 3.** *Obs.* the cap, resembling a cock's comb, formerly worn by professional fools. [var. of *cock's comb*] – **coxcombical** /kɒksˈkɒməkəl, -ˈkoʊmə-/, *adj.*

**coxcombry** /ˈkɒkskoʊmri/, *n., pl.* **-ries. 1.** the manners or behaviour of a coxcomb. **2.** a foppish trait.

**Cox's orange pippin,** *n.* a juicy, crisp variety of apple, with firm flesh and russet skin.

**coxswain** /ˈkɒksən, -sweɪn/, *n.* **1.** the helmsman of a boat. **2.** (on a ship) one who has charge of a boat and its crew. Also, **cockswain.** [ME *cock* ship's boat + SWAIN servant]

**coy** /kɔɪ/, *adj.* **1.** shy; modest (now usu. of girls). **2.** affectedly shy or reserved. **3.** *Obs.* disdainful. **4.** *Obs.* quiet. [ME, from F *coi,* earlier *quei,* from L *quiētus* at rest] – **coyly,** *adv.* – **coyness,** *n.*

**Coy.,** Company.

coyote

**coyote** /kɔɪˈoʊti/, *n.* **1.** a wild, wolf-like animal, *Canis latrans,* of western North America, noted for loud and prolonged howling at night; the prairie wolf. **2.** *U.S.* a contemptible person. [Mex. Sp., from Nahuatl *koyotl*]

**coypu** /ˈkɔɪpu/, *n., pl.* **-pus,** (*esp. collectively*) **-pu.** a large aquatic rodent, *Myocastor* (or *Myopotamus*) *coypus,* yielding the fur nutria, originally from South America but later introduced into Europe, and now officially a pest. [Amer. Sp. *coipu,* from Araucanian *koypu*]

**coz** /kʌz/, *n. Colloq.* cousin.

**coze** /koʊz/, *v.,* **cozed, cozing,** *n. Obs.* *–v.i.* **1.** to converse in a friendly way; chat. *–n.* **2.** a friendly talk; a chat. [F *causer*]

coypu

**cozen** /ˈkʌzən/, *v.t.* to cheat; deceive; beguile. [orig. obscure] – **cozener,** *n.*

**cozenage** /ˈkʌzənɪdʒ/, *n.* **1.** the practice of cozening. **2.** the fact of being cozened. **3.** a fraud; a deception.

**cozy** /ˈkoʊzi/, *adj.,* **-zier, -ziest,** *n., pl.* **-zies.** *U.S.* →**cosy.** – **cozily,** *adv.* – **coziness,** *n.*

**cozzie** /ˈkɒzi/, *n. Colloq.* →**swimming costume.** Also, **cossie.**

**cp.,** compare.

**c.p.,** candlepower.

**cP,** centipoise.

**C.P.** /si ˈpi/, **1.** Communist Party. **2.** Country Party.

**C.P.A.** /si pi ˈeɪ/, Communist Party of Australia.

**C.P.I.** /si pi ˈaɪ/, Consumer Price Index.

**cpl,** corporal.

**C.P.O.** /si pi ˈoʊ/, Chief Petty Officer.

**c.p.s.** /si pi ˈɛs/, **1.** cycles per second. **2.** characters per second.

**CPU** /si pi ˈju/, *n.* that section of a computer which controls arithmetic, logical and control functions. Also, **central processor unit.**

**cr.,** credit.

**Cr,** *Chem.* chromium.

**crab**[1] /kræb/, *n., v.,* **crabbed, crabbing.** *–n.* **1.** any of the stalk-eyed decapod crustaceans constituting the suborder Brachyura (**true crabs**) having a short, broad, more or less flattened body, the abdomen or so-called tail being small and folded under the thorax. **2.** any of various other crustaceans (as the **hermit crab**), or other animals (as the **horseshoe crab**), resembling the true crabs. **3.** (*cap.*) the zodiacal constellation or sign Cancer. **4.** any of various mechanical contrivances for hoisting or pulling. **5.** (*pl.*) a losing throw, as two aces, in the game of hazard. **6.** →**crablouse. 7. catch a crab,** *Rowing.* to make a faulty stroke, as one in which the blade either enters the water at the wrong angle and sinks too deep, or is held at the wrong angle and fails to enter the water at all. *–v.i.* **8.** to move sideways. **9.** *Aeron.* (of an aircraft) to head partly into the crosswind to compensate for drift. **10.** to fish for crabs. *–v.t.* **11.** *Aeron.* to head (an aircraft) partly into the crosswind to compensate for drift. [ME *crabbe,* OE *crabba,* c. G *Krabbe*] – **crablike,** *adj.*

crab

**crab**[2] /kræb/, *n.* **1.** a crab-apple (fruit or tree). **2.** an ill-tempered or grouchy person. [ME *crabbe,* ? var. of d. *scrab* crab-apple. Cf. d. Swed. *skrabba*]

**crab**[3] /kræb/, *v.,* **crabbed, crabbing.** *–v.i.* **1.** (of hawks) to claw each other. **2.** to find fault. *–v.t.* **3.** to claw, as a hawk. **4.** *Colloq.* to find fault with. **5.** *Colloq.* to spoil. **6.** *Colloq.* to impede; impair. **7.** (*pl.*) **draw the crabs,** *Colloq.* to attract the unwelcome attention of an authority, as the police. [cf. MD *krabben* scratch, quarrel; akin to CRAB[1]]

**crab-apple** /ˈkræb-æpəl/, *n.* **1.** a small, sour wild apple. **2.** any of various cultivated species and varieties of apple, small, sour, and astringent or slightly bitter, used for making jelly and preserves. **3.** any tree bearing such fruit.

**crabbed** /kræbd/, *adj.* **1.** perplexing; intricate: *a crabbed author, writings, etc.* **2.** difficult to decipher, as cramped handwriting. **3.** crabby. [ME, from CRAB[1] + -ED[3]] – **crabbedly,** *adv.* – **crabbedness,** *n.*

**crabber** /ˈkræbə/, *n.* **1.** one who fishes for crabs. **2.** a boat used in fishing for crabs.

**crabbing** /ˈkræbɪŋ/, *n.* the finishing process of passing woollen cloth over rollers into hot water or steam, to prevent the formation of creases or uneven shrinkage.

**crabby** /ˈkræbi/, *adj.,* **-bier, -biest.** irritable.

**crabgrass** /ˈkræbgras/, *n.* **1.** a name given to several weedy grasses, esp. grasses of the genus *Digitaria* which have aboveground stems rooting wherever the nodes come into contact with the soil. **2.** →**crowsfoot grass.**

**crabhole** /ˈkræbhoʊl/, *n.* a hole in the ground made by a land-crab.

**crabhole country** /ˈ– ˌkʌntri/, *n.* →**gilgai.**

**crablouse** /ˈkræblaʊs/, *n.* a body louse, *Phthirius pubis,* that generally infects the pubic region and causes severe itching. Also, **crab.**

**crab's eyes** /kræbz aɪz/, *n.* →**Indian liquorice.**

**crab spider** /ˈkræb spaɪdə/, *n.* a well-camouflaged spider, *Synalus angustus,* found on the bark of trees, which does not build a web but catches insects with its spined legs.

**crabstick** /ˈkræbstɪk/, *n.* **1.** a stick, cane, or club made of wood, esp. of the crab-tree. **2.** an ill-tempered, crabbed person.

**crabwise** /ˈkræbwaɪz/, *adv.* in the manner of a crab; (referring esp. to motion) sideways or diagonally. Also, **crabways** /ˈkræbweɪz/.

**crack** /kræk/, *v.i.* **1.** to make a sudden, sharp sound in, or as in, breaking; snap, as a whip. **2.** to break with a sudden, sharp sound. **3.** to break without complete separation of parts; become fissured. **4.** (of the voice) to break abruptly and discordantly, esp. into an upper register. **5.** to fail; give way. **6.** to break with grief. *–v.t.* **7.** to cause to make a sudden sharp sound; making a snapping sound with (a whip, etc.); strike with a sharp noise. **8.** to break without complete separation of parts; break into fissures. **9.** to break with a sudden sharp sound. **10.** *Colloq.* to break into (a safe, vault, etc.). **11.** *Colloq.* to solve (a mystery, etc.). **12.** to deal with successfully: *to crack a wave.* **13.** *Colloq.* to open and drink (a bottle of wine, etc.). **14.** to damage; impair. **15.** to become unsound mentally. **16.** to make (the voice) harsh or unmanageable. **17.** to utter or tell, as a joke. **18.** *Obs.* to boast. **19.** to subject to the process of cracking in the distillation of petroleum, etc. *–v.* **20.** Some special verb phrases are:

**crack a fat,** *Colloq.* to have an erection.

**crack a smile,** to smile, though disinclined.

**crack down on,** *Colloq.* to take severe measures, esp. in enforcing discipline.

**crack hardy** or **hearty,** *Colloq.* to endure with patience; put on a brave front.

**crack it, 1.** *Colloq.* to have or offer sexual intercourse. **2.** *Colloq.* to be successful. **3.** to work as a prostitute.

**crack on, 1.** *Naut.* to carry or set sail boldly, especially in heavy weather. **2.** *Chiefly Naut.* to pursue a course at high speed, especially in adverse conditions.

**crack up, 1.** to suffer a physical, mental or moral breakdown. **2.** to crash. **3.** *Colloq.* to praise; extol.

**get cracking,** *Colloq.* to start an activity, esp. energetically.

*–n.* **21.** a sudden, sharp noise, as of something breaking. **22.** the snap of a whip, etc. **23.** a shot, as with a rifle. **24.** a resounding blow. **25.** a break without complete separation of parts; a fissure; a flaw. **26.** a slight opening, as one between door and doorpost. **27.** a mental flaw. **28.** a broken or changing tone of the voice. **29.** *Mountaineering.* a cleft in rock, narrower than a chimney. **30.** *Colloq.* a try; an opportunity or chance. **31.** an expert: *all the cracks were gathered for the fray.* **32.** *Colloq.* the anus. **33.** *Colloq.* a joke; gibe. **34.** *Colloq.* a moment; instant: *he was on his feet again in a crack.* **35.** *Colloq.* a burglary. **36.** *Colloq.* the female pudendum. **37.** *Colloq.* a prostitute's customer. **38. at first crack,** at dawn. **39. crack of dawn,** the first light of the day. **40. crack of doom,** the end of the world; doomsday. **41. have a crack at,** *Colloq.* to attempt; try. *–adj.* **42.** *Colloq.* of superior excellence; first-rate: *a crack rider.* [unexplained var. of obs. *crake* creak, OE *cracian* resound. See CREAK, CROAK, all probably imitative in orig.]

**crackajack** /ˈkrækədʒæk/, *n., adj.* →**crackerjack.**

**crackbrain** /ˈkrækbreɪn/, *n.* an insane person.

**crackbrained** /ˈkrækbreɪnd/, *adj.* insane; crazy.

**crackdown** /ˈkrækdaʊn/, *n.* an enforcing of regulations, discipline, etc., particularly when sudden: *a police crackdown on gambling clubs.*

**cracked** /krækt/, *adj.* **1.** broken. **2.** broken without separation of parts; fissured. **3.** damaged. **4.** *Colloq.* mentally unsound. **5.** broken in tone, as the voice.

**cracker** /ˈkrækə/, *n.* **1.** a thin, crisp biscuit. **2.** a kind of firework which explodes with a loud report; firecracker. **3.** →**bonbon. 4.** something which has a particular quality in a high degree: *this* (fast) *pace is a cracker; this* (beautiful) *model is a cracker.* **5.** *U.S.* one of a class of poor whites in parts of the south-eastern U.S. **6.** one who or that which cracks, esp. an attachment of cord or horsehair to the end of a whip, allowing a loud report on flexion. **7.** *N.Z.* →**karaka. 8. not to have a cracker,** *Colloq.* to have no money. **9. not worth a cracker,** *Colloq.* of little worth.

**cracker-barrel** /ˈkrækə-bærəl/, *n. U.S.* a barrel of biscuits in the general store of a small community, which is a gathering place for gossip and thence a symbol of parochialism. Cf. **parish pump.**

**crackerjack** /ˈkrækədʒæk/, *n. Colloq.* **1.** a person of marked ability; something exceptionally fine. *–adj.* **2.** *Colloq.* of marked ability; exceptionally fine. Also, **crackajack.**

**cracker night** /ˈkrækə naɪt/, *n.* a night on which fireworks are let off as a celebration; bonfire night.

**crackers** /ˈkrækəz/, *adj. Colloq.* insane; crazy.

**cracker unit** /ˈkrækə junət/, *n.* →**catalytic cracker.**

**cracking** /ˈkrækɪŋ/, *n.* **1.** (in the distillation of petroleum or the like) the process of breaking down certain hydrocarbons into simpler ones of lower boiling points, by means of excess heat, distillation under pressure, etc., in order to give a greater yield of low-boiling products than could be obtained by simple distillation. *–adj.* **2.** fast; vigorous: *a cracking pace.* **3.** done with precision: *a cracking salute.* **4.** *Colloq.* first-rate; fine; excellent.

**crackle** /ˈkrækəl/, *v.,* **-led, -ling,** *n. –v.i.* **1.** to make slight, sudden, sharp noises, rapidly repeated. *–v.t.* **2.** to cause to crackle. **3.** to break with a crackling noise. *–n.* **4.** the act of crackling. **5.** a crackling noise. **6.** a network of fine cracks, as in the glaze of some kinds of porcelain. **7.** pottery ware with a network of fine cracks in the glaze. [frequentative of CRACK]

**crackleware** /ˈkrækəlwɛə/, *n.* →**crackle** (def. 7).

**crackling** /ˈkræklɪŋ/, *n.* **1.** the making of slight cracking sounds rapidly repeated. **2.** the crisp browned skin or rind of roast pork. **3.** (*usu. pl.*) the crisp residue left when fat, esp. that of pigs, is rendered.

**crackly** /ˈkrækli/, *adj.* apt to crackle.

**cracknel** /ˈkræknəl/, *n.* **1.** a hard, brittle cake or biscuit. **2.** (*pl.*) small bits of fat pork fried crisp. [ME *crakenelle,* from F *craquelin,* from MD *crakelinc*]

**crackpot** /ˈkrækpɒt/, *Colloq. –n.* **1.** an eccentric or insane person. *–adj.* **2.** eccentric; insane; impractical.

**cracksman** /ˈkræksmən/, *n., pl.* **-men.** *Colloq.* a burglar.

**crack-up** /ˈkræk-ʌp/, *n.* **1.** a crash; collision. **2.** *Colloq.* a breakdown in health. **3.** collapse; defeat.

**-cracy,** a noun termination meaning 'rule', 'government', 'governing body', as in *autocracy, bureaucracy.* [F *-cratie,* from Gk *-kratia,* from *krátos* rule, strength]

**cradle** /ˈkreɪdəl/, *n., v.,* **-dled, -dling.** *–n.* **1.** a little bed or cot for an infant, usu. built on rockers. **2.** the place where anything is nurtured during its early existence. **3.** any of various contrivances similar to a child's cradle, as the framework on which a ship rests during construction or repair. **4.** a frame that prevents the bedclothes touching an injured part of a bedridden patient. **5.** a plank supported in a sling from above, on which a man may sit, or stand, to carry out work on a vertical surface, as the side of a building or ship. **6.** a flat, movable framework with swivel wheels, on which a mechanic can lie while working beneath a motor vehicle. **7.** *Agric.* **a.** a frame of wood with a row of long curved teeth projecting above and parallel to a scythe, for laying grain in bunches as it is cut. **b.** a scythe together with the cradle in which it is set. **8.** *Agric.* a framework on which animals are held firmly to be shorn or given routine treatment, as marking and branding calves. **9.** a kind of box on rockers used by miners for washing auriferous gravel or sand to separate the gold. **10.** an engraver's tool for laying mezzotint grounds. *–v.t.* **11.** to place or rock in or as in a cradle. **12.** to nurture during infancy. **13.** to cut (grain) with a cradle. **14.** to place in a ship's cradle. **15.** to wash in a miner's cradle. **16.** to receive or hold as a cradle. **17.** *Lacrosse.* to hold (the ball) in the net of the crosse while running with it. *–v.i.* **18.** to lie in, or as in, a cradle. **19.** to cut grain with a cradle-scythe. [ME *cradel,* OE *cradol.* Cf. G *Kratte* basket] – **cradler,** *n.*

cradle

**cradle cap** /ˈ– kæp/, *n. Colloq.* a manifestation of seborrhoea in infancy, characterised by adherent yellowish plaques on the scalp.

**cradle rock** /ˈ– rɒk/, *n.* →**bubblegum music.**

**cradle-scythe** /ˈkreɪdl-saɪð/, *n.* →**cradle** (def. 7b).

**cradle-snatcher** /ˈkreɪdl-snætʃə/, *n.* one who shows romantic or sexual interest in a much younger person.

**cradlesong** /ˈkreɪdlsɒŋ/, *n.* a lullaby.

**cradling** /ˈkreɪdlɪŋ/, *n.* **1.** *Archit.* a framework of wood, fixed round beams or columns to receive a casing. **2.** *Lacrosse.* the technique of swinging the crosse while running so the ball is kept in the net.

**craft** /kraft/, *n.* **1.** skill; ingenuity; dexterity. **2.** skill or art applied to bad purposes; cunning; deceit; guile. **3.** an art, trade, or occupation requiring special skill, esp. manual skill; a handicraft. **4.** the members of a trade or profession collectively; a guild. **5.** (*construed as pl.*) boats, ships, and vessels collectively. **6.** a single vessel. **7.** (*construed as pl.*) aircraft collectively. **8.** a single aircraft. [ME; OE *cræft,* c. G *Kraft*]

**craft award** /ˈ– əwɔd/, *n.* an award of an industrial tribunal relating to a particular craft as distinct from an industry or establishment.

**craft guild** /ˈ– gɪld/, *n.* an association of people working in the same craft.

**craftsman** /ˈkraftsmən/, *n., pl.* **-men. 1.** one who practises a craft; an artisan. **2.** an artist. [*crafts* (possessive of CRAFT) + MAN] – **craftsmanship,** *n.*

**crafty** /ˈkrafti/, *adj.,* **-tier, -tiest. 1.** skilful in underhand or evil schemes; cunning, deceitful; sly. **2.** *Archaic.* skilful; ingenious; dexterous. – **craftily,** *adv.* – **craftiness,** *n.*

**crag** /kræg/, *n.* a steep, rugged rock; a rough, broken, projecting part of a rock. [ME, from Celtic; cf. Welsh *craig* rock] – **cragged** /ˈkrægəd/, *adj.*

**crag-and-tail** /kræg-ən-ˈteɪl/, *n.* a hill or crag, of which one face has a steep slope and the other a gentle slope; commonly formed by glacial action.

**craggy** /ˈkrægi/, *adj.,* **-gier, -giest. 1.** full of crags or broken rocks. **2.** rugged; rough. – **craggily,** *adv.* – **cragginess,** *n.*

**cragsman** /ˈkrægzmən/, *n., pl.* **-men.** one accustomed to or skilled in climbing crags.

**crake** /kreɪk/, *n.* any of various small, widely distributed birds of the family Rallidae, frequenting swamps and reedy margins of lakes as the **spotted crake,** *Porzana fluminea,* of Australia and Tasmania. [ME, from Scand.; cf. Icel. *krāka*]

**cram** /kræm/, *v.,* **crammed, cramming,** *n. –v.t.* **1.** to fill (something) by force with more than it can conveniently hold. **2.** to force or stuff (fol. by *into, down,* etc.). **3.** to fill with or as with excess of food. **4.** to prepare (a person), as for an examination, by hastily storing his memory with facts. **5.** to get a knowledge of (a subject) by so preparing oneself. *–v.i.* **6.** to eat greedily or to excess. **7.** to study for an examination by hastily memorising facts. *–n.* **8.** a crammed state. **9.** the act or result of cramming. [OE *crammian,* from *crimman* insert]

**crambo** /ˈkræmboʊ/, *n.* **1.** a game in which one person or side must find a rhyme to a word or a line of verse given by another. **2.** (*derog.*) rhyme. [earlier *crambe,* from L: lit., cabbage, short for *crambē repetīta* repeated cabbage, dull rhyme]

**cram-full** /kræmˈfʊl, ˈkræmfʊl/, *adj.* full to the utmost;

crammed: *a larder cram-full of food.*

**crammer** /ˈkræmə/, *n.* **1.** one who or that which crams. **2.** *Chiefly Brit.* a person or a school which prepares pupils for examinations by cramming them with facts in a short time. **3.** a pupil studying for an examination. **4.** a textbook from which facts may be crammed. **5.** an apparatus for forcibly feeding poultry to fatten them. **6.** *Colloq.* a lie.

**cramoisy** /ˈkræmɔɪzi, -məzi/, *adj.* **1.** *Archaic.* crimson. *–n.* **2.** *Obs.* crimson cloth. Also, **cramesy.** [F *cramoisi,* from Ar. *qirmizī* CRIMSON]

**cramp**[1] /kræmp/, *n.* **1.** a sudden involuntary, persistent contraction of a muscle or a group of muscles, esp. of the extremities, sometimes associated with severe pain. **2.** (*oft. pl.*) piercing pains in the abdomen. **3. diver's cramps,** →**the bends.** See **bend**[1] (def. 21). **4. writer's cramp,** an occupational disability involving cramp in some muscles of the fingers and hands. *–v.t.* **5.** to affect with, or as with, a cramp. [ME *crampe,* from MD]

**cramp**[2] /kræmp/, *n.* **1.** a small metal bar with bent ends, for holding together planks, masonry, etc.; a cramp iron. **2.** a portable frame or tool with a movable part which can be screwed up to hold things together; clamp. **3.** anything that confines or restrains. **4.** a cramped state or part. *–v.t.* **5.** to fasten or hold with a cramp. **6.** to confine narrowly; restrict; restrain; hamper. **7. cramp one's style,** to hinder a person from showing his best abilities, etc. *–adj.* **8.** cramped. [MD: hook, clamp]

**cramped** /kræmpt/, *adj.* **1.** contracted; narrow. **2.** difficult to decipher or understand.

**cramp iron** /ˈkræmp aɪən/, *n.* a cramp, or piece of iron with bent ends, for holding together pieces of stone, etc.

**crampon** /ˈkræmpən/, *n.* **1.** a grappling iron, esp. one of a pair for raising heavy weights. **2.** *Mountaineering.* a spiked iron plate worn on the shoe to ensure grip. [F, from *crampe* (from Gmc. See CRAMP[2])]

**cranage** /ˈkreɪnɪdʒ/, *n.* **1.** the service performed by a crane, in docks etc. **2.** the charge made for the use of a crane.

**cranberry** /ˈkrænbəri, -bri/, *n., pl.* **-ries. 1.** the red, acid fruit or berry of any plant of the genus *Vaccinium,* as *V. oxycoccus,* used in making sauce, jelly, etc. **2.** the plant itself. [LG *kraanbere;* cf. G *Kran(ich)beere* craneberry. See CRANE]

**crane** /kreɪn/, *n., v.,* **craned, craning.** *–n.* **1.** any of a group of large wading birds (family Gruidae) with very long legs, bill, and neck, and elevated hind toe. **2.** (popularly) any of various similar birds of other families, as the white-faced heron, *Ardea novaehollandiae.* **3.** a device for moving heavy weights, having two motions, one a direct lift and the other a horizontal movement, and consisting in one of its simplest forms of an upright post turning on its vertical axis and bearing a projecting arm on which the hoisting tackle is fitted. **4.** (*pl.*) *Naut.* supports of iron or timber at a vessel's side for stowing boats or spars upon. *–v.t.* **5.** to hoist, lower, or move by or as by a crane. **6.** to stretch (the neck) as a crane does. *–v.i.* **7.** to stretch out one's neck. **8.** *Colloq.* to hesitate at danger, difficulty, etc. **9.** *Hunting.* (of a horse) to pull up at a hedge and look over before jumping. [ME; OE *cran,* c. G *Kran*]

crane

**crane chaser** /ˈ– tʃeɪsə/, *n.* a man employed to sling loads and control their movement when handled by a lifting appliance, as a crane.

**cranefly** /ˈkreɪnflaɪ/, *n.* any of the dipterous insects constituting the family Tipulidae, characterised by very long legs; the daddy-long-legs.

**cranesbill** /ˈkreɪnzbɪl/, *n.* any plant of the genus *Geranium* (see **geranium**) with long, slender, beaked fruit. Also, **crane's-bill.** [CRANE('s) + BILL[2]; 16th-cent. translation of D *kranebek* geranium]

**cranial** /ˈkreɪniəl/, *adj.* of or pertaining to the cranium or skull. **– cranially,** *adv.*

**cranial index** /– ˈɪndɛks/, *n.* the ratio of the greatest breadth of the skull to the greatest length from front to back, multiplied by 100; cephalic index.

**craniate** /ˈkreɪniət, -eɪt/, *adj.* **1.** having a cranium or skull. **2.** belonging to the Craniata, a primary division of vertebrates, comprising those which possess a skull and brain, and including the mammals, birds, reptiles, amphibians, and fishes. *–n.* **3.** a craniate animal.

**cranio-,** a combining form of **cranium.** Also, **crani-.**

**craniology** /kreɪniˈɒlədʒi/, *n.* the science that deals with the size, shape, and other characteristics of skulls. **– craniological** /kreɪniəˈlɒdʒɪkəl/, *adj.* **– craniologist,** *n.*

**craniometer** /kreɪniˈɒmətə/, *n.* an instrument for measuring the external dimensions of skulls.

**craniometry** /kreɪniˈɒmətri/, *n.* the science of measuring skulls. **– craniometric** /kreɪniəˈmɛtrɪk/, **craniometrical,** *adj.* **– craniometrist,** *n.*

**craniotomy** /kreɪniˈɒtəmi/, *n., pl.* **-mies.** the operation of opening the skull, usually for operations on the brain.

**cranium** /ˈkreɪniəm/, *n., pl.* **-nia** /-niə/. **1.** the skull of a vertebrate. **2.** that part of the skull which encloses the brain. [ML, from Gk *krāníon*]

**crank**[1] /kræŋk/, *n.* **1.** *Mach.* a device for communicating motion, or for changing rotary motion into reciprocating motion, or vice versa, consisting in its simplest form of an arm projecting from, or secured at right angles at the end of, the axis or shaft which receives or imparts the motion. **2.** *Colloq.* an eccentric person, or one who holds stubbornly to eccentric views. **3.** *Colloq.* an eccentric notion. **4.** a turn of speech; a verbal conceit. *–v.t.* **5.** to bend into or make in the shape of a crank. **6.** to furnish with a crank. **7.** to cause (a shaft) to revolve by applying force to a crank; turn a crankshaft in (an internal-combustion engine) to start the engine. *–v.i.* **8.** to turn a crank, as in starting a motor-car engine. **9.** to bend. *–adj.* **10.** unstable; shaky; unsteady. **11.** odd, as typical of a crank (def. 2). [ME *cranke,* OE *cranc,* in *crancstæf* weaving implement, crank]

**crank**[2] /kræŋk/, *adj.* liable to lurch or capsize, as a ship. [short for *crank-sided;* cf. D *krengd* careened]

**crankcase** /ˈkræŋkkeɪs/, *n.* (in an internal-combustion engine) the housing which encloses the crankshaft, connecting rods, and allied parts.

**crankpin** /ˈkræŋkpɪn/, *n.* a pin or cylinder at the outer end or part of a crank, as for holding a connecting rod.

**crankshaft** /ˈkræŋkʃaft/, *n.* a shaft driving or driven by a crank, esp. the main shaft of an engine which carries the cranks to which the connecting rods are attached.

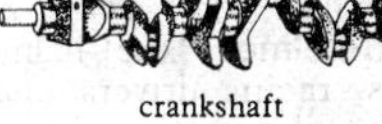
crankshaft

**cranky**[1] /ˈkræŋki/, *adj.,* **-kier, -kiest. 1.** eccentric; queer. **2.** ill-tempered; cross. **3.** shaky; unsteady; out of order. **– crankily,** *adv.* **– crankiness,** *n.*

**cranky**[2] /ˈkræŋki/, *adj.* liable to capsize.

**crannog** /ˈkrænəg/, *n.* an ancient Irish or Scottish lake dwelling, usually built on an artificial island. Also, **crannoge** /ˈkrænədʒ/. [Irish, from *crann* tree, beam]

**cranny** /ˈkræni/, *n., pl.* **-nies.** a small, narrow opening (in a wall, rock, etc.); a chink; crevice; fissure. [ME *crany,* from F *cran* fissure (from *crener* cut away, from L *crēnāre*) + -Y[2]] **– crannied,** *adj.*

**crap** /kræp/, *n., v.,* **crapped, crapping.** *Colloq. –n.* **1.** excrement. **2.** nonsense; rubbish. **3.** junk; odds and ends. *–v.t.* **4.** to make a mess of; bungle (oft. fol. by *up*): *to crap a job up.* **5.** annoy; disgust (fol. by *off*). *–v.i.* **6.** to defecate. **7.** Also, **crap on.** to talk nonsense. **8. crap out,** to fail. [late ME *crappe* chaff, from MD] **– crappy,** *adj.*

**crape** /kreɪp/, *n., v.t.,* **craped, craping.** →**crepe** (esp. defs 4 and 5). [anglicised spelling of CREPE]

**crape fern** /ˈ– fɜn/, *n. N.Z.* →**Prince of Wales feather.**

**crapper** /ˈkræpə/, *n. Colloq.* →**toilet** (def. 1).

**craps** /kræps/, *n.* a gambling game played with two dice, a modern and simplified form of hazard.

**crapshooter** /ˈkræpʃutə/, *n. U.S.* a person who plays the game of craps.

**crapulent** /ˈkræpjələnt/, *adj.* sick from gross excess in drinking or eating. [L *crāpulentus* drunk] **– crapulence,** *n.*

**crapulous** /ˈkræpjələs/, *adj.* **1.** given to or characterised by gross excess in drinking or eating. **2.** suffering from or due to such excess. [LL *crāpulōsus,* from L *crāpula* intoxication] **– crapulousness,** *n.*

**craquelure** /ˈkrækəljuə/, *n.* the fine hairlines that develop on old paintings. [F, from *craqueler* CRACKLE]

**crash**[1] /kræʃ/, *v.t.* **1.** to break in pieces violently and noisily; shatter. **2.** to force or drive with violence and noise. **3.** *Colloq.* to come uninvited to (a party, etc.). **4.** *Colloq.* to enter without buying a ticket: *to crash the gate.* **5.** to damage a car, aircraft, etc. in a collision. *–v.i.* **6.** to break or fall to pieces with noise. **7.** to make a loud, clattering noise as of something dashed to pieces. **8.** to collapse or fail suddenly, as a financial enterprise. **9.** to move or go with a crash; strike with a crash. **10.** of an aircraft, to fall to the ground. **11.** *Colloq.* to defecate. **12.** *Colloq.* to collapse or fall asleep with exhaustion. *–n.* **13.** a breaking or falling to pieces with loud noise. **14.** the shock of collision and breaking. **15.** a sudden and violent falling to ruin. **16.** *Computers.* a complete system malfunction which destroys the content of the computer memory requiring a bootstrap procedure before resumption of operation. **17.** a sudden collapse of a financial enterprise or the like. **18.** a sudden loud noise, as of something dashed to pieces; the sound of thunder, loud music, etc. **19.** of an aircraft, the act of crashing. **20.** *Colloq.* the act of defecating. *–adj.* **21.** *Colloq.* characterised by all-out, intensive effort, esp. to meet an emergency: *a crash program.* [ME; b. CRAZE and MASH] **– crasher,** *n.*

**crash**[2] /kræʃ/, *n.* **1.** a fabric of plain weave, made of rough, irregular, or lumpy yarns. It may be used as linen or cotton towelling, rayon dress fabric, etc. **2.** *U.S.* →**mull**[3] (def.2). [orig. unknown]

**crash barrier** /'– bæriə/, *n.* a strong protective fence erected by the sides of motor-racing tracks and dangerous sections of roads; guardrail.

**crash cart** /'– kat/, *n. Colloq.* a mobile trolley fitted for emergencies and wheeled to hospital wards as needed.

**crash cymbal** /'– sɪmbəl/, *n.* an extremely resonant cymbal.

**crash dive** /'– daɪv/, *n.* a rapid dive by a submarine made at a steep angle, esp. to avoid attack on the surface.

**crash-dive** /'kræʃ-daɪv/, *v.i.* **-dived, -diving.** (of a submarine) to dive rapidly at a steep angle.

**crash-graze** /'kræʃ-greɪz/, *v.t.* to graze a large mob of sheep on a small area to crop the growth rapidly. **– crash-grazing,** *n.*

**crash hat** /'kræʃ hæt/, *n.* →**crash-helmet.**

**crash-helmet** /'kræʃ-hɛlmət/, *n.* a helmet worn by motorcyclists, racing drivers and others, to protect the head in the event of a crash.

**crash-hot** /'kræʃ-hɒt/, *adj. Colloq.* excellent. Also (*in predicative use*), **crash hot** /kræʃ 'hɒt/.

**crashing** /'kræʃɪŋ/, *adj. Colloq.* complete and utter: *a crashing bore.*

**crash-land** /'kræʃ-lænd/, *v.t.* **1.** to land (an aircraft) in an emergency in such a way that the minimum of damage is sustained. *–v.i.* **2.** to land an aircraft in this way. **– crash-landing,** *n.*

**crasis** /'kreɪsəs/, *n., pl.* **-ses** /-siz/. **1.** the mixture or blending of different elements in the constitution of the body; temperament. **2.** *Gram.* the mingling or combination of two vowels. [Gk: a mingling]

**crass** /kræs/, *adj.* **1.** gross; stupid: *crass ignorance.* **2.** thick; coarse. [L *crassus* solid, thick, dense, fat] **– crassly,** *adv.* **– crassness,** *n.*

**crassitude** /'kræsətjud/, *n.* **1.** gross ignorance or stupidity. **2.** thickness; grossness.

**crassulaceous** /ˌkræsju'leɪʃəs/, *adj.* belonging to the Crassulaceae family of plants, mostly fleshy or succulent herbs, including the houseleek, etc. [NL *Crassula* the typical genus (from L *crassus* thick) + -ACEOUS]

**-crat,** a noun termination meaning 'ruler', 'member of a ruling body', 'advocate of a particular form of rule', as in *aristocrat, autocrat, democrat, plutocrat.* Cf. **-cracy.** [F *-crate,* from Gk *kratḗs* ruler]

**crate** /kreɪt/, *n., v.,* **crated, crating.** *–n.* **1.** a box or framework, usu. of wooden slats, for packing and transporting fruit, furniture, etc. **2.** a basket of wickerwork, for the transportation of crockery, etc. **3.** the amount contained by or contents of a crate. **4.** *Colloq.* a motor vehicle, aeroplane, or the like, esp. a dilapidated one. *–v.t.* **5.** to put in a crate. [L *crātis* wicker-work]

**crater** /'kreɪtə/, *n.* **1.** the cup-shaped depression or cavity marking the orifice of a volcano. **2.** (in the surface of the earth, moon, etc.) a rounded hollow formed by the impact of a meteorite. **3.** (on the surface of the moon) a roughly circular depression, almost always containing a central mountain, and often shut in by mountainous walls. **4.** the hole or pit in the ground where a military mine, bomb, or shell has exploded. **5.** a large vessel or bowl used by the ancient Greeks and Romans, originally for mixing wine with water. **6.** (*cap.*) *Astron.* a small southern constellation. *–v.i.* **7.** to form a crater or craters. *–v.t.* **8.** to make a crater or craters in. [L, from Gk *krātḗr,* orig. bowl for mixing wine and water] **– craterlike,** *adj.* **– craterous,** *adj.* **– cratering,** *n.*

**craunch** /krɔntʃ/, *v.t., v.i., n.* →**crunch.** [var. of *scranch, cranch.* Cf. D *schranzen* break]

**cravat** /krə'væt/, *n.* a scarf worn round the neck; neckcloth. [F *cravate;* so called because adopted from the Croats (F *Cravates*)]

**crave** /kreɪv/, *v.,* **craved, craving.** *–v.t.* **1.** to long for or desire eagerly. **2.** to need greatly; require. **3.** to ask earnestly for (something); beg for. **4.** *Obs.* to ask (a person) earnestly for something or to do something. *–v.i.* **5.** to beg or plead (fol. by *for*). **6.** to long (fol. by *for* or *after*). [ME *craven,* OE *crafian.* Cf. Icel. *krefja* demand] **– craver,** *n.* **– cravingly,** *adv.*

**craven** /'kreɪvən/, *adj.* **1.** cowardly; pusillanimous; mean-spirited. *–n.* **2.** a coward. [ME *cravant,* from OF, b. *cra-v(antê)* overthrown and (*recre*)*ant* RECREANT] **– cravenly,** *adv.* **– cravenness,** *n.*

**craving** /'kreɪvɪŋ/, *n.* eager or urgent desire; longing; yearning.

**craw** /krɔ/, *n.* **1.** the crop of a bird or insect. **2.** the stomach of an animal. **3. stick in one's craw,** to irritate or annoy a person. [ME *crawe,* c. D *kraag* neck]

**crawbob** /'krɔbɒb/, *n.* →**yabby.** Also, **craybob.**

**crawchie** /'krɔtʃi/, *n. Qld.* →**yabby.**

**crawfish** /'krɔfɪʃ/, *n., pl.* **-fishes,** (*esp. collectively*) **-fish.** *Chiefly U.S.* →**crayfish** (esp. def. 2).

**crawl**[1] /krɔl/, *v.i.* **1.** to move by dragging the body along the ground, as a worm, or on the hands and knees, as a young child. **2.** to progress slowly, laboriously, or timorously: *the work crawled.* **3.** to go stealthily or abjectly. **4.** to behave abjectly. **5.** to be, or feel as if, over-run with crawling things. *–n.* **6.** the act of crawling; a slow, crawling motion. **7.** Also, **Australian crawl.** *Swimming.* a stroke in prone position characterised by alternate overarm movements and a continuous up and down kick. [ME, from Scand.; cf. Dan. *kravle* creep] **– crawlingly,** *adv.*

Australian crawl

**crawl**[2] /krɔl/, *n.* an enclosure in shallow water on the seacoast, for confining fish, turtles, etc. [D *kraal,* from Sp. *corral* CORRAL]

**crawler** /'krɔlə/, *n.* **1.** one who or that which crawls. **2.** →**caterpillar** (defs 2, 3, and 4). **3.** an abject flatterer. **4.** (*usu. pl.*) →**rompers.** **5.** a person who is slow or lazy, or unfit to work. **6.** an animal which is docile through temperament, old age or weakness. **7.** *Obs.* a shepherd. **8.** a caterpillar tractor, usu. designed for a specific purpose, as a crawler-dozer, crawler-loader, etc.

**crawly** /'krɔli/, *adj. Colloq.* that crawls; imparting the sensation of being overrun with crawling things; creepy.

**cray** /kreɪ/, *n. Colloq.* →**crayfish.**

**craybob** /'kreɪbɒb/, *n.* →**crawbob.**

**crayfish** /'kreɪfɪʃ/, *n., pl.* **-fishes** (*esp. collectively*) **-fish.** **1.** any of various freshwater decapod crustaceans of the family Parastacidae, as the yabby, marron, etc., having characteristically large claws. **2.** any of numerous similar Northern Hemisphere crustaceans of the genera *Astacus* and *Cambarus.* **3.** Also, **sea crayfish.** →**lobster** (def. 1). Also, *Chiefly U.S.,* **crawfish.** [alteration

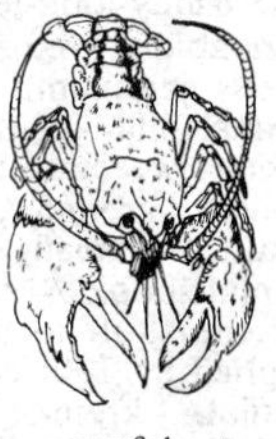

crayfish

i = peat ɪ = pit ɛ = pet æ = pat a = part ɒ = pot ʌ = putt ɔ = port ʊ = put u = pool ɜ = pert ə = apart aɪ = buy eɪ = bay ɔɪ = boy aʊ = how
oʊ = hoe ɪə = here ɛə = hair ʊə = tour g = give θ = thin ð = then ʃ = show ʒ = measure tʃ = choke dʒ = joke ŋ = sing j = you õ = Fr. bon

(by pop. etym.) of ME *crevice,* from OF, from OHG *krebiz* crab]

**crayon** /'kreɪɒn/, *n., v.,* **-oned, -oning.** *–n.* **1.** a pointed stick or pencil of coloured wax, chalk, etc., used for drawing. **2.** a drawing in crayons. *–v.t.* **3.** to draw with a crayon or crayons. **4.** to sketch out (a plan, etc.). [F, from *craie,* from L *crēta* chalk] – **crayoner, crayonist,** *n.*

**craypot** /'kreɪpɒt/, *n.* a trap in which crayfish are caught.

**craze** /kreɪz/, *v.,* **crazed, crazing,** *n.* *–v.t.* **1.** to impair in intellect; make insane. **2.** to make small cracks on the surface of (pottery, etc.); to crackle. *–v.i.* **3.** to become insane. **4.** to become minutely cracked, as the glaze of pottery. **5.** to break; shatter. *–n.* **6.** a mania; a popular fashion, etc., usu. shortlived; a rage. **7.** insanity; an insane condition. **8.** a minute crack in the glaze of pottery, etc. [ME *crase(n)* break, from Scand.; cf. Swed. *krasa*]

**crazed** /kreɪzd/, *adj.* **1.** insane; demented. **2.** having small cracks in the glaze, as pottery.

**crazy** /'kreɪzi/, *adj.,* **-zier, -ziest. 1.** demented; mad. **2.** eccentric; bizarre; unusual. **3.** unrealistic; impractical: *a crazy scheme.* **4.** *Colloq.* intensely enthusiastic or excited. **5.** likely to collapse, fall to pieces, or disintegrate. – **crazily,** *adv.* – **craziness,** *n.*

**crazy bone** /'– boʊn/, *n. U.S.* →**funny bone.**

**crazy paving** /– 'peɪvɪŋ/, *n.* a pavement made up of slabs of various irregular shapes.

**crazy quilt** /'– kwɪlt/, *n.* a patchwork quilt made of irregular patches combined with little or no regard to pattern.

**creak** /krik/, *v.i.* **1.** to make a sharp, harsh, grating, or squeaking sound. **2.** to move with creaking. *–v.t.* **3.** to cause to creak. *–n.* **4.** a creaking sound. [ME *creken.* Cf. OE *crǣcettan,* var. of *crācettan* CROAK]

**creaky** /'kriki/, *adj.,* **-kier, -kiest.** creaking; apt to creak. – **creakily,** *adv.* – **creakiness,** *n.*

**cream** /krim/, *n.* **1.** the fatty part of milk, which rises to the surface when the liquid is allowed to stand. **2.** any dish or delicacy made largely of cream or resembling cream. **3.** any creamlike substance, esp. various cosmetics. **4.** (*usu. pl.*) a soft-centred confection of fondant or fudge coated with chocolate. **5.** a puree or soup containing cream or milk: *cream of tomato soup.* **6.** the best part of anything. **7.** yellowish white; light tint of yellow or buff. *–v.i.* **8.** to form cream. **9.** to froth; foam. *–v.t.* **10.** to work (butter and sugar, etc.) to a smooth, creamy mass. **11.** to prepare (chicken, oysters, vegetables, etc.) with cream, milk, or a cream sauce. **12.** to allow (milk) to form cream. **13.** to skim (milk). **14.** to separate as cream. **15.** to take the cream or best part of. **16.** to use a cosmetic cream on. **17.** to add cream to (coffee, or the like). **18.** *Colloq.* to beat up in a fight. **19. cream one's jeans, a.** *Colloq.* to have an orgasm while dressed. **b.** *Colloq.* to become extremely excited. *–adj.* **20.** cream-coloured. **21.** (of a liqueur) rich and usu. sweet. [ME *creme,* from F, from LL *chrisma* CHRISM]

**cream bun** /– 'bʌn/, *n.* a bun with a split containing cream.

**cream cake** /'– keɪk/, *n.* a cake or other confection with a cream filling.

**cream caramel** /– 'kærəməl/, *n.* →**crème caramel.**

**cream cheese** /– 'tʃiz/, *n.* a soft, white, smooth-textured, unripened cheese made of sweet milk and sometimes cream.

**cream-coloured** /'krim-kʌləd/, *adj.* having a yellowish white colour. Also, *U.S.,* **cream-colored.**

**creamed** /krimd/, *v.* **1.** past participle of **cream.** *–adj. Colloq.* **2.** beaten up in a fight. **3.** wiped off one's surfboard by a wave.

**creamer** /krimə/, *n.* **1.** one who or that which creams. **2.** a small jug, pitcher, etc., for holding cream. **3.** a refrigerator in which milk is placed to facilitate the formation of cream. **4.** a vessel or apparatus for separating cream from milk. **5.** *Colloq.* a coward.

**creamery** /'kriməri/, *n., pl.* **-ries. 1.** an establishment engaged in the production of butter and cheese. **2.** a place for the sale of milk and its products. **3.** a place where milk is set to form cream.

**cream horn** /'krim hɔn/, *n.* a confection consisting of a hollow cone of puff pastry filled with cream.

**creamie** /'krimi/, *n.* **1.** a cream-coloured animal, esp. a horse. **2.** a quarter-caste aboriginal.

**creaming soda** /krimɪŋ 'soʊdə/, *n.* a soft drink made with carbonated water, variously flavoured but esp. with vanilla. Also, **cream soda, creamy soda.**

**cream of tartar** *n.* purified and crystallised potassium bitartrate, used as a baking powder ingredient, etc. See **tartar** (def. 3).

**cream puff** /'krim pʌf/, *n.* **1.** a confection of choux pastry with a cream filling. **2.** *Colloq.* a weak person; an effeminate person; a cissy.

**cream puff pastry,** *n.* →**choux pastry.**

**cream sauce** /krim 'sɔs/, *n.* a sauce made of cream or milk, flour, butter, etc.

**cream sherry** /– 'ʃɛri/, *n.* a rich sweet sherry.

**creamy** /'krimi/, *adj.,* **-mier, -miest. 1.** containing cream. **2.** resembling cream, as in appearance or consistency; soft and smooth. **3.** cream-coloured. – **creaminess,** *n.*

**creance** /'kriəns/, *n.* (in falconry) a cord secured to the leg of a hawk to prevent escape during training. [ME, from F *créance*]

**crease**[1] /kris/, *n., v.,* **creased, creasing.** *–n.* **1.** a line or mark produced in anything by folding; a fold; a ridge; a furrow. **2.** the sharp vertical ridge in the front and at the back of each leg of a pair of trousers, produced by pressing. **3.** *Cricket.* one of three lines marked near each wicket: **a. bowling crease,** beyond which the bowler may not advance when bowling. **b. popping crease,** at which the batsman stands when batting. **c. return crease,** marking the sideways limits of the bowler at each side of the bowling crease. **4.** *Ice Hockey.* a small rectangular area in front of each goal, into which an attacking player may skate only if he has the puck, if the puck is already within the area, or if the goalkeeper is absent. **5.** *Lacrosse.* a semicircle in front of each goal, which no attacking player may enter unless the ball is already within the area. *–v.t.* **6.** to make a crease or creases in or on; wrinkle. **7.** *Colloq.* to strike (a person). *–v.i.* **8.** to become creased. [orig. unknown] – **creaser,** *n.* – **creasy,** *adj.*

**crease**[2] /kris/, *n.* →**kris.**

**crease-resistant** /'kris-rəˌzɪstənt/, *adj.* (of a fabric) able to resist normal wrinkling.

**create** /kri'eɪt/, *v.,* **-ated, -ating,** *adj.* *–v.t.* **1.** to bring into being; cause to exist; produce. **2.** to evolve from one's own thought or imagination. **3.** to be the first to represent (a part or role). **4.** to make by investing with new character or functions; constitute; appoint: *to create a peer.* **5.** to be the cause or occasion of; give rise to. *–v.i.* **6.** to be engaged, often ostentatiously, in creating something, as a work of art: *the painter was creating while we stood by.* **7.** *Colloq.* to make a fuss or an uproar. [L *creātus,* pp. of *creāre* bring into being]

**creatine** /'kriətən/, *n.* an amino acid, a major reserve of chemical energy in muscle. $NH_2C(=NH)NH^+(CH_3)CH_2COO^-$, found mainly in combined form as creatine phosphate, present in the tissues of all vertebrates and some invertebrates.

**creation** /kri'eɪʃən/, *n.* **1.** the act of creating. **2.** the fact of being created. **3. the Creation,** the original bringing into existence of the universe by the Deity. **4.** that which is created. **5.** the world; universe. **6.** creatures collectively. **7.** a product of inventive ingenuity; an original work, esp. of the imaginative faculty. **8.** a strikingly fashionable garment or hat, distinguished by its unique styling. – **creational,** *adj.*

**creationism** /kri'eɪʃənɪzəm/, *n.* **1.** the doctrine that God immediately creates out of nothing a new human soul for each individual born. Cf. **traducianism. 2.** the doctrine that matter and all things were created, substantially as they now exist, by the fiat of an omnipotent Creator, and not gradually evolved or developed. – **creationist,** *n.*

**creative** /kri'eɪtɪv/, *adj.* **1.** having the quality or power of creating. **2.** resulting from originality of thought or expression. **3.** originative; productive (fol. by *of*). – **creatively,** *adv.* – **creativeness,** *n.*

**creative leisure centre,** *n.* a place where people spend their leisure time in productive pursuits, as painting, gymnastics, pottery, etc. Also, **leisure centre.**

**creativity** /kriə'tɪvəti/, *n.* **1.** the state or quality of being creative. **2.** creative ability.

**creator** /kri'eɪtə/, *n.* **1.** one who or that which creates. **2. the**

**Creator,** God. – **creatorship,** *n.*

**creatural** /ˈkritʃərəl/, *adj.* of, pertaining to, or of the nature of a creature or creatures.

**creature** /ˈkritʃə/, *n.* **1.** anything created, animate or inanimate. **2.** an animate being. **3.** an animal, as distinct from man. **4.** a human being (often used in contempt, commiseration, or endearment). **5.** a person owing his rise and fortune to another, or subject to the will or influence of another. [ME, from OF, from LL *creātūra* a thing created]

**creature comforts** /ˈ– kʌmfəts/, *n.pl.* material things which minister to bodily comfort; esp. food, alcoholic drink, etc.

**creaturely** /ˈkritʃəli/, *adj.* →**creatural.**

**creche** /kreɪʃ, krɛʃ/, *n.* **1.** a nursery where children are cared for while their mothers work. **2.** a home for foundlings. **3.** a tableau of Mary, Joseph, and others round the crib of Jesus in the stable at Bethlehem, often built for display at Christmas. Also, **crèche.** [F, from OHG *kripja* crib]

**credence** /ˈkridns/, *n.* **1.** belief: *to give credence to a statement.* **2.** something giving a claim to belief or confidence: *letter of credence.* **3.** Also, **credence table, credenza. a.** a small side table, shelf, or niche for holding articles used in the Eucharist service. **b.** a sideboard. [ME, from ML *crēdentia* belief, credit, sideboard, from L *crēdens,* ppr., believing]

**credendum** /krəˈdɛndəm/, *n., pl.* **-da** /-də/. that which is to be believed; an article of faith. [L, neut. of *crēdendus,* gerundive of *crēdere* believe]

**credent** /ˈkridnt/, *adj.* **1.** believing. **2.** *Obs.* credible.

**credential** /krəˈdɛnʃəl/, *n.* **1.** that which gives a title to belief or confidence. **2.** (*usu. pl.*) a letter or other testimonial attesting the bearer's right to confidence or authority. –*adj.* **3.** giving a title to belief or confidence. [ML *crēdentia* belief + -AL[1]]

**credibility gap** /krɛdəˈbɪləti gæp/, *n.* the difference between what is said, as by a politician, and what is actually meant or done.

**credible** /ˈkrɛdəbəl/, *adj.* **1.** capable of being believed; believable. **2.** worthy of belief or confidence; trustworthy. [ME, from L *crēdibilis*] – **credibility, credibleness,** *n.* – **credibly,** *adv.*

**credit** /ˈkrɛdət/, *n.* **1.** belief; trust. **2.** influence or authority resulting from the confidence of others or from one's reputation. **3.** trustworthiness; credibility. **4.** repute; reputation. **5.** favourable estimation. **6.** commendation or honour given for some action, quality, etc. **7.** a source of commendation or honour. **8.** the ascription or acknowledgment of something as due or properly attributable to a person, etc. **9.** (*pl.*) a list, appearing at the beginning or end of a film, which shows the names of those who have been associated with its production. **10. a.** official acceptance and recording of the work of a student in a particular course of study. **b.** a unit of a curriculum (short for **credit hour**): *he took the course for four credits.* **11.** time allowed for payment for goods, etc., obtained on trust. **12.** confidence in a purchaser's ability and intention to pay, displayed by entrusting him with goods, etc., without immediate payment. **13.** reputation of solvency and probity, entitling a person to be trusted in buying or borrowing. **14.** power to buy or borrow on trust. **15.** a sum of money due to a person; anything valuable standing on the credit side of an account. **16.** the balance in one's favour in an account. **17.** *Bookkeeping.* **a.** the acknowledgment or an entry of payment or value received, in an account. **b.** the side (right-hand) of an account on which such entries are made (opposed to *debit*). **c.** an entry, or the total shown, on the credit side. **18.** any deposit or sum against which one may draw. **19. on credit,** by deferred payment. **20. do someone credit.** Also, **do credit to someone.** to be a source of honour or distinction to someone. –*v.t.* **21.** to believe; put confidence in; trust; have faith in. **22.** to reflect credit upon; do credit to; give reputation or honour to. **23.** to ascribe (something) to a person, etc.; make ascription of something to (a person, etc.) (fol. by *with*). **24. a.** *Bookkeeping.* to enter upon the credit side of an account; give credit for or to. **b.** to give the benefit of such an entry to (a person, etc.) **25.** to award educational credits to: *credited with three points in history.* [F, from It. *credito,* from L *creditus,* pp., believed]

**creditable** /ˈkrɛdətəbəl/, *adj.* bringing credit, honour, reputation, or esteem. – **creditableness,** *n.* – **creditably,** *adv.*

**credit agency** /ˈkrɛdət ˌeɪdʒənsi/, *n.* an organisation that investigates on behalf of a client the credit worthiness of the client's prospective customers.

**credit card** /ˈ– kad/, *n.* a card which identifies the holder as entitled to obtain without payment of cash, goods, food, services, etc. which are then charged to the holder's account. Also, **credit plate.**

**credit foncier** /– ˈfɒnsiə/, *n.* a method of repayment of a long-term housing loan which is repayed by equal monthly instalments comprising principal and interest.

**credit insurance** /– ɪnˈʃɔrəns/, *n.* insurance coverage designed to minimise loss to creditors when a debtor defaults.

**credit life insurance,** *n.* insurance guaranteeing payment of the unpaid portion of a loan, in the event of the debtor's death.

**credit note** /ˈkrɛdət noʊt/, *n.* a note issued by a trader showing the amount of credit due to a customer, usu. for goods to be taken in lieu of those returned.

**creditor** /ˈkrɛdətə/, *n.* **1.** one who gives credit in business transactions. **2.** one to whom money is due (opposed to *debtor*). **3.** *Bookkeeping.* →**credit** (def. 17b, c).

**credit rating** /ˈkrɛdət reɪtɪŋ/, *n.* an estimation of the extent to which a customer can be granted credit, usu. determined by a credit agency.

**credit slip** /ˈ– slɪp/, *n.* a form completed and signed by a person when paying into the credit of an account.

**credit squeeze** /ˈ– skwiz/, *n.* **1.** restriction by a government of the amount of credit available to borrowers. **2.** the period during which the restrictions are in operation.

**credit standing** /ˈ– stændɪŋ/, *n.* reputation for meeting financial obligations.

**credit transfer** /ˈ– trænsfɜ/, *n.* a system by which credit is paid into a bank for transfer to the payee's account at another bank or branch.

**credit union** /ˈ– junjən/, *n.* a financial organisation for receiving and lending money, usu. formed by workers in some industry or at some place of employment.

**credo** /ˈkreɪdoʊ, ˈkridoʊ/, *n., pl.* **-dos. 1.** any creed or formula of belief. **2.** the Apostles' or the Nicene Creed. **3.** a musical setting of the creed, usu. of the Nicene Creed. [L: I believe, the first word of the Apostles' and the Nicene Creeds in Latin]

**credulity** /krəˈdjuləti/, *n.* a disposition, arising from weakness or ignorance, to believe too readily. [late ME *credulite,* from L *crēdulitas*]

**credulous** /ˈkrɛdʒələs/, *adj.* **1.** ready or disposed to believe, esp. on weak or insufficient evidence. **2.** marked by or arising from credulity. [L *crēdulus* apt to believe] – **credulously,** *adv.* – **credulousness,** *n.*

**creed** /krid/, *n.* **1.** any system of belief or of opinion. **2.** an accepted system of religious belief. **3.** any formula of religious belief, as of a denomination. **4.** the Apostles' Creed. **5.** an authoritative formulated statement of the chief articles of Christian belief, as the Apostles', the Nicene, or the Athanasian Creed. [ME *crede,* OE *crēda,* from L *crēdo* I believe. See CREDO] – **creedal, credal,** *adj.* – **creedless,** *adj.*

**creek** /krik/, *n.* **1.** small stream, as a branch of a river, (originally of unexplored inlets, as def. 2). **2.** a narrow recess in the shore of the sea; a small inlet or bay. **3.** *Obs.* a narrow or winding passage. **4. up the creek** or **up shit creek** *Colloq.* in a predicament; in trouble. [ME *creke,* apparently northern var. of *crike* (short vowel), from Scand.: cf. Icel. *kriki* crack, nook]

**creeker** /ˈkrikə/, *n.* a racehorse which runs well on a sand-track.

**creel** /kril/, *n.* **1.** a wickerwork basket, esp. one used by anglers for holding fish. **2.** a wickerwork trap to catch fish, lobsters, etc. **3.** a framework, esp. one for holding bobbins in a spinning machine. [ME *crele,* ? from F *creil,* from L *crātis* wickerwork. Cf. GRILLE]

**creep** /krip/, *v.,* **crept, creeping** *n.,* –*v.i.* **1.** to move with the body close to the ground, as a reptile or an insect. **2.** to move slowly, imperceptibly, or stealthily. **3.** to enter undetected; to sneak up behind. **4.** to move or behave timidly or servilely. **5.** to move along very slowly, as a motor car in heavy traffic. **6.** to have a sensation as of something creeping over the skin. **7.** to grow along the ground, a wall, etc., as a plant, esp. a creeper (def. 2). **8.** *Naut.* to grapple (usu. fol. by *for*). **9. make (one's) flesh creep,** to frighten; repel. *–n.* **10.** the act of creeping. **11.** (*usu. pl.*) a sensation as of something creeping over the skin. **12.** the slow movement of concrete due to chemical change in concrete over time. **13.** *Engineering.* the deformation of metal caused by heat or stress. **14.** *Geol.* the slow and imperceptible downslope movement of earth or rock. **15.** *Colloq.* an unpleasant, obnoxious, or insignificant person. [ME *crepen,* OE *crēopan,* c. D *kruipen*]

**creeper** /'kripə/, *n.* **1.** one who or that which creeps. **2.** *Bot.* a plant which grows upon or just beneath the surface of the ground, or upon any other surface, sending out rootlets from the stem, as ivy and couch. **3.** →**treecreeper.** **4.** a grappling device for dragging a river, etc. **5.** a spiked piece of iron worn on the heel of the shoe to prevent slipping on ice, etc. **6.** (*pl.*) *Colloq.* thick rubber-soled shoes. **7.** *Cricket.* a ball that moves along the ground instead of bouncing as expected.

**creep feeder** /'krɪp fidə/, *n.* an animal feeding pen constructed to admit young animals while excluding the larger ones.

**creep-graze** /'krip-greɪz/, *v.t.* to allow lambs, or other young, access to fresh pastures while preventing their mothers from grazing there by means of a temporary barrier. **– creep-grazing,** *n.*

**creeping barrage** /kripɪŋ 'bæraʒ/, *n.* a barrage of slowly advancing artillery fire.

**creeping bent grass,** *n.* a perennial stoloniferous grass, *Agrostis stolonifera,* used for fine lawns.

**creeping Jesus** /kripɪŋ 'dʒizəz/, *n. Colloq.* a slinking, fawning person.

**creeping oxalis** /kripɪŋ ɒk'saləs/, *n.* →**yellow wood sorrel.**

**creeping red fescue,** *n.* a variety of red fescue, used extensively for lawns. See **fescue.**

**creeping thistle** /kripɪŋ 'θɪsəl/, *n.* a perennial dioecious herb, *Cirsium arvense,* family Compositae, widespread in Europe and Asia; a naturalised troublesome weed in North America.

**creepy** /'kripi/, *adj.,* **-pier, -piest.** **1.** that creeps, as an insect. **2.** having or causing a creeping sensation of the skin, as from horror: *a creepy silence.* **3.** *Colloq.* (of a person) unpleasant, obnoxious or insignificant. **– creepiness,** *n.*

**creepy-crawly** /kripi-'krɔli/, *Colloq.* *–n.* **1.** an insect. *–adj.* **2.** having or causing a creeping sensation.

**creese** /kris/, *n.* →**kris.**

**cremate** /krə'meɪt/, *v.t.,* **-mated, -mating.** **1.** to reduce (a corpse) to ashes by fire. **2.** to consume by fire; burn. [L *cremātus,* pp., consumed by fire] **– cremation,** *n.*

**cremationist** /krə'meɪʃənəst/, *n.* one who advocates cremation instead of burial of the dead.

**cremator** /krə'meɪtə/, *n.* **1.** one who cremates. **2.** a furnace for cremating corpses. **3.** an incinerator for rubbish, etc. [LL]

**crematorium** /kremə'tɔriəm/, *n.* an establishment for cremating dead bodies.

**crematory** /'kremətri, -ətəri/, *adj., n., pl.* **-ries.** *–adj.* **1.** of or pertaining to cremation. *–n.* **2.** →**crematorium.**

**crème** /krɛm/, *n.* **1.** cream. **2.** one of various liqueurs. [F]

**crème brûlée** /krɛm 'bruleɪ/, *n.* a rich cream custard topped with caramelised sugar. [F: burnt cream]

**crème caramel** /– kærə'mɛl/, *n.* a dessert of baked custard topped with a sauce of caramel. Also, **cream caramel.** [F]

**crème de la crème** /krɛm də la 'krɛm/, *n.* the very best; the flower; the choicest part.

**crème de menthe** /krɛm də 'mɒnθ/, *n.* liqueur flavoured with mint.

**crenate** /'krineɪt/, *adj.* having the margin notched or scalloped so as to form rounded teeth, as a leaf. Also, **crenated.** [NL *crēnātus,* from *crēna* notch] **– crenately,** *adv.*

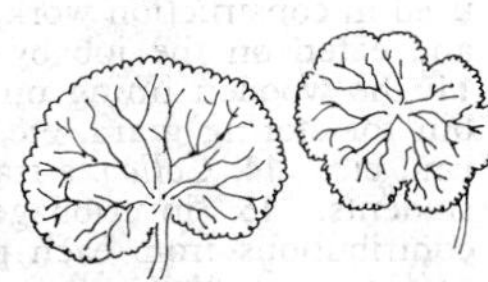
crenate and doubly crenate leaves

**crenation** /krə'neɪʃən/, *n.* **1.** a rounded projection or tooth, as on the margin of a leaf. **2.** crenate state.

**crenature** /'krɛnətjʊə, 'krinə-/, *n.* **1.** a rounded tooth as of a crenate leaf. **2.** a notch between teeth.

**crenel** /'krɛnəl/, *n., v.,* **-elled, -elling,** or (*U.S.*) **-eled, -eling.** *–n.* **1.** one of the open spaces between the merlons of a battlement. **2.** a crenature. *–v.t.* **3.** to crenellate. Also, **crenelle.** [late ME, from MF, diminutive of *cren* notch. See CRENULATE]

**crenellate** /'krɛnəleɪt/, *v.t.,* **-lated, -lating.** **1.** to furnish with crenels or battlements. **2.** *Archit.* to form with square indentations as a moulding. Also, *U.S.,* **crenelate.** [F *créneler* (from *crenel,* diminutive of *cren* notch) + -ATE[1]] **– crenellated,** *adj.*

**crenellation** /krɛnə'leɪʃən/, *n.* **1.** the act of crenellating. **2.** the state of being crenellated. **3.** a battlement. **4.** a notch; indentation. Also, *U.S.,* **crenelation.**

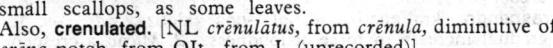

crenellated moulding

**crenelle** /krə'nɛl/, *n., v.t.,* **-nelled, -nelling.** →**crenel.**

**crenulate** /'krɛnjəleɪt, -lət/, *adj.* having the edge cut into very small scallops, as some leaves. Also, **crenulated.** [NL *crēnulātus,* from *crēnula,* diminutive of *crēna* notch, from OIt., from L (unrecorded)]

**crenulation** /krɛnjə'leɪʃən/, *n.* **1.** a minute crenation. **2.** crenulate state.

**creodont** /'kriədɒnt/, *n.* any of the Creodonta, a group of primitive carnivorous mammals, characterised by small brains. Certain creodonts are regarded as the ancestors of the modern carnivores. [NL *Creodonta* (pl.), from Gk *kréas* flesh + *odoús* tooth]

**Creole** /'krioul/, *n.* **1.** (in the West Indies and Spanish America) one born in the region but of European, usu. Spanish, ancestry. **2.** (in Louisiana and elsewhere) a person born in the region but of French ancestry. **3.** a person born in a place but of foreign ancestry, as distinguished from the aborigines and half-breeds. **4.** the French language of Louisiana, esp. that spoken by white persons in New Orleans. **5.** (*l.c.*) a pidgin which has become the primary language of a speech community. **6.** (*l.c.*) a person of mixed Creole and Negro ancestry speaking a form of French or Spanish. **7.** (*l.c.*) a native-born Negro, as distinguished from a Negro brought from Africa. *–adj.* **8.** of, pertaining to, or characteristic of a Creole or the Creoles. **9.** (*l.c.*) of, belonging to, or characteristic of the Creoles: *a creole dialect, creole French.* **10.** bred or growing in a country, but of foreign origin, as an animal or plant. **11.** (*l.c.*) **a.** denoting a savoury dish with a garnish of rice, sweet peppers cooked in oil, and tomatoes. **b.** denoting a sweet dish containing rice. [F, from Sp. *criollo* native to the locality, from Pg. *crioulo,* from *criar* bring up, from L *creāre* create]

**creolised** /'kriəlaɪzd/, *adj.* (of a language) having become a pidgin and then passed into use as a community's native language. Also, **creolized.**

**creosol** /'kriəsɒl/, *n.* a colourless oily liquid, $C_8H_{10}O_2$, with an agreeable smell and burning taste, resembling carbolic acid; obtained from wood tar and guaiacum resin. [CREOS(OTE) + -OL[2]]

**creosote** /'kriəsout/, *n., v.,* **-soted, -soting.** *–n.* **1.** an oily liquid with a burning taste and a penetrating smell, obtained by the distillation of wood tar, and used as a preservative and antiseptic. **2.** →**coal-tar creosote.** *–v.t.* **3.** to treat with creosote. [*creo-* (combining form representing Gk *kréas* flesh) + Gk *sōtḗr* saviour] **– creosotic** /kriə'sɒtɪk/, *adj.*

**creosote bush** /'– bʊʃ/, *n.* an evergreen shrub, *Larrea mexicana,* of northern Mexico and adjacent regions, bearing resinous foliage with a strong smell of creosote.

**crepe** /kreɪp/, *n., v.,* **creped, creping.** *–n.* **1.** a thin, light fabric of silk, cotton, or other fibre, with a finely crinkled or ridged surface. **2.** Also, **crepe paper.** thin paper wrinkled to resemble crepe. **3.** a thin pancake. **4.** a black (or white) silk fabric, used for mourning veils, trimmings, etc. **5.** a band or piece of this material, as for a token of mourning. *–v.t.* **6.** to cover, clothe, or drape with crepe. Also, **crêpe, crape.** [F, from L *crispus* curled]

**crepe de Chine** /– də ˈʃin/, *n.* a light, soft silk or rayon fabric with minute surface irregularities. [F: China crepe]

**crepe hair** /– ˈhɛə/, *n.* false hair, usu. plaited, used in theatrical make-up for beards, etc.

**crepe myrtle** /– ˈmɜtl/, *n.* any cultivated shrub of the genus *Lagerstroemia,* esp. *L. indica* from China, the many horticultural selections of which give clusters of blooms in a variety of shades, esp. pink.

**crepe rubber** /– ˈrʌbə/, *n.* a type of crude rubber, pressed into corrugated sheets, used esp. for making shoe soles.

**crepe suzette** /– suˈzɛt/, *n.* a thin dessert pancake, usu. rolled and served with hot orange or tangerine sauce, often flavoured with curaçao or other liqueurs.

**crepitate** /ˈkrɛpəteɪt/, *v.i.,* **-tated, -tating.** to make a crackling sound; crackle; rattle. [L *crepitātus,* pp.] – **crepitation,** *n.*

**crept** /krɛpt/, *v.* past tense and past participle of **creep.**

**crepuscular** /krəˈpʌskjələ/, *adj.* **1.** of, pertaining to, or resembling twilight; dim; indistinct. **2.** *Zool.* appearing or flying in the twilight.

**crepuscule** /ˈkrɛpəskjul/, *n.* twilight; dusk. [F, from L *crepusculum*]

**cres.,** **1.** *Music.* →**crescendo** (def. 3). **2.** →**crescent.** Also, **cresc.**

**crescendo** /krəˈʃɛndo/, *n., pl.* **-dos** /ˈdoʊz/, *adj.* *–n.* **1.** a gradual increase in force or loudness. **2.** *Music.* a crescendo passage. *–adj.* **3.** gradually increasing in force or loudness. [It., ppr. of *crescere* increase, from L *crescere*]

**crescent** /ˈkrɛsənt, ˈkrɛzənt/, *n.* **1. a.** the biconvex figure of the moon in its first quarter, or the similar figure of the moon in its last quarter, resembling a bow terminating in points. **b.** any of the similar aspects of Venus or Mercury when less than half of the illuminated hemisphere can be seen. **2.** a representation of this. **3.** the emblem of the Turkish Empire. **4.** the symbol of Turkish or Islamic power. **5.** any crescent-shaped object, as a roll of bread. **6.** *U.S.* a percussion instrument used in military bands, consisting of a crescent-shaped metal plate hung with a set of little bells. **7.** a curved street. *–adj.* **8.** shaped like the moon in its first quarter. **9.** increasing; growing. [L *crescens,* ppr., increasing; replacing ME *cressant,* from OF *creissant* (later *croissant*), ppr.]

crescent (def. 1)

**crescograph** /ˈkrɛskəgræf/, *n.* an instrument which makes perceptible the growth of plants. [L *crescere* to grow + -GRAPH]

**cresol** /ˈkrisɒl/, *n.* any of three isomeric methyl phenols, $CH_3C_6H_4OH$, occurring in coal tar and wood tar; used as disinfectants, wood preservatives as of railway sleepers, etc., and in the manufacture of dyestuffs and perfumes.

**cress** /krɛs/, *n.* **1.** any of various plants of the mustard family with pungent-tasting leaves, often used for salad and as a garnish, esp. the **garden cress,** *Lepidium sativum.* **2.** any of various similar plants. [ME and OE *cresse,* c. G *Kresse*]

**cresset** /ˈkrɛsət/, *n.* a metal cup often mounted on a pole or suspended from above, containing oil, pitch, etc., which is burnt for light or as a beacon. [ME, from OF]

**crest** /krɛst/, *n.* **1.** a tuft or other natural growth of the top of an animal's head, as the comb of a cock. **2.** anything resembling or suggesting such a tuft. **3.** the ridge of the neck of a horse, dog, etc. **4.** the mane growing from this ridge. **5.** a plume or other ornament on the top of a helmet. **6.** a helmet. **7.** the apex of a helmet. **8.** *Her.* a figure borne above the escutcheon in a coat of arms, and also used separately as a distinguishing device. **9.** the head or top of anything. **10.** the highest part of a hill or mountain range. **11.** a ridge or ridgelike formation. **12.** *Anat.* a ridge along the surface of a bone. **13.** the foamy top of a wave. **14.** the highest or best of the kind. **15.** pride; high spirit; courage; daring. **16.** *Archit.* a cresting. *–v.t.* **17.** to furnish with a crest. **18.** to serve as a crest for; crown or top. **19.** to reach the crest or summit of (a hill, advertising campaign, etc.). *–v.i.* **20.** to form or rise into a crest, as a wave. [ME *creste,* from OF, from L *crista* tuft] – **crested,** *adj.* – **crestless,** *adj.*

**crested flycatcher** /krɛstəd ˈflaɪkætʃə/, *n.* a North American flycatcher, *Myiarchus crinitus,* known for its use of cast-off snakeskin as nest material.

**crested tern** /krɛstəd ˈtɜn/, *n.* a tern, *Sterna bergii,* with white underparts, grey back wings and tail, and erectile black crown and nape, found around the coast of Australia, and throughout the Indian and Pacific Oceans and south-east Asia.

crested tern

**crested wattle** /krɛstəd ˈwɒtl/, *n.* a small tree, *Albizia lophantha,* native to western Australia, naturalised widely elsewhere in Australia.

**crestfallen** /ˈkrɛstfɔlən/, *adj.* **1.** dejected; dispirited; depressed. **2.** with drooping crest. – **crestfallenly,** *adv.* – **crestfallenness,** *n.*

**cresting** /ˈkrɛstɪŋ/, *n.* the ornamental part which surmounts a roof ridge, wall, etc.

**crest-tailed marsupial mouse,** *n.* a small, carnivorous mouse-like marsupial, *Dasycercus cristicauda,* of the arid Australian interior, having a terminal crest of black hairs on the upper surface of the tail; mulgara; Canning's little dog.

**cretaceous** /krəˈteɪʃəs/, *adj.* **1.** of the nature of, resembling, or containing chalk. **2.** (*cap.*) *Geol.* the third and latest of the periods included in the Mesozoic era. *–n.* **3.** *Geol.* the system of strata deposited during the cretaceous period. [L *crētāceus* chalklike]

**cretin** /ˈkrɛtn/, *n.* **1.** a person afflicted with cretinism. **2.** *Colloq.* a fool; a stupid person. [F, from d. F. *crestin,* from L *Christiānus* Christian] – **cretinous,** *adj.*

**cretinism** /ˈkrɛtənɪzəm/, *n.* a chronic disease, due to absence or deficiency of the normal thyroid secretion, characterised by physical deformity (often with goitre), dwarfism, and idiocy.

**cretonne** /krəˈtɒn/, *n.* a heavy cotton material in printed designs, used esp. for curtains and loose covers. [F, from *Creton,* village in Normandy]

**crevasse** /krəˈvæs/, *n., v.,* **-vassed, -vassing.** *–n.* **1.** a fissure or deep cleft in the ice of a glacier. *–v.t.* **2.** to fissure with crevasses. [F. See CREVICE]

**crevice** /ˈkrɛvəs/, *n.* a crack forming an opening; a cleft; a rift; a fissure. [ME *crevace,* from OF, from *crever* burst, from L *crepāre* crack] – **creviced,** *adj.*

**crew**[1] /kru/, *n.* **1.** a group of persons engaged upon a particular work; a gang. **2. a.** the company of men who man a ship or boat. **b.** the common sailors of a ship's company. **c.** a particular section of a ship's company. **3.** the persons manning an aircraft in flight. **4.** (*oft. derog.*) a company; crowd. *–v.i.* **5.** to act as a member of a crew. *–v.t.* **6.** to provide with a crew. [late ME *crue,* from ONF *creue* increase, from L *crescere* grow]

**crew**[2] /kru/, *v.* past tense of **crow**[2].

**crew cut** /ˈ– kʌt/, *n.* a very closely cropped haircut.

**crewel** /ˈkruəl/, *n.* a fine worsted yarn used for embroidery, etc. [late ME *crule,* of unknown orig.] – **crewelwork,** *n.*

**crew-neck** /ˈkru-nɛk/, *adj.* (of garments) having a plain ribbed neckband fitting closely around the neck.

**crib** /krɪb/, *n., v.,* **cribbed, cribbing.** *–n.* **1.** a child's bed, usu. oval, and often of wickerwork, lined and decorated with muslin, etc. **2.** a stall or pen for cattle. **3.** a rack or manger for fodder, as in a stable or house for cattle. **4.** a tableau of Mary, Joseph, and the others grouped round the holy crib in Bethlehem, often displayed at Christmas. **5.** a small house. **6.** a small room. **7.** any confined space. **8.** a wicker basket. **9.** any of various frameworks, as of logs or timber, used in construction work. **10.** a meal, packed in a container, and eaten on the job by a miner, construction worker, etc. **11.** the wooden lining on the inside of a mine shaft. **12.** a bin for storing grain, etc. **13.** *Colloq.* a petty theft, plagiarism, etc. **14.** *Colloq.* a translation or other illicit aid used by students. **15.** (in cribbage) a set of cards made up by equal contributions from each player's hand, and belonging to the dealer. *–v.t.* **16.** to confine in, or as in, a crib. **17.** to provide with a crib or cribs. **18.** to line with timber or planking. **19.** *Colloq.* to pilfer or steal, as a passage from an author. *–v.i.* **20.** *Colloq.* to use a crib. **21.** →**crib-bite.** [ME *cribbe,* OE *crib(b)*, c. G *Krippe*]

**cribbage** /ˈkrɪbɪdʒ/, *n.* a game at cards, basically for two, but also played by three, or four players, a characteristic feature of which is the crib. [CRIB + -AGE]

**cribbage board** /ˈ– bɔd/, *n.* a board with numbered holes in rows, into which pegs may be inserted to indicate the score in a cribbage game.

**cribber** /ˈkrɪbə/, *n.* **1.** one who cribs. **2.** a horse that practises cribbing.

**cribbing** /ˈkrɪbɪŋ/, *n.* **1.** Also, **crib-biting.** wind-sucking by horses, an injurious habit in which the animal bites his manger and in the process swallows air. **2.** *Mining.* **a.** timber lining, closely spaced, as in a shaft, etc. **b.** pieces of timber for lining a shaft, etc.

**crib-bite** /ˈkrɪb-baɪt/, *v.i.*, **-bit, -bitten** or **-bit, -biting.** to practise cribbing, as a horse. – **crib-biter,** *n.*

**cribriform** /ˈkrɪbrifɔm/, *adj.* sievelike. Also, **cribrous** /ˈkrɪbrəs/. [L *crībrum* sieve + -I- + -FORM]

**crib room** /ˈkrɪb rum/, *n.* a room set aside for employees in which they can store their lunch and other belongings.

**crib-tin** /ˈkrɪb-tɪn/, *n. N.Z.* →**lunch box.**

**cribwork** /ˈkrɪbwɜk/, *n.* structural work used in foundations in loose soil, etc., consisting of layers of logs or beams one above another, with the logs of each layer at right angles to those below.

**crick** /krɪk/, *n.* **1.** a sharp, painful spasm of the muscles, as of the neck or back, making it difficult to move the part. –*v.t.* **2.** to give a crick or wrench to (the neck, etc.). [orig. uncert.]

**cricket**[1] /ˈkrɪkət/, *n.* any of the orthopterous insects comprising the family Gryllidae, characterised by their long antennae, ability to leap, and the ability of the males to produce shrill sounds by friction of their leathery forewings. [ME *criket,* from OF *criquet;* imitative]

**cricket**[2] /ˈkrɪkət/, *n.* **1.** an outdoor game played with ball, bats, and wickets, by two sides of eleven players each. **2.** *Colloq.* fair play: *his behaviour was not cricket.* –*v.i.* **3.** to play cricket. [cf. OF *criquet* stick] – **cricketer,** *n.*

**cricket ball** /ˈ– bɔl/, *n.* a ball specifically made for cricket (usu. of leather sewn around a hard resilient cork-like centre; now often made of synthetic material, as plastic).

**cricko** /ˈkrɪkoʊ/, *n.* →**vigoro.**

**cricoid** /ˈkraɪkɔɪd/, *adj.* **1.** having the shape of a seal ring, as a cartilage at the lower part of the larynx. –*n.* **2.** the cricoid cartilage. [Gk *krikoeidḗs* ring-shaped]

**cri de coeur** /kri də ˈkɜ/, *n.* a cry from the heart. [F]

**crier** /ˈkraɪə/, *n.* **1.** one who cries. **2.** a court or town official who makes public announcements. **3.** one who cries goods for sale in the streets; a hawker.

**crikey** /ˈkraɪki/, *interj. Colloq.* (an expression of surprise; a mild oath). Also, **cricky, crickey.**

**crim** /krɪm/, *Colloq.* –*n.* **1.** a criminal. –*adj.* **2.** of or pertaining to a crime.

**crime** /kraɪm/, *n.* **1.** an act committed or an omission of duty, injurious to the public welfare, for which punishment is prescribed by law, imposed in a judicial proceeding usu. brought in the name of the state. **2.** serious violation of human law: *steeped in crime.* **3.** any offence, esp. one of grave character. **4.** serious wrongdoing; sin. **5.** *Colloq.* a foolish or senseless act: *it's a crime to have to work so hard.* [ME, from OF, from L *crīmen* offence]

**Crimean shirt** /kraɪmiən ˈʃɜt/, *n.* (formerly) a kind of shirt worn in the bush.

**crime of passion,** *n.* a crime committed under the influence of passionate feelings, usu. feelings of sexual jealousy. [translation of F *crime passionel*]

**crime sheet** /ˈkraɪm ʃit/, *n. Mil.* a list of offences against military law.

**criminal** /ˈkrɪmənəl/, *adj.* **1.** of or pertaining to crime or its punishment: *criminal law.* **2.** of the nature of or involving crime. **3.** guilty of crime. –*n.* **4.** a person guilty or convicted of a crime. [L *crīminālis*] – **criminally,** *adv.*

**criminality** /krɪməˈnæləti/, *n., pl.* **-ties.** **1.** the quality of being criminal. **2.** a criminal act or practice.

**criminate** /ˈkrɪməneɪt/, *v.t.,* **-nated, -nating.** **1.** to charge with a crime. **2.** to incriminate. **3.** to censure (an act, etc.) as criminal; condemn. [L *crīminātus,* pp., accused] – **crimination,** *n.*

**criminative** /ˈkrɪmənətɪv/, *adj.* tending to or involving crimination; accusatory. Also, **criminatory** /ˈkrɪmənətri/.

**Criminol.,** Criminology.

**criminology** /ˌkrɪməˈnɒlədʒi/, *n.* the science dealing with the causes and treatment of crimes and criminals. [L *crīmen* crime + -O- + -LOGY] – **criminological** /krɪmənəˈlɒdʒɪkəl/, *adj.* – **criminologist,** *n.*

**crimmer** /ˈkrɪmə/, *n.* →**krimmer.**

**crimp**[1] /krɪmp/, *v.t.* **1.** to press into small regular folds; frill; corrugate; make wavy. **2.** to curl (hair), esp. with a hot iron. **3.** to bend (leather) into shape. **4.** to gash (the flesh of a live fish or of one just killed) with a knife to make it more crisp when cooked. –*n.* **5.** the act of crimping. **6.** crimped condition or form. **7.** (*usu. pl.*) something crimped, as a lock of hair. **8.** the waviness of wool fibres as naturally grown on sheep. **9.** a crease formed in sheet metal or plate metal to make the material less flexible, or for fastening purposes. [ME *crympe(n),* OE *gecrympan* curl (from *crump* crooked), c. LG *krümpen,* Dan. *krympe* shrink] – **crimper,** *n.*

**crimp**[2] /krɪmp/, *n.* **1.** an agent who procures seamen, soldiers, etc., for service, by inducing, swindling, or coercing them. –*v.t.* **2.** to procure (seamen, soldiers, etc.) by such means. [special use of CRIMP[1]]

**crimping iron** /ˈkrɪmpɪŋ aɪən/, *n.* a heated iron, used to crimp hair or material.

**crimple** /ˈkrɪmpəl/, *v.i., v.t.,* **-pled, -pling.** to wrinkle, crinkle, or curl. [frequentative of CRIMP[1]]

**crimplene** /ˈkrɪmplin/, *n.* a modified polyester filament yarn, used for garments, and noted for its crease-resistant qualities. [Trademark]

**crimpy** /ˈkrɪmpi/, *adj.,* **-pier, -piest.** of a crimped form or appearance.

**crimson** /ˈkrɪmzən/, *adj.* **1.** deep purplish red. **2.** sanguinary. –*n.* **3.** a crimson colour, pigment, or dye. –*v.t.* **4.** to make crimson. –*v.i.* **5.** to become crimson; to blush. [ME *cremesin,* from early It. *cremesino,* from *chermisí,* or from Sp. *cremesin,* from *carmesí;* both from Ar. *qirmizī*]

**cringe** /krɪndʒ/, *v.,* **cringed, cringing,** *n.* –*v.i.* **1.** to shrink, bend, or crouch, esp. from fear or servility; cower. **2.** to fawn. –*n.* **3.** servile or fawning obeisance. [ME *crengen,* from OE *cringan* yield, fall (in battle). See CRINKLE, CRANK[1]] – **cringer,** *n.* – **cringingly,** *adj.*

**cringle** /ˈkrɪŋgəl/, *n.* a ring or eye of rope or the like, esp. on the edge of a sail, usu. made up round a metal thimble or grummet. [LG *kringel,* diminutive of *kring* circle, ring]

cringle

**crinite**[1] /ˈkraɪnaɪt/, *adj.* **1.** hairy. **2.** *Bot., Entomol.* having long hairs, or tufts of long, weak hairs. [L *crīnītus,* pp., provided with hair]

**crinite**[2] /ˈkraɪnaɪt, ˈkrɪnaɪt/, *n.* a fossil crinoid. [Gk *krínon* lily + -ITE[1]]

**crinkle** /ˈkrɪŋkəl/, *v.,* **-kled, -kling,** *n.* –*v.i.* **1.** to wind or turn in and out. **2.** to wrinkle; crimple; ripple. **3.** to make slight, sharp sounds; rustle. –*v.t.* **4.** to cause to wrinkle or rustle. –*n.* **5.** a turn or twist; a wrinkle; a ripple. **6.** a crinkling sound. [ME frequentative of OE *crincan* bend, yield. See CRINGE, CRANK[1]] – **crinkly,** *adj.*

**crinoid** /ˈkraɪnɔɪd, ˈkrɪnɔɪd/, *adj.* **1.** lily-like. –*n.* **2.** one of the Crinoidea, a class of echinoderms with radiating arms usu. borne mouth up on an attached stalk, including the sea-lilies, feather-stars and numerous fossil forms. [Gk *krinoeidḗs* lily-like]

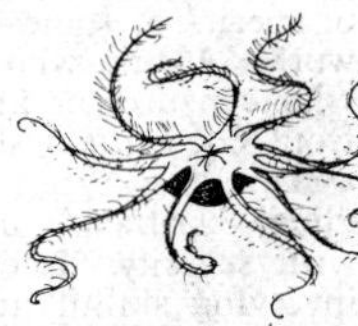

unstalked crinoid (feather-star)

**crinoline** /ˈkrɪnələn/, *n.* **1.** a petticoat of horsehair and flax or other stiff material, formerly worn by women under a full dress skirt. **2.** a hoop skirt. **3.** stiff coarse cotton material for interlining. **4.** netting fitted round a ship as a protection against torpedoes. [F, from It. *crinolino,* from *crino* hair + *lino* thread]

**crinum** /ˈkraɪnəm/, *n.* any plant of the tropical and subtropical genus *Crinum,* comprising tall bulbous plants, usu. with umbels of large, showy flowers. [NL, from Gk *krínon* lily]

**criosphinx** /ˈkraɪəsfɪŋks/, *n., pl.* **-sphinxes, -sphinges** /-sfɪndʒiz/. a sphinx with the head of a ram. [Gk *kriό(s)* ram + *sphinx* sphinx]

**cripes** /kraɪps/, *interj.* (an expression of amazement, disgust, or the like.) [euphemistic var. of *Christ*]

**cripple** /ˈkrɪpəl/, *n., v.,* **-pled, -pling.** *–n.* **1.** one who is partially or wholly deprived of the use of one or more of his limbs; a lame person. **2.** an animal which is disabled by disease, old age, etc., esp. one which cannot keep up with the herd. **3. emotional cripple,** a person who is unable to enter into normal emotional relationships because of inadequate or obsessive responses. *–v.t.* **4.** to make a cripple of; lame. **5.** to disable; impair. [ME *cripel,* OE *crypel;* akin to CREEP] **– crippler,** *n.*

**crisis** /ˈkraɪsəs/, *n., pl.* **-ses** /-siz/. **1.** a decisive or vitally important stage in the course of anything; a turning point; a critical time or occasion: *a political crisis, a business crisis.* **2.** the point in a play or story at which hostile elements are most tensely opposed to each other. **3. a.** the point in the course of a disease at which a decisive change occurs, leading either to recovery or to death. **b.** the change itself. [L, from Gk *krísis* decision]

**crisp** /krɪsp/, *adj.* **1.** hard but easily breakable; brittle: *crisp toast.* **2.** firm and fresh: *crisp leaf of lettuce.* **3.** brisk; sharp; decided: *crisp manner, reply, etc.* **4.** lively; pithy; sparkling: *crisp repartee.* **5.** bracing; invigorating: *crisp air.* **6.** crinkled, wrinkled, or rippled, as skin or water. **7.** in small, stiff or firm curls; curly. *–v.t.* **8.** to make crisp. **9.** to curl. *–v.i.* **10.** to become crisp. *–n.* **11.** a wafer of potato fried, dried, and usu. served cold. **12.** something that is crisp: *burnt to a crisp.* [ME and OE, from L *crispus* curled] **– crisply,** *adv.* **– crispness,** *n.*

**crispate** /ˈkrɪspeɪt, -pət/, *adj.* crisped or curled. Also, **crispated.** [L *crispātus,* pp., curled]

**crispation** /krɪsˈpeɪʃən/, *n.* **1.** the act of crisping or curling. **2.** the state of being crisped. **3.** a slight contraction or undulation.

**crispbread** /ˈkrɪspbrɛd/, *n.* a kind of crisp biscuit, frequently made to be low in kilojoules.

**crisper** /ˈkrɪspə/, *n.* **1.** one who or that which crisps, corrugates, or curls. **2.** the vegetable container of a refrigerator.

**crispy** /ˈkrɪspi/, *adj.,* **-pier, -piest.** **1.** brittle; crisp. **2.** curly or wavy. **3.** brisk.

**crispy-crunchy** /krɪspi-ˈkrʌntʃi/, *adj.* very crisp and crunchy.

**crissal** /ˈkrɪsəl/, *adj.* of or pertaining to the crissum.

**crisscross** /ˈkrɪskrɒs/, *adj.* **1.** in crossing lines; crossed; crossing; marked by crossings. *–n.* **2.** a crisscross mark, pattern, etc. *–adv.* **3.** in a crisscross manner; crosswise. *–v.t.* **4.** to mark with crossing lines. *–v.i.* **5.** to form crossing lines. [var. of CHRISTCROSS]

**crissum** /ˈkrɪsəm/, *n., pl.* **crissa** /ˈkrɪsə/. **1.** the region surrounding the cloacal opening beneath the tail of a bird. **2.** the feathers of this region collectively. [NL, from L *crissāre* move the haunches]

**cristate** /ˈkrɪsteɪt/, *adj.* **1.** having a crest; crested. **2.** forming a crest. Also, **cristated.** [L *cristātus,* from *crista* CREST]

**crit** /krɪt/, *n.* a critique. [abbrev.]

**criterion** /kraɪˈtɪəriən/, *n., pl.* **-teria** /-ˈtɪəriə/, **-terions.** a standard of judgment or criticism; an established rule or principle for testing anything. [Gk *kritḗrion* test, standard]

**critic** /ˈkrɪtɪk/, *n.* **1.** a person skilled in judging the qualities or merits of some class of things, esp. of literary or artistic work. **2.** one who judges captiously or with severity; one who censures or finds fault. **3.** *Obs.* a critique. [L *criticus,* from Gk *kritikós* skilled in judging, decisive, critical (as n., a critic)]

**critical** /ˈkrɪtɪkəl/, *adj.* **1.** inclined to find fault or to judge with severity. **2.** occupied with or skilled in criticism. **3.** involving skilful judgment as to truth, merit, etc.; judicial: *a critical analysis.* **4.** of or pertaining to critics or criticism: *critical essays.* **5.** pertaining to, or of the nature of, a crisis; of decisive importance with respect to the outcome; crucial: *the critical moment.* **6.** involving suspense, risk, peril, etc.; dangerous: *a critical shortage.* **7.** (of an illness, condition, etc.) severe; grave. **8.** *Surfing.* (of a wave) steep and likely to break suddenly. **9.** *Physics.* denoting a constant value, as of temperature, frequency, etc., at which one or more related properties of a substance undergo an abrupt change: *critical pressure.* **10.** *Maths.* indicating a point at which some transition or change takes place. **11.** *Bot. Zool.* (of species) distinguished by slight or questionable differences; uncertain or difficult to determine. **– critically,** *adv.* **– criticalness,** *n.*

**critical altitude** /– ˈæltətʃud/, *n.* the altitude beyond which an aircraft or air-breathing guided missile ceases to perform satisfactorily.

**critical angle** /– ˈæŋgəl/, *n.* **1.** *Optics.* the limiting angle of incidence for total internal reflection. **2.** the angle of attack at which there is a sudden change in the airflow round an aerofoil with subsequent decrease in lift and increase in drag.

**critical apparatus** /– æpəˈratəs/, *n.* the information found in scholarly editions of literary texts, usu. in footnotes, concerning variant texts and interpretations.

**critical constants** /– ˈkɒnstənts/, *n.pl.* the critical temperature, pressure, density, and volume of a substance.

**critical damping** /– ˈdæmpɪŋ/, *n.* damping such that a system reaches equilibrium after an initial displacement in the shortest possible time.

**critical mass** /– ˈmæs/, *n.* the minimum quantity of fissile material necessary for a chain-reaction to take place.

**critical-path analysis** /ˌkrɪtɪkəl-paθ əˈnæləsəs/, *n.* a mathematical method which yields the minimum solution to a problem, given a set of constraints, as logistics of supply, organisation of a factory, production line, etc.

**critical philosophy** /ˌkrɪtɪkəl fəˈlɒsəfi/, *n.* the mature philosophy of Kant, based on a critical examination of the faculty of knowledge.

**critical pressure** /– ˈprɛʃə/, *n.* the pressure of the saturated vapour of a substance at the critical temperature.

**critical state** /– ˈsteɪt/, *n.* the state of a pure stable substance in which two of its phases exist at an identical temperature, pressure and volume.

**critical temperature** /– ˈtɛmprətʃə/, *n.* **1.** *Physics.* (of a gas) the temperature above which a gas cannot be liquefied by pressure alone. **2.** *Metall.* **a.** the highest temperature at which it is possible to separate substances into two fluid phases (the vapour phase and the liquid phase). **b.** the transition temperature of a solid from one allotropic form to another. **3.** Also, **critical point.** the temperature at which magnetic materials lose their magnetic properties.

**critical velocity** /– vəˈlɒsəti/, *n.* the velocity at which the flow of a fluid ceases to be streamline and becomes turbulent.

**critical volume** /– ˈvɒljum/, *n.* the volume occupied by one mole of a substance while in a critical state.

**criticise** /ˈkrɪtəsaɪz/, *v.,* **-cised, -cising.** *–v.i.* **1.** to make judgments as to merits and faults. **2.** to find fault. *–v.t.* **3.** to judge or discuss the merits and faults of. **4.** to find fault with. Also, **criticize. – criticisable,** *adj.* **– criticiser,** *n.*

**criticism** /ˈkrɪtəsɪzəm/, *n.* **1.** the act or art of analysing and judging the quality of a literary or artistic work, etc.: *literary criticism.* **2.** the act of passing judgment as to the merits of something. **3.** the act of passing severe judgment; censure; fault-finding. **4.** a critical comment, article, or essay; a critique. **5.** any of various methods of investigating the origin, meaning, etc., of a book of the Bible: *higher criticism, historical criticism.* **6.** any of various methods of investigation with the purpose of establishing an authentic text corresponding as nearly as possible to an author's intended text: *verbal criticism.*

**critique** /krəˈtik, kri-/, *n.* **1.** an article or essay criticising a literary or other work; a review. **2.** the art or practice of criticism. [F, from Gk *kritikḗ* the critical art, properly fem. of *kritikós*]

**critter** /ˈkrɪtə/, *n. U.S. Colloq.* →**creature.**

**CRO** /kroʊ/, *n.* →**cathode-ray oscilloscope.**

**croak** /kroʊk/, *v.i.* **1.** to utter a low, hoarse, dismal cry, as a frog or a raven. **2.** to speak with a low, hollow voice. **3.** to talk despondently; forebode evil; grumble. **4.** *Colloq.* to die. *–v.t.* **5.** to utter or announce by croaking. **6.** *Colloq.* to kill. *–n.* **7.** the act or sound of croaking. [late ME; back-formation from OE *crăcettan.* Cf. CREAK] **– croaker,** *n.*

**croaky** /ˈkroʊki/, *adj.* making a croaking sound. **– croakily,** *adv.*

**croc** /krɒk/, *n.* a crocodile. [abbrev.]

**crochet** /ˈkroʊʃə, ˈkroʊʃeɪ/, *n., v.,* **-cheted** /-ʃəd, -ʃeɪd/, **-cheting** /-ʃətɪŋ, -ʃeɪɪŋ/. *–n.* **1.** a kind of needlework done with a needle having at one end a small hook for drawing the thread or yarn into intertwined loops. **2.** the work or fabric so made. *–v.t., v.i.* **3.** to form by crochet. [F: hooked implement, diminutive of OF *croche* hook]

**crochet hook** /ˈkroʊʃə hʊk/, *n.* a thin rodlike knitting needle, with a hook at one end, used to crochet.

**crocidolite** /kroʊˈsɪdəlaɪt/, *n.* a mineral of the amphibole group, essentially a sodium iron silicate, occurring in fibres of a delicate blue colour (blue asbestos) and appearing in altered form, as the tiger's eye, which is golden brown, or hawk's eye, which is dark blue. [*crocido-* (combining form representing Gk *krokís* nap, wool) + -LITE]

**crock**[1] /krɒk/, *n.* **1.** an earthen pot, jar, or other vessel. **2.** a potsherd. **3.** a piece of crockery (def. 2). [ME *crokke,* OE *croc(c), crocca* pot. Cf. Icel. *krukka* jug]

**crock**[2] /krɒk/, *n.* **1.** an old ewe. **2.** an old worn-out horse. **3.** *Colloq.* a worn-out, decrepit old person. **4.** *Colloq.* an old motor car. [akin to CRACK, *v.*]

**crockery** /ˈkrɒkəri/, *n.* **1.** crocks or earthen vessels collectively; earthenware. **2.** china in general, esp. as for domestic use.

**crocket** /ˈkrɒkət/, *n.* a medieval ornament in the form of leafage curled out over a knot or knob; placed on the angles of the inclined sides of pinnacles, under cornices, etc. [ME *croket,* from AF. See CROCHET]

**crock-pot** /ˈkrɒk-pɒt/, *n.* an electric appliance which simmers food at a low heat over a long period.

**crocodile** /ˈkrɒkədaɪl/, *n.* **1.** any of the large, thick-skinned reptiles, lizard-like in form, which constitute the genus *Crocodylus* (order Crocodilia), inhabiting the waters of tropical Africa, Asia, Australia, and America, esp. *C. niloticus* of the Nile. **2.** any animal of the order Crocodilia, including the alligators of America and the gavial of India. **3.** the skin of these animals, used for shoes, handbags, etc. **4.** one who makes a hyprocritical show of sorrow. **5.** *Colloq.* a double file of persons, as schoolchildren out for a walk. *–v.i.* **6.** *Colloq.* to swim with another person holding on to one's shoulders. [L *crocodīlus,* from Gk *krokódeilos* lizard; replacing ME *cocodrille,* from OF]

crocodile

**crocodile bird** /ˈ– bɜd/, *n.* an African plover, *Pluvianus aegyptius,* which often sits upon basking crocodiles and feeds on their insect parasites.

**crocodile clip** /ˈ– klɪp/, *n.* a terminal for temporary electrical connections with narrow jaws like those of a crocodile.

**crocodile tears** /ˈ– tɪəz/, *n.pl.* **1.** false or insincere tears, as the tears said to be shed by crocodiles over those they devour. **2.** hypocritical show of sorrow.

**crocodilian** /ˌkrɒkəˈdɪliən/, *n.* **1.** any of the Crocodilia, an order of reptiles including the crocodiles, alligators, etc. *–adj.* **2.** of or pertaining to the crocodile. **3.** pertaining to the crocodilians. **4.** hypocritical.

**crocoite** /ˈkroʊkoʊaɪt/, *n.* a mineral, lead chromate, $PbCrO_4$. Also, **crocoisite** /kroʊˈkoʊəsaɪt, ˈkroʊkwəsaɪt/. [Gk *krokó(eis)* saffron-coloured + -ITE[1]]

**crocus** /ˈkroʊkəs/, *n., pl.* **crocuses. 1.** any of the small plants constituting the genus *Crocus,* much cultivated for their showy, solitary flowers. **2.** the flower or bulb of the crocus. **3.** a deep yellow; orangish yellow; saffron. **4.** a polishing powder consisting of iron oxide. [L, from Gk *krókos* saffron]

**croft** /krɒft/, *n.* **1.** a small piece of enclosed ground for tillage, pasture, etc. **2.** a very small farm, as one worked by a Scottish crofter. [ME and OE. Cf. MD *kroft* field on high land]

**crofter** /ˈkrɒftə/, *n.* one who rents or owns and works a croft, as in parts of Scotland or northern England.

**crofton weed** /ˈkrɒftən wid/, *n.* a tall herbaceous perennial, *Eupatorium adenophorum,* native to America but a troublesome weed in warm coastal parts of Australia.

**croissant** /ˈkrwʌsɒ̃/, *n.* a roll of leavened dough or puff pastry, shaped into a crescent and baked.

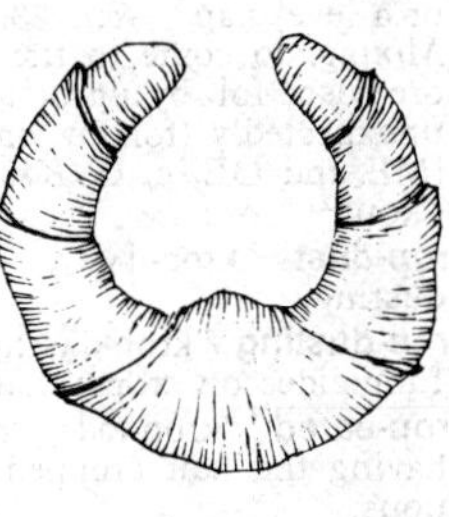
croissant

**Cro-Magnon** /kroʊ-ˈmægnən, -ˈmænjən/, *adj.* of or pertaining to the prehistoric race whose remains were first found at Cro-Magnon, a cave in Dordogne, France, where in 1868 *Homo sapiens* remains were first found in a deposit with upper Paleolithic tools. The remains were characterised by a very long head, low face and orbits and tall stature.

**cromlech** /ˈkrɒmlɛk/, *n.* **1.** a circle of upright stones or monoliths. **2.** →**dolmen.** [Welsh, from *crom* bent, bowed + *llech* flat stone]

**crone** /kroʊn/, *n.* an old woman. [MD *croonje,* from ONF *carogne* carcass]

**cronk** /krɒŋk/, *adj.* **1.** fraudulent. **2.** sick; ailing. [Brit. d. *crank*]

**crony** /ˈkroʊni/, *n., pl.* **-nies.** an intimate friend or companion. [earlier *chrony,* ? from Gk *chrónios* longlasting, from *chrónos* time]

**cronyism** /ˈkroʊniɪzəm/, *n.* unfair partiality shown, esp. in political appointments, for one's friends.

**crook**[1] /krʊk/, *n.* **1.** a bent or curved implement, piece, appendage, etc.; a hook; the hooked part of anything. **2.** an instrument or implement having a bent or curved part, as a shepherd's staff hooked at one end or as the crosier of a bishop or abbot. **3.** the act of crooking or bending. **4.** any bend, turn, or curve. **5.** a dishonest person, esp. a swindler, or thief. **6.** a device on some musical wind instruments for changing the pitch, consisting of a piece of tubing inserted into the main tube. *–v.t.* **7.** to bend; curve; make a crook in. *–v.i.* **8.** to bend; curve. [ME *crok(e),* from Scand.; cf. Icel. *krōkr*]

**crook**[2] /krʊk/, *Colloq. –adj.* **1.** sick; disabled. **2.** bad; inferior. **3.** unpleasant; difficult: *a crook job. –adv.* **4. go crook,** to upbraid noisily (fol. by *at* or *on*). **5. put (one) crook,** to give wrong or bad advice.

**crookback** /ˈkrʊkbæk/, *n.* →**hunchback.** – **crookbacked,** *adj.*

**crooked** /ˈkrʊkəd/, *adj.* **1.** bent; not straight; curved. **2.** deformed. **3. crooked on,** angry with. [OE *gecrōcod*] – **crookedly,** *adv.* – **crookedness,** *n.*

**Crookes dark space,** *n.* the dark space in a vacuum tube between the cathode and the negative glow, occurring when pressure is very low. [named after Sir William *Crookes,* 1832-1919, English chemist and physicist]

**crookie** /ˈkrʊki/, *n.* any thing or person that proves a failure.

**crool** /krul/, *v.t.,* **croolled, croolling.** *Colloq.* →**cruel.**

**croon** /krun/, *v.i.* **1.** to sing softly, esp. with exaggerated feeling. **2.** to utter a low murmuring sound. **3.** *Scot., Irish.* to lament; moan. *–v.t.* **4.** to sing softly, esp. with exaggerated feeling. *–n.* **5.** the act or sound of crooning. [late ME, from MD *krōnen* murmur] – **crooner,** *n.*

**crop** /krɒp/, *n., v.,* **cropped, cropping.** *–n.* **1.** the cultivated produce of the ground, as grain or fruit, while growing or when gathered. **2.** the yield of such produce for a particular season. **3.** the yield of some other product in a season: *the lamb crop.* **4.** a supply produced. **5.** a collection or group of persons or things occurring together: *a crop of lies.* **6.** the stock or handle of a whip. **7.** a short riding whip with a loop instead of a lash. **8.** an entire tanned hide of an animal. **9.** the act of cropping. **10.** a mark produced by clipping the ears, as of an animal. **11.** a style of wearing the hair cut short. **12.** a head of hair so cut. **13.** an outcrop of a vein or seam. **14.** a special pouchlike enlargement of the gullet of many birds, in which food is held, and may undergo partial preparation for digestion. **15.** a digestive organ in other animals; the craw. *–v.t.* **16.** to cut off or remove the head or top of (a plant, etc.). **17.** to cut off the ends or a part of. **18.** to cut short. **19.** to clip the ears, hair, etc., of. **20.** *Photog.* to cut off or mask the unwanted parts of (a print or negative). **21.** to cause to bear a crop or crops. **22.** *Textiles.* to cut or shear the nap of (a fabric) so as to give a smooth face or a level nap. *–v.i.* **23.** to bear or yield a crop or crops. **24.** *Mining.* to come to the surface of the ground, as a vein of ore (usu. fol. by *up* or *out*). **25.** to appear unintentionally or unexpectedly (fol. by *up* or *out*): *a new problem cropped up.* [ME and OE, c. G *Kropf;* orig. meaning protuberance. See CROUP[2]]

**crop-dust** /'krɒp-dʌst/, *v.t.* to subject arable land to crop-dusting.

**crop-dusting** /'krɒp-dʌstɪŋ/, *n.* the spraying of insecticides or fungicides on crops, usu. by an aeroplane.

**crop-eared** /'krɒp-ɪəd/, *adj.* **1.** having the ears cropped. **2.** having the hair cropped short, so that the ears are conspicuous.

**crop lien** /'krɒp liən/, *n.* a lien given over a growing crop or agricultural produce, as security for an advance.

**cropper**[1] /'krɒpə/, *n.* **1.** one who or that which crops. **2.** one who raises a crop. **3.** one who cultivates land for its owner in return for part of the crop. **4.** a plant which furnishes a crop. **5.** a machine that shears the nap of cloth. **6.** a fall. **7. come a cropper,** *Colloq.* **a.** to fall heavily, esp. from a horse. **b.** to fail; collapse, or be struck by misfortune.

**cropper**[2] /'krɒpə/, *n.* one of a breed of pigeons, having the power of distending their crops; a pouter.

**croppy** /'krɒpi/, *n.* **1.** a person with hair cut very short. **2.** a convict, esp. Irish, with such hair.

**crop rotation** /'krɒp roʊ,teɪʃən/, *n.* the system of growing different crops in the same piece of ground in consecutive plantings so as to maintain soil fertility.

**croquet** /'kroʊkeɪ, -ki/, *n., v.,* **-queted** /-keɪd, -kid/, **-queting** /-keɪɪŋ, -kiɪŋ/. *–n.* **1.** an outdoor game played by knocking wooden balls through a series of iron arches by means of mallets. **2.** (in this game) the act of driving away an opponent's ball by striking one's own when the two are in contact. *–v.t.* **3.** to drive away (a ball) by a croquet. [d. F: hockey stick]

**croquette** /kroʊ'kɛt/, *n.* a small mass of minced meat or fish, or of rice potato, or other material, often coated with beaten egg and breadcrumbs and fried in deep fat. [F, from *croquer* crunch]

**crosier** /'kroʊziə/, *n.* **1.** the pastoral staff of a bishop or an abbot, hooked at one end like a shepherd's crook. **2.** *Bot.* the circinate young frond of a fern. Also, **crozier.** [short for *crosier-staff* staff carried by the *crosier* crossbearer (from F *crosier,* from ML *crociārius* crookbearer)]

**cross** /krɒs/, *n.* **1.** a structure consisting essentially of an upright and a transverse piece, upon which persons were formerly put to death. **2. the Cross, a.** the cross upon which Jesus died. **b.** →**Southern Cross. 3.** a figure of the cross as a Christian emblem, badge, etc. **4.** the cross as the symbol of Christianity. **5.** a small cross with a human figure attached to it, as a representation of Jesus crucified; crucifix. **6.** the sign of the cross made with the right hand as an act of devotion. **7.** a structure or monument sometimes in the form of a cross, set up for prayer, as a memorial or a place where proclamations are read. **8.** the place in a town or village where such a monument stands or stood. **9.** any of various conventional representations or modifications of the Christian emblem as used symbolically or for ornament, as in heraldry, art, etc.: *a Latin, Greek, St. George's, or Maltese cross.* **10.** the crucifixion of Jesus as the culmination of His redemptive mission. **11.** any suffering borne for Jesus' sake. **12.** any burden, affliction, responsibility, etc., that one has to bear. **13.** the teaching of redemption gained by Jesus's death. **14.** Christian religion or those who accept it; Christianity; Christendom. **15.** any object, figure, or mark resembling a cross, as two intersecting lines. **16.** such a mark made instead of a signature by a person unable to write. **17.** a four-way joint or connection used in pipe-fitting, the connections being at right angles. **18.** a crossing. **19.** a place of crossing. **20.** *Boxing.* a blow delivered to the head through an opponent's guard, or over his arm. **21.** *Soccer.* a pass (def. 58) from a wing position towards the centre. **22.** an opposing; thwarting. **23.** a crossing of animals or plants; a mixing of breeds. **24.** an animal, plant, breed, etc., produced by crossing; a cross-breed. **25.** something intermediate in character between two things. **26. on the cross,** dishonestly. *–v.t.* **27.** to make the sign of the cross upon or over, as in devotion. **28.** to mark with a cross. **29.** to cancel by marking with a cross or with a line or lines. **30.** to place in the form of a cross or crosswise. **31.** to put or draw (a line etc.) across. **32.** to mark (the face of a cheque) with two vertical parallel lines with or without the words *not negotiable* written between them. **33.** to set (a yard, etc.) in position across a mast. **34.** to lie or pass across; intersect. **35.** to move, pass, or extend from one side to the other side of (a street, river, etc.). **36.** to transport across something. **37.** to meet and pass. **38.** *Archaic.* to encounter. **39.** to oppose; thwart. **40.** to cause (members of different genera, species, breeds, varieties, or the like) to produce offspring; cross-fertilise. **41. cross one's heart,** to pledge; promise; swear. **42. cross one's mind,** to occur to one; come as an idea. **43. cross one's t's and dot one's i's,** to pay punctilious attention to details. **44. cross someone's palm with silver,** to give money to someone to tell one's fortune. **45. cross the floor,** in parliament, to vote with an opposing party. *–v.i.* **46.** to lie or be athwart; intersect. **47.** to move, pass, extend from one side or place to another. **48.** to meet and pass. **49.** to interbreed. *–adj.* **50.** lying or passing crosswise or across each other; athwart; transverse: *cross axes.* **51.** involving interchange; reciprocal. **52.** contrary; opposite. **53.** adverse; unfavourable. **54.** ill-humoured; snappish: *a cross word.* **55.** crossbred; hybrid. **56.** illegal; dishonest. [ME and OE *cros,* from OIrish, from L *crux* (Icel. *kross,* also, from OIrish or ? from OE)] – **crossly,** *adv.* – **crossness,** *n.*

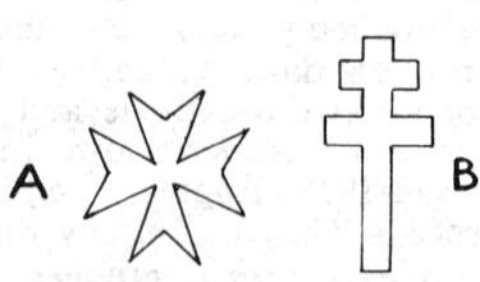

crosses: A, Maltese cross; B, patriarchal cross

**cross-,** a first element of compounds, modifying the second part, meaning: **1.** going across: *crossroad.* **2.** counter: *cross-examination.* **3.** marked with a cross: *hot cross buns.* **4.** cruciform: *crossbones,* etc.

**cross-action** /'krɒs-ækʃən/, *n.* the bringing by the defendant in an action of another action against the plaintiff in respect of the same subject matter.

**cross-banding** /'krɒs-bændɪŋ/, *n.* decorative banding on a piece of furniture, formed by laying the grain crosswise to the grain of the principal surface.

**crossbar** /'krɒsba/, *n.* **1.** a transverse bar, line, or stripe. **2.** a transverse bar between goalposts, as in soccer, rugby football, etc. **3.** a horizontal bar used in gymnastics. **4.** (in athletics) the transverse bar that a high-jumper, pole-vaulter, etc., must clear. **5.** a type of telephone exchange in which a centralised control rapidly routes incoming signals to crossbar switches and so on to their destination.

**crossbar switch** /– 'swɪtʃ/, *n.* a switch used in telephony having ten vertical and ten horizontal paths any one of one set of which may be linked to any one of the other.

**cross-bat** /'krɒs-bæt/, *n. Cricket.* **1.** a bat moving in a horizontal curve, as for a cut. *–adj.* **2.** of a stroke played with a cross-bat. Also, **cross bat.**

**crossbeam** /'krɒsbim/, *n.* transverse beam.

**cross-bearings** /'krɒs-bɛərɪŋz/, *n.pl.* compass bearings of two or more fixed points taken from a ship to determine its position.

**cross-bedded** /krɒs-'bɛdəd/, *adj.* having an arrangement of laminations, as strata of sandstone, inclining transverse or oblique to the main planes of stratification.

**crossbench** /'krɒsbɛntʃ/, *n.* **1.** one of a set of seats, as at the houses of parliament, for those who belong neither to the government nor to opposition parties. **2.** a bench laid crosswise. *–adj.* **3.** independent. – **crossbencher,** *n.*

**crossbill** /'krɒsbɪl/, *n.* any bird of the fringilline genus *Loxia,* characterised by mandibles curved so that the tips cross each other when the bill is closed.

**crossbones** /'krɒsboʊnz/, *n.pl.* two bones placed crosswise, usu. below a skull, symbolising death.

**crossbow** /'krɒsboʊ/, *n.* an old weapon for shooting missiles, consisting of a bow fixed transversely on a stock having a groove or barrel to direct the missile. – **crossbowman** /'krɒsboʊmən/, *n.*

**cross-bow rudder** /'krɒs-ba ,rʌdə/, *n.* (in canoeing) a paddle stroke used to turn the bow in the direction opposite to the bowman's normal paddling side.

**crossbred** /ˈkrɒsbrɛd/, *adj.* **1.** produced by crossbreeding. *–n.* **2.** an animal or group of animals produced by hybridisation.

**crossbreed** /ˈkrɒsbrid/, *v.*, **-bred, -breeding,** *n.* *–v.t.* **1.** to produce (a hybrid) within a species, using two breeds or varieties. *–v.i.* **2.** to undertake or engage in hybridising, esp. within a single species. **3.** a person of mixed race. *–n.* **4.** →**crossbred.**

**cross-buttock** /krɒs-ˈbʌtək/, *n.* (in wrestling) a throw over the hip, using it as a fulcrum.

**crosscheck** /krɒsˈtʃɛk, ˈkrɒstʃɛk/, *v.t.* to determine the accuracy of something by checking from different sources; to recheck.

**cross-country** /ˈkrɒs-kʌntri/, *adj.*, *n;* /krɒs-ˈkʌntri/, *adv.* *–adj.* **1.** directed across fields or open country; not following the main roads. **2.** from one end of the country to the other. **3.** *Skiing.* of or pertaining to skiing which involves long distances and gradual gradients as opposed to alpine skiing. **4.** of or pertaining to flying across the country. *–n.* **5.** a running race which is routed across the country, often on difficult terrain, as opposed to one held on a prepared track. *–adv.* **6.** across open country.

**cross-course** /ˈkrɒs-kɔs/, *n.* a seam or belt of rock, not necessarily a lode, crossing a lode.

**cross-current** /ˈkrɒs-kʌrənt/, *n.* a current, as in a stream, the sea, etc., moving across the main current.

**crosscut** /ˈkrɒskʌt/, *adj.*, *n.*, *v.*, **-cut, -cutting.** *–adj.* **1.** made or used for cutting: *a crosscut saw.* **2.** cut across or transversely. *–n.* **3.** a direct course between two points, as one diagonal to a main way. **4.** a transverse cut or course. **5.** *Mining.* an underground passageway, usu. from shaft to a vein of ore or across a vein of ore. *–v.t.* **6.** to cut across. **7.** to cut with a crosscut saw.

**crosscut chisel** /– ˈtʃɪzəl/, *n.* a cold chisel.

**crosscut file** /– ˈfaɪl/, *n.* a file with two intersecting rows of cuts.

**crosscut saw** /– ˈsɔ/, *n.* any saw designed to cut across the grain, as a handsaw or a panel saw, but esp. a large saw with a handle at each end.

**crosscutter** /ˈkrɒskʌtə/, *n.* *N.Z.* a timberman who uses a crosscut saw.

**cross-drive** /ˈkrɒs-draɪv/, *n.* *Mining.* a drive at right angles to the main drive, usu. short and serving various purposes.

**crosse** /krɒs/, *n.* a long-handled racquet used in the game of lacrosse. [F; of Gmc orig.]

**cross-examine** /krɒs-əgˈzæmən/, *v.t.*, **-ined, -ining. 1.** to examine by questions intended to check a previous examination; examine closely or minutely. **2.** to examine (a witness called by the opposing side), as for the purpose of disproving his testimony. – **cross-examination** /ˌkrɒs-əgzæməˈneɪʃən/, *n.* – **crossexaminer,** *n.*

**cross-eye** /ˈkrɒs-aɪ/, *n.* strabismus, esp. the form in which both eyes turn towards the nose. – **cross-eyed,** *adj.*

**cross-fertilisation** /ˌkrɒs-fɜtəlaɪˈzeɪʃən/, *n.* **1.** *Biol.* the fertilisation of an organism by the fusion of an egg from one individual with a sperm (or male gamete) of a different individual. **2.** *Bot.* fertilisation of one flower or plant by pollen from another (opposed to *self-fertilisation*). **3.** *Colloq.* a productive interchange of ideas. Also, **cross-fertilization.**

**cross-fertilise** /krɒs-ˈfɜtəlaɪz/, *v.t.*, **-lised, -lising.** to cause the cross-fertilisation of. Also, **cross-fertilize.**

**cross-fire** /ˈkrɒs-faɪə/, *n.* **1.** a brisk exchange of words or opinions. **2.** *Mil.* lines of fire from two or more positions, crossing one another, or a single one of such lines.

**cross-gartered** /ˈkrɒs-gatəd/, *adj.* *Archaic.* having garters crossed at the knees.

**cross-grained** /ˈkrɒs-greɪnd/, *adj.* **1.** having the grain running transversely, or diagonally, or having an irregular or gnarled grain, as timber. **2.** perverse; intractable. *–adv.* **3.** across the grain; perversely. – **crossgrainedness,** *n.*

**cross-guard** /ˈkrɒs-gad/, *n.* the transverse guard of a sword set at right angles to the blade.

**crosshair** /ˈkrɒshɛə/, *n.* a fine wire or strand of spider's web or other material, crossing another or others in a focal plane of an optical instrument, serving to define a line of sight; crosswire.

**crosshatch** /ˈkrɒshætʃ/, *v.t.* to hatch or shade with two or more intersecting series of parallel lines. – **crosshatching,** *n.*

**crosshead** /ˈkrɒshɛd/, *n.* **1.** *Print.* a title or heading filling a line or group of lines the full width of the column. **2.** the sliding and bearing member of a diesel, steam, or gas engine, between the piston rod and the connecting rod. **3.** the rod or beam across the head of any of various other mechanisms. – **crossheading,** *n.*

**crossholding** /ˈkrɒshoʊldɪŋ/, *n.* among a group of allied commercial companies, the holding of shares in companies within the group, as a mutually protective device.

**cross-index** /krɒs-ˈɪndɛks/, *n.* **1.** a note, or a group of notes referring the reader to material elsewhere. *–v.t.* **2.** to provide with cross-references. *–v.i.* **3.** to contain cross-references; to refer to related material as in a book, etc.

**crossing** /ˈkrɒsɪŋ/, *n.* **1.** the act of one who or that which crosses. **2.** a place where lines, tracks, etc., cross each other. **3.** the intersection of nave and transept in a cruciform church. **4.** a place at which a road, river, etc., may be crossed. **5.** a railway crossing. **6.** the act of opposing or thwarting; contradiction. **7.** crossbreeding.

**crossing over** /krɒsɪŋ ˈoʊvə/, *n.* the interchange of corresponding chromatid segments of homologous chromosomes with their linked genes.

**crossjack** /ˈkrɒsdʒæk/; *Naut.* /ˈkrɒdʒək/, *n.* a square sail on the lower yard of a mizzenmast.

**crosskick** /ˈkrɒskɪk/, *v.i.* **1.** (in rugby football) to kick the ball across the field to be gathered by another player. *–n.* **2.** such a kick.

**cross-legged** /krɒs-ˈlɛgəd, -ˈlɛgd/, *adj.* having the legs crossed; having one leg placed across the other.

**crosslet** /ˈkrɒslət/, *n.* *Chiefly Her.* a small cross.

**crossness** /ˈkrɒsnəs/, *n.* the condition or quality of being cross or irritable.

**crossopterygian** /krəˌsɒptəˈrɪdʒiən/, *n.* **1.** any fish of the group Crossopterygii, all fossil except *Latimeria chalumnae*, supposed to be ancestral to amphibians and other land vertebrates. *–adj.* **2.** of or pertaining to any fish of this group.

**crossover** /ˈkrɒsoʊvə/, *n.* **1.** the act of crossing over. **2.** *Biol.* a genotype resulting from crossing over. **3.** *Railways.* a system of points, usu. connecting up and down tracks. **4.** →**flyover.**

**crossover network** /– ˌnɛtwɜk/, *n.* an audio circuit device in a radio or record player which sorts the impulses received and channels them into high- or low-frequency loudspeakers.

**crosspatch** /ˈkrɒspætʃ/, *n.* *Colloq.* a cross person.

**crosspiece** /ˈkrɒspis/, *n.* a piece of any material placed across something; a transverse piece.

**cross-ply** /ˈkrɒs-plaɪ/, *adj.* (of a motor tyre) having the fabric cords stretched diagonally, thus bracing the tread.

**cross-pollinate** /krɒs-ˈpɒləneɪt/, *v.t.*, **-nated, -nating.** →**cross-fertilise.** – **crosspollination,** *n.*

**cross-purpose** /krɒs-ˈpɜpəs/, *n.* **1.** an opposing or contrary purpose. **2. be at cross-purposes,** to be involved in a misunderstanding such that each person makes a wrong interpretation of the other's interests or intentions (fol. by *with*).

**cross-question** /krɒs-ˈkwɛstʃən/, *v.t.* **1.** to cross-examine. *–n.* **2.** a question asked by way of cross-examination.

**cross reef** /ˈkrɒs rif/, *n.* a mineral vein in a mine which intersects another such vein.

**cross-refer** /krɒs-rəˈfɜ/, *v.t.*, *v.i.*, **-ferred, -ferring.** →**cross-reference.**

**cross-reference** /krɒs-ˈrɛfrəns/, *n.*, *v.*, **-renced, -rencing.** *–n.* **1.** a reference from one part of a book, etc., to a word, item, etc., in another part. *–v.t.* **2.** to relate (an item, passage in a book, etc.) to another by means of a cross-reference. *–v.i.* **3.** to make a cross-reference.

**cross-relation** /krɒs-rəˈleɪʃən/, *n.* →**false relation.**

**crossroad** /ˈkrɒsroʊd/, *n.* **1.** a road that crosses another road, or one that runs transversely to main roads. **2.** a byroad. **3. a.** (*oft. pl., construed as sing.*) the place where roads intersect. **b.** (*usu. pl.*) a stage at which a vital decision must be made.

**crossruff** /ˈkrɒsrʌf/, *Whist, Bridge.* –*n.* **1.** a play in which each hand of a partnership trumps a different suit; a see-saw. –*v.t.* **2.** to play by means of a crossruff. –*v.i.* **3.** to perform a crossruff.

**cross-section** /ˈkrɒs-sɛkʃən/, *n.* **1.** a section made by a plane cutting anything transversely, esp. at right angles to the longest axis. **2.** a piece so cut off. **3.** the act of cutting anything across. **4.** a typical selection; a sample showing all characteristic parts, etc.: *a cross-section of Australin opinion.* **5.** *Geol.* a profile showing an interpretation of a vertical section of the earth explored by geological and for geophysical methods. **6.** *Physics.* the effective area for the interaction of an atom, nucleus or elementary particle with an incident beam of radiation. **7.** *Survey.* a vertical section of the ground surface taken at right angles to a survey line. –*v.t.* **8.** to cut or make into a cross-section. – **cross-sectional,** *adj.*

**cross-shot** /ˈkrɒs-ʃɒt/, *n.* (in tennis) a shot played diagonally across the court.

**cross-staff** /ˈkrɒs-staf/, *n.* a surveyor's instrument, having two sights at right angles to each other and used for setting out right angles in the field.

**cross-stitch** /ˈkrɒs-stɪtʃ/, *n.* **1.** a kind of stitching employing pairs of diagonal stitches of the same length crossing each other in the middle at right angles. –*v.t.* **2.** to make or embroider with cross-stitches. –*v.i.* **3.** to work in cross-stitch.

**cross-street** /ˈkrɒs-strit/, *n.* a street crossing another street, or one running transversely to main streets.

**cross-talk** /ˈkrɒs-tɔk/, *n.* **1.** unwanted interference between two neighbouring electronic circuits. **2.** *Parl. Proc.* an interchange of remarks across the house between members of different parties.

**cross-town** /ˈkrɒs-taʊn/, *adj.* that runs across the town: *a cross-town bus.*

**crosstree** /ˈkrɒstri/, *n.* one of the horizontal transverse pieces of timber or metal fastened to the head of a lower mast or topmast of a sailing ship in order to support the top, spread the shrouds, etc.

C, crosstree

**cross vine** /ˈkrɒs vaɪn/, *n.* →**bignonia.**

**crossway** /ˈkrɒsweɪ/, *n.* →**crossroad.**

**cross-wind** /ˈkrɒs-wɪnd/, *n.* a wind blowing at right angles to the line of flight of an aircraft.

**crosswire** /ˈkrɒswaɪə/, *n.* →**crosshair.**

**crosswise** /ˈkrɒswaɪz/, *adv.* **1.** across; transversely. **2.** in the form of a cross. **3.** contrarily. Also, **crossways** /ˈkrɒsweɪz/.

**crossword puzzle** /ˈkrɒswɜd pʌzəl/, *n.* a puzzle in which words corresponding to given meanings are to be supplied and fitted into a particular figure divided into spaces, the letters of the words being arranged across the figure, or vertically, or sometimes otherwise.

**crotalaria** /kroʊtəˈlarıə/, *n.* any herb or shrub of the large genus *Crotalaria,* widely distributed in tropical areas and occasionally the cause of stock-poisoning, the flowers of which are pea-shaped and usu. yellow and the pods hard and inflated when dry; rattlepod.

**crotch** /krɒtʃ/, *n.* **1.** a forked piece, part, support, etc. **2.** a forking or place of forking, as of the human body between the legs. **3.** the part of a pair of trousers, pants, etc., formed by the joining of the two legs. **4.** a piece of material, so used in the join. [var. of CRUTCH] – **crotched** /krɒtʃt/, *adj.*

**crotchet** /ˈkrɒtʃət/, *n.* **1.** a hooklike device or part. **2.** *Entomol.* a small hooklike process. **3.** a curved surgical instrument with a sharp hook. **4.** an odd fancy or whimsical notion. **5.** *Music.* a note having one quarter of the time value of a semibreve or half the value of a minim. **6.** *Obs.* a small hook. [ME *crochet,* from OF. See CROCHET]

**crotchety** /ˈkrɒtʃəti/, *adj.* **1.** given to crotchets or odd fancies; full of crotchets. **2.** of the nature of a crotchet. **3.** *Colloq.* irritable, difficult, or cross. – **crotchetiness,** *n.*

**croton** /ˈkroʊtn/, *n.* **1.** any of the chiefly tropical plants constituting the genus *Croton,* many species of which, as *C. tiglium,* have important medicinal properties. **2.** (among florists) any plant of the related genus *Codiaeum* cultivated for its ornamental foliage. [NL, from Gk *krotṓn* a tick, also a plant having ticklike seeds]

**crotonic acid** /kroʊˌtɒnɪk ˈæsəd/, *n.* a colourless, crystalline compound, $CH_3CHCHCOOH$, used in organic synthesis.

**croton oil** /kroʊtn ˈɔɪl/, *n.* a powerful purgative oil from *Croton tiglium,* a shrub or tree of the East Indies.

**crouch** /kraʊtʃ/, *v.i.* **1.** (of people) to lower the body with one or both knees bent, in any position which inclines the trunk forward. **2.** (of animals) to lie close to or on the ground with legs bent as in the position taken when about to spring. **3.** to stoop or bend low. **4.** to bend servilely; cringe. –*v.t.* **5.** to bend low. –*n.* **6.** the act or position of crouching. **7.** Also, **crouch start.** *Athletics.* a method of starting sprint races in which the runner crouches down on all fours. [ME *crouche(n),* from OF *crochir* become bent, from *croche* hook]

**crouchback** /ˈkraʊtʃbæk/, *Archaic.* –*n.* **1.** a crooked or hunched back. **2.** one who has a crooked back; a hunchback. –*adj.* **3.** having a hunched back.

**croup**[1] /krup/, *n. Pathol.* inflammation of the larynx, esp. in children leading to laryngeal spasm, characterised by a hoarse cough and difficulty in breathing. [n. use of *croup,* v. (now dial.), cry hoarsely, b. CROAK and WHOOP]

**croup**[2] /krup/, *n.* the rump or buttocks of certain animals, esp. of a horse. Also, **croupe.** [ME *croupe,* from F, from Gmc; cf. CROP]

**croupade** /kruˈpeɪd/, *n.* (in dressage) a leap in which a horse draws up its hind legs towards the belly.

**croupier** /ˈkrupiə/, *n.* **1.** an attendant who collects and pays the money at a gaming table. **2.** one who at a public dinner sits at the lower end of the table as assistant chairman. [F; orig., one who rides behind on the croup of another's horse]

**croupous** /ˈkrupəs/, *adj.* pertaining to, of the nature of, or resembling croup.

**croupy** /ˈkrupi/, *adj.* **1.** pertaining to or resembling croup. **2.** affected with croup.

**croustade** /kruˈsteɪd, ˈkrusteɪd/, *n.* a shell or case of fried bread, pastry, mashed potatoes, etc., for filling with ragout or the like.

**croute** /krut/, *n.* a piece of fried or toasted bread on which meat dishes or small savouries may be served. [F *croûte* CRUST]

**crouton** /ˈkrutɒn/, *n.* **1.** a small piece of bread, often cube shaped, crispy fried or toasted, for use in soups, minces, etc. **2.** a small croute. [F, diminutive of *croûte* CROUTE]

**crow**[1] /kroʊ/, *n.* **1.** either of two large, lustrous black, Australian birds of the genus *Corvus,* having a characteristic harsh call: **a.** the **Australian crow,** *C. orru.* **b.** the **little crow,** *C. bennetti.* **2.** the wattled *Callaeas* species of New Zealand. **3.** certain other birds of the genus *Corvus* as the **carrion crow** (*C. corone*) of Europe and the **American crow** (*C. brachyrhynchos*). **4.** certain European birds of the family Corvidae as the chough, *Pyrrhocorax pyrrhocorax,* and the **Cornish crow,** *P. graculus.* **5.** →**crowbar.** **6.** *N.Z.* one who pitches sheaves to the stack-builder. **7. as the crow flies,** in a straight line. **8. eat crow,** *Colloq.* to be forced to do or say something very unpleasant or humiliating. **9. starve, stiffen** or **stone the crows,** *Colloq.* (an exclamation of astonishment). **10.** *Colloq.* an unattractive woman. [ME; OE *crawe.* See CROW[2], *v.*]

carrion crow

**crow**[2] /kroʊ/, *v.,* **crowed** (or **crew** *for def. 1*), **crowed, crowing,** *n.* –*v.i.* **1.** to utter the characteristic cry of a cock. **2.** to utter an inarticulate cry of pleasure, as an infant does. **3.** to exult loudly; boast. –*n.* **4.** the characteristic cry of the cock. **5.** an inarticulate cry of pleasure. [ME *crowe(n),* OE *crāwen,* c. D *kraaien,* G *krähen;* imitative]

**crowbar** /ˈkroʊba/, *n.* a bar of iron, often with a wedge-shaped end, for use as a lever, etc.

**crowberry** /ˈkroʊbɛri/, *n., pl.* **-ries.** **1.** the insipid black or reddish berry of an evergreen heathlike shrub, *Empetrum nigrum,* of northern regions. **2.** the plant itself, of the family Empetraceae.

**crow blackbird** /kroʊ ˈblækbɜd/, *n.* any of several North

American birds of the genus *Quiscalus* (family Icteridae), as *Q. quiscula,* the purple grackle, noted for iridescent black plumage and trough-shaped tails.

**crowd**[1] /kraʊd/, *n.* **1.** a large number of persons gathered closely together; a throng. **2.** any large number of persons. **3.** people in general; the masses. **4.** any group or set of persons, as one's circle of acquaintances: *I can't get on with your crowd.* **5.** a large number of things gathered or considered together. *–v.i.* **6.** to gather in large numbers; throng; swarm. **7.** (of a mechanical shovel) to force the bucket into a mass of earth or rock; used chiefly for machines which dig by pushing away from themselves. **8.** to press forward; advance by pushing. *–v.t.* **9.** to push; shove. **10.** to press closely together; force into a confined space. **11.** to fill to excess; fill by crowding or pressing into. **12.** *U.S. Colloq.* to urge; press by solicitation; annoy by urging: *to crowd a debtor for immediate payment.* **13. crowd (on) sail,** *Naut.* to carry as much sail as possible. [ME *crowde(n),* OE *crūdan,* c. MD *kruyden*]

**crowd**[2] /kraʊd/, *n.* an ancient Celtic musical instrument related to the kithara, but bowed. Also, **crwth.** [ME *crowde,* from Welsh *crwth*]

**crowded** /ˈkraʊdəd/, *adj.* **1.** filled to excess; filled with a crowd; packed: *crowded streets.* **2.** uncomfortably close together: *crowded passengers on a bus.* **– crowdedly,** *adv.* **– crowdedness,** *n.*

**crowd-pleaser** /ˈkraʊd-plizə/, *n.* an entertainment, as a film, concert, etc., designed to be popular with the masses.

**crowd-puller** /ˈkraʊd-pʊlə/, *n.* →**drawcard.**

**crowea** /ˈkroʊiə/, *n.* any low pink-flowered shrub of the genus *Crowea* found on sandstone areas of eastern Australia.

**croweater** /ˈkroʊitə/, *n. Colloq.* →**South Australian.**

**crowfoot** /ˈkroʊfʊt/, *n., pl.* **-foots** *for defs 1 and 2,* **-feet** *for defs 3 and 4.* **1.** any plant of the genus *Ranunculus,* esp. one with divided leaves suggestive of a crow's foot; a buttercup. **2.** any of various other plants with leaves or other parts suggestive of a bird's foot as certain species of the genus *Erodium.* **3.** →**caltrop.**

**crow garlic** /kroʊ ˈgalɪk/, *n.* an Old World plant, *Allium vineale,* which often bears bulbils in place of flowers.

**crown** /kraʊn/, *n.* **1.** an ornamental wreath or garland for the head, conferred by the ancients as a mark of victory or distinction. **2.** honorary distinction; reward. **3.** a decorative fillet or covering for the head, worn as a symbol of sovereignty. **4.** the power or dominion of a sovereign. **5. the Crown,** the sovereign as head of the state, or the supreme governing power of a state under a monarchical government. **6.** any crownlike emblem or design, used in a heraldic crest, as a badge of rank in some armies, etc. **7.** a coin of several countries generally bearing a crown or a crowned head on the obverse. **8.** a krone or a krona. **9.** a size of paper, 15 × 20 inches, most commonly in use before metrication. **10.** *Agric.* a grade or quality of dried vine fruit. **11.** something having the form of a crown, as the corona of a flower. **12.** *Bot.* **a.** the leaves and living branches of a tree. **b.** the point at which the root of a seed plant joins the stem. **c.** a circle of appendages on the throat of the corolla, etc.; corona. **13.** the top or highest part of anything, as of the head, a hat, a mountain, etc. **14.** the head itself: *he broke his crown.* **15.** the crest, as of a bird. **16.** *Dentistry.* **a.** that part of a tooth which is covered by enamel. **b.** an artificial substitute, as of gold or porcelain, for the crown of a tooth. **17.** an exalting or chief attribute. **18.** the acme or supreme source of honour, excellence, beauty, etc. **19.** crown glass. **20.** *Naut.* the part of an anchor where the arms join the shank. **21.** the part of a cut gem above the girdle. *–v.t.* **22.** to place a crown or garland upon the head of. **23.** to invest with a regal crown, or with regal dignity and power. **24.** to honour as with a crown; reward; invest with honour, dignity, etc. **25.** to surmount as with a crown; surmount as a crown does. **26.** *Colloq.* to hit on the top of the head. **27.** to complete worthily; bring to a successful or effective conclusion. **28.** (in draughts) to change (a piece) into a king, after it has safely reached the last row, by putting another piece on top of it. [ME *croune, coroune,* from AF, from L *corōna* garland, crown. Cf. CORONA] **– crowner,** *n.*

**crown agent** /– ˈeɪdʒənt/, *n.* an agent for the crown in charge of the finances of a crown colony.

**crown auction** /– ˈɒkʃən/, *n.* the sale of government owned land at public auction.

**crown beard** /ˈ– bɪəd/, *n.* an annual yellow-flowered herb, *Verbesina encelioides,* native to America but often found as a weed in dry areas.

**crown cap** /ˈ– kæp/, *n.* →**crown seal.**

**crown colony** /– ˈkɒləni/, *n.* a colony in which the crown has the entire control of legislation and administration, as distinguished from one having a constitution and representative government.

**crown court** /– ˈkɔt/, *n. Brit.* a court of quarter sessions and assizes.

**crown gall** /ˈ– gɔl/, *n.* a bacterial disease producing abnormal growths on fruit trees and other plants, caused by *Agrobacterium tumefaciens.*

**crown glass** /ˈ– glas/, *n.* **1.** an optical glass of low dispersion and generally low refractive index. **2.** an old form of window glass formed by blowing a globe and whirling it into a disc, composed essentially of soda, lime, and silica.

**crown graft** /ˈ– graft/, *n.* a graft in which the scion is inserted at the crown of the stock.

**crown imperial** /– ɪmˈpɪəriəl/, *n.* a plant, *Fritillaria imperialis,* with an erect stem bearing a whorl of large pendulous flowers near the top.

**crown jewels** /– ˈdʒuəlz/, *n. pl.* the jewels used by the sovereign on state occasions.

**crown land** /– ˈlænd/, *n.* land belonging to the government.

**crown-of-thorns starfish** /ˌkraʊn-əv-θɔnz ˈstafɪʃ/, *n.* a starfish, *Acanthaster planci,* having sharp, stinging spines on the top surface of the body and arms, widely distributed in tropical waters and particularly abundant on the Great Barrier Reef where it is very destructive of certain corals.

**crownpiece** /ˈkraʊnpis/, *n.* **1.** a piece or part forming or fitting the crown or top of anything. **2.** →**crown** (def. 7).

**crown prince** /kraʊn ˈprɪns/, *n.* the heir apparent of a monarch.

**crown princess** /– ˈprɪnsɛs/, *n.* **1.** the heiress apparent of a monarch. **2.** the wife of a crown prince.

**crown roast** /– ˈroʊst/, *n.* a roast of lamb shaped to resemble a crown from two racks of ribs each containing six to eight cutlets.

**crown saw** /ˈ– sɔ/, *n.* a rotary saw consisting of a hollow cylinder with teeth on its end or edge, as the surgeon's trephine.

**crown seal** /– ˈsil/, *n.* a metal cap, usu. lined with cork for stopping bottles of beer, soft drink, etc., and which is fastened to a rim at the mouth of the bottle by crimping its edge over the rim. Also, *U.S.,* **crown cap, crown cork.**

**crown wheel** /ˈ– wil/, *n.* **1.** the larger of the two wheels in a bevel gear. **2.** *Horol.* a wheel next to the winding knob, having two sets of teeth, one at right angles to its plane.

**crown witness** /– ˈwɪtnəs/, *n.* a witness for the Crown in a criminal prosecution.

**crow's-foot** /ˈkroʊz-fʊt/, *n., pl.* **-feet. 1.** (*usu. pl.*) a wrinkle at the outer corner of the eye. **2.** *Tailoring.* a three-pointed embroidered figure used as a finish.

**crowsfoot grass** /ˈkroʊzfʊt gras/, *n.* a coarse, tufted summer annual, *Eleusine indica,* infesting coastal cultivation, pasture areas, lawns, and wastelands.

**crow's-nest** /ˈkroʊz-nɛst/, *n. Naut.* **1.** a box or shelter for the lookout man, secured near the top of a mast. **2.** a similar lookout station ashore.

**crow step** /ˈkroʊ stɛp/, *n.* one of a series of steps on the face of a gable, sometimes used instead of a slope. Also, **corbie step.**

**crow-stepped gable** /kroʊ-stɛpt ˈgeɪbəl/, *n.* a gable with crow steps. Also, **corbie gable.**

**croze** /kroʊz/, *n.* **1.** the groove at the ends of the staves of a barrel, cask, etc., into which the edge of the head fits. **2.** a tool for cutting such a groove. [cf. F *creux* groove]

**crozier** /ˈkroʊziə/, *n.* →**crosier.**

**crt.,** court.

**CRT,** Cathode Ray Tube.

**cru** /kru/, *adj.* of or pertaining to a vineyard of high quality. [F *crû,* from *croître* to grow]

**cruces** /ˈkrusiz/, *n.* plural of **crux.**

**crucial** /ˈkruʃəl/, *adj.* **1.** involving a final and supreme decision; decisive; critical: *a crucial experiment.* **2.** severe; trying. **3.** of the form of a cross; cross-shaped. [*cruci-* (from L, combining form of *crux* cross) + -AL[1]] – **crucially,** *adv.*

**cruciate** /ˈkruʃiət, -eɪt/, *adj.* **1.** cross-shaped. **2.** *Bot.* having the form of a cross with equal arms, as the flowers of mustard, etc. **3.** *Entomol.* crossing each other diagonally in repose, as the wings of an insect. [NL *cruciātus,* from L *crux* CROSS]

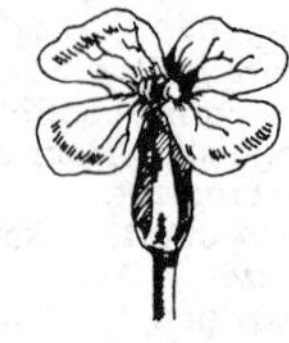
cruciate flower

**crucible** /ˈkrusəbəl/, *n.* **1.** a vessel of metal or refractory material employed for heating substances to high temperatures. **2.** (in a metallurgical furnace) the hollow part at the bottom, in which molten metal collects. **3.** a severe, searching test. [ML *crucibulum* night lamp, melting pot; this ? from *crucibolum* whale oil cruse (cf. L *bālaena* whale). See CRUSE]

**crucible steel** /– ˈstil/, *n.* steel made in a crucible, esp. a highgrade steel prepared by melting selected materials.

**crucifer** /ˈkrusəfə/, *n.* **1.** one who carries a cross, as in ecclesiastical processions. **2.** *Bot.* a plant belonging to the family Cruciferae which includes cabbage, mustard and wallflower. [LL]

**cruciferous** /kruˈsɪfərəs/, *adj.* **1.** bearing a cross. **2.** *Bot.* belonging or pertaining to the family Cruciferae, whose members bear flowers having a crosslike, four-petalled corolla. [LL *crucifer* cross-bearing + -OUS]

**crucifix** /ˈkrusəfɪks/, *n.* **1.** a cross with the figure of Jesus crucified upon it. **2.** any cross. [ME, from LL *crucifixus,* pp., fixed to a cross]

**crucifixion** /krusəˈfɪkʃən/, *n.* **1.** the act of crucifying. **2.** (*cap.*) the death of Jesus by exposure upon a cross. **3.** a picture or other representation of this.

**crucifix orchid** /ˌkrusəfɪks ˈɔkəd/, *n.* a commonly cultivated orchid of garden origin, *Epidendrum* × *obrienianum,* with orange flowers and a three-lobed labellum.

crucifix orchid

**cruciform** /ˈkrusəfɔm/, *adj.* cross-shaped. [L *crux* cross + -I- + -FORM] – **cruciformly,** *adv.*

**crucify** /ˈkrusəfaɪ/, *v.t.,* **-fied, -fying. 1.** to put to death by nailing or binding the body to a cross. **2.** to torment; treat with severity. **3.** to subdue (passion, sin, etc.). [ME *crucifien,* from OF *crucifier,* from LL *crucifigere* fix to a cross. See -FY] – **crucifier,** *n.*

**crud** /krʌd/, *n. Colloq.* anything or anyone regarded as inferior. [Brit. d. *crud* curd] – **cruddy,** *adj.*

**crude** /krud/, *adj.,* **cruder, crudest. 1.** in a raw or unprepared state; unrefined: *crude oil, sugar,* etc. **2.** unripe; not mature. **3.** lacking finish, polish, proper arrangement, or completeness: *a crude summary.* **4.** lacking culture, refinement, tact, etc.: *crude persons, behaviour, speech,* etc. *–n.* **5.** crude oil. [ME, from L *crūdus* raw, crude, rough. Cf. CRUEL] – **crudely,** *adj.* – **crudeness,** *n.*

**crudité** /ˈkrudəteɪ/, *n.* a thinly-cut raw vegetable often served with a dip sauce as an hors d'oeuvre. [F]

**crudity** /ˈkrudəti/, *n., pl.* **-ties. 1.** the state or quality of being crude. **2.** an instance of this; anything crude.

**cruel** /ˈkruəl/, *adj., v.,* **cruelled, cruelling.** *–adj.* **1.** disposed to inflict suffering; indifferent to, or taking pleasure in, the pain or distress of another; hard-hearted; pitiless. **2.** causing, or marked by, great pain or distress: *a cruel remark.* *–v.t.* **3.** *Colloq.* to impair, spoil: *to cruel one's chances.* **4. cruel one's pitch,** *Colloq.* to spoil one's opportunity. [ME, from OF, from L *crūdēlis* hard, cruel, akin to *crudus* CRUDE] – **cruelly,** *adv.* – **cruelness,** *n.*

**cruelty** /ˈkruəlti/, *n., pl.* **-ties. 1.** the state or quality of being cruel. **2.** cruel disposition or conduct. **3.** a cruel act. **4.** *Law.* as a ground for judicial separation or divorce, conduct, habitual for a period of not less than one year, which has caused danger to life, limb or health of a spouse and which gives rise to a reasonable apprehension of danger.

**cruet** /ˈkruət/, *n.* **1.** a set, on a stand, of containers for salt, pepper, and mustard or for vinegar and oil. **2.** an individual container. **3.** any of the contents. **4.** *Eccles.* one of the vessels used in the celebration of the mass for holding wine or water. **5.** *Colloq.* head. **6. do one's cruet,** *Colloq.* lose one's head. [ME, from OF, diminutive of *crue* pitcher, pot, from Gmc; cf. G *Krug* pot]

**cruise** /kruz/, *v.,* **cruised, cruising,** *n.* *–v.i.* **1.** to sail to and fro, or from place to place, as in search of hostile ships, or for pleasure. **2.** (of a car, aeroplane, etc.) to move along easily at a moderate speed. *–v.t.* **3.** to cruise over. *–n.* **4.** the act of cruising; a voyage made by cruising. [D *kruisen* cross, cruise, from *kruis* cross]

**cruiser** /ˈkruzə/, *n.* **1.** one who or that which cruises, as a person or a ship. **2.** one of a class of warships of medium tonnage, designed for high speed and long cruising radius. **3.** a boat, usu. power-driven, adapted for pleasure trips. **4.** a very large beer glass. **5.** the contents of such a glass.

**crumb** /krʌm/, *n.* **1.** a small particle of bread, cake, etc., such as breaks or falls off. **2.** a small particle or portion of anything. **3.** the soft inner portion of bread (distinguished from *crust*). *–v.t.* **4.** to dress or prepare with breadcrumbs; to bread. **5.** to break into crumbs or small fragments. Also, (formerly) **crum.** [ME *crumme,* OE *cruma,* akin to G *Krume*]

**crumble** /ˈkrʌmbəl/, *v.,* **-bled, -bling,** *n.* *–v.t.* **1.** to break into small fragments or crumbs. *–v.i.* **2.** to fall into small pieces; break or part into small fragments. **3.** to decay; disappear piecemeal. *–n.* **4.** something crumbling or crumbled. **5.** a sweet dish containing stewed fruit topped by a crumbly pastry of brown sugar, flour, and butter. [earlier *crimble,* frequentative of OE *gecrymman* crumble (from *cruma* crumb); assimilated in form to CRUMB] – **crumbly,** *adj.*

**crumble-feed** /ˈkrʌmbəl-fid/, *n. Agric.* **1.** feed prepared for poultry in the form of pellets of concentrated food. *–v.i.* **2.** to feed poultry with this preparation.

**crumbly** /ˈkrʌmbli/, *adj.,* **-blier, -bliest.** apt to crumble; friable.

**crumby** /ˈkrʌmi/, *adj.,* **-ier, -iest. 1.** full of crumbs. **2.** soft.

**crumhorn** /ˈkrʌmhɔn/, *n.* a wind-capped double reed instrument of the Renaissance. Also, **krummhorn.**

**crummy** /ˈkrʌmi/, *adj.,* **-mier, -miest.** *Colloq.* very inferior, mean, or shabby.

**crump** /krʌmp/, *n.* the dull, heavy sound of bombs or shells exploding. [imitative]

**crumpet** /ˈkrʌmpət/, *n.* **1.** a kind of light, soft bread, cooked on a griddle or the like, usu. then served toasted and buttered. **2.** *Colloq.* a girl or woman considered as a sexual object. **3.** *Colloq.* the head: *soft in the crumpet.* **4. not worth a crumpet,** *Colloq.* worthless; of little or no value. [short for *crumpet cake* curled cake, ME *crompid,* pp. of obs. *crump,* var. of CRIMP[1]]

**crumple** /ˈkrʌmpəl/, *v.,* **-pled, -pling,** *n.* *–v.t.* **1.** to draw or press into irregular folds; rumple; wrinkle. *–v.i.* **2.** to contract into wrinkles; shrink; shrivel. **3.** to collapse; give way. *–n.* **4.** an irregular fold or wrinkle produced by crumpling. [frequentative of obs. *crump,* var. of CRIMP[1]]

**crunch** /krʌntʃ/, *v.t.* **1.** to crush with the teeth; chew with a crushing noise. **2.** to crush or grind noisily. *–v.i.* **3.** to chew with a crushing sound. **4.** to produce, or proceed with, a crushing noise. *–n.* **5.** the act or sound of crunching. **6.** *Colloq.* a moment of crisis. [b. CRAUNCH and CRUSH]

**crunchie** /ˈkrʌntʃi/, *n. Colloq.* **1.** *Mil.* an infantryman. **2.** a pimple. [CRUNCH + -IE]

**crunchy** /ˈkrʌntʃi/, *adj.,* **-chier, -chiest.** making a crunching sound when eaten, as crisp celery, chips, etc.

**crunode** /ˈkrunoʊd/, *n.* a node (def. 5) at which the tangents to the two curves are real and distinct (opposed to *acnode*). [L *cru(x)* cross + NODE]

**cruor** /ˈkruɔ/, *n. Obs.* coagulated blood, or that portion of the blood which forms the clot. [L: blood, gore]

**crupper** /ˈkrʌpə/, *n.* **1.** a leather strap on the back of the saddle of a harness, which passes in a loop under a horse's tail, to prevent the saddle from slipping forward. **2.** the rump or buttocks of a horse. [ME *cropere,* from OF, from *crope.* See CROUP[2]]

**crural** /ˈkrʊərəl/, *adj.* of or pertaining to the crus, or leg, or the hind limb. [L *crūrālis,* from *crūs* leg]

**crus** /krʊs/, *n., pl.* **crura** /ˈkrʊərə/. **1.** *Anat., Zool.* **a.** that part of the leg or hind limb between the femur or thigh and the ankle or tarsus; the shank. **b.** an elongated process, as of a bone or other structure. **2.** any of various parts likened to a leg. [L: leg]

**crusade** /kruˈseɪd/, *n., v.,* **-saded, -sading.** *–n.* **1.** (*oft. cap.*) any of the military expeditions undertaken by the Christians of Europe in the eleventh, twelfth, and thirteenth centuries for the recovery of the Holy Land from the Muslims. **2.** any war carried on under papal sanction. **3.** any vigorous, aggressive movement for the defence or advancement of an idea, cause, etc. **4.** a campaign to stimulate or increase Christian faith. Cf. **mission.** *–v.i.* **5.** to go on or engage in a crusade. [b. earlier *crusada* (from Sp. *cruzada*) and *croisade* (from F). See CROSS, -ADE[1]] – **crusader,** *n.*

**cruse** /kruz/, *n.* an earthen pot, bottle, etc., for liquids. [MD]

**crush** /krʌʃ/, *v.t.* **1.** to press and bruise between two hard bodies; squeeze out of shape or normal condition. **2.** to break into small fragments or particles, as ore, stone, etc. **3.** to force out by pressing or squeezing. **4.** to put down, overpower, or subdue completely; overwhelm. **5.** to oppress harshly. **6.** *Archaic.* to drink (wine, etc.). **7. crush the price,** *Colloq.* to lay out a bookmaker's money on a horse so that the odds shorten. *–v.i.* **8.** to become crushed. **9.** to advance with crushing; press or crowd forcibly. *–n.* **10.** the act of crushing. **11.** the state of being crushed. **12.** *Colloq.* a great crowd; a crowded social gathering. **13.** a beverage made by expressing the juice from fruit, as from oranges. **14.** a permanent or portable construction, often built from tubular steel, to form a small yard in which individual cattle receive veterinary or routine treatment such as de-horning, drenching, etc. **15.** a narrow, funnel-shaped, fenced passage along which stock, esp. cattle, are driven for handling; race. **16.** *N.Z.* →**crush-pen. 17.** *Colloq.* an infatuation. [ME *crusch(en),* apparently from OF *croissir* crash, gnash, break, crush; probably from Gmc]

**crusher** /ˈkrʌʃə/, *n.* **1.** one who or that which crushes. **2.** *Colloq.* a person employed by a bookmaker to crush the price.

**crush note** /ˈkrʌʃ noʊt/, *n. Music.* →**acciaccatura.**

**crush-pen** /ˈkrʌʃ-pɛn/, *n. N.Z.* narrow pen with wide entrance into which stock may be driven for counting, ear-marking, etc. Also, **crush-yard.**

**crusoe** /ˈkrusoʊ/, *n. Colloq.* one who lives alone on an uninhabited island. [from Robinson *Crusoe,* the marooned seaman in Daniel Defoe's novel *Robinson Crusoe* (1719)]

**crust** /krʌst/, *n.* **1.** the hard outer portion of a loaf of bread (distinguished from *crumb*). **2.** a piece of this. **3.** the outside covering of a pie. **4.** any more or less hard external covering or coating. **5.** the hard outer shell or covering of an animal or plant. **6.** the exterior portion of the earth, accessible to examination. **7.** a scab or eschar. **8.** deposit from wine, as it ripens, on the interior of bottles, consisting of tartar and colouring matter. **9.** *Colloq.* impertinence. **10.** *Colloq.* a livelihood: *what do you do for a crust?* **11. down to the last crust,** destitute. **12. the crust,** *Prison Colloq.* a sentence for vagrancy: *to do the crust. –v.t.* **13.** to cover with or as with a crust; encrust. **14.** to form (something) into a crust. **15.** to charge with vagrancy. *–v.i.* **16.** to form or contract a crust. **17.** to form into a crust. [ME, from L *crusta* rind: replacing ME *crouste,* from OF]

**crustacean** /krʌsˈteɪʃən/, *adj.* **1.** belonging to the Crustacea, a class of (chiefly aquatic) arthropods, including the lobsters, shrimps, crabs, barnacles, woodlice, etc., commonly having the body covered with a hard shell or crust. *–n.* **2.** a crustacean animal. **3. come the uncooked crustacean,** *Colloq.* See **prawn** (def. 2).

**crustaceous** /ˈkrʌsteɪʃəs/, *adj.* **1.** of the nature of or pertaining to a crust or shell. **2.** belonging to the Crustacea. **3.** having a hard covering or crust. [NL *crustāceus* hard-shelled]

**crustal** /ˈkrʌstəl/, *adj.* of or pertaining to a crust, as that of the earth.

**crusty** /ˈkrʌsti/, *adj.,* **crustier, crustiest. 1.** of the nature of or resembling a crust; having a crust. **2.** harsh; surly; crabbed: *crusty person, manner, remark, etc.* – **crustily,** *adv.* – **crustiness,** *n.*

**crutch** /krʌtʃ/, *n.* **1.** a staff or support to assist a lame or infirm person in walking, now usu. with a cross piece at one end to fit under the armpit. **2.** any of various devices resembling this in shape or use. **3.** a forked support or part. **4.** a forked rest for the legs in side-saddle. **5.** the crotch of the human body. **6.** *Naut.* a semicircular support to hold a spar. **7.** *Colloq.* anything relied on, trusted. *–v.t.* **8.** to shear wool from a sheep's breech area and hind legs, to prevent fouling of the wool by excreta. **9.** to immerse (sheep) in a sheep dip by using a crutch. **10.** to support on crutches; prop; sustain. [ME *crucche,* OE *crycc,* c. D *kruk* and G *Krücke.* Cf. CROOK[1$cp2]]

**crutchings** /ˈkrʌtʃɪŋz/, *n.pl.* the wool taken from a sheep by crutching.

**crux** /krʌks/, *n., pl.* **cruxes, cruces** /ˈkrusiz/. **1.** a vital, basic, or decisive point. **2.** a cross. **3.** something that torments by its puzzling nature; a perplexing difficulty. [L: cross, torment, trouble]

**crux ansata** /– ænˈsatə/, *n.* a T-shaped cross with a loop at the top; ankh. [L: cross with a handle]

**cry** /kraɪ/, *v.,* **cried, crying,** *n., pl.* **cries.** *–v.i.* **1.** to utter inarticulate sounds, esp. of lamentation, grief, or suffering, usu. with tears. **2.** to weep; shed tears, with or without sound. **3.** to call loudly; shout. **4.** to give forth vocal sounds or characteristic calls, as animals; yelp; bark. *–v.t.* **5.** to utter or pronounce loudly; call out. **6.** to announce orally in public; sell by outcry. **7.** to beg for or implore in a loud voice. **8.** to disparage; belittle (fol. by *down*). **9.** to break a promise, agreement, etc. (fol. by *off*). **10.** to praise; extol (fol. by *up*). *–n.* **11.** the act or sound of crying; any loud utterance or exclamation; a shout, scream, or wail. **12.** clamour; outcry. **13.** an entreaty; appeal. **14.** *Obs.* an oral proclamation or announcement. **15.** a call of wares for sale, etc., as by a street vendor. **16.** public report. **17.** an opinion generally expressed. **18.** a battle cry. **19.** a political or party slogan. **20.** a fit of weeping. **21.** the utterance or call of an animal. **22.** a pack of hounds. **23. a far cry, a.** quite some distance; a long way. **b.** only remotely related; very different. [ME *crie(n),* from OF *crier,* from L *quirītāre*] – **cryingly,** *adv.*

**cry-baby** /ˈkraɪ-beɪbi/, *n., pl.* **-bies.** *Colloq.* one given to crying like a baby, or to weak display of injured feeling.

**crying** /ˈkraɪɪŋ/, *adj.* **1.** that cries; clamorous; wailing; weeping. **2.** demanding attention or remedy: *a crying evil.*

**cryo-,** a word element meaning 'icy cold', 'frost', 'low temperature'. [Gk *kryo-,* combining form of *krýos*]

**cryobiology** /ˌkraɪoʊbaɪˈɒlədʒi/, *n.* the study of effects of low temperatures on living organisms.

**cryocautery** /kraɪoʊˈkɔtəri/, *n.* the destruction of body tissue by application of extreme cold.

**cryogen** /ˈkraɪədʒən/, *n.* a substance for producing low temperatures; a freezing mixture.

**cryogenics** /kraɪəˈdʒɛnɪks/, *n.* that branch of physics concerned with the properties of materials at very low temperatures. – **cryogenic,** *adj.*

**cryohydrate** /ˌkraɪoʊˈhaɪdreɪt/, *n.* a mixture of ice and another substance in definite proportions such that a minimum melting or freezing point is attained.

**cryolite** /ˈkraɪəlaɪt/, *n.* a mineral, sodium aluminium fluoride, $Na_3AlF_6$, occurring in white masses, used as a flux in the electrolytic production of aluminium and as an insecticide; Greenland spar.

**cryometer** /kraɪˈɒmətə/, *n.* a thermometer for the measurement of low temperatures, as one containing alcohol instead of mercury.

**cryonics** /kraɪˈɒnɪks/, *n.* the practice of storing a dead body at a very low temperature in the hope that some future technology may be able to bring it back to life. – **cryonic,** *adj.*

**cryophilic** /kraɪəˈfɪlɪk/, *adj.* well-adapted to low temperatures, esp. of bacteria developing best at temperatures below 10°C.

**cryophyle** /ˈkraɪəfaɪl/, *n.* a life form well-adapted to low temperatures.

**cryoprecipitate** /ˌkraɪoʊprəˈsɪpətət/, *n.* plasma containing clotting factors, stored in a frozen state, and used to correct coagulation defects, esp. in haemophilia.

**cryoscope** /ˈkraɪəskoʊp/, *n.* an instrument for determining freezing and solidification points.

**cryoscopic method** /ˌkraɪəskɒpɪk ˈmɛθəd/, *n.* a method of determining the molecular weight of a dissolved substance by measuring the depression of the freezing point of the solvent produced by a known concentration of solute.

**cryoscopy** /kraɪˈɒskəpi/, *n.* **1.** the determination of the freezing points of liquids or solutions, or of the lowering of the freezing points by dissolved substances. **2.** *Med.* the determination of the freezing points of certain bodily fluids, as urine, for diagnosis.

**cryostat** /ˈkraɪəstæt/, *n.* an apparatus usu. automatic, maintaining a very low constant temperature.

**cryosurgery** /kraɪoʊˈsɜdʒəri/, *n.* surgery using extreme cold for the destruction of body tissue.

**cryotherapy** /kraɪoʊˈθɛrəpi/, *n.* a form of therapy which consists of local or general refrigeration of the body or part of it.

**cryotron** /ˈkraɪətrɒn/, *n.* a miniature switch which operates at the temperature of liquid helium and which depends on superconductivity.

**cryoturbation** /ˌkraɪoʊtɜˈbeɪʃən/, *n.* the weathering of soil under conditions of extreme cold.

**crypt** /krɪpt/, *n.* **1.** a subterranean chamber or vault, esp. one beneath the main floor of a church, used as a burial place, etc. **2.** *Anat.* a slender pit or recess; a small glandular cavity. [L *crypta,* from Gk *kryptḗ,* properly fem. of *kryptós* hidden] – **cryptal,** *adj.*

**cryptanalysis** /krɪptəˈnæləsəs/, *n.* the art of deciphering secret characters or codes by analysis. – **cryptanalyst,** *n.* – **cryptanalytic,** *adj.*

**cryptic** /ˈkrɪptɪk/, *adj.* **1.** hidden; secret; occult. **2.** mysterious; enigmatic. **3.** *Zool.* fitted for concealing. Also, **cryptical.** – **cryptically,** *adv.*

**crypto** /ˈkrɪptoʊ/, *n. Colloq.* a person who conceals his allegience to a political group.

**crypto-,** a word element meaning 'hidden', as in *cryptocastic.* Also, before vowels, **crypt-.** [combining form representing Gk *kryptós*]

**cryptochannel** /ˈkrɪptoʊtʃænəl/, *n.* a system of secret communication between two or more cryptographers.

**cryptoclastic** /ˌkrɪptoʊˈklæstɪk/, *adj.* composed of extremely fine, broken or fragmental particles barely visible under the microscope.

**cryptocrystalline** /ˌkrɪptoʊˈkrɪstəlaɪn/, *adj.* crystalline but so fine-grained that the individual components cannot be seen with a magnifying glass.

**cryptogam** /ˈkrɪptəgæm/, *n.* **1.** any of the Cryptogamia, an old primary division of plants comprising those without true flowers and seeds, as the ferns, mosses, and thallophytes. **2.** a plant without a true seed (opposed to *phanerogam*). [back-formation from NL *cryptogamia,* from *crypto-* CRYPTO- + Gk *-gamía* married state] – **cryptogamic, cryptogamous** /krɪpˈtɒgəməs/, *adj.*

**cryptogenic** /krɪptoʊˈdʒɛnɪk/, *adj.* of obscure or unknown origin, as a disease.

**cryptogram** /ˈkrɪptəgræm/, *n.* a message or writing in secret characters or otherwise occult; a cryptograph. – **cryptogrammic,** *adj.*

**cryptograph** /ˈkrɪptəgræf, -graf/, *n.* **1.** a cryptogram. **2.** a system of secret writing; a cipher. **3.** a device for translating text into cipher.

**cryptography** /krɪpˈtɒgrəfi/, *n.* **1.** the process or art of writing in or deciphering secret characters or cipher. **2.** anything so written. – **cryptographer, cryptographist,** *n.* – **cryptographic** /krɪptoʊˈgræfɪk/, *adj.*

**cryptology** /krɪpˈtɒlədʒi/, *n.* the science of maintaining the security of communication in and of extracting information from codes.

**cryptonym** /ˈkrɪptənɪm/, *n.* a secret name. [CRYPT- + Gk *ónym(a)* name]

**cryptonymous** /krɪpˈtɒnəməs/, *adj.* anonymous.

**cryptosystem** /ˈkrɪptoʊsɪstəm/, *n.* a method of processing secret information involving both encryption and decryption.

**cryptozoic** /ˌkrɪptəˈzoʊɪk/, *n.* →**Pre-Cambrian.**

**cryptozoite** /krɪptəˈzoʊaɪt/, *n.* the phase in the development of malaria parasites in their vertebrate hosts during which they live in cells other than red corpuscles, as in the human liver.

**cryst.,** crystallography. Also, **crystall.**

**crystal** /ˈkrɪstl/, *n.* **1.** a clear, transparent mineral or glass resembling ice. **2.** the transparent form of crystallised quartz. **3.** *Chem., Mineral.* a solid body having a characteristic internal structure and enclosed by symmetrically arranged plane surfaces, intersecting at definite and characteristic angles. **4.** anything made of or resembling such a substance. **5.** a single grain or mass of a crystalline substance. **6.** glass of a high degree of brilliance. **7.** cut glass. **8.** the glass or plastic cover over the face of a watch. **9.** *Radio.* **a.** the piece of galena, carborundum, or the like, forming the essential part of a crystal detector. **b.** the crystal detector itself. **10.** a crystal ball. **11.** a quartz crystal ground in the shape of a rectangular parallelepiped, which vibrates strongly at one frequency when electric voltages of that frequency are placed across opposite sides. It is used to control the frequency of an oscillator as, for example, the frequency of a radio transmitter. *–adj.* **12.** composed of crystal. **13.** resembling crystal; clear; transparent. **14.** *Radio.* pertaining to or employing a crystal detector. [ME *cristal,* from OF; replacing OE *cristalla,* from L *crystallum,* from Gk *krýstallos* ice, crystal] – **crystal-like,** *adj.*

**crystal ball** /– ˈbɔl/, *n.* a ball into which a fortune-teller looks in order to see distant or future events.

**crystal detector** /– dəˈtɛktə/, *n.* a device used in early radio receiving apparatus for rectifying the alternating currents, consisting essentially of a crystal, as of galena or carborundum, permitting a current to pass freely in one direction only.

**crystal-gazing** /ˈkrɪstl-geɪzɪŋ/, *n.* **1.** looking into a crystal ball. **2.** attempting to predict the future. – **crystal-gazer,** *n.*

**crystall-,** variant of **crystallo-,** used before vowels.

**crystall.,** crystallography.

**crystal lattice** /krɪstl ˈlætəs/, *n.* →**lattice** (def. 3).

**crystalliferous** /krɪstəˈlɪfərəs/, *adj.* bearing, containing, or yielding crystals. [L *crystallum* crystal + -I- + -FEROUS]

**crystalline** /ˈkrɪstəlaɪn/, *adj.* **1.** of or like crystal; clear; transparent. **2.** formed by crystallisation. **3.** composed of crystals, as rocks. **4.** pertaining to crystals or their formation. [Gk *krystállinos*]

**crystalline lens** /– ˈlɛnz/, *n.* a doubly convex, transparent, lenslike body in the eye, situated behind the iris and serving to focus the rays of light on the retina.

**crystallisation** /krɪstəlaɪˈzeɪʃən/, *n.* **1.** the act of crystallising; the process of forming crystals. **2.** a crystallised body or formation. Also, **crystallization.**

**crystallise** /ˈkrɪstəlaɪz/, *v.,* **-lised, -lising.** *–v.t.* **1.** to form into crystals; cause to assume crystalline form. **2.** to give definite or concrete form to. **3.** *Cookery.* to coat (fruit or flower petals) with sugar to give an attractive, edible finish. *–v.i.* **4.** to form crystals; become crystalline in form. **5.** to assume definite or concrete form. Also, **crystallize.** – **crystallisable,** *adj.*

**crystallite** /ˈkrɪstəlaɪt/, *n.* a minute body in igneous rocks, marking an incipient stage in crystallisation. [CRYSTALL- + -ITE[1]]

**crystallo-,** a word element meaning 'crystal', as in *crystallographic.* Also, before vowels, **crystall-.** [Gk *krystallo-,* combining form of *krýstallos*]

**crystallographic** /ˌkrɪstəloʊˈgræfɪk/, *adj.* of or pertaining to crystallography. Also, **crystallographical.** – **crystallographically,** *adv.*

**crystallography** /krɪstəˈlɒgrəfi/, *n.* the science dealing with crystallisation and the forms and structure of crystals. – **crystallographer,** *n.*

**crystalloid** /ˈkrɪstəlɔɪd/, *adj.* **1.** resembling a crystal; of the nature of a crystalloid. *–n.* **2.** a substance (usu. crystallisable) which, when dissolved in a liquid, will diffuse readily through vegetable or animal membranes (contrasted with *colloid*). **3.** *Bot.* one of certain minute crystal-like granules of protein, found in the tissues of various seeds. [Gk *krystalloeidḗs.* See CRYSTAL, -OID] – **crystalloidal,** *adj.*

**crystallomancy** /ˈkrɪstəloʊˌmænsi/, *n.* divination by means of a transparent body, such as a crystal ball, precious stone, or mirror.

**crystal oscillator** /krɪstl ˈɒsəleɪtə/, *n.* a source of electrical oscillations of very constant frequency determined by the physical characteristics of a quartz crystal.

**crystal pick-up** /ˈ– pɪk-ʌp/, *n.* a gramophone pick-up in which a piezoelectric crystal converts stylus vibrations into electric impulses for amplification.

**crystal rectifier** /– ˈrɛktəfaɪə/, *n.* a semiconducting crystal used as a rectifier; a semiconductor diode.

**crystal set** /ˈ– sɛt/, *n.* a simple form of radio receiver based on a crystal detector.

**crystal violet** /– ˈvaɪələt/, *n.* a dye derived from rosaniline, used as an indicator in medicine.

**c/s,** cycle per second.

**Cs,** *Chem.* caesium.

**csabai** /tʃəˈbaɪ, ˈtʃɒbɔɪ/, *n.* a raw smoked sausage, mainly pork, heavily spiced with paprika, black pepper and garlic. [named after district in Hungary]

**csardas** /ˈtʃadæʃ/, *n.* →**czardas.**

**CS gas** /si ɛs ˈgæs/, *n.* a noisome gas, used esp. in riot control, which causes tears, excessive salivation and difficulty in breathing. [from the initials of its U.S. inventors B. *C(arson)* and R. *S(taughton)*]

**C'ship,** Championship.

**C.S.I.R.O.** /ˌsi ɛs aɪ ar ˈoʊ/, Commonwealth Scientific and Industrial Research Organisation. Also, **CSIRO.**

**C.S.M.,** Chief Stipendiary Magistrate.

**C-spring** /ˈsi-sprɪŋ/, *n.* →**cee-spring.**

**cSt,** centistokes.

**CST,** Central Standard Time.

**ct.,** **1.** carat. **2.** caught. **3.** circuit. **4.** court.

**CT,** computerised tomography.

**cteno-,** a word element referring to comb-like scales, as in *ctenophore.* Also, before vowels, **cten-.** [Gk *kteno-,* combining form of *kteís* comb]

**ctenoid** /ˈtɛnɔɪd, ˈtin-/, *adj.* **1.** comb-like or pectinate; rough-edged. **2.** having rough-edged scales. [Gk *ktenoeidḗs* comb-shaped]

**ctenophore** /ˈtɛnəfɔ, ˈti-/, *n.* a member of the Ctenophora, a phylum of marine swimming invertebrates with rounded, oval or band-shaped gelatinous bodies and eight meridional rows of ciliated plates; comb jelly. – **ctenophoran,** *adj., n.*

**ctge.,** **1.** cartage. **2.** cottage.

**ctl,** cental.

**cu.,** **1.** cubic. **2.** cumulus.

**Cu,** *Chem.* cuprum; copper.

**cub** /kʌb/, *n.* **1.** the young of certain animals, as the fox, bear, etc. **2.** (*joc.*) an awkward or uncouth youth. **3.** a novice or apprentice, esp. a cub reporter. **4.** a member of the junior division (ages 8-11) of the Scouts. [var. of COB[1]] – **cubbish,** *adj.* – **cubbishness,** *n.*

**Cuba** /ˈkjubə/, *n.* an island republic in the Caribbean, off the south-eastern coast of North America. – **Cuban,** *adj., n.*

**cubage** /ˈkjubɪdʒ/, *n.* →**cubature.**

**Cuban heel** /kjubən ˈhil/, *n.* a high, uncurved heel on a boot or shoe.

**cubature** /ˈkjubətʃə/, *n.* **1.** the determination of the cubic contents of a thing. **2.** cubic contents. [L *cubus* cube, on model of QUADRATURE]

**cubby** /ˈkʌbi/, *n., pl.* **-bies.** a snug, confined place; a cubbyhouse. [obs. *cub* shed; cf. LG *kübje* shed]

**cubbyhole** /ˈkʌbihoʊl/, *n.* a small enclosed space.

**cubbyhouse** /ˈkʌbihaʊs/, *n.* a children's playhouse.

**cube** /kjub/, *n., v.,* **cubed, cubing.** –*n.* **1.** solid bounded by six equal squares, the angle between any two adjacent faces being a right angle. **2.** a piece of anything of this form. **3.** the third power of a quantity: *the cube of 4 is 4 × 4 × 4, or 64.* **4.** a small block of sugar, concentrated meat or vegetable extract: *sugar cube, beef cube.* –*v.t.* **5.** to make into a cube or cubes. **6.** to measure the cubic contents of. **7.** to raise to the third power; find the cube of. [L *cubus,* from Gk *kýbos* die, cube]

**cubeb** /ˈkjubɛb/, *n.* the spicy fruit or drupe of an East Indian climbing shrub, *Piper cubeba,* dried in an unripe but fully grown state, and used in the treatment of urinary and bronchial disorders. [ME *quibibe,* from F *cubèbe,* from Ar. *kabāba*]

**cube roll** /kjub ˈroʊl/, *n.* →**rib eye.**

**cube root** /– ˈrut/, *n.* the quantity of which a given quantity is the cube: *4 is the cube root of 64.*

**cube sugar** /– ˈʃʊgə/, *n.* granulated crystals of sugar formed into rough cubes by a heat-drying process.

**cubic** /ˈkjubɪk/, *adj.* **1.** of three dimensions; solid, or pertaining to solid content: *a cubic metre* (the volume of a cube whose edges are each a metre long). **2.** having the form of a cube. **3.** *Arith., Alg., etc.,* being of the third power or degree. **4.** *Crystall.* belonging or pertaining to the isometric system of crystallisation. Also, **cubical.** – **cubically,** *adv.* – **cubicalness,** *n.*

**cubicle** /ˈkjubɪkəl/, *n.* **1.** a bedroom, esp. one of a number of small ones in a divided dormitory. **2.** any small space or compartment partitioned off. [L *cubiculum* bedchamber]

**cubic measure** /kjubɪk ˈmɛʒə/, *n.* **1.** the measurement of volume in cubic units. **2.** a system of such units.

**cubiculum** /kjuˈbɪkjələm/, *n., pl.* **-la** /-lə/. a burial chamber, as in catacombs. [L: bedroom]

**cubiform** /ˈkjubəfɔm/, *adj.* formed like a cube.

**cubism** /ˈkjubɪzəm/, *n.* an art movement, initiated in France in 1907, which was concerned with the analysis of forms and their interrelation and whose proponents made surface arrangements of planes, lines and shapes, often overlapping and interlocking, in an attempt to represent solidity and volume on a two-dimensional plane. – **cubist,** *n., adj.* – **cubistic** /kjuˈbɪstɪk/, *adj.* – **cubistically,** *adv.*

**cubit** /ˈkjubət/, *n.* an ancient linear unit based on the length of the forearm, varying in extent, but usu. between 18 and 22 inches, or 460 and 560 mm. [ME, from L *cubitum* elbow, ell]

**cubmaster** /ˈkʌbmastə/, *n.* the adult leader of a pack of Scout cubs.

**cuboid** /ˈkjubɔɪd/, *adj.* **1.** resembling a cube in form. **2.** *Anat.* denoting or pertaining to the outermost bone of the distal row of tarsal bones. –*n.* **3.** *Maths.* a rectangular parallelepiped. **4.** *Anat.* the cuboid bone. – **cuboidal,** *adj.*

**cub reporter** /kʌb rəˈpɔtə/, *n. Colloq.* a reporter without experience.

**cucaracha** /kʊkəˈratʃə/, *n.* a night-club dance originating in Mexico. [named after La *Cucaracha,* The Cockroach, a popular song]

**cucking stool** /ˈkʌkɪŋ stul/, *n.* a former instrument of punishment consisting of a chair in which an offender, esp. a common scold, was strapped, to be jeered at and pelted by the crowd, or, sometimes, to be ducked. See **ducking stool.** [ME *cuking stol* mucking stool; *cucking,* ppr. of obs. v. *cuck* defecate (from Scand.; cf. Icel. *kúka*)]

**cuckold** /ˈkʌkəld/, *n.* **1.** the husband of an unfaithful wife. –*v.t.* **2.** to make a cuckold of (a husband). [ME *cokewold;* orig. uncert.]

**cuckoldry** /ˈkʌkəldri/, *n.* **1.** the act or fact of making a cuckold of one. **2.** the state of being a cuckold.

**cuckoo** /ˈkʊku/, *n.* **1.** any of a number of slim, long-tailed, frequently migratory, Australian birds of the family Cuculidae, noted for their habit of laying eggs in the nests of other birds, as the pallid cuckoo. **2.** any of various other members of the same family esp. *Cuculus canorus,* a common European bird with a characteristic two note call. **3.** the call of the cuckoo, or an imitation of it. **4.** a fool; simpleton. –*v.i.* **5.** to utter the call of the cuckoo or an imitation of it. –*v.t.* **6.** to repeat monotonously. –*adj.* **7.** *Colloq.* crazy; silly; foolish. [ME *cucu* (imitative of its call). Cf. F *coucou,* G *Kuckuk*]

pallid cuckoo

**cuckoo clock** /ˈ– klɒk/, *n.* a clock which announces the hours by a sound like the call of the European cuckoo.

**cuckooflower** /ˈkʊkuflaʊə/, *n.* any of various plants, as the ragged robin.

**cuckoopint** /ˈkʊkupaɪnt/, *n.* a common European species of arum, *Arum maculatum;* wake-robin.

**cuckoo sandstone** /kʊku 'sændstoʊn/, *n.* →**speckled hen.**

**cuckoo scab** /'– skæb/, *n.* (of cattle) a skin disease at the back of the head and ears.

**cuckoo-shrike** /'kʊku-ʃraɪk/, *n.* any of various birds of the mainly tropical family Campephagidae as the **black-faced cuckoo-shrike,** *Coracina novaehollandiae,* and the cicada bird.

black-faced cuckoo-shrike

**cuckoo-spit** /'kʊku-spɪt/, *n.* **1.** a frothy secretion found on plants, exuded as a protective covering by the young of certain insects, as the froghoppers. **2.** an insect secreting this.

**cuckoo wrasse** /'kʊku ræs/, *n.* a common British fish, *Labrus mixtus,* with a marked colour difference between the male and the female.

**cuculiform** /kjə'kjuləfɔm/, *adj.* pertaining to or resembling the order Cuculiformes, containing the cuckoos, roadrunners, etc. [L *cucūlus* cuckoo + -I- + -FORM]

**cucullate** /'kjukəleɪt, -lət/, *adj.* **1.** cowled; hooded. **2.** resembling a cowl or hood. Also, **cucullated.** [LL *cucullātus* hooded]

**cucumber** /'kjukʌmbə/, *n.* **1.** a creeping plant, *Cucumis sativus,* occurring in many cultivated forms, yielding a long fleshy fruit which is commonly eaten green as a salad and used for pickling. **2.** the fruit of this plant. **3.** any of various allied or similar plants or their fruits. **4. cool as a cucumber,** poised and confident. [F (obs.) *cocombre,* from L *cucumis;* replacing ME *cucumer,* from L *cucumis*]

**cucumber orchid** /– 'ɔkəd/, *n.* an epiphytic orchid, *Dendrobium cucumerinum,* of New South Wales and southern Queensland, favouring the Casuarina as host plant.

**cucumber tree** /'– ˌtri/, *n.* **1.** any of several American magnolias, esp. *Magnolia acuminata.* **2.** any of certain other trees, as an East Indian tree of the genus *Averrhoa.*

**cucumiform** /kjə'kjuməfɔm/, *adj.* shaped like a cucumber; approximately cylindrical, with rounded or tapering ends. [L *cucumi(s)* cucumber + -FORM]

**cucurbit** /kju'kɜbət/, *n.* **1.** a gourd. **2.** any cucurbitaceous plant including pumpkins and melons. [ME *cucurbite,* from F, from L *cucurbita* gourd]

**cucurbitaceous** /kjəkɜbə'teɪʃəs/, *adj.* belonging to the Cucurbitaceae, or gourd family of plants which includes the pumpkin, cucumber, muskmelon, watermelon, etc. [L *cucurbita* gourd]

**cud** /kʌd/, *n.* **1.** the portion of food which a ruminating animal returns from the first stomach to the mouth to chew a second time. **2. chew the cud,** to reflect; meditate. [ME; OE *cudu,* var. of *cwidu.* See QUID[1]]

**cudbear** /'kʌdbɛə/, *n.* a violet colouring matter obtained from various lichens, esp. *Ochrolechia tartarea.*

**cuddle** /'kʌdl/, *v.,* **-dled, -dling,** *n.* –*v.t.* **1.** to draw or hold close in an affectionate manner; hug tenderly; fondle. –*v.i.* **2.** to lie close and snug; nestle; curl up in going to sleep. –*n.* **3.** the act of cuddling; a hug; an embrace. [obs. *couth,* adj., comfortable, friendly (OE *cūth* familiar) + *-le,* frequentative suffix. Cf. FONDLE] – **cuddlesome, cuddly,** *adj.*

**cuddle seat** /'– sit/, *n.* **1.** a canvas seat slung over the shoulders, used for carrying babies. **2.** a swing chair (usu. outdoors) with a canopy, often seating only two.

**cuddy**[1] /'kʌdi/, *n., pl.* **-dies. 1.** a small cabin on a ship or boat, esp. one under the poop. **2.** a small room; a cupboard. [orig. unknown]

**cuddy**[2] /'kʌdi/, *n., pl.* **-dies. 1.** a small horse. **2.** *Chiefly Scot.* a donkey. [orig. unknown]

**cudgel** /'kʌdʒəl/, *n., v.,* **-elled, -elling** or (*U.S.*) **-eled, -eling.** –*n.* **1.** a short, thick stick used as a weapon; a club. **2. take up the cudgels,** to engage in a contest. –*v.t.* **3.** to strike with a cudgel; beat. **4. cudgel one's brains,** to think hard. [ME *cuggel,* OE *cycgel,* akin to G *Kugel* ball] – **cudgeller;** *U.S.,* **cudgeler,** *n.*

**cudgerie** /'kʌdʒəri/, *n.* any of several trees, as *Flindersia schottiana,* a large tree of the Australian rainforests with a big woody fruit capsule, or the **blush cudgerie,** *Euroschinus falcatus,* so called because of the pink colour of its wood. [Aboriginal]

**cudweed** /'kʌdwid/, *n.* **1.** any of the woolly herbs constituting the genus *Gnaphalium.* **2.** any of various plants of allied genera.

**cue**[1] /kju/, *n.* **1.** anything said or done on or behind the stage that is followed by a specific line or action: *each line of dialogue is a cue to the succeeding line; an offstage door slam was his cue to enter.* **2.** a hint; an intimation; a guiding suggestion. **3.** the part one is to play; a prescribed or necessary course of action. **4.** *Archaic.* humour; disposition. **5.** the one element in a complex event which is crucial to the perception of the whole. –*v.t.* **6.** to provide with a cue. [? spelling of abbrev. *q.* or *qu.* for L *quando* when]

**cue**[2] /kju/, *n., v.,* **cued, cuing.** –*n.* **1.** a long tapering rod, tipped with a soft leather pad, used to strike the ball in billiards, etc. **2.** a queue of hair. –*v.t.* **3.** to tie into a cue or tail. [var. of *queue,* from F]

**cue ball** /'– bɔl/, *n.* (in billiards, etc.) the ball struck by the cue as distinguished from the other balls on the table.

**cue dot** /'– dɒt/, *n.* a spot mechanically scraped onto a frame of a film, to indicate that the film is about to end.

**cueist** /'kjuəst/, *n.* a billiard-player.

**cuff**[1] /kʌf/, *n.* **1.** a fold, band, or variously shaped piece serving as a trimming or finish for the bottom of a sleeve or trouser leg. **2.** the part of a gauntlet or long glove that extends over the wrist. **3.** a separate or detachable band or piece of linen or other material worn about the wrist, inside or outside the sleeve. **4. off the cuff,** impromptu; extemporaneously; on the spur of the moment: *to speak off the cuff.* **5. on the cuff,** *Colloq.* **a.** on credit. **b.** *N.Z.* excessive; unfair. [ME *cuffe, coffe* glove, mitten; orig. uncert.]

**cuff**[2] /kʌf/, *v.t.* **1.** to strike with the open hand; beat; buffet. –*n.* **2.** a blow with the fist or the open hand; a buffet. **3.** a handcuff. [cf. Swed. *kuffa* thrust, push]

**cufflink** /'kʌflɪŋk/, *n.* a link which fastens a shirt cuff.

**cuica** /'kwikə/, *n.* a South American friction drum used in bossa nova, etc. Also, **quica.**

**cuie** /'kjui/, *n. Colloq.* cucumber, Also, **cu** /kju/, **cuey.** [CU(CUMBER) + -IE]

**cuirass** /kwə'ræs/, *n.* **1.** a piece of defensive armour for the body, combining a breastplate and a piece for the back. **2.** the breastplate alone. **3.** any similar covering, as the protective armour of a ship. **4.** *Zool.* a hard shell or other covering forming an indurated defensive shield. –*v.t.* **5.** to equip or cover with a cuirass. [F *cuirasse,* b. *cuir(ie)* leather armour (from *cuir,* from L *corium* leather) and Pr. *(coir)assa* (from LL *coriācea,* fem., made of leather)]

**cuirassier** /kwɪrə'sɪə/, *n.* a cavalry soldier wearing a cuirass. [F]

**cuisenaire rods** /kwizə'nɛə rɒdz/, *n.pl.* coloured wooden blocks graduated in length, used as an aid in teaching numeracy to children. [named after the inventor, Georges *Cuisenaire,* Belgian educationist]

**cuisine** /kwə'zin/, *n.* **1.** the kitchen; the culinary department of a house, hotel, etc. **2.** style of cooking; cookery. [F, from L *cocīna, coquīna* kitchen. See KITCHEN]

**cuisse** /kwɪs/, *n.* a piece of armour to protect the thigh. Also, **cuish** /kwɪʃ/. [F: thigh, from L *coxa* hip]

**cukie** /'kjuki/, *n. Colloq.* cucumber

**culch** /kʌltʃ/, *n.* **1.** the stones, old shells, etc., forming an oyster bed and furnishing points of attachment for the spawn of oysters. **2.** the spawn. **3.** rubbish; refuse. –*v.t.* **4.** to prepare (an oyster bed) with culch. Also, **cultch.** [cf. OF *culche* bed]

**cul-de-sac** /'kʌl-də-sæk/, *n.* **1.** a street, lane, etc., closed at one end; blind alley. **2.** saclike cavity, tube, or the like, open only at one end, as the caecum. **3.** *Mil.* the situation of a military force hemmed in on all sides except behind. [F: bottom of sack]

**-cule,** a diminutive suffix of nouns, as in *animalcule, molecule.* Also, **-cle.** [F, or from L *-culus, -cula, -culum*]

**culet** /'kjulət/, *n.* **1.** the small flat face forming the bottom of a brilliant. **2.** the part of medieval armour protecting the back of the body below the waist. [F (obs.), diminutive of *cul* bottom, from L *cūlus.* Cf. F *culasse* culet]

**culex** /'kjulɛks/, *n., pl.* **-lices** /-ləsiz/. any mosquito of the genus *Culex,* including the common house mosquito, *Culex* *pipiens.* [L: a gnat]

**culicid** /kju'lısəd/, *n.* **1.** any of the dipterous insects of the family Culicidae; a mosquito. *–adj.* **2.** belonging or pertaining to the Culicidae.

**culinary** /'kʌlənri, -ənəri/, *adj.* pertaining to the kitchen or to cookery; used in cooking. [L *culīnārius,* from *culīna* kitchen]

**cull** /kʌl/, *v.t.* **1.** to choose; select; pick; gather the choice things or parts from. **2.** to collect; gather; pluck. **3.** to remove animals of inferior quality from (a herd or flock). **4.** to kill (noxious animals, as deer, kangaroos, etc.), with a view to controlling numbers. *–n.* **5.** the act of culling. **6.** something culled, esp. an inferior animal withdrawn from a herd or flock. [ME *culle(n),* from OF *coillir,* from L *colligere* COLLECT[1]]

**cullender** /'kʌləndə/, *n.* →**colander.**

**culler** /'kʌlə/, *n.* a professional shooter of noxious animals, esp. deer.

**cullet** /'kʌlət/, *n.* broken or waste glass suitable for remelting.

**cullion** /'kʌliən/, *n. Archaic.* a base or vile fellow. [ME *coillion,* from F *couillon,* from L *cōleus* testicle]

**cully** /'kʌli/, *n., pl.* **-lies,** *v.,* **-lied, -lying.** *Archaic. Colloq.* *–n.* **1.** a dupe. **2.** a man or fellow. **3.** a companion, friend. *–v.t.* **4.** to trick; cheat; dupe. [short for CULLION]

**culm**[1] /kʌlm/, *n.* **1.** coal dust; slack. **2.** anthracite, esp. of inferior grade. [var. of *coom* soot]

**culm**[2] /kʌlm/, *n.* **1.** a stem or stalk, esp. the jointed and usu. hollow stem of grasses. *–v.i.* **2.** to grow or develop into a culm. [L *culmus* stalk. Cf. HAULM]

**culmiferous** /kʌl'mıfərəs/, *adj.* bearing culms.

**culminant** /'kʌlmənənt/, *adj.* culminating; topmost.

**culminate** /'kʌlməneıt/, *v.i.,* **-nated, -nating. 1.** to reach the highest point, the summit, or highest development (usu. fol. by *in*). **2.** *Astron.* (of a celestial body) to be on the meridian, or reach the highest or the lowest altitude. [LL *culminātus,* pp., crowned]

**culmination** /kʌlmə'neıʃən/, *n.* **1.** the act or fact of culminating. **2.** that in which anything culminates; the highest point; the acme. **3.** *Astron.* the position of a celestial body when it is on the meridian.

**culottes** /kə'lɒts/, *n.pl.* a skirt-like garment, separated and sewn like trousers. [F]

**culpable** /'kʌlpəbəl/, *adj.* deserving blame or censure; blameworthy. [L *culpābilis* blameworthy; replacing ME *coupable,* from OF] **– culpability** /kʌlpə'bıləti/, **culpableness,** *n.* **– culpably,** *adv.*

**culpable driving** /– 'draıvıŋ/, *n.* the driving of a motor vehicle whilst under the influence of liquor or a drug, or in a reckless manner, causing the death of or serious injury to a person.

**culprit** /'kʌlprət/, *n.* **1.** a person arraigned for an offence. **2.** one guilty of or responsible for a specified offence or fault. [orig. uncert.; traditionally explained as from L *cul(pābilis),* guilty + AF *pri(s)t* ready, i.e. the prosecution is ready to prove guilt]

**cult** /kʌlt/, *n.* **1.** a particular system of religious worship, esp. with reference to its rites and ceremonies. **2.** an instance of an almost religious veneration for a person or thing, esp. as manifested by a body of admirers: *a cult of Napoleon.* **3.** the object of such devotion. **4.** a popular fashion; fad. [L *cultus* care, worship] **– cultism,** *n.* **– cultist,** *n.*

**cultch** /kʌltʃ/, *n., v.t.* →**culch.**

**cultigen** /'kʌltədʒən/, *n.* any plant found only in cultivation, the origin of which is not known with any certainty.

**cultivable** /'kʌltəvəbəl/, *adj.* capable of being cultivated. Also, **cultivatable** /kʌltə'veıtəbəl/. [F, from *cultiver* cultivate] **– cultivability** /kʌltəvə'bıləti/, *n.*

**cultivar** /'kʌltəva/, *n.* a variety of plant that has been produced only under cultivation. [CULTI(VATED) + VAR(IETY)]

**cultivate** /'kʌltəveıt/, *v.t.,* **-vated, -vating. 1.** to bestow labour upon (land) in raising crops; till; improve by husbandry. **2.** to use a cultivator on. **3.** to promote or improve the growth of (a plant, etc.) by labour and attention. **4.** to produce by culture. **5.** to develop or improve by education or training; train; refine. **6.** to promote the growth or development of (an art, science, etc.); foster. **7.** to devote oneself to (an art, etc.). **8.** to seek to promote or foster (friendship, etc.). **9.** to seek the acquaintance or friendship of (a person). [ML *cultīvātus,* pp. of *cultīvāre;* from *cultīvus* tilled, from L *cultus,* pp. of *colere* till]

**cultivated** /'kʌltəveıtəd/, *adj.* **1.** subjected to cultivation. **2.** produced or improved by cultivation, as a plant. **3.** educated; refined; cultured.

**Cultivated Australian** /ˌkʌltəveıtəd əs'treıljən/, *n.* that pronunciation of Australian English which serves as a prestige form. See **Spectrum of Australian English.**

**cultivation** /kʌltə'veıʃən/, *n.* **1.** the act or art of cultivating. **2.** the state of being cultivated. **3.** culture. **4.** →**cultivation paddock.**

**cultivation paddock** /'– ˌpædək/, *n.* **1.** a paddock which is kept specifically for cropping. **2.** a paddock ploughed, or sown to a crop. Also, **cultivation.**

**cultivator** /'kʌltəveıtə/, *n.* **1.** one who or that which cultivates. **2.** an implement for loosening the earth and destroying weeds when drawn between rows of growing plants.

**cultrate** /'kʌltreıt/, *adj.* sharp-edged and pointed, as a leaf. Also, **cultrated.** [L *cultrātus,* from *culter* knife]

**cultural** /'kʌltʃərəl/, *adj.* of or pertaining to culture or cultivation. **– culturally,** *adv.*

**cultural attache** /– ə'tæʃeı/, *n.* an attache whose special consideration is to promote a cultural exchange between his country and the country to which he is posted.

**cultural cringe** /– 'krındʒ/, *n.* a feeling that one's country's culture is inferior to that of other countries.

**culture** /'kʌltʃə/, *n., v.,* **-tured, -turing.** *–n.* **1.** the action or practice of cultivating the soil; tillage. **2.** the raising of plants or animals, esp. with a view to their improvement. **3.** the product or growth resulting from such cultivation. **4.** development or improvement by education or training. **5.** enlightenment or refinement resulting from such development. **6.** a particular state or stage of civilisation, as in the case of a certain nation or period: *Greek culture.* **7.** *Sociol.* the sum total of ways of living built up by a group of human beings, which is transmitted from one generation to another. **8.** *Biol.* **a.** the cultivation of micro-organisms, as bacteria, or of tissues, for scientific study, medicinal use, etc. **b.** the product or growth resulting from such cultivation. *–v.t.* **9.** to subject to culture; cultivate. **10.** *Biol.* **a.** to develop (micro-organisms, tissues, etc.) in an artifical medium. **b.** to introduce (living material) into a culture medium. [ME, from F, from L *cultūra* tending, cultivation] **– cultureless,** *adj.*

**culture complex** /'– kɒmplɛks/, *n.* a group of culture traits all interrelated and dominated by one essential trait: *political nationalism is a culture complex.*

**cultured** /'kʌltʃəd/, *adj.* **1.** cultivated; artificially nurtured or grown. **2.** enlightened; refined.

**cultured pearl** /– 'pɜl/, *n.* a pearl grown around a speck of foreign matter artificially introduced into the shell of an oyster or clam.

**culture factor** /'kʌltʃə fæktə/, *n.* the whole of a culture at a given time as it affects further cultural development.

**culture pattern** /'– pætən/, *n.* a group of interrelated cultural traits of some continuity.

**culture shock** /'– ʃɒk/, *n.* the disorientation and unhappiness caused by an inability to adapt to a culture which is different from one's own.

**culture-vulture** /'kʌltʃə-vʌltʃə/, *n. Colloq.* (*mildly derog. or joc.*) one who takes excessive interest in the arts.

**culturist** /'kʌltʃərəst/, *n.* **1.** a cultivator. **2.** an advocate or devotee of culture.

**cultus** /'kʌltəs/, *n.* a cult. [L]

**culver** /'kʌlvə/, *n. Poetic.* a dove; a pigeon. [ME *colfre,* OE *culfre*]

**culverin** /'kʌlvərən/, *n.* **1.** a medieval form of musket. **2.** a kind of heavy cannon, used in the 16th and 17th centuries. [F *coulevrine,* from *couleuvre,* from L *colubra* serpent. Cf. COBRA]

**Culver's root** /kʌlvəz 'rut/, *n.* **1.** the root of a tall herb, *Veronicastrum virginicum,* used in medicine as a cathartic and emetic. **2.** the plant. Also, **Culver's physic.**

**culvert** /'kʌlvət/, *n.* a drain or channel crossing under a road, etc.; a sewer; a conduit. [orig. uncert.]

**cum** /kʌm, kʊm/, *prep.* **1.** with; together with; including (used sometimes in financial phrases as *cum dividend, cum rights,* etc., which are often abbreviated simply *cum*). **2.** (in combination) serving a dual function as; the functions being indicated by the preceding and following elements: *the dwelling-cum-workshop was nearby.* [L]

**cum.**, cumulative.

**cumber** /ˈkʌmbə/, *v.t.* **1.** to hinder; hamper. **2.** to overload; burden. **3.** to inconvenience; trouble. *–n.* **4.** hindrance. **5.** that which cumbers. **6.** *Archaic.* embarrassment; trouble. [MFlem. *comber,* c. G *Kummer* trouble] – **cumberer,** *n.*

**cumbersome** /ˈkʌmbəsəm/, *adj.* **1.** burdensome; troublesome. **2.** unwieldy; clumsy. – **cumbersomely,** *adv.* – **cumbersomeness,** *n.*

**cumbrance** /ˈkʌmbrəns/, *n.* **1.** trouble. **2.** encumbrance.

**cumbrous** /ˈkʌmbrəs/, *adj.* cumbersome. – **cumbrously,** *adv.* – **cumbrousness,** *n.*

**cumbungi** /kʌmˈbʌŋgi/, *n.* any tall, marsh plants of the genus *Typha;* bullrush; flag. [orig. uncert.]

**cumin** /ˈkʌmən/, *n.* **1.** a small plant, *Cuminum cyminum,* bearing aromatic seedlike fruit used in cookery and medicine. **2.** the fruit or seeds. [ME *comin,* from OF, from L *cumīnum,* from Gk *kýminon;* replacing OE *cymen*]

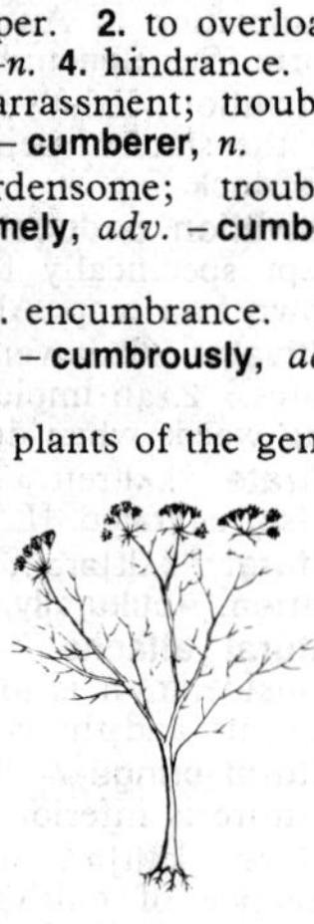

cumin

**cum laude** /kʌm ˈlɔdi, kum ˈlaudeɪ/, with honour (used chiefly in U.S. universities to grant the lowest of three special honours for above-average academic performance). See **magna cum laude** and **summa cum laude.**

**cummerbund** /ˈkʌməbʌnd/, *n.* (in India and elsewhere) a shawl or sash worn as a belt. [Hind. *kamarband,* from Pers.]

**cumquat** /ˈkʌmkwɒt/, *n.* →**kumquat.**

**cumshaw** /ˈkʌmʃɔ/, *n.* (formerly in Chinese ports) a present; gratuity; tip. [Chinese (Amoy d.) *kamsiā* for Mandarin *kan hsieh* grateful thanks]

**cumulate** /ˈkjumjəleɪt/, *v.,* **-lated, -lating;** /ˈkjumjələt, -leɪt/, *adj.* *–v.t.* **1.** to heap up; amass; accumulate. *–adj.* **2.** heaped up. [L *cumulātus,* pp., heaped up]

**cumulation** /kjumjəˈleɪʃən/, *n.* **1.** the act of cumulating; accumulation. **2.** a heap; mass.

**cumulative** /ˈkjumjələtɪv/, *adj.* **1.** increasing or growing by accumulation or successive additions. **2.** formed by or resulting from accumulation or the addition of successive parts or elements. **3.** *Law.* of or pertaining to statutes which provide different remedies, penalties or punishments; it is a matter of construction whether they were intended to be cumulative or whether it was intended that only one apply in a given case. **4.** *Law.* of sentences imposed on a person already convicted and to act after the expiration of other sentences; opposed to *concurrent sentences.* **5.** *Law.* of legacies bequeathed twice; it is a matter of construction whether the legatee is entitled to both or only one. **6.** of or pertaining to experimental error which increases in magnitude with each successive step. – **cumulatively,** *adv.* – **cumulativeness,** *n.*

**cumulative evidence** /– ˈɛvədəns/, *n.* **1.** evidence of which the parts reinforce one another, producing an effect stronger than any part taken by itself. **2.** testimony repetitive of testimony earlier given.

**cumulative preference share,** *n.* a share issued on terms such that should the dividend in any year or years be not paid in whole or in part, the right to receive the unpaid monies remains.

**cumulative voting** /– ˈvoutɪŋ/, *n.* a system which gives each voter as many votes as there are persons to be elected from one representative district, allowing him to accumulate them on one candidate or to distribute them.

**cumuliform** /ˈkjumjələfɔm/, *adj.* having the appearance or character of cumulus clouds.

**cumulonimbus** /ˌkjumjəlouˈnɪmbəs/, *n.* a heavy, tall mass of cloud whose summits rise in the form of mountains or towers, the upper parts having a fibrous texture characteristic of high clouds formed of ice crystals. This cloud is characteristic of thunderstorm conditions.

**cumulous** /ˈkjumjələs/, *adj.* of the form of a cumulus (cloud); composed of cumuli.

**cumulus** /ˈkjumjələs/, *n., pl.* **-li** /-li/. **1.** a heap; pile. **2.** *Meteorol.* a cloud with summit domelike or made up of rounded heaps, and with flat base, seen in fair weather and usu. a brilliant white with a smooth, well-outlined structure.

**cumulus fractus** /– ˈfræktəs/, *n.* a cumulus cloud that is ill-formed, ragged, usu. small, and rapidly changing.

**cuneal** /ˈkjuniəl/, *adj.* wedgelike; wedge-shaped. [L *cuneus* wedge + -AL[1]]

**cuneate** /ˈkjuniət, -eɪt/, *adj.* **1.** wedgeshaped. **2.** (of leaves) triangular and tapering to a point at the base. Also, **cuneated.** [L *cuneātus,* pp., made wedge-shaped]

cuneate leaf

**cuneiform** /ˈkjunəfɔm/, *adj.* **1.** having the form of a wedge; wedge-shaped, as the characters used in writing in ancient Persia, Assyria, etc. **2.** denoting or pertaining to this kind of writing. **3.** *Anat.* denoting or pertaining to any of various wedge-shaped bones, as of the tarsus. *–n.* **4.** cuneiform characters or writing. **5.** a cuneiform bone. [L *cuneus* wedge + -I- + -FORM]

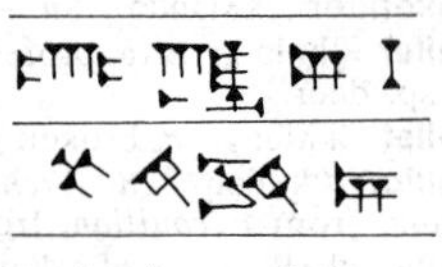

Assyrian cuneiform characters

**cu-nim** /ˈkju-nɪm/, *n.* →**cumulonimbus.**

**cunje** /ˈkʌndʒi/, *n.* →**cunjevoi** (def. 2).

**cunjevoi** /ˈkʌndʒəvɔɪ/, *n.* **1.** a hastate-leaved perennial herb of the Arum family, *Alocasia macrorrhizos,* native to Asia and the Pacific Islands as well as Australia where it is common in rainforest and along coastal river-banks; its poisonous rhizomes were rendered harmless by cooking and eaten by the Aborigines. **2.** Also, **cunje.** a common, Australian, littoral tunicate, *Pyura stolonifera,* popular as a fish bait; sea-squirt. [Aboriginal]

cunjevoi

**Cunnamulla gun** /ˌkʌnəmʌlə ˈgʌn/, *n.* a shearer who claims expertise he does not have. [from *Cunnamulla,* a town in Qld]

**cunnilingus** /kʌnəˈlɪŋgəs/, *n.* oral stimulation of the female genitals. Also, **cunnilinctus** /kʌnəˈlɪŋktəs/. [NL, from L *cunni-,* combining form of *cunnus* vulva + *linctus,* pp., licked]

**cunning** /ˈkʌnɪŋ/, *n.* **1.** ability; skill; expertness. **2.** skill employed in a crafty manner; skilfulness in deceiving; craftiness; guile. *–adj.* **3.** exhibiting or wrought with ingenuity. **4.** artfully subtle or shrewd; crafty; sly. **5.** *Archaic.* skilful; expert. [ME; var. of OE *cunnung,* from *cunnan* know (how). See CAN[1]] – **cunningly,** *adv.* – **cunningness,** *n.*

**cunningham eye** /kʌnɪŋhəm ˈaɪ/, *n.* a hole made in a sail through which a rope may be passed to control the shape of the sail.

**Cunningham's skink** /ˌkʌnɪŋhəmz ˈskɪŋk/, *n.* a common skink, *Egernia cunninghami,* found in rocky areas of south-eastern Australia, similar in size to the blue-tongue lizard but having spiny-ridged scales. [named after Allan *Cunningham,* 1791-1839, explorer]

Cunningham's skink

**cunning kick** /ˈkʌnɪŋ kɪk/, *n.* *Colloq.* a secret reserve of money. [CUNNING + KICK (def. 34)]

**cunt** /kʌnt/, *n.* *Colloq.* **1.** the female pudendum. **2.** woman considered as a sexual object. **3.** (*derog.*) any person. **4.** sexual intercourse.

**cunthook** /ˈkʌnthʊk/, *n.* *N.Z. Colloq.* (*derog.*) an unpleasant or despicable man.

**cunt-struck** /ˈkʌnt-strʌk/, *adj.* *Colloq.* infatuated with women.

**cup** /kʌp/, *n., v.,* **cupped, cupping.** *–n.* **1.** a small, open container, esp. of porcelain or metal, used mainly to drink from. **2.** (*oft. cap.*) an ornamental cup or other article, esp. of precious metal, offered as a prize for a contest: *Melbourne Cup, Davis Cup.* **3.** (*cap.*) the contest in which such a cup is the prize: *he entered in the Cup.* **4.** the containing part of a goblet or the like. **5.** a cup with its contents. **6.** the quantity contained in a cup. **7.** a unit of capacity formerly equal to 8 fluid ounces, now 250 millilitres. **8.** any of various beverages, as a mixture of wine and various ingredients: *claret cup.* **9.** the chalice used in the Eucharist. **10.** the wine of the Eucharist. **11.** something to be partaken of or endured, as suffering. **12.** (*pl.*) the drinking of alcoholic beverages. **13.** (*pl.*) a state of intoxication. **14.** any cuplike utensil, organ, part, cavity, etc. **15.** that part of a bra which is shaped to hold the breast. **16.** the porcelain insulator on power or telephone poles. **17.** that part of a milking-machine which holds the cow's teat. **18.** *Golf.* **a.** the metal receptacle within the hole. **b.** the hole itself. **19.** a cupping glass. **20.** **in one's cups,** intoxicated; tipsy. *–v.t.* **21.** to take or place in or as in a cup: *he cupped his ear with the palm of his hand to hear better.* **22.** to form into the shape of a cup. **23.** to use a cupping glass on. [ME and OE *cuppe,* from LL *cuppa* cup, var. of L *cūpa* tub, cask] – **cuplike,** *adj.*

**cupbearer** /ˈkʌpbɛərə/, *n.* an attendant who fills and hands the cups in which drink is served.

**cupboard** /ˈkʌbəd/, *n.* **1.** an enclosed recess of a room for storing foodstuffs, clothing, etc., usu. having shelves, hooks or the like. **2.** a free-standing article of furniture for any of these or similar purposes. [ME, from CUP + BOARD]

**cupboard love** /ˈ– lʌv/, *n.* love inspired by considerations of material gain.

**cupcake** /ˈkʌpkeɪk/, *n.* a small cake baked in a cup-shaped pan or paper patty pan.

**cupel** /ˈkjupəl, kjuˈpɛl/, *n., v.,* **-pelled, -pelling** or (*U.S.*) **-peled, -peling.** *–n.* **1.** a small cup-like porous vessel, usu. made of bone ash, used in assaying, as for separating gold and silver from lead. **2.** a receptacle or furnace bottom in which silver is refined. *–v.t.* **3.** to heat or refine in a cupel. [F *coupelle,* from LL *cuppa* CUP]

**cupellation** /kjupəˈleɪʃən/, *n.* the process of separating noble metals, esp. gold and silver, from impurities by subjecting the impure metal to a blast of hot air in a cupel.

**cup final** /kʌp ˈfaɪnəl/, *n.* the final match in an eliminating contest, as the Davis Cup competition, after which the winning team is awarded the cup as a symbol of victory.

**cupful** /ˈkʌpfʊl/, *n., pl.* **-fuls.** a quantity sufficient to fill a cup.

**cupid** /ˈkjupəd/, *n.* a winged boy with bow and arrows, or a representation of one, esp. as a symbol of love. [*Cupid,* the Roman god of love, son of Venus; ME *Cupide,* from L *Cupīdo,* lit., desire, passion]

**cupidity** /kjuˈpɪdəti/, *n.* eager or inordinate desire, esp. to possess something. [L *cupiditas* passionate desire]

**cupie** /ˈkjupi/, *n.* →**kewpie**[1].

**cup moth** /ˈkʌp mɒθ/, *n.* any of various Australian moths of family Limacodidae, which pupate in sturdy, cup-shaped cocoons attached to branches and twigs of trees, and whose larvae have rosettes of erectile stinging spines on their backs.

**cupola** /ˈkjupələ/, *n.* **1.** a rounded vault or dome constituting, or built upon a roof; a small dome-like or towerlike structure on a roof. **2.** a dome or relatively small size, esp. when forming part of a minor or decorative element of a larger building. **3.** any of various domelike structures, organs, etc. **4.** *Metall.* a cylindrical, vertical furnace for melting metal, esp. grey iron, by having the charge come in contact with the hot fuel, usu. metallurgical coke. [It.: dome, from LL *cūpula,* diminutive of *cūpa* tub, cask]

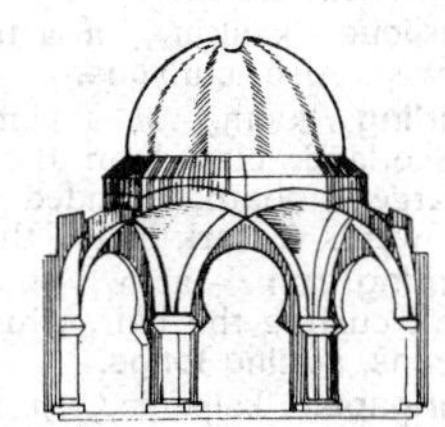
cupola

**cuppa** /ˈkʌpə/, *n. Colloq.* a cup of tea.

**cupped** /ˈkʌpt/, *adj.* hollowed out like a cup; cup-shaped.

**cupper** /ˈkʌpə/, *n.* one who performs the operation of cupping.

**cupping** /ˈkʌpɪŋ/, *n.* the process of drawing blood from the body by scarification and the application of a cupping glass, or by the application of a cupping glass without scarification, as for relieving internal congestion.

**cupping glass** /ˈ– glas/, *n.* a glass vessel in which a partial vacuum is created, as by heat, used in cupping.

**cupr-,** a word element referring to copper. Also, before consonants, **cupri-, cupro-.** [L, combining form of *cuprum*]

**cuprammonium** /kjupräˈmoʊniəm/, *n.* any cation containing copper and ammonia.

**cupreous** /ˈkjupriəs/, *adj.* **1.** copper-coloured; metallic reddish brown. **2.** consisting of or containing copper; copper-like. [L *cupreus* of copper]

**cupressaceous** /ˌkjuprəˈseɪʃəs/, *adj.* belonging to the family Cupressaceae which includes many ornamental trees.

**cupric** /ˈkjuprɪk/, *adj.* of or containing copper, esp. in the divalent state, as *cupric oxide,* CuO.

**cupriferous** /kjuˈprɪfərəs/, *adj.* yielding copper.

**cuprite** /ˈkjupraɪt/, *n.* a mineral, cuprous oxide, $Cu_2O$, occurring in red crystals and granular masses; an ore of copper.

**cupronickel** /kjuproʊˈnɪkəl/, *n.* **1.** an alloy of copper containing nickel. *–adj.* **2.** containing copper and nickel.

**cupro-uranite** /kjuprə-ˈjʊərənaɪt/, *n.* →**copper uranite.**

**cuprous** /ˈkjuprəs/, *adj.* containing monovalent copper, as *cuprous oxide,* $Cu_2O$.

**cuprum** /ˈkjuprəm/, *n.* →**copper**[1]. [L]

**cup tie** /ˈkʌp taɪ/, *n.* a match between two teams in an eliminating contest for a cup.

**cupule** /ˈkjupjul/, *n.* **1.** *Bot.* a cup-shaped structure as the involucre of indurated, cohering bracts in the acorn. **2.** *Zool.* a small cup-shaped sucker or similar organ or part. [L *cūpula,* diminutive of *cūpa* tub, cup]

cupules (def. 1): A, of acorn; B, of fungus

**cur** /kɜ/, *n.* **1.** a snarling, worthless, or outcast dog. **2.** a low, despicable person. [ME *curre;* imitative]

**curable** /ˈkjurəbəl/, *adj.* that may be cured. – **curability** /kjurəˈbɪləti/, **curableness,** *n.* – **curably,** *adv.*

**curaçao** /kjurəˈseɪoʊ/, *n.* a cordial or liqueur flavoured with the peel of the bitter Curaçao orange. Also, **curacao.** [from *Curaçao,* main island of Netherlands Antilles, off the coast of Venezuela]

**curacy** /ˈkjurəsi/, *n., pl.* **-cies.** the office or position of a curate.

**curare** /kjuˈrari/, *n.* **1.** a blackish resin-like substance from *Strychnos toxifera* and other tropical plants of the genus *Strychnos,* and from *Chondrodendron tomentosum,* used by South American Indians for poisoning arrows, and employed in physiological experiments, etc., for arresting the action of the motor nerves. **2.** a plant yielding it. Also, **curari.** [Carib *kurare*]

**curassow** /ˈkjurəsoʊ/, *n.* any of various large, arboreal, gallinaceous South and Central American birds belonging to the family Cracidae, somewhat resembling the turkey and sometimes domesticated. [named after the island of CURAÇAO]

**curate** /ˈkjurət/, *n.* **1.** a clergyman employed as assistant or deputy of a rector or vicar. **2.** *Archaic.* any ecclesiastic entrusted with the cure of souls, as a parish priest. [ME *curat,* from ML *cūrātus,* from *cūra.* See CURE, *n.*]

**curate's egg** /ˌkjurəts ˈɛg/, *n.* an event, object, etc, which is good and bad in spots, or about which one has mixed feelings.

**curative** /ˈkjurətɪv/, *adj.* **1.** serving to cure or heal; pertaining to curing or remedial treatment; remedial. *–n.* **2.** a curative agent; a remedy. – **curatively,** *adv.* – **curativeness,** *n.*

**curator** /kjuˈreɪtə/, *n.* **1.** the person in charge of a museum, art collection, etc.; a custodian. **2.** a manager; overseer; superintendent. **3.** a guardian, as of a minor, lunatic, etc. [L: overseer, guardian; replacing ME *curatour,* from AF] – **curatorial** /kjurəˈtɔriəl/, *adj.* – **curatorship,** *n.* – **curatrix** /ˈkjurətrɪks/, *n., fem.*

**curb** /kɜb/, *n.* **1.** a chain or strap attached to the upper ends of the branches of a bit and passing under the horse's lower jaw, used in restraining the horse. **2.** anything that restrains or controls; a restraint; a check. **3.** an enclosing framework or border. **4.** *Chiefly U.S.* →**kerb.** **5.** *Vet. Sci.* a swelling on the lower part of the back of the hock of a horse, often causing lameness. *–v.t.* **6.** to control as with a curb; restrain; check. **7.** to put a curb on (a horse). [late ME, from F *courbe* curved, from L *curvus* bent, crooked]

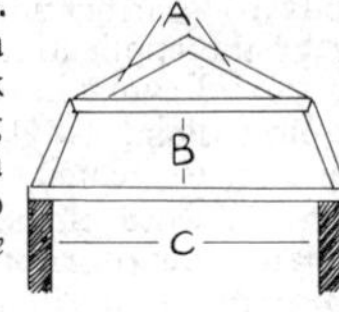

curb roof: A, rafters; B, tie beams; C, walls

**curb bit** /'– bɪt/, *n.* a bit for a horse, which, by slight effort, produces great pressure on the mouth for controlling the animal.

**curbing** /'kɜbɪŋ/, *n. Chiefly U.S.* →**kerbing.**

**curb roof** /– 'ruf/, *n.* a roof with two slopes to each face, the lower being the steeper.

**curbstone** /'kɜbstoʊn/, *n. Chiefly U.S.* →**kerbstone.**

**curculio** /kɜ'kjulioʊ/, *n., pl.* **-lios.** any of certain snout-beetles or weevils of the family Curculionidae, as the **plum curculio,** *Conotrachelus nenuphar,* injurious to fruit. [L: weevil]

**curcuma** /'kɜkjumə/, *n.* any plant of the genus *Curcuma,* of the East Indies, etc., as *C. longa* or *C. zedoaria,* the former yielding turmeric and the latter zedoary. [NL, from Ar. *kurkum* saffron, turmeric]

**curd** /kɜd/, *n.* **1.** (*oft. pl.*) a substance consisting of casein, etc., obtained from milk by coagulation, used for making into cheese or eaten as food. **2.** any substance resembling this. *–v.t.* **3.** to turn into curd. *–v.i.* **4.** to coagulate; congeal. [ME *crud.* Cf. CROWD[1]]

**curd cheese** /– 'tʃiz/, *n.* →**cottage cheese.**

**curdle** /'kɜdl/, *v.,* **-dled, -dling.** *–v.t.* **1.** to change into curd. **2. curdle the blood,** to terrify with horror or fear. *–v.i.* **3.** to coagulate; congeal. [frequentative of CURD]

**curdy** /'kɜdi/, *adj.* like curd; full of or containing curd; coagulated.

**cure** /'kjuə, 'kjʊə/, *n., v.,* **cured, curing.** *–n.* **1.** a method or course of remedial treatment, as for disease. **2.** successful remedial treatment; restoration to health. **3.** a means of healing or curing; a remedy. **4.** the act or a method of curing meat, fish, etc. **5.** spiritual charge of the people in a certain district. **6.** the office or district of one exercising such oversight. *–v.t.* **7.** to restore to health. **8.** to relieve or rid of something troublesome or detrimental, as an illness, a bad habit, etc. **9.** to prepare (meat, fish, etc.) for preservation, by salting, drying, etc. **10.** to prepare, preserve, or finish (a substance), as concrete, by a chemical or physical process. **11.** to vulcanise (rubber). *–v.i.* **12.** to effect a cure. **13.** to become cured. [ME, from OF, from L *cūra* care, treatment, concern, ML an ecclesiastical cure] **– cureless,** *adj.* **– curelessly,** *adv.* **– curer,** *n.*

**curé** /'kjureɪ/, *n.* (in French use) a parish priest. [F, from VL *cūrātus.* See CURATE]

**cure-all** /'kjʊər-ɔl, 'kjuər-ɔl/, *n.* a cure for all ills; a panacea.

**curettage** /kju'rɛtɪdʒ/, *n.* the process of curetting. [F]

**curette** /kju'rɛt/, *n., v.,* **-retted, -retting.** *–n.* **1.** a scoop-shaped surgical instrument used for removing diseased tissue from body cavities such as the uterus, etc. **2.** *Med.* the scraping of a cavity, esp. the uterus, with a curette. *–v.t.* **3.** to scrape with a curette. [F, from *curer* cleanse, from L *curāre*]

**curfew** /'kɜfju/, *n.* **1.** the ringing of a bell at a fixed hour in the evening as a signal for covering or extinguishing fires, as practised in medieval Europe. **2.** the ringing of an evening bell as later practised. **3.** a regulation, as enforced during civil disturbances, which establishes strict controls on movement after nightfall. **4.** the time at which such a bell is rung or such a regulation enforced. **5.** the bell itself. [ME *corfew,* from AF *coeverfu,* var. of OF *cuevre-feu* cover-fire]

**curia** /'kjuriə/, *n., pl.* **curiae** /'kjurii/. **1.** one of the political subdivisions of each of the three tribes of ancient Roman citizens. **2.** the building in which such a division or group met, as for worship or public deliberation. **3.** the senate house in ancient Rome. **4.** the senate of ancient Italian towns. **5.** (*usu. cap.*) the pope and those about him at Rome engaged in the administration of the papal authority (the **Curia Romana**). **6.** (*usu. cap.*) the papal court. [L] **– curial,** *adj.*

**curie** /'kjuri/, *n.* a non-SI unit of measurement of the activity of a radionuclide equal to $37 \times 10^9$ becquerels. [named after Marie *Curie,* 1867-1934, Polish-born physicist]

**curie point** /'– pɔɪnt/, *n.* the temperature at which a ferromagnetic substance becomes merely paramagnetic.

**Curie's law** /'kjuriz lɔ/, *n.* the law that the magnetic susceptibility of a substance is inversely proportional to the absolute temperature. [named after Pierre *Curie,* 1859-1906, French physicist and chemist]

**curio** /'kjurioʊ/, *n., pl.* **curios.** any article, object of art, etc., valued as a curiosity. [short for CURIOSITY]

**curiosa** /kjuri'oʊsə/, *n.pl., Chiefly U.S.* books, pamphlets, etc., dealing with unusual subjects, esp. pornographic ones (a term used by booksellers and collectors); erotica. [L: curious (things)] **– curiosum,** *n. sing.*

**curiosity** /kjuri'ɒsəti/, *n., pl.* **-ties.** **1.** the desire to learn or know about anything; inquisitiveness. **2.** curious or interesting quality, as from strangeness. **3.** a curious, rare, or novel thing. [L *cūriōsitas*]

**curious** /'kjuriəs/, *adj.* **1.** desirous of learning or knowing; inquisitive. **2.** prying; meddlesome. **3.** *Archaic.* made or prepared with skill or art. **4.** marked by special care or pains, as an inquiry or investigation. **5.** exciting attention or interest because of strangeness or novelty. **6.** odd; eccentric. **7.** (of books) indelicate, indecent, or obscene. **8.** *Obs.* marked by intricacy or subtlety. [ME, from OF *curios,* from L *cūriōsus* careful, inquiring, inquisitive] **– curiously,** *adv.* **– curiousness,** *n.*

**curium** /'kjuriəm/, *n.* an element not found in nature, but discovered in 1944 among the products of the bombardment of uranium and plutonium by very energetic helium ions. *Symbol:* Cm; *at. no.:* 96.

**curl** /kɜl/, *v.t.* **1.** to form into ringlets, as the hair. **2.** to form into a spiral or curved shape; coil. **3.** *Obs.* to adorn with, or as with, curls or ringlets. **4. curl one's lip,** to express disdain. *–v.i.* **5.** to form curls or ringlets, as the hair. **6.** to coil. **7.** to become curved or undulated. **8.** *Scot.* to play at curling. **9.** *Colloq.* to shrink away, as in horror or disgust: *the sight of blood always makes me curl.* **10. curl up,** to lie down comfortably: *to curl up with a good book.* **11. make (someone's) hair curl,** to cause someone to be astonished. *–n.* **12.** a ringlet of hair. **13.** anything of a spiral or curved shape. **14.** a coil. **15.** the act of curling. **16.** the state of being curled. **17.** any of various diseases of plants with which the leaves are distorted, fluted, or puffed because of unequal growth. **18. curl the mo,** *Colloq.* **a.** to succeed brilliantly. **b.** (an exclamation indicating surprised admiration). [ME *crolled, crulled,* ppl. adj., from MD or MFlem.]

**curler** /'kɜlə/, *n.* **1.** one who or that which curls. **2.** any of various types of rollers, etc., used by women to curl the hair. **3.** a player at curling.

**curlew** /'kɜlju/, *n.* any of a number of wide-ranging, largely migratory shore-birds of the family Scolopacidae, esp. of genus *Numenius,* having long legs and a long, slender, down-curved bill, as the eastern curlew. [ME *corlewe,* from OF *courlieu;* imitative]

curlew

**curlicue** /'kɜlikju/, *n.* a fantastic curl or twist. Also, **curlycue.**

**curling** /'kɜlɪŋ/, *n.* a game, common in Scotland, played on the ice, in which large, smooth, rounded stones are slid towards a mark called the tee.

**curling iron** /'– aɪən/, *n.* a rod of iron to be used when heated for curling the hair, which is twined around it. Also, **curling irons, curling tongs.**

**curlpaper** /'kɜlpeɪpə/, *n.* a piece of paper on which a lock of hair is rolled up tightly, to remain until the hair has become fixed in a curl.

**curly** /'kɜli/, *adj.,* **curlier, curliest.** **1.** curling or tending to curl. **2.** having curls. **3.** difficult to deal with: *a few curly problems.* **– curliness,** *n.*

**curly brackets** /– 'brækəts/, *n.pl.* See **bracket** (def. 6a).

**curlyhead** /'kɜlihɛd/, *n.* a person, esp. a child, with curly hair.

**curly leaf** /'kɜli lif/, *n.* →**curl** (def. 17).

**curmudgeon** /kɜ'mʌdʒən/, *n.* an irascible, churlish, miserly fellow. – **curmudgeonly,** *adj.*

**currajong** /'kʌrədʒɒŋ/, *n.* →**kurrajong.**

**currant** /'kʌrənt/, *n.* **1.** a small seedless raisin, produced chiefly in California and in the Levant, used in cookery, etc. **2.** the small, edible, acid, round fruit or berry of certain wild or cultivated shrubs of the genus *Ribes,* as *R. sativum* (**redcurrant** and **white currant**) and *R. nigrum* (**blackcurrant**). **3.** the shrub itself. **4.** any of various similar fruits or shrubs. [ME *(raysons of) Coraunte,* from AF *(raisins de) Corauntz* (raisins of) Corinth; so called because orig. from Corinth in Greece]

**currant luncheon** /– 'lʌntʃən/, *n.* a biscuit with dried fruit sandwiched between two thin layers of sweet pastry; garibaldi. [Trademark]

**currawong** /'kʌrəwɒŋ/, *n.* **1.** any of several large black and white or greyish birds of the genus *Strepera,* with solid bodies, large pointed bills, yellow eyes and loud, ringing calls, found in many parts of Australia and Tasmania. **2.** a small tree, *Acacia doratoxylon,* found on dry ridges in inland eastern Australia. **3.** any of certain similar species of the genus *Acacia.* [Aboriginal]

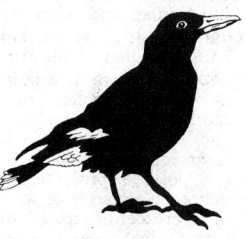

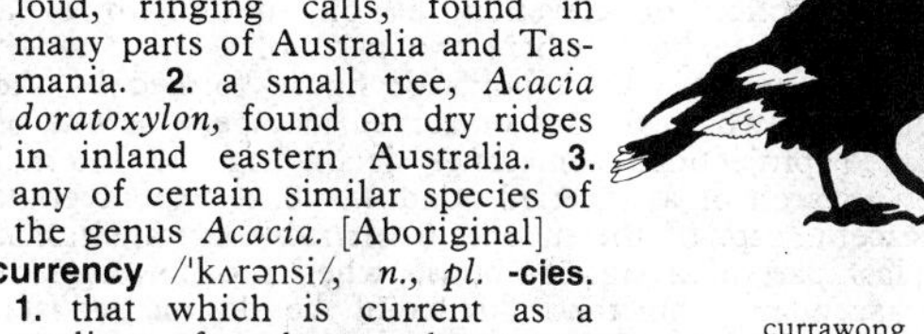
currawong

**currency** /'kʌrənsi/, *n., pl.* **-cies.** **1.** that which is current as a medium of exchange; the money in actual use. **2.** the fact or quality of being passed on, as from person to person. **3.** general acceptance; prevalence; vogue. **4.** the fact or state of passing in time. **5.** circulation, as of coin. **6.** (formerly) one born in Australia. *–adj.* **7.** (formerly) born in Australia, as opposed to *sterling,* one born in Britain or Ireland. **8. currency lad (lass),** (formerly) a man (woman) born in Australia.

**current** /'kʌrənt/, *adj.* **1.** passing in time, or belonging to the time actually passing: *the current month.* **2.** passing from one to another; circulating, as coin. **3.** publicly reported or known. **4.** prevalent. **5.** generally accepted; in vogue. *–n.* **6.** a flowing; flow, as of a river. **7.** that which flows, as a stream. **8.** a portion of a large body of water, or of air, etc., moving in a certain direction. **9. a.** a movement or flow of electric charges. **b.** a measure of the rate of flow. The SI unit of current is the ampere. **10.** course, as of time or events; the main course; the general tendency. [L *currens,* ppr., running; replacing ME *corant,* from OF] – **currently,** *adv.*

**current account** /– ə'kaʊnt/, *n.* →**cheque account.**

**current assets** /– 'æsɛts/, *n.pl.* cash, together with loans and other assets which can be readily converted to cash within a year.

**current collector** /'– kəlɛktə/, *n.* (on an electric train, tramcar, etc.) any device, as a pantograph (def. 2), for maintaining electrical contact between a contact conductor and the electrical circuit of the vehicle on which the collector is mounted.

**current density** /'– dɛnsəti/, *n.* the rate of flow in amperes per unit of cross-sectional area at a given place in a conductor, or more generally, current per unit area.

**current expenses** /– ək'spɛnsəz/, *n.pl.* regularly continuing expenditures for the maintenance and the carrying on of business.

**current liabilities** /– laɪə'bɪlətiz/, *n.pl.* indebtedness within one year.

**curricle** /'kʌrɪkəl/, *n.* a light, two-wheeled, open carriage drawn by two horses abreast. [L *curriculum* a running, course, race, race chariot]

**curriculum** /kə'rɪkjələm/, *n., pl.* **-lums, -la** /-lə/. **1.** the aggregate of courses of study given in a school, college, university, etc. **2.** the regular or a particular course of study in a school, college, etc. [L. See CURRICLE] – **curricular,** *adj.*

**curriculum vitae** /– 'vitaɪ/, *n.* a brief account of one's career to date.

**currier** /'kʌriə/, *n.* **1.** one who dresses and colours leather after it is tanned. **2.** one who curries (a horse, etc.). [ME *corier,* from OF, from L *coriārius* tanner]

**curriery** /'kʌriəri/, *n., pl.* **-eries.** **1.** the occupation or business of a currier. **2.** the place where it is carried on.

**currish** /'kɜrɪʃ/, *adj.* **1.** of or pertaining to a cur. **2.** curlike; snarling; quarrelsome. **3.** contemptible. – **currishly,** *adv.* – **currishness,** *n.*

**curry**[1] /'kʌri/, *n., pl.* **-ries,** *v.,* **-ried, rying.** *–n.* **1.** an Indian sauce or relish in many varieties, containing a mixture of spices, seeds, vegetables, fruits, etc., eaten with rice or combined with meat, fish or other food. **2.** a dish prepared with a curry sauce or with curry powder. **3. give (someone) curry,** to abuse angrily. *–v.t.* **4.** to prepare (food) with a curry sauce or with curry powder. [Tamil *kari* sauce]

**curry**[2] /'kʌri/, *v.t.,* **-ried, -rying.** **1.** to rub and clean (a horse, etc.) with a comb; currycomb. **2.** to dress (tanned hides) by soaking, scraping, beating, colouring, etc. **3.** to beat; thrash. **4. curry favour,** to seek favour by a show of kindness, courtesy, flattery, etc. [ME *cory,* from OF *coreer,* earlier *conreder* put in order, from *con-* CON- + *-reder* make ready (from Gmc)]

**currycomb** /'kʌrikoʊm/, *n.* **1.** a comb, usu. with rows of metal teeth, for currying horses, etc. *–v.t.* **2.** to rub or clean with such a comb.

**curry powder** /'kʌri paʊdə/, *n.* a powdered preparation of spices and other ingredients, notably turmeric, used for making curry sauce or for seasoning food.

**curse** /kɜs/, *n., v.,* **cursed** or **curst, cursing.** *–n.* **1.** the expression of a wish that evil, etc., befall another. **2.** an ecclesiastical censure or anathema. **3.** a profane oath. **4.** evil that has been invoked upon one. **5.** something accursed. **6.** the cause of evil, misfortune, or trouble. **7. the curse,** *Colloq.* menstruation. *–v.t.* **8.** to wish or invoke evil, calamity, injury, or destruction upon. **9.** to swear at. **10.** to blaspheme. **11.** to afflict with great evil. **12.** to excommunicate. *–v.i.* **13.** to utter curses; swear profanely. [ME *curs,* OE *curs,* from *cūrsian,* v., curse, reprove (whence ME *cursen*), from OIrish *cūrsagim* I blame] – **curser,** *n.*

**cursed** /'kɜsəd, kɜst/, *adj.* **1.** under a curse; damned. **2.** deserving a curse; hateful; abominable. **3.** cantankerous; ill-tempered; cross. – **cursedly,** *adj.* – **cursedness,** *n.*

**cursive** /'kɜsɪv/, *adj.* **1.** (of writing or printing type) in flowing strokes, with the letters joined together. *–n.* **2.** a cursive letter or printing type. [ML *cursīvus,* from L *cursus* a running] – **cursively,** *adv.*

**cursor** /'kɜsə/, *n.* **1.** a slider, as the transparent slider forming part of a slide rule on which are marked one or more reference lines. **2.** any movable referrence point or line, esp. vertical, as one on a computer video terminal displaying information in analog form and movable to the part of the display where measurements are to be computed.

**cursorial** /kɜ'sɔriəl/, *adj.* **1.** adapted for running, as the feet and skeleton of dogs, horses, etc. **2.** having limbs adapted for running, as certain birds, insects, etc.

**cursory** /'kɜsəri/, *adj.* going rapidly over something, without noticing details; hasty; superficial. [L *cursōrius* pertaining to a runner or a race] – **cursorily,** *adv.* – **cursoriness,** *n.*

**curst** /kɜst/, *v.* **1.** past tense and past participle of **curse.** *–adj.* **2.** cursed.

**curt** /kɜt/, *adj.* **1.** short; shortened. **2.** brief in speech etc. **3.** rudely brief in speech, manner, etc. [L *curtus* cut short, clipped. Cf. SHORT] – **curtly,** *adv.* – **curtness,** *n.*

**curtail** /kɜ'teɪl/, *v.t.* to cut short; cut off a part of; abridge reduce; diminish. [var. (by association with TAIL[1]) of obs. *curtal,* v., dock, from F *courtault,* from *court* short, from L *curtus*] – **curtailer,** *n.* – **curtailment,** *n.*

**curtail step** /'– stɛp/, *n.* the first or bottom step of a stair, when it is finished in a curved line at its outer end.

**curtain** /'kɜtn/, *n.* **1.** a hanging piece of fabric used to shut out the light from a window, adorn a room, etc. **2.** *Theat.* **a.** a set of hanging drapery, etc., for concealing all or part of the set from the view of the audience. **b.** the act or time of raising or opening a curtain at the start of a performance. **c.** the fall of a curtain at the end of a scene or act. **3.** anything that shuts off, covers, or conceals: *a curtain of artillery fire.* **4.** *Archit.* a flat portion of a wall, connecting two towers, projecting structures, or the like. **5.** *Fort.* the part of a wall or rampart connecting two bastions, towers, or the like. 6. (*pl.*) *Colloq.* the end, esp. of a life. *–v.t.* 7. to provide, shut off, conceal, or adorn with, or as with, a curtain. [ME *curtine,* from OF, from LL *cortīna* curtain]

**curtain call** /'– kɔl/, *n.* the appearance of performers at the conclusion of a performance in response to the applause of the audience.

**curtain lecture** /'– lɛktʃə/, *n.* a private scolding, esp. one by a wife to her husband.

**curtain-raiser** /'kɜtn-reɪzə/, *n.* **1.** an event taking place immediately before another (main) event, as a short play or junior football game. **2.** a prelude or foretaste of something.

**curtain speech** /'kɜtn spitʃ/, *n.* **1.** the final speech in a play or section of a play before the curtain is lowered. **2.** a speech made by someone standing in front of the curtain of a theatre.

**curtain wall** /'– wɔl/, *n.* an exterior wall of a building, having no structural function.

**curtesy** /'kɜtəsi/, *n., pl.* **-sies.** the life tenure formerly enjoyed by a husband in his wife's land inheritance after her death, provided they had issue able to inherit: *a tenancy by the curtesy.* [var. of COURTESY]

**curtilage** /'kɜtəlɪdʒ/, *n.* the area of land occupied by a dwelling and its yard and outbuildings, actually enclosed or considered as enclosed. [ME, from AF, from OF *courtil* little court. See COURT]

**curtsey** /'kɜtsi/, *n., pl.* **-seys,** *v.,* **-seyed, -seying.** →**curtsy.**

**curtsy** /'kɜtsi/, *n., pl.* **-sies,** *v.,* **-sied, -sying.** *–n.* **1.** a bow by women in recognition or respect, consisting of bending the knees and lowering the body. *–v.i.* **2.** to make a curtsy. [var. of COURTESY]

**curvaceous** /kɜ'veɪʃəs/, *adj. Colloq.* (of a woman) having a full and shapely figure. [CURVE + -ACEOUS]

**curvature** /'kɜvətʃə/, *n.* **1.** the act of curving. **2.** curved condition, often abnormal: *curvature of the spine.* **3.** the degree of curving. **4.** something curved. **5.** *Maths.* a measure of the extent to which a line departs from being straight or a surface departs from being plane.

**curve** /kɜv/, *n., v.,* **curved, curving.** *–n.* **1.** a continuously bending line, usu. without angles. **2.** any curved outline, form, thing, or part. **3.** a line on a graph, diagram, etc. representing a continuous variation in force, quantity, etc. **4.** a curved ruler used by draughtsmen. *–v.i.* **5.** to bend in a curve. **6.** to take the course of a curve. *–v.t.* **7.** to bend into a curve. **8.** to cause to take the course of a curve. [L *curvus* bent, curved] – **curvedly** /'kɜvədli/, *adv.* – **curvedness,** *n.*

**curvet** /kɜ'vɛt/, *n., v.,* **-vetted, -vetting** or **-veted, -veting.** *–n.* **1.** a leap of a horse in which the forelegs are raised together and equally advanced, and then, as they are falling, the hindlegs are raised with a spring, so that all the legs are off the ground at once. *–v.i.* **2.** to leap in a curvet, as a horse; cause one's horse to do this. **3.** to leap and frisk. *–v.t.* **4.** to cause to make a curvet. [It. *corvetta,* diminutive of *corvo,* from L *curvus* bent, curved]

**curvi-,** a combining form of **curve.**

**curvilinear** /kɜvə'lɪniə/, *adj.* **1.** consisting of or bounded by curved lines: *a curvilinear figure.* **2.** forming, or moving in a curved line. **3.** formed, or characterised by, curved lines. Also, **curvilineal.**

**curvy** /'kɜvi/, *adj.* having curves; curvaceous.

**cuscus** /'kʌskʌs/, *n.* any of various nocturnal, arboreal marsupials of the genus *Phalanger* of New Guinea and adjacent islands and rainforest areas of northern Queensland, having a round head, small ears, thick, woolly fur and a long, partially scaled, prehensile tail.

cuscus

**cusec** /'kjusɛk/, *n.* a unit of measurement in the imperial system, equal to one cubic foot per second or approx. 0.028 $m^3$/s (as a rate of flow).

**cush** /'kʊʃ/, *adj. in the phrase* **all cush,** *Obs. Colloq.* all right; okay. Also, **cush-n-all, cush-n-andy.**

**cushion** /'kʊʃən/, *n.* **1.** a soft bag of cloth, leather, or rubber, filled with feathers, air, etc., used to sit, kneel, or lie on. **2.** anything similar in appearance or

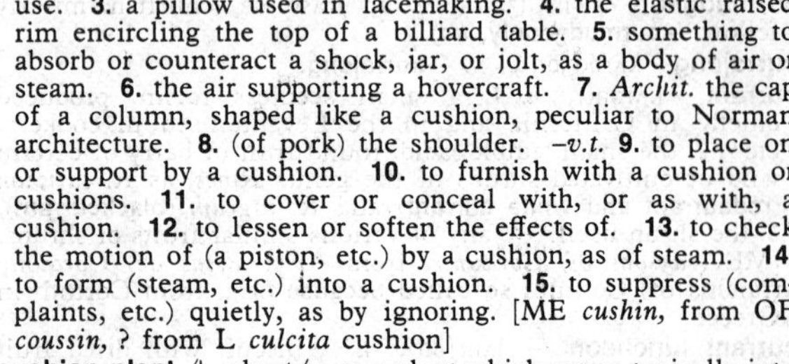

use. **3.** a pillow used in lacemaking. **4.** the elastic raised rim encircling the top of a billiard table. **5.** something to absorb or counteract a shock, jar, or jolt, as a body of air or steam. **6.** the air supporting a hovercraft. **7.** *Archit.* the cap of a column, shaped like a cushion, peculiar to Norman architecture. **8.** (of pork) the shoulder. *–v.t.* **9.** to place on or support by a cushion. **10.** to furnish with a cushion or cushions. **11.** to cover or conceal with, or as with, a cushion. **12.** to lessen or soften the effects of. **13.** to check the motion of (a piston, etc.) by a cushion, as of steam. **14.** to form (steam, etc.) into a cushion. **15.** to suppress (complaints, etc.) quietly, as by ignoring. [ME *cushin,* from OF *coussin,* ? from L *culcita* cushion]

**cushion plant** /'– plænt/, *n.* a plant which grows typically into a cushion-like mound.

**Cushitic** /ku'ʃɪtɪk/, *n.* a group of Hamitic languages, including Somali and other languages of Somaliland and Ethiopia.

**cushy** /'kʊʃi/, *adj.,* **cushier, cushiest.** *Colloq.* easy; pleasant. [Anglo-Indian, from Hind. *khūsh* excellent]

**cusp** /kʌsp/, *n.* **1.** a point; pointed end. **2.** *Anat., Zool., Bot.* a point, projection or elevation, as on the crown of a tooth. **3.** *Maths.* a point where two parts of a curve touch and end. **4.** *Archit., etc.* a point or figure formed by the intersection of two small arcs or curved members, as one of the pointed projections sometimes decorating the internal curve of an arch or a traceried window. **5.** *Astron.* a point of a crescent, esp. of the moon. **6.** *Astrol.* the transitional first or last part of a sign or house when the new sign is gaining ascendancy, but the influence of the old one persists: *to be born on the cusp.* [L *cuspis* point]

**cusped** /kʌspt/, *adj.* having a cusp or cusps; cusp-like. Also, **cuspate** /'kʌspət, -peɪt/, **cuspated.**

**cuspid** /'kʌspəd/, *n.* a tooth with a single projection point or elevation; a canine tooth (*cuspid* is preferred for a human canine tooth). [L *cuspis* point]

**cuspidal** /'kʌspədl/, *adj.* of, like, or having a cusp; cuspidate.

**cuspidate** /'kʌspədeɪt/, *adj.* **1.** having a cusp or cusps. **2.** furnished with or ending in a sharp and stiff point or cusp: *cuspidate leaves, cuspidate tooth.* Also, **cuspidated.** [NL *cuspidātus,* from L *cuspis* point]

**cuspidation** /kʌspə'deɪʃən/, *n.* decoration with cusps, as in architecture.

**cuspidor** /'kʌspədɔ/, *n.* a bowl used as a receptacle for spit. [Pg.: spitter, spittoon, from *cuspir,* from L *conspuere* spit upon]

**cuss** /kʌs/, *Orig. U.S. Colloq. –n.* **1.** a curse. **2.** a person or animal: *a queer but likeable cuss. –v.t.* **3.** to curse. *–v.i.* **4.** to curse. [early var. of CURSE]

**cussed** /'kʌsəd/, *adj. Colloq.* **1.** cursed. **2.** obstinate; perverse. – **cussedly,** *adv.* – **cussedness,** *n.*

**custard** /'kʌstəd/, *n.* **1.** Also, **boiled custard.** a sauce for sweet puddings, fruit, etc., made from milk, eggs and sugar, heated and often thickened with cornflour. **2.** →**baked custard.** [earlier *crustarde* (with loss of first *-r-* by dissimilation), a kind of patty, from OE *croste* CRUST]

**custard-apple** /'kʌstəd-æpəl/, *n.* **1.** the fruit of any of a group of shrubs and trees, native to tropical America, and possessing soft edible pulp; often confined to the single species, *Annona reticulata.* **2.** the tree itself.

custard apple

**custard pie** /kʌstəd 'paɪ/, *n.* a large custard tart.

**custard-pie** /'kʌstəd-paɪ/, *adj.* of or pertaining to slapstick comedy typified by the throwing of custard pies.

**custard powder** /'– paʊdə/, *n.* a commercially-produced powdered mixture used as a base in making custard.

**custard tart** /– 'tat/, *n.* an open pastry case filled with baked custard often sprinkled with spice, as nutmeg.

**custodial** /kʌs'toʊdiəl/, *adj.* of or pertaining to custody.

**custodian** /kʌs'toʊdiən/, *n.* a person who has custody; a keeper; guardian. – **custodianship,** *n.*

**custody** /ˈkʌstədi/, *n., pl.* **-dies.** **1.** keeping; guardianship; care: *in the custody of her father.* **2.** the keeping or charge of officers of the law: *the car was held in the custody of the police.* **3.** imprisonment: *he was taken into custody.* [L *custōdia*]

**custom** /ˈkʌstəm/, *n.* **1.** a habitual practice; the usual way of acting in given circumstances. **2.** habits or usages collectively; convention. **3.** a long-continued habit which is so established that it has the force of law. **4.** such habits collectively. **5.** a customary tax, tribute, or service due by feudal tenants to their lord. **6.** *Sociol.* a group pattern of habitual activity usu. transmitted from one generation to another. **7.** toll; duty. **8.** (*pl.*) customs duties. **9.** (*pl.*) the government department that collects these duties. **10.** habitual patronage of a particular shop, etc.; business patronage. **11.** customers or patrons collectively. **12.** the aggregate of customers. [ME *custume,* from OF, from L *consuētūdo* custom. See CONSUETUDE. Cf. COSTUME]

**customable** /ˈkʌstəməbəl/, *adj.* subject to customs or duties; dutiable.

**customary** /ˈkʌstəməri, -təmri/, *adj., n., pl.* **-aries.** *–adj.* **1.** according to or depending on custom; usual; habitual. **2.** of or established by custom rather than law. **3.** *Law.* defined by long-continued practices: *the customary service due from land in a manor.* *–n.* **4.** a book or document containing the legal customs or customary laws of a locality. **5.** any body of such customs or laws. [ML *customārius,* from OF *custume* CUSTOM] **– customarily,** *adv.* **– customariness,** *n.*

**custom-built** /ˈkʌstəm-bɪlt/, *adj.* made to individual order: *a custom-built limousine.*

**customer** /ˈkʌstəmə/, *n.* **1.** one who purchases goods from another; a buyer; a patron. **2.** *Colloq.* a person one has to deal with; a fellow: *a queer customer.*

**custom feeding** /ˈkʌstəm fidɪŋ/, *n.* the practice of pasturing one's cattle on another farmer's feedlot to have them fattened for slaughter.

**customise** /ˈkʌstəmaɪz/, *v.t.,* **-mised, -mising.** to rebuild or alter the bodywork of (a car, etc.) so as to make it unique.

**custom-made** /ˈkʌstəm-meɪd/, *adj.* made to individual order: *custom-made shoes.*

**customs duties** /ˈkʌstəmz djutiz/, *n.pl.* duties imposed by law on imported or, less commonly, exported goods.

**customs house** /ˈkʌstəmz haʊs/, *n.* a government office, often at a seaport, for collecting customs, clearing vessels, etc. Also, *Chiefly U.S.,* **custom house.**

**customs union** /ˈkʌstəmz junjən/, *n.* an arrangement between independent nations or tariff areas to remove customs barriers between them and to adopt a uniform tariff policy.

**custumal** /ˈkʌstjəməl/, *n.* →**customary.** [ML *custumālis,* Latinisation of OF *costumel* customary]

**cut** /kʌt/, *v.,* **cut, cutting,** *adj., n.* *–v.t.* **1.** to penetrate with, or as with, a sharp-edged instrument: *he cut his finger.* **2.** to strike sharply, as with a whip. **3.** to wound severely the feelings of. **4.** to divide, with or as with, a sharp-edged instrument; sever; carve: *to cut a rope, bread into slices, etc.* **5.** to hew or saw down; fell: *to cut timber.* **6.** to detach with, or as with, a sharp-edged instrument; separate from the main body; lop off. **7.** to reap; mow; harvest: *to cut grain or hay.* **8.** to trim by clipping, shearing, paring, or pruning: *to cut the hair or the nails.* **9.** to castrate. **10.** to intersect; cross: *one line cuts another at right angles.* **11.** to stop; halt the running of, as an engine, a liquid, etc. **12.** to abridge or shorten by omitting a part: *to cut a speech.* **13.** to lower; reduce; diminish (sometimes fol. by *down*): *to cut rates.* **14.** *Radio, T.V.* to stop recording or transmitting (a scene, broadcast, etc.). **15.** *Films, T.V., etc.* to edit (filmed material) by cutting and rearranging pieces of film. **16.** to record (def. 6). **17.** to make or fashion by cutting, as a statue, jewel, garment, etc. **18.** to hollow out; excavate; dig: *cut a trench.* **19.** *Colloq.* to renounce; give up. **20.** *Colloq.* to refuse to recognise socially. **21.** to perform or execute: *to cut a caper.* **22.** *Colloq.* to absent oneself from. **23.** *Cards.* **a.** to divide (a pack of cards) at random into two or more parts, by removing cards from the top. **b.** to take (a card) from a pack. **24.** *Sport.* to hit (a ball) either with the hand or some instrument so as to change its course and often to cause it to spin. **25.** *Cricket.* **a.** in batting, to strike with a cross-bat and dispatch (a ball) on the off side, usu. in a direction between cover and fine third man. **b.** in bowling, to cause (the ball) to deviate on bouncing, usu. by making the seam strike the pitch; to seam. **26.** of sheep, to yield (wool) on being shorn: *the sheep cut a heavy fleece.* **27.** to record a song, etc. on (a record). **28.** to dilute or adulterate (a drug, as heroin, etc.) with other substances, as talcum powder. *–v.i.* **29.** to penetrate or divide something as with sharp-edged instrument; make an incision: *the scissors cut well.* **30.** to allow incision or severing: *butter cuts easily.* **31.** to pass, go, or come, esp. in the most direct way (fol. by *across, through, in,* etc.): *to cut across a field.* **32.** to strike sharply, as with a whip. **33.** (of the teeth) to grow through the gums. **34.** *Cards.* to cut the cards. **35.** *Radio, T.V.* to stop filming or recording. **36.** *Colloq.* to run away; make off. **37.** (of a horse) to interfere. **38.** *Cricket.* to make a cut in batting. *–v.* **39.** Some special verb phrases are:

**cut across, 1.** to take a short cut. **2.** to interrupt.

**cut a dash,** to make an impression by one's ostentatious or flamboyant behaviour or dress.

**cut and run,** to leave unceremoniously and in great haste.

**cut back, 1.** to shorten or reduce. **2.** (in a novel, film, etc.) to return suddenly to earlier events. **3.** *Football.* to reverse direction suddenly by moving in the diagonally opposite course. **4.** *Surfing.* to change the direction of one's board by going out of a wave and coming back into it.

**cut both ways, 1.** (of an argument, proposal, etc.) to support and oppose the same contention. **2.** to be beneficial in some ways and disadvantageous in others.

**cut corners,** to do a job in the shortest possible time as by bypassing regulations or skimping on detail.

**cut down, 1.** to bring down by cutting. **2.** to reduce, esp. expenses, costs, etc.

**cut down to size,** to reduce to the proper status or level, or to the frame of mind in keeping with a person's position.

**cut in, 1.** to interrupt. **2.** (in traffic) to pull in dangerously soon after overtaking. **3.** to allow oneself (or someone else) a share: *he cut his brother in on the deal.* **4.** to stop a dancing couple in order to dance with one of them. **5.** *Elect.* to switch on. **6.** to begin to shear sheep. **7.** to join a cardgame by taking the place of someone who is leaving.

**cut it fine,** to leave only a narrow margin of error.

**cut it out,** *Colloq.* to stop it; desist.

**cut no ice,** to make no impression on (fol. by *with*).

**cut off, 1.** to intercept. **2.** to interrupt. **3.** to bring to a sudden end. **4.** to shut out. **5.** to disinherit. **6.** (in a telephone conversation) to disconnect.

**cut one's coat according to one's cloth,** to live within the limits of one's resources or opportunities.

**cut one's losses,** to abandon a project in which one has already invested some part of one's capital, either material or emotional, for no return, so as not to incur more losses.

**cut one's teeth on,** *Colloq.* to gain experience on.

**cut out, 1.** to omit; delete; excise. **2.** to spend all the money represented by (a cheque). **3.** to oust and replace; supplant (esp. a rival). **4.** to stop; cease: *the shearing cut out on Friday.* **5.** to plan or arrange; prepare. **6.** to fashion or shape; form; make. **7.** to move suddenly out of the lane or path in which one has been driving. **8.** *Print.* to remove the background from an illustration so that the outline of the subject appears on an unprinted background. **9.** (of an electrical device) to switch off, as when overloaded. **10.** to remove individual livestock from a herd or flock. **11.** (of timberland) to clear an area completely. **12.** to leave a cardgame.

**cut out for,** to be fit for.

**cut (someone) dead,** to ignore (someone).

**cut (someone) short,** to interrupt (someone).

**cut teeth,** to have the teeth grow through the gums.

**cut up, 1.** to cut into pieces. **2.** *Colloq.* to criticise severely. **3.** *Colloq.* to upset or cause distress to. **4.** *Horse-racing.* to adopt cutthroat tactics.

**cut up rough** or **nasty,** to behave badly; become unpleasant.

*–adj.* **40.** that has been subjected to cutting; divided into pieces by cutting; detached by cutting: *cut flowers.* **41.** *Bot.* incised; cleft. **42.** fashioned by cutting; having the surface shaped or ornamented by grinding and polishing: cut glass. **43.** reduced by, or as by, cutting: *cut rates.* **44.** *Colloq.* drunk. **45.** diluted; adulterated; impure: *cut heroin.* **46. cut**

**and dried, a.** fixed or settled in advance. **b.** lacking freshness or spontaneity. **47. cut out,** (of shearing) finished. **48. go like a cut cat,** go very fast. *–n.* **49.** the act of cutting; a stroke or a blow as with a knife, whip, etc. **50.** a piece cut off, esp. of meat. **51.** *Butchering.* part of an animal usu. cut as one piece. **52.** *Colloq.* share: *his cut was 20 per cent.* **53.** the quantity cut, as wool or timber. **54.** the result of cutting as an incision, wound, etc.; a passage, channel, etc., made by cutting or digging. **55.** manner or fashion in which anything is cut. **56.** style; manner, kind. **57.** a passage or course straight across: *a short cut.* **58.** a number of sheep or cattle cut out from the herd. **59.** an excision or omission of a part. **60.** a part excised or omitted. **61.** part of a mob of livestock separated from a main mob: *a cut of 300 steers was taken.* **62.** a reduction in price, salary, etc. **63.** an act, speech, etc., which wounds the feelings. **64. a.** a blow from a cane; corporal punishment esp. when administered to schoolchildren. **b. the cuts,** a caning. **65.** an engraved block or place used for printing, or an impression from it. **66.** *Colloq.* a refusal to recognise an acquaintance. **67.** *Sport.* **a.** the act of cutting a ball. **b.** the spin of the ball. **68.** *Cricket.* a batting stroke which cuts (def. 25). **69.** a track on a record. **70.** *Cards.* a cutting of the cards. **71.** one of several pieces of straw, paper, etc. used in drawing lots. **72.** *Films, T.V., etc.* a quick transition from one shot to another. **73.** the quantity of wool shorn: *my cut was thirty bales.* **74. a cut above,** *Colloq.* somewhat superior to another in some respect. **75. cut and thrust, a.** swordplay with the edge as well as the point of the sword. **b.** lively exchange of opinions or arguments: *the cut and thrust of politics.* **76. in for one's cut,** participating in the expectation of a share in the spoils or profit. [ME *cutten, kytten, kitten;* akin to d. Swed. *kata* cut]

**cutaneous** /kju'teɪniəs/, *adj.* of, pertaining to, or affecting the skin. [ML *cutāneus,* from L *cutis* skin]

**cutaway** /'kʌtəweɪ/, *adj.* **1.** (of a coat) having the skirt cut away from the waist in front in a curve. **2.** (of a model of a building, etc.) with part cut away to reveal the interior. *–n.* **3.** a cutaway coat.

**cutback** /'kʌtbæk/, *n.* **1.** reduction to an earlier rate, as in production. **2.** *Surfing.* the act of cutting back. **3.** *U.S.* →**flashback.**

**cutch** /kʌtʃ/, *n.* →**catechu.**

**cute** /kjut/, *adj.*, **cuter, cutest. 1.** *Colloq.* pleasingly pretty or dainty. **2.** clever; shrewd. [aphetic var. of ACUTE] – **cutely,** *adv.* – **cuteness,** *n.*

**cut glass** /kʌt 'glas/, *n.* glass ornamented or shaped by cutting or grinding with abrasive wheels. – **cutglass,** *adj.*

**cuticle** /'kjutɪkəl/, *n.* **1.** the epidermis. **2.** a superficial integument, membrane, or the like. **3.** the non-living epidermis which surrounds the edges of the fingernail or toenail. **4.** *Bot.* a very thin hyaline film covering the surface of plants, and derived from the outer surfaces of the epidermal cells. [L *cutīcula,* diminutive of *cutis* skin] – **cuticular** /kju'tɪkjələ/, *adj.*

**cuticula** /kju'tɪkjələ/, *n., pl.* **-lae** /-li/. the outer non-cellular layer of the arthropod integument, composed of a mixture of chitin and protein, but commonly containing other hardening substances. [L: skin]

**cutie** /'kjuti/, *n. Colloq.* a pleasing person; one with a winning personality, esp. female. Also, **cutey.**

**cutin** /'kjutən/, *n.* a transparent waxy substance constituting together with cellulose the cuticle of plants. [L *cutis* skin + -IN[2]]

**cutinise** /'kjutənaɪz/, *v.*, **-nised, -nising.** *–v.t.* **1.** to make into cutin. *–v.i.* **2.** to become cutin. Also, **cutinize.** – **cutinisation,** *n.*

**cutis** /'kjutəs/, *n.* the corium or true skin, beneath the epidermis. Also, **cutis vera** /'vɪərə/.

**cutlass** /'kʌtləs/, *n.* a short, heavy, slightly curved sword, formerly used esp. at sea. [F *coutelas,* from L *cultellus* small knife]

cutlass

**cutler** /'kʌtlə/, *n.* one who makes, sells, or repairs knives and other cutting instruments. [ME *coteler,* from F *coutelier,* from *coutel* small knife, from L *cultellus*]

**cutlery** /'kʌtləri/, *n.* **1.** the art or business of a cutler. **2.** cutting instruments collectively, esp. those for dinner-table use. [F *coutelerie.* See CUTLER]

**cutlet** /'kʌtlət/, *n.* **1.** a cut of meat, usu. lamb or veal, for grilling, frying or roasting, containing a rib, and cut from the neck of the carcase; a rib chop. **2.** a fish steak. [F *côtelette,* double diminutive of *côte* rib, from L *costa*]

**cut-lunch** /kʌt-'lʌntʃ/, *n.* **1.** a light lunch, usu. sandwiches, prepared at home to be eaten elsewhere. **2. carry a cut-lunch,** *Colloq.* to have an honest job. *–adj.* **3.** amateur.

**cut-lunch commando** /– kə'mændoʊ/, *n.* **1.** *Mil.* a person who has a desk job but who is officious or overbearing in manner. **2.** an amateur or part-time soldier. **3.** an amateur hunter who makes up with bravado for what he lacks in skill.

**cut-lunch revolutionary** /– rɛvəlu'ʃənəri/, *n.* one who professes revolutionary ideals from the safety of his position in the establishment.

**cut-off** /'kʌt-ɒf/, *n.* **1.** a cutting off, or something that cuts off; a shorter passage or way. **2.** a specified point of termination; limit. **3.** →**oxbow** (def. 2). **4.** the arresting of the passage of steam or working fluid to the cylinder of an engine, or the mechanism effecting it. **5.** the negative bias which has to be applied to the control grid of a radio valve in order to reduce the anode current to zero. *–adj.* **6.** of or pertaining to a cut-off.

**cut-off grade** /'– ˌgreɪd/, *n.* the lowest grade of mineralised material that qualifies as ore in a given deposit; the material of the lowest assay that is included in an ore estimate.

**cut-out** /'kʌt-aʊt/, *n.* **1.** something cut out from something else. **2.** *Elect.* an automatic device (usu. electro-magnetic or thermal) for breaking an electric circuit when the current exceeds the predetermined value. **3.** *Print.* an illustration whose subject appears on an unprinted background. **4.** the completion of shearing. **5.** the last of the flock to be shorn.

**cut-price** /'kʌt-praɪs/, *adj.* **1.** (of goods) for sale at a price lower than the suggested retail price. **2.** (of a shop, etc.) dealing in such goods.

**cutpurse** /'kʌtpɜs/, *n.* **1.** (formerly) one who steals by cutting purses from the girdle. **2.** →**pickpocket.**

**cut rate** /kʌt 'reɪt/, *n.* a price, fare, or rate below the standard charge. – **cut-rate,** *adj.*

**cutter** /'kʌtə/, *n.* **1.** one who or that which cuts. **2.** a small sailing boat with one mast, a bowsprit, a gaff, and a boom. **3.** a medium-sized boat for rowing or sailing, or a launch, belonging to a warship. **4.** a light-armed government vessel (**revenue cutter**), used to prevent smuggling and enforce customs regulations. **5.** *Cricket.* a ball which strikes the ground on its seam, and suddenly changes direction.

**cutter-out** /kʌtər-'aʊt/, *n.* a person who separates individual cattle from the herd.

**cutthroat** /'kʌtθroʊt/, *n.* **1.** one who cuts throats; a murderer. **2.** a cutthroat razor. *–adj.* **3.** murderous. **4.** (of a razor) having an open blade. **5.** relentless: *cutthroat competition.* **6.** pertaining to a game participated in by three or more persons, each acting and scoring as an individual. **7.** *Horseracing.* of or pertaining to the tactics of two or more horses which race to the front and race each other, thus dissipating energy and failing to win.

**cutting** /'kʌtɪŋ/, *n.* **1.** the act of one who or that which cuts. **2.** something cut off. **3.** *Hort.* a piece of plant, commonly a root, shoot, or leaf, cut from a plant to reproduce an entire new plant. **4.** a piece clipped out of a newspaper; a clipping. **5.** something produced by cutting; an excavation through high ground, as in constructing a road, etc. **6.** (*pl.*) *Geol.* the fragmental rock samples broken or torn from penetrated rock during the course of drilling. *–adj.* **7.** that cuts; penetrating or dividing by, or as by, a cut. **8.** piercing, as a wind. **9.** wounding the feelings severely; sarcastic. – **cuttingly,** *adv.*

**cutting-grass** /'kʌtɪŋ-gras/, *n.* any of various grasses or sedges with leaves sufficiently hard and rough to inflict cuts, esp. *Gahnia* species.

**cuttlebone** /'kʌtlboʊn/, *n.* the calcareous internal shell or plate of true cuttlefishes, used to make powder for polishing, and fed to canaries to supply the necessary lime, etc.

**cuttlefish** /'kʌtlfɪʃ/, *n., pl.* **-fishes,** (*esp. collectively*) **-fish.** any of various decapod dibranchiate cephalopods, esp. of the genus *Sepia,* having sucker-bearing arms and the power of ejecting a black, inklike fluid when pursued. Also, **cuttle.** [*cuttle* (ME *codulle,* OE *cudele* cuttlefish; akin to COD[1]) + FISH[1]]

cuttlefish

**cutty-grass** /'kʌti-gras/, *n. N.Z.* →**cutting-grass.**

**cutwater** /'kʌtwɔtə/, *n.* **1.** the forepart of a ship's stem or prow, which cuts the water. **2.** the sharp edge of a pier of a bridge, which resists the action of water or ice.

**cutwork** /'kʌtwɜk/, *n.* openwork embroidery in which the ground fabric is cut out about the pattern.

**cutworm** /'kʌtwɜm/, *n.* any of various caterpillars of certain noctuid moths, which feed at night on the young plants of corn, cabbage, etc., cutting them off at or near the ground.

**cuvee** /kju'veɪ/, *n.* **1.** the contents of a wine vat. **2.** a blend of wine. [F *cuver* ferment]

**CWA,** Country Women's Association.

**cwt,** hundredweight.

**-cy,** **1.** a suffix of abstract nouns, usu. paired with adjectives ending in *-t, -te, -tic,* esp. *-nt,* as *democracy, accuracy, expediency, necromancy,* also paired with other adjectives, as *fallacy* (*fallacious*), or with a noun, as *lunacy,* sometimes forming (in extended suffixes) action nouns, as *vacancy* (*vacate*), *occupancy* (*occupy*). **2.** a suffix of nouns denoting a rank or dignity, sometimes attached to the stem of a word rather than the word itself, as *captaincy, colonelcy, magistracy.* [representing F *-cie, -tie,* L *-cia, -tia,* Gk *-kia, -keia, -tia, -teia*]

**cyan-**[1], variant of **cyano-**[1], usu. before vowels and *h,* as in *cyanamide.*

**cyan-**[2], variant of **cyano-**[2], before vowels.

**cyan-**[3], variant of **cyano-**[3], before vowels.

**cyanamide** /saɪ'ænəmaɪd, 'saɪənəmaɪd/, *n.* **1.** a white crystalline compound, $H_2NCN$, obtainable by the action of ammonia on cyanogen chloride or from calcium cyanamide. **2.** an ester or salt of this substance. Also, **cyanamid** /saɪ'ænəməd, 'saɪənəməd/. [CYAN(O)-[3] + AMIDE]

**cyanate** /'saɪəneɪt/, *n.* a salt of cyanic acid.

**cyanic** /saɪ'ænɪk/, *adj.* **1.** blue (applied esp. to a series of colours in flowers, including the blues and colours tending towards blue). **2.** containing, of, or belonging to cyanogen. [CYAN(O)-[1] + -IC]

**cyanic acid** /– 'æsəd/, *n.* a poisonous compound, HOCN, isomeric with fulminic acid, but unstable except at low temperatures.

**cyanide** /'saɪənaɪd/, *n., v.,* **-nided, -niding.** *–n.* **1.** Also, **cyanid.** a salt of hydrocyanic acid, as potassium cyanide, KCN. *–v.t.* **2.** to treat with a cyanide, as an ore in the process of extracting gold. **3.** *N.Z.* to poison (possums) with cyanides.

**cyanide hardening** /'– ˌhadənɪŋ/, *n.* the introduction of carbon and nitrogen into the surface of steel by heating it in contact with molten cyanides; a form of case-hardening.

**cyanide process** /'– ˌproʊsɛs/, *n.* a process for extracting gold from its ores, by dissolving in potassium cyanide, reducing the resulting aurocyanide with zinc, filtering off the product and subjecting it to cupellation.

**cyanine** /'saɪənin/, *n.* any of several groups of dyes which make silver halide photographic plates sensitive to a colour range. Also, **cyanin** /'saɪənən/.

**cyanite** /'saɪənaɪt/, *n.* →**kyanite.**

**cyano-**[1], a word element indicating dark blue colouring. Also, **cyan-**[1]. [Gk *kyano-,* combining form of *kýanos* dark blue]

**cyano-**[2], a combining form of **cyanide.** Also, **cyan-**[2].

**cyano-**[3], a word element referring to the cyanide group, CN. Also, **cyan-**[3]. [combining form representing CYANOGEN]

**cyanocobalamin** /ˌsaɪənoʊkə'bæləmən/, *n.* one of the active forms of vitamin $B_{12}$, occurring as dark red crystals or red powder; a food supplement.

**cyanogen** /'saɪənədʒən/, *n.* **1.** a poisonous, inflammable gas, $C_2N_2$, used in synthesis as a fumigant and as a rocket propellant. **2.** a univalent radical, CN. [CYANO-[2] + -GEN]

**cyanohydrin** /ˌsaɪənoʊ'haɪdrən/, *n.* one of a class of organic compounds which have both the CN and the OH radicals linked to the same carbon atom.

**cyanosis** /saɪə'noʊsəs/, *n.* blueness or lividness of the skin, as from imperfectly oxygenated blood. Also, **cyanopathy** /saɪə'nɒpəθi/. [NL, from Gk *kyánōsis* dark blue colour] – **cyanotic** /saɪə'nɒtɪk/, *adj.*

**cyanotype** /saɪ'ænətaɪp/, *n.* **1.** a process of photographic printing with ferric salts producing blue lines on a white background, used chiefly in printing tracings. **2.** a print made by such a process. [CYANO-[1] + -TYPE]

**cyanuric acid** /saɪəˌnjurɪk 'æsəd/, *n.* a white crystalline acid, $C_3H_3N_3O_3 \cdot 2H_20$, obtained by heating urea or by the action of water on cyanuric chloride; tricyanic acid.

**cyathiform** /'siəθəfɔm, saɪ'æθ-/, *adj.* shaped like a cup; widened at the top.

**cybernetics** /saɪbə'nɛtɪks/, *n.* the scientific study of those methods of control and communication which are common to living organisms and machines, esp. as applied to the analysis of the operations of machines such as computers. [Gk *kybernḗtēs* helmsman + -ICS] – **cybernetic,** *adj.* – **cybernation,** *n.*

**cycad** /'saɪkæd/, *n.* any of the Cycadales, an order of gymnospermous plants intermediate in appearance between ferns and the palms, many species having a thick unbranched columnar trunk bearing a crown of large leathery pinnate leaves. [NL *Cycas* the typical genus, from Gk *kýkās,* late spelling var. of *kóïkās,* acc. pl. of *kóïx* kind of palm]

cycad

**cycl-,** a word element meaning 'cycle', used esp. in the chemical terminology of cyclic compounds, also in referring to wheel turns. Also, **cyclo-.** [Gk *kykl-,* combining form of *kýklos* ring, circle, wheel]

**cyclamate** /'saɪkləmeɪt, -mət/, *n.* any of a group of artificial sweeteners, sometimes used as food additives.

**cyclamen** /'saɪkləmən, 'sɪk-/, *n.* any plant of the genus *Cyclamen* which has tuberous rootstocks and nodding white, purple, pink, or crimson flowers with reflexed petals. [NL, from Gk *kykláminos*]

**cycle** /'saɪkəl/, *n., v.,* **-cled, -cling.** *–n.* **1.** a round of years or a recurring period of time, esp. one in which certain events or phenomena repeat themselves in the same order and at the same intervals. **2.** any round of operations or events; a series which returns upon itself; any complete course or series. **3.** any long period of years; an age. **4.** a series of poetic or prose narratives about some mythical or heroic theme: *the Arthurian cycle.* **5.** any group of poems or songs about a central event, figure, etc. **6.** the aggregate of legendary or traditional matter with a common mythical or heroic theme. **7.** a bicycle, tricycle, etc. **8.** a period pertaining to the recurrence of astronomical phenomena. **9.** *Physics.* any series of changes in or operations performed by a system which brings it back to its original state, as in an alternating electric current or operation of a heat engine. **10.** →**hertz.** *–v.i.* **11.** to ride or travel by a bicycle, etc. **12.** to move or revolve in cycles; pass through cycles. [L *cyclus,* from Gk *kýklos* ring, circle]

**cycle per second,** *n.* →**hertz.** *Symbol:* c/s

**cycleway** /'saɪkəlweɪ/, *n.* a path or section of a road specially designated for the use of bicycle riders.

**cyclic** /'saɪklɪk, 'sɪklɪk/, *adj.* **1.** of or pertaining to a cycle or cycles; revolving or recurring in cycles; characterised by recurrence in cycles. **2.** of or belonging to a cycle of heroic or mythical poems or prose narratives. **3.** *Geom.* (of a figure) one which can be inscribed in a circle: *cyclic quadrilateral.* **4.** *Chem.* of or denoting a compound whose structural formula contains a closed chain or ring of atoms. **5.** *Bot.* **a.** arranged in whorls, as the parts of a flower. **b.** (of a flower) having the parts so arranged. Also, **cyclical.** [L *cyclicus,* from Gk *kyklikós* circular] – **cyclically,** *adv.*

**cyclic adenylic acid,** *n.* the compound produced by many hormones acting on adenyl cyclase; it activates specific enzymes to ultimately produce the response characteristic of the hormone.

**cyclic AMP** /saɪklɪk eɪ em 'pi/, *n.* →**cyclic adenylic acid.**

**cycling lizard** /ˈsaɪklɪŋ lɪzəd/, *n.* →**frill-necked lizard.**

**cyclist** /ˈsaɪkləst/, *n.* one who rides or travels by a bicycle, tricycle, etc. Also, *U.S.,* **cycler.**

**cyclo-**, variant of **cycl-**, before consonants, as in *cyclograph.*

**cyclograph** /ˈsaɪkləgræf, -graf/, *n.* **1.** *Elect.* an instrument in which the position of a beam of light, or a cathode ray, is controlled by two forces at right angles to each other, such that a closed figure is produced on a screen. **2.** →**arcograph.**

**cyclohexane** /ˌsaɪkloʊˈhɛkseɪn, ˌsaɪklə-/, *n.* a colourless, hydrocarbon, ring compound, $C_6H_{12}$, composed of six methylene radicals ($CH_2$) united by single bonds. It is made by hydrogenation of benzene, and also occurs in some petroleum oils.

**cycloid** /ˈsaɪklɔɪd/, *adj.* **1.** resembling a circle; circular. **2.** (of fishes' scales) smooth-edged, more or less circular in form, with concentric striations. **3.** having such scales, as a fish. **4.** *Psychol.* (of a personality type) characterised by variations of mood between excitement and depression. *–n.* **5.** a cycloid fish. **6.** *Geom.* a curve generated by a point on the circumference of a circle which rolls, without slipping, on a straight line in its plane. [Gk *kykloeidḗs* like a circle] – **cycloidal,** *adj.*

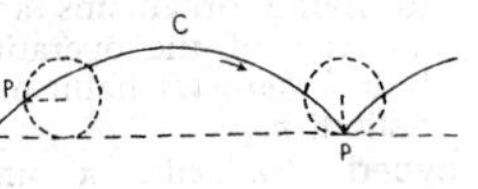

C, cycloid; P, point tracing cycloid on fixed circle

**cyclometer** /saɪˈklɒmətə/, *n.* **1.** an instrument which measures circular arcs. **2.** a device for recording the revolutions of a wheel and hence the distance traversed by a wheeled vehicle, esp. a bicycle.

**cyclonal** /saɪˈkloʊnəl/, *adj.* of or like a cyclone.

**cyclone** /ˈsaɪkloʊn/, *n.* **1.** an atmospheric pressure system characterised by relatively low pressure at its centre, and by clockwise wind motion in the southern hemisphere, anticlockwise in the northern. **2.** a tropical hurricane, esp. in the Indian Ocean. [Gk *kyklôn,* ppr., moving in a circle] – **cyclonic** /saɪˈklɒnɪk/, **cyclonical,** *adj.* – **cyclonically,** *adv.*

**cyclone fence** /– ˈfɛns/, *n.* a fence made from fencing panels. [Trademark]

**cyclonite** /ˈsaɪklənaɪt/, *n.* a white crystalline solid, $(CH_2N \cdot NO_2)_3$ used as an explosive; hexogen; RDX.

**cyclonoscope** /saɪˈkloʊnəˌskoʊp/, *n.* a device for determining the centre of a cyclone.

**cyclopaedia** /saɪkləˈpidiə/, *n.* →**encyclopaedia.** Also, **cyclopedia.** – **cyclopaedic,** *adj.* – **cyclopaedist,** *n.*

**cyclopean** /saɪkləˈpiən, saɪˈklɒpiən/, *adj.* **1.** gigantic; vast. **2.** *Archit.* of, like or denoting an early style of masonry employing massive stones, more or less irregular in shape. [from *Cyclops,* in Gk mythology one of a race of giants with only one circular eye in the middle of the forehead]

**cyclopentane** /ˌsaɪkloʊˈpɛnteɪn/, *n.* a colourless liquid, $C_5H_{10}$, derived from some petroleums.

**cycloplegia** /ˌsaɪkloʊˈplidʒə, ˌsɪkloʊ-/, *n.* paralysis of the intraocular muscles.

**cyclopropane** /ˌsaɪkloʊˈproʊpeɪn/, *n.* a colourless gas, $C_3H_6$, used as an anaesthetic.

**cyclorama** /saɪkləˈramə/, *n.* **1.** a pictorial representation, in natural perspective, of a landscape, a battle, etc., on the inner wall of a cylindrical room or hall, the spectators occupying a position in the centre. **2.** *Theat.* a curved wall or backcloth at the back of a stage used to create the impression of unlimited space or distance, or for lighting effects. [CYCL- + Gk *(h)órama* view] – **cycloramic** /saɪkləˈræmɪk/, *adj.*

**cyclostomatous** /saɪkləˈstɒmətəs, -ˈstoʊmə-, sɪklə-/, *adj.* **1.** having a circular mouth. **2.** belonging or pertaining to the Cyclostomata. See **cyclostome.** Also, **cyclostomate** /saɪˈklɒstəmət, -meɪt/.

**cyclostome** /ˈsaɪkləstoʊm, ˈsɪklə-/, *adj.* **1.** belonging or pertaining to the Cyclostomata, a group or class of eel-like aquatic vertebrates (the lampreys and hagfishes), characterised by pouchlike gills and a circular suctorial mouth without hinged jaws. **2.** having a circular mouth. *–n.* **3.** a cyclostome vertebrate; a lamprey or a hagfish. [CYCLO- + Gk *stóma* mouth]

**cyclostyle** /ˈsaɪkləstaɪl/, *n.* **1.** a manifolding device consisting of a kind of pen with a small toothed wheel at the end which cuts minute holes in a specially prepared paper stretched over a smooth surface, thus forming a stencil from which copies are printed. *–v.t.* **2.** to use a cyclostyle.

**cyclothymia** /ˌsaɪkləˈθaɪmiə/, *n.* the tendency toward alternating periods of elation and depression, which, in extreme, is manifested as manic-depressive psychosis. [CYCLO- + Gk *-thymia* -mindedness (from *thymós* mind)] – **cyclothymic,** *adj.*

**cyclothymiac** /saɪkləˈθaɪmiæk, sɪklə-/, *n.* a person affected with cyclothymia.

**cyclotron** /ˈsaɪklətrɒn/, *n.* a device for imparting very high speed to electrified particles by successive electric impulses at high frequency, space requirements and applied voltage being kept relatively low by causing the particles to move in spiral paths in a strong magnetic field.

**cyclotron frequency** /– ˈfrikwənsi/, *n.* the frequency at which an electron or ion orbits about the magnetic field direction.

**cyder** /ˈsaɪdə/, *n.* →**cider.**

**cygnet** /ˈsɪgnət/, *n.* a young swan. [ME, from L *cygnus* swan (from Gk *kýknos*) + -ET]

**cyl.**, cylinder.

**cylinder** /ˈsɪləndə/, *n.* **1.** *Geom.* **a.** a solid bounded by two parallel planes and the surface generated by a straight line moving parallel to a given straight line, and intersecting a given curve lying in one of the planes. When the given curve is a circle, the solid is called a **right circular cylinder,** if the given line is perpendicular to the planes, and an **oblique circular cylinder** otherwise. **b.** a curved surface generated in this manner. **2.** any cylinder-like object or part, whether solid or hollow. **3.** the rotating part of a revolver, which contains the chambers for the cartridges. **4.** the body of a pump. **5.** the chamber in an engine in which the working medium acts upon the piston. **6.** *Bldg Trades.* a closed circular tank for storing hot water to be drawn off through taps. **7.** (in certain printing presses) **a.** a rotating cylinder which produces the impression, under which a flat forme to be printed from passes. **b.** either of two cylinders, one carrying a curved forme or plate to be printed from, which rotate against each other in opposite directions. **8.** *Archaeol.* a cylindrical or somewhat barrel-shaped stone or clay object, bearing a cuneiform inscription or a carved design, worn by the Babylonians, Assyrians, and kindred peoples as a seal and amulet. *–v.t.* **9.** to furnish with a cylinder or cylinders. **10.** to subject to the action of a cylinder or cylinders. [L *cylindrus,* from Gk *kýlindros* roller, cylinder] – **cylinder-like,** *adj.*

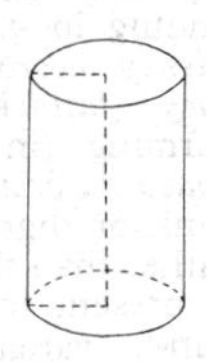
right circular cylinder

**cylinder block** /ˈ– blɒk/, *n.* the casting in which the cylinders of an internal-combustion engine are contained.

**cylinder head** /ˈ– hɛd/, *n.* a detachable portion of an engine fastened securely to the cylinder block containing all or a portion of the combustion chamber.

**cylinder lock** /ˈ– lɒk/, *n.* a lock for an entrance door, opened by key from the outside and by a knob from the inside.

**cylinder press** /ˈ– prɛs/, *n.* →**press**[1] (def. 32a).

**cylindrical** /səˈlɪndrɪkəl/, *adj.* of, pertaining to, or of the form of a cylinder. Also, **cylindric.** – **cylindrically,** *adv.*

**cylindrical projection** /– prəˈdʒɛkʃən/, *n.* a kind of map projection in which the earth's surface is projected on to a surrounding cylinder, which is then opened out.

**cylindroid** /səˈlɪndrɔɪd/, *n.* **1.** a solid having the form of a cylinder with equal and parallel elliptical bases. *–adj.* **2.** resembling a cylinder. [Gk *kylindroeidḗs* cylinder-like. See -OID]

**cylix** /ˈsaɪlɪks/, *n., pl.* **cylices** /ˈsaɪləsiz/. a shallow drinking cup of ancient Greece, usu. with a stem and foot, and two handles. [Gk *kýlix*]

**cyma** /ˈsaɪmə/, *n., pl.* **-mae** /-mi/, **-mas** /-məz/. **1.** *Archit.* a projecting moulding whose profile is a compound biconcave curve. It is called a **cyma recta** when the projective part is concave and a **cyma reversa** when the projecting portion is convex. **2.** *Bot.* →**cyme.** [NL, from Gk *kŷma* something swollen, wave, waved moulding, sprout]

**cymatium** /saɪˈmeɪtiəm/, *n., pl.* **-tia** /-tiə/. the capping moulding of a cornice, placed above the corona commonly having a cyma recta as its most important feature. [L, from Gk *kymátion,* diminutive of *kŷma* wave]

**cymbal** /ˈsɪmbəl/, *n.* one of a pair of concave plates of brass or bronze which are struck together to produce a sharp ringing sound. [OE, from L *cymbalum,* from Gk *kýmbalon,* from *kýmbē* cup, bowl] – **cymbalist,** *n.*

**cymbalo** /ˈsɪmbəloʊ/, *n.* →**dulcimer.**

**cymbidium** /sɪmˈbɪdiəm/, *n.* any species of the widespread orchid genus *Cymbidium* found in Africa, Asia and Australia.

**cyme** /saɪm/, *n.* **1.** an inflorescence in which the primary axis bears a single terminal flower which develops first, the inflorescence being continued by secondary, tertiary, and other axes. **2.** a flat or convex inflorescence of this type. [L *cȳma* sprout, from Gk *kŷma.* See CYMA]

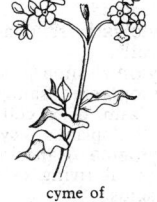

cyme of forget-me-not

**cymene** /ˈsaɪmin/, *n.* a liquid hydrocarbon, $C_{10}H_{14}$, with a pleasant smell, occurring in the volatile oil of the common cumin, *Cuminum cyminum,* and existing in three isomeric forms, *ortho-, meta-,* and *para-cymene.* [*cym-* (combining form representing Gk *kýminon* cumin) + -ENE]

**cymo-,** a word element meaning 'wave'. [Gk *kymo-,* combining form of *kŷma* wave, embryo, sprout]

**cymograph** /ˈsaɪməgræf, -graf/, *n.* →**kymograph.**

**cymophane** /ˈsaɪməfeɪn/, *n.* →**chrysoberyl.** – **cymophanous** /saɪˈmɒfənəs/, *adj.*

**cymose** /ˈsaɪmoʊs/, *adj.* **1.** bearing a cyme or cymes. **2.** of or of the nature of a cyme. [L *cȳmōsus* full of shoots. See CYME] – **cymosely,** *adv.*

**Cymric** /ˈkɪmrɪk/, *adj.* **1.** pertaining to the Cymry. *–n.* **2.** Welsh (the language). Also, **Kymric.** [Welsh *Cymru* Wales or *Cymry* the Welsh + -IC]

**Cymry** /ˈkɪmri/, *n.pl.* the Welsh, or the branch of the Celtic race to which the Welsh belong, comprising also the Cornish people and the Bretons. Also, **Kymry.** [Welsh, pl. *Cymro* Welshman. Cf. Welsh *Cymru* Wales]

**cynic** /ˈsɪnɪk/, *n.* **1.** a sneering faultfinder; one who doubts or denies the goodness of human motives, and who often displays his attitude by sneers, sarcasm, etc. **2.** (*cap.*) one of a sect of Greek philosophers founded by Antisthenes of Athens (born about 444 B.C.), who sought to develop the ethical teachings of Socrates. *–adj.* **3.** cynical. **4.** (*cap.*) of or pertaining to the Cynics or their doctrines. [L *cynicus,* from Gk *kynikós* doglike, churlish, Cynic]

**cynical** /ˈsɪnɪkəl/, *adj.* **1.** like or characteristic of a cynic; distrusting the motives of others. **2.** (*cap.*) →**cynic** (def. 4). – **cynically,** *adv.*

**cynicism** /ˈsɪnəsɪzəm/, *n.* **1.** cynical disposition or character. **2.** a cynical remark. **3.** (*cap.*) the doctrines or practices of the Cynics.

**cynocephalus** /saɪnoʊˈsɛfələs/, *n., pl.* **-cephali** /-ˈsɛfəlaɪ/. **1.** any mammal of the genus *Cynocephalus,* of South East Asia, as the flying lemur or colugo. **2.** the dog-faced baboon. **3.** →**Tasmanian wolf. 4.** any of a mythical race of dog-headed men.

**cynosure** /ˈsɪnəʃʊə/, *n.* **1.** something that strongly attracts attention by its brilliance, etc.: *the cynosure of all eyes.* **2.** something serving for guidance or direction. [L *Cynosūra,* from Gk *Kynósoura,* lit., dog's tail]

**cyperaceous** /saɪpəˈreɪʃəs/, *adj.* pertaining or belonging to, or resembling, the Cyperaceae or the sedge family of monocotyledonous plants, with solid, often triangular, stems and small, coriaceous, achenial fruit. [NL *Cyperus* the typical genus (from Gk *kýpeiros* kind of marsh plant) + -ACEOUS]

**cypher** /ˈsaɪfə/, *n., v.i., v.t.* →**cipher.**

**cy pres** /si ˈpreɪ/, *Law.* **1.** as near as practicable. **2. doctrine of cy pres,** an equitable doctrine (applicable only to cases of charitable trusts or donations) which, in place of an impossible or illegal condition, limitation, or object, allows the nearest practicable one to be substituted. Also, **cypres.** [late AF: as nearly]

**cypress**[1] /ˈsaɪprəs/, *n.* **1.** any of the evergreen trees constituting the coniferous genus *Cupressus,* distinguished by dark green scale-like, overlapping leaves, often a very slender tree with a durable wood. **2.** any of various other allied coniferous trees as of the genera *Chamaecyparis, Taxodium* (**bald cypress**), etc. **3.** any of various other plants in some way resembling the true cypress. **4.** the wood of these trees. [LL *cypressus,* L *cupressus,* from Gk *kypárissos;* replacing ME *cipres,* from OF]

**cypress**[2] /ˈsaɪprəs/, *n. Obs.* a fine, thin fabric resembling lawn or crepe, which was formerly much used in black for mourning garments, etc. Also, **cyprus.** [ME *cipres,* probably from OF; apparently named from CYPRUS]

**cypress pine** /– ˈpaɪn/, *n.* any tree of the mostly Australian genus *Callitris* including several species producing valuable softwood timber.

**Cyprian** /ˈsɪpriən/, *adj.* **1.** pertaining to Cyprus, famous as a centre for the worship of Aphrodite (Venus). **2.** lewd; licentious. *–n.* **3.** a native or inhabitant of Cyprus. **4.** a lewd person, esp. a prostitute. [L *Cyprius* (from Gk *Kýprios* of Cyprus) + -AN]

**cyprinid** /ˈsɪprənɪd, səˈpraɪnɪd/, *n.* **1.** any fish belonging to the Cyprinidae, a large family of freshwater fishes including the carps, minnows and tenches. *–adj.* **2.** of or relating to the Cyprinidae.

**cyprinodont** /səˈprɪnədɒnt, -ˈpraɪnə-/, *n.* any of the Cyprinodontidae, a family of small soft-finned fishes, mostly inhabiting the fresh and brackish waters of North America, including the killifishes, certain top minnows, the guppy, etc. [Gk *kyprînos* carp + *odoús* tooth]

**cyprinoid** /ˈsɪprənɔɪd, səˈpraɪnɔɪd/, *adj.* **1.** resembling or pertaining to a carp or related fish. **2.** belonging to the Cyprinoidea, a group of fishes including the carps, suckers, loaches, etc. *–n.* **3.** a cyprinoid fish.

**Cypriot** /ˈsɪpriət/, *n.* **1.** a native or inhabitant of Cyprus. **2.** the Greek dialect of Cyprus. *–adj.* **3.** Cyprian. Also, **Cypriote** /ˈsɪprioʊt/. [Gk *Kypriṓtēs*]

**cypripedium** /sɪprəˈpidiəm/, *n.* any plant of the genus *Cypripedium,* comprising orchids having large flowers with a protruding sac-like labellum. [NL, from L *Cypri(s)* Venus + *pēs* foot + -IUM]

**cyprus** /ˈsaɪprəs/, *n. Obs.* →**cypress**[2].

**Cyprus** /ˈsaɪprəs/, *n.* an island republic in the Mediterranean.

**cypsela** /ˈsɪpsələ/, *n., pl.* **-lae** /-li/ or **-las.** an achene with an adherent calyx, as in the family Compositae. [NL, from Gk *kypsélē* hollow vessel]

**Cyrillic** /səˈrɪlɪk/, *adj.* of or pertaining to an old Slavic alphabet based mainly on Greek uncials and reputed to have been invented by St Cyril, originally used for writing Old Church Slavonic and adopted with some modifications for the writing of Russian and some other Slavic languages and for some non-Slavic languages of the Soviet Union. [from St. *Cyril,* A.D. 827-869, Greek missionary to the Moravians]

**cyrto-,** a word element meaning 'curved.' [Gk *kyrto-,* combining form of *kyrtós*]

**cyst** /sɪst/, *n.* **1.** *Pathol.* a closed bladder-like sac formed in animal tissues, containing fluid or semifluid morbid matter. **2.** a bladder, sac, or vesicle. **3.** *Bot.* **a.** a spore-like cell with a resistant protective wall. **b.** a cell or cavity enclosing reproductive bodies, etc. **4.** *Zool.* **a.** a sac, usu. spherical, surrounding an animal that has passed into a dormant condition. **b.** such a sac plus the contained animal. [NL *cystis,* from Gk *kýstis* bladder, bag, pouch]

**cyst-,** a combining form representing **cyst.** Also, **cysti-, cysto-.**

**-cyst,** a terminal combining form of **cyst.**

**cystectomy** /sɪsˈtɛktəmi/, *n., pl.* **-mies.** excision of a cyst or bladder, usu. the urinary bladder.

**cysteine** /ˈsɪsteɪn/, *n.* a crystalline amino acid, $HSCH_2CH(NH_3^+)COO^-$, occurring in proteins.

**cysti-,** variant of **cyst-,** as in *cysticercoid.*

**cystic** /ˈsɪstɪk/, *adj.* **1.** pertaining to, of the nature of, or having a cyst or cysts; encysted. **2.** *Anat.* belonging to or relating to the urinary bladder or the gall bladder.

**cysticercoid** /ˌsɪstəˈsɜkɔɪd/, *n.* the larva of certain tapeworms, developing in insects, etc., in which a single head forms without a spacious bladder around it.

**cysticercus** /ˌsɪstəˈsɜkəs/, *n., pl.* **-cerci** /-ˈsɜsi/. the bladder worm larva of certain tapeworms, with a single head (scolex) formed in a large bladder. [NL, from Gk *kysti-* CYSTI- + *kérkos* tail]

**cystic fibrosis** /ˌsɪstɪk faɪˈbroʊsəs/, *n.* a hereditary, chronic disease of the pancreas, lungs, etc., beginning in infancy, in which there is difficulty in breathing and an inability to digest.

**cystine** /ˈsɪstin/, *n.* a sulphur-containing amino acid found in proteins, esp. hair, wool, and horn.

**cystitis** /sɪsˈtaɪtəs/, *n.* inflammation of the urinary bladder.

**cysto-**, variant of **cyst-**, before consonants, as in *cystoscope.*

**cystocarp** /ˈsɪstəkap/, *n.* the mass of carpospores formed as a result of fertilisation in red algae (Rhodophyta), with or without a special envelope (pericarp).

**cystocoele** /ˈsɪstəsil/, *n.* hernia in which the urinary bladder protrudes into the vagina.

**cystoid** /ˈsɪstɔɪd/, *adj.* **1.** resembling a cyst but having no enclosing capsule. *–n.* **2.** a cyst-like formation.

**cystolith** /ˈsɪstəlɪθ/, *n.* a mass of calcium carbonate on the cellulose wall.

**cystoscope** /ˈsɪstəskoʊp/, *n.* a slender, cylindrical instrument for examining the interior of the urinary bladder and for the introduction of medication therein.

**cystotomy** /sɪsˈtɒtəmi/, *n., pl.* **-mies.** the operation of cutting into the urinary bladder.

**cytaster** /saɪˈtæstə, ˈsaɪ-/, *n.* →**aster.**

**-cyte**, a word element referring to cells or corpuscles, as in *leucocyte.* [combining form representing Gk *kýtos* container]

**cytidine** /ˈsaɪtədin/, *n.* a nucleoside of cytosine and ribose, present in all living cells.

**cytidylic acid** /saɪtəˌdɪlɪk ˈæsəd/, *n.* the monophosphate of cytidine, present in all living cells mainly in combined form; one of the monomeric sub-units in ribonucleic acid.

**cyto-**, a word element referring to cells, as in *cytogenesis.* Also, before vowels, **cyt-**. [Gk *kyto-*, combining form of *kýtos* container]

**cytochrome** /ˈsaɪtəkroʊm/, *n.* any of a group of haemoproteins, occurring widely in living cells, all of which take part in biological oxidations.

**cytogenesis** /ˌsaɪtoʊˈdʒɛnəsəs/, *n.* the genesis and differentiation of cells.

**cytogenetics** /saɪtoʊdʒəˈnɛtɪks/, *n.* the part played by cells in causing phenomena of heredity, mutation, and evolution.

**cytokinesis** /ˌsaɪtoʊkəˈnisəs, -kaɪ-/, *n.* the changes in the cytoplasm during mitosis, meiosis, and fertilisation.

**cytology** /saɪˈtɒlədʒi/, *n.* the scientific study of cells, esp. their formation, structure, and functions. – **cytologist,** *n.* – **cytological,** *adj.*

**cytolysis** /saɪˈtɒləsəs/, *n.* the dissolution or degeneration of cells.

**cyton** /ˈsaɪtɒn/, *n.* the body of a nerve cell.

**cytoplasm** /ˈsaɪtəplæzəm/, *n.* the living substance or protoplasm of a cell exclusive of the nucleus. Also, **cytoplast** /ˈsaɪtəplæst/. – **cytoplasmic** /saɪtəˈplæzmɪk/, *adj.*

**cytosine** /ˈsaɪtəsin/, *n.* a pyrimidine base, $C_4H_5N_3O$, present in all living cells, mainly in combined form, as in nucleic acids.

**czar** /za/, *n.* →**tsar.** – **czardom** /ˈzadəm/, *n.*

**czardas** /ˈtʃadæʃ/, *n.* a Hungarian national dance in two movements, one slow and the other fast. [Hung. *csárdás*]

**czarevitch** /ˈzarəvɪtʃ/, *n.* →**tsarevitch.**

**czarevna** /zaˈrɛvnə/, *n.* →**tsarevna.**

**czarina** /zaˈrinə/, *n.* →**tsarina.**

**czarism** /ˈzarɪzəm/, *n.* →**tsarism.**

**czarist** /ˈzarəst/, *n.* →**tsarist.**

**czaritza** /zaˈrɪtsə/, *n.* →**tsaritsa.**

**Czech** /tʃɛk/, *n.* **1.** a member of the most westerly branch of the Slavs, comprising the Bohemians (or Czechs proper), the Moravians, and the Slovaks. **2.** the language of Bohemia and Moravia, a Slavic language similar to Slovak. *–adj.* **3.** of or pertaining to the Czechs or their language. **4.** →**Czechoslovak.**

**Czechoslovak** /tʃɛkəˈsloʊvæk/, *n.* **1.** a member of the branch of the Slavic race comprising the Czechs proper, the Slovaks, etc. *–adj.* **2.** of or pertaining to the Czechoslovaks.

**Czechoslovakia** /tʃɛkəsləˈvakiə/, *n.* a republic in central Europe. – **Czechoslovakian,** *adj., n.*

**Dd** Roman BODONI **Dd** Sans Serif GILL **Dd** Script COMIC **Dd** Decorative PRETORIAN

*Although there are numerous typefaces in the world they can be divided into four main classifications. These are:*

*ROMAN or SERIF. This typeface came into being from the technique of the Roman masons who, working in stone, finished off each letter with a serif or small stroke projecting from the top or bottom. This was done to correct any feeling of unevenness or imbalance they may have created in cutting the characters in stone.*

*SANS SERIF (without serif). This typeface is geometric in design and has straight-edged characters and lines of a regular thickness.*

*SCRIPT. Based on the movement of the hand, this typeface is often italicised or slanted, as if drawn by a brush or quill pen.*

*DECORATIVE. Any typeface that exaggerates the characteristics of any of the other three classifications to a degree that places it outside of them.*

*The dictionary entries in this book use a SANS SERIF typeface called Helvetica (set in a bold face for the head words) and a SERIF typeface Plantin (used throughout the body of the entries).*

**D, d** /di/, *n., pl.* **D's** or **Ds, d's** or **ds. 1.** the fourth letter of the English alphabet. **2.** (used as a symbol) the fourth in order; the fourth in a series. **3.** *Music.* **a.** the second degree of the scale of C, or the fourth degree of the scale of A minor. **b.** a written or printed note representing this tone. **c.** a key, string, or pipe tuned to this note. **d.** (in solmisation) the second note of the scale, called **re.**

**d,** day.

**'d,** contraction of: **1.** had. **2.** would.

**d-,** former abbreviation for **dextro-.**

**d.,** **1.** daughter. **2.** delete. **3.** penny, pence. [L *denarius*] **4.** died. **5.** dialect. **6.** dialectal. **7.** diameter. **8.** dose. **9.** deci-. **10.** density.

**D,** **1.** Roman numeral for 500. **2.** *Chem.* deuterium. **3.** Dutch.

**D**[1] /di/, *n.* a detective. Also, **d.**

**D**[2] /di/, *n.* an iron D-shaped loop fixed in a saddle from which gear, as a water bottle, etc., can be hung. Also, **dee.**

**D-,** a prefix used to describe the configurations of chemical compounds that have the same chirality as D-glyceraldehyde. See **glyceraldehyde.**

**D.,** **1.** Dutch. **2.** Deputy. **3.** Department.

**D/A,** Deposit Account.

**D.A.** /di 'eɪ/, *n. U.S.* District Attorney.

**dab**[1] /dæb/, *v.,* **dabbed, dabbing,** *n.* *–v.t.* **1.** to tap lightly, as with the hand. **2.** to pat or tap gently, as with some soft or moist substance. **3.** to apply (a substance) by light strokes. *–v.i.* **4.** to touch lightly; peck. *–n.* **5.** a quick or light blow; a pat, as with the hand or something soft. **6.** a small moist lump or mass. **7.** a small quantity. **8.** →**dab hand.** [ME. Cf. Norw. *dabba* tap with the foot, G *Tappe* footprint]

**dab**[2] /dæb/, *n.* **1.** a European flatfish, *Limanda limanda.* **2.** a sand-dab or other small flatfish. [orig. unknown]

**dabber** /'dæbə/, *n.* **1.** one who or that which dabs. **2.** a pad for applying ink, etc., used by printers and engravers.

**dabble** /'dæbəl/, *v.,* **-bled, -bling.** *–v.t.* **1.** to wet slightly or repeatedly in or with a liquid; splash; spatter. *–v.i.* **2.** to play in water, as with the hands or feet. **3.** to do anything in a slight or superficial manner: *to dabble in literature.* [Flem. *dabbelen*] – **dabbler,** *n.*

**dabchick** /'dæbtʃɪk/, *n.* **1.** either of two small Australian waterbirds, the **little grebe,** *Podiceps novaehollandiae,* and the **hoary-headed grebe,** *P. poliocephalus.* **2.** a very similar New Zealand bird, *P. rufopectus.* **3.** the coot, *Fulica atra.* **4.** any of various other waterbirds esp. the **little grebe,** *P. fluviatilis,* of Europe, or the **pied-billed grebe,** *Podilymbus podiceps,* of America.

**dab hand** /dæb 'hænd/, *n. Colloq.* a person particularly skilled (usu. fol. by *at*).

**da capo** /da 'kapoʊ/, *adv.* (a musical direction) from the beginning. [It.]

**dace** /deɪs/, *n., pl.* **dace.** **1.** a small freshwater cyprinoid fish, *Leuciscus leuciscus,* of Europe, with a stout, fusiform body. **2.** any of several similar or related fishes of North America [ME *darse,* from OF *dars* DART[2]]

**dacha** /'dætʃə/, *n.* a country villa (in Russia). [Russ.]

**dachshund** /'dæksənd, 'dæʃhənd/, *n.* one of a German breed of small dogs with a long body and very short legs. [G *Dachs* badger + *Hund* dog]

dachshund

**dacoit** /də'kɔɪt/, *n.* a member of a type of robber band formerly active in India and Burma. [Hindi *dakait*]

**D-A converter** /ˌdi-eɪ kən'vɜtə/, *n.* digital to analog converter. Also, **D to A converter.**

**dacron** /'dækrɒn/, *n.* a strong synthetic textile fibre resistant to creases. [Trademark]

**dactyl** /'dæktɪl, -tl/, *n.* **1.** *Zool.* a digit. **2.** *Pros.* a foot of three syllables, one long followed by two short, or in modern verse, one accented followed by two unaccented (¯˘˘), as in 'Gēntlў ănd hūmănlў'. [ME *dactile,* from L *dactylus,* from Gk *dáktylos* finger or toe, date (see DATE[2]), metrical foot]

**dactylic** /dæk'tɪlɪk/, *adj.* **1.** of or characterised by dactyls. **2.** of a dactyl. *–n.* **3.** a dactylic verse.

**dactylology** /dæktə'lɒlədʒi/, *n.* the art of communicating ideas by signs made with the fingers, as in a manual alphabet used by the deaf.

**dactylomancy** /'dæktəloʊˌmænsi/, *n.* divination by means of rings.

**dad** /dæd/, *n.* **1.** father. **2.** *Colloq.* (a form of address to an older man). [earlier *dadde,* nursery substitute for FATHER]

**dada** /'dada/, *n.* a movement in art and literature, originating in Zurich and lasting from about 1915 to 1922, which intended to outrage and offend by deliberately flouting traditional aesthetic standards and social mores. [F *dada* hobbyhorse, symbol of the movement and title of its review]

– **dadaism,** *n.* – **dadaist,** *n.*

**dad and mum,** *n. Colloq.* rum. [rhyming slang]

**daddy** /ˈdædi/, *n., pl.* **-dies. 1.** (*in children's speech*) dad; father. **2.** →**sugar daddy. 3. the daddy of them all,** *Colloq.* the biggest, most powerful, most impressive, etc.

**daddy-long-legs** /ˌdædi-ˈlɒŋ-lɛgz/, *n. sing. and pl.* **1.** a small web-spinning spider of the family Pholcidae, with long, thin legs, frequently found indoors. **2.** →**cranefly. 3.** →**house centipede. 4.** →**harvestman.**

**Dad'n'Dave** /dædnˈdeɪv/, *n.* **1.** *Colloq.* a shave. [rhyming slang] *–adj.* **2.** of or pertaining to anything amusingly or ludicrously countrified. [from two bush characters in the writings of Steele Rudd]

**dado** /ˈdeɪdoʊ/, *n., pl.* **-dos, -does. 1.** the part of a pedestal between the base and the cornice or cap. **2.** the lower broad part of an interior wall finished in wallpaper, a fabric, paint, or the like. **3.** a strip of patterned wallpaper just below the picture rail; the frieze. [It.: die, cube, pedestal, from L *dātus.* See DIE[2]]

pedestal: A, cornice; B, dado; C, base

**daedal** /ˈdeɪdəl/, *adj. Chiefly Poetic.* **1.** skilful or ingenious. **2.** showing skill or artistic cunning. **3.** diversified. [L *daedalus* skilful, from Gk *daídalos*]

**daemon** /ˈdimən, ˈdaɪ-/, *n.* **1.** *Gk Myth.* **a.** a god. **b.** a subordinate deity, as the genius of a place or a man's attendant spirit. **2.** a demon. Also, **daimon.** [L, from Gk *daímōn*] – **daemonic** /dəˈmɒnɪk/, *adj.*

**DAF,** delayed auditory feedback.

**daff** /dæf/, *n. Colloq.* a daffodil.

**daffodil** /ˈdæfədɪl/, *n.* **1.** a plant, *Narcissus pseudo-narcissus,* with single or double yellow nodding flowers, blooming in the spring; Lent lily. **2.** any plant of the genus *Narcissus.* **3.** a light or pale yellow. [unexplained var. of ME *affodille,* from VL *affodillus,* var. of *asphodelus,* from Gk *asphódelos*]

**daffodilly** /ˈdæfədɪli/, *n., pl.* **-lies.** *Poetic.* →**daffodil** (defs 1 and 2). Also, **daffadowndilly** /ˌdæfədaʊnˈdɪli/, **daffydowndilly.**

**daffy** /ˈdæfi/, *adj.,* **daffier, daffiest.** *Colloq.* silly; weak-minded; crazy. [Scot. d. *daff* a fool; akin to DAFT]

**daft** /daft/, *adj.* **1.** simple or foolish. **2.** insane; crazy. [ME *daffte,* OE *gedæfte* mild, meek. Cf. DEFT] – **daftly,** *adv.* – **daftness,** *n.*

**dag**[1] /dæg/, *n., v.,* **dagged, dagging.** *–n.* **1.** wool on a sheep's rear quarters, often dirty with mud and excreta. **2. rattle your dags,** *Colloq.* hurry up. *–v.t.* **3.** to shear dags from (sheep). Also, **daglock.** [ME *dagge;* orig. uncert.] – **dagging,** *n.*

**dag**[2] /dæg/, *v.t.,* **dagged, dagging.** *Horseracing.* **1.** to follow (a jockey) offering assistance in the expectation of receiving racing information. [? from DAG[1]] – **dagger,** *n.*

**dag**[3] /dæg/, *n.* **1.** →**dag picker. 2.** *Colloq.* an odd, eccentric or amusing person. – **daggish,** *adj.*

**dag**[4] /dæg/, *n. Colloq.* **1.** an untidy, slovenly person. **2.** a person who, while neat in appearance and conservative in manners, lacks style or panache. [backformation from DAGGY[1]]

**dagga** /ˈdagə/, *n. S. African.* wild hemp, *Cannabis sativa.* [Afrikaans]

**dagger**[1] /ˈdægə/, *n.* **1.** a short-edged and pointed weapon, like a small sword, used for thrusting and stabbing. **2.** *Print.* a mark (†) used for references, etc.; the obelisk. **3.** (*pl.*) hand shears. **4. look daggers,** to cast angry, threatening, or vengeful glances. *–v.t.* **5.** to stab with a dagger. **6.** *Print.* to mark with a dagger. [ME, from obs. *dag* pierce, stab]

**dagger**[2] /ˈdægə/, *n.* →**dag picker.** [DAG[1] + -ER[1]]

**dagger orchid** /ˈdægər ɔkəd/, *n.* an epiphytic orchid, *Dendrobium pugioniforme,* often forming large masses on trees in coastal forests of New South Wales and southern Queensland.

dagger orchid

**dagger plate** /ˈdægə pleɪt/, *n.* →**centreboard.**

**daggle** /ˈdægəl/, *v.t., v.i.,* **-gled, -gling.** *Obs.* to drag or trail through mud, water, etc.; draggle. [frequentative of d. *dag* bemire. See DAG[1]]

**daggy**[1] /ˈdægi/, *adj. Colloq.* **1.** dirty; slovenly; unpleasant. **2.** conservative and lacking in style, esp. in appearance. [DAG[1] + -Y[1]]

**daggy**[2] /ˈdægi/, *adj. Colloq.* stupid; idiotic; eccentric. [DAG[3] + -Y[1]]

**daglock** /ˈdæglɒk/, *n.* →**dag**[1]. [DAGGLE + LOCK[2]]

**dago** /ˈdeɪgoʊ/, *n., pl.* **-gos, -goes.** *Colloq.* (*derog.*) **1.** a Spaniard or Portuguese. **2.** a person of Latin race. Also, **Dago.** [? Sp. *Diego* James]

**dag picker** /ˈdæg pɪkə/, *n.* a shedhand who sorts wool from dags. Also, **dag boy.**

**daguerreotype** /dəˈgɛrətaɪp/, *n., v.,* **-typed, -typing.** *–n.* **1.** an early photographic process (invented in 1839) in which the impression was made on a silver surface sensitised to the action of light by iodine, and then developed by mercury vapour. **2.** a picture so made. *–v.t.* **3.** to photograph by this process. [named after L. J. M. *Daguerre,* 1789-1851, French inventor. See -TYPE] – **daguerreotyper, daguerreotypist,** *n.*

**dagwood sandwich** /ˌdægwʊd ˈsænwɪtʃ/, *n.* a large sandwich, with a number of different fillings, and sometimes more than two slices of bread. Also, **dagwood.** [from *Dagwood* Bumstead, the hero of a U.S. comic strip 'Blondie' who was given to making sandwiches of this type]

**dagwool** /ˈdægwʊl/, *n.* hindquarter wool clotted with excrement, dirt, etc.

**dahlia** /ˈdeɪljə/, *n.* **1.** any plant of the genus *Dahlia,* native to Mexico and Central America, widely cultivated for its showy, variously coloured flowers. **2.** the flower or tuberous root of a dahlia. [NL; named after A. *Dahl,* died 1789, Swedish botanist]

**Dahomey** /dəˈhoʊmi/, *n.* a republic in West Africa. – **Dahoman,** *adj., n.*

**daily** /ˈdeɪli/, *adj., n., pl.* **-lies,** *adv. –adj.* **1.** of, done, occurring, or issued each day or each weekday. *–n.* **2.** a newspaper appearing each day or each weekday. **3.** a servant, usu. female, who comes to work every day. *–adv.* **4.** every day; day by day: *she phoned the hospital daily.*

**daily double** /– ˈdʌbəl/, *n.* two selected races on the one program on which a starting price double (def. 25) is conducted.

**daimio** /ˈdaɪmjoʊ/, *n., pl.* **-mio, -mios. 1.** the class of greater nobles in Japanese feudalism. Often the daimio were descendants of younger sons of emperors. **2.** a member of this class. Also, **daimyo.** [Jap., from Chinese *dai* great + *mio* name]

**daimon** /ˈdaɪmən/, *n.* →**daemon.** [see DEMON]

**dainty** /ˈdeɪnti/, *adj.,* **-tier, -tiest,** *n., pl.* **-ties.** *–adj.* **1.** of delicate beauty or charm; exquisite. **2.** pleasing to the palate; toothsome; delicious: *dainty food.* **3.** particular in discrimination or taste; fastidious. **4.** too particular; squeamish. *–n.* **5.** something delicious to the taste; a delicacy. [ME *deinte,* from OF, from L *dignitas* worthiness] – **daintily,** *adv.* – **daintiness,** *n.*

**daiquiri** /ˈdaɪkəri, dəˈkɪəri, ˈdækəri/, *n., pl.* **-ris.** a cocktail consisting of rum, lime juice, sugar, and ice.

**dairy** /ˈdɛəri/, *n., pl.* **dairies,** *adj. –n.* **1.** a place, as a room or building, where milk and cream are kept and made into butter and cheese. **2. a.** a shop or company that sells milk, butter, etc. **b.** *N.Z.* →**milk bar. 3.** the business of producing milk, butter, and cheese. **4.** a dairy farm. **5.** the cows on a farm. *–adj.* **6.** pertaining to or made in a dairy. [ME *deierie,* from *dei* female servant, dairymaid (OE *dǣge* breadmaker) + *-erie* -ERY]

**dairy butter** /'– bʌtə/, *n. N.Z.* home-made butter (as distinct from factory-made).

**dairy cattle** /'– kætl/, *n.* cows raised mainly for their milk.

**dairy factory** /'– fæktri/, *n.* a building, often a farmers' co-operative, where dairy produce is processed.

**dairy farm** /'– fam/, *n.* a farm devoted chiefly to the production of milk and milk products. – **dairy farmer,** *n.* – **dairy farming,** *n.*

**dairying** /ˈdɛəriɪŋ/, *n.* the business of a dairy.

**dairymaid** /ˈdɛərimeɪd/, *n.* a female servant employed in a dairy.

**dairyman** /ˈdɛərimən/, *n., pl.* **-men.** one who owns, manages or works in a dairy, or on a dairy farm.

**dairywoman** /ˈdɛəriwʊmən/, *n., pl.* **-men.** a female dairyman.

**dais** /ˈdeɪəs/, *n.* a raised platform, as at the end of a room, for a throne, seats of honour, a lecturer's desk, etc. [ME *deis,* from OF, from LL *discus* table, L disc, dish. See DISCUS]

**daisy** /ˈdeɪzi/, *n., pl.* **-sies,** *adj.* *–n.* **1.** any plant of the family Compositae whose flower heads have a yellow disc and white rays, as the snow daisy or the shasta daisy. **2.** any similar shaped flower of different colours, as the burr daisy. **3.** *Colloq.* something fine or first-rate. **4. push up daisies,** *Colloq.* to be dead and buried. *–adj.* **5.** *Colloq.* fine; first-class; excellent; first-rate. [ME *dayesye,* OE *daegesēage* day's eye] **– daisied,** *adj.*

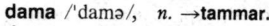

daisy

**daisy-burr** /ˈdeɪzi-bɜ/, *n.* →**burr-daisy.**

**daisy-bush** /ˈdeɪzi-bʊʃ/, *n.* →**olearia.**

**daisy-chain** /ˈdeɪzi-tʃeɪn/, *n.* a garland of daisies joined together by interlinked stems.

**daisy-cutter** /ˈdeɪzi-kʌtə/, *n.* *Colloq.* (in cricket, football, tennis, etc.) a ball which, after being struck or kicked skims along near the ground.

**daisy gun** /ˈdeɪzi gʌn/, *n.* →**BB gun.** [Trademark]

**Dakin's solution** /ˈdeɪkənz səˌluʃən/, *n.* a liquid antiseptic, an approximately neutral solution containing about 0·5 per cent of sodium hypochlorite, used in treating infected wounds. [named after H. D. *Dakin,* 1880-1952, English chemist, the originator]

**daks** /dæks/, *n.pl. Colloq.* trousers. [Trademark]

**dale** /deɪl/, *n.* **1.** a vale; valley. **2.** a small, open, river valley partly enclosed by low hills. [ME; OE *dæl,* c. G *Tal*]

**dalgyte** /ˈdælgaɪt/, *n.* →**bilby.**

**dalliance** /ˈdæliəns/, *n.* **1.** a trifling away of time; dawdling. **2.** amorous toying; flirtation. [ME; from DALLY + -ANCE]

**dally** /ˈdæli/, *v.,* **-lied, -lying.** *–v.i.* **1.** to sport or play, esp. amorously. **2.** to play mockingly; trifle: *dally with danger.* **3.** to waste time; loiter; delay. *–v.t.* **4.** to waste (time) (fol. by *away*). [ME *daly(en),* from OF *dalier* talk; ? of Gmc orig.] **– dallier,** *n.* **– dallyingly,** *adv.*

**Dally** /ˈdæli/, *n. N.Z. Colloq.* **1.** a Dalmation settler, or a descendant. *–adj.* **2.** Dalmatian.

**Dalmatian** /dælˈmeɪʃən/, *adj.* **1.** of or pertaining to Dalmatia or its people. *–n.* **2.** an inhabitant of Dalmatia, esp. a member of the native Slavic-speaking race. **3.** a Romance language formerly spoken in Dalmatia, now extinct. **4.** one of a breed of dogs resembling the pointer, of a white colour profusely marked with small black or liver-coloured spots; coach dog.

Dalmatian (def. 4)

**dalmatic** /dælˈmætɪk/, *n.* **1.** an ecclesiastical vestment worn over the alb by a deacon or bishop, as at the celebration of the mass. **2.** a similar robe worn by kings and emperors at their coronation. [L *dalmatica,* properly fem. of *Dalmaticus* Dalmatian]

**dal segno** /dæl ˈsɛnjoʊ/, *adv.* (a musical direction) go back to the sign and repeat. [It.]

**daltonism** /ˈdɔltənɪzəm/, *n.* colour blindness; esp. inability to distinguish red from green. [named after John *Dalton,* who was so afflicted. See DALTON'S ATOMIC THEORY]

**Dalton's atomic theory,** *n.* the theory that matter is composed of indivisible particles called atoms; the atoms of any particular element being identical in all respects, but differing from those of other elements in their weight. Compounds are formed by the combination of different elements in simple numerical proportions. Although refined by modern discoveries this theory forms the basis of chemistry. [named after John *Dalton,* 1766-1844, English chemist and physicist]

**dam**[1] /dæm/, *n., v.,* **dammed, damming.** *–n.* **1.** a barrier to obstruct the flow of water, esp. one of earth, masonry, etc., built across a stream. **2.** a body of water confined by such a barrier. **3.** any barrier resembling a dam. **4.** →**tank** (def. 2). *–v.t.* **5.** to furnish with a dam; obstruct or confine with a dam. **6.** to stop up; block up. [ME, c. G *Damm*]

**dam**[2] /dæm/, *n.* a female parent (used esp. of quadrupeds). [ME *dam(me),* var. of DAME]

**dama** /ˈdamə/, *n.* →**tammar.**

**damage** /ˈdæmɪdʒ/, *n., v.,* **-aged, -aging.** *–n.* **1.** injury or harm that impairs value or usefulness. **2.** (*pl.*) *Law.* the estimated money equivalent for detriment or injury sustained. **3.** *Colloq.* cost; expense. *–v.t.* **4.** to cause damage to; injure or harm; impair the usefulness of. *–v.i.* **5.** to suffer damage. [ME, from OF *dam* (from L *damnum* harm, loss) + *-age* -AGE] **– damageable,** *adj.* **– damageability** /ˌdæmɪdʒəˈbɪləti/, *n.* **– damager,** *n.* **– damagingly,** *adv.*

**daman** /ˈdæmən/, *n.* **1.** a small mammal, *Procavia syriaca,* of the order Hyracoidea, native to Syria, Palestine, etc. (the *cony* of the English Bible). **2.** any hyrax. [Ar., short for *daman isrāīl* lamb of Israel]

**damascene** /ˈdæməsin, dæməˈsin/, *adj., n., v.,* **-scened, -scening.** *–adj.* **1.** of or pertaining to the art of damascening. *–n.* **2.** work or patterns produced by damascening. *–v.t.* **3.** to produce wavy lines on, as in the welding of iron and steel in the swords of Damascus. **4.** to ornament (objects of iron and steel) by inlaying with precious metals, or by etching. Also, **damaskeen** for defs 3 and 4. [ME, from L *Damascēnus,* from Gk *Damaskēnós* of Damascus]

**Damascus steel** /dəmæskəs ˈstil/, *n.* a kind of steel with a wavy or variegated pattern, originally made in the Near East, chiefly at Damascus, and used for making sword blades.

**damask** /ˈdæməsk/, *n.* **1.** a reversible fabric of linen, silk, cotton, or wool, woven with patterns. **2.** the table linen of this material. **3.** →**Damascus steel. 4.** the peculiar pattern or wavy appearance on its surface. **5.** the pink colour of the damask rose. *–adj.* **6.** made of or like damask: *damask cloth.* **7.** pink (like the damask rose). *–v.t.* **8.** to damascene. **9.** to weave or adorn with elaborate design, as in damask cloth. [ME *damaske,* from L *Damascus,* from Gk *Damaskós* Damascus]

**damaskeen** /dæməˈskin/, *v.t.* →**damascene.**

**damask rose** /dæməsk ˈroʊz/, *n.* a fragrant pink rose, *Rosa damascena.*

**dame** /deɪm/, *n.* **1.** a form of address to any woman of rank or authority. **2.** the legal title of the wife of a knight or baronet. **3.** (*cap.*) (since 1917) the distinctive title employed before the name of a woman who holds the Order of the British Empire. **4.** *Colloq.* a woman. **5.** *Archaic.* the mistress of a household. **6.** *Archaic.* a woman of rank or authority, as a female ruler. **7.** *Hist.* the mistress of a school. **8.** a comic representation of an old woman in a pantomime, usu. played by a man. **9.** See **dom.** [ME, from OF, from L *domina* mistress, lady]

**dame's violet** /deɪmz ˈvaɪələt/, *n.* a branched herb, *Hesperis matronalis,* with scented white or violet flowers, native to Europe and Asia.

**dammar** /ˈdæmə/, *n.* **1.** a copal-like resin chiefly from trees of the family Dipterocarpaceae in southern Asia, esp. Malaya and Sumatra, much used for making colourless varnish. **2.** any of various similar resins from trees of other families. Also, **dammer.** [Malay *damar* resin]

**damn** /dæm/, *v.t.* **1.** to declare (something) to be bad, unfit, invalid, or illegal. **2.** to condemn as a failure: *damn a play.* **3.** to bring condemnation upon; ruin. **4.** to doom to eternal punishment, or condemn to hell. **5.** to swear at or curse, using the word 'damn'. **6. as near as damn it,** *Colloq.* as near as conceivably possible. *–n.* **7.** a negligible amount: *not worth a damn.* **8. not to give a damn,** not to care; be unconcerned. *–interj.* **9.** (an expression of anger, annoyance, or emphasis.) [ME *damne(n),* from OF *damner,* from L *damnāre* condemn, doom]

**damnable** /ˈdæmnəbəl/, *adj.* **1.** worthy of damnation. **2.** detestable, abominable, or outrageous. **3.** hateful, annoying. **– damnableness,** *n.* **– damnably,** *adv.*

**damn-all** /dæm-ˈɔl/, *n. Colloq.* **1.** a negligible amount: *he's done damn-all today.* *–adj.* **2.** very few. **3.** negligible; trifling.

**damnation** /dæmˈneɪʃən/, *n.* **1.** act of damning. **2.** state of being damned. **3.** a cause or occasion of being damned. **4.** *Theol.* sin as incurring or deserving eternal punishment. *–interj.* **5.** (the noun 'damnation', used as an oath expressing anger, disappointment, etc.)

**damnatory** /ˈdæmnətri/, *adj.* conveying or occasioning condemnation; damning.

**damned** /dæmd/, *adj.* **1.** condemned, esp. to eternal punishment. **2.** detestable. *–adv.* **3.** extremely, very.

**damnedest** /ˈdæmdəst/, *n. Colloq.* the limit of personal effort, or an object's or element's natural function: *to do one's damnedest.*

**damnify** /ˈdæmnəfaɪ/, *v.t.*, **-fied, -fying.** *Law.* to cause loss or damage to. [AF *damnifier,* from L *damnificāre* injure]

**damning** /ˈdæmɪŋ/, *adj.* that damns or condemns; incriminating. **– damningly,** *adv.*

**damp** /dæmp/, *adj.* **1.** moderately wet; moist. **2.** *Archaic.* dejected. *–n.* **3.** moisture; humidity; moist air. **4.** a noxious or stifling vapour or gas, esp. in a mine. **5.** depression of spirits; dejection. **6.** a check or discouragement. *–v.t.* **7.** to make damp; moisten. **8.** to check or retard the energy, action, etc., of. **9.** to stifle or suffocate; extinguish. **10.** *Acoustics, Music.* to check or retard the action of (a vibrating string, etc.); dull; deaden. **11.** to furnish (esp. pianos) with a damper or dampers. **12.** *Physics.* to cause a decrease in amplitude of (an oscillation). [ME *domp,* from MFlem.: vapour, c. G *Dampf* steam] **– dampish,** *adj.* **– damply,** *adv.* **– dampness,** *n.*

**dampcourse** /ˈdæmpkɔs/, *n.* a horizontal layer of impervious material laid in a wall to stop moisture rising. Also, **damp-proof course.**

**dampen** /ˈdæmpən/, *v.t.* **1.** to make damp; moisten. **2.** to dull or deaden; depress. *–v.i.* **3.** to become damp. **– dampener,** *n.*

**damper**[1] /ˈdæmpə/, *n.* **1.** one who or that which damps. **2.** a movable plate for regulating the draught in a stove, furnace, ducting system, etc. **3.** *Music.* **a.** a device in stringed keyboard instruments to deaden the vibration of the strings. **b.** the mute of a brass instrument, as a horn. **4.** *Elect.* an attachment to keep the indicator of a measuring instrument from oscillating excessively, usu. a set of vanes in an air space or fluid, or a short-circuited winding in a magnetic field. **5. put a damper on,** *Colloq.* to discourage.

**damper**[2] /ˈdæmpə/, *n.* a bush bread made from a simple flour and water dough with or without a raising agent, cooked in the coals or in a camp oven. [Brit. d.]

**damping** /ˈdæmpɪŋ/, *n. Physics.* **1.** a decrease caused in the amplitude of successive oscillations or waves. *–adj.* **2.** of or pertaining to such a decrease.

**damping-off** /ˌdæmpɪŋ-ˈɒf/, *n.* a disease of plants, esp. seedlings, caused by various fungi, mainly *Pythium debaryanum,* which spread rapidly under conditions of excessive moisture.

**damp-proof** /ˈdæmp-pruf/, *adj.* **1.** resistant to damp. *–v.t.* **2.** to make resistant to damp.

**damp squib** /dæmp ˈskwɪb/, *n.* →**squib** (def. 5).

**damsel** /ˈdæmzəl/, *n. Archaic.* a young woman; a girl; a maiden, originally one of gentle or noble birth. [ME *dameisele,* from OF, from L *domina* mistress, lady. See DAME]

**damselfish** /ˈdæmzəlfɪʃ/, *n.* any small tropical fish of the family Pomacentridae, with a brightly coloured, laterally compressed body.

**damsel fly** /ˈdæmzəl/ flaɪ/, *n.* any of the more fragile insects of the order Odonata, distinguished from the dragonflies by having the wings closed while at rest.

**damson** /ˈdæmzən/, *n.* **1.** the small dark blue or purple fruit of a plum, *Prunus insititia,* introduced into Europe from Asia Minor. **2.** the tree bearing it. [ME *damascene,* representing L (*prunum*) *damascēnum* (plum) of Damascus. See DAMASCENE]

**damson cheese** /ˈ– tʃiz/, *n.* a thick, viscous conserve made of pulped and sieved damsons and sugar.

**Dan**[1] /dæn/, *n. Archaic.* a title of honour, equivalent to *master* or *sir: Dan Chaucer, Dan Cupid.* [ME, from OF, from L *dominus* master, lord]

**Dan**[2] /dæn/, *n. Judo.* **1.** one of the grades into which experienced judo contestants are divided: *there are twelve Dans, but the highest ever achieved is tenth Dan.* **2.** a contestant who has achieved such a grade.

**Dan**[3] /dæn/, *n. Colloq.* a sanitary man. [from the jingle *Dan, Dan the dunny man*]

**Dan.,** **1.** *Bible.* Daniel. **2.** Danish.

**danablu** /deɪnəˈblu/, *n.* →**Danish blue.**

**danbo** /ˈdænboʊ/, *n.* a semi-hard, smooth-faced and even-textured cheese, with small holes spread throughout the surface, originating in Denmark.

**dance** /dæns, dans/, *v.*, **danced, dancing,** *n. –v.i.* **1.** to move with the feet or body rhythmically, esp. to music. **2.** to leap, skip, etc., as from excitement or emotion; move nimbly or quickly. **3.** to bob up and down. *–v.t.* **4.** to perform or take part in (a dance). **5.** to cause to dance. **6. dance attendance,** to attend constantly or solicitously. **7. dance on air,** *Colloq.* to be hanged. **8. dance the night away,** *Colloq.* to spend the night in celebration. *–n.* **9.** a successive group of rhythmical steps, generally executed to music. **10.** an act or round of dancing. **11.** a social gathering for dancing; ball. **12.** a piece of music suited in rhythm to a particular form of dancing. **13.** a series of apparently rhythmic movements as performed by some insects or birds, etc. **14. lead someone a merry dance,** *Colloq.* to frustrate someone, as by constantly changing one's moods, intentions, attitudes, etc. [ME *daunse(n),* from OF *danser;* probably of Gmc orig.] **– danceable,** *adj.* **– dancingly,** *adv.*

**dance band** /ˈ– bænd/, *n.* a band which plays music for dancing.

**dance hall** /ˈ– hɔl/, *n.* a large public hall in which dances may be held.

**dance of death,** *n.* a symbolic dance in which a skeleton Death leads people to their graves. Also, **danse macabre.**

**dancer** /ˈdænsə, ˈdansə/, *n.* **1.** one who dances. **2.** one who dances professionally, as on the stage.

**dancette** /dænˈsɛt/, *n.* **1.** *Her.* a fesse with three indentations. **2.** *Archit.* a zigzag or chevron moulding.

**D and C** /di ən ˈsi/, *n.* dilatation and curettage, a surgical method for the removal of tissue from the uterus by scraping.

**dandelion** /ˈdændilaɪən, -də-/, *n.* **1.** a common plant, *Taraxacum officinale,* abundant as a weed, characterised by deeply toothed or notched leaves and golden yellow flowers. **2.** any other plant of the genus *Taraxacum.* [F *dent de lion* lion's tooth (with allusion to the toothed leaves)]

dandelion

**dandelion clock** /ˈ– klɒk/, *n.* the seed-head of the dandelion. It is said that the number of puffs needed to blow all the seeds off will give the hour of the day.

**dander** /ˈdændə/, *n. Colloq.* anger or temper: *to get one's dander up.* [? fig. use of *dander* DANDRUFF; or fig. use of *dander* ferment]

**Dandie Dinmont** /ˌdændi ˈdɪnmɒnt/, *n.* one of a breed of small terriers with a long body, short legs, and a pepper or mustard-coloured coat. [from *Dandie* (Andrew) *Dinmont,* in Sir Walter Scott's 'Guy Mannering', said to own the progenitors]

**dandify** /ˈdændəfaɪ/, *v.t.*, **-fied, -fying.** to make dandy-like or foppish; dress or fit out like a dandy. **– dandification** /dændəfəˈkeɪʃən/, *n.*

**dandle** /ˈdændəl/, *v.t.*, **-dled, -dling.** **1.** to move lightly up and down, as a child on the knees or in the arms. **2.** to pet. [? from Scand.; cf. Faeroese *danda* dandle] **– dandler,** *n.*

**dandruff** /ˈdændrəf, -rʌf/, *n.* a scurf which forms on the scalp and comes off in small scales. Also, **dandriff.** [orig. unknown]

**dandy**[1] /ˈdændi/, *n., pl.* **-dies,** *adj.,* **-dier, -diest.** *–n.* **1.** a man who is excessively concerned about clothes and appearance; a fop. **2.** *Colloq.* something very fine or first rate. **3.** *Naut.* a yawl with a jigger mast aft on which a mizzen lugsail is set. *–adj.* **4.** foppish. **5.** *Colloq.* fine; first-rate. [? special use of *Dandy,* var. of *Andy* (Andrew)] **– dandyish,** *adj.* **– dandyism,** *n.*

**dandy**[2] /ˈdændi/, *n.* (in the West Indies) dengue. Also, **dandy fever.**

**dandy**[3] /ˈdændi/, *n.* →**dixie** (def. 2).

dandy

**dandy-brush** /ˈdændi-brʌʃ/, *n.* a stiff brush used for grooming horses, made of split whalebone, vegetable fibre, or the like.

**dandy roll** /ˈdændi roʊl/, *n. Print.* a wire mesh cylinder in a paper-making machine which implants a permanent pattern in the paper. Also, **dandy roller.**

**danger** /'deɪndʒə/, *n.* **1.** liability or exposure to harm or injury; risk; peril. **2.** an instance or cause of peril. **3.** the position (of a signal, etc.) indicating danger: *although the signal was at danger, the train did not stop.* **4.** *Obs.* power; jurisdiction; domain. [ME *daunger,* from OF *dangier,* from LL, from *dominium* lordship]

**danger money** /'– mʌni/, *n.* payment over and above normal wages for work where there is some risk involved.

**dangerous** /'deɪndʒərəs/, *adj.* full of danger or risk; causing danger; perilous; hazardous; unsafe. – **dangerously,** *adv.* – **dangerousness,** *n.*

**dangle** /'dæŋgəl/, *v.,* **-gled, -gling.** *n.* –*v.i.* **1.** to hang loosely with a swaying motion. **2.** *Colloq.* to be hanged. **3.** to hang about or follow a person, as if seeking favour. –*v.t.* **4.** to cause to dangle; hold or carry swaying loosely. –*n.* **5.** the act of dangling. **6.** something that dangles. [Scand.; cf. Dan. *dangle* dangle, bob up and down] – **dangler,** *n.*

**dangling participle** /ˌdæŋglɪŋ 'patəsɪpəl/, *n. Gram.* →**misrelated participle.**

**Daniell cell** /'dænjəl sɛl/, *n.* a primary cell producing 1.1 volts, consisting of a zinc anode standing in dilute sulphuric acid, and a copper cathode standing in copper sulphate, the two electrolytes being separated by a porous pot. [named after John *Daniell,* 1790-1845, English physicist]

**Danish** /'deɪnɪʃ/, *adj.* **1.** of or pertaining to the Danes, their country, or their language. –*n.* **2.** a Germanic language, the language of Denmark, closely related to Norwegian, Swedish, and Icelandic.

**Danish blue** /– 'blu/, *n.* a blue veined cheese originally made in Denmark. Also, **danablu.**

**Danish pastry** /– 'peɪstri/, *n.* a confection of sweet yeast dough containing egg and milk, cut into crescents, turnovers, triangles, etc., and filled with almond paste, apple, apricots, lemon curd, sweetened cream cheese, etc., before cooking.

**dank** /dæŋk/, *adj.* unpleasantly moist or humid; damp. [cf. Swed. *dank* marshy place, Icel. *dökk* pool] – **dankly,** *adv.* – **dankness,** *n.*

**Dano-Norwegian** /ˌdeɪnoʊ-nɔ'widʒən/, *n.* →**Bokmål.**

**danse macabre** /dans mə'kabrə/, *n.* →**dance of death.**

**danseur** /dan'sɜ/, *n.* a male ballet dancer. [F, from *danser* DANCE]

**danseuse** /dan'sɜz/, *n., pl.* **-seuses** /-'sɜz/. a female ballet dancer. [F, fem. of *danseur*]

**Dantean** /'dæntiən/, *adj.* **1.** of Dante or his writings. **2.** Dantesque. –*n.* **3.** a scholar devoted to the study of Dante. [orig. with ref. to *Dante* Alighieri, 1265-1321, Italian poet, author of the *Divine Comedy*]

**Dantesque** /dæn'tɛsk/, *adj.* in the style of Dante; suggestive of the experience, particularly the horrors, described by Dante in the *Divine Comedy.*

**danthonia** /dæn'θoʊniə/, *n.* any of the many Australian and New Zealand grasses belonging to the genus *Danthonia;* wallaby grass.

**dap**[1] /dæp/, *v.i.,* **dapped, dapping. 1.** to fish by letting the bait fall lightly on the water. **2.** to dip lightly or suddenly into water. **3.** to bounce on, or as on, the surface of water. [ME *dop.* Cf. DIP]

**dap**[2] /dæp/, *n.* (in building) a groove to receive connectors; occasionally, a notch.

**daphne** /'dæfni/, *n.* **1.** the laurel, *Laurus nobilis.* **2.** any plant of the genus *Daphne,* family Thymeleaceae, of Europe and Asia, comprising small shrubs of which some species, as *D. mezereum,* are cultivated for their fragrant flowers. [L, from Gk: laurel. *Daphne,* a nymph pursued by Apollo, was saved by being changed into a laurel tree]

**daphnia** /'dæfniə/, *n.* any member of the genus *Daphnia* of small freshwater crustaceans, or of one of several closely related genera; water-flea.

**dapper** /'dæpə/, *adj.* **1.** neat; trim; smart. **2.** small and active. [late ME *dapyr* pretty, elegant; cf. G *tapfer* brave] – **dapperly,** *adv.* – **dapperness,** *n.*

**dapple** /'dæpəl/, *n., adj., v.,* **-pled, -pling.** –*n.* **1.** mottled marking, as of an animal's skin or coat. **2.** an animal with a mottled skin or coat. –*adj.* **3.** dappled; spotted: *a dapple horse.* –*v.t.* **4.** to mark with spots. –*v.i.* **5.** to become marked with spots. [orig. uncert. Cf. Icel. *depill* spot, dot]

**dapple-bay** /dæpəl-'beɪ/, *adj.* of a bay colour with ill-defined mottling of a darker shade.

**dappled** /'dæpəld/, *adj.* having spots of different colours or shades; spotted.

**dapple-grey** /dæpəl-'greɪ/, *adj.* grey with ill-defined mottling of a darker shade.

**darbies** /'dabiz/, *n.pl. Prison Colloq.* handcuffs.

**Darby and Joan,** *n.* the typical 'old married couple' happily leading a life of placid domesticity.

**dare** /dɛə/, *v.,* **dared** or **durst, dared, daring,** *n.* –*v.i.* **1.** to have the necessary courage or boldness for something; be bold enough. **2. dare say,** to assume as probable; have no doubt. –*v.t.* **3.** to have the necessary courage for; venture on. **4.** to meet defiantly. **5.** to challenge or provoke to action, esp. by doubting one's courage; defy: *to dare a man to fight.* –*n.* **6.** *Colloq.* a challenge, as to some dangerous act. [ME *dar,* OE *dear(r),* 1st and 3rd pers. sing. pres. ind. of *durran;* akin to OHG *giturran*] – **darer,** *n.*

**daredevil** /'dɛədɛvəl/, *n.* **1.** a recklessly daring person. –*adj.* **2.** recklessly daring.

**daredevilry** /'dɛədɛvəlri/, *n.* recklessness; venturesomeness. Also, *U.S.,* **daredeviltry** /'dɛədɛvəltri/.

**darg** /dag/, *n.* **1.** a day's work. **2.** a production quota. [ME dawerk, OE *dægweorc* day-work]

**dargawarra** /dagə'wɒrə/, *n.* one of the indigenous Australian placental hopping-mice, *Notomys alexis;* spinifex hopping-mouse. [Aboriginal]

**daring** /'dɛərɪŋ/, *n.* **1.** adventurous courage; boldness. –*adj.* **2.** that dares; bold; intrepid; adventurous. – **daringly,** *adv.* – **daringness,** *n.*

**dariole** /'dærioʊl/, *n.* **1.** a type of small, cup-shaped mould. **2.** a dish made in such a mould, as a small cream tart, or a savoury mixture often set in aspic. [ME, from F]

**dark** /dak/, *adj.* **1.** without light; with very little light: *a dark room.* **2.** radiating or reflecting little light: *a dark colour.* **3.** approaching black in hue: *a dark brown.* **4.** not pale or fair: *a dark complexion.* **5.** gloomy; cheerless; dismal. **6.** sullen; frowning. **7.** evil; wicked: *dark thoughts.* **8.** destitute of knowledge or culture; unenlightened. **9.** hard to understand; obscure. **10.** hidden; secret. **11.** silent; reticent. **12.** *Phonet.* (of *l* sounds) resembling a back vowel in quality: *English l is darker than French l.* –*n.* **13.** absence of light; darkness. **14.** night; nightfall. **15.** a dark place. **16.** a dark colour. **17.** obscurity. **18.** secrecy. **19.** ignorance: *in the dark.* –*v.t., v.i. Obs.* **20.** to darken. [ME *derk,* OE *deorc.* Cf. MHG *terken*] – **darkish,** *adj.*

**Dark Ages** /'dak eɪdʒəz/, *n.pl.* **1.** the time in history from about A.D. 476 to about A.D. 1000. **2.** (loosely) the whole of the Middle Ages, the period preceding the Renaissance. **3.** a state of backwardness or unenlightenment: *you're really living in the Dark Ages, aren't you?*

**Dark Continent** /dak 'kɒntənənt/, **The,** *n.* Africa, so called because, until recently, most of the continent was unexplored by Europeans.

**darken** /'dakən/, *v.t.* **1.** to make dark or darker; make obscure. **2.** to make less white or clear in colour. **3.** to make gloomy; sadden. **4.** to make blind. –*v.i.* **5.** to become dark or darker. **6.** to become obscure. **7.** to become less white or clear in colour. **8.** to grow clouded, as with gloom or anger. **9.** to become blind. – **darkener,** *n.*

**dark glasses** /dak 'glasəz/, *n.pl.* **1.** glasses with lenses heavily tinted to reduce the amount of light passing through them. **2.** →**sunglasses.**

**dark horse** /dak 'hɔs/, *n.* **1.** a racehorse, competitor, etc., about whom little is known or who unexpectedly wins. **2.** a person whose capabilities may be greater than they are known to be.

**darkie** /'daki/, *n. Colloq.* **1.** a dark-skinned person, esp. an Aborigine. **2.** →**faeces. 3. drop** or **choke a darkie,** to defecate. **4.** →**luderick.** Also, **darky, darkey.**

**dark lantern** /'dak læntən/, *n.* a lantern whose light can be obscured by a dark slide or cover at the opening.

**darkle** /'dakəl/, *v.i.,* **-kled, -kling. 1.** to appear dark; show indistinctly. **2.** to grow dark, gloomy, etc. [backformation from DARKLING, adv., taken as ppr.]

**darkling** /ˈdaklɪŋ/, *Poetic.* *–adv.* **1.** in the dark. *–adj.* **2.** being or occurring in the dark; dark; obscure. [DARK + -LING[2]]

**darkly** /ˈdakli/, *adv.* **1.** so as to appear dark. **2.** mysteriously; threateningly. **3.** *Archaic.* imperfectly; faintly.

**dark microscope** /dak ˈmaɪkrəskoʊp/, *n.* →**ultramicroscope.** Also, **dark-field microscope.**

**darkness** /ˈdaknəs/, *n.* **1.** the state or quality of being dark. **2.** absence or deficiency of light. **3.** wickedness or evil. **4.** obscurity; concealment. **5.** blindness; ignorance.

**darkroom** /ˈdakrum/, *n.* a room from which the actinic rays of light have been excluded, used in making, handling, and developing photographic film, etc.

**darksome** /ˈdaksəm/, *adj. Poetic.* dark; darkish.

**dark star** /dak ˈsta/, *n.* a star which cannot be seen directly and the presence of which is deduced as from its radio emissions, its gravitational effects, etc.

**dark'un** /ˈdakən/, *n. Wharf Labourer Colloq.* a twenty-four hour shift.

**darky** /ˈdaki/, *n.* →**darkie.** Also, **darkey.**

**darl** /dal/, *n.* →**darling.**

**darling** /ˈdalɪŋ/, *n.* **1.** a person very dear to another; person dearly loved. **2.** a person or thing in great favour. *–adj.* **3.** very dear; dearly loved. **4.** favourite. [ME *derling,* OE *dēorling,* from *dēore* dear + -LING[1]]

**Darling clover** /dalɪŋ ˈkloʊvə/, *n.* a herbaceous Australian species, *Trigonella suavissima,* found in inland areas; a sweet-smelling, clover-like plant which is useful fodder. [from *Darling* River, in western N.S.W.]

**Darling lily** /– ˈlɪli/, *n.* a handsome fragrant lily, *Crinum flaccidum,* found along the inland watercourses of northern and central Australia. [from *Darling* River, in western N.S.W.]

**Darling pea** /– ˈpi/, *n.* **1.** any of a number of herbs of the genus *Swainsona,* esp. *S. galegifolia* and *S. greyana,* with red-purple flowers, widespread esp. in inland areas of Australia and frequently the cause of stock poisoning. **2. get the Darling pea,** *Colloq.* to be insane or behave strangely. [from *Darling* River, in western N.S.W.]

**Darling shower** /– ˈʃaʊə/, *n.* a dust storm. [from *Darling* River, in western N.S.W.]

**darn**[1] /dan/, *v.t.* **1.** to mend (clothes, etc., or a rent or hole) with rows of stitches, sometimes with crossing and interwoven rows to fill up a gap. *–n.* **2.** a darned place in a garment, etc. **3.** the act of darning. [? ME *dernen,* OE *dernan* hide] – **darner,** *n.*

**darn**[2] /dan/, *Colloq.* *–adj., adv.* **1.** →**darned.** *–v.t.* **2.** to confound; curse. *–n.* **3. not give a darn,** to be utterly indifferent. *–interj.* **4.** (a mild expletive). [var. of DAMN]

**darned** /dand/, *Colloq.* *–adj.* **1.** confounded; blessed. *–adv.* **2.** extremely; remarkably.

**darnedest** /ˈdandəst/, *n. in the phrase* **do one's darnedest,** *Colloq.* to exert oneself to the utmost; try very hard.

**darnel** /ˈdanəl/, *n.* an annual grass, *Lolium temulentum,* found as a weed in grain fields. [ME. Cf. d. F *darnelle,* probably of Gmc orig.]

**darning** /ˈdanɪŋ/, *n.* **1.** the act of one who darns. **2.** the result produced. **3.** articles darned or to be darned.

**darning egg** /ˈ– ɛg/, *n.* a rounded support, usu. of wood, on which fabric is held conveniently firm while being darned. Also, **darning mushroom.**

**darning needle** /ˈ– nidəl/, *n.* a long needle with a large eye used in darning.

**darraign** /dəˈreɪn/, *v.t.* →**deraign.**

**dart**[1] /dat/, *n.* **1.** a long, slender, pointed, missile weapon propelled by the hand or otherwise. **2.** something resembling such a weapon, as the sting of an insect. **3.** act of darting; a sudden, swift movement. **4.** (*pl.*) a game in which a pointed missile is thrown at a dartboard. **5.** a seam that is used where a wedge-shaped piece has been cut out to adjust the fit of a garment. **6.** *Colloq.* a cigarette. *–v.i.* **7.** to move swiftly; spring or start suddenly and run swiftly. *–v.t.* **8.** to throw or thrust suddenly and rapidly. **9.** to throw with a sudden thrust, as a dart. [ME, from OF, from Gmc] – **dartingly,** *adv.*

**dart**[2] /dat/, *n.* any of several tropical and semi-tropical marine fishes as the Australian *Trachinotus botla* and the **snub-nosed dart,** *T. blochii.*

**dart**[3] /dat/, *n. Colloq.* **1.** a plan or idea; scheme. **2.** a particular fancy or favourite. [from *dart,* goldmining term for gold-bearing alluvial]

**Dart** /dat/, *n. in the phrase* **the Old Dart,** England. [orig. uncert.]

**dartboard** /ˈdatbɔd/, *n.* the target in the game of darts, marked with concentric circles divided into segments, and having a bull's-eye at the centre.

**darter** /ˈdatə/, *n.* **1.** one who or that which darts or moves swiftly. **2.** any of various fish-eating birds of the genus *Anhinga* having small heads, long slender necks and long, pointed bills, as *A. rufa,* widely distributed in Australia and elsewhere; snakebird.

**Darwinian** /daˈwɪniən/, *n.* **1.** an adherent of Darwinism. **2.** one who was born in Darwin, the capital city of the Northern Territory, or who has come to regard it as his home town. *–adj.* **3.** of or pertaining to Darwinism, or to Charles Darwin. **4.** of or pertaining to the city of Darwin.

**Darwinism** /ˈdawənɪzəm/, *n.* the body of biological doctrine maintained by Charles Darwin, 1809-82, English naturalist, respecting the origin of species as derived by descent, with variation, from parent forms, through the natural selection of those best adapted to survive in the struggle for existence. – **Darwinist,** *n., adj.*

**Darwinite** /ˈdawənaɪt/, *n., adj.* →**Darwinian.**

**dash**[1] /dæʃ/, *v.t.* **1.** to strike violently, esp. so as to break to pieces. **2.** to throw or thrust violently or suddenly. **3.** to splash violently; bespatter (with water, mud, etc.). **4.** to apply roughly as by splashing. **5.** to throw something into so as to produce a mixture; mix; adulterate: *to dash wine with water.* **6.** to ruin or frustrate (hopes, plans, etc.). **7.** to depress or dispirit. **8.** to confound or abash. **9.** to write, make, sketch, etc., hastily (usu. fol. by *off* or *down*). *–v.i.* **10.** to strike with violence. **11.** to move with violence; rush. *–n.* **12.** a violent and rapid blow or stroke. **13.** a check or discouragement. **14.** the throwing or splashing of water, etc., against a thing. **15.** the sound of splashing. **16.** a small quantity of anything thrown into or mixed with something else: *a dash of salt, a dash of pink.* **17.** a hasty stroke, esp. of a pen. **18.** a horizontal line (–) used in writing and printing as a mark of punctuation to indicate an abrupt break or pause in a sentence, to begin and end a parenthetic clause, as an indication of omission of letters, words, etc., as a dividing line between distinct portions of matter, and for other purposes. **19.** *Music.* the sign placed above or below a note to indicate that it is to be played staccato. **20.** *Maths.* an acute accent, used in algebra and in lettering diagrams as a discrimination mark; prime. **21.** an impetuous movement; a rush; a sudden onset. **22.** *Athletics.* a short race or sprint decided in one attempt, not in heats: *a hundred-metre dash.* **23.** spirited action; vigour in action or style. **24.** a dashboard. **25.** *Teleg.* a signal of longer duration than a dot, used in groups of dots and dashes to represent letters, as in morse code. **26. cut a dash,** to create a brilliant impression. **27. do one's dash,** exhaust one's energies or opportunities. [ME *dasche(n),* c. Dan. *daske* slap, flap]

**dash**[2] /dæʃ/, *v.t.* **1.** to confound. *–interj.* **2.** (a mild expletive.)

**dashboard** /ˈdæʃbɔd/, *n.* **1.** the instrument board of a motor car or an aeroplane; fascia. **2.** (formerly) a panel on the front of a vehicle, to prevent mud splashing.

**dasheen** /dæˈʃin/, *n.* the taro plant, *Colocasia esculenta,* native to tropical Asia, grown in the tropics for its edible tubers. [F *de Chine* of China]

**dasher** /ˈdæʃə/, *n.* **1.** one who or that which dashes. **2.** the plunger of a churn. **3.** *Colloq.* a spirited person.

**dashing** /ˈdæʃɪŋ/, *adj.* **1.** impetuous; spirited; lively. **2.** brilliant; showy; stylish. – **dashingly,** *adv.*

**dashpot** /ˈdæʃpɒt/, *n.* a device for damping vibrations, consisting of a piston attached to the part whose movements are to be damped and fitted into a cylinder containing a fluid such as oil.

**dashy** /ˈdæʃi/, *adj.* showy; stylish; dashing.

**dastard** /ˈdæstəd/, *n.* **1.** a mean, sneaking coward. *–adj.* **2.**

mean and sneaking; cowardly. [ME; from *dast* (? var. of *dazed,* pp. of DAZE) + -ARD]

**dastardly** /ˈdæstədli/, *adj.* cowardly; meanly base; sneaking. – **dastardly,** *adv.* – **dastardliness,** *n.*

**dasyure** /ˈdæzijʊə/, *n.* any member of the group of carnivorous Australian marsupials comprising the native cats and the Tasmanian devil. [NL *Dasyūrus,* from *dasy-* (combining form of Gk *dasýs* shaggy) + *-ūrus* (from Gk *ourá* tail)]

**dat.,** dative.

**data** /ˈdeɪtə, ˈdatə/, *n.* **1.** plural of **datum. 2.** (*construed as sing. or pl.*) figures, etc., known or available; information.

**databank** /ˈdeɪtəbæŋk, ˈdatə-/, *n.* →**database.**

**database** /ˈdeɪtəbeɪs, ˈdata-/, *n.* **1.** a large volume of information stored in a computer and organised in categories to facilitate retrieval. **2.** any large collection of information or reference material. Also, **databank.**

**data bus** /ˈdeɪtə bʌs/, *n.* a main connecting channel or path for transferring data between sections of a computer system.

**data-handling system** /ˈdeɪtə-hændlɪŋ ˌsɪstəm/, *n.* a system consisting of electronic or electromechanical units which automatically measure certain quantities at a number of points, and transmit the resultant data to a central location for display or for automatic processing.

**datal** /ˈdeɪtl/, *adj.* chronological; pertaining to a date (of historical documents).

**data processing** /ˈdeɪtə ˌprousɛsɪŋ/, *n.* →**automatic data processing.**

**datary** /ˈdeɪtəri/, *n., pl.* **-ries.** *Rom. Cath. Ch.* **1.** an officer, now cardinal, at the head of a certain office or department of the Curia who investigates the fitness of candidates for benefices in the gift of the papal see. **2.** this office or department. [ML *datārius* (the officer), *datāria* (the office), from *data* DATE[1]]

**date**[1] /deɪt/, *n., v.,* **dated, dating.** –*n.* **1.** a particular point or period of time when something happens or happened. **2.** an inscription on a writing, coin, etc., that shows the time, or time and place, of writing, casting, delivery, etc. **3.** the time or period of an event or to which anything belongs. **4.** the time during which anything lasts; duration. **5.** *Colloq.* an appointment made for a particular time. **6.** *Colloq.* a person, usu. of the opposite sex, with whom one has a social appointment. **7. to date,** to the present time. –*v.i.* **8.** to have a date: *the letter dates from 1873.* **9.** to belong to a particular period; have its origin. **10.** to reckon from some point in time. **11.** *Colloq.* to go out on dates (def. 5) with a person or persons of the opposite sex. –*v.t.* **12.** to mark or furnish with a date. **13.** to ascertain or fix the date or time of; assign a date or time to. **14.** to show to be of a certain age, old-fashioned, or out of date: *that dress dates you.* **15.** *Colloq.* to make a date (def. 5) with; to invite frequently a member of the opposite sex for social engagements. [ME, from F, from ML *data,* properly pp. fem. of L *dāre* give] – **dater,** *n.*

**date**[2] /deɪt/, *n., v.,* **dated, dating.** –*n.* **1.** the oblong, fleshy fruit of the date palm, a staple food in northern Africa, Arabia, etc., and an important export. **2.** the date palm. **3.** *Colloq.* the anus. **4.** *Colloq.* the vagina. **5.** *Colloq.* to have sexual intercourse with. –*v.t.* **6.** *Colloq.* to poke or prod in the buttocks. [ME, from OF, from L *dactylus,* from Gk *dáktylos* date, orig. finger]

**dated** /ˈdeɪtəd/, *adj.* unfashionable; out-of-date.

**dateless** /ˈdeɪtləs/, *adj.* **1.** without a date; undated. **2.** endless. **3.** so old as to be undatable. **4.** of permanent interest regardless of age.

**date line** /ˈdeɪt laɪn/, *n.* **1.** a line in a letter, newspaper article, or the like, giving the date (and often the place) of origin. **2.** Also, **international date line.** a line, theoretically coinciding with the meridian of 180° from Greenwich, England, the regions on either side of which are counted as differing by one day in their calendar dates.

**date loaf** /ˈ– loʊf/, *n.* a cake made in a long narrow loaf-shaped tin, containing dates and nuts, usu. served sliced with butter. Also, **date and nut loaf, nut loaf.**

**date palm** /ˈ– pam/, *n.* the species of palm, *Phoenix dactylifera,* which bears dates, having a stem up to 18 metres high terminating in a crown of pinnate leaves.

**date plum** /ˈ– plʌm/, *n.* a small tree from China and the Himalaya region, *Diospyros lotus,* family Ebenaceae, having small yellow or bluish fruit.

**date stamp** /ˈ– stæmp/, *n.* a device for stamping dates, esp. on postal matter.

**dative** /ˈdeɪtɪv/, *Gram.* –*adj.* **1.** denoting a case, in some inflected languages, having as one function indication of the indirect object of a verb. –*n.* **2.** the dative case. **3.** a word or form in that case, as Latin *regi* in *regi haec dicite* meaning *tell this to the king.* [ME, from L *datīvus* of or pertaining to giving] – **datival** /dəˈtaɪvəl/, *adj.* – **datively,** *adv.*

**dative bond** /ˈ– bɒnd/, *n.* a chemical bond of the covalent type in which the electrons forming the bond are donated by the one atom; coordinate bond.

**dato** /ˈdatoʊ/, *n., pl.* **-tos. 1.** (in the Philippines) a native chief. **2.** the headman of a barrio or tribe in the East Indies. Also, **datto.** [Malay *dātoq* title of respect]

**datum** /ˈdeɪtəm, ˈdatəm/, *n., pl.* **-ta** /-tə/. **1.** any proposition assumed or given, from which conclusions may be drawn. **2.** (*oft. pl.*) any fact assumed to be a matter of direct observation. [L: given (pp. neut.)]

**datum plane** /ˈ– pleɪn/, *n.* a plane, level, line, etc., from which heights and depths are calculated or measured. Also, **datum level, line, point.**

**datura** /dəˈtjurə/, *n.* any plant of the genus *Datura,* the species of which have funnel-shaped flowers, prickly pods, and narcotic properties. [NL, from Hind. *dhatūra,* native name of the plant]

**dau.,** daughter.

**daub** /dɔb/, *v.t.* **1.** to cover or coat with soft, adhesive matter, such as plaster, mud, etc. **2.** to spread (plaster, mud, etc.) on or over something. **3.** to smear, soil, or defile. **4.** to paint unskilfully. –*v.i.* **5.** to daub something. **6.** to paint unskilfully. –*n.* **7.** material, esp. of an inferior kind, for daubing walls, etc. **8.** anything daubed on. **9.** the act of daubing. **10.** a crude, inartistic painting. [ME *daube(n),* from OF *dauber,* from L *dealbāre* whiten, plaster] – **dauber,** *n.*

**daube** /doʊb/, *n.* **1.** *Cookery.* a meat stew with wine, spices or herbs, braised in a sealed earthenware casserole. **2. en daube,** braised in this manner, or in such a casserole. [F]

**daubery** /ˈdɔbəri/, *n.* unskilful painting or work. Also, **daubry.**

**dauerlauf** /ˈdaʊəlaʊf/, *n.* (in skiing) a cross country endurance race. [G, from *dauern* to endure + *lauf,* run]

**daughter** /ˈdɔtə/, *n.* **1.** a female child or person in relation to her parents. **2.** any female descendant. **3.** one related as if by the ties binding daughter to parent: *daughter of the church.* **4.** anything (personified as female) considered with respect to its origin. –*adj.* **5.** denoting first-generation offspring or offshoot, irrespective of sex: *daughter cell.* [var. of ME *doughter,* OE *dohtor,* c. G *Tochter,* Gk *thygátēr*]

**daughter-in-law** /ˈdɔtər-ɪn-lɔ/, *n., pl.* **daughters-in-law.** the wife of one's son.

**daughterly** /ˈdɔtəli/, *adj.* pertaining to, befitting, or like a daughter. – **daughterliness,** *n.*

**daughter product** /ˈdɔtə prɒdʌkt/, *n.* radioactive decay product.

**daunt** /dɔnt/, *v.t.* **1.** to overcome with fear; intimidate. **2.** to lessen the courage of; dishearten. [ME *daunte(n),* from OF *danter,* from L *domāre* tame, subdue]

**dauntless** /ˈdɔntləs/, *adj.* not to be daunted; fearless; intrepid; bold. – **dauntlessly,** *adv.* – **dauntlessness,** *n.*

**dauphin** /ˈdɔfən/, *n.* the distinctive title of the eldest son of the king of France, from 1349 to 1830. [F, apparently orig. a proper name used as a surname; often identified with L *delphīnus* dolphin]

**dauphiness** /ˈdɔfənɛs/, *n.* the wife of the dauphin. Also, **dauphine** /ˈdɔfən, -fin/.

**davenport** /ˈdævənpɔt/, *n.* **1.** a small ornamental writing table. **2.** *U.S.* a large sofa, as one convertible into a bed.

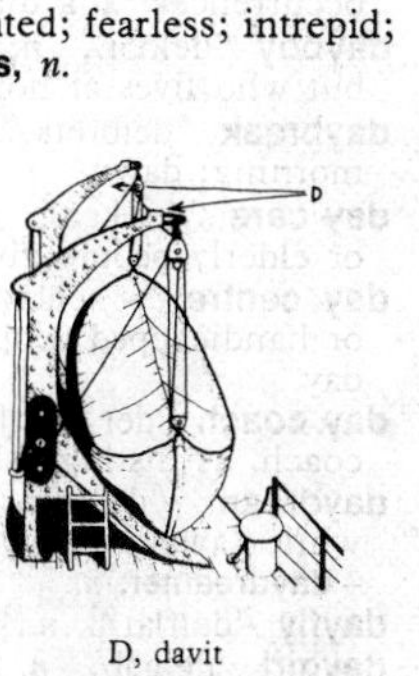

**Davis apparatus** /ˈdeɪvəs æpəˌratəs/, *n.* a device to enable occupants to escape from a disabled submarine; an escape lock. [named after Sir R. H. *Davis,* d. 1965, English inventor]

D, davit

**davit** /ˈdævət/, *n.* a projecting piece of wood or iron (fre-

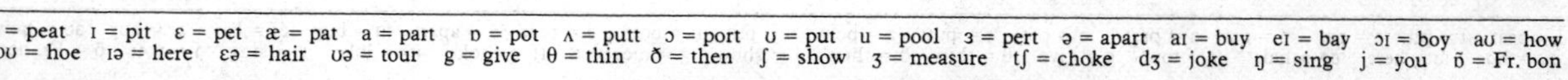
i = peat ɪ = pit ɛ = pet æ = pat a = part ɒ = pot ʌ = putt ɔ = port ʊ = put u = pool ɜ = pert ə = apart aɪ = buy eɪ = bay ɔɪ = boy aʊ = how oʊ = hoe ɪə = here ɛə = hair ʊə = tour g = give θ = thin ð = then ʃ = show ʒ = measure tʃ = choke dʒ = joke ŋ = sing j = you õ = Fr. bon

quently one of a pair) on the side or stern of a vessel, fitted with a tackle, etc., for raising, lowering, or suspending a small boat, anchor, or other weight. [ME *daviot,* from AF, apparently diminutive of *Davi* David]

**Davy Jones** /deɪvi 'dʒoʊnz/, *n.* **1.** the spirit of the sea; the sailors' devil. **2. Davy Jones's locker, a.** the ocean's bottom, esp. as the grave of all who perish at sea. **b.** the ocean.

**Davy lamp** /'– læmp/, *n.* an early safety lamp for miners. [named after Sir Humphry *Davy,* 1778-1829, English chemist]

**daw** /dɔ/, *n.* →**jackdaw.** [ME *dawe.* Cf. OHG *tāha*]

**dawdle** /'dɔdəl/, *v.,* **-dled, -dling.** *–v.i.* **1.** to waste time; idle; trifle. **2.** to walk slowly or lag behind others. *–v.t.* **3.** to waste (time) by trifling (usu. fol. by *away*). [? var. of *daddle* TODDLE] – **dawdler,** *n.*

**dawn** /dɔn/, *n.* **1.** the first appearance of daylight in the morning. **2.** the beginning or rise of anything; advent. *–v.i.* **3.** to begin to grow light in the morning. **4.** to begin to open or develop. **5.** to begin to be perceived (fol. by *on* or *upon*): *the idea dawned on him.* [ME *dawen-* (in *dawening* dawn), apparently from Scand.; cf. Icel. *dögun* dawn] – **dawning,** *n.*

**dawn chorus** /– 'kɔrəs/, *n.* the sound of many birds singing at dawn.

**dawn parade** /'– pəreɪd/, *n.* the ceremony held at dawn on Anzac Day. Also, **dawn service.**

**day** /deɪ/, *n.* **1.** the interval of light between two successive nights; the time between sunrise and sunset. **2.** the light of day; daylight. **3.** *Astron.* **a.** the period during which the earth (or a heavenly body) makes one revolution on its axis. **b.** the average length of this interval, twenty-four hours (**mean solar day**). **c.** the interval of time which elapses between two consecutive returns of the same terrestrial meridian to the sun (**solar day**). **d.** a period reckoned from midnight to midnight and equivalent in length to the mean solar day (**civil day**), as contrasted with a similar period reckoned from noon to noon (**astronomical day**). **e.** the interval of time between the meridional transits of a star, specifically the first point of Aries (**sidereal day**), four minutes shorter than the solar day. **4.** the portion of a day allotted to working: *an eight-hour day.* **5.** a day as a point or unit of time, or on which something occurs. **6.** a day assigned to a particular purpose or observance: *New Year's Day.* **7.** a day of contest, or the contest itself: *to win the day.* **8.** (*oft. pl.*) a particular time or period: *the present day, in days of old.* **9.** (*oft. pl.*) period of life or activity. **10.** period of power or influence: *every dog has his day.* **11. call it a day,** to bring an activity to a close, either temporarily or permanently. **12. day by day,** daily. **13. day in, day out,** for an undetermined succession of days. **14. that'll be the day,** *Colloq.* (an expression indicating disbelief, cynicism, etc.). [ME; OE *dæg,* c. G *Tag*]

**day bed** /'– bɛd/, *n.* **1.** a couch which can be converted to a bed as required. **2.** chaise longue.

**day blindness** /'– blaɪndnəs/, *n.* →**hemeralopia.**

**daybook** /'deɪbʊk/, *n.* **1.** *Bookkeeping.* a book in which the transactions of the day are entered in the order of their occurrence. **2.** a diary.

**dayboy** /'deɪbɔɪ/, *n.* a boy who attends school during the day but who lives at home (opposed to *boarder*).

**daybreak** /'deɪbreɪk/, *n.* the first appearance of light in the morning; dawn.

**day care** /'deɪ kɛə/, *n.* care and supervision of young children or elderly people given daily by trained staff.

**day centre** /'– sɛntə/, *n.* a place where children and elderly or handicapped people may go for social activities during the day.

**day coach** /'deɪ koutʃ/, *n. U.S.* an ordinary railway passenger coach, as distinguished from a sleeper.

**daydream** /'deɪdrim/, *n.* **1.** a visionary fancy indulged in while awake; reverie. *–v.i.* **2.** to indulge in daydreams. – **daydreamer,** *n.*

**dayfly** /'deɪflaɪ/, *n., pl.* **-flies.** →**mayfly.**

**daygirl** /'deɪgɜl/, *n.* a girl who attends school during the day but who lives at home (opposed to *boarder*).

**day labour** /'deɪ leɪbə/, *n.* work, generally unskilled, paid for by the day.

**day labourer** /'– leɪbərə/, *n.* an unskilled worker paid by the day.

**daylight** /'deɪlaɪt/, *n.* **1.** the light of day. **2.** openness; publicity. **3.** daytime. **4.** daybreak.

**daylight factor** /'– ˌfæktə/, *n.* the intensity of light on a horizontal surface inside a building, expressed as a fraction of the intensity when the same horizontal surface is in the open under a sky of uniform brightness.

**daylight robbery** /– 'rɒbəri/, *n.* a shameless attempt to rob, overcharge or cheat someone.

**daylights** /'deɪlaɪts/, *n.pl. in the phrases,* **1. beat the living daylights out of (someone),** *Colloq.* to give (someone) a sound beating. **2. scare the living daylights out of (someone),** *Colloq.* to give (someone) a fright.

**daylight-saving** /ˌdeɪlaɪt-'seɪvɪŋ/, *n.* **1.** a system of reckoning time one or more hours later than the standard time for a country or community, usu. used during summer months to give more hours of daylight to the working day. *–adj.* **2.** of or pertaining to such time.

**day lily** /'deɪ lɪli/, *n.* **1.** any plant of the genus *Hemerocallis,* with yellow or orange flowers which commonly last only for a day. **2.** the flower of this plant.

**daylong** /'deɪlɒŋ/, *adj.* lasting the whole day.

**day nursery** /'deɪ nɜsri/, *n.* a centre for the daytime care of children up to two years of age.

**Day of Atonement,** *n.* a Jewish fast day, Yom Kippur.

**Day of Judgment,** *n.* the day of the Last Judgment, at the end of the world.

**day of reckoning,** *n.* **1.** the time when one has to pay for one's actions, fulfil one's obligations, etc. **2.** (*caps*) →**Day of Judgment.**

**day-patient** /'deɪ-peɪʃənt/, *n.* a patient requiring hospitalisation only during the day.

**day pupil** /'deɪ pjupəl/, *n.* a pupil who lives at home but attends a boarding school.

**day school** /'– skul/, *n.* **1.** a school for pupils living outside the school (distinguished from *boarding school*). **2.** a school held in the daytime (distinguished from *night school*). **3.** a school held on weekdays (distinguished from *Sunday school*).

**day shift** /'– ʃɪft/, *n.* **1.** a work period during the day. **2.** the group of workers working this shift.

**days of grace,** *n.pl.* days (commonly three) allowed by law or custom for payment after a bill or note falls due.

**dayspring** /'deɪsprɪŋ/, *n. Poetic.* dawn; daybreak.

**daystar** /'deɪsta/, *n.* **1.** the morning star. **2.** *Poetic.* the sun.

**daytime** /'deɪtaɪm/, *n.* the time between sunrise and sunset.

**day-to-day** /'deɪ-tə-deɪ/, *adj.* ordinary; happening everyday: *a day-to-day occurrence.*

**daze** /deɪz/, *v.,* **dazed, dazing,** *n.* *–v.t.* **1.** to stun or stupefy with a blow, a shock, etc. **2.** to confuse; bewilder; dazzle. *–n.* **3.** a dazed condition. [ME *dase(n),* from Scand.; cf. Dan. *dase* doze, mope] – **dazedly** /'deɪzədli/, *adv.*

**dazzle** /'dæzəl/, *v.,* **-zled, -zling,** *n.* *–v.t.* **1.** to overpower or dim (the vision) by intense light. **2.** to bewilder by brilliancy or display of any kind. *–v.i.* **3.** to be overpowered by light. **4.** to excite admiration by brilliance. *–n.* **5.** the act or fact of dazzling. **6.** bewildering brightness. **7.** temporary loss of vision, or a temporary reduction of visual acuity, related to the presence of a bright (possibly moving) source of light. [frequentative of DAZE] – **dazzler,** *n.* – **dazzlingly,** *adv.*

**d.b.** /di 'bi/, double-breasted.

**dB,** decibel.

**D.B.E.,** Dame (Commander of the Order) of the British Empire.

**dbl.,** double.

**D/C,** direct current.

**D.C.,** **1.** *Music.* da capo. **2.** diplomatic corps. **3.** direct current. **4.** Double Certificated.

**D. Ch.,** Doctor of Surgery. [NL *Doctor Chīrurgiae*]

**D.C.M.,** Distinguished Conduct Medal; officially, Medal for Distinguished Conduct in the Field.

**D.C.M.** /di si 'ɛm/, *n. Colloq.* discharge from employment; dismissal. [abbrev. for *D(on't) C(ome) M(onday)*]

**d.d.** /di 'di/, *n.* →**deferred delivery share.**

**DD** /di 'di/, Doctor of Divinity.

**D-day** /ˈdi-deɪ/, *n.* the day, usu. unspecified, set for the beginning of a previously planned attack, esp. the day (6 June 1944) of the Allied invasion of Normandy.

**D.D.S.,** Doctor of Dental Surgery.

**DDT** /di di ˈti/, *n.* a very powerful insecticide, dichlorodiphenyltrichloroethane. Also, **D.D.T.**

**de** /də/, *prep.* from; of (much used in French personal names, originally to indicate place of origin). Also, **De;** before vowels, **D', d'.**

**de-,** a prefix meaning: **1.** privation and separation, as in *dehorn, dethrone, detrain.* **2.** negation, as in *demerit, derange.* **3.** descent, as in *degrade, deduce.* **4.** reversal, as in *deactivate.* **5.** intensity, as in *decompound.* [ME, from L, representing *dē*, prep., from, away from, of, out of, etc.; in some words from F, from L *de-*, or from L *dis-* (see DIS-[1])]

**deacon** /ˈdikən/, *n. Eccles.* **1.** originally an officer of the early Christian Church probably concerned with temporal affairs. **2.** (in the Roman Catholic Church) formerly a member of the clerical order next below that of a priest, but since the Second Vatican Council a member of a major order in the hierarchy. **3.** (in the Anglican Church) the rank held before ordination as a priest. **4.** (in other Churches) an appointed or elected officer with variously defined duties. [ME *deacon, deken,* OE *dēacon, diacon,* from LL *diāconus,* from Gk *diākonos* servant, minister, deacon] – **deaconship,** *n.*

**deaconate** /ˈdikənət/, *n. Eccles.* the rank of deacon.

**deaconess** /dikəˈnɛs/, *n.* **1.** (in certain Protestant churches) one of an order of women who carry on educational, hospital, or social work. **2.** a woman elected by a church to assist the clergy.

**deaconry** /ˈdikənri/, *n., pl.* **-ries. 1.** the office of a deacon. **2.** deacons collectively.

**deactivate** /diˈæktəveɪt/, *v.t.,* **-vated, -vating. 1.** to render a bomb, shell, etc. inoperative. **2.** *Phys. Chem.* to return an activated atom, molecule, or substance to its normal state. **3.** *Chem.* to make less active; to return an activated substance (esp. a catalyst) to its normal state. **4.** *Physics.* to lose radioactivity. – **deactivation** /ˌdiæktəˈveɪʃən/, *n.* – **deactivator,** *n.*

**dead** /dɛd/, *adj.* **1.** no longer living; deprived of life. **2.** not endowed with life; inanimate: *dead matter.* **3.** resembling death: *a dead sleep.* **4. a.** bereft of sensation; insensible; numb: *dead to all sense of shame.* **b.** asleep: *dead to the world.* **5.** no longer in existence or use: *dead languages.* **6.** *Law.* deprived of civil rights so that one is in the state of civil death, esp. deprived of the rights of property. **7.** without spiritual life or vigour. **8.** *Colloq.* very tired; exhausted. **9.** infertile; barren. **10.** lacking in vigour, force, motion, etc., or esp. in sport, lacking in or deprived of some other characteristic and desirable quality: *dead market, dead machinery, dead track, dead pitch.* **11. a.** without resonance: *a dead room, a dead sound.* **b.** without resilience or bounce: *a dead ball.* **12.** unproductive: *dead capital.* **13. a dead bat,** *Cricket.* a bat limply held so that the ball drops to the ground after striking it. **14.** extinguished: *a dead fire.* **15.** tasteless or flat, as alcoholic drink. **16.** not glossy, bright, or brilliant. **17.** complete; absolute: *dead loss, dead silence.* **18.** sure; unerring: *a dead shot.* **19.** direct, straight: *a dead line.* **20.** unproductive: *dead capital.* **21.** *Colloq.* empty: *a dead bottle.* **22. a.** *Sport.* out of play: *dead ball.* **b.** *Soccer.* out of play; stationary. **23.** *Golf.* of a ball hit so close to the hole that the success of the next, sinking, shot is assumed. **24.** *Horseracing, etc.* out of the race, either because of an official scratching or because of the unofficial intentions of the owners not to win the race. **25.** having been used or rejected, as type set up or copy for printing. **26.** *Elect.* **a.** free from any electric connection to a source of potential difference and from electric charge. **b.** not having a potential difference from that of the earth. **27.** *Mil.* (of land) not visible; hidden, as by undulations: *dead ground.* **28. a dead horse,** a debt. **29. dead from the neck up,** *Colloq.* lacking intelligence; stupid. **30. work off a dead horse,** to work for money which will go towards paying off a debt. **31. wouldn't be seen dead with (in) (at)** (etc.) *Colloq.* to refuse to have any association with (to wear) (to visit) (etc.) *–n.* **32. the dead, a.** dead persons collectively. **b.** the period of greatest darkness, coldness, etc.: *the dead of night, the dead of winter.* *–adv.* **33.** absolutely; completely: *dead right, dead broke.* **34.** with abrupt and complete stoppage of motion, etc.: *he stopped dead.* **35.** directly; exactly; diametrically: *the wind was dead ahead.* **36. dead set,** *Colloq.* really true. **37. run dead,** *Horseracing.* (of a horse) to be deliberately pulled up so that it does not run at its best. [ME *deed,* OE *dēad,* c. G *tot;* orig. pp. See DIE[1]]

**dead-and-alive** /dɛd-ən-əˈlaɪv/, *adj.* **1.** (of a place) sleepy; backward. **2.** (of a person) dull; unaware.

**dead-and-buried** /dɛd-ən-ˈbɛrid/, *adj.* (of an issue) no longer of interest; finished.

**dead-ball line** /ˈdɛd-bɔl ˌlaɪn/, *n. Rugby Football.* a line behind the goal line, running parallel to it, beyond which the ball passes out of play.

**deadbeat** /ˈdɛdbit/, *Colloq.* *–n.* **1.** a man down on his luck; vagrant. *–adj.* **2.** of or pertaining to the life of a vagrant.

**dead centre** /dɛd ˈsɛntə/, *n.* **1.** (in a reciprocating engine or pump) either of two positions of the crank in which the connecting rod has no power to turn it, occurring when the crank and connecting rod are in the same plane, at each end of a stroke. **Top** (or **inner**) **dead centre** is the position of the piston when it is at the top of its stroke; **bottom** (or **outer**) **dead centre** is the position of the piston at the bottom of its stroke. **2.** *Mach.* a stationary centre which holds the work, as the tailstock of a lathe. **3.** →**dead heart.**

**dead-centre** /dɛd-ˈsɛntə/, *adj.* **1.** completely on target. *–adv.* **2.** right in the middle; accurately.

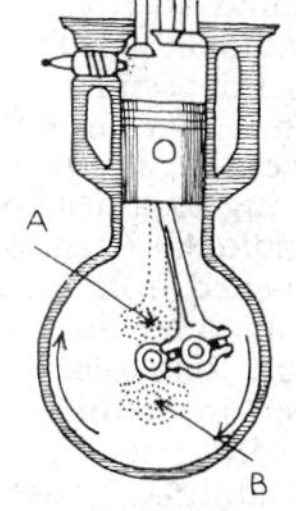

dead centre: A, top dead centre; B, bottom dead centre

**dead draw** /dɛd ˈdrɔ/, *n. Bowls.* a bowl which finishes exactly at the jack.

**dead duck** /– ˈdʌk/, *n.* **1.** a person lacking good prospects; a failure. **2.** something useless, or worthless, or utterly without promise.

**deaden** /ˈdɛdən/, *v.t.* **1.** to make less sensitive, active, energetic, or forcible; dull; weaken: *to deaden sound, the force of a ball, the senses.* **2.** to lessen the velocity of; retard. **3.** to make impervious to sound, as a floor. *–v.i.* **4.** to become dead. – **deadener,** *n.*

**dead end** /dɛd ˈɛnd/, *n.* a road which is closed at one end; a no-through road; cul-de-sac.

**dead-end** /ˈdɛd-ɛnd/, *adj.* **1.** leading nowhere. **2.** offering no future: *dead-end job.* **3.** having no apparent hopes or future, as a juvenile delinquent: *dead-end kid.*

**deadening** /ˈdɛdənɪŋ/, *n.* **1.** a device or material employed to deaden or render dull. **2.** a device or material preventing the transmission of sound. *–adj.* **3.** dulling or rendering less sensitive, as pain, light, sound, etc.

**deadeye** /ˈdɛdaɪ/, *n.* **1.** *Naut.* a round, laterally flattened block encircled by a rope or a metal band and pierced with three holes. **2.** *Colloq.* an accurate shot; marksman.

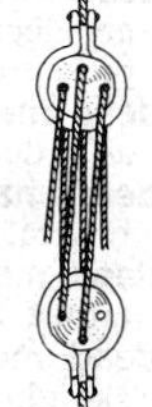
deadeyes

**deadfall** /ˈdɛdfɔl/, *n.* a trap, esp. for large game, in which a weight falls upon and crushes the prey.

**dead finish** /dɛd ˈfɪnɪʃ/, *n.* **1.** any of a number of Australian plant species that form impenetrable thickets, esp. *Acacia tetragonophylla,* a small tree or shrub of spreading habit. **2.** the limit or extreme point (of endurance, success, etc.).

**dead freight** /– ˈfreɪt/, *n.* the sum paid for that part of a vessel not occupied by cargo when the whole vessel is chartered.

**dead hand** /– ˈhænd/, *n.* **1.** an oppressive and retarding influence: *the dead hand of the law.* **2.** →**mortmain. 3.** *Colloq.* (formerly) an expert at doing something.

**deadhead** /ˈdɛdhɛd/, *n. Colloq.* **1.** a dull and ineffectual person. **2.** a spent match[1] (def.1). **3.** a dead or faded flower head.

**dead heart** /dɛd ˈhat/, *n.* the arid central regions of Australia; dead centre.

**dead heat** /– ˈhit/, *n.* a heat or race in which two or more competitors finish together.

**dead horse** /– ˈhɔs/, *n. Colloq.* tomato sauce. [rhyming slang]

**deadhouse** /ˈdɛdhaʊs/, *Colloq. n.* **1.** →**morgue. 2.** a room in a hotel to which drunks are removed to sleep off their intoxication.

**dead ice** /dɛd 'aɪs/, *n.* the ice in a glacier which has ceased to move.

**dead latch** /'– lætʃ/, *n.* →**deadlock**[2].

**dead length** /'– lɛŋθ/, *n. Bowls.* a bowl which stops level with the jack.

**dead letter** /– 'lɛtə/, *n.* **1.** a law, ordinance, etc., which has lost its force, though not formally repealed or abolished. **2.** a letter which lies unclaimed for a certain time at a post office, or which, because of faulty address, etc., cannot be delivered. – **dead-letter,** *adj.*

**dead-letter office** /dɛd-'lɛtər ɒfəs/, *n.* a special division or department of the post office which handles dead letters.

**dead lift** /'dɛd lɪft/, *n. Weightlifting.* a lift in which the barbell is raised from the floor to a position where the competitor is standing upright with straight arms, the barbell held across the thighs.

**deadlight** /'dɛdlaɪt/, *n. Naut.* **1.** a strong wooden or metal shutter for a cabin window or porthole, to prevent water from entering. **2.** a thick pane of glass set in the hull or deck to admit light.

**deadline** /'dɛdlaɪn/, *n.* **1.** a line or limit that must not be passed. **2.** the latest time for finishing something.

**dead load** /'dɛd loud/, *n.* a load that is permanent and immovable, as the weight of a bridge.

**deadlock**[1] /'dɛdlɒk/, *n.* **1.** a state of affairs in which progress is impossible; complete standstill. **2.** *Parl. Proc.* a tied vote on a motion with no chance or opportunity for a change in the allocation of votes that would break the tie. *–v.t.* **3.** to bring to a deadlock. *–v.i.* **4.** to come to a deadlock.

**deadlock**[2] /'dɛdlɒk/, *n.* **1.** a type of lock which can only be opened from inside and outside with a key. *–v.t.* **2.** to secure something in this way: *to deadlock a door.* Also, **dead latch.**

**dead loss** /dɛd 'lɒs/, *n. Colloq.* **1.** a complete failure. **2.** a person or thing that is totally worthless, hopeless, inefficient.

**deadly** /'dɛdli/, *adj.*, **-lier, -liest,** *adv.* *–adj.* **1.** causing or tending to cause death; fatal: *a deadly poison.* **2.** aiming to kill or destroy; implacable: *a deadly enemy.* **3.** involving spiritual death: *a deadly sin.* **4.** like death: *a deadly pallor.* **5.** excessive: *deadly haste.* *–adv.* **6.** in a manner resembling or suggesting death: *deadly pale.* **7.** *Colloq.* excessively: *deadly dull.* – **deadliness,** *n.*

**deadly nightshade** /– 'naɪtʃeɪd/, *n.* **1.** →**belladonna. 2.** →**black nightshade.**

**deadly sins** /– 'sɪnz/, *n.pl.* the sins of pride, covetousness, lust, anger, gluttony, envy, and sloth.

**dead man** /'dɛd mæn/, *n.* any of various objects, as a tree or a log fixed in the ground, used as an anchor in fencing, bridgebuilding, etc.

**dead man's handle,** *n.* a handle for controlling the speed of an electric train or other vehicle which requires the constant pressure of the driver's hand to maintain the power supply.

**dead man's pedal,** a pedal which operates in the same way as a dead man's handle.

**dead march** /'dɛd matʃ/, *n.* a piece of solemn music for a funeral procession, esp. one played at a military funeral.

**dead marine** /– mə'rin/, *n. Colloq.* a bottle which had contained beer, whisky, etc., but is now empty.

**dead meat** /– 'mit/, *n.* (in the meat trade) the carcasses of slaughtered animals, as distinct from live animals yet to be slaughtered for meat.

**dead meat ticket,** *n. Colloq.* →**identity disc.**

**dead men's fingers,** *n.pl.* **1.** the gills of a lobster or crab. **2.** the soft coral, *Alcyonium digitatum,* of European coastal waters. **3.** any of various species of orchid, esp. the European *Orchis latifolia* and *O. maculata.* Also, **dead man's fingers.**

**deadnettle** /'dɛdnɛtl/, *n.* any plant of the genus *Lamium,* superficially like the nettle in appearance, but stingless.

**deadpan** /'dɛdpæn/, *adj. Colloq.* **1.** (of a person or his face) completely lacking expression or reaction. **2.** said without any indication in the speaker's manner or expression that he is aware of the force or implication of what is said: *deadpan humour.* *–adv.* **3.** in a deadpan manner.

**dead point** /dɛd 'pɔɪnt/, *n.* →**dead centre.**

**dead reckoning** /– 'rɛkənɪŋ/, *n. Navig.* **1.** the calculation of a ship's or aircraft's position without astronomical observations, by means of the distances travelled on the various courses with corrections for drift or leeway. **2.** position as so calculated.

**dead-set** /'dɛd-sɛt/, *adj.* certain; assured. Also, *in predicative use,* **dead set.**

**deadshit** /'dɛdʃɪt/, *n. Colloq.* **1.** a mean and contemptible person. **2.** a no-hoper; a dullard. *–adj.* **3.** despicable; mean: *it was a deadshit thing to do.*

**dead shore** /dɛd 'ʃɔ/, *n.* an upright supporting prop or beam.

**dead space** /– 'speɪs/, *n. Mil.* **1.** an area within the maximum range of a weapon, radar, or observer, which cannot be covered by fire or observation from a particular position. **2.** an area or zone which is within range of a radio transmitter, but in which a signal is not received. **3.** the volume of space about and around a gun or guided missile system into which it cannot fire because of mechanical or electronic limitations.

**dead-stick landing** /ˌdɛd-stɪk 'lændɪŋ/, *n. Aeron.* a landing made with a dead engine.

**dead stock** /dɛd 'stɒk/, *n.* **1.** farming equipment, as distinct from livestock. **2.** stock in a business enterprise which is no longer saleable, and is to be written off.

**dead time** /'– taɪm/, *n. Elect.* (in a circuit) the interval time after the circuit has responded to a stimulus during which it cannot respond to a second stimulus.

**dead weight** /– 'weɪt/, *n.* **1.** the heavy, unrelieved weight of anything inert. **2.** a heavy or oppressive burden. **3.** *Naut.* the difference in weight, displacement, etc., between a ship or other vehicle when loaded and when empty. *Abbrev.:* dwt

**deadweight** /'dɛdweɪt/, *adj.* of or pertaining to the dead weight.

**deadweight mass** /'dɛdweɪt mæs/, *n.* the deadweight tonnage, measured in tonnes.

**deadweight tonnage** /'dɛdweɪt tʌnɪdʒ/, *n.* the mass of the cargo, fuel, potable water, boiler feed water, ballast, stores, crew, gear, etc., on a ship.

**deadwood** /'dɛdwʊd/, *n.* **1.** the dead branches on a tree; dead branches or trees. **2.** a person or thing regarded as useless; a hindrance or impediment. **3.** *Naut.* a fin-shaped part of a vessel's keel just forward of the propeller or rudder.

**deadwood fence** /– 'fɛns/, *n.* a fence built of rough logs, fallen branches, etc., heaped together.

**dead wool** /dɛd 'wʊl/, *n.* wool collected in the paddock from dead sheep, of lower quality than plucked wool.

**deaf** /dɛf/, *adj.* **1.** lacking or deprived of the sense of hearing, wholly or partially; unable to hear. **2.** refusing to listen; heedless; inattentive: *deaf to advice, turn a deaf ear to a plea.* *–n.* **3. the deaf,** people unable to hear. [ME *deef,* OE *dēaf,* c. G *taub*] – **deafly,** *adv.* – **deafness,** *n.*

**deaf adder** /'– ædə/, *n.* →**death adder.**

**deaf-aid** /'dɛf-eɪd/, *n.* an electrical or other device used by the deaf to improve their hearing; hearing aid.

**deafen** /'dɛfən/, *v.t.* **1.** to make deaf. **2.** to stun with noise. **3.** to render (a sound) inaudible, esp. by a louder sound. – **deafeningly,** *adv.*

**deaf-mute** /dɛf-'mjut/, *n.* a person who is deaf and dumb, esp. one in whom inability to speak is due to congenital or early deafness.

**deal**[1] /dil/, *v.,* **dealt, dealing,** *n.* *–v.i.* **1.** to occupy oneself or itself (fol. by *with* or *in*): *deal with the first question, botany deals with the study of plants.* **2.** to take action with respect to a thing or person (usu. fol. by *with*): *law courts must deal with lawbreakers.* **3.** to conduct oneself towards persons: *deal fairly.* **4.** to trade or do business: *to deal with a firm, to deal in an article.* **5.** to distribute, esp. the cards required in a game. *–v.t.* **6.** to give to one as his share; apportion (oft. fol. by *out*). **7.** to distribute among a number of recipients, as the cards required in a game. **8.** *Cards.* to give a player (a specific card) in dealing. **9.** to deliver (blows, etc.). *–n.* **10.** *Colloq.* a business transaction. **11.** a bargain or arrangement for mutual advantage, as in commerce or politics, often a secret or underhand one. **12.** treatment; arrangement: *a raw deal, a fair deal.* **13.** a quantity, amount, extent, or degree. **14.** an indefinite but large amount or extent: *a deal of money.* **15.** a unit quantity of marijuana. **16.** act of dealing or distributing. **17.** *Cards.* **a.** the distribution to the players of the cards in a game. **b.** the set of cards in one's hand. **c.**

the turn of a player to deal. **d.** the period of time during which a deal is played. **18.** any undertaking, organisation, etc.; affair. **19.** *Obs.* portion or share. **20. a big deal,** *Colloq.* an important event; a serious matter. **21. big deal!,** *Colloq.* (an ironic exclamation indicating contempt, disbelief, etc.). [ME *delen,* OE *dǣlan* (c. G *teilen,* etc.), from *dǣl* part (c. G *Teil*)]

**deal**[2] /dil/, *n.* **1.** a board or plank, esp. of fir or pine. **2.** such boards collectively. **3.** fir or pine wood. *–adj.* **4.** made of fir or pine wood. **5.** in the form of deal (def. 1). [ME *dele,* from MLG or MD]

**dealer** /ˈdilə/, *n.* **1.** one who buys and sells articles without altering their condition; trader or merchant. **2.** one who buys and sells drugs, as marijuana, heroin, etc., in large quantities. **3.** *Cards.* the player distributing the cards.

**dealfish** /ˈdilfɪʃ/, *n., pl.* **-fishes,** (*esp. collectively*) **-fish.** →**ribbonfish.** [DEAL[2] + FISH[1]]

**dealing** /ˈdilɪŋ/, *n.* **1.** (*usu. pl.*) relations; trading: *business dealings.* **2.** conduct in relation to others; treatment: *honest dealing.*

**dealt** /dɛlt/, *v.* past tense and past participle of **deal**[1].

**dean**[1] /din/, *n.* **1.** *Educ.* **a.** the head of a medical school, university faculty, or the like. **b.** *U.S.* a college or university official in charge of personnel, students, etc. **2.** *Eccles.* **a.** the head of the chapter of a cathedral or a collegiate church. **b.** any of various other ecclesiastical dignitaries, as the head of a division of a diocese. **3.** the senior member, in length of service, of any body; father. [ME *deen,* from OF *deien,* from LL *decānus* chief of ten] – **deanship,** *n.*

**dean**[2] /din/, *n.* →**dene.**

**deaner** /ˈdinə/, *n.* →**deener.**

**deanery** /ˈdinəri/, *n., pl.* **-eries. 1.** the office, jurisdiction, or district of a dean. **2.** the residence of a dean.

**dear**[1] /dɪə/, *adj.* **1.** beloved or loved: *a dear friend of mine.* **2.** (in the salutation of a letter) highly esteemed: *Dear Sirs.* **3.** precious in one's regard: *dear to his heart.* **4.** high-priced; expensive. **5.** charging high prices. **6.** high; excessive: *a dear price to pay.* **7.** *Obs.* worthy. *–n.* **8.** one who is dear. **9.** a beloved one (often used in direct address): *my dear.* *–adv.* **10.** dearly; fondly. **11.** at a high price. *–interj.* **12.** (an exclamation of surprise, distress, etc.) [ME *dere,* OE *dēore,* c. G *teuer*] – **dearly,** *adv.* – **dearness,** *n.*

**dear**[2] /dɪə/, *adj. Archaic.* hard; grievous. Also, **dere.** [ME *dere,* OE *dēor;* cf. Icel. *dȳr* difficult, rigorous]

**dear John** /– ˈdʒɒn/, *n. Colloq.* a letter to a lover ending a relationship.

**dearth** /dɜθ/, *n.* **1.** scarcity or scanty supply; lack. **2.** scarcity and dearness of food; famine. [ME *derthe.* See DEAR[2], -TH[1]]

**deary** /ˈdɪəri/, *n., pl.* **dearies.** (esp. as an affectionate or colloquial term of address by an elderly woman) dear; darling. Also, **dearie.**

**death** /dɛθ/, *n.* **1.** the act of dying; the end of life; the total and permanent cessation of the vital functions of an animal or plant. **2.** (*oft. cap.*) the annihilating power personified, usu. represented as a skeleton: *'O Death, where is thy sting?'* **3.** the state of being dead: *to lie still in death.* **4.** extinction; destruction: *it will mean the death of our hopes.* **5.** the time at which a person dies: *the letters may be published after my death.* **6.** manner of dying: *a hero's death.* **7.** loss or deprivation of civil life. **8.** loss or absence of spiritual life. **9.** bloodshed or murder. **10.** a cause or occasion of death: *you'll be the death of me.* **11.** a pestilence: *the black death.* **12. at death's door,** in danger of death; gravely ill. **13. do to death, a.** to kill. **b.** to repeat until hackneyed. **14. fate worse than death,** *Colloq.* **a.** (*usu. joc.*) a circumstance regarded as particularly horrible. **b.** rape. **c.** (*joc.*) sexual intercourse. **15. in at the death, a.** *Hunting.* present when the hunted animal is caught and killed. **b.** present at the climax or conclusion of a series of events or a situation. **16. like death (warmed up),** *Colloq.* appearing, feeling, extremely ill or exhausted. **17. like grim death,** tenaciously, firmly: *he hung on like grim death.* **18. put to death,** to kill; execute. **19. sick to death,** *Colloq.* irritated or annoyed to an extreme degree. [ME *deeth,* OE *dēath,* c. G *Tod*]

**death adder** /– ædə/, *n.* **1.** Also, **deaf adder.** a venomous viper-like snake, *Acanthopis antarcticus,* of Australia and the island of New Guinea, having a stout body and broad head. **2.** a mean, avaricious person. **3. have a death adder in one's pocket,** *Colloq.* to be mean or parsimonious.

death adder

**deathbed** /ˈdɛθbɛd/, *n.* **1.** the bed on which a person dies. **2.** the last few hours before death.

**death bell** /ˈdɛθ bɛl/, *n.* the bell that announces a death.

**deathblow** /ˈdɛθbloʊ/, *n.* a blow causing death.

**death cell** /ˈdɛθ sɛl/, *n.* a building or part of a prison in which persons condemned to death await execution.

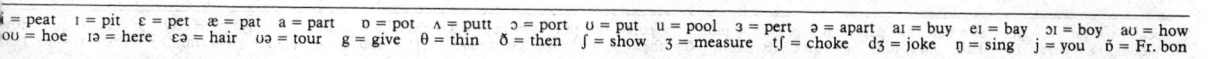

**death certificate** /– səˌtɪfɪkət/, *n.* a certificate issued compulsorily on the death of each person, signed by a qualified medical practitioner to certify death and its cause if known.

**death cup** /ˈ– kʌp/, *n.* **1.** a poisonous toadstool of the genus *Amanita,* part of which persists around the base of the stipe as a definite membranous cup. **2.** the cup.

**death duty** /ˈ– djuti/, *n.* (*usu. pl.*) a tax paid upon the inheritance of property.

**deathful** /ˈdɛθfəl/, *adj.* **1.** fatal. **2.** deathlike.

**death knell** /ˈdɛθ nɛl/, *n.* **1.** death bell. **2.** the harbinger of the death or destruction of a person or thing. **3.** anything which precipitates the end of a plan or action.

**death-knock** /ˈdɛθ-nɒk/, *n. Colloq.* the end; the last minute.

**deathless** /ˈdɛθləs/, *adj.* **1.** not subject to death; immortal. **2.** perpetual. – **deathlessly,** *adv.* – **deathlessness,** *n.*

**deathlike** /ˈdɛθlaɪk/, *adj.* resembling death.

**deathly** /ˈdɛθli/, *adj.* **1.** causing death; deadly; fatal. **2.** like death. **3.** *Poetic.* of death. *–adv.* **4.** in the manner of death. **5.** very; utterly: *deathly afraid.* [ME *dethlich,* OE *dēathlīc*]

**death mask** /ˈdɛθ mask/, *n.* a cast of a person's face taken after death.

**death penalty** /ˈ– pɛnəlti/, *n.* the sentence of death as given to a convicted criminal; capital punishment.

**death rate** /ˈ– reɪt/, *n.* →**mortality rate.**

**death-rattle** /ˈdɛθ-rætəl/, *n.* a sound sometimes produced in the throat immediately before death, caused by the passage of air through collected mucus.

**death ray** /ˈdɛθ reɪ/, *n* a ray able to destroy life from a distance.

**deathroll** /ˈdɛθroʊl/, *n.* a list of persons killed, as in a battle or accident.

**death row** /dɛθ ˈroʊ/, *n. Colloq.* the group of cells in which condemned prisoners are kept, esp. in the U.S.

**death seat** /ˈdɛθ sit/, *n. Colloq.* **1.** the front passenger seat in a motor car. **2.** (in a trotting race) a position on the outside of the leader, from which it is very hard to win.

**death's-head** /ˈdɛθs-hɛd/, *n.* a human skull, esp. as a symbol of mortality.

**death's-head moth** /ˈ– mɒθ/, *n.* a European hawkmoth, *Acherontia atropos,* having markings on the back of the thorax resembling a human skull.

**deathsman** /ˈdɛθsmən/, *n., pl.* **-men.** *Archaic.* an executioner.

**death toll** /ˈdɛθ toʊl/, *n.* the number of people killed, esp. in accidents, natural disasters, etc., at or over a given time.

**deathtrap** /ˈdɛθtræp/, *n.* **1.** a structure or building which is unsafe, and esp. one which is a fire-risk. **2.** any dangerous circumstance or situation.

**death warrant** /ˈdɛθ wɒrənt/, *n.* **1.** an official order authorising the execution of the sentence of death. **2.** anything which ends hope, expectation, etc.

**deathwatch** /ˈdɛθwɒtʃ/, *n.* **1.** a vigil beside a dying or dead person. **2.** a guard set over a condemned person before execution.

**deathwatch beetle** /– ˈbitl/, *n.* any of certain beetles of the family Anobiidae which infest timbers. The ticking sound caused by their heads tapping against wood was thought to presage death.

**death-wish** /ˈdɛθ-wɪʃ/, *n.* **1.** the desire, esp. subconscious, for one's own death, or sometimes for the death of another. **2. have a death-wish,** *Colloq.* to pursue a course of action which is against one's own interests.

**deb** /dɛb/, *n.* →**debutante.** [shortened form]

**deb.,** debenture.

**debacle** /deɪ'bakəl, də-/, *n.* **1.** a general break-up or rout; sudden overthrow or collapse; overwhelming disaster. **2.** a breaking up of ice in a river. **3.** a violent rush of waters. [F, from *débâcler* unbar, clear, from *dé-* DIS-[1] + *bâcler* bar (from L *baculum* stick, rod)]

**debag** /di'bæg/, *v.t.,* **-bagged, -bagging.** *Colloq.* to remove the trousers of, as a joke or punishment.

**debar** /di'ba, də-/, *v.t.,* **-barred, -barring. 1.** to bar out or exclude from a place or condition. **2.** to prevent or prohibit (an action, etc.). [F *débarrer,* OF *desbarrer,* from *des-* DIS-[1] + *barrer* BAR[1], *v.*] – **debarment,** *n.*

**debark** /di'bak/, *v.i.* **1.** to disembark. *–v.t.* **2.** to unload, as from a ship. [F *débarquer,* from *dé-* DIS-[1] + *barque* BARQUE] – **debarkation** /diba'keɪʃən/, *n.*

**debase** /də'beɪs/, *v.t.,* **-based, -basing. 1.** to reduce in quality or value; adulterate. **2.** to lower in rank or dignity. [DE- + obs. *base* (aphetic var. of ABASE)] – **debasement,** *n.* – **debaser,** *n.* – **debasingly,** *adv.*

**debatable** /də'beɪtəbəl/, *adj.* **1.** capable of being debated. **2.** in dispute. Also, **debateable.**

**debate** /də'beɪt/, *n., v.,* **-bated, -bating.** *–n.* **1.** a discussion, esp. of a public question in an assembly. **2.** deliberation; consideration. **3.** a systematic contest of speakers in which two opposing points of view of a proposition are advanced. *–v.i.* **4.** to engage in discussion, esp. in a legislative or public assembly. **5.** to deliberate; consider; discuss or argue. *–v.t.* **6.** to discuss or argue (a question), as in a public assembly. **7.** to dispute about. **8.** to deliberate upon; consider. **9.** *Archaic.* to contend for or over. [ME *debate(n),* from OF *debatre,* from *de-* DE- + *batre* BEAT] – **debater,** *n.*

**debauch** /də'bɔtʃ/, *v.t.* **1.** to corrupt by sensuality, intemperance, etc.; seduce. **2.** to corrupt or pervert; deprave. **3.** *Obs.* to lead away, as from allegiance or duty. *–v.i.* **4.** to indulge in a debauch. *–n.* **5.** a period of debauchery. **6.** debauchery. [F *débaucher,* OF *desbaucher* seduce from duty] – **debauched,** *adj.* – **debaucher,** *n.* – **debauchment,** *n.*

**debauchee** /dəbɔ'tʃi/, *n.* one addicted to excessive indulgence in sensual pleasures; one given to debauchery. [F *débauché,* pp. of *débaucher* DEBAUCH]

**debauchery** /də'bɔtʃəri/, *n., pl.* **-eries. 1.** excessive indulgence in sensual pleasures; intemperance. **2.** *Obs.* seduction from virtue, allegiance, or duty.

**de bene esse** /ˌdeɪ ˌbɛni 'ɛsi/, *adj. Law.* (of evidence) valid for the time being, but to be considered more fully later. It refers esp. to an examination, out of court before trial, of witnesses who are old, dangerously ill or about to leave the country, on the terms that if the witness continues to be ill or absent, their evidence is to be read at the trial, but if they recover or return, their evidence is to be taken in the usual manner. [ML: lit., of well-being]

**debenture** /də'bɛntʃə/, *n.* **1.** a note or certificate acknowledging a debt, as given by an incorporated company; a bond or one of a series of bonds. **2.** a deed containing a charge or mortgage on a company's assets; a mortgage debenture. **3.** a certificate of drawback issued at a customs house. [L *dēbentur* there are owing]

**debenture stock** /'– stɒk/, *n.* a series or group of debentures for a single debt.

**debil-debil** /'dɛbəl-dɛbəl/, *n.* a devil. [Aboriginal pidgin]

**debil-debil country** /'– ˌkʌntri/, *n.* harsh terrain not easily traversed.

**debilitate** /də'bɪləteɪt/, *v.t.,* **-tated, -tating.** to make weak or feeble; weaken; enfeeble. [L *dēbilitātus,* pp., weakened] – **debilitation** /dəbɪlə'teɪʃən/, *n.* – **debilitative** /də'bɪlətətɪv/, *adj.*

**debility** /də'bɪləti/, *n., pl.* **-ties.** the state of being weak or feeble; weakness. [ME *debylite,* from L *dēbilitas* weakness]

**debit** /'dɛbət/, *n.* **1.** the recording of an entry of debt in an account. **2. a.** that which is entered in an account as a debt; a recorded item of debt. **b.** any entry, or the total shown, on the debit side. **c.** the side (left side) of an account on which such entries are made (opposed to *credit*). *–v.t.* **3.** to charge with a debt. **4.** to charge as a debt. **5.** to enter upon the debit side of an account. [L *dēbitum* something owed. See DEBT]

**debonair** /dɛbə'nɛə/, *adj.* **1.** of pleasant manners; courteous. **2.** gay; sprightly. Also, **debonaire, debonnaire.** [ME *debonere,* from OF *debonaire,* orig. phrase *de bon aire* of good disposition] – **debonairly,** *adv.* – **debonairness,** *n.*

**debouch** /də'buʃ/, *v.i.* **1.** to issue or emerge from a narrow opening. *–n.* **2.** →**débouché.** [F *déboucher,* from *dé-* DIS-[1] + *bouche* mouth (from L *bucca* cheek, mouth)]

**débouché** /deɪbu'ʃeɪ/, *n.* **1.** *Fort.* an opening in works for passing troops. **2.** an outlet; an exit. [F]

**debouchment** /də'buʃmənt/, *n.* **1.** the act or fact of debouching. **2.** a mouth or outlet, as of a river or pass.

**debourbage** /də'bɜbɪdʒ/, *n.* (in winemaking) the system of separating the deposits from the must before fermentation. [F: clearing]

**debride** /də'brid/, *v.t.,* **-brided, briding.** (in surgery) to remove lacerated tissue or foreign matter. – **debridement,** *n.*

**debrief** /di'brif/, *v.t. Orig. U.S.* to interrogate (a soldier, astronaut, diplomat, etc.) on return from a mission in order to assess the conduct and results of the mission. – **debriefing,** *n.*

**debris** /'dɛbri, 'deɪbri, də'bri/, *n.* **1.** the remains of anything broken down or destroyed; ruins; fragments; rubbish. **2.** *Geol.* an accumulation of loose fragments of rock, etc. Also, **débris.** [F *débris,* from OF *debrisier* break down, from *de-* DE- + *brisier* break (cf. BRUISE)]

**debt** /dɛt/, *n.* **1.** that which is owed; that which one person is bound to pay to or perform for another. **2.** a liability or obligation to pay or render something. **3.** the condition of being under such an obligation. **4.** *Theol.* an offence requiring reparation; a sin; a trespass. **5. bad debt,** a debt of which there is no prospect of payment. [ME *det,* from OF *dete,* from L *dēbitum* (thing) owed, properly pp. neut.]

**debt of honour,** *n.* a debt which is not legally recoverable, as a gambling debt.

**debtor** /'dɛtə/, *n.* one who is in debt or under obligations to another (opposed to *creditor*).

**debug** /di'bʌg/, *v.t.,* **-bugged, -bugging.** *Colloq.* **1.** to detect and remove faults in (an electronic system). **2.** *Computers.* to remove errors or incompatible logical conditions from a program. **3.** to detect and remove electronic listening devices from (a room or the like). – **debugger,** *n.*

**debunk** /di'bʌŋk/, *v.t. Colloq.* to strip of false sentiment, etc.; to make fun of.

**debus** /di'bʌs/, *v.i.,* **-bussed, -bussing.** *Chiefly Mil.* to alight from any vehicle. – **debussing,** *n.*

**debut** /'deɪbju, -bu, də'bu/, *n.* **1.** a first public appearance on a stage, on television, etc. **2.** a formal introduction and entrance into society. **3.** the beginning of a professional career, etc. [F, from *débuter* make the first stroke in a game, make one's first appearance, from *dé-* DE- + *but* goal, mark]

**debutaniser** /di'bjutənaɪzə/, *n.* that which removes by distillation butanes and butylenes.

**debutante** /'dɛbjətɒnt/, *n.* a girl making a debut, esp. into society. [F, fem. ppr. of *débuter.* See DEBUT] – **debutant,** *n. masc.*

**dec-** /dɛk-/, →**deka-.**

**dec.,** deceased.

**Dec.,** December.

**deca-** /'dɛkə-/, →**deka-.**

**decade** /'dɛkeɪd/, *n.* **1.** a period of ten years. **2.** a group, set, or series of ten. [F, from L *decas,* from Gk *dekás* a group of ten] – **decadal,** *adj.*

**decadence** /'dɛkədəns/, *n.* the act or process of falling into an inferior condition or state, esp. moral; decay; deterioration. Also, **decadency.** [F, from L *dē* DE- + *cadere* fall]

**decadent** /'dɛkədənt/, *adj.* **1.** deteriorating, as morally or aesthetically. *–n.* **2.** one who is decadent. – **decadently,** *adv.*

**decaffeinated** /di'kæfəneɪtəd/, *adj.* having had the caffeine removed: *decaffeinated coffee.*

**decagon** /'dɛkəgɒn, -gən/, *n.* a polygon having ten angles and ten sides. [ML *decagōnum.* See DECA-, -GON] – **decagonal** /də'kægənəl/, *adj.*

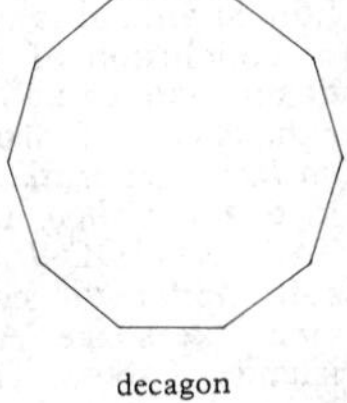
decagon

**decahedron** /dɛkə'hidrən/, *n., pl.* **-drons,**

**-dra** /-drə/. a solid figure having ten faces. – **decahedral,** *adj.*

**decal** /'dikæl/, *n.* **1.** the art or process of transferring pictures or designs from specially prepared paper to wood, metal, china, glass, etc. **2.** the paper bearing such a picture or design. *–v.t.* **3.** to transfer (a design) on to such a surface. [short for DECALCOMANIA]

**decalcify** /di'kælsəfaɪ/, *v.t.,* **-fied, -fying.** to deprive (esp. a bone) of lime or calcareous matter. – **decalcification** /di,kælsəfə'keɪʃən/, *n.*

**decalcomania** /di,kælkə'meɪniə/, *n.* →**decal.** [F *décalcomanie,* from *décalco-* (representing *décalquer* transfer a tracing of) + *manie* MANIA]

**decalescence** /dikə'lɛsəns/, *n.* (in the heating of iron) the sudden absorption of heat observed as it passes a certain temperature. – **decalescent,** *adj.*

**decamp** /di'kæmp/, *v.i.* **1.** to depart from a camp; break camp. **2.** to depart quickly, secretly, or unceremoniously. [F *décamper,* from *dé-* DIS-[1] + *camper* encamp] – **decampment,** *n.*

**decan** /'dɛkæn/, *n. Astrol.* one of three divisions of ten days in each zodiac sign.

**decanal** /də'keɪnəl/, *adj.* **1.** of or pertaining to a dean or his office. *–n.* **2.** →**decani.** [ML *decānus* dean + -AL[1]] – **decanally,** *adv.*

**decane** /'dɛkeɪn/, *n. Chem.* a hydrocarbon, $C_{10}H_{22}$, of the methane series, occurring in several isomeric forms.

**decani** /di'keɪnaɪ/, *n.* the portion of a cathedral choir on the south or dean's side. [ML: gen. of *decānus* dean]

**decant** /də'kænt/, *v.t.* **1.** to pour off gently, as liquor, without disturbing the sediment. **2.** to pour from one container into another. [ML *dēcanthāre.* See DE-, CANT[2]] – **decantation** /dikæn'teɪʃən/, *n.*

**decanter** /də'kæntə/, *n.* **1.** a bottle used for decanting. **2.** a vessel, usu. an ornamental bottle, from which wine, water, etc., are served at table.

**decapitate** /də'kæpəteɪt, di-/, *v.t.,* **-tated, -tating.** to cut off the head of; behead; kill by beheading. [ML *dēcapitātus,* pp. of *dēcapitāre,* from L *caput* head] – **decapitation** /dəkæpə'teɪʃən/, *n.* – **decapitator,** *n.*

**decapod** /'dɛkəpɒd/, *n.* **1.** any crustacean of the order Decapoda, including crabs, lobsters, crayfish, prawns, shrimps, etc., characterised by their five pairs of walking legs. **2.** any ten-armed dibranchiate cephalopod, as the cuttlefish, squid, etc. *–adj.* **3.** belonging to the Decapoda. **4.** having ten limbs. – **decapodous** /də'kæpədəs/, *adj.*

**decarb** /di'kab/, *n. Colloq.* decarbonisation.

**decarbonise** /di'kabənaɪz/, *v.t.,* **-nised, -nising.** to remove the carbon deposit from the walls of the combustion chamber and piston head of an internal-combustion engine. Also, **decarbonize.** – **decarbonisation** /di,kabənaɪ'zeɪʃən/, *n.*

**decarboxylase** /,dika'bɒksəleɪz/, *n.* any enzyme catalysing the loss of carbon dioxide from a substrate.

**decarburise** /di'kabjəraɪz/, *v.t.,* **-rised, -rising.** to remove carbon from the surface of a ferrous alloy or molten steel. Also, **decarburize.** – **decarburisation** /di,kabjəraɪ'zeɪʃən/, *n.*

**decartelise** /di'katəlaɪz/, *v.t.,* **-lised, -lising.** to break up or dissolve (a cartel, def. 1). Also, **decartelize.** – **decartelisation** /di,katəlaɪ'zeɪʃən/, *n.*

**decasualise** /di'kæʒjuəlaɪz/, *v.t.,* **-lised, -lising. 1.** to reduce or eliminate the employment of casual labour in (a firm, industry, etc.). **2.** to change the status of (a casual worker), as to permanent employment. Also, **decasualize.** – **decasualisation** /di,kæʒjuəlaɪ'zeɪʃən/, *n.*

**decasyllabic** /,dɛkəsɪ'læbɪk/, *adj.* **1.** having ten syllables. *–n.* **2.** (*pl.*) decasyllabic verse.

**decasyllable** /,dɛkə'sɪləbəl/, *n.* a line or verse of ten syllables.

**decathlon** /də'kæθlɒn/, *n.* an athletic contest comprising ten different events, and won by the contestant having the highest total score. [DECA- + Gk *âthlon* contest]

**decay** /di'keɪ, də-/, *v.i.* **1.** to fall away from a state of excellence, prosperity, health, etc.; deteriorate; decline. **2.** to become decomposed; rot. **3.** *Physics.* **a.** (of a radioactive substance) to transform into a daughter product. **b.** (of an elementary particle) to transform into a more stable particle. **4.** *Electronics.* (of a current or voltage) to fall away after the source of energy has been removed from the circuit. *–v.t.* **5.** to cause to decay. *–n.* **6.** a gradual falling into an inferior condition; progressive decline. **7.** loss of strength, health, intellect, etc. **8.** decomposition; rotting. **9.** *Physics.* the disintegration of a radioactive substance or the transformation of an elementary particle into one of greater stability. **10.** *Mil.* the decrease in the radiation intensity of any radioactive material with respect to time. **11.** *Obs.* a wasting disease, esp. consumption. [ME *decay(en),* from OF *decair,* from *de-* DE- + *cair* (from L *cadere* fall)]

**decd,** deceased.

**decease** /də'sis/, *n., v.,* **-ceased, -ceasing.** *–n.* **1.** departure from life; death. *–v.i.* **2.** to depart from life; die. [ME *deces,* from OF, from L *dēcessus* departure, death]

**deceased** /də'sist/, *adj.* **1.** dead. *–n.* **2. the deceased,** the dead person or persons.

**deceased estate** /– ə'steɪt/, *n.* →**estate** (def. 2e).

**deceit** /də'sit/, *n.* **1.** the act or practice of deceiving; concealment or perversion of the truth for the purpose of misleading; fraud; cheating. **2.** an act or device intended to deceive; a trick; stratagem. **3.** deceiving quality; falseness. [ME *deceite,* from OF, from *deceveir* DECEIVE]

**deceitful** /də'sitfəl/, *adj.* **1.** full of deceit; given to deceiving. **2.** misleading; fraudulent; deceptive. – **deceitfully,** *adv.* – **deceitfulness,** *n.*

**deceive** /də'siv/, *v.,* **-ceived, -ceiving.** *–v.t.* **1.** to mislead by a false appearance or statement; delude. **2.** to be unfaithful to; commit adultery against. **3.** *Obs.* to beguile or while away (time, etc.). *–v.i.* **4.** to practise deceit; act deceitfully. [ME *deceyve(n),* from OF *deceveir,* from L *dēcipere* catch, ensnare, deceive] – **deceivable,** *adj.* – **deceivableness, deceivability** /dəsivə'bɪləti/, *n.* – **deceiver,** *n.* – **deceivably,** *adv.* – **deceivingly,** *adv.*

**decelerate** /di'sɛləreɪt/, *v.,* **-rated, -rating.** *–v.i.* **1.** to decrease in velocity. *–v.t.* **2.** to decrease the velocity of. [DE- + (AC)CELERATE] – **deceleration** /di,sɛlə'reɪʃən/, *n.* – **decelerator,** *n.*

**December** /də'sɛmbə/, *n.* the twelfth month of the year, containing 31 days. [L: the tenth month of the early Roman year; replacing ME *decembre,* from OF]

**decency** /'disənsi/, *n., pl.* **-cies. 1.** the state or quality of being decent. **2.** conformity to the recognised standards of propriety, good taste, modesty, etc. **3.** something decent or proper. **4.** (*pl.*) the requirements or observances of decent life or conduct.

**decennary** /də'sɛnəri/, *n., pl.* **-ries.** →**decennium.** [L *decennis* of ten years + -ARY[1]]

**decennial** /də'sɛniəl/, *adj.* **1.** of or for ten years. **2.** occurring every ten years. *–n.* **3.** a decennial anniversary. **4.** its celebration. – **decennially,** *adv.*

**decennium** /də'sɛniəm/, *n., pl.* **-cenniums, -cennia** /-'sɛniə/. a period of ten years; a decade. [L, from *decennis* of ten years]

**decent** /'disənt/, *adj.* **1.** fitting; appropriate. **2.** conforming to recognised standards of propriety, good taste, modesty, etc., as in behaviour or speech. **3.** respectable; worthy: *a decent family.* **4.** of seemly appearance: *decent clothes; are you decent?* **5.** fair; tolerable; passable: *a decent wage.* **6.** *Colloq.* kind; obliging: *thanks, that's decent of you.* [L *decens,* ppr., fitting] – **decently,** *adv.* – **decentness,** *n.*

**decentralise** /di'sɛntrəlaɪz/, *v.t.,* **-lised, -lising. 1.** to disperse (industry, population, etc.) from an area of concentration or density, esp. from large cities to relatively undeveloped rural areas. **2.** to undo the centralisation of administrative powers (of an organisation, government, etc.). Also, **decentralize.** – **decentralisation** /di,sɛntrəlaɪ'zeɪʃən/, *n.*

**decentre** /di'sɛntə/, *v.t.,* **-tred, -tring. 1.** to put out of centre. **2.** to make eccentric. Also, *U.S.,* **decenter.**

**deception** /də'sɛpʃən/, *n.* **1.** the act of deceiving. **2.** the state of being deceived. **3.** something that deceives or is intended to deceive; an artifice; a sham; a cheat. [ME *decepcioun,* from LL *dēceptio,* from L *dēcipere* DECEIVE]

**deceptive** /də'sɛptɪv/, *adj.* apt or tending to deceive. [NL *dēceptīvus*] – **deceptively,** *adv.* – **deceptiveness,** *n.*

**decerebrate** /di'sɛrəbreɪt/, *v.t.,* **-brated, -brating.** *Surg.* to interrupt the connection between the brain or a part of the brain and the nervous system.

**decerebration** /disɛrə'breɪʃən/, *n. Surg.* **1.** the interruption of the paths of connection between the brain and the rest of the nervous system. **2.** interruption of the brain's influence on the nervous system by spinal cord transection.

**deci-** /'dɛsi-/, a prefix denoting $10^{-1}$ of a given unit, as in *decigram. Symbol:* d [combining form representing L *decem* ten, *decimus* tenth]

**decibel** /'dɛsəbɛl/, *n.* a unit expressing difference in power, usu. between electric or acoustic signals, or between some particular signal and a reference level understood; equal to one tenth of a bel. *Symbol:* dB

**decid.,** deciduous.

**decide** /də'saɪd/, *v.,* **-cided, -ciding.** *–v.t.* **1.** to determine or settle (a question, controversy, struggle, etc.) by giving victory to one side. **2.** to adjust or settle (anything in dispute or doubt). **3.** to bring (a person) to a decision. *–v.i.* **4.** to settle something in dispute or doubt. **5.** to pronounce a judgment; come to a conclusion. [ME *decide(n),* from L *dēcīdere* cut off, determine] – **decidable,** *adj.*

**decided** /də'saɪdəd/, *adj.* **1.** free from ambiguity; unquestionable; unmistakable. **2.** free from hesitation or wavering; resolute; determined. – **decidedly,** *adv.* – **decidedness,** *n.*

**decider** /də'saɪdə/, *n.* **1.** one who or that which decides. **2.** a decisive action, event, or the like. **3.** an extra race or game to decide a previously level contest.

**decidua** /də'sɪdʒuə/, *n.* the inner mucosal lining of the uterus which in some mammals is cast off at parturition. [NL, properly fem. of L *dēciduus.* See DECIDUOUS] – **decidual,** *adj.*

**deciduous** /də'sɪdʒuəs/, *adj.* **1.** shedding the leaves annually, as trees, shrubs, etc. **2.** falling off or shed at a particular season, stage of growth, etc., as leaves, horns, teeth, etc. **3.** not permanent; transitory. [L *dēciduus* falling down] – **deciduously,** *adv.* – **deciduousness,** *n.*

**decile** /'dɛsaɪl/, *n. Statistics.* one of the values of a variable which divides its distribution into ten groups having equal frequencies. [L *dec(em)* ten + -ILE]

**decimal** /'dɛsəməl/, *adj.* **1.** pertaining to tenths, or to the number ten. **2.** proceeding by tens: *a decimal system.* *–n.* **3.** a decimal fraction. **4.** a decimal number. [L *decimus* tenth + -AL[1]] – **decimally,** *adv.*

**decimal classification** /– klæsəfə'keɪʃən/, *n.* (in libraries) a system of classifying books into ten main subject-classes, with further subdivision by tens in these classes, the divisions being represented by the numbers of a decimal system.

**decimal currency** /– 'kʌrənsi/, *n.* currency in which units are graded in multiples of ten: *1 dollar × $10^2$ becomes $0.01.*

**decimal fraction** /– 'frækʃən/, *n.* a fraction whose denominator is some power of ten, usu. indicated by a dot (the **decimal point**) written before the numerator, as $0.4 = \frac{4}{10}$; $0.126 = \frac{126}{1000}$.

**decimalise** /'dɛsəməlaɪz/, *v.t.,* **-lised, -lising.** to reduce to a decimal system. Also, **decimalize.** – **decimalisation** /ˌdɛsəməlaɪ'zeɪʃən/, *n.*

**decimal number** /ˌdɛsəməl 'nʌmbə/, *n. Maths.* any finite or infinite string of digits containing a decimal point: *1.0, 5.23, 3.14159 . . . are decimal numbers.*

**decimal place** /– 'pleɪs/, *n.* **1.** the position of a digit to the right of a decimal point: *in 9.623, 3 is in the third decimal place.* **2.** the number of digits to the right of a decimal point: *9.623 is a number in three decimal places.*

**decimal point** /– 'pɔɪnt/, *n.* (in the decimal system) a dot preceding the fractional part of a number.

**decimal system** /'– sɪstəm/, *n.* any system of counting or measurement whose units are powers of ten.

**decimate** /'dɛsəmeɪt/, *v.t.,* **-mated, -mating.** **1.** to destroy a great number or proportion of. **2.** to select by lot and kill every tenth man of. **3.** *Obs.* to take a tenth of or from. [L *decimātus,* pp.] – **decimation** /dɛsə'meɪʃən/, *n.* – **decimator,** *n.*

**decinormal** /dɛsi'nɔməl/, *adj. Chem.* (of a solution) containing one tenth of the equivalent weight of the constituent in question in one litre of solution.

**decipher** /də'saɪfə/, *v.t.* **1.** to make out the meaning of (poor or partially obliterated writing, etc.). **2.** to discover the meaning of (anything difficult to trace or understand). **3.** to interpret by the use of a key, as something written in cipher. – **decipherable,** *adj.* – **decipherer,** *n.* – **decipherment,** *n.*

**decision** /də'sɪʒən/, *n.* **1.** the act of deciding; determination (of a question or doubt). **2.** a judgment, as one formally pronounced by a court. **3.** a making up of one's mind. **4.** that which is decided; a resolution. **5.** the quality of being decided; firmness, as of character. [L *dēcīsio* a cutting down, decision]

**decisive** /də'saɪsɪv/, *adj.* **1.** having the power or quality of determining; putting an end to controversy: *a decisive fact, test, etc.* **2.** characterised by or displaying decision; resolute; determined. – **decisively,** *adv.* – **decisiveness,** *n.*

**deck** /dɛk/, *n.* **1.** a horizontal platform extending from side to side of a ship or of part of a ship, forming a covering for the space below and itself serving as a floor. **2.** any platform or part suggesting the deck of a ship, as the top surface of a surfboard. **3.** a floor, platform or tier, as in a bus or bridge. **4.** the horizontal platform on or in a tape-recorder, gramophone, or the like, above which the turntable or spools revolve, and which often incorporates some of the controls. **5.** *Chiefly U.S.* a pack of playing cards. **6. clear the decks, a.** *Naut.* to prepare for combat, as by removing from the deck all unnecessary gear. **b.** *Colloq.* to prepare for action of any kind. **7. hit the deck,** *Colloq.* **a.** to fall to the ground or floor. **b.** to rise from bed. **8. not playing with a full deck,** *Colloq.* insane. **9. on deck,** *Colloq.* **a.** on duty; on hand; present at the time. **b.** alive: *is he still on deck?* *–v.t.* **10.** to clothe or attire in something ornamental; array. **11.** *Naut.* to furnish with or as with a deck, as a vessel. **12.** *Colloq.* to knock (someone) to the ground. [MD *decken* cover, c. G *decken*]

**deck cargo** /'– ˌkagoʊ/, *n.* cargo carried on an open deck of a ship.

**deckchair** /'dɛktʃɛə/, *n.* a portable folding chair with back and seat of canvas or similar material, often in one piece.

**decker** /'dɛkə/, *n.* **1.** one who or that which decks. **2.** a ship, vehicle, bed, etc., having a certain number of levels: *a double decker* (bus), *a three decker* (ship). **3.** a type of hat.

**deckhand** /'dɛkhænd/, *n.* **1.** any sailor, over the age of seventeen, who has served at sea for at least twelve months. **2.** any sailor who works on the deck.

**deck head** /'dɛk hɛd/, *n. Naut.* the underneath of any deck in the compartment below.

**deckhouse** /'dɛkhaʊs/, *n.* a large structure erected on the deck of a ship in which cabins, galley, wheelhouse, etc. are located.

**decking** /'dɛkɪŋ/, *n.* **1.** the material, or a unit or units of the material, composing a deck or roof. **2.** material, as waterproofed paper, for forming a cover or deck. **3.** a flat roof. **4.** the deck of a jetty, quay or bridge. **5.** adornment or embellishment.

**deckle** /'dɛkəl/, *n.* **1.** (in paper making) a frame which forms the paper pulp, fixing the size of a sheet of paper. **2.** deckle edge. [G *Deckel,* diminutive of *Decke* cover]

**deckle edge** /– 'ɛdʒ/, *n.* the untrimmed edge of handmade paper, formerly much used for ornamental effect in fine books.

**deckle-edged** /'dɛkəl-ɛdʒd/, *adj.* having a deckle edge.

**deck officer** /'dɛk ɒfəsə/, *n.* **1.** a ship's officer concerned with navigation, stowage of cargo etc., as distinct from other officers such as engineer.

**deck quoit** /'– kɔɪt/, *n.* one of a set of rope or rubber rings thrown in any of various games known as **deck quoits,** as on the deck of a ship.

**deck tennis** /'– tɛnəs/, *n.* any of several games adapted from tennis for playing in the confined space of a ship's deck.

**decl.,** declension.

**declaim** /də'kleɪm/, *v.i.* **1.** to speak aloud rhetorically; make a formal speech. **2.** to inveigh (fol. by *against*). **3.** to speak or write for oratorical effect, without sincerity or sound argument. *–v.t.* **4.** to utter aloud in a rhetorical manner. [ME *declame(n),* from L *dēclāmāre* cry aloud] – **declaimer,** *n.*

**declamation** /dɛklə'meɪʃən/, *n.* **1.** the act or art of declaiming. **2.** an exercise in oratory or elocution. **3.** speech or writing for oratorical effect.

**declamatory** /də'klæmətəri, -tri/, *adj.* **1.** pertaining to or characterised by declamation. **2.** merely rhetorical; stilted.

i = peat ɪ = pit ɛ = pet æ = pat a = part ɒ = pot ʌ = putt ɔ = port ʊ = put u = pool ɜ = pert ə = apart aɪ = buy eɪ = bay ɔɪ = boy aʊ = how oʊ = hoe ɪə = here ɛə = hair ʊə = tour g = give θ = thin ð = then ʃ = show ʒ = measure tʃ = choke dʒ = joke ŋ = sing j = you õ = Fr. bon

**declarable** /də'klɛərəbəl/, *adj.* **1.** capable of being declared or proved. **2.** (of goods, etc.) required by law to be declared at customs; dutiable.

**declarant** /də'klɛərənt/, *n.* one who makes a declaration, esp. a legal declaration.

**declaration** /dɛklə'reɪʃən/, *n.* **1.** a positive, explicit, or formal statement, announcement, etc. **2.** a proclamation: *a declaration of war.* **3.** that which is proclaimed. **4.** the document embodying the proclamation. **5.** a statement of goods, etc., liable to duty. **6.** *Law.* the decision of a court or judge on a question of law or rights. **7.** *Law. Obs.* **a.** the formal statement in which a plaintiff presents his claim in an action. **b.** a complaint. **8.** *Cricket.* the voluntary closure of an innings before all ten wickets have fallen. **9.** *Cards.* **a.** *Bridge.* a bid, esp. the successful bid. **b.** the statement during the game of the points earned by a player, in bezique or other games.

**declarative** /də'klærətɪv/, *adj.* serving to declare, make clear, or explain; declaratory. – **declaratively,** *adv.*

**declaratory** /də'klærətri/, *adj.* serving to explain rather than pronounce: *the court gave a declaratory judgment, parliament passed a declaratory act.* – **declaratorily** /də'klærətərəli/, *adv.*

**declare** /də'klɛə/, *v.,* **-clared, -claring.** *–v.t.* **1.** to make known, esp. in explicit or formal terms. **2.** to announce officially; proclaim. **3.** to state emphatically; affirm. **4.** to manifest; reveal. **5.** to make due statement of (dutiable goods, etc.). **6.** to make (a dividend) payable. **7.** *Bridge.* to signify (a certain suit) as trumps or to establish the bid at no-trump. *–v.i.* **8.** to make a declaration. **9.** to proclaim oneself. **10.** *Cricket.* to close an innings voluntarily before all ten wickets have fallen. [ME *declar(en),* from L *dēclārāre* make clear] – **declarer,** *n.*

**declared** /də'klɛəd/, *adj.* avowed; professed. – **declaredly** /də'klɛərədli/, *adv.*

**declass** /di'klas/, *v.t.* to remove or degrade from one's class (social or other).

**déclassé** /ˌdeɪkla'seɪ/, *adj.* fallen or lowered in social rank, class, etc. [F] – **déclassée,** *adj. fem.*

**declassify** /di'klæsəfaɪ/, *v.t.,* **-fied, -fying.** to remove the classification (def. 3) from; take off the security list.

**declension** /də'klɛnʃən/, *n.* **1.** *Gram.* **a.** the inflection of nouns, and of words similarly inflected, for categories such as case and number. For example (Latin): *puella, puellam, puellae, puellae, etc.* **b.** the whole set of inflected forms of such a word, or the recital thereof in a fixed order. **c.** a class of such words having similar sets of inflected forms, as the Latin *second declension.* **2.** an act or instance of declining. **3.** a bending, sloping, or moving downward. **4.** deterioration; decline. **5.** deviation, as from a standard. [irregularly from L *dēclīnātio* a bending aside, inflection, probably modelled on *dēscensio* descent] – **declensional,** *adj.*

**declinate** /'dɛklənеɪt/, *adj. Chiefly Bot.* having a downward curve; bending away, as from the horizontal.

**declination** /dɛklə'neɪʃən/, *n.* **1.** *Astron.* the angular distance of a heavenly body from the celestial equator, measured on a great circle passing through the celestial pole and the body. **2.** Also, **magnetic declination, variation.** the horizontal angle between the direction of true north and magnetic north at any place. **3.** a bending, sloping, or moving downward. **4.** *Chiefly U.S.* deterioration; decline. **5.** *U.S.* a swerving or deviating, as from a standard. **6.** *Obs.* a polite refusal.

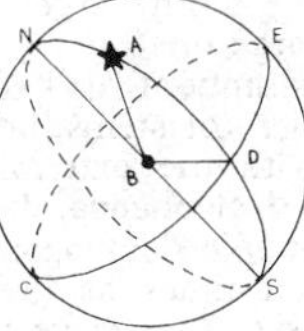

declination: A, star; B, earth; N, north celestial pole; S, south celestial pole; DBA, declination of star; CDE, celestial equator

**declinator** /'dɛklənеɪtə/, *n.* a power-driven machine for transporting goods or people up and down a steep slope.

**declinatory** /də'klaɪnətri/, *adj.* expressing refusal; implying declination.

**declinature** /də'klaɪnətʃə/, *n.* the act or fact of refusing.

**decline** /də'klaɪn/, *v,* **-clined, -clining;** /də'klaɪn, 'diklaɪn/, *n.* *–v.t.* **1.** to withhold consent to do, enter upon, or accept; refuse: *he declined to say more about it, he declined the offer with thanks.* **2.** to cause to slope or incline downward. **3.** *Gram.* **a.** to inflect (a noun, pronoun, or adjective). In Latin, *puella* is declined *puella, puellam, puellae, puellae, puellā* in the five cases of the singular. **b.** to recite or display all, or some subset, of the inflected forms of a noun, pronoun, or adjective in a fixed order. *–v.i.* **4.** to express courteous refusal; refuse. **5.** to bend or slant down; slope or trend downward; descend. **6.** to draw towards the close, as the day. **7.** to fail in strength, vigour, character, value, etc.; deteriorate. **8.** *Gram.* to be characterised by declension. *–n.* **9.** a downward incline or slope. **10.** a failing or gradual loss, as in strength, character, value, etc.; deterioration; diminution. **11.** progress downwards or towards a close, as of the sun or the day. **12.** a gradual diminution of the physical powers, as in later life or in disease. **13.** the last part or phase. [ME *decline(n),* from OF *decliner,* from L *dēclīnāre* bend from, avoid, inflect] – **declinable,** *adj.* – **decliner,** *n.*

**declinometer** /dɛklə'nɒmətə/, *n.* an instrument for measuring magnetic declination. [*declino-* (combining form representing L *dēclīnāre* bend from) + -METER[1]]

**declivitous** /də'klɪvətəs/, *adj.* rather steep.

**declivity** /də'klɪvəti/, *n., pl.* **-ties.** a downward slope, as of ground (opposed to *acclivity*). [L *dēclīvitas* slope]

**declivous** /də'klaɪvəs/, *adj.* sloping downwards.

**declutch** /di'klʌtʃ/, *v.i.* to disengage the clutch of motor vehicles, etc.

**decoct** /də'kɒkt/, *v.t.* to boil (a medicinal substance, etc.) in water, etc.; to extract the essence or principles. [L *dēcoctus,* pp., boiled down]

**decoction** /də'kɒkʃən/, *n.* **1.** the act of boiling in water, in order to extract the peculiar properties or virtues. **2.** an extract obtained by decocting. **3.** water in which a substance, usu. animal or vegetable, has been boiled, and which thus contains the constituents or principles of the substance soluble in boiling water.

**decode** /di'koʊd/, *v.t.,* **-coded, -coding.** to translate from code into the original language or form.

**decoder** /di'koʊdə/, *n.* **1.** one who or that which decodes. **2.** *Computers.* a logic device which converts data from one number system to another.

**decoke** /di'koʊk/, *v.,* **-coked, -coking,** *n. Colloq. –v.t.* **1.** to decarbonise. *–n.* **2.** decarbonisation. [DE- + COKE[1]]

**decollate**[1] /di'kɒleɪt/, *v.t.,* **-lated, -lating.** to behead; decapitate. [L *dēcollātus,* pp., beheaded] – **decollation** /dikɒ'leɪʃən/, *n.* – **decollator,** *n.*

**decollate**[2] /'dɛkəleɪt, dikə'leɪt/, *v.t.,* **-lated, -lating.** to separate (multiple-layered stationery, etc.) into single copies. [DE- + COLLATE] – **decollator,** *n.*

**décolletage** /deɪ'kɒlətaʒ/, *n.* **1.** the neckline of a dress cut low in the front and across the shoulders. **2.** a décolleté garment or dress. [F, from *décolleter.* See DÉCOLLETÉ]

**décolleté** /deɪ'kɒləteɪ/, *adj.* **1.** (of a garment) low-necked. **2.** wearing a low-necked garment. [F, pp. of *décolleter* bare the neck of, from *col* neck]

**decolonise** /di'kɒlənaɪz/, *v.t.,* **-nised, -nising.** to release from the status of a colony; grant self-government or independence to. Also, **decolonize.** – **decolonisation** /diˌkɒlənaɪ'zeɪʃən/, *n.*

**decolour** /di'kʌlə/, *v.t.* **1.** to deprive of colour; bleach. Also, *U.S.,* **decolor.** *–v.i.* **2.** to lose colour. [L *dēcolōrāre* deprive of colour] – **decolouration** /diˌkʌlə'reɪʃən/, *n.*

**decolourant** /di'kʌlərənt/, *adj.* **1.** having the property of removing colour; bleaching. *–n.* **2.** a decolourant substance or agent. Also, **decolorant.**

**decolourise** /di'kʌləraɪz/, *v.t.,* **-ised, -ising.** →**decolour.** Also, **decolorise, -ize, decolourize.** – **decolourisation** /diˌkʌləraɪ'zeɪʃən/, *n.* – **decolouriser,** *n.*

**decompose** /dikəm'poʊz/, *v.,* **-posed, -posing.** *–v.t.* **1.** to separate or resolve into constituent parts or elements; disintegrate. *–v.i.* **2.** to rot; putrefy. [F *décomposer,* from *dé-* DIS-[1] + *composer* COMPOSE] – **decomposable,** *adj.* – **decomposer,** *n.*

decompound leaf

**decomposition** /dikɒmpə'zɪʃən/, *n.* **1.** the act or process of decomposing. **2.** the state of being decomposed; disintegration; decay.

**decompound** /dikəm'paʊnd/, *v.t.* **1.** (of

things already compound) to compound a second or further time. **2.** to decompose. *–adj.* **3.** *Bot.* divided into compound divisions. **4.** composed of things which are themselves compound.

**decompress** /dikəm'prɛs/, *v.t.* **1.** to cause to undergo decompression. **2.** to return a person to normal atmospheric pressure in a decompression chamber. *–v.i.* **3.** to undergo decompression.

**decompression** /dikəm'prɛʃən/, *n.* **1.** the act or process of relieving pressure. **2.** the gradual return of persons, as divers or construction workers, to normal atmospheric pressure after working in deep water or in air under compression.

**decompression chamber** /'– tʃeɪmbə/, *n.* a chamber in which the pressure can be varied, in which persons who have been subjected to abnormal pressure remain while returning gradually to atmospheric pressure; hyperbaric chamber.

**decompression sickness** /'– sɪknəs/, *n.* →**bend**[1] (def. 21).

**decongestant** /dikən'dʒɛstənt/, *n.* **1.** a substance used to relieve congestion esp. in the upper respiratory tract. *–adj.* **2.** relieving congestion.

**deconsecrate** /di'kɒnsəkreɪt/, *v.t.*, **-crated, crating.** to deprive of sanctity acquired through consecration; secularise.

**deconsolidate** /dikən'sɒlədeɪt/, *v.t.* to remove goods from a shipping container and place in a store awaiting acceptance or delivery. – **deconsolidation** /ˌdikənsɒlə'deɪʃən/, *n.*

**decontaminate** /dikən'tæməneɪt/, *v.t.*, **-nated, -nating.** to make (any object or area) safe for unprotected personnel by absorbing, making harmless, or destroying chemicals with which they have been in contact. – **decontamination** /ˌdikəntæmə'neɪʃən/, *n.*

**decontrol** /dikən'troʊl/, *v.*, **-trolled, -trolling,** *n.* *–v.t.* **1.** to remove controls, or from control. *–n.* **2.** removal of control.

**decor** /'deɪkɔ, 'dɛkɔ/, *n.* **1.** decoration in general. **2.** a style of decoration. **3.** *Theat.* scenic decoration; scenery. [F, from *décorer* decorate, from L *decorāre*]

**decorate** /'dɛkəreɪt/, *v.*, **-rated, -rating.** *–v.t.* **1.** to furnish or deck with something becoming or ornamental; embellish. **2.** to plan and execute the design, wallpaper, etc., and sometimes the furnishings of (a house, room, or the like). **3.** to confer distinction upon by a badge, a medal of honour, etc. *–v.i.* **4.** to be engaged in executing the decoration of a house, room, etc. [L *decorātus*, pp.]

**decoration** /dɛkə'reɪʃən/, *n.* **1.** the act of decorating. **2.** adornment; embellishment. **3.** the style in which a house, room, etc., is decorated. **4.** a badge of an order, medal, etc., conferred and worn as a mark of honour.

**decorative** /'dɛkərətɪv, 'dɛkrətɪv/, *adj.* **1.** serving or tending to decorate. **2.** attractive but superficial. – **decoratively,** *adv.* – **decorativeness,** *n.*

**decorator** /'dɛkəreɪtə/, *n.* **1.** one who decorates. **2.** one who professionally decorates houses or buildings, particularly their interior.

**decorator colours** /'– kʌləz/, *n.pl.* clear, bright, fashionable, eyecatching colours judged suitable for interior decoration.

**decorous** /'dɛkərəs/, *adj.* characterised by propriety in conduct, manners, appearance, character, etc. [L *decōrus* becoming, seemly] – **decorously,** *adv.* – **decorousness,** *n.*

**decorticate** /di'kɔtəkeɪt/, *v.t.*, **-cated, -cating.** to remove the bark, husk, or outer covering from. [L *dēcorticātus*, pp.] – **decortication** /dikɔtə'keɪʃən/, *n.* – **decorticator,** *n.*

**decorum** /də'kɔrəm/, *n.* **1.** propriety of behaviour, speech, dress, etc. **2.** that which is proper or seemly; fitness; congruity; propriety. **3.** an observance or requirement of polite society. [L, properly neut. of *decōrus* DECOROUS]

**decouple** /di'kʌpəl/, *v.t.*, **-led, -ling.** (in electronics) to reduce unwanted interference in a system or between two parts of a system.

**decoy** /də'kɔɪ, 'dikɔɪ/, *n.;* /də'kɔɪ/, *v.* *–n.* **1.** one who entices or allures, as into a trap, danger, etc. **2.** anything used as a lure. *–v.t.* **3.** to lure by or as by a decoy. [var. of *coy* (now d.), both from D (*de*) *kooi* (the) cage, from L *cavea* CAGE] – **decoyer,** *n.*

**decrease** /də'kris/, *v.*, **-creased, -creasing;** /'dikris, də'kris/, *n.* *–v.i.* **1.** to diminish gradually in extent, quantity, strength, power, etc. *–v.t.* **2.** to make less; cause to diminish. *–n.* **3.** a process of growing less, or the resulting condition; gradual diminution. **4.** the amount by which a thing is lessened. [ME *decrese(n)*, from OF *decreiss-*, from L *dēcrescere* grow less] – **decreasingly,** *adv.*

**decree** /də'kri/, *n., v.*, **-creed, -creeing.** *–n.* **1.** an ordinance or edict promulgated by civil or other authority. **2.** *Law.* a judicial decision or order. **3.** *Theol.* one of the eternal purposes of God, by which events are fore-ordained. *–v.t.* **4.** to ordain or decide by decree. *–v.i.* **5.** to issue a decree. [ME *decre*, from OF, var. of *decret*, from L *dēcrētum*, properly pp. neut.]

**decree absolute** /– 'æbsəlut/, *n. Law.* See **absolute** (def. 9).

**decree nisi** /– 'naɪsaɪ/, *n. Law.* See **nisi.**

**decrement** /'dɛkrəmənt/, *n.* **1.** the process or fact of decreasing; gradual diminution. **2.** the amount lost by diminution. **3.** *Maths.* a negative increment. *–v.t.* **4.** *Computers.* to reduce the numerical contents of (a counter).

**decrepit** /də'krɛpət/, *adj.* broken down or weakened by old age; feeble; infirm. [L *dēcrepitus*, lit., noiseless] – **decrepitly,** *adv.*

**decrepitate** /də'krɛpəteɪt/, *v.*, **-tated, -tating.** *–v.t.* **1.** to roast or calcine (salt, etc.) so as to cause crackling or until crackling ceases. *–v.i.* **2.** to make a crackling noise, as salt in roasting. [NL *dēcrepitātus* crackled down] – **decrepitation** /dəkrɛpə'teɪʃən/, *n.*

**decrepitude** /də'krɛpətʃud/, *n.* decrepit condition; feebleness, esp. from old age.

**decresc.,** *Music.* decrescendo.

**decrescendo** /dikrə'ʃɛndoʊ/, *adv., n., pl.* **-dos.** *Music.* *–adv.* **1.** gradually reducing force or loudness; diminuendo (opposed to *crescendo*). *–n.* **2.** a gradual reduction in force or loudness. **3.** a passage of music in which there is a decrescendo. [It. *decrescere* DECREASE]

**decrescent** /də'krɛsənt/, *adj.* **1.** decreasing. **2.** waning, as the moon. [L *dēcrescens*, ppr., decreasing]

**decretal** /də'kritl/, *adj.* **1.** pertaining to, of the nature of, or containing a decree or decrees. *–n.* **2.** a papal document authoritatively determining some point of doctrine or church law. [ME *decretale*, from ML, from L *dēcrētum* DECREE]

**decretive** /də'kritɪv/, *adj.* having the force of a decree; pertaining to a decree.

**decretory** /'dɛkrətəri, -tri/, *adj.* **1.** pertaining to or following a decree. **2.** established by a decree; judicial.

**decrial** /də'kraɪəl/, *n.* the act of decrying; disparagement.

**decry** /də'kraɪ/, *v.t.*, **-cried, -crying.** **1.** to speak disparagingly of; censure as faulty or worthless. **2.** to condemn or depreciate by proclamation, as foreign or obsolete coins. [F *décrier*, from *dé-* DIS-[1] + *crier* CRY] – **decrier,** *n.*

**decrypt** /di'krɪpt/, *v.t. Mil.* to convert a cryptogram into plain text by a reversal of the encryption process. This does not include solution by cryptanalysis. – **decryption,** *n.*

**decuman** /'dɛkjumən/, *adj.* **1.** large or immense, as a wave. **2.** every tenth in a series. [L *decumānus*, var. of *decimānus* of the tenth, large (from the notion that every tenth wave is a large one)]

**decumbent** /də'kʌmbənt/, *adj.* **1.** lying down; recumbent. **2.** *Bot.* (of stems, branches, etc.) lying or trailing on the ground with the extremity tending to ascend. [L *dēcumbens*, ppr.] – **decumbence, decumbency,** *n.* – **decumbently,** *adv.*

**decuple** /'dɛkjəpəl/, *adj., n., v.*, **-pled, -pling.** *–adj.* **1.** tenfold; ten times as great. *–n.* **2.** a tenfold quantity or multiple. *–v.t.* **3.** to make ten times as great. [F, from L *decuplus* tenfold]

**decurrent** /də'kʌrənt/, *adj. Bot.* extending down the stem below the place of insertion, as certain leaves. [L *dēcurrens*, ppr., running down] – **decurrently,** *adv.*

**decussate** /di'kʌseɪt, 'dɛkəseɪt/, *v.*, **-sated, -sating;** /di'kʌseɪt, -ət/, *adj.* *–v.t.* **1.** to cross in the form of the letter X. *–v.i.* **2.** to intersect. *–adj.* **3.** in the form of the letter X; crossed; intersected. **4.** *Bot.* (of leaves, etc.) arranged along the stem in pairs, each pair at right angles to the pair next above or below. [L *decussātus*, pp., divided in the form of an X] – **decussately,** *adv.* – **decussation** /dikə'seɪʃən, dɛkə-/, *n.*

decurrent leaf

**dedans** /də'dænz/, *n.* an open gallery at the service end of a royal tennis court.

**dedicate** /'dɛdəkeɪt/, *v.*, **-cated, -cating,** *adj.* *–v.t.* **1.** to set apart and consecrate to a deity or to a sacred purpose. **2.** to give up wholly or earnestly, as to some person or end; set apart or appropriate. **3.** to inscribe or address (a book, piece of music, etc.) to a patron, friend, etc., as in testimony of respect or affection. *–adj.* **4.** *Archaic.* consecrated. [L *dēdicātus,* pp., proclaimed, devoted] **– dedicator,** *n.*

decussate leaf

**dedicated** /'dɛdəkeɪtəd/, *adj.* **1.** wholly committed to something, as an ideal, way of life, etc.: *a dedicated socialist, a dedicated lexicographer.* **2.** *Computers.* of a computer used as a control computer.

**dedication** /dɛdə'keɪʃən/, *n.* **1.** the act of dedicating. **2.** the fact of being dedicated. **3.** an inscription prefixed or attached to a book, etc., dedicating it to some person.

**dedication of way,** *n. Law.* express or implied opening of a way on private land to public use.

**dedicatory** /'dɛdəkeɪtəri, 'dɛdəkətri/, *adj.* of or pertaining to dedication; serving as a dedication. Also, **dedicative.**

**deduce** /də'djus/, *v.t.*, **-duced, -ducing. 1.** to derive as a conclusion from something known or assumed; infer. **2.** to trace the derivation of; trace the course of. [L *dedūcere* lead down, derive] **– deducible,** *adj.*

**deduct** /də'dʌkt/, *v.t.* to take away, as from a sum or amount. [L *dēductus,* pp., led down, withdrawn] **– deductable, deductible,** *adj.*

**deduction** /də'dʌkʃən/, *n.* **1.** the act of deducting; subtraction; abatement. **2.** that which is deducted. **3.** the process of drawing a conclusion from something known or assumed. **4.** inference in which, granted the truth of the premises, the conclusion must be true.

**deductive** /də'dʌktɪv/, *adj.* based on inference from accepted principles; reasoning by deduction. **– deductively,** *adv.*

**dee** /di/, *n.* →**D**[2].

**deed** /did/, *n.* **1.** that which is done, performed, or accomplished; an act. **2.** an exploit or achievement. **3.** action or performance, often as contrasted with words. **4.** *Law.* a writing or document signed, sealed and delivered to effect a conveyance, esp. of real property. [ME *dede,* OE *dēd,* var. of *dæd,* c. G *Tat.* See DO[1]] **– deedless,** *adj.*

**deed poll** /'– poul/, *n.* a deed in the form of a declaration to all the world of the grantor's act and intention, as, for example, to change his name.

**deejay** /'didʒeɪ/, *n.* →**DJ.**

**deem** /dim/, *v.i.* **1.** to form or have an opinion; judge; think. *–v.t.* **2.** to hold as an opinion; think; regard. [ME *demen,* OE *dēman,* c. Goth. *dōmjan.* See DOOM]

**de-emphasise** /di-'ɛmfəsaɪz/, *v.t.*, **-sised, -sising.** to cease to emphasise; to reduce the practice of.

**deener** /'dinə/, *n. Obs. Colloq.* a shilling. Also, **deenah, deaner.** [orig. uncert.]

**deep** /dip/, *adj.* **1.** extending far downwards, inwards, or backwards. **2.** having a specified dimension downwards, inwards, or backwards: *a tank two metres deep.* **3.** situated far or a certain distance down, in, or back. **4.** extending far in width; broad: *a deep border.* **5.** outside the solar system: *deep space.* **6.** extending or advancing far down: *a deep dive.* **7.** coming from far down: *a deep breath.* **8.** lying below a surface. **9.** difficult to penetrate or understand; abstruse. **10.** not superficial; profound. **11.** grave or serious. **12.** heartfelt: *deep sorrow or prayer.* **13.** absorbing: *deep study.* **14.** great in measure; intense: *deep sleep.* **15.** (of colours) intense; dark and vivid: *a deep red.* **16.** low in pitch, as sound. **17.** having penetrating intellectual powers. **18.** profoundly cunning or artful. **19.** much involved: *deep in debt.* **20.** absorbed: *deep in thought.* **21.** *Cricket.* relatively far from the wicket: *the deep field.* **22.** *Tennis.* (of a shot) played from baseline to baseline. **23. go off the deep end,** *Colloq.* **a.** to get into a dither; to become hysterical. **b.** to go to extremes. **24. in deep water,** *Colloq.* in trouble or difficulties. *–n.* **25.** the deep part of the sea, a river, etc. **26.** *Oceanog.* oceanic areas of exceptional depth. **27.** any deep space or place. **28.** the part of greatest intensity, as of winter. **29.** *Naut.* the depth in fathoms estimated between two successive marks on a lead line. **30. the deep,** *Poetic.* the sea or ocean. *–adv.* **31.** to or at a considerable or specified depth. **32.** far on (in time). **33.** profoundly; intensely. [ME *depe,* OE *dēop,* c. G *tief.* See DIP, *v.*] **– deeply,** *adv.* **– deepness,** *n.*

**deep-bosomed** /'dip-bʊzəmd/, *adj.* having large breasts.

**deep-dyed** /'dip-daɪd/, *adj.* (*usu. pejor.*) thorough-going; unmitigated.

**deepen** /'dipən/, *v.t.* **1.** to make deep or deeper. *–v.i.* **2.** to become deep or deeper. **– deepener,** *n.*

**deep freeze** /dip 'friz/, *n.*, *v.*, **-froze, -frozen, -freezing.** *–n.* **1.** a locker or compartment in a refrigerator in which food can be quickly frozen and stored at a very low temperature; freezer. **2. give (someone) the deep freeze,** to ignore or act coldly towards. *–v.t.* **3.** to store or freeze in a deep freeze. [Trademark]

**deep-frier** /dip-'fraɪə/, *n.* a pan containing sufficient fat for deep-frying, and usu. a wire-mesh basket for holding the food being cooked. Also, **deep-fryer.**

**deep-fry** /dip-'fraɪ/, *v.t.*, **-fried, -frying.** to fry in a sufficient quantity of fat or oil to cover the food being cooked.

**deep ground** /dip 'graʊnd/, *n. Mining.* an underground lode, not outcropping on the surface.

**deep knees bend,** *n. Weightlifting.* a lift in which the contestant stands holding the barbell across the back of his shoulders, then squats until the tops of his thighs are parallel with the floor, before straightening up.

**deep-laid** /'dip-leɪd/, *adj.* carefully, cunningly, or secretly made: *deep-laid plot.*

**deep litter** /dip 'lɪtə/, *n. Agric.* a litter (def. 6) for animals and poultry formed on a dry limed sawdust base, into which droppings, feed spills, etc. are trampled, and naturally disinfected.

**deep mid-off** /– mɪd-'ɒf/, *n. Cricket.* →**long-off.**

**deep mid-on** /– mɪd-'ɒn/, *n. Cricket.* →**long-on.**

**deep north** /– 'nɔθ/, *n.* (*sometimes caps*) *Colloq.* Queensland, often so called on analogy with the deep south, because of supposed conservative and racially intolerant attitudes.

**deep-rooted** /'dip-rutəd/, *adj.* deeply rooted; firmly implanted.

**deep-sea** /'dip-si/, *adj.* of, pertaining to, or in the deeper parts of the sea.

**deep-seated** /'dip-sitəd/, *adj.* firmly implanted.

**deep south** /dip 'saʊθ/, *n.* (*also caps*) the south-eastern states of the United States, often cited as an area of racial intolerance.

**deep space** /– 'speɪs/, *n.* outside the solar system.

**deep structure** /'– strʌktʃə/, *n.* **1.** *Linguistics.* in transformational grammar, the grammatical relationships inherent in the elements of a phrase or sentence though not immediately apparent from the surface structure. **2.** the real nature of a problem or situation, as opposed to its superficial appearance.

**deepwater** /'dipwɔtə/, *adj.* **1.** (of a port) having the capacity to accommodate relatively large ships. **2.** ocean-going. **3.** living in the ocean as opposed to the shallow waters offshore.

**deer** /dɪə/, *n.*, *pl.* **deer. 1.** any animal of the family Cervidae, comprising ruminants most of which have solid deciduous horns or antlers (usu. the male only), as *Cervus elaphus* of Europe. **2.** any of the smaller species of this family, as distinguished from the moose, elk, etc. [ME *dere,* OE *dēor,* c. G *Tier* beast]

deer

**deerculler** /'dɪəkʌlə/, *n. N.Z.* a government-employed professional deer hunter.

**deergrass** /'dɪəgras/, *n.* a tufted perennial plant, *Trichophorum caespitosum,* family Cyperaceae, common in wet peaty situations throughout northern temperate regions.

**deerhound** /'dɪəhaʊnd/, *n.* one of a Scottish breed of dogs, allied to and resembling the greyhound but larger and having a shaggy coat.

deerhound

**deerlick** /ˈdɪəlɪk/, *n.* a spot of ground, naturally or artificially salty, where deer come to nibble or lick the earth.

**deer-mouse** /ˈdɪə-maʊs/, *n.* any of several species of mice, family Cricetidae, esp. the widely distributed white-footed mouse, *Peromyscus leucopus,* of North America.

**deer-park** /ˈdɪə-pak/, *n.* a park in which deer are kept.

**deerskin** /ˈdɪəskɪn/, *n.*,**1.** the skin of a deer. **2.** leather made from this. **3.** a garment made of such leather. *–adj.* **4.** made of deerskin.

**deerstalker** /ˈdɪəstɔkə/, *n.* **1.** one who stalks deer. **2.** a sportsman's helmet-shaped hat, having peaks back and front and earflaps. – **deerstalking,** *n.*

**de-escalate** /di-ˈeskəleɪt/, *v.t.,* **-lated, -lating.** to reduce one's commitment to or involvement in (a war, campaign, program, etc.). – **de-escalation** /di-ɛskəˈleɪʃən/, *n.*

**def.,** definition.

**deface** /dəˈfeɪs/, *v.t.,* **-faced, -facing. 1.** to mar the face or appearance of; disfigure. **2.** to blot out; efface. [ME, from F (obs.) *defacer,* earlier *desfacier,* from *des-* DIS-[1] + *face* FACE] – **defaceable,** *adj.* – **defacement,** *n.* – **defacer,** *n.*

**de facto** /di ˈfæktoʊ, də, deɪ/, *adj.* **1.** in fact; in reality. **2.** actually existing, whether with or without right (opposed to *de jure*). *–n.* **3.** Also, **de facto wife.** a woman who lives with a man as his wife, but is not married to him. **4.** Also, **de facto husband.** a man who lives with a woman as her husband, but is not married to her. [L: from the fact]

**defalcate** /ˈdifælkeɪt/, *v.i.,* **-cated, -cating.** *Law.* to be guilty of defalcation. [ML *dēfalcātus,* pp.] – **defalcator,** *n.*

**defalcation** /difælˈkeɪʃən/, *n. Law.* **1.** misappropriation of money, etc., held by a trustee or other fiduciary. **2.** the sum misappropriated.

**defamation** /dɛfəˈmeɪʃən/, *n.* the wrong of injuring another's reputation without good reason or justification; calumny; slander or libel.

**defamatory** /dəˈfæmətri, -ətəri/, *adj.* containing defamation; injurious to reputation; slanderous. – **defamatorily,** *adv.*

**defame** /diˈfeɪm, də-/, *v.t.,* **-famed, -faming. 1.** to attack the good name or reputation of, as by uttering or publishing maliciously anything injurious; slander; libel; calumniate. **2.** *Archaic.* to disgrace. [ME *defamen,* from ML *dēfāmāre;* replacing ME *diffamen,* from OF *diffamer,* from L *diffāmāre*] – **defamer,** *n.*

**default** /dəˈfɔlt/, *n.* **1.** failure to act; neglect. **2.** failure to meet financial obligations. **3.** *Law.* failure to perform an act or obligation legally required, esp. to appear in court or to plead at a time assigned. **4.** failure to participate in or complete anything, as a scheduled match. **5.** want; lack; absence: *owing to default of water. –v.i.* **6.** to fail in fulfilling or satisfying an engagement, claim, or obligation. **7.** to fail to meet financial engagements, or to account properly for money, etc., in one's care. **8.** *Law.* to fail to appear in court. **9. a.** to fail to participate in or complete anything, as a match. **b.** to lose a match by default. *–v.t.* **10.** to fail to perform or pay. **11.** to declare to be in default, esp. legally. **12.** *Law.* to lose by failure to appear in court. **13. a.** to fail to compete in (a game, race, etc.). **b.** to lose by default. [ME *defaute,* from OF, from *defaillir,* after *faute* and *faillir.* See FAULT]

**defaulter** /dəˈfɔltə/, *n.* **1.** one who defaults, or fails to fulfil an obligation, esp. a legal or financial one. **2.** a soldier convicted summarily of a minor offence and sentenced to restriction of privileges.

**default summons** /dəˈfɔlt sʌmənz/, *n. Law.* a summary method in certain inferior courts for the recovery of a debt or liquidated demand.

**defeasance** /dəˈfizəns/, *n. Law.* **1.** a rendering null and void. **2.** a condition on the performance of which a deed or other instrument is defeated or rendered void. **3.** a collateral deed or other writing embodying such a condition. [ME *defesance,* from OF, from *defesant,* ppr. of *de(s)faire* undo. See DEFEAT]

**defeasible** /dəˈfizəbəl/, *adj.* that may be annulled or terminated. – **defeasibleness, defeasibility** *n.*

**defeat** /dəˈfit/, *v.t.* **1.** to overcome in a contest, battle, etc.; vanquish; win or achieve victory over. **2.** to frustrate; thwart. **3.** *Law.* to annul. *–n.* **4.** the act of overcoming in a contest. **5.** an overthrow; vanquishment. **6.** a bringing to naught; frustration. **7.** undoing; destruction; ruin. [ME *defete(n),* from OF *de(s)fait,* pp. of *desfaire* undo, from *des-* DIS-[1] + *faire* (from L *facere* do)] – **defeater,** *n.*

**defeatism** /dəˈfitɪzəm/, *n.* the attitude, policy, or conduct of those who admit or expect defeat, usu. resulting from a premature decision that further struggle or effort is futile. – **defeatist,** *n., adj.*

**defecate** /ˈdɛfəkeɪt/, *v.,* **-cated, -cating.** *–v.i.* **1.** to void excrement. **2.** to become clear of dregs, impurities, etc. *–v.t.* **3.** to clear of dregs, impurities, etc.; purify; refine. [L *dēfaecātus,* pp., cleansed from dregs] – **defecation** /dɛfəˈkeɪʃən/, *n.* – **defecator,** *n.*

**defect** /ˈdifɛkt, dəˈfɛkt/, *n.;* /dəˈfɛkt/, *v.* *–n.* **1.** a falling short; a fault or imperfection. **2.** want or lack, esp. of something essential to perfection or completeness; deficiency. *–v.i.* **3.** to desert a country, cause, etc. [L *dēfectus* want, defect] – **defector,** *n.*

**defection** /dəˈfɛkʃən/, *n.* **1.** a falling away from allegiance, duty, virtue; desertion; backsliding; apostasy. **2.** failure; lack.

**defective** /dəˈfɛktɪv/, *adj.* **1.** having a defect; faulty; imperfect. **2.** *Psychol.* characterised by subnormal intelligence or behaviour. **3.** *Gram.* (of an inflected word or its inflection) lacking one or more of the inflected forms proper to most words of the same class in the language, as English *must* (which occurs only in the present tense). *–n.* **4.** one who or that which is defective. – **defectively,** *adv.* – **defectiveness,** *n.*

**defence** /dəˈfɛns/, *n.* **1.** resistance against attack; protection. **2.** something that defends, esp. a fortification. **3.** the defending of a cause or the like by speech, argument, etc. **4.** a speech, argument, etc., in vindication. **5.** *Law.* **a.** the denial or pleading of the defendant in answer to the claim or charge against him. **b.** the proceedings adopted by a defendant, or his legal agents, for defending himself. **c.** a defendant and his legal agents collectively. **6. a.** the practice or art of defending oneself or one's goal against attack, as in fencing, boxing, soccer, etc. **b.** the players in a team collectively whose primary function is to defend the goal, etc. **c.** a plan or system of defending. Also, *U.S.,* **defense.** [ME, from OF, from LL *dēfensa* prohibition, from L *dēfendere* ward off; replacing ME *defens,* from OF, from L *dēfensum* (thing) forbidden, properly pp. of *dēfendere*] – **defenceless,** *adj.* – **defencelessly,** *adv.* – **defencelessness,** *n.*

**defence mechanism** /ˈ– ˌmɛkənɪzəm/, *n.* **1.** *Physiol.* organic activity, as the formation of an antitoxin, as a defensive measure. **2.** *Psychoanal.* a group of unconscious processes which oppose the entrance into consciousness or the acting out of unacceptable or painful ideas and impulses.

**defend** /dəˈfɛnd/, *v.t.* **1.** to ward off attack from; guard against assault or injury (fol. by *from* or *against*). **2.** to maintain by argument, evidence, etc.; uphold. **3.** to contest (a legal charge, claim, etc.). **4.** to act as counsel for (an accused man). *–v.i.* **5.** *Law.* to enter or make a defence. [ME *defende(n),* from OF *defendre,* from L *dēfendere* ward off] – **defendable,** *adj.* – **defender,** *n.*

**defendant** /dəˈfɛndənt/, *n.* **1.** *Law.* the party against whom a claim or charge is brought in a proceeding. *–adj.* **2.** *Obs.* defensive.

**defenestrate** /diˈfɛnəstreɪt/, *v.t.,* **-strated, -strating.** to throw out of a window. [backformation from DEFENESTRATION]

**defenestration** /diˌfɛnəˈstreɪʃən/, *n.* the act of throwing out of a window. [DE- + L *fenestra* window + -ATION]

**defense** /dəˈfɛns/, *n. U.S.* →**defence.**

**defensible** /dəˈfɛnsəbəl/, *adj.* **1.** capable of being defended against assault or injury. **2.** capable of being defended in argument; justifiable. – **defensibility** /dəfɛnsəˈbɪləti/, **defensibleness,** *n.* – **defensibly,** *adv.*

**defensive** /dəˈfɛnsɪv/, *adj.* **1.** serving to defend; protective: *defensive armour.* **2.** made or carried on for the purpose of resisting attack. **3.** of or pertaining to defence: *a defensive attitude.* *–n.* **4.** something that serves to protect or defend. **5.** defensive position or attitude. – **defensively,** *adv.* – **defensiveness,** *n.*

**defer**[1] /dəˈfɜ/, *v.,* **-ferred, -ferring.** *–v.t.* **1.** to put off (action, etc.) to a future time. *–v.i.* **2.** to put off action; delay. [ME *differre(n),* from L *differre* delay. See DIFFER] – **deferrer,** *n.*

**defer**[2] /dəˈfɜ/, *v.i.* **-ferred, -ferring.** to yield in judgment or opinion (fol. by *to*). [F *déférer,* from L *dēferre* carry from or down, report, accuse]

**deference** /ˈdɛfərəns/, *n.* **1.** submission or yielding to the judgment, opinion, will, etc., of another. **2.** respectful or courteous regard: *in deference to his wishes.*

**deferent**[1] /ˈdɛfərənt/, *adj.* →**deferential.** [L *dēferens,* ppr., bringing down]

**deferent**[2] /ˈdɛfərənt/, *adj.* **1.** *Anat.* conveying away. **2.** *Anat.* pertaining to the vas deferens, the deferent duct of the testes. **3.** *Astron. Obs.* (in the Ptolemaic system) the circle on which the centre of the epicycle moves. [see DEFERENT[1], DEFER[2]]

**deferential** /dɛfəˈrɛnʃəl/, *adj.* marked by or showing deference; respectful. – **deferentially,** *adv.*

**deferment** /dəˈfɜmənt/, *n.* the act of deferring or putting off; postponement.

**deferral** /dəˈfɜrəl/, *n.* →**deferment.**

**deferred** /dəˈfɜd/, *adj.* **1.** postponed or delayed, as property rights which do not vest until some future event has occurred. **2.** suspended or held back for a period: *deferred interest account of shareholders.*

**deferred delivery share,** *n.* a share which can be sold only on the understanding that buyers must accept a delay in delivery of scrip, due to reconstruction of the company's share capital. Also, **deferred share.** *Abbrev.:* d.d.

**deferred dividend** /dəfɜd ˈdɪvədɛnd/, *n.* a dividend to which the holder of a company share is not entitled before a certain lapse of time, unless ordinary shareholders receive more than the stated rate of dividend.

**deferred share** /dəfɜd ˈʃɛə/, *n.* **1.** →**deferred delivery share.** **2.** a share which entitles the holder to a deferred dividend.

**defiance** /dəˈfaɪəns/, *n.* **1.** a daring or bold resistance to authority or to any opposing force. **2.** open disregard: *in defiance of criticism.* **3.** a challenge to meet in combat or contest.

**defiant** /dəˈfaɪənt/, *adj.* characterised by defiance, bold opposition, or antagonism. [F, ppr. of *défier* DEFY] – **defiantly,** *adv.* – **defiantness,** *n.*

**defibrillation** /diˌfɪbrəˈleɪʃən/, *n.* **1.** the separation of fibres. **2.** the stopping of the fibrillation (def. 2) of the heart.

**defibrillator** /diˈfɪbrəleɪtə/, *n.* a medical apparatus which uses an electric shock to restore normal heart rhythm.

**deficiency** /dəˈfɪʃənsi/, *n., pl.* **-cies.** **1.** the state or fact of being deficient; lack; incompleteness; insufficiency. **2.** the amount lacked; a deficit.

**deficiency disease** /ˈ– dəziz/, *n.* an illness due to an insufficient supply of one or more essential dietary constituents.

**deficiency payment** /ˈ– peɪmənt/, *n.* →**subsidy.**

**deficiency payments scheme,** *n.* a plan for support of the price of a produce (esp. by government).

**deficient** /dəˈfɪʃənt/, *adj.* **1.** lacking some element or characteristic; defective. **2.** insufficient; inadequate. [L *dēficiens,* ppr., wanting] – **deficiently,** *adv.*

**deficit** /ˈdɛfəsət/, *n.* the amount by which a sum of money falls short of the required amount. [L: there is wanting]

**defilade** /ˈdɛfəleɪd/, *v.,* **-laded, -lading,** *n.* *Mil.* *–v.t.* **1.** to shield from enemy fire or observation by using natural or artificial obstacles. *–n.* **2.** protection from hostile ground observation and fire provided by an obstacle such as a hill, ridge, or bank. **3.** a vertical distance by which a position is concealed from enemy observation. [F, from *défiler,* orig., unthread, from *dé-* DIS-[1] +*(en)filer* thread (from L *fīlum* a thread)]

**defile**[1] /dəˈfaɪl/, *v.t.,* **-filed, -filing.** **1.** to make foul, dirty, or unclean; pollute; taint. **2.** to violate the chastity of. **3.** to make ceremonially unclean; desecrate. **4.** to sully (a reputation, etc.). [alteration of *befile* (OE *befȳlan* befoul)] – **defilement,** *n.* – **defiler,** *n.*

**defile**[2] /dəˈfaɪl, ˈdifaɪl/, *n., v.,* **-filed, -filing.** *–n.* **1.** any narrow passage, esp. between mountains. *–v.i.* **2.** to march in a line, or by files; file off. [F, n. use of pp. of *défiler* file off]

**define** /dəˈfaɪn/, *v.t.,* **-fined, -fining.** **1.** to state or set forth the meaning of (a word, phrase, etc.). **2.** to explain the nature or essential qualities of; describe. **3.** to determine or fix the boundaries or extent of. **4.** to make clear the outline or form of. **5.** to fix or lay down definitely; specify distinctly. [ME *deffyne(n),* from F *définir,* from L *dēfīnīre* limit, determine, explain, terminate] – **definable,** *adj.* – **definability** /dəfaɪnəˈbɪləti/, *n.* – **definer,** *n.* – **definably,** *adv.*

**definiendum** /dəfɪniˈɛndəm/, *n., pl.* **-da** /-də/. the thing which is to be defined, esp. the word or phrase to be defined in a dictionary entry. [L, neut. ger. of *dēfīnīre* DEFINE]

**definiens** /dəˈfɪniənz/, *n., pl.* **definientia** /dəfɪniˈɛntʃə/. the word or words used to explain the meaning of another word, as in a dictionary definition. [L , ppr. of *dēfīnīre* DEFINE]

**defining clause** /dəˌfaɪnɪŋ ˈklɔz/, *n.* →**restrictive clause.**

**definite** /ˈdɛfənət/, *adj.* **1.** clearly defined or determined; not vague or general; fixed; precise; exact. **2.** having fixed limits; bounded with precision. **3.** defining; limiting. **4.** *Colloq.* certain; sure: *he was quite definite about his intentions.* **5.** *Bot.* (of an inflorescence) determinate. [L *dēfīnītus,* pp., limited, determined] – **definitely,** *adv.* – **definiteness,** *n.*

**definite article** /– ˈatɪkəl/, *n.* the article, as English *the,* which classes as identified the noun it modifies.

**definition** /dɛfəˈnɪʃən/, *n.* **1.** the act of defining or making definite or clear. **2.** the formal statement of the meaning or signification of a word, phrase, etc. **3.** the condition of being definite. **4.** *Optics.* sharpness of the image formed by an optical system. **5.** *Electron.* the accuracy of sound reproduction through a receiver, or picture reproduction in a television receiver.

**definitive** /dəˈfɪnətɪv/, *adj.* **1.** having the function of deciding or settling; determining; conclusive; final. **2.** serving to fix or specify definitely. **3.** having its fixed and final form. *–n.* **4.** a defining or limiting word, as an article, a demonstrative, or the like. – **definitively,** *adv.* – **definitiveness,** *n.*

**definitude** /dəˈfɪnətʃud/, *n.* definiteness; exactitude; precision.

**deflagrate** /ˈdɛfləgreɪt, ˈdiflə-/, *v.,* **-grated, -grating.** *–v.i.* **1.** to burn, esp. suddenly and violently. *–v.t.* **2.** to cause to burn with great heat. [L *dēflagrātus,* pp.] – **deflagration** /dɛfləˈgreɪʃən/, *n.*

**deflate** /dəˈfleɪt/, *v.t.,* **-flated, -flating.** **1.** to release the air or gas from (something inflated, as a tyre). **2.** to reduce (currency, prices, etc.) from an inflated condition. **3.** to reduce in esteem, esp. self-esteem (a person or a person's ego). [L *dēflātus,* pp., blown off]

**deflation** /dəˈfleɪʃən/, *n.* **1.** the act of deflating. **2.** an abnormal decline in the level of commodity prices, esp. one not accompanied by an equal reduction in the costs of production. **3.** *Geol.* the removal of material from a beach or other land surface by wind action.

**deflationary** /dəˈfleɪʃənri/, *adj.* of or pertaining to, or tending to deflation.

**deflect** /dəˈflɛkt/, *v.i.* **1.** to bend or turn aside; swerve. *–v.t.* **2.** to cause to turn from a true course or right line. [L *dēflectere*] – **deflector,** *n.*

**deflection** /dəˈflɛkʃən/, *n.* **1.** the act of deflecting. **2.** the state of being deflected. **3.** amount of deviation. **4.** *Physics.* the deviation or swing of the indicator of an instrument from the position taken as zero. **5.** *Optics.* the bending of rays of light from a straight line. Also, **deflexion.**

**deflective** /dəˈflɛktɪv/, *adj.* causing deflection.

**deflexed** /diˈflɛkst/, *adj.* (of leaves or petals) turned sharply downwards. [L *dēflexus,* pp. of *dēflectere* bend down, DEFLECT]

**defloration** /difləˈreɪʃən/, *n.* the act of deflowering. [ME *defloracion,* from LL *dēflōrātio*]

**deflower** /diˈflaʊə/, *v.t.* **1.** to deprive or strip of flowers. **2.** to deprive (a woman) of virginity; ravish. **3.** to despoil of beauty, freshness, sanctity, etc. [DE- + FLOWER, replacing ME *deflore(n),* from OF *desflorer* remove the flower(s) from, ravish] – **deflowerer,** *n.*

**defluxion** /dəˈflʌkʃən/, *n.* *Pathol.* a copious discharge of fluid matter, as in catarrh.

**defoliant** /dəˈfoʊliənt/, *n.* a chemical preparation used to cause defoliation.

**defoliate** /də'fouliеɪt/, *v.*, **-ated, -ating,** *adj.* *–v.t.* **1.** to strip or deprive (a tree, etc.) of leaves. *–v.i.* **2.** to lose leaves. *–adj.* **3.** having lost its leaves, as a tree; defoliated. [ML *dēfoliātus,* pp. of *dēfoliāre,* from L *folium* leaf] – **defoliation** /dəfouli'eɪʃən/, *n.*

**deforce** /də'fɔs/, *v.t.*, **-forced, -forcing.** *Law.* to withhold (property, esp. land) by force or violence, as from the rightful owner. [AF *deforcer,* from *de-* DE- + *forcer* FORCE, *v.*] – **deforcement,** *n.*

**deforciant** /də'fɔʃənt/, *n. Law.* one who deforces.

**deforest** /di'fɒrəst/, *v.t.* to divest of forests or trees. – **deforestation** /diˌfɒrəst'eɪʃən/, *n.* – **deforester,** *n.*

**deform** /də'fɔm/, *v.t.* **1.** to mar the natural form or shape of; put out of shape; disfigure. **2.** to make ugly, ungraceful, or displeasing; mar the beauty of; spoil. **3.** to change the form of; transform. **4.** to subject to deformation. [ME, from L *dēformāre* disfigure] – **deformer,** *n.*

**deformable** /də'fɔməbəl/, *adj.* capable of being deformed. – **deformability** /dəfɔmə'bɪləti/, *n.*

**deformation** /difɔ'meɪʃən/, *n.* **1.** the act of deforming; distortion; disfigurement. **2.** the result of deforming; change of form, esp. for the worse. **3.** a change in the shape or dimensions of a body resulting from stress; strain. **4.** an altered form.

**deformed** /də'fɔmd/, *adj.* **1.** having the form changed, with loss of beauty, etc.; misshapen; disfigured. **2.** hateful; offensive. **3.** *Mech.* subjected to deformation (def. 3). – **deformedly** /də'fɔmədli/, *adv.*

**deformity** /də'fɔməti/, *n.*, *pl.* **-ties. 1.** the quality or state of being deformed, disfigured, or misshapen. **2.** an abnormally formed part of the body, etc. **3.** a deformed person or thing. **4.** hatefulness; ugliness.

**defraud** /də'frɔd/, *v.t.* to deprive of a right or property by fraud; cheat. [ME *defraude(n),* from L *dēfraudāre.* Cf. FRAUD] – **defraudation** /difrɔd'eɪʃən/, *n.* – **defrauder,** *n.*

**defray** /də'freɪ/, *v.t.* to bear or pay (the costs, expenses, etc.). [F *défrayer,* OF *desfraier* pay costs, from *des-* DIS-$^1$ + *frai* cost, of Gmc orig.] – **defrayable,** *adj.* – **defrayer,** *n.*

**defrayal** /də'freɪəl/, *n.* payment of charges or expenses. Also, **defrayment.**

**defreeze** /di'friz/, *v.* →**defrost.**

**defrock** /di'frɒk/, *v.t.* to unfrock.

**defrost** /di'frɒst, də-/, *v.t.* **1.** to remove the frost or ice from. **2.** to cause (food, etc.) to thaw, as by removing from a refrigerator. *–v.i.* **3.** to thaw; to become free of frost and ice. – **defroster,** *n.*

**deft** /dɛft/, *adj.* dexterous; nimble; skilful; clever. [ME; var. of DAFT] – **deftly,** *adv.* – **deftness,** *n.*

**defunct** /də'fʌŋkt/, *adj.* **1.** deceased; dead; extinct. **2.** no longer operative; not in use. *–n.* **3. the defunct, a.** the dead person. **b.** dead people collectively. [L *dēfunctus,* pp., discharged, finished] – **defunctness,** *n.*

**defunctive** /də'fʌŋktɪv/, *adj.* of or pertaining to the dead; funereal.

**defuse** /di'fjuz/, *v.t.*, **-fused, -fusing. 1.** to remove the fuse from (a bomb). **2.** to calm (a situation or action).

**defy** /də'faɪ/, *v.*, **-fied, -fying.** *–v.t.* **1.** to challenge the power of; resist boldly or openly. **2.** to offer effective resistance to: *a fort which defies attacks.* **3.** to challenge (one) to do something deemed impossible. **4.** *Archaic.* to challenge to a combat or contest. [ME *defye(n),* from OF *defier,* from *de-* DE- + *fier* (from L *fidere* trust)]

**deg.,** degree; degrees.

**dégagé** /deɪga'ʒeɪ/, *adj.* **1.** unconstrained; easy, as in manner. **2.** disinterested. [F, pp. of *dégager* disengage, put at ease]

**degas** /di'gæs/, *v.t.*, **-gassed, -gassing. 1.** to free from gas. **2.** to treat with chemical agents to destroy a gas or its harmful properties. **3.** to complete the evacuation of gases in (a radio valve). – **degasify,** *v.* – **degasification** /digæsəfə'keɪʃən/, *n.* – **degasser,** *n.*

**degauss** /di'gaʊs, -'gɔs/, *v.t.* to demagnetise, esp. to neutralise a ship's magnetic field as a protection against magnetic mines. [DE- + *gauss* (from Karl Friedrich *Gauss,* 1777-1855, German mathematician)] – **degaussing,** *n.*

**degeneracy** /də'dʒɛnərəsi/, *n.* a degenerate state or character; degeneration.

**degenerate** /də'dʒɛnəreɪt/, *v.*, **-rated, -rating;** /də'dʒɛnərət/, *adj., n.* *–v.i.* **1.** to decline in physical, mental, or moral qualities; deteriorate. **2.** *Biol.* to revert to a less highly organised or simpler type. *–adj.* **3.** having declined in physical or moral qualities; deteriorated; degraded: *a degenerate king.* **4.** having lost, or become impaired with respect to, the qualities proper to the race or kind: *a degenerate plant.* **5.** characterised by or associated with degeneracy: *degenerate times.* **6.** *Physics, Astron.* (of a gas) having its constituent atomic nuclei and electrons packed too closely together to permit the evolution of nuclear energy, as in white dwarf stars. *–n.* **7.** one who has retrogressed from a normal type or standard, as in morals or character. **8.** one exhibiting morbid physical and mental traits or tendencies, esp. from birth. [L *dēgenerātus,* pp., departed from its race] – **degenerately,** *adv.* – **degenerateness,** *n.*

**degeneration** /dədʒɛnə'reɪʃən/, *n.* **1.** the process of degenerating. **2.** the state of being degenerate. **3.** *Biol.* reversion to a less highly organised or a simpler type. **4.** *Pathol.* **a.** a process by which a tissue deteriorates, loses functional activity, and may become converted into or replaced by other kinds of tissue. **b.** the morbid condition produced by such a process.

**degenerative** /də'dʒɛnərətɪv/, *adj.* **1.** tending to degenerate. **2.** characterised by degeneration.

**deglamourise** /di'glæməraɪz/, *v.t.*, **-ised, -ising.** to deprive of an aura of glamour.

**deglitch** /di'glɪtʃ/, *v.t.* to remove the glitches from.

**deglutinate** /də'glutəneɪt/, *v.t.*, **-nated, -nating.** to extract the gluten from. [L *dēglūtinātus,* pp., unglued]

**deglutition** /ˌdiglu'tɪʃən/, *n.* the act or process of swallowing. [F, from L *dēglūtīre* swallow down]

**degradation** /dɛgrə'deɪʃən/, *n.* **1.** the act of degrading. **2.** the state of being degraded. **3.** *Phys. Geog.* the general lowering of the surface of the land by erosive processes, esp. by the removal of material through erosion. **4.** *Chem.* the breakdown of a complex compound into simple ones, esp. the conversion of a sucrose into a compound with one less carbon atom.

**degrade** /də'greɪd/, *v.t.*, **-graded, -grading. 1.** to reduce from a higher to a lower rank, degree, etc.; deprive of office, rank, degree, or title as a punishment. **2.** to lower in character or quality; debase; deprave. **3.** to lower in dignity or estimation; bring into contempt. **4.** to reduce in amount, strength, intensity, etc. **5.** *Phys. Geog.* to wear down by erosion. **6.** *Chem.* to disintegrate. [ME *degrade(n),* from ecclesiastical LL *dēgradāre* reduce in rank, from L *gradus* GRADE] – **degradable,** *adj.*

**degraded** /də'greɪdəd/, *adj.* debased; degenerate. – **degradedly,** *adv.* – **degradedness,** *n.*

**degrading** /də'greɪdɪŋ/, *adj.* that degrades; debasing: *degrading obsequiousness.* – **degradingly,** *adv.* – **degradingness,** *n.*

**degrease** /di'gris/, *v.t.*, **-greased, -greasing.** to remove the fat or grease from. – **degreaser,** *n.*

**degree** /də'gri/, *n.* **1.** a step or stage in an ascending or descending scale, or in a course or process. **2.** *Genetics, Law, etc.* a certain distance or remove in the line of descent or consanguinity. **3.** a stage in a scale of rank or dignity; relative rank, station, etc: *a man of high degree.* **4.** a stage in a scale of intensity or amount: *to the last degree.* **5.** the angle between two radii of a circle which cut off on the circumference an arc equal to $\frac{1}{360}$ of that circumference (often indicated by the sign °, as 45°); 17.453 293 × $10^{-3}$ radians. **6.** *Alg.* the sum of the exponents of the variables in an algebraic expression: *$x^3$ and $2x^2y$ are terms of degree three.* **7.** a unit in the measurement of temperature. **8.** a unit on an arbitrary scale of measurement. **9.** *Geog.* **a.** the unit of measurement of latitude or longitude, usu. employed to indicate position on the earth's surface, the position of a line or point being fixed by its angular distance measured in degrees from the equator or a given meridian. **b.** *Astron.* the

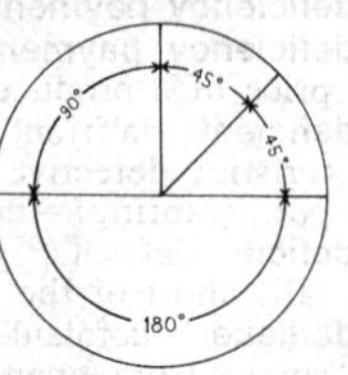

degree (def. 5)

i = peat ɪ = pit ɛ = pet æ = pat a = part ɒ = pot ʌ = putt ɔ = port ʊ = put u = pool ɜ = pert ə = apart aɪ = buy eɪ = bay ɔɪ = boy aʊ = how oʊ = hoe ɪə = here ɛə = hair ʊə = tour g = give θ = thin ð = then ʃ = show ʒ = measure tʃ = choke dʒ = joke ŋ = sing j = you õ = Fr. bon

position of a line or point in the celestial sphere fixed by its angular distance measured from the equator (equinoctial) or a given meridian. **10.** a qualification conferred by a university for successful work, as judged by examination, or as an honorary recognition of achievement. **11.** *Gram.* one of the three parallel formations (positive, comparative, and superlative) of adjectives and adverbs, showing differences in quality, quantity, or intensity in the attribute referred to, as English *low, lower, lowest.* **12.** *Music.* **a.** the interval from one note to another on a stave. **b.** one of the eight progressive intervals from the tonic in an octave. **13.** *U.S.* a classification of certain crimes according to their seriousness: *first degree murder.* **14. by degrees,** gradually. **15. to a degree,** to an undefined but considerable extent. [ME *degre,* from OF, from *de-* DE- + *gre,* from L *gradus* step, degree, GRADE]

**degree of freedom,** *n.* **1.** *Statistics.* the number of independent random variables that together make up a statistic. **2. a.** *Mech.* the number of independent ways a body can be displaced. **b.** *Physics.* the number of independent ways in which a molecule can possess translational, vibrational, or rotational energies. **3.** *Chem.* the least number of variables which must be determined in order to define the state of a system in the phase rule.

**degust** /di'gʌst/, *v.i.* **1.** *Obs.* to taste. **2.** to have a taste. [L *dēgustāre*] – **degustation** /digʌst'eɪʃən/, *n.*

**de gustibus non est disputandum** /deɪ ˌgustibʊs ˌnɒn ɛst ˌdɪspju'tændʊm/, there is no disputing about tastes. [L]

**degut** /di'gʌt/, *v.t.,* **-gutted, -gutting.** to remove the guts, essential parts or elements of (an animal, etc.).

**dehisce** /də'hɪs/, *v.i.,* **-hisced, -hiscing.** to gape; burst open, as capsules of plants. [L *dehiscere*]

**dehiscence** /də'hɪsəns/, *n.* **1.** *Bot.* the natural bursting open of capsules, fruits, anthers, etc., for the discharge of their contents. **2.** *Biol.* the release of materials by the splitting open of an organ or tissue.

**dehiscent** /də'hɪsənt/, *adj.* gaping open; characterised by dehiscence.

**dehorn** /di'hɔn/, *v.t.* to deprive (cattle) of horns. – **dehorner,** *n.*

**dehumanise** /di'hjumənaɪz/, *v.t.,* **-nised, -nising.** to deprive of human character. Also, **dehumanize.** – **dehumanisation** /diˌhjumənaɪ'zeɪʃən/, *n.*

**dehumidify** /dihju'mɪdəfaɪ/, *v.t.,* **-fied, -fying.** to remove moisture from; to reduce the degree of humidity of. – **dehumidification** /dihjuˌmɪdəfə'keɪʃən/, *n.* – **dehumidifier,** *n.*

**dehydrate** /'dihaɪdreɪt/, *v.,* **-drated, -drating.** –*v.t.* **1.** to deprive of water. **2.** to free (vegetables, etc.) of moisture, for preservation. –*v.i.* **3.** to lose water or moisture. [DE- + HYDR-[1] + -ATE[1]] – **dehydration** /dihaɪ'dreɪʃən/, *n.*

**dehydrogenase** /ˌdihaɪ'drɒdʒəneɪz/, *n.* any enzyme that catalyses the dehydrogenation of a substrate.

**dehydrogenise** /di'haɪdrədʒəˌnaɪz/, *v.t.,* **-nised, -nising.** *Chem.* to remove hydrogen from (a compound). Also, **dehydrogenize, dehydrogenate.** – **dehydrogenation, dehydrogenisation** /diˌhaɪdrədʒənaɪ'zeɪʃən/, *n.*

**dehypnotise** /di'hɪpnətaɪz/, *v.t.,* **-tised, -tising.** to bring out of the hypnotic state. Also, **dehypnotize.**

**de-ice** /di-'aɪs/, *v.t.,* **-iced, -icing.** to free or keep free of ice.

**de-icer** /di-'aɪsə/, *n.* a mechanical or exhaust-heat device preventing or removing ice formation.

**deicide** /'diəsaɪd, 'deɪəsaɪd/, *n.* **1.** one who kills a god. **2.** the killing of a god. [L *deus* god + -I- + -CIDE] – **deicidal** /diə'saɪdəl, deɪə-/, *adj.*

**deictic** /'daɪktɪk, deɪ'ɪktɪk/, *adj.* **1.** *Logic.* proving directly. **2.** *Gram.* pointing; demonstrative; manifesting deixis. [Gk *deiktikós*] – **deictically,** *adv.*

**deific** /di'ɪfɪk, deɪ'ɪfɪk/, *adj.* making divine; deifying. [LL *deificus* god-making, sacred]

**deification** /ˌdiɪfə'keɪʃən ˌdeɪ-/, *n.* **1.** the act of deifying. **2.** the state of being deified. **3.** a deified embodiment.

**deiform** /'diəfɔm, 'deɪə-/, *adj.* godlike; divine. [ML *deiformis,* from L *deus* god. See -FORM]

**deify** /'diəfaɪ, 'deɪə-/, *v.t.,* **-fied, -fying.** **1.** to make a god of; exalt to the rank of a deity. **2.** to adore or regard as a deity: *to deify prudence.* [ME *deify(en),* from OF *deifier,* from LL *deificāre*] – **deifier,** *n.*

**deign** /deɪn/, *v.i.* **1.** to think fit or in accordance with one's dignity; condescend. –*v.t.* **2.** to condescend to give or grant: *deigning no reply.* [ME *deine(n),* from OF *deignier,* from L *dignārī* deem worthy]

**deil** /dil/, *n. Scot.* →**devil.**

**deionise** /di'aɪənaɪz/, *v.t.* to deprive of ions, remove the ions from. Also, **deionize.** – **deionisation** /diˌaɪənaɪ'zeɪʃən/, *n.* – **deioniser,** *n.*

**deipnosophist** /daɪp'nɒsəfəst/, *n.* a master of the art of dining, esp. of conversation at table. [Gk *deipnosophistai* (pl.) kitchen-sophists, title of a work by Athenaeus (?A.D. 228)]

**deism** /'diɪzəm, 'deɪ-/, *n.* **1.** belief in the existence of a god on the evidence of reason and nature only, with rejection of supernatural revelation (distinguished from *theism*). **2.** belief in a god who created the world but has since remained indifferent to his creation (distinguished from *atheism, pantheism,* and *theism*). [L *deus* god + -ISM]

**deist** /'diəst, 'deɪ-/, *n.* one who believes in deism. – **deistic** /di'ɪstɪk, deɪ-/, **deistical** /di'ɪstɪkəl, deɪ-/, *adj.* – **deistically** /di'ɪstɪkli, deɪ-/, *adv.*

**deity** /'diəti, 'deɪ-/, *n., pl.* **-ties.** **1.** a god or goddess. **2.** divine character or nature. **3.** the estate or rank of a god. **4.** the character or nature of the Supreme Being. **5. the Deity,** God. [ME *deite,* from OF, from LL *deitās*]

**deixis** /'daɪksəs/, *n. Linguistics.* use of a deictic word; a pointing out (as in the function of pronouns in English). [Gk: reference]

**deja vu** /deɪʒa 'vu/, *n.* **1.** the sense or illusion of having previously experienced something actually being encountered for the first time. –*adj.* **2.** unoriginal; trite. Also, **déjà vu.** [F]

**deject** /də'dʒɛkt/, *v.t.* to depress the spirits of; dispirit; dishearten. [L *dējectus,* pp., thrown down]

**dejected** /də'dʒɛktəd/, *adj.* depressed in spirits; disheartened; low-spirited. – **dejectedly,** *adv.* – **dejectedness,** *n.*

**dejection** /də'dʒɛkʃən/, *n.* depression or lowness of spirits.

**déjeuner** /'deɪʒəneɪ/, *n.* **1.** breakfast. **2.** (in European use) lunch. [F, orig. inf., OF *desjeuner* break one's fast, from *des-* DIS-[1] + *jeun* fasting, from L *jējūnus* jejune]

**de jure** /deɪ 'dʒʊəreɪ, di 'dʒʊəri/, *adv.* by right; according to law. [L]

**deka-** /'dɛkə-/, a prefix denoting 10 times a given unit, as in *dekametre.* Also, **deca-;** before vowels, **dec-, dek-.** *Symbol:* da [Gk *deka-,* combining form of *déka* ten]

**dekerugmatise** /dikə'rʊgmətaɪz/, *v.t.,* **-tised, -tising.** *Theol.* to attempt to express divine truths without such distortion as may have been introduced by the form of their proclamation, as in divine acts, miracles, etc. Also, **dekerygmatise.** [DE- + Gk *kḗrygma* proclamation + -ISE[1]]

**dekko** /'dɛkoʊ/, *n., pl.* **-kos.** *Colloq.* look or view. Also, **dek.** [Hind. *dekho* look!]

**deknacker** /di'nækə/, *v.t. Colloq.* to castrate.

**del,** *Stock Exchange.* delivery not enforceable.

**del.,** **1.** delegate. **2.** delete. [L *delineavit* he drew it] **3.** delivered.

**delaine** /də'leɪn/, *n.* a thin woollen fabric, often having a printed pattern; mousseline de laine.

**delaminate** /di'læməneɪt/, *v.i.,* **-nated, -nating.** to split into laminae or thin layers.

**delamination** /dəlæmə'neɪʃən/, *n.* **1.** a splitting apart into layers. **2.** *Embryol.* the separation of a primitive blastoderm into two layers of cells.

**delate** /də'leɪt/, *v.t.,* **-lated, -lating.** **1.** to inform against; denounce or accuse. **2.** to relate or report (an offence, etc.). [L *dēlātus,* pp., carried from or down, reported, accused] – **delation,** *n.* – **delator,** *n.*

**delay** /də'leɪ, di-/, *v.t.* **1.** to put off to a later time; defer; postpone. **2.** to impede the progress of; retard; hinder. –*v.i.* **3.** to put off action; linger; loiter: *don't delay!* –*n.* **4.** the act of delaying; procrastination; loitering. **5.** an instance of being delayed. **6.** *Electronics.* **a.** the time interval required for a signal to propagate through a circuit. **b.** a circuit whose sole function is to delay or retard a signal by a fixed amount of time. [ME *delaie(n),* from OF *de(s)laier,* from *des-* DIS-[1] + *laier,* var. of *laissier* leave, from L *laxāre* loosen] – **delayer,** *n.*

**delayed action** /dəleɪd 'ækʃən/, *n.* (of an explosive projectile) designed to explode some time after hitting the target or being otherwise primed.

**delayed auditory feedback,** *n.* the return by electronic methods to the ears of a person speaking, of what is being said a split second after it has been said; usu. induces stuttering or some form of speech impairment.

**delayed feedback** /dəleɪd 'fidbæk/, *n.* the return of part of the output of an electronic system to its input with a deliberate time delay; may be used for echo effects in music. See **delayed auditory feedback.**

**delayed neutron** /– 'njutrɒn/, *n.* a neutron, resulting from a nuclear fission, which is emitted after a measurable lapse of time.

**delaying action** /də'leɪɪŋ ækʃən/, *n.* any action taken whose purpose is to gain time, esp. a military action delaying the advance of a superior enemy force by withdrawing while inflicting the maximum damage possible without becoming involved in decisive combat.

**delay line** /də'leɪ laɪn/, *n. Electronics.* a device which introduces a delay into a signal path.

**dele** /'dili/, *v.*, **deled, deleing,** *n., pl.* **deles** /'diliz/. *Print.* *–v.t.* **1.** (usu. imperative) to take out; omit; delete (generally represented by a symbol). *–n.* **2.** the symbol meaning delete. [L]

**delectable** /də'lɛktəbəl/, *adj.* delightful; highly pleasing; enjoyable. [ME, from L *dēlectābilis*] – **delectableness, delectability** /dəlɛktə'bɪləti/, *n.* – **delectably,** *adv.*

**delectate** /də'lɛkteɪt/, *v.t.*, **-tated, -tating.** to please; charm; delight. [L *dēlectātus*, pp., delighted]

**delectation** /ˌdilɛk'teɪʃən/, *n.* →**delight.**

**delegacy** /'dɛləgəsi/, *n., pl.* **-cies. 1.** the position or commission of a delegate. **2.** the sending or appointing of a delegate. **3.** a body of delegates.

**delegate** /'dɛləgət, -geɪt/, *n.;* /'dɛləgeɪt/, *v.* **-gated, -gating.** *–n.* **1.** one delegated to act for or represent another or others; a deputy; a representative, as at a conference, or the like. *–v.t.* **2.** to send or appoint (a person) as deputy or representative. **3.** to commit (powers, functions, etc.) to another as agent or deputy. [L *dēlēgātus*, pp., sent, deputed]

**delegated legislation** /ˌdɛləgeɪtəd ˌlɛdʒəs'leɪʃən/, *n.* subordinate legislation of an essentially subsidiary or procedural character, the power of enactment of which is delegated to the executive by the parliament in order to lessen the load on the legislative machine.

**delegation** /dɛlə'geɪʃən/, *n.* **1.** the act of delegating. **2.** the fact of being delegated. **3.** any group of delegates. **4.** a group of persons officially elected or appointed to represent another, or others: *the delegation from Townsville voted with the opposition.*

**delenda** /də'lɛndə/, *n.pl.* matter which is to be deleted. [L, neut. gerundive of *dēlēre* to delete]

**delete** /də'lit/, *v.t.*, **-leted, -leting.** to strike out or take out (anything written or printed); cancel; erase; expunge. [L *dēlētus*, pp., done away with, destroyed]

**deleterious** /dɛlə'tɪəriəs/, *adj.* **1.** injurious to health. **2.** hurtful; harmful; injurious. [NL *dēlētērius*, from Gk *dēlētērios*] – **deleteriously,** *adv.* – **deleteriousness,** *n.*

**deletion** /də'liʃən/, *n.* **1.** the act of deleting. **2.** the fact of being deleted. **3.** a deleted passage. [L *dēlētio*]

**delft** /dɛlft/, *n.* **1.** a kind of glazed earthenware decorated in colours, esp. in blue, made at Delft a town in the western Netherlands. **2.** any pottery resembling this. Also, **delf** /dɛlf/, **delftware.**

**deli** /'dɛli/, *n. Colloq.* →**dellie.**

**deliberate** /də'lɪbərət/, *adj.;* /də'lɪbəreɪt/, *v.*, **-rated, -rating.** *–adj.* **1.** carefully weighed or considered; studied; intentional. **2.** characterised by deliberation; careful or slow in deciding. **3.** leisurely in movement or action; slow; unhurried. *–v.t.* **4.** to weigh in the mind; consider: *to deliberate a question, a proposition, etc.* *–v.i.* **5.** to think carefully or attentively; reflect. **6.** to consult or confer formally. [L *dēlīberātus*, pp., weighed well] – **deliberately,** *adv.* – **deliberateness,** *n.* – **deliberator,** *n.*

**deliberation** /dəlɪbə'reɪʃən/, *n.* **1.** careful consideration before decision. **2.** formal consultation or discussion. **3.** deliberate quality; leisureliness of movement or action; slowness.

**deliberative** /də'lɪbərətɪv, -lɪbrə-/, *adj.* **1.** having the function of deliberating, as a legislative assembly. **2.** having to do with policy; dealing with the wisdom and expediency of a proposal: *a deliberative speech.* – **deliberatively,** *adv.* – **deliberativeness,** *n.*

**deliberative vote** /– 'voʊt/, *n.* the ordinary vote of a member of a committee or meeting, as distinct from the casting vote of a chairman.

**delicacy** /'dɛləkəsi/, *n., pl.* **-cies. 1.** fineness of texture, quality, etc.; softness: *the delicacy of lace.* **2.** something delightful or pleasing, esp. to the palate. **3.** fineness of perception or feeling; sensitiveness. **4.** the quality of requiring or involving great care or tact: *negotiations of great delicacy.* **5.** nicety of action or operation; minute accuracy: *a surgeon's delicacy of touch.* **6.** fineness of feeling with regard to what is fitting, proper, etc. **7.** bodily weakness; liability to sickness. **8.** gratification; luxury.

**delicate** /'dɛləkət/, *adj.* **1.** fine in texture, quality, construction, etc. **2.** dainty or choice, as food. **3.** soft or faint, as colour. **4.** so fine or slight as to be scarcely perceptible; subtle. **5.** easily damaged; fragile. **6.** requiring great care, caution, or tact. **7.** fine or exquisite in action or execution: *a delicate instrument.* **8.** regardful of what is becoming, proper, etc., or of the feelings of others. **9.** exquisite or refined in perception or feeling; sensitive. **10.** distinguishing subtle differences. **11.** fastidious. [ME, from L *dēlicātus* delightful, luxurious, soft; akin to DELICIOUS] – **delicately,** *adv.* – **delicateness,** *n.*

**delicatessen** /dɛləkə'tɛsən/, *n.* a shop selling cooked or prepared goods ready for serving, usu. having a noticeable proportion of continental or exotic items. [G *Delikatessen*, pl. of *Delikatesse* delicacy, from F *délicatesse*, from It. *delicatezza*, from *delicato* DELICATE]

**delicious** /də'lɪʃəs/, *adj.* **1.** highly pleasing to the senses, esp. to taste or smell. **2.** pleasing in the highest degree; delightful. *–n.* **3.** (*cap.*) certain varieties of eating apples. [ME, from OF, from LL *dēliciōsus*, from L *dēlicia* delight] – **deliciously,** *adv.* – **deliciousness,** *n.*

**delict** /də'lɪkt, di'lɪkt/, *n.* **1.** *Civil Law.* a legal offence. **2.** *Rom. Law.* a civil wrong permitting compensation or punitive damages. **3.** *Common Law.* a tort.

**delight** /də'laɪt/, *n.* **1.** a high degree of pleasure or enjoyment; joy; rapture. **2.** something that gives great pleasure. *–v.t.* **3.** to give great pleasure, satisfaction, or enjoyment to; please highly. *–v.i.* **4.** to have great pleasure; take pleasure (fol. by *in* or an infinitive). [erroneous 16th-cent. sp., after *light*, replacing ME *delit*, from OF, from *delitier*, from L *dēlectāre*, frequentative of *dēlicere* allure] – **delighter,** *n.*

**delighted** /də'laɪtəd/, *adj.* highly pleased. – **delightedly,** *adv.* – **delightedness,** *n.*

**delightful** /də'laɪtfəl/, *adj.* affording delight; highly pleasing. – **delightfully,** *adv.* – **delightfulness,** *n.*

**delightsome** /də'laɪtsəm/, *adj. Archaic.* delightful. – **delightsomely,** *adv.* – **delightsomeness,** *n.*

**Delilah** /də'laɪlə/, *n.* a seductive and treacherous woman. [named after Samson's mistress, who betrayed him to the Philistines (Judges 16)]

**delimit** /di'lɪmət/, *v.t.* to fix or mark the limits of; demarcate. [F *délimiter*, from L *dēlīmitāre*] – **delimitation** /diˌlɪmə'teɪʃən/, *n.* – **delimitative,** *adj.*

**delineable** /də'lɪniəbəl/, *adj.* that can be delineated.

**delineate** /də'lɪnieɪt/, *v.t.*, **-ated, -ating. 1.** to trace the outline of; sketch or trace in outline; represent pictorially. **2.** to portray in words; describe. [L *dēlīneātus*, pp., sketched out]

**delineation** /dəlɪni'eɪʃən/, *n.* **1.** the act or process of delineating. **2.** a chart or diagram; a sketch; a rough draft. **3.** a description. – **delineative** /də'lɪniətɪv/, *adj.*

**delineator** /də'lɪnieɪtə/, *n.* **1.** one who or that which delineates. **2.** a tailor's pattern which can be adjusted for cutting garments of different sizes.

**delinquency** /də'lɪŋkwənsi/, *n., pl.* **-cies. 1.** failure in or neglect of duty or obligation; fault; guilt. **2.** a misdeed or offence, esp. by a young person. **3.** delinquent behaviour or character.

**delinquent** /də'lɪŋkwənt/, *adj.* **1.** failing in or neglectful of a duty or obligation; guilty of a misdeed or offence. **2.** of or pertaining to delinquents: *delinquent taxes.* *–n.* **3.** one who is delinquent, esp. a young person: *juvenile delinquent.* [L *dēlinquens,* ppr.] – **delinquently,** *adv.*

**deliquesce** /dɛlɪ'kwɛs/, *v.i.,* **-quesced, -quescing. 1.** to melt away. **2.** to become liquid by absorbing moisture from the air, as certain salts. [L *dēliquescere* melt away]

**deliquescence** /dɛlɪ'kwɛsəns/, *n.* **1.** the act or process of deliquescing. **2.** the liquid when something deliquesces. – **deliquescent,** *adj.*

**deliration** /dɛlə'reɪʃən/, *n.* mental derangement; raving; delirium. [L *dēlīrātio*]

**delirious** /də'lɪəriəs/, *adj.* **1.** affected with delirium. **2.** characteristic of delirium. **3.** wild with excitement, enthusiasm, etc. – **deliriously,** *adv.* – **deliriousness,** *n.*

**delirium** /də'lɪəriəm/, *n., pl.* **-liriums, -liria** /-'lɪəriə/. **1.** a more or less temporary disorder of the mental faculties, as in fevers, disturbances of consciousness, or intoxication, characterised by restlessness, excitement, delusions, hallucinations, etc. **2.** a state of violent excitement or emotion. [L, from *dēlīrāre* be deranged, lit., go out of the furrow]

**delirium tremens** /– 'trɛmənz/, *n.* a violent restlessness due to excessive indulgence in alcohol, characterised by trembling, terrifying visual hallucinations, etc. [NL: trembling delirium]

**delish** /də'lɪʃ/, *adj. Colloq.* delicious.

**de-list** /di-'lɪst/, *v.t.* **1.** *Stock Exchange.* to cease to quote prices of shares, etc., of a company. **2.** to remove from a list.

**delitescent** /dɛlə'tɛsənt/, *adj.* concealed. [L *dēlitescens,* ppr.] – **delitescence,** *n.*

**deliver** /də'lɪvə/, *v.t.* **1.** to give up or surrender; give into another's possession or keeping. **2.** to carry and pass over (letters, goods, etc.) to the intended recipient or recipients. **3.** to direct; cast; cause to move in a certain direction: *the bowler delivers the ball to the batsman.* **4.** to strike: *to deliver a blow.* **5.** to give forth or produce: *our mines are still delivering 192 million tonnes of coal each year.* **6.** to give forth in words; utter or pronounce: *to deliver a verdict.* **7.** to bring forth (young); give birth to. **8.** to assist (a female) in giving birth. **9.** to assist at the birth of. **10.** to disburden (oneself) of thoughts, opinions, etc. **11.** to set free; liberate. **12.** to release or save: *deliver us from evil.* *–v.i.* **13.** to make a delivery or deliveries. **14.** to give birth. **15.** to provide a delivery service. [ME *delivre(n),* from F *délivrer,* from LL *dēlīberāre* set free] – **deliverable,** *adj.* – **deliverer,** *n.*

**deliverance** /də'lɪvərəns/, *n.* **1.** the act of delivering. **2.** the fact of being delivered. **3.** a thought or judgment expressed; a formal or authoritative pronouncement.

**delivery** /də'lɪvəri/, *n., pl.* **-eries. 1.** the delivering of letters, goods, etc. **2.** a giving up or handing over; surrender. **3.** the utterance or enunciation of words. **4.** vocal and bodily behaviour during the presentation of a speech. **5.** the act or manner of giving or sending forth, as of a ball by the bowler in cricket. **6.** release or rescue. **7.** the being delivered of, or giving birth to a child; parturition. **8.** something delivered. **9.** *Comm.* a shipment of goods from the seller to the buyer. **10.** *Law.* an act sometimes essential to a legally effective transfer of property: *a delivery of deed.* *–adj.* **11.** of or pertaining to one who or that which makes deliveries: *delivery truck, delivery man.*

**delivery not enforceable,** *adj.* indicating a new issue of shares for which scrip has not yet been issued, and which sell for slightly less than existing shares to compensate for the delay in scrip delivery. *Abbrev.:* del

**delivery room** /'– rum/, *n.* a room in a hospital where babies are delivered.

**dell** /dɛl/, *n.* a small valley; a vale, esp. a wooded one. [ME *delle,* OE *dell;* akin to DALE]

**dellie** /'dɛli/, *n. Colloq.* delicatessen. Also, **deli.**

**delmonico steak** /dɛl,mɒnɪkoʊ 'steɪk/, *n.* a small piece of steak, often boned, cut from the front end of the beef short loin. Also, **club steak.** [named after Lorenzo *Delmonico,* 1813-81, New York restaurateur]

**delo** /'dɛloʊ/, *n. Colloq.* a delegate.

**delocalise** /di'loʊkəlaɪz/, *v.t.,* **-lised, -lising.** to remove from the proper or usual locality. Also, **delocalize.** – **delocalisation** /di,loʊkəlaɪ'zeɪʃən/, *n.*

**delouse** /di'laʊs/, *v.t.* **-loused, -lousing.** to free of lice; remove lice from.

**Delphic** /'dɛlfɪk/, *adj.* ambiguous, enigmatic, obscure. Also, **Delphian** /'dɛlfiən/. [L *Delphicus,* from Gk *Delphikós* of Delphi (the ancient city in central Greece, famed for its oracle of Apollo, which was noted for giving ambiguous answers.)] – **Delphically,** *adv.*

**delphinine** /'dɛlfənin, -naɪn/, *n.* a bitter, poisonous, crystalline alkaloid obtained from various species of delphinium, esp. *Delphinium staphisagria.* [DELPHIN(IUM) + -INE[2]]

**delphinium** /dɛl'fɪniəm/, *n.* any of numerous garden varieties of the genus *Delphinium,* having handsome, usu. blue, irregular flowers. [NL, from Gk *delphínion* larkspur, diminutive of *delphín* dolphin; so called from the shape of the nectary]

**delta** /'dɛltə/, *n.* **1.** the fourth letter (Δ, δ, = English *D, d*) of the Greek alphabet. **2.** anything triangular, like the Greek capital Δ. **3.** a nearly flat plain of alluvial deposit between diverging branches of the mouth of a river, often, though not necessarily, triangular: *the delta of the Nile.*

**delta blues** /– 'bluz/, *n. Music.* an early form of blues originating from the Mississippi basin, in which the singing is usu. accompanied by solo guitar.

**delta connection** /– kə'nɛkʃən/, *n.* a form of three-phase circuit arrangement in which three line conductors are connected to terminals of three circuit elements linked to form a triangle or capital delta, Δ.

**deltaic** /dɛl'teɪɪk/, *adj.* **1.** forming a delta. **2.** having a delta. **3.** like a delta; fan-shaped.

**delta iron** /dɛltə 'aɪən/, *n. Metall.* the allotropic form of iron consisting of body-centred cubic crystals which, when pure, exists between approx. 1400°C and the melting point.

**delta ray** /'– reɪ/, *n. Physics.* an electron knocked out of an atom by a fast-moving ionised particle.

**deltiology** /dɛlti'ɒlədʒi/, *n.* the collection and study of postcards. [Gk *deltíon,* diminutive of *déltos* writing-tablet + -LOGY]

**deltoid** /'dɛltɔɪd/, *n.* **1.** a large triangular muscle covering the joint of the shoulder and serving to raise the arm away from the side of the body. *–adj.* **2.** triangular. [Gk *deltoeidḗs* delta-shaped]

**delude** /də'lud, -'ljud/, *v.t.* **-luded, -luding.** to mislead the mind or judgment of; deceive. [L *dēlūdere* play false] – **deluder,** *n.*

deltoid leaf

**deluge** /'dɛljudʒ/, *n., v.,* **-uged, -uging.** *–n.* **1.** a great overflowing of water; inundation; flood; downpour. **2.** anything that overwhelms like a flood. **3. the Deluge,** *Bible.* the great flood in the days of Noah. *–v.t.* **4.** to flood; inundate. **5.** to overrun; overwhelm. [ME, from OF, from L *dīluvium*]

**delusion** /də'luʒən, -'ljuʒən/, *n.* **1.** the act of deluding. **2.** the fact of being deluded. **3.** a false belief or opinion. **4.** *Psychiatry.* a false belief which cannot be modified by reasoning or by demonstration of facts. When persistent, it is characteristic of psychosis. Cf. **illusion** (def. 4), **hallucination.** – **delusional,** *adj.*

**delusive** /də'lusɪv, -'ljusɪv/, *adj.* **1.** tending to delude; deceptive. **2.** of the nature of a delusion; false; unreal. Also, **delusory** /də'lusəri/. – **delusively,** *adv.* – **delusiveness,** *n.*

**deluxe** /də'lʌks/, *adj.* of special elegance, sumptuousness, or fineness. Also, **de luxe.** [F: of luxury]

**delve** /dɛlv/, *v.,* **delved, delving.** *–v.i.* **1.** to carry on intensive or thorough research for information, etc. **2.** to dip; slope suddenly. **3.** *Archaic.* to dig as with a spade. **4.** *Agric.* to clear silt from a drain, esp. in fruit growing areas. *–v.t.* **5.** *Archaic.* to dig. **6.** *Archaic.* to obtain by digging. [ME *delve(n),* OE *delfan,* c. D *delven*]

**delver** /'dɛlvə/, *n. Agric.* **1.** one who delves. **2.** an apparatus developed to clear silt from a drain, esp. in fruit growing areas.

**dem.,** demy.

**demagnetise** /di'mægnətaɪz/, *v.t.,* **-tised, -tising.** to remove magnetic properties from. Also, **demagnetize.** – **demagnetisation** /di,mægnətaɪ'zeɪʃən/, *n.* – **demagnetiser,** *n.*

**demagogic** /dɛmə'gɒgɪk/, *adj.* **1.** characteristic of a demagogue. **2.** of a demagogue. Also, **demagogical.**

**demagogue** /ˈdɛməgɒg/, *n.* **1.** a leader who uses the passions or prejudices of the populace for his own interests; an unprincipled popular orator or agitator. **2.** (historically) a leader of the people. Also, *U.S.*, **demagog.** [Gk *dēmagōgós*, from *dêmos* people + *agōgós* leader]

**demagoguery** /dɛməˈgɒgəri/, *n.* the methods or practices of a demagogue.

**demagoguism** /ˈdɛməgɒgɪzəm/, *n.* →**demagoguery.** Also, **demagogism.**

**demagogy** /ˈdɛməgɒgi/, *n.* **1.** →**demagoguery.** **2.** the character of a demagogue. **3.** a body of demagogues.

**demand** /dəˈmænd, -ˈmand/, *v.t.* **1.** to ask for with authority; claim as a right: *to demand something of or from a person.* **2.** to ask for peremptorily or urgently. **3.** to call for or require as just, proper, or necessary: *a task which demands patience.* **4.** *Law.* to lay formal legal claim to. *–v.i.* **5.** to make a demand; inquire or ask. *–n.* **6.** the act of demanding. **7.** that which is demanded. **8.** an urgent or pressing requirement: *demands upon one's time.* **9.** an inquiry or question. **10.** a requisition; a legal claim. **11.** the state of being in request for purchase or use: *an article in great demand.* **12.** *Econ.* **a.** the desire to purchase and possess, coupled with the power of purchasing. **b.** the quantity of any goods which buyers will take at a particular price. See **supply**[1]. **13. on demand,** subject to payment upon presentation and demand. [F *demander*, from ML *dēmandāre* demand, from L: give in charge, entrust] – **demandable,** *adj.* – **demander,** *n.*

**demandant** /dəˈmændənt, -ˈmand-/, *n. Law.* **1.** the plaintiff in a real action. **2.** any plaintiff.

**demand bill** /dəˈmænd bɪl/, *n.* a bill of exchange, note, etc., payable on demand or presentation. Also, **demand draft, demand note.**

**demand economy** /ˈ– əˌkɒnəmi/, *n.* an economy in which a sellers' market prevails.

**demand feeding** /ˈ– fidɪŋ/, *n.* the breast or bottle feeding of a baby when it cries, rather than according to a set routine.

**demand-pull inflation** /dəmænd-ˌpʊl ɪnˈfleɪʃən/, *n. Econ.* a situation where prices are forced higher because a demand for a product greatly exceeds the manufacturer's ability to supply it. See **cost-push inflation.**

**demarcate** /ˈdimaˌkeɪt/, *v.t.*, **-cated, -cating. 1.** to mark off the boundaries of. **2.** to separate distinctly. [backformation from DEMARCATION]

**demarcation** /dimaˈkeɪʃən/, *n.* **1.** the marking off of the boundaries of something. **2.** a division between things, esp. the division between types of work carried out by members of different trade unions. **3.** separation by distinct boundaries. **4.** the defining of boundaries. Also, **demarkation.** [Latinisation of Sp. *demarcación*, from *demarcar* mark out the bounds of]

**demarcation dispute** /ˈ– dəspjut/, *n.* a dispute between trade unions over the division of types of work carried out by the members of different unions.

**démarche** /ˈdeɪmaʃ/, *n.* **1.** a plan or mode of procedure. **2.** a change in a course of action. **3.** a diplomatic representation made to a foreign government. [F, from *démarcher* march]

**dematerialise** /diməˈtɪəriəlaɪz/, *v.*, **-lised, -lising.** *–v.t.* **1.** to deprive of material character. *–v.i.* **2.** to lose material character or form. Also, **dematerialize.** – **dematerialisation** /diməˌtɪəriəlaɪˈzeɪʃən/, *n.*

**deme** /dim/, *n.* **1.** one of the administrative divisions of ancient Attica and of modern Greece. **2.** a local population made up of closely related organisms and large enough to have evolutionary significance. [Gk *dêmos* district, country, people, commons]

**demean**[1] /dəˈmin/, *v.t.* to lower in dignity or standing; debase. [DE- + MEAN[2], modelled on DEBASE]

**demean**[2] /dəˈmin/, *v.t.* to conduct or behave (oneself) in a specified manner. [ME *demene(n)*, from OF *demener*, from *de-* DE- + *mener* lead, from L *mināre* drive]

**demeanour** /dəˈminə/, *n.* conduct; behaviour; bearing. Also, *U.S.*, **demeanor.** [ME *demenure*, from *demene(n)* DEMEAN[2], *v.*]

**dement** /dəˈmɛnt/, *v.t.* to drive mad or insane. [L *dēmentāre* deprive of mind]

**demented** /dəˈmɛntəd/, *adj.* out of one's mind; crazed; insane; affected with dementia. – **dementedly,** *adv.* – **dementedness,** *n.*

**dementia** /dəˈmɛnʃiə, -ʃə/, *n.* a state of mental disorder characterised by impairment or loss of the mental powers; commonly an end result of several mental or other diseases. [L: madness]

**dementia praecox** /–ˈprikɒks/, *n.* a form of insanity usu. occurring or beginning at puberty and characterised by introversion, dissociation, and odd, distorted behaviour; one of the schizophrenic reactions beginning at puberty. [L: precocious insanity]

**demerara** /dɛməˈrɛərə/, *n.* a brown crystallised cane sugar from the West Indies and nearby countries. [from *Demerara*, a region in Guyana, where it was originally chiefly produced]

**demerit** /diˈmɛrət/, *n.* **1.** censurable or punishable quality; fault. **2.** a mark against a person for misconduct or deficiency. **3.** *Obs.* merit or desert. [ML *dēmeritum* fault, from L *dēmerērī* deserve (esp. well)]

**demersal** /dəˈmɜsəl/, *adj. Zool.* found at or near the sea bottom. [L *dēmersus*, pp., submerged + -AL[2]]

**demesne** /dəˈmeɪn/, *n.* **1.** possession (of land) as one's own. **2.** an estate possessed, or in the actual possession or use of the owner. **3.** the land attached to a manor house, reserved for the owner's use. **4.** the dominion or territory of a sovereign or state; a domain. **5.** a district; region. [ME *demeyne*, from AF. See DOMAIN]

**demi-,** a prefix meaning: **1.** half, as in *demilune.* **2.** inferior, as in *demigod.* [F, representing *demi*, adj. (also n. and adv.), from L *dīmedius*, replacing *dīmidius* half]

**demigod** /ˈdɛmigɒd/, *n.* **1.** one partly divine and partly human; an inferior deity. **2.** a deified mortal. – **demigoddess** /ˈdɛmiˌgɒdɛs/, *n. fem.*

**demijohn** /ˈdɛmidʒɒn/, *n.* a large small-necked bottle, usu. cased in wickerwork. [F *damejeanne*, apparently a popular name, Dame Jane]

demijohn

**demilitarise** /diˈmɪlətəraɪz/, *v.t.*, **-rised, -rising. 1.** to deprive of military character; free from militarism. **2.** to place under civil instead of military control. **3.** to prevent by treaty or force an independent state from arming itself, or maintaining its arms. Also, **demilitarize.** – **demilitarisation** /diˌmɪlətəraɪˈzeɪʃən/, *n.*

**demilitarised zone** /diˈmɪlətəraɪzd ˌzoʊn/, *n. Mil.* a defined area in which the stationing or concentrating of military forces, or the retention or establishment of military installations of any description, is prohibited.

**demilune** /ˈdɛmilun/, *n.* anything crescent-shaped, esp. an outwork of a fortification resembling a bastion. [F: lit., half-moon]

**demimondaine** /ˌdɛmimɒnˈdeɪn/, *n.* a woman of the demimonde. [F]

**demimonde** /ˌdɛmiˈmɒnd/, *n.* **1.** the world or class of women who are maintained by wealthy lovers. **2.** the world of any group on the fringes of social respectability. [F: lit., half-world]

**demipique** /ˈdɛmipik/, *n.* an 18th-century military saddle having a low pommel. [DEMI- + *pique* (pseudo-F sp. of PEAK[1])]

**demirelief** /ˈdɛmirəˌlif/, *n.* sculpture in middle relief, between alto-rilievo and bas-relief; mezzo-rilievo.

**demirep** /ˈdɛmirɛp/, *n.* a woman of doubtful or compromised reputation. [short for *demi-reputation*]

**demise** /dəˈmaɪz/, *n.*, *v.*, **-mised, -mising.** *–n.* **1.** death or decease. **2.** *Law.* **a.** a death or decease occasioning the transfer of an estate. **b.** a conveyance or transfer of an estate. **3.** *Govt.* transfer of sovereignty, as by the death or deposition of the sovereign. *–v.t.* **4.** *Law.* to transfer (an estate, etc.) for a limited time; lease. **5.** *Govt.* to transfer (sovereignty), as by the death or abdication of the sovereign. *–v.i.* **6.** *Law.* to pass by bequest, inheritance, or succession to the Crown. [OF, properly pp. fem. of *desmettre* send or put away] – **demisable,** *adj.*

**demi-sec** /dɛmi-ˈsɛk/, *adj.* (of champagne) half-dry (indicating the dosage of liqueur added as a sweetening agent prior to final corkage). [F: half-dry]

**demisemiquaver** /ˌdɛmiˈsɛmiˌkweɪvə, ˈdɛmiˌsɛmi-/, *n.* a musical note having half the time value of a semiquaver.

**demission** /diˈmɪʃən/, *n.* **1.** abdication. **2.** *Rare.* dismissal. [F. Cf. L *dīmissio* a sending away]

**demister** /diˈmɪstə/, *n.* a device for directing air, usu. heated, onto the windscreen or other windows of a vehicle to clear them of mist or frost.

**demitasse** /dɛmiˈtæs, -ˈtas/, *n.* a small cup for serving black coffee after dinner. [F: half cup]

**demiurge** /ˈdɛmiˌɜdʒ/, *n. Philos.* **a.** (in Platonic philosophy) the artificer of the world. **b.** (in the Gnostic and certain other systems) a supernatural being imagined as creating or fashioning the world in subordination to the Supreme Being, and sometimes regarded as the originator of evil. [Gk *dēmiourgós* worker for the people, artificer, maker] – **demiurgeous** /dɛmiˈɜdʒəs/, **demiurgic** /dɛmiˈɜdʒɪk/, *adj.* – **demiurgically** /dɛmiˈɜdʒɪkli/, *adv.*

**demivolt** /ˈdɛmivoult/, *n.* a half-turn made by a horse with the forelegs raised. Also, **demivolte.** [F *demi-volte.* See DEMI-, VOLT²]

**demo** /ˈdɛmou/, *n. Colloq.* →**demonstration.**

**demo-,** a word element meaning 'people', 'population', 'common people'. [Gk, combining form of *dêmos* DEMOS]

**demob** /diˈmɒb/, *n., v.,* **-mobbed, -mobbing.** *Colloq. –n.* **1.** demobilisation. *–v.t.* **2.** to discharge (a soldier) from the army. [short for DEMOBILISE]

**demobilise** /diˈmoubəlaɪz/, *v.,* **-lised, -lising.** *–v.t.* **1.** to disband (an army, etc.). *–v.i.* **2.** (of an army or its members) to disband. Also, **demobilize.** – **demobilisation** /diˌmoubəlaɪˈzeɪʃən/, *n.*

**democracy** /dəˈmɒkrəsi/, *n., pl.* **-cies.** **1.** government by the people; a form of government in which the supreme power is vested in the people and exercised by them or by their elected agents under a free electoral system. **2.** a state having such a form of government. **3.** (in a restricted sense) a state in which the supreme power is vested in the people and exercised directly by them rather than by elected representatives. See **republic. 4.** a state of society characterised by formal equality of rights and privileges. **5.** political or social equality; democratic spirit. **6.** the common people of a community as distinguished from any privileged class; the common people with respect to their political power. [F *démocratie,* from Gk *dēmokratía* popular government, from *dēmo-* DEMO- + *-kratía* rule, authority]

**democrat** /ˈdɛməkræt/, *n.* **1.** an advocate of democracy. **2.** one who maintains the political or social equality of all people.

**democratic** /dɛməˈkrætɪk/, *adj.* **1.** pertaining to or of the nature of democracy or a democracy. **2.** pertaining to or characterised by the principle of political or social equality for all. **3.** advocating or upholding democracy. Also, **democratical.** – **democratically,** *adv.*

**Democratic Kampuchea** /ˌdɛməkrætɪk kæmpəˈtʃɪə/, *n.* official name of **Kampuchea.**

**Democratic People's Republic of Korea,** *n.* official name of **North Korea.**

**Democratic Yemen** /dɛməˌkrætɪk ˈjɛmən/, *n.* a country on the southern Arabian peninsula.

**democratise** /dəˈmɒkrətaɪz/, *v.,* **-tised, -tising.** *–v.t.* **1.** to make democratic. *–v.i.* **2.** to become democratic. Also, **democratize.** – **democratisation** /dəˌmɒkrətaɪˈzeɪʃən/, *n.*

**demoded** /diˈmoudəd/, *adj.* no longer in fashion.

**demodulate** /diˈmɒdʒəleɪt/, *v.t.,* **-lated, -lating.** *Radio.* to separate (a signal) from the carrier wave in a radio receiver. – **demodulation** /ˌdimɒdʒəˈleɪʃən/, *n.*

**demographic** /dɛməˈgræfɪk/, *adj.* of or pertaining to demography. Also, **demographical.** – **demographically,** *adv.*

**demographics** /dɛməˈgræfɪks/, *n.pl.* demographic data.

**demography** /dəˈmɒgrəfi/, *n.* the science of vital and social statistics, as of the births, deaths, diseases, marriages, etc., of populations. – **demographer, demographist,** *n.*

**demoiselle** /dɛmwaˈzɛl/, *n.* **1.** a damsel. **2.** the Numidian crane, *Anthropoides virgo,* of northern Africa, Asia, and Europe, having long white plumes behind the eyes. **3.** any of various slender-bodied dragonflies. [F]

**demolish** /dəˈmɒlɪʃ/, *v.t.* **1.** to throw or pull down (a building, etc.); reduce to ruins. **2.** to put an end to; destroy; ruin utterly; lay waste. **3.** *Colloq.* to eat or drink greedily. [F *démoliss-,* from *démolir,* from L *dēmōlīrī* throw down, destroy] – **demolisher,** *n.* – **demolishment,** *n.*

**demolition** /dɛməˈlɪʃən/, *n.* **1.** the act of demolishing. **2.** the state of being demolished; destruction.

**demon** /ˈdimən/, *n.* **1.** an evil spirit; a devil. **2.** an evil passion. **3.** an atrociously wicked or cruel person. **4.** a person of great energy, etc. **5.** *Colloq.* (formerly) a convict; bushranger. **6.** *Colloq.* (formerly) a trooper. **7.** *Colloq.* a detective; policeman, esp. a motorcycle policeman. **8.** →**daemon.** [ME, from LL *daemōn* evil spirit, L spirit, from Gk *daímōn* divine power, fate, god]

**demon-,** a word element meaning 'demon'. [Gk, combining form of *daímōn*]

**demonetise** /diˈmʌnətaɪz/, *v.t.,* **-tised, -tising.** **1.** to divest of value, as the monetary standard. **2.** to withdraw from use as money. Also, **demonetize.** – **demonetisation** /diˌmʌnətaɪˈzeɪʃən/, *n.*

**demoniac** /dəˈmouniæk/, *adj.* Also, **demoniacal** /dɛmə-ˈnaɪəkəl/. **1.** of, pertaining to, or like a demon. **2.** possessed by an evil spirit; raging; frantic. *–n.* **3.** one seemingly possessed by a demon or evil spirit. [ME *demoniak,* from LL *daemoniacus,* from Gk *daimoniakós*] – **demoniacally** /dɛməˈnaɪəkəli, -əkli/, *adv.*

**demonian** /dəˈmouniən/, *adj.* pertaining to or of the nature of a demon.

**demonic** /dəˈmɒnɪk/, *adj.* **1.** of, pertaining to, or of the nature of a demon. **2.** inspired as if by a demon, indwelling spirit, or genius. [L *daemonicus,* from Gk *daimonikós*]

**demonise** /ˈdimənaɪz/, *v.t.,* **-nised, -nising.** **1.** to turn into or make like a demon. **2.** to subject to the influence of demons. Also, **demonize.**

**demonism** /ˈdimənɪzəm/, *n.* **1.** belief in demons. **2.** worship of demons. **3.** →**demonology.** – **demonist,** *n.*

**demono-,** variant of **demon-,** before consonants.

**demonolater** /diməˈnɒlətə/, *n.* a demon worshipper.

**demonolatry** /diməˈnɒlətri/, *n.* the worship of demons.

**demonology** /diməˈnɒlədʒi/, *n.* the study of demons or of beliefs about demons. – **demonologist,** *n.*

**demonomancy** /ˈdimənouˌmænsi/, *n.* divination through the aid of demons.

**demonstrable** /dəˈmɒnstrəbəl, ˈdɛmən-/, *adj.* capable of being demonstrated. – **demonstrability** /dəmɒnstrəˈbɪləti/, **demonstrableness,** *n.* – **demonstrably,** *adv.*

**demonstrate** /ˈdɛmənstreɪt/, *v.,* **-strated, -strating.** *–v.t.* **1.** to make evident by arguments or reasoning; prove. **2.** to describe and explain with the help of specimens or by experiment. **3.** to manifest or exhibit. *–v.i.* **4.** to make, give, or take part in, a demonstration. **5.** *Mil.* to attack or make a show of force to deceive the enemy; feint. [L *dēmonstrātus,* pp., showed, proved]

**demonstration** /dɛmənˈstreɪʃən/, *n.* **1.** the proving of anything conclusively, as by arguments, reasoning, evidence, etc. **2.** proof, or anything serving as a proof. **3.** a description or explanation, as of a process, given with the help of specimens or by experiment. **4.** the act of exhibiting and explaining an article or commodity by way of advertising it. **5.** an exhibition, as of feeling; a display; manifestation. **6.** a public exhibition of sympathy, opposition, etc., as a parade or mass meeting. **7.** a show of military force or of offensive operations, made to deceive the enemy. **8.** *Maths.* →**proof** (def. 5). – **demonstrational,** *adj.* – **demonstrationist,** *n.*

**demonstration school** /ˈ– ˌskul/, *n.* a primary or secondary school where student teachers observe lessons conducted by teachers.

**demonstrative** /dəˈmɒnstrətɪv/, *adj.* **1.** characterised by or given to open exhibition or expression of the feelings, etc. **2.** serving to demonstrate; explanatory or illustrative. **3.** serving to prove the truth of anything; indubitably conclusive. **4.** *Gram.* indicating or specifying the thing referred to. *–n.* **5.** *Gram.* a demonstrative word, as *this* or *there.* – **demonstratively,** *adv.* – **demonstrativeness,** *n.*

**demonstrator** /ˈdɛmənstreɪtə/, *n.* **1.** one who or that which demonstrates. **2.** one who takes part in a public demonstration. **3.** one who explains or teaches by practical demonstrations. **4.** one who shows the use and application (of a product, etc.) to prospective customers. **5.** a new motor car which has been used only for demonstration.

**demoralise** /di'mɒrəlaɪz/, *v.t.*, **-lised, -lising. 1.** to corrupt or undermine the morals of. **2.** to deprive (a person, a body of soldiers, etc.) of spirit, courage, discipline, etc. **3.** to reduce to a state of weakness or disorder. Also, **demoralize.** [F *démoraliser*] – **demoralisation** /di,mɒrəlaɪ'zeɪʃən/, *n.* – **demoraliser,** *n.*

**demos** /'dimɒs/, *n.* **1.** the people or commons of an ancient Greek state. **2.** the common people; the populace. [Gk: district, people]

**demote** /də'moʊt, di-/, *v.t.*, **-moted, -moting.** to reduce to a lower grade or class (opposed to *promote*). [DE- + *mote,* modelled on PROMOTE] – **demotion,** *n.*

**demotic** /də'mɒtɪk/, *adj.* **1.** of or pertaining to the common people; popular. **2.** of or pertaining to the ancient Egyptian handwriting of ordinary life, a simplified form of the hieratic characters. **3.** of or pertaining to the Modern Greek vernacular. *–n.* **4.** the demotic script of ancient Egypt. **5.** (*cap.*) the Modern Greek vernacular. [Gk *dēmotikós* popular, plebeian]

**demount** /di'maʊnt/, *v.t.* to remove from its mounting, setting, or place of support, as a gun.

**demountable** /di'maʊntəbəl/, *adj.* **1.** able to be dismantled. **2.** (of a building) able to be dismantled and removed from one site and reassembled on a new location. *–n.* **3.** such a building.

**demulcent** /də'mʌlsənt/, *adj.* **1.** soothing or mollifying, as a medicinal substance. *–n.* **2.** a demulcent (often mucilaginous) substance or agent, as for soothing or protecting an irritated mucous membrane. [L *dēmulcens,* ppr., stroking down, softening]

**demulsify** /di'mʌlsəfaɪ/, *v.t.*, **-fied, -fying.** *Phys. Chem.* to break down (an emulsion) into separate substances, incapable of re-forming the same emulsion.

**demur** /də'mɜ/, *v.*, **-murred, -murring,** *n. –v.i.* **1.** to make objection; take exception; object. **2.** *Law.* to interpose a demurrer. **3.** *Obs.* to linger; hesitate. *–n.* **4.** the act of making objection. **5.** an objection raised. **6.** *Obs., Law.* a demurrer. **7.** *Obs.* hesitation. [ME *demeore(n),* from OF *demeurer,* from L *dēmorārī* linger]

**demure** /də'mjuə, -'mjʊə/, *adj.*, **-murer, -murest. 1.** affectedly or unnaturally modest, decorous, or prim. **2.** sober; serious; sedate; decorous. [ME, from OF *meur* grave, ripe, from L *mātūrus* MATURE] – **demurely,** *adv.* – **demureness,** *n.*

**demurrage** /də'mʌrɪdʒ/, *n. Comm.* **1.** the detention of a vessel, as in loading or unloading, beyond the time agreed upon. **2.** the similar detention of a railway wagon, etc. **3.** a charge for such detention.

**demurral** /də'mɜrəl/, *n.* the act of demurring; demur.

**demurrer** /də'mɜrə/ *for def. 1;* /di'mʌrə/ *for defs 2 and 3,* *n.* **1.** one who demurs; an objector. **2.** *Law.* a pleading in effect that even if the facts are as alleged by the opposite party, they do not sustain the contention based on them. **3.** an objection or demur. [AF, var. of OF *demourer.* See DEMUR]

**demy** /də'mi/, *n.*, *pl.* **-mies.** a size of printing paper, $22\frac{1}{2}$ inches by $17\frac{1}{2}$ inches, most commonly in use before metrication. [free form of DEMI-, with change of final *i* to *y* in accordance with rules of English spelling]

**demyelisation** /di,maɪələ'zeɪʃən/, *n.* a process in which the myelin is lost from nervous tissue. Also, **demyelization, demyelination** /di,maɪələ'neɪʃən/.

**demystify** /di'mɪstəfaɪ/, *v.t.* to remove the aura of mystery or strangeness from: *pledged to demystify the political system.* – **demystification** /di,mɪstəfə'keɪʃən/, *n.*

**demythologise** /dimə'θɒlədʒaɪz/, *v.t.*, **-gised, -gising. 1.** to divest (a writing, person, work of art, etc.) of its legendary or mythological character. **2.** to present (a religious system) in rational terms. Also, **demythologize.**

**den** /dɛn/, *n., v.,* **denned, denning.** *–n.* **1.** a secluded place, as a cave, serving as the habitation of a wild beast. **2.** a cave as a place of shelter, concealment, etc. **3.** a squalid or vile abode or place: *dens of misery.* **4.** a cosy or secluded room for personal use. *–v.i.* **5.** to live in or as in a den. [ME; OE *denn.* Cf. early mod. D *denne* floor, cave, den, G *Tenne* floor]

**denarius** /də'nɛəriəs/, *n.*, *pl.* **-narii** /-'nɛərii/. **1.** a Roman silver coin of varying intrinsic value. **2.** (formerly) (in English monetary reckoning) a penny, hence *d.* [L, orig. adj., containing ten (asses). See DENARY]

**denary** /'dinəri/, *adj.* **1.** containing ten; tenfold. **2.** proceeding by tens; decimal. [L *dēnārius* containing ten, from *dēnī* ten at a time]

**denasalise** /di'neɪzəlaɪz/, *v.t.*, **-lised, -lising.** to remove nasality totally or partially from (a phonetic segment or series of phonetic segments). Also, **denasalize.**

**denasality** /,dineɪ'zæləti/, *n.* a lack of adequate nasal resonance during speech.

**denationalise** /di'næʃənəlaɪz/, *v.t.*, **-lised, -lising. 1.** to deprive of national status, attachments, or characteristics. **2.** to return (an industry, etc.) from state to private ownership. Also, **denationalize.** – **denationalisation** /di,næʃənəlaɪ'zeɪʃən/, *n.*

**denaturalise** /di'nætʃərəlaɪz/, *v.t.*, **-lised, lising. 1.** to deprive of the original nature; make unnatural. **2.** to deprive of the rights and privileges of citizenship or of naturalisation. Also, **denaturalize.** – **denaturalisation** /di,nætʃərəlaɪ'zeɪʃən/, *n.*

**denature** /di'neɪtʃə/, *v.t.*, **-tured, -turing. 1.** to deprive (something) of its peculiar nature. **2.** to render (alcohol, etc.) unfit for drinking or eating by adding a poisonous substance without altering the usefulness for other purposes. **3.** *Biochem.* to treat (a protein, etc.) by chemical or physical means so as to alter its original state. **4.** to render (a fissile material) unsuitable for use in a nuclear weapon by adding another isotope to it. – **denaturant,** *n.* – **denaturation** /dineɪtʃə'reɪʃən/, *n.*

**denaturise** /di'neɪtʃəraɪz/, *v.t.*, **-rised, -rising.** to denature. Also, **denaturize.** – **denaturisation** /di,neɪtʃəraɪ'zeɪʃən/, *n.*

**dendr-,** variant of **dendro-,** before vowels.

**dendriform** /'dɛndrəfɔm/, *adj.* treelike in form. [DENDR- + -I- + -FORM]

**dendrite** /'dɛndraɪt/, *n.* **1.** *Geol.* **a.** a branching figure or marking, resembling moss or a shrub or tree in form, occurring on or in certain stones or minerals, and due to the presence of a foreign material. **b.** any arborescent crystalline growth, as of gold or silver. **2.** *Anat., Physiol.* the branching portion of a neurone which picks up the stimulus and transmits it to the cyton. [Gk *dendrítēs* of a tree]

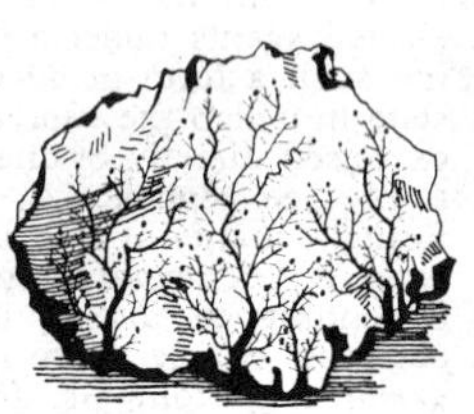
dendrite (def. 1a)

**dendritic** /dɛn'drɪtɪk/, *adj.* **1.** formed or marked like a dendrite. **2.** of a branching form; arborescent. Also, **dendritical.** – **dendritically,** *adv.*

**dendro-,** a word element meaning 'tree', as in *dendrology.* [Gk, combining form of *déndron*]

**dendrobates** /dɛn'drɒbətiz/, *n.* any member of the *Dendrobates,* a South American genus of frogs whose glands exude a poison used by Indians for poisoning their arrowheads; the poison-arrow frog.

**dendrobium** /dɛn'droʊbiəm/, *n.* any species of the very large orchid genus *Dendrobium,* widely distributed in Asia and Australia, as *D. bigibbum,* Cooktown orchid, and *D. speciosum,* rocklily.

**dendrochronology** /,dɛndroʊkrə'nɒlədʒi/, *n.* a method of dating archaeological material by comparison with the ring pattern of timber. [DENDRO- + CHRONOLOGY] – **dendrochronological** /,dɛndroʊ,krɒnə'lɒdʒɪkəl/, *adj.*

**dendroid** /'dɛndrɔɪd/, *adj.* treelike; branching like a tree; arborescent. Also, **dendroidal** /dɛn'drɔɪdl/. [Gk *dendroeidḗs* treelike]

**dendrolatry** /dɛn'drɒlətri/, *n.* the worship of trees.

**dendrology** /dɛn'drɒlədʒi/, *n.* the part of botany that treats of trees and shrubs. – **dendrological** /dɛndrə'lɒdʒɪkəl/, **dendrologous** /dɛn'drɒləgəs/, *adj.* – **dendrologist** /dɛn'drɒlədʒəst/, *n.*

**-dendron,** a word element meaning 'tree', as in *rhododendron.* [representing Gk *déndron* tree]

**dene** /din/, *n.* a bare sandy tract or low sandhill near the sea. Also, **dean.** [ME; orig. uncert.]

**denegation** /dɛnəˈgeɪʃən/, *n.* denial; contradiction. [LL *dēnegātio*]

**dengue** /ˈdɛŋgi/, *n.* an infectious, eruptive, usu. epidemic, fever of warm climates, characterised esp. by severe pains in the joints and muscles; breakbone fever. [Sp., from Swahili *dinga* cramp]

**denial** /dəˈnaɪəl/, *n.* **1.** a contradiction of a statement, etc. **2.** refusal to believe a doctrine, etc. **3.** disbelief in the existence or reality of a thing. **4.** the refusal of a claim, request, etc., or of a person making a request. **5.** refusal to recognise or acknowledge; a disowning or disavowal. **6.** →**self-denial.** [DENY + -AL[2]]

**denier**[1] /dəˈnaɪə/, *n.* one who denies. [ME; from DENY + -ER[1]]

**denier**[2] /ˈdɛniə, ˈdɛnieɪ/, *n.* a unit of weight used to indicate the fineness of silk, nylon, etc. [ME, from OF, from L *dēnārius* DENARIUS]

**denigrate** /ˈdɛnəgreɪt/, *v.t.*, **-grated, -grating. 1.** to sully; defame. **2.** to blacken. [L *dēnigrātus*, pp., blackened] – **denigration** /dɛnəˈgreɪʃən/, *n.* – **denigrator,** *n.*

**denim** /ˈdɛnəm/, *n.* **1.** a heavy twilled cotton for overalls, trousers, etc. **2.** a similar fabric of a finer quality used to cover cushions, etc. **3.** (*pl.*) *Colloq.* denim trousers or overalls. [F, short for *serge de Nîmes* serge of Nîmes]

**denitrify** /diˈnaɪtrəfaɪ/, *v.t.*, **-fied, -fying.** to reduce (nitrates) to nitrites, ammonia, and free nitrogen, as micro-organisms do in soil. – **denitrification** /diˌnaɪtrəfəˈkeɪʃən/, *n.*

**denizen** /ˈdɛnəzən/, *n.* **1.** an inhabitant; resident. **2.** an alien admitted to residence and to certain rights of citizenship in a country. **3.** anything adapted to a new place, condition, etc., as a naturalised foreign word, or an animal or plant not indigenous to a place but successfully naturalised. *–v.t.* **4.** to make a denizen of. [ME *deynseyn*, from AF *deinzein*, from *deinz* within, from L *dē intus*]

**Denmark** /ˈdɛnmak/, *n.* a kingdom in northern Europe.

**denominate** /dəˈnɒməneɪt/, *v.t.*, **-nated, -nating.** to give a name to, esp. to call by a specific name. [L *dēnōminātus*, pp.]

**denomination** /dənɒməˈneɪʃən/, *n.* **1.** a name or designation, esp. one for a class of things. **2.** a class or kind of persons or things distinguished by a specific name. **3.** a religious group. **4.** the act of denominating. **5.** one of the grades or degrees in a series of designations of quantity, value, measure, weight, etc.: *money of small denominations.*

**denominational** /dənɒməˈneɪʃənəl/, *adj.* of or pertaining to a particular religious body or sect; sectarian. – **denominationally,** *adv.*

**denominationalism** /dənɒməˈneɪʃənəlɪzəm/, *n.* denominational or sectarian spirit or policy; the tendency to divide into denominations or sects. – **denominationalist,** *n.*

**denominative** /dəˈnɒmənətɪv/, *adj.* **1.** conferring or constituting a distinctive denomination or name. **2.** *Gram.* (esp. of verbs) formed from a noun, as English *to man* from the noun *man.* *–n.* **3.** *Gram.* a denominative verb or other word.

**denominator** /dəˈnɒməneɪtə/, *n.* **1.** *Maths.* that term of a fraction (usu. under the line) which shows the number of equal parts into which the unit is divided; a divisor placed under a dividend. **2.** one who or that which denominates, or from which a name is derived.

**denotation** /dinoʊˈteɪʃən/, *n.* **1.** the meaning of a term when it identifies something by naming it (distinguished from *connotation*). **2.** the act or fact of denoting; indication. **3.** something that denotes; a mark; symbol. **4.** *Logic.* the class of particulars to which a term is applicable.

**denotative** /diˈnoʊtətɪv/, *adj.* having power to denote. – **denotatively,** *adv.*

**denote** /dəˈnoʊt/, *v.t.*, **-noted, -noting. 1.** to be a mark or sign of; indicate: *a quick pulse often denotes fever.* **2.** to be a name or designation for. **3.** to represent by a symbol; stand as a symbol for. **4.** to impress with a denoting stamp. [F *dénoter*, from L *dēnotāre* mark out] – **denotable,** *adj.*

**denouement** /dəˈnumõ/, *n.* **1.** the final disentangling of the intricacies of a plot, as of a drama or novel. **2.** the place in the plot at which this occurs. **3.** outcome; solution. [F, from *dénouer* untie, from *de(s)-* DE- + *nouer*, from L *nodāre* knot, tie]

**denounce** /dəˈnaʊns/, *v.t.*, **-nounced, -nouncing. 1.** to condemn openly; assail with censure. **2.** to make formal accusation against; inform against. **3.** to give formal notice of the termination of (a treaty, etc.). **4.** to proclaim (something evil). [ME *denounse(n)*, from OF *denoncier*, from L *dēnuntiāre* threaten] – **denouncement,** *n.* – **denouncer,** *n.*

**de novo** /di ˈnoʊvoʊ/, *adv.* from the beginning; anew. [L]

**dense** /dɛns/, *adj.*, **denser, densest. 1.** having the component parts closely compacted together; compact: *a dense forest, dense population.* **2.** thickheaded; obtuse; stupid. **3.** intense: *dense ignorance.* **4.** *Photog.* (of a developed negative) relatively opaque; transmitting little light. [L *densus* thick, thickly set] – **densely,** *adv.* – **denseness,** *n.*

**densimeter** /dɛnˈsɪmətə/, *n.* any instrument for measuring density.

**densitometer** /dɛnsəˈtɒmətə/, *n.* an instrument for measuring the density of photographic negatives.

**density** /ˈdɛnsəti/, *n.*, *pl.* **-ties. 1.** the state or quality of being dense; compactness; closely set or crowded condition. **2.** stupidity. **3.** *Physics.* **a.** the mass per unit of volume. **b.** the amount per unit of volume or per unit of area of any physical quantity, as in *energy density, current density.* **4.** *Photog.* the opacity of any medium, esp. of a photographic plate or negative, which is often expressed logarithmically. **5.** the compactness in a sheep's fleece of fibre growth on a given area of skin. **6.** *Bot.* a quantitative character of a plant community; the average number of individuals per area sampled.

**dent**[1] /dɛnt/, *n.* **1.** a hollow or depression in a surface, as from a blow. *–v.t.* **2.** to make a dent in or on; indent. **3.** to impress as a dent. *–v.i.* **4.** to sink in, making a dent. **5.** to become indented. [ME *dente;* var. of DINT]

**dent**[2] /dɛnt/, *n.* a toothlike projection, as a tooth of a gearwheel. [F, from L *dens* tooth]

**dental** /ˈdɛntl/, *adj.* **1.** of or pertaining to the teeth. **2.** of or pertaining to dentistry. **3.** *Phonet.* **a.** with the tongue tip touching or near the upper front teeth, as French *t.* **b.** alveolar, as English alveolar *t.* *–n.* **4.** *Phonet.* a dental sound. [ML *dentālis*, from L *dens* tooth]

**dental floss** /ˈ– flɒs/, *n.* →**floss** (def. 4).

**dentary** /ˈdɛntəri/, *n.* one of the pair of bones in the lower jaw of some vertebrates, usu. bearing teeth.

**dentate** /ˈdɛnteɪt/, *adj.* having a toothed margin, or toothlike projections or processes. [L *dentātus*, from *dens* tooth] – **dentately,** *adv.*

dentate leaf

**dentation** /dɛnˈteɪʃən/, *n.* **1.** a dentate state or form. **2.** an angular projection of a margin.

**denti-,** a word element meaning 'tooth', as in *dentiform.* Also, before vowels, **dent-.** [L, combining form of *dens*]

**denticle** /ˈdɛntɪkl/, *n.* a small tooth or toothlike part. [ME, from L *denticulus*, diminutive of *dens* tooth]

**denticulate** /dɛnˈtɪkjələt, -leɪt/, *adj.* **1.** finely dentate, as a leaf. **2.** *Archit.* having dentils. Also, **denticulated.** – **denticulately,** *adv.*

**denticulation** /dɛntɪkjəˈleɪʃən/, *n.* **1.** a denticulate state or form. **2.** a denticle. **3.** a series of denticles.

**dentiform** /ˈdɛntəfɔm/, *adj.* having the form of a tooth.

**dentifrice** /ˈdɛntəfrəs/, *n.* a powder, paste, or other preparation for cleaning the teeth. [F, from L *dentifricium* tooth powder. See DENTI-, FRICTION]

**dentil** /ˈdɛntl/, *n.* *Archit.* one of a series of small rectangular blocks arranged like a row of teeth, as in the lower part of a cornice. [F *dentille* (obs.), fem. diminutive of *dent* tooth]

**dentilabial** /dɛntiˈleɪbiəl/, *adj.*, *n.* →**labiodental.**

**dentilingual** /dɛntiˈlɪŋgwəl/, *adj.* **1.** (of speech sounds) uttered with the tongue at the teeth, as the *th* in *thin* and *this.* *–n.* **2.** a dentilingual sound.

**dentine** /ˈdɛntin/, *n.* *Anat.* the hard calcareous tissue beneath the enamel of the crown of the tooth and beneath the cementum of the root of the tooth. It contains less organic substance than cementum or bone and forms the greatest part of a tooth. Also, *Chiefly U.S.*, **dentin.** [DENT(I)- + -INE[2]] – **dentinal,** *adj.*

**dentiphone** /ˈdɛntəfoʊn/, *n.* an instrument held against the teeth to assist hearing by transmitting sound vibrations to the

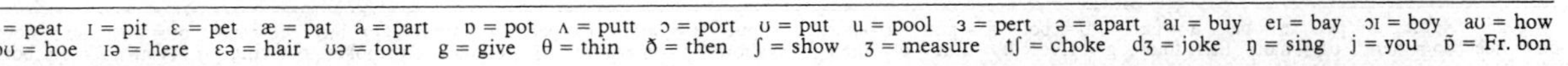

auditory nerve.

**dentirostral** /dɛnti'rɒstrəl/, *adj. Ornith.* having a tooth-like or notched projection on the bill.

**dentist** /'dɛntəst/, *n.* one whose profession is dentistry. [F *dentiste*, from *dent* tooth]

**dentistry** /'dɛntəstri/, *n.* the science or art dealing with the prevention and treatment of oral disease, esp. in relation to the health of the body as a whole, and including such operations as the filling and crowning of teeth, the construction of dentures, etc.

**dentition** /dɛn'tɪʃən/, *n.* **1.** the growing of teeth; teething. **2.** the kind, number, and arrangement of the teeth of an animal, including man. [L *dentītio* teething]

**dentoid** /'dɛntɔɪd/, *adj.* like a tooth.

**denture** /'dɛntʃə/, *n.* an artificial restoration of several teeth (**partial denture**) or of all the teeth of either jaw (**full denture**). [F, from *dent* tooth]

**denuclearise** /di'njukliəraɪz/, *v.t.*, **-rised, -rising.** to remove all nuclear armaments from (an area, country, etc.), in accordance with a declared policy or agreement: *Asia should become a denuclearised zone.*

**denudate** /di'njudeɪt, 'dɛnjədeɪt/, *v.*, **-dated, -dating,** *adj.* *–v.t.* **1.** to denude. *–adj.* **2.** denuded; bare.

**denudation** /,dinju'deɪʃən, ,dɛnjə'deɪʃən/, *n.* **1.** the act of denuding. **2.** denuded or bare condition. **3.** *Geol.* the laying bare of rock by erosive processes.

**denude** /də'njud/, *v.t.*, **-nuded, -nuding.** **1.** to make naked or bare; strip. **2.** *Geol.* to subject to denudation. [L *dēnūdāre* lay bare]

**denumerable** /də'njumərəbəl/, *adj. Maths.* (of a set) finite or countable.

**denunciate** /də'nʌnsieɪt/, *v.t.*, **-ated, -ating.** to denounce; condemn openly. [L *dēnuntiātus*, pp.] **– denunciator,** *n.*

**denunciation** /dənʌnsi'eɪʃən/, *n.* **1.** a denouncing as evil; open and vehement condemnation. **2.** *Obs.* an accusation of crime before a public prosecutor or tribunal. **3.** notice of the termination of an international agreement or part thereof. **4.** announcement of impending evil; threat; warning.

**denunciatory** /də'nʌnsiətəri, -tri/, *adj.* characterised by or given to denunciation. Also, **denunciative. – denunciator,** *n.*

**deny** /də'naɪ/, *v.t.*, **-nied, -nying.** **1.** to assert the negative of; declare not to be true: *I deny the charge, I deny he has done it.* **2.** to refuse to believe (a doctrine, etc.); reject as false or erroneous. **3.** to refuse to grant (a claim, request, etc.): *he denied me this, I was denied this.* **4.** to refuse to recognise or acknowledge; disown; disavow; repudiate. **5.** to refuse access to (one visited). **6.** *Obs.* to refuse to accept. **7.** *Obs.* to refuse (to do something). **8. deny oneself,** to exercise self-denial. [ME *denye(n)*, from F *dénier*, from L *dēnegāre*] **– deniable,** *adj.*

**deodar** /'diədа/, *n.* a species of cedar, *Cedrus deodara*, a large Himalayan tree valued for its beauty and for its durable wood. [Hind., from Skt *devadāra* wood of the gods]

**deodorant** /di'oʊdərənt/, *n.* **1.** an agent for destroying odours. **2.** a substance, often combined with an antiperspirant, for inhibiting or masking perspiration or other bodily odours. *–adj.* **3.** capable of destroying odours.

**deodorise** /di'oʊdəraɪz/, *v.t.*, **-rised, -rising.** to deprive of odour, esp. of the fetid smell arising from impurities. Also, **deodorize. – deodorisation** /di,oʊdəraɪ'zeɪʃən/, *n.* **– deodoriser,** *n.*

**Deo gratias** /,deɪoʊ 'gratias/, *interj.* thanks be to God. [L]

**deontology** /diɒn'tɒlədʒi/, *n.* the science of duty or moral obligation; ethics. [Gk *déon* that which is binding or needful (properly ppr. neut. of *deîn* bind) + -O- + -LOGY] **– deontological** /di,ɒntə'lɒdʒɪkəl/, *adj.* **– deontologist,** *n.*

**Deo volente** /,deɪoʊ və'lɛnti/, God willing (it); if God wills it. [L]

**deoxidise** /di'ɒksədaɪz/, *v.t.*, **-dised, -dising.** to remove oxygen from; reduce from the state of an oxide. Also, **deoxidize. – deoxidisation** /di,ɒksədaɪ'zeɪʃən/, *n.* **– deoxidiser,** *n.*

**deoxy-,** a prefix used in forming names of chemical compounds, and denoting the absence of oxygen from a molecule, as *deoxyribonucleic acid.*

**deoxygenate** /di'ɒksədʒəneɪt/, *v.t.*, **-nated, -nating.** to remove oxygen from. **– deoxygenation** /di,ɒksədʒə'neɪʃən/, *n.*

**deoxygenise** /di'ɒksədʒənaɪz/, *v.t.*, **-nised, -nising.** to deoxygenate. Also, **deoxygenize.**

**deoxyribonuclease** /di,ɒksi,raɪboʊ'njuklieɪz/, *n.* any enzyme which will catalyse the hydrolysis of deoxyribonucleic acid.

**deoxyribonucleic acid** /di,ɒksi,raɪboʊnju,kliɪk 'æsəd, -nju,kleɪɪk/, *n.* one of a class of large molecules which are found mainly in the nuclei of cells and in viruses and which are responsible for the transference of genetic characteristics, usu. consisting of two interwoven helical chains of polynucleotides. Also, **desoxyribonucleic acid.** *Abbrev.:* DNA

**deoxyribonucleotide** /di,ɒksi,raɪboʊ'njukliətaɪd/, *n.* a phosphate ester of a deoxyribonucleoside, from which DNA is formed.

**deoxyribose** /di,ɒksi'raɪboʊz, -boʊs/, *n.* a pentose sugar, $C_5H_{10}O_4$, which in its dextrorotatory form is present in combined form in deoxyribonucleic acids.

**dep.,** deposit.

**depart** /də'pat/, *v.i.* **1.** to go away, as from a place; take one's leave. **2.** to turn aside or away; diverge; deviate (fol. by *from*). **3.** to pass away, as from life or existence. *–v.t.* **4.** *Rare.* to go away from or leave: *to depart this life.* *–n.* **5.** *Obs.* departure; death. [ME *departe(n)*, from OF *departir*, from *de-* DE- + *partir* leave, divide (from L *partīre*)]

**departed** /də'patəd/, *adj.* **1.** deceased; dead. **2.** gone; past. *–n.* **3. the departed, a.** the dead person. **b.** the dead collectively.

**department** /də'patmənt/, *n.* **1.** a distinct part of anything arranged in divisions; a division of a complex whole or organised system. **2.** a division of official business or duties or functions. **3.** one of the (large) districts into which a country, as France, is divided for administrative purposes. **4.** one of the principal branches of a governmental organisation. **5.** one of the sections of a school, college, or university dealing with a particular field of knowledge: *the department of English.* **6.** a section of a retail store selling a particular class or kind of goods. **7.** a sphere or province of activity, knowledge or responsibility. **– departmental** /,dipat'mɛntl/, *adj.* **– departmentally** /,dipat'mɛntəli/, *adv.*

**departmentalise** /,dipat'mɛntəlaɪz/, *v.t.*, **-lised, -lising.** to divide into departments. Also, **departmentalize.**

**departmentalism** /,dipat'mɛntəlɪzəm/, *n.* **1.** division into departments. **2.** advocacy of or strict adherence to such a division.

**department store** /də'patmənt stɔ/, *n.* a large retail shop selling a variety of goods in different departments.

**departure** /də'patʃə/, *n.* **1.** a going away; a setting out or starting. **2.** divergence or deviation. **3.** *Naut.* **a.** the distance due east or west made by a ship when sailing on any course. **b.** a datum point from which a vessel takes a course away from land. **4.** *Archaic.* decease or death.

**depasture** /di'pastʃə/, *v.*, **-tured, -turing.** *–v.t.* **1.** to consume the produce of (land) as pasture. **2.** to pasture (cattle). *–v.i.* **3.** to graze.

**depend** /də'pɛnd/, *v.i.* **1.** to rely; trust: *you may depend on the accuracy of the report.* **2.** to rely for support, maintenance, help, etc.: *children depend on their parents.* **3.** to be conditioned or contingent: *it depends upon himself, his efforts, his knowledge.* **4.** (of a word or other linguistic form) to be subordinate (to another linguistic form in the same construction). **5.** to hang down; be suspended. **6.** to be undetermined or pending. [ME *depend(en)*, from OF *dependre*, from L *dēpendēre* hang upon]

**dependable** /də'pɛndəbəl/, *adj.* that may be depended on; reliable; trustworthy. **– dependability** /dəpɛndə'bɪləti/, **– dependableness,** *n.* **– dependably,** *adv.*

**dependant** /də'pɛndənt/, *n.* Also, **dependent. 1.** one who depends on or looks to another for support, favour, etc. **2.** a person to whom one contributes all or a major amount of necessary financial support. **3.** a retainer; servant. *–adj.* **4.** →**dependent.**

**dependence** /də'pɛndəns/, *n.* **1.** the state of depending for aid, support, etc. **2.** reliance; confidence; trust. **3.** the state of being conditional or contingent on something; natural or logical sequence. **4.** subordination or subjection: *the dependence of the church upon the state.* **5.** an object of reliance or trust.

**dependency** /də'pɛndənsi/, *n.*, *pl.* **-cies.** **1.** the state of being dependent; dependence. **2.** something dependent or subordinate; an appurtenance. **3.** an outbuilding or annexe. **4.** a subject territory which is not an integral part of the ruling country.

**dependent** /də'pɛndənt/, *adj.* Also, *Chiefly U.S.,* **dependant. 1.** depending on something else for aid, support, etc. **2.** conditioned; contingent. **3.** subordinate; subject. **4.** (of linguistic forms) not used in isolation; used only in connection with other forms. **5.** hanging down; pendent. *–n.* **6.** *Chiefly U.S.* →**dependant.**

**dependent clause** /'– klɔz/, *n.* →**subordinate clause.**

**dependent variable** /– 'vɛəriəbəl/, *n.* a variable expressed as a function of other more basic variables called independent variables.

**depersonalise** /di'pɜsənəlaɪz/, *v.t.,* **-lised, -lising. 1.** to make impersonal. **2.** *Psychiatry.* to cause an individual to experience his personality and/or body as unreal. **3.** *Psychol.* to cause an individual to feel himself non-human, a cog in an impersonal machine. Also, **depersonalize.** – **depersonalisation** /di,pɜsənəlaɪ'zeɪʃən/, *n.*

**depict** /də'pɪkt/, *v.t.* **1.** to represent by or as by painting; portray; delineate. **2.** to represent in words; describe. [L *dēpictus,* pp., portrayed] – **depicter,** *n.* – **depiction,** *n.* – **depictive,** *adj.*

**depicture** /də'pɪktʃə/, *v.t.,* **-tured, -turing.** to picture; depict.

**depilate** /'dɛpəleɪt/, *v.t.,* **-lated, -lating.** to remove the hair from. [L *dēpilātus,* pp.] – **depilation** /dɛpə'leɪʃən/, *n.*

**depilatory** /də'pɪlətri/, *adj., n., pl.* **-ries.** *–adj.* **1.** capable of removing hair. *–n.* **2.** a depilatory agent.

**depillar** /di'pɪlə/, *v.t.* to remove the pillars of a mine.

**deplete** /də'plit/, *v.t.,* **-pleted, -pleting.** to deprive of that which fills; decrease the fullness of; reduce the stock or amount of. [L *dēplētus,* pp., emptied out] – **depletion,** *n.* – **depletive, depletory** /də'plitəri/, *adj.*

**deplorable** /də'plɔrəbəl/, *adj.* **1.** causing or being a subject for grief or regret; sad; lamentable. **2.** causing or being a subject for censure or reproach; bad; wretched. – **deplorableness, deplorability** /dəplɔrə'bɪləti/, *n.* – **deplorably,** *adv.*

**deplore** /də'plɔ/, *v.t.,* **-plored, -ploring.** to feel or express deep grief for or in regard to; regret deeply. [L *dēplōrāre* bewail] – **deplorer,** *n.* – **deploringly,** *adv.*

**deploy** /də'plɔɪ/, *v.t.* **1.** to spread out (troops or military units) and form an extended front. **2.** to make careful utilisation of (mineral resources). *–v.i.* **3.** to spread out with extended front. [F *déployer,* from *dé-* DIS-[1] + *ployer,* from L *plicāre* fold] – **deployment,** *n.* – **deployable,** *adj.*

**deplume** /di'plum/, *v.t.,* **-plumed, -pluming. 1.** to deprive of feathers; pluck. **2.** to strip of honour, wealth, etc. [F *déplumer,* from *dé-* DIS-[1] + *plume* (from L *plūma* feather)] – **deplumation** /diplu'meɪʃən/, *n.*

**depolarise** /di'poʊləraɪz/, *v.t.,* **-rised, -rising.** to deprive of polarity or polarisation as in a muscle fibre during excitation. Also, **depolarize.** – **depolarisation** /di,poʊləraɪ'zeɪʃən/, *n.* – **depolariser,** *n.*

**depoliticise** /dipə'lɪtəsaɪz/, *v.t.,* **-cised, -cising.** to remove from the area of political involvement or influence; to make neutral in a political sense.

**depone** /də'poʊn/, *v.,* **-poned, -poning.** *–v.t.* **1.** *Archaic.* to testify under oath. *–v.i.* **2.** to give testimony. [L *dēpōnere* put away or down, ML testify. See DEPOSIT]

**deponent** /də'poʊnənt/, *adj.* **1.** *Gk and Lat. Gram.* (of a verb) appearing only in the passive (or Greek middle) voice forms, but with active meaning. *–n.* **2.** *Law.* one who testifies under oath, esp. in writing. **3.** *Gk and Lat. Gram.* a deponent verb: *a Latin form such as 'loqui' is a deponent.* [L *dēpōnens,* ppr., laying aside, depositing, ML testifying]

**depopulate** /di'pɒpjuleɪt/, *v.t.,* **-lated, -lating.** to deprive of inhabitants, wholly or in part, as by destruction or expulsion. [L *dēpopulātus,* pp., having laid waste] – **depopulation** /dipɒpjə'leɪʃən/, *n.* – **depopulator,** *n.* – **depopulate** /di'pɒpjələt, -leɪt/, *adj.*

**deport** /də'pɔt/, *v.t.* **1.** to transport forcibly, as to a penal colony or a place of exile. **2.** to expel (an undesirable alien) from a country; banish. **3.** to bear, conduct, or behave (oneself) in a particular manner. [F *déporter,* from L *dēportāre* carry away, transport, banish]

**deportation** /,dipɔ'teɪʃən/, *n.* the lawful expulsion of undesirable aliens and other persons from a state.

**deportee** /,dipɔ'ti/, *n.* **1.** one who is deported, as from a country. **2.** a person awaiting deportation. [DEPORT, *v.* + -EE]

**deportment** /də'pɔtmənt/, *n.* **1.** manner of bearing; carriage. **2.** demeanour; conduct; behaviour.

**deposal** /də'poʊzəl/, *n.* deposition, as from office.

**depose** /də'poʊz/, *v.,* **-posed, -posing.** *–v.t.* **1.** to remove from office or position, esp. high office. **2.** to declare or testify, esp. under oath, usu. in writing. *–v.i.* **3.** to bear witness; give sworn testimony, esp. in writing. [ME *depose(n),* from OF *deposer* put down, from *de-* DE- + *poser* POSE[1]] – **deposable,** *adj.* – **deposer,** *n.*

**deposit** /də'pɒzət/, *v.t.* **1.** to put or lay down; place; put. **2.** to throw down or precipitate: *soil deposited by a river.* **3.** to place for safekeeping or in trust. **4.** to give as security or in part payment. *–n.* **5.** anything laid or thrown down, as matter precipitated from a fluid; sediment. **6.** a coating of metal deposited by an electric current. **7.** an accumulation, or occurrence, of ore, oil, etc., of any form or nature. **8.** anything laid away or entrusted to another for safekeeping. **9.** money placed in a bank. **10.** anything given as security or in part payment. [L *dēpositus,* pp., put away or down, deposited, ML testified. See DEPONE]

**deposit account** /'– əkaʊnt/, *n.* a bank account opened for the purpose of saving money and earning interest, as opposed to a current account.

**depositary** /də'pɒzətri, -ətəri/, *n., pl.* **-taries. 1.** one to whom anything is given in trust. **2.** →**depository.**

**deposition** /dɛpə'zɪʃən, dipə-/, *n.* **1.** removal from an office or position. **2.** the act of depositing. **3.** that which is deposited. **4.** *Law.* **a.** the giving of testimony under oath. **b.** the testimony so given. **c.** a statement under oath, taken down in writing, which may be used in court in place of the production of the witness. **5.** *(cap.)* **a.** the removal of Christ's body from the Cross. **b.** a representation of this.

**depositor** /də'pɒzətə/, *n.* **1.** one who or that which deposits. **2.** one who deposits money in a bank.

**depository** /də'pɒzətri, -ətəri/, *n., pl.* **-ries. 1.** a place where anything is deposited or stored for safekeeping; a storehouse. **2.** a depositary; trustee.

**deposit receipt** /də'pɒzət rəsit/, *n.* a written acknowledgment by a bank that it has received from a person named a specified sum as a deposit.

**deposit slip** /'– slɪp/, *n.* a printed form filled in by depositor when he pays an amount of money into his account at a bank.

**depot** /'dɛpoʊ/, *n.* **1.** a depository; storehouse. **2.** a garage where buses or trams are kept. **3.** *U.S.* a railway station. [F *dépôt,* from L *dēpositum* DEPOSIT, *n.*]

**deprave** /də'preɪv/, *v.t.,* **-praved, -praving.** to make bad or worse; vitiate; corrupt. [ME *deprave(n),* from L *dēprāvāre* pervert] – **depravation** /dɛprə'veɪʃən/, *n.* – **depraver,** *n.*

**depraved** /də'preɪvd/, *adj.* corrupt or perverted, esp. morally; wicked.

**depravity** /də'prævəti/, *n., pl.* **-ties. 1.** the state of being depraved. **2.** a depraved act or practice. **3.** *Theol.* the innate sinfulness of man.

**deprecate** /'dɛprəkeɪt/, *v.t.,* **-cated, -cating.** to express earnest disapproval of; urge reasons against; protest against (a scheme, purpose, etc.). [L *dēprecātus,* pp., having prayed against] – **deprecatingly,** *adv.* – **deprecation** /dɛprə'keɪʃən/, *n.* – **deprecator,** *n.*

**deprecatory** /dɛprə'keɪtəri/, *adj.* **1.** of the nature of deprecation; expressing deprecation. **2.** apologetic; expressing apology. – **deprecatorily,** *adv.*

**depreciate** /də'priʃieɪt, də'prisieɪt/, *v.,* **-ated, -ating.** *–v.t.* **1.** to reduce the purchasing value of (money). **2.** to lessen the value of. **3.** to represent as of little value or merit; belittle. *–v.i.* **4.** to decline in value. [LL *dēpretiātus* (ML *dēpreciātus*) undervalued] – **depreciatingly,** *adv.* – **depreciator,** *n.*

**depreciation** /dəpriʃi'eɪʃən, -prisi-/, *n.* **1.** a decrease in value due to wear and tear, decay, decline in price, etc. **2.** the notional amount of money involved in such a decrease, viewed as a cost. **3.** a decrease in the purchasing or exchange value of money. **4.** a lowering in estimation; disparagement.

i = peat ɪ = pit ɛ = pet æ = pat a = part ɒ = pot ʌ = putt ɔ = port ʊ = put u = pool ɜ = pert ə = apart aɪ = buy eɪ = bay ɔɪ = boy aʊ = how oʊ = hoe ɪə = here ɛə = hair ʊə = tour g = give θ = thin ð = then ʃ = show ʒ = measure tʃ = choke dʒ = joke ŋ = sing j = you õ = Fr. bon

**depreciation allowance** /'– əlaʊəns/, *n.* the maximum annual amount allowed by taxation authorities for the owner of capital equipment to deduct from an earlier estimation of the value of his equipment as an acceptable deduction against his income.

**depreciatory** /də'priʃiətri/, *adj.* tending to depreciate. Also, **depreciative.**

**depredate** /'dɛprədeɪt/, *v.*, **-dated, -dating.** *–v.t.* **1.** to prey upon; plunder; lay waste. *–v.i.* **2.** to prey; make depredations. [L *dēpraedātus,* pp., having pillaged] – **depredator,** *n.* – **depredatory** /dɛprə'deɪtəri, də'prɛdətəri, -tri/, *adj.*

**depredation** /dɛprə'deɪʃən/, *n.* a preying upon or plundering; robbery; ravage.

**depress** /də'prɛs/, *v.t.* **1.** to lower in spirits; deject; dispirit. **2.** to lower in force, vigour, etc.; weaken; make dull. **3.** to lower in amount or value. **4.** to put into a lower position: *to depress the muzzle of a gun.* **5.** to press down. **6.** (in music) to lower in pitch. [ME *depresse(n),* from OF *depresser,* from L *dēpressus,* pp., pressed down] – **depressible,** *adj.* – **depressingly,** *adv.*

**depressant** /də'prɛsənt/, *adj.* **1.** having the quality of depressing or lowering the vital activities; sedative. *–n.* **2.** a sedative.

**depressed** /də'prɛst/, *adj.* **1.** dejected; downcast. **2.** pressed down; lower than the general surface. **3.** lowered in force, amount, etc. **4.** *Bot., Zool.* flattened down; broader than high. **5.** economically backward.

**depressed area** /– 'ɛəriə/, *n.* a region where unemployment and a low standard of living prevail.

**depression** /də'prɛʃən/, *n.* **1.** the act of depressing. **2.** the state of being depressed. **3.** a depressed or sunken place or part; a hollow. **4.** dejection of spirits. **5.** *Psychol.* a state of despondency characterised by feelings of inadequacy, lowered activity, sadness and pessimism. **6.** *Psychiatry.* mental disorder characterised by unresponsiveness to stimuli, self-depreciation, delusions of inadequacy and hopelessness. **7.** dullness or inactivity, as of trade. **8.** a period during which there is a general slump in economic activities. **9.** *Pathol.* a low state of vital powers or functional activity. **10.** *Astron., etc.* angular distance below the horizon. **11.** *Survey.* the angle between the line from an observer to an object below him and a horizontal line. **12.** *Meteorol.* an area of low atmospheric pressure. [ME, from L *dēpressio*]

**depressive** /də'prɛsɪv/, *adj.* **1.** tending to depress. **2.** characterised by depression, esp. mental depression. – **depressively,** *adv.* – **depressiveness,** *n.*

**depressomotor** /dəˌprɛsoʊ'moʊtə/, *adj. Physiol., Med.* causing a retardation of motor activity: *depressomotor nerves.*

**depressor** /də'prɛsə/, *n.* **1.** one who or that which depresses. **2.** *Physiol., Anat.* **a.** a muscle that draws down a part. **b.** Also, **depressor nerve.** a nerve from the aorta to the centres controlling heart rate and blood pressure. **3.** *Surg.* an instrument for pressing down a protruding part.

**depressurise** /di'prɛʃəraɪz/, *v.i.*, **-rised, -rising.** to reduce pressure inside a contained space as the cabin of a jet plane with malfunctioning air pressure control, or a decompression chamber, etc. – **depressurisation** /diˌprɛʃəraɪ'zeɪʃən/, *n.*

**deprivation** /dɛprə'veɪʃən/, *n.* **1.** the act of depriving. **2.** the fact of being deprived. **3.** dispossession; loss; bereavement. Also, **deprival** /də'praɪvəl/.

**deprive** /də'praɪv/, *v.t.*, **-prived, -priving. 1.** to divest of something possessed or enjoyed; dispossess; strip; bereave. **2.** to keep (a person, etc.) from possessing or enjoying something withheld. **3.** to remove (an ecclesiastic) from a benefice; to remove from office. [ME *deprive(n),* from OF *depriver,* from *priver,* from L *prīvāre* deprive] – **deprivable,** *adj.* – **depriver,** *n.*

**deprived** /də'praɪvd/, *adj.* (esp. of children) without certain benefits of money or social class; lacking educational opportunities, parental affection, etc.

**de profundis** /deɪ prə'fʊndɪs/, out of the depths (of sorrow, despair, etc.). [L]

**deprogrammer** /di'proʊgræmə/, *n.* one who specialises in reversing the supposed brainwashing of a cult follower.

**depside** /'dɛpsaɪd, -səd/, *n. Chem.* any of a group of esters formed from two or more phenol carboxylic acid molecules. [Gk *dépsein* tan + -IDE]

**dept,** department.

**Deptford pink** /dɛptfəd 'pɪŋk/, *n.* an annual plant, *Dianthus armeria,* found in Europe and Asia and having pale red flowers.

**depth** /dɛpθ/, *n.* **1.** measure or distance downwards, inwards, or backwards. **2.** deepness, as of water, suited to or safe for a person or thing. **3.** abstruseness, as of a subject. **4.** gravity; seriousness. **5.** emotional profundity: *depth of woe.* **6.** (*pl.*) a low intellectual or moral condition. **7.** intensity, as of silence, colour, etc. **8.** lowness of pitch. **9.** extent of intellectual penetration, sagacity, or profundity. **10.** (*usu. pl.*) a deep part or place, as of the sea. **11.** an unfathomable space, or abyss. **12.** the remotest or extreme part, as of space. **13.** a deep or underlying region, as of feeling. **14.** the part of greatest intensity, as of night or winter. **15. beyond** or **out of one's depth, a.** in water too deep for one to touch the bottom. **b.** beyond one's capacity or understanding. **16. in depth,** intensely; thoroughly. [ME *depth(e),* from *dep-* (OE *dēop* DEEP) + -TH[1]]

**depth charge** /'– tʃadʒ/, *n.* a bomb dropped or thrown into the water from a ship or aeroplane which explodes on reaching a certain depth, used to destroy submarines, etc.

**depth of field,** *n. Optics.* the range of distances along the axis of a camera or other optical instrument, in which an object will produce a reasonably clear image. Also, **depth of focus.**

**depurate** /'dɛpjəreɪt/, *v.*, **-rated, -rating.** *–v.t.* **1.** to make free from impurities; purify; cleanse. *–v.i.* **2.** to become cleansed or purified. [ML *dēpūrātus,* pp.] – **depuration** /dɛpjə'reɪʃən/, *n.* – **depurator,** *n.*

**depurative** /'dɛpjəreɪtɪv, 'dɛpjərətɪv/, *adj.* **1.** serving to depurate; purifying. *–n.* **2.** a depurative agent or substance.

**deputation** /dɛpju'teɪʃən/, *n.* **1.** appointment to represent or act for another or others. **2.** the person or (usu.) body of persons so appointed or authorised. Cf. *U.S.* **delegation** (def. 4).

**depute** /də'pjut/, *v.t.*, **-puted, -puting. 1.** to appoint as one's substitute or agent. **2.** to assign (a charge, etc.) to a deputy. [ME *depute(n),* from OF *deputer,* from LL *dēputāre* destine, allot, L count as, reckon]

**deputise** /'dɛpjətaɪz/, *v.*, **-tised, -tising.** *–v.t.* **1.** to appoint as a deputy. *–v.i.* **2.** to act as a deputy. Also, **deputize.**

**deputy** /'dɛpjəti/, *n., pl.* **-ties,** *adj.* *–n.* **1.** a person appointed or authorised to act for another or others. **2.** a person appointed or elected as assistant to a public official as an alderman or (U.S.) a sheriff, serving as successor in the event of a vacancy. **3.** a person representing a constituency in any of certain legislative bodies, as in the French Chamber of Deputies. *–adj.* **4.** acting as deputy for another. [ME *depute,* from OF, properly pp. of *deputer* DEPUTE] – **deputyship,** *n.*

**der.,** **1.** derivation. **2.** derivative. **3.** derived.

**deracinate** /də'ræsəneɪt/, *v.t.*, **-nated, -nating.** to pull up by the roots; uproot; extirpate; eradicate. [F *déraciner* (from *dé-* DIS-[1] + *racine,* from L *rādix* root) + -ATE[1]] – **deracination** /dəræsə'neɪʃən/, *n.*

**deraign** /də'reɪn/, *v.t. Hist.* to dispose troops for (battle). Also, **darraign.** [ME *dereyne(n),* from OF *deraisnier* render an account of, explain, defend, from *de-* DE- + *raisnier* discourse, plead, from *raison,* from L *ratio* reckoning. Cf. ARRAIGN] – **deraignment,** *n.*

**derail** /di'reɪl/, *v.t.* **1.** to cause (a train, etc.) to run off the rails. *–v.i.* **2.** (of a train, etc.) to run off the rails of a track. [F *dérailler,* from *dé-* DIS-[1] + *rail* rail, from E. See RAIL[1]] – **derailment,** *n.*

**derailleur** /di'reɪlə/, *adj.* of or pertaining to gearing mechanism on a pushbike which derails a chain from one sprocket and rerails it onto another, thus allowing a number of possible combinations of front and rear sprockets, all providing different gear ratios.

**derange** /də'reɪndʒ/, *v.t.*, **-ranged, -ranging. 1.** to throw into disorder; disarrange. **2.** to disturb the condition, action, or functions of. **3.** to unsettle the reason of; make insane. [F *déranger,* OF *desrengier,* from *des-* DIS-[1] + *rengier* RANGE, *v.*]

**deranged** /də'reɪndʒd/, *adj.* **1.** disordered. **2.** insane.

**derangement** /də'reɪndʒmənt/, *n.* **1.** the act of deranging. **2.** disarrangement; disorder. **3.** mental disorder; insanity.

**derby** /'dabi, 'dɜbi/; /'dɜbi/ *for def. 4, n., pl.* **-bies. 1.** an important race esp. of horses. **2. local derby,** any sporting contest between teams from the same area. **3.** →**soapbox derby. 4.** *U.S.* a stiff felt hat with rounded crown and brim. Cf. **bowler**[1]. [named after a horserace at Epsom Downs, England, founded 1780 by the Earl of *Derby*]

**derecognise** /di'rɛkəgnaɪz/, *v.t.,* **-nised, -nising.** to withdraw political recognition from.

**deregister** /di'rɛdʒəstə/, *v.t.* to remove from a register, esp. one which is an index of professional competence. – **deregistration** /di,rɛdʒəs'treɪʃən/, *n.*

**derelict** /'dɛrəlɪkt/, *adj.* **1.** left or abandoned, as by the owner or guardian (said esp. of a ship abandoned at sea). **2.** neglected; dilapidated. *–n.* **3.** personal property abandoned or thrown away by the owner. **4.** a ship abandoned at sea. **5.** a person forsaken or abandoned, esp. by society. **6.** *Law.* land left dry by a change of the waterline. [L *dērelictus,* pp., forsaken utterly]

**dereliction** /dɛrə'lɪkʃən/, *n.* **1.** culpable neglect, as of duty; delinquency; fault. **2.** the act of abandoning. **3.** the state of being abandoned. **4.** *Law.* **a.** a leaving dry of land by recession of the waterline. **b.** the land thus left dry.

**derequisition** /,dirɛkwə'zɪʃən/, *n.* **1.** the return from military to civilian control. *–v.t.* **2.** to return to civilian control.

**de rerum natura** /deɪ ,rɛərəm na'tura/, concerning the nature of things. [L]

**derestricted** /dirə'strɪktəd/, *adj.* of a road, area, etc. away from built-up areas, where motorists may drive at speeds up to the maximum permitted on roads.

**deride** /də'raɪd/, *v.t.,* **-rided, -riding.** to laugh at in contempt; scoff or jeer at; mock. [L *dērīdēre* laugh] – **derider,** *n.* – **deridingly,** *adv.*

**de rigueur** /də rɪ'gɜ/, *adj.* strictly required, as by etiquette or usage. [F]

**derisible** /də'rɪzəbəl/, *adj.* subject to or worthy of derision.

**derision** /də'rɪʒən/, *n.* **1.** the act of deriding; ridicule; mockery. **2.** an object of ridicule. [L *dērīsio*]

**derisive** /də'raɪsɪv, də'rɪzɪv/, *adj.* characterised by derision; ridiculing; mocking. Also, **derisory** /də'raɪzəri, də'rɪzəri/. – **derisively,** *adv.* – **derisiveness,** *n.*

**deriv** /də'rɪv/, *n. Chem.* →**derivative.**

**deriv., 1.** derivation. **2.** derivative. **3.** derive. **4.** derived.

**derivate** /'dɛrəvət, -veɪt/, *n.* **1.** something derived; a derivative. *–adj.* **2.** derived.

**derivation** /dɛrə'veɪʃən/, *n.* **1.** the act of deriving. **2.** the fact of being derived. **3.** origination or origin. **4.** that which is derived; derivative. **5.** *Maths.* differentiation. **6.** *Gram.* **a.** the process of composing new words by the addition of prefixes or suffixes to already existing root words as *atomic* from *atom, hardness* from *hard.* **b.** the systematic description of such processes in a particular language, as contrasted with *inflection* which consists of adding prefixes, infixes, or suffixes to make a different form of the same word: *hardness* is an example of derivation; *harder* of inflection. **c.** such processes collectively or in general. **7.** *Gram.* the process of tracing a word back to its earliest known form. – **derivational,** *adj.*

**derivative** /də'rɪvətɪv/, *adj.* **1.** derived. **2.** not original or primitive; secondary. *–n.* **3.** something derived or derivative. **4.** *Gram.* a form derived from another: *atomic* is a derivative of *atom.* **5.** *Chem.* a substance or compound obtained from, or regarded as derived from, another substance or compound. **6.** *Maths.* **a.** the instantaneous rate of change of a function with respect to the variable. **b.** the linear function which best approximates a given function in the vicinity of a given point. – **derivatively,** *adv.*

**derive** /də'raɪv/, *v.,* **-rived, -riving.** *–v.t.* **1.** to receive or obtain from a source or origin (fol. by *from*). **2.** to trace, as from a source or origin. **3.** to obtain by reasoning; deduce. **4.** *Chem.* to produce (a compound) from another compound by replacement of elements or radicals. *–v.i.* **5.** to come from a source; originate. [F *dériver,* from L *dērīvāre* lead off] – **derivable,** *adj.* – **deriver,** *n.*

**derived unit** /dəraɪvd 'junət/, *n.* any unit derived from primary units of length, time, mass, etc.

**-derm,** a word element meaning 'skin', as in *endoderm.* [Gk *-dermos,* etc., having skin, skinned]

**derma** /'dɜmə/, *n.* **1.** the corium or true skin, beneath the epidermis. **2.** the skin in general. [NL, from Gk: skin] – **dermal,** *adj.*

**dermal** /'dɜməl/, *adj.* of or pertaining to skin.

**dermatitis** /dɜmə'taɪtəs/, *n.* inflammation of the skin.

**dermato-,** a word element meaning 'skin', as in *dermatology.* Also, **derm-, dermat-, dermo-.** [Gk, combining form of *dérma*]

**dermatogen** /də'mætədʒən, 'dɜmətoʊdʒən/, *n.* a thin layer of meristem in embryos and growing ends of stems and roots, which give rise to the epidermis.

**dermatographia** /,dɜmətoʊ'græfiə/, *n. Med.* a condition in which touching or lightly scratching the skin causes raised reddish marks. Also, **dermatographism, dermographia** /,dɜmoʊ'græfiə/, **dermographism.**

**dermatoid** /'dɜmətɔɪd/, *adj.* resembling skin; skinlike.

**dermatology** /dɜmə'tɒlədʒi/, *n.* the science of the skin and its diseases. – **dermatological** /dɜmətə'lɒdʒɪkəl/, *adj.* – **dermatologist,** *n.*

**dermatome** /'dɜmətoʊm/, *n.* **1.** *Anat.* an area of the skin that is supplied with the nerve fibres of a single posterior, spinal root. **2.** *Surg.* a mechanical instrument for cutting thin sections of skin for grafting. **3.** *Embryol.* the part of a mesodermal somite contributing to the development of the dermis. – **dermatomic** /dɜmə'tɒmɪk/, *adj.*

**dermatomyositis** /,dɜmətoʊ,maɪə'saɪtəs/, *n.* a degenerative change of skin and muscle causing weakness and pain.

**dermatophyte** /'dɜmətoʊ,faɪt/, *n.* any fungus parasitic on the skin and causing a skin disease, as ringworm.

**dermatoplasty** /'dɜmətoʊ,plæsti/, *n.* plastic surgery of the skin. See **skin grafting.**

**dermatosis** /dɜmə'toʊsəs/, *n., pl.* **-toses** /-'toʊsiz/. any disease of the skin.

**dermis** /'dɜməs/, *n.* →**derma.** [NL; abstracted from EPIDERMIS] – **dermic,** *adj.*

**dermo** /'dɜmoʊ/, *n. Colloq.* dermatitis.

**dermoid** /'dɜmɔɪd/, *adj.* **1.** skinlike; dermatoid. *–n.* **2.** *Pathol.* a congenital cyst containing hair, skin, teeth, etc.

**dernier cri** /,dɛənjeɪ 'kri/, *n.* **1.** the last word. **2.** the latest fashion. [F]

**dero** /'dɛroʊ/, *n. Colloq.* a vagrant, esp. one with a weird or sinister appearance. Also, **derro.** [shortened form of DERELICT]

**derog., 1.** derogative. **2.** derogatory.

**derogate** /'dɛrəgeɪt/, *v.,* **-gated, -gating;** /'dɛrəgət, -geɪt/, *adj.* *–v.i.* **1.** to detract, as from authority, estimation, etc. (fol. by *from*). **2.** to fall away in character or conduct; degenerate (fol. by *from*). [L *dērogātus,* pp., repealed, taken or detracted from] – **derogation,** *n.*

**derogative** /də'rɒgətɪv/, *adj.* lessening; belittling; derogatory. – **derogatively,** *adv.*

**derogatory** /də'rɒgətri, -ətəri/, *adj.* tending to derogate or detract, as from authority or estimation; disparaging; depreciatory. – **derogatorily,** *adv.* – **derogatoriness,** *n.*

**derrick** /'dɛrɪk/, *n.* **1.** any of various devices for lifting and moving heavy weights. **2.** the tower-like framework over an oil-well or the like. **3.** a crane, usu. stationary, carrying lifting tackle at the end of a boom or jib. *–v.t.* **4.** to move (the jib of a crane). [named after *Derrick,* a hangman at Tyburn, London, about 1600]

**derrière** /dɛri'ɛə/, *n. Colloq. (joc.)* the buttocks; the bottom. [F: lit., behind, n. use of prep.]

**derring-do** /,dɛrɪŋ-'du/, *n.* daring deeds; heroic daring. [ME *dorryng don* daring to do; erroneously taken as n. phrase by Spenser]

**derringer** /'dɛrɪndʒə/, *n.* a short-barrelled pistol of large calibre. Also, **deringer.** [named after Henry *Deringer,* 1786-1868, American gunsmith]

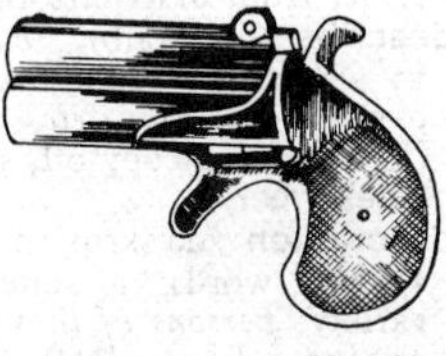

derringer

**derris** /'dɛrəs/, *n.* any plant of the genus *Derris,* of the family Leguminosae, esp. *D. elliptica* and allied species, the roots of which contain rotenone and are used as an insecticide.

**derry** /'dɛri/, *n.* **1.** Also, **derry-down** /'dɛri-daʊn/. a meaningless refrain or chorus in old songs. **2.** an alarm; pursuit, esp. by the police. **3.** *Colloq.* **have a derry on,** to be prejudiced against.

**derv** /dɜv/, *n. Brit.* diesel engine fuel oil. [short for *d(iesel) e(ngined) r(oad) v(ehicle)*]

**DERV,** diesel-engined road vehicle.

**dervish** /'dɜvɪʃ/, *n.* a member of any of various Muslim ascetic orders, some of which carry on ecstatic observances, such as violent dancing and pirouetting (**dancing, spinning,** or **whirling dervishes**) or vociferous chanting or shouting (**howling dervishes**). [Turk., from Pers. *darvish* religious mendicant]

**Derwent duck** /dɜwənt 'dʌk/, *n.* (formerly) a convict at Hobart on the river Derwent.

**Derwent smelt** /– 'smɛlt/, *n.* a fish, *Lovettia sealii,* endemic in northern and eastern Tasmanian waters, which spawns in fresh-water rivers but spends most of its life in the sea, growing to a length of six centimetres; it is often used for whitebait.

**desalinate** /di'sæləneɪt/, *v.t.,* **-nated, -nating.** to subject (sea water) to a process of desalination. Also, **desalinise.**

**desalination** /ˌdisælə'neɪʃən/, *n.* the process of removing the dissolved salts from sea water so that it becomes suitable for drinking water or for agricultural irrigation. Also, **desalinisation.**

**desalinise** /di'sælənaɪz/, *v.t.,* **-nised, -nising.** to desalinate. Also, **desalinize.**

**desc.,** **1.** descendant. **2.** described.

**descant** /'dɛskænt/, *n.;* /dɛs'kænt, dəs-/, *v.* *–n.* **1.** *Music.* **a.** a melody or counterpoint accompanying a simple musical theme and usu. written above it. **b.** (in part music) the soprano. **c.** a song or melody. **2.** a variation upon anything; comment on a subject. *–v.i.* **3.** *Music.* to sing. **4.** to make comments; discourse at length and with variety. Also, **discant.** [ME, from ONF, from *des-* DIS-[1] + *cant* (from L *cantus* song)] – **descanter,** *n.*

**descend** /də'sɛnd/, *v.i.* **1.** to move or pass from a higher to a lower place; go or come down; fall; sink. **2.** to pass from higher to lower in any scale. **3.** to go from generals to particulars. **4.** to slope or tend downward. **5.** to come down by transmission, as from ancestors. **6.** to be derived by birth or extraction. **7.** to come down in a hostile manner, as an army: *to descend upon the enemy.* **8.** to approach or pounce upon, esp. in a greedy or hasty manner (fol. by *on* or *upon*). **9.** to come down from a certain intellectual, moral, or social standard: *he would never descend to baseness.* *–v.t.* **10.** to move or lead downwards upon or along; go down. [ME *descend(en),* from OF *descendre,* from L *dēscendere*]

**descendant** /də'sɛndənt/, *n.* **1.** one descended from an ancestor; an offspring, near or remote. *–adj.* **2.** →**descendent.** [F, ppr. of *descendre* DESCEND]

**descendent** /də'sɛndənt/, *adj.* **1.** descending; going or coming down. **2.** descending from an ancestor. [L *dēscendens,* ppr., descending]

**descender** /də'sɛndə/, *n.* **1.** one who or that which descends. **2.** (in printing) the part of such letters as *p, q, j,* and *y* that goes below the body of most lower-case letters.

**descendible** /də'sɛndəbəl/, *adj.* capable of being transmitted by inheritance. Also, **descendable.**

**descent** /də'sɛnt/, *n.* **1.** the act or fact of descending. **2.** a downward inclination or slope. **3.** a passage or stairway leading down. **4.** derivation from an ancestor; extraction; lineage. **5.** any passing from higher to lower in degree or state. **6.** a sudden incursion or attack. **7.** *Law.* transmission of real property by intestate succession. [ME, from OF *descente,* from *descendre* DESCEND]

**describe** /də'skraɪb/, *v.t.,* **-scribed, -scribing.** **1.** to set forth in written or spoken words; give an account of: *to describe a scene, a person, etc.* **2.** *Geom.* to draw or trace, as an arc. [L *dēscrībere* copy off, sketch off, describe] – **describable,** *adj.* – **describer,** *n.*

**description** /də'skrɪpʃən/, *n.* **1.** representation by written or spoken words; a statement that describes. **2.** sort; kind; variety: *persons of that description.* **3.** *Geom.* the act of describing a figure. [ME, from L *dēscrīptio*]

**descriptive** /də'skrɪptɪv/, *adj.* **1.** having the quality of describing; characterised by description. **2.** *Gram.* **a.** seeking to describe language as it is rather than prescribe what it should be. **b.** (of an adjective) expressing a quality of the noun it modifies (opposed to *limiting* or *demonstrative*), as *fresh* in *fresh milk.* **c.** (of any other expression) acting like such an adjective. – **descriptively,** *adv.* – **descriptiveness,** *n.*

**descriptive clause** /– 'klɔz/, *n.* a relative clause, in English writing usu. set off in commas, which describes or supplements, but does not identify, the antecedent; nonrestrictive clause. In 'this year, *which has been dry,* is bad for crops' the italicised part is a descriptive clause (opposed to *restrictive clause*).

**descriptive geometry** /– dʒi'ɒmətri/, *n.* **1.** the theory of making projections of any accurately defined figure such that from them can be deduced not only its projective, but also its metrical properties. **2.** geometry in general, treated by means of projections.

**descriptive grammar** /– 'græmə/, *n.* a grammar based on observed usage rather than on prescriptive rules (opposed to *prescriptive grammar*).

**descriptive science** /– 'saɪəns/, *n.* a science which classifies and describes the material in a particular field (usu. opposed to *explanatory science,* which gives causes).

**descriptivism** /də'skrɪptəvɪzəm/, *n.* an approach which is characterised by classification or description rather than by explanation. – **descriptivist,** *adj.*

**descry** /dɛs'kraɪ/, *v.t.,* **-scried, -scrying.** **1.** to make out (something distant or unclear) by looking; espy: *the lookout descried land.* **2.** to discover; perceive; distinguish; detect. [ME *descry(en),* apparently from OF *descrier* proclaim. See DECRY] – **descrier,** *n.*

**desecrate** /'dɛsəkreɪt/, *v.t.,* **-crated, -crating.** to divest of sacred or hallowed character or office; divert from a sacred to a profane purpose; treat with sacrilege; profane. [DE- + *-secrate,* modelled on CONSECRATE] – **desecrater, desecrator,** *n.* – **desecration** /dɛsə'kreɪʃən/, *n.*

**desegregate** /di'sɛgrəgeɪt/, *v.,* **-gated, -gating.** *–v.t.* **1.** to eliminate racial segregation from (schools and other public places or institutions). *–v.i.* **2.** to become desegregated.

**desegregation** /ˌdisɛgrə'geɪʃən/, *n.* the process of eliminating racial segregation in schools, public places, railways, the armed forces, etc.

**desensitise** /di'sɛnsətaɪz/, *v.t.,* **-tised, -tising.** **1.** to lessen the sensitiveness of. **2.** *Physiol.* to eliminate the natural or acquired reactivity or sensitivity of (an animal, organ, tissue, etc.) to an external stimulus, as an allergen. **3.** *Photog.* to make less sensitive or wholly insensitive to light, as the emulsion on a film. Also, **desensitize.** – **desensitisation** /diˌsɛnsətaɪ'zeɪʃən/, *n.* – **desensitiser,** *n.*

**desert**[1] /'dɛzət/, *n.* **1.** an area so deficient in moisture as to support only a sparse, widely spaced vegetation, or none at all. **2.** any area in which few forms of life can exist because of lack of water, permanent frost, or absence of soil. **3.** any place lacking in something. *–adj.* **4.** of, pertaining to, or like a desert; desolate; barren. [ME, from OF, from L (Eccl.) *dēsertum,* properly neut. pp. of *dēserere* abandon, forsake]

**desert**[2] /də'zɜt/, *v.t.* **1.** to leave (a person, place, etc.) without intending to return; to abandon or forsake: *he deserted his wife.* **2.** (of a soldier or sailor) to leave or run away from (the service, duty, etc.) with the intention of never returning. **3.** to fail (one): *all hope deserted him.* *–v.i.* **4.** (esp. of a soldier or sailor) to forsake one's duty, etc. [F *déserter,* from LL *dēsertāre,* frequentative of L *dēserere*] – **deserter,** *n.*

**desert**[3] /də'zɜt/, *n.* **1.** that which is deserved; a due reward or punishment. **2.** worthiness of reward or punishment; merit or demerit. **3.** the fact of deserving well; merit; a virtue. [ME, from OF *deserte,* from *deservir* DESERVE]

**desert bandicoot** /ˌdɛzət 'bændikut/, *n.* a long-nosed bandicoot, *Perameles eremiana,* of Australian arid central regions.

**desert boot** /'– but/, *n.* a soft, ankle-length boot, made of suede with a hard sole often of rubber.

**desert chat** /– 'tʃæt/, *n.* a small, ground-dwelling insectivorous bird, *Ashbyia lovensis,* inhabiting the stony arid interior of Australia. Also, **gibber bird.**

**deserted** /də'zɜtəd/, *adj.* **1.** abandoned; forsaken; uninhabited. **2.** lonely; unfrequented.

**desertion** /də'zɜʃən/, *n.* **1.** the act of deserting. **2.** the state of being deserted. **3.** *Law.* wilful abandonment, esp. of one's wife or husband without consent, in violation of legal or moral obligation.

**desert lemon** /dɛzət 'lɛmən/, *n.* a tree of arid regions, *Eremocitrus glauca,* with small, acid fruit.

**desert oak** /– 'oʊk/, *n.* **1.** a tree, *Casuarina decaisneana,* of central and north-western Australia, with timber very resistant to attack by termites. **2.** any other tree of dry areas with oak-like timber, as *Acacia coriacea.*

**desert pea** /– 'pi/, *n.* →**Sturt's desert pea.**

**desert rat** /– 'ræt/, *n.* **1.** →**jerboa.** **2.** *Mil. Colloq.* a member of the various Allied forces who fought in the desert campaigns in North Africa, 1941-42, esp. one who assisted in the defence of Tobruk. [named after the divisional sign, a jerboa, of the British 7th armoured division]

**desert rat-kangaroo** /– 'ræt-kæŋgə,ru/, *n.* a small, rare marsupial, *Caloprymnus campestris,* of the western plains region of Queensland.

**deserve** /də'zɜv/, *v.*, **-served, -serving.** *–v.t.* **1.** to merit (reward, punishment, esteem, etc.) in return for actions, qualities, etc. *–v.i.* **2.** to be worthy of recompense. [ME *deserve(n),* from OF *deservir,* from L *dēservīre* serve zealously] – **deserver,** *n.*

**deservedly** /də'zɜvədli/, *adv.* justly; according to desert, whether of good or evil.

**deserving** /də'zɜvɪŋ/, *adj.* worthy of reward, praise, or help; meritorious (oft. fol. by *of*). – **deservingly,** *adv.* – **deservingness,** *n.*

**de-sex** /di-'sɛks/, *v.t. Colloq.* (of an animal) to spay or castrate.

**desexualise** /di'sɛkʃuəlaɪz/, *v.t.*, **-lised, -lising.** to deprive of sexual characteristics or quality. Also, **desexualize.**

**déshabillé** /,deɪzæ'bieɪ/, *adj.* in dishabille. [F]

**desiccant** /'dɛsəkənt/, *adj.* **1.** desiccating or drying, as a medicine. *–n.* **2.** a desiccant substance or agent.

**desiccate** /'dɛsəkeɪt/, *v.*, **-cated, -cating.** *–v.t.* **1.** to dry thoroughly; dry up. **2.** to preserve by depriving of moisture, as foods. *–v.i.* **3.** to become dry. [L *dēsiccātus,* pp., completely dried] – **desiccation** /dɛsə'keɪʃən/, *n.* – **desiccative** /'dɛsəkətɪv, də'sɪkətɪv/, *n.*

**desiccated** /'dɛsəkeɪtəd/, *adj.* dehydrated or powdered: *desiccated milk or soup.*

**desiccator** /'dɛsəkeɪtə/, *n.* **1.** one who or that which desiccates. **2.** an apparatus for drying fruit, milk, etc., or for absorbing the moisture present in a chemical substance, etc.

**desid.,** desideratum.

**desiderata** /dəzɪdə'ratə, -'reɪtə/, *n.* plural of **desideratum.**

**desiderate** /də'zɪdəreɪt/, *v.t.*, **-rated, -rating.** to feel a desire for; long for; feel the want of. [L *dēsīderātus,* pp., longed for] – **desideration** /dəzɪdə'reɪʃən/, *n.*

**desiderative** /də'zɪdərətɪv/, *adj.* **1.** having or expressing desire. **2.** *Gram.* (of a verb derived from another) expressing desire to perform the action denoted by the underlying verb. For example, Sanskrit *véda,* he knows; *vi-vid-is-ati,* he wishes to know. *– n.* **3.** *Gram.* a desiderative verb.

**desideratum** /dəzɪdə'ratəm, -'reɪtəm/, *n., pl.* **-ta.** something wanted or needed. [L, properly pp. neut.]

**desig.,** designate.

**design** /də'zaɪn/, *v.t.* **1.** to prepare the preliminary sketch or the plans for (a work to be executed). **2.** to plan or fashion artistically or skilfully. **3.** to intend for a definite purpose. **4.** to form or conceive in the mind; contrive; plan: *he is designing a plan to enlarge his garden.* **5.** *Obs.* to mark out, as by a sign; indicate. *–v.i.* **6.** to make drawings, preliminary sketches, or plans. **7.** to plan and fashion a work of art, etc. *–n.* **8.** an outline, sketch, or plan, as of a work of art, an edifice, or a machine to be executed or constructed. **9.** the combination of details or features of a picture, building, etc.; the pattern or device of artistic work. **10.** the art of designing: *a school of design.* **11.** a plan; a project; a scheme. **12.** a hostile plan; crafty scheme. **13.** the end in view; intention; purpose. **14.** evil or selfish intention: *have designs on (or against) a person.* **15.** adaptation of means to a preconceived end. **16.** an artistic work. **17. by design,** deliberately. [F *désigner* designate, from L *dēsignāre* mark out]

**designate** /'dɛzɪgneɪt/, *v.*, **-nated, -nating;** /'dɛzɪgnət, -neɪt/, *adj.* *–v.t.* **1.** to mark or point out; indicate; show; specify. **2.** to name; entitle; style. **3.** to nominate or select for a duty, office, purpose, etc.; appoint; assign. *–adj.* **4.** appointed to an office but not yet in possession of it; designated, as *the ambassador designate.* [L *dēsignātus,* pp., marked out] – **designative,** *adj.* – **designator,** *n.*

**designation** /dɛzɪg'neɪʃən/, *n.* **1.** the act of designating. **2.** the fact of being designated. **3.** that which designates; a name. **4.** nomination; appointment.

**designedly** /də'zaɪnədli/, *adv.* by design; purposely.

**designer** /də'zaɪnə/, *n.* **1.** one who devises or executes designs, as for works of art, decorative patterns, dresses, machines, etc. **2.** a schemer or intriguer.

**designing** /də'zaɪnɪŋ/, *adj.* **1.** contriving schemes; artful. **2.** showing forethought. *–n.* **3.** the act or art of making designs. – **designingly,** *adv.*

**desinence** /'dɛsənəns/, *n.* termination or ending, as a line of verse.

**desirable** /də'zaɪrəbəl/, *adj.* **1.** worthy to be desired; pleasing, excellent, or fine. **2.** arousing desire: *a desirable woman.* **3.** advisable: *a desirable course of action.* *–n.* **4.** one who or that which is desirable. – **desirability** /dəzaɪrə'bɪləti/, **desirableness,** *n.* – **desirably,** *adv.*

**desire** /də'zaɪə/, *v.*, **-sired, -siring,** *n.* *–v.t.* **1.** to wish or long for; crave; want. **2.** to express a wish to obtain; ask for; request: *the king desired that he should return.* *–n.* **3.** a longing or craving. **4.** an expressed wish; request. **5.** something desired. **6.** sexual appetite; lust. [ME *desire(n),* from OF *desirer,* from L *dēsīderāre* want] – **desirer,** *n.*

**desirous** /də'zaɪrəs/, *adj.* having or characterised by desire; desiring.

**desist** /də'zɪst/, *v.i.* to cease, as from some action or proceeding; stop. [OF *desister,* from L *dēsistere* leave off] – **desistance, desistence,** *n.*

**desk** /dɛsk/, *n.* **1.** a table specially adapted for convenience in writing or reading, sometimes made with a sloping top, and generally fitted with drawers and compartments. **2.** a music-stand. **3.** a section of a complex organisation, such as a government department or newspaper, with responsibilities for a particular area of activities: *the China desk at Foreign Affairs.* **4.** the section of a hotel, office, building etc., where clients and visitors may be received and assisted; the reception desk.

**deskwork** /'dɛskwɜk/, *n.* **1.** work done at a desk. **2.** habitual writing, as that of a clerk or an author.

**desman** /'dɛsmən/, *n., pl.* **-mans.** either of two aquatic insectivorous mammals, related to shrews, *Desmana moschata* of Russia, and *Galemys pyrenaica* of the Pyrenees. [Swed., short for *desman-ratta* muskrat]

desman

**desmid** /'dɛsməd/, *n.* any of the microscopic freshwater algae belonging to the family Desmidiaceae. [NL *Desmidium,* typical genus, diminutive of Gk *desmós* band, chain] – **desmidian,** *adj.*

**desmodromic valve** /,dɛzmədrɒmɪk 'vælv/, *n.* a valve allowing fuel to pass into a combustion engine which is mechanically shut as well as opened. [Gk *desmós* band, chain, ligament + Gk *drómos* a running + -IC]

**desmoid** /'dɛsmɔɪd/, *adj. Anat.* **1.** resembling a fascia or fibrous sheet. **2.** resembling a ligament; ligamentous. *–n.* **3.** *Pathol.* a firm and tough tumour of woven fibrous tissue. [Gk *desmós* band, chain, ligament + -OID]

**desolate** /'dɛsələt, 'dɛz-/, *adj.;* /'dɛsəleɪt, 'dɛz-/, *v.* **-lated, -lating.** *–adj.* **1.** barren or laid waste; devastated. **2.** deprived or destitute of inhabitants; deserted. **3.** left alone; lonely. **4.** having the feeling of being abandoned by friends or by hope. **5.** dreary; dismal. *–v.t.* **6.** to lay waste; devastate. **7.** to deprive of inhabitants; depopulate. **8.** to make disconsolate. **9.** to forsake or abandon. [ME, from L *dēsōlātus,* pp., left alone, forsaken] – **desolater, desolator,** *n.* – **desolately,** *adv.* – **desolateness,** *n.*

**desolation** /dɛsə'leɪʃən, dɛz-/, *n.* **1.** the act of desolating. **2.** the state of being desolated. **3.** devastation; ruin. **4.** dreariness; barrenness. **5.** deprivation of companionship or comfort; loneliness; disconsolateness. **6.** a desolate place. [ME, from L *dēsōlātiō*]

**desorb** /di'zɔb/, *v.t.* **1.** to release (a gas or other substance) from a condition of being adsorbed or absorbed. *–v.i.* **2.** (of a gas or other substance) to separate from a surface on which it has been adsorbed. [DE- + *(ad)sorb*] – **desorption,** *n.*

**desp.,** **1.** despatch. **2.** despatched.

**despair** /də'spɛə/, *n.* **1.** loss of hope; hopelessness. **2.** that which causes hopelessness; that of which there is no hope. *–v.i.* **3.** to lose or give up hope; to be without hope (oft. fol. by *of*): *to despair of humanity.* [ME *despeir(en),* from OF *desperer,* from L *dēspērāre* be without hope]

**despairing** /də'spɛərɪŋ/, *adj.* **1.** given to despair or hopelessness. **2.** indicating despair. – **despairingly,** *adv.*

**despatch** /də'spætʃ/, *v.t., v.i., n.* →**dispatch.** – **despatcher,** *n.*

**desperado** /dɛspə'radoʊ/, *n., pl.* **-does, -dos.** a desperate or reckless criminal; one ready for any desperate deed. [probably refashioning of *desperate* after Sp. words in *-ado.* Cf. OSp. *desperado,* from L *dēspērātus* DESPERATE]

**desperate** /'dɛsprət, -pərət/, *adj.* **1.** reckless from despair; ready to run any risk: *a desperate villain.* **2.** leaving little or no hope; very serious or dangerous; extremely bad: *a desperate illness.* **3.** having no hope: *a desperate situation.* **4.** undertaken as a last resort: *a desperate remedy.* [late ME, from L *dēspērātus,* pp., given up, despaired of] – **desperately,** *adv.* – **desperateness,** *n.*

**desperation** /dɛspə'reɪʃən/, *n.* **1.** the state of being desperate; the recklessness of despair. **2.** the act or fact of despairing; despair. **3.** *Colloq.* extreme keenness or urgency, esp. in sport.

**despicable** /də'spɪkəbəl/, *adj.* that is to be despised; contemptible. [LL *dēspicābilis,* from L *dēspicārī* despise] – **despicability** /dəspɪkə'bɪləti/, **despicableness,** *n.* – **despicably,** *adv.*

**despise** /də'spaɪz/, *v.t.,* **-spised, -spising.** to look down upon, as in contempt; scorn; disdain. [ME *despise(n),* from OF *despire,* from L *dēspicere* look down upon, despise] – **despiser,** *n.*

**despite** /də'spaɪt/, *prep.* **1.** in spite of; notwithstanding. *–n.* **2.** contemptuous treatment; insult. **3.** *Archaic.* malice, hatred, or spite. **4. in despite of,** in contempt or defiance of; in spite of; notwithstanding. [orig. *in despite of;* ME *despit,* from OF, from L *dēspectus* a looking down upon]

**despiteful** /də'spaɪtfəl/, *adj. Archaic.* contemptuous; malicious; spiteful. – **despitefully,** *adv.* – **despitefulness,** *n.*

**despiteous** /dəs'pɪtiəs/, *adj. Archaic.* **1.** malicious; spiteful. **2.** contemptuous. – **despiteously,** *adv.*

**despoil** /də'spɔɪl/, *v.t.* to strip of possessions; rob; plunder; pillage. [ME *despoile(n),* from OF *despoillier,* from L *dēspoliāre* plunder, rob] – **despoiler,** *n.* – **despoilment,** *n.*

**despoliation** /dəspoʊli'eɪʃən/, *n.* **1.** the act of despoiling. **2.** the fact of being despoiled.

**despond** /də'spɒnd/, *v.i.* **1.** to lose heart, courage, or hope. *–n.* **2.** *Archaic.* despondency: *slough of despond.* [L *dēspondēre* promise to give, give up, lose (heart)] – **despondingly,** *adv.*

**despondency** /də'spɒndənsi/, *n.* a state of being despondent; depression of spirits from loss of courage or hope; dejection. Also, **despondence.**

**despondent** /də'spɒndənt/, *adj.* desponding; depressed or dejected. [L *dēspondens,* ppr., giving up, despairing] – **despondently,** *adv.*

**despot** /'dɛspɒt/, *n.* **1.** an absolute ruler; an autocrat. **2.** a tyrant or oppressor. **3. benevolent despot,** a ruler who has the interests of his subjects at heart; an enlightened ruler. [Gk *despótēs* master]

**despotic** /dəs'pɒtɪk/, *adj.* of, pertaining to, or of the nature of a despot or despotism; autocratic; arbitrary; tyrannical. – **despotically,** *adv.*

**despotism** /'dɛspətɪzəm/, *n.* **1.** the rule of a despot; the exercise of absolute authority. **2.** an absolute or autocratic government. **3.** absolute power or control; tyranny. **4.** a country ruled by a despot.

**desquamate** /'dɛskwəmeɪt/, *v.i.,* **-mated, -mating.** *Pathol.* to come off in scales, as the skin in certain diseases; peel off. [L *dēsquāmātus,* pp., scaled off] – **desquamation** /dɛskwə'meɪʃən/, *n.* – **desquamatory** /dəs'kwæmətri, -ətəri/, *adj.*

**dessert** /də'zɜt/, *n.* **1.** the final course of a meal including sweet pies, puddings, etc. **2.** a serving of fruits, or some sweet confection, at the end of a meal. [F, from *desservir* clear the table, from *des-* DIS-[1] + *servīr* serve]

**dessertspoon** /də'zɜtspun/, *n.* a spoon, intermediate in size between a tablespoon and a teaspoon, used for eating dessert.

**dessertspoonful** /də'zɜtspun,fʊl/, *n.* as much as a dessertspoon can hold, equal to about two teaspoonfuls.

**destalk** /di'stɔk/, *v.t.* in wine making, to remove the stalks from the berry at the time of crushing.

**desterilise** /di'stɛrəlaɪz/, *v.t.,* **-lised, -lising.** to make unsterile. Also, **desterilize.**

**de stijl** /də 'staɪl/, *adj.* of or pertaining to the ideas, particularly those concerning neoplasticism, propounded in *de Stijl,* a Dutch periodical, 1917-1928, which had influences on the Bauhaus movement and on commercial art. [D: the style]

**destination** /dɛstə'neɪʃən/, *n.* **1.** the predetermined end of a journey or voyage. **2.** the purpose for which anything is destined; ultimate end or design.

**destine** /'dɛstən/, *v.t.,* **-tined, -tining.** **1.** to set apart for a particular use, purpose, etc.; design; intend. **2.** to appoint or ordain beforehand, as by divine decree; foreordain; predetermine. [ME *destenen,* from OF *destiner,* from L *dēstināre* make fast, establish, appoint]

**destined** /'dɛstənd/, *adj.* **1.** bound for a certain destination. **2.** designed; intended. **3.** predetermined.

**destiny** /'dɛstəni/, *n., pl.* **-nies.** **1.** that which is to happen to a particular person or thing; one's lot or fortune. **2.** the predetermined course of events. **3.** the power or agency which determines the course of events. **4.** *(cap.)* this power personified or represented as a goddess. [ME *destinee,* from OF, from *destiner* DESTINE]

**destitute** /'dɛstətjut, -tʃut/, *adj.* **1.** bereft of means or resources; lacking the means of subsistence. **2.** deprived or devoid of (something) (fol. by *of*). **3.** *Obs.* abandoned or deserted. [ME, from L *dēstitūtus,* pp., put away, abandoned] – **destituteness,** *n.*

**destitution** /dɛstə'tjuʃən/, *n.* **1.** want of the means of subsistence; utter poverty. **2.** deprivation. [ME, from L *dēstitūtio*]

**destn,** destination.

**destroy** /də'strɔɪ/, *v.t.* **1.** to reduce to pieces or to a useless form; ruin; spoil; demolish. **2.** to put an end to; extinguish. **3.** to kill; slay. **4.** to render ineffective; nullify; invalidate. [ME *destruy(en),* from OF *destruire,* from LL var. of L *dēstruere* pull down, destroy] – **destroyable,** *adj.*

**destroyer** /də'strɔɪə/, *n.* **1.** one who or that which destroys. **2.** a small, fast warship, originally designed to destroy torpedo boats.

**destroyer escort** /də'strɔɪər ɛskɔt/, *n.* a destroyer or smaller warship (in Australia, a frigate), detailed to protect aircraft carriers and to escort convoys.

**destroy party** /də'strɔɪ pati/, *n. Colloq.* →**destructo** (def. 2).

**destruct** /də'strʌkt/, *v.i.* **1.** to blow up, as a missile that fails to function properly. *–v.t.* **2.** to destroy. *–n.* **3.** the deliberate destruction of a rocket or the like before completion of its mission. [backformation from DESTRUCTION]

**destructible** /də'strʌktəbəl/, *adj.* that may be destroyed; liable to destruction. – **destructibility** /dəstrʌktə'bɪləti/, **destructibleness,** *n.*

**destruction** /də'strʌkʃən/, *n.* **1.** the act of destroying. **2.** the fact or condition of being destroyed; demolition; annihilation. **3.** a cause or means of destroying. [ME, from L *dēstructio*]

**destructionist** /də'strʌkʃənəst/, *n.* an advocate of the destruction of an existing political institution or the like.

**destructive** /dəs'trʌktɪv/, *adj.* **1.** tending to destroy; causing destruction (fol. by *of* or *to*). **2.** tending to overthrow, disprove, or discredit: *destructive criticism.* *–n.* **3.** a destructive agent or force. – **destructively,** *adv.* – **destructiveness, destructivity** /,dɛstrʌk'tɪvəti/, *n.*

**destructive distillation** /– dɪstə'leɪʃən/, *n.* the destruction or decomposition of a substance, as wood, coal, etc., by heat in a closed vessel, and the collection of the volatile matters evolved.

**destructo** /də'strʌktoʊ/, *n. Colloq.* **1.** a person whose behaviour is so wild or outlandish that he is regarded as being suicidal. **2.** a wild, brawling party.

**destructor** /də'strʌktə/, *n.* a furnace for the burning of refuse; an incinerator. [LL, from L *dēstruere* destroy]

**destruct system** /də'strʌkt sɪstəm/, *n.* a system within a missile or similar vehicle which, when operated by external command or preset internal means, destroys that vehicle.

**desuetude** /'dɛswətjud, də'sjuətjud/, *n.* the state of being no longer used or practised. [F, from L *dēsuētūdo*]

**desulphurisation** /ˌdisʌlfəraɪ'zeɪʃən/, *n.* the removal of unwanted sulphur or sulphur compounds as from chimney gases, etc. Also, **desulphurization.**

**desultory** /'dɛsəltri, -təri, 'dɛz-/, *adj.* **1.** veering about from one thing to another; disconnected, unmethodical, or fitful: *desultory reading or conversation.* **2.** random: *a desultory thought.* [L *dēsultōrius* of a leaper, superficial] – **desultorily,** *adv.* – **desultoriness,** *n.*

**Det.,** Detective.

**detach** /də'tætʃ/, *v.t.* **1.** to unfasten and separate; disengage; disunite. **2.** to send away (a regiment, ship, etc.) on a special mission: *men were detached to defend the pass.* [F *détacher,* from OF *tache* (from Rom. *tacca*) nail. Cf. ATTACH] – **detachable,** *adj.* – **detachability** /dətætʃə'bɪləti/, *n.* – **detacher,** *n.*

**detached** /də'tætʃt/, *adj.* **1.** standing apart; separate; unattached (usu. applied to houses): *he lives in a detached house.* **2.** not interested; unconcerned; aloof. **3.** objective; unbiased.

**detachment** /də'tætʃmənt/, *n.* **1.** the act of detaching. **2.** the condition of being detached. **3.** a state of aloofness, as from worldly affairs or from the concerns of others. **4.** freedom from prejudice or partiality. **5.** the act of sending out a detached force of troops or naval ships. **6.** something detached, as a number of troops separated from a main force for some special combat or other task.

**detail** /'diteɪl/, *n.* **1.** an individual or minute part; an item or particular. **2.** particulars collectively; minutiae. **3.** a dealing with or treating part by part or item by item. **4.** fine, intricate decoration. **5.** a detail drawing. **6.** any small section of a larger structure considered as a unit. **7.** a reproduction of a part or section of something, esp. a work of art, often enlarged. **8.** *Mil.* **a.** detailing or telling off, as of a small force or an officer, for a special service. **b.** the party or person so selected. **c.** a particular assignment of duty. **9.** *Archaic.* a narrative or report of particulars. **10. in detail,** circumstantially; item by item. *–v.t.* **11.** to relate or report in particulars; tell fully and distinctly. **12.** *Mil.* to order or appoint for some particular duty, as a patrol, a guard, etc. **13.** to decorate with fine, intricate designs. **14.** to improve the appearance of (a motor vehicle, aeroplane, etc.) before sale by finishing and decorating it, inside and out. [F *détailler* cut in pieces, retail]

**detail drawing** /– 'drɔɪŋ/, *n.* a drawing, on a relatively large scale, of a part of a building, machine, etc., with dimensions or other information for use in construction.

**detailer** /'diteɪlə/, *n.* a person employed to detail a motor vehicle, aeroplane, etc.

**detain** /də'teɪn/, *v.t.* **1.** to keep from proceeding; keep waiting; delay. **2.** to keep under restraint or in custody. **3.** to keep back or withhold, as from a person. [late ME *detaine(n),* from OF *detenir,* from L *dētinēre* keep back] – **detainment,** *n.*

**detainee** /ˌditeɪ'ni, də'teɪni/, *n.* one who is detained or held prisoner or in custody without trial.

**detainer** /də'teɪnə/, *n.* **1.** one who or that which detains. **2.** *Law.* the wrongful detaining or withholding of what belongs to another. **3.** *Law.* a writ for the further detention of a person already in custody. [AF *detener,* var. of OF *detenir*]

**detect** /də'tɛkt/, *v.t.* **1.** to discover or notice a fact, a process, or an action: *to detect someone in a dishonest act.* **2.** to find out the action or character of: *to detect a hypocrite.* **3.** to discover the presence, existence, or fact of. **4.** *Radio.* to subject to the action of a detector. [L *dētectus,* pp., discovered, uncovered] – **detectable, detectible,** *adj.*

**detectaphone** /də'tɛktəfoʊn/, *n.* a device for tapping telephone conversations.

**detection** /də'tɛkʃən/, *n.* **1.** the act of detecting. **2.** the fact of being detected. **3.** discovery, as of error or crime. **4.** *Radio.* extraction of the modulating audio-frequency signal from the radio-frequency carrier; demodulation.

**detective** /də'tɛktɪv/, *n.* **1.** a member of the police force or a private investigator whose job it is to obtain information and evidence, as of offences against the law, and to discover the author of a crime. *–adj.* **2.** pertaining to detection or detectives: *a detective story.* **3.** serving to detect; detecting.

**detector** /də'tɛktə/, *n.* **1.** one who or that which detects. **2.** *Radio.* **a.** a device for detecting electric oscillations or waves. **b.** a device for detection (def. 4). [LL]

**detent**[1] /də'tɛnt/, *n.* a piece of a mechanism which, when disengaged, releases the operating power, or by which the action is prevented or checked; a catch, as in a lock, clock, etc.; a pawl. [F *détente,* from *détendre* relax, from *dé-* DIS-[1] + *tendre* (from L *tendere* stretch)]

**detent**[2] /də'tɛnt/, *n.* holding back or inhibition. [L *dētentus,* pp., detained]

**détente** /deɪ'tɒnt/, *n.* a relaxing, as of international tension. [F]

**detention** /də'tɛnʃən/, *n.* **1.** the act of detaining. **2.** the state of being detained. **3.** a keeping in custody; confinement. **4.** a keeping in (of a pupil) after school hours as a form of punishment. **5.** the withholding of what belongs to or is claimed by another.

**detention centre** /'– sɛntə/, *n. Brit.* a form of prison to which offenders between the ages of 14 and 21 may be committed.

**deter** /də'tɜ/, *v.t.,* **-terred, -terring.** to discourage or restrain (one) from acting or proceeding, through fear, doubt, etc. [L *dēterrēre* frighten from] – **determent,** *n.*

**deterge** /də'tɜdʒ/, *v.t.,* **-terged, -terging.** **1.** to wipe away. **2.** to cleanse by removing foul or morbid matter, as from a wound. [L *dētergēre* wipe off]

**detergence** /də'tɜdʒəns/, *n.* cleansing or purging power. Also, **detergency.**

**detergent** /də'tɜdʒənt/, *adj.* **1.** cleansing; purging. *–n.* **2. a.** any cleaning agent, including soap. **b.** one of a group of synthetic, organic cleaning agents with surface-active properties which, unlike soap, is not produced from fats or oils.

**deteriorate** /də'tɪəriəreɪt/, *v.,* **-rated, -rating.** *–v.t.* **1.** to make worse; make lower in character or quality. *–v.i.* **2.** to become worse. [LL *dēteriōrātus,* pp.] – **deterioration** /dətɪəriə'reɪʃən/, *n.* – **deteriorative,** *adj.*

**determinable** /də'tɜmənəbəl/, *adj.* **1.** capable of being determined. **2.** *Law.* subject to termination.

**determinant** /də'tɜmənənt/, *adj.* **1.** serving to determine; determining. *–n.* **2.** a determining agent or factor. **3.** *Maths.* an algebraic expression in the elements of a square matrix, used in solving linear systems of equations. – **determinantal** /dətɜmə'næntəl/, *adj.*

**determinate** /də'tɜmənət/, *adj.* **1.** having defined limits; definite. **2.** settled; positive. **3.** determined upon; conclusive; final. **4.** determined; resolute. **5.** *Bot.* (of an inflorescence) having the primary and each secondary axis ending in a flower or bud, thus preventing further elongation. [ME, from L *dēterminātus,* pp., determined] – **determinately,** *adv.* – **determinateness,** *n.*

**determination** /dətɜmə'neɪʃən/, *n.* **1.** the act of coming to a decision; the fixing or settling of a purpose. **2.** ascertainment, as after observation or investigation. **3.** a result ascertained; a solution. **4.** the settlement of a dispute, etc., by authoritative decision. **5.** the decision arrived at or pronounced. **6.** the quality of being determined or resolute; firmness of purpose. **7.** a fixed purpose or intention. **8.** the fixing or settling of amount, limit, character, etc. **9.** fixed direction or tendency towards some object or end. **10.** *Chiefly Law.* conclusion or termination. **11.** *Embryol.* the fixation of the nature of morphological differentiation in a group of cells before actual, visible differentiation. **12.** *Logic.* the rendering of a notion more definite by the addition of differentiating characters.

**determinative** /də'tɜmənətɪv/, *adj.* **1.** serving to determine; determining. *–n.* **2.** something that determines. **3.** (in hieroglyphics) an ideographic sign attached to a word as an indication of its meaning. – **determinatively,** *adv.* – **determinativeness,** *n.*

**determine** /də'tɜmən/, *v.,* **-mined, -mining.** *–v.t.* **1.** to settle or decide (a dispute, question, etc.) by an authoritative decision. **2.** to conclude or ascertain, as after reasoning, observation, etc. **3.** *Geom.* to fix the position of. **4.** to fix or decide causally; condition: *demand determines supply.* **5.** to give direction or tendency to; impel. **6.** *Logic.* to limit, as an idea, by adding differentiating characters. **7.** *Chiefly Law.* to put an end to; terminate. **8.** to lead or bring (a person) to a decision: *it finally determined him to do it.* **9.** to decide upon. *–v.i.* **10.** to come to a decision or resolution; decide. **11.** *Chiefly Law.* to come to an end. [ME *determine(n),* from OF *determiner,* from L *dēterminūre* limit] **– determiner,** *n.*

**determined** /də'tɜmənd/, *adj.* **1.** resolute; unflinching; firm. **2.** decided; settled; resolved. **– determinedly,** *adv.* **– determinedness,** *n.*

**determinism** /də'tɜmənɪzəm/, *n.* the doctrine that neither outside events nor human choices are uncaused, but are the results of antecedent conditions, physical or psychological. **– determinist,** *n., adj.* **– deterministic** /dətɜmə'nɪstɪk/, *adj.* **– deterministically** /dətɜmə'nɪstɪkli/, *adv.*

**deterrent** /də'tɛrənt, -'tɜr-/, *adj.* **1.** deterring; restraining. *–n.* **2.** something that deters or is expected to deter, as possession of a nuclear weapon. **– deterrence,** *n.*

**detersive** /də'tɜsɪv/, *adj.* **1.** detergent. *–n.* **2.** a detersive agent or medicine.

**detest** /də'tɛst/, *v.t.* to feel abhorrence of; hate; dislike intensely. [F *détester,* from L *dētestārī,* lit., curse while calling a deity to witness] **– detester,** *n.*

**detestable** /də'tɛstəbəl/, *adj.* deserving to be detested; abominable; hateful. **– detestability** /dətɛstə'bɪləti/, **detestableness,** *n.* **– detestably,** *adv.*

**detestation** /ditɛs'teɪʃən/, *n.* **1.** abhorrence; hatred. **2.** a person or thing detested.

**dethrone** /di'θroun/, *v.t.,* **-throned, -throning.** to remove from the throne; depose. **– dethronement,** *n.* **– dethroner,** *n.*

**detinue** /'dɛtənju/, *n.* an old common-law form of action to recover possession or the value of articles of personal property wrongfully detained. [OF *detenue* detention, orig. pp. fem. of *detenir* DETAIN]

**detonate** /'dɛtəneɪt/, *v.,* **-nated, -nating.** *–v.t.* **1.** to cause to explode. *–v.i.* **2.** to explode, esp. with great noise, suddenness, or violence. [L *dētonātus,* pp., thundered forth]

**detonating gas** /'dɛtəneɪtɪŋ ˌgæs/, *n.* →**electrolytic gas.**

**detonation** /dɛtə'neɪʃən/, *n.* **1.** the act of detonating. **2.** an explosion. **3. a.** *Chem.* very rapid combustion which occurs in a shock wave. **b.** the combustion reactions which cause knocking or pinging in an internal-combustion engine. **c.** the accompanying knocking or pinging sound.

**detonator** /'dɛtəneɪtə/, *n.* **1.** a device, as a percussion cap or an explosive, used to make another substance explode. **2.** something that explodes.

**detour** /'ditʊə, -tuə, -tɔ/, *n.* **1.** a roundabout or circuitous way or course, esp. one used temporarily instead of the main route. *–v.i.* **2.** to make a detour; go by way of a detour. *–v.t.* **3.** to cause to make a detour; send by way of a detour. [F, from *détourner* turn aside, from *dé-* DIS-[1] + *tourner* turn]

**detoxication centre** /ˌditɒksə'keɪʃən sɛntə/, *n.* a centre for the purpose of supervising people in their withdrawal from addictive drugs. Also, **detoxification centre.**

**detoxing gear** /di'tɒksɪŋ gɪə/, *n.* a mechanism on a car designed to reduce the level of toxins in the exhaust.

**detract** /də'trækt/, *v.t.* **1.** to take away (a part); abate (fol. by *from*). **2.** to draw away or divert. *–v.i.* **3.** to take away a part, as from quality, value, or reputation. [L *dētractus,* pp., drawn away or down] **– detractingly,** *adv.* **– detractor,** *n.*

**detraction** /də'trækʃən/, *n.* the act of detracting, or of belittling the reputation or worth of a person; disparagement.

**detractive** /də'træktɪv/, *adj.* tending or seeking to detract; depreciative. Also, **detractory** /də'træktəri/. **– detractively,** *adv.*

**detrain** /di'treɪn/, *Chiefly Mil. –v.i.* **1.** to alight from a railway train. *–v.t.* **2.** to discharge (troops, etc.) from a railway train. **– detrainment,** *n.*

**detribalise** /di'traɪbəlaɪz/, *v.t.,* **-lised, -lising.** to destroy the ethnic and cultural inheritance of the members of a tribal group, mainly through contact with different cultures: *the detribalised Aborigines of the city.* Also, **detribalize.** **– detribalisation** /ˌditraɪbəlaɪ'zeɪʃən/, *n.*

**detriment** /'dɛtrəmənt/, *n.* **1.** loss, damage, or injury. **2.** a cause of loss or damage. [L *dētrīmentum* loss, damage]

**detrimental** /dɛtrə'mɛntl/, *adj.* causing detriment; injurious; prejudicial. **– detrimentally,** *adv.*

**detrital** /də'traɪtl/, *adj.* composed of detritus.

**detrition** /də'trɪʃən/, *n.* the act of wearing away by rubbing.

**detritus** /də'traɪtəs/, *n.* **1.** particles of rock or other material worn or broken away from a mass, as by the action of water or glacial ice. **2.** any disintegrated material; debris. [L: a rubbing away]

**de trop** /də 'troʊ/, *adj.* **1.** in the way; not wanted; superfluous. **2.** inappropriate; out of place. [F: lit., of too much]

**detrude** /di'trud/, *v.t.,* **-truded, -truding.** **1.** to thrust out or away. **2.** to thrust or force down. [L *dētrūdere*]

**detruncate** /di'trʌŋkeɪt/, *v.t.,* **-cated, -cating.** to reduce by cutting off a part; cut down. [L *dētruncātus,* pp.] **– detruncation** /ˌditrʌŋ'keɪʃən/, *n.*

**detrusion** /də'truʒən/, *n.* the act of detruding. [LL *dētrūsio,* from L *dētrūdere* thrust away]

**detumescence** /ˌditju'mɛsəns/, *n.* subsidence of swelling. [L *dētumescere* cease to swell. See TUMESCENT, -ENCE]

**detune** /di'tjun/, *v.t.,* **-tuned, -tuning.** **1.** to adjust a high-performance engine, as in a racing car, so that its performance is reduced but its suitability for general use is increased. **2.** to alter the period of oscillation in a circuit so that it no longer coincides with that of another circuit with which it interacts.

**deuce**[1] /djus/, *n.* **1.** a card, or the side of a dice, having two pips. **2.** *Tennis, etc.* a juncture in a game at which the scores are level and either player (or pair) must gain a lead of two points in order to win the game. [OF *deus,* from L *duōs,* acc. of *duo* two]

**deuce**[2] /djus/, *n. Colloq.* bad luck; the devil (used in mild imprecations and exclamations). [special use of DEUCE[1], probably from LG *de duus!* the deuce, an unlucky throw at dice. Cf. G *der Daus!*]

**deuced** /'djusəd, djust/, *Colloq. –adj.* **1.** confounded; excessive. *–adv.* **2.** Also, **deucedly.** confoundedly; excessively.

**deurbanise** /di'ɜbənaɪz/, *v.t.,* **-nised, -nising.** to deprive (a people or a place) of urban character. Also, **deurbanize.**

**deus ex machina** /ˌdeɪʊs ɛks 'mækənə/, *n.* an improbable, artificial, or unmotivated device for unravelling a plot, esp. in drama. [L: god from a machine]

**deut-,** variant of **deuto-,** before vowels.

**Deut.,** *Bible.* Deuteronomy.

**deuter-,** a form of **deutero-** (def. 1) before a vowel.

**deuterium** /dju'tɪəriəm/, *n.* an isotope of hydrogen, having twice the mass of ordinary hydrogen; heavy hydrogen. *Symbol:* D; *at. no.:* 1; *at. wt.:* 2.01. [NL, from Gk *deutereîon,* neut. sing. of *deutereîos,* adj., having second place]

**deuterium oxide** /– 'ɒksaɪd/, *n.* →**heavy water.**

**deutero-,** a word element: **1.** meaning 'second' or 'later', as in *deuterogamy.* **2.** *Chem.* indicating the presence of deuterium. [Gk, combining form of *deúteros* second]

**deuterogamy** /djutə'rɒgəmi/, *n.* a second marriage, after the death or divorce of a first husband or wife. [Gk *deuterogamía* second marriage] **– deuterogamist,** *n.*

**deuteron** /'djutərɒn/, *n.* a deuterium nucleus.

**deuto-,** **1.** variant of **deutero-.** **2.** *Chem.* a prefix denoting the second in a series. Also, **deut-.**

**deutoplasm** /'djutəplæzəm/, *n. Embryol.* that part of the ovocyte which furnishes the nourishment of the embryo.

**Deutschland** /'dɔɪtʃlʌnt, -lænd/, *n.* German name of **Germany.**

**deutschmark** /'dɔɪtʃmak/, *n.* the monetary unit of West Germany since 1948. *Abbrev.:* DM Also, **deutschemark.**

**deutzia** /'djutsiə/, *n.* any shrub of the genus *Deutzia,* family Saxifragaceae, having mostly white, pink, or purplish flowers. [named after Jan *Deutz,* 1743-88?, Dutch naturalist]

**dev.,** **1.** development. **2.** deviation.

**devaluate** /di'væljueɪt/, *v.t.,* **-ated, -ating.** **1.** to deprive of value; reduce the value of. **2.** to devalue. [DE- + VALUE, *n.* + -ATE[1]]

**devaluation** /ˌdivælju'eɪʃən/, *n.* **1.** an official lowering of the legal exchange value of a country's currency. **2.** a reduction of value, importance, etc.

**devalue** /di'vælju/, *v.*, **-valued, -valuing.** *–v.t.* **1.** to lower the legal value of (a currency); devaluate. **2.** to diminish the worth or value of: *his advice was devalued by recent developments.* *–v.i.* **3.** (of a currency) to decrease in legal value.

**Devanagari** /deɪvə'nagəri/, *n.* the alphabetical script in which Sanskrit is usu. written, also employed for Hindi, and, in a modified form, other modern languages of India. [Skt: lit., Nagari (an alphabet of India) of the gods]

**devastate** /'dɛvəsteɪt/, *v.t.*, **-stated, -stating.** to lay waste; ravage; render desolate. [L *dēvastātus,* pp.]

**devastating** /'dɛvəsteɪtɪŋ/, *adj.* **1.** tending or threatening to devastate. **2.** *Colloq.* (of a remark, description, etc.) highly effective. – **devastatingly,** *adv.*

**devastation** /dɛvə'steɪʃən/, *n.* **1.** act of devastating; destruction. **2.** devastated state; desolation.

**devastavit** /dɛvə'steɪvət/, *n.* any violation or neglect of duty by a personal representative which makes him personally responsible to persons having claims on the assets, as creditors and beneficiaries. [L: he has laid waste]

**develop** /də'vɛləp/, *v.t.* **1.** to bring out the capabilities or possibilities of; bring to a more advanced or effective state. **2.** to cause to grow or expand. **3.** to elaborate or expand in detail. **4.** to bring into being or activity; generate; evolve. **5.** to build on (land). **6.** to prepare (vacant land) for housing by the provision of roads, sewerage, etc. **7.** *Biol.* to cause to go through the process of natural evolution from a previous and lower stage, or from an embryonic state, to a later and more complex or perfect one. **8.** *Maths.* **a.** to express in an extended form, as in a series. **b.** to unroll on to a plane surface. **9.** *Music.* to unfold, by various technical means, the inherent possibilities of (a theme). **10.** *Photog.* **a.** to render visible (the latent image) in the exposed sensitised film of a photographic plate, etc. **b.** to treat (a photographic plate, etc.) with chemical agents so as to bring out the latent image. **11.** *Chess.* to bring a piece into a useful position. *–v.i.* **12.** to grow into a more mature or advanced state; advance; expand. **13.** to come gradually into existence or operation; be evolved. **14.** to be disclosed; become evident or manifest. **15.** *Biol.* to undergo differentiation in ontogeny or progress in phylogeny. **16.** to undergo developing, as a photographic plate. [F *développer,* from *dé-* DIS-[1] + *voluper* wrap. Cf. ENVELOP] – **developable,** *adj.*

**developed** /də'vɛləpt/, *adj.* industrialised.

**developer** /də'vɛləpə/, *n.* **1.** one who or that which develops. **2.** a person who (or company which) acquires land for development projects. **3.** *Photog.* the reducing agent or solution used to develop a photographic film or plate.

**developing** /də'vɛləpɪŋ/, *adj.* (of a country) in the early stages of developing an industrial economy. Also, **less-developed, underdeveloped.**

**development** /də'vɛləpmənt/, *n.* **1.** the act, process or result of developing. **2.** a developed state, form, or product. **3.** evolution, growth, expansion. **4.** a fact or circumstance bringing about a new situation. **5.** a building project, usu. large, as an office block, housing estate, shopping complex, etc. **6.** the preparation of vacant land for building by the provision of roads, sewerage, etc. **7.** *Music.* the part of a movement or composition in which a theme or themes are developed. – **developmental** /dəvɛləp'mɛntl/, *adj.* – **developmentally** /dəvɛləp'mɛntəli/, *adv.*

**development application** /'– æplə,keɪʃən/, *n.* an application to a local government body for permission to develop a land site.

**deviant** /'diviənt/, *adj.* **1.** deviating from an accepted norm, esp. in politics or sex. *–n.* **2.** one who or that which is deviant. – **deviance, deviancy,** *n.*

**deviate** /'divieɪt/, *v.*, **-ated, -ating;** /'diviət/, *adj., n.* *–v.i.* **1.** to turn aside (from a way or course). **2.** to depart or swerve, as from a procedure, course of action, or acceptable standard. **3.** to digress as from a line of thought or reasoning. *–v.t.* **4.** to cause to swerve; turn aside. *–adj., n.* **5.** *Chiefly U.S.* deviant. [LL *dēviātus,* pp. of *dēviāre,* from L *de-* DE- + *via* way] – **deviator,** *n.*

**deviation** /divi'eɪʃən/, *n.* **1.** the act of deviating; divergence. **2.** departure from an accepted standard. **3.** *Statistics.* the difference between one of a set of values and the mean of the set. **4.** *Navig.* the error of a ship's magnetic compass due to local magnetism; the angle between the compass meridian and the magnetic meridian. **5.** a road or rail detour.

**deviationist** /divi'eɪʃənəst/, *n.* (chiefly in Communist ideology) one who departs from accepted party policies or practices. – **deviationism,** *n.*

**device** /də'vaɪs/, *n.* **1.** an invention or contrivance. **2.** a plan or scheme for effecting a purpose. **3.** a crafty scheme; a trick. **4.** an artistic figure or design used as a heraldic bearing (often accompanied by a motto), or as an emblem, badge, trademark, or the like. **5.** a motto. **6.** (*pl.*) will; desire; ingenuity; inclination: *left to his own devices.* **7.** something artistically or fancifully designed. **8.** *Computers.* →**peripheral device.** [b. ME *devis* division, discourse and *devise* heraldic device, will, both from OF, from L *dīvīsus, -a,* pp., divided]

**devil** /'dɛvəl/, *n.*, *v.*, **-illed, -illing** or (*U.S.*) **-iled, -iling.** *–n.* **1.** *Theol.* **a.** (*sometimes cap.*) the supreme spirit of evil; Satan. **b.** a subordinate evil spirit at enmity with God, and having power to afflict man both with bodily disease and with spiritual corruption. **2.** a depiction of the devil as a man with a tail, cloven hoofs, and horns. **3.** an atrociously wicked, cruel, or ill-tempered person. **4.** a person of great cleverness, energy, or recklessness. **5.** the errand boy or the youngest apprentice in a printing office. **6.** *Colloq.* a person, usu. one in unfortunate circumstances. **7.** *Law.* a junior counsel working without a fee. **8.** a hack writer. **9.** *Colloq.* fighting spirit. **10.** a machine designed to do destructive work, esp. with spikes or sharp teeth, as a machine for tearing rags, etc. **11.** any of various portable furnaces or braziers. **12. the devil!** (an emphatic expletive or mild oath used to express disgust, anger, astonishment, negation, etc.) **13. between the devil and the deep blue sea,** faced with two equally distasteful alternatives. **14. devil of a,** *Colloq.* extremely difficult. **15. give the devil his due,** to do justice to or give deserved credit to an unpleasant or disliked person. **16. the devil to pay,** serious trouble to be faced. **17. go to the devil, a.** to fail completely; be ruined. **b.** to become depraved. **c.** an expletive expressing annoyance, disgust, impatience, etc. **18. let the devil take the hindmost,** to leave the least fortunate to suffer unpleasant consequences; abandon or leave to one's fate. **19. play the** (**very**) **devil with,** to ruin; do great harm to. **20. raise the devil,** to make a commotion. **21. speak** or **talk of the devil,** here comes the person who has been the subject of conversation. *–v.t.* **22.** *Colloq.* to harass, torment or pester. **23.** *Cookery.* to prepare food esp. by grilling with hot spices. **24.** to tear (rags, cloth, etc.) with a devil (def. 10). *–v.i.* **25.** to do work, esp. hackwork, for a lawyer or literary man; perform arduous or unpaid work or without recognition of one's services. [ME *devel,* OE *deofol,* from L *diabolus,* from Gk *diábolos* Satan, orig. slanderer]

**devilfish** /'dɛvəlfɪʃ/, *n., pl.* **-fishes,** (*esp. collectively*) **-fish. 1.** Also, **devil ray.** the manta ray, *Manta alfredi,* of the Great Barrier Reef and north Australian waters. **2.** any of several large rays of genera *Manta* and *Mobula,* inhabiting warm seas. **3.** any of various large cephalopods as the octopus.

**devilish** /'dɛvəlɪʃ, 'dɛvlɪʃ/, *adj.* **1.** of, like, or befitting a devil; diabolical; fiendish. **2.** *Colloq.* excessive; very great. *–adv.* **3.** *Colloq.* excessively; extremely. – **devilishly,** *adv.* – **devilishness,** *n.*

**devilkin** /'dɛvəlkən/, *n.* a little devil; an imp.

**devil-may-care** /,dɛvəl-meɪ-'kɛə/, *adj.* reckless; careless; happy-go-lucky.

**devilment** /'dɛvəlmənt/, *n.* devilish action or conduct; mischief.

**devil-on-horseback** /,dɛvəl-ɒn-'hɔsbæk/, *n.* →**angel-on-horseback.**

**devil-on-the-coals** /,dɛvəl-ɒn-ðə-'koʊlz/, *n.* *Colloq.* a small, thin, quickly made damper.

**devil ray** /'dɛvəl reɪ/, *n.* →**devilfish** (def. 1).

**devilry** /'dɛvəlri/, *n., pl.* **-ries. 1.** wicked or reckless mischief. **2.** extreme wickedness. **3.** mischievous or wicked behaviour. **4.** diabolic magic or art. **5.** demonology. Also, **deviltry.**

**devil's advocate** /dɛvəlz 'ædvəkət/, *n.* an advocate of an opposing or bad cause, esp. for the sake of argument. [translation of NL *advocātus diabolī,* in the Rom. Cath.

Church the official appointed to present the arguments on a proposed canonisation]

**devil's claw** /– 'klɔ/, *n.* any of the herbaceous shrubs of the family Martyniaceae, as *Proboscidea louisiana,* an American species with woody fruit tapering to a curved beak about 15 cm long.

**devil's darning needle,** *n.* →**dragonfly.**

**devil's food cake,** *n.* a rich, chocolate cake.

**devil's grip** /'dɛvəlz grɪp/, *n.* a serious defect in conformation in sheep, appearing as a depression immediately behind the withers, and associated with short yolk-stained wool of poor character; the condition sometimes extends down behind the shoulder blades and even right round the girth.

**devil's guts** /'– gʌts/, *n.* →**dodder laurel.** Also, **devil's twine.**

**devil's punchbowl** /– 'pʌntʃboʊl/, *n.* a deep hollow in a hillside.

**devil's twine** /'– twaɪn/, *n.* any of the tangled slender semi-parasitic vines of the genus *Cassytha.* Also, **devil's guts.**

**devil take the hindmost,** *n.* a cycling race over four to eight kilometres in which the rider finishing last in a lap drops out of the race.

**deviltry** /'dɛvəltri/, *n., pl.* **-tries.** →**devilry.**

**devious** /'diviəs/, *adj.* **1.** departing from the direct way; circuitous. **2.** out of the way; remote. **3.** departing from the accepted way; roundabout. **4.** not straightforward; tricky; deceptive; deceitful. [L *dēvius* out of the way] – **deviously,** *adv.* – **deviousness,** *n.*

**devisable** /də'vaɪzəbəl/, *adj.* **1.** capable of being invented or contrived. **2.** capable of being bequeathed or assigned by will.

**devisal** /də'vaɪzəl/, *n.* the act of devising; contrivance.

**devise** /də'vaɪz/, *v.,* **-vised, -vising,** *n.* –*v.t.* **1.** to order or arrange the plan of; think out; plan; contrive; invent. **2.** *Law.* to assign or transmit (property, esp. real property) by will. –*v.i.* **3.** to form a plan; contrive. –*n.* **4.** *Law.* **a.** the act of disposing of property, esp. real property, by will. **b.** a will or clause in a will disposing of property, esp. real property. **c.** the property disposed of. [ME *devise(n),* from OF *deviser,* from LL frequentative of L *dīvidere* separate] – **deviser,** *n.*

**devisee** /dəvaɪ'zi/, *n.* one to whom a devise is made.

**devisor** /də'vaɪzə/, *n.* one who makes a devise.

**devitalise** /di'vaɪtəlaɪz/, *v.t.,* **-lised, -lising.** to deprive of vitality or vital properties; make lifeless or weak. Also, **devitalize.** – **devitalisation** /diˌvaɪtəlaɪ'zeɪʃən/, *n.*

**devitrify** /di'vɪtrəfaɪ/, *v.,* **-fied, -fying.** –*v.t.* **1.** to deprive, wholly or partly, of vitreous character or properties, esp. to process glass so that it develops a minute crystalline structure, with a corresponding loss of transparency. –*v.i.* **2.** *Geol.* (of glassy, igneous rocks) to change into rocks composed of definite and distinct minerals. – **devitrification** /diˌvɪtrəfə'keɪʃən/, *n.*

**devocalise** /di'voʊkəlaɪz/, *v.t.,* **-lised, -lising.** *Phonet.* to make (a voiced speech sound) voiceless. Also, **devocalize.** – **devocalisation** /diˌvoʊkəlaɪ'zeɪʃən/, *n.*

**devoice** /ˌdi'vɔɪs/, *v.t.,* **-voiced, -voicing.** (in phonetics) to make (a voiced sound) voiceless.

**devoid** /də'vɔɪd/, *adj.* empty, not possessing, free from, void, or destitute (fol. by *of*). [orig. pp. of obs. *devoid,* v., from OF *desvuidier* empty out, from *des-* DIS-[1] + *vuidier,* v., empty, void]

**devoir** /də'vwa/, *n.* **1.** an act of civility or respect. **2.** (*pl.*) respects or compliments. **3.** *Archaic.* duty. [F, orig. inf., from L *dēbēre* owe]

**devolution** /divə'luʃən/, *n.* **1.** the act or fact of devolving; passage onward from stage to stage. **2.** the passing on to a successor of an unexercised right. **3.** *Law.* the passing of property, as upon death or bankruptcy. **4.** *Biol.* degeneration; retrograde evolution (opposed to *evolution*). **5.** the transfer or delegation of power or authority. – **devolutionary,** *adj.*

**devolve** /də'vɒlv/, *v.,* **-volved, -volving.** –*v.t.* **1.** to transfer or delegate (a duty, responsibility, etc.) to or upon another; pass on. **2.** *Law.* to pass by inheritance or legal succession. **3.** *Archaic.* to roll downward; roll. –*v.i.* **4.** to fall as a duty or responsibility on a person. **5.** to be transferred or passed on from one to another. **6.** *Archaic.* to roll down. [L *dēvolvere* roll down] – **devolvement,** *n.*

**Devon** /'dɛvən/, *n.* **1.** a breed of dairy and beef cattle, usu. red, originating in Devonshire. **2.** a breed of sheep, with brown face and legs, and long wool. **3.** (*l.c.*) a large, smooth, bland sausage, usu. sliced thinly and eaten cold.

**Devonian** /də'voʊniən/, *adj.* **1.** pertaining to a geological period or a system of rocks following the Silurian and preceding the Carboniferous. –*n.* **2.** the Devonian period or system.

**Devonshire cream** /dɛvənʃə 'krim, -ʃɪə/, *n.* →**clotted cream.**

**Devonshire tea** /– 'ti/, *n.* a light meal of scones, jam and cream, usu. served with tea.

**devote** /də'voʊt/, *v.,* **-voted, -voting,** *adj.* –*v.t.* **1.** to give up or appropriate to or concentrate on a particular pursuit, occupation, purpose, cause, person, etc.: *devoting himself to science, evenings devoted to reading.* **2.** to appropriate by or as by a vow; set apart or dedicate by a solemn or formal act; consecrate. [L *dēvōtus,* pp., vowed]

**devoted** /də'voʊtəd/, *adj.* **1.** zealous or ardent in attachment: *a devoted friend.* **2.** dedicated; consecrated. – **devotedly,** *adv.* – **devotedness,** *n.*

**devotee** /dɛvə'ti/, *n.* **1.** one ardently devoted to anything; an enthusiast. **2.** one zealously or fanatically devoted to religion.

**devotement** /də'voʊtmənt/, *n.* devotion; dedication.

**devotion** /də'voʊʃən/, *n.* **1.** dedication; consecration. **2.** earnest attachment to a cause, person, etc. **3.** a giving over or appropriating to any purpose, cause, etc. **4.** *Theol.* the ready will to perform what belongs to the service of God. **5.** (*oft. pl.*) *Eccles.* religious observance or worship; a form of prayer or worship for special use. [ME, from L *dēvōtio*]

**devotional** /də'voʊʃənəl/, *adj.* characterised by devotion; used in devotions. – **devotionally,** *adv.*

**devour** /də'vaʊə/, *v.t.* **1.** to swallow or eat up voraciously or ravenously. **2.** to consume destructively, recklessly, or wantonly. **3.** to swallow up or engulf. **4.** to take in greedily with the senses or intellect. **5.** to absorb or engross wholly: *devoured by fears.* [ME *devoure(n),* from OF *devorer,* from L *dēvorāre* swallow down] – **devourer,** *n.* – **devouringly,** *adv.*

**devout** /də'vaʊt/, *adj.* **1.** devoted to divine worship or service; pious; religious. **2.** expressing devotion or piety: *devout prayer.* **3.** earnest or sincere; hearty. [ME, from OF *devot,* from L *dēvōtus,* pp., devoted] – **devoutly,** *adv.* – **devoutness,** *n.*

**dew** /dju/, *n.* **1.** moisture condensed from the atmosphere, esp. at night, and deposited in the form of small drops upon any cool surface. **2.** something likened to dew, as serving to refresh or as suggestive of morning. **3.** moisture in small drops on a surface, as tears, perspiration, etc. –*v.t.* **4.** to wet with or as with dew. [ME; OE *dēaw,* c. G *Tau*] – **dewless,** *adj.*

**Dewar flask** /'djuə flask/, *n.* a double-walled silvered-glass flask in which the space between the walls is evacuated, used for storing liquids at a low temperature, esp. liquid air. [named after Sir James *Dewar,* 1842-1923, Scottish chemist and physicist who invented it]

**dewberry** /'djubɛri, -bri/, *n., pl.* **-ries. 1.** the fruit of several species of running, trailing blackberries, as *Rubus roribaccus* in North America, and *Rubus caesius* in Europe. **2.** a plant bearing such fruit.

**dewclaw** /'djuklɔ/, *n.* **1.** a functionless inner claw or digit in the foot of some dogs, not reaching the ground in walking. **2.** an analogous false hoof of deer, pigs, etc.

**dewdrop** /'djudrɒp/, *n.* **1.** a drop of dew. **2.** *Colloq.* a drop at the end of a person's nose.

**Dewey decimal classification,** *n.* See **decimal classification.** [named after Melvil *Dewey,* 1851-1931, U.S. librarian]

**dewfish** /'djufɪʃ/, *n.* →**tandan.**

**dewlap** /'djulæp/, *n.* **1.** a pendulous fold of skin under the throat of cattle. **2.** any similar part, as the loose skin under the throat of some dogs, the wattle of fowls, etc. **3.** any loose skin on the human throat. [from *dew,* of

D: dewlap (def. 1)

uncert. meaning + *lap,* OE *læppa* pendulous piece. Cf. Dan. *doglæp*] – **dewlapped,** *adj.*

**dewpoint** /ˈdjupɔɪnt/, *n.* the temperature of the air at which dew begins to be deposited; the temperature at which a given sample of air will have a relative humidity of 100 per cent.

**dewy** /ˈdjui/, *adj.,* **dewier, dewiest. 1.** moist with or as with dew. **2.** having the quality of dew: *dewy tears.* **3.** *Poetic.* falling gently, or refreshing like dew: *dewy sleep.* **4.** of dew. – **dewily,** *adv.* – **dewiness,** *n.*

**dewy-eyed** /ˈdjui-aɪd/, *adj.* credulous; naive; trusting.

**dexamphetamine** /ˌdɛksæmˈfɛtəmin/, *n.* →**dextroamphetamine.**

**dexedrine** /ˈdɛksədrin/, *n.* (*also cap.*) →**dextroamphetamine.** [Trademark]

**dexter** /ˈdɛkstə/, *adj.* **1.** on the right side; right. **2.** *Her.* situated to the right of the bearer and hence to the left of the spectator (opposed to *sinister*). **3.** *Obs.* favourable. [L: right, favourable]

**dexterity** /dɛksˈtɛrəti/, *n.* **1.** adroitness or skill in using the hands or body. **2.** mental adroitness or skill; cleverness. **3.** right-handedness. [DEXTER + -ITY]

**dexterous** /ˈdɛkstrəs, -stərəs/, *adj.* **1.** skilful or adroit in the use of the hands or body. **2.** having mental adroitness or skill; clever. **3.** done with dexterity. **4.** right-handed. Also, **dextrous.** – **dexterously,** *adv.* – **dexterousness,** *n.*

**dextral** /ˈdɛkstrəl/, *adj.* **1.** of, pertaining to, or on the right-hand side; right (opposed to *sinistral*). **2.** right-handed. **3.** *Zool.* (of certain shells) coiling from left to right. – **dextrally,** *adv.* – **dextrality** /dɛksˈtræləti/, *n.*

**dextran** /ˈdɛkstrən/, *n.* a white gummy material, produced from milk, molasses, etc., by bacterial action. [DEXTR(O)- + -AN(E)]

**dextrin** /ˈdɛkstrən/, *n.* a soluble gummy substance formed from starch by the action of heat, acids, or enzymes, occurring in various forms and having dextrorotatory properties; used chiefly as a thickening agent in printing inks and food, as a substitute for gum arabic and as a mucilage; starch-gum. Also, **dextrine.** [F *dextrine,* from L *dexter* right]

**dextro** /ˈdɛkstroʊ/, *adj.* turning clockwise.

**dextro-,** a word element meaning: **1.** right. **2.** *Chem.* denoting a substance that rotates the plane of plane polarised light to the right. *Symbol:* + Also, **dextr-.** [L, combining form of *dexter* right]

**dextroamphetamine** /ˌdɛkstroʊæmˈfɛtəmin/, *n.* a white, crystalline, water-soluble solid, $C_6H_5CH_2CH(NH_2)CH_3$, used in the treatment of obesity.

**dextroglucose** /ˈdɛkstroʊglukoʊz, -oʊs/, *n.* See **glucose.**

**dextrogyrate** /dɛkstroʊˈdʒaɪrət, -reɪt/, *adj.* →**dextrorotatory.**

**dextrorotation** /ˌdɛkstroʊroʊˈteɪʃən/, *n.* a turning of the plane of polarisation of light to the right.

**dextrorotatory** /ˌdɛkstroʊroʊˈteɪtəri, -ˈroʊtətəri/, *adj.* turning the plane of polarisation of light to the right, as certain crystals and compounds. Also, **dextrorotary.**

**dextrorse** /ˈdɛkstrɔs, dɛksˈtrɔs/, *adj.* rising spirally from left to right (from a point of view at the centre of the spiral), as a stem (opposed to *sinistrorse*). Also, **dextrorsal.** [L *dextrorsum* towards the right] – **dextrorsely,** *adv.*

**dextrose** /ˈdɛkstroʊz, -oʊs/, *n.* dextroglucose, commercially obtainable from starch by acid hydrolysis. See **glucose.** [DEXTR(O)- + (GLUC)OSE]

**dextrotocopherol** /ˌdɛkstroʊtəˈkɒfərɒl/, *n.* the most potent form of vitamin E, $C_{29}H_{50}O_2$, known to be required by certain mammals for normal reproduction.

**dextrous** /ˈdɛkstrəs/, *adj.* →**dexterous.** – **dextrously,** *adv.* – **dextrousness,** *n.*

**dezincification** /diˌzɪŋkəfəˈkeɪʃən/, *n.* a process of corrosion in which the zinc of copper-zinc alloys becomes absorbed by the environment.

**d.f.,** dead freight.

**DF,** double-fronted. Also, **df.**

**D/F,** direction finding.

**D.F.,** Defender of the Faith. [L *Dēfensor Fideī*]

**D.F.C.,** Distinguished Flying Cross.

**D.F.M.** /di ɛf ˈɛm/, Distinguished Flying Medal.

**dft, 1.** defendant. **2.** draft.

**dg,** decigram; decigrams.

**d-glucose** /di-ˈglukoʊz, -oʊs/, *n.* →**dextroglucose.**

**d.h.,** dead heat.

**dhal** /dal/, *n.* **1.** an Indian name for lentils or pulses. **2.** a cooked dish of lentils. [Hind.]

**dharma** /ˈdamə/, *n.* (in Hinduism and Buddhism) **1.** essential quality or character. **2.** law, esp. religious law. **3.** conformity to law; propriety. **4.** virtue. **5.** religion. **6.** the doctrine or teaching of the Buddha. [Skt: decree, custom]

**dhobi** /ˈdoʊbi/, *n.* an Indian washerman or laundry-boy. [Hind.]

**dhole** /doʊl/, *n.* an Indian wild dog, a fierce, red-coated species, *Cuon rutilus,* hunting in packs, and capable of running down large game. [orig. uncert.]

**dhoti** /ˈdoʊti/, *n., pl.* **-tis.** a long loincloth worn by male Hindus. Also, **dhooti** /ˈduti/. [Hind.]

**dhow** /daʊ/, *n.* an Arab coasting vessel, usu. lateen-rigged. [Ar. *dāwa, dau,* probably of Indic orig.]

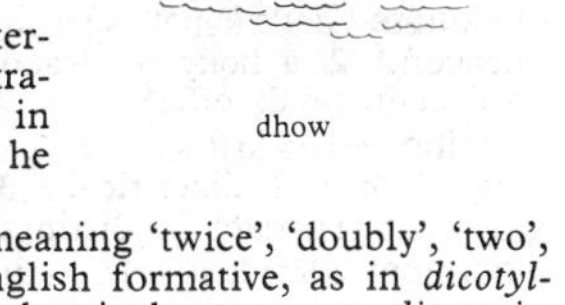

dhow

**dhrupad** /ˈdrupæd/, *n.* a form of north Indian classical vocal music, typically in a slow tempo, which develops various parts of the raga.

**dhufish** /ˈdjufɪʃ/, *n.* →**tandan.**

**dhyana** /daɪˈanə/, *n.* an uninterrupted state of mental concentration upon a single object, as in yoga. [Skt *dhyāna,* from *dhyāti* he thinks]

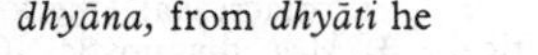

**di-**[1], a prefix of Greek origin, meaning 'twice', 'doubly', 'two', freely used (like *bi-*) as an English formative, as in *dicotyledon, dipolar,* and in many chemical terms, as *diatomic, disulphide.* Also, **dis-**[2]. Cf. **mono-.** [Gk, representing *dis* twice, doubly; akin to Gk *dýo* two. See BI-]

**di-**[2], variant of **dis-**[1], before *b, d, l, m, n, r, s,* and *v,* and sometimes *g* and *j,* as in *divide.*

**di-**[3], variant of **dia-,** before vowels, as in *diocese, diorama.*

**Di,** *Chem.* didymium.

**dia-,** a prefix of learned words meaning: **1.** passing through, as in *diathermy.* **2.** thoroughly; completely, as in *diagnosis.* **3.** going apart, as in *dialysis.* **4.** opposed in moment, as in *diamagnetism.* Also, **di-**[3]. [Gk, representing *diá,* prep., through, between, across, by, of; akin to *dýo* two, and *di-* DI-[1]]

**dia., 1.** diagram. **2.** dialect. **3.** diameter.

**diabase** /ˈdaɪəbeɪs/, *n.* **1.** a dark igneous rock consisting essentially of augite and felspar, an altered dolerite. **2.** *U.S.* a dark igneous rock occurring as minor intrusives composed essentially of labradorite and pyroxene. **3.** *Obs.* diorite. [F, from *dia-* (erroneously for *di-* two) + *base* BASE[1]] – **diabasic** /daɪəˈbeɪsɪk/, *adj.*

**diabetes** /daɪəˈbitiz/, *n.* **1.** a disease in which the ability of the body to use sugar is impaired and sugar appears abnormally in the urine (**diabetes mellitus**). **2.** a disease in which there is a persistent abnormal amount of urine (**diabetes insipidus**). [NL, from Gk: lit., a passer through]

**diabetic** /daɪəˈbɛtɪk/, *adj.* **1.** of or pertaining to diabetes. **2.** having diabetes. –*n.* **3.** a person who has diabetes.

**diable** /diˈablə/, *adj.* of or pertaining to food which is cooked with hot spices; devilled. Also, **à la diable.** [F]

**diablerie** /diˈabləri/, *n.* **1.** diabolic magic or art; sorcery. **2.** the domain or realm of devils. **3.** the lore of devils; demonology. **4.** reckless mischief; devilry. Also, **diablery.** [F, from *diable* DEVIL]

**diabolic** /daɪəˈbɒlɪk/, *adj.* **1.** having the qualities of a devil; fiendish; outrageously wicked: *a diabolic plot.* **2.** pertaining to or actuated by the devil or a devil. **3.** *Colloq.* difficult; unpleasant; very bad. Also, **diabolical** (esp. for def. 3). [LL *diabolicus,* from Gk *diabolikós*] – **diabolically,** *adv.* – **diabolicalness,** *n.*

**diabolise** /daɪˈæbəlaɪz/, *v.t.,* **-lised, -lising. 1.** to make diabolical or devilish. **2.** to represent as diabolical. **3.** to subject to diabolical influences. Also, **diabolize.**

**diabolism** /daɪˈæbəlɪzəm/, *n.* **1. a.** action aided or caused by the devil; sorcery; witchcraft. **b.** the character or condition of a devil. **c.** doctrine concerning devils; belief in or worship of devils. **2.** action befitting the devil; devilry. – **diabolist,** *n.*

**diabolo** /di'æbəloʊ/, *n.* **1.** a game in which a top is spun, thrown and caught by or balanced on and whirled along a string attached to two sticks, held one in each hand. **2.** the top itself.

**diacaustic** /daɪə'kɒstɪk, -'kɔstɪk/, *adj.* **1.** denoting a caustic surface or curve formed by refraction of light. See **catacaustic.** *–n.* **2.** a diacaustic surface or curve.

**diacetylmorphine** /ˌdaɪəsitl'mɔfin/, *n.* →**heroin.** Also, **diamorphine.**

**diachronic** /daɪə'krɒnɪk/, *adj.* of or pertaining to changes or developments over a period of time (esp. of language). Cf. **synchronic.** [Gk *diá* DIA- + *chrónos* time] – **diachronically,** *adv.*

**diachylon** /daɪ'ækəlɒn/, *n.* an adhesive plaster consisting essentially of lead oxide and oil. Also, **diachylum.** [L, from Gk *dià chȳlôn* (something) made of juices; also Latinised as *diachylum,* whence E sp. with *-um;* replacing ME *diaculon,* from ML, and ME *diaquilon,* from F, both from L *diachȳlōn*]

**diacid** /daɪ'æsəd/, *adj.* **1.** capable of combining with two molecules of a monobasic acid. **2.** (of an acid or a salt) having two replaceable hydrogen atoms.

**diaconal** /daɪ'ækənəl/, *adj.* pertaining to a deacon. [LL *diāconālis,* from *diāconus* DEACON]

**diaconate** /daɪ'ækənət, -neɪt/, *n.* **1.** the office or dignity of a deacon. **2.** a body of deacons. **3.** the period during which a deacon holds office.

**diacritic** /daɪə'krɪtɪk/, *n.* **1.** a diacritical mark, point, or sign. *–adj.* **2.** diacritical. **3.** *Med.* diagnostic. [Gk *diakritikós* that separates or distinguishes]

**diacritical** /daɪə'krɪtɪkəl/, *adj.* **1.** serving to distinguish; distinctive. **2.** capable of distinguishing. **3.** denoting a mark, point, or sign added or attached to a letter or character to distinguish it from another of similar form, to give it a particular phonetic value, to indicate stress, etc. – **diacritically,** *adv.*

**diactinic** /ˌdaɪæk'tɪnɪk/, *adj.* capable of transmitting the actinic rays of light. – **diactinism** /daɪ'æktənɪzəm/, *n.*

**diadelphous** /daɪə'dɛlfəs/, *adj.* **1.** (of stamens) united into two sets by their filaments. **2.** (of plants) having the stamens so united. [DI-[1] + Gk *adelphós* brother + -OUS]

**diadem** /'daɪədɛm/, *n.* **1.** a crown. **2.** a cloth headband, sometimes adorned with jewels, formerly worn by oriental kings. **3.** royal dignity or authority. *–v.t.* **4.** to adorn with, or as if with, a diadem; crown. [L *diadēma,* from Gk: fillet, band; replacing ME *dyademe,* from OF]

**diadem spider** /– 'spaɪdə/, *n.* the common garden spider, *Araneus diademata,* of Europe and North Asia.

**diadochokinesis** /daɪˌædəkoʊkə'nisəs/, *n.* the normal power of performing, in rapid succession, alternating bodily movements, such as tapping a finger or opening and closing the jaws. [Gk *diádochos* successor + *kínēsis* motion]

**diaeresis** /daɪ'ɛrəsəs/, *n., pl.* **-ses** /-siz/. →**dieresis.**

**diag.,** diagram.

**diageotropic** /ˌdaɪədʒiə'trɒpɪk/, *adj.* growing at right angles to the direction of gravity. – **diageotropically,** *adv.* – **diageotropism** /ˌdaɪədʒi'ɒtrəpɪzəm/, *n.*

**diagnose** /'daɪəgnoʊz/, *v.,* **-nosed, -nosing.** *–v.t.* **1.** to identify by diagnosis (a case, disease, etc.). *–v.i.* **2.** to make a diagnosis.

**diagnosis** /daɪəg'noʊsəs/, *n., pl.* **-ses** /-siz/. **1.** *Med.* **a.** the process of determining by examination the nature and circumstances of a diseased condition. **b.** the decision reached from such an examination. **2.** *Biol.* scientific determination; a description which classifies precisely. **3.** any analogous examination or analysis. [NL, from Gk: a distinguishing]

**diagnostic** /daɪəg'nɒstɪk/, *adj.* **1.** pertaining to a diagnosis. **2.** having value in diagnosis. *–n.* **3.** →**diagnosis** (def. 1a, b). **4.** a symptom or characteristic of value in diagnosis. [Gk *diagnōstikós*] – **diagnostically,** *adv.*

**diagnostician** /ˌdaɪəgnɒs'tɪʃən/, *n.* an expert or specialist in making diagnoses.

**diagnostics** /daɪəg'nɒstɪks/, *n.* the art or science of diagnosis. [pl. of DIAGNOSTIC]

**diagonal** /daɪ'ægənəl/, *adj.* **1.** *Maths.* **a.** connecting, as a straight line, two non-adjacent angles or vertices of a quadrilateral, polygon, or polyhedron. **b.** extending, as a plane, from one edge of a solid figure to an opposite edge. **2.** having an oblique direction. **3.** having oblique lines, ridges, etc. *–n.* **4.** a diagonal line or plane. **5.** a diagonal row, plank, part, etc. **6.** diagonal cloth. [L *diagōnālis,* from Gk *diagṓnios* from angle to angle] – **diagonally,** *adv.*

**diagonal cloth** /– 'klɒθ/, *n.* a twilled fabric with a diagonal weave.

**diagram** /'daɪəgræm/, *n., v.,* **-grammed, -gramming** or (*esp. U.S.*) **-gramed, -graming.** *–n.* **1.** a figure, or set of lines, marks, etc., to accompany a geometrical demonstration, give the outlines or general features of an object, show the course or results of a process, etc. **2.** a drawing or plan that outlines and explains, the parts, operation, etc., of something. **3.** a chart, plan, or scheme. *–v.t.* **4.** to represent by a diagram; make a diagram of. [L *diagramma,* from Gk: that which is marked out by lines]

**diagrammatic** /daɪəgrə'mætɪk/, *adj.* **1.** in the form of a diagram. **2.** pertaining to diagrams. Also, **diagrammatical.** – **diagrammatically,** *adv.*

**diagrammatise** /daɪə'græmətaɪz/, *v.t.,* **-tised, tising.** →**diagram** (def. 4). Also, **diagrammatize.**

**diagraph** /'daɪəgræf, -graf/, *n.* **1.** a device for drawing, used in reproducing outlines, plans, etc., mechanically on any desired scale. **2.** a combined protractor and scale. [F *diagraphe,* from Gk *diagráphein* mark out by lines. See DIAGRAM]

**diakinesis** /daɪəkə'nisəs, -kaɪ-/, *n.* the prophase of the first meiotic division of a spermatocyte or ovocyte. [NL, from *dia-* DIA- + Gk *kínēsis* movement]

**dial** /'daɪəl/, *n., v.,* **dialled, dialling** or (*esp. U.S.*) **dialed, dialing.** *–n.* **1.** a face upon which time is indicated by hands, pointers, or shadows. **2.** a plate or disc with graduations or figures, as for the indication of pressure, number of revolutions, etc., as by the movements of a pointer. **3.** a rotatable plate or disc used for tuning a radio station in or out. **4.** a plate or disc with letters and numbers, used in making telephone connections. **5.** *Mining.* a compass used for underground surveying. **6.** *Colloq.* the human face. *–v.t.* **7.** to measure with or as with a dial. **8.** to regulate, select, or tune in by means of a dial, as on a radio. **9.** to indicate on a telephone dial. **10.** to call by means of a telephone dial. **11.** *Mining.* to survey with a dial (def. 5) and chain. *–v.i.* **12.** to use a telephone dial. [ME, from ML *diālis* daily, from L *dies* day]

**dial.,** **1.** dialect. **2.** dialectal.

**dialect** /'daɪəlɛkt/, *n.* **1.** the language of a particular district or class, esp. as distinguished from the standard language, as a provincial or rural substandard form of a language. **2.** a special variety or branch of a language, as Afrikaans if considered as a branch of Dutch. **3.** a language considered as one of a number of related languages: *the Roman dialects.* [L *dialectus,* from Gk *diálektos* discourse, language, dialect]

**dialectal** /daɪə'lɛktl/, *adj.* **1.** of a dialect. **2.** characteristic of a dialect. – **dialectally,** *adv.*

**dialect atlas** /'daɪəlɛkt ætləs/, *n.* an atlas showing how the distinctive features of a dialect or dialects are distributed geographically. Also, **linguistic atlas.**

**dialect geography** /ˌdaɪəlɛkt dʒi'ɒgrəfi/, *n.* the study of the geographical distribution of the distinctive features of a dialect or dialects; linguistic geography.

**dialectic** /daɪə'lɛktɪk/, *adj.* **1.** of, pertaining to, or of the nature of logical argumentation. **2.** dialectal. **3.** proceeding by or as if by debate between conflicting points of view. *–n.* **4.** a process of change that results from an interplay between opposite tendencies. **5.** logical argumentation. **6.** (*oft. pl.*) **a.** logic or a branch of logic. **b.** any formal system of reasoning or thought. **7.** See **Hegelian dialectic.** **8.** →**dialectical materialism.** **9.** (in Kantian philosophy) the use of the principles of understanding in an attempt to determine objects beyond the limits of experience. [L *dialectica,* from Gk *dialektikḗ* (*tech‍nḗ*) argumentative (art); replacing ME *dialetike,* from OF]

**dialectical** /daɪə'lɛktɪkəl/, *adj.* **1.** of or pertaining to the Hegelian dialectic. **2.** dialectal.

**dialectical materialism** /– mə'tɪəriəlɪzəm/, *n.* a theory of reality developed chiefly by Karl Marx, combining elements of traditional materialist philosophy and the method of Hegelian dialectic. – **dialectical materialist,** *n.*

**dialectician** /daɪəlɛk'tɪʃən/, *n.* **1.** one skilled in dialectic; a logician. **2.** one who studies dialects.

**dialecticism** /daɪə'lɛktəsɪzəm/, *n.* **1.** dialectal speech or influence. **2.** a dialectal word or expression.

**dialectics** /daɪə'lɛktɪks/, *n.* →**dialectic** (def. 6).

**dialectology** /daɪəlɛk'tɒlədʒi/, *n.* the study of dialects. – **dialectologist,** *n.*

**dial gauge** /'daɪəl geɪdʒ/, *n.* an instrument in which small displacements of a plunger are indicated on a dial.

**dialling** /'daɪəlɪŋ, 'daɪlɪŋ/, *n.* **1.** the art of constructing sundials. **2.** the measurement of time by means of dials. **3.** surveying by means of a dial. Also, *U.S.,* **dialing.**

**dialling code** /'– koʊd/, *n.* →**area code.** Also, **dial code.**

**dialogism** /daɪ'ælədʒɪzəm/, *n.* the discussion of a subject in an imaginary dialogue. [Gk *dialogismós* consideration]

**dialogist** /daɪ'ælədʒəst/, *n.* **1.** a speaker in a dialogue. **2.** a writer of dialogue. – **dialogistic** /daɪələ'dʒɪstɪk/, *adj.*

**dialogue** /'daɪəlɒg/, *n., v.,* **-logued, -loguing.** *–n.* **1.** conversation between two or more persons. **2.** the conversation between characters in a novel, drama, etc. **3.** an exchange of ideas or opinions on a particular issue. **4.** a literary work in the form of a conversation. **5.** (esp. in diplomacy) a state of communication between parties, countries, etc., in which cautious goodwill may lead to formal agreements: *we need dialogue with China.* **6.** to carry on a dialogue; converse. *–v.t.* **7.** to put into the form of a dialogue. Also, *U.S.,* **dialog.** [F, from L *dialogus,* from Gk *diálogos; replacing* ME *dialoge,* from OF] – **dialoguer,** *n.*

**dial tone** /'daɪəl toʊn/, *n.* the sound which a functioning telephone makes, indicating that the user may dial a number.

**dialyse** /'daɪəlaɪz/, *v.t.,* **-lysed, -lysing** or *(esp. U.S.)* **-lyzed, -lyzing.** to subject to dialysis; separate or procure by dialysis. – **dialyser,** *n.*

**dialyser** /'daɪəlaɪzə/, *n.* →**dialysis machine.**

**dialysis** /daɪ'æləsəs/, *n., pl.* **-ses** /-siz/. **1.** the separation of smaller molecules from larger ones, or of crystalloids from colloids in a solution by selective diffusion through a semipermeable membrane. **2.** (in cases of defective kidney function) the removal of waste products from the blood by causing them to diffuse through a semipermeable membrane; haemodialysis. [Gk: separation, dissolution]

**dialysis machine** /'– məʃin/, *n.* an apparatus in which dialysis is performed. Also, **dialyser.**

**diam.,** diameter.

**diamagnetic** /daɪəmæg'nɛtɪk/, *adj.* denoting or pertaining to a class of substances, as bismuth and copper, whose permeability is less than that of a vacuum. In a magnetic field their induced magnetism is in a direction opposite to that of iron (opposed to *paramagnetic* and *ferromagnetic*). – **diamagnetically,** *adv.* – **diamagnetism** /daɪə'mægnətɪzəm/, *n.*

**diamanté** /daɪə'mɒnti, diə-/, *n.* **1.** a fabric made to sparkle by covering with glittering particles. **2.** such a glittering particle. *–adj.* **3.** (of a fabric) sparkling. [F, orig. adj.]

**diamantiferous** /daɪəmən'tɪfərəs/, *adj.* containing diamonds. Also, **diamondiferous.** [see DIAMOND, -FEROUS]

**diamantine** /daɪə'mæntaɪn/, *adj.* resembling diamonds or the properties of diamonds. [F *diamantin,* from *diamant* DIAMOND]

**diameter** /daɪ'æmətə/, *n.* **1.** *Geom.* **a.** a straight line passing through the centre of a circle or sphere and terminated at each end by the circumference or surface. **b.** a straight line passing from side to side of any figure or body, through its centre. **2.** the length of such a line; thickness. [ME *diametre,* from OF, from L *diametros,* from Gk: diagonal, diameter]

**diametral** /daɪ'æmətrəl/, *adj.* **1.** of a diameter. **2.** forming a diameter. – **diametrally,** *adv.*

**diametrical** /daɪə'mɛtrɪkəl/, *adj.* **1.** pertaining to a diameter; along a diameter. **2.** direct; complete; absolute: *diametrical opposites.* Also, **diametric.** – **diametrically,** *adv.*

**diamine** /'daɪəmin, -mən, daɪə'min/, *n.* a compound containing two $NH_2$ radicals.

**diamond** /'daɪəmənd, 'daɪmənd/, *n.* **1.** a pure or nearly pure form of carbon, crystallised in the isometric system, of extreme hardness and, when used as a precious stone, of great brilliancy. **2.** a piece of this stone. **3.** a tool provided with an uncut diamond, used for cutting glass. **4.** an equilateral quadrilateral, esp. as placed with its diagonals vertical and horizontal; a lozenge or rhombus. **5. a.** a red lozenge-shaped figure on a playing card. **b.** a card of the suit bearing such figures. **c.** *(pl.)* the suit. **6.** a baseball field or the space enclosed within the baselines. **7.** a $4\frac{1}{2}$-point type of a size between gem and pearl. *–adj.* **8.** made of or with a diamond or diamonds. **9.** indicating the 75th, or sometimes the 60th, event of a series, as a wedding anniversary. **10.** shaped like a diamond (def. 4). *–v.t.* **11.** to adorn with or as with diamonds. [ME *diamant,* from OF, from LL *diamas,* alteration of L *adamas* adamant, diamond. See ADAMANT]

**diamondback** /'daɪəməndbæk/, *n.* a common venomous rattlesnake, *Crotalus adamantus,* of the southern United States. Also, **diamondback rattlesnake.**

**diamondback moth** /– 'mɒθ/, *n.* a moth, *Plutella maculipennis,* the male of which has diamond-shaped yellow spots on the wing; the larvae breed on leaves of Cruciferae and are therefore a major pest.

**diamond beetle** /'daɪəmənd bitl/, *n.* one of the weevil genus, *Entimus,* of Brazil, noted for its iridescent colouration.

**diamond bird** /'– bɜd/, *n.* any of various pardalotes having distinctive diamond-like markings, as the spotted pardalote.

**diamond drill** /'– drɪl/, *n.* a drill having a hollow, cylindrical bit set with diamonds, used for obtaining cores of rock samples for geological or mineralogical examination.

**diamond dust** /'– dʌst/, *n.* pulverised diamonds, used as an abrasive.

**diamond firetail** /– 'faɪəteɪl/, *n.* a small Australian finch, *Zonaeginthus guttatus,* brownish above with a conspicuous crimson rump and prominent white spotting on the flanks; spotted-sided finch. Also, **diamond sparrow.**

**diamond fish** /'– fɪʃ/, *n.* →**devilfish** (def. 1).

**diamondiferous** /daɪəmən'dɪfərəs/, *adj.* diamond bearing.

**diamond point** /'daɪəmənd pɔɪnt/, *n.* **1.** a tool tipped with diamond, used in engraving. **2.** *(pl.)* the set of points where two lines of rails intersect obliquely without communicating.

**diamond saw** /'– sɔ/, *n.* a circular saw, with carbonadoes set in its perimeter used for cutting stone.

**diamond snake** /'– sneɪk/, *n.* a large Australian python, *Morelia spilotes spilotes,* greenish-black in colour with yellow diamond spots on the sides.

**diamond sparrow** /'– spæroʊ/, *n.* →**diamond firetail.**

**diamorphine** /daɪə'mɔfin/, *n.* →**heroin.**

**diandrous** /daɪ'ændrəs/, *adj.* **1.** (of a flower) having two stamens. **2.** (of a plant) having flowers with two stamens. [NL *diandrus.* See DI-[1], -ANDROUS]

**dianella** /daɪə'nɛlə/, *n.* any perennial herb of the genus *Dianella* with nodding blue flowers, as *D. tasmanica* of the highlands of south-eastern Australia.

**dianoetic** /daɪənoʊ'ɛtɪk/, *adj.* pertaining to thought or reasoning, esp. discursive reasoning. [Gk *dianoētikós*]

**dianthus** /daɪ'ænθəs/, *n.* any plant of the genus *Dianthus,* family Caryophyllaceae, as the carnation or the sweet william. [NL, from Gk *Di(ós)* of Zeus + *ánthos* flower]

**diap.,** diapason.

**diapason** /daɪə'peɪzən, -sən/, *n.* **1.** a melody or strain. **2.** the compass of a voice or instrument. **3.** a fixed standard of pitch. **4.** either of two principal timbres or stops of a pipe organ: **a.** the **open diapason,** giving full, majestic tones. **b.** the **stopped diapason,** giving powerful flutelike tones. **5.** any of several other organ stops. **6.** a tuning fork. [L, from Gk, short for *dià pasôn chordôn symphōnía* concord through all notes (of the scale)] – **diapasonic** /daɪəpeɪ'zɒnɪk/, *adj.*

**diapause** /'daɪəpɔz/, *n.* **1.** a period of quiescence during the development of insects, etc. **2.** a sexually quiescent period in an adult insect.

**diaper** /'daɪəpə, 'daɪpə/, *n.* **1.** *U.S.* a baby's nappy. **2.** a linen or cotton fabric with a woven pattern of small constantly repeated figures, as diamonds. **3.** such a pattern (originally used in medieval weaving of silk and gold), used as a decoration for walls, etc. *–v.t.* **4.** to ornament with a diaper-like pattern. [ME *diapre,* from OF, var. of *diaspre,* from MGk *diaspros* pure white]

**diaper shirt** /'– ʃɜt/, *n.* a baby's shirt which reaches only to the top of the nappy.

**diaphaneity** /daɪəfə'niəti/, *n.* transparency.

**diaphanous** /daɪ'æfənəs/, *adj.* transparent; translucent. [ML *diaphanus,* from Gk *diaphanḗs*] – **diaphanously,** *adv.* – **diaphanousness,** *n.*

**diaphone** /'daɪəfoun/, *n.* all the variant forms of a phoneme that are found in the regional and social dialects of a language. [DIA- + PHONE²] – **diaphonic** /daɪə'fɒnɪk/, *adj.*

**diaphoresis** /daɪəfə'risəs/, *n.* perspiration, esp. when artificially produced. [LL, from Gk: a sweat]

**diaphoretic** /daɪəfə'rɛtɪk/, *adj.* **1.** producing perspiration. –*n.* **2.** a diaphoretic medicine.

**diaphragm** /'daɪəfræm/, *n.* **1.** *Anat.* **a.** a muscular, membranous or ligamentous wall separating two cavities or limiting a cavity. **b.** the partition separating the thoracic cavity from the abdominal cavity in mammals. **2.** *Phys. Chem., etc.* **a.** a porous plate separating two liquids, as in a galvanic cell. **b.** a semi-permeable membrane or the like. **3.** a vibrating membrane or disc, as in a telephone or microphone. **4.** a contraceptive membrane worn in the vagina covering the cervix. **5.** *Optics.* a ring, or a plate pierced with a circular hole so arranged as to fall in the axis of the instrument, used in optical instruments to control the amount of light entering the instrument, as in a camera or a telescope. **6.** *Civ. Eng.* a plate for strengthening metal-framed constructions. [LL *diaphragma,* from Gk: midriff, barrier]

**diaphragmatic** /ˌdaɪəfræg'mætɪk/, *adj.* **1.** of the diaphragm. **2.** like a diaphragm. – **diaphragmatically,** *adv.*

**diaphysis** /daɪ'æfəsəs/, *n., pl.* **-ses** /-siz/. the shaft of a long bone. [NL, from Gk: a growing through] – **diaphysial** /daɪə'fɪziəl/, *adj.*

**diapophysis** /daɪə'pɒfəsəs/, *n., pl.* **-ses** /-siz/. the transverse process proper of a vertebra. [NL. See DI-³, APOPHYSIS] – **diapophysial** /daɪəpə'fɪziəl/, *adj.*

**diarchy** /'daɪˌaki/, *n., pl.* **-chies.** government or a government in which power is vested in two rulers or authorities. Also, **dyarchy.** [DI-¹ + Gk *archía* rule] – **diarchal, diarchic,** *adj.*

**diarist** /'daɪərəst/, *n.* one who keeps a diary.

**diarrhoea** /daɪə'riə/, *n.* an intestinal disorder characterised by morbid frequency and fluidity of faecal evacuations. Also, **diarrhea.** [LL, from Gk *diárrhoia* a flowing through] – **diarrhoeal, diarrhoeic,** *adj.*

**diarthrosis** /daɪa'θrousəs/, *n., pl.* **-ses** /-siz/. a type of bone articulation which permits movement in any direction, the opposing bones being held in opposition. [NL, from Gk: division by joints. See DIA-, ARTHRO-, -OSIS] – **diarthrodial** /daɪa'θroudiəl/, *adj.*

**diary** /'daɪəri/, *n., pl.* **-ries. 1.** a daily record, esp. of the writer's own experiences or observations. **2.** a book for keeping such a record, or for noting appointments and engagements. [L *diārium* daily allowance, journal]

**diaspora** /daɪ'æspərə/, *n.* **1.** a dispersion, as of a people of common national origin or beliefs. **2.** the people dispersed. [Gk: a scattering; orig. applied to the Jews scattered among the Gentiles after the Babylonian captivity]

**diaspore** /'daɪəspɔ/, *n.* a natural hydrated aluminium oxide, $Al_2O_3 \cdot H_2O$, occurring in bauxite and with corundum and dolomite, used as a refractory or an abrasive.

**diastalsis** /daɪə'stælsəs/, *n.* the peristaltic downward movement of the small intestine during digestion. [DIA- + (PERI)STALSIS]

**diastase** /daɪə'steɪz/, *n.* an enzyme (amylase) present in germinated barley, potatoes, etc., which converts starch into dextrin and maltose. [F, from Gk *diástasis* separation]

**diastasis** /daɪ'æstəsəs/, *n. Pathol.* **1.** any simple separation of parts normally joined together esp. the separation of the epiphysis from the body of the bone, without fracture. **2.** *Physiol.* the final phase of diastole. [Gk: separation]

**diastatic** /daɪə'stætɪk/, *adj.* **1.** pertaining to diastase; having the properties of diastase: *diastatic action.* **2.** *Med., Physiol.* of or pertaining to diastasis. Also, **diastazic** /daɪə'stæzɪk/. [Gk *diastatikós* separating]

**diaster** /daɪ'æstə/, *n.* a stage in mitosis at which the chromosomes, after their division and separation, are grouped near the poles of the spindle. [DI-¹ + -ASTER²] – **diastral,** *adj.*

**diastole** /daɪ'æstəli/, *n.* **1.** *Physiol., etc.* the normal rhythmical relaxation and dilatation of the heart, esp. that of the ventricles. **2.** *Pros.* the lengthening of a syllable regularly short, esp. before a pause or at the ictus. [LL, from Gk: a putting asunder, dilatation, lengthening]

**diastolic** /daɪə'stɒlɪk/, *adj.* pertaining to or produced by diastole.

**diastrophism** /daɪ'æstrəˌfɪzəm/, *n.* **1.** the action of the forces which cause the earth's crust to be deformed, producing continents, mountains, changes of level, etc. **2.** any such deformation. [Gk *diastrophḗ* distortion + -ISM] – **diastrophic** /daɪə'strɒfɪk/, *adj.*

**diathermancy** /daɪə'θɜmənsi/, *n.* the property of transmitting radiant heat; quality of being diathermanous. [F *diathermansie,* from *dia-* DIA- + Gk *thérmansis* heating]

**diathermanous** /daɪə'θɜmənəs/, *adj.* permeable to radiant heat.

**diathermic** /daɪə'θɜmɪk/, *adj.* **1.** *Med.* pertaining to diathermy. **2.** *Physics.* diathermanous. [F *diathermique,* from *dia-* DIA- + Gk *thérmē* heat + *-ique* -IC]

**diathermy** /'daɪəθɜmi/, *n.* the therapeutic use of heat produced by high frequency electric current. Also, **diathermia** /daɪə'θɜmiə/.

**diathesis** /daɪ'æθəsəs/, *n., pl.* **-eses** /-əsiz/. a constitutional predisposition or tendency, as to a particular disease or pathological condition. [NL, from Gk: arrangement, disposition] – **diathetic** /daɪə'θɛtɪk/, *adj.*

**diatom** /'daɪətəm, -tɒm/, *n.* any of numerous microscopic, unicellular, marine or freshwater algae having siliceous cell walls. [NL *Diatoma,* a genus of diatoms, from LGk *diátomos,* verbal adj. of Gk *diatémnein* cut through]

**diatomaceous** /daɪətə'meɪʃəs/, *adj.* consisting of or containing diatoms or their fossil remains.

**diatomaceous earth** /– 'ɜθ/, *n.* a fine siliceous earth composed chiefly of cell walls of diatoms, used in filtration, as an abrasive, etc.; kieselguhr. Also, **diatomite** /daɪ'ætəmaɪt/.

**diatomic** /daɪə'tɒmɪk/, *adj.* **1.** having two atoms in the molecule. **2.** containing two replaceable atoms or groups; bivalent.

**diatonic** /daɪə'tɒnɪk/, *adj.* involving only the tones, intervals, or harmonies of a major or minor scale without chromatic alteration. [LL *diatonicus,* from Gk *diatonikós,* for *diátonos*] – **diatonically,** *adv.*

**diatribe** /'daɪətraɪb/, *n.* a bitter and violent denunciation, attack, or criticism. [L *diatriba,* from Gk *diatribḗ* pastime, study, discourse]

**diatropism** /daɪ'ætrəpɪzəm/, *n.* the tendency of some plant organs to take a transverse position to the line of action of an outside stimulus. – **diatropic** /daɪə'trɒpɪk/, *adj.*

**diazine** /'diəzin, di'æzin, -ən/, *n.* any of a group of three isomeric hydrocarbons, $C_4H_4N_2$, containing a ring of four carbon and two nitrogen atoms. Also, **diazin** /'diəzən, di'æzən/.

**diazo-,** a combining form denoting a diazo compound. [DI-¹ + AZO-]

**diazo compound** /daɪ'æzou ˌkɒmpaund/, *n.* a compound containing a group of two nitrogen atoms, $N_2$, united with one hydrocarbon radical or with one hydrocarbon radical and another atom or group of atoms.

**diazole** /'daɪəzoul, daɪ'æzoul/, *n.* any of a group of organic compounds containing three carbon and two nitrogen atoms arranged in a ring.

**diazomethane** /daɪˌæzou'miθeɪn/, *n.* an odourless, yellow gas, $CH_2N_2$, which is poisonous, used as a methylating agent in organic syntheses.

**diazonium salts** /daɪəˌzouniəm 'sɒlts/, *n.pl.* a group of salts formed by the combination of the diazonium radical ($Ar.N \equiv N$-, where Ar. is an aryl group) and an acid radical, important intermediates in the manufacture of dyes.

**diazotisation** /daɪˌæzətaɪ'zeɪʃən/, *n.* the preparation of a diazo compound, as by treating an amine with nitrous acid. Also, **diazotization.**

**diazotise** /daɪ'æzətaɪz/, *v.t.,* **-tised, -tising.** to treat so as to convert into a diazonium salt. Also, **diazotize.**

**dib** /dɪb/, *v.i.,* **dibbed, dibbing.** to fish by letting the bait bob lightly on the water. [b. DIP and BOB¹]

**dibasic** /daɪ'beɪsɪk/, *adj.* **1.** containing two replaceable or ionisable hydrogen atoms, as *dibasic acid.* **2.** having two univalent, basic atoms, as *dibasic sodium phosphate,* $Na_2HPO_4$.

**dibble** /ˈdɪbəl/, *v.t.*, **-bled, -bling.** to make a hole in (the ground) with or as with a dibbler (def. 2).

**dibbler** /ˈdɪblə/, *n.* **1.** one who or that which dibbles. **2.** an implement for making holes in the ground for planting seeds, bulbs, etc. **3.** a marsupial mouse, *Antechinus apicalis,* of the Albany region of Western Australia; thought to be extinct but rediscovered in 1967. Also, **dibber.**

**dibranchiate** /daɪˈbræŋkiət, -kieɪt/, *Zool. –adj.* **1.** belonging or pertaining to the Dibranchiata, a subclass or order of cephalopods with two gills, including the decapods and octopods. *–n.* **2.** a dibranchiate cephalopod. [NL *Dibranchiāta,* pl. See DI-[1], BRANCHIATE]

**dibs** /dɪbz/, *n. pl. Colloq.* **1.** →**marbles** (def. 7). **2.** a stake in a game. **3.** funds or money: *in the dibs.* **4.** winnings. **5. dibs in,** taking part; included, esp. in a game. **6. play for dibs,** to play with the object of keeping what has been won. [from *dibstones,* formerly a children's game played with small stones; var. of DAB[1]]

**dicarboxylic acid** /daɪˌkabɒkˌsɪlɪk ˈæsəd/, *n.* any of the organic compounds which have two carboxyl radicals, -COOH.

**dice** /daɪs/, *n. pl., sing.* **die,** *v.,* **diced, dicing.** *–n.* **1.** small cubes of plastic, ivory, bone, or wood, marked on each side with a different number of spots (1 to 6), usu. used in pairs in games of chance or in gambling. **2.** any of various games, esp. gambling games, played by shaking the dice (in the cupped hand or in a receptacle) and throwing them on to a flat surface. **3.** any small cubes. **4. no dice,** *Colloq.* of no use; unsuccessful; out of luck. *–v.t.* **5.** to cut into small cubes. **6.** to decorate with cube-like figures. **7.** *Colloq.* to throw away, reject. *–v.i.* **8.** to play at dice. **9. dice with death,** *Colloq.* to act dangerously or take a risk. [see DIE[2]] **– dicer,** *n.*

**dicephalous** /daɪˈsɛfələs/, *adj.* having two heads. [Gk *diképhalos*]

**dicey** /ˈdaɪsi/, *adj. Colloq.* dangerous; risky; tricky.

**dichasium** /daɪˈkeɪziəm/, *n., pl.* **-sia** /-ziə/. a form of cymose inflorescence in which each axis produces a pair of lateral axes. [NL, from Gk *díchasis* division + -IUM] **– dichasial,** *adj.*

**dichlamydeous** /ˌdaɪkləˈmɪdiəs/, *adj.* (of a flower) having both a calyx and a corolla.

**dichlorodifluoromethane** /daɪˌklɔroudaɪˌfluərouˈmiθeɪn/, *n.* a colourless, non-inflammable gas, $CCl_2F_2$, used as a refrigerant, and as a propellant in aerosols and fire-extinguishers.

**dichlorodiphenyltrichloroethane** /daɪˌklɔroudaɪˌfɛnəltraɪˌklɔrouˈiθeɪn/, *n.* a white powdery compound having a faint, pleasant smell, used as a contact insecticide, commonly known as DDT.

**dichloromethane** /daɪˌklɔrouˈmiθeɪn/, *n.* a colourless liquid, $CH_2Cl_2$, used as an industrial solvent; methylene chloride.

**dicho-,** a word element meaning in 'two parts', 'in pairs'. [Gk, combining form of *dícha* in two, asunder]

**dichogamous** /daɪˈkɒgəməs/, *adj.* having the stamens and pistils maturing at different times (thus preventing self-fertilisation), as a monoclinous flower (opposed to *homogamous*). Also, **dichogamic** /ˌdaɪkouˈgæmɪk/.

**dichogamy** /daɪˈkɒgəmi/, *n.* dichogamous condition.

**dichotomise** /daɪˈkɒtəmaɪz/, *v.,* **-mised, -mising.** *–v.t.* **1.** to divide or separate into two parts. **2.** to divide into pairs. *–v.i.* **3.** to be or become separated or divided into two parts. Also, **dichotomize. – dichotomist,** *n.* **– dichotomisation** /daɪˌkɒtəmaɪˈzeɪʃən/, *n.*

**dichotomous** /daɪˈkɒtəməs/, *adj.* divided or dividing into two parts. Also, **dichotomic** /ˌdaɪkouˈtɒmɪk/. **– dichotomously,** *adv.*

**dichotomy** /daɪˈkɒtəmi/, *n., pl.* **-mies. 1.** division into two parts or into twos; subdivision into halves or pairs. **2.** *Logic.* classification by division, or by successive subdivision, into two groups or sections. **3.** *Bot.* a mode of branching by constant bifurcation as in some stems, in veins of leaves, etc. **4.** *Astron.* the phase of the moon, or of an inferior planet, when half of its disc is visible. [Gk *dichotomía* a cutting in two]

**dichroic** /daɪˈkrouɪk/, *adj.* **1.** characterised by dichroism: *a dichroic crystal.* **2.** dichromatic. Also, **dichroitic** /ˌdaɪkrouˈɪtɪk/. [Gk *díchroos* of two colours + -IC]

**dichroism** /ˈdaɪkrouˌɪzəm/, *n.* **1.** *Crystall.* a property possessed by many doubly refracting crystals of exhibiting different colours when viewed in different directions. **2.** *Chem.* the exhibition of essentially different colours by certain solutions in different degrees of dilution or concentration. [Gk *díchroos* of two colours + -ISM]

**dichromate** /daɪˈkroumeɪt, -mət/, *n.* a salt of a hypothetical acid, $H_2Cr_2O_7$, as potassium dichromate, $K_2Cr_2O_7$.

**dichromatic** /ˌdaɪkrouˈmætɪk/, *adj.* **1.** having or showing two colours; dichromic. **2.** of or having dichromatism (def. 2). **3.** *Zool.* exhibiting two colour phases within a species not due to age or season. [DI-[1] + Gk *chrōmatikós* pertaining to colour]

**dichromaticism** /ˌdaɪkrouˈmætəsɪzəm/, *n.* →**dichroism** (def. 1).

**dichromatism** /daɪˈkroumətɪzəm/, *n.* **1.** dichromatic condition. **2.** dichromic condition of vision.

**dichromic**[1] /daɪˈkroumɪk/, *adj.* of or embracing two colours only. [Gk *díchrōmos* two-coloured + -IC]

**dichromic**[2] /daɪˈkroumɪk/, *adj.* of a compound containing two atoms of chromium. [DI-[1] + CHROM(IUM) + -IC]

**dichromic acid** /– ˈæsəd/, *n.* the hypothetical acid, $H_2Cr_2O_7$, from which the dichromates (sometimes called bichromates) are derived.

**dichromic vision** /– ˈvɪʒən/, *n.* colour-blindness in which only two of the three primary colours are perceived.

**dichroscope** /ˈdaɪkrəskoup/, *n.* an instrument for testing the dichroism (or pleochroism) of crystals. [Gk *díchroos* of two colours + -SCOPE]

**dicing** /ˈdaɪsɪŋ/, *n.* **1.** gambling or playing dice. **2.** ornamentation, esp. of leather, with squares or diamonds.

**dick**[1] /dɪk/, *n. Colloq.* a detective. [shortened form of DETECTIVE; ? influenced by DICK[2]]

**dick**[2] /dɪk/, *n. Colloq.* **1.** the penis. **2.** a foolish, unattractive person; dickhead. **3. clever dick,** a smart aleck. **4. have had the dick,** to be finished or ruined.

**dicken** /ˈdɪkən/, *interj. Colloq.* **1.** (a questioning interjection) is it true?; really? **2.** (an affirmative interjection) it is true!; really! Also, **dickon.** [var. of DICKENS]

**dickens** /ˈdɪkənz/, *n., interj.* (prec. by *the*) devil; deuce (often used in exclamations and as a mild imprecation).

**dicker**[1] /ˈdɪkə/, *n. Hist.* a quantity of ten, esp. hides or skins. [ME *dyker;* akin to *decury,* from L *decuria* a company of ten]

**dicker**[2] /ˈdɪkə/, *Chiefly U.S. –v.i.* **1.** to trade by barter or by petty bargaining; haggle. **2.** *Politics.* to try to arrange matters by mutual bargaining. **3.** to vacillate. *–v.t.* **4.** to trade; exchange. *–n.* **5.** a petty bargain; barter. **6.** *Politics.* a deal. [? v. use of DICKER[1]]

**dickey** /ˈdɪki/, *n., pl.* **-eys.** →**dicky**[1].

**dickhead** /ˈdɪkhɛd/, *n.* a fool; idiot: *country people are scornful of Sydney dickheads.*

**dickie** /ˈdɪki/, *n.* (*in children's speech*) a penis.

**dickon** /ˈdɪkən/, *interj.* →**dicken.**

**dicky**[1] /ˈdɪki/, *n., pl.* **-ies. 1.** a detachable shirt front, or blouse front. **2.** a pinafore or apron. **3.** a donkey, esp. a male. **4.** Also, **dicky-seat.** a small additional seat at the outside or back of a vehicle; rumble seat. Also, **dickey, dickie.** [application of *Dicky,* diminutive of *Dick,* proper name]

**dicky**[2] /ˈdɪki/, *adj. Colloq.* **1.** unsteady, shaky; in bad health; in poor condition. **2.** difficult; untenable: *a dicky position.*

**dickybird** /ˈdɪkibɜd/, *n.* (*in children's speech*) a bird.

**diclinous** /daɪˈklaɪnəs, ˈdaɪklənəs/, *adj.* **1.** (of a plant species, etc.) having the stamens and the pistils in separate flowers, either on the same plant or on different plants; either monoecious or dioecious. **2.** (of a flower) having only stamens or only pistils; unisexual. [DI-[1] + Gk *klī́nē* bed + -OUS]

**dicotyledon** /ˌdaɪkɒtəˈlidn/, *n.* **1.** a plant with two cotyledons. **2.** a member of the group Dicotyledones, one of the two subclasses of angiospermous plants, characterised by producing seeds with two cotyledons or seed leaves, and by an exogenous mode of growth. Cf. **monocotyledon.**

**dicotyledonous** /ˌdaɪkɒtəˈlidənəs/, *adj.* having two cotyledons; belonging or pertaining to the Dicotyledones. See **dicotyledon** (def. 2).

**dicoumarol** /daɪˈkumərɒl/, *n.* a drug occurring in spoiled clover and also synthesised, used to prevent the coagulation of blood and in the treatment of arterial thrombosis. [DI-[1] + COUMAR(IN) + -OL]

**dicrotic** /daɪ'krɒtɪk/, *adj.* **1.** having two arterial beats for one heartbeat, as certain pulses. **2.** pertaining to such a pulse. [Gk *díkrotos* double-beating + -IC] – **dicrotism** /'daɪkrətɪzəm/, *n.*

**dict.**, dictionary.

**dicta** /'dɪktə/, *n.* a plural of **dictum.**

**dictaphone** /'dɪktəfoʊn/, *n.* an instrument that records and reproduces dictation. [Trademark; from DICTA(TE) + -PHONE]

**dictate** /dɪk'teɪt/, *v.*, **-tated, -tating;** /'dɪkteɪt/, *n.* –*v.t.* **1.** to say or read aloud (something) to be taken down in writing or recorded mechanically. **2.** to prescribe positively; command with authority. –*v.i.* **3.** to say or read aloud something to be taken down. **4.** to give orders. –*n.* **5.** an authoritative order or command. **6.** a guiding or ruling principle, requirement, etc. [L *dictātus,* pp., pronounced, dictated, composed, prescribed]

**dictation** /dɪk'teɪʃən/, *n.* **1.** the act of dictating for reproduction in writing, etc. **2.** words dictated, or taken down as dictated. **3.** the act of commanding positively or authoritatively. **4.** something commanded.

**dictator** /dɪk'teɪtə, 'dɪkteɪtə/, *n.* **1.** a person exercising absolute power, esp. one who assumes absolute control in a government without hereditary right or the free consent of the people. **2.** (in ancient Rome) a person constitutionally invested with supreme authority during a crisis, the regular magistracy being subordinated to him until the crisis was met. **3.** a person who authoritatively prescribes conduct, usage, etc.; a domineering or overbearing person. **4. benevolent dictator,** a dictator who has the interests of the people he governs at heart. [L] – **dictatress** /dɪk'teɪtrəs/, **dictatrix** /'dɪktətrɪks/, *n. fem.*

**dictatorial** /dɪktə'tɔriəl/, *adj.* **1.** of or pertaining to a dictator or a dictatorship. **2.** appropriate to, or characteristic of, a dictator; absolute; unlimited. **3.** inclined to dictate or command; imperious; overbearing: *a dictatorial tone.* Also, **dictatory.** – **dictatorially,** *adv.* – **dictatorialness,** *n.*

**dictatorship** /dɪk'teɪtəʃɪp/, *n.* **1.** a country, government, or the form of government in which absolute authority is exercised by a dictator. **2.** absolute or imperious power. **3.** the office or position held by a dictator. **4.** the period of a dictator's tenure of office. Also, **dictature** /'dɪktətʃə/.

**diction** /'dɪkʃən/, *n.* **1.** style of speaking or writing as dependent upon choice of words: *good diction, a Latin diction.* **2.** the degree of distinctness with which speech sounds are uttered; enunciation. [L *dictio* saying]

**dictionary** /'dɪkʃənri, 'dɪkʃənəri/, *n., pl.* **-aries. 1.** a book containing a selection of the words of a language, usu. arranged alphabetically, with explanations of their meanings, pronunciations, etymologies, and other information concerning them, expressed either in the same or in another language; lexicon; glossary. **2.** a book giving information on particular subjects or a particular class of words, names or facts, usu. under alphabetically arranged headings: *a biographical dictionary.* [ML *dictiōnārium,* lit., a word-book, from LL *dictio* word. See DICTION]

**dictograph** /'dɪktəgræf, -graf/, *n.* **1.** a telephonic device with a highly sensitive transmitter obviating the necessity of a mouthpiece, much used for secretly listening to conversations or obtaining a record of them. **2.** (*cap.*) a trademark for this device. [L *dictum* something said + -O- + -GRAPH]

**dictum** /'dɪktəm/, *n., pl.* **-ta** /-tə/, **-tums. 1.** an authoritative pronouncement; judicial assertion. **2.** a saying; maxim. **3.** →**obiter dictum.** [L: something said, a saying, a command, properly pp. neut. of *dīcere* say]

**dicyandiamide** /daɪˌsaɪəndaɪ'æmaɪd/, *n.* a polymerisation product of cyanamide, $(H_2NCN)_2$, used in the manufacture of plastics and resins and as a chemical intermediate.

**did**[1] /dɪd/, *v.* **1.** past tense of **do. 2. that did it,** *Colloq.* that was the limit of endurance, patience, etc.

**did**[2] /dɪd/, *n. Colloq.* a toilet. Also, **diddy.** [U.S. colloq. (children's speech) modification of DIAPER]

**didactic** /daɪ'dæktɪk, də-/, *adj.* **1.** intended for instruction; instructive: *didactic poetry.* **2.** inclined to teach or lecture others too much: *a didactic old lady.* [Gk *didaktikós* apt at teaching] – **didactically,** *adv.* – **didacticism,** *n.*

**didactics** /daɪ'dæktɪks, də-/, *n.* the art or science of teaching.

**didapper** /'daɪdæpə/, *n.* →**dabchick.** [for *divedapper*]

**diddle** /'dɪdl/, *v.t.*, **-dled, -dling.** *Colloq.* to cheat; swindle; victimise. [orig. uncert.] – **diddler,** *n.*

**diddums** /'dɪdəmz/, *interj.* (an exclamation indicating that the speaker thinks that the person addressed is being childish and petulant). [in speech to children *did he (she)*]

**diddy**[1] /'dɪdi/, *n.* →**did**[2].

**diddy**[2] /'dɪdi/, *n. Colloq.* a woman's breast or nipple. [var. of TITTY]

**didgeridoo** /ˌdɪdʒəri'du/, *n.* an Aboriginal wind instrument consisting of a wooden pipe about two metres long and five centimetres in diameter on which complex rhythmic patterns are played more or less on one note. Also, **didjeridu.** [Aboriginal]

didgeridoo

**didn't** /'dɪdnt, 'dɪdn/, *v.* contraction of *did not.*

**didst** /dɪdst/, *v. Archaic or Poetic.* 2nd person singular past tense of **do.**

**didymium** /daɪ'dɪmiəm, də-/, *n.* a mixture of neodymium and praseodymium, formerly supposed to be an element (and called the 'twin brother of lanthanum'). [NL, from Gk *dídymos* twin + *-ium* -IUM]

**didymous** /'dɪdəməs/, *adj.* occurring in pairs; paired; twin. [Gk *dídymos* double, twin]

**die**[1] /daɪ/, *v.i.*, **died, dying. 1.** to cease to live; undergo the complete and permanent cessation of all vital functions. **2.** (of something inanimate) to cease to exist: *the secret died with him.* **3.** to lose force, strength, or active qualities: *traditions die slowly.* **4.** to cease to function; stop: *the engine died.* **5.** to pass gradually; fade or subside gradually (usu. fol. by *away, out,* or *down*): *the storm slowly died down.* **6.** to lose spiritual life. **7.** to faint or languish. **8.** to suffer as if dying. **9.** to pine with desire, love, longing, etc. **10.** *Colloq.* to desire or want keenly or greatly: *I'm dying for a drink.* **11. die away,** (of a sound) to become weaker or fainter and then cease: *the music gradually died away.* **12. die back,** (of a plant, etc.) to wither from the top downwards to the stem or root. **13. die down, a.** to become calm or quiet; subside. **b.** (of a plant, etc.) to die above the ground, leaving only the root. **14. die hard, a.** to die only after a bitter struggle. **b.** to cling stubbornly to a belief, theory, etc.; refuse to yield. **15. die off,** to die one after another until the number is greatly reduced. **16. die on (someone), a.** to die, in circumstances where the death leaves a possibly unexpected responsibility or obligation to (someone). **b.** to fall asleep while in the company of (someone). **17. die out,** to become extinct; disappear. [early ME *deghen,* c. Icel. *deyja.* Cf. DEAD, DEATH]

**die**[2] /daɪ/, *n., pl.* **dies** *for defs 1, 2, 4,* **dice** *for def. 3; v.,* **died, dieing.** –*n.* **1. a.** any of various devices for cutting or forming material in a press or a stamping or forging machine. **b.** a hollow device of steel, often composed of several pieces, to be fitted into a stock, for cutting the threads of bolts, etc. **c.** one of the separate pieces of such a device. **d.** a steel block or plate with small conical holes through which wire, plastic rods, etc., are drawn. **2.** an engraved stamp for impressing a design, etc., upon some softer material, as in coining money. **3.** singular of **dice. 4.** *Archit.* the dado of a pedestal, esp. when cubical. **5. the die is cast,** the decision has been irrevocably made. –*v.t.* **6.** to impress, shape, or cut with a die. [ME *de,* from OF, from L *datum,* orig. pp. neut., lit., given (apparently in sense of given by fortune)]

**dieback** /'daɪbæk/, *n.* a condition of plants, shrubs, etc., which starts at the tips of the shoots and works downwards causing progressive lifelessness; in forest trees it may be caused by the fungus *Phytophthera cinnamoni.*

**die-casting** /'daɪ-kastɪŋ/, *n.* **1.** a process in which metal is forced into metallic moulds under hydraulic pressure. **2.** an article made by this process. –*adj.* **3.** Also, **diecast.** of or pertaining to this process.

**diecious** /daɪ'iʃəs/, *adj. U.S.* →**dioecious.**

**diehard** /'daɪhad/, *n.* **1.** one who resists vigorously to the last, esp. a bigoted conservative. –*adj.* **2.** resisting vigorously to the last.

**dieldrin** /ˈdildrən/, *n.* an organochlorine compound, highly toxic to animal life and used as a systemic insecticide. [Trademark]

**dielectric** /daɪəˈlɛktrɪk/, *Elect.* –*adj.* **1.** non-conducting. **2.** conveying electric effects otherwise than by conduction, as a medium through which electricity acts in the process of induction. –*n.* **3.** a dielectric substance; insulator. [DI-[3] + ELECTRIC] – **dielectrically,** *adv.*

**dielectric constant** /– ˈkɒnstənt/, *n.* the ratio of the capacitance of a capacitator when its plates are separated by the given dielectric, to the capacitance when its plates are separated by air.

**dielectric heating** /– ˈhitɪŋ/, *n.* a form of heating in which a non-conductor is heated by being subjected to an alternating electric field.

**dielectric strength** /– ˈstrɛŋθ/, *n.* the maximum voltage that can be applied to a unit thickness of a dielectric material without causing electrical breakdown.

**diencephalon** /daɪɛnˈsɛfəlɒn/, *n.* the posterior section of the prosencephalon; the interbrain or middle brain; thalamencephalon. [DI-[3] + ENCEPHALON]

**-dienes,** a suffix designating a compound containing two double bonds. [DI-[1] + -ENE + *-s* (pl.)]

**dieresis** /daɪˈɛrəsəs/, *n., pl.* **-ses** /-siz/. **1.** the separation of two adjacent vowels. **2.** a sign (¨) placed over the second of two adjacent vowels to indicate separate pronunciation, as in *Alcinoüs.* **3.** *Pros.* the division made in a line of verse by coincidence of the end of a foot and the end of a word. Also, **diaeresis.** [L, from Gk *diaíresis* separation, division]

**diesel** /ˈdizəl/, *n.* **1.** →**diesel engine. 2.** a locomotive, truck, ship or the like driven by a diesel engine. **3.** diesel oil.

**diesel cycle** /ˈ– saɪkəl/, *n.* an engine cycle, usu. four strokes, as intake, compression, power, and exhaust, in which ignition occurs at constant pressure, and heat is rejected at constant volume.

**diesel-electric** /dizəl-əˈlɛktrɪk/, *adj.* having an electric motor powered by a diesel engine.

**diesel engine** /ˈdizəl ɛndʒən/, *n.* (*sometimes cap.*) an ignition-compression type of internal-combustion engine in which fuel oil is sprayed into the cylinder after the air in it has been compressed to about 550°C, thus causing the ignition of the oil, at substantially constant pressure. Also, **diesel motor.** [named after Rudolf *Diesel,* 1858-1913, German inventor]

**dieseline** /dizəˈlin/, *n.* →**diesel oil.** Also, **diesoline.**

**dieselise** /ˈdizəlaɪz/, *v.t.,* **-lised, -lising.** to change (a railway system) from steam traction to diesel-electric traction. – **dieselisation** /dizəlaɪˈzeɪʃən/, *n.*

**diesel oil** /ˈdizəl ɔɪl/, *n.* the oil which remains after petrol and kerosene have been distilled from crude petroleum; used as a fuel for diesel engines and for carburetting water gas; distillate. Also, **dieseline, gas oil.**

**die-sinker** /ˈdaɪ-sɪŋkə/, *n.* an engraver of dies for stamping or embossing. – **die-sinking,** *n.*

**diesis** /ˈdaɪəsəs/, *n., pl.* **-ses** /-siz/. **1.** *Music.* the difference between a major and a minor semitone. **2.** *Print.* the mark ‡; double dagger. [L, from Gk: a sending through]

**dies non** /ˌdaɪiz ˈnoʊn/, *n.* a day on which no courts can be held or no legal business transacted. [short for L *dies nōn jūridicus* a day not juridical]

**die-stamping** /ˈdaɪ-stæmpɪŋ/, *n.* the process by which a design is inked and raised in relief simultaneously.

**diestock** /ˈdaɪstɒk/, *n.* a device for holding the dies used in cutting threads on a rod or pipe.

**diet**[1] /ˈdaɪət/, *n., v.,* **-eted, -eting.** –*n.* **1.** food considered in terms of its qualities, composition, and its effects on health: *milk is a wholesome article of diet.* **2.** a particular selection of food, esp. as prescribed to improve the physical condition, regulate weight, or cure a disease. **3.** the usual or regular food or foods a person eats most frequently. **4.** anything that is habitually provided. **5. be on a diet,** to be following a prescribed diet, esp. so as to lose weight. –*v.t.* **6.** to regulate the food of, esp. in order to improve the physical condition or regulate weight. –*v.i.* **7.** to select or limit the food one eats to improve one's physical condition or lose weight. [ME *diete,* from OF, from L *diaeta,* from Gk *díaita* way of living, diet] – **dieter,** *n.*

**diet**[2] /ˈdaɪət/, *n.* a formal assembly for discussing or acting upon public or state affairs, as (formerly) the general assembly of the estates of the Holy Roman Empire, the German Reichstag, Japan, etc. [late ME, from ML *diēta, diaeta* public assembly, apparently the same word as L *diaeta* (see DIET[1]), with sense affected by L *dies* day]

**dietarian** /daɪəˈtɛəriən/, *n.* one who strictly follows a prescribed diet.

**dietary** /ˈdaɪətri, -təri/, *adj., n., pl.* **-taries.** –*adj.* **1.** pertaining to diet: *dietary laws.* –*n.* **2.** a regulated allowance of food. **3.** a system or course of diet.

**diet chart** /ˈdaɪət tʃat/, *n.* a chart listing the number of kilojoules in specified quantities of foods, and sometimes recommending certain combinations and quantities of foods to be eaten when on a diet.

**dietetic** /daɪəˈtɛtɪk/, *adj.* pertaining to diet or to regulation of the use of food. Also, **dietetical.** [L *diaetēticus,* from Gk *diaitētikós*] – **dietetically,** *adv.*

**dietetics** /daɪəˈtɛtɪks/, *n.* the art or science concerned with the regulation of diet.

**diethylmalonate** /ˌdaɪɛθəlˈmæləneɪt/, *n. Chem.* →**malonic ester.**

**diethylstilboestrol** /daɪˌɛθəlstɪlˈbistrɒl/, *n.* a synthetic substance, $[HOC_6H_4C(C_2H_5)_2=]_2$, not itself an oestrogen but having a more potent oestrogenic activity than oestrone, used in the treatment of menopausal symptoms, etc.

**dietitian** /daɪəˈtɪʃən/, *n.* one versed in the regulation of diet, or in the planning or supervision of meals. Also, **dietician.** [from DIET[1], modelled on PHYSICIAN]

**diff** /dɪf/, *n.* **1.** difference. **2.** →**differential** (def. 6).

**differ** /ˈdɪfə/, *v.i.* **1.** to be unlike, dissimilar, or distinct in nature or qualities (oft. fol. by *from*). **2.** to disagree in opinion, belief, etc.; be at variance (oft. fol. by *with* or *from*). [F *différer,* from L *differre* bear apart, put off, delay (see DEFER[1]), be different]

**difference** /ˈdɪfrəns/, *n., v.,* **-enced, -encing.** –*n.* **1.** the state or relation of being different; dissimilarity. **2.** an instance or point of unlikeness or dissimilarity. **3.** a significant change in or effect upon a situation. **4.** a distinguishing characteristic; distinctive quality or feature. **5.** the degree in which one person or thing differs from another. **6.** the act of distinguishing; discrimination; distinction. **7.** a disagreement in opinion; dispute; quarrel. **8.** *Maths.* the amount by which one quantity is greater or less than another. **9.** *Logic.* a differentia. **10.** *Her.* the descent of a younger branch from the main line of a family. **11. split the difference, a.** to compromise. **b.** to divide the remainder equally. –*v.t.* **12.** to cause or constitute a difference in or between; make different. **13.** to perceive the difference in or between; discriminate. **14.** *Her.* to make an addition (to a coat of arms) to identify a particular branch of a family. [ME, OE, from L *differentia*]

**different** /ˈdɪfrənt/, *adj.* **1.** differing in character; having unlike qualities; dissimilar. **2.** not identical; separate or distinct. **3.** various; several. **4.** unusual; not ordinary; striking. [ME, from OF, from L *differens,* ppr. of *differre.* See DIFFER] – **differently,** *adv.*

**differentia** /dɪfəˈrɛnʃiə/, *n., pl.* **-tiae** /-ʃii/. the character or attribute by which one species is distinguished from all others of the same genus. [L: difference]

**differentiable** /dɪfəˈrɛnʃjəbəl/, *adj.* capable of being differentiated.

**differential** /dɪfəˈrɛnʃəl/, *adj.* **1.** of or pertaining to difference or diversity. **2.** constituting a difference; distinguishing; distinctive: *a differential feature.* **3.** exhibiting or depending upon a difference or distinction. **4.** *Physics, Mach., etc.* pertaining to or involving the difference of two or more notions, forces, etc.: *a differential gear.* **5.** *Maths.* pertaining to or involving differentials. –*n.* **6.** *Mach.* an epicyclic train of gears designed to permit two or more shafts to revolve at different speeds when driven by a third shaft; esp. a set of gears in a motor car which permit the driving wheels to revolve at different speeds when the car is turning. **7.** *Elect.* a coil of wire in which the polar action produced is opposite to that of another coil. **8.** *Maths.* **a.** →**derivative** (def. 6 b). **b.** the approximate change in value of a function calculated by using the derivative instead of the function itself. [ML *differentiālis,* from L *differentia* difference] – **differentially,** *adv.*

**differential calculus** /– 'kælkjələs/, *n.* the branch of mathematics which studies the properties and applications of derivatives and differentials.

**differential coefficient** /– koʊə'fɪʃənt/, *n. Maths.* →**derivative** (def. 6a).

**differential equation** /– ə'kweɪʒən/, *n. Maths.* an equation involving differentials or derivatives.

**differential gear** /– 'gɪə/, *n. Mach.* **1.** →**differential** (def. 6). **2.** any of various analogous arrangements of gears.

**differential rate** /– 'reɪt/, *n.* a special lower rate, as one charged by one of two or more competing businesses.

**differential thermometer** /– θə'mɒmətə/, *n.* a thermometer with two linked bulbs, for measuring changes in temperature.

**differential windlass** /– 'wɪndləs/, *n.* a windlass with a barrel composed of two parts of different diameter, its power being determined by the difference in the two diameters.

**differentiate** /dɪfə'rɛnʃieɪt/, *v.,* **-ated, -ating.** *–v.t.* **1.** to mark off by differences; distinguish; alter; change. **2.** to perceive the difference in or between; discriminate. **3.** to make different by modification, as a biological species. **4.** *Maths.* to obtain the derivative of. *–v.i.* **5.** to become unlike or dissimilar; change in character. **6.** to make a distinction; discriminate. **7.** *Biol.* (of cells or tissues) to change from relatively generalised to specialised kinds, during development. – **differentiation** /dɪfərɛnʃi'eɪʃən/, *n.* – **differentiator,** *n.*

**difficult** /'dɪfəkəlt/, *adj.* **1.** hard to do, perform, or accomplish; not easy; requiring much effort: *a difficult task.* **2.** hard to understand or solve: *a difficult problem.* **3.** hard to deal with or get on with. **4.** hard to please or induce. **5.** disadvantageous; hampering; involving hardships. [backformation from DIFFICULTY] – **difficultly,** *adv.*

**difficultness** /'dɪfəkəltnəs/, *n.* contrariness; ill temper and obstinacy.

**difficulty** /'dɪfəkəlti/, *n., pl.* **-ties. 1.** the fact or condition of being difficult. **2.** (*oft. pl.*) an embarrassing situation, esp. of financial affairs. **3.** a trouble. **4.** a cause of trouble or embarrassment. **5.** reluctance; unwillingness. **6.** a demur; objection. **7.** that which is hard to do, understand, or surmount. [ME *difficulte,* from L *difficultas*]

**diffidence** /'dɪfədəns/, *n.* **1.** lack of confidence in one's own ability, worth, or fitness; timidity; shyness. **2.** restraint or reserve in manner, conduct, etc.

**diffident** /'dɪfədənt/, *adj.* **1.** lacking confidence in one's own ability, worth or fitness; timid; shy. **2.** restrained or reserved in manner, conduct, etc. **3.** *Rare.* distrustful. [L *diffidens,* ppr., mistrusting] – **diffidently,** *adv.*

**diffluent** /'dɪfluənt/, *adj.* tending to flow apart; readily dissolving. [L *diffluens,* ppr., flowing away] – **diffluence,** *n.*

**diffract** /də'frækt/, *v.t.* to break up or bend by diffraction. [L *diffractus,* pp., broken in pieces]

**diffraction** /də'frækʃən/, *n.* **1.** a modification that light or other radiation undergoes when it passes by the edge of an opaque body, or is sent through small apertures, resulting in the formation of a series of light and dark bands, prismatic colours, or spectra. This effect is an interference phenomenon due to the wave nature of radiation. **2.** the analogous modification produced upon soundwaves when passing by the edge of a building or other large body.

**diffraction grating** /'– ˌgreɪtɪŋ/, *n.* a band of equidistant parallel lines (from 4 000 to 12 000 or more to the centimetre), ruled on a surface of glass or polished metal, used for obtaining optical spectra.

**diffractive** /də'fræktɪv/, *adj.* causing or pertaining to diffraction. – **diffractively,** *adv.* – **diffractiveness,** *n.*

**diffuse** /də'fjuz/, *v.,* **-fused, -fusing;** /də'fjus/, *adj.* *–v.t.* **1.** to pour out and spread, as a fluid. **2.** to spread or scatter widely or thinly; disseminate. **3.** *Physics.* to spread by diffusion. *–v.i.* **4.** to spread. **5.** *Physics.* to intermingle or pass by diffusion. *–adj.* **6.** characterised by great length or discursiveness in speech or writing; wordy. **7.** widely spread or scattered; dispersed. **8.** *Bot.* widely or loosely spreading. [ME, from L *diffūsus,* pp., poured out] – **diffusely** /də'fjusli/, *adv.* – **diffuseness,** *n.*

**diffused** /də'fjuzd/, *adj.* **1.** spread widely. **2.** (of lighting) distributed evenly, without glare. – **diffusedly,** *adv.*

**diffuser** /də'fjuzə/, *n.* **1.** one who or that which diffuses. **2.** (in any of various machines or mechanical systems, as centrifugal pumps or compressors) a device for utilising part of the kinetic energy of a fluid passing through a machine by gradually increasing the cross-sectional area of the channel or chamber through which it flows so as to decrease its speed and increase its pressure. **3.** (in a lighting fixture) any of a variety of translucent materials for filtering glare from the light source. **4.** a pierced plate or similar device for distributing compressed air for aeration of sewerage. **5.** a wedge or cone placed in front of an open-diaphragm loudspeaker to avoid focusing of the high-frequency soundwaves. **6.** *Photog.* a frame enclosing a fine silk or lightly ground glass screen which can be placed over the lens of a camera to soften the lighting. Also, **diffusor.**

**diffusible** /də'fjuzəbəl/, *adj.* capable of being diffused. – **diffusibility** /dəfjuzə'bɪləti/, *n.*

**diffusion** /də'fjuʒən/, *n.* **1.** the act of diffusing. **2.** the state of being diffused. **3.** diffuseness or prolixity of speech or writing. **4.** *Physics.* **a.** the gradual permeation of any region by a fluid, owing to the thermal agitation of its particles or molecules. **b.** the process of being scattered. See **scatter** (def. 3). **5.** *Anthrop., Sociol.* the transmission of elements from one culture to another.

**diffusion pump** /'– pʌmp/, *n.* a pump for obtaining a high vacuum in which mercury or oil is forced through an orifice; gas molecules from the vessel to be exhausted diffuse through the mercury or oil vapour around the orifice and are entrained by the issuing jet; condensation pump.

**diffusive** /də'fjusɪv/, *adj.* **1.** tending to diffuse. **2.** characterised by diffusion. **3.** diffuse; prolix. – **diffusively,** *adv.* – **diffusiveness,** *n.*

**diffusivity** /ˌdɪfju'sɪvəti/, *n.* the property of a substance indicative of the rate at which a thermal disturbance will be transmitted.

**diffy** /'dɪfi/, *n. N.Z. Colloq.* →**differential** (def. 6).

**dig** /dɪg/, *v.,* **dug** or **digged, digging,** *n.* *–v.i.* **1.** to break up, turn over, or remove earth, etc., as with a spade; make an excavation. **2.** to make one's way by, or as by, digging. *–v.t.* **3.** to break up and turn over, or penetrate and loosen (the ground) with a spade, etc. (oft. fol. by *up*). **4.** to make (a hole, tunnel, etc.) by removing material. **5.** to obtain or remove by digging (oft. fol. by *up* or *out*). **6.** to find or discover by effort or search. **7.** to thrust, plunge, or force (fol. by *into*): *he dug his heel into the ground.* **8.** *Colloq.* **a.** to understand or find to one's taste. **b.** to take notice of; pay attention to. **9. dig in, a.** to dig trenches, as in order to defend a position in battle. **b.** to maintain one's position or opinion firmly. **c.** *Colloq.* to apply oneself vigorously. **10. dig into,** *Colloq.* to apply oneself vigorously to (work, eating, etc.). **11. dig out** or **up, a.** to discover in the course of digging. **b.** *Colloq.* to discover, find, reveal. *–n.* **12.** thrust; poke. **13.** a cutting, sarcastic remark. **14.** an archaeological site undergoing excavation. **15.** *Colloq.* a digger (def. 5) (a common form of address among men). **16.** (*pl.*) lodgings. **17.** *Cricket.* an innings. [ME *diggen,* probably from F *diguer,* of Gmc orig.]

**digamma** /daɪ'gæmə/, *n.* a letter of the Greek alphabet, but early in disuse, corresponding in form to *F* and having much the same sound as English *w.* [L, from Gk, from *di-* DI-[1] + *gámma* gamma; from its likeness to two gammas (Γ) one above the other]

**digamy** /'dɪgəmi/, *n.* second marriage; the practice of marrying again after the death or divorce of the first spouse. [LL *digamia,* from Gk] – **digamous,** *adj.*

**digastric** /daɪ'gæstrɪk/, *adj.* **1.** *Anat.* having two fleshy bellies with an intervening tendinous part, as certain muscles. *–n.* **2.** a muscle of the lower jaw (so called because in man it has two bellies).

**digenesis** /daɪ'dʒɛnəsəs/, *n.* reproduction in alternate generations by different processes, one sexual and one asexual. – **digenetic** /daɪdʒə'nɛtɪk/, *adj.*

**digest** /də'dʒɛst, daɪ-/, *v.;* /'daɪdʒɛst/, *n.* *–v.t.* **1.** to prepare (food) in the alimentary canal for assimilation into the system. **2.** to promote the digestion of (food). **3.** to assimilate mentally; obtain mental nourishment or improvement from. **4.** to arrange methodically in the mind; think over: *to digest a plan.* **5.** to bear with patience; endure. **6.** to arrange in convenient or methodical order; reduce to a system; classify. **7.** to condense, abridge, or summarise. **8.** *Chem.* to keep (a substance) in contact with a liquid to soften or to disintegrate it. *–v.i.* **9.** to digest food. **10.** to undergo digestion, as food. *–n.* **11.** a collection or summary, esp. of literary, historical, legal, or scientific matter, often classified or condensed. **12.** *Law.* **a.** a systematic abstract of some body of law. **b. the Digest,** a collection in fifty books, of excerpts compiled by order of Justinian in the sixth century, the largest part of the Corpus Juris Civilis; the Pandects. [ME, from L *dīgestus,* pp., separated, arranged, dissolved] **– digestedly,** *adv.* **– digestedness,** *n.*

**digestant** /də'dʒɛstənt, daɪ-/, *n.* a medicinal agent that promotes digestion.

**digester** /də'dʒɛstə, daɪ-/, *n.* **1.** one who or that which digests. **2.** an apparatus in which substances are reduced or prepared by moisture and heat, chemical action, etc.

**digestible** /də'dʒɛstəbəl, daɪ-/, *adj.* capable of being digested; easily digested. **– digestibility** /dədʒɛstə'bɪləti/, **digestibleness,** *n.* **– digestibly,** *adv.*

**digestion** /də'dʒɛstʃən, daɪ-/, *n.* **1.** the process by which food is digested. **2.** the function or power of digesting food. **3.** the act of digesting. **4.** the resulting state.

**digestive** /də'dʒɛstɪv, daɪ-/, *adj.* **1.** serving for or pertaining to digestion; having the function of digesting food. **2.** promoting digestion. *–n.* **3.** an agent or medicine promoting digestion. **– digestively,** *adv.*

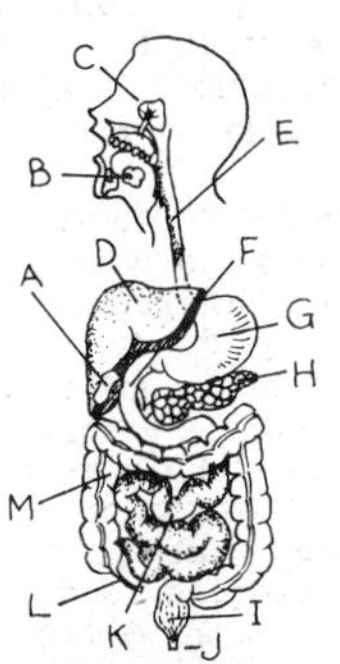

digestive system: A, gall bladder; B, submaxillary gland; C, parotid gland; D, liver; E, oesophagus; F, duodenum; G, stomach; H, pancreas; I, rectum; J, anus; K, small intestine; L, vermiform appendix; M, large intestine

**digestive biscuit** /– 'bɪskət/, *n.* a biscuit made from wholemeal flour.

**digger** /'dɪgə/, *n.* **1.** a person or an animal that digs. **2.** a tool, part of a machine, etc., for digging. **3.** a miner, esp. a gold-miner. **4.** *Colloq.* an Australian soldier esp. one who served in World War I. **5.** (a term of address among men) cobber; mate. **6.** *N.Z. Prison Colloq.* a punishment cell.

**digger's speedwell** /ˌdɪgəz 'spidwɛl/, *n.* a soft-wooded shrub with purplish-blue flowers, *Parahebe perfoliata,* characterised by stem-clasping leaves, common esp. in tableland areas of eastern Australia. Also, **digger's delight.** [from the erroneous supposition that it grows only on auriferous soil]

**digger wasp** /'dɪgə wɒsp/, *n.* any of the solitary wasps of the family Sphecidae which excavate holes in the ground and provision them with caterpillars, etc.

**diggings** /'dɪgɪŋz/, *n.pl.* **1.** a place where digging is carried on. **2.** a mining operation or locality. **3.** that which is dug out. **4.** *Colloq.* living quarters; lodgings.

**digging stick** /'dɪgɪŋ stɪk/, *n.* (among tribal aborigines) a specially shaped stick used by women for digging for roots, yams, etc.

**dight** /daɪt/, *v.t.,* **dight** or **dighted, dighting.** *Archaic.* **1.** to make ready; prepare. **2.** to equip; furnish. **3.** to dress; adorn. [ME *dighte(n),* OE *dihtan* compose, arrange, from L *dictāre* DICTATE. Cf. G *dichten* compose, Icel. *dikta* to write Latin]

**digit** /'dɪdʒət/, *n.* **1.** a finger or toe. **2.** the breadth of a finger used as a unit of linear measure. **3.** any of the Arabic figures 0, 1 . . . 9. **4.** *Astron.* the twelfth part of the diameter of the sun or moon. [L *digitus* finger, toe]

**digital** /'dɪdʒətl/, *adj.* **1.** of or pertaining to a digit. **2.** resembling a digit or finger. **3.** having digits or digit-like parts. **4.** *Electronics.* of or pertaining to information represented by patterns made up from qualities existing in two states only, on and off, as pulses (opposed to *analog*): *digital signals.* *–n.* **5.** one of the keys or finger levers of instruments of the organ or piano class.

**digital clock** /– 'klɒk/, *n.* a clock which uses a digital display to represent the time.

**digital computer** /– kəm'pjutə/, *n.* See **computer.**

**digital controller** /– kən'troʊlə/, *n.* →**control computer.**

**digital display** /– də'spleɪ/, *n.* a display in which information is represented in digital rather than analog form; readout.

**digitalin** /dɪdʒə'teɪlən/, *n.* **1.** a glucoside obtained from digitalis. **2.** any of several extracts of mixtures of glucosides obtained from digitalis.

**digitalis** /dɪdʒə'taləs/, *n.* **1.** any plant of the genus *Digitalis,* esp. the common foxglove, *D. purpurea.* **2.** the dried leaves of the common foxglove, used in medicine, esp. as a heart stimulant. [NL, the genus name (after G name *Fingerhut* thimble; from the shape of the corolla), special use of L *digitālis* pertaining to the finger]

**digitalise** /'dɪdʒətəlaɪz/, *v.t.,* **-lised, -lising.** to administer digitalis to (a person suffering from a heart disorder) until the required physiological adjustment is made. **– digitalisation** /ˌdɪdʒətəlaɪ'zeɪʃən/, *n.*

**digitalism** /'dɪdʒətəlɪzəm/, *n.* the morbid result of over-consumption of digitalis.

**digital-to-analog converter** /dɪdʒətl-tu-ˌænəlɒg kən'vɜtə/, *n.* an electronic device for converting digital signals to analogue signals. **– digital-to-analog conversion,** *n.*

**digital watch** /dɪdʒətl 'wɒtʃ/, *n.* a watch which uses a digital display to represent the time.

**digitate** /'dɪdʒəteɪt/, *adj.* **1.** *Zool.* having digits or digit-like processes. **2.** *Bot.* having radiating divisions or leaflets resembling the fingers of a hand. **3.** like a digit or finger. Also, **digitated. – digitately,** *adv.*

**digitation** /dɪdʒə'teɪʃən/, *n. Biol.* **1.** digitate formation. **2.** a digit-like process or division.

**digitiform** /'dɪdʒətəfɔm/, *adj.* finger-like.

**digitigrade** /'dɪdʒətəgreɪd/, *Zool.* *–adj.* **1.** walking on the toes, as most quadruped mammals. *–n.* **2.** an animal that walks on its toes. See **plantigrade.** [F, from L *digitus* finger + -I- + -GRADE]

**digitise** /'dɪdʒətaɪz/, *v.t.,* **-tised, -tising.** to express (analog information) in digital form.

**digitoxin** /dɪdʒə'tɒksən/, *n.* a cardiac glucoside obtained from digitalis.

**diglot** /'daɪglɒt/, *adj.* **1.** bilingual. *–n.* **2.** a bilingual book or edition. [Gk *díglōttos* speaking two languages] **– diglottic** /daɪ'glɒtɪk/, *adj.*

**dignified** /'dɪgnəfaɪd/, *adj.* marked by dignity of aspect or manner; noble; stately: *dignified conduct.* **– dignifiedly,** *adv.*

**dignify** /'dɪgnəfaɪ/, *v.t.,* **-fied, -fying.** **1.** to confer honour or dignity upon; honour; ennoble. **2.** to give highsounding title or name to; confer unmerited distinction upon. [ML *dignificāre,* from L *digni-* worthy + *-ficāre* make]

**dignitary** /'dɪgnətri, -nətəri/, *n., pl.* **-taries.** one who holds a high rank or office, esp. in the church.

**dignity** /'dɪgnəti/, *n., pl.* **-ties.** **1.** nobility of manner or style; stateliness; gravity. **2.** nobleness or elevation of mind; worthiness: *dignity of sentiments.* **3.** honourable place; elevated rank. **4.** degree of excellence, either in estimation or in the order of nature: *man is superior in dignity to brutes.* **5.** relative standing; rank. **6.** a high office or title. **7.** the person holding it. **8.** *Astrol.* a position within a sign which lends a heightened influence to a planet. **9. beneath one's dignity,** too humiliating to consider. **10. stand on one's dignity,** to refuse to enter into an action considered to be unworthy. [L *dignitas* worthiness, rank; replacing ME *dignete,* from OF]

**digraph** /'daɪgræf, -graf/, *n.* a pair of letters representing a single speech sound, as *ea* in *meat,* or *th* in *path.*

**digress** /daɪ'grɛs/, *v.i.* to deviate or wander away from the main purpose in speaking or writing, or from the principal line of argument, study, etc. [L *dīgressus,* pp., having departed] **– digresser,** *n.*

**digression** /daɪ'grɛʃən/, *n.* **1.** the act of digressing. **2.** a portion of a discourse, etc., deviating from the main theme. **– digressional,** *adj.*

**digressive** /daɪ'grɛsɪv/, *adj.* tending to digress; departing from the main subject. **– digressively,** *adv.* **– digressiveness,** *n.*

**digs** /dɪgz/, *n.pl. Colloq.* living quarters; lodgings; diggings.

**dihedral** /daɪ'hidrəl/, *adj. Maths.* **1.** having, or formed by, two planes: *a dihedral angle.* **2.** pertaining to or having a dihedral angle or angles. **3.** (of an aircraft) having the wings sloping, esp. upwards. See **anhedral.** *–n.* **4.** Also, **dihedral angle.** *Maths.* the figure made by two planes which intersect. **5.** *Aeron.* the inclination, esp. upwards, of the wings, etc. of an aeroplane to the horizontal. [DI-[1] + Gk *hédra* seat, base + -AL[1]]

**dihedron** /daɪ'hidrən/, *n.* →**dihedral** (def. 3).

**dihydro-** a prefix denoting an additional two hydrogen atoms in the molecule.

**dihydroxyphenylalanine** /ˌdaɪhaɪˌdrɒksifɛnəl'ælənin/, *n.* a non-protein amino acid, $(OH)_2 \cdot C_6H_3 \cdot CH_2 \cdot CH(NH^+_3)\ COO^-$; dopa.

**dik-dik** /'dɪk-dɪk/, *n.* any diminutive antelope of the genera *Madoqua* and *Rhynchotragus,* native to eastern and southwestern Africa. [? some Cushitic language]

**dike** /daɪk/, *n., v.,* **diked, diking.** →**dyke**[1]. **– diker,** *n.*

**diketone** /daɪ'kitoun/, *n.* a compound containing two CO groups.

**diktat** /'dɪktat/, *n.* **1.** a harsh settlement imposed on a defeated group. **2.** a dogmatic pronouncement. [G, from L *dictātum,* pp. neut. of *dictāre* DICTATE]

**dil.,** dilute.

**dilacerate** /də'læsəreɪt, daɪ-/, *v.t.,* **-ated, -ating.** to rend asunder; tear in pieces. [L *dīlacerātus,* pp.] **– dilaceration** /dəlæsə'reɪʃən, daɪ-/, *n.*

**dilapidate** /də'læpədeɪt/, *v.,* **-dated, -dating.** *–v.t.* **1.** to bring (a building, etc.) into a ruinous condition, as by misuse or neglect. **2.** to squander; waste. *–v.i.* **3.** to fall into ruin or decay. [L *dīlapidātus,* pp., thrown away, lit., scattered (orig. referring to stones)]

**dilapidated** /də'læpədeɪtəd/, *adj.* reduced to, or fallen into, ruin or decay.

**dilapidation** /dəlæpə'deɪʃən/, *n.* **1.** a state of ruin or decay; the process of becoming or causing to become dilapidated. **2.** (*pl.*) *Law.* the extent of the repairs necessary to premises at the end of a tenancy. **3.** the wearing away of rocks as a result of natural causes.

**dilatancy theory** /daɪ'leɪtənsi θɪəri/, *n.* a theory for predicting earthquakes which depends upon measurements of wave motions set up when rocks dilate.

**dilatant** /daɪ'leɪtnt, də-/, *adj.* **1.** dilating; expanding. *–n.* **2.** →**dilator** (def. 3). **– dilatancy,** *n.*

**dilatation** /daɪlə'teɪʃən/, *n.* →**dilation.**

**dilate** /daɪ'leɪt, də-/, *v.,* **-lated, -lating.** *–v.t.* **1.** to make wider or larger; cause to expand. *–v.i.* **2.** to spread out; expand. **3.** to speak at length; expatiate (fol. by *upon* or *on* or used absolutely). [L *dīlātāre* spread out] **– dilatable,** *adj.* **– dilatability** /daɪˌleɪtə'bɪləti, də-/, *n.*

**dilation** /daɪ'leɪʃən, də-/, *n.* **1.** the act of dilating. **2.** the state of being dilated. **3.** a dilated formation or part. **4.** *Pathol.* **a.** an abnormal enlargement of an aperture or a canal of the body, or one made for the purposes of surgical or medical treatment. **b.** a restoration to normal potency of an abnormally small body opening or passageway, as the anus or oesophagus. Also, **dilatation.**

**dilative** /daɪ'leɪtɪv, də-/, *adj.* serving or tending to dilate.

**dilatometer** /dɪlə'tɒmətə/, *n.* an instrument for measuring the expansion of substances.

**dilator** /daɪ'leɪtə, də-/, *n.* **1.** one who or that which dilates. **2.** *Anat.* a muscle that dilates some cavity of the body. **3.** *Surg.* an instrument for dilating body canals, orifices, or cavities. Also, **dilatator.**

**dilatory** /'dɪlətri, -təri/, *adj.* **1.** inclined to delay or procrastinate; slow; tardy; not prompt. **2.** intended to bring about delay, gain time, or defer decision: *a dilatory strategy.* **3.** **dilatory plea,** *Law.* a form of pleading having the effect of delaying proceedings. [L *dīlātōrius,* from *dīlātor* delayer] **– dilatorily,** *adv.* **– dilatoriness,** *n.*

**dildo** /'dɪldou/, *n., pl.* **-dos.** an artificial erect penis. Also, **dildoe.**

**dilemma** /də'lɛmə, daɪ-/, *n.* **1.** a situation requiring a choice between equally undesirable alternatives; an embarrassing or perplexing situation. **2.** *Logic.* a form of argument in which two or more alternatives (**the horns of the dilemma**) are presented, each of which is indicated to have consequences (usu. unfavourable) for the one who must choose. [LL, from Gk: double proposition] **– dilemmatic** /dɪlə'mætɪk/, *adj.*

**dilettante** /dɪlə'tænti, 'dɪlətænt/, *n., pl.* **-ti** /-ti/, **-tes,** *adj.* *–n.* **1.** one who pursues an art or science desultorily or merely for amusement; a dabbler. **2.** a lover of an art or science, esp. of a fine art. *–adj.* **3.** of or pertaining to dilettantes. [It., properly ppr. of *dilettare,* from L *dēlectāre* DELIGHT, *v.*] **– dilettantish,** *adj.*

**dilettantism** /dɪlə'tæntɪzəm/, *n.* the practice or characteristics of a dilettante. Also, **dilettanteism** /ˌdɪlə'tæntiɪzəm/.

**diligence**[1] /'dɪlədʒəns/, *n.* constant and earnest effort to accomplish what is undertaken; persistent exertion of body or mind. [ME, from L *dīligentia*]

**diligence**[2] /'dɪlədʒəns/, *n.* a public stagecoach, esp. in France. [F, short for *carrosse de diligence* speed coach]

**diligent** /'dɪlədʒənt/, *adj.* **1.** constant and persistent in an effort to accomplish something. **2.** pursued with persevering attention; painstaking. [ME, from L *dīligens,* properly ppr., choosing, liking] **– diligently,** *adv.*

**dill**[1] /dɪl/, *n.* **1.** a plant *Anethum graveolens,* bearing a seedlike fruit used in medicine and for flavouring pickles, etc. **2.** its aromatic seeds or leaves. [ME *dille, dile,* OE *dile-;* akin to G *Dill(e),* Swed. *dill*]

**dill**[2] /dɪl/, *n. Colloq.* a fool; an incompetent. Also, **dillpot.** [? backformation from DILLY[1]]

**dill cucumber** /– 'kjukʌmbə/, *n.* →**dill pickle.**

**dill pickle** /– 'pɪkəl/, *n.* a pickled cucumber flavoured with dill.

**dill water** /'– wɔtə/, *n.* a medicinal drink prepared from dill.

**dillwynia** /dɪl'wɪniə/, *n.* any ericoid shrub of the endemic Australian genus *Dillwynia,* family Papilionaceae, bearing small yellow to orange-red flowers; parrot pea.

**dilly**[1] /'dɪli/, *adj.* queer; mad; crazy. [D(AFT) + (S)ILLY]

**dilly**[2] /'dɪli/, *n.* something remarkable of its kind; a delightful or excellent person or thing: *that's a dilly of an idea.* [DEL(IGHTFUL) or DEL(ICIOUS) + -Y[2]]

**dillybag** /'dɪlibæg/, *n.* **1.** any small bag for carrying food or personal belongings. **2.** an Aboriginal bag of twisted grass or fibre. Also, **dilly.** [Aboriginal *dilly* + BAG]

dillybag (def. 2)

**dillydally** /'dɪlidæli/, *v.i.,* **-dallied, -dallying.** to waste time, esp. by indecision; trifle; loiter. [dissimilated reduplication of DALLY. Cf. SHILLYSHALLY]

**diluent** /'dɪljuənt/, *adj.* **1.** diluting; serving for dilution. *–n.* **2.** a diluting substance, esp. one that dilutes the blood. [L *dīluens,* ppr., washing away]

**dilute** /daɪ'lut, -'ljut/, *v.,* **-luted, -luting,** *adj.* *–v.t.* **1.** to make thinner or weaker by the addition of water or the like. **2.** to make (a colour, etc.) fainter. **3.** to reduce the strength, force, or efficiency of by admixture. **4.** to increase the proportion (in a labour force) of unskilled to skilled. *–v.i.* **5.** to become diluted. *–adj.* **6.** reduced in strength, as a chemical by admixture; weak: *a dilute solution.* [L *dīlūtus,* pp., washed to pieces, dissolved, diluted] **– diluter,** *n.*

**dilutee** /daɪ'luti/, *n. Colloq.* **1.** a man, ineligible for service in World War II, who was trained at a trade by means of a crash course and certificated after the war. **2.** (*derog.*) any inadequately trained or otherwise incompetent tradesman.

**dilution** /daɪ'luʃən/, *n.* **1.** the act of diluting. **2.** the state of being diluted. **3.** something diluted; a diluted form of anything. **4.** *Chem.* the reciprocal of concentration; the volume of solvent (usu. in litres) in which a unit quantity (usu. a gram-molecule) of solute is dissolved.

**diluvial** /daɪ'luviəl, də-/, *adj.* **1.** pertaining to a deluge or flood, esp. the flood described in Genesis. **2.** *Geol.* pertaining to or consisting of diluvium. Also, **diluvian.** [L *dīluviālis*]

**diluvium** /daɪ'luviəm, də-/, *n., pl.* **-via** /-viə/. a coarse superficial deposit formerly attributed to a general deluge but now regarded as glacial drift. [L: deluge]

**dim** /dɪm/, *adj.,* **dimmer, dimmest,** *v.,* **dimmed, dimming.**

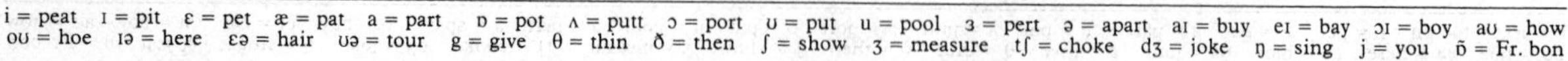

*–adj.* **1.** not bright; obscure from lack of light; somewhat dark: *a dim room.* **2.** not clearly seen; indistinct: *a dim object.* **3.** not clear to the mind; vague: *a dim idea.* **4.** not brilliant; dull in lustre: *a dim colour.* **5.** faint: *a dim sound.* **6.** not seeing clearly: *eyes dim with tears.* **7.** not clearly understanding. **8.** disparaging; adverse: *to take a dim view.* **9.** *Colloq.* (of a person), stupid; lacking in intelligence. *–v.t.* **10.** to make dim. *–v.i.* **11.** to become or grow dim. [ME *dim(e)*, OE *dim(m)*, c. OFris. *dim,* Icel. *dimmr*] **– dimly,** *adv.* **– dimness,** *n.*

**dim.,** **1.** diminuendo. **2.** diminutive. Also, **dimin.**

**dime** /daɪm/, *n.* a silver coin of the U.S., of the value of 10 cents or $\frac{1}{10}$ dollar. [ME, from OF, var. of *disme,* from L *decima* tenth part, tithe, properly fem. of *decimus* tenth]

**dime novel** /– ˈnɒvəl/, *n. U.S.* a cheap and usu. sensational novel.

**dimension** /dəˈmɛnʃən/, *n.* **1.** magnitude measured in a particular direction, or along a diameter or principal axis. **2.** (*usu. pl.*) measure; extent; size; magnitude; scope; importance. **3.** an aspect; appearance: *the conference took on a more interesting dimension.* **4.** the number of magnitudes needed to specify extent: *a room has three dimensions – length, breadth and height.* [L *dīmensio* a measuring] **– dimensional,** *adj.* **– dimensionless,** *adj.*

**dimension stone** /ˈ– stoʊn/, *n.* stone cut to size for use in building.

**dimer** /ˈdaɪmə/, *n.* a substance composed of molecules formed from two molecules of a monomer.

**dimercaprol** /ˌdaɪmɜˈkæprɒl/, *n.* a colourless, oily, viscous liquid, $CH_2(SH)CH(SH)CH_2OH$, used as an antidote to lewisite, and in treating bismuth, gold, mercury, and arsenic poisoning. [alteration of *dimercaptopropanol*]

**dimerous** /ˈdɪmərəs/, *adj.* **1.** consisting of or divided into two parts. **2.** *Bot.* (of flowers) having two members in each whorl. [Gk *dimerḗs* bipartite + -OUS] **– dimerism,** *n.*

**dimeter** /ˈdɪmətə/, *n. Pros.* a verse or line of two measures or feet. For example: *He is gone on the mountain,/ He is lost to the forest.* [LL, from Gk *dímetros* of two measures]

**dimethoxymethane** /ˌdaɪmɛθɒksiˈmiθeɪn/, *n.* →**methylal.**

**dimidiate** /dəˈmɪdieɪt/, *v.,* **-ated, -ating;** /dəˈmɪdiət/, *adj.* *–v.t.* **1.** to divide into halves; reduce to half. *–adj.* **2.** divided into halves. **3.** *Biol.* having only one side or one half fully developed. [L *dīmidiātus,* pp., halved] **– dimidiation** /dəˌmɪdiˈeɪʃən/, *n.*

**diminish** /dəˈmɪnɪʃ/, *v.t.* **1.** to make, or cause to seem, smaller; lessen; reduce. **2.** to cause to taper. **3.** to make smaller by a semitone than the corresponding perfect or minor interval. **4.** to detract from; disparage. *–v.i.* **5.** to lessen; decrease. [b. earlier *diminue* (from ML *dīminuere,* for L *dēminuere* make smaller) and *minish* (from OF *menuisier* make small, from Rom. *minūtiāre,* from L *minūtus* MINUTE[2]] **– diminishable,** *adj.* **– diminishingly,** *adv.*

**diminished responsibility** /dəˌmɪnɪʃt rəspɒnsəˈbɪləti/, *n.* limitation of a person's criminal responsibility in killing or being a party to the killing of another on the ground of mental weakness or abnormality; not available as a mitigating factor in all jurisdictions.

**diminished seventh chord,** *n.* (in music) a diminished triad with an added diminished seventh.

**diminishing returns** /dəˌmɪnɪʃɪŋ rəˈtɜnz/, *n.pl.* the fact, often stated as a law or principle, that as any factor in production (as labour, capital, etc.) is increased, the output per unit factor will eventually decrease.

**diminuendo** /dəˌmɪnjuˈɛndoʊ/, *adj., n., pl.* **-dos** /-doʊz/. *Music.* *–adj.* **1.** gradually reducing in force or loudness; decrescendo (opposed to *crescendo*). *–n.* **2.** a gradual reduction of force or loudness. **3.** a diminuendo passage. *Symbol:* > [It., ppr. of *diminuire.* See DIMINISH]

**diminution** /dɪməˈnjuʃən/, *n.* **1.** the act, fact or process of diminishing; lessening; reduction. **2.** *Music.* the repetition or imitation of a subject or theme in notes of shorter duration than those first used. [ME *diminucion,* from AF *diminuciun,* from L *dīminūtio*]

**diminutive** /dəˈmɪnjətɪv/, *adj.* **1.** small; little; tiny: *a diminutive house.* **2.** *Gram.* pertaining to or productive of a form denoting smallness, familiarity, affection, or triviality, as the suffix *-let,* in *droplet* from *drop.* *–n.* **3.** a small thing or person. **4.** *Gram.* a diminutive element or formation. **5.** *Her.* a charge smaller in length or breadth than the usual. [ME, from ML *dīminutīvus,* from L *dī-, dēminūtus,* pp., lessened] **– diminutively,** *adj.* **– diminutiveness,** *n.*

**dimissory letter** /dəˈmɪsəri ˌlɛtə/, *n.* a letter issued by a bishop, abbot, etc., permitting a subject to be ordained by another bishop. Also, **dimissorial letter.** [ME *dymyssories* (pl.), from L (*litterae*) *dīmissōriae* dimissory (letter), from *dīmissus,* pp., sent away]

**dimity** /ˈdɪməti/, *n., pl.* **-ties.** a thin cotton fabric, white, dyed, or printed, woven with a stripe or check of heavier yarn. [late ME *demyt,* from It. *dimito* coarse cotton, from Gk *dímitos* of double thread]

**dimmer** /ˈdɪmə/, *n.* **1.** one who or that which dims. **2.** Also, **dimmer switch,** a rheostat, or similar device, by which the intensity of illumination, esp. in stage lighting, is varied.

**dimorph** /ˈdaɪmɔf/, *n.* (in crystallography) either of the two forms assumed by a dimorphous substance.

**dimorphism** /daɪˈmɔfɪzəm/, *n.* **1.** *Zool.* the occurrence of two forms distinct in structure, colouration, etc., among animals of the same species. **2.** *Bot.* the occurrence of two different forms of flowers, leaves, etc., on the same plant or on distinct plants of the same species. **3.** *Crystall.* the property of some substances of crystallising in two chemically identical but crystallographically distinct forms.

**dimorphotheca** /daɪˌmɔfəˈθikə/, *n.* any plant of the small southern African genus *Dimorphotheca,* two species of which, *D. sinuata* with orange flowers and *D. pluvialis* with white and violet-blue flowers, are grown in gardens.

**dimorphous** /daɪˈmɔfəs/, *adj.* exhibiting dimorphism. Also, **dimorphic.** [Gk *dímorphos*]

**dim-out** /ˈdɪm-aʊt/, *n. U.S.* a reduction or concealment of night lighting, as of a city, a ship, etc., to make it less visible from the air or sea.

**dimple** /ˈdɪmpəl/, *n., v.,* **-pled, -pling.** *–n.* **1.** a small natural hollow, permanent or transient, in some soft part of the human body, esp. one produced in the cheek in smiling. **2.** any slight depression like this. *–v.t.* **3.** to mark with, or as with, dimples; produce dimples in. *–v.i.* **4.** to form dimples. [ME *dympull,* c. MHG *tümpfil* pool] **– dimply,** *adj.*

**dim sim** /dɪm ˈsɪm/, *n.* a dish of Chinese origin, made of seasoned meat wrapped in thin dough and steamed or fried. [? Cantonese *tim-sam* snack]

**dimwit** /ˈdɪmwɪt/, *n. Colloq.* a stupid or slow-thinking person. **– dimwitted,** *adj.*

**din** /dɪn/, *n., v.,* **dinned, dinning.** *–n.* **1.** a loud, confused noise; a continued loud or tumultuous sound; noisy clamour. *–v.t.* **2.** to assail with din. **3.** to sound or utter with clamour or persistent repetition. *–v.i.* **4.** to make a din. [ME *din(e),* OE *dyne, dynn,* c. Icel. *dynr*]

**din.,** dining-room.

**dinar** /ˈdina/, *n.* a unit of currency of greatly varying value used in various Arab countries and Yugoslavia. *Abbrev.:* Din., D., d. [Ar., from LGk *dēnárion,* from L *dēnārius* DENARIUS]

**din-din** /ˈdɪn-dɪn/, *n.* (*in children's speech and joc.*) dinner. Also, **din-dins.**

**dine** /daɪn/, *v.,* **dined, dining.** *–v.i.* **1.** to eat the principal meal of the day; have dinner. **2.** to take any meal. **3. dine at the Y,** *Colloq.* to engage in cunnilingus. **4. dine out,** to eat dinner away from home. **5. dine out on, a.** to be invited to places where one might not otherwise have gone on the strength of (a particular ability, qualification, etc.). **b.** to entertain with (a particular joke, anecdote, etc.) at a dinner or other social occasion. *–v.t.* **6.** to entertain at dinner. [ME *dine(n),* from F *dîner,* from LL *disjējūnāre* breakfast]

**diner** /ˈdaɪnə/, *n.* **1.** one who dines. **2.** a railway restaurant car. **3.** a cafeteria.

**dinette** /daɪˈnɛt/, *n.* a part of a kitchen or other room set apart for meals.

**ding**[1] /dɪŋ/, *v.i.* **1.** to strike or beat. **2.** to sound, as a bell; ring, esp. with wearisome continuance. **3.** to keep repeating; impress by reiteration. *–v.t.* **4.** to cause to ring, as by striking. **5.** to hammer at someone with repetitious talk. **6.** *Colloq.* to throw away. **7.** *Colloq.* to smash; damage. *–n.* **8.** a blow or stroke. **9.** the sound of a bell or the like. **10.** *Colloq.* a damaged section on a car, bike, surfboard, etc. **11.** *Colloq.* a minor accident involving a car, bike, surfboard, etc. **12.** *Colloq.* an argument. **13.** *Colloq.* the penis. **14.** *Colloq.* (*derog.*) a foreigner, esp. an Italian or Greek. **15.** Also, **dinger.** the buttocks; arse. [imitative]

**ding**[2] /dɪŋ/, *n. Colloq.* a party, esp. a wild or successful one. [short for WING-DING]

**ding-a-ling** /ˈdɪŋ-ə-lɪŋ/, *n. Colloq.* a fool; idiot; eccentric person.

**dingbat** /ˈdɪŋbæt/, *n. Colloq.* **1.** an eccentric or peculiar person. **2. the dingbats, a.** delirium tremens. **b.** a fit of madness or rage.

**dingbats** /ˈdɪŋbæts/, *adj. Colloq.* peculiar; odd; crazy.

**ding-dong** /ˈdɪŋ-dɒŋ/, *n.* **1.** the sound of a bell. **2.** any similar sound of repeated strokes. **3.** a loud and vigorous argument. *–adj.* **4.** repeated in succession or alternation. **5.** *Colloq.* vigorously fought with alternating success: *a ding-dong contest.* [imitative]

**dinger** /ˈdɪŋə/, *n.* **1.** who or that which dings. **2.** *Colloq.* the buttocks; arse. **3.** *Colloq.* a shanghai; catapult.

**dinghy** /ˈdɪŋgi/, *n., pl.* **-ghies. 1.** a small rowing or sailing boat or ship's tender. **2.** an inflatable rubber boat for aircraft. **3.** any of various boats for rowing or sailing used in the East Indies. Also, **dingey, dingy, dinky.** [Hind. *dīngī*]

**dingle** /ˈdɪŋgəl/, *n. Chiefly Poetic.* a deep narrow cleft between hills; a shady dell.

**dingo** /ˈdɪŋgoʊ/, *n., pl.* **-goes, gos,** *v.* *–n.* **1.** the Australian wild dog, *Canis familiaris,* introduced by the Aborigines, often tawny-yellow in colour, with erect ears, a bushy tail and distinctive gait, and with a call resembling a howl or yelp rather than a bark. **2. a.** a contemptible person; coward. **b.** one who shirks responsibility or evades difficult situations. *–v.i.* **3.** to act in a cowardly manner. **4. dingo on (someone),** to betray (someone). *–v.t.* **5.** to shirk, evade, or avoid; to spoil or ruin. [Aboriginal]

dingo

**dingy**[1] /ˈdɪndʒi/, *adj.,* **-gier, -giest.** of a dark, dull, or dirty colour or aspect; lacking brightness or freshness; shabby; disreputable. [orig. uncert.] – **dingily,** *adv.* – **dinginess,** *n.*

**dingy**[2] /ˈdɪŋgi/, *n.* →**dinghy.**

**dining car** /ˈdaɪnɪŋ ka/, *n.* a carriage on a passenger train with restaurant or cafeteria-style facilities. Also, **restaurant car.**

**dining hall** /ˈ– hɔl/, *n.* a large room, as at a college or other institution where dinner and other meals are eaten.

**dining room** /ˈ– rum/, *n.* a room in which dinner and other meals are taken.

**dining table** /ˈ– teɪbəl/, *n.* a table on which meals, esp. the more formal meals, are served.

**dinitrobenzene** /daɪˌnaɪtroʊˈbɛnzin, -bɛnˈzin/, *n.* one of three isomeric compounds, $C_6H_4(NO_2)_2$, the most important of which is made by nitration of benzene or nitrobenzene and used in the manufacture of azo dyes.

**dink** /dɪŋk/, *Colloq. –v.t.* **1.** →**double** (def. 41). *–n.* **2.** →**double** (def. 29). **3.** a minor injury (on a surfboard or in a car).

**dinkum** /ˈdɪŋkəm/, *Colloq. –adj.* **1.** Also, **dinky-di.** true; honest; genuine: *dinkum Aussie.* **2.** seriously interested in a proposed deal, scheme, etc. *–adv.* **3.** truly. See **fair dinkum.** *–n.* **4.** an excellent or remarkable example of its kind: *you little dinkum.* **5.** *Obs.* a definite amount of work; darg. Also, **dink, dinky.** [Brit. d.]

**dinkus** /ˈdɪŋkəs/, *n.* a small drawing used to decorate a page, or to break up a block of type. Also, *U.S.,* **dingus.** [coined by an artist in the *Bulletin* c. 1920; ? from DINKY[1]]

**dinky**[1] /ˈdɪŋki/, *adj.,* **dinkier, dinkiest,** *n., pl.* **dinkies.** *Colloq. –adj.* **1.** of small size. **2.** neat; dainty; smart. *–n.* **3.** a small tricycle. **4.** →**dinghy.** [Brit. d.]

**dinky**[2] /ˈdɪŋki/, *adj., adv., n.* →**dinkum.**

**dinky-di** /ˈdɪŋki-daɪ/, *adj.* →**dinkum.** [alteration of DINKUM]

**dinner** /ˈdɪnə/, *n.* **1.** the main meal, taken either about noon or in the evening. **2.** a formal meal in honour of some person or occasion. **3. done like a dinner,** *Colloq.* completely defeated or outwitted. [ME *diner,* from F, orig. inf. See DINE] – **dinnerless,** *adj.*

**dinner-dance** /ˈdɪnə-dæns/, *n.* a social function at which dinner is served and dancing takes place.

**dinner jacket** /ˈdɪnə dʒækət/, *n.* a jacket worn by men on formal or semi-formal occasions.

**dinner napkin** /ˈ– næpkən/, *n.* →**serviette.**

**dinner set** /ˈ– sɛt/, *n.* a set of china or pottery articles used in serving dinner, including plates of various sizes, cups, saucers, etc. Also, **dinner service.**

**dinner suit** /ˈ– sut/, *n.* a man's suit of evening clothes, usu. black, generally distinguished by its short jacket and black tie. Cf. **dress suit.**

**dinner table** /ˈ– teɪbəl/, *n.* →**dining table.**

**dinnertime** /ˈdɪnətaɪm/, *n.* **1.** the time in the evening when dinner is eaten. **2.** lunchtime. *–adj.* **3.** denoting, pertaining to, or taking place at either of these times.

**dinnies** /ˈdɪniz/, *n.pl. Colloq.* dinner.

**dinnyhayser** /ˌdɪniˈheɪzə/, *n. Colloq.* anything superior or excellent. [from *Dinny Hayes,* pugilist]

**dino-,** a word element meaning 'terrible', as in *dinothere.* [Gk *deino-,* combining form of *deinós*]

**dinoceras** /daɪˈnɒsərəs/, *n.* any member of an extinct genus, *Dinoceras,* comprising the huge horned ungulate mammals of the Eocene of North America; uintatherium. [NL, from *dino-* DINO- + Gk *kéras* horn]

**dinornis** /daɪˈnɔnəs/, *n.* an ostrich-sized flightless bird of the genus *Dinornis* of New Zealand, now extinct; moa.

**dinosaur** /ˈdaɪnəsɔ/, *n.* any member of extinct groups of Mesozoic reptiles, mostly of gigantic size, known in modern classifications as the Saurischia and the Ornithischia. [NL *dīnosaurus.* See DINO-, -SAUR]

**dinosaurian** /daɪnəˈsɔriən/, *adj.* pertaining to or of the nature of a dinosaur.

**dinothere** /ˈdaɪnəθɪə/, *n.* any animal of the extinct genus *Dinotherium,* comprising elephant-like mammals of the later Tertiary of Europe and Asia, characterised by downward curving tusks in the lower jaw. [NL *dinotherium,* from *dino-* DINO- + Gk *thēríon* wild beast]

**dint** /dɪnt/, *n.* **1.** force; power: *by dint of argument.* **2.** a dent. **3.** *Obs.* a blow; stroke. *–v.t.* **4.** to make a dint or dints in. **5.** to impress or drive in with force. [ME; OE *dynt,* c. Icel. *dyntr*] – **dintless,** *adj.*

**diocesan** /daɪˈɒsəsən/, *adj.* **1.** of or pertaining to a diocese. *–n.* **2.** one of the clergy or people of a diocese. **3.** the bishop in charge of a diocese.

**diocese** /ˈdaɪəsəs/, *n., pl.* **dioceses** /ˈdaɪəsəsəz, ˈdaɪəsiz/. the district, with its population, falling under the pastoral care of a bishop. [ME *diocise,* from OF, from ML *diocēsis,* for L *dioecēsis* district, from Gk *dioíkēsis* housekeeping, administration, province, diocese]

**diode** /ˈdaɪoʊd/, *n.* a device with two terminals which can conduct a current in one direction only. [DI-[1] + -ODE[2]]

**dioecious** /daɪˈiʃəs/, *adj.* (esp. of plants) having the male and female organs in separate and distinct individuals; having separate sexes. [NL *dioecia* genus name (from Gk *di-* DI-[1] + *oikíon* little house) + -OUS]

**dioestrum** /daɪˈistrəm/, *n.* the period between the rutting periods, esp. of female animals. [NL. See DI-[1], OESTRUS]

**Dionysian** /daɪəˈnɪsiən, -ˈnɪz-/, *adj.* **1.** pertaining to Dionysus or Bacchus. **2.** (*l.c.*) wild; orgiastic. [named after *Dionysus,* in Greek mythology the young and beautiful god of wine and the drama, identified with the Roman god Bacchus]

**diopside** /daɪˈɒpsaɪd/, *n.* a common variety of pyroscene, calcium magnesium metasilicate, $CaMgSi_2O_6$, occurring in various colours, often greenish, usu. in crystals. [F, from *di-* DI-[1] + Gk *ópsis* appearance]

**dioptase** /daɪˈɒpteɪz, -eɪs/, *n.* a mineral, hydrous copper silicate, $CuSiO_3H_2O$, occurring in emerald green crystals; emerald copper. [F, from Gk *di-* DI-[3] + *optasía* view]

**dioptometer** /daɪɒpˈtɒmətə/, *n.* an instrument for measuring the eye's refraction.

**dioptre** /daɪˈɒptə/, *n.* a unit of the refractive power of a lens, expressed as the reciprocal of the focal length in metres. Also, *U.S.,* **diopter.** [L *dioptra,* from Gk: kind of levelling instrument]

**dioptric** /daɪˈɒptrɪk/, *adj.* **1.** *Optics.* pertaining to dioptrics: *dioptric images.* **2.** *Ophthalm.* assisting vision by refractive correction. Also, **dioptrical.** [Gk *dioptrikós* pertaining to the use of the *dióptra.* See DIOPTRE] – **dioptrically,** *adv.*

**dioptrics** /daɪ'ɒptrɪks/, *n.* the branch of geometrical optics dealing with the formation of images by lenses.

**diorama** /daɪə'rama/, *n.* **1.** a miniature scene reproduced in three dimensions with the aid of lights, colours, etc. **2.** a spectacular picture, partly translucent, for exhibition through an aperture, made more realistic by various illuminating devices. **3.** a building where such scenes or pictures are exhibited. [F, from *di-* DI-[3] + Gk *(h)órama* view] – **dioramic** /daɪə'ræmɪk/, *adj.*

**diorite** /'daɪəraɪt/, *n.* a granular igneous rock consisting essentially of plagioclase felspar and hornblende. [F, from Gk *dior(ízein)* distinguish + *-ite* -ITE[1]] – **dioritic** /daɪə'rɪtɪk/, *adj.*

**diosma** /daɪ'ɒzmə/, *n.* **1.** any heath-like shrub of the southern African genus *Diosma.* **2.** a related plant *Coleonema pulchrum* with small pink flowers, grown in gardens.

**diosmose** /daɪ'ɒsmoʊs, -'ɒz-/, *v.t.,* **-mosed, -mosing.** →**osmose.** – **diosmosis** /daɪɒs'moʊsəs, -ɒz-/, *n.*

**dioxan** /daɪ'ɒksən/, *n.* a colourless liquid, a cyclic ether with a faint, pleasant smell, $C_4H_8O_2$, used in the varnish and silk industries and as a dehydrator in histology. Also, **dioxane** /daɪ'ɒkseɪn/.

**dioxide** /daɪ'ɒksaɪd/, *n.* **1.** an oxide containing two atoms of oxygen per molecule, as *manganese dioxide,* $MnO_2$. **2.** (loosely) peroxide. [DI-[1] + OXIDE]

**dip.,** diploma.

**dip** /dɪp/, *v.,* **dipped, dipping,** *n.* *–v.t.* **1.** to plunge temporarily into a liquid, as to wet or to take up some of the liquid. **2.** to raise or take up by dipping action; lift by bailing or scooping: *to dip water out of a boat.* **3.** to lower and raise: *to dip a flag in salutation.* **4.** to baptise by immersion. **5.** to immerse (a sheep, etc.) in a solution to destroy germs, parasites, or the like. **6.** to make (a candle) by repeatedly dipping a wick into melted tallow. **7.** to moisten or wet as if by immersion. **8.** to direct (motor-car headlights) downwards, as to avoid dazzling oncoming drivers. **9. to dip one's lid to (someone),** pay honour to or congratulate (someone). *–v.i.* **10.** to plunge into water or other liquid and emerge quickly. **11.** to plunge the hand, a dipper, etc., into water, etc., esp. in order to remove something. **12.** to sink or drop down, as if plunging into water. **13.** to incline or slope downwards. **14.** to engage slightly in a subject. **15.** to read here and there in a book. **16. dip into one's pocket,** to spend money; pay. **17. dip out,** *Colloq.* **a.** to remain uninvolved; avoid (fol. by *on*). **b.** to miss out. **c.** to fail: *he dipped out in his exams.* *–n.* **18.** the act of dipping; a plunge into water, etc. **19.** that which is taken up by dipping. **20.** a liquid into which something is dipped. **21.** →**sheep dip. 22.** a lowering momentarily; a sinking down. **23.** a soft savoury mixture into which biscuits, potato crisps, or the like, are dipped before being eaten, usu. served with cocktails. **24.** →**doughboy** (def. 2). **25.** downward extension, inclination, or slope. **26.** the amount of such extension. **27.** a hollow or depression in the land. **28.** *Geol., Mining.* the downward inclination of a stratum, vein, fault, joint or other planar surface referred to a horizontal plane. **29.** *Survey.* the angular amount by which the horizon lies below the level of the eye. **30.** the angle which a freely poised magnetic needle makes with the plane of the horizon; inclination. **31.** a short downward plunge of an aeroplane or the like. **32.** a depression built into a road to lead away surface water; spoon drain. **33.** *Colloq.* a short swim. **34.** a candle made by repeatedly dipping a wick into melted tallow. **35.** *Gymnastics.* an exercise on parallel bars in which a person bends his elbows until his chin is on a level with the bars, then elevates himself by straightening out his arms. **36.** *Prison Colloq.* a pickpocket. [ME *dippe(n),* OE *dyppan;* akin to G *taufen* baptise, and DEEP]

**dipartite** /daɪ'pataɪt/, *adj.* divided into several parts.

**dip circle** /'dɪp sɜkəl/, *n.* →**dip needle.**

**Dip. Ed.** /dɪp 'ɛd/, Diploma of Education.

**dipetalous** /daɪ'pɛtələs/, *adj.* →**bipetalous.**

**diphase** /'daɪfeɪz/, *adj.* →**quarter-phase.** Also, **diphasic** /daɪ'feɪzɪk/.

**diphenyl** /daɪ'fɛnəl, -'finəl/, *n.* →**biphenyl.**

**diphenylamine** /daɪfɛnələ'min, -'æmən, daɪfinəl-/, *n.* an aromatic crystalline benzene derivative, $(C_6H_5)_2NH$, used in the preparation of various dyes, as a reagent for oxidising agents, and as a stabliser in nitrocellulose propellants.

**diphosgene** /daɪ'fɒsdʒin/, *n.* a poison gas, $ClCOOCCl_3$ used in World War I.

**diphtheria** /dɪf'θɪəriə/, *n.* a febrile infectious disease caused by a specific bacillus and characterised by the formation of a false membrane in the air passages, esp. the throat. [NL, from Gk *diphthéra* skin, leather + *-ia,* -IA]

**diphtheritic** /dɪfθə'rɪtɪk/, *adj.* **1.** pertaining to diphtheria. **2.** affected by diphtheria. Also, **diphtherial** /dɪf'θɪəriəl/, **diphtheric** /dɪf'θɛrɪk/.

**diphtheroid** /'dɪfθərɔɪd/, *adj.* resembling diphtheria or the diphtheria organism.

**diphthong** /'dɪfθɒŋ/, *n.* **1.** a speech sound consisting of a glide from the articulatory position of one vowel towards that of another, and having only one syllabic peak, as *ei* in *vein.* **2.** a digraph as *ea* in *each.* **3.** a ligature representing a vowel, as *æ* or *œ.* [LL *diphthongus,* from Gk *díphthongos,* lit., having two sounds] – **diphthongal** /'dɪfθɒŋəl, -θɒŋgəl/, *adj.*

**diphthongise** /'dɪfθɒŋaɪz, -θɒŋgaɪz/, *v.,* **-ised, -ising.** *–v.t.* **1.** to change into or pronounce as a diphthong. *–v.i.* **2.** to become a diphthong. Also, **diphthongize.** – **diphthongisation** /dɪfθɒŋaɪ'zeɪʃən, -θɒŋg-/, *n.*

**diphyllous** /daɪ'fɪləs/, *adj.* having two leaves.

**diphyodont** /'dɪfiədɒnt/, *adj.* having two successive sets of teeth, as most mammals. [Gk *diphyḗs* double + -ODONT]

**diplacusis** /dɪplə'kjusəs/, *n.* the perception of a single tone as two tones differing in pitch, due to a pathological condition resulting in unequal performance of each ear.

**diplegia** /daɪ'plidʒə/, *n.* paralysis of similar parts on both sides of the body. [NL, from Gk *di-* DI-[1] + *plēgḗ* stroke]

**diplex** /'daɪplɛks/, *adj.* denoting or pertaining to a system of telegraphic or radio communication for sending two messages simultaneously in the same direction over a single wire or communications channel. [DI-[1] + *-plex,* modelled on DUPLEX] – **diplexer,** *n.*

**Dip. Lib.** /dɪp 'lɪb/, Diploma in Librarianship.

**diplo-,** a word element referring to pairs, doubles, as in *diplocardiac.* Also, before vowels, **dipl-.** [Gk, combining form of *diplóos* twofold]

**diploblastic** /dɪploʊ'blæstɪk/, *adj.* of or pertaining to embryos and lower invertebrates such as the sponges and jellyfish which have bodies developed from only two cellular layers. [DIPLO- + BLAST(O)- + -IC]

**diplocardiac** /dɪploʊ'kadiæk/, *adj.* pertaining to a heart, divided into two separated sides, one pumping venous blood to the lungs and the other the freshly oxygenated blood from the lungs to the other parts of the body, as in birds and mammals.

**diplococcus** /dɪplə'kɒkəs/, *n., pl.* **-cocci** /-'kɒksaɪ, -'kɒkaɪ/. any of certain bacterial species whose organisms occur in pairs, as in *diplococcus pneumoniae,* etc. [NL. See DIPLO-, COCCUS]

**diplodocus** /daɪ'plɒdəkəs/, *n.* any animal of the extinct genus *Diplodocus,* comprising gigantic dinosaurs of the upper Jurassic of western North America. [NL, from *diplo-* DIPLO- + Gk *dokós* beam]

**diploe** /'dɪploʊi/, *n.* (in anatomy) the cancellate bony tissue between the hard inner and outer walls of the bones of the cranium. [Gk: a fold]

**diploid** /'dɪplɔɪd/, *adj.* **1.** double. **2.** *Biol.* having two similar complements of chromosomes. *–n.* **3.** *Biol.* an organism or cell with double the basic (haploid) number of chromosomes. **4.** *Crystall.* a solid belonging to the isometric system, with 24 trapezoidal planes.

**diploma** /də'ploʊmə/, *n., pl.* **-mas,** *v.,* **-maed, -maing.** *–n.* **1.** a document as one stating a candidate's success in an examination or some other qualification, etc., usu. of a lower standard or more specialised character than a degree. **2.** a public or official document. *–v.t.* **3.** to furnish with a diploma. [L, from Gk: paper folded double, letter of recommendation, licence, etc.]

**diplomacy** /də'ploʊməsi/, *n., pl.* **-cies. 1.** the conduct by government officials of negotiations and other relations between states. **2.** the science of conducting such negotiations. **3.** skill in managing any negotiations; artful management. [F *diplomatie* (with *t* pron. as *s*), from *diplomate* diplomat]

**diplomat** /ˈdɪpləmæt/, *n.* one employed or skilled in diplomacy; a diplomatist.

**diplomate** /ˈdɪpləmeɪt/, *n.* one who has received a diploma; esp. a doctor, engineer, etc., who has been certified as a specialist by a board within his profession. [DIPLOM(A) + -ATE[1]]

**diplomatic** /dɪpləˈmætɪk/, *adj.* **1.** of, pertaining to, or engaged in diplomacy. **2.** skilled in diplomacy; tactful. **3.** of or pertaining to diplomatics. – **diplomatically,** *adv.*

**diplomatic corps** /ˈ– kɔ/, *n.* the body of diplomats accredited and resident at a court or capital. Also, **diplomatic body.**

**diplomatic immunity** /– əˈmjunəti/, *n.* the immunity from local jurisdiction, taxation, etc., which is the privilege of official representatives of a foreign state.

**diplomatics** /dɪpləˈmætɪks/, *n.* the phase of palaeography devoted to ancient documents.

**diplomatist** /dəˈploʊmətəst/, *n.* **1.** a diplomat. **2.** one who is astute and tactful in any negotiation.

**diplopia** /dəˈploʊpiə/, *n.* a morbid condition of vision in which a single object appears double. [NL. See DIPL(O)-, -OPIA] – **diplopic** /dəˈplɒpɪk/, *adj.*

**diplopod** /ˈdɪpləpɒd/, *adj.* **1.** of or pertaining to the Diplopoda, a class of arthropods having tracheae, consisting of the millipedes. –*n.* **2.** any member of the Diplopoda; a millipede. [DIPLO- + -POD]

**diploscope** /ˈdɪpləskoʊp/, *n.* an operating microscope with eye pieces for two surgeons.

**diplosis** /dəˈploʊsəs/, *n.* (in biology) the doubling of the chromosome number by the union of the haploid sets in the union of gametes. [Gk: a doubling]

**diplostemonous** /ˌdɪploʊˈstimənəs, -ˈstɛmə-/, *adj.* having two series of stamens, or twice as many stamens as petals.

**dip needle** /ˈdɪp nidl/, *n.* an instrument for measuring dip (def. 30) consisting of a magnetised needle suspended on a horizontal pivot and a counter arm to control the sensitivity and position of the needle. Also, **dip circle, dipping needle.**

**dipnoan** /dɪpˈnoʊən/, *adj.* **1.** belonging or pertaining to the Dipnoi, a class or group of fishes having both gills and lungs. –*n.* **2.** a dipnoan fish. [NL *Dipnoi,* pl., genus type (from Gk *dípnoos* (sing.) having two breathing apertures) + -AN]

**dipody** /ˈdɪpədi/, *n., pl.* **-dies.** a group of two metrical feet.

**dipole** /ˈdaɪpoʊl/, *n.* **1.** a pair of equal and opposite electric charges or magnetic poles, forces, etc., as on the surfaces of a body or in a molecule. **2.** a molecule having the effective centre of the positive and negative charges separated. **3.** a radio antenna consisting of two conductors. – **dipolar,** *adj.*

**dipole moment** /– ˈmoʊmənt/, *n.* a physical quantity which determines the moment or torque experienced by a dipole when placed in an electric or magnetic field.

**dip-pen** /ˈdɪp-pɛn/, *n.* a pen designed to be dipped into ink, as opposed to a fountain pen.

**dipper** /ˈdɪpə/, *n.* **1.** one who or that which dips. **2.** a container with a handle, used for taking up liquids. **3.** any of various diving birds, esp. of the genus *Cinclus,* as *C. aquaticus,* the common European water ouzel. **4.** *Geol.* **a.** a digging bucket rigidly attached to a stick or arm on an excavating machine. **b.** the complete excavating machine. **5.** (*chiefly pl.*) *N.Z. Colloq.* a member of any revivalist sect which practises baptism by total immersion. – **dipperful** /ˈdɪpəfʊl/, *n.*

**dipping needle** /ˈdɪpɪŋ nidl/, *n.* →**dip needle.**

**dippy** /ˈdɪpi/, *adj. Colloq.* stupid; foolish.

**diprotodont** /daɪˈproʊtəˌdɒnt/, *n.* one of a group of marsupials having fewer than three upper incisor teeth on each side of the jaw, and including kangaroos and wombats. [DI-[1] + PROT- + -ODONT]

**dipsacaceous** /dɪpsəˈkeɪʃəs/, *adj.* belonging to the Dipsacaceae, or teasel family of plants. [NL *Dipsacus,* typical genus (from Gk *dípsakos* teasel) + -ACEOUS]

**dipso** /ˈdɪpsoʊ/, *Colloq.* –*n.* **1.** a dipsomaniac. –*adj.* **2.** dipsomaniacal.

**dipsomania** /dɪpsəˈmeɪniə/, *n.* an irresistible, generally periodic, craving for intoxicating drink. [NL, from Gk *díp-so(s)* thirst + *manía* MANIA]

**dipsomaniac** /dɪpsəˈmeɪniæk/, *n.* one who suffers from an irresistible and insatiable craving for intoxicants. – **dipsomaniacal** /dɪpsəməˈnaɪəkəl/, *adj.*

**dip stick** /ˈdɪp stɪk/, *n.* a stick or rod inserted into a tank or motor-car sump to measure the level of liquid which it contains.

**dip switch** /ˈ– swɪtʃ/, *n.* a switch that lowers the beams of a vehicle's headlights. Also, **dipper switch.**

**dipteral** /ˈdɪptərəl/, *adj.* **1.** *Archit.* having two rows of columns on all sides. **2.** *Biol.* →**dipterous.**

**dipteran** /ˈdɪptərən/, *adj.* **1.** →**dipterous.** –*n.* **2.** a dipterous insect.

**dipterous** /ˈdɪptərəs/, *adj.* **1.** *Entomol.* belonging or pertaining to the order Diptera, that includes the common houseflies, gnats, mosquitoes, etc., characterised typically by a single pair of membranous wings. **2.** *Bot.* having two winglike appendages, as seeds, stems, etc. [NL *dīpterus* two-winged, from Gk *dípteros*]

**diptych** /ˈdɪptɪk/, *n.* **1.** a hinged two-leaved tablet used by the ancients for writing on with the stylus. **2.** a pair of pictures or carvings on two panels hinged together. [LL *diptycha,* neut. pl., double-folded, from Gk]

**dire** /ˈdaɪə/, *adj.,* **direr, direst. 1.** causing or attended with great fear or suffering; dreadful; awful: *a dire calamity.* **2.** **in dire straits,** in extreme difficulty; in danger. [L *dīrus*]

**direct** /dəˈrɛkt, daɪ-/, *v.t.* **1.** to guide with advice; regulate the course of; conduct; manage; control. **2.** to give authoritative instructions to; command; order or ordain (something): *I directed him to do it, or that he do it.* **3.** to tell or show (a person) the way to a place, etc. **4.** to organise and supervise the artistic production of a play or film. **5.** to point or aim towards a place or an object; cause to move, act, or work towards a certain object or end. **6.** to address (words, etc.) to a person. **7.** to mark (a letter, etc.) as intended for or sent to a particular person. –*v.i.* **8.** to act as a guide or director. **9.** to give commands or orders. –*adj.* **10.** proceeding in a straight line or by the shortest course; straight; undeviating; not oblique. **11.** proceeding in an unbroken line of descent; lineal, not collateral. **12.** following the natural order, as in mathematics. **13.** without intervening agency; immediate; personal. **14.** going straight to the point; straightforward; downright. **15.** absolute; exact: *the direct contrary.* **16.** *Gram.* (of quotation or speech) consisting exactly of the words originally used (opposed to *reported*): *He said 'I am coming'.* **17.** *Govt.* of or by action of voters, which takes effect without any intervening agency such as representatives. **18.** *Elect.* of or pertaining to direct current. **19.** *Astron.* **a.** moving in an orbit in the same direction as the earth in its revolution round the sun. **b.** appearing to move in the zodiac according to the natural order of the signs, or from west to east (opposed to *retrograde*). **20.** *Dyeing.* working without the use of a mordant; substantive. –*adv.* **21.** in a direct manner; directly; straight. [ME *direct(en),* from L *directus,* pp.] – **directness,** *n.*

**direct action** /– ˈækʃən/, *n.* any method of directly pitting the strength of organised workers or any other large group against employers or capitalists or government, as by strikes, picketing, sabotage, working strictly to rule, civil disobedience, etc. – **direct-actionist** *n.*

**direct carving** /– ˈkavɪŋ/, *n.* the art of carving directly in stone or wood without a finished model as a guide or template.

**direct current** /– ˈkʌrənt/, *n.* (in electronics) a relatively steady current in one direction in a circuit; a continuous stream of electrons through a conductor. Cf. **alternating current.**

**direct evidence** /– ˈɛvədəns/, *n.* evidence of a witness who testifies to the truth of the fact to be proved (contrasted with *circumstantial evidence*).

**direct fire** /– ˈfaɪə/, *n.* gunfire delivered on a target, using the target itself as a point of aim for either the gun or the director.

**direct heating** /– ˈhitɪŋ/, *n.* the heating of a room by means of a heat source within that room.

**direction** /dəˈrɛkʃən, daɪ-/, *n.* **1.** the act of directing, pointing, aiming, etc. **2.** the line along which anything lies, faces, moves, etc., with reference to the point or region towards which it is directed. **3.** the point or region itself. **4.** a line of action, tendency, etc. **5.** guidance; instruction. **6.** order; command. **7.** management; control. **8.** a directorate. **9.** the superscription on a letter, etc., giving the name and address of the intended recipient. **10.** decisions in a stage or film production as to stage business, speaking of lines, lighting, and general presentation. **11.** a symbol or phrase in a musical score which indicates the correct tempo, style of performance, mood, etc.

**directional** /dəˈrɛkʃənəl, daɪ-/, *adj.* **1.** of or pertaining to direction in space. **2.** *Radio.* adapted for determining the direction of signals received, or for transmitting signals in a given direction: *a directional antenna.*

**direction-finder** /dəˈrɛkʃən-faɪndə/, *n.* a contrivance on a radio receiver usu. based on a loop antenna rotating on a vertical axis, which ascertains the direction of incoming radio waves.

**directive** /dəˈrɛktɪv, daɪ-/, *adj.* **1.** serving to direct; directing. *–n.* **2.** an authoritative instruction or direction.

**direct labour** /dərɛkt ˈleɪbə/, *n.* the direct employment of labour in the building industry by the promoter of the work instead of through a contractor.

**directly** /dəˈrɛktli, daɪ-/, *adv.* **1.** in a direct line, way, or manner; straight. **2.** without delay; immediately. **3.** presently. **4.** absolutely; exactly; precisely. *–conj.* **5.** as soon as: *directly he arrived, he mentioned the subject.*

**direct memory access,** *n.* a data path to a computer memory in which the Central Processing Unit does not intervene; used for high speed transfer of large volumes of data. Also, **direct memory channel.**

**direct method** /dərɛkt ˈmɛθəd/, *n.* a method of teaching a foreign language without reference to the learner's native tongue.

**direct object** /– ˈɒbdʒɛkt/, *n.* (in English and some other languages) the person or thing upon which the action of the verb is expended or towards which it is directed, in English expressed by a noun or pronoun without a preposition and generally coming after the verb: *he hit the horse* has *the horse* as the direct object.

**director** /dəˈrɛktə, daɪ-/, *n.* **1.** one who or that which directs. **2.** *Comm.* one of a body of persons chosen to control or govern the affairs of a company or corporation. **3.** the permanent head in certain government departments. **4.** the manager of the interpretative aspects of a stage or film production who supervises such elements as the acting, photography, etc. **5.** *Mil.* a device used in field-gunnery for measuring angles in the horizontal and vertical planes. **– directorship,** *n.* **– directress, directrix,** *n. fem.*

**directorate** /dəˈrɛktərət, -trət, daɪ-/, *n.* **1.** the office of a director. **2.** a body of directors.

**director-general** /dərɛktə-ˈdʒɛnrəl/, *n.* the permanent head in certain government departments.

**directorial** /dərɛkˈtɔriəl, daɪrɛk-/, *adj.* pertaining to a director or directorate.

**directory** /dəˈrɛktəri, -tri/, *n., pl.* **-ries,** *adj.* *–n.* **1.** a book or the like containing an alphabetical list of the names and addresses of people in a city, district, building, etc., or of a particular class of persons, etc. **2.** a book containing an alphabetical list of telephone subscribers and their numbers. **3.** a book of directions. *–adj.* **4.** serving to direct; directing. [L *dīrectōrius* that directs (ML *directōrium,* n.)]

**direct painting** /dərɛkt ˈpeɪntɪŋ/, *n.* →**alla prima.**

**directrix** /dəˈrɛktrɪks/, *n., pl.* **-trices** /-trəsiz/. **1.** *Maths.* a fixed line used in the description of certain curves or surfaces. **2.** a directress. [NL]

**direct tax** /dərɛkt ˈtæks/, *n.* a compulsory monetary contribution such as income tax, demanded by a government for its support and levied directly on the persons who will bear the burden of it.

**direct wave** /– ˈweɪv/, *n.* →**ground wave.** Also, **direct ray.**

**direful** /ˈdaɪəfʊl/, *adj.* dreadful; awful; terrible. **– direfully,** *adv.* **– direfulness,** *n.*

**direttissimo** /dɪrəˈtɪsimoʊ/, *n.* a straight or nearly straight route up a mountain face, regardless of difficulty. [It: most direct]

**dirge** /dɜdʒ/, *n.* **1.** a funeral song or tune, or one expressing mourning. **2.** *Eccles.* the office of the dead, or the funeral service as sung. [L, syncopated var. of *dīrige* (imperative of *dīrigere* direct), first word of the antiphon sung in the L office of the dead]

**dirigible** /ˈdɪrɪdʒəbəl, dəˈrɪdʒəbəl/, *n.* **1.** an airship. *–adj.* **2.** that may be controlled, directed, or steered. [L *dīrigere* DIRECT, *v.* + -IBLE]

**diriment** /ˈdɪrəmənt/, *adj.* **1.** that renders absolutely void; nullifying. **2.** *Rom. Cath. Ch.* rendering marriage null and void from the very beginning. [L *dirimens,* ppr., separating, breaking off]

**dirk** /dɜk/, *n.* **1.** a stabbing weapon; a dagger, esp. as used in the Highlands of Scotland. *–v.t.* **2.** to stab with a dirk. [orig. uncert.]

**dirndl** /ˈdɜndl/, *n.* **1.** a type of woman's dress with full skirt and close-fitting bodice, commonly of colourful and strikingly patterned material, derived from Tyrolean peasant use. **2.** a skirt in such a style. [G: girl]

**dirt** /dɜt/, *n.* **1.** earth or soil, esp. when loose. *n.* **2.** any foul or filthy substance, as excrement, mud, etc. **3.** something vile, mean, or worthless. **4.** moral filth; vileness. **5.** abusive or scurrilous language. **6.** unsavoury or malicious gossip. **7.** *Mining.* **a.** crude broken ore or waste. **b.** (in placer mining) the material from which the gold is separated by washing. **8.** **do (someone) dirt,** *Colloq.* to behave unfairly or wrongly towards (someone). **9.** **eat dirt,** to accept insult without complaint. *–adj.* **10.** consisting of dirt: *a dirt road.* [metathetic var. of ME *drit,* from Scand.; cf. Icel. *drit* excrement]

**dirt-cheap** /ˈdɜt-tʃip/, *adj.* very inexpensive.

**dirt money** /ˈdɜt mʌni/, *n.* **1.** a disability allowance paid to a worker for working in esp. dirty conditions. **2.** very little money; underpayment.

**dirt road** /– ˈroʊd/, *n.* an unsealed road, esp. a gravel road.

**dirt track** /ˈ– træk/, *n.* an oval or circular track surfaced with cinders, used for motor-cycle speedway racing.

**dirty** /ˈdɜti/, *adj.,* **dirtier, dirtiest,** *v.,* **dirtied, dirtying.** *–adj.* **1.** soiled with dirt; foul; unclean. **2.** imparting dirt; soiling. **3.** vile; mean. **4.** morally unclean; indecent. **5.** *Sport.* characterised by rough, unfair play, frequent fouls, etc. **6.** (of devices capable of producing nuclear reactions) having the quality of generating unwanted radioactive by-products: *a dirty bomb.* **7.** stormy; squally, as the weather: *it looks dirty to windward.* **8.** appearing as if soiled; dark-coloured; dingy. **9.** *Colloq.* angry. **10.** **be dirty on,** *Colloq.* to be angry with. **11.** to make dirty. *–v.i.* **12.** to become dirty. *–n.* **13.** **do the dirty on,** *Colloq.* to behave unfairly or wrongly towards. *–adv.* **14.** *Colloq.* very; extremely: *dirty big.* **– dirtily,** *adv.* **– dirtiness,** *n.*

**dirty dog** /– ˈdɒg/, *n.* an unprincipled person.

**dirty float** /ˈ– floʊt/, *n.* a devaluation or revaluation of a currency brought about by a government intervention in the international money market, as by buying or selling foreign exchange.

**dirty linen** /– ˈlɪnən/, *n.* **1.** soiled laundry. **2.** **wash one's dirty linen in public,** *Colloq.* reveal or discuss matters of a scandalous nature from one's private life.

**dirty look** /– ˈlʊk/, *n. Colloq.* an angry or sullen expression: *she gave him a dirty look.*

**dirty tricks** /– ˈtrɪks/, *n.pl.* underhand activities designed to discredit or smear a political opponent.

**dirty weekend** /– wikˈɛnd/, *n. Colloq.* a weekend spent with a lover in sensual delights.

**dirty wind** /– ˈwɪnd/, *n.* →**backwind.**

**dirty word** /– ˈwɜd/, *n.* **1.** a vulgar word. **2.** something one doesn't mention because it is as objectionable as if it were a vulgar word: *work is a dirty word around here.*

**dirty work** /ˈ– wɜk/, *n.* **1.** work of an unusually dirty or offensive nature for which employees are paid a special rate as compensation. **2.** **do someone's dirty work,** *Colloq.* to take over an unpleasant task for another person usu. without reward or thanks.

**dis-**[1], a prefix of Latin origin meaning 'apart', 'asunder', 'away', 'utterly', or having a privative, negative, or reversing force (see **de-** and **un-**[2]), used freely, esp. with these latter significations, as an English formative, as in *disability, disaffirm, disbar, disbelief, discontent, disentangle, dishearten,* *disinfect, dislike, disown, disrelish.* Also, **di-**. [L (akin to L *bis,* Gk *dis* twice); before *f, dif-;* before some consonants, *di-;* often replacing obs. *des-,* from OF]

**dis-**[2], variant of **di-**[1], as in *dissyllable.*

**disability** /dɪsə'bɪləti/, *n., pl.* **-ties. 1.** lack of competent power, strength, or physical or mental ability; incapacity. **2.** to make legally incapable; disqualify.

**disability allowance** /'– əlaʊəns/, *n.* an amount of money paid for working under certain unpleasant conditions.

**disability insurance** /'– ɪnʃɔrəns/, *n.* a type of insurance where a policy remains in full force without payment of additional premiums if the holder becomes totally or permanently disabled.

**disable** /dɪs'eɪbəl/, *v.t.,* **-bled, -bling. 1.** to make unable; weaken or destroy the capability of; cripple; incapacitate. **2.** to make legally incapable; disqualify. **– disablement,** *n.*

**disabuse** /dɪsə'bjuz/, *v.t.,* **-bused, -busing.** to free from deception or error; set right. [DIS-[1] + ABUSE, *v.*]

**disaccharide** /daɪ'sækəraɪd/, *n.* any of a group of carbohydrates which are formed from two monosaccharides which may be the same (maltose) or different (sucrose). [DI-[1] + SACCHARIDE]

**disaccord** /dɪsə'kɔd/, *v.i.* **1.** to disagree. *–n.* **2.** disagreement.

**disaccredit** /dɪsə'krɛdət/, *v.t.* take away the credentials of; cause to be no longer authorised.

**disaccustom** /dɪsə'kʌstəm/, *v.t.* to cause to lose a habit.

**disadvantage** /dɪsəd'væntɪdʒ/, *n., v.,* **-taged, -taging.** *–n.* **1.** absence or deprivation of advantage; any unfavourable circumstance or condition. **2.** injury to interest, reputation, credit, profit, etc.; loss. *–v.t.* **3.** to subject to disadvantage.

**disadvantaged** /dɪsəd'væntɪdʒd/, *v.* **1.** past tense and past participle of **disadvantage.** *–adj.* **2.** low in socio-economic rank or background: *a disadvantaged suburb.* **3.** deprived of financial security, educational background, opportunity, etc., as a result of discrimination.

**disadvantageous** /ˌdɪsædvæn'teɪdʒəs/, *adj.* attended with disadvantage; unfavourable; detrimental. **– disadvantageously,** *adv.* **– disadvantageousness,** *n.*

**disaffect** /dɪsə'fɛkt/, *v.t.* to alienate the affection of; make ill-affected, discontented, or disloyal.

**disaffection** /dɪsə'fɛkʃən/, *n.* absence or alienation of affection or goodwill; estrangement; disloyalty.

**disaffiliate** /dɪsə'fɪlieɪt/, *v.i.,* **-ated, -ating.** to sever an alliance with; cease membership of.

**disaffirm** /dɪsə'fɜm/, *v.t.* **1.** to deny; contradict. **2.** *Law.* to annul; reverse; repudiate. **– disaffirmance, disaffirmation** /dɪsæfə'meɪʃən/, *n.*

**disafforest** /dɪsə'fɒrəst/, *n.* to strip of forests. [ML *disafforestāre*]

**disagree** /dɪsə'gri/, *v.i.,* **-greed, -greeing. 1.** to fail to agree; differ (fol. by *with*): *the conclusions disagree with the facts.* **2.** to differ in opinion; dissent. **3.** to quarrel. **4.** to conflict in action or effect: *food that disagrees with one.*

**disagreeable** /dɪsə'griəbəl/, *adj.* **1.** contrary to one's taste or liking; unpleasant; offensive; repugnant. **2.** unpleasant in manner or nature; unamiable. **– disagreeableness,** *n.* **– disagreeably,** *adv.*

**disagreement** /dɪsə'grimənt/, *n.* **1.** the act, state, or fact of disagreeing. **2.** lack of agreement; diversity; unlikeness. **3.** difference of opinion; dissent. **4.** dissension; quarrel. **5.** unwholesome action or effect, as of food.

**disallow** /dɪsə'laʊ/, *v.t.* **1.** to refuse to allow. **2.** to refuse to admit the truth or validity of. **– disallowable,** *adj.* **– disallowance,** *n.*

**disambiguate** /dɪsæm'bɪgjueɪt/, *v.t.,* **-ated, -ating. 1.** to remove the ambiguity from. **2.** to identify the possible interpretations of a phrase or sentence, and to choose the preferred one. **– disambiguation** /ˌdɪsæmbɪgju'eɪʃən/, *n.*

**disannul** /dɪsə'nʌl/, *v.t.,* **-nulled, -nulling.** to annul utterly; make void. [DIS-[1] (intensive) + ANNUL] **– disannulment,** *n.*

**disanoint** /dɪsə'nɔint/, *v.t.* to invalidate the consecration of.

**disappear** /dɪsə'pɪə/, *v.i.* **1.** to cease to appear or to be seen; vanish from sight. **2.** to cease to exist or be known; pass away; end gradually. **3.** *Colloq.* to go away; depart.

**disappearance** /dɪsə'pɪərəns/, *n.* the act of disappearing; a ceasing to appear or to exist.

**disappoint** /dɪsə'pɔɪnt/, *v.t.* **1.** to fail to fulfil the expectations or wishes of (a person): *his conduct disappointed us.* **2.** to defeat the fulfilment of (hopes, plans, etc.); thwart; frustrate. [OF *desappointer,* from *des-* DIS-[1] + *appointer* APPOINT] **– disappointer,** *n.* **– disappointingly,** *adv.*

**disappointment** /dɪsə'pɔɪntmənt/, *n.* **1.** the act or fact of disappointing: *he has lost hope because of frequent disappointments.* **2.** state or feeling of being disappointed: *great was his disappointment.* **3.** something that disappoints: *the play was a disappointment.*

**disapprobation** /ˌdɪsæprə'beɪʃən/, *n.* →**disapproval. – disapprobative** /dɪsə'proʊbətɪv/, *adj.* **– disapprobatory** /dɪsə'proʊbətri, -təri/, *adj.*

**disapproval** /dɪsə'pruvəl/, *n.* the act or state of disapproving; a condemnatory feeling or utterance; censure.

**disapprove** /dɪsə'pruv/, *v.,* **-proved, -proving.** *–v.t.* **1.** to think wrong or reprehensible; censure or condemn in opinion. **2.** to withhold approval from; decline to sanction: *the court disapproved the verdict.* *–v.i.* **3.** to have an unfavourable opinion (fol. by *of*). **– disapprover,** *n.* **– disapprovingly,** *adv.*

**disarm** /dɪs'am/, *v.t.* **1.** to deprive of arms. **2.** to deprive of means of attack or defence. **3.** to divest of hostility, suspicion, etc.; make friendly. *–v.i.* **4.** to lay down arms. **5.** (of a country) to reduce or limit the size, equipment, armament, etc., of the army, navy, or air forces. *–n.* **6.** (in fencing) the act of disarming an opponent. [OF *desarmer,* from *des-* DIS-[1] + *armer* ARM[2]] **– disarmer,** *n.*

**disarmament** /dɪs'aməmənt/, *n.* **1.** the act of disarming. **2.** the state of being disarmed, as in fencing. **3.** the reduction or limitation of the size, equipment, armament, etc., of the army, navy, or air forces.

**disarming** /dɪs'amɪŋ/, *adj.* **1.** removing or likely to remove antagonsim, suspicion, or the like. **2.** winning, endearing. **– disarmingly,** *adv.*

**disarrange** /dɪsə'reɪndʒ/, *v.t.,* **-ranged, -ranging.** to disturb the arrangement of; disorder; unsettle. **– disarrangement,** *n.* **– disarranger,** *n.*

**disarray** /dɪsə'reɪ/, *v.t.* **1.** to put out of array or order; throw into disorder. **2.** to undress. *–n.* **3.** disorder; confusion. **4.** disorder of apparel; disorderly dress.

**disarticulate** /dɪsa'tɪkjəleɪt/, *v.,* **-lated, -lating.** *–v.t.* **1.** to take apart at the joints. *–v.i.* **2.** to come apart at the joints. **– disarticulation** /dɪsaˌtɪkjə'leɪʃən/, *n.* **– disarticulator,** *n.*

**disassemble** /dɪsə'sɛmbəl/, *v.t.,* **-bled, -bling.** to take apart.

**disassembly** /dɪsə'sɛmbli/, *n.* **1.** the act of disassembling. **2.** state of being disassembled.

**disassociate** /dɪsə'soʊʃieɪt, -sieɪt/, *v.t.,* **-ated, -ating.** →**dissociate. – disassociation** /ˌdɪsəsoʊʃi'eɪʃən, -soʊsi-/, *n.*

**disaster** /də'zastə/, *n.* **1.** any unfortunate event, esp. a sudden or great misfortune. **2.** *Colloq.* a total failure, as of a person, machine, plan, etc. [It. *disastro,* from *disastrato* not having a (lucky) star, from *dis-* DIS-[1] + *astr(o)* star + *-ato,* properly, ppl. ending]

**disaster area** /'dəzastər ɛəriə/, *n.* **1.** an area so nominated in which there is a breakdown of communications, supplies and services, as a result of some catastrophe. **2.** *Colloq.* a person who seems overwhelmed by misfortune. **3.** *Colloq.* an untidy place.

**disastrous** /də'zastrəs/, *adj.* **1.** causing great distress or injury; ruinous; unfortunate; calamitous. **2.** *Archaic.* foreboding disaster. **– disastrously,** *adv.* **– disastrousness,** *n.*

**disavow** /dɪsə'vaʊ/, *v.t.* to disclaim knowledge of, connection with, or responsibility for; disown; repudiate. [ME *desavoue(n),* from OF *desavouer,* from *des-* DIS-[1] + *avouer* AVOW] **– disavower,** *n.*

**disavowal** /dɪsə'vaʊəl/, *n.* a disowning; repudiation; denial.

**disband** /dɪs'bænd/, *v.t.* **1.** to break up or disorganise (a band or company); dissolve (a military force) by dismissing from service. *–v.i.* **2.** to break up, as a band or company. [MF *desbander,* from *des-* DIS-[1] + *bander* tie] **– disbandment,** *n.*

**disbar** /dɪs'ba/, *v.t.,* **-barred, -barring.** to expel from the legal profession or from the bar. [DIS-[1] + BAR[1]] **– disbarment,** *n.*

**disbelief** /dɪsbə'lif/, *n.* refusal or inability to believe.

**disbelieve** /dɪsbə'liv/, *v.,* **-lieved, -lieving.** *–v.t.* **1.** to reject as false: *I disbelieve your statement.* *–v.i.* **2.** to have no faith in (fol. by *in*): *I disbelieve in man-made solutions.*

**disbranch** /dɪsˈbræntʃ/, *v.t.* **1.** to deprive of branches, as a tree. **2.** to cut or break off, as a branch.

**disbud** /dɪsˈbʌd/, *v.t.*, **-budded, -budding.** to remove leaf or flower buds from (a plant, etc.), to improve the quality or shape of what remains.

**disburden** /dɪsˈbɜdn/, *v.t.* **1.** to remove a burden from; rid of a burden. **2.** to relieve of anything oppressive or annoying. **3.** to get rid of (a burden); discharge. *–v.i.* **4.** to unload a burden. – **disburdenment,** *n.*

**disburse** /dɪsˈbɜs/, *v.t.*, **-bursed, -bursing.** to pay out (money); expend. [OF *desbourser,* from *des-* DIS-[1] + *bourse* purse (from LL *bursa.* See BURSA)] – **disbursable,** *adj.* – **disburser,** *n.*

**disbursement** /dɪsˈbɜsmənt/, *n.* **1.** the act of disbursing. **2.** that which is disbursed; money expended.

**disc** /dɪsk/, *n.* **1.** any thin, flat, circular plate or object. **2.** a round, flat area. **3.** the apparently flat surface of the sun, etc. **4.** a gramophone record. **5.** a disc brake. **6.** *Archaic.* a discus. **7.** *Bot., Zool., etc.* any of various roundish, flat structures or parts, as a plate of tissue between whorls of floral parts. **8.** *Bot.* (in composite plants) the central portion of the flower head, composed of tubular florets. **9.** *Anat., Zool.* **a. interarticular disc,** a plate of cartilage interposed between the articulating ends of bones. **b. intervertebral disc,** the plate of fibrocartilage interposed between the bodies of adjacent vertebrae. **10.** *Bowls.* one of two circles enscribed on each side of the bowl, the smaller of which indicates the bias side. **11.** →**magnetic disc.** *–v.t.* **12.** to prepare (soil) with a disc harrow. Also, *Chiefly U.S.,* **disk.** [L *discus* DISCUS] – **discal,** *adj.* – **disclike,** *adj.*

**disc.,** **1.** discipline. **2.** discount. **3.** discovered.

**discalced** /dɪsˈkælst/, *adj.* without shoes; unshod; barefooted; specifically applied to a branch of the Carmelite monks known as **Discalceati** (the barefooted). Also, **discalceate** /dɪsˈkælsiət, -eɪt/.

**discant** /ˈdɪskænt/, *n.;* /dɪsˈkænt/, *v.i.* →**descant.**

**discard** /dɪsˈkad/, *v.;* /ˈdɪskad/, *n.* *–v.t.* **1.** to cast aside; reject; dismiss, esp. from use. **2.** *Cards.* **a.** to throw out (a card or cards) from one's hand. **b.** to play (a card, not a trump, of a different suit from that of the card led). *–v.i.* **3.** *Cards.* to discard a card or cards. *–n.* **4.** the act of discarding. **5.** one who or that which is cast out or rejected. **6.** *Cards.* the card or cards discarded. – **discarder,** *n.*

**disc brake** /ˈdɪsk breɪk/, *n.* a brake, commonly used on the road wheels of motor vehicles and the landing wheels of aircraft, in which friction is obtained by the action of pads on a flat disc attached to the rotating part to be slowed down.

**discern** /dəˈsɜn/, *v.t.* **1.** to perceive by the sight or some other sense or by the intellect; see, recognise, or apprehend clearly. **2.** to distinguish mentally; recognise as distinct or different; discriminate: *he discerns good and bad, good from bad.* *–v.i.* **3.** to distinguish or discriminate. [ME *discerne(n),* from F *discerner,* from L *discernere*] – **discerner,** *n.*

**discernible** /dəˈsɜnəbəl/, *adj.* capable of being discerned; distinguishable. – **discernibleness,** *n.* – **discernibly,** *adv.*

**discerning** /dəˈsɜnɪŋ/, *adj.* showing discernment; discriminating. – **discerningly,** *adv.*

**discernment** /dəˈsɜnmənt/, *n.* **1.** faculty of discerning; discrimination; acuteness of judgment. **2.** the act of discerning.

**disc file** /ˈdɪsk faɪl/, *n.* (in computers) a set of circular discs with magnetic coating, which revolve at high speed and act as a memory unit providing large storage and fast access.

**discharge** /dɪsˈtʃadʒ/, *v.,* **-charged, -charging;** /ˈdɪstʃadʒ/, *n.* *–v.t.* **1.** to relieve of a charge or load; unload (a ship, etc.). **2.** to remove, send forth, or get rid of (a charge, lead, etc.). **3.** to fire; shoot: *discharge a gun, bow, bullet, etc.* **4.** to pour forth, as water. **5.** to relieve oneself of (an obligation, etc.). **6.** to relieve of obligation, responsibility, etc. **7.** to fulfil, perform, or execute (a duty, function, etc.). **8.** to relieve or deprive of office, employment, etc.; dismiss from service. **9.** to send away or allow to go (fol. by *from*). **10.** to pay (a debt). **11.** *Law.* to release, as bail or a defendant. **12.** *Elect.* to rid (something) of a charge of electricity: *a short circuit may discharge a battery.* **13.** *Dyeing.* to free from a dye, as by chemical bleaching. *–v.i.* **14.** to get rid of a burden or load. **15.** to deliver a charge or load. **16.** to come or pour forth. **17.** to blur; run. **18.** *Elect.* to lose, or give up, a charge of electricity. *–n.* **19.** the act of discharging a ship, load, etc. **20.** act of firing a missile weapon, as a bow by drawing and releasing the string, or a gun by exploding the charge of powder. **21.** a sending or coming forth, as of water from a pipe; ejection; emission. **22.** rate or amount of issue. **23.** something discharged or emitted. **24.** a relieving or ridding, or a getting rid, of something of the nature of a charge. **25.** *Law.* **a.** acquittal or exoneration. **b.** annulment, as of a court order. **c.** freeing of one held under legal process. **26.** a relieving or being relieved of obligation or liability; the fulfilling of an obligation. **27.** the payment of a debt. **28.** release or dismissal from office, employment, etc. **29.** a certificate of release, as from obligation or liability. **30.** *Elect.* **a.** the withdrawing or transference of an electric charge. **b.** the equalisation of the difference of potential between two terminals or the like. **31.** *Elect.* →**gas discharge.** [ME *descharge(n),* from OF *descharger.* See DIS-[1], CHARGE] – **dischargeable,** *adj.* – **discharger,** *n.*

**disc harrow** /ˈdɪsk hæroʊ/, *n.* a harrow having a number of sharp-edged concave discs set at such an angle that as the machine is drawn along they pulverise and turn the soil, and destroy weeds. Also, **disc plough.**

**disci-,** a combining form of **disc.**

**discifloral** /dɪsiˈflɔrəl/, *adj.* having flowers in which the receptacle is expanded into a conspicuous disc.

**disciple** /dəˈsaɪpəl/, *n.* **1.** one of the twelve personal followers of Jesus Christ. **2.** any follower of Christ. **3.** an adherent of the doctrines of another; a follower. [ME, from OF, from L *discipulus;* replacing ME *deciple,* from OF; replacing OE *discipul,* from L (as above)] – **discipleship,** *n.*

**disciplinable** /ˈdɪsəˌplɪnəbəl/, *adj.* **1.** subject to or meriting correction. **2.** capable of being instructed.

**disciplinal** /ˈdɪsəplənəl, dɪsəˈplaɪnəl/, *adj.* of, pertaining to, or of the nature of discipline.

**disciplinant** /ˈdɪsəplənənt/, *n.* one who subjects himself to discipline.

**disciplinarian** /dɪsəpləˈnɛəriən/, *n.* **1.** one who enforces or advocates discipline. *–adj.* **2.** disciplinary.

**disciplinary** /ˈdɪsəplənri/, *adj.* of or for discipline; promoting discipline.

**discipline** /ˈdɪsəplən/, *n., v.,* **-plined, -plining.** *–n.* **1.** training to act in accordance with rules; drill: *military discipline.* **2.** instruction and exercise designed to train to proper conduct or action. **3.** punishment inflicted by way of correction and training. **4.** the training effect of experience, adversity, etc. **5.** subjection to rules of conduct of behaviour; a state of order maintained by training and control: *good discipline in an army.* **6.** a set or system of rules and regulations. **7.** *Eccles.* the system of government regulating the practice of a church as distinguished from its doctrine. **8.** a branch of instruction or learning. **9.** a form of sexual play in which one partner submits to being punished by the other. *–v.t.* **10.** to train by instruction and exercise; drill. **11.** to bring to a state of order and obedience by training and control. **12.** to subject to discipline or punishment; correct; chastise. [ME, from L *disciplīna* instruction] – **discipliner,** *n.*

**disc jockey** /ˈdɪsk dʒɒki/, *n.* one who comperes radio programs of gramophone records.

**disclaim** /dɪsˈkleɪm/, *v.t.* **1.** to repudiate or deny interest in or connection with; disavow; disown: *disclaiming all participation.* **2.** *Law.* to renounce a claim or right to. **3.** to reject the claims or authority of. *–v.i.* **4.** *Law.* to renounce or repudiate a legal claim or right. **5.** *Obs.* to disavow interest. [AF *disclaimer, desclamer,* from *des-* DIS-[1] + *clamer* CLAIM]

**disclaimer** /dɪsˈkleɪmə/, *n.* **1.** the act of disclaiming; the renouncing, repudiating, or denying of a claim; disavowal. **2.** one who disclaims. [AF]

**disclamation** /dɪskləˈmeɪʃən/, *n.* the act of disclaiming; renunciation; disavowal.

**disclose** /dəsˈkloʊz/, *v.,* **-closed, -closing.** *–v.t.* **1.** to cause to appear; allow to be seen; make known; reveal: *to disclose a plot.* **2.** to uncover; lay open to view. [ME *disclose(n), desclose(n),* from OF *desclos-,* stem of *desclore* unclose, from *des-* DIS-[1] + *clore* (from L *claudere* CLOSE)] – **discloser,** *n.*

**disclosing tablet** /dəsˈkloʊzɪŋ ˌtæblət/, *n.* a dental preparation taken to reveal plaque (def. 4) left on a tooth.

**disclosure** /dəs'kloʊʒə/, *n.* **1.** the act of disclosing; exposure; revelation. **2.** that which is disclosed; a revelation.

**disco** /'dɪskoʊ/, *n.* **1.** →**discotheque.** –*adj.* **2.** of or pertaining to music specifically written for use in discotheques.

**discobolus** /dɪs'kɒbələs/, *n., pl.* **-li** /-laɪ/. a thrower of the discus. [L, from Gk *diskobólos*]

**discography** /dɪs'kɒgrəfi/, *n.* **1.** a listing of selected gramophone records as those made by one particular artist, orchestra, etc. **2.** the study of gramophone records. – **discographer,** *n.*

**discoid** /'dɪskɔɪd/, *adj.* **1.** having the form of a discus or disc; flat and circular. **2.** *Bot.* consisting of disc florets only as in some composite plants. [LL *discoīdēs*, from Gk *diskoeidḗs*]

**discoidal** /dɪs'kɔɪdl/, *adj.* →**discoid.**

**discolour** /dɪs'kʌlə/, *v.t.* **1.** to change the colour of; spoil the colour of; stain. –*v.i.* **2.** to change colour; become faded or stained. Also, *U.S.,* **discolor.** [ME *discolour(en)*, from OF *descolorer*, from L *dis-* DIS-[1] + *color* colour]

**discolouration** /dɪskʌlə'reɪʃən/, *n.* **1.** the act or fact of discolouring. **2.** the state of being discoloured. **3.** a discoloured marking; a stain. Also, **discoloration, discolourment.**

**discombobulate** /dɪskəm'bɒbjuleɪt/, *v.t.,* **-lated, -lating.** *Colloq.* to upset, confuse (a person). [mock-Latin formation, ? from DISCOMPOSE or DISCOMFORT]

**discomfit** /dɪs'kʌmfət/, *v.t.* **1.** to defeat utterly; rout. **2.** to frustrate the plans of; thwart; foil. **3.** to throw into perplexity and dejection; disconcert. [ME, from OF *desconfit*, pp. of *desconfire*, from *des-* DIS-[1] + *confire* make, accomplish (from L *conficere*)]

**discomfiture** /dɪs'kʌmfətʃə/, *n.* **1.** defeat in battle; rout. **2.** frustration of hopes or plans. **3.** disconcertion; confusion.

**discomfort** /dɪs'kʌmfət/, *n.* **1.** absence of comfort or pleasure; uneasiness; disturbance of peace; pain. **2.** anything that disturbs the comfort. –*v.t.* **3.** to disturb the comfort or happiness of; make uncomfortable or uneasy. [ME *discomfort(en)*, from OF *desconforter*, from *des-* DIS-[1] + *conforter* COMFORT]

**discommend** /dɪskə'mɛnd/, *v.t.* **1.** to express disapproval of. **2.** to bring into disfavour. – **discommendable,** *adj.* – **discommendation** /dɪskɒmɛn'deɪʃən/, *n.* – **discommender,** *n.*

**discommode** /dɪskə'moʊd/, *v.t.,* **-moded, -moding.** to put to inconvenience; trouble; incommode. [DIS-[1] + L *commodāre* make fit]

**discommodity** /dɪskə'mɒdəti/, *n., pl.* **-ties.** **1.** inconvenience; disadvantageous. **2.** a source of inconvenience or trouble; disadvantage.

**discompose** /dɪskəm'poʊz/, *v.t.,* **-posed, -posing.** **1.** to bring into disorder; disarrange; unsettle. **2.** to disturb the composure of; agitate; perturb. – **discomposedly,** *adv.* – **discomposingly,** *adv.*

**discomposure** /dɪskəm'poʊʒə/, *n.* the state of being discomposed; disorder; agitation; perturbation.

**disco music** /'dɪskoʊ ˌmjuzɪk/, *n.* music specifically written for use in discotheques.

**disconcert** /dɪskən'sɜt/, *v.t.* **1.** to disturb the self-possession of; confuse; perturb; ruffle. **2.** to throw into disorder or confusion; disarrange. – **disconcertingly,** *adv.* – **disconcertion, disconcertment,** *n.*

**disconcerted** /dɪskən'sɜtəd/, *adj.* confused; abashed. – **disconcertedly,** *adv.* – **disconcertedness,** *n.*

**disconformity** /dɪskən'fɔməti/, *n., pl.* **-ties.** **1.** the lack of conformity; refusal or failure to conform. **2.** *Geol.* an erosion surface between two nearly horizontal sets of strata representing a long time interval between deposition of the underlying beds and deposition of the upper sequence.

**disconnect** /dɪskə'nɛkt/, *v.t.* to sever or interrupt the connection of or between; detach.

**disconnected** /dɪskə'nɛktəd/, *adj.* **1.** not connected; disjointed; broken. **2.** incoherent. – **disconnectedly,** *adv.* – **disconnectedness,** *n.*

**disconnection** /dɪskə'nɛkʃən/, *n.* **1.** the act of disconnecting. **2.** the state of being disconnected; lack of union. Also, **disconnexion.**

**disconsolate** /dɪs'kɒnsələt/, *adj.* **1.** without consolation or solace; unhappy; inconsolable. **2.** characterised by or causing discomfort; cheerless; gloomy. [ML *disconsōlātus*, from *dis-* DIS-[1] + L *consōlātus*, pp., having consoled] – **disconsolately,** *adv.* – **disconsolation** /dɪsˌkɒnsə'leɪʃən/, **disconsolateness,** *n.*

**discontent** /dɪskən'tɛnt/, *adj.* **1.** not content; dissatisfied; discontented. –*n.* **2.** Also, **discontentment.** lack of content; dissatisfaction. –*v.t.* **3.** to deprive of content; dissatisfy; displease.

**discontented** /dɪskən'tɛntəd/, *adj.* uneasy in mind; dissatisfied; restlessly unhappy. – **discontentedly,** *adv.* – **discontentedness,** *n.*

**discontinuance** /dɪskən'tɪnjuəns/, *n.* **1.** lack of continued connection or cohesion of parts; lack of union; disruption. **2.** *Law.* the termination of a suit by the act of the plaintiff, as by notice in writing, or by neglect to take the proper adjournments to keep it pending.

**discontinuation** /dɪskəntɪnju'eɪʃən/, *n.* breach or interruption of continuity or unity.

**discontinue** /dɪskən'tɪnju/, *v.,* **-tinued, -tinuing.** –*v.t.* **1.** to cause to cease; put an end to. **2.** to cease to take, use, etc.: *to discontinue a newspaper.* **3.** *Law.* to terminate or abandon (a suit, etc.). –*v.i.* **4.** to come to an end or stop; cease; desist. – **discontinuer,** *n.*

**discontinuity** /ˌdɪskɒntən'juəti/, *n.* lack of continuity, uninterrupted connection, or cohesion.

**discontinuous** /dɪskən'tɪnjuəs/, *adj.* not continuous; broken; interrupted; intermittent. – **discontinuously,** *adv.* – **discontinuousness,** *n.*

**discophil** /'dɪskəfɪl/, *n.* one who studies and collects gramophone records, esp. rare ones or a particular type of record. Also, **discophile** /'dɪskəfaɪl/.

**discord** /'dɪskɔd/, *n.* **1.** lack of concord or harmony between persons or things; disagreement of relations. **2.** difference of opinions. **3.** strife; dispute; war. **4.** (in music) an inharmonious combination of musical notes sounded together. **5.** any confused or harsh noise; dissonance. [ME *discord(en)*, from OF *discorder*, from L *discordāre* be at variance]

**discordance** /dɪs'kɔdns/, *n.* discordant character; disagreement; discord. Also, **discordancy.**

**discordant** /dɪs'kɔdnt/, *adj.* **1.** being at variance; disagreeing; incongruous: *discordant opinions.* **2.** disagreeable to the ear; dissonant; harsh. – **discordantly,** *adv.*

**discotheque** /'dɪskətɛk/, *n.* a place of public entertainment or a club in which patrons may dance, esp. to recorded music. Also, **discothèque, disco.** [F]

**discount** /'dɪskaʊnt/ *for defs 1-3 and 7,* /dɪs'kaʊnt/ *for defs 4-6, v.;* /'dɪskaʊnt/, *n.* –*v.t.* **1.** to deduct, as a certain amount in settling a bill; make a reduction of. **2.** to advance money with deduction of interest on (not immediately payable). **3.** to purchase or sell (a bill or note) before maturity at a reduction based on the interest for the time it still has to run. **4.** to leave out of account; disregard. **5.** to make a deduction from; allow for exaggeration in (a statement, etc.). **6.** to take (an event, etc.) into account in advance, esp. with loss of value, effectiveness, etc. –*v.i.* **7.** to advance money after deduction of interest. –*n.* **8.** the act of discounting. **9.** amount deducted for prompt payment or other special reason. **10.** any deduction from the nominal value. **11.** the amount of interest obtained by one who discounts. **12. at a discount, a.** *Comm.* below par. **b.** in low esteem or regard. **c.** not in demand. [OF *desconter*, from *des-* DIS-[1] + *conter* COUNT[1]] – **discountable,** *adj.* – **discounter,** *n.*

**discount broker** /'– broʊkə/, *n.* a merchant who cashes bills of exchange at a discount, or lends money at a discount on securities.

**discounted cash flow,** *n.* the current value of all the future cash to be generated by a development project.

**discountenance** /dɪs'kaʊntənəns/, *v.,* **-nanced, -nancing,** *n.* –*v.t.* **1.** to put out of countenance; disconcert; abash. **2.** to show disapproval of; treat with disfavour. –*n.* **3.** disapproval. [F (obs.) *descontenancer*, from *des-* DIS-[1] + *contenancer* COUNTENANCE, *v.*]

**discount house** /'dɪskaʊnt ˌhaʊs/, *n.* **1.** the place of business of a discount broker. **2.** Also, **discount store.** a store selling practically all its merchandise at a price often considerably below the usual or advertised retail price.

**discount rate** /'– ˌreɪt/, *n.* rate of interest charged by a banker for discounting bills of exchange.

**discourage** /dɪsˈkʌrɪdʒ/, *v.t.*, **-raged, -raging.** **1.** to deprive of courage; dishearten; dispirit. **2.** to dissuade (fol. by *from*). **3.** to obstruct by opposition or difficulty; hinder: *low prices discourage industry.* **4.** to express disapproval of: *to discourage the expression of enthusiasm.* [OF *descoragier,* from *des-* DIS-[1] + *corage* COURAGE] – **discourager,** *n.* – **discouragingly,** *adv.*

**discouragement** /dɪsˈkʌrɪdʒmənt/, *n.* **1.** the act of discouraging. **2.** the state of being discouraged. **3.** something that discourages.

**discourse** /ˈdɪskɔs, dɪsˈkɔs/, *n.*; /dɪsˈkɔs/, *v.* **-coursed, -coursing.** –*n.* **1.** communication of thought by words; talk; conversation. **2.** a formal discussion of a subject in speech or writing, as a dissertation, treatise, sermon, etc. –*v.i.* **3.** to communicate thoughts orally; talk; converse. **4.** to treat of a subject formally in speech or writing. –*v.t.* **5.** to utter or give forth (musical sounds). [ME *discours,* from F, from L *discursus*] – **discourser,** *n.*

**discourteous** /dɪsˈkɜtiəs/, *adj.* lacking courtesy; impolite; uncivil; rude. – **discourteously,** *adv.* – **discourteousness,** *n.*

**discourtesy** /dɪsˈkɜtəsi/, *n., pl.* **-sies.** **1.** lack or breach of courtesy; incivility; rudeness. **2.** a discourteous or impolite act.

**discover** /dəsˈkʌvə/, *v.t.* **1.** to get knowledge of, learn of, or find out; gain sight or knowledge of (something previously unseen or unknown). **2.** *Archaic.* to act so as to manifest unconsciously or unintentionally; betray. **3.** *Archaic.* to make known; reveal. [ME *discover(en),* from OF *descovrir,* from *des-* DIS-[1] + *covrir* COVER] – **discoverable,** *adj.* – **discoverer,** *n.*

**discovery** /dəsˈkʌvəri/, *n., pl.* **-eries.** **1.** the act of discovering. **2.** something discovered. **3.** *Law.* compulsory disclosure, as of facts or documents.

**discredit** /dɪsˈkrɛdət/, *v.t.* **1.** to injure the credit or reputation of. **2.** to show to be undeserving of credit or belief; destroy confidence in. **3.** to give no credit to; disbelieve: *the report is discredited.* –*n.* **4.** loss or lack of belief, of confidence; disbelief; distrust. **5.** loss or lack of repute or esteem; disrepute. **6.** something that damages a good reputation. [DIS-[1] + CREDIT, *v.*]

**discreditable** /dɪsˈkrɛdətəbəl/, *adj.* such as to bring discredit; disgraceful. – **discreditably,** *adv.*

**discreet** /dəsˈkrit/, *adj.* **1.** wise or judicious in avoiding mistakes or faults; prudent; circumspect; cautious; not rash. **2.** not given to careless talk; restrained. [ME *discret,* from OF, from L *discrētus,* pp., separated] – **discreetly,** *adv.* – **discreetness,** *n.*

**discrepancy** /dɪsˈkrɛpənsi/, *n., pl.* **-cies.** **1.** the state or quality of being discrepant; difference; inconsistency. **2.** an instance of difference or inconsistency. Also, **discrepance.**

**discrepant** /dɪsˈkrɛpənt/, *adj.* differing; disagreeing; discordant; inconsistent. [L *discrepans,* ppr., being discordant] – **discrepantly,** *adv.*

**discrete** /dɪsˈkrit/, *adj.* **1.** detached from others; separate; distinct. **2.** consisting of or characterised by distinct or individual parts; discontinuous. [L *discrētus* separated] – **discretely,** *adv.* – **discreteness,** *n.*

**discretion** /dɪsˈkrɛʃən/, *n.* **1.** power or right of deciding, or of acting according to one's own judgment; freedom of judgment or choice. **2.** the quality of being discreet; discernment of what is judicious or expedient, esp. with reference to one's own actions or speech; prudence. **3. at discretion,** as one wishes or decides.

**discretional** /dɪsˈkrɛʃənəl/, *adj.* →**discretionary.** – **discretionally,** *adv.*

**discretionary** /dɪsˈkrɛʃənri, -ənəri/, *adj.* **1.** subject or left to one's discretion. **2.** of or pertaining to discretion. **3. discretionary trust,** *Law.* one in which the trustees have absolute discretion as to the application of the trust capital and income.

**discretion statement** /dɪsˈkrɛʃən ˌsteɪtmənt/, *n.* (formerly) a sealed statement lodged by a petitioner for a divorce asking the court to exercise its discretion in his or her favour and to grant a divorce notwithstanding his or her own admitted adultery.

**discriminate** /dəsˈkrɪməneɪt/, *v.,* **-nated, -nating;** /dəsˈkrɪmənət/, *adj.* –*v.i.* **1.** to make a distinction, as in favour of or against a person or thing: *to discriminate against a minority.* **2.** to note or observe a difference; distinguish accurately: *to discriminate between things.* **3.** *Electronics.* to extract a desired frequency from unwanted frequency components in a radio signal. –*v.t.* **4.** to make or constitute a distinction in or between; differentiate: *to discriminate one thing from another.* **5.** to note or distinguish as different. **6.** *Electronics.* to extract (a desired frequency) from unwanted frequency components in a radio signal. –*adj.* **7.** marked by discrimination; making nice distinctions. [L *discrimīnātus,* pp., divided, distinguished] – **discriminately,** *adv.* – **discriminator,** *n.*

**discriminating** /dəsˈkrɪməneɪtɪŋ/, *adj.* **1.** differentiating; distinctive. **2.** perceiving differences or distinctions with nicety; possessing discrimination. **3.** differential, as a tariff. – **discriminatingly,** *adv.*

**discrimination** /dəskrɪməˈneɪʃən/, *n.* **1.** the act of discriminating. **2.** the resulting state. **3.** the making of a difference in particular cases, as in favour of or against a person or thing. **4.** the power of making nice distinctions; discriminating judgment. **5.** *Electronics.* the extraction of a desired frequency from a signal containing many frequencies, esp. in radio receivers.

**discriminative** /dəsˈkrɪmənətɪv/, *adj.* **1.** that marks distinction; constituting a difference; characteristic: *the discriminative features of men.* **2.** making distinctions; discriminating. **3.** (of a tariff, etc.) differential. – **discriminatively,** *adv.*

**discriminatory** /dəsˈkrɪmənətəri, -tri/, *adj.* exhibiting prejudice; showing discrimination.

**disc storage** /dɪsk ˈstɔrɪdʒ/, *n.* a method of high-speed bulk storage of computer programs and data, whereby they are stored on a rotating circular plate coated with a magnetic material, as iron oxide.

**discursive** /dɪsˈkɜsɪv/, *adj.* **1.** passing rapidly or irregularly from one subject to another; rambling; digressive. **2.** proceeding by reasoning or argument; not intuitive. – **discursively,** *adv.* – **discursiveness,** *n.* – **discursion,** *n.*

**discus** /ˈdɪskəs/, *n., pl.* **discuses, disci** /ˈdɪsaɪ/. **1.** a circular stone or metal plate for throwing, as among the ancient Greeks and Romans. **2.** a similar object, thrown by modern athletes, usu. made of wood rimmed with metal. **3.** the exercise or competition of throwing it. [L, from Gk *dískos* discus, disc, DISH]

**discuss** /dəsˈkʌs/, *v.t.* **1.** to examine by argument; sift the considerations for and against; debate; talk over. **2.** *Rare.* to try the quality of (food or drink) by consuming. [ME *discusse(n),* from L *discussus,* pp., struck asunder] – **discusser,** *n.* – **discussible, discussable,** *adj.*

**discussant** /dəsˈkʌsənt/, *n.* a person who takes part in a discussion, esp. at a conference.

**discussion** /dəsˈkʌʃən/, *n.* the act of discussing; critical examination by argument; debate.

**disc wheel** /ˈdɪsk wil/, *n.* a spokeless vehicular wheel, esp. on motor cars, having a heavy, circular disc of pressed steel mounted on the hub and supporting the tyre rim on its outer edge.

**disdain** /dɪsˈdeɪn/, *v.t.* **1.** to look upon or treat with contempt; despise; scorn. **2.** to think unworthy of notice, performance, etc.; consider beneath oneself. –*n.* **3.** a feeling of contempt for anything regarded as unworthy; haughty contempt; scorn. [ME *desdaine(n),* from OF *desdeignier,* from *des-* DIS-[1] + *deignier* DEIGN]

**disdainful** /dɪsˈdeɪnfəl/, *adj.* full of or showing disdain; scornful. – **disdainfully,** *adv.* – **disdainfulness,** *n.*

**disease** /dəˈziz/; /dɪsˈiz/ *for def. 4, n.*; /dəˈziz/, *v.* **-seased, -seasing.** –*n.* **1.** a morbid condition of the body, or of some organ or part; illness; sickness; ailment. **2.** a similar disorder in plants. **3.** any deranged or depraved condition, as of the mind, affairs, etc. **4.** uneasiness; anxiety. –*v.t.* **5.** to affect with disease; make ill. [ME *disese,* from OF *desaise,* from *des-* DIS-[1] + *aise* EASE]

**diseconomy** /dɪsəˈkɒnəmi/, *n.* **1.** the lack of economy; a faulty economy. **2. diseconomies of scale,** a situation where a manufacturer finds that any increase in his capital outlay in plant and machinery results in higher costs per unit of production.

**disembark** /dɪsəmˈbak/, *v.t.* **1.** to put on shore from a ship;

land. *–v.i.* **2.** to go on shore; land. – **disembarkation** /dɪsˌɛmbaˈkeɪʃən/, *n.*

**disembarrass** /dɪsəmˈbærəs/, *v.t.* **1.** to free from embarrassment. **2.** to relieve; rid. **3.** to disentangle; extricate. – **disembarrassment,** *n.*

**disembody** /dɪsəmˈbɒdi/, *v.t.,* **-bodied, -bodying.** to divest (a soul, etc.) of the body: *disembodied spirit.* – **disembodiment,** *n.*

**disembogue** /dɪsəmˈboʊg/, *v.,* **-bogued, -boguing.** *–v.i.* **1.** to empty or discharge by pouring forth the contents. **2.** (of a river, stream, etc.) to flow out or discharge at the mouth. **3.** *Geol.* to debouch. *–v.t.* **4.** to discharge; cast forth. [Sp. *desembocar,* from *des-* DIS-[1] + *embocar* enter by the mouth, from *en-* in- + *boca* mouth (from L *bucca* cheek)] – **disemboguement,** *n.*

**disembowel** /dɪsəmˈbaʊəl/, *v.t.,* **-elled, -elling** or (*U.S.*) **-eled, -eling.** to remove the bowels or entrails from; eviscerate. – **disembowelment,** *n.*

**disembroil** /dɪsəmˈbrɔɪl/, *v.t.* to free from embroilment, entanglement, or confusion.

**disenable** /dɪsəˈneɪbəl/, *v.t.,* **-bled, -bling.** to deprive of ability; make unable; prevent.

**disenchant** /dɪsənˈtʃænt/, *v.t.* to free from enchantment; disillusion. – **disenchanter,** *n.* – **disenchantment,** *n.*

**disencumber** /dɪsənˈkʌmbə/, *v.t.* to free from encumbrance; disburden.

**disenfranchise** /dɪsənˈfræntʃaɪz/, *v.t.,* **-chised, -chising.** →**disfranchise.** – **disenfranchisement** /dɪsənˈfræntʃəzmənt/, *n.*

**disengage** /dɪsənˈgeɪdʒ/, *v.,* **-gaged, -gaging.** *–v.t.* **1.** to release from attachment or connection; loosen; unfasten. **2.** to free from engagement, pledge, obligation, etc. **3.** to break off action with (an enemy). *–v.i.* **4.** to become disengaged; free oneself.

**disengagement** /dɪsənˈgeɪdʒmənt/, *n.* **1.** the act or process of disengaging, or state of being disengaged. **2.** freedom from obligation or occupation; leisure.

**disentail** /dɪsənˈteɪl/, *v.t.* to free (an estate) from entail. – **disentailment,** *n.*

**disentangle** /dɪsənˈtæŋgəl/, *v.,* **-gled, -gling.** *–v.t.* **1.** to free from entanglement; untangle; extricate (fol. by *from*). *–v.i.* **2.** to become free from entanglement. – **disentanglement,** *n.*

**disentitle** /dɪsənˈtaɪtl/, *v.t.,* **-tled, -tling.** to deprive of title or right.

**disentomb** /dɪsənˈtum/, *v.t.* to take from the tomb; disinter. – **disentombment,** *n.*

**disentrance** /dɪsənˈtræns/, *v.t.,* **-tranced, -trancing.** to bring out of an entranced condition. – **disentrancement,** *n.*

**disentwine** /dɪsənˈtwaɪn/, *v.t., v.i.,* **-twined, -twining.** to bring or come out of an entwined or intertwined state; untwine.

**disepalous** /daɪˈsɛpələs/, *adj.* having two sepals.

**disestablish** /dɪsəsˈtæblɪʃ/, *v.t.* **1.** to deprive of the character of being established. **2.** to withdraw exclusive state recognition or support from (a church). – **disestablishment,** *n.*

**disestablishmentarian** /ˌdɪsəsˌtæblɪʃmənˈtɛəriən/, *n.* **1.** one who favours the disestablishment of the state church. *–adj.* **2.** of, pertaining to, or in favour of the disestablishment of the state church. – **disestablishmentarianism,** *n.*

**disesteem** /dɪsəˈstim/, *v.t.* **1.** to hold in low esteem; think slightingly of. *–n.* **2.** lack of esteem; disregard.

**disfavour** /dɪsˈfeɪvə/, *n.* **1.** unfavourable regard; displeasure; disesteem: *the minister incurred the king's disfavour.* **2.** lack of favour; state of being regarded unfavourably: *in disfavour at court.* **3.** an act of disregard, dislike, or unkindness: *to dispense disfavours.* *–v.t.* **4.** to regard or treat with disfavour. Also, *U.S.,* **disfavor.**

**disfeature** /dɪsˈfitʃə/, *v.t.,* **-tured, -turing.** to mar the features of; disfigure. – **disfeaturement,** *n.*

**disfigure** /dɪsˈfɪgə/, *v.t.,* **-ured, -uring.** **1.** to mar the figure, appearance, or beauty of; deform; deface. **2.** to mar the effect or excellence of. [ME *disfigure(n),* from OF *desfigurer,* from *des-* DIS-[1] + *figurer,* from *figure* FIGURE, *n.*] – **disfigurer,** *n.*

**disfigurement** /dɪsˈfɪgəmənt/, *n.* **1.** the act of disfiguring. **2.** disfigured condition. **3.** something that disfigures. Also, **disfiguration** /dɪsˌfɪgjəˈreɪʃən/.

**disforest** /dɪsˈfɒrəst/, *v.t.* →**disafforest.** – **disforestation** /dɪsˌfɒrəsˈteɪʃən/, *n.*

**disfranchise** /dɪsˈfræntʃaɪz/, *v.t.,* **-chised, -chising.** **1.** to deprive (persons) of rights of citizenship, as of the right to vote. **2.** to deprive of a franchise, privilege, or right. – **disfranchisement** /dɪsˈfræntʃəzmənt, ˌdɪsfrænˈtʃaɪzmənt/, *n.*

**disfrock** /dɪsˈfrɒk/, *v.t.* →**unfrock.**

**disfurnish** /dɪsˈfɜnɪʃ/, *v.t.* to deprive of something with which a person or thing is furnished; strip. – **disfurnishment,** *n.*

**disgorge** /dɪsˈgɔdʒ/, *v.,* **-gorged, -gorging.** *–v.t.* **1.** to eject or throw out from or as from the gorge or throat; to vomit; discharge. **2.** to give up unwillingly. *–v.i.* **3.** to disgorge something. [late ME, from OF *desgorger,* from *des-* DIS-[1] + *gorge* throat] – **disgorgement,** *n.* – **disgorger,** *n.*

**disgrace** /dəsˈgreɪs/, *n., v.,* **-graced, -gracing.** *–n.* **1.** the state of being in dishonour; ignominy; shame. **2.** a cause of shame or reproach; that which dishonours. **3.** the state of being out of favour; exclusion from favour, confidence, or trust. *–v.t.* **4.** to bring or reflect shame or reproach upon. **5.** to dismiss with discredit; put out of grace or favour; treat with disfavour. [F, from It. *disgrazia.* See DIS-[1], GRACE] – **disgracer,** *n.*

**disgraceful** /dəsˈgreɪsfəl/, *adj.* bringing or deserving disgrace; shameful; dishonourable; disreputable. – **disgracefully,** *adv.* – **disgracefulness,** *n.*

**disgruntle** /dɪsˈgrʌntl/, *v.t.,* **-tled, -tling.** to put into a state of sulky dissatisfaction; make discontented. [DIS-[1] + *gruntle* complain, frequentative of GRUNT] – **disgruntlement,** *n.*

**disgruntled** /dɪsˈgrʌntld/, *v.* **1.** past tense and past participle of **disgruntle.** *–adj.* **2.** mildly upset; discontented.

**disguise** /dəsˈgaɪz/, *v.,* **-guised, -guising,** *n.* *–v.t.* **1.** to change the guise or appearance of, so as to conceal identity or to mislead; conceal the identity of by means of a misleading garb, etc. **2.** to conceal or cover up the real state or character of by a counterfeit form or appearance; misrepresent: *to disguise one's intentions.* *–n.* **3.** that which disguises; something that serves or is intended for concealment of identity, character, or quality; a deceptive covering, condition, manner, etc. **4.** the make-up, mask or costume of an entertainer. **5.** the act of disguising. **6.** the state of being disguised. [ME *desgise(n),* from OF *desguiser,* from *des-* DIS-[1] + *guise* GUISE] – **disguisable,** *adj.* – **disguisedly,** *adv.* – **disguiser,** *n.*

**disgust** /dəsˈgʌst/, *v.t.* **1.** to cause nausea or loathing in. **2.** to offend the good taste, moral sense, etc., of; cause aversion or impatient dissatisfaction in. *–n.* **3.** strong distaste; nausea; loathing. **4.** repugnance caused by something offensive; strong aversion; impatient dissatisfaction. [MF *desgouster,* from *des-* DIS-[1] + *gouster* taste, relish] – **disgustedly,** *adv.*

**disgustful** /dəsˈgʌstfəl/, *adj.* *Archaic.* causing disgust; nauseous; offensive. – **disgustfully,** *adv.*

**disgusting** /dəsˈgʌstɪŋ/, *adj.* causing disgust; offensive to the physical, moral, or aesthetic taste. – **disgustingly,** *adv.*

**dish** /dɪʃ/, *n.* **1.** an open, more or less shallow container of pottery, glass, metal, wood, etc., used for various purposes, esp. for holding or serving food. **2.** that which is served or contained in a dish. **3.** a particular article or preparation of food. **4.** as much as a dish will hold; a dishful. **5.** anything like a dish in form or use. **6.** concave state, or the degree of concavity, as of a wheel. **7.** *Colloq.* an attractive girl or man. *–v.t.* **8.** to put into or serve in a dish, as food (oft. fol. by *up*): *to dish up food.* **9.** to fashion like a dish; make concave. **10.** *Colloq.* to defeat; frustrate; cheat, (oft. fol. by *up*). **11.** to abandon; discard; sack. **12. dish out,** to distribute; share out. [ME; OE *disc* dish, plate, bowl (cf. G *Tisch* table), from L *discus* dish, DISCUS]

**dishabille** /dɪsəˈbil/, *n.* **1.** the state of being undressed, partly dressed, or dressed negligently or carelessly. **2.** a garment worn in undress. **3.** a loose morning dress. [from F *déshabillé,* properly pp. of *déshabiller* undress, from *dés-* DIS-[1] + *habiller* dress]

**dishallow** /dɪsˈhæloʊ/, *v.t.* to profane; desecrate.

**disharmonious** /dɪshaˈmoʊniəs/, *adj.* inharmonious; discordant.

**disharmonise** /dɪsˈhamənaɪz/, *v.,* **-nised, -nising.** *–v.t.* **1.** to cause disharmony. *–v.i.* **2.** to be inharmonious. Also, **disharmonize.**

**disharmony** /dɪsˈhaməni/, *n., pl.* **-nies.** discord; lack of harmony between persons or things.

**dishcloth** /ˈdɪʃklɒθ/, *n.* a cloth for use in washing dishes. Also, **dishrag.**

**dishcloth gourd** /ˈ– gʊəd/, *n.* →**loofah.**

**dishearten** /dɪsˈhatn/, *v.t.* to depress the spirits of; discourage. – **dishearteningly,** *adv.* – **disheartenment,** *n.*

**dished** /dɪʃt/, *adj.* **1.** concave: *a dished face.* **2.** *Colloq.* defeated; frustrated; cheated. **3.** (of parallel wheels) farther apart at the top than at the bottom.

**dishelm** /dɪsˈhɛlm/, *Archaic.* –*v.t.* **1.** to divest of the helmet. –*v.i.* **2.** to take off one's helmet.

**dishevel** /dɪˈʃɛvəl/, *v.t.,* **-elled, -elling.** or (*U.S.*) **-eled, -eling.** to let down (the hair); let hang in loose disorder. [ME *dischevelen,* from OF *descheveler,* from *des-* DIS-[1] + *chevel* hair (from L *capillus*)] – **dishevelment,** *n.*

**dishevelled** /dɪˈʃɛvəld/, *adj.* **1.** hanging loosely or in disorder; unkempt: *dishevelled hair.* **2.** untidy; disarranged: *dishevelled appearance.* Also, *U.S.* **disheveled.**

**dishful** /ˈdɪʃfʊl/, *n.* the amount contained in a dish.

**dishonest** /dɪsˈɒnəst/, *adj.* **1.** not honest; disposed to lie, cheat, or steal: *a dishonest person.* **2.** proceeding from or exhibiting lack of honesty; fraudulent. – **dishonestly,** *adv.*

**dishonesty** /dɪsˈɒnəsti/, *n., pl.* **-ties. 1.** lack of honesty; a disposition to lie, cheat, or steal. **2.** a dishonest act as a fraud or theft.

**dishonour** /dɪsˈɒnə/, *n.* **1.** lack of honour; dishonourable character or conduct. **2.** disgrace; ignominy; shame. **3.** an indignity; insult. **4.** a cause of shame; a disgrace. **5.** failure or refusal of the drawee or acceptor of a bill of exchange or cheque to accept it, or, if it is accepted, to honour his liability by payment. –*v.t.* **6.** to deprive of honour; disgrace; bring reproach or shame on. **7.** to fail or refuse to honour (a draft, etc.) by payment. Also, *U.S.,* **dishonor.** [ME *dishonour,* from OF *deshonor,* from *des-* DIS-[1] + *honor* honour (from L)] – **dishonourer,** *n.*

**dishonourable** /dɪsˈɒnrəbəl, -ərəbəl/, *adj.* **1.** showing lack of honour; ignoble; base; disgraceful; shameful: *a dishonourable act.* **2.** having no honour or good repute: *a dishonourable man.* Also, *U.S.,* **dishonorable.** – **dishonourableness,** *n.* – **dishonourably,** *adv.*

**dish rack** /ˈdɪʃ ræk/, *n.* a rack for holding plates and other crockery, esp. for draining after washing.

**dishrag** /ˈdɪʃræg/, *n.* →**dishcloth.**

**dishwasher** /ˈdɪʃwɒʃə/, *n.* **1.** one who washes dishes, plates, etc. **2.** an electric machine which automatically washes and sometimes dries dishes, plates, etc.

**dishwater** /ˈdɪʃwɔtə/, *n.* **1.** water in which dishes are, or have been, washed. **2.** *Colloq.* any weak drink. **3. dull as dishwater,** *Colloq.* very boring.

**dishy** /ˈdɪʃi/, *adj. Colloq.* (of persons or things) attractive.

**disillusion** /dɪsəˈluʒən/, *v.t.* **1.** to free from illusion; disenchant. –*n.* **2.** a freeing or a being freed from illusion; disenchantment. – **disillusionment,** *n.* – **disillusive** /dɪsəˈlusɪv/, *adj.*

**disimpassioned** /dɪsɪmˈpæʃənd/, *adj.* calm; dispassionate; passionless.

**disincentive** /ˌdɪsɪnˈsɛntɪv/, *n.* **1.** anything that deters from action, etc. –*adj.* **2.** discouraging, as from action; disheartening.

**disinclination** /ˌdɪsɪnkləˈneɪʃən/, *n.* the absence of inclination; averseness; distaste; unwillingness.

**disincline** /ˌdɪsɪnˈklaɪn/, *v.,* **-clined, -clining.** –*v.t.* **1.** to make averse. –*v.i.* **2.** to be averse or indisposed.

**disinfect** /ˌdɪsɪnˈfɛkt/, *v.t.* to cleanse (rooms, clothing, etc.) from infection; destroy disease germs in. – **disinfector,** *n.*

**disinfectant** /dɪsənˈfɛktənt/, *n.* **1.** any chemical agent that destroys bacteria. –*adj.* **2.** disinfecting.

**disinfection** /ˌdɪsɪnˈfɛkʃən/, *n.* the process of disinfecting.

**disinfest** /ˌdɪsɪnˈfɛst/, *v.t.* to rid of vermin, esp. lice or rats. – **disinfestation** /dɪsɪnˌfɛsˈteɪʃən/, *n.*

**disinflation** /ˌdɪsɪnˈfleɪʃən/, *n.* a reduction of prices generally with attendant increase in the purchasing power of money.

**disingenuous** /ˌdɪsɪnˈdʒɛnjuəs/, *adj.* not ingenuous; lacking in frankness, candour, or sincerity; insincere: *disingenuous persons.* – **disingenuously,** *adv.* – **disingenuousness,** *n.*

**disinherit** /ˌdɪsɪnˈhɛrət/, *v.t.* **1.** to exclude from inheritance (an heir or a next of kin). **2.** to deprive of the right to inherit. – **disinheritance,** *n.*

**disintegrate** /dɪsˈɪntəgreɪt/, *v.,* **-grated, -grating.** –*v.t.* **1.** to reduce to particles, fragments, or parts; break up or destroy the cohesion of: *rocks are disintegrated by frost and rain.* –*v.i.* **2.** to separate into its component parts; break up. **3.** (of a person) to lose one's judgment, memory, mental grasp, etc., as through senility. – **disintegrable** /dɪsˈɪntəgrəbəl/, *adj.* – **disintegration** /dɪsˌɪntəˈgreɪʃən/, *n.* – **disintegrator,** *n.*

**disinter** /dɪsɪnˈtɜ/, *v.t.,* **-terred, -terring. 1.** to take out of the place of interment; exhume; unearth. **2.** to bring from obscurity into view. – **disinterment,** *n.*

**disinterest** /dɪsˈɪntərəst, -trəst/, *n.* **1.** absence of personal involvement or bias. –*v.t.* **2.** to divest of interest or concern.

**disinterested** /dɪsˈɪntrəstəd/, *adj.* **1.** unbiased by personal involvement or advantage; not influenced by selfish motives. **2.** *Colloq.* uninterested. – **disinterestedly,** *adv.* – **disinterestedness,** *n.*

**disject** /dɪsˈdʒɛkt/, *v.t.* to cast asunder; scatter; disperse. [L *disjectus,* pp., thrown asunder]

**disjoin** /dɪsˈdʒɔɪn/, *v.t.* **1.** to undo or prevent the junction or union of; disunite; separate. –*v.i.* **2.** to become disunited; separate. [ME *desjoyne(n),* from OF *desjoindre,* from L *disjungere*]

**disjoint** /dɪsˈdʒɔɪnt/, *v.t.* **1.** to separate or disconnect the joints or joinings of. **2.** to put out of order; derange. –*v.i.* **3.** to come apart. **4.** to be dislocated; to put out of joint. –*adj.* **5.** *Maths.* (of two sets) having no elements in common. [OF *desjoint,* pp. of *desjoindre,* from L *disjungere*]

**disjointed** /dɪsˈdʒɔɪntəd/, *adj.* **1.** having the joints or connections separated: *a disjointed fowl.* **2.** disconnected; incoherent: *a disjointed discourse.* – **disjointedly,** *adv.* – **disjointedness,** *n.*

**disjunct** /dɪsˈdʒʌŋkt/, *adj.* **1.** disjointed; separated. **2.** *Music.* progressing melodically by intervals larger than a second. **3.** *Entomol.* having the head, thorax, and abdomen separated by deep constrictions. [L *disjunctus,* pp., disjoined]

**disjunction** /dɪsˈdʒʌŋkʃən/, *n.* **1.** the act of disjoining. **2.** the state of being disjoined. **3.** *Logic.* **a.** the relation of the terms of a complex proposition where alternatives are in juxtaposition, as p or q or both (inclusive), p or q but not both (exclusive). **b.** the statement of such a proposition. **c.** a set of alternative possibilities.

**disjunctive** /dɪsˈdʒʌŋktɪv/, *adj.* **1.** serving or tending to disjoin; separating; dividing; distinguishing. **2.** *Gram.* **a.** syntactically setting two or more expressions in opposition to each other, as *but* in *poor but happy,* or expressing an alternative, as *or* in *this or that.* **b.** not syntactically dependent upon some particular expression. **3.** *Logic.* characterising propositions which are disjunctions. –*n.* **4.** a statement, etc., involving alternatives. **5.** *Gram.* a disjunctive word. – **disjunctively,** *adv.*

**disjuncture** /dɪsˈdʒʌŋktʃə/, *n.* **1.** the act of disjoining. **2.** the state of being disjoined.

**disk** /dɪsk/, *n.* →**disc.**

**dislike** /dɪsˈlaɪk/, *v.,* **-liked, -liking,** *n.* –*v.t.* **1.** not to like; regard with displeasure or aversion: *I dislike him, I dislike having to work.* –*n.* **2.** the feeling of disliking; distaste: *I have taken a strong dislike to him.* – **dislikeable,** *adj.*

**dislocate** /ˈdɪsləkeɪt/, *v.t.,* **-cated, -cating. 1.** to put out of place; displace; put out of proper relative position. **2.** to put out of joint or out of position, as a limb or an organ. **3.** to throw out of order; derange; upset; disorder. [ML *dislocātus,* pp. of *dislocāre,* from L *dis-* DIS-[1] + *locāre* place]

**dislocation** /dɪsləˈkeɪʃən/, *n.* **1.** the act of dislocating. **2.** the state of being dislocated. **3.** a dislocated joint. **4.** *Geol.* a fault. **5.** *Crystall.* a plane defect in a crystal.

**dislodge** /dɪsˈlɒdʒ/, *v.,* **-lodged, -lodging.** –*v.t.* **1.** to remove or drive from a place of rest or lodgment; drive from a position occupied. –*v.i.* **2.** to go from a place of lodgment. – **dislodgment,** *n.*

**disloyal** /dɪsˈlɔɪəl/, *adj.* not loyal; false to one's obligations or allegiance; faithless; treacherous. [OF *desloial,* from *des-* DIS-[1] + *loial* law-abiding (from L *lēgālis*)] – **disloyally,** *adv.*

**disloyalty** /dɪsˈlɔɪəlti/, *n., pl.* **-ties. 1.** the quality of being disloyal; unfaithfulness. **2.** violation of allegiance or duty, as to a government. **3.** a disloyal act.

**dismal** /'dɪzməl/, *adj.* **1.** causing gloom or dejection; gloomy; dreary; cheerless; melancholy. **2.** terrible; dreadful. *–n.* **3.** (*usu. pl.*) *Colloq.* gloom; melancholy; dumps: *in the dismals.* **4.** something dismal. [ME *dismall;* orig. uncert.] **– dismally,** *adv.* **– dismalness,** *n.*

**dismantle** /dɪs'mæntl/, *v.t.,* **-tled, -tling. 1.** to deprive or strip of apparatus, furniture, equipments, defences, etc.: *to dismantle a ship or a fortress.* **2.** to pull down; take apart; take to pieces. **3.** to divest of dress, covering, etc. [F (obs.) *desmanteler.* See DIS-¹, MANTLE] **– dismantlement,** *n.*

**dismast** /dɪs'mast/, *v.t.* to deprive of masts; break off the masts of. **– dismastment,** *n.*

**dismay** /dɪs'meɪ/, *v.t.* **1.** to break down the courage of utterly, as by sudden danger or trouble; dishearten utterly; daunt. **2.** to cause to feel strong displeasure or disappointment. *–n.* **3.** sudden or complete loss of courage; utter disheartenment. **4.** disappointment; consternation. [ME *desmaien,* probably from OF; cf. OF *esmaier* dismay]

**dismember** /dɪs'mɛmbə/, *v.t.* **1.** to deprive of members or limbs; divide limb from limb. **2.** to separate into parts; divide and distribute the parts of (a kingdom, etc.). [ME *dismembre(n),* from OF *desmembrer,* from *des-* DIS-¹ + *membre* MEMBER] **– dismemberer,** *n.* **– dismemberment,** *n.*

**dismiss** /dɪs'mɪs/, *v.t.* **1.** to direct or allow (an assembly of persons, etc.) to disperse. **2.** to bid or allow (a person) to go; give permission to depart. **3.** to send forth (a thing); let go. **4.** to discharge or remove, as from office or service. **5.** *Cricket.* **a.** (of a bowler) to cause a batsman to conclude his innings by clean-bowling him, having him caught out, etc. **b.** (of a team) to cause the opposing team to conclude their innings. **6.** to discard or reject. **7.** to put off or away; lay aside, esp. to put aside from consideration. **8.** to have done with (a subject) after summary treatment. **9.** *Law.* to put out of court, as a complaint or appeal. *–n.* **10.** *Mil.* a command for soldiers to drop out of their ranks and disperse. [ML *dismissus,* pp., sent away, for L *dīmissus*] **– dismissible,** *adj.*

**dismissal** /dɪs'mɪsəl/, *n.* **1.** the act of dismissing. **2.** state of being dismissed. **3.** a spoken or written order of discharge. Also, **dismission** /dɪs'mɪʃən/.

**dismissive** /dɪs'mɪsɪv/, *adj.* **1.** expressing dismissal, disregard, or rejection. **2.** expressing contempt. Also, **dismissory.**

**dismount** /dɪs'maʊnt/, *v.i.* **1.** to get off or alight from a horse, bicycle, etc. *–v.t.* **2.** to bring or throw down, as from a horse; unhorse. **3.** to remove (a thing) from its mounting, support, setting, etc. **4.** to take (a piece of mechanism) to pieces. *–n.* **5.** the act or manner of dismounting. **– dismountable,** *adj.*

**dismounted drill** /dɪs,maʊntəd 'drɪl/, *n.* drill (def. 2) performed by infantry.

**disnature** /dɪs'neɪtʃə/, *v.t.,* **-tured, -turing.** to deprive of its proper nature; make unnatural.

**disobedience** /dɪsə'bidiəns/, *n.* lack of obedience; neglect or refusal to obey.

**disobedient** /dɪsə'bidiənt/, *adj.* neglecting or refusing to obey; refractory. **– disobediently,** *adv.*

**disobey** /dɪsə'beɪ/, *v.t.* **1.** to neglect or refuse to obey (an order, person, etc.). *–v.i.* **2.** to be disobedient. [ME *disobey(en),* from OF *desobeir,* from *des-* DIS-¹ + *obeir* OBEY] **– disobeyer,** *n.*

**disoblige** /dɪsə'blaɪdʒ/, *v.t.,* **-bliged, -bliging. 1.** to refuse or neglect to oblige; act contrary to the desire or convenience of; fail to accommodate. **2.** to give offence to; affront. **– disobliging,** *adj.* **– disobligingly,** *adv.* **– disobligingness,** *n.*

**disodium cromoglycate** /daɪ,soʊdiəm kroʊmoʊ'glaɪkeɪt/, *n.* →**Intal.**

**disoperation** /dɪsɒpə'reɪʃən/, *n.* the conscious or unconscious behaviour of organisms living together and producing a result which is disadvantageous or harmful to the organisms concerned.

**disorder** /dɪs'ɔdə/, *n.* **1.** lack of order or regular arrangement; disarrangement; confusion. **2.** an irregularity. **3.** breach of order; disorderly conduct; a public disturbance. **4.** a derangement of physical or mental health or functions. *–v.t.* **5.** to destroy the order or regular arrangement of; disarrange. **6.** to derange the physical or mental health or functions of.

**disordered** /dɪs'ɔdəd/, *adj.* **1.** in confusion. **2.** mentally ill.

**disorderly** /dɪs'ɔdəli/, *adj.* **1.** characterised by disorder; irregular; untidy; confused. **2.** unruly; turbulent; tumultuous. **3.** *Law.* violating, or opposed to, constituted order; contrary to public order or morality. *–adv.* **4.** without order, rule, or method; irregularly; confusedly. **– disorderliness,** *n.*

**disorderly conduct** /– 'kɒndʌkt/, *n.* any of various petty disdemeanours, generally including nuisances, breaches of the peace, offensive or immoral conduct in public, etc.

**disorderly house** /– 'haʊs/, *n.* **1.** a house of prostitution; brothel. **2.** a gambling place.

**disorderly person** /– 'pɜsən/, *n.* a person guilty of disorderly conduct or of separate offences as loitering in public, vagrancy, etc.

**disorganisation** /dɪs,ɔgənaɪ'zeɪʃən/, *n.* **1.** a breaking up of order or system; disunion or disruption of constituent parts. **2.** the absence of organisation or orderly arrangement; disarrangement; disorder. Also, **disorganization.**

**disorganise** /dɪs'ɔgənaɪz/, *v.t.* **-nised, -nising.** to destroy the organisation, systematic arrangement, or orderly connection of; throw into confusion or disorder. Also, **disorganize.** **– disorganiser,** *n.*

**disorientate** /dɪs'ɒriənteɪt/, *v.t.,* **-tated, -tating. 1.** to confuse as to direction. **2.** to turn away from east. **3.** to perplex; to confuse. Also, **disorient.** **– disorientation** /dɪs,ɒriən'teɪʃən/, *n.*

**disown** /dɪs'oʊn/, *v.t.* to refuse to acknowledge as belonging or pertaining to oneself; deny the ownership of or responsibility for; repudiate; renounce. **– disowner,** *n.* **– disownment,** *n.*

**disp.,** dispensed.

**disparage** /dəs'pærɪdʒ/, *v.t.,* **-raged, -raging. 1.** to bring reproach or discredit upon; lower the estimation of. **2.** to speak of or treat slightingly; depreciate; belittle. [ME *desparage(n),* from OF *desparagier* match unequally, from *des-* DIS-¹ + *parage* equality, from *parer* equalise (from L *pariāre*)] **– disparager,** *n.* **– disparagingly,** *adv.*

**disparagement** /dəs'pærɪdʒmənt/, *n.* **1.** the act of disparaging. **2.** something that causes loss of dignity or reputation.

**disparate** /'dɪspərət/, *adj.* distinct in kind; essentially different; dissimilar; unlike; having no common genus. [L *disparātus,* pp., separated] **– disparately,** *adv.* **– disparateness,** *n.*

**disparity** /dɪs'pærəti/, *n., pl.* **-ties.** lack of similarity or equality; inequality; difference: *a disparity in age, rank, condition, etc.*

**dispassion** /dɪs'pæʃən/, *n.* freedom from passion; unemotional state or quality.

**dispassionate** /dɪs'pæʃənət/, *adj.* free from or unaffected by passion; devoid of personal feeling or bias; impartial; calm: *a dispassionate critic.* **– dispassionately,** *adv.* **– dispassionateness,** *n.*

**dispatch** /dəs'pætʃ/, *v.t.* **1.** to send off; put under way: *to dispatch a messenger, telegram, etc.* **2.** to put to death; kill. **3.** to transact or dispose of (business, etc.) promptly or speedily; execute quickly; settle. *–v.i.* **4.** *Archaic.* to hasten; be quick. **5.** *Obs.* to settle a matter. *–n.* **6.** the sending off of a messenger, letter, etc., to a destination. **7.** a putting to death; killing. **8.** prompt or speedy transaction, as of business. **9.** expeditious performance, promptitude, or speed: *proceed with all possible dispatch.* **10. a.** a method of effecting a speedy delivery of goods. **b.** a conveyance or organisation for the expeditious transmission of merchandise, etc. **11.** a written message sent in haste. **12.** a state paper as a diplomatic or military communication, sent by special messenger. **13. mentioned in dispatches,** named in military reports for special bravery or acts of service. **14.** a news account transmitted by a reporter to his newspaper or other agency. **15.** a telegram. Also, **despatch.** [It. *dispacciare* hasten, speed, or from Sp. *despachar*] **– dispatcher,** *n.*

**dispatch box** /'– bɒks/, *n.* a sealed and locked box in which confidential government papers are carried by special messengers.

**dispatch case** /'– keɪs/, *n.* →**briefcase.**

**dispatch note** /'– noʊt/, *n. Chiefly Brit.* **1.** a notification sent in advance of a parcel to notify the recipient of its pending arrival. **2.** a document attached to a parcel to be sent abroad, containing details of the contents.

**dispatch rider** /'– raɪdə/, *n.* an official messenger, esp. military, who carries dispatches by motorcycle.

**dispel** /dɪsˈpɛl/, *v.*, **-pelled, -pelling.** *–v.t.* **1.** to drive off in various directions; scatter; disperse; dissipate: *to dispel vapours, fear, etc.* *–v.i.* **2.** to be scattered; melt away. [L *dispellere* drive asunder] – **dispeller,** *n.*

**dispend** /dɪsˈpɛnd/, *v.t. Archaic.* to pay out; expend; spend. [ME *despende(n)*, from OF *despendre*, from L *dispendere* weigh out]

**dispensable** /dɪsˈpɛnsəbəl/, *adj.* **1.** that may be dispensed with or done without; unimportant. **2.** capable of being dispensed or administered. **3.** admitting of dispensation, as an offence or a sin. **4.** that may be declared not binding. – **dispensability** /dɪspɛnsəˈbɪləti/, *n.*

**dispensary** /dɪsˈpɛnsəri, -sri/, *n., pl.* **-saries.** **1.** a place where something is dispensed, esp. medicines. **2.** a charitable or public institution where medicines are furnished and medical advice is given gratuitously or for a small fee.

**dispensation** /ˌdɪspɛnˈseɪʃən/, *n.* **1.** the act of dispensing; distribution; administration; management. **2.** that which is distributed or given out. **3.** a certain order, system, or arrangement. **4.** *Theol.* **a.** the divine ordering of the affairs of the world. **b.** an appointment or arrangement, as by God. **c.** a divinely appointed order or system: *the old, Mosaic, or Jewish dispensation; the new, gospel, or Christian dispensation.* **5.** a dispensing with, doing away with, or doing without something. **6.** *Rom. Cath. Ch.* **a.** the relaxation of a law by a competent superior in a specific case directly affecting physical matters. **b.** the document containing this. – **dispensational,** *adj.*

**dispensator** /ˈdɪspɛnˌseɪtə/, *n.* one who dispenses; a distributor; an administrator.

**dispensatory** /dɪsˈpɛnsətəri, -sətri/, *n., pl.* **-ries.** a book in which the composition, preparation, and uses of medicinal substances are described; a non-official pharmacopoeia.

**dispense** /dɪsˈpɛns/, *v.*, **-pensed, -pensing,** *n.* *–v.t.* **1.** to deal out; distribute: *to dispense justice, wisdom, etc.* **2.** to administer (laws, etc.). **3.** *Pharm.* to put up and distribute (medicine), esp. on prescription. **4.** (in some Christian churches) to grant a dispensation to, for, or from. **5.** to administer (the Eucharist): *the sacrament will be dispensed.* *–v.i.* **6.** to grant dispensation. **7. dispense with, a.** to do without; forgo. **b.** to do away with (a need, etc.). **c.** to grant exemption from (a law, promise, etc.). [ME *dispense(n)*, from OF *dispenser*, from L *dispensāre* weigh out, frequentative of L *dispendere*]

**dispenser** /dɪsˈpɛnsə/, *n.* **1.** one who or that which dispenses. **2.** a container that dispenses a certain measure of a commodity, as toothpaste, soap, etc.

**dispermous** /daɪˈspɜməs/, *adj.* two-seeded.

**dispersal** /dəsˈpɜsəl/, *n.* →**dispersion** (defs 1 and 2).

**disperse** /dəsˈpɜs/, *v.*, **-persed, -persing.** *–v.t.* **1.** to scatter abroad; send or drive off in various directions. **2.** to spread; diffuse: *the wise disperse knowledge.* **3.** to dispel; cause to vanish: *the fog is dispersed.* *–v.i.* **4.** to separate and move apart in different directions without order or regularity; become scattered: *the company dispersed at 10 o'clock.* **5.** to be dispelled; be scattered out of sight; vanish. [F *disperser*, from L *dispersus*, pp., scattered] – **dispersedly,** *adv.* – **disperser,** *n.*

**disperse phase** /ˈ– feɪz/, *n.* the suspended particles in a colloidal solution.

**dispersion** /dəsˈpɜʒən, -ʃən/, *n.* **1.** the act of dispersing. **2.** the state of being dispersed. **3.** *Physics.* **a.** the variation of the refractive index (of a medium) with the wavelength of electromagnetic radiation passing through it, as of light in glass or radio waves in the ionosphere. **b.** the separation of light into colours produced by this. **4.** *Statistics.* the scattering of values of a variable round the mean or median of a distribution. **5.** *Chem.* a system of dispersed particles suspended in a fluid. **6.** the scattering of bombs, etc., released under apparently identical conditions.

**dispersion error** /ˈ– ɛrə/, *n.* a measure of the accuracy potential of a firearm based on the largest distance between the centre of impact of a group of shots and the fall of one shot.

**dispersion medium** /ˈ– ˌmidiəm/, *n.* the solvent in a colloidal solution.

**dispersive** /dəsˈpɜsɪv/, *adj.* serving or tending to disperse.

**dispirit** /dɪsˈpɪrət/, *v.t.* to deprive of spirit; depress the spirits of; discourage; dishearten. – **dispirited,** *adj.* – **dispiriting,** *adj.* – **dispiritedly,** *adv.* – **dispiritingly,** *adv.* – **dispiritedness,** *n.*

**dispiteous** /dɪsˈpɪtiəs/, *adj. Archaic.* cruel; pitiless.

**displace** /dɪsˈpleɪs/, *v.t.*, **-placed, -placing.** **1.** to put out of the usual or proper place: *to displace a bone.* **2.** to take the place of; replace. **3.** to remove from a position, office, etc. – **displaceable,** *adj.*

**displaced person** /dɪsˌpleɪst ˈpɜsən/, *n.* a civilian who is involuntarily outside the national boundaries of his country.

**displacement** /dɪsˈpleɪsmənt/, *n.* **1.** the act of displacing. **2.** the state of being displaced. **3.** *Physics.* the displacing or replacing of one thing by another, as of water by something immersed or floating in it. **4.** the weight or the volume of fluid displaced by a floating or submerged body, equivalent to the weight of the floating body or to the volume of the submerged body: *a ship with a displacement of 10 000 tonnes.* **5.** *Mach.* (of a cylinder) the volume swept out by the piston. **6.** *Geol.* offset of rocks due to movement along a fault. **7.** *Psychoanal.* the transfer of an emotion from the object about which it was originally experienced to another object.

**displacement activity** /ˈ– ækˌtɪvəti/, *n. Psychol.* an activity, usu. irrelevant to the situation, by which the focus in an area of psychological conflict can be transferred to something more acceptable to the ego.

**displacement hull** /ˈ– hʌl/, *n.* a hull designed to pass through the water, rather than to skim over the surface.

**displacement ton** /ˈ– tʌn/, *n.* →**ton**[1] (def. 4).

**display** /dɪsˈpleɪ/, *v.t.* **1.** to show; exhibit; make visible: *to display a flag.* **2.** to reveal; betray: *to display fear.* **3.** to unfold; open out; spread out: *to display a sail.* **4.** to show ostentatiously. **5.** *Print.* to give special prominence to (words, etc.) by choice and arrangement of type, etc. *–n.* **6.** the act of displaying; exhibition; show: *a display of goods, skill, etc.* **7.** an ostentatious show: *a vulgar display of wealth.* **8.** a pattern of behaviour used by birds as visual communication, often associated with mating. **9.** *Print.* **a.** the giving of prominence to particular words, etc., by the choice and arrangement of types and position, as in an advertisement, headline, or news story. **b.** printed matter thus displayed. **10.** an electronic system capable of representing information visibly, as on a cathode ray tube. [ME *desplay(en)*, from OF *despleier, desploier* DEPLOY] – **displayer,** *n.*

**display van** /ˈ– væn/, *n.* a railway carriage fitted with visual displays showing aspects of railway facilities, usu. sent to country depots.

**displease** /dɪsˈpliz/, *v.*, **-pleased, -pleasing.** *–v.t.* **1.** to cause dissatisfaction to; offend; annoy. *–v.i.* **2.** to be unpleasant; cause displeasure. – **displeasingly,** *adv.*

**displeasure** /dɪsˈplɛʒə/, *n., v.*, **-ured, -uring.** *–n.* **1.** dissatisfaction; annoyance; anger. **2.** *Archaic.* discomfort, uneasiness, or pain. **3.** *Archaic.* a cause of offence, annoyance, or injury. *–v.t.* **4.** *Archaic.* to displease.

**disport** /dɪsˈpɔt/, *v.t.* **1.** to divert or amuse (oneself); exercise or display (oneself) in a sportive manner. *–v.i.* **2.** to divert oneself; sport. *–n.* **3.** *Archaic.* diversion; amusement; play; sport. [ME *desporte(n)*, from OF *desporter, deporter*, from *des-* DIS-[1], *de-* DE- + *porter* carry (from L *portāre*)]

**disposable** /dəsˈpoʊzəbəl/, *adj.* capable of being disposed of; subject to disposal; inclined.

**disposable income** /–ˈɪŋkʌm/, *n.* that part of a person's income which remains after the deduction of income tax, etc.

**disposal** /dəsˈpoʊzəl/, *n.* **1.** the act of disposing, or of disposing of, something; arrangement. **2.** a disposing of as by gift or sale; bestowal or assignment. **3.** power or right to dispose of a thing; control: *left to his disposal.* **4.** *Aus. Rules.* ability to handpass or kick the ball to a team-mate.

**disposals store** /dəsˈpoʊzəlz stɔ/, *n.* →**army surplus store.** Also, **disposal store.**

**dispose** /dəsˈpoʊz/, *v.*, **-posed, -posing,** *n.* *–v.t.* **1.** to put in a particular or the proper order or arrangement; adjust by arranging the parts. **2.** to put in a particular or suitable place. **3.** to give a tendency or inclination to; incline. *–v.i.* **4.** to arrange or decide matters. **5. dispose of, a.** to deal with definitely; get rid of. **b.** to make over or part with, as by gift or sale. [ME *dispose(n)*, from OF *disposer*, from *dis-*

DIS-[1] + *poser* POSE[1], but associated with L *dispōnere* (cf. DISPOSITION)] – **disposer,** *n.*

**disposed** /dəs'poʊzd/, *adj.* inclined or minded, esp. favourably (usu. fol. by *to* or infinitive).

**disposition** /dɪspə'zɪʃən/, *n.* **1.** mental or moral constitution; turn of mind. **2.** mental inclination; willingness. **3.** physical inclination or tendency. **4.** arrangement, as of troops or buildings. **5.** final settlement of a matter. **6.** *Archaic.* regulation; appointment; dispensation. **7.** bestowal, as by gift or sale. **8.** power to dispose of a thing; control. [L *dispositio*] – **dispositional,** *adj.*

**dispossess** /dɪspə'zɛs/, *v.t.* to put (a person) out of possession, esp. of real property; oust. – **dispossession,** *n.* – **dispossessor,** *n.* – **dispossessory** /dɪspə'zɛsəri/, *adj.*

**disposure** /dəs'poʊʒə/, *n. Rare.* disposal; disposition.

**dispraise** /dɪs'preɪz/, *v.,* **-praised, -praising,** *n.* –*v.t.* **1.** to speak of as undeserving; censure; disparage. –*n.* **2.** act of dispraising; censure. – **dispraiser,** *n.* – **dispraisingly,** *adv.*

**dispread** /dɪs'prɛd/, *v.t., v.i.,* **-spread, -spreading.** *Archaic.* to spread out; extend.

**disprin** /'dɪsprən/, *n.* (*also cap.*) a soluble form of aspirin. [Trademark]

**disprize** /dɪs'praɪz/, *v.t.,* **-prized, -prizing.** *Archaic.* to hold in small esteem; disdain.

**disproof** /dɪs'pruf/, *n.* the act of disproving; proof to the contrary; refutation.

**disproportion** /dɪsprə'pɔʃən/, *n.* **1.** lack of proportion; want of due relation, as in size, number, etc. **2.** something out of proportion. –*v.t.* **3.** to make disproportionate. – **disproportionable,** *adj.* – **disproportionableness,** *n.* – **disproportionably,** *adv.*

**disproportionate** /dɪsprə'pɔʃənət/, *adj.* not proportionate; out of proportion, as in size, number, etc. Also, **disproportional.** – **disproportionately,** *adv.* – **disproportionateness,** *n.*

**disprove** /dɪs'pruv/, *v.t.,* **-proved, -proving.** to prove (an assertion, claim, etc.) to be false or wrong; refute; invalidate. [ME *disprove(n),* from OF *desprover,* from *des-* DIS-[1] + *prover* PROVE] – **disprovable,** *adj.* – **disproval,** *n.*

**disputable** /dɪs'pjutəbəl, 'dɪspjətəbəl/, *adj.* that may be disputed; liable to be called in question; questionable. – **disputability** /dɪs,pjutə'bɪləti/, disputableness, *n.* – **disputably,** *adv.*

**disputant** /dɪs'pjutənt, 'dɪs-/, *adj.* **1.** disputing. –*n.* **2.** one who disputes; a debater.

**disputation** /dɪspju'teɪʃən/, *n.* **1.** the act of disputing or debating; verbal controversy; a discussion or debate. **2.** an academic exercise consisting of the arguing of a thesis between its maintainer and his opponents. **3.** *Obs.* conversation.

**disputatious** /dɪspju'teɪʃəs/, *adj.* given to disputation; argumentative; contentious. Also, **disputative** /dɪs'pjutətɪv/. – **disputatiously,** *adv.* – **disputatiousness,** *n.*

**dispute** /dəs'pjut/, *v.,* **-puted, -puting,** *n.* –*v.i.* **1.** to engage in argument or discussion. **2.** to argue vehemently; wrangle or quarrel. –*v.t.* **3.** to argue or debate about; discuss. **4.** to argue against; call in question. **5.** to quarrel or fight about; contest. **6.** to strive against; oppose: *to dispute an advance.* –*n.* **7.** argumentation; verbal contention; a debate or controversy; a quarrel. [ME, from L *disputāre;* replacing ME *despute(n),* from OF] – **disputer,** *n.*

**disqualification** /dɪs,kwɒləfə'keɪʃən/, *n.* **1.** the act of disqualifying. **2.** the state of being disqualified. **3.** something that disqualifies.

**disqualify** /dɪs'kwɒləfaɪ/, *v.,* **-fied, -fying.** –*v.t.* **1.** to deprive of qualification or fitness; render unfit; incapacitate. **2.** to deprive of legal or other rights or privileges; pronounce unqualified. **3.** *Sport.* to deprive of the right to engage or compete in a match because the rules have been broken.

**disquiet** /dɪs'kwaɪət/, *v.t.* **1.** to deprive of quiet, rest, or peace; disturb; make uneasy. –*n.* **2.** lack of quiet; disturbance; unrest; uneasiness. – **disquietly,** *adv.*

**disquieting** /dɪs'kwaɪətɪŋ/, *adj.* causing disquiet; disturbing.

**disquietude** /dɪs'kwaɪətjud/, *n.* a state of disquiet; uneasiness.

**disquisition** /dɪskwə'zɪʃən/, *n.* a formal discourse or treatise in which a subject is examined and discussed; a dissertation. [L *disquīsītio* inquiry]

**disrate** /dɪs'reɪt/, *v.t.,* **-rated, -rating.** to reduce to a lower rating, as a petty officer, or a non-commissioned officer of marines. Cf. **degrade.**

**disregard** /dɪsrə'gad/, *v.t.* **1.** to pay no attention to; leave out of consideration. **2.** to treat without due regard, respect, or attentiveness. –*n.* **3.** lack of regard or attention; neglect. **4.** lack of due or respectful regard. – **disregarder,** *n.*

**disregardful** /dɪsrə'gadfəl/, *adj.* neglectful; careless.

**disrelish** /dɪs'rɛlɪʃ/, *v.t.* **1.** to have a distaste for; dislike. –*n.* **2.** distaste; dislike.

**disremember** /dɪsrə'mɛmbə/, *Colloq.* –*v.t.* **1.** to forget. –*v.i.* **2.** to fail to remember.

**disrepair** /dɪsrə'pɛə/, *n.* the state of being out of repair; impaired condition.

**disreputable** /dɪs'rɛpjətəbəl/, *adj.* **1.** not reputable; having a bad reputation. **2.** discreditable; dishonourable. – **disreputability** /dɪs,rɛpjətə'bɪləti/, **disreputableness,** *n.* – **disreputably,** *adv.*

**disrepute** /dɪsrə'pjut/, *n.* ill repute; discredit (usu. prec. by *in, into*): *that policy is in disrepute; this would bring the administration of justice into disrepute.* Also, *Archaic,* **disreputation** /dɪs,rɛpjə'teɪʃən/.

**disrespect** /dɪsrə'spɛkt/, *n.* **1.** lack of respect; disesteem; rudeness. –*v.t.* **2.** to regard or treat without respect; regard or treat with contempt or rudeness.

**disrespectable** /dɪsrə'spɛktəbəl/, *adj.* not respectable. – **disrespectability** /dɪsrə,spɛktə'bɪləti/, *n.*

**disrespectful** /dɪsrə'spɛktfəl/, *adj.* characterised by disrespect; having or showing disrespect. – **disrespectfully,** *adv.* – **disrespectfulness,** *n.*

**disrobe** /dɪs'roʊb/, *v.* **-robed, -robing.** –*v.i.* **1.** to undress. –*v.t.* **2.** to undress (someone). **3.** to divest of official robes; remove from office. – **disrobement,** *n.* – **disrober,** *n.*

**disrupt** /dɪs'rʌpt/, *v.t.* **1.** to break or rend asunder. –*v.i.* **2.** to break up. –*adj.* **3.** disrupted; rent asunder. [L *disruptus,* pp.] – **disrupter, disruptor,** *n.*

**disruption** /dɪs'rʌpʃən/, *n.* **1.** forcible separation or division into parts. **2.** a disrupted condition.

**disruptive** /dɪs'rʌptɪv/, *adj.* disrupting; pertaining to disruption.

**disruptive discharge** /– 'dɪstʃadʒ/, *n.* the sudden and large increase in current through an insulating medium due to complete failure of the medium under electrostatic stress.

**diss.,** **1.** dissertation. **2.** dissolved.

**dissatisfaction** /,dɪssætəs'fækʃən/, *n.* lack of satisfaction; state of not being satisfied.

**dissatisfactory** /,dɪssætəs'fæktri, -əri/, *adj.* causing dissatisfaction.

**dissatisfied** /dɪs'sætəsfaɪd/, *adj.* **1.** discontented; not pleased; offended. **2.** showing dissatisfaction: *a dissatisfied look.* – **dissatisfiedly,** *adv.*

**dissatisfy** /dɪs'sætəsfaɪ/, *v.t.,* **-fied, -fying.** to make ill-satisfied, ill-pleased, or discontented.

**disseat** /dɪs'sit/, *v.t.* →**unseat.**

**dissect** /də'sɛkt, daɪ-/, *v.t.* **1.** to cut apart (an animal body, plant, etc.) to examine the structure, relation of parts, or the like. **2.** to examine minutely part by part; analyse. [L *dissectus,* pp., cut asunder] – **dissectible,** *adj.* – **dissector,** *n.*

**dissected** /də'sɛktəd, daɪ-/, *adj.* **1.** *Bot.* deeply cut into numerous segments, as a leaf. **2.** *Phys. Geog.* (of land surface) cut by erosion into hills and valleys or into flat upland areas separated by valleys. **3.** (of a map) cut into sections and mounted on linen, enabling it to be folded and carried without damage.

**dissection** /də'sɛkʃən, daɪ-/, *n.* **1.** the act of dissecting. **2.** something that has been dissected.

**disseise** /dɪs'siz/, *v.t.,* **-seised, -seising.** to deprive (a person) of seisin, or of the possession, of a freehold interest in land, esp. wrongfully or by force; oust. Also, **disseize.** [ME *disseyse(n),* from AF *disseisir* dispossess, from *dis-* DIS-[1] + *saisir* SEIZE] – **disseisor,** *n.*

**dissemblance**[1] /də'sɛmbləns/, *n. Archaic.* dissimilarity; unlikeness. [OF *dessemblance,* from *dessembler* be unlike, from *des-* DIS-[1] + *sembler* seem (from L *simulāre*)]

**dissemblance**[2] /də'sɛmbləns/, *n. Archaic.* dissembling; dissimulation. [DISSEMBLE + -ANCE]

**dissemble** /də'sɛmbəl/, *v.,* **-bled, -bling.** –*v.t.* **1.** to give a false semblance to; conceal the real nature of. **2.** to put on the appearance of; feign. **3.** *Archaic.* to let pass unnoticed; ignore. *–v.i.* **4.** to conceal one's motives, etc., under some pretence; speak or act hypocritically. [DIS-[1] + *-semble,* modelled on RESEMBLE] **– dissembler,** *n.* **– dissemblingly,** *adv.*

**disseminate** /də'sɛməneɪt/, *v.t.,* **-nated, -nating.** to scatter, as seed in sowing; spread abroad; diffuse; promulgate. [L *dissēminātus,* pp.] **– dissemination** /dəsɛmə'neɪʃən/, *n.* **– disseminative,** *adj.* **– disseminator,** *n.*

**disseminated sclerosis** /də,sɛməneɪtəd sklə'roʊsəs/, *n.* →**multiple sclerosis.**

**dissension** /də'sɛnʃən/, *n.* **1.** violent disagreement; discord; a contention or quarrel. **2.** difference in sentiment or opinion; disagreement.

**dissent** /də'sɛnt/, *v.i.* **1.** to differ in sentiment or opinion; disagree; withhold assent (fol. by *from*). **2.** to differ in religious opinion; reject the doctrines or authority of an established church. *–n.* **3.** difference in sentiment or opinion. **4.** separation from an established church; nonconformity. [ME *dissente(n),* from L *dissentīre* differ in opinion] **– dissenting,** *adj.* **– dissentingly,** *adv.*

**dissenter** /də'sɛntə/, *n.* **1.** one who dissents in any matter; one who disagrees with any opinion. **2.** (*sometimes cap.*) a person, now esp. a Protestant, who dissents from the established church.

**dissentient** /də'sɛntiənt/, *adj.* **1.** dissenting, esp. from the opinion of the majority. *–n.* **2.** one who dissents. **– dissentience,** *n.*

**dissentious** /də'sɛnʃəs/, *adj.* contentious; quarrelsome.

**dissepiment** /də'sɛpəmənt/, *n.* **1.** a partition or septum. **2.** *Bot.* one of the partitions formed within ovaries and fruits by the coherence of the sides of the constituent carpels. [L *dissaepīmentum* that which separates] **– dissepimental** /dəsɛpə'mɛntl/, *adj.*

**dissert** /də'sɜt/, *v.i. Obs.* to discourse on a subject. [L *dissertus,* pp., examined, discussed]

**dissertate** /'dɪsəteɪt/, *v.i.,* **-tated, -tating.** to treat of a subject in discourse; make a dissertation. [L *dissertātus,* pp., discussed] **– dissertator,** *n.*

**dissertation** /dɪsə'teɪʃən/, *n.* **1.** a written essay, treatise, or thesis. **2.** *Chiefly U.S.* a thesis written by a candidate for a doctorate. **3.** a formal discourse. **– dissertational,** *adj.*

**disserve** /dɪs'sɜv/, *v.t.,* **-served, -serving.** to serve ill; do an ill turn to.

**disservice** /dɪs'sɜvəs/, *n.* harm; injury; an ill turn. **– disserviceable,** *adj.*

**dissever** /dɪ'sɛvə/, *v.t.* **1.** to sever; separate. **2.** to divide into parts. *–v.i.* **3.** to part; separate. **– disseverance, disseverment, disseveration** /dɪ,sɛvə'reɪʃən/, *n.*

**dissidence** /'dɪsədəns/, *n.* disagreement.

**dissident** /'dɪsədənt/, *adj.* **1.** differing; disagreeing; dissenting. *–n.* **2.** one who differs; a dissenter, esp. against a particular political system. [L *dissidens,* ppr., differing, sitting apart]

**dissilient** /də'sɪliənt/, *adj.* flying or bursting asunder. [L *dissiliens,* ppr.] **– dissilience, dissiliency,** *n.*

**dissimilar** /dɪ'sɪmələ/, *adj.* not similar; unlike; different. **– dissimilarly,** *adv.*

**dissimilarity** /,dɪsɪmə'lærəti/, *n., pl.* **-ties. 1.** unlikeness; difference. **2.** a point of difference.

**dissimilate** /dɪ'sɪməleɪt/, *v.t.,* **-lated, -lating.** to change (a speech sound) so that it is less like another sound in a neighbouring syllable, as in *marble,* which derives from the French *marbre.* **– dissimilative** /dɪ'sɪmələtɪv/, *adj.*

**dissimilation** /dɪsɪmə'leɪʃən/, *n.* **1.** a making or becoming unlike. **2.** *Phonet.* the act or process of dissimilating speech sounds. **3.** *Biol.* →**catabolism.**

**dissimilitude** /,dɪsɪ'mɪlətjud/, *n.* **1.** unlikeness; difference. **2.** a point of difference.

**dissimulate** /də'sɪmjəleɪt/, *v.,* **-lated, -lating.** *–v.t.* **1.** to disguise or conceal under a false semblance; dissemble. *–v.i.* **2.** to use dissimulation; dissemble. [L *dissimulātus,* pp.] **– dissimulative** /də'sɪmjələtɪv/, *adj.* **– dissimulator,** *n.*

**dissimulation** /dəsɪmjə'leɪʃən/, *n.* **1.** the act of dissimulating; feigning; hypocrisy. **2.** *Psychiatry.* the ability or the tendency to appear mentally normal when actually suffering from disorder, a characteristic of the paranoiac. Cf. **simulation.**

**dissipate** /'dɪsəpeɪt/, *v.,* **-pated, -pating.** *–v.t.* **1.** to scatter in various directions; disperse; dispel; disintegrate. **2.** to scatter wastefully or extravagantly; squander. *–v.i.* **3.** to become scattered or dispersed; be dispelled; disintegrate. **4.** to indulge in extravagant, intemperate, or dissolute pleasure; practise dissipation. [L *dissipātus,* pp., scattered, demolished] **– dissipater,** *n.* **– dissipative,** *adj.*

**dissipated** /'dɪsəpeɪtəd/, *adj.* **1.** indulging in or characterised by excessive devotion to pleasure; intemperate; dissolute. **2.** dispersed; scattered; dispelled. **– dissipatedly,** *adv.* **– dissipatedness,** *n.*

**dissipation** /dɪsə'peɪʃən/, *n.* **1.** the act of dissipating. **2.** the state of being dissipated; dispersing; disintegration. **3.** a wasting by misuse. **4.** mental distraction; a diversion. **5.** dissolute mode of living; intemperance or debauchery.

**disso** /'dɪsoʊ/, *n. Colloq.* a wharf labourer suffering from disability or advanced age, who is fit only for work on the wharf, not on the ship.

**dissociable** /dɪ'soʊʃəbəl, -'soʊsiəbəl/, *adj.* **1.** capable of being dissociated; separable. **2.** unsociable. **3.** incongruous; not reconcilable.

**dissocial** /dɪ'soʊʃəl/, *adj.* unsocial; disinclined to or unsuitable for society.

**dissocialise** /dɪ'soʊʃəlaɪz/, *v.t.,* **-lised, -lising.** to make unsociable. Also, **dissocialize.**

**dissociate** /dɪ'soʊʃieɪt, -'soʊsieɪt/, *v.,* **-ated, -ating.** *–v.t.* **1.** to sever the association of; disunite; separate. **2.** *Chem.* to subject to dissociation. *–v.i.* **3.** to withdraw from association. **4.** *Chem.* to undergo dissociation. [L *dissociātus,* pp.] **– dissociative** /dɪ'soʊʃətɪv, -'soʊsiətɪv/, *adj.*

**dissociation** /dɪsoʊsi'eɪʃən/, *n.* **1.** the act of dissociating. **2.** the state of being dissociated; disunion. **3.** *Phys. Chem.* **a.** the reversible resolution or decomposition of a complex substance into simpler constituents, due to variation in the physical conditions, as when water gradually decomposes into hydrogen and oxygen under great heat, in such a way that when the temperature is lowered the liberated elements recombine to form water. **b.** electrolytic dissociation. **4.** *Psychiatry.* the splitting off of certain mental processes from the main body of consciousness, with varying degrees of autonomy resulting.

**dissoluble** /dɪ'sɒljəbəl/, *adj.* capable of being dissolved. **– dissolubility** /dɪ,sɒljə'bɪləti/, **dissolubleness,** *n.*

**dissolute** /'dɪsəlut/, *adj.* indifferent to moral restraints; given over to dissipation; licentious. [L *dissolūtus,* pp., loosened] **– dissolutely,** *adv.* **– dissoluteness,** *n.*

**dissolution** /dɪsə'luʃən/, *n.* **1.** the act of resolving into parts or elements. **2.** the resulting state. **3.** the undoing or breaking up of a tie, bond, union, etc. **4.** the breaking up of an assembly or organisation; dismissal; dispersal. **5.** *Govt.* an order issued by the head of the state terminating a parliament and necessitating a new election. **6.** death or decease. **7.** a bringing or coming to an end; destruction. **8.** the legal termination of business activity, including the distribution of assets and the fixing of liabilities. **9.** *Chem.* solution in a liquid substance. **– dissolutive** /'dɪsəlutɪv/, *adj.*

**dissolve** /də'zɒlv/, *v.,* **-solved, -solving,** *n.* *–v.t.* **1.** to make a solution of in a solvent. **2.** to undo (a tie or bond); break up (a connection, union, etc.). **3.** to break up (an assembly or organisation); dismiss; disperse. **4.** *Govt.* to order the termination of a parliament, usu. at constitutionally prescribed intervals, or in the event of the government being defeated. **5.** to bring to an end; destroy; dispel. **6.** to resolve into parts or elements; disintegrate. **7.** to destroy the binding power of: *dissolve a spell.* **8.** *Law.* to deprive of force; annul: *to dissolve a marriage or injunction.* *–v.i.* **9.** to become dissolved, as in a solvent. **10.** to break up or disperse. **11.** to lose force or strength; lose binding force. **12.** to disappear gradually; fade from sight or apprehension. **13.** *Films.* to fade out one shot while simultaneously fading in the next shot, overlapping the two shots during the process. *–n.* **14.** *Films.* a scene made by dissolving. [ME *dissolve(n),* from L *dissolvere* loosen, disunite] **– dissolvability** /dəzɒlvə'bɪləti/, **dissolvableness,** *n.* **– dissolvable,** *adj.* **– dissolver,** *n.*

**dissolvent** /də'zɒlvənt/, *adj., n.* →**solvent.**

**dissonance** /'dɪsənəns/, *n.* **1.** an inharmonious or harsh sound; discord. **2.** *Music.* a simultaneous combination of notes conventionally accepted as being in a state of unrest and needing resolution (opposed to *consonance*). **3.** disagreement or incongruity. Also, **dissonancy.**

**dissonant** /ˈdɪsənənt/, *adj.* **1.** disagreeing or harsh in sound; discordant. **2.** out of harmony; incongruous; at variance. [L *dissonans,* ppr., disagreeing in sound] – **dissonantly,** *adv.*

**dissuade** /dɪˈsweɪd/, *v.t.,* **-suaded, -suading.** **1.** to deter by advice or persuasion; persuade not to do something (fol. by *from*): *dissuade him from leaving home.* **2.** to advise or urge against (an action, etc.). [L *dissuādēre* advise against] – **dissuader,** *n.*

**dissuasion** /dɪˈsweɪʒən/, *n.* the act of dissuading.

**dissuasive** /dɪˈsweɪsɪv/, *adj.* tending to dissuade. – **dissuasively,** *adv.*

**dissymetric** /dɪsəˈmɛtrɪk/, *adj.* **1.** lacking symmetry. **2.** of or pertaining to two objects which are disposed in opposite directions. **3.** *Chem.* of or pertaining to a molecule which may have some axes of symmetry but which is so structured that its mirror image is not superimposable upon itself. – **dissymmetrical,** *adj.*

**dissymmetry** /dɪˈsɪmətri/, *n.* **1.** absence of symmetry. **2.** symmetry between two objects disposed in opposite directions.

**dist.,** distance.

**distaff** /ˈdɪstaf/, *n.* **1.** a staff with a cleft end, formerly used for holding the wool, flax, etc., from which the thread was drawn in spinning by hand. **2.** an analogous part of a spinning wheel, for holding flax to be spun. **3.** the female sex. **4.** a female heir; a woman. [ME *distaf,* OE *distæf,* from *dis-,* akin to LG *diesse* bunch of flax on a distaff + *stæf* STAFF[1]]

D, distaff on spinning wheel

**distaff side** /ˈ– saɪd/, *n.* the female side of a family.

**distain** /dɪˈsteɪn/, *v.t. Archaic.* to discolour; stain; sully. [ME *disteyne(n),* from OF *desteindre,* from *des-* DIS-[1] + *teindre* wet, dye (from L *tingere*)]

**distal** /ˈdɪstl/, *adj.* situated away from the point of origin or attachment, as of a limb or bone; terminal (opposed to *proximal*). [DIST(ANT) + -AL[1]] – **distally,** *adj.*

**distance** /ˈdɪstns, ˈdɪstəns/, *n., v.,* **-tanced, -tancing.** *–n.* **1.** the extent of space intervening between things or points. **2.** the state or fact of being distant, as of one thing from another; remoteness. **3.** the interval between two points of time. **4.** progress; advance: *our business has come a good distance in a year.* **5.** remoteness in any respect. **6.** a distant point, place or region. **7.** the distant part of a landscape, etc. **8.** reserve or aloofness; one's proper degree of aloofness: *to keep one's distance.* **9.** *Horseracing, etc.* **a.** the official length to be run, usu. measured in kilometres, formerly in furlongs. **b.** the length by which a horse is said to have won a race, as a head, neck, etc. **10.** **go the distance,** to complete a proposed undertaking, as of a horse able to complete a course, a boxer able to last the proposed number of rounds, a student able to gain his award, etc. **11.** *Obs.* disagreement or dissension; a quarrel. *–v.t.* **12.** to leave behind at a distance, as at a race; surpass. **13.** to place at a distance. **14.** to cause to appear distant.

**distance receptor** /ˈ– rəsɛptə/, *n.* →**teleceptor.**

**distant** /ˈdɪstənt/, *adj.* **1.** far off or apart in space; not near at hand; remote (fol. by *from*). **2.** separate or apart in space: *a place a kilometre distant.* **3.** apart or far off in time. **4.** far apart in any respect: *a distant relative.* **5.** reserved; not familiar or cordial. **6.** to a distance: *a distant journey.* [F, from L *distans,* ppr., being distant, standing apart] – **distantly,** *adv.*

**distant early warning system,** *n. Chiefly U.S.* a network of radar stations intended to give warning of a missile attack.

**distant signal** /ˈ– sɪgnəl/, *n.* a railway caution signal fixed at braking distance from a home signal.

**distant work** /– ˈwɜk/, *n.* work which is not performed at a fixed working place, and for travelling to which employees may be paid additional amounts to compensate for the inconvenience and expense involved.

**distaste** /dɪsˈteɪst/, *n., v.,* **-tasted, -tasting.** *–n.* **1.** dislike; disinclination. **2.** disrelish for food or drink. *–v.t.* **3.** *Archaic.* to dislike.

**distasteful** /dɪsˈteɪstfəl/, *adj.* **1.** causing dislike. **2.** unpleasant to the taste. – **distastefully,** *adv.* – **distastefulness,** *n.*

**distemper**[1] /dɪsˈtɛmpə/, *n.* **1.** *Vet. Sci.* **a.** a specific infectious disease of young dogs caused by a filterable virus. **b.** a disease of horses; strangles. **c.** (formerly) any of several diseases characterised by fever and catarrhal symptoms. **2.** deranged condition of mind or body; a disorder or disease. **3.** disorder or disturbance. **4.** ill humour; discontent. *–v.t.* **5.** to derange physically or mentally. [ME *distempre(n),* from ML *distemperāre.* See DIS-[1], TEMPER]

**distemper**[2] /dɪsˈtɛmpə/, *n.* **1.** a water paint used for the decoration of interior walls and ceilings, esp. one in which the binding medium consists essentially of glue, casein, or a similar sizing material. *–v.t.* **2.** to paint with distemper. [OF *destemprer,* from *des-* DIS-[1] + *temprer* dilute, soak (from L *temperāre*)]

**distend** /dəsˈtɛnd/, *v.i.* **1.** to become stretched, or bloated; to swell, as something hollow or elastic. *–v.t.* **2.** to stretch apart or asunder. **3.** to exaggerate, or magnify the importance of. [L *distendere*]

**distensible** /dəsˈtɛnsəbəl/, *adj.* capable of being distended. – **distensibility** /dəstɛnsəˈbɪləti/, *n.*

**distensile** /dəsˈtɛnsaɪl/, *adj.* **1.** distensible. **2.** capable of causing distension.

**distension** /dəsˈtɛnʃən/, *n.* **1.** the act of distending. **2.** the state of being distended. Also, **distention.**

**distich** /ˈdɪstɪk/, *n.* **1.** a group of two lines of verse, usu. making complete sense; a couplet. **2.** a rhyming couplet. [L *distichon,* from Gk, neut. of *dístichos* of two rows or lines] – **distichal,** *adj.*

**distichous** /ˈdɪstɪkəs/, *adj.* arranged alternately in two vertical rows on opposite sides of an axis, as leaves. [L *distichus* of two rows. See DISTICH] – **distichously,** *adv.*

**distil** /dəsˈtɪl/, *v.,* **-tilled, -tilling.** *–v.t.* **1.** to subject to a process of vaporisation and subsequent condensation, as for purification or concentration. **2.** to extract the volatile components of by distillation; transform by distillation. **3.** to extract or obtain by distillation. **4.** to drive (*off* or *out*) by distillation. **5.** to let fall in drops; give forth in or as in drops. *–v.i.* **6.** to undergo distillation. **7.** to become vaporised and then condensed in distillation. **8.** to drop, pass, or condense as a distillate. **9.** to fall in drops; trickle; exude. Also, *U.S.,* **distill.** [ME *distille(n),* from L *distillāre,* var. of *dēstillāre* drip down] – **distillable,** *adj.*

**distillate** /ˈdɪstələt, -leɪt/, *n.* **1.** the product obtained from the condensation of vapours in distillation. **2.** →**diesel oil.**

**distillation** /dɪstəˈleɪʃən/, *n.* **1.** the volatilisation or evaporation and subsequent condensation of a liquid, as when water is boiled in a retort and the steam is condensed in a cool receiver. **2.** the purification or concentration of a substance; the obtaining of the essence or volatile properties contained in it, or the separation of one substance from another, by such a process. **3.** a product of distilling; a distillate. **4.** the act or process of distilling. **5.** the fact of being distilled. – **distillatory** /dəsˈtɪlətəri, -tri/, *adj.*

**distilled** /dəsˈtɪld/, *adj.* obtained or produced by distillation.

**distiller** /dəsˈtɪlə/, *n.* **1.** an apparatus for distilling, as a condenser, or esp., one for distillation of salt water at sea. **2.** one whose business it is to extract alcoholic spirits by distillation.

**distillery** /dəsˈtɪləri/, *n., pl.* **-eries.** a place or establishment where distilling, esp. the distilling of alcoholic spirits, is carried on.

**distilment** /dəsˈtɪlmənt/, *n.* **1.** the act or process of distilling. **2.** the product of distilling. Also, *U.S.,* **distillment.**

**distinct** /dəsˈtɪŋkt/, *adj.* **1.** distinguished as not being the same; not identical; separate (fol. by *from* or used absolutely). **2.** different in nature or qualities; dissimilar. **3.** clear to the senses or intellect; plain; definite; unmistakable. **4.** distinguishing clearly, as the vision. **5.** more than usually notable; pronounced; effective: *his book is a distinct enrichment of our literature.* – **distinctness,** *n.*

**distinction** /dəsˈtɪŋkʃən/, *n.* **1.** a marking off or distinguishing as different. **2.** the recognising or noting of differences;

discrimination. **3.** a discrimination made between things as different. **4.** the condition of being different; a difference. **5.** a distinguishing characteristic. **6.** a distinguishing or treating with special attention or favour. **7.** a mark of special favour. **8.** marked superiority; note; eminence. **9.** (in certain examinations) the highest awarded grade. **10.** distinguished appearance. **11.** division.

**distinctive** /dəs'tɪŋktɪv/, *adj.* **1.** distinguishing; serving to distinguish; characteristic. **2.** *Linguistics.* phonemically significant: *distinctive features.* – **distinctively,** *adv.* – **distinctiveness,** *n.*

**distinctly** /dəs'tɪŋktli/, *adv.* **1.** a distinct manner; clearly. **2.** without doubt; unmistakeably.

**distingué** /dɪ'stæŋgeɪ/, *adj.* distinguished; having an air of distinction. [F, pp. of *distinguer* distinguish] – **distinguée,** *adj. fem.*

**distinguish** /dəs'tɪŋgwɪʃ/, *v.t.* **1.** to mark off as different (fol. by *from*). **2.** to recognise as distinct or different; discriminate. **3.** to perceive clearly by sight or other sense; discern; recognise. **4.** to serve to separate as different; be a distinctive characteristic of; characterise. **5.** to make prominent, conspicuous, or eminent: *to distinguish oneself in battle.* **6.** to divide into classes; classify. **7.** *Archaic.* to single out for or honour with special attention. *–v.i.* **8.** to indicate or show a difference (fol. by *between*). **9.** to recognise or note differences; discriminate. [L *distinguere* separate, distinguish + -ISH[2], modelled on EXTINGUISH] – **distinguishable,** *adj.* – **distinguishableness,** *n.* – **distinguishably,** *adv.* – **distinguisher,** *n.* – **distinguishingly,** *adv.*

**distinguished** /dəs'tɪŋgwɪʃt/, *adj.* **1.** conspicuous; marked. **2.** noted; eminent; famous. **3.** having an air of distinction; distingué.

**distort** /dəs'tɔt/, *v.t.* **1.** to twist awry or out of shape; make crooked or deformed. **2.** to pervert; misrepresent. **3.** *Electronics.* to change (a signal waveform) so that the information is degraded. [L *distortus,* pp.] – **distorted,** *adj.* – **distortedly,** *adv.* – **distortedness,** *n.* – **distorter,** *n.*

**distortion** /dəs'tɔʃən/, *n.* **1.** the act of distorting. **2.** the state of being distorted. **3.** anything distorted. **4.** *Electronics.* a change in the waveform of a signal which degrades the information. – **distortional,** *adj.*

**distortion box** /'– bɒks/, *n.* an electronic device which distorts amplified sound and is used for special effects in some modern music.

**distract** /dəs'trækt/, *v.t.* **1.** to draw away or divert, as the mind or attention. **2.** to divide (the mind, attention, etc.) between objects. **3.** to entertain; amuse; divert. **4.** to disturb or trouble greatly in mind. **5.** to rend by dissension or strife. [L *distractus,* pp., pulled asunder. Cf. DISTRAUGHT] – **distracted,** *adj.* – **distractedly,** *adv.* – **distracter,** *n.* – **distracting,** *adj.* – **distractingly,** *adv.*

**distraction** /dəs'trækʃən/, *n.* **1.** the act of distracting. **2.** the state of being distracted. **3.** amusement; recreation; entertainment. **4.** violent disturbance of mind; mental derangement or madness. **5.** division or disorder due to dissension; tumult.

**distractive** /dəs'træktɪv/, *adj.* tending to distract.

**distrain** /dəs'treɪn/, *Law. –v.t.* **1.** to constrain by seizing and holding goods, etc., in pledge for rent, damages, etc., or in order to obtain satisfaction of a claim. **2.** to levy a distress upon. *–v.i.* **3.** to levy a distress. [ME *destreyne(n),* from OF *destreindre* constrain, from L *distringere* draw asunder, detain, hinder] – **distrainable,** *adj.* – **distrainment,** *n.* – **distrainer, distrainor,** *n.* – **distraint,** *n.*

**distrait** /dəs'treɪ/, *adj.* abstracted in thought; absent-minded. [F, pp. of *distraire,* from L *distrahere* pull asunder. See DISTRACT] – **distraite** /dɪs'treɪt/, *adj. fem.*

**distraught** /dəs'trɔt/, *adj.* **1.** distracted; bewildered; deeply agitated. **2.** crazed. [var. of obs. *distract,* adj., by association with *straught,* pp. of STRETCH] – **distraughtly,** *adv.*

**distress** /dəs'trɛs/, *n.* **1.** great pain, anxiety, or sorrow; acute suffering; affliction; trouble. **2.** acute poverty; physical exhaustion. **3.** a state of extreme necessity. **4.** the state of a ship requiring immediate assistance, as because of accident. **5.** *Law.* **a.** an act of distraining; the legal seizure and detention of the goods of another as security or satisfaction for debt, etc. **b.** the thing seized in distraining. *–v.t.* **6.** to afflict with pain, anxiety, or sorrow; trouble sorely; worry; bother. **7.** to subject to pressure, stress, or strain; embarrass or exhaust by strain. **8.** *Archaic.* to constrain. [ME *destresse,* from OF *destrece,* from L *districtus,* pp., distrained] – **distressing,** *adj.* – **distressingly,** *adv.*

**distress call** /'– kɔl/, *n.* **1.** an international code sign inferring that the sender is in danger or difficulty, as *Mayday* or *SOS.* **2.** any communication indicating distress: *the police sent out a distress call for blood donors.*

**distressed area** /də,strɛst 'ɛəriə/, *n.* →**depressed area.**

**distressful** /də'strɛsfəl/, *adj.* **1.** causing or involving distress. **2.** full of distress; feeling or indicating distress. – **distressfully,** *adv.* – **distressfulness,** *n.*

**distress rocket** /dəs'trɛs rɒkət/, *n.* a rocket used to make a distress signal.

**distress signal** /'– sɪgnəl/, *n.* a signal by persons in danger summoning aid and indicating their position by rocket, radio code, flag, or any other means.

**distributary** /dəs'trɪbjətəri, -tri/, *n.* **1.** a branch of a distributing system. **2.** a branch of a river flowing from the main river and not rejoining it, as in a delta.

**distribute** /dəs'trɪbjut/, *v.t.,* **-uted, -uting. 1.** to divide and bestow in shares; deal out; allot. **2.** to disperse through a space or over an area; spread; scatter. **3.** to divide into parts of distinct character. **4.** to divide into classes: *these plants are distributed into 22 classes.* **5.** *Print.* to separate the type that has been used for printing and replace in its proper compartments. **6.** *Logic.* to employ (a term) so as to refer to all the individuals denoted by it: *the term 'men' is distributed in 'all men are mortal' but not in 'some men are old'.* [L *distribūtus,* pp.] – **distributable,** *adj.*

**distribution** /dɪstrə'bjuʃən/, *n.* **1.** the act of distributing. **2.** the state or manner of being distributed. **3.** arrangement; classification. **4.** that which is distributed. **5.** the places where things of any particular category occur: *the distribution of coniferous forests in the world.* **6.** the transporting, marketing, merchandising, and selling of a product. **7.** *Econ.* **a.** the division of the aggregate income of any society among its members, or among the factors of production. **b.** the system of dispersing goods throughout a community. **8.** *Statistics.* a set of values or measurements of a set of elements, each measurement being associated with an element. – **distributional,** *adj.*

**distribution curve** /'– kɜv/, *n.* the curve or line of a graph whose axes or data are based upon a specific frequency distribution. See **frequency distribution.**

**distributive** /dəs'trɪbjətɪv/, *adj.* **1.** that distributes; characterised by or pertaining to distribution. **2.** *Gram.* treating the members of a group individually, as the adjectives *each* and *every.* **3.** *Logic.* (of a term) distributed in a given proposition. *–n.* **4.** a distributive word or expression. – **distributively,** *adv.* – **distributiveness,** *n.*

**distributor** /dəs'trɪbjətə/, *n.* **1.** one who or that which distributes. **2.** *Comm.* one engaged in the general distribution or marketing of some article or class of goods. **3.** *Mach.* a device in a multicylinder engine which distributes the igniting voltage to the sparking plugs in a definite sequence. Also, **distributer. 4.** a major arterial road, usu. a freeway, designed to take traffic quickly from the centre of the city towards the outer suburbs.

**distributorship** /dəs'trɪbjətəʃɪp/, *n.* the right to act as a distributor or selling agent.

**district** /'dɪstrɪkt/, *n.* **1.** a region or locality. **2.** an area of land delineated for some administrative or other purpose. **3.** *S.A.* →**shire** (def. 1). **4.** *Brit.* a sub-division of a town, city, or county often reflecting old and now non-existent boundaries. [ML *districtus* territory under jurisdiction, special use of L *districtus,* pp., constrained]

**district allowance** /'– əlaʊəns/, *n.* an allowance paid above the usual rate of pay as compensation for hardships arising from working in a particular district, as isolation, heat, etc.

**district attorney** /– ə'tɜni/, *n. U.S.* the public prosecutor for a specific district.

**District Court** /dɪstrɪkt 'kɔt/, *n.* a middle court between the Court of Petty Sessions and the Supreme Court with statutory jurisdiction, presided over by a Judge, not a Justice.

**district hospital** /dɪstrɪkt 'hɒspətəl/, *n.* a hospital, usu. metropolitan, which serves the needs of a particular locality.

**district nurse** /– 'nзs/, *n.* a state-registered nurse appointed to visit and look after the health of people in a certain area, esp. mothers and babies, the old and sick.

**district school** /'– skul/, *n.* →**central school.**

**district surveyor** /– sə'veɪə/, *n.* an officer, usu. a qualified surveyor, employed by the government to supervise all survey work in a specified district.

**distrust** /dɪs'trʌst/, *v.t.* **1.** to feel distrust of; regard with doubt or suspicion. *–n.* **2.** lack of trust; doubt; suspicion. **– distruster,** *n.*

**distrustful** /dɪs'trʌstfəl/, *adj.* full of distrust; doubtful; suspicious. **– distrustfully,** *adv.* **– distrustfulness,** *n.*

**disturb** /də'stзb/, *v.t.* **1.** to interrupt the quiet, rest, or peace of. **2.** to interfere with; interrupt; hinder. **3.** to throw into commotion or disorder; agitate; disorder; disarrange; unsettle. **4.** to perplex; trouble. [L *disturbāre* throw into disorder, disturb] **– disturber,** *n.* **– disturbingly,** *adv.*

**disturbance** /də'stзbəns/, *n.* **1.** the act of disturbing. **2.** the state of being disturbed. **3.** an instance of this; commotion. **4.** something that disturbs. **5.** an outbreak of disorder; a breach of public peace. **6.** *Geol.* **a.** the bending or faulting of rock from its original position. **b.** a mountain-making movement of the earth's crust, of moderate intensity and somewhat restricted geographic extent. **7.** *Law.* infringement of an incorporeal right.

**disulphate** /daɪ'sʌlfeɪt/, *n.* **1.** a salt of pyrosulphuric acid, as sodium disulphate, $Na_2S_2O_7$. See **pyro-**. **2.** bisulphate. Also, *U.S.,* **disulfate.** [DI-[1] + SULPHATE]

**disulphide** /daɪ'sʌlfaɪd/, *n.* a sulphide containing two atoms of sulphur, as carbon disulphide, $CS_2$. Also, *U.S.,* **disulfide.**

**disulphuric** /ˌdaɪsʌl'fjurɪk/, *n.* →**pyrosulphuric.** See **pyro-**. Also, *U.S.,* **disulfuric.**

**disulphuric acid** /– 'æsəd/, *n.* →**fuming sulphuric acid.**

**disunion** /dɪs'junjən/, *n.* **1.** severance of union; separation; disjunction. **2.** lack of union; dissension.

**disunite** /dɪsju'naɪt/, *v.,* **-nited, -niting.** *–v.t.* **1.** to sever the union of; separate; disjoin. **2.** to set at variance, or alienate. *–v.i.* **3.** to part; fall asunder.

**disunity** /dɪs'junəti/, *n., pl.* **-ties.** lack of unity.

**disuse** /dɪs'jus/, *n.;* /dɪs'juz/, *v.,* **-used, -using.** *–n.* **1.** discontinuance of use or practice. *–v.t.* **2.** to cease to use.

**disutility** /ˌdɪsju'tɪləti/, *n.* the quality of causing inconvenience or harm; injuriousness.

**disvalue** /dɪs'vælju/, *v.t.,* **-ued, -uing.** *Rare.* to depreciate; disparage.

**disyllable** /dɪ'sɪləbəl/, *n.* a word of two syllables, as *virtue.* [L *disyllabus,* from Gk *disýllabos.* See SYLLABLE] **– disyllabic** /dɪsɪ'læbɪk/, *adj.* **– disyllabification** /dɪsɪˌlæbəfə'keɪʃən/, *n.* **– disyllabism** /dɪ'sɪləbɪzəm/, *n.*

**disyoke** /dɪs'joʊk/, *v.t.,* **-yoked, -yoking.** to free from or as from a yoke.

**dita** /'ditə/, *n.* a shrub or tree, *Alstonia scholaris,* family Apocynaceae, of the Old World tropics with large, glossy, whorled leaves.

**ditch** /dɪtʃ/, *n.* **1.** a long, narrow hollow made in the earth by digging, as one for draining or irrigating land; a trench. **2.** any open passage or trench, as a natural channel or waterway. **3.** the border of a bowling green. **4. last ditch,** *Colloq.* the last defence; utmost extremity. **5.** *Colloq.* the sea. *–v.t.* **6.** to dig a ditch or ditches in. **7.** *U.S.* to cause to be thrown into or as into a ditch, as a motor car in a crash. **8.** *Colloq.* to get rid of; get away from. **9.** *Colloq.* to crash-land (an aeroplane), esp. in the sea. *–v.i.* **10.** *Colloq.* to crash-land an aeroplane. [ME *dīch,* OE *dīc,* c. G *Teich.* See DIKE]

**ditcher** /'dɪtʃə/, *n.* **1.** one who or that which digs ditches. **2.** *Bowls.* a bowl which goes into the ditch (def. 3) having touched neither the jack nor any other bowl in play.

**ditheism** /'daɪθiˌɪzəm/, *n.* **1.** the doctrine of, or belief in, two supreme gods. **2.** belief in the existence of two independent antagonistic principles, one good and the other evil. [DI-[1] + Gk *theós* god + -ISM] **– ditheist,** *n.* **– ditheistic** /daɪθi'ɪstɪk/, *adj.*

**dither** /'dɪðə/, *n.* **1.** a trembling; vibration. **2.** *Colloq.* a state of trembling excitement or vacillation. *–v.i.* **3.** to be vacillating; uncertain. **4.** to tremble with excitement or fear. [var. of *didder,* ME *diddir;* orig. obscure. Cf. DODDER[1]] **dithery,** *adj.*

**dithionate** /daɪ'θaɪəneɪt/, *n.* a salt of diothionic acid containing the ion $S_2O_6^{2-}$.

**dithionic acid** /daɪˌθaɪənɪk 'æsəd/, *n.* a moderately strong, stable acid, $H_2S_2O_6$.

**dithionite** /daɪ'θaɪənaɪt/, *n.* a salt of diothionous acid containing the ion $S_2O_4^{2-}$.

**dithionous acid** /daɪˌθaɪənəs 'æsəd/, *n.* an acid, $H_2S_2O_4$, known only in solution and as salts called dithionites, hydrosulphites, hyposulphites. Also, **hyposulphurous acid.**

**dithyramb** /'dɪθəræm, -ræmb/, *n.* **1.** a choral song or hymn of vehement or wild character and usu. irregular in form, originally in honour of Dionysus or Bacchus. **2.** any poem or other composition having similar characteristics. [L *dīthyrambus,* from Gk *dīthýrambos*]

**dithyrambic** /dɪθə'ræmbɪk/, *adj.* **1.** of, pertaining to, or of the nature of a dithyramb. **2.** wildly irregular in form. **3.** wildly enthusiastic.

**dittander** /də'tændə/, *n.* a perennial herb, *Lepidium latifolium,* found mainly in coastal regions of Europe and formerly used as a condiment.

**dittany** /'dɪtəni/, *n., pl.* **-nies. 1.** a plant, *Origanum dictamnus* (**dittany of Crete**), family Labiatae, formerly in high repute for its alleged medicinal virtues. **2.** a plant, *Cunila origanoides,* family Labiatae, of North America, bearing clusters of purplish flowers. **3.** a plant, *Dictamnus albus,* family Rutaceae, cultivated for its showy flowers. [ME *ditonye,* from OF *ditan,* from L *dictamnus,* from Gk *díktamnon,* said to be so called from Mt *Dicte* in Crete, where it abounded]

**ditto** /'dɪtoʊ/, *n., pl.* **-tos,** *adv., v.,* **-toed, -toing.** *–n.* **1.** the aforesaid; the same (used in accounts, lists, etc., to avoid repetition). *Symbol:* " ; *abbrev.:* do. **2.** the same thing repeated. **3.** *Colloq.* a duplicate or copy. *–adv.* **4.** as already stated; likewise. *–v.t.* **5.** to duplicate; copy. [It.: said, aforesaid, from L *dictus,* pp., said]

**dittography** /dɪ'tɒgrəfi/, *n.* **1.** unintentional repetition of one or more symbols in writing, as in copying a manuscript. **2.** the resulting passage or reading. [Gk *dittó(s)* double + -GRAPHY] **– dittographic** /dɪtə'græfɪk/, *adj.*

**ditto marks** /'dɪtoʊ maks/, *n.pl.* two small marks (") indicating the repetition of something, usu. placed beneath the thing repeated.

**ditty** /'dɪti/, *n., pl.* **-ties. 1.** a poem intended to be sung. **2.** a short, simple song. [ME *dite,* from OF, from L *dictātum* thing composed or recited]

**ditty-bag** /'dɪti-bæg/, *n.* a bag used by sailors to hold sewing implements and other necessaries.

**ditty-box** /'dɪti-bɒks/, *n.* a small box used as a ditty-bag.

**diuresis** /ˌdaɪju'risəs/, *n.* excessive discharge of urine. [NL, from Gk *di-* DI-[3] + *oúrēsis* urination]

**diuretic** /ˌdaɪju'rɛtɪk/, *adj.* **1.** increasing the volume of the urine, as a medicinal substance. *–n.* **2.** a diuretic medicine or agent. [LL *diūrēticus* promoting urine, from Gk *diourētikós*]

**diuris** /daɪ'jurəs/, *n.* any plant of the orchid genus *Diuris,* a group largely restricted to Australia and characterised by long lateral sepals; double tails.

**diurnal** /daɪ'зnəl/, *adj.* **1.** of or pertaining to each day; daily. **2.** of or belonging to the daytime. **3.** *Bot.* showing a periodic alteration of condition with day and night, as certain flowers which open by day and close by night. **4.** active by day, as certain birds and insects. *–n.* **5.** *Liturgy.* a service-book containing offices for the daily hours of prayer. **6.** *Archaic.* a diary. **7.** *Archaic.* a daily or other newspaper. [LL *diurnālis* daily] **– diurnally,** *n.*

**diurnal parallax** /– 'pærəlæks/, *n.* →**parallax** (def. 2).

**div.,** **1.** dividend. **2.** division.

**diva** /'divə/, *n., pl.* **-vas, -ve** /-vi/. a distinguished female singer; a prima donna. [It., from L: goddess]

**divagate** /'daɪvəgeɪt/, *v.i.,* **-gated, -gating. 1.** to wander; stray. **2.** to digress in speech. [L *dīvagātus,* pp., having wandered] **– divagation** /daɪvə'geɪʃən/, *n.*

**divalent** /daɪ'veɪlənt, 'daɪveɪlənt/, *adj.* having a valency of two, as the ferrous ion, $Fe^{++}$.

**divan** /də'væn/, *n.* **1.** a low bed with no headboard or tailboard. **2.** a sofa or couch. **3.** a long, cushioned seat against a wall, as in Middle Eastern countries. **4.** (formerly) a council of state in Turkey and other Middle Eastern countries. **5.** any council, committee, or commission. **6.** (formerly in the Middle East) **a.** a council chamber, judgment hall, audience chamber, or bureau of state. **b.** a large building used for some public purpose, as a customs house. **7.** a smoking room, as in connection with a tobacco shop. **8.** *Obs.* a collection of oriental lyric verse, esp. poems by one author. [Turk., from Pers. *dēvān* (now *dīwān*)]

**divaricate** /daɪˈværəkeɪt/, *v.*, **-cated, -cating;** /daɪˈværəkət, keɪt/, *adj.* *–v.t.* **1.** to spread apart. *–v.i.* **2.** to branch; diverge. **3.** *Bot., Zool.* to branch at a wide angle. *–adj.* **4.** spread apart; widely divergent. **5.** *Bot., Zool.* branching at a wide angle. [L *dīvāricātus*, pp., spread apart] **– divaricately,** *adv.* **– divarication** /daɪˌværəˈkeɪʃən/, *n.* **– divaricator,** *n.*

**dive** /daɪv/, *v.*, **dived** or (*U.S. Colloq.*) **dove, dived, diving,** *n.* *–v.i.* **1.** to plunge, esp. head first, as into water. **2.** to go below the surface of the water, as a submarine. **3.** to plunge deeply. **4.** (of an aeroplane) to plunge downward at a greater angle than when gliding. **5.** to penetrate suddenly into anything, as with the hand. **6.** to dart. **7.** to enter deeply into (a subject, business, etc.) *–n.* **8.** the act of diving. **9.** *Colloq.* a disreputable place, as for drinking, gambling, etc., esp. a cellar or basement. **10.** a sharp fall: *a dive in net profit.* **11.** *Boxing.* a pretended knockout (pre-arranged between two boxers): *he took a dive in the third round.* [ME *dive(n)* dive, dip, OE *dȳfan*, v.t., dip (causative of *dūfan*, v.i., dive, sink), c. Icel. *dȳfa* dip]

**dive-bomb** /ˈdaɪv-bɒm/, *v.t.* **1.** *Aeron.* to bomb by diving at a steep angle so that the pilot sights the target through his gun sights and releases the bombs just before pulling out. *–v.i.* **2.** *Colloq.* to jump into water, as a swimming pool, creek, etc., with the knees tucked under the chin. *–n.* **3.** *Colloq.* the action of dive-bombing.

**dive-bomber** /ˈdaɪv-bɒmə/, *n.* an aeroplane of the pursuit type which drops its bombs while diving at the target.

**diver** /ˈdaɪvə/, *n.* **1.** one who or that which dives. **2.** one who makes a business of diving, as for pearl oysters, to examine sunken vessels, etc. **3.** any of various birds which habitually dive, as loons, grebes, etc.

**diverge** /daɪˈvɜdʒ/, *v.i.*, **-verged, -verging.** **1.** to move or lie in different directions from a common point; branch off. **2.** to differ in opinion or character; deviate. **3.** to digress, from a plan, discussion, etc. **4.** *Maths.* (of an infinite sequence of numbers) to not converge. [NL *dīvergere*, from L *dī-* DIS-[1] + *vergere* incline, VERGE[2]]

**divergence** /daɪˈvɜdʒəns/, *n.* **1.** the act, fact, or amount of diverging. **2.** *Meteorol.* a condition brought about by a net flow of air from a given region. Also, **divergency.**

**divergent** /daɪˈvɜdʒənt/, *adj.* **1.** diverging; deviating. **2.** pertaining to divergence. **– divergently,** *adv.*

**divers** /ˈdaɪvəz/, *adj.* several, sundry (sometimes used pronominally): *divers of them.* [ME, from OF, from L *dīversus*, pp., lit., turned different ways]

**diverse** /daɪˈvɜs, ˈdaɪvɜs/, *adj.* **1.** of a different kind, form, character, etc.; unlike. **2.** of various kinds or forms; multiform. [var. of DIVERS, but now associated more directly with L *dīversus*] **– diversely,** *adv.* **– diverseness,** *n.*

**diversification** /daɪˌvɜsəfəˈkeɪʃən, də-/, *n.* **1.** the state or act of diversifying. **2.** the art of manufacturing a number of different articles; selling a number of different goods, or putting money into a number of different investments in order to diminish the effects of a possible financial failure of one part.

**diversified** /daɪˈvɜsəfaɪd, də-/, *adj.* **1.** distinguished by various forms, or by a variety of objects. **2.** varied; distributed among several types: *diversified investments.*

**diversiform** /daɪˈvɜsəfɔm/, *adj.* differing in form; of various forms. [L *dīversus* various + -I- + -FORM]

**diversify** /daɪˈvɜsəfaɪ, də-/, *v.*, **-fied, -fying.** *–v.t.* **1.** to make diverse, as in form or character; give variety or diversity to; variegate. **2.** to vary (investments); invest in different types of (securities). *–v.i.* **3.** to extend one's activities, esp. in business, over more than one field. [F *diversifier*, from ML *dīversificāre*, from L *dīversi-* diverse + *-ficāre* make] **– diversifiable,** *adj.*

**diversion** /daɪˈvɜʒən, də-/, *n.* **1.** the act of diverting or turning aside, as from a course. **2.** a compulsory detour on a road or motorway, to avoid an obstacle, bottleneck, etc. **3.** distraction from business, care, etc.; recreation; entertainment; amusement; a pastime. **4.** *Mil.* a feint intended to draw off attention from the point of main attack. **– diversionary,** *adj.*

**diversionary therapy** /daɪˌvɜʒənri ˈθɛrəpi/, *n.* a method of therapy which aims at providing mental diversion or relaxation for a patient.

**diversionist** /dəˈvɜʒənəst/, *n.* a saboteur, esp. one who plots against a communist government.

**diversity** /daɪˈvɜsəti, də-/, *n., pl.* **-ties.** **1.** the state or fact of being diverse; difference; unlikeness. **2.** variety; multiformity. **3.** a point of difference.

**divert** /daɪˈvɜt, də-/, *v.t.* **1.** to turn aside or form a path or course; deflect. **2.** to set (traffic) on a detour. **3.** to draw off to a different object, purpose, etc. **4.** to distract from serious occupation; entertain or amuse. [OF *divertir*, from L *dīvertere* turn aside, separate] **– diverter,** *n.* **– divertible,** *adj.*

**diverticulitis** /daɪvəˈtɪkjulaɪtəs/, *n.* the inflammation of one or more diverticula, esp. of the intestines.

**diverticulum** /daɪvəˈtɪkjələm/, *n., pl.* **-la** /-lə/. a blind tubular sac or process, branching off from a canal or cavity, as the intestine. [L: byway] **– diverticular,** *adj.*

**divertimento** /dɪvɜtəˈmɛntoʊ/, *n., pl.* **-ti** /-ti/. an instrumental composition in several movements, light and diverting in character. [It.]

**diverting** /daɪˈvɜtɪŋ, də-/, *adj.* that diverts; entertaining; amusing. **– divertingly,** *adv.*

**divertissement** /dɪˈvɜtɪsmɒ̃/, *n.* **1.** a diversion or entertainment. **2.** *Music.* a divertimento. **3.** a short ballet or other performance given between or in the course of acts or longer pieces. **4.** a series of such performances. [F, from *divertiss-*, stem of *divertir* DIVERT]

**divertive** /daɪˈvɜtɪv/, *adj.* diverting; amusing.

**divest** /daɪˈvɛst/, *v.t.* **1.** to strip of clothing etc.; disrobe. **2.** to strip or deprive of anything; dispossess. **3.** *Law.* to take away or alienate (property, etc.). [ML *dīvestīre*, var. of *disvestīre* (Latinisation of OF *desvestir*)]

**divestible** /daɪˈvɛstəbəl/, *adj.* capable of being divested, as an estate in land.

**divestiture** /daɪˈvɛstɪtʃə/, *n.* **1.** the act of divesting. **2.** the state of being divested. Also, **divestment, divesture.**

**dividable** /dəˈvaɪdəbəl/, *adj.* →**divisible.**

**divide** /dəˈvaɪd/, *v.*, **-vided, -viding,** *n.* *–v.t.* **1.** to separate into parts. **2.** to separate or part from each other or from something else; sunder; cut off. **3.** to deal out in parts; apportion; share. **4.** to separate in opinion or feeling; cause to disagree. **5.** to distinguish the kinds of; classify. **6.** *Maths.* **a.** to separate into equal parts by the process of division. **b.** to be a divisor of, without a remainder. **c.** to graduate (a rule, etc.). **7.** *Parl. Proc.* to separate (a legislature, etc.) into two groups in ascertaining the vote on a question. *–v.i.* **8.** to become divided or separated. **9.** to share something with others. **10.** to branch; diverge; fork. **11.** *Maths.* to go through the process of division. **12.** *Parl. Proc.* to vote by separating into two groups. *–n.* **13.** *Colloq.* act of dividing; a division. **14.** *Phys. Geog.* a watershed: *the Great Divide.* [ME *divide(n)*, from L *dīvidere* force asunder, cleave, part, distribute]

**divided** /dəˈvaɪdəd/, *adj.* **1.** separated; separate; disunited; shared. **2.** *Bot.* (of a leaf) cut into distinct portions by incisions extending to the midrib or the base.

**divided road** /– ˈroʊd/, *n.* a major road on which the lanes of traffic moving in opposite directions are separated by a strip of grass, trees, etc.

**dividend** /ˈdɪvədɛnd/, *n.* **1.** *Maths.* a number to be divided by another number (the divisor). **2.** *Law.* a sum out of an insolvent estate to be divided among the creditors. **3.** *Finance.* **a.** a pro-rata share in an amount to be distributed. **b.** a sum of money paid to shareholders of a company or trading concern out of earnings. **c.** interest payable on public funds. **4.** a percentage of the purchasing money spent over a period in a cooperative store, etc., returned to the purchaser at the end of that period. **5.** a payment to creditors and shareholders in a liquidated company. **6.** *Insurance.* a distribution of profit by a company to an assured. **7.** a share of anything divided. **8.** the totalisator payout on a racing bet.

[L *dīvidendum* (thing) to be divided, neut. ger. of *dīvidere* DIVIDE]

**dividend cover** /'– kʌvə/, *n.* the number of times that the declared dividend is covered by a company's net profit.

**dividend rate** /'– reɪt/, *n. Stock Exchange.* the dividend shown as a percentage of the par value.

**dividend warrant** /'– wɒrənt/, *n.* an order issued by a company in favour of a shareholder for payment of the dividend due to him.

**dividend yield** /'– jild/, *n. Stock Exchange.* the dividend shown as a percentage of the last sale price.

**divider** /də'vaɪdə/, *n.* **1.** one who or that which divides. **2.** (*pl.*) a pair of compasses as used for dividing lines, measuring, etc.

dividers

**divi-divi** /dɪvi-'dɪvi/, *n.* **1.** a shrub or small tree, *Caesalpinia coriaria,* of tropical America, the astringent pods of which are much used in tanning and dyeing. **2.** the related species. **3.** the pods of either plant. [Carib]

**dividual** /də'vɪdʒuəl/, *adj. Archaic.* **1.** divisible or divided. **2.** separate; distinct. **3.** distributed; shared. [L *dīviduus* divisible + -AL[1]] – **dividually,** *adv.*

**divination** /dɪvə'neɪʃən/, *n.* **1.** the discovering of what is obscure or the foretelling of future events, as by supernatural means. **2.** augury; a prophecy. **3.** instinctive prevision. [L *dīvīnātio,* from *dīvīnāre* DIVINE, *v.*] – **divinatory** /dɪ'vɪnətəri, -tri/, *adj.*

**divine** /də'vaɪn/, *adj., n., v.,* **-vined, -vining.** *–adj.* **1.** of or pertaining to a god, esp. the Supreme Being. **2.** addressed or appropriated to God; religious; sacred. **3.** proceeding from God. **4.** godlike; characteristic of or befitting a deity. **5.** heavenly; celestial. **6.** being a god, or God. **7.** pertaining to divinity or theology. **8.** of superhuman or surpassing excellence. **9.** *Colloq.* excellent. *–n.* **10.** one versed in divinity; a theologian. **11.** a priest or clergyman. *–v.t.* **12.** to discover (water, metal, etc.,) by a divining rod. **13.** to discover or declare (something obscure or future), as by supernatural means; prophesy. **14.** to perceive by intuition or insight; conjecture. **15.** *Obs. or Archaic.* to portend. *–v.i.* **16.** to use or practise divination; prophesy. **17.** to have perception by intuition or insight; conjecture. [ME, from L *dīvīnus;* replacing ME *devine,* from OF] – **divinely,** *adv.* – **divineness,** *n.*

**divine office** /'– ɒfəs/, *n.* (*sometimes caps*) →**office** (def. 13b).

**diviner** /də'vaɪnə/, *n.* **1.** one who divines; a soothsayer; a prophet; a conjecturer. **2.** one who searches for and finds hidden water, metal, or oil, by means of a divining rod.

**divine right of kings,** *n.* a belief formerly held that a king's right to rule derives directly from God, not from the people, and that he should therefore be obeyed in all things.

**divine service** /də'vaɪn sɜvəs/, *n.* a service in a Christian church.

**diving beetle** /'daɪvɪŋ bitl/, *n.* any of the predacious beetles that constitute the family Dytiscidae, adapted for swimming and diving.

**diving bell** /'– bɛl/, *n.* a hollow vessel filled with air under pressure, in which persons may work under water.

**diving board** /'– bɔd/, *n.* a plank or board placed beside or projecting over a swimming pool from which swimmers may dive.

**diving petrel** /– 'pɛtrəl/, *n.* any of various birds of the family Pelecanoididae, esp. the common diving petrel, *Pelecanoides urinatrix,* a small, short-tailed bird, black above and white underneath, with brown eyes, black beak and cobalt blue legs, common in south-eastern Australian seas.

**diving suit** /'– sut/, *n.* a watertight garment, consisting of a rubber or metal body covering and a helmet with an air-supply line attached, worn by divers. Also, **diving dress.**

**divining rod** /də'vaɪnɪŋ ˌrɒd/, *n.* a rod used in divining, esp. a forked stick, commonly of hazel, said to tremble or move when held over a spot where water, metal, etc., is underground.

**divinise** /'dɪvənaɪz/, *v.t.,* **-nised, -nising.** to make divine; deify. Also, **divinize.** – **divinisation** /dɪvənaɪ'zeɪʃən/, *n.*

**divinity** /də'vɪnəti/, *n., pl.* **-ties.** **1.** the quality of being divine; divine nature. **2.** deity; godhood. **3.** a divine being; a god. **4.** a deity below God but above man. **5.** the science of divine things; theology. **6.** godlike character; supreme excellence.

**divisi** /də'visi/, *adv.* (a musical direction) divided, as of strings, etc., playing parts. [It.] – **divisi,** *adj.*

**divisibility** /dəvɪzə'bɪləti/, *n.* **1.** capability of being divided. **2.** *Maths.* the capacity of being exactly divided, without remainder.

**divisible** /də'vɪzəbəl/, *adj.* capable of being divided. – **divisibleness,** *n.* – **divisibly,** *adv.*

**division** /də'vɪʒən/, *n.* **1.** the act of dividing; partition. **2.** the state of being divided. **3.** a distribution; a sharing-out. **4.** *Maths.* the operation inverse to multiplication; the finding of a quantity (the quotient) which, when multiplied by a given quantity (the divisor) gives another given quantity (the dividend). *Symbol:* ÷ **5.** something that divides; a dividing line or mark. **6.** one of the parts into which a thing is divided; a section. **7.** separation by difference of opinion or feeling; disagreement; dissension. **8.** *Bot.* one of the major groupings of the plant kingdom. **9.** *Govt.* the separation of the members of a legislature, etc., into two groups, in taking a vote. **10.** one of the parts into which a country or an organisation is divided for political, administrative, judicial, military, or other purposes. **11.** a semi-independent, but ultimately subordinate administrative unit in industry or government. **12.** *Sport.* a category or section containing all teams or competitors divided according to weight, skill, age, or some other criterion. **13.** *Mil.* a major administrative and tactical formation, larger than a regiment or brigade, and smaller than a corps, usu. commanded by a major general. **14.** one of a number of trains needed to run on the same service at approximately the same time to meet unusual demand: *the Brisbane Limited 2nd division.* [L *dīvīsio;* replacing ME *devisioun,* from OF] – **divisional, divisionary,** *adj.* – **divisionally,** *adv.*

**divisionism** /də'vɪʒənɪzəm/, *n.* →**pointillism.**

**division sign** /də'vɪʒən saɪn/, *n.* the symbol (÷) placed between two expressions, denoting division of the first by the second.

**divisive** /də'vɪzɪv, -'vaɪsɪv/, *adj.* **1.** forming or expressing division or distribution. **2.** creating division or discord. – **divisively,** *adv.* – **divisiveness,** *n.*

**divisor** /də'vaɪzə/, *n. Maths.* **1.** a number by which another number (the dividend) is divided. **2.** a number contained in another given number a certain number of times, without a remainder.

**divorce** /də'vɔs/, *n., v.,* **-vorced, -vorcing.** *–n.* **1.** the dissolution of the marriage contract. **2.** any formal separation of man and wife according to established custom. **3.** a complete separation of any kind. *–v.t.* **4.** to separate; cut off. [ME *divors,* from F *divorce,* from L *dīvortium* separation, dissolution] – **divorceable,** *adj.* – **divorcer,** *n.*

**divorcee** /dəvɔ'si/, *n.* a divorced person.

**divorcement** /də'vɔsmənt/, *n.* divorce.

**divot** /'dɪvət/, *n.* **1.** *Golf, Cricket, etc.* a piece of turf cut out with a club or bat making a stroke. **2.** *Scot.* a piece of turf; a sod.

**divulgate** /də'vʌlgeɪt/, *v.t.,* **-gated, -gating.** to make publicly known; publish. [L *dīvulgātus,* pp., divulged] – **divulgater, divulgator,** *n.* – **divulgation** /ˌdivʌl'geiʃən/, *n.*

**divulge** /daɪ'vʌldʒ, də-/, *v.t.,* **-vulged, -vulging.** to disclose or reveal (something private, secret, or previously unknown). [L *dīvulgāre* make common] – **divulgement,** *n.* – **divulger,** *n.* – **divulgence,** *n.*

**divulsion** /daɪ'vʌlʃən/, *n.* a tearing asunder; violent separation. [F, from L *dīvulsio*] – **divulsive,** *adj.*

**divvy**[1] /'dɪvi/, *n., pl.* **-vies.** *Colloq.* **1.** →**dividend.** **2.** (*pl.*) rewards; profits; gains. *–v.t.* **3.** to share out (fol. by *up*). **4.** to share with (fol. by *with*). [shortened form of DIVIDEND]

**divvy**[2] /'dɪvi/, *n. Colloq.* →**divot** (def. 1).

**dixie** /'dɪksi/, *n.* **1. a.** a large iron pot in which stew, tea, etc. is made. **b.** a mess tin. **2.** a small container of ice-cream; bucket; dandy. [Hind. *degachī*]

**Dixie** /'dɪksi/, *n.* the southern U.S.

**Dixieland** /'dɪksilænd/, *n.* a style of jazz composition and performance characterised by vigorous improvisation.

**D.I.Y.,** do-it-yourself.
**dizygotic** /ˌdaɪzaɪˈgɒtɪk/, *adj.* (of twins) produced from two zygotes; fraternal.
**dizzy** /ˈdɪzi/, *adj.,* **-zier, -ziest,** *v.,* **-zied, -zying.** *–adj.* **1.** affected with a sensation of whirling, with tendency to fall; giddy; vertiginous. **2.** bewildered; confused. **3.** causing giddiness: *a dizzy height.* **4.** heedless; thoughtless. **5.** *Colloq.* foolish or stupid. *–v.t.* **6.** to make dizzy. [ME and OE *dysig* foolish, c. LG *düsig* stupefied] – **dizzily,** *adv.* – **dizziness,** *n.*
**DJ** /di ˈdʒeɪ/, *n.* →**disc jockey.**
**djelwuck** /ˈdʒɛlwʌk/, *n.* a tall shrub or small tree, *Hedycarya angustifolia,* found in or near rainforest in eastern Australia.
**Djibouti** /dʒəˈbuti/, *n.* a republic near the southern entrance to the Red Sea.
**djinn** /dʒɪn/, *n.* →**jinn.**
**dL,** decilitre.
**D. Litt.** /di ˈlɪt/, **1.** Doctor of Letters. **2.** Also, **D. Lit.** Doctor of Literature. [L *Doctor Litterārum*]
**DLP** /di ɛl ˈpi/, Democratic Labor Party.
**DM,** Deutsche Mark.
**DMA,** direct memory access.
**DMC,** direct memory channel. See **direct memory access.**
**DMR** /di ɛm ˈa/, Department of Main Roads.
**D.Mus.** /di ˈmʌs/, Doctor of Music.
**DMZ** /di ɛm ˈzɛd/, demilitarised zone.
**DNA** /di ɛn ˈeɪ/, *Biochem.* deoxyribonucleic acid.
**D-notice** /ˈdi-noʊtəs/, *n.* a classification for books, films, etc., which are considered to be in breach of the national security act.
**do**[1] /du/, *v., pres. sing.* 1 **do,** 2 **do** or (*Archaic*) **doest** or **dost,** 3 **does** or (*Archaic*) **doeth** or **doth;** *pl.* **do;** *pt.* **did;** *pp.* **done;** *ppr.* **doing;** *n.* *–v.t.* **1.** to perform (acts, duty, penance, a problem, a part, etc.). **2.** to execute (a piece or amount of work, etc.). **3.** to accomplish; finish. **4.** to put forth; exert: *do your best.* **5.** to be the cause of (good, harm, credit, etc.); bring about; effect. **6.** to render (homage, justice, etc.). **7.** to deal with (anything) as the case may require: *to do* (*cook*) *meat, do* (*wash*) *the dishes.* **8.** to cover; traverse: *we did thirty kilometres today.* **9.** to travel at a specified speed: *the car was doing 50 km/h.* **10.** to serve a period of time in a prison. **11.** to make; create; form: *she will do your portrait.* **12.** to study: *he is doing German.* **13.** to visit as a tourist or sightseer: *they did Spain last year.* **14.** *Colloq.* to serve; suffice for: *this will do us for the present.* **15.** *Colloq.* to provide; prepare: *this pub does lunches.* **16.** *Colloq.* to cheat or swindle. **17.** *Colloq.* to use up; expend: *he did his money at the races.* **18.** *Colloq.* to treat violently; beat up. **19.** *Colloq.* to have sexual intercourse with. **20.** to spay or castrate (an animal). *–v.i.* **21.** to act, esp. effectively; be in action. **22.** to behave or proceed (wisely, etc.). **23.** to get along or fare (well or ill); manage (with; without, etc.). **24.** to be as to health: *how do you do?* **25.** to serve or be satisfactory, as for the purpose; suffice; be enough: *will this do?* **26.** to deal; treat (fol. by *by*): *to do well by a man.* *–aux. v.* **27.** (used without special meaning in interrogative, negative, and inverted constructions, in imperatives with *you* or *thou* expressed and occasionally as a metric expedient in verse): *do you think so? I don't agree.* **28.** (used to lend emphasis to a principal verb): *do come!* **29.** (used to avoid repetition of a full verb or verb expression): *I think as you do. Did you see him? I did.*
*–v.* **30.** Some special verb phrases are:
**can** or **could do with,** to require or be likely to benefit from: *I could do with more sleep.*
**do a freeze,** *Colloq.* to be very cold.
**do a perish,** *Colloq.* **1.** to die. **2.** to be very cold.
**do a slow burn,** *Colloq.* to smoulder with anger.
**do a (someone),** *Colloq.* to imitate (someone): *he did a Whitlam.*
**do away with, 1.** to put an end to; abolish. **2.** to kill.
**do down,** *Colloq.* to get the better of; cheat.
**do for, 1.** to accomplish the defeat, ruin, death, etc., of. **2.** *Colloq.* to cook and keep house for. **3.** to provide or manage for. **4.** *Colloq.* to charge with a certain offence: *I've been done for speeding again.*
**do in,** *Colloq.* **1.** to kill; murder. **2.** to exhaust; tire out. **3.** to ruin. **4.** to spend, lose, esp. money.
**do one proud,** *Colloq.* to treat lavishly.
**do one's block** or **nana,** *Colloq.* to lose one's temper.
**do one's dough, 1.** to lose money on a bad buy or bet. **2.** to throw away a last chance.
**do one's nuts over,** *Colloq.* to become infatuated with.
**do one's thing,** *Colloq.* to act according to one's own self-image.
**do or die,** to make a supreme effort.
**do out of,** *Colloq.* to deprive, cheat, or swindle of.
**do over, 1.** to redecorate; renovate: *to do a room over.* **2.** to assault. **3.** *Colloq.* to have sexual intercourse with.
**do time,** to serve a term in prison.
**do up, 1.** to wrap and tie up. **2.** to fasten. **3.** to comb out and pin up (hair). **4.** to renovate. **5.** to dress up, esp. in fancy costume.
**do without, 1.** to dispense with; give up: *to do without luxuries.* **2.** to manage without; get along in the absence of: *the shop was closed, so we had to do without sweets.*
**have to do with,** to be connected with: *smoking has a lot to do with cancer.*
**make do,** to get along with the resources available.
*–n.* **31.** *Colloq.* a swindle. **32.** *Colloq.* a festivity or treat: *we're having a big do next week.* **33.** (*pl.*) rules; customs; etc.: *dos and don'ts.* **34.** *N.Z.* a success: *make a do of something.* [ME; OE *dōn,* c. D *doen,* G *tun;* akin to L *-dere,* Gk *tithénai*]
**do**[2] /doʊ/, *n.* **1.** the syllable used for the first note of the scale in solfège. See **solfège. 2.** →**doh.** [see GAMUT]
**do.,** ditto.
**D.O.A.** /di oʊ ˈeɪ/, dead on arrival.
**doab** /ˈdoʊəb/, *n.* an alluvial tract of land between two adjacent rivers, as that between the Ganges and the Jumna rivers.
**doable** /ˈduəbəl/, *adj.* that may be done.
**do-all** /ˈdu-ɔl/, *n.* →**factotum.**
**doat** /doʊt/, *v.i.* →**dote.**
**dob** /dɒb/, *v.,* **dobbed, dobbing.** *Colloq.* *–v.t.* **1.** to betray, report (someone), as for a misdemeanour (fol. by *in*). **2.** to nominate (someone absent) for an unpleasant task (fol. by *in*). **3.** *Football.* to kick, usu. accurately, esp. in shooting for goal: *he's dobbed another goal.* **4. dob in,** to contribute. **5. dob on,** to inform against; betray. *–v.i.* **6. dob in,** to contribute money to a common fund: *we'll all dob in and buy him a present.*
**D.O.B.,** date of birth.
**dobber** /ˈdɒbə/, *n. Colloq.* an informer; telltale.
**dobbin** /ˈdɒbən/, *n.* horse, esp. a workhorse. [var. of *Robin,* familiar var. of *Robert,* man's name]
**dobby** /ˈdɒbi/, *n.* a loom attachment for the weaving of small, sometimes geometric, figures. Also, **dobbie.**
**Doberman pinscher** /doʊbəmən ˈpɪntʃə/, *n.* a breed of large smooth-coated terriers, usu. black-and-tan or brown, with long forelegs, and wide hindquarters. Also, **Doberman.**
**doc** /dɒk/, *n. Colloq.* a doctor.
**docent** /ˈdoʊsənt/, *n. U.S.* a lecturer in certain colleges and universities, with a rank inferior to that of professor. [G *Dozent,* from L *docens,* ppr. of *docēre* teach]
**docile** /ˈdoʊsaɪl/, *adj.* **1.** readily trained or taught; teachable. **2.** easily managed or handled; tractable. [late ME, from L *docilis*] – **docilely,** *adv.* – **docility** /doʊˈsɪləti/, *n.*
**dock**[1] /dɒk/, *n.* **1.** a wharf. **2.** the space or waterway between two piers or wharves, as for receiving a ship while in port. **3.** such a waterway, enclosed or open, together with the surrounding piers, wharves, etc. **4.** dry dock. **5.** a semi-enclosed structure which a plane, truck, etc., can enter for the purpose of loading, repair, maintenance, etc. **6.** →**scene dock. 7.** *Colloq.* **in dock, a.** (of equipment, etc.) out of order and being fixed. **b.** (of a person) ill; laid up. *–v.t.* **8.** to bring into a dock; lay up in a dock. **9.** to put into a dry dock for repairs, cleaning, or painting. **10.** *Aerospace.* to close and lock (one spacecraft) into another while in orbit. *–v.i.* **11.** to come or go into a dock or dry dock. **12.** *Aerospace.* to close and lock two spacecraft together in orbit. [cf. D *dok;* orig. uncert.]
**dock**[2] /dɒk/, *n.* **1.** the solid or fleshy part of an animal's tail, as distinguished from the hair. **2.** the part of a tail left after cutting or clipping. *–v.t.* **3.** to cut off the end of (a tail, etc.). **4.** to deduct a part from (wages, etc.). **5.** to cut short the tail of. **6.** to deduct from the wages of. [ME *dok,* OE

*-docca,* in *fingerdocca* finger muscle]

**dock**[3] /dɒk/, *n.* an enclosed place in a courtroom where the accused is placed during trial. [cf. Flem. *dok* cage]

**dock**[4] /dɒk/, *n.* **1.** any of various plants of the genus *Rumex,* as *R. crispus* **(curled dock)** and *R. obtusifolius* **(broad-leaved dock),** mostly troublesome weeds with long taproots. **2.** any of various other plants, mostly coarse weeds. [ME *dokke,* OE *docce,* c. MD *docke*]

**dockage**[1] /ˈdɒkɪdʒ/, *n.* **1.** a charge for the use of a dock. **2.** docking accommodations. **3.** act of docking a vessel. [DOCK[1] + -AGE]

**dockage**[2] /ˈdɒkɪdʒ/, *n.* **1.** curtailment; deduction, as from wages. **2.** waste material in wheat and other grains which is easily removed. [DOCK[2] + -AGE]

**dock-dues** /ˈdɒk-djuz/, *n.* payments for use of a dock; dockage.

**docker**[1] /ˈdɒkə/, *n.* a man employed on the wharves of a port, as in loading and unloading vessels; a wharf labourer. [DOCK[1] + -ER[1]]

**docker**[2] /ˈdɒkə/, *n.* one who or that which docks, cuts short, or cuts off. [DOCK[2] + -ER[1]]

**docket** /ˈdɒkət/, *n.* **1.** an official memorandum or entry of proceedings in a legal cause, or a register of such entries. **2.** the abstract of the contents of proposed letters patent. **3.** *U.S.* the list of business to be transacted by court or assembly; the agenda; a list of projects or cases awaiting action. **4.** *U.S.* a list of causes in court for trials, or the names of the parties who have causes pending. **5.** *U.S.* a writing on a letter or document, stating its contents; any statement of particulars attached to a package, etc.; a label or ticket. **6.** a warrant certifying payment of customs duty. **7.** a receipt: *can I have a docket please?* *–v.t.* **8.** *Law.* to make an abstract or summary of the heads of, as a document; abstract and enter in a book: *judgments regularly docketed.* **9.** to endorse (a letter, etc.) with a memorandum. [ME *doket;* orig. obscure]

**docking**[1] /ˈdɒkɪŋ/, *n.* a supportive platform used in maintenance, esp. for aircraft. [DOCK[1] + -ING[1]]

**docking**[2] /ˈdɒkɪŋ/, *n.* a short piece left over when a length of timber is cut to size. [DOCK[2] + -ING[1]]

**docking saw** /ˈ– sɔ/, *n.* a motorised circular saw fitted to a bench, and used in a saw mill to cut across logs of timber.

**dock labourer** /ˈdɒk leɪbərə/, *n.* →**docker**[1].

**dockyard** /ˈdɒkjad/, *n.* a naval establishment containing docks, shops, warehouses, etc., where ships are built, fitted out, and repaired.

**doco** /ˈdɒkoʊ/, *n. Colloq.* documentary. [shortened form]

**doctor** /ˈdɒktə/, *n.* **1.** a person licensed to practise medicine, or some branch of medicine; a physician or medical practitioner other than a surgeon. **2.** a person who has received the highest degree conferred by a faculty of a university. **3.** (*cap.*) a conventional title of respect for such a person. **4.** the academic title possessed by such a person, originally implying qualification to teach, now generally based on at least three years of advanced study and research beyond the bachelor's degree. **5.** a man of great learning. **6.** any of various mechanical contrivances, designed to remedy an emergency situation or to fulfil a special function. **7. Doctor of the Church,** one of the few teachers, as St Augustine, recognised as having a major formative influence on Christian thinking. **8.** *Colloq.* an expert; one who makes the final decision: *you're the doctor.* **9.** a strong, fresh breeze, as the Albany, Esperance, Fremantle doctor. **10.** *Colloq.* **a.** ship's cook. **b.** a sheep-station cook. **11. go for the doctor, a.** to bet all one's money on a race. **b.** to make an effort that consumes all one's resources. **12. just what the doctor ordered,** *Colloq.* something agreeable; the perfect solution. *–v.t.* **13.** to treat medicinally. **14.** *Colloq.* to repair or mend. **15.** *Colloq.* to tamper with; falsify; adulterate. **16.** *Colloq.* to castrate or spay. *–v.i.* **17.** to practise medicine. [L: teacher; replacing ME *doctour,* from OF] – **doctoral,** *adj.* – **doctoress, doctress** /ˈdɒktrəs/, (*Rare*) *n. fem.*

**doctorate** /ˈdɒktərət/, *n.* the degree of doctor.

**doctor fish** /ˈdɒktə fɪʃ/, *n.* →**tench.**

**Doctor of Philosophy,** *n.* a higher university degree awarded for original research in various subjects. *Abbrev.:* Ph.D., D.Phil., D.Ph.

**doctrinaire** /dɒktrəˈnɛə/, *n.* **1.** one who tries to apply some doctrine or theory without a sufficient regard to practical considerations; an impractical theorist. *–adj.* **2.** dogmatic. **3.** theoretic and unpractical. **4.** of a doctrinaire. [F, from *doctrine* DOCTRINE] – **doctrinarism,** *n.* – **doctrinarian,** *n.*

**doctrinal** /dɒkˈtraɪnəl/, *adj.* of, pertaining to, or concerned with, doctrine. – **doctrinally,** *adv.*

**doctrine** /ˈdɒktrən/, *n.* **1.** a particular principle taught or advocated. **2.** that which is taught; teachings collectively. **3.** a body or system of teachings relating to a particular subject. [ME, from F, from L *doctrīna* teaching, learning] – **doctrinism,** *n.*

**doctrine of affection,** *n.* the theory that classifies musical effects used to express particular concepts and emotions such as joy, sorrow, languor, etc. [G *Affectenlehre* doctrine of emotional expression]

**document** /ˈdɒkjəmənt/, *n.;* /ˈdɒkjuˌmɛnt/, *v.* *–n.* **1.** a written or printed paper furnishing information or evidence, a legal or official paper. **2.** *Obs.* evidence; proof. *–v.t.* **3.** to furnish with documents, evidence, or the like. **4.** to support by documentary evidence. [ME, from L *documentum* lesson, example]

**documentary** /dɒkjuˈmɛntəri, -tri/, *adj., n., pl.* **-ries.** *–adj.* **1.** Also, **documental** /dɒkjuˈmɛntl/. pertaining to, consisting of, or derived from documents. *–n.* **2.** a factual presentation of a real event, person's life, etc., in a television or radio program, film, etc.

**documentary bill** /– ˈbɪl/, *n.* a bill of exchange to which are attached various documents, as a policy of insurance, invoice, etc.

**documentary credit** /– ˈkrɛdət/, *n.* a credit established by a banker at the request of an importer, under which the banker lends his name as drawee of bills of exchange covering the cost of goods sold to the importer, such bills to be accompanied by shipping documents.

**documentation** /ˌdɒkjumɛnˈteɪʃən/, *n.* **1.** the use of documentary evidence. **2.** a furnishing with documents. **3.** the recording of an event, as by the media.

**dodder**[1] /ˈdɒdə/, *v.i.* to shake; tremble; totter. [cf. DITHER, TOTTER] – **dodderer,** *n.* – **doddery,** *adj.*

**dodder**[2] /ˈdɒdə/, *n.* any of the leafless parasitic plants comprising the genus *Cuscuta,* with yellowish, reddish, or white threadlike stems that twine about clover, flax, etc. [ME *doder,* c. G *Dotter*]

**doddered** /ˈdɒdəd/, *adj.* infirm; feeble.

**doddering** /ˈdɒdərɪŋ/, *adj.* that dodders; shaking; tottering; feeble-minded from age; senile.

**dodder laurel** /dɒdə ˈlɒrəl/, *n.* a twining plant of the genus *Cassytha,* with slender, yellowish stems and small rounded fruit.

**dodeca-,** a word element meaning 'twelve'. Also, before vowels, **dodec-.** [Gk *dōdeka-,* combining form of *dṓdeka*]

**dodecagon** /doʊˈdɛkəgən/, *n.* a polygon having twelve angles and twelve sides. [Gk *dōdekágōnon.* See DODECA-, -GON] – **dodecagonal** /doʊdəˈkægənəl/, *adj.*

**dodecahedron** /ˌdoʊdɛkəˈhidrən/, *n., pl.* **-drons, -dra** /-drə/. a solid figure having twelve faces. [Gk *dōdekáedron*] – **dodecahedral,** *adj.*

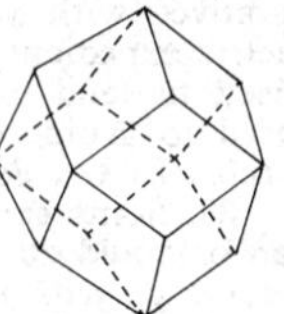
rhombic dodecahedron

**dodecaphonic** /ˌdoʊdɛkəˈfɒnɪk/, *adj.* pertaining to serial music; twelve-tone. – **dodecaphonist,** *n.* – **dodecaphony,** *n.*

**dodge** /dɒdʒ/, *v.,* **dodged, dodging,** *n.* *–v.i.* **1.** to move aside or change position suddenly, as to avoid a blow or to get behind something. **2.** to use evasive methods; prevaricate. *–v.t.* **3.** to elude by a sudden shift of position or by strategy. *–n.* **4.** an act of dodging; a spring aside. **5.** *Colloq.* an ingenious expedient or contrivance; a shifty trick. **6.** (in change-ringing) the ringing of a bell one place out of its regular ascending or descending order. [orig. uncert.]

**dodgem** /ˈdɒdʒəm/, *n.* a small, low-powered, electrically driven vehicle driven on a special rink at carnivals, shows, etc., for the amusement of bumping other dodgems. Also, **dodgem car.** [? b. DODGE + THEM]

**dodger**[1] /ˈdɒdʒə/, *n.* **1.** one who dodges. **2.** a shifty person. **3.** a small handbill. **4.** *Naut.* a sheltering screen on a ship's bridge, made of canvas and light timber.

**dodger**[2] /ˈdɒdʒə/, *n. Colloq.* food, esp. bread. [Brit. d.]

**dodge tide** /ˈdɒdʒ taɪd/, *n.* a tide during which, as a result of a particular combination of gravitational forces, the level of the water remains somewhere about its mid-point for an unusually long period of time.

**dodgy** /ˈdɒdʒi/, *adj.* **1.** artful. **2.** *Colloq.* difficult; awkward; tricky.

**dodo** /ˈdoʊdoʊ/, *n., pl.* **-does, -dos.** **1.** a clumsy flightless bird of the genera *Raphus* and *Pezophaps,* about the size of a goose, formerly inhabiting the islands of Mauritius, Reunion, and Rodriguez, but now extinct. **2.** *Colloq.* a silly or slow-witted person. **3. dead as a dodo,** *Colloq.* inanimate and beyond possibility of revival. [Pg. *doudo* silly]

dodo

**doe** /doʊ/, *n.* **1.** the female of the deer and antelope. **2.** the female of certain other animals, as the kangaroo, goat, and rabbit. [ME *do,* OE *dā.* Cf. L *dāma, damma* deer]

**doer** /ˈduə/, *n.* **1.** one who or that which does something; a performer; an actor. **2.** an amusing or odd person. **3.** a hard worker. **4.** any animal or poultry which gains weight or rapidly improves in condition.

**does** /dʌz/; *weak form* /dəz/ *v.* **1.** 3rd person singular present indicative of **do**[1]. **2. that does it!** (an exclamation indicating exasperation, defeat, etc.).

**doeskin** /ˈdoʊskɪn/, *n.* **1.** the skin of a doe. **2.** leather made from this. **3.** (*pl.*) gloves made of skin. **4.** a smoothly finished, closely woven, finely twilled woollen cloth.

**doesn't** /ˈdʌzənt/, *v.* contraction of *does not.*

**doeth** /ˈduəθ/, *v. Archaic.* (now only in poetic or liturgical use) 3rd person singular present of **do**[1].

**doff** /dɒf/, *v.t.* **1.** to put or take off, as dress. **2.** to remove (the hat) in salutation. **3.** to throw off; get rid of. [contraction of *do off.* Cf. DON[2]] – **doffer,** *n.*

**dog** /dɒg/, *n., v.,* **dogged, dogging.** *–n.* **1.** a domesticated carnivore, *Canis familiaris,* bred in a great many varieties. **2.** any animal belonging to the same family, Canidae, including the wolves, jackals, foxes, etc. **3.** the male of such an animal (opposed to *bitch*). **4.** any of various animals suggesting the dog, as the prairie dog. **5.** a despicable fellow. **6.** a fellow in general: *a gay dog.* **7.** any of various mechanical devices, as for gripping or holding something. **8.** an andiron. **9.** (*pl.*) *Colloq.* greyhound racing. **10.** (*pl.*) *Colloq.* feet. **11.** *Colloq.* an informer. **12. a dog tied up,** *Colloq.* an outstanding account. **13. go to the dogs,** *Colloq.* to go to ruin. **14. hot dog,** *Orig. U.S.* a frankfurter in a roll. **15. lame dog,** an unfortunate person; a helpless person. **16. lead a dog's life,** to have a harassed existence; to be continuously unhappy. **17. let sleeping dogs lie,** to refrain from action which might alter the existing situation. **18. put on (the) dog,** *Orig. Colloq.* to behave pretentiously; put on airs. **19. the dog's disease,** *Colloq.* a cold; influenza, esp. when the symptom of nasal catarrh is evident. *–v.t.* **20.** to follow or track like a dog, esp. with hostile intent; hound. **21.** to drive or chase with a dog or dogs. [ME *dogge,* OE *docga;* orig. unknown]

**dogbane** /ˈdɒgbeɪn/, *n.* any plant of the genus *Apocynum,* esp. *A. androsaemifolium,* a perennial herb abounding in an acrid milky juice and having an intensely bitter root that has been used in medicine.

**dogberry**[1] /ˈdɒgbəri/, *n.* any ignorant and blundering official. [from *Dogberry,* a constable in Shakespeare's *Much Ado About Nothing*] – **dogberryism,** *n.*

**dogberry**[2] /ˈdɒgberi, -bəri/, *n., pl.* **-ries.** **1.** the berry or fruit of any of various plants, as the European dogwood, *Cornus sanguinea,* or the North American chokeberry, *Aronia arbutifolia.* **2.** the plant itself. **3.** any of several other northern hemisphere plants.

**dogbox** /ˈdɒgbɒks/, *n.* **1.** a compartment in a passenger train or tram to which there is no access from within the carriage, as by a corridor. **2.** *N.Z. Colloq.* cramped quarters; a kennel-like room. **3. in the dogbox,** *N.Z. Colloq.* in disfavour (fol. by *with*).

**dogbox carriage** /– kærɪdʒ/, *n.* a railway carriage in which there is no access by corridor from one passenger compartment to another.

**dogcart** /ˈdɒgkat/, *n.* **1.** a light horse-drawn, two-wheeled vehicle with two transverse seats back to back. **2.** a cart drawn by dogs.

dogcart

**dog catcher** /ˈdɒg kætʃə/, *n.* a local government employee whose task is to round up stray dogs and take them to the local pound.

**dog-collar** /ˈdɒg-kɒlə/, *n.* **1.** a collar to identify or control a dog. **2.** a stiff collar, fastened behind, worn by certain clergymen or priests; a clerical collar. **3.** →**choker** (def. 2).

**dog days** /ˈdɒg deɪz/, *n. pl.* **1.** a sultry part of the summer. **2.** (*sing.*) a particularly hot day. [so called from their association in the northern hemisphere with the time of the heliacal rising of one of the Dog Stars]

**doge** /doʊdʒ/, *n.* the chief magistrate of the old republics of Venice and Genoa. [It., from L *dux* leader] – **dogeship,** *n.*

**dog-ear** /ˈdɒg-ɪə/, *n.* **1.** the corner of a page in a book folded over like a dog's ear, as by careless use or to mark a place. *–v.t.* **2.** to disfigure with dog-ears. – **dogeared,** *adj.*

**dog-eat-dog** /ˌdɒg-it-ˈdɒg/, *adj.* extremely competitive: *dog-eat-dog society.*

**dog-fancier** /ˈdɒg-fænsiə/, *n.* **1.** a breeder or seller of dogs. **2.** an expert or connoisseur of dogs.

**dog fence** /ˈdɒg fɛns/, *n.* a fence constructed so as to keep out dingoes or wild dogs from a property.

**dog fennel** /– ˈfɛnəl/, *n.* →**mayweed.**

**dogfight** /ˈdɒgfaɪt/, *n.* **1.** a fierce fight between two dogs. **2.** a violent engagement of fighter planes at close quarters. **3.** any rough-and-tumble physical battle.

**dogfish** /ˈdɒgfɪʃ/, *n., pl.* **-fishes,** (*esp. collectively*) **-fish.** **1.** any of various small sharks, as the Australian *Squalus megalops,* which prey on food fishes. **2.** any of various other fishes, as the bowfin.

**dog fox** /ˈdɒg fɒks/, *n.* a male fox.

**dogged** /ˈdɒgəd/, *adj.* having the pertinacity of a dog; obstinate. [DOG + -ED[3]. Cf. CRABBED] – **doggedly,** *adv.* – **doggedness,** *n.*

**dogger**[1] /ˈdɒgə/, *n.* a two-masted Dutch fishing vessel with a blunt bow, used in the North Sea. [ME *doggere.* Cf. Icel. *dugga* small fishing vessel]

**dogger**[2] /ˈdɒgə/, *n.* a person who hunts wild dogs and dingoes on which there is a bounty.

**dogger**[3] /ˈdɒgə/, *n.* **1.** a concretion of ironstone or silica in sands and clays. **2.** (*cap.*) a subdivision of the European Jurassic period, characterised by this rock formation.

**doggerel** /ˈdɒgərəl/, *adj.* **1.** (of verse) comic or burlesque, and usu. loose or irregular in measure. **2.** rude; crude; poor. *–n.* **3.** doggerel verse. Also, **dogrel** /ˈdɒgrəl/. [ME; orig. uncert.]

**doggery** /ˈdɒgəri/, *n., pl.* **-eries.** **1.** doggish behaviour or conduct; mean or mischievous action. **2.** dogs collectively. **3.** rabble; canaille.

**doggie** /ˈdɒgi/, *n., adj.,* **-gier, -giest.** *–n.* **1.** a little dog. **2.** a pet term for any dog. **3.** →**spotted mackerel.** *–adj.* **4.** of or pertaining to a dog. **5.** fond of dogs. **6.** of or pertaining to short, coarse, straight wool of nondescript type, frequently found on old sheep. Also, **doggy.**

**doggie bag** /ˈ– bæg/, *n.* a bag provided by a restaurant or the like, for carrying home leftovers, as for a dog. Also, **doggy bag.**

**dogging** /ˈdɒgɪŋ/, *n.* the hunting of dingoes or wild dogs.

**doggish** /ˈdɒgɪʃ/, *adj.* **1.** canine. **2.** surly. – **doggishly,** *adv.* – **doggishness,** *n.*

**doggo** /ˈdɒgoʊ/, *adv. Colloq.* **1.** out of sight. **2. lie doggo,** to hide; remain in concealment.

**doggone** /ˈdɒgɒn/, *U.S. Colloq.* *–adj.* **1.** darned; damn. *–adv.* **2.** very; extremely: *he's doggone rich.*

**doghouse** /ˈdɒghaus/, *n.* **1.** a kennel. **2.** a wretched house or dwelling. **3.** the raised section at the after end of the cabin on a yacht. **4. in the doghouse,** in disfavour.

**dog in the manger,** *n.* a person who, like the dog in Aesop's fable, churlishly keeps something of no particular use to himself so that others cannot use it.

**dog Latin** /dɒg 'lætn/, *n.* mongrel or spurious Latin.

**dogleg** /'dɒglɛg/, *n.* **1.** an angle in a road, track, etc., resembling that of a dog's hind leg. *–adj.* **2.** Also, **dog-legged.** having such a bend.

**dogleg fence** /– 'fɛns/, *n.* **1.** a fence in which the members supporting the uprights and the top rail form doglegs. **2.** a single fence consisting of logs interlaced on a zigzag course.

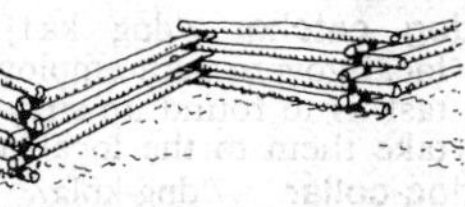
dogleg fence (def. 2)

**dogma** /'dɒgmə/, *n., pl.* **-mas, -mata** /-mətə/. **1.** a system of principles or tenets, as of a church. **2.** a tenet or doctrine authoritatively laid down, as by a church. **3.** prescribed doctrine. **4.** a settled opinion; a belief; a principle. [L, from Gk]

**dogman** /'dɒgmən/, *n.* a construction worker who works with cranes, often travelling up and down with the load or on the crane hook; rigger.

**dogmatic** /dɒg'mætɪk/, *adj.* **1.** of, pertaining to, or of the nature of a dogma or dogmas; doctrinal. **2.** asserting opinions in an authoritative, positive, or arrogant manner; positive; opinionated. Also, **dogmatical.** – **dogmatically,** *adv.*

**dogmatics** /dɒg'mætɪks/, *n.* the science which treats of the arrangement and statement of religious doctrines, esp. of the doctrines received in and taught by the Christian church; doctrinal theology.

**dogmatise** /'dɒgmətaɪz/, *v.,* **-tised, -tising.** *–v.i.* **1.** to make dogmatic assertions; speak or write dogmatically. *–v.t.* **2.** to assert or deliver as a dogma. Also, **dogmatize.** [ML *dogmatizāre,* from Gk *dogmatízein*] – **dogmatisation** /dɒgmətaɪ'zeɪʃən/, *n.* – **dogmatiser,** *n.*

**dogmatism** /'dɒgmətɪzəm/, *n.* dogmatic character; authoritative, positive, or arrogant assertion of opinions.

**dogmatist** /'dɒgmətəst/, *n.* **1.** one who asserts positively his own opinions; a dogmatic person. **2.** one who lays down dogmas.

**dog nail** /'dɒg neɪl/, *n.* **1.** →**dog spike.** **2.** →**ceiling dog.**

**dog net** /'– nɛt/, *n.* a fence which keeps out dogs, esp. dingoes.

**do-gooder** /'du-gʊdə/, *n. Colloq.* a well-intentioned, but often clumsy social reformer.

**dog paddle** /'dɒg pædl/, *n.* a simple, very slow swimming stroke, in which the arms and legs are flicked below water.

**dogrose** /'dɒgroʊz/, *n.* **1.** →**bauera.** **2.** a thorny shrub, *Rosa canina,* family Rosaceae, of temperate Eurasia, having pink or white flowers, used as a stock for grafting hybrid roses.

**dog run** /'dɒg rʌn/, *n.* a long wire stretched from one point to another, to which a dog's chain is attached allowing it a certain amount of freedom.

**dogsbody** /'dɒgzbɒdi/, *n. Colloq.* an overworked drudge, esp. one who is imposed on.

**dog's breakfast** /dɒgz 'brɛkfəst/, *n. Colloq.* a mess; a confused state of affairs. Also, **dog's dinner.**

**dog's cock** /'– kɒk/, *n. Colloq.* an exclamation mark.

**dog's eye** /'dɒgz aɪ/, *n. Colloq.* a meat pie. [rhyming slang]

**dog shark** /'dɒg ʃak/, *n.* →**dogfish.**

**dogshore** /'dɒgʃɔ/, *n.* one of the timbers holding a small vessel temporarily before launching.

**dog's mercury** /dɒgz 'mɜkjəri/, *n.* a euphorbiaceous creeping perennial, *Mercuralis perennis,* with small unisexual flowers, common in woods of Europe and south-western Asia.

**dog spike** /'dɒg spaɪk/, *n.* a heavy nail which spikes a rail to a sleeper in the permanent way. Also, **dog nail.**

**dog squad** /'dɒg skwɒd/, *n. Prison Colloq.* undercover police.

**dog's-tail** /'dɒgz-teɪl/, *n.* any grass of the Old World genus *Cynosurus,* the species of which have the spikes fringed on one side only, esp. *C. cristatus* (**crested dog's-tail**). Also, **dog's-tail grass.**

**dogstick** /'dɒgstɪk/, *n.* →**sprag** (def. 1).

**dog's-tongue** /'dɒgz-tʌŋ/, *n.* →**hound's-tongue.**

**dog's-tooth grass** /'dɒgz-tuθ ˌgras/, *n.* →**couch**[2].

**dog tag** /'dɒg tæg/, *n.* →**identity disc.**

**dog-tired** /dɒg-'taɪəd/, *adj.* very tired.

**dogtooth** /'dɒgtuθ/, *n., pl.* **-teeth** /-tiθ/. **1.** a canine tooth. **2.** *Archit.* a toothlike medieval ornament, or a moulding cut in projecting teeth. **3.** Also, **dog's tooth.** →**hound's-tooth.**

**dog-tooth tuna** /– 'tjunə/, *n.* a white-fleshed tuna, *Gymnosarcha nuda,* of northern Australian waters.

**dogtooth violet** /ˌdɒgtuθ 'vaɪələt/, *n.* **1.** a bulbous plant, *Erythronium dens-canis,* of Europe, bearing purple flowers. **2.** any of several American plants of the same genus. Also, **dog's-tooth violet, dogviolet.**

**dog trailer** /'dɒg treɪlə/, *n.* a trailer of large capacity towed behind a truck, as for carrying ore. Cf. **semitrailer.**

**dogtrot** /'dɒgtrɒt/, *n.* a gentle trot, like that of a dog.

**dog-tucker** /'dɒg-tʌkə/, *Colloq.* *–n.* **1.** meat used for dog food. *–adj.* **2.** (of a sheep) fit only to be used as dog food.

**dogvane** /'dɒgveɪn/, *n.* →**telltale** (def. 6).

**dogwatch** /'dɒgwɒtʃ/, *n.* **1.** *Naut.* either of two short watches on shipboard, from 4 to 6 p.m. and from 6 to 8 p.m. introduced to effect changes in watches kept on consecutive days. **2.** the night shift, as in a colliery.

**dogwhelk** /'dɒgwɛlk/, *n.* any of several whelks of the class Gastropoda, as *Plicarcularia thersites* of northern Australia and other areas of the Indo-Pacific.

**dogwood** /'dɒgwʊd/, *n.* **1.** any tree or shrub of the genus *Cornus,* esp. *C. sanguinea,* a deciduous shrub of calcareous soil in Europe, family Cornaceae. **2.** the wood of any such tree. **3.** a name used for various unrelated plants which emit a foetid odour when burning.

**doh** /doʊ/, *n.* the syllable used for the first note of the scale in solfa. Also, **do.** See **solfa.**

**doily** /'dɔɪli/, *n., pl.* **-lies.** **1.** a small ornamental mat, as of embroidery or lace, paper or plastic, often placed under cakes, sandwiches, etc., on a plate. **2.** *Archaic.* a small ornamental napkin used at the table at dessert, etc. Also, **doiley.** [named after a 17th-cent. draper of London]

**doing** /'duɪŋ/, *n.* **1.** action; performance; execution: *it's all in the doing.* **2.** (*pl.*) deeds; proceedings. **3.** (*pl.*) the materials or ingredients for a meal. **4.** *Colloq.* a scolding; a beating. **5. nothing doing,** (an exclamation indicating refusal). **6. take a bit of** or **a lot of** or **some doing,** to require great effort.

**do-it-yourself** /du-ət-jə'sɛlf/, *adj. Colloq.* of or designed for use by amateurs without special training: *a do-it-yourself kit for building a radio.* – **do-it-yourselfer,** *n.*

**dol.,** dollar.

**dolabriform** /doʊ'læbrəfɔm/, *adj. Bot., Zool.* shaped like an axe or a cleaver. [L *dolābra* pickaxe, axe + -I- + -FORM]

**Dolbyised** /'dɒlbiaɪzd/, *adj.* subjected to the Dolby system.

**Dolby system** /'dɒlbi sɪstəm/, *n.* either of two systems, Dolby A and Dolby B, by means of which noise is reduced in recording and playback of magnetic tapes; Dolby A treats all sections of the sound spectrum while Dolby B treats only the high frequency end of the spectrum. [Trademark]

dolabriform leaf

**dolce** /'dɒltʃeɪ/, *adv.* **1.** (a musical direction) sweetly; softly. **2.** a soft-toned organ stop. [It.: sweet, from L *dulcis*] – **dolce,** *adj.*

**dolce vita** /– 'vitə/, *n.* sweet life; life dedicated to the pursuit of pleasure. [It.]

**doldrums** /'dɒldrəmz/, *n.pl.* **1. a.** the region of relatively calm winds near the equator. **b.** the calms or weather variations characteristic of those parts. **2. in the doldrums,** a period of dullness, depression, etc. [orig. uncert.]

**dole**[1] /doʊl/, *n., v.,* **doled, doling.** *–n.* **1.** a portion of money, food, etc., given, esp. in charity or for maintenance. **2.** a dealing out or distributing, esp. in charity. **3.** a payment by a government to an unemployed person. **4. go** or **be on the dole,** to receive such payments. **5.** *Archaic.* one's fate or destiny. *–v.t.* **6.** to distribute in charity. **7.** to give out sparingly or in small quantities (fol. by *out*). [ME; OE *dāl* part, portion. See DEAL[1]]

**dole**[2] /doʊl/, *n. Archaic.* grief or sorrow; lamentation. [ME *dol, doel,* from OF, from L *dolēre* grieve]

**dole bludger** /ˈdoʊl blʌdʒə/, *n. Colloq.* (*derog.*) one who is unemployed and lives on social security payments without making proper attempts to find employment.

**doleful** /ˈdoʊlfəl/, *adj.* full of grief; sorrowful; gloomy. – **dolefully,** *adv.* – **dolefulness,** *n.*

**dolente** /dɒˈlɛnteɪ/, *adv.* (a musical direction) sadly; plaintively. [It.]

**dolerite** /ˈdɒləraɪt/, *n.* **1.** a coarse-grained variety of basalt. **2.** any of various other igneous rocks, as diabase. **3.** any igneous rock resembling basalt whose composition cannot be determined without microscopic examination. [F, from Gk *dolerós* deceptive + -ITE[1]] – **doleritic** /dɒləˈrɪtɪk/, *adj.*

**doley** /ˈdoʊli/, *n. Colloq.* a person in receipt of the dole.

**dolichocephalic** /ˌdɒləkoʊsəˈfælɪk/, *adj.* **1.** long-headed; having a breadth of head small in proportion to the length from front to back (opposed to *brachycephalic*). **2.** having a cephalic index of 75 or less. Also, **dolichocephalous** /ˌdɒləkoʊˈsɛfələs/. [Gk *dolichó(s)* long + Gk *kephalḗ* head + -IC] – **dolichocephalism** /ˌdɒləkoʊˈsɛfəlɪzəm/, *n.* – **dolichocephaly,** *n.*

**dolichocranic** /dɒləkoʊˈkreɪnɪk/, *adj.* **1.** long-skulled; having a breadth of skull small in proportion to length from front to back (opposed to *brachycranic*). **2.** having a cranial index of 75 or less.

**dolichos** /ˈdɒlikɒs/, *n.* →**lablab.**

**doline** /ˈdɒlin/, *n.* a shallow depression, either funnel- or saucer-shaped, and having its floor covered by cultivated soil, formed by solution in mountain limestone country. Also, **dolina** /dɒˈlinə/. [Serbo-Croat *dolina*]

**doll** /dɒl/, *n.* **1.** a toy puppet representing a child or other human being; a child's toy baby. **2.** a pretty but expressionless or unintelligent woman. **3.** *Colloq.* an attractive woman, esp. one who is young. *–v.i.* **4.** *Colloq.* to dress in a smart or showy manner (fol. by *up*). *–v.t.* **5.** to dress (oneself) up rather too smartly or too much (fol. by *up*). [from *Doll, Dolly,* for *Dorothy,* woman's name] – **dollish,** *adj.* – **dollishly,** *adv.* – **dollishness,** *n.*

**dollar** /ˈdɒlə/, *n.* **1.** the monetary unit of Australia, equal to 100 cents. *Symbol:* $ **2.** any of various units elsewhere, as in the U.S., Hong Kong, etc. **3. bottom dollar,** the last of a person's money: *down to his bottom dollar.* [earlier *daler,* from LG and early mod. D, c. HG *Thaler,* for *Joachimsthaler* coin of Joachimsthal, town in Bohemia where they were coined]

**dollar area** /ˈdɒlər ɛəriə/, *n.* those countries in which the U.S. dollar is the international unit of currency.

**dollar bird** /ˈdɒlə bɜd/, *n.* an insectivorous bird, *Eurystomus orientalis,* with conspicuous pale patches on the underwings, which breeds in summer in Australia and migrates to New Guinea and islands further north.

**dollar diplomacy** /– dəˈploʊməsi/, *n. U.S.* **1.** diplomacy dictated by financial interest. **2.** diplomacy in the field of foreign relations employing financial means to increase another country's security, or increase political power in another country. **3.** a government policy of promoting the business interests of its citizens in other countries.

**dollar spot** /ˈ– spɒt/, *n.* a disease of turf grasses, appearing as small dollar-shaped, yellowish patches caused by a soil-inhabiting fungus.

**dollop** /ˈdɒləp/, *n. Colloq.* a lump; a mass.

**doll's house** /ˈdɒlz haʊs/, *n.* **1.** a toy house for dolls. **2.** a small, pretty house, built in a conventional style. Also, *U.S.,* **dollhouse.**

**dolly**[1] /ˈdɒli/, *n., pl.* **dollies. 1.** a child's name for a doll. **2. a.** a low truck with small wheels for moving loads too heavy to be carried by hand. **b.** *Films, Television.* a small, mobile platform for carrying cameras, directors, etc., and often running on tracks. **3.** *Mach.* a tool for receiving and holding the head of a rivet while the other end is being headed. **4.** *Bldg Trades.* an extension piece placed on the lead of a pile while being driven. **5.** any of a number of devices thought to resemble a doll or which derives from one, such as **a.** a short wooden pole with arms or handles attached toward the top and prongs or paddles toward the bottom which was formerly used to agitate or pound clothes being washed; posser. **b.** a similar implement used in scouring wool, washing ore, breaking and mixing clay in a puddling tub, etc. **c.** (in panel beating, etc.) a hand tool with one end made very heavy as by lead, and used to form sheet metal, reshape a dented pipe, etc. **6.** an early form of stamping machine for crushing gold-bearing rock. **7.** Also, **dolly bird.** *Colloq.* a girl, esp. a young, attractive one, who is not particularly intelligent. **8. up to dolly's wax,** up to one's neck. *–v.i.* **9.** *Films, Television.* to move the dolly forwards or backwards while shooting film. *–v.t.* **10.** to reshape or form metal using a dolly (def. 5c). **11.** *Mining.* to crush (gold-bearing rock) by means of a dolly. **12.** *Colloq.* to falsify evidence against: *the police dollied Joe.*

**dolly**[2] /ˈdɒli/, *n.* a doughnut-shaped hand fishing reel, usu. made of wood or plastic.

**dolly catch** /ˈ– kætʃ/, *n.* (in cricket) a simple, easily taken catch.

**dollying** /ˈdɒliɪŋ/, *n.* (in mining) an operation applied in the field in which vein or reef material is first reduced to a powder so that its free gold content can be tested.

**dolly mixture** /ˈdɒli mɪkstʃə/, *n.* a variety of miniature sweets designed for children.

**dolly mop** /ˈ– mɒp/, *n.* a dish mop.

**dolly pot** /ˈ– pɒt/, *n.* a tub in which a dolly (def. 5) is used. Also, **dolly tub.**

**Dolly Varden** /dɒli ˈvadn/, *n.* **1.** a style of gay-flowered print gown. **2.** a broad-brimmed, flower-trimmed hat, formerly worn by women. [named after a character in Dickens's *Barnaby Rudge*]

**dolmades** /dɒlˈmadiz/, *n. pl.* (in cookery) blanched vine leaves with a stuffing of minced lamb and cooked rice, rolled into balls or packets and braised in a little stock with oil and lemon juice. Also, **dolmas.**

dolman

**dolman** /ˈdɒlmən/, *n., pl.* **-mans. 1.** a woman's mantle with capelike arm pieces instead of sleeves. **2.** a long outer robe worn by Turks. **3.** a hussar's jacket, worn over the shoulder like a cape, with one or both sleeves hanging loosely. [Turk *dōlāmān*]

**dolman sleeve** /– ˈsliv/, *n.* a sleeve tapering to the wrist from a wide armhole, used in women's clothes.

**dolmas** /ˈdɒlməz/, *n.pl.* →**dolmades.**

**dolmen** /ˈdɒlmən/, *n.* a structure usu. regarded as a tomb, consisting of two or more large upright stones set with a space between and capped by a horizontal stone. Cf. **cromlech.** [F, made up by French writers as if from Breton *taol, tol* table + *men* stone]

dolmen

**dolomite** /ˈdɒləmaɪt/, *n.* **1.** a very common mineral, calcium magnesium carbonate, $CaMg(CO_3)_2$, occurring in crystals and in masses (called **dolomite marble** when coarse-grained); pearl spar. **2.** a rock consisting essentially or largely of this mineral. [named after D. G. de *Dolomieu,* 1750-1801, French geologist] – **dolomitic** /dɒləˈmɪtɪk/, *adj.*

**doloroso** /dɒləˈroʊsoʊ/, *adv.* (a musical direction) with pain or sadness; plaintively. [It.] – **doloroso,** *adj.*

**dolorous** /ˈdɒlərəs/, *adj.* full of, expressing, or causing pain or sorrow; distressed; grievous; mournful. – **dolorously,** *adv.* – **dolorousness,** *n.*

**dolour** /ˈdɒlə, ˈdoʊlə/, *n.* sorrow or grief. Also, *U.S.,* **dolor.** [ME *doloure,* from OF *dolour,* from L *dolor* pain, grief]

**dolphin** /ˈdɒlfən/, *n.* **1.** any of various cetaceans of the family Delphinidae, some of which are commonly called porpoises, esp. *Delphinus delphis,* which has a long, sharp nose and abounds in the Mediterranean and the temperate Atlantic. **2.** either of two fishes of tropical and temperate seas *Coryphaena hippurus* and *C. equisetis,* noted for their rapid colour changes when dying. **3.** *Naut.* a post, pile cluster, or buoy to which

dolphin

to moor a vessel. [ME *dalphyne,* from OF *daulphin,* from L *delphīnus,* from Gk *delphís.* Cf. DAUPHIN]

**dolphin kick** /'– kɪk/, *n.* a kick, usu. performed in the butterfly stroke, in which the legs are held together and moved up and down by bending and straightening them at the knee twice in quick succession.

**dolphin striker** /'– straɪkə/, *n. Naut.* →**martingale** (def. 2).

**dolt** /doʊlt/, *n.* a dull, stupid fellow; a blockhead. – **doltish,** *adj.* – **doltishly,** *adv.* – **doltishness,** *n.*

**dom** /dɒm/, *n.* **1.** (*oft. cap.*) the title of a monk in some orders, esp. the Benedictines. **2.** (formerly) a title of nobility in Portugal.

**-dom,** a noun suffix meaning: **1.** domain, as in *kingdom.* **2.** collection of persons, as in *officialdom.* **3.** rank or station, as in *earldom.* **4.** general condition, as in *freedom.* [OE *-dōm,* suffix, representing *dōm,* n. See DOOM]

**dom.,** **1.** domestic. **2.** domicile. **3.** dominant.

**d.o.m.** /di oʊ 'ɛm/, *n. Colloq.* dirty old man.

**domain** /də'meɪn/, *n.* **1.** *Law.* ultimate ownership and control over the use of land. **2.** an estate; any land held in possession. **3.** a territory under rule or influence; a realm. **4.** (*oft. cap.*) a public park, a recreation ground: *the Sydney Domain.* **5.** a field of action, thought, etc.: *the domain of commerce or of science.* **6.** the scope or range of any sphere of personal knowledge. **7.** a region with specific characteristics, types of growth, animal life, etc. **8.** *Physics.* a small region of a ferromagnetic substance in which the constituent atoms or molecules have a common direction of magnetisation. **9.** *Maths.* (of a function) the set of values of the independent variables for which the function is defined. [F *domaine,* OF *demeine* (see DEMESNE), from L *dominicum,* orig. neut. of *dominicus* of a lord]

**domatium** /doʊ'meɪʃəm/, *n.* a small cavity usu. on a leaf in the axil of a vein, and often giving shelter to microfauna.

**dome** /doʊm/, *n., v.,* **domed, doming.** –*n.* **1.** *Archit.* **a.** a large, hemispherical, approximately hemispherical, or spheroidal vault, its form produced by rotating an arch on its vertical radius. **b.** a roof of domical shape. **c.** a vault or curved roof on a polygonal plan, as an octagonal dome. **2.** a large, impressive, or fanciful structure. **3.** anything shaped like a dome. **4.** *Crystall.* a form whose planes intersect the vertical axis but are parallel to one of the lateral axes. **5.** *Geol.* a roughly symmetrical upfold, the beds dipping in all directions, more or less equally, from a point. **6.** *Geol.* a smoothly-rounded rock-capped mountain summit, roughly resembling the dome or cupola of a building. **7.** →**press-stud.** **8.** *Colloq.* a person's head. –*v.t.* **9.** to cover with or as with a dome. **10.** to shape like a dome. –*v.i.* **11.** to rise or swell as a dome. [L *domus* house; partly through F *dôme* cathedral church, from It. *duomo* cupola, dome, from Pr. *doma* cupola, from Gk: house] – **domelike,** *adj.*

**domestic** /də'mɛstɪk/, *adj.* **1.** of or pertaining to the home, the household, or household affairs. **2.** devoted to home life or affairs. **3.** living with man; tame: *domestic animals.* **4.** of or pertaining to one's own or a particular country as apart from other countries. **5.** belonging, existing, or produced within a country; not foreign: *domestic trade.* –*n.* **6.** a hired household servant. **7.** *Colloq.* an argument with one's spouse. **8.** (*pl.*) home manufacturers or goods. [L *domesticus* belonging to the household] – **domestically,** *adv.*

**domesticate** /də'mɛstəkeɪt/, *v.t., v.i.,* **-cated, -cating.** **1.** to convert to domestic uses; tame. **2.** to attach to home life or affairs. **3.** to cause to be or feel at home; naturalise. – **domestication** /dəmɛstə'keɪʃən/, *n.* – **domesticator,** *n.*

**domestic help** /də,mɛstɪk 'hɛlp/, *n.* **1.** one hired to provide assistance in the house, esp. with cleaning. **2.** the assistance provided.

**domesticity** /,dɒmɛs'tɪsəti/, *n., pl.* **-ties.** **1.** the state of being domesticated; domestic or home life. **2.** (*pl.*) domestic affairs; home conditions and arrangements.

**domestic science** /də,mɛstɪk 'saɪəns/, *n.* the academic study of cookery, needlework, and housework.

**domical** /'doʊməkəl, 'dɒməkəl/, *adj.* **1.** domelike. **2.** having a dome or domes. – **domically,** *adv.*

**domicile** /'dɒməsaɪl/, *n., v.,* **-ciled, -ciling.** –*n.* **1.** a place of residence; an abode; a house or home. **2.** *Law.* a permanent legal residence. **3.** *Comm.* a place at which a bill of exchange is made payable other than the acceptor's private or business address. –*v.t.* **4.** to establish in a domicile. –*v.i.* **5.** to have one's domicile; dwell (fol. by *at, in,* etc.). **6.** to name the place at which a bill of exchange will be payable. [F, from L *domicilium* habitation, dwelling]

**domiciliary** /dɒmə'sɪliəri, -'sɪljəri/, *adj.* of or pertaining to a domicile.

**domiciliate** /dɒmə'sɪlieɪt/, *v.t., v.i.,* **-ated, -ating.** →**domicile.** – **domiciliation** /,dɒməsɪli'eɪʃən/, *n.*

**dominance** /'dɒmənəns/, *n.* **1.** rule; control; authority; ascendancy. **2.** the condition of being dominant. Also, **dominancy.**

**dominant** /'dɒmənənt/, *adj.* **1.** ruling; governing; controlling; most influential. **2.** occupying a commanding position: *the dominant points of the globe.* **3.** main; major; chief: *steel production is the dominant industry in Newcastle.* **4.** *Genetics.* pertaining to or exhibiting a dominant, as opposed to a recessive. **5.** *Music.* pertaining to or based on the dominant: *the dominant chord.* –*n.* **6.** *Genetics.* a hereditary character resulting from a gene with a greater biochemical activity than another, termed the recessive. The dominant masks the recessive. **7.** *Music.* the fifth note of a scale. [F, from L *dominans,* ppr.] – **dominantly,** *adv.*

**dominant seventh chord,** *n.* (in music) a major triad with an added minor seventh, often used as a dominant chord. Also, **seventh chord.**

**dominant tenement** /dɒmənənt 'tɛnəmənt/, *n.* (in law) land in favour of which an easement or other servitude exists over another's land (the **servient tenement**). Also, **dominant estate.**

**dominate** /'dɒməneɪt/, *v.,* **-nated, -nating.** –*v.t.* **1.** to rule over; govern; control. **2.** to tower above; overshadow. –*v.i.* **3.** to rule; exercise control; predominate. **4.** to occupy a commanding position. [L *dominātus,* pp.] – **dominator,** *n.,* – **dominative,** *adj.*

**domination** /dɒmə'neɪʃən/, *n.* **1.** the act of dominating. **2.** rule or sway, often arbitrary. **3.** (*pl.*) an order of angels. See **angel** (def. 1).

**domineer** /dɒmə'nɪə/, *v.i.* **1.** to govern arbitrarily; tyrannise. **2.** to command haughtily; behave arrogantly. **3.** to tower (over or above). –*v.t.* **4.** to rule or command (someone) arrogantly or arbitrarily. [D *domineren,* from F *dominer,* from L *dominārī* rule]

**domineering** /dɒmə'nɪərɪŋ/, *adj.* inclined to domineer; overbearing; tyrannical. – **domineeringly,** *adv.* – **domineeringness,** *n.*

**dominical** /də'mɪnɪkəl/, *adj.* **1.** of or pertaining to Jesus Christ as Lord. **2.** of or pertaining to the Lord's Day, or Sunday. [ML *dominicālis* of or pertaining to the Lord or the Lord's Day (ML *dominica*), from L *dominicus* belonging to a lord or (LL) the Lord]

**Dominican Republic** /də,mɪnɪkən rə'pʌblɪk/, *n.* a republic in the West Indies occupying the eastern part of the island of Hispaniola.

**dominie** /'dɒməni/, *n.* **1.** *Chiefly Scot.* a schoolmaster. **2.** a clergyman, pastor, or parson (a title used specifically in the reformed churches.). [L *domine,* vocative of *dominus* master, lord]

**dominion** /də'mɪnjən/, *n.* **1.** the power or right of governing and controlling; sovereign authority. **2.** rule or sway; control or influence. **3.** a territory, usu. of considerable size, in which a single rulership holds sway. **4.** lands or domains subject to sovereignty or control. **5.** a territory constituting a self-governing commonwealth and being one of a number of such territories united in a community of nations, or empire (formerly applied to self-governing divisions of the British Empire, as Canada, New Zealand, etc.). **6.** (*pl.*) *Theol.* domination (def. 3). [ME, from F (obs.), from L *dominium* lordship, ownership]

**dominium** /də'mɪnjəm/, *n. Law.* complete power to use, to enjoy, and to dispose of property at will. [L. See DOMINION]

**domino**[1] /'dɒmənoʊ/, *n., pl.* **-noes, -nos.** **1.** a large, loose cloak, usu. hooded, worn with a small mask by persons in masquerade. **2.** the mask. **3.** a person wearing such dress. [Sp., from L, dative of *dominus* master]

**domino**[2] /'dɒmənoʊ/, *n., pl.* **-noes.** **1.** (*pl. construed as sing.*) any of various games played with flat, oblong pieces of ivory, bone, or wood, the face of which is divided into two parts, each left blank or marked with pips, usu. from one to six. **2.** one of these pieces. **3.** *Obs. Colloq.* the last in a succession of things, pleasant or unpleasant. **4.** *Obs. Colloq.* the last lash in a flogging. [orig. unknown]

**domino theory** /'– θɪəri/, *n.* a theory that a particular political development or event in one country will lead to its repetition in others, as a Communist takeover of one South-East Asian country leading to a similar takeover of neighbouring countries.

**domra** /'dɒmrə/, *n.* a Russian folk-instrument, usu. with three strings, which are plucked.

**don**[1] /dɒn/, *n.* **1.** (*cap.*) a Spanish title prefixed to the Christian name of a man of a high rank. **2.** a Spanish lord or gentleman. **3.** a person of great importance. **4.** (in British universities) a head, fellow, or tutor of a college. **5.** the leader of a Mafia family. [Sp., from L *dominus* master, lord]

**don**[2] /dɒn/, *v.t.,* **donned, donning.** to put on (clothing, etc.). [contraction of *do on.* Cf. DOFF]

**donah** /'doʊnə/, *n. Colloq.* (formerly) a girl, sweetheart. [Sp. *doña,* from L *domina* mistress, lady]

**donary** /'doʊnəri/, *n.* a votive offering; a thing given to sacred use.

**donate** /doʊ'neɪt/, *v.t.,* **-nated, -nating.** to present as a gift; make a gift or donation of, as to a fund or cause. [back-formation from DONATION] – **donator,** *n.*

**donation** /doʊ'neɪʃən/, *n.* **1.** the act of presenting something as a gift. **2.** a gift, as to a fund; a contribution. [L *dōnātio,* from *dōnāre* give]

**donative** /'doʊnətɪv/, *n.* **1.** a gift or donation; a largess. *–adj.* **2.** of the nature of a donation; vested or vesting by donation.

**done** /dʌn/, *v.* **1.** past participle of **do**[1]. **2. have** or **be done with,** to finish relations or connections with. *–adj.* **3.** executed; completed; finished; settled. **4.** cooked. **5.** worn out; used up. **6.** in conformity with fashion and good taste: *it isn't done.* **7. done for,** *Colloq.* **a.** dead. **b.** close to death. **c.** utterly exhausted. **d.** deprived of one's means of livelihood, etc.; ruined. **8. done in,** *Colloq.* very tired; exhausted. **9. done out,** *Colloq.* cheated; tricked (fol. by *of*). **10. done up,** *Colloq.* **a.** dressed smartly. **b.** finished; ruined. *–interj.* **11.** agreed; settled.

**donee** /doʊ'ni/, *n. Law.* **1.** one to whom a gift is made. **2.** one who has a power of appointment in property. [DON(OR) + -EE]

**dong** /dɒŋ/, *v.t.* **1.** *Colloq.* to hit, punch. *–v.i.* **2.** (of a bell, etc.) to ring. *–n.* **3.** a heavy blow. **4.** *Colloq.* the penis.

**donga** /'dɒŋgə/, *n.* **1.** a shallow gully or dried-out watercourse. **2.** a makeshift shelter. **3.** *Chiefly Papua New Guinea.* a house. **4. the donga,** *Colloq.* the bush; the outback. *–v.i. Colloq.* **5.** to loaf; bludge. [Afrikaans: watercourse, from Zulu *udonga*]

**donger** /'dɒŋə/, *n.* **1.** a club (for stunning fish, etc.). **2.** *Colloq.* the penis.

**donjon** /'dʌndʒən, 'dɒn-/, *n.* the inner tower, keep, or stronghold of a castle. [archaic var. of DUNGEON]

**Don Juan** /dɒn 'dʒuən, – 'wan/, *n.* a seducer of women; rake. [named after *Don Juan,* a legendary Spanish nobleman of dissolute habits]

**donk**[1] /dɒŋk/, *n. Colloq.* **1.** →**donkey engine. 2.** any engine.

**donk**[2] /dɒŋk/, *n. Colloq.* **1.** a donkey. **2.** a racehorse.

**donkey**[1] /'dɒŋki/, *n., pl.* **-keys,** *adj.* *–n.* **1.** a domesticated ass, *Equus asinus,* used as a beast of burden. **2.** a stupid, silly or obstinate person. **3. donkey's years,** a long time. *–adj.* **4.** *Mach.* auxiliary: *donkey pump.* [? familiar var. of *Duncan,* man's name]

**donkey**[2] /'dɒŋki/, *v., n. S.A. Colloq.* *–v.t.* **1.** →**double** (def. 41). *–n.* **2.** →**double** (def. 29).

**donkey deep** /'– dip/, *adj. N.Z. Colloq.* deeply immersed or versed in.

**donkey drop** /'– drɒp/, *n. Colloq.* (in cricket) a slow, high ball which looks easy to hit.

**donkey engine** /'– ɛndʒən/, *n.* a small, usu. subsidiary, steam engine.

**donkey jacket** /'– dʒækət/, *n. Brit.* **1.** a hip-length thick jacket, in the style of a reefer, but usu. with a leather or imitation leather panel across the shoulders. **2.** →**reefer**[1].

**donkey-lick** /'dɒŋki-lɪk/, *v.t. Horseracing, etc., Colloq.* to defeat (another contestant in a race) with ease.

**donkey orchid** /'dɒŋki ɔkəd/, *n.* a terrestrial orchid, *Diuris longifolia,* with yellow and brown flowers, widespread in southern Australia.

**donkey vote** /'– voʊt/, *n.* **1.** in a compulsory preferential system of voting, a vote in which the voter's apparent order of preference among the candidates listed on the ballot paper corresponds with the order in which the names appear in the list, so that he probably is not expressing any preference at all. **2.** the proportion of such votes to the total ballot.

**donkey work** /'– wɜk/, *n. Colloq.* drudgery; hard, tedious work.

**donna** /'dɒnə/, *n.* **1.** a lady. **2.** (*cap.*) a title of respect for a lady. [It., from L *domina* lady, mistress. See DON[1]]

**donnish** /'dɒnɪʃ/, *adj.* resembling or characteristic of a university don; stuffy or pedantic. – **donnishly,** *adv.* – **donnishness,** *n.*

**donny** /'dɒni/, *n. N.Z. Colloq.* →**donnybrook.**

**donnybrook** /'dɒnibrʊk/, *n.* a fight or argument; a brawl. Also, **donneybrook.** [orig. with ref. to a fair held annually until 1855 at *Donnybrook,* Dublin, and famous for rioting and dissipation]

**donor** /'doʊnə/, *n.* **1.** one who gives or donates. **2.** *Med.* **a.** a person or animal furnishing blood for transfusion. **b.** a person furnishing body organs, as a kidney or heart, for transplant surgery. **3.** *Law.* one who gives property by gift, legacy, or devise, or who confers a power of appointment. **4.** *Chem.* the atom which supplies both electrons in a dative bond. **5.** *Electronics.* an imperfection or impurity in a semiconductor which causes conduction by electrons. [ME *donour,* from AF, from *doner* give, from L *dōnāre*]

**donor bond** /'– bɒnd/, *n. Chem.* →**semipolar bond.**

**donor card** /'– kad/, *n.* a card carried by one who has given permission for his body to be used for transplant surgery after his death.

**don't** /doʊnt/, *v.* contraction of *do not.*

**donut** /'doʊnʌt/, *n.* →**doughnut** (def. 1).

**donzel** /'dɒnzəl/, *n. Archaic.* a young gentleman not yet knighted; a squire; a page. [It. *donzello,* from Pr. *donsel,* from LL *domnicellus,* diminutive of L *dominus* master]

**donzella** /dɒn'zɛlə/, *n. Archaic.* a young lady of noble birth.

**doob** /dub/, *n. Colloq.* a dope, ignoramus. – **dooby,** *adj.*

**doodackie** /'dudæki/, *n. N.Z. Colloq.* →**thingummyjig.**

**doodad** /'dudæd/, *n. Colloq.* any trifling ornament or bit of decorative finery.

**doodah** /'duda/, *n. Colloq.* →**thingummyjig.**

**doodie** /'dudi/, *n. Colloq.* a pipe[1] (def. 3).

**doodle** /'dudl/, *v.,* **-dled, -dling,** *n.* *–v.t.* **1.** to draw a design, figure, etc., while preoccupied. *–v.i.* **2.** to scribble idly. *–n.* **3.** a scribbled design, figure, etc., drawn idly.

**doodlebug** /'dudlbʌg/, *n.* **1.** a divining rod or similar device supposedly useful in locating water, oil, minerals, etc., underground. **2.** *Colloq.* →**buzzbomb.**

**doofer** /'dufə/, *n.* →**doover.**

**doohickie** /'duhɪki/, *n. Colloq.* →**thingummyjig.**

**doolan** /'dulən/, *n. N.Z. Colloq.* an Irish Catholic; a Roman Catholic. Also, **dooly, Mickey Doolan.** – **dooly,** *adj.*

**doom** /dum/, *n.* **1.** fate or destiny, esp. adverse fate. **2.** ruin; death. **3.** a judgment, decision, or sentence, esp. an unfavourable one. *–v.t.* **4.** to destine, esp. to an adverse fate. **5.** to pronounce judgment against; condemn. **6.** to ordain or fix as a sentence or fate. [ME *dome,* OE *dōm* judgment, sentence, law, authority, c. OHG *tuom,* Icel. *dōmr,* Goth. *dōms,* orig., that which is put or set; akin to DO[1], *v.,* -DOM, suffix]

**doomsday** /'dumzdeɪ/, *n.* **1.** the day of the Last Judgment, at the end of the world. **2.** any day of sentence or condemnation. [ME *domes dai,* OE *dōmes dæg* day of judgment]

**doomsdayman** /'dumzdeɪˌmæn/, *n.* →**doomwatcher.**

**doomwatcher** /'dumwɒtʃə/, *n.* one pessimistic about the future of the world, esp. the exploitation of its natural resources.

**doona** /'dunə/, *n.* a quilted eiderdown with a down filling. [Trademark]

**door** /dɔ/, *n.* **1.** a movable barrier of wood or other material, commonly turning on hinges or sliding in a groove, for closing and opening a passage or opening into a building, room, cupboard, etc. **2.** a doorway. **3.** the building, etc., to which a door belongs: *two doors down the street.* **4.** any means of approach or access, or of exit. **5. lay at the door of,** to attribute to; to impute blame for. **6. next door to, a.** in the next house to. **b.** very near; bordering upon. **7. out of doors,** in the open air; outside a building. **8. show one the door,** to dismiss from the house; turn out. [ME *dore,* OE *duru.* Cf. G *Tür,* Icel. *dyrr,* also OE *dor* gate, c. G *Tor;* akin to L *foris,* Gk *thýra*]

**doorbell** /'dɔbɛl/, *n.* a bell at a door or connected with a door, rung by persons outside seeking admittance.

**doorframe** /'dɔfreɪm/, *n.* the surrounds of a door, including a lintel and two jambs.

**doorhandle** /'dɔhændl/, *n.* a handle, upon which pressure is applied in order to release the latch to open a door.

**doorjamb** /'dɔdʒæm/, *n.* a side or vertical piece of a door supporting the lintel.

**doorkeeper** /'dɔkipə/, *n.* **1.** one who keeps or guards a door or entrance. **2.** a porter.

**doorknob** /'dɔnɒb/, *n.* a knob, the turning of which releases the latch to open a door.

**doorknock** /'dɔnɒk/, *v.i.* **1.** to go from house to house seeking funds for some charity, support for some political party, etc. *–n.* **2.** a campaign of doorknocking: *the Heart Foundation is holding a doorknock.* *–adj.* **3.** of or pertaining to such a campaign: *a doorknock appeal.*

**doorknocker** /'dɔnɒkə/, *n.* a knocker on or near a door, used by persons outside to gain admittance.

**doorman** /'dɔmæn, -mən/, *n., pl.* **-men** /-mɛn, -mən/. →**commissionaire.**

**doormat** /'dɔmæt/, *n.* **1.** a mat, placed in front of a door, for scraping mud or dirt from shoes. **2.** *Colloq.* an uncomplaining person who meekly accepts ill-treatment or bullying.

**doormoney** /'dɔmʌni/, *n.* a payment made for admission to a place of entertainment.

**doornail** /'dɔneɪl/, *n.* **1.** a large-headed nail formerly used for strengthening or ornamenting doors. **2. dead as a doornail,** dead beyond any doubt.

**doorplate** /'dɔpleɪt/, *n.* a plate on the door of a house or room, bearing a name, number, or the like.

**doorpost** /'dɔpoʊst/, *n.* the jamb or upright sidepiece of a doorway.

**doorsill** /'dɔsɪl/, *n.* the sill of a doorway.

**doorstep** /'dɔstɛp/, *n.* **1.** a step at a door, raised above the level of the ground outside; one of a series of steps leading from the ground to a door. **2.** *Colloq.* an extremely thick slice of bread.

**doorstop** /'dɔstɒp/, *n.* **1.** a device, often heavy, to keep a door open. **2.** a device, often rubber or plastic, to prevent a door from hitting a wall. Also, **doorstopper.**

**door-to-door** /'dɔ-tə-dɔ/, *adj.* **1.** direct from one specified point to another: *door-to-door delivery.* **2.** making direct contact with customers or the like in their homes: *a door-to-door salesman.*

**doorway** /'dɔweɪ/, *n.* **1.** the passage or opening into a building, room, etc., closed and opened by a door. **2.** the means of access; the start of something.

**doover** /'duvə/, *n. Colloq.* any object (often used jocularly in place of the usual name). Also, **doovah, doofer.** [? alteration of *do for* in such phrases as *that will do for now*]

**dooverlackie** /'duvəlæki/, *n. Colloq.* →**doover.** Also, **doovahlackie.**

**doozey** /'duzi/, *n. Colloq.* anything especially pleasing.

**dopa** /'doʊpə/, *n.* a non-protein amino acid, the precursor of adrenaline and melanin; used in the treatment of Parkinson's disease. Also, **DOPA.** [*d(ihydr)o(xy)p(henyl)a(lanine)*]

**dope** /doʊp/, *n., v.,* **doped, doping.** *–n.* **1.** any thick liquid or pasty preparation, as a sauce, lubricant, etc. **2.** an absorbent material used to absorb and hold a liquid, as in the manufacture of dynamite. **3. a.** any of various varnish-like products for coating the cloth fabric of aeroplane wings or the like, in order to make it waterproof, stronger, etc. **b.** a similar product used to coat the fabric of a balloon to reduce gas leakage. **4.** *Colloq.* a molasses-like preparation of opium used for smoking. **5.** *Colloq.* any drug, esp. a narcotic. **6.** *Colloq.* a stimulating drug, as one illegally given to a racehorse to induce greater speed. **7.** *Colloq.* information or data. **8.** *Colloq.* a stupid person. *–v.t.* **9.** *Colloq.* to affect with dope or drugs. **10.** *Electronics.* to add a small quantity of impurity to (a semiconductor) to achieve a particular characteristic. [D *doop* a dipping, sauce, from *doopen* dip, baptise. See DIP] – **doper,** *n.*

**dope fiend** /'– find/, *n. Colloq.* a person addicted to drugs, esp. narcotics.

**dope-pedlar** /'doʊp-pɛdlə/, *n.* a person who sells illegal drugs.

**dopey** /'doʊpi/, *adj.,* **dopier, dopiest.** *Colloq.* **1.** affected by or as by a stupefying drug. **2.** slow-witted; stupid. Also, **dopy.**

**doppelgänger** /'dɒpəlgɛŋə, -gæŋə/, *n.* an apparitional double or counterpart of a living person. Also, **doubleganger.** [G: double-goer. Cf. D *Dubbelganger*]

**doppio movimento** /ˌdɒpioʊ muvə'mɛntoʊ/, *adv.* (a musical direction) twice as fast. [It.]

**Doppler effect** /'dɒplər əfɛkt/, *n.* the apparent change in frequency and wavelength of a train of sound or light waves if the distance between the source and the receiver is changing. [named after C. J. *Doppler,* 1803-53, Austrian physicist]

**Doppler radar** /ˌdɒplə 'reɪda/, *n.* a radar system which differentiates between fixed and moving targets by detecting the apparent change in frequency of the reflected wave due to motion of the target or the observer.

**dor** /dɔ/, *n.* any of various insects that fly with a buzzing or droning noise. Also, **dorr.** [ME *dor(r)e,* OE *dora*]

**Doradillo** /dɔrə'dɪloʊ/, *n.* a white grape variety used for making cheap wines for popular consumption.

**dorbeetle** /'dɔbitl/, *n.* any of various beetles that fly with a droning sound, esp. a common European dung beetle, *Geotrupes stercorarius.* [DOR + BEETLE[1]]

**Dorian** /'dɔriən/, *adj.* **1.** of or pertaining to Doris, a division of ancient Greece, or the race named from it, one of the principal divisions of the ancient Greeks. *–n.* **2.** a Dorian Greek. [L *Dōrius* (from Gk *Dṓrios* Dorian) + -AN]

**Dorian mode** /– 'moʊd/, *n.* a scale, represented by the white keys of a keyboard instrument, beginning on D.

**Doric** /'dɒrɪk/, *adj.* **1.** of or pertaining to Doris, an ancient region in central Greece, its inhabitants, or their dialect. **2.** rustic, as a dialect. **3.** *Archit.* denoting or pertaining to the simplest of the three Greek orders of architecture, distinguished by low proportions, shaft without base, saucer-shaped capital (echinus) and frieze of metopes and triglyphs. [L *Dōricus,* from Gk *Dōrikós*]

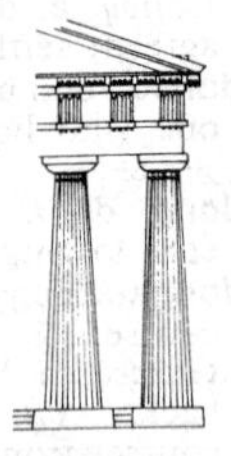

Doric order

**dorm** /dɔm/, *n. Colloq.* a dormitory.

**dormancy** /'dɔmənsi/, *n.* the state of being dormant.

**dormant** /'dɔmənt/, *adj.* **1.** lying asleep or as if asleep; inactive as in sleep; torpid. **2.** in a state of rest or inactivity; quiescent; inoperative; in abeyance. **3.** (of a volcano) not erupting. **4.** *Bot.* temporarily inactive: *dormant buds, dormant seeds.* **5.** *Her.* (of an animal) lying down with its head on its forepaws, as if asleep. [ME, from OF, ppr. of *dormir,* from L *dormīre* sleep, be inactive]

**dormer** /'dɔmə/, *n.* **1.** Also, **dormer window.** a vertical window in a projection built out from a sloping roof. **2.** the whole projecting structure. [orig., a sleeping chamber; cf. OF *dormeor,* from L *dormītōrium* DORMITORY]

**dormered** /'dɔməd/, *adj.* having dormer windows.

**dormient** /'dɔmiənt/, *adj.* sleeping; dormant. [L *dormiens,* ppr.]

dormer

**dormitory** /'dɔmətri/, *n., pl.* **-tories. 1.** a room for sleeping, usu. large and containing many beds, sometimes in cubicles, for the inmates of a school or other institution. **2.** a mental or spiritual resting-place. **3.** Also, **dormitory suburb.** a suburb in which a high proportion of the inhabitants are commuters. **4.** *U.S.* a building containing a number of sleeping rooms. [L *dormītōrium,* properly neut. of *dormītōrius* of sleeping]

**dormouse** /ˈdɔmaʊs/, *n., pl.* **-mice** /-maɪs/. any of the small, furry-tailed rodents of Europe, Asia and Africa which constitute the family Gliridae, resembling small squirrels in appearance and habits. [? DOR(MANT) + MOUSE]

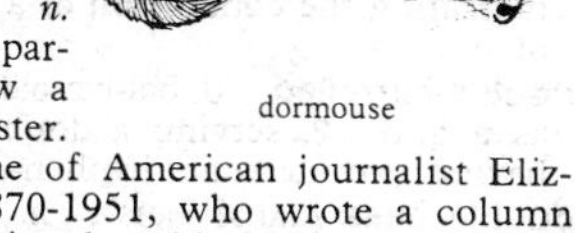
dormouse

**dormy** /ˈdɔmi/, *adj.* (of a player or side in golf) being in the lead by as many holes as are still to be played.

**dorothy dixer** /ˌdɒrəθi ˈdɪksə/, *n. Colloq.* a question asked in parliament specifically to allow a propagandist reply by a minister. [from *Dorothy Dix,* pen name of American journalist Elizabeth Meriwether Gilmer, 1870-1951, who wrote a column of advice to people with emotional problems; it was thought that she wrote her more intriguing letters herself]

**dorr** /dɔ/, *n.* →**dor.**

**dorsal** /ˈdɔsəl/, *adj.* **1.** *Zool.* of, pertaining to, or situated on the back, as of an organ or part: *dorsal nerves.* **2.** *Bot.* pertaining to the surface away from the axis, as of a leaf; abaxial. [ML *dorsālis,* from L *dorsum* back] – **dorsally,** *adv.*

**dorsal fin** /ˈ– fɪn/, *n.* the fin or finlike integumentary expansion generally developed on the back of aquatic vertebrates.

**dorsel** /ˈdɔsəl/, *n.* →**dossal.**

**Dorset Horn** /dɔsət ˈhɔn/, *n.* one of a British breed of horned short wool sheep, popular in Australia for crossing with the Merino for fat lamb raising. [orig. from Dorsetshire, England]

**dorsi-,** a combining form of **dorsal, dorsum,** as in *dorsiferous.* Also, **dorso-.**

**dorsifixed** /ˈdɔsifɪkst/, *adj.* attached at or by the back, as anthers.

**dorsiventral** /dɔsiˈvɛntrəl/, *adj.* **1.** *Bot.* having distinct dorsal and ventral sides, as most foliage leaves. **2.** *Zool.* →**dorsoventral.**

**dorsoventral** /dɔsoʊˈvɛntrəl/, *adj.* **1.** *Zool.* pertaining to the dorsal and ventral aspects of the body; extending from the dorsal to the ventral side: *the dorsoventral axis.* **2.** *Bot.* →**dorsiventral.**

**dorsum** /ˈdɔsəm/, *n., pl.* **-sa** /-sə/. **1.** the back, as of the body. **2.** the back or outer surface of an organ, part, etc. [L]

**dory**[1] /ˈdɔri/, *n., pl.* **-ries.** a boat with a narrow, flat bottom, high ends, and flaring sides. [first used in W Indies; native Central American name for a dugout]

**dory**[2] /ˈdɔri/, *n., pl.* **-ries.** **1.** a flattened, deep-bodied, spiny-rayed, marine food fish, *Zeus faber* (the **John Dory**), found both in European and in Australian seas. **2.** any of several related species. [ME *dore,* from F *dorée,* lit., gilded]

dory[1]

**dos-à-dos** /ˌdoʊz-a-ˈdoʊ/, *adv., n., pl.* **-dos** /-doʊz/. *–adv.* **1.** back to back. *–n.* **2.** a seat designed so that the occupants sit back to back. [F]

**dosage** /ˈdoʊsɪdʒ/, *n.* **1.** the administration of medicine in doses. **2.** the amount of a medicine to be given. **3.** the sugar syrup added to champagne to produce secondary fermentation or to sweeten it. **4.** *Physics.* →**dose** (def. 4).

**dose** /doʊs/, *n., v.,* **dosed, dosing.** *–n.* **1.** a quantity of medicine prescribed to be taken at one time. **2.** a definite quantity of anything analogous to medicine, esp. of something nauseous or disagreeable. **3.** *Colloq.* venereal disease. **4.** *Physics.* the amount of ionising radiation absorbed by a given quantity of material, usu. measured in rads; dosage. *–v.t.* **5.** to administer in or apportion for doses. **6.** to give doses to. [F, from ML *dosis,* from Gk: giving, portion, dose]

**dosh** /dɒʃ/, *n. Colloq.* money.

**dosido** /ˌdoʊsiˈdoʊ/, *n.* a dance movement in reels, etc., in which two persons advance, pass round each other back to back, and return to their places. Also, **dosedo.** [F *dos-à-dos* back to back]

**dosimeter** /doʊˈsɪmətə/, *n.* **1.** an apparatus for measuring minute quantities of liquid; a drop meter. **2.** an instrument for measuring doses of ionising radiation (esp. X-rays). Also, **dosemeter.**

**dosimetry** /doʊˈsɪmətri/, *n.* **1.** the measurement of the doses of medicines. **2.** the measurement of doses of ionising radiation (esp. X-rays). – **dosimetric** /doʊsəˈmɛtrɪk/, *adj.*

**doss** /dɒs/, *Colloq. –n.* **1.** a place to sleep, esp. in a cheap lodging house. **2.** sleep. *–v.i.* **3.** to sleep in a dosshouse. **4.** to make a temporary sleeping place for oneself (oft. fol. by *down*). [F *dos* back, through LL, from L *dorsum*]

**dossal** /ˈdɒsəl/, *n.* **1.** Also, **dorsal.** an ornamental hanging placed at the back of an altar or at the sides of the chancel, made obsolete in Roman Catholic churches by the introduction of more altars after the Second Vatican Council, but still found in some Anglo-Catholic churches. **2.** *Archaic.* →**dosser**[1] (def. 2). Also, **dossel.** [ML *dossālis* for *dorsālis,* L *dorsuālis* of the back]

**dosser**[1] /ˈdɒsə/, *n.* **1.** a basket for carrying objects on the back; a pannier. **2.** an ornamental covering for the back of a seat, esp. a throne, etc. **3.** a hanging, sometimes richly embroidered, for the walls of a hall or for the back or sides of a chancel. [ME *doser,* from OF *dossier,* from *dos* back, from L *dorsum*]

**dosser**[2] /ˈdɒsə/, *n.* one who sleeps in a dosshouse.

**dosshouse** /ˈdɒshaʊs/, *n.* a cheap lodging house; usu. for men only.

**dossier** /ˈdɒsiə/, *n.* a bundle of documents on the same subject, esp. information about a particular person. [F: a bundle of papers with a label on the back. See DOSSER[1]]

**dossil** /ˈdɒsəl/, *n.* a plug of lint for a wound; a folded bandage used as a compress.

**dost** /dʌst/, *v. Archaic.* 2nd person singular present indicative of **do**[1].

**dot**[1] /dɒt/, *n., v.,* **dotted, dotting.** *–n.* **1.** a minute or small spot on a surface; a speck. **2.** a small, roundish mark made with or as with a pen. **3.** anything relatively small or specklike. **4.** *Music.* **a.** a point placed after a note or rest, to indicate that the duration of the note or rest is to be increased one half. A double dot further increases the duration by one half the value of the single dot. **b.** a point placed under or over a note to indicate that it is to be played staccato, i.e., shortened. **5.** *Teleg.* a signal of shorter duration than a dash, used in groups of dots, dashes, and spaces, to represent letters in Morse or a similar code. **6.** a full stop; a decimal point. **7. in the year dot,** *Colloq.* long ago. **8. on the dot,** *Colloq.* punctual; exactly on time. *–v.t.* **9.** to mark with or as with a dot or dots. **10.** to stud or diversify, as dots do. **11.** to place like dots. **12.** *Colloq.* to hit; punch. *–v.i.* **13.** to make a dot or dots. **14. dot and carry one,** *Colloq.* **a.** to walk with a limp. **b.** (in simple mathematics) to set down the unit and carry over the tens to the next column. **15. dot one's i's and cross one's t's,** *Colloq.* to be meticulous; to particularise minutely. [OE *dott* head of a boil. Cf. D *dot* kind of knot] – **dotter,** *n.*

**dot**[2] /dɒt/, *n. Civil Law.* →**dowry.** [F, from L *dōs*] – **dotal,** *adj.*

**dotage** /ˈdoʊtɪdʒ/, *n.* **1.** feebleness of mind, esp. resulting from old age; senility. **2.** excessive fondness; foolish affection. [DOTE, *v.* + -AGE]

**dotard** /ˈdoʊtəd/, *n.* one who is weak-minded, esp. from old age.

**dote** /doʊt/, *v.i.,* **doted, doting.** **1.** to bestow excessive love or fondness (fol. by *on* or *upon*). **2.** to be weak-minded, esp. from old age. Also, **doat.** [ME *doten,* c. MD *doten.* Cf. D *dutten* doze, dote, Icel. *dotta* nod from sleep, MHG *totzen* take a nap] – **doter,** *n.*

**doth** /dʌθ/, *v. Archaic.* 3rd person singular present indicative of **do**[1].

**doting** /ˈdoʊtɪŋ/, *adj.* **1.** extravagantly fond. **2.** weak-minded, esp. from old age. – **dotingly,** *adv.*

**dotted** /ˈdɒtəd/, *adj.* **1.** covered with dots; stippled. **2. sign on the dotted line,** to conclude an agreement.

**dotterel** /ˈdɒtərəl/, *n.* any of a number of small, wading birds of the family Charadriidae frequenting seashores and open marshy areas, widely distributed and often migratory, as the **red-capped dotterel,** *Charadrius ruficapillus,* of temperate and tropical coasts of Australia. Also, **dottrel.** [DOTE + -REL]

**dottle** /ˈdɒtl/, *n.* the plug of half-smoked tobacco in the bottom of a pipe after smoking. Also, **dottel.** [diminutive of DOT[1]]

**dotty** /ˈdɒti/, *adj.*, **-tier, -tiest. 1.** *Colloq.* crazy; eccentric. **2.** *Colloq.* feeble or unsteady in gait. **3.** marked with dots; placed like dots. [DOT[1], *n.* + -Y[1]]

**doubah** /ˈduba/, *n.* a slender, twining plant, *Leichhardtia leptophylla,* widely distributed throughout Australia.

**double** /ˈdʌbəl/, *adj., n., v.,* **-led, -ling,** *adv.* *–adj.* **1.** twice as great, heavy, strong, etc.: *double pay, a double portion.* **2.** twofold in form, size, amount, extent, etc.; of extra size or weight: *a double blanket.* **3.** composed of two like parts or members; paired: *a double cherry.* **4.** *Bot.* (of flowers) having the number of petals largely increased. **5.** (of musical instruments) producing a tone an octave lower than the notes indicate. **6.** twofold in character, meaning, or conduct; ambiguous: *a double interpretation.* **7.** deceitful; hypocritical; insincere. **8.** folded over once; folded in two; doubled. **9.** duple, as time or rhythm. **10.** *Print.* **a.** denoting a size of paper of twice the area of the size specified. **b.** a doublet (def. 5). **11. live** or **lead a double life,** to conduct one's life in an apparently blameless fashion while secretly involved in a dishonourable, immoral, or socially disapproved activity. *–n.* **12.** a twofold size or amount; twice as much. **13.** a duplicate; a counterpart. **14.** a sudden backward turn or bend. **15.** a shift or artifice. **16.** *Eccles.* one of the more important feasts of the year, so called because the antiphon is doubled, i.e., sung in full before each psalm as well as after (except for little hours). **17.** *Films, etc.* a substitute actor who takes another's place, as in difficult or dangerous scenes. **18.** *Theat.* an actor with two parts in one play. **19.** *Mil.* double time. **20.** *Tennis.* two successive faults in serving. **21.** (*pl.*) a game in which there are two players on each side. **22.** in bridge or other card games, a challenge by an opponent that declarer cannot fulfil his contract, increasing the points to be won or lost. **23.** *Bridge.* **a.** a hand which warrants such a challenge. **b.** a conventional bid informing partner that a player's hand is of certain strength. **24.** (in darts) **a.** a narrow space between two parallel circles on the outer edge of a dartboard. **b.** a throw which places a dart there. **25.** a bet on two horses, in different races, any winnings and the stake from the first bet being placed on the second horse: *feature double, daily double.* **26.** a ticket (usu. for a dance or ball) for two people. **27.** *Colloq.* a two-barrelled shotgun. **28.** the performance of a cricketer who has scored a thousand runs and taken a hundred wickets in one season. **29.** a ride obtained from being doubled (def. 41). **30. at** or **on the double, a.** in double time. **b.** *Colloq.* fast; quickly; at a run. **31.** *Colloq.* **come the double on,** deceive; doublecross. *–v.t.* **32.** to make double or twice as great: *to double a sum, size, etc.* **33.** *Films, etc.* to act as a double or substitute for another actor. **34.** to be or have twice as much as. **35.** to bend or fold with one part upon another (oft. fol. by *over, up, back,* etc.) **36.** to clench (the fist). **37.** to sail or go round: *to double Cape Horn.* **38.** to couple; associate. **39.** *Music.* to reduplicate by means of a note in another part, either at the unison or at an octave above or below. **40.** *Bridge.* **a.** to increase (the points) to be won or lost on a declaration. **b.** to make increased, as a bid. **41.** to convey a second person on a horse, bicycle or motorcycle. *–v.i.* **42.** to become double. **43.** to double a stake in gambling or the like (oft. fol. by *up*). **44.** to bend or fold (oft. fol. by *up*). **45.** to turn back on a course (oft. fol. by *back*). **46.** to share quarters, etc. (fol. by *up*). **47.** *Mil.* to march at the double-time pace. **48.** to serve in two capacities, as, **a.** *Theat.* to play two stage roles in a small company. **b.** *Music.* to play two instruments in a band. **49.** *Bridge.* to become increased, as a bid. *–adv.* **50.** twofold; doubly. **51. double or quits,** *Colloq.* **a.** a bet in which a debtor stands to double his debt if he loses or be excused if he wins. **b.** any of various gambling games based on this principle. [ME, from OF *duble,* from L *duplus*] – **doubleness,** *n.* – **doubler,** *n.*

**double-acting** /ˈdʌbəl-æktɪŋ/, *adj.* (of any reciprocating machine or implement) acting effectively in both directions (distinguished from *single-acting*).

**double adapter** /dʌbəl əˈdæptə/, *n.* a plug-in connector by which two electrical appliances may be operated simultaneously from a single power-point.

**double agent** /– ˈeɪdʒənt/, *n.* a secret agent working simultaneously for two opposed employers as countries, governments, etc., usu. without either of them knowing of his association with the other.

**double-bank** /dʌbəl-ˈbæŋk/, *v.t.* **1.** to double (def. 41). **2.** to double (an order for goods, etc.) in error. *–n.* **3.** a double (def. 29).

**double-banked** /ˈdʌbəl-bæŋkt/, *adj.* **1.** having two rowers at each oar. **2.** having two tiers of oars, one above the other, in ancient vessels. **3.** carrying guns on two decks.

**double bar** /dʌbəl ˈba/, *n.* a double vertical line on a stave indicating the conclusion of a piece of music or a subdivision of it.

**double-barrelled** /ˈdʌbəl-bærəld/, *adj.* **1.** having two barrels, as a gun. **2.** serving a double purpose. **3.** (of a surname) having two elements hyphenated. Also, *U.S.* **double-barreled.**

**double bass** /dʌbəl ˈbeɪs/, *n.* **1.** the largest instrument of the violin family, having four strings and played resting vertically on the floor. **2.** →**contrabass.**

**double-bass** /ˈdʌbəl-beɪs/, *adj.* of or pertaining to that member of any family of musical instruments which is below the bass.

**double bassoon** /dʌbəl bəˈsun/, *n.* a bassoon an octave lower in pitch than the ordinary bassoon; the largest and deepest-toned instrument of the oboe class; contrabassoon.

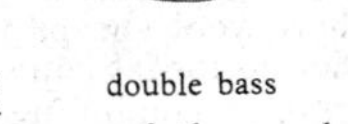
double bass

**double-bass viol** /ˌdʌbəl-beɪs ˈvaɪɒl/, *n.* a six-stringed musical instrument tuned an octave below the bass viol; an ancestor of the modern double bass.

**double bed** /dʌbəl ˈbɛd/, *n.* a bed large enough for two people to sleep in.

**double bill** /– ˈbɪl/, *n.* a program, esp. at a cinema, on which there are two main items.

**double bind** /– ˈbaɪnd/, *n.* a situation which presents alternatives which are equally unattractive.

**double blind** /– ˈblaɪnd/, *n.* a stratagem employed in an experiment in which neither the subject nor the person carrying out the test is aware of the particulars of the test items, thus avoiding bias on either side.

**double bluff** /– ˈblʌf/, *n.* a cover for masking action or purpose, consisting of two separate strategems or decoys, one of which is intended to be discovered, thereby giving greater chance of success to the other.

**double boiler** /– ˈbɔɪlə/, *n.* a pair of interlocking pans, the bottom one containing water which while boiling gently heats the food in the upper pan. Also, **double saucepan.**

**double bond** /– ˈbɒnd/, *n.* two covalent bonds linking two atoms of a molecule together; characteristic of unsaturated organic compounds.

**double-breasted** /ˈdʌbəl-brɛstəd/, *adj.* (of a garment) overlapping sufficiently to form two thicknesses of considerable width on the breast. See **single-breasted.**

**double bunger** /dʌbəl ˈbʌŋə/, *n.* an extremely loud, large bunger.

**double-bunk** /dʌbəl-ˈbʌŋk/, *v.i.* **1.** to sleep two to a single bed. *–n.* **2.** two single beds mounted one above the other.

**double-check** /dʌbəl-ˈtʃɛk/, *v.t., v.i.* to check twice or again; recheck. – **double-check,** *n.*

**double chin** /dʌbəl ˈtʃɪn/, *n.* a fold of fat beneath the chin.

**double cloth** /– ˈklɒθ/, *n.* a fabric woven of two sets of yarns, as double-faced coating or Jacquard blanket.

**double concerto** /– kənˈtʃɜtoʊ/, *n.* a concerto in which there are two solo instruments.

**doublecross** /dʌbəlˈkrɒs/, *v.t. Colloq.* to prove treacherous to; betray. – **double-crosser,** *n.*

**double dagger** /dʌbəl ˈdægə/, *n.* a mark (‡) used for references, etc.; the diesis.

**double-dealing** /dʌbəl-ˈdilɪŋ/, *n.* **1.** duplicity. *–adj.* **2.** using duplicity; treacherous. – **double-dealer,** *n.*

**double-decker** /dʌbəl-ˈdɛkə/, *n.* something with two decks, tiers, or the like, as a ship with two decks above the waterline, or a bus or tram having two floors for passengers. – **double deck, double decker,** *adj.*

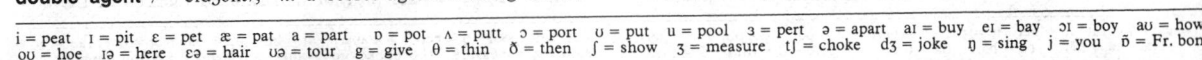

**ouble-declutch** /dʌbəl-di'klʌtʃ/, *v.i., n.* →**double-shuffle.**

**ouble decomposition** /dʌbəl ˌdikɒmpə'zɪʃən/, *n.* a chemical reaction between two compounds in which both decompose and two new compounds are formed; metathesis.

**Ɩouble-dink** /dʌbəl-'dɪŋk/, *v.t.* →**double** (def. 41).

**Ɩouble dissolution** /dʌbəl dɪsə'luʃən/, *n.* an order issued by a governor-general dissolving both houses of parliament and necessitating a new election for all senators and members.

**Ɩouble drummer** /– 'drʌmə/, *n.* a black or dark brown cicada with clear orange markings, *Thopha saccata,* having a heavy, thickset body and, in the male, large swollen drum covers; Union Jack.

**Ɩouble-dutch** /dʌbəl-'dʌtʃ/, *n. Colloq.* nonsense; gibberish; incomprehensible speech.

**Ɩouble-dyed** /'dʌbəl-daɪd/, *adj.* **1.** dyed twice. **2.** deeply imbued with guilt.

**Ɩouble eagle** /dʌbəl 'igəl/, *n.* **1.** an eagle with two heads, as represented in the old arms of Russia and Austria. **2.** *U.S.* (formerly) a gold coin worth two eagles, or $20.

**Ɩouble-edged** /'dʌbəl-ɛdʒd/, *adj.* **1.** having two cutting edges. **2.** acting in two ways: *a double-edged reform.*

**double-ender** /dʌbəl-'ɛndə/, *n.* **1.** a vehicle, esp. a boat, which can be driven from both ends. **2.** →**stump-tailed skink.**

**Ɩouble entendre** /ˌdublɒ̃'tɒ̃drə/, *n.* **1.** a double meaning. **2.** a word or expression with two meanings, one often indelicate. [F (obs.)]

**double entry** /dʌbəl 'ɛntri/, *n.* a bookkeeping method in which each transaction is entered twice in the ledger, once to the debit of one account, and once to the credit of another. Cf. **single entry.**

**double exposure** /– əks'poʊʒə/, *n.* **1.** the taking of two pictures on one frame of film. **2.** a photograph so obtained consisting of pictures superimposed, thus making one photograph.

**double-faced** /'dʌbəl-feɪst/, *adj.* **1.** practising duplicity; hypocritical. **2.** having two faces or aspects.

**double-fault** /dʌbəl-'fɔlt/, *n.* (in tennis and squash) two serving faults in succession, resulting in the loss of a point to the server.

**double-feature** /dʌbəl-'fitʃə/, *n.* a cinema program in which two full-length films are shown.

**double first** /dʌbəl 'fɜst/, *n.* **1.** first class honours degree at a university, gained in two subjects. **2.** one who has achieved this.

**double flat** /–'flæt/, *n.* **1.** a symbol (♭♭) on a music score that lowers a note by two semitones. **2.** a note marked and affected by this symbol.

**double fleece** /– 'flis/, *n.* **1.** a fleece of wool consisting of two years' growth. **2.** →**double fleecer.**

**double fleecer** /– 'flisə/, *n.* a sheep carrying two years' growth of fleece.

**double glazing** /– 'gleɪzɪŋ/, *n.* glazing in which two layers of glass are separated by a dead air space.

**double happy** /– 'hæpi/, *n. N.Z.* a firecracker. [Trademark]

**double-headed hawk** /ˌdʌbəl-hɛdəd 'hɔk/, *n.* the eastern Australian hawk-moth, *Coequosa triangularis,* whose large green larva appears to possess a second head at its posterior end.

**double-header** /dʌbəl-'hɛdə/, *n.* **1.** a double-headed coin. **2.** a double amount of serving (esp. two standard nips of spirits). **3.** an ice-cream cone designed to carry two scoops of ice-cream.

**double helical gear,** *n.* →**herringbone gear.**

**double helix** /dʌbəl 'hilɪks/, *n.* any two interlocking spirals, esp. the structure of DNA where two chains are held together by hydrogen bonds in a double spiral.

**double-hung** /'dʌbəl-hʌŋ/, *adj.* (of a window) having two sashes, each balanced by sash cords and weights in order to move up and down to open and close the window.

**double image** /dʌbəl 'ɪmɪdʒ/, *n.* (in cases of diplopia) that which is seen when the images from the two eyes cannot be united.

**double-jointed** /dʌbəl-'dʒɔɪntəd/, *adj.* naving unusually flexible joints which enable the appendages and spine to curve in extraordinary ways.

**double-lock** /dʌbəl-'lɒk/, *v.t.* to turn a key in a lock twice, so as to shoot a second bolt.

**double magnum** /dʌbəl 'mægnəm/, *n.* a wine bottle four times the normal size.

**double-minded** /dʌbəl-'maɪndəd/, *adj.* wavering or undecided in mind. – **double-mindedness,** *n.*

**doubleness** /'dʌbəlnəs/, *n.* **1.** the quality or condition of being double. **2.** deception or dissimulation.

**double option** /dʌbəl 'ɒpʃən/, *n. Stock Exchange.* a privilege consisting of a put and a call combined, giving the holder the right, at his option, either of delivering a certain amount of stock, etc., at a specified price, or of buying a certain amount of stock, etc., at another specified price within a stipulated period.

**double-page spread** /ˌdʌbəl-peɪdʒ 'sprɛd/, *n.* →**double-spread.**

**double-park** /dʌbəl-'pak/, *v.t.* **1.** to park (a car) alongside another, making a double row alongside the kerb. *–v.i.* **2.** to park a car in this manner.

**double pneumonia** /dʌbəl nju'moʊnjə, njə-/, *n.* pneumonia affecting both lungs.

**double-quick** /dʌbəl-'kwɪk/, *adj.* **1.** very quick or rapid. *–adv.* **2.** in a quick or rapid manner. *–n.* **3.** double time.

**doubler** /'dʌblə/, *n.* a ram over six months old, counted as two sheep in a shearer's tally.

**double-reed** /dʌbəl-'rid/, *adj.* of or pertaining to wind instruments producing sounds through two reeds fastened and beating together, as the oboe.

**double refraction** /dʌbəl rə'frækʃən/, *n.* the separation of a ray of light into two unequally refracted rays, as in passing through certain crystals.

**double room** /– 'rum/, *n.* a bedroom for two people, usu. with a double bed, in a motel, hotel, etc.

**doubles** /'dʌbəlz/, *n.pl.* **1.** a form of betting in which the punter is required to select the winners of two nominated races. **2.** a game, esp. tennis, played by opposing teams of two players.

**double salt** /dʌbəl 'sɒlt/, *n.* a salt which crystallises as a single substance, but when dissolved ionises as two distinct salts.

**double saucepan** /– 'sɔspən/, *n.* →**double boiler.**

**double scull** /– 'skʌl/, *n.* a rowing boat built to accommodate two oarsmen.

**double sharp** /dʌbəl 'ʃap/, *n.* **1.** a symbol (𝄪) on a music score that raises a note by two semitones. **2.** a note marked and affected by this symbol.

**double-shuffle** /dʌbəl-'ʃʌfəl/, *v.,* **-fled, -fling,** *n.* *–v.i.* **1.** to change gear, by moving first into neutral and then into the desired gear, releasing the clutch-pedal between each movement. *–n.* **2.** an act or instance of double-shuffling. Also, **double-declutch.**

**double-spread** /dʌbəl-'sprɛd/, *n.* a pair of facing pages of a book, magazine, or the like, viewed as a whole. Also, **double-page spread.**

**double standard** /dʌbəl 'stændəd/, *n.* **1.** a moral code more lenient towards men than towards women. **2.** any rule, judgment, principle, etc., which permits greater freedom to one person or group than to another.

**double star** /'– sta/, *n.* two stars so near to each other in the sky that they appear as one under certain conditions. **Optical double stars** are two stars at greatly different distances but nearly in line with each other and the observer. **Physical double stars** or **binary stars** are a physical system whose two components are at nearly the same distance from the earth.

**double-stop** /dʌbəl-'stɒp/, *v.i.,* **-stopped, -stopping.** to play simultaneously two stopped notes (on a stringed instrument).

**doublet** /'dʌblət/, *n.* **1.** a close-fitting outer body garment, with or without sleeves, formerly worn by men. **2.** a pair of like things; a couple. **3.** one of a pair of like things; a duplicate. **4.** one of two words in the same language, representing the same original, as the English *coy* and *quiet,* one taken from Old French, the other

Elizabethan doublet

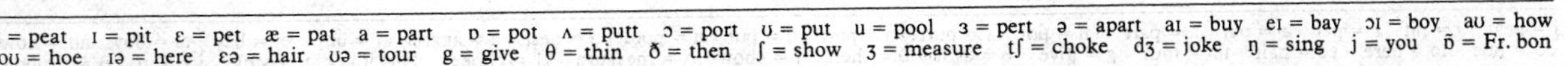
i = peat ɪ = pit ɛ = pet æ = pat a = part ɒ = pot ʌ = putt ɔ = port ʊ = put u = pool ɜ = pert ə = apart aɪ = buy eɪ = bay ɔɪ = boy aʊ = how
oʊ = hoe ɪə = here ɛə = hair ʊə = tour g = give θ = thin ð = then ʃ = show ʒ = measure tʃ = choke dʒ = joke ŋ = sing j = you õ = Fr. bon

from Latin. 5. *Print.* an unintentional repetition in printed matter or proof. 6. (*pl.*) two dice on each of which the same number of spots turns up at a throw. 7. *Jewellery.* a counterfeit gem made by the welding of two pieces of a different nature, as a thin bar of opal with a potch or plastic backing. [ME, from OF *double* DOUBLE, *adj.* + *-et* -ET]

**double tails** /'dʌbəl teɪlz/, *n.pl.* any plant of the orchid genus *Diuris,* a group largely restricted to Australia, characterised by long lateral sepals.

**double take** /– 'teɪk/, *n.* a second look, either literally or figuratively given to a person, event, etc., whose significance is suddenly understood.

**doubletalk** /'dʌbəltɔk/, *n. Colloq.* 1. speech using nonsense syllables together with words in a rapid patter. 2. evasive or ambiguous language.

**doublethink** /'dʌbəlθɪŋk/, *n.* the ability to accept two contradictory facts simultaneously, and to discipline the mind to ignore the conflict between them. [coined by George Orwell in *Nineteen Eighty-Four* (1949)]

**double-throw** /dʌbəl-'θroʊ/, *adj.* (of a switch) capable of engaging with two alternative sets of fixed contacts.

**double time** /dʌbəl 'taɪm/, *n.* 1. double wages paid to persons who remain at work on certain occasions, such as public holidays, etc. 2. *U.S. Army.* the fastest rate of marching troops, a slow jog in which 180 paces are taken in a minute. 3. a slow run by troops in step. 4. *Colloq.* a run at any speed. 5. **in doubletime,** with speed; quickly.

**double-time** /dʌbəl-'taɪm/, *v.,* **-timed, -timing.** *–v.t.* 1. to march (troops) in double time. *–v.i.* 2. to march in double time. 3. to proceed quickly.

**double-tongue** /'dʌbəl-tʌŋ/, *v.i.,* **-tongued, -tonguing.** (in playing the flute, cornet, etc.) to apply the tongue rapidly to the teeth and the hard palate alternately, so as to ensure a brilliant execution of a staccato passage.

**double-tongued** /'dʌbəltʌŋd/, *adj.* deceitful.

**double wedding** /dʌbəl 'wɛdɪŋ/, *n.* a wedding ceremony in which two couples are married at the same time.

**double-yolker** /dʌbəl-'joʊkə/, *n.* an egg having two yolks.

**doubloon** /dʌb'lun/, *n.* a former Spanish gold coin. [F *doublon,* or from Sp. *doblón,* augmentative of *doble* DOUBLE, *adj.*]

**doublure** /dub'ljʊə/, *n.* an ornamental lining of a book cover. [F, from *doubler* to line, DOUBLE]

**doubly** /'dʌbli/, *adv.* 1. in a double manner, measure, or degree. 2. in two ways. 3. *Obs. or Archaic.* with duplicity.

**doubt** /daʊt/, *v.t.* 1. to be uncertain in opinion about; hold questionable; hesitate to believe. 2. to distrust. 3. *Archaic.* to fear; suspect. *–v.i.* 4. to feel uncertainty as to something; be undecided in opinion or belief. *–n.* 5. undecidedness of opinion or belief; a feeling of uncertainty. 6. distrust; suspicion. 7. a state of affairs such as to occasion uncertainty. 8. *Obs.* fear; dread. 9. **beyond a shadow of doubt,** for certain; definitely. 10. **in doubt,** in uncertainty; in suspense. 11. **no doubt, a.** probably. **b.** certainly. 12. **without doubt,** without question; certainly. [ME *douten,* from OF *douter,* from L *dubitāre* hesitate, doubt] **– doubtable,** *adj.* **– doubter,** *n.* **– doubtingly,** *adv.*

**doubtful** /'daʊtfəl/, *adj.* 1. admitting of or causing doubt; uncertain; ambiguous. 2. of uncertain issue. 3. of questionable character. 4. undecided in opinion or belief; hesitating. **– doubtfully,** *adv.* **– doubtfulness,** *n.*

**doubting Thomas** /daʊtɪŋ 'tɒməs/, *n.* one who refuses to believe without proof. [from *Thomas,* the Apostle who doubted Christ's resurrection]

**doubtless** /'daʊtləs/, *adv.* 1. without doubt; unquestionably. 2. probably or presumably. *–adj.* 3. free from doubt or uncertainty. **– doubtlessly,** *adv.* **– doubtlessness,** *n.*

**douc** /duk/, *n.* a colourful leaf-eating monkey, *Pygathrix nemaus,* of forest regions of South East Asia. Also, **douc langur.**

**douceur** /du'sɜ/, *n.* 1. a gratuity, fee, or tip. 2. a conciliatory gift or bribe. 3. sweetness; agreeableness. [F, from *douce* (fem.) sweet, from L *dulcis*]

**douche** /duʃ/, *n., v.,* **douched, douching.** *–n.* 1. a jet or current of water applied to a body part, organ, or cavity for medicinal, hygienic, or contraceptive purposes. 2. the application of such a jet. 3. an instrument for administering it. 4. a bath administered by such a jet. *–v.t.* 5. to apply a douche to; douse. *–v.i.* 6. to receive a douche. [F, from It *doccia* conduit, shower, from L *dūcere* lead]

**dough** /doʊ/, *n.* 1. flour or meal combined with water, milk, etc., in a mass for baking into bread, cake, etc.; paste of bread. 2. any soft, pasty mass. 3. *Colloq.* money. 4. **do one's dough,** *Colloq.* to lose one's money, esp. in some speculation or gamble. [ME *dogh,* OE *dāh,* c. D *deeg,* G *Teig*]

**doughboy** /'doʊbɔɪ/, *n.* 1. *U.S. Colloq.* an infantryman. 2. a rounded lump of dough boiled or steamed as a dumpling.

**doughie** /'doʊi/, *n. Colloq.* a stupid person.

**doughnut** /'doʊnʌt/, *n.* 1. a small ring-shaped cake of sweetened or, sometimes, of unsweetened dough fried in deep fat. 2. *Physics.* the toroidal vacuum chamber of a particle of accelerator. [DOUGH + NUT, in allusion to the original shape]

**doughty** /'daʊti/, *adj.,* **-tier, -tiest.** strong; hardy; valiant. [ME; OE *dohtig,* unexplained var. of *dyhtig,* from *dugan* be good, avail, c. G *tüchtig*] **– doughtily,** *adv.* **– doughtiness,** *n.*

**doughy** /'doʊi/, *adj.,* **doughier, doughiest.** of or like dough; half-baked; soft and heavy; pallid and flabby.

**Douglas fir** /dʌgləs 'fɜ/, *n.* a coniferous tree, *Pseudotsuga menziesii* or *P. glauca,* of western North America, often over 60 metres high, and yielding a strong, durable timber. Also, **Douglas pine, Douglas spruce.** [named after David *Douglas,* 1798-1834, Scottish botanist and traveller]

**Douglas Scale** /'– skeɪl/, *n.* the international sea and swell scale. [from the originator, Sir Henry Percy *Douglas,* 1876-1939, director of British Naval Meteorological Service]

**doum-palm** /'dum-pam/, *n.* any African palm of the genus *Hyphaene* which has branched stems and fan-shaped leaves, esp. the Egyptian *H. thebaica* with a hard wood used for making implements.

**dour** /'daʊə, dʊə/, *adj.* 1. sullen; gloomy; sour. 2. hard; severe; stern. [Scot. d. (? from ME *doure),* from L *dūrus* hard] **– dourly,** *adv.* **– dourness,** *n.*

**doura** /'dʊərə/, *n.* →**durra.** Also, **dourah.**

**dourine** /'durin/, *n. Vet. Sci.* an infectious disease of horses, affecting chiefly the genitals and hind legs, caused by a protozoan parasite, *Trypanosoma equiperdum.* [F *dourin*]

**douroucouli** /duru'kuli/, *n., pl.* **-lis.** the night ape or owl monkey, *Aotus trivergatus,* native to Central and South America, and the only true monkey that is nocturnal.

**douse** /daʊs/, *v.,* **doused, dousing.** *–v.t.* 1. to plunge into water or the like; drench: *to douse someone with water.* 2. *Colloq.* to put out or extinguish (a light). 3. *Colloq.* to take off or doff. 4. *Naut.* to lower in haste, as a sail; slacken suddenly. *–v.i.* 5. to plunge or be plunged into a liquid. Also, **dowse.** [orig. obscure] **– douser,** *n.*

**dove** /dʌv/, *n.* 1. any bird of the pigeon family Columbidae, as the native peaceful dove, *Geopelia striata,* a blue-grey bird with bars and scallops of black, or the introduced spotted turtledove, *Steptophelia chinensis.* 2. (in literature) this bird as the symbol of innocence, gentleness, tenderness and peace. 3. (*cap.*) the Holy Ghost. 4. an innocent, gentle, or tender person. 5. a politician or political adviser who favours conciliatory policies as a solution to armed conflict. 6. *Colloq.* a term of endearment. [ME; OE *dūfe-,* c. D *duif,* G *Taube,* Icel. *dūfa,* Goth. *dubō* dove, lit., diver; akin to DIVE, *v.*]

**dove colour** /'– kʌlə/, *n.* a warm grey with a slight purplish or pinkish tint. **– dove-coloured,** *adj.*

**dovecot** /'dʌvkɒt/, *n.* a structure, usu. at a height above the ground, for domestic pigeons. Also, **dovecote** /'dʌvkoʊt/.

**dovekie** /'dʌvki/, *n.* →**little auk.**

**dovelike** /'dʌvlaɪk/, *adj.* like a dove; innocent; tender.

**dover** /'doʊvə/, *n.* 1. a pocket knife. 2. hand shears. 3. **flash one's dover,** *Colloq.* to prepare to eat. 4. **the run of one's dover,** *Colloq.* as much to eat as one wants. [orig. from brand name on blade of both knife and shears]

**Dover's powder** /'doʊvəz paʊdə/, *n.* a medicinal powder containing ipecacuanha and opium, used as an anodyne, diaphoretic, and antispasmodic. [named after Dr Thomas *Dover,* 1660-1742, English physician]

**dovetail** /'dʌvteɪl/, *n.* 1. *Carp.* a joint or fastening formed by one or more tenons and mortises spread in the shape of a dove's tail. *–v.t.* 2. *Carp.* to join together by means of a dovetail or dovetails. **3.** to join together compactly or harmoniously. *–v.i.* **4.** to fit together by means of or as with dovetails.

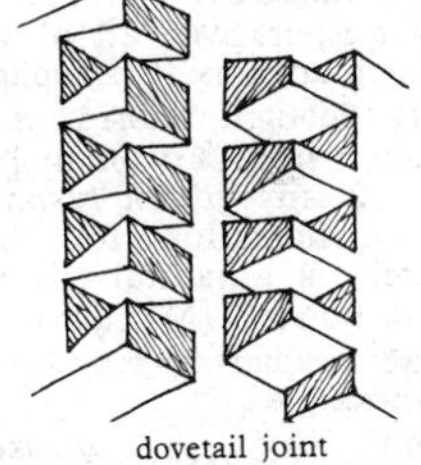
dovetail joint

**dovish** /ˈdʌvɪʃ/, *adj.* (of a politician or political adviser) conciliatory; favouring peaceful solutions.

**dowable** /ˈdaʊəbəl/, *adj. Law.* entitled to dower.

**dowager** /ˈdaʊədʒə/, *n.* **1.** a woman who holds some title or property from her deceased husband, esp. the widow of a king, duke, or the like; often added to her title to distinguish her from the wife of the present king, duke, or the like. **2.** *Colloq.* a dignified elderly lady. *–adj.* **3.** like, pertaining to, or characteristic of a dowager. [MF *douagiere,* from *douage* dower, from *douer* endow, from L *dōtāre*]

**dowager's hump** /daʊədʒəz ˈhʌmp/, *n.* →**widow's hump.**

**dowdy** /ˈdaʊdi/, *adj.,* **-dier, -diest,** *n., pl.* **-dies.** *–adj.* **1.** ill-dressed; not trim, smart, or stylish. *–n.* **2.** an ill-dressed woman. [earlier *dowd,* ME *doude;* orig. obscure] **– dowdily,** *adv.* **– dowdiness,** *n.* **– dowdyish,** *adj.*

**dowel** /ˈdaʊəl/, *n., v.,* **-elled, -elling** or (*U.S.*) **-eled, -eling.** *Carp. –n.* **1.** Also, **dowel pin.** a pin, usu. round, fitting into corresponding holes in two adjacent pieces to prevent slipping or to align the two pieces. *–v.t.* **2.** to reinforce with dowels; furnish with dowels. [cf. G *Döbel* peg, plug, pin]

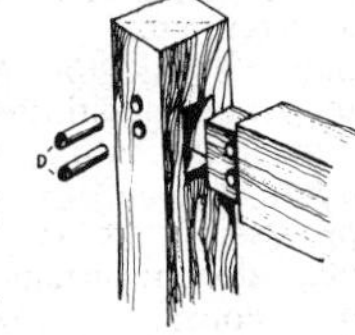
D, dowel pins

**dowel screw** /ˈ– skru/, *n.* a wood screw with a thread at each end, used esp. for picture frames.

**dower** /ˈdaʊə/, *n.* **1.** the portion of a deceased husband's real property allowed by the law to his widow for her life. **2.** →**dowry** (def. 1). **3.** a natural gift or endowment. *–v.t.* **4.** to provide with a dower or dowry. **5.** to give as a dower or dowry. [ME, from OF *douaire,* from LL *dōtārium,* from L *dōs* dowry] **– dowerless,** *adj.*

**dower house** /ˈ– haʊs/, *n.* **1.** a house set apart for a widow, often a small house on her deceased husband's estate. **2.** any small house, once on the estate of a country-house.

**dowery** /ˈdaʊəri/, *n., pl.* **-eries.** →**dowry.**

**Dow-Jones index** /ˌdaʊ-dʒoʊnz ˈɪndɛks/, *n.* an index of ordinary share prices on the U.S. share market, based on the daily average price of selected lists of industrial, railroad and utility companies in the U.S. [named after C.H. *Dow* and E.D. *Jones,* American financial statisticians]

**dowlas** /ˈdaʊləs/, *n.* **1.** a coarse linen fabric originally used for clothing in the 16th century. **2.** a rough cotton fabric often used for roller towels and cheap sheets. [named after *Daoulas,* village in Brittany]

**down**[1] /daʊn/, *adv.* **1.** from higher to lower; in descending direction or order; into or in a lower position or condition. **2.** on or to the ground. **3.** to a point of submission, inactivity, etc. **4.** to or in a position spoken of as lower, as the south, the country, a business district, etc. **5.** to or at a low point, degree, rate, pitch, volume, etc. **6.** from an earlier to a later time. **7.** from a greater to a less bulk, degree of consistency, strength, etc.: *to boil down syrup.* **8.** in due position or state: *to settle down to work.* **9.** on paper or in a book: *to write down.* **10.** in cash; at once: *pay $40 down.* **11. sent down, a.** *Colloq.* expelled from university. **b.** sent to prison. **12.** *Colloq.* in a prostrate, depressed, or degraded condition. **13.** *Boxing.* touching the ring floor with some part of the body other than the feet. **14. down to earth,** practical, realistic. **15. down with,** towards a lower position or total abolition. **16. go down on (someone),** *Colloq.* to practise fellatio. *–prep.* **17.** to, towards, or at a lower place on or in: *down the stairs.* **18.** to, towards, near, or at a lower station, condition, or rank in. **19.** away from the source, origin, etc., of: *down the river.* **20.** in the same course or direction as: *to sail down the wind.* **21. down south,** *Colloq.* **a.** in the south. **b.** (of money) not to be spent, but put in the bank: *put it all down south.* *–adj.* **22.** downwards; going or directed downwards. **23.** travelling away from a terminus. **24.** confined to bed through illness. **25.** not in activity: *the wind is down.* **26.** (esp. of a computer) not operational. **27.** *Colloq.* in prison: *he is down for a few months.* **28.** being a portion of the full price of an article bought on an instalment plan or mortgage, etc., that is paid at the time of purchase. **29.** losing or having lost money at gambling: *he was $10 down after a day at the races.* **30.** *Games.* losing or behind an opponent by a specified number of points, holes, etc. **31.** depressed; unhappy. **32. down and out, a.** *Colloq.* without friends, money, or prospects. **b.** *Boxing.* touching the flat canvas with some part of the body other than the feet. **33. down at heel,** poor; shabby; seedy. **34. down in the mouth,** discouraged; depressed. **35. down on,** over-severe; unnecessarily ready to detect faults and punish harshly. **36. down on one's luck,** suffering a period of poverty, destitution, etc. **37. down time,** *Colloq.* time lost. *–n.* **38.** a downward movement; a descent. **39.** a reverse· *the ups and downs of fortune.* **40.** *Colloq.* a grudge; a feeling of hostility: *he has a down on me.* *–v.t.* **41.** to put or throw down; subdue. **42.** to drink down: *to down a schooner of beer.* **43. down tools,** (of workers) to cease to work, as in starting a strike. *–v.i.* **44.** to go down; fall. *–interj.* **45.** (a command, esp. to a dog, to cease jumping, etc.): *down Rover!* **46.** (a command to take cover, or duck). [ME *doune,* late OE *dūne,* aphetic var. of *adūne,* earlier *of dūne* from (the) hill. See DOWN[3]]

**down**[2] /daʊn/, *n.* **1.** the first feathering of young birds. **2.** the soft under-plumage of birds as distinct from the contour feathers. **3.** a soft hairy growth as the hair on the human face when first beginning to appear. **4.** *Bot.* **a.** a fine soft pubescence upon plants and some fruits. **b.** the light feather pappus or coma upon seeds by which they are borne upon the wind, as in the dandelion and thistle. [ME *downe,* from Scand.; cf. Icel. *dūnn*]

**down**[3] /daʊn/, *n.* **1.** (*usu. pl.*) open, rolling, upland country with fairly smooth slopes usu. covered with grass. **2.** *Archaic.* a hill; a sand hill or dune. **3.** any breed of sheep belonging to the short wool group. [ME; OE *dūn* hill, c. OD *dūna.* See DUNE. Not connected with OIrish *dūn* walled town]

**down-and-out** /daʊn-ən-ˈaʊt/, *n. Colloq.* a person, usu. of disreputable appearance, without friends, money, or prospects.

**down-beat** /ˈdaʊn-bit/, *n.* **1.** a downward movement of the conductor's baton indicating the first beat of the bar in a piece of music. **2.** the first beat of a bar.

**down-bow** /ˈdaʊn-boʊ/, *n.* (in bowing on a stringed instrument) a stroke bringing the tip of the bow towards the strings, indicated in scores by the symbol ⊓ (opposed to *up-bow*).

**downcast** /ˈdaʊnkast/, *adj.* **1.** directed downwards, as the eyes. **2.** dejected in spirit; depressed. *–n.* **3.** Also, **downcast shaft.** a shaft down which air passes, as into a mine. **4.** *Geol.* a fault which throws a coal seam down.

**downcomer** /ˈdaʊnkʌmə/, *n.* a pipe, tube or passage for conducting material downwards.

**down draught** /ˈdaʊn draft/, *n.* a descending current of air.

**downer** /ˈdaʊnə/, *n. Colloq.* **1.** a depressant or tranquilliser, as valium, etc. **2.** a depressing experience.

**downfall** /ˈdaʊnfɔl/, *n.* **1.** descent to a lower position or standing; overthrow; ruin. **2.** a cause of this. **3.** a fall, as of rain or snow. **– downfallen,** *adj.*

**downgrade** /daʊnˈgreɪd/, *v.,* **-graded, -grading,** *n., adj., adv.* *–v.t.* **1.** to assign (a person, job or the like) to a lower status, usu. with a smaller salary. **2.** to reduce the security classification of (a classified document, article, etc.). **3.** to denigrate or belittle: *he attempted to downgrade his rival's victory.* *–n.* **4.** a downward slope. **5. on the downgrade,** heading for poverty, ruin, etc. *–adj., adv.* **6.** downhill.

**downhaul** /ˈdaʊnhɔl/, *n.* a rope for hauling down a sail, flag, etc.

**downhearted** /daʊnˈhatəd/, *adj.* dejected; depressed; discouraged. **– downheartedly,** *adv.* **– downheartedness,** *n.*

**downhill** /daʊnˈhɪl/, *adv.;* /ˈdaʊnhɪl/, *adj., n.* *–adv.* **1.** down the slope of a hill; downwards into a deteriorating or declining position, condition, etc. *–adj.* **2.** going or tending downwards on or as on a hill. *–n.* **3.** *Skiing.* a high-speed race downhill in which skiers compete in turn, the winner being the competitor who completes the course in the fastest time.

**downland** /ˈdaʊnlænd/, *n.* hilly pasture; undulating country, esp. rolling grasslands.

**down-market** /ˈdaʊn-makət/, *adj.* **1.** of or pertaining to commercial services and goods of inferior status, quality and price. **2.** inferior in style or production. See **up-market.**

**down payment** /daʊn ˈpeɪmənt/, *n.* the initial deposit on a purchase made on an instalment plan or mortgage.

**downpipe** /ˈdaʊnpaɪp/, *n.* a pipe for conveying rainwater from roofs to the drain or the ground; spouting.

**downpour** /ˈdaʊnpɔ/, *n.* a heavy, continuous fall of water, rain, etc.

**down-railer** /ˈdaʊn-reɪlə/, *n.* a surfboard with the edges turned down.

**downright** /ˈdaʊnraɪt/, *adj.* **1.** thorough; absolute; out-and-out. **2.** direct; straightforward. **3.** *Archaic.* directed straight downwards: *a downright blow.* *–adv.* **4.** completely or thoroughly: *he is downright angry.* – **downrightly,** *adv.* – **downrightness,** *n.*

**downriver** /ˈdaʊnrɪvə/, *adj.* along a river in the direction of its current. Cf. **upriver.**

**downsize** /ˈdaʊnsaɪz/, *v.t.,* **-sized, -sizing.** to scale down in size.

**Down's syndrome** /ˈdaʊnz sɪndroʊm/, *n.* a chromosomal abnormality which results in mental retardation and certain physical characteristics as slanting eyes; Mongolism. [from John Langdon-*Down,* 1828-96, English physician]

**downstage** /daʊnˈsteɪdʒ/, *adv.;* /ˈdaʊnsteɪdʒ/, *adj., n.* *–adv.* **1.** at or towards the front of the stage in a theatre. *–adj.* **2.** pertaining to the front of the stage. *–n.* **3.** the front of a stage.

**downstairs** /daʊnˈstɛəz/, *adv.;* /ˈdaʊnstɛəz/, *adj., n.* *–adv.* **1.** down the stairs. **2.** to or on a lower floor. *–adj.* **3.** Also, **downstair.** pertaining to or situated on a lower floor. *–n.* **4.** the lower floor of a house.

**downstream** /daʊnˈstrim/, *adv.;* /ˈdaʊnstrim/, *adj.* *–adv.* **1.** with or in the direction of the current of a stream. *–adj.* **2.** farther down a stream; moving with the current.

**downswing** /ˈdaʊnswɪŋ/, *n.* **1.** a swing downward. **2.** *Golf.* in driving a ball, the downward swing of a golf club. **3.** a decline in business activity.

**down-the-line shooting** /ˌdaʊn-ðə-laɪn ˈʃutɪŋ/, *n.* a form of trapshooting in which five or more shooters stand in a line firing in turn at the targets as they are released.

**downthrow** /ˈdaʊnθroʊ/, *n.* **1.** a throwing down or being thrown down; an overthrow. **2.** *Geol.* the downward displacement of strata by a fault. – **downthrown,** *adj.*

**down-to-earth** /ˈdaʊn-tu-ɜθ/, *adj.* sensible; without pretensions; realistic.

**downtown** /daʊnˈtaʊn/, *adv.;* /ˈdaʊntaʊn/, *adj.* *–adv.* **1.** to or in the business section of a city. *–adj.* **2.** of, pertaining to, or situated in the business section of a city.

**downtrodden** /ˈdaʊntrɒdn/, *adj.* trodden down; trampled upon; tyrannised over. Also, **downtrod.**

**downturn** /ˈdaʊntɜn/, *n.* a decline, deterioration: *a downturn in prosperity.*

**down-under** /daʊn-ˈʌndə/, *n.* *Colloq.* a term applied usu. in the Northern Hemisphere to Australia, New Zealand, and adjacent Pacific islands.

**down-value** /daʊn-ˈvælju/, *v.t.,* **-ued, -uing.** to reduce in value.

**downward** /ˈdaʊnwəd/, *adj.* **1.** moving or tending to a lower place or condition. **2.** descending or deriving from a head, source, or beginning. *–adv.* **3.** downwards. – **downwardly,** *adv.* – **downwardness,** *n.*

**downwards** /ˈdaʊnwədz/, *adv.* **1.** from a higher to a lower place or condition. **2.** down from a head, source, or beginning. **3.** from more ancient times to the present day. Also, **downward.**

**downwash** /ˈdaʊnwɒʃ/, *n.* the air deflected downwards by an aerofoil.

**downwind** /daʊnˈwɪnd/, *adv.;* /ˈdaʊnwɪnd/, *adj.* *–adv.* **1.** in the direction of the wind; with the wind. **2.** towards the leeward side. *–adj.* **3.** going downwind. **4.** situated leeward.

**downy** /ˈdaʊni/, *adj.,* **downier, downiest.** **1.** of the nature of or resembling down; fluffy; soft. **2.** made of down. **3.** covered with down. **4.** soft; soothing; calm. **5. downy bird,** *Colloq.* a canny person. – **downiness,** *n.*

**downy mildew** /– ˈmɪldju/, *n.* fungi belonging to the family Peronosporaceae, all of which are obligate parasites of vascular plants, as *Plasmopara viticola,* downy mildew of grapes.

**dowry** /ˈdaʊəri, ˈdaʊri/, *n., pl.* **-ries.** **1.** the money, goods, or estate which a woman brings to her husband at marriage; dot. **2.** any gift or reward given to or for a bride by a man in consideration for the marriage. **3.** *Obs.* a widow's dower. **4.** a natural gift or endowment; talent: *a noble dowry.* Also, **dowery.** [ME *dowerie,* from AF. See DOWER]

**dowse**[1] /daʊs/, *v.t., v.i.,* **dowsed, dowsing.** →**douse.** – **dowser,** *n.*

**dowse**[2] /daʊz/, *v.i.,* **dowsed, dowsing.** to search for subterranean supplies of water, ore, etc., by the aid of a divining rod. [orig. unknown] – **dowser,** *n.*

**dowsing rod** /ˈdaʊzɪŋ rɒd/, *n.* →**divining rod.**

**doxology** /dɒkˈsɒlədʒi/, *n., pl.* **-gies.** a hymn or form of words containing an ascription of praise to God, as the Gloria in Excelsis (**great doxology** or **greater doxology**), the Gloria Patri (**lesser doxology**), or the metrical formula beginning 'Praise God from whom all blessings flow'. [ML *doxologia,* from Gk: a praising] – **doxological** /dɒksəˈlɒdʒəkəl/, *adj.* – **doxologically** /dɒksəˈlɒdʒəkli/, *adv.*

**doxy**[1] /ˈdɒksi/, *n., pl.* **doxies.** **1.** opinion; doctrine. **2.** religious views. Also, **doxie.** [abstracted from ORTHODOXY, HETERODOXY, etc.]

**doxy**[2] /ˈdɒksi/, *n., pl.* **doxies.** *Archaic.* a mistress or paramour; a prostitute. [MFlem. *docke* doll + *-sy,* affectionate diminutive suffix]

**doyen** /ˈdɔɪən/, *n.* the senior member of a body, class, profession, etc. [F. See DEAN] – **doyenne,** *n. fem.*

**doz.,** dozen; dozens.

**doze** /doʊz/, *v.,* **dozed, dozing,** *n.* *–v.i.* **1.** to sleep lightly or fitfully. **2.** to fall into a light sleep unintentionally (oft. fol. by *off*). **3.** to be dull or half asleep. *–v.t.* **4.** to pass or spend (time) in drowsiness (oft. fol. by *away*). *–n.* **5.** a light or fitful sleep. [cf. OE *dwǣsian* become stupid, Dan. *döse* make dull, heavy, drowsy] – **dozer,** *n.*

**dozen** /ˈdʌzən/, *n., pl.* **dozen, dozens.** **1.** a group of twelve units or things. **2. daily dozen,** daily physical exercises. [ME *dozein,* from OF *dozeine,* from *douze* twelve, from L *duodecim*]

**dozer** /ˈdoʊzə/, *n.* →**bulldozer.**

**dozy** /ˈdoʊzi/, *adj.,* **dozier, doziest.** **1.** drowsy; half asleep. **2.** (of wood) waterlogged and soft. – **dozily,** *adv.* – **doziness,** *n.*

**D.P.** /di ˈpi/, displaced person. Also, **DP.**

**D.Phil.** /di ˈfɪl/, Doctor of Philosophy.

**dpt,** department.

**dr.,** dram.

**Dr,** **1.** Doctor. **2.** debtor. **3.** Drive (in street names).

**drab**[1] /dræb/, *adj.,* **drabber, drabbest,** *n.* *–adj.* **1.** having a dull grey colour. **2.** dull; cheerless. *–n.* **3.** dull grey; dull brownish or yellowish grey. [F *drap* cloth. See DRAPE] – **drably,** *adv.* – **drabness,** *n.*

**drab**[2] /dræb/, *n., v.,* **drabbed, drabbing.** *–n.* **1.** a dirty, untidy woman; a slattern. **2.** a prostitute. *–v.i.* **3.** to associate with drabs. [? LG or D. Cf. D *drab* dregs, LG *drabbe* mire. Cf. also d. E *drabbletail* slattern (with DRABBLE, *v.*) and its synonym *draggletail*]

**drabbet** /ˈdræbət/, *n.* a coarse drab linen fabric used for making tea-towels, etc. [DRAB[1] + -ET]

**drabble** /ˈdræbəl/, *v.t., v.i.,* **-bled, -bling.** to draggle; make or become wet and dirty. [ME *drabelen,* ? from LG]

**dracaena** /drəˈsinə/, *n.* **1.** any tree of the genus *Dracaena,* native to tropical regions. **2.** any tree of the closely related genus *Cordyline.* [NL, from Gk *drákaina* she-dragon]

**drachm** /dræm/, *n.* **1.** a unit of apothecaries' weight in the imperial system, equal to $\frac{1}{8}$ ounce or 3.887 9346 × $10^{-3}$ kg. **2.** See **fluid drachm.** **3.** →**drachma.** [L *drachma,* from Gk *drachmḗ* an Attic weight and coin]

**drachma** /ˈdrækmə/, *n. pl.* **-mas, -mae.** /-mi/. **1.** the monetary unit of modern Greece. **2.** the principal silver coin of the ancient Greeks, varying in weight and value. **3.** a small ancient Greek weight, approximately corresponding to the apothecaries' drachm. [L, from Gk *drachmḗ,* lit., handful]

**drack** /dræk/, *adj. Colloq.* unattractive; dressed in a slovenly manner: *a drack sort.*

**draco lizard** /ˌdreɪkoʊ ˈlɪzəd/, *n.* any of the lizards of the genus *Draco,* esp. *D. volans,* the flying dragon of the Malay Peninsula, which has wings like membranes enabling it to glide from tree to tree, etc.

**draconian** /drəˈkoʊniən/, *adj.* harsh; rigorous; severe. Also, **draconic** /drəkɒnɪk/. [from *Draco,* fl. 7th-cent. B.C., Athenian statesman] – **draconically,** *adv.*

**draconic** /drəˈkɒnɪk/, *adj.* of or like a dragon. [L *draco* DRAGON + -IC]

**draff** /dræf/, *n.* refuse, esp. of malt after brewing; lees; dregs. – **draffy,** *adj.*

**draft** /draft/, *n.* **1.** a drawing, sketch, or design. **2.** a first or preliminary form of any writing, subject to revision and copying. **3.** the act of drawing; delineation. **4.** *U.S.* the taking of supplies, forces, money, etc., from a given source. **5.** conscription. **6.** (formerly) a selection of persons already in service, to be sent from one post or organisation to another, in either the army or the navy; a detachment. **7.** a written order drawn by one person upon another; a writing directing the payment of money on account of the drawer; a bill of exchange. **8.** a drain or demand made on anything. **9.** *Foundry.* the slight taper given to a pattern so that it may be drawn from the sand without injury to the mould. **10.** *Masonry.* the narrow band worked along the margin or margins of a rough-faced stone, so that it can be accurately placed. **11.** the sectional area of the openings in a turbine wheel or in a sluice gate. **12.** an animal or animals selected and separated from the herd or flock. **13.** *Chiefly U.S.* →**draught** (esp. defs 3 and 4). *–v.t.* **14.** to draw the outlines or plan of, or sketch. **15.** to draw up in written form, as a first draft. **16.** to conscript. **17.** *Masonry.* to cut a draft on. **18.** to separate livestock from the herd or flock for a particular purpose, as branding. [ME *draht,* later *draught, droft,* (cf. OE *droht* pull, draught), verbal abstract of *draw* (OE *dragan*), c. G *Tracht.* See DRAUGHT] – **drafter,** *n.*

**draft card** /ˈ– kad/, *n.* a card officially notifying a person of his liability for conscription into the armed forces.

**draft dodger** /ˈ– dɒdʒə/, *n.* one who evades or attempts to evade conscription into the armed forces.

**draftee** /drafˈti/, *n. U.S.* →**conscript.**

**drafting gate** /ˈdraftɪŋ geɪt/, *n.* →**swing gate.**

**drafting race** /ˈ– reɪs/, *n.* a narrow race leading to a drafting yard.

**drafting yard** /– ˈjad/, *n.* a yard in which sheep or cattle are sorted. Also, **drafting pen.**

**draftsman** /ˈdraftsmən/, *n., pl.* **-men. 1.** one who draws up documents. **2.** →**draughtsman** (defs 1 and 2). – **draftsmanship,** *n.*

**draft tube** /ˈdraft tjub/, *n.* the flared passage leading vertically from a water turbine to its tailrace.

**drag** /dræg/, *v.,* **dragged, dragging,** *n.* *–v.t.* **1.** to draw with force, effort, or difficulty; pull heavily or slowly along; haul; trail. **2.** to search with a drag, grapnel, or the like. **3.** to introduce, as an irrelevant matter (fol. by *in*). **4.** to protract or pass tediously (oft. fol. by *out* or *on*). **5. drag one's feet,** to hang back deliberately; be recalcitrant. **6. drag the chain,** *Colloq.* to hinder others by doing something slowly. *–v.i.* **7.** to be drawn or hauled along. **8.** to trail on the ground. **9.** to move heavily or with effort. **10.** to proceed or pass with tedious slowness. **11.** to use a drag or grapnel; dredge. *–n.* **12.** something used by or for dragging as a dragnet or a dredge. **13.** a grapnel, net, or other apparatus dragged through water in searching, as for dead bodies. **14.** a heavy harrow. **15.** a four-horse sporting and passenger coach with seats inside and on top. **16.** a metal shoe to receive a wheel of heavy wagons and serve as a wheel lock on steep grades. **17.** anything that retards progress. **18.** act of dragging. **19.** slow, laborious movement or procedure; retardation. **20.** the force due to the relative airflow exerted on an aeroplane or other body tending to reduce its forward motion. **21.** *Hunting.* **a.** the scent or trail of a fox, etc. **b.** something, as aniseed, dragged over the ground to leave an artificial scent. **c.** a hunt with such a scent. **22.** *Angling.* **a.** a brake on a fishing reel. **b.** the sideways pull on a fishline as caused by a cross current. **23.** *Colloq.* somebody or something that is extremely boring. **24.** *Colloq.* a puff or a pull on a cigarette. **25.** *Colloq.* women's clothes, worn by men; transvestite costume. **26.** *Prison Colloq.* a prison sentence of three month's duration. **27.** *Colloq.* →**drag-race. 28.** *Colloq.* a road or street: *the main drag.* **29. have a drag,** *U.S. Colloq.* influence (fol. by *with*): *he has a drag with the managing director.* [late ME; cf. MLG *dragge* grapnel]

drag (def. 15)

**drag-anchor** /ˈdræg-æŋkə/, *n.* →**sea-anchor.**

**draggle** /drægəl/, *v.,* **-gled, -gling.** *–v.t.* **1.** to soil by dragging over damp ground or in the mud. *–v.i.* **2.** to hang trailing; become draggled. **3.** to follow slowly; straggle. [DRAG + *-le,* frequentative suffix]

**draggletail** /ˈdrægəlteɪl/, *n.* a bedraggled or untidy person; slut; slattern.

**draggletailed** /ˈdrægəlteɪld/, *adj.* having the garments draggled as from trailing in the wet and dirt.

**draghound** /ˈdræghaʊnd/, *n.* a hound trained to follow a drag or artificial scent.

**drag hunt** /ˈdræg hʌnt/, *n.* a hunt with a drag or artificial scent.

**dragline** /ˈdræglaɪn/, *n.* **1.** →**dragrope. 2.** a type of excavating equipment which casts a rope-hung bucket a considerable distance, collects the material by pulling the bucket towards itself on the ground by a second rope, elevates the bucket and dumps the material where required.

**draglink** /ˈdræglɪŋk/, *n.* a link for connecting the cranks of two shafts.

**dragnet** /ˈdrægnɛt/, *n.* **1.** a net to be drawn along the bottom of a river, pond, etc., or along the ground, to catch something. **2.** anything that serves to catch or drag in, as a police system.

**dragoman** /ˈdrægəmən/, *n., pl.* **-mans, -men.** (in Middle Eastern countries) a professional interpreter. [F, from LGk *dragoúmanos,* from Ar. *targumān* interpreter]

**dragon** /ˈdrægən/, *n.* **1.** a mythical monster variously represented, generally as a huge winged reptile with crested head and terrible claws, and often spouting fire. **2.** *Rare.* a huge serpent or snake. **3.** *Bible.* a large serpent, a crocodile, a great marine animal, or a jackal. **4.** a name for Satan. **5.** a fierce, violent person. **6. a.** a severely watchful woman; a duenna. **b.** a formidable woman. **7.** any of the small flying lizards of the East Indian region. **8.** →**komodo dragon. 9.** any of various agamid lizards, as the frill-necked lizard, *Chlamydosaurus kingi* of northern Australia. [ME, from OF, from L *draco,* from Gk *drákōn* serpent] – **dragoness,** *n. fem.* – **dragonish,** *adj.*

dragon (def. 9): dragon lizard

**dragonet** /ˈdrægənət/, *n.* **1.** a little or young dragon. **2.** any fish of the family Callionymidae comprising small shore fishes which are often brightly coloured. [ME, from OF, diminutive of *dragon* DRAGON]

**dragonfly** /ˈdrægənflaɪ/, *n., pl.* **-flies.** any of the larger, harmless insects of the order Odonata, which feed on mosquitoes and other insects, and whose immature forms are aquatic.

**dragon's blood** /ˈdrægənz blʌd/, *n.* **1.** a red resin exuding from the fruit of species of *Daemonorops,* as *D. draco,* palms of the Malay Archipelago, formerly used in medicine, but now chiefly in the preparation of varnishes, etc. **2.** any of various similar resins from other trees.

**dragon tree** /ˈdrægən tri/, *n.* a tree, *Dracaena draco,* of the Canary Islands, yielding a variety of dragon's blood.

**dragoon** /drəˈgun/, *n.* **1.** a cavalryman of certain regiments. **2.** *Obs.* a mounted infantryman armed with a short musket. *–v.t.* **3.** to set dragoons or soldiers upon; to persecute by armed force; to oppress; harass. **4.** to force by rigorous and oppressive measures; coerce. [F *dragon* dragoon (orig., dragon), referring first to the hammer of a pistol, then to the firearm and then to the troops carrying it]

**dragoon bird** /ˈ– bɜd/, *n.* →**noisy pitta.**

**drag race** /ˈdræg reɪs/, *n.* a race between cars starting from a standstill, the winner being the car that can accelerate fastest. Also, **drag.** – **dragracer,** *n.*

**drag-race** /ˈdræg-reɪs/, *v.i.,* **-raced, -racing.** to race cars to see which can accelerate most rapidly from a standing start. – **drag-racing,** *n.*

**dragrope** /ˈdrægroʊp/, *n.* **1.** a rope for dragging something, as a piece of artillery. **2.** a rope dragging from something, as the guide rope from a balloon.

**dragsail** /ˈdrægseɪl/, *n.* →**sea-anchor.** Also, **drag-sheet** /ˈdrægʃit/.

**dragster** /ˈdrægstə/, *n.* **1.** a car designed for drag-racing. **2.** a bicycle with high handlebars and an extension of the framework behind the seat. **3.** a bicycle with high handlebars, a long saddle, a sissy bar and smaller than average wheels.

**drag strip** /ˈdræg strɪp/, *n.* a straight piece of road suitable for drag racing.

**drain** /dreɪn/, *v.t.* **1.** to draw off gradually, as a liquid; remove by degrees, as by filtration. **2.** to draw off or take away completely. **3.** to withdraw liquid gradually from; make empty or dry by drawing off liquid. **4.** to deprive of possessions, resources, etc., by gradual withdrawal; exhaust. **5. drain the dragon,** *Colloq.* to urinate. *–v.i.* **6.** to flow off gradually. **7.** to become empty or dry by the gradual flowing off of moisture. *–n.* **8.** that by which anything is drained, as a pipe or conduit. **9.** *Electronics.* one of the three electrodes of a field effect transistor. **10.** *Surg.* a material or appliance for maintaining the opening of a wound to permit free exit of fluid contents. **11.** gradual or continuous outflow, withdrawal, or expenditure. **12.** the cause of a continual outflow, withdrawal, or expenditure. **13.** act of draining. **14.** *Colloq.* a small drink. **15. go down the drain,** *Colloq.* **a.** to be wasted. **b.** to become worthless. **16. laugh like a drain,** *Colloq.* to laugh loudly. [OE *drēnian, drēahnian* drain, strain out; akin to DRY] – **drainable,** *adj.* – **drainer,** *n.*

**drainage** /ˈdreɪnɪdʒ/, *n.* **1.** the act or process of draining. **2.** a system of drains, artificial or natural. **3.** drainage basin. **4.** that which is drained off. **5.** *Surg.* the draining of body fluids (bile, urine, etc.) or of pus and other morbid products from a wound.

**drainage basin** /ˈ– beɪsən/, *n.* the entire area drained by a river and all its tributaries. Also, **drainage area.**

**drainer** /ˈdreɪnə/, *n.* one who installs the drains and fittings of a sewage, sullage or stormwater drainage system outside or under a building.

**draining-board** /ˈdreɪnɪŋ-bɔd/, *n.* a gently sloping board, etc., usu. having runnels, beside a sink on which crockery is placed after washing to dry.

**draining pen** /ˈdreɪnɪŋ pɛn/, *n.* a pen where sheep which have just been dipped stand until the surplus dip has drained back into the reservoir.

**drainpipe** /ˈdreɪnpaɪp/, *n.* **1.** a pipe receiving the discharge of waste pipes and soil pipes. **2.** (*pl.*) *Colloq.* tight, narrow trousers.

**drake** /dreɪk/, *n.* the male of any bird of the duck kind. [ME, c. d. G *draak;* cf. OHG *an(u)trahho*]

**drake stone** /ˈ– stoʊn/, *n.* a smooth flat stone suitable for skimming over the surface of water.

**dram** /dræm/, *n.* **1.** a unit of measurement in the imperial system, equal to $\frac{1}{16}$ ounce avoirdupois weight (27.34 grains) or approx. 1.772 × $10^{-3}$ kg. **2.** *U.S.* →**drachm** (def. 1). **3.** →**fluid drachm.** **4.** a small drink of liquor. **5.** a small quantity of anything. [ME *drame,* from OF, from L *drachma* DRACHMA]

**drama** /ˈdramə/, *n.* **1.** a composition in prose or verse presenting in dialogue or pantomime a story involving conflict or contrast of character, esp. one intended to be acted on the stage; a play. **2.** the branch of literature having such compositions as its subject; dramatic art or representation. **3.** that art which deals with plays from their writing to their final production. **4.** any series of events having dramatic interest or results. [LL: a play, from Gk: deed, play]

**dramamine** /ˈdræməmin/, *n.* (*also cap.*) a synthetic antihistamine, used in the treatment of allergic disorders and as a preventive for seasickness and airsickness. [Trademark]

**drama queen** /ˈdramə kwin/, *n.* a person who is overly theatrical and emotional.

**dramatic** /drəˈmætɪk/, *adj.* **1.** of or pertaining to the drama. **2.** employing the form or manner of the drama. **3.** characteristic of or appropriate to the drama; involving conflict or contrast. Also, *Rare,* **dramatical.** – **dramatically,** *adv.*

**dramatic irony** /– ˈaɪrəni/, *n.* →**irony**[1] (def. 4).

**dramatics** /drəˈmætɪks/, *n.* **1.** (*construed as sing. or pl.*) the art of producing or acting dramas. **2.** (*construed as pl.*) dramatic productions, esp. by amateurs. **3.** (*construed as pl.*) dramatic behaviour.

**dramatic soprano** /drəˌmætɪk səˈpranoʊ/, *n.* a soprano with a large, untiring voice best suited to those female roles of grand opera which require greatest stamina and dramatic expressiveness.

**dramatisation** /dræmətaɪˈzeɪʃən/, *n.* **1.** the act of dramatising. **2.** construction or representation in dramatic form. **3.** a dramatised version, of another form of literature or of historic facts. Also, **dramatization.**

**dramatise** /ˈdræmətaɪz/, *v.t.,* **-tised, -tising. 1.** to put into dramatic form. **2.** to express or represent dramatically: *he dramatises his woes.* Also, **dramatize.** – **dramatiser,** *n.*

**dramatis personae** /ˌdræmətɪs pɜˈsoʊnaɪ/, *n.pl.* **1.** the persons or characters in a drama. **2.** *Colloq.* the people who are the key figures in any situation. [L]

**dramatist** /ˈdræmətəst/, *n.* a writer of dramas or dramatic poetry; a playwright.

**dramaturge** /ˈdræmətɜdʒ/, *n.* →**dramatist.** Also, **dramaturgist.**

**dramaturgy** /ˈdræmətɜdʒi/, *n.* **1.** the science of dramatic composition. **2.** the dramatic art. **3.** dramatic representation. [Gk *drāmatourgía* composition of dramas] – **dramaturgic** /dræməˈtɜdʒɪk/, **dramaturgical** /dræməˈtɜdʒɪkəl/, *adj.*

**drank** /dræŋk/, *v.* past tense and former past participle of **drink.**

**drape** /dreɪp/, *v.,* **draped, draping,** *n.* *–v.t.* **1.** to cover or hang with cloth or some fabric, esp. in graceful folds; adorn with drapery. **2.** to adjust (hangings, clothing, etc.) in graceful folds. **3.** *Colloq.* to position in a casual manner: *he draped his legs over the arms of the chair.* *–v.i.* **4.** to fall in folds, as drapery. *–n.* **5.** manner or style of hanging. **6.** (*pl.*) curtains. [F *draper,* from *drap* cloth, from LL *drappus*]

**draper** /ˈdreɪpə/, *n.* a dealer in textiles and cloth goods, etc. [ME, from AF, var. of F *drapier*]

**drapery** /ˈdreɪpəri/, *n., pl.* **-peries. 1.** cloths or textile fabrics collectively. **2.** the business of a draper. **3.** coverings, hangings, clothing, etc., of some fabric, esp. as arranged in loose, graceful folds. **4.** *Art.* hangings, clothing, etc., so arranged as represented in sculpture or painting. – **draperied,** *adj.*

**drastic** /ˈdræstɪk/, *adj.* acting with force or violence; violent. [Gk *drastikós* efficacious] – **drastically,** *adv.*

**drat** /dræt/, *v.,* **dratted, dratting,** *interj.* *–v.t.* **1.** *Colloq.* to confound; to damn. *–interj.* **2.** (a mild exclamation of vexation.)

**dratted** /ˈdrætəd/, *adj. Colloq.* confounded.

**draught** /draft/, *n.* **1.** a current of air, esp. in a room, chimney, stove, or any enclosed space. **2.** a device for regulating the flow of air in a stove, fireplace, etc. **3.** *Naut.* the fullness of a sail created by the sailmaker. **4.** an act of drawing or pulling, or that which is drawn; a pull; haul. **5.** an animal, or team of animals used to pull a load. **6.** the drawing of a liquid from its receptacle, as of ale from a cask. **7.** drinking, or a drink. **8.** an amount drunk as a continuous act. **9.** a dose of medicine. **10.** a catch or take of fish. **11. a.** the action of displacing water with a vessel. **b.** the depth of water a vessel needs to float it. **12.** (*pl. construed as sing.*) a game played by two people each with twelve pieces on a chequered board. **13.** one of the pieces in this game. **14. feel the draught,** *Colloq.* feel or be harmed by conditions becoming unfavourable. **15.** →**draft** (esp. defs 1-3). *–adj.* **16.** being on draught; drawn as required; draught ale. **17.** used or suited for drawing loads. [ME *draht,* c. D *dragt,* G *Tracht,* Icel. *drāttr.* See DRAFT]

**draught beer** /– 'bɪə/, *n.* beer drawn from a cask or keg.

**draughtboard** /'draftbɔd/, *n.* a board marked off into sixty-four squares of two alternating colours, on which draughts and chess are played. Also, **draughtsboard.**

**draughthorse** /'drafthɔs/, *n.* a strong heavily built horse, 15 hands or over in height, used for pulling heavy loads.

**draughtsman** /'draftsmən/, *n., pl.* **-men. 1.** one who draws sketches, plans, or designs. **2.** one employed in making mechanical drawings, as of machines, structures, etc. **3.** →**draftsman** (def. 1). **4.** one of the pieces used in draughts, usu. a small coloured disc. – **draughtsmanship,** *n.*

**draughty** /'drafti/, *adj.,* **draughtier, draughtiest.** characterised by or causing draughts of air. – **draughtiness,** *n.*

**Dravidian** /drə'vɪdiən/, *n.* **1.** a great linguistic family of India, including Tamil, Telugu, Kanarese, and Malayalam, and, in Baluchistan, Brahui. It is wholly distinct from Indo-European. **2.** a member of a race of people speaking these languages, occupying much of southern India and parts of Ceylon. *–adj.* **3.** Also, **Dravidic.** of or pertaining to this people or their language.

**draw** /drɔ/, *v.,* **drew** /dru/ **drawn, drawing,** *n. –v.t.* **1.** to cause to come in a particular direction as by a pulling force; pull; drag; lead (oft. fol. by *along, away, in, out, off,* etc.). **2.** to bring or take out, as from a receptacle, or source: *to draw water, blood, tears, teeth.* **3.** to bring towards oneself or itself, as by inherent force or influence; attract. **4.** to pick or choose at random. **5. a.** to be dealt or take a card from the pack. **b.** *Bridge.* to remove trumps, or outstanding cards of a given suit, from an opponent's hand. **6.** to sketch in lines or words; delineate; depict: *to draw a picture.* **7.** to mark out; trace. **8.** to frame or formulate as a distinction. **9.** to take in, as by sucking or inhaling. **10.** to get; derive; deduce: *to draw a conclusion.* **11.** to disembowel (a fowl, etc.). **12.** to drain (a pond, etc., by a channel, etc.). **13.** to pull out to full or greater length; stretch; make by attenuating, as wire. **14.** to wrinkle or shrink by contraction. **15.** *Med.* to digest and cause to discharge: *to draw an abscess by a poultice.* **16.** to write or sign an order, draft, or bill of exchange. **17.** *Naut.* (of a boat) to displace (a certain depth of water). **18.** *Sport.* to leave (a contest) undecided. **19.** *Sport.* to be placed in a certain position for the start of a race: *to draw a good position.* **20.** *Archery.* to pull back the bowstring and arrow preparatory to shooting the arrow. **21.** *Billiards.* to cause to recoil after impact, as if pulled back. **22.** to search (covert) for game. **23.** *Curling.* to toss (the stone) gently. **24.** (of tea) to infuse. *–v.i.* **25.** to exert a pulling, moving, or attracting force: *a sail draws by being filled with wind and properly trimmed.* **26.** to be drawn; move as under a pulling force (oft. fol. by *on, off, out,* etc.): *the day draws near.* **27.** to take out a sword, pistol, etc., for action (oft. fol. by *on*). **28.** to use or practise the art of tracing figures; practise drawing. **29.** to shrink or contract. **30.** *Med.* to act as an irritant or to cause blisters. **31.** to produce or have a draught of air, etc., as in a pipe or flue. **32.** *Games.* to leave a contest undecided. **33.** *Hunting.* **a.** (of a hound) to advance carefully towards the game, after indicating it by pointing. **b.** (of a hound) to follow the game animal by its scent. *–v.* **34.** Some special verb phrases are:

**draw a blank, 1.** to draw from a lottery an unmarked counter, one not associated with any prize. **2.** to be unsuccessful, esp. when looking for someone or something.

**draw on, 1.** to approach; to near. **2.** to pull on (a garment). **3.** to call on or make a demand on: *to draw on supplies, etc.* **4.** to make a levy or call on for money, supplies, etc.

**draw out, 1.** to extract. **2.** to lengthen or prolong. **3.** to encourage or persuade somebody to talk.

**draw stumps,** *Cricket.* to pull up the stumps as a sign that the day's play has ended.

**draw the lead,** *Boxing.* to force an opponent to lead, and then counter-punch through his guard.

**draw the line,** *Colloq.* **1.** to fix a limit. **2.** to decline.

**draw the teeth of,** *Colloq.* to render harmless.

**draw up, 1.** to bring to, or come to a halt. **2.** to prepare, or set out a document, plan, etc. **3.** to arrange, esp. in military formation.

*–n.* **35.** the act of drawing. **36.** something that draws or attracts. **37.** that which is drawn, as a lot. **38.** the distance from the bottom of a mine pit to the top. **39.** *Sport.* a drawn or undecided contest. **40.** *Lacrosse.* the starting or restarting movement of a game, in which the crosses of two opposing players are pulled apart, having previously been placed back to back with the ball between them. **41.** *Bowls.* the path taken by a bowl after delivery. **42.** *Canoeing.* a stroke used to propel the canoe sideways. **43.** *Bowls.* the extent of the curve in the path a bowl takes, as a result of its inbuilt bias. [ME *drawen,* OE *dragan,* c. Icel. *draga* draw, G *tragen* carry, bear. Cf. DRAG]

**drawback** /'drɔbæk/, *n.* **1.** a hindrance or disadvantage. **2.** *Comm.* an amount paid back from a charge made. **3.** *Govt.* refund of excise or import duty, as when imported goods are re-exported. See **rebate**[1]. **4.** the full inhalation of tobacco smoke into the lungs.

**drawbar** /'drɔba/, *n.* a metal bar which connects a steam engine to the tender, or the two bogies of some electric locomotives.

**drawbore** /'drɔbɔ/, *v.,* **-bored, -boring,** *n. –v.t.* **1.** to bore a hole (in a tenon) slightly out of alignment, so that when a pin is driven in, the mortised and tenoned parts are drawn snugly together. *–n.* **2.** a hole thus made.

**drawbridge** /'drɔbrɪdʒ/, *n.* a bridge of which the whole or a part may be drawn up or aside to prevent access or to leave a passage open for boats, etc.

**drawcard** /'drɔkad/, *n.* a person, act, entertainment, occasion, etc., that can be relied upon to produce a large attendance; crowd puller.

**drawee** /drɔ'i/, *n.* one on whom an order, draft, or bill of exchange is drawn.

**drawer** /drɔ/ *for defs 1 and 2;* /'drɔə/ *for defs 3-5. –n.* **1.** a sliding compartment, as in a piece of furniture, that may be drawn out in order to get access to it. **2.** (*pl.*) a garment for the lower part of the body, with a separate portion for each leg; underpants. **3.** one who or that which draws. **4.** *Finance.* one who draws an order, draft, or bill of exchange. **5.** *Archaic.* a tapster.

**drawing** /'drɔɪŋ, 'drɔrɪŋ/, *n.* **1.** the act of a person or thing that draws. **2.** representation by lines; delineation of form without reference to colour. **3.** a sketch, plan, or design, esp. one made with pen, pencil, or crayon. **4.** the art of making these.

**drawing account** /'– əkaʊnt/, *n. U.S. Banking, etc.* →**cheque account.**

**drawing board** /'– bɔd/, *n.* **1.** a rectangular board to which paper can be affixed for drawing on. **2. on the drawing board,** in preparation. **3. back to the drawing board,** back to the basic essentials; back to the start.

**drawing paper** /'– peɪpə/, *n.* a rough-surfaced paper, particularly suited to pencil, crayon or charcoal drawing, as its surface gives a grained effect.

**drawing-pin** /'drɔɪŋ-pɪn/, *n.* a short broad-headed tack designed to be pushed in by the thumb. Also, **thumbtack.**

**drawing room** /'drɔɪŋ rum/, *n.* **1.** a room for the reception and entertainment of visitors; a living room. **2.** a formal reception, esp. at court. **3.** *U.S.* a private compartment in a railway carriage. [obs. *drawing* withdrawing + ROOM]

**drawings-back** /drɔɪŋz-'bæk/, *n.* →**forcings-back.**

**drawknife** /'drɔnaɪf/, *n.* a knife with a handle at each end at right angles to the blade, used by drawing over a surface.

drawknife

**drawl** /drɔl/, *v.t., v.i.* **1.** to say or speak with slow, lingering utterance. *–n.* **2.** the act or utterance of one who drawls. [apparently a frequentative form connected with DRAW. Cf. D *dralen,* LG *draueln* loiter] – **drawler,** *n.* – **drawlingly,** *adv.* – **drawly,** *adj.*

**drawn** /drɔn/, *v.* **1.** past participle of **draw.** *–adj.* **2.** haggard; tired; tense. **3.** pulled together; closed. **4.** equal in score, as a game. **5.** eviscerated, as a fowl. **6.** (of a weapon) unsheathed. **7. (hung), drawn and quartered, a.** punished for treason by being dragged to a place of execution, there hung, and subsequently cut into four pieces for public display. **b.** *Colloq.* punished severely.

**drawnet** /'drɔnɛt/, *n.* a net with a drawstring in various weights and meshes, used for trapping animals.

**drawn-thread work** /drɔn-ˈθrɛd wɜk/, *n.* ornamental work done by drawing threads from a fabric, the remaining portions usu. being formed into lacelike patterns by needlework. Also, **drawn work.**

**drawplate** /ˈdrɔpleɪt/, *n.* a die plate with conical holes through which to draw wire and thus to regulate its size and shape.

**drawshave** /ˈdrɔʃeɪv/, *n.* →**drawknife.**

**drawsheet** /ˈdrɔʃit/, *n.* a sheet that can be pulled from under a patient in bed.

**drawstring** /ˈdrɔstrɪŋ/, *n.* a string, cord, etc., which tightens or closes an opening, as of a bag, clothing, etc., when one or both ends are pulled.

**draw table** /ˈdrɔ teɪbəl/, *n.* a table with one or more leaves which slide out to form an extension.

**drawtube** /ˈdrɔtjub/, *n.* a tube sliding within another tube, as the tube carrying the eyepiece in a microscope.

**draw-well** /ˈdrɔ-wɛl/, *n.* a well from which water is drawn by a bucket suspended by a rope.

**dray** /dreɪ/, *n.* **1.** a low, strong cart without fixed sides, for carrying heavy loads. **2.** a sledge. *–v.t.* **3.** to convey on a dray. [ME *draye* sledge without wheels. Cf. OE *dræg-* in *drægnett* dragnet, from OE *dragan* draw]

**drayage** /ˈdreɪɪdʒ/, *n.* **1.** conveyance by dray. **2.** a charge made for it.

**dray-horse** /ˈdreɪ-hɔs/, *n.* a strong carthorse; a powerful horse used to draw a dray.

**drayman** /ˈdreɪmən/, *n., pl.* **-men.** a man who drives a dray.

**dread** /drɛd/, *v.t.* **1.** to fear greatly; be in shrinking apprehension or expectation of: *to dread death.* **2.** *Obs.* to hold in respectful awe. *–v.i.* **3.** *Obs.* to be in great fear. *–n.* **4.** terror or apprehension as to something future; great fear. **5.** deep awe or reverence. **6.** a person or thing dreaded. *–adj.* **7.** greatly feared; frightful; terrible. **8.** held in awe; revered. [ME *drede(n)*, OE *drǣdan,* aphetic var. of *adrǣdan, ondrǣdan,* c. OHG *intrātan* fear]

**dreadful** /ˈdrɛdfəl/, *adj.* **1.** causing great dread, fear, or terror; terrible: *a dreadful storm.* **2.** venerable; awe-inspiring. **3.** *Colloq.* extremely bad, unpleasant, ugly, great, etc. *–n. Colloq.* **4.** Also, **penny-dreadful.** a cheap, lurid story, as of crime or adventure. **5.** a periodical given to highly sensational matter. – **dreadfully,** *adv.* – **dreadfulness,** *n.*

**dreadnought** /ˈdrɛdnɔt/, *n.* **1.** (formerly) a type of battleship. **2.** one who fears nothing. **3.** an outer garment of heavy woollen cloth. **4.** *Colloq.* a heavyweight boxer. **5.** *Colloq.* (formerly) a heavy type of tramcar used in Sydney.

**dream** /drim/, *n., v.,* **dreamed** or **dreamt, dreaming.** *–n.* **1.** a succession of images or ideas present in the mind during sleep. **2.** the sleeping state in which this occurs. **3.** an object seen in a dream. **4.** an involuntary vision occurring to one awake: *a waking dream.* **5.** a vision voluntarily indulged in while awake; daydream; reverie. **6.** a wild or vain fancy. **7.** something or somebody of an unreal beauty or charm. **8.** a hope; an inspiration; an aim. **9.** *Prison Colloq.* a period of imprisonment of six months. *–v.i.* **10.** to have a dream or dreams. **11.** to indulge in daydreams or reveries. **12.** to think or conceive of something in a very remote way (fol. by *of*). *–v.t.* **13.** to see or imagine in sleep or in a vision. **14.** to imagine as if in a dream; fancy; suppose. **15.** to pass or spend (time, etc.) in dreaming (oft. fol. by *away*). **16. dream up,** *Colloq.* to invent; to form or plan an idea in the imagination. [ME *dreem* dream, OE *drēam* mirth, noise; change of meaning probably due to Scand. influence. Cf. Icel. *draumr* dream] – **dreamer,** *n.* – **dreamful,** *adj.* – **dreamingly,** *adv.* – **dreamless,** *adj.* – **dreamlessly,** *adv.* – **dreamlessness,** *n.* – **dreamlike,** *adj.*

**dreamboat** /ˈdrimbout/, *n. Colloq.* **1.** an overwhelmingly attractive member of the opposite sex. **2.** anything greatly desired.

**dreaming** /ˈdrimɪŋ/, *n.* **1.** an Aboriginal's awareness and knowledge of the Dreamtime. **2.** (*cap.*) **the Dreaming,** →**Dreamtime.** [from the Aboriginal notion that in a dreaming state one is receptive to this form of awareness]

**dreamland** /ˈdrimlænd/, *n.* the land of imagination or fancy; the region of reverie.

**dreamt** /drɛmt/, *v.* a past tense and past participle of **dream.**

**Dreamtime** /ˈdrimtaɪm/, *n.* (in Aboriginal mythology) the time in which the earth received its present form and in which the patterns and cycles of life and nature were initiated.

**dream world** /ˈdrim wɜld/, *n.* the world of fancy, rather than of objective reality.

**dreamy** /ˈdrimi/, *adj.,* **dreamier, dreamiest. 1.** full of dreams; characterised by or causing dreams. **2.** of the nature of or characteristic of dreams; visionary. **3.** vague; dim. **4.** soothing; quiet; gentle. **5.** *Colloq.* marvellous; extremely pleasing. – **dreamily,** *adv.* – **dreaminess,** *n.*

**dreary** /ˈdrɪəri/, *adj.,* **drearier, dreariest. 1.** causing sadness or gloom. **2.** dull. **3.** *Archaic.* sad; sorrowful. Also, *Poetic,* **drear.** [ME *drery,* OE *drēorig* gory, cruel, sad] – **drearily,** *adv.* – **dreariness,** *n.*

**dredge**[1] /drɛdʒ/, *n., v.,* **dredged, dredging.** *–n.* **1.** a dragnet or other contrivance for gathering material or objects from the bed of a river, etc. **2.** any of various powerful machines for dredging up or removing earth, etc., as from the bottom of a river, by means of a scoop, a series of buckets, a suction pipe, or the like. *–v.t.* **3.** to clear out with a dredge; remove sand, silt, mud, etc., from the bottom of. **4.** to take, catch, or gather with a dredge; obtain or remove by a dredge. *–v.i.* **5.** to use a dredge. **6.** to find, usu. with some difficulty (fol. by *up*): *to dredge up an argument.* [late ME *dreg,* akin to OE *dragan* DRAW]

**dredge**[2] /drɛdʒ/, *v.t.,* **dredged, dredging.** (in cooking) to sprinkle or coat with some powdered substance, esp. flour. [apparently v. use of *dredge* mixed grain]

**dredger**[1] /ˈdrɛdʒə/, *n.* **1.** a machine for dredging. **2.** one who uses a dredge. **3.** a barge, boat, etc., equipped for dredging.

**dredger**[2] /ˈdrɛdʒə/, *n.* a container with a perforated top for sprinkling flour, etc. [DREDGE[2] + -ER[1]]

**dredging machine** /ˈdrɛdʒɪŋ məʃin/, *n.* →**dredge**[1] (def. 2).

**dreg** /drɛg/, *n.* **1.** (*usu. pl.*) the sediment of wine or other drink; lees; grounds. **2.** (*usu. pl.*) any waste or worthless residue. **3.** a small remnant or quantity. [ME, from Scand.; cf. Icel. *dreggjar* dregs] – **dreggy,** *adj.*

**drench** /drɛntʃ/, *v.t.* **1.** to wet thoroughly; steep; soak: *garments drenched with rain, swords drenched in blood.* **2.** *Archaic.* to cause to drink. **3.** *Vet. Sci.* to administer a draught of medicine to (an animal), esp. by force: *to drench a horse.* *–n.* **4.** the act of drenching. **5.** something that drenches: *a drench of rain.* **6.** a preparation for drenching or steeping. **7.** *Obs.* a large drink or draught. **8.** a draught of medicine, esp. one administered to an animal by force. [ME *drenche(n)*, OE *drencan,* causative of *drincan* drink] – **drencher,** *n.*

**drenching-gun** /ˈdrɛntʃɪŋ-gʌn/, *n.* a device for administering a drench to animals.

**Dresden china** /ˌdrɛzdən ˈtʃaɪnə/, *n.* a delicate porcelain ware made in Meissen, near Dresden, Eastern Germany. Also, **Dresden.**

**dress** /drɛs/, *n., adj., v.,* **dressed** or **drest, dressing.** *–n.* **1.** the chief outer garment worn by women, consisting of a skirt and a bodice, made either separately or together. **2.** clothing; apparel; garb. **3.** fine clothes; formal costume: *full dress.* **4.** outer covering, as the plumage of birds. *–adj.* **5.** of or for a dress or dresses. **6.** of or for a formal occasion: *a dress suit, a dress uniform.* *–v.t.* **7.** to equip with clothing, ornaments, etc.; deck; attire. **8.** to put formal or evening clothes on. **9.** to arrange a display in; ornament or adorn: *to dress a shop window.* **10.** to prepare (fowl, game, skins, fabrics, timber, stone, ore, etc.) by special processes. **11.** to comb out and do up (hair). **12.** to cultivate (land, etc.). **13.** to treat (wounds or sores). **14.** to make straight; bring (troops) into line: *to dress ranks.* **15.** *Colloq.* to scold severely; upbraid and rebuke (fol. by *down*). **16. dress ship,** *Naut.* to decorate a ship by hoisting lines of flags running the full length of the ship. *–v.i.* **17.** to clothe or attire oneself, esp. in formal or evening clothes: *she is dressing for dinner.* **18.** to come into line, as troops. **19. dress up, a.** to put on best clothes. **b.** to put on fancy dress, costume, or guise. [ME *dres(en)*, from OF *dresser* arrange, from L *dīrectus* straight. See DIRECT, *v.*]

**dressage** /ˈdrɛsaʒ/, *n.* the art of training of a horse in obedience, deportment, and responses.

**dress circle** /ˈdrɛs sɜkəl/, *n.* a circular or curving division of seats in a theatre, cinema, etc., usu. the first gallery above the floor, originally set apart for spectators in evening dress.

**ress coat** /ˈ– koʊt/, *n.* a man's close-fitting evening coat, with open front and with the skirts cut away over the hips.

**ressed weight** /drɛst ˈweɪt/, *n.* the weight of a carcass when skin and offal are removed.

**dresser**[1] /ˈdrɛsə/, *n.* **1.** one who dresses. **2.** one employed to help to dress actors, etc., at a theatre. **3.** any of several tools or devices used in dressing materials. **4.** an assistant to a surgeon. **5.** a window-dresser. [DRESS + -ER[1]]

**dresser**[2] /ˈdrɛsə/, *n.* **1.** a kitchen sideboard with a set of shelves and drawers for dishes and cooking utensils. **2.** *Obs.* a table or sideboard on which food is dressed for serving. [ME *dressour,* from OF *dresseur,* from *dresser* DRESS]

dresser[2]

**dressing** /ˈdrɛsɪŋ/, *n.* **1.** the act of one who or that which dresses. **2.** that with which something is dressed. **3.** a sauce for food: *salad dressing.* **4.** stuffing for a fowl. **5.** an application for a wound. **6.** manure, compost, or other fertilisers for land. **7.** (*usu. pl.*) *Archit.* worked or dressed stones, esp. those around window or door openings or at the angle of a building. **8.** the grooming of a horse.

**dressing-down** /drɛsɪŋ-ˈdaʊn/, *n.* **1.** a severe reprimand; scolding. **2.** a thrashing; beating.

**dressing floor** /ˈdrɛsɪŋ flɔ/, *n.* the place where ore is sorted on the floor of a mine; a strake.

**dressing-gown** /ˈdrɛsɪŋ-gaʊn/, *n.* a loose gown or robe generally worn over night attire.

**dressing-room** /ˈdrɛsɪŋ-rum/, *n.* a room for use in getting dressed, esp. backstage in a theatre.

**dressing station** /ˈdrɛsɪŋ steɪʃən/, *n. Mil.* a post or centre close to the combat area, which gives first aid to the wounded.

**dressing-table** /ˈdrɛsɪŋ-teɪbəl/, *n.* **1.** a table or stand, usu. surmounted by a mirror. **2.** a small desk-like table, with drawers beneath often screened by curtains.

**dressmaker** /ˈdrɛsmeɪkə/, *n.* one whose occupation is the making of women's dresses, coats, etc. – **dressmaking,** *n.*

**dress parade** /ˈdrɛs pəreɪd/, *n. Mil.* a ceremonial parade at which dress uniforms are worn.

**dress rehearsal** /ˈdrɛs rəhɜsəl/, *n.* a rehearsal of a play in costume and with scenery, properties, and lights arranged and operated as for a performance; the final rehearsal.

**dress shield** /ˈ– ʃild/, *n.* a pad worn under the arms beneath the clothing to keep perspiration from showing or staining.

**dress suit** /ˈ– sut/, *n.* a man's suit, either black or coloured, for formal or semi-formal wear.

**dress uniform** /ˈ– junəfɔm/, *n.* the special outfit worn by the military at functions and parades.

**dressy** /ˈdrɛsi/, *adj.* **1.** smart; stylish. **2.** suitable for formal occasions. **3.** excessively elaborate. – **dressily,** *adv.* – **dressiness,** *n.*

**drest** /drɛst/, *v. Archaic.* past tense and past participle of **dress.**

**drew** /dru/, *v.* past tense of **draw.**

**dribble** /ˈdrɪbəl/, *v.,* **-bled, -bling,** *n.* –*v.i.* **1.** to fall or flow in drops or small quantities; trickle. **2.** to drivel; slaver. **3.** *Soccer, Hockey, etc.* to advance a ball by a series of short kicks or pushes. **4.** (in netball and basketball) to move about a court while bouncing a ball. –*v.t.* **5.** to let fall in drops. **6.** *Sport.* **a.** (in soccer, hockey, etc.) to move (the ball) along by a rapid succession of short kicks, pushes, or hits. **b.** (in netball and basketball) to bounce a ball. –*n.* **7.** a small trickling stream. **8.** a drop. **9.** a small quantity of anything. **10.** *Sport.* the act of dribbling. [frequentative of obs. *drib* drip, in some senses influenced by DRIVEL] – **dribbler,** *n.* – **dribbly,** *adj.*

**driblet** /ˈdrɪblət/, *n.* **1.** a small portion or part. **2.** a small or petty sum. Also, **dribblet.** [DRIBBLE + -ET]

**dribs and drabs** /drɪbz ən ˈdræbz/, *n. pl.* small and often irregular amounts.

**dried** /draɪd/, *v.* past tense and past participle of **dry.**

**dried fruits** /– ˈfruts/, *n.pl.* assorted fruit, as raisins, sultanas, apricots, apples, which has been dried in the sun.

**drier** /ˈdraɪə/, *adj.* **1.** comparative of **dry.** –*n.* Also, **dryer. 2.** one who or that which dries. **3.** any substance added to paints, varnishes, etc., to make them dry quickly. **4.** a mechanical contrivance for removing moisture.

**driest** /ˈdraɪəst/, *adj.* superlative of **dry.**

**drift** /drɪft/, *n.* **1.** a driving movement or force; impulse; impetus; pressure. **2.** *Navig.* movement or course under the impulse of water currents, wind, etc. **3.** *Phys. Geog.* a broad and shallow current which advances at a rate of 15 to 25 kilometres a day, like that which crosses the middle Atlantic. **4.** *Naut.* the direction and distance that a ship is carried by a current at sea. **5.** *Aeron.* deviation of an aircraft from a set course, due to cross-winds. **6.** the course of anything; tendency; aim: *the drift of an argument.* **7.** something driven, or formed by driving. **8.** a heap of any matter driven together: *a drift of sand.* **9.** *Geol.* **a.** a deposit of detritus. **b.** the deposit of a continental ice-sheet. **10.** the state or process of being driven. **11.** Also, **drift bolt.** a tapering steel rod, used to bring two holes into alignment for riveting or bolting. **12.** *Mach.* a round, tapering piece of steel for enlarging holes in metal, or for bringing holes in line to receive rivets, etc. **13.** *Civ. Eng.* a secondary tunnel between two main tunnels or shafts. **14.** *Mining.* an approximately horizontal passageway in underground mining, etc. –*v.i.* **15.** to be carried along by currents of water or air, or by the force of circumstances. **16.** to wander aimlessly. **17.** to be driven into heaps: *drifting sand.* –*v.t.* **18.** to carry along: *the current drifted the boat to sea.* **19.** to drive into heaps: *drifted snow.* **20.** *Agric.* to move (sheep) from one paddock to another, ensuring that ewes which have freshly lambed are left behind undisturbed. [ME *drift* act of driving, verbal abstract from OE *drīfan* drive] – **drifter, drifting,** *n.*

**driftage** /ˈdrɪftɪdʒ/, *n.* **1.** the action or amount of drifting. **2.** drifted matter. **3.** *Naut.* the amount of deviation from a ship's course due to leeway. **4.** windage.

**drift anchor** /ˈdrɪft æŋkə/, *n.* a sea-anchor or drag.

**drift bolt** /ˈdrɪft boʊlt/, *n.* →**drift** (def. 11).

**drifter** /ˈdrɪftə/, *n.* **1.** one who or that which drifts. **2.** *Colloq.* a shiftless person. **3.** a fishing boat that uses a driftnet.

**drift ice** /ˈdrɪft aɪs/, *n.* detached floating ice in masses which drift with the wind or ocean currents, as in the polar seas.

**drift mining** /ˈ– maɪnɪŋ/, *n.* mining by means of horizontal or slightly inclined tunnels or drifts, as against the use of vertical shafts.

**driftnet** /ˈdrɪftnɛt/, *n.* a fine-mesh fishing net, weighted at the bottom, and supported with floats at the top, which drifts with the tide or current.

**drift sail** /ˈdrɪft seɪl/, *n.* a sail dropped in the sea and used as a sea anchor, to help lessen the drift of a ship in a storm.

**driftwood** /ˈdrɪftwʊd/, *n.* wood floating on, or cast ashore by, the water.

**drifty** /ˈdrɪfti/, *adj.* of the nature of, or characterised by, drifts.

**drill**[1] /drɪl/, *n.* **1.** a tool or machine for drilling or boring cylindrical holes. **2.** *Mil.* **a.** training in formal marching or other precise military or naval movements. **b.** an exercise in such training: *gun drill.* **3.** any strict, methodical training, instrument, or exercise. **4.** *Colloq.* correct procedure; routine. **5.** a gastropod, *Urosalpinx cinera,* destructive to oysters. –*v.t.* **6.** to pierce or bore a hole in (anything). **7.** to make (a hole) by boring. **8.** *Mil.* to instruct and exercise in formation marching and movement, the carrying of arms during formal marching, and the formal handling of arms for ceremonies and guard work. **9.** to impart (knowledge) by strict training or discipline. –*v.i.* **10.** to pierce or bore with a drill. **11.** to go through exercise in military or other training. [D *drillen* bore, drill] – **drillable,** *adj.* – **driller,** *n.*

**drill**[2] /drɪl/, *n.* **1.** a small furrow made in the soil in which to sow seeds. **2.** →**seed drill. 3.** a row of seeds or plants thus sown. –*v.t.* **4.** to sow (seed) or raise (crops) in drills. **5.** to plant (ground) in drills. [orig. uncert.] – **driller,** *n.*

**drill**[3] /drɪl/, *n.* strong twilled cotton for a variety of uses. [short for DRILLING[2], from G: triplet, confused with *Drillich* ticking (*dri* three + *-lich*), from L *trilix* with three threads, *tri-* being translated]

**drill**[4] /drɪl/, *n.* a baboon, *Papio leucophaeus,* of western Africa, smaller than the mandrill. [orig. unknown]

**drilling**[1] /'drɪlɪŋ/, *n.* the act of a person or thing that drills. [DRILL[1], *v.* + -ING[1]]

**drilling**[2] /'drɪlɪŋ/, *n.* →**drill**[3].

**drillmaster** /'drɪlmastə/, *n.* **1.** one who trains others in anything, esp. in a mechanical or repetitious manner. **2.** *Mil.* an instructor in marching, etc.

**drill press** /'drɪl prɛs/, *n.* a machine tool for boring holes with a drill or drills.

**drill sergeant** /'– sadʒənt/, *n.* a sergeant specially employed in instructing drill.

**drill stem test,** *n.* a test of the productive capacity of an oil or gas well when still full of drilling mud.

**drill string** /'drɪl strɪŋ/, *n.* the assemblage of equipment for drilling comprising items as rods, bits, etc.

**drill team** /'– tim/, *n.* a team of drilled men, trained in ceremonial drill for exhibitions, etc.

**drily** /'draɪli/, *adv.* →**dryly.**

**drink** /drɪŋk/, *v.*, **drank** (formerly also **drunk**); **drunk** (sometimes **drank,** formerly or as pred. adj. **drunken**); **drinking;** *n.* –*v.i.* **1.** to swallow water or other liquid; imbibe. **2.** to imbibe alcoholic beverages, esp. habitually or to excess; tipple. **3.** to salute in drinking; drink in honour of (fol. by *to*). **4. drink with the flies,** *Colloq.* to drink alone. –*v.t.* **5.** to swallow (a liquid). **6.** to take in (a liquid) in any manner; absorb. **7.** to take in through the senses, esp. with eagerness and pleasure. **8.** to swallow the contents of (a cup, etc.). **9.** to drink in honour of or with good wishes for: *to drink one's health.* –*n.* **10.** any liquid which is swallowed to quench thirst, for nourishment, etc.; a beverage. **11.** alcoholic liquor. **12.** excessive indulgence in alcoholic liquor. **13.** a draught of liquid; a potion. **14.** (*pl.*) a small informal party: *do come over for drinks.* **15. the drink,** *Colloq.* the sea or a large lake. [ME *drinke(n),* OE *drincan,* c. G *trinken*]

**drinkable** /'drɪŋkəbəl/, *adj.* **1.** that may be drunk; suitable for drinking. –*n.* **2.** (*usu. pl.*) something drinkable; a liquid for drinking.

**drink-drive** /'drɪŋk-draɪv/, *adj.* of or pertaining to the driving of a motor car while under the influence of alcohol: *a drink-drive offence.*

**drink-driving** /drɪŋk-'draɪvɪŋ/, *n.* the driving of a motor car whilst one is under the influence of alcohol.

**drinker** /'drɪŋkə/, *n.* **1.** one who drinks. **2.** one who drinks alcoholic liquors habitually or to excess. **3.** a drinking trough.

**drinking fountain** /'drɪŋkɪŋ faʊntn/, *n.* a fountain which ejects water suitable for drinking. Also, **bubbler.**

**drinking-house** /'drɪŋkɪŋ-haʊs/, *n.* a building principally used to provide accommodation for the sale and consumption of alcoholic beverages.

**drinking song** /'– sɒŋ/, *n.* a hearty song, often in praise of liquor, suitable to be sung by a group engaged in friendly drinking.

**drinking water** /'– wɔtə/, *n.* water suitable to be drunk by humans without boiling first.

**drink waiter** /'drɪŋk weɪtə/, *n.* a waiter who serves beer, wine, etc., at tables in a hotel or restaurant. Also, **drinks waiter.**

**driography** /draɪ'ɒgrəfi/, *n.* a process of lithographic printing in which special inks are used, and water completely dispensed with. [DRY + -O- + -GRAPHY, after LITHOGRAPHY]

**drip** /drɪp/, *v.*, **dripped** or **dript, dripping,** *n.* –*v.i.* **1.** to let fall drops; shed drops. **2.** to fall in drops, as a liquid. –*v.t.* **3.** to let fall in drops. –*n.* **4.** the act of dripping. **5.** the liquid that drips. **6.** the sound made by the fall of liquid drops. **7.** *Med.* the continuous slow infusion of fluid containing nutrients or drugs to a patient, esp. after surgery. **8.** *Archit.* **a.** a projecting part of a cornice or the like, so shaped as to throw off rainwater and thus protect the parts below. **b.** a projecting metal strip or a groove having the same function. **9.** *Colloq.* an insipid or colourless person; a fool. [late ME *dryppe,* from Scand.: cf. Dan. *dryppe*]

**drip coffee** /'– kɒfi/, *n.* coffee prepared by having boiling water pass down through finely ground coffee beans.

**drip-dry** /'drɪp-draɪ/, *adj., v.,* **-dried, -drying.** –*adj.* **1.** (of a fabric) drying in its desired shape, when hung dripping wet after being rinsed. –*n.* **2.** a garment which dries in this way. –*v.t.* **3.** to hang a fabric article after rinsing, while still dripping wet, and allow it to dry and assume its desired shape with no ironing. –*v.i.* **4.** (of a fabric) to dry in this way.

**drip-feed** /'drɪp-fid/, *n., v.,* **-fed, -feeding.** –*n.* **1.** nourishment given via a tube into the stomach or a vein. –*v.t.* **2.** to feed by such means.

**drip irrigation** /ˌdrɪp ɪrə'geɪʃən/, *n.* the process of irrigating by allowing water to leak slowly from pipes.

**dripolator** /'drɪpəleɪtə/, *n.* a coffee-making machine in which boiling water is allowed to pass down slowly through finely ground coffee beans.

**drip painting** /'drɪp peɪntɪŋ/, *n.* **1.** a painting technique used esp. in action painting whereby the artist uses calligraphic movements to manipulate colour as it is dripped or poured onto the painting surface. **2.** a painting so executed.

**dripping** /'drɪpɪŋ/, *n.* **1.** the act of anything that drips. **2** (*oft. pl.*) the liquid that drips. **3.** fat exuded from meat in cooking and used as shortening, for making gravy, or for basting.

**dripping pan** /'– pæn/, *n.* a pan used under roasting meat to receive the dripping.

**drippy** /'drɪpi/, *adj. Colloq.* (of a person) colourless; insipid; stupid.

**drip ring** /'drɪp rɪŋ/, *n.* a ring of rubber, leather, etc., on the shaft of an oar or paddle to prevent water running on to the handles.

**dripstone** /'drɪpstoʊn/, *n.* calcium carbonate, $CaCo_3$, occurring in the form of stalactites and stalagmites.

**drive** /draɪv/, *v.*, **drove** or (*Archaic*) **drave; driven; driving;** *n., adj.* –*v.t.* **1.** to send along, away, off, in, out, back, etc., by compulsion; force along: *to drive someone to desperation, out of one's senses, to do something.* **2.** to overwork; overtask. **3.** to cause and guide the movement of (an animal, vehicle, etc.). **4.** to convey in a vehicle. **5.** to keep (machinery) going. **6.** to impel; constrain; urge; compel. **7.** to carry (business, a bargain, etc.) vigorously through. **8.** *Mining, etc.* to excavate horizontally (or nearly so). **9.** *Tennis, Cricket, Golf, Bowls, etc.* to hit or throw (the ball) very swiftly. **10.** *Hunting.* to chase (game). **11. drive a coach and four (through),** to go through easily, without opposition or hindrance: *you could drive a coach and four through that argument.* **12. drive (someone) up the wall,** *Colloq.* to exasperate (someone). –*v.i.* **13.** to go along before an impelling force; be impelled: *the ship drove before the wind.* **14.** to rush or dash violently. **15.** to make an effort to reach or obtain; aim (fol. by *at*): *the idea he was driving at, what is he driving at?* **16.** to act as driver. **17.** to go or travel in a driven vehicle: *to drive away, back, in, out, from, to, etc.* –*n.* **18.** the act of driving. **19.** an impelling along, as of game, cattle, or floating logs, in a particular direction. **20.** (in tree-felling) a line of trees on a hillside partly cut so as to fall when the uppermost tree is felled. **21.** the animals, logs, etc., thus driven. **22.** *Psychol.* a source of motivation: *the sex drive.* **23.** *Sport.* a propelling or forceful action, esp. a powerful battery stroke in cricket, tennis, etc., or a forcible delivery in bowls. **24.** a vigorous onset or onward course. **25.** a strong military offensive. **26.** a united effort to accomplish some purpose, esp. to raise money for a government loan or for some charity. **27.** vigorous pressure or effort, as in business. **28.** energy and initiative. **29.** a trip in a driven vehicle. **30.** a road for driving, esp. a private access road to a private house. **31.** *Mining.* a horizontal tunnel or shaft. **32.** *Mach.* a driving mechanism, as of a motor car: *gear drive, chain drive.* **33.** *Motor Vehicles.* point or points of power application to the roadway: *front drive, rear drive, four-wheel drive.* **34.** *Comm. Colloq.* an attempt to force down the market price of a commodity by offering a quantity at a low price. –*adj.* **35.** pertaining to a part of a machine used in its propulsion. [ME *driven,* OE *drīfan,* c. G *treiben*]

**drive-in** /'draɪv-ɪn/, *n.* **1.** a cinema so designed that patrons drive in to a large area in front of an outdoor screen and view the film while seated in their cars. –*adj.* **2.** (of any shop, food outlet, etc.) catering for customers in cars.

**drive-it-in** /'draɪv-ət-ɪn/, *n. Colloq.* a drive-in cinema.

**drivel** /'drɪvəl/, *v.*, **-elled, -elling** or (*U.S.*) **-eled, -eling,** *n.* –*v.i.* **1.** to let saliva flow from the mouth or mucus from the nose; slaver. **2.** to issue like spittle. **3.** to talk childishly or idiotically. *–v.t.* **4.** to utter childishly or idiotically. **5.** to waste foolishly. *–n.* **6.** childish, idiotic, or silly talk; twaddle. [ME *dryvele, drevel(en),* OE *dreflian*] – **driveller,** *n.*

**driven** /ˈdrɪvən/, *v.* **1.** past participle of **drive. 2.** (of snow) drifted: *pure as the driven snow.*

**driver** /ˈdraɪvə/, *n.* **1.** one who or that which drives. **2.** one who drives an animal or animals, a vehicle, etc.; coachman, drover, chauffeur, etc. **3.** one whose job is to drive and control railway engines. **4.** *Mach.* a part that transmits force or motion. **5.** a golf club with a long shaft, used for making long shots, as from the tee. **6.** a strap through which the hand is passed to hold hand shears when shearing sheep. – **driverless,** *adj.*

**driver ant** /ˈdraɪvər ænt/, *n.* any of the ants of the subfamily Dorylinae, occurring in tropical Africa and America, which live in temporary nests and travel as vast armies in long files, preying on other animals, chiefly insects. Also, **army ant.**

**drive shaft** /ˈdraɪv ʃaft/, *n.* any rotating shaft that transmits power from an engine to that part which is to be driven, as wheels, etc.

**drive system** /ˈdraɪv sɪstəm/, *n.* a system of felling trees in which one tree, when felled, initiates a chain reaction which brings down a number of trees.

**drive tree** /ˈ– tri/, *n.* the tree which when felled will bring down all the other trees in a drive system.

**driveway** /ˈdraɪvweɪ/, *n.* **1.** a passage along which vehicles may be driven, esp. outside a private house. **2.** the area in the front of a service station adjacent to the petrol pumps.

**driving** /ˈdraɪvɪŋ/, *adj.* **1.** (of a person) effective in eliciting work from others; energetic. **2.** violent; having tremendous force. **3.** relaying or transmitting power. **4.** rhythmic; urgent; in a fast tempo.

**driving licence** /ˈ– laɪsəns/, *n.* a permit, issued by a licensing authority, allowing one to drive certain vehicles on public roads.

**driving test** /ˈ– tɛst/, *n.* a test of the fitness and ability of a person to drive a vehicle on public roads.

**driving wheel** /ˈ– wil/, *n.* **1.** *Mach.* a main wheel which communicates motion to others. **2.** one of the propelling wheels of a locomotive; any wheel used to transform the force of the locomotive cylinder into tractive effort. **3.** one of the road wheels of a motor vehicle which transmits the drive.

**drizzle** /ˈdrɪzəl/, *v.,* **-zled, -zling,** *n.* *–v.i.* **1.** to rain gently and steadily in fine drops; sprinkle. *–n.* **2.** a very light rain; mist. **3.** *Meteorol.* precipitation consisting of numerous, minute droplets of water less than 0.5 mm in diameter. [possibly diminutive and frequentative form of rare ME *dresen,* OE *drēosan* fall] – **drizzly,** *adj.*

**drogher** /ˈdroʊgə/, *n.* a slow, clumsy type of sailing vessel, usu. intended for sheltered water. Also, **droger, droguer.** [D *droger,* lit., drier (i.e. of herring), from *drogen* to dry]

**drogue** /droʊg/, *n.* **1.** a bucket-like contrivance used as a sea-anchor. **2.** *Aerospace.* a small parachute used to pull out the main canopy of a parachute brake.

**drogue target** /ˈ– tagət/, *n. Mil.* a fabric cone or sleeve used as an airborne towed target.

**droit** /drɔɪt/, *n.* **1.** a legal right or claim. **2.** that to which one has a legal right or claim. **3.** *Finance.* duty; custom. **4.** *Obs.* the body of rules constituting the law. [F, from Rom. *dērectum,* from L *dīrectum* right, properly neut. of L *dīrectus* straight. See DIRECT, *adj.*]

**droll** /droʊl/, *adj.* amusingly queer; comical; waggish. [F *drôle,* from MD *drolle* little man] – **drollness,** *n.* – **drolly,** *adv.*

**drollery** /ˈdroʊləri/, *n., pl.* **-eries. 1.** something amusingly queer or funny. **2.** a jest; a facetious tale. **3.** droll quality; humour. **4.** the action or behaviour of a buffoon or wag; jesting.

**drome** /droʊm/, *n. Colloq.* an aerodrome. Also, **'drome.**

**-drome,** a word element meaning 'running', 'course', 'racecourse', as in *hippodrome.* [combining form representing Gk *drómos*]

**dromedary** /ˈdrɒmədɛri, -dri/, *n., pl.* **-daries.** the one-humped or Arabian camel, *Camelus dromedarius,* light swift types of which are bred for racing. [ME *dromedarye,* from LL *dromedārius,* from L *dromas* dromedary, from Gk: running]

**dromond** /ˈdrɒmənd, ˈdrʌm-/, *n.* a large, fast-sailing vessel of the Middle Ages. [ME *dromon,* from LL *dromo,* from LGk *drómōn* light vessel, from Gk *drómos* a running]

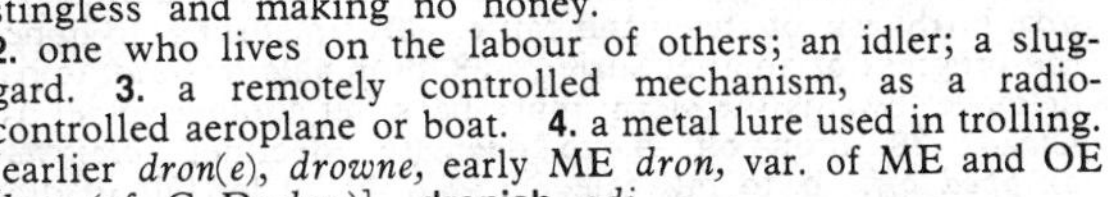

dromedary

**dromos** /ˈdrɒmɒs/, *n.* **1.** a passage or entrance-way, as to an ancient subterranean tomb. **2.** a racecourse or track in ancient Greece. [Gk]

**-dromous,** an adjective termination corresponding to **-drome.** [-DROME + -OUS]

**drone**[1] /droʊn/, *n.* **1.** the male of the honey bee and other bees, stingless and making no honey. **2.** one who lives on the labour of others; an idler; a sluggard. **3.** a remotely controlled mechanism, as a radio-controlled aeroplane or boat. **4.** a metal lure used in trolling. [earlier *dron(e), drowne,* early ME *dron,* var. of ME and OE *dran* (cf. G *Drohne*)] – **dronish,** *adj.*

**drone**[2] /droʊn/, *v.,* **droned, droning,** *n.* *–v.i.* **1.** to make a dull, continued, monotonous sound; hum; buzz. **2.** to speak in a monotonous tone. *–v.t.* **3.** to say in a dull, monotonous tone. *–n.* **4.** *Music.* **a.** a continuous low tone produced by the bass pipes or bass strings of musical instruments. **b.** the pipes (esp. of the bagpipe) or strings producing this tone. **c.** a bagpipe equipped with such pipes. **5.** a monotonous tone; a humming; a buzzing. **6.** a monotonous speaker. [cf. DRONE[1]; akin to ME *droun* roar] – **droningly,** *adv.*

**drongo**[1] /ˈdrɒŋgoʊ/, *n., pl.* **-gos. 1.** →**spangled drongo. 2.** any of the oscinine passerine birds of the African, Asiatic and Australian family Dicruridae, usu. black in colour, with long forked tails, and insectivorous habits. [Malagasy]

**drongo**[2] /ˈdrɒŋgoʊ/, *n. Colloq.* **1.** a slow-witted or stupid person. **2.** a raw recruit. [perhaps from *Drongo,* the name of a racehorse in the early 1920s which never won a race]

drongo[2]: 1920s cartoon of racehorse *Drongo*

**droob** /drub/, *n. Colloq.* **1.** a minute portion of anything: *he didn't get a droob.* **2.** a weak, ineffectual or slow-witted person. – **drooby,** *adj.*

**drool** /drul/, *n. Colloq.* **1.** →**drivel.** *–v.i.* **2.** →**drivel** (def. 1). **3.** to show excessive pleasure at an object or at the prospect of enjoying something (fol. by *over*).

**droop** /drup/, *v.i.* **1.** to sink, bend, or hang down, as from weakness or exhaustion. **2.** *Poetic.* to sink; descend, as the sun. **3.** to fall into a state of physical weakness; flag; fail. **4.** to lose spirit or courage. *–v.t.* **5.** to let sink or drop. *–n.* **6.** the condition or action of drooping. **7.** a flap on an aeroplane; aileron. [ME *droupe(n),* from Scand.; cf. Icel. *drūpa;* akin to DROP] – **droopingly,** *adv.* – **droopy,** *adj.*

**drooping sedge** /drupɪŋ ˈsɛdʒ/, *n.* →**Bergalia tussock.**

**drop** /drɒp/, *n., v.,* **dropped** or **dropt, dropping.** *–n.* **1.** a small quantity of liquid which falls or is produced in a more or less spherical mass; a liquid globule. **2.** the quantity of liquid contained in such a mass. **3. a.** a very small quantity of liquid. **b.** a small drink, usu. alcoholic. **4.** a minute quantity of anything. **5.** (*usu. pl.*) liquid medicine given in drops. **6.** something like or likened to a drip. **7.** a lozenge (confection). **8.** a pendant. **9.** act of dripping; fall; descent. **10.** the distance or depth to which anything drips or falls. **11.** a steep slope. **12.** a fall in degree, amount, value, etc.: *a drop in price.* **13.** that which drips or is used for dropping. **14.** a drop curtain. **15.** a trapdoor. **16.** gallows. **17. long drop,** *Colloq.* Also, **high jump.** execution by hanging. **18. a.** a stick of parachutists. **b.** a descent by parachute. **19. a.** the total yield of lambs from a flock of sheep. **b.** the lambing season. **20.** *Colloq.* a fence (def. 17). **21.** *Naut.* the vertical length of a course. See **hoist. 22. get** or **have the drop on,** *U.S. Colloq.* **a.** to pull and aim a gun, etc., before an antagonist can. **b.** to get or have at a disadvantage. *–v.i.* **23.** to fall in globules or small portions, as water or other liquid: *rain drops from the clouds.* **24.** to fall vertically like a drop; have an abrupt descent. **25.** to sink to the ground as if inanimate. **26.** to fall wounded, dead, etc. **27.** to come to an end; cease; lapse: *there the matter dropped.* **28.** to withdraw; disappear (fol. by *out*). **29.** to squat or crouch, as a dog at the sight of game. **30.** to fall lower in condition, degree, etc.; sink: *the prices dropped sharply.* **31.** to pass without effort into some condition: *to drop asleep, drop into the habit of doing it.* **32.** to move down gently, as with the tide or a light wind. **33.** to fall or move (back, behind, to the rear, etc.). **34.** to come or go casually or unexpectedly into a place; to visit informally (fol. by *in, by, across,* etc.): *he dropped in on us occasionally.* **35.** (of an unborn child) to change position in the womb so that the head becomes engaged before labour. **36.** (of animals) to give birth, esp. of sheep and cattle. **37.** (in surfing) to impede the progress of another surfer. **38. drop astern,** *Naut.* to pass or move towards the stern; move back; let another vessel pass ahead. **39. drop off, a.** to decrease; decline: *sales have dropped off.* **b.** to fall asleep. *–v.t.* **40.** to let fall in drops or small portions: *drop a tear.* **41.** *Archaic.* to sprinkle with or as with drops. **42.** to let fall; allow to sink to a lower position; lower: *to drop anchor.* **43.** to give birth to (young). **44.** to utter or express casually or incidentally, as a hint. **45.** to send or post (a note, etc.): *drop me a line.* **46.** to bring to the ground by a blow or shot. **47.** to set down, as from a ship, car, etc. (fol. by *off*). **48.** to omit (a letter or syllable) in pronunciation or writing: *he dropped his h's.* **49.** to lengthen by lowering: *to drop a hem.* **50.** to lower (the voice) in pitch or loudness. **51.** to cease to keep up or have to do with: *I dropped the subject.* **52.** to cease to employ; to dismiss. **53.** *Colloq.* to take (drugs) in tablet or capsule form. **54.** *Rugby Football, etc.* to score (a goal) by a drop kick. **55.** *Naut.* to outdistance; pass out of sight of. **56.** *Colloq.* to stop, cease: *drop it!* **57.** *Colloq.* to fell (a tree, etc.). **58.** *Prison Colloq.* to inform on (someone) (sometimes fol. by *in*). **59. drop a bundle,** *Colloq.* **a.** to give birth. **b.** to reveal startling news, information, etc. **c.** to suffer a heavy monetary loss as the result of gambling, investment, etc. **60. drop one's bundle,** *Colloq.* to give up; to yield to oppressive circumstances. [ME *drope,* OE *dropa,* c. Icel. *dropi*] **– droppable,** *adj.*

**drop ceiling** /– 'silɪŋ/, *n.* a false ceiling suspended below the real ceiling for acoustic or architectural reasons or to give space for service pipes.

**drop curtain** /'– kɜtn/, *n.* a theatre curtain which is lowered into position from the flies.

**drop-forge** /'drɒp-fɔdʒ/, *v.t.,* **-forged, -forging.** *Metall.* to forge by the impact of a falling mass or weight, the hot piece of metal usu. being placed between dies and subjected to the blow of a drop hammer or the like. **– drop-forging,** *n.*

**drop goal** /'drɒp goʊl/, *n. Rugby Football.* **→field goal.**

**drop hammer** /'– hæmə/, *n.* an apparatus for forging, etc., in which a heavy weight is made to drop on the metal to be worked, which is placed on an anvil or in dies.

**drop kick** /'– kɪk/, *n.* **1.** *Football.* a kick given the ball just as it rises from the ground after being dropped by the kicker. **2.** *N.Z. Colloq.* an obnoxious person.

**drop-kick** /'drɒp-kɪk/, *v.i., v.t. Football.* to give a drop kick (to). **– drop-kicker,** *n.*

**drop leaf** /'drɒp lif/, *n.* an extension attached to the end or side of a table and folded vertically when not needed. **– drop-leaf,** *adj.*

**droplet** /'drɒplət/, *n.* a little drop.

**droplight** /'drɒplaɪt/, *n.* an electric lamp connected with a fixture above by a tube or wire which enables it to be brought down to a lower level.

**dropline** /'drɒplaɪn/, *n. Angling.* a long line set diagonally between the surface and the bottom.

**drop meter** /'drɒp mitə/, *n.* **→dosimeter** (def. 1).

**drop noseband** /drɒp 'noʊzbænd/, *n.* that part of a bridle which goes over the nose and below the bit, preventing a horse from opening its mouth too far.

**drop-off** /'drɒp-ɒf/, *n.* an underwater cliff.

**drop-out** /'drɒp-aʊt/, *n.* **1.** one who decides to opt out of conventional society, a given social group or an educational institution: *student drop-outs became more numerous in the sixties.* **2.** *Rugby Football.* a drop kick made from a defending player's quarter line or goal line after the ball has crossed the try line or has been touched down. **3.** *Photog.* a high-contrast line print. **4. a.** *Computers.* a loss of information stored on magnetic tape files, caused by dust or lint specks or by a damaged or imperfect tape. **b.** (of tape-recording) a similarly caused brief loss of or reduction in the sound recorded. Also, **dropout.**

**dropper** /'drɒpə/, *n.* **1.** one who or that which drops. **2.** Also, **eye-dropper.** a glass tube with an elastic cap at one end and a small orifice at the other, for drawing in a liquid and expelling it in drops. **3.** a batten fixed to a fence to keep the wires apart.

**droppie** /'drɒpi/, *n. Colloq.* a drop kick.

**dropping** /'drɒpɪŋ/, *n.* **1.** act of one who or that which drops. **2.** that which drops or falls in drops. **3.** (*pl.*) dung of animals.

**dropping flock** /'– flɒk/, *n.* a flock of ewes in lamb.

**drop-punt** /'drɒp-pʌnt/, *n.* **1.** a punt kick executed so that the football moves through the air with a backwards lengthwise spin, as a drop kick. *–v.t.* **2.** to kick (a football) thus.

**drop-rail** /'drɒp-reɪl/, *n.* a makeshift farmgate, a pole slotted into both gate posts.

**drop scene** /'drɒp sin/, *n.* **1. →drop curtain. 2.** a final scene in an act or play.

**drop scone** /'– skɒn/, *n.* **→pikelet.**

**dropseed** /'drɒpsid/, *n.* any of four main species of slender, short-lived perennial grasses of the widely distributed genus *Sporobulus,* as fairy grass.

**drop shipment** /'drɒp ʃɪpmənt/, *n.* an order shipped by a seller to the customer or his distributor, as a shipment by a manufacturer to a retailer that is invoiced to a wholesaler.

**drop shot** /'– ʃɒt/, *n.* **1.** shot made in a shot tower. **2.** *Tennis.* a stroke which causes a ball to fall abruptly after clearing the net. **3.** a ball so played.

**dropsical** /'drɒpsəkəl, -sɪkəl/, *adj.* of, like, or affected with dropsy. **– dropsically,** *adv.*

**dropsy** /'drɒpsi/, *n.* an excessive accumulation of serous fluid in a serous cavity or in the subcutaneous cellular tissue. [ME *(y)dropesie,* from OF *idropisie,* from L *hydrōpsis,* from Gk *hýdrōps*] **– dropsied** /'drɒpsid/, *adj.*

**dropt** /drɒpt/, *v.* past tense and past participle of **drop.**

**drop tank** /'drɒp tæŋk/, *n.* a tank, usu. for extra fuel, which can be dropped from an aircraft after the contents have been used.

**drop test** /'drɒp tɛst/, *n.* (*joc.*) a putative attempt to fix a faulty piece of equipment, usu. electronic, by dropping it.

**drop window** /'– wɪndoʊ/, *n.* a sash-window descending completely into a space below the sill.

**droshky** /'drɒʃki/, *n., pl.* **-kies. 1.** a light, low, four-wheeled, open vehicle, used in Russia, in which the passengers sit astride or sideways on a long, narrow bench. **2.** any of various other vehicles, as the ordinary carriage, used elsewhere. Also, **drosky** /'drɒski/. [Russ. *drozhki,* diminutive of *drogi* wagon]

**drosometer** /drɒ'sɒmətə/, *n.* an instrument for measuring the amount of dew formed on a surface.

**drosophila** /drə'sɒfələ/, *n., pl.* **-lae** /-li/. a fly of the genus *Drosophila,* esp. *D. melanogaster,* which is widely used in laboratory studies of heredity. [NL, from Gk *dróso(s)* dew + *phílos* loving]

**dross** /drɒs/, *n.* **1.** a waste product taken off molten metal during smelting, essentially metallic in character. **2.** waste matter; refuse. [ME and OE *drōs,* c. MD *droes* dregs. Cf. G *Drusen* dregs, husks] **– drossy,** *adj.* **– drossiness,** *n.*

**drought** /draʊt/, *n.* **1.** dry weather; lack of rain. **2.** scarcity. Also, **drouth** /draʊθ/. [ME *drought(h),* etc., OE *drūgath,* akin to *drȳge* dry]

**drought-feed** /'draʊt-fid/, *n.* **1.** a basic drought survival ration fed to stock once or twice a week, the object of which is to save all the stock, not to fatten some and starve others. *–v.t.* **2.** to feed (stock) this ration. Also, **survival level feeding.**

**Droughtmaster** /'draʊtmastə/, *n.* one of a breed of cattle, half Brahman and half Shorthorn/Devon, bred to withstand heat and drought conditions.

**drought-resistant** /ˈdraʊt-rəzɪstənt/, *adj.* **1.** (of breeds of cattle) bred to have greater resistance to drought conditions. **2.** (of varieties of plants, esp. cereals) developed to withstand drought conditions.

**droughty** /ˈdraʊti/, *adj.* **1.** dry. **2.** lacking rain. Also, **drouthy** /ˈdraʊθi/.

**drove**[1] /droʊv/, *v.* past tense of **drive.**

**drove**[2] /droʊv/, *n., v.,* **droved, droving.** *–n.* **1.** a number of oxen, sheep, or swine driven in a group; herd; flock. **2.** a large crowd of human beings, esp. in motion. **3.** *Bldg Trades.* **a.** Also, **drove chisel.** a stonemason's chisel, used in making droved work. **b.** →**drove work.** **4.** a road along which animals are driven. *–v.t.* **5.** to drive herds of cattle or flocks of sheep, usu. over long distances, to market. **6.** *Bldg Trades.* to work or smooth (stone, etc.) as with a stonemason's drove. [ME; OE *drāf* act of driving, herd, company. See DRIVE]

**drover** /ˈdroʊvə/, *n.* one who drives cattle, sheep, etc., to market, usu. over long distances.

**drove work** /ˈdroʊv wɜk/, *n.* the surface of stone worked with a drove.

**drown** /draʊn/, *v.i.* **1.** to be suffocated by immersion in water or other liquid. *–v.t.* **2.** to suffocate (a person, etc.) by immersion in water or other liquid. **3.** to destroy; get rid of. **4.** to flood; inundate. **5.** to overwhelm as by a flood; overpower. **6.** to make inaudible; muffle; obscure. [var. of obs. *drunken,* OE *druncnian;* ME *drounne* shows loss of *c* between the nasals; length of nasal later shifted to vowel]

**drowned valley** /draʊnd ˈvæli/, *n.* a submerged valley, flooded by sea or lake.

**drowse** /draʊz/, *v.,* **drowsed, drowsing,** *n.* *–v.i.* **1.** to be sleepy; be half asleep. **2.** to be dull or sluggish. *–v.t.* **3.** to make sleepy. **4.** to pass or spend (time) in drowsing. *–n.* **5.** a sleepy condition; state of being half asleep. [OE *drūsian* droop, become sluggish]

**drowsy** /ˈdraʊzi/, *adj.,* **-sier, -siest.** **1.** inclined to sleep; half asleep. **2.** marked by or resulting from sleepiness. **3.** dull; sluggish. **4.** inducing sleepiness. – **drowsily,** *adv.* – **drowsiness,** *n.*

**drub** /drʌb/, *v.,* **drubbed, drubbing,** *n.* *–v.t.* **1.** to beat with a stick or the like; cudgel; flog; thrash: *to drub something into or out of a person.* **2.** to defeat decisively. **3.** to stamp (the feet). *–n.* **4.** a blow with a stick or the like. [? Ar. *darb* stroke] – **drubber,** *n.*

**drubbing** /ˈdrʌbɪŋ/, *n.* a beating; a decisive defeat.

**drudge** /drʌdʒ/, *n., v.,* **drudged, drudging.** *–n.* **1.** one who labours at servile or uninteresting tasks; a hard toiler. *–v.i.* **2.** to perform servile, distasteful, or hard work. [OE *Drycg-* bearer (in proper name)] – **drudger,** *n.* – **drudgingly,** *adv.*

**drudgery** /ˈdrʌdʒəri/, *n., pl.* **-eries.** tedious, hard, or uninteresting work.

**drug** /drʌg/, *n., v.,* **drugged, drugging.** *–n.* **1.** a chemical substance given with the intention of preventing or curing disease or otherwise enhancing the physical or mental welfare of men or animals. **2.** a habit-forming medicinal substance; a narcotic. **3.** (formerly) any ingredient used in chemistry, pharmacy, dyeing, or the like. **4.** a commodity that is overabundant, or in excess of demand, in the market. *–v.t.* **5.** to mix (food or drink) with a drug, esp. a narcotic or poisonous drug. **6.** to stupefy or poison with a drug. **7.** to administer anything nauseous to; surfeit. [ME *drogges* (pl.), from OF *drogue,* ? from D *drog* dry thing]

**drugget** /ˈdrʌgət/, *n.* a rug made of coarse hair with cotton or jute. [F *droguet,* from *drogue* drug, cheap article]

**druggie** /ˈdrʌgi/, *n. Colloq.* one who takes drugs habitually.

**druggist** /ˈdrʌgəst/, *n. U.S.* a pharmacist; dispensing chemist.

**drug of dependence,** *n.* any drug which tends to produce in the person taking it an appetite or need for it in further regular quantities, as nicotine, heroin, alcohol, etc.

**drugola** /drʌgˈoʊlə/, *n.* a bribe in the form of drugs rather than money. [DRUG + (PAY)OLA]

**drugstore** /ˈdrʌgstɔ/, *n. U.S.* a chemist's shop where cigarettes, light meals, etc., are also sold.

**Druid** /ˈdruəd/, *n.* (*oft. l.c.*) **1.** one of an order of priests or ministers of religion among the ancient Celts of Gaul, Britain, and Ireland. **2.** a member of one of several modern movements to revive druidism, which meet seasonally in special costume to conduct their ceremonies. **3.** an official at an eisteddfod. [F *druide,* from L *druidae,* pl.] – **Druidess** /ˈdruədəs/, *n. fem.* – **druidic** /druˈɪdɪk/, **druidical** /druˈɪdɪkəl/, *adj.*

**druidism** /ˈdruədɪzəm/, *n.* the religion or rites of the Druids.

**drum** /drʌm/, *n., v.,* **drummed, drumming.** *–n.* **1.** a musical instrument consisting of a hollow body covered at one or both ends with a tightly stretched membrane, or head, which is struck with the hand, a stick, or a pair of sticks. **2.** any hollow tree or similar device used in this way. **3.** the sound produced by either of these. **4.** any noise suggestive of it. **5.** one who plays the drum. **6.** a natural organ by which an animal produces a loud or bass sound. **7.** something resembling a drum in shape or structure, or in the noise it produces. **8.** *Computers.* a magnetically coated drum revolving at high speed, and similar in function to a disc-file. **9.** *Archit.* the supporting wall, circular in plan, upon which a dome sits. **10.** *Archit.* one section of a circular column. **11.** *Anat., Zool.* the eardrum or tympanic membrane. **12.** a cylindrical part of a machine. **13.** a magnetic drum. **14.** a cylindrical box or receptacle. **15.** a brothel. **16.** drumfish. **17.** *Colloq.* information or advice usu. confidential or profitable: *to give someone the drum.* *–v.i.* **18.** to beat or play a drum. **19.** to beat on anything rhythmically. **20.** to make a sound like that of a drum; resound. **21.** (of partridges and other birds) to produce a sound resembling drumming. *–v.t.* **22.** to beat rhythmically; perform (a tune) by drumming. **23.** to call or summon by, or as by, beating a drum. **24.** to drive or force by persistent repetition: *to drum an idea into someone.* **25.** to expel or dismiss in disgrace to the beat of a drum (fol. by *out*). **26.** to solicit or obtain (trade, customers, etc.) (oft. fol. by *up*). **27.** to give advice or information (usu. fol. by *up*). [? shortening of 16th-cent. E *drumslade* drummer, from LG *trommelslag* drumbeat; or from MD *tromme*]

**drumbeat** /ˈdrʌmbit/, *n.* the sound or rhythm of a drum.

**drum brake** /ˈdrʌm breɪk/, *n.* a brake, the operation of which involves a brake drum.

**drumfire** /ˈdrʌmfaɪə/, *n.* gunfire so heavy and continuous as to sound like the beating of drums.

**drumhead** /ˈdrʌmhɛd/, *n.* **1.** the membrane stretched upon a drum. **2.** the top part of a capstan.

**drumhead court martial,** *n.* a court martial held (originally round an upturned drum for a table) for the summary trial of charges of offences committed during military operations.

**drumlin** /ˈdrʌmlən/, *n.* a long narrow or oval hill of unstratified glacial drift smoothly rounded by the movement of glacier ice. [? var. of *drumling,* diminutive of Irish, Scot. *drum* long, narrow hill, ridge] – **drumlinoid,** *adj., n.*

**drum-major** /drʌm-ˈmeɪdʒə/, *n.* a person (in the army usu. of the rank of sergeant major) in command of a corps of drums, who also commands both the band and corps of drums on parade.

**drum-majorette** /ˌdrʌm-meɪdʒəˈrɛt/, *n.* a girl who marches in front of a band in a parade twisting a baton.

**drummer** /ˈdrʌmə/, *n.* **1.** one who plays a drum. **2.** (formerly) a commercial traveller or travelling salesman. **3.** →**swagman.** **4.** a learner, or the slowest shearer, in a shearing gang. **5.** Also, **pig drummer.** any of a number of sound-producing fish of the family Kyphosidae.

**drummy** /ˈdrʌmi/, *n.* a cement or plaster surface which is not bonded to the substrate and which emits a sound like a drum when tapped.

**drumstick** /ˈdrʌmstɪk/, *n.* **1.** a stick for beating a drum. **2.** the lower part of the leg of a cooked chicken, duck, turkey, etc.

**drumsticks** /ˈdrʌmstɪks/, *n.* any shrub of the Australian genus *Isopogon,* family Proteaceae.

**drunk** /drʌŋk/, *adj.* (*used predicatively*) **1.** intoxicated with, or as with, strong drink: *drunk with joy, success.* *–n. Colloq.* **2.** a drunken person. **3.** a spree; a drinking party. *–v.* **4.** past participle and former past tense of **drink.**

**drunkard** /ˈdrʌŋkəd/, *n.* one who is frequently drunk.

**drunken** /ˈdrʌŋkən/, *adj.* **1.** intoxicated; drunk. **2.** given to drunkenness. **3.** pertaining to, proceeding from, or marked by intoxication: *a drunken quarrel.* –**drunkenly,** *adv.* –**drunkenness,** *n.*

**drupaceous** /dru'peɪʃəs/, *adj.* **1.** resembling or relating to a drupe; consisting of drupes. **2.** producing drupes.

**drupe** /drup/, *n.* a fruit, as the peach, cherry, plum, etc., consisting of an outer skin (epicarp), a (generally) pulpy and succulent layer (mesocarp), and a hard and woody inner shell or stone (endocarp) which encloses usu. a single seed. [NL *drūpa* drupe, L *drūpa, druppa* overripe olive, from Gk *drýppa*]

**drupelet** /'druplət/, *n.* a little drupe, as one of the individual pericarps composing the blackberry. Also, **drupel** /'drupəl/.

**druse** /druz/, *n.* **1.** *Geol.* **a.** a crust of small crystals lining the sides of a cavity, usu. of the same minerals as in the enclosing rock. **b.** a cavity of this sort. **2.** *Bot.* a mass of small crystals of sodium oxalate which forms around some plant cells. [F, from G *Druse* weathered ore]

**druthers** /'drʌðəz/, *n.pl. Colloq.* choice; preference. [contracted form of *I'd rather*]

**dry** /draɪ/, *adj.,* **drier, driest,** *v.,* **dried, drying,** *n., pl.* **dries.** –*adj.* **1.** free from moisture; not moist; not wet. **2.** having little or no rain: *a dry climate or season.* **3.** characterised by absence, deficiency, or failure of natural or ordinary moisture. **4.** not under, in, or on water: *dry land.* **5.** not yielding water or other liquid: *a dry well.* **6.** not yielding milk: *a dry cow.* **7.** free from tears: *dry eyes.* **8.** wiped or drained away; evaporated: *a dry river.* **9.** desiring drink; thirsty. **10.** causing thirst: *dry work.* **11.** without butter or the like: *dry toast.* **12.** (of a biscuit) not sweet. **13.** *Art.* hard and formal in outline; precisely executed. **14.** *Bldg Trades.* (of an interior wall, ceiling, etc.) finished without the use of plastering. **15.** plain; bald; unadorned: *dry facts.* **16.** dull; uninteresting: *a dry subject.* **17.** humorous or sarcastic in an unemotional or impersonal way: *dry humour.* **18.** indifferent; cold; unemotional: *a dry answer.* **19.** (of wines) not sweet. **20.** of or pertaining to non-liquid substances or commodities: *dry measure.* **21.** characterised by or favouring prohibition of the manufacture and sale of alcoholic liquor for use as beverages: *a dry ship.* **22.** (of a sheep) not rearing a lamb. **23.** **declare dry,** to declare sheep to be sufficiently unaffected by rain to enable shearing to continue. –*v.t.* **24.** to make dry; to free from moisture: *dry your eyes.* **25. dry out,** to subject (an alcoholic or other drug addict) to a systematic process of detoxification. –*v.i.* **26.** to become dry; lose moisture. **27.** **dry out,** (of alcoholics, and other drug addicts) to rid the body of the drug of dependence. **28. dry up, a.** to become completely dry. **b.** to become intellectually barren. **c.** *Colloq.* to stop talking. –*n.* **29.** a dry state, condition, or place. **30.** *Colloq.* dry ginger ale: *brandy and dry.* **31.** *Mining.* a change house usu. equipped with baths, lockup cubicles and means of drying wet clothing. **32.** *U.S. Colloq.* a prohibitionist. **33.** **the dry,** (*sometimes cap.*) the rainless season in central and northern Australia and in the tropics generally; May to November. [ME *drie,* OE *drȳge,* akin to LG *drög,* G *trocken*] –**dryly, drily,** *adv.* –**dryness,** *n.*

**dryad** /'draɪəd, -æd/, *n., pl.* **-ads, -ades** /-ədiz/. (*oft. cap.*) in Greek mythology, a deity or nymph of the woods; a nymph supposed to reside in trees or preside over woods. [L *Dryas* (pl. *Dryades*), from Gk, from *drŷs* tree, oak] –**dryadic** /draɪ'ædɪk/, *adj.*

**dryandra** /draɪ'ændrə/, *n.* any of several species of small trees of the family Proteaceae, common in western Australia, which have large brightly-coloured flowers of various hues.

**Dryasdust** /'draɪəzdʌst/, *n.* one who deals with dry, uninteresting subjects; a dull pedant. [from Dr Jonas *Dryasdust,* a fictitious character to whom Sir Walter Scott, 1771-1832, dedicated some of his novels]

**dry battery** /'draɪ bætri/, *n.* a dry cell, or voltaic battery consisting of a number of dry cells.

**dry-blow** /'draɪ-bloʊ/, *v.i.* to separate gold from other material by winnowing.

**dry-blower** /'draɪ-bloʊə/, *n.* a miner employing the method of dry-blowing.

**dry cell** /'draɪ sɛl/, *n.* a primary cell in which the electrolyte exists in the form of a paste or is absorbed in a porous medium, or is otherwise restrained from flowing from its original position.

**dry-clean** /draɪ-'klin/, *v.t.* to clean (garments, etc.) with benzine, chemical solvents, etc., rather than water. –**drycleaner,** *n.*

**dry-cleaning** /draɪ-'klinɪŋ/, *n.* **1.** the process of cleaning (garments, etc.) with benzene, chemical solvents, etc. **2.** the articles cleaned by this process.

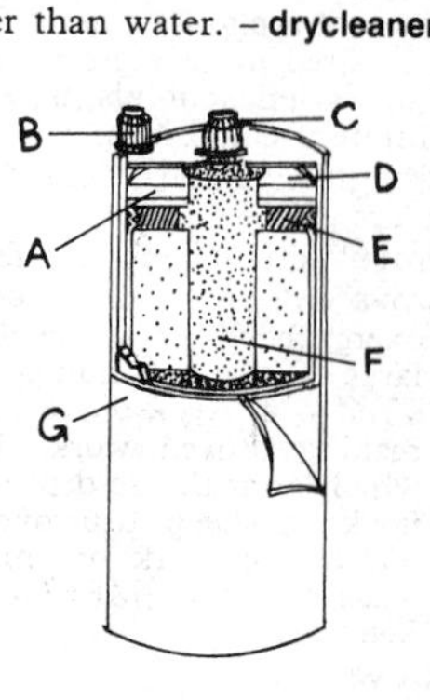

**dry distillation** /'draɪ dɪstə,leɪʃən/, *n.* →**destructive distillation.**

**dry dock** /'draɪ dɒk/, *n.* **1.** a basin-like structure from which the water can be removed after the entrance of a ship, used when making repairs on a ship's bottom, etc. **2.** a floating structure which may be partially submerged to permit a vessel to enter, and then raised to lift the vessel out of the water for repairs, etc.

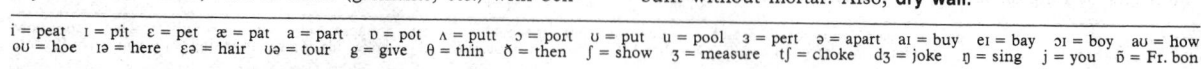

dry cell: A, asphalt inner seal; B, negative terminal; C, positive terminal; D, expansion chamber; E, depolarising mix; F, carbon electrode; G, zinc can

**dry-dock** /'draɪ-dɒk/, *v.t.* **1.** to place in a dry dock. –*v.i.* **2.** to go into dry dock.

**dryer** /'draɪə/, *n.* →**drier.**

**dry farming** /draɪ 'famɪŋ/, *n.* a mode of farming practised in regions of slight or insufficient rainfall, depending largely upon tillage methods which render the soil more receptive of moisture and reduce evaporation. –**dry farmer,** *n.*

**dry fly** /'draɪ flaɪ/, *n.* a lure resembling a fly, which floats on the water, and is used in fishing, esp. for trout and salmon. –**dry-fly** /'draɪ-flaɪ/, *adj.*

**dry fry** /draɪ 'fraɪ/, *n.* →**pan fry.**

**dry goods** /'– gʊdz/, *n.pl.* textile fabrics and related articles of trade, as distinct from groceries, hardware, etc.

**dry ice** /– 'aɪs/, *n.* solid carbon dioxide, having a temperature of minus 78°C at atmospheric pressure.

**drying oil** /'draɪɪŋ ɔɪl/, *n.* an animal or vegetable oil which hardens to a tough film when a thin layer is exposed to the air.

**dry kiln** /draɪ 'kɪln/, *n.* an oven for the controlled drying of cut wood.

**dry martini** /– ma'tini/, *n.* a cocktail largely of gin with a quarter or less of dry vermouth.

**dry measure** /– 'mɛʒə/, *n.* the system of units of capacity formerly used in Britain, Australia and the U.S. for measuring dry commodities, as grain, fruit, etc.

**dry nurse** /– 'nɜs/, *n.* a nurse who takes care of a child but does not suckle it.

**dry-nurse** /draɪ-'nɜs/, *v.t.,* **-nursed, -nursing.** to act as a dry nurse to.

**dry pan** /'draɪ pæn/, *n. Colloq.* →**sanitary can.**

**dry plate** /'– pleɪt/, *n.* a glass plate coated with a sensitive emulsion of silver bromide and silver iodide in gelatine, upon which a negative or positive can be produced by exposure (as in a camera) and development.

**dry point** /'– pɔɪnt/, *n.* **1.** a stout, sharp-pointed needle used for ploughing into copper plates to produce furrows with raised edges that print with a fuzzy, velvety black. **2.** the process of engraving in this way. **3.** an engraving so made.

**dry rot** /– 'rɒt/, *n.* **1.** a decay of seasoned timber causing it to become brittle and to crumble to a dry powder, due to various fungi. **2.** any of various diseases of vegetables in which the dead tissue is dry, caused in timber by *Merulius lacrymans,* in potatoes by *Fusarium caeruleum,* and in swedes, turnips, etc., by *Phoma lingam.*

**dry run** /– 'rʌn/, *n.* a test exercise or rehearsal.

**dry-shell** /draɪ-'ʃɛl/, *v.i.* to collect shells from reefs exposed at low tide.

**dry-shod** /'draɪ-ʃɒd/, *adj.* having or keeping the shoes dry.

**dry-ski training** /draɪ-'ski ,treɪnɪŋ/, *n.* pre-season training for skiing on a matting or plastic surface.

**dry socket** /draɪ 'sɒkət/, *n.* a painful tooth socket which has become infected and inflamed after the extraction of the tooth.

**dry-stone wall** /,draɪ-stoʊn 'wɔl/, *n.* a rubble or stone wall built without mortar. Also, **dry wall.**

**D.S.,** *Music.* dal segno.
**D.Sc.** /ˌdi ɛs ˈsi/, Doctor of Science.
**D.S.C.** /di ɛs ˈsi/, Distinguished Service Cross.
**D.S.M.** /ˌdi ɛs ˈɛm/, Distinguished Service Medal.
**D.S.O.** /ˌdi ɛs ˈoʊ/, Distinguished Service Order.
**dtella** /ˈdɛlə/, *n.* the commonest Australian gecko, *Gehyra variegata,* small and grey and having adhesive pads on the toes.
**D.Th.** /ˌdi ti ˈeɪtʃ/, Doctor of Theology. Also, **D. Theol.**
**D to A** /ˌdi tu ˈeɪ/, *adj.* digital to analog.
**d.t.'s** /di ˈtiz/, *n.* →**delirium tremens.** Also, **d.t.**
**Du.,** Dutch.
**duad** /ˈdjuæd/, *n.* a group of two. [b. DUAL and DYAD]
**dual** /ˈdjuəl/, *adj.* **1.** of or pertaining to two. **2.** composed or consisting of two parts; twofold; double: *dual ownership, dual controls on a plane.* **3.** *Gram.* (in some languages) designating a number category which implies two persons or things. *–n.* **4.** *Gram.* **a.** the dual number. **b.** a form therein, as Greek *anthrṓpō* two men, nominative dual of *ánthrōpos* man, cf. *ánthrōpoi* three or more men, or Old English *git* 'you two' as contrasted with *ge,* 'you' referring to three or more. [L *duālis* containing two] – **dually,** *adv.*
**dual carriageway** /– ˈkærɪdʒweɪ/, *n.* →**divided road.**
**dualism** /ˈdjuəlɪzəm/, *n.* **1.** the state of being dual or consisting of two parts; division into two. **2.** *Philos.* a theory holding that there are two, and only two, basic and irreducible principles, as mind and body. **3.** *Theol.* **a.** the doctrine that there are two independent divine beings or eternal principles, one good and the other evil. **b.** the belief that man embodies two parts, such as body and soul. – **dualist,** *n.*
**dualistic** /djuəˈlɪstɪk/, *adj.* **1.** of, pertaining to, or of the nature of dualism. **2.** dual. – **dualistically,** *adv.*
**duality** /djuˈæləti/, *n.* dual state or quality.
**dual-purpose** /djuəl-ˈpɜpəs/, *adj.* **1.** serving two functions. **2.** (of sheep) bred and selected for the economic production of both wool and mutton. **3.** (of cattle) bred for the production of beef and milk.
**dub**[1] /dʌb/, *v.t.,* **dubbed, dubbing. 1.** to strike lightly with a sword in the ceremony of conferring knighthood; make, or designate as, a knight: *the king dubbed him knight.* **2.** to invest with any dignity or title; style; name; call: *he dubbed me charlatan.* **3.** to strike, cut, rub, etc., in order to make smooth, or of an equal surface: *to dub leather, timber.* **4.** to dress (a fly) for fishing. [ME *dubben,* OE *dubbian,* c. Icel. *dubba* equip, dub; akin to DOWEL]
**dub**[2] /dʌb/, *v.,* **dubbed, dubbing,** *n.* *–v.t., v.i.* **1.** to thrust; poke. *–n.* **2.** a thrust; poke. **3.** a drumbeat. [see DUB[1]. Cf. LG *dubben* thrust, beat]
**dub**[3] /dʌb/, *v.,* **dubbed, dubbing,** *n.* *–v.t.* **1.** to change the soundtrack (of a film or videotape), as in substituting a dialogue in another language. **2.** to add new sounds on to an existing recording. **3.** to transfer recorded sound on to a new record or tape; rerecord. *–n.* **4.** →**dubbing**[2]. [short for DOUBLE]
**dubbing**[1] /ˈdʌbɪŋ/, *n.* the conferring of knighthood; accolade.
**dubbing**[2] /ˈdʌbɪŋ/, *n.* **1.** alteration of, or addition to, the soundtrack of a film, or other recording. **2.** a record or tape made from an existing recording, not from an original source of sound.
**dubbing**[3] /ˈdʌbɪŋ/, *n.* a preparation of oil and tallow used for softening and waterproofing leather. Also, **dubbin.**
**dubbo** /ˈdʌboʊ/, *Colloq.* *–adj.* **1.** stupid; imbecilic. *–n.* **2.** an idiot or imbecile.
**dubersome** /ˈdjubəsəm/, *adj.* (formerly) doubtful. [Brit. d.]
**dubiety** /djuˈbaɪəti/, *n., pl.* **-ties. 1.** doubtfulness; doubt. **2.** a matter of doubt. Also, **dubiosity** /djubiˈɒsəti/.
**dubious** /ˈdjubiəs/, *adj.* **1.** doubtful; marked by or occasioning doubt: *a dubious question.* **2.** of doubtful quality or propriety; questionable: *a dubious transaction, a dubious compliment.* **3.** of uncertain outcome: *in dubious battle.* **4.** wavering or hesitating in opinion; inclined to doubt. [L *dubiōsus* doubtful] – **dubiously,** *adv.* – **dubiousness,** *n.*
**dubitable** /ˈdjubətəbəl/, *adj.* that may be doubted; doubtful; uncertain. – **dubitably,** *adv.*
**dubitation** /djubəˈteɪʃən/, *n.* doubt. [L *dubitātio,* from *dubitāre* doubt]
**dubitative** /ˈdjubətətɪv/, *adj.* **1.** doubting; doubtful. **2.** expressing doubt. [LL *dubitātīvus* doubtful] – **dubitatively,** *adv.*
**ducal** /ˈdjukəl/, *adj.* of or pertaining to a duke. [LL *ducālis,* from *dux* leader. See DUKE] – **ducally,** *adv.*
**ducat** /ˈdʌkət/, *n.* **1.** any of various gold coins formerly in wide use in European countries. **2.** an old silver coin of varying value; an old Venetian money of account. [ME, from F, from It. *ducato* a coin (orig. one issued in 1140 by Roger II of Sicily as Duke of Apulia), also duchy, from *duca* DUKE]
**duces tecum** /dutʃiz ˈteɪkəm/, *n.* an order to a person to appear in court bringing with him certain documents; he is liable to a penalty if he fails to do so. [L *sub poenā dūcēs tēcum* under penalty, you shall bring with you]
**duchess** /ˈdʌtʃɛs, ˈdʌtʃəs/, *n.* **1.** the wife or widow of a duke. **2.** *Hist.* a woman who holds in her own right the sovereignty or titles of a duchy. **3.** *Colloq.* a woman of showy demeanour or appearance. *–v.t.* **4.** *Colloq.* to treat in an obsequious fashion in order to improve one's social or political standing. [ME *duchesse,* from F, from *duc* DUKE]
**duchesse** /ˈdʌtʃɛs/, *adj.* **1.** of or pertaining to a dressing table, chest of drawers, etc., with a swing mirror. *–n.* **2.** such a piece of furniture.
**duchesse lace** /ˈdʌtʃəs leɪs/, *n.* a fine bobbin lace of Flemish origin featuring delicate floral designs joined by bobbin-made brides.
**duchesse set** /ˈ– sɛt/, *n.* a matching set, usu. three in number, of doilies to go under the usual accessories as brush, trinket box, etc., on the top of a duchesse.
**duchy** /ˈdʌtʃi/, *n., pl.* **duchies.** the territory ruled by a duke or duchess. [ME *duche,* from OF, from *duc* DUKE]
**duck**[1] /dʌk/, *n.* **1.** any of numerous wild or domesticated web-footed swimming birds of the family Anatidae, esp. of the genus *Anas* and allied genera, including the black duck and the mallard, characterised by a broad, flat bill, short legs, and depressed body. **2.** the female of this fowl, as distinguished from the male (or *drake*). **3.** the flesh of a duck, eaten as food. **4.** *Colloq.* a darling; pet. **5.** *Colloq.* a woman: *an old duck.* [ME *duk, doke,* OE *dūce,* lit., diver; akin to DUCK[2], *v.*]

Burdekin duck

**duck**[2] /dʌk/, *v.i.* **1.** to plunge the whole body or the head momentarily under water. **2.** to stoop suddenly; bob. **3.** to avoid a blow, unpleasant task, etc. **4.** to go away, often in the expectation of an early return (fol. by *out* or *up*): *just ducked out to the shops for a few minutes.* *–v.t.* **5.** to plunge or dip in water momentarily. **6.** to lower (the head, etc.) suddenly. **7.** to avoid (a blow, unpleasant task, etc.). *–n.* **8.** the act of ducking. [ME *duke, douke,* c. MLG *duken,* G *tauchen* dive] – **ducker,** *n.*
**duck**[3] /dʌk/, *n.* **1.** heavy plain cotton fabric for tents, clothing, bags, mechanical uses, etc., in many weights and widths. **2.** (*pl.*) clothes, esp. trousers, made of it. [D *doek* cloth, c. G *Tuch*]
**duck**[4] /dʌk/, *n.* a military vehicle for amphibious use. [from *DUKW,* its code name in World War II]
**duck**[5] /dʌk/, *n.* *Cricket.* a batsman's score of nought. Also, **duck's egg.**
**duckbill** /ˈdʌkbɪl/, *n.* →**platypus.** Also, **duck-billed platypus.**
**duckboard** /ˈdʌkbɔd/, *n.* a board, or a section or structure of boarding, laid as a floor or track over wet or muddy ground.
**duckhawk** /ˈdʌkhɔk/, *n.* **1.** a small, dark, extremely fast falcon, *Falco longipennis,* frequenting open and lightly timbered country and mountain ranges in Australia and Tasmania. **2.** the American peregrine falcon, *Falco peregrinus anatum,* well known for its speed and audacity.
**ducking stool** /ˈdʌkɪŋ stul/, *n.* a stool or chair in which offenders were formerly punished by being tied and plunged into water. See **cucking stool.**
**duckling** /ˈdʌklɪŋ/, *n.* a young duck.
**ducks and drakes,** *n.pl.* **1.** *Brit.* →**skipping stones. 2. make ducks and drakes of, play (at) ducks and drakes with,** to handle recklessly; squander.
**ducks and geese,** *n.pl.* *Colloq.* the police. [rhyming slang]
**duckshove** /ˈdʌkʃʌv/, *v.,* **-shoved, -shoving.** *Colloq.* *–v.i.* **1.**

to use unfair methods; to be unscrupulous in dealings. **2.** (of a taxi driver) to solicit passengers along the roadside, rather than waiting in turn at a rank. – **duckshover,** *n.*

**ducktail** /ˈdʌkteɪl/, *n.* **1.** the tail feathers of a duck. **2.** the swept up hair at the back of the head where hair combed back on each side meets.

**duckweed** /ˈdʌkwid/, *n.* **1.** any member of the family Lemnaceae, esp. of the genus *Lemna,* comprising small aquatic plants which float free on still water. **2.** a native weed, *Hydrocotyle tripartita,* with small leaves and creeping stems, esp. troublesome on lawns; waterweed. Also, **duck weed.** [so called because it is eaten by ducks]

**ducky** /ˈdʌki/, *adj., n., pl.* **duckies.** *Colloq. –adj.* **1.** dear; darling. *–n.* **2.** darling; dear; pet. Also, **duckie.**

**duco** /ˈdjukoʊ/, *n.* **1.** a type of paint, esp. as applied to the body work of a motor vehicle. *–v.t.* **2.** to spray or otherwise coat (a vehicle) with duco. [Trademark]

**duct** /dʌkt/, *n.* **1.** any tube, canal, or conduit by which fluid or other substances are conducted or conveyed. **2.** *Anat., Zool.* a tube, canal, or vessel conveying a body fluid, esp. a glandular secretion or excretion. **3.** *Bot.* a cavity or vessel formed by elongated cells or by many cells. **4.** *Elect.* a pipe for enclosing electric cables. [L *ductus* leading, conduct, conduit]

**ducted heating** /dʌktəd ˈhitɪŋ/, *n.* a system of heating in which hot air is circulated through the building by means of ducts.

**ductile** /ˈdʌktaɪl/, *adj.* **1.** capable of being drawn out into wire or threads, as gold. **2.** capable of being hammered out thin, as certain metals. **3.** able to stand deformation under a load without fracture. **4.** capable of being moulded or shaped; plastic. **5.** susceptible; compliant; tractable. [ME *ductil,* from L *ductilis* that may be led] –**ductility** /dʌkˈtɪləti/, *n.*

**ductless gland** /dʌktləs ˈglænd/, *n.* a gland which possesses no excretory duct, but whose secretion is absorbed directly into the blood or lymph, as the thyroid, adrenals, pituitary gland, and parathyroids.

**dud** /dʌd/, *Colloq. –n.* **1.** any thing or person that proves a failure. **2.** *Mil.* a shell that fails to explode after being fired. *–v.t.* **3.** to cause someone to fail (fol. by *up*). **4.** to misinform someone deliberately (fol. by *up*). *–adj.* **5.** useless; defective. [orig. uncert.]

**dud-dropper** /ˈdʌd-drɒpə/, *n. Colloq.* one who sells inferior goods as superior goods, in a manner suggesting that they are high-priced goods being sold cheaply because they are stolen.

**dude** /djud, dud/, *n. Chiefly U.S. Colloq.* **1.** an affected or fastidious man; fop. **2.** a person brought up in a large city. **3.** a city-dweller holidaying on a ranch. **4.** an adult male; fellow.

**dudeen** /duˈdin/, *n.* an Irish short clay tobacco pipe.

**dude ranch** /djud ˈræntʃ/, *n. U.S.* a ranch operated also as a holiday resort.

**dudgeon** /ˈdʌdʒən/, *n.* a feeling of offence or resentment; anger: *we left in high dudgeon.* [orig. unknown]

**duds** /dʌdz/, *n.pl. Colloq.* **1.** trousers. **2.** clothes; (often) old or ragged clothes. **3.** belongings in general. [ME *dudde,* akin to LG *dudel* a coarse sackcloth]

**due** /dju/, *adj.* **1.** immediately payable. **2.** owing, irrespective of whether the time of payment has arrived. **3.** rightful; proper; fitting: *due care, in due time.* **4.** adequate; sufficient: *a due margin for delay.* **5.** attributable, as to a cause: *a delay due to an accident.* **6.** under engagement as to time; expected to be ready, be present, or arrive. *–n.* **7.** that which is due or owed. **8.** (*usu. pl.*) a payment due, as a charge, a fee, a membership subscription, etc. **9. give a person his due,** to ascribe proper credit to. *–adv.* **10.** directly or straight: *he sailed due east.* **11.** *Archaic.* duly. [ME *dew,* from OF *deü,* orig. pp. of *devoir,* from L *dēbēre* owe]

**duecento** /duəˈtʃɛntoʊ/, *n.* the 13th century, used commonly with reference to Italian art and literature of that period. Also, **dugento.** [It.: two hundred, short for *mille duecento* one thousand two hundred]

**duel** /ˈdjuəl/, *n., v.,* **-elled, -elling** or (*U.S.*) **-eled, -eling.** *–n.* **1.** a prearranged combat between two persons, fought with deadly weapons according to an accepted code of procedure, esp. to settle a private quarrel. **2.** any contest between two persons or parties. *–v.i.* **3.** to fight in a duel. [ML *duellum* a combat between two] – **dueller, duellist,** *n.*

**duello** /djuˈɛloʊ/, *n., pl.* **-los. 1.** the practice or skill of duelling. **2.** the code of rules regulating it. [It.]

**duenna** /djuˈɛnə/, *n.* **1.** (in Spain and Portugal) an older woman serving as escort or protector of a young lady. **2.** a governess; chaperon. [Sp. *dueña,* from L *domina* mistress]

**duet** /djuˈɛt/, *n.* a musical composition for two voices or performers. [It. *duetto,* diminutive of *duo* two] – **duettist,** *n.*

**duff**[1] /dʌf/, *n.* **1.** *Brit.* a flour pudding boiled, or sometimes steamed, in a bag, as plum duff. **2. up the duff,** *Colloq.* **a.** pregnant. **b.** ruined; broken. *–v.t.* **3.** *Colloq.* to make pregnant. [var. of DOUGH]

**duff**[2] /dʌf/, *n.* **1.** a ground surface consisting of matted peaty materials in forested soils. **2.** coal dust. [fig. use of DUFF[1]]

**duff**[3] /dʌf/, *v.t.* **1.** to steal (cattle, sheep, etc.), usu. altering brands in the process. **2.** to recondition or change the appearance of (esp. old or stolen goods). [backformation from DUFFER[1]]

**duff**[4] /dʌf/, *v.t.* **1.** *Golf.* to strike (a ball) clumsily by hitting the ground behind the ball. **2.** *Sport.* to fail to play (a shot) successfully. [backformation from DUFFER[2]]

**duffer**[1] /ˈdʌfə/, *n.* **1.** *Brit. Colloq.* a pedlar, esp. one who sells cheap, flashy goods as valuable items under false pretences. **2.** one who steals cattle, sheep, etc., esp. by altering the brand. [Brit. thieves' slang]

**duffer**[2] /ˈdʌfə/, *n.* **1.** a plodding, stupid, or incompetent person. **2.** *Mining.* **a.** a shaft yielding no payable ore. **b.** a mine, claim, etc., producing little or no payable ore. **3.** anything inferior or useless. [? from DUFF[3]; perhaps from DUFF[1]; or from Scot. *duffar, duffart, dowfart* a stupid, inactive fellow; c. ON *daufr* deaf]

**duffle** /ˈdʌfəl/, *n.* a coarse woollen cloth having a thick nap. Also, **duffel.** [after *Duffel,* town near Antwerp, N Belgium]

**duffle bag** /ˈ– bæg/, *n.* a cylindrical canvas bag used for carrying personal effects. Also, **duffel bag.**

**duffle coat** /ˈ– koʊt/, *n.* a heavy woollen coat, knee-length or three-quarter-length, usu. with a hood and toggles. Also, **duffel coat.**

**dug**[1] /dʌg/, *v.* past tense and past participle of **dig.**

**dug**[2] /dʌg/, *n.* the breast, udder or nipple of a female. [cf. Swed. *dägga,* Dan. *dægge* suckle]

**dugento** /duˈgɛntoʊ/, *n.* →**duecento.**

**dugite** /ˈdugaɪt/, *n.* a medium-sized, venomous snake, *Pseudonaja affinis,* of central and western areas of Australia, related to the common brown snake.

**dugong** /ˈdugɒŋ/, *n.* an aquatic herbivorous mammal, *Dugong dugon,* of the order Sirenia, found in tropical coastal areas of the Indian Ocean, having forelimbs adapted as flippers, no hind limbs, and a horizontal lobed tail; sea-cow. [Malay *dūyong*]

dugong

**dugout** /ˈdʌgaʊt/, *n.* **1.** a rough shelter or dwelling formed by an excavation in the ground or in the face of a bank. **2.** *Mining.* an abandoned opal working which has been turned into living quarters. **3.** a boat made by hollowing out a log.

**D.U.I.** /di ju ˈaɪ/, *n.* a charge made by police against a person who is observed to be driving under the influence of alcohol. [*D*(*riving*) *U*(*nder the*) *I*(*nfluence*)]

dugout canoe

**duiker** /ˈdaɪkə/, *n.* **1.** Also, **duyker, duikerbok** /ˈdaɪkəbɒk/. any of the small African antelopes with spikelike horns (usu. on the males only) which plunge through and under bushes instead of leaping over them and which are included in two genera, *Cephalophus* and *Sylvicapra.* **2.** any of various diving seabirds of southern Africa, family Sulidae, having all four toes webbed. **3.** →**tropic bird.** [Afrikaans: diver]

i = peat ɪ = pit ɛ = pet æ = pat a = part ɒ = pot ʌ = putt ɔ = port ʊ = put u = pool ɜ = pert ə = apart aɪ = buy eɪ = bay ɔɪ = boy aʊ = how oʊ = hoe ɪə = here ɛə = hair ʊə = tour g = give θ = thin ð = then ʃ = show ʒ = measure tʃ = choke dʒ = joke ŋ = sing j = you õ = Fr. bon

**duke** /djuk/; /duk/ *for def. 4, n.* **1.** a sovereign prince, the ruler of a small state called a duchy. **2.** (in Britain) a nobleman of the highest rank after that of a prince and ranking next above marquess. **3.** a nobleman of corresponding rank in certain other countries. **4.** (*chiefly pl.*) *Colloq.* the hand or fist. [ME *duc,* from OF, from L *dux* leader, ML duke]

**dukedom** /ˈdjukdəm/, *n.* **1.** the state or territory ruled by a duke. **2.** the office or rank of a duke.

**Duke of Kent,** *n. Colloq.* rent. [rhyming slang]

**dulcet** /ˈdʌlsət/, *adj.* **1.** agreeable to the feelings, the eye, or, esp., the ear; pleasing; soothing; melodious. **2.** *Archaic.* sweet to the taste or smell. *–n.* **3.** an organ stop resembling the dulciana, but an octave higher. [ME *doucet,* from OF, diminutive of *dous* sweet, from L *dulcis*]

**dulciana** /dʌlsiˈanə/, *n.* an organ stop having metal pipes, and giving thin, incisive, somewhat stringlike tones. [NL, from L *dulcis* sweet]

**dulcify** /ˈdʌlsəfaɪ/, *v.t.,* **-fied, -fying. 1.** to make more agreeable; mollify; appease. **2.** to sweeten. [LL *dulcificāre,* from L *dulci-* sweet + *-ficāre* make] **– dulcification** /dʌlsəfəˈkeɪʃən/, *n.*

**dulcimer** /ˈdʌlsəmə/, *n.* **1.** a trapezoidal zither with metal strings struck by light hammers; a cembalo; a cymbalo. **2.** *U.S.* a modern folk instrument related to the guitar and plucked with the fingers. [late ME *dowcemer,* from OF *doulcemer,* var. of *doulcemele*]

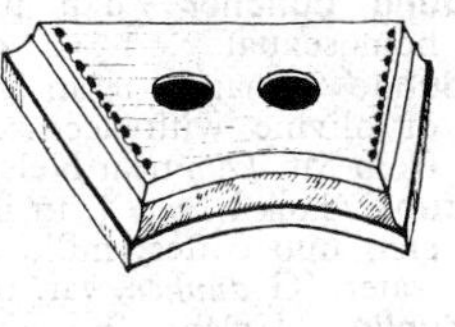

dulcimer

**dulcinea** /dʌlsəˈniə/, *n.* a ladylove; a sweetheart. [from *Dulcinea* (from Sp. *dulce,* from L *dulcis* sweet), name given by Don Quixote to his peasant ladylove in the romance by Cervantes, 1547-1616, Spanish novelist]

**dulia** /djuˈlaɪə/, *n. Rom. Cath. Theol.* veneration and invocation given to saints as the servants of God and friends of God. See **hyperdulia** and **latria.** [ML, from Gk *douleía* servitude, service]

**dull** /dʌl/, *adj.* **1.** slow of understanding; obtuse; stupid. **2.** lacking keenness of perception in the senses or feelings; insensible; unfeeling. **3.** not intense or acute: *a dull pain.* **4.** slow in motion or action; not brisk; sluggish. **5.** listless; spiritless. **6.** causing ennui or depression; tedious; uninteresting: *a dull sermon.* **7.** not sharp; blunt: *a dull knife.* **8.** having very little depth of colour; lacking in richness or intensity of colour. **9.** not bright, intense, or clear; dim: *a dull day or sound.* *–v.t., v.i.* **10.** to make or become dull. [ME *dul, dull;* akin to OE *dol* foolish, stupid, G *toll* mad] **– dullish,** *adj.* **– dulness, dullness,** *n.* **– dully,** *adv.*

**dullard** /ˈdʌləd/, *n.* a dull or stupid person. [DULL, *adj.* + -ARD]

**dullsville** /ˈdʌlsvɪl/, *n. U.S. Colloq.* an activity or place which is boring or tedious. [DULL + *-s-* + -VILLE]

**dulse** /dʌls/, *n.* coarse, edible, red seaweed, *Rhodymenia palmata.* [Irish and Gaelic *duileasg*]

**duly** /ˈdjuli/, *adv.* **1.** in a due manner; properly; fitly. **2.** in due season; punctually. **3.** adequately.

**duma** /ˈduma/, *n.* (in Russia prior to 1917) **1.** a council or official assembly. **2.** (*cap.*) an elective legislative assembly, constituting the lower house of parliament, which was established in 1905 by Nicholas II. Also, **douma.** [Russ.]

**dumaresq** /djuˈmærɪk/, *n.* a device which gauges the rate at which an enemy ship, missile, etc., is moving. [named after its inventor, Rear-Admiral John Saumarlz *Dumaresq,* 1873-1922, Australian naval officer]

**dumb** /dʌm/, *adj.* **1.** without the power of speech. **2.** bereft of the power of speech temporarily: *dumb with astonishment.* **3.** that does not speak or is little addicted to speaking. **4.** made, done, etc., without speech. **5.** lacking some usual property, characteristic, etc.: *dumb ague.* **6.** stupid; dull-witted. **7.** of or pertaining to a machine which cannot operate independently but is reliant on a computerised machine. [OE, c. G *dumm* stupid] **– dumbly,** *adv.* **– dumbness,** *n.*

**dumb ague** /dʌm ˈeɪgju/, *n.* an irregular form of intermittent malarial fever, lacking the usual chill.

**dumbbell** /ˈdʌmbɛl/, *n.* a gymnasium hand apparatus made of wood or metal, consisting of two balls joined by a barlike handle, used as weights, usu. in pairs.

**dumbcluck** /ˈdʌmklʌk/, *n. Colloq.* a fool; idiot.

**dumb Dora** /dʌm ˈdɔrə/, *n.* a dull or stupid girl or woman.

**dumbfound** /ˈdʌmfaʊnd/, *v.t.* to strike dumb with amazement. Also, **dumfound.** [b. DUMB and CONFOUND] **– dumbfounder,** *n.*

**dumb piano** /dʌm piˈænoʊ/, *n.* a small and silent keyboard instrument with neither hammers nor strings, intended for practice.

**dumb show** /ˈdʌm ʃoʊ/, *n.* **1.** a part of a dramatic representation given in pantomime, common in the early English drama. **2.** gesture without speech.

**dumb waiter** /dʌm ˈweɪtə/, *n.* **1.** a small stand placed near a dining table. **2.** *Brit.* →**lazy Susan. 3.** a conveyor consisting of a framework with shelves, drawn up and down in a shaft.

**dumdum**[1] /ˈdʌmdʌm/, *n.* a kind of hollow-nosed bullet that expands on impact, inflicting a severe wound. Also, **dumdum bullet.** [named after *Dum-Dum,* town in W Bengal, a former ammunition factory]

**dumdum**[2] /ˈdʌmdʌm/, *n. Colloq.* (*esp. in children's speech*) a stupid person. [reduplication of DUMB]

**dummy** /ˈdʌmi/, *n., pl.* **-mies,** *adj.* *–n.* **1.** an imitation or copy of something, as for display, to indicate appearance, exhibit clothing, etc. **2.** *Colloq.* a stupid person; dolt. **3.** one who has nothing to say or who takes no active part in affairs. **4.** (esp. in buying land) one put forward to act for others while ostensibly acting for himself. **5.** a dumb person; a mute. **6.** *Cards.* **a.** (in bridge) the dealer's partner whose hand is exposed and played by the dealer. **b.** the cards so exposed. **c.** a game so played. **d.** an imaginary player represented by an exposed hand which is played by and serves as partner to one of the players. **7.** a rubber teat, etc., given to a baby to suck. **8.** a new fence post put in alongside an old one. **9.** *Print.* sheets folded and made up to show the size, shape, form, sequence, and general style of a contemplated piece of printing. **10.** *Football.* Also, **dummy pass.** a feigned or pretended manoeuvre. **11.** the open car in a cable tram which has the grip (def. 8) and in which the driver sits, thus appearing to contain some means of propulsion as an engine. **12.** a machine which is dumb (def. 7). **13.** *N.Z. Prison Colloq.* a punishment cell; digger. **14. sell a dummy,** *Football.* to make a dummy pass. *–adj.* **15.** acting for others while ostensibly acting for oneself, esp. in buying land. **16.** counterfeit; sham; imitation. **17.** *Cards.* played with a dummy. **18.** of or pertaining to a new fence post put in alongside an old one. *–v.t.* **19.** to put in dummy fence posts. **20.** to prepare a dummy of (a book, etc.). *–v.i.* **21.** *Football.* to make a dummy pass.

**dummy half** /– ˈhaf/, *n.* (in Rugby League) the player who acts as a half, gathering and distributing the ball after it has been played following a tackle, etc.

**dummy run** /– ˈrʌn/, *n.* a trial; an exploratory attempt.

**dumortierite** /duˈmɔtiəˌraɪt/, *n.* a mineral, aluminium borosilicate, used in making refractories. [named after Eugène *Dumortier,* 19th-cent. French palaeontologist. See -ITE[1]]

**dump**[1] /dʌmp/, *v.t.* **1.** to throw down in a mass; fling down or drop heavily. **2.** to empty out, as from a cart by tilting. **3.** to get rid of; hand over to somebody else. **4.** *Computers.* to print out, with minimal editing, the content of computer memory, usu. for diagnostic purposes in debugging. **5.** to compress (two bales of wool) together. **6.** *Comm.* **a.** to put (goods) on the market in large quantities and at a low price, esp. to a large or favoured buyer. **b.** to market (goods) thus in a foreign country, as at a price below that charged in the home country. **7.** *Football.* to tackle heavily. **8.** (of a wave) to hurl a body-surfer onto the churned-up sand at the bottom of the wave. *–v.i.* **9.** to fall or drop down suddenly. **10.** to unload. **11.** to offer for sale at a low price, esp. to offer low prices to favoured buyers. *–n.* **12.** anything as rubbish dumped or thrown down. **13.** a place where it is deposited. **14.** *Mil.* a collection of ammunition, stores, etc., deposited at some point, as near a battle front, to be distributed for use. **15.** the act of dumping. **16.** *Mining.* **a.** a runway or embankment, equipped with tripping devices, from which low-grade ore, rock, etc., are dumped. **b.** the pile of ore so dumped. **17.** two bales of wool compressed into one. **18.** *Mining.* mullock and dirt heaped around mine shafts. **19.** *Colloq.* a place, house, or town that is poorly kept up, and generally of wretched appearance. **20. sell the dump,** *Colloq.* **a.** *Football.* to pass the ball to (another player) to avoid being tackled (fol. by *to*). **b.** to pass on something worthless, or the object of some dispute to (someone else) to avoid trouble (fol. by *to*). [ME, from Scand.; cf. Dan. *dumpe* fall plump]

**dump**[2] /dʌmp/, *n.* **1.** (formerly) a clumsy leaden counter used by boys in games. **2.** (formerly) a round piece cut from the centre of a silver dollar, and used as a coin. Cf. **holey dollar.** [orig. uncert.; ? akin to DUMPY[2]]

dump[2] (def. 2): holey dollar and dump

**dumped wool** /dʌmpt ˈwʊl/, *n.* a package of wool compressed tightly for shipment and held by metal bands or wires.

**dumper** /ˈdʌmpə/, *n.* **1.** one who or that which dumps. **2.** *Surfing.* a wave which, in shallow water, instead of breaking evenly from the top, crashes violently down, throwing surfers to the bottom. **3.** *Colloq.* →**tip-truck.**

**dumping cash security,** *n.* a cash deposit required to be placed with customs by an Australian importer when it is considered likely that the goods are being dumped in Australia.

**dumpish** /ˈdʌmpɪʃ/, *adj.* depressed; sad. – **dumpishly,** *adv.* – **dumpishness,** *n.*

**dumpling** /ˈdʌmplɪŋ/, *n.* **1.** a rounded mass of steamed dough (often served with stewed meat, etc.). **2.** a kind of pudding consisting of a wrapping of dough enclosing an apple or other fruit, and boiled or baked. **3.** →**quenelle.** [history obscure; ? orig. *lumpling* (from LUMP[1] + -LING[1]) with *d-* by dissimilation]

**dump rake** /ˈdʌmp reɪk/, *n.* a power-driven or tractor-drawn rake which gathers hay into windrows or heaps.

**dumps** /dʌmps/, *n.pl. Colloq.* a dull, gloomy state of mind: *down in the dumps.* [Brit. obs. *dump* a slow dance, sad tune. Cf. MD *domp* haze]

**dump truck** /ˈdʌmp trʌk/, *n.* →**tip-truck.**

**dumpty** /ˈdʌmpti/, *n.* **1.** a low stuffed seat, or cushion. **2.** *Colloq.* a toilet. *–adj.* **3.** short and stout; dumpy.

**dumpy**[1] /ˈdʌmpi/, *adj.,* **dumpier, dumpiest.** dumpish; dejected; sulky. [Brit. obs. *dump* a slow dance, sad tune + -Y[1]]

**dumpy**[2] /ˈdʌmpi/, *adj.,* **dumpier, dumpiest.** short and stout; squat: *a dumpy woman.* [? akin to DUMPLING] – **dumpily,** *adv.* – **dumpiness,** *n.*

**dumpy level** /ˈ– lɛvəl/, *n.* a surveying instrument consisting of a spirit level mounted under and parallel to a telescope, the latter being rigidly attached to its supports.

**dun**[1] /dʌn/, *v.,* **dunned, dunning,** *n. –v.t.* **1.** to make repeated and insistent demands upon, esp. for the payment of a debt. *–n.* **2.** one who duns; an importunate creditor. **3.** a demand for payment, esp. a written one. [special use of obs. *dun* din, from Scand.; cf. Icel. *duna* boom, roar]

**dun**[2] /dʌn/, *adj.* **1.** dull or greyish brown. **2.** dark; gloomy. *–n.* **3.** dun colour. **4.** a mayfly. **5.** a dun fly. **6.** a dun-coloured horse. [ME *dun(ne),* OE *dunn,* c. OS *dun* reddish brown]

**dunce** /dʌns/, *n.* a dull-witted or stupid person; a dolt. [from John *Duns* Scotus, *c.* 1265-*c.* 1308, scholastic theologian; his system was attacked as foolish by the humanists]

**dunce's cap** /ˈdʌnsəz kæp/, *n.* a tall paper cone, formerly put on the head of a slow or lazy student. Also, **dunce cap.**

**dunderhead** /ˈdʌndəhɛd/, *n.* a dunce; blockhead. Also, **dunderpate** /ˈdʌndəpeɪt/. – **dunderheaded,** *adj.*

**dundreary** /dʌnˈdrɪəri/, *n., pl.* **-ries.** (*usu. pl.*) long side-whiskers worn without a beard. [from Lord *Dundreary,* a character in the play *Our American Cousin* (1858) by Tom Taylor, 1817-80, English dramatist]

**dune** /djun/, *n.* a sand hill or sand ridge formed by the wind, usu. in desert regions or near lakes and oceans. [F, from MD, c. OE *dūn.* See DOWN[3]]

**dune buggy** /ˈ– ˌbʌgi/, *n.* →**beach buggy.**

**dun fly** /ˈdʌn flaɪ/, *n.* a dun-coloured artificial fishing fly attached to the leader to mimic the larval stage of certain flies.

**dung** /dʌŋ/, *n.* **1.** manure; excrement, esp. of animals. *–v.t.* **2.** to manure (ground) with, or as with, dung. [ME *dunge,* OE *dung,* c. G *Dung*] – **dungy,** *adj.*

**dungaree** /dʌŋgəˈri/, *n.* **1.** a coarse cotton fabric of East Indian origin, used esp. for sailors' clothing. **2.** (*pl.*) work clothes, overalls, etc., made of this fabric. [Hind. *dungrī*]

**dungaree settler** /– ˈsɛtlə/, *n.* a small farmer in the early Australian colonial period who was too poor to wear anything but faded blue Indian cotton garments.

**dung beetle** /ˈdʌŋ bitl/, *n.* any of various scarabaeid beetles that feed upon or breed in dung, as the sacred Egyptian scarab *Scarabaeus sacer.*

**dungeon** /ˈdʌndʒən/, *n.* any strong, close cell, esp. underground; donjon. [ME, from OF *donjon,* from LL *dominio* dominion, tower, from L *dominus* master, lord]

**dunghill** /ˈdʌŋhɪl/, *n.* **1.** a heap of dung. **2.** a mean or vile place, abode, condition, or person.

**dung puncher** /ˈdʌŋ pʌntʃə/, *n. Colloq.* an active male homosexual.

**dunite** /ˈdʌnaɪt/, *n.* an igneous rock composed almost entirely of olivine with accessory pyroxene and chromite. [named from Mt. *Dun* near Nelson, N.Z., where it was first identified]

**dunk** /dʌŋk/, *v.t.* **1.** to immerse in water. **2.** to dip (biscuits, etc.) into coffee, milk, etc. *–v.i.* **3.** to submerge oneself in water. [G *dunken,* var. of *tunken* dip] – **dunker,** *n.*

**dunlin** /ˈdʌnlən/, *n.* a widely distributed sandpiper, *Erolia alpina,* which breeds in northern parts of the Northern Hemisphere, and which has been seen on rare occasions in Australia. [d. var. of *dunling,* from DUN[2] + -LING[1]]

**dunlop** /ˈdʌnlɒp/, *n.* a pressed Scottish cheese, creamy white in colour and having a mild flavour and creamy texture.

**dunnage** /ˈdʌnɪdʒ/, *n.* **1.** baggage or personal effects. **2.** *Naut.* loose material laid beneath or wedged among cargo to prevent injury from water or chafing: *dried brush for dunnage.* [D *dunnetjes* loosely together]

**dunnart** /ˈdʌnat/, *n.* any of the narrow-footed marsupial mice of genus *Sminthopsis.* [Aboriginal]

**dunno** /dəˈnoʊ, dʌˈnoʊ/, *v.* (*not generally regarded as standard usage*) contraction of *don't know.*

**dunnock** /ˈdʌnək/, *n.* the common hedge sparrow, *Prunella modularis,* of Europe. [DUN[2] + -OCK]

**dunny** /ˈdʌni/, *n. Colloq.* **1.** an outside toilet, found in unsewered areas, usu. at some distance from the house it serves and consisting of a small shed furnished with a lavatory seat placed over a sanitary can: *all alone like a country dunny.* **2.** a toilet. **3.** a sanitary can. [short for Brit. d. *dunnakin, dunnaken,* from *dannaken,* from *danna* dung + *ken* place]

**dunny can** /ˈ– kæn/, *n. Colloq.* a sanitary can.

**dunny cart** /ˈ– kat/, *n. Colloq.* a sanitary cart.

**duo** /ˈdjuoʊ/, *n., pl.* **duos, dui** /ˈdjui/. **1.** *Music.* a duet. **2.** a pair of singers, entertainers, etc. [It., from L: two]

**duo-,** a word element meaning 'two', as in *duologue.* [L, combining form of *duo*]

**duodecimal** /djuoʊˈdɛsəməl/, *adj.* **1.** pertaining to twelfths, or to the number twelve. **2.** proceeding by twelves. *–n.* **3.** one of a system of numerals the base of which is twelve. **4.** one of twelve equal parts. [L *duodecimus* twelfth + -AL[1]] – **duodecimally,** *adv.*

**duodecimo** /djuoʊˈdɛsimoʊ/, *n., pl.* **-mos,** *adj. –n.* **1.** a book size determined by printing on sheets folded to form twelve leaves or twenty-four pages. *Abbrev.:* 12mo or 12° *–adj.* **2.** in duodecimo. [L (*in*) *duodecimō* in twelfth]

**duoden-,** a combining form representing **duodenum,** as in *duodenitis.* Also, **duodeno-.**

**duodenal** /djuəˈdinəl/, *adj.* of or pertaining to the duodenum.

**duodenary** /djuəˈdinəri/, *adj.* duodecimal. [L *duodēnārius* containing twelve]

**duodenitis** /ˌdjuoʊdəˈnaɪtəs/, *n.* inflammation of the duodenum.

**duodenum** /djuəˈdinəm/, *n.* the first portion of the small intestine, from the stomach to the jejunum. [ML, from L

i = peat ɪ = pit ɛ = pet æ = pat a = part ɒ = pot ʌ = putt ɔ = port ʊ = put u = pool ɜ = pert ə = apart aɪ = buy eɪ = bay ɔɪ = boy aʊ = how oʊ = hoe ɪə = here ɛə = hair ʊə = tour g = give θ = thin ð = then ʃ = show ʒ = measure tʃ = choke dʒ = joke ŋ = sing j = you õ = Fr. bon

*duodēnī* twelve each; so called from its length, about twelve finger breadths]

**duologue** /ˈdjuəlɒg/, *n.* **1.** a conversation between two persons; a dialogue. **2.** a dramatic performance or piece in the form of a dialogue limited to two speakers. [DUO- + *-logue*, modelled on MONOLOGUE]

**duopoly** /djuˈɒpəli/, *n.* a market situation where two competing sellers hold control over a product or service. [DUO- + (MONO)POLY] – **duopolistic** /djuɒpəˈlɪstɪk/, *adj.*

**duopsony** /djuˈɒpsəni/, *n., pl.* **-nies.** a market situation where two rival buyers control the demand for a product or service. [DUO- + Gk *opsōnía* purchase of victuals, catering]

**duotone** /ˈdjuətoʊn/, *adj.* **1.** of or pertaining to a half tone illustration printed in two colours from two plates made from the same original but usu. with different screen angles. *–n.* **2.** such an illustration.

**dup.,** duplicate.

**dupe** /djup/, *n., v.,* **duped, duping.** *–n.* **1.** a person who is imposed upon or deceived; a gull. *–v.t.* **2.** to make a dupe of; deceive; delude; trick. [F: properly, hoopoe, from L *upupa*] – **dupable,** *adj.* – **dupability** /djupəˈbɪləti/, *n.* – **duper,** *n.*

**dupery** /ˈdjupəri/, *n., pl.* **-eries. 1.** the act or practice of duping. **2.** the state of one who is duped.

**duple** /ˈdjupəl/, *adj.* double; twofold. [L *duplus* double]

**duplet** /ˈdjuplət/, *n.* **1.** *Chem.* a pair of electrons, shared between two atoms, forming a covalent bond. **2.** *Music.* a group of two notes which are to be played in the time of three notes.

**duple time** /ˈdjupəl taɪm/, *n.* (of music) characterised by two beats to the bar.

**duplex** /ˈdjuplɛks/, *adj.* **1.** twofold; double. **2.** *Mach.* including two identical working parts in a single framework, though one could operate alone. *–n.* **3.** a T-bar lift with two parallel sets of towing cables and T-bars. **4.** a two-storey block of flats or home units, one flat occupying each floor.

**duplexer** /ˈdjuplɛksə/, *n.* a radio system which permits simultaneous transmission and reception of signals.

**duplicate** /ˈdjupləkət/ *adj., n.;* /ˈdjupləkeɪt/ *v.,* **-cated, -cating.** *–adj.* **1.** exactly like or corresponding to something else. **2.** double; consisting of or existing in two corresponding parts. **3.** *Cards.* denoting a game in which a team tries for the best result on hands also played by competing partnerships: *duplicate bridge. –n.* **4.** a copy exactly like an original. **5.** anything corresponding in all respects to something else. **6.** *Cards.* a duplicate game. **7. in duplicate,** in two copies, exactly alike. *–v.t.* **8.** to make an exact copy of; repeat. **9.** to double; make twofold. **10.** to reproduce by asexual means, as by cloning. [L *duplicātus*, pp., doubled] – **duplicative** /ˈdjupləkətɪv/, *adj.*

**duplicating paper** /ˈdjupləkeɪtɪŋ ˌpeɪpə/, *n.* paper specially treated or prepared for use in a duplicator.

**duplication** /djupləˈkeɪʃən/, *n.* **1.** the act of duplicating. **2.** the state of being duplicated. **3.** a duplicate.

**duplicator** /ˈdjupləkeɪtə/, *n.* a machine for making multiple copies of printed or handwritten documents by means of an inking apparatus and a specially prepared master copy. Also, **duplicating machine.**

**duplicity** /djuˈplɪsəti/, *n., pl.* **-ties. 1.** the quality or state of being double. **2.** deceitfulness in speech or conduct; speaking or acting in two different ways concerning the same matter with intent to deceive; double-dealing. **3.** *Law.* the objectionable legal procedure of presenting a pleading which contains more than one claim, defence, etc. [LL *duplicitas* doubleness, from L *duplex*. See DUPLEX]

**dur** /dʊə/, *adj. Music.* major. [G]

**dura** /ˈdjurə/, *n.* →**dura mater.** – **dural,** *adj.*

**durable** /ˈdjurəbəl/, *adj.* **1.** having the quality of lasting or enduring; not easily worn out, decayed, etc. **2.** of or pertaining to goods which will be good for some time, as opposed to those intended to be used or consumed immediately. *–n.* **3.** (*pl.*) goods which are durable. [ME, from L *dūrābilis* lasting, from *dūrāre* endure] – **durability** /djurəˈbɪləti/, **durableness,** *n.* – **durably,** *adv.*

**duralumin** /djuˈræljəmən/, *n.* an alloy comparable in strength and hardness to soft steel. [Trademark]

**dura mater** /djurə ˈmatə/, *n.* the tough, fibrous membrane forming the outermost of the three coverings of the brain and spinal cord. See **arachnoid** and **pia mater.** Also, **dura.** [ML: lit., hard mother]

**durance** /ˈdjurəns/, *n.* **1.** forced confinement; imprisonment: *in durance vile.* [late ME, from MF: duration, from *durer*, from L *dūrāre* last]

**duration** /djuˈreɪʃən/, *n.* **1.** continuance in time. **2.** the length of time anything continues. **3. for the duration,** for a long time. [ME, from LL *dūrātio*, from L *dūrāre* last]

**durative** /ˈdjurətɪv/, *adj.* denoting a verb aspect, as in Russian, expressing incompleted, or continued, action, etc. Compare English *beat* (which implies duration or continued action) with *strike;* also *walk*, durative, with *step.*

**durbar** /ˈdɜba/, *n.* (in India before 1947) **1.** the court of a native ruler. **2.** a public audience or levee held by a native prince or a British governor or viceroy; an official reception. **3.** the hall or place of audience. **4.** the audience itself. [Hind., Pers. *darbār* court]

**duress** /djuˈrɛs/, *n.* **1.** constraint; compulsion. **2.** forcible restraint of liberty; imprisonment. **3.** *Law.* such constraint or coercion as will render void a contract or other legal act entered or performed under its influence. [ME *duresse*, from OF, from L *dūritia* hardness]

**durex** /ˈdjurɛks/, *n.* **1.** →**sticky tape. 2.** *Brit.* contraceptive sheath. Also, **durex tape.** [Trademark]

**durian** /ˈdjuriən/, *n.* **1.** the edible fruit, with a hard, prickly rind, of a tree, *Durio zibethinus*, of south-eastern Asia which has a distinctive flavour and smell. **2.** the tree itself. Also, **durion.** [Malay, from *duri* thorn]

**during** /ˈdjurɪŋ/, *prep.* **1.** throughout the continuance of. **2.** in the course of. [ME, from F *durer*, from L *dūrāre* endure]

**durmast** /ˈdɜmast/, *n.* a European oak, *Quercus petraea*, with a heavy, elastic wood highly valued by the builder and the cabinet-maker.

**durobby** /djuˈrɒbi/, *n.* →**robby.**

**durra** /ˈdʌrə/, *n.* a type of grain sorghum with slender stalks, cultivated in Asia, etc.; Indian millet; Guinea corn. Also, **doura, dourah.** [Ar. *dhura*]

**durry** /ˈdʌri/, *n., pl.* **-ries.** *Colloq.* a cigarette.

**durst** /dɜst/, *v.* a past tense of **dare.**

**durule** /ˈdjurul/, *n.* →**time-release capsule.**

**durum wheat** /ˈdjurəm wit/, *n.* an important species or variety of wheat, *Triticum durum*, the flour from which is largely used for macaroni, etc. Also, **durum.** [L *dūrus* hard]

**dusk** /dʌsk/, *n.* **1.** partial darkness; a state between light and darkness; twilight; shade; gloom. **2.** the darker stage of twilight. *–adj.* **3.** dark; tending to darkness. *–v.i.* **4.** to become dusk; darken. *–v.t.* **5.** to make dark. [metathetic var. of OE *dux, dox* dark, c. L *fuscus* dark brown] – **duskish,** *adj.*

**dusky** /ˈdʌski/, *adj.,* **duskier, duskiest. 1.** somewhat dark; dark-coloured. **2.** deficient in light; dim. **3.** gloomy. – **duskily,** *adv.* – **duskiness,** *n.*

**dusky moorhen** /– ˈmɔhɛn/, *n.* a rail, *Gallinula tenebrosa*, brownish black with white patches on the tail-coverts and a red frontal shield, found mainly in swamps and parklands of eastern Australia.

**dust** /dʌst/, *n.* **1.** earth or other matter in fine, dry particles. **2.** any finely powdered substance, as sawdust. **3.** a cloud of finely powdered earth or other matter in the air. **4.** that to which anything, as the human body, is reduced by disintegration or decay. **5.** the mortal body of man. **6.** *Archaic.* a single particle or grain. **7.** ashes, refuse, etc. **8.** a low or humble condition. **9.** anything worthless. **10.** gold dust. **11.** *Obs. Colloq.* flour. **12.** disturbance; turmoil. **13. bite the dust,** to be killed or wounded. **14. raise the dust,** *Colloq.* make a fuss; cause a disturbance. **15. lick the dust,** *Colloq.* **a.** to be killed or wounded. **b.** to grovel; humble oneself abjectly. **16. shake the dust off one's feet,** to depart with scorn. **17. throw dust in one's eyes,** to mislead. *–v.t.* **18.** to free from dust; wipe the dust from: *to dust (or dust off) the table.* **19.** to sprinkle with dust or powder: *to dust plants with powder.* **20.** to strew or sprinkle as dust: *dust powder over plants.* **21.** to soil with dust; make dusty. *–v.i.* **22.** to wipe dust from a table, room, etc. **23.** to become dusty. [ME *doust*, OE *dūst*, c. G *Dunst* vapour] – **dustless,** *adj.*

**dust bath** /ˈ– baθ/, *n.* the practice adopted by a bird of forcing dust through its feathers, possibly as a control against parasites.

**dustbin** /ˈdʌstbɪn/, *n. Brit.* →**garbage bin.** Also, *U.S.,* **ash can.**

**dust bowl** /ˈdʌst boʊl/, *n.* an area of sparse vegetation subject to dust storms.

**dustcart** /ˈdʌstkat/, *n. Brit.* →**garbage truck.**

**dustcoat** /ˈdʌstkoʊt/, *n.* a long, light overgarment worn to protect clothing from dust. Also, *U.S.,* **duster.**

**dustcover** /ˈdʌstkʌvə/, *n.* **1.** a large cloth or sheet placed over furniture to protect it from dust. **2.** →**dust jacket.**

**dust devil** /ˈdʌst dɛvəl/, *n.* a miniature whirlwind of considerable intensity that picks up dust and rubbish and carries it some distance into the air.

**duster** /ˈdʌstə/, *n.* **1.** one who or that which dusts. **2.** a cloth, brush, etc., for removing dust. **3.** a felt pad mounted on a wooden block, used in schools for cleaning the blackboard. **4.** an apparatus for sprinkling dust or powder on something. **5.** *U.S.* a dust coat.

**dusting** /ˈdʌstɪŋ/, *n.* **1.** a light coating, as of powder. **2.** *Colloq.* a beating; thrashing.

**dust jacket** /ˈdʌst dʒækət/, *n.* a jacket (def. 3) for a book. Also, **dust cover.**

**dustman** /ˈdʌstmən/, *n., pl.* **-men.** *Brit.* →**garbageman.**

**dustpan** /ˈdʌstpæn/, *n.* a shovel-like utensil with a short handle into which dust is swept for removal.

**dustproof** /ˈdʌstpruf/, *adj.* impervious to dust.

**dustsheet** /ˈdʌstʃit/, *n.* →**dustcover.**

**dust-shot** /ˈdʌst-ʃɒt/, *n.* the smallest size of shot for a shotgun.

**dust squall** /dʌst skwɔl/, *n.* a squall which throws up a great deal of dust.

**dust storm** /ˈ– stɔm/, *n.* a storm of wind which raises dense masses of dust into the air, as in a desert region.

**dust-up** /ˈdʌst-ʌp/, *n. Colloq.* a commotion; fight; scuffle.

**dusty** /ˈdʌsti/, *adj.,* **dustier, dustiest. 1.** filled, covered, or clouded with dust. **2.** of the nature of dust; powdery. **3.** of the colour of dust; grey. **4. not so dusty,** *Colloq.* not too bad; quite good. **– dustily,** *adv.* **– dustiness,** *n.*

**dusty miller** /– ˈmɪlə/, *n.* **1.** a creeping perennial herb, *Cerastium tomentosum,* covered with dense white hairs, native to south-eastern Europe, and commonly grown in rock gardens; snow-in-summer. **2.** any of certain unrelated species with foliage bearing white hairs.

**dutch** /dʌtʃ/, *n. Brit. Colloq.* wife. [shortened form of DUCHESS]

**Dutch** /dʌtʃ/, *adj.* **1.** of, pertaining to, or characteristic of the natives or inhabitants of the Netherlands or Holland, or their country or language. **2. go Dutch,** *Colloq.* to have each person pay his or her own expenses. *–n.* **3.** the people of the Netherlands or Holland. **4.** a Germanic language, the language of the Netherlands. **5. in dutch with,** in trouble, in disfavour with. **6.** *Obs.* the German language. [MD *dutsch* German, Dutch, c. G *deutsch* German, orig., popular, national, translation of L *vulgāris* vernacular]

**Dutch auction** /– ˈɒkʃən/, *n.* an auction in which the price is gradually lowered until a bid is made.

**Dutch barn** /– ˈban/, *n.* a steel-framed building without walls and with a curved roof, often used for storing hay on farms.

**Dutch cap** /– ˈkæp/, *n.* →**diaphragm** (def. 4).

**Dutch cheese** /– ˈtʃiz/, *n.* **1.** a small, globular, hard cheese made from skimmed milk. **2.** cottage cheese.

**Dutch clover** /– ˈkloʊvə/, *n.* the common white clover.

**Dutch courage** /– ˈkʌrɪdʒ/, *n.* courage inspired by alcoholic drink.

**Dutch doll** /– ˈdɒl/, *n.* a jointed wooden doll.

**Dutch door** /– ˈdɔ/, *n.* →**stable door.**

**Dutch elm disease,** *n.* an often fatal fungal disease of elm trees spread by the bark beetle, and characterised by withering of leaves and branches.

**Dutch gold** /– ˈgoʊld/, *n.* an alloy of copper and zinc in the form of thin sheets, used as a cheap imitation of gold leaf. Also, **Dutch foil, Dutch leaf, Dutch metal.**

**Dutchman** /ˈdʌtʃmən/, *n., pl.* **-men. 1.** a native or inhabitant of Holland. **2.** *Carp., etc.* a piece or wedge inserted to hide the fault in a badly made joint, stop an opening, etc.

**Dutchman's-pipe** /dʌtʃmənz-ˈpaɪp/, *n.* a climbing vine, *Aristolochia macrophylla,* with large leaves and flowers of a curved form suggesting a tobacco pipe.

**Dutch oven** /dʌtʃ ˈʌvən/, *n.* **1.** a large, heavy pot with a close-fitting lid used for slow cooking. **2.** a metal utensil, open in front, for roasting before an open fire. **3.** a brick oven in which the walls are preheated for cooking.

**Dutch rush** /– ˈrʌʃ/, *n.* a widespread horsetail, *Equisetum hyemale,* the long, scarcely branched siliceous stems of which were formerly used for scouring pots and pans.

**Dutch treat** /– ˈtrit/, *n.* a meal or entertainment in which each person pays for himself. Also, **Dutch shout.**

**Dutch uncle** /– ˈʌŋkəl/, *n.* a person who criticises or reproves with unsparing severity and frankness.

**Dutch wife** /–ˈ waɪf/, *n.* a bolster or wicker frame to be placed between the legs for comfort while sleeping, esp. in certain tropical countries.

**duteous** /ˈdjutiəs/, *adj.* dutiful; obedient; submissive. **– duteously,** *adv.* **– duteousness,** *n.*

**dutiable** /ˈdjutiəbəl/, *adj.* subject to duty, as imported goods.

**dutiful** /ˈdjutəfəl/, *adj.* **1.** performing the duties required of one; obedient: *a dutiful child.* **2.** required by duty; proceeding from or expressive of a sense of duty: *dutiful attention.* **– dutifully,** *adv.* **– dutifulness,** *n.*

**duty** /ˈdjuti/, *n., pl.* **-ties. 1.** that which one is bound to do by moral or legal obligation. **2.** the binding or obligatory force of that which is morally right; moral obligation. **3.** action required by one's position or occupation; office; function: *the duties of a soldier or clergyman.* **4.** the conduct due to a superior; homage; respect. **5.** an act of respect, or an expression of respectful consideration. **6.** a specific or *ad valorem* levy imposed by law on the import, export, sale, or manufacture of goods, the transference of property, the legal recognition of deeds and documents, etc. **7.** a payment, service, etc., imposed and enforceable by law or custom. **8.** *Mach.* **a.** the amount of work done by an engine per unit amount of fuel consumed. **b.** the measure of effectiveness of any machine. **9.** *Agric.* the amount of water necessary to provide for the crop in a given area. **10. do duty for,** be a substitute for; serve the same function as. **11. off duty,** not at work. **12. on duty,** at work. [ME *duete,* from AF, from *du, due* DUE]

**duty-bound** /ˈdjuti-baʊnd/, *adj.* morally obliged.

**duty-free** /djuti-ˈfri/, *adj.* free of customs duty.

**duty-free shop** /ˌdjuti-ˈfri ʃɒp/, *n.* a shop, often at an airport, where duty-free goods can be bought.

**duty officer** /ˈdjuti ɒfəsə/, *n.* the officer rostered to be on duty at a particular time and place.

**duty solicitor** /ˈdjuti səlɪsətə/, *n.* a solicitor who is rostered to appear at a court to advise or represent, subject to a means test, anyone who is appearing in court that day and who does not have legal representation.

**duumvir** /ˈdjuəmvɪə/, *n., pl.* **-virs, -viri** /-vɪəri/. a member of a duumvirate. [L, backformation from *duum virum,* gen. pl., of two men]

**duumvirate** /djuˈʌmvərət/, *n.* **1.** a union of two men in the same office. **2.** the office or government of two such persons.

**duvet** /djuˈveɪ/, *n.* any of various things stuffed with down, as a kind of quilt. [F: lit., down]

**duvetyn** /ˈdjuvətən/, *n.* a napped fabric, in a twilled or plain weave, of cotton, wool, silk, or rayon. Also, **duvetine, duvetyne.** [F, from *duvet* DUVET + *-yn* -INE[2]]

**dux** /dʌks/, *n.* the top pupil academically in some division of a school. [L: leader]

**duyker** /ˈdaɪkə/, *n.* →**duiker.**

**D.V.,** Deo volente.

**dvandva** /ˈdvandva, dəˈvandəva/, *adj.* **1.** denoting a compound word neither element of which is subordinate to the other, as *bittersweet, Anglo-Saxon.* *–n.* **2.** a dvandva compound. [Skt, nasalised reduplication of *dva* TWO]

**dwale** /dweɪl/, *n.* the deadly nightshade, *Atropa belladonna.*

**dwarf** /dwɔf/, *n.* **1.** a human being much below the ordinary stature or size; a pygmy. **2.** an animal or plant much below the ordinary size of its kind or species. **3.** *Myth.* a small, manlike being, commonly associated with elves and goblins. *–adj.* **4.** of unusually small stature or size; diminutive. *–v.t.* **5.** to cause to appear or seem small in size, extent, character, etc. **6.** to make dwarf or dwarfish; prevent the due development of. *–v.i.* **7.** to become stunted or smaller. [ME *dwerf,* OE *dweorg,* c. D *dwerg,* G *Zwerg*]

**dwarfish** /ˈdwɔfɪʃ/, *adj.* like a dwarf; below the ordinary stature or size; diminutive. – **dwarfishly,** *adv.* – **dwarfishness,** *n.*

**dwarfism** /ˈdwɔfɪzəm/, *n.* the pathological condition of being a dwarf.

**dwarf mallow** /dwɔf ˈmæloʊ/, *n.* a European herb, *Malva neglecta,* with roundish leaves and small pinkish white flowers.

**dwarf star** /ˈ– sta/, *n.* a star of relatively small volume and low luminosity, but often of high density.

**dwell** /dwɛl/, *v.,* **dwelt** or **dwelled, dwelling,** *n.* *–v.i.* **1.** to abide as a permanent resident. **2.** to continue for a time. **3.** to linger over in thought, speech, or writing; to emphasise (oft. fol. by *on* or *upon*): *to dwell upon a subject, a point in argument.* *–n.* **4.** *Mach.* a pause occurring regularly when a machine is in operation. **5.** a flat part on a cam which, during part of the cycle, keeps a part in a specific position. [ME *dwellen* delay, tarry, abide, OE *dwellan, dwelian* lead astray, hinder, delay, c. Icel. *dvelja*] – **dweller,** *n.*

**dwelling** /ˈdwɛlɪŋ/, *n.* **1.** a place of residence or abode; a house. **2.** continued or habitual residence.

**dwelling house** /ˈ– haʊs/, *n.* a house occupied, or intended to be occupied, as a residence.

**dwelling place** /ˈ– pleɪs/, *n.* a place of residence or abode.

**dwelt** /dwɛlt/, *v.* past tense and past participle of **dwell.**

**dwindle** /ˈdwɪndl/, *v.,* **-dled, -dling.** *–v.i.* **1.** to become smaller and smaller; shrink; waste away: *his vast fortune has dwindled away.* **2.** to fall away, as in quality; degenerate. *–v.t.* **3.** to make smaller and smaller; cause to shrink: *failing health dwindles ambition.* [diminutive of DWINE]

**dwine** /dwaɪn/, *v.i.,* **dwined, dwining.** *Archaic.* to waste away; fade. [OE *dwīnan* languish]

**dwt,** pennyweight. [*d,* for DENARIUS (see def. 2) + *wt* weight]

**Dy,** *Chem.* dysprosium.

**dyad** /ˈdaɪæd/, *n.* **1.** a group of two; a couple. **2.** *Biol.* **a.** a secondary morphological unit, consisting of two monads: *chromosome dyad.* **b.** the double chromosomes resulting from the splitting of a tetrad. **3.** *Chem.* an element, atom, or radical having a valency of two. *–adj.* **4.** dyadic. [LL *dyas,* from Gk: the number two]

**dyadic** /daɪˈædɪk/, *adj.* of two parts; pertaining to the number two.

**dyarchy** /ˈdaɪaki/, *n., pl.* **-chies.** →**diarchy.** – **dyarchic** /daɪˈakɪk/, **dyarchical** /daɪˈakɪkəl/, *adj.*

**dye** /daɪ/, *n., v.,* **dyed, dyeing.** *–n.* **1.** a colouring material or matter. **2.** a liquid containing colouring matter for imparting a particular hue to cloth, etc. **3.** colour or hue, esp. as produced by dyeing. **4. of the deepest** or **blackest dye,** of the worst kind. [ME *die,* OE *dēag*] *–v.t.* **5.** to colour or stain; treat with a dye; colour (cloth, etc.) by soaking in a liquid containing colouring matter: *to dye cloth red.* **6.** to impart (colour) by means of a dye. *–v.i.* **7.** to impart colour, as a dye: *this brand dyes well.* **8.** to become coloured when treated with a dye: *this cloth dyes easily.* [ME *dien,* OE *dēagian*] – **dyer,** *n.*

**dyed-in-the-wool** /ˌdaɪd-ɪn-ðə-ˈwʊl/, *adj.* **1.** dyed before weaving. **2.** through-and-through; complete; inveterate: *a dyed-in-the-wool Liberal.*

**dyeing** /ˈdaɪɪŋ/, *n.* process of colouring fibres, yarns, or fabrics.

**dyeline** /ˈdaɪlaɪn/, *n.* a proof produced by photographic means.

**dyer's greenweed** /daɪəz ˈgrinwid/, *n.* a small shrub, *Genista tinctoria,* with yellow flowers and yielding a yellow dye, widespread in rough grassland in Europe and western Asia.

**dyer's rocket** /– ˈrɒkət/, *n.* a biennial herb, *Reseda luteola,* with long spikes of yellowish or green flowers, widespread in Europe and western Asia and formerly cultivated for a yellow dye it contains.

**dyestuff** /ˈdaɪstʌf/, *n.* a material yielding, or used as, a dye.

**dyewood** /ˈdaɪwʊd/, *n.* any wood yielding a colouring matter used for dyeing.

**dying** /ˈdaɪɪŋ/, *adj.* **1.** ceasing to live; approaching death: *a dying man.* **2.** pertaining to or associated with death: *a dying hour.* **3.** given, uttered, or manifested just before death: *dying words.* **4.** drawing to a close: *the dying year.* *–n.* **5.** death.

**dyke**[1] /daɪk/, *n., v.,* **dyked, dyking,** *adj.* *–n.* **1.** an embankment for restraining the waters of the sea or a river. **2.** a ditch. **3.** a ridge or bank of earth as thrown up in excavating. **4.** a causeway. **5.** an obstacle; barrier. **6.** *Geol.* a tabular body of igneous rock which cuts across the structure of adjacent rocks or cuts massive rocks; formed by intrusion of magma. **7.** *Colloq.* a lavatory. *–v.t.* **8.** to furnish or drain with a dyke. **9.** to enclose, restrain, or protect by a dyke: *to dyke a tract of land.* Also, **dike.** [ME, from Scand.; cf. Icel. *dīk, dīki* ditch; akin to DITCH]

**dyke**[2] /daɪk/, *n. Colloq.* a lesbian. [orig. unknown]

**dyn.,** dyne.

**dyna-,** a word element referring to power, as in *dynameter.* Also, **dynam-.** [Gk, combining form of *dýnamis* power, *dýnasthai* be able]

**dynameter** /daɪˈnæmətə/, *n.* an instrument for determining the magnifying power of telescopes. [DYNA- + -METER[1]; or shortened form of DYNAMOMETER]

**dynamic** /daɪˈnæmɪk/, *adj.* **1.** of or pertaining to force not in equilibrium (opposed to *static*) or to force in any state. **2.** pertaining to dynamics. **3.** pertaining to or characterised by energy or effective action; active; forceful. Also, **dynamical.** [Gk *dynamikós* powerful]

**dynamics** /daɪˈnæmɪks/, *n.* **1.** *Physics.* the branch of mechanics concerned with those forces which cause or affect the motion of bodies. **2.** the science or principles of forces acting in any field. **3.** (*construed as pl.*) the forces, physical or moral, at work in any field. **4.** *Music.* variations in the volume of sound.

**dynamic similarity** /daɪˌnæmɪk sɪməˈlærəti/, *n.* a principle whereby model aeroplanes, ships, and hydraulic structures are operated for test purposes under conditions exactly simulating fullscale performance.

**dynamism** /ˈdaɪnəmɪzəm/, *n.* **1.** the force or active principle on which a thing, person or movement operates. **2.** *Philos.* the doctrine that all things are essentially active.

**dynamite** /ˈdaɪnəmaɪt/, *n., v.,* **-mited, -miting.** *–n.* **1.** a high explosive consisting of nitroglycerine mixed with some absorbent substance such as kieselguhr. **2.** *Colloq.* anything or anyone potentially dangerous and liable to cause trouble. **3.** *Colloq.* anything or anyone exceptional. *–v.t.* **4.** to blow up, shatter, or destroy with dynamite. **5.** to mine or charge with dynamite. – **dynamitic** /daɪnəˈmɪtɪk/, *adj.*

**dynamiter** /ˈdaɪnəmaɪtə/, *n.* one who uses dynamite, esp. for revolutionary purposes. Also, **dynamitist.**

**dynamo** /ˈdaɪnəmoʊ/, *n., pl.* **-mos.** **1.** any rotating machine in which mechanical energy is converted into electrical energy, esp. a direct current generator. **2.** *Colloq.* a forceful, energetic person.

**dynamo-,** variant of **dyna-,** as in *dynamometer.*

**dynamoelectric** /ˌdaɪnəmoʊəˈlɛktrɪk/, *adj.* pertaining to the conversion of mechanical energy into electric energy, or vice versa: *a dynamoelectric machine.* Also, **dynamoelectrical.**

**dynamometer** /daɪnəˈmɒmətə/, *n.* a device for measuring force or power. [DYNAMO + -METER[1]]

**dynamometry** /daɪnəˈmɒmətri/, *n.* the study or practice of the construction or use of dynamometers. – **dynamometric** /ˌdaɪnəmoʊˈmɛtrɪk/, **dynamometrical** /ˌdaɪnəmoʊˈmɛtrɪkəl/, *adj.*

**dynamotor** /ˈdaɪnəmoʊtə/, *n.* a machine which combines both motor and generator action in one magnetic field either with two armatures or with one armature having two separate windings.

**dynast** /ˈdɪnəst, ˈdɪnæst/, *n.* a ruler or potentate, esp. a hereditary ruler. [L *dynastēs,* from Gk: lord, chief]

**dynasty** /ˈdɪnəsti/, *n., pl.* **-ties.** **1.** a sequence of rulers from the same family or stock. **2.** the rule of such a sequence. – **dynastic** /dəˈnæstɪk, daɪ-/, **dynastical** /dəˈnæstɪkəl, daɪ-/, *adj.* – **dynastically** /dəˈnæstɪkli, daɪ-/, *adv.*

**dynatron** /ˈdaɪnətrɒn/, *n.* a radio valve consisting of three electrodes, in which as the plate voltage increases there is a decrease in the plate current because of emission of electrons from the plate. It is frequently used as an oscillator in radio.

**dyne** /daɪn/, *n.* the unit of force in the centimetre-gram-second system, equal to $10 \times 10^{-6}$ newtons. *Symbol:* dyn [F, from Gk *dýnamis* force]

**dys-**, a prefix, esp. medical, indicating difficulty, poor condition, as in *dysphoria.* [Gk: hard, bad, unlucky; akin to Skt *dus-, dur-,* OE *tō-,* HG *zer-*]

**dysarthria** /dɪs'aθriə/, *n.* impairment of articulation due to some dysfunction of the central nervous system. [DYS- + Gk *árthron* joint]

**dyscalculia** /ˌdɪskæl'kjuliə/, *n.* impairment in ability to calculate.

**dysentery** /'dɪsəntri/, *n.* an infectious disease marked by inflammation and ulceration of the lower part of the bowels, with diarrhoea that becomes mucous and haemorrhagic. [L *dysenteria,* from Gk; replacing ME *dissenterie,* from OF] – **dysenteric** /dɪsən'tɛrɪk/, *adj.*

**dysfunction** /dɪs'fʌŋkʃən/, *n.* malfunctioning, as of a structure of the body.

**dysgenic** /dɪs'dʒɛnɪk/, *adj.* pertaining to or causing degeneration in the type of offspring produced (opposed to *eugenic*).

**dysgenics** /dɪs'dʒɛnɪks/, *n.* the study of the operation of factors that cause degeneration in offspring.

**dysgraphia** /dɪs'græfiə/, *n.* impairment in the ability to write.

**dyslalia** /dɪs'leɪliə/, *n.* defective articulation due to faulty learning or structural abnormalities of the speech organs. [NL, from Gk *dys-* DYS- + *lāliá* talking]

**dyslectic** /dɪs'lɛktɪk/, *n.* **1.** one who suffers from dyslexia. *–adj.* **2.** suffering from dyslexia. Also, **dyslexic** /dɪs'lɛksɪk/.

**dyslexia** /dɪs'lɛksiə/, *n.* impairment in reading ability, often associated with other disorders esp. in writing and co-ordination.

**dyslogistic** /dɪslə'dʒɪstɪk/, *adj.* conveying disapproval or censure; opprobrious; not eulogistic. [DYS- + (EU)LOGISTIC] – **dyslogistically,** *adv.*

**dysmenorrhoea** /dɪsˌmɛnə'riə/, *n.* painful menstruation. Also, *Chiefly U.S.,* **dysmenorrhea.**

**dyspareunia** /dɪspə'runiə/, *n.* painful intercourse.

**dyspepsia** /dɪs'pɛpsiə/, *n.* deranged or impaired digestion indigestion (opposed to *eupepsia*). Also, **dyspepsy** /dɪs'pɛpsi/ [L, from Gk]

**dyspeptic** /dɪs'pɛptɪk/, *adj.* **1.** pertaining to, subject to, or suffering from dyspepsia. **2.** morbidly gloomy or pessimistic. *–n.* **3.** a person subject to or suffering from dyspepsia. Also, **dyspeptical.** – **dyspeptically,** *adv.*

**dysphagia** /dɪs'feɪdʒiə/, *n.* difficulty in swallowing – **dysphagic** /dɪs'feɪdʒɪk/, *adj.*

**dysphasia** /dɪs'feɪʒə, -'feɪziə/, *n.* →**aphasia.**

**dysphemia** /dɪs'fimiə/, *n.* disturbance of phonation, articulation or hearing due to psychological disorders. [Gk: ill language]

**dysphemism** /'dɪsfəmɪzəm/, *n.* **1.** the substitution of a harsh, disparaging or offensive expression for a mild or agreeable one (opposed to *euphemism*). **2.** the expression so substituted: *dead meat tickets is a dysphemism for identity discs.*

**dysphonia** /dɪs'founiə/, *n.* disturbance of the normal functioning in the production of sound. [NL, from Gk: roughness of sound] – **dysphonic** /dɪs'fɒnɪk/, *adj.*

**dysphoria** /dɪs'fɔriə/, *n.* a state of dissatisfaction, anxiety, restlessness, or fidgeting. [NL, from Gk: agitation]

**dysplasia** /dɪs'pleɪʒə, -'pleɪziə/, *n.* abnormal development of bodily parts. [NL, from *dys-* DYS- + *-plasia,* from Gk *plásis* a shaping] – **dysplastic** /dɪs'plæstɪk/, *adj.*

**dyspnoea** /dɪsp'niə/, *n.* difficult or laboured breathing (opposed to *eupnoea*). Also, *Chiefly U.S.,* **dyspnea.** [L, from Gk *dýspnoia* difficulty of breathing] – **dyspnoeal, dyspnoeic,** *adj.*

**dysprosium** /dɪs'prousiəm/, *n.* a rare-earth metallic element found in small amounts in certain minerals together with other rare earths. *Symbol:* Dy; *at. wt:* 162.50; *at. no.:* 66. [NL, from Gk *dysprósitos* hard to get at]

**dystocia** /dɪs'toukiə/, *n.* slow or difficult labour or delivery. Also, **dystokia.** [Gk *dystokía*]

**dysuria** /dɪs'juəriə/, *n.* difficult or painful urination. [LL, from Gk *dysouría*]

**Ee** Roman TIMES **Ee** Sans Serif ERAS

Script ALICE

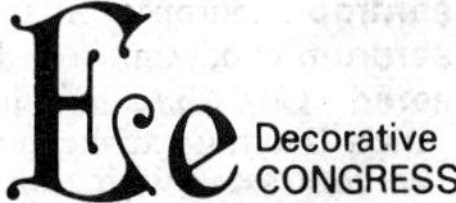
Decorative CONGRESS

*Although there are numerous typefaces in the world they can be divided into four main classifications. These are:*

*ROMAN or SERIF. This typeface came into being from the technique of the Roman masons who, working in stone, finished off each letter with a serif or small stroke projecting from the top or bottom. This was done to correct any feeling of unevenness or imbalance they may have created in cutting the characters in stone.*

*SANS SERIF (without serif). This typeface is geometric in design and has straight-edged characters and lines of a regular thickness.*

*SCRIPT. Based on the movement of the hand, this typeface is often italicised or slanted, as if drawn by a brush or quill pen.*

*DECORATIVE. Any typeface that exaggerates the characteristics of any of the other three classifications to a degree that places it outside of them.*

*The dictionary entries in this book use a SAN SERIF typeface called Helvetica (set in a bold face for the head words) and a SERIF typeface Plantin (used throughout the body of the entries).*

**E, e** /i/, *n., pl.* **E's** or **Es, e's** or **es.** **1.** the fifth letter of the English alphabet. **2.** *Music.* **a.** the third degree in the scale of C major or the fifth in the relative minor scale of A minor. **b.** a written or printed note representing this tone. **c.** a string, key, or pipe, tuned to this note. **d.** (in solmisation) the third note of the scale, called **mi.**

**e,** *Maths.* a transcendental constant equal to 2.718 2818..., used as the base of natural logarithms.

**e-,** variant of **ex-**[1], used in words of Latin origin before consonants except *c, f, p, q, s,* and *t,* as in *emit.*

**E,** **1.** east. **2.** eastern. **3.** English.

**ea.,** each.

**each** /itʃ/, *adj.* **1.** every, of two or more considered individually or one by one: *each stone in the building.* **2. bet each way,** *Colloq.* **a.** to place an each-way bet. **b.** to be undecided or neutral. *–pron.* **3.** each one: *each went his way.* *–adv.* **4.** apiece: *they cost a dollar each.* [ME *ech(e),* etc., OE *ǣlc,* etc., from *ā* ever + *(ge)līc* like, c. OHG *ēo-gilīh*]

**each other** /– ˈʌðə/, *n.* each the other; used to describe a reciprocal relation or action between two or more people, objects, etc.: *they hit each other.*

**each-way** /itʃ-ˈweɪ/, *adj.* (of a bet in horseracing, etc.) staked on a place (second or third) as well as on a win.

**eager** /ˈigə/, *adj.,* **1.** keen or ardent in desire or feeling; impatiently longing: *I am eager for or about it, eager to do it.* **2.** characterised by great earnestness. [ME *egre,* from OF *aigre,* from L *ācer* sharp] – **eagerly,** *adv.* – **eagerness,** *n.*

eagle

**eager beaver** /– ˈbivə/, *n. Colloq.* **1.** a diligent and zealous person. **2.** one over-eager for work.

**eagle** /ˈigəl/, *n.* **1.** any of certain large, diurnal birds of prey of the family Accipitridae, as the wedge-tail eagle, noted for their size, strength, powerful flight and keenness of vision. **2.** *Golf.* a score two below par on any but par-three holes. **3.** a former gold coin of the U.S., of the value of ten dollars, having a figure of an eagle on the reverse. [ME *egle,* from OF, from L *aquila*]

**eagle-eyed** /ˈigəl-aɪd/, *adj.* sharp-sighted.

**eaglehawk** /ˈigəlhɔk/, *n.* **1.** a large brown eagle, *Uroaëtus audax,* with a broad wing-span and a wedge-shaped tail; wedge-tailed eagle. *–v.i.* **2.** to pluck wool from a dead sheep.

**eagle owl** /ˈigəl aʊl/, *n.* a large, rapacious owl, *Bubo bubo,* of Europe.

**eaglet** /ˈiglət/, *n.* a young eagle. [F *aiglette,* diminutive of *aigle* EAGLE]

**eaglewood** /ˈigəlwʊd/, *n.* a tree from India and the Malay Peninsula, *Aquilaria agallocha,* the wood of which yields a resin used as a perfume. [translation of Pg. *pāo d'aguila* wood of agalloch, by confusion with Pg. *águia* eagle. See AGALLOCH]

**eagre** /ˈeɪgə/, *n.* →**bore**[3]. [perhaps from OE *ēagor* flood]

**ear**[1] /ɪə/, *n.* **1.** the organ of hearing, in man and mammals usu. consisting of three parts (**external ear, middle ear,** and **internal ear**). **2.** the external part alone. **3.** the sense of hearing. **4.** nice perception of the differences of sound, esp. sensitiveness to the quality and correctness of musical sounds: *an ear for music.* **5.** attention; heed, esp. favourable attention: *gain a person's ear.* **6.** any object resembling or suggestive of the external ear, as the handle of a pitcher or the part of a bell by which it is hung. **7.** *Journalism.* either of the small spaces or boxes in the upper corners of the front page of a newspaper, containing displayed matter, as an indication of the edition, an advertisement, etc. **8. be all ears,** to listen attentively. **9. bend (someone's) ear,** *Colloq.* to harangue (someone). **10. by ear,** without dependence upon or reference to written music. **11. do on one's ear,** do without difficulty. **12. fall on deaf ears,** to pass unheeded. **13. have an ear to the ground,** to be well informed about gossip or trends. **14. go in one ear and out the other,**

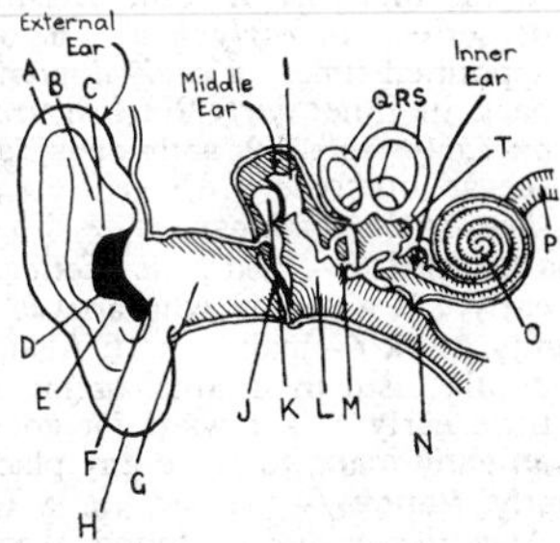


transverse section of a human ear

external ear: A, helix; B, fossa of antihelix; C, antihelix; D, concha; E, antitragus; F, tragus; G, external auditory meatus; H, lobe

middle ear: I, incus; J, tympanic membrane; K, malleus; L, tympanum; M, staples; N, Eustachian tube

inner ear: O, cochlea; P, internal auditory meatus; Q, R, S, anterior, external, posterior, semicircular canals; T, vestibule

to be heard but ignored; to make no impression. **15. out on one's ear,** dismissed summarily. **16. set by the ears,** to cause to disagree or quarrel. **17. turn a deaf ear,** to refuse to help or consider helping. **18. up to one's ears,** deeply involved; extremely busy. **19. wet behind the ears,** naive; immature. [ME *ere,* OE *ēare,* c. G *Ohr;* akin to L *auris,* Gk *oûs*] – **earless,** *adj.* – **earlike,** *adj.*

**ear**[2] /ɪə/, *n.* **1.** that part of a cereal plant, as wheat or barley, which contains the flowers and hence the fruit, grains, or kernels. –*v.i.* **2.** to form or put forth ears. [ME *ere,* OE *ēar,* c. G *Ähre*]

**earache** /ˈɪəreɪk/, *n.* pain in the ear; otalgia.

**earbash** /ˈɪəbæʃ/, *v.t.* **1.** to harangue (someone). –*v.i.* **2.** to talk insistently and for a long time. – **earbasher,** *n.* – **earbashing,** *n.*

**ear canal** /ˈɪə kənæl/, *n.* →**auditory canal.**

**eardrop** /ˈɪədrɒp/, *n.* an earring with a pendant.

**eardrum** /ˈɪədrʌm/, *n.* the tympanic membrane.

**eared** /ɪəd/, *adj.* having ears or earlike appendages, as **eared owls** (having earlike feathers), **eared seals** (having outer ears as contrasted with those which do not).

**ear fish** /ˈɪə fɪʃ/, *n.* →**abalone.**

**earflap** /ˈɪəflæp/, *n.* one of a pair of pieces attached to a cap, for covering the ears in cold weather.

**earful** /ˈɪəfʊl/, *n. Colloq.* **1.** a quantity of oral advice, esp. unsolicited advice. **2.** a stern rebuke, esp. lengthy or abusive.

**earing** /ˈɪərɪŋ/, *n.* a small rope attached to a cringle of a sail and used in reefing, etc. [? EAR[1] + -ING[1]]

**earl** /ɜl/, *n.* a British nobleman ranked immediately below a marquess and immediately above a viscount, the title now being unconnected with territorial jurisdiction. [ME *erl,* OE *eorl* (c. Icel. *jarl* JARL), orig., man, warrior, esp. one of good birth (contrasted with *ceorl* simple freeman, CHURL)]

**earlap** /ˈɪəlæp/, *n.* **1.** earflap. **2.** the lobe of the ear. **3.** the whole external ear.

**earldom** /ˈɜldəm/, *n.* **1.** the rank or title of an earl. **2.** *Obs.* the territory or jurisdiction of an earl. [EARL + -DOM]

**early** /ˈɜli/, *adv.,* **-lier, -liest,** *adj.* –*adv.* **1.** in or during the first part of some division of time, or of some course or series: *early in the year.* **2.** before the usual or appointed time; in good time: *come early.* **3.** far back in time. **4. early on,** after very little time has elapsed; before the main part of a project, game, etc., has been completed. –*adj.* **5.** occurring in the first part of some division of time, or of some course or series: *an early hour.* **6.** occurring before the usual or appointed time: *an early dinner.* **7.** belonging to a period far back in time: *early English architecture.* **8.** occurring soon: *an early reply.* **9. early days,** too soon to form an opinion or see an outcome. [ME *erli,* etc., OE *ærlīce* (from *ær* soon + *-līce* -LY)] – **earliness,** *n.*

**early bird** /ˈ– bɜd/, *n. Colloq.* **1.** a person who gets up early. **2.** a person who arrives before others.

**early mark** /ˈ– mak/, *n.* **1.** Also, **early minutes.** permission for pupils, usu. in infants' or primary school, to leave a class a little early as a reward for good behaviour or work. **2. take an early mark,** to leave any place of work early.

**early Nancy** /– ˈnænsi/, *n.* a wildflower of the lily family, *Anguillaria dioica,* found throughout Australia, the white flower of which has a purple band around the base of each segment, together forming a purple ring; blackman's potatoes.

**early opener** /– ˈoʊpnə/, *n.* a hotel which opens for bar trading before normal hours.

**early warning system,** *n.* a radar system intended to give warning of the approach of hostile bombers or guided missiles.

**earlywood** /ˈɜliwʊd/, *n.* →**springwood.**

**earmark** /ˈɪəmak/, *n.* **1.** a mark of identification made on the ear of an animal. **2.** any identifying or distinguishing mark or characteristic. –*v.t.* **3.** to mark with an earmark. **4.** to set aside for a specific purpose or use: *to earmark goods for export.*

**earmuff** /ˈɪəmʌf/, *n.* one of a pair of adjustable coverings for protecting the ears in cold weather.

**earn** /ɜn/, *v.t.* **1.** to gain by labour or service: *to earn one's living.* **2.** to merit as compensation, as for service; deserve: *to receive more than one has earned.* **3.** to get as one's desert or due: *to earn a reputation for honesty.* **4.** to gain as due return or profit: *defence bonds earn interest.* **5.** to bring or procure as deserved: *fair dealing earns confidence.* –*n.* **6.** *Prison Colloq.* proceeds of a robbery. [ME *ernie(n),* OE *earnian;* akin to OHG *arnēn* earn] – **earner,** *n.*

**earnest**[1] /ˈɜnəst/, *adj.* **1.** serious in intention, purpose, or effort; sincerely zealous: *an earnest worker.* **2.** showing depth and sincerity of feeling: *earnest words.* **3.** having serious importance, or demanding serious attention: *'Life is real! Life is earnest!'* –*n.* **4.** seriousness, as of intention or purpose, as opposed to jest, play, or trifling: *in earnest.* [ME *erneste,* OE *eornost,* c. D and G *ernst*] – **earnestly,** *adv.* – **earnestness,** *n.*

**earnest**[2] /ˈɜnəst/, *n.* **1.** a portion of something, given or done in advance as a pledge of the remainder. **2.** *Law.* earnest money. **3.** anything that gives pledge, promise, assurance, or indication of what is to follow. [ME *ernes,* alteration of earlier *erles* (orig., a pl. form, from OF), apparently by association with suffix *-ness*]

**earnest money** /ˈ– mʌni/, *n.* money given to bind a contract.

**earning** /ˈɜnɪŋ/, *n.* **1.** the act of one who earns. **2.** (*pl.*) money earned; wages; profits. [ME *erning,* OE *earnung*]

**earnings per share,** *n.* a company's net profit divided by the total number of shares in the company, usu. expressed as cents per share. *Abbrev.:* e.p.s.

**earnings yield** /ˈɜnɪŋz jild/, *n.* the fraction calculated by dividing a company's earnings per share by its share price, expressed as a percentage.

**earphone** /ˈɪəfoʊn/, *n.* a small device for converting electric signals into soundwaves, so designed that it is meant to fit into the ear or to be held close to it.

**earpiece** /ˈɪəpis/, *n.* the earphone of a telephone receiver or the like.

**ear-piercing** /ˈɪə-pɪəsɪŋ/, *adj.* **1.** shrill; extremely harsh to the ears. –*n.* **2.** the piercing of the ear lobe to take an earring.

**earplug** /ˈɪəplʌg/, *n.* a piece of soft material, as wax, inserted into the outer ear to keep out water, noise, etc.

**earring** /ˈɪəˌrɪŋ/, *n.* a ring or other ornament worn in or on the lobe of the ear.

**earshot** /ˈɪəʃɒt/, *n.* reach or range of hearing: *within earshot.*

**ear-splitting** /ˈɪə-splɪtɪŋ/, *adj.* shrill; extremely harsh to the ears.

**ear stone** /ˈɪə stoʊn/, *n.* →**otolith.**

**earth** /ɜθ/, *n.* **1.** (*oft. cap.*) the planet which we inhabit, the third in order from the sun. **2.** the inhabitants of this planet: *the whole earth rejoiced.* **3.** this planet as the habitation of man, often in contrast to heaven and hell. **4.** the surface of this planet. **5.** the solid matter of this planet; the dry land; the ground. **6.** the softer part of the land, as distinguished from rock; soil. **7.** the hole of a burrowing animal. **8.** any hole in the ground where a fox seeks shelter when being chased. **9.** *Chem.* any of several metallic oxides which are not easily reduced, as alumina, zirconia, etc. Cf. **alkaline earth** and **rare earth. 10.** *Elect.* **a.** a conducting connection between an electric circuit or equipment and the ground or some similar large conducting body. **b.** the terminal to which the earthing connection is attached. **11. cost the earth,** to cost a great deal. **12. down to earth,** practical; plain; blunt. **13. on earth,** (used as an intensive): *what on earth are you doing?* **14. run to earth, a.** to pursue (an animal) to its burrow or hole. **b.** to hunt down; track down. **15. want the earth,** to have excessive demands or expectations. –*v.t.* **16.** *Elect.* to establish an earth for (a device, circuit, etc.); join (a conductor) to earth. [ME *erthe,* OE *eorthe,* c. G *Erde*]

**earthborn** /ˈɜθbɔn/, *adj.* **1.** born or sprung from the earth; of earthly origin. **2.** mortal.

**earthbound** /ˈɜθbaʊnd/, *adj.* **1.** firmly fixed in the earth. **2.** having only earthly interests. **3.** (of the spirit of a dead person) tied to the earth and their previous existence.

**earth closet** /ˈɜθ klɒzət/, *n.* **1.** a privy in which earth is used as a covering or deodorising agent. **2.** a privy, usu. in rural areas, which is basically a deep hole in the ground.

**earthen** /ˈɜθən/, *adj.* **1.** composed of earth. **2.** made of baked clay.

**earthenware** /ˈɜθənwɛə/, *n.* **1.** earthen pottery; vessels, etc., of baked or hardened clay. **2.** the material of such vessels (usu. the coarse, opaque varieties, the finer, translucent kinds being called *porcelain*).

**earthflow** /ˈɜθfloʊ/, *n.* an avalanche of loose surface material on the ground, made unstable, esp. as a result of heavy rain.

**earthiness** /ˈɜθinəs/, *n.* **1.** earthy nature or properties. **2.** the quality of being down to earth or direct. **3.** coarseness; crudity. **4.** unrefined, straightforward sensuality, esp. sexuality.

**earthlight** /ˈɜθlaɪt/, *n.* →**earthshine.**

**earthling** /ˈɜθlɪŋ/, *n.* **1.** an inhabitant of earth; a mortal. **2.** one attached to earthly or worldly things.

**earth loop** /ˈɜθ lup/, *n.* electronic circuitry which allows two paths to earth instead of one; a source of unwanted hum esp. in audio systems.

**earthly** /ˈɜθli/, *adj.*, **-lier, -liest. 1.** of or pertaining to the earth, esp. as opposed to heaven; worldly. **2.** possible or conceivable: *no earthly use.* **3. not have an earthly,** to have no idea. [ME *erthly,* OE *eorthlīc*] – **earthliness,** *n.*

**earth magnetism** /ɜθ ˈmægnətɪzəm/, *n.* →**terrestrial magnetism.**

**earthman** /ˈɜθmæn/, *n.* a native of the planet earth (used chiefly in science fiction).

**earthmother** /ˈɜθmʌðə/, *n.* **1.** a goddess associated with the earth, considered as the source and spiritual mother of all living things. **2.** *Colloq.* any woman seen to embody attributes as sensuality, generosity and motherly concern.

**earthnut** /ˈɜθnʌt/, *n.* a slender umbelliferous perennial, *Conopodium majus,* with an edible underground tuber, of western Europe; pignut.

**earth pillar** /ˈɜθ pɪlə/, *n.* a column of soft earthy material or rock capped by a stone or boulder which has protected it from complete erosion while adjacent material has been removed.

**earthquake** /ˈɜθkweɪk/, *n.* tremors or earth movements in the earth's crust when fracturing rocks send out a series of three distinct sets of shock waves (earthquake waves).

**earth return** /ˈɜθ rətɜn/, *n.* an electrical path which completes a circuit through the earth, or through a body at the same potential as the earth.

**earth satellite** /– ˈsætəlaɪt/, *n.* **1.** a man-made satellite (def. 5) which orbits the earth. **2.** the moon.

**earth-shaking** /ˈɜθ-ʃeɪkɪŋ/, *adj.* of the greatest importance; tending to cause great upheaval. Also, **earth-shattering.**

**earthshine** /ˈɜθʃaɪn/, *n.* the faint light on the part of the moon not illuminated by the sun, due to the light which the earth reflects on the moon. Also, **earthlight.**

**earthstar** /ˈɜθsta/, *n.* a fungus of the genus *Geaster,* with an outer covering which splits into the form of a star.

**earth station** /ˈɜθ steɪʃən/, *n.* a facility on the surface of the earth for the receipt of messages from satellites.

**earth wax** /ˈɜθ wæks/, *n. Chem.* →**ozokerite.**

**earthwolf** /ˈɜθwʊlf/, *n.* →**aardwolf.**

**earthwork** /ˈɜθwɜk/, *n.* (*usu. pl.*) **1.** the excavating and embanking of earth involved in engineering construction. **2.** a construction formed chiefly of earth, used in military operations. **3.** (*pl.*) →**land art.**

**earthworm** /ˈɜθwɜm/, *n.* **1.** any one of numerous annelid worms that burrow in soil and feed on soil and decaying organic matter. **2.** a mean or grovelling person.

**earthy** /ˈɜθi/, *adj.*, **earthier, earthiest. 1.** of the nature of or consisting of earth or soil. **2.** characteristic of earth: *an earthy smell.* **3.** (of the flavour of a wine) suggestive of the soil in which the grapes were grown. **4.** worldly. **5.** coarse or unrefined. **6.** direct; robust; unaffected. **7.** sensual in a natural way; unashamedly sexual.

**ear trumpet** /ˈɪə trʌmpət/, *n.* a device for collecting and intensifying sounds, held to the ear as an aid in defective hearing.

**earwax** /ˈɪəwæks/, *n.* →**cerumen.**

**earwig** /ˈɪəwɪg/, *n.*, *v.*, **-wigged, -wigging.** –*n.* **1.** any insect of the order Dermaptera, characterised by the forceps or pincers at the end of the abdomen. These harmless insects were popularly supposed to injure the human ear. **2.** *Colloq.* an eavesdropper; stickybeak. –*v.t.* **3.** to fill the mind of (someone) with prejudice by insinuations. –*v.i.* **4.** to eavesdrop. [ME *erwyge,* OE *ēarwicga* ear insect]

**earwitness** /ˈɪəwɪtnəs/, *n.* **1.** one who can give testimony of something heard. –*adj.* **2.** delivered by an earwitness.

**ease** /iz/, *n.*, *v.*, **eased, easing.** –*n.* **1.** freedom from labour, pain, or physical annoyance of any kind; tranquil rest; comfort: *to take one's ease.* **2.** freedom from concern, anxiety, or solicitude; a quiet state of mind: *be at ease.* **3.** freedom from difficulty or great labour; facility: *it can be done with ease.* **4.** freedom from stiffness, constraint, or formality; unaffectedness: *ease of manner, at ease with others.* **5. at ease,** *Mil.* a position of rest in which soldiers may relax, but may not leave their place or talk. –*v.t.* **6.** to give rest or relief to; make comfortable. **7.** to free from anxiety or care: *to ease one's mind.* **8.** to mitigate, lighten, or lessen: *to ease the pain.* **9.** to release from pressure, tension, or the like: *to ease off a rope.* **10.** (in sewing, etc.) to join two pieces of material whose edges are of unequal length in such a way that the extra fullness of the larger section is distributed evenly along the join. **11.** to render less difficult; facilitate. **12.** to move slowly and with great care. **13.** to insert slowly and with care (fol. by *in*). **14.** *Naut.* **a.** to bring (the helm) slowly towards midships. **b.** to give (a ship) leeward helm or trim sails so as to present the bow to a wave. –*v.i.* **15.** to reduce severity, pressure, tension, etc. (oft. fol. by *off* or *up*). **16.** to become less painful or burdensome, etc. **17.** to move with great care (oft. fol. by *along*). **18.** to take one's time over commencing (fol. by *into*). [ME *eise,* from OF *aise,* from LL *adjacens* near]

**easeful** /ˈizfəl/, *adj.* comfortable; quiet; peaceful; restful. – **easefully,** *adv.* – **easefulness,** *n.*

**easel** /ˈizəl/, *n.* a frame in the form of a tripod, for supporting an artist's canvas, a blackboard, or the like. [D *ezel,* c. G *Esel* easel, lit., ass; akin to ASS]

**easement** /ˈizmənt/, *n.* **1.** an easing; relief. **2.** something that gives ease; a convenience. **3.** *Law.* a right held by one person to make use of the land of another.

**easer** /ˈizə/, *n.* one who or that which eases.

**easies** /ˈiziz/, *n. pl. N.Z.* →**step-ins.**

easel

**easily** /ˈizəli/, *adv.* **1.** in an easy manner; with ease; without trouble. **2.** beyond question: *easily the best.* **3.** probably; likely.

**easiness** /ˈizinəs/, *n.* **1.** the quality or condition of being easy. **2.** ease of manner; carelessness; indifference.

**east** /ist/, *n.* **1.** a cardinal point of the compass (90 degrees to the right of north), corresponding to the point where the sun is seen to rise. **2.** the direction in which this point lies. **3.** (*l.c. or cap.*) a quarter or territory situated in this direction. **4. the East, a.** the parts of Asia collectively (as lying east of Europe) where civilisation has existed from early times, including Asia Minor, Syria, Arabia, India, China, etc.; the Orient. **b.** eastern Australia. –*adj.* **5.** directed or proceeding towards the east: *the east route.* **6.** coming from the east: *an east wind.* **7.** lying towards or situated in the east: *the east side.* **8.** *Eccles.* towards the altar as situated with respect to the nave. –*adv.* **9.** towards or in the east: *he went east.* **10.** from the east. [ME *est,* OE *ēast,* c. MHG *ōst,* G *Osten,* n. See EASTER]

**eastbound** /ˈistbaʊnd/, *adj.* travelling towards the east.

**east by north,** *n.* 11°15′ (one point) north of east; 78° 45′ from due north. *Abbrev.:* E by N

**east by south,** *n.* 11° 15′ (one point) south of east; 101° 15′ from due south. *Abbrev.:* E by S

**Easter** /ˈistə/, *n.* **1.** an annual Christian festival in commemoration of the resurrection of Jesus Christ, observed on the first Sunday after the full moon that occurs on or next after 21 March. **2.** Also, **Easter Day, Easter Sunday.** the day on which this festival is celebrated. [ME *ester,* OE *ēastre,* pl. *ēastron* (c. G *Ostern,* pl.), orig., name of goddess; akin to L *aurōra* dawn, Gk *eōs.* Cf. EAST]

**Easter egg** /ˈistər ɛg/, *n.* a coloured egg, or chocolate imitation of one, used at Easter as a gift or decoration.

**easterly** /ˈistəli/, *adj.* **1.** moving, directed, or situated towards the east: *an easterly course.* **2.** coming from the east: *an* *easterly wind.* *–adv.* **3.** towards the east. **4.** from the east.

**eastern** /ˈistən/, *adj.* **1.** lying towards or situated in the east: *the eastern seaboard.* **2.** directed or proceeding towards the east: *an eastern route.* **3.** coming from the east: *an eastern wind.* **4.** (*usu. cap.*) of or pertaining to the East: *the Eastern Church.* **5.** (*sometimes cap.*) oriental. [ME *esterne,* OE *ēasterne*]

**eastern brush wallaby,** *n.* →**red wallaby.**

**Eastern Church** /ˈistən tʃɜtʃ/, *n.* **1.** the Christian Church of the countries formerly comprising the Eastern Roman Empire, the eastern division of the Roman Empire, and, after A.D. 476, the Roman Empire with its capital at Constantinople. **2.** any body of Christians owing allegiance to the Orthodox Church and observing the Greek rite rather than the Roman.

**eastern curlew** /istən ˈkɜlju/, *n.* a large curlew, *Numenius madagascariensis,* which flies from Siberia to Australia in August and September, and returns about April; while in Australia it lives on estuaries, mud flats and sandy beaches on the eastern coast.

**easterner** /ˈistənə/, *n.* (*oft. cap.*) a native or inhabitant of an eastern area.

**eastern grip** /ˈistən grɪp/, *n.* a grip used to hold the racquet in a forehand shot with the palm behind the handle. Also, **handshake grip.**

**Eastern Hemisphere** /istən ˈhɛməsfɪə/, *n.* the part of the world lying east of the Greenwich Meridian, including Asia, Africa, Australia, and Europe.

**easternmost** /ˈistənmoʊst/, *adj.* farthest east.

**eastern spinebill** /istən ˈspaɪnbɪl/, *n.* a small eastern Australian nectar-feeding bird, *Acanthorhynchus tenuirostris,* with a long, slender, downward curving bill; cobbler's awl.

**Eastern Standard Time,** *n.* a time zone lying on the 150th meridian including Queensland, New South Wales, Victoria and Tasmania, ten hours ahead of *Greenwich Mean Time* and a half-hour ahead of *Central Standard Time* and two hours ahead of *Western Standard Time.*

**Eastern Stater** /istən ˈsteɪtə/, *n. W.A.* (*usu. pejor.*) a person who comes from any of the eastern States of Australia.

**Eastern States** /istən ˈsteɪts/, *n.pl. W.A.* those states of Australia which are east of the Nullabor desert, esp. South Australia, Victoria and New South Wales.

**Eastertide** /ˈistətaɪd/, *n.* **1.** Easter time. **2.** the week ushered in by and following Easter. **3.** the fifty days between Easter and Whitsuntide.

**East Germany** /ist ˈdʒɜməni/, *n.* a country in central Europe, formed after World War II as the Soviet zone of occupation. Official name: **German Democratic Republic.**

**easting** /ˈistɪŋ/, *n.* **1.** the difference in longitude between two positions on a map as a result of progress to the east. **2.** progress in an easterly direction. **3.** the east coordinate which together with the northing identifies a position on a map.

**east-north-east** /ist-nɔθ-ˈist/, *n.* **1.** the point of the compass midway between east and north-east; 67° 30′ from north. *–adj.* **2.** lying or situated in this direction. *–adv.* **3.** to, in, or from this direction. *Abbrev.:* ENE Also, *esp. Naut.,* **east-nor'-east** /ist-nɔ-ˈist/.

**east-south-east** /ist-saʊθ-ˈist/, *n.* **1.** the point of the compass midway between east and south-east; 112° 30′ from north. *–adj.* **2.** lying or situated in this direction. *–adv.* **3.** to, in, or from this direction. *Abbrev.:* ESE Also, *esp. Naut.,* **east-sou'-east** /ist-saʊ-ˈist/.

**eastward** /ˈistwəd/, *adj.* **1.** moving, bearing, facing, or situated towards the east. *–adv.* **2.** eastwards.

**eastwardly** /ˈistwədli/, *adj.* **1.** having an eastward direction or situation. **2.** coming from the east: *an eastwardly wind.* *–adv.* **3.** towards the east. **4.** from the east.

**eastwards** /ˈistwədz/, *adv.* towards the east. Also, **eastward.**

**easy** /ˈizi/, *adj.,* **easier, easiest,** *adv., v.,* **easied, easying.** *–adj.* **1.** not difficult; requiring no great labour or effort: *easy to read, an easy victory.* **2.** free from pain, discomfort, worry, or care: *he is resting easier this morning, easy in one's mind.* **3.** conducive to ease or comfort: *an easy stance.* **4.** fond of or given to ease; easygoing. **5.** not harsh or strict; lenient: *an easy master.* **6.** not burdensome or oppressive: *easy terms.* **7.** not difficult to influence; compliant. **8.** *Colloq.* having no firm preferences in a particular matter: *I'm easy.* **9.** free from formality, constraint, or embarrassment: *easy style; easy manners.* **10.** not tight; fitting loosely: *an easy fit.* **11.** not forced or hurried; moderate: *an easy pace.* **12.** *Comm.* **a.** (of a commodity) not difficult to obtain; in plentiful supply and (often) weak in price. **b.** (of the market) not characterised by eager demand. **13. easy on the eyes,** attractive; good looking. **14. on easy street,** with plenty of money; in a comfortable financial position. *–adv.* **15.** *Colloq.* in an easy manner; comfortably: *take it easy.* **16. go easy on,** *Colloq.* **a.** to be lenient with. **b.** to use sparingly: *go easy on the honey.* **17. go easy with,** *Colloq.* to handle carefully: *go easy with that valuable jar.* *–v.t.* **18.** *Rowing.* stop the motion of (the oars). *–v.i.* **19.** *Rowing.* to stop rowing. [ME *aisie,* from OF, pp. of *aisier* EASE, *v.*]

**easychair** /ˈizitʃɛə/, *n.* an armchair in which to relax at ease.

**easygoing** /ˈizigoʊɪŋ/, *adj.* **1.** taking matters in an easy way; comfortably unconcerned. **2.** going easily, as a horse.

**easy rider** /izi ˈraɪdə/, *n. Colloq.* **1.** *U.S.* a lover who is sexually satisfying. **2.** *U.S.* a guitar. **3.** an easyrider motorbike.

**easyrider** /ˈiziraɪdə/, *adj.* of or pertaining to a motorbike with a seat sloping up at the back and large enough to seat two people.

**easy wicket** /izi ˈwɪkət/, *n.* **1.** *Cricket.* a pitch of slow pace which favours the batsman. **2.** *Colloq.* an easy task; a comfortable position in life: *the manager is on an easy wicket here.*

**eat** /it/, *v.,* **ate** /eɪt, ɛt/, or (*Archaic*) **eat; eaten** /ˈitn/ or (*Archaic*) **eat** /ɛt, it/; **eating;** *n.* *–v.t.* **1.** to take into the mouth and swallow for nourishment; esp. to masticate and swallow, as solid food. **2.** to consume by or as by devouring. **3.** to ravage or devastate. **4.** to wear or waste away; corrode. **5.** to make (a hole, passage, etc.) as by gnawing or corrosion. **6.** *Colloq.* to cause to worry; trouble: *what's eating you?* **7. eat one's heart out,** to pine. **8. eat one's words,** to take back what one has said. *–v.i.* **9.** to consume food; take a meal. **10.** to make a way as by gnawing or corrosion. **11.** to be eatable; taste: *these pears eat well.* **12.** *Colloq.* to perform fellatio or cunnilingus with. **13. eat fit to bust,** to eat with good appetite. **14. eat out,** to dine out of one's home at a restaurant, club, hotel, etc. **15. eat out of someone's hand,** to be uncritically compliant and trusting, often in a servile or sycophantic manner. *–n.* **16.** (*pl.*) *Colloq.* food. [ME *eten,* OE *etan,* c. G *essen,* akin to L *edere,* Gk *édein*]

**eatable** /ˈitəbəl/, *adj.* **1.** edible. *–n.* **2.** (*usu. pl.*) an article of food.

**eater** /ˈitə/, *n.* **1.** one who or that which eats. **2.** *Colloq.* a fruit suitable for eating, esp. raw.

**eatery** /ˈitəri/, *n. Colloq.* an eating house.

**eating** /ˈitɪŋ/, *n.* **1.** the act of one who or that which eats. **2.** food with reference to the quality perceived when eaten: *this fish is delicious eating.* *–adj.* **3.** suitable to be eaten, esp. raw.

**eating house** /ˈ– haʊs/, *n.* a cafe or restaurant, esp. a cheap one.

**eating irons** /ˈ– aɪənz/, *n. pl. Colloq.* eating utensils.

**eau de Cologne** /oʊ də kəˈloʊn/, *n.* cologne. [Trademark]

**eau de Nil** /oʊ də ˈnil/, *n.* a dull green colour. [F: lit., water of the Nile]

**eau de vie** /oʊ də ˈvi/, *n.* brandy, esp. the coarser and less purified varieties. [F: lit., water of life]

**eaves** /ivz/, *n. pl.* the overhanging lower edge of a roof. [ME *eves,* OE *efes,* c. OHG *obisa* hall]

**eavesdrop** /ˈivzdrɒp/, *v.i.,* **-dropped, -dropping.** to listen clandestinely. [lit., be on the *eavesdrop* (of a house), earlier *eavesdrip* ground on which falls the drip from the eaves, OE *yfesdrype*] – **eavesdropper,** *n.*

eaves

**ebb** /ɛb/, *n.* **1.** the reflux or falling of the tide (opposed to *flood* and *flow*). **2.** a flowing backwards or away; decline or decay. **3.** a point of decline: *his fortunes were at a low ebb.* *–v.i.* **4.** to flow back or away, as the water of a tide (opposed to *flow*). **5.** to decline or decay; waste or fade away: *his life is ebbing.* [ME *ebbe,* OE *ebba,* c. D *ebbe, eb*]

**ebb tide** /'– taɪd/, *n.* the reflux of the tide; the retiring tide.

**E-boat** /'i-boʊt/, *n.* a very fast unarmoured motor boat armed with torpedoes and guns. [short for *enemy boat*]

**ebon** /'ɛbən/, *Poetic.* –*n.* **1.** →**ebony.** –*adj.* **2.** made of ebony.

**ebonise** /'ɛbənaɪz/, *v.t.,* **-nised, -nising.** to stain or finish in imitation of ebony. Also, **ebonize.**

**ebonist** /'ɛbənəst/, *n.* a worker in ebony.

**ebonite** /'ɛbənaɪt/, *n.* →**vulcanite.** [EBON(Y) + -ITE[1]]

**ebony** /'ɛbəni/, *n., pl.* **-onies,** *adj.* –*n.* **1.** a hard, heavy durable wood, most highly prized when black, from various tropical trees of the genus *Diospyros,* as *D. ebenum* of southern India and Ceylon, used for cabinetwork, etc., and *Maba humilis* of Queensland used for musical instruments. **2.** any tree yielding such wood. **3.** any of various similar woods or trees. –*adj.* **4.** made of ebony. **5.** like ebony; black. Also, *Poetic,* **ebon.** [ME *hebenyf,* irregularly from L *hebeninus,* from Gk *ebéninos* made of ebony]

**ebracteate** /ə'bræktiɛɪt, -tiət/, *adj.* without bracts.

**ebracteolate** /ə'bræktiəleɪt, -lət/, *adj.* without bracteoles.

**ebriety** /ə'braɪəti/, *n.* the habit or state of drunkenness.

**ebullience** /ə'bʊljəns, ə'bʌl-, ə'bjul-/, *n.* **1.** a boiling over; overflow. **2.** fervour; enthusiasm; excitement. Also, **ebulliency.**

**ebullient** /ə'bʊljənt, ə'bʌl-, ə'bjul-/, *adj.* **1.** seething or overflowing with fervour, enthusiasm, excitement, etc. **2.** boiling; bubbling like a boiling liquid. [L *ēbulliens,* ppr., boiling out or up] – **ebulliently,** *adv.*

**ebullioscopy** /əˌbʊli'ɒskəpi/, *n.* the method of determining the molecular weight of a substance by observing the boiling point of a solvent in which it is dissolved.

**ebullition** /ɛbə'lɪʃən/, *n.* **1.** a seething or overflowing, as of passion or feeling; an outburst: *ebullition of feeling.* **2.** an ebullient state. **3.** the act or process of boiling. **4.** a rushing forth of water, lava, etc., in a state of agitation. [L *ēbullītio*]

**eburnation** /ibə'neɪʃən, ɛbə-/, *n.* a morbid change in a tooth or bone, by which it becomes very hard and dense, like ivory. [L *eburnus* of ivory + -ATION]

**eburnean** /ə'bɜniən/, *adj.* of or like ivory.

**ec-,** variant of **ex-**[3], before consonants, as in *eccentric.*

**ecad** /'ikæd, 'ɛkæd/, *n.* **1.** a habitat form of an organism showing characteristics which are imposed by habitat conditions and are non-heritable. Cf. **variety. 2.** an acquired characteristic.

**écarté** /eɪ'kateɪ/, *n.* a game at cards for two persons. [F, properly pp. of *écarter* discard]

**ecbolic** /ɛk'bɒlɪk/, *adj.* promoting labour; oxytocic.

**eccentric** /ək'sɛntrɪk/, *adj.* **1.** deviating from the recognised or usual character, practice, etc.; irregular; peculiar; odd; queer: *eccentric conduct, an eccentric person.* **2.** not having the same centre, as two circles or spheres of which one is within the other or which intersect; not concentric. **3.** not situated in the centre, as an axis. **4.** *Mach.* having the axis or support away from the centre, as a wheel. **5.** *Astron.* deviating from a circular form, as an orbit. –*n.* **6.** one who or that which is unusual, peculiar, odd. **7.** *Mach.* a device for converting circular into reciprocating rectilinear motion, consisting of a disc fixed somewhat out of centre to a revolving shaft, and working freely in a surrounding collar (**eccentric strap**), to which a rod (**eccentric rod**) is attached. **8.** *Astron.* in the Ptolemaic system, the circle on which the sun moves about the earth which is slightly off centre. [LL *eccentricus,* from Gk *ékkentros* out of the centre] – **eccentrically,** *adv.*

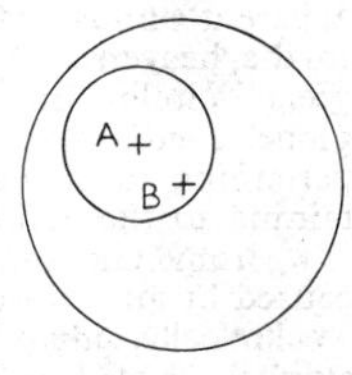

eccentric circles: A, centre of small circle; B, centre of large circle

**eccentricity** /ɛksən'trɪsəti/, *n., pl.* **-ties. 1.** an oddity or peculiarity, as of conduct. **2.** the quality of being eccentric. **3.** the amount by which anything is eccentric. **4.** *Mach.* the throw of an eccentric. **5.** *Maths.* the ratio of the distance from a point on a conic to a focus and the distance from that point to a directrix.

**ecchymosis** /ɛkə'moʊsəs/, *n., pl.* **-ses** /-siz/. a discolouration due to extravasation of blood, as in a bruise. [NL, from Gk *ekchýmōsis,* from *ekchymoûsthai* extravasate blood] – **ecchymosed** /'ɛkəmoʊzd, -moʊst/, **ecchymotic** /ɛkə'mɒtɪk/, *adj.*

**Eccl.,** *Bible.* Ecclesiastes. Also, **Eccles.**

**eccles.,** ecclesiastical. Also, **eccl.**

**ecclesia** /ə'kliziə/, *n., pl.* **-siae** /-zii/. **1.** an assembly, esp. the popular assembly of ancient Athens. **2.** a congregation; a church. [L: assembly of the people, LL church, from Gk *ekklēsía*]

**ecclesiarch** /ə'kliziak/, *n.* **1.** a prince of the church, esp. in the Eastern Roman Empire. **2.** *Orthodox Church.* a sacristan.

**ecclesiast** /ə'kliziæst/, *n. Archaic.* an ecclesiastic.

**ecclesiastic** /əklizi'æstɪk/, *n.* **1.** a clergyman, or person in orders. –*adj.* **2.** ecclesiastical. [LL *ecclēsiasticus,* from Gk *ekklēsiastikós* of the assembly or church]

**ecclesiastical** /əklizi'æstəkəl/, *adj.* of or pertaining to the church or the clergy; churchly; clerical; not secular; not lay: *ecclesiastical discipline, affairs, ecclesiastical courts.* – **ecclesiastically,** *adv.*

**ecclesiasticism** /əˌklizi'æstəsɪzəm/, *n.* **1.** ecclesiastical principles, practices, or spirit. **2.** devotion to the principles or interests of the church.

**ecclesiolatry** /əklizi'ɒlətri/, *n.* worship of the church; excessive reverence for churchly forms and traditions. [ECCLESI(A) + -(O)LATRY]

**ecclesiology** /əklizi'ɒlədʒi/, *n.* **1.** the science of church architecture and decoration. **2.** the study of church history and doctrine. [ECCLESI(A) + -O- + -LOGY] – **ecclesiologic** /əkliziə'lɒdʒɪk/, **ecclesiological** /əkliziə'lɒdʒɪkəl/, *adj.* – **ecclesiologist,** *n.*

**eccrinology** /ɛkrə'nɒlədʒi/, *n.* the branch of physiology relating to secretions.

**eccrisis** /'ɛkrəsəs/, *n.* the expulsion of waste matter from the body.

**eccritic** /ɛ'krɪtɪk/, *adj.* **1.** having the property of expelling waste matter. –*n.* **2.** something, as a medicine, that causes eccrisis.

**ecdemic** /ɛk'dɛmɪk/, *adj.* denoting or pertaining to a disease that originates outside the area in which it occurs (opposed to *epidemic* and *endemic*).

**ecdysis** /'ɛkdəsəs/, *n., pl.* **-ses** /-siz/. the shedding or casting off of an outer coat or integument by snakes, crustaceans, etc. [NL, from Gk *ékdysis* a getting out]

**ecdysone** /ɛk'daɪsoʊn/, *n.* the steroid hormone causing ecdysis in crustaceans and insects.

**ecesis** /ə'sisəs/, *n.* the establishment of an immigrant plant in a new environment. [NL, from Gk *oíkēsis* an inhabiting] – **ecesic,** *adj.*

**ECG** /i si 'gi/, **1.** electrocardiogram. **2.** electrocardiograph.

**echelon** /'ɛʃəlɒn/, *n.* **1.** a level of command: *in the higher echelons.* **2.** a formation of troops, ships, aeroplanes, etc., in which groups are disposed in parallel lines, each to the right or left of the one in front, so that the whole presents the appearance of steps. **3.** one of the groups of a command so disposed. **4.** any steplike formation, esp. of people in movement. **5.** Also, **echelon grating.** *Physics.* a type of diffraction grating used in spectroscopy when high resolution is required, consisting of a series of plates of equal thickness arranged in stepwise formation with a constant offset. –*v.t., v.i.* **6.** to form in echelon. [F: lit., ladder rung, from *échelle* ladder, from L *scāla* SCALE[3]]

**echidna** /ə'kɪdnə/, *n., pl.* **-nas, -nae** /-ni/. any of the spine-covered insectivorous monotreme mammals with claws and a slender snout, occurring in two genera, the curved-beaked echidna, *Zaglossus* (or *Proechidna*), of New Guinea, and the smaller, straight-beaked echidna, *Tachyglossus,* represented by several species in Australia, Tasmania, and southern New Guinea; spiny anteater. [NL, from Gk: viper]

echidna

**echinate** /ˈɛkəneɪt/, *adj.* spiny; bristly. Also, **echinated.**

**echinococcosis** /ˌɛkənoʊkɒˈkoʊsəs/, *n.* infestation of man with the tapeworm, *Echinococcus granulosus,* in its larval or hydatid stage.

**echinoderm** /əˈkaɪnədɜm, əˈkɪnə-/, *n.* any of the Echinodermata, a phylum of marine animals such as starfishes, sea-urchins, sea-cucumbers, etc., having a radiating arrangement of parts and a body wall stiffened by calcareous pieces that may protrude as spines. [NL *Echinodermata.* See ECHINUS, -DERM]

**echinodermatous** /əkaɪnoʊˈdɜmətəs/, *adj.* belonging to or pertaining to the echinoderms.

**echinoid** /əˈkaɪnɔɪd, ˈɛkənɔɪd/, *adj.* **1.** belonging to the Echinoidea, a class of echinoderms of rounded form covered with projecting spines, including the sea-urchins, etc. **2.** resembling a sea-urchin. *–n.* **3.** one of the Echinoidea; a sea-urchin. [ECHIN(US) + -OID]

**echinus** /əˈkaɪnəs/, *n., pl.* **-ni** -/naɪ/. **1.** a sea-urchin of the genus *Echinus.* **2.** *Archit.* a rounded moulding, as that supporting the abacus of a Doric capital. [L, from Gk *echînos,* orig., hedgehog]

**echo** /ˈɛkoʊ/, *n., pl.* **echoes,** *v.,* **echoed, echoing.** *–n.* **1.** a repetition of sound, produced by the reflection of soundwaves from an obstructing surface. **2.** a sound heard again near its source, after reflection. **3.** any repetition or close imitation, as of the ideas or opinions of another. **4.** one who reflects or imitates another. **5.** a sympathetic response, as to sentiments expressed. **6.** *Music.* **a.** a part **(echo organ)** or stop **(echo stop)** of a large organ for the production of echo-like effects. **b.** the manual controlling this. **7.** *Cards.* (esp. in bridge or whist) a signal, as by a card played, to a partner that the player wishes the suit continued. **8.** *Electronics.* the reflection of a radio wave such as is used in radar or the like. *–v.i.* **9.** to emit an echo; resound with an echo. **10.** to be repeated by or as by an echo. *–v.t.* **11.** to repeat by or as by an echo; emit an echo of: *the hall echoes even faint sounds.* **12.** to repeat or imitate the words, sentiments, etc., of (a person). **13.** to repeat or imitate (words, sentiments, etc.). [L, from Gk: sound, echo; in classical mythology personified as the mountain nymph who pined away for love of Narcissus until only her voice remained] **–echoer,** *n.* **–echoless,** *adj.* **–echolike,** *adj.*

**echo chamber** /ˈ– tʃeɪmbə/, *n.* a room with sound-reflective walls, or a device, for creating echoes; used in sound recording, etc.

**echoic** /ɛˈkoʊɪk/, *adj.* **1.** echo-like. **2.** →**onomatopoeic.**

**echoism** /ˈɛkoʊɪzəm/, *n.* →**onomatopoeia.**

**echolalia** /ɛkoʊˈleɪliə/, *n.* an immediate, involuntary, and senseless repetition of words heard, occurring in some types of mental derangement. **–echolalic** /ɛkoʊˈlælɪk/, *adj.*

**echolocation** /ˌɛkoʊloʊˈkeɪʃən/, *n.* the general method of locating objects by determining the time for an echo to return and the direction from which it returns, either by radar or by sonar.

**echopraxia** /ɛkoʊˈpræksiə/, *n.* an immediate, involuntary, and senseless repetition of the movements of others, occurring in some types of mental derangement. Also, **echopraxis** /ɛkoʊˈpræksəs/. **–echopractic** /ɛkoʊˈpræktɪk/, *adj.*

**echo ranging** /ˈɛkoʊ reɪndʒɪŋ/, *n.* a method of locating solid underwater objects by measuring the time required for the echo of a pulse of soundwaves to return to the point of observation.

**echoscope** /ˈɛkoʊskoʊp/, *n.* a machine which uses high frequency sound waves in order to visualise internal organs of the body.

**echo sounder** /ˈɛkoʊ saʊndə/, *n.* a device for measuring the depth of water below a ship by observing the time taken for a pulse of soundwaves to reach the seabed and for its echo to return; sonar.

**echo sounding** /ˈ– saʊndɪŋ/, *n.* **1.** a method of measuring the depth of water below a ship by the use of an echo sounder. **2.** a measurement so obtained.

**echo unit** /ˈ– junət/, *n.* an electronic device which repeats an audio signal after a short and usu. programmable interval, thus producing an echo effect.

**ECHO virus** /ˈɛkoʊ vaɪrəs/, *n.* a strain of viruses which are transient inhabitants of the alimentary canal, some of which cause diseases, as aseptic meningitis. [E(*nteric*) C(*ytopathic*) H(*uman*) O(*rphan*)]

**eclair** /eɪˈklɛə, ə-/, *n.* a light, finger-shaped cake made of choux pastry, filled with cream or custard, and coated with (usu. chocolate) icing. Also, **éclair.** [F: lit., lightning, from *éclairer* lighten. Cf. L *exclārāre*]

**eclampsia** /əˈklæmpsiə/, *n.* a form of convulsions, esp. of a recurrent nature, as during pregnancy or parturition. [NL, from Gk *eklámpein* shine forth] **–eclamptic,** *adj.*

**eclat** /eɪˈkla/, *n.* **1.** brilliance of success, reputation, etc.: *the eclat of a great achievement.* **2.** ostentatious or elaborate display. **3.** applause; acclaim. Also, **éclat.** [F: fragment, also burst (of light, etc.)]

**eclectic** /ɛˈklɛktɪk/, *adj.* **1.** selecting; choosing from various sources. **2.** made up of what is selected from diverse sources. **3.** not following any one system, as of philosophy, medicine, etc., but selecting and using whatever is considered best in all systems. *–n.* **4.** one who follows an eclectic method, as in philosophy. [Gk *eklektikós* selective] **–eclectically,** *adv.*

**eclecticism** /ɛˈklɛktəsɪzəm/, *n.* **1.** the use or advocacy of an eclectic method. **2.** an eclectic system.

**eclipse** /əˈklɪps, i-/, *n., v.,* **eclipsed, eclipsing.** *–n.* **1.** *Astron.* **a.** the obscuration of the light of a satellite by the intervention of its primary planet between it and the sun, as in a **lunar eclipse** when the moon is partially or wholly within the earth's shadow. **b. solar eclipse,** the interception of the light of the sun by the intervention of the moon between it and the observer. **c.** (in an eclipsing binary system) the partial or complete interception of the light of one component by the other. **2.** any obscuration of light. **3.** any obscuration or overshadowing; loss of brilliance or splendour. *–v.t.* **4.** to cause to suffer eclipse: *the moon eclipses the sun.* **5.** to cast a shadow upon; obscure; darken. **6.** to make dim by comparison; surpass. [ME, from OF, from L *eclīpsis,* from Gk *ékleipsis,* lit., a failing] **–eclipser,** *n.*

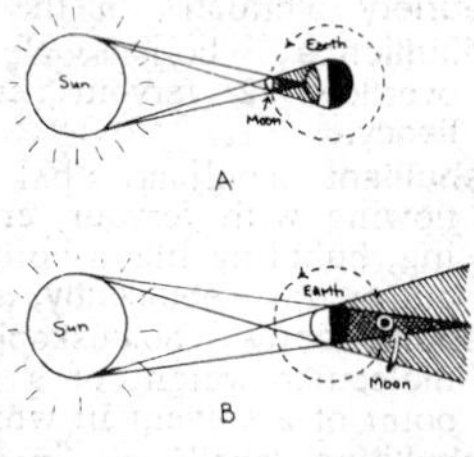


A, solar eclipse; B, lunar eclipse

**eclipsing variable** /əklɪpsɪŋ ˈvɛəriəbəl/, *n.* a variable star whose changes in brightness are caused by periodic eclipses of two stars in a binary system.

**ecliptic** /əˈklɪptɪk, i-/, *n.* **1.** the great circle formed by the intersection of the plane of the earth's orbit with the celestial sphere; the apparent annual path of the sun in the heavens. **2.** an analogous great circle on a terrestrial globe. *–adj.* Also, **ecliptical. 3.** pertaining to an eclipse. **4.** pertaining to the ecliptic. [L *eclipticus,* from Gk *ekleiptikós* of or caused by an eclipse. See ECLIPSE] **–ecliptically,** *adv.*

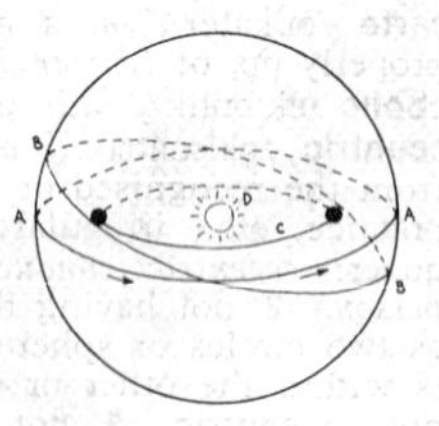


diagram of ecliptic: A, ecliptic; B, celestial equator; C, orbit of earth; D, sun

**eclogite** /ˈɛklədʒaɪt/, *n.* a rock consisting of granular aggregate of green pyroxene and red garnet, often also containing kyanite, silvery mica, quartz, and pyrite. [Gk *eklogḗ* selection + -ITE[1]]

**eclogue** /ˈɛklɒg/, *n.* a short poem, esp. pastoral or idyllic. [L *ecloga,* from Gk *eklogḗ* a selection]

**eco-freak** /ˈikoʊ-frik, ˈɛk-/, *n. Chiefly U.S.* →**eco-nut.**

**ecol.,** ecology.

**ecology** /əˈkɒlədʒi/, *n.* **1.** the branch of biology which treats of the relations between organisms and their environment; bionomics. **2.** the branch of sociology concerned with the spacing of people and of institutions and their resulting interdependence. [Gk *oîko(s)* house + -LOGY] **–ecological** /ikəˈlɒdʒɪkəl/, **ecologic** /ikəˈlɒdʒɪk/, *adj.* **–ecologically** /ikəˈlɒdʒɪkli/, *adv.* **–ecologist,** *n.*

**econ.,** **1.** economic. **2.** economics. **3.** economy.

**econometrics** /əkɒnəˈmɛtrɪks, ikɒn-/, *n.* the analysis by statistical and mathematical methods of economic data, theories, etc. –**econometric, econometrical,** *adj.* –**econometrician** /əkɒnəməˈtrɪʃən/, **econometrist,** *n.*

**economic** /ɛkəˈnɒmɪk, ikə-/, *adj.* **1.** pertaining to the production, distribution, and use of income and wealth. **2.** of or pertaining to the science of economics. **3.** pertaining to an economy, or system of organisation or operation, esp. of the process of production. **4.** pertaining to the means of living; utilitarian: *economic entomology, botany, etc.* **5.** *Colloq.* economical. **6.** *Colloq.* cheap. [L *oeconomicus,* from Gk *oikonomikós,* from *oikonomía.* See ECONOMY]

**economical** /ɛkəˈnɒmɪkəl, ikə-/, *adj.* **1.** avoiding waste or extravagance; thrifty. **2.** economic.

**economically** /ɛkəˈnɒmɪkli, ikə-/, *adv.* **1.** with economy; with frugality or moderation. **2.** as regards the efficient use of income and wealth.

**economics** /ɛkəˈnɒmɪks, ikə-/, *n.* **1.** the science treating of the production, distribution, and consumption of goods and services, or the material welfare of mankind; political economy. **2.** (*construed as pl.*) economically significant aspects.

**economise** /əˈkɒnəmaɪz/, *v.,* **-mised, -mising.** –*v.t.* **1.** to manage economically; use sparingly or frugally. –*v.i.* **2.** to practise economy; avoid waste or extravagance. Also, **economize.** –**economisation** /əˌkɒnəmaɪˈzeɪʃən/, *n.* –**economiser,** *n.*

**economist** /əˈkɒnəməst/, *n.* **1.** one versed in the science of economics. **2.** an economical person.

**economy** /əˈkɒnəmi/, *n., pl.* **-mies. 1.** thrifty management; frugality in the expenditure or consumption of money, materials, etc. **2.** an act or means of thrifty saving; a saving. **3.** the management, or science of management, of the resources of a community, etc., with a view to productiveness and avoidance of waste: *national economy.* **4.** the disposition or regulation of the parts or functions of any organic whole; an organised system or method. **5.** the efficient, sparing, and concise use of something: *economy of effort.* **6.** *Theol.* **a.** the divine plan for man, his creation, redemption, and final beatitude. **b.** the method of divine administration, as at a particular time or for a particular race. **7.** *Archaic.* the management of household affairs. [L *oeconomia,* from Gk *oikonomía* management of a household or of the state]

**economy class** /ˈ– klas/, *n.* **1.** a type of lower-priced accommodation, as in a hotel, or for travel, as on a train. –*adj.* **2.** of or pertaining to such accommodation or travel.

**eco-nut** /ˈikoʊ-nʌt, ˈɛk-/, *n. Colloq.* a person who is deeply concerned with ecology and environment issues.

**ecophene** /ˈikoʊfin, ˈɛk-/, *n.* →**ecotype.**

**ecospecies** /ˈikoʊˌspisiz, ˈɛk-/, *n.* a group of plants comprising one or more ecotypes whose members can reproduce amongst themselves without loss of fertility in offspring. Also, **species** (def. 2).

**ecosphere** /ˈikoʊsfɪə, ˈɛk-/, *n.* the part of the atmosphere of a planet or other heavenly body which can sustain life.

**écossaise** /ɛkɒˈseɪz, eɪk-/, *n.* **1.** a kind of country dance in quick 2/4 time. **2.** the music for such a dance. [F: Scottish (fem.)]

**ecosystem** /ˈikoʊˌsɪstəm, ˈɛk-/, *n.* a community of organisms, interacting with one another, plus the environment in which they live and with which they also interact, as a pond, a forest.

**ecotone** /ˈikoʊtoʊn, ˈɛk-, -kə-/, *n.* the transition zone between two plant communities, as that between rainforest and sclerophyll forest. [Gk *oîko(s)* home + *tónos* stress]

**ecotype** /ˈikoʊtaɪp, ˈɛk-, -kə-/, *n.* a subspecies which has become specially adapted to certain environmental conditions.

**écraseur** /eɪkraˈzɜ/, *n.* a surgical instrument used in an operation where haemorrhage is feared, as in removing certain types of tumours, consisting of a chain or wire loop which is gradually tightened. [F, from *écraser* crush]

**ecru** /ˈɛkru, ˈeɪkru/, *adj.* **1.** very light brown in colour, as raw silk, unbleached linen, etc. –*n.* **2.** ecru colour. [F: raw, unbleached, from *é-* thoroughly (from L *ex-* EX-[1]) + *cru* raw, from L *crūdus*]

**ecstasy** /ˈɛkstəsi/, *n., pl.* **-sies. 1.** overpowering emotion or exaltation; a sudden access of intense feeling. **2.** rapturous delight. **3.** the frenzy of poetic inspiration. **4.** mental transport or rapture from the contemplation of divine things. [ME *extasie,* from OF, from ML *extasis,* from Gk *ékstasis* displacement, distraction of mind]

**ecstatic** /ɛkˈstætɪk/, *adj.* **1.** of, pertaining to, or characterised by ecstasy. **2.** subject to or in a state of ecstasy; transported; rapturous. –*n.* **3.** one subject to fits of ecstasy. **4.** (*pl.*) ecstatic transports; raptures. –**ecstatically,** *adv.*

**ECT** /i si ˈti/, electroconvulsive therapy. Also, **E.C.T.**

**ecthlipsis** /ɛkˈθlɪpsəs/, *n., pl.* **-ses** /-siz/. the suppression of a sound, esp. (in Latin prosody) of a final syllable ending in *m* before a vowel or *h.*

**ecthyma** /ˈɛkθəmə/, *n.* a contagious virus disease of sheep and goats marked by vesicular and pustular lesions on the lips, and occasionally affecting man; sore mouth.

**ecto-,** a prefix (chiefly in biological words) meaning 'outside', 'outer', 'external', 'lying upon' (opposed to *endo- ento-*), as in *ectoderm.* [Gk *ekto-,* combining form of *ektós* outside]

**ectoblast** /ˈɛktoʊblæst, ˈɛktə-/, *n.* the prospective ectoderm, before the separation of the germ layers. –**ectoblastic** /ɛktoʊˈblæstɪk, ɛktə-/, *adj.*

**ectoderm** /ˈɛktoʊdɜm, ˈɛktə-/, *n.* the outer germ layer in the embryo of any metazoan. –**ectodermal** /ɛktoʊˈdɜməl, ɛktə-/, **ectodermic** /ɛktoʊˈdɜmɪk, ɛktə-/, *adj.*

**ectogenous** /ɛkˈtɒdʒənəs/, *adj.* (of bacteria) able to live and develop outside the host. –**ectogenesis** /ɛktoʊˈdʒɛnəsəs/, *n.*

**ectomere** /ˈɛktoʊmɪə, ˈɛktə-/, *n.* any one of the blastomeres which participate in the development of the ectoderm.

**ectomorph** /ˈɛktoʊmɔf, ˈɛktə-/, *n.* a person of ectomorphic type.

**ectomorphic** /ɛktoʊˈmɔfɪk, ɛktə-/, *adj.* having a thinly built body characterised by the relative prominence of structures developed from the embryonic ectoderm (distinguished from *endomorphic, mesomorphic*).

**-ectomy,** a combining form attached to the name of a part of the body and producing a word meaning an operation for the excision of that part. [*ec-* (from Gk *ek-,* prefix form of *ek, ex* out of) + -TOMY]

**ectoparasite** /ɛktoʊˈpærəsaɪt, ɛktə-/, *n.* an external parasite (opposed to *endoparasite*).

**ectopia** /ɛkˈtoʊpiə/, *n.* the morbid displacement of a bodily organ or part.

**ectopic** /ɛkˈtɒpɪk/, *adj.* in an abnormal position or place, as in pregnancy outside the womb, talipes, etc. [Gk *éktop(os)* displaced + -IC]

**ectoplasm** /ˈɛktoʊplæzəm, ˈɛktə-/, *n.* **1.** *Biol.* the outer layer of the cytoplasm in a protozoan or vegetable cell (opposed to *endoplasm*). **2.** *Spiritualism.* the supposed emanation from the body of a medium. –**ectoplasmic** /ɛktoʊˈplæzmɪk, ɛktə-/, *adj.*

**ectosarc** /ˈɛktoʊsak, ˈɛktə-/, *n.* the ectoplasm of a protozoan (opposed to *endosarc*).

**ectosteal** /ˈɛktoʊstil, ˈɛktə-/, *adj.* pertaining to or situated on the outside of the bone.

**ectostosis** /ɛktɒsˈtoʊsəs/, *n.* the ossification of cartilage proceeding from without inward. [NL; from ECT(O)- + *ostosis* as in EXOSTOSIS]

**ectotrophic** /ɛktoʊˈtrɒfɪk, -ˈtroʊfɪk, ɛktə-/, *adj.* of, denoting, or pertaining to a type of mycorrhizal association, found particularly in forest trees, in which the fungal hyphae form a dense layer on the surface of the roots.

**ectype** /ˈɛktaɪp/, *n.* a reproduction or copy (opposed to *prototype*). [Gk *éktypos* wrought in relief, formed in outline] –**ectypal,** *adj.*

**Ecuador** /ˈɛkwədɔ/, *n.* a republic in north-western South America. –**Ecuadorian** /ɛkwəˈdɔriən/, *adj., n.*

**ecumenical** /ikjəˈmɛnəkəl, ɛk-/, *adj.* **1.** general; universal. **2.** pertaining to the whole Christian Church. **3.** tending or intended to promote Christian unity, esp. the unification of all Christian Churches: *the ecumenical movement.* Also, **ecumenic, oecumenical.** [LL *oecumenicus* (from Gk *oikoumenikós* general, universal) + -AL[1]] –**ecumenically,** *adv.*

**ecumenicalism** /ikjəˈmɛnəkəlɪzəm, ɛk-/, *n.* the doctrines and practices of the ecumenical movement.

**eczema** /ˈɛksəmə/, *n.* an inflammatory disease of the skin attended with itching and the exudation of serous matter. [NL, from Gk: a cutaneous eruption] –**eczematous** /ɛkˈsɛmətəs/, *adj.*

**-ed**[1], a suffix forming the past tense, as in *he crossed the river.* [OE *-de, -ede, -ode, -ade*]

**-ed**[2], a suffix forming: **1.** the past participle, as in *he had crossed the river.* **2.** participial adjectives indicating a condition or quality resulting from the action of the verb, as *inflated balloons.* [OE *-ed, -od, -ad*]

**-ed**[3], a suffix serving to form adjectives from nouns, as *bearded, moneyed, tender-hearted.* [OE *-ede*]

**ed.** /ɛd/, **1.** edited. **2.** edition. **3.** *pl.* **eds.** editor.

**edacious** /ə'deɪʃəs/, *adj.* devouring; voracious; consuming. [EDACI(TY) + -OUS] – **edaciously,** *adv.* – **edaciousness,** *n.*

**edacity** /ə'dæsəti/, *n.* good appetite. [L *edācitas* gluttony]

**edam** /'idəm, 'ɛdəm/, *n.* a hard, round yellow cheese, sometimes spiced, with a red wax rind. [named after *Edam,* in Holland, where it originated]

**edaphic** /ə'dæfɪk/, *adj.* due to soil or topography rather than climate. [Gk *édaphos* bottom + -IC] – **edaphically,** *adv.*

**eddo** /'ɛdoʊ/, *n., pl.* **eddoes** /'ɛdoʊz/. the edible root of the taro, or of any of several related plants; dasheen. [? Ibo *edè*]

**eddy** /'ɛdi/, *n., pl.* **eddies,** *v.,* **eddied, eddying.** *–n.* **1.** a current at variance with the main current in a stream of liquid or gas, esp. one having a rotary or whirling motion. **2.** any similar current, as of air, dust, fog, etc. *–v.i.* **3.** to move in eddies. *–v.t.* **4.** to whirl in eddies. [OE *ed-* turning + *ēa* stream. Cf. Icel. *idha*]

**eddy current** /'– kʌrənt/, *n.* an electric current induced in a mass of conducting material, esp. the iron cores of electromagnets, by a varying magnetic field; Foucault current.

**eddy current heating,** *n.* →**induction heating.**

**edelweiss** /'eɪdəlvaɪs/, *n.* **1.** a small composite herb, *Leontopodium alpinum,* having white woolly leaves and flowers, growing at high altitudes on the European Alps and some other mountain ranges of Eurasia. **2.** any of various related herbs thought to resemble this, as Australian edelweiss. [G, from *edel* noble + *weiss* white]

**edema** /ə'dimə/, *n., pl.* **-mata** /-mətə/. *U.S.* →**oedema.** – **edematous** /ə'dɛmətəs/, **edematose** /ə'dɛmətoʊs/, *adj.*

**Eden** /'idn/, *n.* **1.** the garden which was the first home of Adam and Eve. **2.** any delightful region or abode. **3.** a state of perfect happiness. [Heb.: lit., pleasure, delight] – **Edenic** /i'dɛnɪk/, *adj.*

**edentate** /i'dɛnteɪt/, *adj.* **1.** belonging or pertaining to the Edentata, an order of New World mammals, comprising the armadillos, the sloths, and the South American anteaters. **2.** toothless. *–n.* **3.** an edentate mammal. [L *ēdentātus,* pp., deprived of teeth]

**Edgar Britt** /ɛdgə 'brɪt/, *n. Colloq.* the act of defecating. [rhyming slang, *Edgar Britt* shit]

**edge** /ɛdʒ/, *n., v.,* **edged, edging.** *–n.* **1.** the border or part adjacent to a line of division; a brim or margin: *the horizon's edge.* **2.** a brink or verge: *the edge of a precipice.* **3.** one of the narrow surfaces of a thin, flat object: *a book with gilt edges.* **4.** the line in which two surfaces of a solid object meet: *the edge of a box.* **5.** the thin, sharp side of the blade of a cutting instrument or weapon. **6.** the sharpness proper to a blade. **7.** sharpness or keenness of language, argument, appetite, desire, etc. **8.** *Skiing.* a steel edge fitted to skis to make control easier on ice or hard snow. **9.** *Cricket.* a stroke off the edge of the bat, usu. unintentional; a snick. **10. have the edge,** *Colloq.* to have the advantage (usu. fol. by *over*). **11. on edge, a.** acutely uncomfortable or sensitive: *nerves on edge, to set the teeth on edge.* **b.** eager or impatient. **12. over the edge,** →**unbalanced** (def. 3). *–v.t.* **13.** to put an edge on; sharpen. **14.** to machine to a straight line or a desired curve. **15.** to provide with an edge or border; border. **16.** to move edgeways; move or force gradually: *to edge one's way through a crowd, to edge a rival off the track.* **17.** *Skiing.* to force the edges of the skis into the slope to prevent side slipping. **18.** *Cricket.* to play the ball from the edge of the bat, usu. unintentionally; snick. *–v.i.* **19.** to move edgeways; advance gradually. [ME *egge,* OE *ecg,* c. G *Ecke,* Icel. *egg;* akin to L *aciēs* edge, point] – **edged,** *adj.* – **edgeless,** *adj.* – **edger,** *n.*

**edgebone** /'ɛdʒboʊn/, *n.* →**aitchbone.**

**edger** /'ɛdʒə/, *n.* an instrument for cutting the edges of lawns.

**edge tool** /'ɛdʒ tul/, *n.* a tool with a cutting edge.

**edgeways** /'ɛdʒweɪz/, *adv.* **1.** with the edge forwards; in the direction of the edge. **2.** with a sideways movement. **3. get a word in edgeways,** to succeed in forcing one's way into an animated conversation or in making a remark when a voluble person is for a moment silent. Also, **edgewise** /'ɛdʒwaɪz/.

**edging** /'ɛdʒɪŋ/, *n.* **1.** the act of one who edges. **2.** something that serves for an edge; trimming for edges.

**edgy** /'ɛdʒi/, *adj.,* **-ier, -iest.** **1.** sharp-edged; sharply defined, as outlines. **2.** on edge; irritable. – **edginess,** *n.*

**edh** /ɛð/, *n.* →**eth.**

**edible** /'ɛdəbəl/, *adj.* **1.** fit to be eaten as food; eatable; esculent. *–n.* **2.** (*usu. pl.*) anything edible; an eatable. [LL *edibilis,* from L *edere* eat] – **edibility** /ɛdə'bɪləti/, **edibleness,** *n.*

**edict** /'idɪkt/, *n.* **1.** a decree issued by a sovereign or other authority. **2.** any authoritative proclamation or command. [L *ēdictum,* properly pp. neut., declared, proclaimed; replacing ME *edit,* from OF] – **edictal** /i'dɪktəl/, *adj.* – **edictally** /i'dɪktəli/, *adv.*

**edification** /ɛdəfə'keɪʃən/, *n.* **1.** the act of edifying. **2.** the state of being edified. **3.** moral improvement. – **edificatory,** *adj.*

**edifice** /'ɛdəfəs/, *n.* a building, esp. one of large size or imposing appearance: *a spacious edifice of brick.* [F, from L *aedificium* building] – **edificial** /ɛdə'fɪʃəl/, *adj.*

**edify** /'ɛdəfaɪ/, *v.t.,* **-fied, -fying.** to build up or increase the faith, morality, etc., of; instruct or benefit, esp. morally. [ME *edifie(n),* from OF *edifier,* from L *aedificāre* build] – **edifier,** *n.* – **edifyingly,** *adv.*

**Edison accumulator** /ɛdəsən ə'kjumjəleɪtə/, *n.* an accumulator in which the positive plate is nickel hydroxide and the negative plate is iron; the electrolyte is a 20 per cent solution of potassium hydroxide; Ni-Fe accumulator. [named after Thomas Alva *Edison,* 1847-1931, U.S. inventor]

**edit** /'ɛdət/, *v.t.* **1.** to supervise or direct the preparation of (a newspaper, magazine, etc.); act as editor of; direct the policies of. **2.** to collect, prepare, and arrange (materials) for publication. **3.** to revise and correct. **4.** to make (a cinema or television film, sound recording, or any part of a film or recording) from rushes, by cutting and arranging them, synchronising soundtrack, etc. [partly from L *ēditus,* pp., given forth; partly backformation from EDITOR]

**edit.,** **1.** edited. **2.** edition. **3.** editor.

**edition** /ə'dɪʃən/, *n.* **1.** one of a number of printings of the same book, newspaper, etc., issued at different times, and differing from another by alterations, additions, etc. (as distinguished from *impression*). **2.** the format in which a literary work is published: *a one-volume edition of Shakespeare.* **3.** the whole number of impressions or copies of a book, newspaper, etc., printed from one set of type at one time. **4.** *Colloq.* any version of anything, esp. one resembling an earlier version. [L *ēditio*]

**editor** /'ɛdətə/, *n.* **1.** one who edits written material for publication. **2.** a person responsible for the content of a newspaper, magazine, or the like, usu. one who presents his opinion or comment in the name of the paper. **3.** a person responsible for one aspect of a newspaper's activities: *fashion editor.* **4.** a person responsible for the content and sometimes the policy of the publications of a publishing house. **5.** one who edits films, recordings, etc. [L]

**editorial** /ɛdə'tɔriəl/, *n.* **1.** an article, in a newspaper or the like, presenting the opinion or comment of an editor or a leader-writer in the name of the paper; a leader (def. 5). *–adj.* **2.** of or pertaining to an editor. **3.** written by an editor.

**editorialise** /ɛdə'tɔriəlaɪz/, *v.i.,* **-lised, -lising.** to set forth one's position or opinion on some subject in, or as if in, an editorial. Also, **editorialize.**

**editorialist** /ɛdə'tɔriələst/, *n.* one who writes editorials.

**editorially** /ɛdə'tɔriəli/, *adv.* **1.** in an editorial manner; as an editor does. **2.** in an editorial.

**editorship** /'ɛdətəʃɪp/, *n.* **1.** the office or function of an editor. **2.** editorial direction.

**EDP** /i di 'pi/, electronic data processing.

**Educ.**, Education.
**educable** /ˈɛdʒəkəbəl/, *adj.* capable of being educated. – **educability** /ɛdʒəkəˈbɪləti/, *n.*
**educate** /ˈɛdʒəkeɪt/, *v.t.*, **-cated, -cating.** **1.** to develop the faculties and powers of by teaching, instruction, or schooling; qualify by instruction or training for a particular calling, practice, etc.; train: *to educate someone for something or to do something.* **2.** to provide education for; send to school. **3.** to develop or train (the ear, taste, etc.). [L *ēducātus,* pp., brought up, trained, educated]
**educated** /ˈɛdʒəkeɪtəd/, *adj.* **1.** having undergone education. **2.** characterised by or displaying qualities of culture and learning.
**education** /ɛdʒəˈkeɪʃən/, *n.* **1.** the act or process of educating; the imparting or acquisition of knowledge, skill, etc.; systematic instruction or training. **2.** the result produced by instruction, training, or study. **3.** the science or art of teaching; pedagogics.
**educational** /ɛdʒəˈkeɪʃənəl/, *adj.* **1.** pertaining to education. **2.** tending to educate. – **educationally,** *adv.*
**educationalist** /ɛdʒəˈkeɪʃənələst/, *n.* an expert in theories and methods of education. Also, **educationist.**
**education week** /ɛdʒəˈkeɪʃən wik/, *n.* a week set aside each year during which special school displays, functions, etc., are held in order to foster community involvement and interest in schools.
**educative** /ˈɛdʒəkətɪv/, *adj.* **1.** serving to educate: *educative knowledge.* **2.** pertaining to education: *the educative process.*
**educator** /ˈɛdʒəkeɪtə/, *n.* one who or that which educates; a teacher. [L]
**educatory** /ˈɛdʒəkətri, ɛdʒəˈkeɪtəri/, *adj.* serving to educate.
**educe** /əˈdjus, i-/, *v.t.*, **educed, educing.** to draw forth or bring out; elicit; develop. [L *ēdūcere* lead forth, bring up] – **educible,** *adj.*
**educt** /ˈidʌkt/, *n.* **1.** something educed. **2.** *Chem.* one substance extracted unchanged from another (distinguished from a *product*). [L *ēductus,* pp., educed]
**eduction** /əˈdʌkʃən, i-/, *n.* **1.** the act of educing. **2.** something educed. **3.** *Mech.* the exhaust from a steam engine, or sometimes from an internal-combustion engine.
**eductive** /əˈdʌktɪv, i-/, *adj.* serving to educe.
**eductor** /əˈdʌktə, i-/, *n.* one who or that which educes.
**Edwardian** /ɛdˈwɔdiən/, *adj.* pertaining to the time of Edward VII, a period now often regarded as ornate, opulent, and leisurely. – **Edwardianism,** *n.*
**-ee,** a suffix of nouns denoting one who is the object of some action, or undergoes or receives something (often as opposed to the person acting), as in *assignee, donee, employee.* [F *-é,* pp. ending, from L *-ātus* -ATE[1]]
**EEC** /i i ˈsi/, European Economic Community; the Common Market.
**EEG** /i i ˈdʒi/, **1.** electroencephalogram. **2.** electroencephalograph.
**eel** /il/, *n.* **1.** any of various elongate, snakelike, freshwater or marine fishes of the order Apodes, as *Anguilla reinhardtii* of eastern Australian rivers or *A. anguilla* of Europe. **2.** any of several similar but unrelated fishes as the lamprey. [ME *ele,* from OE *ēl,* replacing OE *ǣl,* c. D *aal,* G *Aal*]
**eelgrass** /ˈilgras/, *n.* **1.** any of various marine or freshwater plants with ribbon-like leaves, as *Zostera marina* and *Vallisneria spiralis.* **2.** →**seagrass.**

eel

**eelpout** /ˈilpaʊt/, *n.* **1.** any of the blenny-like marine fishes constituting the family Zoarcidae. **2.** →**burbot.** [OE *ǣlepūte*]
**eelspear** /ˈilspɪə/, *n.* a broad-pronged instrument used for catching eels.
**eelworm** /ˈilwɜm/, *n.* any small nematode worm of the family Anguillulidae.
**eely** /ˈili/, *adj.* eel-like; wriggling.
**e'en**[1] /in/, *adv. Poetic.* even.
**e'en**[2] /in/, *n. Poetic.* evening.
**e'er** /ɛə/, *adv. Poetic.* ever.
**-eer,** a suffix of nouns denoting one who is concerned with, or employed in connection with, or busies himself with something, as in *auctioneer, engineer, profiteer.* Also, **-ier.** [F *-ier,* from L *-ārius.* See -ARY[1] and -ER[2]]
**eerie** /ˈɪəri/, *adj.*, **eerier, eeriest.** inspiring fear; weird, strange, or uncanny. Also, **eery.** [ME *eri,* d. var. of obs. *argh,* OE *earg* cowardly, c. G *arg* bad] – **eerily,** *adv.* – **eeriness,** *n.*
**ef-,** variant of **ex-** (by assimilation) before *f,* as in *efferent.*
**eff** /ɛf/, *v.t., v.i. Colloq.* (*euph.*) fuck: *eff off.* – **effing,** *adj.*
**effable** /ˈɛfəbəl/, *adj.* utterable; expressible. [F, from L *effābilis,* from *effāri* to utter, from *ex-* EX-[1] + *fāri* to speak]
**efface** /əˈfeɪs/, *v.t.*, **effaced, effacing.** **1.** to wipe out; destroy; do away with: *to efface a memory.* **2.** to rub out, erase, or obliterate (outlines, traces, inscriptions, etc.). **3.** to make inconspicuous or not noticeable: *to efface oneself.* [late ME, from F *effacer,* from *ef-* (from L *ex-* EX-[1]) + *face* FACE] – **effaceable,** *adj.* – **effacement,** *n.* – **effacer,** *n.*
**effect** /əˈfɛkt, i-/, *n.* **1.** that which is produced by some agency or cause; a result; a consequence: *the effect of heat.* **2.** power to produce results; efficacy; force; validity; weight: *of no effect.* **3.** the state of being operative; operation or execution; accomplishment or fulfilment: *to bring a plan into effect.* **4.** a mental impression produced, as by a painting, speech, etc. **5.** the result intended; purport or intent; tenor or significance: *he wrote to that effect.* **6.** (of stage properties) a sight, sound or, occasionally, smell simulated by artificial means to give a particular impression in a theatre. **7.** (*pl.*) goods; movables; personal property. **8. for effect,** for the sake of a desired impression; with histrionic intent. **9. in effect, a.** in fact or reality. **b.** in operation, as a law. **10. take effect,** to operate or begin to operate. *–v.t.* **11.** to produce as an effect; bring about; accomplish; make happen. **12.** to produce or make. [ME, from L *effectus,* from *efficere* bring about] – **effecter,** *n.* – **effectible,** *adj.*
**effective** /əˈfɛktɪv, i-/, *adj.* **1.** serving to effect the purpose; producing the intended or expected result: *effective measures, effective steps towards peace.* **2.** actually in effect: *the law becomes effective at midnight.* **3.** producing a striking impression; striking: *an effective picture.* *–n.* **4.** a soldier or sailor fit for duty or active service. **5.** the effective total of a military force. – **effectively,** *adv.* – **effectiveness,** *n.*
**effective resistance** /– rəˈzɪstəns/, *n.* the resistance of a conductor to alternating current; in addition to d.c. resistance it includes any losses caused by the current and is expressed as the ratio of the total loss to the square of the r.m.s. of the current.
**effector** /əˈfɛktə, i-/, *n.* an organ tissue or cell that carries out a response to a nerve impulse, such as a muscle or gland. [L]
**effectual** /əˈfɛktʃuəl, i-/, *adj.* **1.** producing, or capable of producing, an intended effect; adequate. **2.** valid or binding, as an agreement or document. [LL *effectuālis*] – **effectuality** /əfɛktʃuˈæləti, i-/, **effectualness,** *n.* – **effectually,** *adv.*
**effectuate** /əˈfɛktʃueɪt, i-/, *v.t.*, **-ated, -ating.** to bring about; effect. [LL *effectuātus.* See -ATE[1]] – **effectuation** /əfɛktʃuˈeɪʃən/, *n.*
**effeminacy** /əˈfɛmənəsi, i-/, *n.* the state or quality of being effeminate.
**effeminate** /əˈfɛmənət, i-/, *adj.* **1.** (of a man) soft or delicate to an unmanly degree in traits, tastes, habits, etc.; womanish. **2.** characterised by unmanly softness, delicacy, self-indulgence, etc.: *an effeminate life.* *–n.* **3.** a male homosexual. [L *effēminātus,* pp., made womanish] – **effeminately,** *adv.* – **effeminateness,** *n.*
**effeminise** /əˈfɛmənaɪz, i-/, *v.t.*, **-nised, -nising.** to make effeminate. Also, **effeminize.**
**effendi** /əˈfɛndi/, *n., pl.* **-dis.** (formerly) a Turkish title of respect for government officials, etc. [Turk. *efendī,* from Gk *authéntēs* master, actual doer. See AUTHENTIC]
**efferent** /ˈɛfərənt/, *adj.* carrying away (opposed to *afferent*): *efferent impulses from the brain.* [L *efferens,* ppr., bringing out, raising]
**effervesce** /ɛfəˈvɛs/, *v.i.*, **-vesced, -vescing.** **1.** to give off bubbles of gas, as fermenting liquors; bubble and hiss. **2.** to issue forth in bubbles. **3.** to exhibit fervour, excitement,

i = peat ɪ = pit ɛ = pet æ = pat a = part ɒ = pot ʌ = putt ɔ = port ʊ = put u = pool ɜ = pert ə = apart aɪ = buy eɪ = bay ɔɪ = boy aʊ = how oʊ = hoe ɪə = here ɛə = hair ʊə = tour g = give θ = thin ð = then ʃ = show ʒ = measure tʃ = choke dʒ = joke ŋ = sing j = you õ = Fr. bon

liveliness, etc. [L *effervescere* boil up] – **effervescence, effervescency,** *n.* – **effervescible,** *adj.*

**effervescent** /ɛfə'vɛsənt/, *adj.* **1.** effervescing; bubbling. **2.** gay; lively; sparkling. – **effervescently,** *adv.*

**effete** /ə'fit/, *adj.* **1.** that has lost its vigour or energy; exhausted; worn out. **2.** unable to produce. [L *effētus* exhausted] – **effetely,** *adv.* – **effeteness,** *n.*

**efficacious** /ɛfə'keɪʃəs/, *adj.* having or showing efficacy; effective as a means, measure, remedy, etc. [L *efficācia* efficacy + -OUS] – **efficaciously,** *adv.* – **efficaciousness,** *n.*

**efficacy** /'ɛfəkəsi/, *n., pl.* **-cies.** capacity for serving to produce effects; effectiveness. [L *efficācia*]

**efficiency** /ə'fɪʃənsi, i-/, *n., pl.* **-cies. 1.** the fact or quality of being efficient; competency in performance. **2.** the ratio of the work done or energy developed by a machine, engine, etc., to the energy supplied to it.

**efficiency bar** /'– ba/, *n.* a level on a salary scale beyond which increments are dependent on certified efficiency.

**efficient** /ə'fɪʃənt, i-/, *adj.* **1.** adequate in operation or performance; having and using the requisite knowledge, skill, and industry; competent; capable. **2.** producing an effect, as a cause; causative. [L *efficiens,* ppr., accomplishing] – **efficiently,** *adv.*

**effigy** /'ɛfədʒi/, *n., pl.* **-gies. 1.** a representation or image, esp. sculptured, as on a monument or coin. **2.** a doll or crude representation of a person, esp. one made as an expression of hatred, or to be used in witchcraft. **3. burn** or **hang in effigy,** to burn or hang an image of a person as an expression of public indignation, ridicule, or hatred. [F *effigie,* from L *effigies* copy of an object]

**effigy-mound** /'ɛfədʒi-maʊnd/, *n.* a mound of earth dating from prehistoric times, shaped like an animal.

**effleurage** /'ɛflɜraʒ/, *n.* a massaging movement of the hands along the muscles.

**effloresce** /ɛflə'rɛs/, *v.i.,* **-resced, -rescing. 1.** to burst into bloom; blossom. **2.** (of a crystal) to change on the surface to a powder, upon exposure to air, as a result of loss of water or crystallisation. **3.** (of a rock or mineral) to become encrusted with fine-grain crystals as a result of evaporation or chemical change. [L *efflōrescere* blossom]

**efflorescence** /ɛflə'rɛsəns/, *n.* **1.** the state or period of flowering. **2.** *Chem., Mineral.* **a.** the act or process of efflorescing. **b.** the resulting powdery substance or encrustation. **3.** *Pathol.* a rash or eruption.

**efflorescent** /ɛflə'rɛsənt/, *adj.* **1.** efflorescing; blossoming. **2.** *Chem., Mineral.* **a.** subject to efflorescence. **b.** covered with or forming an efflorescence. [L *efflōrescens,* ppr.]

**effluence** /'ɛfluəns/, *n.* **1.** outward flow; efflux. **2.** something that flows out; an emanation. [modelled on *affluence.* See EFFLUENT]

**effluent** /'ɛfluənt/, *adj.* **1.** flowing out or forth. –*n.* **2.** that which flows out or forth; outflow. **3.** a stream flowing out of another stream, a lake, etc. **4.** the outflow from sewage during purification. **5.** liquid industrial waste. **6.** the radioactive waste from nuclear power stations, etc. [L *effluens,* ppr.]

**effluvium** /ə'fluviəm/, *n., pl.* **-via** /-viə/, **-viums.** a slight or invisible exhalation or vapour, esp. one that is disagreeable or noxious. [L: a flowing out] – **effluvial,** *adj.*

**efflux** /'ɛflʌks/, *n.* **1.** outward flow, as of water. **2.** that which flows out; an effluence. **3.** *Aeron.* the mixture of combustion products and air which constitutes the propulsive gases in a jet, or rocket engine. Also, **effluxion.**

**effort** /'ɛfət/, *n.* **1.** exertion of power, physical or mental: *an effort to reform.* **2.** an attempt. **3.** something done by exertion; an achievement, as in literature or art. **4.** *Mech. Eng.* a measured amount of force exerted on a mechanism, as a lever. [F, from OF *esforcier,* from *es-* (from L *ex-* EX-[1]) + *force* strength, from L *fortis* strong] – **effortful,** *adj.*

**effortless** /'ɛfətləs/, *adj.* **1.** requiring or involving no effort; easy. **2.** making no effort; passive. – **effortlessly,** *adv.* – **effortlessness,** *n.*

**effrontery** /ə'frʌntəri, i-/, *n., pl.* **-teries.** shameless or impudent boldness; barefaced audacity. [F *effronterie,* from OF *esfronte* shameless, from *es-* (from L *ex-* EX-[1]) + *front* brow (from L *frons*) + *-e* -ed]

**effulge** /ə'fʌldʒ, i-/, *v.,* **-fulged, -fulging.** –*v.i.* **1.** to shine brilliantly. –*v.t.* **2.** to send forth (beams of light, etc.). [L *effulgēre* shine forth]

**effulgent** /ə'fʌldʒənt, i-/, *adj.* shining forth brilliantly; radiant. – **effulgence,** *n.* – **effulgently,** *adv.*

**effuse** /ə'fjuz, i-/, *v.,* **-fused, -fusing;** /ə'fjus, i-/, *adj.* –*v.t.* **1.** to pour out or forth; shed; disseminate. –*v.i.* **2.** to exude. **3.** *Physics.* (of gas) to flow gradually through porous material or one or more tiny apertures. –*adj.* **4.** *Bot.* spread out loosely. **5.** (of certain shells) having the lips separated by a gap or groove. [L *effūsus,* pp., poured forth]

**effusion** /ə'fjuʒən, i-/, *n.* **1.** the act of effusing or pouring forth. **2.** that which is effused. **3.** unrestrained expression of feelings, etc.: *poetic effusions.* **4.** *Pathol.* **a.** the escape of a fluid from its natural vessels into a body cavity. **b.** the fluid which escapes.

**effusive** /ə'fjusɪv, -zɪv, i-/, *adj.* **1.** unduly demonstrative; without reserve: *effusive emotion, an effusive person.* **2.** *Geol.* of or pertaining to volcanic rocks which are poured out at the earth's surface as distinct from intrusive rocks injected at depth. – **effusively,** *adv.* – **effusiveness,** *n.*

**EFT** /i ɛf 'ti/, Electronic Funds Transfer.

**e.g.** /i 'dʒi/, for example. [L *exempli gratia*]

**egad** /i'gæd/, *interj.* (an expletive or mild oath): *egad, that's true.* [alteration of *A God* oh God!]

**egalitarian** /əgælə'tɛəriən, i-/, *adj.* **1.** asserting the equality of all people. –*n.* **2.** one who asserts the equality of all people. [from F *égal* EQUAL; replacing EQUALITARIAN] – **egalitarianism,** *n.*

**egest** /i'dʒɛst/, *v.t.* to discharge, as from the body; void (opposed to *ingest*). [L *ēgestus,* pp., brought out] – **egestive,** *adj.*

**egesta** /i'dʒɛstə/, *n. pl.* matter egested from the body, as excrement. [L, neut. pl. of *ēgestus,* pp., brought out]

**egestion** /i'dʒɛstʃən/, *n.* the process of egesting; the voiding of the waste of digestion.

**egg**[1] /ɛg/, *n.* **1.** the roundish reproductive body produced by the female of animals, consisting of the female reproductive cell and its envelopes. The envelopes may be albumen jelly, membranes, egg case, or shell, according to species. **2.** the body of this sort produced by birds, esp. the domestic hen. **3.** anything resembling a hen's egg. **4.** Also, **egg cell.** the ovum or female reproductive cell. **5. bad egg,** a person of reprehensible character. **6. have egg on one's face,** *Colloq.* to be exposed in an embarassing situation. **7. in the egg,** in the planning stages. **8. put all one's eggs in one basket,** to devote all one's resources to or risk all one's possessions, etc., on a single undertaking. **9. tread on eggs,** to be very cautious. –*v.t.* **10.** to prepare (food) by dipping in beaten egg. [Scand. (cf. Icel. *egg*); replacing ME *ey,* OE *ǣg,* c. G *Ei.* Cf. L *ōvum,* Gk *ōión*]

**egg**[2] /ɛg/, *v.t.* to incite or urge; encourage (usu. fol. by *on*). [Scand.; cf. Icel. *eggja,* from *egg* EDGE]

**egg and dart, egg and tongue, egg and anchor,** *n.* an egg-shaped ornament alternating with a dart-like, tongue-like, or anchor-like ornament, used to enrich a moulding.

egg-and-dart moulding

**egg-and-spoon race** /ɛg-ən-'spun reɪs/, *n.* a race in which contestants have to pick up an egg in a spoon and balance it while running.

**eggar** /'ɛgə/, *n.* →**egger.**

**egg-beater** /'ɛg-bitə/, *n.* **1.** a utensil with rotating blades used for beating eggs, whipping cream, etc. **2.** *Colloq.* a helicopter.

**eggbound** /'ɛgbaʊnd/, *adj.* unable to expel an egg. – **egg-binding** /'ɛgbaɪndɪŋ/, *n.*

**egg-carton** /'ɛg-katən/, *n.* a moulded cardboard box in which eggs are packaged and sold.

**egg coddler** /'ɛg kɒdlə/, *n.* a closed container, usu. egg-shaped, in which an egg may be coddled.

**eggcosy** /'ɛgkoʊzi/, *n.* a cover to put over a boiled egg to keep it warm until it is eaten.

**eggcup** /ˈɛgkʌp/, *n.* a small cup for holding a boiled egg upright.

**egger** /ˈɛgə/, *n.* any of various species of moths of the family Lasiocampidae. Also, **eggar.**

**eggflip** /ˈɛgflɪp/, *n.* a milk drink containing whipped raw egg, sugar, and sometimes flavouring.

**eggfruit** /ˈɛgfrut/, *n.* →**eggplant.**

**egghead** /ˈɛghɛd/, *n. Colloq.* an intellectual; highbrow.

**eggnog** /ˈɛgnɒg/, *n.* eggflip, with the addition of spices and alcohol, served hot or cold. [EGG[1] + *nog* strong ale]

**eggplant** /ˈɛgplænt/, *n.* **1.** a plant, *Solanum melongena,* probably originally of Central Asia, cultivated for its edible, more or less egg-shaped fruit, dark purple (or sometimes white or yellow) in colour; aubergine. **2.** the fruit, used as a table vegetable. Also, **eggfruit.**

**egg roll** /ɛg ˈroʊl/, *n.* **1.** a roll (def. 54) with an egg filling. **2.** *Colloq. (derog.)* a stupid person; idiot.

**eggs-and-bacon** /ɛgz-ən-ˈbeɪkən/, *n.* →**bacon-and-eggs.**

**eggs Benedict** /ɛgz ˈbɛnədɪkt/, *n.pl.* poached eggs on slices of ham and toast covered with hollandaise sauce. [named after Commodore E. C. *Benedict,* 1834-1920, American banker and yachtsman, who invented the dish]

**egg-shaped** /ˈɛg-ʃeɪpt/, *adj.* having oval form, esp. with one end broader than the other.

**eggshell** /ˈɛgʃɛl/, *n.* **1.** the shell of a bird's egg, consisting of keratin fibres and calcite crystals. **2.** a pale yellow colour. *–adj.* **3.** like an eggshell; thin and delicate; very brittle. **4.** (of a paint) having an almost matt finish resembling the surface texture of an eggshell; having very little gloss. **5.** pale yellow.

**eggshell blonde** /– ˈblɒnd/, *n. Colloq.* a bald person.

**eggshell china** /– ˈtʃaɪnə/, *n.* very thin, translucent porcelain.

**eggslice** /ˈɛgslaɪs/, *n.* a utensil for removing fried eggs, etc., from a pan.

**eggspoon** /ˈɛgspun/, *n.* a spoon, smaller than a teaspoon, used for eating boiled eggs.

**eggtimer** /ˈɛgtaɪmə/, *n.* a small hourglass running for about three minutes, used to time the boiling of an egg.

**egg tooth** /ˈɛg tuθ/, *n.* a calcareous point on the tip of the beak or upper jaw, by which an unhatched bird or reptile breaks through the eggshell on hatching.

**eggwhisk** /ˈɛgwɪsk/, *n.* →**whisk**[2] (def. 3).

**eggwhite** /ˈɛgwaɪt/, *n.* the white of an egg; albumen.

**egis** /ˈidʒəs/, *n.* →**aegis.**

**eglantine** /ˈɛgləntin, -aɪn/, *n.* any of various plants of the genus *Rosa,* family Rosaceae, mainly of northern temperate and sub-tropical regions, esp. sweetbriar. Also, **eglatere** /ˈɛglətɪə/. [ME *eglentine,* from F *églantine,* from OF *aiglent* sweetbriar, from L *acus* needle]

**ego** /ˈigoʊ/, *n., pl.* **egos.** **1.** the 'I' or self of any person; a person as thinking, feeling, and willing, and distinguishing itself from the selves of others and from objects of its thought. **2.** (*oft. cap.*) *Philos.* the enduring and conscious element which knows experience. **3.** *Psychoanal.* that part of the psychic apparatus which experiences the outside world and reacts to it, thus mediating between the primitive drives of the id and the demands of the social and physical environment. **4.** *Colloq.* conceit; egotism. [L: I]

**egocentric** /ˈɛgoʊsɛntrɪk, ˈigoʊ-/, *adj.* **1.** having or regarding self as the centre of all things, esp. as applied to the known world. **2.** self-centred. *–n.* **3.** an egocentric person. **–egocentricity** /ˌɛgoʊsɛnˈtrɪsəti, ˌigoʊ-/, *n.*

**ego ideal** /igoʊ aɪˈdil/, *n. Psychol.* a more or less conscious criterion of personal excellence towards which an individual strives. It is derived from a composite image of the characteristics of persons (initially the parents) with whom the individual identifies himself.

**egoism** /ˈɛgoʊɪzəm, ˈigoʊ-/, *n.* **1.** the habit of valuing everything only in reference to one's personal interest; pure selfishness. **2.** egotism or self-conceit. **3.** *Ethics.* the doctrine that the individual and his self-interest are the basis of all behaviour. [EGO + -ISM]

**egoist** /ˈɛgoʊəst, ˈigoʊ-/, *n.* **1.** a self-centred or selfish person. **2.** an egotist. **3.** an adherent of the metaphysical principle of the ego or self; a solipsist. [EGO + -IST] **–egoistic** /ɛgoʊˈɪstɪk, igoʊ-/, **egoistical** /ɛgoʊˈɪstɪkəl, igoʊ-/, *adj.* **–egoistically** /ɛgoʊˈɪstɪkli, igoʊ-/, *adv.*

**egomania** /ˌɛgoʊˈmeɪniə, ˌigoʊ-/, *n.* morbid egotism. [EGO + -MANIA] **–egomaniac,** *n.*

**egotism** /ˈɛgətɪzəm, ˈigoʊ-, ˈigə-/, *n.* **1.** the habit of talking too much about oneself; self-conceit; boastfulness. **2.** selfishness. [EGO + hiatus-filling *-t-* + -ISM]

**egotist** /ˈɛgətəst, ˈigə-/, *n.* **1.** a conceited, boastful person. **2.** an egoist. **–egotistic** /ɛgəˈtɪstɪk, igə-/, **egotistical** /ɛgəˈtɪstɪkəl, igə-/, *adj.* **–egotistically** /ɛgəˈtɪstɪkli, igə-/, *adv.*

**ego trip** /ˈigoʊ trɪp/, *n. Colloq.* behaviour intended to attract attention and admiration, for the sake of boosting one's own ego.

**ego-trip** /ˈigoʊ-trɪp/, *v.i.,* **-tripped, -tripping.** *Colloq.* to indulge in an ego trip.

**egregious** /əˈgridʒiəs, -dʒəs/, *adj.* **1.** remarkably or extraordinarily bad; flagrant: *an egregious lie, an egregious fool.* **2.** *Obs.* distinguished or eminent. [L *ēgregius* distinguished, lit., (standing) out from the herd] **–egregiously,** *adv.* **–egregiousness,** *n.*

**egress** /ˈigrɛs/, *n.* **1.** the act of going or passing out, esp. from an enclosed place. **2.** a means or place of going out; an exit. **3.** the right of going out. [L *ēgressus,* from *ēgredī* go out] **–egression** /iˈgrɛʃən/, *n.*

**egret** /ˈigrət/, *n.* **1.** any of various herons occurring throughout the world and bearing long plumes in the breeding season, as the **white egret,** *Egretta alba,* a large graceful white bird, found beside rivers, lakes, or dams. **2.** the plume of an egret; aigrette. **3.** the feathery pappus of the dandelion, thistle, and other plants; aigrette. [ME *egrete,* from OF, var. of *aigrette*]

egret

**Egypt** /ˈidʒəpt, ˈidʒɪpt/, *n.* a republic in north-eastern Africa. Official name: **Arab Republic of Egypt.**

**Egypt.,** Egyptian.

**Egyptian** /əˈdʒɪpʃən/, *adj.* **1.** of or pertaining to Egypt or its people: *Egyptian architecture.* **2.** of or pertaining to the gipsies. *–n.* **3.** a native or inhabitant of Egypt. **4.** a gipsy. **5.** the language of the ancient Egyptians, an extinct Hamitic language.

**Egyptology** /ˌidʒɪpˈtɒlədʒi/, *n.* the science or study of Egyptian antiquities. **–Egyptological** /əˌdʒɪptəˈlɒdʒɪkəl/, *adj.* **–Egyptologist,** *n.*

**eh** /eɪ/, *interj.* (an interrogative utterance, sometimes expressing surprise or doubt): *wasn't it lucky, eh?*

**EHF** /i eɪtʃ ˈɛf/, *Radio.* extremely high frequency.

**ehoa** /ˈɛhoʊə/, *n. N.Z.* friend, as a term of address. [Maori]

**eider** /ˈaɪdə/, *n.* any of several large sea-ducks of the genus *Somateria* and allied genera of the Northern Hemisphere, generally black and white, and yielding eiderdown. Also, **eider duck.** [Icel. *æ̅dhur,* from Old Norse *æ̅dhr*]

eider duck

**eiderdown** /ˈaɪdədaʊn/, *n.* **1.** down or soft feathers from the breast of the eider duck. **2.** a heavy quilt, properly one filled with eiderdown (def. 1). **3.** *U.S.* a fabric of cotton with wool nap. [from Icel. *æ̅dardūn* (18th-cent. spelling) down of the eider (gen. sing.); spelling *eider-* follows (18th-cent.) Swed. or G, representing Icel. *æ̅* with *ei*]

**eidetic** /aɪˈdɛtɪk/, *adj.* **1.** of, pertaining to, constituting or having a vivid and persistent type of imagery or memory, esp. during childhood. **2.** pertaining to an image that recreates a recent optical impression with hallucinatory clarity.

**eidolon** /aɪˈdoʊlɒn/, *n., pl.* **-la** /-lə/. an image; a phantom; an apparition. [Gk: image. Cf. IDOL]

**eight** /eɪt/, *n.* **1.** a cardinal number, seven plus one. **2.** a symbol for this number, as 8 or VIII. **3.** a set of this many persons or things. **4.** a playing card bearing eight pips. **5.** *Rowing.* **a.** a crew of eight oarsmen. **b.** a racing boat for a crew of eight and a cox. *–adj.* **6.** amounting to eight in number. [ME *eighte, ehte,* OE *eahta,* c. D and G *acht;* akin to L *octō,* Gk *oktō*]

i = peat ɪ = pit ɛ = pet æ = pat a = part ɒ = pot ʌ = putt ɔ = port ʊ = put u = pool ɜ = pert ə = apart aɪ = buy eɪ = bay ɔɪ = boy aʊ = how
oʊ = hoe ɪə = here ɛə = hair ʊə = tour g = give θ = thin ð = then ʃ = show ʒ = measure tʃ = choke dʒ = joke ŋ = sing j = you õ = Fr. bon

**eighteen** /eɪ'tin/, *n.* **1.** a cardinal number, ten plus eight. **2.** a symbol for this number, as 18 or XVIII. **3.** a team in Australian Rules football: *the Carlton eighteen.* **4.** a large keg of beer (a kilderkin), formerly approx. 18 gallons, now 79 litres. *–adj.* **5.** amounting to eighteen in number. [ME *ehtetene,* OE *eahtatēne.* See EIGHT, -TEEN] – **eighteenth,** *adj.*

**eighteenmo** /eɪ'tinmoʊ/, *n.* →**octodecimo.**

**eightfold** /'eɪtfoʊld/, *adj.* **1.** comprising eight parts or members; eight times as great or as much. *–adv.* **2.** in eightfold measure.

**eighth** /eɪtθ/, *adj.* **1.** next after the seventh. **2.** being one of eight equal parts. *–n.* **3.** the eighth one of a series. **4.** an eighth part. **5.** *Music.* an octave.

**eighth note** /'– noʊt/, *n. U.S.* →**quaver.**

**eight-hour day** /ˌeɪt-aʊə 'deɪ/, *n.* a day in which eight hours are spent at work, eight hours asleep and eight hours in recreational and other activities; formerly the goal of social reformers fighting against overlong working hours.

**eight-second rule** /eɪt-'sɛkənd rul/, *n.* an amateur boxing rule which makes mandatory an eight second count before a knocked-down boxer may resume the bout, whatever his condition.

**eightsome** /'eɪtsəm/, *n.* **1.** *Rare.* a group of eight things or persons. **2.** Also, **eightsome reel.** a lively Scottish reel in which eight or a multiple of eight persons dance together.

**eightvo** /'eɪtvoʊ/, *n., pl.* **-vos,** *adj.* →**octavo.**

**eighty** /'eɪti/, *n., pl.* **eighties,** *adj.* *–n.* **1.** a cardinal number, ten times eight. **2.** a symbol for this number, as 80 or LXXX or XXC. **3.** (*pl.*) the numbers from 80 to 89 of a series, esp. with reference to the years of a person's age, or the years of a century. *–adj.* **4.** amounting to eighty in number. [ME *eighteti,* OE *eahtatig*] – **eightieth** /'eɪtiəθ/, *adj., n.*

**eikon** /'aɪkɒn/, *n.* →**icon.**

**einkorn** /'aɪnkɔn/, *n.* a wheat, *Triticum monococcum,* family Poaceae, probably originally from south east Europe and south west Asia, cultivated by Neolithic man and still grown on rocky mountainous ground in southern Europe.

**einsteinium** /aɪn'staɪniəm/, *n.* a synthetic, radioactive, metallic element. *Symbol:* Es; *at. no.:* 99. [Albert *Einstein,* 1879-1955, German physicist, + -IUM]

**Einstein shift** /ˌaɪnstaɪn 'ʃɪft/, *n.* a slight displacement, towards the red, of lines of the spectrum of the sun and other dense stars due to their gravitational field, originally predicted by Albert Einstein.

**Einstein theory** /'– θɪəri/, *n.* See **relativity.**

**Eire** /'ɛərə/, *n.* former name of the **Republic of Ireland;** still its official Gaelic name.

**eisteddfod** /ə'stɛdfəd/, *n.* **1.** any competitive music festival. **2.** (*cap.*) a congress of Welsh bards and minstrels. [Welsh: session, from *eistedd* sit]

**either** /'aɪðə, 'iðə/, *adj.* **1.** one or the other of two: *you may sit at either end of the table.* **2.** each of the two; the one and the other: *there are trees on either side of the river.* *–pron.* **3.** one or the other; not both: *take either; either is correct.* *–conj.* **4.** (used as one of two coordinate alternatives): *either come or write.* *–adv.* **5.** (used after negative sentences coordinated by *and, or, nor*): *he is not fond of parties and I am not either, I am going and nobody can prevent it either;* after a negative subordinate clause: *if you do not come, he will not come either.* [ME; OE *ǣgther,* contraction of *ǣghwæther* each of two, both, from *ā* always + *gehwæther* each of two. See WHETHER]

**either-or** /aɪðər-'ɔ, iðər-'ɔ/, *adj.* of or pertaining to a choice of one of two possible courses: *an either-or situation.*

**ejaculate** /ə'dʒækjəleɪt, i-/, *v.,* **-lated, -lating.** *–v.t.* **1.** to utter suddenly and briefly; exclaim. **2.** to eject suddenly and swiftly; discharge. *–v.i.* **3.** to discharge seminal fluid. [L *ējaculātus,* pp., having cast out] – **ejaculator,** *n.*

**ejaculation** /ədʒækjə'leɪʃən, i-/, *n.* **1.** an abrupt, exclamatory utterance. **2.** the act of ejaculating. **3.** the rhythmic discharge of seminal fluid from the male passages; an emission.

**ejaculatory** /ə'dʒækjələtri, i-/, *adj.* pertaining to or of the nature of an ejaculation or exclamatory utterance. Also, **ejaculative.**

**eject** /ə'dʒɛkt, i-/, *v.;* /'idʒɛkt/, *n.* *–v.t.* **1.** to drive or force out; expel, as from a place or position. **2.** to dismiss, as from office, occupancy, etc. **3.** to evict, as from property. *–n.* **4.** *Psychol.* something whose existence is inferred as a reality, but which is outside of, and inaccessible to, the consciousness of the one making the inference. [L *ējectus,* pp. thrown out]

**ejecta** /ə'dʒɛktə, i-/, *n.pl.* matter ejected, as from a volcano in eruption. [L, neut. pl. of *ējectus.* See EJECT]

**ejection** /ə'dʒɛkʃən, i-/, *n.* **1.** the act of ejecting. **2.** the state of being ejected. **3.** something ejected, as lava.

**ejective** /ə'dʒɛktɪv, i-/, *adj.* **1.** serving to eject. **2.** *Phonet.* (of a stop or fricative) produced with air compressed above the closed glottis. *–n.* **3.** *Phonet.* an ejective stop or fricative.

**ejectment** /ə'dʒɛktmənt, i-/, *n.* **1.** the act of ejecting. **2.** *Law.* an action for the recovery of land wherein the title of real property may be tried and the possession recovered, wherever the party claiming has a right of entry (abolished 1852 in Britain; available in other common law jurisdictions till much later).

**ejector** /ə'dʒɛktə, i-/, *n.* **1.** one who or that which ejects. **2.** the mechanism in a firearm or gun which, after firing, throws out the empty cartridge or shell from the weapon.

**ejusdem generis rule** /ədʒuzdəm 'dʒɛnərəs rul/, *n. Law.* a rule of construction that when particular words used in an instrument or statute are followed by general words, the latter should be interpreted as being limited to the same sense as the former. [L: of the same kind]

**eka-,** a prefix primarily used to indicate an element which stands or is assumed to stand in the same family of the periodic table as a specified element esp. when not yet isolated: *ekasilicon.*

**eke**[1] /ik/, *v.t.,* **eked, eking. 1.** *Archaic.* to increase; enlarge; lengthen. **2. eke out, a.** to supply what is lacking to; supplement. **b.** to contrive to make (a living) or support (existence) by various makeshifts. [var. of obs. *ēche.* OE *ēcan,* with *k* from obs. n. *eke* addition (OE *ēaca*). Cf. *ēacen* augmented. Akin to Icel. *auka,* Goth. *aukan,* L *augēre* increase]

**eke**[2] /ik/, *adv., conj. Archaic.* also. [ME *eek,* from OE *ēc;* replacing OE *ēac,* c. G *auch*]

**ekistics** /i'kɪstɪks/, *n.* the science of human settlements. [coined by C. A. Doxiadis, 1913-75, Greek architect and planner, from Gk *oikizein* to settle, colonise, from *oîkos* house]

**elaborate** /ə'læbərət/, *adj.;* /ə'læbəreɪt, i-/, *v.* **-rated, -rating.** *–adj.* **1.** worked out with great care and nicety of detail; executed with great minuteness: *elaborate preparations, care, etc.* *–v.t.* **2.** to work out carefully or minutely; work up to perfection. **3.** to produce or develop by labour. **4.** *Physiol.* to convert (food, plasma, etc.) by means of chemical processes into a substance more suitable for use within the body. *–v.i.* **5.** to add details in writing, speaking, etc.; give additional or fuller treatment (fol. by *on* or *upon*): *to elaborate upon a theme or an idea.* **6.** to become elaborate. [L *ēlabōrātus,* pp., worked out] – **elaborately,** *adv.* – **elaborateness,** *n.* – **elaborator,** *n.* – **elaborative,** *adj.*

**elaboration** /əlæbə'reɪʃən, i-/, *n.* **1.** the act of elaborating. **2.** the state of being elaborated; elaborateness. **3.** something elaborated. **4.** *Physiol.* the process by which substances are built up in the bodies of animals or plants.

**elan** /eɪ'læn, -'lõ/, *n.* dash; impetuous ardour. [F, from *élancer* hurl, rush forth]

**eland** /'ilənd/, *n.* either of two large, heavily built African antelopes, *Taurotragus oryx* and *T. derbianus,* having spirally twisted horns in both sexes. [Afrikaans, special use of D *eland* elk, from G *Elend,* from Lithuanian *élnis* elk]

eland

**elapid** /'ɛləpɪd/, *n.* **1.** any snake of the family Elapidae, of warm regions, characterised by fixed venomous fangs at the front of the jaw, and including many Australian snakes, as the taipan and tiger snake, as well as cobras, mambas and kraits. *–adj.* **2.** of or pertaining to the Elapidae family of snakes.

**elapse** /ə'læps, i-/, *v.*, **elapsed, elapsing,** *n.* *–v.i.* **1.** (of time) to slip by or pass away. *–n.* **2.** the passing (of time); lapse. [L *ēlapsus,* pp.]

**elasmobranch** /ə'læzməbræŋk, i-/, *adj.* **1.** of the Elasmobranchii, the group of vertebrates including the sharks and rays, with cartilaginous skeletons and five to seven pairs of gill openings. *–n.* **2.** an elasmobranch fish. [NL *Elasmobranchii,* pl., from Gk *elasmó(s)* metal plate + *bránchia* gills]

**elastance** /ə'læstəns, i-/, *n.* the reciprocal of electrical capacitance.

**elastase** /ə'læsteɪz, -eɪs/, *n.* an enzyme, usu. isolated from the pancreas, which breaks up elastin.

**elastic** /ə'læstɪk, i-/, *adj.* **1.** having the property of recovering shape after deformation, as solids. **2.** spontaneously expansive, as gases. **3.** flexible, yielding, or accommodating: *an elastic conscience.* **4.** springing back or rebounding; springy: *an elastic step.* **5.** readily recovering from depression or exhaustion; buoyant: *an elastic temperament.* *–n.* **6.** webbing, or material in the form of a band, made elastic with strips of rubber. **7.** a piece of this material. **8.** *U.S.* a rubber band. [NL *elasticus,* from Gk *elastikós* propulsive] – **elastically,** *adv.*

**elastic band** /– 'bænd/, *n.* →**rubber band.**

**elastic bitumen** /– 'bɪtʃəmən/, *n.* →**mineral caoutchouc.**

**elastic collision** /– kə'lɪʒən/, *n.* **1.** an ideal collision between bodies in which their total kinetic energy before collision equals their total kinetic energy after collision. **2.** a collision between a particle and an atomic nucleus in which the nucleus is neither broken up nor excited.

**elasticise** /ə'læstəsaɪz, i-/, *v.t.*, **-cised, -cising.** to weave with elastic thread or make with elastic sections. Also, **elasticize.**

**elasticity** /əlæs'tɪsəti, i-/, *n.* **1.** the state or quality of being elastic. **2.** flexibility: *elasticity of meaning.* **3.** buoyancy; ability to resist or overcome depression.

**elastic limit** /əlæstɪk 'lɪmət/, *n.* the limiting value of the stress which can be applied to a body, or substance, without causing its permanent deformation.

**elastic modulus** /– 'mɒdʒələs/, *n.* a measure of the ratio of stress to strain in a given material.

**elastics** /ə'læstɪks, i-/, *n.* a game in which children jump in sets of patterns over stretched pieces of elastic.

**elastic sides** /əlæstɪk 'saɪdz/, *n.pl.* boots similar to riding boots, with a piece of elastic inset into the sides.

**elastin** /ə'læstɪn, i-/, *n.* a protein constituting the basic substance of elastic tissue. [ELAST(IC) + -IN[2]]

**elastomer** /ə'læstəmə, i-/, *n.* an elastic, rubber-like substance occurring naturally (natural rubber) or produced synthetically (butyl rubber, neoprene, etc.). [ELAST(IC) + -O- + Gk *mér(os)* part] – **elastomeric** /əlæstə'merɪk, i-/, *adj.*

**elastoplast** /ə'læstəplæst, -plast/, *n.* an adhesive dressing for superficial wounds, usu. supplied in long strips. [Trademark]

**elastration** /ˌilæs'treɪʃən/, *n.* a method of castrating male calves and lambs and of removing tails of lambs by placing an antiseptic rubber band about the testes or on the tail which cuts off the blood supply, and causes the part to die and fall off.

**elastrator** /ˌilæs'treɪtə/, *n.* an instrument used in elastration.

**elate** /ə'leɪt, i-/, *v.*, **elated, elating,** *adj.* *–v.t.* **1.** to put in high spirits; make proud. *–adj.* **2.** elated. [ME, from L *ēlātus,* pp., brought out, raised, exalted]

**elated** /ə'leɪtəd, i-/, *adj.* in high spirits; proud; jubilant. – **elatedly,** *adv.* – **elatedness,** *n.*

**elater** /'elətə/, *n.* **1.** *Bot.* an elastic filament serving to disperse spores of some algae, fungi, etc. **2.** *Zool.* →**elaterid.** [NL, from Gk: driver]

**elaterid** /ə'lætərəd/, *n.* **1.** any of the click beetles constituting the family Elateridae, most of which have the power of springing up when laid on their backs. *–adj.* **2.** of or pertaining to the Elateridae.

**elaterin** /ə'lætərən, i-/, *n.* a white crystalline substance obtained from and constituting the active principle of elaterium, used as a cathartic.

**elaterite** /ə'lætəraɪt, i-/, *n.* →**mineral caoutchouc.**

**elaterium** /elə'tɪəriəm/, *n.* a cathartic obtained from the juice of *Ecballium elaterium,* the squirting cucumber. [L, from Gk *elatḗrion* an opening medicine]

**elation** /ə'leɪʃən, i-/, *n.* exaltation of spirit, as from joy or pride; exultant gladness; high spirits.

**elative** /ə'leɪtɪv/, *adj.* **1.** having a superlative or intensive function. **2.** denoting a grammatical case used in some languages to express motion away from. *–n.* **3.** a superlative or intensive.

**E-layer** /'i-leɪə/, *n.* →**Heaviside layer.**

**elbow** /'elboʊ/, *n.* **1.** the bend or joint of the arm between upper arm and forearm. **2.** something bent like the elbow, as a sharp turn in a road or river, or a piece of pipe bent at an angle. **3. at one's elbow,** near at hand. **4. out at elbows** or **out at the elbow,** ragged or impoverished. **5. up to the elbows,** very busy with; wholly engaged or engrossed. **6. bend,** or **raise one's elbow,** to drink (esp. beer). *–v.t.* **7.** to push with or as with the elbow; jostle. **8.** to make (one's way) by so pushing. *–v.i.* **9.** to push; jostle. [ME *elbowe,* OE *elneboga,* c. G *Ellenbogen,* orig., arm bow. See ELL, BOW[1]]

**elbow grease** /'– gris/, *n.* vigorous, continuous exertion; hard physical labour.

**elbow orchid** /'– ɔkəd/, *n.* any of several species of the terrestrial orchid genus *Spiculaea* of Australia and New Guinea, characterised by an elbow-like joint in the column.

**elbow-room** /'elboʊ-rum/, *n.* sufficient room or scope.

**el cheapo** /el 'tʃipoʊ/, *Colloq.* *–adj.* **1.** of or pertaining to that which is cheap and inferior, as a restaurant, amplifier, record, etc. *–n.* **2.** any such article. **3.** a cheap restaurant. [imitative of Sp. nominal form]

**elder[1]** /'eldə/, *adj.* **1.** older. **2.** senior: *an elder officer.* **3.** earlier: *in elder times.* *–n.* **4.** a person who is older than oneself; one's senior. **5.** an aged person. **6.** one of the older and more influential men of a tribe or community, often a chief or ruler. **7.** →**presbyter. 8.** (in certain Protestant churches) a governing officer, often with teaching or pastoral functions. **9.** (in the Mormon Church) one holding the higher or Melchizedek priesthood. [ME; OE *eldra,* etc. (comparative of *ald, eald* OLD), c. G *älter*] – **eldership,** *n.*

**elder[2]** /'eldə/, *n.* **1.** any plant of the genus *Sambucus* of the northern hemisphere, which is composed of shrubs or trees with clusters of small, usu. white, flowers and black to red fruit. **2.** any of various unrelated species, as ground elder, *Aegopodium podagraria* and box elder, *Acer negundo.* [ME *eldre, elrene, ellerne,* OE *ellærn,* c. MLG *ellern, elderne*]

**elderberry** /'eldəberi/, *n.*, *pl.* **-ries. 1.** the drupaceous fruit of the elder, used in making wine, jelly, etc. **2.** →**elder[2]**.

**elderly** /'eldəli/, *adj.* **1.** somewhat old; between middle and old age. **2.** of or pertaining to persons in later life. – **elderliness,** *n.*

**elder statesman** /eldə 'steɪtsmən/, *n.*, *pl.* **-men.** an influential elderly citizen, as a retired politician, whose advice is sought, esp. on matters of national importance.

**eldest** /'eldəst/, *adj.* oldest; now surviving only in *the eldest brother, sister,* and *eldest hand.* [OE *eldest(a),* superlative of *ald, eald* OLD, c. G *ältest(e)*]

**el dorado** /el də'radoʊ/, *n.* a legendary treasure city; a place of reputed fabulous wealth. [Sp.: the gilded]

**eldritch** /'eldrɪtʃ/, *adj.* *Orig. Scot.* weird; unearthly.

**elecampane** /eləkæm'peɪn/, *n.* a plant, *Inula helenium,* with large yellow flowers and aromatic leaves and root. [earlier *elena* (OE *elene*) *campana,* for ML *enula* (in L *inula*) *campāna,* probably, inula (L name of plant) of the fields]

**elect** /ə'lekt, i-/, *v.t.* **1.** to select by vote, as for an office. **2.** to determine in favour of (a course of action, etc.). **3.** to pick out or choose. **4.** (of God) to select for divine mercy or favour, esp. for salvation. *–adj.* **5.** selected for an office, but not yet inducted (usu. after the noun): *the president-elect.* **6.** picked out; chosen. **7.** select or choice. **8.** chosen by God, esp. for eternal life. *–n.* **9.** a person or the persons chosen or worthy to be chosen. **10.** those chosen by God, esp. for eternal life. [late ME, from L *ēlectus,* pp., chosen, picked out]

**elect.,** **1.** electric. **2.** electrical. **3.** electricity. Also, **elec.**

**election** /ə'lekʃən, i-/, *n.* **1.** the selection of a person or persons for office by vote. **2.** a public vote upon a proposition submitted. **3.** the act of electing. **4.** the choice by God of individuals, as for a particular work, or esp. for salvation of eternal life. **5.** *Law.* the choice between alternative rights or claims; (in Equity) a doctrine that he who takes a benefit under an instrument must accept the instrument as a whole.

**electioneer** /ə'lɛkʃənɪə, i-/, *v.i.* to work for the success of a candidate, party, etc., in an election. – **electioneerer,** *n.* – **electioneering,** *adj., n.*

**elective** /ə'lɛktɪv, i-/, *adj.* **1.** pertaining to the principle of electing to office, etc. **2.** appointed by election, as an officer. **3.** bestowed by or derived from election, as an office. **4.** having the power of electing to office, etc., as a body of persons. **5.** open to choice; optional; not required: *an elective subject in high school or university.* **6.** *Chem.* selecting for combination or action: *elective attraction* (tendency to combine with certain substances in preference to others). –*n.* **7.** an optional study; a study which a student may select from among alternatives. – **electively,** *adv.* – **electiveness, electivity** /ilɛk'tɪvəti/, *n.*

**elector** /ə'lɛktə, i-/, *n.* one who elects or may elect, esp. a qualified voter. – **electorship,** *n.*

**electoral** /ə'lɛktərəl, -trəl, i-/, *adj.* **1.** pertaining to electors or election. **2.** consisting of electors.

**electoral college** /'– ˌkɒlɪdʒ/, *n. U.S.* a body of electors chosen by voters in each state to elect the president and vice-president of the United States.

**electoral officer** /'– ɒfəsə/, *n.* an officer responsible for the conduct of elections and the maintenance of electoral rolls.

**electoral roll** /'– roʊl/, *n.* a register of all persons entitled to vote in a constituency. Also, **electoral register.**

**electorate** /ə'lɛktərət, -trət, i-/, *n.* **1.** a body of constituents; the body of voters, or, loosely, of residents, in a district represented by an elected member of the legislature. **2.** the district itself. **3.** the body of persons entitled to vote in an electorate.

**electr-,** variant of **electro-**, before vowels, as in *electrode.*

**Electra complex** /ə'lɛktrə ˌkɒmplɛks/, *n.* the unresolved desire of a daughter for sexual gratification from her father. [from the Greek legend of *Electra,* daughter of Agamemnon and Clytemnestra, who invited her brother Orestes to avenge the murder of their father by their mother]

**electret** /əlɛk'trɛt/, *n.* a dielectric possessing a permanent electric dipole moment.

**electric** /ə'lɛktrɪk/, *adj.* **1.** pertaining to, derived from, produced by, or involving electricity: *an electric current, an electric shock.* **2.** producing, transmitting, or operated by electric currents: *an electric bell.* **3.** electrifying; thrilling; exciting; stirring. **4.** of or pertaining to musical instruments which are amplified by means of a built-in electronic device attached directly to some sounding section of the instrument, as electric guitar, electric bass, etc. [NL *ēlectricus,* from L *ēlectrum,* from Gk *ḗlektron* amber (as a substance that develops electricity under friction)]

**electrical** /ə'lɛktrɪkəl/, *adj.* **1.** electric. **2.** concerned with electricity: *an electrical engineer.* – **electrically,** *adv.*

**electrical engineer** /– ɛndʒə'nɪə/, *n.* one who practises electrical engineering.

**electrical engineering** /– ɛndʒə'nɪərɪŋ/, *n.* the branch of engineering concerned with the design, construction, and maintenance of electrical machinery, power transmission equipment, and communication systems.

**electrical storm** /'– stɔm/, *n.* →**thunderstorm.**

**electric blanket** /əlɛktrɪk 'blæŋkət/, *n.* a blanket containing an electric heating element, usu. thermostatically controlled.

**electric blue** /– 'blu/, *n.* a steely blue colour.

**electric car** /– 'ka/, *n.* a car which has an electric motor.

**electric cell** /– 'sɛl/, *n.* See **cell** (def. 7).

**electric chair** /– 'tʃɛə/, *n.* **1.** an electrified chair used to execute criminals sentenced to death. **2.** the electrocution.

**electric charge** /– 'tʃadʒ/, *n.* **1.** a property of matter which determines its behaviour in electric and magnetic fields. **2.** a quantity of electricity; the SI unit of electric charge is the coulomb.

**electric current** /– 'kʌrənt/, *n.* a flow of electricity. See **current** (def. 9).

**electric dipole** /– 'daɪpoʊl/, *n.* a pair of equal and opposite electrical charges.

**electric eel**[1] /– 'il/, *n.* an eel-like freshwater fish, *Electrophorus electricus,* of northern South America, having the power of giving strong electric discharges.

**electric eel**[2] /– 'il/, *n.* a mechanically driven, rotating, cutting device for cleaning blocked drainage pipes; sewermat.

**electric eye** /– 'aɪ/, *n.* →**photoelectric cell.**

**electric fence** /– 'fɛns/, *n.* **1.** a fence through which an electric current passes, used to deter intruders. **2.** a fence, one or two wires of which are periodically energised by a high tension voltage to keep animals back. Also, **electrified fence.**

**electric field** /– 'fild/, *n.* a condition of space in the vicinity of an electric charge, a varying electric current, or a moving magnet which manifests itself as a force on an electric charge within that space.

**electric field strength,** *n.* the strength of an electric field, in SI units measured in volts per metre.

**electric furnace** /əlɛktrɪk 'fɜnəs/, *n.* a furnace in which the heat required is produced through electricity.

**electric guitar** /– gə'ta/, *n.* a guitar with a device attached to its bridge for transmitting the sounds produced through an amplifier to a loudspeaker.

**electric hare** /– 'hɛə/, *n.* (in greyhound racing) a model of a rabbit, propelled electrically, which the dogs chase. Also, **electric rabbit.**

**electrician** /əlɛk'trɪʃən, ɛlɛk-, ilɛk-/, *n.* **1.** one who installs, operates, maintains, or repairs electrical devices. **2.** a student of the science of electricity.

**electric intensity** /əlɛktrɪk ɪn'tɛnsəti/, *n.* the strength of an electric field at any given point; electric field strength.

**electricity** /əlɛk'trɪsəti, ɛlɛk-, ilɛk-/, *n.* **1.** an agency producing various physical phenomena, as attraction and repulsion, luminous and heating effects, shock to the body, chemical decomposition, etc., which were originally thought to be caused by a kind of fluid, but are now regarded as being due to the presence and movements of electrons, protons, and other electrically charged particles. **2.** the science dealing with this agency. **3.** electric current.

**electric jug** /əlɛktrɪk 'dʒʌg/, *n.* an earthenware jug fitted with an electric heating element, for boiling water.

**electric light** /– 'laɪt/, *n.* **1.** illumination produced by the use of electricity. **2.** →**bulb** (def. 3).

**electric logging** /– 'lɒgɪŋ/, *n.* the process of recording the rock formations penetrated by a drill based on the electrical properties of the rocks measured by a recording device lowered down the drill hole.

**electric motor** /– 'moʊtə/, *n.* a motor powered by electricity.

**electric organ** /– 'ɔgən/, *n.* **1.** *Zool.* an anatomical feature in certain fishes, as the electric eel, which generates and discharges electricity, mainly for defensive purposes. **2.** *Music.* **a.** →**organ** (def. 2). **b.** a pipe organ which is operated electrically.

**electric potential** /– pə'tɛnʃəl/, *n.* →**potential** (def. 8).

**electric ray** /– 'reɪ/, *n.* a ray of the family Torpedinidae which possesses a peculiar organ enabling it to stun its prey with electric shock.

**electric shock** /– 'ʃɒk/, *n.* the effect of the passage of an electric current through the body.

**electric welding** /– 'wɛldɪŋ/, *n.* →**arc welding.**

**electrify** /ə'lɛktrəfaɪ, i-/, *v.t.,* **-fied, -fying. 1.** to charge with or subject to electricity; to apply electricity to. **2.** to equip for the use of electric power, as a railway. **3.** to startle greatly; excite or thrill: *to electrify an audience.* [ELECTR(IC) + -(I)FY] – **electrifiable,** *adj.* – **electrification** /əlɛktrəfə'keɪʃən/, *n.* – **electrifier,** *n.*

**electro** /ə'lɛktroʊ/, *n., pl.* **-tros. 1.** →**electroplate. 2.** →**electrotype.**

**electro-,** a word meaning 'pertaining to or caused by electricity', as in *electromagnet, electrotype, electrochemistry, electrolysis, electrocute.* Also, **electr-.** [Gk *ēlektro-,* combining form of *ḗlektron* amber]

**electroanalysis** /əˌlɛktroʊə'næləsəs, i-/, *n.* chemical analysis by electrolysis. – **electroanalytic** /əˌlɛktroʊænə'lɪtɪk/, *adj.*

**electrobiology** /əˌlɛktroʊbaɪ'ɒlədʒi, i-/, *n.* the science of electrical phenomena in living organisms.

**electrocardiogram** /əˌlɛktroʊ'kadiəgræm, i-/, *n.* the graphic record produced by an electrocardiograph. *Abbrev.:* ECG Also, **cardiogram.** [ELECTRO- + CARDIO- + -GRAM[1]]

**electrocardiograph** /əˌlɛktroʊ'kadiəgræf, i-/, *n.* a device which detects and records the minute differences in potential caused by heart action and occurring between different parts of the body; used in the diagnosis of heart disease. *Abbrev.:* ECG Also, **cardiograph.** [ELECTRO- + CARDIO- + -GRAPH] – **electrocardiographic** /əˌlɛktroʊˌkadiəˈgræfɪk, i-/, *adj.* – **electrocardiographically** /əˌlɛktroʊˌkadiəˈgræfɪkli, i-/, *adv.* – **electrocardiography** /əˌlɛktroʊˌkadiˈɒgrəfi/, *n.*

**electrochemical equivalent** /əlɛktroʊˌkɛmɪkəl əˈkwɪvələnt, i-/, *n.* the mass of a substance liberated or deposited during electrolysis by 1 coulomb, usu. expressed in grams.

**electrochemical series** /– ˈsɪəriz/, *n. Chem* →**electromotive series.**

**electrochemistry** /əlɛktroʊˈkɛməstri, i-/, *n.* the branch of chemistry that deals with the chemical changes produced by electricity and the production of electricity by chemical changes. – **electrochemical,** *adj.* – **electrochemically,** *adv.* – **electrochemist,** *n.*

**electroconvulsive therapy** /əˌlɛktroʊkənˌvʌlsɪv ˈθɛrəpi, i-/, *n.* a type of psychiatric therapy in which an electric shock is administered to the brain, used mainly in treatment of depression; shock treatment. *Abbrev.:* ECT

**electrocute** /əˈlɛktrəkjut, i-/, *v.t.*, **-cuted, -cuting. 1.** to kill by electricity. **2.** to execute (a criminal) by electricity. [ELECTRO- + *-cute* in EXECUTE] – **electrocution** /əlɛktrəˈkjuʃən/, *n.*

**electrode** /əˈlɛktroʊd, i-/, *n.* a conductor of electricity belonging to the class of metallic conductors, but not necessarily a metal, through which a current enters or leaves an electrolytic cell, arc generator, radio valve, gaseous discharge tube, or any conductor of the non-metallic class. [ELECTR(O)- + -ODE[2]]

**electrodeposit** /əˌlɛktroʊdəˈpɒzət, i-/, *v.t.* **1.** to deposit (a metal, etc.) by electrolysis. *–n.* **2.** a deposit, as of metal, produced by electrolysis.

**electrodessication** /əˌlɛktroʊˌdɛsəˈkeɪʃən, i-/, *n.* (in medicine) the destruction of small growths esp. of skin, cervix, etc., by diathermy.

**electrodynamic** /əˌlɛktroʊdaɪˈnæmɪk, i-/, *adj.* **1.** pertaining to the force of electricity in motion. **2.** pertaining to electrodynamics. Also, **electrodynamical.**

**electrodynamics** /əˌlɛktroʊdaɪˈnæmɪks, i-/, *n.* the branch of electricity that deals with the mutual action of electric currents and the interaction of currents and magnets.

**electrodynamometer** /əˌlɛktroʊˌdaɪnəˈmɒmətə, i-/, *n.* an instrument in which the mechanical reactions between two parts of the same circuit are used for detecting or measuring an electric current.

**electroencephalogram** /əˌlɛktroʊɛnˈsɛfələgræm, i-/, *n.* the graphic record produced by an electroencephalograph. *Abbrev.:* EEG [ELECTRO- + ENCEPHALO- + -GRAM[1]]

**electroencephalograph** /əˌlɛktroʊɛnˈsɛfələgræf, i-/, *n.* a device which detects and records the electrical activity of the brain. *Abbrev.:* EEG [ELECTRO- + ENCEPHALO- + -GRAPH] – **electroencephalographic** /əˌlɛktroʊɛnˌsɛfələˈgræfɪk, i-/, *adj.* – **electroencephalographically** /əˌlɛktroʊɛnˌsɛfələˈgræfɪkli, i-/, *adv.* – **electroencephalography** /əˌlɛktroʊɛnˌsɛfəˈlɒgrəfi, i-/, *n.*

**electroextraction** /əˌlɛktroʊəkˈstrækʃən, i-/, *n.* the recovery of a metal from a solution of its salts by electrolysis.

**electroform** /əˈlɛktrəfɔm, i-/, *v.t.* to produce or reproduce (metallic articles) by electrodeposition. – **electroforming,** *n.*

**electrograph** /əˈlɛktrəgræf, i-/, *n.* **1.** a curve automatically traced, forming a record of the indications of an electrometer. **2.** an apparatus for engraving metal plates on cylinders used in printing. **3.** an apparatus used to transmit pictures, etc., electrically. – **electrographic** /əlɛktrəˈgræfɪk, i-/, *adj.* – **electrographically** /əlɛktrəˈgræfɪkli, i-/, *adv.* – **electrography** /əlɛkˈtrɒgrəfi, i-/, *n.*

**electrokinetic potential** /əˌlɛktroʊkənɛtɪk pəˈtɛnʃəl, i-, -kaɪ-/, *n.* →**zetapotential.**

**electrokinetics** /əˌlɛktroʊkəˈnɛtɪks, i-, -kaɪ-/, *n.* the branch of electricity that deals with currents. – **electrokinetic,** *adj.*

**electroless plating** /əlɛktrələs ˈpleɪtɪŋ, i-/, *n.* an immersion plating process in which a chemical reducing agent changes metal ions to metal.

**electroluminescence** /əˌlɛktroʊˌluməˈnɛsəns, i-/, *n.* the property of emitting light on activation by an alternating current. – **electroluminescent,** *adj.*

**electrolyse** /əˈlɛktrəlaɪz, i-/, *v.t.*, **-lysed, -lysing.** to decompose by electrolysis. Also, *U.S.*, **electrolyze.** – **electrolysation** /əˌlɛktrəlaɪˈzeɪʃən, i-/, *n.* – **electrolyser,** *n.*

**electrolysis** /əlɛkˈtrɒləsəs, i-, ˌɛləkˈtrɒləsəs/, *n.* **1.** the decomposition of a chemical compound by an electric current. **2.** *Surg.* the destruction of tumours, hair roots, etc., by an electric current.

**electrolyte** /əˈlɛktrəlaɪt, i-/, *n.* **1.** an electricity conducting medium in which the flow of current is accompanied by the movement of matter. **2.** *Chem.* any substance which dissociates into ions when dissolved in a suitable medium or when melted, thus forming a conductor of electricity.

**electrolytic** /əlɛktrəˈlɪtɪk, i-/, *adj.* **1.** pertaining to or derived by electrolysis. **2.** pertaining to an electrolyte. Also, **electrolytical.** – **electrolytically,** *adv.*

**electrolytic cell** /– ˈsɛl/, *n.* See **cell** (def. 8).

**electrolytic condenser** /– kənˈdɛnsə/, *n.* a capacitor of fixed capacitance in which one electrode consists of a metal foil coated with a thin layer of the metal oxide, and the other electrode is a non-corrosive salt solution or paste. Also, **electrolytic capacitor.**

**electrolytic dissociation** /– dəsoʊʃiˈeɪʃən/, *n.* the separation of the molecule of an electrolyte into its constituent atoms.

**electrolytic gas** /– ˈgæs/, *n.* a gas produced by the electrolysis of water, consisting of a mixture of hydrogen and oxygen in the ratio 2:1 by volume; detonating gas.

**electrolytic rectifier** /– ˈrɛktəfaɪə/, *n.* a rectifier consisting of an electrolytic cell which depends for its action on the properties of certain metals and electrolytes to allow current to flow only in one direction.

**electromagnet** /əˌlɛktroʊˈmægnət, i-/, *n.* a device consisting of an iron or steel core which is magnetised by electric current in a coil which surrounds it.

electromagnet: A, armature; B, core; C, coil carrying current; L, load

**electromagnetic** /əˌlɛktroʊmægˈnɛtɪk, i-/, *adj.* **1.** pertaining to an electromagnet. **2.** pertaining to electromagnetism. – **electromagnetically,** *adv.*

**electromagnetic field** /– ˈfild/, *n.* the field produced by the propagation of electromagnetic waves through space (or a conducting medium), and characterised by the presence of both an electric and magnetic field distribution varying in both time and space.

**electromagnetic induction** /– ɪnˈdʌkʃən/, *n.* the induction of an electromotive force in a circuit by a change in the magnetic flux linked with it.

**electromagnetic pump** /– ˈpʌmp/, *n.* a pump used for liquid metals consisting of a flattened tube placed between the poles of an electromagnet. When a current is passed through the liquid metal in the tube it is subjected to a force along the axis of the tube.

**electromagnetic radiation** /– reɪdiˈeɪʃən/, *n.* radiation consisting of electromagnetic waves.

**electromagnetic spectrum** /– ˈspɛktrəm/, *n.* the whole range of frequencies over which electromagnetic waves can be propagated, ranging from radio waves to cosmic radiation and including light.

**electromagnetic tape** /– ˈteɪp/, *n.* →**magnetic tape.**

**electromagnetic unit** /– ˈjunət/, *n.* a unit in a system of units within the c.g.s. system, used for measuring electric currents and magnetisation, based on the unit magnetic pole which repels a similar pole placed 1 cm distant with a force of 1 dyne. *Abbrev.:* emu, E.M.U.

**electromagnetic wave** /– ˈweɪv/, *n.* a moving disturbance in space produced by the acceleration of an electric charge; consisting of an electric field and a magnetic field at right-angles to each other, both moving at the same velocity in a direction at right angles to the plane of the two fields.

**electromagnetism** /əˌlɛktroʊˈmægnəˌtɪzəm, i-/, *n.* **1.** the phenomena collectively resting upon the relations between electric currents and magnetism. **2.** the science that deals with these relations.

**electromechanical** /əˌlɛktroʊmə'kænɪkəl, i-/, *adj.* containing both electrical and mechanical elements.

**electrometallurgy** /əˌlɛktroʊ'mɛtəˌlɜdʒi, i-/, *n.* the refining of metals and ores by an electric current. – **electrometallurgical** /əˌlɛktroʊˌmɛtə'lɜdʒɪkəl, i-/, *adj.* – **electrometallurgist,** *n.*

**electrometer** /ɛlək'trɒmətə, əlɛk-, ilɛk-/, *n.* an instrument for detecting or measuring a potential difference by means of the mechanical forces exerted between electrically charged bodies. – **electrometric** /əˌlɛktroʊ'mɛtrɪk/, **electrometrical** /əlɛktroʊ'mɛtrɪkəl/, *adj.* – **electrometrically** /əlɛktroʊ'mɛtrɪkli/, *adv.*

**electromotive** /əˌlɛktroʊ'moʊtɪv, i-/, *adj.* pertaining to, producing, or tending to produce a flow of electricity.

**electromotive force** /– 'fɔs/, *n.* a measure of the intensity of a source of electrical energy which produces an electric current in a circuit. The SI unit is the volt. *Abbrev.:* e.m.f., E.M.F., emf, EMF

**electromotive series** /– 'sɪəriz/, *n.* the metals arranged in the order in which they will replace each other from their salts. Hydrogen is also included, and metals above hydrogen in the series will liberate it from acids. Also, **electrochemical series.**

**electromotor** /əˌlɛktroʊ'moʊtə, i-/, *n.* →**electric motor.**

**electromyography** /əˌlɛktroʊmaɪ'ɒgrəfi, i-/, *n.* a method of investigating the action of muscles by tracking the electrical activity associated with this action, which makes use of electrodes either placed on the skin over the muscles or inserted as needles into the muscles. *Abbrev.:* E.M.G.

**electron** /ə'lɛktrɒn, i-/, *n.* an elementary particle which is a constituent of all atoms, with a minute mass of $9.1083 \times 10^{-28}$ grams. It has a negative electric charge of approximately $1.6 \times 10^{-19}$ coulombs. The positively charged electron is called a *positron.* [ELECTR(IC) + (I)ON]

**electron beam** /– 'bim/, *n.* a stream of electrons.

**electronegative** /əˌlɛktroʊ'nɛgətɪv, i-/, *adj.* **1.** containing negative electricity; tending to pass to the positive pole in electrolysis. **2.** assuming negative potential when in contact with a dissimilar substance. **3.** nonmetallic.

**electron gun** /ə'lɛktrɒn ˌgʌn/, *n.* the cathode in a cathode-ray tube which emits electrons, and the surrounding electrostatic or electromagnetic apparatus which controls and focuses the electron stream.

**electronic** /ɛlək'trɒnɪk, əlɛk'trɒnɪk, i-/, *adj.* **1.** of or pertaining to electrons. **2.** of, pertaining to, or concerned with electronics or any devices or systems based on electronics.

**electronic computer** /– kəm'pjutə/, *n.* See **computer.**

**electronic data processing,** *n.* the use of digital computers to handle information. *Abbrev.:* EDP

**electronic flash** /ɛləktrɒnɪk 'flæʃ/, *n.* (in photography) a device for producing a very bright flash of light by an electric discharge through a gas-filled tube.

**electronic media** /– 'midiə/, *n.* that section of the media which uses electronic means of communication, as radio and television.

**electronic music** /ɛləkˌtrɒnɪk 'mjuzɪk/, *n.* music produced by electronic means, which may include organised non-musical sounds. Also, **electrophonic music.**

**electronic organ** /– 'ɔgən/, *n.* →**organ** (def. 2).

**electronics** /əlɛk'trɒnɪks, i-, ɛlək-/, *n.* the investigation and application of phenomena involving the movement of electrons in valves and semiconductors.

**electronic video recording,** *n.* any of various systems of recording and duplicating video programs, usu. on electron sensitive film, for domestic playback.

**electron lens** /əlɛktrɒn 'lɛnz, i-/, *n.* a combination of static or varying electric and magnetic fields used to focus streams of electrons in a manner similar to that of an optical lens.

**electron micrograph** /– 'maɪkroʊgræf/, *n.* a photograph of an object or collection of objects obtained with an electron microscope.

**electron microscope** /– 'maɪkrəskoʊp/, *n.* a microscope of extremely high power which uses beams of electrons focused by electron lenses instead of rays of light, the magnified image being formed on a fluorescent screen or recorded on a photographic plate. Its magnification is substantially greater than that of any optical microscope.

**electron-pair** /əˌlɛktrɒn-'pɛə/, *n.* two electrons occupying the same region in space in relation to one nucleus or more and spinning in opposite directions.

**electron paramagnetic resonance,** *n. Physics.* a phenomenon exhibited by paramagnetic substances in which the spin of an unpaired electron aligns itself with a magnetic field. Used in molecular structure analysis. *Abbrev.:* EPR Also, **electron spin resonance.**

**electron probe microanalysis,** *n.* a method of analysing tiny quantities of a substance by bombarding it with a narrow beam of electrons and examining the resulting X-ray emission spectrum.

**electron spin resonance,** *n.* →**electron paramagnetic resonance.** *Abbrev.:* ESR

**electron spin resonance spectroscopy,** *n.* a method of locating electrons within a molecule and so providing information about the molecule's structure. It depends on a property of paramagnetic substances which results from their unpaired electrons.

**electron tube** /əlɛktrɒn 'tjub, i-/, *n. U.S. Electronics.* →**valve** (def. 7).

**electronuclear machine** /əˌlɛktroʊˌnjukliə mə'ʃin, i-/, *n.* a device for the production of very high energy beams of particles (protons, electrons, etc.) by acceleration in electric and magnetic fields. Examples are the cyclotron, synchrotron, cosmotron, etc.

**electronvolt** /əlɛktrɒn'voʊlt/, *n.* a unit of energy used in X-rays, gamma rays, atomic and nuclear physics; 1 electron-volt equals $160.219 \times 10^{-21}$ joules. *Symbol:* eV

**electrophonic** /əˌlɛktroʊ'fɒnɪk, i-/, *adj.* (of musical instruments) based on oscillating electric currents. – **electrophonically,** *adv.*

**electrophonic music** /– 'mjuzɪk/, *n.* →**electronic music.**

**electrophoresis** /əˌlɛktroʊfə'risəs, i-/, *n.* the motion of colloidal particles suspended in a fluid medium, under the influence of an electric field. [ELECTRO- + Gk *phórēsis* a carrying]

**electrophorus** /əlɛk'trɒfərəs, i-/, *n., pl.* **-ri** /-raɪ/. an instrument for generating static electricity by means of induction. [NL. See ELECTRO-, -PHOROUS]

**electroplate** /ə'lɛktrəpleɪt, i-/, *v.,* **-plated, -plating,** *n.* –*v.t.* **1.** to plate or coat with a metal by electrolysis. –*n.* **2.** electroplated articles or ware. – **electroplater,** *n.* – **electroplating,** *n.*

**electropositive** /əˌlɛktroʊ'pɒzətɪv, i-/, *adj.* **1.** containing positive electricity; tending to pass to the negative pole in electrolysis. **2.** assuming positive potential when in contact with another substance. **3.** basic, as an element or radical.

**electroscope** /ə'lɛktrəskoʊp, i-/, *n.* a device for detecting the presence of electricity, and whether it is positive or negative, by means of electric attraction and repulsion. – **electroscopic** /əlɛktrə'skɒpɪk/, *adj.*

**electrostatic** /əlɛktroʊ'stætɪk, i-/, *adj.* of or pertaining to static electricity.

**electrostatic generator** /– 'dʒɛnəreɪtə/, *n.* a machine for the production of electrical charges at high potential, such as the Wimshurst machine and the Van de Graaff generator.

**electrostatic precipitation** /– prəsɪpə'teɪʃən/, *n.* a method of removing small particles of dust, smoke, oil, etc., from a gas, esp. air, by first giving the particles an electrostatic charge and then passing the gas between two charged plates to which the particles are attracted.

**electrostatics** /əlɛktroʊ'stætɪks, i-/, *n.* the science of static electricity.

**electrostatic unit** /əˌlɛktroʊstætɪk 'junət/, *n.* a unit in a system of units, within the c.g.s. system, based on the unit of charge, which is defined as that quantity of electricity which will repel an equal quantity 1 cm distant with a force of 1 dyne. *Abbrev.:* e.s.u., E.S.U., esu

**electrostriction** /əlɛktroʊ'strɪkʃən, i-/, *n.* the elastic deformation of a dielectric when placed in an electric field.

**electrotherapeutics** /əˌlɛktroʊˌθɛrə'pjutɪks, i-/, *n.* therapeutics based upon the curative use of electricity. – **electrotherapeutic, electrotherapeutical,** *adj.*

**electrotherapist** /əlɛktroʊ'θɛrəpəst, i-/, *n.* one versed in electrotherapeutics. Also, **electrotherapeutist** /əˌlɛktroʊθɛrə'pjutəst, i-/.

**electrotherapy** /əˌlɛktroʊ'θɛrəpi, i-/, *n.* treatment of diseases by means of electricity; electrotherapeutics.

**electrotonus** /əlɛk'trɒtənəs, i-/, *n.* the altered state of a nerve during the passage of an electric current through it. [NL, from Gk *ēlektro-* ELECTRO- + *tónos* tension] – **electrotonic** /əlɛktrou'tɒnɪk, i-/, *adj.*

**electrotype** /ə'lɛktrətaɪp, i-/, *n., v.,* **-typed, -typing.** *–n.* **1.** a facsimile, for use in printing, of a block of type, an engraving, or the like, consisting of a thin shell of metal (copper or nickel), deposited by electrolytic action in a wax, lead, or plastic mould of the original and backed with lead alloy. *–v.t.* **2.** to make an electrotype or electrotypes of. – **electrotyper,** *n.*

**electrovalency** /əlɛktrou'veɪlənsi, i-/, *n.* the valency of an ion; equal to the number of electrons lost or gained by the atom which becomes the ion. Also, *U.S.,* **electrovalence.** – **electrovalent,** *adj.*

**electrovalent bond** /əlɛktrou,veɪlənt 'bɒnd/, *n.* a chemical bond formed by the transfer of one or more electrons from one atom to another, the resulting ions being held together by electrostatic attraction. Also, **ionic bond, polar bond.**

**electrowinning** /ə'lɛktrou,wɪnɪŋ/, *n.* the recovery of pure metal from impure concentrates by electrolysis.

**electrum** /ə'lɛktrəm, i-/, *n.* an amber-coloured alloy of gold and silver. [L, from Gk *ēlektron* amber, also gold-silver alloy. See ELECTRIC]

**electuary** /ə'lɛktʃuəri, i-/, *n., pl.* **-aries.** a medicine composed usu. of a powder mixed into a pasty mass with syrup or honey. [ME, from LL *ēlectuārium.* Cf. Gk *ekleiktón* electuary, from *ekleíchein* lick up (in passive, be taken as an electuary)]

**eleemosynary** /ɛlə'mouzənəri, ɛli-/, *adj.* **1.** of or pertaining to alms, charity, or charitable donations; charitable. **2.** derived from or provided by charity. **3.** dependent on or supported by charity. [ML *eleēmosynārius,* from LL *eleēmosyna* alms. See ALMS]

**elegance** /'ɛləgəns, 'ɛlɪ-/, *n.* **1.** elegant quality: *elegance of dress.* **2.** something elegant; a refinement.

**elegancy** /'ɛləgənsi, 'ɛlɪ-/, *n., pl.* **-cies.** →**elegance.**

**elegant** /'ɛləgənt, 'ɛlɪ-/, *adj.* **1.** tastefully fine or luxurious in dress, manners, etc.: *elegant furnishings.* **2.** gracefully refined, as in tastes, habits, literary style, etc. **3.** nice, choice, or pleasingly superior in quality or kind, as a contrivance, preparation, or process. **4.** *Colloq.* excellent; fine; superior. [L *ēlegans* fastidious, nice, fine, elegant] – **elegantly,** *adv.*

**elegiac** /ɛlə'dʒaɪək/, *adj.* Also, **elegiacal.** **1.** *Class. Pros.* denoting a distich the first line of which is a dactylic hexameter and the second a pentameter, or a verse differing from the hexameter by suppression of the arsis or metrically unaccented part of the third and the sixth foot. **2.** belonging to an elegy or to elegy; having to do with elegies. **3.** expressing sorrow or lamentation: *elegiac strains.* *–n.* **4.** an elegiac or distich verse. **5.** a poem or poems in such distichs or verses. [LL *elegīacus,* from Gk *elegeiakós*]

**elegise** /'ɛlədʒaɪz/, *v.,* **-gised, -gising.** *–v.t.* **1.** to lament in or as in an elegy. *–v.i.* **2.** to compose an elegy. Also, **elegize.**

**elegist** /'ɛlədʒəst/, *n.* the author of an elegy.

**elegit** /'ɛlədʒət/, *n.* a writ of execution against a judgment debtor's goods or property held by the judgment creditor until payment of the debt. [L: he has chosen]

**elegy** /'ɛlədʒi/, *n., pl.* **-gies.** **1.** a mournful, melancholy, or plaintive poem, esp. a funeral song or a lament for the dead, as Milton's *Lycidas.* **2.** poetry or a poem written in elegiac metre. **3.** a sad or funeral composition, vocal or instrumental, whether actually commemorative or not. [L *elegīa,* from Gk *elegeía,* properly neut. pl. of *elegeîos* elegiac, from *élegos* lament]

**element** /'ɛləmənt/, *n.* **1.** a component or constituent part of a whole. **2.** *(pl.)* the rudimentary principles of an art, science, etc.: *the elements of grammar.* **3.** one of the simple substances, usu. earth, water, air, and fire, regarded by Aristotle as constituting the material universe. **4.** one of these four substances regarded as the natural habitat of something. **5.** the sphere or environment adapted to any person or thing: *to be in one's element.* **6.** *(pl.)* atmospheric agencies or forces: *exposed to the elements.* **7.** *Chem.* one of a class of substances which consist entirely of atoms of the same atomic number. **8.** *Astron.* any of the data required for the solution of a problem: *the elements of a planetary orbit,* which determine the orientation, size, and shape of the orbit, and the position of the planet in the orbit at any time. **9.** *Elect.* **a.** the resistance wire, and the former to which it is attached, of an electric heater or other domestic appliance containing a heating unit. **b.** one of the electrodes of a cell or radio valve. **10.** *Maths.* **a.** a member of a set. **b.** a part of a geometric figure. **c.** any one of the units which go to make up an array. **11.** *Gram.* any word, group of words, or part of a word, which recurs in various contexts in a language with relatively constant meaning. **12.** *(pl.)* the bread and wine used in the Eucharist. [ME, from L *elementum* a first principle, rudiment]

**elemental** /ɛlə'mɛntl/, *adj.* **1.** of the nature of an ultimate constituent; simple; uncompounded. **2.** pertaining to rudiments or first principles. **3.** of, pertaining to, or of the nature of the four elements or any one of them. **4.** pertaining to the agencies, forces, or phenomena of physical nature: *elemental gods, elemental worship.* **5.** comparable to the great forces of nature, as with reference to their power: *elemental grandeur.* **6.** pertaining to chemical elements. – **elementally,** *adv.*

**elementary** /ɛlə'mɛntri, -təri/, *adj.* **1.** pertaining to or dealing with elements, rudiments, or first principles: *elementary education, an elementary grammar.* **2.** of the nature of an ultimate constituent; simple or uncompounded. **3.** pertaining to the four elements or to the great forces of nature; elemental. – **elementarily,** *adv.* – **elementariness,** *n.*

**elementary particle** /– 'patɪkəl/, *n.* any of a class of entities which used to be thought to be the indivisible units of which all matter is composed; fundamental particle; ultimate particle.

**elemi** /'ɛləmi/, *n., pl.* **-mis.** any of various fragrant resins used in medicine, varnish making, etc. [cf. F *élémi,* Sp. *elemí,* from Ar. *allāmi*]

**elenchus** /ə'lɛŋkəs/, *n., pl.* **-chi** /-kaɪ/. **1.** a logical refutation; an argument which refutes another argument by proving the contrary of its conclusion. **2.** a false refutation; a sophistical argument. [L, from Gk *élenchos* cross-examination] – **elenctic,** *adj.*

African elephant

**eleoptene** /ɛli'ɒptin/, *n.* the liquid portion of volatile oils (opposed to the solid part, *stearoptene*). [Gk *élaio(n)* oil + *ptēnós* winged, volatile]

**elephant** /'ɛləfənt/, *n.* **1.** either of two very large, herbivorous mammals of the family Elephantidae, the *Loxodonta africana* of Africa and the somewhat smaller *Elephas maximus* of India and neighbouring regions, having thick, almost hairless skin, a long, prehensile trunk, upper incisors prolonged into long curved tusks and, in the African species, large, flapping ears. **2.** an animal of the order Proboscidea, as a mammoth. **3.** *Obs.* a very large paper size. **4.** any book larger than 53 x 53cm. **5.** See **white elephant.** **6.** See **pink elephant.** [L *elephantus,* also *elephās,* from Gk *eléphas* elephant, ivory; replacing ME *olifaunt,* from OF *olifant*] – **elephantoid,** *adj.*

Indian elephant

**elephant gun** /'– gʌn/, *n.* **1.** a rifle of large calibre, designed for hunting elephants. **2.** *Colloq.* a surfboard used for riding big waves.

**elephantiasis** /ɛləfən'taɪəsəs, -fæn-/, *n.* a chronic disease, due to lymphatic obstruction, characterised by enormous enlargement of the parts affected. [L, from Gk, from *eléphas* elephant]

**elephantine** /ɛlə'fæntaɪn/, *adj.* **1.** pertaining to or resembling an elephant. **2.** huge; ponderous; clumsy.

**elephants** /'ɛləfənts/, *adj. Colloq.* drunk. [rhyming slang, *elephant's trunk,* drunk]

**elephant seal** /ˈɛləfənt sil/, *n.* either of two species of large earless seals, the males of which have an inflatable trunk-like proboscis, *Mirounga leonina* of Antarctic regions and *M. angustirostris* of North America.

**elephant's-ear** /ˈɛləfənts-ɪə/, *n.* **1.** →**taro.** **2.** any plant of the genus *Begonia,* family Begoniaceae, of tropical regions. **3.** any of various other plants whose leaves resemble the ears of an elephant.

**elephant shrew** /ˈɛləfənt ʃru/, *n.* any of several rat-sized, jumping insectivores of the family Macroscelididae of Africa, having a long, scaly tail and flexible, trunk-like snout.

**elevate** /ˈɛləveɪt/, *v.,* **-vated, -vating.** *–v.t.* **1.** to move or raise to a higher place or position; lift up. **2.** to raise to a higher state or station; exalt. **3.** to raise the spirits of; put in high spirits. [ME *elevat,* from L *ēlevātus,* pp.]

**elevated** /ˈɛləveɪtəd/, *adj.* **1.** raised, esp. above the ground: *an elevated platform.* **2.** exalted or noble: *elevated thoughts.* **3.** elated; joyful. **4.** slightly drunk.

**elevation** /ɛləˈveɪʃən/, *n.* **1.** altitude above sea or ground level. **2.** an elevated place; an eminence. **3.** loftiness; grandeur or dignity; nobleness. **4.** the act of elevating. **5.** the state of being elevated. **6.** *Archit.* **a.** a drawing or design which represents an object or structure as being projected geometrically on a vertical plane parallel to its chief dimension. **b.** one of the external faces of a building; facade. **7.** *Survey.* the angle between the line from an observer to an object above him and a horizontal line. **8.** the ability of a dancer to stay in the air while executing a step. **9.** *Rom. Cath. Ch.* (*usu cap.*) the lifting up of the bread and wine after consecration by the priest, in the view of the congregation.

**elevator** /ˈɛləveɪtə/, *n.* **1.** one who or that which elevates or raises. **2.** a mechanical device for raising articles. **3.** → **lift** (def. 23). **4.** a building for storing grain, the grain being handled by means of mechanical lifting and conveying devices. **5.** a hinged horizontal plane on an aeroplane, etc., used to control the longitudinal inclination, generally placed at the tail end of the fuselage. **6.** *Anat.* a muscle for raising part of the body. [LL]

**eleven** /əˈlɛvən/, *n.* **1.** a cardinal number, ten plus one. **2.** a symbol for this number, as 11 and XI. **3.** a set of this many persons or things. **4.** a team of eleven players, as in soccer, cricket, hockey, etc. *–adj.* **5.** amounting to eleven in number. [ME *elleven(e),* etc., OE *ellefne, endleofan,* etc., lit., one left (after counting ten). Cf. OHG *einlif,* MHG *eilf,* G *elf*] **– eleventh,** *adj., n.*

**eleven-plus** /əlɛvən-ˈplʌs/, *n. Brit.* an examination taken by some British primary school children at the age of about eleven, the result of which determines the type of state secondary education for which they are eligible.

**elevenses** /əˈlɛvənzəz/, *n. Brit. Colloq.* a light mid-morning snack, usu. taken at about 11 o'clock.

**eleventh hour** /əlɛvənθ ˈaʊə/, *n.* the last possible moment for doing something. [from the parable (Matthew 20: 1-16) in which the workers hired at the eleventh hour received the same wages as those hired earlier] **– eleventh-hour,** *adj.*

**elf** /ɛlf/, *n., pl.* **elves** /ɛlvz/. **1.** one of a class of imaginary beings, esp. from mountainous regions, with magical powers, given to capricious interference in human affairs, and usu. imagined to be a diminutive being in human form; a sprite; a fairy. **2.** a dwarf or a small child. **3.** a small, mischievous person. [ME, backformation from *elven,* OE *elfen* nymph (feminine elf), representing OE *ælf,* c. G *Alp* nightmare (def. 3), incubus] **– elflike,** *adj.*

**elfchild** /ˈɛlftʃaɪld/, *n.* →**changeling.**

**elfin** /ˈɛlfən/, *adj.* **1.** of or like elves. **2.** small, mischievous, sprightly, bright. *–n.* **3.** an elf.

**elfish** /ˈɛlfɪʃ/, *adj.* **1.** elf-like. **2.** small and mischievous. Also, **elvish. – elfishly,** *adv.* **– elfishness,** *n.*

**elflock** /ˈɛlflɒk/, *n.* a tangled lock of hair.

**elicit** /əˈlɪsət/, *v.t.* to draw or bring out or forth; educe; evoke: *to elicit the truth.* [L *ēlicitus,* pp.] **– elicitation** /əlɪsəˈteɪʃən/, *n.* **– elicitor,** *n.*

**elide** /əˈlaɪd, i-/, *v.t.,* **elided, eliding.** to omit (a vowel, consonant, or syllable) in pronunciation. [L *ēlīdere* crush out]

**eligibility** /ɛlədʒəˈbɪləti/, *n.* **1.** worthiness or fitness to be chosen. **2.** legal qualification for election or appointment.

**eligible** /ˈɛlədʒəbəl/, *adj.* **1.** fit or proper to be chosen; worthy of choice; desirable. **2.** legally qualified to be elected or appointed to office. **3.** of a single person, the desirable object of matrimonial designs: *an eligible bachelor.* [F, from L *ēligere* pick out] **– eligibly,** *adv.*

**eliminate** /əˈlɪməneɪt, i-/, *v.t.,* **-nated, -nating.** **1.** to get rid of; expel; remove: *to eliminate errors.* **2.** to omit as irrelevant or unimportant; ignore. **3.** *Physiol.* to void or expel from an organism. **4.** *Maths.* to remove (a quantity) from an equation by elimination. [L *ēlīminātus,* pp., turned out of doors] **– eliminability** /əlɪmənəˈbɪləti/, *n.* **– eliminator,** *n.* **– eliminable,** *adj.* **– eliminative,** *adj.* **– eliminatory,** *adj.*

elk

**elimination** /əlɪməˈneɪʃən, i-/, *n.* **1.** the act of eliminating. **2.** the state of being eliminated. **3.** *Maths.* the process of solving a system of linear equations by a procedure in which variables are successively removed. *–adj.* **4.** of or pertaining to a competition in which losing players are removed at the end of each round until only the winner remains.

**elision** /əˈlɪʒən, i-/, *n.* the omission of a vowel, consonant, or syllable in writing or pronunciation. [L *ēlīsio* a striking out]

**elite** /əˈlit, eɪ-, i-/, *n.* **1.** the choice or best part, as of a body or class of persons. **2.** (*construed as pl.*) persons of the highest class. **3.** a group of persons exercising the major share of authority or control within a larger organisation. **4.** a small type, approximately 10-point, used in typewriters and having about one character every 2 mm. [F, from *élire* choose, from L *ēligere*]

**elitism** /əˈlitɪzəm, eɪ-, i-/, *n.* **1.** practice of or belief in rule by an elite. **2.** consciousness of or pride in belonging to a select or favoured group. **3.** *Colloq.* snobbery; anti-democratic sentiment. **– elitist,** *n., adj.*

**elixir** /əˈlɪksə, ɛ-, i-/, *n.* **1.** an alchemic preparation formerly believed to be capable of transmuting base metals into gold, or of prolonging life: *elixir vitae,* or *elixir of life.* **2.** a sovereign remedy; panacea; cure-all. **3.** the quintessence or absolute embodiment of anything. **4.** *Pharm.* **a.** a tincture with more than one base, or some similar compound medicine. **b.** an aromatic, sweetened alcoholic liquid containing medicinal agents, or used as a vehicle for them. [ME, from ML, from Ar. *el, al* the + *iksīr* philosopher's stone, probably from LGk *xḗrion* a drying powder for wounds]

**Elizabethan** /əlɪzəˈbiθən, i-/, *adj.* **1.** of or pertaining to Elizabeth I, queen of England 1558-1603, or to her times. *–n.* **2.** one who lived in England during the Elizabethan period, esp. a poet or dramatist.

**elk** /ɛlk/, *n., pl.* **elks** *or* **elk.** **1.** the largest existing European and Asiatic deer, *Alces alces,* closely related to the moose, having a large head with broad, overhanging muzzle, and large palmate antlers in the male. **2.** (in America) the wapiti. **3.** a pliable leather used for sports shoes, made originally of elk hide but now of calfskin or cowhide tanned and smoked to resemble elk hide. [apparently from OE *ealh* elk (c. G *Elch*) + *-k* suffix]

**elkhorn fern** /ˈɛlkhɔn ˌfɜn/, *n.* →**staghorn fern.**

**elkhound** /ˈɛlkhaʊnd/, *n.* one of a large, strong breed of dogs with a thick grey coat, originally a Norwegian hunting dog. Also, **Norwegian elkhound.**

**ell** /ɛl/, *n.* a former measure of length, varying in different countries, but often about 115 cm. [ME and OE *eln,* c. D *el,* G *Elle;* orig. meaning arm, forearm (see ELBOW), and akin to L *ulna,* Gk *ōlénē*]

**Ellangowan poison bush,** *n.* a shrub, *Myoporum desertii,* family Myoporaceae, of the drier parts of Australia, having small white flowers and succulent yellowish fruits, and having foliage known to have poisoned stock; turkey bush.

**ellipse** /əˈlɪps, i-/, *n.* a plane curve such that the sums of the distances of each point in its periphery from two fixed points, the foci, are equal. It is a conic section formed by the intersection of a right circular cone by a plane which cuts obliquely the axis and the opposite sides of the cone. [L *ellipsis.* See ELLIPSIS]

**ellipsis** /ə'lɪpsɪs, i-/, *n., pl.* **-ses** /-siz/. **1.** *Gram.* the omission from a sentence of a word or words which would complete or clarify the construction. **2.** *Print.* a mark or marks as — or . . . or * * *, to indicate an omission or suppression of letters or words. [L, from Gk *élleipsis* omission]

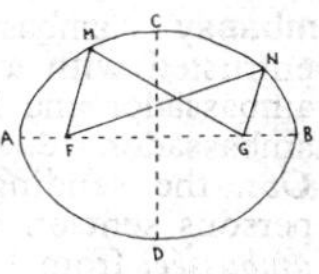

ellipse: AB, CD, axes of ellipse; F, G, foci; FM + GM equals FN + GN, M and N being any points in the curve

**ellipsoid** /ə'lɪpsɔɪd, i-/, *n.* **1.** a solid figure all plane sections of which are ellipses or circles. *–adj.* **2.** ellipsoidal.

**ellipsoidal** /əlɪp'sɔɪdl, ˌilɪp-/, *adj.* pertaining to, or having the form of, an ellipsoid.

**elliptical** /ə'lɪptɪkəl, i-/, *adj.* **1.** pertaining to or having the form of an ellipse. **2.** pertaining to or marked by grammatical ellipses. **3.** extremely or excessively concise or condensed. Also, **elliptic.**

**elliptically** /ə'lɪptɪkli, i-/, *adv.* **1.** in the form of an ellipse. **2.** in an elliptical manner; with an ellipsis.

**elliptical stern** /ə'lɪptɪkəl ˌstɜn, i-/, *n.* →**counter stern.**

**ellipticity** /əlɪp'tɪsəti, ˌilɪp-/, *n.* the degree of divergence of an ellipse from the circle.

**elm** /ɛlm/, *n.* **1.** any tree, mostly deciduous, of the genus *Ulmus,* family Ulmaceae, of northern temperate regions and mountains of tropical Asia, as English elm, *U. procera,* a large tree probably once endemic in England, now widely cultivated for shade and ornament, and Chinese elm, *U. parvifolia,* of China, Japan, Korea and Taiwan. **2.** the wood of any such tree. [ME and OE, c. OHG *elm;* akin to Icel. *álmr,* L *ulmus*]

**elocution** /ɛlə'kjuʃən/, *n.* **1.** manner of speaking or reading in public. **2.** the study and practice of spoken delivery, including the management of voice and gesture. [L *ēlocūtio* a speaking out] – **elocutionary** /ɛlə'kjuʃənri, -ʃənəri/, *adj.* – **elocutionist,** *n.*

**elodea** /ɛlə'diə/, *n.* any species of the submerged water plant genus *Elodea,* esp. *E. canadensis,* a troublesome weed of waterways.

**eloign** /ə'lɔɪn/, *v.t.* to remove (oneself) to a distance. Also, **eloin.** [AF *esloignier,* from OF *es-* (see EX-[1]) + *loign* far away (from L *longē*)]

**elongate** /'ilɒŋgeɪt/, *v.,* **-gated, -gating,** *adj.* *–v.t.* **1.** to draw out to greater length; lengthen; extend. *–v.i.* **2.** to increase in length. *–adj.* **3.** elongated. [LL *ēlongātus,* pp., removed, prolonged]

**elongation** /ilɒŋ'geɪʃən/, *n.* **1.** the act of elongating. **2.** the state of being elongated. **3.** that which is elongated; an elongated part. **4.** *Astron.* the angular distance measured from the earth, between a planet or the moon and the sun, or between a satellite and the planet about which it revolves.

**elope** /ə'loʊp, i-/, *v.i.,* **eloped, eloping.** **1.** to run away with a lover, usu. in order to marry without parental consent. **2.** to abscond or escape. [ME **alopen,* from *a-* A-[3] + *lopen* LOPE. Cf. AF *aloper* ravish (a woman), elope (with a man)] – **elopement,** *n.* – **eloper,** *n.*

**eloquence** /'ɛləkwəns/, *n.* **1.** the action, practice, or art of using language with fluency, power, and aptness. **2.** eloquent language or discourse: *a flow of eloquence.*

**eloquent** /'ɛləkwənt/, *adj.* **1.** having or exercising the power of fluent, forcible, and appropriate speech: *an eloquent orator.* **2.** characterised by forcible and appropriate expression: *an eloquent speech.* **3.** movingly expressive: *eloquent looks.* [ME, from L *ēloquens,* ppr., speaking out] – **eloquently,** *adv.*

elouera

**elouera** /ɛ'lauərə/, *n.* a stone implement of uncertain use but possibly a scraper, in the form of a triangular-sectioned blade, resembling a segment of an orange, often with a glossy surface acquired apparently by use, and typical of the Eloueran period.

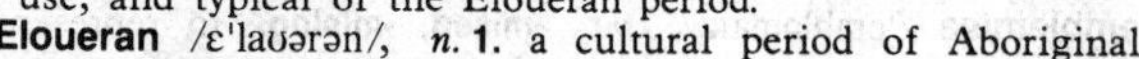

**Eloueran** /ɛ'lauərən/, *n.* **1.** a cultural period of Aboriginal development recognised in eastern Australia, which follows the Bondaian period and extends to the present. *–adj.* **2.** of, or pertaining to this period.

**El Salvador** /ɛl 'sælvədɔ/, *n.* a republic in Central America.

**else** /ɛls/, *adv.* **1.** (following as an appositive an indef. or interrog. pronoun). **a.** other than the person or the thing mentioned; instead: *somebody else; who else?* **b.** in addition: *what else shall I do? who else is going?* **2.** (following an indef. or interrog. pronoun and forming with it an indef. or compound pronoun with inflection at the end): *somebody else's child, nobody else's business, who else's child could it be?* **3.** otherwise: *run, or else you will be late.* [ME and OE *elles* (c. OHG *elles*) adv. gen. of a pre-E word, c. L *alius* other]

**elsewhere** /'ɛlswɛə, ɛls'wɛə/, *adv.* somewhere else; in or to some other place.

**elucidate** /ə'lusədeɪt, i-/, *v.t.,* **-dated, -dating.** to make lucid or clear; throw light upon; explain. [LL *ēlūcidātus,* pp., made light] – **elucidation** /əlusə'deɪʃən, i-/, *n.* – **elucidator,** *n.* – **elucidative, elucidatory,** *adj.*

**elude** /ə'lud, i-/, *v.t.,* **eluded, eluding.** **1.** to avoid or escape by dexterity or artifice: *to elude pursuit.* **2.** to slip away from; evade: *to elude vigilance.* **3.** to escape the mind; baffle. [L *ēlūdere* finish play, deceive] – **eluder,** *n.*

**elusion** /ə'luʒən, i-/, *n.* the act of eluding; evasion; clever escape. [ML *ēlūsio.* See ELUDE]

**elusive** /ə'lusɪv, i-/, *adj.* **1.** eluding clear perception hard to express or define. **2.** dexterously evasive. Also, **elusory** /ə'lusəri, i-/. – **elusively,** *adv.* – **elusiveness,** *n.*

**elutriate** /ə'lutrieɪt, i-/, *v.t.,* **-ated, -ating.** **1.** to purify by washing and straining or decanting. **2.** to separate the light and heavy particles of by suspending in a current of water or air. [L *ēlūtriātus,* pp.] – **elutriator,** *n.* – **elutriation** *n.*

**eluviation** /ə'luvieɪʃən, i-/, *n.* the removal of material in solution or suspension from the uppermost horizon of a soil to a lower horizon by the downward percolation of water.

**eluvium** /ə'luviəm, i-/, *n., pl.* **-via** /-viə/. a deposit of soil, dust, etc., originating in the place where found as through decomposition of rock (distinguished from *alluvium*). [NL, from L *ēluere* wash out] – **eluvial,** *adj.*

**elvan** /'ɛlvən/, *n.* a granular, igneous rock found most often in dykes and composed essentially of quartz and orthoclase. Also, **elvanite** /'ɛlvənaɪt/.

**elver** /'ɛlvə/, *n.* a young eel, particularly when running up a stream from the ocean. [var. of *eel-fare* (from EEL + FARE) passage of young eels up a river]

**elves** /ɛlvz/, *n.* plural of **elf.**

**elvish** /'ɛlvɪʃ/, *adj.* →**elfish.** – **elvishly,** *adv.*

**Elysian** /ə'lɪziən, i-/, *adj.* **1.** pertaining to, or resembling, Elysium. **2.** blissful; delightful.

**Elysium** /ə'lɪziəm, i-/, *n.* **1.** any place or state of perfect happiness. **2.** an abode or state of the dead. [L, from Gk, short for *Elýsion* (*pedíon*) Elysian (plain or field), the abode of the blessed after death]

**elytra** /'ɛlətrə/, *n.* plural of **elytron, elytrum.**

**elytral** /'ɛlətrəl/, *adj.* of or pertaining to an elytron.

**elytriform** /ɛ'lɪtrəfɔm/, *adj.* shaped like an elytron.

**elytroid** /'ɛlətrɔɪd/, *adj.* like an elytron.

**elytron** /'ɛlətrɒn/, *n., pl.* **-tra** /-trə/. one of the pair of hardened forewings of certain insects, as beetles, forming a protective covering for the posterior wings. Also, **elytrum** /'ɛlətrəm/. [NL, from Gk: cover, sheath] – **elytral,** *adj.*

**elytrous** /'ɛlətrəs/, *adj.* having elytra.

**elytrum** /'ɛlətrəm/, *n., pl.* **-tra** /-trə/. →**elytron.**

**em**[1] /ɛm/, *n., pl.* **ems.** **1.** the letter M, m. **2.** *Print.* the square of the body size of any type (originally the portion of a line occupied by the letter M). **3.** *Print.* the unit of measurement of the printing on a page equal to 12 points; pica. *–adj.* **4.** having the size of an em: *em quad.* [name of the letter M]

**em**[2] /əm/, *pron. pl. Colloq.* them (occurs only in unstressed position). Also, **'em.** [ME *hem,* dat. and acc. pl. of HE; now taken for weak form of THEM]

**em-**[1], variant of **en-**[1], before *b, p,* and sometimes *m,* as in *embalm.* Cf. **im-**[1].

**em-**[2], variant of **en-**[2], before *b, m, p, ph,* as in *embolism, emphasis.*

**emaciate** /ə'meɪsieɪt, i-/, *v.t.*, **-ated, -ating.** to make lean by a gradual wasting away of flesh. [L *ēmaciātus*, pp.]

**emaciation** /əmeɪsi'eɪʃən, i-/, *n.* abnormal thinness, caused by lack of nutrition or by disease.

**emanate** /'ɛmәneɪt/, *v.i.*, **-nated, -nating.** to flow out, issue, or proceed as from a source or origin; come forth; originate. [L *ēmānātus*, pp.] – **emanative, emanatory,** *adj.*

**emanation** /ɛmə'neɪʃən/, *n.* **1.** the act or fact of emanating. **2.** something that emanates. **3.** *Chem.* a gaseous product of radioactive disintegration including radon, thoron, and actinon; emanon.

**emancipate** /ə'mænsəpeɪt, i-/, *v.t.*, **-pated, -pating. 1.** to free from restraint of any kind, esp. the inhibitions of tradition. **2.** to free (a slave). **3.** *Roman and Civil Law.* to terminate paternal control over. [L *ēmancipātus*, pp.] – **emancipative,** *adj.*

**emancipated convict** /ə,mænsəpeɪtəd 'kɒnvɪkt, i-/, *n.* →**emancipist** (def. 2). Also, **emancipated colonist, emancipated man.**

**emancipation** /əmænsə'peɪʃən, i-/, *n.* **1.** the act of emancipating. **2.** the fact of being emancipated; freedom.

**emancipationist** /əmænsə'peɪʃənəst/, *n.* one who supports or brings about emancipation.

**emancipator** /ə'mænsəpeɪtə, i-/, *n.* one who emancipates. [LL]

**emancipist** /ə'mænsəpəst/, *n.* **1.** an emancipationist. **2.** (formerly) a freed convict, esp. one who received a conditional or absolute pardon from a colonial governor in Australia as a reward for good conduct.

**emanon** /'ɛmənɒn/, *n.* →**emanation** (def. 3).

**emarginate** /ə'madʒəneɪt/, *adj.* **1.** notched at the margin. **2.** *Bot.* notched at the apex, as a petal or leaf. Also, **emarginated.** [L *ēmarginātus*, pp., deprived of an edge]

emarginate leaves

**emasculate** /ə'mæskjəleɪt, i-/, *v.*, **-lated, -lating;** /ə'mæskjələt, i-, -leɪt/, *adj.* –*v.t.* **1.** to castrate. **2.** to deprive of strength or vigour; weaken; render effeminate. –*adj.* **3.** emasculated; effeminate. [L *ēmasculātus*, pp.] – **emasculation** /əmæskjə'leɪʃən, i-/, *n.* – **emasculator,** *n.* – **emasculatory, emasculative,** *adj.*

**embalm** /ɛm'bam/, *v.t.* **1.** to treat (a dead body) with balsams, spices, etc., or (now usu.) with drugs or chemicals, in order to preserve from decay. **2.** to preserve from oblivion; keep in memory. **3.** *Poetic.* to impart a balmy fragrance to. [ME *enbaume(n)*, from F *embaumer*, from *em-* EM-[1] + *baume* BALM] – **embalmer,** *n.* – **embalmment,** *n.*

**embank** /ɛm'bæŋk/, *v.t.* to enclose, confine, or protect with a bank, mound, dyke, or the like.

**embankment** /ɛm'bæŋkmənt, ə-/, *n.* **1.** a bank, mound, dyke, or the like, raised to hold back water, carry a road, etc. **2.** the act of embanking.

**embarcation** /ɛmba'keɪʃən/, *n.* →**embarkation.**

**embargo** /ɛm'bagoʊ/, *n.*, *pl.* **-goes,** *v.*, **-goed, -going.** –*n.* **1.** an order of a government prohibiting the movement of merchant vessels from or into its ports. **2.** any restriction imposed upon commerce by law. **3.** a restraint or hindrance; a prohibition. –*v.t.* **4.** to impose an embargo on. [Sp., from *embargar* restrain, from Rom. *barra* BAR[1]]

**embark** /ɛm'bak/, *v.i.* **1.** to board a ship, as for a voyage. **2.** to engage in an enterprise, business, etc. –*v.t.* **3.** to put or receive on board a ship. **4.** to involve (a person) in an enterprise; venture or invest (money, etc.) in an enterprise. [F *embarquer*, from *em-* EM-[1] (from L *in-*) + *barque* BARQUE]

**embarkation** /ɛmba'keɪʃən/, *n.* the act or process of embarking. Also, **embarcation.**

**embarrass** /ɛm'bærəs/, *v.t.* **1.** to disconcert; abash; make uncomfortable, self-conscious, etc.; confuse. **2.** to make difficult or intricate, as a question or problem; complicate. **3.** to put obstacles or difficulties in the way of; impede. **4.** to beset with financial difficulties; burden with debt. –*v.i.* **5.** to become disconcerted, abashed. [F *embarrasser*, lit., block, obstruct, from *embarras* obstacle] – **embarrassing,** *adj.* – **embarrassingly,** *adv.*

**embarrassment** /ɛm'bærəsmənt/, *n.* **1.** embarrassed state; disconcertion; abashment. **2.** the act of embarrassing. **3.** that which embarrasses. **4.** superabundance; excess.

**embassy** /'ɛmbəsi/, *n.*, *pl.* **-sies. 1.** a body of persons entrusted with a mission to a sovereign or government; an ambassador and his staff. **2.** the official headquarters of an ambassador. **3.** the function or office of an ambassador. **4.** *Obs.* the sending of ambassadors. **5.** *Colloq.* the body of persons sent on any undertaking. [var. of *ambassy*, from MF *ambassée*, from LL *ambactia* office]

**embattle**[1] /ɛm'bætl/, *v.t.*, **-tled, -tling. 1.** to arrange in order of battle; prepare for battle; arm. **2.** *Archaic.* to fortify (a town, etc.). [ME *embataile(n)*, from OF *embataillier*, from *em-* EM-[1] + *bataille* BATTLE]

**embattle**[2] /ɛm'bætl/, *v.t.*, **-tled, -tling.** to furnish with battlements. [ME, from EM-[1] + OF *bataillier;* see BATTLEMENT]

**embay** /ɛm'beɪ/, *v.t.* to enclose in or as in a bay; surround.

**embayment** /ɛm'beɪmənt/, *n.* **1.** a bay. **2.** *Phys. Geog.* **a.** an indentation in a shoreline forming an open bay. **b.** the formation of a bay. **3.** *Phys. Geog.* a continental border area which subsides concurrently with deposition of sediment.

**embed** /ɛm'bɛd/, *v.t.*, **-bedded, -bedding. 1.** to fix firmly in a surrounding mass. **2.** to lay in or as in a bed. **3.** *Linguistics.* to insert (a relative clause, etc.) within a main clause. Also, **imbed.** – **embedding, embedment,** *n.*

**embellish** /ɛm'bɛlɪʃ/, *v.t.* **1.** to beautify by or as by ornamentation; ornament; adorn. **2.** to enhance (a statement or narrative) with fictitious additions; embroider. [ME *embelyss(en)*, from OF *embelliss-*, stem of *embellir*, from *em-* EM-[1] + *bel* handsome] – **embellisher,** *n.*

**embellishment** /ɛm'bɛlɪʃmənt/, *n.* **1.** an ornament or decoration. **2.** a fictitious addition, as in a statement. **3.** the act of embellishing. **4.** *Music.* any pattern of decorative notes unessential to the implied harmony.

**ember**[1] /'ɛmbə/, *n.* **1.** a small live coal, brand of wood, etc., as in a dying fire. **2.** (*pl.*) the smouldering remains of a fire. [ME *eemer, emeri*, OE *ǣmerge*, c. Icel. *eimyrja*]

**ember**[2] /'ɛmbə/, *adj.* pertaining to the three-day period of prayer and fasting that comes once in each season of the liturgical year. [ME *ymber* (attrib.), OE *ymbren*, special use of OE *ymbrene, ymbryne* circuit, course, from *ymb* around + *ryne* a running]

**embezzle** /ɛm'bɛzəl/, *v.t.*, **-zled, -zling.** to appropriate fraudulently to one's own use, as money or property entrusted to one's possession. [ME *enbesyl(en)*, from AF *enbesiler*, from *en-* EM-[1] + *beseler* destroy, dissipate] – **embezzlement,** *n.* – **embezzler,** *n.*

**embitter** /ɛm'bɪtə/, *v.t.* to make bitter or more bitter. – **embitterer,** *n.* – **embitterment,** *n.*

**emblaze**[1] /ɛm'bleɪz/, *v.t. Archaic.* **1.** to illuminate; light up. **2.** to kindle.

**emblaze**[2] /ɛm'bleɪz/, *v.t.* **1.** to adorn with heraldic devices. **2.** *Archaic.* to celebrate; render famous.

**emblazon** /ɛm'bleɪzən/, *v.t.* **1.** to portray or inscribe on or as on a heraldic shield; to embellish or decorate. **2.** to proclaim; celebrate or extol. – **emblazoner,** *n.*

**emblazonment** /ɛm'bleɪzənmənt/, *n.* **1.** the act of emblazoning. **2.** that which is emblazoned.

**emblazonry** /ɛm'bleɪzənri/, *n.* **1.** the act or art of emblazoning; heraldic decoration. **2.** brilliant representation or embellishment.

**emblem** /'ɛmbləm/, *n.* **1.** an object, or a representation of it, symbolising a quality, state, class of persons, etc.; a symbol. **2.** an allegorical drawing or picture, often with explanatory writing. [L *emblēma* inlaid work, ornamentation, from Gk: an insertion]

**emblematic** /ɛmblə'mætɪk/, *adj.* pertaining to, of the nature of, or serving as an emblem; symbolic. Also, **emblematical.** – **emblematically,** *adv.*

**emblematise** /ɛm'blɛmətaɪz/, *v.t.*, **-tised, -tising.** to serve as an emblem of; represent by an emblem. Also, **emblematize.**

**emblematist** /ɛm'blɛmətəst/, *n.* a designer, maker, or user of emblems.

**emblements** /'ɛmbləmənts/, *n. pl.* the products or profits of land which has been sown or planted. [AF *emblaement*, from *emblaer*, from *em-* EM-[1] + *blé* grain (from Gmc. Cf. MD *blaad*, OE *blǣd*)]

**emblemise** /'ɛmbləmaɪz/, *v.t.*, **-mised, -mising.** to represent by an emblem; emblematise. Also, **emblemize.**

**embodiment** /ɛm'bɒdimənt/, *n.* **1.** the act of embodying. **2.** the state of being embodied. **3.** that in which something is embodied; an incarnation. **4.** something embodied.

**embody** /ɛm'bɒdi/, *v.t.*, **-bodied, -bodying. 1.** to invest with a body, as a spirit; incarnate; make corporeal. **2.** to give a concrete form to; express or exemplify (ideas, etc.) in concrete form. **3.** to collect into or include in a body; organise; incorporate. **4.** to embrace or comprise.

**embolden** /ɛm'bouldn/, *v.t.* to make bold or more bold; hearten or encourage. – **emboldener,** *n.*

**embolectomy** /ɛmbə'lɛktəmi/, *n., pl.* **-mies.** the removal of an embolus from an artery, which it is obstructing, by surgery. [EMBOL(US) + -ECTOMY]

**embolic** /ɛm'bɒlɪk/, *adj.* **1.** *Pathol.* pertaining to an embolus or to embolism. **2.** *Embryol.* developing inwardly; related to a process of invagination.

**embolism** /'ɛmbəlɪzəm/, *n.* **1.** intercalation, as of a day in a year. **2.** a period of time intercalated. **3.** an extension and elaboration of the last petition in the Lord's Prayer, as in the canon of the Roman Catholic liturgy. **4.** *Pathol.* the occlusion of a blood vessel by an embolus. [LL *embolismus* intercalation, from Gk *embállein* throw in. See EMBLEM] – **embolismic,** *adj.*

**embolus** /'ɛmbələs/, *n., pl.* **-li** /-laɪ/. undissolved material carried by the blood current and impacted in some part of the vascular system, as thrombi or fragments of thrombi, tissue fragments, clumps of bacteria, protozoan parasites, fat globules, gas bubbles. [L: piston, from Gk *émbolos* peg, stopper]

**emboly** /'ɛmbəli/, *n.* a gradual embedding of one part into another, as in the formation of certain gastrulae. [Gk *embolḗ* throwing in, invasion]

**embonpoint** /õmbõ'pwa/, *n.* exaggerated plumpness; stoutness. [F: lit., in good condition]

**embosom** /ɛm'bʊzəm/, *v.t.* **1.** to enfold, envelop, or enclose. **2.** to take into or hold in the bosom; embrace. **3.** to cherish; foster.

**emboss** /ɛm'bɒs/, *v.t.* **1.** to raise or represent surface designs in relief. **2.** to cause to bulge out; make protuberant; make umbonate. **3.** to raise a design on a fabric by pressing. **4.** to cover or ornament with bosses or studs. [ME *embosse(n)*, from OF *embocer* swell in protuberances, from *em-* EM-[1] + *boce* swelling, BOSS[2]] – **embosser,** *n.* – **embossment,** *n.*

**embouchure** /'ɒmbuʃʊə/, *n.* **1.** the mouth of a river. **2.** the opening out of a valley into a plain. **3.** *Music.* **a.** the mouthpiece of a wind instrument, esp. when of metal. **b.** the adjustment of a player's mouth to such a mouthpiece. [F, from *emboucher* put into the mouth, discharge by a mouth or outlet, from *em-* EM-[1] + *bouche* mouth (from L *bucca* cheek, mouth)]

**embowel** /ɛm'baʊəl/, *v.t.*, **-elled, -elling** or (*U.S.*) **-eled, -eling.** →**disembowel.**

**embower** /ɛm'baʊə/, *v.t.* to shelter in or as in a bower; cover or surround with foliage.

**embrace** /ɛm'breɪs/, *v.*, **-braced, -bracing,** *n.* –*v.t.* **1.** to take or clasp in the arms; press to the bosom; hug. **2.** to take or receive (an idea, etc.) gladly or eagerly; accept willingly. **3.** to avail oneself of (an opportunity, etc.). **4.** to adopt (a profession, a religion, etc.). **5.** to take in with the eye or the mind. **6.** to encircle; surround; enclose. **7.** to include or contain. –*v.i.* **8.** to join in an embrace. –*n.* **9.** an act of embracing; a hug. [ME *enbrace(n)*, from OF *embracier*, from *em-* EM-[1] + *bras* arm (from L *bracchium*)] – **embraceable,** *adj.* – **embracement,** *n.* – **embracer,** *n.* – **embracive,** *adj.*

**embraceor** /ɛm'breɪsə/, *n.* a person guilty of embracery. Also, **embracer.**

**embracery** /ɛm'breɪsəri/, *n., pl.* **-eries.** the offence of attempting to influence a judge or jury corruptly. [ME *embracerie*, from OF *embraser* instigate, lit., set fire to]

**embranchment** /ɛm'bræntʃmənt, -'brantʃ-/, *n.* **1.** a branching or ramification. **2.** a branch.

**embrangle** /ɛm'bræŋgəl/, *v.t.*, **-gled, -gling.** to confuse; entangle; perplex. Also, **imbrangle.** [EM-[1] + *brangle* (b. BRAWL[1] and WRANGLE)] – **embranglement,** *n.*

**embrasure** /ɛm'breɪʒə/, *n.* **1.** an opening in a wall or parapet through which a gun may be fired, constructed with sides which flare outward. **2.** *Archit.* an enlargement of the aperture of a door or window, at the inside face of the wall, by means of splayed sides. [F, from *embraser, ébraser* to splay (an opening)]

**embrocate** /'ɛmbrəkeɪt/, *v.t.*, **-cated, -cating.** to moisten and rub with a liniment or lotion. [ML *embrocātus*, pp. of *embrocāre*, from LL *embrocha*, from Gk *embrochḗ* lotion]

**embrocation** /ɛmbrə'keɪʃən/, *n.* **1.** the act of embrocating a bruised or diseased part of the body. **2.** the liquid for this; a liniment or lotion.

**embroider** /ɛm'brɔɪdə/, *v.t.* **1.** to decorate with ornamental needlework. **2.** to produce or form in needlework. **3.** to adorn or embellish rhetorically, esp. with fictitious additions. –*v.i.* **4.** to do embroidery. **5.** to provide rhetorical embellishment, esp. by fictitious additions. [apparently from EM-[1] + BROIDER] – **embroiderer,** *n.*

**embroidery** /ɛm'brɔɪdəri, -dri/, *n., pl.* **-deries. 1.** the art of working, with a needle, raised and ornamental designs in threads of silk, cotton, gold, silver, or other material, upon any woven fabric, leather, paper, etc. **2.** embroidered work or ornamentation. **3.** *Colloq.* embellishment by invented or exaggerated detail.

**embroil** /ɛm'brɔɪl, əm-/, *v.t.* **1.** to bring into a state of discord; involve in contention or strife. **2.** to throw into confusion; complicate. [F *embrouiller*, from *em-* EM-[1] + *brouiller* BROIL[2]] – **embroiler,** *n.* – **embroilment,** *n.*

**embrown** /ɛm'braʊn/, *v.t.* **1.** to make brown or dark. –*v.i.* **2.** to become brown or dark.

**embrute** /ɛm'brut/, *v.t., v.i.*, **-bruted, -bruting.** →**imbrute.**

**embryectomy** /ɛmbri'ɛktəmi/, *n., pl.* **-mies.** removal of an embryo by surgery. [EMBRY(O) + -ECTOMY]

**embryo** /'ɛmbrioʊ/, *n., pl.* **-os. 1.** an organism in the earlier stages of its development, as before emergence from the egg or before metamorphosis. **2.** (among mammals and other viviparous animals) a young animal during its earlier stages within the mother's body (including, in man, the developmental stages up to the end of the seventh week). **3.** the rudimentary plant usu. contained in the seed. **4.** the beginning or rudimentary stage of anything. –*adj.* **5.** embryonic. [ML, from Gk *émbryon*]

**embryogeny** /ɛmbri'ɒdʒəni/, *n.* the formation and development of the embryo, as a subject of scientific study. Also, **embryogenesis** /ˌɛmbrioʊ'dʒɛnəsəs/. [EMBRYO + -GENY] – **embryogenetic** /ˌɛmbrioʊdʒə'nɛtɪk/, *adj.*

**embryol.**, embryology.

**embryology** /ɛmbri'ɒlədʒi/, *n.* the science of the embryo, its genesis, development, etc. [EMBRYO + -LOGY] – **embryological** /ˌɛmbriə'lɒdʒɪkəl/, **embryologic** /ˌɛmbriə'lɒdʒɪk/, *adj.* – **embryologist,** *n.*

**embryonic** /ɛmbri'ɒnɪk/, *adj.* **1.** pertaining to or in the state of an embryo. **2.** rudimentary; undeveloped. Also, **embryonal** /'ɛmbriənəl/.

**embryo sac** /'ɛmbrioʊ sæk/, *n.* the megaspore of a seed-bearing plant, being situated within the ovule, giving rise to the endo-sperm or supposed female prothallium, and forming the cell in which the embryo is developed.

**embryotomy** /ɛmbri'ɒtəmi/, *n.* the dismemberment of a foetus to effect an otherwise impossible delivery.

**embryulcia** /ɛmbri'ʌlsiə/, *n.* the mechanical removal of an embryo or foetus from the uterus.

**embuggerance** /ɛm'bʌgərəns/, *n. Mil. Colloq.* **1.** an unnecessary or irrelevant interruption in the completion of a task. **2.** an insignificant or irksome factor which will not prevent the achievement of the overall objective. – **embuggery,** *n.* – **embuggerist,** *n.*

**embus** /ɛm'bʌs/, *v.*, **-bussed, -bussing.** –*v.i.* **1.** *Chiefly Mil.* to board a bus. –*v.t.* **2.** to put aboard a bus. – **embussing,** *adj.*

**emeer** /ɛ'mɪə/, *n.* →**emir.**

**emend** /ə'mɛnd, i-/, *v.t.* **1.** to free from faults or errors; correct. **2.** to amend (a text) by removing errors. [L *ēmendāre* correct] – **emendable,** *adj.*

**emendate** /'imɔndeɪt/, *v.t.*, **-dated, -dating.** to emend (a text). – **emendator,** *n.*

**emendation** /imən'deɪʃən/, *n.* **1.** a correction. **2.** the act of emending. – **emendatory** /i'mɛndətri, -təri/, *adj.*

**emerald** /ˈɛmrəld, ˈɛmərəld/, *n.* **1.** a rare green variety of beryl, highly valued as a gem. **2.** clear bright green. **3.** a printing type (6½ point) of a size between nonpareil and minion. *–adj.* **4.** having a clear, bright green colour. [ME *emeraude,* from OF, from L *smaragdus* a green precious stone, from Gk *smáragdos*]

**emerald copper** /– ˈkɒpə/, *n.* →**dioptase.**

**Emerald Isle** /ɛmrəld ˈaɪl/, *n. Poetic.* Ireland.

**emerge** /əˈmɜdʒ, i-/, *v.i.,* **emerged, emerging. 1.** to rise or come forth from or as from water or other liquid. **2.** to come forth into view or notice, as from concealment or obscurity. **3.** to come up or arise, as a question or difficulty. [L *ēmergere* rise out]

**emergence** /əˈmɜdʒəns, i-/, *n.* **1.** the act or fact of emerging. **2.** an outgrowth, as a prickle, on the surface of an organ.

**emergency** /əˈmɜdʒənsi, i-/, *n., pl.* **-cies. 1.** an unforeseen occurrence; a sudden and urgent occasion for action. **2. a.** one who stands by in case of emergency. **b.** *Aus. Rules.* a player who is not selected in a team, as one of the eighteen, or as a reserve, but is kept ready to play in case one of the team should be unavailable at the last minute. [ML *ēmergentia* a coming up]

**emergent** /əˈmɜdʒənt, i-/, *adj.* **1.** emerging; rising from a liquid or other surrounding medium. **2.** (of a nation) recently independent or newly formed as a political entity, and generally in an early stage of economic development. **3.** coming into view or notice; issuing. **4.** arising casually or unexpectedly. **5.** calling for immediate action; urgent. **– emergently,** *adv.*

**emergent evolution** /– ˈɛvəluʃən/, *n.* the appearance of entirely new properties at certain critical stages or levels in the course of evolution, e.g. the origin of multicellular organisms, of nervous systems, psychic processes, etc.

**emeritus** /əˈmɛrətəs, i-/, *adj., n., pl.* **-ti** /-ti/. *–adj.* **1.** retired or honourably discharged from active duty because of age, infirmity, or long service, but retained on the rolls: *a professor emeritus.* *–n.* **2.** an emeritus professor, etc. [L, pp.: having served out one's time]

**emersed** /əˈmɜst, i-/, *adj.* **1.** having emerged. **2.** *Bot.* risen or standing out of water, surrounding leaves, etc. [L *ēmersus,* pp., emerged + -ED[2]]

**emersion** /əˈmɜʒən, i-/, *n.* **1.** the act or fact of emerging; emergence. **2.** *Astron.* the reappearance of a heavenly body after an eclipse or occultation. [modelled on IMMERSION (see def. 5)]

**emery** /ˈɛməri/, *n.* a granular mineral substance consisting typically of corundum mixed with magnetite or haematite, used powdered, crushed, or consolidated for grinding and polishing. [F *émeri,* from Gk *smêris*]

**emery board** /ˈ– bɔd/, *n.* a small stiff strip, as of cardboard, or wood, covered with crushed emery and used to file fingernails.

**emery cloth** /ˈ– klɒθ/, *n.* emery-coated cloth used as an abrasive.

**emery paper** /ˈ– peɪpə/, *n.* emery-coated paper used as an abrasive.

**emery wheel** /ˈ– wil/, *n.* a wheel for grinding or polishing, consisting mostly of or faced with emery.

**emesis** /ˈɛməsəs/, *n.* vomiting. [NL, from Gk]

**emetic** /əˈmɛtɪk/, *adj.* **1.** inducing vomiting, as a medicinal substance. *–n.* **2.** an emetic medicine or agent. [L *emeticus,* from Gk *emetikós*]

**emetine** /ˈɛmətin, -taɪn/, *n.* a colourless crystalline, or white powdery substance, $C_{29}H_{40}N_2O_4$, principal ingredient of ipecacuanha, a specific against amoebic dysentery. Also, **emetin** /ˈɛmətən/. [Gk *émetos* vomiting + -INE[2]]

**emeu** /ˈimju/, *n.* →**emu.**

**emf** /i ɛm ˈɛf/, electromotive force. Also, **e.m.f., EMF, E.M.F.**

**-emia,** variant of **-aemia,** as in *hyperemia.*

**emigrant** /ˈɛməgrənt/, *n.* **1.** one who emigrates, as from a native land. *–adj.* **2.** emigrating. [L *ēmigrans,* ppr.]

**emigrate** /ˈɛməgreɪt/, *v.i.,* **-grated, -grating.** to leave one country or region to settle in another; migrate. [L *ēmigrātus,* pp.]

**emigration** /ɛməˈgreɪʃən/, *n.* **1.** the act of emigrating. **2.** a body of emigrants; emigrants collectively. **– emigrational,** *adj.*

**émigré** /ˈɛməgreɪ/, *n., pl.* **-grés** /-greɪz/. an emigrant, esp. one who flees from his native land to escape political persecution. [F, pp. of *émigrer,* from L *ēmigrāre* emigrate]

**eminence** /ˈɛmənəns/, *n.* **1.** high station, rank, or repute. **2.** a high place or part; a hill or elevation; height. **3.** (*cap.*) *Rom. Cath. Ch.* the title of honour of a cardinal: *your Eminence.*

**éminence grise** /ɛmənəns ˈgriz/, *n.* a person who wields power unseen and unofficially, usu. through another official person; grey eminence. [F]

**eminent** /ˈɛmənənt/, *adj.* **1.** high in station, rank, or repute; distinguished. **2.** conspicuous, signal, or noteworthy: *eminent services, eminent fairness.* **3.** lofty; high. **4.** prominent; projecting; protruding. [L *ēminens,* ppr., standing out] **– eminently,** *adv.*

**eminent domain** /– dəˈmeɪn/, *n.* the power of the state to acquire land for works of public utility without the consent of its owner.

**emir** /ɛˈmɪə, ˈɛmɪə/, *n.* **1.** a Muslim or Arabian chieftain or prince. **2.** a title of honour of the descendants of Mohammed. **3.** a former title of certain Turkish officials. Also, **emeer.** [var. of AMIR]

**emirate** /ˈɛmərеɪt/, *n.* a territory under the control of an emir.

**emissary** /ˈɛməsəri, -əsri/, *n., pl.* **-saries. 1.** an agent sent on a mission. **2.** an agent sent on a mission of a secret nature. [L *ēmissārius* sent out (adj.), scout (n.)]

**emission** /əˈmɪʃən, i-/, *n.* **1.** the act of emitting. **2.** that which is emitted; a discharge; an emanation. **3.** the act of issuing. **4.** *Electronics.* a measure of the number of electrons emitted by the heated filament or cathode of a vacuum tube. **5.** a discharge of fluid from the body, specifically a discharge of semen. **6.** the fluid discharged. [L *ēmissio*]

**emission spectrum** /ˈ– spɛktrəm/, *n.* the spectrum observed when light or other electromagnetic radiation coming directly from a source is examined with a spectroscope.

**emissive** /əˈmɪsɪv, i-/, *adj.* **1.** serving to emit. **2.** pertaining to emission.

**emissivity** /iməˈsɪvəti, ɛmə-/, *n.* the relative ability of a surface to emit radiant energy compared to an ideal black body at the same temperature and with the same area.

**emit** /əˈmɪt, i-/, *v.t.,* **emitted, emitting. 1.** to send forth; give out or forth (liquid, light, heat, sound, etc.); discharge. **2.** to issue, as an order or a decree. **3.** to issue formally for circulation. **4.** to utter, as opinions. [L *ēmittere* send out]

**emittance** /əˈmɪtəns, i-/, *n.* the luminous flux emitted by a source per unit area; luminous emittance.

**emitter** /əˈmɪtə, i-/, *n.* **1.** one who or that which emits. **2.** *Electronics.* an electrode that emits charge, esp. in a transistor.

**emmenagogue** /əˈmɛnəgɒg, əˈminə-/, *n.* a medicine that promotes the menstrual discharge. [Gk *émmēn(a)* menses + -AGOGUE] **– emmenagogic** /əmɛnəˈgɒdʒɪk, əminə-/, *adj.*

**Emmenthaler** /ˈɛməntalə/, *n.* a firm, pale yellow or whitish cheese containing many holes, made usu. from cows' milk half skimmed. Also, **Emmental, Emmentaler, Emmenthal.** [named after *Emmenthal,* a valley in Switzerland; see -ER[1]]

**emmer** /ˈɛmə/, *n.* a form of wheat, *Triticum dicoccum,* cultivated in the Mediterranean region since Neolithic times and still grown in Eurasia to a limited extent.

**emmetropia** /ɛməˈtroupiə/, *n.* the normal refractive condition of the eye, in which the rays of light are accurately focused on the retina. [NL, from Gk *émmetros* in measure + *-ōpía* eye state] **– emmetropic** /ɛməˈtrɒpɪk/, *adj.*

**emolliate** /əˈmɒlieɪt, -ˈmou-/, *v.t.,* **-ated, -ating. 1.** to soften. **2.** to render effeminate. **– emollition** /ɛməˈlɪʃən/, *n.*

**emollient** /əˈmɒliənt, -ˈmou-/, *adj.* **1.** having the power of softening or relaxing living tissues, as a medicinal substance; soothing, esp. to the skin. *–n.* **2.** *Med.* an emollient medicine or agent. [L *ēmolliens,* ppr.]

**emolument** /əˈmɒljəmənt/, *n.* profit arising from office or employment; compensation for services; salary or fees. [L *ēmolumentum, ēmolimentum* profit]

**emote** /iˈmout, ə-/, *v.i.,* **emoted, emoting.** *Colloq.* **1.** to show or affect emotion. **2.** to behave theatrically; to act a part, esp. without talent. [backformation from EMOTION]

**emotion** /ə'moʊʃən, i-/, *n.* **1.** an affective state of consciousness in which joy, sorrow, fear, hate, or the like, is experienced (distinguished from cognitive and volitional states of consciousness). **2.** any of the feelings of joy, sorrow, fear, hate, love, etc. **3.** a state of agitation of the feelings actuated by experiencing fear, joy, etc. [F, from *émouvoir* excite, OF *esmovoir,* from L *ēmovēre*] – **emotionless,** *adj.*

**emotional** /ə'moʊʃənəl, i-/, *adj.* **1.** pertaining to emotion or the emotions. **2.** subject to or easily affected by emotion. **3.** appealing to the emotions. **4.** effected or determined by emotion rather than reason: *an emotional decision.* **5.** overwrought; displaying undue emotion. – **emotionally,** *adv.*

**emotionalise** /ə'moʊʃənəlaɪz, i-/, *v.t.,* **-lised, -lising.** to make emotional; treat as a matter of emotion. Also, **emotionalize.**

**emotionalism** /ə'moʊʃənəlɪzəm, i-/, *n.* **1.** emotional character. **2.** appeal to the emotions. **3.** tendency to emotion, esp. morbid emotion. **4.** expression of emotion.

**emotionalist** /ə'moʊʃənələst, i-/, *n.* **1.** one who appeals to the emotions, esp. unduly. **2.** one easily affected by emotion.

**emotionality** /əmoʊʃə'næləti, i-/, *n.* emotional state or quality.

**emotive** /ə'moʊtɪv, i-/, *adj.* **1.** characterised by or pertaining to emotion. **2.** exciting emotion. – **emotively,** *adv.* – **emotiveness, emotivity** /ˌimoʊ'tɪvəti/, *n.*

**empale** /ɛm'peɪl/, *v.t.,* **-paled, -paling.** →**impale.**

**empanel** /ɛm'pænəl/, *v.t.,* **-elled, -elling** or (*U.S.*) **-eled, -eling.** to enter on a panel or list for jury duty. Also, **impanel.** – **empanelment,** *n.*

**empathetic** /ɛmpə'θɛtɪk/, *adj.* feeling in close sympathy; in accord. [EMPA(THY) + (SYMPA)THETIC]

**empathise** /'ɛmpəθaɪz/, *v.i.,* **-thised, -thising.** to experience empathy (fol. by *with*). Also, **empathize.**

**empathy** /'ɛmpəθi/, *n.* mental entering into the feeling or spirit of a person or thing; appreciative perception or understanding. [Gk *empátheia.* Cf. G *Einfühlung,* lit., infeeling] – **empathic** /ɛm'pæθɪk/, *adj.* – **empathically** /ɛm'pæθɪkli/, *adv.*

**empennage** /ɛm'pɛnɪdʒ/, *n.* the rear part of an aeroplane or airship, usu. comprising stabiliser, elevator, vertical fin, and rudder. [F, from *empenner,* v., feather, from *em-* EM-[1] + *penne* (from L *penna* feather)]

**emperor** /'ɛmpərə/, *n.* **1.** the sovereign or supreme ruler of an empire. **2.** a title of dignity given to certain kings not rulers of empires. **3.** any of various Australian fishes of the family Lethrinidae, resembling bream but having pointed heads and scaleless cheeks. [ME *emperour(e),* from OF *empereor,* from L *imperātor* ruler] – **emperorship,** *n.*

**emperor gum moth,** *n.* a common and large saturniid moth, *Antheraea eucalypti,* of eastern Australia.

**emperor moth** /'– mɒθ/, *n.* any of various large moths of the family Saturniidae having stout bodies, long antennae and prominent eyespots on the wings.

**emperor penguin** /– 'pɛŋgwən/, *n.* the largest of the penguins, *Aptendoytes forsteri,* of the Antarctic, noted for its habit of holding its egg or young between the feet in a fold of abdominal skin resembling a pouch.

**empery** /'ɛmpəri/, *n., pl.* **-peries.** *Poetic.* **1.** absolute dominion; empire. **2.** the territory of an emperor. [ME *emperie,* from OF, from *emperer* to rule, from L *imperāre*]

**emphasis** /'ɛmfəsəs/, *n., pl.* **-ses** /-siz/. **1.** stress laid upon, or importance or significance attached to anything. **2.** anything upon which great stress is laid. **3.** *Rhet.* **a.** special and significant stress of voice laid on particular words or syllables. **b.** stress laid on particular words, by means of position, repetition, or other indication. **4.** intensity or force of expression, action, etc. **5.** prominence, as of outline. [L, from Gk]

**emphasise** /'ɛmfəsaɪz/, *v.t.,* **-sised, -sising.** to give emphasis to; lay stress upon; stress. Also, **emphasize.**

**emphatic** /ɛm'fætɪk/, *adj.* **1.** uttered, or to be uttered, with emphasis; strongly expressive. **2.** using emphasis in speech or action. **3.** forcibly significant; strongly marked; striking. **4.** *Phonet.* having a secondary velar articulation, as certain dental consonants in Arabic. *–n.* **5.** *Phonet.* an emphatic consonant. [Gk *emphatikós,* var. of *emphantikós* expressive] – **emphatically,** *adv.*

**emphysema** /ɛmfə'simə/, *n.* abnormal distension of an organ or a part of the body with air or other gas, esp. pulmonary emphysema which causes severe restriction of respiratory function. [NL, from Gk: inflation] – **emphysematous** /ɛmfə'sɛmətəs, -'simə-/, *adj.*

**empire** /'ɛmpaɪə/, *n.* **1.** an aggregate of nations or peoples ruled over by an emperor or other powerful sovereign or government; usu. a territory of greater extent than a kingdom ruled by a single sovereign: *the Roman empire.* **2.** a government under an emperor: *the first French empire.* **3.** supreme power in governing; imperial power; sovereignty. **4.** supreme control; absolute sway. **5.** *Colloq.* a large and powerful enterprise or group of enterprises controlled by a single person or group of people. *–adj.* **6.** (*cap.*) developed or in vogue during the First Empire in France (1804-15), applied esp. to certain styles of interior decoration, furniture, etc., and of women's dress (implying esp. a high waistline, with skirts hanging straight and loose.) **7.** →**empire sausage.** [ME, from F, from L *imperium* a command, authority, realm]

**empire builder** /'– bɪldə/, *n.* one who sets out to increase his influence, area of control, and reputation to the greatest possible extent.

**empire sausage** /– 'sɒsɪdʒ/, *n.* →**devon** (def. 3). Also, **empire.**

**empiric** /ɛm'pɪrɪk/, *n.* **1.** anyone who follows an empirical method. **2.** *Obs.* a quack; a charlatan. *–adj.* **3.** empirical. [L *empīricus,* from Gk *empeirikós,* from *empeiría* experience]

**empirical** /ɛm'pɪrɪkəl/, *adj.* **1.** derived from or guided by experience or experiment. **2.** depending upon experience or observation alone, without using science or theory, esp. in medicine. – **empirically,** *adv.*

**empirical formula** /– 'fɔmjulə, -jələ/, *n.* **1.** *Chem.* a chemical formula indicating the number of each kind of atom in the molecule, as $CH_2O$. **2.** any mathematical or engineering formula which is obtained on the basis of experimental results rather than pure theory.

**empiricism** /ɛm'pɪrəsɪzəm/, *n.* **1.** empirical method or practice. **2.** *Philos.* the doctrine that all knowledge is derived from experience. **3.** undue reliance upon experience; quackery. **4.** an empirical conclusion. – **empiricist,** *n., adj.*

**emplace** /ɛm'pleɪs/, *v.t.,* **-placed, -placing.** to place or position.

**emplacement** /ɛm'pleɪsmənt/, *n.* **1.** *Fort.* the space, platform, or the like for a gun or battery and its accessories. **2.** a putting in place or position; location.

**emplane** /ɛm'pleɪn/, *v.t., v.i.,* **-planed, -planing.** →**enplane.**

**employ** /ɛm'plɔɪ/, *v.t.* **1.** to use the services of (a person); have or keep in one's service; keep busy or at work: *this factory employs thousands of men.* **2.** to make use of (an instrument, means, etc.); use; apply. **3.** to occupy or devote (time, energies, etc.): *I employ my spare time in reading.* *–n.* **4.** employment; service: *to be in someone's employ.* [F *employer,* from L *implicāre* enfold] – **employable,** *adj.*

**employee** /ɛm'plɔɪi, ɛmplɔɪ'i/, *n.* a person working for another person or a business firm for pay. Also, **employe, employé.** [EMPLOY, *v.* + -EE; replacing *employe,* from F, pp. of *employer* employ]

**employer** /ɛm'plɔɪə/, *n.* one who employs people, esp. for wages.

**employment** /ɛm'plɔɪmənt/, *n.* **1.** the act of employing. **2.** the state of being employed; employ; services. **3.** that on which one is employed; work; occupation; business.

**employment service** /'– sɜvəs/, *n.* a government department with offices for finding employment for the unemployed and for paying unemployment benefits.

**empoison** /ɛm'pɔɪzən/, *v.t.* **1.** to corrupt. **2.** to poison. [ME *empoyson(en),* from F *empoisoner,* from *em-* EM-[1] + *poison* POISON]

**emporium** /ɛm'pɔriəm/, *n., pl.* **-poriums, -poria** /-'pɔriə/. a large store selling a great variety of articles. [L, from Gk *empórion* a trading place]

**empower** /ɛm'paʊə/, *v.t.* **1.** to give power or authority to; authorise: *I empowered him to make the deal for me.* **2.** to enable or permit. – **empowerment,** *n.*

**empress** /'ɛmprəs/, *n.* **1.** a woman ruler of an empire. **2.** the consort of an emperor. **3.** a supreme or sovereign ruler: *empress of the seas.* [ME *empresse,* from OF *emper(er)esse,* replacing *empereris,* from L *imperātrix*]

**emprise** /ɛm'praɪz/, *n. Archaic.* **1.** an adventurous enterprise. **2.** knightly daring or prowess. [ME, from OF, n. use of fem. pp. of *emprendre* undertake, from *em-* EM-[1] + *prendre* take (from L *prehendere*)]

**empty** /ˈɛmpti, ˈɛmti/, *adj.*, **-tier, -tiest,** *v.*, **-tied, -tying,** *n., pl.* **-ties.** *–adj.* **1.** containing nothing; void of the usual or appropriate contents: *an empty bottle.* **2.** vacant; unoccupied: *an empty house.* **3.** without burden or load: *an empty wagon.* **4.** destitute of some quality or qualities; devoid (fol. by *of*): *a life now as empty of happiness as it was full of it.* **5.** without force, effect, or significance; unsatisfactory; meaningless: *empty compliments, empty pleasures.* **6.** *Colloq.* hungry. **7.** without knowledge or sense; frivolous; foolish. **8.** *Colloq.* drained of emotion; spent. *–v.t.* **9.** to make empty; deprive of contents; discharge the contents of: *to empty a bucket.* **10.** to discharge (contents): *empty the water out of a bucket.* *–v.i.* **11.** to become empty: *the room emptied rapidly after the lecture.* **12.** to discharge contents, as a river: *the river empties into the sea.* *–n.* **13.** *Colloq.* something empty, as a bottle, can, or the like. [ME; OE *ǣmtig,* var. of *ǣmettig,* from *ǣmetta* leisure + *-ig* -Y[1]] – **emptily,** *adv.* – **emptiness,** *n.*

**empty-handed** /ɛmpti-ˈhændəd, ɛmti-/, *adj.* **1.** having nothing in the hands. **2.** bringing or taking nothing; having gained nothing.

**empty-headed** /ɛmpti-ˈhɛdəd, ɛmti-/, *adj.* brainless; foolish.

**empty set** /ɛmpti ˈsɛt/, *n.* →**null set.**

**empurple** /ɛmˈpɜpəl/, *v.t.*, **-pled, -pling.** to tinge or colour with purple.

**empyema** /ɛmpaɪˈimə/, *n.* a collection of pus in some cavity of the body, esp. in the pleural cavity. [NL, from Gk: suppuration] – **empyemic,** *adj.*

**empyreal** /ɛmpaɪˈriəl/, *adj.* **1.** pertaining to the highest heaven; empyrean. **2.** pertaining to the sky; celestial. **3.** formed of pure fire or light. [LL *empyreus* (from Gk *empýrios* fiery) + -AL[1]]

**empyrean** /ɛmpaɪˈriən/, *n.* **1.** the highest heaven, supposed by the ancients to contain the pure element of fire. **2.** the visible heavens; the firmament. *–adj.* **3.** empyreal.

**em rule** /ˈɛm rul/, *n.* a rule (def. 8c) which is an em in length; dash (def. 18).

**emu** /ˈimju/, *n.* **1.** Also, **emeu.** either of two large, flightless, three-toed Australian birds of the ratite genus *Dromaius, D. novae-hollandiae* and *D. diemenianus,* closely related to the ostrich, but smaller. The former species has the skin of the head and the throat blue, and long, drooping, brownish plumage; the latter species is now extinct. **2.** *Racing Colloq.* one who frequents racecourses, trotting and dog tracks, and TAB branches, and collects discarded betting tickets in the hope of finding some which will pay. [Pg. *ema* ostrich, cassowary]

emu

**E.M.U.** /i em ˈju/, electromagnetic unit. Also, **emu**

**emu-apple** /ˈimju-æpəl/, *n.* **1.** Also, **emu-apple tree.** a small tree, *Owenia acidula,* with a rounded crown of dark green leaves, and small rounded, red, highly acidic fruits, found in the north-eastern parts of Australia. **2.** the fruit of this tree.

**emu-bobber** /ˈimju-bɒbə/, *n.* a person employed to pick up sticks lying around on land which has been cleared or burnt off; stick-picker. – **emu-bobbing,** *n.*

**emu bush** /ˈimju bʊʃ/, *n.* any of a number of shrubs of the endemic Australian genus *Eremophila,* family Myoporaceae, having fruits which are eaten by emus, esp. the berrigan.

**emulate** /ˈɛmjuleɪt, -je-/, *v.t.*, **-lated, -lating.** **1.** to try to equal or excel; imitate with effort to equal or surpass. **2.** to rival with some degree of success. [L *aemulātus,* pp., having rivalled] – **emulative** /ˈɛmjələtɪv/, *adj.* – **emulator,** *n.*

**emulation** /ɛmjuˈleɪʃən, -jə-/, *n.* effort or desire to equal or excel others.

**emulous** /ˈɛmjələs/, *adj.* **1.** desirous of equalling or excelling; filled with emulation. **2.** arising from or of the nature of emulation, as actions, etc. [L *aemulus*] – **emulously,** *adv.* – **emulousness,** *n.*

**emulsify** /əˈmʌlsəfaɪ/, *v.t.*, **-fied, -fying.** to make into an emulsion. – **emulsification** /əmʌlsəfəˈkeɪʃən/, *n.* – **emulsifier,** *n.*

**emulsion** /əˈmʌlʃən/, *n.* **1.** a liquid preparation of the colour and consistency of milk. **2.** any colloidal suspension of a liquid in another liquid. **3.** *Pharm.* a liquid preparation consisting of minute particles of an oily, fatty, resinous, or other substance held in suspension in an aqueous fluid by means of a gum or other viscous matter. **4.** *Photog.* the light-sensitive layer on a photographic film, plate, or paper, consisting of one or more of the silver halides in gelatine. [NL *ēmulsio,* from L *ēmulsus,* pp., milked out] – **emulsive,** *adj.*

**emulsion paint** /ˈ– peɪnt/, *n.* a paint in which the pigment is dispersed in an emulsion, or an emulsion-like dispersion of an organic binding material in water.

**emulsoid** /əˈmʌlsɔɪd/, *n.* a sol in which the disperse phase is a liquid.

**emunctory** /əˈmʌŋktəri/, *n., pl.* **-ries,** *adj.* *–n.* **1.** a part or organ of the body, as the skin, a kidney, etc., carrying off waste products. *–adj.* **2.** excretory. [NL, from L *ēmunctōrium* a pair of snuffers]

**emu parade** /ˈimju pəreɪd/, *n.* the picking up of litter in a camping area, school playground, etc., by a group of people organised for this purpose.

**emu wren** /ˈ– rɛn/, *n.* any of several small, brown warblers of the genus *Stipiturus* having long, loosely-barbed tail feathers, similar to those of the emu.

**en** /ɛn/, *n.* **1.** the letter N, n. **2.** *Print.* half of the width of an em; N quad.

**en-**[1], a prefix meaning primarily 'in', 'into', first occurring in words from French, but now used freely as an English formative: **1.** with the old concrete force of putting the object into or on something or of bringing the object into the specified condition, often serving to form transitive verbs from nouns or adjectives, as in *enable, enact, endear, engulf, enshrine, enslave.* **2.** prefixed to verbs, to make them transitive, or, if already transitive, to give them the transitive sign, as in *enkindle, entwine, engild, engird, engrave, enshield.* Also, **em-**[1]. Cf. **in-**[2], **im-**[1]. [F, from L *in-,* representing *in,* prep., in, into, on, to]

**en-**[2], a prefix representing Greek *en-,* corresponding to **en-**[1] and occurring chiefly in combinations already formed in Greek, as *energy, enthusiasm.* Also, **em-**[2].

**-en**[1], a suffix, forming transitive and intransitive verbs from adjectives, as in *fasten, harden, sweeten,* or from nouns, as in *heighten, lengthen, strengthen.* [abstracted from old verbs like *fasten* (contrast *listen,* where *-en* has kept its non-morphemic character)]

**-en**[2], a suffix of adjectives indicating 'material', 'appearance', as in *ashen, golden, oaken.* [OE]

**-en**[3], a suffix used to mark the past participle in many strong and some weak verbs, as in *taken, proven.* [OE]

**-en**[4], a suffix forming the plural of some nouns, as in *brethren, children, oxen,* and other words, now mostly archaic, as *eyen, hosen.* [ME; OE *-an,* case ending of weak nouns, as in *oxan,* oblique sing. and nom. and acc. pl. of *oxa* ox]

**-en**[5], a diminutive suffix, as in *maiden, kitten,* etc. [OE]

**enable** /ɛnˈeɪbəl, ən-/, *v.t.*, **-bled, -bling.** **1.** to make able; give power, means, or ability to; make competent; authorise: *this will enable him to do it.* **2.** to make possible or easy.

**enabling** /ɛnˈeɪblɪŋ, ən-/, *adj.* (of an act, statute, or bill) enabling a person or a company to do something otherwise illegal.

**enact** /ɛnˈækt, ən-/, *v.t.* **1.** to make into an act or statute. **2.** to ordain; decree. **3.** to represent on or as on the stage; act the part of: *to enact Hamlet.* – **enactor,** *n.*

**enactive** /ɛnˈæktɪv, ən-/, *adj.* having power to enact or establish, as a law.

**enactment** /ɛnˈæktmənt, ən-/, *n.* **1.** the act of enacting. **2.** the state or fact of being enacted. **3.** that which is enacted; a law; a statute. **4.** a section or part of a section in an act.

**enactory** /ɛnˈæktəri, ən-/, *adj.* of or pertaining to an enactment which creates new rights and obligations.

**enallage** /ɛnˈælədʒi, ən-/, *n.* the substitution of one grammatical form for another. [Gk]

**enamel** /əˈnæməl/, *n., v.*, **-elled, -elling** or (*U.S.*) **-eled, -eling.** *–n.* **1.** a glassy substance, usu. opaque, applied by fusion to the surface of metal, pottery, etc., as an ornament or for protection. **2.** any of various enamel-like varnishes, paints, etc. **3.** any enamel-like surface with a bright lustre. **4.** an artistic work executed in enamel. **5.** *Anat., Zool.* the hard, glossy, calcareous outer structure of the crowns of the teeth, containing only a slight amount of organic substance. **6.** a coating applied to the nails to create a smooth and glossy surface, and often to colour them. *–v.t.* **7.** to inlay or overlay with enamel. **8.** to form an enamel-like surface upon: *to enamel metal.* **9.** to decorate as with enamel; variegate with colours. [ME *enamayl,* from AF, from *en-* EN-[1] + *amayl,* OF *esmail,* c. It. *smalto* SMALT; akin to SMELT[1]] – **enameller,** *n.* – **enamellist,** *n.* – **enamelwork,** *n.*

**enamelling** /ə'næməlɪŋ/, *n.* **1.** the act or work of one who enamels. **2.** a decoration or coating of enamel. Also, *U.S.,* **enameling.**

**enamel orchid** /ə'næməl ɔkəd/, *n.* any of various terrestrial orchids of the genera *Glossodia* and *Elythranthera,* of Australia, having flowers with spreading glossy petals and sepals.

**enamelware** /ə'næməlwɛə/, *n.* equipment or utensils, usu. for kitchen use, which are enamelled.

**enamour** /ɛn'æmə, ən-/, *v.t.* to inflame with love; charm; captivate (usu. passive fol. by *of*): *to be enamoured of a lady.* Also, *U.S.* **enamor.** [ME *enamor(en),* from OF *enamourer,* from *en-* EN-[1] + *amour* (from L *amor* love)]

**enantiomer** /ɛ'næntiəmə/, *n.* one of two forms in which a dissymetric molecule can exist, which is a non-superimposable mirror image of the other; each form rotates polarised light in a different direction.

**enantiomorph** /ɛ'næntiə,mɔf/, *n.* →**enantiomer.** – **enantiomorphic, enantiomorphous,** *adj.*

**enantiomorphism** /ɛn,æntiə'mɔ,fɪzəm/, *n.* the property of certain substances which exist in two non-superimposable crystalline forms, one being a mirror image of the other. – **enantiomorphic, enantiomorphous,** *adj.*

**enantiosis** /ɛ,nænti'oʊsəs/, *n.* a form of words in which the meaning to be conveyed is the opposite of what is stated. Cf. **irony.** [Gk]

**enantiotropy** /ɛnænti'ɒtrəpi/, *n.* the property of certain substances which exist in two crystalline forms, one being stable below a certain temperature, the other above it. – **enantiotropic** /ɛ,næntiə'trɒpɪk/, *adj.*

**enargite** /ən'adʒaɪt, 'ɛnədʒaɪt/, *n.* a mineral used as a source of copper, consisting of a copper and arsenic sulphide, $Cu_3AsS_4$, which occurs as black orthorhombic crystals.

**enarthrosis** /ɛna'θroʊsəs/, *n., pl.* **-ses** /-siz/. a joint, as at the shoulder, in which a convex end of one bone is socketed in a concavity of another; a ball-and-socket joint. [NL, from Gk: jointing in] – **enarthrodial,** *adj.*

**en bloc** /ɒn 'blɒk/, *adv.* as a whole.

**encaenia** /ɛn'siniə, ən-/, *n.pl.* festive ceremonies commemorating the founding of a city or the consecration of a church. [L, from Gk *enkaínia* consecration feast]

**encage** /ɛn'keɪdʒ, ən-/, *v.t.,* **-caged, -caging.** to confine in or as in a cage; coop up.

**encamp** /ɛn'kæmp, ən-/, *v.i., v.t.* to settle or lodge in a camp.

**encampment** /ɛn'kæmpmənt, ən-/, *n.* **1.** the act of encamping; lodgment in a camp. **2.** the place or quarters occupied in camping; a camp.

**encapsulate** /ɛn'kæpsjəleɪt, ən-, -ʃə-/, *v.t.,* **-lated, -lating.** to enclose in or as in a capsule. – **encapsulation** /ɛn,kæpsjə'leɪʃən, -ʃə-/, *n.*

**encarnalise** /ɛn'kanəlaɪz, ən-/, *v.t.,* **-lised, -lising.** to invest with a carnal or fleshly form. Also, **encarnalize.**

**encase** /ɛn'keɪs, ən-/, *v.t.,* **-cased, -casing.** to enclose in or as in a case. Also, **incase.** [EN-[1] + CASE[2]] – **encasement,** *n.*

**encaustic** /ɛn'kɒstɪk, ən-/, *adj.* **1.** painted with wax colours fixed with heat, or with any process in which colours are burnt in. *–n.* **2.** a work of art produced by an encaustic process. [L *encausticus* of burning in, from Gk *enkaustikós*]

**-ence,** a noun suffix equivalent to **-ance,** and corresponding to **-ent** in adjectives, as in *abstinence, consistence, dependence, difference.* [F, alteration of *-ance* -ANCE by etymological association with L *-entia,* noun suffix]

**enceinte**[1] /ɒn'sænt/, *adj.* pregnant; with child. [F, from LL *incincta,* pp. fem., ungirt]

**enceinte**[2] /ɒn'sænt/, *n.* **1.** a wall or enclosure, as of a fortified place. **2.** the place enclosed. [F, from *enceindre,* from L *incingere* enclose, as with a girdle]

**encephalic** /ɛnsə'fælɪk/, *adj.* of or pertaining to the encephalon or brain.

**encephalin** /ɛn'sɛfələn/, *n.* a chemical generated by the brain which has properties like those of narcotics. Also, **enkephalin** /ɛn'kɛfələn/.

**encephalitis** /ɛnsɛfə'laɪtəs, ɛnkɛf-, ən-/, *n.* inflammation of the substance of the brain. [NL; see ENCEPHAL(O)-, -ITIS] – **encephalitic** /ɛnsɛfə'lɪtɪk, ɛnkɛf-, ən-/, *adj.*

**encephalitis lethargica** /- lə'θadʒɪkə/, *n.* →**sleeping sickness.**

**encephalo-,** a word element meaning 'brain', as in *encephalomyelitis.* Also, **encephal-.** [Gk *enkephalo-,* combining form of *enképhalos*]

**encephalogram** /ɛn'sɛfələgræm, ɛnkɛf-/, *n.* an X-ray photograph of the ventricles and subarachnoid space of the brain.

**encephalograph** /ɛn'sɛfələgræf, ɛnkɛf-/, *n.* **1.** →**encephalogram. 2.** →**electroencephalograph.** [ENCEPHALO- + -GRAPH]

**encephalography** /ɛn,sɛfə'lɒgrəfi, ɛn,kɛfə-/, *n.* the production of encephalograms after the introduction of air or oxygen into the ventricles and subarachnoid space by means of a lumbar or asternal puncture.

**encephaloma** /ɛn,sɛfə'loʊmə, ɛn,kɛf-/, *n., pl.* **-mata** /-mətə/. **1.** a brain tumour. **2.** hernia of the brain.

**encephalomyelitis** /ɛn,sɛfəloʊ,maɪə'laɪtəs, ɛn,kɛf-/, *n.* any of the several inflammatory diseases of the brain and spinal cord.

**encephalon** /ɛn'sɛfəlɒn, ɛn'kɛf-/, *n., pl.* **-la** /-lə/. the brain. [NL, from Gk *encéphalos* the brain]

**encephalopathy** /ɛn,sɛfə'lɒpəθi, ɛn,kɛf-/, *n.* any disease of the brain.

**encephalosis** /ɛn,sɛfə'loʊsəs, ɛn,kɛf-/, *n.* any degenerative disease of the brain.

**encephalotomy** /ɛn,sɛfə'lɒtəmi, ɛn,kɛf-/, *n.* a surgical incision of the brain.

**enchain** /ɛn'tʃeɪn, ən-/, *v.t.* **1.** to fasten with or as with a chain or chains; fetter; restrain. **2.** to hold fast, as the attention. [ME *encheinen,* from OF *enchainer,* from *en-* EN-[1] + *chaine* CHAIN] – **enchainment,** *n.*

**enchant** /ɛn'tʃænt, ən-, -'tʃant/, *v.t.* **1.** to subject to magical influence; cast a spell over; bewitch. **2.** to impart a magic quality or effect to. **3.** to delight in a high degree; charm. [ME *enchaunt(en),* from OF *enchanter,* from L *incantāre* chant a magic formula against]

**enchanter** /ɛn'tʃæntə, ən-, -'tʃant-/, *n.* **1.** one who enchants. **2.** a magician.

**enchanter's nightshade** /ɛn,tʃæntəz 'naɪtʃeɪd, ən-, -,tʃant-/, *n.* any of several species of northern temperate perennial herbs belonging to the genus *Circaea,* esp. *C. lutetiana,* having small white flowers.

**enchanting** /ɛn'tʃæntɪŋ, ən, -'tʃant-/, *adj.* charming; bewitching. – **enchantingly,** *adv.*

**enchantment** /ɛn'tʃæntmənt, ən-, -'tʃant-/, *n.* **1.** the act or art of enchanting. **2.** that which enchants.

**enchantress** /ɛn'tʃæntrəs, ən-, -'tʃant-/, *n.* **1.** a woman who enchants; a sorceress. **2.** a fascinating woman.

**enchase** /ɛn'tʃeɪs, ən-/, *v.t.,* **-chased, -chasing. 1.** to place (gems) in an ornamental setting. **2.** to decorate with inlay, embossing, or engraving. [F *enchâsser,* from *en-* EN-[1] + *châsse* shrine (from L *capsa* box). See CASE[2]]

**enchiridion** /ɛnkaɪ'rɪdiən/, *n., pl.* **-ridions, -ridia** /-'rɪdiə/. a handbook; a manual. [Gk, from *en-* EN-[2] + *cheír* hand + *-idion,* diminutive suffix]

**enchondroma** /ɛnkən'droʊmə/, *n., pl.* **-mata** /-mətə/, **-dromas.** a tumour which consists essentially of cartilage. [EN-[2] + Gk *chóndros* cartilage + -OMA] – **enchondromatous** /ɛnkən'drɒmətəs, -'droʊmə-/, *adj.*

**enchorial** /ɛn'kɔriəl/, *adj.* (esp. of demotic writing) belonging to or used in a particular country; native; domestic. Also, **enchoric** /ɛn'kɔrɪk, -'kɒrɪk/. [Gk *enchṓrios* in or of a country + -AL[1]]

**encincture** /ɛn'sɪŋktʃə, ən-/, *v.,* **-tured, -turing,** *n. –v.t.* **1.** to girdle; surround or encompass as with a girdle. *–n.* **2.** the act or fact of being encompassed.

**encipher** /ɛn'saɪfə, ən-/, *v.t.* →**encrypt.**

**encircle** /ɛn'sɜkəl, ən-/, *v.t.*, **-cled, -cling.** **1.** to form a circle round; surround; encompass. **2.** to make a circling movement about; make the circuit of. – **encirclement,** *n.*

**enclave** /'ɛnkleɪv/, *n.* a country, or, esp., an outlying portion of a country, entirely or mostly surrounded by the territory of another country. [F, from *enclaver* shut in, from Rom. *inclāvāre*]

**enclitic** /ɛn'klɪtɪk/, *adj.* **1.** (of a word) so closely connected with a preceding word as to have no independent accent. –*n.* **2.** an enclitic word, as *que* (and) in Latin: *arma virumque,* arms and the man. [LL *encliticus,* from Gk *enklitikós,* lit., leaning on] – **enclitically,** *adv.*

**enclose** /ɛn'kloʊz, ən-/, *v.t.*, **-closed, -closing.** **1.** to shut in; close in on all sides. **2.** to surround as with a fence or wall: *to enclose land.* **3.** to insert in the same envelope, etc., with the main letter, etc.: *he enclosed a cheque.* **4.** to contain (the thing transmitted): *his letter enclosed a cheque.* Also, *Law or Archaic,* **inclose.** [EN-[1] + CLOSE, *v., after OF enclos,* pp. of *enclore*]

**enclosure** /ɛn'kloʊʒə, ən-/, *n.* **1.** the act of enclosing. **2.** the separation and appropriation of land, esp. of common land, by means of a fence. **3.** a tract of land surrounded by a fence. **4.** that which encloses, as a fence or wall. **5.** the cabinet, etc., in which a loudspeaker or group of loudspeakers is mounted. **6.** that which is enclosed, as a paper sent in a letter. **7.** a section of a sports ground reserved for spectators, or for a certain section of the spectators. Also, *Law or Archaic,* **inclosure.**

**encode** /ɛn'koʊd/, *v.t.*, **-coded, -coding.** to put into coded form, as of a message, computer program, etc.

**encolpion** /ɛn'kɒlpiən/, *n., pl.* **-pia** /-piə/. a reliquary, cross, or the like, worn on the breast of bishops of the Eastern Church. [MGk, n. use of Gk adj. *enkólpios* in the bosom, from *kólpos* bosom]

**encomiast** /ɛn'koʊmiæst/, *n.* one who utters or writes an encomium; a eulogist. [Gk *enkōmiastḗs*]

**encomiastic** /ɛnkoʊmi'æstɪk/, *adj.* →**eulogistic.** Also, **encomiastical.**

**encomium** /ɛn'koʊmiəm, ən-/, *n., pl.* **-miums, -mia** /-miə/. a formal expression of praise; a eulogy. [L, from Gk *enkṓmion* eulogy, properly neut. of *enkṓmios* belonging to a Bacchic revel]

**encompass** /ɛn'kʌmpəs, ən-/, *v.t.* **1.** to form a circle about; encircle; surround. **2.** to enclose; contain. **3.** *Obs.* to outwit. – **encompassment,** *n.*

**encore** /'ɒnkɔ, 'ɒŋkɔ/, *interj., n., v.*, **-cored, -coring.** –*interj.* **1.** again; once more (used by an audience in calling for a repetition of a song, etc., or for an additional number or piece). –*n.* **2.** a demand, as by applause, for a repetition of a song, etc., or for an additional number or piece. **3.** that which is given in response to such a demand. –*v.t.* **4.** to call for a repetition of. **5.** to call for an encore from (a performer). [F: still, yet, besides, from L *hanc hōram* within this hour]

**encore surgery** /– 'sɜdʒəri/, *n. Colloq.* surgery which is not urgently required but which is undertaken while a patient is being operated on for another reason.

**encounter** /ɛn'kaʊntə, ən-/, *v.t.* **1.** to come upon; meet with, esp. unexpectedly. **2.** to meet with or contend against (difficulties, opposition, etc.). **3.** to meet (a person, military force, etc.) in conflict. –*n.* **4.** a meeting with a person or thing, esp. casually or unexpectedly. **5.** a meeting in conflict or opposition; a battle; a combat. [ME *encountre(n)* from OF *encontrer,* from LL *incontrāre,* from L *in-* IN-[2] + *contrā* against]

**encounter group** /'– grup/, *n.* a number of people who meet together to understand and study interpersonal relationships.

**encourage** /ɛn'kʌrɪdʒ, ən-/, *v.*, **-raged, -raging,** *n.* –*v.t.* **1.** to inspire with courage, spirit, or confidence. **2.** to stimulate by assistance, approval, etc. –*n.* **3.** →**encourage handicap. 4.** →**encourage horse.** [ME *encorage(n),* from OF *encoragier,* from *en-* EN-[1] + *corage* COURAGE] – **encourager,** *n.* – **encouragingly,** *adv.*

**encourage handicap** /– 'hændikæp/, *n.* a restricted race for horses which are specified as being in the encourage class in accordance with the rules operating in each State of Australia.

**encourage horse** /– 'hɔs/, *n.* a horse eligible to run in an encourage handicap. Also, **encourage-class horse.**

**encouragement** /ɛn'kʌrɪdʒmənt, ən-/, *n.* **1.** the act of encouraging. **2.** the state of being encouraged. **3.** that which encourages.

**encrinite** /'ɛnkrənaɪt/, *n.* **1.** a fossil crinoid. **2.** any crinoid. [EN-[2] + Gk *krínon* lily + -ITE[1]]

**encroach** /ɛn'kroʊtʃ, ən-/, *v.i.* **1.** to advance beyond proper limits; make gradual inroads. **2.** to trespass upon the property or rights of another, esp. stealthily or by gradual advances. [ME *encroche(n),* from OF *encrochier,* from *en-* EN-[1] + *croc* hook] – **encroacher,** *n.* – **encroachingly,** *adv.*

**encroachment** /ɛn'kroʊtʃmənt, ən-/, *n.* **1.** the act of encroaching. **2.** anything taken by encroaching.

**en croute** /ɒn 'krut, õ/, *adv.* cooked in a pastry crust. [F: in a crust]

**encrust** /ɛn'krʌst, ən-/, *v.t.* **1.** to cover or line with a crust or hard coating. **2.** to form into a crust. **3.** to deposit as a crust. –*v.i.* **4.** to form a crust. Also, **incrust.** [L *incrustāre*]

**encrustation** /ɛnkrʌs'teɪʃən/, *n.* **1.** an encrusting or being encrusted. **2.** a crust or coat of anything on the surface of a body; a covering, coating, or scale. **3.** the inlaying or addition of enriching materials on a surface. **4.** the inlaid or added enriching materials to a surface or an object. Also, **incrustation.**

**encrypt** /ɛn'krɪpt, ən-/, *v.t.* to convert (a plain-text message) into unintelligible language by means of a cipher or cryptosystem. – **encryption,** *n.*

**enculturation** /ɛn,kʌltʃə'reɪʃən/, *n.* →**socialisation.**

**encumber** /ɛn'kʌmbə, ən-/, *v.t.* **1.** to impede or hamper; retard; embarrass. **2.** to block up or fill with what is obstructive or superfluous. **3.** to burden with obligations, debt, etc. **4.** to burden or impede with or as with parcels, etc. Also, **incumber.** [ME *encombre(n),* from OF *encombrer,* from *en-* EN-[1] + *combre* barrier (from LL *combrus,* from Gallic *comberos* a bringing together)]

**encumbrance** /ɛn'kʌmbrəns, ən-/, *n.* **1.** that which encumbers; something useless or superfluous; a burden; a hindrance. **2.** a dependent person, esp. a child. **3.** *Law.* a burden or claim on property, as a mortgage. Also, **incumbrance.**

**encumbrancer** /ɛn'kʌmbrənsə, ən-/, *n. Law.* one who holds an encumbrance.

**encyclical** /ɛn'sɪklɪkəl, ən-/, *n.* **1.** a letter addressed by the Pope to all the bishops of the world in communion with the Holy See. –*adj.* **2.** intended for wide or general circulation; general. Also, **encyclic.** [LL *encyclicus* (replacing L *encyclius,* from Gk *enkýklios* circular, general) + -AL[1]]

**encyclopaedia** /ɛn,saɪklə'pidɪə, ən-/, *n.* **1.** a work treating separately various topics from all branches of knowledge, usu. in alphabetical arrangement. **2.** a work treating exhaustively one art or science esp. in articles arranged alphabetically; a cyclopaedia. **3.** (*cap.*) the French work edited by Diderot and D'Alembert, published in the 18th century, distinguished by its advanced or radical character. Also, **encyclopedia.** [LL, from pseudo-Gk (occurring in mss. of Quintilian, Pliny, and Galen) *enkyklopaideía,* for *enkýklios paideía* general education, complete round or course of learning. See ENCYCLICAL, CYCLOPAEDIA]

**encyclopaedic** /ɛn,saɪklə'pidɪk, ən-/, *adj.* **1.** pertaining to or of the nature of an encyclopaedia; relating to all branches of knowledge. **2.** embracing all or much human learning. Also, **encyclopedic.**

**encyclopaedism** /,ɛnsaɪklə'pidɪzəm, ən-/, *n.* **1.** encyclopaedic learning. **2.** (*oft. cap.*) the doctrines and influence of the Encyclopaedists. Also, **encyclopedism.**

**encyclopaedist** /,ɛnsaɪklə'pidəst, ən-/, *n.* **1.** a compiler of or contributor to an encyclopaedia. **2.** (*oft. cap.*) one of the collaborators in the French Encyclopaedia. Also, **encyclopedist.**

**encyst** /ɛn'sɪst, ən-/, *v.t.* **1.** to enclose in a cyst. –*v.i.* **2.** to become enclosed in a cyst. – **encystment, encystation,** /,ɛnsɪs'teɪʃən/, *n.*

**end** /ɛnd/, *n.* **1.** an extremity of anything that is longer than it is broad: *the end of a street, rope, rod, etc.* **2.** an extreme or farthermost part of anything extended in space: *the ends* *of the earth.* **3.** anything that bounds an object at one of its extremities; a limit. **4.** a place or section adjacent to an extremity or limit: *at the far end of the room.* **5.** the act of coming to an end; termination. **6.** the concluding part. **7.** a purpose or aim: *to gain one's end.* **8.** the object for which a thing exists: *the happiness of the people is the end of government.* **9.** issue or result. **10.** termination of existence; death. **11.** a cause of death, destruction, or ruin. **12.** a remnant or fragment: *odds and ends.* **13.** a part or share of something: *her end of the work.* **14.** a district or locality, esp. part of a town: *the West End.* **15.** *Cricket.* a wicket: *the batting end, the bowling end.* **16.** *Football, etc.* the half of the field which is defended by one team and attacked by the other. **17.** *Bowls.* a part of the game during which the players all deliver their bowls to one end of the green; at the completion of one end the direction of play may reverse. **18. at a loose end,** Also, **at loose ends. a.** unoccupied; with nothing to do. **b.** in disorder. **19. end on,** with the end facing, or next to. **20. end to end,** (of two objects) having the ends adjacent. **21. get one's end in,** *Colloq.* (of a male) to have sexual intercourse. **22. go off the deep end,** *Colloq.* to become violently agitated; lose control of emotions. **23. in the end,** as an outcome; at last; finally. **24. keep one's end up,** *Colloq.* to see that one's contribution to a joint undertaking is adequately performed. **25. make (both) ends meet,** to keep expenditure within one's means. **26. no end,** *Colloq.* very much; greatly. **27. on end, a.** upright. **b.** continuously. **28. the (living) end, a.** the worst possible. **b.** a person who is incompetent or insufferable in every way. *–v.t.* **29.** to bring to an end or natural conclusion. **30.** to put an end to by force. **31.** to form the end of. *–v.i.* **32.** to come to an end; terminate; cease: *he ended by settling down.* **33.** to issue or result: *extravagance ends in want.* **34.** *Colloq.* to reach a final condition, circumstance, goal (oft. fol. by *up*): *you'll end up in prison.* [ME and OE *ende*, c. G *Ende.* See AND] – **ender,** *n.*

**end-,** variant of **endo-,** before vowels, as in *endamoeba.*

**endamoeba** /ɛndəˈmibə/, *n.* a protozoan, genus *Endamoeba,* one species of which causes dysentery and liver abscess. Also, *U.S.,* **endameba.** [END- + AMOEBA]

**endanger** /ɛnˈdeɪndʒə, ən-/, *v.t.* to expose to danger; imperil. – **endangerment,** *n.*

**endarch** /ˈɛndak/, *adj.* denoting a strand or cylinder of primary xylem in a stem or root with the protoxylem on its inner edge.

**end-blown** /ˈɛnd-bloʊn/, *adj.* (of a flute) having a mouth-piece at the end of the tube, so that the player's breath is directed into the instrument.

**end brain** /ˈɛnd breɪn/, *n.* →**telencephalon.**

**endear** /ɛnˈdɪə, ən-/, *v.t.* to make dear, esteemed, or beloved: *he endeared himself to his mother.* – **endearingly,** *adv.*

**endearment** /ɛnˈdɪəmənt, ən-/, *n.* **1.** the act of endearing. **2.** the state of being endeared. **3.** an action or utterance manifesting affection; a caress or an affectionate term.

**endeavour** /ɛnˈdɛvə, ən-/, *v.i.* **1.** to exert oneself to do or effect something; make an effort; strive. *–v.t.* **2.** to attempt; try: *he endeavours to keep things nice about his place.* *–n.* **3.** a strenuous effort; an attempt. Also, *U.S.,* **endeavor.** [ME *endever(en)* to exert oneself, from the phrase *putten en deveren* to make it one's duty. Cf. F *en devoir* in duty] – **endeavourer,** *n.*

**endemic** /ɛnˈdɛmɪk/, *adj.* **1.** Also, **endemical.** peculiar to a particular people or locality, as a disease. *–n.* **2.** an endemic disease. [Gk *éndēmos* belonging to a people + -IC] – **endemically,** *adv.* – **endemism** /ˈɛndəmɪzəm/, **endemicity** /ɛndəˈmɪsəti/, *n.*

**endermic** /ɛnˈdɜmɪk/, *adj.* acting through the skin, as a medicine. [EN-[2] + DERM(A) + -IC]

**en déshabillé** /õ dɛˈzabijeɪ/, *adj.* in dishabille or undress. [F]

**endgame** /ˈɛndgeɪm/, *n.* the final stage of a game of chess, played with few surviving pieces, leading to checkmate or stalemate.

**end-grain** /ˈɛnd-greɪn/, *n.* the outward grain of the end of a piece of wood.

**ending** /ˈɛndɪŋ/, *n.* **1.** a bringing or coming to an end; termination; close. **2.** the final or concluding part. **3.** death. **4.** *Gram.* an inflectional morpheme at the end of a word form, as *-s* in *cuts.* **5.** (in popular use) any final word part, as the *-ow* of *widow.* [ME; OE *endung*]

**endive** /ˈɛndaɪv/, *n.* a herb, *Cichorium endivia,* probably of Indian origin, now widely cultivated for its finely divided curled leaves used in salads and as a cooked vegetable. [ME, from F, from ML *endivia,* from MGk *indivi,* from L *intibus, intibum*]

**endless** /ˈɛndləs/, *adj.* **1.** having no end, limit, or conclusion; boundless; infinite; interminable; incessant. **2.** made continuous, as by joining the two ends of a single length: *an endless chain or belt.* – **endlessly,** *adv.* – **endlessness,** *n.*

**endman** /ˈɛndmæn/, *n.* **1.** a man at one end of a row or line. **2.** a man at either end of the line of performers of a minstrel troupe, who plays on the bones or tambourine and carries on humorous dialogue with the interlocutor.

**end matter** /ˈɛnd mætə/, *n.* the parts of a book which follow its principle contents, as the index, glossary, etc.

**endmost** /ˈɛndmoʊst/, *adj.* →**farthest.**

**end note** /ˈɛnd noʊt/, *n.* supplementary material printed at the end of a chapter, article or text.

**endo-,** a word element meaning 'internal', as in *endocardial.* Also, **end-.** [Gk, combining form of *éndon* within]

**endoblast** /ˈɛndoʊblæst/, *n.* the prospective endoderm; the blastemic cells which are to form the endoderm. – **endoblastic** /ˌɛndoʊˈblæstɪk/, *adj.*

**endocardial** /ɛndoʊˈkadiəl/, *adj.* **1.** within the heart; intracardiac. **2.** pertaining to the endocardium.

**endocarditis** /ˌɛndoʊkaˈdaɪtəs/, *n.* inflammation of the endocardium. [NL, from ENDOCARD(IUM) + -ITIS] – **endocarditic** /ˌɛndoʊkaˈdɪtɪk/, *adj.*

**endocardium** /ɛndoʊˈkadiəm/, *n.* the delicate serous membrane which lines the cavities of the heart and aids in forming the valves by duplication. [NL, from *endo-* ENDO- + *cardium* (combining form representing Gk *kardía* heart)]

**endocarp** /ˈɛndoʊkap/, *n.* the inner layer of a pericarp, as the stone of certain fruits.


fruit of peach: A, endocarp; B, epicarp; C, mesocarp; ABC, pericarp

**endocentric** /ˌɛndoʊˈsɛntrɪk/, *adj.* having the same function in a sentence as one of its immediate constituents. *Cold water* is an endocentric construction since it functions in the same way as would the noun *water.* Cf. **exocentric.**

**endocrine** /ˈɛndəkrən, -krin, -kraɪn/, *n.* **1.** an endocrine gland or organ. **2.** an internal secretion. *–adj.* **3.** of or pertaining to the endocrine glands or their secretions: *endocrine function.* [ENDO- + Gk *krínein* separate] – **endocrinal** /ɛndəˈkraɪnəl/, **endocrinic** /ɛndəˈkrɪnɪk/, **endocrinous** /ɛnˈdɒkrənəs/, *adj.*

**endocrine gland** /ˈ– glænd/, *n.* any of various glands or organs (as the thyroid gland, suprarenal bodies, pituitary body, etc.) which produce certain important internal secretions (products given up directly to the blood or lymph) acting upon particular organs, and which, through improper functioning, may cause grave disorders or death; ductless gland.

**endocrinology** /ˌɛndoʊkrəˈnɒlədʒi/, *n.* the science that deals with the endocrine glands, esp. in their relation to bodily changes. – **endocrinologist,** *n.*

**endoderm** /ˈɛndoʊdɜm/, *n.* the inner germ layer in the embryo of a metazoan. Also, **entoderm.** – **endodermal** /ɛndoʊˈdɜməl/, **endodermic** /ɛndoʊˈdɜmɪk/, *adj.*

**endodermis** /ɛndoʊˈdɜməs/, *n.* a specialised uniseriate layer of cells delimiting the stele of vascular plants.

**endodontist** /ˈɛndoʊdɒntəst/, *n.* a dentist who specialises in the treatment of the roots of teeth.

**endoergic** /ˌɛndoʊˈɜdʒɪk/, *adj.* (of a process or reaction, esp. a nuclear one) consuming energy; endothermic.

**endogamous** /ɛnˈdɒgəməs/, *adj.* **1.** marrying customarily within the tribe or other social unit. **2.** pertaining to such marriage (opposed to *exogamous*). Also, **endogamic** /ɛndoʊˈgæmɪk/.

**endogamy** /ɛnˈdɒgəmi/, *n.* marriage within the tribe or other social unit (opposed to *exogamy*).

**endogen** /ˈɛndoʊdʒɛn/, *n.* any plant of the obsolete class Endogenae, including the monocotyledons, whose stems were erroneously supposed to grow from within.

**endogenous** /ɛn'dɒdʒənəs/, *adj.* **1.** growing or proceeding from within; originating within. **2.** *Anat.* autogenous. – **endogenously,** *adv.*

**endolymph** /'ɛndoʊlɪmf/, *n.* the fluid contained within the membranous labyrinth of the ear.

**endometriosis** /ˌɛndoʊˌmitri'oʊsəs/, *n.* the presence of uterine lining in other organs, most commonly the ovary, characterised by cyst formation, adhesions, and menstrual pain. – **endometrial,** *adj.*

**endometritis** /ˌɛndoʊmə'traɪtəs/, *n.* inflammation of the lining of the uterus.

**endometrium** /ˌɛndoʊ'mitriəm/, *n., pl.* **-tria** /-triə/. the mucous membrane lining the uterus.

**endomorph** /'ɛndoʊmɔf/, *n.* **1.** *Mineral.* a mineral enclosed within another mineral. **2.** *Physiol.* a person of endomorphic type.

**endomorphic** /ɛndoʊ'mɔfɪk/, *adj.* **1.** *Mineral.* occurring in the form of an endomorph. **2.** *Mineral.* of or relating to endomorphs. **3.** of or pertaining to those phases of contact metamorphism that are developed in the intrusive rock itself. **4.** *Physiol.* having a heavily built body characterised by the relative prominence of structures developed from the embryonic endoderm (distinguished from *ectomorphic, mesomorphic*).

**endomorphism** /ɛndoʊ'mɔfɪzəm/, *n.* a change within the mass of an intrusive igneous rock brought about by the rock's own magma.

**endoparasite** /ˌɛndoʊ'pærəsaɪt/, *n.* an internal parasite (opposed to *ectoparasite*).

**endoperidium** /ˌɛndoʊpə'rɪdiəm/, *n.* See **peridium.**

**endophyte** /'ɛndoʊfaɪt/, *n.* a plant living within an animal or another plant, usu. as a parasite.

**endoplasm** /'ɛndoʊplæzəm/, *n.* the inner portion of the cytoplasm in the cell of a protozoan or vegetable cell (opposed to *ectoplasm*). – **endoplasmic** /ˌɛndoʊ'plæzmɪk/, *adj.*

**endopleura** /ˌɛndoʊ'pluərə/, *n.* the inner coat of a seed, the tegmen.

**endoreic** /ˌɛndə'riɪk/, *adj.* having internal flow, as of drainage basins which have no outlet to the sea.

**end organ** /'ɛnd ɔgən/, *n.* one of several specialised structures found at the peripheral end of sensory or motor nerve fibres.

**endorse** /ɛn'dɔs, ən-/, *v.t.,* **-dorsed, -dorsing. 1.** to write (something) on the back of a document, etc. **2.** to sign one's name on (a commercial document or other instrument). **3.** to designate (another) as payee by one's endorsement. **4.** to acknowledge (payment) by placing one's signature on a bill, draft, etc. **5.** to add a modifying statement to (a document). **6.** to record a conviction for a motoring offence on (a driving licence). **7.** (of a branch of a political party) to select as a candidate for an election: *he's the endorsed Labor candidate for Bradfield.* Also, **indorse.** [partial Latinisation of ME *endosse,* from OF *endosser,* from *en-* on + *dos* (from L *dorsum* back)] – **endorsable,** *adj.* – **endorser,** *n.*

**endorsee** /ɛndɔ'si, ən-/, *n.* one to whom a negotiable document is endorsed. Also, **indorsee.**

**endorsement** /ɛn'dɔsmənt, ən-/, *n.* **1.** approval or sanction. **2.** the placing of one's signature, etc., on a document. **3.** the signature, etc., placed on the reverse of a commercial document which assigns the interest therein to another. **4.** a clause under which the stated coverage of an insurance policy may be altered. **5.** any statement subsequently added to a document to indicate some modification of its original terms.

**endosarc** /'ɛndoʊsak/, *n.* the endoplasm of a protozoan (opposed to *ectosarc*).

**endoscope** /'ɛndoʊskoʊp/, *n.* a slender tubular instrument used to examine the interior of a body cavity or hollow viscus. – **endoscopic,** *adj.* – **endoscopy** /ɛn'dɒskəpi/, *n.*

**endoskeleton** /ˌɛndoʊ'skɛlətn/, *n.* the internal skeleton or framework of the body of an animal (opposed to *exoskeleton*). – **endoskeletal,** *adj.*

**endosmosis** /ˌɛndɒz'moʊsəs, -dɒs-/, *n.* **1.** osmosis from without inwards. **2.** (in osmosis) the flow of that fluid which passes with the greater rapidity into the other (opposed to *exosmosis*). [NL] – **endosmotic** /ɛndɒz'mɒtɪk, -dɒs-/, *adj.* – **endosmotically** /ɛndɒz'mɒtɪkli, -dɒs-/, *adv.*

**endosperm** /'ɛndoʊspɜm/, *n.* nutritive matter in seed plant ovules, derived from the embryo sac. – **endospermic,** *adj.*

**endospore** /'ɛndoʊspɔ/, *n.* **1.** *Bot.* the inner coat of a spore. **2.** *Bacteriol.* a spore formed within a cell of a rod-shaped organism. **3.** a fungal spore formed within a reproductive structure, i.e. an endogenous spore.

**endosteum** /ɛn'dɒstiəm/, *n., pl.* **-tea** /-tiə/. the vascular membrane lining the medullary cavity of a bone. [NL, from Gk *end-* END- + *ostéon* bone]

**endostosis** /ˌɛndɒs'toʊsəs/, *n.* bone formation beginning in the substance of cartilage. [END(O)- + OSTOSIS]

**endothecium** /ɛndoʊ'θiʃiəm, -siəm/, *n., pl.* **-cia** /-ʃiə, -siə/. **1.** the sub-epidermal cell layer of an anther which causes it to open when mature, often having special thickenings. **2.** the inner tissues of bryophyte capsules which give rise to the spores and other structures. [NL, from Gk *endo-* ENDO- + *thēkíon* little case]

**endothelial** /ɛndoʊ'θiliəl/, *adj.* pertaining to endothelium.

**endothelioid** /ɛndoʊ'θiliɔɪd/, *adj.* resembling endothelium.

**endothelioma** /ˌɛndoʊˌθili'oʊmə/, *n., pl.* **-mata** /-mətə/, **-mas.** a tumour (malignant or benign) originating from the endothelium. [ENDOTHELI(UM) + -OMA]

**endothelium** /ɛndoʊ'θiliəm/, *n., pl.* **-lia** /-liə/. the tissue which lines blood vessels, lymphatics, serous cavities, and the like; a form of epithelium (in the broad sense). [NL, from Gk *endo-* ENDO- + *thēlḗ* nipple + *-ion*]

**endothermic** /ɛndoʊ'θɜmɪk/, *adj.* denoting or pertaining to a chemical change which is accompanied by an absorption of heat (opposed to *exothermic*).

**endotoxin** /ˌɛndoʊ'tɒksən/, *n.* the toxic protoplasm of a micro-organism which is liberated and causes its toxic action when the organism dies or disintegrates as of *Eberthella typhi,* the causative agent in typhoid fever.

**endotoxin shock syndrome,** *n.* a cardiovascular collapse caused by a fulminating bacterial infection, esp. in older people and women of menstrual age. Cf. **toxic shock syndrome.**

**endotrophic** /ˌɛndoʊ'trɒfɪk, -'troʊfɪk/, *adj.* of, denoting, or pertaining to a type of mycorrhizal association, as found in orchids, in which the fungal hyphae occur within the root tissue.

**endow** /ɛn'daʊ, ən-/, *v.t.* **1.** to provide with a permanent fund or source of income: *to endow a college.* **2.** to furnish as with some gift, faculty, or quality; equip: *Nature has endowed him with great ability.* **3.** *Archaic.* to provide with a dower. [ME *endow(en),* from OF *endouer,* from *en-* EN-[1] + *douer,* from L *dōtāre* endow] – **endower,** *n.*

**endowment** /ɛn'daʊmənt, ən-/, *n.* **1.** the act of endowing. **2.** that with which an institution, person, etc., is endowed, as property or funds. **3.** (*usu. pl.*) an attribute of mind or body; a gift of nature. **4.** →**child endowment.**

**endowment insurance** /– ɪn'ʃɔrəns/, *n.* a form of insurance providing for the payment of a fixed sum to the insured person at a specified time, or to his heirs, or a person designated, should he die before the time named.

**endpaper** /'ɛndpeɪpə/, *n.* a sheet of strong paper, half of which is pasted on to the inside of the cover of a book, the other half forming the flyleaf.

**end pin** /'ɛnd pɪn/, *n.* the usu. adjustable pin attached to the end of a cello and on which it rests on the floor.

**endplay** /'ɛndpleɪ/, *n.* towards the end of a game, a contrived set of manoeuvres designed to disadvantage an opponent.

**end point** /'ɛnd pɔɪnt/, *n.* the point in a volumetric titration denoting the completion of a reaction, usu. marked by a change in colour of an indicator.

**end product** /'– prɒdʌkt/, *n.* final or resulting product.

**end-stopped** /'ɛnd-stɒpt/, *adj.* of lines of verse at the end of each of which there is a pause.

**endue** /ɛn'dju, ən-/, *v.t.,* **-dued, -duing. 1.** to invest or endow with some gift, quality, or faculty: *endued with life.* **2.** to put on; assume. **3.** to clothe (fol. by *with*). Also, **indue.** [ME *endew(en),* from OF *enduire,* from L *indūcere* lead into, confused with L *induere* put on]

**endurable** /ɛn'djurəbəl, ən-/, *adj.* that may be endured. – **endurableness,** *n.* – **endurably,** *adv.*

**endurance** /ɛn'djurəns, ən-/, *n.* **1.** the fact or power of enduring or bearing anything. **2.** lasting quality; duration.

3. something endured, as a hardship. **4.** *Aeron.* the time an aircraft can continue flying under given conditions without refuelling.

**endurance limit** /– lɪmət/, *n.* (in fatigue testing) the maximum stress which a material will withstand without breaking.

**endure** /ɛn'djuə/, *v.,* **-dured, -during.** *–v.t.* **1.** to hold out against; sustain without impairment or yielding; undergo. **2.** to bear without resistance or with patience; tolerate: *I cannot endure to listen to that any longer.* *–v.i.* **3.** to continue to exist; last. **4.** to support adverse force or influence of any kind; suffer without yielding; suffer patiently. **5.** to retain a certain stature; maintain recognition of merit. [ME *endure(n),* from OF *endurer,* from L *indūrāre* harden, ML endure]

**enduring** /ɛn'djurɪŋ, ən-/, *adj.* **1.** lasting; permanent. **2.** long-suffering; patient. – **enduringly,** *adv.* – **enduringness,** *n.*

**endways** /'ɛndweɪz/, *adv.* **1.** on end. **2.** with the end upwards or forwards. **3.** towards the ends or end; lengthways. **4.** end to end. Also, **endwise** /'ɛndwaɪz/.

**-ene,** **1.** a noun suffix used in chemistry, in names of hydrocarbons, as *anthracene, benzene, naphthalene,* specifically those of the olefine or ethylene series, as *butylene.* **2.** a generalised suffix used in trademarks for substances, often implying synthetic manufacture. [special use of *-ene,* adj. suffix (as in *terrene*), from L *-ēnus* (in Gk *-ēnos*)]

**ENE,** east-north-east. Also, **E.N.E.**

**enema** /'ɛnəmə/, *n., pl.* **enemas, enemata** /ə'nɛmətə, i-/. **1.** a fluid injected into the rectum, as to evacuate the bowels. **2.** an instrument for doing this. **3.** the injection of the fluid. [Gk: injection, clyster]

**enemy** /'ɛnəmi/, *n., pl.* **-mies,** *adj.* *–n.* **1.** one who cherishes hatred or harmful designs against another; an adversary or opponent. **2.** an armed foe; an opposing military force. **3.** a hostile nation or state. **4.** a subject of such a state. **5.** something harmful or prejudicial. *–adj.* **6.** belonging to a hostile power or to any of its nationals: *enemy property.* [ME, from OF *enemi,* from L *inimīcus* unfriendly, hostile]

**energetic** /ɛnə'dʒɛtɪk/, *adj.* **1.** possessing or exhibiting energy; forcible; vigorous. **2.** powerful in action or effect; effective. [Gk *energētikós* active] – **energetically,** *adv.*

**energetics** /ɛnə'dʒɛtɪks/, *n.* the science of the laws of energy. [pl. of ENERGETIC. See -ICS]

**energise** /'ɛnədʒaɪz/, *v.,* **-gised, -gising.** *–v.t.* **1.** to give energy to; rouse into activity. *–v.i.* **2.** to be in operation; put forth energy. Also, **energize.** – **energiser,** *n.*

**energumen** /ɛnɜ'gjumən/, *n.* **1.** one possessed by an evil spirit; a demoniac. **2.** a fanatical enthusiast. [LL *energūmenus,* from Gk *energoúmenos,* ppr. pass. of *energeîn* operate, influence]

**energy** /'ɛnədʒi/, *n., pl.* **-gies.** **1.** capacity or habit of vigorous activity. **2.** the actual exertion of power; operation; activity. **3.** power as exerted. **4.** ability to produce action or effect. **5.** vigour or forcefulness of expression. **6.** *Physics.* the capacity for doing work which exists in various forms, as kinetic energy, nuclear energy, etc.; the derived SI unit of energy is the joule. [LL *energīa,* from Gk *enérgeia* agency, force]

**energy level** /'– lɛvəl/, *n.* one of a number of quantised energy states in which a nucleus, atom, or molecule can exist. Transitions between different levels involve the loss or gain of a finite quantity of energy. Also, **energy state.**

**enervate** /'ɛnəveɪt/, *v.,* **-vated, -vating,** *adj.* *–v.t.* **1.** to deprive of nerve, force, or strength; destroy the vigour of; weaken. *–adj.* **2.** enervated. [L *ēnervātus,* pp.] – **enervation** /ɛnə'veɪʃən/, *n.* – **enervator,** *n.* – **enervative,** *adj.*

**enface** /ɛn'feɪs, ən-/, *v.t.,* **-faced, -facing.** **1.** to write, print, or stamp something on the face of (a note, draft, etc.). **2.** to write, print, or stamp (something) on the face of a note, draft, etc. – **enfacement,** *n.*

**en famille** /õ fa'mi, fæ'mi/, *adv.* with one's family; within the family circle; at home. [F: in the family]

**enfant terrible** /õfõ tə'riblə/, *n.* **1.** an embarrassing child; one who is impolite or uncontrollable. **2.** a precociously talented person whose ideas or behaviour appear outlandish or iconoclastic to others in his milieu or profession. [F]

**enfeeble** /ɛn'fibəl, ən-/, *v.t.,* **-bled, -bling.** to make feeble; weaken. [ME *enfeble(n),* from OF *enfeblir,* from *en-* EN-[1] + *feble* FEEBLE] – **enfeeblement,** *n.* – **enfeebler,** *n.*

**enfeoff** /ɛn'fif, -'fɛf/, *v.t.* **1.** to invest with a fief or fee. **2.** to give as a fief. **3.** to surrender. [ME *enfeoffe(n),* from AF *enfeoffer.* See EN-[1], FIEF] – **enfeoffment,** *n.*

**enfetter** /ɛn'fɛtə, ən-/, *v.t.* to bind with or as with fetters.

**Enfield rifle** /ɛnfild 'raɪfəl/, *n.* any of various breech-loading, bolt-action rifles, first made at Enfield, England. Also, **Enfield.**

**enfilade** /'ɛnfəleɪd/, *n.;* /ɛnfə'leɪd/ *v.,* **-laded, -lading.** *Mil.* *–n.* **1.** a situation of works, troops, etc., making them subject to a sweeping fire from along the length of a line of works, trenches, batteries, etc., so that they are taken in the flank. **2.** the fire thus directed. *–v.t.* **3.** to attack with an enfilade. [F, from *enfiler* to thread, string, go through, rake with fire, from *en-* EN-[1] + *fil* a thread]

**enfold** /ɛn'foʊld, ən-/, *v.t.* **1.** to wrap up; envelop: *enfolded in a magic mantle.* **2.** to clasp; embrace. **3.** to surround with or as with folds. **4.** to form into a fold or folds: *a cambium layer deeply enfolded where it extends downwards.* Also, **infold.** – **enfolder,** *n.* – **enfoldment,** *n.*

**enforce** /ɛn'fɔs, ən-/, *v.t.,* **-forced, -forcing.** **1.** to put or keep in force; compel obedience to: *to enforce laws or rules.* **2.** to obtain (payment, obedience, etc.) by force or compulsion. **3.** to impose (a course of action) upon a person. **4.** to support (a demand, etc.) by force. **5.** to impress or urge (an argument, etc.) forcibly; lay stress upon. [ME *enforce(n),* from OF *enforcier,* from L *in-* IN-[1] + *fortis* strong] – **enforceable,** *adj.* – **enforcedly,** *adv.* – **enforcer,** *n.*

**enforcement** /ɛn'fɔsmənt, ən-/, *n.* **1.** the act or process of enforcing. **2.** *Archaic.* that which enforces.

**enfranchise** /ɛn'fræntʃaɪz, ən-/, *v.t.,* **-chised, -chising.** **1.** to grant a franchise to; admit to citizenship, esp. to the right of voting. **2.** *Law.* to invest with the right of being represented in Parliament. **3.** to set free; liberate, as from slavery. [MF *enfranchiss-,* stem of *enfranchir,* from *en-* EN-[1] + *franc* free, FRANK] – **enfranchisement** /ən'fræntʃəzmənt/, *n.* – **enfranchiser,** *n.*

**eng.,** **1.** engine. **2.** engineer. **3.** engineering. **4.** engraved. **5.** engraver. **6.** engraving.

**engage** /ɛn'geɪdʒ, ən-/, *v.,* **-gaged, -gaging.** *–v.t.* **1.** to occupy the attention or efforts of (a person, etc.): *he engaged her in conversation.* **2.** to secure for aid, employment, use, etc.; hire: *to engage a workman, to engage a room.* **3.** to attract and hold fast: *to engage the attention, interest, etc.* **4.** to reserve or secure. **5.** to attract or please: *his good nature engages everybody to him.* **6.** to bind as by pledge, promise, contract, or oath; make liable: *he engaged, verbally or in writing, to do it.* **7.** to betroth (usu. used in the passive). **8.** to bring (troops) into conflict; enter into conflict with: *our army engaged the enemy.* **9.** *Mech.* to cause to become interlocked; interlock with: *engage first gear.* **10.** *Archaic.* to entangle or involve. **11.** *Archaic.* to attach or secure. *–v.i.* **12.** to occupy oneself; become involved: *to engage in business, politics.* **13.** to take employment. **14.** to pledge one's word; assume an obligation. **15.** to cross weapons; enter into conflict. **16.** *Mech.* to interlock. [F *engager,* from *en-* EN-[1] + *gage* pledge, GAGE[1]] – **engager,** *n.*

**engaged** /ɛn'geɪdʒd, ən-/, *adj.* **1.** busy or occupied; involved. **2.** under engagement; pledged. **3.** betrothed. **4.** entered into conflict with. **5.** *Mech.* **a.** interlocked. **b.** (of wheels) in gear with each other. **6.** *Archit. Sculpture, etc.* secured to, or (actually or apparently) partly sunk into, something else, as a column with respect to a wall. **7.** of a telephone line, inaccessible because already in use. **8.** of a person whose telephone is being dialled, inaccessible because the line is already in use. **9.** of a signal emitted by a telephone indicating that the line is already in use.

**engagement** /ɛn'geɪdʒmənt, ən-/, *n.* **1.** the act of engaging. **2.** the state of being engaged. **3.** a pledge; an obligation or agreement. **4.** betrothal. **5,** employment, or a period or post of employment. **6.** an appointment or arrangement, often of a business nature. **7.** an encounter, conflict, or battle. **8.** *Mech.* the act or state of interlocking. **9.** *Fencing.* the state of having the blades in contact.

**engagement ring** /'– rɪŋ/, *n.* a ring given in token of an engagement by a man to his fiancée, usu. worn on the third finger of the left hand.

**engaging** /ɛn'geɪdʒɪŋ, ən-/, *adj.* winning; attractive; pleasing. – **engagingly,** *adv.* – **engagingness,** *n.*

**engender** /ɛn'dʒɛndə, ən-/, *v.t.* **1.** to produce, cause, or give rise to: *hatred engenders violence.* **2.** to beget; procreate. *–v.i.* **3.** to be produced or caused; come into existence. [ME *engendre(n)*, from OF *engendrer,* from L *ingenerāre* beget] – **engenderer,** *n.* – **engenderment,** *n.*

**engine** /'ɛndʒən/, *n.* **1.** any mechanism or machine designed to convert energy into mechanical work: *a steam engine, internal-combustion engine, etc.* **2.** a railway locomotive. **3.** any mechanical contrivance. **4.** a machine or instrument used in warfare, as a battering ram, catapult, piece of artillery, etc. **5.** *Obs.* an instrument of torture, esp. the rack. [ME *engin,* from OF, from L *ingenium* nature, invention]

**engine-driver** /'ɛndʒən-draɪvə/, *n.* one who drives a locomotive.

**engineer** /ɛndʒə'nɪə/, *n.* **1.** one versed in the design, construction, and use of engines or machines, or in any of the various branches of engineering: *a mechanical engineer, an electrical, civil, etc., engineer.* **2.** one who manages a ship's engines. **3.** a member of the armed forces esp. trained in engineering work. **4.** a skilful manager. **5.** *U.S.* an engine-driver. *–v.t.* **6.** to plan, construct, or manage as an engineer. **7.** to arrange, manage or carry through by skilful or artful contrivance.

**engineering** /ɛndʒə'nɪərɪŋ/, *n.* **1.** the art or science of making practical application of the knowledge of pure sciences such as physics, chemistry, biology, etc. **2.** the action, work, or profession of an engineer. **3.** skilful or artful contrivance; manoeuvring.

**engineer officer** /ɛndʒə'nɪər ˌɒfəsə/, *n.* a marine officer in charge of the engines on a ship, usu. a watchkeeping officer in the engine-room.

**engineer's chain** /ˌɛndʒənɪəz 'tʃeɪn/, *n.* See **chain** (def. 9).

**engine-house** /'ɛndʒən-haʊs/, *n.* a building in which an engine is kept.

**engineman** /'ɛndʒənmən/, *n., pl.* **-men** /-mən/. a driver or fireman of a railway locomotive.

**engine-room** /'ɛndʒən-rum/, *n.* **1.** the room in a vessel in which a ship's engines are situated. **2.** any room housing an engine.

**engine-room artificer** /– a'tɪfəsə/, *n.* a junior naval officer whose duty is to assist the engineer officer.

**enginery** /'ɛndʒənri/, *n.* **1.** engines collectively. **2.** engines of war. **3.** skilful or artful contrivance.

**engine turning** /'ɛndʒən tɜnɪŋ/, *n.* the engraving of any symmetrical pattern on a metallic surface by machinery.

**engird** /ɛn'gɜd, ən-/, *v.t.,* **-girt** or **-girded, -girding.** to encircle; encompass.

**engirdle** /ɛn'gɜdəl, ən-/, *v.t.,* **-dled, -dling.** →**engird.**

**englacial** /ɛn'gleɪsiəl, ən-/, *adj.* **1.** within the ice of a glacier. **2.** believed to have been formerly within the ice of a glacier or ice-sheet: *englacial debris.*

**englacial stream** /– 'strim/, *n.* a stream of melt-water which flows through a tunnel within an ice-sheet or glacier.

**England** /'ɪŋglənd/, *n.* the largest division of the United Kingdom, occupying all of the main island of Great Britain except Scotland and Wales. [ME *Engeland,* OE *Englaland* land of the English]

**Englander** /'ɪŋgləndə/, *n.* **1.** *Rare.* a native of England. **2.** **little Englander, a.** *Colloq.* an opponent of imperialism, esp. one advocating isolationist policies in the late 19th century. **b.** *Colloq.* an opponent of Britain's joining the common market, preferring to see Britain less influential but independent.

**English** /'ɪŋglɪʃ, 'ɪŋlɪʃ/, *adj.* **1.** of, pertaining to, or characteristic of England or its inhabitants, institutions, etc. **2.** belonging or pertaining to, or spoken or written in, the English language. *–n.* **3.** the people of England collectively, esp. as distinguished from the Scots, Welsh, and Irish. **4.** the Germanic language of the British Isles, widespread and standard also in Australia and many other countries, esp. those colonised by Britain. It is historically termed Old English or Anglo-Saxon (to 1150), Middle English (to 1450) and Modern English. **5.** (*l.c.*) *U.S.* →**side** (def. 15). **6.** a printing type (14 point) or a size between pica and two-line brevier. **7.** straightforward and simple language. **8. the Queen's (King's) English,** (supposedly) educated or correct English speech or usage. *–v.t.* **9.** to translate into English. **10.** to adopt (a foreign word) into English. **11.** (*l.c.*) *U.S. Billiards.* to impart english or side to (a ball). [ME; OE *Englisc,* from *Engle, Angle* the English]

**English bond** /– 'bɒnd/, *n.* a common arrangement of brickwork in which alternate courses of bricks are headers and stretchers, i.e., they show the short ends or the long faces of the bricks. Cf. **Flemish bond.**

**English couch grass,** *n.* →**couch**[2].

**English elm** /ɪŋglɪʃ 'ɛlm/, *n.* →**elm.**

**English horn** /– 'hɔn/, *n.* →**cor anglais.**

**Englishman** /'ɪŋglɪʃmən/, *n., pl.* **-men. 1.** a person native to or resident in England. **2.** an English ship. – **Englishwoman,** *n.*

**Englishness** /'ɪŋglɪʃnəs/, *n.* the quality of being English.

**English rose** /– 'roʊz/, *n.* a pretty girl with very fair and blushing complexion, the stereotype of English beauty.

**English setter** /– 'sɛtə/, *n.* one of a breed of long-haired gun dogs, usu. tan-and-white, white with liver flecks, or pure white, with a rangy body.

English setter

**English springer spaniel,** *n.* one of the two breeds of springer spaniel, slightly larger than the Welsh springer spaniel, and having a black-and-white or liver-and-white coat.

**engorge** /ɛn'gɔdʒ, ən-/, *v.t.,* **-gorged, -gorging. 1.** to swallow greedily; glut or gorge. **2.** *Pathol.* to congest with blood. [F *engorger,* from *en-* EN-[1] + *gorge* GORGE] – **engorgement,** *n.*

**engraft** /ɛn'graft, ən-/, *v.t.* to insert, as a scion of one tree or plant into another, for propagation: *to engraft a peach on a plum.* Also, **ingraft.** – **engraftation** /ɛngraf'teɪʃən/, *n.* – **engraftment,** *n.*

**engrail** /ɛn'greɪl, ən-/, *v.t.* **1.** to ornament the edge of with curved indentations. **2.** (on a coin or medal) to form the decorative margin of a ring of dots. [ME *engrele(n),* from OF *engresler,* from *en-* EN-[1] + *gresle* hail] – **engrailment,** *n.*

**engrain** /ɛn'greɪn, ən-/, *v.t.;* /'ɛngreɪn/, *adj.* →**ingrain.** [ME, from EN-[1] + GRAIN. Cf. F *en graine* where *graine* means cochineal dye]

**engram** /'ɛngræm/, *n.* **1.** *Biol.* the durable mark caused by a stimulus upon protoplasm. **2.** *Psychol.* →**trace**[1] (def. 4).

**engrave** /ɛn'greɪv, ən-/, *v.t.,* **-graved, -graving. 1.** to incise (letters, designs, etc.) on a hard surface, as of metal, stone, or the end grain of wood. **2.** to print from such a surface. **3.** to mark or ornament with incised letters, designs, etc. **4.** to impress deeply; infix. [EN-[1] + GRAVE[3], *v.*, modelled on F *engraver*] – **engraver,** *n.*

**engraving** /ɛn'greɪvɪŋ, ən-/, *n.* **1.** the act or art of one who or that which engraves. **2.** the art of forming designs by cutting, corrosion by acids, a photographic process, etc., on the surface of metal plates or of blocks of wood, etc., for the purpose of taking off impressions or prints of the design so formed. **3.** the design engraved. **4.** an engraved plate or block. **5.** an impression or print from this.

**engross** /ɛn'groʊs, ən-/, *v.t.* **1.** to occupy wholly, as the mind or attention; absorb. **2.** to write or copy in a fair, large hand or in a formal manner, as a public document or record. **3.** to acquire the whole of (a commodity), in order to control the market; monopolise. [ME *engross(en),* from AF *engrosser* write large; also from OF, from *en gros* in large quantities, from L *in-* IN-[2] + LL *grossus* thick, GROSS] – **engrosser,** *n.*

**engrossing** /ɛn'groʊsɪŋ, ən-/, *adj.* **1.** fully occupying the mind or attention; absorbing. **2.** acquiring overall control; monopolising. – **engrossingly,** *adv.*

**engrossment** /ɛn'groʊsmənt, ən-/, *n.* **1.** the act of engrossing. **2.** an engrossed copy of a document.

**engulf** /ɛn'gʌlf, ən-/, *v.t.* **1.** to swallow up in or as in a gulf. **2.** to plunge or immerse. Also, **ingulf.** – **engulfment,** *n.*

**enhance** /ɛn'hæns, -'hans, ən-/, *v.t.,* **-hanced, -hancing. 1.** to raise to a higher degree; intensify; magnify. **2.** to raise the value or price of. [ME *enhaunce(n),* from AF *enhauncer,* nasalised var. of OF *enhaucier,* from *en-* EN-[1] + *haucier* raise. See HAWSER] – **enhancement,** *n.* – **enhancer,** *n.* – **enhancive,** *adj.*

**enharmonic** /ˌɛnha'mɒnɪk/, *adj.* having the same pitch in the tempered scale but written in different notation, as G-sharp and A-flat. [LL *enharmonicus* in accord, from Gk *enarmonikós*] – **enharmonically,** *adv.*

**enigma** /ə'nɪgmə/, *n.* **1.** somebody or something puzzling or inexplicable. **2.** a saying, question, picture, etc., containing a hidden meaning; a riddle. [L *aenigma,* from Gk *aínigma* riddle]

**enigmatic** /ɛnɪg'mætɪk/, *adj.* resembling an enigma; perplexing; mysterious. Also, **enigmatical.** – **enigmatically,** *adv.*

**enjambment** /ɛn'dʒæmmənt, ən-/, *n.* the running on of the thought from one line or couplet to the next. Also, **enjambement.** [F *enjambement,* from *enjamber* stride over, project, from *en-* EN-[1] + *jambe* leg]

**enjoin** /ɛn'dʒɔɪn, ən-/, *v.t.* **1.** to order or direct (a person, etc.) to do something; prescribe (a course of action, etc.) with authority or emphasis. **2.** *Law.* to prohibit or restrain by an injunction. [ME *enjoyn(en),* from OF *enjoindre,* from L *injungere* join into or to, impose, enjoin] – **enjoiner,** *n.* – **enjoinment,** *n.*

**enjoy** /ɛn'dʒɔɪ, ən-/, *v.t.* **1.** to experience with joy; take pleasure in. **2.** to have and use with satisfaction; have the benefit of. **3.** to find or experience pleasure for (oneself). **4.** to undergo (an improvement). **5.** to have sexual intercourse with (a woman). *–v.i.* **6.** to have a good time: *let's forget our troubles and enjoy.* [ME *enjoye(n),* from OF *enjoir,* from *en-* EN-[1] + *joir* JOY, *v.*] – **enjoyer,** *n.*

**enjoyable** /ɛn'dʒɔɪəbəl, ən-/, *adj.* that may be enjoyed; affording enjoyment. – **enjoyableness,** *n.* – **enjoyably,** *adv.*

**enjoyment** /ɛn'dʒɔɪmənt, ən-/, *n.* **1.** the possession, use, or occupancy of anything with satisfaction or pleasure. **2.** a particular form or source of pleasure. **3.** *Law.* the exercise of a right: *the enjoyment of an estate.*

**enkindle** /ɛn'kɪndl, ən-/, *v.t., v.i.,* **-dled, -dling.** to kindle into flame, ardour, activity, interest, etc. – **enkindler,** *n.*

**enlace** /ɛn'leɪs, ən-/, *v.t.,* **-laced, -lacing.** **1.** to bind or encircle as with a lace or cord. **2.** to interlace; intertwine. [ME *enlase(n),* from F *enlacer,* from *en-* EN-[1] + *lacier* LACE, *v.*] – **enlacement,** *n.*

**enlarge** /ɛn'ladʒ, ən-/, *v.,* **-larged, -larging.** *–v.t.* **1.** to make larger; increase in extent, bulk, or quantity; add to. **2.** to increase the capacity or scope of; expand. **3.** *Photog.* to make (a print) larger than the negative, by projection printing. *–v.i.* **4.** to grow larger; increase; expand. **5.** to speak or write at large; expatiate: *to enlarge upon a point.* **6.** *Law.* to extend time (within which an appeal may be brought). **7.** *Law.* to increase an estate, as a limited interest in land being increased into a fee simple. [ME *enlargen,* from OF *enlarger,* from *en-* EN-[1] + *large* LARGE] – **enlargeable,** *adj.* – **enlarger,** *n.*

**enlargement** /ɛn'ladʒmənt, ən-/, *n.* **1.** the act of enlarging; increase; expansion; amplification. **2.** anything, as a photograph, that is an enlarged form of something else. **3.** anything that enlarges something else; an addition.

**enlighten** /ɛn'laɪtn, ən-/, *v.t.* **1.** to give intellectual or spiritual light to; instruct; impart knowledge to. **2.** *Archaic or Poetic.* to shed light upon. – **enlightener,** *n.* – **enlighteningly,** *adv.*

**enlightened** /ɛn'laɪtnd, ən-/, *adj.* **1.** instructed; well-informed; not bound by prejudice and superstition. **2.** tempered with reason: *enlightened despotism.*

**enlightenment** /ɛn'laɪtnmənt, ən-/, *n.* **1.** the act of enlightening. **2.** the state of being enlightened. **3. the Enlightenment,** an 18th-century philosophical movement characterised by rationalism. **4.** (in Hinduism and Buddhism) the condition that revelation brings to the believer who has striven for its attainment, making him henceforth separated from the rest of mankind.

**enlist** /ɛn'lɪst, ən-/, *v.i.* **1.** to engage for military or naval service by enrolling after mutual agreement. **2.** to enter into some cause, enterprise, etc. *–v.t.* **3.** to engage for military or naval service. **4.** to secure (a person, services, etc.) for some cause, enterprise, etc. – **enlister,** *n.*

**enlisted man** /ɛn'lɪstəd mæn, ən-/, *n. U.S.* a serviceman who is not a commissioned officer or a warrant officer, or cadet.

**enlistment** /ɛn'lɪstmənt, ən-/, *n.* the act of enlisting; state of being enlisted.

**enliven** /ɛn'laɪvən, ən-/, *v.t.* **1.** to make vigorous or active; invigorate. **2.** to make sprightly, gay, or cheerful; brighten. [obs. *enlive* enliven (from EN-[1] + LIVE[2], *adj.*) + -EN[1]] – **enlivener,** *n.* – **enlivenment,** *n.*

**en masse** /ɒn 'mæs/, *adv.* in a mass or body; all together. [F]

**enmesh** /ɛn'mɛʃ, ən-/, *v.t.* to catch, as in a net; entangle. Also, **immesh, inmesh.** – **enmeshment,** *n.*

**enmity** /'ɛnməti/, *n., pl.* **-ties.** a feeling or condition of hostility; hatred; ill will; animosity; antagonism. [ME *enemyte,* from OF *ennemistie,* from L *inimīcus* enemy]

**ennead** /'ɛniəd/, *n.* **1.** a group of nine persons or things. **2.** (*cap.*) a group of nine gods in Egyptian religion. [Gk *enneás,* from *ennéa* nine] – **enneadic** /ˌɛni'ædɪk/, *adj.*

**enneagon** /'ɛniəgən/, *n.* →**nonagon.**

**ennoble** /ɛ'noʊbəl, ə-/, *v.t.,* **-bled, -bling.** **1.** to elevate in degree, excellence, or respect; dignify; exalt. **2.** to confer a title of nobility on. – **ennoblement,** *n.* – **ennobler,** *n.*

**ennui** /ɒn'wi/, *n.* a feeling of weariness and discontent resulting from satiety or lack of interest; boredom. [F, from L *in odiō.* See ANNOY, *n.*]

**enol** /'inɒl/, *n.* an organic compound containing a hydroxyl group attached to a doubly linked carbon atom, as in C=C–OH. [apparently from Gk *(h)én* (neut. of *heîs* one) + -OL[1]] – **enolic** /i'nɒlɪk/, *adj.*

**enormity** /ə'nɔməti, i-/, *n., pl.* **-ties.** **1.** enormousness; hugeness of size, scope, extent, etc. **2.** outrageous or heinous character; atrociousness: *the enormity of his offences.* **3.** something outrageous or heinous, as an offence. [L *ēnormitas* hugeness, irregularity]

**enormous** /ə'nɔməs, i-/, *adj.* **1.** greatly exceeding the common size, extent, etc.; huge; immense. **2.** outrageous or atrocious: *enormous wickedness.* [L *ēnormis* huge] – **enormously,** *adv.* – **enormousness,** *n.*

**enosis** /'ɛnoʊsəs/, *n.* the demand by Greek Cypriots for the political union of Cyprus with Greece. [MGk: union]

**enough** /ə'nʌf, i-/, *adj.* **1.** adequate for the want or need; sufficient for the purpose or to satisfy desire: *I've had enough of it, noise enough to wake the dead.* *–n.* **2.** an adequate quantity or number; a sufficiency. *–adv.* **3.** in a quantity or degree that answers a purpose or satisfies a need or desire; sufficiently. **4.** fully or quite: *ready enough.* **5.** tolerably or passably: *he sings well enough.* *–interj.* **6.** (an exclamation indicating frustration, anger, extreme irritation, etc.). [ME *enogh,* OE *genōh,* c. G *genug*]

**enounce** /i'naʊns/, *v.t.,* **enounced, enouncing.** **1.** to announce, declare, or proclaim. **2.** to state definitely, as a proposition. **3.** to utter or pronounce, as words. [F *énoncer,* from L *ēnuntiāre*] – **enouncement,** *n.*

**en papillote** /ˌɒ̃ pæpi'joʊt, -jɒt/, *adj., adv.* baked in a paper case. [F]

**en passant** /ɒ̃ 'pasɒ̃, pa'sɒ̃/, *adv.* **1.** in passing; by the way. *–n.* **2.** *Chess.* a rule according to which a pawn, after making the optional initial move over two squares, may be taken by an adversary's pawn, which makes the capture exactly as if the initial move had been over only one square. [F]

**enplane** /ɛn'pleɪn/, *v.i., v.t.* **-planed, -planing.** *Chiefly Mil.* to go or take on board an aeroplane.

**en prise** /ɒ̃ 'priz/, *adj.* (in chess) in line for capture; likely to be captured. [F]

**enquire** /ɪn'kwaɪə, ən-, ɛn-/, *v.,* **-quired, -quiring.** *–v.i.* **1.** to seek information by questioning; ask. *–v.t.* **2.** to seek to learn by asking. Also, **inquire.** – **enquirer,** *n.*

**enquiry** /ɪn'kwaɪri, ən-, ɛn-/, *n., pl.* **-quiries.** **1.** a seeking for truth, information, or knowledge. **2.** a question or query. Also, **inquiry.**

**enrage** /ɛn'reɪdʒ, ən-/, *v.t.,* **-raged, -raging.** to put into a rage; infuriate. [MF *enrager,* from *en-* EN-[1] + *rage* RAGE]

**en rapport** /ɒ̃ rə'pɔ/, *adj.* in sympathy or accord; in agreement; congenial. [F]

**enrapt** /ɛn'ræpt, ən-/, *adj.* rapt; transported; enraptured.

**enrapture** /ɛn'ræptʃə, ən-/, *v.t.,* **-tured, -turing.** to move to rapture; delight beyond measure.

**enrich** /ɛn'rɪtʃ, ən-/, *v.t.* **1.** to supply with riches, wealth, abundant or valuable possessions, etc.: *commerce enriches a nation.* **2.** to supply with abundance of anything desirable:

*to enrich the mind with knowledge.* **3.** to adorn; make splendid with costly decoration. **4.** to make finer in quality as by supplying desirable elements or ingredients: *to enrich bread or soil.* **5.** to enhance; make finer in flavour, colour, or significance. **6.** *Physics.* to increase the abundance of a particular isotope in a mixture of isotopes, esp. of a fissile isotope in a nuclear fuel, as enriching uranium with the isotope U-235. [ME *enrich(en),* from OF *enrichir,* from *en-* EN-[1] + *riche* RICH]

**enriched uranium** /ɛn,rɪtʃt ju'reɪniəm/, *n.* uranium ore which has been processed to increase the percentage of uranium oxide $U_3O_8$ from its mined grade. The usual increase is from 0.71% U-235 to 3% U-235.

**enrichment** /ɛn'rɪtʃmənt, ən-/, *n.* **1.** the act of enriching. **2.** the state of being enriched. **3.** something that enriches.

**enrobe** /ɛn'roʊb, ən-/, *v.,* **-robed, -robing.** *–v.t.* **1.** to put ceremonial garments on (someone). *–v.i.* **2.** to dress in ceremonial garments.

**enrol** /ɛn'roʊl, ən-/, *v.t.,* **-rolled, -rolling. 1.** to write (a name) or insert the name of (a person) in a roll or register; place upon a list. **2.** to enlist (oneself). **3.** to put in a record; record. **4.** to roll or wrap up. *–v.i.* **5.** to enrol oneself. Also, *Chiefly U.S.,* **enroll.** [ME *enroll(en),* from OF *enroller,* from *en-* EN-[1] + *rolle* ROLL, *n.*] – **enroller,** *n.*

**enrolment** /ɛn'roʊlmənt, ən-/, *n.* **1.** the act of enrolling; process of being enrolled. **2.** the number of persons enrolled, as for a course or in a school. Also, *Chiefly U.S.,* **enrollment.**

**enroot** /ən'rut, ən-/, *v.t.* **1.** to fix by the root. **2.** to fix fast; implant deeply.

**en route** /ɒn 'rut/, *adv.* on the way. [F]

**en rule** /'ɛn rul/, *n.* a rule (def. 8c) which is an en in length.

**ens** /ɛnz/, *n., pl.* **entia** /'ɛnʃiə/. being, considered in the abstract. [LL, ppr. neut. of *esse* be]

**ensanguine** /ɛn'sæŋgwən, ən-/, *v.t.,* **-guined, -guining.** to stain or cover with or as with blood. [EN-[1] + SANGUINE]

**ensconce** /ɛn'skɒns, ən-/, *v.t.,* **-sconced, -sconcing. 1.** to cover or shelter; hide securely. **2.** to settle securely or snugly: *ensconced in an armchair.* [EN-[1] + SCONCE[2]]

**ensemble** /ɒn'sɒmbəl/, *n.* **1.** all the parts of a thing taken together, so that each part is considered only in relation to the whole. **2.** the entire costume of an individual, esp. when all the parts are in harmony. **3.** the general effect, as of a work of art. **4. a.** the united performance of the full number of singers, musicians, etc. **b.** the group so performing: *a string ensemble.* **c.** tightness of performance. **5.** a group of supporting singers, actors, dancers, etc., in a theatrical production. *–adv.* **6.** *Obs.* together. [ME, from F, from LL *insimul* at the same time]

**enshrine** /ɛn'ʃraɪn, ən-/, *v.t.,* **-shrined, -shrining. 1.** to enclose in or as in a shrine. **2.** to cherish as sacred. Also, **inshrine.** – **enshrinement,** *n.*

**enshroud** /ɛn'ʃraʊd, ən-/, *v.t.* to shroud; conceal.

**ensiform** /'ɛnsəfɔm/, *adj.* (of plant and animal organs) sword-shaped, as a gladiolus leaf; xiphoid. [L *ensi(s)* sword + -FORM]

ensiform leaves of an iris

**ensign** /'ɛnsaɪn/; *Naval* /'ɛnsən/ *n.* **1.** a flag or banner, as of a nation. **2.** a badge of office or authority. **3.** any sign, token, or emblem. **4.** a standard-bearer. **5.** (formerly) the lowest commissioned rank in the British infantry. **6.** *U.S. Navy.* the lowest ranking commissioned officer. [ME *ensaigne,* from OF *enseigne,* from L *insignia* INSIGNIA] – **ensignship, ensigncy,** *n.*

**ensilage** /'ɛnsələdʒ/, *n., v.,* **-laged, -laging.** *–n.* **1.** the preservation of green fodder in a silo or pit. **2.** fodder thus preserved. *–v.t.* **3.** →**ensile.** [F, from *ensiler* ENSILE]

**ensile** /ɛn'saɪl, 'ɛnsəl/, *v.t.,* **-siled, -siling. 1.** to preserve (green fodder) in a silo. **2.** to make into ensilage. Also, **ensilage.** [F *ensiler,* from Sp. *ensilar,* from *en-* EN-[1] + *silo* SILO]

**enslave** /ɛn'sleɪv, ən-/, *v.t.,* **-slaved, -slaving.** to make a slave of; reduce to slavery. – **enslavement,** *n.* – **enslaver,** *n.*

**ensnare** /ɛn'snɛə, ən-/, *v.t.,* **-snared, -snaring.** to capture in, or involve as in, a snare. – **ensnarement,** *n.* – **ensnarer,** *n.*

**enstatite** /'ɛnstətaɪt/, *n.* a mineral of the pyroxene group consisting of magnesium silicate, occurring as an important constituent of basic igneous rocks. [Gk *enstátēs* adversary + -ITE[1]; so called because of its refractory nature]

**ensue** /ɛn'sju, ən-/, *v.i.,* **-sued, -suing. 1.** to follow in order; come afterwards, esp. in immediate succession. **2.** to follow as a consequence; result. [ME *ensewe(n),* from OF *ensuivre,* from L *insequī* follow close upon]

**en suite** /ɒn 'swit/, *n.* **1.** in succession; in a series or set. *–n.* **2.** a small bathroom attached to a bedroom. [F]

**ensure** /ɛn'ʃɔ, ən-/, *v.t.,* **-sured, -suring. 1.** to secure, or bring surely, as to a person: *this letter will ensure you a hearing.* **2.** to make sure or certain to come, occur, etc.: *measures to ensure the success of an undertaking.* **3.** to make secure or safe, as from harm. [ME *ensure(n),* from AF *ensurer,* from *en-* EN-[1] + OF *seur* SURE]

**enswathe** /ɛn'sweɪð, ən-/, *v.t.,* **-swathed, -swathing.** →**swathe**[1]. Also, **inswathe.** – **enswathement,** *n.*

**-ent,** a suffix equivalent to **-ant,** in adjectives and nouns, as in *ardent, dependent, different, expedient.* [L, stem ending of ppr. in vbs. of conjugations 2, 3, 4]

**E.N.T.** /i ɛn 'ti/, *Med.* Ear, Nose, and Throat.

**entablature** /ɛn'tæblətʃə/, *n.* **1.** that part of a classic architectural order which rests horizontally upon the columns and consists of the architrave, frieze, and cornice. **2.** a similar part in other constructions. [It. *intavolatura,* from *intavolare* board up]

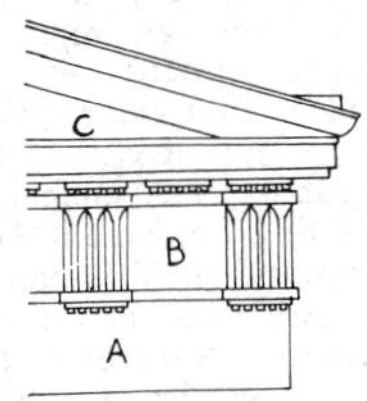

entablature: A, architrave, B, frieze; C, cornice

**entail** /ɛn'teɪl, ən-/, *v.t.* **1.** to bring on or involve by necessity or consequences: *a loss entailing no regret.* **2.** to impose as a burden. **3.** to limit the inheritance of (a landed estate) to a specified line of heirs, so that it cannot be alienated, devised, or bequeathed. **4.** to cause (anything) to descend to a fixed series of possessors. **5.** *Logic.* the relation by which one proposition is deducible logically from another: *being a bachelor entails being unmarried. –n.* **6.** the act of entailing. **7.** the state of being entailed. **8.** any predetermined order of succession, as to an office. **9.** that which is entailed, as an estate. **10.** the rule of descent settled for an estate. [EN-[1] + TAIL[2]] – **entailer,** *n.* – **entailment,** *n.*

**entangle** /ɛn'tæŋgəl, ən-/, *v.t.,* **-gled, -gling. 1.** to make tangled; complicate (usu. used in the passive). **2.** to involve in anything like a tangle; ensnare; enmesh. **3.** to involve in difficulties; embarrass; perplex. – **entangler,** *n.*

**entanglement** /ɛn'tæŋgəlmənt, ən-/, *n.* **1.** the act of entangling. **2.** the state of being entangled. **3.** that which entangles; a snare; an embarrassment; a complication.

**entasis** /'ɛntəsəs/, *n. Archit.* the swelling or outward curve of the shaft of a column. [NL, from Gk: a stretching]

**entelechy** /ɛn'tɛləki, ən-/, *n., pl.* **-chies. 1.** a realisation or actuality as opposed to a potentiality. **2.** (in vitalist philosophy) the vital force or principle directing growth and life. [LL *entelechīa,* from Gk, from *en télei échein* be in fulfilment or completion]

**entellus** /ɛn'tɛləs, ən-/, *n.* →**hanuman.** [NL; apparently named after *Entellus,* character (elderly man) in Virgil's *Aeneid*]

**entente** /ɒn'tɒnt/, *n.* **1.** understanding. **2.** the parties to an understanding. [F]

**entente cordiale** /– kɔdi'al/, *n.* a friendly understanding, esp. between two governments. [F]

**enter** /'ɛntə/, *v.i.* **1.** to come or go in. **2.** to make an entrance, as on the stage. **3.** to be admitted. **4.** to make a beginning (oft. fol. by *on* or *upon*). **5. enter into, a.** to take an interest or part in; engage in. **b.** to take up the consideration of (a subject); investigate. **c.** to sympathise with (a person's feelings, etc.). **d.** to assume the obligation of. **e.** to become a party to. **f.** to make a beginning in. **g.** to form a constituent part or ingredient of: *lead enters into the composition of pewter.* **h.** to penetrate; plunge deeply into. **i.** to go into a specific state: *enter into a state of hypnosis.* –*v.t.* **6.** to come or go into. **7.** to penetrate or pierce: *the bullet entered the flesh.* **8.** to put in or insert: *to enter a wedge.* **9.** to become a member of, or join. **10.** to cause to be admitted, as into a school, competition, etc. **11.** to make a beginning of or in, or begin upon; engage or become involved in. **12.** to make a record of; record or register. **13.** *Law.* **a.** to place in regular form before a court, as a writ. **b.** to occupy or to take possession of (lands); make an entrance, entry, ingress in, under claim of a right to possession. **14.** to register formally; submit; put forward: *to enter an objection.* **15.** to report (a vessel, etc.) at the customs house. [ME *entre(n),* from OF *entrer,* from L *intrāre* go into] – **enterable,** *adj.* – **enterer,** *n.*

**enteric** /ɛn'tɛrɪk/, *adj.* **1.** pertaining to the enteron; intestinal. **2.** typhoid. [Gk *enterikós,* from *énteron* intestine]

**enteric fever** /– 'fivə/, *n.* →**typhoid fever.**

**enteritis** /ɛntə'raɪtəs/, *n.* inflammation of the intestines.

**entero-**, a word element meaning 'intestine', as in *enterotoxaemia.* [Gk, combining form of *énteron*]

**enteron** /'ɛntərɒn/, *n., pl.* **-tera** /-tərə/. the alimentary canal; the digestive tract. [NL, from Gk: intestine]

**enterostomy** /ɛntə'rɒstəmi/, *n., pl.* **-mies.** the making of an artificial opening into the small intestine, which opens on to the abdominal wall, for feeding or drainage.

**enterotoxaemia** /ˌɛntəroʊtɒk'simiə/, *n.* a disease of sheep caused by severe systematic poisoning from bacterial toxins in the intestinal tract. Also, *U.S.,* **enterotoxemia.**

**enterovirus** /ɛntəroʊ'vaɪrəs/, *n.* any of the viruses of the gastrointestinal tract.

**enterprise** /'ɛntəpraɪz/, *n.* **1.** a project undertaken or to be undertaken, esp. one that is of some importance or that requires boldness or energy. **2.** engagement in such projects. **3.** boldness or readiness in undertaking, adventurous spirit, or energy. **4.** a company organised for commercial purposes. [ME, from OF *entreprise,* from *entreprendre* take in hand, from *entre* INTER- + *prendre* seize, take (from L *prehendere*)]

**enterpriser** /'ɛntəpraɪzə/, *n.* one who undertakes an enterprise.

**enterprising** /'ɛntəpraɪzɪŋ/, *adj.* ready to undertake projects of importance or difficulty, or untried schemes; energetic and daring in carrying out any undertaking. – **enterprisingly,** *adv.*

**entertain** /ɛntə'teɪn/, *v.t.* **1.** to hold the attention of agreeably; divert; amuse. **2.** to receive as a guest, esp. at one's table; show hospitality to. **3.** to give admittance or reception to. **4.** to admit into the mind; consider. **5.** to hold in the mind; harbour; cherish. **6.** to maintain or keep up. –*v.i.* **7.** to exercise hospitality; entertain company; provide entertainment for guests. [late ME *entertene(n),* from F *entretenir,* from *entre-* INTER- + *tenir* (from L *tenēre* hold)]

**entertainer** /ɛntə'teɪnə/, *n.* **1.** one who entertains. **2.** a singer, reciter, or the like, who gives, or takes part in, public entertainments.

**entertaining** /ɛntə'teɪnɪŋ/, *adj.* affording entertainment; amusing; diverting. – **entertainingly,** *adv.* – **entertainingness,** *n.*

**entertainment** /ɛntə'teɪnmənt/, *n.* **1.** the act of entertaining; agreeable occupation for the mind; diversion, or amusement. **2.** something affording diversion or amusement, esp. an exhibition or performance of some kind. **3.** hospitable provision for the wants of guests.

**enthalpy** /'ɛnθəlpi, ɛn'θælpi, ən-/, *n.* a thermodynamic property of a substance or system equal to the sum of its internal energy and the product of its pressure and volume; heat content; total heat.

**enthetic** /ɛn'θɛtɪk, ən-/, *adj.* introduced from without, as diseases propagated by inoculation. [Gk *enthetikós* fit for implanting]

**enthral** /ɛn'θrɔl, ən-/, *v.t.,* **-thralled, -thralling.** **1.** to captivate; charm. **2.** to put or hold in thraldom; subjugate. Also, *Chiefly U.S.,* **enthrall.** – **enthraller,** *n.* – **enthralment,** *U.S.,* **enthrallment,** *n.*

**enthrone** /ɛn'θroʊn, ən-/, *v.t.,* **-throned, -throning.** **1.** to place on or as on a throne. **2.** to invest with sovereign or episcopal authority. **3.** to exalt. – **enthronement, enthronisation** /ɛnˌθroʊnə'zeɪʃən, ən-/, *n.*

**enthuse** /ɛn'θuz, -'θjuz, ən-/, *v.,* **-thused, -thusing.** –*v.i.* **1.** to become enthusiastic; show enthusiasm. –*v.t.* **2.** to move to enthusiasm. [backformation from ENTHUSIASM]

**enthusiasm** /ɛn'θuziæzəm, -'θjuz-, ən-/, *n.* **1.** absorbing or controlling possession of the mind by any interest or pursuit; lively interest. **2.** extravagant religious emotion. [LL *enthūsiasmus,* from Gk *enthousiasmós*]

**enthusiast** /ɛn'θuziæst, -iəst, -'θjuz-, ən-/, *n.* **1.** one who is filled with enthusiasm for some principle, pursuit, etc.; a person of ardent zeal. **2.** a religious visionary or fanatic.

**enthusiastic** /ɛnˌθuzi'æstɪk, -ˌθjuz-, ən-/, *adj.* **1.** full of or characterised by enthusiasm; ardent. **2.** pertaining to or of the nature of enthusiasm. – **enthusiastically,** *adv.*

**enthymeme** /'ɛnθəmim/, *n.* (in logic) a syllogism in which one premise is unexpressed. [L *enthȳmēma,* from Gk: thought, argument] – **enthymematic** /ɛnθəmi'mætɪk/, **enthymematical** /ɛnθəmi'mætɪkəl/, *adj.*

**entice** /ɛn'taɪs, ən-/, *v.t.,* **-ticed, -ticing.** to draw on by exciting hope or desire; inveigle. [ME *entyce(n),* from OF *enticier* incite, from L *titio* firebrand] – **enticer,** *n.* – **enticingly,** *adv.*

**enticement** /ɛn'taɪsmənt, ən-/, *n.* **1.** the act or practice of enticing, esp. to evil. **2.** the state of being enticed. **3.** that which entices; an allurement. **4.** *Law.* the tort of inducing or persuading, without lawful justification, one spouse to leave another.

**entire** /ɛn'taɪə, ən-/, *adj.* **1.** having all the parts or elements; whole; complete. **2.** not broken, mutilated, or decayed; intact. **3.** unimpaired or undiminished. **4.** being wholly of one piece; undivided; continuous. **5.** *Bot.* without notches or indentations, as leaves. **6.** full or thorough: *entire freedom of choice.* **7.** not gelded: *an entire horse.* **8.** *Obs.* wholly of one kind; unmixed or pure. –*n.* **9.** the whole; entirety. **10.** an entire horse; a stallion. [ME *enter,* from OF *entier,* from L *integrum,* acc. of *integer* untouched, whole] – **entireness,** *n.*

**entirely** /ɛn'taɪəli, ən-/, *adv.* **1.** wholly or fully; completely or unreservedly. **2.** solely or exclusively.

**entirety** /ɛn'taɪrəti, ən-/, *n., pl.* **-ties.** **1.** the state of being entire; completeness. **2.** that which is entire; the whole.

**entitle** /ɛn'taɪtl, ən-/, *v.t.,* **-tled, -tling.** **1.** to give (a person or thing) a title, right, or claim to something; furnish with grounds for laying claim. **2.** to call by a particular title or name; name. **3.** to designate (a person) by an honorary title. [ME *entitle(n),* from OF *entituler,* from LL *intitulāre,* from L *in-* IN-$^2$ + *titulus* TITLE]

**entitlement issue** /ɛn'taɪtlmənt ɪʃu/, *n.* a method of raising capital whereby existing shareholders may buy new shares, usu. below market price, which are usu. issued in a predetermined ratio to current shareholdings, and cannot be sold or transferred; non-renounceable issue.

**entity** /'ɛntəti/, *n., pl.* **-ties.** **1.** something that has a real existence; a thing. **2.** being or existence. **3.** essential nature. [LL *entitas*]

**ento-**, variant of **endo-**. [Gk, combining form of *entós* within]

**entoblast** /'ɛntoʊblæst, -blast/, *n.* **1.** →**endoderm.** **2.** →**hypoblast.**

**entoderm** /'ɛntoʊdɜm/, *n.* →**endoderm.**

**entoleter** /'ɛntəlitə/, *n.* a machine used in flour processing which destroys insect eggs remaining in the sifted flour. [Trademark] – **entoleted,** *adj.*

**entomb** /ɛn'tum, ən-/, *v.t.* **1.** to place in a tomb; bury; inter. **2.** to serve as a tomb for. [OF *entomber,* from *en-* EN-$^1$ + *tombe* TOMB] – **entombment,** *n.*

**entomic** /ɛn'tɒmɪk, ən-/, *adj.* of or pertaining to insects.

**entomo-**, a word element meaning 'insect'. Also, before vowels, **entom-**. [combining form representing Gk *éntoma* insects, from *éntomos* cut up]

**entomol.**, entomology. Also, **entom.**

**entomologise** /ɛntə'mɒlədʒaɪz/, *v.i.,* **-gised, -gising.** **1.** to study entomology. **2.** to gather entomological specimens. Also, **entomologize.**

**entomology** /ɛntə'mɒlədʒi/, *n.* the branch of zoology that treats of insects. – **entomological** /ɛntəmə'lɒdʒɪkəl/, **entomologic** /ɛntəmə'lɒdʒɪk/, *adj.* – **entomologically** /ɛntəmə'lɒdʒɪkli/, *adv.* – **entomologist,** *n.*

**entomophagous** /ɛntə'mɒfəgəs/, *adj.* feeding on insects; insectivorous.

**entomophilous** /ɛntəˈmɒfələs/, *adj.* (of a plant) pollinated by insects. – **entomophily,** *n.*

**entomostracan** /ɛntəˈmɒstrəkən/, *adj.* **1.** belonging to the Entomostraca, a subclass of mostly small crustaceans. –*n.* **2.** an entomostracan crustacean. [ENTOM(O)- + Gk *óstrakon* shell + -AN] – **entomostracous,** *adj.*

**entophyte** /ˈɛntoʊfaɪt/, *n.* a plant growing within an animal or another plant, usu. as a parasite. [ENTO- + -PHYTE] – **entophytic** /ɛntəˈfɪtɪk/, *adj.*

**entopic** /ɛnˈtɒpɪk/, *adj. Anat.* occurring in the usual place.

**entoptic** /ɛnˈtɒptɪk/, *adj.* lying or originating within the eyeball.

**entotic** /ɛnˈtɒtɪk/, *adj.* of or pertaining to the interior of the ear.

**entourage** /ɒntuˈradʒ, -raʒ/, *n.* **1.** attendants, as of a person of rank. **2.** any group of people accompanying or assisting someone. **3.** surroundings; environment. [F, from *entourer* surround. See EN-[1], TOUR]

**en-tout-cas** /ɒn-tu-ˈka/, *n.* a tennis court surface which can be used in all weather. [Trademark, from F: in every case]

**entozoa** /ɛntəˈzoʊə/, *n.pl., sing.* **-zoon** /-ˈzoʊən/. *Biol.* animals, esp. intestinal worms, living as parasites within the body of another animal. – **entozoan,** *adj., n.*

**entozoic** /ɛntəˈzoʊɪk/, *adj. Biol.* living parasitically within the body of an animal.

**entr'acte** /ˈɒntrækt/, *n.* **1.** the interval between two consecutive acts of a theatrical or operatic performance. **2.** a performance, as of music or dancing, given during such an interval. **3.** a piece of music or the like for such a performance. [F: between-act]

**entrails** /ˈɛntreɪlz/, *n.pl.* **1.** the internal parts of the trunk of an animal body. **2.** the intestines or bowels. **3.** the internal parts of anything. [ME *entraile,* from F *entrailles,* from LL *intrālia* intestines, from L *inter* within]

**entrain** /ɛnˈtreɪn, ən-/, *v.t.* **1.** to put aboard a train. **2.** (of a fluid) to carry (particles) along by its flow. –*v.i.* **3.** to go aboard a train. – **entrainment,** *n.*

**entrammel** /ɛnˈtræməl, ən-/, *v.t.,* **-elled, elling** or (*U.S.*) **-eled, -eling.** to trammel; fetter; entangle.

**entrance**[1] /ˈɛntrəns/, *n.* **1.** the act of entering, as into a place or upon new duties. **2.** a point or place of entering; an opening or passage for entering. **3.** power or liberty of entering; admission. **4.** admission fee. **5.** in a play, the moment during the performance, or the place in the script, at which an actor comes on the stage. [OF, from *entrer* ENTER]

**entrance**[2] /ɛnˈtræns, -ˈtrans, ən-/, *v.t.,* **-tranced, -trancing. 1.** to fill with delight enrapture. **2.** to put into a trance. [EN-[1] + TRANCE, *v.*] – **entrancement,** *n.* – **entrancingly,** *adv.*

**entrant** /ˈɛntrənt/, *n.* **1.** one who enters. **2.** a new member, as of an association, a university, etc. **3.** a competitor in a contest. [F, ppr. of *entrer* ENTER]

**entrap** /ɛnˈtræp, ən-/, *v.t.,* **-trapped, -trapping. 1.** to catch in or as in a trap; ensnare. **2.** to bring unawares into difficulty or danger. **3.** to draw into contradiction or damaging admission. [OF *entraper,* from *en-* EN-[1] + *trape* trap] – **entrapment,** *n.* – **entrapper,** *n.*

**entreasure** /ɛnˈtrɛʒə, ən-/, *v.t.,* **-ured, -uring.** to lay up in or as in a treasury.

**entreat** /ɛnˈtrit, ən-/, *v.t.* **1.** to make supplication to (a person); beseech; implore: *to entreat a person for something.* **2.** to ask earnestly for (something). –*v.i.* **3.** to make an earnest request or petition. Also, **intreat.** [ME *entrete(n),* from OF *entraitier,* from *en-* EN-[1] + *traitier* TREAT] – **entreatingly,** *adv.*

**entreaty** /ɛnˈtriti, ən-/, *n., pl.* **-treaties.** earnest request or petition; supplication.

**entrechat** /ɒntrəˈʃa/, *n.* (in ballet) a jump during which the dancer crosses his feet a number of times while in the air. [F, from It. (*capriola*) *intrecciata* complicated (caper), from *in-* IN-[2] + *treccia* tress, plait]

**entrecote** /ɒntrəˈkoʊt/, *n.* a steak cut from between the ribs. Also, **rib steak.** [F]

**entree** /ˈɒntreɪ/, *n.* **1.** a dish served at dinner before the main course. **2.** the right or privilege of entering. Also, **entrée.** [F. See ENTRY]

**entremets** /ɒntrəˈmeɪ/, *n., pl.* **-mets** /-ˈmeɪz/. a dish served at dinner between the principal courses or with the roast; a side dish. [F: lit., between-dish]

**entrench** /ɛnˈtrɛntʃ, ən-/, *v.t.* **1.** to dig trenches for defensive purposes around (oneself, a military position, etc.). **2.** to place in a position of strength; establish firmly: *the soldiers entrenched themselves behind a thick concrete wall.* **3.** to establish so strongly or securely as to make any change very difficult: *the clauses concerning human rights are entrenched in the new constitution.* –*v.i.* **4.** to dig in. **5.** to trench or encroach; trespass; infringe (fol. by *on* or *upon*): *to entrench on the domain or rights of another.* **6.** to verge (fol. by *on* or *upon*): *proceedings entrenching on impiety.* Also, **intrench.** – **entrencher,** *n.*

**entrenchment** /ɛnˈtrɛntʃmənt, ən-/, *n.* **1.** the act of entrenching. **2.** an entrenched position. **3.** (*usu. pl.*) an earth breastwork or ditch for protection against enemy fire. Also, **intrenchment.**

**entre nous** /ɒntrə ˈnu/, *adj.* between ourselves; confidentially. [F]

**entrepot** /ˈɒntrəpoʊ/, *n.* **1.** a warehouse. **2.** a commercial centre for the collection, distribution, and transhipment of goods. Also, **entrepôt.** [F, from OF *entreposer* store up, from *entre-* INTER- + *poser* place (from L *pausāre* rest)]

**entrepreneur** /ɒntrəprəˈnɜ/, *n.* **1.** one who organises and manages any enterprise, esp. one involving considerable risk (often in theatrical context). **2.** an employer of productive labour; a contractor. [F, from *entreprendre* undertake. See ENTERPRISE] – **entrepreneurial,** *adj.*

**entresol** /ˈɒntrəsɒl/, *n. Archit.* a low storey between two other storeys of greater height, usu. one immediately above the chief or ground floor; a mezzanine. [F: between-floor]

**entropy** /ˈɛntrəpi/, *n.* a measure of the unavailable energy in a thermodynamic system; it may also be regarded as a measure of the state of disorder of a system. A change of entropy in a reversible process is the ratio of heat absorbed to the absolute temperature. [Gk *en-* EN-[2] + *tropḗ* transformation]

**entrust** /ɛnˈtrʌst, ən-/, *v.t.* **1.** to invest with a trust or responsibility; charge with a specified office or duty involving trust. **2.** to commit (something) in trust (*to*); confide, as for care, use, or performance: *to entrust a secret, money, powers, or work to another.* **3.** to commit as if with trust or confidence: *to entrust one's life to a frayed rope.* Also, **intrust.** – **entrustment,** *n.*

**entry** /ˈɛntri/, *n., pl.* **-tries. 1.** an act of entering; entrance. **2.** a place of ingress or entrance, esp. an entrance hall or vestibule. **3.** permission or right of entry; access. **4.** the act of entering or recording something in a book, register, list, etc. **5.** the statement, etc., so entered or recorded. **6.** one entered in a contest or competition. **7.** *Law.* the act of taking possession of lands or tenements by entering or setting foot on them. **8.** *Music.* a point in a musical performance where a member of an orchestra or choir or a soloist begins to play or sing after being silent for some time. **9.** the giving of an account of a ship's cargo at a customs house to obtain permission to land the goods. **10.** *Bookkeeping.* **a.** See **double entry. b.** See **single entry.** [ME *entree,* from F, *entrer* ENTER]

**entwine** /ɛnˈtwaɪn, ən-/, *v.t., v.i.,* **-twined, -twining.** to twine with, about, around, or together. Also, **intwine.** – **entwinement,** *n.*

**entwist** /ɛnˈtwɪst, ən-/, *v.t.* to twist together or about. Also, **intwist.**

**enucleate** /əˈnjuklieɪt, i-/, *v.,* **-ated, -ating;** /əˈnjukliət, -ieɪt, i-/, *adj.* –*v.t.* **1.** *Biol.* to deprive of the nucleus. **2.** to remove (a kernel, tumour, eyeball, etc.) from its enveloping cover. **3.** to bring out; disclose. –*adj.* **4.** having no nucleus. [L *ēnucleātus,* pp.] – **enucleation** /ənjukliˈeɪʃən, i-/, *n.*

**enumerable** /əˈnjumərəbəl, i-/, *adj. Maths.* capable of being enumerated.

**enumerate** /əˈnjuməreɪt, i-/, *v.t.,* **-rated, -rating. 1.** to mention separately as if in counting; name one by one; specify as in a list. **2.** to ascertain the number of; count. [L *ēnumerātus,* pp., counted out] – **enumerative** /əˈnjumərətɪv, i-/, *adj.* – **enumerator,** *n.*

**enumeration** /ənjuməˈreɪʃən, i-/, *n.* **1.** the act of enumerating. **2.** a catalogue or list.

**enunciate** /ə'nʌnsieɪt, i-/, *v.*, **-ated, -ating.** *–v.t.* **1.** to utter or pronounce (words, etc.), esp. in a particular manner: *he enunciates his words distinctly.* **2.** to state or declare definitely, as a theory. **3.** to announce or proclaim. *–v.i.* **4.** to pronounce words, esp. in an articulate or a particular manner. [L *ēnuntiātus,* pp.] – **enunciable,** *adj.* – **enunciability** /ə,nʌnsiə'bɪləti, i-/, *n.* – **enunciatively,** *adv.* – **enunciator,** *n.*

**enunciation** /ə,nʌnsi'eɪʃən, i-/, *n.* **1.** the act or the manner of enunciating. **2.** utterance or pronunciation. **3.** a formal announcement; a formal statement, as of a proposition or doctrine.

**enure** /ən'juə/, *v.t., v.i.,* **-ured, -uring.** →**inure.**

**enuresis** /ɛnju'risəs/, *n. Pathol.* incontinence or involuntary discharge of urine; bed-wetting. [NL, from Gk *enoureîn* make water in] – **enuretic,** *adj.*

**envelop** /ɛn'vɛləp, ən-/, *v.;* /'ɛnvəloup, 'ɒn-/, *n.* *–v.t.* **1.** to wrap up in or as in a covering. **2.** to serve as a wrapping or covering for. **3.** to surround entirely. **4.** to obscure or conceal: *mountains enveloped in mist.* *–n.* **5.** →**envelope.** [ME *envolupe(n),* from OF *envoluper,* from *en-* EN-[1] + *voluper* wrap. Cf. DEVELOP] – **enveloper** /ɛn'vɛləpə, ən-/, *n.*

**envelope** /'ɛnvəloup, 'ɒn-/, *n.* **1.** a cover for a letter or the like, usu. so made that it can be sealed or fastened. **2.** that which envelops; a wrapper, integument, or surrounding cover. **3.** *Bot.* a surrounding or enclosing part, as of leaves. **4.** *Geom.* a curve or surface tangent to each member of a family of curves or surfaces. **5.** the fabric structure enclosing the gasbag of a balloon or airship. **6.** the gasbag itself. **7.** the airtight glass or metal container of a vacuum tube. **8.** the shape of the amplitude frequency spectrum which defines the quality of a sound at a given point in time. [F *enveloppe*]

**envelopment** /ɛn'vɛləpmənt, ən-/, *n.* **1.** the act of enveloping. **2.** the state of being enveloped. **3.** a wrapping or covering.

**envenom** /ɛn'vɛnəm, ən-/, *v.t.* **1.** to impregnate with venom; make poisonous. **2.** to embitter. [ME *envenime(n),* from OF *envenimer,* from *en-* EN-[1] + *venim* VENOM]

**enviable** /'ɛnviəbəl/, *adj.* that is to be envied; worthy to be envied; highly desirable. – **enviableness,** *n.* – **enviably,** *adv.*

**envious** /'ɛnviəs/, *adj.* full of, feeling, or expressing envy: *envious of a person's success, an envious attack.* [ME, from AF, var. of OF *envieus,* from *envie* ENVY] – **enviously,** *adv.* – **enviousness,** *n.*

**environ** /ɛn'vaɪrən, ən-/, *v.t.* to form a circle or ring round; surround; envelop. [ME *environ(en),* from F *environner,* from *environ* around]

**environment** /ɛn'vaɪrənmənt, ən-/, *n.* **1.** the aggregate of surrounding things, conditions, or influences. **2.** the act of environing. **3.** the state of being environed. **4.** that which environs. **5.** an art form related to assemblage, consisting typically of a large indoor or outdoor construction made from junk materials, pieces of sculpture, painted panels, etc., which is designed to be viewed and touched while the spectator moves around, over, under and through it. – **environmental,** *adj.*

**environmental impact study,** *n.* a study undertaken in order to assess the effect on a specified environment of the introduction of any new factor which may upset the ecological balance.

**environmentalism** /ɛn,vaɪrən'mɛntəlɪzəm, ən-/, *n.* **1.** the theory that environmental factors, both physical and cultural, have paramount influence on the development of animals and humans, both individually and socially. Cf. **hereditarianism.** **2.** the advocacy of the protection and conservation of the natural environment.

**environmentalist** /ɛn,vaɪrən'mɛntələst, ən-/, *n.* **1.** an advocate of environmentalism. **2.** one who studies and is committed to the protection and conservation of the natural environment.

**environs** /ɛn'vaɪrənz, ən-/, *n.pl.* immediate neighbourhood; surrounding parts or districts, as of a city; outskirts; suburbs. [F]

**envisage** /ɛn'vɪzədʒ, -zɪdʒ, ən-/, *v.t.,* **-aged, -aging.** **1.** to contemplate; visualise. **2.** to look in the face of; face. [F *envisager,* from *en-* EN-[1] + *visage* VISAGE] – **envisagement,** *n.*

**envision** /ɛn'vɪʒən, ən-/, *v.t.* to picture mentally, esp. some future event or events.

**envoy**[1] /'ɛnvɔɪ/, *n.* **1.** a diplomatic agent of the second rank, next in dignity after an ambassador, commonly called minister (title in full: **envoy extraordinary and minister plenipotentiary**). **2.** a diplomatic agent. **3.** any accredited messenger or representative. [F *envoyé,* properly pp. of *envoyer* send. See ENVOY[2]]

**envoy**[2] /'ɛnvɔɪ/, *n.* **1.** a short stanza concluding a poem in certain archaic metrical forms. **2.** a postscript to a poetical or prose composition, sometimes serving as a dedication. Also, **envoi.** [ME *envoye,* from OF, from *envoier* send, from *en voie* on the way]

**envy** /'ɛnvi/, *n., pl.* **-vies,** *v.,* **-vied, -vying.** *–n.* **1.** a feeling of discontent or mortification, usu. with ill will, at seeing another's superiority, advantages, or success. **2.** desire for some advantage possessed by another. **3.** an object of envious feeling. *–v.t.* **4.** to regard with envy; be envious of. [ME *envie,* from OF, from L *invidia*] – **envier,** *n.* – **envyingly,** *adv.*

**enwall** /ɛn'wɔl, ən-/, *v.t.* to enclose with a wall.

**enweave** /ɛn'wiv, ən-/, *v.t.,* **-wove** or **-weaved; -woven** or **-weaved; -weaving.** **1.** to weave in or together. **2.** to introduce into or as into a fabric in weaving. **3.** to combine or diversify with something woven in. Also, **inweave.**

**enwind** /ɛn'waɪnd, ən-/, *v.t.,* **-wound, -winding.** to wind or coil about; encircle. Also, **inwind.**

**enwomb** /ɛn'wum, ən-/, *v.t.* to enclose in or as in the womb.

**enwrap** /ɛn'ræp, ən-/, *v.t.,* **-wrapped, -wrapping.** **1.** to wrap or envelop in something: *enwrapped in leaves.* **2.** to engross; preoccupy. Also, **inwrap.**

**enwreathe** /ɛn'rið, ən-/, *v.t.,* **-wreathed, -wreathing.** to surround with or as if with a wreath. Also, **inwreathe.**

**Enzed** /ɛn'zɛd/, *n., adj. Colloq.* New Zealand.

**Enzedder** /ɛn'zɛdə/, *n. Colloq.* a New Zealander.

**enzootic** /ɛnzou'ɒtɪk/, *adj.* **1.** (of diseases) prevailing among or afflicting animals in a particular locality. Cf. **endemic.** *–n.* **2.** an enzootic disease. [EN-[2] + ZO(O)- + -OTIC, modelled on EPIZOOTIC]

**enzymatic** /ɛnzaɪ'mætɪk/, *n.* →**enzymic.**

**enzyme** /'ɛnzaɪm/, *n.* **1.** the leavened bread of the Eucharist in the Greek Orthodox Church. **2.** any protein capable of catalysing a chemical reaction necessary to the cell. [MGk *énzymos* leavened, from *en-* EN-[2] + Gk *zýmē* leaven]

**enzymic** /ɛn'zaɪmɪk/, *adj.* of or pertaining to an enzyme. Also, **enzymatic** /,ɛnzaɪ'mætɪk/.

**enzymogen** /ɛn'zaɪmədʒən/, *n.* the inactive form in which many enzymes are made and stored, as trypsinogen; zymogen.

**enzymology** /ɛnzaɪ'mɒlədʒi/, *n.* the study of enzymes and their properties. – **enzymological** /ɛnzaɪmə'lɒdʒɪkəl/, *adj.* – **enzymologist,** *n.*

**enzymolysis** /ɛnzaɪ'mɒləsəs/, *n.* fermentation or other lytic reactions produced by an enzyme.

**eo-,** a word element meaning 'early', 'primeval', as in *Eocene.* [Gk, combining form of *ēṓs* dawn]

**Eocene** /'iousin, 'iə-/, *adj.* **1.** pertaining to the second principal subdivision of the Tertiary period or system. *–n.* **2.** an early Tertiary epoch or series succeeding Palaeocene and preceding Oligocene.

**Eogene** /'ioudʒin, 'iə-/, *adj. Geol.* **1.** pertaining to a division of the Tertiary period or system that comprises Palaeocene, Eocene and Oligocene. *–n.* **2.** the time or rocks representing the earlier half of the Tertiary period or system.

**eohippus** /iou'hɪpəs/, *n.* a horse of a fossil genus, *Eohippus,* from the Lower Eocene of the western U.S., the oldest type of the family Equidae, about as large as a fox, with four complete toes on each forefoot and three hoofed toes on each hindfoot. [NL, from Gk *ēō-* EO- + *híppos* horse]

eohippus: reconstruction based on fossil remains

**Eolian** /i'ouliən/, *adj., n.* →**Aeolian**[1].

**Eolic** /i'oulɪk/, *n., adj.* →**Aeolic**[1].

**eolith** /'iouliθ, 'iə-/, *n.* a crude flint implement characteristic of

i = peat ɪ = pit ɛ = pet æ = pat a = part ɒ = pot ʌ = putt ɔ = port ʊ = put u = pool ɜ = pert ə = apart aɪ = buy eɪ = bay ɔɪ = boy aʊ = how
oʊ = hoe ɪə = here ɛə = hair ʊə = tour g = give θ = thin ð = then ʃ = show ʒ = measure tʃ = choke dʒ = joke ŋ = sing j = you õ = Fr. bon

the earliest stage of human culture, shaped by, rather than for, use.

**eolithic** /iou'lıθık, iə-/, *adj.* denoting or pertaining to the earliest stage of human culture, characterised by the use of amorphous stone implements.

**eon** /'iɒn/, *n.* →**aeon.**

**eonism** /'iənızəm/, *n.* the adoption of female clothing, mannerisms, etc., by a man; transvestism. [named after the Chevalier d'*Eon,* d. 1810, Frenchman who dressed as a woman]

**eosin** /'iousən, 'iə-/, *n.* **1.** a coal-tar product, $C_{20}H_8Br_4O_5$, used for dyeing silk, etc., rose red. **2.** any of a variety of eosin-like dyes. Also, **eosine** /'iousin, -saın, 'iə-/. [Gk *ēṓs* dawn + -IN[2]] – **eosin-like,** *adj.*

**eosinophil** /iou'sınəfəl, iə-/, *n.* a cell containing granules staining with acid dyes, whose numbers increase in allergic diseases and certain parasitic infections. Also, **eosinophile.** [EOSIN + -O- + -PHIL]

**eosinophilic** /ˌiousınə'fılık, ˌiə-/, *adj.* **1.** pertaining to an eosinophil or eosinophilia. **2.** associated with an increased number of eosinophils.

**-eous,** variant of **-ous,** occurring in adjectives taken from Latin or derived from Latin nouns. [L *-eus*]

**Eozoic** /iou'zouık, iə-/, *n.* a division of pre-Cambrian time and rocks characterised by the dawn of life on the earth. [EO- + ZO(O)- + -IC]

**ep-,** variant of **epi-,** before vowels, as in *epaxial.*

**EP** /i 'pi/, *adj.* **1.** denoting a gramophone record impressed with a double set of microgrooves that revolves at 45 r.p.m. *–n.* **2.** such a record. [initials of *extended play*]

**epacris** /ə'pækrəs/, *n.* any shrub of the genus *Epacris,* family Epacridaceae, of Australia and New Zealand, characterised by bell-shaped or cylindrical flowers as heath, *E. impressa* of south-eastern Australia. Also, **epacrid.**

**epact** /'ipækt/, *n.* **1.** the excess in days of a solar year over a lunar year. **2.** the age in days of the calendar moon at the beginning of the year (1 January). [LL *epacta,* from Gk *epaktḗ,* properly fem. of *epaktós,* vbl. adj., added]

**epagoge** /'ɛpəgoudʒi/, *n.* the induction of a general proposition from particular propositions. [Gk *epagōgḗ* argument by induction] – **epagogic** /ɛpə'gɒdʒık/, *adj.*

**eparch** /'ɛpak/, *n.* **1.** the prefect or governor of an eparchy. **2.** *Greek Orthodox Church.* a bishop or metropolitan of an eparchy. [Gk *éparchos* commander]

**eparchy** /'ɛpaki/, *n., pl.* **-chies. 1.** (in modern Greece) one of the administrative subdivisions of a province. **2.** (in ancient Greece) a province. **3.** *Greek Orthodox Church.* a diocese or archdiocese. – **eparchial** /ɛ'pakiəl/, *adj.*

**epaulet** /'ɛpəlɛt, -lət/, *n.* an ornamental shoulder piece worn on uniforms, chiefly by military and naval officers. Also, **epaulette.** [F *épaulette,* from *épaule* shoulder, from L *spatula* blade]

**epaxial** /ɛp'æksiəl/, *adj. Anat.* above or posterior to an axis. – **epaxially,** *adv.*

**épée** /'ɛpeı, 'eı-/, *n.* **1.** a sharp-pointed duelling sword. **2.** (in fencing) a long, narrow sword with a blunted point. [F: sword, from L *spatha,* from Gk *spáthē* blade]

**épéeist** /'ɛpeıəst, 'eı-/, *n.* one who uses an épée.

**epeirogeny** /ɛpə'rɒdʒəni/, *n. Geol.* vertical or tilting movement of the earth's crust affecting broad areas of the continents or ocean basins. Also, **epeirogenesis** /ɛpərə'dʒɛnəsəs/, **epirogeny.** [Gk *ḗpeiro(s)* land, mainland, continent + -GENY] – **epeirogenic** /ɛpərə'dʒɛnık/, *adj.*

**epencephalon** /ɛpɛn'sɛfəlɒn, -'kɛf-/, *n., pl.* **-la** /-lə/. *Anat.* the hindbrain. – **epencephalic** /ˌɛpɛnsə'fælık, -kə-/, *adj.*

**epenthesis** /ɛ'pɛnθəsəs/, *n., pl.* **-ses** /-siz/. (in linguistic process) the insertion of one or more sounds in the middle of a word, as the schwa in the pronunciation /'fıləm/ of *film.* [LL, from Gk: insertion] – **epenthetic** /ɛpɛn'θɛtık/, *adj.*

**epergne** /i'pɜn/, *n.* an ornamental piece for the centre of a dinner table, often elaborate in design, for holding fruit, flowers, etc. [? F *épargne* saving, treasury]

**epexegesis** /əpɛksə'dʒisəs/, *n. Rhet.* **1.** the addition of a word or words to explain a preceding word or sentence. **2.** the word or words so added.

**epexegetic** /əpɛksə'dʒɛtık/, *adj.* of or like an epexegesis. Also, **epexegetical.** – **epexegetically,** *adv.*

**eph-,** variant of **-epi-,** before an aspirate, as in *ephemera.*

**Eph.,** *Bible.* Ephesians.

**ephedrine** /'ɛfədrin, -draın/, *n.* a crystalline alkaloid, $C_{10}H_{15}NO$, found in some plants of the genus *Ephedra,* family Gnetaceae, of the Northern Hemisphere, used esp. for colds, asthma, and hay fever. Also, **ephedrin** /'ɛfədrən/. [NL *ephedra* (L horsetail, a plant, from Gk) + -INE[2]]

**ephemera** /ə'fɛmərə, i-/, *n., pl.* **-eras, -erae** /-əri/. **1.** anything short-lived or transitory. **2.** →**ephemerid.** [NL, orig., pl. of *ephḗmeron* (from Gk, neut. sing. of *ephḗmeros* of or for only one day), but now treated as sing.]

**ephemeral** /ə'fɛmərəl, i-/, *adj.* **1.** lasting only a day or a very short time; short-lived; transitory. *–n.* **2.** an ephemeral entity, as certain insects. – **ephemerally,** *adv.*

**ephemerid** /ə'fɛmərəd, i-/, *n.* →**mayfly.** [NL *Ephēmeridae.* See EPHEMERA]

**ephemeris** /ə'fɛmərəs, i-/, *n., pl.* **ephemerides** /ɛfə'mɛrədiz/. **1.** a table showing the positions of a heavenly body on a number of dates in an orderly sequence. **2.** an astronomical almanac containing such tables. **3.** *Obs.* an almanac or calendar. [L, from Gk: diary, calendar, record]

**ephemeris time** /'– ˌtaım/, *n. Astron.* time measured by the orbital motions of the earth, the moon, and the planets. The **ephemeris second** is the fundamental unit and is defined as a precise fraction of the tropical year 1900.

**ephemeron** /ə'fɛmərən, i-/, *n., pl.* **-era** /-ərə/, **-erons.** anything short-lived or ephemeral. [Gk: a short-lived insect. See EPHEMERA]

**ephod** /'ifɒd/, *n.* a kind of Hebrew priestly vestment, esp. that worn by the high priest. [Heb.; in some passages apparently meaning 'idol']

**epi-,** a prefix meaning 'on', 'to', 'against', 'above', 'near', 'after', 'in addition to', sometimes used as an English formative, chiefly in scientific words, as *epiblast, epicalyx, epizoon.* Also, **ep-, eph-.** [Gk, representing *epí,* prep. and adv., *ep-* before vowel, *eph-* before aspirate]

**epiblast** /'ɛpiblæst, -blast/, *n.* the outer layer of a gastrula, consisting of ectoblast and various portions of mesoblast and endoblast, according to species. – **epiblastic** /ɛpi'blæstık/, *adj.*

**epiboly** /ɛ'pıbəli, ə-/, *n. Embryol.* the development of one part so that it surrounds another. [Gk *epibolḗ* a throwing on] – **epibolic** /ˌɛpi'bɒlık/, *adj.*

**epic** /'ɛpık/, *adj.* Also, **epical. 1.** denoting or pertaining to poetic composition in which a series of heroic achievements or events, usu. of a hero, is dealt with at length as a continuous narrative in elevated style: *Homer's 'Iliad' is an epic poem.* **2.** resembling or suggesting such poetry. **3.** heroic; imposing; impressive. *–n.* **4.** an epic poem. **5.** any novel or film resembling an epic, esp. one dealing with the adventures and achievements of a single individual. **6.** something worthy to form the subject of an epic: *the epic of the defence of Stalingrad.* **7.** (*cap.*) Also, **Homeric.** the Greek dialect represented in the *Iliad* and the *Odyssey.* [L *epicus,* from Gk *epikós,* from *épos* EPOS] – **epically,** *adv.* – **epic-like,** *adj.*

**epicalyx** /ɛpi'keılıks, -'kælıks/, *n., pl.* **-calyxes, -calyces** /-'keıləsiz, -kæl-/. (in a flower) an involucre resembling an outer calyx as in the hibiscus.

E, epicalyx

**epicanthus** /ɛpi'kænθəs/, *n., pl.* **-thi** /-θaı/. a fold of skin extending from the eyelid over the inner canthus of the eye, characteristic in members of the Mongolian race. – **epicanthic,** *adj.*

**epicardium** /ɛpi'kadiəm/, *n., pl.* **-dia** /-diə/. the inner serous layer of the pericardium, lying directly upon the heart. [NL, from *epi-* EPI- + *-cardium* (combining form representing Gk *kardía* heart)] – **epicardial,** *adj.*

**epicarp** /'ɛpikap/, *n.* the outermost layer of a pericarp, as the rind or peel of certain fruits; exocarp.

**epicedium** /ɛpi'sidiəm, ɛpə-/, *n., pl.* **-cedia** /-'sidiə/. a funeral song. [L, from Gk *epikḗdeion,* properly neut. adj., of or for a funeral] – **epicedial, epicedian,** *adj.*

**epicene** /'ɛpisin, 'ɛpə-/, *adj.* **1.** belonging to, or partaking of the characteristics of, both sexes. **2.** (of Greek and Latin nouns) of the same gender class regardless of the sex of the being referred to, as Latin *vulpēs,* fox or vixen, always grammatically feminine. *–n.* **3.** an epicene person. [L *epicoenus,* from Gk *epíkoinos* common]

**epicentre** /ˈɛpisɛntə/, *n.* a point from which earthquake waves seem to go out, directly above the true centre of disturbance. Also, **epicentrum,** *U.S.,* **epicenter.** [NL *epicentrum,* from Gk *epíkentros* on the centre] – **epicentral** /ɛpiˈsɛntrəl/, *adj.*

**epiclesis** /ɛpiˈklisəs, ɛpə-/, *n.* an invocation included in the canon of the Eucharist either to God that He will send the Holy Spirit, or to the Holy Spirit directly, so that the consecration of the bread and wine may take place. [Gk *epíklēsis,* from *epikaleîn* to invoke]

**epicotyl** /ɛpiˈkɒtl/, *n.* (in the embryo of a plant) that part of the stem above the cotyledons.

**epicrisis** /ˈɛpikraɪsəs/, *n.* a crisis in the course of a disease which is secondary to the primary crisis and comes after it. [EPI- + CRISIS]

**epicritic** /ɛpiˈkrɪtɪk/, *adj.* referring or pertaining to cutaneous nerve fibres perceiving fine sensational variations, or to such perception (opposed to *protopathic*). [Gk *epikritikós* determining]

**epic theatre** /ˌɛpɪk ˈθɪətə/, *n.* a style of drama, developed by the German playwright Bertolt Brecht (1898-1956), which emphasises the need for the audience to become emotionally detached from the action, and which dispenses with many of the traditional stage devices for audience involvement and excitement.

**epicure** /ˈɛpɪkjuə, ˈɛpə-/, *n.* **1.** one who cultivates a refined taste, as in food, drink, art, music, etc. **2.** one given up to sensuous enjoyment; a glutton or sybarite. **3.** a pale yellow New Zealand cheese, of the cheddar type, with a strong, sharp flavour, and a crumbly texture. [orig. anglicised form of *Epicurus,* Greek philosopher, 342?-270 B.C.]

**epicurean** /ɛpikjuˈriən, ɛpə-/, *adj.* **1.** given or adapted to luxury, or indulgence in sensuous pleasures; of luxurious tastes or habits, esp. in eating and drinking. **2.** fit for an epicure. *–n.* **3.** one devoted to the pursuit of pleasure or luxury; an epicure. **4.** (*cap.*) a disciple of Epicurus.

**Epicureanism** /ɛpikjuˈriənɪzəm, ɛpə-/, *n.* **1.** the philosophical system of Epicurus, Greek philosopher, or attachment to his doctrines, the chief of which were that the external world resulted from a fortuitous concourse of atoms, and that the highest good in life is pleasure, which consists in freedom from disturbance or pain. **2.** (*l.c.*) epicurean indulgence or habits. Also, **Epicurism** /ˈɛpikjurɪzəm/.

**epicycle** /ˈɛpisaɪkəl/, *n.* **1.** a small circle the centre of which moves round in the circumference of a larger circle, used in Ptolemaic astronomy to account for observed periodic irregularities in planetary motions. **2.** *Maths.* a circle which rolls (externally or internally), without slipping, on another circle, generating an epicycloid or a hypocycloid. [LL *epicyclus,* from Gk *epikýklos*]

**epicyclic** /ɛpiˈsaɪklɪk/, *adj.* of or pertaining to an epicycle. Also, **epicyclical.**

**epicyclic train** /– ˈtreɪn/, *n. Mach.* any train of gears, the axes of the wheels of which revolve around a common centre. Also, **epicyclic gear.**

**epicycloid** /ɛpiˈsaɪklɔɪd/, *n. Geom.* a curve generated by the motion of a point on the circumference of a circle which revolves, usu. externally, on the circumference of a larger circle. – **epicycloidal** /ˌɛpisaɪˈklɔɪdl/, *adj.*

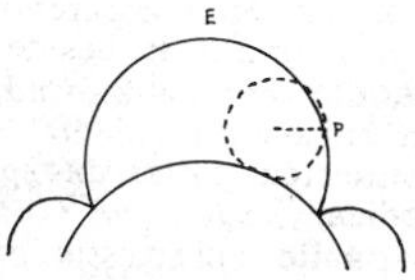

E

P

E, epicycloid; P, point tracing epicycloid on fixed circle

**epicycloidal gear** /ɛpisaɪˌklɔɪdl ˈgɪə/, *n.* one of the wheels in an epicyclic train. Also, **epicycloidal wheel.**

**epideictic** /ɛpiˈdaɪktɪk/, *adj.* displaying the skill of the speaker: *epideictic orations.* Also, **epidictic** /ɛpiˈdɪktɪk/. [Gk *epideiktikós* displaying]

**epidemic** /ɛpəˈdɛmɪk/, *adj.* **1.** Also, **epidemical.** affecting at the same time a large number of people in a locality, and spreading from person to person, as a disease not permanently prevalent there. *–n.* **2.** a temporary prevalence of a disease. [obs. *epidemy,* from LL *epidēmia,* from Gk: prevalence of an epidemic] – **epidemical,** *adj.* – **epidemically,** *adv.* – **epidemicity** /ɛpədəˈmɪsəti/, *n.*

**epidemiology** /ɛpəˌdimiˈɒlədʒi/, *n.* the branch of medicine dealing with epidemic diseases. – **epidemiological** /ɛpəˌdimiəˈlɒdʒɪkəl/, *adj.* – **epidemiologist,** *n.*

**epidermis** /ɛpiˈdɜməs, ɛpə-, ˈɛpidɜməs/, *n.* **1.** *Anat.* the outer, non-vascular, non-sensitive layer of the skin, covering the true skin or corium (dermis). **2.** *Zool.* the outermost living layer of an animal, usu. composed of one or more layers of cells. **3.** *Bot.* the superficial cell layer of the primary regions of vascular plants. [LL, from Gk: outer skin] – **epidermal, epidermic,** *adj.*

**epidermoid** /ɛpiˈdɜmɔɪd, ɛpə-/, *adj.* resembling epidermis. Also, **epidermoidal** /ˌɜpidɛˈmɔɪdl/.

**epidiascope** /ɛpiˈdaɪəskoup/, *n.* a projector for throwing an enlarged image of either an opaque object or a transparency on a screen. Also, **episcope** /ˈɛpiskoup/.

**epidictic** /ɛpiˈdɪktɪk/, *adj.* →**epideictic.**

**epididymis** /ɛpiˈdɪdəməs/, *n., pl.* **-didymides** /-dɪˈdɪmədiz/. an elongated organ applied to the posterior surface of a testis, in which the spermatozoa ripen; chiefly the convoluted beginning of the deferent duct. [NL, from Gk] – **epididymal,** *adj.*

**epidote** /ˈɛpidout/, *n.* a mineral, calcium aluminium iron silicate, $Ca_2(Al, Fe)_3Si_3O_{12}$ (OH), occurring in yellowish green prismatic crystals. [F, from Gk *epididónai* increase] – **epidotic** /ɛpiˈdɒtɪk/, *adj.*

**epidural** /ɛpiˈdjurəl/, *adj.* **1.** situated on or over the dura. *–n.* **2.** →**epidural anaesthetic.**

**epidural anaesthetic** /– ænəsˈθɛtɪk/, *n.* the injection of an agent into the epidural space of the spinal cord to produce regional anaesthesia, esp. in childbirth.

**epifocal** /ɛpiˈfoukəl/, *adj. Geol.* →**epicentral.**

**epigamic** /ɛpiˈgæmɪk/, *adj. Zool.* tending to attract the opposite sex during the mating season, as the colours of certain birds.

**epigastric** /ɛpiˈgæstrɪk/, *adj.* lying upon, distributed over, or pertaining to, the abdomen or the stomach.

**epigastrium** /ɛpiˈgæstriəm/, *n.* the upper and median part of the abdomen, lying over the stomach. [NL, from Gk *epigástrion* over the belly]

**epigeal** /ɛpiˈdʒiəl/, *adj.* **1.** of an insect, living near the surface of the ground, as on low herbs or on other surface vegetation. **2.** →**epigeous.** Also, **epigean.** [EPIGE(OUS) + -AL[1]]

**epigene** /ˈɛpidʒin/, *adj. Geol.* formed or originating on the earth's surface (opposed to *hypogene*). [F, from Gk *epigenḗs* growing after or later]

**epigenesis** /ɛpiˈdʒɛnəsəs/, *n.* **1.** *Biol.* a theoretical concept of generation according to which the embryo is formed by a series of new formations or successive differentiations (opposed to *preformation*). **2.** *Geol.* the processes of ore deposition effective during a period subsequent to the original formation of the enclosing rock. – **epigenesist, epigenist** /ɛˈpɪdʒənəst/, *n.* – **epigenetic** /ɛpidʒəˈnɛtɪk/, *adj.* – **epigenetically** /ɛpidʒəˈnɛtɪkli/, *adv.*

**epigenous** /ɛˈpɪdʒənəs/, *adj. Bot.* growing on the surface, esp. the upper surface, as fungi on leaves.

**epigeous** /ɛpiˈdʒiəs/, *adj. Bot.* **1.** growing on or close to the ground. **2.** (of cotyledons) lifted above ground in germination. [Gk *epígeios* on earth]

**epiglottis** /ɛpiˈglɒtəs, ˈɛpiglɒtəs/, *n.* a thin, valvelike cartilaginous structure that covers the glottis during swallowing, preventing the entrance of food and drink into the larynx. [NL, from Gk] – **epiglottal, epiglottic,** *adj.*

**epigone** /ˈɛpigoun/, *n.* an inferior imitator or follower of an important writer, painter, etc. Also, **epigon** /ˈɛpigɒn/. [L *epigonus,* from Gk *epígonos* born afterwards]

**epigram** /ˈɛpigræm, ˈɛpə-/, *n.* **1.** any witty, ingenious, or pointed saying tersely expressed. **2.** epigrammatic expression. **3.** a short poem dealing concisely with a single subject, usu. ending with a witty or ingenious turn of thought, and often satirical. [L *epigramma,* from Gk: an inscription]

**epigrammatic** /ɛpigrəˈmætɪk, ˈɛpə-/, *adj.* **1.** of or like an epigram; terse and ingenious in expression. **2.** given to epigrams. – **epigrammatically,** *adv.*

**epigrammatise** /ɛpiˈgræmətaɪz, ɛpə-/, *v.t., v.i.,* **-tised, -tising.**

to express by epigrams, or make epigrams. Also, **epigrammatize.**

**epigrammatism** /ɛpiˈgræmətɪzəm, ɛpə-/, *n.* epigrammatic character or style.

**epigrammatist** /ɛpiˈgræmətəst, ɛpə-/, *n.* a maker of epigrams.

**epigraph** /ˈɛpigræf, -graf, ˈɛpə-/, *n.* **1.** an inscription, esp. on a building, statue, or the like. **2.** an apposite quotation at the beginning of a book, chapter, etc. [Gk *epigraphḗ*]

**epigraphic** /ɛpiˈgræfɪk, ɛpə-/, *adj.* **1.** pertaining to epigraphs. **2.** pertaining to epigraphy. Also, **epigraphical.** – **epigraphically,** *adv.*

**epigraphy** /ɛˈpɪgrəfi, ə-/, *n.* **1.** the study or science of epigraphs or inscriptions. **2.** inscriptions collectively. – **epigraphist, epigrapher,** *n.*

**epigynous** /ɛˈpɪdʒənəs, ə-/, *adj.* (of a flower) having or pertaining to the sepals, petals and stamens inserted above the ovary. [EPI- + Gk *gynḗ* woman, female + -OUS]

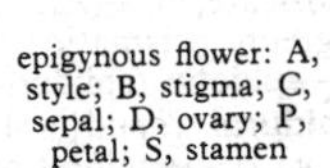

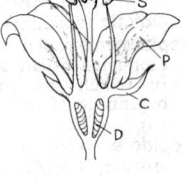

epigynous flower: A, style; B, stigma; C, sepal; D, ovary; P, petal; S, stamen

**epigyny** /ɛˈpɪdʒəni, ə-/, *n.* an epigynous condition.

**epilate** /ˈɛpəleɪt/, *v.t.*, **-lated, -lating.** to pluck out, remove (hair); depilate. – **epilation** /ɛpəˈleɪʃən/, *n.* – **epilator,** *n.*

**epilepsy** /ˈɛpəlɛpsi/, *n.* a nervous disease usu. characterised by convulsions and almost always by loss of consciousness. [LL *epilēpsia,* from Gk: lit., a seizure]

**epileptic** /ɛpəˈlɛptɪk/, *adj.* **1.** pertaining to epilepsy: *epileptic state.* –*n.* **2.** one affected with epilepsy. – **epileptically,** *adv.*

**epileptoid** /ɛpəˈlɛptɔɪd/, *adj.* resembling epilepsy. Also, **epileptiform.**

**epilogist** /ɛˈpɪlədʒəst, ə-/, *n.* the writer or speaker of an epilogue.

**epilogue** /ˈɛpilɒg, ˈɛpə-/, *n.* **1.** a speech, usu. in verse, by one of the actors after the conclusion of a play. **2.** the person or persons speaking this. **3.** a concluding part added to a literary work. **4.** the final program, esp. one with a religious content, of a day's broadcasting on radio or television. [F, from L *epilogus,* from Gk *epílogos* a conclusion]

**epimer** /ˈɛpəmə/, *n. Chem.* either of a pair of isomeric compounds which differ from each other in the positions of H and OH groups; common in aldoses. Also, **epimeride.** – **epimeric** /ɛpiˈmɛrɪk/, *adj.*

**epimerise** /ˈɛpəməraɪz/, *v.t.*, **-rised, -rising.** to convert into an epimer. Also, **epimerize.** – **epimerisation** /ˌɛpəməraɪˈzeɪʃən/, *n.*

**epimorphosis** /ˌɛpimɔˈfousəs/, *n.* a form of development in segmented animals in which body segmentation is completed before hatching.

**epinasty** /ˈɛpənæsti/, *n.* (of a plant) increased growth on the upper surface of an organ, esp. a leaf, causing it to bend downwards. [EPI- + Gk *nastós* pressed close, compact + -Y[3]] – **epinastic** /ɛpəˈnæstɪk/, *adj.* – **epinastically** /ɛpəˈnæstɪkli/, *adv.*

**epinephrine** /ɛpiˈnɛfrən, -rin/, *n.* →**adrenaline.** Also, **epinephrin.** [EPI- + Gk *nephrós* kidney + -INE[2]]

**epineurium** /ɛpiˈnjuriəm, ɛpə-/, *n., pl.* **-neuria** /-ˈnjuriə/. the dense sheath of connective tissue which surrounds the trunk of a nerve. [NL, from Gk *epi-* EPI- + *neûron* sinew, tendon]

**epipetalous** /ɛpiˈpɛtələs, ɛpə-/, *adj.* **1.** (of stamens) inserted on the petals and appearing to originate from them. **2.** (of a flower) having the stamens inserted on the corolla.

**epiphany** /əˈpɪfəni/, *n.* **1.** an appearance, revelation, or manifestation of a divine being. **2.** the manifestation of Christ to the Magi. **3.** the Christian festival on 6 January, celebrating this. **4.** a season of the Church year. **5.** a revelation of the basic nature of something; a perception of some essential truth. [Gk *epiphaneia,* lit., appearance, manifestation, from *epiphanḗs* coming to light, appearing, from *epiphaínein* to manifest]

**epiphenomenalism** /ɛpifəˈnɒmənəlɪzəm/, *n.* the doctrine that conscious processes, though distinct from physical processes, have no distinct causal properties; automatism.

**epiphenomenon** /ˌɛpifəˈnɒmənən/, *n., pl.* **-na** /-nə/. **1.** *Pathol.* a secondary or additional symptom or complication arising during the course of a malady. **2.** any secondary phenomenon.

**epiphyll** /ˈɛpifɪl, ˈɛpə-/, *n.* an epiphyte that grows on the surface, esp. the upper surface, of leaves, as a lichen. – **epiphyllous** /ɛpiˈfɪləs, ɛpə-/, *adj.*

**epiphysis** /ɛˈpɪfəsəs/, *n., pl.* **-ses** /-siz/. **1.** a part or process of a bone which is separated from the main body of the bone by a layer of cartilage, and which finally becomes united with the bone through further ossification. **2.** the pineal body of the brain. [NL, from Gk: an outgrowth] – **epiphysial** /ɛpiˈfiziəl ɛpə-/, *adj.*

**epiphyte** /ˈɛpifaɪt, ˈɛpə-/, *n.* a plant which grows upon another but does not get food, water, or minerals from it. – **epiphytic** /ɛpiˈfɪtɪk, ɛpə-/, **epiphytical** /ɛpiˈfɪtɪkəl, ɛpə-/, *adj.* – **epiphytically** /ɛpiˈfɪtɪkli, ɛpə-/, *adv.*

**epiphytotic** /ɛpifaɪˈtɒtɪk, ɛpə-/, *adj.* (of a disease or parasite) epidemic on plants. [EPI- + -PHYT(E) + -OTIC]

**epiploon** /əˈpɪplouən/, *n. Anat.* the great omentum. – **epiploic** /ɛpiˈplouɪk, ɛpə-/, *adj.*

**epirogeny** /ɛpiˈrɒdʒəni/, *n.* →**epeirogeny.** – **epirogenic** /ˌɛpirouˈdʒɛnɪk/, *adj.*

**Episc.,** **1.** Episcopal. Also, **Epis.**

**episcopacy** /əˈpɪskəpəsi/, *n., pl.* **-cies.** **1.** government of the church by bishops; church government in which there are three distinct orders of ministers, namely bishops, priests or presbyters, and deacons. **2.** the office or incumbency of a bishop. **3.** the order of bishops.

**episcopal** /əˈpɪskəpəl/, *adj.* **1.** pertaining to a bishop. **2.** based on or recognising an order of bishops exercising pastoral authority and discipline: *the Methodist Episcopal Church.* **3.** *Chiefly U.S.* designating or pertaining to the Anglican Church, or a branch of it. [LL *epīscopālis,* from *epīscopus* bishop]

**Episcopalian** /əpɪskəˈpeɪliən/, *adj.* **1.** pertaining or adhering to the Episcopal Church (of the Anglican communion). **2.** (*l.c.*) pertaining or adhering to the episcopal form of church government. –*n.* **3.** a member of the Episcopal Church. **4.** (*l.c.*) an adherent of the episcopal system of church government. – **Episcopalianism,** *n.*

**episcopalism** /əˈpɪskəpəlɪzəm/, *n.* the theory of church polity according to which the supreme ecclesiastical authority is vested in the episcopal order as a whole, and not in any individual except by delegation.

**episcopate** /əˈpɪskəpət, -peɪt/, *n.* **1.** the office and dignity of a bishop; a bishopric. **2.** the order or body of bishops. **3.** the incumbency of a bishop.

**episcope** /əˈpɪskəpi/, *n.* →**episcopacy** (def. 2).

**episcopise** /əˈpɪskəpaɪz/, *v.*, **-pised, -pising.** –*v.t.* **1.** to make a bishop of. **2.** to convert to Episcopalianism. –*v.i.* **3.** to act as a bishop. Also, **episcopize.**

**episode** /ˈɛpəsoud/, *n.* **1.** an incident in the course of a series of events, in a person's life or experience, etc. **2.** an incidental narrative or digression in the course of a story, poem, or other writing. **3.** any of a number of loosely connected but generally related scenes or stories comprising a literary work. **4.** a part in an old Greek tragedy between two choric songs. **5.** *Music.* an intermediate or digressive passage, esp. in a contrapuntal composition. **6.** (in radio, television, etc.) any of the separate programs constituting a serial. [Gk *epeisódion* a parenthetic addition, properly neut. of *epeisódios* coming in besides]

**episodic** /ɛpəˈsɒdɪk/, *adj.* **1.** pertaining to or of the nature of an episode; incidental. **2.** divided into separate or loosely connected parts: *an episodic novel.* Also, **episodical.** – **episodically,** *adv.*

**epispastic** /ɛpiˈspæstɪk, ɛpə-/, *adj.* **1.** raising a blister. –*n.* **2.** a blistering agent; a vesicatory. [Gk *epispastikós,* lit., drawing towards]

**epistasis** /ɛˈpɪstəsəs/, *n. Med.* **1.** suppression of a secretion or discharge. **2.** a film which forms on the surface of urine after it has been left standing for some time. [Gk] – **epistatic** /ɛpiˈstætɪk/, *adj.*

**epistaxis** /ɛpiˈstæksəs/, *n.* bleeding from the nose. [NL, from Gk *epistázein* drop on]

**epistemic** /ɛpiˈstɛmɪk/, *adj.* relating to our knowledge of things rather than to the nature of the things themselves.

**epistemology** /əpɪstəˈmɒlədʒi/, *n.* the branch of philosophy which investigates the origin, nature, methods, and limits of human knowledge. [Gk *epistēmē* knowledge + -o- + -LOGY] – **epistemological** /əpɪstəmə'lɒdʒɪkəl/, *adj.* – **epistemologically** /əpɪstəmə'lɒdʒɪkli/, *adv.* – **epistemologist**, *n.*

**episternum** /ɛpi'stɜnəm/, *n., pl.* **-na** /-nə/. **1.** (in mammals) the upper part of the sternum. **2.** *Entomol.* the principal anterior subdivision of a thoracic pleuron. – **episternal**, *adj., n.*

**epistle** /ə'pɪsəl/, *n.* **1.** a written communication; a letter, esp. one of formal or didactic character. **2.** (*usu. cap.*) one of the apostolic letters found in the New Testament. **3.** (*oft. cap.*) an extract, usu. from one of the Epistles of the New Testament, forming part of the Eucharistic service in certain churches. [ME; OE *epistol,* from L *epistola,* from Gk *epistolḗ* message, letter]

**epistler** /ə'pɪslə, ə'pɪstlə/, *n.* **1.** a writer of an epistle. **2.** the one who reads the epistle in the Eucharistic service. Also, **epistoler** /ə'pɪstələ/, **epistolist.**

**epistle side** /ə'pɪsəl saɪd/, *n.* the right-hand side of a church facing the altar. Cf. **gospel side.**

**epistolary** /ə'pɪstələri/, *adj.* **1.** contained in or carried on by letters. **2.** of or pertaining to letters. Also, **epistolatory** /-lətri/.

**epistyle** /'ɛpistaɪl, 'ɛpə-/, *n. Archit.* →**architrave.** [L *epistȳlium,* from Gk *epistȳlion*]

**epitaph** /'ɛpitaf, 'ɛpə-/, *n.* **1.** a commemorative inscription on a tomb or mortuary monument. **2.** any brief writing resembling such an inscription. [ME *epitaphe,* from L *epitaphium,* from Gk *epitáphion* funeral oration, neut. of *epitáphios* over or at a tomb] – **epitaphic** /ɛpi'tæfɪk/, *adj.* – **epitaphist,** *n.*

**epitasis** /ə'pɪtəsəs/, *n.* (in ancient drama) the main part of the play, following the protasis. [L, from Gk]

**epitaxy** /'ɛpitæksi, 'ɛpə-/, *n. Electronics.* the growth of a second crystal on the surface of a first, as in the manufacture of transistors and integrated circuits. – **epitaxial** /ɛpi'tæksiəl, ɛpə-/, *adj.*

**epithalamion** /ɛpiθə'leɪmiən, ɛpə-/, *n., pl.* **-mia** /-miə/. →**epithalamium.**

**epithalamium** /ɛpiθə'leɪmiəm, ɛpə-/, *n., pl.* **-miums, -mia** /-miə/. a nuptial song or poem; a poem in honour of a bride and bridegroom. [L, from Gk *epithalámion* (neut. adj.) nuptial] – **epithalamic** /ɛpiθə'læmɪk, ɛpə-/, *adj.*

**epithelial** /ɛpi'θiliəl, ɛpə-/, *adj.* pertaining to epithelium.

**epithelioid** /ɛpi'θiliɔɪd, ɛpə-/, *adj.* resembling epithelium.

**epithelioma** /ɛpiθili'oumə/, *n., pl.* **-mata** /-mətə/, **-mas.** a cancer or malignant growth consisting chiefly of epithelial cells. [NL, from EPITHELI(UM) + -OMA] – **epitheliomatous,** *adj.*

**epithelium** /ɛpi'θiliəm, ɛpə-/, *n., pl.* **-liums, -lia** /-liə/. *Biol.* any tissue which covers a surface, or lines a cavity or the like, and which performs protective, secreting, or other functions, as the epidermis, the lining of blood vessels, etc. [NL, from Gk *epi-* EPI- + *thēlḗ* nipple + *-ion,* diminutive suffix]

**epithermal** /ɛpi'θɜməl/, *adj. Physics.* having energy slightly above the energy of thermal agitation and comparable with chemical bond energies.

**epithet** /'ɛpəθɛt, ɛpi-, -θət/, *n.* **1.** an adjective or other term applied to a person or thing to express an attribute, as in Alexander *the Great.* **2.** a word or phrase expressing abuse or contempt: *she hurled choice epithets at his departing figure.* [L *epitheton,* from Gk, properly neut. of *epíthetos* added] – **epithetic** /ɛpə'θɛtɪk, ɛpi-/, **epithetical** /ɛpə'θɛtɪkəl/, *adj.*

**epitome** /ə'pɪtəmi/, *n.* **1.** a summary or condensed account, esp. of a literary work; an abstract. **2.** a condensed representation or typical characteristic of something: *the epitome of all mankind.* [L, from Gk, from *epitémnein* cut into, abridge] – **epitomic** /ɛpi'tɒmɪk/, **epitomical** /ɛpi'tɒmɪkəl/, *adj.*

**epitomise** /ə'pɪtəmaɪz/, *v.t.,* **-mised, -mising. 1.** to make an epitome of. **2.** to contain in small compass. Also, **epitomize.** – **epitomiser,** *n.*

**epitrachelion** /ɛpitrə'kiliən/, *n.* a stole worn by priests and bishops of the Greek Orthodox Church.

**epizoic** /ɛpi'zouɪk, ɛpə-/, *adj. Zool.* externally parasitic.

**epizoon** /ɛpi'zouən, ɛpə-/, *n., pl.* **-zoa** /-'zouə/. an external parasite; an ectozoon. [EPI- + ZOON]

**epizootic** /ɛpizou'ɒtɪk/, *adj.* **1.** (of diseases) prevalent temporarily among animals. *–n.* **2.** an epizootic disease. [EPI- + ZO(O)- + -OTIC. Cf. F *épizootique*] – **epizootically,** *adv.*

**epizooty** /ɛpi'zouəti, ɛpə-/, *n., pl.* **-ties.** an epizootic disease.

**epoch** /'ipɒk, 'ɛpɒk/, *n.* **1.** a particular period of time as marked by distinctive character, events, etc. **2.** the beginning of any distinctive period in the history of anything. **3.** a point of time distinguished by a particular event, or state of affairs. **4.** *Geol.* the main division of a geological period, representing the time required for making a geological series. **5.** *Astron.* **a.** an arbitrarily fixed instant of time or date (usu. the beginning of a century or half-century) used as a reference in giving the elements of a planetary orbit or the like. **b.** the mean longitude of a planet as seen from the sun at such an instant or date. [ML *epocha,* from Gk *epochḗ* check, pause, position, epoch]

**epochal** /'ɛpəkəl/, *adj.* **1.** of or pertaining to an epoch or epochs. **2.** of the nature of an epoch. **3.** epoch-making.

**epoch-making** /'ipɒk-meɪkɪŋ/, *adj.* opening a new era, as in human history, thought, or knowledge: *an epoch-making discovery.*

**epode** /'ɛpoud/, *n.* **1.** a kind of lyric poem, invented by Archilochus (about 650 B.C.), in which a long verse is followed by a short one. **2.** the part of a lyric ode following the strophe and antistrophe. [F, from L *epōdos,* from Gk *epōidós* after song, incantation]

**eponym** /'ɛpənɪm/, *n.* **1.** a person, real or imaginary, from whom a tribe, place, institution, etc., takes, or is supposed to take, its name, as *Britons* from *Brut* (supposed to be the grandson of Aeneas). **2.** any official in ancient times whose name was used to designate his year of office. [Gk *epṓnymon* (neut.) named after] – **eponymic** /ɛpou'nɪmɪk/, *adj.*

**eponymous** /ə'pɒnəməs/, *adj.* giving one's name to a tribe, place, etc. [Gk *epṓnymos*]

**eponymy** /ə'pɒnəmi/, *n.* the derivation of names from eponyms. [Gk *epōnymía* surname]

**épopée** /'ɛpɒpeɪ/, *n.* **1.** an epic. **2.** epic poetry. Also, **epopoeia** /ɛpɒ'peɪə/. [F, from Gk *epopoiía* epic poetry]

**epos** /'ɛpɒs/, *n.* **1.** an epic. **2.** epic poetry. **3.** a body of poems, transmitted orally, dealing with the traditions of a people, esp. poems treating parts of a common epic theme. **4.** a series of events worthy of treatment in epic poetry. [L, from Gk: word, tale, song; pl. epic poetry]

**epoxy** /i'pɒksi, ə-/, *adj., n., pl.* **epoxies.** *–adj.* **1.** containing an oxygen atom that bridges two connected atoms, as in *epoxy ethene.* *–n.* **2.** Also, **epoxy** or **epoxide resin.** any of a class of substances derived by polymerisation from certain viscous liquid or brittle solid compounds, used chiefly in adhesives, coatings, electrical insulation, solder mix, in the casting of tools and dyes, and in experimental sculpture. [EPI- + OXY-[2]]

**EPR** /i pi 'a/, ethylene-propylene rubber.

**e.p.s.** /i pi 'ɛs/, earnings per share.

**epsilon** /'ɛpsələn, -lɒn/, *n.* the fifth letter (E, ε, English short E, e) of the Greek alphabet. [Gk *è psīlón* e simple]

**Epsom salts** /ɛpsəm 'sɒlts/, *n.pl.* hydrated magnesium sulphate, used as a cathartic, etc. [so called because first prepared from the water of the mineral springs at *Epsom,* England]

**equable** /'ɛkwəbəl/, *adj.* **1.** free from variations; uniform, as motion or temperature. **2.** uniform in operation or effect, as laws. **3.** tranquil, even, or not easily disturbed, as the mind. [L *aequābilis* that can be made equal] – **equability** /ɛkwə'bɪləti/, **equableness,** *n.* – **equably,** *adv.*

**equal** /'ikwəl/, *adj., n., v.,* **equalled, equalling** or (*U.S.*) **equaled, equaling.** *–adj.* **1.** as great as another (fol. by *to* or *with*): *the velocity of sound is not equal to that of light.* **2.** like or alike in quantity, degree, value, etc.; of the same rank, ability, merit, etc. **3.** evenly proportioned or balanced: *an equal mixture, an equal contest.* **4.** uniform in operation or effect: *equal laws.* **5.** adequate or sufficient in quantity or degree: *the supply is equal to the demand.* **6.** having adequate powers, ability, or means: *he was not equal to the task.* **7.** level, as a plain. **8.** *Archaic.* tranquil or undisturbed. **9.** *Archaic.* impartial or equitable. *–n.* **10.** one who or that which is equal. *–v.t.* **11.** to be or become equal to; match. **12.** to make or do something equal to. **13.** to recompense fully: *he will equal your losses.* [L *aequālis* like, equal]

**equalisation reserve** /ikwəlaɪˌzeɪʃən rə'zɜv/, *n.* a reserve held by an insurer to cover an underwriting loss in whole or in part.

**equalise** /ˈikwəlaɪz/, *v.t.*, **-ised, -ising. 1.** to make equal: *to equalise tax burdens.* **2.** to make uniform. **3.** *Sport.* to reach a score equal to that of an opponent. **4.** to alter (sound) by cutting out certain parts of the sound spectrum or by boosting others. Also, **equalize.** – **equalisation** /ˌikwəlaɪˈzeɪʃən/, *n.*

**equaliser** /ˈikwəlaɪzə/, *n.* **1.** one who or that which equalises. **2.** any of various devices or appliances for equalising strains, pressures, etc. **3.** an electrical connection established between two points in a network to secure some constant relation between the two points, as potential, impedance, etc. **4.** *Colloq.* a gun. Also, **equalizer.**

**equalitarian** /ikwɒləˈtɛəriən, ə-/, *adj.* →**egalitarian.** – **equalitarianism,** *n.*

**equality** /iˈkwɒləti, ə-/, *n., pl.* **-ties. 1.** the state of being equal; correspondence in quality, degree, value, rank, ability, etc. **2.** uniform character, as of motion or surface.

**equally** /ˈikwəli/, *adv.* in an equal manner or degree.

**equals sign** /ˈikwəlz saɪn/, *n.* the symbol =, used to show that two things are equal. Also, **equal sign.**

**equanimity** /ikwəˈnɪməti, ɛkwə-/, *n.* evenness of mind or temper; calmness; composure. [L *aequanimitas,* from *aequanimis* of an even mind]

**equate** /iˈkweɪt, ə-/, *v.t.,* **equated, equating. 1.** to state the equality of or between; put in the form of an equation. **2.** to reduce to an average; make such correction or allowance in as will reduce to a common standard of comparison. **3.** to regard, treat, or represent as equivalent. [L *aequātus,* pp., made equal]

**equation** /iˈkweɪʒən, ə-, -ʃən/, *n.* **1.** the act of making equal; equalisation. **2.** equally balanced state; equilibrium. **3.** *Maths.* **a.** an expression of, or a proposition asserting, the equality of two quantities, employing the sign = between them. **b.** a mathematical formula interpreted as a question asking for what values of a variable two expressions in that variable are equal, as $3x^2 - 2x + 4 = 0$. **4.** *Chem.* a symbolic representation of a reaction. **5.** →**personal equation.** – **equational,** *adj.*

**equation of state,** *n.* any equation connecting the pressure, volume and temperature of a substance.

**equator** /əˈkweɪtə, i-/, *n.* **1.** that great circle of a sphere or any heavenly body which has a centre at each pole and lies equidistant between them, its plane being perpendicular to the axis of the sphere or heavenly body. **2.** the great circle of the earth, equidistant from the North and South Poles. **3.** a circle separating a surface into two congruent parts. [ME, from LL *aequātor,* lit., equaliser (of day and night, as when the sun is on the equator)]

**equatorial** /ɛkwəˈtɔriəl/, *adj.* **1.** of, pertaining to, or near an equator, esp. the equator of the earth. **2.** of or like the regions at the earth's equator: *equatorial vegetation.* –*n.* **3.** a telescope mounting having two axes of motion, one parallel to the earth's axis, and one at right angles to it. **4.** *Aerospace.* an orbit in the plane of the equator.

**equatorial climate** /– ˈklaɪmət/, *n.* a type of climate characterised by consistently high temperatures and rainfall throughout the year; roughly between latitudes 5°N and 5°S.

**Equatorial Guinea** /ˌɛkwətɔriəl ˈgɪni/, *n.* a country in western Africa.

**equerry** /ˈɛkwəri/, *n., pl.* **-ries. 1.** an officer of a royal or similar household, charged with the care of the horses. **2.** an officer who attends on the British sovereign or governor. [F *écurie,* OF *escuirie,* from *escuier* SQUIRE]

**equestrian** /əˈkwɛstriən, i-/, *adj.* **1.** of or pertaining to horsemen or horsemanship. **2.** mounted on horseback. **3.** of or pertaining to the Roman equites: *the equestrian order.* **4.** representing a person on horseback: *an equestrian statue.* **5.** pertaining to or composed of knights. –*n.* **6.** a rider or performer on horseback. [L *equestri(s)* of a horseman + -AN] – **equestrianism,** *n.*

**equestrienne** /əkwɛstriˈɛn, i-/, *n.* a female rider or performer on horseback. [pseudo-F fem. of EQUESTRIAN]

**equi-,** a word element meaning 'equal', as in *equidistant, equivalent.* [combining form representing L *aequus* equal]

**equiangular** /ikwiˈæŋgjələ, ɛ-/, *adj.* having all the angles equal.

**equidistance** /ikwiˈdɪstəns, ikwə-, ɛ-/, *n.* equal distance.

**equidistant** /ikwiˈdɪstənt, ikwə-, ɛ-/, *adj.* equally distant. – **equidistantly,** *adv.*

**equilateral** /ikwəˈlætərəl/, *adj.* **1.** having all the sides equal. –*n.* **2.** a figure having all its sides equal. **3.** a side equivalent or equal to others. [LL *aequilaterālis*] – **equilaterally,** *adv.*

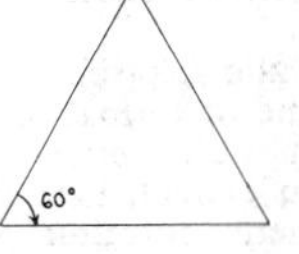

equilateral triangle

**equilibrant** /əˈkwɪləbrənt, i-/, *n.* a counterbalancing force or system of forces.

**equilibrate** /əˈkwɪləbreɪt, i-/, *v.,* **-brated, -brating.** –*v.t.* **1.** to balance equally; keep in equipoise or equilibrium. **2.** to be in equilibrium with; counterpoise. –*v.i.* **3.** to balance. [LL *aequilībrātus* in equilibrium, from L *aequi-* EQUI- + *lībrātus* balanced] – **equilibration** /əkwɪləˈbreɪʃən, i-/, *n.* – **equilibrator,** *n.*

**equilibrist** /əˈkwɪləbrəst, i-/, *n.* one who practises balancing in unnatural positions and hazardous movements, as a rope-dancer. [EQUILIBR(IUM) + -IST] – **equilibristic** /əkwɪləˈbrɪstɪk, i-/, *adj.*

**equilibrium** /ikwəˈlɪbriəm, ɛ-/, *n.* **1.** a state of rest due to the action of forces that counteract each other. **2.** equal balance between any powers, influences, etc.; equality of effect. **3.** mental or emotional balance. **4.** *Chem.* the condition of a mixture of reagents in which some of them are reacting to produce certain others (forward reaction) and these others are reacting to reform the original ones (reverse reaction) so that the rates of the forward and reverse reactions under the given conditions are the same, the mixture remaining effectively constant in composition.

**equilibrium constant** /– ˈkɒnstənt/, *n.* a number which for a given chemical reaction in equilibrium under certain conditions, expresses the proportion of the concentrations of those chemicals which are the end products of the forward reaction to the concentrations of those which are the end products of the reverse reaction. *Symbol:* K

**equimolecular** /ikwiməˈlɛkjələ, ɛ-/, *adj.* containing equal numbers of molecules.

**equine** /ˈɛkwaɪn, i-/, *adj.* **1.** of or resembling a horse. –*n.* **2.** a horse. [L *equīnus,* from *equus* horse] – **equinity** /ɛˈkwɪnəti/, *n.*

**equinoctial** /ikwəˈnɒkʃəl, ɛ-/, *adj.* **1.** pertaining to an equinox or the equinoxes, or to the equality of day and night. **2.** pertaining to the celestial equator. **3.** occurring at or about the time of an equinox: *an equinoctial storm.* **4.** *Bot.* (of a flower) opening regularly at a certain hour. –*n.* **5.** →**equinoctial line. 6.** a gale or storm at or near the time of an equinox. [ME, from L *aequinoctiālis,* from *aequinoctium* EQUINOX]

**equinoctial line** /– ˈlaɪn/, *n.* the celestial equator. Also, **equinoctial circle.**

**equinoctial point** /– ˈpɔɪnt/, *n.* either of the two points in which the celestial equator and the ecliptic intersect each other, reached by the sun's centre at the equinoxes.

**equinox** /ˈikwənɒks, ɛ-/, *n.* **1.** the time when the sun crosses the plane of the earth's equator, making night and day all over the earth of equal length, occurring about 21 March and 22 September. **2.** either of the equinoctial points. [ML *equinoxium,* L *aequinoctium* equality between day and night]

**equip** /əˈkwɪp, i-/, *v.t.,* **equipped, equipping. 1.** to furnish or provide with whatever is needed for services or for any undertaking; to fit out, as a ship, office, kitchen, etc. **2.** to dress out; array. [F *équipper,* OF *esquiper,* probably from Scand.; cf. Icel. *skipa* put in order, arrange, man (a ship, etc.)] – **equipper,** *n.*

**equipage** /ˈɛkwəpɪdʒ, ˈi-/, *n.* **1.** a carriage. **2.** a completely equipped carriage, with horses and servants. **3.** outfit, as of a ship, an army, or a soldier; equipment. **4.** a set of small household articles, as of china. **5.** a collection of articles for personal ornament or use.

**equipment** /əˈkwɪpmənt, i-/, *n.* **1.** anything used in or provided for equipping. **2.** the act of equipping. **3.** the state of being equipped. **4.** a person's knowledge and skill necessary for a task, etc.: *a man's equipment for the law, for medicine.* **5.** a collection of necessary implements (such as tools).

**equipoise** /'ikwəpɔɪz, 'ɛ-/, *n.* **1.** an equal distribution of weight; even balance; equilibrium. **2.** →**counterpoise.**

**equipollent** /ikwə'pɒlənt, ɛ-/, *adj.* **1.** equal in power, effect, etc.; equivalent. **2.** *Logic.* (of two propositons, etc.) logically deducible from each other, as 'All men are mortal' and 'No men are immortal'. *–n.* **3.** an equivalent. [L *aequipollens* of equal value] – **equipollence, equipollency,** *n.*

**equiponderance** /ˌikwi'pɒndərəns, ˌɛ-/, *n.* equality of weight; equipoise. Also, **equiponderancy.** – **equiponderant,** *adj.*

**equiponderate** /ˌikwi'pɒndəreɪt, ˌɛ-/, *v.t.,* **-ated, -ating.** to equal or offset in weight, force, importance, etc.; counterbalance. [ML *aequiponderātus,* pp. of *aequiponderāre,* from L *aequi-* EQUI- + *ponderāre* weigh]

**equipotent** /ikwɪ'poʊtənt, ɛ-/, *adj.* equal in power.

**equipotential** /ikwipə'tɛnʃəl, ɛ-/, *adj.* **1.** of the same potential. **2.** *Physics.* at every point having the same potential.

**equisetum** /ɛkwɪ'sitəm/, *n., pl.* **-tums, -ta** /-tə/. any of the perennial herbaceous plants of the genus *Equisetum,* widely distributed except in Australia and New Zealand, including the horsetails and the scouring rushes. [NL, L *equisaetum,* from *equi-* horse + *saeta* bristle] – **equisetic,** *adj.*

**equitable** /'ɛkwətəbəl/, *adj.* **1.** characterised by equity or fairness; just and right; fair; reasonable. **2.** *Law.* pertaining to or valid in equity, as distinguished from the common law. – **equitableness,** *n.* – **equitably,** *adv.*

**equitant** /'ɛkwətənt/, *adj.* straddling or overlapping, as leaves whose bases overlap the leaves above or within them. [L *equitans,* ppr., riding]

**equitation** /ɛkwə'teɪʃən/, *n.* the act or art of riding a horse. [L *equitātio,* from *equitāre* ride]

**equity** /'ɛkwəti/, *n., pl.* **-ties. 1.** the quality of being fair or impartial; fairness; impartiality. **2.** that which is fair and just. **3.** *Law.* **a.** the application of the dictates of conscience or the principles of natural justice to the settlement of controversies. **b.** a system of jurisprudence or a body of doctrines and rules developed in England and followed in other common law countries, serving to supplement and remedy the limitations and the inflexibility of the common law. **c.** an equitable right or claim. **d.** an equity of redemption. **4.** the interest of a shareholder of common stock in a company. **5.** (*pl.*) stocks and shares not bearing fixed interest. **6.** the amount by which the market value of a debtor's securities exceeds his indebtedness. **7.** (*cap.*) the actors' trade union. [ME *equite,* from L *aequitas* equality, justice]

**equity of redemption,** *n.* the right of a mortgagor to redeem the mortgaged property by paying the debt, within a certain time after the due date.

**equiv.,** equivalent.

**equivalence** /ə'kwɪvələns i-/, *n.* **1.** the state or fact of being equivalent; equality in value, force, significance, etc. **2.** *Chem.* the quality of having equal valency. Also, **equivalency.**

**equivalence relation** /'– rəleɪʃən/, *n. Logic, Maths.* a reflexive, symmetric and transitive relation, that establishes any two elements in the set as equivalent or non-equivalent. Also, **equivalence.**

**equivalent** /ə'kwɪvələnt, i-/, *adj.* **1.** equal in value, measure, force, effect, significance, etc. **2.** corresponding in position, function, etc. **3.** *Chem.* having the same capacity to combine or react chemically. *–n.* **4.** that which is equivalent. [ME, from LL *aequivalens,* ppr., having equal power] – **equivalently,** *adv.*

**equivalent weight** /– 'weɪt/, *n.* the weight of an element, radical, or compound which will combine with, or replace, 1.007 97 grams of hydrogen or 8 grams of oxygen; for an element, the atomic weight divided by the valency.

**equivocal** /ə'kwɪvəkəl, i-/, *adj.* **1.** of uncertain significance; not determined: *an equivocal attitude.* **2.** of doubtful nature or character; questionable; dubious; suspicious. **3.** having different meanings equally possible, as a word or phrase; susceptible of double interpretation; ambiguous. [ME *equivoc* (from LL *aequivocus* ambiguous) + -AL[1]] – **equivocally,** *adv.* – **equivocalness,** *n.*

**equivocate** /ə'kwɪvəkeɪt, i-/, *v.i.,* **-cated, -cating.** to use equivocal or ambiguous expressions, esp. in order to mislead; prevaricate. [backformation from EQUIVOCATION] – **equivocatingly,** *adv.* – **equivocator,** *n.* – **equivocatory,** *adj.*

**equivocation** /əkwɪvə'keɪʃən, i-/, *n.* **1.** the use of equivocal or ambiguous expressions, esp. in order to mislead; prevarication. **2.** an equivocal or ambiguous expression; equivoque. **3.** *Logic.* a fallacy depending on the double meaning of a word. [ME, from LL *aequivocātio*]

**equivoque** /'ɛkwəvoʊk/, *n.* **1.** an equivocal term; an ambiguous expression. **2.** a play upon words; a pun. **3.** double meaning; ambiguity. Also, **equivoke.** [F, replacing ME *equivoc.* See EQUIVOCAL]

**er** /ə, ɜ/, *interj.* (the written representation of an inarticulate sound made by a speaker when hesitating.)

**-er**[1], a suffix: **1.** forming nouns designating persons from the object of their occupation or labour, as in *hatter, tiler, tinner, moonshiner,* or from their place of origin or abode, as in *Icelander, southerner, villager,* or designating either persons or things from some special characteristic or circumstances, as in *two-seater, three-master, teetotaller, fiver, tenner.* **2.** serving as the regular English formative of agent nouns (being attached to verbs of any origin), as in *bearer, creeper, employer, harvester, teacher, theoriser.* [OE *-ere,* c. G *-er,* etc.; akin to L *-ārius*]

**-er**[2], a suffix of nouns denoting persons or things concerned or connected with something, as in *butler, grocer, officer, garner.* [ME, from AF, OF *-er, -ier,* from L *-ārius,* neut. *-ārium.* Cf. -ARY[1]]

**-er**[3], a termination of certain nouns denoting action or process, as in *dinner, rejoinder, remainder, trover.* [F; orig. inf. termination]

**-er**[4], a suffix forming the comparative degree of adjectives, as in *harder, smaller.* [OE *-ra, -re,* c. G *-er*]

**-er**[5], a suffix forming the comparative degree of adverbs, as in *faster.* [OE *-or,* c. OHG *-or,* G *-er*]

**-er**[6], a suffix forming frequentative verbs, as *flicker, flutter, glimmer, patter.* [OE *-r-,* c. G *-(e)r-*]

**Er,** *Chem.* erbium.

**E.R.,** Queen Elizabeth. [L *Elizabeth Regina*]

**era** /'ɪərə/, *n.* **1.** a period of time marked by distinctive character, events, etc.: *an era of progress.* **2.** the period of time to which anything belongs or is to be assigned. **3.** a system of chronological notation reckoned from a given date. **4.** a period during which years are numbered and dates reckoned from a particular point of time in the past: *the Christian era.* **5.** a point of time from which succeeding years are numbered, as at the beginning of a system of chronology. **6.** a date or an event forming the beginning of any distinctive period. **7.** a major division of geological time: *Palaeozoic era.* [LL, var. of *aera* number or epoch by which reckoning is made, era, probably the same word as L *aera* counters, pl. of *aes* copper, bronze]

**eradiate** /ə'reɪdieɪt, i-/, *v.,* **-ated, -ating.** →**radiate.**

**eradiation** /ə'reɪdieɪʃən, i-/, *n.* the act or process of shooting forth (light rays, etc); radiation.

**eradicable** /ə'rædəkəbəl, i-/, *adj.* that may be eradicated.

**eradicate** /ə'rædəkeɪt, i-/, *v.t.,* **-cated, -cating. 1.** to remove or destroy utterly; extirpate. **2.** to pull up by the roots. [L *ērādīcātus,* pp. rooted out] – **eradication** /ərædə'keɪʃən, i-/, *n.* – **eradicator,** *n.* – **eradicative,** *adj.*

**erase** /ə'reɪz, i-/, *v.t.,* **erased, erasing. 1.** to rub or scrape out, as letters or characters written, engraved, etc.; efface. **2.** to obliterate material recorded on an electromagnetic tape by demagnetising it. [L *ērāsus,* pp., scratched out] – **erasable,** *adj.* – **erasion,** *n.*

**eraser** /ə'reɪzə, i-/, *n.* **1.** an instrument, as a piece of rubber or cloth, for erasing marks made with pen, pencil, chalk, etc. **2.** one who, or that which erases.

**erasure** /ə'reɪʒə, i-/, *n.* **1.** the act of erasing. **2.** a place, or mark remaining where something has been erased.

**erbium** /'ɜbiəm/, *n.* a rare-earth metallic element, having pink salts. [NL, from *(Ytt)erb(y)* (see YTTERBIUM) + *-ium* -IUM]

**erbo** /'ɜboʊ/, *n.* a processed cheese made from gruyere and blue vein, with a mild, distinctive flavour.

**ere** /ɛə/, *prep., conj. Archaic.* before. [ME; OE *ǣr, ēr* (c. G *eher*), comparative of OE *ār* soon, early, c. Goth. *air.* See ERST, EARLY]

**erect** /ə'rɛkt, i-/, *adj.* **1.** upright in position or posture: *to stand or sit erect.* **2.** raised or directed upwards: *a dog with* *ears erect.* **3.** *Bot.* vertical throughout; not spreading or declined: *an erect stem, an erect leaf or ovule.* **4.** *Optics.* (of an image) having the same position as the object; not inverted. *–v.t.* **5.** to build; construct; raise: *to erect a house.* **6.** to raise and set in an upright or perpendicular position: *to erect a telegraph pole.* **7.** *Geom.* to draw or construct (a line or figure) upon a given line, base, or the like. **8.** *Optics.* to change (an inverted image) to a normal position. **9.** to set up or establish, as an institution; found. **10.** *Mach.* to assemble; make ready for use. [ME, from L *ērectus,* pp., set upright, built] **–erectable,** *adj.* **–erecter,** *n.* **–erectness,** *n.* **–erectly,** *adv.*

**erectile** /əˈrɛktaɪl, i-/, *adj.* **1.** capable of being erected or set upright. **2.** *Anat.* susceptible of being distended with blood and becoming rigid, as tissue. **–erectility** /ərɛkˈtɪləti/, *n.*

**erection** /əˈrɛkʃən, i-/, *n.* **1.** the act of erecting. **2.** the state of being erected. **3.** something erected, as a building or other structure. **4.** *Physiol.* **a.** a distended and rigid state of an organ or part containing erectile tissue. **b.** an erect penis.

**erective** /əˈrɛktɪv, i-/, *adj.* tending to erect.

**erector** /əˈrɛktə, i-/, *n.* **1.** one who or that which erects. **2.** *Anat.* a muscle which erects the body or one of its parts. Also, **erecter.**

**erelong** /ɛəˈlɒŋ/, *adv. Archaic.* before long; soon.

**eremite** /ˈɛrəmaɪt/, *n.* a religious solitary; a hermit. [ME, from LL *erēmīta,* from Gk *erēmítēs* HERMIT] **–eremitic** /ɛrəˈmɪtɪk/, **eremitical** /ɛrəˈmɪtɪkəl/, **eremitish** /ˈɛrəˌmaɪtɪʃ/, *adj.* **–eremitism** /ˈɛrəmətɪzəm/, *n.*

**erenow** /ɛəˈnaʊ/, *adv. Archaic.* before this time.

**erepsin** /əˈrɛpsən, i-/, *n.* a mixture of proteolytic enzymes, consisting mainly of peptidases, produced by the wall of the small intestine of vertebrates.

**erethism** /ˈɛrəθɪzəm/, *n.* an unusual or excessive degree of irritability or stimulation in an animal organ or tissue. [Gk *erethismós* irritation] **–erethismic** /ɛrəˈθɪzmɪk/, **erethistic** /ɛrəˈθɪstɪk/, **erethitic** /ɛrəˈθɪtɪk/, *adj.*

**erewhile** /ɛəˈwaɪl/, *adv. Archaic.* formerly.

**erg**[1] /ɜg/, *n.* a unit of work or energy in the centimetre-gram-second system, equal to $0.1 \times 10^{-6}$ joules. *Symbol:* erg [Gk *érgon* work. See WORK, *n.*]

**erg**[2] /ɜg/, *n.* any vast area covered deeply with sand in the form of shifting dunes, as parts of the Sahara Desert. [F, from Hamitic]

**ergate** /ˈɜgeɪt/, *n.* the worker ant. [Gk *ergátēs* worker]

**ergative** /ˈɜgətɪv/, *adj. Gram.* causative. In a sentence like *John moved the table,* John is the agent or cause of the action, and the word *John* is the ergative subject. Cf. *the table moved.*

**ergo** /ˈɜgoʊ/, *conj., adv.* therefore; consequently. [L]

**ergograph** /ˈɜgəgræf, ˈɜgoʊ-, -graf/, *n.* an instrument that measures and records the amount of work done when a muscle contracts.

**ergometer** /ɜˈgɒmətə/, *n.* a device for measuring the work performed by a group of muscles under controlled conditions, as to time, rate, or resistance.

**ergometrine maleate** /ɜgoʊˌmɛtrin ˈmælieɪt/, *n.* an alkaloid derived from ergot which has a powerful oxytocic action.

**ergonomics** /ɜgəˈnɒmɪks, ɜgoʊ-/, *n.* the study of the engineering aspects of the relationship between human workers and their working environment.

**ergophobia** /ˌɜgoʊˈfoʊbiə/, *n.* the fear of work.

**ergosterol** /ɜˈgɒstərɒl/, *n.* a sterol derived from cholesterol and contained in yeast and in small amounts in the fats of animals, converted into vitamin D by exposure to ultraviolet rays. [ERGO(T) + STEROL]

**ergot** /ˈɜgət, -gɒt/, *n.* **1.** any fungus of the genus *Claviceps* which causes a disease of rye and other grasses, resulting in the replacement of the seed with a long, hard, hornlike, dark-coloured sclerotium. **2.** the disease caused by such a fungus. **3.** the sclerotium produced by such a fungus, esp. of *C. purpurea,* growing on rye, which is used medicinally as a haemostatic and which is a source of lysergic acid.

**ergotamine tartrate** /ɜˌgɒtəmin ˈtatreɪt/, *n.* an alkaloid derived from ergot, used to treat migraine.

**ergotism** /ˈɜgətɪzəm/, *n.* a disease due to eating food prepared from rye, etc., affected with ergot.

**erica** /ˈɛrɪkə/, *n.* any of various shrubs of the genus *Erica,* family Ericaceae, esp. those of southern Africa, cultivated for their showy flowers.

**ericaceous** /ɛrəˈkeɪʃəs, ɛri-/, *adj.* belonging to the Ericaceae, or heath family of plants, which includes the heath, arbutus, azalea, rhododendron, American laurel, etc. [NL *Erīcāceae* (from *Erīca* the heath genus, from Gk *ereíkē* heath) + -OUS]

**ericoid** /ˈɛrəkɔɪd, ˈɛri-/, *adj.* (of a leaf) small and sharp-pointed, as the leaf of an erica or other heath.

**erigeron** /əˈrɪdʒərən, əˈrɪg-/, *n.* any plant of the genus *Erigeron,* family Compositae, including some common weeds; fleabane. [L, from Gk: groundsel]

**Erin** /ˈɛrɪn, ˈɛərɪn, -ən/, *n. Poetic.* Ireland. [OIrish *Erinn,* dative of *Eriu,* later *Eire* Ireland]

**erinaceous** /ɛrəˈneɪʃəs/, *adj.* of the hedgehog kind or family.

**eringo** /ɛˈrɪŋgoʊ/, *n.* →**eryngo.**

**Erinoid** /ˈɛrənɔɪd/, *n.* a thermoplastic material made from casein and formaldehyde. [Trademark]

**eriostemon** /ɛriˈɒstəmən/, *n.* any shrub of the genus *Eriostemon,* family Rutaceae, a group almost confined to temperate Australia and characterised by white or pink waxy flowers; waxflower.

**eristic** /ɛˈrɪstɪk/, *adj.* **1.** Also, **eristical.** pertaining to controversy or disputation; controversial. *–n.* **2.** one who engages in disputation; controversialist. **3.** the art of disputation. [Gk *eristikós,* from *erízein* wrangle]

**Erlenmeyer flask** /ˈɜlənmaɪə ˌflask/, *n.* a flat-bottomed, conical flask with a narrow neck, widely used in chemical laboratories. [named after E. *Erlenmeyer,* d. 1909, German chemist]

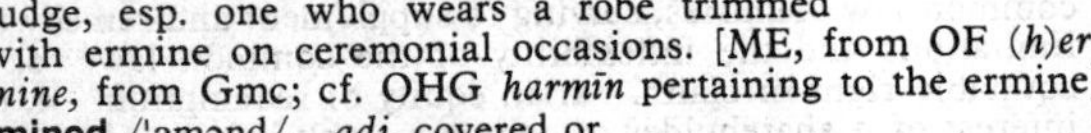

Erlenmeyer flask

**ermine** /ˈɜmən/, *n., pl.* **-mines,** (*esp. collectively*) **-mine.** **1.** a weasel, *Mustela erminea* of northern regions, which turns white in winter. The brown summer phase is called the stoat. **2.** the lustrous white winter fur of the ermine, having a black tail tip. **3.** the rank, office, or dignity of a king, nobleman, or judge, esp. one who wears a robe trimmed with ermine on ceremonial occasions. [ME, from OF *(h)ermine,* from Gmc; cf. OHG *harmīn* pertaining to the ermine]

**ermined** /ˈɜmənd/, *adj.* covered or adorned with ermine.

**-ern,** *n.* an adjectival suffix occurring in *northern,* etc. [ME and OE *-erne*]

**erne** /ɜn/, *n.* →**sea-eagle.** Also, **ern.** [ME; OE *earn,* c. MLG *arn* eagle]

ermine

**erode** /əˈroʊd, i-/, *v.t.,* **eroded, eroding.** **1.** to eat out or away; destroy by slow consumption. **2.** to form (a channel, etc.) by eating or wearing away (used esp. in geology, to denote the action of all the forces of nature that wear away the earth's surface). [L *ērōdere* gnaw off]

**erodent** /əˈroʊdənt, i-/, *adj.* eroding; erosive: *the erodent power of wind.*

**erogenous** /əˈrɒdʒənəs, ɛ-, i-/, *adj.* arousing or tending to arouse sexual desire. Also, **erogenic** /ɛrəˈdʒɛnɪk/. **–erogeneity** /ˌɛrədʒəˈniəti/, *n.*

**erogenous zone** /ˈ– zoʊn/, *n.* any area of the body, the stimulation of which produces sexual excitement or pleasure.

**eros** /ˈɪərɒs, ˈɛrɒs/, *n.* **1.** earthly or sexual love. **2.** *Psychol.* the self-preserving instincts as opposed to the self-destructive instincts. **3.** libido; sexual drive. [from *Eros,* the Greek god of love; L, from Gk: lit., love]

**erose** /əˈroʊs, i-/, *adj.* **1.** uneven as if gnawed away. **2.** *Bot.* having the margin irregularly incised as if gnawed, as a leaf. [L *ērōsus,* pp., gnawed off]

**erosion** /əˈroʊʒən, i-/, *n.* **1.** the act of eroding. **2.** the state of being eroded. **3.** the process by which the surface of the earth is worn away by the action of water, glaciers, winds, waves, etc.

**erosive** /əˈroʊsɪv, i-/, *adj.* serving to erode; causing erosion.

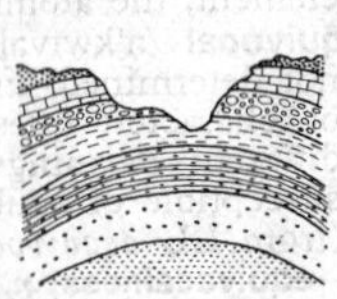

erosion: section of stratified rock bent into a low anticline by erosion

**erotic** /ə'rɒtɪk, ɛ-, i-/, *adj.* **1.** of or pertaining to sexual love; amatory. **2.** arousing or satisfying sexual desire. **3.** subject to or marked by strong sexual desires. *–n.* **4.** an erotic poem. **5.** an erotic person. [Gk *erōtikós* pertaining to love. See EROS]

**erotica** /ə'rɒtɪkə, ɛ-, i-/, *n.* literature or art dealing with sexual love.

**eroticise** /ə'rɒtəsaɪz, ɛ-, i-/, *v.t.*, **-cised, -cising.** to make erotic; to stimulate sexually. **– eroticisation** /əˌrɒtəsaɪ'zeɪʃən, ɛ-, i-/, *n.*

**eroticism** /ə'rɒtəsɪzəm, ɛ-, i-/, *n.* **1.** erotic character or tendency. **2.** *Psychol.* morbid sexual desires or instincts.

**eroticist** /ə'rɒtəsəst, ɛ-, i-/, *n.* a person who engages in erotic activities.

**erotise** /'ɛrətaɪz/, *v.t.*, **-tised, -tising.** to translate (emotion, etc.) into sexual feeling.

**erotism** /'ɛrətɪzəm/, *n.* the arousal and satisfaction of sexual desires.

**erotogenic** /əˌrɒtoʊ'dʒɛnɪk/, *adj.* productive of, or produced by, sexual stimulation.

**erotology** /ɛrə'tɒlədʒi/, *n.* the study of erotic behaviour. **– erotologist,** *n.* **– erotological** /ɛˌrɒtoʊ'lɒdʒɪkəl/, *adj.*

**erotomania** /ərɒtə'meɪniə/, *n.* abnormally strong or persistent sexual desire. **– erotomaniac,** *n.*

**err** /ɜ/, *v.i.* **1.** to go astray in thought or belief; be mistaken; be incorrect. **2.** to go astray morally; sin. **3.** to deviate from the true course, aim, or purpose. [ME *erre(n)*, OF *errer*, from L *errāre* wander]

**errand** /'ɛrənd/, *n.* **1.** a trip to convey a message or execute a commission; a short journey for a specific purpose: *he was sent on an errand.* **2.** a special business entrusted to a messenger; a commission. **3.** the purpose of any trip or journey: *his errand was to bribe the chieftain into releasing the captives.* [ME; OE *ærende*, c. OHG *ārunti*. Cf. OE *ār* messenger]

**errant** /'ɛrənt/, *adj.* **1.** journeying or travelling, as a medieval knight in quest of adventure; roving adventurously. **2.** deviating from the regular or proper course; erring. **3.** moving in an aimless or quickly changing manner. [ME *erraunte*, from F *errant*, properly ppr. of *errer*, OF *esrer* travel (from VL *iterāre* journey), but b. with F *errant*, ppr. of *errer* ERR] **– errantly,** *adv.*

**errantry** /'ɛrəntri/, *n., pl.* **-tries.** conduct or performance like that of a knight-errant.

**errata** /ə'ratə, ɛ-/, *n.* plural of **erratum.**

**erratic** /ə'rætɪk, i-/, *adj.* **1.** deviating from the proper or usual course in conduct or opinion; eccentric. **2.** having no certain course; wandering; not fixed: *erratic winds.* **3.** *Geol.* **a.** (of boulders, etc.) transported from the original site to an unusual location, as by glacial action. **b.** pertaining to such boulders, etc. *–n.* **4.** an erratic or eccentric person. **5.** *Geol.* an erratic boulder or block of rock. [ME, from L *errāticus*, from *errāre* wander, ERR] **– erratically,** *adv.*

**erratum** /ə'ratəm, ɛ-/, *n., pl.* **-ta** /-tə/. an error in writing or printing. [L, properly pp. neut., erred]

**errhine** /'ɛraɪn, -ɪn/, *adj.* **1.** designed to be snuffed into the nose. **2.** occasioning discharges from the nose. *–n.* **3.** a medicine to be snuffed up the nostrils to promote sneezing and increased discharges. [NL *errhīnum*, from Gk *érrhīnon*, from *en-* EN-[2] + *rhís* nose]

**erring** /'ɜrɪŋ/, *adj.* **1.** going astray; in error; wrong. **2.** sinning. **– erringly,** *adv.*

**erron.,** **1.** erroneous. **2.** erroneously.

**erroneous** /ə'roʊniəs/, *adj.* containing error; mistaken; incorrect. [ME, from L *errōneus* straying] **– erroneously,** *adv.* **– erroneousness,** *n.*

**error** /'ɛrə/, *n.* **1.** deviation from accuracy or correctness; a mistake, as in action, speech, etc. **2.** belief in something untrue, the holding of mistaken opinions. **3.** the condition of believing what is not true: *in error about the date.* **4.** a moral offence; wrongdoing. **5.** *Physics., etc.* the difference between the observed or approximately determined value and the true value of a quantity. [L; replacing ME *errour*, from OF] **– errorless,** *adj.*

**error of closure,** *n. Survey.* **1.** the amount by which a closed traverse fails to satisfy the requirements of a true mathematical figure, as the length of line joining the true and computed position of the same point. **2.** the ratio of this linear error to the perimeter of the traverse. **3.** (for angles) the amount by which the sum of the observed angles fails to equal the true sum. **4.** (in levelling) the amount by which an elevation determined by a series of levels fails to agree with an established elevation.

**ersatz** /'ɜzæts, 'ɛəz-, -zats/, *adj* **1.** serving as a substitute: *an ersatz meat dish made of aubergine and oatmeal.* *–n.* **2.** a substitute. [G]

**Erse** /ɜs/, *n.* **1.** Gaelic, esp. Scottish Gaelic. *–adj.* **2.** of or pertaining to the Celts in the Highlands of Scotland or their language. [Scot. var. of IRISH]

**erst** /ɜst/, *adv. Archaic.* before the present time; formerly. [ME; OE *ǣrst*, syncopated var. of *ǣrest* (c. G *erst*), superl. of *ǣr*. See ERE]

**erstwhile** /'ɜstwaɪl/, *adj.* **1.** former: *erstwhile enemies.* *–adv.* **2.** *Archaic.* formerly; erst.

**erubescent** /ɛru'bɛsənt/, *adj.* becoming red or reddish; blushing. [L *ērubescens*, ppr., reddening] **– erubescence,** *n.*

**eruct** /ə'rʌkt, i-/, *v.i.* **1.** to belch. *–v.t.* **2.** to belch (wind from the stomach). **3.** to emit (fumes, matter, etc.) violently, as from a volcano. [L *ēructāre* belch forth]

**eructate** /ə'rʌkteɪt, i-/, *v.t., v.i.*, **-tated, -tating.** →**eruct.** **– eructation** /irʌk'teɪʃən/, *n.*

**erudite** /'ɛrədaɪt/, *adj.* characterised by erudition; learned or scholarly: *an erudite professor, an erudite commentary.* [L *ērudītus*, pp., instructed] **– eruditely,** *adv.* **– eruditeness,** *n.*

**erudition** /ɛrə'dɪʃən/, *n.* acquired knowledge, esp. in literature, languages, history, etc.; learning; scholarship.

**erumpent** /ə'rʌmpənt, i-/, *adj.* **1.** bursting forth. **2.** *Bot.* prominent, as if bursting through the epidermis.

**erupt** /ə'rʌpt, i-/, *v.i.* **1.** to burst forth, as volcanic matter. **2.** (of a volcano, geyser, etc.) to eject matter. **3.** (of teeth) to break through surrounding hard and soft tissues and become visible in the mouth. **4.** to break out suddenly or violently, as if from restraint. **5.** to break out with or as with a skin rash. *–v.t.* **6.** to cause to burst forth. **7.** (of a volcano, etc.) to eject (matter). [L *ēruptus*, pp.] **– eruptible,** *adj.*

**eruption** /ə'rʌpʃən, i-/, *n.* **1.** an issuing forth suddenly and violently; an outburst; an outbreak. **2.** *Geol.* the ejection of molten rock, water, etc., as from a volcano, geyser, etc. **3.** that which is erupted or ejected, as molten rock, etc. **4.** *Pathol.* **a.** the breaking out of a rash, acne, etc. **b.** a rash or exanthema. [L *ēruptio*] **– eruptional,** *adj.*

**eruptive** /ə'rʌptɪv, i-/, *adj.* **1.** bursting forth, or tending to burst forth. **2.** pertaining to or of the nature of an eruption. **3.** *Geol.* (of rocks) formed by the eruption of molten material. **4.** *Pathol.* causing or attended with an eruption or rash. *–n.* **5.** *Geol.* an eruptive rock.

**-ery,** a suffix of nouns denoting occupation, business, calling, or condition, place or establishment, goods or products, things collectively, qualities, actions, etc., as in *archery, bakery, cutlery, fishery, grocery, nunnery, pottery, finery, foolery, prudery, scenery, tracery, trickery, witchery.* [ME, from OF *-erie*, from *-ier* -ER[2] + *-ie* -Y[3]]

**eryngo** /ə'rɪŋgoʊ/, *n., pl.* **-goes.** any of various spiny herbs of the umbelliferous genus *Eryngium*, of temperate and subtropical regions, numerous in South America, as *E. maritimum*, the sea-holly of European coasts, and *E. rostratum*, blue devil. Also, **eringo.** [It. *eringio*, from L *ēryngion*, from Gk, diminutive of *éryngos*]

**erysipelas** /ɛrə'sɪpələs/, *n.* an acute, febrile, infectious disease, due to a specific streptococcus, and characterised by diffusely spreading, deep red inflammation of the skin or mucous membranes. [L, from Gk; replacing ME *herisipila*, etc., from ML] **– erysipelatous** /ɛrəsɪ'pɛlətəs/, *adj.*

**erysipeloid** /ɛrə'sɪpəlɔɪd/, *n.* a disease of man contracted by contact with the bacillus that causes erysipelas in pigs, sheep, turkeys and other animals kept in captivity, and characterised by a painful local ulcer, generally on one of the hands.

**erythema** /ɛrə'θimə/, *n.* abnormal redness of the skin due to local congestion, as in inflammation. [NL, from Gk: redness or flush] **– erythematic** /ɛrəθə'mætɪk/, **erythematous** /ɛrə'θimətəs/, *adj.*

**erythraemia** /ɛrə'θrimiə/, *n.* **1.** an excess of red blood cells. **2.** any disease with this characteristic.

**erythrism** /əˈrɪθrɪzəm/, *n.* abnormal redness, as of plumage or hair. – **erythrismal** /ˌɛrɪθˈrɪzməl/, *adj.*

**erythrite** /əˈrɪθraɪt/, *n.* **1.** →**cobalt bloom. 2.** →**erythritol.**

**erythritol** /əˈrɪθrətɒl/, *n.* a tetrahydric crystalline alcohol $(CH_2OHCHOH)_2$, related to carbohydrates, and derived from certain lichens.

**erythro-,** a word element meaning 'red', as in *erythrocyte.* Also, **erythr-.** [Gk, combining form of *erythrós*]

**erythroblast** /əˈrɪθroʊˌblæst, -ˌblast/, *n.* a nucleated cell in the bone marrow from which red blood cells develop.

**erythrocyte** /əˈrɪθrəsaɪt, əˈrɪθroʊ-/, *n.* one of the red corpuscles of the blood; red blood cell.

**erythrocytometer** /əˌrɪθroʊsaɪˈtɒmətə/, *n.* a laboratory instrument using the light diffraction principle to measure the diameter of red cells (or other microscopic particles) in a thin film.

**erythroderma** /əˌrɪθroʊˈdɜmə/, *n.* abnormal redness of skin.

**erythrogenesis** /əˌrɪθroʊˈdʒɛnəsəs/, *n.* the production of erythrocytes; erythropoiesis.

**erythromycin** /əˌrɪθrəˈmaɪsən, ərɪθroʊ-/, *n.* an antibiotic effective against diseases caused by bacteria, including several against which penicillin is ineffective. Its use is reserved for the treatment of resistant staphylococcal infections.

**erythrophobia** /əˌrɪθroʊˈfoʊbiə/, *n.* **1.** *Pathol.* morbid flushing. **2.** *Psychol.* morbid aversion to red.

**erythropoiesis** /əˌrɪθroʊpɔɪˈisəs/, *n.* the formation of erythrocytes. – **erythropoietic,** *adj.*

**erythrosine** /əˈrɪθroʊˌsin, əˈrɪθrə-, -ˌsaɪn/, *n.* sodium (or potassium) salt of iodeosin, $C_{20}H_6I_4Na_2O_5$; a brown powder colourant which gives a cherry red solution in water.

**-es,** a variant of **-s**[2] and **-s**[3] after *s, z, ch, sh,* and in those nouns ending in *-f* which have *-v-* in the plural. Cf. **-ies.**

**es-.** For words with prefix **es-**, see also **aes-** and **oes-**.

**E.S.,** Eastern States.

**escadrille** /ˈɛskədrɪl/, *n.* **1.** *Obs.* a small naval squadron. **2.** *U.S.* a squadron or divisional unit of aeroplanes: *the Lafayette Escadrille of World War I.* [F, from Sp. *escadrilla,* diminutive of *escuadra* squadron, from It. *squadra* square, from *squadrare* to square, from L *exquadrāre*]

**escalade** /ɛskəˈleɪd/, *n., v.,* **-laded, -lading.** *–n.* **1.** a scaling or mounting by means of ladders, esp. in an assault upon a fortified place. *–v.t.* **2.** to mount, pass, or enter by means of ladders. [F, from It. *scalata,* from *scalare* climb, from *scala* steps, SCALE[3]] – **escalader,** *n.*

**escalate** /ˈɛskəleɪt/, *v.,* **-lated, -lating.** *–v.t.* **1.** to enlarge; intensify, esp. a war. *–v.i.* **2.** to grow in size or intensity; develop or increase by stages: *food prices are escalating.* [backformation from ESCALATOR] – **escalation** /ɛskəˈleɪʃən/, *n.*

**escalation clause** /ɛskəˈleɪʃən klɔz/, *n.* a provision in a contract allowing for adjustments up or down under specific economic conditions, as in the cost of living in a wage agreement. Also, **escalator clause.**

**escalator** /ˈɛskəleɪtə/, *n.* a continuously moving staircase for carrying passengers up or down. [b. ESCALADE and ELEVATOR]

**escalator clause** /ˈ– klɔz/, *n.* →**escalation clause.**

**escallop** /ɛsˈkɒləp, -ˈkæl-/, *n.* **1.** *Her.* a decoration in the form of a scallop-shell. *–v.t.* **2.** →**scallop** (def. 8).

**escalope** /ˈɛskəlɒp/, *n.* a thin slice of veal, pork, or beef coated in egg and breadcrumbs and fried.

**escapade** /ˈɛskəpeɪd, ɛskəˈpeɪd/, *n.* **1.** a reckless proceeding; a wild prank. **2.** an escape from confinement or restraint. [F, from Sp. *escapada,* from *escapar* escape, or from It. *scappata* (from *scappare*)]

**escape** /əsˈkeɪp/, *v.,* **-caped, -caping,** *n. –v.i.* **1.** to slip or get away, as from confinement or restraint; gain or regain liberty. **2.** to slip away from pursuit or peril; avoid capture, punishment, or any threatened evil. **3.** to issue from a confining enclosure, as a fluid. **4.** *Bot.* (of an introduced plant) to grow wild. *–v.t.* **5.** to slip away from or elude (pursuers, captors, etc.). **6.** to succeed in avoiding (any threatened or possible danger or evil). **7.** to elude (notice, search, etc.). **8.** to fail to be noticed or recollected by (a person). **9.** to slip from (a person) inadvertently, as a remark. *–n.* **10.** an act or instance of escaping. **11.** the fact of having escaped. **12.** a means of escaping: *a fire escape.* **13.** avoidance of reality. **14.** leakage, as of water, gas, etc. **15.** *Bot.* a plant originally cultivated, now growing wild. [ME *escape(n),* from ONF *escaper,* from L *ex-* EX-[1] + *cappa* cloak] – **escapable,** – **escapeless,** *adj.* – **escaper,** *n.*

**escapee** /ɛskəˈpi/, *n.* one who has escaped, as from internment, imprisonment, etc.

**escape lock** /əsˈkeɪp lɒk/, *n.* →**Davis apparatus.**

**escape mechanism** /ˈ– mɛkənɪzəm/, *n.* a means, as daydreaming, etc., of avoiding unpleasant realities.

**escapement** /əsˈkeɪpmənt/, *n.* **1.** *Archaic.* **a.** an act of escaping. **b.** a way of escape; an outlet. **2.** the portion of a watch or clock which measures beats and controls the speed of the time train. **3.** a mechanism consisting of a notched wheel and ratchet for regulating the motion of a typewriter carriage.

escapement (def. 2): anchor escapement

**escape velocity** /əskeɪp vəˈlɒsəti/, *n.* the minimum velocity that a body needs in order to overcome the gravitational field of a planet or satellite.

**escape wheel** /ˈ– wil/, *n.* a revolving toothed wheel in a watch or clock which transmits impulses to a vibrating fork. Also, **scapewheel.**

**escapism** /əsˈkeɪpɪzəm/, *n.* the avoidance of reality by absorption of the mind in entertainment, or in an imaginative situation, activity, etc. – **escapist,** *adj., n.*

**escapology** /ɛskəˈpɒlədʒi/, *n.* the technique of escaping from a confining device, prison, etc. – **escapologist,** *n.*

**escargot** /əsˈkagoʊ, ɛskaˈgoʊ/, *n.* an edible snail. [F]

**escarp** /əsˈkap/, *n.* **1.** *Fort.* the inner slope or wall of the ditch surrounding a rampart. **2.** any similar steep slope. *–v.t.* **3.** to make into an escarp; give a steep slope to; furnish with escarps. [F *escarpe,* from It. *scarpa,* of Gmc orig. See SHARP, and cf. SCARP]

**escarpment** /əsˈkapmənt/, *n.* **1.** a long, cliff-like ridge of rock, or the like, commonly formed by faulting or fracturing of the earth's crust. **2.** ground cut into an escarp about a fortification or defensive position.

**-esce,** a suffix of verbs meaning to begin to be or do something, become, grow, or be somewhat (as indicated by the rest of the word), as in *convalesce, deliquesce.* [L *-escere,* with inchoative force]

**-escence,** a suffix of nouns denoting action or process, change, state, or condition, etc., and corresponding to verbs ending in *-esce* or adjectives ending in *-escent,* as in *convalescence, deliquescence, luminescence, recrudescence.* [L *-escentia.* See -ESCE, -ENCE]

**-escent,** a suffix of adjectives meaning beginning to be or do something, becoming or being somewhat (as indicated), as in *convalescent, deliquescent, recrudescent,* often associated with verbs ending in *-esce* or nouns ending in *-escence.* [L *-escens,* ppr. ending]

**eschalot** /ˈɛʃəlɒt, ɛʃəˈlɒt/, *n.* →**shallot.**

**eschar** /ˈɛska/, *n.* a hard crust or scab formed on the skin, as from a burn. [LL *eschara,* from Gk: hearth, scar]

**escharotic** /ɛskəˈrɒtɪk/, *adj.* **1.** producing an eschar, as a medicinal substance; caustic. *–n.* **2.** a caustic application. [LL *escharōticus,* from Gk *escharōtikós*]

**eschatology** /ɛskəˈtɒlədʒi/, *n.* **1.** the doctrines of the last or final things, as death, the judgment, the future state, etc. **2.** the branch of theology dealing with them. [Gk *éschato(s)* last + -LOGY] – **eschatological** /ɛskætəˈlɒdʒɪkəl/, *adj.* – **eschatologist,** *n.*

**escheat** /əsˈtʃit/, *n.* **1.** the reversion of property to the owner or to the crown when there is a failure of persons legally qualified to inherit or to claim. **2.** property or a possession which reverts by escheat. **3.** the right to take property subject to escheat. *–v.i.* **4.** to revert by escheat, as to the crown or the state. *–v.t.* **5.** to make an escheat of; confiscate. [ME *eschette,* from OF, from *escheoir* fall to one's share, from *es-* EX-[1] + *cheoir* (from L *cadere* fall)] – **escheatable,** *adj.* – **escheatment,** *n.*

**escheatage** /əsˈtʃitɪdʒ/, *n.* the right of succeeding to an escheat.

**escheator** /əsˈtʃitə/, *n.* an officer in charge of escheats.

**eschew** /əsˈtʃu, ɛs-/, *v.t.* to abstain from; shun; avoid: *to* *eschew evil.* [ME *eschewen,* from OF *eschiver,* from Gmc; cf. SHY[1] and see SKEW[1]] – **eschewal,** *n.* – **eschewer,** *n.*

**escort** /ˈɛskɔt/, *n.;* /əsˈkɔt, ɛs-/, *v.* –*n.* **1.** a body of persons, or a single person, ship or ships, etc., accompanying another or others for protection, guidance, or courtesy. **2.** an armed guard. **3.** protection, safeguard, or guidance on a journey. **4.** a person accompanying another to a dance, party, etc.; partner. –*v.t.* **5.** to attend or accompany as an escort. [F *escorte,* from It. *scorta,* from *scorgere* guide, from s- (from L *ex-*) + *-corgere* (from L *corrigere* correct)]

**escort agency** /ˈ– ˌeɪdʒənsi/, *n.* an establishment which hires out a partner for an outing, social occasion, etc.

**escort return** /ˈ– rəˌtɜn/, *n.* (formerly) the amount of gold sent from a goldfield to the city under the care of the government escort, used as a statistic of production.

**escribe** /əsˈkraɪb, i-/, *v.t.,* **escribed, escribing.** to draw (a circle) touching one side of a triangle externally and the other two sides produced.

**escritoire** /ɛskrɪˈtwa/, *n.* a writing desk. [F, from LL *scriptōria,* for *scriptōrium.* See SCRIPTORIUM]

escritoire: Louis XVI marquetry escritoire

**escrow** /ˈɛskroʊ, əsˈkroʊ, ɛs-/, *n.* **1.** a contract, deed, bond, or other written agreement deposited with a third person, by whom it is to be delivered to the grantee or promisee on the fulfilment of some condition. **2.** the state of remaining ineffective until certain conditions are met. **3. in escrow,** (of money, goods, etc.) held in trust or as security. [AF *escrowe,* OF *escroe* piece of cloth, parchment, SCROLL; of Gmc orig.; akin to SHRED]

**escudo** /ɛsˈkjudoʊ/, *n., pl.* **-dos** /-doʊz/. **1.** the monetary unit of Portugal. **2.** a coin of this value. **3.** the monetary unit of Chile. **4.** a banknote of this value. **5.** any of various gold and silver coins of Spain, Spanish America, and Portugal. [Sp., Pg., from L *scūtum* shield]

**escuerzo** /ɛsˈkwɛəzoʊ/, *n.* a large frog of the genus *Ceratophrys* living in and around the Amazon basin.

**esculent** /ˈɛskjulənt/, *adj.* **1.** suitable for use as food; edible. –*n.* **2.** something edible, esp. a vegetable. [L *ēsculentus* good to eat]

**escutcheon** /əsˈkʌtʃən/, *n.* **1.** the shield or shield-shaped surface, on which armorial bearings are depicted. **2. blot on the escutcheon,** a stain on one's honour or reputation. **3.** a plate for protecting the keyhole of a door, or to which the handle is attached. **4.** the panel on a ship's stern bearing her name. [AF *escuchon,* from L *scūtum* shield] – **escutcheoned,** *adj.*

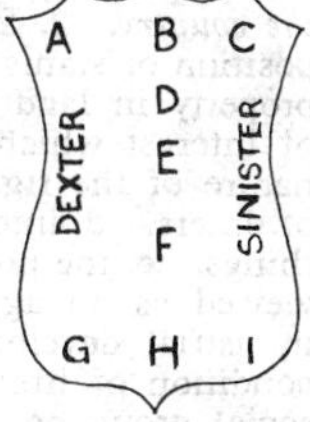

escutcheon: A, dexter chief; B, middle chief; C, sinister chief; D, honour point; E, fess point; F, nombril point; G, dexter base; H, middle base; I, sinister base

**-ese,** a noun and adjective suffix referring to locality, nationality, language, literary style, etc., as in *Japanese, journalese.* [OF *-eis,* from L *-ēnsis*]

**ESE,** east-south-east. Also, **E.S.E.**

**esker** /ˈɛskə/, *n.* a serpentine ridge of gravelly and sandy drift, formed by streams under or in glacial ice. Also, **eskar** /ˈɛska, -kə/. [Irish *eiscir*]

**Eskimo** /ˈɛskəmoʊ, ˈɛskɪ-/, *n., pl.* **-mos, -mo,** *adj.* –*n.* **1.** one of a race or people, characterised by short stature, muscular build, light brown complexion, and broad, flat face, inhabiting areas of Greenland, northern Canada, Alaska, and north-eastern Siberia. **2.** their language, of Eskimoan stock. –*adj.* **3.** of or pertaining to the Eskimos or their language. [Dan., from F *Esquimaux* (pl.), from Algonquian name for the people, meaning eaters of raw flesh]

**Eskimoan** /ɛskəˈmoʊən, ɛskɪ-/, *adj.* **1.** of or pertaining to the Eskimos or their language. –*n.* **2.** a linguistic stock including Eskimo and Aleut. Also, **Eskimauan.**

**Eskimo dog** /ˈɛskəmoʊ dɒg/, *n.* one of a breed of strong dogs used by the Eskimos to draw sledges.

**eskimo roll** /ˈɛskəmoʊ roʊl/, *n.* the rolling over, or capsizing, of a canoe, with the paddler remaining in place, and the subsequent righting of the canoe at the completion of the roll.

**esky** /ˈɛski/, *n.* a portable icebox; chillybin. [Trademark]

**esophageal** /əsɒfəˈdʒiəl, i-/, *adj. U.S.* →**oesophageal.**

**esophagus** /əˈsɒfəgəs, i-/, *n., pl.* **-gi** /-gi/. *U.S.* →**oesophagus.**

**esoteric** /ɛsəˈtɛrɪk, ɛsoʊ-/, *adj.* **1.** understood by or meant for a select few; profound; recondite. **2.** belonging to the select few. **3.** private; secret; confidential. **4.** (of philosophical doctrine, etc.) intended to be communicated only to the initiated. [Gk *esōterikós* inner] – **esoterically,** *adv.* – **esotericism, esotery** /ˈɛsətəri/, *n.*

**esp.,** especially.

**ESP** /i ɛs ˈpi/, *n.* extrasensory perception; perception or communication outside of normal sensory activity, as in telepathy and clairvoyance. Also, **e.s.p.**

**espadrille** /ɛspəˈdrɪl/, *n.* a rope-soled sandal. [F, from Pr. *espardilho,* diminutive of *espart* ESPARTO]

**espalier** /əsˈpæljə/, *n.* **1.** a trellis or framework on which fruit trees, vines or shrubs are trained to grow flat. **2.** a plant trained on such a trellis or framework, or on a fence or wall. –*v.t.* **3.** to train on an espalier. **4.** to furnish with an espalier. [F, from It. *spalliera* support, from *spalla* shoulder]

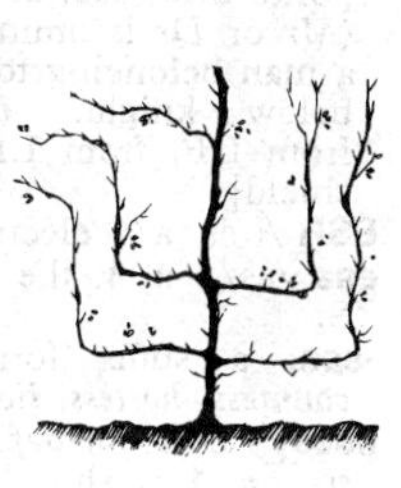
espalier

**esparto** /ɛsˈpatoʊ/, *n.* any of several grasses, esp. *Stipa tenacissima,* of southern Europe and northern Africa, used for making paper, cordage, etc. Also, **esparto grass.** [Sp., from L *spartum,* from Gk *spárton* a rope made of *spártos* a broomlike plant]

**espec.,** especially.

**especial** /əsˈpɛʃəl/, *adj.* **1.** special; exceptional; outstanding: *of no especial importance, an especial friend.* **2.** of a particular kind, or peculiar to a particular one: *your especial case.* [ME, from OF, from L *speciālis* pertaining to a particular kind]

**especially** /əsˈpɛʃəli/, *adv.* particularly; principally; unusually: *be especially watchful.*

**esperance** /ˈɛspərəns/, *n. Obs.* hope. [ME *esperaunce,* from OF *esperance,* from *esperer,* from L *spērāre* hope]

**Esperance doctor** /ɛspərəns ˈdɒktə/, *n.* a strong, cool wind blowing after a hot day in Esperance, a town in Western Australia.

**Esperance waxflower** /– ˈwæksflaʊə/, *n.* a shrub, *Chamelaucium megalopetalum,* with white flowers, found on the southern coast of western Australia. Also, **Esperance wax.**

**Esperanto** /ɛspəˈræntoʊ/, *n.* an artificial language invented in 1887 by L. L. Zamenhof and intended for international auxiliary use. It is based on the commonest words in the most important European languages. [Sp. *esperanza* hope, used by Zamenhof as a pseudonym] – **Esperantist,** *n., adj.*

**espial** /əsˈpaɪəl/, *n.* **1.** the act of spying or espying. **2.** keeping watch; observation.

**espionage** /ˈɛspiənaʒ, -nadʒ/, *n.* **1.** the practice of spying on others. **2.** the systematic use of spies by a government to discover the military and political secrets of other nations. [F *espionnage,* from *espionner* spy upon, from *espion* spy, from It. *spione,* augmentative of *spia,* from Gmc; cf. G *spähen* to scout, reconnoitre]

**esplanade** /ˈɛspləneɪd, -nad/, *n.* any open level space serving for public walks or drives, esp. one by the sea. [F, from Sp. *esplanada,* from *esplanar,* from L *explānāre* to level]

**espousal** /əsˈpaʊzəl/, *n.* **1.** adoption or advocacy, as of a cause or principle. **2.** (*sometimes pl.*) a marriage (or sometimes an engagement) ceremony. [ME *espousaile,* from OF, from L *spōnsālia,* neut. pl. of *spōnsālis* pertaining to betrothal]

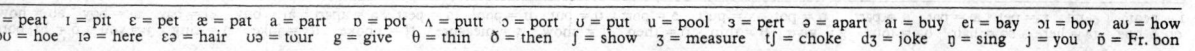

**espouse** /əsˈpaʊz, ɛs-/, *v.t.,* **-poused, -pousing. 1.** to make one's own, adopt, or embrace, as a cause. **2.** to take in marriage; marry. **3.** *Obs.* to give (a woman) in marriage. [MF *espouser,* from L *spōnsāre* betroth, espouse] – **espouser,** *n.*

**espresso** /ɛs'prɛsoʊ/, *n.* coffee made by forcing steam under pressure or boiling water through ground coffee beans. Also, **expresso.** [It.: expressed (coffee)]

**espresso bar** /'– ba/, *n.* a coffee bar serving espresso coffee. Also, **expresso bar.**

**esprit** /əs'pri, ɛs-/, *n.* wit; sprightliness; lively intelligence. [F, from L *spīritus* SPIRIT]

**esprit de corps** /əs,pri də 'kɔ/, *n.* a sense of union and of common interests and responsibilities, as developed among a group of persons associated together.

**espy** /əs'paɪ, ɛs-/, *v.t.*, **-pied, -pying.** to see at a distance; catch sight of; detect. [ME *espy(en),* from OF *espier,* from Gmc; cf. G *spähen* to scout, reconnoitre] – **espier,** *n.*

**Esq.,** Esquire.

**-esque,** an adjective suffix indicating style, manner, or distinctive character, as in *arabesque, picturesque, statuesque.* [F, from It. *-esco;* of Gmc orig. Cf. -ISH[1]]

**esquimautage** /ɛskəmoʊ'taʒ/, *n.* the manoeuvre of righting a canoe using the eskimo roll. [F]

**esquire** /əs'kwaɪə, 'ɛs-/, *n., v.,* **-quired, -quiring.** *–n.* **1.** a polite title (usu. abbreviated to *Esq.*) after a man's last name (*Mr* or *Dr* is omitted when it is used): *John Smith, Esq.* **2.** a man belonging to the order of English gentry ranking next below a knight. *–v.t.* **3.** to address as 'Esquire'. [ME *esquier,* from OF, from LL *scūtārius* shield-bearer, from L *scūtum* shield]

**ESR** /i ɛs 'a/, electron spin resonance.

**ess** /ɛs/, *n.* **1.** the letter S, s. **2.** something shaped like an S.

**-ess,** a suffix forming distinctively feminine nouns, as *countess, hostess, lioness.* [F *-esse,* from L *-issa,* from Gk]

**essay** /'ɛseɪ/ *for def. 1,* /'ɛseɪ, ɛ'seɪ/ *for defs 2 and 3, n.;* /ɛ'seɪ/, *v.* *n.* **1.** a short literary composition on a particular subject. **2.** an effort to perform or accomplish something; an attempt. **3.** a tentative effort. *–v.t.* **4.** to try; attempt. **5.** to put to the test; make trial of. [MF *essai,* from LL *exagium* a weighing. Cf. ASSAY] – **essayer,** *n.* – **essayistic,** *adj.*

**essayist** /'ɛseɪəst/, *n.* **1.** a writer of essays. **2.** *Rare.* one who makes essays or trials.

**essence** /'ɛsəns/, *n.* **1.** intrinsic nature; important elements or features of a thing. **2.** a substance obtained from a plant, drug, or the like, by distillation or other process, and containing its characteristic properties in concentrated form. **3.** an alcoholic solution of an essential oil. **4.** a perfume. **5.** *Philos.* the inward nature, true substance, or constitution of anything. **6.** something that is, esp. a spiritual or immaterial entity. [ME, from L *essentia*]

**essential** /ə'sɛnʃəl/, *adj.* **1.** absolutely necessary; indispensable: *discipline is essential in an army.* **2.** pertaining to or constituting the essence of a thing. **3.** having the nature of an essence of a plant, etc. **4.** being such by its very nature, or in the highest sense: *essential happiness, essential poetry.* *–n.* **5.** an indispensable element; a chief point: *concentrate on essentials rather than details.* [ME, from LL *essentiālis.* See ESSENCE] – **essentially,** *adv.* – **essentialness,** *n.*

**essential amino acid,** *n.* any amino acid which cannot be produced by the body, but must be supplied in the diet.

**essential fatty acid,** *n.* a fatty acid which cannot be produced by the body but must be supplied in the diet.

**essentiality** /əsɛnʃi'æləti/, *n., pl.* **-ties. 1.** the quality of being essential; essential character. **2.** an essential element or point.

**essential oil** /əsɛnʃəl 'ɔɪl/, *n.* any of a class of oils obtained from plants, possessing the smell and other properties of the plant, and volatilising completely when heated, used in making perfumes, flavours, etc.

**essonite** /'ɛsənaɪt/, *n.* →**hessonite.**

**-est,** a suffix forming the superlative degree of adjectives and adverbs, as in *warmest, fastest, soonest.* [OE *-est, -ost.* Cf. Gk *-isto-*]

**est., 1.** established. **2.** estimated.

**EST,** Eastern Standard Time.

**estab.,** established.

**establish** /əs'tæblɪʃ/, *v.t.* **1.** to set up on a firm or permanent basis; institute; found: *to establish a government, a business, a university, etc.* **2.** to settle or install in a position, business, etc.: *to establish one's son in business.* **3.** to settle (oneself) as if permanently. **4.** to cause to be permanently accepted: *to establish a custom or a precedent.* **5.** to show to be valid or well grounded; prove: *to establish a fact, theory, claim, etc.* **6.** to appoint or ordain for permanence, as a law; fix unalterably. **7.** to set up or bring about permanently: *establish order.* **8.** to make (a church) a national or state institution. **9.** *Cards.* to obtain control of (a suit) so that one can win all the subsequent tricks in that suit. [ME *establisse(n),* from OF *establiss-,* stem of *establir,* from L *stabilīre* make stable] – **establisher,** *n.*

**established church** /ə,stæblɪʃt 'tʃɜtʃ, ɛs-/, *n.* a church recognised and sometimes partly supported by the state.

**establishment** /əs'tæblɪʃmənt, ɛs-/, *n.* **1.** the act of establishing. **2.** the state or fact of being established. **3.** something established; a constituted order or system. **4. the Establishment,** a loosely defined grouping of people in a community or interest group, whose joint opinions and values have a strong influence on the existing power structure of the community. **5.** a place of business or residence and everything connected with it (as furniture, fixtures, grounds, employees). **6.** a permanent civil, military, or other force or organisation. **7.** institution. **8.** the recognition by the state of a church as the state church. **9.** the church so recognised, esp. the Church of England. **10.** *Archaic.* fixed allowance or income.

**establishmentarian** /əstæblɪʃmən'tɛəriən/, *adj.* **1.** advocating and maintaining the principle of an established church, esp. the Church of England. *–n.* **2.** one who supports, or is an adherent of the established church.

**establishment award** /əs'tæblɪʃmənt əwɔd, ɛs-/, *n.* an industrial award covering all employees, whatever their classification, in a particular establishment and generally designed to provide for a degree of uniformity in conditions throughout that establishment.

**estaminet** /əs'tæmənei, ɛs-/, *n.* a bar; cafe; bistro. [F, from Walloon *staminé,* from *stamon* post, from Gmc; cf. G *Stamm* STEM[1]]

**estancia** /əs'tænsjə, ɛs-/, *n.* (in Spanish America) a landed estate; a cattle farm.

**estapol** /'ɛstəpɒl/, *n.* **1.** a varnish for wooden floors and furniture. *–v.t.* **2.** to treat (a floor, etc.) with estapol. [Trademark]

**estate** /ə'steɪt, ɛs-/, *n., v.,* **-tated, -tating.** *–n.* **1.** a piece of landed property, esp. one of large extent: *to have an estate in the country.* **2.** *Law.* **a.** property or possessions. **b.** the legal position or status of an owner, considered with respect to his property in land or other things. **c.** the degree or quantity of interest which a person has in land with respect to the nature of the right, its duration, or its relation to the rights of others. **d.** interest, ownership, or property in land or other things. **e.** the property of a deceased person, a bankrupt, etc., viewed as an aggregate. **3.** a housing development. **4.** an industrial development area; a trading estate. **5.** period or condition of life: *to attain to man's estate.* **6.** a political or social group or class, as in France, the clergy, nobles, and commons, or in the Britain, the lords spiritual, lords temporal, and commons (the three **estates of the realm**). **7.** condition or circumstances with reference to worldly prosperity, estimation, etc.; social status or rank. **8.** high rank or dignity. **9.** *Archaic.* pomp or state. *–adj.* **10.** denoting the wine from one particular estate or vineyard. *–v.t.* **11.** *Obs.* to establish in or as in an estate. [ME, from OF *estat,* from L *status.* See STATE]

**estate agent** /'– eɪdʒənt/, *n.* **1.** one who acts as an intermediary between the buyer and the seller of properties, houses, land, etc.; land agent.

**estate car** /'– ka/, *n. Brit.* →**station wagon.**

**estate duty** /'– djuti/, *n.* tax paid on a deceased person's property and other assets before they can pass into the hands of his beneficiaries.

**esteem** /əs'tim/, *v.t.* **1.** to regard as valuable; regard highly or favourably: *I esteem him highly.* **2.** to consider as of a certain value; regard: *I esteem it worthless.* **3.** to set a value on; value: *to esteem lightly.* *–n.* **4.** favourable opinion or judgment; respect or regard: *to hold a person or thing in high* *esteem.* **5.** *Archaic.* opinion or judgment of merit or demerit; estimation. [late ME *estyme(n)*, from MF *estimer,* from L *aestimāre.* See ESTIMATE, and cf. AIM]

**ester** /ˈɛstə/, *n.* a compound formed by the reaction between an acid and an alcohol with the elimination of a molecule of water. [coined by L. Gmelin, 1788-1853, German chemist]

**esterase** /ˈɛstəreɪz/, *n.* an enzyme which hydrolyses an ester.

**ester gum** /ˈɛstə gʌm/, *n.* a hard resin obtained by esterifying rosin, or other natural gums, with a polyhydric alcohol (esp. glycerol); used in the manufacture of paints and varnishes.

**esterify** /əsˈtɛrəfaɪ, ɛs-/, *v.*, **-fied, -fying.** *–v.t.* **1.** to convert (a compound) into an ester. *–v.i.* **2.** to change into an ester. – **esterification** /əstɛrəfəˈkeɪʃən, ɛs-/, *n.*

**Esth.**, *Bible.* Esther.

**esthesia** /əsˈθiziə, -ˈθiʒə/, *n. U.S.* →**aesthesia.**

**esthesis** /əsˈθisəs/, *n. U.S.* →**aesthesis.**

**esthete** /əsˈθit, ˈisθit, ˈɛsθit/, *n. U.S.* →**aesthete.**

**esthetic** /əsˈθɛtɪk, is-/, *adj. U.S.* →**aesthetic.**

**esthetical** /əsˈθɛtɪkəl, is-/, *adj. U.S.* →**aesthetical.**

**esthetically** /əsˈθɛtɪkli, is-/, *adv. U.S.* →**aesthetically.**

**esthetician** /isθəˈtɪʃən/, *n. U.S.* →**aesthetician.**

**estheticism** /əsˈθɛtəsɪzəm, is-/, *n. U.S.* →**aestheticism.**

**esthetics** /əsˈθɛtɪks, is-/, *n. U.S.* →**aesthetics.**

**estimable** /ˈɛstəməbəl/, *adj.* **1.** worthy of esteem; deserving respect. **2.** capable of being estimated. – **estimableness,** *n.* – **estimably,** *adv.*

**estimate** /ˈɛstəmeɪt/, *v.*, **-mated, -mating;** /ˈɛstəmət/, *n.* *–v.t.* **1.** to form an approximate judgment or opinion regarding the value, amount, size, weight, etc., of; calculate approximately. **2.** to form an opinion of; judge. *–v.i.* **3.** to submit approximate figures, as of the cost of work to be done. *–n.* **4.** an approximate judgment or calculation, as of the value, amount, etc., of something. **5.** a judgment or opinion, as of the qualities of a person or thing; estimation or judgment. **6.** an approximate statement of what would be charged for certain work to be done, submitted by one ready to undertake the work. [L *aestimātus,* pp., valued, rated. Cf. ESTEEM] – **estimator,** *n.*

**estimation** /ɛstəˈmeɪʃən/, *n.* **1.** judgment or opinion: *in my estimation.* **2.** esteem; respect: *to hold in high estimation.* **3.** approximate calculation; estimate: *to make an estimation of one's resources.*

**estimative** /ˈɛstəmətɪv/, *adj.* **1.** capable of estimating. **2.** based upon or pertaining to estimation.

**estipulate** /əˈstɪpjulət, -leɪt/, *adj.* →**exstipulate.**

**estival** /ˈɛstəvəl, ɛsˈtaɪvəl, əs-/, *adj. Chiefly U.S.* →**aestival.**

**estivate** /ˈɛstəveɪt/, *v.i.*, **-vated, -vating.** *Chiefly U.S.* →**aestivate.**

**estivation** /ɛstəˈveɪʃən/, *n. Chiefly U.S.* →**aestivation.**

**estoc** /ˈɛstɒk, ɛsˈtɒk/, *n.* a short stabbing sword. [ME, from OF]

**estop** /əsˈtɒp/, *v.t.*, **-topped, -topping.** **1.** *Law.* to hinder or prevent by estoppel. **2.** (formerly) to stop. [OF *estoper* stop up, AF *estopper* (in law), from OF *estoupe,* from L *stuppa* tow. Cf. STOP, *v.*]

**estoppage** /əsˈtɒpɪdʒ/, *n.* condition of being estopped.

**estoppel** /əsˈtɒpəl/, *n. Law.* a bar or impediment preventing a party from asserting a fact or a claim inconsistent with a position he previously took, either by conduct or words, esp. where a representation has been relied or acted upon by others. [cf. OF *estoupail* stopper, from *estouper* ESTOP]

**estovers** /əsˈtoʊvəz, ɛs-/, *n.pl. Law.* necessaries allowed by law, as wood and timber to a tenant, alimony to a wife, etc. [AF: necessities, properly *estover,* inf., be necessary, from Rom. *estopēre,* from L *est opus* it is necessary]

**estradiol** /ɛstrəˈdiɒl, is-/, *n. U.S.* →**oestradiol.**

**estragon** /ˈɛstrəgən/, *n.* →**tarragon.**

**estrange** /əˈstreɪndʒ/, *v.t.*, **estranged, estranging.** **1.** to turn away in feeling or affection; alienate the affections of. **2.** to remove to or keep (usu. oneself) at a distance. **3.** to divert from the original use or possessor. [late ME, from MF *estrangier,* from L *extrāneāre,* from *extrāneus* foreign. See STRANGE] – **estrangement,** *n.* – **estranger,** *n.*

**estrapade** /ɛstrəˈpeɪd/, *n.* an attempt by a horse to throw its rider by rearing and kicking.

**estray** /əsˈtreɪ/, *n.* **1.** anything strayed away. **2.** *Law.* a domestic animal, as a horse or a sheep, found wandering or without an owner. *–v.i.* **3.** *Archaic.* to stray. [AF. See STRAY, *v.*]

**estreat** /əsˈtrit/, *Law.* *–n.* **1.** a true copy or extract of an original writing or record, as of a fine. *–v.t.* **2.** to make an estreat of (a fine, etc.) for prosecution. **3.** to levy (fines) under an estreat; exact (anything) by way of fine or levy. [AF *estrete,* var. of *estraite,* properly fem. pp. of *estraire,* from L *extrahere.* See EXTRACT]

**estriol** /ˈɛstriɒl, ˈis-/, *n. U.S.* →**oestriol.**

**estrogen** /ˈɛstrədʒən, ˈis-/, *n. U.S.* →**oestrogen.** – **estrogenic** /ɛstrəˈdʒɛnɪk, is-/, *adj.*

**estrone** /ˈɛstroʊn, ˈis-/, *n. U.S.* →**oestrone.**

**estrous** /ˈɛstrəs, ˈis-/, *adj. U.S.* →**oestrous.**

**estrous cycle** /ˈ– saɪkəl/, *n. U.S.* →**oestrous cycle.**

**estrus** /ˈɛstrəs, ˈis-/, *n. U.S.* →**oestrus.**

**estuarine** /ˈɛstʃuərin, -raɪn/, *adj.* **1.** formed in an estuary. **2.** found in estuaries.

**estuary** /ˈɛstʃuəri, ˈɛstʃəri/, *n., pl.* **-aries.** **1.** that part of the mouth or lower course of a river in which its current meets the sea's tides, and is subject to their effects. **2.** an arm or inlet of the sea. [L *aestuārium,* from *aestus* a heaving motion, surge, tide] – **estuarial** /ɛstʃuˈɛəriəl/, *adj.*

**estufado system** /ɛstəˈfadoʊ ˌsɪstəm/, *n.* a method of accelerating the maturation of wine by placing it in casks in hot rooms. [Sp. *estufa* stove]

**e.s.u.** /i ɛs ˈju/, *Physics.* See **electrostatic unit.** Also, **E.S.U.**

**esurient** /əˈsjuriənt, i-/, *adj.* hungry; greedy. [L *ēsuriens,* ppr., desiring to eat] – **esurience, esuriency,** *n.* – **esuriently,** *adv.*

**-et,** a noun suffix having properly a diminutive force (now lost in many words), as in *islet, bullet, facet, midget, owlet, plummet.* [OF *-et* masc., *-ette* fem.]

**Et,** *Chem.* ethyl.

**eta** /ˈitə/, *n.* the seventh letter (H, η, English long E, e) of the Greek alphabet.

**e.t.a.** /i ti ˈeɪ/, estimated time of arrival. Also, **E.T.A.**

**étagère** /eɪtəˈʒɛə/, *n.* a series of open shelves for bric-a-brac, etc. Also, **etagere.** [F]

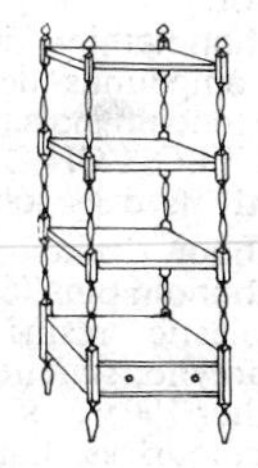
étagère

**et al** /ɛt ˈæl/, and others. [L *et alii*]

**etalon** /ˈɛtəlɒn/, *n.* an interferometer used for studying the hyperfine structure of atomic spectra; the interference effect is produced by multiple reflection between fixed, parallel, half-silvered glass or quartz plates. [F; MF *estalon* standard, from OF *estal* place, from Gmc]

**etc.,** →**et cetera.**

**et cetera** /ət ˈsɛtrə, ɛt-, -ərə/, and others; and so forth; and so on (used to indicate that more of the same sort or class might have been mentioned, but for shortness are omitted). *Abbrev.:* etc. [L *et cētera* and the rest]

**etceteras** /ətˈsɛtrəz, ɛt-, -ərəz/, *n.pl.* **1.** other things or persons unspecified. **2.** extras or sundries.

**etch** /ɛtʃ/, *v.t.* **1.** to cut, bite, or corrode with an acid or the like; engrave (metals, etc.) with an acid or the like, esp. to form a design in furrows which when charged with ink will give an impression on paper. **2.** to produce or copy by this method, as on copper. **3.** to portray or outline clearly (a character, features, etc.). **4.** to fix in the memory; to root firmly in the mind. **5.** to cut, as a geographical feature, by erosion, etc. *–v.i.* **6.** to practise the art of etching. [D *etsen,* from G *ätzen* feed, corrode, etch; akin to EAT] – **etcher,** *n.*

**etching** /ˈɛtʃɪŋ/, *n.* **1.** a process of making designs or pictures on a metal plate, glass, etc., by the corrosion of an acid instead of by a burin. **2.** an impression, as on paper, taken from an etched plate. **3.** the design produced. **4.** the plate on which such a design is etched.

**eternal** /əˈtɜnəl, i-/, *adj.* **1.** lasting throughout eternity; without beginning or end: *eternal life.* **2.** perpetual; ceaseless: *eternal quarrelling, chatter, etc.* **3.** enduring; immutable: *eternal principles.* **4.** *Metaphys.* existing outside of all relations of time; not subject to change. **5. the Eternal City,** Rome. *–n.* **6.** that which is eternal. **7. the Eternal,** God. [ME, from LL *aeternālis,* from L *aeternus.* See ETERNE] – **eternally,** *adv.* – **eternalness,** *n.*

**eternalise** /ə'tɜnəlaɪz, i-/, *v.t.*, **-lised, -lising.** **1.** to make eternal. **2.** to immortalise. Also, **eternalize.**

**eternal triangle** /əˌtɜnəl 'traɪæŋgəl/, *n. Colloq.* the relationship of husband, wife, and mistress or lover, considered as a constantly recurring social phenomenon.

**eterne** /i'tɜn/, *adj. Archaic.* eternal. [ME, from OF, from L *aeternus*, for *aeviternus* eternal]

**eternise** /i'tɜnaɪz, ə-/, *v.t.*, **-nised, -nising.** **1.** to make eternal; perpetuate. **2.** to immortalise. Also, **eternize.**

**eternity** /ə'tɜnəti, i-/, *n., pl.* **-ties.** **1.** infinite time; duration without beginning or end. **2.** eternal existence, esp. as contrasted with mortal life. **3.** an endless or seemingly endless period of time. [ME *eternite*, from OF, from L *aeternitas*, from *aeternus*. See ETERNE]

**eternity ring** /'– rɪŋ/, *n.* a ring worn, usu. by a woman, as a symbol of everlasting love.

**etesian** /ə'tiʒən/, *adj.* recurring annually (applied to certain Mediterranean winds). [L *etēsius* (from Gk *etēsios*, lit., annual) + -AN]

**eth** /ɛθ/, *n.* the name of a letter formerly used in the English alphabet, and still used in Icelandic and in phonetic alphabets. It is a crossed *d* in form (ð), and represents in Old English both unvoiced and voiced *th*, but in present use, the voiced *th* only. See **thorn** (def. 5). Also, **edh.**

ð

eth

**-eth**[1], an ending of the third person singular present indicative of verbs, now occurring only in archaic forms or used in solemn or poetic language, as in *doeth* or *doth, hath, hopeth, sitteth.* [OE *-eth, -ath, -oth, -th;* akin to L *-t*]

**-eth**[2], the form of *-th*, the ordinal suffix, after a vowel, as in *twentieth, thirtieth,* etc. See **-th**[2].

**ethanal** /'iθənæl, 'ɛθ-/, *n. Chem.* →**acetaldehyde.**

**ethane** /'iθeɪn/, *n.* an odourless, gaseous hydrocarbon, $C_2H_6$, of the methane series, present in illuminating gas and crude petroleum. [ETH(ER) + -ANE]

**ethanol** /'iθənɒl, 'ɛθ-/, *n. Chem.* →**ethyl alcohol.** [ETHAN(E) + -OL[1]]

**ethanolamine** /iθə'nɒləmin, ɛθ-, -maɪn/, *n.* one of a group of compounds derived from ethyl alcohol and amino groups; **monoethanolamine,** $NH^2CH_2CH_2OH$, **diethanolamine,** $NH(CH_2CH_2OH)_2$, and **triethanolamine,** $N(CH_2CH_2OH)_3$, are all used as solvents and in the manufacture of detergents.

**ethene** /'ɛθin/, *n. Chem.* →**ethylene.**

**ethenoid plastics** /ˌɛθənɔɪd 'plæstɪks/, *n.pl.* a group of thermoplastic resins containing a double bond; usu. includes acrylic, styrene and vinyl resins.

**ether** /'iθə/, *n.* **1.** *Chem.* **a.** a highly volatile and inflammable colourless liquid (**ethyl ether**), $(C_2H_5)_2O$, obtained by the action of sulphuric acid on alcohol, and used as a solvent and anaesthetic; sulphuric ether; diethyl ether. **b.** one of a class of organic compounds in which any two organic radicals are attached directly to oxygen, having the general formula $R_2O$, as ethyl ether $(C_2H_5)_2O$. **2.** the upper regions of space; the clear sky; the heavens. **3.** the medium supposed by the ancients to fill the upper regions. **4.** an all-pervading medium postulated for the transmission of light, heat, etc., by the older elastic solid theory. Also, **aether** (for defs 2-4). **5.** (*usu. pl.*) certain undefined properties of wine which result in fine flavour and bouquet. [L *aether*, from Gk *aithḗr* upper air, sky]

**ethereal** /ə'θɪəriəl, i-/, *adj.* **1.** light, airy or tenuous. **2.** extremely delicate or refined: *ethereal beauty.* **3.** heavenly or celestial. **4.** of the ether or upper regions of space. **5.** *Chem.* pertaining to, containing, or resembling ethyl ether. Also, **aethereal** (for defs 1-4). – **ethereality** /əθɪəri'æləti, i-/, **etherealness,** *n.* – **ethereally,** *adv.*

**etherealise** /ə'θɪəriəlaɪz, i-/, *v.t.*, **-lised, -lising.** to make ethereal. Also, **etherealize.** –**ethereally,** *adv.*

**etherify** /'iθərəfaɪ, i'θɛrəfaɪ/, *v.t.*, **-fied, -fying.** *Chem.* to convert into an ether. – **etherification** /iˌθɛrəfə'keɪʃən/, *n.*

**etherise** /'iθəraɪz/, *v.t.*, **-rised, -rising.** to put under the influence of ether. Also, **etherize.** – **etherisation** /ˌiθəraɪ'seɪʃən/, *n.* – **etheriser,** *n.*

**ethic** /'ɛθɪk/, *adj.* **1.** pertaining to morals; ethical. –*n.* **2.** *Rare.* →**ethics. 3.** an overall emphasis on moral matters: *the puritan ethic.* [L *ēthicus*, from Gk *ēthikós* of morals, moral]

**ethical** /'ɛθɪkəl/, *adj.* **1.** pertaining to or dealing with morals or the principles of morality; pertaining to right and wrong in conduct. **2.** in accordance with the rules or standards for right conduct or practice, esp. the standards of a profession: *it is not considered ethical for doctors to advertise.* **3.** a medicine which cannot be bought over the counter but must be prescribed by a doctor. – **ethically,** *adv.* – **ethicalness,** *n.*

**ethicise** /'ɛθəsaɪz/, *v.t.*, **-cised, -cising.** to make ethical; treat or regard as ethical. Also, **ethicize.**

**ethics** /'ɛθɪks/, *n.pl.* **1.** a system of moral principles, by which human actions and proposals may be judged good or bad or right or wrong. **2.** the rules of conduct recognised in respect of a particular class of human actions: *medical ethics.* **3.** moral principles, as of an individual.

**ethine** /'ɛθaɪn/, *n. Chem.* →**acetylene.** Also, **ethyne.**

**ethionamide** /ɛθi'ɒnəmaɪd/, *n.* a drug used to treat pulmonary tuberculosis.

**Ethiop** /'iθiɒp/, *adj., n.* →**Ethiopian.** [L *Aethiops*, from Gk *Aithíops*]

**Ethiopia** /iθi'oupiə/, *n.* a state in eastern Africa.

**Ethiopian** /iθi'oupiən/, *adj.* **1.** pertaining to Ethiopia or to its inhabitants. **2.** *Archaic.* Negro. **3.** *Archaic.* belonging to Africa south of the Tropic of Cancer. –*n.* **4.** a native of Ethiopia. **5.** *Archaic.* a Negro.

**Ethiopian realm** /– 'rɛlm/, *n.* a biogeographical realm comprising Africa and Arabia south of the Tropic of Cancer. Endemic mammals include the chimpanzee and gorilla; two notable fish are the primitive bichis and the African lungfish.

**ethmoid** /'ɛθmɔɪd/, *adj.* **1.** designating or pertaining to a bone of the skull at the root of the nose, containing numerous perforations for the filaments of the olfactory nerve. –*n.* **2.** the ethmoid bone. [Gk *ethmoeidḗs* sievelike] – **ethmoidal,** *adj.*

**ethnarch** /'ɛθnak/, *n.* the ruler of a people, tribe, or nation. [Gk *ethnárchēs.* See ETHNO-, -ARCH]

**ethnarchy** /'ɛθnaki/, *n., pl.* **-chies.** the government, office, or jurisdiction of an ethnarch.

**ethnic** /'ɛθnɪk/, *adj.* **1.** pertaining to or peculiar to a population, esp. to a speech group, loosely also to a race. **2.** referring to the origin, classification, characteristics, etc., of such groups. **3.** of or pertaining to members of the community who are migrants or the descendants of migrants and whose native language is not English. **4.** recognisable as coming from an identifiable culture: *ethnic music.* **5.** for the use of ethnic groups: *ethnic radio.* **6.** *Colloq.* (*sometimes derog.*) **a.** of those who seek an older and more simple life style, usu. involving the practice of handicrafts and supposed folk ways. **b.** of the life style itself. **c.** odd; quaint. –*n.* **7.** a member of an ethnic group. **8.** (a term of abuse or derision). Also, **ethnical.** [ME, from LL *ethnicus*, from Gk *ethnikós* national, gentile, heathen, from *éthnos* nation] – **ethnically,** *adv.*

**ethnic group** /'– grup/, *n.* a group of people, racially or historically related, having a common and distinctive culture.

**ethno** /'ɛθnou/, *n. Colloq.* (*derog.*) a migrant.

**ethno-,** a word element meaning 'race', 'nation', as in *ethnology.* [Gk, combining form of *éthnos*]

**ethnocentrism** /ɛθnou'sɛntrɪzəm/, *n.* the belief in the inherent superiority of one's own group and culture accompanied by a feeling of contempt for other groups and cultures. – **ethnocentric,** *adj.*

**ethnocide** /'ɛθnousaɪd/, *n.* the destruction of an ethnic group.

**ethnog.,** ethnography.

**ethnogeny** /ɛθ'nɒdʒəni/, *n.* the branch of ethnology which studies the origin of distinctive populations or races.

**ethnography** /ɛθ'nɒgrəfi/, *n.* **1.** the scientific description and classification of the various cultural and racial groups of mankind. **2.** ethnology, esp. as descriptive. – **ethongrapher,** *n.* – **ethnographic** /ɛθnə'græfɪk/, **ethnographical** /ɛθnə'græfɪkəl/, *adj.* – **ethnographically** /ɛθnə'græfɪkli/, *adv.*

**ethnol.,** **1.** ethnological. **2.** ethnology.

**ethnology** /ɛθ'nɒlədʒi/, *n.* the science that treats of the distinctive subdivisions of mankind, their origin, relations, speech, institutions, etc. – **ethnological** /ɛθnə'lɒdʒɪkəl/, **ethnologic** /ɛθnə'lɒdʒɪk/, *adj.* – **ethnologically** /ɛθnə'lɒdʒɪkli/, *adv.* – **ethnologist,** *n.*

**ethnomusicology** /ˌɛθnoʊˌmjuzə'kɒlədʒi/, *n.* **1.** the study of music outside the European art music tradition. **2.** the sociological study of the range of musics found in a particular locale.

**ethology** /i'θɒlədʒi/, *n.* the scientific study of the behaviour of animals in relation to their normal environments. – **ethologic** /ɛθə'lɒdʒɪk/, **ethological** /ɛθə'lɒdʒɪkəl/, *adj.* – **ethologically** /ɛθə'lɒdʒɪkli/, *adv.*

**ethos** /'iθɒs/, *n.* **1.** character or disposition. **2.** *Sociol.* the fundamental spiritual characteristics of a culture. **3.** *Art.* the inherent quality of a work which produces, or is fitted to produce, a high moral impression, noble, dignified, and universal (opposed to *pathos*). [NL, from Gk: character]

**ethyl** /'ɛθəl, 'iθaɪl/, *n.* **1.** *Chem.* a univalent radical, $C_2H_5$, from ethane. **2.** a type of anti-knock fluid, containing lead tetraethyl and other ingredients for a more even combustion. **3.** petrol to which this fluid has been added. [ETH(ER) + -YL] – **ethylic** /ə'θɪlɪk/, *adj.*

**ethyl acetate** /– 'æsəteɪt/, *n.* a colourless liquid with a fruity smell, $CH_3COOC_2H_5$; used as a solvent for paints and varnishes, as a flavouring and in perfume.

**ethyl alcohol** /– 'ælkəhɒl/, *n.* See **alcohol.**

**ethylate** /'ɛθəleɪt/, *v.*, **-lated, -lating,** *n.* –*v.t.* **1.** to introduce one or more ethyl radicals into (a compound). –*n.* **2.** a metallic derivative of ethyl alcohol, as potassium ethylate ($KOC_2H_5$).

**ethyl carbamate** /ˌɛθəl 'kabəmeɪt, ˌiθaɪl/, *n. Chem.* →**urethane.**

**ethylene** /'ɛθəlin/, *n.* a colourless, inflammable gas, $C_2H_4$, with an unpleasant smell, the first member of the ethylene series. Also, **ethene.**

**ethylene diamine** /– daɪ'æmaɪn/, *n.* a colourless volatile liquid, $NH_2CH_2CH_2NH_2$, with an ammoniacal odour, used chiefly as a solvent and in organic synthesis.

**ethylene dichloride** /– daɪ'klɔraɪd/, *n.* a colourless oily liquid, $C_2H_4Cl_2$, used in the synthesis of vinyl chloride.

**ethylene glycol** /– 'glaɪkɒl/, *n. Chem.* →**glycol.**

**ethylene group** /'– grup/, *n.* the bivalent radical, $-CH_2CH_2-$, derived from ethylene or ethane.

**ethylene-propylene rubber** /ˌɛθəlin-'proʊpəlin rʌbə/, *n.* a fully saturated, stereoregular, synthetic rubber made by the polymerisation of approximately equal proportions of ethylene and propylene. *Abbrev.*: EPR

**ethylene series** /'ɛθəlin ˌsɪəriz/, *n.* a series of unsaturated aliphatic hydrocarbons having one double bond, with the general formula, $C_nH_{2n}$.

**ethyl ether** /ɛθəl 'iθə, iθaɪl/, *n.* See **ether** (def. 1a).

**ethyl nitrate** /– 'naɪtreɪt/, *n.* a colourless, explosive liquid, $C_2H_5ONO_2$, used in organic synthesis. Also, **nitric ether.**

**ethyl nitrite** /– 'naɪtraɪt/, *n.* a colourless, volatile liquid, $C_2H_5ONO$, used in medicine and in organic synthesis. Also, **nitrous ether.**

**ethyne** /'ɛθaɪn/, *n. Chem.* →**ethine.**

**ethynyl group** /ɛ'θaɪnəl ˌgrup/, *n.* the univalent group, $HC \equiv C-$, derived from acetylene.

**etiolate** /'itioʊleɪt/, *v.*, **-lated, -lating.** –*v.t.* **1.** to cause (a plant) to whiten by excluding light. –*v.i.* **2.** to become blanched or whitened, as when grown without sunlight. [F *étioler* blanch + -ATE[1]] – **etiolation** /itiə'leɪʃən/, *n.*

**etiology** /iti'ɒlədʒi/, *n. U.S.* →**aetiology.**

**etiquette** /'ɛtikət/, *n.* **1.** conventional requirements as to social behaviour; proprieties of conduct as established in any class or community or for any occasion. **2.** a prescribed or accepted code of usage in matters of ceremony, as at a court or in official or other formal observances. **3.** conventional and accepted standards and practices in certain professions, as medicine. [F, in OF *estiquette* TICKET, of Gmc orig.; cf. STICK[2]]

**etna** /'ɛtnə/, *n.* a small vessel for heating liquids, consisting of a cup for the liquid with a fixed saucer surrounding it in which alcohol is burnt.

**Eton collar** /itn 'kɒlə/, *n.* a broad stiff collar folded outside an Eton jacket.

**Eton crop** /– 'krɒp/, *n.* a woman's hairstyle in which the hair is cut short at the back and worn generally in a mannish fashion.

**Eton jacket** /– 'dʒækət/, *n.* **1.** a boy's short jacket reaching to the waist as worn by students at Eton College, a boys' school in England founded in 1440 by Henry VI. **2.** a similar short jacket worn by women.

**Etruscan** /ə'trʌskən/, *adj.* **1.** pertaining to Etruria, its inhabitants, civilisation, art, or language. –*n.* **2.** an inhabitant of ancient Etruria. **3.** the extinct language of Etruria. Also, **Etrurian** /ə'truriən/. [L *Etruscus* of Etruria + -AN]

**Etruscology** /itrʌs'kɒlədʒi/, *n.* the scientific study of ancient Etruscan civilisation. – **Etruscologist,** *n.*

**et seq.,** *pl.* **et seqq., et sqq.** and the following. [L *et sequens*]

**-ette,** a noun suffix, the feminine form of *-et,* occurring esp.: **1.** with the original diminutive force, as in *cigarette.* **2.** as a distinctively feminine ending, as in *coquette,* and various colloquial formations, as *usherette.* **3.** in trademarks of imitations or substitutes, as in *leatherette.* [F, fem. of *-et* -ET]

**étude** /eɪ'tjud/, *n.* **1.** a musical composition intended mainly for the practice of some point of technique. **2.** a musical composition performed for its aesthetic appeal which also embodies a specific technical exercise. [F. See STUDY, *n.*]

**etui** /ɛ'twi, eɪ-/, *n., pl.* **etuis.** a small case, esp. one for small objects, as needles, toilet articles, etc. Also, *Chiefly U.S.,* **etwee.** [F *étui,* from OF *etuier* keep, from L *studiāre* care for]

**etym.,** **1.** etymological. **2.** etymology. Also, **etymol.**

**etymologise** /ɛtə'mɒlədʒaɪz/, *v.*, **-gised, -gising.** –*v.t.* **1.** to trace the history of (a word). –*v.i.* **2.** to study etymology. **3.** to give or suggest the etymology of words. Also, **etymologize.**

**etymology** /ɛtə'mɒlədʒi/, *n., pl.* **-gies. 1.** the study of historical linguistic change, esp. as applied to individual words. **2.** an account of the history of a particular word. **3.** the derivation of a word. [L *etymologia,* from Gk. See ETYMON, -LOGY] – **etymological** /ɛtəmə'lɒdʒɪkəl/, **etymologic** /ɛtəmə'lɒdʒɪk/, *adj.* – **etymologically** /ɛtəmə'lɒdʒɪkli/, *adv.* – **etymologist,** *n.*

**etymon** /'ɛtəmɒn/, *n., pl.* **-mons, -ma** /-mə/. a primary linguistic form, from which derivatives are formed. [L, from Gk: the original sense, form, or element of a word, properly neut. of *étymos* true, real]

**eu-,** a prefix meaning 'good', 'well', occurring chiefly in words of Greek origin, as in *eupepsia.* [Gk, combining form of *eús,* adj., good, neut. *eú* (used as adv., well)]

**Eu,** *Chem.* europium.

**eucaine** /'jukeɪn/, *n.* **1.** a crystalline organic compound used as a local anaesthetic as a substitute for cocaine, $C_{19}H_{27}NO_4$ (**alpha-eucaine**). **2.** a similar but less used compound, $C_{15}H_{21}NO_2$ (**beta-eucaine**); benzamine. [EU- + (CO)CAINE]

**eucalypt** /'jukəlɪpt/, *n.* any tree of the genus *Eucalyptus.*

**eucalyptol** /jukə'lɪptɒl/, *n. Chem.* →**cineol.** [EUCALYPT(US) + -OL[2]]

**eucalyptus** /jukə'lɪptəs/, *n., pl.* **-tuses, -ti** /-taɪ/, *adj.* –*n.* **1.** any member of the myrtaceous genus *Eucalyptus,* including many tall trees, native to the Australian region and cultivated elsewhere, many yielding valuable timber and some an oil, used in medicine as a germicide and expectorant. –*adj.* **2.** of or pertaining to a preparation, confection, etc., containing eucalyptus oil. [NL, from *eu-* EU- + Gk *kalyptós* covered (with allusion to the cap covering the buds)]

eucalyptus (def. 1)

**eucalyptus oil** /'– ɔɪl/, *n.* an essential oil distilled from the leaves of certain trees of the genus *Eucalyptus,* used in medicine as a germicide and expectorant.

**eucharis** /'jukərɪs/, *n.* any species of the genus *Eucharis,* some of which are cultivated for their large, fragrant white flowers. [NL, from Gk: pleasing]

**Eucharist** /'jukərəst/, *n.* **1.** the sacrament of the Lord's Supper; the communion; the sacrifice of the mass. **2.** the consecrated elements of the Lord's Supper, esp. the bread. **3.** (*l.c.*) the giving of thanks; thanksgiving. [LL *eucharistia,* from Gk: gratefulness, thanksgiving, the eucharist] – **Eucharistic** /jukə'rɪstɪk/, **Eucharistical** /jukə'rɪstɪkəl/, *adj.* – **Eucharistically** /jukə'rɪstɪkli/, *adv.*

**euchre** /ˈjukə/, *n., v.,* **-chred, -chring.** *U.S. –n.* **1.** *Cards.* a game played usu. by two, three, or four persons, with the 32 (or 28 or 24) highest cards in the pack. **2.** an instance of euchring or being euchred. *–v.t.* **3.** to get the better of (an opponent) in a hand at euchre by his failure to win three tricks after having made the trump. **4.** *Colloq.* to outwit; get the better of, as by scheming. [orig. uncert.]

**euchred** /ˈjukəd/, *adj. Colloq.* beaten; exhausted.

**euclasite** /ˈjukləsaɪt/, *n.* a green or blue mineral, beryllium aluminium silicate, $BeAl\ S_1O_4(OH)$, occurring in prismatic crystals. Also, **euclase.** [F, from *eu-* EU- + Gk *klásis* a breaking + -ITE[1]]

**Euclidean** /juˈklɪdiən/, *adj.* of or pertaining to Euclid, Greek geometrician of Alexandria, fl. 300 B.C., or adopting his postulates: *Euclidean geometry.* Also, **Euclidian.**

**eudemon** /juˈdimən/, *n.* a good demon or spirit. Also, **eudaemon.** [Gk *eudaímōn* happy, from *eu-* EU- + *daímōn* spirit, destiny]

**eudemonia** /judəˈmoʊniə/, *n.* **1.** happiness; welfare. **2.** (in Aristotelian philosophy) happiness as the result of an active life governed by reason. Also, **eudaemonia.** [Gk *eudaimonía*]

**eudemonic** /judəˈmɒnɪk/, *adj.* **1.** pertaining or conducive to happiness. **2.** pertaining to eudemonics. Also, **eudaemonic.**

**eudemonics** /judəˈmɒnɪks/, *n.* **1.** the science of happiness. **2.** →**eudemonism.** Also, **eudaemonics.**

**eudemonism** /juˈdimənɪzəm/, *n.* the system of ethics which holds that the basis of moral obligations lies in their relation to the production of happiness. Also, **eudaemonism.** [EUDEMON(IA) + -ISM] – **eudemonist,** *n.* – **eudemonistic** /judiməˈnɪstɪk/, **eudemonistical** /judiməˈnɪstɪkəl/, *adj.*

**eudiometer** /judiˈɒmətə/, *n.* a graduated glass measuring tube for gas analysis. [Gk *eúdio(s)* fine, clear, as weather + -METER[1]] – **eudiometric** /judiəˈmɛtrɪk/, **eudiometrical** /judiəˈmɛtrɪkəl/, *adj.* – **eudiometrically** /judiəˈmɛtrɪkli/, *adv.*

**eudiometry** /judiˈɒmətri/, *n.* the measurement and analysis of gases with a eudiometer.

**eugenic** /juˈdʒinɪk, -ˈdʒɛn-/, *adj.* **1.** of or bringing about improvement in the type of offspring produced. **2.** having good inherited characteristics. Also, **eugenical.** [Gk *eugénēs* well born + -IC] – **eugenically,** *adv.*

**eugenicist** /juˈdʒinəsəst, -ˈdʒɛn-/, *n.* **1.** a specialist in eugenics. **2.** an advocate of eugenic measures. Also, **eugenist** /ˈjudʒənəst/.

**eugenics** /juˈdʒinɪks, -ˈdʒɛn-/, *n.* **1.** the science of improving the qualities of the human race, esp. the careful selection of parents. **2.** the science of improving offspring.

**eugenol** /ˈjudʒənɒl/, *n.* a colourless, aromatic, oily compound, $C_{10}H_{12}O_2$, contained in certain essential oils, as that of cloves. [NL *Eugen(ia)* genus of myrtaceous plants + -OL[2]]

**euglena** /juˈglinə/, *n.* a green type of flagellate protozoan of the genus *Euglena,* with one flagellum and a red eyespot, much used for class and experimental study.

**euhemerise** /juˈhimərаɪz/, *v.t., v.i.,* **-rised, -rising.** to treat or explain (myths) by euhemerism. Also, **euhemerize.**

**euhemerism** /juˈhimərɪzəm/, *n.* **1.** the theory held by Euhemerus, ? 300 B.C., Greek writer, that polytheistic mythology arose out of the deification of dead heroes. **2.** mythological interpretation which reduces the gods to the level of distinguished men; the derivation of mythology from history. – **euhemerist,** *n.* – **euhemeristic** /juhiməˈrɪstɪk/, *adj.* – **euhemeristically** /juhiməˈrɪstɪkli/, *adv.*

**eulachon** /ˈjuləkɒn/, *n.* →**candlefish.**

**eulogia** /juˈloʊdʒiə/, *n.* **1.** the unconsecrated bread not needed in the Eucharist, but blessed and distributed among those members of the congregation who did not commune. This custom still exists in the Greek Church. **2.** *Eccles.* the Eucharist. **3.** alms; any gift. [Eccl. L, from Gk. See EULOGY]

**eulogise** /ˈjulədʒaɪz/, *v.t.,* **-gised, -gising.** to praise highly; speak or write a eulogy about. Also, **eulogize.** – **eulogiser,** *n.*

**eulogist** /ˈjulədʒəst/, *n.* one who eulogises.

**eulogistic** /juləˈdʒɪstɪk/, *adj.* pertaining to or containing eulogy; laudatory. Also, **eulogistical.** – **eulogistically,** *adv.*

**eulogium** /juˈloʊdʒiəm/, *n., pl.* **-giums, -gia** /-dʒiə/. **1.** eulogy. **2.** eulogistic language. [ML. See EULOGY]

**eulogy** /ˈjulədʒi/, *n., pl.* **-gies. 1.** a speech or writing in praise of a person or thing, esp. a set oration in honour of a deceased person. **2.** high praise or commendation. [ML *eulogium,* var. of *eulogia* (from Gk: praise), by association with *ēlogium* short saying]

**eumung** /ˈjumʌŋ/, *n.* any of several species of the genus *Acacia,* as *A. stenophylla* of inland eastern Australia. Also, **eumong** /ˈjumɒŋ/. [Aboriginal]

**eunuch** /ˈjunək/, *n.* a castrated man, esp. one formerly employed as a harem attendant or officer of state by oriental rulers. [ME *eunuchus,* from L, from Gk *eunoûchos* chamber attendant]

**euonymus** /juˈɒnəməs/, *n.* any of the widespread genus *Euonymus,* of shrubs and small trees, usu. bearing crimson or rose-coloured capsules which on opening disclose the seed. Also, **evonymus.** [NL, from Gk *euṓnymos* spindle tree, lit., of good name]

**eupatorium** /jupəˈtɔriəm/, *n.* any plant of the large genus *Eupatorium,* mostly American, with heads of white or purplish flowers; several species are cultivated, some have become weeds, as *E. adenophorum,* crofton weed. [NL, from Gk *eupatórion;* named after Mithridates *Eupator,* king of Pontus, 120?-63 B.C.]

**eupatrid** /juˈpætrɪd/, *n., pl.* **-patridae, -patrids. 1.** one of the hereditary aristocrats of ancient Athens and other states of Greece, who at one time formed the ruling class. **2.** any aristocrat or patrician. [NL, from Gk *eupatrídēs*]

**eupepsia** /juˈpɛpsiə/, *n.* good digestion (opposed to *dyspepsia*). Also, **eupepsy.** [NL, from Gk: good digestion] – **eupeptic,** *adj.*

**euph.,** **1.** euphemism. **2.** euphemistic.

**euphemise** /ˈjufəmaɪz/, *v.,* **-mised, -mising.** *–v.t.* **1.** to refer to by means of euphemism. *–v.i.* **2.** to employ euphemism. Also, **euphemize.**

**euphemism** /ˈjufəmɪzəm/, *n.* **1.** the substitution of a mild, indirect, or vague expression for a harsh or blunt one. **2.** the expression so substituted: *'to pass away' is a euphemism for 'to die'.* **3.** *Colloq.* the toilet. [Gk *euphēmismós,* from *euphēmízein* use fair words] – **euphemist,** *n.* – **euphemistic** /jufəˈmɪstɪk/, **euphemistical** /jufəˈmɪstɪkəl/, *adj.* – **euphemistically** /jufəˈmɪstɪkli/, *adv.*

**euphonic** /juˈfɒnɪk/, *adj.* pertaining to or characterised by euphony. Also, **euphonical.** – **euphonically,** *adv.* – **euphonicalness,** *n.*

**euphonious** /juˈfoʊniəs/, *adj.* characterised by euphony, well-sounding; agreeable to the ear. – **euphoniously,** *adv.* – **euphoniousness,** *n.*

**euphonise** /ˈjufənaɪz/, *v.t.,* **-nised, -nising.** to make euphonious. Also, **euphonize.**

**euphonium** /juˈfoʊniəm/, *n.* a tenor tuba mainly used in brass bands. [NL, from Gk *eúphōnos* well-sounding]

**euphony** /ˈjufəni/, *n., pl.* **-nies. 1.** agreeableness of sound; pleasing effect to the ear, esp. of speech sounds as uttered or as combined in utterance. **2.** a tendency to change speech sounds for ease and economy of utterance, a former explanation of phonetic change. [LL *euphōnia,* from Gk, from *eúphōnos* well-sounding]

**euphorbia** /juˈfɔbiə/, *n.* any of the plants of the widespread genus *Euphorbia* which vary greatly, but consist mostly of herbs and shrubs with an acrid milky juice; a spurge. [ME *euforbia,* for L *euphorbea* an African plant; named after *Euphorbus,* a Greek physician]

**euphorbiaceous** /jufɔbiˈeɪʃəs/, *adj.* belonging to the Euphorbiaceae, or spurge family of plants, which includes the spurges, cascarilla, castor oil, and cassava plants.

**euphoria** /juˈfɔriə/, *n.* a feeling or state of well-being, esp. one of unnatural elation. [NL, from Gk, from *eúphoros* bearing well] – **euphoric** /juˈfɒrɪk/, *adj.*

**euphotic zone** /juˈfoʊtɪk zoʊn/, *n.* the zone, about one hundred metres deep from the surface of the sea, in which enough light penetrates to allow active photosynthesis.

**euphrasy** /ˈjufrəsi/, *n.* →**eyebright** (def. 1). [late ME, from ML *euphrasia,* from Gk: delight]

**euphroe** /ˈjufroʊ, -vroʊ/, *n. Naut.* an oblong or oval piece of wood perforated with holes through which small lines are rove, forming a crowfoot, from which an awning is suspended. Also, **uphroe.** [D, pseudo-learned spelling of *juffrouw,* lit., young woman]

**euphuism** /ˈjufjuɪzəm/, *n.* **1.** an affected style in imitation of that of John Lyly, 1554? - 1606, author of *Euphues, Anatomy of Wit* (1579) and *Euphues and his England* (1580), fashionable in England about the end of the 16th century, characterised chiefly by long series of antitheses, frequent similes relating to myths and natural history, alliteration, etc. **2.** any similar ornate style of writing or speaking; highflown language. **3.** an instance of such style or language. – **euphuist,** *n.* – **euphuistic** /jufju'ɪstɪk/, **euphuistical** /jufju'ɪstɪkəl/, *adj.* – **euphuistically** /jufju'ɪstɪkli/, *adv.*

**euplastic** /ju'plæstɪk/, *adj.* capable of being transformed into organised tissue. [Gk *eúplastos* easy to mould + -IC]

**euploid** /'juplɔɪd/, *adj.* having each of the different chromosomes of the set present in the same number; an exact multiple of the haploid chromosome number.

**eupnoea** /jup'niə/, *n.* easy or normal breathing (opposed to *dyspnoea*). [NL, from Gk *eúpnoia,* from *eúpnoos* breathing well]

**Eur.,** **1.** Europe. **2.** European.

**eurabbie** /ju'ræbi/, *n.* a tree found in Victoria and New South Wales, *Eucalyptus globulus* subsp. *bicostata,* with striking waxy bluish juvenile foliage and white flowers; blue gum.

**Eurasia** /ju'reɪʒə/, *n.* Europe and Asia considered as a whole.

**Eurasian** /ju'reɪʒən/, *adj.* **1.** pertaining to Europe and Asia taken together. **2.** of mixed European and Asian descent. *–n.* **3.** a person one of whose parents is European and the other Asian.

**eureka** /ju'rikə/, *interj.* **1.** I have found (it) (the reputed exclamation of Archimedes, 287?-212 B.C., mathematician, physicist and inventor, when, after long study, he discovered a method of detecting the amount of alloy in the crown of the king of Syracuse). **2.** an exclamation of triumph at a discovery or supposed discovery. [Gk *heúrēka*]

**eureka flag** /ju,rikə 'flæg/, *n.* a flag bearing a white cross, with a star at the end of each arm, on a blue field; first raised at the Eureka Stockade in 1854 and more recently associated with the move to make Australia a republic.

**eurhythmic** /ju'riðmɪk/, *adj.* **1.** characterised by a pleasing rhythm; harmoniously ordered or proportioned. **2.** of or pertaining to eurhythmics. Also, **eurythmic.**

**eurhythmics** /ju'rɪðmɪks/, *n.* the art of interpreting in bodily movements the rhythm of musical compositions, with the aim of developing the sense of rhythm and symmetry; invented by Emile Jacques-Dalcroze. Also, **eurythmics.**

**eurhythmy** /ju'rɪðmi/, *n.* rhythmical movement or order; harmonious proportion. Also, **eurythmy.** [Gk *eurhythmía* rhythmical order]

**euripus** /ju'ripəs/, *n., pl.* **-pi** /-paɪ/. a strait, esp. one in which the flow of water in both directions is violent, as (*cap.*) that between the island of Euboea and Boeotia in Greece. [L, from Gk *eúrīpos,* from *eu-* EU- + *rhīpḗ* impetus, rush]

**euro** /'juroʊ/, *n.* →**wallaroo.**

**Euro-,** (*sometimes l.c.*) a prefix meaning 'European'. Also, *before a vowel,* **Eur-.**

**eurobond** /'juroʊbɒnd/, *n.* certificate of ownership of a long term Eurodollar debt due from a government or corporation.

**Eurodollar** /'juroʊdɒlə/, *n.* funds held in Europe as American dollars rather than in less stable local currencies.

**Europe** /'jurəp/, *n.* the continent which is the western part of the Eurasian landmass.

**European** /jurə'piən/, *adj.* **1.** pertaining to Europe or its inhabitants. **2.** native to or derived from Europe. *–n.* **3.** a native or inhabitant of Europe. **4.** a person of European descent or connections.

**Europeanise** /jurə'piənaɪz/, *v.t.,* **-nised, -nising.** to make European. Also, **Europeanize.** – **Europeanisation** /,jurəpiənaɪ'zeɪʃən/, *n.*

**Europeanism** /jurə'piənɪzəm/, *n.* **1.** European characteristics, ideas, methods, sympathies, etc. **2.** a European trait or practice.

**europium** /ju'roʊpiəm/, *n.* a rare-earth metallic element with light pink salts. *Symbol:* Eu; *at. wt:* 151.96; *at. no.:* 63. [NL, from L *Eurōpa* Europe]

**eury-,** a word element meaning 'broad', as in *eurypterid.* [Gk, combining form of *eurýs*]

**eurypterid** /ju'rɪptərɪd/, *n.* any of the Eurypterida, a group of Palaeozoic arthropods resembling in some respects the horseshoe crabs. [NL *Eurypterida,* pl., from Gk *eury-* EURY- + Gk *pterón* wing + *-ida* (see -ID[2])]

**eurythmic** /ju'rɪðmɪk/, *adj.* →**eurhythmic.** – **eurythmics,** *n.* – **eurythmy,** *n.*

**eusol** /'jusɒl/, *n.* an antiseptic solution obtained from chlorinated lime and boric acid. [*E*(*dinburgh*) *U*(*niversity*) *S*(*olution*) *O*(*f*) *L*(*ime*)]

**eusporangiate** /,juspɔ'rændʒiət/, *adj.* (of a fern) having sporangia derived from a group of cells.

**Eustachian tube** /ju'steɪʃən tjub/, *n.* a canal extending from the middle ear to the pharynx; auditory canal. [*Eustachian,* from Bartolommeo *Eustachio* d. 1574, Italian anatomist, + -AN]

**eustatic movement** /ju,stætɪk 'muvmənt/, *n.* a world-wide change in sea-level due to an increase or decrease in the volume of water in the seas, which may be caused by the melting of icesheets; no movement of the land is involved. Also, **eustatic change.**

**eutaxy** /'jutæksi/, *n.* good or right order. [F *eutaxie,* from Gk *eutaxía* good arrangement]

**eutectic** /ju'tɛktɪk/, *adj. Chem.* **1.** of greatest fusibility (said of an alloy or mixture whose melting point is lower than that of any other alloy or mixture of the same ingredients). **2.** denoting or pertaining to such a mixture or its properties: *a eutectic melting point.* *–n.* **3.** a eutectic substance. [Gk *eútēktos* easily melted + -IC]

**eutectoid** /ju'tɛktɔɪd/, *adj.* **1.** resembling a eutectic. *–n.* **2.** eutectoid alloy. [EUTECT(IC) + -OID]

**euthanasia** /juθə'neɪʒə/, *n.* **1.** painless death. **2.** the putting of a person to death painlessly, esp. a person suffering from an incurable and painful disease. [NL, from Gk: an easy death]

**euthenics** /ju'θɛnɪks/, *n.* the science of bettering the environment or living conditions, esp. to improve the race. [Gk *euthēnía* plenty, well-being + -ICS]

**eutherian** /ju'θɪəriən/, *adj.* belonging to the most highly evolved group of mammals, in which the young are nourished before birth by means of a placenta. [NL *Eutheria,* from EU- + Gk *thería,* pl. of *thēríon* beast]

**euxenite** /'juksənaɪt/, *n.* a brownish black mineral of complex composition, containing yttrium, columbium, titanium, uranium, etc. [Gk *eúxenos* hospitable (in allusion to its many constituents) + -ITE[1]]

**eV,** electronvolt.

**evacuant** /ə'vækjuənt/, *adj.* **1.** evacuating; promoting evacuation, esp. from the bowels. *–n.* **2.** an evacuant medicine or agent.

**evacuate** /ə'vækjueɪt/, *v.,* **-ated, -ating.** *–v.t.* **1.** to leave empty; vacate. **2.** to move (persons or things) from a threatened place, disaster area, etc., to a place of greater safety. **3.** *Mil.* **a.** to remove (troops, wounded soldiers, inhabitants, etc.) from a place. **b.** to withdraw from or quit (a town, fort, etc., which has been occupied). **4.** *Physiol.* to discharge or eject as through the excretory passages, esp. from the bowels. **5.** *Phys. Chem.* to pump out, creating a vacuum; exhaust: *the apparatus was evacuated before being filled with oxygen.* *–v.i.* **6.** to leave a town because of air-raid threats, etc.: *they evacuated when the air raids began.* [L *ēvacuātus,* pp., emptied out] – **evacuator,** *n.*

**evacuation** /əvækju'eɪʃən/, *n.* **1.** the act or process of evacuating. **2.** the condition of being evacuated. **3.** a making empty of contents; expulsion, as of contents. **4.** *Physiol.* discharge, as of waste matter through the excretory passages, esp. from the bowels. **5.** that which is evacuated or discharged. **6.** the removal of persons or things from a disaster or danger area, etc., to a place of greater safety. **7.** *Mil.* **a.** clearance by removal of troops, etc. **b.** the withdrawal or removal of troops, wounded soldiers, inhabitants, etc. – **evacuative** /ə'vækjuətɪv/, *adj.*

**evacuee** /əvækju'i/, *n.* a person who is withdrawn or removed from a place of danger.

**evade** /ə'veɪd, i-/, *v.,* **evaded, evading.** *–v.t.* **1.** to escape from by trickery or cleverness: *evade pursuit.* **2.** to get round by trickery: *evade the law, the rules.* **3.** to avoid doing or fulfilling: *evade a duty, obligation, etc.* **4.** to avoid answering directly: *evade a question.* **5.** to baffle; elude: *a word that evades definition, the solution evaded him.* *–v.i.* **6.** to practise evasion. [L *ēvādere* pass over, go out] – **evadable, evadible,** *adj.* – **evader,** *n.* – **evadingly,** *adv.*

**evaginate** /əˈvædʒəneɪt, i-/, *v.t.,* **-nated, -nating.** to turn inside out, or cause to protrude by eversion, as a tubular organ. [L *ēvāgīnātus,* pp., unsheathed] – **evagination** /əvædʒəˈneɪʃən, i-/, *n.*

**evaluate** /əˈvæljueɪt, i-/, *v.t.,* **-ated, -ating. 1.** to ascertain the value or amount of; appraise carefully. **2.** *Maths.* to ascertain the numerical value of. [F *évaluer* (from OF *value,* pp. of *valoir* be worth, from L *valēre*) + -ATE[1]] – **evaluation** /əvæljuˈeɪʃən, i-/, *n.*

**evanesce** /ɛvəˈnɛs/, *v.i.,* **-nesced, -nescing.** to disappear gradually; vanish; fade away. [L *ēvānescere*] – **evanescence,** *n.*

**evanescent** /ɛvəˈnɛsənt/, *adj.* **1.** vanishing; passing away; fleeting. **2.** tending to become imperceptible; scarcely perceptible. – **evanescently,** *adv.*

**evangel**[1] /əˈvændʒəl, i-/, *n.* **1.** the good tidings of the redemption of the world through Jesus Christ; the gospel. **2.** (*usu. cap.*) any of the four Gospels. **3.** doctrine taken as a guide or regarded as of prime importance. [LL *ēvangelium,* from Gk *euangélion* good tidings; replacing ME *evangile,* from OF]

**evangel**[2] /əˈvændʒəl, i-/, *n.* an evangelist. [Gk *euángelos* good messenger]

**evangelical** /ivænˈdʒɛləkəl/, *adj.* **1.** pertaining to the gospel and its teachings. **2.** related to those Christian bodies which emphasise the teachings and authority of the Scriptures, in opposition to that of the church itself or of reason. **3.** pertaining to certain movements in the 18th and 19th centuries which stressed the importance of personal experience of guilt for sin, and of reconciliation to God through Christ. **4.** evangelistic. *–n.* **5.** an adherent of evangelical doctrines or a member of an evangelical church or party, esp. of the Low Church party in the Church of England. – **evangelically,** *adv.*

**evangelicalism** /ivænˈdʒɛləkəlɪzəm/, *n.* **1.** evangelical doctrines or principles. **2.** adherence to them, or to an evangelical church or party.

**evangelise** /əˈvændʒɛlaɪz, i-/, *v.,* **-lised, -lising.** *–v.t.* **1.** to preach the gospel to. **2.** to convert to Christianity. *–v.i.* **3.** to preach the gospel; act as an evangelist. Also, **evangelize.** – **evangelisation** /əvændʒəlaɪˈzeɪʃən, i-/, *n.* – **evangeliser,** *n.*

**evangelism** /əˈvændʒəlɪzəm, i-/, *n.* **1.** the preaching or promulgation of the gospel; the work of an evangelist. **2.** →**evangelicalism.**

**evangelist** /əˈvændʒələst, i-/, *n.* **1.** a preacher of the gospel. **2.** (*cap.*) any of the writers (Matthew, Mark, Luke, and John) of the four Gospels. **3.** one of a class of teachers in the early church, next in rank after apostles and prophets. **4.** a revivalist. **5.** an occasional or itinerant preacher. **6.** (*cap.*) *Mormon Ch.* a patriarch.

**evangelistic** /əvændʒəˈlɪstɪk, i-/, *adj.* **1.** pertaining to evangelists, or preachers of the gospel. **2.** evangelical. **3.** seeking to evangelise; striving to convert sinners. **4.** designed or fitted to evangelise. **5.** (*oft. cap.*) of or pertaining to the four Evangelists. – **evangelistically,** *adv.*

**evanish** /əˈvænɪʃ, i-/, *v.i. Archaic.* **1.** to vanish or disappear. **2.** to cease to be. – **evanishment,** *n.*

**evaporable** /əˈvæpərəbəl, i-/, *adj.* capable of being converted to gas by evaporation. – **evaporability** /əvæpərəˈbɪləti, i-/, *n.*

**evaporate** /əˈvæpəreɪt, i-/, *v.,* **-rated, -rating.** *–v.i.* **1.** to turn to vapour; pass off in vapour. **2.** to give off moisture. **3.** to disappear; vanish; fade: *as soon as his situation became clear to him, his hopes quickly evaporated.* *–v.t.* **4.** to convert into a gaseous state or vapour; drive off or extract in the form of vapour. **5.** to extract moisture or liquid from, as by heat, so as to make dry or to reduce to a denser state: *to evaporate fruit.* **6.** to cause to fade or disappear. [LL *ēvapōrātus,* pp., dispersed in vapour] – **evaporator,** *n.*

**evaporated milk** /əˌvæpəreɪtəd ˈmɪlk/, *n.* thick, unsweetened, tinned milk made by removing some of the water from whole milk.

**evaporation** /əvæpəˈreɪʃən, i-/, *n.* **1.** the act or process of evaporating. **2.** the state of being evaporated. **3.** matter, or the quantity of matter, evaporated or passed off in vapour. – **evaporative** /əˈvæpərətɪv, i-/, *adj.*

**evasion** /əˈveɪʒən, i-/, *n.* **1.** the act of escaping something by trickery or cleverness: *evasion of one's duty, responsibilities, etc.* **2.** the avoiding of an argument, accusation, question, or the like, as by a subterfuge. **3.** a means of evading; a subterfuge; an excuse or trick to avoid or get round something. **4.** tax evasion. [late ME, from LL *ēvāsio*]

**evasive** /əˈveɪsɪv, i-/, *adj.* **1.** tending or seeking to evade; characterised by evasion: *an evasive answer.* **2.** elusive or evanescent. – **evasively,** *adv.* – **evasiveness,** *n.*

**eve** /iv/, *n.* **1.** the evening, or often the day, before a church festival, and hence before any date or event. **2.** the period just preceding any event, etc.: *the eve of a revolution.* **3.** *Archaic.* the evening. [var. of EVEN[2]]

**evection** /əˈvɛkʃən, i-/, *n.* a periodic inequality in the moon's motion caused by the attraction of the sun. [L *ēvectio,* from *ēvehere* carry forth or up] – **evectional,** *adj.*

**even**[1] /ˈivən/, *adj.* **1.** level; flat; without irregularities; smooth: *an even surface, even country.* **2.** on the same level; in the same plane or line; parallel: *even with the ground.* **3.** free from variations or fluctuations; regular: *even motion.* **4.** uniform in action, character, or quality: *an even colour, to hold an even course.* **5.** equal in measure or quantity: *even quantities of two substances.* **6.** same: *letters of even date.* **7.** divisible by 2, thus, 2, 4, 6, 8, 10, and 12 are *even* numbers (opposed to *odd,* as 1, 3, etc.). **8.** denoted by such a number: *the even pages of a book.* **9.** exactly expressible in integers, or in tens, hundreds, etc., without fractional parts: *an even kilometre, an even hundred.* **10.** exactly balanced on each side; equally divided. **11.** leaving no balance of debt on either side, as accounts; square, as one person with another. **12.** calm; placid; not easily excited or angered: *an even temper.* **13.** equitable, impartial, or fair: *an even bargain, an even chance.* *–adv.* **14.** evenly. **15.** still; yet (used to emphasise a comparative): *even more suitable.* **16.** (used to suggest that something mentioned as a possibility constitutes an extreme case, or one that might not be expected): *the slightest noise, even, disturbs him: even if he goes, he may not take part.* **17.** just: *even now.* **18.** fully or quite: *even to death.* **19.** indeed (used as an intensive for stressing identity or truth of something): *he is willing, even eager, to do it.* **20.** *Archaic.* exactly or precisely: *it was even so.* **21. break even,** to have one's credits or profits equal one's debits or losses. **22. get even,** to get one's revenge; square accounts. *–v.t.* **23.** to make even; level; smooth. **24.** to place in an even state as to claim or obligation; balance: *to even, or even up, accounts.* *–v.i.* **25.** to become even (fol. by *out* or *off*). [ME; OE *efen,* c. G *eben*] – **evener,** *n.* – **evenness,** *n.* – **evenly,** *adv.*

**even**[2] /ˈivən/, *n. Archaic.* evening; eve. [ME; OE *ēfen, ǣfen;* akin to G *Abend*]

**evenfall** /ˈivənfɔl/, *n. Archaic.* the beginning of evening.

**even-handed** /ˈivən-hændəd/, *adj.* impartial; equitable: *even-handed justice.* – **even-handedness,** *n.*

**evening** /ˈivnɪŋ/, *n.* **1.** the latter part of the day and the early part of the night. **2.** the period from sunset to bedtime. **3.** any concluding or declining period: *the evening of life.* **4.** an evening's reception or entertainment. **5.** *Qld.* the period of the day after midday. *–adj.* **6.** of or pertaining to evening. **7.** occurring or seen in the evening. [ME; OE *ǣfnung,* from *ǣfnian* draw towards evening]

**evening college** /ˈ– ˌkɒlɪdʒ/, *n.* a place, usu. a school, where classes are held outside normal working hours in a wide variety of subjects to provide further education, esp. for adults in the community.

**evening dress** /ˈ– drɛs/, *n.* formal evening clothes.

**evening gown** /ˈ– gaʊn/, *n.* a woman's formal or semi-formal dress, esp. one with a floor-length skirt.

**evening primrose** /– ˈprɪmroʊz/, *n.* **1.** a plant, *Oenothera biennis,* family Onagraceae, with yellow flowers that open at nightfall. **2.** any of various plants of the same or related genera, displaying similar behaviour.

**evenings** /ˈivnɪŋz/, *adv. Colloq.* during or in the evening regularly.

**evening star** /ivnɪŋ ˈsta/, *n.* a bright planet seen in the west after sunset, esp. Venus.

**evening suit** /ˈ– sut/, *n.* →**dress suit.**

**even-minded** /ˈivən-maɪndəd/, *adj.* not easily ruffled, disturbed, prejudiced, etc.; calm; equable. – **even-mindedness,** *n.*

**even money** /ivən ˈmʌni/, *n.* **1.** an equal sum bet by each backer. **2.** paying out as winnings (of a bet) the same amount as staked.

**evens** /ˈivənz/, *adv.* **1.** (of a bet staked) evenly; with even money. **2. be evens,** to be on a par; be equal. *–n.* **3.** (*usu. construed as sing.*) →**even money.**

**Evensong** /ˈivənsɒŋ/, *n.* **1.** *C. of E.* a form of worship appointed to be said or sung at evening; Evening Prayer. **2.** *Rom. Cath. Ch.* →**vespers. 3.** *Archaic.* evening. [ME; OE *ǣfensang,* from *ǣfen* evening + *sang* song]

**event** /əˈvɛnt, i-/, *n.* **1.** anything that happens or is regarded as happening; an occurrence, esp. one of some importance. **2.** the fact of happening (chiefly in the phrase *in the event of*). **3.** the outcome, issue, or result of anything (chiefly in the phrase *after the event*). **4.** *Philos.* something which occurs in a certain place during a particular interval of time. **5.** *Sport.* each of the items in a program of one sport or a number of sports. **6. at all events** or **in any event,** whatever happens; in any case. [L *ēventus* occurrence, issue] **–eventless,** *adj.*

**even-tempered** /ˈivən-tɛmpəd/, *adj.* not easily ruffled or disturbed; calm.

**eventful** /əˈvɛntfəl, i-/, *adj.* **1.** full of events or incidents, esp. of a striking character: *an eventful period.* **2.** having important issues or results; momentous. **–eventfully,** *adv.* **–eventfulness,** *n.*

**eventide** /ˈivəntaɪd/, *n. Archaic.* evening.

**eventu-,** a word element meaning 'event'. [combining form representing L *ēventus*]

**eventual** /əˈvɛntʃəl, -tʃuəl/, *adj.* **1.** pertaining to the event or issue; consequent; ultimate. **2.** depending upon uncertain events; contingent.

**eventuality** /əvɛntʃuˈæləti/, *n., pl.* **-ties. 1.** a contingent event; a possible occurrence or circumstance. **2.** the state or fact of being eventual; contingent character.

**eventually** /əˈvɛntʃəli, -tʃuəli/, *adv.* finally; ultimately.

**eventuate** /əˈvɛntʃueɪt/, *v.i.,* **-ated, -ating. 1.** to have issue; result. **2.** to come about. **–eventuation** /əvɛntʃuˈeɪʃən/, *n.*

**ever** /ˈɛvə/, *adv.* **1.** at all times: *he is ever ready to excuse himself.* **2.** continuously: *ever since then.* **3.** at any time: *did you ever see anything like it?* **4.** (with emphatic force, in various idiomatic constructions and phrases) in any possible case; by any chance; at all: *how ever did you manage to do it?* **5. ever and again** or **ever and anon,** every now and then; continually. **6. ever so,** to whatever extent or degree; greatly; exceedingly: *ever so long, be he ever so bold.* **7. for ever,** for eternity; eternally; always; continually. **8. for ever and a day,** for ever; eternally. [ME; OE *ǣfre,* probably akin to *ā* ever. See AY[2]]

**everglade** /ˈɛvəgleɪd/, *n. U.S.* a tract of low, swampy land characterised by clumps of tall grass and numerous branching waterways.

**evergreen** /ˈɛvəgrin/, *adj.* **1.** (of trees, shrubs, etc.) having living leaves throughout the entire year, the leaves of the past season not being shed until after the new foliage has been completely formed. **2.** (of leaves) belonging to such a plant. **3. a.** retaining youthful characteristics in maturity: *an evergreen tennis player.* **b.** retaining popularity from an earlier period: *an evergreen play.* *–n.* **4.** an evergreen plant. **5. a.** one who retains the vigour or prowess of his youth. **b.** that which retains its popularity from an earlier period. **6.** (*pl.*) *Chiefly U.S.* twigs or branches from evergreen plants used for decoration.

**everlasting** /ˈɛvəlastɪŋ/, *adj.* **1.** lasting for ever; eternal. **2.** lasting or continuing indefinitely. **3.** incessant; constantly recurring. **4.** wearisome: *to tire of someone's everlasting puns.* *–n.* **5.** eternal duration; eternity. **6. the Everlasting,** the Eternal Being; God. **7.** Also, **everlasting flower,** any of various plants or flowers which retain their shape, colour, etc., when dried, as certain species of the genera *Helichrysum* and *Helipterum.* **–everlastingly,** *adv.* **–everlastingness,** *n.*

**evermore** /ɛvəˈmɔ/, *adv.* **1.** always, for ever; eternally (oft. prec. by *for*). **2.** at all times; continually.

**eversible** /iˈvɜsəbəl/, *adj.* capable of being everted.

**eversion** /iˈvɜʒən/, *n.* a turning or being turned outwards, or inside out.

**evert** /iˈvɜt/, *v.t.* to turn outwards, or inside out. [L *ēvertere* overturn]

**every** /ˈɛvri/, *adj.* **1.** each (referring one by one to all the members of an aggregate): *we go there every day, be sure to remember every word he says.* **2.** all possible; the greatest possible degree of: *every prospect of success.* **3. every bit,** *Colloq.* in every respect; in all points: *every bit as good.* **4. every man and his dog,** a lot of people; the general public. **5. every now and then** or **every now and again** or **every once in a while,** occasionally; from time to time. **6. every other,** every second; every alternate. **7. every which way,** in all directions. [ME *every, everich,* etc., OE *ǣfre ǣlc* EVER EACH]

**everybody** /ˈɛvribɒdi/, *pron.* **1.** every person. **2. everybody who is anybody,** *Colloq.* everyone important.

**everyday** /ˈɛvrideɪ/, *adj.* **1.** of or pertaining to every day; daily: *an everyday occurrence.* **2.** of or for ordinary days, as contrasted with Sundays or special occasions: *everyday clothes.* **3.** such as is met with every day; ordinary; commonplace: *an everyday scene.*

**everyman** /ˈɛvrimæn/, *n.* **1.** a common or ordinary man as representative of mankind. *–pron.* **2.** everybody; every person. [from *Everyman,* a 15th-cent. English morality play]

**everyone** /ˈɛvriwʌn/, *pron.* every person; everybody. Also, **every one.**

**everything** /ˈɛvriθɪŋ/, *pron.* **1.** every thing or particular of an aggregate or total; all. **2.** something extremely important: *this news means everything to us.*

**everyway** /ˈɛvriweɪ/, *adv.* in every way; in every direction, manner, or respect.

**everywhere** /ˈɛvriwɛə/, *adv.* in every place or part; in all places.

**evict** /əˈvɪkt, i-/, *v.t.* **1.** to expel (a person, esp. a tenant) from land, a building, etc., by legal process. **2.** to recover (property, etc.) by virtue of superior legal title. [L *ēvictus,* pp., overcome completely, (property) recovered by judicial decision] **–eviction,** *n.* **–evictor,** *n.*

**evidence** /ˈɛvədəns/, *n., v.,* **-denced, -dencing.** *–n.* **1.** ground for belief; that which tends to prove or disprove something; proof. **2.** something that makes evident; an indication or sign. **3.** *Law.* the data, in the form of testimony of witnesses, or of documents or other objects (such as a photograph, a revolver, etc.) identified by witnesses, offered to the court or jury in proof of the facts at issue. **4. in evidence,** in a situation to be readily seen; plainly visible; conspicuous. **5. turn queen's, king's,** or **state's evidence,** (of an accomplice in a crime) to become a witness for the prosecution against the others involved. *–v.t.* **6.** to make evident or clear; show clearly; manifest. **7.** to support by evidence.

**evident** /ˈɛvədənt/, *adj.* plain or clear to the sight or understanding: *an evident mistake.* [L *ēvidens*]

**evidential** /ɛvəˈdɛnʃəl/, *adj.* of or having the nature of, serving as, or based on evidence. **–evidentially,** *adv.*

**evidentiary** /ɛvəˈdɛnʃəri/, *adj.* **1.** of or pertaining to evidence. **2.** furnishing or constituting evidence.

**evidently** /ˈɛvədəntli/, *adv.* obviously; apparently.

**evil** /ˈivəl/, *adj.* **1.** violating or inconsistent with the moral law; wicked: *evil deeds, an evil life.* **2.** harmful; injurious: *evil laws.* **3.** characterised or accompanied by misfortune or suffering; unfortunate; disastrous: *to be fallen on evil days.* **4.** due to (actual or imputed) bad character or conduct: *an evil reputation.* **5.** characterised by anger, irascibility, etc. **6. the evil one,** the devil; Satan. *–n.* **7.** that which is evil; evil quality, intention, or conduct: *to choose the lesser of two evils.* **8.** (*sometimes cap.*) the force which governs and brings about wickedness and sin. **9.** that part of someone or something that is wicked. **10.** harm; mischief; misfortune: *to wish one evil.* **11.** anything causing injury or harm. **12.** a disease: *king's evil* (scrofula). *–adv.* **13.** in an evil manner; badly; ill: *it went evil with his house.* [ME; OE *yfel,* c. G *übel*] **–evilly,** *adv.* **–evilness,** *n.*

**evildoer** /ˈivəlduə/, *n.* one who does evil. **–evildoing,** *adj., n.*

**evil eye** /ivəl ˈaɪ/, *n.* the power superstitiously attributed to certain persons of inflicting injury or bad luck by a look. **–evil-eyed,** *adj.*

**evil-minded** /ˈivəl-maɪndəd/, *adj.* **1.** having an evil mind; malignant. **2.** *Colloq.* (*joc.*) excessively preoccupied with sex.

**evince** /əˈvɪns, i-/, *v.t.,* **evinced, evincing. 1.** to show clearly; make evident or manifest; prove. **2.** to reveal the possession of (a quality, trait, etc.). [L *ēvincere* overcome completely, prove, demonstrate] – **evincible,** *adj.*

**evincive** /ə'vɪnsɪv, i-/, *adj.* serving to evince; indicative.

**eviscerate** /ə'vɪsəreɪt, i-/, *v.*, **-rated, -rating,** *adj.* *–v.t.* **1.** to disembowel. **2.** to deprive of vital or essential parts. *–adj.* **3.** *Surg.* disembowelled. [L *ēviscerātus,* pp., disembowelled] – **evisceration** /əvɪsə'reɪʃən, i-/, *n.*

**evitable** /'ɛvətəbəl/, *adj.* avoidable. [L *ēvitābilis* avoidable]

**evocable** /'ɛvəkəbəl/, *adj.* that may be evoked.

**evocate** /'ɛvəkeɪt, 'ivə-/, *v.t.*, **-cated, -cating.** to call up, as from the dead.

**evocation** /ɛvə'keɪʃən, 'ivə-/, *n.* the act of evoking; a calling forth. [L *ēvocātio,* from *ēvocāre* call forth]

**evocative** /ə'vɒkətɪv/, *adj.* tending to evoke.

**evocator** /'ɛvəkeɪtə, 'ivə-/, *n.* **1.** *Embryol.* a morphogenic substance, or a piece of tissue, generally not living, which contains morphogenic substances. **2.** one who evokes, esp. one who calls up spirits.

**evoke** /ə'voʊk, i-/, *v.t.*, **evoked, evoking.** **1.** to call up, or produce (memories, feelings, etc.): *to evoke a memory, a smile, etc.* **2.** to provoke, or elicit. **3.** to call up; cause to appear; summon: *to evoke a spirit from the dead.* [L *ēvocāre* call forth] – **evoker,** *n.*

**evoked response audiometry,** *n.* the monitoring by means of electrodes, etc., of the response in the auditory nervous system made to an auditory stimulus in the ear canal.

**evolute** /'ivəlut, 'ɛvə-/, *n. Geom.* the locus of the centres of curvature of, or the envelope of the normals to, another curve (called the *involute*). [L *ēvolūtus,* pp., rolled out]

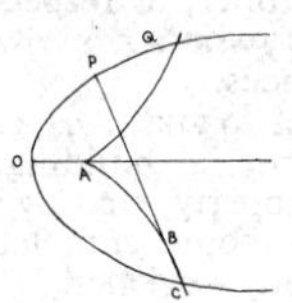

ABC, evolute of parabolic arc OPQ

**evolution** /ɛvə'luʃən, ivə-/, *n.* **1.** any process of formation or growth; development: *the evolution of man, the drama, the aeroplane, etc.* **2.** something evolved; a product. **3.** *Biol.* the continuous genetic adaptation of organisms or species to the environment by the integrating agencies of selection, hybridisation, inbreeding, and mutation. **4.** a motion incomplete in itself, but combining with coordinated motions to produce a single action, as in a machine. **5.** an evolving or giving off of gas, heat, etc. **6.** *Maths.* the extraction of roots from powers (the inverse of *involution*). [L *ēvolūtio,* from *ēvolvere* roll out] – **evolutional,** *adj.* – **evolutionally,** *adv.*

**evolutionary** /ɛvə'luʃənri, ivə-, -nəri/, *adj.* **1.** pertaining to evolution or development; developmental: *the evolutionary origin of species.* **2.** in accordance with the theory of evolution. **3.** pertaining to or performing evolutions.

**evolutionist** /ɛvə'luʃənəst, ivə-/, *n.* a believer in the theory of evolution.

**evolutionistic** /ɛvə,luʃə'nɪstɪk, ivə-/, *adj.* **1.** tending to support the theory of evolution. **2.** tending to cause evolution.

**evolve** /ə'vɒlv, i-/, *v.*, **evolved, evolving.** *–v.t.* **1.** to develop gradually: *to evolve a scheme, a plan, a theory, etc.* **2.** *Biol.* to develop, as by a process of differentiation, to a more highly organised condition. **3.** to give off or emit, as smells, vapours, etc. *–v.i.* **4.** to come forth gradually into being; develop; undergo evolution. [L *ēvolvere* roll out, unroll, unfold] – **evolvable,** *adj.* – **evolvement,** *n.* – **evolver,** *n.*

**evonymus** /ə'vɒnəməs/, *n.* →**euonymus.**

**evulsion** /i'vʌlʃən/, *n.* **1.** the act of plucking or pulling out; forcible extraction. **2.** the forcible tearing away of a part. [L *ēvulsio,* from *ēvellere* pluck out]

**ewe** /ju/, *n.* a female sheep. [ME and OE, c. D *ooi;* akin to L *ovis,* Gk *óis,* Skt *avi* sheep]

**Ewe** /'iwi/, *n.* **1.** a language of West Africa, spoken in parts of Togo and Ghana. **2.** the people speaking this language.

**ewe-neck** /'ju-nɛk/, *n.* a thin hollow neck, low in front of the shoulder, as of a horse or other animal. – **ewe-necked,** *adj.*

**ewer** /'juə/, *n.* **1.** a pitcher with a wide spout, esp. one to hold water for ablutions. **2.** a decorative vessel having a spout and handle, esp. a tall, slender vessel with a base. [ME, from AF, from L *aquāria* vessel for water]

ewer and basin

**ex**[1] /ɛks/, *prep.* **1.** *Finance.* without, not including, or without the right to have: *ex dividend, ex interest, ex rights.* **2.** *Comm.* out of; free out of: *ex warehouse, ex ship, etc.* (free of charges until the time of removal out of the warehouse, ship, etc.). *–n.* **3.** *Colloq.* one's former husband or wife. **4.** *Colloq.* one's former boy friend or girl friend. [L. See EX-[1]]

**ex**[2] /ɛks/, *n.* the letter X, x.

**ex-**[1], a prefix meaning 'out of', 'from', and hence 'utterly', 'thoroughly', and sometimes serving to impart a privative or negative force or to indicate a former title, status, etc.; freely used as an English formative, as in *exstipulate, exterritorial,* and esp. in such combinations as *ex-president* (former president), *ex-member, ex-wife;* occurring before vowels and *c, p, q, s, t.* Also, **e-, ef-.** [L, combining form of *ex, ē,* prep., out of, from, beyond]

**ex-**[2], variant of **exo-.**

**ex-**[3], a prefix identical in meaning with **ex-**[1], occurring before vowels in words of Greek origin, as in *exarch, exegis.* Also, **ec-.** [Gk, also before consonants *ek-* EC-; becoming *ec-* in L derivatives]

**ex.,** **1.** examination. **2.** examined. **3.** example. **4.** except. **5.** exception. **6.** exchange. **7.** excursion. **8.** executed. **9.** executive.

**Ex.,** *Bible.* Exodus.

**exa-** /'ɛksə-/, a prefix denoting $10^{18}$ of a given unit, as in *exahertz. Symbol:* E

**exacerbate** /ɛk'sæsəbeɪt/, *v.t.*, **-bated, -bating.** **1.** to increase the bitterness or violence of (disease, ill feeling, etc.); aggravate. **2.** to embitter the feelings of (a person); irritate; exasperate. [L *exacerbātus,* pp., irritated]

**exacerbation** /ɛk,sæsə'beɪʃən/, *n.* **1.** the action of exacerbating; the condition of being exacerbated. **2.** *Med.* a paroxysmal increase in severity.

**exact** /əg'zækt, ɛg-/, *adj.* **1.** strictly accurate or correct: *an exact likeness, description, or translation.* **2.** precise, as opposed to approximate: *the exact sum due, the exact date.* **3.** admitting of no deviation, as laws, discipline, etc.; strict or rigorous. **4.** characterised by or using strict accuracy or precision: *exact instruments, an exact thinker.* *–v.t.* **5.** to call for, demand, or require: *to exact obedience, respect.* **6.** to force or compel the payment, yielding, or performance of: *to exact money, tribute, etc.* [L *exactus,* pp., forced out, required, measured by a standard] – **exactable,** *adj.* – **exacter, exactor,** *n.* – **exactness,** *n.*

**exacting** /əg'zæktɪŋ, ɛg-/, *adj.* **1.** severe or rigid in demands or requirements, as a person. **2.** requiring close application, as a task. **3.** given to or characterised by exaction; extortionate. – **exactingly,** *adv.* – **exactingness,** *n.*

**exaction** /əg'zækʃən, ɛg-/, *n.* **1.** the act of exacting; extortion. **2.** something exacted.

**exactitude** /əg'zæktətjud, ɛg-/, *n.* the quality of being exact; exactness; preciseness; accuracy.

**exactly** /əg'zæktli, ɛg-/, *adv.* **1.** in an exact manner; precisely, according to rule, measure, fact, etc., accurately. **2.** just: *she does exactly as she likes.* **3.** quite so; that's right.

**exact science** /əgzækt 'saɪəns, ɛg-/, *n.* a science (such as mathematics) which permits of accurate analysis.

**exaggerate** /əg'zædʒəreɪt, ɛg-/, *v.*, **-rated, -rating.** *–v.t.* **1.** to magnify beyond the limits of truth; overstate; represent disproportionately: *to exaggerate one's importance, the difficulties of a situation, the size of one's house, etc.* **2.** to increase or enlarge abnormally. *–v.i.* **3.** to employ exaggeration, as in speech or writing: *a person who is always exaggerating.* [L *exaggerātus,* pp., heaped up] – **exaggeratingly,** *adv.* – **exaggerator,** *n.*

**exaggerated** /əg'zædʒəreɪtəd, ɛg-/, *adj.* **1.** unduly magnified: *to have an exaggerated opinion of oneself.* **2.** abnormally increased or enlarged: *a heart greatly exaggerated by disease.* – **exaggeratedly,** *adv.*

**exaggerated stereo** /– 'stɛrioʊ/, *n.* →**hyperstereoscopy.**

**exaggeration** /əgzædʒə'reɪʃən, ɛg-/, *n.* **1.** the act of exaggerating. **2.** the state of being exaggerated. **3.** an exaggerated statement.

**exaggerative** /əg'zædʒərətɪv, ɛg-/, *adj.* given to or characterised by exaggeration. Also, **exaggeratory** /-reɪtəri, ɛg-/.

**exalt** /əg'zɔlt, ɛg-/, *v.t.* **1.** to elevate in rank, honour, power, character, quality, etc.: *exalted to the position of president.* **2.** to praise; extol: *to exalt someone to the skies.* **3.** *Obs.* to elate, as with pride or joy. **4.** to stimulate, as the imagination. **5.** to intensify, as a colour. **6.** *Archaic.* to raise up. [L *exaltāre* lift up] – **exalter,** *n.*

**exaltation** /ˌɛgzɔl'teɪʃən/, *n.* **1.** the act of exalting. **2.** the state of being exalted. **3.** elation of mind, or feeling, sometimes abnormal or morbid in character; rapture. **4.** *Astrol.* the position of a planet in the zodiac in which it is considered to exert its greatest influence.

**exalted** /əg'zɔltəd, ɛg-/, *adj.* **1.** elevated, as in rank or character; of high station: *an exalted personage.* **2.** noble or elevated, lofty: *an exalted style.* **3.** rapturously excited. – **exaltedly,** *adv.* – **exaltedness,** *n.*

**exam** /əg'zæm, ɛg-/, *n.* an examination.

**exam.,** **1.** examination. **2.** examined. **3.** examinee. **4.** examiner.

**examen** /əg'zeɪmən, ɛg-/, *n. Eccles.* an examination, as of conscience. [L: a weighing, consideration]

**examinant** /əg'zæmənənt, ɛg-/, *n.* an examiner.

**examination** /əgzæmə'neɪʃən, ɛg-/, *n.* **1.** the act of examining; inspection; inquiry; investigation. **2.** the state of being examined. **3.** the act or process of testing pupils, candidates, etc., as by questions. **4.** the test itself; list of questions asked. **5.** the statements, etc., made by one examined. **6.** *Law.* formal interrogation. [L *exāminātio*] – **examinational,** *adj.*

**examine** /əg'zæmən, ɛg-/, *v.t.,* **-ined, -ining.** **1.** to inspect or scrutinise carefully; inquire into or investigate. **2.** to test the knowledge, reactions, or qualifications of (a pupil, candidate, etc.), as by questions or assigned tasks. **3.** to subject to legal inquisition; put to question in regard to conduct or to knowledge of facts; interrogate: *to examine a witness or a suspected person.* [ME *examine(n),* from F *examiner,* from L *exāmināre* weigh accurately, test] – **examinable,** *adj.* – **examiner,** *n.*

**examinee** /əgzæmə'ni, ɛg-/, *n.* one who is examined.

**example** /əg'zæmpəl, ɛg-/, *n., v.,* **-pled, -pling.** *–n.* **1.** one of a number of things, or a part of something, taken to show the character of the whole. **2.** something to be imitated; a pattern or model: *to set a good example.* **3.** an instance serving for illustration; a specimen. **4.** an instance illustrating a rule or method, as a mathematical problem proposed for solution. **5.** an instance, esp. of punishment, serving for a warning; a warning. **6.** a precedent; a parallel case: *an action without example.* *–v.t.* **7.** to give or be an example of (chiefly in pp.). [ME, from OF *essample,* from L *exempla,* pl. of *exemplum*]

**exanimate** /əg'zænəmət, -meɪt, ɛg-/, *adj.* **1.** inanimate or lifeless. **2.** spiritless; disheartened. [L *exanimātus,* pp., deprived of breath, life, or spirit] – **exanimation** /əgzænə'meɪʃən, ɛg-/, *n.*

**exanthema** /ɛksæn'θimə/, *n., pl.* **-themata** /-'θimətə/. **1.** *Pathol.* an eruption or rash on the skin, esp. one attended with fever. **2.** See **vesicular exanthema.** [LL, from Gk: a bursting into flower] – **exanthematic** /ɛksænθə'mætɪk/, **exanthematous** /ɛksæn'θimətəs/, *adj.*

**exarch**[1] /'ɛksak/, *n.* **1.** (in the Eastern Church) **a.** a patriarch's deputy. **b.** (formerly) a bishop ranking below a patriarch and above a metropolitan. **2.** the ruler of a province in the Byzantine Empire. [LL *exarchus,* from Gk *éxarchos* leader]

**exarch**[2] /'ɛksak/, *adj.* denoting or pertaining to a strand or cylinder of primary xylem in a stem or root with the protoxylem on its outer edge. [EX-[2] + Gk *archē* beginning]

**exarchate** /'ɛksakeɪt, ɛk'sakeɪt/, *n.* the office, jurisdiction, or province of an exarch.

**exasperate** /əg'zæspəreɪt, ɛg-/, *v.t.,* **-rated, -rating.** to irritate to a high degree; annoy extremely; infuriate. [L *exasperātus,* pp., roughened] – **exasperatedly,** *adv.* – **exasperatingly,** *adv.* – **exasperator,** *n.*

**exasperation** /əgzæspə'reɪʃən, ɛg-/, *n.* **1.** the act of exasperating; provocation. **2.** the state of being exasperated; irritation; extreme annoyance.

**exc.,** **1.** except. **2.** exception. **3.** excursion.

**ex cathedra** /ɛks kə'θidrə/, *adv.* from the seat of authority; with authority, used esp. of those pronouncements of the pope which are considered infallible. [L: from the chair] – **ex-cathedra,** *adj.*

**excaudate** /ɛks'kɔdeɪt/, *adj.* (of animals) tailless. [EX-[1] + CAUDATE]

**excavate** /'ɛkskəveɪt/, *v.t.,* **-vated, -vating.** **1.** to make hollow by removing the inner part; make a hole or cavity in; form into a hollow, as by digging. **2.** to make (a hole, tunnel, etc.) by removing material. **3.** to dig or scoop out (earth, etc.). **4.** to expose or lay bare by digging; unearth: *to excavate an ancient city.* [L *excavātus,* pp., hollowed out]

**excavation** /ɛkskə'veɪʃən/, *n.* **1.** the act of excavating. **2.** a hole or cavity made by excavating. **3.** the site of archaeological investigation by digging.

**excavator** /'ɛkskəveɪtə/, *n.* **1.** one who or that which excavates. **2.** a power-driven machine for digging, moving, or transporting loose gravel, sand, or soil.

**exceed** /ək'sid, ɛk-/, *v.t.* **1.** to go beyond the bounds or limits of: *to exceed one's powers.* **2.** to go beyond in quantity, degree, rate, etc.: *to exceed the speed limit.* **3.** to surpass; be superior to; excel. *–v.i.* **4.** to be greater, as in quantity or degree. **5.** to surpass others, excel, or be superior. [ME *excede(n),* from F *excéder,* from L *excēdere* go out] – **exceeder,** *n.*

**exceeding** /ək'sidɪŋ, ɛk-/, *adj.* **1.** extraordinary; excessive. *–adv.* **2.** *Archaic.* exceedingly.

**exceedingly** /ək'sidɪŋli, ɛk-/, *adv.* to an unusual degree; extremely.

**excel** /ək'sɛl, ɛk-/, *v.,* **-celled, -celling.** *–v.t.* **1.** to surpass; be superior to; outdo. *–v.i.* **2.** to surpass others or be superior in some respect. [L *excellere*]

**excellence** /'ɛksələns/, *n.* **1.** the fact or state of excelling; superiority; eminence. **2.** an excellent quality or feature. **3.** (*usu. cap.*) →**excellency** (def. 1).

**excellency** /'ɛksələnsi/, *n., pl.* **-cies.** **1.** (*usu. cap.*) a title of honour given to certain high officials, as governors and ambassadors. **2.** (*usu. cap.*) a person so entitled. **3.** excellence. [L *excellentia*]

**excellent** /'ɛksələnt/, *adj.* **1.** possessing excellence or superior merit; remarkably good. **2.** *Obs.* extraordinary; superior. [ME, from L *excellens,* ppr.] – **excellently,** *adv.*

**except**[1] /ək'sɛpt, ɛk-/, *prep.* **1.** with the exclusion of; excluding; save; but: *they were all there except me.* *–conj.* **2.** with the exception (that): *parallel cases except that A is younger than B.* **3.** otherwise than; but (fol. by an adv., phrase, or clause): *well fortified except here.* **4.** *Archaic.* unless. [L *exceptus,* pp., taken out]

**except**[2] /ək'sɛpt, ɛk-/, *v.t.* **1.** to exclude; leave out: *present company excepted.* *–v.i.* **2.** to object: *to except against a statement, a witness, etc.* [ME *excepte(n),* from F *excepter,* from L *exceptus,* pp.]

**excepting** /ək'sɛptɪŋ, ɛk-/, *prep.* **1.** excluding; barring; saving; except. *–conj.* **2.** *Archaic.* except; unless; save.

**exception** /ək'sɛpʃən, ɛk-/, *n.* **1.** the act of excepting. **2.** the fact of being excepted. **3.** something excepted; an instance or case not conforming to the general rule. **4.** an adverse criticism, esp. on a particular point; opposition of opinion; objection; demurral: *a statement liable to exception.* **5. take exception, a.** to make objection; demur with respect to something (usu. fol. by *to*). **b.** to take offence (oft. fol. by *at*). [L *exceptio*]

**exceptionable** /ək'sɛpʃənəbəl, ɛk-/, *adj.* liable to exception or objection; objectionable. – **exceptionableness,** *n.* – **exceptionably,** *adv.*

**exceptional** /ək'sɛpʃənəl, ɛk-/, *adj.* forming an exception or unusual instance; unusual; extraordinary. – **exceptionally,** *adv.* – **exceptionalness,** *n.*

**exceptive** /ək'sɛptɪv, ɛk-/, *adj.* **1.** that excepts; making an exception. **2.** disposed to take exception; objecting.

**excerpt** /'ɛksɜpt/, *n.;* /ɛk'sɜpt/, *v.* *–n.* **1.** a passage taken out of a book or the like; an extract. *–v.t.* **2.** to take out (a passage) from a book or the like; extract. [L *excerptus,* pp., picked out] – **excerption,** *n.*

**excess** /ək'sɛs, 'ɛk-/, *n.;* /'ɛksɛs/, *adj.* *–n.* **1.** the fact of exceeding something else in amount or degree. **2.** the amount or degree by which one thing exceeds another. **3.** an extreme or excessive amount or degree; superabundance: *have an excess of energy.* **4.** a going beyond ordinary or proper limits. **5.** immoderate indulgence; intemperance in eating and drinking. *–adj.* **6.** more than or above what is necessary, usual, or specified; extra: *excess baggage, excess profits.* [ME *excesse,* from L *excessus* a departure]

**excessive** /əkˈsɛsɪv, ɛk-/, *adj.* exceeding the usual or proper limit or degree; characterised by excess: *excessive charges, excessive indulgence.* – **excessively,** *adv.* – **excessiveness,** *n.*

**exch.,** **1.** exchange. **2.** exchequer.

**exchange** /əksˈtʃeɪndʒ, ɛk-/, *v.,* **-changed, -changing,** *n.* *–v.t.* **1.** to part with for some equivalent; give up (something) for something else. **2.** to replace by another or something else; change for another: *to exchange a purchase.* **3.** to give and receive reciprocally; interchange: *to exchange blows, gifts, etc.* **4.** to part with in return for some equivalent; transfer for a recompense; barter: *to exchange dollars for pounds.* **5.** *Chess.* to capture (an enemy piece) in return for a capture by the opponent generally of a piece or pieces of equal value. *–v.i.* **6.** to make an exchange. **7.** to pass or be taken in exchange or as an equivalent. *–n.* **8.** the act or process of exchanging: *an exchange of gifts, prisoners of war, etc.* **9.** that which is given or received in exchange or substitution for something else: *the car was a fair exchange.* **10.** a place for buying and selling commodities, securities, etc., typically open only to members. **11.** a central office or central station: *a telephone exchange.* **12.** the method or system by which debits and credits in different places are settled without the actual transference of money, by means of documents representing money values. **13.** the discharge of obligations in different places by the transfer of credits. **14.** the reciprocal transference of equivalent sums of money, as in the currencies of two different countries. **15.** the giving or receiving of a sum of money in one place for a bill ordering the payment of an equivalent sum in another. **16.** the varying rate or sum, in one currency, given for a fixed sum in another currency; rate of exchange. **17.** the amount of the difference in value between two or more currencies, or between the values of the same currency at two or more places. **18.** the cheques, drafts, etc., exchanged at a clearing house. **19.** *Chess.* the reciprocal capture of pieces, generally of equal value, in a single series of moves. **20.** →**transfusion** (def. 2a). **21.** →**stock exchange.** [ME *eschaunge,* from AF, from LL *excambium*] – **exchanger,** *n.*

**exchangeable** /əksˈtʃeɪndʒəbəl, ɛk-/, *adj.* that can be exchanged. – **exchangeability** /əkstʃeɪndʒəˈbɪləti, ɛk-/, *n.*

**exchange force** /əksˈtʃeɪndʒ fɔs/, *n.* **1.** strong nuclear force; a force which holds the nucleons together within an atomic nucleus as a result of the exchange of mesons. **2.** a force which occurs in ferromagnetic materials causing the alignment of all the individual magnetic moments of large groups of atoms.

**exchange rate** /ˈ– reɪt/, *n.* in international money markets, the rate of exchange of one currency for another.

**exchequer** /əksˈtʃɛkə/, *n.* **1.** a treasury, as of a state or nation. **2.** (in Britain) **a.** (*oft. cap.*) the government department in charge of the public revenues. **b.** (formerly) an office which administered the royal revenues and determined all cases affecting them. **c.** (*cap.*) an ancient common-law court of civil jurisdiction (**Court of Exchequer**) in which all cases affecting the revenues of the crown were tried. **3.** *Colloq.* funds; finances. [ME *escheker,* from OF *eschequier* chess board (so called with reference to the table-cover marked with squares on which accounts were reckoned with counters). See CHEQUER]

**excide** /ɛkˈsaɪd/, *v.t.,* **-cided, -ciding.** to cut out; excise.

**excipient** /əkˈsɪpiənt, ɛk-/, *n.* a more or less inert substance, as sugar, jelly, etc., used as the medium or vehicle for the administration of an active medicine. [L *excipiens,* ppr., taking out]

**excisable**[1] /ɛkˈsaɪzəbəl/, *adj.* subject to excise duty.

**excisable**[2] /ɛkˈsaɪzəbəl/, *adj.* capable of being excised or cut out.

**excise**[1] /ɛkˈsaɪz, ˈɛksaɪz/, *n.;* /ɛkˈsaɪz/ *v.,* **-cised, -cising.** *–n.* **1.** an inland tax or duty on certain commodities, as spirits, tobacco, etc., levied on their manufacture, sale, or consumption within the country. **2.** a tax levied for a licence to carry on certain employments, pursue certain sports, etc. **3.** that branch of the civil service which collects excise duties. *–v.t.* **4.** to impose an excise on. [MD *excijs,* from OF *acceis* a tax, from LL *accēnsāre* tax] – **excision** /ɛkˈsɪʒən/, *n.*

**excise**[2] /ɛkˈsaɪz/, *v.t.,* **-cised, -cising.** **1.** to expunge, as a passage or sentence. **2.** to cut out or off, as a tumour. [L *excīsus,* pp., cut out]

**excitability** /əksaɪtəˈbɪləti, ɛk-/, *n.* **1.** the quality of being excitable. **2.** *Physiol.* irritability.

**excitable** /əkˈsaɪtəbəl, ɛk-/, *adj.* capable of being excited; easily excited. – **excitableness,** *n.* – **excitably,** *adv.*

**excitant** /əkˈsaɪtənt, ɛk-, ˈɛksətənt/, *adj.* **1.** exciting; stimulating. *–n.* **2.** *Physiol.* something that excites; a stimulant.

**excitation** /ɛksaɪˈteɪʃən/, *n.* **1.** the act of exciting. **2.** means of exciting; that which excites. **3.** the state of being excited. **4.** *Elect.* the relative strength of the magnetic field in a dynamo: *normal excitation.* **5.** *Physics.* a process in which an atom, nucleus, or molecule is raised to a higher energy state than normal.

**excitative** /əkˈsaɪtətɪv, ɛk-/, *adj.* tending to excite. Also, **excitatory** /ɛksaɪˈteɪtəri, -tri/.

**excite** /əkˈsaɪt, ɛk-/, *v.t.,* **-cited, -citing.** **1.** to arouse or stir up the feelings of: *to excite jealousy or hatred.* **2.** to cause; awaken: *to excite interest or curiosity.* **3.** to stir to action; stir up: *to excite a dog.* **4.** *Physiol.* to stimulate: *to excite a nerve.* **5.** *Elect.* to produce electric activity or a magnetic field in: *to excite a dynamo.* **6.** *Physics.* to raise (an atom, nucleus, or molecule) to a higher energy state than the normal. [ME *excite(n),* from L *excitāre,* frequentative of *exciēre* call forth, rouse]

**excited** /əkˈsaɪtəd, ɛk-/, *adj.* **1.** stirred emotionally; agitated. **2.** stimulated to activity; brisk. **3.** *Physics.* (of an atom or nucleus) in a state of higher energy than the normal state. – **excitedly,** *adv.*

**excitement** /əkˈsaɪtmənt, ɛk-/, *n.* **1.** an excited state or condition. **2.** something that excites.

**exciter** /əkˈsaɪtə, ɛk-/, *n.* **1.** one who or that which excites. **2.** *Elect.* an auxiliary generator which supplies energy for the excitation of another electric machine.

**exciting** /əkˈsaɪtɪŋ, ɛk-/, *adj.* producing excitement; stirring. – **excitingly,** *adv.*

**excitor** /əkˈsaɪtə, ɛk-, -tɔ/, *n.* **1.** *Physiol.* a nerve whose stimulation excites greater action. **2.** →**exciter.**

**excl.,** excluding.

**exclaim** /əksˈkleɪm, ɛks-/, *v.i.* **1.** to cry out or speak suddenly and vehemently, as in surprise, strong emotion, protest, etc. *–v.t.* **2.** to cry out; say loudly or vehemently. [earlier *exclame,* from L *exclāmāre* call out] – **exclaimer,** *n.*

**exclamation** /ɛkskləˈmeɪʃən/, *n.* **1.** the act of exclaiming; an outcry; a loud complaint or protest. **2.** →**interjection.**

**exclamation mark** /ˈ– ˌmak/, *n.* **1.** a punctuation mark (!) used after an exclamation. **2.** *Brit.* a road sign bearing a symbol resembling this mark, placed to give advance warning of some hazard. Also, **exclamation point.**

**exclamatory** /əksˈklæmətri, ɛks-, -təri/, *adj.* **1.** using, containing, or expressing exclamation. **2.** pertaining to exclamation. – **exclamatorily,** *adv.*

**exclave** /ˈɛkskleɪv/, *n.* a part of a country separated from it geographically and surrounded by alien territory: *West Berlin is an exclave of West Germany.* [EX-[1] + *-clave* of ENCLAVE]

**exclude** /əksˈklud, ɛks-/, *v.t.,* **-cluded, -cluding.** **1.** to shut or keep out; prevent the entrance of. **2.** to shut out from consideration, privilege, etc. **3.** to expel and keep out; thrust out; eject. [ME *exclude(n),* from L *exclūdere*] – **excludable,** *adj.* – **excluder,** *n.*

**excluded middle, law of,** *n. Logic.* the law which states that a proposition is either true or false, or that a thing either has or does not have a given property.

**exclusion** /əksˈkluʒən, ɛks-/, *n.* **1.** the act of excluding. **2.** the state of being excluded. **3.** *Physiol.* a keeping apart; the blocking of an entrance. [L *exclūsio*]

**exclusion clause** /ˈ– klɔz/, *n.* a clause in an insurance policy stipulating risks not covered in the policy.

**exclusionism** /əksˈkluʒənɪzəm, ɛks-/, *n.* the principle, policy, or practice of exclusion, as from rights or privileges.

**exclusionist** /əkˈskluʒənəst, ɛk-/, *n.* **1.** one who advocates exclusionism. **2.** (formerly) a free Australian immigrant who opposed admitting emancipists to full civil rights. Also, **exclusivist.**

**exclusion principle** /əksˈkluʒən ˌprɪnsəpəl/, *n.* the principle that no two electrons, protons, or neutrons in a given system can be characterised by the same set of quantum numbers. Also, **Pauli's exclusion principle.**

**exclusive** /əksˈklusɪv, ɛks-/, *adj.* **1.** not admitting of something else; incompatible: *mutually exclusive ideas.* **2.** excluding from consideration or account, as from 100 to 121 exclusive (excluding 100 and 121, and including from 101 to 120). **3.** limited to the object or objects designated: *exclusive attention to business.* **4.** shutting out all others from a part or share: *an exclusive grant.* **5.** shutting out all other activities: *an exclusive occupation.* **6.** in which no others have a share: *exclusive information.* **7.** single or sole: *the exclusive means of communication between two places.* **8.** available through only one channel of marketing. **9.** disposed to resist the admission of outsiders to association, intimacy, etc.: *an exclusive clique.* **10.** *Colloq.* fashionable: *an exclusive club.* **11.** *Logic.* such that only one of a range of possibilities can be correct or true, as an exclusive disjunction. *–n.* **12.** a story which is in the possession of only one newspaper. **13.** an item of clothing which is sold with the guarantee that it is not mass-produced. **14.** (formerly) a person who was opposed to giving full civil rights to emancipists. [ML *exclūsīvus,* pp., excluded] – **exclusively,** *adv.* – **exclusiveness,** *n.*

**exclusivist** /əksˈklusəvəst, ɛks-/, *n.* →**exclusionist.**

**exclusory** /əksˈkluzəri, ɛks-/, *adj.* having the power or function of excluding; exclusive.

**excogitate** /ɛksˈkɒdʒəteɪt/, *v.t.,* **-tated, -tating.** to think out; devise; invent. [L *excōgitātus,* pp., found out by thinking] – **excogitation** /ɛkskɒdʒəˈteɪʃən/, *n.* – **excogitative** /ɛksˈkɒdʒətətɪv/, *adj.* – **excogitator,** *n.*

**excommunicable** /ɛkskəˈmjunɪkəbəl/, *adj.* **1.** liable or deserving to be excommunicated, as a person. **2.** punishable by excommunication, as an offence.

**excommunicate** /ɛkskəˈmjunəkeɪt/, *v.,* **-cated, -cating,** *n., adj.* *–v.t.* **1.** to cut off from communion or membership, esp. from the sacraments and fellowship of the church by ecclesiastical sentence. *–n.* **2.** an excommunicated person. *–adj.* **3.** excommunicated. [LL *excommūnicātus,* pp., lit., put out of the community] – **excommunicator,** *n.*

**excommunication** /ˌɛkskəmjunəˈkeɪʃən/, *n.* **1.** the act of excommunicating. **2.** the state of being excommunicated. **3.** the ecclesiastical sentence by which a person is excommunicated.

**excommunicative** /ɛkskəˈmjunəkətɪv/, *adj.* disposed or serving to excommunicate.

**excommunicatory** /ɛkskəˈmjunəkətri, -təri/, *adj.* relating to or causing excommunication.

**excoriate** /əksˈkɔrieɪt, ɛks-/, *v.t.,* **-ated, -ating.** **1.** to strip off or remove the skin from. **2.** to flay verbally; denounce; censure. [L *excoriātus,* pp. of *excoriāre* strip off the hide]

**excoriation** /əkskɔriˈeɪʃən, ɛks-/, *n.* **1.** the act of excoriating. **2.** the state of being excoriated. **3.** an excoriated place on the body.

**excorticate** /əksˈkɔtəkeɪt, ɛks-/, *v.t.,* **-cated, -cating.** to remove the mark, husk or outer covering from; decorticate. – **excortication** /əkskɔtəˈkeɪʃən, ɛks-/, *n.*

**excrement** /ˈɛkskrəmənt/, *n.* waste matter discharged from the body, esp. the faeces. [L *excrēmentum* what is evacuated] – **excremental** /ɛkskrəˈmɛntl/, *adj.* – **excrementally** /ɛkskrəˈmɛntəli/, *adv.*

**excrementitious** /ɛkskrəmenˈtɪʃəs/, *adj.* of or like excrement. – **excrementitiously,** *adv.*

**excrescence** /ɛksˈkrɛsəns/, *n.* **1.** abnormal growth or increase. **2.** an abnormal outgrowth, usu. harmless, on an animal or vegetable body. **3.** a normal outgrowth such as hair. **4.** any disfiguring addition.

**excrescency** /əksˈkrɛsənsi, ɛks-/, *n., pl.* **-cies.** the state of being excrescent.

**excrescent** /əksˈkrɛsənt, ɛks-/, *adj.* **1.** growing abnormally out of something else; superfluous. **2.** *Phonet.* added without grammatical or historical justification, as the *t* in against (ME *ageyns*). [L *excrescens,* ppr., growing out]

**excreta** /əksˈkritə, ɛks-/, *n.pl.* excreted matter, as sweat, urine, etc. [L, neut. pl. of *excrētus,* pp., separated] – **excretal,** *adj.*

**excrete** /əksˈkrit, ɛks-/, *v.t.,* **-creted, -creting.** to separate and eliminate from an organic body; separate and expel from the blood or tissues, as waste or harmful matters. [L *excrētus,* pp., sifted out, discharged] – **excretive,** *adj.*

**excretion** /əksˈkriʃən, ɛks-/, *n.* **1.** the act of excreting. **2.** the substance excreted, as sweat or urine, or certain plant products.

**excretory** /əksˈkritəri, ɛks-/, *adj.* pertaining to or concerned in excretion; having this function of excreting.

**excruciate** /əksˈkruʃieɪt, ɛks-/, *v.t.,* **-ated, -ating.** to inflict severe pain upon; torture. [L *excruciātus,* pp., tortured greatly]

**excruciating** /əksˈkruʃieɪtɪŋ, ɛks-/, *adj.* extremely painful; causing extreme suffering; torturing. – **excruciatingly,** *adv.*

**excruciation** /əkskruʃiˈeɪʃən, ɛks-/, *n.* **1.** the act of excruciating. **2.** the state of being excruciated. **3.** an instance of this; torture.

**exculpate** /ˈɛkskʌlpeɪt, ɛksˈkʌlpeɪt/, *v.t.,* **-pated, -pating.** to clear from a charge of guilt or fault; free from blame; vindicate. [EX-[1] + L *culpa* fault, blame + -ATE[1]] – **exculpable** /əkˈskʌlpəbəl, ɛk-/, *adj.* – **exculpation** /ɛkskʌlˈpeɪʃən/, *n.*

**exculpatory** /əksˈkʌlpətri, ɛks-, -təri/, *adj.* tending to clear from a charge of fault or guilt.

**excurrent** /ɛksˈkʌrənt/, *adj.* **1.** running out or forth. **2.** *Zool.* giving passage outwards; affording exit, as the excurrent canal of certain sponges. **3.** *Bot.* **a.** having the axis prolonged so as to form an undivided main stem or trunk, as the stem of the spruce. **b.** projecting beyond the apex, as the midrib in certain leaves. [L *excurrens,* ppr., running out]

**excurse** /əkˈskɜs, ɛk-/, *v.i.,* **-cursed, -cursing.** **1.** to go on an excursion. **2.** to digress; wander.

**excursion** /əkˈskɜʃən, ɛk-/, *n.* **1.** a short journey or trip to some point for a special purpose: *a pleasure excursion, a scientific excursion.* **2.** a trip in a coach, train, etc., at a reduced rate: *weekend excursions to seashore or mountain resorts.* **3.** the persons who make such a journey. **4.** deviation or digression. **5.** *Physics.* the departure of a body from its mean position or proper course. **6.** *Mach.* **a.** the range of stroke of any moving part. **b.** the stroke itself. **7.** *Obs.* a sally or raid. [L *excursio* a running out]

**excursionist** /əkˈskɜʃənəst, ɛk-/, *n.* one who goes on an excursion.

**excursion ticket** /əkˈskɜʃən tɪkət/, *n.* a return ticket for off-peak travel at a reduced rate, as to a resort, etc.

**excursive** /əkˈskɜsɪv, ɛk-/, *adj.* **1.** given to making excursions; wandering; digressive. **2.** of the nature of an excursion; rambling; desultory. – **excursively,** *adv.* – **excursiveness,** *n.*

**excursus** /ɛkˈskɜsəs/, *n., pl.* **-suses, -sus.** **1.** a detailed discussion of some point in a book (usu. added as an appendix). **2.** an incidental discussion, or digression, as in a narrative. [L, from *excurrere* run out]

**excusatory** /əkˈskjuzətri, ɛk-, -təri/, *adj.* serving or intended to excuse.

**excuse** /əkˈskjuz, ɛk-/, *v.,* **-scused, -scusing;** /əkˈskjus/, *n.* *–v.t.* **1.** to regard or judge with indulgence; pardon or forgive; overlook (a fault, etc.). **2.** to offer an apology for; apologise for; seek to remove the blame of. **3.** to serve as an apology or justification for; justify: *ignorance of the law excuses no man.* **4. a.** to release from an obligation or duty: *to be excused from attending a meeting.* **b.** to allow to leave a place, or cease an activity: *to be excused from the room.* **5.** to seek or obtain exemption or release for (oneself): *to excuse oneself from duty.* **6.** to refrain from exacting; remit; dispense with: *to excuse a fine.* *–n.* **7.** that which is offered as a reason for being excused; a plea offered in extenuation of a fault, or for release from an obligation, etc. **8.** something serving to excuse; a ground or reason for excusing. **9.** the act of excusing. **10.** a pretext or subterfuge. **11.** an inferior or inadequate example of something specified: *she was shabbily dressed and wearing a poor excuse for a hat.* [ME *excuse(n),* from L *excūsāre* allege in excuse] – **excusable,** *adj.* – **excusableness,** *n.* – **excusably,** *adv.* – **excusal,** *n.* – **excuseless,** *adj.* – **excuser,** *n.* – **excusive,** *adj.*

**excuse-me** /əksˈkjuz-mi/, *n.* *Brit.* a dance in which one may take the partner of another dancer.

**ex date** /'ɛks deɪt/, *n. Stock Exchange.* the date on which shares change from being quoted *cum* (*dividend*) to *ex* (*dividend*).

**ex-directory** /'ɛks-dərɛktəri/, *adj.* →**unlisted** (def. 3).

**ex dividend** /ɛks 'dɪvədɛnd/, *adj. Stock Exchange.* without dividend; the buyer of the stock being not entitled to the dividend.

**exeat** /'ɛksiæt/, *n.* formal leave of absence, esp. for a student to leave school or institution where his presence would normally be required. [L: 3rd pers. pres. subjunctive of *exīre* to go out]

**exec.** /əg'zɛk/, **1.** executive. **2.** executor.

**execrable** /'ɛksəkrəbəl/, *adj.* **1.** deserving to be execrated; detestable; abominable. **2.** *Colloq.* very bad: *an execrable pun.* – **execrably,** *adv.*

**execrate** /'ɛksəkreɪt/, *v.,* **-crated, -crating.** *–v.t.* **1.** to detest utterly; abhor; abominate. **2.** to curse; imprecate evil upon. *–v.i.* **3.** to utter curses. [L *ex(s)ecrātus,* pp., having cursed] – **execrator,** *n.*

**execration** /ɛksə'kreɪʃən/, *n.* **1.** the act of execrating. **2.** a curse or imprecation. **3.** the object execrated; a thing held in abomination.

**execrative** /'ɛksəkreɪtɪv/, *adj.* **1.** pertaining to or characterised by execration. **2.** prone to execrate. – **execratively,** *adv.*

**execratory** /'ɛksəkreɪtəri/, *adj.* **1.** pertaining to execration. **2.** having the nature of or containing an execration.

**executant** /əg'zɛkjətənt, ɛg-/, *n.* one who executes or performs, esp. musically.

**execute** /'ɛksəkjut/, *v.t.,* **-cuted, -cuting.** **1.** to carry out; accomplish: *to execute a plan or order.* **2.** to perform or do: *to execute a manoeuvre or gymnastic feat.* **3.** to inflict capital punishment on; put to death according to law. **4.** to produce in accordance with a plan or design: *to execute a statue or a picture.* **5.** to perform or play (a piece of music). **6.** *Law.* **a.** to give effect or force to (a law, decree, judicial sentence, etc.). **b.** to carry out the terms of (a will). **c.** to transact or carry through (a contract, mortgage, etc.) in the manner prescribed by law; complete and give validity to (a legal instrument) by fulfilling the legal requirements, as by signing, sealing, etc. [ME *execute(n),* from ML *execūtāre,* from L *ex(s)ecūtus,* pp., having followed out] – **executable,** *adj.* – **executer,** *n.*

**execution** /ɛksə'kjuʃən/, *n.* **1.** the act or process of executing. **2.** the state or fact of being executed. **3.** the infliction of capital punishment, or, formerly, of any legal punishment. **4.** the process of performing a judgment or sentence of a court. **5.** mode or style of performance; technical skill, as in music. **6.** effective action, esp. of weapons, or the result attained by it (usu. prec. by *do*): *every shot did execution.* **7.** *Law.* a judicial writ directing the enforcement of a judgment.

**executioner** /ɛksə'kjuʃənə/, *n.* **1.** one who executes. **2.** an official who inflicts capital punishment in pursuance of a legal warrant.

**executive** /əg'zɛkjətɪv, ɛg-/, *adj., n., v.,* **-tived, -tiving.** *–adj.* **1.** suited for execution or carrying into effect; of the kind requisite for practical performance or direction: *executive ability.* **2.** charged with or pertaining to execution of laws, or administration of affairs. **3.** designed for or used by executives: *an executive aircraft.* *–n.* **4.** a person or body having administrative authority as in a company. **5.** →**ministry** (def. 4). **6.** the body of people, members of the governing party or parties, drawn from both houses of parliament, who form policy and control the appropriate government departments and instrumentalities, and who are responsible to parliament for such administration. **7.** →**executive council.** *–v.t.* **8.** *Colloq.* to murder or assassinate, often through the agency of a hired killer. – **executively,** *adv.*

**executive council** /– 'kaʊnsəl/, *n.* a government executive body comprising the ministry and the governor-general or governor.

**executor** /əg'zɛkjətə, ɛg-/, *n.* **1.** one who executes, or carries out, performs, fulfils, etc. **2.** *Law.* a person named by a testator in his will to carry out the provisions of his will. [ME *executour,* from AF, from L *ex(s)ecūtor,* lit., one who follows out] – **executorial** /əgzɛkjə'tɔriəl, ɛg-/, *adj.* – **executorship,** *n.*

**executor de son tort,** *n. Law.* one who takes it upon himself to act as executor or administrator without any expressed authority. [F]

**executory** /əg'zɛkjətri, ɛg-/, *adj.* **1.** →**executive.** **2.** *Law.* that remains to be carried into effect.

**executrix** /əg'zɛkjətrɪks, ɛg-/, *n., pl.* **executrices** /əgzɛkjə'trisiz, ɛg-/. a female executor.

**exedra** /'ɛksədrə, ɛk'sidrə/, *n.* a semicircular or rectangular recess with raised seats originating in classical architecture.

**exegesis** /ɛksə'dʒisəs/, *n., pl.* **-ses** /-siz/. critical explanation or interpretation, esp. of Scripture. [NL, from Gk: explanation]

**exegete** /'ɛksədʒit/, *n.* one skilled in exegesis.

**exegetic** /ɛksə'dʒɛtɪk/, *adj.* pertaining to exegesis; expository. Also **exegetical.** [Gk *exēgētikós* explanatory] – **exegetically,** *adv.*

**exegetics** /ɛksə'dʒɛtɪks/, *n.* the science of exegesis; exegetical theology.

**exempla** /əg'zɛmplə/, *n.* plural of **exemplum.**

**exemplar** /əg'zɛmplə, ɛg-, -pla/, *n.* **1.** a model or pattern to be copied or imitated. **2.** an example; typical instance. **3.** an original or archetype. **4.** a copy of a book or text. [L: copy, model; replacing ME *exemplaire,* from OF]

**exemplary** /əg'zɛmpləri, ɛg-/, *adj.* **1.** worthy of imitation; commendable: *exemplary conduct.* **2.** such as may serve as a warning: *an exemplary penalty.* **3.** serving as a model or pattern. **4.** serving as an illustration or specimen; illustrative; typical. **5.** of, pertaining to, or consisting of exempla. – **exemplarily,** *adv.* – **exemplariness,** *n.*

**exemplification** /əgzɛmpləfə'keɪʃən, eg-/, *n.* **1.** the act of exemplifying. **2.** that which exemplifies; an illustration or example. **3.** *Law.* an attested copy of a document, under official seal.

**exemplificative** /əg'zɛmpləfəkeɪtɪv, ɛg-/, *adj.* serving to exemplify.

**exemplify** /əg'zɛmpləfaɪ, ɛg-/, *v.t.,* **-fied, -fying.** **1.** to show or illustrate by example. **2.** to furnish, or serve as, an example of. **3.** *Law.* to transcribe or copy; make an attested copy of (a document) under seal. [ME *exemplyfy(en),* from ML *exemplificāre,* from L *exempli-* example + *ficāre* make] – **exemplifier,** *n.*

**exempli gratia** /ɛgzɛmpli 'gratia/, *adv.* for the sake of example; for example. *Abbrev.:* e.g. [L]

**exemplum** /əg'zɛmpləm, ɛg-/, *n., pl.* **-pla** /-plə/. **1.** an anecdote designed to point a moral, esp. in a medieval sermon. **2.** an example. [L]

**exempt** /əg'zɛmpt, ɛg-/, *v.t.* **1.** to free from an obligation or liability to which others are subject; release: *to exempt someone from military service, from an examination, etc.* *–adj.* **2.** released from, or not subject to, an obligation, liability, etc.: *exempt from taxes.* *–n.* **3.** one who is exempt from, or not subject to, an obligation, duty, etc. [ME, from L *exemptus,* pp.] – **exemptible,** *adj.*

**exemption** /əg'zɛmpʃən, ɛg-/, *n.* **1.** the act of exempting. **2.** the state of being exempted; immunity.

**exenterate** /əg'zɛntəreɪt, ɛg-/, *v.* **-rated, -rating;** /əg'zɛntəreɪt, ɛg, -rət/, *adj.* *–v.t.* **1.** to remove the contents of; disembowel; eviscerate. *–adj.* **2.** disembowelled.

**exequatur** /ɛksə'kweɪtə/, *n.* **1.** a written recognition of a consul by the government of the state in which he is stationed authorising him to exercise his powers. **2.** an authorisation granted by a secular ruler for the publication of papal bulls or other ecclesiastical enactments to give them binding force. [L: let him execute]

**exequies** /'ɛksəkwiz/, *n.pl., sing.* **-quy** /-kwi/. funeral rites or ceremonies. [ME *exequies* (pl.), from OF, from L *exequiae* funeral procession] – **exequial,** *adj.*

**exercise** /'ɛksəsaɪz/, *n., v.,* **-cised, -cising.** *–n.* **1.** bodily or mental exertion, esp. for the sake of training or improvement. **2.** something done or performed as a means of practice or training, to improve a specific skill or to acquire competence in a particular field: *exercises in French grammar, exercises for the piano.* **3.** a putting into action, use, operation, or effect: *the exercise of caution or care, the exercise of willpower.* **4.** a composition or work of art executed for practice or to illustrate a specific technical point. **5.** a literary, artistic, or musical performance of technical rather than aesthetic value. **6.** a written school task. **7.** (*pl.*) military drill or manoeuvres. **8.** (*oft. pl.*) *U.S.* a ceremony; formal proceeding. **9.** a religious observance or act of worship. **10.** an academic disputation. *–v.t.* **11.** to put through exercises, or forms of practice or exertion, designed to train, develop, condition, etc.: *to exercise troops, a horse, the voice, etc.* **12.** to put (faculties, rights, etc.) into action, practice, or use: *to exercise one's strength, one's sight, etc.* **13.** to use or display in one's action or procedure: *to exercise caution, patience, judgment.* **14.** to make use of (one's privileges, powers, etc.): *to exercise one's rights.* **15.** to discharge (a function); perform: *to exercise the duties of one's office.* **16.** to have as an effect: *to exercise an influence on someone.* **17.** to worry; make uneasy; annoy: *to be much exercised about one's health.* *–v.i.* **18.** to go through exercises; take bodily exercise. [ME *exercise,* from OF, from L *exercitium*] – **exercisable,** *adj.* – **exerciser,** *n.*

**exercitation** /əgzɜsəˈteɪʃən, ɛg-/, *n.* **1.** exercise or exertion, as of faculties or powers. **2.** practice or training. **3.** a performance. **4.** a disquisition or discourse. [ME *exercitacion,* from L *exercitātio* exercise, practice]

**exergue** /ɛkˈsɜg/, *n.* the space below the base line on a coin or medal. [F, from Gk *ex-* EX-[3] + *érgon* work] – **exergual,** *adj.*

**exert** /əgˈzɜt, ɛg-/, *v.t.* **1.** to put forth, as power; exercise, as ability or influence; put into vigorous action. **2. exert oneself,** to put forth one's powers; use one's efforts; strive. [L *ex(s)ertus,* pp.] – **exertive,** *adj.*

**exertion** /əgˈzɜʃən, ɛg-/, *n.* **1.** vigorous action or effort. **2.** an effort. **3.** exercise, as of power or faculties. **4.** an instance of this.

**exeunt** /ˈɛksiʊnt/, (a stage direction indicating that the actors named go out or off stage). [L]

**exeunt omnes** /– ˈɒmneɪz/, (a stage direction indicating that all actors go out or off stage). [L]

**exfoliate** /ɛksˈfoʊlieɪt/, *v.,* **-ated, -ating.** *–v.t.* **1.** to throw off in scales. *–v.i.* **2.** to throw off scales or flakes; peel off in thin fragments: *the exfoliating bark of a tree.* **3.** *Geol.* **a.** to split or swell into a scaly aggregate, as certain minerals when heated. **b.** to separate into rudely concentric layers or sheets, as certain rocks during weathering. **4.** *Surg.* to separate and come off in scales, as scaling skin or any structure separating in flakes. [LL *exfoliātus,* pp., stripped of leaves] – **exfoliative,** *adj.*

**exfoliation** /ɛksfoʊliˈeɪʃən/, *n.* **1.** the act or process of exfoliating. **2.** the state of being exfoliated. **3.** that which is exfoliated, or scaled off.

**ex-govie** /ɛks-ˈgʌvi/, *n. A.C.T.* **1.** a house built by the Commonwealth Government but now privately owned. *–adj.* **2.** of or pertaining to such a house.

**ex gratia** /ɛks ˈgreɪʃə/, *adj.* (of something granted) as a favour and not because of a legal obligation. [L]

**exhalant** /ɛksˈheɪlənt/, *adj.* **1.** exhaling; emitting. *–n.* **2.** that which exhales.

**exhalation** /ɛkshəˈleɪʃən, ɛksəˈleɪʃən/, *n.* **1.** the act of exhaling. **2.** that which is exhaled; a vapour; an emanation.

**exhale** /ɛksˈheɪl/, *v.,* **-haled, -haling.** *–v.i.* **1.** to emit breath or vapour. **2.** to pass off as vapour; pass off as an effluence. *–v.t.* **3.** to breathe out; emit (air, etc.). **4.** to give off as vapour. **5.** to draw out as a vapour or effluence; evaporate. [ME *exhale(n),* from F *exhaler,* from L *exhālāre* breathe out] – **exhalable, exhalative,** *adj.*

**exhaust** /əgˈzɔst, ɛg-/, *v.t.* **1.** to empty by drawing out the contents. **2.** to create a vacuum in. **3.** to draw out or drain off; draw or drain off completely. **4.** to use up or consume completely; expend the whole of. **5.** to drain of strength or energy; wear out, or fatigue greatly, as a person: *I have exhausted myself working.* **6.** to draw out all that is essential in (a subject, topic, etc.); treat or study thoroughly. **7.** to deprive wholly of useful or essential properties, possessions, resources, etc. **8.** to deprive of ingredients by the use of solvents, as a drug. **9.** to destroy the fertility of (soil), as by intensive cultivation. *–v.i.* **10.** to pass out or escape, as spent steam from the cylinder of an engine. *–n.* **11.** *Mach.* the escape of gases from the cylinder of an engine after ignition and expansion. **12.** the steam or gases ejected. **13.** the parts of an engine through which the exhaust is ejected. **14.** *Bldg Trades.* to install a ventilation system in a building. [L *exhaustus,* pp., drained out] – **exhauster,** *n.* – **exhaustible,** *adj.* – **exhaustibility** /əgzɔstəˈbɪləti, eg-/, *n.*

**exhaust fan** /ˈ– fæn/, *n.* the fan in a ventilation system used to remove vitiated or excess air.

**exhaustion** /əgˈzɔstʃən, ɛg-/, *n.* **1.** the act or process of exhausting. **2.** the state of being exhausted. **3.** extreme weakness or fatigue.

**exhaustive** /əgˈzɔstɪv, ɛg-/, *adj.* **1.** exhausting a subject, topic, etc.; comprehensive; thorough. **2.** tending to exhaust or drain, as of resources or strength. – **exhaustively,** *adv.* – **exhaustiveness,** *n.*

**exhaustive ballot** /– ˈbælət/, *n.* a method of election where, if no candidate has an absolute majority, votes are recast until one does.

**exhaustless** /əgˈzɔstləs, ɛg-/, *adj.* →**inexhaustible.** – **exhaustlessly,** *adv.* – **exhaustlessness,** *n.*

**exhaust pipe** /əgˈzɔst paɪp/, *n.* a pipe for releasing waste gases from an internal-combustion engine.

**exhibit** /əgˈzɪbət, ɛg-/, *v.t.* **1.** to offer or expose to view; present for inspection. **2.** to manifest or display: *to exhibit anger.* **3.** to place on show: *to exhibit paintings.* **4.** *Law.* to submit (a document, etc.) in evidence in a court of law. *–v.i.* **5.** to make or give an exhibition; present something to public view. *–n.* **6.** an exhibiting or exhibition. **7.** that which is exhibited. **8.** an object or a collection of objects shown in an exhibition, fair, etc. **9.** *Law.* a document or other object exhibited in court and referred to and identified in written evidence. [L *exhibitus,* pp.] – **exhibitor, exhibiter,** *n.*

**exhibition** /ɛksəˈbɪʃən/, *n.* **1.** an exhibiting, showing, or presenting to view. **2.** a public display of feats of skill, athletic prowess, etc., as a boxing bout in which no decision is reached. **3.** a public show or display. **4.** an allowance or grant made to a student at a university, usu. upon the result of a competitive examination. **5. make an exhibition of oneself,** to behave foolishly or so as to excite ridicule.

**exhibitionism** /ɛksəˈbɪʃənɪzəm/, *n.* **1.** a tendency to display one's abilities or to behave in such a way as to attract attention. **2.** *Psychiatry.* an abnormal tendency to make a display of oneself; (in a more severe form) with exposure of the genitals.

**exhibitionist** /ɛksəˈbɪʃənəst/, *n.* **1.** one who desires to make an exhibition of himself or his powers, personality, etc. **2.** *Psychiatry.* one affected with the compulsions of exhibitionism. – **exhibitionistic** /ˌɛksəbɪʃəˈnɪstɪk/, *adj.*

**exhibitive** /əgˈzɪbətɪv, ɛg-/, *adj.* serving for exhibition; tending to exhibit.

**exhibitory** /əgˈzɪbətri, ɛg-, -təri/, *adj.* pertaining to or intended for exhibition or display.

**exhilarant** /əgˈzɪlərənt, ɛg-/, *adj.* **1.** exhilarating. *–n.* **2.** something that exhilarates.

**exhilarate** /əgˈzɪləreɪt, ɛg-/, *v.t.,* **-rated, -rating.** **1.** to make cheerful or merry. **2.** to enliven; stimulate; invigorate. [L *exhilarātus,* pp.] – **exhilarating,** *adj.* – **exhilaratingly,** *adv.* – **exhilarator,** *n.*

**exhilaration** /əgzɪləˈreɪʃən, ɛg-/, *n.* **1.** exhilarated condition or feeling. **2.** the act of exhilarating.

**exhilarative** /əgˈzɪlərətɪv, ɛg-/, *adj.* tending to exhilarate. Also, **exhilaratory.**

**exhort** /əgˈzɔt, ɛg-/, *v.t.* **1.** to urge, advise, or caution earnestly; admonish urgently. *–v.i.* **2.** to make exhortation; give admonition. [ME *exhort(en),* from L *exhortārī* urge, encourage] – **exhorter,** *n.*

**exhortation** /ɛgzɔˈteɪʃən/, *n.* **1.** the act or process of exhorting. **2.** an utterance, discourse, or address conveying urgent advice or recommendations.

**exhortative** /əgˈzɔtətɪv, ɛg-/, *adj.* **1.** serving or intended to exhort. **2.** pertaining to exhortation. Also, **exhortatory.**

**exhume** /ɛksˈhjum/, *v.t.,* **-humed, -huming.** to dig (something buried, esp. a dead body) out of the earth; disinter. [ML *exhumāre,* from L *ex-* EX-[1] + *humus* earth, ground] – **exhumation** /ɛkshjuˈmeɪʃən/, *n.* – **exhumer,** *n.*

**exigency** /əgˈzɪdʒənsi, ɛg-, ˈɛksədʒənsi/, *n., pl.* **-cies.** **1.** exigent state or character; urgency. **2.** (*usu. pl.*) a circumstance that renders prompt action necessary; the need, demand, or requirement of a particular occasion. **3.** a case or situation which demands prompt action or remedy; an emergency. Also, **exigence.**

**exigent** /ˈɛksədʒənt/, *adj.* **1.** requiring immediate action or aid; urgent; pressing. **2.** requiring a great deal, or more than is reasonable. [L *exigens,* ppr., requiring, lit., driving out] – **exigently,** *adv.*

**exigible** /ˈɛksədʒəbəl/, *adj.* that may be exacted; requirable.

**exiguous** /əgˈzɪgjuəs, ɛg-/, *adj.* scanty; small; slender. [L *exiguus*] – **exiguity** /ɛksəˈgjuəti/, **exiguousness,** *n.* – **exiguously,** *adv.*

**exile** /ˈɛgzaɪl, ˈɛksaɪl/, *n., v.,* **-iled, -iling.** *–n.* **1.** prolonged separation from one's country or home, as by stress of circumstances. **2.** anyone separated from his country or home. **3.** expulsion from one's native land by authoritative decree. **4.** the fact or state of such expulsion. **5.** a person banished from his native land. *–v.t.* **6.** to separate from country, home, etc. **7.** to expel or banish (a person) from his country; expatriate. [ME *exil,* from OF, from L *ex(s)ilium* banishment]

**exist** /əgˈzɪst, ɛg-, ɪg-/, *v.i.* **1.** to have actual being; be. **2.** to have life or animation; live. **3.** to continue to be or to live. **4.** to have being in a specified place or under certain conditions; be found; occur. [L *ex(s)istere* stand forth, arise, be]

**existence** /əgˈzɪstəns, ɛg-, ɪg-/, *n.* **1.** the state or fact of existing; being. **2.** continuance in being or life; life: *a struggle for existence.* **3.** mode of existing. **4.** all that exists. **5.** something that exists, an entity, or a being.

**existent** /əgˈzɪstənt, ɛg-, ɪg-/, *adj.* **1.** existing; having existence. **2.** now existing. *–n.* **3.** one who or that which exists.

**existential** /ɛgzɪsˈtɛnʃəl/, *adj.* **1.** pertaining to existence. **2.** *Philos.* of or pertaining to existentialism. **3.** *Logic.* (of a proposition) involving the actual existence of the objects the proposition is about. – **existentially,** *adv.*

**existentialism** /ɛgzɪsˈtɛnʃəlɪzəm/, *n.* any of a group of doctrines, some theistic, some atheistic, deriving from Kierkegaard, which stress the importance of existence, as such, and of the freedom and responsibility of the finite human individual. – **existentialist,** *adj., n.*

**existential psychology** /ɛgzɪsˌtɛnʃəl saɪˈkɒlədʒi/, *n.* **1.** a school of psychology based on the study of introspective data as themselves existing. **2.** the psychological aspect of existentialism.

**exit** /ˈɛgzət, -zɪt, ˈɛksət, -sɪt/, *n.* **1.** a way or passage out. **2.** a going out or away; a departure: *to make one's exit.* **3.** the departure of a player from the stage as part of the action of a play. *–v.i.* **4.** he (or she, or the person named) goes out (used in the text of plays, with reference to an actor). **5.** to depart; go away. **6.** to die. [special use of stage direction *exit* he goes out, influenced by association with L *exitus* a going out]

**ex lib.,** ex libris.

**ex libris** /ɛks ˈlibrəs/, (a phrase inscribed in or on a book, before the name of the owner). [L: from the books]

**ex-librist** /ɛks-ˈlibrəst/, *n.* a collector of bookplates. – **exlibrism,** *n.*

**exo-,** a prefix meaning 'external'. Also, **ex-**[2]. [Gk: outside]

**exocarp** /ˈɛksoukap/, *n.* →**epicarp.**

**exocentric** /ɛksouˈsɛntrɪk/, *adj.* not having the same function in a sentence as any one of its immediate constituents. *In the garden* is an exocentric construction, since it does not function in the same way as the noun *garden.* Cf. **endocentric.**

**exocrine** /ˈɛksoukraɪn, -rɪn/, *adj.* **1.** (of a gland, organ, etc.) having external secretion. **2.** pertaining to the secretion of such a gland.

**Exod.,** *Bible.* Exodus.

**exodermis** /ɛksouˈdɜməs/, *n.* (of a plant) the outer layer or layers of the cortex of primary roots which become suberised after the epidermis has been lost.

**exodontia** /ɛksouˈdɒntiə/, *n.* the branch of dentistry dealing with the extraction of teeth. Also, **exodontics.** [NL, from Gk *ex-* EX-[3] + *odoús* tooth + *-ia* -IA. Cf. Gk *exodontízomai* have one's teeth removed] – **exodontist,** *n.*

**exodus** /ˈɛksədəs/, *n.* a going out; a departure or emigration, usu. of a large number of people. [reference to *Exodus,* the book of the Bible which describes the departure of the Israelites from Egypt under Moses; ME, from L, from Gk *éxodos* a going out]

**exoergic** /ˌɛksouˈɜdʒɪk/, *adj.* (of a process or reaction) giving off energy, esp. of a nuclear process; exothermic.

**ex officio** /ɛks əˈfɪsiou, əˈfɪʃiou/, *adv.* by virtue of office or official position. [L: from office] – **ex-officio,** *adj.*

**exogamy** /ɛkˈsɒgəmi/, *n.* **1.** the custom of marrying outside the tribe or other social unit (opposed to *endogamy*). **2.** *Biol.* the union of gametes of parents not closely related. – **exogamous, exogamic** /ɛksouˈgæmɪk/, *adj.*

**exogenesis** /ˌɛksouˈdʒɛnəsəs/, *n.* the origin (of a disease) from causes external to the body.

**exogenetic** /ˌɛksoudʒəˈnɛtɪk/, *adj.* **1.** having an external origin. **2.** *Med.* (of a disease) caused by external factors. **3.** *Geol.* (of rock movement or processes) occurring at the earth's surface.

**exogenous** /əkˈsɒdʒənəs/, *adj.* **1.** having its origin external; derived externally. **2.** *Bot.* (of plants, as the dicotyledons) having stems which grow by the addition of an annual layer of wood to the outside beneath the bark. **3.** *Physiol., Biochem.* of or denoting the metabolic assimilation of proteins, in which the elimination of nitrogenous catabolites is in direct proportion to the amount of protein taken in. [NL *exōgenus* growing on the outside. See EXO-, -GENOUS] – **exogenic** /ɛksəˈdʒɛnɪk/, *adj.* – **exogenously,** *adv.*

**exonerate** /əgˈzɒnəreɪt, ɛg-/, *v.t.,* **-rated, -rating. 1.** to clear, as of a charge; free from blame; exculpate. **2.** to relieve, as from an obligation, duty, or task. [L *exonerātus,* pp., disburdened] – **exoneration** /əgzɒnəˈreɪʃən, ɛg-/, *n.* – **exonerative,** *adj.* – **exonerator,** *n.*

**exoperidium** /ˌɛksoupəˈrɪdiəm/, *n.* →**peridium.**

**exophthalmos** /ˌɛksɒfˈθælməs/, *n.* protrusion of the eyeball from the orbit, caused by disease or injury. Also, **exophthalmus, exophthalmia.** [NL, from Gk: as adj., with prominent eyes] – **exophthalmic,** *adj.*

**exorable** /ˈɛksərəbəl/, *adj.* susceptible of being persuaded or moved by entreaty. [L *exōrābilis*] – **exorability** /ɛksərəˈbɪləti/, *n.*

**exorbitance** /əgˈzɔbətəns, ɛg-/, *n.* the quality of being exorbitant; excessiveness. Also, **exorbitancy.**

**exorbitant** /əgˈzɔbətənt, ɛg-/, *adj.* exceeding the bounds of custom, propriety, or reason, esp. in amount or extent: *to charge an exorbitant price for something.* [LL *exorbitans,* ppr., going out of the track] – **exorbitantly,** *adv.*

**exorcise** /ˈɛksɔsaɪz/, *v.t.,* **-cised, -cising. 1.** to seek to expel (an evil spirit) by adjuration or religious or solemn ceremonies. **2.** to deliver (a person, place, etc.) from evil spirits or malignant influences. Also, **exorcize.** [LL *exorcīzāre,* from Gk *exorkízein*] – **exorcisement,** *n.* – **exorciser,** *n.*

**exorcism** /ˈɛksɔsɪzəm/, *n.* **1.** the act or process of exorcising. **2.** the ceremony or the formula used.

**exorcist** /ˈɛksɔsəst, -səsəst/, *n.* **1.** one who exorcises. **2.** *Rom. Cath. Church.* a member of one of the minor orders.

**exordium** /ɛkˈsɔdiəm/, *n., pl.* **-diums, -dia** /-diə/. **1.** the beginning of anything. **2.** the introductory part of an oration or discourse. [L: a beginning] – **exordial,** *adj.*

**exoreic** /ɛksəˈriɪk/, *adj.* having external flow as of drainage basins which carry drainage to the sea.

**exoskeleton** /ˌɛksouˈskɛlətən/, *n.* an external protective covering or integument, esp. when hard, as the shell of crustaceans, the scales and plates of fishes, etc. (opposed to *endoskeleton*). – **exoskeletal,** *adj.*

**exosmosis** /ɛksɒzˈmousəs/, *n.* **1.** osmosis from within outwards. **2.** (in osmosis) the flow of that fluid which passes with the lesser rapidity into the other (opposed to *endosmosis*). Also, **exosmose** /ˈɛksɒzmous/. [EX-[3] + OSMOSIS] – **exosmotic** /ɛksɒzˈmɒtɪk/, **exosmic** /ɛkˈsɒzmɪk/, *adj.*

**exosphere** /ˈɛksousfɪə/, *n.* the outermost region of the atmosphere where collisions between molecular particles are so rare that only the force of gravity will return escaping molecules to the upper atmosphere.

**exospore** /ˈɛksouspɔ/, *n.* (of a plant) the outer coat of a spore.

**exostosis** /ɛksɒsˈtousəs/, *n., pl.* **-ses** /-siz/. the morbid formation of bone, or a morbid bony growth, on a bone. [NL, from Gk: outgrowth of bone]

**exoteric** /ɛksouˈtɛrɪk/, *adj.* **1.** suitable for or communicated

i = peat ɪ = pit ɛ = pet æ = pat a = part ɒ = pot ʌ = putt ɔ = port ʊ = put u = pool ɜ = pert ə = apart aɪ = buy eɪ = bay ɔɪ = boy aʊ = how
oʊ = hoe ɪə = here ɛə = hair ʊə = tour g = give θ = thin ð = then ʃ = show ʒ = measure tʃ = choke dʒ = joke ŋ = sing j = you õ = Fr. bon

to the general public. **2.** not belonging or pertaining to the inner or select circle, as of disciples. **3.** popular; simple; commonplace. **4.** of or pertaining to the outside; exterior; external. [LL *exōtericus* external, from Gk *exōterikós*] – **exoterically,** *adv.* – **exotericism,** *n.*

**exothermic** /ɛksoʊ'θɜmɪk/, *adj.* denoting or pertaining to a chemical change which is accompanied by a liberation of heat (opposed to *endothermic*).

**exotic** /əg'zɒtɪk, ɛg-/, *adj.* **1.** of foreign origin or character; not native; introduced from abroad, but not fully naturalised or acclimatised. **2.** strikingly unusual or colourful in appearance or effect; strange; exciting. **3.** *Physics.* (of an atom) with an electron or electrons replaced by muons, antiprotons, etc. –*n.* **4.** anything exotic, as a plant. [L *exōticus,* from Gk *exōtikós* foreign, alien] – **exotically,** *adv.*

**exotica** /əg'zɒtɪkə, ɛg-/, *n.pl.* possessions, artifacts, etc., characterised by the quality of being unusual or exotic.

**exoticism** /əg'zɒtəsɪzəm, ɛg-/, *n.* **1.** tendency to adopt what is exotic. **2.** exotic quality or character. **3.** anything exotic, as a foreign word or idiom.

**exotoxin** /ɛksoʊ'tɒksən/, *n.* a toxin secreted during the life of an organism, either in the body tissues or in food.

**exp.,** **1.** expenses. **2.** expired. **3.** export. **4.** exportation. **5.** exported. **6.** exporter. **7.** express. **8.** experienced.

**expand** /ək'spænd, ɛk-/, *v.t.* **1.** to increase in extent, size, volume, scope, etc.: *heat expands metal.* **2.** to spread or stretch out; unfold: *a bird expands its wings.* **3.** to express in fuller form or greater detail; develop: *to expand a short story into a novel.* –*v.i.* **4.** to increase or grow in extent, bulk, scope, etc.: *most metals expand with heat, the mind expands with experience.* **5.** to spread out; unfold; develop: *the buds had not yet expanded.* [L *expandere* spread out] – **expandable,** *adj.* – **expander,** *n.*

**expanded** /ək'spændəd, ɛk-/, *adj.* **1.** increased in area, bulk, or volume; enlarged. **2.** spread out; extended. **3.** (of printing type) wider than usual for its height.

**expanded metal** /– 'mɛtl/, *n.* sheet metal which has been cut and stretched so that it forms a network giving greater rigidity than wire netting.

**expanding universe** /ˌəkspændɪŋ 'junəvɜs/, *n.* →**big bang theory.**

**expanse** /ək'spæns, ɛk-/, *n.* **1.** that which is spread out, esp. over a large area. **2.** an uninterrupted space or area; a wide extent of anything: *an expanse of water, of sky, etc.* **3.** expansion; extension.

**expansible** /ək'spænsəbəl, ɛk-/, *adj.* capable of being expanded. – **expansibility** /əkspænsə'bɪləti, ɛk-/, *n.*

**expansile** /ək'spænsaɪl, ɛk-/, *adj.* **1.** capable of expanding; such as to expand. **2.** pertaining to expansion.

**expansion** /ək'spænʃən, ɛk-/, *n.* **1.** the act of expanding. **2.** the state of being expanded. **3.** the amount or degree of expanding. **4.** an expanded, dilated, or enlarged portion or form of a thing. **5.** anything spread out; an expanse. **6.** *Maths.* the development at length of an expression indicated in a contracted form. **7.** *Mach.* that part of the operation of an engine in which the volume of the working medium increases and its pressure decreases. [LL *expansio*]

**expansionism** /ək'spænʃənɪzəm, ɛk-/, *n.* the policy of expansion, esp. of territorial expansion. – **expansionist,** *n.*

**expansive** /ək'spænsɪv, ɛk-/, *adj.* **1.** tending to expand or capable of expanding. **2.** causing expansion. **3.** having a wide range or extent; comprehensive; extensive. **4.** (of a person's character, or speech) effusive, unrestrained, free, or open. **5.** *Psychiatry.* marked by an abnormal euphoristic state and by delusions of grandeur. – **expansively,** *adv.* – **expansiveness,** *n.*

**ex parte** /ɛks 'pati/, *adv., adj.* from or on one side only, as in a controversy; in the interest of one party. [L]

**expatiate** /əks'peɪʃieɪt, ɛk-/, *v.i.,* **-ated, -ating.** **1.** to enlarge in discourse or writing; be copious in description or discussion: *to expatiate upon a theme.* **2.** to move or wander about intellectually, imaginatively, etc., without restraint. [L *ex(s)patiātus,* pp., extended, spread out] – **expatiation** /əkspeɪʃi'eɪʃən, ɛk-/, *n.* – **expatiator,** *n.*

**expatriate** /ɛks'pætrieɪt/, *v.,* **-ated, -ating;** /ɛks'pætriət, -rieɪt/, *adj., n.* –*v.t.* **1.** to banish (a person) from his native country. **2.** to withdraw (oneself) from residence in one's native country. **3.** to withdraw (oneself) from allegiance to one's country. –*adj.* **4.** expatriated; exiled. –*n.* **5.** an expatriated person. [LL *expatriātus,* pp.] – **expatriation** /ɛksˌpætri'eɪʃən/, *n.*

**expect** /ək'spɛkt, ɛk-/, *v.t.* **1.** to look forward to; regard as likely to happen; anticipate the occurrence or the coming of: *I expect to do it, I expect him to come, I expect that he will come.* **2.** to look for with reason or justification: *we cannot expect obedience, expect him to do that.* –*v.i.* **3.** *Colloq.* to suppose or surmise. **4.** *Colloq.* to be pregnant: *my wife is expecting again.* [L *ex(s)pectāre* look for]

**expectancy** /ək'spɛktənsi, ɛk-/, *n., pl.* **-cies.** **1.** the quality or state of expecting; expectation; anticipatory belief or desire. **2.** the state of being expected. **3.** an object of expectation; something expected. Also, **expectance.**

**expectant** /ək'spɛktənt, ɛk-/, *adj.* **1.** having expectations; expecting. **2.** expecting the birth of a child: *an expectant mother.* **3.** characterised by expectations. **4.** expected or anticipated; prospective. –*n.* **5.** one who expects; one who waits in expectation. – **expectantly,** *adv.*

**expectation** /ˌɛkspɛk'teɪʃən/, *n.* **1.** the act of expecting. **2.** the state of expecting: *wait in expectation.* **3.** the state of being expected. **4.** an expectant mental attitude. **5.** something expected; a thing looked forward to. **6.** (*oft. pl.*) a prospect of future good or profit: *to have great expectations.* **7.** the degree of probability of the occurrence of something.

**expectation of life,** *n.* the average duration of life beyond a person's attained age, as shown by mortality tables.

**expectative** /ək'spɛktətɪv, ɛk-/, *adj.* **1.** of or pertaining to expectation. **2.** characterised by expectation.

**expectorant** /ək'spɛktərənt, ɛk-/, *adj.* **1.** promoting expectoration from the respiratory tract. –*n.* **2.** an expectorant medicine.

**expectorate** /ək'spɛktəreɪt, ɛk-/, *v.,* **-rated, -rating.** –*v.t.* **1.** to eject or expel (phlegm, etc.) from the throat or lungs by coughing or hawking and spitting; spit. –*v.i.* **2.** to spit. [L *expectorātus,* pp., banished from the breast] – **expectorator,** *n.*

**expectoration** /əkspɛktə'reɪʃən, ɛk-/, *n.* **1.** the act of expectorating. **2.** matter that is expectorated.

**expediency** /ək'spidiənsi, ɛk-/, *n., pl.* **-cies.** **1.** the quality of being expedient; advantageousness; advisability. **2.** a regard for what is politic or advantageous rather than for what is right or just; a sense of self-interest. **3.** something expedient. Also, **expedience.**

**expedient** /ək'spidiənt, ɛk-/, *adj.* **1.** tending to promote some proposed or desired object; fit or suitable for the purpose; proper in the circumstances: *it is expedient that you go.* **2.** conducive to advantage or interest, as opposed to right. **3.** acting in accordance with expediency. –*n.* **4.** a means to an end. **5.** a means devised or employed in an exigency; a resource; a shift: *to resort to expedients to achieve one's purpose.* [ME, from L *expediens,* ppr., dispatching] – **expediently,** *adv.*

**expediential** /əkspidi'ɛnʃəl, ɛk-/, *adj.* pertaining to or regulated by expediency.

**expedite** /'ɛkspədaɪt/, *v.,* **-dited, -diting,** *adj.* –*v.t.* **1.** to speed up the progress of; hasten: *to expedite matters.* **2.** to accomplish promptly, as a piece of business; dispatch. **3.** to issue officially, as a document. –*adj.* **4.** *Obs.* ready; alert. [L *expedītus,* pp., extricated, helped forwards, sent off or dispatched] – **expediter,** *n.*

**expedition** /ɛkspə'dɪʃən/, *n.* **1.** an excursion, journey, or voyage made for some specific purpose, as of war or exploration. **2.** the body of persons or ships, etc., engaged in it. **3.** promptness or speed in accomplishing something.

**expeditionary** /ɛkspə'dɪʃənri, -ʃənəri/, *adj.* pertaining to or composing an expedition: *an expeditionary force.*

**expeditious** /ɛkspə'dɪʃəs/, *adj.* quick; characterised by promptness. – **expeditiously,** *adv.* – **expeditiousness,** *n.*

**expel** /ək'spɛl, ɛk-/, *v.t.,* **-pelled, -pelling.** **1.** to drive or force out or away; discharge or eject: *to expel air from the lungs, an invader from a country.* **2.** to cut off from membership or relations: *to expel a pupil from a school.* [ME *expelle(n),* from L *expellere* drive out] – **expellable,** *adj.* – **expellee** /ɛkspɛl'i/, *n.* – **expeller,** *n.*

**expellant** /ək'spɛlənt, ɛk-/, *adj.* **1.** expelling or having the power to expel. –*n.* **2.** an expellant medicine. Also, **expellent.**

**expend** /ək'spɛnd, ɛk-/, *v.t.* **1.** to use up: *to expend energy, time, care, etc., on something.* **2.** to pay out; disburse; spend. [L *expendere* weigh out, pay out] – **expender,** *n.*

**expendable** /ək'spɛndəbəl, ɛk-/, *adj.* **1.** capable of being expended. **2.** (of an item of equipment or supply) normally consumed in use. **3.** (of men, equipment, etc.) capable of being sacrificed to achieve an objective.

**expenditure** /ək'spɛndətʃə, ɛk-/, *n.* **1.** the act of expending; disbursement; consumption. **2.** that which is expended; expense.

**expense** /ək'spɛns, ɛk-/, *n.* **1.** cost or charge. **2.** a cause or occasion of spending: *owning a car is a great expense.* **3.** the act of expending; expenditure. **4.** loss or injury due to any detracting cause (prec. by *at*): *quantity at the expense of quality.* **5.** (*pl.*) *Comm.* **a.** charges incurred in the execution of an undertaking or commission. **b.** money paid as reimbursement for such charges: *to receive a salary and expenses.* [ME, from AF, from LL *expensa,* properly pp. fem., paid or weighed out]

**expense account** /'– əkaʊnt/, *n.* a record of expenditure incurred by an employee in the course of business to be refunded by the employer or claimed against tax.

**expensive** /ək'spɛnsɪv, ɛk-/, *adj.* entailing great expense; costly. – **expensively,** *adv.* – **expensiveness,** *n.*

**experience** /ək'spɪəriəns, ɛk-/, *n., v.,* **-enced, -encing.** *–n.* **1.** a particular instance of personally encountering or undergoing something: *a strange experience.* **2.** the process or fact of personally observing, encountering, or undergoing something: *business experience.* **3.** the observing, encountering, or undergoing of things generally as they occur in the course of time: *to learn from experience, the range of human experience.* **4.** knowledge or practical wisdom gained from what one has observed, encountered, or undergone: *men of experience.* **5.** *Philos.* the totality of the cognitions given by perception; all that is perceived, understood, and remembered. *–v.t.* **6.** to have experience of; meet with; undergo; feel. **7.** to learn by experience. [ME, from OF, from L *experientia* trial, proof, knowledge]

**experienced** /ək'spɪəriənst, ɛk-/, *adj.* **1.** having had experience. **2.** having learned through experience; taught by experience. **3.** wise or skilful through experience: *an experienced teacher, general, etc.*

**experience table** /ək'spɪəriəns teɪbəl/, *n.* a table compiled from statistical information on the basis of which expectation of life, etc., can be predicted.

**experiential** /əkspɛri'ɛnʃəl, ɛk-/, *adj.* pertaining to or derived from experience. – **experientially,** *adv.*

**experientialism** /əkspɛri'ɛnʃəlɪzəm, ɛk-/, *n.* a doctrine that maintains that all knowledge is derived from experience. – **experientialist,** *n.*

**experiment** /ək'spɛrəmənt, ɛk-/, *n.;* /ək'spɛrəmɛnt, ɛk-/, *v.* *–n.* **1.** a test or trial; a tentative procedure; an act or operation for the purpose of discovering something unknown or testing a principle, supposition, etc.: *a chemical experiment.* **2.** the conducting of such operations; experimentation: *a product that is the result of long experiment.* *–v.i.* **3.** to try or test in order to find something out: *to experiment with drugs in order to find a cure for a certain disease.* [ME, from L *experīmentum* a trial, test] – **experimenter,** *n.*

**experimental** /əkspɛrə'mɛntl, ɛk-/, *adj.* **1.** pertaining to, derived from, or founded on experiment: *an experimental science.* **2.** based on or derived from experience; empirical: *experimental religion.* **3.** of the nature of an experiment; tentative. **4.** functioning as an experiment or used as a means of experimentation: *an experimental aeroplane, an experimental theatre.* – **experimentalist,** *n.* – **experimentally,** *adv.*

**experimentalism** /əkspɛrə'mɛntəlɪzəm, ɛk-/, *n.* systematic reliance upon experimentation; empiricism.

**experimentation** /əkspɛrəmɛn'teɪʃən, ɛk-/, *n.* the act or practice of making experiments; the process of experimenting.

**expert** /'ɛkspɜt/, *n.* **1.** a person who has special skill or knowledge in some particular field; a specialist; authority: *a language expert, an expert on mining.* **2.** *Shearing.* the man who sharpens the shearers' cutters. *–adj.* **3.** possessing special skill or knowledge; trained by practice; skilful or skilled (oft. fol. by *in* or *at*): *an expert driver, to be expert at driving a car.* **4.** pertaining to, coming from, or characteristic of an expert: *expert work, expert advice.* [ME, from L *expertus,* pp., having tried] – **expertly,** *adv.* – **expertness,** *n.*

**expertise** /ɛkspɜ'tiz/, *n.* expert skill or knowledge; expertness.

**expiable** /'ɛkspiəbəl/, *adj.* capable of being expiated.

**expiate** /'ɛkspieɪt/, *v.t.,* **-ated, -ating.** to atone for; make amends or reparation for. [L *expiātus,* pp.] – **expiator,** *n.*

**expiation** /ɛkspi'eɪʃən/, *n.* **1.** the act of expiating. **2.** the means by which atonement or reparation is made; atonement.

**expiatory** /ˌɛkspi'eɪtri, ɛk'spiətri, -təri/, *adj.* able to make atonement or expiation; offered by way of expiation.

**expiration** /ɛkspə'reɪʃən/, *n.* **1.** →**expiry.** **2.** the act of expiring, or breathing out; emission of air from the lungs. **3.** *Obs.* death.

**expiratory** /ək'spɪrətri, ɛk-, -təri/, *adj.* pertaining to the expiration of air from the lungs.

**expire** /ək'spaɪə, ɛk-/, *v.,* **-pired, -piring.** *–v.i.* **1.** to come to an end; terminate. **2.** to die out, as a fire. **3.** to emit the last breath; die. *–v.t.* **4.** to breathe out; emit (air) from the lungs. **5.** to emit or eject. [ME *expire(n),* from F *expirer,* from L *ex(s)pīrāre* breathe out] – **expirer,** *n.*

**expiree** /ɛkspaɪ'ri/, *n.* (formerly) a convict in the early period of the colonisation of Australia, whose sentence had expired.

**expiry** /ɛk'spaɪri/, *n., pl.* **-ries.** **1.** a coming to an end; termination; close. *–adj.* **2.** of or pertaining to the time at which something terminates.

**explain** /ək'spleɪn, ɛk-/, *v.t.* **1.** to make plain or clear; render intelligible: *to explain an obscure point.* **2.** to make known in detail: *to explain how to do something, to explain a process.* **3.** to assign a meaning to; interpret. **4.** to make clear the cause or reason of; account for. **5.** to dispel (difficulties, etc.) by explanation; nullify the significance, or the apparent significance, of (words, facts, occurrences, etc.) by explanation (fol. by *away*). *–v.i.* **6.** to give an explanation. [L *explānāre* make plain, flatten out] – **explainable,** *adj.* – **explainer,** *n.*

**explanation** /ɛksplə'neɪʃən/, *n.* **1.** the act or process of explaining. **2.** that which explains; a statement made to clarify something and make it understandable; an exposition. **3.** a meaning or interpretation: *to find an explanation of a mystery.* **4.** a mutual declaration of the meaning of words spoken, actions, motives, etc., with a view to adjusting a misunderstanding or reconciling differences. [L *explānātio*]

**explanatory** /ək'splænətri, ɛk-, -təri/, *adj.* serving to explain. Also, **explanative.** – **explanatorily,** *adv.*

**explant** /ɛks'plænt, '-plant/, *v.t.* **1.** to take living material from an animal or plant and place it in a culture medium. *–n.* **2.** a piece of explanted tissue. [EX-[1] + PLANT]

**expletive** /ək'splitɪv, ɛk-/, *adj.* **1.** Also, **expletory.** added merely to fill out a sentence or line, give emphasis, etc. *–n.* **2.** an expletive syllable, word, or phrase. **3.** an interjectory word or expression, frequently profane; an exclamatory oath. [LL *explētīvus* serving to fill out] – **expletively,** *adv.*

**explicable** /əks'plɪkəbəl, ɛk-/, *adj.* capable of being explained.

**explicate** /'ɛkspləkeɪt/, *v.t.,* **-cated, -cating.** **1.** to develop (a principle, etc.). **2.** to make plain or clear; explain; interpret. [L *explicātus,* pp., unfolded]

**explication** /ɛksplə'keɪʃən/, *n.* **1.** the act of explicating. **2.** an explanation; interpretation.

**explicative** /ək'splɪkətɪv, ɛk-/, *adj.* explanatory; interpretative. Also, **explicatory.**

**explicit** /ək'splɪsət, ɛk-/, *adj.* **1.** leaving nothing merely implied; clearly expressed; unequivocal: *an explicit statement, instruction, etc.* **2.** clearly developed or formulated: *explicit knowledge or belief.* **3.** definite and unreserved in expression; outspoken: *he was quite explicit on that point.* **4.** *Maths.* (of a function) having the dependent variable expressed directly in terms of the independent variables. See **implicit** (def. 4). [L *explicitus,* var. of *explicātus,* pp., unfolded] – **explicitly,** *adv.* – **explicitness,** *n.*

**explode** /ək'sploʊd, ɛk-/, *v.,* **-ploded, -ploding.** *–v.i.* **1.** to expand with force and noise because of rapid chemical change or decomposition, as gunpowder, nitroglycerine, etc. **2.** to burst, fly into pieces, or break up violently with a loud report, as a boiler from excessive pressure of steam. **3.** to burst forth violently, esp. with noise, laughter, violent speech, etc. 4. *Phonet.* (of stop consonants) to end with a plosion so that the aspiration at the end of the consonant is audible, as *t* in *ten.* *–v.t.* 5. to cause (gunpowder, a boiler, etc.) to explode. 6. to cause to be rejected; destroy the reputation of; discredit or disprove: *to explode a theory.* 7. *Phonet.* to end with a plosion. [L *explōdere* drive out by clapping] – **exploder,** *n.*

**exploded** /ək'sploʊdəd, ɛk-/, *adj.* (of a design, model, etc.) showing all its parts separately, but in their proper positions relative to the whole.

**exploded view** /– 'vju/, *n.* a drawing of a complicated mechanism showing the individual parts still in their relative positions but moved outward and apart.

**exploit**[1] /'ɛksplɔɪt/, *n.* 1. a striking or notable deed; a feat; a spirited or heroic act. 2. *Colloq.* an unusual event or experience. [ME *esploit,* from OF, from L *explicitum,* pp. neut., unfolded]

**exploit**[2] /ək'splɔɪt, ɛk-/, *v.t.* 1. to turn to practical account; utilise for profit, esp. natural resources. 2. to use selfishly for one's own ends. [ME *expleiten,* from OF *expleiter,* from L *explicāre* unfold] – **exploitable,** *adj.* – **exploitative,** *adj.*

**exploitation** /ɛksplɔɪ'teɪʃən/, *n.* 1. utilisation for profit. 2. selfish utilisation.

**exploiter** /ək'splɔɪtə, ɛk-/, *n.* one who exploits.

**exploration** /ɛksplə'reɪʃən/, *n.* 1. the act of exploring. 2. the investigation of unknown regions.

**exploration licence** /'– laɪsəns/, *n.* a licence granted for a specific time to explore a large section of country with a view to prospecting.

**exploratory** /ək'splɒrətri, ɛk-, -təri/, *adj.* 1. pertaining to or concerned with exploration. 2. inclined to make explorations. Also, **explorative.**

**explore** /ək'splɔ, ɛk-/, *v.,* **-plored, -ploring.** *–v.t.* 1. to traverse or range over (a region, etc.) for the purpose of discovery. 2. to look into closely; scrutinise; examine. 3. *Surg.* to investigate, esp. mechanically, as with a probe. 4. *Obs.* to search for; search out. *–v.i.* 5. to engage in exploration. 6. **explore every avenue,** to try every means. [L *explōrāre*]

**explorer** /ək'splɔrə, ɛk-/, *n.* 1. one who or that which explores, esp. one who investigates unknown regions. 2. any instrument used in exploring or sounding a wound, or a cavity in a tooth, etc.

**explosion** /ək'sploʊʒən, ɛk-/, *n.* 1. the act of exploding; a violent expansion or bursting with noise, as of gunpowder or a boiler. 2. the noise itself. 3. a violent outburst of laughter, anger, etc. 4. any sudden, rapid, or large increase: *the population explosion.* 5. the burning of fuel with air in an internal-combustion engine. 6. *Phonet.* →**plosion.** [L *explōsio* a driving off by clapping]

**explosive** /ək'sploʊzɪv, ɛk-, -sɪv/, *adj.* 1. tending or serving to explode: *an explosive substance.* 2. pertaining to or of the nature of an explosion. 3. *Phonet.* →**plosive.** *–n.* 4. an explosive agent or substance, as dynamite. 5. *Phonet,* →**plosive.** – **explosively,** *adv.* – **explosiveness,** *n.*

**explosive rivet** /– 'rɪvət/, *n.* a rivet containing a small explosive charge for expanding the shank in positions which would otherwise be inaccessible.

**expo** /'ɛkspoʊ/, *n.* a large exhibition of technology, arts and crafts, industrial products, etc., often accompanied by shows, dances, festivals, displays, etc. [short for EXPOSITION (def. 1)]

**exponent** /ək'spoʊnənt, ɛk-/, *n.* 1. one who or that which expounds, explains, or interprets. 2. one who or that which stands as a representative, type, or symbol of something: *the exponent of democratic principles.* 3. *Maths.* a symbol placed above and at the right of another symbol (the base), to denote to what power the latter is to be raised, as in $x^3$. [L *expōnens,* ppr., putting forth]

**exponential** /ɛkspə'nɛnʃəl/, *adj.* 1. of or pertaining to an exponent or exponents. 2. *Maths.* a. of or pertaining to the constant *e.* b. having the unknown quantity or variable as an exponent. 3. *Colloq.* marked by a rapid increase in magnitude, number, etc. *–n.* 4. *Maths.* an exponential quantity or function, esp. the constant *e* raised to the power of a given expression containing a variable. – **exponentially,** *adv.*

**exponential horn** /– 'hɔn/, *n.* a loudspeaker horn whose cross-sectional area increases exponentially with the distance from the throat.

**exponible** /ək'spoʊnəbəl, ɛk-/, *adj.* (in logic, esp. of an obscure proposition) admitting or requiring exposition.

**export** /ək'spɔt, ɛk-, 'ɛkspɔt/, *v.;* /'ɛkspɔt/, *n., adj.* *–v.t.* 1. to send (commodities) to other countries or places for sale, exchange, etc. *–n.* 2. the act of exporting; exportation. 3. that which is exported; an article exported. *–adj.* 4. a. of or pertaining to the export of goods: *export income.* b. of or pertaining to products good enough in quality to be exported and better than those kept for home consumption: *export beef.* [L *exportāre* carry away] – **exportable,** *adj.* – **exporter,** *n.*

**exportation** /ɛkspɔ'teɪʃən/, *n.* 1. the act of exporting; the sending of commodities out of a country, typically in trade. 2. *U.S.* something exported.

**export reject** /ɛkspɔt 'ridʒɛkt/, *n.* an item, esp. a foodstuff, which is of insufficient excellence for export but which can be sold locally.

**exposal** /ək'spoʊzəl, ɛk-/, *n.* →**exposure.**

**expose** /ək'spoʊz, ɛk-/, *v.t.,* **-posed, -posing.** 1. to lay open to danger, attack, harm, etc.: *to expose soldiers to gunfire, to expose one's character to attack.* 2. to lay open to something specified: *to expose oneself to misunderstanding.* 3. to uncover or bare to the air, cold, etc.: *to expose one's head to the rain.* 4. to present to view; exhibit; display: *the beggar who exposes his sores.* 5. (*reflexive*) (of a man) to display the genitals: *to expose oneself.* 6. to make known, disclose, or reveal (intentions, secrets, etc.) 7. to reveal or unmask (crime, fraud, an imposter, etc.). 8. to hold up to public reprehension or ridicule. 9. to leave in an unsheltered or open place, as (in primitive societies) an unwanted child to die. 10. *Photog.* to subject (a plate, film or paper) to the action of light or other actinic rays. [OF *exposer,* from *ex-* EX-[1] + *poser* put (see POSE[1]), but associated with derivative of L *expōnere* set forth]

**exposé** /ɛkspoʊ'zeɪ/, *n.* 1. a formal explanation or exposition. 2. an exposure, as of something discreditable. [F, orig. pp. of *exposer* expose]

**exposed** /ək'spoʊzd, ɛk-/, *adj.* 1. left or being without shelter or protection; vulnerable; open to attack. 2. laid open to view; unconcealed. – **exposedness** *n.*

**exposition** /ɛkspə'zɪʃən/, *n.* 1. an exhibition or show, as of the products of art and manufacture. 2. an act of expounding, setting forth, or explaining. 3. a detailed statement or explanation; an explanatory treatise. 4. the act of presenting to view; display. 5. the state of being exposed. 6. *Music.* that part of a fugue or a sonata form, in which the subject or main themes are initially stated.

**expositor** /ək'spɒzətə, ɛk-/, *n.* one who expounds, or gives an exposition. [L; replacing ME *exposit(o)ur,* from AF]

**expository** /ək'spɒzətri, ɛk-, -təri/, *adj.* serving to expound, set forth, or explain. Also, **expositive.**

**ex post facto** /ɛks poʊst 'fæktoʊ/, *adv., adj.* from or by subsequent action; subsequently; retrospectively. [L]

**ex post facto law,** *n.* one passed after an alleged crime has been committed which, if applied in the case of an accused person, would work to his disadvantage.

**expostulate** /ək'spɒstʃuleɪt, ɛk-/, *v.i.,* **-lated, -lating.** to reason earnestly with a person against something he intends to do or has done; remonstrate (*on,* or *upon*): *to expostulate with him on the impropriety.* [L *expostulātus,* pp.] – **expostulatingly,** *adv.* – **expostulator,** *n.*

**expostulation** /əkspɒstʃu'leɪʃən, ɛk-/, *n.* 1. the act of expostulating; remonstrance; earnest and kindly protest. 2. an expostulatory remark or address.

**expostulatory** /ək'spɒstʃulətri, ɛk-, -təri/, *adj.* expostulating; conveying expostulation. Also, **expostulative.**

**exposure** /ək'spoʊʒə, ɛk-/, *n.* 1. the act of exposing. 2. disclosure, as of something private or secret. 3. revealing or unmasking, as of crime, fraud, an imposter, etc. 4. presentation to view, esp. in an open or public manner. 5. a laying open or subjecting to the action or influence of something: *exposure to the weather, to danger, or to ridicule.* 6. *Photog.* a. the act of presenting a sensitive material as film, plate, or paper, to the action of light or other actinic rays. b. the duration of this exposure. 7. a putting out without shelter or protection, as of an abandoned child. 8. a state of being exposed. 9. situation with regard to sunlight or wind; aspect: *a southern exposure.* 10. something exposed, as to view; an exposed surface. [EXPOS(E) + -URE]

**exposure meter** /'– mitə/, *n.* →**light meter.**

**expound** /ək'spaʊnd, ɛk-/, *v.t.* **1.** to set forth or state in detail: *to expound theories, principles, etc.* **2.** to explain; interpret. [ME *expoune(n), expounde(n),* from OF *espondre,* from L *expōnere* put out, expose, set forth, explain] – **expounder,** *n.*

**express** /ək'sprɛs, ɛk-/, *v.t.* **1.** to put (thought) into words: *to express an idea clearly.* **2.** to show, manifest, or reveal: *to express one's feelings.* **3.** to set forth the opinions, feelings, etc., of (oneself), as in speaking, writing, painting. **4.** to represent by a symbol, character, figure, or formula. **5.** to press or squeeze out: *to express the juice of grapes.* **6.** to exude or emit (a liquid, smell, or the like) as if under pressure. **7.** *Chiefly U.S.* to send express: *to express a package or merchandise.* *–adj.* **8.** clearly indicated; distinctly stated (rather than implied); definite; explicit; plain. **9.** special; particular; definite: *an express purpose.* **10.** duly or exactly formed or represented: *an express image.* **11.** pertaining to an express: *an express agency.* **12.** specially direct or fast, as a train, etc. *–adv.* **13.** by express; by express train or messenger; unusually fast. **14.** specially; for a particular purpose. *–n.* **15.** an express train, bus or, occasionally, a long-distance motor coach. **16.** a messenger or a message specially sent. **17.** a system or method for the speedy dispatch of parcels, money, etc.: *to send a parcel by express.* **18.** a company engaged in this business. **19.** that which is sent by express. [ME *expresse,* from L *expressus,* pp., pressed out, described] – **expresser,** *n.* – **expressible,** *adj.*

**expressage** /ək'sprɛsɪdʒ, ɛk-/, *n.* **1.** the business of transmitting parcels, money, etc., by express. **2.** the charge for such transmission.

**express delivery** /əksprɛs də'lɪvəri/, *n.* rapid delivery by special messenger.

**expression** /ək'sprɛʃən, ɛk-/, *n.* **1.** the act of expressing or setting forth in words: *the expression of opinions, facts, etc.* **2.** a particular word, phrase, or form of words: *archaic expressions.* **3.** the manner or form in which a thing is expressed in words; wording; phrasing. **4.** the power of expressing in words: *joy beyond expression.* **5.** indication of feeling, spirit, character, etc., as on the face, in the voice, or in artistic execution. **6.** a look or intonation as expressing feeling, etc.: *a sad expression.* **7.** the quality or power of expressing feeling, etc.: *a face that lacks expression.* **8.** the act of expressing or representing, as by symbols. **9.** *Maths.* a symbol or a combination of symbols serving to express something. **10.** the act of expressing or pressing out. – **expressionless,** *adj.*

**expressionism** /ək'sprɛʃənɪzəm, ɛk-/, *n.* a theory of art esp. that originating in Europe about the time of World War I, which emphasises free expression of the artist's emotional reactions rather than the representation of the natural appearance of objects. – **expressionist,** *n., adj.* – **expressionistic** /əksprɛʃə'nɪstɪk, ɛk-/, *adj.*

**expression mark** /ək'sprɛʃən mak/, *n.* one of a set of directions in a piece of music indicating how it should be played.

**expressive** /ək'sprɛsɪv, ɛk-/, *adj.* **1.** serving to express; indicative of power to express: *a look expressive of gratitude.* **2.** full of expression, as the face or voice. **3.** of, pertaining to, or concerned with expression. – **expressively,** *adv.* – **expressiveness,** *n.* – **expressivity** /ɛksprɛs'ɪvəti/, *n.*

**express letter** /ək'sprɛs lɛtə/, *n.* a letter sent by special delivery.

**expressly** /ək'sprɛsli, ɛk-/, *adv.* **1.** in an express manner; explicitly. **2.** for the express purpose; specially.

**expresso** /ɛk'sprɛsoʊ/, *n.* →**espresso.**

**expressway** /ək'sprɛsweɪ, ɛk-/, *n.* a road designed for high speed traffic. Also, **freeway.**

**expropriate** /ɛks'proʊprieɪt/, *v.t.,* **-ated, -ating. 1.** to take, esp. for public use by the right of eminent domain, thus divesting the title of the private owner. **2.** to dispossess (a person) of ownership. [LL *expropriātus,* pp., deprived of property, from L *ex-* EX-[1] + *proprium* property] – **expropriation** /ɛksproʊpri'eɪʃən/, *n.* – **expropriator,** *n.*

**ex-pug** /ɛks-'pʌg/, *n. Colloq.* a retired boxer.

**expugnable** /ɛk'spʌgnəbəl/, *adj.* capable of being overcome, defeated, conquered, etc.

**expulsion** /ək'spʌlʃən, ɛk-/, *n.* **1.** the act of driving out or expelling. **2.** the state of being expelled. [L *expulsio*]

**expulsive** /ək'spʌlsɪv, ɛk-/, *adj.* tending or serving to expel.

**expunction** /ək'spʌŋkʃən, ɛk-/, *n.* the act of expunging; an erasure. [L *expunctus,* pp., struck out + -ION]

**expunge** /ək'spʌndʒ, ɛk-/, *v.t.,* **-punged, -punging. 1.** to strike or blot out; erase; obliterate. **2.** to efface; wipe out or destroy. [L *expungere* prick out, strike out] – **expunger,** *n.*

**expurgate** /'ɛkspɜgeɪt, -pəgeɪt/, *v.t.,* **-gated, -gating. 1.** to amend by removing offensive or objectionable matter: *to expurgate a book.* **2.** to purge or cleanse. [L *expurgātus,* pp., purged] – **expurgation** /ɛkspɜ'geɪʃən, -pə'geɪʃən/, *n.* – **expurgator,** *n.*

**expurgatorial** /ɛkspɜgə'tɔriəl/, *adj.* pertaining to an expurgator or to expurgation.

**expurgatory** /ɛk'spɜgətri, -təri/, *adj.* serving to expurgate; of or pertaining to expurgation.

**exquisite** /'ɛkskwəzət, ək'skwɪzət, ɛk-/, *adj.* **1.** of peculiar beauty or charm, or rare and appealing excellence, as a face, a flower, colouring, music, poetry, etc. **2.** extraordinarily fine, admirable, or consummate. **3.** intense, acute, or keen, as pleasure, pain, etc. **4.** keenly or delicately sensitive or responsive: *an exquisite ear for music.* **5.** of rare excellence of production or execution, as works of art, workmanship, or the artist or worker. **6.** of peculiar refinement or elegance, as taste, manners, etc., or persons. **7.** *Obs.* carefully sought out, chosen, ascertained, devised, etc. *–n.* **8.** a person, esp. a man, who is too much concerned about his clothes, etc.; a dandy; a coxcomb. [ME, from L *exquīsītus,* pp., sought out] – **exquisitely,** *adv.* – **exquisiteness,** *n.*

**exsanguination** /əksæŋgwə'neɪʃən, ɛk-/, *n.* **1.** expulsion of blood from a part. **2.** the state of being deprived of blood. – **exsanguinous** /ək'sæŋgwənəs, ɛk-/, *adj.*

**exsanguine** /ək'sæŋgwɪn, ɛk-/, *adj.* →**anaemic.**

**exscind** /ɛk'sɪnd/, *v.t.* to cut out or off. [L *exscindere*]

**exsect** /ɛk'sɛkt/, *v.t.* to cut out. [L *exsectus,* pp.] – **exsection,** *n.*

**exsert** /ɛk'sɜt/, *v.t.* **1.** to thrust out. *–adj.* **2.** →**exserted.** [L *exsertus,* pp., put forth] – **exsertion,** *n.*

**exserted** /ɛk'sɜtəd/, *adj.* (of a plant or animal part) projecting beyond the surrounding parts, as a stamen.

**exsertile** /ɛk'sɜtaɪl/, *adj.* capable of being exserted or protruded, as a lizard's tongue.

**ex-service** /ɛk-'sɜvəs/, *adj.* **1.** having formerly served in the armed forces. **2.** Also **ex-services.** of or pertaining to a group, society, club, etc. for returned servicemen.

**ex-serviceman** /ɛk-'sɜvəsmən/, *n., pl.* **-men** /-mən/. one who has served in one of the armed services, esp. during wartime.

**exsiccate** /'ɛksəkeɪt/, *v.t.,* **-cated, -cating. 1.** to dry or remove the moisture from, as a substance. **2.** to dry up, as moisture. [L *exsiccātus,* pp.] – **exsiccation** /ɛksə'keɪʃən/, *n.* – **exsiccative** /'ɛksəkətɪv/, *adj.* – **exsiccator,** *n.*

**exstipulate** /ɛk'stɪpjələt, -leɪt/, *adj.* (of a petiole) without stipules. Also, **estipulate.**

**ext.,** **1.** extension. **2.** external. **3.** extinct. **4.** extra.

**extant** /ɛk'stænt, 'ɛkstənt/, *adj.* **1.** in existence; still existing; not destroyed or lost. **2.** *Archaic.* standing out; protruding. [L *ex(s)tans,* ppr., standing out]

**extemporal** /ək'stɛmpərəl, ɛk-/, *adj. Obs. or Archaic.* extemporaneous; extempore. [L *extemporālis*]

**extemporaneous** /əkstɛmpə'reɪniəs, ɛk-/, *adj.* **1.** done or spoken extempore; impromptu: *an extemporaneous speech.* **2.** speaking or performing extempore. **3.** made for the occasion, as a shelter. [LL *extemporāneus,* replacing L *extemporālis*] – **extemporaneously,** *adv.* – **extemporaneousness,** *n.*

**extemporary** /ək'stɛmpərəri, ɛk-, -prəri/, *adj.* **1.** extemporaneous; extempore. **2.** *Obs.* sudden; unexpected. – **extemporarily,** *adv.* – **extemporariness,** *n.*

**extempore** /ək'stɛmpəri, ɛk-/, *adv.* **1.** on the spur of the moment; without premeditation or preparation; offhand. **2.** without notes: *to speak extempore.* **3.** (of musical performance) by improvisation. *–adj.* **4.** extemporaneous; impromptu. [L *ex tempore,* lit., out of the time]

**extemporise** /ək'stɛmpəraɪz, ɛk-/, *v.,* **-rised, -rising.** *–v.i.* **1.** to speak extempore. **2.** to sing, or play an instrument, composing the music as one proceeds; improvise. *–v.t.* **3.** to make or devise for the occasion. **4.** *Music.* to compose while playing; improvise. Also, **extemporize.** – **extemporisation** /əkstɛmpəraɪˈzeɪʃən, ɛk-/, *n.* – **extemporiser,** *n.*

**extend** /əkˈstɛnd, ɛk-/, *v.t.* **1.** to stretch out; draw out to the full length. **2.** to stretch, draw, or arrange in a given direction, or so as to reach a particular point, as a cord or a line of troops. **3.** to stretch forth or hold out, as the arm or hand. **4.** to place at full length, esp. horizontally, as the body, limbs, etc. **5.** to increase the length or duration of; lengthen; prolong. **6.** to stretch out in various or all directions; expand; spread out in area. **7.** to enlarge the scope of, or make more comprehensive, as operations or influence. **8.** to hold forth as an offer or grant; offer; grant; give. **9.** *Finance.* to postpone (the payment of a debt) beyond the time originally agreed upon. **10.** *Comm.* to transfer (figures) from one column to another in bookkeeping, invoices, etc. **11.** *Law.* **a.** to assess or value. **b.** to make a seizure or levy upon, as land, by a writ of elegit or a writ of extent. **12.** *Obs.* to take by seizure. –*v.i.* **13.** to be or become extended; stretch out; to be continued in length or duration, or in various or all directions. **14.** to reach, as to a particular point. **15.** to increase in length, area, scope, etc. [ME *extend(en),* from L *extendere*] – **extendible, extendable,** *adj.*

**extended** /əkˈstɛndəd, ɛk-/, *adj.* **1.** stretched out. **2.** continued or prolonged. **3.** spread out. **4.** widespread or extensive; having extension or spatial magnitude. **5.** outstretched. **6.** *Print.* (of type) expanded. – **extendedly,** *adv.*

**extended family** /– ˈfæmli/, *n.* a family group or unit comprising not only parents and children but also immediate relatives, and sometimes people not related to the group; responsibility for all the children is shared by all the older members of the group. See **nuclear family.**

**extended play** /– ˈpleɪ/, *adj.* →**EP**

**extender** /əkˈstɛndə, ɛk-/, *n.* **1.** an inorganic powder added to paints to improve film formation and to minimise settlement on storage. **2.** a substance added to synthetic resins, glues, or elastomers either to reduce their cost or to some extent to modify their properties.

**extensible** /əkˈstɛnsəbəl, ɛk-/, *adj.* capable of being extended. – **extensibility** /əkstɛnsəˈbɪləti, ɛk-/, **extensibleness,** *n.*

**extensile** /ɛkˈstɛnsaɪl/, *adj. Chiefly Zool., Anat.* capable of being extended; adapted for stretching out; extensible; protrusible.

**extensimeter** /ˌɛkstɛnˈsɪmətə/, *n.* →**extensometer.**

**extension** /əkˈstɛnʃən, ɛk-/, *n.* **1.** the act of extending. **2.** the state of being extended. **3.** that by which something is extended; a prolongation, as an addition to a house. **4.** something extended; an extended object or space. **5.** range of extending; degree of extensiveness; extent. **6.** an extra telephone connected to the same line as a main telephone. **7.** *Comm.* a written engagement on the part of a creditor, allowing a debtor further time to pay a debt. **8.** *Physics., etc.* that property of a body by which it occupies a portion of space. **9.** *Anat.* **a.** the act of straightening a limb. **b.** the position which a limb assumes when it is straightened. **10.** *Logic.* the class of things to which a term is applicable; denotation: *the extension of the term 'man' consists of the class of such individuals as 'Socrates', 'Plato', 'Aristotle', etc.* –*adj.* **11.** of or pertaining to a course, lecture, service, etc., which is outside the normal function of an organisation: *the department of agriculture offers an extension service to farmers.* [L *extensio*] – **extensional,** *adj.* – **extensionally,** *adv.*

**extension course** /ˈ– kɔs/, *n.* (in many universities and colleges) a course of study for persons not regularly enrolled as students, frequently provided through evening classes or by correspondence.

**extension worker** /ˈ– wɜkə/, *n. N.Z.* a trained worker paid to give expert or practical field-advice in agriculture, farming, forestry, etc.

**extensity** /əkˈstɛnsəti, ɛk-/, *n.* **1.** the quality of having extension. **2.** *Psychol.* that attribute of sensation from which the perception of extension is developed.

**extensive** /əkˈstɛnsɪv, ɛk-/, *adj.* **1.** of great extent; wide; broad; covering a great area; large in amount: *an extensive forest, an extensive influence.* **2.** far-reaching; comprehensive; thorough; lengthy; detailed: *extensive knowledge, extensive enquiries.* **3.** of or having extension. **4.** pertaining to a system of agriculture involving the use or cultivation of large areas of land (as where land is cheap) with a minimum of labour and expense (opposed to *intensive*). – **extensively,** *adv.* – **extensiveness,** *n.*

**extensometer** /ˌɛkstɛnˈsɒmətə/, *n.* an apparatus for measuring minute degrees of expansion, contraction, or deformation. Also, **extensimeter.** [L *extensus,* pp., extended + -o- + -METER[1]]

**extensor** /əkˈstɛnsə, ɛk-, -sɔ/, *n.* a muscle which serves to extend or straighten a part of the body (opposed to *flexor*). [LL: one who or that which stretches]

**extent** /əkˈstɛnt, ɛk-/, *n.* **1.** the space or degree to which a thing extends; length, area, or volume: *the extent of a line, to the full extent of his power.* **2.** something extended; an extended space; a particular length, area, or volume; something having extension. **3.** *English Law.* **a.** a writ to recover debts of record due to the crown, under which land, etc., may be seized. **b.** a seizure made under such a writ. **4.** *U.S. Law.* a writ, or a levy, by which a creditor has his debtor's lands valued and transferred to himself, absolutely or for a term of years. **5.** *Hist.* assessment or valuation, as of land. **6.** *Logic.* →**extension** (def. 10). [ME *extente,* from AF, from L *extendere* extend]

**extenuate** /əkˈstɛnjueɪt, ɛk-/, *v.t.,* **-ated, -ating. 1.** to represent (fault, offence, etc.) as less serious: *to extenuate a crime.* **2.** to serve to make (fault, offence, etc.) seem less serious: *extenuating circumstances.* **3.** to underestimate, underrate, or make light of. **4.** *Archaic.* **a.** to make thin, lean, or emaciated. **b.** to reduce the consistency or density of. [L *extenuātus,* pp., made thin] – **extenuatingly,** *adv.* – **extenuative,** *adj.* – **extenuator,** *n.*

**extenuation** /əkstɛnjuˈeɪʃən, ɛk-/, *n.* **1.** the act of extenuating. **2.** the state of being extenuated. **3.** that which extenuates; a partial excuse.

**extenuatory** /əkˈstɛnjuətri, ɛk-, -təri/, *adj.* tending to extenuate; characterised by extenuation.

**exterior** /əkˈstɪəriə, ɛk-/, *adj.* **1.** outer; being on the outer side: *the exterior side or surface, exterior decorations.* **2.** situated or being outside; pertaining to or connected with what is outside: *the exterior possessions of a country.* **3.** *Geom.* (of an angle) outer, as an angle formed outside two parallel lines when cut by a third line. –*n.* **4.** the outer surface or part; the outside; outward form or appearance. **5.** *Films, Television.* a sequence shot out-of-doors. [L, comparative of *exter, exterus* outer, outward] – **exteriority** /əkstɪəriˈɒrəti, ɛk-/, *n.* – **exteriorly,** *adv.*

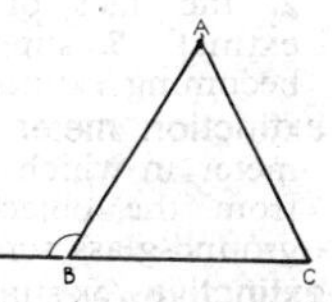

ABD, exterior angle of triangle ABC

**exteriorise** /əkˈstɪəriəˌraɪz/, *v.t.* **1.** →**externalise. 2.** (of an occultist) to abandon the physical body for a short period of time, while retaining full consciousness and awareness. **3.** *Surg.* to expose (an attached organ, etc.) outside a body cavity, esp. to remove it from the field of operation. – **exteriorisation,** *n.*

**exterminate** /əkˈstɜməneɪt, ɛk-/, *v.t.,* **-nated, -nating.** to get rid of by destroying; destroy totally; extirpate. [L *exterminātus,* pp., driven beyond the boundaries] – **exterminable,** *adj.* – **extermination** /əkstɜməˈneɪʃən, ɛk-/, *n.* – **exterminator,** *n.*

**exterminatory** /əkˈstɜmənətri, ɛk-, -təri/, *adj.* serving or tending to exterminate. Also, **exterminative.**

**extern** /ˈɛkstɜn, əkˈstɜn/, *n.* a person connected with an institution but not residing in it. Also, **externe.** [L *externus* outward]

**external** /əkˈstɜnəl, ɛk-/, *adj.* **1.** of or pertaining to the outside or outer part; outer. **2.** to be applied to the outside of a body, as a remedy. **3.** situated or being outside something; acting or coming from without. **4.** pertaining to the outward or visible appearance or show: *external acts of worship.* **5.** pertaining to or concerned with what is outside or foreign: *external commerce.* **6.** *Zool., Anat.* on the side farthest away from the body, from the median line, or from the centre of a radially symmetrical form. **7.** *Metaphys.* belonging or pertaining to the world of things, considered as independent of the perceiving mind. **8.** *Educ.* studying or studied outside the campus of a university or similar institution: *an external degree.* –*n.* **9.** the outside; outer surface. **10.** that which is external. **11.** (*pl.*) external or non-essential features, circumstances, etc.: *the externals of religion.* [EXTERN + -AL[1]] – **externally,** *adv.*

**external-combustion** /əkstɜnəl-kəm'bʌstʃən/, *adj.* of or pertaining to an engine in which the ignition of the fuel mixture takes place outside the engine cylinder (as distinct from an *internal-combustion engine*).

**external ear** /ɛk'stɜnəl ɪə/, *n.* that section of the ear which is made up of its projecting outer portion and the ear canal.

**externalise** /ək'stɜnəlaɪz, ɛk-/, *v.t.,* **-lised, -lising.** **1.** to make external; embody in an outward form. **2.** *Psychol.* to attribute (one's own emotions) to the outside world. Also, **externalize.** – **externalisation** /ək,stɜnəlaɪ'zeɪʃən, ɛk-/, *n.*

**externalism** /ək'stɜnəlɪzəm, ɛk-/, *n.* attention or devotion to externals; excessive attention to externals, esp. in religion. – **externalist,** *n.*

**externality** /ɛkstɜ'nælәti/, *n., pl.* **-ties.** **1.** the state or quality of being external. **2.** something external; an outward feature. **3.** excessive attention to externals.

**exteroceptive** /ɛkstəroʊ'sɛptɪv/, *adj.* pertaining to exteroceptors, the stimuli impinging upon them, and the nerve impulses initiated by them. [*extero-* (combining form of L *exterus* exterior) + *-ceptive,* as in RECEPTIVE]

**exteroceptor** /'ɛkstəroʊsɛptə/, *n.* an end organ in or near the skin or mucous membrane, responding to and conveying stimuli from the external environment. [*extero-* + -CEPTOR. See EXTEROCEPTIVE]

**exterritorial** /,ɛkstɛrə'tɔriəl/, *adj.* →**extraterritorial.** – **exterritoriality** /,ɛkstɛrətɔri'æləti/, *n.* – **exterritorially,** *adv.*

**extinct** /əks'tɪŋkt, ɛk-/, *adj.* **1.** extinguished; quenched; having ceased eruption, as a volcano. **2.** obsolete, as an institution. **3.** having come to an end; without a living representative, as a species. [ME *extincte,* from L *extinctus,* pp., destroyed, put out]

**extinction** /ək'stiŋkʃən, ɛk-/, *n.* **1.** the act of extinguishing. **2.** the fact of being extinguished; condition of being extinct. **3.** suppression; abolition; annihilation. **4.** *Biol.* a becoming extinct; a coming to an end or dying out.

**extinction meter** /'– mitə/, *n.* (in photography) an exposure meter in which the reading is made by attenuating the light from the object until the point when the image on a ground-glass screen becomes indistinguishable.

**extinctive** /ək'stiŋktɪv, ɛk-/, *adj.* tending or serving to extinguish.

**extinguish** /ək'stɪŋgwɪʃ, ɛk-/, *v.t.* **1.** to put out (a fire, light, etc.); put out the flame of (something burning or alight). **2.** to put an end to or bring to an end; wipe out of existence: *to extinguish a hope, a life, etc.* **3.** to obscure or eclipse, as by superior brilliancy. **4.** *Law.* to discharge (a debt), as by payment. [L *ex(s)tinguere* put out, quench, destroy + -ISH[2]] – **extinguishable,** *adj.* – **extinguishment,** *n.*

**extinguisher** /ək'stɪŋgwɪʃə, ɛk-/, *n.* **1.** one who or that which extinguishes. **2.** any of various portable apparatuses for extinguishing fire: *a chemical extinguisher.*

**extirpate** /'ɛkstɜpeɪt, -stə-/, *v.t.,* **-pated, -pating.** **1.** to remove utterly; destroy totally; exterminate; do away with. **2.** to pull up by the roots; root up. [L *ex(s)tirpātus,* pp., rooted out] – **extirpation** /ɛkstɜ'peɪʃən, -stə-/, *n.* – **extirpative,** *adj.* – **extirpator,** *n.*

**extol** /ək'stoʊl, ɛk-/, *v.t.,* **-tolled, -tolling.** to praise highly; laud; eulogise. Also, **extoll.** [L *extollere,* lit., lift out or up] – **extoller,** *n.* – **extolment,** *n.*

**extort** /ək'stɔt, ɛk-/, *v.t.* **1.** to wrest or wring (something) from a person by violence, intimidation, or abuse of authority; obtain (money, information, etc.) by force, torture, threat, or the like. **2.** to take illegally under cover of office. [L *extortus,* pp., twisted or wrested out] – **extorter,** *n.* – **extortive,** *adj.*

**extortion** /ək'stɔʃən, ɛk-/, *n.* **1.** the act of extorting. **2.** *Law.* the crime of obtaining money or other things of value under colour of office, when none is due or not so much is due, or before it is due. **3.** oppressive or illegal exaction, as of excessive price or interest. **4.** anything extorted. [ME, from L *extortio*]

**extortionary** /ək'stɔʃənri, ɛk-, -ʃənəri/, *adj.* characterised by or given to extortion.

**extortionate** /ək'stɔʃənət, ɛk-/, *adj.* **1.** exorbitant; grossly excessive: *extortionate prices.* **2.** characterised by extortion, as persons. – **extortionately,** *adv.*

**extortioner** /ək'stɔʃənə, ɛk-/, *n.* one who practises extortion. Also, **extortionist.**

**extra** /'ɛkstrə/, *adj.* **1.** beyond or more than what is usual, expected, or necessary; additional: *an extra edition of a newspaper, an extra price.* **2.** better than what is usual: *extra fineness.* **3.** *Colloq.* extraordinarily good. *–n.* **4.** something extra or additional. **5.** an additional expense. **6.** an edition of a newspaper other than the regular edition or editions. **7.** *U.S.* something of superior quality. **8.** *Films.* a person hired by the day to play a minor part, as a member of a mob or crowd. **9.** *U.S.* an additional worker. **10.** (*usu. pl.*) *Cricket.* a score or run not made from the bat, as a bye or a wide; sundry. **11.** an additional period taught by a teacher because of the absence of a colleague. *–adv.* **12.** in excess of the usual or specified amount: *an extra high price.* **13.** beyond the ordinary degree; unusually; uncommonly: *done extra well.* [probably orig. short for EXTRAORDINARY. Cf. EXTRA-]

**extra-,** a prefix meaning 'outside', 'beyond', 'besides', freely used as an English formative, as in *extrajudicial, extraterritorial,* and many other words mostly self explanatory, as *extra-atmospheric,* etc. Also, **extro-.** [L, combining form of *extrā,* adv. and prep., outside (of), without]

**extrabold** /ɛkstrə'boʊld/, *n.* unusually heavy bold-face print.

**extracanonical** /ɛkstrəkə'nɒnɪkəl/, *adj.* not included in the canon of Scripture.

**extracellular** /ɛkstrə'sɛljələ/, *adj.* outside a cell or cells.

**extra-condensed** /ɛkstrə-kən'dɛnst/, *adj.* (of type) having an extremely narrow face.

**extra cover** /ɛkstrə 'kʌvə/, *n. Cricket* **1.** the position of a fielder between mid-off and cover-point. **2.** a fielder occupying this position. Also, **extra cover-point.**

**extract** /ək'strækt, ɛk-/, *v.;* /'ɛkstrækt/, *n.* *–v.t.* **1.** to draw forth or get out by force: *to extract a tooth.* **2.** to deduce (a doctrine, principle, etc.). **3.** to derive or obtain (pleasure, comfort, etc.) from a particular source. **4.** to take or copy out (matter from a book, etc.), or make excerpts from (the book, etc.). **5.** to extort (information, money, etc.). **6.** to separate or obtain (a juice, ingredient, principle, etc.) from a mixture by pressure, distillation, treatment with solvents, or the like. **7.** *Metall.* to separate a metal from its ore by any process. **8.** *Maths.* to determine (the root of a quantity). *–n.* **9.** something extracted. **10.** a passage taken from a book, etc.; an excerpt; a quotation. **11.** a solution or preparation containing the active principles of a drug, plant juice, or the like. **12.** a solid or viscid substance extracted from a drug, plant, or the like. **13.** *Textiles.* a material made from old woollen and worsted fabrics with the addition of cotton or rayon. [L *extractus,* pp., drawn out] – **extractable, extractible,** *adj.*

**extraction** /ək'strækʃən, ɛk-/, *n.* **1.** the act of extracting. **2.** the state or fact of being extracted. **3.** descent or lineage. **4.** something extracted; an extract.

**extractive** /ək'stræktɪv, ɛk-/, *adj.* **1.** tending or serving to extract. **2.** that may be extracted. **3.** of or of the nature of an extract. *–n.* **4.** something extracted.

**extractor** /ək'stræktə, ɛk-/, *n.* **1.** a person or a thing that extracts. **2.** the mechanism in a firearm or cannon which, after firing, pulls an empty or unfired cartridge or shell case out of the chamber of the weapon and brings it into place for action by the ejector.

**extracurricular** /ɛkstrəkə'rɪkjələ/, *adj.* outside the regular curriculum.

**extraditable** /'ɛkstrədaɪtəbəl/, *adj.* **1.** capable of being extradited; subject to extradition. **2.** capable of incurring extradition.

**extradite** /'ɛkstrədaɪt/, *v.t.,* **-dited, -diting.** **1.** to give up (a fugitive or prisoner) to another nation, state, or authority. **2.** to obtain the extradition of. [backformation from EXTRADITION]

**extradition** /ɛkstrə'dɪʃən/, *n.* the surrender of a fugitive from justice or a prisoner by one state or authority to another. [F, from L *ex-* EX-[1] + *trāditio* a giving over]

**extrados** /ɛk'streɪdɒs/, *n.* the exterior curve or surface of an arch or vault. [F, from L *extra-* EXTRA- + F *dos* back (from L *dorsum*)]

**extragalactic** /ɛkstrəgə'læktɪk/, *adj.* outside the galaxy.

**extrajudicial** /ˌɛkstrədʒu'dɪʃəl/, *adj.* outside the normal course of judicial procedure; beyond the action or authority of a court. – **extrajudicially,** *adv.*

**extramarital** /ɛkstrə'mærətl/, *adj.* of or pertaining to sexual relations with someone other than one's spouse.

**extrametrical** /ɛkstrə'mɛtrəkəl/, *adj.* containing more syllables than those required by the metre.

**extramundane** /ɛkstrə'mʌndeɪn/, *adj.* beyond our world or the material universe.

**extramural** /ɛkstrə'mjurəl/, *adj.* **1.** outside the walls or boundaries, as of a city or town. **2.** outside the confines of a school or university; connected with a school or university but not under its direct control: *extramural studies, extramural activities.*

**extraneous** /ək'streɪniəs, ɛk-/, *adj.* introduced or coming from without; not belonging or proper to a thing; external; foreign; not essential. [L *extrāneus* that is without, foreign] – **extraneously,** *adv.* – **extraneousness,** *n.*

**extraordinary** /ək'strɔdənri, ɛk-/, *adj.* **1.** beyond what is ordinary; out of the regular or established order: *extraordinary power or expenses.* **2.** exceptional in character, amount, extent, degree, etc.; unusual; remarkable: *extraordinary weather, weight, speed, an extraordinary man or book.* **3.** (of officials, etc.) outside of, additional to, or ranking below an ordinary one: *an extraordinary professor.* [L *extrāordinārius* out of the common order] – **extraordinarily,** *adv.* – **extraordinariness,** *n.*

**extraordinary ray** /– 'reɪ/, *n.* the part of a doubly refracted ray which does not obey the ordinary laws of refraction. See **ordinary ray.**

**extrapolate** /ɛk'stræpəleɪt/, *v.,* **-lated, -lating.** *–v.t.* **1.** *Statistics.* to estimate a quantity which depends on one or more variables by extending the variables beyond their established ranges. **2.** to infer (what is not known) from that which is known; conjecture. *–v.i.* **3.** to perform extrapolation. [EXTRA- + *-polate* of INTERPOLATE] – **extrapolation** /ɛkstræpə'leɪʃən/, *n.*

**extraprofessional** /ɛkstrəprə'fɛʃənəl/, *adj.* outside ordinary limits of professional interest or duty.

**extrasensory** /ɛkstrə'sɛnsəri/, *adj.* outside the normal sense perception. See ESP.

**extra-special** /ɛkstrə-'spɛʃəl/, *n.;* /'ɛkstrə-spɛʃəl/, *adj.* *–n.* **1.** a special extra edition of a newspaper. *–adj.* **2.** exceptionally good or unusual. – **extra-specially,** *adv.*

**extrasystole** /ɛkstrə'sɪstəli/, *n.* a heart beat occurring before its normal time in the heart rhythm and followed by a compensatory pause; premature beat.

**extraterrestrial** /ɛkstrətə'rɛstriəl/, *adj.* outside or originating outside the earth.

**extraterritorial** /ˌɛkstrətɛrə'tɔriəl/, *adj.* **1.** beyond local territorial jurisdiction, as the status of persons resident in a country but not subject to its laws. **2.** pertaining to such persons. Also, **exterritorial.** [NL *extrā territōri(um)* outside the domain + -AL[1]] – **extraterritorially,** *adv.*

**extraterritoriality** /ˌɛkstrətɛrətɔri'æləti/, *n.* the possession or exercise of political rights by a foreign power within a state having its own government.

**extra time** /ɛkstrə 'taɪm/, *n.* (in a sporting match) additional time allowed for play to make up for time lost by injury, etc., or to allow a tie (def. 27) to be broken.

**extrauterine** /ɛkstrə'jutəraɪn, -in/, *adj.* being beyond or outside the uterus.

**extravagance** /ək'strævəgəns, ɛk-/, *n.* **1.** excessive expenditure or outlay of money. **2.** an instance of this. **3.** unrestrained or fantastic excess, as of actions, opinions, etc. **4.** an extravagant action, notion, etc.

**extravagancy** /ək'strævəgənsi, ɛk-/, *n., pl.* **-cies.** extravagance.

**extravagant** /ək'strævəgənt, ɛk-/, *adj.* **1.** going beyond prudence or necessity in expenditure; wasteful: *an extravagant person.* **2.** excessively high; exorbitant: *extravagant expenses or prices.* **3.** exceeding the bounds of reason, as actions, demands, opinions, passions, etc. **4.** exceedingly elaborate; flamboyant: *an extravagant dress.* **5.** *Obs.* wandering beyond bounds. [ME, from ML *extrāvagans,* ppr. of *extrāvagārī* wander beyond, from L *extrā-* EXTRA- + *vagārī* wander] – **extravagantly,** *adv.* – **extravagantness,** *n.*

**extravaganza** /əkstrævə'gænzə, ɛk-/, *n.* **1.** a musical or dramatic composition, as comic opera or musical comedy, marked by wildness and irregularity in form and feeling and elaborateness in staging and costume. **2.** extravagant behaviour or speech. [b. EXTRAVAGANCE and It. *stravaganza* queer behaviour]

**extravagate** /ək'strævəgeɪt, ɛk-/, *v.i.,* **-gated, -gating.** **1.** to wander beyond bounds; stray; roam at will. **2.** to go beyond the bounds of propriety or reason.

**extravasate** /ək'strævəseɪt, ɛk-/, *v.,* **-sated, -sating.** *–v.i.* **1.** *Pathol.* to force out from the proper vessels, as blood, esp. so as to diffuse through the surrounding tissues. **2.** *Geol.* to pour out molten or liquid matter from the earth as lava from a vent, water from a geyser, etc. *–v.i.* **3.** *Pathol.* to be extravasated, as blood. **4.** *Geol.* (of molten or liquid matter) to pour forth from the earth. [EXTRA + L *vās* vessel + -ATE[1]]

**extravasation** /əkstrævə'seɪʃən, ɛk-/, *n.* **1.** the act of extravasating. **2.** the matter extravasated.

**extravascular** /ɛkstrə'væskjələ/, *adj.* situated outside a blood vessel or vessels.

**extravehicular activity** /ˌɛkstrəvəˌhɪkjələ æk'tɪvəti/, *n.* any operation carried out by an astronaut outside his spacecraft, either in space or on the moon. Also, **EVA.**

**extraversion** /'ɛkstrəvɜʒən/, *n.* →**extroversion.**

**extravert** /'ɛkstrəvɜt/, *n.* →**extrovert.**

**extreme** /ək'strim, ɛk-/, *adj.* **-tremer, -tremist,** *n.* *–adj.* **1.** of a character or kind farthest removed from the ordinary or average: *an extreme case, extreme measures.* **2.** utmost or exceedingly great in degree: *extreme joy.* **3.** farthest from the centre or middle; outermost; endmost. **4.** farthest, utmost, or very far in any direction. **5.** going to the utmost lengths, or exceeding the bounds of moderation: *extreme fashions.* **6.** going to the utmost or very great lengths in action, habit, opinion, etc.: *an extreme socialist.* **7.** last or final: *extreme unction.* *–n.* **8.** the utmost or highest degree, or a very high degree: *showy in the extreme, to an extreme.* **9.** one of two things as remote or different from each other as possible: *the extremes of joy and grief.* **10.** the farthest or utmost length, or an excessive length, beyond the ordinary or average: *to go to extremes in dress.* **11.** *Logic.* the subject or the predicate of the conclusion of a syllogism; either of two terms which are separated in the premises and brought together in the conclusion. **12.** *Obs.* the utmost point, or extremity of something. [ME, from L *extrēmus,* superl. of *exter* outer, outward] – **extremeness,** *n.*

**extremely** /ək'strimli, ɛk-/, *adv.* in an extreme degree; exceedingly.

**extremely high frequency,** *n.* a radio frequency of between 30 000 and 300 000 megacycles per second. *Abbrev.:* EHF

**extreme unction** /əkstrim 'ʌŋkʃən/, *n.* a sacrament of the Roman Catholic church in which a dying person is anointed with oil by a priest for the health of his soul and body.

**extremism** /ək'strimɪzəm, ɛk-/, *n.* a tendency or disposition to go to extremes, esp. in political matters.

**extremist** /ək'striməst, ɛk-/, *n.* **1.** one who goes to extremes, esp. in political matters. **2.** a supporter of extreme doctrines or practices. *–adj.* **3.** belonging or pertaining to extremists.

**extremity** /ək'strɛməti, ɛk-/, *n., pl.* **-ties.** **1.** the extreme or terminal point, limit, or part of something. **2.** a limb of the body. **3.** (*chiefly pl.*) the end part of a limb, as a hand or foot. **4.** (*oft. pl.*) a condition, or circumstances, of extreme need, distress, etc. **5.** the utmost or any extreme degree: *the extremity of joy.* **6.** (*chiefly pl.*) an extreme measure: *to be forced to extremities.* **7.** extreme character, as of views. **8.** (*chiefly pl.*) a person's last moments.

**extricable** /'ɛkstrɪkəbəl, ək'strɪkəbəl, ɛk-/, *adj.* that may be extricated.

**extricate** /'ɛkstrəkeɪt/, *v.t.,* **-cated, -cating.** **1.** to disentangle; disengage; free: *to extricate one from a dangerous or embarrassing situation.* **2.** to liberate (gas, etc.) from combination, as in a chemical process. [L *extrīcātus,* pp., disentangled] – **extrication** /ɛkstrə'keɪʃən/, *n.*

**extrinsic** /ɛks'trɪnzɪk/, *adj.* **1.** extraneous; not inherent; unessential. **2.** being outside a thing; outward or external; operating or coming from without. **3.** *Anat.* (of certain muscles, nerves, etc.) originating outside the anatomical limits of a part. Also, **extrinsical.** [EX-[1] + (IN)TRINSIC. Cf. F *extrinsèque,* adj., L *extrinsecus,* adv.] – **extrinsically,** *adv.*

**extrinsic semiconductor** /– sɛmikən'dʌktə/, *n.* a semiconductor in which the carrier density results mainly from the presence of impurities or other imperfections, as opposed to an intrinsic semiconductor in which the material is unmodified.

**extro-,** variant of **extra-** (used to contrast with **intro-**).

**extrorse** /ɛk'strɔs/, *adj.* turned or facing outwards, as anthers which open towards the perianth. [LL *extrorsus* in an outward direction] – **extrorsely,** *adv.*

**extroversion** /ɛkstrə'vɜʒən/, *n.* **1.** Also, **extraversion.** interest directed outwards or to things outside the self (opposed to *introversion*). **2.** *Pathol.* a turning inside out, as of the eyelids or of the bladder. **3.** the act of extroverting. **4.** an extroverted state. – **extroversive,** *adj.*

**extrovert** /'ɛkstrəvɜt/, *n.* **1.** one characterised by extroversion; a person concerned chiefly with what is external or objective (opposed to *introvert*). *–adj.* **2.** marked by extroversion. *–v.t.* **3.** to direct (the mind, etc.) outwards, or to things outside the self. Also, **extravert.** [EXTRO- + L *vertere* turn. See INTROVERT]

**extrude** /ɛk'strud/, *v.,* **-truded, -truding.** *–v.t.* **1.** to thrust out; force or press out; expel. **2.** (in moulding or making metals, plastics, etc.) to form into a desired cross-sectional shape by ejecting through a shaped opening: *to extrude tubing.* *–v.i.* **3.** to protrude. [L *extrūdere* thrust out] – **extruder,** *n.* – **extrusion,** *n.*

**extruded protein** /ɛk͵strudəd 'proʊtin/, *n.* vegetable protein which has been extruded and dried to form a powdered protein additive.

**extrusive** /ɛk'struziv, -sɪv/, *adj.* **1.** tending to extrude. **2.** pertaining to extrusion. **3.** *Geol.* **a.** (of rocks) having been forced out in a molten or plastic condition at the surface of the earth. **b.** denoting or pertaining to volcanic rocks.

**exuberance** /əg'zjubərəns, ɛg-/, *n.* **1.** Also, **exuberancy.** the state of being exuberant. **2.** an instance of this.

**exuberant** /əg'zjubərənt, ɛg-/, *adj.* **1.** lavish; effusive: *an exuberant welcome.* **2.** full of vigour; abounding in high spirits: *the soldiers were exuberant after their victory.* **3.** profuse in growth or production; luxuriant; superabundant: *exuberant vegetation.* [L *exūberans,* ppr., being fruitful] – **exuberantly,** *adv.*

**exuberate** /əg'zjubəreɪt, ɛg-/, *v.i.,* **-rated, -rating.** to be exuberant; superabound; overflow.

**exudate** /'ɛksjudeɪt/, *n.* a substance exuded; exudation.

**exudation** /ɛksju'deɪʃən/, *n.* **1.** the act of exuding. **2.** that which is exuded. **3.** a sweatlike issue or discharge through pores or small openings. – **exudative** /əg'zjudətɪv, ɛg-/, *adj.*

**exude** /əg'zjud, ɛg-/, *v.,* **-uded, -uding.** *–v.i.* **1.** to come out gradually in drops like sweat through pores or small openings; ooze out. *–v.t.* **2.** to send out like sweat; emit through pores or small openings. [L *ex(s)ūdāre*]

**exult** /əg'zʌlt, ɛg-/, *v.i.* **1.** to show or feel a lively or triumphant joy; rejoice exceedingly; be highly elated; be jubilant (fol. by *in, at, over,* or an infinitive): *he exulted to find that he had won.* **2.** *Obs.* to leap, esp. for joy. [L *ex(s)ultāre,* frequentative of *exsilire* leap out or up] – **exultingly,** *adv.*

**exultant** /əg'zʌltənt, ɛg-/, *adj.* exulting; highly elated; triumphant. – **exultantly,** *adv.*

**exultation** /ɛgzəl'teɪʃən/, *n.* the act of exulting; lively or triumphant joy, as over success or victory. Also, **exultance, exultancy** /əg'zʌltənsi, ɛg-/.

**exurb** /'ɛksɜb/, *n.* a residential area outside the limits of the city and its suburbs, usu. for the wealthy. – **exurban** /ɛks'ɜbən/, *adj.*

**exurbanite** /ɛks'ɜbənaɪt/, *n.* a resident of an exurb.

**exurbia** /ɛks'ɜbiə/, *n.* exurbs viewed collectively.

**exuviae** /əg'zjuvii, ɛg-/, *n. pl.* the cast skins, shells, or other coverings of animals. [L: garments stripped off, skins of animals] – **exuvial,** *adj.*

**exuviate** /əg'zjuvieɪt, ɛg-/, *v.,* **-ated, -ating.** *–v.t.* **1.** to cast off or shed (a covering, as a skin). *–v.i.* **2.** to cast off or shed exuviae; moult. – **exuviation** /əgzjuvi'eɪʃən, ɛg-/, *n.*

**-ey**[1], variant of **-y**[1], used esp. after *y,* as in *clayey.*

**-ey**[2], variant of **-y**[2], used esp. after *y.*

**eyas** /'iəs/, *n.* a nestling. [ME, var. of *nyas, nias* (*a nyas* being taken as *an eyas*), from F *niais* a nestling, from L *nīdus* nest]

**eye** /aɪ/, *n., pl.* **eyes;** *v.,* **eyed, eyeing** or **eying.** *–n.* **1.** the origin of sight or vision. **2.** all the structures situated within or near the orbit which assist the organ of vision. **3.** this organ with respect to the colour of the iris: *blue eyes.* **4.** the region surrounding the eye: *a black eye.* **5.** sight; vision. **6.** power of seeing; appreciative or discriminating visual perception: *an eye for colour.* **7.** (*oft. pl.*) look, glance, or gaze: *to cast one's eye on a thing.* **8.** (*oft. pl.*) attentive look, close observation, or watch: *to keep an eye on a person, to be all eyes.* **9.** regard, respect, view, aim, or intention: *to have an eye to one's own advantage, with an eye to winning favour.* **10.** (*oft. pl.*) manner or way of looking at a thing, estimation, or opinion: *in the eyes of the law.* **11.** mental view: *in my mind's eye.* **12.** a centre of light, intelligence, influence, etc. **13.** something resembling or suggesting the eye in appearance, shape, etc., as the bud of a tuber, the central spot of a target, the lens of a camera, one of the round spots on the tail feathers of a peacock, the hole of a needle, a hole pierced in a thing for the insertion of some object, a metal or other ring as for a rope to pass through, or the loop into which a hook is inserted (forming together with the hook a **hook and eye**). **14.** *Meteorol.* the central region of low pressure in a tropical hurricane, where calm conditions prevail, often with clear skies. **15.** *Naut.* the precise direction from which the wind is blowing. **16.** *Naut.* the foremost part of the bows of a ship. **17.** Some special noun phrases are:

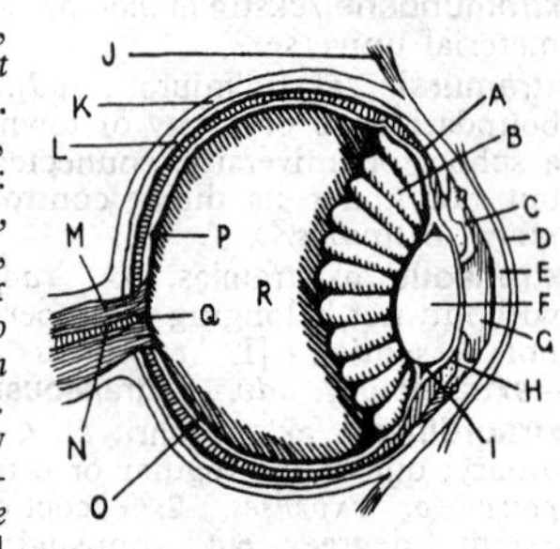

human eye: A, ciliary muscle; B, ciliary processes; C, iris; D, conjunctiva; E, cornea; F, crystalline lens; G, anterior chamber; H, posterior chamber; I, suspensory ligament; J, ocular muscles; K, sclera; L, choroid; M, optic nerve; N, retinal artery; O, retina; P, yellow spot; Q, blind spot; R, vitreous humour

**all my eye,** *Colloq.* nonsense.

**(all) my eye and Betty Martin,** (an expression of disbelief or scepticism).

**an eye for an eye,** repayment in kind, as revenge for an injustice.

**before (under) one's very eyes,** in one's presence.

**catch someone's eye,** to attract someone's attention.

**cry one's eyes out,** to weep copiously.

**do in the eye,** *Colloq.* to take advantage of; cheat; swindle.

**easy on the eye,** attractive to look at.

**eye of the day,** *Poetic.* the sun.

**get one's eye in, 1.** (in cricket and other ball games) to be able, through practice, to follow the movement of the ball. **2.** *Colloq.* to adapt oneself to a situation; become accustomed.

**give someone the glad eye,** to look amorously at.

**go eyes out,** to work very hard.

**have an eye for,** to be discerning; be a good judge of.

**have eyes only for, a.** to look at nothing else but. **b.** to desire nothing else but.

**in the public eye,** often seen in public; well known.

**keep an eye on,** to watch attentively; mind.

**keep an eye out for,** to be watchful, or on the lookout for.

**keep one's eyes open (skinned) (peeled),** to be especially watchful.

**lay, clap,** or **set eyes on,** to catch sight of; see.

**make eyes at,** to gaze flirtatiously at.

**make someone open his eyes,** to astonish; cause to stare in surprise.

**open the eyes of,** to make (a person) aware of the truth of something or of something previously unknown; to enlighten.

**pick the eyes out of,** to select the best parts, pieces, etc., of (a collection).

**pipe one's eye,** *Brit.* (*Colloq.*) to weep.

**run one's eye over,** to glance at briefly.

**see eye to eye,** to have the same opinion; agree.

**see with half an eye,** to see easily; realise immediately.

**shut** or **close one's eyes to,** to refuse to see; disregard.
**sight for sore eyes,** a welcome sight; an agreeable surprise.
**turn a blind eye on** or **to,** to pretend not to see; ignore.
**up to the eyes in,** very busy with; deeply involved.
**with one's eyes open,** fully aware of potential risks.
*–v.t.* **18.** to fix the eyes upon; view. **19.** to observe or watch narrowly. **20.** to make an eye in: *to eye a needle.* [ME; OE *ēge,* d. var. of *ēage,* c. G *Auge.* Cf. L *oculus*]

**eyeball** /ˈaɪbɔl/, *n.* **1.** the ball or globe of the eye. **2. eyeball to eyeball,** aggressively face to face; in confrontation. **3. greasy eyeball,** *Colloq.* a disdainful look: *he gave her the greasy eyeball.* *–v.t.* **4.** to look at, inspect, esp. mathematical data. **5.** to inspect (an object) directly as with the naked eye or through a telescope, as opposed to indirect inspection, as by reading the traces from a radio telescope, a spectroscope, etc.

**eyebath** /ˈaɪbaθ/, *n.* a vessel specially shaped for applying lotion to or bathing the eye. Also, **eyecup.**

**eyebeam** /ˈaɪbim/, *n.* a beam or glance of the eye.

**eye bolt** /ˈaɪ boʊlt/, *n.* a metal bar with a screw-thread at one end and bent or forged into a circle at the other; used to secure ropes, etc.

**eyebright** /ˈaɪbraɪt/, *n.* **1.** any of various herbs of the genus *Euphrasia,* as *E. officinalis* of Europe, formerly used for diseases of the eye. **2.** any of several other small herbs.

**eyebrow** /ˈaɪbraʊ/, *n.* **1.** the arch or ridge forming the upper part of the orbit of the eye. **2.** the fringe of hair growing upon it.

**eye-catching** /ˈaɪ-kætʃɪŋ/, *adj.* attracting attention; attractive or noticeable. – **eye-catcher,** *n.*

**eyeclip** /ˈaɪklɪp/, *n.* the wool cut from around a sheep's eyes. Also, **eyewool.**

**eyed** /aɪd/, *adj.* **1.** having eyes. **2.** having eyelike spots.

**eye dog** /ˈaɪ dɒg/, *n.* a trained sheepdog which controls sheep by its gaze or eye.

**eye-dropper** /ˈaɪ-drɒpə/, *n.* →**dropper** (def. 2).

**eye fillet** /ˈaɪ fɪlət/, *n.* →**fillet** (def. 6b).

**eyeful** /ˈaɪfʊl/, *n.* **1.** an amount of dust, etc., blown or thrown into the eye. **2.** as much as one wants to see or as much as the eye can take in at a glance. **3.** *Colloq.* a person of striking appearance, esp. a beautiful woman.

**eyeglass** /ˈaɪglas/, *n.* **1.** the eyepiece of an optical instrument; an ocular. **2.** →**eyebath. 3.** →**glass** (def. 4).

**eyehole** /ˈaɪhoʊl/, *n.* **1.** →**eye socket. 2.** a hole to look through, as in a mask or a curtain. **3.** a circular opening for the insertion of a pin, hook, rope, etc.

**eyelash** /ˈaɪlæʃ/, *n.* one of the short, thick, curved hairs growing as a fringe on the edge of an eyelid.

**eyeless** /ˈaɪləs/, *adj.* **1.** lacking eyes. **2.** blind.

**eyelet** /ˈaɪlət/, *n.* **1.** a small, typically round hole, esp. one finished at the edge, as in cloth or leather, for the passage of a lace or cord, or in embroidery, for ornament. **2.** a metal ring for lining a small hole. **3.** an eyehole in a wall, mask, etc. **4.** a small eye. *–v.t.* **5.** to make eyelets (holes) in. **6.** to insert metal eyelets in. [ME *oilet,* from F *œillet,* diminutive of *œil* eye]

**eyeleteer** /aɪləˈtɪə/, *n.* a small pointed instrument for making eyelet holes.

**eyelid** /ˈaɪlɪd/, *n.* **1.** the movable lid of skin which serves to cover and uncover the eyeball. **2.** the movable parts at the exhaust end of a jet engine designed to alter the direction of the exhaust flow; clamshell.

**eyeliner** /ˈaɪlaɪnə/, *n.* **1.** dark lines, usu. black or brown, applied for cosmetic purposes to the edges of the eyelids or as the user wishes. **2.** the chemical, pencil, etc., which is used to apply the dark lines.

**eyen** /ˈaɪən/, *n. Archaic.* plural of **eye.**

**eye-opener** /ˈaɪ-oʊpənə/, *n.* **1.** something that causes the eyes to open, as an enlightening or startling disclosure or experience. **2.** *Colloq.* →**heart-starter.**

**eyepiece** /ˈaɪpis/, *n.* (in an optical instrument) the lens or combination of lenses to which the eye is applied.

**eye rhyme** /ˈaɪ raɪm/, *n.* a rhyme in which two words are similar in spelling rather than sound: *a tough with a cough.*

**eye-service** /ˈaɪ-sɜvəs/, *n.* homage paid with the eyes; admiring looks.

**eyeshade** /ˈaɪʃeɪd/, *n.* a visor worn over the head or forehead to protect the eyes from overhead light.

**eye shadow** /ˈaɪ ʃædoʊ/, *n.* a cosmetic material applied to the eyelids.

**eyeshot** /ˈaɪʃɒt/, *n.* **1.** range of vision; view. **2.** a glance.

**eyesight** /ˈaɪsaɪt/, *n.* **1.** the power or faculty of seeing. **2.** the action or fact of seeing. **3.** the range of the eye.

**eye socket** /ˈaɪ sɒkət/, *n.* the socket or orbit of the eye.

**eyesore** /ˈaɪsɔ/, *n.* something unpleasant to look at: *the broken window was an eyesore to the neighbours.*

**eye splice** /ˈaɪ splaɪs/, *n.* a splice made in a rope by turning back one end and interweaving it with the main body of the rope so as to form a loop.

**eyespot** /ˈaɪspɒt/, *n.* **1.** a sensory organ of lower animals, having a light-perceiving function. **2.** an eyelike spot, as on the tail of a peacock.

**eyes right** /aɪz ˈraɪt/, *n.* **1.** the command given to turn the head and eyes to the right or to the left as a salute while marching in formation. **2.** the action of turning the eyes and head to the right or to the left.

**eyestalk** /ˈaɪstɔk/, *n.* the stalk or peduncle upon which the eye is borne in lobsters, shrimps, etc.

**eyestone** /ˈaɪstoʊn/, *n.* a small calcareous body, flat on one side and convex on the other, passed between the eye and the eyelid to bring out cinders, etc.

**eyestrain** /ˈaɪstreɪn/, *n.* a sensation of discomfort produced in the eyes by their excessive or faulty use.

**Eyetalian** /aɪˈtæljən/, *n. Colloq. (joc.)* an Italian.

**eyetie** /ˈaɪtaɪ/, *n. Colloq.* an Italian. Also, **eytie, Itie.**

**eyetooth** /ˈaɪtuθ/, *n., pl.* **-teeth** /-tiθ/. **1.** a canine tooth, esp. of the upper jaw (so named from its position under the eye). **2. cut one's eyeteeth,** to become old and experienced enough to understand things. **3. give one's eyeteeth for,** *Colloq.* to desire greatly.

**eyewash** /ˈaɪwɒʃ/, *n.* **1.** Also, **eyewater** /ˈaɪwɔtə/. a lotion for the eyes. **2.** *Colloq.* a deception intended to mislead a person into thinking something is good or correct. **3.** *Colloq.* nonsense.

**eyewink** /ˈaɪwɪŋk/, *n.* **1.** a wink of the eye. **2.** a look or glance.

**eyewitness** /ˈaɪwɪtnəs/, *n.* **1.** one who actually beholds some act or occurrence, and hence can give testimony concerning it. *–adj.* **2.** given by an eyewitness.

**eyne** /aɪn/, *n. Archaic.* plural of **eye.**

**eyra** /ˈɛərə, ˈaɪərə/, *n.* a jaguarondi in its reddish-brown colour phase. [Tupi]

**eyrie** /ˈɪəri, ˈɛəri/, *n.* **1.** the nest of a bird of prey, as an eagle or a hawk. **2.** a lofty nest of any large bird. **3.** an elevated habitation or situation. Also, **aerie, aery, eyry.** [var. of AERIE, influenced by ME *ey* egg]

**Ezek.,** *Bible.* Ezekiel.

**Ff** Roman TRUMP **Ff** Sans Serif FRANKLIN GOTHIC **Ff** Script ONDINE **Ff** Decorative UNBELIEVABLE

*Although there are numerous typefaces in the world they can be divided into four main classifications. These are:*

*ROMAN or SERIF. This typeface came into being from the technique of the Roman masons who, working in stone, finished off each letter with a serif or small stroke projecting from the top or bottom. This was done to correct any feeling of unevenness or imbalance they may have created in cutting the characters in stone.*

*SANS SERIF (without serif). This typeface is geometric in design and has straight-edged characters and lines of a regular thickness.*

*SCRIPT. Based on the movement of the hand, this typeface is often italicised or slanted, as if drawn by a brush or quill pen.*

*DECORATIVE. Any typeface that exaggerates the characteristics of any of the other three classifications to a degree that places it outside of them.*

*The dictionary entries in this book use a SAN SERIF typeface called Helvetica (set in a bold face for the head words) and a SERIF typeface Plantin (used throughout the body of the entries).*

**F, f** /ɛf/, *n., pl.* **F's** or **Fs, f's** or **fs.** **1.** the sixth letter of the English alphabet. **2.** the sixth in order or in a series. **3.** *Music.* **a.** the fourth degree in the scale of C major or the sixth in the relative scale of A minor. **b.** a printed or written note indicating this tone. **c.** a string, key, or pipe tuned to this note. **d.** (in solmisation) the fourth note of the scale of C, called fa.

**f** /ɛf/, *v.t., v.i.,* **f'ed, f'ing.** (to swear at by using the word *fuck*): *he f'ed all and sundry.* Also, **eff.** – **f'ing,** *adj.*

**f.,** **1.** *Music.* forte. **2.** *Maths.* function (of). **3.** *Elect.* farad. **4.** (*pl.* **ff**) folio. **5.** following. **6.** franc. **7. the big f,** (*euph.*) any of various vulgar, taboo, or obscene words beginning with f, as *fart, fuck.*

**F,** **1.** Fahrenheit. **2.** *Elect.* farad. **3.** *Phonet.* formant; $F_1$ is the first formant, $F_2$ the second, etc., but $F_0$ is the fundamental frequency. **4.** *Genetics.* (with a subscript number following) a generation of filial offspring from a given parent, $F_1$ is the first generation of offspring, $F_2$ is the second, etc. **5.** *Chem.* fluorine. **6.** French. **7.** freeway.

**F.,** *Photog.* See **f number.** Also, **f, F:, f:, F/, f/, f/.**

**fa** /fa/, *n.* **1.** the syllable used for the fourth note of the scale in solfège. See **solfège.** **2.** fah. [see GAMUT]

**F.A.** /ɛf 'eɪ/, *n.* →**sweet F.A.**

**F.A.** /ɛf 'eɪ/, Football Association.

**fab** /fæb/, *adj.* marvellous; wonderful. [short for FABULOUS]

**Fabergé** /'fæbəʒeɪ/, *n.* gold and enamel ware made in St Petersburg, Russia, in the late 19th and early 20th centuries. [named after Peter Carl *Fabergé,* 1846-1920, Russian jeweller]

**Fabian** /'feɪbiən/, *adj.* **1.** avoiding battle; purposely delaying; cautiously dilatory: *Fabian policy.* **2.** (of the Fabian Society) a socialist society founded in England in 1884 favouring gradual spread of socialism by peaceful means. *–n.* **3.** a member of or sympathiser with the Fabian Society. [from Quintus *Fabius* Maximus, d. 203 B.C., Roman general who harassed Hannibal's army without risking pitched battle] – **Fabianism,** *n.* – **Fabianist,** *n., adj.*

**fable** /'feɪbəl/, *n., v.,* **-bled, -bling.** *–n.* **1.** a short tale to teach a moral, often with animals or inanimate objects as characters; apologue: *the fable of the tortoise and the hare.* **2.** a story not founded on fact. **3.** a story about supernatural or extraordinary persons or incidents; a legend. **4.** legends or myths collectively: *classical fable.* **5.** an untruth; a falsehood. **6.** *Archaic.* the plot of an epic, a dramatic poem, or a play. **7.** *Archaic.* idle talk: *old wives' fables.* *–v.i.* **8.** to tell or write fables. **9.** to speak falsely; lie. *–v.t.* **10.** to invent (stories); talk about as if true. [ME *fabul,* from L *fābula* narrative] – **fabler,** *n.*

**fabled** /'feɪbəld/, *adj.* **1.** celebrated as fables; mythical; legendary: *fabled goddess of the wood.* **2.** having no real existence; fictitious: *fabled chest of gold.*

**fabliau** /'fæbliou/, *n., pl.* **-aux** /-ouz/. one of the short metrical tales of the medieval French poets, usu. rough and humorous. [F, orig. d., diminutive of *fable* FABLE]

**fabric** /'fæbrɪk/, *n.* **1.** a cloth made by weaving, knitting, or felting fibres: *woollen fabrics.* **2.** the texture of the woven, knitted, or felted material: *cloths of different fabric.* **3.** framework; structure: *fabric of society.* **4.** a building; edifice. **5.** the method of construction. **6.** *Geol.* the orientation in space of the elements of which a rock is composed. **7.** *Geol.* that factor of the texture of a crystalline rock which depends on the relative sizes, shapes and arrangement of the component crystals. [late ME *fabrike,* from L *fabrica* workshop, art, fabric]

**fabricant** /'fæbrəkənt/, *n.* a maker; artisan.

**fabricate** /'fæbrəkeɪt/, *v.t.,* **-cated, -cating.** **1.** to make by art and labour; construct. **2.** to make by assembling standard parts or sections. **3.** to devise or invent (a legend, lie, etc.). **4.** to fake; forge (a document). [L *fabricātus,* pp., having made] – **fabricator,** *n.*

**fabrication** /fæbrə'keɪʃən/, *n.* **1.** the process of fabricating; manufacture. **2.** something fabricated, esp. an untruthful statement.

**fabulist** /'fæbjuləst/, *n.* **1.** a person who invents or relates fables. **2.** a liar.

**fabulous** /'fæbjuləs/, *adj.* **1.** almost unbelievable: *a fabulous price.* **2.** *Colloq.* wonderful; exceptionally pleasing. **3.** told about in fables; not true or real: *the fabulous exploits of Hercules.* **4.** known about only through myths or legends: *the fabulous age in Greek history.* **5.** based on fables. [L *fābulōsus*] – **fabulously,** *adv.* – **fabulousness,** *n.*

**faburden** /'fæbədən/, *n.* →**fauxbourdon.**

**fac.,** **1.** facsimile. **2.** factor.

**facade** /fə'sad, fæ-/, *n.* **1.** *Archit.* a face or front, or the principal face, of a building. **2.** an appearance, esp. a misleading one: *behind his facade of benevolence he hides a cruel nature.* Also, **façade.** [F, from *face,* after It. *facciata,* from *faccia* FACE]

**face** /feɪs/, *n., v.,* **faced, facing.** *–n.* **1.** the front part of the head, from the forehead to the chin. **2.** sight; presence: *to* *one's face.* **3.** a look or expression on the face: *sad face.* **4.** an expression, indicating ridicule, disgust, etc.: *to make faces.* **5.** make-up: *to put a face on.* **6.** *Colloq.* boldness; impudence: *to have the face to ask.* **7.** outward appearance: *old problems with new faces.* **8.** outward show; pretence: *to put a good face on the matter.* **9.** good name; prestige: *to save one's face, lose face.* **10.** a well-known person, esp. one on whom a publicity drive, campaign, etc., depends; identity. **11.** (of a document) the manifest sense or express terms. **12.** the geographic characteristics or general appearance (of a land surface). **13.** an aspect of a hill, mountain, etc.: *the sheep were on the southern face.* **14.** the surface: *face of the earth.* **15.** the side or part of a side upon which the use of a thing depends: *the face of a cloth, document, playing card, watch, etc.* **16.** the most important side; the front: *the face of a building, arch, etc.* **17.** the acting, striking, or working surface of an implement, tool, bat, club, etc. **18.** *Geom.* any one of the bounding surfaces of a solid figure: *a cube has six faces.* **19.** *Mining.* the front or end of a drift or excavation, where the material is being or was last mined. **20.** *Print.* **a.** the working surface of a type, plate, etc. **b.** the style or appearance of type; typeface: *broad* or *narrow face.* **21.** *Fort.* either of the two outer sides which form the salient angle of a bastion or the like. **22.** *Crystall.* crystal face. **23. face to face, a.** opposite. **b.** confronted (fol. by *with*): *to come face to face with death.* **24. in (the) face of, a.** notwithstanding: *in the face of many obstacles.* **b.** when confronted with: *to keep up prices in the face of a falling market.* **25. look one in the face,** to meet without fear or embarrassment. **26. off one's face, a.** mad; insane. **b.** incapacitated as a result of taking drugs, alcohol, etc. **27. on the face of it,** to all appearances; seemingly. **28. put on one's face,** to put on make-up. **29. set one's face against,** to oppose implacably. **30. show one's face,** to make an appearance; be seen. *–v.t.* **31.** to look towards: *face the light.* **32.** to have the front towards or in the direction of: *the statue faces the park.* **33.** to meet face to face; confront: *faced with a problem.* **34.** to see a matter through despite embarrassment: *to face a thing out.* **35.** to oppose confidently or defiantly: *to face fearful odds.* **36.** to cover or partly cover with a different material in front: *a brick house faced with wood.* **37.** to cover some part of (a garment) with another material. **38.** to turn the face of (a playing card) upwards. **39.** to dress or smooth the surface of (a stone, etc.). **40.** to cause (soldiers) to turn to the right, left, or in the opposite direction. **41.** *Ice Hockey.* (of the referee) to put (the puck) in play by dropping it between two opposing players. **42. face it out,** to ignore or defy blame, hostility, etc. **43. face (one) out, a.** to stare out. **b.** to cause (another) to concede by adhering consistently to a particular version. *–v.i.* **44.** to be turned (oft. fol. by *to, towards*). **45.** to be placed (fol. by *on, to, towards*). **46.** to turn to the right, left, or in the opposite direction. **47. face off,** *Ice Hockey.* to start play by dropping the puck between two opposing players. **48. face up to,** to meet courageously; acknowledge; deal with. [ME, from F, from VL *facia,* replacing L *facies* form, face] **–faceable,** *adj.*

**face-ache** /ˈfeɪs-eɪk/, *n.* **1.** facial pains; neuralgia. **2.** *Colloq.* an extremely ugly or irritating person.

**face brick** /ˈfeɪs brɪk/, *n.* a brick specially moulded and fired so as to present an attractive face in colour or texture.

**face-card** /ˈfeɪs-kad/, *n.* →**court card.**

**face-centred** /ˈfeɪs-sɛntəd/, *adj.* (of a crystal structure) having atomic or ionic centres at the middle of the faces of each cubic cell as well as at the corners (distinguished from *body-centred*).

**facecloth** /ˈfeɪsklɒθ/, *n.* **1.** →**washer** (def. 4). **2.** a cloth used to cover the face of a dead person.

**face edge** /ˈfeɪs ɛdʒ/, *n.* →**working edge.**

**face flannel** /ˈ– flænəl/, *n.* →**washer** (def. 4).

**face fungus** /ˈ– fʌŋgəs/, *n.* *Colloq.* (*joc.*) facial hair, as a moustache, beard, etc.

**face gear** /ˈ– gɪə/, *n.* a gearwheel in which the teeth are on the face of the wheel instead of around its edge.

**faceguard** /ˈfeɪsgad/, *n.* (in fencing, etc.) a mask to protect the face.

**faceless** /ˈfeɪsləs/, *adj.* **1.** having no face. **2.** without discernible individuality; anonymous: *faceless officials.* **–facelessness,** *n.*

**faceless men** /– ˈmɛn/, *n. pl.* men who exercise political power without having to take personal or public responsibility for their actions.

**facelift** /ˈfeɪslɪft/, *n.* **1.** a session or course of plastic surgery on the face for the elimination of wrinkles, etc. **2.** any improvement in appearance: *to give an ancient building a facelift.* **–facelifting,** *n., adj.*

**face mask** /ˈfeɪs mask/, *n.* a cosmetic preparation left on the face for a number of minutes to tighten and clear the skin. Also, **facial mask.**

**face-off** /ˈfeɪs-ɒf/, *n.* (in ice hockey) the process by which play is commenced, in which the referee drops the puck between two opposing players.

**face-pack** /ˈfeɪs-pæk/, *n.* a paste or cream used by women to improve the complexion and free the skin from impurities.

**face paint** /ˈfeɪs peɪnt/, *n.* make-up for theatrical use.

**face-plate** /ˈfeɪs-pleɪt/, *n.* a circular plate, which may be attached to the mandrel of a lathe, provided with slots and holes for securing work of an irregular shape.

**face powder** /ˈfeɪs paʊdə/, *n.* a cosmetic powder used by women on the face.

**facer** /ˈfeɪsə/, *n.* **1.** one who or that which faces, esp. a cutter for smoothing a surface. See **face** (defs 36, 39). **2.** *Colloq.* a sudden and severe check; a disconcerting difficulty, problem, etc. **3.** *Colloq.* a blow in the face.

**face-saver** /ˈfeɪs-seɪvə/, *n.* one who or that which saves one's prestige. **–face-saving,** *adj.*

**face side** /ˈfeɪs saɪd/, *n.* →**working face.**

**facet** /ˈfæsət/, *n., v.,* **-eted, -eting.** *–n.* **1.** one of the small plane polished surfaces of a cut gem. **2.** aspect; phase: *a facet of the mind.* **3.** *Archit.* a filled-in flute sometimes seen at the bottom of columnar shafts. **4.** *Zool.* one of the corneal lenses of a compound arthropod eye. *–v.t.* **5.** to cut facets on. [F *facette,* diminutive of *face* FACE]

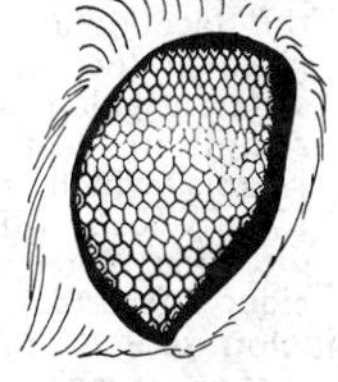
compound eye of a housefly showing facets (highly magnified)

**facete** /fəˈsit/, *adj.* *Archaic.* facetious; witty. [L *facētus* fine, elegant, witty]

**facetiae** /fəˈsiʃii/, *n.pl.* **1.** amusing writing or witty remarks. **2.** coarsely witty books. [L, pl. of *facētia* a witticism. See FACETE]

**facetious** /fəˈsiʃəs/, *adj.* **1.** intended to be amusing: *his facetious remarks are often merely offensive.* **2.** trying to be amusing: *a facetious person.* **3.** *Obs.* pleasantly humorous. [FACETI(AE) + -OUS] **–facetiously,** *adv.* **–facetiousness,** *n.*

**face value** /ˈfeɪs vælju/, *n.* **1.** par value; the value stated on the face of a financial instrument or document. **2.** apparent value: *accept promises at face value.*

**face washer** /ˈ– wɒʃə/, *n.* →**washer.**

**facia** /ˈfeɪʃə/, *n.* **1.** the panel on which instruments, control knobs, etc. are mounted, as in a motor car, a piece of electronic equipment, etc. **2.** *Brit.* the demarcated surface above or beside a shop-front on which the occupier's name, etc., is written. Also, **fascia.** [var. of FASCIA]

**facia board** /ˈ– bɔd/, *n.* material, usu. layered plastic, specially designed for use as a facia.

**facial** /ˈfeɪʃəl/, *adj.* **1.** of the face: *facial expression.* **2.** for the face: *a facial cream.* *–n.* **3.** *Colloq.* a massage or treatment for the face. **4. give (someone) a facial,** *Prison Colloq.* to slash (someone's) face with a knife, razor, etc. **–facially,** *adv.*

**facial angle** /– ˈæŋgəl/, *n.* the angle formed on the face of a skull by a line from nasion to prosthion at its intersection with Reid's base-line.

**facial eczema** /– ˈɛksəmə/, *n.* a contagious disease in sheep.

**facial index** /– ˈɪndɛks/, *n.* the ratio of the breadth of a face to its height.

**-facient,** a suffix forming adjectives meaning 'that makes or causes (something)' and nouns meaning 'one that makes or causes (something)', as in *absorbefacient,* noun and adjective. [L *faciens,* ppr., doing, making]

**facies** /ˈfeɪʃiiz/, *n.* **1.** a general appearance of something naturally occurring, as a particular flora, fauna or ecological community. **2.** *Med.* the facial expression indicative of a particular illness: *peptic ulcer facies.* **3.** *Geol.* the total properties of a sedimentary deposit, including mineral composition, texture, type of bedding, faunal content, reflecting the conditions and environment of formation. [L]

**facile** /ˈfæsaɪl/, *adj.* **1.** moving, acting, working, proceeding, etc., with ease: *a facile hand, tongue, pen, etc.* **2.** easily done, performed, used, etc.: *a facile victory, method, etc.* **3.** easy or unconstrained, as manners or persons; affable, agreeable, or complaisant; easily influenced. **4.** glib: *a facile expression.* [L *facilis* easy to do, easy] – **facilely,** *adv.* – **facileness,** *n.*

**facilitate** /fəˈsɪləteɪt/, *v.t.,* **-tated, -tating. 1.** to make easier or less difficult; help forward (an action, a process, etc.). **2.** *Archaic.* to assist the progress of (a person).

**facilitation** /fəsɪləˈteɪʃən/, *n.* **1.** the act or process of facilitating. **2.** *Psychol.* the tendency of a stimulus to reinforce another stimulus.

**facility** /fəˈsɪləti/, *n., pl.* **-ties. 1.** something that makes possible the easier performance of any action; advantage: *transport facilities, to afford someone every facility for doing something.* **2.** freedom from difficulty; ease: *facility of understanding.* **3.** readiness because of skill or practice; dexterity: *compose with great facility.* **4.** an easy-flowing manner: *facility of style.* **5.** ready compliance. **6.** a rocket base for non-military missiles. **7.** (*pl.*) Also, **toilet facilities.** bathroom and toilet. **8.** a building or complex of buildings, designed for a specific purpose, as for the holding of sporting contests. [L *facilitas.* See FACILE]

**facing** /ˈfeɪsɪŋ/, *n.* **1.** a covering in front, for ornament, protection, etc., as an outer layer of different stone forming the face of a wall. **2.** material applied on the edge of a garment for ornament or protection. **3.** (*pl.*) coverings of a different colour applied on the collar, cuffs, or other parts of a uniform coat, as the different colours on officers' mess jackets which signify different corps, regiments, etc. **4.** *Chiefly U.S. Mil.* the act of turning to face in a given direction in response to a command. **5.** *N.Z.* an open hillside; a face (def. 13).

**facing tool** /ˈ– tul/, *n.* a lathe tool for smoothing a plane surface at right angles to the axis of rotation.

**facinorous** /fəˈsɪnərəs/, *adj. Archaic.* atrociously wicked. [L *facinorōsus,* from *facinus* (bad) deed]

**facsim.,** facsimile.

**facsimile** /fækˈsɪməli/, *n., adj., v.,* **-led, -leing.** *–n.* **1.** an exact copy. **2.** *Radio.* **a.** a method of transmitting pictures by radio telegraph. See **phototelegraphy. b.** a picture so sent. *–adj.* **3.** of a facsimile. **4.** producing facsimiles. *–v.t.* **5.** to reproduce in facsimile; make a facsimile of. [L *fac,* impv., make + *simile* (neut.) like]

**fact** /fækt/, *n.* **1.** what has really happened or is the case; truth; reality: *in fact rather than theory, the fact of the matter is.* **2.** something known to have happened; a truth known by actual experience or observation: *scientists working with facts.* **3.** something said to be true or supposed to have happened: *the facts are as follows.* **4.** *Law.* **a.** an actual or alleged physical or mental event or existence, as distinguished from a legal effect or consequence. Thus, whether certain words were spoken is *a question of fact;* whether, if spoken, they constituted a binding promise, is usu. *a question of law.* **b.** an evil deed (now only in certain legal phrases): *before the fact, after the fact.* **5. in fact,** really; indeed. [L *factum* (thing) done, properly pp. neut.]

**fact-finding** /ˈfækt-faɪndɪŋ/, *adj.* of or pertaining to an enquiry, mission, etc., intended to ascertain the truth or provide detailed information.

**factice** /ˈfæktəs/, *n.* a rubber-like substance produced by vulcanising vegetable oils with sulphur or sulphur chloride. [F, from L *factītius* artificial]

**faction** /ˈfækʃən/, *n.* **1.** a smaller group of people within a larger group, often one using unscrupulous methods to accomplish selfish purposes. **2.** party strife or intrigue: *faction has no regard for national interests.* [L *factio* a doing or making, action, party] – **factionary, factionist,** *n.*

**factional** /ˈfækʃənəl/, *adj.* of a faction or factions; self-interested; partisan. – **factionalism,** *n,* – **factionalist,** *adj.*

**factionalise** /ˈfækʃənəlaɪz/, *v.t.,* **-lised, -lising.** to divide into polarised groups or factions.

**factious** /ˈfækʃəs/, *adj.* **1.** acting only in the interests of a group or faction: *factious opposition.* **2.** caused by factional spirit or strife: *factious quarrels.* [L *factiōsus*] – **factiously,** *adv.* – **factiousness,** *n.*

**factitious** /fækˈtɪʃəs/, *adj.* **1.** artificial; not spontaneous or natural: *a factitious value, factitious enthusiasm.* **2.** made; manufactured. [L *factītius* made by art] – **factitiously,** *adv.* – **factitiousness,** *n.*

**factitive** /ˈfæktətɪv/, *adj.* designating verbs which convey the idea of making or rendering according to order or specification; such verbs are accompanied not only by the direct object but by an additional word indicating the result of the process. For example: They *made* him their *ruler;* to *paint* the house *red.* [NL *factitīvus,* from L *factitāre* declare (a person) to be, frequentative of *facere* do, make] – **factitively,** *adv.*

**fact of life,** *n.* **1.** an event, development, situation, etc., which must be faced as an unalterable reality in life. **2. facts of life,** the details concerning sexual behaviour and reproduction, esp. as explained to children.

**factoid** /ˈfæktɔɪd/, *n.* a contrived fact.

**factor** /ˈfæktə/, *n.* **1.** one of the elements that contribute to bringing about any given result. **2.** *Maths.* one of two or more numbers, algebraic expressions, or the like, which when multiplied together produce a given product; a divisor: *6 and 3 are factors of 18.* **3.** *Genetics.* a gene, allele, or determiner for hereditary characters. **4.** one who acts, or transacts business, for another. **5.** an agent entrusted with possession of goods for sale. **6.** the steward or bailiff of an estate. *–v.t.* **7.** to factorise. [L: doer, maker] – **factorship,** *n.*

**factor analysis** /fæktər ənˈæləsəs/, *n.* a technique for determining which among a set of variables, for which statistics are held, exert the greatest influence on the matter being investigated.

**factorial** /fækˈtɔriəl/, *n.* **1.** *Maths.* the product of an integer multiplied by all the lower integers: *the factorial of 4* (*written 4! or* (*Obs.*) $\underline{4|}$) *is* $4 \times 3 \times 2 \times 1 = 24$. *–adj.* **2.** *Maths.* of or pertaining to factors or factorials. **3.** of or pertaining to a factor or a factory.

**factoring** /ˈfæktərɪŋ/, *n.* the business of purchasing and collecting accounts receivable.

**factorise** /ˈfæktəraɪz/, *v.t.,* **-rised, -rising.** to resolve into factors. Also, **factorize.** – **factorisation** /fæktəraɪˈzeɪʃən/, *n.*

**factor of safety,** *n.* the ratio between the maximum stress that a structural part can withstand and the safe permissible stress which it may be expected to experience in use.

**factory** /ˈfæktri, -təri/, *n., pl.* **-ries. 1.** a building or group of buildings, usu. with equipment, where goods are manufactured. **2.** (formerly) a prison, as that for women at Parramatta in the early days of the colony at New South Wales. [ML *factōria,* from L *factor*] – **factory-like,** *adj.*

**factory farm** /ˈ– fam/, *n.* a farm in which industrial procedures are adopted as mechanical feeding, battery accommodation, etc.

**factory floor** /– ˈflɔ/, *n.* **1.** the floor of a factory. **2.** an industrial workplace or the people who work there, when viewed as separate from management, administration, promotions, etc: *productivity can only be improved by incentives offered to the factory floor.*

**factory ship** /ˈ– ʃɪp/, *n.* a whaling ship equipped to process killed whales and to store and transport the oil and by-products.

**factotum** /fækˈtoutəm/, *n.* one employed to do all kinds of work for another. [ML, from L *fac,* impv., do + *tōtum* (neut.) all]

**factual** /ˈfæktʃuəl/, *adj.* pertaining to facts; of the nature of fact; real. – **factually,** *adv.* – **factualness,** *n.*

**factualism** /ˈfæktʃuəlɪzəm/, *n.* emphasis and reliance on facts, esp. scientific facts. – **factualist,** *n.*

**factum** /ˈfæktʊm/, *n., pl.* **-tums** or **-ta.** *Law.* a thing done; a deed. [L]

**facture** /ˈfæktʃə/, *n.* **1.** the act, process, or manner of making anything; construction. **2.** the thing made. [ME, from L *factūra,* from *facere* do, make]

**facula** /ˈfækjələ/, *n., pl.* **-lae** /-li/. one of the irregular patches on the sun's disc, brighter than the general surface. [L, diminutive of *fax* torch] – **facular,** *adj.*

**facultative** /ˈfækəltətɪv/, *adj.* **1.** conferring a faculty, privilege, or permission, or the power of doing or not doing something: *a facultative enactment.* **2.** left to one's option or choice; optional. **3.** that may or may not take place; that may or may not assume a specified character. **4.** *Biol., Bacteriol.* having the capacity to live under more than one specific set of environmental conditions, as an animal or plant that can lead either a parasitic or a non-parasitic life (opposed to *obligate*).

**faculty** /ˈfækəlti/, *n., pl.* **-ties. 1.** an ability, natural or acquired, for a particular kind of action. **2.** one of the powers of the mind, as memory, reason, speech, etc.: *the mental faculties, be in full possession of all one's faculties.* **3.** an inherent capability of the body: *the faculties of sight and hearing.* **4.** *Educ.* **a.** one of the branches of learning, as arts, law, or medicine, in a university. **b.** the teaching body, sometimes with the students, in any of these branches. **c.** *U.S.* the entire teaching and administrative force of a university or other educational institution. **5.** the members of a learned profession, esp. the medical profession. **6.** a power or privilege conferred. **7.** *Eccles.* a dispensation, licence, or authorisation. [ME *faculte,* from L *facultas* ability, means]

**fad** /fæd/, *n.* a temporary, usu. irrational, pursuit, fashion, etc., by numbers of people of some action that excites attention and has prestige. [n. use of d. *fad, v.,* be busy about trifles, itself backformation from obs. *faddle,* v., fondle. Cf. FIDDLE, *v.,* and FIDDLE-FADDLE]

**faddish** /ˈfædɪʃ/, *adj.* **1.** resembling a fad. **2.** given to fads. – **faddishness,** *n.*

**faddist** /ˈfædəst/, *n.* one who has a fad or is given to fads.

**faddy** /ˈfædi/, *adj.,* **-dier, -diest.** →**faddish.**

**fade** /feɪd/, *v.,* **faded, fading,** *n.* –*v.i.* **1.** to lose freshness, vigour, strength, or health: *the flower faded.* **2.** to lose brightness or vividness, as light or colour. **3.** to disappear or die gradually (oft. fol. by *away* or *out*): *a fading smile, sound, etc.* **4.** *Television, Radio, Films.* to cause sound and/or vision gradually and progressively to increase (fol. by *in* or *up*) or decrease (fol. by *out*). **5.** to ease oneself out of a difficult situation (fol. by *out*). **6.** (of radio signals) to lose strength due to interference phenomena. **7.** to change the direction of a surfboard towards the breaking part of the wave. –*v.t.* **8.** to cause to fade: *sunshine faded the tapestry.* –*n.* **9. do a fade,** *Colloq.* →**fade** (def. 5) [ME *fade(n),* from OF *fader,* from *fade* pale, weak, from b. L *vapidus* flat and *fatuus* insipid] – **fader,** *n.*

**fade-in** /ˈfeɪd-ɪn/, *n.* a film, television or radio technique used to open a scene, consisting of the progressive introduction of sound and/or vision.

**fadeless** /ˈfeɪdləs/, *adj.* unfading. – **fadelessly,** *adv.*

**fade-out** /ˈfeɪd-aʊt/, *n.* **1.** a film, television or radio technique used to close a scene, consisting of the gradual loss of sound and/or vision. **2.** a disappearance, esp. a gradual one.

**fade switch** /ˈfeɪd swɪtʃ/, *n.* a variable control governing lights or sounds which fade (def. 4).

**fadge** /fædʒ/, *n.* **1.** an irregular package of wool in a container made of hessian, sewn to form bags. **2.** a loosely filled wool bale.

**fadge frame** /ˈ– freɪm/, *n.* a frame made to hold a wool pack upright in a shearing shed.

**faecal pellets** /fikəl ˈpɛləts/, *n.pl.* excreta, mainly of invertebrates, present mainly in modern marine sediments but also as fossils in sedimentary rocks.

**faeces** /ˈfisiz/, *n.pl.* **1.** waste matter discharged from the intestines; excrement. **2.** dregs; sediment. Also, *Chiefly U.S.,* **feces.** [L, pl. of *faex* dregs] – **faecal** /ˈfikəl, ˈfisəl/, *adj.*

**faerie** /ˈfɛəri/, *n.* **1.** fairyland. **2.** *Archaic.* a fairy. –*adj.* **3.** *Archaic.* fairy. Also, **faery.** [var. of FAIRY]

**Faeroese** /fɛəroʊˈiz/, *n., pl.* **-ese,** *adj.* –*n.* **1.** an inhabitant of the Faeroes, an island group in the North Atlantic belonging to Denmark. **2.** the language spoken there, closely related to Icelandic. –*adj.* **3.** of or pertaining to the Faeroes, the people, or their language. Also, **Faroese.**

**faery** /ˈfɛəri/, *n., pl.* **-ries,** *adj.* →**faerie.**

**fag** /fæg/, *v.,* **fagged, fagging,** *n.* –*v.i.* **1.** to work till wearied; work hard: *to fag away at French.* **2.** to act as a fag. –*v.t.* **3.** to tire by labour; exhaust (oft. fol. by *out*): *we were fagged out.* **4.** to make a fag of. –*n.* **5.** drudgery; toil. **6.** *Brit.* a younger boy at a public school required to perform certain services for an older pupil. **7.** a drudge. **8.** a fag-end, as of cloth. **9.** *Colloq.* a cigarette. **10.** *Colloq.* a homosexual. [special use of obs. *fag,* n., flap, which occurs only in expression *fag feathers,* ? for *wag feathers* by alliterative assimilation]

**fag-end** /fæg-ˈɛnd/, *n.* **1.** the last part or very end of something, esp. a remnant. **2.** the unfinished end of a piece of cloth. **3.** the stub of a finished cigarette.

**faggot** /ˈfægət/, *n.* **1.** a bundle of sticks, twigs, or small branches, etc. bound together, used for fuel, as a fascine for revetment, etc. **2.** a bundle of pieces of iron or steel to be welded. **3.** a bundle or bunch of anything. **4.** a ball of chopped meat, esp. pork offal, mixed with herbs, bread, or oats, etc., and eaten fried, or baked. **5.** →**bouquet garni. 6.** *Colloq.* a male homosexual. –*v.t.* **7.** to bind or make into a faggot. **8.** to ornament with faggoting. Also, *U.S.* **fagot.** [ME, from OF; orig. uncert.] – **faggotly,** *adv.*

**faggoting** /ˈfægətɪŋ/, *n.* a type of decorative joining used to combine cloth or lace. Also, *U.S.,* **fagoting.**

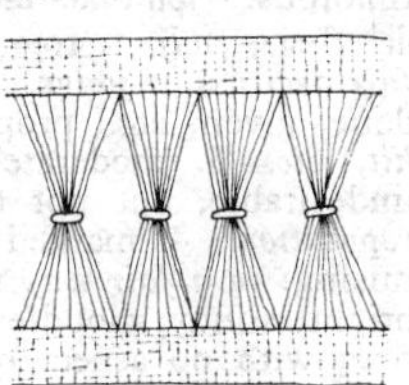
faggoting

**fagotto** /fəˈgɒtoʊ/, *n.* →**bassoon.** – **fagottist,** *n.*

**fah** /fa/, *n. Music.* the syllable used for the fourth note of the scale in solfa. See **solfa.** Also, **fa.**

**Fahrenheit** /ˈfærənhaɪt/, *adj.* **1.** denoting or pertaining to a thermometric scale in which the melting point of ice is 32 degrees above zero (32°F) and the boiling point of water is 212 degrees above zero (212°F). The relation of the degree Fahrenheit to the degree Celsius (°C) is expressed by the formula $°F = \frac{9}{5}°C + 32$. –*n.* **2.** the Fahrenheit scale. [named after Gabriel *Fahrenheit,* 1686-1736, German physicist, who devised this scale and introduced the use of mercury in thermometers]

**faible** /ˈfeɪbəl/, *n.* →**foible** (def. 2).

**faïence** /ˈfaɪɒns/, *n.* glazed earthenware or pottery, esp. a fine variety with highly coloured designs. [F, orig. pottery of *Faenza,* a town in Italy]

**fail** /feɪl/, *v.i.* **1.** to come short or be wanting in action, detail, or result; disappoint or prove lacking in what is attempted, expected, desired, or approved. **2.** to be or become deficient or lacking; fall short; be insufficient or absent: *our supplies failed.* **3.** to fall off; dwindle; pass or die away. **4.** to lose strength or vigour; become weaker. **5.** to become unable to meet one's engagements, esp. one's debts or business obligations; become insolvent or bankrupt. –*v.t.* **6.** to neglect to perform or observe: *he failed to come.* **7.** to prove of no use or help to, as some expected or usual resource: *his friends failed him, words failed him.* **8.** to take (an examination, etc.) without passing. **9.** to declare (a person) unsuccessful in a test, course of study, etc. –*n.* **10. without fail,** for certain; with certainty. [ME *faile(n),* from OF *faillir,* from var. of L *fallere* deceive, disappoint]

**failing** /ˈfeɪlɪŋ/, *n.* **1.** the act or state of one who or that which fails; failure. **2.** a defect; shortcoming; weakness. –*prep.* **3.** in the absence or default of: *failing payment, we shall sue.* – **failingly,** *adv.*

**faille** /feɪl/, *n.* a soft, transversely ribbed silk or rayon fabric. [F]

**fail-safe** /ˈfeɪl-seɪf/, *adj.* ensuring safety in the event of failure or accident: *a fail-safe system.*

**failure** /ˈfeɪljə/, *n.* **1.** an act of failing; a proving unsuccessful; lack of success: *his effort ended in failure, the campaign was a failure.* **2.** non-performance of something due or required: *a failure to do what one has promised, a failure to appear.* **3.** running short; insufficiency: *failure of crops, of supplies.* **4.** loss of strength, vigour, etc.: *the failure of health.* **5.** the condition of being bankrupt by reason of insolvency. **6.** a becoming insolvent or bankrupt: *the failure of a bank.* **7.** one who or that which proves unsuccessful. [AF *failer,* orig. inf., var. of OF *faillir* FAIL]

**fain** /feɪn/, *adv. Archaic.* **1.** gladly; willingly (only with *would,* fol. by simple infinitive): *I would fain be with you.* –*adj.* **2.** content; willing (fol. by an infinitive). **3.** constrained; obliged. **4.** glad; pleased. **5.** desirous; eager. [ME; OE *fægn,* var. of *fægen.* Cf. Icel. *feginn* glad]

**faineant** /ˈfeɪniənt/, *adj.* **1.** that does nothing; idle; indolent. *–n.* **2.** an idler. Also, **fainéant.** [F, from *faire* do + *néant* nothing] – **faineance,** *n.*

**faint** /feɪnt/, *adj.* **1.** lacking brightness, vividness, clearness, loudness, strength, etc.: *a faint light, colour, resemblance.* **2.** feeble; half-hearted: *faint resistance, faint praise.* **3.** feeling weak, dizzy, or exhausted; about to swoon: *faint with hunger.* **4.** lacking courage; cowardly; timorous: *faint heart.* *–v.i.* **5.** to lose consciousness temporarily; swoon. **6.** *Rare.* to lose brightness, vividness, etc. **7.** *Archaic.* to grow weak; lose spirit or courage. *–n.* **8.** temporary loss of consciousness; a swoon. [ME *faint, feint,* from OF: feigned, hypocritical, sluggish, spiritless, pp. of *feindre* FEIGN] – **fainter,** *n.* – **faintish,** *adj.* – **faintly,** *adv.* – **faintness,** *n.*

**faint-hearted** /feɪnt-ˈhatəd/, *adj.* lacking courage; cowardly; timorous. – **faint-heartedly,** *adv.* – **faint-heartedness,** *n.*

**fair**[1] /fɛə/, *adj.* **1.** free from bias, dishonesty, or injustice: *a fair decision or judge.* **2.** that is legitimately sought, pursued, done, given, etc.; proper under the rules: *fair game, stroke, hit, etc.* **3.** moderately good, large, or satisfactory; not undesirable, but not excellent: *a fair income, appearance, reputation.* **4.** marked by favouring conditions; likely; promising: *in a fair way to succeed.* **5.** *Meteorol.* **a.** (of the sky) bright; sunny; cloudless to half-cloudy. **b.** (of the weather) fine; with no aspect of rain, snow, or hail; not stormy. **6.** unobstructed; not blocked up. **7.** without irregularity or unevenness: *a fair surface.* **8.** free from blemish, imperfection, or anything that impairs the appearance, quality, or character: *a fair copy.* **9.** clear; easy to read: *fair handwriting.* **10.** of a light hue; not dark: *fair skin.* **11.** beautiful; pleasing in appearance; attractive. **12.** seemingly good or sincere but not so: *fair promises.* **13.** courteous; civil: *fair words.* **14. a fair cop,** *Colloq.* the discovery of a wrongdoer in the act or with his guilt apparent. **15. a fair treat,** *Colloq.* excessively. **16. fair and square,** honest; just; straightforward. (Cf. def. 20). **17. fair crack of the whip,** *Colloq.* →**fair go. 18. fair to middling,** *Colloq.* tolerably good; so-so. **19. in a fair way to,** likely to; on the way to: *you're in a fair way to becoming an alcoholic, the amount you drink.* *–adv.* **20.** in a fair manner: *he doesn't play fair.* **21.** straight; directly, as in aiming or hitting. **22.** favourably; auspiciously: *to bid fair, speak fair.* **23.** *Colloq.* completely: *I was fair flabbergasted.* **24. fair and square, a.** directly; accurately: *I hit him fair and square on the chin.* **b.** honestly; justly; straightforwardly. *–n.* **25.** *Archaic.* that which is fair. **26.** *Archaic.* a woman. **27.** *Archaic.* a beloved woman, sweetheart. **28. fair's fair** (an exclamation offered as a plea for fair play). *–v.t.* **29.** *Shipbuilding.* to adjust or test the lines of curve of a hull, design, etc. **30.** *Obs.* to make fair. [ME; OE *fæger,* c. OHG *fagar*] – **fairness,** *n.*

**fair**[2] /fɛə/, *n.* **1.** an amusement show, originally as accompanying a sale of livestock; now usu. travelling from place to place, having sideshows, merry-go-rounds, dodgems, etc. **2.** a periodic gathering of buyers and sellers, as of livestock, books, antiques, etc., in an appointed place. **3.** an exhibition, esp. an international one, for the display of national industrial and other achievements: *World's Fair, International Trade Fair.* [ME *feire,* from OF, from LL *fēria* holiday]

**fair buck** /fɛə ˈbʌk/, *n., interj. N.Z. Colloq.,* →**fair go.**

**fair catch** /– ˈkætʃ/, *n.* (in Rugby Union) a clean catch of the ball made by a stationary defending player who calls for a mark and is thus entitled to a kick from the spot where the ball was taken.

**fair comment** /– ˈkɒmɛnt/, *n.* a defence to an action for defamation; the defendant must show that the statement, if not published maliciously, was fair comment on a matter of public interest and was substantially true.

**fair copy** /– ˈkɒpi/, *n.* **1.** a copy of a document made after final correction. **2.** the condition of such a copy.

**fair dinkum** /– ˈdɪŋkəm/, *Colloq.* *–adj.* **1.** true, genuine, dinkum: *are you fair dinkum?* *–interj.* **2.** Also, **fair dink.** (an assertion of truth or genuineness): *it's true, mate, fair dinkum.*

**fair do** /– ˈdu/, *n., interj. N.Z. Colloq.* →**fair go.**

**fair enough** /fɛər əˈnʌf/, *Colloq.* *–adj.* **1.** acceptable; passable. *–interj.* **2.** (a statement of acquiescence, or agreement).

**fair game** /fɛə ˈgeɪm/, *n.* a legitimate, suitable, or likely subject of attack.

**fair go** /– ˈgoʊ/, *Colloq.* *–n.* **1.** a fair or reasonable course of action: *do you think that's a fair go?* *–interj.* **2.** (an appeal for fairness or reason): *fair go, mate!*

**fairground** /ˈfɛəgraʊnd/, *n.* (*oft. pl.*) a place where fairs, etc., are held.

**fair-haired** /ˈfɛə-hɛəd/, *adj.* **1.** having light-coloured hair. **2.** *U.S. Colloq.* blue-eyed; favourite.

**fairies' closet** /fɛəriz ˈklɒzət/, *n.* →**net fungus.**

**fairing** /ˈfɛərɪŋ/, *n.* an exterior part of an aeroplane, motorcycle, or the like, which reduces eddying and resulting drag. [FAIR[1], *adj.* (def. 7) + -ING[1]]

**fairish** /ˈfɛərɪʃ/, *adj.* moderately good, large, or well.

**Fair Isle** /ˈfɛər aɪl/, *n.* (*also l.c.*) an intricate pattern originally knitted with Shetland wool in many colours, embellishing a neutral-coloured garment at the neck, waist, or cuffs. [named after *Fair Isle,* an island off Scotland]

**fairlead** /ˈfɛəlid/, *n.* a fitting on a ship, such as a ring, thimble, or block, or a strip of board with holes in it, through which running rigging is passed to be guided and kept clear of obstructions and chafing. Also, **fair-leader.** [FAIR[1], *adj.* (def. 7) + LEAD[1]]

fairlead

**fairly** /ˈfɛəli/, *adv.* **1.** in a fair manner; justly; impartially. **2.** moderately; tolerably: *fairly good.* **3.** actually; completely: *the wheels fairly spun.* **4.** properly; legitimately. **5.** clearly; distinctly. **6.** *Obs.* courteously.

**fair-minded** /ˈfɛə-maɪndəd/, *adj.* fair in mind or judgment; impartial; unprejudiced: *a wise and fair-minded judge.* – **fair-mindedness,** *n.*

**fair play** /fɛə ˈpleɪ/, *n.* **1.** *Sport.* play according to the rules. **2.** *Colloq.* action conforming to generally accepted ideas of what is fair or acceptable, in competition, etc.

**fair rent** /– ˈrɛnt/, *n.* a periodical payment from a tenant to his landlord, held by a tribunal to be the just rental for the premises.

**fair sex** /ˈ– sɛks/, *n.* women.

**fair-spoken** /ˈfɛə-spoʊkən/, *adj.* courteous, civil, or plausible in speech; well-spoken; smooth-tongued.

**fair-stitching** /ˈfɛə-stɪtʃɪŋ/, *n.* stitching that appears on the edge of a welt shoe to ornament and to bind the outer sole to the welt. – **fair-stitcher,** *n.*

**fair trade** /fɛə ˈtreɪd/, *n.* **1.** *Brit.* the imposition of duties on imports from foreign countries in direct proportion to the duties imposed by those countries on home exports. **2.** *U.S.* →**resale price maintenance.**

**fair-trade** /fɛə-ˈtreɪd/, *v.,* **-traded, -trading,** *adj., adv. U.S.* *–v.t.* **1.** to market a product subject to resale price maintenance. *–adv.* **2.** by way of resale price maintenance. – **fair-trade,** *adj.*

**fairway** /ˈfɛəweɪ/, *n.* **1.** an unobstructed passage or way. **2.** *Golf.* that part of the links between tees and putting greens where the grass is kept short. **3.** *Naut.* **a.** (in a harbour, river, etc.) the navigable portion or channel for vessels. **b.** the usual course taken by vessels.

**fair-weather** /ˈfɛə-wɛðə/, *adj.* **1.** for fair weather only. **2.** weakening or failing in time of trouble: *he was surrounded by fair-weather friends.*

**fairy** /ˈfɛəri/, *n., pl.* **-ries,** *adj.* *–n.* **1.** one of a class of supernatural beings, generally conceived as of diminutive human form, having magical powers capriciously exercised for good or evil in human affairs. **2.** such beings collectively. **3.** *Colloq.* an effeminate male, usu. a homosexual. **4. shoot a fairy,** *Colloq.* to fart. *–adj.* **5.** having to do with fairies. **6.** of the nature of a fairy; fairy-like. [ME, from OF *faerie,* from *fae* FAY[1]] – **fairy-like,** *adj.*

**fairy bread** /ˈ– brɛd/, *n.* **1.** buttered bread sprinkled with hundreds and thousands. **2.** Also, **fairy toast.** very thinly sliced bread baked in the oven until crisp; Melba toast.

**fairy cake** /ˈ– keɪk/, *n.* a small decorated, individual sponge cake.

**fairy floss** /ˈ– flɒs/, *n.* spun sugar, usu. brightly coloured, and often served spun on to a stick. Also, **candy floss.**

**fairy godmother** /– ˈgɒdmʌðə/, *n.* any benefactress, as one who befriended Cinderella in the fairytale of that name.

**fairy grass** /ˈ– gras/, *n.* a tufted, slender, perennial dropseed, *Sporobolus caroli,* often leafy at the base, with numerous grey spikelets crowded on thin, hair-like stalks, found throughout the Australian mainland; yakka grass.

**fairyhood** /ˈfɛərihʊd/, *n.* **1.** fairy state or nature. **2.** fairies collectively.

**fairyism** /ˈfɛəriɪzəm/, *n.* **1.** fairy-like quality. **2.** belief in fairies.

**fairyland** /ˈfɛərilænd/, *n.* **1.** the imaginary realm of the fairies. **2.** any enchanting, beautiful region.

**fairy lanterns** /fɛəri ˈlæntənz/, *n.* a saprophytic plant species, *Thismia rodwayi,* found in leaf mould in forests of south-eastern Australia and New Zealand.

**fairy lights** /ˈ– laɪts/, *n.pl.* small coloured electric lights or candles, used to illuminate gardens or distributed around a Christmas tree for decoration.

**fairy penguin** /– ˈpɛŋgwən/, *n.* →**little penguin.**

**fairy prion** /– ˈpraɪɒn/, *n.* a small prion, *Pachyptila turtur,* of Australasian and subarctic coasts, with a bluish bill and bluish feet.

**fairy ring** /ˈ– rɪŋ/, *n.* a circle formed on the grass in a field by the growth of certain fungi, formerly supposed to be caused by fairies in their dances.

**fairy shrimp** /ˈ– ʃrɪmp/, *n.* a crustacean of the genus *Chirocephalus,* primitive in the retention on the body segments of unspecialised appendages.

**fairytale** /ˈfɛəriteɪl/, *n.* **1.** a tale, usu. involving fairies and folklore, as told to children. **2.** a statement or account of something imaginary or incredible. **3.** a lie; fabrication. *–adj.* **4.** pertaining to or likely to occur in a fairytale; unreal.

**fairy tern** /ˈfɛəri tɜn/, *n.* a tern, *Sterna nereis,* white with pale grey back, wings and tail, a black crown, a white forehead, and orange bill and legs, found on the west and south coasts of Australia, and in New Zealand and New Caledonia.

**fairy toast** /ˈ– toʊst/, *n.* →**fairy bread** (def. 2)

**fait accompli** /ˌfeɪt əkɒmˈpli/, *n.* an accomplished fact; a thing already done. [F]

**faith** /feɪθ/, *n.* **1.** confidence or trust in a person or thing. **2.** belief which is not based on proof. **3.** belief in the doctrines or teachings of religion. **4.** the doctrines which are or should be believed. **5.** a system of religious belief: *the Christian faith, the Jewish faith.* **6.** the obligation of loyalty or fidelity (to a person, promise, engagement, etc.): *to keep or break faith with.* **7.** the observance of this obligation: *to act in good or bad faith.* **8.** *Theol.* that trust in God and in his promises as made through Christ by which man is justified or saved. **9. in faith,** *Archaic.* in truth; indeed. [ME, from OF *feit,* from L *fides*]

**faith cure** /ˈ– kjuə/, *n.* →**faith-healing.**

**faithful** /ˈfeɪθfəl/, *adj.* **1.** strict or thorough in the performance of duty. **2.** true to one's word, promises, vows, etc. **3.** full of or showing loyalty or fidelity. **4.** that may be relied upon, trusted, or believed. **5.** adhering or true to fact or an original: *a faithful account, a faithful copy.* **6.** *Obs.* full of faith; believing. *–n.* **7.** the body of loyal members of any party or group. **8. the faithful,** the believers, esp. **a.** the believing members of the Christian Church or of some branch of it. **b.** the adherents of the Muslim faith. **– faithfully,** *adv.* **– faithfulness,** *n.*

**faith-healer** /ˈfeɪθ-hilə/, *n.* one who claims to effect healing by religious faith.

**faith-healing** /ˈfeɪθ-hilɪŋ/, *n.* **1.** the practice of attempting to cure disease by prayer and religious faith. **2.** an instance of this.

**faithless** /ˈfeɪθləs/, *adj.* **1.** not adhering to allegiance, promises, vows, or duty: *a faithless wife or servant.* **2.** that cannot be relied on or trusted: *faithless coward.* **3.** without trust or belief. **4.** without religious faith. **5.** (among Christians) without Christian faith. **– faithlessly,** *adv.* **– faithlessness,** *n.*

**fake**[1] /feɪk/, *v.,* **faked, faking,** *n., adj. Colloq. –v.t.* **1.** to get up, prepare, or make (something specious, deceptive, or fraudulent). **2.** to conceal the defects of, usu. in order to deceive. **3.** to pretend; simulate: *to fake illness. –v.i.* **4.** to fake something; pretend. **5.** *Theat., Jazz.* to improvise. *–n.* **6.** something faked up; anything made to appear otherwise than it actually is. **7.** one who fakes. *–adj.* **8.** designed to deceive or cheat. [orig. obscure; ? var. of obs. *feak, feague,* from D *vegen* furbish up]

**fake**[2] /feɪk/, *n.* →**flake**[4]. [orig. obscure]

**fakement** /ˈfeɪkmənt/, *n.* (formerly) a dodge, contrivance. [Brit. d.]

**faker** /ˈfeɪkə/, *n. Colloq.* **1.** one who fakes. **2.** *U.S.* a petty swindler. **3.** *U.S.* a pedlar or street vendor.

**fakir** /ˈfeɪkɪə/, *n.* **1.** a Muslim or Hindu religious ascetic or mendicant monk. **2.** a member of any Islamic religious order. Also, **fakeer.** [Ar. *faqīr* poor]

**fa-la** /fa-ˈla/, *n.* **1.** a text or refrain in old songs. **2.** a kind of part-song or madrigal of the 16th and 17th centuries. Also, **fal la.**

**falafel** /fəˈlʌfəl, -ˈlæf-/, *n.* →**felafel.**

**falbala** /ˈfælbələ/, *n.* a flounce; furbelow. [F; orig. uncert.]

**falcate** /ˈfælkeɪt/, *adj.* hooked; curved like a scythe or sickle; falciform: *a falcate part or organ.* [L *falcātus,* from *falx* sickle]

**falchion** /ˈfɔltʃən, -ʃən/, *n.* **1.** a broad, short sword having a convex edge curving sharply to the point. **2.** *Archaic.* any sword. [It. *falcione* (from *falce* sickle, from L *falx*); replacing ME *fauchoun,* from OF]

**falciform** /ˈfælsəfɔm/, *adj.* sickle-shaped; falcate. [L *falx* sickle + -I- + -FORM]

**falcon** /ˈfælkən, ˈfɔlkən, ˈfɔkən/, *n.* **1.** any of various diurnal birds of prey of the family Falconidae, esp. of the genus *Falco,* as the **peregrine falcon** (*F. peregrinus*), having long, pointed wings and a notched bill, and taking its quarry as it moves. **2.** any of various hawks used in falconry, and trained to hunt other birds and game (properly, the female only, the male being known as a tercel). [LL *falco* (from L *falx* sickle); replacing ME *faucon,* from OF]

falcon

**falconer** /ˈfælkənə, ˈfɔl-, ˈfɔkənə/, *n.* **1.** one who hunts with falcons; one who follows the sport of hawking. **2.** one who breeds and trains hawks for hunting.

**falconet**[1] /ˈfælkənɛt, ˈfɔlkə-, ˈfɔkə-/, *n.* any of several very small Asiatic birds of prey principally of the genus *Microhierax.* [FALCON + -ET]

**falconet**[2] /ˈfælkənɛt, ˈfɔlkə-, ˈfɔkə-/, *n.* an old kind of light cannon. [It. *falconetto,* diminutive of *falcone* FALCON]

**falcon-gentle** /fælkən-ˈdʒɛntl/, *n.* **1.** the female of the peregrine falcon. **2.** any female falcon. [translation of F *faucon gentil*]

**falconiform** /fælˈkoʊnəfɔm/, *adj.* of or belonging to the family Falconidae, which includes falcons, hawks, etc. [FALCON + -I- + -FORM]

**falconine** /ˈfælkənaɪn/, *adj.* of, belonging to, or resembling the family Falconiformes or the falcons; falconiform.

**falconry** /ˈfælkənri, ˈfɔlkən-, ˈfɔkən-/, *n.* **1.** the art of training falcons to attack wild fowl or game. **2.** the sport of hawking.

**falderal** /ˈfældəræl/, *n.* **1.** meaningless syllables forming the refrain of various old songs. **2.** mere nonsense. **3.** a trifle; gewgaw. Also, **falderol, folderol.**

**faldstool** /ˈfɔldstul/, *n.* **1.** a chair or seat, originally one capable of being folded, used by a bishop or other prelate when officiating in his own church away from the throne, or in a church not his own. **2.** a movable folding stool or desk at which worshippers kneel during certain acts of devotion. **3.** such a stool placed at the south side of the altar, at which the kings or queens of England kneel at their coronation. **4.** a desk at which the litany is said or sung. [OE *fealdestōl,* c. OHG *faltistuol* folding chair. See FOLD[1], STOOL]

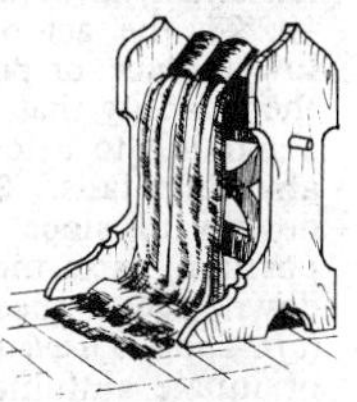

faldstool

**fall** /fɔl/, *v.,* **fell, fallen, falling,** *n. –v.i.* **1.** to descend from a higher to a lower place or position through loss or lack of support; drop. **2.** to come down suddenly from a standing or erect position: *to fall on one's knees.* **3.** to become less or lower: *the temperature fell ten degrees.* **4.** to hang down; extend downwards: *her hair falls from her shoulders.* **5.** to be cast down, as the eyes. **6.** to succumb to temptation. **7.** to lose high position, dignity, character, etc. **8.** to succumb to attack: *the city fell to the enemy.* **9.** to be overthrown, as a government. **10.** to drop down wounded or dead; be slain: *to fall in battle.* **11.** to pass into some condition or relation: *to fall asleep, in love, into ruin.* **12.** to become: *to fall sick, lame, vacant, due.* **13.** to become pregnant. **14.** to come as if by dropping, as stillness, night, etc. **15.** to come by lot or chance: *their choice fell upon him.* **16.** to come by chance into a particular position: *to fall among thieves.* **17.** to come to pass; occur; happen: *Christmas falls on a Monday this year.* **18.** to have proper place: *the accent falls on the first syllable.* **19.** come by right: *the inheritance fell to the only surviving relative.* **20.** (of speech, etc.) to issue or proceed: *the words that fall from his lips.* **21.** to be naturally divisible (fol. by *into*). **22.** to lose animation, as the face. **23.** to slope, as land. **24.** to be directed, as light, sight, etc., on something. **25.** to come down in fragments, as a building. *–v.t.* **26.** to fell (trees, etc.) *–v.* **27.** Some special verb phrases are:

**fall about,** *Colloq.* to laugh immoderately.

**fall away, 1.** to withdraw support or allegiance. **2.** to decline; decay; perish. **3.** to lose flesh; become lean. **4.** *Naut.* to deviate from the course to which the head of the ship is directed: *fall to leeward.*

**fall back,** to recede; give way; retreat.

**fall back on, 1.** *Mil.* to retreat to. **2.** to have recourse to.

**fall behind,** to slacken in pace or progress; lag: *to fall behind in work, payments, etc.*

**fall down,** *Colloq.* to fail: *to fall down on the job.*

**fall flat,** to fail to have a desired effect: *his jokes fell flat.*

**fall for,** *Colloq.* **1.** to be deceived by. **2.** to fall in love with.

**fall foul, 1.** to come into collision, as ships; become entangled. **2.** to come into conflict; have trouble. **3.** to make an attack.

**fall in, 1.** to sink inwards; fall to pieces inwardly. **2.** to take one's proper place in line, as a soldier. **3.** to agree. **4.** *Colloq.* to make a mistake, esp. when tricked into doing so.

**fall in with, 1.** to meet and become acquainted with. **2.** to agree to.

**fall off, 1.** to drop off. **2.** to separate or withdraw. **3.** to become estranged; withdraw from allegiance. **4.** to decline in vigour, interest, etc. **5.** to decrease in number, amount, intensity, etc.; diminish.

**fall on** or **upon, 1.** to assault; attack. **2.** to light upon; chance upon.

**fall on one's feet,** to emerge from a difficult or adverse situation without serious harm.

**fall out, 1.** to drop out of one's place in line, as a soldier. **2.** to disagree; quarrel. **3.** to occur; happen; turn out.

**fall over oneself, 1.** to become confused in attempting to take some action. **2.** to be excessively enthusiastic (fol. by *infinitive*).

**fall short, 1.** to fail to reach a particular amount, degree, standard, etc. **2.** to prove insufficient; give out.

**fall through,** to come to naught; fail; miscarry.

**fall to, 1.** to betake or apply oneself; begin: *to fall to work, argument, blows, etc.* **2.** to begin to eat.

**fall under,** to be classed as; be included in.

*–n.* **28.** the act of falling, or dropping from a higher to a lower place or position; descent, as of rain, snow, etc. **29.** the quantity that descends. **30.** a becoming less; a lowering; a sinking to a lower level. **31.** the distance through which anything falls. **32.** (*usu. pl.*) a cataract or waterfall. **33.** downward slope or declivity. **34.** a falling from an erect position, as to the ground: *to have a bad fall.* **35.** a hanging down. **36.** a succumbing to temptation; lapse into sin. **37.** (*oft. cap.*) *Theol.* the lapse of mankind into a state of natural or innate sinfulness through the transgression of Adam and Eve: *the fall of man.* **38.** surrender or capture, as of a city. **39.** proper place: *the fall of an accent on a syllable.* **40.** *Wrestling.* **a.** the fact or a method of being thrown on one's back by an opponent and held down with both shoulders on the canvas for a specific period of time, usu. a count of three; a pinfall. **b.** a bout, or one of the best of three victories which go to make up a bout: *to try a fall.* **41.** a loosely hanging veil or the like. **42.** a woman's hair piece with long, loose hair. **43.** a piece of leather at the end of a whiplash to which the cracker is attached. **44.** *Mach., etc.* the part of the rope of a tackle to which the power is applied in hoisting. **45.** (*pl.*) *Naut.* the apparatus used in lowering or hoisting a ship's boat. **46.** *Hunting.* →**deadfall. 47.** *Chiefly U.S.* autumn. **48.** a stand of trees suitable for felling. [ME *falle(n),* OE *feallan,* c. G *fallen*]

**fal la** /fa 'la/, *n.* →**fa-la.**

**fallacious** /fə'leɪʃəs/, *adj.* **1.** deceptive: *fallacious evidence.* **2.** containing a fallacy; logically unsound: *fallacious arguments, etc.* **3.** disappointing; delusive: *a fallacious peace.* **– fallaciously,** *adv.* **– fallaciousness,** *n.*

**fallacy** /'fæləsi/, *n., pl.* **-cies. 1.** a deceptive, misleading, or false notion, belief, etc.: *a popular fallacy.* **2.** a misleading or unsound argument. **3.** deceptive, misleading, or false nature. **4.** *Logic.* any of various types of erroneous reasoning that render arguments logically unsound. **5.** *Obs.* deception. [ME *falacye,* from L *fallācia* deceit; replacing ME *fallace,* from OF]

**fallal** /fæl'læl/, *n.* **1.** a bit of finery; a showy article of dress. **2.** a piece of ribbon, worn with streaming ends as an ornament in the 17th century. *–adj.* **3.** *Obs.* finicky; foppish; trifling. [? var. of FALBALA]

**fallalery** /fæl'lælǝri/, *n.* fallals collectively; finery.

**fallen** /'fɔlən/, *v.* **1.** past participle of **fall.** *–adj.* **2.** that has dropped or come down from a higher place or level, or from an upright position. **3.** on the ground; prostrate; down flat. **4.** degraded: *a fallen woman.* **5.** overthrown; destroyed: *a fallen city.* **6.** dead: *fallen in battle.*

**fallen arch** /– 'atʃ/, *n.* an insufficient arching of the underside of the foot leading to flat feet.

**faller** /'fɔlə/, *n.* **1.** one who or that which falls. **2.** any of various devices that operate by falling. **3.** one who fells trees.

**fall guy** /'fɔl gaɪ/, *n. Colloq.* an easy victim; scapegoat.

**fallible** /'fæləbəl/, *adj.* **1.** liable to be deceived or mistaken; liable to err. **2.** liable to be erroneous or false. [ML *fallibilis,* from L *fallere* deceive] **– fallibility** /fælə'bɪləti/, **fallibleness,** *n.* **– fallibly,** *adv.*

**falling sickness** /'fɔlɪŋ sɪknəs/, *n. Archaic.* →**epilepsy.**

**falling star** /– 'sta/, *n.* an incandescent meteor; a shooting star.

**fall line** /'fɔl laɪn/, *n.* **1.** an imaginary line denoting the edge of a plateau or highland area where near-parallel rivers descend to a lowland by falls or rapids; it is often marked by a series of industrial centres where waterfalls have been tapped for power. **2.** *Skiing, Surfing.* the quickest route from the peak of a slope or a wave to the base, used for building up speed.

**Fallopian tubes** /fə'loʊpiən tʃubz/, *n.pl.* the uterine tubes, a pair of slender oviducts leading from the body cavity to the uterus, for transport and fertilisation of ova. [named after Gabriello *Fallopio,* 1523-62, Italian anatomist]

**fallout** /'fɔlaʊt/, *n.* **1.** the descent of airborne particles of dust, soot, or, more particularly, of radioactive materials resulting from a nuclear explosion. **2.** the radioactive particles themselves. **3.** the indirect effects of a decision, event, etc.

**fallout contour** /'– ˌkɒntʊə/, *n.* a line joining points which have the same radiation intensity that define a fallout pattern, represented in terms of roentgens per hour.

**fallout pattern** /'– pætn/, *n.* the distribution of fallout as portrayed by fallout contours.

**fallow**[1] /'fæloʊ/, *adj.* **1.** ploughed and left unseeded for a season or more; uncultivated. *–n.* **2.** land that has lain unseeded for a season or more after ploughing and harrowing. **3.** the method of allowing land to lie for a season or more untilled in order to increase its productivity. *–v.t.* **4.** to make (land) fallow for agricultural purposes. [ME *falwe,* OE *fealga,* pl., fallow land] **– fallowness,** *n.*

**fallow**[2] /'fæloʊ/, *adj.* pale yellow; light brown; dun. [ME *fal(o)we,* OE *fealu,* c. G *fahl, falb* fallow]

**fallow deer** /'– dɪə/, *n.* a deer, *Dama dama,* of Europe and Asia, with a fallow or yellowish coat.

**false** /fɔls, fɒls/, *adj.,* **falser, falsest,** *adv.* *–adj.* **1.** not true or correct; erroneous: *a false statement or accusation.* **2.** uttering or declaring what is untrue: *false prophets, a false witness.* **3.** deceitful; treacherous; faithless: *a false friend.* **4.** deceptive; used to deceive or mislead: *false weights, to give a false impression.* **5.** not genuine; *a false signature, false diamonds, false teeth.* **6.** substitute or supplementary, esp. temporarily: *false supports for a bridge.* **7.** *Biol.* improperly so called, as from deceptive resemblance to something that properly bears the name: *the false acacia.* **8.** not properly adjusted, as a balance. **9.** inaccurate in pitch, as a musical note. *–adv.* **10. play one false,** to behave disloyally towards a person. [ME and OE *fals,* from L *falsus* feigned, deceptive, false, orig. pp.] **– falsely,** *adv.* **– falseness,** *n.*

**false acacia** /– əˈkeɪʃə/, *n.* →**locust** (def. 2).

**false alarm** /– əˈlam/, *n.* anything that gives rise to unfounded alarm or other expectations.

**false bottom** /– ˈbɒtəm/, *n.* a horizontal partition in the lower part of a box, trunk, etc., esp. one forming a secret section.

**false brome** /– ˈbroʊm/, *n.* any grass of the genus *Brachypodium* as the **slender false brome,** *B. distachyum,* widespread in temperate Europe and Asia.

**false card** /– ˈkad/, *n.* (in bridge) a card played to deceive an opponent about the nature of one's hand.

**false-card** /ˈfɔls-kad/, *v.i.* (in bridge) to play a false card.

**false ceiling** /fɔls ˈsiling/, *n.* a ceiling constructed at a level below general ceiling height, sometimes suspended from the original ceiling.

**false cirrus** /– ˈsɪrəs/, *n.* cirrus-like clouds found over thunder clouds.

**false colours** /– ˈkʌləz/, *n.pl.* **1.** the flag of another country. **2.** deceptive appearance; pretence. **3. fly** or **sail under false colours. a.** of a ship, to display, for purposes of deception, the flag of another country. **b.** to deceive; to adopt, for purposes of deception, a role different from one's usual role.

**false dawn** /– ˈdɔn/, *n.* zodiacal light appearing before sunrise.

**false face** /– ˈfeɪs/, *n.* a mask.

**false-hearted** /fɔls-ˈhatəd/, *adj.* having a false or treacherous heart; deceitful; perfidious.

**falsehood** /ˈfɔlshʊd/, *n.* **1.** lack of conformity to truth or fact. **2.** something false; an untrue idea, belief, etc. **3.** a false statement; a lie. **4.** the act of lying or making false statements. **5.** *Obs.* deception.

**false horizon** /fɔls həˈraɪzən/, *n.* **1.** →**artificial horizon. 2.** a line resembling the visible horizon but above or below it.

**false imprisonment** /– ɪmˈprɪzənmənt/, *n.* the imprisonment of a person contrary to law.

**false keel** /– ˈkil/, *n.* a narrow extension of the keel, to protect a ship's bottom and reduce the leeway.

**false labour** /– ˈleɪbə/, *n.* painful contractions of the uterus, often erratic, during late pregnancy, not resulting in actual birth. Also, **pre-labour.**

**false origin** /– ˈɒrədʒən/, *n.* a fixed point to the south and west of a grid zone, on a map from which grid distances are measured eastward and northward.

**false position** /– pəˈzɪʃən/, *n.* a situation in which a person's motives are liable to be misconstrued.

**false-pretencer** /fɔls-prəˈtɛnsə/, *n.* →**con man.** Also, **falser.**

**false pretences** /fɔls prəˈtɛnsəz/, *n.pl.* the obtaining of money or property by the use of false representations, forged documents, or similar illegal device.

**false quantity** /– ˈkwɒntəti/, *n.* (in scansion) a vowel of a length other than that needed for the rhythmic pattern.

**false rail** /– ˈreɪl/, *n.* (in horseracing) a fence placed further onto the actual track on wet days to protect the inside portion of the track from being cut up by the horses' hooves.

**false relation** /– rəˈleɪʃən/, *n.* the relationship between two clashing semitones occurring in parts simultaneously or in immediate succession, where each note is part of a musically coherent melodic line.

**false ribs** /– ˈrɪbz/, *n. pl.* the five lower pairs of ribs, which are not attached to the sternum.

**false sarsaparilla** /– saspəˈrɪlə/, *n.* a trailing plant, *Hardenbergia violacea,* with purple pea-shaped flowers.

**false stage** /– ˈsteɪdʒ/, *n.* a stage built above the actual stage.

**false start** /– ˈstat/, *n.* a start in which one or more competitors in a race cross the starting line, etc., before the signal is given.

**false step** /– ˈstɛp/, *n.* **1.** a stumble. **2.** an unwise act.

**false swamp-rat** /– ˈswɒmp-ræt/, *n.* a small, dark-grey, rare native rat, *Xeromys myoides,* of Queensland and the Northern Territory.

**false teeth** /– ˈtiθ/, *n. pl.* a set of removable dentures.

**falsetto** /fɔlˈsɛtoʊ/, *n., pl.* **-tos,** *adj., adv.* *–n.* **1.** an unnaturally or artificially high-pitched voice or register, esp. in a man. **2.** one who sings with such a voice. *–adj.* **3.** of, or having the quality and compass of, such a voice. **4.** singing in a falsetto. *–adv.* **5.** in a falsetto: *to speak falsetto.* [It., diminutive of *falso* FALSE]

**false vampire** /fɔls ˈvæmpaɪə/, *n.* **1.** →**ghost bat. 2.** a bat of either of the two Old World genera, *Megaderma* and *Macroderma,* large carnivorous forms erroneously reputed to suck blood.

**falsies** /ˈfɔlsiz/, *n.pl. Colloq.* **1.** pads, usu. of foam rubber, worn to enlarge the outline of the breasts. **2.** a brassiere with padded cups. **3.** false eyelashes. **4.** false teeth.

**falsify** /ˈfɔlsəfaɪ/, *v.,* **-fied, -fying.** *–v.t.* **1.** to make false or incorrect, esp. so as to deceive. **2.** to alter fraudulently. **3.** to represent falsely; misrepresent. **4.** to show or prove to be false; disprove. *–v.i.* **5.** *U.S.* to make false statements. [late ME *falsifie,* from LL *falsificāre,* from L *falsificus* that acts falsely] **– falsifiable,** *adj.* **– falsification** /fɔlsəfəˈkeɪʃən/, *n.* **– falsifier,** *n.*

**falsity** /ˈfɔlsəti/, *n., pl.* **-ties. 1.** the quality of being false; incorrectness; untruthfulness; treachery. **2.** something false; a falsehood. [L *falsitas;* replacing ME *falste,* from OF *falsete*]

**faltboat** /ˈfæltboʊt/, *n.* a folding boat similar to a kayak but more easily carried about. Also, **foldboat.** [G, part translation of *Faltboot*]

**falter** /ˈfɔltə/, *v.i.* **1.** to hesitate or waver in action, purpose, etc.; give way. **2.** to speak hesitatingly or brokenly. **3.** to become unsteady in movement, as a person, an animal, or the legs, steps, etc.: *with faltering steps.* *–v.t.* **4.** to utter hesitatingly or brokenly. *–n.* **5.** the act of faltering; an unsteadiness of gait, voice, action, etc. **6.** a faltering sound. [ME, ? from Scand.; cf. Icel. *faltrask,* reflexive, be cumbered] **– falteringly,** *adv.*

**falx** /fælks/, *n., pl.* **falces** /ˈfælsiz/. *Anat.* a sickle-shaped part or process, as of the dura mater. [L]

**fame** /feɪm/, *n., v.,* **famed, faming.** *–n.* **1.** widespread reputation, esp. of a favourable character: *literary fame, to seek fame.* **2.** reputation; common estimation; opinion generally held. *–v.t.* **3.** to spread the fame of; make famous: *this place is famed throughout the world.* [ME, from obs. F, from L *fāma* report, fame] **– fameless,** *adj.*

**famed** /feɪmd/, *adj.* famous.

**familial** /fəˈmɪliəl/, *adj.* **1.** of or pertaining to a family. **2.** appearing in individuals by heredity: *a familial disease.*

**familiar** /fəˈmɪljə/, *adj.* **1.** commonly or generally known or seen: *a familiar sight, a sight familiar to us all.* **2.** well-acquainted; thoroughly conversant: *to be familiar with a subject, book, method, tool, etc.* **3.** easy; informal; unceremonious; unconstrained: *to write in a familiar style.* **4.** closely intimate: *a familiar friend, to be on familiar terms.* **5.** unduly intimate; taking liberties; presuming. **6.** domesticated; tame. **7.** *Rare.* of or pertaining to a family or household. *–n.* **8.** a familiar friend or associate. **9.** a familiar spirit. [L *familiāris* belonging to a household; replacing ME *familier,* from OF] **– familiarly,** *adv.*

**familiarise** /fəˈmɪljəraɪz/, *v.,* **-rised, -rising.** *–v.t.* **1.** to make (a person) familiarly acquainted or conversant, as with something. **2.** to make (something) well known; bring into common knowledge or use. **3.** *Rare.* to make familiar; establish (a person) in friendly intimacy. *–v.i.* **4.** *Obs.* to associate in a familiar way. Also, **familiarize. – familiarisation** /fəmɪljəraɪˈzeɪʃən/, *n.*

**familiarity** /fəmɪliˈærəti/, *n., pl.* **-ties. 1.** close acquaintance; thorough knowledge of (a thing, subject, etc.). **2.** undue intimacy; freedom of behaviour justified only by the most intimate friendly relations. **3.** (*oft. pl.*) an instance or manifestation of such freedom, as in action or speech. **4.** absence of formality or ceremony: *to be on terms of familiarity with someone.*

**familiar spirit** /fəmɪljə 'spɪrət/, *n.* a supernatural spirit or demon supposed to attend on or serve a person.

**family** /'fæməli, 'fæmli/, *n., pl.* **-lies.** **1.** parents and their children, whether dwelling together or not. **2.** one's children collectively. **3.** any group of persons closely related by blood, as parents, children, uncles, aunts, and cousins. **4.** all those persons descended from a common progenitor. **5.** descent, esp. good or noble descent: *young men of family.* **6.** the group of persons who form a household under one head, including parents, children, servants, etc. **7.** the staff, or body of assistance, of an official. **8.** *Colloq.* (formerly) the criminal fraternity. **9.** *U.S.* an independent unit of the Mafia. **10.** *Biol.* the usual major subdivision of an order or suborder, commonly comprising several genera, as Equidae (horses), Formicidae (ants), Orchidaceae (orchids). Names of animal families end in *-idae,* of plant families in *-aceae.* **11.** any group of related things. **12.** (in the classification of languages) a number of languages all of which are more closely related to each other than any of them are to any language outside the group, usu. a major grouping admitting of subdivisions: *English is of the Indo-European family.* *–adj.* **13.** of, pertaining to, or used by a family. **14.** (of a film, television program, etc.) of a type suitable in subject matter and moral tone for all members of the family to see. **15. in the family way,** *Colloq.* pregnant. [ME *familie,* from L *familia* the servants of a household, household, family]

**family allowance** /– ə'lauəns/, *n.* any of various government payments to assist in the rearing of children, as child endowment.

**family Bible** /– 'baɪbəl/, *n.* a large Bible kept in one family for generations, usu. with pages on which are recorded family events, as births, marriages, and deaths.

**family circle** /– 'sɜkəl/, *n.* the closely related members of a family as a group: *a scandal known only within the family circle.*

**family court** /– kɔt/, *n.* a court which administers family law.

**family doctor** /– 'dɒktə/, *n.* a general practitioner, esp. considered as the consultant and adviser of a family.

**family law** /– 'lɔ/, *n.* that body of federal law which pertains to the rights of parents and their children, esp. at the time of the break-up of the family unit.

**family man** /'– mæn/, *n.* **1.** a man who has or wishes to have a family. **2.** one whose interests are closely bound up with his family: *a good family man.*

**family name** /– 'neɪm/, *n.* **1.** the hereditary surname of a family. **2.** a frequent Christian, or first name, in a family.

**family planning** /– 'plænɪŋ/, *n.* the regulation of the number of children born into a family by the use of various methods of birth control.

**family-size** /'fæmli-saɪz/, *adj.* large; suitable for a family: *a family-size car.*

**family skeleton** /fæməli 'skɛlətən/, *n.* a hidden source of shame to a family.

**family tree** /– 'tri/, *n.* a genealogical chart showing the ancestry, descent, and relationship of the members of a family, as of people, animals, languages, etc.

**famine** /'fæmən/, *n.* **1.** extreme and general scarcity of food. **2.** any extreme and general scarcity. **3.** extreme hunger; starvation. [ME, from F, from *faim* hunger, from L *fames*]

**famish** /'fæmɪʃ/, *Archaic.* *–v.i.* **1.** to suffer extreme hunger; starve. **2.** to starve to death. *–v.t.* **3.** to cause to suffer extreme hunger. [ME *fame(n)* famish (from L *fames* hunger) + -ISH[2]] – **famishment,** *n.*

**famished** /'fæmɪʃt/, *adj.* very hungry.

**famous** /'feɪməs/, *adj.* **1.** celebrated in fame or public report; renowned; well known: *a famous victory.* **2.** *Colloq.* first-rate; excellent. **3.** *Obs.* notorious (in an unfavourable sense). [ME, from AF, from L *fāmōsus,* from *fāma* fame] – **famously,** *adv.* – **famousness,** *n.*

**fan**[1] /fæn/, *n., v.,* **fanned, fanning.** *–n.* **1.** any device for causing a current of air by the movement of a broad surface or a number of such surfaces. **2.** an object of feathers, leaves, paper, cloth, etc., for causing a cooling current of air. **3.** anything resembling such an implement, as the tail of a bird. **4.** any of various devices consisting essentially of a series of radiating vanes or blades attached to and revolving with a central hublike portion, and used to produce a current of air. **5.** a series of revolving blades supplying air for winnowing or cleaning grain. **6.** *Geol.* a fan-shaped shingle, deposit, etc. *–v.t.* **7.** to move or agitate (the air) with, or as with, a fan. **8.** to cause air to blow upon, as from a fan; cool or refresh with, or as with, a fan. **9.** to stir to activity with, or as with, a fan: *fan a flame, emotions, etc.* **10.** (of a breeze, etc.) to blow upon, as if driven by a fan. **11.** to spread out like a fan. **12.** *Agric.* to winnow, esp. by an artificial current of air. *–v.i.* **13.** to spread out like a fan (fol. by *out*). [ME; OE *fann,* from L *vannus* fan for winnowing grain]

**fan**[2] /fæn/, *n.* *Colloq.* an enthusiastic devotee or follower: *a football fan, a film fan.* [short for FANATIC]

**fanatic** /fə'nætɪk/, *n.* **1.** a person with an extreme and unreasoning enthusiasm or zeal, esp. in religious matters. *–adj.* **2.** fanatical. [L *fānāticus* pertaining to a temple, inspired by a divinity, frantic]

**fanatical** /fə'nætəkəl/, *adj.* **1.** actuated or characterised by an extreme, unreasoning enthusiasm or zeal, esp. in religious matters. **2.** pertaining to or characteristic of a fanatic. – **fanatically,** *adv.*

**fanaticise** /fə'nætəsaɪz/, *v.,* **-cised, -cising.** *–v.t.* **1.** to make fanatical. *–v.i.* **2.** to act with or show fanaticism. Also, **fanaticize.**

**fanaticism** /fə'nætəsɪzəm/, *n.* fanatical character, spirit, or conduct.

**fanbelt** /'fænbɛlt/, *n.* the belt which drives the cooling fan of a motor, esp. a car motor.

**fancied** /'fænsid/, *adj.* **1.** imaginary: *fancied grievances.* **2.** expected to achieve something, as winning a race: *a much-fancied horse.*

**fancier** /'fænsiə/, *n.* **1.** a person having a liking for or interest in something, as some class of animals or plants. **2.** one who breeds and sells birds, dogs, etc. **3.** one who is under the influence of his fancy.

**fanciful** /'fænsəfəl/, *adj.* **1.** exhibiting fancy; quaint or odd in appearance: *a fanciful design.* **2.** suggested by fancy; imaginary; unreal. **3.** led by fancy rather than by reason and experience; whimsical: *a fanciful mind.* – **fancifully,** *adv.* – **fancifulness,** *n.*

**fanciless** /'fænsiləs/, *adj.* without fancy or imagination.

**fan club** /'fæn klʌb/, *n.* a club, usu. having as its purpose the adulation of a well-known personality or group in the entertainment industry.

**fancy** /'fænsi/, *n., pl.* **-cies,** *adj.,* **-cier, -ciest,** *v.,* **-cied, -cying,** *interj.* *–n.* **1.** imagination, esp. as exercised in a capricious or desultory manner. **2.** the faculty of creating illustrative or decorative imagery, as in poetical or literary composition, as distinct from the power of producing ideal creations consistent with reality (imagination). **3.** a mental image or conception. **4.** an idea or opinion with little foundation; a hallucination. **5.** a caprice; whim; vagary. **6.** capricious preference; inclination; a liking: *to take a fancy to something.* **7.** critical judgment; taste. **8.** the breeding of animals to develop points of beauty or excellence. **9.** people collectively with a deep and particular interest in something, esp. a sport. **10.** *Horseracing, etc.* a horse, dog, etc., expected to win a race. *–adj.* **11.** adapted to please the taste or fancy; of delicate or refined quality: *fancy goods, fruits, etc.* **12.** ornamental. **13.** imaginative. **14.** depending on fancy or caprice; whimsical; irregular. **15.** bred to develop points of beauty or excellence, as an animal. *–v.t.* **16.** to form a conception of; picture to oneself: *fancy living with him all your life!* **17.** to believe without being sure or certain. **18.** to take a liking to; like. **19.** to place one's hopes or expectations on: *I fancy him for our next M.P.* **20.** to breed to develop a special type of animal. **21. fancy oneself,** *Colloq.* to hold an excessively good opinion of one's own merits. *–interj.* **22.** (an expression of mild surprise). [contraction of FANTASY]

**fancy cake** /'– keɪk/, *n.* a small cake, esp. of sponge, with an elaborate topping of icing, etc.

**fancy dress** /'– drɛs/, *n.* **1.** dress chosen in accordance with the wearer's fancy, for wear at a ball or the like, as that characteristic of a particular period or place, class of persons, or historical or fictitious character. **2.** any bizarre or unusual costume.

**fancy-dress ball** /ˌfænsi-drɛs 'bɔl/, *n.* a ball at which fancy dress is worn.

**fancy-free** /fænsi-'fri/, *adj.* free from any influence, esp. that of love.

**fancy man** /'fænsi mæn/, *n. Colloq.* **1.** a pimp. **2.** a lover.

**fancy meat** /– 'mit/, *n.* the internal organs of animals used for food, including brains, heart, kidney, liver, tripe, sweetbreads, tongue, cheek, tail or spleen; offal.

**fancy woman** /'– wʊmən/, *n. Colloq.* **1.** a mistress. **2.** a prostitute.

**fancywork** /'fænsiwɜk/, *n.* ornamental needlework.

**fan dance** /'fæn dæns/, *n.* an erotic dance in which large, often feathered, fans are used to reveal and conceal the body.

**fandangle** /fæn'dæŋgəl/, *n. Colloq.* **1.** a hanging decorative appendage; elaborate ornament. **2.** nonsense; tomfoolery. [perhaps alteration (modelled on NEWFANGLE(D)) of FANDANGO, which was occasionally used earlier in this sense; cf. d. *fandangs* trinkets]

**fandango** /fæn'dæŋgoʊ/, *n., pl.* **-gos.** **1.** a lively Spanish or Latin-American dance in triple time. **2.** a piece of music for such a dance or with its rhythm. **3.** *U.S.* a ball or dance. [Sp., from W Ind.]

**fan delta** /'fæn dɛltə/, *n.* a partially submerged alluvial fan at the mouth of a river.

**fane** /feɪn/, *n. Archaic.* **1.** a temple. **2.** a church. [L *fānum* temple]

**fanfare** /'fænfɛə/, *n.* **1.** a flourish or short air played on trumpets or the like. **2.** an ostentatious flourish or parade. [F, from *fanfarer* blow a fanfare, from *fanfaron* FANFARON]

**fanfaron** /'fænfərɒn/, *n.* **1.** a braggart. **2.** a fanfare. [F, from Sp. *fanfarrón,* from Ar. *farfâr* talkative]

**fanfaronade** /fænfərə'neɪd/, *n.* bragging; bravado; bluster. [F *fanfaronnade,* from Sp. *fanfarronada,* from *fanfarrón* FANFARON]

**fan-flower** /'fæn-flaʊə/, *n.* any plant of the genus *Scaevola,* family Goodeniaceae, characterised by an oblique corolla, slit on one side to the base.

**fanfold** /'fænfoʊld/, *n.* paper for computer or machine use, the sheets of which are joined so that they fall together in a zig-zag pattern like the folds of a fan. Also, **fanfold stationery.**

**fang**[1] /fæŋ/, *n.* **1.** one of the long, sharp, hollow or grooved teeth of a snake, by which venom is injected. **2.** a canine tooth. **3.** the root of a tooth. **4.** a doglike tooth. **5.** a pointed tapering part of a thing. **6.** *Mach.* a tang of a tool. **7.** one of the chelicerae of a spider. **8.** *Colloq.* a tooth. **9.** *Colloq.* the penis. **10.** *Colloq.* **put the fangs** or **nips into,** to attempt to borrow from; to make demands on. *–v.t.* **11.** to borrow money from; to cadge from. **12.** to importune aggressively: *we were fanged for a donation.* **13.** *Obs.* to seize. [ME and OE, c. G *Fang* something caught] **–fanged,** *adj.* **–fangless,** *adj.* **–fanglike,** *adj.*

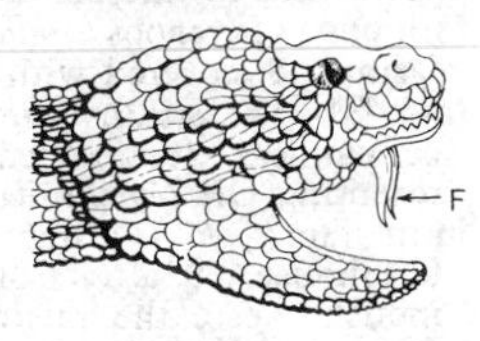

F, fang

**fang**[2] /fæŋ/, *v.i.* **1.** to drive one's car at a very great speed, (oft. fol. by *around*). *–n.* **2.** such a drive. [from Juan *Fangio,* b. 1911, Argentinian racing-car driver]

**fangle** /'fæŋgəl/, *n. Obs.* a fashion: *new fangles of dress.* See **newfangled.**

**fanion** /'fænjən/, *n.* a small flag used to mark surveying stations.

**fanlight** /'fænlaɪt/, *n.* a fan-shaped or other window above a door or other opening.

fanlight

**fan mail** /'fæn meɪl/, *n.* adulatory letters received by a well-known personality in the sporting world, entertainment industry, etc.

**fanner** /'fænə/, *n.* one who or that which fans.

**fanning mill** /'fænɪŋ mɪl/, *n. U.S.* →**winnowing machine.**

**fanny** /'fæni/, *n., pl.* **-nies.** *Colloq.* **1.** the buttocks. **2.** the female pudenda.

**fanon** /'fænən/, *n. Eccles.* **1.** a maniple. **2.** a striped scarf-like vestment worn by the pope over the alb when celebrating solemn pontifical mass. [ME, from F, from ML *fano,* from OHG: flag, cloth, c. VANE]

**fan palm** /'fæn pam/, *n.* any palm with fan-shaped leaves, as the talipot and numerous others.

**fantabulous** /fæn'tæbjuləs/, *adj. Colloq.* marvellous; wonderful. [b. FANTASTIC + FABULOUS]

**fantail** /'fænteɪl/, *n.* **1.** a tail, end, or part shaped like a fan. **2.** a fancy breed of domestic pigeons with a fan-shaped tail. **3.** any of various small birds of the genus *Rhipidura,* having fanlike tails, as the Willie wagtail. **4.** an artificially bred variety of goldfish with double anal and caudal fins. **5.** *Archit.* **a.** a member, or piece of a construction, having the shape of a fan. **b.** a substructure of radiating supports, as of an arch. **6.** a gas burner with a fan-shaped jet. **7.** an auxiliary sail on a windmill for turning it into the wind.

**fan-tan** /'fæn-tæn/, *n.* a Chinese gambling game in which a pile of coins or counters is placed under a bowl and bets are made on what the remainder will be after they have been divided by four. [Chinese (Mandarin) *fan t'an* repeated divisions]

**fantasia** /fæn'teɪziə, -'teɪʒə/, *n.* **1.** *Music.* **a.** a composition in fanciful or irregular rather than strict form or style. **b.** a potpourri of well-known airs arranged with interludes and florid decorations. **2.** a literary work that is not curbed by a fixed plan. [It., from L *phantasia.* See FANTASY]

**fantasise** /'fæntəsaɪz/, *v.i.,* **-sised, -sising.** to indulge in an extended and elaborate daydream.

**fantasm** /'fæntæzəm/, *n.* →**phantasm.**

**fantast** /'fæntæst/, *n.* a visionary.

**fantastic** /fæn'tæstɪk/, *adj.* **1.** odd, quaint, eccentric, or grotesque in conception, design, character, movement, etc.: *fantastic ornaments.* **2.** fanciful or capricious, as persons or their ideas, actions, etc. **3.** imaginary; groundless; not real: *fantastic fears.* **4.** extravagantly fanciful; irrational: *fantastic reasons.* **5.** incredibly great: *a fantastic sum of money.* **6.** grossly impractical: *a fantastic scheme.* **7.** *Colloq.* very good; fine; wonderful: *a fantastic pop song.* Also, **fantastical.** [ME *fantastik,* from ML *fantasticus* imaginary, LL *phantasticus,* from Gk *phantastikós* able to present (to the mind)] **–fantastically,** *adv.* **–fantasticalness, fantasticality** /fænˌtæstə'kæləti/, *n.*

**fantasy** /'fæntəsi, -zi/, *n., pl.* **-sies.** **1.** imagination, esp. when unrestrained. **2.** the forming of grotesque mental images. **3.** a mental image, esp. when grotesque. **4.** *Psychol.* an imaginative sequence fulfilling a psychological need; a daydream. **5.** a hallucination. **6.** a supposition based on no solid foundation; a visionary idea. **7.** caprice; whim. **8.** an ingenious or odd thought, design, or invention. **9.** *Music, Lit.* a fantasia. Also, **phantasy.** [ME *fantasie,* from OF, from L *phantasia* idea, fancy, from Gk: impression, image]

**fantasy land** /'– lænd/, *n.* a world of daydreams.

**fantoccini** /fæntə'tʃini/, *n.pl.* **1.** puppets operated by concealed wires or strings. **2.** dramatic representations in which they are used. [It., pl. of *fantoccino,* diminutive of *fantoccio* puppet, from *fante* boy, from L *infans* child]

**fan tracery** /fæn 'treɪsəri/, *n.* tracery which rises from a capital or a corbel and diverges like the folds of a fan, spreading over the surface of a vault.

**fan vaulting** /– 'vɔltɪŋ/, *n.* a complicated mode of roofing, in which the vault is covered by ribs and veins of tracery, diverging from a single point.

**fanwise** /'fænwaɪz/, *adj.* in the shape of an open fan.

**fan-worm** /'fæn-wɜm/, *n.* any of several tube-living polychaete worms having feathery gills. Also, **feather-worm.**

**fanzine** /'fænzin/, *n. Colloq.* a magazine publishing photographs and adulatory articles about a film star, pop star, etc.

**F.A.Q.** /ɛf eɪ 'kju/, of reasonable or average quality, esp. applied to products as wheat, meat, etc. Also, **f.a.q.**

**far** /fa/, *adv., adj.,* **further** *or (esp. defs 1, 6-8)* **farther, furthest** *or (esp. defs 1, 6-8)* **farthest.** *–adv.* **1.** at or to a great distance; a long way off; to a remote point: *far ahead.* **2.** to or at a remote time, etc.: *to see far into the future.* **3.** to a great

degree; very much: *far better, worse, different.* **4.** at or to a definite distance, point of progress, or degree. **5.** Some special adverb phrases are:
**as far as,** to the distance, extent, or degree that.
**by far,** very much.
**far and away,** very much.
**far and near,** over great distances.
**far and wide,** over great distances.
**far be it from me,** I do not wish or dare.
**far gone, 1.** in an advanced or extreme state. **2.** *Colloq.* extremely mad. **3.** *Colloq.* extremely drunk.
**far out!,** *Colloq.* (an exclamation indicating astonishment, admiration, etc.).
**few and far between,** rare; infrequent.
**go far, 1.** to be successful; do much. **2.** to tend greatly.
**how far,** to what distance, extent, or degree.
**in so far,** to such an extent.
**so far, 1.** up to now. **2.** up to a certain point, extent, etc.
**so far so good,** no trouble yet.
*–adj.* **6.** at a great distance; remote in place. **7.** extending to a great distance. **8.** more distant of the two: *the far side.* **9.** remote in time, degree, scope, purpose, etc. **10.** greatly different or apart. **11. a far cry,** very different. [ME *far, fer,* etc., OE *feor,* c. OHG *fer;* akin to Gk *pérā* further] – **farness,** *n.*

**farad** /ˈfærəd/, *n.* the derived SI unit of the electric capacitance that exists between two conductors when the transfer of an electric charge of one coulomb from one to the other changes the potential difference between them by one volt. *Symbol:* F [named after Michael *Faraday.* See FARADAY]

**faraday** /ˈfærədeɪ/, *n.* a former unit of quantity used in electrolysis, equal to about 96 500 coulombs. [named after Michael *Faraday,* 1791-1867, English physicist and chemist]

**Faraday disc** /ˈ– dɪsk/, *n.* →**homopolar generator.**

**Faraday effect** /ˈ– əfɛkt/, *n.* the rotation of the plane of polarisation of plane-polarised light on traversing an isotropic, transparent medium placed in a magnetic field which processes a component in the direction of the light ray.

**Faraday's law** /ˈfærədeɪz ˌlɔ/, *n.* either of two laws relating to electrolysis which state that: **1.** the chemical action of an electric current is proportional to the quantity of electricity passing. **2.** the weight of substances liberated or deposited by a given quantity of electricity is proportional to their chemical equivalents.

**faradic** /fəˈrædɪk/, *adj.* of or pertaining to electrical induction or the phenomena connected with it. [var. of *faradaic,* from FARADAY]

**faradise** /ˈfærədaɪz/, *v.t.,* **-dised, -dising.** *Chiefly U.S.* to give faradic stimulation to (a muscle). Also, **faradize.** – **faradisation** /færədaɪˈzeɪʃən/, *n.* – **faradiser,** *n.*

**faradism** /ˈfærədɪzəm/, *n.* **1.** induced electricity. **2.** *Med.* its application for therapeutic purposes.

**faradmeter** /ˈfærədmitə/, *n.* an instrument for measuring capacitance.

**farand** /ˈfærənd/, *adj.* →**farrand.**

**farandole** /ˈfærəndoʊl/, *n.* **1.** a lively dance, of Provençal origin, in which all the dancers join hands and execute various figures. **2.** the music for this dance. [F, from Pr. *farandoulo,* probably from *fa* make + *roundelo* round dance, from L *rotundus* round]

**faraway** /ˈfarəweɪ/, *adj.* **1.** distant; remote. **2.** abstracted or dreamy, as a look.

**farce** /fas/, *n., v.,* **farced, farcing.** *–n.* **1.** a light, humorous play in which the plot depends upon situation rather than character. **2.** that branch of drama which is concerned with this form of composition. **3.** foolish show; mockery; a ridiculous sham. **4.** *Obs.* →**forcemeat.** *–v.t. Obs.* **5.** to season (a speech or composition), as with scraps of wit. **6.** to stuff (poultry) for roasting. [ME *farse(n),* from F *farcir,* from L *farcīre* stuff]

**farcemeat** /ˈfasmit/, *n.* →**forcemeat.**

**farceur** /faˈsɜ/, *n.* **1.** a writer or player of farces. **2.** a joker or wag. [F] – **farceuse** /faˈsɜz/, *n. fem.*

**farci** /ˈfasi/, *adj.* stuffed, as of poultry, etc. [F]

**farcical** /ˈfasəkəl/, *adj.* **1.** pertaining to or of the nature of farce. **2.** resembling farce; ludicrous; absurd. – **farcicality** /fasəˈkæləti/, **farcicalness,** *n.* – **farcically,** *adv.*

**farcify** /ˈfasəfaɪ/, *v.t.,* **-fied, -fying.** to turn into a farce; make a mockery of.

**farcy** /ˈfasi/, *n.* a form of the disease glanders, chiefly affecting the superficial lymphatics and the skin of horses and mules. [var. of *farcin,* from F, from L *farcīminum* disease of horses]

**farcy bud** /ˈ– bʌd/, *n.* an ulcerated swelling, produced in farcy. Also, **farcy button.**

**fardel** /ˈfadl/, *n.* **1.** *Archaic.* a bundle; a burden. **2.** →**omasum.** [ME, from OF, diminutive of *farde* pack, from Ar. *farda* bundle]

**fare** /fɛə/, *n., v.,* **fared, faring.** *–n.* **1.** the price of conveyance or passage. **2.** the person or persons who pay to be conveyed in a vehicle. **3.** food. **4.** *Archaic.* state of things. *–v.i.* **5.** to be entertained, esp. with food and drink. **6.** to experience good or bad fortune, treatment, etc.; get on: *he fared well.* **7.** to go; turn out; happen (used impersonally): *it fared ill with him.* **8.** *Archaic.* to go; travel. [ME *fare(n),* OE *faran,* c. G *fahren;* akin to Gk *perân* pass, *póros* passage] – **farer,** *n.*

**Far East** /far ˈist/, *n.* the countries of eastern and south-eastern Asia, as China, Japan, Korea, Thailand, etc.

**farewell** /fɛəˈwɛl/, *interj.* **1.** goodbye; adieu; may you fare well. *–n.* **2.** an expression of good wishes at parting. **3.** leave-taking; departure: *a fond farewell. –adj.* **4.** parting; valedictory: *a farewell sermon. –v.t.* **5.** to say goodbye to. **6.** to honour a person who is retiring or leaving, esp. at a ceremonial occasion. [orig. two words, *fare well.* See FARE, *v.*]

**farfel** /ˈfafəl/, *n., pl.* **-fel.** small pellets or crumbs of some solid foodstuff such as matzos or noodles, used esp. in Jewish cooking. [Yiddish, from MHG *vanelen* noodles]

**far-fetched** /ˈfa-fɛtʃt/, *adj.* remotely connected; forced; strained: *a far-fetched example.*

**far-flung** /ˈfa-flʌŋ/, *adj.* flung or extending over a great distance: *our far-flung battle line.*

**farina** /fəˈrinə/, *n.* **1.** flour or meal made from cereal grains, cooked as cereal or used in puddings, etc. **2.** →**starch. 3.** →**pollen.** [L, from *far* spelt]

**farinaceous** /færəˈneɪʃəs/, *adj.* **1.** consisting or made of flour or meal, as food. **2.** containing or yielding starch, as seeds. **3.** mealy in appearance or nature.

**far infra-red** /ˌfar ɪnfrə-ˈrɛd/, *n.* **1.** the part of the electromagnetic spectrum with wavelengths approximately between about 20 micrometres and about 1 millimetre. *–adj.* **2.** of or pertaining to this part of the electromagnetic spectrum.

**farinose** /ˈfærənoʊs/, *adj.* **1.** yielding farina. **2.** resembling farina. **3.** covered with a mealy powder.

**farl** /fal/, *n.* a thin cake, originally quadrant-shaped, of flour or oatmeal. [contracted form of ME *fardel* quarter, representing OE *fēortha dæl* fourth part]

**farm** /fam/, *n.* **1.** a tract of land devoted to agriculture. **2.** a farmhouse. **3.** a tract of land or water devoted to some other industry, esp. the raising of livestock, fish, etc.: *a chicken farm, an oyster farm.* **4.** the system, method, or act of collecting revenue by letting out a territory in districts. **5.** *Rare.* a country or district let out for the collection of revenue. **6.** a fixed amount accepted from a person in lieu of taxes or the like which he is authorised to collect. **7.** *Eng. Hist.* **a.** the rent or income from leased property or rights such as lands or revenues. **b.** the state of leased properties or rights; a lease; possession under lease. **8.** *Obs.* a fixed yearly amount payable in the form of rent, taxes, or the like. **9. buy back the farm,** to reverse a trend towards excessive foreign ownership of companies, by means of legislation or other government control. *–v.t.* **10.** to cultivate (land). **11.** to raise (livestock, fish, etc.) on a farm (def. 3). **12.** to take the proceeds or profits of (a tax, undertaking, etc.) on paying a fixed sum. **13.** to let or lease (taxes, revenues, an enterprise, etc.) to another for a fixed sum or a percentage (oft. fol. by *out*). **14.** to let or lease the labour or services of (a person) for hire. **15.** to contract for the maintenance of (a person, institution, etc.). **16.** to distribute (responsibilities, duties, etc.) (usu. fol by *out*): *he farmed out the difficult questions to the supervisor.* **17. farm the strike,** *Cricket.* (of a batsman) to manoeuvre to receive most of the balls bowled. *–v.i.* **18.** *Geol.* to obtain drilling and exploration rights in an area controlled by another company on the basis of sharing any profitable discoveries (fol. by *in*). **19.** *Geol.* to make an area available to another company for mineral exploration, particularly drilling, in return for a share of profits in any discoveries (fol. by *out*). **20.** to cultivate the soil; operate a farm. [ME *ferme,* from F, from *fermer* fix, from L *firmāre*] – **farmable,** *adj.*

**farm constable** /'– kʌnstəbəl/, *n.* (formerly) a convict constable supervising other convicts employed in agricultural work.

**farm consultant** /– kən'sʌltənt/, *n.* a professional advisor on agricultural techniques, usu. one in private practice.

**farmer** /'famə/, *n.* **1.** one who farms; one who cultivates land or operates a farm. **2.** one who undertakes the collection of taxes, etc., paying a fixed sum for the privilege of retaining them.

**Farmer Giles** /famə 'dʒaɪlz/, *n. Colloq.* piles; haemorrhoids. [rhyming slang]

**farmers' cooperative** /,faməz koʊ'ɒprətɪv/, *n.* an organisation of farmers for marketing their products or buying supplies.

**farmhand** /'famhænd/, *n.* a person who works on a farm.

**farmhouse** /'famhaʊs/, *n.* **1.** the chief house on a farm, usu. where the owner or tenant lives and from which the farm is managed. **2.** Also, **farmhouse loaf.** a rectangular loaf of white bread.

**farming** /'famɪŋ/, *n.* **1.** the business of operating a farm. **2.** the practice of letting or leasing taxes, revenue, etc., for collection. **3.** the business of collecting taxes. *–adj.* **4.** of, for, or pertaining to farms: *farming skills.*

**farmland** /'famlænd/, *n.* land subject to or suitable for farming.

**farmstead** /'famsted/, *n.* a farm with its buildings.

**farmyard** /'famjad/, *n.* **1.** a yard or enclosure surrounded by or connected with farm buildings. *–adj.* **2.** of, belonging to, or suitable for a farmyard: *farmyard animals.*

**farmyard confetti** /– kən'feti/, *n.* →**cowyard confetti.**

**farnesol** /'fanəsɒl/, *n.* an extract, $C_{15}H_{25}OH$, from the flowers of the acacia, cassia oil, etc., used in the perfume industry.

**faro** /'fɛəroʊ/, *n.* a gambling game in which the players bet on the cards of the dealer's or banker's pack; common in the U.S. [alteration of PHARAOH]

**Faroese** /fɛəroʊ'iz/, *n., pl.* **-ese,** *adj.* →**Faeroese.**

**far-off** /'far-ɒf/, *adj.* distant; remote.

**farouche** /fə'ruʃ/, *adj.* **1.** fierce. **2.** unsociable; shy. **3.** sullen. [F, alteration of *farasche,* from L *forasticus* foreign, from *foras* outside]

**far-out** /'far-aʊt/, *adj. Colloq.* **1.** fantastic; wonderful. **2.** extremely unconventional. Also, *in predicative use,* **far out.**

**farraginous** /fə'rædʒənəs/, *adj.* formed of various materials; confused. [L *farrāgo* mixed fodder + -OUS]

**farrago** /fə'ragoʊ/, *n., pl.* **-goes.** a confused mixture; a hotchpotch; a medley: *a farrago of doubts, fears, hopes, wishes.* [L: mixed fodder, medley]

**farrand** /'færənd/, *adj.* having a specific nature or appearance. Also, **farand.** [ME *farand* comely, orig. ppr. (N d.) of FARE, *v.*]

**far-reaching** /'fa-ritʃɪŋ/, *adj.* extending far in influence, effect, etc.

**farrier** /'færiə/, *n.* **1.** a blacksmith who shoes horses. **2.** a doctor for horses; a veterinary surgeon. **3.** *Mil.* an NCO specially trained in shoeing horses and minor veterinary duties. [MF *ferrier,* from L *ferrārius,* from *ferrum* iron]

**farriery** /'færiəri/, *n., pl.* **-ries.** the art or the establishment of a farrier.

**farrow**[1] /'færoʊ/, *n.* **1.** a litter of pigs. *–v.t.* **2.** (of swine) to bring forth (young). *–v.i.* **3.** to produce a litter of pigs. [ME *far,* OE *fearh;* akin to G *Ferkel* piglet, L *porcus*]

**farrow**[2] /'færoʊ/, *adj.* (of a cow) not pregnant. [orig. uncert. Cf. Flem. *verwekoe* barren cow]

**farrowing house** /'færoʊɪŋ haʊs/, *n.* a sty or pen in which pigs produce litters.

**far-seeing** /'fa-siɪŋ/, *adj.* **1.** having foresight; sagacious; discerning. **2.** able to see far; far-sighted.

**far-sighted** /'fa-saɪtəd/, *adj.* **1.** seeing to a great distance. **2.** seeing objects at a distance more clearly than those near at hand; long-sighted; hypermetropic. **3.** foreseeing future results wisely: *a far-sighted statesman.* – **far-sightedly,** *adv.* – **far-sightedness,** *n.*

**fart** /fat/, *Colloq.* *–n.* **1.** an emission of wind from the anus, esp. an audible one. **2.** a foolish or ineffectual person. *–v.i.* **3.** to emit wind from the anus. **4.** to behave stupidly or waste time (fol. by *around* or *about*). [ME *ferten,* OE *feortan,* c. OHG *ferzan*]

**fart-arse** /'fat-as/, *n., v.,* **-arsed, -arsing.** *Colloq.* *–n.* **1.** an ineffectual person. *–v.i.* **2.** to waste time, to idle (usu. fol. by *about*).

**farther** /'faðə/, *compar. of* **far.** *–adv.* **1.** at or to a greater distance. **2.** at or to a more advanced point. **3.** to a greater degree or extent; further. **4.** additionally; further. *–adj.* **5.** more distant or remote. **6.** extending or tending to greater distance. **7.** additional; further. [ME *ferther;* orig. var. of *further,* but now taken as an irreg. formed compar. (properly *farrer*) of *far,* with superl. *farthest*]

**farthermost** /'faðəmoʊst/, *adj.* most distant or remote; farthest.

**farthest** /'faðəst/, *superl. of* **far.** *–adj.* **1.** most distant or remote. **2.** longest. *–adv.* **3.** to or at the greatest distance. [ME *ferthest,* orig. var. of *furthest.* See FARTHER]

**farthing** /'faðɪŋ/, *n.* **1.** a former British coin of bronze, worth one quarter of a penny, which ceased to be legal tender from 1 January, 1961. **2.** something of very small value. [ME *ferthing,* OE *fēorthung,* from *fēortha* fourth]

**farthingale** /'faðɪŋgeɪl/, *n.* a kind of hoop skirt or framework for expanding a woman's skirt, worn in the 16th and 17th centuries. [MF *verdugale,* from Sp. *verdugado,* from *verdugo* shoot, rod]

farthingale

**farting** /'fatɪŋ/, *adj. N.Z. Colloq.* trivial.

**fart machine** /'fat məʃin/, *n. Colloq.* →**skidoo.**

**fart sack** /'fat sæk/, *n. Colloq.* a bed or a sleeping bag. Also, **farter.**

**F.A.S.,** →**free alongside ship.** Also, **f.a.s.**

**fasces** /'fæsiz/, *n.pl., sing.* **fascis.** a bundle of rods containing an axe, borne before Roman magistrates as an emblem of power. [L] –**fascial** /'fæʃiəl/, *adj.*

**fascia** /'feɪʃə/; *Med.* /'fæʃiə/, *n., pl.* **fasciae** /'fæʃii/. **1.** a band or fillet. **2.** *Archit.* **a.** a long, flat member or band. **b.** a triple horizontal division of an architrave in Ionic, Corinthian, and composite orders. **3.** *Anat., Zool.* **a.** a band or sheath of connective tissue investing, supporting, or binding together internal organs or parts of the body. **b.** tissue of this kind. **4.** *Chiefly Zool.* a distinctly marked band of colour. **5.** →**facia.** [L: band] – **fascial,** *adj.*

**fasciate** /'fæʃieɪt/, *adj.* **1.** bound with a band, fillet, or bandage. **2.** *Bot.* **a.** compressed into a band or bundle. **b.** grown together, as stems. **3.** *Zool.* **a.** composed of bundles. **b.** bound together in a bundle. **c.** marked with a band or bands. Also, **fasciated.** [L *fasciātus,* pp., enveloped with bands]

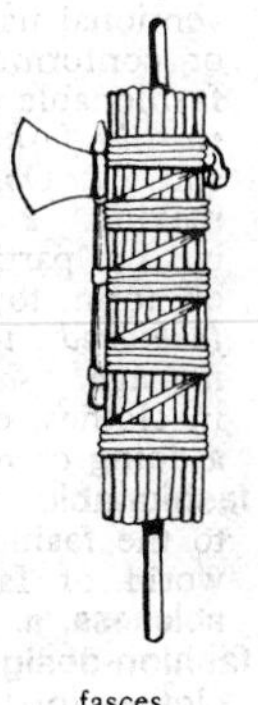
fasces

**fasciation** /fæʃi'eɪʃən/, *n.* **1.** the act or an instance of binding up. **2.** *Bot.* an abnormality of growth resulting in the fusion of several stems to form a flat plate. **3.** the process of becoming fasciate. **4.** the resulting state.

**fascicle** /'fæsəkəl/, *n.* **1.** a small bundle. **2.** a part of a printed work; a number of printed or written sheets bound together, as an instalment for convenience in publication. **3.** *Bot.* a close cluster, as of flowers or leaves. **4.** *Anat.* a small bundle of fibres within a nerve or the central nervous system. [L *fasciculus,* diminutive of *fascis* bundle] – **fascicled,** *adj.*

**fascicular** /fə'sɪkjulə/, *adj.* pertaining to or forming a fascicle; fasciculate.

**fasciculate** /fə'sɪkjulət, -leɪt/, *adj.* arranged in a fascicle or fascicles. Also, **fasciculated.** – **fasciculately,** *adv.*

**fasciculation** /fəsɪkju'leɪʃən/, *n.* **1.** fascicular condition. **2.** spontaneous contractions or twitching of a number of muscle fibres supplied by a single motor nerve filament.

**fascicule** /'fæsɪkjul/, *n.* a fascicle, esp. of a book. [L *fasciculus* little bundle]

**fasciculus** /fə'sɪkjuləs/, *n., pl.* **-li.** **1.** a fascicle, as of nerve or muscle fibres. **2.** a fascicle of a book. [L: little bundle]

**fascinate** /'fæsəneɪt/, *v.t.*, **-nated, -nating.** **1.** to attract and hold irresistibly by delightful qualities. **2.** to deprive of the power of resistance or movement, as through terror. **3.** *Obs.* to bewitch. **4.** *Obs.* to cast under a spell by a look. *–v.i.* **5.** to hold the attention. [L *fascinātus,* pp., enchanted]

**fascinating** /'fæsəneɪtɪŋ/, *adj.* bewitching; captivating; of overwhelming interest: *a fascinating idea.* – **fascinatingly,** *adv.*

**fascination** /fæsə'neɪʃən/, *n.* **1.** the act of fascinating. **2.** the state of being fascinated. **3.** fascinating quality; powerful attraction; charm.

**fascinator** /'fæsəneɪtə/, *n.* **1.** one who or that which fascinates. **2.** a kind of scarf of crochet work, lace, etc., narrowing towards the ends, worn as a head covering.

**fascine** /fæ'sin, fə-/, *n.* **1.** a faggot. **2.** a long bundle of sticks bound together, used in building earthworks and batteries, in strengthening ramparts, as a protective facing for river banks, etc. [F, from L *fascīna* bundle of sticks]

**fascism** /'fæʃɪzəm/, *n.* **1.** (*oft. cap.*) a governmental system with strong centralised power, permitting no opposition or cricitism, controlling all affairs of the nation (industrial, commercial, etc.), emphasising an aggressive nationalism, and (often) anticommunist. **2.** (*oft. cap.*) the philosophy, principles, or methods of fascism; a fascist movement, esp. the one established in Italy by Mussolini in 1922, whence its influence spread to Germany and elsewhere; dissolved in Italy in 1943. **3.** *Colloq.* (*pejor.*) any extreme right-wing ideology, esp. one involving racialism. [It. *Fascismo,* from *fascio* group, bundle, from L *fascis* a bundle of rods containing an axe, a Roman emblem of official power, later adopted by the Italian Fascist party]

**fascist** /'fæʃəst/, *n.* **1.** anyone who believes in or sympathises with fascism. **2.** a member of a fascist movement or party, esp. (*cap.*) in Italy. **3.** *Colloq.* a dictatorial person. **4.** *Colloq.* anyone with extreme right-wing views, esp. with regard to race. *–adj.* **5.** of or like fascism or fascists.

**fashion** /'fæʃən/, *n.* **1.** a prevailing custom or style of dress, etiquette, procedure, etc.: *the latest fashion in hats.* **2.** conventional usage in dress, manners, etc., esp. of polite society, or conformity to it: *dictates of fashion, out of fashion.* **3.** fashionable people collectively. **4.** manner; way; mode: *in a warlike fashion.* **5.** the make or form of anything. **6.** a kind; sort. **7.** *Obs.* workmanship. **8.** *Obs.* the act or process of making. **9. after** or **in a fashion,** in some manner or other, but not particularly well. *–v.t.* **10.** to give a particular shape or form to; make. **11.** to accommodate; adapt: *doctrines fashioned to the varying hour.* **12.** *Obs.* to contrive; manage. *–adj.* **13.** pertaining to or displaying new fashions in clothes, etc. [ME *facioun,* from OF *façon,* from L *factio* a doing or making]

**fashionable** /'fæʃənəbəl/, *adj.* **1.** observant of or conforming to the fashion. **2.** of, characteristic of, or patronised by the world of fashion. *–n.* **3.** a fashionable person. – **fashionableness,** *n.* – **fashionably,** *adv.*

**fashion-designer** /'fæʃən-dəzaɪnə/, *n.* one who designs clothes for the commercial fashion market.

**fashioner** /'fæʃənə/, *n.* **1.** one who fashions, forms, or gives shape to anything. **2.** *Obs.* a tailor or modiste.

**fashion house** /'fæʃən haʊs/, *n.* a firm which designs and manufactures fashionable clothing primarily for the very rich.

**fashion journal** /'– dʒɜnəl/, *n.* a trade magazine or catalogue, written by and usu. aimed at those involved in the fashion industry.

**fashion magazine** /'– mægəzin/, *n.* a magazine discussing and advertising developments in clothing fashions.

**fashion model** /'– mɒdl/, *n.* one employed to pose dressed in the latest fashions for the purposes of photography, advertising, fashion parades, etc.

**fashion parade** /'– pəreɪd/, *n.* a presentation of clothes, fabrics, etc., usu. the latest styles, where the clothes are worn by live models.

**fashion plate** /'– pleɪt/, *n.* **1.** a pictorial design showing a prevailing or new mode of dress. **2.** *Colloq.* a person who wears the latest style in dress.

**fast**[1] /fast/, *adj.* **1.** moving or able to move quickly; quick; swift; rapid: *a fast horse.* **2.** done in comparatively little time: *a fast race, fast work.* **3.** indicating a time in advance of the correct time, as a clock. **4.** adapted to or productive of rapid movement: *a fast track.* **5.** extremely energetic and active, esp. in pursuing pleasure immoderately or without restraint, as a person. **6.** characterised by such energy or pursuit of pleasure, as a mode of life. **7.** resistant: *acid-fast.* **8.** firmly fixed in place; not easily moved; securely attached: *to make fast.* **9.** that cannot escape or be extricated. **10.** firmly tied, as a knot. **11.** closed and made secure, as a door. **12.** such as to hold securely: *to lay fast hold on a thing.* **13.** firm in adherence: *fast friends.* **14.** permanent; lasting: *a fast colour.* **15.** deep or sound, as sleep. **16.** deceptive, insincere, inconstant, or unreliable. **17.** *Photog.* permitting very short exposure, as by having a wide shutter opening or high film sensitivity: *a fast lens or film.* **18.** (of the surface of a cricket pitch, racecourse, etc.) hard and dry, and therefore conducive to fast movement. **19. pull a fast one,** *Colloq.* to act unfairly or deceitfully. *–adv.* **20.** tightly: *to hold fast.* **21.** soundly: *fast asleep.* **22.** quickly, swiftly, or rapidly. **23.** in quick succession. **24.** in an energetic or dissipated way. **25.** *Archaic.* close; near: *fast by.* **26. play fast and loose with,** to behave in an inconsiderate, inconstant, or irresponsible manner towards. *–n.* **27.** something that fastens, as a rope that holds a ship to its moorings. [ME; OE *fæst,* c. D *vast,* Icel. *fastr* fast, firm]

**fast**[2] /fast/, *v.i.* **1.** to abstain from all food. **2.** to eat only sparingly or of certain kinds of food, esp. as a religious observance. *–n.* **3.** a fasting; an abstinence from food, or a limiting of one's food, esp. when voluntary and as a religious observance. **4.** a day or period of fasting. [ME *faste(n),* OE *fæstan,* c. G *fasten*] – **faster,** *n.*

**fastback** /'fastbæk/, *adj.* **1.** (of the rear of a car) designed to give the best aerodynamic flow; sloping uniformly from the back of the roof to a point above the bumper. *–n.* **2.** the rear of a car so designed. **3.** a car having such features.

**fast bowler** /fast 'boʊlə/, *n.* a bowler who delivers a fast ball.

**fast breeder reactor,** *n.* →**breeder** (def. 3).

**fast buck** /fast 'bʌk/, *n. Colloq.* money made quickly and often irresponsibly.

**fast day** /'– deɪ/, *n.* a day on which fasting is observed, esp. such a day appointed by some ecclesiastical or civil authority.

**fasten** /'fasən/, *v.t.* **1.** to make fast; fix firmly or securely in place or position; attach securely to something else. **2.** to make secure, as an article of dress with buttons, clasps, etc., or a door with a lock, bolt, etc. **3.** to enclose securely, as a person or an animal (fol. by *in*). **4.** to attach by any connecting agency: *to fasten a nickname or a crime upon one.* **5.** to direct (the eyes, thoughts, etc.) intently. *–v.i.* **6.** to become fast, fixed, or firm. **7.** to take firm hold; seize (usu. fol. by *on*). **8.** (of the eyes, thoughts, etc.) to be directed intently. [ME *fasten(en), fastne(n),* OE *fæstnian,* from *fjæst,* adj., FAST[1]] – **fastener,** *n.*

**fastening** /'fasənɪŋ/, *n.* something that fastens, as a lock or clasp.

**fast food** /fast 'fud/, *n.* food for sale, as chicken, chips, hamburgers, etc., which can be provided without delay.

**fastidious** /fæs'tɪdiəs/, *adj.* hard to please; excessively critical: *a fastidious taste.* [L *fastīdiōsus,* from *fastīdium* loathing, disgust] – **fastidiously,** *adv.* – **fastidiousness,** *n.*

**fastie** /'fasti/, *n. Colloq.* **1.** a deceitful practice; a cunning act. **2. pull (put over) a fastie,** to deceive; to take an unfair advantage.

**fastigiate** /fæs'tɪdʒiət, -eɪt/, *adj.* **1.** rising to a pointed top. **2.** *Zool.* joined together in a tapering adhering group. **3.** *Bot.* **a.** erect and parallel, as branches. **b.** having such branches. Also, **fastigiated.** [L *fastīgium* gable top, summit, slope + -ATE[1]]

**fast lane** /'fast leɪn/, *n.* **1.** the right-hand lane on a highway, often used for overtaking. **2. in the fast lane,** *Colloq.* (of a lifestyle, etc.) conducted at a hectic pace.

**fastness** /'fastnəs/, *n.* **1.** a secure or fortified place. **2.** the state of being fixed or firm. **3.** the state of being rapid. **4.** the quality of being energetic or dissipated.

**fast neutron** /fast 'njutrɒn/, *n.* a neutron arising from nuclear fission which has lost little energy by collision and therefore travels through space very rapidly; a neutron with energy in excess of about 0.1 MeV.

**fast reactor** /– ri'æktə/, *n.* a nuclear reactor in which most of the fissions are caused by fast neutrons.

**fast road** /'- roud/, *n.* a stretch of road or a highway on which cars are able to drive at high speed.

**fast-talk** /'fast-tɔk/, *v.t.* to confuse or deceive by rapid and often irrelevant talk. – **fast-talking,** *n.*

**fat** /fæt/, *adj.,* **fatter, fattest,** *n., v.,* **fatted, fatting.** –*adj.* **1.** having much flesh other than muscle; fleshy; corpulent; obese. **2.** having much edible flesh; well-fattened: *to kill a fat lamb.* **3.** consisting of, resembling, or containing fat. **4.** abounding in a particular element: *fat pine* (pine rich in resin). **5.** (of paint) having a comparatively high oil content. **6.** fertile, as land. **7.** profitable, as an office. **8.** affording good opportunities: *a fat profit.* **9.** (of spirits, and sometimes of wine) not delicate, clean, fine or pure; containing many different constituents. **10.** thick; broad; extended. **11.** plentiful. **12.** plentifully supplied. **13.** dull; stupid. **14. a fat chance,** *Colloq.* little or no chance. **15. a fat lot,** *Colloq.* little or nothing. –*n.* **16.** any of several white or yellowish substances, greasy to the touch, forming the chief part of the adipose tissue of animals and also found in plants. When pure, the fats are odourless, tasteless, and colourless, and may be either solid or liquid. They are insoluble in water or cold alcohol but easily soluble in ether, chloroform, or benzene. They are compound esters of various fatty acids with glycerol, the pure fats being composed of carbon, hydrogen, and oxygen. **17.** animal tissue containing much of this substance. **18.** the richest or best part of anything. **19.** esp. profitable or advantageous work. **20.** (*pl.*) livestock fattened for sale. **21.** action or lines in a dramatic part which permit an actor to display his abilities. **22.** *Print.* matter that is easily and profitably composed. **23.** *Colloq.* a marble. **24.** *Colloq.* an erection. **25.** *Colloq.* overtime. **26. chew the fat,** *Colloq.* to talk, gossip. **27. crack a fat,** *Colloq.* to have an erection. **28. live on one's fat,** to consume reserves; live on capital. **29. stick fats, a.** to keep one's marble in its present position. **b.** not to shift from one's position. **30. the fat is in the fire,** an irrevocable (and often disastrous) step has been taken, resulting in dire consequences. **31. the fat of the land,** great luxury. –*v.t.* **32.** to make fat; fatten. –*v.i.* **33.** to become fat. [ME; OE *fætt,* orig. pp., fatted, c. G *Feist*]

**fatal** /'feɪtl/, *adj.* **1.** causing death: *a fatal accident.* **2.** causing destruction or ruin: *an action that is fatal to the success of a project.* **3.** decisively important; fateful: *the fatal day finally arrived.* **4.** influencing fate: *the fatal sisters.* **5.** proceeding from or decreed by fate; inevitable. **6.** *Obs.* doomed. **7.** *Obs.* prophetic. [ME, from L *fātālis* of or belonging to fate] – **fatalness,** *n.*

**fatalism** /'feɪtəlɪzəm/, *n.* **1.** the doctrine that all events are subject to fate or inevitable predetermination. **2.** the acceptance of all things and events as inevitable; submission to fate. – **fatalist,** *n.* – **fatalistic** /feɪtə'lɪstɪk/, *adj.* – **fatalistically** /feɪtə'lɪstɪkli/, *adv.*

**fatality** /fə'tæləti/, *n., pl.* **-ties. 1.** a disaster resulting in death; a calamity or misfortune. **2.** one who is killed in an accident or disaster. **3.** the quality of causing death or disaster; deadliness; a fatal influence. **4.** predetermined liability to disaster. **5.** the quality of being predetermined by or subject to fate. **6.** the fate or destiny of a person or thing. **7.** a fixed, unalterably predetermined course of things.

**fatally** /'feɪtəli/, *adv.* **1.** in a manner leading to death or disaster. **2.** by a decree of fate or destiny; by inevitable predetermination.

**fatback** /'fætbæk/, *n.* the fat, usu. salted and dried, from the upper part of a side of pork.

**fat cat** /'fæt kæt/, *n. Colloq.* (*derog.*) **1.** a person who expects special comforts and privileges because of his position or wealth: *the fat cats of the Public Service.* **2.** a wealthy contributor to a political campaign.

**fate** /feɪt/, *n., v.,* **fated, fating.** –*n.* **1.** fortune; lot; destiny. **2.** a divine decree or a fixed sentence by which the order of things is prescribed. **3.** that which is inevitably predetermined; destiny. **4.** a prophetic declaration of what must be. **5.** death, destruction, or ruin. –*v.t.* **6.** to predetermine as by the decree of fate; destine (now only in the passive). [ME, from L *fātum* a prophetic declaration, fate, properly pp. neut., (thing) said]

**fated** /'feɪtəd/, *adj.* **1.** subject to, guided by, or predetermined by fate. **2.** destined. **3.** doomed.

**fateful** /'feɪtfəl/, *adj.* **1.** involving momentous consequences; decisively important. **2.** fatal, deadly, or disastrous. **3.** controlled by irresistible destiny. **4.** prophetic; ominous. – **fatefully,** *adv.* – **fatefulness,** *n.*

**fathead** /'fæthɛd/, *n.* a stupid person. – **fatheaded,** *adj.*

**fat-hen** /'fæt-hɛn/, *n.* a common chenopodiaceous annual weed, *Chenopodium album,* with dark green mealy leaves, widespread in temperate regions.

**father** /'faðə/, *n.* **1.** a male parent. **2.** any male ancestor, esp. the founder of a race, family, or line. **3.** *Colloq.* a father-in-law, stepfather, or adoptive father. **4.** one who exercises paternal care over another; a fatherly protector or provider: *a father to the poor.* **5.** a title of respect for an old man. **6.** the oldest or sometimes chief member of a society, profession, etc. **7.** one of the leading men of a city, etc. **8.** a person or thing who originates or establishes something. **9.** (*cap.*) *Theol.* the Supreme Being and Creator; God. **10. the Father,** the first person of the Trinity. **11.** any of the chief early Christian writers, whose works are the main sources for the history, doctrines, and observances of the Church in the early ages. **12.** *Eccles.* **a.** (*oft. cap.*) a title of reverence, as for Church dignitaries, officers of monasteries, monks, confessors, and priests. **b.** a person bearing this title. **13. the father and mother of a (something),** the biggest; a very big (something). –*v.t.* **14.** to beget. **15.** to originate; be the author of. **16.** to act as a father towards. **17.** to acknowledge oneself the father of. **18.** to assume as one's own; take the responsibility of. [ME *fader,* OE *fæder,* c. G *Vater;* akin to L *pater,* Gk *patḗr*]

**Father Christmas** /faðə 'krɪsməs/, *n.* **1.** →**Santa Claus. 2.** →**beardy.**

**father confessor** /faðə kən'fɛsə/, *n.* →**confessor.**

**father-figure** /'faðə-fɪgə/, *n.* **1.** a man who evokes from another person the filial emotions and attitudes usu. associated with actual fatherhood. **2.** *Colloq.* any elderly man of impressive presence.

**fatherhood** /'faðəhʊd/, *n.* the state of being a father.

**father-in-law** /'faðər-ɪn-lɔ/, *n., pl.* **fathers-in-law. 1.** the father of one's husband or wife. **2.** *Colloq.* a stepfather.

**fatherland** /'faðəlænd/, *n.* **1.** one's native country. **2.** the land of one's ancestors.

**fatherless** /'faðələs/, *adj.* **1.** without a living father. **2.** without a known or legally responsible father.

**fatherly** /'faðəli/, *adj.* **1.** of, like, or befitting a father. –*adv.* **2.** in the manner of a father. – **fatherliness,** *n.*

**Father's Day** /'faðəz deɪ/, *n.* a day set aside in many countries usu. in September, for the honouring of fathers.

**fathom** /'fæðəm/, *n., pl.* **fathoms,** (*esp. collectively*) **fathom,** *v.* –*n.* **1.** a unit of depth in the imperial system equal to 6 ft or 1.8288 m, used in nautical measurements. *Symbol:* fm –*v.t.* **2.** to reach in depth by measurement in fathoms; sound; try the depth of; penetrate to or find the bottom or extent of. **3.** to measure the depth of by sounding. **4.** to penetrate to the bottom of; understand thoroughly. [ME *fathme,* OE *fæthm,* c. G *Faden;* akin to Gk *pétalos* spreading] – **fathomable,** *adj.* – **fathomer,** *n.*

**fathometer** /fə'ðɒmətə/, *n.* an instrument for measuring the depth of water; depends on measurement of the time taken for a sound to reach the seabed and for its echo to return.

**fathomless** /'fæðəmləs/, *adj.* impossible to fathom. – **fathomlessly,** *adv.*

**fatidic** /fə'tɪdɪk, fæ-/, *adj.* prophetic. Also, **fatidical.** [L *fātidicus* prophesying]

**fatigable** /'fætɪgəbəl/, *adj.* easily fatigued or tired.

**fatigue** /fə'tig/, *n., v.,* **-tigued, -tiguing,** *adj.* –*n.* **1.** weariness from bodily or mental exertion. **2.** a cause of weariness; labour; exertion. **3.** *Physiol.* temporary diminution of the excitability or functioning of organs, tissues, or cells after excessive exertion or stimulation. **4.** *Mech.* the weakening of material subjected to stress, esp. a continued series of stresses. **5.** Also, **fatigue duty.** *Mil.* **a.** labour of a generally non-military kind done by soldiers, such as cleaning up an area, or digging drainage ditches, or raking up leaves. **b.** the state of being engaged in such labour: *on fatigue.* **c.** (*pl.*) →**fatigue dress.** –*v.t.* **6.** to weary with bodily or mental exertion; exhaust the strength of. –*adj.* **7.** of or pertaining to fatigue: *fatigue detail.* [F, from *fatiguer,* from L *fatīgāre* tire]

**fatigued** /fə'tigd/, *adj.* wearied.

**fatigue dress** /fə'tig drɛs/, *n.* a soldier's uniform for fatigue duty.

**fatigue life** /'– laɪf/, *n.* the number of applications of a given stress which a sample of material will withstand before failing.

**fatigue party** /'– pati/, *n.* a group of soldiers on fatigue.

**fatigue test** /'– tɛst/, *n.* a test made on a sample of a material to determine the range of alternating stress which it will withstand before failing.

**fat lamb** /'fæt læm/, *n.* **1.** a lamb bred for its tender meat, esp. one bred from a border Leicester cross Merino ewe and a British Dorset-horn ram. **2.** a very young lamb, about 4 months old and still a suckling.

**fatling** /'fætlɪŋ/, *n.* a young animal, as a calf or a lamb, fattened for slaughter. [FAT + -LING[1]]

**fatly** /'fætli/, *adv.* **1.** in a fat manner; plumply. **2.** clumsily. **3.** plentifully; richly; profitably.

**fat mouse** /'fæt maʊs/, *n.* any of the short-tailed mice of the genus *Steatomys* of southern Africa, eaten by the Africans as a delicacy.

**fatness** /'fætnəs/, *n.* **1.** condition of being fat. **2.** corpulence. **3.** oiliness. **4.** richness; fertility.

**fatso** /'fætsoʊ/, *n. Colloq.* a fat person.

**fat-soluble** /'fæt-sɒljubəl/, *adj.* soluble in oils or fats.

**fatted** /'fætəd/, *adj.* **1.** fattened. **2. kill the fatted calf,** to make lavish preparation, esp. of food, for a guest.

**fatten** /'fætn/, *v.t.* **1.** to make fat. **2.** to feed for slaughter. **3.** to enrich; make fertile. **4.** *Poker.* to increase the number of chips in (a pot). *–v.i.* **5.** *Chiefly U.S.* to grow fat. **– fattener,** *n.*

**fattish** /'fætɪʃ/, *adj.* somewhat fat.

**fatty** /'fæti/, *adj.*, **-tier, -tiest,** *n.* *–adj.* **1.** consisting of, containing, or resembling fat: *fatty tissue.* **2.** *Pathol.* characterised by overproduction or excessive accumulation of fat. **3.** *Bldg Trades.* (of mortar) easily workable. *–n.* **4.** *Colloq.* a fat person: *he's a real fatty.* **– fattiness,** *n.*

**fatty acid** /– 'æsəd/, *n.* any of a class of aliphatic acids, esp. one such as palmitic, stearic, oleic, etc., present as glycerides in animal and vegetable fats and oils.

**fatty degeneration** /– dədʒɛnə'reɪʃən/, *n.* deterioration of the cells of the body accompanied by the formation of fat globules within the diseased cells.

**fatty tumour** /– 'tjumə/, *n.* →**lipoma.**

**fatuitous** /fə'tjuətəs/, *adj.* characterised by fatuity.

**fatuity** /fə'tjuəti/, *n., pl.* **-ties. 1.** foolishness; complacent stupidity. **2.** something foolish. [L *fatuitas*]

**fatuous** /'fætʃuəs/, *adj.* **1.** foolish, esp. in an unconscious, complacent manner; silly. **2.** unreal; illusory. [L *fatuus*] **– fatuously,** *adv.* **– fatuousness,** *n.*

**fat-witted** /'fæt-wɪtəd/, *adj.* dull; stupid.

**faubourg** /'foʊbɜg/, *n.* a part of a city outside (or once outside) the walls; suburb. [F]

**faucal** /'fɔkəl/, *adj.* **1.** pertaining to the fauces or opening of the throat. **2.** *Phonet.* **a.** (of the explosion of a stop) produced by lowering the velum, the *t* of *button* has faucal explosion if no vowel is pronounced before the *n.* **b.** laryngeal. [L *fauces* throat + -AL[1]]

**fauces** /'fɔsiz/, *n.pl.* the cavity at the back of the mouth, leading into the pharynx. [L] **– faucial** /'fɔʃəl/, *adj.*

**faucet** /'fɔsət/, *n. Chiefly U.S.* any device for controlling the flow of liquid from a pipe or the like by opening or closing an orifice; a tap; a cock. [ME, from OF *fausset,* from *fausser* force in, damage, from L *falsāre* falsify]

**faugh** /fɔ/, *interj.* (an exclamation of disgust.)

**fault** /fɔlt, fɒlt/, *n.* **1.** a defect or imperfection; a flaw; a failing. **2.** an error or mistake. **3.** a misdeed or transgression. **4.** delinquency; culpability; cause for blame. **5.** *Geol., Mining.* a break in the continuity of a body of rock or of a vein, with dislocation along the plane of fracture. **6.** *Elect.* a partial or total local failure, in the insulation or continuity of a conductor, or in the functioning of an electric system. **7.** *Tennis, etc.* **a.** a failure to serve the ball legitimately within the prescribed limits. **b.** a ball which when served does not land in the proper section of the opponent's court. **8.** *Showjumping.* a scoring unit used in recording improper execution of jumps by contestants. **9.** *Hunting.* a break in the line of scent; a losing of the scent. **10.** *Obs.* lack; want. **11. at fault, a.** open to censure; blamable. **b.** puzzled; astray. **c.** (of hounds) unable to pick up a lost scent. **12. in fault,** open to censure; blamable. **13. find fault,** find something wrong; complain. **14. to a fault,** excessively. *–v.i.* **15.** *Geol.* to undergo a fault or faults. **16.** to commit a fault. *–v.t.* **17.** *Geol.* to cause a fault in. **18.** to find fault with, blame, or censure. [ME *faute,* from OF, from LL *fallita,* from L *fallere* deceive]

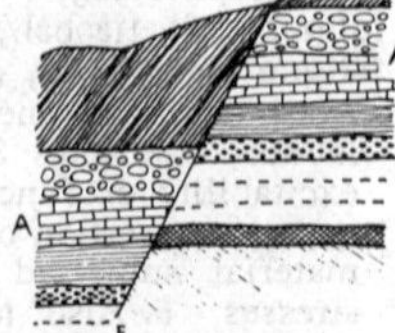

fault (def. 5) showing section of strata displaced by a fault: F, fault line; A and A, former continuous mass of rock

**fault-finder** /'fɔlt-faɪndə/, *n.* one who finds fault; one who complains or objects.

**fault-finding** /'fɔlt-faɪndɪŋ/, *n.* **1.** the act of pointing out faults; carping; picking flaws. *–adj.* **2.** given to finding fault; disposed to complain or object.

**faultless** /'fɔltləs/, *adj.* without fault or defect; perfect. **– faultlessly,** *adv.* **– faultlessness,** *n.*

**fault plane** /'fɔlt pleɪn/, *n.* the plane of fracture in a geological fault.

**faulty** /'fɔlti/, *adj.,* **faultier, faultiest. 1.** having faults or defects: *faulty workmanship.* **2.** *Rare.* of the nature of a fault; morally blamable: *whatever is faulty with the Church.* **3.** *Obs.* culpable; at fault. **– faultily,** *adv.* **– faultiness,** *n.*

**faun** /fɔn/, *n.* (in Roman mythology) one of a class of rural deities represented as men with the ears, horns, and tail, and later also the hind legs, of a goat. [ME, from L] **– faunlike,** *adj.*

**fauna** /'fɔnə/, *n., pl.* **-nas, -nae. 1.** the animals of a given region or period, taken collectively (as distinguished from the plants or *flora*). **2.** a treatise on the animals of a given region or period. [NL, special use of *Fauna,* name of sister of *Faunus,* in Roman mythology a woodland deity identified with Pan] **– faunal,** *adj.*

**fauvism** /'foʊvɪzəm/, *n.* (*oft. cap.*) an art movement centred in Paris and lasting from 1905 to 1908, characterised by flat patterns, violent colour, and distortion of form. [F *fauve* wild beast, used to describe the artists of the movement] **– fauve** /foʊv/, *n., adj.* **– fauvist** /'foʊvəst/, *n., adj.*

**fauxbourdon** /'fæbədən/, *n.* **1.** an ancient compositional style employing three voices harmonising in fourths and sixths. **2.** harmony in progressions of parallel sixths. [F]

**faux pas** /'foʊ pa/, *n., pl.* **faux pas** /'foʊ paz, -pa/. a false step; a slip in manners; a breach of etiquette. [F]

**faveolate** /fə'viəleɪt, -lət/, *adj.* honeycombed; alveolate; pitted. [NL *faveolus* (diminutive of L *favus* honeycomb) + -ATE[1]]

**favonian** /fə'voʊniən/, *adj.* **1.** of or pertaining to the west wind. **2.** mild; favourable; propitious. [L *favōniānus,* from *Favōnius* the west wind]

**favorite son** /feɪvərət 'sʌn/, *n. U.S. Politics.* a candidate for national office proposed by a local or state delegation, with local rather than national support: *Iowa's governor stood as a favorite son in the Democratic primaries for the presidency.* Also, **favourite son.**

**favour** /'feɪvə/, *n.* **1.** a kind act; something done or granted out of goodwill, rather than from justice or for remuneration: *ask a favour.* **2.** kindness; kind approval. **3.** a state of being approved, or held in regard: *in favour, out of favour.* **4.** excessive kindness; unfair partiality: *show undue favour to someone.* **5.** a gift bestowed as a token of goodwill, kind regard, love, etc. **6.** a ribbon, badge, etc., worn in evidence of goodwill or loyalty. **7.** (*pl.*) consent to sexual intimacy. **8.** *Obs.* a letter, esp. a commercial one. **9. in favour of, a.** in support of; on the side of. **b.** to the advantage of. **c.** (of a cheque, etc.) payable to. *–v.t.* **10.** to regard with favour. **11.** to have a preference for; treat with partiality. **12.** to show favour to; oblige. **13.** to be favourable to; facilitate. **14.** *Rare.* to deal with gently: *favour a lame leg.* **15.** to aid or support. Also, *U.S.,* **favor.** [ME, from OF, from L *favor*] **– favourer,** *n.* **– favouringly,** *adv.* **– favourless,** *adj.*

**favourable** /'feɪvərəbəl, -vrəbəl/, *adj.* **1.** affording aid, advantage, or convenience: *a favourable position.* **2.** manifesting favour; inclined to aid or approve. **3.** (of an answer) granting what is desired. **4.** promising well: *the signs are favourable.* Also, *U.S.*, **favorable.** – **favourableness,** *n.* – **favourably,** *adv.*

**favoured** /ˈfeɪvəd/, *adj.* **1.** regarded or treated with favour. **2.** enjoying special advantages. **3.** of specified appearance, used in combination, as in *ill-favoured.* Also, *U.S.*, **favored.**

**favourite** /ˈfeɪvərət, -vrət/, *n.* **1.** a person or thing regarded with special favour or preference. **2.** *Sport.* a competitor considered likely to win. **3.** *Racing.* the horse, dog, etc., which is most heavily backed. **4.** a person treated with special (esp. undue) favour, as by a ruler. *–adj.* **5.** regarded with particular favour or preference: *a favourite child.* Also, *U.S.*, **favorite.** [F *favorit,* var. of *favori,* from It. *favorito,* from *favore* favour, from L *favor*]

**favouritism** /ˈfeɪvərətɪzəm, -vrə-/, *n.* **1.** the favouring of one person or group over others having equal claims. **2.** the state of being a favourite. **3.** the state of being the favourite in a race, competition, etc.: *suffering from favouritism, the horse ran at low odds.* Also, *U.S.*, **favoritism.**

**fawn**[1] /fɔn/, *n.* **1.** a young deer. **2.** a buck or doe of the first year. **3.** a fawn colour. *–adj.* **4.** light yellowish brown. *–v.i.* **5.** (of deer) to bring forth young. [ME *foun,* from OF *faon,* from L *fētus* offspring, young] – **fawnlike,** *adj.*

fawn of Virginia deer

**fawn**[2] /fɔn/, *v.i.* **1.** to seek notice or favour by servile demeanour. **2.** to show fondness by crouching, wagging the tail, licking the hand, etc. (said esp. of dogs). [ME *faghne(n),* OE *fagnian,* var. of *fægnian* rejoice, fawn, from *fægen* glad, fain] – **fawner,** *n.* – **fawningly,** *adv.*

**fay**[1] /feɪ/, *n.* a fairy. [ME, from OF *fae, fee,* from L *fāta* the Fates, pl. of *fātum* FATE]

**fay**[2] /feɪ/, *v.t.* **1.** to fit, esp. together closely, as timbers in shipbuilding. *–v.i.* **2.** to be fitted or joined closely. [ME *feien, fey,* OE *fēgan,* c. G *fügen*]

**fayalite** /ˈfeɪəlaɪt, faɪˈalaɪt/, *n.* a black, greenish, or brownish mineral of the olivine group, ferrous orthosilicate, $Fe_2SiO_4$; iron olivine. [*Fayal* Faial, island in N Atlantic + -ITE[1]]

**faze** /feɪz/, *v.t.*, **fazed, fazing.** *Colloq.* to disturb; discomfit; daunt. [var. of obs. *feeze* disturb, worry]

**fazzo** /ˈfæzoʊ/, *adj.* *(esp. in children's speech)* fabulous; wonderful.

**FBI** /ɛf bi ˈaɪ/, *U.S.* Federal Bureau of Investigation.

**FCL** /ɛf si ˈɛl/, *Shipping.* full container load. Also, **f.c.l.**

**F clef** /ˈɛf klɛf/, *n.* →**bass clef.**

**fcp,** foolscap.

**F.C.T.,** Federal Capital Territory (now Australian Capital Territory).

**F.D.,** →**Fidei Defensor.**

**Fe,** *Chem.* iron. [L *ferrum*]

**fealty** /ˈfiəlti/, *n., pl.* **-ties.** **1.** *Hist.* **a.** fidelity to a lord. **b.** the obligation or the engagement to be faithful to a lord, usu. sworn to by the vassal. **2.** *Archaic.* fidelity; faithfulness. [ME *feaute,* from OF, from L *fidēlitas* fidelity]

**fear** /fɪə/, *n.* **1.** a painful feeling of impending danger, evil, trouble, etc.; the feeling or condition of being afraid. **2.** a specific instance of such a feeling. **3.** anxiety; solicitude. **4.** reverential awe, esp. towards God. **5.** a cause for fear. **6. for fear of,** in order to avoid or prevent. **7. no fear!** *Colloq.* certainly not. *–v.t.* **8.** to regard with fear; be afraid of. **9.** to have reverential awe of. **10.** *Archaic.* to be afraid (used reflexively). **11.** *Archaic.* to frighten. *–v.i.* **12.** to have fear; be afraid. [ME *fere,* OE *fǣr* sudden attack, sudden danger, c. OS *fār* ambush; akin to G *Gefahr* danger] – **fearer,** *n.*

**fearful** /ˈfɪəfəl/, *adj.* **1.** causing, or apt to cause, fear. **2.** feeling fear, dread, or solicitude: *I am fearful of him doing it.* **3.** full of awe or reverence. **4.** showing or caused by fear. **5.** *Colloq.* extremely bad, large, etc. – **fearfully,** *adv.* – **fearfulness,** *n.*

**fearless** /ˈfɪələs/, *adj.* without fear; bold. – **fearlessly,** *adv.* – **fearlessness,** *n.*

**fearsome** /ˈfɪəsəm/, *adj.* **1.** causing fear. **2.** afraid; timid. – **fearsomely,** *adv.* – **fearsomeness,** *n.*

**feasibility study** /fizəˈbɪləti ˌstʌdi/, *n.* a survey or analysis of the need, value, and practicability of a proposed enterprise.

**feasible** /ˈfizəbəl/, *adj.* **1.** capable of being done, effected, or accomplished: *a feasible plan.* **2.** likely; probable: *a feasible theory, a feasible excuse.* [ME *fesable,* from OF, from *faire,* from L *facere* do, make] – **feasibility** /fizəˈbɪləti/, **feasibleness,** *n.* – **feasibly,** *adv.*

**feast** /fist/, *n.* **1.** a periodical celebration, or day or time of celebration, of religious or other character, in commemoration of some event or person, or having some other special significance: *feasts of the Church, the medieval feast of fools, the Chinese feast of lanterns.* **2.** a sumptuous entertainment or meal for many guests. **3.** any rich or abundant meal. **4.** something highly agreeable. *–v.i.* **5.** to have, or partake of, a feast; eat sumptuously. **6.** to dwell with gratification or delight, as on a picture. *–v.t.* **7.** to provide or entertain with a feast. **8.** to gratify; delight. [ME *feste,* from OF, from L *festa,* fem. sing. of *festus* festal] – **feaster,** *n.* – **feasting,** *n.*

**feast-day** /ˈfist-deɪ/, *n.* a day on which a religious feast is celebrated.

**feat**[1] /fit/, *n.* **1.** a noteworthy or extraordinary act or achievement, usu. displaying boldness, skill, etc. **2.** an action; deed. [ME *fait,* from OF, from L *factum* (thing) done, properly pp. neut.]

**feat**[2] /fit/, *adj.* *Archaic.* **1.** apt; skilful; dexterous. **2.** suitable. **3.** neat. [ME *fete,* apparently from OF *fait,* pp. of *faire,* from L *facere* do, make]

**feather** /ˈfɛðə/, *n.* **1.** one of the epidermal appendages which together constitute the plumage of birds, being typically made up of a hard, tubelike portion (the quill) attached to the body of the bird, which passes into a thinner, stemlike distal portion (the rachis) bearing a series of slender processes (barbs) which unite in a bladelike structure (web) on each side. **2.** plumage. **3.** attire. **4.** condition, as of health, spirits, etc.: *in fine feather, in high feather.* **5.** kind or character: *birds of a feather flock together.* **6.** something like a feather, as a tuft or fringe of hair. **7.** a feather-like flaw, as in a precious stone. **8.** *Archery.* **a.** a feather or feathers attached to the nock (rear) end of an arrow to direct its flight. **b.** the feathered end or string end of an arrow. **9.** something very light, weak, or small. **10.** *Rowing.* the act of feathering. **11. a feather in one's cap,** a mark of distinction; an honour. **12. make the feathers fly,** to cause confusion; create disharmony. **13. show the white feather,** to show cowardice. *–v.t.* **14.** to provide with feathers, as an arrow. **15.** to clothe or cover with, or as with, feathers. **16.** *Rowing.* to turn (an oar) after a stroke so that the blade becomes nearly horizontal, and hold it thus as it is moved back into position for the next stroke. **17.** *Aeron.* to stop (an engine) and hold its propeller in a position that offers least wind resistance. **18.** to touch the controls of (a machine) lightly so as to cause it to respond gently and evenly. **19. feather one's nest,** to provide for or enrich oneself. *–v.i.* **20.** to grow feathers. **21.** to be or become feathery in appearance. **22.** (of a wave off the shore) to break very slowly, developing a white cap. **23.** to move like feathers. **24.** *Rowing.* to feather an oar. **25.** *Shooting.* to shoot feathers off (a bird) without killing it. [ME and OE *fether,* c. G *Feder;* akin to Gk *pterón* wing] – **featherless,** *adj.* – **feather-like,** *adj.*

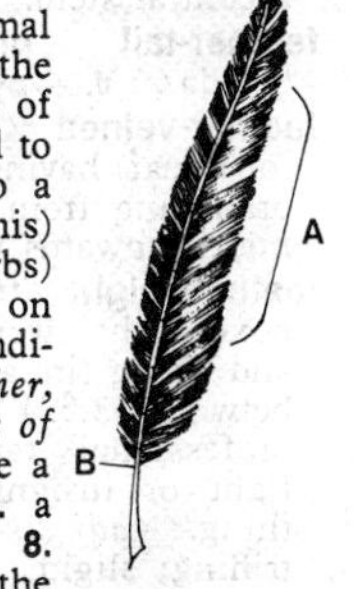

feather: A, vane; B, rachis

**featherbed** /ˈfɛðəbɛd/, *n., v.,* **-bedded, -bedding.** *–n.* **1.** a mattress filled with feathers. **2.** luxury; a pampered state generally. *–v.t.* **3.** to pamper; shield from hardship. **4.** to subsidise. **5.** to limit the work done in (a factory, industry, etc.) in order to avoid dismissing redundant workers. – **featherbedder,** *n.*

**featherbedder** /ˈfɛðəbɛdə/, *n.* a person accustomed to physical and intellectual comfort.

**featherbone** /ˈfɛðəboʊn/, *n.* a substitute for whalebone, made from the quills of domestic fowls.

**featherbrain** /ˈfɛðəbreɪn/, *n.* an irresponsible or weak-minded person. – **featherbrained,** *adj.*

**feather duster** /fɛðə 'dʌstə/, *n.* a brush of feathers, used for dusting.

**feathered** /'fɛðəd/, *adj.* **1.** clothed, covered, or provided with feathers. **2.** winged; swift. **3. feathered friend,** a bird.

**feather-edge** /'fɛðər-ɛdʒ/, *n.* **1.** an edge which thins out like a feather. **2.** the thinner edge of a wedge-shaped board or plank. – **feather-edged,** *adj.*

**feathered paddle** /fɛðəd 'pædl/, *n.* a double-bladed paddle with the blades at right angles.

**feather flower** /'fɛðə flaʊə/, *n.* any of numerous species of *Verticordia,* western Australian plants with fringed petals or sepals.

**feather-grass** /'fɛðə-gras/, *n.* **1.** a densely tufted grass, *Stipa pennata,* of Europe and Asia, the dried feathery inflorescences of which are used for ornament. **2.** any of various species of the grass genus *Pennisetum.*

**featherhead** /'fɛðəhɛd/, *n.* **1.** a silly or light-headed person. **2.** a light or empty head. – **featherheaded,** *adj.*

**feathering** /'fɛðərɪŋ/, *n.* **1.** plumage; a feather-like fringe. **2.** *Music.* a very light and delicate use of the violin bow.

**feather-star** /'fɛðə-sta/, *n.* →**crinoid.**

**featherstitch** /'fɛðəstɪtʃ/, *n.* **1.** an embroidery stitch producing work in which a succession of branches extend alternately on each side of a central stem. *–v.t.* **2.** to ornament by featherstitch.

featherstitch

**feather-tail glider** /fɛðə-teɪl 'glaɪdə/, *n.* →**pygmy glider.**

feather-tail glider

**feather-veined** /'fɛðə-veɪnd/, *adj.* (of a leaf) having a series of veins branching from each side of the midrib towards the margin.

**featherweight** /'fɛðəweɪt/, *n.* **1.** a boxer who weighs between 54 and 57 kg (in amateur ranks) or between 53.521 and 57.153 kg (in professional ranks). **2.** a very light or insignificant person or thing. *–adj.* **3.** belonging to the class of featherweights. **4.** trifling; slight. **5.** Also, **featherweighted.** *Horseracing.* of or pertaining to the horse in the race assigned the least weight by the handicapper.

**featherwood** /'fɛðəwʊd/, *n.* a small tree, *Polyosma cunninghamii,* found in forests of eastern Australia.

**feather-worm** /'fɛðə-wɜm/, *n.* →**fan-worm.** Also, **feather-duster worm.**

**feathery** /'fɛðəri/, *adj.* **1.** clothed or covered with feathers; feathered. **2.** resembling feathers; light; airy; unsubstantial. – **featheriness,** *n.*

**featly** /'fitli/, *adv. Archaic.* **1.** in a feat manner; fitly. **2.** skilfully; nimbly. **3.** neatly; elegantly. [FEAT[2] + -LY] – **featliness,** *n.*

**feature** /'fitʃə/, *n., v.,* **-tured, -turing.** *–n.* **1.** any part of the face, as the nose, chin, etc. **2.** (*pl.*) the face. **3.** the form or cast of the face. **4.** a prominent or conspicuous part or characteristic. **5.** the main film in a cinema program, usu. of more than 60 minutes duration. **6.** a special article, column, cartoon, etc., in a newspaper or magazine. **7.** a non-fiction radio or television program designed to entertain and inform. **8.** *Obs. or Archaic.* make, form, or shape. *–v.t.* **9.** to be a feature or distinctive mark of. **10.** to make a feature of, or give prominence to: *to feature a story or picture in a newspaper.* **11.** *Theat.* to present; give prominence to. **12.** to delineate the features of; depict; outline. *–v.i.* **13.** *Colloq.* to have sexual intercourse (usu. followed by *with*). **14.** to be prominent (fol. by *in*). [ME *feture,* from OF, from L *factūra* making, formation]

**featured** /'fitʃəd/, *adj.* **1.** made a feature of; given prominence; presented. **2.** having features, or a certain cast of features often used in combination: *sharp-featured, ill-featured.*

**feature double** /fitʃə 'dʌbəl/, *n.* a double (def. 25) conducted on two major horseraces, not necessarily run on the same day.

**feature-length** /'fitʃə-lɛŋθ/, *adj.* of a film, television play, documentary, etc., which is as long as a feature (def. 5) but is not classified as one.

**featureless** /'fitʃələs/, *adj.* without distinctive features; uninteresting.

**feature story** /'fitʃə stɔri/, *n.* a story printed for reasons other than its news value.

**featurism** /'fitʃərɪzəm/, *n.* a fashion in design esp. in architecture, interior decorating, etc., which relies on drawing attention to a prominent element, as one wall of a room in an obtrusively different colour. [? coined by Robin Boyd, 1919-71, Australian architect]

**Feb.,** February.

**febri-,** a word element meaning 'fever', as in *febrifuge.* [L, combining form of *febris*]

**febricity** /fə'brɪsəti/, *n.* feverishness.

**febricula** /fə'brɪkjələ/, *n.* a slight and short fever, esp. when of obscure causation. [L, diminutive of *febris* fever]

**febrifacient** /fɛbrə'feɪʃənt/, *adj.* **1.** producing fever. *–n.* **2.** something that produces fever.

**febriferous** /fə'brɪfərəs/, *adj.* **1.** producing fever. **2.** carrying fever.

**febrific** /fə'brɪfɪk/, *adj.* producing or marked by fever. [FEBRI- + -FIC]

**febrifugal** /fɛbrə'fjugəl, fə'brɪfjəgəl/, *adj.* of or like a febrifuge.

**febrifuge** /'fɛbrəfjudʒ/, *adj.* **1.** serving to dispel or reduce fever, as a medicine; antifebrile. *–n.* **2.** a febrifuge medicine or agent. **3.** a cooling drink. [F, from L *febrifugia,* from *febri-* FEBRI- + *-fugia* -FUGE]

**febrile** /'fɛbraɪl, fi-/, *adj.* pertaining to or marked by fever; feverish. [L *febrīlis* pertaining to fever]

**February** /'fɛbruəri/, *n.* the second month of the year, containing ordinarily 28 days, in leap years 29. [L *Februārius,* from *februa,* pl., the Roman festival of purification, celebrated 15 Feb. replacing ME *feverer,* from OF, and OE *Februarius,* from L]

**fec.,** fecit.

**feces** /'fisiz/, *n.pl. Chiefly U.S.* →**faeces.** – **fecal** /fikəl/, *adj.*

**fecit** /'feɪkət/, *v.* he (or she) made (it, as a work of art). [L]

**feckless** /'fɛkləs/, *adj.* **1.** ineffective; feeble. **2.** spiritless; worthless. [Scot. *feck,* var. of *fect,* aphetic var. of EFFECT] – **fecklessly,** *adv.* – **fecklessness,** *n.*

**fecula** /'fɛkjulə/, *n., pl.* **-lae** /-li/. starch obtained by washing the comminuted roots, grains, or other parts of plants. [L *faecula* crust of wine, diminutive of *faex* dregs]

**feculent** /'fɛkjulənt/, *adj.* abounding in dregs or foul matter; turbid; muddy; foul. [L *faeculentus* abounding in dregs, impure] – **feculence,** *n.*

**fecund** /'fɛkənd, 'fik-/, *adj.* capable of producing offspring, or fruit, vegetation, etc., in abundance; prolific; fruitful; productive. [L *fēcundus* fruitful; replacing ME *fecounde,* from OF *fecond*]

**fecundate** /'fɛkəndeɪt, 'fikən-/, *v.t.,* **-dated, -dating.** **1.** to make prolific or fruitful. **2.** *Biol.* to impregnate. [L *fēcundātus,* pp., made fruitful] – **fecundation** /fɛkən'deɪʃən, fikən-/, *n.*

**fecundity** /fə'kʌndəti/, *n.* **1.** the quality of being fecund; the capacity, esp. in female animals, of producing young in great numbers. **2.** fruitfulness or fertility, as of the earth. **3.** capacity of abundant production: *fecundity of imagination.*

**fed**[1] /fɛd/, *v.* **1.** past tense and past participle of **feed.** *–adj.* **2. fed up (to the back teeth),** *Colloq.* annoyed; frustrated (fol. by *with*).

**fed**[2] /fɛd/, *n. Colloq.* **1.** a federal police officer. **2.** any policeman.

**Fed.** /fɛd/, Federal.

**federacy** /'fɛdərəsi/, *n.* →**confederacy.**

**federal** /'fɛdərəl, 'fɛdrəl/, *adj.* **1.** of or pertaining to a compact or a league, esp. a league between nations or states. **2. a.** pertaining to or of the nature of a union of states under a central government distinct from the individual governments of the separate states: *the Federal Government of Australia.* **b.** favouring a strong central government in such a union. **c.** pertaining to such a central government: *federal offices.* *–n.* **3.** an advocate of federation or federalism. **4.** (*cap.*) *U.S. Hist.* **a.** a Federalist. **b.** an adherent of the Unionist. **c.** a soldier in the Federal army. [earlier *foederal,* from L *foedus* compact, league (akin to *fides* faith) + -AL[1]] – **federally,** *adv.*

**federal district** /– 'dɪstrɪkt/, *n.* a district in which the national government of a country is situated, esp. one in Latin America.

**federalise** /'fɛdərəlaɪz, 'fɛdrə-/, *v.t.,* **-lised, -lising.** to make federal; unite in a federal union, as different states. Also, **federalize.** – **federalisation** /fɛdərəlaɪ'zeɪʃən, fɛdrə-/, *n.*

**federalism** /'fɛdərəlɪzəm, 'fɛdrə-/, *n.* **1.** the federal principle of government. **2.** Also, **new federalism.** the belief that the rights and powers of individual states in a federation should not be diminished by or subsumed under a central government.

**federalist** /'fɛdərələst, 'fɛdrə-/, *n.* **1.** an advocate of federalism. *–adj.* **2.** Also, **federalistic.** of Federalism or the Federalists.

**Federal Republic of Germany,** *n.* official name of **West Germany.**

**federal system** /'fɛdərəl sɪstəm/, *n.* a system of government in which responsibilities are divided between several parliaments with one parliament having responsibility for the nation as a whole and the respective parliaments having responsibility for prescribed areas within the nation. In Australia the division is between the State Governments and the Federal Government and the distribution of power and responsibilities between these governments is effected by the Constitution of the Commonwealth. Cf. **unitary system.**

**federal territory** /– 'tɛrətri/, *n.* a region or district under the control of a central government.

**federal theology** /– θi'ɒlədʒi/, *n.* a theological system based on the idea of two covenants between God and man, of Works and of Grace. Also, **covenant theology.**

**federate** /'fɛdəreɪt/, *v.,* **-rated, -rating;** /'fɛdərət, 'fɛdrət/, *adj.* *–v.t.* **1.** to join or bring together in a league or federation. **2.** to organise on a federal basis. *–v.i.* **3.** to unite in a federation. *–adj.* **4.** allied; federated: *federate nations.* – **federator,** *n.*

**federation** /fɛdə'reɪʃən/, *n.* **1.** the act of federating, or uniting in a league. **2.** the formation of a political unity, with a central government, out of a number of separate states, etc., each of which retains control of its own internal affairs. **3.** a league or confederacy. **4.** a federated body formed by a number of states, societies, etc., each retaining control of its own internal affairs.

**federation star** /'– sta/, *n.* the large white six-pointed star on the flag approved for the Commonwealth of Australia in 1903, in which each point represented one of the six federating States, modified in 1908 to the Commonwealth star.

**Federation wheat** /fɛdə'reɪʃən wit/, *n.* a variety of wheat developed by William Farrer as an early-maturing, drought-resistant wheat. [first made available to farmers in 1902-03, just after the federation of the States of Australia]

**federative** /'fɛdərətɪv/, *adj.* **1.** pertaining to or of the nature of a federation. **2.** inclined to federate. – **federatively,** *adv.*

**fedora** /fə'dɔrə/, *n. U.S.* →**trilby.** [said to be from *Fedora,* drama by Viktorien Sardou, 1831-1908, French dramatist]

**fee** /fi/, *n., v.,* **feed, feeing.** *–n.* **1.** a payment for services: *a doctor's fee.* **2.** a sum paid for a privilege: *an admission fee.* **3.** a charge allowed by law for the service of a public officer. **4.** *Law.* **a.** an estate of inheritance in land, either absolute and without limitation to any particular class of heirs (**fee simple**) or limited to a particular class of heirs (**fee tail**). **b.** an estate in land held of a feudal lord on condition of the performing of certain services. **c.** a territory held in fee. **5. hold in fee, a.** to have full ownership in (land, etc.). **b.** *Poetic.* to have absolute mastery over: *Once did she hold the gorgeous East in fee.* *–v.t.* **6.** to give a fee to. [ME, from AF; of Gmc orig.] – **feeless,** *adj.*

**feeble** /'fibəl/, *adj.,* **-bler, -blest. 1.** physically weak, as from age, sickness, etc. **2.** weak intellectually or morally: *a feeble mind.* **3.** lacking in volume, loudness, brightness, distinctness, etc.: *a feeble voice, light.* **4.** lacking in force, strength, or effectiveness: *feeble resistance, arguments, barriers.* [ME *feble,* from OF, from L *flēbilis* lamentable] – **feebleness,** *n.* – **feeblish,** *adj.* – **feebly,** *adv.*

**feeble-minded** /'fibəl-maɪndəd/, *adj.* **1.** feeble in intellect; lacking the normal mental powers. **2.** lacking firmness of mind. – **feeble-mindedness,** *n.*

**feed** /fid/, *v.,* **fed, feeding,** *n.* *–v.t.* **1.** to give food to; supply with nourishment. **2.** →**breastfeed. 3.** to provide with the requisite materials for development, maintenance, or operation. **4.** to yield, or serve as, food for. **5.** to provide as food. **6.** to furnish for consumption. **7.** to satisfy; minister to; gratify. **8.** to supply for maintenance or to be operated upon, as to a machine. **9.** to use (land) as pasture. **10.** *Colloq.* to provide cues to (an actor, esp. a comedian). *–v.i.* **11.** to take food; eat; graze. **12.** to be nourished or gratified; subsist. *–n.* **13.** food, esp. for cattle, etc. **14. a.** milk, or other liquid preparations, for an unweaned baby. **b.** the act of feeding such a baby. **15.** *Colloq.* a meal. **16.** an act of feeding. **17.** the act or process of feeding a furnace, machine, etc. **18.** the material, or the amount of it, so fed or supplied. **19.** a feeding mechanism. **20.** the rate of advance of a cutting mechanism, as a drill or cutting tool. **21.** *Theat. Colloq.* a cue to an actor, esp. a comedian. [ME *fede(n),* OE *fēdan,* akin to OE *fōda* FOOD]

**feedback** /'fidbæk/, *n.* **1.** the returning of a part of the output of any system, esp. a mechanical, electronic, or biological one, as input, esp. for correction or control purposes, to alter the characteristic sound of conventional musical instruments, etc. **2.** an indication of the reaction of the recipient, as of an audience. **3.** *Electronics.* the return of part of the energy of the anode circuit of a radio valve to the grid circuit, either to oppose the input (**negative feedback**) or to reinforce it (**positive feedback**). **4.** the input of a signal into a microphone from the output of the same system, usu. causing a high-pitched screech. *–adj.* **5.** of, involving, or denoting a feedback.

**feedbag** /'fidbæg/, *n.* **1.** a bag which can be hung over a horse's head and which contains feed. **2. put on the feedbag,** to have a meal.

**feed conversion rate,** *n.* the rate at which any food eaten by an animal is converted to energy, growth and development.

**feeder** /'fidə/, *n.* **1.** one who or that which supplies food or feeds something. **2.** one who or that which takes food or nourishment. **3.** a person or device that feeds a machine, printing press, etc. **4.** a tributary stream, a secondary road, a branch of a railway or airline system, etc. **5.** *Elect.* a conductor, or group of conductors, connecting primary equipment in an electric power system. **6.** →**bib** (def. 1).

**feeder school** /'– skul/, *n.* a school which sends its students for further study to another school, as a primary school to a high school.

**feed grain** /'fid greɪn/, *n.* grain grown primarily for animal consumption.

**feeding bottle** /'fidɪŋ bɒtl/, *n.* **1.** Also, **baby's bottle.** a bottle equipped with a teat used to feed liquids to babies. **2.** a similar bottle for use with very young animals.

**feedlot** /'fidlɒt/, *n.* an area of land on which cattle are stocked in large numbers and hand-fed in order to fatten them just prior to selling them.

**feedpipe** /'fidpaɪp/, *n.* a pipe for supplying material, as fuel, to machines.

**feedwater** /'fidwɔtə/, *n.* water which has been treated to remove impurities, for feeding to a boiler to be converted into steam.

**feel** /fil/, *v.,* **felt, feeling,** *n.* *–v.t.* **1.** to perceive or examine by touch. **2.** to have a sensation (other than sight, hearing, taste, and smell) of. **3** to find or pursue (one's way) by touching, groping, or cautious moves. **4.** to be or become conscious of. **5.** to be emotionally affected by: *to feel one's disgrace keenly.* **6.** to experience the effects of: *the whole region felt the storm.* **7.** to have a particular sensation or impression of (fol. by an adjunct or complement): *to feel oneself slighted.* **8.** to have a general or thorough conviction of. **9. feel (someone) out,** to make exploratory moves in order to assess possible reaction. **10. feel (someone) up,** *Colloq.* (usu. of a man) to attempt the manual sexual stimulation of a woman. *–v.i.* **11.** to have perception by touch or by any nerves of sensation other than those of sight, hearing, taste, and smell. **12.** to make examination by touch; grope. **13.** to have mental sensations or emotions. **14.** to be consciously, in emotion, opinion, etc.: *to feel happy, angry, sure.* **15.** to have sympathy or compassion (fol. by *with* or *for*). **16.** to have a sensation of being: *to feel warm, free.* **17.** to seem in the impression produced: *how does it feel to be rich?* **18. feel like,** to have a desire or inclination for. **19. to feel oneself,** to be in one's usual mental or physical state. **20. feel up to,** *Colloq.* to be well enough to be capable of; to be able to cope with. *–n.* **21.** a quality of an object that is perceived by feeling or touching: *a soapy feel.* **22.** an act of feeling. **23.** a sensation of something felt; a vague mental impression or feeling. **24.** the sense of touch: *soft to the feel.* **25.** *Music.* stylistic subtleties which differentiate a number of otherwise very similar musical performances, or performers. [ME *fele(n)*, OE *fēlan*, c. G *fühlen*]

**feeler** /ˈfilə/, *n.* **1.** one who or that which feels. **2.** a proposal, remark, hint, etc., designed to bring out the opinions or purposes of others. **3.** *Zool.* an organ of touch, as an antenna or a tentacle. **4.** (*pl.*) →**feeler gauge.**

**feeler gauge** /ˈ– geɪdʒ/, *n.* a gauge consisting of thin strips of steel of known thickness fixed like penknife blades; used for measuring small distances, as the gap in a spark plug. Also, **feelers.**

**feeling** /ˈfilɪŋ/, *n.* **1.** the function or the power of perceiving by touch; physical sensation not connected with sight, hearing, taste, or smell. **2.** a particular sensation of this kind: *a feeling of warmth, pain, or drowsiness.* **3.** *Psychol.* consciousness itself without regard to thought or a perceived object, as excitement-calm, strain-relaxation. **4.** a consciousness or impression: *a feeling of inferiority.* **5.** an intuition or premonition: *a feeling that something is going to happen.* **6.** an emotion: *a feeling of joy, sorrow, fear.* **7.** capacity for emotion; pity. **8.** a sentiment; opinion: *to have a feeling that something will succeed, the general feeling was in favour of the proposal.* **9.** Also, **bad feeling, ill feeling.** bitterness; collective or mutual hostility or ill will: *there is a certain amount of feeling between them; there was bad feeling over his promotion.* **10.** (*pl.*) sensibilities; susceptibilities: *to hurt one's feelings.* **11.** fine emotional endowment. **12.** *Music, etc.* **a.** emotional or sympathetic perception revealed by an artist in his work. **b.** the general impression conveyed by a work. **c.** sympathetic appreciation, as of music. *–adj.* **13.** that feels; sentient; sensitive, as nerves. **14.** accessible to emotion; sympathetic: *a feeling heart.* **15.** indicating emotion: *a feeling retort.* – **feelingly,** *adv.*

**fee simple** /fi ˈsɪmpəl/, *n.* See **fee** (def. 4a).

**feet** /fit/, *n.* plural of **foot.** – **feetless,** *adj.*

**fee tail** /fi ˈteɪl/, *n.* See **fee** (def. 4a).

**Fehling's solution** /ˌfeɪlɪŋz səˈluʃən/, *n.* a solution of copper sulphate and Rochelle salt in alkali, which is used for the detection and quantitative estimation of sugars and other reducing agents. [named after Hermann *Fehling*, 1812-85, German chemist]

**feign** /feɪn/, *v.t.* **1.** to invent fictitiously or deceptively, as a story or an excuse. **2.** to represent fictitiously; put on an appearance of: *to feign sickness.* **3.** to imitate deceptively: *to feign another's voice.* *–v.i.* **4.** to make believe; pretend: *she feigns to be ill.* [ME *feigne(n)*, from OF *feign-*, stem of *feindre*, from L *fingere* form, conceive, devise] – **feigner,** *n.* – **feigningly,** *adv.*

**feigned** /feɪnd/, *adj.* **1.** pretended; sham; counterfeit. **2.** assumed, as a name. **3.** disguised, as a voice. **4.** fictitiously invented. – **feignedly** /ˈfeɪnədli/, *adv.*

**feijoa** /fiˈdʒoʊə/, *n.* a South American bushy evergreen shrub, *Feijoa sellowiana,* with a green fruit similar to guava in texture and taste; pineapple guava.

**feint**[1] /feɪnt/, *n.* **1.** a movement made with the object of deceiving an adversary; appearance of aiming at one part or point when another is the real object of attack. **2.** a feigned or assumed appearance. *–v.i.* **3.** to make a feint. [F *feinte*, from *feindre* FEIGN]

**feint**[2] /feɪnt/, *n.* **1.** the lightest weight of line used in printing ruled paper. *–adj.* **2.** ruled with a line of such weight. [var. of FAINT]

**feints** /feɪnts/, *n.pl.* the impure spirit which comes over first and last in distilling whisky, etc.

**feisty** /ˈfaɪsti/, *adj. U.S.* **1.** excitable; quarrelsome. **2.** frisky; high-spirited. [d. *fist* a small dog, shortened var. of *fisting* (*dog*), from obs. *fist* to break wind]

**felafel** /fəˈlʌfəl, -ˈlæf-/, *n.* fried balls of spiced ground chick-peas and hot peppers soaked in a relish and chilli sauce. Also, **falafel, filafil.** [Ar. *felāfil*]

**feldspar** /ˈfɛldspa, ˈfɛlspa/, *n.* →**felspar.**

**felicific** /filəˈsɪfɪk/, *adj.* making happy; productive of happiness. [L *fēlīcificus* making happy]

**felicitate** /fəˈlɪsəteɪt/, *v.,* **-tated, -tating.** *–v.t.* **1.** to compliment upon a happy event; congratulate: *to felicitate a friend on his good fortune.* **2.** *Archaic.* to make happy. [LL *fēlīcitātus,* pp. of *fēlīcitāre* make happy, from L *fēlix* happy] – **felicitator,** *n.*

**felicitation** /fəlɪsəˈteɪʃən/, *n.* expression of good wishes; congratulation.

**felicitous** /fəˈlɪsətəs/, *adj.* **1.** apt or appropriate, as action, manner, or expression. **2.** apt in manner or expression, as a person. – **felicitously,** *adv.* – **felicitousness,** *n.*

**felicity** /fəˈlɪsəti/, *n., pl.* **-ties.** **1.** the state of being happy, esp. in a high degree. **2.** an instance of this. **3.** a source of happiness. **4.** a skilful faculty: *felicity of expression.* **5.** an instance or display of this. **6.** *Archaic.* good fortune. [ME *felicite,* from L *fēlīcitas* happiness]

**felid** /ˈfiləd/, *n.* one of the cat family, Felidae.

**feline** /ˈfilaɪn/, *adj.* **1.** belonging or pertaining to the cat family, Felidae, which includes, besides the domestic cat, the lions, tigers, leopards, lynxes, jaguars, etc. **2.** catlike; characteristic of animals of the cat family: *feline softness of step.* **3.** sly; spiteful; stealthy; treacherous. *–n.* **4.** an animal of the cat family. [L *fēlīnus* of a cat] – **felinely,** *adv.* – **felineness, felinity** /fəˈlɪnəti/, *n.*

**feline agranulocytosis** /– əˌgrænjəloʊsaɪˈtoʊsəs/, *n.* a highly fatal, contagious virus disease of domestic cats characterised by fever, somnolence, and diarrhoea; distemper.

**feline enteritis** /– ɛntəˈraɪtəs/, *n.* a highly infectious, often fatal, virus disease of cats.

**fell**[1] /fɛl/, *v.* past tense of **fall.**

**fell**[2] /fɛl/, *v.t.* **1.** to cause to fall; knock, strike, or cut down: *to fell an elephant, a tree, etc.* **2.** *Sewing.* to finish (a seam) by sewing the edge down flat. **3.** *Sewing.* a seam finished by felling. [ME *felle(n)*, OE *fellan,* causative of *feallan* fall] – **feller,** *n.*

**fell**[3] /fɛl/, *adj.* **1.** fierce; cruel; dreadful. **2.** destructive; deadly: *fell poison or disease.* [ME, from OF *fel* base. See FELON[1]] – **fellness,** *n.*

**fell**[4] /fɛl/, *n.* the skin or hide of an animal; a pelt. [ME and OE, c. G *Fell;* akin to L *pellis* skin]

**fell**[5] /fɛl/, *n. Scot.* a stretch of elevated waste land or pasture; a down. [ME, from Scand.; cf. Icel. *fiall* mountain]

**fellable** /ˈfɛləbəl/, *adj.* capable of being or fit to be felled.

**fellah** /ˈfɛlə/, *n., pl.* **fellahs** or **fellahin, fellaheen** /ˈfɛləhin/. a native peasant or labourer in Egypt, Syria, etc. [Ar.: husbandman]

**fellatio** /fəˈleɪʃioʊ/, *n.* oral stimulation of the male genitals. Also, **fellation** /fəˈleɪʃən/. [L]

**feller** /ˈfɛlə/, *n. Colloq.* **1.** fellow. **2.** (a form of address, usu. aggressive, amongst men). Also, **fella.**

**fellmonger** /ˈfɛlmʌŋgə/, *n.* **1.** a dealer in skins or hides of animals, esp. sheepskins. *–v.t.* **2.** to remove wool from the pelt of a dead sheep by treatment with chemicals. – **fellmongering,** *n.*

**felloe** /ˈfɛloʊ/, *n.* the circular rim, or a part of the rim of a wheel, into which the outer ends of the spokes are inserted. Also, **felly.** [ME *fely, felwe,* OE *felg,* c. G *Felge*]

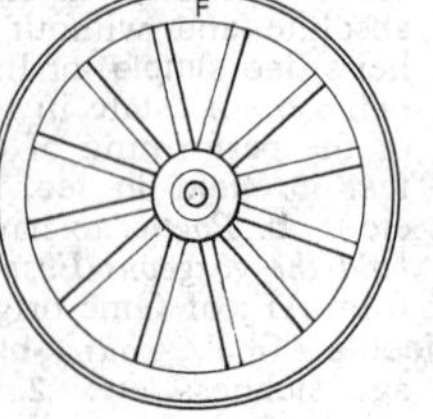

F, felloe

**fellow** /ˈfɛloʊ/, *n.* **1.** *Colloq.* a man; boy. **2.** *Colloq.* a person; suitor; boy friend. **3.** a companion; comrade: *my dear fellow.* **4.** one belonging to the same class; an equal; peer. **5.** one of a pair; a mate or match. **6.** (*usu. cap.*) a member of any of certain learned or professional societies: *a Fellow of the Royal Australian College of Surgeons.* **7.** *Educ.* **a.** a scholar or postgraduate student in a college or university engaged primarily in research rather than undergraduate teaching. **b.** a member of a university or other college, entitled to certain privileges and with certain responsibilities. *–adj.* **8.** belonging to the same class or group; united by the same occupation, interests, etc.; being the same condition: *fellow students, citizens, etc., fellow sufferers.* [ME *felowe, felawe,* late OE *fēolaga,* from Scand.; cf. Icel. *fēlagi* companion (from *fē* money + *-lagi* one who lays (something) down)]

**fellow creature** /– 'kritʃə/, *n.* a creature produced by the same Creator (now used chiefly of human beings): *he was ashamed of his fellow creatures.*

**fellow feeling** /– 'filɪŋ/, *n.* **1.** sympathetic feeling; sympathy. **2.** sense of joint interest.

**fellow servant** /– 'sɜvənt/, *n. Law.* one of a group of workers engaged by the same employer.

**fellowship** /'fɛloʊʃɪp/, *n., v.,* **-shipped, -shipping.** *–n.* **1.** the condition or relation of being a fellow. **2.** community of interest, feeling, etc. **3.** communion, as between members of the same church. **4.** friendliness. **5.** an association of persons having similar tastes, interests, etc. **6.** a company; a guild or corporation. **7.** *Educ.* **a.** the body of fellows in a college or university. **b.** the position or emoluments of a fellow of a university, etc., or the sum of money he receives. **c.** a foundation for the maintenance of a fellow in a college or university.

**fellow traveller** /fɛloʊ 'trævələ/, *n.* **1.** one who travels in company with another. **2.** a non-member who supports or sympathises with a political party, usu. the Communist Party. **3.** a person who without officially belonging to a group, society, organisation, etc., sympathises with it or supports its aims, aspirations or beliefs.

**felly** /'fɛli/, *n., pl.* **-lies.** →**felloe.**

**felo-de-se** /filoʊ-di-'si, fɛloʊ-/, *n., pl.* **felones-de-se** /fɛloʊniz-di-'si/ or **felos-de-se** /filoʊz-di-'si, fɛloʊz-/. *Law.* **1.** one who commits suicide. **2.** suicide. [Anglo-L: a felon with respect to oneself]

**felon**[1] /'fɛlən/, *n.* **1.** *Law.* one who has committed a felony. **2.** *Obs.* a wicked person. **3.** a convict. *–adj.* **4.** *Archaic.* wicked; malicious; treacherous. [ME *feloun,* from OF *felon* base, ? from L *fel* gall, bile]

**felon**[2] /'fɛlən/, *n.* an acute and painful inflammation of the deeper tissues of a finger or toe, usu. near the nail; a form of whitlow. [orig. uncert. Cf. FELON[1]]

**felonious** /fə'loʊniəs/, *adj.* **1.** *Law.* pertaining to, of the nature of, or involving a felony. **2.** *Rare.* wicked; base. **–feloniously,** *adv.* **–feloniousness,** *n.*

**felonry** /'fɛlənri/, *n.* **1.** the whole body or class of felons. **2.** the convict population of a penal colony.

**felony** /'fɛləni/, *n., pl.* **-nies.** *Law.* **1.** any of various indictable offences, as murder, burglary, etc., of graver character than those called misdemeanours. **2.** (in early English law) any crime punishable by loss of life or member and forfeiture of goods and chattels, and which could be prosecuted by appeal.

**felsic** /'fɛlsɪk/, *adj.* **1.** of or pertaining to light coloured rocks containing an abundance of such minerals as felspar, felspathoid and silica. **2.** of or pertaining to the minerals themselves such as quartz, felspars, felspathoids and muscovite. [b. FELSPAR + SILICA]

**felsite** /'fɛlsaɪt/, *n.* a dense, igneous rock consisting typically of felspar and quartz, both of which may appear as phenocrysts. [FELS(PAR) + -ITE[1]] **–felsitic** /fɛl'sɪtɪk/, *adj.*

**felspar** /'fɛlspa/, *n.* any of a group of minerals, principally aluminosilicates of potassium, sodium, and calcium, and characterised by two cleavages at nearly right angles. They are among the most important constituents of igneous rocks. Also, **feldspar.** [half-taken, half-translated from G *Feldspath*] **–felspathic** /fɛl'spæθɪk/, *adj.*

**felspathoid** /'fɛlspəθɔɪd/, *n.* any of a group of minerals, as leucite, which are similar in composition to felspars but contain less silica than the corresponding felspar.

**felspathose** /'fɛlspəθoʊs/, *adj.* of, pertaining to, consisting of, or containing felspar.

**felt**[1] /fɛlt/, *v.* past tense and past participle of **feel.**

**felt**[2] /fɛlt/, *n.* **1.** a non-woven fabric of wool, fur, or hair, matted together by pressure. **2.** any matted fabric or material. *–adj.* **3.** pertaining to or made of felt. *–v.t.* **4.** to make into felt; mat or press together. **5.** to cover with, or as with felt. *–v.i.* **6.** to become matted together. [ME and OE; akin to G *Filz.* See FILTER]

**felting** /'fɛltɪŋ/, *n.* **1.** felted material. **2.** the act or process of making felt. **3.** the materials of which felt is made.

**felt pen** /fɛlt 'pɛn/, *n.* a pen with a felt tip. Also, **felt-tip pen.**

**felucca** /fɛ'lʌkə/, *n.* a long, narrow vessel propelled by oars or lateen sails, or both, used in the Mediterranean. [It., from Ar.]

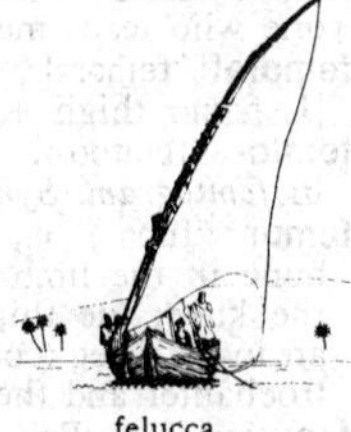
felucca

**fem.,** **1.** female. **2.** feminine.

**female** /'fimeɪl/, *n.* **1.** a human being of the sex which conceives and brings forth young; a woman or girl. **2.** any animal of corresponding sex. **3.** *Bot.* a pistillate plant. *–adj.* **4.** belonging to the sex which brings forth young, or any division or group corresponding to it. **5.** pertaining to or characteristic of this sex; feminine. **6.** composed of females: *a female cricket team.* **7.** *Bot.* **a.** designating or pertaining to a plant or its reproductive structure which produces or contains elements that need fertilisation. **b.** (of seed plants) pistillate. **8.** *Mech.* designating some part, etc., into which a corresponding part fits: *a female outlet.* **9.** *Obs.* womanish; weakly. [ME *female* (a form due to association with *male*), var. of *femelle,* from OF, from L *fēmella,* diminutive of *fēmina* woman] **–femalely,** *adv.* **–femaleness,** *n.*

**female factory** /– ˌfæktri/, *n.* (formerly) a place where female convicts were detained and kept in suitable employment, as the female factory at Parramatta, New South Wales.

**female impersonator** /– ɪm'pɜsəneɪtə/, *n.* a male entertainer who assumes the dress, character and role of a woman.

**female rhyme** /– 'raɪm/, *n.* →**feminine rhyme.**

**feme** /fɛm/, *n. Law.* a woman or wife. [AF, from L *fēmina* woman, wife; cf. F *femme*]

**feme covert** /– 'kʌvət/, *n. Law.* a married woman. [AF: a woman covered, i.e., protected]

**feme sole** /– 'soʊl/, *n. Law.* **1.** an unmarried woman, whether spinster, widow, or divorcee. **2.** a married woman who is independent of her husband with respect to property. [AF: a woman alone]

**femineity** /fɛmə'niəti/, *n.* feminine nature; womanliness. Also, **femality** /fə'mæləti/, **feminality** /fɛmə'næləti/. [L *fēmineus* feminine + -ITY]

**feminie** /'fɛməni/, *n. Archaic.* women collectively. [ME, from OF, from L *fēmina* woman]

**feminine** /'fɛmənən/, *adj.* **1.** pertaining to a woman. **2.** weak; gentle. **3.** effeminate. **4.** belonging to the female sex. **5.** *Gram.* denoting or pertaining to one of the three genders of Latin, Greek, German, etc., or one of the two of French, Spanish, etc., including most nouns denoting females (e.g. in Latin *puella* 'girl' and in German *Frau* 'woman' are feminine) and other nouns (e.g. in Latin *stella* 'star' and in German *Zeit* 'time'). *–n.* **6.** *Gram.* **a.** the feminine gender. **b.** a noun of that gender. **c.** another element marking that gender, as *la* (the feminine article in French and Spanish). [ME, from L *fēminīnus,* from *fēmina* woman] **–femininely,** *adv.* **–feminineness,** *n.*

**feminine cadence** /– 'keɪdəns/, *n.* a cadence in music in which the final chord falls on a weak beat.

**feminine ending** /– 'ɛndɪŋ/, *n.* **1.** *Pros.* an ending in which a line closes with an extra unaccented syllable in addition to the normal accented syllable. **2.** *Gram.* a termination or final syllable marking a feminine word: *'-ā' in Latin is a feminine ending for the ablative case in the singular.*

**feminine rhyme** /– 'raɪm/, *n.* a rhyme of two syllables of which the second is unstressed: *motion, notion* (double rhyme), or of three syllables of which the second and third are unstressed: *fortunate, importunate* (triple rhyme).

**femininity** /fɛmə'nɪnəti/, *n.* **1.** the quality of being feminine; womanliness. **2.** women collectively; womankind.

**feminise** /'fɛmənaɪz/, *v.t., v.i.,* **-nised, -nising.** to make or become feminine. Also, **feminize.** **–feminisation** /fɛmənaɪ'zeɪʃən/, *n.*

**feminism** /'fɛmənɪzəm/, *n.* advocacy of equal rights and opportunities for women, esp. the extension of their activities in social and political life.

**feminist** /ˈfɛmənəst/, *n.* **1.** a supporter of feminism. *–adj.* **2.** of or pertaining to the activities, literature, etc., of feminism.

**femme** /fɛm, fʌm/, *n.* **1.** a woman. **2.** the more passive or feminine partner in a lesbian relationship.

**femme fatale** /– fəˈtal/, *n.* an extremely alluring woman, esp. one who leads men into compromising situations. [F]

**femoral** /ˈfɛmərəl/, *adj.* of or pertaining to the thigh or femur. [L *femur* thigh + -AL[1]]

**femto-** /ˈfɛmtoʊ-/, a prefix denoting $10^{-15}$ of a given unit, as in *femtogram. Symbol:* f [Dan. *femten* fifteen]

**femur** /ˈfimə/, *n., pl.* **femurs, femora** /ˈfɛmərə/. **1.** *Anat.* a bone in the limb of an animal extending from the pelvis to the knee; the thighbone. **2.** *Entomol.* the third segment of an insect's leg (counting from the base), situated between the trochanter and the tibia. [L: thigh]

**fen** /fɛn/, *n. Brit.* low land covered wholly or partially with water; boggy land; a marsh. [ME and OE, c. Icel. *fen* quagmire]

**fence** /fɛns/, *n., v.,* **fenced, fencing.** *–n.* **1.** an enclosure or barrier, usu. of wire or wood, as around or along a field, garden, etc. **2.** the act, practice, or art of fencing; swordplay. **3.** skill in argument, repartee, etc. **4. a.** a person who receives and disposes of stolen goods. **b.** *Colloq.* the place of business of such a person. **5.** *Mach.* a guard or guide, as for regulating the movements of a tool or machine. **6.** *Aeron.* a projection on the wing of an aeroplane, parallel to the airstream, to prevent air flowing along the span. **7.** an obstacle to be jumped in show-jumping or steeplechasing. **8. over the fence,** not reasonable, immoderate. **9. sit on the fence,** to remain neutral; to avoid a conflict. **10. rush one's fences,** to act precipitately. *–v.t.* **11.** to enclose by some barrier, thus asserting exclusive right to possession. **12.** to separate by, or as by, a fence or fences. **13.** *Archaic.* to ward off; keep out. **14.** to defend; protect; guard. *–v.i.* **15.** to use a sword, foil, etc., in defence and attack or in exercise or exhibition of skill in that art. **16.** to parry arguments; strive to evade giving direct answers. **17.** (of a horse) to leap over a fence. **18.** *Colloq.* to receive stolen goods. [aphetic var. of DEFENCE] **–fenceless,** *adj.* **–fencelessness,** *n.* **–fencelike,** *adj.*

**fenced-in** /fɛnst-ˈɪn/, *adj.* enclosed by a fence.

**fence lizard** /ˈfɛns lɪzəd/, *n.* →**garden lizard.**

**fencer** /ˈfɛnsə/, *n.* **1.** one who fences. **2.** one who practises the art of fencing with a sword, foil, etc. **3.** a maker or mender of fences. **4.** a horse trained to jump.

**fence-sitter** /ˈfɛns-sɪtə/, *n.* a person who habitually avoids stating his view or attitude, or who vacillates in an argument.

**fencing** /ˈfɛnsɪŋ/, *n.* **1.** the act, practice, or art of using a sword, foil, etc., for defence and attack. **2.** a parrying of arguments; an evading of direct answers. **3.** an enclosure or railing. **4.** fences collectively. **5.** material for fences. **6.** *Colloq.* the receiving of stolen goods.

**fencing panel** /ˈ– pænəl/, *n.* a panel of chain wire or weldmesh, a number of which can be joined together to make a fence.

**fencing wire** /ˈ– waɪə/, *n.* heavy-gauge wire, sometimes barbed, strands of which are pulled taut between two strainers and supported by a number of posts to make a fence.

**fend** /fɛnd/, *v.t.* **1.** to ward off (oft. fol. by *off*): *to fend off blows.* **2.** *Archaic.* to defend. *–v.i.* **3.** to make defence; offer resistance. **4.** to parry. **5.** *Colloq.* to provide for: *to fend for oneself.* **6.** *Football.* to ward off by means of the open hand. [aphetic var. of DEFEND]

**fender** /ˈfɛndə/, *n.* **1.** one who or that which wards something off. **2.** a device on the front of a railway engine, or the like, for clearing the track of obstructions. **3.** *U.S.* a mudguard of a motor vehicle. **4.** Also, **pudding fender.** *Naut.* a piece of timber, bundle of rope, or the like, hung over the side of a vessel to lessen shock or prevent chafing. **5.** a low metal guard before an open fireplace, to keep back falling coals. [aphetic var. of DEFENDER]

**fenestella** /fɛnəsˈtɛlə/, *n., pl.* **-tellae** /-ˈtɛli/. *Archit.* **1.** a small window or window-like opening. **2.** a small window-like niche in the wall on the south side of an altar, containing the piscina, and frequently also the credence. [L, diminutive of *fenestra* window]

**fenestra** /fəˈnɛstrə/, *n., pl.* **-trae** /-tri/. **1.** *Anat., Zool.* a small opening or perforation, as in a bone. **2.** *Entomol.* a transparent spot in an otherwise opaque surface, as in the wings of certain butterflies and moths. **3.** *Archit.* a window-like opening. [L: window] **–fenestral,** *adj.*

**fenestrated** /fəˈnɛstreɪtəd, ˈfɛnə-/, *adj.* **1.** *Archit.* having windows; windowed; characterised by windows. **2.** pierced, perforated. Also, **fenestrate.** [L *fenestrātus,* pp., furnished with windows + -ED[2]]

**fenestration** /fɛnəsˈtreɪʃən/, *n.* **1.** *Archit.* the arrangement of windows in a building. **2.** *Surg.* any operation which creates a small opening; Lempert operation.

**fennec** /ˈfɛnɛk/, *n.* a small North African fox, *Vulpes zerda,* of a pale fawn colour, and having large pointed ears. [Ar. *fenek*]

**fennel** /ˈfɛnəl/, *n.* **1.** an umbelliferous plant, *Foeniculum vulgare,* having yellow flowers, and bearing aromatic fruits used in cookery and medicine. **2.** the fruits (**fennel seed**) of this plant. **3.** any of various more or less similar plants, as *Ferula communis* (**giant fennel**), a tall ornamental herb. [ME *fenel,* etc., OE *fenol,* etc. from VL *fēnuclum,* var. of L *faeniculum* fennel, diminutive of *faenum* hay]

**fennelflower** /ˈfɛnəlflaʊə/, *n.* **1.** any of the herbs constituting the genus *Nigella,* esp. *N. sativa,* whose seeds are used in the East as a condiment and medicine. **2.** the flower of this plant.

**fenny** /ˈfɛni/, *adj. Brit.* **1.** marshy; boggy. **2.** inhabiting, or growing in, fens. [ME; OE *fennig,* from *fenn* fen]

**fenugreek** /ˈfɛnjugrik/, *n.* a plant, *Trigonella foenumgraecum,* indigenous to western Asia, but extensively cultivated elsewhere, chiefly for forage and for its mucilaginous seeds, which are used in medicine. [ME *fenegrek,* OE *fenogræcum,* from L *faenugraecum,* for *faenum graecum* Greek hay]

**feoff** /fif/, *n.;* /fɛf, fif/, *v.* *–n.* **1.** a fee or feud, or estate in land held of a feudal lord; a tenure of land subject to feudal obligations. **2.** a territory held in fee. *–v.t.* **3.** to invest with a fief or fee; enfeoff. [ME *feoff(en),* from AF *feoffer,* var. of OF *fefier, fieffer,* from *fieu* FEE] **–feoffment,** *n.* **–feoffor, feoffer,** *n.*

**feoffee** /fɛfˈi, fifˈi/, *n.* a person invested with a fief.

**-fer,** a noun suffix meaning 'bearing', 'producing', 'yielding', 'containing', 'conveying', with a corresponding adjective in *-ferous,* as *conifer* (a coniferous tree). [L: bearing, from *ferre* bear]

**ferae naturae** /ˌfɛraɪ ˈnætʃəraɪ/, *adj. Law.* term applied to all animals of those species generally accepted as wild even though the animal in question may itself be tame. [L: of wild nature]

**feral**[1] /ˈfɛrəl, ˈfiərəl/, *adj.* **1.** wild, or existing in a state of nature, as animals (or, sometimes, plants). **2.** having reverted to the wild state, as from domestication. **3.** of or characteristic of wild animals: *the feral state.* [L *fera* wild beast (properly feminine of *ferus* wild) + -AL[1]]

**feral**[2] /ˈfɛrəl, ˈfiərəl/, *adj. Archaic.* **1.** deadly, fatal. **2.** gloomy, funereal. [L *fērālis*]

**ferbam** /ˈfɜbæm/, *n.* a black insoluble powder, $[(CH_3)_2NCSS]_3Fe$, used as a fungicide; ferric dimethyldithiocarbamate.

**ferberite** /ˈfɜbəraɪt/, *n.* a mineral of the wolframite group, theoretically pure ferrous tungstate, but frequently some of the iron is replaced by manganese.

**fer-de-lance** /fɜ-də-ˈlæns, -ˈlans/, *n.* a large, very venomous snake, *Trimeresurus atrox,* of tropical America. [F: lit., iron (head) of a lance]

**feretory** /ˈfɛrətri, -təri/, *n., pl.* **-ries.** **1.** a shrine, usu. portable, designed to hold the relics of saints. **2.** a room or chapel in which shrines were kept. [b. L *ferē(trum)* bier and (REPOSI)TORY; replacing ME *fertre,* from OF]

**feria** /ˈfɛriə, ˈfɪə-/, *n. Eccles.* a weekday not set apart for the observance of any specific feast.

**ferial** /ˈfɛriəl, ˈfɪə-/, *adj.* **1.** pertaining to a holiday. **2.** *Eccles.* pertaining to weekdays not set apart as festivals. [ML *fēriālis,* from L *fēria* holiday]

**ferine** /ˈfɛrin, -aɪn/, *adj.* →**feral**[1]. [L *ferīnus*]

**ferity** /ˈfɛrəti/, *n.* **1.** a wild, untamed, or uncultivated state. **2.** savagery; ferocity. [L *feritas* wildness]

**fermata** /fɜ'matə/, *n., pl.* **-tas.** →**pause** (def. 6). [It.]

**ferment** /'fɜmɛnt/, *n.;* /fə'mɛnt, fɜ-/, *v.* –*n.* **1.** any of various agents or substances which cause fermentation, esp.: **a.** any of various living organisms **(organised ferments),** as yeasts, moulds, certain bacteria, etc. **b.** any of certain complex substances derived from living cells **(unorganised ferments** or **enzymes),** as pepsin, etc. **2.** fermentation. **3.** agitation; excitement; tumult. –*v.t.* **4.** to act upon as a ferment. **5.** to cause to undergo fermentation. **6.** to inflame; foment. **7.** to agitate; excite. –*v.i.* **8.** to be fermented; undergo fermentation. **9.** to seethe with agitation or excitement. [L *fermentum* leaven, agitation] – **fermentable,** *adj.*

**fermentation** /fɜmɛn'teɪʃən/, *n.* **1.** the act or process of fermenting. **2.** *Biochem.* a change brought about by a ferment, such as yeast enzymes which convert grape sugar into ethyl alcohol, etc. **3.** agitation; excitement.

**fermentative** /fɜ'mɛntətɪv/, *adj.* **1.** tending to produce or undergo fermentation. **2.** pertaining to or of the nature of fermentation.

**Fermi-Dirac statistics** /ˌfɜmi-dəræk stə'tɪstɪks, ˌfɛəmi-/, *n.* the branch of quantum statistics used with systems of identical particles whose wave function changes sign if any two particles are interchanged. [named after Enrico *Fermi,* 1901-54, Italian physicist, and Paul *Dirac,* b. 1902, English physicist]

**fermion** /'fɜmiən, 'fɛə-/, *n.* any elementary particle which conforms to Fermi-Dirac statistics and has half integral spin, as a proton or neutron.

**fermium** /'fɜmiəm/, *n.* a synthetic, radioactive element. *Symbol:* Fm; *at. no.:* 100. [from Enrico *Fermi,* 1901-54, Italian physicist, + -IUM]

**fern** /fɜn/, *n.* any of the pteridophytes constituting the order Filicales, distinguished from other pteridophytes in having few leaves, large in proportion to the stems, and bearing sporangia on the undersurface or margin. [ME *ferne,* OE *fearn,* c. G *Farn;* akin to Skt *parna* feather] – **fernlike,** *adj.*

**fernbird** /'fɜnbɜd/, *n.* a small brown and white New Zealand bird, *Bowdleria punctata,* with loosely-barbed tail feathers.

**fernery** /'fɜnəri/, *n., pl.* **-ries.** a place or a glass case in which ferns are grown for ornament.

**fernickety** /fə'nɪkəti/, *adj.* →**pernickety.**

**fern land** /'fɜn lænd/, *n. N.Z.* land covered or originally covered with bracken.

**Fernleaf** /'fɜnlif/, *n. Colloq.* a New Zealander. [from the silver fern leaf, emblem of New Zealand]

**fern seed** /'fɜn sid/, *n.* the spores of ferns, formerly supposed to have the power to make persons invisible.

**ferny** /'fɜni/, *adj.* **1.** pertaining to, consisting of, or like ferns. **2.** abounding in or overgrown with ferns.

**ferocious** /fə'roʊʃəs/, *adj.* savagely fierce, as a wild beast, person, action, aspect, etc.; violently cruel. [FEROCI(TY) + -OUS] – **ferociously,** *adv.* – **ferociousness,** *n.*

**ferocity** /fə'rɒsəti/, *n.* ferocious quality or state; savage fierceness. [L *ferōcitas*]

**-ferous,** an adjective suffix meaning 'bearing', 'producing', 'yielding', 'containing', 'conveying', as in *auriferous, balsamiferous, coniferous, pestiferous.* [-FER producing + -OUS]

**ferrate** /'fɛreɪt/, *n.* a salt of the hypothetical ferric acid. [L *ferrum* iron + -ATE[2]]

**ferrel** /'fɛrəl/, *n., v.t.,* **-relled, -relling** or (*U.S.*) **-reled, -reling.** →**ferrule.**

**Ferrel's law** /fɛrəlz 'lɔ/, *n.* the law that all bodies moving on the earth's surface are deflected to the right in the northern hemisphere and to the left in the southern hemisphere. [named after William *Ferrel,* 1817-91, U.S. meteorologist]

**ferret**[1] /'fɛrət/, *n.* **1.** a domesticated, albinistic, red-eyed form of the polecat, used for hunting rabbits and rats in their burrows. **2.** *Cricket.* a very poor batsman (one who goes in after the rabbits). **3.** a wild species, *Mustela nigripes* (**black-footed ferret**), yellowish brown with the tip of the tail and the legs black, inhabiting prairie regions of the United States as the plains of Nebraska and Kansas, and feeding largely on prairie dogs. –*v.t.* **4.** to drive out by, or as by, means of a ferret. **5.** to hunt with ferrets. **6.** to search out or bring to light: *to ferret out the facts.* –*v.i.* **7.** to search about. [ME *fyrette,* from OF *fuiret,* from L *fūr* thief] – **ferreter,** *n.* – **ferrety,** *adj.*

ferret

**ferret**[2] /'fɛrət/, *n.* a narrow tape or ribbon, as of silk or cotton, used for binding, etc. [It. *fioretto,* diminutive of *fiore,* from L *flōs* flower; conformed to FERRET[1]]

**ferret badger** /'– bædʒə/, *n.* any of the small carnivores constituting the genus *Helictis,* of southern and eastern Asia.

**ferri-,** a word element meaning 'iron', implying esp. combination with ferric iron or ferrites. [var. of FERRO-]

**ferriage** /'fɛriədʒ, -ɪdʒ/, *n.* **1.** conveyance by a ferryboat or the like. **2.** the price charged for ferrying.

**ferric** /'fɛrɪk/, *adj.* of or containing iron, esp. in the trivalent state. [FERR(I)- + -IC]

**ferric oxide** /– 'ɒksaɪd/, *n.* a dark red crystalline solid, $Fe_2O_3$, occurring naturally as haematite; used as a pigment, a mordant, and in polishing compounds.

**ferriferous** /fɛ'rɪfərəs/, *adj.* producing or yielding iron.

**ferrimagnetic** /ˌfɛrimæg'nɛtɪk, ˌfɛraɪ-/, *adj.* pertaining to the type of magnetism, occurring in such materials as ferrites (def. 3), in which the magnetic moments of adjacent atoms are antiparallel and of unequal strength, or in which unequal numbers of magnetic moments are orientated in opposite directions. – **ferrimagnetism** /fɛri'mægnətɪzəm, fɛraɪ-/, *n.*

**Ferris wheel** /'fɛrəs wil/, *n.* an amusement device at fairs, etc., consisting of a large upright wheel rotating about a fixed axis with seats suspended at intervals around its rim. Also, **ferris wheel.** [named after G. W. G. *Ferris,* 1859-96, U.S. engineer]

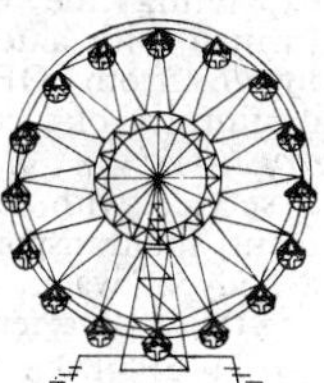

Ferris wheel

**ferrite** /'fɛraɪt/, *n.* **1.** *Chem.* a compound formed when ferric oxide is combined with a more basic metallic oxide, as $NaFeO_2$. **2.** *Metall.* the pure alpha iron occurring in iron-carbon alloys, or any solid solution of which alpha iron is the solvent. **3.** one of a group of ceramic substances with the general formula $MO \cdot Fe_2O_3$ where M is a divalent metal; used, because of their ferrimagnetic (or, in some cases, ferromagnetic) properties, in computers and the electrical equipment of aircraft. **4.** *Elect.* →**core** (def. 3c). – **ferritic** /fɛ'rɪtɪk/, *adj.*

**ferrite-rod aerial** /ˌfɛraɪt-rɒd 'ɛəriəl/, *n.* a radio aerial, esp. of portable radios, consisting of a coil of wire running around a short rod of ferrite.

**ferritin** /'fɛrətən/, *n.* a protein which contains iron; found in the liver and spleen and believed to act as a reservoir of iron for the whole body.

**ferro-,** a word element meaning 'iron'. In chemistry, *ferro-* implies esp. combination with ferrous iron as opposed to ferric iron. Also, **ferri-.** [combining form representing L *ferrum* iron]

**ferrochromium** /fɛroʊ'kroʊmiəm/, *n.* an alloy of iron and up to 70 per cent chromium. Also, **ferrochrome.**

**ferroconcrete** /fɛroʊ'kɒŋkrit/, *n.* →**reinforced concrete.**

**ferroelectric** /ˌfɛroʊə'lɛktrɪk/, *adj.* **1.** pertaining to a non-magnetic substance which possesses spontaneous electric polarisation such that the polarisation can be reversed by an electric field. –*n.* **2.** a ferroelectric substance.

**ferromagnesian** /fɛroʊmæg'niziən, -'niʒən/, *adj.* **1.** (of minerals and rocks) containing iron and magnesium. –*n.* **2.** an iron-magnesium mineral.

**ferromagnetic** /ˌfɛroʊmæg'nɛtɪk/, *adj.* pertaining to a substance, such as iron, which possesses magnetic properties in the absence of an external magnetic field. – **ferromagnetism** /fɛroʊ'mægnətɪzəm/, *n.*

**ferromanganese** /ˌfɛroʊˌmæŋgə'niz/, *n.* an alloy of iron containing up to 90 per cent manganese.

**ferromolybdenum** /ˌfɛroʊmə'lɪbdənəm/, *n.* an alloy of iron containing up to 65 per cent molybdenum.

**ferronickel** /fɛroʊ'nɪkəl/, *n.* a nickel-steel alloy used for making rheostats and coils.

**ferrosilicon** /fɛroʊ'sɪləkən/, *n.* an alloy of iron containing up to 90 per cent silicon.

**ferrotitanium** /ˌfɛroʊtaɪ'teɪniəm, -tə'teɪ-/, *n.* an alloy of iron containing up to 45 per cent titanium.

**ferrotungsten** /fɛroʊ'tʌŋstən/, *n.* an alloy of iron containing up to 80 per cent tungsten.

**ferrotype** /'fɛroʊtaɪp/, *v.*, **-typed, -typing,** *n.* *–v.t.* **1.** to put a glossy surface on (a print) by pressing it while wet on a metal sheet (**ferrotype tin**). *–n.* **2.** a photograph taken on a sensitised sheet of enamelled iron or tin; a tintype. **3.** the process itself.

**ferrous** /'fɛrəs/, *adj.* of or containing iron, esp. in the divalent state.

**ferrous sulphate** /– 'sʌlfeɪt/, *n.* a green, soluble, crystalline solid, $FeSO_4 \cdot 7H_2O$, used in dyeing, tanning, inks, pigments, photography, fertilisers, and medicine; copperas. Also, **iron sulphate.**

**ferrovanadium** /ˌfɛroʊvə'neɪdiəm/, *n.* an alloy of iron containing up to 55 per cent vanadium.

**ferrozirconium** /ˌfɛroʊzɜ'koʊniəm/, *n.* an alloy of iron containing up to 40 per cent zirconium.

**ferruginous** /fɛ'rudʒənəs/, *adj.* **1.** iron-bearing; containing iron. **2.** *Bot.* of the colour of rusty iron. [L *ferrūginus*, from *ferrūgo* iron rust]

**ferrule** /'fɛrul, -rəl/, *n.*, *v.*, **-ruled, -ruling.** *–n.* **1.** a metal ring or cap put round the end of a post, stick, handle, etc., for strength or protection. **2.** (in steam boilers) a bush for expanding the end of a flue. *–v.i.* **3.** to furnish with a ferrule. Also, **ferrel.** [late ME *vyrell*, from OF *virelle*, from L *viriola*, diminutive of *viriae* bracelets]

ferrule on the end of a paintbrush

**ferry** /'fɛri/, *n.*, *pl.* **-ries,** *v.*, **-ried, -rying.** *–n.* **1.** a service with terminals and floating equipment, for transport from shore to shore across a body of water, usu. narrow, as a river, lake or strait. **2.** a ferryboat. **3.** the legal right to ferry passengers, etc., and to charge toll for the service. *–v.t.* **4.** to carry or convey over water in a boat or plane. *–v.i.* **5.** to pass over water in a boat or by ferry. [ME *feri(en)*, OE *ferian*, akin to *faran* fare]

**ferryboat** /'fɛriboʊt/, *n.* a boat used to convey passengers, vehicles, etc., across a river or the like.

**ferryman** /'fɛrimən/, *n.*, *pl.* **-men.** one who owns or runs a ferry.

**fertile** /'fɜtaɪl/, *adj.* **1.** bearing or capable of bearing vegetation, crops, etc., abundantly, as land or soil. **2.** bearing offspring freely; prolific. **3.** abundantly productive or inventive: *a fertile imagination.* **4.** able to produce offspring. **5.** producing an abundance (fol. by *in*): *land fertile in wheat.* **6.** conducive to productiveness: *fertile showers.* **7.** *Biol.* **a.** fertilised, as an egg or ovum. **b.** capable of growth or development, as seeds or eggs. **8.** *Bot.* **a.** capable of producing sexual reproductive structures. **b.** capable of causing fertilisation, as an anther with fully developed pollen. **c.** having spore-bearing organs, as a frond. **9.** *Physics.* (of an isotope, element, or substance) transformable into a fissile material. [ME, from L *fertilis* fruitful] – **fertilely,** *adv.* – **fertileness,** *n.*

**fertilisation** /fɜtəlaɪ'zeɪʃən/, *n.* **1.** the act or process of fertilising. **2.** the state of being fertilised. **3.** *Biol.* **a.** the union of male and female gametic nuclei. **b.** fecundation or impregnation of animals or plants. **4.** the enrichment of soil for the production of crops, etc. Also, **fertilization.**

**fertilise** /'fɜtəlaɪz/, *v.t.*, **-lised, -lising. 1.** *Biol.* **a.** to render (an egg, ovum, or female cell) capable of development by union with the male element, or sperm. **b.** to fecundate or impregnate (an animal or plant). **2.** to make fertile; enrich (soil, etc.) for crops, etc. **3.** to make productive. Also, **fertilize.** – **fertilisable,** *adj.*

**fertiliser** /'fɜtəlaɪzə/, *n.* **1.** any material used to fertilise the soil, esp. a commercial or chemical manure. **2.** one who or that which fertilises an animal or plant. Also, **fertilizer.**

**fertility** /fɜ'tɪləti/, *n.* **1.** the state or quality of being fertile. **2.** *Biol.* the ability to produce offspring; power of reproduction. **3.** (of soil) the quality of supplying nutrients in proper amounts for plant growth when other factors are favourable.

**fertility cult** /'– kʌlt/, *n.* any of various primitive forms of worship in a settled agricultural community centred on the performance of magical rituals to ensure the continuance and abundance of crops, appropriate weather, and the perpetuity of the tribe.

**fertility symbol** /'– sɪmbəl/, *n.* a symbol or object used in a fertility cult, esp. a phallic symbol.

**ferula** /'fɛrələ/, *n.*, *pl.* **-lae** /-li/. **1.** *Bot.* any plant of an umbelliferous genus, *Ferula*, chiefly of the Mediterranean region and central Asia, generally tall and coarse with dissected leaves, many of the Asian species yielding strongly-scented, medicinal gum resins. **2.** a rod; a ferule. [L: rod, giant fennel]

**ferulaceous** /fɛrə'leɪʃəs/, *adj.* pertaining to reeds or canes; having a stalklike reed: *ferulaceous plants.* [L *ferulāceus*, from *ferula* giant fennel]

**ferule** /'fɛrul, -rəl/, *n.*, *v.*, **-ruled, -ruling.** *–n.* **1.** a rod, cane, or flat piece of wood for the punishment of children, by striking them, esp. on the hand. *–v.t.* **2.** to punish with a ferule. [OE *ferele* rod, from L *ferula*]

**fervency** /'fɜvənsi/, *n.* warmth or intensity of feeling; ardour.

**fervent** /'fɜvənt/, *adj.* **1.** having or showing great warmth and earnestness of feeling: *a fervent admirer, plea, etc.* **2.** hot; burning; glowing. [ME, from L *fervens*, ppr., boiling, glowing] – **fervently,** *adv.* – **ferventness,** *n.*

**fervid** /'fɜvəd/, *adj.* **1.** heated or vehement in spirit, enthusiasm, etc.: *a fervid orator.* **2.** burning; glowing; hot. [L *fervidus* burning] – **fervidly,** *adv.* – **fervidness,** *n.*

**fervour** /'fɜvə/, *n.* **1.** great warmth and earnestness of feeling: *to speak with great fervour.* **2.** intense heat. Also, *U.S.*, **fervor.** [ME, from OF, from L *fervor* heat, passion]

**Fescennine** /'fɛsənin, -naɪn/, *adj.* scurrilous; licentious; obscene: *Fescennine verse.* [L *Fescenninus* pertaining to *Fescennia* in Etruria]

**fescue** /'fɛskju/, *n.* **1.** any grass of the genus *Festuca*, some species of which, esp. Chewings fescue and creeping red fescue, are cultivated for pasture or lawns. **2.** any of several grasses belonging to other related genera, as *Vulpia*, rat's-tail fescue. **3.** *Obs.* a small stick, twig, etc., used to point out the letters in teaching children to read. [ME *festue*, from OF, from L *festūca* stalk, straw]

**fess** /fɛs/, *n.* *Her.* a wide horizontal band across the middle of an escutcheon. Also, **fesse.** [late ME *fesse*, from AF, from L *fascia* band]

**fess point** /'– pɔɪnt/, *n.* *Her.* the central point of an escutcheon. Also, **fesse point.**

**fesswise** /'fɛswaɪz/, *adv.* *Her.* in the manner of a fess; across the shield. Also, **fessewise.**

**-fest,** a suffix indicating a period of festive or enthusiastic activity in the thing named: *lovefest, musicfest, talkfest.*

**festa** /'fɛstə/, *n.* a feast, festival, or holiday. [It.]

**festal** /'fɛstl/, *adj.* **1.** pertaining to or befitting a feast, festival, or gala occasion. **2.** of or pertaining to academic dress for formal occasions: *a festal gown.* [late ME, from OF, from L *festum* a festival, feast] – **festally,** *adv.*

**fester** /'fɛstə/, *v.i.* **1.** to generate purulent matter; suppurate. **2.** to cause ulceration, or rankle, as a foreign body in the flesh. **3.** to putrefy or rot. **4.** to rankle, as a feeling of resentment. *–v.t.* **5.** to cause to fester. *–n.* **6.** an ulcer; a rankling sore. **7.** a small, purulent, superficial sore. [ME *festre*, from OF, from L *fistula* ulcer]

**festina lente** /ˌfɛstinə 'lɛnteɪ/, make haste slowly; more haste less speed. [L]

**festination** /fɛstə'neɪʃən/, *n.* a type of gait marked by an involuntary hurrying in walking, observed in certain nervous diseases. [L *festīnātio* haste]

**festival** /'fɛstəvəl/, *n.* **1.** a periodic religious or other feast: *the festival of Christmas.* **2.** any time of feasting; an anniversary for festive celebration. **3.** a public festivity, with performances of music, processions, exhibitions, etc., often timed to coincide with some natural event, as spring, the blossoming of certain trees, etc: *Moomba festival.* **4.** a series of musical, dramatic, or other performances. **5.** *Archaic.* merry-making; revelry. *–adj.* **6.** of, pertaining to, or befitting a feast or holiday; festal. [ME, from ML *festīvālis*, from L *festīvus* FESTIVE]

**festive** /'fɛstɪv/, *adj.* **1.** pertaining to or suitable for a feast or festival. **2.** joyful; merry. [L *festīvus* merry, lively] – **festively,** *adv.* – **festiveness,** *n.*

**festivity** /fɛs'tɪvəti/, *n., pl.* **-ties.** **1.** a festive celebration or occasion. **2.** (*pl.*) festive proceedings. **3.** festive character; festive gaiety or pleasure.

**festoon** /fɛs'tun/, *n.* **1.** a string or chain of flowers, foliage, ribbon, etc., suspended in a curve between two points. **2.** a decorative representation of this, as in architectural work or on pottery. **3.** the curvature of the gum margin around the teeth. *–v.t.* **4.** to adorn with, or as with, festoons. **5.** to form into festoons. **6.** to connect by festoons. [F *feston,* from It. *festone,* from *festa* festival, FEAST]

**festoonery** /fɛs'tunəri/, *n.* **1.** a decoration of festoons. **2.** festoons collectively.

**festschrift** /'fɛstʃrɪft/, *n., pl.* **-schriften** /-ʃrɪftən/, **-schrifts.** a commemorative collection of articles, learned papers, etc., contributed by a number of authors, usu. published in honour of a colleague. [G, lit., a festival writing]

**festuca** /fɛs'tjukə/, *n.* any of various grasses, usu. perennial and tufted, of the genus *Festuca.* See **fescue.**

**FET** /fɛt/, *n.* a transistor employing one type of carrier, in which the current is controlled by an electric field. Also, **field effect transistor.**

**feta** /'fɛtə/, *n.* →**fetta.**

**fetal** /fitl/, *adj. Chiefly U.S.* →**foetal.**

**fetation** /fi'teɪʃən/, *n. Chiefly U.S.* →**foetation.**

**fetch** /fɛtʃ/, *v.t.* **1.** to go and return with, or bring to or from a particular place: *to fetch a book from another room.* **2.** to cause to come to a particular place or condition; succeed in bringing: *to fetch a doctor.* **3.** to realise or bring in (a price, etc.). **4.** *Colloq.* to charm; captivate. **5.** to take (a breath). **6.** to utter (a sigh, groan, etc.). **7.** to deal or deliver (a stroke, blow, etc.). **8.** to perform or execute (a movement, step, leap, etc.). **9.** to start (a pump) by pouring water into the tap above the plunger; prime. **10.** *Chiefly Naut.* to reach; arrive at. **11.** *Hunting.* (as a command to a dog) to retrieve (game). **12.** **fetch up, a.** to bring to a sudden stop. **b.** *U.S.* to bring up (a child, etc.). *–v.i.* **13.** to go and bring things. **14.** *Naut.* to move, go, or take a course: *to fetch about.* **15.** *Hunting.* to retrieve game. **16.** **fetch and carry,** to do minor menial jobs. **17.** **fetch up,** *Colloq.* **a.** to reach as a goal or final state; end up: *you'll fetch up in prison.* **b.** to vomit. **c.** to come to a sudden stop, as a ship running aground, or a walker suddenly pausing. *–n.* **18.** the act of fetching. **19.** the distance of fetching. **20.** the reach or stretch of a thing (specifically the uninterrupted distance travelled by a wave on the sea). **21.** a trick; dodge. **22.** the apparition of a living person; a wraith. **23.** *Archaic.* a stroke; effort: *a fetch of the imagination.* [ME *fecche(n),* OE *feccan,* probably variant of *fetian*] **– fetcher,** *n.*

**fetching** /'fɛtʃɪŋ/, *adj.* charming; captivating. **– fetchingly,** *adv.*

**fete** /feɪt/, *n., v.,* **feted, feting.** *–n.* **1.** a function to raise money for charity, church, school, etc., frequently outdoor and combining the activities of bazaar and fair. **2.** a feast or festival. **3.** a festal day; a holiday. **4.** the festival of the saint after whom a child is named. *–v.t.* **5.** to entertain at or honour with a fete. **6.** to give a hospitable public reception to (someone); lionise. Also, **fête.** [F. See FEAST]

**fete day** /'– deɪ/, *n.* a festival day.

**fetichism** /'fɛtɪʃɪzəm, 'fit-, -təʃ-/, *n.* →**fetishism.** **– fetichist,** *n.* **– fetichistic** /fɛtə'ʃɪstɪk, fi-/, *adj.*

**fetid** /'fɛtəd, 'fitəd/, *adj.* having a strong, offensive smell; stinking. Also, **foetid.** [L *fētidus,* var. of *foetidus*] **– fetidly,** *adv.* **– fetidness, fetidity** /fə'tɪdəti/, *n.*

**fetish** /'fɛtɪʃ, 'fit-/, *n.* **1.** a material, commonly an inanimate object, regarded with awe as being the embodiment or habitation of a potent spirit, or as having magical potency because of the materials and methods used in compounding it. **2.** any object of blind reverence. **3.** an incantation or rite of fetish-worshippers. **4.** an obsession or fixation, usu. expressed in ritualistic behaviour. **5.** *Psychol.* a non-sexual part of the body, an action, or an inanimate object, which gives sexual stimulation. Also, **fetich.** [F *fétich,* from Pg. *feitiço,* originally adj., artificial, from L *factīcius* factitious] **– fetishlike,** *adj.*

**fetishism** /'fɛtɪʃɪzəm, 'fit-, -təʃ-/, *n.* **1.** belief in or use of fetishes. **2.** *Psychol.* the compulsive use of some inanimate object in attaining sexual gratification, such as a shoe, a lock of hair, stockings, underclothes, a neck-piece, etc. **3.** blind devotion. Also, **fetichism.** **– fetishistic** /fɛtə'ʃɪstɪk, fi-/, *adj.*

**fetishist** /'fɛtɪʃəst, 'fit-, -təʃ-/, *n.* a user of fetishes. Also, **fetichist.**

**fetlock** /'fɛtlɒk/, *n.* **1.** a part of a horse's leg situated behind the joint between the cannon bone and the great pastern bone, and bearing a tuft of hair. **2.** this tuft of hair. **3.** the joint at this point (**fetlock joint**). [ME *fet(e)lok,* etc., c. d. G *Fissloch;* orig. obscure]

**fetology** /fi'tɒlədʒi/, *n. Chiefly U.S.* →**foetology.** **– fetologist,** *n.*

**fetor** /'fitɔ, -tə/, *n.* any strong offensive smell; a stench. Also, **foetor.** [L]

**fetta** /'fɛtə/, *n.* a soft, ripened white cheese, from Greece, made originally from goat's or ewe's milk and now from cow's milk, cured in brine. Also, **feta.** [Modern Gk *phéta,* from It. *fetta* slice, cut, from L *offitta,* diminutive of *offa* mouthful, bite]

**fetter** /'fɛtə/, *n.* **1.** a chain or shackle placed on the feet. **2.** (*usu. pl.*) anything that confines or restrains. *–v.t.* **3.** to put fetters upon. **4.** to confine; restrain. [ME and OE *feter,* c. OHG *fezzera;* akin to FOOT]

**fetterless** /'fɛtələs/, *adj.* without fetters; unfettered.

**fetterlock** /'fɛtəlɒk/, *n.* →**fetlock.**

**fettle** /'fɛtl/, *n.* **1.** state; condition: *in fine fettle.* *–v.t.* **2.** *Mech.* to remove the roughness from a casting and to verify that it is free from flaws, by hanging in chains and striking with a hammer. **3.** *Metall.* to line a furnace with loose material. **4.** *Archaic.* to put in order, put a finishing touch to. [ME *fetlen,* from OE *fetel* belt]

**fettler** /'fɛtlə/, *n.* a person, usu. one of a group, responsible for maintaining ballast, condition of sleepers and condition of running rail for a particular section of a railway line; permanent-way man.

**fettling** /'fɛtlɪŋ/, *n.* the material with which the hearth of a puddling furnace or the like is lined, as a substance rich in oxides of iron.

**fettuccine** /'fɛtətʃini/, *n.* pasta cut into wide strips. [It., diminutive of *fetta.* See FETTA]

**fetus** /'fitəs/, *n. Chiefly U.S.* →**foetus.** **– fetal,** *adj.*

**feud**[1] /fjud/, *n.* **1.** a bitter, continuous hostility, esp. between two families, clans, etc. **2.** a quarrel or contention. *–v.i.* **3.** to conduct a feud. [var. of *fead* (*a* being misread as *u*), ME *fede,* from OF *fe(i)de,* from OHG *fēhida* (G *Fehde*), c. OE *fǣhth* enmity. Cf. FOE]

**feud**[2] /fjud/, *n. Law.* →**fee** (def. 4). [ML *feudum,* var. of *feodum.* See FEE]

**feudal** /'fjudl/, *adj.* **1.** of, pertaining to, or of the nature of a feoff or fee: *a feudal estate.* **2.** of or pertaining to the holding of land in a feoff or fee. **3.** of or pertaining to the feudal system: *feudal law.* **– feudally,** *adv.*

**feudal investiture** /– ɪn'vɛstətʃə/, *n.* (in the feudal system) the public grant of the land by the lord to the tenant.

**feudalise** /'fjudəlaɪz/, *v.t.,* **-lised, -lising.** to make feudal; bring under the feudal system. Also, **feudalize.** **– feudalisation** /fjudəlaɪ'zeɪʃən/, *n.*

**feudalism** /'fjudəlɪzəm/, *n.* the feudal organisation, or its principles and practices. **– feudalist,** *n.* **– feudalistic,** /fjudə'lɪstɪk/, *adj.*

**feudality** /fju'dæləti/, *n., pl.* **-ties.** **1.** the state or quality of being feudal. **2.** the principles and practices of feudalism. **3.** a fief or fee.

**feudal system** /'fjudl sɪstəm/, *n.* the organisation in Europe during the Middle Ages, based on the holding of lands in fief or fee, and on the resulting relations between lord and vassal.

**feudatory** /'fjudətəri, -tri/, *n., pl.* **-ries,** *adj.* *–n.* **1.** one who holds his lands by feudal tenure; a feudal vassal. **2.** a fief or fee. *–adj.* **3.** (of a person) owing feudal allegiance to another. **4.** (of a kingdom) under the overlordship of an outside sovereign.

**feudist**[1] /'fjudəst/, *n.* a person who fights in a feud. [FEUD[1] + -IST]

**feudist**[2] /'fjudəst/, *n.* a writer or authority on feudal law. [FEUD[2] + -IST]

**feuilleton** /'fɜjətən, -tõ/, *n.* **1.** a part of a newspaper (usu. the bottom of one or more pages, marked off by a rule) devoted to light literature, fiction, criticism, etc. **2.** an item printed in the feuilleton. [F: small leaf]

**fever** /ˈfivə/, *n.* **1.** a morbid condition of the body characterised by undue rise of temperature, quickening of the pulse, and disturbance of various bodily functions. **2.** any of a group of diseases in which high temperature is a prominent sympton: *scarlet fever.* **3.** intense nervous excitement. **4. fever pitch,** the height of excitement (esp. of crowds). *–v.t.* **5.** to affect with or as with fever. [ME; OE *fefer,* from L *febris*] **– fevered,** *adj.* **– feverless,** *adj.*

**feverfew** /ˈfivəfju/, *n.* a perennial plant, *Chrysanthemum parthenium,* bearing small white flowers, formerly used as a febrifuge. [ME *fevyrfue,* OE *feferfug(i)e,* from LL *febrifugia* kind of plant, from L *febri(s)* fever + *-fugia.* See -FUGE]

**fever heat** /ˈfivə hit/, *n.* **1.** the heat of fever; bodily heat exceeding 37.0° C. **2.** feverish excitement.

**feverish** /ˈfivərɪʃ/, *adj.* **1.** excited or restless, as if from fever. **2.** having fever, esp. a slight degree of fever. **3.** pertaining to, of the nature of, or resembling fever. **4.** infested with fever, as a region. **5.** having a tendency to produce fever, as food. **– feverishly,** *adv.* **– feverishness,** *n.*

**feverous** /ˈfivərəs/, *adj.* →**feverish. – feverously,** *adv.*

**fever-root** /ˈfivə-rut/, *n.* a North American herb, *Triosteum perfoliatum,* having a purgative and emetic root.

**fever-tree** /ˈfivə-tri/, *n.* **1.** any of several trees which produce or are supposed to produce a febrifuge, as *Pinckneya pubens,* a small tree of the south-eastern United States, whose bark is used as a tonic and febrifuge. **2.** a tall, deciduous tree, *Acacia xanthophloea,* of southern Africa, bearing yellow, scented flowers, and usu. found in swampy places.

**few** /fju/, *adj.* **1.** not many; a small number (of). *–n.* **2. the few,** the minority. **3. a few,** a small number. **4. quite a few, a good few, some few,** *Colloq.* a fairly large number. [ME; OE *fēawe,* pl., c. OHG *fōhe;* akin to L *paucus,* Gk *paûros* little, in pl., few] **– fewness,** *n.*

**fewer** /ˈfjuə/, *adj., comp. of* **few.** a smaller number of.

**fey** /feɪ/, *adj.* **1.** as if enchanted, under a spell, aware of supernatural influences. **2.** light-headed; eccentric; slightly crazy. **3.** fated to die. **4.** dying; in the state of heightened awareness formerly supposed to presage death. [ME, OE *fǣge* doomed to die, timid, c. G *feige* cowardly] **– feyly,** *adv.* **– feyness,** *n.*

**fez** /fɛz/, *n., pl.* **fezzes.** a felt cap, usu. of a red colour, having the shape of a truncated cone, and ornamented with a long black tassel, formerly the national headdress of the Turks. [Turk.; named after the town of *Fez,* in Morocco]

fez

**ff.,** *Music.* →**fortissimo.**

**f.f.a.,** **1.** *Chem.* free fatty acid. **2.** free from alongside (ship).

**f. furn,** fully furnished.

**f-hole** /ˈɛf-hoʊl/, *n.* either of a pair of holes in the table of a violin, shaped like an *f.*

**fiacre** /fiˈakrə/, *n.* →**hackney-coach.** [F, named after the Hôtel de St *Fiacre* in Paris]

**fiancée** /fiˈɒnseɪ/, *n.* a woman engaged to be married. [F, pp. of *fiancer* betroth, from *fier* trust, from L *fīdere*] **– fiancé,** *n. masc.*

**fiasco** /fiˈæskoʊ/, *n., pl.* **-cos. 1.** an ignominious failure. **2.** a bottle or flask. [It.: lit., bottle; sense development obscure]

**fiat** /ˈfiæt, ˈfiət/, *n.* **1.** an authoritative decree, sanction, or order. **2.** a formula containing the word *fiat,* by which a person in authority gave his sanction. [L: let it be done, or made]

**fiat lux** /– ˈlʊks/, let there be light. [L]

**fib**[1] /fɪb/, *n., v.,* **fibbed, fibbing.** *–n.* **1.** a trivial falsehood. *–v.i.* **2.** to tell a fib. [short for *fibble-fable,* reduplication of FABLE]

**fib**[2] /fɪb/, *v.t.,* **fibbed, fibbing.** *Colloq.* to beat; give (someone) a rapid succession of blows, as in boxing. [orig. uncert.]

**fibber** /ˈfɪbə/, *n.* one who tells fibs; fibster.

**fibr-,** a word element meaning 'fibre', as in *fibrin. Also,* **fibri-, fibro-.** [combining form representing L *fibra*]

**fibre** /ˈfaɪbə/, *n.* **1.** a fine threadlike piece, as of cotton, jute, or asbestos. **2.** a slender filament. **3.** filaments collectively. **4.** matter composed of filaments. **5.** fibrous structure. **6.** character: *moral fibre.* **7. a.** filamentous matter from the bast tissue or other parts of plants, used for industrial purposes. **b.** a slender, threadlike root of a plant. **c.** a slender, threadlike bast cell. **8.** *Chem.* vulcanised fibre. Also, *U.S.,* **fiber.** [ME *fibre,* from F, from L *fibra* fibre, filament] **– fibred,** *adj.* **– fibreless,** *adj.*

**fibre ball** /ˈ– bɔl/, *n.* a cylindrical or round aggregation of fibre from marine angiosperms, as *Posidonia australis,* formed on beaches by the action of waves.

**fibreboard** /ˈfaɪbəbɔd/, *n.* **1.** a building material made of wood or other plant fibres compressed and cemented into rigid sheets. **2.** a sheet of fibreboard. Also, *U.S.,* **fiberboard.**

**fibreglass** /ˈfaɪbəglas/, *n.* a material consisting of extremely fine filaments of glass which are combined in yarn and woven into fabrics, or are used in masses as an insulator or used embedded in plastic as a construction material for boat hulls, light car bodies, etc.; glass fibre. Also, *U.S.,* **fiberglass, fiberglas.** [Trademark]

**fibre-optic** /faɪbər-ˈɒptɪk/, *adj.* of or pertaining to a device making use of fibre-optics: *fibre-optic gastroscope.*

**fibre optics** /faɪbər ˈɒptɪks/, *n.* **1.** the process of passing light along bundles of very fine fibres by internal reflection. **2.** the study of this process.

**fibri-,** variant of **fibro-.**

**fibriform** /ˈfaɪbrəfɔm, ˈfɪb-/, *adj.* of the form of a fibre or fibres. [FIBRI- + -FORM]

**fibril** /ˈfaɪbrəl, ˈfɪb-/, *n.* a small or fine fibre. [NL *fibrilla,* diminutive of L *fibra* fibre]

**fibrillar** /ˈfaɪbrɪlə, ˈfɪb-/, *adj.* of, pertaining to, or of the nature of fibrils.

**fibrillate** /ˈfaɪbrɪleɪt, ˈfɪb-/, *v.i.* to undergo fibrillation.

**fibrillation** /ˈfaɪbrəleɪʃən, ˈfɪb-/, *n.* **1.** the process of becoming arranged in fibrils. **2.** an incoordinate quivering movement in the fibrils of a muscle, esp. of the heart.

**fibrilliform** /faɪˈbrɪləfɔm, fɪ-/, *adj.* of the form of a fibril.

**fibrillose** /ˈfaɪbrəloʊs, ˈfɪ-/, *adj.* composed of or furnished with fibrils.

**fibrin** /ˈfaɪbrən/, *n.* **1.** *Biochem., Physiol.* a white, rough, fibrous protein, formed in the clotting of blood. **2.** *Bot.* a substance like fibrin found in some plants; gluten. [FIBR- + -IN[2]]

**fibrino-,** a word element representing **fibrin.**

**fibrinogen** /faɪˈbrɪnədʒən/, *n.* a globulin occurring in blood and yielding fibrin in the coagulation of blood.

**fibrinogenic** /ˌfaɪbrənoʊˈdʒɛnɪk/, *adj.* producing fibrin. Also, **fibrinogenous** /faɪbrəˈnɒdʒənəs/.

**fibrinogenopoenia** /ˌfaɪbrənoʊˌdʒɛnoʊˈpiniə/, *n.* a state of decreased fibrinogen in the blood.

**fibrinous** /ˈfaɪbrənəs/, *adj.* containing, composed of, or of the nature of fibrin.

**fibro** /ˈfaɪbroʊ/, *n.* **1.** compressed asbestos and cement used for building materials as wall-board, corrugated roofing, pipes, etc. *–adj.* **2.** of or pertaining to this material: *a fibro house.* Also, **fibrocement.** [Trademark]

**fibro-,** variant of **fibr-,** before consonants.

**fibroid** /ˈfaɪbrɔɪd/, *adj.* **1.** resembling fibre or fibrous tissue. **2.** composed of fibres, as a tumour. *–n.* **3.** *Pathol.* a tumour largely composed of smooth muscle and fibrous tissue.

**fibroin** /ˈfaɪbroʊən/, *n.* an insoluble protein, a principal component of spiders' webs and silk.

**fibrolite** /ˈfaɪbrəlaɪt/, *n.* →**sillimanite.**

**fibroma** /faɪˈbroʊmə/, *n., pl.* **-mata** /-mətə/, **-mas.** a tumour consisting essentially of fibrous tissue. [NL, from L *fibra* fibre + *-oma* -OMA]

**fibroplasia** /faɪbroʊˈpleɪʒə, -ziə/, *n.* the formation of fibrous tissue, as occurs in the healing of wounds.

**fibrose** /ˈfaɪbroʊz/, *v.i.,* **fibrosed, fibrosing.** to form fibrous tissue.

**fibrosis** /faɪˈbroʊsəs/, *n.* the development in an organ of excess fibrous connective tissue. [NL, from L *fibra* fibre + *-osis* -OSIS]

**fibrositis** /faɪbrəˈsaɪtəs/, *n.* an inflammatory change in fibrous tissue, as muscle sheaths, ligament tendons, fasciae, and the

i = peat ɪ = pit ɛ = pet æ = pat a = part ɒ = pot ʌ = putt ɔ = port ʊ = put u = pool ɜ = pert ə = apart aɪ = buy eɪ = bay ɔɪ = boy aʊ = how oʊ = hoe ɪə = here ɛə = hair ʊə = tour g = give θ = thin ð = then ʃ = show ʒ = measure tʃ = choke dʒ = joke ŋ = sing j = you õ = Fr. bon

like, causing pain and difficulty in movement.

**fibrous** /ˈfaɪbrəs/, *adj.* containing, consisting of, or resembling fibres. [NL *fibrōsus,* from L *fibra* fibre] – **fibrously,** *adv.* – **fibrousness,** *n.*

**fibrous plaster** /– ˈplastə/, *n.* plaster made with added fibres of hemp, flax, etc., to strengthen it.

**fibrovascular** /ˌfaɪbroʊˈvæskjələ/, *adj.* (of a conducting strand in a leaf or stem) composed of phloem, xylem, and associated fibres which are frequently in the form of a complete or partial sheath.

**fibster** /ˈfɪbstə/, *n.* →**fibber.**

**fibula** /ˈfɪbjulə, -jələ/, *n., pl.* **-lae** /-li/, **-las.** **1.** *Anat.* the outer and thinner of the two bones of the lower leg, extending from the knee to the ankle. **2.** *Zool.* a corresponding bone (often rudimentary, or ankylosed with the tibia) of the leg or hind limb of other animals. **3.** *Archaeol.* a clasp or brooch, usu. more or less ornamented. [L: clasp, buckle, pin] – **fibular,** *adj.*

**-fic,** an adjective suffix meaning 'making', 'producing', 'causing', as in *colorific, frigorific, horrific, pacific, prolific, soporific.* [L *-ficus* making. Cf. F *-fique*]

**-fication,** a suffix of nouns of action or state corresponding to verbs ending in *-fy,* as in *deification, pacification.* [L *-ficātio,* from *-ficāre.* See -FY]

**fichu** /ˈfiʃu/, *n.* a kind of scarf of muslin, lace, or the like, generally triangular in shape, worn about the neck by women, with the ends drawn together or crossed in front. [F, from *ficher* to throw on in haste]

fichu

**fickle** /ˈfɪkəl/, *adj.* likely to change from caprice, irresolution, or instability. [ME *fikel,* OE *ficol* deceitful, treacherous, akin to *gefic* deceit, *befician* deceive, *ficung* fraud] – **fickleness,** *n.* – **fickly,** *adv.*

**fico** /ˈfikoʊ/, *n., pl.* **-coes.** *Archaic.* the merest trifle. [It., from L *fīcus* fig]

**fict.,** fiction.

**fictile** /ˈfɪktaɪl/, *adj.* **1.** capable of being moulded; plastic. **2.** moulded into form by art. **3.** made of earth, clay, etc., by a potter. **4.** having to do with pottery. [L *fictilis,* from *fingere* form]

**fiction** /ˈfɪkʃən/, *n.* **1.** the branch of literature comprising works of imaginative narration, esp. in prose form. **2.** works of this class, as novels or short stories. **3.** something feigned, invented, or imagined; a made-up story. **4.** *Law.* a statement or supposition which is known to be untrue, made by authority of law to bring a case within the operation of a rule of law. [ME, from L *fictio* a making, fashioning, feigning]

**fictional** /ˈfɪkʃənəl/, *adj.* of, pertaining to, or of the nature of fiction. – **fictionally,** *adv.*

**fictionist** /ˈfɪkʃənəst/, *n.* a writer of fiction.

**fictitious** /fɪkˈtɪʃəs/, *adj.* **1.** counterfeit; false; not genuine: *fictitious names.* **2.** pertaining to or consisting of fiction; imaginatively produced or set forth; created by the imagination: *a fictitious hero.* [L *fictīcius* artificial] – **fictitiously,** *adv.* – **fictitiousness,** *n.*

**fid** /fɪd/, *n.* **1.** *Naut.* a stout piece of wood or metal passed through the heel of a topmast to keep the mast in position. **2.** a conical wooden pin used to open strands of rope in splicing. **3.** a pin used for enlarging holes, stippling and tightening lacing in leatherwork. [orig. uncert.]

**-fid,** an adjective suffix meaning 'divided', 'lobed', as in *bifid, trifid, multifid, pinnatifid.* [L *-fidus,* from *findere* cleave]

**Fid. Def.,** Fidei Defensor.

**fiddle** /ˈfɪdl/, *n., v.,* **-dled, -dling.** *–n.* **1.** a stringed musical instrument of the viol class, esp. a violin. **2.** *Naut.* a device to prevent things from rolling off the table in bad weather. **3. fit as a fiddle,** in excellent health. **4. have a face as long as a fiddle,** to look dismal. **5. on the fiddle,** manipulating or covering up illicit money-making schemes. **6. play second fiddle,** to take a minor part. **7.** *Colloq.* an illegal or underhand transaction or contrivance. *–v.i.* **8.** *Colloq.* to play on the fiddle. **9.** to make aimless movements, as with the hands. **10.** to trifle. **11.** to profit or gain by surreptitious crookedness. *–v.t.* **12.** *Colloq* to play (a tune) on a fiddle. **13.** to trifle: *to fiddle time away.* **14.** to contrive by illegal or underhand means. [ME (and probably OE) *fithele* (see FIDDLER), c. G *Fiedel,* Icel. *fidhla.* Cf. ML *vitula, vidula* VIOL]

**fiddle-back** /ˈfɪdl-bæk/, *n.* **1.** a chair-back shaped like a fiddle. **2.** *Timber Industry Colloq.* the grain in some timbers which has a marking in the shape of a violin. **3.** →**fiddler beetle. 4.** →**brown spider.**

**fiddle bow** /fɪdl ˈboʊ/, *n.* a bow strung with horsehair with which the strings of the violin or a similar instrument are set in vibration.

**fiddle-de-dee** /fɪdl-di-ˈdi/, *interj.* nonsense.

**fiddle-faddle** /ˈfɪdl-fædl/, *n., v.,* **-dled, -dling.** *Colloq. –n.* **1.** nonsense; something trivial. *–v.i.* **2.** to fuss with trifles. [reduplication of FIDDLE, *v.*]

**fiddlehead** /ˈfɪdlhɛd/, *n.* an ornament at the bow of a ship, containing a scroll somewhat like that at the head of a violin.

**fiddler** /ˈfɪdlə/, *n.* **1.** one who plays the fiddle. **2.** one who trifles, makes aimless movements, etc. **3.** *Colloq.* a cheat or rogue. [ME and OE *fithelere,* c. Icel. *fithlari*]

**fiddler beetle** /ˈ– bitl/, *n.* an Australian scarab beetle, *Eupoecila australasiae,* marked with violin pattern on the elytra.

**fiddler crab** /ˈ– kræb/, *n.* any small Indo-Pacific burrowing crab of the genus *Uca,* the male of which has one greatly enlarged claw.

fiddler crab

**fiddlestick** /ˈfɪdlstɪk/, *n.* **1.** a fiddle bow. **2.** a mere nothing.

**fiddlesticks** /ˈfɪdlstɪks/, *interj.* **1.** nonsense. *–n. pl.* **2.** a game of skill, usu. for children, in which small sticks are removed separately from a disordered pile without disturbing the remainder.

**fiddlewood** /ˈfɪdlwʊd/, *n.* **1.** the heavy, hard, durable wood of various West Indian and other trees. **2.** any of the trees.

**fiddley** /ˈfɪdli/, *n., pl.* **fiddlies.** *Colloq.* (formerly) a one pound note (£). Also, **fid.** [rhyming slang, *fiddley-did* quid]

**fiddling** /ˈfɪdlɪŋ/, *adj.* trifling; trivial.

**fiddly** /ˈfɪdli/, *adj. Colloq.* difficult or exacting, as something small done with the hands.

**Fidei Defensor** /ˌfɪdeɪ diˈfɛnsɔ/, *n.* Defender of the Faith, one of the titles of English sovereigns, conferred on Henry VIII by Pope Leo X for his pamphlet attacking Luther, 1521. [L]

**fideism** /fɪˈdeɪˌɪzəm/, *n.* a doctrine which, discounting reason and the intellect, regards faith or revelation as the source of all or some knowledge. [L *fidēs* faith + -ISM]

**fidelity** /fəˈdɛləti/, *n., pl.* **-ties. 1.** the strict observance of promises, duties, etc. **2.** loyalty. **3.** conjugal faithfulness. **4.** strict adherence to truth or fact; (of persons) honesty, truthfulness; (of descriptions, copies, etc.) correspondence with the original. **5.** the ability of an electronic system, as an amplifier, transmitter etc. to reproduce accurately in its output the desired characteristics of its input. **6.** *Bot.* the character of a plant community indicative of the degree with which a species is restricted to a particular kind of community. The five fidelity classes range from 1 for plants which appear accidentally within a community to 5 for plants found completely in only one community. [L *fidēlitas* faithfulness]

**fidget** /ˈfɪdʒət/, *v.i.* **1.** to move about restlessly or impatiently; be uneasy. *–v.t.* **2.** to cause to fidget; make uneasy. *–n.* **3.** (*oft. pl.*) condition of restlessness or uneasiness. **4.** one who fidgets. [frequentative of obs. *fidge,* var. of d. *fitch,* c. Icel. *fikja* move restlessly, be eager]

**fidgety** /ˈfɪdʒəti/, *adj.* restless; uneasy. – **fidgetiness,** *n.*

**fiducial** /fɪˈdjuʃiəl/, *adj.* **1.** *Physics, etc.* accepted as a fixed basis of reference or comparison: *a fiducial point.* **2.** based on or having truth: *fiducial dependence upon God.* [ML *fīdūciālis,* from L *fīdūcia* trust] – **fiducially,** *adv.*

**fiduciary** /fɪˈdjuʃəri/, *adj., n., pl.* **-ries.** *–adj.* **1.** *Law.* of or pertaining to the relation between a fiduciary and his principal: *a fiduciary capacity, a fiduciary duty.* **2.** depending on public confidence for value or currency. *–n.* **3.** *Law.* a person to whom property is entrusted to hold, control, or manage for another.

**fie** /faɪ/, *interj.* an exclamation expressing: **1.** disgust, disapprobation, etc. **2.** humorous pretence of being shocked. [ME *fi*, from OF, from L *fi*, but cf. Icel. *fý*]

**fief** /fif/, *n.* a feoff or fee. [F. See FEE]

**field** /fild/, *n.* **1.** a piece of open or cleared ground, esp. one suitable for pasture or tillage. **2.** a piece of ground devoted to sports or contests. *–n.* **3.** *Sport.* **a.** all the runners in a race. **b.** the runners in a race other than the leaders. **c.** all the participants in any competition. **4.** →**airfield.** **5.** *Horseracing.* all the contestants not individually favoured in betting: *to bet on the field.* **6.** *Hunting.* those following the hounds. **7.** *Cricket, etc.* that part of the ground on which the fielders play. **8.** *Cricket, etc.* the fielders collectively. **9.** *Mil.* **a.** the scene or area of active military operations. **b.** a battlefield. **c.** a battle. **10.** an expanse of anything: *a field of ice.* **11.** any region characterised by a particular feature or product: *a goldfield.* **12.** the surface of a canvas, shield, etc., on which something is portrayed. **13.** (in a flag) the ground of each division. **14.** a sphere, or range of activity, interest, opportunity, study, etc. **15.** a place of investigation, work, etc., away from one's office, laboratory, study, etc., esp. one where basic data and original material are gathered for later analysis. **16.** *Her.* the surface of a shield or escutcheon, or a single section of a quartered shield. **17.** *Physics.* a region of space influenced by some agent: *electric field, magnetic field, gravitation field.* **18.** *Optics.* the entire area visible through or projected by an optical instrument at a given time. **19.** *Elect.* **a.** the main magnetic field of an electric motor or generator. **b.** the structure in a dynamo designed to establish magnetic lines of force in an armature. **20.** *Maths.* a number system which has the same properties relative to the operations of addition, subtraction, multiplication, and division as the number system of all real numbers: *the field of all real numbers.* **21.** *Computers.* a unit of information, as a group of columns on a punched card into which a unit of information is punched. **22.** a mining district separated from other mining districts by a non-mineralised area. **23.** open country: *beasts of the field.* *–v.t.* **24.** *Cricket, etc.* **a.** to stop, or catch, and throw (the ball) as a fielder. **b.** to place (a player or group of players) into the field to play. **25.** to deal or cope with: *he fielded difficult questions.* **26.** to choose (a person or team) to play; to send into a game or on to the field. **27. field a book,** to be a bookmaker (def. 2). *–v.i.* **28.** *Cricket, etc.* **a.** to act as a fielder; field. **b.** to take the field. *–adj.* **29.** *Sport, etc.* of, or happening or contested on, a field rather than a track: *discus, pole vault and long jump are field events.* **30.** *Mil.* of or pertaining to campaign and active combat service as distinguished from service in rear areas or at headquarters: *a field soldier.* **31.** of, pertaining to, or conducted in, the open air or close to primary sources of data or information. [ME and OE *feld*, c. G *Feld*]

**field allowance** /'– əlauəns/, *n.* extra pay for military officers on active service.

**field ambulance** /'– ˌæmbjuləns/, *n.* a medical unit to give emergency treatment on the battlefield.

**field artillery** /'– aˌtɪləri/, *n.* artillery mobile enough to accompany troops in the field.

**field battery** /'– bætəri/, *n.* a battery of field-guns.

**field book** /'– bʊk/, *n.* **1.** a surveyor's book for recording measurements. **2. a.** a book for preserving specimens while in the field. **b.** *Bot., Zool.* a notebook for recording observations in the field. **c.** a guide to the flora or fauna or one aspect of one.

**field capacity** /'– kəˌpæsəti/, *n.* the amount of water held in a soil by capillary action after gravitational water has percolated downward and drained away; expressed as the ratio of the weight of water retained to the weight of dry soil.

**field coil** /'– kɔɪl/, *n.* a coil of wire used for producing a magnetic field as in a dynamo.

**field cricket** /'– krɪkət/, *n.* a shiny black cricket, *Teleogryllus commodus,* which is injurious to crops and pastures.

**field day** /'– deɪ/, *n.* **1.** a day devoted to outdoor activities or sports. **2.** a day on which a hunt meets. **3.** a day when explorations, investigations by a society, etc., are carried on in the field. **4.** *Mil.* **a.** a day on which operations in the field are practised. **b.** a day of display of manoeuvres, etc. **5.** an occasion of unrestricted enjoyment, amusement, success, etc. **6.** a day of brilliant or exciting events.

**field effect transistor,** *n.* →**FET.**

**field emission** /'fild əmɪʃən/, *n.* the emission of electrons from an unheated conductor as a result of an electric field.

**fielder** /'fildə/, *n.* **1.** *Cricket, etc.* a player who fields the ball. **2.** any member of the team which is fielding, as opposed to the one which is batting. **3.** *Horseracing Colloq.* →**bookmaker.**

**field event** /'fild əvɛnt/, *n.* an athletic event which does not take place on a track, as a jumping or throwing event.

**field-glasses** /'fild-glasəz/, *n. pl.* a compact binocular telescope for use out of doors. See **binoculars.**

**field goal** /'fild goʊl/, *n.* (in Rugby Football, etc.) a goal scored by drop-kicking the ball over the opponents' goal during play; drop goal.

**field guidance** /'– gaɪdns/, *n.* guidance of an aeronautical missile to a point within a natural (e.g. gravitational) or artificial (e.g. radio) field by means of the properties of that field.

**field-gun** /'fild-gʌn/, *n.* a cannon mounted on a carriage for service in the field.

**field-gunnery** /'fild-gʌnəri/, *n.* the act or practice of firing field-guns.

**field hockey** /'fild hɒki/, *n.* →**hockey** (as distinguished from *ice hockey*).

**field hospital** /'– hɒspətl/, *n.* a temporary hospital on or near a battlefield.

**field lens** /'– lɛnz/, *n.* the lens in the eyepiece of an optical instrument which is farthest from the eye.

**field madder** /'– mædə/, *n.* a small annual weed with pale mauve flowers, *Sherardia arvensis,* widespread in non-tropical regions.

**field magnet** /'– mægnət/, *n.* a magnet which is used to produce a magnetic field.

**field marshal** /'– maʃəl/, *n.* an officer of the highest military rank in the Australian and certain other armies, and of the second highest rank in the French army.

**fieldmouse** /'fildmaʊs/, *n.* any of various short-tailed mice or voles inhabiting fields and meadows.

**field officer** /'fild ɒfəsə/, *n.* an officer of the rank of major, lieutenant colonel, or colonel.

**field of force,** *n. Physics.* →**field** (def. 17).

**field pea** /'fild pi/, *n.* a legume, *Pisum sativum* var. *arvense,* grown for fodder, or to be ploughed back as green manure.

**field-piece** /'fild-pis/, *n.* →**field-gun.**

**fieldsman** /'fildzmən/, *n., pl.* **-men.** (in cricket) a fielder.

**field study** /'fild stʌdi/, *n.* a planned study depending on first-hand observations and (in sociology) on inquiries and interviews. See **field work.**

**field trial** /'– traɪəl/, *n.* a trial of animals, as hunting dogs, in actual performance in the field.

**field trip** /'– trɪp/, *n.* an investigation away from the classroom, laboratory, office, etc.

**field umpire** /'– ˌʌmpaɪə/, *n.* (in Aus. Rules) the umpire in control of the game; central umpire.

**field winding** /'– waɪndɪŋ/, *n.* the electrically conducting circuit, usu. a number of coils wound on individual poles and connected in series, which produces excitation in a motor or generator.

**field work** /'– wɜk/, *n.* work done in the field, as by a geologist, or a field study, as by a sociologist. **– field worker,** *n.*

**fieldwork** /'fildwɜk/, *n.* a temporary fortification constructed in the field.

**field-wren** /'fild-rɛn/, *n.* a small, brown bird, *Sericornis fuliginosus,* found in varied habitats throughout southern Australia.

**fiend** /find/, *n.* **1.** Satan; the devil. **2.** any evil spirit. **3.** a diabolically cruel or wicked person. **4.** *Colloq.* a person or thing that causes mischief or annoyance. **5.** *Colloq.* one who is devoted or addicted to some game, sport, etc.: *a bridge fiend.* [ME *feend*, OE *fēond*, c. G *Feind*, all orig. ppr. of a verb meaning hate; cf. OE *fēo(ga)n*] **– fiendlike,** *adj.*

**fiendish** /'findɪʃ/, *adj.* **1.** resembling, or characteristic of, a fiend. **2.** diabolically cruel and wicked. **– fiendishly,** *adv.* **– fiendishness,** *n.*

**fierce** /fɪəs/, *adj.*, **fiercer, fiercest.** **1.** wild or vehement in temper, appearance, or action: *fierce animals, fierce looks.* **2.** violent in force, intensity, etc.: *fierce winds.* **3.** furiously eager or intense: *fierce competition.* **4.** *Colloq.* extreme; unreasonable: *the prices are fierce.* [ME *fers, fiers,* from OF, from L *ferus* wild, fierce, cruel] – **fiercely,** *adv.* – **fierceness,** *n.*

**fierce snake** /'– sneɪk/, *n.* →**broad-headed snake.**

**fiery** /'faɪəri/, *adj.*, **fierier, fieriest.** **1.** consisting of, attended with, characterised by, or containing fire: *a fiery discharge.* **2.** intensely hot, as winds, desert sands, etc. **3.** like or suggestive of fire: *a fiery heat, a fiery red.* **4.** flashing or glowing, as the eye. **5.** intensely ardent, impetuous, or passionate: *fiery courage, zeal, speech, etc.* **6.** easily angered; irritable. **7.** inflammable, as gas in a mine. **8.** containing inflammable gas, as a mine. **9.** inflamed, as a tumour or sore. **10.** causing a burning sensation, as liquors or condiments. – **fierily,** *adv.* – **fieriness,** *n.*

**fiery cross** /– 'krɒs/, *n.* **1.** a wooden cross, charred or dipped in blood, formerly sent among Highlanders as a call to arms. **2.** a burning cross, the emblem of several organisations, notably the Ku Klux Klan.

**fiesta** /fi'ɛstə/, *n.* **1.** a religious celebration; a saint's day. **2.** a holiday or festival. [Sp., from L *festus* festive]

**fife** /faɪf/, *n.*, *v.*, **fifed, fifing.** –*n.* **1.** a high-pitched flute much used in military music. –*v.i.* **2.** to play on a fife. [G *Pfeife* PIPE[1]] – **fifer,** *n.*

fife

**fife rail** /'– reɪl/, *n.* a rail round the lower part of a mast of a ship, for holding belaying pins.

**FIFO** /'faɪfoʊ/, *n.* a method of storing and retrieving items from a stack, table or list on the principle that first in is first out. [*F(irst) I(n) F(irst) O(ut)*]

**fifteen** /fɪf'tin/, *n.* **1.** a cardinal number, ten plus five. **2.** a symbol for this number, as 15 or XV. **3.** a set or group of fifteen, as a rugby union team. –*adj.* **4.** amounting to fifteen in number. [ME and OE *fiftene,* from *fif* FIVE + *-tēne* -TEEN]

**fifteenth** /fɪf'tinθ/, *adj.* **1.** next after the fourteenth. **2.** being one of fifteen equal parts. –*n.* **3.** a fifteenth part, esp. of one ($\frac{1}{15}$). **4.** the fifteenth member of a series.

**fifth** /fɪfθ/, *adj.* **1.** next after the fourth. **2.** being one of five equal parts. –*n.* **3.** a fifth part, esp. of one ($\frac{1}{5}$). **4.** the fifth member of a series. **5.** *Music.* **a.** a note on the fifth degree from another note (counted as the first). **b.** the interval between such notes. **c.** the harmonic combination of such notes. [earlier *fift,* ME *fifte,* OE *fīfta;* mod. *-th* from *fourth,* etc.] – **fifthly,** *adv.*

**fifth column** /– 'kɒləm/, *n.* **1.** a body of persons residing in a country who are in sympathy with its enemies, and who are serving enemy interests or are ready to assist an enemy attack. **2.** (originally) Franco sympathisers in Madrid during the civil war (in allusion to a statement in 1936 that the insurgents had four columns marching on Madrid and a fifth column of sympathisers in the city ready to rise and betray it). – **fifth columnist,** *n.*

**fifth position** /– pə'zɪʃən/, *n.* a standing position in ballet, similar to the first, but with the left foot in front, the heel and toe of the left foot adjacent to the toe and heel of the right foot.

**fifth wheel** /– 'wil/, *n.* **1.** a horizontal ring (or segment of a ring) consisting of two bands which slide on each other, placed above the front axle of a carriage and designed to support the forepart of the body while allowing it to turn freely in a horizontal plane. **2.** an extra wheel for a four-wheeled vehicle. **3.** any extra or superfluous thing or person: *like the fifth wheel of a coach.*

**fifty** /'fɪfti/, *n.*, *pl.* **-ties,** *adj.* –*n.* **1.** a cardinal number, ten times five. **2.** a symbol for this number, as 50 or L. **3.** a set of fifty persons or things. **4.** (*pl.*) the numbers from 50 to 59 of a series, esp. with reference to years of age or the years of a century, esp. the 20th. **5.** *Colloq.* →**fifty-fifty.** –*adj.* **6.** amounting to fifty in number. [ME; OE *fiftig,* from *fif* FIVE + *-tig* -TY[1]] – **fiftieth,** *adj.*, *n.*

**fifty-fifty** /fɪfti-'fɪfti/, *Colloq.* –*adv.* **1.** with profits, responsibilities, etc. equally shared. –*adj.* **2.** in equal quantities: *a fifty-fifty mixture.* **3.** of or pertaining to an arrangement, the profits, responsibilities, etc., of which are equally shared. –*n.* **4.** a glass of beer, half old and half new.

**fig** /fɪg/, *n.* **1.** any tree or shrub of the moraceous genus *Ficus,* esp. a small tree, *F. carica,* native to south-western Asia, bearing a turbinate or pear-shaped fruit which is eaten fresh or preserved or dried. **2.** the fruit of such a tree or shrub, or of any related species. **3.** any of various plants having a fruit somewhat resembling the fig. **4.** the value of a fig; the merest trifle; the least bit. **5.** a gesture of contempt; a fico. [ME *fige,* from OF, from OPr. *figa,* from L *ficus*]

**fig.,** **1.** figurative. **2.** figuratively. **3.** figure; figures.

**figbird** /'fɪgbɜd/, *n.* a colourful bird, *Sphecotheres viridis,* of coastal districts of northern and eastern Australia, the male of the species having a bright orange and the female a blue-grey naked facial patch; it eats fruit and berries, as figs, mulberries, bananas, etc.

**fight** /faɪt/, *n.*, *v.*, **fought, fighting.** –*n.* **1.** a battle or combat. **2.** any quarrel, contest, or struggle. **3.** ability or inclination to fight: *there was no fight left in him, to show fight.* **4.** *Navy.* a bulkhead or other screen for the protection of the men during a battle. –*v.i.* **5.** to engage in battle or in single combat; attempt to defeat, subdue, or destroy an adversary. **6.** to contend in any manner; strive vigorously for or against something. –*v.t.* **7.** to contend with or in battle or combat; war against. **8.** to contend with or against in any manner. **9.** to carry on (a battle, duel, etc.). **10.** to maintain (a cause, quarrel, etc.) by fighting or contending. **11.** to make (one's way) by fighting or striving. **12.** to cause or set (a boxer, dog, etc.) to fight. **13.** to manage or manoeuvre (troops, ships, guns, planes, etc.) in battle. **14.** **fight down,** to repress or overcome. **15.** **fight it out,** to struggle till a decisive result is obtained. **16.** **fight off,** to struggle against; drive away. **17.** **fight shy of,** to keep carefully aloof from (a person, affair, etc.). **18.** **fight like Kilkenny cats,** to fight ferociously. [ME; OE *fe(o)htan,* c. G *fechten*] – **fightable,** *adj.*

**fighter** /'faɪtə/, *n.* **1.** one who fights. **2.** *Mil.* an aircraft designed to seek out and destroy enemy aircraft in the air, and to protect bomber aircraft.

**fighter-bomber** /faɪtə-'bɒmə/, *n.* an aircraft that combines the functions of a fighter and a bomber.

**fighting chance** /faɪtɪŋ 'tʃæns/, *n.* a possibility of success.

**fighting cock** /'– kɒk/, *n.* **1.** →**gamecock.** **2.** *Colloq.* a pugnacious person.

**fighting drunk** /– 'drʌŋk/, *adj.* **1.** excessively pugnacious while drunk. –*n.* **2.** a person in such a state.

**fighting fish** /'– fɪʃ/, *n.* a small brilliantly coloured aquarium fish, a species of *Betta,* noted for the fighting habits of the males.

**fighting fit** /– 'fɪt/, *adj.* in very good physical condition.

**fighting top** /'– tɒp/, *n.* (in sailing warships) the fore, main, and mizzen tops, which were platforms built round the lower masts, just above the lower yard. They were fighting stations manned by marksmen armed with muskets, who fired on those on the decks of enemy warships.

**fig leaf** /'fɪg lif/, *n.* **1.** the leaf of a fig tree, esp. in allusion to the first covering of Adam and Eve. **2.** something designed to conceal what is shameful or indecorous.

**figment** /'fɪgmənt/, *n.* **1.** a mere product of the imagination; a pure invention. **2.** a feigned, invented, or imagined story, theory, etc. [L *figmentum* image, fiction, anything made]

**fig-parrot** /'fɪg-pærət/, *n.* any of three species of birds of the family Oppsittidae, which are small and brightly-coloured, and which live in tropical rainforests, feeding chiefly on wild figs.

**figural** /'fɪgjərəl, 'fɪgərəl/, *adj.* of, or pertaining to, figures.

**figurant** /'fɪgjərənt/, *n.* **1.** a ballet dancer who dances only with others in groups or figures. **2.** *Theat.* a minor character on the stage who has little or nothing to say. [F, ppr. of *figurer,* from L *figūrāre* form] – **figurante** /fɪgjə'rɒnt/, *n. fem.*

**figurate** /'fɪgjərət/, *adj.* **1.** of a certain determinate figure or shape. **2.** *Music.* characterised by the use of passing notes or other embellishments; florid. [L *figūrātus,* pp., figured]

**figuration** /fɪgjə'reɪʃən, fɪgə-/, *n.* **1.** the act of shaping into a particular figure. **2.** the resulting figure or shape. **3.** the act of representing figuratively. **4.** a figurative representation.

5. the act of marking or adorning with designs. 6. *Music.* a. the employment of passing notes or other embellishments. b. the figuring of a bass part.

**figurative** /'fɪgjərətɪv, 'fɪgə-/, *adj.* 1. of the nature of or involving a figure of speech, esp. a metaphor; metaphorical; not literal: *a figurative expression.* 2. metaphorically so called: *this remark was a figurative boomerang.* 3. abounding in or addicted to figures of speech. 4. representing by means of a figure or likeness, as in drawing or sculpture. 5. representing by a figure or emblem; emblematic. – **figuratively,** *adv.* – **figurativeness,** *n.*

**figure** /'fɪgə/, *n., v.,* **-ured, -uring.** *–n.* 1. a written symbol other than a letter. 2. a numerical symbol, esp. an Arabic numeral. 3. an amount or value expressed in numbers. 4. (*pl.*) the use of numbers in calculating: *poor at figures.* 5. form or shape, as determined by outlines or exterior surfaces: *round, square, or cubical in figure.* 6. the bodily form or frame: *a slender or graceful figure.* 7. an individual bodily form, or a person with reference to form or appearance: *a tall figure stood in the doorway.* 8. a person as he appears or as presented before the eyes of the world: *political figures.* 9. a character or personage, esp. one of distinction: *a figure in society.* 10. the appearance or impression made by a person, or sometimes a thing. 11. a diagram or pictorial representation in a book, esp. a textbook. 12. a representation, pictorial or sculptured, of something, esp. of the human form. 13. an emblem or type: *the dove is a figure of peace.* 14. *Rhet.* a figure of speech. 15. a device or pattern, as in cloth. 16. a movement, pattern, or series of movements in skating. 17. a distinct movement or division of a dance. 18. *Music.* a short succession of musical notes, either as melody or as a group of chords, which produces a single, complete and distinct impression. 19. *Geom.* a combination of geometrical elements disposed in a particular form or shape: *the circle, square, and polygon are plane figures; the sphere, cube, and polyhedron are solid figures.* 20. *Logic.* any of the forms of the syllogism with respect to the relative position of the middle term. 21. *Optics.* the precise curve required on the surface of an optical element, esp. the mirror of a reflecting telescope. *–v.t.* 22. to compute or calculate. 23. to express in figures. 24. to mark or adorn with figures, or with a pattern or design. 25. to portray by speech or action. 26. to represent or express by a figure of speech. 27. to represent by a pictorial or sculptured figure, a diagram, or the like; picture or depict; trace (an outline, etc.). 28. to conclude, judge, reason, reflect. 29. *Music.* a. to embellish with passing notes or other decorations. b. to write figures above or below (a bass part) to indicate accompanying chords. 30. to solve; understand; make out; (oft. fol. by *out*). *–v.i.* 31. to compute or work with numerical figures. 32. to make a figure or appearance; be conspicuous: *his name figures in the report.* 33. *Colloq.* to be in accordance with expectations or reasonable likelihood. 34. **figure on,** *Colloq.* a. to count or rely on. b. to take into consideration. 35. play a specific role; fit. [ME, from F, from L *figūra* form, shape] – **figureless,** *adj.* – **figurer,** *n.*

**figured** /'fɪgəd/, *adj.* 1. formed or shaped. 2. represented by a pictorial or sculptured figure. 3. ornamented with a device or pattern: *figured silk, figured wallpaper.* 4. *Music.* a. florid. b. having the accompanying chords indicated by figures. 5. figurative, as language.

**figured bass** /– 'beɪs/, *n.* a bass part in a musical score with numbers added under the notes to indicate the chords to be played.

**figurehead** /'fɪgəhɛd/, *n.* 1. a person who is nominally the head of a society, community, etc., but has no real authority or responsibility. 2. *Naut.* an ornamental figure, as a statue or bust, placed over the cutwater of a ship.

**figure of eight,** *n.* 1. a kind of knot made in the shape of a figure 8. 2. a representation in outline of a figure 8 as traced in dancing, ice-skating, etc.

**figure of speech,** *n.* a literary mode of expression, as a metaphor, simile, personification, antithesis, etc., in which words are used out of their literal sense, or out of ordinary locutions, to suggest a picture or image, or for other special effect; a trope.

**figurine** /'fɪgjurin/, *n.* a small ornamental figure of pottery, metalwork, etc.; statuette. [F, from It. *figurina,* diminutive of *figura* FIGURE]

**figwort** /'fɪgwɜt/, *n.* any of numerous, usu. coarse and strong-smelling herbs of the genus *Scrophularia,* found in temperate regions.

**Fiji** /fi'dʒi/, *n.* a country in the South Pacific, north of New Zealand. – **Fijian,** *adj., n.*

**filafil** /fə'lʌfəl, -'læf-/, *n.* →**felafel.**

**filagree** /'fɪləgri/, *n., adj., v.t.* →**filigree.**

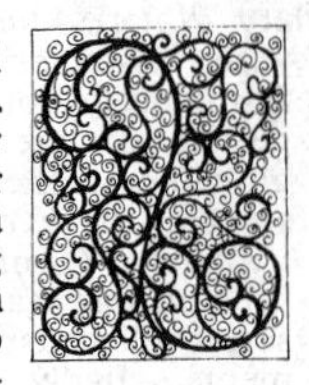
filigree

**filament** /'fɪləmənt/, *n.* 1. a very fine thread or threadlike structure; a fibre or fibril. 2. a single element of textile fibre (as silk), or mechanically produced fibre (as rayon or nylon). 3. *Bot.* a. the stalklike portion of a stamen, supporting the anther. b. a long slender cell or series of attached cells, as in some algae, fungi, etc. 4. *Ornith.* the barb of a down feather. 5. *Elect.* (in an incandescent lamp) the threadlike conductor in the bulb which is raised to incandescence by the passage of current. 6. *Electron.* the heating element (sometimes also acting as a cathode) of a radio valve. It resembles an incandescent electric-lamp filament. 7. *Pathol.* a threadlike substance sometimes contained in urine, or in fluids of inflammation. [LL *filāmentum,* from L *filum* thread]

**filamentary** /fɪlə'mɛntri, -təri/, *adj.* pertaining to or of the nature of a filament or filaments.

**filamentous** /fɪlə'mɛntəs/, *adj.* 1. composed of or containing filaments. 2. resembling a filament. 3. bearing filaments. 4. pertaining to filaments.

**filar** /'faɪlə/, *adj.* 1. of or pertaining to a thread or threads. 2. having threads or the like. [L *filum* thread + -AR[1]]

**filaria** /fə'lɛəriə/, *n., pl.* **-lariae** /-'lɛərii/. any of the slender, threadlike nematode worms (family Filariidae), parasitic as adults in the blood or tissues of vertebrates, and developing as larvae in insects, etc., which become infected by sucking the embryos from the blood. [NL, from L *filum* thread]

**filarial** /fə'lɛəriəl/, *adj.* 1. belonging to the genus *Filaria* and allied genera of the family Filariidae. 2. pertaining to infection by filariae: *filarial disease.*

**filariasis** /fɪlə'raɪəsəs, fəlɛəri'eɪsəs/, *n.* the presence of filarial worms in the blood and lymph channels, in the lymph glands, and other tissues. [NL. See FILARIA, -ASIS]

**filasse** /fə'læs/, *n.* any of various vegetable fibres, other than cotton, processed for manufacture into yarn.

**filature** /'fɪlətʃə/, *n.* 1. the act of forming into threads. 2. a reel for drawing off silk from cocoons. 3. the reeling of silk from cocoons. 4. an establishment for reeling silk. [F, from LL *filāre* spin]

**filbert** /'fɪlbət/, *n.* 1. the thick-shelled, edible nut of certain cultivated varieties of hazel, esp. of *Corylus avellana.* 2. a tree or shrub bearing such nuts. [ME; short for *filbert nut,* nut of (St) Philibert, so called because ripe about this saint's day, 22 August]

**filch** /fɪltʃ/, *v.t.* to steal (esp. something of small value); pilfer. [orig. unknown] – **filcher,** *n.*

**file**[1] /faɪl/, *n., v.,* **filed, filing.** *–n.* 1. any device, as a cabinet, in which papers, etc., are arranged or classified for convenient reference. 2. a collection of papers so arranged or classified; any orderly collection of papers, etc. 3. *Computers.* a memory storage device, other than a core store, as disc file, magnetic tape file, etc. 4. a string or wire on which papers are strung for preservation and reference. 5. **on file,** on or in a file, or in orderly arrangement for convenient reference, as papers. 6. a line of persons or things arranged one behind another, esp. a group of soldiers moving in formation; Indian file; single file. 7. one of the vertical lines of squares on a chessboard. 8. a list or roll. *–v.t.* 9. to place in a file. 10. to arrange (papers, records, official documents, etc.) methodically for preservation and convenient reference. 11. to place on record, register (a petition, etc.). 12. *Law.* to bring (a suit) before a court of law. 13. *Journalism.* to send (newspaper copy) to a newspaper or news agency. *–v.i.* 14. to march in a file or line, one after another, as soldiers. [representing F *fil* thread, string (from L *filum*) and F *file* file, row, from L *filum* thread] – **filer,** *n.*

**file**[2] /faɪl/, *n., v.,* **filed, filing.** *–n.* 1. a metal (usu. steel) tool of varying size and form, with numerous small cutting ridges or teeth on its surface, for smoothing or cutting metal and other substances. *–v.t.* **2.** to reduce, smooth, cut, or remove with or as with a file. [ME; d. OE *fīl,* replacing OE *fēol,* c. G *Feile*] **– filer,** *n.*

**filefish** /ˈfaɪlfɪʃ/, *n., pl.* **-fishes,** (*esp. collectively*) **-fish. 1.** any of various fishes with rough, granular skin, as *Balistoides conspicillum,* found in tropical waters of northern Australia. **2.** →**triggerfish.**

**filet** /ˈfɪlət, ˈfɪleɪ/, *n., v.t.* →**fillet** (defs 6, 10).

**filet lace** /ˈ– leɪs/, *n.* a square mesh net or lace, originally knotted by hand but now copied by machine.

**filet mignon** /fɪleɪ ˈmɪnjɒn/, *n.* a small, tender fillet of beef.

**filial** /ˈfɪljəl, -iəl/, *adj.* **1.** pertaining to or befitting a son or daughter: *filial obedience.* **2.** bearing the relation of a child to a parent. **3.** *Genetics.* indicating the sequence of generations from an original parent. First filial is shown as $F_1$, second filial as $F_2$, etc. [LL *fīliālis,* from L *fīlius* son, *fīlia* daughter + *-ālis* -AL[1]] **– filially,** *adv.* **– filialness,** *n.*

**filiate** /ˈfɪlieɪt/, *v.t.,* **-ated, -ating. 1.** →**affiliate. 2.** *Law.* to determine judicially the paternity of, as a bastard child. [LL *fīliātus,* pp. of *fīliāre* have a child, from L *fīlius* son, *fīlia* daughter. Cf. AFFILIATE]

**filiation** /fɪliˈeɪʃən/, *n.* **1.** the fact of being the child of a certain parent. **2.** descent as if from a parent; derivation. **3.** *Law.* the judicial determination of the paternity of a child, especially of an illegitimate one. **4.** the relation of one thing to another from which it is derived. **5.** the act of filiating. **6.** the state of being filiated. **7.** an affiliated branch, as of a society. [LL *fīliātio,* from *fīliāre* have a child]

**filibeg** /ˈfɪləbɛg/, *n.* the kilt or plaited skirt worn by Scottish Highlanders. Also, **fillibeg, philibeg.** [Gaelic *feileadh-beag* small kilt (as distinguished from the large one formerly worn)]

**filibuster** /ˈfɪləbʌstə/, *n.* **1.** the use of obstructive tactics, such as making prolonged speeches or using irrelevant material, in order to delay legislative action. **2.** an instance of the use of such tactics. **3.** an irregular military adventurer; a freebooter or buccaneer. **4.** one who engages in an unlawful military expedition into a foreign country to inaugurate or to aid a revolution. *–v.i.* **5.** to impede legislation by using obstructive tactics, esp. by making long speeches. **6.** to act as a freebooter, buccaneer, or irregular military adventurer. [Sp. *filibustero,* from D *vrijbuiter* freebooter] **– filibusterer** /fɪləˈbʌstərə/, *n.* **– filibusterism** /fɪləˈbʌstərɪzəm/, *n.* **– filibusterous** /fɪləˈbʌstərəs/, *adj.*

**filicide** /ˈfɪləsaɪd/, *n.* **1.** one who kills his son or daughter. **2.** the act of killing one's son or daughter. [L *fīlius* son, *fīlia* daughter + -CIDE] **– filicidal** /fɪləˈsaɪdəl/, *adj.*

**filiform** /ˈfɪləfɔm, fɪlə-/, *adj.* threadlike; filamentous. [L *fīlum* thread + -I- + -FORM]

**filigree** /ˈfɪləgri/, *n., adj., v.,* **-greed, -greeing.** *–n.* **1.** ornamental work of fine wires, esp. lacy jewellers' work of scrolls and arabesques. **2.** anything very delicate or fanciful. *–adj.* **3.** composed of or resembling filigree. *–v.t.* **4.** to adorn with or form into filigree. Also, **filagree, fillagree.** [var. of *filigrane,* from F, from It. *filigrana.* See FILE[1], GRAIN]

**filigreed** /ˈfɪləgrid/, *adj.* having filigree decorations.

**filing cabinet** /ˈfaɪlɪŋ kæbnət/, *n.* a case with sliding drawers designed to hold filing cards, collections of papers or documents, etc.

**filing card** /ˈ– kad/, *n.* a rectangular piece of thin cardboard on which information may be written and kept for convenient reference along with other such cards in a suitable filing system.

**filing clerk** /ˈ– klak/, *n.* an employee in an office who is chiefly concerned with the filing of letters, records, etc.

**filings** /ˈfaɪlɪŋz/, *n.pl.* particles removed by a file.

**Filipine** /ˈfɪləpin, ˈfɪləpaɪn/, *adj.* →**Philippine.**

**Filipino** /fɪləˈpinoʊ/, *n., pl.* **-nos** /-noʊz/, *adj.* *–n.* **1.** a native of the Philippine Islands, esp. a member of a Christianised native tribe. *–adj.* **2.** →**Philippine.** [Sp., from *Felipe* Philip]

**fill** /fɪl/, *v.t.* **1.** to make full; put as much as can be held into. **2.** to occupy to the full capacity: *water filled the basin, the crowd filled the hall.* **3.** to supply to fullness or plentifully: *to fill a house with furniture, to fill the heart with joy.* **4.** to satisfy, as food does. **5.** to put, as contents, into a receptacle. **6.** to be plentiful throughout: *fish filled the rivers.* **7.** to extend throughout; pervade completely: *the perfume filled the room.* **8.** to furnish (a vacancy or office) with an occupant or incumbent. **9.** to occupy and perform the duties of (a position, post, etc.). **10.** to execute (a business order). **11.** to supply (a blank space) with written matter, decorative work, etc. **12.** to meet (requirements, etc.) satisfactorily: *the book fills a long-felt want.* **13.** to make up or compound (a medical prescription). **14.** to stop up or close: *to fill a tooth or a crevice.* **15.** *Naut.* **a.** to distend (a sail) by pressure of the wind so as to impart headway to a vessel. **b.** to brace (a yard) so that the sail will catch the wind on its after side. **16.** to adulterate: *filled soaps.* **17.** *Civ. Eng.* to build up with fill (def. 24): *to fill low ground with gravel, sand, or earth.* *–v.i.* **18.** to become full: *the hall filled rapidly, her eyes filled with tears.* **19.** to become distended, as sails with the wind. **20.** to fill a cup or other receptacle; pour out drink, as into a cup. *–v.* **21.** Some special verb phrases are:

**fill away,** *Naut.* **1.** to fall off the wind and proceed on a board. **2.** to brace the yards, so that sails which have been aback will stand full.

**fill in, 1.** to fill (a hole, hollow, blank, etc.) with something put in. **2.** to complete (a document, design, etc.) by filling blank spaces. **3.** to put in or insert so as to fill: *to fill in omitted names.* **4.** to occupy, spend (time). **5.** to act as a substitute, replace.

**fill out, 1.** to distend (sails, etc.). **2.** to become larger, fuller, grow fat, expand, as the figure, etc. **3.** to complete the details of (a plan, design, etc.).

**fill the bill,** *Colloq.* to satisfy the requirements of the case; be or do what is wanted.

**fill up,** to fill completely.

*–n.* **22.** a full supply; enough to satisfy want or desire: *to eat one's fill.* **23.** an amount of something sufficient for filling; a charge. **24.** a mass of earth, stones, etc., used to fill a hollow, etc. **25.** *Music.* a solo drum-kit pattern used to end one musical phrase and act as an upbeat to the next. [ME *fille(n),* OE *fyllan,* c. G *füllen;* from FULL[1]]

**fillagree** /ˈfɪləgri/, *adj., v.t.* →**filigree.**

**filled gold** /ˈfɪld goʊld/, *n.* a gold plate mechanically welded to a backing of brass or other base metal and rolled, in which the gold is $\frac{1}{20}$ or more of the total weight.

**filler** /ˈfɪlə/, *n.* **1.** one who or that which fills. **2.** a thing or quantity of a material put in to fill something, or to fill in a gap. **3.** a liquid, paste, or paintlike substance used to fill in pores or cracks before painting or varnishing. **4.** a solid substance added to plastics, paints and elastomers either to modify their properties or reduce their cost; an extender. **5.** the tobacco forming the body of a cigar, as distinguished from the wrapper. **6.** *Journalism.* something used to fill a vacant space. **7.** *Bldg Trades, etc.* a sheet or plate inserted in a gap between two structural members. **8.** an implement used in filling, as a funnel. [FILL + -ER[1]]

**fillet** /ˈfɪlət/, *n.* **1.** a narrow band of ribbon or the like bound round the head or hair. **2.** any narrow strip, as wood or metal. **3.** a strip of any material used for binding. **4.** *Bookbinding.* **a.** a decorative line impressed on a book's cover, usu. at the top and bottom of the back. **b.** a rolling tool for impressing such lines. **5.** *Archit., etc.* **a.** a relatively narrow moulding with a plane face, as between other mouldings. **b.** the flat top of the ridge between two flutes of a column. **6.** *Cookery.* **a.** a strip or long (flat or thick) piece of fish, esp. such as is easily detached from the bones or adjoining parts. **b.** the standard cut of beef or pork which is the portion from the underside of the rump and sirloin, containing little fat. **7.** *Anat.* (formerly) a band of fibres, esp. of white nerve fibres in the brain; lemniscus. **8.** a raised rim or ridge, as a ring on the muzzle of a gun. *–v.t.* **9.** to bind or adorn with or as with a fillet. **10.** *Cookery.* **a.** to cut or prepare (meat or fish) as a fillet. **b.** to cut fillets from. Also, **filet** for defs 6, 10. [ME *filet,* from F, diminutive of *fil* thread, string, from L *fīlum*]

**fillibeg** /ˈfɪləbɛg/, *n.* →**filibeg.**

**fill-in** /ˈfɪl-ɪn/, *n.* **1.** a substitute; stopgap. *–adj.* **2.** temporary: *a fill-in job during the summer vacation.*

**filling** /ˈfɪlɪŋ/, *n.* **1.** that which is put in to fill something: *the filling of a pie.* **2.** a substance in plastic form, as cement, amalgam, or gold foil, used to close a cavity in a tooth. **3.** the act of one who or that which fills; a making or becoming full.

**filling station** /ˈ– steɪʃən/, *n.* →**service station.**

**fillip** /ˈfɪləp/, *v.t.* **1.** to strike with the nail of a finger snapped from the end of the thumb. **2.** to tap or strike smartly. **3.** to drive by or as by a fillip. *–v.i.* **4.** to make a fillip with the fingers. *–n.* **5.** the act or movement of filliping; a smart tap or stroke. **6.** anything that tends to rouse, excite, or revive; a stimulus. [apparently imitative. Cf. FLIP[1]]

**fillister** /ˈfɪləstə/, *n.* a rebates or groove, as one on a window sash to hold the glass and putty.

**fillister plane** /ˈ– pleɪn/, *n.* a plane for cutting rebates or grooves.

**fill-up** /ˈfɪl-ʌp/, *n.* the act of filling up, charging, or replenishing, as the petrol tank of a motor car with petrol.

**filly** /ˈfɪli/, *n., pl.* **-lies. 1.** a female horse not past its fourth birthday; a young mare. **2.** *Colloq.* a girl. [Scand.; cf. Icel. *fylja* female foal. See FOAL]

**film** /fɪlm/, *n.* **1.** a thin layer or coating. **2.** a thin sheet of any material. **3.** *Photog.* **a.** the sensitive coating, as of gelatine and silver bromide, on a photographic plate. **b.** a strip or roll of cellulose nitrate or cellulose acetate composition coated with a sensitive emulsion, used instead of a photographic plate. **4.** *Films.* **a.** a film strip containing consecutive pictures or photographs of objects in motion presented to the eye, esp. by being thrown on to a screen by a projector so rapidly as to give the illusion that the objects or actors are moving. **b.** such a film strip representing an event, play, story, etc. **c.** (*pl.*) such film strips, or the stories, etc., contained on them, collectively. **5.** a thin skin or membrane. **6.** a delicate web of filaments or fine threads. *–v.t.* **7.** to cover with a film, or thin skin or pellicle. **8.** *Films.* **a.** to photograph with a film camera. **b.** to reproduce in the form of a film or films: *to film a novel.* *–v.i.* **9.** to become covered by a film. **10.** *Films.* **a.** to be reproduced in a film, esp. in a specific manner: *this story films easily.* **b.** to direct, make, or otherwise engage in the production of films. [ME *fylme,* OE *filmen;* akin to FELL[4]]

**filmable** /ˈfɪlməbəl/, *adj.* (of a novel, play, etc.) suitable for filming.

**film badge** /ˈfɪlm bædʒ/, *n.* a badge containing a masked photographic film, worn by workers who may come in contact with ionising radiation, and used to indicate the extent of their exposure to these radiations.

**film clip** /ˈ– klɪp/, *n.* a short extract from a film, usu. shown as part of promotional material.

**filmic** /ˈfɪlmɪk/, *adj.* of, or like, a cinema film.

**film library** /fɪlm ˈlaɪbri/, *n.* an organised collection of films for private or public use, including reproductions of printed materials on film, slides, etc.

**filmset** /ˈfɪlmsɛt/, *v.,* **-set, -setting,** *adj.* *Print.* *–v.t.* **1.** to set (type matter) photographically, without the use of hot metal. *–adj.* **2.** set photographically. **– filmsetter,** *n.*

**filmsetting** /ˈfɪlmsɛtɪŋ/, *n.* →**photocomposition.**

**film star** /ˈfɪlm sta/, *n.* a leading actor or actress who is or has been the star of many films.

**film strip** /ˈ– strɪp/, *n.* a length of film containing a series of transparencies for projection on to a screen.

**film theatre** /ˈ– θɪətə/, *n.* →**cinema.**

**filmy** /ˈfɪlmi/, *adj.,* **filmier, filmiest.** of the nature of, resembling, or covered with a thin layer or film. **– filmily,** *adv.* **– filminess,** *n.*

**filmy fern** /– ˈfɜn/, *n.* any fern of the family Hymenophyllaceae found in tropical and temperate regions.

**filoplume** /ˈfɪləplum, ˈfaɪlə-/, *n.* a feather with a shaft but few or no barbs.

**filose** /ˈfaɪlous/, *adj.* **1.** threadlike. **2.** ending in a threadlike process. [L *filum* thread + -OSE[2]]

**filter** /ˈfɪltə/, *n.* **1.** any device in which cloth, paper, porous porcelain, or a layer of charcoal or sand, is held and through which liquid is passed to remove suspended impurities or to recover solids. **2.** any of various analogous devices, as for removing dust from air, impurities from tobacco smoke, or eliminating certain kinds of light rays. **3.** *Colloq.* a filter tip. **4.** *Photog.* a screen of dyed gelatine or glass used to control the rendering of colour or to diminish the intensity of light. **5.** *Physics.* a device for selecting waves or currents of certain frequencies only out of an aggregation including others. *–v.t.* **6.** to remove by the action of a filter. **7.** to act as a filter for. **8.** to pass through, or as through, a filter. *–v.i.* **9.** to percolate; pass through or as through a filter. **10.** (of a line of motor vehicles) to move in a certain direction independently of the general flow of traffic. [ME *filtre,* from OF, from ML *feltrum* felt (used as a filter), from Gmc; cf. FELT[2]] **– filterer,** *n.*

**filterable** /ˈfɪltərəbəl/, *adj.* **1.** capable of being filtered. **2.** *Bacteriol.* capable of passing through bacteria-retaining filters: *a filterable virus.* Also, **filtrable** /ˈfɪltrəbəl/.

**filter bed** /ˈfɪltə bɛd/, *n.* a pond or tank having a false bottom covered with sand, and serving to filter river or pond waters.

**filter cloth** /ˈ– klɒθ/, *n.* a coarse heavy material used in filtering.

**filter paper** /ˈ– peɪpə/, *n.* pure cellulose paper used in filtering.

**filter press** /ˈ– prɛs/, *n.* an apparatus used for filtering on an industrial scale, consisting of a series of metal or wooden frames covered with filter cloth between which the liquid to be filtered is pumped.

**filter tip** /ˈ– tɪp/, *n.* **1.** a cigarette or cigar tip with a means of filtering the smoke. **2.** a cigarette or cigar provided with such a tip. **– filter-tipped,** *adj.*

**filth** /fɪlθ/, *n.* **1.** foul matter; offensive or disgusting dirt. **2.** foul condition. **3.** moral impurity, corruption, or obscenity. **4.** foul language. [ME; OE *fȳlth,* from *fūl* foul]

**filthy** /ˈfɪlθi/, *adj.,* **filthier, filthiest. 1.** foul with, characterised by, or having the nature of filth; disgustingly dirty. **2.** vile; obscene. **3.** (as a general epithet of strong condemnation) highly offensive or objectionable: *filthy lucre.* **4.** *Colloq.* very unpleasant: *filthy weather.* *–adv.* **5. filthy rich,** very rich. **– filthily,** *adv.* **– filthiness,** *n.*

**filtrate** /ˈfɪltreɪt/, *v.,* **-trated, -trating,** *n.* *–v.t., v.i.* **1.** →**filter.** *–n.* **2.** liquid which has been passed through a filter. **– filtration** /fɪlˈtreɪʃən/, *n.*

**filum** /ˈfaɪləm/, *n., pl.* **-la** /-lə/. a threadlike structure or part; a filament. [L]

**fimble** /ˈfɪmbəl/, *n.* the male or staminate plant of hemp, which is harvested before the female or pistillate plant. [LG *fimel,* from F (*chanvre*) *femelle,* lit., female hemp]

**fimbria** /ˈfɪmbriə/, *n., pl.* **-briae** /-brii/. (*oft. pl.*) a fringe or fringed border. [LL: border, fringe] **– fimbrial,** *adj.*

**fimbriate** /ˈfɪmbriət, -eɪt/, *adj.* *Bot., Zool.* fringed; bordered with hairs or with filiform processes. Also, **fimbriated.**

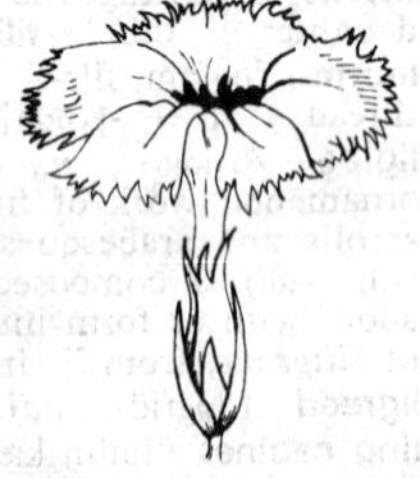

fimbriate petals

**fimbriation** /fɪmbriˈeɪʃən/, *n.* *Bot., Zool.* **1.** fimbriate or fringed condition. **2.** a fringe or fringelike part.

**fimbrillate** /ˈfɪmbrələt, -eɪt/, *adj.* *Bot., Zool.* bordered with, or having, a small or fine fringe. [NL *fimbrilla* (diminutive of LL *fimbria* FIMBRIA) + -ATE[1]]

**fin** /fɪn/, *n., v.,* **finned, finning.** *–n.* **1.** a membranous wing-like or paddle-like organ attached to any of various parts of the body of fishes and certain other aquatic animals, used for propulsion, steering, or balancing. **2.** *Naut.* **a.** a fin-shaped plane on a submarine or boat. **b.** a fin keel. **c.** a submarine conning tower. **3.** Also, *Chiefly U.S.,* **vertical stabiliser.** *Aeron.* any of certain small, subsidiary planes on an aircraft, in general placed parallel to the plane of symmetry. **4.** a small, fin-shaped attachment on the rear underside of a surfboard. **5.** →**flipper. 6.** an external rib for cooling, used on radiators, the cylinders of air-cooled internal-combustion engines, etc. **7.** any part, as of a mechanism, resembling a fin. **8.** *Colloq.* the arm or hand. *–v.t.* **9.** to cut off the fins from (a fish); carve or cut up, as a chub. *–v.i.* **10.** to move the fins; lash the water with the fins, as a whale when dying. [ME *finne,* OE *finn,* c. D *vin,* LG *finne.* Cf. L *pinna*] **– finless,** *adj.* **– finlike,** *adj.*

**fin.**, financial.

**finable** /ˈfaɪnəbəl/, *adj.* →**fineable.**

**finagle** /fəˈneɪgəl/, *v.*, **-gled, -gling.** *Colloq.* *–v.i.* **1.** to practise deception or fraud. *–v.t.* **2.** to trick or cheat (a person); get (something) by guile or trickery. **3.** to wangle: *to finagle free tickets.* [var. of *fainaigue;* orig. uncert.] – **finagler,** *n.*

**final** /ˈfaɪnəl/, *adj.* **1.** pertaining to or coming at the end; last in place, order, or time. **2.** ultimate: *the final goal.* **3.** conclusive or decisive. **4.** *Law.* **a.** precluding further controversy on the questions passed upon: *the decision of the Arbitration Court is final.* **b.** determining completely the rights of the parties, so that no further decision upon the merits of the issues is necessary: *a final judgment or decree.* **5.** constituting the end or purpose: *a final result.* **6.** pertaining to or expressing end or purpose: *a final clause.* **7.** *Phonet.* coming at the end of a word or syllable: *'t' is final in the word 'fit'.* *–n.* **8.** that which is last; that which forms an end or termination of a series. **9.** (*oft. pl.*) something final, as a decisive game or contest after preliminary ones. **10.** →**preliminary final.** **11.** (*pl.*) an examination at the end of a course. **12.** the last edition of a newspaper during the day. **13.** *Music.* the tonic note of a church mode. [ME, from LL *fīnālis,* from L *fīnis* end]

**final causes** /– ˈkɔzəz/, *n.pl.* the philosophical doctrine that the course of events in the universe is explicable mainly by reference to ends or purposes by which all events are controlled.

**finale** /fəˈnali/, *n.* **1.** the last piece, division, or movement of a concert, opera, or musical composition. **2.** the concluding part of any performance, course of proceedings, etc. [It., adj. used as n. See FINAL]

**finalise** /ˈfaɪnəlaɪz/, *v.t.*, **-lised, -lising.** to put into final form; conclude, settle. Also, **finalize.** – **finalisation** /faɪnəlaɪˈzeɪʃən/, *n.*

**finalism** /ˈfaɪnəlɪzəm/, *n.* the philosophical doctrine that nothing exists or was made except for a determinate end; the doctrine of final causes; teleology. – **finalistic** /faɪnəˈlɪstɪk/, *adj.*

**finalist** /ˈfaɪnələst/, *n.* one who is entitled to take part in the final trial or round, as of an athletic contest.

**finality** /faɪˈnæləti/, *n.*, *pl.* **-ties.** **1.** the state, quality, or fact of being final; conclusiveness or decisiveness. **2.** something that is final; a final act, utterance, etc.

**finally** /ˈfaɪnəli/, *adv.* **1.** at the final point or moment; in the end. **2.** in a final manner; conclusively or decisively.

**finance** /ˈfaɪnæns, fəˈnæns/, *n.*, *v.*, **-nanced, -nancing.** *–n.* **1.** the management of public revenues; the conduct or transaction of money matters generally, esp. such as affect the public, as in the fields of banking and investment. **2.** (*pl.*) pecuniary resources, as of a sovereign, state, company, or an individual; revenue. *–v.t.* **3.** to supply with means of payment; provide capital for; to obtain or furnish credit for. **4.** to manage financially. *–v.i.* **5.** to conduct financial operations; manage finances. [ME, from OF: ending, payment, revenue, from OF *finer* finish, settle, pay, from *fin* end, settlement. See FINE²]

**finance bill** /ˈ– bɪl/, *n.* a bill or act of a legislature to obtain public funds.

**finance company** /ˈ– kʌmpəni/, *n.* a company which arranges loans.

**finance editor** /ˈ– ɛdətə/, *n.* (on a newspaper, etc.) the editor in charge of the financial and commercial news.

**financial** /fəˈnænʃəl, faɪ-/, *adj.* **1.** pertaining to monetary receipts and expenditures; pertaining or relating to money matters; pecuniary: *financial operations.* **2.** of or pertaining to those commonly engaged in dealing with money and credit. **3.** *Colloq.* having ready money: *to be financial.* – **financially,** *adv.*

**financial year** /– ˈjɪə/, *n.* any twelve-monthly period at the end of which a government, company, etc., balances its accounts and determines its financial condition. Also, **fiscal year.**

**financier** /fəˈnænsiə, faɪ-/, *n.* **1.** one skilled or engaged in financial operations, whether public, corporate, or individual. *–v.t.* **2.** to finance. [F, from *finance* FINANCE]

**finback** /ˈfɪnbæk/, *n.* any whalebone whale of the genus *Balaenoptera* having a prominent dorsal fin, as *B. musculus* of the northern Atlantic, or *B. physalus,* which attains a length of 18 or even 24 metres; a rorqual. Also, **finback whale, finner, finwhale.**

**finch** /fɪntʃ/, *n.* **1.** any of numerous small, often strikingly coloured passerine birds of the family Estrildidae, the grass-finches, as the **red-browed finch,** *Estrilda temporalis,* of eastern Australia. **2.** any of various small, passerine birds of the family Fringillidae, including the buntings, linnets, crossbills, etc., many having heavy, conical, seed-cracking bills and some of which, as the goldfinch and the greenfinch, have been introduced into Australia. **3.** →**weaver-bird.** [ME; OE *finc,* c. D *vink,* G *Fink*]

finch

**find** /faɪnd/, *v.*, **found, finding,** *n.* *–v.t.* **1.** to come upon by chance; meet. **2.** to learn, attain, or obtain by search or effort. **3.** to discover. **4.** to recover (something lost). **5.** to gain or regain the use of: *to find one's tongue.* **6.** to succeed in attaining; gain by effort: *to find safety in flight, to find occasion for revenge.* **7.** to discover by experience or to perceive: *to find something to be true, to find something new to be developing.* **8.** to ascertain by study or calculation: *to find the sum of several numbers.* **9.** *Law.* **a.** to determine after judicial inquiry: *to find a person guilty.* **b.** to pronounce as an official act (an indictment, verdict, or judgment). **10.** to provide or furnish. **11. find fault,** to find cause of blame or complaint; express dissatisfaction. **12. find oneself,** to discover one's true vocation; learn one's abilities and how to use them. **13. find one's feet, a.** to be able to stand and walk. **b.** to be able to act independently without the help of others. **14. find out, a.** to discover in the course of time or experience; discover by search or inquiry; ascertain by study. **b.** to detect, as in an offence; discover the actions or character of; discover or detect (a fraud, imposture, etc.). **c.** to discover the identity of (a person). *–v.i.* **15.** to determine an issue after judicial inquiry: *the jury found for the plaintiff.* **16.** *Hunting.* to come upon game. *–n.* **17.** the act of finding; a discovery. **18.** something found; a discovery, esp. a valuable or gratifying discovery: *our cook was a real find.* [ME *finde(n),* OE *findan,* c. G *finden*] – **findable,** *adj.*

**finder** /ˈfaɪndə/, *n.* **1.** one who or that which finds. **2.** *Photog.* →**viewfinder.** **3.** *Astron.* a small telescope attached to a larger for the purpose of finding an object more readily. **4. finders keepers,** (an expression said by someone who has found something, claiming his right to keep it).

**fin de siècle** /fæn də siˈɛɪklə/, *n.* **1.** end of the century. **2.** a period comparatively free from social and moral traditions or conventions. [F]

**fin-de-siècle** /fæn-də-siˈeɪklə/, *adj.* **1.** of or pertaining to the period at the close of a century, esp. the end of the 19th century. **2.** decadent. [F]

**finding** /ˈfaɪndɪŋ/, *n.* **1.** the act of one who or that which finds; discovery. **2.** that which is found or ascertained. **3.** *Law.* a decision or verdict after judicial inquiry. **4.** (*pl.*) tools, materials, etc., used by artisans.

**fine**¹ /faɪn/, *adj.*, **finer, finest,** *adv.*, *v.*, **fined, fining.** *–adj.* **1.** of the highest or of very high grade or quality. **2.** free from imperfections or impurities. **3. a.** (of weather) sunny. **b.** *Meteorol.* (of weather) without rain. **4.** choice, excellent, or admirable: *a fine sermon.* **5.** consisting of minute particles: *fine sand.* **6.** very thin or slender: *fine thread.* **7.** keen or sharp, as a tool. **8.** *Naut.* (of a hull form) of a low block coefficient with pointed bow and stern (opposed to *bull*). **9.** delicate in texture: *fine linen.* **10.** delicately fashioned. **11.** highly skilled or accomplished: *a fine musician.* **12.** characterised by or affecting refinement or elegance: *a fine lady.* **13.** trained down to the proper degree, as an athlete. **14.** polished or refined: *fine manners.* **15.** ornate or elegant: *fine writing.* **16.** delicate or subtle: *a fine distinction.* **17.** showy or smart; smartly dressed. **18.** good-looking or handsome. **19.** (of gold, silver, etc.) having a high proportion of pure metal, or having the proportion as specified. **20.** *Cricket.* towards fine leg. **21.** in good health; well: *I'm feeling fine.* *–adv.* **22.** *Colloq.* in a fine manner; excellently or very well;

elegantly; delicately; with nicety. **23.** *Billiards.* in such a way that the driven ball barely touches the object ball in passing. *–v.i.* **24.** to become fine or finer. *–v.t.* **25.** to make fine or finer. **26.** (of weather) to become fine (fol. by *up*). **27.** to clarify (wines or spirits) by filtration. *–n.* **28.** (*pl.*) the extremely small particles which may be present in a powder. **29.** *Mining.* **a.** very small material produced in breaking large lumps, as of ore or coal. **b.** in general, the smallest particles of coal or mineral in any classification process or sample of ore material. [ME *fin,* from OF, from Common Rom. *fino,* backformation from L *fīnīre* FINISH]

**fine**[2] /faɪn/, *n., v.,* **fined, fining.** *–n.* **1.** a sum of money exacted as a penalty for an offence or dereliction; a mulct. **2.** *Law.* **a.** a fee paid by a feudal tenant to the landlord, as on the renewal of tenure. **b.** a sum of money paid by a tenant on the commencement of his tenancy so that his rent may be small or nominal. **3.** *Law.* a conveyance of land through decree of a court, based upon a simulated lawsuit. **4.** *Archaic.* a penalty of any kind. **5. in fine,** finally; in short. *–v.t.* **6.** to subject to a fine, or pecuniary penalty; punish by a fine. [ME *fin,* from OF, from L *fīnis* boundary, end, ML settlement, fine]

**fine**[3] /ˈfineɪ/, *n.* **1.** the end of a repeated section of a musical composition, whether *da capo* or *dal segno.* **2.** the end of a composition comprising several movements. [It.: end]

**fineable** /ˈfaɪnəbəl/, *adj.* subject or liable to a fine. Also, **finable.**

**fine arts** /faɪn ˈats/, *n.pl.* those arts which seek expression through beautiful or significant modes, as architecture, sculpture, painting, music, and engraving.

**fine-cut** /ˈfaɪn-kʌt/, *adj.* cut into very thin strips.

**fine-draw** /faɪn-ˈdrɔ/, *v.t.,* **-drew, -drawn, -drawing. 1.** *Sewing.* to sew together or up so finely or nicely that the joining is not noticeable. **2.** to draw out to extreme fineness, tenuity, or subtlety.

**fine-drawn** /faɪn-ˈdrɔn/, *adj.* drawn out to extreme fineness or thinness: *a fine-drawn wire or distinction.*

**fine-grain** /ˈfaɪn-greɪn/, *adj. Photog.* **1.** (of an image) having an inconspicuous grain. **2.** (of a developer or film) permitting the grain of an image to be inconspicuous.

**fine leg** /faɪn ˈlɛg/, *n. Cricket.* **1.** a leg-side fielding position almost directly behind the wicket. **2.** a fielder in this position.

**finely** /ˈfaɪnli/, *adv.* in a fine manner; excellently; elegantly; delicately; minutely; nicely; subtly.

**fineness** /ˈfaɪnnəs/, *n.* **1.** the state or quality of being fine. **2.** the proportion of pure metal (gold or silver) in an alloy, often expressed by the number of parts in 1000.

**fine print** /faɪn ˈprɪnt/, *n.* the small print in a contract, etc., establishing conditions and matters of detail.

**finery**[1] /ˈfaɪnəri/, *n., pl.* **-ries. 1.** fine or showy dress, ornaments, etc. **2.** *Rare.* smartness or elegance. [FINE[1], *adj.* + -ERY]

**finery**[2] /ˈfaɪnəri/, *n., pl.* **-ries.** a hearth on which cast iron is converted into wrought iron. [F *finerie,* from *finer* FINE[1], *v.*]

**fines herbes** /finz ˈɜb/, *n.pl.* a combination of finely chopped herbs for flavouring soups, sauces, omelettes, etc. [F]

**fine-spun** /ˈfaɪn-spʌn/, *adj.* **1.** spun or drawn out to a fine thread. **2.** highly or excessively refined or subtle.

**finesse** /fəˈnɛs/, *n., v.,* **-nessed, -nessing.** *–n.* **1.** delicacy of execution; subtlety of discrimination. **2.** artful management; craft; strategy. **3.** an artifice or stratagem. **4.** *Croquet.* a strategic move whereby a player seems to waste a turn in order to gain a future advantage. **5.** *Bridge, etc.* an attempt to win a trick by bluffing the opposition into withholding their winning card, allowing a low card to win. **6.** (of wine) fineness of character; elegance. *–v.i.* **7.** to use finesse or artifice. **8.** to make a finesse at cards. *–v.t.* **9.** to accomplish by finesse or artifice. **10.** to make a finesse with (a card). [F, from *fin* FINE[1], *adj.*]

**finetune** /faɪnˈtjun/, *v.,* **-tuned, -tuning. 1.** to make small adjustments to the tuning of (a radio, television, etc.). **2.** to make small adjustments in the tune-up of a (motor vehicle). **3.** to make small changes in the administrative structure of (an organisation).

**finetuner** /faɪnˈtjunə/, *n.* **1.** a device which makes very small adjustments to the tuning of a radio, television, etc. **2.** on the tail of stringed musical instruments, a device incorporating a metal screw whereby a string may be tuned more finely than by adjusting its peg.

**finfoot** /ˈfɪnfʊt/, *n., pl.* **-foots.** any of certain pinnatiped or lobately webbed aquatic birds, family Heliornithidae, of South America, Asia, and Africa, related to the rails and coots.

**fin-footed** /fɪn-ˈfʊtəd/, *adj. Ornith.* **1.** web-footed. **2.** having feet whose toes are separately furnished with flaps, as the finfoots and coots.

**finger** /ˈfɪŋgə/, *n.* **1.** any of the terminal members of the hand, esp. one other than the thumb. **2.** a part of a glove made to receive a finger. **3.** the breadth of a finger as a unit of length; digit. **4.** the length of a finger, 12 cm, or approximately that. **5.** something like or likened to a finger, or serving the purpose of a finger: *the finger of a clock.* **6.** any of various projecting parts of machines. **7.** *Colloq.* a single or branched projection forming a concourse building at an airport. **8.** Some special noun phrases are:

**burn one's fingers,** to get hurt or suffer loss from meddling with or engaging in anything.

**have a finger in the pie,** to have a share in the doing of something.

**keep one's fingers crossed,** to wish for good luck, or success in a particular enterprise.

**lay** or **put one's finger on,** to indicate exactly.

**not lift a finger,** to do nothing; make no attempt.

**pull one's finger out,** *Colloq.* to become active; hurry.

**put the finger on,** *Colloq.* **1.** to inform against or identify (a criminal) to the police. **2.** to designate a victim, as of murder or other crime.

**slip through one's fingers,** to elude one, as a missed opportunity.

**snap one's fingers at,** to show disdain or contempt for.

**twist round one's little finger,** to dominate; influence easily.

*–v.t.* **9.** to touch with the fingers; handle; toy or meddle with. **10.** to stimulate (a woman) erotically with the fingers (fol. by *up*). **11.** to pilfer; filch. **12.** *Colloq.* to point out; accuse. **13.** *Music.* **a.** to play on (an instrument) with the fingers. **b.** to perform or mark (a passage of music) with a certain fingering (def. 2b). *–v.i.* **14.** to touch or handle something with the fingers. **15.** *Music.* **a.** to have its keys arranged for playing with the fingers, as a piano, clarinet, etc. **b.** to use the fingers in playing. [ME and OE; c. G *Finger;* akin to FIVE, FIST] **–fingerer,** *n.* **–fingerless,** *adj.*

**fingerboard** /ˈfɪŋgəbɔd/, *n.* **1.** (in a violin, guitar, etc.) the strip of wood on the neck against which the strings are stopped by the fingers. **2.** (in a piano, organ, etc.) the keyboard.

**fingerbowl** /ˈfɪŋgəboʊl/, *n.* a small bowl to hold water for rinsing the fingers at table.

**fingerbreadth** /ˈfɪŋgəbrɛdθ, -brɛtθ/, *n.* the breadth of a finger, about 20 millimetres. Also, **finger's breadth.**

**finger cherry** /ˈfɪŋgə tʃɛri/, *n.* an Australian tropical tree, *Rhodomyrtus macrocarpa,* with highly poisonous fruit.

**finger food** /ˈ– fud/, *n.* **1.** savouries, canapes, etc. **2.** food suitable for eating with the fingers, esp. food for children, as cheese, celery, carrot, sandwiches, etc.

**fingergrass** /ˈfɪŋgəgras/, *n.* a grass of southern Africa, *Digitaria eriantha,* of summer rainfall areas of the veld. Also, **krulgras.**

**fingering**[1] /ˈfɪŋgərɪŋ/, *n.* **1.** the act of one who fingers. **2.** *Music.* **a.** the action or method of using the fingers in playing an instrument. **b.** the indication of the way the fingers are to be used in performing a piece of music.

**fingering**[2] /ˈfɪŋgərɪŋ/, *n.* a kind of woollen yarn used in the manufacture of stockings.

**fingerling** /ˈfɪŋgəlɪŋ/, *n.* **1.** a young or small fish, esp. a very small salmon or a small trout. **2.** something very small. [FINGER + -LING[1]. Cf. G *Fingerling* thimble]

**fingermark** /ˈfɪŋgəmak/, *n.* a mark, esp. a smudge or stain, made by a finger.

**fingernail** /ˈfɪŋgəneɪl/, *n.* the nail at the end of a finger.

**fingerpick** /ˈfɪŋgəpɪk/, *n.* →**plectrum.**

**fingerplate** /ˈfɪŋgəpleɪt/, *n.* a plate fixed near the latch of a door to protect the surface from being soiled by fingermarks.

**fingerpost** /ˈfɪŋgəpoʊst/, *n.* a signpost with an arm terminating in the shape of an index finger.

**fingerprint** /ˈfɪŋgəprɪnt/, *n.* **1.** an impression of the markings of the inner surface of the last joint of the thumb or a finger. **2.** such an impression made with ink for purposes of identification. *–v.t.* **3.** to take the fingerprints of.

**fingerstall** /ˈfɪŋgəstɔl/, *n.* a covering used to protect a finger.

**fingertip** /ˈfɪŋgətɪp/, *n.* **1.** the tip of a finger. **2.** a covering used to protect the end of a finger. **3. at one's fingertips, a.** close at hand, within easy reach. **b.** readily at one's disposal, as a result of complete familiarity with the subject.

**finger-wave** /ˈfɪŋgə-weɪv/, *n.* a wave set by impressing the fingers into hair dampened with lotion.

**finial** /ˈfaɪniəl/, *n. Archit.* **1.** the ornamental termination of a pinnacle, gable, etc., usu. foliated. **2.** a vertical termination; a cast, carved, or turned ornament capping another form. [ME, from L *finis* end + -IAL]

**finical** /ˈfɪnɪkəl/, *adj.* **1.** excessively fastidious; too particular or fussy. **2.** (of things) overelaborate; containing too much unimportant detail. [FINE[1] + -ICAL] – **finicality** /fɪnəˈkæləti/, **finicalness,** *n.* – **finically,** *adv.*

**finicky** /ˈfɪnɪki/, *adj.* finical. Also, **finikin, finicking.** [unexplained var. of FINICAL]

**fining** /ˈfaɪnɪŋ/, *n.* **1.** the process by which fused glass becomes free from undissolved gases. **2.** the process of clarifying or filtering a wine or spirit to render it brilliant in appearance. **3.** (*pl.*) a substance used in this process. [FINE[1], *v.*]

**finis** /fɪˈnɪs/, *n.* end; conclusion (often used at the end of a book). [L]

**finish** /ˈfɪnɪʃ/, *v.t.* **1.** to bring (action, speech, work, affairs, etc.) to an end or to completion. **2.** to come to the end of (a course, period of time, etc.). **3.** to use up completely (oft. fol. by *up* or *off*): *to finish a plate of food.* **4.** to overcome completely; destroy or kill (oft. fol. by *off*). **5.** to complete and perfect in detail; put the final touches on. **6.** to put the last treatment or coating on (wood, metal, etc.). **7.** to perfect (a person) in education, accomplishments, social graces etc. *–v.i.* **8.** to come to an end. **9.** to complete a course, etc. **10.** *Obs.* to die. *–n.* **11.** the end or conclusion; the last stage. **12.** the end of a hunt, race, etc. **13.** a decisive ending: *a fight to the finish.* **14.** the quality of being finished or completed with smoothness, elegance, etc. **15.** (of wine) the lingering aftertaste. **16.** educational or social polish. **17.** the manner in which a thing is finished in preparation, or an effect imparted in finishing: *a soft or dull finish.* **18.** the surface coating or texture of wood, metal, etc. **19.** something used or serving to finish, complete, or perfect a thing. **20.** woodwork, etc., esp. in the interior of a building, not essential to the structure but used for purposes of ornament, neatness, etc. **21.** a final coat of plaster or paint. **22.** a material for application in finishing. **23.** *Rowing.* the point in the stroke when the oar handle is closest to the chest. [ME *finisch(en)*, from F *finiss-*, stem of *finir*, from L *fīnīre* bound, end] – **finisher,** *n.*

**finished** /ˈfɪnɪʃt/, *adj.* **1.** ended or completed. **2.** completed or perfected in all details, as a product. **3.** polished to the highest degree of excellence: *a finished poem.* **4.** highly accomplished, as a person. **5.** *Agric.* of or pertaining to stock which has reached the right condition for sale.

**finishing school** /ˈfɪnɪʃɪŋ ˌskul/, *n.* a school for completing the education of young women and preparing them for entrance into society.

**finite** /ˈfaɪnaɪt/, *adj.* **1.** having bounds or limits; not too great or too small to be measurable. **2.** subject to limitations or conditions, as of space, time, circumstances, or the laws of nature: *finite existence.* *–n.* **3. the finite, a.** that which is finite. **b.** finite things collectively. [L *fīnītus*, pp., bounded] – **finitely,** *adv.* – **finiteness,** *n.*

**finite verb** /– ˈvɜb/, *n.* a verb limited by person, number, tense, mood, and aspect (opposed to the infinite forms, participle, infinitive, and gerund, which have only a few limitations).

**finitude** /ˈfɪnətʃud/, *n.* the state of being finite.

**fink** /fɪŋk/, *n. Colloq.* **1.** a strike-breaker or blackleg. **2.** a contemptible or undesirable person, esp. one who reneges on an undertaking.

**fin keel** /ˈfɪn kil/, *n.* a finlike projection extending downwards from the keel of a sailing boat, serving to prevent lateral motion and acting as additional ballast.

**Finland** /ˈfɪnlænd/, *n.* a republic in northern Europe. – **Finlander,** *n.*

**finlet** /ˈfɪnlət/, *n.* a small detached finlike appendage in certain fishes, as the mackerel.

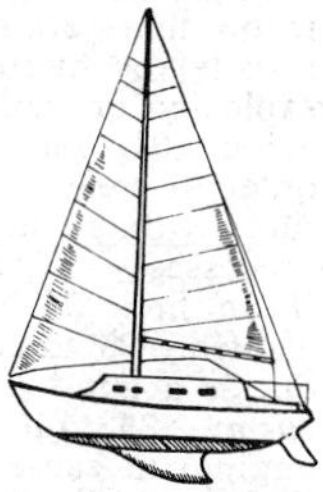

**Finn** /fɪn/, *n.* **1.** an inhabitant or native of Finland. **2.** any native speaker of Finnish, as in America or Russia. **3.** a speaker of any Finnic language.

**finnan haddock** /fɪnən ˈhædək/, *n.* smoked haddock. Also, **finnan haddie** /fɪnən ˈhædi/. [lit., haddock of *Findhorn,* fishing port in Scotland]

**finned** /fɪnd/, *adj.* having a fin or fins.

**finner** /ˈfɪnə/, *n.* →**finback.**

fin keel

**Finnic** /ˈfɪnɪk/, *adj.* **1.** designating Finnish and the languages most closely related to it, as Estonian, Lapp, and some minor languages of the northwestern Soviet Union. **2.** designating all Finno-Ugric languages except the Ugric, or all except Ugric and Permian.

**Finnish** /ˈfɪnɪʃ/, *n.* **1.** the principal language of Finland, a Finno-Ugric language, closely related to Estonian. *–adj.* **2.** of or pertaining to Finland or its inhabitants. **3.** Finnic.

**Finno-Ugric** /ˌfɪnoʊ-ˈjugrɪk/, *n.* a linguistic family of eastern Europe and western Siberia, including Finnish, Estonian, and Lapp, farther east the Zyrian and Votyak, and also the Ugric languages, such as Hungarian and Vogul. It is related to Samoyed.

**finny** /ˈfɪni/, *adj.* **1.** pertaining to or abounding in fish. **2.** having fins; finned. **3.** finlike.

**fino** /ˈfinoʊ/, *adj.* (of sherry) extremely dry. [Sp.: sharp]

**finwhale** /ˈfɪnweɪl/, *n.* →**finback.**

**fiord** /ˈfiɔd/, *n.* a long, relatively narrow arm of the sea, bordered by steep cliffs, as on the coast of Norway. Also, **fjord.** [Norw. See FIRTH]

**fipple** /ˈfɪpəl/, *n.* (in music) a plug, stopping the upper end of a pipe.

**fipple flute** /ˈ– flut/, *n.* a flute equipped with a fipple.

**fir** /fɜ/, *n.* **1.** any of the pyramidal coniferous trees constituting the genus *Abies,* as *A. balsamea,* the balsam fir. **2.** the wood of such a tree. [ME *firr(e)*, OE *fyrh.* Cf. OE *furh(wudu)* pine, Icel. *fura* fir; akin to L *quercus* oak]

**fire** /ˈfaɪə/, *n., v.,* **fired, firing.** *–n.* **1.** the active principle of burning or combustion, manifested by the evolution of light and heat. **2.** a burning mass of material, as on a hearth or in a furnace. **3.** the destructive burning of a building, town, forest, etc.; a conflagration. **4.** a composition or device for producing a conflagration or a fiery display: *Greek fire.* **5.** flashing light; luminous appearance. **6.** brilliance, as of a gem. **7.** burning passion; ardour; enthusiasm. **8.** liveliness of imagination. **9.** fever; inflammation. **10.** severe trial or trouble. **11.** exposure to fire by way of torture or ordeal. **12.** heating quality, as of strong drink. **13.** a spark or sparks. **14.** the discharge of firearms: *to open fire.* **15.** the effect of firing military weapons: *to place fire upon the enemy.* **16.** *Archaic.* lightning, or a thunderbolt. **17.** *Poetic.* a luminous object, as a star: *heavenly fires.* **18.** Some special noun phrases are:

**between two fires,** being attacked from both sides.

**catch fire,** to become ignited.

**go through fire and water,** to face any hardship or danger.

**hang fire, 1.** to be slow in exploding. **2.** to be irresolute, postponed or delayed.

**lay a fire,** to arrange fuel to be lit.

**on fire, 1.** ignited; burning. **2.** eager; ardent; zealous.

**play with fire,** to meddle carelessly or lightly with a dangerous matter.

**set fire to** or **set on fire, 1.** to cause to burn. **2.** to excite violently; inflame.

**take fire, 1.** to become ignited. **2.** to become filled with enthusiasm or zeal.

**under fire, 1.** exposed to enemy fire. **2.** under criticism or attack.

*–v.t.* **19.** to set on fire. **20.** to supply (a furnace, etc.) with fuel; attend to the fire of (a boiler, etc.). **21.** to expose to the

action of fire; subject to heat. **22.** to apply heat in a kiln for baking or glazing; burn. **23.** to heat very slowly for the purpose of drying, as tea. **24.** to inflame, as with passion; fill with ardour. **25.** to inspire. **26.** to light or cause to glow as if on fire. **27.** to discharge, as a gun. **28.** to project (a missile) by discharging from a gun, etc. **29.** to subject to explosion or explosive force, as a mine. **30.** to dismiss from a job. **31.** *Vet. Sci.* to apply a heated iron to (the skin) in order to create a local inflammation of the superficial structures, thus favourably affecting deeper inflammatory processes. *–v.i.* **32.** to take fire; be kindled. **33.** to glow as if on fire. **34.** to become inflamed with passion; become excited. **35.** to perform with enthusiasm and flair. **36.** to go off, as a gun. **37.** to discharge a gun, etc.: *fire at a fleeing enemy.* **38.** to hurl a missile. **39.** (of an internal-combustion engine) to cause ignition of the air-fuel mixture in the cylinder or cylinders. **40. fire away,** *Colloq.* to begin speaking. [ME; OE *fȳr,* c. D *vuur,* G *Feuer;* akin to Gk *pŷr*] – **fireable,** *adj.*

**fire alarm** /ˈfaɪər əlam/, *n.* **1.** a visible or audible notice that a fire has started. **2.** an apparatus for giving this notice.

**fire-and-brimstone** /ˌfaɪər-ən-ˈbrɪmstoun/, *adj.* pertaining to a preacher who or sermon which puts emphasis on hell and its eternal torments.

**firearm** /ˈfaɪəram/, *n.* a small arms weapon from which a projectile is discharged by an explosion.

**fireback** /ˈfaɪəbæk/, *n.* **1.** the rear part of a fireplace. **2.** a decorated plate, esp. of cast iron, lining the rear of a fireplace.

**fireball** /ˈfaɪəbɔl/, *n.* **1.** a ball filled with explosive or combustible material, used as a projectile, to injure the enemy by explosion or to set fire to their works. **2.** a ball of fire, as the sun. **3.** a luminous meteor, sometimes exploding. **4.** lightning having the appearance of a globe of fire. **5.** *Mil.* the luminous sphere of hot gases which forms at the detonation of a nuclear weapon and immediately starts expanding and cooling. **6.** a ball of flaming gas flying through the air and formed from the vaporisation of oils in trees, esp. eucalyptus, during a bush fire.

**fire bay** /ˈfaɪə beɪ/, *n.* that section of a fire trench occupied by riflemen, usu. one squad to a bay.

**firebird** /ˈfaɪəbɜd/, *n.* →**oriole.**

**fireboat** /ˈfaɪəbout/, *n.* a powered vessel equipped for fighting fires.

**fire bomb** /ˈfaɪə bɒm/, *n.* an incendiary bomb.

**firebox** /ˈfaɪəbɒks/, *n.* **1.** the box or chamber in which the fire of a fuel stove, steam-boiler, etc., is placed. **2.** the furnace of a steam-engine, where coal, oil or other fuel is burned for the purpose of generating steam. **3.** *Obs.* →**tinderbox.**

**firebrand** /ˈfaɪəbrænd/, *n.* **1.** a piece of burning wood or other material. **2.** one who or that which kindles strife, inflames the passions, etc.

**firebrat** /ˈfaɪəbræt/, *n.* a small insect, *Thermobia domestica,* found in warm places around furnaces, boilers, etc.

**firebreak** /ˈfaɪəbreɪk/, *n.* a strip of ploughed or cleared land made to check the spread of fire.

**firebrick** /ˈfaɪəbrɪk/, *n.* a brick made of fireclay.

**fire brigade** /ˈfaɪə brəgeɪd/, *n.* a body of firemen.

**firebug** /ˈfaɪəbʌg/, *n. Colloq.* →**incendiary.**

**fireclay** /ˈfaɪəkleɪ/, *n.* a kind of clay capable of resisting high temperature, used for making crucibles, firebricks, etc.

**fire-control** /ˈfaɪə-kəntroul/, *n.* technical supervision of artillery fire or naval gunfire.

**firecracker** /ˈfaɪəkrækə/, *n.* →**cracker** (def. 2).

**firecrest** /ˈfaɪəkrɛst/, *n.* a small European bird, *Regulus ignicapillus,* with a bright red crest.

**fire-curtain** /ˈfaɪə-kɜtn/, *n.* in a theatre, a fireproof screen which can be lowered to separate the stage from the body of the hall.

**firedamp** /ˈfaɪədæmp/, *n.* **1.** a combustible gas, consisting chiefly of methane, formed esp. in coalmines, and dangerously explosive when mixed with certain proportions of atmospheric air. **2.** the explosive mixture itself.

**fire-direction** /ˈfaɪə-dərɛkʃən/, *n.* tactical supervision of artillery fire.

**firedog** /ˈfaɪədɒg/, *n.* →**andiron.**

**firedrake** /ˈfaɪədreɪk/, *n.* a mythical dragon. [OE *fȳrdraca,* from *fȳr* fire + *draca* dragon]

**fire drill** /ˈfaɪə drɪl/, *n.* **1.** a practice drill for firemen, the passengers and crew of a ship, etc., to accustom them to their duties in case of fire. **2.** a drill for pupils in a school, employees in a factory, etc., to train them how to leave the building in case of fire.

**fire-eater** /ˈfaɪər-itə/, *n.* **1.** an entertainer who pretends to eat fire. **2.** one who seeks occasion to fight or quarrel. Also, **fire-swallower.** – **fire-eating,** *adj.*

**fire-engine** /ˈfaɪər-ɛndʒən/, *n.* a motor vehicle equipped for fire fighting, now usu. having a motor-driven pump for shooting water from fire hydrants, etc., or chemical solutions at high pressure.

**fire-escape** /ˈfaɪər-əskeɪp/, *n.* a fire-proof staircase, or some other apparatus or structure, used to escape from a burning building.

**fire-extinguisher** /ˈfaɪər-əkstɪŋgwɪʃə/, *n.* a portable device, usu. containing water or chemicals under pressure, for putting out fires.

**firefighter** /ˈfaɪəfaɪtə/, *n.* **1.** one whose activity or employment is to extinguish fires, esp. bushfires. **2.** *Colloq.* →**troubleshooter.** – **firefighting,** *adj.*

**firefly** /ˈfaɪəflaɪ/, *n., pl.* **-flies. 1.** any of the soft-bodied, nocturnal beetles of the family Lampyridae, which possess abdominal light-producing organs; lightning bug. The luminous larvae or wingless females are called **glow-worms. 2.** a fly (def. 27) designed to protect a camp-fire.

**fireguard** /ˈfaɪəgad/, *n.* a framework of wire placed in front of a fireplace as a protection.

**fire hazard** /ˈfaɪə hæzəd/, *n.* →**firetrap.**

**firehouse** /ˈfaɪəhaus/, *n. U.S.* →**fire station.**

**fire hydrant** /ˈfaɪə haɪdrənt/, *n.* a hydrant used as an emergency water supply for extinguishing fires.

**fire insurance** /ˈfaɪər ɪnʃɔrəns/, *n.* insurance covering loss or damage through fire.

**fire irons** /ˈ– aɪənz/, *n.pl.* implements used for tending a domestic fire, such as tongs, poker, etc.

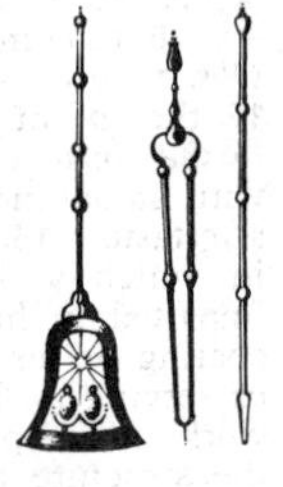

fire irons

**fireless** /ˈfaɪələs/, *adj.* **1.** lacking fire; without a fire. **2.** without life or animation.

**firelight** /ˈfaɪəlaɪt/, *n.* the light from a fire, as on a hearth.

**firelighter** /ˈfaɪəlaɪtə/, *n.* any highly inflammable material used for kindling fires.

**firelock** /ˈfaɪəlɒk/, *n.* **1.** the flintlock musket, in whose lock the priming is ignited by sparks struck from flint and steel. **2.** (formerly) a soldier armed with such a gun.

**fireman** /ˈfaɪəmən/, *n., pl.* **-men. 1.** a man employed to extinguish or prevent fires. **2.** a man employed to tend fires; a stoker. **3.** *Railways.* **a.** one who tends the fire of a steam locomotive and assists the driver. **b.** the assistant to the driver on a diesel or electric locomotive. **4.** *Mining.* a colliery official responsible for precautions against fire.

**firemark** /ˈfaɪəmak/, *n.* a metal plate formerly attached to a building by insurance companies to indicate that it was insured.

**fire office** /ˈfaɪər ɒfəs/, *n.* the office of a fire-insurance company.

**fire opal** /– ˈoupəl/, *n.* a red opal, often with a colour play.

**fireplace** /ˈfaɪəpleɪs/, *n.* **1.** that part of a chimney which opens into a room and in which fuel is burnt. **2.** any open structure, usu. of masonry, for containing fire, as at a camp site.

**fireplug** /ˈfaɪəplʌg/, *n. Chiefly U.S.* →**fire hydrant.**

**fire point** /ˈfaɪə pɔɪnt/, *n.* the lowest temperature at which a substance ignites when a flame is put to it and continues to burn. Also, **firing point.**

**fire policy** /ˈ– pɒləsi/, *n.* an insurance policy covering loss by fire.

**firepower** /ˈfaɪəpauə/, *n.* **1.** the capacity of a military unit, weapon, etc., to deliver fire. **2.** the amount of fire delivered by a unit or weapon.

**firepower umbrella** /ˈfaɪəpauər ʌmˌbrɛlə/, *n.* the specified distance within which the fire of naval ships' anti-aircraft weapons can endanger enemy aircraft.

**fireproof** /ˈfaɪəpruf/, *adj.* **1.** proof against fire; comparatively incombustible. *–v.t.* **2.** to make fireproof.

**fireproofing** /ˈfaɪəprufɪŋ/, *n.* **1.** the act or process of rendering fireproof. **2.** material for use in making anything fireproof.

**firer** /ˈfaɪərə/, *n.* **1.** one who fires, sets on fire, treats with fire or heat, discharges a firearm, etc. **2.** a firearm with reference to its firing: *a single-firer, a rapid-firer.*

**fire-raising** /ˈfaɪə-reɪzɪŋ/, *n.* →**arson.** – **fire-raiser,** *n.*

**fire-rate** /ˈfaɪə-reɪt/, *v.t.*, **-rated, -rating.** to classify (building materials), indicating in hours how long they can withstand the heat of a fire before collapsing.

**fire-resistance** /ˈfaɪə-rəzɪstəns/, *n.* the extent to which a material or building is resistant to fire. – **fire-resistant,** *adj.*

**fire risk** /ˈfaɪə rɪsk/, *n.* **1.** a building, structure or object considered especially likely to catch fire, or one which would be especially unsafe in a fire. **2.** the risk of loss by fire. **3.** the obligation of an insurer to cover the loss caused by a fire.

**firescreen** /ˈfaɪəskrin/, *n.* a screen placed in front of a fireplace for protection or decoration.

**fire ship** /ˈfaɪə ʃɪp/, *n.* a vessel loaded with combustibles and explosives and set adrift to destroy an enemy's ships, etc.

**fireside** /ˈfaɪəsaɪd/, *n.* **1.** the space about a fire or hearth. **2.** home; home life.

**fire station** /ˈfaɪə steɪʃən/, *n.* a building in which fire-fighting equipment and often firemen are housed.

**fire step** /ˈ– stɛp/, *n.* a board or narrow ledge above the bottom of a fire trench from which men can fire, observe enemy movements, etc.

**firestick** /ˈfaɪəstɪk/, *n.* **1.** a lighted stick carried in a smouldering condition from camp to camp by Aboriginals, esp. those in Tasmania, for lighting fires. **2.** a stick that is used to make fire by friction.

**firestone** /ˈfaɪəstoun/, *n.* a fire-resisting stone, esp. a kind of sandstone used in fireplaces, furnaces, etc. [OE *fȳrstān,* from *fȳr* fire + *stān* stone]

**firestorm** /ˈfaɪəstɔm/, *n.* an atmospheric phenomenon caused by a large fire, as after the mass bombing of a city, in which a rising column of air above the fire draws in strong winds often accompanied by rain.

**fire-swallower** /ˈfaɪə-swɒlouə/, *n.* →**fire-eater.**

**firetail** /ˈfaɪəteɪl/, *n.* any of a number of species of grass finch which have crimson upper tail-coverts.

**firethorn** /ˈfaɪəθɔn/, *n.* **1.** an evergreen bushy shrub or tree, *Pyracantha coccinea,* of southern Europe and Asia Minor. **2.** any other species of *Pyracantha* many of which are cultivated for their attractive berries.

**fire trail** /ˈfaɪə treɪl/, *n.* a permanent track cleared through bush to provide firefighters with access to bushfires.

**firetrap** /ˈfaɪətræp/, *n.* a building which, because of the material or arrangement of the structure, is especially dangerous in case of fire.

**fire trench** /ˈfaɪə trɛntʃ/, *n.* a trench from which men can fire rifles and other small arms and in which they are relatively well-protected.

**fire-tube boiler** /ˈfaɪə-tjub ˌbɔɪlə/, *n.* a boiler in which the combustion products pass through tubes immersed in the water space on their way to the chimney. See **water-tube boiler.**

**firewalking** /ˈfaɪəwɔkɪŋ/, *n.* a religious rite or demonstration in which a person walks barefoot through fire, esp. red-hot glowing embers, stones, etc. – **firewalker,** *n.*

**firewall** /ˈfaɪəwɔl/, *n.* a wall made of fireproof material, designed to prevent the spread of a fire, as in buildings, aircraft, motor vehicles, etc.

**firewarden** /ˈfaɪəwɔdən/, *n.* a person having authority in the prevention or extinguishing of fires, as in towns or camps.

**firewatcher** /ˈfaɪəwɒtʃə/, *n.* one who watches for fires, esp. bushfires.

**firewater** /ˈfaɪəwɔtə/, *n.* strong alcoholic drink.

**fireweed** /ˈfaɪəwid/, *n.* **1.** a short-lived native perennial, *Senecio lautus,* commonly found as a low-spreading bush with yellow, daisy-like flowers growing on recently cultivated or poorly grassed land; variable groundsel. **2.** any of various plants appearing in recently burnt clearings or districts, as the rosebay willowherb.

**firewheel tree** /ˈfaɪəwil ˌtri/, *n.* a tree, *Stenocarpus sinuatus,* native to rainforests in New South Wales and Queensland, which bears wheel-like whorls of bright red flowers.

**firewood** /ˈfaɪəwud/, *n.* wood for fuel.

**firework** /ˈfaɪəwɜk/, *n.* **1.** (*usu. pl.*) a combustible or explosive device for producing a striking display of light or a loud noise, often also used in signalling at night, etc. **2.** (*pl.*) **a.** a pyrotechnic display. **b.** a display of anger or bad temper. **c.** an exciting spectacle or performance.

**fire-zone** /ˈfaɪə-zoun/, *n.* an area of concentrated gunfire.

**firing** /ˈfaɪərɪŋ/, *n.* **1.** the act of one who or that which fires. **2.** material for a fire; fuel. **3.** the act of baking ceramics or glass.

**firing line** /ˈ– laɪn/, *n.* **1.** the positions at which troops are stationed to fire upon the enemy or targets. **2.** the troops firing from this line. **3.** the forefront of any activity.

**firing order** /ˈ– ɔdə/, *n.* the sequence in which the cylinders of an internal-combustion engine fires.

**firing party** /ˈ– pati/, *n.* **1.** a military detachment assigned to fire a salute at the burial of a person being honoured. **2.** →**firing squad.**

**firing pin** /ˈ– pɪn/, *n.* a plunger in the firing mechanism of a gun that strikes the primer and thus ignites the propelling charge of a projectile.

**firing squad** /ˈ– skwɒd/, *n.* a military detachment assigned to execute a condemned person by shooting.

**firkin** /ˈfɜkən/, *n.* **1.** a barrel or container in the imperial system holding 9 gallons (40.5 litres). **2.** a small wooden vessel for butter, etc. [ME *ferdekyn,* from MD *ferdelkijn,* diminutive of *ferdel* firkin (lit., fourth part)]

**firm**[1] /fɜm/, *adj.* **1.** comparatively solid, hard, stiff or rigid: *firm ground, flesh, texture.* **2.** securely fixed in place. **3.** steady; not shaking or trembling: *a firm hand or voice.* **4.** fixed, settled, or unalterable, as a belief or conviction, a decree, etc. **5.** steadfast or unwavering, as persons or principles. **6.** indicating firmness: *a firm countenance.* **7.** not fluctuating or falling, as prices or the market. *–v.t.* **8.** to make firm. *–v.i.* **9.** to become firm. **10.** of share prices, rates of exchange, etc., to increase slightly in value. *–adv.* **11.** firmly: *stand firm.* [L *firmus;* replacing ME *ferme,* from OF] – **firmly,** *adv.* – **firmness,** *n.*

**firm**[2] /fɜm/, *n.* **1.** a business organisation or partnership. **2.** the name or title under which associated parties transact business: *the firm of Jones & Co.* **3.** a team of medical officers in or attached to a hospital, headed by a physician or surgeon, specialising in one aspect or branch of medicine. [It., Sp. *firma* signature, from L *firmāre* confirm]

**firmament** /ˈfɜməmənt/, *n.* the vault of heaven; the sky. [ME, from LL *firmāmentum* firmament, L a support, prop] – **firmamental,** *adj.*

**firmer chisel** /ˈfɜmə tʃɪzəl/, *n.* a carpenter's chisel with a blade thin in proportion to its width, fixed to the handle by a tang, usu. pushed by the hand and not driven with a mallet. [*firmer,* from F *fermoir,* b. *formoir* former (from *former* form, from L *formāre*) and *fermer* make firm (from L *firmāre*)]

**firmware** /ˈfɜmwɛə/, *n.* programs fixed into a computer's memory, which cannot be altered without changing the hardware, esp. subroutines which are to last for the life of the computer.

**firn** /fɪən/, *n.* →**névé.** [G: (properly adj.) of last year]

**firry** /ˈfɜri/, *adj.* **1.** of or pertaining to the fir. **2.** made of fir. **3.** abounding in firs.

**first** /fɜst/, *adj.* **1.** being before all others with respect to time, order, rank, importance, etc. (used as the ordinal number of *one*). **2.** *Music.* highest or chief among several voices or instruments of the same class: *first alto, first horn.* **3.** *Motor Vehicles.* of or pertaining to low transmission gear ratio. **4. at first blush,** at the first view; on first consideration. **5. at first hand,** from the first or original source. **6. draw first blood, a.** in physical combat, to inflict the first injury. **b.** in non-physical competition, to gain the initial advantage. **7. first thing,** before anything else; at once; early. *–adv.* **8.** before all others or anything else in time, order, rank, etc. **9.** before some other thing, event, etc. **10.** for the first time. **11.** in preference to something else; rather; sooner. **12.** in the first place; firstly. **13. first up,** at the first attempt. **14. first and last,** altogether; in all. *–n.* **15.** that which is first in time, order, rank, etc. **16.** the beginning.

17. the first part; the first member of a series. **18.** *Music.* **a.** the voice or instrument that takes the highest or chief part in its class, esp. in an orchestra or chorus. **b.** a leader of a group of performers. **19.** *Motor Vehicles.* the lowest forward gear ratio; first gear. **20.** the first place in a race, etc. **21.** a first-class degree. **22.** (*pl.*) the best quality of certain articles of commerce. **23. at (the) first,** at the beginning or outset. **24. from the first,** from the beginning or outset. [ME; OE *fyrst,* c. OHG *furist,* G *Fürst* prince; a superlative form akin to FORE[1]]

**first aid** /– 'eɪd/, *n.* emergency aid or treatment given to persons suffering from accident, etc., until the services of a doctor can be obtained.

**first base** /– 'beɪs/, *n.* **1.** *Baseball.* **a.** the first of the bases from the home plate. **b.** the person playing this position. **2. get to first base,** *Colloq.* to make a slight amount of progress.

**firstborn** /'fɜstbɔn/, *adj.;* /fɜst'bɔn, 'fɜstbɔn/, *n.* *–adj.* **1.** first in the order of birth; eldest. *–n.* **2.** a firstborn child. **3.** a first result or product.

**first cause** /fɜst 'kɔz/, *n.* a cause which does not depend upon another: *God is the first cause.*

**first class** /– 'klas/, *n.* the most luxurious class of accommodation for passengers on a ship, train, aircraft, etc.

**first-class** /'fɜst-klas/, *adj.;* /fɜst-'klas/, *adv.* *–adj.* **1.** of the highest or best class or quality. **2.** best-equipped and most expensive: *a first-class carriage.* **3.** denoting a degree bearing the highest class of honours in a university examination. *–adv.* **4.** by first-class conveyance: *to travel first-class.*

**first cost** /fɜst 'kɒst/, *n.* cost not including profit.

**first cousin** /'– kʌzən/, *n.* See **cousin.**

**first cousin once removed,** *n.* See **cousin.**

**first-day cover** /fɜst-deɪ 'kʌvə/, *n.* an envelope bearing a newly-issued stamp, posted and franked on the day of issue.

**first-degree** /'fɜst-dəgri/, *adj.* of a degree which is at the extreme end of a scale, either as the lowest (*first-degree burn*) or the highest (*first-degree murder*).

**first five-eighth** /'fɜst faɪv-eɪtθ/, *n.* *N.Z.* →**five-eighth** (def. 1). Also, **first five.**

**First Fleet** /– 'flit/, *n.* the ships which took the first convicts to Australia in 1788.

**First Fleeter** /– 'flitə/, *n.* a person whose family can be traced back to someone who came to Australia with the First Fleet in 1788.

**first floor** /– 'flɔ/, *n.* **1.** the floor above the ground floor of a building. **2.** *Orig. U.S.* the ground floor of a building.

**first foot** /fɜst 'fʊt/, *n.* *Scot.* the first person to enter a house on New Year's Day, traditionally an omen for the householder. Also, **first footer.**

**first-foot** /fɜst-'fʊt/, *Scot.* *–v.t.* **1.** to enter (a house) first on New Year's Day. *–v.i.* **2.** to be the first to enter a house on New Year's Day. **3.** to go round making visits as a first foot. **– first-footing,** *n.*

**first fruit** /– 'frut/, *n.* (*usu. pl.*) **1.** the earliest fruit of the season. **2.** the first product or result of anything.

**first-generation** /'fɜst-dʒɛnə,reɪʃən/, *adj.* of or pertaining to a citizen of a country who is either foreign-born and naturalised, or born of foreign parents: *a first-generation Australian.*

**first-hand** /fɜst-'hænd/, *adv.;* /'fɜst-hænd/, *adj.* *–adv.* **1.** from the first or original source. *–adj.* **2.** of or pertaining to the first or original source. **3.** direct from the original source.

**first lady** /fɜst 'leɪdi/, *n.* the wife of a head of government, or of a head of state.

**first light** /– 'laɪt/, *n.* morning twilight.

**firstling** /'fɜstlɪŋ/, *n.* **1.** the first of its kind to be produced or to appear. **2.** first offspring. **3.** the first product or result.

**firstly** /'fɜstli/, *adv.* in the first place; first.

**first mortgage** /fɜst 'mɔgɪdʒ/, *n.* a mortgage having priority over all other mortgages on property.

**first name** /'– neɪm/, *n.* Christian name; forename.

**first night** /– 'naɪt/, *n.* the first public performance of a play, etc.

**first-nighter** /fɜst-'naɪtə/, *n.* one who habitually attends a first night.

**first offender** /fɜst ə'fɛndə/, *n.* one convicted of an offence in law for the first time.

**first officer** /– 'ɒfəsə/, *n.* **1.** →**mate**[2] (def. 6). **2.** in an aircrew, the officer next in seniority to the captain.

**first-past-the-post** /,fɜst-past-ðə-'poʊst/, *adj.* of or pertaining to an electoral system in which the candidate who gains the largest number of votes wins.

**first person** /fɜst 'pɜsən/, *n.* the class of a pronoun or verb in which the speaker is the subject. See **person** (def. 11a).

**first position** /– pə'zɪʃən/, *n.* (in ballet) a position of the feet in which the heels are back to back and the toes point out to the sides.

**first principle** /– 'prɪnsəpəl/, *n.* any law, axiom, or concept which represents the highest degree of generalisation and which depends on fundamental principles.

**first-rate** /'fɜst-reɪt/, *adj.;* /fɜst-'reit/, *adv.* *–adj.* **1.** of the first rate or class. **2.** excellent; very good. *–adv.* **3.** *Colloq.* excellently.

**first reading** /fɜst 'ridɪŋ/, *n.* (in parliament) the introduction and first consideration of a bill.

**first refusal** /fɜst rə'fjuzəl/, *n.* the right of a customer to buy or refuse goods before they can be sold to anyone else.

**first strike** /– 'straɪk/, *n.* an initial attack with nuclear weapons.

**first string** /– 'strɪŋ/, *n.* **1.** →**first violinist.** **2.** the most proficient player in a sporting team. **3. the first string in one's bow,** one's chief skill, asset, etc. **– first-string,** *adj.*

**first-up** /fɜst-'ʌp/, *adj.* **1.** first. *–n.* **2.** a first attempt. **3.** *Horseracing.* the first race a horse runs after being spelled.

**first violinist** /fɜst vaɪə'lɪnəst/, *n.* **1.** the violinist among the first violins who is the leader of the orchestra. **2.** one of the first violins in an orchestra.

**first violins** /– vaɪə'lɪnz/, *n.pl.* the group of violinists in an orchestra who play the first or chief part for the violin.

**first water** /fɜst 'wɔtə/, *n.* **1.** the highest degree of fineness in a diamond or other precious stone. **2.** the highest rank, quality or degree: *he is a musician of the first water.* [? translation of Ar. *mā'* water, lustre]

**firth** /fɜθ/, *n.* *Chiefly Scot.* a long, narrow indentation of the seacoast. Also, **frith.** [Scand.; cf. Icel. *firdh-,* stem of *fjördhr* firth. Cf. FIORD]

**fisc** /fɪsk/, *n.* a royal or state treasury; an exchequer. [L *fiscus* basket, purse, treasury]

**fiscal** /'fɪskəl/, *adj.* **1.** of or pertaining to the public treasury or revenues. **2.** pertaining to financial matters in general. *–n.* **3.** (in some countries) an official having the function of public prosecutor. [L *fiscālis* belonging to the state treasury] **– fiscally,** *adv.*

**fiscal year** /– 'jɪə/, *n.* →**financial year.**

**Fischer-Tropsch process** /,fɪʃə-,trɒpʃ 'proʊsɛs/, *n.* any of several processes for the manufacture of hydrocarbons, or their derivatives, by the catalytic hydrogenation of carbon monoxide under high temperatures and pressures. [named after Franz *Fischer,* 1877-1947, and H. *Tropsch,* d. 1935, German chemists]

**fish**[1] /fɪʃ/, *n., pl.* **fishes,** (*esp. collectively*) **fish** (Note: in technical usage, *fishes* usu. refers to several species, while *fish* refers to only one species.), *v.* *–n.* **1.** any of various cold-blooded, completely aquatic vertebrates, having gills, commonly fins, and typically an elongated body usu. covered with scales. **2.** any of various other aquatic animals. **3.** the flesh of fishes used as food. **4. the Fishes,** the zodiacal constellation or sign Pisces. **5.** *Colloq.* (with an adjective) a person: *a queer fish, a poor fish.* **6. cry stinking fish,** *Archaic.* to disparage oneself or one's efforts. **7. drink like a fish,** to drink alcoholic liquors to excess. **8. feed the fishes, a.** to be seasick. **b.** to drown. **9. fish out of water,** out of one's proper environment, ill at ease in unfamiliar surroundings. **10. neither fish nor fowl.** Also, **neither fish, flesh, fowl, nor good red herring.** neither one thing nor the other. **11. other fish to fry,** other matters requiring attention. **12. a fine (pretty) kettle of fish,** trouble; confusion. *–v.t.* **13.** to

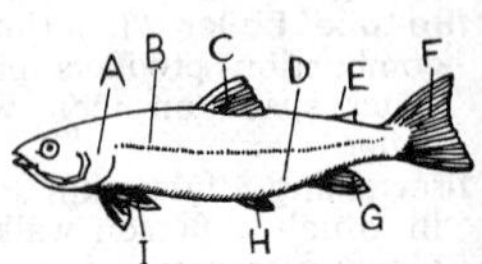

fish: A, operculum; B, lateral line; C, dorsal fin; D, anus; E, adipose fin; F, caudal fin; G, anal fin; H, pelvic fin; I, pectoral fin

catch or attempt to catch (fish or the like). **14.** to try to catch fish in (a stream, etc.). **15.** to draw as by fishing (fol. by *up, out,* etc.). **16.** to search through as by fishing. **17.** *Naut.* to hoist the flukes of (an anchor) up to the gunwale or rail by means of a tackle, to secure it to the deck. **18. fish out, a.** to exhaust of fish by fishing. **b.** to obtain by careful search or by artifice. *–v.i.* **19.** to catch or attempt to catch fish, as by angling or drawing a net. **20.** to search for or attempt to catch on to something under water, in mud, etc., by the use of a dredge, rake, hook, or the like. **21.** to seek to obtain something by artifice or indirectly: *to fish for compliments, information, etc.* **22. fish in troubled waters,** take advantage of uncertain conditions; profit from the difficulties of others. [ME; OE *fisc,* c. D *visch,* G *Fisch;* akin to L *piscis*] – **fishable,** *adj.* – **fishless,** *adj.* – **fishlike,** *adj.*

**fish**[2] /fɪʃ/, *n.* **1.** *Naut.* a long strip of wood, iron, etc., used to strengthen a mast, joint, spar, etc. *–v.t.* **2.** *Naut.* to strengthen or repair (a mast, joint, spar, etc.) by means of a fish. [OF *ficher* to fix]

**fish and chips,** *n.* fish fillets coated with batter, and potato chips, both fried in deep fat or oil.

**fishbolt** /ˈfɪʃboʊlt/, *n.* a bolt that secures a fishplate to the rail in a railway track.

**fishbone fern** /ˌfɪʃboʊn ˈfɜn/, *n.* a commonly grown fern, *Nephrolepis exaltata,* with fronds having numerous pinnae.

fishbone fern

**fishbowl** /ˈfɪʃboʊl/, *n.* a glass bowl in which an ornamental fish is kept.

**fishcake** /ˈfɪʃkeɪk/, *n.* a fried ball or cake of shredded fish, esp. salt cod, and mashed potato. Also, **fish ball.**

**fish cocktail** /fɪʃ ˈkɒkteɪl/, *n.* a small piece of fish prepared in batter, designed to be served as a savoury.

**fisher** /ˈfɪʃə/, *n.* **1.** a fisherman. **2.** an animal that catches fish for food. **3.** a dark brown or blackish, somewhat foxlike marten, *Martes pennanti,* of northern North America. **4.** its fur.

**fisherman** /ˈfɪʃəmən/, *n., pl.* **-men. 1.** one engaged in fishing, whether for profit or pleasure. **2.** a vessel employed in fishing.

**fisherman's bend** /fɪʃəmənz ˈbɛnd/, *n.* a knot consisting of two round turns and a half-hitch round them and the standing part, used commonly to bend a rope to an anchor or similar object.

fisherman's bend

**fishery** /ˈfɪʃəri/, *n., pl.* **-ries. 1.** the occupation or industry of catching fish or taking other products of the sea or streams from the water. **2.** a place where such an industry is regularly carried on. **3.** a fishing establishment. **4.** *Law.* the right of fishing in certain waters.

**fish-eye lens** /fɪʃ-aɪ ˈlɛnz/, *n.* a camera lens in the shape of a protuding fish's eye, which can take in a view of almost 180°, but with considerable linear distortion.

**fish finger** /fɪʃ ˈfɪŋgə/, *n.* a piece of filleted fish cut into a finger-sized rectangle and crumbed ready for frying, grilling or baking.

**fish glue** /ˈ– glu/, *n.* **1.** any glue prepared from fish skins, bladders, or bones. **2.** →**isinglass.**

**fish head** /ˈ– hɛd/, *n.* a dull, spiritless, apathetic person.

**fishhook** /ˈfɪʃhʊk/, *n.* a barbed hook used in fishing.

**fishing** /ˈfɪʃɪŋ/, *n.* **1.** the art or practice of catching fish. **2.** a place or facilities for catching fish.

**fishing frog** /ˈ– frɒg/, *n.* →**angler** (def. 2).

**fishing line** /ˈ– laɪn/, *n.* a line used in fishing.

**fishing rod** /ˈ– rɒd/, *n.* a long rod, usu. flexible, supporting a fishing line.

**fishing smack** /ˈ– smæk/, *n.* a sloop-rigged fishing vessel fitted with a well to keep the catch alive.

**fishing tackle** /ˈ– tækəl/, *n.* the equipment used to catch fish.

**fishjoint** /ˈfɪʃdʒɔɪnt/, *n.* a splice formed by fastening one or more fishplates to the sides of rails, beams, etc., which meet end to end; used esp. in connecting railway lines.

**fish kettle** /ˈfɪʃ kɛtl/, *n.* a deep oval container, usu. having a perforated grid in the bottom, for poaching salmon, etc., sterilising fruit, etc.

**fish knife** /ˈ– naɪf/, *n.* a blunt, broad-bladed knife used for parting or cutting fish at table.

**fish ladder** /ˈ– lædə/, *n.* a series of ascending pools constructed so as to enable fish to swim upstream past a weir or dam.

**fish-louse** /ˈfɪʃ-laʊs/, *n., pl.* **-lice** /-laɪs/. any of numerous small crustaceans, esp. certain copepods, parasitic on fish.

**fishmeal** /ˈfɪʃmil/, *n.* a highly nutritious mealy food produced from fish and used as animal feed and fertiliser.

**fishmonger** /ˈfɪʃmʌŋgə/, *n.* a dealer in fish.

**fish-net** /ˈfɪʃ-nɛt/, *adj.* (of fabric, clothing, etc.) made in a loose open weave.

**fish oil** /ˈfɪʃ ɔɪl/, *n.* a fatty oil obtained from the bodies of fishes and sea mammals and used for rust-proofing motor vehicle bodies, in paint and varnish manufacture, soapmaking, etc.

**fishpaste** /ˈfɪʃpeɪst/, *n.* an edible paste flavoured with ground seafood.

**fishplate** /ˈfɪʃpleɪt/, *n.* one of the splicing plates used in a fishjoint.

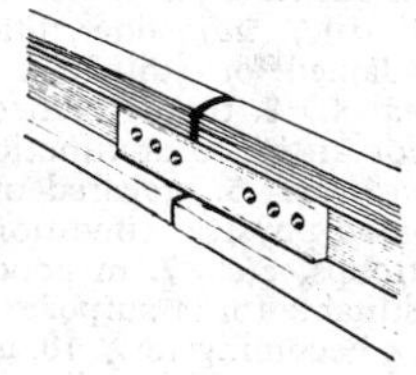
rail fishplate

**fishslice** /ˈfɪʃslaɪs/, *n.* **1.** a broad-bladed kitchen implement with a long handle, for turning fish in frying. **2.** a broad-bladed implement for serving fish at table.

**fish spear** /ˈfɪʃ spɪə/, *n.* a spear or lance, often with several tines, for spearing fish through ice or from a boat or shore.

**fishtail** /ˈfɪʃteɪl/, *v.i.* **1.** to slow an aeroplane by causing its tail to move rapidly from side to side. **2.** (of a ship, boat, etc.) to move forward through the water with a side to side whipping motion of the stern. *–n.* **3.** such a manoeuvre. **4.** a roughly triangular device attached to a Bunsen burner to give a flat, thin flame. **5.** a roughly triangular device attached to a car exhaust pipe, usu. decorative.

**fishwife** /ˈfɪʃwaɪf/, *n., pl.* **-wives. 1.** a woman who sells fish. **2.** a coarse-mannered woman who uses abusive language.

**fishy** /ˈfɪʃi/, *adj.,* **fishier, fishiest. 1.** fishlike in shape, smell, taste, etc. **2.** consisting of fish. **3.** abounding in fish. **4.** *Colloq.* improbable, as a story. **5.** *Colloq.* of questionable character. **6.** dull and expressionless: *fishy eyes.* – **fishily,** *adv.* – **fishiness,** *n.*

**fissi-,** a word element meaning 'cleft'. [L, combining form of *fissus,* pp.]

**fissile** /ˈfɪsaɪl/, *adj.* **1.** capable of being split or divided; cleavable. **2.** *Physics.* (of an atom, isotope, or nucleus) capable of undergoing nuclear fission, esp. of an isotope which is capable of undergoing fission upon impact with a slow neutron. Also, *U.S.,* **fissionable** /ˈfɪʃənəbəl/. [L *fissilis*]

**fission** /ˈfɪʃən/, *n.* **1.** the act of cleaving or splitting into parts. **2.** *Biol.* the division of an organism into new organisms as a process of reproduction. **3.** *Physics.* the splitting of the nucleus of a heavy atom, as uranium, to form the nuclei of lighter atoms. [L *fissio* a cleaving]

**fission bomb** /ˈ– bɒm/, *n.* an atomic weapon which depends on nuclear fission.

**fissiparous** /fɪˈsɪpərəs/, *adj.* reproducing by fission.

**fissirostral** /fɪsiˈrɒstrəl/, *adj. Ornith.* **1.** having a broad, deeply cleft beak or bill, as the swallows and goatsuckers. **2.** (of the bill) deeply cleft.

fissirostral bill of swallow

**fissure** /ˈfɪʃə/, *n., v.,* **-sured, -suring.** *–n.* **1.** a narrow opening produced by cleavage or separation of parts; a cleft. **2.** act of cleaving. **3.** the state of being cleft; cleavage. **4.** *Surg., Anat.* a natural division or groove between adjoining parts of like substance. *–v.t.* **5.** to make fissures in; cleave; split. *–v.i.* **6.** to open fissures; become split. [F, from L *fissūra* a cleft]

**fist** /fɪst/, *n.* **1.** the hand closed tightly, with the fingers doubled into the palm. **2.** *Colloq.* the hand. **3.** *Colloq.* a person's handwriting. **4. make a (good, poor) fist of,** to perform a task (well, badly). **5.** *Print.* the index sign. *–v.t.* **6.** to strike with the fist. **7.** to grasp with the fist. [ME *fiste,* OE *fȳst,* c. G *Faust*]

**fistful** /'fɪstfʊl/, *n.* →**handful.**

**fistic** /'fɪstɪk/, *adj.* of boxing; pugilistic: *fistic heroes.*

**fisticuff** /'fɪstikʌf/, *n.* **1.** a cuff or blow with the fist. **2.** (*pl.*) combat with the fists. *–v.t.* **3.** to strike with the fists. *–v.i.* **4.** to fight with the fists. **– fisticuffer,** *n.*

**fistula** /'fɪstʃʊlə/, *n., pl.* **-las, -lae** /-li/. **1.** *Pathol.* a narrow passage or duct formed by disease or injury, as one leading from an abscess to a free surface, or from one cavity to another. **2.** *Vet. Sci.* any of various suppurative inflammations, as in the withers of a horse, characterised by the formation of passages or sinuses through the tissues and to the surface of the skin. **3.** *Obs.* a pipe, as a flute. [L: pipe, tube, reed, ulcer. Cf. FESTER]

**fistulous** /'fɪstʃʊləs/, *adj.* **1.** *Pathol.* pertaining to or of the nature of a fistula. **2.** tubelike; tubular. **3.** containing tubes or tubelike parts. Also, **fistular.**

**fit**[1] /fɪt/, *adj.,* **fitter, fittest,** *v.,* **fitted, fitting,** *n. –adj.* **1.** well adapted or suited: *a fit choice or opportunity, fit to be eaten.* **2.** proper or becoming. **3.** qualified or competent, as for an office or function. **4.** worthy or deserving: *not fit to be seen.* **5.** prepared or ready: *crops fit for gathering.* **6.** in good physical condition, as an athlete, a race horse, military troops, etc. **7.** in good health. *–v.t.* **8.** to be adapted to or suitable for (a purpose, object, occasion, etc.). **9.** to be proper or becoming for. **10.** to be of the right size or shape for. **11.** to conform or adjust to something: *to fit a ring to the finger.* **12.** to make qualified or competent: *qualities that fit one for leadership.* **13.** to prepare. **14.** to put with precise adjustment (fol. by *in, into, on, over, together,* etc.). **15.** to provide; furnish; equip: *fit a door with a new handle.* **16.** *Colloq.* to bring a person before the law on a trivial or trumped-up charge while really intending to victimise him: *he had been trying to fit Chilla for years.* **17. fit like a glove,** to be a perfect fit. **18. fit out** or **up,** to furnish with clothing, equipment, furniture, fixtures, or other requisites. **19. fit the bill,** to suit; be what is required. **20. fit to be tied,** *Colloq.* very angry. *–v.i.* **21.** to be suitable or proper. **22.** to be of the right size or shape, as a garment for the wearer, or any object or part for a thing to which it is applied. **23. fit in,** to be well adapted to. *–n.* **24.** the manner in which a thing fits: *a perfect fit.* **25.** something that fits: *that coat is a poor fit.* **26.** the process or a process of fitting. **27.** *Colloq.* the equipment used to prepare and inject drugs. [late ME *fȳt;* orig. uncert.] **– fitness,** *n.*

**fit**[2] /fɪt/, *n.* **1.** a sudden, acute attack or manifestation of a disease: *fit of epilepsy.* **2.** an access, spell or period of emotion or feeling, inclination, activity, idleness, etc. **3.** convulsion. **4. by** or **in fits (and starts),** by irregular spells; fitfully; intermittently. **5. throw a fit,** to become very excited or angry. [ME; OE *fitt* fight, struggle]

**fit**[3] /fɪt/, *n.* **1.** a song, ballad, or story. **2.** a division of a song, ballad, or story. [ME; OE *fitt*]

**fitch** /fɪtʃ/, *n.* **1.** the European polecat, *Mustela putorius.* **2.** its fur, esp. **yellow fitch** which is often dyed to imitate other furs. **3.** a small brush made of this hair or of hog's hair. Also, **fitchet** /'fɪtʃət/, **fitchew** /'fɪtʃu/. [MD *vitsche* polecat]

**fitchered** /'fɪtʃəd/, *adj.* (of a mining drill hole) irregular or obstructed, thus jamming the drill. [Cornish d., from F *ficher* to fix]

**fitful** /'fɪtfəl/, *adj.* coming, appearing, acting, etc., in fits or by spells; irregularly intermittent. [FIT[2] + -FUL] **– fitfully,** *adv.* **– fitfulness,** *n.*

**fitly** /'fɪtli/, *adv.* **1.** in a fit manner. **2.** at a fit time.

**fitment** /'fɪtmənt/, *n.* **1.** equipment; furnishing, esp. that built to conform to the shape of a room. **2.** accessory; detachable part.

**fitted** /'fɪtəd/, *adj.* **1.** made so as to conform to the shape of something else. **2.** (of carpets) extending from wall to wall. **3.** provided or equipped with accessories.

**fitter** /'fɪtə/, *n.* **1.** one who or that which fits. **2.** one who fits garments. **3.** one who fits together or adjusts the parts of machinery. **4.** one who supplies and installs fittings or fixtures. **5.** one who furnishes or equips with whatever is necessary for some purpose.

**fitting** /'fɪtɪŋ/, *adj.* **1.** suitable or appropriate; proper or becoming. *–n.* **2.** the act of one who or that which fits. **3.** an act or instance of trying on clothes which are being made to determine proper fit. **4.** (of clothes) size. **5.** anything provided as equipment, parts, accessories, etc. **6.** (*pl.*) furnishings, fixtures, etc. **– fittingly,** *adv.* **– fittingness,** *n.*

**fitting room** /'– rum/, *n.* a room in a dress shop or a tailor's where customers can try on clothes.

**Fitzgerald-Lorentz contraction** /ˌfɪtsdʒerəld-'lɒrənts kənˌtrækʃən/, *n.* an explanation of the negative result of the Michelson-Morley experiment put forward independently by Fitzgerald (1893) and Lorentz (1895). It assumes that bodies moving at a high velocity suffer a contraction in length. This contraction was later shown to be a consequence of the theory of relativity. [named after G. F. *Fitzgerald,* 1851-1901, Irish physicist, and H. A. *Lorentz,* 1853-1928, Dutch physicist]

**five** /faɪv/, *n.* **1.** a cardinal number, four plus one. **2.** a symbol for this number, as 5 or V. **3.** a set of this many persons or things. **4.** a playing card, etc., with five pips. **5. take five,** *Colloq.* to take a break, originally of five minutes, for rest or refreshment, esp. as of a performing group in rehearsal. *–adj.* **6.** amounting to five in number. [ME; OE *fīf,* c. D *vijf,* G *fünf;* akin to L *quinque,* Gk *pénte*]

**five-corners** /faɪv-'kɔnəz/, *n.* →**styphelia.**

**five-day week** /faɪv-deɪ 'wik/, *n.* an arrangement of ordinary hours of work in which the work is performed on five days, Monday to Friday.

**five-eighth** /faɪv-'eɪtθ/, *n. Rugby Football.* **1.** the back who is stationed between the half-back and the centre three-quarters; fly-half; stand-off half. **2.** *N.Z.* either of the two players positioned outside the half-back, either the five-eighth (def. 1) or the inside-centre. Also, **five-eight, five-eighths.**

**five-finger** /'faɪv-fɪŋgə/, *n.* **1.** any of certain species of potentilla with leaves of five leaflets, as *Potentilla canadensis.* **2.** →**bird's-foot trefoil. 3.** →**oxlip. 4.** →**Virginia creeper.** *–adj.* **5.** for five fingers, as a piano exercise.

**five-finger discount** /– 'dɪskaʊnt/, *n. Colloq.* stealing; shoplifting.

**five-finger exercise** /– 'ɛksəsaɪz/, *n.* something easy, as an elementary piano exercise.

**fivefold** /'faɪvfoʊld/, *adj.* **1.** comprising five parts or members. **2.** five times as great or as much. *–adv.* **3.** in fivefold measure.

**five hundred** /faɪv 'hʌndrəd/, *n.* a form of euchre in which a joker and a widow are included and in which 500 points win.

**five o'clock shadow,** *n.* the dark stubble of a man's beard, apparent in the late afternoon, even though he has shaved in the morning.

**fivepins** /'faɪvpɪnz/, *n.pl.* **1.** (*construed as sing.*) a game played with five wooden pins at which a ball is bowled to knock them down. **2.** (*construed as pl.*) the pins used in this game. **– fivepin,** *adj.*

**fiver** /'faɪvə/, *n. Colloq.* **1.** (formerly) a five-pound note. **2.** anything that counts as five.

**fives** /faɪvz/, *n.* a ball game played with the hands or a bat in a walled court.

**five-star** /'faɪv-sta/, *adj. Brit.* of excellent quality. [from the highest rating in a system of grading hotels, restaurants, etc.]

**five-stones** /'faɪv-stoʊns/, *n.* a child's game played with a set of five small square pieces of stone, which are tossed on the palm of the hand and caught on the back of the hand.

**five-to-two** /faɪv-tə-'tu/, *n.* a Jew. [rhyming slang]

**fix** /fɪks/, *v.,* **fixed** or **fixt, fixing,** *n. –v.t.* **1.** to make fast, firm, or stable. **2.** to place definitely and more or less permanently. **3.** to settle definitely; determine: *to fix a price.* **4.** to direct (the eyes, the attention, etc.) steadily. **5.** to attract and hold (the eye, the attention, etc.). **6.** to make set or rigid. **7.** to put into permanent form. **8.** to put or place (responsibility, blame, etc.) on a person. **9.** to assign or refer to a definite place, time, etc. **10.** to repair. **11.** to put in order or in good condition; adjust or arrange. **12.** to provide or supply with (something needed or wanted): *How are you fixed for money?* **13.** *Colloq.* to arrange matters with, or with respect to, esp. privately or dishonestly, so as to secure favourable action: *to fix a jury or a game.* **14.** *U.S.* to get (a meal); prepare (food). **15.** *Colloq.* to put in a condition or position to make no further trouble. **16.** *Colloq.* to get even with; get revenge upon. **17.** *Chem.* **a.** to make stable in consistency or condition; reduce from fluidity or volatility to a more permanent state. **b.** to convert atmospheric nitrogen into nitrates for use as fertilisers. **18.** *Photog.* to remove the light-sensitive silver halides from (a photographic image), rendering it permanent. **19.** *Microscopy.* to kill, make rigid, and preserve for microscopic study. **20.** to castrate or spay (oft. fol. by *up*), usu. of dogs and cats. **21. fix on.** Also, **fix upon.** to decide on, single out, choose. **22. fix up, a.** to arrange, organise, or decide on. **b.** to put right; solve. **23. fix (someone) up,** to attend to (someone's) needs. *–v.i.* **24.** to become fixed. **25.** to become set; assume a rigid or solid form. **26.** to become stable or permanent. **27.** to settle down. *–n.* **28.** *Colloq.* a position from which it is difficult to escape; a predicament. **29.** *Colloq.* the determining of a position, as of an aeroplane by mathematical, electronic, or other means. **30.** *Colloq.* a shot of heroin or other drug. **31.** *Colloq.* a bribe. **32.** *Colloq.* any dishonest device or trick. [late ME, from ML *fixāre,* frequentative of L *figere* fix] **– fixable,** *adj.* **– fixer,** *n.*

**fixate** /ˈfɪkseɪt/, *v.,* **-ated, -ating.** *–v.t.* **1.** *Psychol.* to fix; make stable, as a sensation. *–v.i.* **2.** to become fixed. [apparently backformation from FIXATION]

**fixated** /ˈfɪkseɪtəd, fɪkˈseɪtəd/, *adj.* **1.** *Psychol.* partially arrested in emotional and instinctual development. **2.** *Colloq.* obsessed (fol. by *on*).

**fixation** /fɪkˈseɪʃən/, *n.* **1.** the act of fixing. **2.** the state of being fixed. **3.** *Chem.* **a.** a reduction from a volatile or fluid to a stable or solid form. **b.** the process of converting atmospheric nitrogen into a useful compound, as a nitrate fertiliser. **4.** *Psychol.* a partial arrest of emotional and instinctual development at an early point in life, due to a severe traumatic experience or an overwhelming gratification. [ME, from ML *fixātio,* from *fixāre,* frequentative of L *figere* fix]

**fixative** /ˈfɪksətɪv/, *adj.* **1.** serving to fix; making fixed or permanent. *–n.* **2.** a fixative substance, esp.: **a.** a liquid preservative sprayed on a drawing or pastel to prevent blurring. **b.** a solution for killing, hardening, and preserving material for microscopic study.

**fixed** /fɪkst/, *adj.* **1.** made fast or firm; firmly implanted. **2.** rendered stable or permanent, as colour. **3.** set or intent upon something; steadily directed; set or rigid. **4.** definitely and permanently placed: *a fixed buoy.* **5.** definite; not fluctuating or varying: *fixed prices.* **6.** put in order. **7.** *Colloq.* arranged with, or arranged, privately or dishonestly. **8.** *Chem.* **a.** (of an element) taken into a compound from its free state. **b.** non-volatile, or not easily volatilised: *a fixed oil.* **– fixedly** /ˈfɪksədli/, *adv.* **– fixedness,** *n.*

**fixed assets** /– ˈæsɛts/, *n.pl.* any long-term assets which are held solely for use and not for conversion into cash, as land, buildings, machinery, etc. Also, **capital assets.**

**fixed capital** /– ˈkæpətl/, *n.* capital which has been used to acquire property, execute permanent constructions, or erect plant and machinery intended for retention and employment with a view to making profits (as opposed to *circulating capital*).

**fixed charge** /– ˈtʃadʒ/, *n.* **1.** a legal charge on specific property, as contrasted with a floating charge, both of which are usu. contained in a debenture. **2.** an expense which must be met. **3.** periodic obligation, as taxes, interest on shares, etc. **4.** (*pl.*) such charges as depreciation, rent, interest, etc., arising out of the maintenance of fixed assets.

**fixed idea** /–aɪˈdɪə/, *n.* **1.** a persistent or obsessive idea, often delusional, from which a person cannot escape. **2.** *Psychol.* a delusional idea which dominates the mind in certain forms of insanity.

**fixed interest** /– ˈɪntrəst/, *n.* an interest rate which is payable on a loan and which is fixed for the entire period of the loan.

**fixed liability** /– laɪəˈbɪləti/, *n.* a long-term liability, as a mortgage, debenture.

**fixed oil** /– ˈɔɪl/, *n.* a natural oil which is fixed (def. 8b), as lard oil, linseed oil, etc. Fixed oils occur in the cellular membranes, etc., of animals, and in the seeds, capsules, etc., of plants.

**fixed point** /– ˈpɔɪnt/, *n.* any accurately reproducible equilibrium temperature, as ice point, steam point, sulphur point and the triple point.

**fixed satellite** /– ˈsætəlaɪt/, *n.* an artificial earth satellite in a synchronous orbit.

**fixed star** /– ˈsta/, *n.* any of the stars which apparently always retain the same position with respect to one another.

**fixed trust** /– ˈtrʌst/, *n.* a unit trust whose trust deed provides for a fixed portfolio of investments during the lifetime of the trust, save in exceptional circumstances (opposed to *flexible trust*).

**fixed-wing aircraft** /fɪkst-ˌwɪŋ ˈɛəkraft/, *n.* any aircraft which gains lift by means of fixed aerofoils.

**fixing** /ˈfɪksɪŋ/, *n.* **1.** the act of one who or that which fixes. **2.** (*pl.*) *Colloq.* appliances; trimmings.

**fix-it man** /ˈfɪks-ət mæn/, *n.* a handyman.

**fixity** /ˈfɪksəti/, *n., pl.* **-ties.** **1.** the state or quality of being fixed; stability; permanence. **2.** something fixed.

**fixt** /fɪkst/, *v.* a past tense and past participle of **fix.**

**fixture** /ˈfɪkstʃə/, *n.* **1.** something securely fixed in position; a permanently attached part or appendage of a house, etc.: *an electric-light fixture.* **2.** a person or thing long established in the same place or position. **3.** *Mach.* a device for holding the work in a machine tool, esp. where the machining is to be done in straight surfaces, as in a planer or a milling machine. **4.** *Law.* a moveable chattel (such as a machine, heating plant, etc.) which, by reason of annexation to real property and of adaptation to continuing use in connection with the realty, is considered a part of the realty. **5.** a sporting event to be held on a date arranged in advance, as a football match. **6.** an act of fixing. [var. of *fixure* (from LL *fixūra*) modelled on MIXTURE] **– fixtureless,** *adj.*

**fizgig** /ˈfɪzgɪg/, *n.* **1.** a frivolous, gadding girl or woman. **2.** a kind of hissing firework. **3.** a kind of whirling toy that makes a whizzing noise. **4.** a fish spear. [orig. uncert.]

**fizz** /fɪz/, *v.i.* **1.** to make a hissing or sputtering sound. *–n.* **2.** a hissing sound; effervescence. **3. a.** soda-water or other effervescent water. **b.** *Orig. U.S.* an iced mixed drink made of alcohol, lemon juice, sugar, and soda-water. **4.** champagne. [backformation from FIZZLE]

**fizzer** /ˈfɪzə/, *n. Colloq.* **1.** a firecracker which fails to explode. **2.** a failure; fiasco.

**fizzle** /ˈfɪzəl/, *v.,* **-zled, -zling,** *n.* *–v.t.* **1.** to make a hissing or sputtering sound, esp. one that dies out weakly. **2.** *Colloq.* to fail ignominiously after a good start (oft. fol. by *out*). *–n.* **3.** a fizzling, hissing, or sputtering. **4.** *Colloq.* a fiasco; a failure. [obs. *fise* (from Scand.; cf. Icel. *fīsa* break wind) + *-le,* frequentative and diminutive suffix] **– fizzler,** *n.*

**fizzy** /ˈfɪzi/, *adj.,* **-zier, -ziest.** **1.** that fizzes; fizzing. **2.** (of a soft drink or beverage) carbonated.

**fjeld** /fjɛld/, *n.* a high, bleak plateau on the Scandinavian peninsula. [Norw. See FELL[5]]

**fjord** /ˈfiɔd/, *n.* →**fiord.**

**fl.,** flourished. [L *floruit*]

**flab** /flæb/, *n. Colloq.* bodily fat; flabbiness.

**flabbergast** /ˈflæbəgæst, -gast/, *v.t.* to overcome with surprise and bewilderment; astound. [? FLABB(Y) + AGHAST]

**flabby** /ˈflæbi/, *adj.,* **-bier, -biest.** **1.** hanging loosely or limply, as flesh, muscles, etc. **2.** having such flesh. **3.** lacking firmness, as character, persons, principles, utterances, etc.; feeble. [cf. earlier *flappy* (from FLAP + -Y[1]) in same sense] **– flabbily,** *adv.* **– flabbiness,** *n.*

**flabellate** /ˈflæbəleɪt, fləˈbɛl-, -ət/, *adj.* fan-shaped. Also, **flabelliform** /fləˈbɛləfɔm/.

**flabellum** /fləˈbɛləm/, *n., pl.* **-bella** /-ˈbɛlə/. **1.** a fan, esp. one used in religious ceremonies. **2.** a fan-shaped part. [L: fan]

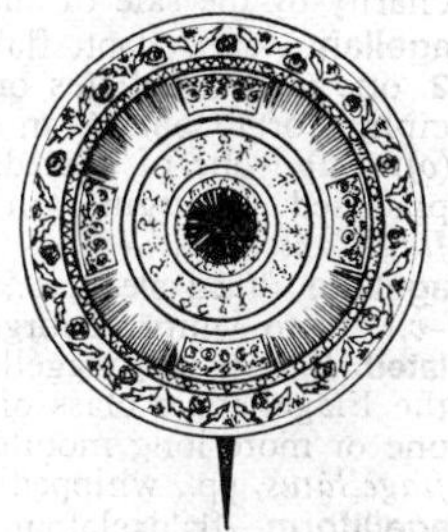
flabellum (def. 1)

**flaccid** /ˈflæsəd/, *adj.* soft and drooping; flabby; limp; not firm: *flaccid muscles.* [L *flaccidus*] – **flaccidity** /flə'sɪdəti/, **flaccidness,** *n.* – **flaccidly,** *adv.*

**flack** /flæk/, *n. Orig. U.S. Colloq.* a publicity agent; press secretary; public relations officer. Also, **flak.**

**flag**[1] /flæg/, *n., v.,* **flagged, flagging.** *–n.* **1.** a piece of cloth, commonly bunting, of varying size, shape, colour, and device, usu. attached by one edge to a staff or cord, and used as an ensign, standard, symbol, signal, decoration, display, etc. **2.** *Naut.* a ship carrying an admiral's flag; a flagship. **3.** *Ornith.* the tuft of long feathers on the leg of falcons and most other hawks; the lengthened feathers on the crus or tibia. **4.** *Hunting.* the tail of a deer or of a setter dog. **5.** *Journalism.* →**masthead** (def. 2). **6.** *Print.* a mark made by a proof corrector indicating an omission. **7.** a slip of paper used as a bookmark. **8.** an attachment to the meter of a taxi showing whether the taxi is engaged or not. **9.** Also, **Australian flag.** *Colloq.* part of a shirt, which has come untucked and hangs out over the trousers. **10. flag of convenience,** the flag of a country with which merchant ships owned by persons of other countries are registered in order to avoid taxes, etc. **11. flag of distress,** a flag displayed as a signal of distress, generally at half-mast or upside down. **12. flag of truce,** a white flag displayed as an invitation to the enemy to confer, or carried as a sign of peaceful intention by one sent to deal with the enemy. **13. have the flags out,** *Colloq.* **a.** to celebrate or welcome. **b.** to be menstruating. **14. hoist the flag,** *Prison Colloq.* to appeal against a conviction or the severity of a sentence. **15. keep the flag flying,** to appear courageous and cheerful in the face of difficulty. **16. show the flag, a.** to assert one's claim or interest, esp. by the physical presence of troops, etc. **b.** *Colloq.* to put in an appearance. **17. strike (lower) the flag, a.** to relinquish command, as of a ship. **b.** to submit or surrender. *–v.t.* **18.** to place a flag or flags over or on; decorate with flags. **19.** to signal or warn (a person, motor vehicle, etc.) with, or as with a flag (sometimes fol. by *down*). **20.** to communicate (information) by, or as by, a flag. **21.** to decoy, as game, by waving a flag or the like to excite attention or curiosity. [apparently b. FLAP, *n.,* and obs. *fag,* n., flap, flag; corresponding words in G, D, etc., from E] – **flagless,** *adj.*

flag[1]: flag of the Commonwealth of Australia

**flag**[2] /flæg/, *n.* **1.** any of various plants with long, sword-shaped leaves, as the **flag lily,** *Iris germanica,* or the cumbungi. **2.** the long, slender leaf of such a plant or of a cereal. [ME *flagge;* orig. uncert. Cf. D *vlag*]

**flag**[3] /flæg/, *v.i.,* **flagged, flagging. 1.** to hang loosely or limply; droop. **2.** to fall off in vigour, energy, activity, interest, etc. [apparently b. FLAP, *v.,* and FAG, *v.,* in obs. sense of droop. See FLAG[1], *n.*]

**flag**[4] /'flæg/, *n. v.,* **flagged, flagging.** *–n.* **1.** a flat slab of stone used for paving, etc. **2.** (*pl.*) a walk paved with such slabs. *–v.t.* **3.** to pave with flags. [late ME *flagge* turf, probably from Scand.; cf. Icel. *flag, flaga*] – **flagless,** *adj.*

**flag captain** /'– kæptn/, *n.* the commanding officer of a flagship.

**flag day** /'– deɪ/, *n.* a day on which money is collected for charity by the sale of small flags.

**flagellant** /'flædʒələnt, flə'dʒɛlənt/, *n.* **1.** one who flagellates. **2.** one who flagellates or scourges himself for religious discipline or to obtain an emotional or sexual experience. **3.** (*oft. cap.*) one of a medieval European sect of fanatics that practised scourging in public. *–adj.* **4.** flagellating. [L. *flagellans,* ppr.]

**flagellate** /'flædʒəleɪt/, *v.,* **-lated, -lating;** /'flædʒələt/, *adj., n.* *–v.t.* **1.** to whip; scourge; flog; lash. *–adj.* **2.** Also, **flagellated.** *Biol.* having flagella. See **flagellum.** *–n.* **3.** *Zool.* any of the Flagellata, a class of protozoans distinguished by having one or more long mobile filaments as locomotory organs. [L *flagellātus,* pp., whipped] – **flagellation,** *n.* – **flagellator,** *n.*

**flagelliform** /flə'dʒɛləfɔm/, *adj.* long, slender, and flexible, like the lash of a whip. [L *flagellum* a whip + -I- + -FORM]

**flagellum** /flə'dʒɛləm/, *n., pl.* **-gella, -gellums. 1.** a long, lashlike appendage serving as an organ of locomotion in certain reproductive bodies, bacteria, protozoans, etc. **2.** a whip or lash. [L: whip, scourge]

**flageolet** /flædʒə'lɛt/, *n.* a small end-blown flute with four fingerholes in front and two in the rear. [F, diminutive of OF *flajol* flute, from L *flāre* blow]

flageolet

**flag fall** /'flæg fɔl/, *n.* an initial fee for hiring a taxi, registered automatically on its meter.

**flaggie** /'flægi/, *n. Colloq.* a flagman.

**flagging**[1] /'flægɪŋ/, *adj.* drooping; weakening; failing. [FLAG[3] + -ING[2]] – **flaggingly,** *adv.*

**flagging**[2] /'flægɪŋ/, *n.* **1.** flagstones collectively. **2.** a pavement of flagstones. [FLAG[4] + -ING[1]]

**flaggy**[1] /'flægi/, *adj.* flagging; drooping; limp. [FLAG[3] + -Y[1]]

**flaggy**[2] /'flægi/, *adj.* consisting of or resembling flags or flagstone; laminate. [FLAG[4] + -Y[1]]

**flaggy**[3] /'flægi/, *adj.* abounding in, consisting of, or resembling the plants called flags. [FLAG[2] + -Y[1]]

**flagitious** /flə'dʒɪʃəs/, *adj.* **1.** shamefully wicked, as persons, actions, times, etc. **2.** heinous or flagrant, crime; infamous. [ME, from L *flāgitiōsus*] – **flagitiously,** *adv.* – **flagitiousness,** *n.*

**flag lieutenant** /'flæg lɛf,tɛnənt/, *n.* an aide to a flag officer.

**flagman** /'flægmən/, *n., pl.* **-men.** one who signals with a flag.

**flag of convenience** *n.* the flag of a country in which a ship has been registered only to gain some financial or legal advantage.

**flag officer** /'flæg ɒfəsə/, *n.* a naval officer, as an admiral, vice-admiral, or rear admiral entitled to display a flag showing his rank.

**flagon** /'flægən/, *n.* **1.** a large bottle for wine, etc., esp. one which is squat and of large circumference. **2.** a vessel for holding liquids, as for use at table, esp. one with a handle, a spout, and usu. a cover. [ME *flakon,* from OF *fla(s)con;* cf. ML *flasca* FLASK[1]]

**flagpole** /'flægpoʊl/, *n.* a staff or pole on which a flag is displayed. Also, **flagstaff** /'flægstaf/.

**flagrant** /'fleɪgrənt/, *adj.* **1.** glaring; notorious; scandalous: *a flagrant crime, a flagrant offender.* **2.** *Rare.* blazing, burning, or glowing. [L *flagrans,* ppr., blazing, burning] – **flagrance, flagrancy,** *n.* – **flagrantly,** *adv.*

**flagrante delicto** /flə,grænti də'lɪktoʊ/, *adv.* while the crime is, or was, being committed. [L]

**flagship** /'flægʃɪp/, *n.* a ship which carries a flag officer of a fleet, squadron, or the like, and displays his flag.

**flag smut** /'flæg smʌt/, *n.* →**stripe smut.**

**flagstone** /'flægstoʊn/, *n.* **1.** a flat slab of stone used for paving, etc. **2.** (*pl.*) a walk paved with such slabs. **3.** rock, such as sandstone, shale, etc., which can be split up into slabs for paving.

**flag-wagging** /'flæg-wægɪŋ/, *n.* **1.** *Naut.* signalling by the use of hand flags, esp. at sea. **2.** excessive patriotic zeal; flag-waving. *–adj.* **3.** flag-waving.

**flag-waving** /'flæg-weɪvɪŋ/, *n.* **1.** an emotional, aggressive, or excessive display of patriotism. *–adj.* **2.** of, pertaining to, or denoting an excess of patriotism.

**flail** /fleɪl/, *n.* **1.** an instrument for threshing grain by hand, consisting of a staff or handle to one end of which is attached a freely swinging stick or bar. **2.** *Mil.* an implement derived from the threshing flail used as a weapon of war in the Middle Ages. *–v.t.* **3.** to strike with, or as if with, a flail. [ME *flegl,* OE *flygel;* akin to FLY]

**flair** /flɛə/, *n.* **1.** talent; aptitude; keen perception. **2.** *Hunting.* scent; sense of smell. [F, from *flairer* smell, from L *frāgrāre*]

**flak** /flæk/, *n.* **1.** anti-aircraft fire, esp. as experienced by the crews of military aircraft at which the fire is directed. **2.** heavy criticism; abuse. **3.** →**flack.** [properly *Fl.A.K.,* from G, abbrev. of *Flieger-Abwehr-Kanone* anti-aircraft gun]

**flake**[1] /fleɪk/, *n., v.,* **flaked, flaking.** *–n.* **1.** a small, flat, thin piece of anything. **2.** a small, detached piece or mass: *a flake of cloud.* **3.** a stratum or layer. *–v.i.* **4.** to peel off or separate in flakes. **5.** to fall in flakes, as snow. **6.** Also, **flake out.** *Colloq.* to collapse, faint, or fall asleep, esp. as a result of complete exhaustion, or influence of alcohol, drugs, etc.

–*v.t.* **7.** to remove in flakes. **8.** to break flakes or chips from. **9.** to cover with or as with flakes. **10.** to form into flakes. [ME, apparently from OE *flac-*, which occurs in *flacor* flying (said of arrows). Cf. also Icel. *flakka* be loose]

**flake**[2] /fleɪk/, *n.* a frame, as for drying fish. [ME *flake, fleke.* Cf. Icel. *flaki, fleki* hurdle, wickerwork shield]

**flake**[3] /fleɪk/, *n.* the flesh of various sharks and rays, often the flaps of the skate, commonly sold in fish shops.

**flake**[4] /fleɪk/, *v.*, **flaked, flaking,** *n.* –*v.t.* **1.** to lay out a rope, cable, etc., in a series of parallel lines for inspection or to prepare it for running. –*n.* **2.** one of the windings of a flaked cable or hawser. Also, **fake.** [var. of FAKE[2]]

**flakers** /'fleɪkəz/, *adj. Colloq.* unconscious; dead drunk.

**flake white** /fleɪk 'waɪt/, *n.* a pigment made from pure white lead.

**flaky** /'fleɪki/, *adj.*, **flakier, flakiest. 1.** of or like flakes. **2.** lying or cleaving off in flakes or layers. [FLAKE[1] + -Y[1]] – **flakily,** *adv.* – **flakiness,** *n.*

**flaky pastry** /– 'peɪstri/, *n.* →**puff pastry.**

**flambé** /flɒm'beɪ/, *adj.* (of food) dressed or served in flaming spirits, esp. brandy. [F, pp. of *flamber* to flame]

**flambeau** /flɒm'boʊ/, *n., pl.* **-beaux** /-boʊz/, **-beaus. 1.** a flaming torch. **2.** a torch for use at night in illuminations, processions, etc. **3.** a large decorated candle-stick, as of bronze. [F, from OF *flambe* flame, earlier *flamble,* from L *flammula,* diminutive of *flamma* flame]

**flamboyant** /flæm'bɔɪənt/, *adj.* **1.** flaming; gorgeous: *flamboyant colours.* **2.** florid; ornate; showy: *flamboyant rhetoric.* –*n.* **3.** Also, **flamboyante.** a flowering tree bearing brilliant red flowers, *Delonix regia,* of eastern Africa and Madagascar. [F, ppr. of *flamboyer* to flame, flare, from OF *flambe* small flame. See FLAMBEAU] – **flamboyance, flamboyancy,** *n.* – **flamboyantly,** *adv.*

**flame** /fleɪm/, *n., v.,* **flamed, flaming.** –*n.* **1.** burning gas or vapour, as from wood, etc., undergoing combustion; a portion of ignited gas or vapour. **2.** (*oft. pl.*) state or condition of blazing combustion: *to burst into flames.* **3.** any flamelike condition; glow; inflamed condition. **4.** brilliant light; scintillating lustre. **5.** bright colouring; a streak or patch of colour. **6.** heat or ardour, as of zeal or passion. **7.** *Colloq.* an object of the passion of love; sweetheart. –*v.i.* **8.** to burn with a flame or flames; burst into flames; blaze. **9.** to glow like flame; shine brilliantly; flash. **10.** to burn as with flame, as passion; break into open anger, indignation, etc.; blush violently (oft. fol. by *up*). –*v.t.* **11.** to subject to the action of flame or fire. [ME, from OF *flamme,* from L *flamma*] – **flameless,** *adj.*

**flame colour** /'– kʌlə/, *n.* bright reddish orange. – **flame-coloured,** *adj.*

**flame-gum** /'fleɪm-gʌm/, *n.* a small tree, *Eucalyptus ficifolia,* of western Australia, widely cultivated for its bright red flowers.

**flame-hardening** /'fleɪm-hadnɪŋ/, *n.* the rapid heating of the surface of iron or steel, by means of a flame, followed by quenching in order to harden the surface.

**flame-holder** /'fleɪm-hoʊldə/, *n.* a device in certain jet engines that provides a sheltered zone for flame stabilisation.

**flame lily** /'fleɪm lɪli/, *n.* a bulbous plant with deep orange perianth segments, *Gloriosa superba,* of tropical Asia and Africa.

**flamenco** /flə'meŋkoʊ/, *n., pl.* **-cos.** a kind of Spanish music or dance, esp. of the gipsy style.

**flame-out** /'fleɪm-aʊt/, *n.* the failure of a jet engine as a result of an interruption in the fuel supply or imperfect combustion.

**flameproof** /'fleɪmpruf/, *adj.* **1.** not easily combustible. **2.** (of an electrical apparatus) designed so that an explosion within the apparatus will not ignite any inflammable gas outside it. **3.** (of glass and other cooking vessels) safe for use on the top of the stove, or above an open flame.

**flame-resistant** /'fleɪm-rəzɪstənt/, *adj.* of or pertaining to that which cannot be ignited easily as of certain types of fabric. – **flame-resistance,** *n.*

**flame test** /'fleɪm tɛst/, *n.* a qualitative chemical test for detecting the presence of certain elements in substances by noting the coloration they impart to a flame.

**flamethrower** /'fleɪmθroʊə/, *n.* a weapon that projects ignited incendiary fuel, as napalm.

**flame-trap** /'fleɪm-træp/, *n.* any device in a fuel line, or the induction system of an engine, which prevents the flame from igniting the combustible mixture at the wrong time or place.

**flame-tree** /'fleɪm-tri/, *n.* an ornamental tree, *Brachychiton acerifolium,* of Australia, with scarlet, bell-shaped flowers. Also, **Illawarra flame-tree.**

**flaming** /'fleɪmɪŋ/, *adj.* **1.** emitting flames; blazing; fiery. **2.** glowing; brilliant. **3.** violent; vehement; passionate. **4.** *Colloq.* (an intensive): *a flaming bore.* **5.** *Colloq.* (a euphemism for various expletives): *stone the flaming crows.* – **flamingly,** *adv.*

**flamingo** /flə'mɪŋgoʊ/, *n., pl.* **-gos, -goes. 1.** any of the aquatic birds constituting the family Phoenicopteridae, with very long neck and legs, webbed feet, bills bent downwards, and pinkish to scarlet plumage. **2.** a dark shade of pinkish orange. [Pg., from Sp. *flamenco,* from Pr. *flamenc,* from *flama* (from L *flamma* FLAME) + suffix *-enc* (from Gmc *-ing*)]

flamingo

**flammable** /'flæməbəl/, *adj.* easily set on fire; combustible; inflammable. – **flammability** /flæmə'bɪləti/, *n.*

**flamy** /'fleɪmi/, *adj.* of or like flame.

**flan** /flæn/, *n.* **1.** an open tart containing cheese, cream, or fruit. **2.** a piece of metal shaped ready to form a coin, but not yet stamped by the die. **3.** the metal of which a coin is made, as distinct from its design. [F]

**flan-case** /'flæn-keɪs/, *n.* a crust of pastry baked before a flan filling is added.

**Flanders poppy** /flændəz 'pɒpi, flan-/, *n.* →**corn poppy.**

**flange** /flændʒ/, *n., v.,* **flanged, flanging.** –*n.* **1.** a projecting rim, collar, edge, ridge, or the like, on an object, for keeping it in place, attaching it to another object, strengthening it, etc. **2.** the horizontal portion or portions of steel shapes, such as the top and bottom flange of an I-beam. **3.** a device or tool for making flanges. –*v.i.* **4.** to project like, or take the form of, a flange. [var. of *flanch,* n., from *flanch,* v., from OF *flanchir* bend, b. *flanc* FLANK and *flechier* (from Rom. *flecticāre,* from L *flectere*)] – **flangeless,** *adj.*

flange

**flank** /flæŋk/, *n.* **1.** the side of an animal or a human being between the ribs and hip. **2.** the thin piece of flesh, constituting this part. **3.** a slice of meat from the flank. **4.** the side of anything, as of a building. **5.** *Mil., Navy.* the extreme right or left side of an army or fleet, or a subdivision of an army or fleet. **6.** *Fort.* **a.** the right or left side of a work or fortification. **b.** a part of a work that defends another work by a fire along the outside of its parapet. **c.** the part of a bastion which extends from the curtain to the face, etc. **7.** *Mach.* **a.** the part of the profile of a gearwheel which lies within the pitch circle or line. **b.** the working surface of a cam. **8. a.** *Rugby Union., Aus. Rules.* an outside position, as half-forward flank, half-back flank, breakaway. **b.** *Aus. Rules,* one who plays in the flank position. –*v.t.* **9.** to stand or be placed or posted at the flank or side of. **10.** to defend or guard at the flank. **11.** to pass round or turn the flank of. –*v.i.* **12.** to occupy a position at the flank or side. **13.** to present the flank or side. [ME *flanke,* OE *flanc,* from OF, from Gmc; cf. OHG *hlancha*]

**flanker** /'flæŋkə/, *n.* **1.** one who or that which flanks. **2.** *Mil.* one of a body of soldiers employed on the flank of an army to guard a line of march. **3.** *Fort.* a fortification projecting so as to defend another work, or to command the flank of an assailing body. **4.** *Chiefly Brit., N.Z. Rugby Union.* →**breakaway.** (def. 6). **5.** *Aus. Rules.* a player in an outside position, as half-back and half-forward flanks.

**flank forward** /flæŋk 'fɔwəd/, *n. Chiefly N.Z. Rugby Union.* →**breakaway** (def. 6).

**flank girth** /'– gɜθ/, *n.* a girth on a saddle used to go around the flanks of a horse rather than the belly.

**flannel** /ˈflænəl/, *n., v.,* **-elled, -elling** or (*U.S.*) **-eled, -eling.** *–n.* **1.** a warm, soft fabric of wool or blends of wool and cotton, wool and rayon, or cotton warp with wool filling. **2.** →**washer** (def. 4). **3.** (*pl.*) an outer garment, esp. trousers, made of flannel. **4.** (*pl.*) *Obs.* woollen undergarments. **5.** *Brit. Colloq.* evasive or flattering talk. *–v.t.* **6.** to cover or clothe with flannel. **7.** to rub with flannel. **8.** *Brit. Colloq.* to flatter or talk evasively to (oft. fol. by *up*). [orig. uncert.] – **flannelly,** *adj.*

**flannelette** /flænəˈlɛt/, *n.* a cotton fabric, plain or printed, napped on one side to imitate flannel.

**flannel flower** /ˈflænəl flaʊə/, *n.* an Australian plant, *Actinotus helianthi,* having white, flannel-like bracts below the flower.

flannel flower

**flap** /flæp/, *v.,* **flapped, flapping,** *n.* *–v.i.* **1.** to swing or sway about loosely, esp. with noise: *a curtain or flag flaps in the wind.* **2.** to move up and down, as wings; flap the wings, or make similar movements. **3.** to strike a blow with something broad and flexible. **4.** *Colloq.* to panic, become flustered. *–v.t.* **5.** to move (arms, wings, etc.) up and down. **6.** to cause to swing or sway loosely, esp. with noise. **7.** to strike with something broad and flexible. **8.** *Colloq.* to toss, fold, shut, etc., smartly, roughly, or noisily. *–n.* **9.** a flapping motion. **10.** the noise produced by something that flaps. **11.** a blow given with something broad and flexible. **12.** something broad and flexible, or flat and thin, that hangs loosely, attached at one side only. **13.** *Surg.* a portion of skin or flesh partially separated from the body which may subsequently be transposed by grafting. **14.** *Aeron.* a wing surface that can be lifted in flight to modify lift and drag. **15.** *Colloq.* a state of panic or nervous excitement: *in a flap.* [ME *flappe(n),* probably of imitative orig.; cf. D *flappen* clap] – **flapless,** *adj.*

**flapdoodle** /ˈflæpdudl/, *n. Colloq.* nonsense; bosh.

**flapdragon** /ˈflæpdrægən/, *n.* **1.** (formerly) a pastime in which the players snatched raisins, plums, etc., out of burning brandy, and ate them. **2.** the object so caught and eaten.

**flapjack** /ˈflæpdʒæk/, *n.* a kind of pancake.

**flapper** /ˈflæpə/, *n.* **1.** something broad and flat for striking with, or for making a noise by striking. **2.** broad, flat, hinged or hanging piece; flap. **3.** a young bird just learning to fly. **4.** a young woman during the 1920s, esp. one freed from the traditional social and moral restraints.

**flapping** /ˈflæpɪŋ/, *v.* **1.** present participle of **flap.** *–adj.* **2. with one's ears flapping,** *Colloq.* with keen interest or astonishment, esp. when listening to a conversation not meant to be overheard. *–n.* **3.** the practice of directing traffic flow by the use of movable lane markers.

**flap speed** /ˈflæp spid/, *n.* the speed of an aeroplane with the wing flaps down.

**flare** /flɛə/, *v.,* **flared, flaring.** *n.* *–v.i.* **1.** to burn with an unsteady, swaying flame, as a torch or candle in the wind. **2.** to blaze with a sudden burst of flame (oft. fol by *up*). **3.** to start up or burst out in sudden fierce activity, passion, anger, etc. (sometimes fol. by *up* or *out*). **4.** to shine or glow. **5.** to spread gradually outwards as the end of a trumpet, or a ship's sides or bows. *–v.t.* **6.** to cause (a candle, etc.) to burn with a swaying flame. **7.** to display conspicuously or ostentatiously. **8.** to signal by flares of fire or light. **9.** to cause (something) to spread gradually outwards in form. **10.** *Metall.* to heat (a high-zinc brass) to such a high temperature that the zinc vapours begin to burn. *–n.* **11.** a flaring or swaying flame or light as of torches in the wind. **12.** a sudden blaze or burst of flame. **13.** a sudden blaze of fire or light used as a signal or for illumination or guidance, etc. **14.** a device or substance used to produce such a blaze of fire or light. **15.** a sudden burst, as of zeal or of temper. **16.** a gradual spread outwards in form; outward curvature: *the flare of a skirt.* **17.** something that spreads out. **18.** *Optics.* light reflected by the surfaces of an optical system. **19.** →**Hawaiian flare. 20.** (*pl.*) trousers having the lower parts of the legs flared. [orig. meaning spread out, display; b. FLY[1] and BARE[1], but cf. Norw. *flara* blaze]

**flare-path** /ˈflɛə-paθ/, *n.* an illuminated runway at an airport to enable aircraft to land or take off when normal visibility is inadequate.

**flare-up** /ˈflɛər-ʌp/, *n.* **1.** a sudden flaring up of flame or light. **2.** *Colloq.* a sudden outburst of anger.

**flaring** /ˈflɛərɪŋ/, *adj.* **1.** that flares; flaming; blazing. **2.** glaringly bright or showy. **3.** spreading gradually outwards in form. – **flaringly,** *adv.*

**flash** /flæʃ/, *n.* **1.** a sudden, transitory outburst of flame or light: *a flash of lightning.* **2.** a sudden, brief outburst or display of joy, wit, etc. **3.** the time occupied by a flash of light; an instant: *to do something in a flash.* **4.** ostentatious display. **5.** a distinctive mark, an emblem, as on a soldier's uniform to identify his unit. **6.** *Journalism.* a brief telegraphic dispatch, usu. transmitting preliminary news of an important story or development. **7.** *Photog.* **a.** →**flash photography. b.** →**flashgun. 8.** *Obs.* the cant or jargon of thieves, vagabonds, etc. **9.** *Naut., etc.* **a.** an extra volume or rush of water, as that produced by a dam or sluiceway, utilised to float a boat over shoals or for other purposes. **b.** the device, as a lock or sluice, used for this purpose. **10.** *Colloq.* a momentary sensation of pleasure following the injection of certain narcotic drugs. **11.** *Mining.* an opal reflecting a single flash in a large patch of colour. **12. flash in the pan,** something which begins promisingly but has no lasting significance. *–v.i.* **13.** to break forth into sudden flame or light, esp. transiently or intermittently; to gleam. **14.** to speak or behave with sudden anger: *he flashed crimson with rage.* **15.** to burst suddenly into view or perception: *the answer flashed into his mind.* **16.** to move like a flash. **17.** to break into sudden action. **18.** *Colloq.* to make a flash or sudden display. *–v.t.* **19.** to emit or send forth (fire or light) in sudden flashes. **20.** to cause to flash, as powder by ignition or flashes. **21.** to send forth like a flash. **22.** to communicate instantaneously, as by telegraph. **23.** *Colloq.* to make a sudden or ostentatious display of: *to flash one's diamonds.* **24.** to expose (def. 5) briefly and unexpectedly. **25.** to increase the flow of water in (a river, etc.). **26.** *Obs.* to dash or splash (water). **27.** *Glassmaking.* **a.** to coat (plain glass or a glass object) with a film of coloured, opal, or white glass. **b.** to apply (such a coating). **28.** *Bldg Trades.* to protect by use of a flashing (def. 1). *–adj.* **29.** showy or ostentatious. **30.** counterfeit or sham. **31.** belonging or pertaining to sporting men. **32.** (formerly) belonging to or connected with thieves, vagabonds, etc., or their cant or jargon: *flash mob.* [ME *flasche(n)* rush (said of tidal waters); b. FLOW (or FLOOD) and WASH]

**flashback** /ˈflæʃbæk/, *n.* **1.** a representation, during the course of a novel, film, etc., of some event or scene which occurred at a previous time. **2.** a sudden remembering of someone or something from the past. **3.** an unexpected reoccurrence of psychedelic phenomena previously induced by drugs. **4.** *Mining.* →**spontaneous combustion.** *–v.i.* **5.** to interrupt a story or film to insert a sequence from an earlier time. **6.** (of a person) to have a flashback (defs 2 and 3).

**flash blindness** /flæʃ ˈblaɪndnəs/, *n.* temporary or permanent impairment of vision resulting from an intense flash of light, esp. suffered as a wartime injury.

**flashboard** /ˈflæʃbɔd/, *n.* a board, or one of a series of boards, as on a milldam, used to increase the depth of the impounded water.

**flashbulb** /ˈflæʃbʌlb/, *n.* a glass bulb filled with oxygen and a thin sheet of magnesium or aluminium, giving a momentary bright light when fired, used as a light source, in photography.

**flash burn** /ˈflæʃ bɜn/, *n.* a burn from a very brief exposure to great heat as from an explosion.

**flashcard** /ˈflæʃkad/, *n.* **1.** a card held up briefly to elicit immediate response to the material written on it from a class of experimental subjects. **2.** a card used similarly by teachers in drilling students esp. in elementary spelling, etc.

**flashcube** /ˈflæʃkjub/, *n.* a camera attachment consisting of four flashbulbs contained in a cube, which turns so that four photographs can be taken without reloading. [Trademark]

**flasher** /ˈflæʃə/, *n.* **1.** *Colloq.* a man who briefly exposes his private parts in public. **2.** *Chiefly Brit.* →**trafficator.**

**flash flood** /flæʃ 'flʌd/, *n.* a sudden, destructive rush of water down a narrow gully or over a sloping surface in desert regions, due to heavy rains in the mountains or foothills.

**flashgun** /'flæʃgʌn/, *n.* a device which discharges a flashbulb in synchronisation with a camera shutter, or which produces a flash by electronic means.

**flashing** /'flæʃɪŋ/, *n.* **1.** *Bldg Trades.* a piece of sheet metal, etc., used to keep out water, and to cover and protect certain joints or angles, as where a roof comes in contact with a wall or chimney. **2.** *Bldg Trades.* a method of burning bricks to give them varied colours. **3.** the act of creating an artificial flood in a conduit or stream, as in a sewer for cleansing it.

**flashlight** /'flæʃlaɪt/, *n.* **1.** any source of artificial light as used in flash photography. **2.** a flash of light, or a light that flashes. **3.** an electric torch.

**flashover** /'flæʃoʊvə/, *n.* **1.** a disruptive electrical discharge around or over the surface of a solid or liquid insulator. *–v.i.* **2.** to establish a flashover.

**flash photography** /'flæʃ fə,tɒgrəfi/, *n.* the use of a flashgun as a light source in photography. Also, **flashlight photography.**

**flash picture** /'– pɪktʃə/, *n.* a photograph taken by flash photography.

**flashpoint** /'flæʃpɔɪnt/, *n.* **1.** the lowest temperature at which a volatile oil will give off explosive or ignitable vapours. **2.** *Colloq.* the point or moment at which an explosion takes place or control is lost: *tempers reached flashpoint after the chairman's speech.*

**flashy** /'flæʃi/, *adj.*, **flashier, flashiest. 1.** sparkling or brilliant, esp. in a superficial way or for the moment. **2.** pretentiously smart; showy; gaudy. **3.** *Rare.* flashing with light. – **flashily,** *adv.* – **flashiness,** *n.*

**flask**[1] /flask/, *n.* **1.** a bottle-shaped container made of glass, metal, etc.: *a flask of oil, a brandy flask.* **2.** an iron container for shipping mercury. **3.** (in foundry work) a moulding box which holds the sand into which molten metal is poured. [OE *flasce, flaxe.* Cf. FLAGON]

**flask**[2] /flask/, *n.* **1.** the armoured plates making up the sides of a guncarriage trail. **2.** *Obs.* the bed of a guncarriage. [d. F *flasque* cheek of a guncarriage, from LL *flasca* FLASK[1], from Gmc. See FLAGON]

**flasket** /'flaskət/, *n.* **1.** a small flask. **2.** a long, shallow basket. [ME *flaskett,* from OF *flasquet* small flask, from *flasque* FLASK[1]]

**flat**[1] /flæt/, *adj.*, **flatter, flattest,** *adv., n., v.,* **flatted, flatting.** *–adj.* **1.** level, even, or without inequalities of surface, as land, etc. **2.** horizontally level: *a flat roof.* **3.** comparatively lacking in projection or depression of surface: *a broad flat face.* **4.** (of a sea, harbour, etc.) unbroken by waves with little or no swell. **5.** lying at full length, as a person. **6.** lying wholly on or against something: *a ladder flat against a wall.* **7.** thrown down, laid low, or level with the ground, as fallen trees or buildings. **8.** (of a race) run on a level course or track, without obstacles to be jumped. **9.** having a generally level shape or appearance; not deep or thick: *a flat plate.* **10.** (of the heel of a shoe) low and broad. **11.** (of feet) having little or no arch. See **flatfoot. 12.** spread out, as an unrolled map, the open hand, etc. **13.** collapsed; deflated: *a flat tyre.* **14.** without qualification; unqualified, downright, or positive: *a flat denial, that's flat, flat broke.* **15.** without modification: *a flat rate, a flat price.* **16.** uninteresting, dull, or tedious. **17.** (of wine) lacking substance and body; low in acidity. **18.** stale; tasteless or insipid, as food. **19.** (of beer, etc.) having lost its effervescence. **20.** pointless, as a remark, joke, etc. **21.** commercially dull, as trade or the market. **22.** lacking relief, contrast, or shading, as a painting. **23.** not giving the effect of perspective: *the flat quality of medieval painting.* **24.** *Painting.* without gloss; matt. **25.** not clear, sharp, or ringing, as sound, a voice, etc. **26.** *Music.* **a.** (of a note) lowered a semitone in pitch: *B flat.* **b.** below an intended pitch, as a note; too low (opposed to *sharp*). **c.** (of an interval) diminished. **27.** *Colloq.* (formerly) honest (opposed to *sharp*). **28.** *Gram.* derived without change in form, as English *to brush* from the noun *brush,* and adverbs which do not add *-ly* to the adjective form, as *fast.* **29.** *Naut.* (of a sail) **a.** cut with little or no fullness. **b.** trimmed as nearly fore-and-aft as possible, for sailing to windward. **30.** of or pertaining to a race run on a course without obstacle: *a flat race.* **31. flat a,** the sound of 'a' in 'fat', contrasted with broad 'a', the sound of 'a' in 'father'. Some words may be pronounced with either the broad or flat 'a', as *dance, chance,* etc. **32. flat as a tack,** exhausted. *–adv.* **33.** in a flat position; horizontally; levelly. **34.** positively; absolutely. **35.** exactly. **36.** *Music.* below the true pitch. **37.** *Finance.* without interest. **38. brace a yard flat aback,** *Naut.* to set a yard so that the wind is nearly at right angles to the forward surface of the sail. **39. fall flat,** to fall completely; fail to succeed in attracting interest, etc. **40. flat out,** *Colloq.* **a.** as fast as possible. **b.** very busy. **c.** lying prone: *flat out like a lizard drinking.* **d.** exhausted; unable to proceed. *–n.* **41.** something flat. **42.** a flat surface, side or part of anything: *the flat of a blade, the flat of the hand.* **43.** flat or level ground; a flat area. **44.** a marsh. **45.** a shallow. **46.** *Colloq.* (formerly) an honest man. **47.** *Colloq.* a policeman. **48.** *Music.* **a.** (in musical notation) the character ♭, which when attached to a note or a stave degree lowers its significance one chromatic semitone. **b.** a note one chromatic semitone below another. **c.** (on keyboard instruments, with reference to any given key) the key next below or to the left. **49.** a flat-heeled shoe. **50.** *Theat.* a piece of scenery consisting of a wooden frame, usu. rectangular, covered with lightweight board or fabric. **51.** a working space below decks: *a steering flat.* **52.** *Horseracing.* **a.** that part of a racecourse not occupied by grandstands: *the Flat.* **b.** Also, **flat enclosure.** the area in the centre of a racecourse. **c.** a race run on a course without obstacles (opposed to the *steeplechase*). **d.** *Brit.* (*oft. cap.*) the season, from March to October, when such races are run. **53.** *Engineering.* an iron or steel bar of rectangular section. **54.** *N.Z. Colloq.* →**flatfish. 55.** *Prison Colloq.* tobacco other than that officially issued. *–v.t.* **56.** *Music.* to lower (a pitch) esp. one semitone. [ME, from Scand.; cf. Icel. *flatr,* Swed. *flat;* akin to OE *flet* floor. See FLAT[2]]

**flat**[2] /flæt/, *n., v.,* **flatted, flatting.** *–n.* **1.** a suite of rooms, usu. on one floor only, forming a complete residence, and usu. rented. **2.** *Obs.* a floor or storey of a building. *–v.i.* **3.** to live in a flat. [var. of obs. *flet,* OE *flet* floor, house, hall; akin to FLAT[1]]

**flat-bed** /'flæt-bɛd/, *adj.* (of a motor truck) having a tray (def. 3).

**flat-bed cylinder press,** *n.* →**press**[1] (def. 32).

**flatboat** /'flætboʊt/, *n.* a large flat-bottomed boat for use in shallow water, esp. for floating down a river.

**flat chat** /flæt 'tʃæt/, *adv.* at full speed: *he drove flat chat down the road.* Also, **full chat.**

**flat-chat** /flæt-'tʃæt/, *v.i.,* **flat-chatted, flat-chatting.** to travel at full speed, esp. in a motor vehicle.

**flatette** /flæt'ɛt/, *n.* a small flat (**flat**[2]). Cf. **bachelor flat.**

**flatfish** /'flætfɪʃ/, *n., pl.* **-fishes,** (*esp. collectively*) **-fish.** any of a group of fishes (often considered as constituting the suborder Heterosomata), including the halibut, flounder, sole, etc., having a greatly compressed body, and swimming on one side, and (in the adult) having both eyes on the upper side.

**flat floor** /'flæt flɔ/, *n.* (of auditoriums) a level floor often without fixed seating to retain flexibility of use, opposed to a *raked* or *stepped floor.*

**flatfoot** /'flætfʊt/, *n., pl.* **-feet. 1. a.** a condition in which the arch of the foot is flattened so that the entire sole rests upon the ground. **b.** a foot with such an arch. **2.** *Colloq.* a policeman.

**flat-footed** /flæt-'fʊtəd/, *adj.* **1.** having flat feet. **2.** *Colloq.* clumsy and tactless. **3.** *Colloq.* unprepared, unable to react quickly. – **flat-footedly,** *adv.* – **flat-footedness,** *n.*

**flathead** /'flæthɛd/, *n.* **1.** any of numerous species of elongate, bottom-dwelling fishes with depressed, ridged heads, belonging esp. to the family Platycephalidae, found in the Indian and Pacific Oceans and commercially important as food fishes. **2.** *N.Z.* a flat-headed nail. **3.** *Colloq.* a fool or simpleton.

**flatiron** /'flætaɪən/, *n.* **1.** an iron heated externally (on a fire, stove, etc.), and used for pressing clothes. **2.** a kind of shallow boat, wide in the beam and with low upper works.

**flatlet** /'flætlət/, *n.* a small flat.

**flatling** /'flætlɪŋ/, *Archaic.* *–adv.* **1.** in a flat position; with the flat side, as of a sword. **2.** flatly or positively. *–adj.* **3.** dealt with the flat side.

**flatmate** /ˈflætmeɪt/, *n.* the fellow occupant of a flat, house, etc.

**flat-pea** /flæt-ˈpi/, *n.* any shrub of the Australian genus *Platylobium,* family Papilionaceae, with pea-shaped flowers and flat pods.

**flat racing** /ˈflæt reɪsɪŋ/, *n.* horseracing on courses without jumps.

**flat-sawn** /ˈflæt-sɔn/, *adj.* denoting a tree or timber that has been sawn up into flat slices, as distinct from being radially or tangentially sawn.

**flat spin** /flæt ˈspɪn/, *n.* **1.** *Aeron.* the descent of an aircraft in a spiral, with the fuselage more or less horizontal; often becoming uncontrollable. **2.** *Colloq.* a state of great confusion.

**flat spot** /ˈ– spɒt/, *n.* an unresponsive point in motor acceleration, due to a weakening of the mixture in the carburettor at a certain throttle opening.

**flat-tail mullet** /flæt-teɪl ˈmʌlət/, *n.* an Australian fish, *Liza dussunier,* of northern waters, having an elongated silver body with a grey-green back. Also, **brown-banded mullet.**

**flatten** /ˈflætn/, *v.t.* **1.** to make flat. **2.** *Colloq.* to knock (someone) out. **3.** *Colloq.* to crush or disconcert. *–v.i.* **4.** to become flat. **5.** *Aeron.* to fly into a horizontal position, as after a dive. – **flattener,** *n.*

**flatter**[1] /ˈflætə/, *v.t.* **1.** to seek to please by complimentary speech or attentions; compliment or praise, esp. insincerely. **2.** to represent too favourably, as in portrayal. **3.** to show to advantage. **4.** to play upon the vanity or susceptibilities of; cajole, wheedle, or beguile. **5.** to gratify by compliments or attentions, or as a compliment does: *to feel flattered by an invitation.* **6.** to beguile with hopes; encourage (hopes); please (oneself) with the thought or belief (fol. by *that* and a clause): *he flattered himself* (*that*) *he might become the head of the school.* *–v.i.* **7.** to use flattery. [? ME *flat(t)eren* float, flutter, assimilated in sense to OF *flat(t)er* caress with the hand, smooth, flatter, of Frankish orig.] – **flatterer,** *n.* – **flatteringly,** *adv.*

**flatter**[2] /ˈflætə/, *n.* **1.** one who or that which makes something flat. **2.** a hammer with a broad face, used by smiths. **3.** a drawplate with a flat orifice for drawing flat metal strips, as for watch springs, etc. [FLAT[1], *v.* + -ER[1]]

**flattery** /ˈflætəri/, *n., pl.* **-teries. 1.** the act of flattering. **2.** a flattering compliment or speech; excessive, insincere praise. [ME *flaterie,* from OF, from *flatere* a flatterer, from *flater.* Cf. FLATTER[1]]

**flattie** /ˈflæti/, *n. Colloq.* **1.** a flat-bottomed dinghy. **2.** →**flathead** (def. 1). **3.** a flat-heeled shoe. Also, **flatty.**

**flatties** /ˈflætiz/, *n. pl. Colloq.* a pair of shoes with low heels.

**flattish** /ˈflætɪʃ/, *adj.* somewhat flat.

**flat-top** /ˈflæt-tɒp/, *n.* **1.** an aircraft carrier. **2.** a railway freight car with a flat decking, suited to the transportation of wheeled vehicles, etc.

**flatulent** /ˈflætʃələnt/, *adj.* **1.** generating gas in the alimentary canal. **2.** attended with or caused by, or suffering from, such an accumulation of gas. **3.** pretentious; empty. Also, *Obs.,* **flatuous** /ˈflætʃuəs/. [F, from L *flātus* a blowing] – **flatulence, flatulency,** *n.* – **flatulently,** *adv.*

**flatus** /ˈfleɪtəs/, *n.* an accumulation of gas in the stomach or intestines. [L: a blowing]

**flatways** /ˈflætweɪz/, *adv.* with the flat side (not the edge) foremost or in contact. Also, **flatwise** /ˈflætwaɪz/.

**flat weed** /ˈflæt wid/, *n.* →**cat's-ear.** Also, **flatweed.**

**flat white** /– ˈwaɪt/, *n.* black coffee with milk added (opposed to *cappucino*).

**flatworm** /ˈflætwɜm/, *n.* →**platyhelminth.**

**flaunt** /flɔnt/, *v.i.* **1.** to parade or display oneself conspicuously or boldly. **2.** to wave conspicuously in the air. *–v.t.* **3.** to parade or display ostentatiously. *–n.* **4.** the act of flaunting. [Scand.; cf. Norw. *flanta* gad about, from *flana* roam; akin to Gk *plánē* roaming (see PLANET)] – **flaunter,** *n.* – **flauntingly,** *adv.* – **flaunty,** *adj.*

**flautist** /ˈflɔtəst/, *n.* a flute player. Also, *Chiefly U.S.,* **flutist.** [It. *flautista,* from *flauto* flute]

**flavescent** /fləˈvɛsənt/, *adj.* turning yellow; yellowish. [L *flāvescens,* ppr.]

**flavin** /ˈfleɪvən/, *n.* **1.** any of various natural yellow pigments, found in plant and animal tissues as a coenzyme of several flavoproteins. **2.** →**quercetin. 3.** acriflavin hydrochloride, a bacteriostatic agent. Also, **flavine.** [L *flāvus* yellow + -IN[2]]

**-flavin,** a word element indicating any of a number of natural derivatives of flavin, as *riboflavin.* Also, **-flavine.**

**flavin adenine dinucleotide** /ˌfleɪvən ˌædənin daɪˈnjukliətaɪd/, *n.* a cofactor involved in some biochemical reactions catalysed by dehydrogenases, as succinate dehydrogenase in the citric acid cycle. *Abbrev.:* FAD

**flavin mononucleotide** /fleɪvən mɒnoʊˈnjukliətaɪd/, *n.* a cofactor involved in some biochemical reactions catalysed by dehydrogenases. *Abbrev.:* FMN

**flavo-,** a word element meaning 'yellow', as in *flavo-protein.* Also, before vowels, **flav-.** [combining form representing L *flāvus*]

**flavone** /ˈfleɪvoʊn/, *n.* **1.** an organic compound, $C_{15}H_{10}O_2$, the parent substance of various yellow dyes. **2.** a derivative of this compound.

**flavoprotein** /fleɪvoʊˈproʊtin/, *n.* an enzyme, containing riboflavin and covalently linked with a protein, active in the oxidation of substrates in animal cells.

**flavopurpurin** /ˌfleɪvoʊˈpɜpjərən/, *n.* a yellowish crystalline compound, $C_{14}H_8O_5$ (isomeric with purpurin), used in dyeing.

**flavorous** /ˈfleɪvərəs/, *adj.* **1.** full of flavour. **2.** pleasant to the smell or taste.

**flavour** /ˈfleɪvə/, *n.* **1.** taste, esp. a characteristic taste, or a noticeable element in the taste, of a thing. **2.** a flavouring substance or extract. **3.** the characteristic quality of a thing: *a book which catches the flavour of the sea.* **4.** a particular quality noticeable in a thing: *language with a strong nautical flavour.* *–v.t.* **5.** to give flavour. Also, *U.S.,* **flavor.** [ME, from OF *flaur,* from L *frāgāre* emit an odour] – **flavourer,** *n.* – **flavourful,** *adj.* – **flavourless,** *adj.*

**flavouring** /ˈfleɪvərɪŋ/, *n.* something that gives flavour; a substance or preparation used to give a particular flavour to food or drink. Also, *U.S.,* **flavoring.**

**flavoursome** /ˈfleɪvəsəm/, *adj.* having a full, rich, pleasant flavour; tasty; flavourful.

**flaw**[1] /flɔ/, *n.* **1.** a marring feature; a defect; a fault. **2.** a defect impairing legal soundness or validity: *flaw in a lease or a will.* **3.** a crack, break, breach, or rent. *–v.t.* **4.** to produce a flaw in. *–v.i.* **5.** to contract a flaw; become cracked or defective. [ME, from Scand.; cf. Swed. *flaga* flake, flaw] – **flawless,** *adj.* – **flawlessly,** *adv.* – **flawlessness,** *n.*

**flaw**[2] /flɔ/, *n.* **1.** a sudden gust or brief sharp storm of wind. **2.** a short spell of rough weather. **3.** *Obs.* a burst of feeling, fury, etc. [Scand.; cf. Swed. *flaga* gust] – **flawy,** *adj.*

**flax** /flæks/, *n.* **1.** any plant of the genus *Linum,* esp. *L. usitatissimum,* a slender, erect annual plant with narrow, lance-shaped leaves and blue flowers, much cultivated for its fibre and seeds. **2.** the fibre of this plant, manufactured into linen yarn for thread or woven fabrics. **3.** any of various plants or fibres resembling flax, as *Phormium tenax,* New Zealand flax, or the Australian settler's flax. [ME; OE *fleax,* c. D and LG *vlas,* G *Flachs*]

**flax-cutter** /ˈflæks-kʌtə/, *n.* one who cuts flax (def. 3) for sale.

**flaxen** /ˈflæksən/, *adj.* **1.** made of flax. **2.** resembling flax. **3.** pertaining to flax. **4.** of the pale yellowish colour of dressed flax. Also, **flaxy.**

**flax honey** /ˈflæks hʌni/, *n. N.Z.* honey produced by bees which feed on the flowers of flax (def. 3).

**flaxie** /ˈflæksi/, *n. N.Z. Colloq.* a person who works in a flax mill. Also, **flax, flaxy.**

**flax mill** /ˈflæks mɪl/, *n.* an establishment producing fibre from flax (def. 3).

**flaxseed** /ˈflækssid/, *n.* the seed of flax, yielding linseed oil; linseed.

**flax-stick** /ˈflæks-stɪk/, *n.* the flower stem of flax (def. 3).

**flay** /fleɪ/, *v.t.* **1.** to strip off the skin or outer covering of. **2.** to criticise or reprove with scathing severity. **3.** to strip of money or property; fleece. [ME *flen,* etc.,

dog flea

OE *flēan*, c. MD *vlaen*, Icel. *flā*] – **flayer,** *n.*

**fl dr,** fluid drachm.

**flea** /fli/, *n.* **1.** any of numerous small, wingless, blood-sucking insects of the order Siphonaptera, parasitic upon mammals and birds, and noted for their powers of leaping. **2.** any of various small beetles and crustaceans which leap like a flea, or swim in a jumpy manner, as the water-flea and beach flea. **3. flea in one's ear,** *Colloq.* **a.** a discomforting rebuke or rebuff; a sharp hint. **b.** a blow to the ear; a cuff. [ME *fle*, OE *flēah, flēa*, c. G *Floh;* akin to FLEE]

**fleabag** /'flibæg/, *n. Colloq.* **1.** a sleeping bag. **2.** a worthless creature ridden with fleas. **3.** an old hag. **4.** *Colloq.* a person, esp. a child, who fidgets.

**fleabane** /'flibeɪn/, *n.* any of various plants of the family Compositae, esp. of the genus *Erigeron,* reputed to destroy or drive away fleas.

**flea-beetle** /'fli-bitl/, *n.* any of certain leaf beetles, noted for their ability to leap.

**fleabite** /'flibaɪt/, *n.* **1.** the bite of a flea. **2.** the red spot caused by it. **3.** a trifling wound, annoyance, etc.

**flea-bitten** /'fli-bɪtn/, *adj.* **1.** bitten by a flea or fleas. **2.** infested with fleas. **3.** (of a horse, etc.) having small reddish spots or streaks upon a lighter ground. **4.** *Colloq.* shabby; dirty.

**flea collar** /'fli kɒlə/, *n.* a collar for cats and dogs which has been impregnated with insecticide and is worn specifically to kill fleas.

**fleam** /flim/, *n.* **1.** the angle of rake between the cutting edge of a saw tooth and the plane of the blade. *–adj.* **2.** (of a saw tooth) having the shape of an isosceles triangle. [OF *flieme,* from LL *phlebotomus* lancet, from Gk *phlebotómos* opening veins. Cf. PHLEBOTOMY]

**flea market** /'fli makət/, *n.* a market where usu. second-hand or cheap articles are sold.

**fleapit** /'flipɪt/, *n. Colloq.* a shabby, dirty room or building, esp. a cinema.

**flea rake** /'fli reɪk/, *n. Colloq.* a comb.

**fleas-'n'-itches** /fliz-ən-'ɪtʃəz/, *n. Colloq.* pictures; the cinema. [rhyming slang]

**fleawort** /'fliwɜt/, *n.* **1.** a rough-leaved herb of Europe, *Inula conyza.* **2.** a European plantain, *Plantago indica,* whose seeds resemble fleas and are used in medicine.

**flèche** /fleɪʃ/, *n., pl.* **flèches** /'fleɪʃəz/. **1.** *Archit.* **a.** a spire, esp. a small light spire decorating a roof. **b.** a slender spire rising from the junction of the nave and transepts of a church, or sometimes crowning the apse. **2.** *Fort.* a fieldwork consisting of two faces forming a salient angle, open at the gorge. **3.** *Fencing.* a method of running attack. [F: arrow, probably from Gmc; cf. FLY[1]]

**fleck** /flɛk/, *n.* **1.** a spot or mark on the skin, as a freckle. **2.** any spot or patch of colour, light, etc. **3.** a speck; a small bit. [n. use of FLECK, *v.*, or backformation from *flecked,* ppl. adj., ME *flekked;* cf. G *Fleck* spot] *–v.t.* **4.** to mark with a fleck or flecks; spot; dapple. [Scand.; cf. Icel. *flekka*]

**fleckless** /'flɛkləs/, *adj.* without flecks or spots. – **flecklessly,** *adv.*

**flection** /'flɛkʃən/, *n.* **1.** the act of bending. **2.** the state of being bent. **3.** a bend; a bent part. **4.** *Anat.* →**flexion. 5.** *Gram.* →**inflection.** Also, **flexion** for defs 1-3. [L *flexio* a bending] – **flectional,** *adj.* – **flectionless,** *adj.*

**fled** /flɛd/, *v.* past tense and past participle of **flee.**

**fledge** /flɛdʒ/, *v.,* **fledged, fledging,** *adj.* *–v.t.* **1.** to bring up (a young bird) until it is able to fly. **2.** to furnish with or as with feathers or plumage; feather (an arrow). *–v.i.* **3.** (of a young bird) to acquire the feathers necessary for flight. *–adj.* **4.** *Archaic.* (of young birds) able to fly; having the wings developed for flight. [ME *flegge,* OE *-fligge,* in *unfligge* unfledged]

**fledgling** /'flɛdʒlɪŋ/, *n.* **1.** a young bird just fledged. **2.** an inexperienced person. Also, **fledgeling.**

**fledgy** /'flɛdʒi/, *adj.,* **fledgier, fledgiest.** *Rare.* feathered or feathery.

**flee** /fli/, *v.,* **fled, fleeing.** *–v.i.* **1.** to run away, as from danger, pursuers, etc.; take flight. **2.** to move swiftly; fly; speed. *–v.t.* **3.** to run away from (a place, person, etc.). [ME *flee(n),* OE *flēon,* c. G *fliehen*]

**fleece** /flis/, *n., v.,* **fleeced, fleecing.** *–n.* **1.** the coat of wool that covers a sheep or some similar animal. **2.** the wool shorn from a sheep at one time. **3.** something resembling a fleece: *a fleece of hair.* **4.** a fabric with a soft, silky pile, used for warmth, as for lining garments. **5.** the soft nap or pile of such a fabric. *–v.t.* **6.** to deprive (a sheep) of the fleece. **7.** to strip of money or belongings; plunder; swindle. **8.** to overspread or line with or as with a fleece. [ME *flees,* OE *flēos,* c. G *Vliess*] – **fleeceable,** *adj.*

**fleece-oh** /'flis-oʊ/, *n.* →**piece-picker.**

**fleece-picker** /'flis-pɪkə/, *n.* **1.** →**piece-picker. 2.** *N.Z.* →**picker-up.** Also, **fleecy.**

**fleeceroller** /'flisroʊlə/, *n.* →**woolroller.**

**fleecy** /'flisi/, *adj.,* **fleecier, fleeciest,** *n.* *–adj.* **1.** covered with, consisting of, or resembling a fleece or wool. *–n.* **2.** Also, **fleecie.** →**piece-picker.** – **fleecily,** *adv.* – **fleeciness,** *n.*

**fleer**[1] /'flɪə/, *v.i.* **1.** to grin or laugh coarsely or mockingly. *–v.t.* **2.** to fleer at; deride. *–n.* **3.** a fleering look; a jeer or gibe. [ME *flery(e), flire.* Cf. Norw. *flire* grin] – **fleeringly,** *adv.*

**fleer**[2] /'fliə/, *n.* one who flees. [FLEE + -ER[1]]

**fleet**[1] /flit/, *n.* **1.** the largest organised unit of naval ships grouped for tactical or other purposes. **2.** the largest organisation of warships under the command of a single officer. **3.** a number of naval vessels, or vessels carrying armed men. **4.** the vessels, aeroplanes or vehicles collectively of a single transport company or undertaking. **5.** a number of aeroplanes, motor vehicles, etc., moving or operating in company. [ME *flete,* OE *flēot* ship, craft, from *flēotan* float]

**fleet**[2] /flit/, *adj.* **1.** swift; rapid: *fleet of foot, a fleet horse.* *–v.i.* **2.** to move swiftly; fly. **3.** *Naut.* to change the position of a ship, cable, etc., esp. in a fore-and-aft direction. **4.** *Archaic.* to glide away like a stream. **5.** *Archaic.* to fade; vanish. **6.** *Obs.* to float; drift. **7.** *Obs.* to swim; sail. *–v.t.* **8.** *Archaic.* to cause (time) to pass lightly or swiftly. **9.** *Naut.* to change the position of; shift. [ME *flete(n),* v., OE *flēotan* float, c. G *fliessen* flow] – **fleetly,** *adv.* – **fleetness,** *n.*

**Fleet Admiral** /'flit ædmərəl/, *n.* the highest ranking officer in the U.S. Navy, ranking next above admiral.

**fleet-footed** /'flit-fʊtəd/, *adj.* swift of foot.

**fleet in being,** *n.* a naval fleet which avoids decisive action but which draws the enemy strength away from another engagement or location.

**fleeting** /'flitɪŋ/, *adj.* gliding swiftly away; passing swiftly; transient; transitory. – **fleetingly,** *adv.* – **fleetingness,** *n.*

**Fleet Street** /'flit strit/, *n.* the British print media. [from *Fleet Street,* a street in London in which many newspapers have their offices]

**Flem.,** Flemish.

**Fleming's rules** /'flɛmɪŋz rulz/, *n.pl.* a set of rules relating the direction of motion, flux, and electromotive force in electrical machines. If the forefinger, second finger, and thumb of the right hand are extended at right angles to each other, the forefinger indicates the direction of the flux, the second finger the direction of the electromotive force, and the thumb the direction of motion in a generator. If the left hand is used the digits indicate directions in a motor. [named after Sir John Ambrose *Fleming,* 1849-1945, English electrical engineer]

**Flemington confetti** /flɛmɪŋtən kən'feti/, *n.* →**cowyard confetti.**

**Flemish** /'flɛmɪʃ/, *adj.* **1.** of or pertaining to Flanders, its people, or their language. **2.** of or denoting a school of painting developed in Flanders and northern France in the 15th century, characterised by cool, clear colours, sharply delineated forms, and accurate proportions and perspective. *–n.* **3.** the language of the Flemings, one of the official languages of Belgium, and a Germanic language closely related to Dutch. **4.** the people of Flanders collectively; the Flemings. [MFlem. *Vlamisch* (D *Vlaamsch*)]

**Flemish bond** /– 'bɒnd/, *n.* a common arrangement in brickwork in which headers and stretchers alternate in every course. Cf. **English bond.**

**flense** /flɛns/, *v.t.,* **flensed, flensing. 1.** to strip the blubber or the skin from (a whale, seal, etc.). **2.** to strip off (blubber or skin). Also, **flench** /'flɛntʃ/, **flinch.** [D *flensen*]

**flesh** /flɛʃ/, *n.* **1.** the soft substance of an animal body, consisting of muscle and fat. **2.** muscular tissue. **3.** fatness; weight: *to put on flesh.* **4.** such substance of animals as an article of food, usu. excluding fish and sometimes fowl; meat. **5.** the body, esp. as distinguished from the spirit or soul. **6.** man's physical or animal nature. **7.** mankind. **8.** living creatures generally. **9.** one's kindred or family, or a member of it. **10.** the soft pulpy portion of a fruit, vegetable, etc., as distinguished from the core, skin, shell, etc. **11.** the surface of the body, esp. with respect to colour. **12.** flesh colour; pinkish white with a tinge of yellow; pinkish cream. **13. in the flesh, a.** alive. **b.** in bodily form; in person. **14. pound of flesh,** a person's right or due, insisted on mercilessly with a total disregard for others. *–v.t.* **15.** to plunge (a weapon) into the flesh. **16.** *Hunting.* to feed (a hound or hawk) with flesh in order to make it more eager for the chase. **17.** *Archaic.* to incite and accustom (persons) to bloodshed or battle by an initial experience. **18.** *Archaic.* to inflame the ardour or passions of by a taste of indulgence. **19. flesh out, a.** to clothe (a skeleton, etc.) with flesh; make fleshy. **b.** to explain, amplify. **20.** to remove adhering flesh from (hides), for leather and for manufacture. [ME; OE *flǣsc,* c. G *Fleisch*] – **fleshless,** *adj.*

**flesh and blood,** *n.* **1.** offspring or relatives: *one's own flesh and blood.* **2.** human nature: *more than flesh and blood can endure.*

**flesh colour** /ˈflɛʃ kʌlə/, *n.* a pinkish-white colour with a tinge of yellow; a pinkish-cream colour. – **flesh-coloured,** *adj.*

**flesh-eater** /ˈflɛʃ-itə/, *n.* →**carnivore.** – **flesh-eating,** *adj.*

**flesher** /ˈflɛʃə/, *n.* **1.** one who fleshes hides. **2.** a tool for fleshing hides.

**flesh-fly** /ˈflɛʃ-flaɪ/, *n., pl.* **-flies.** any fly of the dipterous family Sarcophagidae which deposits its larvae in the flesh of living animals.

**fleshhook** /ˈflɛʃhʊk/, *n.* **1.** a hook for use in lifting meat, as from a pot. **2.** a hook to hang meat on.

**fleshly** /ˈflɛʃli/, *adj.,* **-lier, -liest. 1.** of or pertaining to the flesh or body; bodily, corporeal, or physical. **2.** carnal; sensual. **3.** worldly, rather than spiritual. **4.** *Obs.* having much flesh; fleshy. – **fleshliness,** *n.*

**fleshpots** /ˈflɛʃpɒts/, *n.pl.* places in which luxury or sensual gratification is obtained.

**flesh wound** /ˈflɛʃ wund/, *n.* a wound which does not extend beyond the flesh; a slight wound.

**fleshy** /ˈflɛʃi/, *adj.,* **fleshier, fleshiest. 1.** having much flesh; plump; fat. **2.** consisting of or resembling flesh. **3.** *Bot.* consisting of fleshlike substance; pulpy, as a fruit; thick and tender, as a leaf. – **fleshiness,** *n.*

**fletch** /flɛtʃ/, *v.t.* to provide an arrow with a feather or some artificial substitute.

**fletcher** /ˈflɛtʃə/, *n.* one who makes or deals in arrows, or bows and arrows. [OF *flechier,* from *flèche* arrow]

**fletching** /ˈflɛtʃɪŋ/, *n.* **1.** the act of one who fletches. **2.** the real or artificial feathers of an arrow.

**fleur-de-lis** /flɜ-də-ˈli/, *n., pl.* **fleurs-de-lis** /flɜ-də-ˈliz/. **1.** a heraldic device somewhat resembling three petals or floral segments of an iris tied by an encircling band. **2.** the distinctive bearing of the royal family of France. **3.** the iris (flower or plant). [F: lily flower; replacing ME *flour-de-lys,* from OF]

fleur-de-lis

**fleuron** /ˈflɜrɒn/, *n.* an ornamental flower-like design, used in printing, architecture, pastry-garnishing, etc.

**fleury** /ˈflɜri/, *adj.* **1.** bearing fleurs-de-lis. **2.** terminating in a fleur-de-lis: *a cross fleury.* Also, **flory.**

**flew**[1] /flu/, *v.* past tense of **fly**[1].

**flew**[2] /flu/, *n.* →**flue**[3].

**flews** /fluz/, *n. pl.* the large pendulous upper lip of certain dogs, as bloodhounds.

**flex**[1] /flɛks/, *v.t.* **1.** to bend (something pliant or jointed, as a part of the body). *–v.i.* **2.** to bend. *–n.* **3.** a small, flexible insulated electric cable or wire esp. for supplying power to movable domestic appliances. [L *flexus,* pp.]

**flex**[2] /flɛks/, *v.i.* to absent oneself from work under a flexitime scheme (fol. by *off*). Also, **flexi.** [short for FLEXITIME]

**flexible** /ˈflɛksəbəl/, *adj.* **1.** capable of being bent; easily bent. **2.** susceptible of modification or adaptation; adaptable. **3.** willing or disposed to yield. [L *flexibilis*] – **flexibility** /flɛksəˈbɪləti/, **flexibleness,** *n.* – **flexibly,** *adv.*

**flexible trust** /– ˈtrʌst/, *n.* a unit trust whose trust deed provides for changes being made in the portfolio of investments at the discretion of the management company, usu. after approval by the trustee company (opposed to *fixed trust*).

**flexiday** /ˈflɛksideɪ/, *n.* a day taken off from work under a flexitime scheme.

**flexile** /ˈflɛksaɪl/, *adj.* flexible; pliant; tractable; adaptable. [L *flexilis*]

**flexion** /ˈflɛkʃən/, *n.* **1.** *Anat.* **a.** the motion of a joint which brings the connected parts continually nearer together; the action of any flexor muscle (opposed to *extension*). **b.** the state of a part so moved. **2.** →**flection** (defs 1-3). [L *flexio* a bending] – **flexional,** *adj.* – **flexionless,** *adj.*

**flexitime** /ˈflɛksitaɪm/, *n.* an arrangement of ordinary hours of work in which employees may elect to vary their commencing, ceasing, and meal-break times while still maintaining the total number of hours worked. Also, **gliding time.**

**flexography** /flɛksˈɒgrəfi/, *n.* a printing process using rubber or plastic plates.

**flexor** /ˈflɛksə/, *n.* a muscle which serves to flex or bend a part of the body (opposed to *extensor*). [NL. See FLEX[1], -OR[2]]

**flexuosity** /flɛkʃuˈɒsəti/, *n.* quality or condition of being flexuous.

**flexuous** /ˈflɛkʃuəs/, *adj.* full of bends or curves; winding; sinuous. Also, **flexuose** /ˈflɛkʃuoʊs/. [L *flexuōsus,* from *flexus* a bending] – **flexuously,** *adv.*

**flexure** /ˈflɛkʃə/, *n.* **1.** the act of flexing or bending. **2.** the state of being flexed or bent. **3.** the part bent; a bend; a fold. [L *flexūra* a bending] – **flexural,** *adj.*

**flibbertigibbet** /ˈflɪbətidʒɪbət/, *n.* **1.** a chattering or flighty person, usu. a young girl. **2.** (*cap.*) *Obs.* the name of a fiend.

**flicflac** /ˈflɪkflæk/, *n.* a step in dancing in which the feet strike rapidly together. [F; imitative of the sound]

**flick** /flɪk/, *n.* **1.** a sudden light blow or stroke, as with a whip or the finger. **2.** the sound thus made. **3.** something thrown off with or as with a jerk: *a flick of spray.* **4.** *Boxing.* a punch with a part-open glove, which usu. scores no points. **5.** *Soccer.* a light movement of the foot or head to deflect the ball. **6.** (*usu. pl.*) *Colloq.* **a.** a cinema film. **b.** the cinema. *–v.t.* **7.** to strike lightly with a whip, the finger, etc. **8.** to remove with such a stroke: *to flick dust from one's coat, to flick away a crumb.* **9.** to move (something) with a sudden stroke or jerk. *–v.i.* **10.** to move with a jerk or jerks. **11.** to flutter. [late ME *flykke;* apparently imitative]

**flickback** /ˈflɪkbæk/, *n.* (in Rugby Football) a quick pass in which the ball is gathered and passed in the one movement to a player stationed behind the play.

**flicker** /ˈflɪkə/, *v.i.* **1.** to burn unsteadily; shine with a wavering light. **2.** to wave to and fro; vibrate; quiver. **3.** to flutter. *–v.t.* **4.** to cause to flicker. *–n.* **5.** an unsteady flame or light. **6.** (*usu. pl.*) →**trafficator. 7.** a flickering; flickering movement. **8.** a brief spark: *a flicker of hope.* [ME *flickeren,* OE *flicorian* flutter] – **flickeringly,** *adv.*

**flicker pictures** /ˈ– pɪktʃəz/, *n.pl.* pictures on a set of cards which simulate motion when the cards are released by the thumb or finger so that they each pass rapidly before the eye.

**flick-knife** /ˈflɪk-naɪf/, *n.* a knife the blade of which springs out at the press of a button on the handle; switchblade.

**flick-off** /ˈflɪk-ɒf/, *n.* the action of pulling a surfboard back from a wave before it breaks.

**flick pass** /flɪk ˈpas/, *n.* (in Australian Rules) a handpass in which the ball is struck with an open hand instead of a clenched fist.

**flick-roll** /ˈflɪk-roʊl/, *n.* →**snap-roll.**

**flier** /ˈflaɪə/, *n.* **1.** something that flies, as a bird or insect. **2.** one who or that which moves with great speed. **3.** an aviator. **4.** some part of a machine having a rapid motion. **5.** *Colloq.* a flying jump or leap. **6.** *Archit.* a rectangular tread in a stair forming part of a straight flight of steps. **7.** a small leaflet. Also, **flyer. 8.** *Golf.* a short lofted shot used to get the ball out of the rough. **9.** *Cricket.* a bumper.

**flies** /flaɪz/, *n.* **1.** plural of **fly. 2. there are no flies on (him),**

(he) is shrewd, cunning, and alert.

**flight**[1] /flaɪt/, *n.* **1.** the act, manner, or power of flying. **2.** the distance covered or the course pursued by a flying object. **3.** a number of beings or things flying or passing through the air together: *a flight of swallows.* **4.** a journey by air, esp. by aeroplane. **5.** a scheduled trip on an airline. **6.** the basic tactical unit of military airforces, consisting of two or more aircraft. **7.** the act, principles, or art of flying an aeroplane. **8.** the progress of a spacecraft into space and, sometimes, back. **9.** swift movement in general. **10.** a soaring above or transcending ordinary bounds: *a flight of fancy.* **11.** *Athletics.* a specific number, usu. ten, of hurdles in a race. **12.** the real or artificial feathers at the back of an arrow, dart, etc., designed to make it fly straight. **13.** *Archit.* **a.** the series of steps or stairs between two adjacent landings. **b.** a series of steps, etc., ascending without change of direction. **14.** *Archery.* **a.** a light arrow for long-distance shooting. **b.** the distance covered by such an arrow. **c.** the type of shooting using special tackle in which the aim is to shoot as far as possible. **15. in the first flight,** excellent; one of the best. *–v.i.* **16.** (of wild fowl) to fly in flights (def. 3). *–v.t.* **17.** to deliver (a cricket ball, dart, etc.) in a certain manner, esp. so that it flies comparatively slowly. **18.** to shoot (a bird) in flight. **19.** to attach feathers as flights to (arrows, darts, etc.). [ME; OE *flyht,* c. D *vlucht;* akin to FLY[1], *v.*]

**flight**[2] /flaɪt/, *n.* **1.** the act of fleeing; hasty departure. **2. put to flight,** to force to flee; rout. **3. take (to) flight,** to flee. [ME; c. G *Flucht;* akin to FLEE]

**flight arrow** /'– ærou/, *n.* **1.** an arrow having a conical or pyramidal head without barbs. **2.** a long and light arrow in general; a shaft or arrow for the longbow, as distinguished from the bolt.

**flight attendant** /'– ətɛndənt/, *n.* one whose job is to attend to passengers on an aircraft, serving meals, giving information, etc. See **air hostess, steward.**

**flight control** /'– kəntroul/, *n.* **1.** the organisation and activity which guides the movement of aircraft, esp. from a central tower or look-out at an airport. **2.** (*pl.*) the instruments which control the movement of an aircraft.

**flight deck** /'– dɛk/, *n.* **1.** the compartment of an aeroplane where the controls are situated. **2.** the upper deck of an aircraft-carrier, constructed and equipped for the landing and take-off of aircraft.

**flight engineer** /– ɛndʒə'nɪə/, *n.* the member of an aircrew responsible for the successful operation of the aircraft's systems and engines during flight.

**flight envelope** /'– ɛnvəloup/, *n.* the limiting range of speeds, altitudes, manoeuvres, etc., possible for a particular type of aircraft.

**flight feather** /'– fɛðə/, *n.* one of the large, stiff feathers which form most of the extent of a bird's wing, and which are essential to flight.

**flight formation** /'– fɔmeɪʃən/, *n.* two or more aeroplanes flying in some set arrangement.

**flight indicator** /'– ɪndəkeɪtə/, *n.* an instrument, as an artificial horizon, which indicates the altitude of an aircraft.

**flightless** /'flaɪtləs/, *adj.* incapable of flying.

**flight lieutenant** /'flaɪt lɛftɛnənt/, *n.* **1.** a commissioned rank in the Royal Australian Air Force above that of flying officer and below that of squadron-leader, equivalent to captain in the army, or lieutenant in the navy. **2.** a similar rank in any of various other airforces. **3.** an officer of this rank.

**flightlog** /'flaɪtlɒg/, *n.* →**log** (def. 5).

**flight number** /'flaɪt nʌmbə/, *n.* a number used to identify an aircraft flight, esp. referring to commercial airline arrivals and departures.

**flight path** /'– paθ/, *n.* the actual or intended line of flight of an aircraft.

**flight plan** /'– plæn/, *n.* a detailed outline in writing of a proposed airflight route.

**flight recorder** /'– rəkɔdə/, *n.* a box containing recording equipment which collects information about an aircraft's flight, used esp. to determine the cause of a crash; black box.

**flight shooting** /'– ʃutɪŋ/, *n.* the sport of shooting wild fowl while they are on the wing.

**flight simulator** /'– sɪmjəleɪtə/, *n.* an apparatus which creates flight conditions, used for the training of aircraft pilots.

**flighty** /'flaɪti/, *adj.*, **-tier, -tiest. 1.** given to flights or sallies of fancy, caprice, etc.; volatile; frivolous. **2.** slightly delirious; light-headed; mildly crazy. **3.** emotionally unreliable; flirtatious. **4.** *Rare.* swift or fleet. [FLIGHT[1] + -Y[1]] – **flightily,** *adv.* – **flightiness,** *n.*

**flim-flam** /'flɪm-flæm/, *n., v.,* **-flammed, -flamming,** *adj. Colloq.* *–n.* **1.** a piece of nonsense; mere nonsense. **2.** a trick or deception; humbug. *–v.t.* **3.** to trick; delude; humbug; cheat. *–adj.* **4.** nonsensical; worthless. [cf. Icel. *flimska* mockery] – **flim-flammer,** *n.*

**flimsy** /'flɪmzi/, *adj.*, **-sier, -siest,** *n., pl.* **-sies.** *–adj.* **1.** without material strength or solidity: *a flimsy material, a flimsy structure.* **2.** weak; inadequate; not carefully thought out: *a flimsy excuse or argument.* *–n.* **3.** a thin kind of paper, esp. for use in making several copies of a writing, telegraphic dispatch, etc., at once, as in newspaper work. **4.** a copy of a report or dispatch on such paper. [FILM (by metathesis) + *-sy,* adj. suffix] – **flimsily,** *adv.* – **flimsiness,** *n.*

**flinch**[1] /flɪntʃ/, *v.i.* **1.** to draw back or shrink from what is dangerous, difficult, or unpleasant. **2.** to shrink under pain; wince. *–v.t.* **3.** to draw back or withdraw from. *–n.* **4.** the act of flinching. [? nasalised var. of d. *flitch* flit, shift (one's) position] – **flincher,** *n.* – **flinchingly,** *adv.*

**flinch**[2] /flɪntʃ/, *v.t.* →**flense.** [var. of FLENSE]

**flinders** /'flɪndəz/, *n. pl.* splinters; small pieces or fragments. [cf. Norw. *flindra* splinter]

**Flinders bar** /'flɪndəz ba/, *n.* a cylindrically shaped bar of soft iron, placed vertically in brass holders on the fore or aft side of the binnacle to compensate the error to the compass caused by the vertically induced magnetism in the ship. [named after Matthew *Flinders,* 1774-1814, English navigator and explorer]

**Flinders grass** /'– gras/, *n.* any of various native annuals of the genus *Iseilema,* being dry-weather resistant, and highly nutritional for livestock; plentiful in inland areas of Australia.

**fling** /flɪŋ/, *v.,* **flung, flinging,** *n.* *–v.t.* **1.** to throw, cast, or hurl; throw with force or violence; throw with impatience, disdain, etc. **2.** to put suddenly or violently: *to fling one into gaol.* **3.** to send forth suddenly and rapidly: *to fling fresh troops into a battle.* **4.** to throw aside or off. **5.** to throw to the ground, as in wrestling or from horseback. *–v.i.* **6.** to move with haste or violence; rush; dash. **7.** to fly into violent and irregular motions, as a horse; throw the body about, as a person. **8.** to utter harsh or abusive language (usu. fol. by *out*). *–n.* **9.** the act of flinging. **10.** a spell of unrestrained indulgence of one's impulses: *to have one's fling.* **11.** an attack upon or attempt at something, as in passing. **12.** a severe or contemptuous remark or gibe. **13.** a lively Scottish dance characterised by flinging movements of the legs and arms (commonly called **Highland fling**). **14. (at) full fling,** at full speed; with reckless abandon. [ME. Cf. Swed. *flänga* fly, race] – **flinger,** *n.*

**flint** /flɪnt/, *n.* **1.** a hard kind of stone, a form of silica resembling chalcedony but more opaque, less pure, and less lustrous. **2.** a piece of this, esp. as used for striking fire. **3.** something very hard or obdurate. **4.** the source of the spark in an automatic cigarette lighter, usu. an alloy of such metals as iron and cerium. *–v.t.* **5.** to furnish with a flint. [ME and OE, c. MD *vlint,* Dan. *flint.* Cf. PLINTH]

**flint glass** /'– glas/, *n.* **1.** any colourless glass other than flat glass. **2.** glass of high dispersion made for optical purposes. Also, **optical flint glass.**

**flintlock** /'flɪntlɒk/, *n.* **1.** a gunlock in which a piece of flint striking against steel produces sparks which ignite the priming. **2.** a firearm with such a lock.

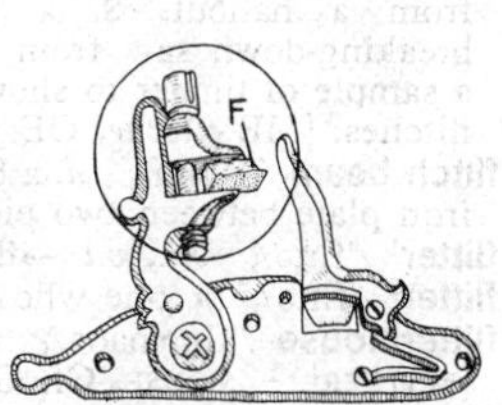

flintlock (circled): F, flint

**flinty** /'flɪnti/, *adj.* **flintier, flintiest. 1.** composed of, containing, or resembling flint; hard as flint. **2.** obdurate; cruel; unmerciful: *a flinty heart.* **3.** (of wine) having a very dry finish. – **flintily,** *adv.* – **flintiness,** *n.*

**flip**[1] /flɪp/, *v.*, **flipped, flipping,** *n.* *–v.t.* **1.** to toss or put in motion with a snap of a finger and thumb; fillip; flick. **2.** to move (something) with a jerk or jerks. **3. flip one's lid,** *Colloq.* to become angry. **4. flip (oneself) off,** *Colloq.* →**masturbate.** *–v.i.* **5.** to make a fillip; strike smartly at something. **6.** to move with a jerk or jerks. *–n.* **7.** a fillip; a smart tap or strike. **8.** a sudden jerk. **9.** a somersault. **10.** *Colloq.* short flight, esp. for pleasure, in an aeroplane. **11.** *Colloq.* an irresponsible person. [probably imitative]

**flip**[2] /flɪp/, *n.* →**eggflip.** [? n. use of FLIP[1]]

**flip**[3] /flɪp/, *adj.*, **flipper, flippest.** *Colloq.* pert; flippant. [adj. use of FLIP[1]]

**flip-flop** /ˈflɪp-flɒp/, *n.* **1.** an electronic circuit which alternates polarity. **2.** *Computers.* an electronic device used to store a binary digit. **3.** →**thong** (def. 34). **4.** a banging to and fro. *–adv.* **5.** to and fro with banging; with repeated flapping.

**flippant** /ˈflɪpənt/, *adj.* **1.** clever or pert in speech. **2.** characterised by a shallow or disrespectful levity. **3.** *Obs.* voluble; talkative. **4.** *Obs.* nimble, limber, or pliant. [orig. obscure, but cf. Icel. *fleipa* babble] – **flippancy, flippantness,** *n.* – **flippantly,** *adv.*

**flip pass** /ˈflɪp pas/, *n.* **1.** (in ice hockey) a pass made by lifting the puck from the ice over an opponent's stick to a team mate. *–v.i.* **2.** to make such a pass.

**flipper** /ˈflɪpə/, *n.* **1.** a broad, flat limb, as of a seal, whale, etc., especially adapted for swimming. **2.** a device resembling in form an animal's flipper, usu. made of rubber, used as an aid in swimming. **3.** *Colloq.* the hand. **4.** *Cricket.* a type of ball which rises rapidly from the pitch with top spin.

**flipper window** /ˈ– wɪndoʊ/, *n.* *Colloq.* →**quarter-vent window.**

**flipping** /ˈflɪpɪŋ/, *adj.* *Colloq.* (an intensifier expressing disgust, annoyance, etc., often used as a euphemism for *fucking*): *a flipping headache.*

**flip side** /ˈflɪp saɪd/, *n.* *Colloq.* the reverse of a gramophone record, usu. carrying a song, etc., of less interest, or popularity.

**flirt** /flɜt/, *v.i.* **1.** to trifle in love; play at love; coquet. **2.** to trifle or toy (with an idea, etc.). **3.** to move with a jerk or jerks; dart about. *–v.t.* **4.** to give a sudden or brisk motion to; wave smartly, as a fan. **5.** to throw or propel with a toss or jerk; fling suddenly. *–n.* **6.** a person given to flirting. **7.** a quick throw or toss; a sudden jerk; a darting motion. **8.** *Archery.* an arrow which flies off course. [imitative] – **flirter,** *n.* – **flirtingly,** *adv.*

**flirtation** /flɜˈteɪʃən/, *n.* **1.** the act or practice of flirting; coquetry. **2.** a love affair which is not serious.

**flirtatious** /flɜˈteɪʃəs/, *adj.* **1.** given to flirtation. **2.** pertaining to flirtation. Also, **flirty.** – **flirtatiously,** *adv.* – **flirtatiousness,** *n.*

**flit** /flɪt/, *v.*, **flitted, flitting,** *n.* *–v.i.* **1.** to move lightly and swiftly; fly, dart, or skim along. **2.** to flutter, as a bird. **3.** to pass away quickly, as time. **4.** *Colloq.* to change one's residence, esp. quickly and surreptitiously. **5.** *Colloq.* to elope. **6.** *Obs.* to depart or die. *–v.t.* **7.** *Archaic.* to remove; transfer; oust or dispossess. *–n.* **8.** a light, swift movement; a flutter. **9.** *Colloq.* a removal, esp. a surreptitious one; an elopement: *a moonlight flit.* **10.** *Chiefly U.S. Colloq.* a male homosexual. [ME *flitten,* from Scand.; cf. Icel. *flytja* carry, convey]

**flitch** /flɪtʃ/, *n.* **1.** the side of a hog (or, formerly, some other animal) salted and cured: *a flitch of bacon.* **2.** a steak cut from a halibut. **3.** a large balk of timber cut by a breaking-down saw from which finished boards are cut. **4.** a sample of timber to show to customers. *–v.t.* **5.** to cut into flitches. [ME *flicche,* OE *flicce,* c. MLG *vlike,* Icel. *flikki*]

**flitch beam** /ˈ– bim/, *n.* a beam formed by sandwiching a thin iron plate between two pieces of timber. Also, **flitched beam.**

**flitter**[1] /ˈflɪtə/, *v.i., v.t.* →**flutter.** [frequentative of FLIT]

**flitter**[2] /ˈflɪtə/, *n.* one who or that which flits. [FLIT, *v.* + -ER[1]]

**flittermouse** /ˈflɪtəmaʊs/, *n., pl.* **-mice.** *Obs.* a bat (animal). [FLITTER[1] + MOUSE. Cf. G *Fledermaus*]

**flitting** /ˈflɪtɪŋ/, *adj.* moving lightly and swiftly; passing quickly; fluttering. – **flittingly,** *adv.*

**flivver** /ˈflɪvə/, *n.* **1.** *Orig. U.S. Colloq.* something of unsatisfactory quality or inferior grade. **2.** an old cheap car. **3.** a cart for use on railway lines, propelled by pumping a handle attached to a crank. **4.** a child's three-wheeled toy conveyance, similarly propelled. [orig. meaning a failure; b. *flopper* (from FLOP) and *fizzler* (from FIZZLE)]

**flixweed** /ˈflɪkswid/, *n.* an annual herb, *Descurainia sophia,* a native of temperate Europe and Asia, widely introduced elsewhere.

**float** /floʊt/, *v.i.* **1.** to rest on the surface of a liquid; be buoyant. **2.** to move gently on the surface of a liquid; drift along. **3.** to rest or move in or as in a liquid, the air, etc. **4.** to move or hover before the eyes or in the mind. **5.** to pass from one to another, as a rumour. **6.** to move or drift about free from attachment. **7.** to be launched or floated, as a company, scheme, etc. **8.** *Comm.* to be in circulation, as an acceptance; be awaiting maturity. *–v.t.* **9.** to cause to float. **10.** to cover with water; flood; irrigate. **11.** to launch (a company, scheme, etc.); set going. **12.** to sell on the market, as a stock or a bond. **13.** to make smooth or level, as the surface of plaster. **14.** (of currency) to allow the rate of exchange of a currency to find its own level in a foreign exchange market. *–n.* **15.** something that floats, as a raft. **16.** something for buoying up. **17.** an inflated bag to sustain a person in water; a life jacket. **18.** *Plumbing, Mach., etc.* (in certain apparatus, cisterns, etc.) a device, as a hollow ball, which through its buoyancy automatically regulates the level, supply, or outlet of a liquid. **19.** →**pontoon**[1] (def. 2). **20.** →**paddle**[1] (def. 2). **21.** *Aeron.* a hollow, boatlike part under the wing or fuselage of an aeroplane enabling it to float on water. **22.** *Angling.* a piece of cork or hollow plastic for supporting a baited line in the water and showing by its movement when a fish bites. **23.** *Zool.* an inflated organ that supports an animal in the water. **24.** a platform on wheels, bearing a display, and drawn in a procession. **25.** *Brit.* a low-bodied vehicle for transporting goods, esp. one powered by batteries: *a milk float.* **26.** →**horse float.** **27.** any of various tools for smoothing, levelling, or the like, as a kind of file, a plasterer's trowel, etc. **28.** the loose yarn on the back of cloth due to a figure weave or brocading. **29.** a quantity of money used by shopkeepers and others to provide change at the start of any transactions; the equivalent sum should remain at the finish of the proceedings. **30.** the total value of cheques written but still not presented at one's bank. **31.** (*pl.*) *Theat.* the footlights. [ME *flotie(n),* OE *flotian,* c. Icel. *flota,* MD *vloten.* See FLEET[2], *v.*]

**floatable** /ˈfloʊtəbəl/, *adj.* **1.** capable of floating; that may be floated. **2.** that can be floated on, as a river. – **floatability** /floʊtəˈbɪləti/, *n.*

**floatage** /ˈfloʊtɪdʒ/, *n.* →**flotage.**

**floatation** /floʊˈteɪʃən/, *n.* →**flotation.**

**floatboard** /ˈfloʊtbɔd/, *n.* a board of an undershot paddlewheel.

**float chamber** /ˈfloʊt tʃeɪmbə/, *n.* the petrol reservoir in a carburettor, in which the petrol level is kept constant by means of an induction valve operated by a float within the chamber.

**floater** /ˈfloʊtə/, *n.* **1.** one who or that which floats. **2.** a meat pie served in pea soup. **3.** *Mining.* loose pieces of ore found at the surface and sometimes indicating better ore at depth. **4.** a loose piece of rock which can be moved by a bulldozer as against a large rock formation which must be drilled and blasted out. **5.** *Colloq.* a cheque which is not honoured. **6.** Also, **butterfly.** *Colloq.* (in two-up) a coin which when tossed fails to spin. **7.** *Prison Colloq.* a book, magazine, etc., the property of a prisoner, circulated throughout the jail. **8.** *Cricket.* →**inswinger.** **9.** *Television.* a piece of film used over a narrator's comments. **10.** *Colloq.* one who often changes his job; a temporary employee; one of the floating population. [FLOAT + -ER[1]]

**float-feed** /ˈfloʊt-fid/, *adj.* equipped with a float to control the feed, as in a carburettor.

**floating** /ˈfloʊtɪŋ/, *adj.* **1.** that floats. **2.** free from attachment, or having but little attachment. **3.** *Pathol.* **a.** freely movable. **b.** unduly movable, as certain organs, esp. the spleen or kidney. **4.** not fixed or settled in a definite place or state: *floating population.* **5.** *Finance.* **a.** in circulation or use, or not permanently invested, as capital. **b.** composed of sums due within a short time and not requiring frequent renewal or refinancing: *a floating debt.* **6.** *Mach.* having a vibration-free suspension; working smoothly. – **floatingly,** *adv.*

**floating assets** /– 'æsɛts/, *n.pl.* assets which are continually changing, as cash, stock in trade, bills of exchange, etc.

**floating bridge** /– 'brɪdʒ/, *n.* **1.** a bridge supported by boats, pontoons, etc. **2.** a car ferry.

**floating charge** /– 'tʃadʒ/, *n.* an equitable charge on the assets of a going concern, which does not become fixed and remains dormant until the company is wound up or breaks some condition, thus permitting the person(s) in whose favour the charge is created to intervene to protect his interests.

**floating currency** /– 'kʌrənsi/, *n.* currency whose value is influenced by rises and falls in the value of other currencies.

**floating dock** /– 'dɒk/, *n.* a floating structure which may be lowered in the water to admit a ship and then raised to leave the ship dry for repairs, etc.; a floating dry dock.

**floating heart** /– 'hat/, *n.* any of certain perennial aquatic herbs of the genus *Nymphoides,* esp. *N. lacunosum,* with floating, more or less heart-shaped leaves.

**floating island** /– 'aɪlənd/, *n.* a floating island-like mass of earth and partly decayed vegetation held together by interlacing roots, sometimes built artificially on wooden platforms as in Asia, or resulting naturally from the accumulation of plant litter on a water surface.

**floating point arithmetic,** *n.* arithmetic involving floating point numbers.

**floating point number,** *n.* a number represented by a decimal number multiplied by a power of 10.

**floating policy** /'floʊtɪŋ pɒləsi/, *n.* a marine insurance policy which insures the goods stated in the policy in whatever ship they may travel.

**floating rib** /'– rɪb/, *n.* one of the two lowest pairs of ribs in man, which are attached neither to the sternum nor to the cartilages of other ribs.

**floating stock** /– 'stɒk/, *n.* stock not held for permanent investment and hence available for speculation; stock held by brokers and speculators rather than investors.

**floating vote** /– 'voʊt/, *n.* floating voters collectively.

**floating voter** /– 'voʊtə/, *n.* →**swinging voter.**

**float plane** /'floʊt pleɪn/, *n.* a small seaplane designed to land on lakes, etc.

**floatstone** /'floʊtstoʊn/, *n.* an abrasive stone used by artisans for rubbing down masonry, concrete, etc.

**floaty** /'floʊti/, *adj.* **1.** able to float; buoyant. **2.** (of a boat) drawing little water. **3.** appearing to float: *a floaty chiffon dress.*

**floc** /flɒk/, *n.* →**flock**[2] (def. 4). [short for FLOCCULE]

**floccillation** /flɒksə'leɪʃən/, *n.* a picking at the bedclothes observed in those suffering great exhaustion, fever, etc.; carphology. [**floccillus* (assumed diminutive of L *floccus* flock of wool) + -ATION]

**floccose** /'flɒkoʊs, flɒ'koʊs/, *adj.* **1.** *Bot.* consisting of or bearing woolly tufts or long soft hairs. **2.** →**flocculent.** [LL *floccōsus,* from L *floccus* flock of wool]

**flocculant** /'flɒkjələnt/, *n.* a substance added to solutions to produce flocculation of suspended particles.

**flocculate** /'flɒkjəleɪt/, *v.*, **-lated, -lating.** *–v.t.* **1.** to form into flocculent masses. *–v.i.* **2.** to form flocculent masses, as cloud, a chemical precipitate, etc.; form aggregated or compound masses of particles. – **flocculation** /flɒkjə'leɪʃən/, *n.*

**floccule** /'flɒkjul/, *n.* **1.** something resembling a small flock or tuft of wool. **2.** a bit of flocculent matter, as in a liquid. [NL *flocculus.* See FLOCCULUS]

**flocculent** /'flɒkjələnt/, *adj.* **1.** like a flock or flocks of wool; covered with a soft woolly substance. **2.** consisting of or containing loose woolly masses. **3.** flaky. – **flocculence,** *n.* – **flocculently,** *adv.*

**flocculent precipitate** /– prə'sɪpəteɪt/, *n.* a woolly-looking precipitate, like that of aluminium hydroxide, from the solution of an aluminium salt to which ammonia is added.

**flocculus** /'flɒkjələs/, *n., pl.* **-li** /-laɪ/. **1.** →**floccule. 2.** *Astron.* one of the bright or dark patches which mottle the sun's chromosphere, visible in spectroheliograms. **3.** *Anat.* a small outgrowth on the anterior part of the undersurface of each cerebellar hemisphere. [NL, diminutive of L *floccus* flock of wool]

**floccus** /'flɒkəs/, *n., pl.* **flocci** /'flɒksaɪ/. **1.** a small tuft of woolly hairs. **2.** the covering or down of unfledged birds. [L]

**flock**[1] /flɒk/, *n.* **1.** a number of animals of one kind keeping, feeding, or herded together, now esp. of sheep or goats, or of birds. **2.** a crowd; large number of people. **3.** (in New Testament and ecclesiastical use) **a.** the Christian Church in relation to Christ. **b.** a single congregation in relation to its pastor. **4.** *Rare.* a band or company of persons. *–v.i.* **5.** to gather or go in a flock, company, or crowd. [ME; OE *floc,* c. Icel. *flokkr*] – **flockless,** *adj.*

**flock**[2] /flɒk/, *n.* **1.** a lock or tuft of wool, hair, etc. **2.** (*pl. or sing.*) wool refuse, shearings of cloth, old cloth torn to pieces, etc., used for stuffing mattresses, upholstering furniture, etc. **3.** (*sing. or pl.*) finely powdered wool, cloth, etc., used in making wallpaper. **4.** a tuftlike mass, as in a chemical precipitate. *–v.t.* **5.** to stuff with flock, as a mattress. **6.** to cover or coat with flock, as wallpaper. [ME *flokke,* apparently from OF *floc,* from L *floccus* flock of wool. Cf. OHG *floccho*]

**flock dot** /'– dɒt/, *n.* a pattern of dots or figures not woven but fastened to cloth with adhesive.

**flock ewe** /'– ju/, *n.* a ewe that is retained for the purpose of wool growing, or lamb raising, and is not a stud animal.

**flock paper** /'– peɪpə/, *n.* wallpaper in which the embellishment consists of fine flock adhering to a previously prepared pattern.

**flock pigeon** /'– pɪdʒən/, *n.* **1.** a medium-sized, nomadic pigeon, *Histriophaps histrionicus,* with a brown back, greyish underparts and a black and white face, usu. found in flocks in open plain country in parts of Queensland and the Northern Territory but more widely dispersed in favourable seasonal conditions. **2.** →**topknot pigeon.**

**flock ram** /'– ræm/, *n.* a pure bred ram of not such a high standard as a stud ram, used for mating with a flock ewe.

**flocky** /'flɒki/, *adj.*, **-kier, -kiest.** like flocks or tufts; flocculent.

**floe** /floʊ/, *n.* **1.** a field of floating ice formed on the surface of the sea, etc. **2.** a detached floating portion of such a field. [? Norw. *flo.* Cf. Icel. *flō*]

**flog** /flɒg/, *v.t.*, **flogged, flogging. 1.** to beat hard with a whip, stick, etc.; whip. **2.** *Colloq.* to sell or attempt to sell. **3.** to steal. **4. flog a dead horse,** to make useless efforts, as in attempting to raise interest in a dead issue. [? b. FLAY and *jog,* var. of JAG[1], *v.*, prick, slash (but cf. FLAGELLATE)] – **flogger,** *n.*

**flogging** /'flɒgɪŋ/, *n.* punishment by beating or whipping.

**flong** /flɒŋ/, *n.* (in printing) paper or other material from which a stereotype mould is made.

**flood** /flʌd/, *n.* **1.** a great flowing or overflowing of water, esp. over land not usu. submerged. **2.** any great outpouring or stream: *a flood of words, tears, light, lava, etc.* **3.** the flowing in of the tide (opposed to *ebb*). *–v.t.* **4.** to overflow in or cover with a flood; fill to overflowing. **5.** to cover as with a flood. **6.** to overwhelm with an abundance of something. *–v.i.* **7.** to flow or pour in or as in a flood. **8.** to rise in a flood; overflow. **9.** *Med.* **a.** to suffer uterine haemorrhage. **b.** to have an excessive menstrual flow. [ME; OE *flōd,* c. G *Flut*] – **floodable,** *adj.* – **floodless,** *adj.* – **flooder,** *n.*

**floodbank** /'flʌdbæŋk/, *n.* →**levee**[1] (defs 1, 2).

**flood control** /'– kəntroʊl/, *n.* the technique of controlling river flow with dams, dykes, artificial channels, etc., so as to minimise the occurrence of floods.

**floodgate** /'flʌdgeɪt/, *n.* **1.** a gate designed to regulate the flow of water. **2.** anything serving to control indiscriminate flow or passage. **3.** *N.Z.* a free-hanging fence across a gully or creek which floats above an occasional flood.

**flood irrigation** /flʌd ɪrə'geɪʃən/, *n.* a method of irrigation in which **a.** water is run on a paddock to the depth of a few centimetres to supply sufficient moisture for the growth of the crop, or **b.** water is made to overflow the natural banks of a levee so as to inundate nearby regions.

**floodlight** /'flʌdlaɪt/, *n., v.*, **-lighted** or **-lit, -lighting.** *–n.* **1.** an artificial light so directed or diffused as to give a comparatively uniform illumination over a given area. **2.** a floodlight lamp or projector. *–v.t.* **3.** to illuminate with or as with a floodlight.

**floodlight projector** /– prə'dʒɛktə/, *n.* a powerful lamp having a reflector curved to produce a floodlight.

**floodmark** /'flʌdmak/, *n.* a mark or line indicating the highest point of a flood, usu. with a date beside it.

**flood plain** /ˈflʌd pleɪn/, *n.* a nearly flat plain along the course of a stream that is naturally subject to flooding at high water.

**flood tide** /ˈ– taɪd/, *n.* **1.** the inflow of the tide; the rising tide. **2.** high tide.

**floodwater** /ˈflʌdwɔtə/, *n.* the water that overflows in a flood; excess water.

**floodway** /ˈflʌdweɪ/, *n.* →**stormwater channel.**

**flookan** /ˈflukæn/, *n. Mining.* **1.** a vein of clayey material. **2.** a vein of fine material and water which will run into underground workings if not stopped. Also, **flucan.** [Cornish d.]

**floor** /flɔ/, *n.* **1.** that part of a room or the like which forms its lower enclosing surface, and upon which one walks. **2.** a storey of a building. Cf. **first floor. 3.** a level supporting surface in any structure: *the floor of a bridge.* **4.** a platform or prepared level area for a particular use: *a threshing floor.* **5.** the flat bottom of any more or less hollow place: *the floor of a cave.* **6.** any more or less flat extent of surface. **7.** *Colloq.* the ground. **8.** the part of a legislative chamber, etc., where the members sit, and from which they speak. **9.** the right of one member to speak from such a place in preference to other members: *to get or have the floor.* **10.** the main part of a stock exchange or the like, as distinct from galleries, etc. **11.** *Mining.* **a.** the bottom of a horizontal passageway. **b.** an underlying stratum, as of ore, usu. flat. **12.** *Naut.* that part of the bottom of a vessel on each side of the keelson which is most nearly horizontal. **13.** the bottom, base, or minimum charged or paid: *a price or wage floor.* **14. wipe the floor with,** *Colloq.* to overcome or vanquish totally. *–v.t.* **15.** to cover or furnish with a floor. **16.** to bring down to the floor or ground; knock down. **17.** *Colloq.* to beat or defeat. **18.** *Colloq.* to confound or nonplus: *to be floored by a problem.* [ME *flore,* OE *flōr,* c. G *Flur*] **–floorless,** *adj.*

**floorage** /ˈflɔrɪdʒ/, *n.* the floor space of a building.

**floorboard** /ˈflɔbɔd/, *n.* a plank in a timber floor.

**floorcloth** /ˈflɔklɒθ/, *n.* a cloth for washing or wiping floors.

**floorer** /ˈflɔrə/, *n.* **1.** one who lays floors. **2.** a person or thing, as a blow, that knocks to the floor. **3.** *Colloq.* something that beats, overwhelms, or confounds.

**flooring** /ˈflɔrɪŋ/, *n.* **1.** a floor. **2.** floors collectively. **3.** materials for making or covering floors.

**floor manager** /ˈflɔ mænədʒə/, *n.* **1.** the person in charge of the area of the set (def. 72) in a television production. **2.** a person in charge of a floor of a department store, etc.

**floor plan** /ˈ– plæn/, *n.* a drawing showing the layout of rooms, etc., on each floor of a building.

**floor price** /ˈflɔ praɪs/, *n.* the price at which goods are bought, as of wool at an auction, electrical equipment in a show-room etc., without allowing for usual additional costs as for transport, installation, etc.

**floor show** /ˈ– ʃoʊ/, *n.* an entertainment given in a nightclub or cabaret, usu. consisting of a series of singing, dancing, or comic episodes.

**floor space** /ˈ– speɪs/, *n.* **1.** space available on a floor. **2.** selling space in a shop, as opposed to space for staff or storage purposes.

**floor-space index** /ˈflɔ-speɪs ˌɪndɛks/, *n.* a ratio of the maximum area on a site which may be built on, to the total area of the site; plot ratio; site index. Also, **floor-space ratio.**

**floor stop** /ˈflɔ stɒp/, *n.* →**doorstop** (def. 2).

**floorwalker** /ˈflɔwɔkə/, *n.* →**shopwalker.**

**floozy** /ˈfluzi/, *n., pl.* **-zies.** *Colloq.* a worthless woman; harlot. Also, **floosy, floosie, floozie.**

**flop** /flɒp/, *v.,* **flopped, flopping,** *n. Colloq. –v.i.* **1.** to fall or plump down suddenly, esp. with noise; drop or turn with a sudden bump or thud. **2.** to fall flat on the surface of water. **3.** to yield or break down suddenly; fail. **4.** to flap, as in the wind. **5.** *U.S.* to change suddenly, as from one side or party to another (oft. fol. by *over*). *–v.t.* **6.** to drop, throw, etc., with a sudden bump or thud. **7.** to flap clumsily and heavily, as wings. *–n.* **8.** the act of flopping. **9.** the sound of flopping; a thud. **10.** a failure. [var. of FLAP] **–flopper,** *n*

**flophouse** /ˈflɒphaʊs/, *n.* →**dosshouse.**

**flopping** /ˈflɒpɪŋ/, *adj. Colloq.* →**flipping.**

**floppy** /ˈflɒpi/, *adj.,* **-pier, -piest.** *Colloq.* tending to flop. **–floppily,** *adv.* **–floppiness,** *n.*

**floppy disc** /– ˈdɪsk/, *n.* a flexible magnetically coated disc used for storing data; diskette.

**flor** /flɔ/, *n.* **1.** a film-forming yeast responsible for the development of character in fino sherries. *–adj.* **2.** of or pertaining to wine produced this way, as flor sherry. [Sp.: mould, flower, from L *flōs*]

**flor.,** flourished. [L *floruit*]

**flora** /ˈflɔrə/, *n., pl.* **floras, florae** /ˈflɔri/. **1.** the plants of a particular region or period, listed by species. **2.** a work systematically describing such plants. [NL, from L *Flora* goddess of flowers, from *flōs* FLOWER]

**flora and fauna reserve,** *n.* →**sanctuary** (def. 6).

**floral** /ˈflɒrəl, ˈflɔrəl/, *adj.* pertaining to or consisting of flowers. [L *flōs* flower] **–florally,** *adv.*

**floral envelope** /– ˈɛnvəloʊp/, *n.* the calyx and corolla of a flower.

**floreated** /ˈflɒrieɪtəd/, *adj.* →**floriated.**

**Florence flask** /ˈflɒrəns ˌflask/, *n.* a flat-bottomed, round flask with a long neck; used in laboratory experiments.

**Florentine** /ˈflɒrəntaɪn, -tin/, *adj.* **1.** of or pertaining to Florence: *the Florentine painters.* **2.** *Cookery.* served with spinach. *–n.* **3.** a native or inhabitant of Florence, a city in central Italy. **4.** a biscuit containing nuts, fruit, etc., and topped with chocolate.

**florescence** /fləˈrɛsəns/, *n.* the act, state, or period of flowering; bloom. [NL *flōrescentia,* from L *flōrescens,* ppr., beginning to flower] **–florescent,** *adj.*

**floret** /ˈflɒrət/, *n.* **1.** a small flower. **2.** the flower of grasses together with the palea and lemma. **3.** one of the clusters of flowers making the head of a compound flower as in the daisy. [cf. OF *florete,* diminutive of *flor,* from L *flōs* flower]

**floriated** /ˈflɒrieɪtəd/, *adj.* decorated with floral ornamentation: *floriated columns.* Also, **floreated.**

**floribunda** /flɒrəˈbʌndə/, *n., pl.* **-das.** a group of hybrid cultivated roses bearing flowers in large sprays.

**floriculture** /ˈflɒrəkʌltʃə/, *n.* the cultivation of flowers or flowering plants, esp. under glass. [L *flōri-* (combining form of *flōs* flower) + CULTURE] **–floricultural** /flɒrəˈkʌltʃərəl/, *adj.* **–floriculturist** /flɒrəˈkʌltʃərəst/, *n.*

**florid** /ˈflɒrəd/, *adj.* **1.** highly coloured or ruddy, as complexion, cheeks, etc. **2.** flowery; excessively ornate; showy: *a florid prose style, florid music.* **3.** *Archit.* abounding in decorative features, as in baroque or rococo styles. **4.** *Archaic.* abounding in or consisting of flowers. [L *flōridus* flowery] **–floridity** /flɒˈrɪdəti/, **floridness,** *n.* **–floridly,** *adv.*

**Florida moss** /ˈflɒrədə mɒs/, *n.* →**Spanish moss.**

**floriferous** /fləˈrɪfərəs/, *adj.* flower-bearing. [L *flōrifer* bearing flowers + -OUS]

**florin** /ˈflɒrən/, *n.* a silver coin worth two shillings; a former unit of currency. [ME, from F, from It. *fiorino* a Florentine coin stamped with a lily, from *fiore,* from L *flōs* flower]

**florist** /ˈflɒrəst/, *n.* a retailer of flowers, ornamental plants, etc.

**floristic** /fləˈrɪstɪk/, *adj.* pertaining to flowers or a flora. **–floristically,** *adv.*

**-florous,** an adjectival suffix meaning 'flower', as in *uniflorous.* [L *-flōrus* flowered]

**flory** /ˈflɔri/, *adj.* →**fleury.**

**flos ferri** /flɒs ˈfɛri/, *n.* an arborescent variety of aragonite. [L: flower of iron]

**floss** /flɒs/, *n.* **1.** the cottony fibre yielded by the silk-cotton trees. **2.** silk filaments with little or no twist, used in weaving as brocade or in embroidery. **3.** any silky filamentous matter, as the silk of maize. **4.** Also, **dental floss.** soft, waxed thread used for cleaning between the teeth. Also, (for defs 1-3), **floss silk.** [Scand.; cf. Icel. *flos* shag of velvet]

**flossy** /ˈflɒsi/, *adj.,* **flossier, flossiest.** made of or resembling floss.

**flotage** /ˈfloʊtɪdʒ/, *n.* **1.** the act of floating. **2.** the state of floating. **3.** floating power; buoyancy. **4.** anything that floats; flotsam. **5.** the ships, etc., afloat on a river. **6.** the part of a ship above the water line. Also, **floatage.** [FLOAT, *n.* + -AGE. Cf. F *flottage*]

**flotation** /floʊˈteɪʃən/, *n.* **1.** the act or state of floating. **2.** the floating or launching of a commercial venture, a loan, etc. **3.** *Metall.* a process for separating the different crystalline phases in a mass of powdered ore based on their ability to sink in, or float on, a given liquid. **4.** the science of floating bodies. Also, **floatation.** [var. of FLOATATION. Cf. F *flottaison* (see FLOTSAM)]

**flote-grass** /ˈfloʊt-gras/, *n.* a perennial grass, *Glyceria fluitans,* growing in shallow water throughout northern temperate regions; manna grass.

**flotilla** /fləˈtɪlə/, *n.* **1.** number of small naval vessels; a subdivision of a fleet. **2.** a small fleet. [Sp., diminutive of *flota* fleet, from F *flotte,* from OE *flota*]

**flotsam** /ˈflɒtsəm/, *n.* such part of the wreckage of a ship and its cargo as is found floating on the water. Cf. **jetsam.** [AF *floteson,* from *floter* float, from OE *flotian*]

**flotsam and jetsam,** *n.* **1.** the wreckage of a ship and its cargo found either floating upon the sea or washed ashore. **2.** odds and ends.

**flounce**[1] /flaʊns/, *v.,* **flounced, flouncing,** *n.* *–v.i.* **1.** to go with an impatient or angry fling of the body (oft. fol. by *away, off, out,* etc.): *to flounce out of a room in a rage.* **2.** to throw the body about, as in floundering or struggling; twist; turn; jerk. *–n.* **3.** action of flouncing; a flouncing movement. [Scand.; cf. Norw. *flunsa* hurry]

**flounce**[2] /flaʊns/, *n., v.,* **flounced, flouncing.** *–n.* **1.** a strip of material, wider than a ruffle, gathered and attached at one edge and with the other edge left hanging, used for trimming, esp. on women's skirts. *–v.t.* **2.** to trim with a flounce or flounces. [var. of obs. *frounce,* from OF *fronce* a wrinkle, fold, from Gmc]

**flouncing** /ˈflaʊnsɪŋ/, *n.* **1.** material for flounces. **2.** trimming consisting of a flounce.

**flounder**[1] /ˈflaʊndə/, *v.i.* **1.** to struggle with stumbling or plunging movements (oft. fol. by *along, on, through,* etc.). **2.** to struggle clumsily or helplessly in embarrassment or confusion. *–n.* **3.** the action of floundering; a floundering movement. [? b. FLOUNCE[1] and FOUNDER[2]]

**flounder**[2] /ˈflaʊndə/, *n., pl.* **-der.** **1.** any of numerous species of flatfishes, belonging to the families Bothidae and Pleuronectidae, found in coastal Australian and New Zealand waters. **2.** a European marine flatfish, *Platichthys flesus,* widely caught for food. **3.** any of a number of similar or related flatfishes, other than soles. [ME, from AF *floundre,* from Scand.; cf. Norw. *flundra*]

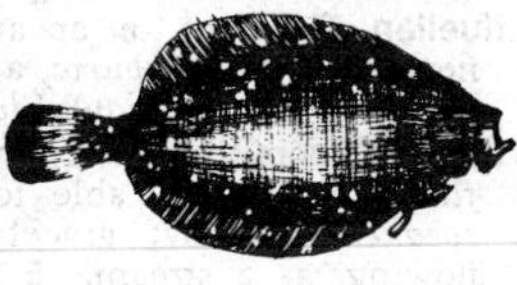
flounder[2]

**flour** /ˈflaʊə/, *n.* **1.** the finely ground meal of wheat or other grain, esp. the finer meal separated by bolting. **2.** any fine, soft powder: *flour of emery.* *–v.t.* **3.** to make (grain, etc.) into flour; grind and bolt. **4.** to sprinkle or dredge with flour, as food or utensils in cookery. **5.** to break up (mercury, in amalgamation) into fine globules, which, owing to some impurity, do not unite with a precious metal. [ME; special use of FLOWER. Cf. F *fleur de farine* the flower or finest part of the meal] – **flourless,** *adj.* – **flourlike,** *adj.*

**flourbag** /ˈflaʊəbæg/, *n.* a large hessian bag for conveying flour in bulk.

**flourish** /ˈflʌrɪʃ/, *v.i.* **1.** to be in a vigorous state; thrive; prosper; be successful: *during this period art flourished.* **2.** to be in its or one's prime; be at the height of fame or excellence. **3.** to grow luxuriantly, or thrive in growth, as a plant. **4.** to make strokes or flourishes with a brandished weapon or the like. **5.** to make a parade or ostentatious display. **6.** to add embellishments or flourishes to writing, letters, etc. **7.** to speak or write in flowery or pretentious language. **8.** *Music.* **a.** to play a showy passage. **b.** to play in a showy manner. **c.** to sound a trumpet call or fanfare. *–v.t.* **9.** to brandish or wave (a sword, a stick, the limbs, etc.) about in the air. **10.** to parade, flaunt, or display ostentatiously: *to flourish one's wealth.* **11.** to embellish (writing, etc.) with sweeping or fanciful curves or lines. **12.** to adorn with decorative designs, colour, etc. *–n.* **13.** a brandishing or waving, as of a sword, a stick, or the like. **14.** a parade or ostentatious display. **15.** a decoration or embellishment in writing. **16.** *Rhet.* a parade of fine language; an expression used merely for effect. **17.** *Music.* **a.** an elaborate passage or addition largely for display. **b.** a trumpet call or fanfare. **18.** *Rare.* the condition of flourishing or thriving: *in full flourish.* **19.** *Obs.* the state of flowering. [ME *florish(en),* from OF *floriss-,* stem of *florir,* from L *flōrēre* bloom] – **flourisher,** *n.*

**flourishing** /ˈflʌrɪʃɪŋ/, *adj.* that flourishes; vigorous in growth; thriving; prosperous. – **flourishingly,** *adv.*

**flour mill** /ˈflaʊə mɪl/, *n.* a mill for making flour.

**floury** /ˈflaʊəri/, *adj.* **1.** of, pertaining to, or resembling flour. **2.** covered or white with flour. **3.** (of fruit) lacking crispness and flavour.

**floury baker** /– ˈbeɪkə/, *n. Colloq.* a common cicada of eastern Australia, *Abricta curvicosta,* dark brown with orange markings and a superficial whitish covering resembling flour. Also, **floury miller.**

**flout** /flaʊt/, *v.t.* **1.** to mock; scoff at; treat with disdain or contempt. *–v.i.* **2.** to mock, gibe, or scoff (oft. fol. by *at*). *–n.* **3.** a flouting speech or action; a mocking insult; a gibe. [ME *floute(n),* var. of FLUTE, *v.* Cf. D *fluiten* play the flute, mock, impose upon] – **flouter,** *n.* – **floutingly,** *adv.*

**flow** /floʊ/, *v.i.* **1.** to move along in a stream, as a liquid; circulate, as the blood. **2.** to stream or well forth; issue or proceed from a source; discharge a stream, as of blood. **3.** to come or go as in a stream, as persons or things. **4.** to proceed continuously and smoothly, like a stream, as thought, speech, or verse. **5.** to fall or hang loosely at full length, as hair. **6.** to overflow or abound with something: *a land flowing with milk and honey.* **7.** to rise and advance, as the tide (opposed to *ebb*). *–v.t.* **8.** to cause or permit to flow. **9.** to cover with water or other liquid; flood. *–n.* **10.** the act of flowing. **11.** movement in or as in a stream; any continuous movement, as of thought, speech, trade, etc., like that of a stream of water. **12.** the rate of flowing. **13.** the volume of fluid that flows through a passage of any given section in a unit of time. **14.** that which flows; a stream. **15.** an outpouring or discharge of something, as in a stream: *a flow of blood.* **16.** an overflowing. **17.** the rise of the tide; flood (opposed to *ebb*). **18.** *Scot.* an inlet of the sea. **19.** *Scot.* a flat, marshy tract of land. [ME *flowen,* OE *flōwan,* c. LG *flojen,* Icel. *flōa*]

**flowage** /ˈfloʊɪdʒ/, *n.* **1.** the act of flowing; flow; the state of being flooded. **2.** the flowing or overflowing liquid. **3.** *Mech.* gradual internal motion or deformation, without fracture, of a viscous solid such as asphalt.

**flow chart** /ˈfloʊ tʃat/, *n.* a diagram showing the step-by-step operation of a system. Also, **flow diagram, flow sheet.**

**flower** /ˈflaʊə/, *n.* **1.** the blossom of a plant. **2.** *Bot.* **a.** the sexual reproductive structure of the angiosperm usu. consisting of gynoecium, androecium and perianth. **b.** an analogous reproductive structure in other plants, as the mosses. **3.** a plant considered with reference to its blossom or cultivated for its floral beauty. **4.** the state of efflorescence or bloom: *plants in flower.* **5.** an ornament or decorative symbol representing a flower; fleuron. **6.** any ornament or adornment. **7.** a figure of speech. **8.** the finest or most flourishing state or period, as of life or beauty. **9.** the best or finest member or part of a number, body, or whole: *the flower of chivalry.* **10.** the finest or choicest product or example. **11.** (*pl.*) *Chem.* a substance in the form of a fine powder, esp. as obtained by sublimation: *flowers of sulphur.* **12. see the flowers,** *Colloq.* (*euph.*) to be menstruating. *–v.i.* **13.** to produce flowers, or blossom, as a plant; to come to full bloom. **14.** to abound in flowers. **15.** to reach the stage of full development. *–v.t.* **16.** to cover or deck with flowers. **17.** to decorate with a floral design. [ME *flour,* from OF, from L *flōs*] – **flower-like,** *adj.*

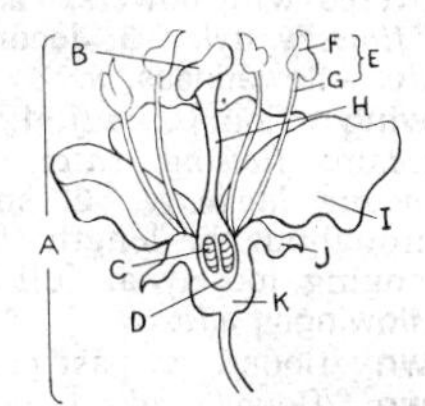

stylised section of a flower: A, pistil; B, stigma; C, ovule; D, ovary; E, stamen; F, anther; G, filament; H, style; I, petal; J, sepal; K, receptacle

**flowerage** /ˈflaʊərɪdʒ/, *n.* **1.** flowers collectively. **2.** floral ornament or decoration. **3.** *Rare.* the process or state of flowering.

**flower arrangement** /ˈflaʊər əreɪndʒmənt/, *n.* a decorative design made with flowers.

**flowerbed** /ˈflaʊəbɛd/, *n.* a plot of ground, esp. in a garden, where flowering plants are cultivated.

**flowerbox** /ˈflaʊəbɒks/, *n.* a box-shaped container with drainage holes at the bottom, designed for growing flowers.

**flowerchild** /ˈflaʊətʃaɪld/, *n.* →**hippie.**

**flower-de-luce** /flaʊə-də-ˈlus/, *n.* **1.** the iris (flower or plant). **2.** *Archaic.* the lily. [old var. of *fleur-de-lis* influenced by FLOWER]

**flowered** /ˈflaʊəd/, *adj.* **1.** having flowers. **2.** decorated with flowers, or a floral pattern.

**flowerer** /ˈflaʊərə/, *n.* a plant that flowers at a specific time, in a specific manner, etc.: *a late flowerer, an abundant flowerer.*

**floweret** /ˈflaʊərət/, *n.* a small flower; a floret.

**flower garden** /ˈflaʊə gadən/, *n.* a garden in which flowering plants, rather than vegetables or grass, are cultivated.

**flower girl** /ˈ– gɜl/, *n.* **1.** a very young girl attending a bride. **2.** *Brit.* a woman selling flowers in the street.

**flower head** /ˈ– hɛd/, *n.* **1.** *Bot.* an inflorescence consisting of a dense cluster of sessile florets; a capitulum. **2.** a cluster of flowers, an inflorescence.

**flowering** /ˈflaʊərɪŋ/, *adj.* bearing flowers.

**flowering dogwood** /– ˈdɒgwʊd/, *n.* a deciduous shrub, *Cornus florida,* native to the eastern U.S., widely planted for its pink and white flowers.

**flowering rush** /– ˈrʌʃ/, *n.* an aquatic herb of the family Butomaceae, with long narrow leaves and umbels of pink flowers, *Butomus umbellatus,* of Europe and temperate Asia.

**flowerless** /ˈflaʊələs/, *adj.* **1.** without flowers. **2.** *Bot.* without a true seed; cryptogamic.

**flower of Jove,** *n.* a perennial herb of the family Caryophyllaceae from the central European Alps, *Lychnis flos-jovis,* often cultivated for its grey woolly foliage and bright red flowers.

**flowerpot** /ˈflaʊəpɒt/, *n.* a pot to hold earth for a plant to grow in.

**flower power** /ˈflaʊə paʊə/, *n.* the force for good seen by the hippy cult of the 1960s in advocating peace, cooperation and love, to be symbolised by the flower.

**flower wasp** /ˈflaʊə wɒsp/, *n.* any of various wasplike insects of the predominantly Australian family Thynnidae, as the blue ant.

**flowery** /ˈflaʊəri/, *adj.,* **-rier, -riest.** **1.** abounding in or covered with flowers. **2.** containing highly ornate language: *a flowery style.* **3.** decorated with floral designs. – **flowerily,** *adv.* – **floweriness,** *n.*

**flowing** /ˈfloʊɪŋ/, *adj.* **1.** that flows; moving in or as in a stream: *flowing water.* **2.** proceeding smoothly or easily: *flowing language.* **3.** smoothly and gracefully continuous throughout the length: *flowing lines or curves.* **4.** falling or hanging loosely at full length: *flowing hair, draperies, etc.* – **flowingly,** *adv.*

**flown**[1] /floʊn/, *v.* past participle of **fly**[1].

**flown**[2] /floʊn/, *adj.* **1.** decorated by means of colour freely blended or flowed, as a glaze. **2.** *Archaic.* filled to excess. [ME *flowen,* OE *flōwen,* pp. of *flōwan* flow]

**flow-on** /ˈfloʊ-ɒn/, *n.* the wider application of changes in wages, costs, etc., which have arisen in one part of the community.

**flow sheet** /ˈfloʊ ʃit/, *n.* →**flow chart.**

**flowthrough** /ˈfloʊθru/, *n.* **1.** the movement of air, liquid, etc., passing through a confined space. **2.** the consequence of a previous event or condition: *the flowthrough from wage indexation.* –*adj.* **3.** of or pertaining to flowthrough: *indexation flowthrough effects.*

**flowthrough ventilation** /– vɛntəˈleɪʃən/, *n.* the system of ventilating the interiors of motor cars, etc., in which air enters through ducts at the front and leaves through ducts in the rear, the windows being shut.

**fl oz,** fluid ounce.

**Flt Lt,** Flight Lieutenant.

**flu** /flu/, *n. Colloq.* →**influenza.**

**flub** /flʌb/, *v.t.,* **flubbed, flubbing.** **1.** to bungle; make a mess of. –*n.* **2.** something badly performed.

**fluctuant** /ˈflʌktʃuənt/, *adj.* **1.** fluctuating; varying. **2.** *Med.* having a soft or liquid centre, as a boil, abscess, etc.

**fluctuate** /ˈflʌktʃueɪt/, *v.,* **-ated, -ating.** –*v.i.* **1.** to change continually, as by turns, from one course, position, condition, amount, etc., to another, as the mind, opinion, policy, prices, temperature, etc.; vary irregularly; be unstable. **2.** to move in waves or like waves. –*v.t. Rare.* **3.** to cause to fluctuate. [L *fluctuātus,* pp., undulated]

**fluctuation** /flʌktʃuˈeɪʃən/, *n.* **1.** continual change from one course, position, condition, etc., to another; alternating variation; vacillation; wavering; instability. **2.** wavelike motion. **3.** a rise or fall in price, value, etc. **4.** *Genetics.* a body variation which is not inherited.

**fludrocortisone** /ˌfludroʊˈkɔtəzoʊn/, *n.* a type of hydrocortisone containing a fluorine group which has the actions of hydrocortisone but is more potent and causes salt retention.

**flue**[1] /flu/, *n.* **1.** the smoke passage in a chimney. **2.** any duct or passage for air, gases, or the like. **3.** (in certain steam boilers) any of the pipes or tubes through which hot gases, etc., are conveyed in order to heat surrounding or adjacent water. **4.** *Music.* **a.** →**fluepipe. b.** the air passage in a fluepipe between the blowing end and the lateral hole. [earlier *flew,* ? representing OE *flēwsa* a flowing, the form *flews* being taken for a plural]

**flue**[2] /flu/, *n.* downy matter; fluff. [? OE *flug-* in *flugol* swift, fleeting (akin to FLY[1], *v.*). Cf. LG *flug*] – **fluey,** *adj.*

**flue**[3] /flu/, *n.* a kind of fishing net. Also, **flew.** [ME *flowe.* Cf. MD *vluwe* fishing net]

**flue**[4] /flu/, *n.* **1.** a barb of a feather. **2.** the fluke of an anchor. [orig. obscure. Cf. Swed. *fly*]

**flue**[5] /flu/, *v.i.,* **flued, fluing.** (at the sides of a fireplace, etc.) to splay. [ME d. *flew* shallow]

**flue gas** /ˈ– gæs/, *n.* the gaseous combustion products from a boiler furnace consisting of a mixture of carbon dioxide, carbon monoxide, nitrogen, oxygen, and steam.

**fluellen** /fluˈɛlən/, *n.* an annual herb with yellow and purple flowers, *Kickxia spuria,* a common weed in European cereal crops. [Welsh (*llysiau*) *Llewelyn* herbs of Llewelyn]

**fluent** /ˈfluənt/, *adj.* **1.** flowing smoothly and easily: *to speak fluent French.* **2.** able to speak or write readily: *a fluent speaker.* **3.** easy; graceful: *fluent motion, curves, etc.* **4.** flowing, as a stream. **5.** *Rare.* capable of flowing, or fluid, as liquids or gases. **6.** *Rare.* not fixed or stable in form. [L *fluens,* ppr., flowing] – **fluency, fluentness,** *n.* – **fluently,** *adv.*

**fluepipe** /ˈflupaɪp/, *n.* **1.** *Music.* an organ pipe in which a current of air striking a mouth or aperture produces the note. **2.** *Bldg Trades.* a pipe of some heat-resistant material leading smoke from a stove to a flue.

**fluestop** /ˈflustɒp/, *n.* an organ stop whose sound is produced by fluepipes; any stop which is not a reedstop.

**fluff** /flʌf/, *n.* **1.** light, downy particles, as of cotton. **2.** a downy mass; something downy or fluffy. **3.** *Colloq.* a blunder or error in execution, performance, etc. **4. bit of fluff,** a girl, esp. one who is superficially attractive. **5.** *Colloq.* a fart. –*v.t.* **6.** to make into fluff; shake or puff out (feathers, hair, etc.) into a fluffy mass. **7.** *Colloq.* to fail to perform properly: *to fluff a golf stroke, an examination, lines of a play.* –*v.i.* **8.** to become fluffy, move, float, or settle down like fluff. **9.** *Colloq.* to blunder; fail in performance or execution. **10.** *Colloq.* to break wind. **11.** to lie; bluff. [? b. FLUE[2] and PUFF]

**fluffy** /ˈflʌfi/, *adj.* **fluffier, fluffiest.** of, like, or covered with fluff. – **fluffily,** *adv.* – **fluffiness,** *n.*

**fluffy glider** /– ˈglaɪdə/, *n.* one of the larger gliding possums of north-eastern Australia, *Petaurus australis,* having length of about 75 cm. Also, **yellow-bellied glider.**

**flugelhorn** /ˈflugəlhɔn/, *n.* a keyed brass instrument with cup mouthpiece and of conical bore, used mainly in brass bands. [G *Flügelhorn,* lit., wing-horn]

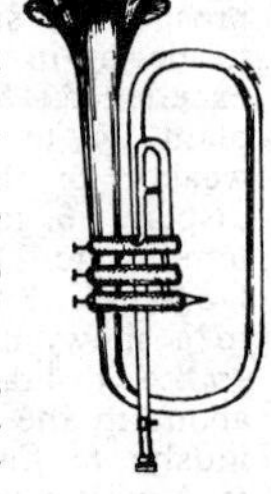
flugelhorn

**fluid** /ˈfluəd/, *n.* **1.** a substance which is capable of flowing and offers no permanent resistance to changes of shape; a liquid or a gas. *–adj.* **2.** capable of flowing; liquid or gaseous. **3.** consisting of or pertaining to fluids. **4.** changing readily; shifting, not fixed, stable, or rigid. [L *fluidus,* from *fluere* flow] **– fluidal, fluidic** /flu'ɪdɪk/, *adj.* **– fluidity,** /flu'ɪdəti/, **fluidness,** *n.* **– fluidly,** *adv.*

**fluid drachm** /– 'dræm/, *n.* a unit of capacity in the imperial system equal to one eighth of a fluid ounce or approx. $3.552 \times 10^{-6}$ m$^3$. *Symbol:* fl dr

**fluid drive** /'– draɪv/, *n.* a device for transmitting torque from one shaft to another, esp. for providing a smooth coupling between the engine of a motor vehicle and the transmission; consists of two vaned rotors in a sealed casing filled with oil. The driven rotor transmits its momentum to oil which in turn drives the second rotor; hydraulic torque converter. Also, **fluid flywheel.**

**fluid extract** /– 'ɛkstrækt/, *n.* an alcoholic solution of a vegetable drug when 1 cubic centimetre of the preparation is equivalent, in activity, to one gram of the drug in powdered form.

**fluidics** /flu'ɪdɪks/, *n.* the branch of computing which uses hydraulic systems to simulate problems and manipulate data. Fluidic systems are slow in operation compared with electronic circuits but are suitable for specialised applications. **– fluidic,** *adj.*

**fluidise** /'fluədaɪz/, *v.t.,* **-dised, -dising. 1.** to handle solid particles as if they were liquids by transporting them in a stream of gas. **2.** to make fluid. Also, **fluidize. – fluidisation** /fluədaɪ'zeɪʃən/, *n.* **– fluidiser,** *n.*

**fluid mechanics** /fluəd mə'kænɪks/, *n.* an applied science embodying the basic principles of both gaseous and liquid flow.

**fluid ounce** /– 'aʊns/, *n.* a unit of volume in the imperial system, equal to $\frac{1}{20}$ of a pint (28.413 062 5 $\times 10^{-3}$ litres) or, in the U.S., $\frac{1}{16}$ of a pint (29.573 529 562 5 $\times 10^{-3}$ litres).

**fluid pressure** /'– prɛʃə/, *n.* the pressure exerted by a fluid, equal in all directions around a point and acting in a perpendicular direction to any surface.

**fluid tablet** /'– tæblət/, *n. Colloq.* a diuretic tablet.

**fluke**[1] /fluk/, *n.* **1.** the flat triangular piece at the end of each arm of an anchor, which catches in the ground. **2.** a barb, or the barbed head, of a harpoon, etc. **3.** either half of the triangular tail of a whale. [? special use of FLUKE[3]]

F

F, fluke[1] (def. 1)

**fluke**[2] /fluk/, *n., v.,* **fluked, fluking.** *–n.* **1.** any accidental advantage; a lucky chance. **2.** an accidentally successful stroke in billiards or other sports. *–v.t.* **3.** *Colloq.* to hit, make, or gain by a fluke. [orig. unknown. Cf. d. E *fluke* a guess]

**fluke**[3] /fluk/, *n.* **1.** the flounder, *Platichtys flesus.* **2.** any flounder. **3.** →**trematode.** [ME, var. of *flook,* OE *flōc*]

**fluky** /'fluki/, *adj.,* **flukier, flukiest. 1.** *Colloq.* obtained by chance rather than skill. **2.** uncertain, as a wind. Also, **flukey.** [FLUKE[2] + -Y[1]] **– flukiness,** *n.*

**flume** /flum/, *n., v.,* **flumed, fluming.** *U.S. –n.* **1.** a deep narrow defile, esp. one containing a mountain torrent. **2.** an artificial channel or trough for conducting water, as one in which logs, etc., are transported. *–v.t.* **3.** to transport, as timber, in a flume. **4.** to divert (a river, etc.) by a flume. [ME, from OF *flum,* from L *flūmen* stream]

**flummery** /'flʌməri/, *n., pl.* **-ries. 1.** a fruit flavoured jelly mixture, sometimes thickened with flour, beaten until fluffy and allowed to set. **2.** a soft jelly made by boiling oatmeal or flour with water, straining and allowing to set. **3.** any light, fluffy sweet, as a cream custard or jelly whipped up with egg whites. **4.** agreeable humbug; empty compliment. **5.** superficial or useless ornaments; trivia. [Welsh *llymru*]

**flummox** /'flʌməks/, *Colloq. –v.t.* **1.** to bewilder; confuse. *–v.i.* **2.** to become bewildered or unsure of what to do.

**flump** /flʌmp/, *Colloq. –v.i.* **1.** to plump down suddenly or heavily; flop. *–v.t.* **2.** to set or throw down with a dull noise. *–n.* **3.** act or sound of flumping. [b. FALL and PLUMP[2]]

**flung** /flʌŋ/, *v.* past tense and past participle of **fling.**

**flunk** /flʌŋk/, *Colloq. –v.i.* **1.** to fail, as a student in an examination. **2.** to give up; back out (fol. by *out*). *–v.t.* **3.** to fail in (an examination, etc.). **4.** to remove (a student) as unqualified from a school, course, etc. *–n.* **5.** a failure, as in a recitation or examination. [? akin to FLINCH[1], FUNK[1]]

**flunkey** /'flʌŋki/, *n., pl.* **-keys. 1.** a male servant in livery; a lackey. **2.** a servile follower; a toady. [? alteration of FLANKER] **– flunkeydom, flunkeyism,** *n.* **– flunkeyish,** *adj.*

**flunky** /'flʌŋki/, *n., pl.* **-kies.** →**flunkey.**

**fluon** /'fluɒn/, *n.* a plastic with non-adhesive surface properties, polytetrafluorethylene; used as a coating on non-stick cooking utensils. [Trademark]

**fluor** /'fluɔ/, *n.* →**fluorspar.** [L: a flowing (so called from its use as a flux)]

**fluor-**[1], a word element indicating the presence of fluorine. [combining form of FLUORINE]

**fluor-**[2], a word element indicating fluorescence. [combining form of FLUORESCENCE]

**fluorene** /'fluərin, flu-/, *n.* a white crystalline aromatic hydrocarbon, $C_{13}H_{10}$, used in the manufacture of resins and dyes; ortho-diphenylene methane.

**fluoresce** /fluə'rɛs, flə-/, *v.i.,* **-resced, -rescing.** to exhibit the phenomena of fluorescence.

**fluorescein** /'fluərəsin, 'flu-/, *n.* an orange-red water-insoluble compound, $C_{20}H_{12}O_5$, whose solutions in alkalis produce an orange colour and a green fluorescence. It is used as an indicator and in dyes. Also, **fluoresceine.**

**fluorescence** /fluə'rɛsəns, flə-/, *n.* **1.** the property possessed by certain substances of emitting light upon exposure to external radiation or bombardment by a stream of particles. **2.** the light or luminosity so produced.

**fluorescent** /fluə'rɛsənt, flə-/, *adj.* possessing the property of fluorescence; exhibiting fluorescence.

**fluorescent tube** /– 'tjub/, *n.* an electric discharge tube in which light is produced by passage of electricity through a metallic vapour or gas enclosed in a tube or bulb.

**fluoric** /'fluərɪk, 'flu-/, *adj.* **1.** *Chem.* pertaining to or obtained from fluorine. **2.** *Mineral.* pertaining to or obtained from fluor. [F *fluorique,* from *fluor* fluid acid, from L: a flowing]

**fluoridate** /'fluərədeɪt, 'flu-/, *v.t.* to treat by means of fluoridation. [backformation from FLUORIDATION]

**fluoridation** /fluərə'deɪʃən, 'flu-/, *n.* the addition to toothpaste, public water supplies, etc. of fluoride compounds to prevent tooth decay in the populace. [FLUORID(E) + -ATION]

**fluoride** /'fluəraɪd, 'flu-/, *n.* **1.** a salt of hydrofluoric acid. **2.** an organic compound with one or more hydrogen atoms substituted by fluorine atoms, as methyl fluoride. *–adj.* **3.** of or pertaining to a substance containing fluoride, as toothpaste.

**fluorinate** /'fluərəneɪt, 'flu-/, *v.t.,* **-nated, -nating.** to treat or combine with fluorine. **– fluorination** /fluərə'neɪʃən, flu-/, *n.*

**fluorine** /'fluərin, 'flu-/, *n.* a non-metallic element, a pale yellow corrosive gas, occurring combined, esp. in fluorspar, cryolite, phosphate rock, and other minerals. *Symbol:* F; *at. wt:* 18.9984; *at. no.:* 9.

**fluorine dating** /'– deɪtɪŋ/, *n.* a method of determining the age of objects of plant or animal origin by means of their content of fluorine absorbed from surrounding ground water.

**fluorite** /'fluəraɪt, 'flu-/, *n.* →**fluorspar.**

**fluoroborate** /ˌfluəroʊ'bɔreɪt, ˌfluroʊ-/, *n.* a salt of fluoroboric acid. Also, **fluoborate** /ˌfluoʊ'bɔreɪt/.

**fluoroboric acid** /ˌfluəroʊbɔrɪk 'æsəd, ˌfluroʊ-/, *n.* a colourless liquid $HBF_4$, used in the synthesis of fluoroborates. Also, **hydrofluoboric acid** /ˌhaɪdroʊfluəˌbɔrɪk 'æsəd/, **fluoboric acid** /ˌfluoʊbɔrɪk 'æsəd/.

**fluorocarbon** /ˌfluəroʊ'kabən, ˌfluroʊ-/, *n.* any of a class of compounds made by substituting fluorine for hydrogen in a hydrocarbon and characterised by great chemical stability. They are used as lubricants, fire-extinguishers, and in industrial applications in which resistance to heat, radioactivity, etc., is essential.

**fluorophosphate** /ˌfluəroʊ'fɒsfeɪt, ˌfluroʊ-/, *n.* a salt or ester of flurophosphoric acid. Also, **fluophosphate** /ˌfluoʊ'fɒsfeɪt/.

**fluorophosphoric acid** /ˌfluəroʊfɒsfɒrɪk 'æsəd, ˌfluroʊ-/, *n.* any of the three acids $H_2PO_3F$ (*mono-*), $HPO_2F_2$ (*di-*), or $HPF_6$ (*hexa-*). Also, **fluophosphoric acid** /ˌfluoʊfɒsfɒrɪk 'æsəd/.

**fluoroscope** /'flurəskoʊp/, *n.* a tube or box, fitted with a screen coated with a fluorescent substance, used for viewing objects exposed to X-rays or other radiation directed to, or focused upon, the screen. [FLUOR-² + -O- + -SCOPE]

**fluoroscopic** /fluərə'skɒpɪk, flu-/, *adj.* pertaining to the fluoroscope or to fluoroscopy. – **fluoroscopically,** *adv.*

**fluoroscopy** /fluə'rɒskəpi, flu-/, *n.* the act of using the fluoroscope, or of examining by means of a fluorescent screen, the shadows of bodies shown up by X-rays; screening.

**fluorosilicate** /ˌfluəroʊ'sɪləkeɪt, ˌfluroʊ-, -kət/, *n.* a salt of fluorosilicic acid. Also, **fluosilicate** /fluoʊ'sɪləkeɪt, -kət/.

**fluorosilicic acid** /ˌfluəroʊsəlɪsɪk 'æsəd, ˌfluroʊ-/, *n.* an unstable acid, $H_2SiF_6$, used in aqueous solution or in the form of its salts as a wood preservative, disinfectant, and hardening agent.

**fluorspar** /'fluəspa/, *n.* a common mineral, calcium fluoride, $CaF_2$, occurring in colourless, green, blue, purple, and yellow crystals, usu. in cubes. It is the principal source of fluorine, and is also used as a flux in metallurgy and for ornamental purposes. Also, **fluor;** *Chiefly U.S.,* **fluorite.**

**fluothane** /'fluəθeɪn/, *n.* halothane, a general inhalant anaesthetic. [Trademark]

**flurry** /'flʌri/, *n., pl.* **-ries,** *v.,* **-ried, -rying.** *–n.* **1.** a sudden gust of wind. **2.** a light gusty shower or snowfall. **3.** commotion; sudden excitement or confusion; nervous hurry. **4.** *Stock Exchange.* a brief agitation in prices. *–v.t.* **5.** to put (a person) into a flurry; make nervous; confuse; fluster. [b. FLUTTER and HURRY]

**flush¹** /flʌʃ/, *n.* **1.** a blush; a rosy glow. **2.** a rushing or overspreading flow, as of water. **3.** a rush of emotion; elation: *the first flush of success, of victory.* **4.** glowing freshness or vigour: *the flush of youth.* **5.** the hot stage of a fever, esp. hot flushes; waves of heat, as during fever, menopause, etc. **6.** *Colloq.* an arrangement or mechanism for flushing drains, etc. *–v.t.* **7.** to redden; cause to blush or glow. **8.** to flood with water, as for cleansing purposes; wash out (a sewer, etc.). **9.** to animate or elate. *–v.i.* **10.** to blush; redden. **11.** to flow with a rush; flow and spread suddenly. [from FLUSH³] – **flusher,** *n.*

**flush²** /flʌʃ/, *adj.* **1.** even or level, as with a surface; in one plane. **2.** well-supplied, as with money; affluent; prosperous. **3.** abundant or plentiful, as money. **4.** flushed with colour; blushing. **5.** full of vigour; lusty. **6.** quite full; full to overflowing. **7.** *Naut.* (of a deck) unbroken by deckhouses, etc., and having an even surface fore and aft or from stem to stern. **8.** *Print.* even or level with the right or left margins of the type page; without an indentation. *–adv.* **9.** so as to be flush or even. **10.** squarely; full on: *I hit him flush on the face.* *–v.t.* **11.** to make flush or even. **12.** to fill or cover with mortar or cement. **13.** *Agric.* to place (ewes about to be mated) on good pasture or give them extra food for a short period to induce the maturation of a greater number of ova. *–v.i.* **14.** to send out shoots, as plants in spring. *–n.* **15.** a fresh growth, as of shoots and leaves. [special use of FLUSH¹]

**flush³** /flʌʃ/, *v.t.* **1. a.** to disturb a game bird or hunted animal so that it moves from its cover into view suddenly. **b.** to cause others to reveal themselves (oft. fol. by *out*): *this should flush out the fellow travellers.* *–v.i.* **2.** to fly out into view or start up suddenly. *–n.* **3.** a flushed bird or flock of birds. [ME *flussh,* orig. uncert.; perhaps imitative]

**flush⁴** /flʌʃ/, *adj.* **1.** consisting entirely of cards of one suit: *a flush hand.* *–n.* **2.** a hand or set of cards all of one suit. See **royal flush, straight flush.** [cf. F (obs.) *flus,* var. of *flux* flow, flush (cf. E *run* of cards), from L *fluxus* FLUX]

**fluster** /'flʌstə/, *v.t.* **1.** to confuse; make nervous. **2.** to excite and confuse with drink. *–v.i.* **3.** to become confused; become agitated or flurried. *–n.* **4.** confusion; flurry; nervous excitement. [cf. Icel. *flaustr* hurry, bustle and cf. BLUSTER]

**flustrate** /'flʌstreɪt/, *v.t.,* **-trated, -trating.** *Colloq.* →**fluster.** – **flustration** /flʌs'treɪʃən/, *n.*

**flute** /flut/, *n., v.,* **fluted, fluting.** *–n.* **1.** a musical wind instrument consisting of a tube with a series of fingerholes or keys, in which the wind is directed against a sharp edge, either directly, as in the modern orchestral transverse flute, or through a flue, as in the recorder. **2.** an organ stop with wide flue pipes, having a flutelike tone. **3.** one who plays the flute; a flautist. **4.** *Archit., etc.* a channel or furrow with a rounded section, as in a pillar. **5.** a groove in any material, as in a woman's ruffle. **6.** a groove in a tool, as in a twist drill, funnel, etc. **7.** *Colloq.* a topic; subject. **8.** **have the flute,** *Colloq.* to monopolise a conversation. **9.** **pass the flute (kip),** *Colloq.* to allow someone else an opportunity to speak. *–v.i.* **10.** to produce or utter flutelike sounds. **11.** to play a flute. *–v.t.* **12.** to utter in flutelike tones. **13.** to form longitudinal flutes or furrows in. [ME *flowte,* from OF *fleüte,* from Pr. *flauta,* from L *flātus,* pp., blown] – **flutelike,** *adj.*

flute

**fluted** /'flutəd/, *adj.* **1.** having flutes or grooves, as a pillar. **2.** fine, clear and mellow; flutelike: *fluted notes.*

**fluter** /'flutə/, *n.* **1.** one who makes flutings. **2.** *Obs.* a flautist. **3.** *Colloq.* a garrulous person.

**flutiness** /'flutinəs/, *n.* the quality of being fluty.

**fluting** /'flutɪŋ/, *n.* **1.** fluted work; furrows up and down, as on a Corinthian column. **2.** a flute, groove, or furrow. **3.** the act of making flutes. **4.** the act of playing on the flute. **5.** the sound made by such playing; a flutelike sound.

**fluting iron** /'– aɪən/, *n.* a specially shaped iron for pressing ruffles, etc., into a fluted form.

**flutist** /'flutəst/, *n. Chiefly U.S.* →**flautist.**

**flutter** /'flʌtə/, *v.i.* **1.** to flap or wave lightly in air, as a flag. **2.** (of birds, etc.) to flap or attempt to flap the wings, or fly with flapping movements. **3.** to move in quick, irregular motions. **4.** to beat fast and irregularly, as the heart. **5.** to be tremulous or agitated. **6.** to go with irregular motions or aimless course. **7.** *Swimming.* (of the feet) to move alternately up and down as a means of propulsion, as in the crawl and backstroke. *–v.t.* **8.** to cause to flutter; vibrate; agitate. **9.** to confuse; throw into a state of nervous excitement, mental agitation, or tremulous excitement. **10.** *Swimming.* to cause (the feet) to flutter. **11.** *Colloq.* to wager (a small amount). *–n.* **12.** a fluttering movement. **13.** a state of nervous excitement or mental agitation. **14.** sensation; stir: *to cause or make a flutter.* **15.** a rapid variation in pitch fidelity resulting from fluctuations in the speed of a recording. **16.** *Swimming.* →**flutter-kick. 17.** *Colloq.* a small wager or bet. [ME *floteren,* OE *floterian,* frequentative of *flotian* float] – **flutterer,** *n.* – **flutteringly,** *adv.*

**flutter-by** /'flʌtə-baɪ/, *n. Colloq.* →**butterfly.**

**flutter heart** /'flʌtə hat/, *n.* a cardiac arrhythmia in which the atrial contractions are very rapid but rhythmic and of uniform amplitude; atrial flutter.

**flutter-kick** /'flʌtə-kɪk/, *n.* (in swimming) a kick, usu. performed as part of the crawl, in which the legs are held straight and moved up and down alternately.

**flutter-tongue** /'flʌtə-tʌŋ/, *n.* a musical effect caused by trilling on wind instruments such as the flute and trumpet.

**fluttery** /'flʌtəri/, *adj.* fluttering; apt to flutter.

**fluty** /'fluti/, *adj.,* **-tier, -tiest.** flutelike, as in tone.

**fluvial** /'fluviəl/, *adj.* of, pertaining to, or produced by a river. [L *fluviālis,* from *fluvius* river]

**fluviatile** /'fluviətaɪl, -təl/, *adj.* pertaining or peculiar to rivers; found in or near rivers. [L *fluviātilis,* from *fluvius* river]

**fluvioglacial** /ˌfluvioʊ'gleɪʃəl/, *adj.* pertaining to streams flowing from glaciers or to the deposits made by such streams.

**flux** /flʌks/, *n.* **1.** a flowing or flow. **2.** the flowing in of the tide. **3.** continuous passage; continuous change: *to be in a state of flux.* **4.** *Pathol.* **a.** an abnormal or morbid discharge of blood or other matter from the body. **b.** dysentery (**bloody flux**). **5.** *Physics.* **a.** the rate of flow of a fluid, heat, or the like. **b.** luminous flux. **c.** →**magnetic flux. d.** electric flux. **e.** (in nuclear physics) the product of the number of particles per unit volume and their average velocity. **6.** (in metal refining) a material used to remove undesirable substances like sand, ash or dirt, as a molten mixture. **7.** →**fusion.** *–v.t.* **8.** to melt; fuse; make fluid. **9.** *Obs.* to purge. *–v.i.* **10.** to flow. [ME, from L *fluxus* a flowing]

**flux density** /'– dɛnsəti/, *n.* the magnetic or electric flux per unit of cross-sectional area.

**fluxgate** /'flʌksgeɪt/, *n.* a device which gives out an electric signal proportional to the intensity of the magnetic field acting along its axis; used to indicate the direction of the terrestial magnetic field in the fluxgate compass.

**fluxion** /ˈflʌkʃən/, *n. Obs.* **1.** the act of flowing; a flow or flux. **2.** *Maths. Obs.* the derivative relative to the time, the rate of change of a varying quantity. – **fluxional, fluxionary** /ˈflʌkʃənri/, *adj.* – **fluxionally,** *adv.*

**fluxmeter** /ˈflʌksmitə/, *n.* an instrument for measuring magnetic flux.

**fluxus** /ˈflʌksəs/, *n.* a festival or occasion similar to a happening (def. 2) which incorporates elements of theatre, music, literature, etc., not in their traditional forms. [L: flowing]

**fly**[1] /flaɪ/, *v.,* **flew, flown, flying,** *n., pl.* **flies.** *–v.i.* **1.** to move through the air on wings, as a bird. **2.** to be borne through the air by the wind or any other force or agency. **3.** to float or flutter in the air, as a flag, the hair, etc. **4.** to travel through the air in an aircraft or as an aircraft does. **5.** to move or pass swiftly; move with a start or rush. **6.** to make an attack by flying, as a hawk does. **7.** to change rapidly and unexpectedly from one state to another: *to fly open.* **8.** to flee. **9. fly high, a.** to be ambitious. **b.** *Colloq.* to be in a state of euphoria, as induced by drugs. **10. fly in the face of,** to defy insultingly. **11. fly off the handle,** *Colloq.* to lose one's temper, esp. unexpectedly. **12. fly out,** *Colloq.* to lose one's temper; become suddenly violently angry. **13. let fly,** to make an attack. *–v.t.* **14.** to cause to fly: *to fly a model aeroplane, a kite, a hawk.* **15.** to operate (an aircraft or spacecraft). **16.** to hoist aloft or bear aloft: *to fly a flag.* **17.** to travel over by flying. **18.** to transport by flying. **19.** to avoid; flee from. **20.** *Theat.* **a.** to raise (scenery) into the flies. **b.** to suspend (scenery) above a stage from the flies by means of wire rigging, etc. **21. fly a kite, a.** *Colloq.* to attempt to obtain reactions to a proposal for a course of action by allowing it to be circulated as a rumour or unconfirmed report. **b.** *Colloq.* to undertake some other activity: *go fly a kite.* **22. fly at,** to attack. **23. let fly, a.** to throw or propel. **b.** to give free rein to, esp. in attacking: *he let fly his pent-up anger.* **c.** *Naut.* to release (a line) quickly so that wind is completely spilled from a sail. *–n.* **24.** a strip sewn along one edge of a garment, to aid in concealing the buttons or other fasteners. **25.** such a strip used to hide the opening on a pair of trousers, or the fastening itself. **26.** a flap forming the door of a tent. **27.** a piece of canvas extending over the ridgepole of a tent and forming an outer roof. **28.** a light tent. **29.** the act of flying; a flight. **30.** *U.S.* the course of a flying object, as a ball. **31.** (formerly) a light, single-horsed public carriage for passengers. **32.** *Mach.* →**flywheel. 33.** *Horol.* a regulating device for chime and striking mechanisms, consisting of an arrangement of vanes on a revolving axis. **34.** *Print.* **a.** a contrivance for receiving and delivering separately printed sheets from a press. **b.** (formerly) one who removed printed matter from a press. **35.** the extent of a flag from the staff to the outer end, or the outer end itself. **36.** *(pl.) Theat.* the space and apparatus above the stage. **37. on the fly,** *U.S.* **a.** while still in flight; on the volley. **b.** hurriedly. **38.** *Colloq.* an attempt: *give it a fly.* **39.** a children's running and jumping game played with sticks spaced out on the ground. [ME *flien,* OE *flēogan,* c. D *vliegen,* G *fliegen*]

**fly**[2] /flaɪ/, *n., pl.* **flies. 1.** any of the two-winged insects constituting the order Diptera **(true flies),** esp. one of the family Muscidae, as the common housefly, *Musca domestica.* **2.** any of a number of other winged insects, as the mayfly or firefly. **3.** *Angling.* a fishhook dressed with silk, tinsel, etc., to resemble an insect. **4. fly in the ointment,** a slight flaw that greatly diminishes the value or pleasure of something. **5. no flies on** or **about,** *Colloq.* **a.** not easily tricked; wary. **b.** *Obs.* honest. **6. with the flies,** alone: *drinking with the flies.* [ME *flye,* OE *flēoge, flȳge,* c. G *Fliege*] – **flyless,** *adj.*

**fly**[3] /flaɪ/, *adj. Colloq.* knowing; sharp. [? special use of FLY[1]]

**flyable** /ˈflaɪəbəl/, *adj.* capable of being flown.

**fly agaric** /flaɪ ˈægərɪk, -əˈgærɪk/, *n.* a very poisonous mushroom, *Amanita muscaria,* sometimes used for making a poison for flies.

**fly-ash** /ˈflaɪ-æʃ/, *n.* the fine ash produced from burning pulverised coal, found to have cement-like qualities in concrete and also sometimes used in brick-making.

**fly-away** /ˈflaɪ-əweɪ/, *adj.* **1.** fluttering; streaming. **2.** flighty; volatile; frivolous.

**flyback** /ˈflaɪbæk/, *n.* **1.** any instrument or device which resets itself rapidly, as a stopwatch. **2.** the act of resetting or returning to zero, as the return of the electron beam in a cathode-ray tube to its starting point after the completion of a line or trace.

**fly ball** /ˈflaɪ bɔl/, *n.* (in cricket, baseball, etc.) a ball hit high into the air.

**flyblow** /ˈflaɪbloʊ/, *v.,* **-blew, -blown, -blowing,** *n. –v.t.* **1.** to deposit eggs or larvae on (meat). *–n.* **2.** the egg or young larva (maggot) of a blowfly, deposited on meat, etc.

**flyblown** /ˈflaɪbloʊn/, *adj.* **1.** tainted with flyblows. **2.** spoilt; corrupt. **3.** *Colloq.* broke; penniless.

**flyboat** /ˈflaɪboʊt/, *n.* a fast vessel, esp. one designed for use on canals. [D *vlieboot*]

**flybook** /ˈflaɪbʊk/, *n.* a booklike case for artificial flies for fishing.

**fly-by-night** /ˈflaɪ-baɪ-naɪt/, *Colloq. –adj.* **1.** irresponsible; unreliable. *–n.* **2.** a person who leaves secretly at night, as in order to avoid paying his debts. **3.** one who leads a gay night-life.

**fly-camp** /ˈflaɪ-kæmp/, *n. N.Z.* a temporary or makeshift camp.

**flycatcher** /ˈflaɪkætʃə/, *n.* **1.** any of numerous small, insectivorous birds of the Old World family Muscicapidae, as the Australian Jacky winter, or the European **spotted flycatcher,** *Muscicapa grisola.* **2.** any bird of the family Monarchidae, often highly coloured and long-tailed, found in many parts of the world, as the satin flycatcher.

**flyer** /ˈflaɪə/, *n.* →**flier.**

**fly-fish** /ˈflaɪ-fɪʃ/, *v.i.* to fish with artificial flies as bait. – **fly-fisher,** *n.* – **fly-fishing,** *n.*

**fly-floor** /ˈflaɪ-flɔ/, *n.* a gallery in a theatre running alongside the flies, where lines controlling the scenery, etc., are worked. Also, **fly-gallery** /ˈflaɪ-gæləri/.

**fly half** /flaɪ ˈhaf/, *n. N.Z., Brit.* →**five-eighth** (def. 1).

**fly honeysuckle** /flaɪ ˈhʌnisʌkəl/, *n.* a deciduous shrub with yellowish paired flowers, *Lonicera xylosteum,* growing in woods and hedges throughout Europe and northern and western Asia.

flying buttress

flying buttress

**flying** /ˈflaɪɪŋ/, *adj.* →**1.** that flies; making flight or passing through the air: *a flying insect.* **2.** floating, fluttering or waving, or hanging or moving freely, in the air: *flying banners, flying hair.* **3.** extending through the air. **4.** moving swiftly. **5.** made while moving swiftly. **6.** hasty: *a flying trip.* **7.** designed for swiftness. **8.** fleeing, running away, or taking flight. **9.** *Naut.* (of a sail) having none of its edges bent to spars or stays. *–n.* **10.** the act of moving through the air on wings; flight.

**flying boat** /ˈ– boʊt/, *n.* an aircraft, whose main body consists of a single hull or boat, that can take off and land on water.

**flying bomb** /ˈ– bɒm/, *n.* a gyroscopically steered, winged bomb, powered by a pulse jet, used in World War II.

**flying bridge** /ˈ– brɪdʒ/, *n.* a bridge of a ship projecting over the ship's edge to provide good visibility of the ship's side when docking, etc.

**flying buttress** /– ˈbʌtrəs/, *n.* a segmental arch which carries the thrust of a wall over a space to a solid pier buttress.

**flying circus** /– ˈsɜkəs/, *n. Colloq.* a group of aircraft operating together performing aerobatic manoeuvres.

**flying coachman** /– ˈkoʊtʃmən/, *n.* →**regent honeyeater.**

**flying colours** /– ˈkʌləz/, *n.pl.* →**1.** flags borne aloft. **2.** triumphant success.

**flying column** /ˈ– kɒləm/, *n.* (formerly) a force of troops equipped and organised to move swiftly and independently of a principal unit to which it is attached.

**flying doctor** /– ˈdɒktə/, *n.* a medical practitioner operating in connection with an aerial service, and providing medical aid to remote parts of Australia.

flying-duck orchid

**flying dragon** /– ˈdrægən/, *n.* →**flying lizard.**

**flying-duck orchid** /ˈflaɪɪŋ-ˈdʌk ɔkəd/, *n.* a terrestrial orchid, *Caleana major,* of eastern Australia, characterised by flowers resembling a duck in flight.

**Flying Dutchman** /flaɪɪŋ ˈdʌtʃmən/, *n.* a class of yacht. [named after the *Flying Dutchman,* a legendary spectral Dutch ship whose captain was condemned to sail the sea, beating against the wind, till the Day of Judgment]

**flying field** /ˈflaɪɪŋ fild/, *n.* →**airfield.**

**flying fish** /ˈ– fɪʃ/, *n.* any of certain fishes with winglike pectoral fins which help them to glide for some distance through the air after leaping from the water, esp. of the family Exocoetidae, as *Exocoetus volitans.*

flying fish

**flying fox** /ˈ– fɒks/, *n.* **1.** any of various large bats of the suborder Megachiroptera, esp. of the genus *Pteropus,* of Australia, tropical Asia and Africa, having a foxlike head and feeding on fruit and blossom. **2.** a cable-operated carrier over watercourses or difficult terrain.

flying fox (def. 1)

**flying gurnard** /– ˈgɜnəd/, *n.* any of several fishes of the family Dactylopteridae, as *Dactylopena orientalis* of eastern Australian waters, having wing-like pectoral fins though apparently not able to fly.

**flying handicap** /– ˈhændikæp/, *n.* a sprinting race for horses carrying not less than 48 kg.

**flying jib** /– ˈdʒɪb/, *n.* a triangular sail set forward of the jib.

**flying kites** /ˈ– kaɪts/, *n.pl.* the lightest and highest sails on a sailing ship, set only in light or moderate winds.

flying fox (def. 2)

**flying lemur** /– ˈlimə/, *n.* a lemur-like mammal having a broad fold of skin on each side of the body to act as a wing in gliding from tree to tree. The species *Cynocephalus temminckii* is distributed over South East Asia and the East Indies, *Cynocephalus volans* in the Philippine area. They are the only representatives of the order Dermoptera.

**flying lizard** /ˈ– lɪzəd/, *n.* any of the arboreal lizards of the genus *Draco* of south-eastern Asia and the East Indies, with extensible membranes along the sides by means of which they make long gliding leaps from tree to tree; flying dragon.

**flying machine** /ˈ– məʃin/, *n.* a contrivance which sustains itself in, and propels itself through, the air; an aeroplane or the like.

**flying mare** /– ˈmɛə/, *n.* a method of attack in which a wrestler grasps the wrist or head of his opponent, turns in the opposite direction, and throws him over his shoulder and down.

**flying mouse** /– ˈmaʊs/, *n.* →**pygmy glider.**

**flying officer** /ˈ– ɒfəsə/, *n.* a commissioned rank in the Australian and some other Air Forces above that of pilot officer and below flight lieutenant; equivalent to army lieutenant, or sub-lieutenant in the navy.

flying phalanger

**flying possum** /– ˈpɒsəm/, *n.* →**gliding possum.** Also, **flying phalanger.**

**flying saucer** /– ˈsɔsə/, *n.* any of various disc-shaped objects allegedly seen flying at high speeds and altitudes.

**flying shore** /– ˈʃɔ/, *n.* a horizontal supporting prop or beam between two vertical structures.

**flying spot scanner,** *n.* a device for scanning the object to be transmitted in a television system, using a spot of light which is generated by a cathode-ray tube and received by a photo-sensitive multiplier.

**flying squad** /ˈflaɪɪŋ skwɒd/, *n.* **1.** a detachment of police organised for special tasks, esp. in emergencies. **2.** a special detachment of any other organisation.

**flying squirrel** /– ˈskwɪrəl/, *n.* **1.** →**gliding possum. 2.** a squirrel-like animal, esp. of the genus *Glaucomys,* as *G. volans* of the eastern U.S., with folds of skin connecting the fore and hind legs, enabling it to take long gliding leaps.

flying squirrel

**flying start** /– ˈstat/, *n.* **1.** a start to a race by which competitors may approach the starting line at speed, but are disqualified or recalled if they cross it before the starting signal is given. **2.** *Colloq.* a great advantage: *his first-hand knowledge of Italy gave him a flying start over other candidates.*

**flying tackle** /– ˈtækəl/, *n.* a dive through the air at a person, esp. an opponent in sport, in order to bring him to the ground.

**flying trapeze** /– trəˈpiz/, *n.* a trapeze, usu. with longer ropes and suspended many metres above the ground, for use in circus acts, etc.

**flying wing** /ˈ– wɪŋ/, *n.* an aircraft in which the fuselage forms an integral part of the wing structure.

**flyleaf** /ˈflaɪlif/, *n., pl.* **-leaves** /-livz/. a blank leaf in the front or at the back of a book.

**fly line** /ˈflaɪ laɪn/, *n.* a line used in fly-fishing.

**fly-loft** /ˈflaɪ-lɒft/, *n.* the portion of a theatre building above the stage into which scenery may be raised.

**flyman** /ˈflaɪmən/, *n., pl.* **-men.** a stagehand, esp. one who operates the apparatus in the flies.

**fly-net** /ˈflaɪ-nɛt/, *n.* a fringe or net worn around the hat or face as protection from flies.

**flyover** /ˈflaɪoʊvə/, *n. Brit.* →**overpass.**

**flypaper** /ˈflaɪpeɪpə/, *n.* paper prepared to destroy flies by poisoning them or by catching them on its sticky surface.

**fly-past** /ˈflaɪ-past/, *n.* a ceremonial flight of aircraft over a given point.

**fly rail** /ˈflaɪ reɪl/, *n.* a bracket that swings out to support the drop leaf of a table.

**fly rod** /ˈ– rɒd/, *n.* a light, flexible rod used in fly-fishing, usu. made up in three pieces.

**flyscreen** /ˈflaɪskrin/, *n.* **1.** a frame (containing fine mesh) fitted to a door or window to keep out insects. *–v.t.* **2.** to install flyscreens on windows, etc.

**flyspeck** /ˈflaɪspɛk/, *n.* **1.** a speck or tiny stain from the excrement of a fly. **2.** a minute spot. *–v.t.* **3.** to mark with flyspecks.

**flystrike** /ˈflaɪstraɪk/, *n.* →**blowfly strike.**

**fly-struck** /ˈflaɪ-strʌk/, *adj.* infested with fly maggots.

**flyswat** /ˈflaɪswɒt/, *n.* a handheld device for killing flies, as a flap of wire mesh on a handle. Also, **flyswatter.**

**flytrap** /ˈflaɪtræp/, *n.* **1.** any of various plants which entrap insects, esp. Venus's flytrap. **2.** a trap for flies.

**flyveil** /ˈflaɪveɪl/, *n.* netting hung from a hat to protect the face from flies.

**flyweight** /ˈflaɪweɪt/, *n.* a boxer weighing between 48 and 51 kg (in the amateur ranks) or no more than 50.80 kg (in the professional ranks).

**flywheel** /ˈflaɪwil/, *n.* **1.** a heavy wheel which by its momentum tends to equalise the speed of machinery with which it is connected. **2.** a wheel used to carry the piston over dead centre.

**flywire** /ˈflaɪwaɪə/, *n.* very fine wire mesh designed to keep out flies and other insects.

**fm,** **1.** fathom. **2.** from.

**Fm,** *Chem.* fermium.

**FM** /ɛf ˈɛm/, frequency modulation.

**F.M.,** field marshal.

**f number** /ˈɛf nʌmbə/, *n.* the ratio of the focal length of a lens system to its effective diameter, used to number aperture openings in a camera.

**F.O.,** **1.** field officer. **2.** flying officer.

**F.O.** /ɛf ˈoʊ/, *n. Colloq.* →**foreign order.**

**foal** /foʊl/, *n.* **1.** the young of a horse, or other equine animal, of either sex, when not yet past its first birthday (officially 1 August for all Australian horses). *–v.t.* **2.** to bring forth (a foal). *–v.i.* **3.** to bring forth a foal. [ME *fole,* OE *fola,* c. OHG *folo*]

**foam** /foʊm/, *n.* **1.** an aggregation of minute bubbles formed on the surface of a liquid by agitation, fermentation, etc. **2.** the froth of perspiration formed on the skin of a horse or other animal from great exertion. **3.** froth formed in the mouth, as in epilepsy and rabies. **4.** a substance which on being discharged from a fire-extinguisher forms a layer of small stable bubbles. **5.** a light material, in either spongy or rigid form, produced by foaming. *–v.i.* **6.** to form or gather foam; emit foam. **7. foam at the mouth,** to be speechless with some emotion, esp. with rage, etc. *–v.t.* **8.** to cause to foam. **9.** to introduce gas bubbles into (a substance, as plastic or resin) to form a light material. [ME *fome,* OE *fām,* c. G *Feim*] – **foamingly,** *adv.* – **foamless,** *adj.*

**foam rubber** /– ˈrʌbə/, *n.* rubber so processed that it is light, firm, and spongy, used for mattresses, in furniture, for protective cushioning, etc.

**foamy** /ˈfoʊmi/, *adj.,* **foamier, foamiest. 1.** covered with or full of foam. **2.** consisting of foam. **3.** resembling foam. **4.** pertaining to foam. – **foamily,** *adv.* – **foaminess,** *n.*

**fob**[1] /fɒb/, *n.* **1.** Also, **fob pocket.** a small pocket just below the waistline in trousers or breeches (formerly in the waistband) to hold a watch, etc. **2.** a short chain or ribbon with a seal or the like, attached to a watch and worn hanging from the pocket. [orig. unknown. Cf. d. HG *fuppe* pocket, *fuppen* to pocket stealthily]

**fob**[2] /fɒb/, *v.t.,* **fobbed, fobbing. 1.** to palm off (fol. by *off*): *to fob off an inferior watch on a person.* **2.** to put off (fol. by *off*): *to fob one off with promises.* **3.** *Archaic.* to cheat; deceive. [akin to FOB[1]. Cf. G *foppen* deceive]

**f.o.b.,** free on board.

**focal** /ˈfoʊkəl/, *adj.* of or pertaining to a focus. – **focally,** *adv.*

**focal infection** /ˈ– ɪnfɛkʃən/, *n.* an infection in which the bacteria are localised in some region, as the tissue round a tooth or a tonsil, from which they often spread to some other organ or structure of the body.

**focalise** /ˈfoʊkəlaɪz/, *v.t.,* **-lised, -lising.** →**focus.** Also, **focalize.** – **focalisation** /foʊkəlaɪˈzeɪʃən/, *n.*

**focal length** /ˈfoʊkəl lɛŋθ/, *n.* **1.** (of a mirror or lens) the distance from the optical centre to the focal point. **2.** (of a telescope) the distance between the object lens and its corresponding focal plane.

**focal plane** /ˈ– pleɪn/, *n.* **1.** the plane normal to the principal axis of a lens (or system of lenses) or a mirror, which passes through the focal point. **2.** the plane in which light rays from an external object are focused in a camera. **3.** the transverse plane in a telescope where the real image of a distant view is in focus.

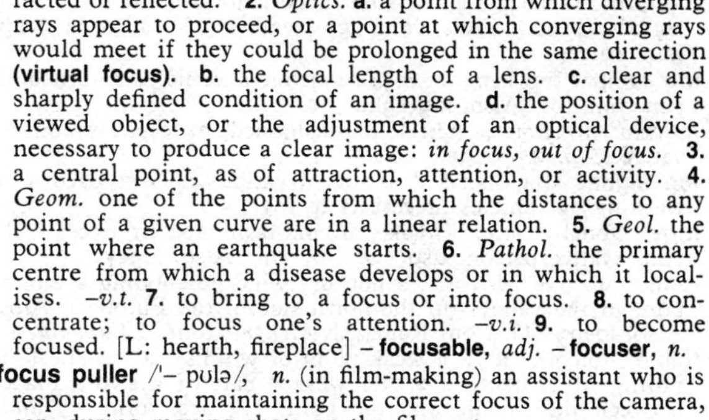


F, focus; L, focal length; A, convex lens; B, concave lens

**focal plane shutter,** *n.* a camera shutter, consisting of a roller blind with a slot in it, which is situated as close to the plate or film as possible.

**focal point** /ˈ– pɔɪnt/, *n.* **1.** the focus for a beam of light rays parallel to the principal axis of a lens or mirror; principal focus. **2.** *Colloq.* the main point of interest, agreement, disagreement, etc.

**focsle** /ˈfoʊksəl/, *n.*→**forecastle.** Also, **fo'c'sle.**

**focus** /ˈfoʊkəs/, *n., pl.* **-ci** /-saɪ, -kaɪ/, **-cuses,** *v.,* **-cused, -cusing,** or **-cussed, -cussing.** *–n.* **1.** *Physics.* a point at which rays of light, heat, or other radiation, meet after being refracted or reflected. **2.** *Optics.* **a.** a point from which diverging rays appear to proceed, or a point at which converging rays would meet if they could be prolonged in the same direction **(virtual focus). b.** the focal length of a lens. **c.** clear and sharply defined condition of an image. **d.** the position of a viewed object, or the adjustment of an optical device, necessary to produce a clear image: *in focus, out of focus.* **3.** a central point, as of attraction, attention, or activity. **4.** *Geom.* one of the points from which the distances to any point of a given curve are in a linear relation. **5.** *Geol.* the point where an earthquake starts. **6.** *Pathol.* the primary centre from which a disease develops or in which it localises. *–v.t.* **7.** to bring to a focus or into focus. **8.** to concentrate; to focus one's attention. *–v.i.* **9.** to become focused. [L: hearth, fireplace] – **focusable,** *adj.* – **focuser,** *n.*

**focus puller** /ˈ– pʊlə/, *n.* (in film-making) an assistant who is responsible for maintaining the correct focus of the camera, esp. during moving shots on the film set.

**fodder** /ˈfɒdə/, *n.* **1.** food for livestock, esp. dried food, as hay, straw, etc. *–v.t.* **2.** to feed with or as with fodder. [ME; OE *fodder, fōdor,* c. G *Futter;* akin to FOOD]

**fodder roller** /ˈ– roʊlə/, *n.* a machine which rolls fodder into weatherproof rolls to be left in the paddock for animals to feed on.

**foe** /foʊ/, *n.* **1.** one who entertains enmity, hatred, or malice against another; an enemy. **2.** an enemy in war; hostile army. **3.** one belonging to a hostile army or nation. **4.** an opponent in a game, or contest. **5.** a person who is opposed in feeling, principle, etc., to something: *a foe to progress.* **6.** a thing that is opposed to or destructive of: *cleanliness is a foe to infection.* [ME *foo,* OE *(ge)fā(h)* enemy (absolute use of adj. meaning hostile). See FEUD[1]]

**foehn** /fɜn/, *n.* →**föhn.**

**foetal** /ˈfitl/, *adj.* of, pertaining to, or having the character of a foetus. Also, *Chiefly U.S.,* **fetal.**

**foetation** /fiˈteɪʃən/, *n.* pregnancy; gestation. Also, *Chiefly U.S.,* **fetation.**

**foeticide** /ˈfitəsaɪd/, *n.* the destruction of a foetus. Also, *Chiefly U.S.,* **feticide.** [L *foetus* + -I- + -CIDE] – **foeticidal** /fitəˈsaɪdəl/, *adj.*

**foetid** /ˈfitəd/, *adj.* →**fetid.**

**foetology** /fiˈtɒlədʒi/, *n.* the study of the foetus. – **foetologist,** *n.*

**foetor** /ˈfitə/, *n.* →**fetor.**

**foetus** /ˈfitəs/, *n.* the young of an animal in the womb or in the egg, esp. in its later stages. Also, *Chiefly U.S.,* **fetus.** [L: a bringing forth, offspring, young]

**fog**[1] /fɒg/, *n., v.,* **fogged, fogging.** *–n.* **1.** a cloudlike mass or layer of minute globules of water in the air near the earth's surface; thick mist. **2.** any darkened state of the atmosphere, or the diffused substance which causes it. **3.** a state of mental confusion or obscurity: *a fog of doubt.* **4.** *Photog.* a darkening of the whole or of parts of a developed plate or print from sources other than image-forming light in the camera. **5.** *Phys., Chem.* a colloidal system consisting of liquid particles dispersed in a gaseous medium. *–v.t.* **6.** to envelop with, or as with fog. **7.** *Photog.* to affect (a negative or print) by fog. **8.** to confuse; perplex; bewilder. **9.** *Agric.* to fumigate (commercial poultry-raising buildings) using various chemicals in aerosol form. **10.** *Agric.* to treat (cattle) for cattle tick using a fine spray. *–v.i.* **11.** to become enveloped or obscured with, or as with, fog. **12.** *Photog.* to be affected by fog. [backformation from FOGGY. See FOG[2]] – **fogless,** *adj.*

**fog**[2] /fɒg/, *n.* **1.** a second growth of grass, as after mowing. **2.** any of several species of the genus *Holcus.* [ME *fogge,* from Scand.; cf. Norw. *fogg* long grass on damp ground, and obs. E *foggy* marshy]

**fogbank** /ˈfɒgbæŋk/, *n.* a stratum of fog as seen from a distance.

**fogbound** /ˈfɒgbaʊnd/, *adj.* immobilised or obscured by fog.

**fogey** /ˈfoʊgi/, *n., pl.* **-geys.** →**fogy.**

**foggy** /ˈfɒgi/, *adj.,* **-gier, -giest. 1.** abounding in or thick with fog; misty. **2.** resembling fog; dim; obscure. **3.** *Photog.* affected by fog. **4. not have the foggiest,** *Colloq.* not to have the least idea. [from FOG[2]; orig. meaning marshy, thick, murky] – **foggily,** *adv.* – **fogginess,** *n.*

**foghorn** /ˈfɒghɔn/, *n.* **1.** *Naut.* a horn for sounding warning signals, as to vessels, in foggy weather. **2.** *Colloq.* a deep, loud voice.

**fog lamp** /ˈfɒg læmp/, *n.* a lamp on a vehicle, designed to penetrate fog. Also, **fog light.**

**fogram** /ˈfougrəm/, *adj.* **1.** old-fashioned; excessively conservative. –*n.* **2.** →**fogy.**

**fog signal** /ˈfɒg sɪgnəl/, *n.* any of various devices used as a warning by vehicles or vessels in fog.

**fogy** /ˈfougi/, *n., pl.* **-gies.** an old-fashioned or excessively conservative person (usu. prec. by *old*). Also, **fogey.**

**föhn** /fɜn/, *n. Meteorol.* a hot, dry wind descending a mountain, in the valleys on the north side of the European Alps. Also, **foehn.** [G, from Romansh *favugn,* from L *Favōnius*]

**foible** /ˈfɔɪbəl/, *n.* **1.** a weak point or whimsy; a weakness or failing of character. **2.** the weaker part of a sword blade, between the middle and the point. [F, obs. form of *faible* FEEBLE]

**foie gras** /fwa ˈgra/, *n.* →**pâté de foie gras.**

**foil**[1] /fɔɪl/, *v.t.* **1.** to frustrate (a person, an attempt, a purpose); baffle; balk. **2.** *Archaic.* to defeat; repulse; check. –*n.* **3.** *Archaic.* a defeat; check; repulse. [ME *foile(n),* from OF *fuler* trample. See FULL[2]]

**foil**[2] /fɔɪl/, *n.* **1.** a metallic substance formed into very thin sheets by rolling and hammering: *gold, tin, aluminium, or lead foil.* **2.** the metallic backing applied to glass to form a mirror. **3.** a thin layer of metal placed under a gem in a closed setting, to improve its colour or brilliancy. **4.** anything that serves to set off another thing distinctly or to advantage by contrast. **5.** *Archit.* an arc or a rounded space between cusps, as in the tracery of a window or in other ornamentation. The number of foils varies, as in **trefoil** and **multifoil.** –*v.t.* **6.** to cover or back with foil. **7.** *Archit.* to ornament with foils. **8.** to set off by contrast. [ME *foile,* from OF *foil,* from L *folium* leaf; akin to Gk *phýllon*]

foil[2] (def. 5)

**foil**[3] /fɔɪl/, *n.* **1.** a flexible, thin sword with a button at the point, for use in fencing. **2.** (*pl.*) the art of exercise or fencing with such swords. [orig. uncert.]

**foil printing** /ˈ– prɪntɪŋ/, *n.* a printing process similar to letterpress, the ink being replaced by a foil, usu. of metal.

**foilsman** /ˈfɔɪlzmən/, *n., pl.* **-men.** one who is expert at fencing with foils.

**foison** /ˈfɔɪzən/, *n. Archaic.* **1.** abundance; plenty. **2.** abundant harvest. [ME, from OF, from L *fūsio* a pouring out]

**foist** /fɔɪst/, *v.t.* **1.** to palm off or impose fraudulently or unwarrantably (fol. by *on* or *upon*): *to foist inferior goods on a customer.* **2.** to bring or put surreptitiously or fraudulently (fol. by *in* or *into*). [probably from D *vuisten* to take in hand]

**fol.,** **1.** folio. **2.** followed. **3.** following.

**fold**[1] /fould/, *v.t.* **1.** to double or bend (cloth, paper, etc.) over upon itself. **2.** to bring into a compact form, or shut, by bending and laying parts together (oft. fol. by *up*): *to fold up a map.* **3.** to bring together (the arms, hands, legs, etc.) with one round another: *to fold one's arms on one's chest.* **4.** to bend or wind (fol. by *about, round,* etc.): *to fold one's arms about a person's neck.* **5.** to bring (the wings) close to the body, as a bird on alighting. **6.** to enclose; wrap: *to fold something in paper.* **7.** to clasp or embrace: *to fold someone in one's arms.* **8.** *Cookery.* to mix (*in*), as beaten eggwhites added to a batter or the like, by gently turning one part over another with a spoon, etc. –*v.i.* **9.** to be folded or be capable of folding: *the doors fold back.* **10.** to be closed or brought to an end, usu. with financial loss, as a business enterprise or theatrical production. **11. fold up, a.** to collapse. **b.** to fail in business. –*n.* **12.** a part that is folded; pleat; layer: *to wrap something in folds of cloth.* **13.** a hollow made by folding: *to carry something in the fold of one's dress.* **14.** a crease made by folding. **15.** a hollow place in undulating ground: *a fold of the hills or mountains.* **16.** *Geol.* a portion of strata which is folded or bent (as an anticline or syncline), or which connects two horizontal or parallel portions of strata of different levels (as a monocline). **17.** a coil of a serpent, string, etc. **18.** an act of folding or doubling over. [ME *folde(n),* from OE *faldan,* replacing OE *fealdan,* c. G *falten*]

**fold**[2] /fould/, *n.* **1.** an enclosure for domestic animals, esp. sheep. **2.** the sheep contained in it. **3.** a flock of sheep. **4.** a church or congregation. **5. return to the fold,** to return, as to an accepted standard of behaviour. –*v.t.* **6.** to confine (sheep, etc.) in a fold. [ME *folde,* OE *fald, falod,* c. LG *falt* enclosure, yard]

**-fold,** a suffix attached to numerals and other quantitative words or stems to denote multiplication by or division into a certain number, as in *twofold, manifold.* [ME; d. OE *-fald,* replacing OE *-feald,* c. G *-falt;* akin to Gk *-paltos,* as in *dípaltos* double]

**foldaway** /ˈfouldəweɪ/, *adj.* of or pertaining to a bed, table, etc., which can be folded up and put away when not in use.

**foldboat** /ˈfouldbout/, *n.* →**faltboat.**

**folder** /ˈfouldə/, *n.* **1.** one who or that which folds. **2.** a folded printed sheet, as a circular or a timetable. **3.** an outer cover, usu. a folded sheet of light cardboard, for papers.

**folderol** /ˈfɒldərɒl/, *n.* →**falderal.**

**folding doors** /ˌfouldɪŋ ˈdɔz/, *n.pl.* a set of doors hinged together to fold flat against one another when opened.

**folding money** /ˈ– mʌni/, *n. Colloq.* banknotes. Also, **folding stuff.**

**fold mountains** /ˈfould mauntənz/, *n.* mountains formed by massive folding and uplift as a result of compression in the earth's crust.

**fold-out** /ˈfould-aut/, *n.* →**gatefold.**

**folia** /ˈfouliə/, *n.* plural of **folium.**

**foliaceous** /fouliˈeɪʃəs/, *adj.* **1.** of the nature of a leaf; leaf-like. **2.** bearing leaves or leaf-like parts. **3.** pertaining to or consisting of leaves. **4.** consisting of leaf-like plates or laminae; foliated. [L *foliāceus* leafy]

**foliage** /ˈfouliɪdʒ/, *n.* **1.** the leaves of a plant, collectively; leafage. **2.** leaves in general. **3.** the representation of leaves, flowers, and branches in architectural ornament, etc. [F, alteration (to conform to L *folium*) of *feuillage,* from *feuille,* from L *folium* leaf] – **foliaged,** *adj.*

**foliar** /ˈfouliə/, *adj.* of, pertaining to, or having the nature of a leaf or leaves.

**foliate** /ˈfouliət, -eɪt/, *adj.;* /ˈfoulieɪt/ *v.,* **-ated, -ating.** –*adj.* **1.** having or covered with leaves. **2.** leaf-like. **3.** *Archit.* foliated (def. 3). –*v.i.* **4.** to put forth leaves. **5.** to split into thin leaf-like layers or laminae. –*v.t.* **6.** to shape like a leaf or leaves. **7.** to decorate with foils or foliage. **8.** to form into thin sheets. **9.** to spread over with a thin metallic backing. **10.** to number leaves (not pages) of (a book). [L *foliātus* leafy]

**foliated** /ˈfoulieɪtəd/, *adj.* **1.** shaped like a leaf or leaves. **2.** *Crystall.* consisting of thin and separable laminae. **3.** *Archit.* Also, **foliate. a.** ornamented with or composed of foils. **b.** ornamented with representations of foliage.

**foliation** /fouliˈeɪʃən/, *n.* **1.** the act of foliating or putting forth leaves. **2.** the state of being in leaf. **3.** *Bot.* the arrangement of leaves within the bud. **4.** leaves or foliage. **5.** the consecutive numbering of the leaves (not pages) of a book or manuscript. **6.** the total number of such leaves. **7.** (of rocks) the laminated pattern resulting from the segregation of different minerals into parallel layers by metamorphic processes. **8.** ornamentation with foliage, or an arrangement of foliage. **9.** *Archit.* ornamentation with foils, or tracery so formed. **10.** formation into thin sheets. **11.** the application of foil to glass.

**foliature** /ˈfouliətʃə/, *n.* a cluster of leaves; foliage.

**folic acid** /foulɪk ˈæsəd/, *n.* one of the B complex of vitamins that is used in the treatment of certain types of anaemia. [*fol(ium)* leaf + -IC]

**folio** /ˈfouliou/, *n., pl.* **-lios,** *adj., v.,* **-lioed, -lioing.** –*n.* **1.** a sheet of paper folded once to make two leaves (four pages) of a book. **2.** a volume having pages of the largest size. **3.** a leaf of a manuscript or book numbered only on the front side. **4.** *Print.* the page number of a book. **5.** *Bookkeeping.* a page of an account book or a left-hand page and a right-hand page facing each other and having the same serial number. **6.** *Law.* a certain number of words, usu. 72, taken as a unit for computing the length of a document. *-adj.* **7.** pertaining to or having the format of a folio: *a folio volume.* *-v.t.* **8.** to number the leaves of (a book) on one side only. **9.** *Law.* to mark each folio in (a pleading, etc.) with the proper number. [L, ablative of *folium* leaf]

**foliolate** /ˈfoʊliəleɪt, foʊˈliələt, -leɪt/, *adj.* pertaining to or consisting of leaflets (often used in compounds, as *bifoliolate, trifoliolate,* etc.). [NL *foliolātus,* from *foliolum* a leaflet, diminutive of L *folium* leaf]

**foliose** /ˈfoʊlioʊs/, *adj.* leafy. [L *foliōsus*]

**-folious,** an adjective suffix meaning 'leafy'. [L *foliōsus*]

**folium** /ˈfoʊliəm/, *n., pl.* **-lia** /-liə/. **1.** a thin leaf-like stratum or layer; a lamella. **2.** *Geom.* a loop; part of a curve terminated at both ends by the same node. [L: leaf. See FOIL[2]]

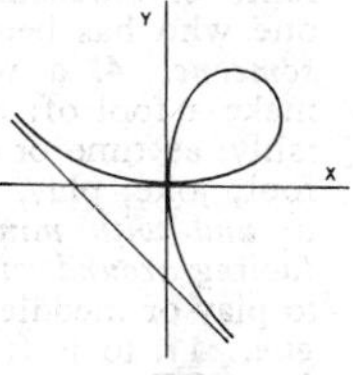

folium: equation of folium is $x^3 + y^3 = 3axy$, where *a* is constant

**folk** /foʊk/, *n., pl.* **folk, folks,** *adj.* *-n.* **1.** people in general, esp. the common people. **2.** (*usu. pl.*) people of a specified class or group: *poor folks.* **3.** (*pl.*) *Colloq.* the persons of one's own family; one's relatives. **4.** *Archaic.* a people or tribe. *-adj.* **5.** originating among the common people. **6.** of or pertaining to a folk song or folk singer. [ME; OE *folc,* c. D *volk,* G *Volk,* Swed. and Dan. *folk* people]

**folk dance** /ˈ- dæns, dans/, *n.* **1.** a dance which originated among, and has been transmitted through, the common people. **2.** a piece of music for such a dance. – **folk dancing,** *n.*

**folk etymology** /- ɛtəˈmɒlədʒi/, *n.* a type of pseudo-learned modification of linguistic forms according to a falsely assumed etymology, as in *Welsh rarebit* from *Welsh rabbit.*

**folkie** /ˈfoʊki/, *n. Colloq.* one who likes or performs folk music.

**folklore** /ˈfoʊklɔ/, *n.* **1.** the lore of the common people; the traditional beliefs, legends, customs, etc., of a people. **2.** the study of such lore. – **folklorist,** *n.* – **folkloristic** /foʊklɔˈrɪstɪk/, *adj.*

**folk mass** /ˈfoʊk mæs/, *n.* **1.** a church mass the music for which is in the style of folk music, or is played by the instruments commonly associated with pop music, as electric guitar, etc.

**folk medicine** /ˈ- mɛdəsən/, *n.* the traditional cures for illness which are not administered by a medical practitioner.

**folk memory** /ˈ- mɛməri/, *n.* the knowledge of past events which is retained among members of a particular community independently of its written records.

**folk music** /ˈ- mjuzɪk/, *n.* **1.** music, usu. of simple character, originating and handed down among the common people. **2.** music originating in the urban American beat generation of the 1940s and 1950s which concentrates on lyrics of social comment. Also, **folk.**

**folk remedy** /ˈ- rɛmədi/, *n.* a remedy used in folk medicine.

**folk-rock** /foʊk-ˈrɒk/, *n.* folk music influenced by rock.

**folk singer** /ˈfoʊk sɪŋə/, *n.* one who sings folk songs.

**folk song** /ˈ- sɒŋ/, *n.* **1.** a song, usu. of simple or artless character, originating and handed down among the common people. **2.** a song in imitation of this type.

**folksy** /ˈfoʊksi/, *adj. Colloq.* **1.** rustic or imitative of the rustic. **2.** *U.S.* sociable; friendly; unceremonious.

**folktale** /ˈfoʊkteɪl/, *n.* a tale or legend originating and handed down among the common people. Also, **folk story.**

**folkways** /ˈfoʊkweɪz/, *n.pl.* the ways of living and acting in a human group, built up without conscious design but serving as compelling guides of conduct.

**foll.,** following.

**follicle** /ˈfɒlɪkəl/, *n.* **1.** *Bot.* a dry one-celled seed vessel consisting of a single carpel, and dehiscent only by the ventral suture, as the fruit of larkspur. **2.** *Anat.* a small cavity, sac, or gland. [L *folliculus,* diminutive of *follis* bellows, bag]

**follicular** /fəˈlɪkjələ/, *adj.* **1.** pertaining to, consisting of, or resembling a follicle or follicles; provided with follicles. **2.** *Pathol.* pertaining to a follicle. Also, **folliculate, folliculated.**

**folliculin** /fəˈlɪkjələn/, *n.* →**oestrone.**

**follow** /ˈfɒloʊ/, *v.t.* **1.** to come after in natural sequence, order of time, etc.; succeed. **2.** to go or come after; move behind in the same direction: *go on ahead and I'll follow you.* **3.** to accept as a guide or leader; accept the authority or example of, or adhere to, as a person. **4.** to conform to, comply with, or act in accordance with: *to follow a person's advice.* **5.** to imitate or copy. **6.** to move forward along (a path, etc.). **7.** to come after as a result or consequence; result from: *it follows from this that he must be innocent.* **8.** to go after or along with (a person, etc.) as a companion. **9.** to go in pursuit of: *to follow an enemy.* **10.** to endeavour to obtain or to attain to. **11.** to engage in or be concerned with as a pursuit: *to follow the sea.* **12.** to watch the movements, progress, or course of. **13.** to keep up to date with; observe the development of: *to follow the news.* **14.** to keep up with and understand (an argument, etc.): *do you follow me?* **15. follow out,** to execute; carry out to a conclusion. **16. follow through, a.** to carry out completely as a stroke in tennis or golf. **b.** to pursue an endeavour to its conclusion. **17. follow suit, a.** *Cards.* to play a card of the same suit as that first played. **b.** to follow the example of another. **18. follow up, a.** to pursue closely. **b.** to pursue to a conclusion. **c.** to take further action, investigation, etc., after the elapse of an interval of time; reopen. **d.** to increase the effect of by further action. *-v.i.* **19.** to come next after something else in natural sequence, order of time, etc. **20.** to happen or occur after something else; come next as an event. **21.** to attend. **22.** to go or come after a person or thing in motion: *go on ahead and I'll follow.* **23.** to result as an effect; occur as a consequence. *-n.* **24.** an act of following. **25.** *Billiards.* a stroke causing the player's ball to roll after the ball struck by it. [ME *folwe(n),* OE *folgian,* c. G *folgen*]

**follower** /ˈfɒloʊə/, *n.* **1.** one who or that which follows. **2.** one who follows another in regard to his ideas or belief; disciple or adherent. **3.** a person who copies or imitates: *a dedicated follower of fashion.* **4.** an attendant or servant. **5.** *Obs.* a male admirer of a young woman. **6.** *Aus. Rules.* a ruckman, or, sometimes, a rover. **7.** a supporter of a particular football team. **8.** *Mach.* a part of a machine that receives motion from, or follows the motion of, another part.

**following** /ˈfɒloʊɪŋ/, *n.* **1.** a body of followers, attendants, adherents, etc. **2. the following,** things, lines, pages, etc., that follow. *-adj.* **3.** that follows. **4.** that comes after or next in order or time: *the following day.* **5.** that is now to follow; now to be mentioned, described, related, or the like.

**follow-on** /fɒloʊ-ˈɒn/, *n.* an immediate second batting innings forced on a cricket team which in the first innings scores less than half the runs scored by the opposing team.

**follow-the-job occupation** /ˌfɒloʊ-ðə-ˈdʒɒb ˌɒkjəˌpeɪʃən/, *n.* an occupation which is not carried out at a fixed working place and which, for continuity of employment, requires an employee to move to different sites from time to time.

**follow-the-leader** /ˌfɒloʊ-ðə-ˈlidə/, *n.* a children's game in which the players follow the actions and speech of the leader. Also, **follow-my-leader.**

**follow-through** /fɒloʊ-ˈθru/, *n.* **1.** the completion of a motion, as in the stroke of a tennis racket or golf club. **2.** the portion of such a motion after the ball has been hit.

**follow-up** /ˈfɒloʊ-ʌp/, *n.* **1.** the act of following up. **2.** a letter or circular sent to a person to increase the effectiveness of a previous one, as in advertising. **3.** *Journalism.* a story providing further information on a news item already published. **4.** *Med.* an examination of a patient some time after initial treatment, in order to assess progress. *-adj.* **5.** (of business letters, etc.) sent to a prospective customer to obtain an additional order or offer.

**folly** /ˈfɒli/, *n., pl.* **-lies. 1.** the state or quality of being foolish; lack of understanding or sense. **2.** a foolish action, practice, idea, etc.; an absurdity. **3.** *Archit.* a useless but costly structure, often in the form of a sham Gothic or classical ruin; esp. popular in 18th-century England. **4.** (*pl.*) a theatrical revue. **5.** *Obs.* wickedness; wantonness. [ME *folie,* from OF, from *fol* mad. See FOOL[1]]

**foment** /fəˈmɛnt/, *v.t.* **1.** to promote the growth or development of; instigate or foster (discord, rebellion, etc.). **2.** to apply warm water or medicated liquid, cloths dipped in such liquid, or the like, to (the surface of the body). [LL *fōmentāre,* from L *fōmentum* a warm application] – **fomenter,** *n.*

**fomentation** /ˌfoʊmɛnˈteɪʃən/, *n.* **1.** instigation; encouragement of discord, rebellion, etc. **2.** the application of warm liquid, etc., to the surface of the body. **3.** the liquid, etc., so applied.

**fomes** /ˈfoʊmiz/, *n., pl.* **fomites** /ˈfoʊmətiz/. a substance, as bedding or clothing (but not food), capable of transmitting infection. [L: touchwood, tinder]

**fond**[1] /fɒnd/, *adj.* **1.** liking (fol. by *of*): *fond of children, fond of drink.* **2.** loving: *give someone a fond look.* **3.** foolishly tender; over-affectionate; doting: *a fond parent.* **4.** cherished with strong or unreasoning affection: *nourish fond hopes.* **5.** *Archaic.* foolishly credulous or trusting. **6.** *Archaic.* foolish or silly. [ME *fonned,* pp. of *fonnen* be foolish; orig. uncert. Cf. FUN]

**fond**[2] /fɒnd/, *n.* **1.** a background or groundwork, esp. of lace. **2.** *Obs.* fund; stock. [F. See FUND]

**fondant** /ˈfɒndənt/, *n.* **1.** a thick, creamy sugar paste, the basis of many sweets and icings. **2.** a sweet made of this paste. [F, properly ppr. of *fondre* melt]

**fondle** /ˈfɒndl/, *v.,* **-dled, -dling.** *–v.t.* **1.** to handle or touch fondly; caress. **2.** *Obs.* to treat with fond indulgence. *–v.i.* **3.** to show fondness, as by manner, words, or caresses. [frequentative of obs. *fond,* v.] – **fondler,** *n.*

**fondly** /ˈfɒndli/, *adv.* **1.** in a fond manner; lovingly or affectionately. **2.** with complacent credulity.

**fondness** /ˈfɒndnəs/, *n.* **1.** the state or quality of being fond. **2.** affectionateness or tenderness. **3.** doting affection. **4.** instinctive liking. **5.** *Archaic.* complacent credulity.

**fondue** /ˈfɒndju/, *n.* **1.** a dish of melted cheese and white wine, heated over a small burner at the table, into which pieces of bread are dipped before being eaten. **2.** any similar dish of oil or flavoured stock (def. 30) in which pieces of fish, meat, vegetable or fruit are cooked at the table on individual skewers before being eaten. [F, fem. pp. of *fondre* melt]

**fondue fork** /ˈ– fɔk/, *n.* a long-handled fork for dipping pieces of bread, etc., in a fondue.

**font**[1] /fɒnt/, *n.* **1.** a receptacle, usu. of stone, as in a baptistery or church, for the water used in baptism. **2.** a receptacle for holy water; stoup. **3.** the reservoir for oil in a lamp. **4.** *Archaic.* a fountain. [ME and OE, from L *fons* baptismal font, spring, fountain]

font[1] (def. 1)

**font**[2] /fɒnt/, *n.* a complete assortment of printing type of one style and size. Also, **fount.** [F *fonte,* from *foundre* melt, cast. See FOUND[3]]

**fontal** /ˈfɒntl/, *adj.* **1.** pertaining to or issuing as from a fount or spring. **2.** pertaining to or being the source of something. **3.** of or pertaining to a font, as of baptism.

**fontanelle** /fɒntəˈnɛl/, *n.* one of the spaces, closed by membrane, between the bones of the foetal or young skull. Also, *Chiefly U.S.,* **fontanel.** [F, (fem.) diminutive of *fontaine* FOUNTAIN]

**food** /fud/, *n.* **1.** what is eaten, or taken into the body, for nourishment. **2.** more or less solid nourishment (as opposed to *drink*). **3.** a particular kind of solid nourishment: *a breakfast food.* **4.** whatever supplies nourishment to organic bodies: *the food of plants.* **5.** anything serving as material for consumption or use: *food for thought.* [ME *fode,* OE *fōda.* Cf. FEED, FODDER, FOSTER] – **foodless,** *adj.*

**food chain** /ˈ– tʃeɪn/, *n.* a series of organisms interrelated in their feeding habits, the smallest being eaten by a larger one, which in turn is eaten by a still larger one, etc.

**food fish** /ˈ– fɪʃ/, *n.* a fish which is caught for food, esp. commercially (opposed to *game fish*).

**food grain** /ˈ– greɪn/, *n.* grain grown primarily for human consumption.

**food poisoning** /ˈ– ˌpɔɪzənɪŋ, ˌpɔɪznɪŋ/, *n.* **1.** an acute illness caused by eating contaminated food, usu. presenting gastrointestinal symptoms. It may be due to the ingestion of organisms, as salmonellae or toxins, formed by organisms as in staphylococcal food poisoning, or due to organic insecticides present in the food. **2.** an illness caused by eating naturally poisonous substances such as poisonous mushrooms and berries.

**foodstuff** /ˈfudstʌf/, *n.* a substance or material suitable for food.

**food value** /ˈfud vælju/, *n.* the nutritional worth of any foodstuff.

**food web** /ˈ– wɛb/, *n.* a series of organisms related by predator-prey activities; a series of interrelated food chains.

**fool**[1] /ful/, *n.* **1.** one who lacks sense; a silly or stupid person. **2.** a professional jester, formerly kept by a person of rank for amusement. **3.** one who is made to appear a fool; one who has been imposed on by others: *to make a fool of someone.* **4.** a weak-minded or idiotic person. *–v.t.* **5.** to make a fool of; impose on; trick; deceive. **6.** to spend foolishly, as time or money (fol. by *away*). *–v.i.* **7.** to act like a fool; joke; play. **8.** to potter, aimlessly; waste time: *to fool around with minor details.* **9.** to philander, or trifle with: *fooling around with a woman old enough to be his mother.* **10.** to play or meddle foolishly (fol. by *with*): *to fool with a loaded gun.* **11.** to jest; make believe: *I was only fooling.* [ME *fol,* from OF (n. and adj.), from LL *follis* empty-headed fellow, L bellows]

**fool**[2] /ful/, *n.* a dish made of fruit stewed, made into a puree, and mixed with thick cream or custard: *gooseberry fool.* [probably special use of FOOL[1]]

**foolery** /ˈfuləri/, *n., pl.* **-eries. 1.** foolish action or conduct. **2.** a foolish action, performance, or thing.

**foolhardy** /ˈfulhadi/, *adj.,* **-dier, -diest.** bold without judgment; foolishly rash or venturesome. – **foolhardily,** *adv.* – **foolhardiness,** *n.*

**foolish** /ˈfulɪʃ/, *adj.* **1.** silly; without sense: *a foolish person.* **2.** resulting from or evidencing folly; ill-considered; unwise: *a foolish action, speech, etc.* **3.** *Obs. or Archaic.* trifling, insignificant, or paltry. – **foolishly,** *adv.* – **foolishness,** *n.*

**foolproof** /ˈfulpruf/, *adj. Colloq.* **1.** involving no risk or harm, even when tampered with. **2.** never-failing: *a foolproof method.*

**fool's cap** /ˈfulz kæp/, *n.* a kind of cap or hood, usu. hung with bells, formerly worn by professional jesters.

**foolscap** /ˈfulzkæp/, *n.* **1.** a printing paper size, 13½ × 17 inches, most commonly in use before metrication (so called from its former watermark, the outline of a fool's cap). **2.** *U.S.* writing paper, usu. folded, varying in size from 12 × 15 to 12 × 16 inches. **3.** →**fool's cap.**

**fool's errand** /ˈfulz ɛrənd/, *n.* an absurd or useless errand.

**fool's gold** /ˈ– goʊld/, *n.* iron pyrites, sometimes mistaken for gold.

**fool's paradise** /– ˈpærədaɪs/, *n.* a state of illusory happiness; enjoyment based on false beliefs or hopes.

**fool's parsley** /– ˈpasli/, *n.* a fetid, poisonous umbelliferous herb, *Aethusa cynapium,* resembling parsley.

**fool's watercress** /– ˈwɔtəkrɛs/, *n.* an aquatic, perennial, umbelliferous herb, *Apium nodiflorum,* widely distributed in temperate regions and sometimes mistaken for the true watercress.

**foot** /fʊt/, *n., pl.* **feet** or (*oft. for def. 22*) **foots,** *v. –n.* **1.** (in vertebrates) the terminal part of the leg, below the ankle joint, on which the body stands and moves. **2.** (in invertebrates) any part similar in position or function. **3.** such a part considered as the organ of locomotion. **4.** a unit of length in the imperial system, derived from the length of the human foot. It is divided into 12 inches and equal to 0.3048 m. **5.** See **foot of water. 6.** See **superficial foot. 7.** *Music.* **a.** a unit of measurement of a vibrating air column. **b.** the sound produced by such a length, as an eight-foot tone. **8.** infantry. **9.** walking or running motion. **10.** step; pace. **11.** any thing or part resembling a foot, as in function. **12.** (of furniture) a shaped or ornamented part terminating the leg. **13.** the flaring base or rim of a glass, teapot, etc. **14.** the part of a stocking, etc., covering the foot. **15.** the lowest part, or bottom, as of a hill, ladder, page, sail, etc. **16.** the part of anything opposite the top or head. **17.** the end of a bed, grave, etc., towards which the feet are placed. **18.** *Print.* the part of the type body which forms the sides of the groove, at the base. **19.** the last, as of a series. **20.** *Obs.* that which is written at the bottom, as the total of an account. **21.** *Pros.*

a group of syllables constituting a metrical unit of a verse. **22.** (*pl. oft.* **foots**) sediment or dregs. **23.** Some special noun phrases are:

**a foot in the mouth,** *Colloq.* an embarassing blunder.

**at one's feet, 1.** captive; at one's mercy. **2.** utterly devoted to one.

**fall on one's feet,** to be lucky.

**feet first,** *Colloq.* **1.** dead. **2.** thoughtlessly; impetuously.

**feet of clay,** an imperfection or blemish on what would otherwise have been perfection.

**get off on the right (wrong) foot,** to have a good (bad) start.

**get one's feet wet,** *Colloq.* to obtain first-hand and practical experience.

**have one foot in the grave,** to be near death.

**keep one's feet,** to keep one's balance.

**keep one's feet on the ground,** to retain a sensible and practical outlook.

**on foot, 1.** on one's feet, rather than riding or sitting. **2.** in motion; astir. **3.** in active existence or operation.

**put one's best foot forward, 1.** to make as good an impression as possible. **2.** to do one's very best. **3.** to walk as fast as possible.

**put one's feet up,** *Colloq.* to relax or rest, esp. by lying down.

**put one's foot down,** to take a firm stand.

**put one's foot in it,** *Colloq.* to make an embarrassing blunder.

**put** or **set someone on his feet, 1.** to enable someone to act without help from others; make someone financially independent. **2.** to restore someone to a former position or condition.

**set foot in,** to enter; go in.

**set on foot,** to start (something) going; originate.

**stand on one's own feet,** to be self-sufficient.

**sweep off one's feet, 1.** to cause someone to lose a footing, as a wave, etc. **2.** to impress or overwhelm.

*–v.i.* **24.** to walk; go on foot (oft. fol. by indefinite *it*). **25.** to move the feet to measure or music, or dance (oft. fol. by indefinite *it*). **26.** to total, as an account (fol. by *up*). *–v.t.* **27.** to set foot on; walk or dance on. **28.** to traverse on foot. **29.** to make or attach a foot to: *to foot a stocking.* **30.** *Colloq.* to add, as a column of figures, and set the sum at the foot (fol. by *up*). **31.** *Colloq.* to pay or settle, as a bill. **32.** to seize with talons, as a hawk. **33.** to establish. **34.** *Obs.* to kick. *–interj.* **35. my foot!** nonsense! (used as an exclamation of disbelief). [ME; OE *fōt*, c. G *Fuss;* akin to L *pēs*, Gk *poús*]

**footage** /ˈfʊtɪdʒ/, *n.* **1.** *Mining.* **a.** payment by the running foot of work done. **b.** amount so paid. **c.** the number of feet of borehold drilled per unit of time, or that required to complete a specific project or contract. **2.** length or extent in feet: *the footage of timber.* **3.** a length of film; the film used for a scene or scenes.

**foot-and-mouth disease** /fʊt-ən-ˈmaʊθ dəziz/, *n.* a contagious virus disease of cattle and other cloven-hoofed animals, characterised by a vesicular eruption about the hoofs and mouth. The disease very rarely affects man.

**football** /ˈfʊtbɔl/, *n.* **1.** any game in which the kicking of a ball has a large part, as Australian Rules, Rugby Union, Rugby League, Soccer, American Football, etc. **2.** the ball used in such games. **3.** *Colloq.* an amphetamine pill.

**footballer** /ˈfʊtbɔlə/, *n.* **1.** a person who plays football. **2.** *Colloq.* a person who fights with his feet.

**football pools** /ˈfʊtbɔl pulz/, *n.pl.* organised gambling on the results of football matches; the pools.

**footbath** /ˈfʊtbaθ/, *n.* **1.** the act of bathing the feet. **2.** an apparatus for this purpose.

**footboard** /ˈfʊtbɔd/, *n.* **1.** a board or small platform on which to support the foot or feet. **2.** an upright piece across the foot of a bedstead. **3.** →**treadle.**

**footboy** /ˈfʊtbɔɪ/, *n.* a boy in livery employed as a servant; page; lackey.

**footbrake** /ˈfʊtbreɪk/, *n.* a brake which is applied by pressure on a foot pedal.

**footbridge** /ˈfʊtbrɪdʒ/, *n.* a bridge intended for pedestrians only.

**foot-candela** /fʊt-kænˈdilə/, *n.* a unit of illumination in the imperial system, equivalent to that produced by a standard candle at a distance of one foot; equal to 10.763 91 lux. Also, **foot-candle.** *Symbol:* ft cd

**footcloth** /ˈfʊtklɒθ/, *n.* **1.** *Archaic.* a carpet or rug. **2.** *Obs.* a richly ornamented caparison for a horse, hanging down to the ground.

**footdrop** /ˈfʊtdrɒp/, *n.* abnormal dropping of the foot, due to paralysis of the anterior leg muscles.

**footed** /ˈfʊtəd/, *adj.* provided with a foot or feet: *a four-footed animal.*

**footer** /ˈfʊtə/, *n.* **1.** one who goes on foot; a walker. **2.** (with a numeral prefixed) a person or thing of the height or length in feet indicated: *a six-footer.* **3.** (with a numeral prefixed) a racing yacht with an unenclosed hull of the length in feet indicated: *that yacht is a sixteen-footer.* **4.** *Colloq.* →**football.**

**footfall** /ˈfʊtfɔl/, *n.* **1.** a footstep. **2.** the sound of footsteps.

**foot-fault** /ˈfʊt-fɔlt/, *n.* **1.** *Tennis.* a service fault in which the server allows one or both feet to cross or touch the base line. **2.** *Bowls.* a failure to keep one foot on or above the mat and the other in front of the rear line of the mat while delivering.

**footgear** /ˈfʊtgɪə/, *n.* →**footwear.**

**foothill** /ˈfʊthɪl/, *n.* a minor elevation at the base of a mountain or mountain range.

**foothold** /ˈfʊthoʊld/, *n.* **1.** a hold or support for the feet; a place where one may stand or tread securely. **2.** firm footing; secure position.

**footie** /ˈfʊti/, *n. Colloq.* →**football.** Also, **footy.**

**footing** /ˈfʊtɪŋ/, *n.* **1.** a secure position; foothold. **2.** the basis or foundation on which anything is established. **3.** a place or support for the feet; surface to stand on. **4.** the act of one that foots, or moves on foot, as in walking or dancing. **5.** a firm placing or stable position of the feet. **6.** the part of the foundation of wall, column, etc., that is in direct contact with the ground. **7.** position or status assigned to a person, etc., in estimation or treatment. **8.** mutual standing; reciprocal relation: *to be on a friendly footing with someone.* **9.** entrance into a new position or relationship. **10.** a fee demanded from a person upon his entrance into a trade, society, etc. **11.** the act of putting a foot to anything, as a stocking. **12.** that which is added as a foot. **13.** the act of adding up a column of figures. **14.** the amount of such a column as footed up.

**foot-lambert** /fʊt-ˈlæmbət/, *n.* a unit of luminance in the imperial system, equal to approx. 3.426 26 candelas per square metre.

**footle** /ˈfutl/, *v.*, **-tled, -tling,** *n.* *–v.t.* **1.** to talk or act in a silly way. *–n.* **2.** nonsense; silliness. [orig. obscure]

**footless** /ˈfʊtləs/, *adj.* **1.** without a foot or feet. **2.** unsupported or unsubstantial. **3.** *U.S. Colloq.* awkward, helpless, or inefficient.

**footlights** /ˈfʊtlaɪts/, *n.pl.* **1.** *Theat.* a row of lights at the front of the stage, nearly on a level with the feet of the performers. **2.** *Colloq.* the stage; acting profession.

**footling** /ˈfutlɪŋ/, *adj. Colloq.* foolish; silly; trifling. [FOOTLE, *v.* + -ING[2]]

**footloose** /ˈfʊtlus/, *adj.* free to go or travel about; not confined by responsibilities, etc.: *footloose and fancy-free.*

**footman** /ˈfʊtmən/, *n., pl.* **-men. 1.** a male servant in livery who attends the door or the carriage, waits at table, etc. **2.** a metal stand before a fire, to keep something hot. **3.** *Obs.* a foot soldier.

**footmark** /ˈfʊtmak/, *n.* →**footprint.**

**footnote** /ˈfʊtnoʊt/, *n., v.,* **-noted, -noting.** *–n.* **1.** a note or comment at the foot of a page, referring to a specific part of the text on the page. **2.** an added comment, of less importance than the main text. *–v.t.* **3.** to add footnotes to a text.

**foot of water,** *n.* a unit of pressure in the imperial system, equal to 2983.6992 pascals.

**footpace** /ˈfʊtpeɪs/, *n.* **1.** a walking pace. **2.** a raised portion of a floor, as for a teacher; dais. **3.** a landing or resting place at the end of a short flight of steps.

**footpad** /ˈfʊtpæd/, *n.* a highwayman who robs on foot.

**footpass** /ˈfʊtpas/, *v.i. Aus. Rules.* to kick a ball directly to a team-mate.

**footpath** /ˈfʊtpaθ/, *n.* a path for pedestrians only; pavement.

**footplate** /ˈfʊtpleɪt/, *n.* a platform in a locomotive on which the crew stand.

**foot-plateman** /ˈfʊt-pleɪtmən/, *n., pl.* **-men** /-mən/. *Brit.* a driver or fireman of a railway locomotive.

**foot-pound-second system** /fʊt-paʊnd-ˈsɛkənd sɪstəm/, *n.* a system of imperial units employed in science, based on the foot, pound, and second as the fundamental units of length, mass, and time. *Abbrev.:* f.p.s. (system).

**footprint** /ˈfʊtprɪnt/, *n.* a mark left by the foot.

**footrace** /ˈfʊtreɪs/, *n.* a running or walking race.

**footrest** /ˈfʊtrɛst/, *n.* a low bench or stool used to support one's feet.

**footrope** /ˈfʊtroʊp/, *n.* **1.** the portion of the boltrope to which the lower edge of a sail is sewn. **2.** a rope extended under a yard, for the men to stand on while reefing or furling.

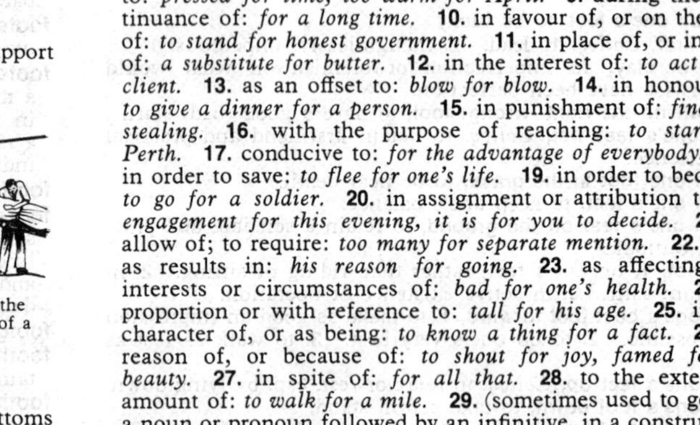
footrope: sailors using the footrope in the furling of a sail

**footrot** /ˈfʊtrɒt/, *n.* **1.** *Vet. Sci.* an infection of the feet of sheep, causing inflammatory changes of the toes and lameness. *–v.t.* **2.** to clean sheep of footrot.

**foot rule** /ˈfʊt rul/, *n.* a ruler one foot in length.

**foot-scraper** /ˈfʊt-skreɪpə/, *n.* a metal grid set in a frame for cleaning mud off the bottoms of shoes before entering a house.

**footslog** /ˈfʊtslɒg/, *v.i.*, **-slogged, -slogging.** *Colloq.* to march or tramp; slog on foot.

**footslogger** /ˈfʊtslɒgə/, *n. Colloq.* one who footslogs, but esp. an infantryman.

**foot soldier** /ˈfʊt soʊldʒə/, *n.* an infantryman.

**footsore** /ˈfʊtsɔ/, *adj.* having sore or tender feet, as from much walking.

**footstalk** /ˈfʊtstɔk/, *n.* **1.** →**pedicel. 2.** →**peduncle.**

**footstall** /ˈfʊtstɔl/, *n.* **1.** the stirrup of a woman's side-saddle. **2.** *Archit.* the plinth or base of a pillar.

**footstep** /ˈfʊtstɛp/, *n.* **1.** a step or tread of the foot, or the sound produced by it; footfall. **2.** the distance traversed by the foot in stepping; a pace. **3.** →**footprint. 4.** a step by which to ascend or descend. **5. follow in one's footsteps,** to succeed or imitate another.

**footstock** /ˈfʊtstɒk/, *n.* →**tailstock.**

**footstool** /ˈfʊtstul/, *n.* a low stool upon which to rest one's feet.

**footsy** /ˈfʊtsi/, *n., pl.* **-sies.** *Colloq.* **1.** (*esp. in children's speech*) a foot. **2. play footsies, a.** to touch in secret a person's feet, knees, etc., with one's feet, esp. as part of amorous play (fol. by *with*). **b.** to flirt (fol. by *with*): *he is playing footsies with the vicar's wife.*

**foot-up** /ˈfʊt-ʌp/, *n.* the illegal raising of the hooker's foot in a rugby scrum before the ball has been put in.

**footwall** /ˈfʊtwɔl/, *n.* the rock base underlying a mineral vein, reef or fault.

**foot-warmer** /ˈfʊtwɔmə/, *n.* any of various contrivances for keeping the feet warm.

**footway** /ˈfʊtweɪ/, *n.* a way or path for pedestrians only.

**footwear** /ˈfʊtwɛə/, *n.* articles for wearing on the feet, esp. boots, shoes, slippers, etc. Also, **footgear.**

**footwork** /ˈfʊtwɜk/, *n.* **1.** the use of the feet, as in tennis, boxing, etc. **2.** skilful manoeuvring.

**footworn** /ˈfʊtwɔn/, *adj.* **1.** worn by the feet: *a footworn pavement.* **2.** footsore.

**footy** /ˈfʊti/, *n. Colloq.* →**footie.**

**foozle** /ˈfuzəl/, *v.*, **-zled, -zling,** *n.* *–v.t.* **1.** to bungle: *to foozle a stroke in golf.* *–v.i.* **2.** to play clumsily. *–n.* **3.** an act of foozling, esp. a bad stroke in golf. [cf. d. G *fuseln* work badly]

**fop** /fɒp/, *n.* a man who is excessively concerned about his manners and appearance. [orig. uncert. Cf. FOB[2]]

**foppery** /ˈfɒpəri/, *n., pl.* **-peries. 1.** the manners, actions, dress, etc., of a fop. **2.** something foppish.

**foppish** /ˈfɒpɪʃ/, *adj.* resembling or befitting a fop. **– foppishly,** *adv.* **– foppishness,** *n.*

**for** /fɔ/; *weak forms* /fə, f/, *prep.* **1.** with the object or purpose of: *to go for a walk.* **2.** intended to belong to, suit the purposes or needs of, or be used in connection with: *a book for children, a box for gloves.* **3.** in order to obtain: *a suit for damages.* **4.** with inclination or tendency towards: *to long for a thing, to have an eye for beauty.* **5.** (as expressing a wish or desire for something to be obtained): *O for the wings of a dove.* **6.** in consideration of, or in return for: *three for a dollar, to be thanked for one's efforts.* **7.** appropriate or adapted to: *a subject for speculation.* **8.** with regard or respect to: *pressed for time, too warm for April.* **9.** during the continuance of: *for a long time.* **10.** in favour of, or on the side of: *to stand for honest government.* **11.** in place of, or instead of: *a substitute for butter.* **12.** in the interest of: *to act for a client.* **13.** as an offset to: *blow for blow.* **14.** in honour of: *to give a dinner for a person.* **15.** in punishment of: *fined for stealing.* **16.** with the purpose of reaching: *to start for Perth.* **17.** conducive to: *for the advantage of everybody.* **18.** in order to save: *to flee for one's life.* **19.** in order to become: *to go for a soldier.* **20.** in assignment or attribution to: *an engagement for this evening, it is for you to decide.* **21.** to allow of; to require: *too many for separate mention.* **22.** such as results in: *his reason for going.* **23.** as affecting the interests or circumstances of: *bad for one's health.* **24.** in proportion or with reference to: *tall for his age.* **25.** in the character of, or as being: *to know a thing for a fact.* **26.** by reason of, or because of: *to shout for joy, famed for its beauty.* **27.** in spite of: *for all that.* **28.** to the extent or amount of: *to walk for a mile.* **29.** (sometimes used to govern a noun or pronoun followed by an infinitive, in a construction equivalent to a clause with *that* and the auxiliary *should,* etc.): *it is time for him to go,* meaning *it is time that he should go.* **30. for it,** *Colloq.* about to suffer some punishment, injury, setback, or the like. **31. for to,** *Archaic.* in order to; to. *–conj.* **32.** seeing that; since. **33.** because. [ME and OE; c. OS *for;* akin to *fore,* adv. and prep.]

**for-,** a prefix meaning 'away', 'off', 'to the uttermost', 'extremely', 'wrongly', or imparting a negative or privative force, occurring in words of Old or Middle English origin, many of which are now obsolete or archaic, as in *forswear, forbid.* [ME and OE. Cf. G *ver-,* Gk *peri-,* L *per-*]

**f.o.r.,** free on rail.

**forage** /ˈfɒrɪdʒ/, *n., v.*, **-raged, -raging.** *–n.* **1.** food for horses and cattle; fodder; provender. **2.** the seeking or obtaining such food. **3.** the act of searching for provisions of any kind. **4.** a raid. *–v.i.* **5.** to wander in search of supplies. **6.** to hunt or search about. **7.** to make a raid. *–v.t.* **8.** to collect forage from; strip of supplies; plunder. **9.** to supply with forage. **10.** to obtain by foraging. [ME, from F *fourrage,* from OF *fuerre* fodder, from Gmc (see FODDER)] **– forager,** *n.*

**forage cap** /ˈ– kæp/, *n.* an undress military cap.

**foramen** /fəˈreɪmən/, *n., pl.* **-ramina** /-ˈræmənə/. an opening, orifice, or short passage, as in a bone or in the integument of the ovule of a plant. [L: hole]

**foramen magnum** /– ˈmægnəm/, *n.* the great hole in the occipital bone forming the passage from the cranial cavity to the spinal canal. [L: lit., great hole]

**foraminate** /fəˈræmənət, -neɪt/, *adj.* full of holes or foramina. Also, **foraminous.**

**foraminifer** /fɒrəˈmɪnəfə/, *n.* any of the Foraminifera, an extensive order of small, mostly marine rhizopods commonly having a calcareous shell perforated in many species by small holes or pores. [L *forāmen* hole + -I- + -FER] **– foraminiferal** /fɒrəməˈnɪfərəl/, **foraminiferous** /fɒrəməˈnɪfərəs/, *adj.*

**forasmuch** /fɔrəzˈmʌtʃ/, *conj.* in view of the fact that; seeing that; since (fol. by *as*).

**foray** /ˈfɒreɪ, ˈfɔ-/, *n.* **1.** a raid for the purpose of taking plunder. *–v.i.* **2.** to make a raid; forage; pillage. *–v.t.* **3.** to ravage in search of plunder. [ME *forrei(en),* backformation from *forreier* FORAYER]

**forayer** /ˈfɒreɪə, fɔˈreɪə/, *n.* →**marauder.** [ME *forreier,* from OF *forrier* forager]

**forb** /fɔb/, *n.* a herbaceous plant other than a grass, esp. a broad-leaved herb growing in a field, etc.

**forbade** /fəˈbeɪd/, *v.* past tense of **forbid.** Also, **forbad** /fəˈbæd/.

**forbear**[1] /fɔˈbɛə/, *v.*, **-bore, -borne, -bearing.** *–v.t.* **1.** to refrain from; desist from; cease. **2.** to refrain from using, etc.; keep back; withhold. **3.** *Archaic.* to endure. *–v.i.* **4.** to refrain; hold back. **5.** to be patient; show forbearance. [ME *forbere(n),* OE *forberan.* See FOR-, BEAR[1]] **– forbearer,** *n.* **– forbearingly,** *adv.*

**forbear**[2] /'fɔbɛə/, *n.* →**forebear.**

**forbearance** /fɔ'bɛərəns/, *n.* **1.** the act of forbearing; a refraining from something. **2.** forbearing conduct or quality; patient endurance; lenity. **3.** an abstaining from the enforcement of a right. **4.** *Obs.* a creditor's giving of indulgence after the day originally fixed for payment.

**forbid** /fə'bɪd/, *v.t.*, **-bade** or **-bad, -bidden** or **-bid, -bidding. 1.** to command (a person, etc.) not to do, have, use, etc., something, or not to enter some place. **2.** to put an interdiction against (something); prohibit. **3.** to hinder or prevent; make impossible. **4.** to exclude; repel. [ME *forbede(n)*, OE *forbēodan*] – **forbidder,** *n.*

**forbiddance** /fə'bɪdəns/, *n. Rare.* **1.** the act of forbidding. **2.** the state of being forbidden.

**forbidden** /fə'bɪdn/, *v.* **1.** past participle of **forbid.** *–adj.* **2.** prohibited.

**forbidden fruit** /– 'frut/, *n.* **1.** the fruit of the tree of knowledge, eaten by Adam and Eve in defiance of God. **2.** unlawful pleasure, esp. illicit sexual pleasure.

**forbidding** /fə'bɪdɪŋ/, *adj.* **1.** causing dislike or fear: *a forbidding countenance.* **2.** repellent; dangerous-looking: *forbidding cliffs, clouds, etc.* – **forbiddingly,** *adv.* – **forbiddingness,** *n.*

**forbore** /fɔ'bɔ/, *v.* past tense of **forbear**[1].

**forborne** /fɔ'bɔn/, *v.* past participle of **forbear**[1].

**force** /fɔs/, *n., v.,* **forced, forcing.** *–n.* **1.** strength; impetus; intensity of effect. **2.** might, as of a ruler or realm; strength for war. **3.** strength or power exerted upon an object; physical coercion; violence: *to use force in order to do something, to use force on a person.* **4.** *Agric.* the ability of a dog to control stock: *the dog has a lot of force.* **5.** *Law.* violence offered to persons or things, as the use of force in breaking into a house. **6.** power to influence, affect, or control; power to convince: *the force of an argument, the force of circumstances.* **7.** mental or moral strength; power of effective action or of overcoming resistance. **8.** (*oft. pl.*) a large body of armed men; an army. **9.** any body of persons combined for joint action: *an office force.* **10.** an organisation of police: *the police force.* **11.** intensity or power of effect: *the force of her playing.* **12.** operation: *a law now in force.* **13.** *Physics.* **a.** an influence which produces or tends to produce motion or change of motion. **b.** the intensity of such an influence. **14.** any influence or agency analogous to physical force: *social forces.* **15.** binding power, as of an agreement. **16.** value; significance; meaning. *–v.t.* **17.** to compel; constrain, or oblige (oneself or someone) to do something: *force someone to confess.* **18.** to drive or propel against resistance. **19.** to bring about or effect by force; bring about of necessity or as a necessary result: *force a passage, to force a smile, etc.* **20.** to put or impose (something) forcibly on or upon a person: *force something on someone's attention.* **21.** to compel by force; overcome the resistance of. **22.** to obtain or draw forth by or as by force; extort: *force a confession.* **23.** to overpower; enter or take by force. **24.** to break open (a door, lock, etc.). **25.** to cause (plants, fruits, etc.) to grow or mature at an increased rate by artificial means. **26.** to press, urge, or exert to violent effort or to the utmost. **27.** to use force upon. **28.** *Cards.* **a.** to compel (a player) to trump by leading a suit of which he has no cards. **b.** to compel a player to play (a particular card). **c.** to compel (a player) to play so as to make known the strength of his hand. **29.** *Agric.* to keep (stock) moving through a race or yard, usu. using a dog. **30.** *Obs.* to enforce (a law, etc.). **31.** *Obs.* to give force to; strengthen; reinforce. [ME, from F, from VL *fortia*, from L *fortis* strong] – **forceless,** *adj.* – **forcer,** *n.*

**forced** /fɔst/, *adj.* **1.** enforced or compulsory: *forced labour.* **2.** strained, unnatural, or affected: *a forced smile.* **3.** subjected to force. **4.** emergency: *forced landing of an aeroplane.* **5.** *Maths.* denoting a change in a system caused by an outside agency. – **forcedly** /'fɔsədli/, *adv.* – **forcedness,** *n.*

**forced march** /– 'matʃ/, *n.* any march longer than troops are usu. expected to travel, and maintained with little time for resting or for servicing vehicles.

**force-feed** /'fɔs-fid/, *n., v.,* **-fed, -feeding.** *–n.* **1.** a means of lubrication used in most internal-combustion engines, characterised by the use of a pressure pump. *–v.t.* **2.** to compel to take food.

**force-field** /'fɔs-fild/, *n.* (in science fiction) a protective shield consisting of the field of some usu. undefined energy source, so-called by analogy with magnetic field or electric field.

**forceful** /'fɔsfəl/, *adj.* **1.** full of force; powerful; vigorous; effective. **2.** acting or driven with force. – **forcefully,** *adv.* – **forcefulness,** *n.*

**force majeure** /fɔs ma'ʒɜ/, *n.* **1.** a superior force. **2.** *Law.* **a.** an unexpected and disruptive event operating to excuse a party from a contract. **b.** (of a clause) providing that a party to a contract shall be excused in case of war, strikes, etc. [F]

**forcemeat** /'fɔsmit/, *n.* meat chopped fine and seasoned, used in cooking as stuffing, etc. Also, **farcemeat.** [*force*, var. of obs. *farce* stuffing + MEAT]

**forceps** /'fɔsəps/, *n., pl.* **-ceps, -cipes** /-səpiz/. **1.** an instrument, as pincers or tongs, for seizing and holding objects, as in surgical operations. **2.** *Zool.* a grasping organ resembling a forceps. [L] – **forcepslike,** *adj.*

artery forceps

**forceps delivery** /'– dəlɪvəri/, *n.* the delivery of a baby involving the use of forceps.

**force-pump** /'fɔs-pʌmp/, *n.* any pump which delivers a liquid under pressure, so as to eject it forcibly (opposed to *lift-pump*).

**force-ripen** /'fɔs-raɪpən/, *v.t.* to cause prematurely picked fruit to become ripe, as by storing them in particular gases, in warm temperatures, etc.

**forcible** /'fɔsəbəl/, *adj.* **1.** effected by force. **2.** having force; producing a powerful effect; effective. **3.** convincing, as reasoning. **4.** characterised by the use of force or violence. – **forcibleness, forcibility** /fɔsə'bɪləti/, *n.* – **forcibly,** *adv.*

**forcible entry** /– 'ɛntri/, *n.* the criminal offence of entering with threats, force, etc., and taking possession of land or tenements.

**forcing dog** /'fɔsɪŋ dɒg/, *n.* a dog skilled in moving stock in the direction it wishes.

**forcing pen** /'– pɛn/, *n.* a specially designed pen from which stock are forced into other pens for handling.

**forcings-back** /fɔsɪŋz-'bæk/, *n.* a children's game in which each team must remain behind a ball being kicked between them, the object being to kick the ball so far that the opposing team is forced further and further back.

**ford** /fɔd/, *n.* **1.** a place where a river or other body of water may be crossed by wading. *–v.t.* **2.** to cross (a river, etc.) by a ford. [ME and OE, c. G *Furt;* akin to FARE, PORT[1]] – **fordable,** *adj.* – **fordless,** *adj.*

**fordigraph** /'fɔdəgræf/, *n.* **1.** a duplicator of special type for producing copies of material typed, written or drawn onto a master sheet. *–v.t.* **2.** to make copies of something on such a duplicator. [Trademark] – **fordigraphic,** *adj.*

**fordo** /fɔ'du/, *v.t.,* **-did, -done, -doing.** *Archaic.* **1.** to do away with; kill; destroy. **2.** to ruin; undo. Also, **foredo.** [ME, OE *fordon.* See FOR-, DO[1]]

**fordone** /fɔ'dʌn/, *adj. Archaic.* exhausted with fatigue.

**fore**[1] /fɔ/, *adj.* **1.** situated at or towards the front, as compared with something else. **2.** first in place, time, order, rank, etc.; forward; earlier. *–adv.* **3.** *Naut.* at or towards the bow. **4.** *Obs.* before. *–n.* **5.** the forepart of anything; the front. **6.** *Naut.* the foremast. **7. to the fore, a.** to or at the front; to or in a conspicuous place or position. **b.** ready at hand. **c.** still alive. *–prep. and conj.* **8.** *Obs.* before. [special use of FORE-, detached from words like *forepart, forefather,* etc.]

**fore**[2] /fɔ/, *interj.* a cry of warning to persons on a golf course who are liable to be struck by the ball. [probably aphetic var. of BEFORE]

**fore-,** a prefix form of **before** meaning 'front', (*forehead, forecastle*), 'ahead of time' (*forecast, foretell*), 'superior' (*foreman*), etc. [ME and OE *for(e)*]

**fore-and-aft** /fɔr-ən-'aft/, *adj.* **1.** parallel to the longitudinal axis of a ship. **2.** denoting a rig in which the principal sails are set on gaffs, stags, or masts, on the centre line of the vessel. *–adv.* **3.** Also, **all fore-and-aft.** from stem to stern.

**fore-and-after** /fɔr-ən-'aftə/, *n.* a vessel with fore-and-aft sails, as a schooner.

i = peat ɪ = pit ɛ = pet æ = pat a = part ɒ = pot ʌ = putt ɔ = port ʊ = put u = pool ɜ = pert ə = apart aɪ = buy eɪ = bay ɔɪ = boy aʊ = how oʊ = hoe ɪə = here ɛə = hair ʊə = tour g = give θ = thin ð = then ʃ = show ʒ = measure tʃ = choke dʒ = joke ŋ = sing j = you õ = Fr. bon

**fore-and-aft sail** /fɔr-ən-aft 'seɪl/, *n.* any sail not set on a yard, usu. bent to a gaff or set on a stay in the centre line. See **sail** (def. 1).

**forearm**[1] /'fɔram/, *n.* the part of the arm between the elbow and the wrist. [FORE- + ARM[1]]

**forearm**[2] /fɔr'am/, *v.t.* to arm beforehand. [FORE- + ARM[2]]

**forebear** /'fɔbɛə/, *n.* (*usu. pl.*) an ancestor; forefather. Also, **forbear.** [ME (Scot.); from FORE- + *bear* being (var. of *beer,* from BE, *v.* + -ER[1])]

**forebode** /fɔ'boʊd/, *v.*, **-boded, -boding.** *–v.t.* **1.** to foretell or predict; portend; be an omen of; indicate beforehand: *clouds that forbode a storm.* **2.** to have a presentiment of (esp. evil). *–v.i.* **3.** to prophesy. **4.** to have a presentiment. – **foreboder,** *n.*

**foreboding** /fɔ'boʊdɪŋ/, *n.* **1.** a prediction; portent. **2.** a presentiment. *–adj.* **3.** that forbodes, esp. evil. – **forebodingly,** *adv.*

**forebrain** /'fɔbreɪn/, *n.* **1.** that portion of the adult brain which develops from the prosencephalon. **2.** →**prosencephalon.**

**forecast** /'fɔkast/, *v.*, **-cast** or **-casted, -casting,** *n.* *–v.t.* **1.** to conjecture beforehand; predict. **2.** to make a forecast of (the weather, etc.). **3.** to serve as, a forecast of; foreshadow. **4.** to cast, contrive, or plan beforehand; prearrange. *–v.i.* **5.** to conjecture beforehand; make a forecast. **6.** to plan or arrange beforehand. *–n.* **7.** a conjecture as to something in the future. **8.** a prediction, esp. as to the weather. **9.** the act, practice, or faculty of forecasting. **10.** foresight in planning. – **forecaster,** *n.*

**forecastle** /'foʊksəl/, *n.* **1.** the seamen's quarters in the forward part of a merchant vessel. **2.** Also, **forecastle head.** a short raised deck in the forepart of a ship. Also, **fo'c'sle.**

F

diagram of a ship's bow: F, forecastle (def. 1)

**forecast quinella** /ˌfɔkast kwə'nɛlə/, *n.* See **quinella.**

**forecited** /'fɔsaɪtəd/, *adj.* previously cited.

**foreclose** /fɔ'kloʊz/, *v.*, **-closed, -closing.** *–v.t.* **1.** *Law.* **a.** to deprive (a mortgagor or pledgor) of the right to redeem his property. **b.** to take away the right to redeem (a mortgage or pledge). **2.** to shut out; exclude or bar. **3.** to hinder or prevent, as from doing something. **4.** to establish an exclusive claim to. **5.** to close, settle, or answer beforehand. *–v.i.* **6.** to foreclose a mortgage or pledge. [ME *forclose(n),* from OF *forclos,* pp. of *forclore* exclude, from *for-* out + *clore* shut, from L *claudere*] – **foreclosable,** *adj.*

**foreclosure** /fɔ'kloʊʒə/, *n.* the act of foreclosing a mortgage or pledge.

**forecourse** /'fɔkɔs/, *n.* the course set on the foremast (the foresail in a square-rigged sailing vessel).

**forecourt** /'fɔkɔt/, *n.* **1.** a court in front of a building or a group of buildings. **2.** *Brit.* →**driveway** (def. 2).

**foredate** /fɔ'deɪt/, *v.t.*, **-dated, -dating.** →**antedate.**

**foredeck** /'fɔdɛk/, *n.* the forward part of the spar deck of a ship.

**foredo** /fɔ'du/, *v.t.*, **-did, -done, -doing.** →**fordo.**

**foredoom** /fɔ'dum/, *v.*; /'fɔdum/, *n.* *–v.t.* **1.** to doom beforehand. *–n.* **2.** a doom ordained beforehand.

**fore edge** /'fɔr ɛdʒ/, *n.* the front outer edge of a book, opposite the bound edge.

**forefather** /'fɔfaðə/, *n.* an ancestor.

**forefeel** /fɔ'fil/, *v.*, **-felt, -feeling,** *n.* *–v.t.* **1.** to feel or perceive beforehand; have a presentiment of. *–n.* **2.** a feeling beforehand.

**forefend** /fɔ'fɛnd/, *v.t.* →**forfend.**

**forefinger** /'fɔfɪŋgə/, *n.* the first finger, next to the thumb; the index finger.

**forefoot** /'fɔfʊt/, *n., pl.* **-feet** /-fit/. **1.** *Zool.* one of the front feet of a quadruped, or of an insect, etc. **2.** *Naut.* the forward end of the keel.

**forefront** /'fɔfrʌnt/, *n.* the foremost part or place.

**foregather** /fɔ'gæðə/, *v.i.* →**forgather.**

**foregift** /'fɔgɪft/, *n.* a premium sometimes paid in consideration of the granting of a lease.

**forego**[1] /fɔ'goʊ/, *v.*, **-went, -gone, -going.** *–v.i.* **1.** to go before. *–v.t.* **2.** to precede. [OE *foregān* go before, from *fore-* FORE- + *gān* go] – **foregoer,** *n.*

**forego**[2] /fɔ'goʊ/, *v.t.*, **-went, -gone, -going.** →**forgo.** – **foregoer,** *n.*

**foregoing** /'fɔgoʊɪŋ/, *adj.* going before; preceding: *the foregoing passage.*

**foregone** /fɔ'gɒn, 'fɔgɒn/, *adj.* that has gone before; previous; past. – **foregoneness,** *n.*

**foregone conclusion** /– kən'kluʒən/, *n.* **1.** an inevitable conclusion or result. **2.** a conclusion, opinion, or decision formed in advance.

**foreground** /'fɔgraʊnd/, *n.* the ground or parts situated, or represented as situated, in the front; the nearer portion of a scene (opposed to *background*).

**foregrounding** /'fɔgraʊndɪŋ/, *n.* the use of grammatical devices in a sentence in order to place in the foreground of attention those parts of the sentence which are to be taken as new information.

**foregut** /'fɔgʌt/, *n.* the upper part of the embryonic digestive canal from which the pharynx, oesophagus, stomach, and part of the duodenum develop.

**forehand** /'fɔhænd/, *adj.* **1.** made to the right side of the body (when the player is right-handed). **2.** being in front or ahead. **3.** foremost or leading. **4.** done beforehand; anticipative; given or made in advance, as a payment. *–n.* **5.** position in front or above; superior position; adventure. **6.** *Tennis, etc.* **a.** forehand stroke. **b.** that type of playing, or the stance taken when making such strokes. **7.** *Bowls.* a delivery of a bowl by a righthanded player in a right hand direction with the bias side inwards. **8.** the part of a horse which is in front of the rider.

**forehanded** /'fɔhændəd/, *adj.* **1.** forehand, as a stroke in tennis, etc. **2.** *U.S.* providing for the future; prudent; thrifty. **3.** *U.S.* in easy circumstances; well-to-do. – **forehandedness,** *n.*

**forehead** /'fɒrəd/, *n.* **1.** the fore or front upper part of the head; the part of the face above the eyes; the brow. **2.** the fore or front part of anything. [ME *forehe(v)ed,* OE *forhēafod,* from *for(e)-* FORE- + *hēafod* head]

**foreign** /'fɒrən/, *adj.* **1.** pertaining to, characteristic of, or derived from another country or nation; not native or domestic. **2.** pertaining to relations or dealings with other countries. **3.** external to one's own country or nation: *a foreign country.* **4.** carried on abroad, or with other countries: *foreign trade.* **5.** belonging to or coming from another district, province, society, etc. **6.** situated outside a district, province, etc. **7.** *Law.* outside the legal jurisdiction of the state; alien. **8.** belonging to or proceeding from other persons or things: *a statement supported by foreign testimony.* **9.** not belonging to the place or body where found: *a foreign substance in the eye.* **10.** not related to or connected with the thing under consideration: *foreign to our discussion.* **11.** alien in character; irrelevant or inappropriate; remote. **12.** strange or unfamiliar. [ME *forene,* from OF *forain,* from L *foras* out of doors, outside] – **foreignness,** *n.*

**foreign affairs** /– ə'fɛəz/, *n.pl.* international relations; activities of a nation arising from its dealings with other nations.

**foreign aid** /– 'eɪd/, *n.* financial and other aid given to underdeveloped countries by technologically more advanced ones.

**foreign bill** /– 'bɪl/, *n.* any bill of exchange other than an inland bill.

**foreign body** /– 'bɒdi/, *n.* **1.** a substance found in but not belonging to the human body. **2.** any unwanted object.

**foreign correspondent** /– 'kɒrəspɒndənt/, *n.* a correspondent, as of a newspaper, etc., sent abroad to write articles and news dispatches from a foreign country for publication in his own country.

**foreigner** /ˈfɒrənə/, *n.* **1.** a person not native or naturalised in the country or jurisdiction under consideration; an alien. **2.** a thing produced in or coming from a foreign country.

**foreign exchange** /fɒrən əksˈtʃeɪndʒ/, *n.* **1.** the buying and selling of the money of other countries. **2.** the money of other countries.

**foreign exchange market,** *n.* part of the money market which deals with the trading of one currency for another.

**foreign exchange rate,** *n.* the rate at which the money of one country is exchanged for that of another.

**foreignism** /ˈfɒrənɪzəm/, *n. U.S.* **1.** a foreign custom, etc. **2.** any trait or deviation from accepted speech standards that comes from the influence of a foreign language. **3.** imitation of anything foreign. **4.** foreign quality.

**foreign legion** /fɒrən ˈlidʒən/, *n.* **1.** a military body in the service of a state, including foreign volunteers. **2.** (*caps*) a military body in the French Army, consisting of foreigners of all nationalities, and including Frenchmen, used mainly for military operations and duties outside France, formerly in northern Africa.

**foreign office** /ˈ– ɒfəs/, *n. Brit.* the government department concerned with the conduct of international relations.

**foreign order** /– ˈɔdə/, *n.* (in a work shop, laboratory, etc.) a job, repair, etc., carried out by employees for themselves or their clients, and not as part of the regular work required by their employers. Also, **F.O., foreigner.**

**foreign relations** /– rəˈleɪʃənz/, *n. pl.* **1.** the relationship between nations arising out of their dealings with each other. **2.** the field of foreign affairs.

**foreign secretary** /– ˈsɛkrətri/, *n. Brit.* the minister for foreign affairs.

**forejudge**[1] /fɔˈdʒʌdʒ/, *v.t.*, **-judged, -judging.** to judge beforehand; prejudge. [FORE- + JUDGE, *v.*]

**forejudge**[2] /fɔˈdʒʌdʒ/, *v.t.*, **-judged, -judging.** →**forjudge.**

**foreknow** /fɔˈnoʊ/, *v.t.*, **-knew, -known, -knowing.** to know beforehand. – **foreknowable,** *adj.* – **foreknowingly,** *adv.*

**foreknowledge** /fɔˈnɒlɪdʒ/, *n.* knowledge of a thing before it exists or happens; prescience.

**foreland** /ˈfɔlænd/, *n.* **1.** a cape, headland, or promontory. **2.** land or territory lying in front. **3.** *Geol.* the region in front of a series of overthrust sheets. **4.** *Geol.* the resistant block towards which geosynclinal sediments move when compressed.

**foreleg** /ˈfɔlɛg/, *n.* one of the front legs of a quadruped, or of an insect, etc.

**forelimb** /ˈfɔlɪm/, *n.* a front limb of an animal.

**forelock**[1] /ˈfɔlɒk/, *n.* **1.** the lock of hair that grows from the forepart of the head. **2.** a prominent or somewhat detached lock above the forehead. **3. take time by the forelock,** *Colloq.* to seize an opportunity. **4. touch (tug) (pull) one's forelock,** *Colloq.* to touch or tug one's forelock as a gesture of servility. [FORE- + LOCK[2]]

**forelock**[2] /ˈfɔlɒk/, *n.* **1.** a round or flat wedge of iron passed through a hole in the inner end of a bolt to prevent its withdrawal when a strain is placed on it. *–v.t.* **2.** to fasten by means of a forelock. [FORE- + LOCK[1]]

**foreloin** /ˈfɔlɔɪn/, *n.* a cut of pork which is that portion of the forequarter containing the shoulder blade.

**foreman** /ˈfɔmən/, *n., pl.* **-men. 1.** a man in charge of a group of workers. **2.** the spokesman of a jury. – **foremanship,** *n.*

**foremast** /ˈfɔmast, -məst/, *n.* the mast nearest the bow of a ship.

**foremost** /ˈfɔmoʊst/, *adj.* **1.** first in place, order, rank, etc. *–adv.* **2.** first. [FORE[1], *adj.* + -MOST, replacing ME and OE *formest,* from *forma* first (var. of *frum(a).* Cf. L *prīmus*) + -EST]

**forename** /ˈfɔneɪm/, *n.* a name that precedes the family name or surname; a first name.

**forenamed** /ˈfɔneɪmd/, *adj.* named before; mentioned before in the same writing or discourse.

**forenoon** /ˈfɔnun/, *n.* **1.** the period of daylight before noon. **2.** the latter part of the morning, esp. the part ordinarily employed in transacting business. *–adj.* **3.** of or pertaining to the forenoon.

**forensic** /fəˈrɛnsɪk, -zɪk/, *adj.* **1.** pertaining to, connected with, or used in courts of law or public discussion and debate. **2.** adapted or suited to argumentation; argumentative. [L *forens(is)* of the forum + -IC] – **forensically,** *adv.*

**forensic medicine** /– ˈmɛdəsən/, *n.* →**medical jurisprudence.**

**foreordain** /fɔrɔˈdeɪn/, *v.t.* to ordain or appoint beforehand; predestinate. – **foreordainment,** *n.*

**foreordination** /fɔrɔdəˈneɪʃən/, *n.* previous ordination or appointment; predestination.

**forepart** /ˈfɔpat/, *n.* the fore, front, or early part.

**forepaw** /ˈfɔpɔ/, *n.* either of the front feet of an animal that has paws.

**forepeak** /ˈfɔpik/, *n.* the part of the hold in the angle formed by the bow of a ship.

**foreplay** /ˈfɔpleɪ/, *n.* stimulation preceding sexual intercourse.

**forequarter** /ˈfɔkwɔtə/, *n.* (in cutting meat) the forward end of half of a carcass.

**forereach** /fɔˈritʃ/, *v.i.* **1.** to gain, as one ship on another. *–v.t.* **2.** to gain upon; overhaul and pass.

**forerun** /fɔˈrʌn/, *v.t.*, **-ran, -run, -running. 1.** to run in front of; precede; be the precurser of. **2.** to anticipate or forestall. **3.** *Obs.* to outrun or outstrip.

**forerunner** /ˈfɔrʌnə/, *n.* **1.** a predecessor; ancestor. **2.** one who or that which foreruns; a herald or harbinger. **3.** a prognostic or portent.

**foresaid** /ˈfɔsɛd/, *adj.* aforementioned; aforesaid.

**foresail** /ˈfɔseɪl, -səl/, *n.* **1.** the sail bent to the foreyard of a square-rigged vessel. **2.** the principal sail on the foremast of a schooner. **3.** the forestay sail of a sloop, cutter, etc.

**foresee** /fɔˈsi/, *v.*, **-saw, -seen, -seeing.** *–v.t.* **1.** to see beforehand; have prescience of; foreknow. *–v.i.* **2.** to exercise foresight. [ME; OE *foresēon,* from *fore-* FORE- + *sēon* SEE[1]] – **foreseeable,** *adj.* – **foreseer,** *n.*

**foreshadow** /fɔˈʃædoʊ/, *v.t.* to show or indicate beforehand; prefigure. – **foreshadower,** *n.*

**foresheet** /ˈfɔʃit/, *n.* **1.** a sheet of a foresail. **2.** (*pl.*) the forward part of an open boat.

**foreshock** /ˈfɔʃɒk/, *n.* a lesser shock preceding the main shock of an earthquake.

**foreshore** /ˈfɔʃɔ/, *n.* **1.** the forepart of the shore; the part of the shore between the ordinary high-water mark and low-water mark. **2.** the ground between the water's edge and the land cultivated or built upon.

**foreshorten** /fɔˈʃɔtn/, *v.t.* to reduce the length of (a line, part, object, or the like, which lies in a plane not perpendicular to the line of sight) in order to give the proper impression to the eye by means of perspective. – **foreshortening,** *n.*

**foreshow** /fɔˈʃoʊ/, *v.t.*, **-showed, -shown, -showing.** to show beforehand; foretell; foreshadow. [ME *forescewen,* OE *forescēawian,* from *fore-* FORE- + *scēawian* show]

**foreside** /ˈfɔsaɪd/, *n.* **1.** the front side or part. **2.** the upper side. **3.** *U.S.* a stretch of land fronting the sea.

**foresight** /ˈfɔsaɪt/, *n.* **1.** care or provision for the future; provident care. **2.** the act or power of foreseeing; prevision; prescience. **3.** the act of looking forward. **4.** perception gained by or as by looking forward; prospect; a view into the future. **5.** *Survey.* **a.** a sight or reading taken on a forward point. **b.** (in levelling) a rod reading on a point the elevation of which is to be determined. **6.** a sight on the muzzle of a gun. – **foresighted,** *adj.* – **foresightedness,** *n.*

**foreskin** /ˈfɔskɪn/, *n.* →**prepuce.**

**forest** /ˈfɒrəst/, *n.* **1.** a large tract of land covered with trees: *Kioloa State Forest.* **2.** the trees alone: *to cut down a forest.* **3.** *Brit.* a tract of woody grounds and pastures, generally belonging to the sovereign, set apart for game. **4.** *Brit.* an area, once extensively wooded, now more or less cultivated: *Ashdown Forest.* **5.** a thick cluster of many things. *–v.t.* **6.** to cover with trees; convert into a forest. [ME, from OF, from VL *forestis* an unenclosed wood (as opposed to a park), from L *foris* outside. See FOREIGN] – **forested,** *adj.* – **forestless,** *adj.* – **forest-like,** *adj.*

**forestage** /ˈfɔsteɪdʒ/, *n.* that part of a stage in a theatre which is nearest to the audience, often extending in front of the curtain.

**forestall** /fɔˈstɔl/, *v.t.* **1.** to prevent, hinder, or thwart by action in advance; take measures concerning or deal with (a thing) in advance. **2.** to deal with, meet, or realise in advance of the natural or proper time; be beforehand with or get ahead of (a person, etc.) in action. **3.** to buy up (goods) in advance, in order to enhance the price. **4.** to prevent sales at (a fair, market, etc.) by buying up or diverting goods. [ME *forstalle,* from OE *foresteall* intervention (to defeat justice), waylaying. See FORE-, STALL[2]] – **forestaller,** *n.* – **forestalment,** *n.*

**forestation** /fɒrəsˈteɪʃən/, *n.* the planting of forests.

**forestay** /ˈfɔsteɪ/, *n.* a strong rope (now generally of wire) extending forward from the head of the foremast to the knightheads or stem to support the mast.

**forestay sail** /ˈ– seɪl, səl/, *n.* a triangular sail set on the forestay, being the first sail in front of the forward (or single) mast.

**forester** /ˈfɒrəstə/, *n.* **1.** one who practises, or is versed in, forestry. **2.** an officer having charge of a forest. **3.** *Zool.* an animal of the forest. **4.** →**great grey kangaroo. 5.** any of various moths of the family Zygaenidae, as *Procris statices,* a moth whose larva feeds on sorrel.

**forest oak** /fɒrəst ˈoʊk/, *n.* a tree, *Casuarina torulosa,* with slender drooping branchlets, often found on hillsides in forests of eastern New South Wales.

**forestry** /ˈfɒrəstri/, *n.* **1.** the science of planting and taking care of forests. **2.** the act of establishing and managing forests. **3.** forest land.

**foretaste** /ˈfɔteɪst/, *n.;* /fɔˈteɪst/, *v.,* **-tasted, -tasting.** *–n.* **1.** a taste beforehand; anticipation. *–v.t.* **2.** to taste beforehand; enjoy by anticipation.

**foretell** /fɔˈtɛl/, *v.,* **-told, -telling.** *–v.t.* **1.** to tell of beforehand; predict or prophesy. **2.** (of things) to foreshow. *–v.i.* **3.** to utter a prediction or a prophecy. – **foreteller,** *n.*

**forethought** /ˈfɔθɔt/, *n.* **1.** provident care; prudence. **2.** a thinking of something beforehand; previous consideration; anticipation.

**forethoughtful** /fɔˈθɔtfəl/, *adj.* full of or having forethought; provident. – **forethoughtfully,** *adv.* – **forethoughtfulness,** *n.*

**foretime** /ˈfɔtaɪm/, *n.* former or past time; the past.

**foretoken** /ˈfɔtoʊkən/, *n.;* /fɔˈtoʊkən/, *v.* *–n.* **1.** a premonitory token or sign. *–v.t.* **2.** to foreshadow. [ME *foretokne,* OE *foretācn,* from *fore-* FORE- + *tācn* token]

**foretop** /ˈfɔtɒp/; *for def. 1 also* /-təp/, *n.* **1.** *Naut.* a platform at the head of a foremast. **2.** the forelock of an animal, esp. a horse. **3.** *Obs.* a human forelock, or a lock of hair on the front of a wig.

**fore-topgallant** /ˌfɔ-tɒpˈgælənt, -təˈgæl-/, *adj.* (of a mast, sail, yard, etc.) next above the foretopmast.

**fore-topgallant mast** /ˈ– mast/, *n.* the mast on a ship next above the fore-topmast.

**fore-topmast** /fɔ-ˈtɒpmast, -məst/, *n.* the mast erected at the head of the foremast, above the foretop on a ship.

**fore-topsail** /fɔ-ˈtɒpseɪl, -səl/, *n.* the sail set on the fore-topmast.

**for ever** /fər ˈɛvə/, *adv.* **1.** eternally; without ever ending: *to last for ever, go away for ever.* **2.** continually; incessantly: *he's for ever complaining.* Also, *U.S.,* **forever.**

**forevermore** /fərɛvəˈmɔ/, *adv.* for ever hereafter. Also, **for ever more.**

**forewarn** /fɔˈwɔn/, *v.t.* to warn beforehand.

**forewing** /ˈfɔwɪŋ/, *n.* either wing of the anterior pair of an insect's two pairs of wings.

**forewoman** /ˈfɔwʊmən/, *n., pl.* **-women.** a woman in charge of a group of employees.

**foreword** /ˈfɔwɜd/, *n.* a preface or introductory statement in a book, etc.

**foreyard** /ˈfɔjad/, *n.* the lower yard on the foremast of a ship.

**forfeit** /ˈfɔfət/, *n.* **1.** a fine; a penalty. **2.** the act of forfeiting; forfeiture. **3.** something to which the right is lost by the commission of a crime or misdeed, the neglect of a duty, a breach of contract, etc. **4.** an article deposited in a game because of a mistake and redeemable by a fine or penalty. **5.** (*pl.*) a game so played. *–v.t.* **6.** to lose as a forfeit. **7.** to lose, or become liable to lose, in consequence of crime, fault, breach of engagement, etc. *–adj.* **8.** forfeited. [ME *forfet,* from OF, pp. of *forfaire,* from *for-* outside, wrongly + *faire* do] – **forfeitable,** *adj.* – **forfeiter,** *n.*

**forfeiture** /ˈfɔfətʃə/, *n.* **1.** the act of forfeiting. **2.** that which is forfeited; a fine mulct.

**forfend** /fɔˈfɛnd/, *v.t.* **1.** *U.S.* to defend, secure, or protect. **2.** *Archaic.* to fend off, avert, or prevent. Also, **forefend.** [ME; from FOR- + FEND]

**forficate** /ˈfɔfəkət, -keɪt/, *adj.* deeply forked, as the tail of certain birds. [L *forfex* scissors + -ATE[1]]

**forgather** /fɔˈgæðə/, *v.i.* **1.** to gather together; convene; assemble. **2.** to encounter or meet, esp. by accident. **3.** to associate or fraternise (fol. by *with*). Also, **foregather.**

**forgave** /fəˈgeɪv/, *v.* past tense of **forgive.**

**forge**[1] /fɔdʒ/, *n., v.,* **forged, forging.** *–n.* **1.** the special fireplace, hearth, or furnace in which metal is heated before shaping. **2.** →**smithy.** *–v.t.* **3.** to form by heating and hammering; beat into shape. **4.** to form or make in any way. **5.** to invent (a fictitious story, a lie, etc.). **6.** to imitate (a signature, etc.) fraudulently; fabricate by false imitation. *–v.i.* **7.** to commit forgery. **8.** to work at a forge. [ME, from OF, from L *fabrica* workshop] – **forgeable,** *adj.* – **forger,** *n.*

**forge**[2] /fɔdʒ/, *v.i.,* **forged, forging.** to move ahead slowly, with difficulty, or by mere momentum (usu. fol. by *ahead*). [orig. uncert.]

**forgery** /ˈfɔdʒəri/, *n., pl.* **-geries. 1.** the making of a fraudulent imitation of a thing, or of something spurious which is put forth as genuine, as a coin, a work of art, a literary production, etc. **2.** something, as a coin, a work of art, a writing, etc., produced by forgery. **3.** *Law.* the false making or alteration of a writing by which the legal rights or obligations of another person are apparently affected; simulated signing of another person's name to any such writing (whether or not it is also the forger's name). **4.** the act of fabricating or producing falsely. **5.** *Archaic.* fictitious invention or deception.

**forget** /fəˈgɛt/, *v.,* **-got** or (*Archaic*) **-gat; -gotten** or **-got; -getting.** *–v.t.* **1.** to cease to remember; fail to remember; be unable to recall. **2.** to omit or neglect unintentionally (to do something). **3.** to omit to take; leave behind inadvertently: *to forget one's keys.* **4.** to omit to mention; leave unnoticed. **5.** to omit to think of; take no note of. **6.** to neglect wilfully; overlook, disregard, or slight. **7. forget it,** to drop the subject. **8. forget oneself, a.** to say or do something improper. **b.** to fail to remember one's station, position, or character. **c.** to become absent-minded. **d.** to lose consciousness, as in sleep. *–v.i.* **9.** to cease or omit to think of something. [FOR- + GET; replacing ME *foryete(n),* OE *forg(i)etan*] – **forgettable,** *adj.* – **forgetter,** *n.*

**forgetful** /fəˈgɛtfəl/, *adj.* **1.** apt to forget; that forgets: *a forgetful person.* **2.** heedless or neglectful (oft. fol. by *of*): *to be forgetful of others.* **3.** *Poetic.* causing to forget. – **forgetfully,** *adv.* – **forgetfulness,** *n.*

**forget-me-not** /fəˈgɛt-mi-nɒt/, *n.* any small plant of the family Boraginaceae, esp. of the genera *Myosotis* and *Cynoglossum,* a light blue flower, regarded as an emblem of constancy.

**forging** /ˈfɔdʒɪŋ/, *n.* **1.** something forged; a piece of forged work in metal. **2.** (in horses) the act of striking and injuring the forelegs with the shoes of the hind legs while racing.

**forgive** /fəˈgɪv/, *v.,* **-gave, -given, -giving.** *–v.t.* **1.** to grant free pardon for or remission of (an offence, debt, etc.); pardon. **2.** to give up all claim on account of; remit (a debt, etc.). **3.** to grant free pardon to (a person). **4.** to cease to feel resentment against: *to forgive one's enemies.* *–v.i.* **5.** to pardon an offence or an offender. [FOR- + GIVE; replacing ME *foryiven,* OE *forgiefan*] – **forgivable,** *adj.* – **forgivably,** *adv.*

**forgiveness** /fəˈgɪvnəs/, *n.* **1.** the act of forgiving. **2.** the state of being forgiven. **3.** disposition or willingness to forgive.

**forgiving** /fəˈgɪvɪŋ/, *adj.* that forgives; disposed to forgive; indicating forgiveness. – **forgivingly,** *adv.* – **forgivingness,** *n.*

**forgo** /fɔˈgoʊ/, *v.t.,* **-went, -gone, -going. 1.** to abstain or refrain from; do without; give up, renounce, or resign. **2.** *Archaic.* to neglect or overlook. **3.** *Archaic.* to quit or leave. **4.** *Obs.* to go or pass by. Also, **forego.** [ME *forgon,* OE *forgān.* See FOR-, GO] – **forgoer,** *n.*

**forgot** /fəˈgɒt/, *v.* past tense and past participle of **forget.**

**forgotten** /fəˈgɒtn/, *v.* past participle of **forget.**

**forjudge** /fɔˈdʒʌdʒ/, *v.t.,* **-judged, -judging.** to exclude, expel, dispossess, or deprive by a legal judgment. Also, **forejudge.** [ME *forjuge(n),* from OF *forjugier,* from *for-* out + *jugier* JUDGE, *v.*]

**fork** /fɔk/, *n.* **1.** an instrument having two or more prongs or tines, for holding, lifting, etc., as any of various agricultural tools, or an implement for handling food at table or in cooking. **2.** something resembling or suggesting this in form. **3.** →**tuning fork.** **4.** a forking, or dividing into branches. **5.** the point or part at which a thing, as a river or a road, divides into branches. **6.** each of the branches into which a thing forks. **7.** *Chiefly U.S.* a principal tributary of a river. **8.** *Colloq.* a jockey. **9.** *Obs.* the barbed head of an arrow. *–v.t.* **10.** to make fork-shaped. **11.** to pierce, raise, pitch, dig, etc., with a fork. **12.** *Chess.* to assail (two pieces) at the same time. **13.** *Colloq.* to hand over; pay (fol. by *over* or *out*). **14.** to mount (a horse) by vaulting onto the saddle. *–v.i.* **15.** to form a fork; divide into branches. *–v.t.* [ME *forke,* OE *forca,* from L *furca*] – **forkful,** *n.* – **forkless,** *adj.* – **forklike,** *adj.*

**fork dinner** /'– dɪnə/, *n.* a dinner comprising fork dishes.

**fork dish** /'– dɪʃ/, *n.* a dish, esp. a savoury one, designed to be eaten with a fork.

**forked** /fɔkt/, *adj.* **1.** having a fork or forking branches. **2.** zigzag, as lightning. – **forkedly** /'fɔkədli/, *adv.* – **forkedness,** *n.*

**forked lightning** /– 'laɪtnɪŋ/, *n.* lightning visible in wavy, zigzag, or broken lines.

**fork hoist** /'fɔk hɔɪst/, *n. N.Z.* →**fork-lift.**

**fork-lift** /'fɔk-lɪft/, *n.* an electric truck with two power-operated, parallel, horizontal arms for lifting and carrying goods, esp. in a warehouse or factory. Also, **fork-lift truck.**

**fork luncheon** /fɔk 'lʌntʃən/, *n.* a buffet luncheon spread on tables or sideboards from which the guests serve themselves. Also, **fork lunch.**

**forlorn** /fə'lɔn/, *adj.* **1.** abandoned, deserted, or forsaken (sometimes fol. by *of*). **2.** desolate or dreary; unhappy or miserable, as in feeling, condition, or appearance. **3.** desperate or hopeless. **4.** bereft (fol. by *of*). [var. of *forlore(n),* pp. of (obs.) *forlese,* v., OE *forlēosan* lose, destroy. See FOR-, LORN] – **forlornly,** *adv.* – **forlorness,** *n.*

**forlorn hope** /– 'houp/, *n.* **1.** a vain hope; an undertaking almost certain to fail. **2.** a perilous or desperate enterprise. [D, alteration of *verloren hoop,* lit., lost troop]

**form** /fɔm/, *n.* **1.** definite shape; external shape or appearance considered apart from colour or material; configuration. **2.** the shape of a thing or person. **3.** a body, esp. that of a human being. **4.** something that gives or determines shape; a mould. **5.** a particular structural condition, character, or mode of being exhibited by a thing: *water in the form of ice.* **6.** the manner or style of arranging and coordinating parts for a pleasing or effective result, as in literary or musical composition. **7.** the formal structure of a work of art; the organisation and relationship of lines or colours in a painting or volumes and voids in a sculpture so as to create a coherent image. **8.** any assemblage of similar things constituting a component of a group, esp. of a zoological group. **9.** *Crystall.* the combination of all the like faces possible on a crystal of given symmetry. **10.** due or proper shape; orderly arrangement of parts; good order. **11.** *Maths.* a homogeneous polynomial in two or more variables. **12.** *Philos.* **a.** the structure, pattern, organisation, or essential nature of anything. **b.** form or pattern considered in distinction from matter. **c.** (in Platonic use) an idea (def. 7c). **d.** (in Aristotelian use) that which gives to a thing its particular species or kind. **13.** *Logic.* the abstract relations of terms in a proposition, and of propositions to one another. **14.** a set, prescribed, or customary order or method of doing something. **15.** a set order of words, as for use in religious ritual or in a legal document. **16.** a document with blank spaces to be filled in with particulars before it is executed: *a tax form.* **17.** a typical document to be used as a guide in framing others for like cases: *a form for a deed.* **18.** a conventional method of procedure or behaviour. **19.** a formality or ceremony, often with implication of absence of real meaning. **20.** procedure, according to a set order or method. **21.** formality; ceremony; conformity to the usages of society. **22.** mere outward formality or ceremony; conventional observance of social usages. **23.** procedure or conduct, as judged by social standards. **24.** manner or method of performing something. **25.** condition, esp. good condition, with reference to fitness for performing. **26.** *Gram.* **a.** any word, part of a word, or group of words arranged in a construction, which recurs in various contexts in a language with relatively constant meaning. **b.** a particular shape of a form (def. 26a) when it occurs in several ways: *in 'I'm', ''m' is a form of 'am'.* **c.** a word with a particular inflectional ending or other modification, as *goes* is a form of *go.* **27. a.** a single division of a school containing pupils of about the same age or of the same level of scholastic progress. **b.** the pupils themselves in such a division. **28.** a bench or long seat. **29.** the bed, nest, or lair of a hare. **30.** *Mil.* a movement in dismounted drill by which a body of troops changes its direction of movement but not its formation. **31.** *Horseracing, etc.* the record of an entrant's past performance by which chances of success in a race are assessed. **32.** *Colloq.* a person's record or reputation. **33. a matter of form,** a routine activity, esp. a procedural matter. *–v.t.* **34.** to construct or frame. **35.** to make or produce; to serve to make up, or compose; serve for, or constitute. **36.** to place in order; arrange; organise. **37.** to frame (ideas, opinions, etc.) in the mind. **38.** to contract (habits, friendships, etc.). **39.** to give form or shape to; shape; fashion. **40.** to give a particular form to, or fashion in a particular manner. **41.** to mould by discipline or instruction. **42.** *Gram.* to stand in relation to (a particular derivative or other form) by virtue of the absence or presence of an affix or other grammatical element or change: *'man' forms its plural by the change of -a- to -e-.* **43.** *Mil.* to draw up in lines or in formation (fol. by *up*). *–v.i.* **44.** to take or assume form. **45.** to be formed or produced. **46.** to take a particular form or arrangement. [ME *forme,* from OF, from L *forma* form, figure, model, mould, sort, ML seat]

**-form,** a suffix meaning 'having the form of', as in *cruciform.* [L *-formis*]

**formal** /'fɔməl/, *adj.* **1.** being in accordance with conventional requirements; conventional. **2.** marked by form or ceremony: *a formal occasion.* **3.** observant of form, as persons; ceremonious. **4.** excessively ceremonious. **5.** being a matter of form only; perfunctory. **6.** made or done in accordance with forms ensuring validity: *a formal vote.* **7.** being in accordance with prescribed or customary forms: *a formal siege.* **8.** *Fine Arts.* of or pertaining to the composition and the organisation of the constituent elements in a work of art. **9.** *Educ.* acquired in a recognised place of learning: *a formal education.* **10.** excessively regular or symmetrical. **11.** denoting language whose grammar and syntax are correct, and speech whose sounds are carefully formed without sounding stilted: *the language and speech of formal occasions.* See **informal** (def. 4). **12.** *Philos.* **a.** pertaining to form. **b.** (in Aristotelian use) not material; essential. **13.** pertaining to the form, shape, or mode of being of a thing, esp. as distinguished from the matter. **14.** being such in form, esp. in mere outward form. *–n.* **15.** a dance or ball, at which formal evening dress is to be worn. **16.** (*pl.*) a man's formal dress. – **formalness,** *n.*

**formaldehyde** /fɔ'mældəhaɪd/, *n.* a gas, HCHO, used most often in the form of a 40 per cent aqueous solution, as a disinfectant and preservative, and in the manufacture of various resins and plastics; methanal. Also, **formaldehyd.** [FORM(IC ACID) + ALDEHYDE]

**formal dress** /fɔməl 'drɛs/, *n.* attire suitable for a formal occasion as an evening dress, military dress uniform, etc.

**formalin** /'fɔmələn/, *n.* an aqueous solution of formaldehyde used as a sterilising solution for non-boilable material, in the treatment of warts, and as a preservative for biological specimens.

**formalise** /'fɔməlaɪz/, *v.,* **-lised, -lising.** *–v.t.* **1.** to make formal. **2.** to give a definite form or shape to. *–v.i.* **3.** to be formal; act with formality. Also, **formalize.** – **formalisation** /fɔməlaɪ'zeɪʃən/, *n.*

**formalism** /'fɔməlɪzəm/, *n.* **1.** strict adherence to or observance of prescribed or customary forms. **2.** (in religion) excessive attachment to external forms and observances. – **formalist,** *n.* – **formalistic** /fɔmə'lɪstɪk/, *adj.*

**formality** /fɔ'mæləti/, *n., pl.* **-ties. 1.** the condition or quality of being formal; accordance with prescribed, customary, or due forms; conventionality. **2.** rigorously methodical character. **3.** excessive regularity, or stiffness. **4.** observance of form or ceremony. **5.** marked or excessive ceremoniousness. **6.** an established order or mode of proceeding: *the formalities of judicial process.* **7.** a formal act or observance. **8.** something done merely for form's sake; a requirement of custom or etiquette.

**formal logic** /fɔməl 'lɒdʒɪk/, *n.* the branch of logic concerned exclusively with the principles of deductive reasoning and in consequence with the forms (as distinct from the content) of propositions.

**formally** /'fɔməli/, *adv.* **1.** in a formal manner. **2.** as regards form; in form.

**formant** /'fɔmənt/, *n.* any of several frequency regions of relatively greater intensity in a sound spectrum, which together determine the characteristic quality of a vowel sound. [G *Formant,* from L *formans,* ppr. of *formāre* to form]

**format** /'fɔmæt/, *n.* **1.** the shape and size of a book or the like as determined by the number of times the original sheet has been folded to form the leaves. See **folio** (def. 2), **quarto, octavo, duodecimo,** etc. **2.** the general physical appearance of a book, newspaper, or magazine, etc., such as the typeface, binding, quality of paper, margins, etc. **3.** the plan or style of something: *the format of a television series.* **4.** the size and shape of a negative or the print from it. **5.** *Computers.* an orderly arrangement of data elements to form a larger entity, as a list, table, file, etc. *–v.t.* **6.** *Computers.* to organise the output data into appropriate patterns by column, line, etc. [F, from L (*liber*) *formātus* (a book) formed (in a certain way)]

**formate** /'fɔmeɪt/, *n.* a salt or ester of formic acid. [FORM(IC ACID) + -ATE²]

**formation** /fɔ'meɪʃən/, *n.* **1.** the act or process of forming. **2.** the state of being formed. **3.** the manner in which a thing is formed; disposition of parts; formal structure or arrangement. **4.** *Mil.* a particular disposition of troops. **5.** a group of two or more aircraft flying as a unit according to a fixed plan. **6.** a team of ballroom dancers, gymnasts, etc., performing according to a previously arranged sequence. **7.** something formed. **8.** *Geol.* **a.** a succession of beds of rock of one dominant lithology, produced during a single period of deposition and capable of being mapped on a regional scale. **b.** the process of depositing material of a particular composition or origin. **9.** *Biol.* climax community of plants extending over a very large natural area, the nature of which is determined by climate, as rain forest, mallee country.

**formative** /'fɔmətɪv/, *adj.* **1.** giving form or shape; forming; shaping; fashioning; moulding. **2.** pertaining to formation or development: *the formative period of a nation.* **3.** *Biol.* **a.** capable of developing new cells or tissue by cell division and differentiation: *formative tissue.* **b.** concerned with the formation of an embryo, organ, or the like. **4.** *Gram.* pertaining to a formative. *–n.* **5.** *Gram.* a derivational affix, particularly one which determines the part of speech of the derived word, such as *-ness,* in *loudness, hardness,* etc. **– formatively,** *adv.* **– formativeness,** *n.*

**formative element** /'– ɛləmənt/, *n.* **1.** a morpheme which serves as an affix, not as a base (or root) in word formation. **2.** any non-inflectional morpheme, whether base or affix.

**form class** /'fɔm klas/, *n.* a class of words or forms in a language with one or more grammatical features in common, as (in Latin) all masculine nouns in the nominative singular, or all masculine singular nouns, or all masculine nouns, or all singular nouns, or all nouns.

**form criticism** /'– krɪtəsɪzəm/, *n.* a method of criticism of the Old and New Testaments, which is based on the belief that the writers often collected, arranged and edited units of literary material circulating in the early church and which, by noting these units, their arrangement, and the changes made in them, seeks to discuss the evolution of religious thought and idea.

**forme** /fɔm/, *n.* an assemblage of type and blocks locked up in the chase preparatory to printing.

**former¹** /'fɔmə/, *adj.* **1.** preceding in time; prior or earlier. **2.** past, long past, or ancient. **3.** preceding in order; being the first of two. **4.** being the first mentioned of two. **5.** having held a particular office in the past: *a former president.* [ME, from obs. *forme* (OE *forma* first) + -ER⁴. Cf. ME and OE *formest* foremost]

**former²** /'fɔmə/, *n.* **1.** one who or that which forms or serves to form. **2.** *Elect.* a tool for giving a coil or winding a specified shape. **3.** a member of a specified form, in a high school: *sixth-former; first-former.*

**formerly** /'fɔməli/, *adv.* in time past; heretofore; of old.

**formica** /fɔ'maɪkə/, *n.* a thermosetting plastic usu. used in transparent or printed sheets as a chemical-proof and heat-resistant covering for furniture, wall panels, etc. [Trademark]

**formic acid** /fɔmɪk 'æsəd/, *n.* a colourless irritant liquid, HCOOH, once obtained from ants and other insects, but now manufactured synthetically; methanoic acid. [L *formīca* ant]

**formicate** /'fɔməkeɪt/, *v.i.,* **-cated, -cating.** to swarm with moving beings, as ants. [L *formīcātus,* pp. of *formīcāre* creep like ants]

**formiciasis** /,fɔməsi'eɪsəs/, *n.* a morbid condition caused by ant bites.

**formidable** /'fɔmədəbəl, fɔ'mɪdəbəl/, *adj.* **1.** that is to be feared or dreaded, esp. in encounters or dealings. **2.** of alarming strength, size, difficulty, etc. **3.** such as to inspire apprehension of defeat or failure. [F, from L *formīdābilis* causing fear] **– formidableness, formidability** /fɔmɪdə'bɪləti/, *n.* **– formidably,** *adv.*

**formless** /'fɔmləs/, *adj.* wanting form or shape; shapeless; without a determinate or regular form. **– formlessly,** *adv.* **– formlessness,** *n.*

**form letter** /'fɔm lɛtə/, *n.* a letter printed, duplicated, or typed, copies of which are sent to a number of people.

**form master** /'– mastə/, *n.* a male teacher in charge of and responsible for the progress of a form.

**form mistress** /'– mɪstrəs/, *n.* a female teacher in charge of a form.

**Formosa** /fɔ'moʊsə/, *n.* former name of **Taiwan.**

**formula** /'fɔmjələ/, *n., pl.* **-las, -lae** /-li/. **1.** a set form of words, as for stating or declaring something definitely or authoritatively, for indicating procedure to be followed, or for prescribed use on some ceremonial occasion. **2.** *Maths.* a rule or principle frequently expressed in algebraic symbols. **3.** a fixed and successful method of doing something: *his book followed the usual formula of sex, sadism, and spying.* **4.** *Chem.* an expression of the constituents of a compound by symbols and figures, as an **empirical formula,** which merely indicates the number of each kind of atom in the molecule, as $CH_2O$, or a **structural formula,** which represents diagrammatically the linkage of each atom in the molecule, as H–O–H. **5.** a recipe or prescription. **6.** one of the sets of specifications to which racing motor cars must conform to classify for particular races. **7.** a formal statement of religious doctrine. [L, diminutive of *forma* FORM, *n.*]

**formularise** /'fɔmjələraɪz/, *v.t.,* **-rised, -rising.** →**formulate.** Also, **formularize. – formularisation** /fɔmjələraɪ'zeɪʃən/, *n.*

**formulary** /'fɔmjələri/, *n., pl.* **-ries,** *adj.* *–n.* **1.** a collection or system of formulas. **2.** a set form of words; formula. **3.** a book containing a comprehensive guide to drugs and medicines, and their prescription.

**formulate** /'fɔmjəleɪt/, *v.t.,* **-lated, -lating. 1.** to express in precise form; state definitely or systematically. **2.** to reduce to or express in a formula. **– formulation** /fɔmjə'leɪʃən/, *n.* **– formulator,** *n.*

**formulise** /'fɔmjəlaɪz/, *v.t.,* **-lised, -lising.** →**formulate.** Also, **formulize. – formulisation** /fɔmjəlaɪ'zeɪʃən/, *n.* **– formuliser,** *n.*

**formulism** /'fɔmjəlɪzəm/, *n.* **1.** adherence to or systematic use of formulas. **2.** a system of formulas. **– formulistic** /fɔmjə'lɪstɪk/, *adj.*

**formwork** /'fɔmwɜk/, *n.* (in building) the temporary structure into which concrete is poured which defines its shape once it has cured. Also, **forms.**

**formyl** /'fɔməl/, *n.* the radical, HCO, derived from formic acid; methanoyl. [FORM(IC ACID) + -YL]

**fornicate** /'fɔnəkeɪt/, *v.i.,* **-cated, -cating.** to commit fornication. [LL *fornicātus,* pp. of *fornicārī,* from L *fornix* (underground) brothel, arch, vault] **– fornicator,** *n.*

**fornication** /fɔnə'keɪʃən/, *n.* **1.** voluntary sexual intercourse between unmarried persons. **2.** *Bible.* **a.** adultery. **b.** idolatry.

**fornix** /'fɔnɪks/, *n., pl.* **-nices** /-nəsiz/. any of various arched or vaulted structures, as an arching fibrous formation in the brain. [L: arch, vault]

**forsake** /fə'seɪk/, *v.t.*, **-sook, -saken, -saking. 1.** to desert or abandon: *forsake one's friends.* **2.** to give up or renounce (a habit, way of life, etc.). [ME *forsake(n)*, OE *forsacan* deny, give up, from *for-* FOR- + *sacan* dispute]

**forsaken** /fə'seɪkən/, *v.* **1.** past participle of **forsake.** *-adj.* **2.** deserted; abandoned; forlorn. **-forsakenly,** *adv.* **-forsakenness,** *n.*

**forsook** /fə'sʊk/, *v.* past tense of **forsake.**

**forsooth** /fə'suθ/, *adv. Archaic.* in truth; in fact; indeed (now used ironically or derisively). [ME *forsooth(e)*, OE *forsōth* for sooth]

**forsterite** /'fɒstəraɪt/, *n.* a mineral of the olivine group, a silicate of magnesium, $Mg_2SiO_4$, occurring usu. as white, greenish, or yellowish grains in basic igneous rocks. [named after J. R. *Forster,* 1729-98, German naturalist. See -ITE[1]]

**forswear** /fɔ'swɛə/, *v.*, **-swore, -sworn, -swearing.** *-v.t.* **1.** to reject or renounce upon oath or with protestations. **2.** to deny upon oath or with strong asseveration. **3.** to perjure (oneself). *-v.i.* **4.** to swear falsely; commit perjury. [ME *forsweren,* OE *forswerian;* see FOR-, SWEAR] **-forswearer,** *n.*

**forsworn** /fɔ'swɔn/, *v.* **1.** past participle of **forswear.** *-adj.* **2.** perjured.

**forsythia** /fɔ'saɪθiə/, *n.* any shrub of the genus *Forsythia,* native to China and south-eastern Europe, species of which are much cultivated for their showy yellow flowers appearing before the leaves in early spring. [NL, named after W. *Forsyth,* 1737-1804, English horticulturist]

**fort** /fɔt/, *n.* **1.** a strong or fortified place; any armed place surrounded by defensive works and occupied by troops; a fortification; a fortress. **2.** (in North America) a trading post. **3. hold the fort,** to maintain the existing position or state of affairs. [F, from L *fortis* strong]

**fort.,** **1.** fortification. **2.** fortified.

**fortalice** /'fɔtələs/, *n.* a small fort; an outwork. [ME, from ML *fortalitia, fortalitium,* from L *fortis* strong]

**forte**[1] /'fɔteɪ/ *for def. 1;* /fɔt/ *for def. 2, n.* **1.** a strong point, as of a person; that in which one excels. **2.** the stronger part of a sword blade between the middle and the hilt (opposed to *foible*). [F *fort,* n. use of *fort,* adj. See FORT]

**forte**[2] /'fɔteɪ/, *adv.* **1.** (a musical direction) loudly (opposed to *piano*). *-adj.* **2.** loud; forceful. *-n.* **3.** a passage that is loud and forcible, or is intended to be so. [It., from L *fortis* strong]

**forte piano** /– pi'anoʊ/, *adv.* (a musical direction) loud and then immediately soft.

**fortepiano** /fɔteɪpi'ænoʊ/, *n.* a small-toned keyboard instrument, a forerunner of the pianoforte which, unlike a harpsichord, allowed gradations of loudness as the keys were struck more forcibly.

**fortescue** /'fɔtəskju/, *n.* a small brown-banded fish of the Scorpion family, *Centropogon australis,* having spiny fins and spines on the sides of the head capable of inflicting a painful wound.

**forth** /fɔθ/, *adv.* **1.** forwards; onwards or outwards in place or space. **2.** onwards in time, in order, or in a series: *from that day forth.* **3.** out, as from concealment or inaction; into view or consideration. **4.** away, as from a place or country; abroad. **5. and so forth,** and so on; and others; et cetera. *-prep.* **6.** *Archaic.* out of; forth from. [ME and OE, c. G *fort;* akin to FURTHER]

**forthcoming** /'fɔθkʌmɪŋ/, *adj.* **1.** coming forth, or about to come forth; about to appear; approaching in time. **2.** ready or available when required or expected. *-n.* **3.** a coming forth; appearance.

**forthright** /'fɔθraɪt/, *adj.* **1.** going straight to the point; outspoken. **2.** proceeding in a straight course; direct; straightforward. *-adv.* **3.** straight or directly forward; in a direct manner. **4.** *Archaic.* straightaway; at once; immediately. *-n.* **5.** *Archaic.* a straight course or path. **-forthrightness,** *n.*

**forthwith** /fɔθ'wɪθ, -'wɪð/, *adv.* **1.** immediately; at once; without delay. **2.** as soon as can reasonably be expected.

**fortieth** /'fɔtiəθ/, *adj.* **1.** next after the thirty-ninth. **2.** being one of forty equal parts. *-n.* **3.** a fortieth part, esp. of one ($\frac{1}{40}$). **4.** the fortieth member of a series.

**fortification** /fɔtəfə'keɪʃən/, *n.* **1.** the act of fortifying or strengthening. **2.** that which fortifies or protects. **3.** the art or science of constructing defensive military works. **4.** (*oft. pl.*) a military work constructed for the purpose of strengthening a position; fortified place; fort; castle.

**fortify** /'fɔtəfaɪ/, *v.*, **-fied, -fying.** *-v.t.* **1.** to strengthen against attack; surround with defences; provide with defensive military works; protect with fortifications. **2.** to furnish with a means of resisting force or standing strain, wear, etc. **3.** to make strong; impart strength or vigour to, as the body. **4.** to enrich and increase the effectiveness as of food, by adding further ingredients. **5.** to strengthen mentally or morally. **6.** to confirm or corroborate. **7.** to add alcohol to (wines, etc.) to stop fermentation or to increase the strength. *-v.i.* **8.** to set up defensive works; erect fortifications. [ME *fortifie(n),* from F *fortifier,* from LL *fortificāre,* from *forti-* strong + *-ficāre* make] **-fortifiable,** *adj.* **-fortifier,** *n.*

**Fortin's barometer** /fɔtənz bə'rɒmətə/, *n.* a type of mercury barometer for making accurate readings of the pressure of the atmosphere; contains an adjustable mercury cistern. [named after J. *Fortin,* 1750-1831, French physicist]

**fortis** /'fɔtəs/, *adj., n., pl.* **-tes** /-tiz/. *-adj.* **1.** pronounced with considerable muscular tension and breath pressure, resulting in a strong fricative or explosive sound: *f* and *p* are fortis, as compared to lenis *v* and *b.* *-n.* **2.** a fortis consonant. [L: strong]

**fortissimo** /fɔ'tɪsɪmoʊ/, *adv.* **1.** (a musical direction) very loudly. *-adj.* **2.** very loud. [It., superl. of *forte.* See FORTE[2]]

**fortitude** /'fɔtətʃud/, *n.* patient courage under affliction, privation, or temptation; moral strength or endurance. [L *fortitūdo*]

**fortitudinous** /fɔtə'tjudənəs/, *adj.* having fortitude.

**fortnight** /'fɔtnaɪt/, *n.* the space of fourteen nights and days; two weeks. [ME *fourtenight,* contraction of OE *fēowertēne niht* fourteen nights]

**fortnightly** /'fɔtnaɪtli/, *adj., adv., n., pl.* **-lies.** *-adj.* **1.** occurring or appearing once a fortnight. *-adv.* **2.** once a fortnight. *-n.* **3.** a periodical issued every two weeks.

**FORTRAN** /'fɔtræn/, *n.* a computer language for scientific calculations in which instructions are expressed in an algebraic notation. Also, **Fortran.** [FOR(MULA) + TRAN(SLATION)]

**fortress** /'fɔtrəs/, *n.* **1.** a large fortified place; a fort or group of forts, often including a town. **2.** any place of security. *-v.t.* **3.** *Rare.* to furnish with or defend by a fortress: *the city is heavily fortressed.* [ME *forterresse,* from OF, from *fort* strong]

**Fortress Australia** /fɔtrəs ɒs'treɪljə/, *n.* a defence policy which states that in time of war Australia must be defended in its approaches, and which is therefore opposed to having defence forces stationed outside Australia (opposed to *forward defence*).

**fortuitism** /fɔ'tjuətɪzəm/, *n.* the doctrine or belief that adaptations in nature come about by chance, and not by design. **-fortuitist,** *n., adj.*

**fortuitous** /fɔ'tjuətəs/, *adj.* happening or produced by chance; accidental. [L *fortuītus* casual] **-fortuitously,** *adv.* **-fortuitousness,** *n.*

**fortuity** /fɔ'tjuəti/, *n., pl.* **-ties. 1.** fortuitous character; the fact of being accidental or casual. **2.** accident or chance. **3.** an accidental occurrence.

**fortunate** /'fɔtʃənət/, *adj.* **1.** having good fortune; receiving good from uncertain or unexpected sources; lucky. **2.** bringing or presaging good fortune; resulting favourably; auspicious. [ME, from L *fortūnātus,* pp., made prosperous or happy] **-fortunately,** *adv.* **-fortunateness,** *n.*

**fortune** /'fɔtʃən/, *n., v.*, **-tuned, -tuning.** *-n.* **1.** position in life as determined by wealth: *to make one's fortune, a man of fortune.* **2.** amount or stock of wealth. **3.** great wealth; ample stock of wealth. **4.** chance; luck. **5.** (*oft. pl.*) that which falls or is to fall to one as his portion in life or in any particular proceeding. **6.** lot; destiny. **7.** (*oft. cap.*) chance personified, commonly regarded as a goddess distributing arbitrarily or capriciously the lots of life. **8.** good luck; success; prosperity. **9.** *Colloq.* a person of wealth, esp. a woman; an heiress. **10. tell someone's fortune,** to profess to foretell coming events in a person's life. [ME, from F, from L *fortūna* chance, luck, fortune] **-fortuneless,** *adj.*

**fortune cookie** /'– kuki/, *n.* a thin layer of dough folded and baked around a slip of paper on which words are printed offering pithy comment or predicting the future; associated principally with the Chinese.

**fortune-hunter** /ˈfɔtʃən-hʌntə/, *n.* one who seeks to win a fortune, esp. through marriage. – **fortune-hunting,** *adj.*

**fortune-teller** /ˈfɔtʃən-tɛlə/, *n.* one who professes to tell people what will happen in the future. – **fortune-telling,** *adj., n.*

**forty**[1] /ˈfɔti/, *n., pl.* **-ties,** *adj.* –*n.* **1.** a cardinal number, ten times four. **2.** a symbol for this number, as 40 or XL or XXXX. **3.** (*pl.*) the numbers from 40 to 49 of a series, usu. with reference to the years of a person's age, or the years of a century, esp. the 20th. **4. roaring forties,** those parts of the oceans in the southern hemisphere between latitudes 40° and 60° where north-westerly winds are constant throughout the year; noted for their gales. –*adj.* **5.** amounting to forty in number. [ME *fourti,* OE *fēowertig,* from *fēower* four + *-tig* -TY[1]]

**forty**[2] /ˈfɔti/, *n. Colloq.* a thief; scoundrel. [from the Fitzroy *Forty,* a Melbourne gang of thieves named after Ali Baba and the Forty thieves, in *The Arabian Nights*]

**forty-five** /fɔti-ˈfaɪv/, *n.* a gramophone record which revolves forty-five times a minute when being played.

**forty winks** /– ˈwɪŋks/, *n. pl.* a short nap, esp. in the daytime.

**forum** /ˈfɔrəm/, *n., pl.* **forums, fora** /ˈfɔrə/. **1.** the marketplace or public square of an ancient Roman city, the centre of judicial and other business and a place of assembly for the people. **2.** a court or tribunal: *the forum of public opinion.* **3.** an assembly for the discussion of questions of public interest. [L]

**forward** /ˈfɔwəd/; *for def. 11 also* /ˈfɔrəd/, *adj.* **1.** directed towards a point in advance, moving ahead; onward: *a forward motion.* **2.** being in a condition of advancement; well-advanced. **3.** ready, prompt, or eager. **4.** presumptuous, pert, or bold. **5.** situated in the front or forepart. **6.** lying in advance; fore. **7.** of or pertaining to the future: *forward buying.* **8.** radical or extreme, as persons or opinions. –*n.* **9.** *Soccer, Hockey, etc.* a player stationed in advance of other members of his team; any player in the forward line. **10. a.** *Aus. Rules.* one of six players occupying the three full-forward and three half-forward positions who constitute the forward line, the main attacking force of the team. **b.** *Rugby Union.* one of the eight players in a team who form the scrum, stand in line-outs, and act as a pack in rushing the ball forward and getting it to the three-quarters. **c.** *Rugby League.* one of six players with similar functions. –*adv.* **11.** towards the bow or the front part of a ship or aeroplane. **12.** forwards. –*v.t.* **13.** to send forward; transmit, esp. to a new address: *to forward a letter.* **14.** to advance or help onwards; hasten; promote. **15.** *Bookbinding.* to prepare (a book) for the finisher. See **forwarding.** [ME and OE *for(e)ward.* See FORE[1], -WARD] – **forwardly,** *adv.*

**forward defence** /– dəˈfɛns/, *n.* a defence policy which supports the stationing of Australian forces at strategic points in the region, thereby averting any threat to Australia, and which relies necessarily on the involvement of allies.

**forward delivery** /– dəˈlɪvəri/, *n.* delivery (of parcels, goods, etc.) at a future date.

**forwarder** /ˈfɔwədə/, *n.* one who forwards or sends forward.

**forward exchange** /fɔwəd əksˈtʃeɪndʒ/, *n.* foreign currency bought or sold for future delivery.

**forwarding** /ˈfɔwədɪŋ/, *n.* **1.** *Bookbinding.* a stage which involves stitching, fitting the back, pasting, etc., just before the pages are placed in the completed book cover. **2.** the act of one who forwards; the business of a forwarding agent.

**forwarding agent** /ˈ– eɪdʒənt/, *n.* an agent who organises the collection, forwarding and delivery of goods.

**forward line** /ˈfɔwəd laɪn/, *n. Soccer, Hockey, etc.* the five attacking players of a team; outside left, outside right, centre-forward, inside left, and inside right.

**forwardness** /ˈfɔwədnəs/, *n.* **1.** over-readiness to push oneself forward; presumption; boldness; lack of due modesty. **2.** cheerful readiness; promptness; eagerness. **3.** the condition of being forward or in advance.

**forward pass** /fɔwəd ˈpas/, *n.* (in Rugby football) a pass in which the ball is illegally thrown towards the opponent's goal.

**forward pocket** /– ˈpɒkət/, *n. Aus. Rules.* **1.** either of the two positions on either side of full forward. **2.** a player occupying such a position.

**forward quotation** /– kwoʊˈteɪʃən/, *n.* the price quoted on a forward delivery. Also, **forward price.**

**forward rate** /ˈ– reɪt/, *n.* the price of forward exchange.

**forward roll** /– ˈroʊl/, *n.* a type of somersault usual in gymnastics in which the body pivots while the back of the neck and usu. the hands briefly touch the ground. Also, **neck roll.**

**forwards** /ˈfɔwədz/, *adv.* **1.** towards or at a place, point, or time in advance; onwards; ahead: *to move forwards, from this day forwards, to look forwards.* **2.** towards the front. **3.** out; forth; into view or consideration. Also (esp. in figurative senses), **forward.**

**forward sell** /fɔwəd ˈsɛl/, *v.t.* to sell the wool from a flock of sheep before it is shorn.

**forward short leg,** *n. Cricket.* **1.** a fielding position in front of the wicket on the leg side close to the batsman. **2.** a fielder in this position.

**forward store condition,** *n.* the condition of an animal which is in good store condition, but needs final fattening, before being slaughtered.

**forwent** /fɔˈwɛnt/, *v.* past tense of **forgo.**

**forwhy** /fɔˈwaɪ/, *Archaic.* (*sometimes joc.*). –*adv.* **1.** why. –*conj.* **2.** because.

**forzando** /fɔtˈsændoʊ/, *adv., adj. Music.* →**sforzando.** [It., ger. of *forzare* force]

**Fosbury flop** /fɒzbəri ˈflɒp/, *n.* a style of high jumping in which the athlete clears the jump facing upwards with his back to the bar, and lands on his back on the mat. [named after *Fosbury,* an American athlete]

**fossa** /ˈfɒsə/, *n., pl.* **fossae** /ˈfɒsi/. **1.** *Anat.* a pit, cavity, or depression in a bone, etc. **2.** the most primitive member of the civet family, *Cryptoprocta ferox,* of Madagascar. [L: ditch, trench]

**fosse** /fɒs/, *n.* **1.** a moat or defensive ditch in a fortification, usu. filled with water. **2.** any ditch, trench, or canal. Also, **foss.** [ME, from F, from L *fossa* ditch]

**fossick** /ˈfɒsɪk/, *v.i.* **1. a.** to search unsystematically or in a small way for mineral deposits, usu. over ground previously worked by others. **b.** to search similarly for small items: *to fossick through a drawer for scissors.* **2.** to search for an object by which to make gain: *to fossick for clients.* **3.** *Mining.* to undermine another's digging. –*v.t.* **4.** to dig, hunt (fol. by *out*). [Cornish d. *fossick* troublesome person, *fussick* bustle about, from FUSS + *-ick,* var. of -OCK] – **fossicker,** *n.*

**fossil** /ˈfɒsəl/, *n.* **1.** any remains, impression, or trace of an animal or plant of a former geological age, as a skeleton or a footprint. **2.** *Colloq.* an outdated or old-fashioned person or thing. **3.** *Obs.* anything dug out of the earth. –*adj.* **4.** of the nature of a fossil: *fossil insects.* **5.** obtained from below the earth's surface: *fossil salt.* **6.** belonging to a past epoch or discarded system; antiquated. [L *fossilis* dug up; replacing earlier *fossile,* from F] – **fossil-like,** *adj.*

**fossil fuel** /ˈ– fjul/, *n.* the remains of organisms (or their products) embedded in the earth, with high carbon and/or hydrogen contents, which are used by man as fuels; esp. coal, oil and natural gas.

**fossiliferous** /fɒsəˈlɪfərəs/, *adj.* bearing or containing fossils, as rocks or strata.

**fossilise** /ˈfɒsəlaɪz/, *v.,* **-lised, -lising.** –*v.t.* **1.** *Geol.* to convert into a fossil; replace organic substances with mineral in the remains of an organism. **2.** to change as if into mere lifeless remains or traces of the past. **3.** to make rigidly antiquated, as persons, ideas, etc. –*v.i.* **4.** to become a fossil. Also, **fossilize.** – **fossilisation** /fɒsəlaɪˈzeɪʃən/, *n.*

**fossorial** /fɒˈsɔriəl/, *adj.* **1.** digging or burrowing. **2.** adapted for digging, as the hands, feet, and skeleton of moles, armadillos, and aardvarks. [LL *fossōrius* (from L *fossor* digger) + -AL[1]]

**foster** /ˈfɒstə/, *v.t.* **1.** to promote the growth or development of; further; encourage: *to foster foreign trade.* **2.** to bring up or rear, as a foster-child. **3.** to care for or cherish. **4.** to place (a child) in a foster home. **5.** *Obs.* to feed or nourish. –*n.* **6.** a foster-child. [ME; OE *fōster* nourishment, *fōstrian* nourish; akin to FOOD] – **fosterer,** *n.*

**fosterage** /ˈfɒstərɪdʒ/, *n.* **1.** the act of fostering or rearing another's child as one's own, esp. as a temporary measure until the child is claimed by the natural parent or adopted. **2.** the condition of being a foster-child. **3.** the act of promoting or encouraging.

**foster-brother** /ˈfɒstə-brʌðə/, *n.* a boy brought up with another child of different parents.

**foster care** /ˈfɒstə kɛə/, *n.* the upbringing or the supervision of the upbringing of foster-children, in a private home or a public institution.

**foster-child** /ˈfɒstə-tʃaɪld/, *n., pl.* **-children.** a child brought up by someone not its own mother or father.

**foster-daughter** /ˈfɒstə-dɔtə/, *n.* a girl brought up like one's own daughter, though not such by birth.

**foster-father** /ˈfɒstə-faðə/, *n.* one who takes the place of a father in raising a child.

**foster home** /ˈfɒstə hoʊm/, *n.* a household in which a child is raised by a person or persons other than its natural father or mother.

**fosterling** /ˈfɒstəlɪŋ/, *n.* a foster-child. [ME; OE *fōstorling.* See FOSTER, *n.*, -LING[1]]

**foster-mother** /ˈfɒstə-mʌðə/, *n.* **1.** a woman who takes the place of the mother in bringing up a child. **2.** a nurse.

**foster-parent** /ˈfɒstə-pɛərənt/, *n.* a foster-father or foster-mother.

**foster-sister** /ˈfɒstə-sɪstə/, *n.* a girl brought up with another child of different parents.

**foster-son** /ˈfɒstə-sʌn/, *n.* a boy brought up like one's own son, though not such by birth.

**fother** /ˈfɒðə/, *v.i.* **1.** to stop a leak in a wooden hull by covering it with a sail or tarpaulin containing a thrumming of rope yarns and oakum. *–v.t.* **2.** to cover (a sail, etc.) with such a thrumming. [? D *voederen* to line, or LG *fodern* to line]

**Foucault current** /fukoʊ ˈkʌrənt/, *n.* →**eddy current.**

**Foucault pendulum** /– ˈpɛndʒələm/, *n.* a long thin pendulum which demonstrates the rotation of the earth by changing its plane of oscillation during the course of a day. [demonstrated by Jean Bernard Léon *Foucault,* 1819-68, French physicist]

**foudroyant** /fuˈdrɔɪənt/, *adj.* **1.** striking as with lightning; sudden and overwhelming in effect; stunning; dazzling. **2.** *Pathol.* (of disease) beginning in a sudden and severe form. [F, ppr. of *foudroyer* strike with lightning, from *foudre* lightning, from L *fulgur*]

**fought** /fɔt/, *v.* past tense and past participle of **fight.**

**foul** /faʊl/, *adj.* **1.** grossly offensive to the senses; disgustingly loathsome; noisome: *a foul smell.* **2.** charged with or characterised by offensive or noisome matter: *foul air.* **3.** filthy or dirty, as places, vessels, or clothes. **4.** muddy, as a road. **5.** clogged or obstructed with foreign matter: *a foul chimney.* **6.** unfavourable or stormy, as weather. **7.** contrary, as the wind. **8.** grossly offensive in a moral sense. **9.** abominable, wicked, or vile, as deeds, crime, slander, etc. **10.** scurrilous, profane, or obscene, as language. **11.** contrary to the rules or established usages, as of a sport or game; unfair. **12.** *Sport.* pertaining to a foul ball; an infringement of a rule. **13.** in collision or obstructing contact: *a ship foul of a rock.* **14.** entangled, caught, or jammed: *a foul anchor.* **15.** abounding in errors or in marks of correction, as a printer's proof. **16.** not fair; ugly or unattractive. *–adv.* **17.** in a foul manner; foully; unfairly. **18. fall foul of, a.** (of ships) to collide with. **b.** to quarrel with; come into conflict with. *–n.* **19.** that which is foul. **20.** a collision or entanglement. **21.** a violation of the rules of a sport or game. *–v.t.* **22.** to make foul; defile; soil. **23.** to clog or obstruct, as a chimney or the bore of a gun. **24.** to collide with. **25.** to cause to become entangled or caught, as a rope. **26.** to defile; dishonour; disgrace. **27.** *Naut.* to encumber (a ship's bottom) with seaweed, barnacles, etc. **28. foul up,** *Colloq.* to bungle or spoil; to cause confusion. *–v.i.* **29.** to become foul. **30.** *Naut.* to come into collision, as two boats. **31.** to become entangled or clogged: *the rope fouled.* **32.** *Sport.* to make a foul play; give a foul blow. [ME; OE *fūl,* c. G *faul;* akin to L *pūs* pus, *pūtēre* to stink] – **foully,** *adv.*

**foulard** /fuˈlad/, *n.* a soft lightweight silk or rayon of twill weave with printed design, for ties, trimmings, etc. [F, from Swiss F *foulat* fulled cloth, c. F *fouler* to full, from L *fullāre*]

**foul-minded** /ˈfaʊl-maɪndəd/, *adj.* having unclean thoughts. – **foul-mindedness,** *n.*

**foul-mouthed** /ˈfaʊl-maʊðd/, *adj.* using scurrilous, profane, or obscene language; given to filthy or abusive speech.

**foulness** /ˈfaʊlnəs/, *n.* **1.** the state or quality of being foul. **2.** that which is foul; foul matter; filth. **3.** wickedness. [ME; OE *fūlness.* See FOUL, *adj.*, -NESS]

**foul play** /faʊl ˈpleɪ/, *n.* **1.** any unfair or treacherous dealing, often such as involves murder. **2.** unfair conduct in a game.

**fouls** /faʊlz/, *n.* an infection of the feet of cattle causing a foul-smelling inflammation between the toes and round the coronary band.

**foul-up** /ˈfaʊl-ʌp/, *n.* a condition of confusion.

**found**[1] /faʊnd/, *v.* **1.** past tense and past participle of **find. 2. all found,** inclusive of necessary provisions, etc.; with everything provided. [ME; OE *funde, fundon* pt., *funden* pp.]

**found**[2] /faʊnd/, *v.t.* **1.** to set up or establish on a firm basis or for enduring existence: *to found a dynasty.* **2.** to lay the lowest part of, fix, or build (a structure) on a firm base or ground: *a house founded upon a rock.* **3.** to base or ground (fol. by *on* or *upon*): *a story founded on fact.* **4.** to afford a basis or ground for. *–v.i.* **5.** to be founded or based (fol. by *on* or *upon*). **6.** to base one's opinion (fol. by *on* or *upon*). [ME *founde(n),* from OF *fonder,* from L *fundāre* lay the bottom of, found]

**found**[3] /faʊnd/, *v.t.* **1.** to melt and pour (metal, glass, etc.) into a mould. **2.** to form or make (an article) of molten material in a mould; cast. [ME *fond(en),* from OF *fondre* melt, cast, from L *fundere* pour, melt, cast]

**foundation** /faʊnˈdeɪʃən/, *n.* **1.** that on which something is founded. **2.** the basis or ground of anything. **3.** the natural or prepared ground or base on which some structure rests. **4.** the lowest division of a building, wall, or the like, usu. of masonry and partly or wholly below the surface of the ground. **5.** the act of founding, setting up, establishing, etc. **6.** the state of being founded. **7.** a donation or legacy for the support of an institution; an endowment. **8.** an endowed institution. **9.** →**foundation cream.** *–adj.* **10.** of or pertaining to one associated with the beginning: *a foundation member.*

**foundation cream** /ˈ– krim/, *n.* a cosmetic cream or lotion used as a base for powder or facial make-up.

**foundation garment** /ˈ– gamənt/, *n.* an undergarment, as a corset, corselet or girdle, worn by women to give support or contours to the figure.

**foundation stone** /ˈ– stoʊn/, *n.* **1.** one of the stones forming the foundation of a building. **2.** a stone, set in a building near ground level, usu. bearing the date of setting and some commemorative inscription.

**founder**[1] /ˈfaʊndə/, *n.* one who founds or establishes. [FOUND[2] + -ER[1]]

**founder**[2] /ˈfaʊndə/, *v.i.* **1.** to fill with water and sink, as a ship. **2.** to fall or sink down, as buildings, ground, etc. **3.** to suffer wreck, or fail utterly. **4.** to stumble, break down, or go lame, as a horse. **5.** *Vet. Sci.* (of a horse) to suffer from founder. *–v.t.* **6.** to cause to fill with water and sink, as a ship. **7.** *Vet. Sci.* to cause (a horse, etc.) to break down, go lame, or suffer from founder. *–n.* **8.** *Vet. Sci.* →**laminitis.** [ME *foundren,* from OF *fondrer,* from L *fundus* bottom]

**founder**[3] /ˈfaʊndə/, *n.* one who founds or casts metal, etc. [FOUND[3] + -ER[1]]

**founders' shares** /ˈfaʊndəz ʃɛəz/, *n.pl.* shares created in order to remunerate the founder or promoter of a company; often receiving a large share of the net profit after certain fixed dividends have been paid on the ordinary and other classes of stock.

**founders' type** /ˈ– taɪp/, *n.* printing type cast in individual characters for setting by hand.

**founding father** /ˌfaʊndɪŋ ˈfaðə/, *n.* one of the originators of an organisation, first settlers of a town, etc.

**foundling** /ˈfaʊndlɪŋ/, *n.* an infant found abandoned; a child without a parent or guardian. [ME *found(e)ling,* from *founde(n),* pp. of FIND, *v.* + -LING[1]]

**found object** /ˌfaʊnd ˈɒbdʒɛkt/, *n.* an object of any kind, as a piece of household debris, chosen by an artist for inclusion in an assemblage where it gains a new significance from its effect in the whole composition.

**foundry** /ˈfaʊndri/, *n., pl.* **-dries.** **1.** an establishment for the production of castings, in which molten metal is poured into moulds to shape the castings. **2.** the founding of metal, etc. **3.** things made by founding; castings. [F *fonderie,* from *fondre* FOUND³]

**foundry proof** /ˈ– pruf/, *n.* a proof pulled for a final checking before printing plates are made.

**fount¹** /faʊnt/, *n.* **1.** a spring of water; fountain. **2.** a source or origin. [short for FOUNTAIN]

**fount²** /fɒnt/, *n.* →**font².** [F *fonte,* from *fondre* melt, cast. See FOUND³]

**fountain** /ˈfaʊntn/, *n.* **1.** a spring or source of water; the source or head of a stream. **2.** the source or origin of anything. **3.** a jet or stream of water (or other liquid) made by mechanical means to spout or rise from an opening or structure, as to afford water for use, or to cool the air, or to serve for ornament. **4.** a structure for discharging such a jet or a number of jets, often an elaborate or artistic work with basins, sculptures, etc. **5.** a soda fountain. **6.** a reservoir for a liquid to be supplied gradually or continuously. [late ME *fontayne,* from OF *fontaine,* from LL *fontāna,* properly fem. of L *fontānus* of or from a spring] – **fountainless,** *adj.* – **fountain-like,** *adj.*

**fountainhead** /ˈfaʊntnhɛd/, *n.* **1.** a fountain or spring from which a stream flows; the head or source of a stream. **2.** a primary source.

**fountain pen** /ˈfaʊntn pɛn/, *n.* a pen with a reservoir for supplying ink to the point of the nib.

**four** /fɔ/, *n.* **1.** a cardinal number, three plus one. **2.** a symbol of this number, 4 or IV or IIII. **3.** a set of this many persons or things. **4.** →**foursome. 5.** a playing card, etc., with four pips. **6.** *Rowing.* **a.** a crew of four oarsmen. **b.** a racing boat for a crew of four and sometimes a cox. **7.** *Cricket.* a hit scoring four runs, when the ball is hit to the boundary, but first touches the ground inside the boundary. **8. on all fours,** on the hands and feet (or knees). **9. on all fours with,** corresponding exactly to. *–adj.* **10.** amounting to four in number. [ME; OE *fēower,* c. D and G *vier* four; akin to L *quattuor,* Gk *téttares*]

**four-by** /ˈfɔ-bi/, *n. Colloq.* →**four-by-two¹.**

**four-by-two¹** /fɔ-bi-ˈtu/, *n.* **1.** a piece of wood, the cross section of which measured about four inches by two inches. **2.** a small piece of cloth attached to a pull-through to clean a rifle.

**four-by-two²** /fɔ-bi-ˈtu/, *n. Colloq.* a Jew. [rhyming slang]

**four-by-two³** /fɔ-bi-ˈtu/, *n. Prison Colloq.* a prison warder. [rhyming slang, *four-by-two* screw (def. 12)]

**fourchette** /fɔˈʃɛt/, *n.* **1.** *Anat.* the fold of skin which forms the posterior margin of the vulva. **2.** *Ornith.* the furcula or united clavicles of a bird; the wishbone of a fowl. **3.** *Zool.* the frog of an animal's foot. **4.** a strip of leather or fabric joining front and back sections of a glove finger. [F, diminutive of *fourche,* from L *furca* fork]

**four-colour** /ˈfɔ-kʌlə/, *adj.* of or pertaining to a process of colour reproduction in photography or printing in which four colours (magenta, green-blue, yellow and black) are variously combined.

**four-dimensional** /fɔ-dəˈmɛnʃənəl, -daɪ-/, *adj.* exhibiting or requiring four dimensions for unique determination, esp. the three spatial dimensions and the fourth temporal dimension.

**four-dimensional continuum** /– kənˈtɪnjuəm/, *n.* →**continuum** (def. 3).

**four-eyes** /ˈfɔr-aɪz/, *n.* **1.** any of several species of fishes with eyes adapted for seeing above and below water, esp. the genus *Anableps.* **2.** *Colloq.* a person who wears glasses.

**four-flush** /ˈfɔ-flʌʃ/, *n.* **1.** *Poker.* four cards of a possible flush, which, with one card of a different suit, make up a hand; an imperfect flush. **2.** *Colloq.* a bluff. *–v.i.* **3.** to act as a four-flusher.

**four-flusher** /fɔ-flʌʃə/, *n. Colloq.* one who makes pretensions that he cannot or does not bear out.

**fourfold** /ˈfɔfoʊld/, *adj.* **1.** comprising four parts or members. **2.** four times as great or as much. *–adv.* **3.** in fourfold measure.

**four foot** /ˈfɔ fʊt/, *n.* the space between railway lines.

**four-footed** /ˈfɔ-fʊtəd/, *adj.* having four feet.

**four-four time** /fɔ-ˈfɔ taɪm/, *n.* →**quadruple time.**

**four-handed** /ˈfɔ-hændəd/, *adj.* **1.** involving four hands or players, as a game at cards. **2.** intended for four hands, as a piece of music for the piano. **3.** having four hands, or four feet adapted for use as hands; quadrumanous.

**Fourier analysis** /furiə əˈnæləsəs/, *n.* the decomposition of any periodic function such as a complex sound or electromagnetic wave-form into the sum of a number of sine and cosine functions. [named after Jean Baptiste Joseph *Fourier,* 1768-1830, French mathematician and physicist]

**Fourierism** /ˈfuriərɪzəm/, *n.* the communal social system propounded by François Marie Charles Fourier, under which society was to be organised into phalanxes or associations, each large enough for all industrial and social requirements. – **Fourierist, Fourierite,** *n.* – **Fourieristic** /furiəˈrɪstɪk/, *adj.*

**four-in-hand** /fɔr-ɪn-ˈhænd/, *n.* **1.** a long scarf or tie to be tied in a flat slipknot with the ends left hanging. **2.** a vehicle drawn by four horses and driven by one person. **3.** a team of four horses. *–adj.* **4.** having to do with a four-in-hand.

**four-leaf clover** /fɔ-lif ˈkloʊvə/, *n.* **1.** a cloverleaf having four leaflets instead of the usual three; it is said to bring good luck. **2.** →**cloverleaf** (def. 2).

**four-legged kangaroo** /fɔ-lɛgəd kæŋgəˈru/, *n.* (*joc.*) a cow, bull, etc.; beast.

**four-letter word** /fɔ-lɛtə ˈwɜd/, *n.* **1.** any of a number of short words, often of four letters, held to be vulgar or offensive because of reference to sex or excrement. **2.** anything which is distasteful or unpleasant: *housework is a four-letter word.*

**four-masted** /ˈfɔ-mastəd/, *adj.* (of a boat) carrying four masts.

**four-o'clock** /fɔr-əˈklɒk/, *n.* **1.** a common garden plant, *Mirabilis jalapa,* with red, white, yellow, or variegated flowers which open late in the afternoon. **2.** →**noisy friar-bird.**

**four of a kind,** *n.* a set of four cards of the same denomination, as four kings, four tens, etc.

**four-on-the-floor** /ˌfɔr-ɒn-ðə-ˈflɔ/, *n. Colloq.* a gearlever situated on the floor of a motor vehicle with four forward gears (opposed to a *column shift*).

**four-poster** /fɔ-ˈpoʊstə/, *n.* a bed with four posts supporting a canopy over the bed, sometimes with curtains.

**fourscore** /ˈfɔskɔ/, *adj.* four times twenty; eighty.

**four-seater** /fɔ-ˈsitə/, *n.* a vehicle seating four people.

**foursome** /ˈfɔsəm/, *n.* **1.** *Golf, etc.* a match played by four persons, two on each side. **2.** a company or set of four. *–adj.* **3.** consisting of four; performed by four persons together. See **eightsome.** [FOUR + -SOME²]

**foursquare** /fɔˈskwɛə/, *adj.* **1.** square. **2.** firm; steady. **3.** frank; blunt. *–adv.* **4.** without equivocation. – **foursquarely,** *adv.* – **foursquareness,** *n.*

**four-stroke** /ˈfɔ-stroʊk/, *adj.* **1.** denoting or pertaining to an internal-combustion engine cycle in which one piston stroke out of every four is a power stroke. **2.** powered by such an engine. *–n.* **3.** a four-stroke engine or vehicle.

**fourteen** /fɔˈtin/, *n.* **1.** a cardinal number, ten plus four. **2.** a symbol for this number, as 14 or XIV or XIIII. *–adj.* **3.** amounting to fourteen in number. [ME *fourtene,* OE *fēowertēne.* See FOUR, -TEEN]

**fourteenth** /fɔˈtinθ/, *adj.* **1.** next after the thirteenth. **2.** being one of fourteen equal parts. *–n.* **3.** a fourteenth part, esp. of one ($\frac{1}{14}$). **4.** the fourteenth member of a series.

**fourth** /fɔθ/, *adj.* **1.** next after the third. **2.** being one of four equal parts. *–n.* **3.** a fourth part, esp. of one ($\frac{1}{4}$). **4.** the fourth member of a series. **5.** *Music.* **a.** a note on the fourth degree from a given note (counted as the first). **b.** the interval between such notes. **c.** the harmonic combination of such notes. [ME; OE *fēo(we)rtha.* See FOUR, -TH²]

**fourth dimension** /– dəˈmɛnʃən/, *n.* the dimension of time, which is required in addition to the three dimensions of space, in order to locate a point in space-time. – **fourth-dimensional,** *adj.*

**fourth estate** /– əsˈteɪt/, *n.* the public press, the newspapers or journalists collectively.

**fourthly** /ˈfɔθli/, *adv.* in the fourth place.

**fourtrella** /fɔˈtrɛlə/, *n. S.A.* →**quadrella.**

**four-wheel** /ˈfɔ-wil/, *adj.* **1.** having four wheels. **2.** pertaining to the arrangement whereby all four wheels of a motor vehicle are connected to the source of power: *four-wheel drive.*

**four-wheel drive** /– 'draɪv/, *n.* **1.** the mechanism which connects all four wheels of a motor vehicle to the source of power. **2.** a motor vehicle which has such a mechanism. *Abbrev:* 4WD

**four-wheeler** /fɔ-'wilə/, *n.* **1.** a four-wheeled vehicle. **2. a.** →**four-wheel drive** (def. 2). **b.** *Colloq.* the driver of a four-wheel drive (def. 2).

**fovea** /'foʊviə/, *n., pl.* **-veae** /-vii/. a small pit or depression in a bone or other structure. [L: small pit] – **foveal,** *adj.*

**fovea centralis** /– sɛn'traləs/, *n.* a small pit or depression at the back of the retina forming the point of sharpest vision. [L]

**foveate** /'foʊviət, -eɪt/, *adj.* having foveae; pitted.

**foveola** /fə'viələ/, *n., pl.* **-lae** /-li/. a small fovea; a very small pit or depression. Also, **foveole.** [NL, diminutive of L *fovea.* See FOVEA]

**foveolate** /fə'viəleɪt, -lət/, *adj.* having foveolae, or very small pits. Also, **foveolated.**

**fowl** /faʊl/, *n., pl.* **fowls,** (*esp. collectively*) **fowl,** *v.* –*n.* **1.** the domestic or barnyard hen or cock (**domestic fowl**), a gallinaceous bird (often designated as *Gallus domesticus*) of the pheasant family, descended from wild species of *Gallus* (**jungle fowl**). **2.** any of various other gallinaceous or similar birds, as the turkey or duck. **3.** (in market and household use) a full-grown domestic fowl for food purposes (as distinguished from a chicken, or young fowl). **4.** the flesh or meat of a domestic fowl. **5.** any bird (now chiefly in combination): *waterfowl, wildfowl.* –*v.i.* **6.** to hunt or take wildfowl. [ME *foule,* OE *fugel,* c. G *Vogel*]

**fowler** /'faʊlə/, *n.* one who hunts, shoots, or snares birds, for sport or for a living.

**fowling** /'faʊlɪŋ/, *n.* the practice or sport of shooting or snaring birds.

**fowling net** /'– nɛt/, *n.* a net for catching birds.

**fowling-piece** /'faʊlɪŋ-pis/, *n.* a shotgun for shooting wildfowl.

**fox** /fɒks/, *n.* **1.** any of certain carnivores of the dog family, Canidae, esp. those constituting the genus *Vulpes,* smaller than the wolves, characterised by pointed muzzle, erect ears, and long, bushy tail. **2.** the fur of this animal. **3.** a cunning or crafty person. **4.** *Naut.* a seizing made by twisting several rope yarns together and rubbing them down. **5.** *Bible.* (sometimes) the jackal. –*v.t.* **6.** *Colloq.* to deceive or trick. **7.** *Obs.* to intoxicate or befuddle. **8.** to cause (papers, etc.) to discolour with reddish brown spots of mildew. **9.** *Colloq.* to fetch (often said to a dog as a command): *Fox it!* **10.** to repair or make (a shoe) with leather or other material applied so as to cover or form part of the upper front. –*v.i.* **11.** to act cunningly or craftily. **12.** (of papers, etc.) to become foxed. [ME and OE, c. G *Fuchs.* See VIXEN] – **foxlike,** *adj.*

fox

**fox-bat** /'fɒks-bæt/, *n.* **1.** →**flying fox. 2.**→**fruit-bat.**

**fox brush** /'fɒks brʌʃ/, *n.* the bushy tail of a fox.

**foxglove** /'fɒksglʌv/, *n.* any plant of the genus *Digitalis,* esp. *D. purpurea,* the common foxglove, a native of Europe, bearing drooping, tubular, purple or white flowers, and leaves that are used medicinally. See **digitalis.** [ME *foxes glove,* OE *foxes glōfa*]

English foxhound

**foxgrape** /'fɒksgreɪp/, *n.* either of two species of grape, *Vitis labrusca* of the northern U.S. or *V. rotundifolia* of the southern U.S., from which various cultivated varieties have been derived.

**foxhole** /'fɒkshoʊl/, *n.* **1.** a fox's lair. **2.** a small pit, usu. for one or two men, used for cover in a battle area.

**foxhound** /'fɒkshaʊnd/, *n.* one of a breed of fleet, keen-scented hounds trained to hunt foxes.

**fox-hunting** /'fɒks-hʌntɪŋ/, *n.* a sport in which the hunters follow a fox that is being pursued by a hound or hounds. – **fox-hunter,** *n.*

**foxie** /'fɒksi/, *n. Colloq.* a fox terrier.

**foxtail** /'fɒksteɪl/, *n.* any of various grasses with soft, brush-like spikes of flower, as species of the genus *Alopecurus.*

**fox terrier** /fɒks 'tɛriə/, *n.* one of a breed of small, active terriers, formerly used to drive foxes from their holes, having a coat which is either smooth and dense or harsh and wiry, according to variety, and is usu. white with dark markings.

smooth-haired fox terrier

**foxtrot** /'fɒkstrɒt/, *n., v.,* **-trotted, -trotting.** –*n.* **1.** a ballroom dance, in 4/4 time, characterised by various combinations of short, quick steps. **2.** a pace, as of a horse, consisting of a series of short steps, as in slackening from a trot to a walk. –*v.i.* **3.** to dance a foxtrot.

**foxy** /'fɒksi/, *adj.,* **foxier, foxiest,** *n.* –*adj.* **1.** foxlike; cunning or crafty. **2.** discoloured or foxed. **3.** yellowish or reddish brown; of the colour of the common red fox. **4.** impaired or defective in quality. **5.** (esp. of a painting) having an excessively reddish tone. **6.** (of wines) having the pronounced flavour natural to native American grape varieties, as that of foxgrape. –*n.* **7.** *Colloq.* a fox terrier. Also, **foxie.**

**foxy lady** /– 'leɪdi/, *n.* a sexy, sophisticated lady of independent spirit.

**foyer** /'fɔɪə/, *n.* **1.** (in theatres and cinemas) the area between the outer lobby and the auditorium. **2.** a hall or anteroom, esp. in a hotel. [F: hearth, fireside (orig. a room to which theatre audiences went for warmth between the acts), from Rom. *focārium,* from L *focus* hearth]

**fp,** forte piano.

**f.p.,** freezing point.

**f.p.s.** /ɛf pi 'ɛs/, *n.* **1.** →**foot-pound-second (system). 2.** feet per second.

**Fr,** **1.** Father. **2.** *Chem.* francium.

**Fr.,** **1.** frater[1]. **2.** French.

**Fra** /fra/, *n.* brother (a title of a friar): *Fra Giovanni.* [It., abbrev. of *frate* brother]

**fracas** /'frækа, -kəs/, *n.* a disorderly noise, disturbance, or fight; uproar. [F, from It. *fracasso,* from *fracassare* smash, from *fra-* (from L *infrā* among) completely + *cassare* (from L *quassāre* to shake)]

**fraction** /'frækʃən/, *n.* **1.** *Maths.* **a.** one or more parts of a unit or whole number; the ratio between any two numbers. **b.** a ratio of algebraic quantities analogous to the arithmetical vulgar fraction and similarly expressed. **2.** a part as distinct from the whole of anything: *only a fraction of the population is literate.* **3.** a piece broken off; fragment or bit. **4.** the act of breaking. **5.** *Eccles.* the breaking of bread in the Eucharistic service. **6.** *Chem.* a component of a chemical mixture, esp. when it has been separated from the mixture. –*v.t.* **7.** to divide into fractions. [ME, from LL *fractio,* from L *frangere* break]

**fractional** /'frækʃənəl/, *adj.* **1.** pertaining to fractions; comprising a part or the parts of a unit; constituting a fraction: *fractional numbers.* **2.** partial, inconsiderable, or insignificant. **3.** *Chem.* of or denoting a process, as distillation, crystallisation, or oxidation, by which the component substances of a mixture are separated according to differences in certain of their properties, as boiling point, critical temperature, solubility, etc. Also, **fractionary** /'frækʃənri/ for defs 1, 2. – **fractionally,** *adv.*

**fractional currency** /– ˌkʌrənsi/, *n.* coins or paper money of a smaller denomination than the monetary unit.

**fractional distillation** /– dɪstə'leɪʃən/, *n.* a process in which the components of a liquid mixture, as crude petroleum, are separated by distilling the mixture at different temperatures and condensing the components separately.

**fractional fitting** /– 'fɪtɪŋ/, *n.* a sizing system for shoes, providing a number of variations in width in each length size.

**fractionate** /'frækʃəneɪt/, *v.t.,* **-nated, -nating. 1.** to separate (a mixture) into its ingredients, or into portions having different properties, as by distillation or crystallisation; subject to fractional distillation, crystallisation, or the like. **2.** to obtain by such a process. – **fractionation** /frækʃən'eɪʃən/, *n.* – **fractionator,** *n.*

**fractionating column** /ˌfrækʃəneɪtɪŋ 'kɒləm/, *n.* a long vertical column forming part of a still, containing rings, plates or bubble caps, as used in fractional distillation.

**fractionise** /'frækʃənaɪz/, *v.t.,* **-nised, -nising.** to divide into fractions. Also, **fractionize.**

**fractious** /'frækʃəs/, *adj.* **1.** cross, fretful, or peevish. **2.** refractory or unruly. [FRACTI(ON) (in obs. sense of discord) + -OUS, modelled on CAPTIOUS, etc.] – **fractiously,** *adv.* – **fractiousness,** *n.*

**fracto-,** a word element meaning 'broken'. [combining form representing L *fractus,* pp.]

**fractocumulus** /ˌfræktoʊ'kjumjələs/, *n., pl.* **-li** /-laɪ/. very low, ragged clouds, slightly cumuliform, which often appear beneath nimbostratus clouds during active precipitation.

**fractostratus** /ˌfræktoʊ'streɪtəs/, *n., pl.* **-ti** /-taɪ/. very low, ragged clouds of stratiform appearance which often appear beneath nimbostratus clouds during active precipitation; scud.

**fracture** /'fræktʃə/, *n., v.,* **-tured, -turing.** *–n.* **1.** the breaking of a bone, cartilage, etc., or the resulting condition (in a bone, called *simple* when the bone does not communicate with the exterior, and *compound* when there is also a laceration of the integuments permitting communication with the exterior). **2.** the characteristic manner of breaking. **3.** the characteristic appearance of a broken surface, as of a mineral. **4.** the act of breaking. **5.** the state of being broken. **6.** a break, breach, or split. *–v.t.* **7.** to break or crack. **8.** to cause or to suffer a fracture in (a bone, etc.). *–v.i.* **9.** to undergo fracture; break. [F, from L *fractūra* breach] – **fractural,** *adj.*

**fracture filling** /'– fɪlɪŋ/, *n.* material found in cracks in fissured rock; it is commonly of siliceous or carbonate composition and may have traces of ore minerals in it.

**fracture zone** /'– zoʊn/, *n.* an area of a rock mass in which the fabric of the rock is disturbed by earth movement.

**frae** /freɪ/, *prep., adv. Scot.* from.

**fraenulum** /'frinjələm, 'frɛn-/, *n., pl.* **-la** /-lə/. **1.** *Anat., Zool.* a small fraenum. **2.** *Entomol.* a strong spine or group of bristles on the hind wing of moths and butterflies projecting beneath the forewing and serving to hold the two wings together in flight. Also, **frenulum.** [NL, diminutive of L *frænum* curb]

**fraenum** /'frinəm/, *n., pl.* **-na** /-nə/. a small fold of membrane which checks or restrains the motion of a part, as the one which binds down the underside of the tongue. Also, **frenum.** [L]

**fragile** /'frædʒaɪl/, *adj.* easily broken, shattered, or damaged; delicate; brittle; frail. [L *fragilis*] – **fragilely,** *adv.* – **fragility** /frə'dʒɪləti/, **fragileness,** *n.*

**fragment** /'frægmənt/, *n.* **1.** a part broken off or detached: *scattered fragments of rock.* **2.** a portion that is unfinished or incomplete: *fragments of a letter.* **3.** an odd piece, bit, or scrap. [L *fragmentum*]

**fragmental** /fræg'mɛntl/, *adj.* **1.** fragmentary. **2.** *Geol.* →**clastic.**

**fragmentary** /'frægməntri, -təri/, *adj.* composed of fragments; broken; disconnected; incomplete: *fragmentary evidence, remains, etc.* – **fragmentarily,** *adv.* – **fragmentariness,** *n.*

**fragmentation** /frægmən'teɪʃən/, *n.* **1.** the act or process of fragmenting. **2.** the disintegration or breakdown of norms of thought, behaviour, or social relationship. **3.** the fragments from an exploded bomb or hand grenade.

**fragmentation bomb** /'– bɒm/, *n.* a bomb which, when exploded, breaks into many small fragments which scatter at high speed.

**fragmentation weapon** /'– wɛpən/, *n.* a weapon which when exploded or discharged causes a scattering of small fragments at high speed.

**fragmented** /fræg'mɛntəd/, *adj.* **1.** reduced to fragments. **2.** disorganised; broken down.

**fragrance** /'freɪgrəns/, *n.* fragrant quality or odour; sweet scent. Also, **fragrancy.**

**fragrant** /'freɪgrənt/, *adj.* **1.** having a pleasant odour; sweet-smelling; sweet-scented. **2.** delightful; pleasant: *fragrant memories.* [L *frāgrans,* ppr., emitting an odour, smelling sweet] – **fragrantly,** *adv.*

**fraidy-cat** /'freɪdi-kæt/, *n. Colloq.* (*esp. in children's speech*) a coward; scaredy-cat. [(A)FRAID + -Y[1]]

**frail**[1] /freɪl/, *adj.* **1.** weak; not robust; having delicate health. **2.** easily broken or destroyed; fragile. **3.** morally weak; not strong against temptation. [ME *frele,* from OF, var. of *fraile,* from L *fragilis* fragile] – **frailly,** *adv.* – **frailness,** *n.*

**frail**[2] /freɪl/, *n.* **1.** a large flexible basket made of rushes, used esp. for dried fruits, as dates, figs, or raisins. **2.** a quantity of raisins contained in such a basket. [ME *frayel,* from OF *fraiel*]

**frailty** /'freɪlti/, *n., pl.* **-ties. 1.** the quality or state of being frail. **2.** moral weakness; liability to yield to temptation. **3.** a fault proceeding from moral weakness.

**fraise** /freɪz/, *n.* **1.** *Fort.* a defence consisting of pointed stakes projecting from the ramparts in a horizontal or an inclined position. **2.** a ruff worn round the neck in the 16th century. [F, from *fraiser* to frizzle, curl, from Pr. *frezar,* from a Gmc word; cf. OE *frīs* curled]

**framboesia** /fræm'biʒə, -ziə/, *n.* →**yaws.** Also, **frambesia.** [NL, Latinisation of F *framboise* raspberry, from Rom. *frambosia,* contraction of *frāga ambrosia* ambrosia strawberry]

**frame** /freɪm/, *n., v.,* **framed, framing.** *–n.* **1.** an enclosing border or case, as for a picture. **2.** anything composed of parts fitted and joined together; a structure. **3.** the sustaining parts of a structure fitted and joined together; framework skeleton. **4.** the body, esp. the human body, with reference to its make or build. **5.** a structure for admitting or enclosing something. **6.** any of various machines operating on or within a framework. **7.** a machine or part of a machine used in textile production. **8.** the rigid part of a bicycle. **9.** a particular state, as of the mind: *an unhappy frame of mind.* **10.** form, constitution, or structure in general; system; order. **11.** *Shipbuilding.* **a.** one of the transverse structural members of a ship's hull, extending from the gunwale to the bilge or to the keel. **b. square frame,** a frame set perpendicularly to the vertical plane of the keel. **c. cant frame,** a frame set at an acute angle to the vertical plane of the keel. **12.** a structure placed in a beehive on which bees build a honeycomb. **13.** *Colloq.* (in baseball) an inning. **14.** *Snooker.* **a.** the triangular form used to set up the balls for a game. **b.** the balls as so set up. **c.** the period of play required to pocket them. **15.** one of the successive small pictures on a strip of film. **16.** *Electronics.* a quantity of information which is transmitted as a unit. **17.** *Colloq.* (of livestock) an emaciated animal. **18.** *Colloq.* →**frame-up.** *–v.t.* **19.** to form or make, as by fitting and uniting parts together; construct. **20.** to contrive, devise, or compose, as a plan, law, poem, etc. **21.** to conceive or imagine, as ideas, etc. **22.** to fashion or shape. **23.** to shape or to prearrange fraudulently or falsely, as a plot, a race, etc. **24.** *Colloq.* to incriminate unjustly by a plot, as a person. **25.** to provide with or put into a frame, as a picture. **26. frame a book,** *Horseracing.* to set oneself up as a bookmaker. **27.** *Obs.* to direct, as one's steps. *–v.i.* **28.** to betake oneself, or resort. **29.** to prepare, attempt, give promise, or manage to do something. [ME *frame(n),* OE *framian* avail, profit, from *fram* forward] – **frameless,** *adj.* – **framer,** *n.*

**framed building** /freɪmd 'bɪldɪŋ/, *n.* a construction in which a framework (usu. metal or wood) forms the supporting structure.

**frame house** /'freɪm haʊs/, *n.* a sawn timber house sheathed outside with weatherboards or shingles.

**frame of reference,** *n.* **1.** *Sociol.* a set of standards to which individuals or groups refer, and which determine and sanction their behaviour and attitudes, esp. in norm formation. **2.** *Maths.* a system of coordinates within which a particular set of conditions can be defined. **3.** *Physics.* a set of coordinates or reference axes for defining the position of a point or body. **4.** a context, a set of considerations, factors, etc., in the light of which a present concern is to be considered.

**frame pack** /ˈfreɪm pæk/, *n.* a rucksack set on a frame to fit the carrier's back, used by bushwalkers, etc.

**framesaw** /ˈfreɪmsɔ/, *n.* →**gangsaw.**

**frame-up** /ˈfreɪm-ʌp/, *n. Colloq.* that which is framed, as a plot, or a contest whose result is fraudulently prearranged. Also, **frame.**

**framework** /ˈfreɪmwɜk/, *n.* **1.** a structure composed of parts fitted and united together. **2.** one designed to support or enclose something; frame or skeleton. **3.** frames collectively. **4.** work done in, on, or with a frame.

**framework operations** /– ɒpəˈreɪʃənz/, *n.pl.* military operations designed to clear and hold an area of immediate guerilla influence and re-establish civil control.

**framing** /ˈfreɪmɪŋ/, *n.* **1.** the act, process, or manner of constructing anything. **2.** the act of providing with a frame. **3.** framed work; a frame or a system of frames.

**franc** /fræŋk/, *n.* **1.** the monetary unit of France, Belgium, Switzerland, and various other countries. **2.** a former silver coin of France. [ME *frank,* from OF *franc,* so called from the ML legend *Francorum rex* king of the Franks (or French), on the first coin]

**France** /fræns, frans/, *n.* a republic in western Europe.

**franchise** /ˈfræntʃaɪz/, *n.* **1.** the rights of a citizen, esp. the right to vote. **2.** a privilege arising from the grant of a sovereign or government, or from prescription, which presupposes a grant. **3.** a privilege of a public nature conferred on an individual or body of individuals by a governmental grant. **4.** permission granted by a manufacturer to a distributor or retailer to sell his products. **5.** *Rare.* the district or jurisdiction to which the privilege of an individual or corporation extends. **6.** (formerly) a legal immunity or exemption from a particular burden, exaction, or the like. **7.** *Insurance.* an amount or percentage specified in a policy, below which the insurer accepts no liability for any claim. [ME, from OF, from *franc* free, FRANK]

**franchisee** /ˌfræntʃaɪˈzi/, *n.* one who receives a franchise.

**francium** /ˈfrænsiəm/, *n.* a radioactive element of the alkali metal group. *Symbol:* Fr; *at. no.:* 87. [FRANC(E), where first identified + -IUM]

**Franco-**, a word element meaning 'French' or 'France', as in *Franco-German.* [combining form representing ML *Francus* a Frank, a Frenchman]

**francolin** /ˈfræŋkələn/, *n.* any of various gallinaceous birds of the genus *Francolinus* of Europe, Africa and Asia, related to and resembling quails and partridges. [F, from It. *francolino*]

**Francophile** /ˈfræŋkoʊfaɪl/, *adj.* (*sometimes l.c.*) **1.** friendly to France or the French. *–n.* **2.** one who is friendly to France or the French. Also, **Francophil** /ˈfrænkəfəl/.

**Francophobe** /ˈfræŋkoʊfoʊb/, *adj.* (*sometimes l.c.*). **1.** fearing or hating France. *–n.* **2.** one who fears or hates France.

**francophone** /ˈfræŋkoʊfoʊn/, *adj.* French-speaking.

**franc-tireur** /frɒnk-tɪəˈrɜ/, *n.* **1.** a sharpshooter; sniper. **2.** an irregular soldier; guerrilla fighter. [F: lit., free-shooter]

**franger** /ˈfræŋə/, *n. Colloq.* →**contraceptive sheath.**

**frangible** /ˈfrændʒəbəl/, *adj.* **1.** capable of being broken; breakable. **2.** of or pertaining to telegraph poles, etc., designed to detach from a solid base at ground level upon the impact of a motor vehicle. *–n.* **3.** a telegraph pole which is frangible. [ME *frangebyll,* from OF *frangible,* from L *frangere* break] **– frangibility** /frændʒəˈbɪləti/, *n.*

**frangipane** /ˈfrændʒəˌpeɪn/, *n.* a pastry filling made with cream, almonds and sugar, and flavoured with frangipanni. [See FRANGIPANNI]

**frangipanni** /frændʒəˈpæni/, *n., pl.* **-nies.** **1.** a shrub or tree, of the genus *Plumeria,* with thick, fleshy branches, cultivated for its strongly scented yellow and white, occasionally pink, flowers. **2.** a perfume prepared from, or imitating this scent. Also, **frangipani.** [F *frangipane,* from (*gants de*) *frangipane,* (gloves with) frangipani, after the Marquis *Frangipani* of Rome, who invented a perfume for scenting gloves in the 16th century]

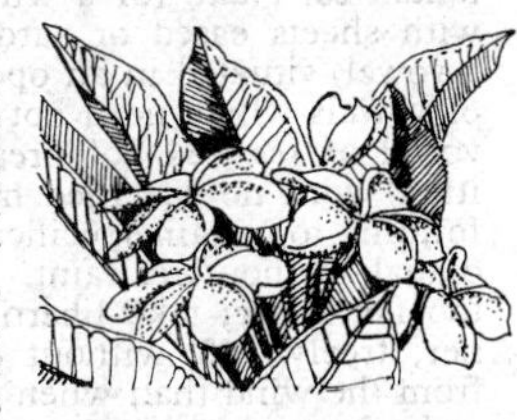
frangipanni

**franglais** /frɒŋˈgleɪ/, *n.* (*derog.*) that type of contemporary French which makes use of imported English words. [b. F *français* French + *anglais* English]

**frank** /fræŋk/, *adj.* **1.** open or unreserved in speech; candid or outspoken; sincere. **2.** undisguised; avowed; downright: *frank mutiny.* *–n.* **3.** a signature or mark affixed by special privilege to a letter, parcel, or the like, to ensure its transmission free of charge, as by post. **4.** the privilege of franking letters, etc. **5.** a franked letter, parcel, etc. *–v.t.* **6.** to mark (a letter, parcel, etc.) for transmission free of the usual charge, by virtue of official or special privilege; send free of charge, as mail. **7.** to facilitate the coming of (a person). **8.** convey (a person) free of charge. **9.** to secure exemption for. **10.** to enable to pass or go freely. [ME, from OF *franc,* from LL *francus* free, orig. Frank] **– frankable,** *adj.* **– franker,** *n.*

**Frank** /fræŋk/, *n.* **1.** a member of a group of ancient Germanic peoples dwelling in the regions of the Rhine. **2.** (in the Levant) any native or inhabitant of western Europe. [ME *Franke,* OE *Franca,* c. OHG *Franko;* usually said to be from the name of the national weapon. Cf. OE *franca* spear, javelin. See FRANK]

**Frankenstein** /ˈfræŋkənstaɪn/, *n.* **1.** one who creates a monster or a destructive agency that he cannot control or that brings about his own ruin. **2.** the monster or destructive agency itself. [from the hero of Mary Shelley's novel, *Frankenstein,* a student who created such a monster]

**frankfurt** /ˈfræŋkfət/, *n.* a reddish variety of sausage made of beef or pork, commonly cooked by steaming or boiling. Also, **frankfurter, frank.** [from *Frankfurt,* a town in W Germany]

**frankincense** /ˈfræŋkənsɛns/, *n.* an aromatic gum resin from various Asiatic and African trees of the genus *Boswellia,* esp. *B. carteri,* used chiefly for burning as incense or ceremonially. [ME *franke ensens,* from OF *franc encens* pure incense. See FRANK, INCENSE[1]]

**franklin** /ˈfræŋklən/, *n.* (in the late Middle Ages) a landowner of free but not noble birth. [ME *frankeleyn,* from ML *francus* free, FRANK]

**franklinite** /ˈfræŋklənaɪt/, *n.* a mineral of the spinel group, an oxide of zinc, manganese, and iron, occurring in black octahedral crystals or in masses; an ore of zinc. [named after *Franklin,* town in New Jersey, U.S.A., where it is found. See -ITE[1]]

**frankly** /ˈfræŋkli/, *adv.* in a frank manner; freely; openly; unreservedly; candidly; plainly.

**frankness** /ˈfræŋknəs/, *n.* plainness of speech; candour; openness.

**frantic** /ˈfræntɪk/, *adj.* **1.** wild with excitement, passion, fear, pain, etc.; frenzied; characterised by or pertaining to frenzy. **2.** *Archaic.* insane or mad. [ME *frentik,* from OF *frenetique,* from L *phrenēticus* delirious, from Gk *phrenētikós*] **– frantically, franticly,** *adv.* **– franticness,** *n.*

**frap** /fræp/, *v.t.,* **frapped, frapping.** *Naut.* to bind securely. [ME *frap(en),* from OF *fraper* strike]

**frappé** /ˈfræpeɪ/, *n.* **1.** a fruit juice mixture frozen to a puree. **2.** a drink consisting of a liqueur poured over crushed ice. *–adj.* **3.** frozen; chilled; iced. [F, pp. of *frapper* ice (drinks), orig., beat, from Gmc; cf. RAP[1]]

**fratch** /frætʃ/, *v.i. Colloq.* to fret; complain.

**frater**[1] /ˈfreɪtə/, *n.* a brother; comrade. [L: brother]

**frater**[2] /ˈfreɪtə/, *n.* the refectory of a religious house. Also, **fratry.** [ME *freitur,* from OF *fraitur,* short for *refreitor,* representing ML *refectōrium* REFECTORY]

**fraternal** /frəˈtɜnəl/, *adj.* **1.** of or befitting a brother or brothers; brotherly. **2.** of or being a society of men associated in brotherly union, as for mutual aid or benefit: *a fraternal society.* [L *frāternus* brotherly + -AL[1]] **– fraternalism,** *n.* **– fraternally,** *adv.*

**fraternal twin** /– ˈtwɪn/, *n.* one of twins produced from two different eggs, each fertilised by a different sperm. Also, **dizygotic twin.**

**fraternise** /ˈfrætənaɪz/, *v.,* **-nised, -nising.** *–v.i.* **1.** to associate in a fraternal or friendly way. **2.** to associate intimately with citizens of an enemy or conquered country. *–v.t.* **3.** *Rare.* to bring into fraternal association or sympathy. Also, **fraternize.** **– fraternisation** /ˌfrætənaɪˈzeɪʃən/, *n.* **– fraterniser,** *n.*

**fraternity** /frəˈtɜnəti/, *n., pl.* **-ties.** **1.** a body of persons associated as by ties of brotherhood. **2.** any body or class of persons having common purposes, interest, etc: *the medical fraternity.* **3.** an organisation of laymen for pious or charitable purposes. **4.** the relation of persons associated on the footing of brothers: *liberty, equality, and fraternity.* **5.** the relation of a brother or between brothers; brotherhood. **6.** *U.S.* a student society organised for social and other purposes, and designated by two or more letters of the Greek alphabet. [ME *fraternite,* from OF, from L *frāternitas* brotherhood]

**fratricide** /ˈfrætrəsaɪd/, *n.* **1.** one who kills his or her brother. **2.** the act of killing one's brother. [L *frātricīda* (def. 1), *frātricīdium* (def. 2). See -CIDE] – **fratricidal** /frætrəˈsaɪdəl/, *adj.*

**Frau** /fraʊ/, *n., pl.* **Frauen** /ˈfraʊən/. **1.** a German woman. **2.** a conventional German form of address to a married woman (as title, equivalent to *Mrs*). [G]

**fraud** /frɔd/, *n.* **1.** deceit, trickery, sharp practice, or breach of confidence, by which it is sought to gain some unfair or dishonest advantage. **2.** a particular instance of such deceit or trickery: *election frauds.* **3.** any deception, artifice, or trick. **4.** one who makes deceitful pretences; impostor. **5.** *Law.* advantage gained by unfair means; a false representation of fact made knowingly, or without belief in its truth, or recklessly, not knowing whether it is true or false. In equity, fraud is an infraction of the rules of fair dealing. [ME *fraude,* from OF, from L *fraus* cheating, deceit]

**fraudulent** /ˈfrɔdʒələnt/, *adj.* **1.** given to or using fraud, as a person; cheating; dishonest. **2.** characterised by, involving, or proceeding from fraud, as actions, enterprise, methods, gains, etc. [ME, from L *fraudulentus* cheating] – **fraudulence, fraudulency,** *n.* – **fraudulently,** *adv.*

**fraught** /frɔt/, *adj.* **1.** involving; attended (with); full (of): *an undertaking fraught with danger, a heart fraught with grief.* **2.** *Archaic or Poetic.* filled or laden (with): *ships fraught with precious wares.* –*n.* **3.** *Obs.* a load; cargo; freight (of a ship). **4.** *Colloq.* upset; anxious; tense. [ME, from MD or MLG *vracht* freight money, FREIGHT. Cf. OHG *frēht* earnings]

**Fräulein** /ˈfrɔlaɪn, ˈfrɔɪ-/, *n., pl.* **Fräulein.** **1.** an unmarried German woman. **2.** a conventional German title of respect and form of address for an unmarried woman (equivalent to *Miss*).

**Fraunhofer diffraction** /ˌfraʊnhoʊfə dəˈfrækʃən/, *n.* the class of diffraction phenomena in which both the light source and the receiving screen are effectively at an infinite distance from the diffracting system. See also **Fresnel diffraction.** [named after Joseph von *Fraunhofer,* 1787-1826, German optician and physicist]

**Fraunhofer lines** /ˈ– ˌlaɪnz/, *n.pl.* the dark lines of the solar spectrum. [See FRAUNHOFER DIFFRACTION]

**fraxinella** /fræksɪˈnɛlə/, *n.* →**dittany** (def. 3). [NL, diminutive of L *fraxinus* ash tree]

**fray**[1] /freɪ/, *n.* **1.** a noisy quarrel; contest; brawl; fight, skirmish, or battle. **2.** *Archaic.* fright. [aphetic var. of AFFRAY]

**fray**[2] /freɪ/, *v.t.* **1.** to wear (cloth, rope, etc.) to loose, ravelled threads or fibres at the edge or end; cause to unravel. **2.** to wear by rubbing (sometimes fol. by *through*). **3.** to strain (a person's temper); exasperate; upset. –*v.i.* **4.** to become frayed, as cloth, etc.; ravel out. **5.** to rub against something. –*n.* **6.** a frayed part, as in cloth. [F *frayer,* from L *fricāre* rub]

**frazil** /ˈfreɪzəl/, *n.* small spikes of ice which form in water moving with sufficient turbulence to prevent the formation of a sheet of ice.

**frazzle** /ˈfræzəl/, *v.,* **-zled, -zling,** *n.* –*v.i., v.t.* **1.** to fray; wear to threads or shreds. **2.** to weary; tire out. –*n.* **3.** a state of being frazzled or worn out. **4.** a remnant; shred. [b. FRAY[2] and *fazzle,* ME *faselin* unravel, c. G *faseln*]

**freak**[1] /frik/, *n.* **1.** a sudden and apparently causeless change or turn of events, the mind, etc.; a capricious notion, occurrence, etc. **2.** any abnormal product or curiously unusual object; monstrosity. **3.** a person or animal on exhibition as an example of some strange deviation from nature. **4.** a person who does not conform to orthodox, conservative forms of behaviour, as by being a homosexual, by taking illicit drugs, by wearing unconventional dress, etc. **5.** *Colloq.* a person who is enthused about a particular thing: *a Jesus freak, a drug freak.* –*adj.* **6.** unusual; odd; irregular: *a freak copy of a book.* –*v.i.* **7.** Also, **freak out.** *Colloq.* **a.** to have an extreme reaction, either favourable or adverse, to something, esp. a drug-induced experience. **b.** to panic (usu. fol. by *on*). –*v.t.* **8.** to terrify, as an experience produced by hallucinogenic drugs. [? akin to OE *frīcian* dance]

**freak**[2] /frik/, *v.t.* **1.** to fleck, streak, or variegate. –*n.* **2.** a fleck or streak of colour. [? v. use of FREAK[1]; apparently coined by Milton]

**freakish** /ˈfrikɪʃ/, *adj.* **1.** given to or full of freaks; whimsical; capricious. **2.** resembling a freak; queer; odd; grotesque. – **freakishly,** *adv.* – **freakishness,** *n.*

**freak-out** /ˈfrik-aʊt/, *n. Colloq.* **1.** an extreme experience, usu. terrifying, produced by hallucinogenic drugs. **2.** any unusual or unexpected experience.

**freaky** /ˈfriki/, *adj.,* **-kier, -kiest.** →**freakish.** – **freakiness,** *n.*

**freckle** /ˈfrɛkəl/, *n., v.,* **-led, -ling.** –*n.* **1.** a small brownish spot in the skin, esp. on the face, neck, or arms. **2.** any small spot or discoloration. **3.** *Colloq.* →**anus.** –*v.t.* **4.** to cover with freckles or produce freckles on. –*v.i.* **5.** to become freckled. [b. obs. *frecken* freckle (from Scand.; cf. Icel. *freknur,* pl.) and SPECKLE, *n.*] – **freckled,** *adj.*

**freckly** /ˈfrɛkli, -kəli/, *adj.* covered with freckles.

**Fred Nerk** /frɛd ˈnɜk/, *n.* an imaginary person regarded as the archetypal fool or simpleton.

**free** /fri/, *adj.,* **freer, freest,** *adv., v.,* **freed, freeing,** *n.* –*adj.* **1.** enjoying personal rights or liberty, as one not in slavery. **2.** pertaining to or reserved for those who enjoy personal liberty. **3.** possessed of, characterised by, or existing under civil liberty as opposed to arbitrary or despotic government, as a country or state, or its citizens, institutions, etc. **4.** enjoying political liberty or independence, as a people or country not under foreign rule. **5.** exempt from external authority, interference, restriction, etc., as a person, the will, thought, choice, action, etc.; independent; unfettered. **6.** at liberty, permitted, or able at will (to do something): *free to choose.* **7.** not subject to special regulation or restrictions, as trade: *free trade.* **8.** not literal, as a translation. **9.** not subject to rules, set forms, etc.: *the free song of a bird, free verse.* **10.** clear of obstructions or obstacles, as a corridor. **11.** available; unoccupied; not in use: *the managing director is now free.* **12.** exempt or released from something specified that controls, restrains, burdens, etc. (fol. by *from* or *of*): *free from matrimonial ties, free of taxes.* **13.** having immunity or being safe (usu. fol. by *from*): *free from criticism.* **14.** uncombined chemically: *free oxygen.* **15.** that may be used by or open to all: *a free port, a free market.* **16.** general: *a free fight.* **17.** unimpeded, as motion or movements; easy, firm, or swift in movement: *a free step.* **18.** loose, or not held fast or attached: *to get one's arm free.* **19.** not joined to or in contact with something else: *a free surface.* **20.** acting without self-restraint or reserve: *too free with one's tongue.* **21.** frank and open; unconstrained, unceremonious, or familiar. **22.** unrestrained by decency; loose or licentious. **23.** ready in giving, liberal, or lavish: *to be free with one's advice.* **24.** given readily or in profusion, or unstinted. **25.** given without consideration of a return, as a gift. **26.** provided without, or not subject to, a charge or payment: *free milk.* **27.** admitted to entry and enjoyment at will (fol. by *of*): *to be free of a friend's house.* **28.** easily worked, as stone or land. **29.** *Naut.* (of a wind) blowing so that a boat can sail with sheets eased or yards squared; fair. **30.** *Phonet.* **a.** (of a vowel) situated in an open syllable. **b.** belonging to a class of vowels which need not be followed by a consonant, as the vowel of *see.* **31.** (of firearms used in international competition) with no specified trigger pressure, but otherwise conforming to certain specifications. **32. free and easy,** informal; casual; without restraint. **33. make free with,** to treat or use too familiarly; take liberties with. –*adv.* **34.** in a free manner; freely. **35.** without cost or charge. **36.** *Naut.* farther from the wind than when close-hauled: *to sail free.* –*v.t.* **37.** make free; set at liberty; release from bondage, imprisonment, or restraint. **38.** to exempt or deliver (fol. by *from*). **39.** to relieve or rid (usu. fol. by *of*). **40.** to disengage (fol. by *from* or *of*). –*n.* **41.** *Colloq.* →**free kick.** **42. for free,** *Colloq.* for nothing; gratis. [ME; OE *frēo*, c. G *frei*, orig., dear, favoured. Cf. FRIEND]

**free agent** /– 'eɪdʒənt/, *n.* one who has the power to act freely and without constraint, and is not responsible to anyone for his actions.

**free air overpressure,** *n.* the pressure, in excess of the ambient atmospheric pressure, created in the air by the blast wave from an explosion.

**free alongside ship,** *adj.* (a term of sale meaning that the seller agrees to deliver the merchandise alongside ship without extra charge to the buyer).

**free-associate** /fri-ə'souʃieɪt/, *v.*, **-ated, -ating.** –*v.i.* **1.** to elaborate a train of thought suggested by a spontaneous reaction to a word, image, thought, etc. –*v.t.* **2.** to link (words, ideas, etc.) which may not appear to have any connection; improvise verbally upon.

**free association** /fri əsousi'eɪʃən/, *n.* **1.** the first association called forth by each of a series of stimulus words. **2.** a train of thought elicited in response to a single word.

**freebie** /'fribi/, *n. Colloq.* a service or item provided without charge.

**freeboard** /'fribɔd/, *n.* **1.** the distance between the water surface and the freeboard deck of a vessel. **2.** the minimum such dimension permitted by law for given regions and seasons.

**freeboard deck** /'– dɛk/, *n.* **1.** the lowest continuous deck of a vessel; the deck below which bulkheads are watertight, and from which freeboard is measured.

**freeboot** /'fribut/, *v.i.* to act as a freebooter.

**freebooter** /'fributə/, *n.* one who goes about in search of plunder; a pirate or buccaneer. [D *vrijbuiter*, from *vrij* free + *buit* booty + *-er* -ER[1]]

**freeborn** /'fribɔn/, *adj.* **1.** born free, rather than in slavery, bondage, or vassalage. **2.** pertaining to or befitting persons born free.

**Free Church** /'fri tʃɜtʃ/, *n.* **1.** the churches collectively which did not conform to the Church of England or accept the legislation passed to enforce uniformity in religion; the nonconformist churches. **2.** any such Protestant church in Britain or elsewhere. –*adj.* **3.** of or pertaining to such a church.

**free city** /fri 'sɪti/, *n.* a city having an independent government and forming a sovereign state by itself.

**free diver** /'– daɪvə/, *n.* a diver who does not use any artificial breathing apparatus.

**freedman** /'fridmæn/, *n., pl.* **-men.** a man who has been freed from slavery. – **freedwoman,** *n. fem.*

**freedom** /'fridəm/, *n.* **1.** civil liberty, as opposed to subjection to an arbitrary or despotic government. **2.** political or national independence. **3.** a particular immunity or other privilege enjoyed, as by a city or corporation. **4.** personal liberty, as opposed to bondage or slavery. **5.** the state of being at liberty rather than in confinement or under physical restraint. **6.** exemption from external control, interference, regulation, etc. **7.** power of determining one's or its own action. **8.** *Philos.* the condition of the will as the volitional instigator of human actions; relative self-determination. **9.** absence of or release from ties, obligations, etc. **10.** exemption or immunity: *freedom from taxation.* **11.** exemption from the presence of anything specified (fol. by *from*): *freedom from fear.* **12.** ease or facility of movement or action. **13.** frankness of manner or speech. **14.** absence of ceremony or reserve; familiarity. **15.** a liberty taken. **16.** the right of enjoying all the privileges or peculiar rights of citizenship, membership, or the like: *the freedom of the city.* **17.** the right of frequenting, enjoying, or using at will: *to have the freedom of a friend's library.* [ME; OE *frēodōm.* See FREE, -DOM]

**freedom fighter** /'– faɪtə/, *n.* one who joins in organised resistance, usu. armed, against the established government, or the domination of his country by a foreign power.

**freedom of the seas,** *n.* **1.** the doctrine that ships of neutral countries may sail anywhere on the high seas without interference by warring powers. **2.** the possession or exercise of that freedom.

**freedom ride** /'fridəm raɪd/, *n.* an organised bus ride to places where racial discrimination is practised, by people who wish to protest against the practice. – **freedom rider,** *n.*

**free energy** /fri 'ɛnədʒi/, *n.* that portion of the energy of a system which is the maximum available for doing work.

**free enterprise** /– 'ɛntəpraɪz/, *n.* the doctrine or practice of a minimum amount of government control of private business and industry.

**free fall** /'– fɔl/, *n.* **1.** the motion of any unpowered body travelling in a gravitational field. **2.** the part of a parachute descent before the parachute opens.

**free-fall** /'fri-fɔl/, *v.i.*, **-fell, -fallen, -falling.** to execute a free fall.

**free flight** /fri 'flaɪt/, *n.* the flight of an object moving without the assistance of an engine: *after the rocket failure the missile moved forward in free flight.*

**free-for-all** /fri-fər-'ɔl/, *n.* **1.** Also, **free fight.** a fight, game, contest, etc., open to everyone. **2.** a brawl. **3.** any event which becomes chaotic, usu. as a result of the number of people involved.

**free form** /'fri fɔm/, *n.* a linguistic form which occurs sometimes or always by itself, not having the limitation of a bound form (which see), as *fire.*

**free-form** /'fri-fɔm/, *adj.* having an asymmetrical shape or outline, usu. flowing, free of formal or traditional lines.

**free hand** /fri 'hænd/, *n.* unrestricted freedom or authority.

**freehand** /'frihænd/, *adj.* done by the hand without guiding instruments, measurements, or other aids: *a freehand drawing.*

**free-handed** /'fri-hændəd/, *adj.* **1.** open-handed; generous; liberal. **2.** having the hands free. – **free-handedness,** *n.*

**free-hearted** /'fri-hatəd/, *adj.* having a free heart; light-hearted; spontaneous; frank; generous.

**free hit** /fri 'hɪt/, *n.* a stroke awarded to a hockey player because of an infringement of the rules by a member of the opposing team.

**freehold** /'frihould/, *n.* **1. a.** a tenure of real property by which an estate of inheritance in fee simple or fee tail or for life is held. **b.** an estate held by such tenure. Cf. **leasehold.** –*adj.* **2.** of or pertaining to such tenure or property in such tenure. –*adv.* **3.** by right of such tenure.

**freeholder** /'frihouldə/, *n.* the owner of a freehold.

**free house** /'fri haus/, *n.* a public house which is not bound to obtain all its supplies of beer, etc., from one brewing firm (distinguished from *tied house*).

**free kick** /– 'kɪk/, *n.* (in football) a kick awarded to a team after a mark or after an infringement by the opposing side.

**freelance** /'frilæns/, *n., v.*, **-lanced, -lancing,** *adj., adv.* –*n.* **1.** a journalist, commercial artist, editor, etc., who does not work on a regular salaried basis for any one employer. **2.** a politician who is not attached to any particular political party. **3.** a mercenary soldier or military adventurer of the Middle Ages, often of knightly rank, who offered his services to any state, party, or cause. –*v.i.* **4.** to act or work as a freelance. –*adj.* **5.** of or pertaining to a freelance. –*adv.* **6.** in the manner of a freelance. – **freelancer,** *n.*

**free-liver** /fri-'lɪvə/, *n.* one who in his mode of life freely indulges his appetites. – **free-living,** *adj., n.*

**freeload** /'friloud/, *v.i.* to contrive to take food, benefits, etc., without paying or contributing; cadge. – **freeloader,** *n.*

**free love** /fri 'lʌv/, *n.* the doctrine or practice of free choice in sexual relations, without restraint of legal marriage or of any continuing obligations independent of one's will.

**freely** /'frili/, *adv.* in a free manner.

**freeman** /'frimən/, *n., pl.* **-men. 1.** a man who is free; a man who enjoys personal, civil, or political liberty. **2.** one who enjoys or is entitled to citizenship, franchise, or other peculiar privilege.

**freemartin** /'frimatn/, *n.* a generally sterile heifer calf twin-born with a bull. [orig. uncert.]

**Freemason** /'frimeɪsən/, *n.* **1.** Also, **Mason.** a member of a widely distributed secret order (**Free and Accepted Masons**), having for its object mutual assistance and the promotion of brotherly love among its members. **2.** (*l.c.*) *Hist.* **a.** one of a class of skilled stoneworkers of the Middle Ages, possessed of secret signs and passwords. **b.** a member of a society composed of such workers, with honorary members (known as *accepted masons*) who were not connected with the building trades. – **freemasonic** /frimə'sɒnɪk/, *adj.*

**freemasonry** /'frimeɪsənri/, *n.* **1.** secret or tacit brotherhood; instinctive sympathy. **2.** (*cap.*) the principles, practices, and institutions of Freemasons.

**freeness** /'frinəs/, *n.* the state or quality of being free.

**free of the country,** *adj.* (formerly) of or pertaining to convicts freed from custody but not permitted to leave Australia. Also, **free on the ground.**

**free on board,** *adj.* (a term of sale meaning that the seller agrees to deliver the merchandise aboard the carrier without extra charge to the buyer).

**free port** /'fri pɔt/, *n.* **1.** a port open under equal conditions to all traders. **2.** a part or all of a port not included in customs territory so as to expedite transhipment of what is not to be imported.

**free radical** /– 'rædɪkəl/, *n.* a radical (def. 12) which exists independently for short periods during the course of a chemical reaction, or for larger periods under special conditions.

**free-range** /'fri-reɪndʒ/, *adj.* **1.** of, pertaining to, or denoting chickens reared in an open or free environment rather than in a battery. **2.** of or denoting the eggs of such chickens.

**free selection** /fri sə'lɛkʃən/, *n.* (formerly) land selected, esp. for agricultural use and taken up by lease or licence under various land acts, or after crown auction, as opposed to land granted by the Crown or taken by squatting.

**free selector** /– sə'lɛktə/, *n.* a farmer who took up land under free selection.

**freesia** /'friʒə/, *n.* any plant of the genus *Freesia,* native to southern Africa, cultivated for its fragrant white, yellow, or sometimes coloured, tubular flowers. [NL; named after E.M. *Fries,* 1794-1878, Swedish botanist]

**free space** /fri 'speɪs/, *n.* a perfect vacuum. See **vacuum** (def. 1).

**free speech** /– 'spitʃ/, *n.* the right to voice one's opinions in public.

**free-spoken** /'fri-spoʊkən/, *adj.* given to speaking freely or without reserve. – **free-spokenness,** *n.*

**freestanding** /'fristændɪŋ/, *adj.* free of attachment or support; standing independently: *a freestanding house.*

**freestone** /'fristoʊn/, *n.* **1.** any stone, as sandstone, which can be freely worked or quarried, esp. one which cuts well in all directions without splitting. **2.** Also, **slipstone.** a freestone fruit, esp. a peach or plum. *–adj.* **3.** made of freestone: *a freestone house.* **4.** Also, **slipstone.** having a stone from which the pulp is easily separated, as certain peaches and plums.

**free store** /'fri stɔ/, *n.* a warehouse licensed under the Customs Act for the storage of goods which are not subject to any tariff or on which customs duties have been paid.

**freestyle** /'fristaɪl/, *n.* **1.** *Swimming.* a race in which the competitors may use any stroke they choose, usu. the crawl. **2. a.** the style of swimming used in such a race. **b.** →**crawl**[1] (def. 7). **3.** *Wrestling.* a style of wrestling in which almost every kind of hold is permitted; all-in wrestling. *–adj.* **4.** of or pertaining to freestyle.

**free-swimmer** /'fri-swɪmə/, *n.* an animal, as a fish, that swims about freely.

**free-swimming** /'fri-swɪmɪŋ/, *adj.* (of aquatic animals) not fixed or attached; capable of swimming about freely.

**freethinker** /fri'θɪŋkə/, *n.* **1.** one who forms his opinions independently of authority or tradition, esp. in matters of religion. **2.** one who asserts the rational basis of atheism. – **freethinking,** *n., adj.*

**free thought** /fri 'θɔt/, *n.* **1.** thought unrestrained by deference to authority, esp. in matters of religion. **2.** the school of thought which maintains that, in questions of religion, atheism is the only rationally acceptable conclusion.

**free throw** /– 'θroʊ/, *n.* a throw awarded in basketball for an infringement.

**free trade** /– 'treɪd/, *n.* **1.** trade between different countries, free from governmental restrictions or duties. **2.** international trade free from protective duties, etc., and subject only to such tariffs as are needed for revenue. **3.** the system, principles, or maintenance of such trade. **4.** *Obs.* smuggling.

**free-trader** /fri-'treɪdə/, *n.* **1.** an advocate of free trade. **2.** *Obs.* a smuggler.

**free verse** /fri 'vɜs/, *n.* verse unhampered by fixed metrical forms, in extreme instances consisting of little more than rhythmic prose in lines of irregular length.

**free vote** /– 'voʊt/, *n.* in a house of parliament, a vote on a motion in which members are free to vote according to their own judgment without being bound by any party policy or decision; conscience vote.

**freeway** /'friweɪ/, *n.* a road designed for high speed traffic. Also, **expressway.**

**freewheel** /'friwil/, *n.* **1.** an overrunning clutch device in connection with the transmission gearbox of a motor vehicle which automatically disengages the drive shaft whenever it tends to rotate more rapidly than the shaft driving it. **2.** a form of rear bicycle wheel which has a device freeing it from the driving mechanism, as when the pedals are stopped in coasting. *–v.i.* **3.** to coast in a motor car, bicycle, etc., with the wheels disengaged from the driving mechanism. **4.** *Colloq.* to act independently, particulary in personal, social matters. **5.** *Colloq.* to discuss matters or to act in a wide-ranging, uninhibited manner, as of a politician. *–adj.* **6.** of or pertaining to a freewheel device: *a freewheel bicycle.* *–adv.* **7.** in a manner involving a freewheel device: *he was racing down the hill freewheel.*

**free will** /fri 'wɪl/, *n.* **1.** free choice; voluntary decision. **2.** the doctrine that the conduct of human beings expresses personal choice and is not simply determined by physical or divine forces.

**free-will** /'fri-wɪl/, *adj.* **1.** made or done freely or of one's own accord; voluntary: *a free-will offering.* **2.** of or pertaining to the metaphysical doctrine of the freedom of the will: *the free-will controversy.*

**freeze** /friz/, *v.,* **froze, frozen, freezing,** *n.* *–v.i.* **1.** to become hardened into ice or into a solid body; to change from the liquid to the solid state by loss of heat. **2.** to become hard or rigid because of loss of heat, as objects containing moisture. **3.** to become obstructed by the formation of ice, as pipes. **4.** to become fixed to something by or as by the action of frost. **5.** to be of the degree of cold at which water freezes. **6.** to be extremely cold: *the weather is freezing.* **7.** to suffer the effects of intense cold; have the sensation of extreme cold. **8.** to die of frost or cold. **9.** to lose warmth of feeling; be chilled with fear, etc. **10. freeze over,** to become coated with ice. **11.** to stop suddenly; become immobilised, as through fear, shock, etc. *–v.t.* **12.** to congeal; harden into ice; change from a fluid to a solid state by loss of heat. **13.** to form ice on the surface of, as a river or pond. **14.** to obstruct or close by the formation of ice, as pipes (oft. fol. by *up*). **15.** to fix fast in ice. **16.** to harden or stiffen by cold, as objects containing moisture. **17.** to subject (something) to a freezing temperature, as in a refrigerator. **18.** to cause to suffer the effects of intense cold; produce the sensation of extreme cold in. **19.** to kill by frost or cold. **20.** to congeal as if by cold; chill with fear; dampen the enthusiasm of. **21.** to cause (someone) to become immobilised, as through fear, shock, etc. **22.** to exclude, or compel to withdraw, from society, business, etc., as by chilling behaviour, severe competition, etc. (fol. by *out*). **23.** *Finance.* to render impossible of liquidation or collection: *bank loans are frozen in business depressions.* **24.** to fix (wages, prices, etc.) at a specific level, usu. by government order. **25.** to make insensitive (a part of the body) by artificial freezing, as for surgery. *–n.* **26.** the act of freezing. **27.** the state of being frozen. **28.** *Meteorol.* a period during which temperatures remain constantly below 0°C. **29.** a frost. **30.** legislative action by a government to fix wages, prices, etc., at a specific level. **31. do a freeze,** *Colloq.* to be very cold. **32.** (in films) an arresting of the motion by printing one frame many times. [ME *frese(n),* OE *frēosan,* c. G *frieren*] – **freezable,** *adj.*

**freeze-brand** /'friz-brænd/, *v.t.* to brand stock by using dry ice (frozen $CO_2$) on a shaven area of skin in place of extreme heat. – **freeze-branding,** *n.*

**freeze-dry** /'friz-draɪ/, *v.t.,* **-dried, -drying.** to dry (food, blood, serum, etc.) while frozen and under high vacuum, as for prolonged storage. – **freeze-drying,** *n.*

**freezer** /ˈfrizə/, *n.* **1.** one who or that which freezes or chills. **2.** a machine containing cold brine, etc., for freezing ice-cream mixture or the like. **3.** a refrigerated cabinet held at or below 0°C. **4.** a compartment of a refrigerator held at or below 0°C. **5.** *Agric.* a sheep or other animal bred for the frozen meat export trade, or killed for that purpose.

**freezer-burn** /ˈfrizə-bɜn/, *n.* an unattractive mark found on frozen dressed poultry and other meat which has been stored in improperly controlled conditions and which makes the meat pale, detracting from its flavour.

**freeze-up** /ˈfriz-ʌp/, *n.* a spell of freezing weather.

**freezing chamber** /ˈfrizɪŋ ˌtʃeɪmbə/, *n.* the chamber of a freezing works where meat is frozen.

**freezing mixture** /ˈ– mɪkstʃə/, *n.* a mixture of two (or more) substances, esp. salt and ice, which produce a temperature below 0°C.

**freezing point** /ˈ– pɔɪnt/, *n.* the temperature at which a liquid freezes: *the freezing point of water is 0°C.*

**freezing works** /ˈ– wɜks/, *n.pl.* (*construed as sing.*) meatworks where meat is frozen, usu. for export. – **freezing-worker,** *n.*

**freight** /freɪt/, *n.* **1.** cargo or lading carried for pay either by land, water, or air. **2. a.** the cargo or lading, or any part of the cargo or lading, of a ship. **b.** merchandise transported by water or air. **3.** the transporting of goods by water. **4.** the charge made for transporting goods. **5.** a goods train. –*v.t.* **6.** to load; burden. **7.** to load or lade with goods or merchandise for transport. **8.** to transport as freight; send by freight. [ME *freyght,* from MD or MLG *vrecht,* var. of *vracht.* See FRAUGHT, *n.*] – **freightless,** *adj.*

**freightage** /ˈfreɪtɪdʒ/, *n.* **1.** that which is freighted; cargo; lading. **2.** charge for the conveyance of freight.

**freight car** /ˈfreɪt ka/, *n. U.S.* a goods wagon; luggage van.

**freighter** /ˈfreɪtə/, *n.* **1.** one who charters and loads ships. **2.** one whose occupation it is to receive and forward freight. **3.** a cargo ship. **4.** an aircraft that carries merchandise.

**freight terminal** /ˈfreɪt tɜmənəl/, *n.* →**goods yard.**

**freight ton** /ˈ– tʌn/, *n.* See **ton**[1] (def. 2).

**freight train** /ˈ– treɪn/, *n.* →**goods train.**

**Fremantle doctor** /frəˌmæntəl ˈdɒktə/, *n. Colloq.* a strong, cool wind blowing after a hot day in Fremantle, a town in Western Australia.

**fremitus** /ˈfrɛmətəs/, *n.* a vibration of the body perceptible on palpation. [L: a roaring, murmuring]

**French** /frɛntʃ/, *adj.* **1.** of, pertaining to, or characteristic of France, its inhabitants, or their language. –*n.* **2.** the people of France and their immediate descendants elsewhere, collectively. **3.** a Romance language, the language of France, official also in Belgium, Switzerland, and Canada. **4.** *Colloq.* (*joc.*) mild swear words: *pardon my French.* [ME; OE *Frencisc,* from *Franca* FRANK]

French doors

**French bean** /ˈ– ˈbin/, *n.* a small twining or bushy annual herb, *Phaseolus vulgaris,* often cultivated for its slender green edible pods. Also, **kidney bean, haricot bean.**

**French bread** /ˈ– ˈbrɛd/, *n.* white bread, usu. in long, slender loaves with a crisp crust and tapering ends.

**French Canadian** /ˈ– kəˈneɪdiən/, *n.* **1.** a French settler in Canada; a French-speaking descendant of such a settler. **2.** the language of French Canadians. –*adj.* **3.** of or pertaining to French Canadians, or the areas in which they constitute a majority.

**French chalk** /ˈ– ˈtʃɔk/, *n.* a talc for marking lines on cloth, etc.

**French combing** /ˈ– ˈkoumɪŋ/, *n.* combing wool suitable for continental machinery.

**French cricket** /ˈ– ˈkrɪkət/, *n.* a game played with a ball and a cricket bat, in which the batsman holds the bat in front of his legs, and can only be dismissed if the ball hits his legs or he is caught.

**French curve** /ˈ– ˈkɜv/, *n.* a flat celluloid or wooden drawing instrument consisting of a number of different curves, used to guide the pen or pencil in drawing curves of varying radii; railway curve.

**French doors** /ˈ– ˈdɔz/, *n.pl.* a pair of doors, often glazed, hinged to the doorjambs and opening in the middle.

**French dressing** /ˈ– ˈdrɛsɪŋ/, *n.* a salad dressing prepared from oil, vinegar, salt, spices, etc.

**French fried potatoes,** *n.pl.* thin strips of potatoes fried in deep fat; chips. Also, **French fries.**

**French-fry** /frɛntʃ-ˈfraɪ/, *v.t.* to fry (sliced potatoes, onions, etc.) in fat.

**French grey** /frɛntʃ ˈgreɪ/, *n.* a light greenish-grey colour.

**French Guiana** /ˈ– giˈanə/, *n.* an overseas department of France on the northeast coast of South America.

**French horn** /ˈ– ˈhɔn/, *n.* a mellow-toned brass wind instrument derived from the hunting horn and consisting of a long, coiled tube ending in a flaring bell.

**Frenchify** /ˈfrɛntʃəfaɪ/, *v.t.,* **-fied, -fying.** (*sometimes l.c.*) to make French; imbue with French qualities.

**French kiss** /frɛntʃ ˈkɪs/, *n. Colloq.* a kiss in which the tongue enters the partner's mouth.

**French knife** /ˈ– ˈnaɪf/, *n.* a heavy sharp knife with a large wedge-shaped pointed blade, used esp. for cutting meat and poultry.

**French knot** /ˈ– ˈnɒt/, *n.* a type of embroidery stitch forming a decorative knot.

**French leave** /ˈ– ˈliv/, *n.* departure without ceremony, permission, or notice.

**French letter** /ˈ– ˈlɛtə/, *n.* →**contraceptive sheath.**

**French moult** /ˈ– ˈmoult/, *n.* a congenital feather disorder of budgerigars and some parrots causing patchy feather growth and poor development of wing and tail quills.

**French mustard** /ˈ– ˈmʌstəd/, *n.* a mild mustard made with vinegar.

**French onion soup,** *n.* onion soup poured over slices of white bread, covered with grated cheese and browned in an oven.

**French pancake** /frɛntʃ ˈpænkeɪk/, *n.* a thin, light pancake, usu. having a sweet or savoury filling.

**French pastry** /ˈ– ˈpeɪstri/, *n.* a short pastry, as used for piecrusts and filled with rich creams, fruit preparations, etc.

**French polish** /ˈ– ˈpɒlɪʃ/, *n.* a solution of shellac in methylated spirits with or without the addition of some colouring material; used as a high-quality furniture finish.

**French-polish** /frɛntʃ-ˈpɒlɪʃ/, *v.t.* to finish (a piece of furniture) with French polish. – **French-polisher,** *n.* – **French-polishing,** *n.*

**French pox** /frɛntʃ ˈpɒks/, *n.* →**pox** (def. 2).

**French salad** /ˈ– ˈsæləd/, *n.* a green salad with French dressing.

**French seam** /ˈ– ˈsim/, *n.* a seam in which the edges of the cloth are sewn first on the right side, then on the wrong, so as to be completely enclosed.

**French toast** /ˈ– ˈtoust/, *n.* sliced bread soaked in a milk and egg batter and lightly fried.

**French window** /ˈ– ˈwɪndou/, *n.* a glazed folding door serving as both a window and a door, and usu. opening on to a garden or balcony.

**Frenchy** /ˈfrɛntʃi/, *adj.,* **Frenchier, Frenchiest,** *n., pl.* **-ies.** *Colloq.* –*adj.* **1.** characteristic or suggestive of the French. –*n.* **2.** a Frenchman. **3.** (*oft. l.c.*) →**French letter.**

**frenetic** /frəˈnɛtɪk/, *adj.* frantic; frenzied. Also, **phrenetic.** [var. of PHRENETIC] – **frenetically,** *adv.*

**frenulum** /ˈfrɛnjələm/, *n., pl.* **-la** /-lə/. →**fraenulum.**

**frenum** /ˈfrinəm/, *n., pl.* **-na** /-nə/. →**fraenum.**

**frenzied** /ˈfrɛnzid/, *adj.* wildly excited or enthusiastic; frantic; mad. Also, **phrensied.**

**frenzy** /ˈfrɛnzi/, *n., pl.* **-zies,** *v.,* **-zied, -zying.** –*n.* **1.** violent mental agitation; wild excitement or enthusiasm. **2.** the violent excitement of a paroxysm of mania; mental derangement; delirium. –*v.t.* **3.** to drive to frenzy; make frantic. Also, **phrensy.** [ME *frenesie,* from OF, from LL *phrenēsis,* from LGk, replacing Gk *phrenîtis*]

**freon** /ˈfriɒn/, *n.* any of various derivatives of ethane which are chemically unreactive; used in refrigerants, aerosols, etc.

**freq.,** **1.** frequent. **2.** frequentative. **3.** frequently.

**frequency** /ˈfrikwənsi/, *n., pl.* **-cies.** **1.** Also, **frequence.** the state or fact of being frequent; frequent occurrence. **2.** rate of recurrence. **3.** *Physics.* the number of cycles, oscillations, or vibrations of a wave motion or oscillation in unit time; the derived SI unit of frequency is the hertz. **4.** *Maths.* the number of times an event occurs. **5.** *Statistics.* the number of items occurring in a given category. See **relative frequency.** **6.** *Bot.* a quantitative character of a plant community; an expression of the percentage of sample plots in which a particular species occurs. **7.** *Med.* a condition which causes frequent urination. [L *frequentia*]

**frequency band** /'– bænd/, *n.* (esp. in radio) a continuous set of frequencies between two nominated frequencies.

**frequency distribution** /'– dɪstrə,bjuʃən/, *n.* the set of frequencies associated with the different categories, intervals, or values to which items in a statistical group belong.

**frequency modulation** /'– mɒdʒə,leɪʃən/, *n.* a broadcasting system, relatively free from static, in which the frequency of the transmitted wave is modulated or varied in accordance with the amplitude and pitch of the signal (distinguished from *amplitude modulation*). *Abbrev.: FM*

**frequent** /'frikwənt/, *adj.;* /frə'kwɛnt/, *v.* *–adj.* **1.** happening or occurring at short intervals: *to make frequent trips to a place.* **2.** constant, habitual, or regular: *a frequent guest.* **3.** at short distances apart: *a coast with frequent lighthouses.* *–v.t.* **4.** to visit often; go often to; be often in. [L *frequens* crowded] – **frequenter,** *n.*

**frequentation** /frikwɛn'teɪʃən/, *n.* the practice of frequenting; habit of visiting often.

**frequentative** /frə'kwɛntətɪv/, *adj.* **1.** (of a derived verb, or of an aspect of verb inflection) expressing repetition of the action denoted by the underlying verb. *–n.* **2.** a frequentative or iterative verb. **3.** the frequentative or iterative aspect. **4.** a verb therein, as *wrestle* from *wrest.*

**frequently** /'frikwəntli/, *adv.* often; many times; at short intervals.

**frère** /frɛə/, *n., pl.* **frères** /frɛə/. **1.** brother; fellow member of an organisation. **2.** friar; monk. [F]

**fresco** /'frɛskoʊ/, *n., pl.* **-coes, -cos,** *v.,* **-coed, -coing.** *–n.* **1.** the art of painting on fresh lime plaster, as on a wall or ceiling, so that the pigments are absorbed (**true fresco**), or, less properly, on dried plaster, (**dry fresco**). **2.** a picture or design so painted. *–v.t.* **3.** to paint in fresco. [It.: cool, FRESH; from Gmc] – **frescoer,** *n.*

**fresh** /frɛʃ/, *adj.* **1.** newly made or obtained, etc.: *fresh footprints.* **2.** newly arrived: *fresh from school.* **3.** new; not previously known, met with, etc.; novel. **4.** additional or further: *fresh supplies.* **5.** not salt: *fresh water.* **6.** retaining the original properties unimpaired; not deteriorated. **7.** not canned or frozen; not preserved by pickling, salting, drying, etc. **8.** not fatigued; brisk; vigorous. **9.** not faded, worn, obliterated, etc. **10.** looking youthful and healthy. **11.** pure, cool, or refreshing, as air. **12.** inexperienced. **13.** forward or presumptuous; cheeky. *–n.* **14.** the fresh part or time. **15.** a freshet. *–adv.* **16.** freshly. [ME; OE *fersc,* c. G *frisch*] – **freshly,** *adv.* – **freshness,** *n.*

**fresh breeze** /– 'briz/, *n.* **1.** a wind of Beaufort scale force 5, with average wind speed of 17 to 21 knots, or 29 to 38 kmh. **2.** any light or moderate wind which has a freshening, cooling or bracing effect.

**freshen** /'frɛʃən/, *v.t.* **1.** to make fresh; refresh, revive, or renew. **2.** to remove saltiness from. **3.** *Naut.* to relieve, as a rope, by altering the position of a part exposed to friction. *–v.i.* **4.** to become or grow fresh. **5.** to make oneself fresh, as by washing, etc. (usu. fol. by *up*). – **freshener,** *n.*

**fresher** /'frɛʃə/, *n.* **1.** a student in the first year of the course at a university or college. **2.** a novice. Also, **freshman.**

**fresher bashing** /'– bæʃɪŋ/, *n.* the undue persecution of a student in his first year by more senior students under the fresher system.

**fresher system** /'– sɪstəm/, *n.* the imposition on a first year student at a college, university and less frequently a school, of locally determined behaviour patterns such as the performance of particular chores or the submission to initiation ceremonies, trials, etc.

**freshet** /'frɛʃət/, *n.* **1.** a sudden rise in the level of a stream, or a flood, due to heavy rains or the rapid melting of snow and ice. **2.** a freshwater stream flowing into the sea. [diminutive of FRESH, used as n.]

**freshette** /frɛʃ'ɛt/, *n.* a female fresher.

**freshman** /'frɛʃmən/, *n.* →**fresher.**

**freshwater** /'frɛʃwɔtə/, *adj.* **1.** of or living in water that is fresh, or not salt (opposed to *salt-water* or *marine*). **2.** accustomed to fresh water only, and not to the sea. **3.** having little experience.

**freshwater bream** /– 'brɪm/, *n.* →**golden perch.**

**freshwater flathead** /– 'flæthɛd/, *n.* →**congolli.**

**freshwater herring** /– 'hɛrɪŋ/, *n.* **1.** a small fish of eastern Australian coastal rivers *Potamalosa richmondia.* **2.** any of various species of *Fluvialosa* or related genera, as the bony bream. **3.** the powan, *Coregonus clupeoides,* found in certain lakes of Britain. **4.** a cisco (whitefish), *Leucichthys artedi,* of the Great Lakes and small glacial lakes of eastern North America.

**Fresnel diffraction** /,frɛznəl də'frækʃən, ,freɪnəl/, *n.* the class of diffraction phenomena in which the light source or the receiving screen (or both) are at finite distances from the diffracting system. See **Fraunhofer diffraction.** [named after Augustin Jean *Fresnel,* 1788-1827, French physicist]

**fret**[1] /frɛt/, *v.,* **fretted, fretting,** *n.* *–v.i.* **1.** to give oneself up to feelings of irritation, resentful discontent, regret, worry, or the like. **2.** to cause corrosion; gnaw. **3.** to make a way by gnawing or corrosion. **4.** to become eaten, worn, or corroded. **5.** *Civ. Eng.* to scab. **6.** to move in agitation or commotion, as water. *–v.t.* **7.** to torment; irritate, annoy, or vex. **8.** to wear away or consume by gnawing, friction, rust, corrosives, etc. **9.** to form or make by wearing away a substance. **10.** to agitate (water). *–n.* **11.** an irritated state of mind; annoyance; vexation. **12.** erosion; corrosion; gnawing. **13.** a worn or eroded place. [ME *frete(n),* OE *fretan,* c. G *fressen* eat]

**fret**[2] /frɛt/, *n., v.,* **fretted, fretting.** *–n.* **1.** an interlaced, angular design; fretwork. **2.** an angular design of bands within a border. *–v.t.* **3.** to ornament with a fret or fretwork. [ME *frette,* of uncert. orig.; cf. OF *frete* interlaced work, OE *frettewian,* var. of *fretwian, frætwian* adorn]

fret[2] (def. 2): Greek frets

**fret**[3] /frɛt/, *n., v.,* **fretted, fretting.** *–n.* **1.** any of the ridges of wood, metal, or string, set across the fingerboard of a lute or similar instrument which help the fingers to stop the strings at the correct points. *–v.t.* **2.** to provide with frets. [orig. uncert.]

**fretful** /'frɛtfəl/, *adj.* disposed to fret; irritable or peevish. – **fretfully,** *adv.* – **fretfulness,** *n.*

**fretsaw** /'frɛtsɔ/, *n.* a long, narrow-bladed saw used to cut ornamental work from thin wood.

**fretted** /'frɛtəd/, *adj.* ornamented with frets.

**fretwork** /'frɛtwɜk/, *n.* **1.** ornamental work consisting of interlacing parts, esp. work in which the design is formed by perforation. **2.** any pattern of dark and light, such as that of perforated fretwork.

**Freudian** /'frɔɪdiən/, *adj.* **1.** of or pertaining to Sigmund Freud, 1856-1939, physician and psychoanalyst, or to his doctrines, esp. in respect to the causes and treatment of neurotic and psychopathic states, the interpretation of dreams, etc. *–n.* **2.** an adherent of the essential doctrines of Freud. – **Freudianism,** *n.*

**Freudian slip** /– 'slɪp/, *n.* a slip of the tongue by which the speaker actually says something apposite or revealing, which was not primarily intended, but is taken to reveal the speaker's true or subconscious thoughts.

**Fri.,** Friday.

**friable** /'fraɪəbəl/, *adj.* easily crumbled or reduced to powder; crumbly: *friable rock.* [L *friābilis*] – **friability** /fraɪə'bɪləti/, **friableness,** *n.*

**friar** /'fraɪə/, *n.* a brother or member of one of certain Christian religious orders, esp. the mendicant orders of Franciscans (**Grey Friars**), Dominicans (**Black Friars**), Carmelites (**White Friars**), and Augustinians (**Austin Friars**). [ME *frere,* from OF, from L *frāter* brother]

**friar-bird** /'fraɪə-bɜd/, *n.* any of certain honey-eating birds of the genus *Philemon* of Australia and adjacent areas, having the head partly naked like a friar, as the noisy friar-bird.

**friar's balsam** /fraɪəz 'bɔlsəm/, *n.* a tincture of benzoin.

**friar's lantern** /– 'læntən/, *n.* →**ignis fatuus.**

**friary** /'fraɪəri/, *n., pl.* **-ries.** **1.** a convent of friars. **2.** a brotherhood of friars.

**frib** /frɪb/, *n.* a small piece of wool clinging to a fleece, as a second cut. [orig. unknown] – **fribby,** *adj.*

**fricandeau** /'frɪkəndoʊ/, *n., pl.* **-deaus, -deaux** /-doʊz/. a loin of veal, larded and braised, or roasted. [F]

**fricassee** /frɪkə'si, 'frɪkəsi/, *n., v.,* **-seed, -seeing.** *–n.* **1.** meat, esp. chicken or veal, stewed, and served in a white sauce made of its own stock. *–v.t.* **2.** to prepare as a fricassee. [F, from *fricasser* to sauté and serve with sauce, from Pr. *fricassá,* from *fricar* fry, from Rom. *frīgicāre,* intensive of L *frīgere*]

**fricative** /'frɪkətɪv/, *adj.* **1.** (of consonants) characterised by a noise produced by air being forced through an opening, as in *f, v, s,* etc. *–n.* **2.** a fricative consonant. [NL *fricātīvus,* from L *fricāre* rub] – **frication** /frɪ'keɪʃən/, *n.*

**friction** /'frɪkʃən/, *n.* **1.** clashing or conflict, as of opinions, etc. **2.** *Mech., Physics.* the resistance to the relative motion (sliding or rolling) of surfaces of bodies in contact. **3.** the rubbing of the surface of one body against that of another. [L *frictio* a rubbing]

**frictional** /'frɪkʃənəl/, *adj.* **1.** of, pertaining to, or of the nature of friction. **2.** moved, worked, or produced by friction. – **frictionally,** *adv.*

**friction clutch** /'frɪkʃən klʌtʃ/, *n.* a clutch in which one rotating member turns another by the friction between them.

**friction drum** /'– drʌm/, *n.* a type of drum which has a stick attached to the drum membrane, and which is made to sound by rubbing the stick.

**friction match** /'– mætʃ/, *n.* (formerly) a match ignited by striking on a rough surface; lucifer; lucifer match.

**Friday** /'fraɪdeɪ, -di/, *n.* the sixth day of the week, following Thursday. [ME; OE *Frīgedæg* Freo's day, from *Frīge,* gen. sing. of *Frēo* (OE goddess identified with Venus) + *dæg* day; *Frēo* is identical with OE adj. *frēo* free]

**fridge**[1] /frɪdʒ/, *n. Colloq.* →**refrigerator.**

**fridge**[2] /frɪdʒ/, *n. Colloq.* a frigid girl or woman. Also, **fridgie** /'frɪdʒi/. [from FRIGID]

**fried** /fraɪd/, *adj.* **1.** cooked in fat or oil. *–v.* **2.** past tense and past participle of **fry**[1].

**fried egg** /– 'ɛg/, *n.* **1.** an egg cooked by frying. **2.** *Colloq.* →**traffic dome.**

**fried rice** /– 'raɪs/, *n.* a dish of Chinese origin in which cooked rice is fried in oil, usu. seasoned with soya sauce, and garnished with onion, barbecued pork, pieces of cooked egg, etc.

**friend** /frɛnd/, *n.* **1.** one attached to another by feelings of affection or personal regard. **2.** a well-wisher, patron, or supporter. **3.** one who is on good terms with another; one not hostile. **4.** a member of the same nation, party, etc. **5.** (*cap.*) a member of the Society of Friends; Quaker. **6.** (*cap.*) one who supports an institution, charity, etc., with money or honorary services. [ME; OE *frēond,* c. D *vriend,* G *Freund,* Goth. *frijonds,* all orig. ppr. of a verb meaning love (in OE, *frēogan*). Cf. FRIDAY, FREE] – **friendless,** *adj.* – **friendlessness,** *n.*

Friesian

**friendly** /'frɛndli/, *adj.,* **-lier, -liest,** *adv. –adj.* **1.** characteristic of or befitting a friend; showing friendship: *a friendly greeting.* **2.** like a friend; kind. **3.** favourably disposed; inclined to approve, help, or support. **4.** not hostile or at variance; amicable. **5.** *Sport.* of a match which does not entail points in a competition. *–n.* **6.** *Sport.* a friendly match. *–adv.* **7.** in a friendly manner; like a friend. [ME *frendly,* OE *frēondlīc*] – **friendlily,** *adv.* – **friendliness,** *n.*

**Friendly Islands** /'frɛndli aɪləndz/, *n.pl.* **Tonga.**

**friendly society** /'frɛndli səsaɪəti/, *n.* a society which by voluntary subscriptions provides for the relief or maintenance of its members and their families in sickness, old age, etc.

**friendship** /'frɛndʃɪp/, *n.* **1.** friendly feeling or disposition. **2.** the state of being a friend; association as friends. **3.** a friendly relation or intimacy.

**frier** /'fraɪə/, *n.*→**fryer.**

**Friesian** /'friʒən/, *n.* **1.** one of a breed of dairy cattle, usu. black and white in colouring. *–adj.* **2.** of or pertaining to this breed of cattle. [var. of FRISIAN]

**frieze** /friz/, *n.* **1.** that part of an entablature between the architrave and the cornice, commonly ornamented with sculpture. **2.** any similar decorative band or feature, as on a wall. [F *frise,* ? from ML *frisium, frigium* embroidery, from L *Phrygium* (*opus*) Phrygian (work)] – **friezing,** *n.*

**frig**[1] /frɪg/, *v.,* **frigged, frigging.** *Colloq. –v.i.* **1.** to masturbate. **2.** to have sexual intercourse. **3.** to behave in a stupid or aimless manner (oft. fol. by *around*). *–v.t.* **4.** to confuse; muddle (fol by *up*). **5.** to break or make cease to function: *you've frigged the radiator.* [L *fricāre* rub]

**frig**[2] /frɪdʒ/, *n. Colloq.* →**refrigerator.**

**frigate** /'frɪgət/, *n.* **1.** (formerly) a naval vessel next in size to a ship of the line. **2.** a general-purpose warship of about 2700 tonnes, used as an escort vessel. [F *frégate,* from It. *fregata*]

**frigatebird** /'frɪgətbɜd/, *n.* any of several species of large, rapacious, tropical seabirds with huge wings, forked tails and small legs and feet, noted for their powers of flight, as the greater frigatebird, *Fregata minor;* man-o'-war bird.

**frigging** /'frɪgɪŋ/, *adj., adv. Colloq.* →**fucking.**

**fright** /fraɪt/, *n.* **1.** sudden and extreme fear; a sudden terror. **2.** a person or thing of shocking, grotesque, or ridiculous appearance: *she looked a fright.* *–v.t.* **3.** *Poetic.* to frighten. [ME *frighte,* OE *fryhto,* metathetic var. of *fyrhto;* akin to G *Furcht*]

**frighten** /'fraɪtn/, *v.t.* **1.** to throw into a fright; terrify; scare. **2.** to drive (fol. by *away, off,* etc.) by scaring. – **frightener,** *n.* – **frighteningly,** *adv.*

**frightened** /'fraɪtnd/, *adj.* **1.** thrown into a fright. **2.** afraid (fol. by *of*).

**frightful** /'fraɪtfəl/, *adj.* **1.** such as to cause fright; dreadful, terrible, or alarming. **2.** horrible, shocking, or revolting. **3.** unpleasant; disagreeable: *we had a frightful time.* **4.** *Colloq.* very great. – **frightfully,** *adv.* – **frightfulness,** *n.*

**frigid** /'frɪdʒəd/, *adj.* **1.** very cold in temperature: *a frigid climate.* **2.** without warmth of feeling; without ardour or enthusiasm. **3.** stiff or formal. **4.** sexually unresponsive. [L *frīgidus*] – **frigidity** /frɪ'dʒɪdəti/, **frigidness,** *n.* – **frigidly,** *adv.*

**Frigid Zone** /'frɪdʒəd zoʊn/, *n.* either of the two regions between the poles and the polar circles.

**frigorific** /frɪgə'rɪfɪk/, *adj.* causing or producing cold. [L *frīgorificus* cooling]

**frig-up** /'frɪg-ʌp/, *n. Colloq.* a confusion; muddle; mess.

**frijol** /'frihoʊl/, *n., pl.* **frijoles** /'frihoʊlz/. a cultivated bean of the genus *Phaseolus,* much used for food in Mexico, etc. Also, **frihole** /fri'hoʊli/. [Sp.]

**frill** /frɪl/, *n.* **1.** a trimming consisting of a strip of material or lace, gathered at one edge and left loose at the other; a ruffle. **2.** something resembling such a trimming, as the fringe of hair on the chest of some dogs. **3.** *Colloq.* affectation of manner, style, etc. **4.** something superfluous or useless. **5.** *Photog.* a wrinkling or loosening of an emulsion at the edges. *–v.t.* **6.** to trim or ornament with a frill or frills. **7.** to form into a frill. *–v.i.* **8.** *Photog.* (of an emulsion) to become wrinkled or loose. **9.** to make a single cut around the circumference of a tree so as to kill it prior to clearing the land. [? Flemish *frul* frill (of a collar), *frullen* have frills] – **frilly,** *adj.*

frill-necked lizard

**frilled dragon** /frɪld 'drægən/, *n.*→**frill-necked lizard.**

**frilled lizard** /– 'lɪzəd/, *n.* **1.**→**frill-necked lizard.** **2.**→**bearded lizard.**

**frillie** /'frɪli/, *n. Colloq.*→**frill-necked lizard.**

**frilling** /'frɪlɪŋ/, *n.* frilled edging.

**frill-necked lizard** /ˌfrɪl-nɛkt 'lɪzəd/, *n.* **1.** Also, **bicycle lizard.**

an agamid or dragon lizard, *Chlamydosaurus kingi,* of northern Australia possessing a large, ruff-like, erectable frill behind the head and using hind legs for propulsion. **2.** frequently, but incorrectly, the bearded lizard, *Amphibolurus barbatus,* of which the beard or frill is comparatively small. Also, **frilled lizard, frilled dragon, bearded dragon.**

**fringe** /frɪndʒ/, *n., v.,* **fringed, fringing,** *adj.* *–n.* **1.** an ornamental bordering having projecting lengths of thread, cord, etc., either loose or variously arranged or combined. **2.** anything resembling or suggesting this: *a fringe of trees about a field.* **3.** hair falling over the brow. **4.** border; margin; outer part or extremity. **5.** *Optics.* one of the alternate light and dark bands produced by diffraction or interference. *–v.t.* **6.** to furnish with or as with a fringe. **7.** to serve as a fringe for. *–adj.* **8.** accessory; supplementary: *fringe benefits.* **9.** of or pertaining to a person or group living on the outskirts of social acceptibility. [ME *frenge,* from OF, from LL *fimbria* border, fringe] **– fringeless,** *adj.* **– fringelike,** *adj.* **– fringy,** *adj.*

**fringe benefit** /– ˈbɛnəfət/, *n.* any remuneration received in addition to one's wage, as a pension, travel allowance, etc.

**fringed lily** /frɪndʒd ˈlɪli/, *n.* a small perennial herbaceous plant of the genus *Thysanotus,* family Liliaceae, having a bright mauve or violet flower of distinctive type, with three broad petals bearing a prominent fringe along their margins. Also, **fringed violet.**

**fringed waterlily** /– ˈwɔtəlɪli/, *n.* any species of the genus *Nymphoides* of the family Menyanthaceae, with floating leaves and small groups of yellow flowers, widespread in ponds and slow-flowing rivers.

**fringe dweller** /ˈfrɪndʒ dwɛlə/, *n.* **1.** a person who lives, usu. in miserable conditions, on the fringe of a town or settlement. **2.** a person who attaches himself to a group, etc., in order to benefit from the social advantages or prestige which naturally accrue to that group.

**fringe-myrtle** /frɪndʒ-ˈmɜtl/, *n.* any shrub of the Australian genus *Calytrix,* esp. *C. tetragona,* with a wide distribution in the southern half of the continent.

**fringe pin** /ˈfrɪndʒ pɪn/, *n.* a piece of thin bent wire for pinning hair in position.

**fringe tree** /ˈ– tri/, *n.* a shrub or small tree, *Chionanthus virginicus,* of the southern United States, bearing panicles of white flowers with long, narrow petals.

**fringilline** /ˈfrɪndʒəlaɪn, -ɪn/, *adj.* belonging or pertaining to the Fringillidae, the finch family, which includes the sparrows, canaries, linnets, etc., as well as various finches. [L *fringilla* kind of bird + -INE[1]]

**frippery** /ˈfrɪpəri/, *n., pl.* **-ries.** **1.** finery in dress, esp. when tawdry. **2.** empty display; ostentation. **3.** trifles. [F *friperie,* OF *freperie,* from *frepe* rag]

**Fris.,** Frisian.

**frisbee** /ˈfrɪzbi/, *n.* a saucer-shaped toy of coloured plastic, which if thrown with a horizontal spin stays aloft for some time. [Trademark]

**frisé** /ˈfrizeɪ/, *n.* a rug or upholstery fabric made with pile in uncut loops or in a combination of cut and uncut.

**Frisian** /ˈfrɪziən, -ʒən/, *adj.* **1.** of or pertaining to Friesland, its inhabitants, or their language. *–n.* **2.** one of the people of Friesland. **3.** the Germanic language most closely related to English, spoken in Friesland and nearby islands.

**frisk** /frɪsk/, *v.i.* **1.** to dance, leap, skip, or gambol, as in frolic. *–v.t.* **2.** *Colloq.* to search (a person) for concealed weapons, etc., by feeling his clothing. **3.** *Colloq.* to steal something from (someone) in this way. *–n.* **4.** a leap, skip, or caper. **5.** a frolic. [orig. adj., from OF *frisque,* from Gmc; cf. G *frisch* lively] **– frisker,** *n.*

**frisket** /ˈfrɪskət/, *n.* an iron frame to hold in place a sheet of paper to be printed.

**frisky** /ˈfrɪski/, *adj.,* **friskier, friskiest.** lively; frolicsome; playful. **– friskily,** *adv.* **– friskiness,** *n.*

**frit** /frɪt/, *n., v.,* **fritted, fritting.** *–n.* **1. a.** a fused or partially fused material used as a basis for glazes or enamels. **b.** the composition from which artificial soft porcelain is made. **2.** the material from which the glazed portion of artificial teeth is made. **3.** (in medieval glass-making) fused or calcined material, ready to serve as part of the batch for glass-making. *–v.t.* **4.** to fuse (materials) in making a frit. [F *fritte,* from It. *fritta,* from *friggere* (from L *frīgere*) roast, fry]

**frith** /frɪθ/, *n. Chiefly Scot.*→**firth.** [metathetic var. of FIRTH]

**fritillary** /frəˈtɪləri/, *n., pl.* **-ries.** **1.** any of several orange-brown butterflies which are silver-spotted beneath, of the genus *Argynnis* and allied species. **2.** any plant of the liliaceous genus *Fritillaria,* esp. *F. meleagris,* with solitary, nodding chequered purple or white flowers, occurring in damp pastures in Europe but frequently cultivated. [NL *fritillāria,* from L *fritillus* dicebox]

**fritter**[1] /ˈfrɪtə/, *v.t.* **1.** to disperse or squander piecemeal, or waste little by little (usu. fol. by *away*): *to fritter away one's money.* **2.** to break or tear into small pieces or shreds. *–n.* **3.** a small piece, fragment, or shred. [earlier *fitter,* from *fit* part] **– fritterer,** *n.*

**fritter**[2] /ˈfrɪtə/, *n.* a small cake of batter, sometimes containing fruit or some other ingredient, fried in deep fat or sautéed in a frying pan. [ME *frytour,* from OF *friture,* from *frire* FRY[1]]

**fritz** /frɪts/, *n. in the phrase,* **on the fritz,** *Colloq.* broken; not in working order.

**Fritz** /frɪts/, *n. Colloq.* **1.** a German, esp. a German soldier. **2.** Germans or a German army collectively. **3.** (*l.c.*) Also, **pork fritz.** a large bland pre-cooked sausage eaten cold; devon.

**Friulian** /friˈuliən/, *n.* **1.** a Rhaeto-Romanic language spoken by about half a million people in north-eastern Italy. **2.** a native of the Friuli region of north eastern Italy. Also, **Friulan** /friˈulən/.

**frivolity** /frəˈvɒləti/, *n., pl.* **-ties.** **1.** the quality or state of being frivolous. **2.** a frivolous act or thing.

**frivolous** /ˈfrɪvələs/, *adj.* **1.** of little or no weight, worth, or importance; not worthy of serious notice: *a frivolous objection.* **2.** characterised by lack of seriousness or sense: *frivolous conduct.* **3.** given to trifling or levity, as persons. [L *frīvolus* silly, trifling, paltry] **– frivolously,** *adv.* **– frivolousness,** *n.*

**frizz** /frɪz/, *v.,* **frizzed, frizzing,** *n., pl.* **frizzes.** *–v.t.* **1.** to make into small, crisp curls or little tufts. *–v.i.* **2.** to form into such curls. *–n.* **3.** the state of being frizzed. **4.** something frizzed; frizzed hair. Also, **friz.** [backformation from FRIZZLE[1]]

**frizzle**[1] /ˈfrɪzəl/, *v.,* **-zled, -zling,** *n.* *–v.t.* **1.** to frizz. *–n.* **2.** a short, crisp curl. [orig. obscure. Cf. OE *frīs* curled] **– frizzler,** *n.*

**frizzle**[2] /ˈfrɪzəl/, *v.,* **-zled, -zling.** *–v.i.* **1.** to make a sizzling or sputtering noise in frying or the like. *–v.t.* **2.** to crisp (meat, etc.) by frying. [b. FRY[1] and FIZZLE]

**frizzy** /ˈfrɪzi/, *adj.* curly: *frizzy hair.* Also, *U.S.,* **frizzly** /ˈfrɪzli/.

**fro** /froʊ/, *adv.* **1.** *Obs.* from; back. **2.** **to and fro, a.** back and forth. **b.** hither and thither. [ME, earlier *frā,* from Scand.; cf. Icel. *frā,* c. OE *fram* from]

frockcoat

**frock** /frɒk/, *n.* **1.** a dress, esp. for a small girl. **2.** a loose outer garment worn by peasants and workmen; smock. **3.** a coarse outer garment with large sleeves, worn by monks. *–v.t.* **4.** to provide with or clothe in a frock. **5.** to invest with priestly or clerical office. [ME *froke,* from OF *froc,* of Gmc orig.] **– frockless,** *adj.*

**frockcoat** /ˈfrɒkkoʊt/, *n.* a man's close-fitting coat, usu. double-breasted, extending to about the knees.

**frog**[1] /frɒg/, *n., v.,* **frogged, frogging.** *–n.* **1.** any of various tailless amphibians, order Salientia, esp. of the web-footed aquatic species constituting the genus *Rana* and allied genera, typically having a smooth skin and long hind legs adapted for leaping. **2.** any of various froglike amphibians. **3.** a slight hoarseness due to mucus on the vocal cords: *a frog in the throat.* **4.** (*cap.*) (*derog.*) Frenchman. **5.** a French letter; sheath (def. 6). **6.** a small, heavy holder placed in a bowl or vase to hold flower stems in position. **7.** an indentation on a brick. **8.** an attachment suspended from a belt for supporting a sword. **9.** (formerly) a pound; £,l. *–v.i.* **10.** to catch, or search for, frogs. [ME *frogge,* OE *frogga;*

frog[1]: Australian bullfrog

i = peat ɪ = pit ɛ = pet æ = pat a = part ɒ = pot ʌ = putt ɔ = port ʊ = put u = pool ɜ = pert ə = apart aɪ = buy eɪ = bay ɔɪ = boy aʊ = how oʊ = hoe ɪə = here ɛə = hair ʊə = tour g = give θ = thin ð = then ʃ = show ʒ = measure tʃ = choke dʒ = joke ŋ = sing j = you õ = Fr. bon

akin to G *Frosch*] – **froglike,** *adj.*

**frog**[2] /frɒg/, *n.* **1.** an ornamental fastening for the front of a coat, consisting of a button and a loop through which it passes. **2.** a device at the intersection of two railway tracks, to permit the wheels and flanges on one track to cross or branch from the other, or a similar device on a system of overhead wires as on a tramway or electric railway. [? Pg. *froco,* from L *floccus* FLOCK[2]]

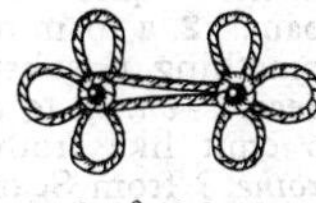
frog[2] (def. 1)

**frog**[3] /frɒg/, *n.* a triangular mass of elastic, horny substance in the middle of the sole of the foot of a horse or related animal. [special use of FROG[1]]

**frog and toad,** *n. Colloq.* a road. [rhyming slang]

**frog crab** /ˈfrɒg kræb/, *n.* an Indo-Pacific crab, *Ranina ranina,* having an enlarged thorax and a small abdomen not curled under the thorax; spanner crab.

**frogfish** /ˈfrɒgfɪʃ/, *n., pl.* **-fishes,** (*esp. collectively*) **-fish. 1.** any of the thick-headed, wide-mouthed fishes constituting the family Batrachoididae, as *Batrachomoeus dubius,* of warm seas around Australia and elsewhere. **2.** →**angler** (def. 2).

**frogged** /frɒgd/, *adj.* with frogs (**frog**[2] def. 1): *a frogged coat.*

**froghopper** /ˈfrɒghɒpə/, *n.* any of various small, leaping, homopterous insects, family Cercopidae, whose young live in a spittle-like secretion on plants; spittle insect; cuckoo-spit.

**frog kick** /ˈfrɒg kɪk/, *n.* a type of swimming kick in which the legs are bent at the knees, extended outwards, and then brought together forcefully, as in breaststroke.

**frogman** /ˈfrɒgmən/, *n., pl.* **-men.** a swimmer specially equipped for swimming underwater, esp. with wetsuit, flippers, aqualung, etc.

**frogmarch** /ˈfrɒgmatʃ/, *v.t.* **1.** to force a person to walk by applying a half nelson or seizing him by the scruff of the neck and the trousers belt, and forcing him forward. **2.** *Brit. U.S.* to carry a person face downwards, four men holding each one limb.

**frogmouth** /ˈfrɒgmaʊθ/, *n.* any of various species of nocturnal birds of the family Podargidae, with wide bills, soft wings and silent flight, found throughout Australia and in various parts of Asia, as the tawny frogmouth.

**frog plaster** /ˈfrɒg plastə/, *n.* a plaster which encases a child from armpit to ankles, with legs sideways and at an angle to the body, used to treat congenital dislocation of the hip.

**frog's eggs** /ˈfrɒgz ɛgz/, *n.pl. Colloq.* boiled sago or tapioca, esp. as served in institutions.

**frogspawn** /ˈfrɒgspɒn/, *n.* **1.** frogs' eggs; the spawn of frogs or a frog. **2.** any member of the genus of red algae *Batrachospermum.*

**frogspit** /ˈfrɒgspɪt/, *n.* any of several filamentous fresh-water green algae forming floating masses. Also, **frogspittle** /ˈfrɒgspɪtl/.

**frolic** /ˈfrɒlɪk/, *n., v.,* **-icked, -icking,** *adj.* –*n.* **1.** merry play; gay prank; gaiety; fun. **2.** a merrymaking. –*v.i.* **3.** to play merrily; have fun; play merry pranks. –*adj.* **4.** gay; merry; full of mirth or pranks; full of fun. [D *vrolijk* joyful (c. G *fröhlich*), from *vro* glad + *lijk* like] – **frolicker,** *n.*

**frolicsome** /ˈfrɒlɪksəm/, *adj.* merrily playful; full of fun. – **frolicsomely,** *adv.* – **frolicsomeness,** *n.*

**from** /frɒm/; *weak form* /frəm/, *prep.* a particle specifying a starting point, and hence used to express removal or separation in space, time, order, etc., discrimination or distinction, source or origin, instrumentality, and cause or reason: *a train running west from Sydney, from that time onwards, to wander from one's purpose, to refrain from laughing, sketches drawn from nature.* [ME and OE, var. of *fram,* prep., from, as adv., forwards, forth, c. OHG and Goth. *fram,* prep. and adv., Icel. *frā,* prep. (cf. FRO), *fram,* adv.]

**fromenty** /ˈfroʊmənti/, *n.* →**frumenty.**

**frond** /frɒnd/, *n.* **1.** a finely divided leaf, often large (properly applied to the ferns and some of the palms). **2.** a leaf-like expansion not differentiated into stem and foliage, as in lichens. [L *frons* leafy branch] – **fronded,** *adj.* – **frondless,** *adj.*

**frondescence** /frɒnˈdɛsəns/, *n.* **1.** the process or period of coming into leaf. **2.** foliage. [NL *frondescentia,* from L *frondescens,* ppr. of *frondescere,* frequentative of *frondēre* put forth leaves] – **frondescent,** *adj.*

**frons** /frɒnz/, *n.* the facial area of an insect's head above or behind the clypeus. [L; see FRONT]

**front** /frʌnt/, *n.* **1.** the foremost part or surface of anything. **2.** the part or side of anything, as a house, which seems to look out or be directed forwards. **3.** any side or face, as of a house. **4.** a place or position directly before anything. **5.** *Mil.* **a.** the foremost line or part of an army, etc. **b.** a line of battle. **c.** the place where active operations are carried on. **6.** land facing a road, river, etc. **7.** a seaside promenade. **8.** someone or something which serves as a cover for another activity, esp. an illegal or disreputable one. **9.** outward impression of rank, position, or wealth. **10.** bearing or demeanour in confronting anything: *a calm front.* **11.** cool assurance, or impudence. **12.** the forehead, or the entire face. **13.** a coalition or movement to achieve a particular end, usu. political: *people's front.* **14.** something attached or worn at the forepart, as a shirt-front, a dicky, etc. **15.** *Meteorol.* a surface of discontinuity separating two dissimilar air-masses. **16. up front,** in advance: *they paid a thousand dollars up front.* –*adj.* **17.** of or pertaining to the front. **18.** situated in or at the front. **19.** *Phonet.* pronounced with the tongue relatively far forward in the mouth: the vowels of 'beet' and 'bat' are front vowels. –*v.t.* **20.** to have the front towards; face: *our house fronts the lake.* **21.** to meet face to face; confront. **22.** to face in opposition, hostility, or defiance. **23.** to furnish or supply with a front. **24.** to serve as a front to. –*v.i.* **25.** to have or turn the front in some specified direction: *our house fronts on to the lake.* **26.** *Colloq.* to appear before a court on a charge. **27.** Also, **front up.** *Colloq.* to arrive, turn up. [ME, from L *frons* forehead, front] – **frontless,** *adj.*

**frontage** /ˈfrʌntɪdʒ/, *n.* **1.** the front of a building or plot of land. **2.** the lineal extent of this front. **3.** the direction it faces. **4.** land abutting on a river, street, etc. **5.** the space lying between a building and the street, etc.

**frontal** /ˈfrʌntl/, *adj.* **1.** of, in, or at the front: *a frontal attack.* **2.** *Anat.* denoting or pertaining to the bone (or pair of bones) forming the forehead, or to the forehead in general. **3.** *Meteorol.* of or pertaining to the division between dissimilar air-masses. **4.** viewed from the front: *a frontal nude.* –*n.* **5.** *Eccles.* a movable cover or hanging for the front of an altar. **6.** *Anat.* a bone of the forehead; frontal bone. **7. full frontal,** a view of a naked body from the front. [LL *frontālis,* from L *frons* front; replacing ME *frountel,* from OF *frontel*] – **frontally,** *adv.*

**frontbencher** /ˈfrʌntbɛntʃə, frʌntˈbɛntʃə/, *n.* a member of parliament who is a government minister or opposition spokesman. – **frontbench,** *adj.*

**front-end** /ˈfrʌnt-ɛnd/, *adj.* of or pertaining to the beginning of a project, plan, etc.

**front-end loader** /ˌfrʌnt-ɛnd ˈloʊdə/, *n.* a small tractor (usu. with rubber wheels) having a hydraulically operated scoop at the front; tractor shovel.

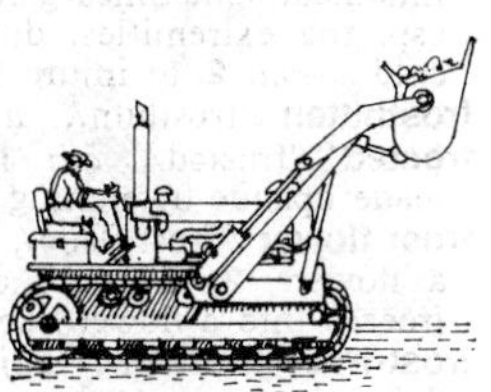
front-end loader

**frontier** /frʌnˈtɪə, ˈfrʌntɪə/, *n.* **1.** that part of a country which borders another country; boundary; border; extreme limit. **2.** *U.S.* that part of a country which forms the border of its settled or inhabited regions. **3.** (oft. *pl.*) the incompletely developed region of a field of knowledge, etc.: *frontiers of philosophy.* –*adj.* **4.** of or on the frontier: *a frontier town.* [ME *frountere,* from OF *frontiere,* from *front* in sense of opposite side]

**frontiersman** /frʌnˈtɪəzmən/, *n., pl.* **-men.** a man who lives on the frontier.

**frontispiece** /ˈfrʌntəspis/, *n.* **1.** an illustrated leaf preceding the titlepage of a book. **2.** *Archit.* **a.** the most richly decorated and usu. central portion of the principal face of a building. **b.** the pediment over a door, gate, etc. [alteration (conformed to *piece*) of earlier *frontispice,* from F, from ML *frontispicium,* from L *fronti-* front + *-spicium* look]

**frontlet** /ˈfrʌntlət/, *n.* **1.** the forehead of an animal or bird. **2.**

an ornament or band worn on the head as a phylactery. **3.** a cloth hanging over the upper part of an altar frontal. [ME *frontlette,* from OF *frontelet,* diminutive of *frontel* FRONTAL, *n.*]

**front line** /frʌnt 'laɪn/, *n.* **1.** →**front** (def. 5). **2.** in a jazz band, the solo players.

**front-line** /'frʌnt-laɪn/, *adj.* **1.** foremost; in front. **2.** prominent; renowned.

**front man** /'frʌnt mæn/, *n.* **1.** a man who takes public responsibility for, or handles public enquiries and complaints about a project, organisation, etc. **2.** →**linkman.** **3.** a person who, appearing in a position of responsibility in an organisation, gives a false respectability to that organisation's underhand or illegal activities.

**front of house,** *n.* the parts of a theatre used by the audience.

**frontogenesis** /,frʌntoʊ'dʒenəsəs/, *n.* the development, or marked intensification, of a front (def. 15).

**frontolysis** /frʌn'tɒləsəs/, *n.* the disappearance, or marked weakening of a front (def. 15).

**front-page** /'frʌnt-peɪdʒ/, *adj.* **1.** pertaining to the front page of a newspaper. **2.** of consequence; worth putting on the first page of a newspaper.

**front rank** /frʌnt 'ræŋk/, *n.* **1.** the highest rank or grade. *–adj.* **2.** Also, **front ranking.** of high quality; pre-eminent; best. **– front-ranker,** *n.*

**front-runner** /'frʌnt-rʌnə/, *n.* **1.** *Horseracing.* a horse that leads all the way in a race. **2.** anyone who is or appears to be leading in a competition. **3.** a contestant who runs best when in the lead.

**front stop** /'frʌnt stɒp/, *n.* (in rowing) a wooden block placed at the stern end of the seat slide to prevent it running off the tracks.

**frontwards** /'frʌntwədz/, *adv.* towards the front. Also, **frontward.**

**frost** /frɒst/, *n.* **1.** the atmospheric condition which causes the freezing of water. **2. degrees of frost,** degrees below freezing point: *we had ten degrees of frost (i.e., -10°C).* **3.** a covering of minute ice needles, formed from the atmosphere at night on cold surfaces when the dewpoint is below freezing point (**white frost** or **hoarfrost**). Cf. **black frost.** **4.** the act or process of freezing. **5.** crushed glass of paper thickness, used for decorative purposes. **6.** a coolness between persons; an icy manner. **7.** *Colloq.* something which is received coldly; a failure. **8.** *Colloq.* a swindle. *–v.t.* **9.** to cover with frost. **10.** to give a frostlike surface to (glass, etc.). **11.** to ice (a cake, etc.). *–v.i.* **12.** to freeze or become covered with frost (oft. fol. by *up* or *over*). [ME and OE *frost, forst,* c. D *vorst,* G *Frost,* Icel. *frost,* akin to FREEZE] **– frostless,** *adj.* **– frostlike,** *adj.*

**frostbite** /'frɒstbaɪt/, *n., v.,* **-bit, -bitten, -biting.** *–n.* **1.** the inflamed, sometimes gangrenous effect on a part of the body, esp. the extremities, due to excessive exposure to extreme cold. *–v.t.* **2.** to injure by frost or extreme cold.

**frostbitten** /'frɒstbɪtn/, *adj.* injured by frost or extreme cold.

**frosted** /'frɒstəd/, *adj.* **1.** covered with frost. **2.** (of glass) made opaque by etching or sandblasting. **3.** (of a cake) iced.

**frost flower** /'frɒst flaʊə/, *n.* **1.** an ice-crystal which looks like a flower. **2.** moisture on the outside of a window which freezes into a flower-like frost pattern.

**frost-free** /'frɒst-fri/, *adj.* of a refrigerator that never needs defrosting.

**frostie** /'frɒsti/, *n. Colloq.* a cold bottle or can of beer. Also, **frosty.**

**frosting** /'frɒstɪŋ/, *n.* **1.** a preparation of sugar, water, egg-whites, and cream of tartar; a fluffy icing used to cover and decorate cakes. **2.** any kind of cake icing. **3.** a lustreless finish, as of metal or glass. **4.** a material used for decorative work, as signs, etc., made from coarse, powdered glass flakes.

**frost point** /'frɒst pɔɪnt/, *n.* →**hoarfrost point.**

**frostwork** /'frɒstwɜk/, *n.* **1.** the delicate tracery formed by frost, esp. on glass. **2.** similar ornamentation, as on metal.

**frosty** /'frɒsti/, *adj.,* **-tier, -tiest.** **1.** attended with or producing frost; freezing; very cold: *frosty weather.* **2.** consisting of or covered with a frost. **3.** lacking warmth of feeling. **4.** resembling frost; white or grey, as hair. **5.** of or characteristic of old age. **6.** →**frostie.** **– frostily,** *adv.* **– frostiness,** *n.*

**frosty face** /'– feɪs/, *n.* an occasional defect of merino sheep consisting of chalky harsh white hairs covering the face.

**froth** /frɒθ/, *n.* **1.** an aggregation of bubbles, as on a fermented liquid or at the mouth of a hard-driven horse; foam. **2.** a foam of saliva or fluid resulting from disease. **3.** something unsubstantial or evanescent, as idle talk; trivial ideas. *–v.t.* **4.** to cover with froth. **5.** to cause to foam. **6.** to emit like froth. *–v.i.* **7.** to give out froth; foam. [ME *frothe,* ? from Scand.; cf. Icel. *frodha.* Cf. also OE *āfrēothan* form froth]

**froth flotation** /'– floʊ,teɪʃən/, *n.* a process for separating a mixture of finely divided minerals by agitating them in a froth of water and oil, so that some float and others sink.

**frothy** /'frɒθi/, *adj.,* **-ier, -iest.** **1.** of, like, or having froth; foamy. **2.** unsubstantial; trifling; shallow. **– frothily,** *adv.* **– frothiness,** *n.*

**frottage** /'frɒtɪdʒ/, *n.* **1.** *Psychiatry.* one clothed body being brought into contact with the clothed body of another, for sexual gratification. **2.** *Art.* the technique of taking a rubbing from a rough surface, as wood. [F: rubbing, friction, from *frotter* to rub]

**frottola** /'frɒtələ/, *n.* a secular Italian song of the 15th and 16th centuries, that is largely homophonic and has a repeated refrain.

**froufrou** /'frufru/, *n.* a rustling, particularly the rustling of silk, as in a woman's dress. [F]

**froward** /'froʊəd/, *adj.* perverse; wilfully contrary; refractory; not easily managed. [ME. See FRO, -WARD] **– frowardly,** *adv.* **– frowardness,** *n.*

**frown** /fraʊn/, *v.i.* **1.** to contract the brow as in displeasure or deep thought; scowl. **2.** to look displeased; have an angry look. **3.** to look disapprovingly (fol. by *on* or *upon*): *to frown upon a scheme.* *–v.t.* **4.** to express by a frown. *–n.* **5.** a frowning look; scowl. **6.** any expression or show of disapproval. [ME *froune(n),* from OF *froignier,* from *froigne* surly expression; of Celtic orig.] **– frowner,** *n.* **– frowningly,** *adv.*

**frowsty** /'fraʊsti/, *adj.* ill-smelling; musty; close-smelling. [orig. unknown]

**frowzy** /'fraʊzi/, *adj.,* **-zier, -ziest.** **1.** dirty and untidy; slovenly. **2.** ill-smelling; musty. Also, **frowsy, frouzy.** [akin to FROWSTY] **– frowzily,** *adv.* **– frowziness,** *n.*

**froze** /froʊz/, *v.* past tense of **freeze.**

**frozen** /'froʊzən/, *v.* **1.** past participle of **freeze.** *–adj.* **2.** congealed by cold; covered with ice, as a stream. **3.** frigid; very cold. **4.** injured or killed by frost or cold. **5.** obstructed by ice, as pipes. **6.** (of food) preserved by refrigeration. **7.** chilly or cold in manner; unfeeling: *a frozen stare.* **8.** *Finance.* rendered impossible of liquidation, as by business conditions: *frozen loans.* [pp. of FREEZE] **– frozenly,** *adv.* **– frozenness,** *n.*

**F.R.S.** /,ɛf ar 'ɛs/, Fellow of the Royal Society.

**frt,** freight.

**fructiferous** /frʌk'tɪfərəs, frʊk-/, *adj.* fruit-bearing; producing fruit. [L *fructifer* fruit-bearing + -OUS]

**fructification** /,frʌktəfə'keɪʃən, frʊk-/, *n.* **1.** the act of fructifying; the fruiting of a plant. **2.** the fruit of a plant. **3.** the organs of fruiting.

**fructify** /'frʌktəfaɪ, frʊk-/, *v.,* **-fied, -fying.** *–v.i.* **1.** to bear fruit. *–v.t.* **2.** to make fruitful or productive; fertilise. [ME *fructifie(n),* from F *fructifier,* from L *fructificāre* bear fruit]

**fructivorous** /frʌk'tɪvərəs, frʊk-/, *adj.* (of animals) having a diet of fruit, as the flying fox. [L *fructus* fruit + -VOROUS]

**fructose** /'frʊktoʊz, -toʊs, 'frʌk-/, *n.* a laevorotatory ketose sugar, $C_6H_{12}O_6$, which is an intensely sweet carbohydrate occurring naturally in honey and invert sugar; dextrofructose is the naturally occurring isomer; laevulose. [L *fructus* fruit + -OSE[2]]

**fructuous** /'frʌktʃuəs, 'frʊk-/, *adj.* fruitful; profitable. **– fructuously,** *adv.* **– fructuousness,** *n.*

**frug** /frʌg/, *n., v.,* **frugged, frugging.** *–n.* **1.** a dance derived from the twist. *–v.i.* **2.** to dance the frug.

**frugal** /'frugəl/, *adj.* **1.** economical in use or expenditure; prudently saving or sparing. **2.** entailing little expense; costing little; scanty; meagre. [L *frūgālis* economical] **– frugality** /fru'gæləti/, **frugalness,** *n.* **– frugally,** *adv.*

**fruit** /frut/, *n.* **1.** any product of vegetable growth useful to men or animals. **2.** *Bot.* **a.** the developed ovary of a seed plant with its contents and accessory parts, as the peapod, nut, tomato, pineapple, etc. **b.** the edible part of a plant developed from a flower, with any accessory tissues, as the peach, mulberry, banana, etc. **c.** the spores and accessory organs of a cryptogam. **3.** anything produced or accruing; product, result or effect; return or profit. **4.** *Colloq.* a male homosexual. **5.** *Brit.* (formerly a form of address to a friend): *hello, old fruit!* **6.** **fruit for (on) the sideboard, a.** something extra; a luxury item. **b.** an additional source of income. *–v.i.* **7.** to bear or bring to bear fruit. [ME, from OF, from L *fructus* enjoyment, proceeds, fruit] **– fruitlike,** *adj.*

**fruitage** /ˈfrutɪdʒ/, *n.* **1.** the bearing of fruit. **2.** fruits collectively. **3.** product or result.

**fruitarian** /fruˈtɛəriən/, *n.* one whose diet consists mainly of fruit. [FRUIT + -ARIAN, modelled on VEGETARIAN]

**fruit-bat** /ˈfrut-bæt/, *n.* any of various fruit-eating bats of the suborder Megachiroptera, including the flying foxes.

**fruit cake** /ˈfrut keɪk/, *n.* **1.** a rich cake containing currants, nuts, lemon peel, etc. **2.** *Colloq.* a ratbag. **3.** **nutty as a fruitcake,** foolish, very eccentric.

**fruit cocktail** /– ˈkɒkteɪl/, *n.* an assortment of fruits served in a glass or cup as an appetiser or dessert.

**fruit cup** /ˈ– kʌp/, *n.* a non-alcoholic drink made from the juice of one or more fruits, often with pieces of fruit added. Also, **fruit punch.**

**fruiter** /ˈfrutə/, *n.* **1.** a ship employed in transporting fruit. **2.** a fruit-grower.

**fruiterer** /ˈfrutərə/, *n.* a dealer in fruit; greengrocer.

**fruit-fly** /ˈfrut-flaɪ/, *n.* **1.** any of various small, dipterous flies which lay their eggs in developing fruit and are serious destructive pests, esp., in Australia, the Queensland fruit fly, *Dacus tryoni.* **2.** any member of the genus *Drosophila,* the vinegar flies.

**fruitful** /ˈfrutfəl/, *adj.* **1.** abounding in fruit, as trees or other plants; bearing fruit abundantly. **2.** producing an abundant growth, as of fruit. **3.** productive of results; profitable: *fruitful investigations.* **– fruitfully,** *adv.* **– fruitfulness,** *n.*

**fruit gum** /ˈfrut gʌm/, *n.* a soft but resilient fruit-flavoured confection.

**fruit-ice** /ˈfrut-aɪs/, *n.* a fruit flavoured iceblock on a stick containing a minimum of five per cent of fruit.

**fruition** /fruˈɪʃən/, *n.* **1.** attainment of anything desired; attainment of maturity; realisation of results: *the fruition of one's labours.* **2.** enjoyment, as of something attained or realised. **3.** the state of bearing fruit. [ME, from LL *fruitio* enjoyment]

**fruit knife** /ˈfrut naɪf/, *n.* a small knife used for cutting and paring fruit at table.

**fruitless** /ˈfrutləs/, *adj.* **1.** useless; unproductive; vain; without results. **2.** without fruit; barren. **– fruitlessly,** *adv.* **– fruitlessness,** *n.*

**fruit machine** /ˈfrut məʃin/, *n.* *Chiefly Brit. and U.S.* a poker machine, originally displaying its score in the form of replicas of various fruits.

**fruit salad** /– ˈsæləd/, *n.* **1.** a salad composed of various kinds of fruit cut up and mixed together. **2.** *Mil. Colloq.* a large collection of medal ribbons.

**fruit salad plant,** *n.* →**monstera deliciosa.**

**fruit saline** /ˈfrut səlin/, *n.* a fruit-flavoured saline (def. 3).

**fruit slice** /ˈ– slaɪs/, *n.* →**garibaldi.**

**fruit sugar** /ˈ– ʃʊgə/, *n.* →**fructose.**

**fruit tree** /ˈ– tri/, *n.* a tree bearing edible fruit.

**fruity** /ˈfruti/, *adj.,* **-tier, -tiest.** **1.** resembling fruit; having the taste or flavour of fruit. **2.** (of wine) having body and fullness of flavour. **3.** (of a voice) mellow, florid. **4.** sexually suggestive; salacious. **5.** smelly. **6.** *Colloq.* homosexual.

**frumentaceous** /ˌfrumɛnˈteɪʃəs/, *adj.* of the nature of or resembling wheat or other grain. [LL *frūmentāceus* of grain]

**frumenty** /ˈfrumənti/, *n.* hulled wheat boiled in milk and seasoned with sugar, etc. Also, **fromenty, furmenty, furmety, furmity.** [ME *frumentee,* from OF, from *frument,* from L *frūmentum* grain]

**frump** /frʌmp/, *n.* a dowdy, drably dressed woman. [orig. unknown]

**frumpish** /ˈfrʌmpɪʃ/, *adj.* dowdy and unattractive. **– frumpishly,** *adv.* **– frumpishness,** *n.*

**frumpy** /ˈfrʌmpi/, *adj.,* **-pier, -piest.** →**frumpish. – frumpily,** *adv.* **– frumpiness,** *n.*

**frustrate** /frʌsˈtreɪt/, *v.,* **-trated, -trating.** *–v.t.* **1.** to make (plans, efforts, etc.) of no avail; defeat; baffle; nullify. **2.** to disappoint or thwart (a person). [L *frustrātus,* pp., having disappointed or deceived]

**frustration** /frʌsˈtreɪʃən/, *n.* **1.** the state or quality of being frustrated. **2.** *Law.* premature and unexpected determination of a valid contract by the happening subsequent to its making of some event which makes performance legally or physically impossible.

**frustule** /ˈfrʌstʃul/, *n.* the siliceous cell wall of a diatom. [LL *frustulum,* diminutive of L *frustum* piece, bit]

**frustum** /ˈfrʌstəm/, *n., pl.* **-ta** /-tə/, **-tums.** **1.** the part of a conical solid left after cutting off a top portion on a plane parallel to the base. **2.** the part of a conical solid between two cutting planes. [L: piece, bit]

F, frustum of a cone

**frutescent** /fruˈtɛsənt/, *adj.* tending to be shrublike; shrubby. [L *frut(ex)* shrub, bush + -ESCENT] **– frutescence,** *n.*

**fruticose** /ˈfrutəkoʊs/, *adj.* having the form of a shrub; shrublike. [L *fruticōsus* bushy]

**fry**[1] /fraɪ/, *v.,* **fried, frying,** *n., pl.* **fries.** *–v.t.* **1.** to cook in fat, oil, etc., usu. over direct heat. *–v.i.* **2.** to undergo cooking in fat, oil, etc. *–n.* **3.** a dish of something fried. **4.** *U.S.* an occasion at which the chief food is fried, frequently outdoors: *a fish fry.* [ME *frye(n),* from F *frire,* from L *frīgere*]

**fry**[2] /fraɪ/, *n., pl.* **fry.** **1.** the young of fishes, or of some other animals, as frogs. **2.** young or small fishes or other young creatures, as children, collectively. **3.** **small fry,** unimportant or insignificant people; young children. [ME; cf. Icel. *frjō,* Swed. *frö,* Goth. *fraiw* seed]

**fryer** /ˈfraɪə/, *n.* one who or that which fries. Also, **frier.**

**frying pan** /ˈfraɪɪŋ pæn/, *n.* **1.** a shallow pan with a long handle, in which food is fried. *–adj.* **2.** *Colloq.* of no account; small-time.

**fryingpan brand** /ˈfraɪɪŋpæn ˌbrænd/, *n.* *Colloq.* a large brand used by cattle thieves to cover the rightful owner's brand.

**frypan** /ˈfraɪpæn/, *n.* a frying pan, esp. an electric one.

**ft,** **1.** feet. **2.** foot.

**ft cd,** foot-candela.

**fubsy** /ˈfʌbzi/, *adj.* *Colloq.* short and fat; stumpy. [orig. unknown]

**fuchsia** /ˈfjuʃə/, *n.* **1.** any plant of the genus *Fuchsia,* which includes many varieties cultivated for their handsome drooping flowers. **2.** any of various unrelated species with flowers thought to resemble those of the fuchsia, as *Eremophila maculata.* [NL, named after Leonhard *Fuchs,* 1501-66, German botanist. See -IA]

**fuchsine** /ˈfuksaɪn, -sin/, *n.* a germicidal, coal-tar dye obtained by oxidising a mixture of aniline and the toluidines; magenta. The dye is a greenish solid which forms deep red solutions. Also, **fuchsin** /ˈfuksən/. [FUCHS(IA) + -INE[2]; so named from its likeness to the flower in colour]

**fuchsite** /ˈfuksaɪt/, *n.* a green variety of muscovite in which some of the aluminium is replaced by chromium. [named after J. N. von *Fuchs,* 19th-century German geologist]

**fuck** /fʌk/, *Colloq.* *–v.t.* **1.** to have sexual intercourse with. **2.** to treat (someone) unfairly, deceive, or cause inconvenience, distress, etc. to (oft. fol. by *about, around,* etc.). **3.** **fuck up,** to make a mess of; ruin. *–v.i.* **4.** to have sexual intercourse. **5.** to behave stupidly or inanely (oft. fol. by *about, around* etc.). **6.** **fuck off,** (*oft. offensive*) to go away; depart. *–n.* **7.** a person, as the object of the sexual act: *a good fuck.* **8.** the act of sexual intercourse. **9.** **not give a fuck,** not to care at all. **10.** **the fuck,** (an intensive): *who the fuck are you?* *–interj.* **11.** (an offensive exclamation of disgust or annoyance, often used as a mere intensive). **12.** **what the fuck!** (an exclamation of contempt, dismissal, or the like). **13.** (an exclamation of wonder or delight). [? ME, of uncert. orig.; but cf. G *ficken,* lit., to strike, F *foutre,* L *futuere,* Gk *phyteúein*]

**fuckable** /ˈfʌkəbəl/, *adj. Colloq.* sexually desirable.

**fuck-all** /fʌk-ˈɔl, ˈfʌk-ɔl/, *n. Colloq.* very little, nothing: *they've done fuck-all all day.*

**fucked** /fʌkt/, *adj. Colloq.* **1.** exhausted. **2.** ruined, done for. **3.** broken; out of order. **4. get fucked,** (*offensive*) go away; leave (one) alone.

**fucker** /ˈfʌkə/, *n. Colloq.* **1.** one who fucks; one much given to fucking. **2.** a contemptible person or thing. **3.** (*not necessarily offensive*) any person.

**fucking** /ˈfʌkɪŋ/, *Colloq.* –*adj.* **1.** (an intensive signifying approval, as in *it's a fucking marvel* or disapproval, as in *fucking bastard*). –*adv.* **2.** very; extremely: *fucking ridiculous.*

**fuck-up** /ˈfʌk-ʌp/, *n. Colloq.* confusion; ruin; miscalculation; mistake.

**fuckwit** /ˈfʌkwɪt/, *n. Colloq.* a nincompoop.

**fuckwitted** /ˈfʌkwɪtəd/, *adj. Colloq.* foolish; stupid.

**fucoid** /ˈfjukɔɪd/, *adj.* **1.** resembling, or allied to, seaweeds of the genus *Fucus.* See **fucus.** –*n.* **2.** a fucoid seaweed. [FUC(US) + -OID]

**fucus** /ˈfjukəs/, *n., pl.* **-ci** /-saɪ/. any seaweed of the genus *Fucus,* olive brown algae with branching fronds and often air-bladders. [L: rock lichen]

**fuddle** /ˈfʌdl/, *v.,* **-dled, -dling.** –*v.t.* **1.** to intoxicate. **2.** to muddle or confuse. –*v.i.* **3.** to tipple. –*n.* **4.** an intoxicated or confused state.

**fuddy-duddy** /ˈfʌdi-dʌdi/, *n.* a fussy, stuffy, or old-fashioned person.

**fudge**[1] /fʌdʒ/, *n.* a kind of soft sweet composed of sugar, butter, milk, chocolate, or the like. [orig. uncert.]

**fudge**[2] /fʌdʒ/, *n., v.,* **fudged, fudging.** –*n.* **1.** nonsense or bosh (sometimes used as a contemptuous interjection). –*v.i.* **2.** to talk nonsense. [orig. unknown]

**fudge**[3] /fʌdʒ/, *n., v.,* **fudged, fudging.** –*n.* **1.** a small stereotype or a few lines of specially prepared type which may replace a detachable part of the page plate of a newspaper in order to admit a late bulletin without replating the whole page. **2.** the bulletin thus printed, often in colour. **3.** a machine or attachment for printing such a bulletin. –*v.t.* **4.** to put together in a makeshift, clumsy, or dishonest way; fake. **5.** (in marbles) to play one's shot improperly by edging the marble over the line. –*v.i.* **6.** (in games and contests) to gain advantage improperly. [var. of FADGE]

**fuel** /ˈfjuəl, fjul/, *n., v.,* **-elled, -elling,** or (*U.S.*) **-eled, -eling.** –*n.* **1.** combustible matter used to maintain fire, as coal, wood, oil, etc. **2.** a fissile material used in a nuclear reactor to produce energy. **3.** the means of sustaining or increasing passion, ardour, etc. **4.** food; those elements in food which enable the body to produce energy. **5. add fuel to the fire,** to aggravate. –*v.t.* **6.** to supply with fuel. –*v.i.* **7.** to procure or take in fuel. (oft. fol. by *up*). [ME *fuelle,* from OF *feuaile,* from L *focus* hearth, fireplace]

**fuel cell** /ˈ– sɛl/, *n.* **1.** a continuously fed battery in which a chemical reaction is used directly to produce electricity. **2.** one of a number of fuel tanks.

**fuel element** /ˈ– ɛləmənt/, *n.* an element of nuclear fuel for use in a nuclear reactor, esp. uranium encased in a canister.

**fuel-injection** /ˈfjuəl-ɪndʒɛkʃən/, *n.* a method of spraying liquid fuel directly into the cylinders of an internal-combustion engine instead of using a carburettor. – **fuel-injector,** *n.*

**fuel oil** /ˈfjuəl ɔɪl/, *n.* an oil used for fuel, esp. one used as a substitute for coal, as crude petroleum.

**fuel stove** /– ˈstoʊv/, *n.* a stove which burns wood, coal, coke, or other solid fuel to generate heat for cooking, room-warming, etc.

**fug** /fʌg/, *n.* a stuffy or smoky atmosphere. – **fuggy,** *adj.*

**fugacious** /fjuˈgeɪʃəs/, *adj.* **1.** *Bot.* falling or fading early. **2.** fleeting; transitory. [obs. *fugacy* flight (from L *fugāx* apt to flee) + -OUS] – **fugaciously,** *adv.* – **fugacity** /fjuˈgæsəti/, *n.*

**fugal**[1] /ˈfjugəl/, *adj.* of or pertaining to a fugue, or composed in the style of a fugue. – **fugally,** *adv.*

**fugal**[2] /ˈfjugəl/, *n.* →**whizzer** (def. 2).

**fugato** /fjuˈgatoʊ/, *adv.* **1.** in fugue style, but not according to strict rules. –*n.* **2.** music in this style. [It.]

**-fuge,** a word element referring to 'flight', as in *refuge.* [combining form representing L *-fugia,* from *fugāre* put to flight]

**fugitive** /ˈfjudʒətəv, -ɪv/, *n.* **1.** a person who is fleeing; a runaway. –*adj.* **2.** having taken flight, or run away: *a fugitive slave.* **3.** fleeting; transitory. **4.** dealing with subjects of passing interest, as writings; ephemeral. **5.** difficult to define or retain; elusive. **6.** wandering, roving, or vagabond. [L *fugitīvus* fleeing; replacing ME *fugitif,* from F] – **fugitively,** *adv.* – **fugitiveness,** *n.*

**fugleman** /ˈfjugəlmən/, *n., pl.* **-men.** **1.** a well-drilled soldier placed in front of a military company as a model for others. **2.** anyone serving as an example. [G *Flügelmann,* lit., wing man]

**fugue** /fjug/, *n.* **1.** *Music.* a polyphonic composition based upon one, two, or even more themes, which are enunciated by the several voices or parts in turn, subjected to contrapuntal treatment, and gradually built up into a complex form having somewhat distinct divisions or stages of development and a marked climax at the end. **2.** *Psychol.* a period of loss of memory, when the individual disappears from his usual haunts. [F, from It. *fuga,* from L *fuga* flight] – **fuguelike,** *adj.*

**Führer** /ˈfjurə/, *n.* **1.** leader. **2. der** /dɛə/ **Führer,** the leader (applied esp. to Adolf Hitler). Also, **Fuehrer.** [G]

**-ful,** a suffix meaning: **1.** full of or characterised by: *shameful, beautiful, careful, thoughtful.* **2.** tending or able to: *wakeful, harmful.* **3.** as much as will fill: *spoonful, handful.* [ME and OE *-full, -ful,* representing *full, ful* FULL[1]]

**fulcrum** /ˈfʊlkrəm/, *n., pl.* **-crums, -cra** /-krə/. **1.** the support, or point of rest, on which a lever turns in moving a body. **2.** a prop. [L: bedpost]

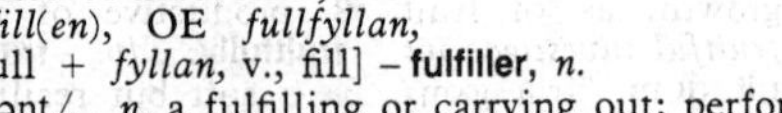

F, fulcrum

**fulfil** /fʊlˈfɪl/, *v.t.,* **-filled, -filling.** **1.** to carry out, or bring to consummation, as a prophecy, promise, etc. **2.** to perform or do, as duty; obey or follow, as commands. **3.** to satisfy (requirements, etc.) **4.** to bring to an end, finish, or complete, as a period of time. Also, *U.S.* **fulfill.** [ME *fulfill(en),* OE *fullfyllan,* from *full,* adj., full + *fyllan,* v., fill] – **fulfiller,** *n.*

**fulfilment** /fʊlˈfɪlmənt/, *n.* a fulfilling or carrying out; performance; completion; realisation; satisfaction. Also, *U.S.,* **fulfillment.**

**fulgent** /ˈfʌldʒənt/, *adj.* shining brightly; resplendent. [ME, from L *fulgens,* ppr.] – **fulgently,** *adv.*

**fulgurant** /ˈfʊlgjurənt, ˈfʌl-/, *adj.* flashing like lightning. [L *fulgurans,* ppr.]

**fulgurate** /ˈfʊlgjəreɪt, ˈfʌl-/, *v.,* **-rated, -rating.** –*v.i.* **1.** to flash or dart like lightning. –*v.t.* **2.** *Med.* to destroy (esp. an abnormal growth) by electrodessication. [L *fulgurātus,* pp.] – **fulguration** /fʊlgjəˈreɪʃən, fʌl-/, *n.*

**fulgurating** /ˈfʊlgjəreɪtɪŋ, ˈfʌl-/, *adj.* (of pains) sharp and intermittent, like flashes of lightning.

**fulgurite** /ˈfʊlgjuraɪt, ˈfʌl-/, *n.* a tube formed in sand or rock by lightning. [L *fulgur* lightning + -ITE[1]]

**fulgurous** /ˈfʊlgjərəs, ˈfʌl-/, *adj.* resembling lightning.

**fuliginous** /fjuˈlɪdʒənəs/, *adj.* **1.** sooty; smoky. **2.** dull or brownish dark grey. [LL *fūlīginōsus* full of soot]

**full**[1] /fʊl/, *adj.* **1.** filled; containing all that can be held; filled to utmost capacity: *a full cup.* **2.** complete; entire; maximum: *a full supply.* **3.** of the maximum size, amount, extent, volume, etc.: *a full kilometre, full pay, the full moon.* **4.** (of garments, etc.) wide, ample, or having ample folds. **5.** filled or rounded out, as in form. **6.** *Music.* ample and complete in volume or richness of sound. **7.** (of wines) having considerable body. **8.** (of a horse) still ungelded. **9.** being fully or entirely such: *a full brother.* **10.** *Colloq.* intoxicated. **11.** *Naut.* (of a hull form) with bluff bow and stern, and almost square mid section. **12. full and by,** *Naut.* with the sails full and sailing close to the wind. **13. full of,** engrossed with or absorbed in. **14. full of oneself,** conceited; egoistic. **15. full up, a.** filled to capacity. **b.** *Colloq.* (of a person) replete; having eaten enough. **c.** *N.Z. Colloq.* exasperated; disgruntled. **16. full as a boot** (**bull**), (**tick**), *Colloq.* very drunk. **17. in full cry,** in hot pursuit, as dogs in the chase. **18. in full force,** with no-one missing. –*adv.* **19.** completely or entirely. **20.** exactly or directly: *the blow struck him full* *in the face.* **21.** *Archaic.* very: *full well.* *–v.t.* **22.** *Sewing.* to ease one side of a seam into the other, by gathers or tucks. *–v.i.* **23.** to become full. *–n.* **24. in full, a.** without reduction; to or for the full amount: *a receipt in full.* **b.** without abbreviation or contraction. **25. on the full,** (of a ball) in flight before bouncing. **26. to the full,** in full measure; to the utmost extent. **27.** (of the moon) the stage of complete illumination. [ME and OE *full, ful,* c. G *voll;* akin to L *plēnus,* Gk *plḗrēs*] – **fully,** *adv.*

**full**[2] /fʊl/, *v.t.* **1.** to cleanse and thicken (cloth, etc.) by special processes in manufacture. *–v.i.* **2.** (of cloth, etc.) to become compacted or felted. [ME *fulle(n),* backformation from FULLER[1]]

**full age** /– 'eɪdʒ/, *n.* adulthood, after one's minority; the age of 18.

**full-back** /fʊl-'bæk, 'fʊl-bæk/, *n.* **1.** *Aus. Rules.* **a.** the central position on the back line nearest to the defenders' goal. **b.** one who plays in this position. **2.** *Soccer, Rugby, Hockey, etc.* a player whose main purpose is to defend his own goal.

**Full Bench** /fʊl 'bɛntʃ/, *n.* a sitting of a court consisting of more than one judge, which is deemed to represent all of the judges of the Court.

**full binding** /fʊl 'baɪndɪŋ/, *n.* a complete binding of a volume in any one material, generally leather.

**full blood** /'– blʌd/, *n.* **1.** an individual of unmixed ancestry esp. for dark-skinned peoples as Aborigines, negroes, etc. **2.** purebred, esp. of horses.

**full-blooded** /'fʊl-blʌdəd/, *adj.* **1.** of unmixed ancestry; thoroughbred. **2.** vigorous; virile; hearty.

**full-blown** /'fʊl-bloʊn/, *adj.* **1.** in full bloom: *a full-blown rose.* **2.** completely developed.

**full board** /fʊl 'bɔd/, *n.* **1.** (in a hotel or the like) the provision of sleeping accommodation and all main meals. **2.** a complete number of shearers for the season.

**full-bodied** /'fʊl-bɒdid/, *adj.* with maximum flavour and strength.

**full bore** /fʊl 'bɔ/, *adv.* **1.** with maximum effort; with the greatest possible speed or productivity. *–n.* **2.** the maximum production (of oil or gas from a drill hole). **3. the full bore,** *Colloq.* the maximum: *give it the full bore.*

**full-bottomed** /'fʊl-bɒtəmd/, *adj.* of or pertaining to a wig which is long at the back.

**full brick** /– 'brɪk/, *adj.* **1.** of or pertaining to a building all the walls of which are brick. **2.** such a building.

**full brother** /– 'brʌðə/, *n.* a brother both of whose parents are the same as one's own. Also, **whole brother.**

**full chat** /– 'tʃæt/, *adv.* →**flat chat.**

**full container load,** *n.* the contents of a shipping or other container which has been hired by one shipper with the complete contents consigned to one consignee.

**full cousin** /'fʊl kʌzən/, *n.* See **cousin.**

**full dress** /fʊl 'drɛs/, *n.* **1.** a uniform worn on ceremonial or formal occasions, with all appropriate accoutrements. **2.** ceremonial or formal evening attire.

**full-dress** /'fʊl-drɛs/, *adj.* **1.** denoting, pertaining to, or requiring full dress. **2.** formal and of some importance.

**fuller**[1] /'fʊlə/, *n.* one who fulls cloth. [ME; OE *fullere,* from L *full(o)* fuller + *-ere* -ER[1]]

**fuller**[2] /'fʊlə/, *n.* a half-round set hammer used for grooving and spreading iron. [apparently from FULL[1], *v.,* to make full + -ER[1]]

**fuller's earth** /fʊləz 'ɜθ/, *n.* an absorbent clay, used for removing grease from cloth, etc., in fulling, as a filter, medically, as a dusting powder, and in paints as an extender.

**fuller's teasel** /– 'tizəl/, *n.* a teasel, *Dipsacus fullonum,* of which the dried heads were used for raising the nap on cloth.

**full-faced** /'fʊl-feɪst/, *adj.* **1.** having a plump or round face. **2.** facing squarely towards the spectator or in a given direction. **3.** *Print.* (of type) bold-faced.

**full-forward** /fʊl-'fɔwəd/, *n. Aus. Rules.* **1.** the central position on the forward line nearest to the goal which is being attacked. **2.** one who plays in such a position.

**full-frontal** /'fʊl-frʌntəl/, *adj.* **1.** giving a complete view of a naked person from the front. **2.** with every detail exposed. *–n.* **3.** a full-frontal picture.

**full-grown** /'fʊl-groʊn/, *adj.* fully grown; mature.

**full house** /fʊl 'haʊs/, *n.* **1.** a poker hand consisting of three of a kind and a pair, as three queens and two tens. **2.** a theatre or cinema filled to capacity. **3.** (in housie-housie) a fully covered card. Also, **full hand.**

**full-length** /'fʊl-lɛŋθ/, *adj.* **1.** fully stretched. **2.** (of a portrait) showing the whole figure. **3.** unabridged. **4.** of standard length.

**full moon** /fʊl 'mun/, *n.* →**moon** (def. 2c).

**full-mouth** /'fʊl-maʊθ/, *adj.* **1.** a sheep that has all its permanent incisor teeth. *–n.* **2.** such a sheep.

**full nelson** /fʊl 'nɛlsən/, *n.* a wrestling hold, illegal under most rules, in which both arms pass from behind under the opponent's armpits and the hands are joined behind his neck.

**fullness** /'fʊlnəs/, *n.* **1.** the state of being full. **2. the fullness of time,** the proper or destined time. Also, *Chiefly U.S.,* **fulness.**

**full out** /'fʊl aʊt/, *adj.* **1.** written out in full. **2.** *Print.* not indented.

**full pitch** /– 'pɪtʃ/, *n.* →**full toss.**

**full point** /– 'pɔɪnt/, *n.* →**full stop.**

**full points** /– 'pɔɪnts/, *n.pl. Colloq.* (in Australian Rules) a goal.

**full radiator** /– 'reɪdieɪtə/, *n.* →**black body** (def. 1).

**full-rigged** /'fʊl-rɪgd/, *adj.* **1.** *Naut.* having three or more masts and with square sails on all masts. **2.** having all equipment.

**full sail** /fʊl 'seɪl/, *adv.* **1.** with all sails set. **2.** Also, **at full sail.** moving rapidly: *she burst into the room full sail.*

**full-scale** /'fʊl-skeɪl/, *adj.* **1.** (of a drawing, etc.) identical in size to the original. **2.** large; important; thorough: *a full-scale attack.*

**full score** /fʊl 'skɔ/, *n.* a musical score in which every part (for voice or instrument) is written on a separate stave.

**full sister** /– 'sɪstə/, *n.* a sister both of whose parents are the same as one's own. Also, **whole sister.**

**full stop** /– 'stɒp/, *n.* the point or character (.) used to mark the end of a complete declarative sentence, indicate an abbreviation, etc.; a period. Also, **full point.**

**full tilt** /– 'tɪlt/, *adj. Colloq.* at top speed: *the bus was going full tilt for the station.*

**full-time** /'fʊl-taɪm/, *adj.* **1.** of, or pertaining to, or taking all the normal working hours (opposed to *part-time*). **2.** of, or pertaining to, something which occupies a person all the time. **3.** *Sport.* of or pertaining to the time at which play is to end: *the full-time whistle.* *–adv.* **4.** during all normal working hours. *–n.* **5.** *Sport.* the time at which play is to end.

**full toss** /fʊl 'tɒs/, *n. Cricket.* a ball bowled which travels the whole way to the batsman without touching the ground. Also, **full pitch.**

**fully-fashioned** /'fʊli-fæʃənd/, *adj.* (of knitted garments, etc.) shaped to fit closely.

**fully-fledged** /'fʊli-flɛdʒd/, *adj.* **1.** able to fly. **2.** fully developed. **3.** of full rank or standing. **4.** fully qualified or established: *a fully-fledged professor.*

**fully-paid** /'fʊli-peɪd/, *adj.* **1.** of or pertaining to shares or stock on which the face-value of the capital represented has been paid in full. *–n.* **2.** such a share or stock.

**fulmar** /'fʊlmə/, *n.* any of certain oceanic birds of the petrel family, as *Fulmar glacioloides,* a gull-like Antarctic species. [? lit., foul gull (with allusion to its stench), from Scand.; cf. Icel. *fūll* foul, *mār* gull]

**fulminant** /'fʊlmənənt, 'fʌl-/, *adj.* **1.** fulminating. **2.** *Pathol.* developing or progressing suddenly, severely and rapidly. [L *fulminans,* ppr., lightning]

**fulminate** /'fʊlməneɪt, 'fʌl-/, *v.,* **-nated, -nating,** *n.* *–v.i.* **1.** to explode with a loud noise; detonate. **2.** to issue denunciations or the like (oft. fol. by *against*). *–v.t.* **3.** to cause to explode. *–n.* **4.** *Chem.* one of a group of unstable explosive compounds derived from fulminic acid, esp. the mercury salt of fulminic acid which is a powerful detonating agent. [L *fulminātus,* pp., struck by lightning] – **fulminator,** *n.* – **fulminatory,** *adj.*

**fulminating compound** /fʊlməneɪtɪŋ 'kɒmpaʊnd/, *n.* →**fulminate.**

**fulminating gold** /– 'goʊld/, *n.* the explosive, yellow precipitate formed when ammonia is added to a solution of gold chloride.

**fulminating powder** /– 'paudə/, *n.* **1.** powder which explodes by percussion. **2.** →**fulminate.**

**fulmination** /fulmə'neɪʃən, fʌl-/, *n.* **1.** a violent denunciation or censure. **2.** violent explosion.

**fulminic acid** /fʊl,mɪnɪk 'æsəd/, *n.* an acid, HONC, an isomer of cyanic acid, found only in its salts, the fulminates.

**fulminous** /'fʊlmənəs, 'fʌl-/, *adj.* connected with, or resembling, thunder and lightning.

**fulsome** /'fʊlsəm/, *adj.* **1.** offensive to good taste, esp. as being excessive; gross; insincere: *fulsome praise.* **2.** disgusting, nauseating. **3.** copious; abundant. [ME *fulsum,* from FULL[1] + -SOME[1]; evidence of association with FOUL] – **fulsomely,** *adv.* – **fulsomeness,** *n.*

**fulvous** /'fʊlvəs/, *adj.* tawny; dull yellowish grey or brown. [L *fulvus* deep yellow]

**fumaric acid** /fju,mærɪk 'æsəd/, *n.* a dibasic acid, HOOCCH:CHCOOH, isomeric with maleic acid, occurring in small amounts in almost all living cells as a component of the citric acid cycle and in greater amounts in several plants.

**fumarole** /'fjumərouI/, *n.* a hole in or near a volcano, from which vapour issues. [F *fumerolle,* from LL *fūmāriolum,* diminutive of L *fūmārium* smoke chamber]

**fumble** /'fʌmbəl/, *v.,* **-bled, -bling,** *n.* –*v.i.* **1.** to feel or grope about clumsily (fol. by *at, with, after, for*). **2.** to hesitate in speaking; to speak indistinctly. **3.** *Sport.* to fumble the ball. –*v.t.* **4.** to handle clumsily. **5.** *Sport.* to fail to catch and hold (a ball) or to catch and hold (it) clumsily. **6.** *Colloq.* to touch, fondle, embrace, etc.,the body of another as a means to sexual stimulation. –*n.* **7.** the act of fumbling. **8.** a bungling attempt at something. [LG *fummeln;* cf. Swed. *fumla* grope] – **fumbler,** *n.* – **fumbling,** *adj., n.* – **fumblingly,** *adv.*

**fume** /fjum/, *n., v.,* **fumed, fuming.** –*n.* **1.** (*oft. pl.*) any smokelike or vaporous exhalation from matter or substances. **2.** an odorous exhalation as from flowers. –*v.t.* **3.** to send forth as fumes. **4.** to disperse or drive away in vapours; send up as vapour. **5.** to treat with fumes, to fumigate. –*v.i.* **6.** (of smoke, a vapour, etc.) to rise or pass off. **7.** to emit fumes. **8.** to show irritation or anger. [ME, from OF *fum,* from L *fūmus* smoke, steam, fume] – **fumeless,** *adj.* – **fumelike,** *adj.* – **fumingly,** *adv.*

**fume cupboard** /'– kʌbəd/, *n.* a cupboard with forced ventilation designed for conducting experiments which involve noxious or harmful gases.

**fumed** /fjumd/, *adj.* darkened or coloured by exposure to ammonia fumes, as oak and other wood.

**fumet** /'fjumeɪ/, *n.* a strong, well-reduced stock made from fish or game. [F *fumer* smoke]

**fumigant** /'fjuməgənt/, *n.* any chemical, as hydrogen cyanide and ethylene oxide, which is used in fumigation.

**fumigate** /'fjuməgeɪt/, *v.t.,* **-gated, -gating.** to expose to smoke or fumes, as in disinfecting. [L *fūmigātus,* pp., smoked] – **fumigation** /fjumə'geɪʃən/, *n.*

**fumigator** /'fjuməgeɪtə/, *n.* **1.** one who or that which fumigates. **2.** a structure in which plants are fumigated to destroy insects.

**fuming sulphuric acid,** *n.* a solution of sulphur trioxide in sulphuric acid, $H_2S_2O_7$, forming crystals below 35°C; oleum; pyrosulphuric acid; disulphuric acid.

**fumitory** /'fjumətri, -təri/, *n., pl.* **-ries.** any plant of the genus *Fumaria,* of the family Fumariaceae, esp. a delicate herb, *F. officinalis,* with finely dissected leaves and racemes of purplish flowers, formerly used medicinally. [ME *fumeter,* from OF *fumeterre,* from ML *fūmus terrae* smoke of the earth]

**fumy** /'fjumi/, *adj.,* **-mier, -miest.** composed of or full of fumes; fumelike.

**fun** /fʌn/, *n., v.,* **funned, funning.** –*n.* **1.** mirthful sport or diversion; merry amusement; joking; playfulness. **2. for** or **in fun,** as a joke; playfully; not seriously. **3. like fun,** *Colloq.* not at all. **4. make fun of, poke fun at,** to ridicule. –*v.i.* **5.** *Colloq.* to make fun; joke. –*adj.* **6.** *Colloq.* of, or pertaining to fun; amusing. **7.** *Colloq.* entertaining; lively: *Brisbane is a fun city.* [? d. var. of obs. *fon,* v., befool. See FOND[1]]

**funambulist** /fju'næmbjələst/, *n.* a tightrope walker. [L *fūnambulus* rope-dancer + -IST] – **funambulism,** *n.*

**fun and games,** *n.pl. Colloq.* **1.** inconsequential activity. **2.** (*ironic*) amatory play. **3.** (*ironic*) problems and difficulties.

**function** /'fʌŋkʃən/, *n.* **1.** the kind of action or activity proper to a person, thing, or institution. **2.** any ceremonious public or social gathering or occasion. **3.** *Maths.* a mathematical quantity whose value depends upon the values of other quantities, called the arguments or independent variables of the function. **4.** *Gram.* **a.** the grammatical role which a linguistic form plays, or the position which it occupies in a particular construction. **b.** the grammatical roles or the positions of a linguistic form or form class collectively. **5.** any basic computer operation. –*v.i.* **6.** to perform a function; act; serve; operate; carry out normal work, activity, or processes. **7.** *Gram.* to have or exercise a function: *in earlier English the present tense often functioned as the future.* [L *functio* performance] – **functionless,** *adj.*

**functional** /'fʌŋkʃənəl/, *adj.* **1.** of or pertaining to a function or functions. **2.** designed or adapted primarily to perform some operation or duty: *a functional building.* **3.** capable of operating or functioning. **4.** pertaining to an algebraic operation: *a functional symbol.* – **functionality** /fʌŋkʃə'nælәti/, *n.* – **functionally,** *adv.*

**functional disease** /– də'ziz/, *n.* a disease in which there is a morbid change in the function of an organ, but no structural alteration in the tissues involved often implying a psychosomatic disease (opposed to *organic disease*).

**functionalise** /'fʌŋkʃənəlaɪz/, *v.t.,* **-lised, -lising.** **1.** to make functional or more functional. **2.** to place or assign to some function or office. Also, **functionalize.**

**functionalism** /'fʌŋkʃənəlɪzəm/, *n.* **1.** the doctrine or practice in furniture design, architecture, etc., under which such factors as material and form are determined primarily by functional considerations. **2.** any doctrine or its application stressing purpose, practicality, utility.

**functionary** /'fʌŋkʃənri, -ʃənəri/, *n., pl.* **-ries.** →**official.**

**function word** /'fʌŋkʃən wɜd/, *n. Linguistics.* a word, like *the* or *of,* which may add meaning to, or show relationships between, content words in a given sentence but do not refer the mind to any entity outside the sentence.

**fund** /fʌnd/, *n.* **1.** a stock of money or pecuniary resources. **2.** a store or stock of something, now often of something immaterial: *a fund of knowledge.* **3.** (*pl.*) money in hand; pecuniary resources. **4.** (*pl.*) various stocks of the national debt in which the general public may invest. **5.** (*pl., usu. cap.*) consols and other government securities. –*v.t.* **6.** to put into a fund or store. **7.** to convert (a floating debt or debts) into a more or less permanent debt or loan, represented by interest-bearing bonds. **8.** to arrange for (a debt or debts) to be on a long-term basis. **9.** to invest (money) in a fund or funds. **10.** to provide a fund to pay the interest or principle of (a debt). [L *fundus* bottom, estate; replacing FOND[2] in most of its meanings]

**fundament** /'fʌndəmənt/, *n.* →**anus.** [L *fundāmentum* foundation; replacing ME *fondement,* from OF]

**fundamental** /fʌndə'mɛntl/, *adj.* **1.** serving as, or being a component part of, a foundation or basis; basic; underlying: *fundamental principles.* **2.** of or affecting the foundation or basis: *a fundamental change.* **3.** essential; primary; original. **4.** *Music.* (of a chord) having its root as its lowest note. –*n.* **5.** a leading or primary principle, rule, law, or the like, which serves as the groundwork of a system; essential part. **6.** Also, **fundamental note** or **tone.** *Music.* **a.** the root of a chord. **b.** the primary note of the harmonic series. **7.** →**fundamental frequency.** [NL *fundāmentālis,* from L *fundāmentum* foundation] – **fundamentality** /fʌndəmɛn'tæləti/, *n.* – **fundamentally,** *adv.*

**fundamental bass** /– 'beɪs/, *n.* a fictitious bass line consisting of the roots of the chords employed.

**fundamental constant** /– 'kɒnstənt/, *n.* the value of one of certain basic physical quantities, such as the charge and mass of an electron, the masses of a proton and a neutron, the velocity of light, Planck's constant, Boltzmann's constant, gravitational constant, etc., upon which the numerical values of all physical phenomena depend.

**fundamental frequency** /– 'frikwənsi/, *n.* the component of lowest frequency in a complex sound of musical type.

**fundamentalism** /fʌndəˈmɛntəlɪzəm/, *n.* **1.** a movement in American Protestantism which stresses the inerrancy of the Bible not only in matters of faith and morals but also as literal historical record and prophecy, e.g., of creation, the virgin birth of Christ, his second advent, etc. (opposed to *modernism*). **2.** the faith in the Bible so stressed. – **fundamentalist,** *n., adj.*

**fundamental particle** /ˌfʌndəmɛntl ˈpatɪkəl/, *n.* →**elementary particle.**

**fundamental unit** /– ˈjunət/, *n.* one of the units (esp. those of mass, length, and time) taken as a basis for a system of units.

**funded debt** /ˈfʌndəd dɛt/, *n.* a government debt, not repayable before twelve months, for the repayment of which a sinking fund has been established.

**fundraise** /ˈfʌndreɪz/, *v.i.*, **-raised, -raising.** to collect money for a specific group or purpose as for a charity, a political party, a building appeal, etc. – **fundraising,** *n.*

**fund-raiser** /ˈfʌnd-reɪzə/, *n.* **1.** a person who is employed to raise funds. **2.** a social event organised to raise funds.

**fundus** /ˈfʌndəs/, *n.* the base of an animal organ, or the part opposite to or remote from an aperture. [L: bottom]

**funeral** /ˈfjunrəl, ˈfjunərəl/, *n.* **1.** the ceremonies connected with the disposition of the body of a dead person; obsequies. **2.** a funeral procession. **3.** *Colloq.* business; worry; concern: *that's his funeral.* *–adj.* **4.** of or pertaining to a funeral. [ME, from ML *fūnerālis,* from L *fūnus* funeral, death]

**funeral director** /ˈ– dərɛktə/, *n.* →**undertaker.**

**funeral parlour** /ˈ– palə/, *n.* an undertaker's place of business, sometimes containing a small chapel as well as the rooms where the dead are prepared for burial or cremation.

**funerary** /ˈfjunərəri/, *adj.* of or pertaining to a funeral or burial: *a funerary urn.*

**funereal** /fjuˈnɪəriəl/, *adj.* **1.** of or pertaining to a funeral. **2.** mournful; gloomy; dismal. [L *fūnereus* of a funeral + -AL[1]] – **funereally,** *adv.*

**funfair** /ˈfʌnfɛə/, *n.* an outdoor entertainment with sideshows, mechanical amusements, etc.; a fair.

**fungal** /ˈfʌŋgəl/, *adj.* **1.** →**fungous.** *–n.* **2.** →**fungus.**

**fungate** /ˈfʌŋgeɪt/, *v.i.*, **-ated, -ating.** to grow in fungus-like masses.

**fungi** /ˈfʌŋgi/, *n.* plural of **fungus.**

**fungible** /ˈfʌndʒəbəl/, *adj.* **1.** of such a nature that one unit or portion may be replaced by another in respect of function, office, or use: usu. confined to goods. *–n.* **2.** a fungible thing, as money or grain. [ML *fungibilis,* from L *fungī* fulfil the office of]

**fungicide** /ˈfʌŋgəsaɪd/, *n.* an agent, such as a spray or dust, used for destroying fungi. [*fungi-* (combining form of FUNGUS) + -CIDE] – **fungicidal** /fʌŋgəˈsaɪdəl/, *adj.*

**fungiform** /ˈfʌŋgəfɔm/, *adj.* having the form of a fungus or mushroom. [*fungi-* (combining form of FUNGUS) + -FORM]

**fungoid** /ˈfʌŋgɔɪd/, *adj.* **1.** resembling a fungus; of the nature of a fungus. **2.** *Pathol.* characterised by fungus-like morbid growths.

**fungous** /ˈfʌŋgəs/, *adj.* **1.** of, pertaining to, or caused by fungi. **2.** of the nature of or resembling a fungus. [ME, from L *fungōsus,* from *fungus* sponge, mushroom, fungus]

**fungus** /ˈfʌŋgəs/, *n., pl.* **fungi** /ˈfʌŋgi/, **funguses,** *adj.* *–n.* **1.** any of the Fungi, a group of thallophytes including the mushrooms, moulds, mildews, rusts, smuts, etc., characterised chiefly by absence of chlorophyll and which subsist upon dead or living organic matter. **2.** *Pathol.* a spongy morbid growth, as proud flesh formed in a wound. *–adj.* **3.** →**fungous.** [L: mushroom, fungus] – **fungus-like,** *adj.*

**fungus fly** /ˈ– flaɪ/, *n.* any of numerous small, two-winged flies of the family Mycetophilidae, that breed in fungi, some of which have light-producing larvae.

**funicle** /ˈfjunɪkəl/, *n.* (in plants) the stalk of an ovule or seed. [L *fūniculus,* diminutive of *fūnis* rope]

**funicular** /fəˈnɪkjələ/, *adj.* **1.** of or pertaning to a rope or cord, or its tension. **2.** worked by a rope or the like. *–n.* **3.** →**funicular railway.** [L *fūniculus* little rope + -AR[1]]

**funicular railway** /ˈ– reɪlweɪ/, *n.* a railway system of short length operating up steep gradients, in which cable-linked cars or trains move up and down simultaneously, thus minimising the pull of gravity.

**funiculate** /fjuˈnɪkjələt, -leɪt/, *adj.* having a funicle.

**funiculus** /fjuˈnɪkjələs/, *n., pl.* **-li** /-laɪ/. **1.** *Anat.* a cordlike structure, esp. one of the three main nerve tracts of each half of the spinal cord. **2.** *Bot.* →**funicle.** [L, diminutive of *fūnis* rope]

**funk**[1] /fʌŋk/, *Colloq. –n.* **1.** cowering fear; state of fright or terror. **2.** one who funks; a coward. *–v.t.* **3.** to be afraid of. **4.** to frighten. **5.** to shrink from; try to shirk. *–v.i.* **6.** to shrink or quail in fear. [? Flemish *fonck*]

**funk**[2] /fʌnk/, *n.* **1.** an up-tempo style of soul music originating on the west coast of America and distinguished by much syncopation. **2.** *U.S.* a strong smell or stink. [F, akin to d. *funquer* to give off smoke]

**funk art** /– ˈat/, *n.* a style of art originating on the west coast of America which reacted against the more rigid New York style of abstract expressionism, and sought freer, more human forms of expression; a regional variant of pop art.

**funk-hole** /ˈfʌŋk-hoʊl/, *n. Colloq.* a place of refuge from something feared. [FUNK[1] + HOLE]

**funky** /ˈfʌŋki/, *adj.* **1.** exciting, satisfying or pleasurable. **2.** *Music.* pertaining to or in the style of funk. **3.** of or pertaining to a style of dress, reminiscent of the period identified by the emergence of jazz. **4.** *U.S.* having an unpleasant smell. [FUNK[2] + -Y[1]]

**funnel** /ˈfʌnəl/, *n., v.*, **-nelled, -nelling** or (*U.S.*) **-neled, -neling.** *–n.* **1.** a cone-shaped utensil with a tube at the apex, for conducting liquid, etc., through a small opening, as into a bottle. **2.** a metal chimney, esp. of a ship or a steam-engine. **3.** a flue, tube, or shaft, as for ventilation. *–v.t.* **4.** to converge or concentrate: *to funnel all one's energies into a job.* [ME *fonel,* from OF, from LL *fundibulum,* L *infundibulum*] – **funnel-like,** *adj.*

funnel

**funnel cloud** /ˈ– klaʊd/, *n.* a funnel-shaped cloud formed from the core of a waterspout or tornado.

**funnel-web** /ˈfʌnəl-wɛb/, *n.* **1.** either of two species of large, aggressive, venomous, eastern Australian spiders of the genus *Atrax,* which construct a silken, tube-like lair sometimes expanded into a funnel shape at the entrance. **2.** any other species of the genus *Atrax.*

funnel-web spider

**funnies** /ˈfʌniz/, *n.pl. Colloq.* **1.** comic strips. **2.** the section of a newspaper containing them.

**funny** /ˈfʌni/, *adj.*, **-nier, -niest.** **1.** affording fun; amusing; comical. **2.** curious; strange; queer; odd. **3.** *Colloq.* insolent. *–n.* **4.** *Colloq.* a joke. [FUN, *n.* + -Y[1]] – **funnily,** *adv.* – **funniness,** *n.*

**funny bone** /ˈ– boʊn/, *n.* the part of the elbow where the ulnar nerve passes by the internal condyle of the humerus, which when struck causes a peculiar tingling sensation in the arm and hand. Also, *U.S.,* **crazy bone.**

**funny business** /ˈ– bɪznəs/, *n. Colloq.* **1.** foolish behaviour. **2.** underhand, dubious, or dishonest dealings. **3.** sexual intercourse or any amorous behaviour.

**funny farm** /ˈ– fam/, *n. Colloq.* (*joc.*) a lunatic asylum; psychiatric hospital.

**fun park** /ˈfʌn pak/, *n.* →**amusement park.**

**fun parlour** /ˈ– palə/, *n.* a shop with various coin-operated devices for entertainment, as pin ball machines, etc.

**fur,** furlong.

**fur** /fɜ/, *n., v.*, **furred, furring.** *–n.* **1.** the skin of certain animals (as the sable, ermine, beaver, etc.), covered with a fine, soft, thick, hairy coating. **2.** the cured and treated skin of certain of these animals used for lining or trimming garments or for entire garments. **3.** (*usu. pl.*) an article of dress made of or with such material, as a fur coat or stole. **4.** any coating resembling or suggesting fur, as one of morbid matter

i = peat ɪ = pit ɛ = pet æ = pat a = part ɒ = pot ʌ = putt ɔ = port ʊ = put u = pool ɜ = pert ə = apart aɪ = buy eɪ = bay ɔɪ = boy aʊ = how oʊ = hoe ɪə = here ɛə = hair ʊə = tour g = give θ = thin ð = then ʃ = show ʒ = measure tʃ = choke dʒ = joke ŋ = sing j = you õ = Fr. bon

on the tongue. **5.** the gritty insoluble deposit formed on the inside of boilers, kettles, etc., when hard water is boiled, consisting of calcium, magnesium, and iron carbonates. **6.** *Her.* any of several patterns that are classified as tinctures. **7.** **make the fur fly,** *Colloq.* to quarrel noisily; make a scene or disturbance. *–v.t.* **8.** to line, face, or trim (a garment, etc.) with fur. **9.** to clothe (a person) with fur. **10.** to coat with foul or deposited matter. **11.** *Bldg Trades.* to apply furring to (a wall, etc.) *–adj.* **12.** of or pertaining to fur. [ME *furre,* from OF *forrer* line with fur, orig. encase, from *forre* sheath, from Gmc; cf. G *Futter* sheath] – **furless,** *adj.*

**furan** /ˈfjuræn, fjəˈræn/, *n.* a colourless liquid, $C_4H_4O$, an unsaturated five-membered ring compound derived from furfural. Also, **furfuran.** [var. of FURFURAN]

**furbelow** /ˈfɜbəloʊ/, *n.* **1.** a pleated or gathered trimming on a woman's gown or the like; flounce. **2.** any bit of showy trimming or finery. *–v.t.* **3.** to ornament with or as with furbelows. [var. of FALBALA]

**furbish** /ˈfɜbɪʃ/, *v.t.* **1.** to restore to freshness of appearance or condition (oft. fol. by *up*). **2.** to remove rust from (armour, weapons, etc.); polish; burnish. [ME *furbish(en),* from OF *forbiss-,* stem of *forbir* polish, clean, from Gmc; cf. OHG *furban*] – **furbisher,** *n.*

**furburger** /ˈfɜbɜgə/, *n.* *Colloq.* simultaneous fellatio and cunnilingus; sixty-nine.

**furcate** /ˈfɜkeɪt, -kət/, *adj;* /ˈfɜkeɪt/, *v.,* **-cated, -cating.** *–adj.* **1.** forked. *–v.i.* **2.** to form a fork; divide into branches. [ML *furcātus* cloven, from L *furca* fork] – **furcation** /fɜˈkeɪʃən/, *n.*

**furcula** /ˈfɜkjələ/, *n., pl.* **-lae** /-li/. the forked clavicular bone of a bird; wishbone. [L, diminutive of *furca* fork] – **furcular,** *adj.*

**furculum** /ˈfɜkjələm/, *n., pl.* **-la** /-lə/. →**furcula.** [NL, incorrectly formed diminutive of L *furca* fork]

**furfur** /ˈfɜfə/, *n., pl.* **-fures** /-fjuriz, -fəriz/. **1.** →**dandruff.** **2.** *Physiol.* any epidermal scale. **3.** the bran of grain. [L]

**furfuraceous** /fɜfjuˈreɪʃəs/, *adj.* **1.** branlike. **2.** scaly; scurfy. [LL *furfurāceus*]

**furfural** /ˈfɜfəræl/, *n.* an oily liquid aldehyde, $C_4H_3O \cdot CHO$, with an aromatic odour, obtained by distilling bran, sugar, wood, etc., with dilute sulphuric acid, used in the manufacture of plastics and in refining lubricating oils. [L *furfur* bran + AL(DEHYDE)]

**furfuran** /ˈfɜfəræn/, *n.* →**furan.** [G, from L *furfur* bran + *-an* -ANE]

**furious** /ˈfjuriəs/, *adj.* **1.** full of fury, violent passion, or rage. **2.** intensely violent, as wind, storms, etc. **3.** of unrestrained energy, speed, etc.: *furious activity.* [ME, from L *furiōsus* raging] – **furiously,** *adv.* – **furiousness,** *n.*

**furl** /fɜl/, *v.t.* **1.** to draw into a compact roll, as a sail against a spar or a flag against its staff. *–v.i.* **2.** to become furled. *–n.* **3.** the act of furling or state of being furled. **4.** a roll resulting from being furled. [cf. F *ferler,* OF *ferlier,* from *fer* firm (from L *firmus*) + *lier* to bind (from L *ligāre*)]

**furlong** /ˈfɜlɒŋ/, *n.* a unit of distance, in the imperial system, equal to 220 yards or 201.168 m. *Symbol:* fur [ME; OE *furlang,* from *furh* furrow + *lang* long]

**furlough** /ˈfɜloʊ/, *n.* leave of absence from official duty usu. for a longish period. [var. of *furloff,* from D *verlof* leave. Cf. G *Verlaub* permission; pronunciation by association with *dough, though*]

**furmenty** /ˈfɜmənti/, *n.* →**frumenty.** Also, **furmety, furmity** /ˈfɜməti/.

**furn.,** furnished.

**furnace** /ˈfɜnəs/, *n.* **1.** a structure or apparatus in which to generate heat, as for heating buildings, smelting ores, producing steam, etc. **2.** a place of burning heat. [ME *furneise,* from OF *fornais, fornaise,* from L *fornax* oven] – **furnace-like,** *adj.*

**furnish** /ˈfɜnɪʃ/, *v.t.* **1.** to provide or supply. **2.** to fit up (a house, room, etc.) with necessary appliances, esp. furniture. [ME *furnisshe(n),* from OF *furniss-,* stem of *furnir* accomplish, furnish, from Gmc; cf. OHG *frumjan* provide] – **furnisher,** *n.*

**furnishing** /ˈfɜnəʃɪŋ/, *n.* **1.** that with which anything is furnished. **2.** (*pl.*) fittings, appliances, articles of furniture, etc., for a house or room.

**furnit.,** furniture.

**furniture** /ˈfɜnətʃə/, *n.* **1.** the movable articles, as tables, chairs, bedsteads, desks, cabinets, etc., required for use or ornament in a house, office, or the like. **2.** fittings, apparatus, or necessary accessories for something. **3.** *Print.* pieces of wood or metal, less than type-high, set in and about pages of type to fill them out and hold the type in place. [F *fourniture,* from *fournir* FURNISH]

**furore** /ˈfjurɔ/, *n.* **1.** a general outburst of enthusiasm or excited disorder. **2.** fury; rage; madness. Also, **furor.** [L: a raging; replacing late ME *fureur,* from F]

**furphy** /ˈfɜfi/, *n., pl.* **-phies.** a rumour; a false story. [from John *Furphy,* manufacturer in Victoria of water and sanitation carts, which during World War I were centres of gossip]

furphy: water cart made by John Furphy

**furred** /fɜd/, *adj.* **1.** having fur. **2.** made with or of fur, as garments. **3.** clad in fur or furs, as persons. **4.** coated with morbid matter, as the tongue.

**furrier** /ˈfʌriə/, *n.* a dealer in or dresser of furs.

**furriery** /ˈfʌriəri/, *n., pl.* **-eries. 1.** furs in general. **2.** the business or trade of a furrier.

**furring** /ˈfɜrɪŋ/, *n.* **1.** the act of lining, trimming, or clothing with fur. **2.** the fur used. **3.** the formation in a kettle, etc. of a coating of matter on something, as on the tongue. **4.** *Bldg Trades.* **a.** the nailing on of thin strips of board, as to furnish a level surface for lathing or plastering, to provide airspace between a wall and plastering, etc. **b.** materials so used.

**furrow** /ˈfʌroʊ/, *n.* **1.** a narrow trench made in the ground, esp. by a plough. **2.** a narrow, trenchlike depression in any surface. **3.** a groove, as in the skin of the forehead, etc. *–v.t.* **4.** to make a furrow or furrows in; plough (land, etc.). **5.** to make wrinkles in (the face, etc.). [ME *forwe, furgh(e),* OE *furh,* c. G *Furche;* akin to L *porca* ridge between furrows] – **furrower,** *n.*

**furrow horse** /ˈ– hɔs/, *n.* a plough horse trained not to deviate from a furrow once he is set in it.

**furry** /ˈfɜri/, *adj.,* **-rier, -riest. 1.** made of or with fur. **2.** covered with fur; wearing fur. **3.** consisting of or resembling fur. – **furriness,** *n.*

**fur seal** /ˈfɜ sil/, *n.* any of various species of eared seal, of the genera *Callorhinus* and *Arctocephalus,* which have under the outer hair a thick coat of fur of great commercial value (distinguished from *hair seal*).

**further** /ˈfɜðə/, *compar. adv. and adj., superl.* **furthest,** *v.* *–adv.* **1.** at or to a greater distance; farther. **2.** at or to a more advanced point; to a greater extent; farther. **3.** in addition; moreover. *–adj.* **4.** more distant or remote; farther. **5.** more extended. **6.** additional; more. *–v.t.* **7.** to help forward (a work, undertaking, cause, etc.); promote; advance; forward. [ME *further(e), furthra,* OE *furthor* (orig. compar. of **forth* FORTH); c. G *vordere* more advanced] – **furtherer,** *n.*

**furtherance** /ˈfɜðərəns/, *n.* the act of furthering; promotion; advancement.

**further education** /ˌfɜðər ɛdʒəˈkeɪʃən/, *n.* any form of education beyond the school system, as the formal education of universities and colleges, or the informal adult education programs.

**furthermore** /fɜðəˈmɔ/, *adv.* moreover; in addition.

**furthermost** /ˈfɜðəmoʊst/, *adj.* most distant.

**furthest** /ˈfɜðəst/, *adj., adv.* superlative of **further.** [ME, coined as a superl. of FURTHER. Cf. FARTHEST]

**furtive** /ˈfɜtɪv/, *adj.* **1.** taken, done, used, etc., by stealth; secret: *a furtive glance.* **2.** sly; shifty: *a furtive manner.* [L *furtīvus* stolen] – **furtively,** *adv.* – **furtiveness,** *n.*

**furuncle** /ˈfjurʌŋkəl/, *n.* a boil or inflammatory sore. [L *fūrunculus* a petty thief, a boil] – **furuncular** /fjuˈrʌŋkjələ/, *adj.* – **furunculous** /fjuˈrʌŋkjələs/, *adj.*

**furunculosis** /fjuˌrʌŋkjəˈloʊsəs/, *n.* the morbid state charac-

i = peat ɪ = pit ɛ = pet æ = pat a = part ɒ = pot ʌ = putt ɔ = port ʊ = put u = pool ɜ = pert ə = apart aɪ = buy eɪ = bay ɔɪ = boy aʊ = how oʊ = hoe ɪə = here ɛə = hair ʊə = tour g = give θ = thin ð = then ʃ = show ʒ = measure tʃ = choke dʒ = joke ŋ = sing j = you õ = Fr. bon

terised by the presence of furuncles.

**fury** /ˈfjuri/, *n., pl.* **-ries.** **1.** frenzied or unrestrained violent passion, esp. anger. **2.** violence; vehemence; fierceness. **3.** a fierce and violent person, esp. a woman. **4. like fury,** *Colloq.* furiously; violently. [ME, from L *furia* rage, madness]

**furze** /fɜz/, *n.* →**gorse.** [ME *furse, firse,* OE *fyrs*]

**furzy** /ˈfɜzi/, *adj.* **1.** of or pertaining to furze. **2.** overgrown with furze.

**fusain** /fjuˈzeɪn/, *n.* **1.** a fine charcoal used in drawing, made from the wood of the spindle tree. **2.** a drawing made with it. **3.** a charcoal-like constituent of coal consisting of plant remains from which the volatile matter has been eliminated. [F: spindle tree, charcoal made from its wood, from L *fūsus* spindle]

**fuse**[1] /fjuz/, *n., v.,* **fused, fusing.** *–n.* **1.** *Elect.* a device for preventing an excessive current from passing through a circuit, consisting of a piece of wire which breaks the circuit by melting if the current exceeds a specified value. **2.** a tube, ribbon, or the like, filled or saturated with combustible matter, for igniting an explosive. **3.** a mechanical or electronic device to detonate an explosive charge. **4. blow a fuse,** *Colloq.* to lose one's temper. *–v.i.* **5.** to blow a fuse. [It. *fuso,* from L *fūsus* spindle]



plug fuse[1]: A, conducting metal shell; B, screw thread insulating body; C, glass window; D, solder; E, conducting rivet; F, fusible element

**fuse**[2] /fjuz/, *v.,* **fused, fusing.** *–v.t.* **1.** to combine or blend by melting together; melt. **2.** to unite or blend into a whole, as if by melting together. *–v.i.* **3.** to become liquid under the action of heat; melt. **4.** to become united or blended, as if by melting together. [L *fūsus,* pp., poured, melted, cast]

**fuse box** /ˈ– bɒks/, *n.* a box, containing the fuses for the electrical circuits of a house, car, etc.

**fused silica** /fjuzd ˈsɪləkə/, *n.* →**silica glass.**

**fusee** /fjuˈzi/, *n.* **1.** a kind of match with a large head, for outdoor use. **2.** *Horol.* a spirally grooved, conical pulley and chain arrangement for counteracting the diminishing power of the uncoiling mainspring. **3.** a tumour on the bone of a horse's leg. **4.** →**fuse**[1]. [F *fusée* spindleful of thread, from OF *fus* spindle, from L *fūsus*]

**fuselage** /ˈfjuzəlaʒ, -lɪdʒ/, *n.* the body of an aircraft. [F, from *fuselé* spindle-shaped, from *fuseau* spindle, from L *fūsus*]

**fuse link** /ˈfjuz lɪŋk/, *n.* an electrical element, made of fusible wire or cast from fusible metal, inserted in a fuse (def. 1).

**fusel oil** /ˈfjuzəl ɔɪl/, *n.* a mixture of amyl alcohols obtained as a by-product in the fermentation of grains. [*fusel,* from G: inferior liquor or spirits]

**fuse wire** /ˈfjuz waɪə/, *n.* wire used as a fuse. See **fuse**[1] (def. 1).

**fusibility** /fjuzəˈbɪləti/, *n.* **1.** the quality of being fusible, or convertible from a solid to a fluid state by heat. **2.** the degree to which a substance is fusible.

**fusible** /ˈfjuzəbəl/, *adj.* capable of being fused or melted. – **fusibleness,** *n.*

**fusible metal** /ˈ– mɛtl/, *n.* any of various alloys, as one of bismuth, lead, and tin, which melt at comparatively low temperatures, and hence can be used for making various safety devices. Also, **fusible alloy.**

**fusible plug** /ˈ– plʌg/, *n.* a safety device consisting of a low-melting alloy which is designed to release pressure, in a piece of industrial or domestic equipment, at a predetermined temperature.

**fusiform** /ˈfjuzəfɔm/, *adj.* spindle-shaped; rounded and tapering from the middle towards each end, as some roots. [L *fūsus* spindle + -I- + -FORM]

**fusil**[1] /ˈfjuzəl/, *n.* a light musket or firelock. [F, in OF *foisil* steel for striking fire, from L *focus* hearth]

**fusil**[2] /ˈfjuzəl/, *n. Her.* a bearing in the form of an elongated lozenge. [MF *fusel,* from L *fūsus* spindle. Cf. FUSE[1]]

**fusilier** /fjuzəˈlɪə/, *n.* **1.** a term used in the names of certain British regiments. **2.** formerly a soldier armed with a fusil. Also, **fusileer.** [F, from *fusil* musket]

**fusillade** /fjuzəˈleɪd, -ˈlad/, *n., v.,* **-laded, -lading.** *–n.* **1.** a simultaneous or continuous discharge of firearms. **2.** an execution carried out by this means. **3.** a general discharge or outpouring of anything: *a fusillade of questions.* *–v.t.* **4.** to attack (a plane) or shoot down (persons) by a fusillade. [F, from *fusiller* shoot, from *fusil* musket, FUSIL[1]]

**fusion** /ˈfjuʒən/, *n.* **1.** the act or process of fusing. **2.** the state of being fused. **3.** that which is fused. **4.** *Politics.* **a.** the coalition of parties or factions. **b.** the body resulting from such coalition. **5.** *Physics.* a thermonuclear reaction in which nuclei of light atoms join to form nuclei of heavier atoms, as the combination of deuterium atoms to form helium atoms, and usu. with the release of large amounts of energy. **6.** *Psychol.* the combination of two or more stimuli into an unanalysed, and sometimes unanalysable impression. [L *fūsio* a pouring out]

**fusion bomb** /ˈ– bɒm/, *n.* →**hydrogen bomb.**

**fusion energy** /ˈ– ɛnədʒi/, *n.* the energy released from a fusion reaction.

**fusionism** /ˈfjuʒənɪzəm/, *n.* the principle, policy, or practice of forming coalitions of political parties or groups. – **fusionist,** *n., adj.*

**fusion reaction** /ˈfjuʒən riækʃən/, *n.* →**fusion** (def. 5).

**fusion reactor** /ˈ– riæktə/, *n.* a nuclear reactor in which fusion (def. 5) takes place.

**fuss** /fʌs/, *n.* **1.** an excessive display of anxious activity; needless or useless bustle. **2.** a commotion, argument, or dispute. **3.** a person given to fussing. **4. make a fuss of,** to treat with special care and affection. *–v.i.* **5.** to make a fuss; make much ado about trifles; to move fussily about. **6. fuss over,** to pay excessive attention to. *–v.t.* **7.** to put into a fuss; disturb with trifles; bother. [orig. unknown] – **fusser,** *n.*

**fuss-budget** /ˈfʌs-bʌdʒət/, *n. Chiefly U.S.* a complaining person who constantly makes an issue of trifling matters.

**fusspot** /ˈfʌspɒt/, *n. Colloq.* a fussy person; one who is over-particular.

**fussy** /ˈfʌsi/, *adj.,* **-sier, -siest. 1.** excessively busy with trifles; anxious or particular about petty details. **2.** (of clothes, etc.) elaborately made or trimmed. **3.** full of excessive detail. – **fussily,** *adv.* – **fussiness,** *n.*

**fustian** /ˈfʌstiən/, *n.* **1.** a stout fabric of cotton and flax. **2.** a stout twilled cotton fabric with a short nap or pile. **3.** inflated or turgid language in writing or speaking; bombast; rant; claptrap. *–adj.* **4.** made of fustian. **5.** pompous or bombastic, as language. **6.** worthless; cheap. [ME, from OF *fustaigne,* from ML *fustāneum* (from L *fustis* cudgel), translation of Gk *xýlinon* cotton, from *xýlon* wood]

**fustic** /ˈfʌstɪk/, *n.* **1.** the wood of a large tree (**old fustic**), *Chlorophora tinctoria,* of tropical America, yielding a light yellow dye. **2.** the tree itself. **3.** a small European shrub (**young fustic**), *Cotinus coggygria,* from which a yellow dye is extracted. **4.** the dye of either. **5.** any of several other dyewoods. [F *fustoc,* from Sp., from Ar. *fustuq;* akin to Gk *pistákē* pistachio tree, from Pers.]

**fustigate** /ˈfʌstəgeɪt/, *v.t.,* **-gated, -gating.** *Archaic.* to cudgel; beat; punish. [L *fustīgātus,* pp., cudgelled to death] – **fustigation** /fʌstəˈgeɪʃən/, *n.* – **fustigator,** *n.*

**fusty** /ˈfʌsti/, *adj.,* **-tier, -tiest. 1.** mouldy; musty; having a stale smell; stuffy. **2.** old-fashioned; fogyish. **3.** stubbornly old-fashioned and out-of-date. [ME, from OF *fust* wine cask, log, from L *fustis* cudgel] – **fustily,** *adv.* – **fustiness,** *n.*

**fut** /fʌt, fʊt/, *adv., interj.* →**phut.**

**fut.,** future.

**futah** /ˈfutə/, *n.* **1.** a kind of material originally from India. **2.** a kind of short skirt or loin-cloth worn esp. by Arabs.

**futhorc** /ˈfuθɔk/, *n.* the runic alphabet. Also, **futhork, futharc** /ˈfuθak/, **futhark.** [name consisting of its first six letters]

**futile** /ˈfjutaɪl/, *adj.* **1.** incapable of producing any result; ineffective; useless; not successful. **2.** *Obs.* trifling; not important. [L *fut(t)ilis* untrustworthy, vain, lit., that easily pours out] – **futilely,** *adv.* – **futileness,** *n.*

**futilitarian** /fjutɪləˈtɛəriən/, *adj.* **1.** believing that human hopes are vain and human strivings unjustified. *–n.* **2.** one who holds this belief. **3.** one who devotes himself to profitless pursuits. [from FUTILITY, modelled on UTILITARIAN]

**futility** /fjuˈtɪləti/, *n., pl.* **-ties. 1.** the quality of being futile;

ineffectiveness; uselessness. **2.** unimportance. **3.** a futile act or event.

**futter** /ˈfʌtə/, *n. N.Z.* (formerly) a storehouse, esp. on a sheep-station, raised on posts like a whata. Also, **futtah.** [alteration of WHATA]

**futtock** /ˈfʌtək/, *n.* one of the curved timbers in a frame or rib of a wooden ship. [orig. unknown]

**futtock band** /ˈ– bænd/, *n.* an iron band fitted round the lower mast, abreast of the lower yard, to which the truss of the yard is anchored. It also serves to secure the lower ends of the futtock shrouds. Also, **futtock hoop.**

**futtock plank** /ˈ– plæŋk/, *n.* the plank of the ceiling of a ship (the wooden surface at the bottom of the hold) next to the keelson.

**futtock plate** /ˈ– pleɪt/, *n.* an iron plate, fitted round the edge of the lower top, to which the lower ends of the topmast rigging and the upper ends of the futtock shrouds are secured.

**futtock shrouds** /ˈ– ʃraʊdz/, *n.pl.* short lengths of iron or steel rods, or wire, extending from the futtock band to the futtock plate and fitted with eyes at either end.

**future** /ˈfjutʃə/, *n.* **1.** time that is to be or come hereafter. **2.** what will exist or happen in future time. **3.** a future condition, esp. of success or prosperity. **4. a.** the future tense. **b.** a form therein. **5.** (*pl.*) →**futures contract.** –*adj.* **6.** that is to be or come hereafter: *future events, at some future date.* **7.** pertaining to or connected with time to come: *one's future prospects, future hopes.* **8.** *Gram.* designating a tense denoting an action or state which will take place in the future. For example, in the sentence, *I will go to Canberra next week, will go* is in the future tense. [ME *futur,* from L *futūrus,* future participle of *esse* be]

**future estate** /fjutʃər əsˈteɪt/, *n. Law.* **1.** estate that may be acquired in the future, as a contingent remainder. **2.** existing estate to take effect in possession in the future, as reversion and vested remainder.

**futureless** /ˈfjutʃələs/, *adj.* without a future; having no prospect of future betterment or prosperity.

**future life** /fjutʃə ˈlaɪf/, *n.* a form of life which is believed to follow mortal death; afterlife.

**future perfect** /– ˈpɜfəkt/, *adj. Gram.* **1.** perfect with respect to a temporal point of reference in the future. **2.** designating a tense which usu. denotes an action or state which will have been completed and past at some future point in time. For example, in the sentence *John will have seen her by then, will have* seen is in the future perfect tense. –*n.* **3. a.** the future perfect tense. **b.** a form therein, as *he will have come.*

**futures contract** /ˈfjutʃəz ˌkɒntrækt/, *n.* a purchase or sale of commodities for future receipt or delivery.

**futures exchange** /ˈ– əkstʃeɪndʒ/, *n.* a market place where futures contracts are traded. Also, **futures market.**

**future shock** /fjutʃə ˈʃɒk/, *n.* a type of neurosis occurring among people whose sense of stability is affected by an accelerated rate of technological and social change.

**futurism** /ˈfjutʃərɪzəm/, *n.* an artistic and literary movement, originating in Italy in 1909, whose adherents aimed to represent the movement and speed of the contemporary mechanised age by portraying machines and figures in dynamic motion.

**futurist** /ˈfjutʃərəst/, *adj.* **1.** of or pertaining to work of futurism. –*n.* **2.** a futurist artist or writer. **3.** *Theol.* one who believes in the fulfilment of the prophecies in the Bible.

**futuristic** /fjutʃəˈrɪstɪk/, *adj.* **1.** of or pertaining to futurism. **2.** *Colloq.* (of a work of art or the like) in a modern style; without reference to traditional forms, etc. **3.** (of design in clothes, furniture, etc.) anticipating the space age; avant-garde.

**futurity** /fjuˈtjurəti/, *n., pl.* **-ties. 1.** future time. **2.** a future state or condition; a future event. **3.** the quality of being future. **4.** a futurity race.

**futurity race** /ˈ– reɪs/, *n.* a horserace for which the entries are nominated long before the running.

**futurologist** /fjutʃəˈrɒlədʒəst/, *n.* one who forecasts future trends.

**futurology** /fjutʃəˈrɒlədʒi/, *n.* the prediction of the future as a result of systematic analysis, esp. by the study of present day trends in human affairs.

**fuzz** /fʌz/, *n.* **1.** loose, light, fibrous, or fluffy matter. **2.** a mass or coating of such matter. **3.** *Colloq.* a blur. **4.** *Colloq.* frizzy hair. **5.** *Colloq.* the police force or a policeman. [cf. D *voos* spongy]

**fuzz box** /ˈ– bɒks/, *n.* an electronic device attached to a sound amplifier which overloads the signal causing deliberate distortion in sound.

**fuzzy** /ˈfʌzi/, *adj.,* **-zier, -ziest. 1.** of the nature of or resembling fuzz. **2.** covered with fuzz. **3.** indistinct; blurred. –**fuzzily,** *adv.* –**fuzziness,** *n.*

**fuzzy wuzzy** /ˈ– wʌzi/, *n. Colloq.* **1.** native inhabitant of Papua New Guinea. **2.** (*offensive*) a native, esp. of Africa. [used orig. of Sudanese tribesmen]

**fuzzy wuzzy angel,** *n. Colloq.* any native of Papua New Guinea who helped the Australians, esp. the wounded, during World War II.

**f.v.,** on the back of the page. [L *folio verso*]

**fwd,** forward.

**FX** /ɛf ˈɛks/, *n.pl. Radio, Film, Television etc.* **1.** sound effects. **2.** special visual effects as bombs exploding, snow-falling, etc.

**-fy,** a suffix meaning: **1.** to make; cause to be; render: *simplify, beautify.* **2.** to become; be made: *liquefy.* Also, **-ify.** [F *-fier,* from L *-ficāre* do, make]

**fylfot** /ˈfɪlfɒt/, *n.* →**swastika.** [? var. of *fill-foot* foot-filler]

**Gg** Roman HAWTHORN **Gg** Sans Serif NEWS *Gg* Script MADRID **Gg** Decorative TYPEWRITER

*Although there are numerous typefaces in the world they can be divided into four main classifications. These are:*

*ROMAN or SERIF. This typeface came into being from the technique of the Roman masons who, working in stone, finished off each letter with a serif or small stroke projecting from the top or bottom. This was done to correct any feeling of unevenness or imbalance they may have created in cutting the characters in stone.*

*SANS SERIF (without serif). This typeface is geometric in design and has straight-edged characters and lines of a regular thickness.*

*SCRIPT. Based on the movement of the hand, this typeface is often italicised or slanted, as if drawn by a brush or quill pen.*

*DECORATIVE. Any typeface that exaggerates the characteristics of any of the other three classifications to a degree that places it outside of them.*

*The dictionary entries in this book use a SAN SERIF typeface called Helvetica (set in a bold face for the head words) and a SERIF typeface Plantin (used throughout the body of the entries).*

**G, g** /dʒi/, *n., pl.* **G's** or **Gs, g's** or **gs. 1.** the seventh letter of the English alphabet. **2.** the seventh in order of a series. **3.** *Music.* **a.** the fifth degree in the scale of C major or the seventh in the relative minor scale of A minor. **b.** a written or printed note representing this tone. **c.** a key, string, or pipe tuned to this note. **d.** (in solmisation) the fifth note of the scale, called **sol.**

**g, 1.** gram. **2.** *Physics.* the gravitational acceleration at earth's surface which varies slightly according to latitude, altitude, and the composition of rocks beneath the surface. The internationally accepted figure for standard g is 9.806 65 metres per second squared.

**g., 1.** *Elect.* conductance. **2.** gauge. **3.** gender. **4.** genitive. **5.** (formerly) guinea.

**G** /dʒi/, **1.** *Colloq.* (of films) for general exhibition. **2.** gauss. **3.** giga-. **4.** *Physics.* the constant of gravitation. **5.** *U.S.* (grand) a thousand dollars. **6.** German.

**G., 1.** (specific) gravity. **2.** Gulf.

**Ga,** *Chem.* gallium.

**gab** /gæb/, *v.,* **gabbed, gabbing,** *n. Colloq. –v.i.* **1.** to talk idly; chatter. *–n.* **2.** idle talk; chatter. **3.** glib speech: *the gift of the gab.* [var. of GOB[2] mouth, from Gaelic or Irish] **– gabber,** *n.*

**gabardine** /gæbə'din, 'gæbədin/, *n.* →**gaberdine.**

**gabble** /'gæbəl/, *v.,* **-bled, -bling,** *n. –v.i.* **1.** to talk rapidly and unintelligibly; jabber. **2.** (of geese, etc.) to cackle. *–v.t.* **3.** to utter rapidly and unintelligibly. *–n.* **4.** rapid, unintelligible talk. [frequentative of GAB] **– gabbler,** *n.*

**gabbro** /'gæbroʊ/, *n., pl.* **-bros.** a granular igneous rock, a mixture of labradorite, augite, etc. [It., from L *glaber* smooth, hairless] **– gabbroic** /gæ'broʊɪk/, *adj.* **– gabbroidal** /gæ'brɔɪdl/, *adj.* **– gabbroitic** /,gæbroʊ'ɪtɪk/, *adj.* **– gabbroid,** *adj., n.*

**gabby** /'gæbi/, *adj.,* **-bier, -biest.** *Colloq.* garrulous; loquacious. **– gabbiness,** *n.*

**gaberdine** /gæbə'din, 'gæbədin/, *n.* **1.** a closely woven twill fabric of worsted, cotton or spun rayon. **2.** a man's long, loose cloak or frock, worn in the Middle Ages. Also, **gabardine.** [Sp. *gabardina,* from MHG *wallevart* pilgrimage]

**gabfest** /'gæbfɛst/, *n. Colloq.* a prolonged session of conversation or speeches; conference. [GAB + -FEST]

**gabion** /'geɪbiən/, *n.* **1.** a cylinder of wickerwork filled with earth, used as a military defence. **2.** a cylinder filled with stones and sunk in water, used in laying the foundations of a dam or jetty. [F, from It. *gabbione* large cage, augmentative of *gabbia* cage, from L *cavea* cavity]

**gabionade** /geɪbiə'neɪd/, *n.* **1.** a work formed of or with gabions. **2.** a row of gabions sunk in a stream to control the current. [F. See GABION]

**gable** /'geɪbəl/, *n., v.,* **-bled, -bling.** *–n.* **1.** the triangular wall enclosed by the two slopes of a roof and a horizontal line across the eaves. **2.** any architectural feature shaped like a gable. *–v.t.* **3.** to build with a gable or gables; form as a gable. [ME, probably from Scand.; cf. Icel. *gafl.* Cf. also OHG *gabala,* G *Gabel* fork] **– gabled,** *adj.*

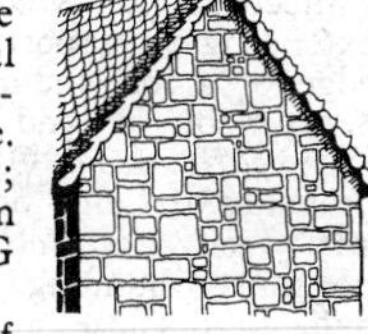
gable (def. 1)

**gable end** /'– ɛnd/, *n.* the end wall of a building where it is surmounted by a gable.

**gable roof** /– 'ruf/, *n.* a ridged roof terminating at one or both ends in a gable.

**gablet** /'geɪblət/, *n.* a little gable.

**gable window** /geɪbəl 'wɪndoʊ/, *n.* **1.** a window in or under a gable. **2.** a window having its upper part shaped like a gable.

**Gabon** /ga'bɒn/, *n.* a republic in south-western equatorial Africa.

**Gabonese** /gæbə'niz/, *adj., n., pl.* **-nese.** *–adj.* **1.** of or pertaining to Gabon or the Gabonese. *–n.* **2.** an inhabitant of Gabon.

**gad**[1] /gæd/, *v.,* **gadded, gadding.** *–v.i.* **1.** to move restlessly or idly from place to place, esp. in search of pleasure (fol. by *about*). [backformation from obs. *gadling* companion, from OE *gædeling*]

**gad**[2] /gæd/, *n., v.,* **gadded, gadding.** *–n.* **1.** a goad for driving cattle. **2.** a pointed mining tool for breaking up rock, coal, etc. *–v.t.* **3.** to break up with a mining gad. [ME, from Scand.; cf. Icel. *gaddr* spike, from Gmc *gazdaz* rod; cf. YARD[1]]

**Gad** /gæd/, *n., interj. Archaic.* a euphemistic form of *God* used as a mild oath. Also, **gad.**

**gadabout** /'gædəbaʊt/, *n. Colloq.* one who gads; a restless person, esp. one who leads an active social life.

**gadfly** /'gædflaɪ/, *n., pl.* **-flies. 1.** any fly that goads or stings domestic animals, as many voracious, bloodsucking flies of the dipterous family Tabanidae. **2.** someone, as a journalist or political agitator, who by his provocative criticisms and actions, unsettles complacent opinions or entrenched interests. [from GAD[2] + FLY[2]]

**gadget** /ˈgædʒət/, *n.* a mechanical contrivance or device; any ingenious article. [orig. uncert. Cf. F *gâchette*]

**gadgetry** /ˈgædʒətri/, *n.* gadgets collectively.

**Gadhelic** /gəˈdɛlɪk/, *adj., n.* →**Goidelic.**

**gadid** /ˈgeɪdɪd/, *n.* a fish of the cod family, Gadidae. [NL *gadus* cod + -ID[2]]

**gadoid** /ˈgeɪdɔɪd/, *adj.* **1.** belonging to or resembling the Anacanthini, an order of soft-finned fishes including the cod, haddock, etc. *–n.* **2.** a gadoid fish. [NL *gadus* cod (from Gk *gádos* kind of fish) + -OID]

**gadolinite** /ˈgædələnaɪt/, *n.* a silicate ore from which the rare-earth metals gadolinium, holmium, and rhenium are extracted. [named after J. *Gadolin*, 1760-1852, Finnish chemist. See -ITE[1]]

**gadolinium** /gædəˈlɪniəm/, *n.* a rare-earth metallic element. *Symbol:* Gd; *at. wt:* 157 25; *at. no.:* 64. [from GADOLIN(ITE) + -IUM]

**gadroon** /gəˈdrun/, *n.* **1.** *Archit.* an elaborately carved or indented convex moulding. **2.** a decorative series of curved inverted flutings, or of convex and concave flutings, as on silversmith's work. [F *godron*, from *goder* crease, pucker] **– gadrooned,** *adj.*

**gadzooks** /gædˈzuks/, *interj. Archaic.* (a mild oath). [? var. of *God's hooks* (by) the nails of Christ]

**Gael** /geɪl/, *n.* **1.** a Scottish Celt or Highlander. **2.** *Rare.* an Irish Celt. [Scot. Gaelic *Gaidheal*, O Irish *Gaidel*]

**Gael.,** Gaelic.

**Gaelic** /ˈgeɪlɪk/, *n.* **1.** the Celtic language of ancient Ireland and any of the languages that developed from it (Irish Gaelic, Scottish Gaelic and Manx). **2.** →**Goidelic.** *–adj.* **3.** of or pertaining to the Gaels or their language.

**gaff**[1] /gæf/, *n.* **1.** a strong hook with a handle, used for landing large fish. **2.** a metal spur for a gamecock. **3.** *Naut.* the spar extending or supporting the upper edge of a fore-and-aft sail. *–v.t.* **4.** to hook or land with a gaff. [ME *gaffe*, from OF: boathook, probably of Celtic orig.]

G, gaff[1] (def. 3)

**gaff**[2] /gæf/, *n. Colloq.* **1.** *Rare.* nonsense; humbug. **2. blow the gaff,** to disclose a secret. [orig. obscure]

**gaffe** /gæf/, *n.* a social blunder. [F]

**gaffer** /ˈgæfə/, *n.* **1.** *Brit. Archaic.* an old man. **2.** *Brit. Colloq.* father. **3.** *Chiefly Brit. Colloq.* an owner, senior partner, foreman, or the like. **4.** *Films, Television.* the chief lighting electrician. [var. of late ME *godfar* (contracted form of GODFATHER)]

**gaff rig** /ˈgæf rɪg/, *n.* a fore-and-aft rig on a sailing boat in which the sails have a quadrilateral shape because of the gaff.

**gaff-topsail** /gæf-ˈtɒpsəl/, *n.* a light triangular sail set between the upper part of a mast and a gaff.

**gag**[1] /gæg/, *v.,* **gagged, gagging,** *n. –v.t.* **1.** to stop up the mouth so as to prevent sound or speech. **2.** to restrain by force or authority from freedom of speech or expression. **3.** (in parliament) to close (a debate) when some members still wish to speak. **4.** to fasten open the jaws of, as in surgical operations. *–v.i.* **5.** to heave with nausea. *–n.* **6.** something thrust into or bound around the mouth to prevent speech. **7.** forceful or authoritative suppression of freedom of speech. **8.** (in parliament) closure of debate when some members still wish to speak. **9.** a surgical instrument for holding the jaws open. [probably imitative of the sound of choking] **– gagger, gagster,** *n.*

**gag**[2] /gæg/, *v.,* **gagged, gagging,** *n. Colloq. –v.t.* **1.** to deceive; hoax. *–v.i.* **2.** to introduce interpolations or gags in acting. **3.** to play on one's credulity by false stories, etc. **4.** to make jokes. *–n.* **5.** a joke. **6.** an interpolation introduced by an actor into his part. **7.** any contrived piece of word play or horseplay. [orig. uncert.] **– gagger,** *n.*

**gaga** /ˈgaga/, *adj. Colloq.* **1.** senile. **2.** mad; fatuously eccentric. **3.** besotted: *he is gaga about his new car.* [F: senile, a senile person (probably imitative)]

**gagaku** /gagaˈku/, *n.* the ancient orchestral court music of Japan. [Jap.]

**gage**[1] /geɪdʒ/, *n., v.,* **gaged, gaging.** *–n.* **1.** something, as a glove, thrown down in token of challenge to combat. **2.** a challenge. **3.** a pledge or pawn; security. *–v.t.* **4.** *Archaic.* to pledge, stake, or wager. [ME, from OF: pledge, security; of Gmc orig. Cf. WAGE]

**gage**[2] /geɪdʒ/, *n., v.t.,* **gaged, gaging.** →**gauge. – gager,** *n.*

**gage**[3] /geɪdʒ/, *n.* any of several plums, varieties of *Prunus domestica.* [short for GREENGAGE]

**gaggle** /ˈgægəl/, *v.,* **-gled, -gling,** *n. –v.i.* **1.** to cackle. *–n.* **2.** a flock of geese. **3.** any disorderly group. **4.** a cackle. [imitative]

**gagroot** /ˈgægrut/, *n.* a plant, *Lobelia inflata,* with emetic properties; Indian tobacco.

**gahnite** /ˈganaɪt/, *n.* a dark green to black mineral of the spinel group, zinc aluminate, $ZnAl_2O_4$; zinc-spinel. [named after J. G. *Gahn*, 1745-1818, Swedish chemist. See -ITE[1]]

**gaiety** /ˈgeɪəti/, *n., pl.* **-ties. 1.** the state of being gay or cheerful; gay spirits. **2.** (*oft. pl.*) merrymaking or festivity: *the gaieties of the New Year season.* **3.** showiness; finery: *gaiety of dress.* [F *gaieté, gaité*, from *gai* GAY]

**gaillardia** /geɪˈladiə, gə-/, *n.* any plant of the American genus *Gaillardia*, several species of which are cultivated for their showy flowers. [NL, named after M. *Gaillard* de Marentonneau, 18th-century French botanist]

**gaily** /ˈgeɪli/, *adv.* **1.** merrily. **2.** showily.

**gain**[1] /geɪn/, *v.t.* **1.** to obtain; secure (something desired); acquire: *gain time.* **2.** to win; get in competition: *gain the prize.* **3.** to acquire as an increase or addition: *to gain weight, speed, etc.* **4.** to obtain as a profit: *he gained ten dollars by that transaction.* **5.** to reach by effort; get to; arrive at: *to gain a good harbour.* *–v.i.* **6.** to improve; make progress; advance. **7.** to get nearer, as in pursuit (fol. by *on* or *upon*). **8.** to get farther away (from pursuers). **9. gain ground, a.** to make an advance, as in the face of opposition. **b.** to obtain an advantage. **10. gain time,** to delay; achieve a postponement. *–n.* **11.** profit; advantage. **12.** (*pl.*) profits; winnings. **13.** an increase or advance. **14.** the act of gaining; acquisition. **15.** *Electronics.* an increase in a signal parameter, as voltage, current, or power, expressed as the ratio of the output to the input. **16.** (of an amplifier) volume. [F *gagner*, from OF *gaaigner* to get possession of, from Gmc *waithanjan* to plunder]

**gain**[2] /geɪn/, *n.* **1.** a notch or dado cut across the edge of a board, usu. made to support a cross board. *–v.t.* **2.** to make a gain or gains in. [orig. uncert.]

**gainer** /ˈgeɪnə/, *n.* **1.** one who or that which gains. **2.** a type of dive in which the diver takes off facing forwards, and jumps upwards and backwards, completing a back somersault so as to enter the water feet first and facing away from the board.

**gainful** /ˈgeɪnfəl/, *adj.* profitable; lucrative. **– gainfully,** *adv.* **– gainfulness,** *n.*

**gainsay** /geɪnˈseɪ/, *v.t.,* **-said, -saying. 1.** to deny. **2.** to speak or act against. [*gain-* against + SAY] **– gainsayer,** *n.*

**'gainst** /gɛnst, geɪnst/, *prep., conj.* →**against.** Also, **gainst.**

**gait** /geɪt/, *n.* **1.** a particular manner of walking. **2.** any of the characteristic rhythms of locomotion of a horse, as the walk, trot, canter or gallop. *–v.t.* **3.** to teach a gait to (a horse). [Scot. and N. Eng. spelling of GATE in various senses, including those above]

**gaited** /ˈgeɪtəd/, *adj.* having a specified gait: *slow-gaited, heavy-gaited oxen.*

**gaiter** /ˈgeɪtə/, *n.* a covering for the ankle and instep, and sometimes also the lower leg, made of cloth or leather and worn over the shoe. [F *guêtre*]

**gal,** gallon; gallons.

**gal**[1] /gæl/, *n. Colloq.* a girl.

**gal**[2] /gæl/, *n. Colloq.* galvanised iron.

**gal**[3] /gæl/, *n.* a unit of acceleration in the centimetre-gram-second system, equal to $10 \times 10^{-3}$ m/s$^2$.

**Gal,** gallon.

**Gal.,** *Bible.* Galatians.

**gala** /ˈgalə/, *adj.* **1.** festive; festal; showy: *his visits were* *always gala occasions.* –*n.* **2.** a celebration; festive occasion. **3.** festal pomp or dress. [F, from It.: festal pomp, finery, from OF *gale* joy, pleasure, from MD *wale* riches]

**galactagogue** /gə'læktəgɒg/, *adj.* **1.** increasing the amount of milk collected, either with or without increasing the amount secreted. –*n.* **2.** a galactagogue agent or medicine. [Gk *galakt-* milk (stem of *gála*) + *-agōgós* bringing]

**galactan** /gə'læktən/, *n.* any of the anhydrides of galactose, composing several gums, agar, and fruit pectins.

**galactic** /gə'læktɪk/, *adj.* **1.** *Astron.* pertaining to a galaxy, esp. the Milky Way. **2.** *Physiol.* pertaining to or stimulating the secretion of milk. [Gk *galaktikós* milky]

**galactic circle** /– 'sɜkəl/, *n.* the great circle of the celestial sphere which most nearly coincides with the middle of the Milky Way. Also, **galactic equator.**

**galactic coordinate** /– koʊ'ɔdɪnət/, *n.* one of a system of coordinates for defining the position of a celestial body with reference to the Milky Way, based on galactic latitude and longitude.

**galactic equator** /– ə'kweɪtə/, *n.* →**galactic circle.**

**galactic latitude** /– 'lætətʃud/, *n.* →**latitude** (def. 3b).

**galactic longitude** /– 'lɒŋgətʃud/, *n.* →**longitude** (def. 2).

**galactic plane** /– 'pleɪn/, *n.* the plane of the galactic circle.

**galactic poles** /– 'poʊlz/, *n.pl.* the two opposite points on the celestial sphere that are farthest north and south of the Milky Way.

**galactopoietic** /gə,læktoʊpɔɪ'ɛtɪk/, *adj.* **1.** increasing the secretion of milk, though not necessarily the amount collected. –*n.* **2.** a galactopoietic agent or medicine. [Gk *galakto-* milk (combining form of *gála*) + *poiētikós* making]

**galactose** /gə'læktoʊz, -toʊs/, *n.* a hexose sugar, $C_6H_{12}O_6$, either laevorotatory or dextrorotatory, the latter being derived from milk sugar by hydrolysis. [Gk *gála* milk + -OSE[2]]

**galah** /gə'la/, *n.* **1.** a common small cockatoo, *Cacatua roseicapilla,* pale grey above and deep pink below, found in open areas in most parts of Australia. **2.** *Colloq.* a fool; simpleton. [Aboriginal]

galah

**Galahad** /'gæləhæd/, *n.* a man of ideal purity of heart and life. [from Sir *Galahad,* the noblest and purest knight of the Round Table in the Arthurian legend]

**galah session** /gə'la sɛʃən/, *n.* *Colloq.* a time set aside for the women of isolated outback areas to converse with one another by radio.

**galangal** /gə'læŋgəl/, *n.* the aromatic, medicinal rhizome of certain plants of the ginger family, esp. *Languas galanga* and *L. officinarum,* of China and the East Indies. [var. of GALINGALE]

**galantine** /'gæləntin/, *n.* a dish of meat or poultry, boned, spiced, jellied and served cold.

**galavant** /'gæləvænt, gælə'vænt/, *v.i.* →**gallivant.**

**galaxias** /gə'læksiəs/, *n.* a genus comprising some twenty-six species of Australian freshwater fish often referred to as native trout.

**galaxy** /'gæləksi/, *n., pl.* **-axies.** **1.** *Astron.* any large system of stars held together by mutual gravitation and separated from any other similar system by vast regions of space. **2.** any brilliant or splendid assemblage, as of filmstars, etc. [ME *galaxye,* from ML *galaxia,* var. of *galaxias,* from Gk, from *gála* milk]

**galbanum** /'gælbənəm/, *n.* a gum resin with a peculiar disagreeable odour, obtained from certain Asiatic plants of the genus *Ferula,* used in medicine and the arts. [ME, from L, from Gk *chalbánē* (Septuagint), from Heb. *ḥelbĕnāh*]

**gale**[1] /geɪl/, *n.* **1.** a strong wind. **2.** *Meteorol.* a wind of Beaufort scale force 8, with average speed of 34 to 40 knots, or 62 to 74 km/h **3.** a noisy outburst: *a gale of laughter.* **4.** *Archaic.* a gentle breeze: *Where'er you walk, cool gales shall fan the glade.* [orig. uncert.]

**gale**[2] /geɪl/, *n.* →**bog myrtle.** [ME *gayl,* OE *gagel,* c. D *gagel,* G *Gagel*]

**galea** /'geɪliə/, *n., pl.* **-leae** /-lii/. any part of the calyx or corolla in the form of a helmet, as the upper lip of the perianth of the greenhood orchid. [L: helmet]

**galeate** /'geɪlieɪt, -ət/, *adj.* having a galea. Also, **galeated.**

**galeiform** /'geɪliəfɔm/, *adj.* helmet-shaped; resembling a galea. [L *galea* helmet + -I- + -FORM]

**galena** /gə'linə/, *n.* a very common heavy (sp. gr. 7.6) mineral, lead sulphide, PbS, occurring in lead-grey crystals, usu. cubes, and cleavable masses; the principal ore of lead. Also, **galenite** /gə'linaɪt/. [L: lead ore]

**Galibi** /gə'libi/, *n.* **1.** a member of a Carib people of French Guiana. **2.** the language of this people.

**Galilean** /gælə'liən/, *adj.* **1.** of or pertaining to Galilee, a hilly region of northern Palestine. –*n.* **2.** a native or inhabitant of Galilee. **3.** *Rare.* a Christian. **4. the Galilean,** Jesus. [*Galile(e)* + -AN]

**galilee** /'gæləli/, *n.* a porch or vestibule, often on the ground floor of a tower, at the entrance of some English churches. [MF, from ML *galilaea,* a galilee, orig. (L) the province of Galilee in northern Palestine; said to refer to the 'Galilee of the Gentiles' in Matt. 4:15]

**galingale** /'gælɪŋgeɪl/, *n.* a tall perennial, *Cyperus longus,* found in wet places in the Mediterranean region and occasionally in southern Britain. [ME, from OF *galingal,* from Ar. *khalanjān,* said to be (through Pers.) from Chinese *Ko-liang-kiang,* lit., wild ginger from Ko, a prefecture in Canton province]

**galipot** /'gælipɒt/, *n.* a kind of turpentine exuded on the stems of certain species of pine. Also, **gallipot.** [F, earlier *garipot* resin, probably from D *harpuis,* c. MLG *harpois* boiled and skimmed resin]

**gall**[1] /gɔl/, *n.* **1.** bile. **2.** something very bitter or severe. **3.** bitterness of spirit; rancour. **4.** impudence; effrontery. [ME; d. OE *galla,* replacing OE *gealla,* c. G *Galle;* akin to L *fel,* Gk *cholḗ* gall, bile]

**gall**[2] /gɔl/, *n.* **1.** a sore on the skin, esp. of a horse, caused by rubbing. **2.** *Archaic.* something irritating. **3.** *Archaic.* a state of irritation. –*v.t.* **4.** to make sore by rubbing; chafe severely. **5.** to irritate or infuriate. [special use of GALL[1]]

**gall**[3] /gɔl/, *n.* any abnormal vegetable growth or excrescence on plants, caused by various agents, including insects, nematodes, fungi, bacteria, viruses, chemicals, and mechanical injuries. [ME *galle,* from F, from L *galla* the oak apple, gallnut]

**gall.,** gallon.

**gallant** /'gælənt, gə'lænt/, *adj.* **1.** brave and dashing: *gallant young men.* **2.** noticeably polite and attentive to women. **3.** generous or sporting: *a gallant gesture.* **4.** amorous. **5.** *Archaic.* splendid and stirring: *a gallant sight.* –*n.* *Archaic.* **6.** a brave and dashing man. **7.** a fashionable young man. **8.** an amorous young man. **9.** a woman's lover. –*v.i.* **10.** *Archaic.* to play the gallant. [OF *galant* splendid, magnificent, from *galer* to rejoice] – **gallantly,** *adv.* – **gallantness,** *n.*

**gallantry** /'gæləntri/, *n., pl.* **-tries.** **1.** dashing courage; heroic bravery. **2.** gallant or courtly attention to women. **3.** a gallant action or speech.

**gallant soldier** /gælənt 'soʊldʒə/, *n.* a small annual herb, *Galinsoga parviflora,* native to South America, but now a widespread weed.

**gall bladder** /'gɔl blædə/, *n.* a vesicle attached to the liver which receives bile from the hepatic ducts, concentrates it, and discharges it after meals.

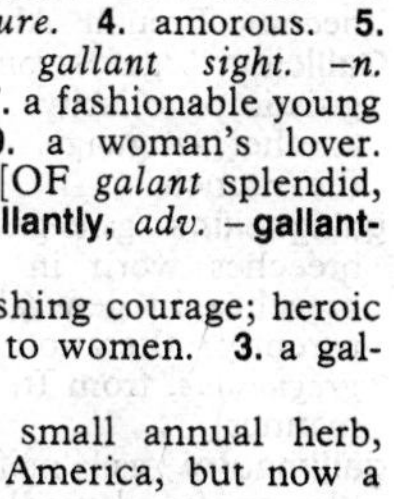

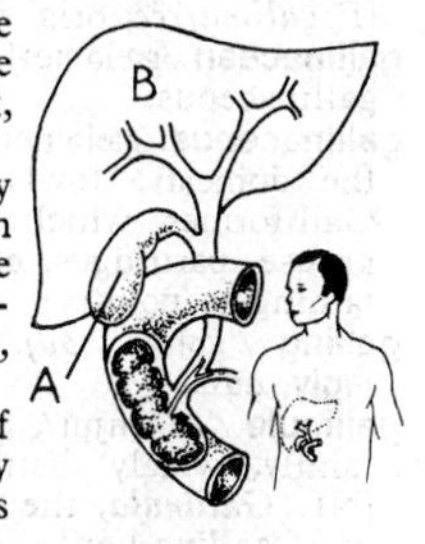

A, gall bladder; B, liver

**galleass** /'gæliəs/, *n.* a large war galley used in the Mediterranean in the 15th to 18th centuries, generally with three masts and rowed by slaves. Also, **galliass.** [MF *galeace,* from It. *galeaza,* augmentative of *galea* GALLEY]

**galleon** /'gæliən, 'gæljən/, *n.* a kind of large sailing vessel formerly used by Spain and other countries, both as warships and as merchant ships. [Sp. *galeón* large galley, augmentative of *galea* GALLEY]

**gallery** /ˈgæləri/, *n., pl.* **-leries.** **1.** a long, narrow, covered walk, open at one or both sides. **2.** a corridor, usu. large and with ornate walls and ceiling. **3.** a raised platform or passageway along the outside or inside of the wall of a building; balcony. **4.** a platform projecting from the interior walls of a church, theatre, etc., to provide seats or room for a part of the audience. **5.** the highest of such platforms in a theatre, usu. containing the cheapest seats. **6.** the occupants of such a platform in a theatre. **7.** any body of spectators or auditors. **8. play to the gallery,** to seek applause by playing to popular taste rather than considered judgment. **9.** a room, series of rooms, or building devoted to the exhibition of works of art. **10.** a collection of art for exhibition. **11.** a room or building in which to take pictures, practise shooting, etc. **12.** *Naut.* a balcony-like structure or platform at the stern or quarter of old ships; admiral's walk. **13.** a passageway made by an animal. **14.** any of various tunnels or passages, as an underground passage in a fortification, a tunnel within the body of a dam, etc. **15.** *Mining.* a level or drift. [It. *galleria,* from ML *galilaea* GALILEE] – **galleried,** *adj.*

**galley** /ˈgæli/, *n., pl.* **-leys. 1.** an early seagoing vessel propelled by oars or by oars and sails. **2.** a large rowing boat, formerly used in England. **3.** the kitchen of a ship or airliner. **4.** *Print.* **a.** a long, narrow tray, usu. of metal, for holding type which has been set. **b.** galley proof. [ME *galeie,* from ML *galeia,* from LGk *galaîa*]

**galley proof** /ˈ– pruf/, *n.* a typographical proof, typically of a single column, before it has been made up into pages.

**galley slave** /ˈ– sleɪv/, *n.* **1.** a person condemned to row in a galley. **2.** an overworked person; drudge.

**galifly** /ˈgɔlflaɪ/, *n., pl.* **-flies.** →**gall wasp.**

**galliard** /ˈgæliad, -iəd, ˈgæljad, -jəd/, *n.* **1.** a spirited dance for two dancers in triple rhythm, common in the 16th and 17th centuries. **2.** a piece of music for this dance. *–adj.* **3.** *Archaic.* lively or gay. [ME, from OF, probably from Celtic **galli-* might, ability]

**gallic**[1] /ˈgælɪk/, *adj.* of or containing gallium, in the trivalent state. [GALL(IUM) + -IC]

**gallic**[2] /ˈgælɪk/, *adj.* pertaining to or derived from plant galls: *gallic acid.* [GALL[3] + -IC]

**Gallic** /ˈgælɪk/, *adj.* **1.** pertaining to the Gauls or Gaul. **2.** pertaining to the French or France. [L *Gallicus,* from *Gallus* a Gaul]

**gallic acid** /gælɪk ˈæsəd/, *n.* an acid, $C_6H_2(OH)_3CO_2H$, a white or yellowish crystalline powder found in nut-galls, mangoes, and other plants.

**Gallicise** /ˈgæləsaɪz/, *v.,* **-cised, -cising.** (*sometimes l.c.*) *–v.t.* **1.** to make French in language, culture, etc. *–v.i.* **2.** to become French. Also, **Gallicize.**

**Gallicism** /ˈgæləsɪzəm/, *n.* (*sometimes l.c.*) **1.** a French linguistic peculiarity. **2.** a French idiom or expression used in another language. **3.** anything considered characteristic of the French.

**galligaskins** /gæləˈgæskənz/, *n. pl.* **1.** a kind of loose hose or breeches worn in the 16th and 17th centuries. **2.** loose breeches in general. **3.** leggings or gaiters of leather. [apparently alteration of F *garguesque,* metathetic var. of *greguesque,* from It. *grechesa,* from *alla grechesa* in the Greek manner]

**gallimaufry** /gæləˈmɔfri/, *n., pl.* **-fries. 1.** a hotchpotch; jumble; confused medley. **2.** *U.S.* a hash made from leftovers. [F *galimafrée,* orig. unknown]

**gallinacean** /gæləˈneɪʃən/, *n.* **1.** a gallinaceous bird. *–adj.* **2.** gallinaceous.

**gallinaceous** /gæləˈneɪʃəs/, *adj.* **1.** pertaining to or resembling the domestic fowls. **2.** belonging to the group or order Galliformes, which includes the domestic fowls, pheasants, grouse, partridges, etc. Also, **gallinacean.** [L *gallīnāceus* pertaining to poultry]

**galling** /ˈgɔlɪŋ/, *adj.* chafing; irritating; exasperating. – **gallingly,** *adv.*

**gallinule** /ˈgælənjul/, *n.* any of certain aquatic birds of the rail family, widely distributed in swampy regions; swamphen. [NL *Gallīnula,* the typical genus (LL: chicken) diminutive of L *gallīna* hen]

**gallipot**[1] /ˈgælipɒt/, *n.* a small glazed pot used by pharmacists for medicines, etc. [? GALLEY + POT[1] (as if brought or imported in galleys)]

**gallipot**[2] /ˈgælipɒt/, *n.* →**galipot.**

**gallium** /ˈgæliəm/, *n.* a rare, bluish white, easily fusible trivalent metallic element, used in high-temperature thermometers on account of its high boiling point (1700°C) and low melting point (30°C). *Symbol:* Ga; *at. wt:* 69.72; *at. no.:* 31; *sp. gr.:* 5.91 at 20°C. [NL, said to be from L *gallus* cock, translation of F *coq,* from the name of the discoverer, *Lecoq* de Boisbaudran]

**gallivant** /ˈgæləvænt/, *v.i.* to go from place to place in a rollicking, frivolous or flirtatious manner. Also, **galavant.** [? humorous alteration of GALLANT]

**gall midge** /ˈgɔl mɪdʒ/, *n.* any small fly of the family Cecidomyidae which makes galls on plants.

**gallnut** /ˈgɔlnʌt/, *n.* a nutlike gall on plants.

**Gallo-,** a word element meaning 'Gallic'. [L, combining form of *Gallus* a Gaul]

**galloglass** /ˈgæloʊˌglas/, *n.* one of a class of soldiers or retainers maintained by Irish chiefs in the 16th century and earlier. Also, **gallowglass.** [Irish *gallóglach,* from *gall* foreigner + *óglach* servant, warrior]

**gallon** /ˈgælən/, *n.* **1.** a unit of capacity in the imperial system, for the measurement of liquids and dry goods, defined as the volume occupied by 10 lbs of distilled water under specified conditions; equal to 4.546 09 × $10^{-3}$ $m^3$ (4.546 09 litres); imperial gallon. **2.** a U.S. measure of liquid commodities only, defined in the U.S. as 231 cubic inches; equal to 3.785 litres. One imperial gallon equals 1.200 94 U.S. gallons. [ME *galun,* from ONF *galon,* perhaps of Celtic orig.]

**galloon** /gəˈlun/, *n.* a braid or trimming of worsted, silk or rayon tinsel, gold or silver, etc. [F *galon,* from *galonner* trim with GALLOON, orig. adorn (the head or hair) with bands or ribbons, from OF *gale* GALA]

**galloot** /gəˈlut/, *n.* →**galoot.**

**gallop** /ˈgæləp/, *v.i.* **1.** to ride a horse at a gallop; ride at full speed. **2.** to run rapidly by leaps, as a horse; go at a gallop. **3.** to go fast, race, or hurry, as a person, the tongue, time, etc. *–v.t.* **4.** to cause (a horse, etc.) to gallop. *–n.* **5.** a fast gait of the horse (or other quadruped) in which in the course of each stride all four feet are off the ground at once. **6.** a run or ride at this gait. **7.** a rapid rate of going, or a course of going at this rate. **8.** (*oft. pl.*) a track where racehorses are exercised. **9. the gallops,** *Colloq.* horseracing (opposed to *the trots, the dogs*). [F *galoper,* from OLG *wala hlōpan* run well] – **galloper,** *n.*

**gallopade** /gæləˈpeɪd/, *n.* **1.** a sprightly kind of dance, originally Hungarian. **2.** the music for it. [F *galopade,* from *galoper* GALLOP]

**galloping** /ˈgæləpɪŋ/, *adj.* **1.** moving at a gallop or quickly. **2.** advancing or encroaching rapidly: *galloping inflation.*

**Gallo-Roman** /ˌgæloʊ-ˈroʊmən/, *adj.* **1.** of or pertaining to the culture of Roman Gaul. **2.** of or pertaining to the dialect of Latin spoken in Roman Gaul. *–n.* **3.** a Gaul of Roman culture. **4.** the dialect of Latin spoken in Roman Gaul.

**Gallo-Romance** /ˌgæloʊ-roʊˈmæns/, *n.* **1.** the hypothetical early Romance language spoken by the inhabitants of Gaul after the end of the Roman empire, forming a transition between Gallo-Roman and Old French but not historically attested. *–adj.* **2.** of or pertaining to this language.

**gallous** /ˈgæləs/, *adj.* containing divalent gallium.

**Galloway** /ˈgæləweɪ/, *n.* **1.** one of a breed of beef cattle originating in Scotland, with a coat of curly black hair. **2.** one of a breed of small strong horses. [named after *Galloway,* a region in Scotland]

**gallowglass** /ˈgæloʊglas/, *n.* →**galloglass.**

**gallows** /ˈgæloʊz/, *n., pl.* **-lows, -lowses. 1.** a wooden frame, consisting of a crossbeam on two uprights, on which condemned persons were, and in certain countries still are, executed by hanging. **2.** a similar structure, as for suspending something or for gymnastic exercise. **3.** execution by hanging. **4.** a device on which slaughtered animals, as cattle, are hung. [ME *galwes,* OE *galgan,* pl. of *g(e)alga* gallows, c. G *Galgen*]

**gallows bird** /ˈ– bɜd/, *n. Colloq.* one who deserves to be hanged.

**gallows bitts** /ˈ– bɪts/, *n. pl.* vertical frames on the deck of

a ship for supporting spare spars.
**gallows humour** /'– hjumə/, *n.* macabre, ironic humour.
**gallows top** /'– tɒp/, *n.* timbers placed across the top of the gallows bitts to secure spare spars.
**gallows tree** /'– tri/, *n. Archaic.* →**gallows.**
**gallstone** /'gɔlstoʊn/, *n.* a calculus or stone formed in the bile ducts or gall bladder.
**gallup poll** /'gæləp poʊl/, *n.* the questioning of a representative cross-section of the population in order to assess public opinion, as of voting intentions. [after George Horace *Gallup,* b. 1901, American statistician]
**gall wasp** /'gɔl wɒsp/, *n.* any of various wasps, as those of the family Cymipidae, whose larvae cause galls on plants.
**galoot** /gə'lut/, *n. Colloq.* an awkward, silly fellow: *silly galoot.* Also, **galloot.**
**galop** /'gæləp/, *n.* **1.** a lively round dance in duple time. **2.** music for, or in the rhythm of, this dance. [F]
**galore** /gə'lɔ/, *adv.* (*used only after nouns*) in abundance: *there was food galore.* [Irish *go leōir* (Gaelic *gu leōir*) to sufficiency]
**galosh** /gə'lɒʃ/, *n., pl.* **-loshes. 1.** a piece of leather running round the lower part of boot or shoe uppers. **2.** *Obs.* a rustic shoe, clog or sandal. Also, **galoche, golosh.** [ME *galoche,* from F, probably from L *gallicula* Gallic (sandal), b. *gallica* Gallic and *caligula* soldier's boot]
**galoshes** /gə'lɒʃəz/, *n.pl.* a pair of over-shoes of rubber or other waterproof substance for protection against wet, cold, etc. Also, **goloshes.** [pl. GALOSH]
**gals,** gallons.
**galumph** /gə'lʌmpf, -'lʌmf/, *v.i.* **1.** to bound exultantly. **2.** to move clumsily, as through an excess of enthusiasm. [b. GALLOP + TRIUMPH; coined by Lewis Carroll]
**galvanic** /gæl'vænɪk/, *adj.* **1.** pertaining to or produced by galvanism; producing or caused by electricity. **2.** affecting or affected as if by galvanism. [from Luigi *Galvani,* 1737-98, Italian physiologist, + -IC]
**galvanic battery** /– 'bætəri/, *n.* →**voltaic battery.**
**galvanic cell** /– 'sɛl/, *n.* an electrolytic cell capable of producing electric energy by electrochemical action.
**galvanise** /'gælvənaɪz/, *v.t.,* **-nised, -nising. 1.** to stimulate by or as by a galvanic current. **2.** to startle into sudden activity. **3.** to coat (iron or steel) with zinc. Also, **galvanize.** – **galvanisation** /gælvənaɪ'zeɪʃən/, *n.* – **galvaniser,** *n.*
**galvanised** /'gælvənaɪzd/, *adj.* **1.** (of iron or steel) coated with zinc. –*n.* **2.** galvanised iron or steel sheeting.
**galvanised burr** /– 'bɜ/, *n.* an Australian plant, *Bassia birchii,* whose spiny fruits are especially troublesome because they become entangled in sheep's fleeces.
**galvanised iron** /– 'aɪən/, *n.* **1.** iron coated with zinc to prevent rust. **2.** such iron formed into corrugated sheets, and used for roofing, etc., esp. in rural buildings or outhouses.
**galvanism** /'gælvənɪzəm/, *n.* **1.** electricity produced by chemical action. **2.** the therapeutic application of electricity to the body.
**galvano-,** a combining form representing **galvanic, galvanism,** as in *galvanocautery.*
**galvanocautery** /ˌgælvənoʊ'kɔtəri, gælˌvænoʊ-/, *n., pl.* **-ries. 1.** a cautery heated by a galvanic current. **2.** cauterisation by such means.
**galvanometer** /gælvə'nɒmətə/, *n.* an instrument for detecting the existence and determining the strength and direction of an electric current.
**galvanometry** /gælvə'nɒmətri/, *n.* the process by which the strength of electric currents is determined. – **galvanometric** /ˌgælvənoʊ'mɛtrɪk, gælˌvænə-/, *adj.*
**galvanoscope** /'gælvənəˌskoʊp, gæl'vænə-/, *n.* an instrument used for detecting the existence, and determining the direction of an electric current. – **galvanoscopic** /ˌgælvənə'skɒpɪk, gælˌvænə-/, *adj.*
**galvanotropism** /ˌgælvə'nɒtrəpɪzəm/, *n.* the movements in growing plant organs induced by the passage of electric currents.
**galvo** /'gælvoʊ/, *n. Colloq.* galvanised iron or steel sheeting.
**galyak** /'gæljæk/, *n.* a fur from the pelt of lambs or kids. [Uzbek]
**gam**[1] /gæm/, *n., v.,* **gammed, gamming.** –*n.* **1.** a herd or school of whales. **2.** *Naut. and U.S.* a social meeting, visit, or the like, as between vessels at sea. –*v.i.* **3.** (of whales) to congregate in a school. **4.** *Naut. and U.S.* to have a gam; meet socially. –*v.t.* **5.** *Naut. and U.S.* to have a gam with. [var. of GAME[1]]
**gam**[2] /gæm/, *n. Colloq.* a leg. [var. of obs. *gamb,* from ONF *gambe.* Cf. OF *jambe* leg]
**gamba** /'gæmbə/, *n.* **1.** an organ stop intended to have a stringlike tone. **2.** →**viola da gamba.**
**gambado**[1] /gæm'beɪdoʊ/, *n., pl.* **-dos, -does. 1.** one of a pair of large protective boots or gaiters fixed to a saddle instead of stirrups. **2.** any long gaiter or legging. [It. *gamba* leg + suffix *-ado*]
**gambado**[2] /gæm'beɪdoʊ/, *n.* **1.** a bound or leap by a horse. **2.** an escapade. Also, **gambade** /gæm'beɪd/. [F *gambade,* influenced by GAMBADO[1]. Cf. GAMBOL]
**gambeson** /'gæmbəsən/, *n.* a medieval military garment of leather or quilted cloth, padded, and worn under mail, but also worn as the principal garment of defence. [ME *gambisoune,* from OF *gambison,* of Gmc orig.]

gambeson

**Gambia** /'gæmbiə/, *n.* a country in western Africa. – **Gambian,** *adj., n.*
**gambier** /'gæmbiə/, *n.* an astringent extract similar to catechu, obtained from the leaves and young shoots of *Uncaria gambir,* a tropical Asiatic shrub, and used in medicine, dyeing, tanning, etc. Also, **gambir.** [Malay *gambir*]
**gambit** /'gæmbət/, *n.* **1.** an opening in chess, in which the player seeks by sacrificing a pawn or other piece to obtain some advantage. **2.** any act or course of action by which one seeks to obtain some advantage. [F, from It. *gambetto* a tripping-up, from *gamba* leg]
**gamble** /'gæmbəl/, *v.,* **-bled, -bling,** *n.* –*v.i.* **1.** to play at any game of chance for stakes. **2.** to stake or risk money, or anything of value, on the outcome of something involving chance. **3.** to act on favourable hopes or assessment: *in calling the general election, the prime minister is gambling on public acceptance of his policies to date.* –*v.t.* **4.** to lose or squander by betting (usu. fol. by *away*). **5.** to risk or venture. –*n.* **6.** any matter or thing involving risk or uncertainty. **7.** a venture in or as in gambling. [? d. var. of ME *gamenen,* OE *gamenian* to sport, play] – **gambler,** *n.* – **gambling,** *n.*
**gamboge** /gæm'boʊdʒ, -'buʒ/, *n.* **1.** Also, **cambogia.** a gum resin from various trees of the genus *Garcinia,* esp. *G. hanburyi,* of Cambodia, Thailand, etc., used as a yellow pigment and as a cathartic. **2.** yellow or yellow-orange. [NL *gambogium,* from *Camboja* CAMBODIA]
**gambol** /'gæmbəl/, *v.,* **-bolled, -bolling** or (*U.S.*) **-boled, -boling,** *n.* –*v.i.* **1.** to skip about, as in dancing or playing; frolic. –*n.* **2.** a skipping or frisking about; frolic. [earlier *gambald,* from F *gambade* a leap, from It. *gambata* a kick, from *gamba* leg]
**gambrel** /'gæmbrəl/, *n.* **1.** the hock of an animal, esp. of a horse. **2.** Also, **cambrel.** a curved rod which pierces both hind shanks of a carcass of beef, lamb, etc., so that the carcass can be hung symmetrically. [ONF **gamberel* butcher's cambrel, from *gambe,* from LL *gamba* hoof, leg]
**gambrel roof** /'– ruf/, *n.* **1.** a roof having a small gablet at the summit of a hipped end. **2.** *U.S.* a mansard roof. – **gambrel-roofed,** *adj.*

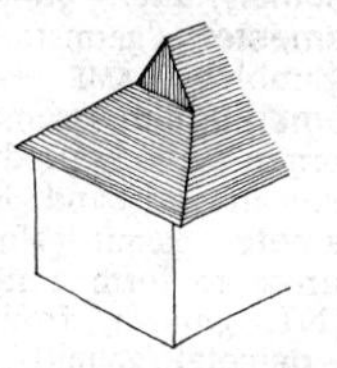
gambrel roof (def. 1)

**game**[1] /geɪm/, *n., adj.,* **gamer, gamest,** *v.,* **gamed, gaming.** –*n.* **1.** an amusement or pastime: *children's games.* **2.** the apparatus employed in playing any of certain games: *a shop selling toys and games.* **3.** a contest for amusement in the form of a trial of chance, skill, or endurance, according to set rules; a match: *games of football, golf, etc.* **4.** a single contest at play, or a definite portion of play in a particular game: *a rubber of three games in bridge.* **5.** the number of points required to win a game. **6.** a particular manner or style of playing a game. **7.** a proceeding carried on according to set rules as in a game: *the game of diplomacy.* **8.** *Colloq.* business or profession. **9.** a trick; strategy: *to see through someone's game.* **10.** sport of any kind; joke: *to make game of a person.* **11.** wild animals, including birds and fishes, such as are hunted or taken for sport or profit. **12.** the flesh of wild animals or game, used for food. **13.** any object of pursuit or attack; prey. **14.** fighting spirit; pluck. **15. game, set and match,** a convincing victory; complete triumph (fol. by *to*). **16. give the game away, a.** to reject or abandon. **b.** to reveal some strategy or secret. **17. have the game sewn up,** to be master of the situation. **18. off one's game,** not giving one's best performance; out of form. **19. play the game,** to act fairly or justly, or in accordance with recognised rules. **20. the game,** *Colloq.* **a.** sexual intercourse. **b.** prostitution. **21. two can play at that game,** *Colloq.* others can act in a like manner (usu. indicating intended retaliation by another person). *–adj.* **22.** pertaining to animals hunted or taken as game. **23.** with fighting spirit; plucky; resolute: *as game as Ned Kelly.* **24.** *Colloq.* willing to undertake something hazardous or challenging (oft. fol. by *for* or by an infinitive): *I'm game to go bushwalking.* *–v.i.* **25.** to play games of chance for stakes; gamble. *–v.t.* **26.** to squander in gaming (fol. by *away*). [ME; OE *gamen,* c. OHG *gaman* glee] **– gamely,** *adv.* **– gameness,** *n.*

**game**[2] /geɪm/, *adj. Colloq.* lame: *a game leg.* [orig. uncert.]

**gamebag** /ˈgeɪmbæg/, *n.* a strong bag of canvas, leather, or the like, for holding game birds or other game.

**game bird** /ˈgeɪm bɜd/, *n.* **1.** a bird hunted for sport, profit, or food. **2.** such a bird, which is usu. wild, raised for food, as pheasant, goose, etc.

**gamecock** /ˈgeɪmkɒk/, *n.* a cock bred and trained for fighting, or one of a fighting breed.

**game fish** /ˈgeɪm fɪʃ/, *n.* an edible fish capable of affording sport to the angler in its capture.

**game fowl** /ˈ– faʊl/, *n.* **1.** a fowl of any species regarded as game or the object of hunting. **2.** a domestic fowl of a breed used for fighting.

**gamekeeper** /ˈgeɪmkipə/, *n.* a person employed, as on an estate, to take care of game, prevent poaching, etc.

**gamelan** /ˈgæməlæn/, *n.* **1.** a South-East Asian tuned percussion instrument. **2.** an orchestra comprising a number of gamelans, with some woodwind and strings. [Malay]

**game laws** /ˈgeɪm lɔz/, *n.pl.* the body of laws enacted for the preservation of game, as by restricting open seasons and the manner of hunting.

**game point** /ˈ– pɔɪnt/, *n.* (in a tennis match, etc.) a point that could decide the game if scored by the leading player.

**game reserve** /ˈ– rəzɜv/, *n.* an area of land set aside for the preservation of wild animals.

**game show** /ˈ– ʃoʊ/, *n.* a program, esp. on television, where people selected to participate compete in the studio for prizes.

**gamesman** /ˈgeɪmzmən/, *n., pl.* **-men. 1. a.** a man (or, sometimes, any person) who plays games. **b.** one who plays games well. **2.** one adept at winning an advantage for himself by gambits, plays, or outright cheating.

**gamesmanship** /ˈgeɪmzmənʃɪp/, *n.* the art or practice of winning games, or gaining advantages without actually cheating, by disconcerting the opponent.

**gamesome** /ˈgeɪmsəm/, *adj.* full of play; frolicsome. **– gamesomely,** *adv.* **– gamesomeness,** *n.*

**gamester** /ˈgeɪmstə/, *n.* a person who gambles habitually; gambler. [GAME[1] + -STER]

**gametangium** /gæməˈtændʒiəm/, *n., pl.* **-gia** /-dʒiə/. a plant organ or body producing gametes. [NL, from Gk *gametḗ* wife, *gamétēs* husband + *angeîon* vessel]

**gamete** /ˈgæmit, gəˈmit/, *n.* either of the two germ cells which unite to form a new organism; a mature reproductive cell. [NL *gameta,* from Gk *gametḗ* wife or *gamétēs* husband] **– gametal** /gəˈmitl/, **gametic** /gəˈmɛtɪk/, *adj.*

**gametocyte** /gəˈmitoʊˌsaɪt/, *n.* a cell that produces gametes.

**gametogenesis** /gæmətoʊˈdʒɛnəsəs/, *n.* the development of gametes.

**gametophore** /gəˈmitoʊfɔ/, *n.* a plant part or structure producing gametes.

**gametophyte** /gəˈmitoʊfaɪt/, *n.* the sexual form of a plant in the alternation of generations (opposed to *sporophyte*).

**game warden** /ˈgeɪm wɔdən/, *n.* an official who enforces game laws.

**gamey** /ˈgeɪmi/, *adj.* →**gamy.**

**gamic** /ˈgæmɪk/, *adj.* sexual (opposed to *agamic*). [Gk *gamikós* of or for marriage]

**gamin** /ˈgæmən/, *n.* **1.** a neglected boy left to run about the streets; street Arab. **2.** a mischievous boy. *–adj.* **3.** (of a person's appearance, or hairstyle) elfin. [F; orig. uncert.]

**gamine** /ˈgæmin/, *n.* **1.** a female street Arab. **2.** a mischievous, boylike girl or woman, esp. one of small stature. [F, fem. of GAMIN]

**gaming** /ˈgeɪmɪŋ/, *n.* gambling.

**gamma** /ˈgæmə/, *n.* **1.** the third letter (Γ, γ, = English G, g) of the Greek alphabet. **2.** the third of any series (used esp. in scientific classification). **3.** a unit of weight equal to one microgram. **4.** the third highest examination mark, usu. the lowest mark awarded. **5.** *Geol.* a unit of magnetic intensity equal to $10^{-5}$ oersted.

**gammadion** /gæˈmadiən/, *n.* an ornamental figure consisting of combinations of the Greek capital gamma, esp. in the form of a swastika or fylfot, or of a voided Greek cross. [MGk, var. of *gammátion,* diminutive of Gk *gámma* gamma]

**gamma globulin** /gæmə ˈglɒbjulən/, *n.* a protein fraction of blood plasma containing antibodies.

**gamma iron** /ˈ– aɪən/, *n.* a form of iron which is nonmagnetic and which, when pure, exists between approx. 900°C and 1400°C; consists of face-centred cubic crystals.

**gamma radiation** /– reɪdiˈeɪʃən/, *n.* radiation consisting of streams of gamma particles; gamma rays.

**gamma rays** /ˈ– reɪz/, *n.pl.* rays similar to X-rays, but of higher frequency and penetrating power, forming part of the radiation of radioactive substance.

**gammon**[1] /ˈgæmən/, *n.* **1.** the game of backgammon. **2.** *Backgammon.* a victory in which the winner throws off all his men before his opponent throws off any. *–v.t.* **3.** *Backgammon.* to win a gammon over. [? special use of ME and OE *gamen.* See GAME[1]]

**gammon**[2] /ˈgæmən/, *n.* **1.** a smoked or cured ham. **2.** the lower end of a side of bacon. [ME *gambon,* from ONF: ham, from *gambe* hoof, leg, from LL *gamba*]

**gammon**[3] /ˈgæmən/, *Colloq.* *–n.* **1.** deceitful nonsense; bosh. *–v.i.* **2.** to talk gammon. **3.** to make pretence. *–v.t.* **4.** to deceive with nonsense. [see GAMMON[1]]

**gammon**[4] /ˈgæmən/, *v.t.* to fasten (a bowsprit) to the stem of a ship. [? akin to GAMMON[2]]

**gammy** /ˈgæmi/, *adj. Colloq.* →**game**[2].

**gamo-,** a word element meaning 'sexual union'. [combining form representing Gk *gámos* marriage]

**gamogenesis** /gæməˈdʒɛnəsəs/, *n.* sexual reproduction. **– gamogenetic** /ˌgæmoʊdʒəˈnɛtɪk/, *adj.* **– gamogenetically** /gæmoʊdʒəˈnɛtɪkli/, *adv.*

**gamopetalous** /ˌgæmoʊˈpɛtələs/, *adj.* (of a flower) having the petals united; sympetalous.

**gamophyllous** /ˌgæmoʊˈfɪləs/, *adj.* having leaves united by their edges.

**gamosepalous** /ˌgæmoʊˈsɛpələs/, *adj.* having the sepals united.

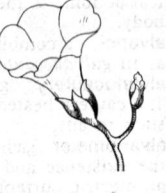

gamopetalous flower

**-gamous,** an adjectival word element corresponding to the noun element **-gamy,** as in *polygamous.* [Gk *-gamos* marrying]

**gamp** /gæmp/, *n. Brit. Colloq.* an umbrella. [said to be from the umbrella of Mrs Sarah *Gamp* in Dickens's *Martin Chuzzlewit*]

**gamut** /ˈgæmət/, *n.* **1.** the whole scale or range. **2.** *Music.* **a.** the whole series of recognised musical notes. **b.** the major scale. [ML, contraction of *gamma ut,* from *gamma,* used to represent the first or lowest tone (G) in the medieval scale + *ut* (later *do*); the notes of the scale being named from a L hymn to St John: *Ut* queant laxis *re*sonare fibris, *Mi*ra gestorum *fa*muli tuorum, *Sol*ve polluti *la*bi reatum, Sancte Iohannes]

**gamy** /ˈgeɪmi/, *adj.,* **gamier, gamiest. 1.** having the flavour of game, esp. game kept uncooked until slightly high, as preferred by connoisseurs: *the meat had a gamy flavour.* **2.**

plucky; brave. Also, **gamey.** – **gamily,** *adv.* – **gaminess,** *n.*

**-gamy,** 1. a word element meaning 'marriage', as in *polygamy.* 2. *Biol.* a word element meaning 'sexual union', as in *allogamy.* [Gk *-gamía,* from *-gamos* marrying, married]

**gan** /gæn/, *v. Archaic.* →**began.**

**gander** /'gændə/, *n.* 1. the male of the goose. 2. *Colloq.* a look at something. [ME; OE *gan(d)ra,* c. MLG *ganre,* D *gander,* from Vernerian var. of Gmc *gans-* goose]

**gang**[1] /gæŋ/, *n.* 1. a band or group: *a gang of boys.* 2. a group of persons working together; squad; shift: *a gang of labourers; iron gang; road gang.* 3. (formerly) a party of convicts employed on public works: *road gang; wood cutting gang.* 4. a group of persons, usu. considered disreputable, violent or criminal, associated for a particular purpose: *a gang of thieves.* 5. a set of tools, etc., arranged to work together or simultaneously. [ME and OE; orig. 'a going'; sense of 'group' from OE *gang* in *gangdæg* processional day] –*v.t.* 6. to arrange in gangs; form into a gang. –*v.i.* 7. *Colloq.* to form or act as a gang. 8. *Scot.* to walk; go. 9. **gang up on,** to attack in a gang; combine against. [ME *gong(e), gang(en),* OE *gongan, gangan,* c. OHG *gangan*]

**gang**[2] /gæŋ/, *n.* →**gangue.**

**ganga** /'gʌndʒə/, *n.* →**cannabis.** Also, **ganja.** [Hindi *gānjhā*]

**gang bang** /'– bæŋ/, *n. Colloq.* an occasion on which a number of males have sexual intercourse with one female. Also, **gangie, gang slash, gang splash.** – **gang banger,** *n.*

**gangboard** /'gæŋbɔd/, *n.* a raised narrow walk on a boat, connecting the forecastle directly with the quarter deck.

**gang cultivator** /'gæŋ kʌltəveɪtə/, *n.* a cultivator having several tines mounted to be operated as a gang.

**ganger** /'gæŋə/, *n.* the foreman of a gang of labourers.

**gang-fight** /'gæŋ-faɪt/, *n.* a fight between two or more gangs of bikies, skinheads, etc.

**gang-gang** /'gæŋ-gæŋ/, *n.* a greyish cockatoo, *Callocephalon fimbriatum,* of south-eastern Australia, the male of which has a red head and crest. [Aboriginal]

**ganghook** /'gæŋhʊk/, *n.* a fishhook made by joining back-to-back the shanks of two or three hooks.

**gangie** /'gæŋi/, *n. Colloq.* →**gang bang.**

**gangland** /'gæŋlænd/, *n.* →**underworld** (def. 1).

**ganglia** /'gæŋgliə/, *n.* plural of **ganglion.**

**gangliated** /'gæŋglieɪtəd/, *adj.* having ganglia. Also, **gangliate** /'gæŋgliət, -eɪt/.

**gangling** /'gæŋglɪŋ/, *adj.* awkwardly tall and spindly; lank and loosely built. Also, **gangly** /'gæŋgli/. [akin to obs. *gangrel* gangling person, from GANG[1]]

**ganglion** /'gæŋgliən/, *n., pl.* **-glia** /-gliə/, **-glions.** 1. *Anat.* grey matter outside the brain and spinal cord. 2. *Pathol.* a cyst or enlargement in connection with the sheath of a tendon, usu. at the wrist. 3. a centre of intellectual or industrial force, activity, etc. [LL: kind of swelling, from Gk: tumour under the skin, on or near a tendon] – **ganglionic** /,gæŋgli'ɒnɪk/, *adj.*

**ganglionectomy** /,gæŋgliə'nɛktəmi/, *n., pl.* **-mies.** the excision of a ganglion.

**gangmill** /'gæŋmɪl/, *n.* a sawmill in which several saws, fitted in a reciprocating frame, cut simultaneously.

**gang nail** /'gæŋ neɪl/, *n.* a piece of sheet metal with sharp triangular projections, used as a connecting piece in timber construction.

**gangplank** /'gæŋplæŋk/, *n.* a plank, often having cleats, used as a temporary bridge in passing into and out of a ship, etc.

**gang plough** /'gæŋ plaʊ/, *n.* 1. a plough with several blades producing parallel furrows. 2. a combination of ploughs in one frame.

**gangrene** /'gæŋgrin/, *n., v.,* **-grened, -grening.** –*n.* 1. the dying of tissue, as from interruption of circulation; mortification. –*v.t.* 2. to affect with gangrene. –*v.i.* 3. to become affected with gangrene. [L *gangraena,* from Gk *gángraina* an eating sore] – **gangrenous** /'gæŋgrənəs/, *adj.*

**gangsaw** /'gæŋsɔ/, *n.* one of the several blades fitted in a frame forming part of a gangmill. Also, **framesaw.**

**gang slash** /'gæŋ slæʃ/, *n.* →**gang bang.** Also, **gang splash.**

**gangster** /'gæŋstə/, *n.* 1. a member of a gang of criminals. 2. *N.Z. Colloq.* a tough but likeable character.

**gangue** /gæŋ/, *n.* the stony or earthy minerals occurring with the metallic ore in a vein or deposit. Also, **gang.** [F, from G *Gang* mineral vein, lode]

**gang warfare** /gæŋ 'wɔfɛə/, *n.* continuous fighting or feuding between different gangs of criminals, bikies, sharpies, etc.

**gangway** /'gæŋweɪ/, *n.* 1. a passageway. 2. *Naut.* **a.** any of various passageways on a ship, as that between the rail and the cabins or houses on the deck. **b.** an opening or removable section of a ship's rail for the gangplank. **c.** →**gangplank. d.** a platform and ladder or stairway slung over the side of a ship. 3. an aisle in a theatre. 4. a temporary path of planks, as at a building site. 5. *Mining.* a main passage or level. 6. *Mining.* a main haulage road underground. 7. the ramp up which logs are moved into a sawmill; logway. –*interj.* 8. clear the way! [OE *gangweg*]

**ganister** /'gænəstə/, *n.* a highly refractory, siliceous rock, used to line furnaces, sometimes artificially made by mixing ground quartz with a bonding material. [orig. uncert.]

**gannet** /'gænət/, *n.* any of several large pelagic birds of the family Sulidae, as the **Australian gannet,** *Morus serrator.* [ME and OE *ganet,* akin to D *gent* gander]

**ganoid** /'gænɔɪd/, *adj.* 1. belonging or pertaining to the Ganoidei, a group of fishes, many of which have hard, smooth scales, as the sturgeons, etc. 2. (of fish scales) having a smooth, shining surface. –*n.* 3. a ganoid fish. [Gk *gános* brightness + -OID]

**gantlet**[1] /'gæntlət, 'gɔnt-/, *n. Chiefly U.S.* →**gauntlet**[1].

**gantlet**[2] /'gæntlət, 'gɔnt-/, *n., v.t. U.S.* →**gauntlet**[2].

**gantline** /'gæntlaɪn, -lən/, *n.* a rope temporarily made fast or rove through a block, as for hoisting rigging on a ship, raising a man to the rigging, etc. [alteration of *girtline*]

**Gantrisin** /'gæntrəzən, -sən/, *n.* a sulpha drug used as an antibacterial agent to treat infections. [Trademark]

**gantry** /'gæntri/, *n., pl.* **-tries.** 1. a spanning framework, as a bridgelike portion of certain cranes, a structure holding railway signals above the tracks, etc. 2. a frame supporting something, as a missile, standing vertical before blast-off. 3. a simple frame holding a barrel or cask. Also, **gauntry.** [d. *gawn* (contraction of GALLON) + *-tree* supporting frame]

**Ganymede** /'gænimid/, *n. Colloq.* 1. a young waiter. 2. a young male homosexual. [from *Ganymede,* a Trojan youth carried off by Zeus, to be his lover and cupbearer]

**gaol** /dʒeɪl/, *n.* 1. a prison. –*v.t.* 2. to take into or hold in custody; imprison. Also, **jail.** [ME *gay(h)ole, gaile,* from ONF *gaiole, gaole,* from L *cavea* cavity, enclosure, cage. See JAIL]

**gaol-bait** /'dʒeɪl-beɪt/, *n. Colloq.* a girl below the legal age of consent. Also, **jail-bait.**

**gaolbird** /'dʒeɪlbɜd/, *n.* one who is or has been confined in gaol; a criminal. Also, **jailbird.**

**gaolbreak** /'dʒeɪlbreɪk/, *n.* an escape from prison by means of force. Also, **jailbreak.**

**gaol delivery** /'dʒeɪl dəlɪvəri/, *n.* 1. a deliverance of imprisoned persons, esp. by force. 2. the act of clearing a gaol of prisoners by bringing them to trial, as at the assizes. Also, **jail delivery.**

**gaoler** /'dʒeɪlə/, *n.* one in charge of a gaol; prison warder. Also, **jailor, jailer.**

**gaol fever** /'dʒeɪl fivə/, *n.* →**typhus.** Also, **jail fever.**

**gaol gang** /'– gæŋ/, *n.* (formerly) those convicts confined to gaol and allowed no free time. Also, **jail gang.**

**gaolhouse** /'dʒeɪlhaʊs/, *n., pl.* **-houses** /-haʊzəz/. →**jailhouse.**

**gaolie** /'dʒeɪli/, *n. Colloq.* →**gaolbird.** Also, **jailie.**

**gap** /gæp/, *n., v.t.,* **gapped, gapping.** –*n.* 1. a break or opening, as in a fence, wall, or the like; breach. 2. a vacant space or interval. 3. a wide divergence. 4. a deep, sloping ravine or cleft cutting a mountain ridge. 5. *Aeron.* the distance between the wings of a biplane. 6. *Colloq.* a divergence, contradiction, disparity, or imbalance: *credibility gap, generation gap, missile gap.* –*v.t.* 7. to make a gap, opening, or breach in. [ME, from Scand.; cf. Swed. *gap* opening, chasm, *gapa* GAPE] – **gapless,** *adj.*

**gape** /geɪp/, *v.,* **gaped, gaping,** *n.* –*v.i.* 1. **a.** to stare with open mouth, as in wonder. **b.** to stare as with open mouth. 2. to open the mouth wide, either intentionally or involuntarily. 3. to open as a gap; split or become open wide. –*n.* 4. a breach or rent; wide opening. 5. the act of gaping. 6. *Zool.* the width of the open mouth. [ME *gapen,* from Scand.; cf. Icel. and Swed. *gapa* open the mouth, c. G *gaffen*] – **gaper,** *n.* – **gapingly,** *adv.*

**gapes** /'geɪps/, *n.pl.* (*construed as sing.*) **1.** *Vet. Sci.* a disease of poultry and other birds, attended with frequent gaping, due to infestation of the trachea and bronchi with gapeworms. **2.** a fit of yawning: *he has the gapes.*

**gapeworm** /'geɪpwɜm/, *n.* a nematode worm, *Syngamus trachea,* which causes gapes.

**gap-toothed** /'gæp-tuθt/, *adj.* having a gap between the teeth, esp. the two front teeth. Also, **gat-toothed.**

**GAQ** /dʒi eɪ 'kju/, *adj.* top quality, esp. of products as meat. [*G*(*ood*) *A*(*verage*) *Q*(*uality*)]

**gar** /ga/, *n., pl.* **-gars,** (*esp. collectively*) **gar. 1.** a seawater fish, *Rhamphistoma belone,* of the North Atlantic, having both jaws prolonged into a beak. **2.** a predacious fish of the genus *Lepisosteus* (including several species, all of North American fresh waters), covered with very hard diamond-shaped ganoid scales and having a beak armed with large teeth. **3.** →**needlefish** (def. 1). Also, **garfish, garpike.** [short for GARFISH]

**gar.,** garage.

**garage** /'gæraʒ, -radʒ, gə'raʒ, -'radʒ/, *n., v.* **-raged, -raging.** –*n.* **1.** a building for sheltering a motor vehicle or vehicles. **2.** an establishment where motor vehicles are repaired, petrol is sold, etc. –*v.t.* **3.** to put or keep in a garage. [F, from *garer* put in shelter, from Pr. *garar* keep, heed, from Gmc; cf. OHG *warōn* heed]

**garage sale** /'– seɪl/, *n.* sale of miscellaneous, usu. second-hand goods, for private gain or for charity.

**garam masala** /gærəm 'mæsələ/, *n.* a fragrant powder of Indian origin consisting of ground cinnamon, cardamon, black pepper, cloves, etc. used to add aroma and flavour to foods just before cooking is complete. [Hind.]

**garb**[1] /gab/, *n.* **1.** fashion or mode of dress, esp. of a distinctive kind. **2.** clothes. **3.** covering, semblance, or form. –*v.t.* **4.** to dress; clothe. [F *garbe,* from It. *garbo* grace, from Gmc; cf. MHG *garwe* GEAR]

**garb**[2] /gab/, *n.* a sheaf of wheat as a heraldic device.

**garbag** /'gabæg/, *n.* a large, strong plastic bag used in place of a garbage bin for collection by garbagemen. [GAR(BAGE) + BAG]

**garbage** /'gabɪdʒ/, *n.* **1.** refuse animal and vegetable matter. **2.** household, esp. kitchen, waste; rubbish; refuse. **3.** anything worthless, undesirable, or unnecessary.

**garbage bin** /'– bɪn/, *n.* a container in which household rubbish is kept until collection or disposal.

**garbage compactor** /'– kəmpæktə/, *n.* a device which compresses garbage esp. as in a garbage truck.

**garbage disposal unit,** *n.* an electric device fitted into a kitchen sink which grinds food waste into a form in which it can be disposed down the waste water system.

**garbageman** /'gabɪdʒmən, -ˌmæn/, *n., pl.* **men** /-mən, -ˌmɛn/. one employed to collect garbage.

**garbage truck** /'gabɪdʒ trʌk/, *n.* a motor vehicle, usu. specially designed, for the collection of domestic refuse.

**garble** /'gabəl/, *v.,* **-bled, -bling,** *n.* –*v.t.* **1.** to make unfair or misleading selections from (facts, statements, writings, etc.); corrupt. **2.** to make incomprehensible. –*n.* **3.** the process of garbling. [It. *garbellare,* from Ar. *gharbala* sift, ? from LL *crēbellāre,* from *cērbellum* little sieve] – **garbler,** *n.*

**garbo** /'gaboʊ/, *n. Colloq.* **1.** →**garbageman. 2.** a garbage container.

**garboard** /'gabɔd/, *n.* the strake of planks laid next to the keel of a ship. Also, **garboard strake.** [D *gaarboord*]

**garcon** /ga'sɒ̃/, *n.* **1.** a male employee or servant. **2.** a waiter. Also, **garçon.** [F: boy, waiter]

**gardant** /'gadənt/, *adj. Her.* →**guardant.**

**garden** /'gadn/, *n.* **1.** a plot of ground devoted to the cultivation of useful or ornamental plants. **2.** a piece of ground, or other space, commonly with ornamental plants, trees, etc., used as a place of recreation: *a botanical garden, a roof garden.* **3.** a fertile and delightful spot or region. –*adj.* **4.** pertaining to or produced in a garden. **5.** (of recent urban developments) deliberately planned so as to have many garden-like open spaces: *a garden city.* **6. lead up the garden path,** *Colloq.* to mislead, hoax, or delude. –*v.i.* **7.** to lay out or cultivate a garden. **8.** *Cricket.* of a batsman, to smooth out bumps and other unevennesses in the pitch by patting or prodding the turf with the bat. –*v.t.* **9.** to cultivate as a garden. [ME *gardin,* from ONF, of Gmc orig.; cf. G *Garten*] – **gardenless,** *adj.* – **gardenlike,** *adj.*

**garden centre** /'– sɛntə/, *n.* a place where requisites for the garden are sold, as plants, fertilisers, hoses, etc.

**gardener** /'gadənə/, *n.* **1.** a person employed to take care of a garden. **2.** one who gardens.

**garden flat** /'gadn flæt/, *n.* a self-contained flat, either part of a house or detached from it, opening onto the garden.

**garden gnome** /– 'noʊm/, *n.* a small statue of a gnome, usu. displayed as a garden decoration.

**gardenia** /ga'dinjə, -niə/, *n.* any of the evergreen trees and shrubs of the genus *Gardenia,* native to the warmer parts of the eastern hemisphere, including species cultivated for their fragrant, waxlike, white flowers. [NL; named after Dr Alexander *Garden,* 1730-91]

**gardening** /'gadnɪŋ, -dənɪŋ/, *n.* **1.** the act of cultivating a garden. **2.** the work or art of a gardener.

**garden lizard** /'gadn lɪzəd/, *n.* the commonest of the small Australian lizards, *Leiolopisma guichenoti.* Also, **sun lizard, fence lizard.**

**garden orach** /'– ɒrɪtʃ/, *n.* See **orach.**

**garden party** /'– pati/, *n.* a party held on a lawn.

**garden setting** /'– sɛtɪŋ/, *n.* a set of matching items of furniture, often a table with chairs, for use outside the house.

**garden-wall bond** /gadn-'wɔl bɒnd/, *n.* an arrangement of brickwork, two bricks thick, in which the bricks are laid with a row of headers every fourth course.

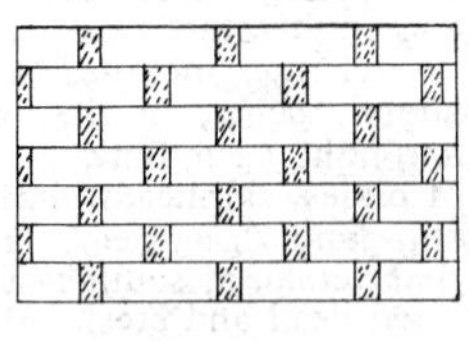

garden-wall bond

**garden warbler** /gadn 'wɔblə/, *n.* any of various small birds esteemed in Italy as a table delicacy, as the warblers of the family Sylvidae, esp. *Sylvia hortensis.*

**garderobe** /'gadroʊb/, *n. Archaic.* **1.** a wardrobe. **2.** a private bedroom. **3.** a latrine; privy. **4.** an armoury.

**gare** /gɛə/, *n.* a straight, coarse, glossy fibre of wool which grows in the fleece.

**garefowl** /'gɛəfaʊl/, *n.* →**great auk.** [from Scand.; cf. Icel. *geir-fugl*]

**garfish** /'gafɪʃ/, *n., pl.* **-fishes,** (*esp. collectively*) **-fish. 1.** any of numerous fishes found in Australian marine and estuarine waters, having a slender body and the lower jaw produced as a needle-like point, as the widely distributed sea garfish *Hemirhamphus australis.* **2.** →**gar.** [ME *garfysshe,* from *gar* (OE *gār* spear) + *fysshe* FISH[1]]

**Gargantuan** /ga'gæntʃuən/, *adj.* gigantic; prodigious. [from *Gargantua,* the amiable giant king who consumed enormous quantities of food and drink, in *Gargantua and Pantagruel* (1534) by François Rabelais]

**garget** /'gadʒət/, *n.* **1.** inflammation of the udder of cows, etc., caused by bacteria; mastitis. **2.** *Obs.* an inflammation of the throat in cattle, pigs, etc. [? ME, from OF *gargate* throat]

**gargle** /'gagəl/, *v.,* **-gled, -gling,** *n.* –*v.t.* **1.** to wash or rinse (the throat or mouth) with a liquid held in the throat and kept in motion by a stream of air from the lungs. –*v.i.* **2.** to gargle the throat or mouth. –*n.* **3.** any liquid used for gargling. **4.** *Colloq.* a drink, usu. alcoholic. [F *gargouiller,* from *gargouille* throat. Cf. L *gurgulio* gullet]

**gargoyle** /'gagɔɪl/, *n.* a spout, often terminating in a grotesque head (animal or human) with open mouth, projecting from the gutter of a building for carrying off rainwater. [ME *gargulye,* from OF *gargouille, gargoule,* apparently the same word as *gargouille* throat. See GARGLE]

gargoyle

**garial** /'gæriəl/, *n.* →**gavial.**

**garibaldi** /gærə'bɔldi/, *n.* →**currant luncheon.**

**garish** /'gɛərɪʃ, 'gar-/, *adj.* **1.** glaring, or excessively bright.

**2.** crudely gay or showy, as dress, etc. **3.** excessively ornate, as structures, writings, etc. [earlier *gaurish,* from obs. *gaure* stare, frequentative of ME *gawe* stare] – **garishly,** *adv.* – **garishness,** *n.*

**garland** /ˈgalənd/, *n.* **1.** a wreath or string of flowers, leaves, or other material, worn for ornament or as an honour, or hung on something as a decoration. **2.** a representation of such a wreath or festoon. **3.** a collection of short literary pieces, usu. poems and ballads; a miscellany. **4.** *Naut.* a band, collar, or grummet, as of rope, for various purposes. –*v.t.* **5.** to crown with a garland; deck with garlands. [ME *garlande,* from OF] – **garlandless,** *adj.* – **garland-like,** *adj.*

**garlic** /ˈgalɪk/, *n.* **1.** a hardy plant, *Allium sativum,* whose strong-scented pungent bulb is used in cookery and medicine. **2.** any of various other species of the same genus. **3.** the bulb of any such plant. **4.** →**garlic sausage.** –*adj.* **5.** seasoned with or containing garlic. [ME *garlec,* OE *gārlēac,* from *gār* spear + *lēac* leek]

**garlic bread** /ˈ– brɛd/, *n.* bread, usu. a French roll, sliced and buttered with garlic butter, and heated in the oven.

**garlic butter** /– ˈbʌtə/, *n.* garlic-flavoured butter.

**garlicky** /ˈgalɪki/, *adj.* like or containing garlic.

**garlic mustard** /galɪk ˈmʌstəd/, *n.* a biennial herb, *Alliaria petiolata,* with a strong-smelling root and small white flowers, widespread in shady places throughout northern temperate regions.

**garlic salt** /– ˈsɒlt/, *n.* garlic-flavoured salt.

**garlic sausage** /– ˈsɒsɪdʒ/, *n.* a variety of devon which is flavoured with garlic.

**garment** /ˈgamənt/, *n.* **1.** any article of clothing. **2.** outer covering; outward appearance. –*v.t.* **3.** to clothe. [ME, from OF *garnement,* from *garnir* equip. See GARNISH] – **garmentless,** *adj.*

**garn** /gan/, *interj. Colloq.* (an expression of incredulity). [contraction of *go on* (GO def. 38)]

**garner** /ˈganə/, *v.t.* **1.** to collect or deposit in or as in a garner; hoard. –*n.* **2.** a granary. **3.** a store of anything. [ME, from OF *gernier, grenier,* from L *grānārium* GRANARY]

**garnet**[1] /ˈganət/, *n.* **1.** any of a group of hard, vitreous minerals, silicates of calcium, magnesium, iron, or manganese with aluminium or iron, varying in colour. A deep red transparent variety is used as a gem and as an abrasive **(garnet paper). 2.** deep red, as of a garnet. [ME *gernet,* from OF *grenat,* from ML *grānātum* garnet, also pomegranate, properly neut. of *grānātus* having grains or seeds] – **garnet-like,** *adj.*

**garnet**[2] /ˈganət/, *n.* a form of hoisting tackle. [ME *garnett,* ? from MD *garnaat*]

**garnet**[3] /ˈganət/, *v.t.* to recover wool fibres from (rags, etc.), by tearing them up between toothed rollers rotating in opposite directions.

**garnierite** /ˈganiəraɪt/, *n.* a mineral, hydrous nickel magnesium silicate, occurring in earthy, green masses, which is an important ore of nickel. [named after Jules *Garnier,* d. 1904, French geologist. See -ITE[1]]

**garnish** /ˈganɪʃ/, *v.t.* **1.** to fit out with something that adorns or decorates. **2.** to decorate (a dish) for the table. **3.** *Law.* **a.** to warn; give notice. **b.** *Obs.* to summon as party to litigation already pending between others. **c.** to attach, as money due or property belonging to a debtor, while it is in the hands of a third person, by warning the latter not to pay it over or surrender it. **4.** *Brit. Colloq.* to exact money from. –*n.* **5.** something placed round or added to a dish for decorative effect or relish. **6.** adornment or decoration. **7.** *Brit. Colloq.* money extracted from a prisoner or worker by his fellow prisoners, boss, etc. [ME *garnisshe(n),* from OF *garniss-,* stem of *garnir* prepare, WARN; of Gmc orig.] – **garnisher,** *n.*

**garnishee** /ganəˈʃi/, *v.,* **-sheed, -sheeing,** *n.* –*v.t.* **1.** to attach (money or property) by garnishment. **2.** to make (a person) a garnishee. –*n.* **3.** a person served with a garnishment.

**garnishment** /ˈganɪʃmənt/, *n.* **1.** adornment; decoration. **2.** *Law.* **a.** a warning or notice. **b.** a summons to appear in litigation pending between others. **c.** a warning served on a person, at the suit of a creditor plaintiff, to hold, subject to the court's direction, money or property of the defendant in his possession.

**garniture** /ˈganɪtʃə/, *n.* anything that garnishes; decoration; adornment. [F, from *garnir.* See GARNISH]

**garotte** /gəˈrɒt/, *n., v.t.,* **-rotted, -rotting.** →**garrotte.**

**garpike** /ˈgapaɪk/, *n.* →**gar.**

**garret** /ˈgærət/, *n.* →**attic** (def. 1). [ME *garite,* from OF: watchtower, from *garir* defend. See GARRISON]

**garreteer** /gærəˈtɪə/, *n.* a person living in a garret, esp. a literary hack.

**garrison** /ˈgærəsən/, *n.* **1.** a body of troops stationed in a fortified place. **2.** the place where they are stationed. –*v.t.* **3.** to provide (a fort, town, etc.) with a garrison. **4.** to occupy (a fort, post, station, etc.). **5.** to put on duty in a fort, post, station, etc. [ME *garison,* from OF: defence, from *garir* defend, of Gmc orig.]

**garrison town** /ˈ– taʊn/, *n.* a town in which a garrison is stationed.

**garron** /ˈgærən/, *n.* a small and inferior kind of horse, bred and used chiefly in Ireland and Scotland. [Gaelic *gearran*]

**garrotte** /gəˈrɒt/, *n., v.,* **-rotted, -rotting.** –*n.* **1.** a Spanish mode of capital punishment, originally by means of an instrument causing death by strangulation, later by one injuring the spinal column at the base of the brain. **2.** the instrument used. **3.** strangulation or throttling, esp. for the purpose of robbery. –*v.t.* **4.** to execute by the garrotte. **5.** to throttle, esp. for the purpose of robbery. Also, **garotte, garrote.** [Sp.: orig. a stick (formerly used in drawing a cord tight), from Pr. *garrot* cudgel, stick for twisting a cord tight, from Celtic *garra* leg] – **garrotter,** *n.*

**garrulity** /gəˈruləti/, *n.* the quality of being garrulous; talkativeness; loquacity.

**garrulous** /ˈgærələs/, *adj.* **1.** given to much talking, esp. about trifles. **2.** wordy or diffuse, as speech. [L *garrulus* talkative] – **garrulously,** *adv.* – **garrulousness,** *n.*

**garryowen** /gæriˈoʊən/, *n. Chiefly Brit. Rugby Union.* →**up-and-under.** [from *Garryowen* Rugby Club, Ireland, famous for its use of this kick]

**garter** /ˈgatə/, *n.* **1.** a fastening, often in the form of a band passing round the leg, to keep up the stocking. –*v.t.* **2.** to fasten with a garter. [ME, from ONF *gartier,* from *garet* the bend of the knee, from Celtic *garra* leg]

**garter belt** /ˈ– bɛlt/, *n. U.S.* →**suspender belt.**

**garter stitch** /ˈ– stɪtʃ/, *n.* **1.** a plain stitch in knitting. **2.** the pattern produced by this.

**garth** /gaθ/, *n.* **1.** the open court enclosed by a cloister (in full, **cloister-garth**). **2.** *Archaic.* a yard or garden. [ME, from Scand.; cf. Icel. *gardhr,* c. YARD[2]]

**gas**[1] /gæs/, *n., pl.* **gases,** *v.,* **gassed, gassing.** –*n.* **1.** *Physics.* a substance consisting of atoms or molecules which are sufficiently mobile for it to occupy the whole of the space in which it is contained. **2.** any such fluid substance or mixture of substances, other than air. **3.** any such fluid substances used as a fuel for heating or lighting, esp. coal gas or natural gas. **4.** any such fluid substance or mixture of substances used as an anaesthetic. **5.** *Coal Mining.* an explosive mixture of firedamp with air. **6.** an aeriform fluid, or a mistlike assemblage of fine particles suspended in air, used in warfare to asphyxiate, poison, or stupefy the enemy. **7.** *Colloq.* empty talk. **8.** *Colloq.* something great, wonderful. –*adj.* **9.** pertaining to, derived from, produced by, or involving gas: *a gas stove.* **10.** *Colloq.* great, wonderful: *a gas idea.* –*v.t.* **11.** to supply with gas. **12.** to affect, overcome, or asphyxiate with gas or fumes. **13.** to treat or impregnate with gas. **14.** *Colloq.* to talk nonsense or speak boastfully to. –*v.i.* **15.** to give off gas, as a storage battery being charged. **16.** *Colloq.* to indulge in empty talk idly. [coined by J.B. van Helmont, 1577-1644, Flemish chemist; suggested by Gk *cháos* chaos] – **gasless,** *adj.*

**gas**[2] /gæs/, *n. Chiefly U.S. Colloq.* **1.** petrol. **2. step on the gas,** to hurry. [shortened form of GASOLINE]

**gas attack** /ˈ– ətæk/, *n.* an attack in which asphyxiating or poisonous gases are employed, as by liberating the gases, and allowing the wind to carry the fumes, or by gas shells.

**gasbag** /ˈgæsbæg/, *n., v.,* **-bagged, -bagging.** –*n.* **1.** a bag for holding gas, as in a balloon or dirigible. **2.** *Colloq.* an empty, voluble talker; a windbag. –*v.i.* **3.** to talk volubly; chatter.

**gas black** /ˈgæs blæk/, *n.* the soot of a natural gas flame, used in paints; fine carbon.

**gas bracket** /'– brækət/, *n.* a gas pipe with burners projecting from a wall.

**gas burner** /'– bɜnə/, *n.* the tip, jet, or end piece of a gas fixture, from which the gas issues to be ignited.

**gas carbon** /'– kabən/, *n.* a hard deposit of almost pure carbon which forms inside coal-gas retorts, used for making carbon electrodes.

**gas chamber** /'– tʃeɪmbə/, *n.* an airtight room in which animals or human beings are killed by means of a poisonous gas. Also, **gas oven.**

**gas chromatography** /– kroʊmə'tɒgrəfi/, *n.* a very sensitive method of analysing a complex mixture of volatile substances, which depends on the relative speeds with which the various components of the mixture pass through a long, narrow tube packed with an inert material which can be coated with a non-volatile liquid. *Abbrev.:* G.C. Also, **gas-liquid chromatography, vapour-phase chromatography.**

**gas coal** /'– koʊl/, *n.* a soft coal suitable for making gas.

**gasconade** /gæskə'neɪd/, *n., v.,* **-naded, -nading.** *–n.* **1.** extravagant boasting; boastful talk. *–v.i.* **2.** to boast extravagantly; bluster. [F *gasconnade,* from *Gascon,* a native of Gascony, former province of south-west France, the inhabitants of which were noted for their boastfulness]

**gas constant** /gæs 'kɒnstənt/, *n.* the constant in the gas laws, equal to approx. 8.31 joules per kelvin mole. Also, **universal gas constant.**

**gas cooker** /'– kʊkə/, *n.* →**gas stove.**

**gas-cut mud** /'gæs-kʌt mʌd/, *n.* (in oil-well drilling) mud, introduced into the hole, which has been lowered in effective density by natural gas rising from the strata traversed.

**gas-cylinder** /'gæs-sɪləndə/, *n.* a cylinder for storing gas in a pressurised form.

**gas discharge** /gæs 'dɪstʃadʒ/, *n.* the passage of current between two electrodes in an evacuated tube, often accompanied by the emission of light.

**gas engine** /'– ɛndʒən/, *n.* an internal-combustion engine which is driven by a mixture of gas and air.

**gaseous** /'gæsiəs, 'geɪ-/, *adj.* having the nature of, in the form of, or pertaining to gas. – **gaseousness,** *n.*

**gaseous diffusion** /– də'fjuʒən/, *n.* the gradual permeation of the molecules of one substance by the molecules of a gas, as a result of random molecular movement.

**gas field** /'gæs fild/, *n.* a region in which natural gas occurs.

**gas fire** /'– faɪə, – 'faɪə/, *n.* a fire in which heat is supplied by gas.

**gas-fired** /'gæs-faɪəd/, *adj.* fuelled or heated by gas.

**gas fitter** /'gæs fɪtə/, *n.* a person who installs gas pipes and gas-operated equipment.

**gas fitting** /'– fɪtɪŋ/, *n.* **1.** the work or business of a gas fitter. **2.** (*pl.*) fittings for the employment of gas for illuminating and heating purposes.

**gas fixture** /'– fɪkstʃə/, *n.* a permanent fixture attached to a gas pipe in the ceiling or wall of a room, as a more or less ornamental pipe (without or with branches) bearing a burner (or burners) and regulating devices.

**gas gangrene** /'– gæŋgrin/, *n.* a gangrenous infection developing in wounds, esp. deep wounds with closed spaces, due to bacteria which form gases in the subcutaneous tissues.

**gash** /gæʃ/, *n.* **1.** a long, deep wound or cut, esp. in the flesh; a slash. **2.** *Colloq.* a second helping of food; anything superfluous or extra. **3.** *Colloq.* the vagina. **4.** *Colloq.* a woman as a sex object. *–v.t.* **5.** to make a long, deep cut in; slash. [earlier *garsh,* from ONF *garser* scarify]

**gas helmet** /'gæs hɛlmət/, *n.* a type of gasmask.

**gas holder** /'gæs hoʊldə/, *n.* →**gasometer.**

**gas hydrate** /– 'haɪdreɪt/, *n.* a clathrate compound formed by a gas (both noble and reactive) and water, usu. forming only at low temperatures and high pressures to give water-insoluble crystalline solids.

**gasiform** /'gæsəfɔm/, *adj.* →**gaseous.**

**gasify** /'gæsəfaɪ/, *v.,* **-fied, -fying.** *–v.t.* **1.** to convert into a gas. *–v.i.* **2.** to become a gas. – **gasification** /gæsəfə'keɪʃən/, *n.*

**gas jet** /'gæs dʒɛt/, *n.* →**gas burner.**

**gasket** /'gæskət/, *n.* **1.** anything used as a packing or jointing material for making joints fluid-tight. **2.** a suitably punched asbestos sheet, usu. sandwiched between thin sheets of copper, for making a gastight joint, esp. between the cylinder block and the cylinder head of an internal-combustion engine. **3.** *Naut.* one of several bands or lines used to bind a furled sail to a yard, etc. **4. blow a gasket,** to lose one's temper. [orig. uncert. Cf. It. *gassetta* gasket]

**gaskin** /'gæskən/, *n.* that part of a horse's hind leg from knee to hip joint; the second thigh.

**gas lamp** /'gæs læmp/, *n.* a lamp in which the illumination is provided by the burning of gas.

**gas laws** /'– lɔz/, *n.pl.* laws, esp. Boyle's law and Charles's law, which relate the pressure, volume, and temperature of a gas. The combined ideal gas law states that for 1 mole of an ideal gas the product of the pressure and the volume is equal to the product of the absolute temperature and a constant known as the **gas constant.**

**gaslight** /'gæslaɪt/, *n.* **1.** light produced by the combustion of illuminating gas. **2.** →**gas burner.**

**gas-liquid chromatography** /gæs-,lɪkwəd kroʊmə'tɒgrəfi/, *n.* →**gas chromatography.** *Abbrev.:* G.L.C.

**gas main** /'gæs meɪn/, *n.* a large pipe for distributing gas from the gasworks to industrial or domestic consumers.

**gasman** /'gæsmæn/, *n.* **1.** a man who works for a gas undertaking, esp. one who reads household gas meters. **2.** a gas fitter.

**gas mantle** /'gæs mæntl/, *n.* a chemically prepared, incombustible network hood for a gas jet which, when the jet is lit, becomes incandescent and gives a brilliant light.

**gasmask** /'gæsmask/, *n.* a masklike device worn to protect against noxious gases, fumes, etc., as in warfare or in certain industries, the air inhaled by the wearer being filtered through charcoal and chemicals.

**gas meter** /'gæs mitə/, *n.* an apparatus for measuring and recording the amount of gas produced or consumed.

**gas oil** /'– ɔɪl/, *n.* →**diesel oil.**

**gasolier** /gæsə'lɪə/, *n.* a chandelier for gas lamps. [GAS[1] + -O- + *-lier* in CHANDELIER]

**gasoline** /'gæsəlin/, *n. Chiefly U.S.* →**petrol.** Also, **gasolene.** [GAS[1] + -OL[2] + -INE[2]]

**gasometer** /gæ'sɒmətə, gə-/, *n.* **1.** a large tank or reservoir for storing gas, esp. at a gasworks. **2.** a laboratory apparatus for measuring or storing gas. [F *gazomètre.* See GAS METER] – **gasometric** /gæsə'mɛtrɪk/, **gasometrical** /gæsə'mɛtrɪkəl/, *adj.*

**gas oven** /gæs 'ʌvən, 'gæs ʌvən/, *n.* **1.** the oven of a gas stove. **2.** a gas chamber.

**gasp** /gæsp, gasp/, *n.* **1.** a sudden, short breath; convulsive effort to breathe. **2.** a short, convulsive utterance, esp. as a result of fear or surprise. *–v.i.* **3.** to catch the breath, or struggle for breath, with open mouth, as from exhaustion; breathe convulsively. **4.** to long with breathless eagerness; desire; crave (fol. by *for* or *after*). *–v.t.* **5.** to utter with gasps (oft. fol. by *out, forth, away,* etc.). **6.** to breathe or emit with gasps (oft. fol. by *away*). [ME *gaspe(n), gayspe(n),* from Scand.; cf. Icel. *geispa,* metathetic var. of *geipsa* yawn; akin to OE *gipian* yawn, *gipung* open mouth]

**gasper** /'gæspə, gaspə/, *n.* **1.** *Brit. Colloq.* a cigarette. **2.** one who or that which gasps.

**gas pipe** /'gæs paɪp/, *n.* a pipe for conveying gas.

**gas range** /'– reɪndʒ/, *n.* a gas stove.

**gas ring** /'– rɪŋ/, *n.* a hollow iron ring with perforations or jets supplied with gas under pressure, used for cooking.

**gasser** /'gæsə/, *n.* **1.** one who or that which gasses. **2.** a well or boring yielding natural gas. **3.** *Colloq.* →**gas**[1] (def. 8).

**gas shell** /'gæs ʃɛl/, *n.* an explosive shell containing a liquid or other material which, when the shell bursts, is converted into an asphyxiating or poisonous gas or vapour.

**gassing** /'gæsɪŋ/, *n.* **1.** the act of one who or that which gasses. **2.** an affecting or overcoming with gas or fumes, as in battle. **3.** the evolution of gases during electrolysis. **4.** a process by which a material is gassed.

**gas stove** /gæs 'stoʊv, 'gæs stoʊv/, *n.* a stove for cooking by gas.

**gassy** /'gæsi/, *adj.,* **-sier, -siest. 1.** full of or containing gas. **2.** like gas. **3.** *Colloq.* given to frivolous or empty-headed chatter. – **gassiness,** *n.*

**gastero-,** variant of **gastro-.**

**gasteropod** /ˈgæstərəpɒd, -trəpɒd/, *n.* →**gastropod.**

**gas thermometer** /gæs θəˈmɒmətə/, *n.* a device for measuring temperature by observing the change in either pressure or volume of an enclosed gas.

**gastight** /ˈgæstaɪt/, *adj.* **1.** not penetrable by a gas. **2.** not admitting a gas under a given pressure.

**gastr-,** variant of **gastro-**, before vowels, as in *gastralgia.*

**gastralgia** /gæsˈtrældʒə/, *n.* **1.** neuralgia of the stomach. **2.** any stomach pain. [GASTR- + -ALGIA]

**gastrectomy** /gæsˈtrɛktəmi/, *n., pl.* **-mies.** the surgical excision of the stomach.

**gastric** /ˈgæstrɪk/, *adj.* pertaining to the stomach.

**gastric juice** /– ˈdʒus/, *n.* the digestive fluid secreted by the glands of the stomach, and containing pepsin and other enzymes.

**gastric ulcer** /– ˈʌlsə/, *n.* an erosion of the stomach's inner wall.

**gastrin** /ˈgæstrən/, *n.* a hormone produced in the pyloric mucosa which stimulates secretion by the gastric glands.

**gastritis** /gæsˈtraɪtəs/, *n.* inflammation of the stomach, esp. of its mucous membrane. [GASTR- + -ITIS] – **gastritic** /gæsˈtrɪtɪk/, *adj.*

**gastro** /ˈgæstroʊ/, *n. Colloq.* →**gastroenteritis.**

**gastro-,** a word element meaning 'stomach', as in *gastropod, gastrology.* Also, **gastero-, gastr-.** [Gk, combining form of *gastḗr*]

**gastroenteritis** /ˌgæstroʊɛntəˈraɪtəs/, *n.* inflammation of the stomach and intestines. [GASTRO- + ENTER(O)- + -ITIS]

**gastroentero-,** a combining form meaning 'gastric and enteric', as in *gastroenterology.* [GASTRO- + ENTERO-]

**gastroenterology** /ˌgæstroʊɛntəˈrɒlədʒi/, *n.* the study of the structure and diseases of digestive organs.

**gastroenterostomy** /ˌgæstroʊɛntəˈrɒstəmi/, *n., pl.* **-mies.** the making of a new opening by surgery between the stomach and the small intestine.

**gastrointestinal** /ˌgæstroʊɪnˈtɛstənəl/, *adj.* of or pertaining to the stomach and intestines.

**gastrolith** /ˈgæstrəlɪθ/, *n.* a calculus or stony concretion in the stomach.

**gastrology** /gæsˈtrɒlədʒi/, *n.* **1.** the study of the structure, functions, and diseases of the stomach. **2.** cookery or good eating. – **gastrologer,** *n.* – **gastrological** /gæstrəˈlɒdʒɪkəl/, *adj.*

**gastronome** /ˈgæstrənoʊm/, *n.* a gourmet; epicure. Also, **gastronomer** /gæsˈtrɒnəmə/. [F, from *gastronomie* GASTRONOMY]

**gastronomy** /gæsˈtrɒnəmi/, *n.* the art or science of good eating. [F *gastronomie,* from Gk *gastronomía*] – **gastronomic** /gæstrəˈnɒmɪk/, **gastronomical** /gæstrəˈnɒmɪkəl/, *adj.* – **gastronomically** /gæstrəˈnɒmɪkli/, *adv.* – **gastronomist,** *n.*

**gastropod** /ˈgæstrəpɒd/, *n.* any of the Gastropoda, a class of molluscs comprising the snails, having a shell of a single valve, usu. spirally coiled, and a ventral muscular foot on which they glide about. Also, **gasteropod.** [NL *Gastropoda,* pl. See GASTRO-, -POD]

**gastroscope** /ˈgæstrəskoʊp/, *n.* a medical instrument for direct visual inspection of the interior of the stomach. – **gastroscopic** /gæstrəˈskɒpɪk/, *adj.*

**gastroscopy** /gæsˈtrɒskəpi/, *n.* examination with a gastroscope to detect disease.

**gastrostomy** /gæsˈtrɒstəmi/, *n., pl.* **-mies.** the operation of cutting into the stomach and leaving a more or less permanent opening for feeding or drainage.

**gastrotomy** /gæsˈtrɒtəmi/, *n., pl.* **-mies.** surgical incision into the stomach.

**gastrotrich** /ˈgæstrətrɪk/, *n.* one of the microscopic multicellular worms belonging to the Gastrotricha, having bands of cilia on the ventral side of the body.

**gastrovascular** /ˌgæstroʊˈvæskjələ/, *adj.* serving for digestion and circulation, as a cavity.

**gastrula** /ˈgæstrələ/, *n., pl.* **-lae** /-li/. the developing embryo when it consists of the three germ layers, occupying their characteristic positions. [NL, diminutive of Gk *gastḗr* belly, stomach] – **gastrular,** *adj.*

**gastrulate** /ˈgæstrəleɪt/, *v.i.,* **-lated, -lating.** to undergo gastrulation.

**gastrulation** /gæstrəˈleɪʃən/, *n.* **1.** the formation of a gastrula. **2.** any process (as that of invagination) by which a blastula or other form of embryo is converted into a gastrula.

**gas turbine** /gæs ˈtɜbaɪn/, *n.* See **turbine** (def. 2).

**gas welding** /– ˈwɛldɪŋ/, *n.* a form of welding in which gas is used as a source of heat.

**gas well** /ˈ– wɛl/, *n.* a well which yields natural gas rather than oil.

**gasworks** /ˈgæswɜks/, *n.* an industrial plant which produces coal gas or any other type of heating or illuminating gas, as well as the other by-products of coal gasification.

**gat**[1] /gæt/, *v. Archaic.* past tense of **get.**

**gat**[2] /gæt/, *n.* an opening between sandbanks; a strait.

**gat**[3] /gæt/, *n. Colloq.* a gun, pistol, or revolver. [shortened form of GATLING GUN]

**gate**[1] /geɪt/, *n., v.,* **gated, gating.** –*n.* **1.** a movable barrier, as a swinging frame, in a fence or wall, or across a passageway. **2.** an opening for passage into an enclosure such as a fenced yard or walled city. **3.** a structure built about such an opening and containing the barrier. **4.** any narrow means of access or entrance. **5.** a broad low gap in land of high relief as the Cassilis Gate in the eastern highlands of New South Wales; often on a political boundary. **6.** a device for regulating the passage of water, steam, or the like, as in a dam, pipe, etc.; valve. **7.** →**starting gate. 8.** the number of persons who pay for admission to an athletic contest or other exhibition. **9.** →**gate money** (def. 1). **10.** payment at a tollgate. **11.** *Motor Vehicles.* the H-shaped arrangement of slots controlling the movement of a gearlever. **12.** a sash or frame for a saw or gang of saws. **13.** *Elect.* **a.** an electronic circuit which controls the passage of information signals according to the state of one or more control signals. **b.** a control electrode on a field effect transistor, silicon controlled rectifier, etc. **14.** *Foundry.* a channel or opening in a mould through which molten metal enters the mould cavity to form a casting. **15.** that part of a camera or projector in which each frame of film is held during exposure or projection. –*v.t.* **16.** to punish by restricting (a student) within the college or school gates. [ME *gat, gate,* OE *gatu* gates, pl. of *geat* opening in a wall, c. LG and D *gat* hole, breach] – **gateman** /ˈgeɪtmən/, *n.*

**gate**[2] /geɪt/, *n. Archaic.* a way, road, or path.

**gateau** /ˈgætoʊ/, *n., pl.* **-teaux** /-toʊz, -toʊ/. an elaborate cake or dessert having a base of sponge, biscuit, or pastry, on top of which fruit, jelly, cream, etc., are added as garnish. Also, **gâteau.** [F *gâteau* cake]

**gatecrash** /ˈgeɪtkræʃ/, *v.t.* to attend (a party) uninvited, or to attend (a public entertainment, etc.) without a ticket. – **gatecrasher,** *n.*

**gatefold** /ˈgeɪtfoʊld/, *n.* a folded insert in a publication exceeding the size of the other pages in the publication; fold-out.

**gatehouse** /ˈgeɪthaʊs/, *n.* **1.** a house at or over a gate, used as the keeper's quarters, a fortification, etc. **2.** →**valve house.**

**gatekeeper** /ˈgeɪtkipə/, *n.* one in charge of a gate.

**gate-leg table** /ˌgeɪt-lɛg ˈteɪbəl/, *n.* a table having drop leaves which are supported when open by legs which swing out and are usu. connected by crosspieces. Also, **gate-legged table.**

**gate money** /ˈgeɪt mʌni/, *n.* **1.** the receipts taken for admission to an athletic contest or other exhibition. **2.** *Colloq.* money given a prisoner on release from prison.

**gatepost** /ˈgeɪtpoʊst/, *n.* the post on which a gate is hung, or the one against which it is closed.

**gate-takings** /ˈgeɪt-teɪkɪŋz/, *n.pl.* →**gate money** (def. 1).

**gateway** /ˈgeɪtweɪ/, *n.* **1.** a passage or entrance which is closed by a gate. **2.** a frame or arch in which a gate is hung; structure built at or over a gate. **3.** any means of entering or leaving a place. **4.** a location through which one has access to an area: *Cooma, gateway to the Snowy Mountains.*

**gather** /ˈgæðə/, *v.t.* **1.** to bring (persons, animals, or things) together into one company or aggregate. **2.** to get together from various places or sources; collect gradually. **3.** to learn or infer from observation: *I gather that he'll be leaving.* **4.** to pick (any crop or natural yield) from its place of growth or formation: *to gather grain, fruit, or flowers.* **5.** to wrap or draw around or close to someone or something: *to gather a person into one's arms.* **6.** to pick up piece by piece. **7.** to attract: *to gather a crowd.* **8.** to take by selection from among other things; sort out; cull. **9.** to assemble or collect (one's energies or oneself) as for an effort (oft. fol. by *up*). **10.** to contract (the brow) into wrinkles. **11.** to draw up (cloth) on a thread in fine folds or puckers by running a thread through. **12.** *Bookbinding.* to assemble (the printed sheets of a book) in their proper sequence to be bound. **13.** to increase (speed, etc.) as a moving vehicle. **14.** *Football.* to pick the ball up from the ground, or catch it in the air. **15.** *Naut.* to gain (way) from a dead stop or extremely slow speed. *–v.i.* **16.** to come together or assemble: *to gather round a fire, to gather in crowds.* **17.** to collect or accumulate. **18.** to grow as by accretion; increase. **19.** to come to a head, as a sore in suppurating. **20. be gathered to one's fathers,** to die. *–n.* **21.** a drawing together; contraction. **22.** (*usu. pl.*) a fold or pucker in gathered cloth, etc. [ME *gader(en)*, OE *gaderian*, from *geador* together, akin to *gæd* fellowship. Cf. TOGETHER, GOOD] – **gatherable,** *adj.* – **gatherer,** *n.*

**gathering** /ˈgæðərɪŋ/, *n.* **1.** the act of one who or that which gathers. **2.** that which is gathered together. **3.** an assembly or meeting; a crowd. **4.** a collection or assemblage of anything. **5.** an inflamed and suppurating swelling. **6.** a gather or series of gathers in cloth. **7.** *Bookbinding.* a section in a book.

**gating signal** /ˈgeɪtɪŋ ˌsɪgnəl/, *n.* a signal which controls the passage of other signals by means of an electronic gate.

**Gatling gun** /ˈgætlɪŋ gʌn/, *n.* an early type of machine gun consisting of a revolving cluster of barrels round a central axis, each barrel being automatically loaded and fired during every revolution of the cluster. [named after R. J. *Gatling*, 1818-1903, American inventor]

**gat-toothed** /ˈgæt-tuθt/, *adj.* →**gap-toothed.**

**gauche** /goʊʃ/, *adj.* awkward; clumsy; tactless: *her apology was as gauche as if she had been a schoolgirl.* [F. See GAUCHERIE] – **gaucheness,** *n.*

**gaucherie** /ˈgoʊʃəri/, *n.* **1.** awkwardness; clumsiness; tactlessness. **2.** an awkward or tactless movement, act, etc. [F, from *gauche* awkward, lit., left (hand)]

**gaucho** /ˈgaʊtʃoʊ/, *n., pl.* **-chos** /-tʃoʊz/. **1.** a native cowboy of the South American pampas, of mixed Spanish and Indian descent. **2.** (*pl.*) flared pants ending just below the knee, worn by women. [Sp.]

**gaud** /gɔd/, *n.* a showy ornament. [ME *gaude*, ? from AF, from *gaudir* rejoice, jest, from L *gaudēre*]

**gaudery** /ˈgɔdəri/, *n., pl.* **-ries. 1.** ostentatious show. **2.** finery; fine or showy things: *she stood in the doorway resplendent in her gaudery.*

**gaudy**[1] /ˈgɔdi/, *adj.,* **-dier, -diest. 1.** brilliant; excessively showy. **2.** showy without taste; vulgarly showy; flashy. [orig. attributive use of GAUDY[2] large bead of rosary, feast; later taken as from GAUD, *n.*] – **gaudily,** *adv.* – **gaudiness,** *n.*

**gaudy**[2] /ˈgɔdi/, *n., pl.* **-dies.** *Brit.* a festival or merrymaking, esp. an annual college feast. [ME, from L *gaudium* joy]

**gauffer** /ˈgoʊfə/, *n., v.t.* →**goffer.**

**gauge** /geɪdʒ/, *v.,* **gauged, gauging,** *n.* *–v.t.* **1.** to appraise, estimate, or judge. **2.** to determine the dimensions, capacity, quantity, or force of; measure, as with a gauge. **3.** to make conformable to a standard. **4.** to cut or rub (bricks or stones) to a uniform size or shape. **5.** to mark off or set out (a measurement, or measured distance). **6.** to gather (cloth). *–n.* **7.** a standard of measure; standard dimension or quantity. **8.** a means of estimating or judging; criterion; test. **9.** extent; scope; capacity. **10.** any instrument for measuring pressure, volume, or dimensions, as a pressure gauge, micrometer gauge, etc. **11.** *Ordn.* the internal diameter of a gun bore. **12.** the thickness or diameter of various (usu. thin) objects. **13.** the distance between the rails in a railway system; **standard gauge** is 1435mm; **broad gauge** is wider, and **narrow gauge** narrower, than this. **14.** the position of one ship with reference to another and to the wind. Also, **gage.** [late ME, from ONF *gauger*, from *gal-* measuring rod; of Celtic orig.] – **gaugeable,** *adj.*

**gauge pressure** /ˈ- prɛʃə/, *n.* the pressure as indicated by a pressure gauge; i.e., the extent to which the pressure being measured exceeds the pressure of the atmosphere (opposed to *absolute pressure.* See **absolute** (def. 8c).

**gauger** /ˈgeɪdʒə/, *n.* **1.** one who or that which gauges. **2.** an exciseman. Also, **gager.**

**Gaulish** /ˈgɔlɪʃ/, *n.* **1.** the extinct language of ancient Gaul, a Celtic language. *–adj.* **2.** of or pertaining to Gaul, its inhabitants, or their language.

**gaultheria** /gɔlˈθɪəriə/, *n.* any of the aromatic evergreen shrubs constituting the genus *Gaultheria.* [NL; named after J.F. *Gaultier*, d. 1756, Canadian botanist]

**gaunt** /gɔnt/, *adj.* **1.** abnormally thin; emaciated; haggard. **2.** bleak, desolate, or grim, as places or things. [ME, from F *gaunet* yellowish] – **gauntly,** *adv.* – **gauntness,** *n.*

**gauntlet**[1] /ˈgɔntlət/, *n.* **1.** a medieval glove, as of mail or plate, to protect the hand. **2.** a glove with a cuff-like extension for the wrist. **3.** the cuff itself. **4. take up the gauntlet,** to accept a challenge, originally to a duel. **5. throw down the gauntlet,** to extend a challenge, originally to a duel. Also, **gantlet.** [ME, from OF *gantelet*, diminutive of *gant* glove, from Gmc; cf. OSwed. *wante*]

**gauntlet**[2] /ˈgɔntlət/, *n.* **1. run the gauntlet, a.** to be forced to run between two rows of men who strike at one with switches or other weapons as one passes (formerly a common military punishment). **b.** to undertake an extremely hazardous operation. **2.** a section of interlaced railway or tramway tracks. *–v.t.* **3.** to lay down as a gauntlet: *to gauntlet tracks.* Also, *U.S.,* **gantlet.** [alteration by association with GAUNTLET[1] of earlier *gantlope*, from Swed. *gatlopp*, lit., lane run, from *gata* way, lane + *lopp* a running course]

**gauntry** /ˈgɔntri/, *n., pl.* **-tries.** →**gantry.**

**gaur** /gaʊə/, *n.* the largest of all wild cattle, *Bos gaurus*, living in forest areas of India, Burma, and Malaya.

**gauss** /gaʊs/, *n. Elect.* **1.** a unit of magnetic induction in the centimetre-gram-second system, equal to $0{\cdot}1 \times 10^{-3}$ teslas. **2.** *Obs.* →**oersted** (def. 1). *Symbol:* Gs, G [named after K.F. *Gauss*, 1777-1855, German mathematician]

**Gaussian distribution** /ˈgaʊsiən dɪstrəˌbjuʃən/, *n.* →**normal distribution.**

**gauze** /gɔz/, *n.* **1.** any thin transparent fabric made from any fibre in a plain or leno weave. **2.** some similar open material, as of wire. **3.** a thin haze. *–v.t.* **4.** to cover with gauze. *–v.i.* **5.** to become misty. [F *gaze*, named after *Gaza*, a seaport in southern Palestine, where it was supposed to be made] – **gauzelike,** *adj.*

**gauzy** /ˈgɔzi/, *adj.,* **-zier, -ziest.** like gauze; thin as gauze. – **gauziness,** *n.*

**gavage** /gəˈvaʒ, ˈgævaʒ/, *n.* forced feeding, as of poultry or human beings, as by a flexible tube. [F, from *gaver* to gorge]

**gave** /geɪv/, *v.* past tense of **give.**

**gavel** /ˈgævəl/, *n.* **1.** a small mallet used by a presiding officer to signal for attention or order. *–v.i.* **2.** to hammer, as with a gavel. [orig. unknown]

**gavelkind** /ˈgævəlkaɪnd/, *n. Law Obs.* **1.** a customary system of land tenure, whose chief feature was equal division of inherited land among the heirs. **2.** a tenure of land in which the tenant was liable for money rent rather than labour or military service. **3.** the land so held. [ME *gavelkynde, gavelikind*, from OE *gafol* tax, tribute + *gecynd* KIND[2]]

**gavial** /ˈgeɪviəl/, *n.* a large Indian crocodile, *Gavialis gangeticus*, with elongated jaws. Also, **garial.** [F, from Hind. *ghariyāl*]

**gavotte** /gəˈvɒt/, *n.* **1.** an old French dance in moderately quick 4/4 time. **2.** a piece of music for, or in the rhythm of, this dance, often forming one of the movements in the classical suite, usu. following the saraband. Also, **gavot.** [F, from Pr. *gavoto* dance of the Gavots (Alpine mountaineers), from pre-Rom. *gav-* mountain stream]

**gawk** /gɔk/, *n.* **1.** an awkward, foolish person. *–v.i.* **2.** *Colloq.* to act like a gawk; stare stupidly. [apparently representing OE word meaning fool, from *gagol* foolish + *-oc* -OCK; used attributively in *gawk hand, gallock hand* left hand]

**gawky** /ˈgɔki/, *adj.,* **-kier, -kiest.** awkward; ungainly; clumsy. – **gawkily,** *adv.* – **gawkiness,** *n.*

**gawp** /gɔp/, *v.i.* to look at something wonderingly or stupidly (oft. fol. by *at*): *I stood there gawping.*

**gay** /geɪ/, *adj.,* **gayer, gayest,** *n.* *–adj.* **1.** having or showing a joyous mood: *gay spirits, music, scenes, etc.* **2.** bright or showy: *gay colours, flowers, ornaments, etc.* **3.** given to or abounding in social or other pleasures: *a gay social season.*

4. dissipated; licentious. **5.** *Colloq.* camp; homosexual. *–n.* **6.** a vain or affected person. **7.** a homosexual. [ME, from OF *gai;* orig. uncert.]

**Gay-Lussac's law** /ˌgaɪ-ləsæks 'lɔ/, *n.* the law which states that when gases combine they do so in a simple ratio by volume to each other and to the gaseous product. [named after J. L. *Gay-Lussac,* 1778-1850, French chemist and physicist]

**gaz.,** **1.** gazette. **2.** gazetteer.

**gazania** /gə'zeɪniə/, *n.* a sprawling perennial herb, *Gazania rigens,* with brightly coloured flowers, mainly yellow and bronze, widely cultivated in gardens.

**gaze** /geɪz/, *v.,* **gazed, gazing,** *n.* *–v.i.* **1.** to look steadily or intently; look with curiosity, wonder, etc. *–n.* **2.** a steady or intent look. [ME, from Scand.; cf. Swed. *gasa* gape, stare] **– gazer,** *n.*

**gazebo** /gə'ziboʊ/, *n., pl.* **-bos, -boes.** a structure commanding an extensive prospect, esp. a turret, pavilion, or summerhouse. [? pseudo-Latin coinage on GAZE, *v.,* after L *vidēbō* I shall see]

**gazehound** /'geɪzhaʊnd/, *n.* a hound that hunts by sight rather than scent.

**gazelle** /gə'zɛl/, *n.* any of various small antelopes of the genus *Gazella* and allied genera, noted for their graceful movements and lustrous eyes. [F, from Ar. *ghazāl*] **– gazelle-like,** *adj.*

gazelle

**gazettal** /gə'zɛtl/, *n.* publication (of laws, ordinances, notices, etc.) in an official government journal.

**gazette** /gə'zɛt/, *n., v.,* **-zetted, -zetting.** *–n.* **1.** a newspaper (now common only in newspaper titles). **2.** an official government journal, containing lists of government appointments and promotions, bankruptcies, etc. *–v.t.* **3.** to publish, announce, or list in a gazette. [F, from It. *gazzetta,* var. of Venetian *gazeta,* orig. a Venetian coin (the price of the gazette), diminutive of *gaza* magpie]

**gazetteer** /gæzə'tɪə/, *n.* **1.** a geographical dictionary. **2.** a journalist, esp. one appointed and paid by the government. [F (obs.) *gazettier*]

**gazob** /gə'zɒb/, *n. Colloq.* a stupid person; a blunderer.

**gazoo** /gə'zu/, *n.* **→kazoo.**

**gazpacho** /gæz'patʃoʊ/, *n.* a Spanish iced soup consisting of uncooked ripe tomatoes, chopped onion, cucumber and green peppers with oil, vinegar, water, and cummin seeds. Also, **gaspacho.**

**gazump** /gə'zʌmp/, *v.t.* (of a vendor before entering upon a binding contract) to force a buyer to accept a price higher than that previously agreed upon.

**gazunder** /gə'zʌndə/, *n. Colloq.* **1. →chamber-pot.** **2.** *Cricket.* a low ball. Also, **gezunder, gozunder.** [contraction of *goes under*]

**G.B.,** Great Britain.

**G.B.E.,** Knight (or Dame) Grand Cross of (the Order of) the British Empire.

**gbejna** /'ʒɪbnə/, *n.* a soft white cheese, with a delicate flavour originally made in Malta, from goats' milk often sold coated in peppercorns. [Maltese: one]

**G.B.H.** /dʒi bi 'eɪtʃ/, *n.* severe hurt or injury inflicted by one person on the body of another. [*G(rievous) B(odily) H(arm)*]

**G.C.,** **1.** George Cross. **2.** *Chem.* gas-chromatography.

**G.C.B.,** Knight Grand Cross of (the Order of) the Bath.

**G clef** /'dzi klɛf/, *n.* a sign on a musical score indicating the position of G above middle C; treble clef.

**G.C.M.G.,** Knight Grand Cross of (the Order of) St Michael and St George.

**G.C.V.O.,** Knight (or Dame) Grand Cross of the (Royal) Victorian Order.

**gd.,** **1.** good. **2.** granddaughter. **3.** ground.

**Gd,** *Chem.* gadolinium.

**G.D.P.,** Gross Domestic Product.

**gds,** goods.

**Ge,** *Chem.* germanium.

**gean** /gin/, *n.* a deciduous tree, *Prunus avium,* native to Europe and western Asia, from which many varieties of cultivated sweet cherries have been derived.

**geanticline** /dʒi'æntəklaɪn/, *n.* an anticline extending over a relatively large part of the earth's surface. [Gk *gê* earth + ANTICLINE]

**gear** /gɪə/, *n.* **1.** *Mach.* **a.** a mechanism for transmitting or changing motion, as by toothed wheels. **b.** a toothed wheel which engages with another wheel or part. **c.** the connection or engagement of toothed wheels with each other: *in gear, out of gear, in high gear, in low gear.* **d.** a group of parts in a complex machine that operates for a single purpose. **2.** implements, tools, or apparatus, esp. as used for a particular operation; harness; tackle. **3.** *Naut.* **a.** the ropes, blocks, etc., belonging to a particular sail or spar. **b.** the tools and equipment used on a ship. **4.** movable property; goods; personal possessions. **5.** *Colloq.* clothes. **6.** *Colloq.* **a.** marijuana. **b.** drugs generally. **7.** ancillary apparatus used to prepare and inject drugs, esp. heroin, intravenously. **8.** *Archaic.* armour or arms. **9.** *Colloq.* external genitalia. *–adj.* **10.** *Brit. Colloq.* fashionable, delightful, or excellent. *–v.t.* **11.** to provide with gearing; connect by gearing; put (machinery) into gear. **12.** to provide with gear; supply; fit; harness. **13.** to prepare, adjust, orientate (someone or something) to a particular situation. **14.** *Econ.* to borrow money in order to increase the amount of total liabilities in relation to the equity capital. *–v.i.* **15.** to fit exactly, as one part of gearing into another; come into or be in gear. **16. gear up,** to make ready; prepare. [ME *gere,* from Scand.; cf. Icel. *gervi, görvi* gear, apparel; akin to OE *gearwe,* pl., equipment, *gearu* ready]

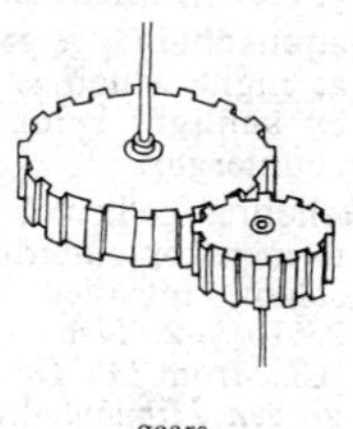
gears

**gearbox** /'gɪəbɒks/, *n.* the casing in which gears are enclosed, esp. in a motor vehicle.

**gearing** /'gɪərɪŋ/, *n.* **1.** the parts collectively by which motion is transmitted in machinery, esp. a train of toothed wheels. **2.** the installation of such gears. **3.** *Stock Exchange.* the relationship of total invested capital to equity capital. A company with high gearing has a high amount of fixed capital compared with ordinary capital.

**gear-ratio** /'gɪə-reɪʃioʊ/, *n.* **1.** the ratio of the speed of the shaft driving a gear assembly or assemblies to that of the assembly or assemblies which the shaft drives. **2.** the ratio of the number of engine revolutions to the number of revolutions of the rear wheel of a motor car.

**gearstick** /'gɪəstɪk/, *n.* a device for selecting or connecting gears for transmitting power, esp. in a motor vehicle. Also, **gearlever** /'gɪəlivə/, **gearshift** /'gɪəʃɪft/.

**gearwheel** /'gɪəwil/, *n.* a wheel having teeth or cogs which engage with those of another wheel or part; cogwheel.

**gecko** /'gɛkoʊ/, *n., pl.* **-os, -oes.** a small, harmless lizard of the family Geckonidae, mostly nocturnal, many with adhesive pads on the toes. [Malay *gēkoq;* imitative]

gecko

**gee**[1] /dʒi/, *interj., n.* (a word of command to horses, etc., directing them to go faster (fol. by *up*).)

**gee**[2] /dʒi/, *interj.* (a mild exclamation of surprise or delight.) [a euphemistic var. of JESUS]

**geebung** /'dʒibʌŋ/, *n.* **1.** any shrub or tree of the genus *Persoonia.* **2.** the small succulent fruit of this tree. [Aboriginal]

**gee-gaw** /'gi-gɔ/, *n.* **→gewgaw.**

**gee-gee** /'dʒi-dʒi/, *n.* (*in children's speech*) a horse.

**geek** /gik/, *n. Colloq.* a look: *have a geek at this.* Also, **geez, gig, gink.** [? Brit. d. *geck* to toss the head]

**geese** /gis/, *n.* plural of **goose.**

**geest** /gist/, *n. Geol.* old deposits produced by flowing water. [LG: dry or sandy soil]

**gee whiz** /dʒi 'wɪz/, *interj. Colloq.* (an exclamation expressing surprise, admiration, etc.). Also, **gee whizz.** [a euphemistic var. of JESUS]

**geezer** /'gizə/, *n. Colloq.* an odd character. Also, **geeser.** [var. of *guiser* (from GUISE (def. 4) + -ER[1]), representing d. pronunciation]

**gefillte fish** /gə'fɪltə ˌfɪʃ/, *n.* fish cooked, chopped, with crumbs, eggs and seasonings, and stuffed back into the skin of the fish or made into dumplings and served chilled. [Yiddish: filled fish]

**gegenschein** /'geɪgənʃaɪn/, *n.* a faint illumination of the sky at night which is sometimes seen opposite the sun; caused by sunlight being reflected by meteoric dust in space. [G: counterglow]

**Gehenna** /gə'hɛnə/, *n.* **1.** *Old Testament.* any place of extreme torment or suffering, esp. the valley of Hinnom, near Jerusalem, regarded as a place of abomination (II Kings 23:10). **2.** *New Testament and Rabbinical Literature.* hell. [LL, from Gk *Géenna,* from Heb. *Gē-Hinnōm* hell, short for *gē ben Hinnōm,* lit., valley of the son of Hinnom. See Jer. 19:5]

**gehlenite** /'geɪlənaɪt/, *n.* a mineral silicate of aluminium and calcium, $Ca_2Al_2SiO_7$, occurring in green or brown prismatic crystals. [named after A.F. *Gehlen,* 1775-1815, German chemist. See -ITE[1]]

**Geiger counter** /'gaɪgə kaʊntə/, *n.* an instrument for detecting and counting ionising particles, consisting of a tube which conducts electricity when the gas within is ionised by such a particle. It is used in measuring the degree of radioactivity in an area left by the explosion of an atom bomb, in investigations of cosmic rays, etc. Also, **Geiger-Müller counter.** [named after Hans *Geiger,* 1882-1947, German physicist]

**geisha** /'geɪʃə/, *n., pl.* **-sha, -shas.** a Japanese girl, trained to entertain men with singing, dancing, and conversation. [Jap.]

**Geissler tube** /'gaɪslə tjub/, *n.* a sealed glass tube with platinum connections at the ends, containing rarefied gas made luminous by an electrical discharge. [named after H. *Geissler,* 1814-79, German mechanic]

**gel** /dʒɛl/, *n., v.,* **gelled, gelling.** *–n.* **1.** *Phys. Chem.* a semirigid colloidal dispersion of a solid with a liquid or gas, as jelly, glue, or silica gel. **2.** a clear, liquid jelly, sometimes tinted, used for cosmetic purposes. *–v.i.* **3.** to form or become a gel. [short for GELATINE]

**gelada** /'dʒɛlədə, dʒə'ladə, 'gɛl-, gə-/, *n.* a hairy baboon, *Theropithecus gelada,* of north-east Africa.

**gelatine** /'dʒɛlətin, dʒɛlə'tin/, *n.* **1.** a brittle, nearly transparent, faintly yellow, odourless, and almost tasteless organic substance, obtained by boiling in water the ligaments, bones, skin, etc., of animals, and forming the basis of jellies, glues, and the like. **2.** any of various similar substances, as vegetable gelatine. **3.** a preparation or product in which gelatine (defs. 1 or 2) is the essential constituent. Also, **gelatin** /'dʒɛlətən/. [F *gélatine,* from It. *gelatina,* from *gelata* jelly, from L *gelāta,* pp. fem., frozen, congealed]

**gelatinise** /dʒə'lætənaɪz/, *v.,* **-nised, -nising.** *–v.t.* **1.** to make gelatinous. **2.** to coat with gelatine, as paper. *–v.i.* **3.** to become gelatinous. Also, **gelatinize.** – **gelatinisation** /dʒəˌlætənaɪ'zeɪʃən/, *n.*

**gelatinoid** /dʒə'lætənɔɪd/, *adj.* **1.** resembling gelatine; gelatinous. *–n.* **2.** a gelatinoid substance.

**gelatinous** /dʒə'lætənəs/, *adj.* **1.** having the nature of jelly; jelly-like. **2.** pertaining to or consisting of gelatine. – **gelatinously,** *adv.* – **gelatinousness,** *n.*

**gelation** /dʒə'leɪʃən/, *n.* **1.** solidification by cold; freezing. **2.** the process of forming a gel. [L *gelātio* freezing]

**gelato** /dʒə'latoʊ, -'læt-/, *n.* an iced confection made from cream, milk or water in any combination, with fruit or nut flavouring, and whipped at a very low temperature. [It.]

**geld**[1] /gɛld/, *v.t.,* **gelded** or **gelt, gelding.** to castrate (esp. animals). [ME *gelde(n),* from Scand.; cf. Icel. *gelda*]

**geld**[2] /gɛld/, *n. Eng. Hist.* **1.** a payment; tax. **2.** a tax paid to the crown by landholders under Saxon and Norman kings. [ML *geldum,* from OE *geld, gield, gyld* payment, tribute, c. D *geld* and G *Geld* money; akin to YIELD, *v.*]

**gelding** /'gɛldɪŋ/, *n.* a castrated animal, esp. a horse. [ME, from Scand.; cf. Icel. *geldingr*]

**gelid** /'dʒɛləd/, *adj.* very cold; icy. [L *gelidus* icy cold] – **gelidity** /dʒə'lɪdəti/, **gelidness,** *n.* – **gelidly,** *adv.*

**gelignite** /'dʒɛləgnaɪt/, *n.* an explosive consisting of nitroglycerine, nitrocellulose, potassium nitrate, and wood pulp which is used for blasting.

**gelt**[1] /gɛlt/, *v.* a past tense and past participle of **geld.**

**gelt**[2] /gɛlt/, *n. Colloq.* money. Also, **gilt.** [D *geld*]

**gem** /dʒɛm/, *n., v.,* **gemmed, gemming.** *–n.* **1.** a stone used in jewellery, fashioned to bring out its beauty. **2.** something likened to, or prized as, a gem because of its beauty or worth, esp. something small: *the gem of the collection.* **3.** a printing type (4 point) between brilliant and diamond. *–v.t.* **4.** to adorn with or as with gems. [ME, from F *gemme,* from L *gemma* bud, jewel; replacing OE *gim* (c. OHG *gimma*), from L] – **gemlike,** *adj.* – **gemmy,** *adj.*

**geminate** /'dʒɛməneɪt/, *v.,* **-nated, -nating;** /'dʒɛmənət, -neɪt/, *adj.* *–v.t.* **1.** to make double or paired. *–v.i.* **2.** to become double. *–adj.* **3.** twin; combined in pairs; coupled. [L *geminātus,* pp., doubled] – **geminately,** *adv.*

**gemination** /dʒɛmə'neɪʃən/, *n.* **1.** a doubling; duplication; repetition. **2.** *Phonetics.* the doubling of a single consonant.

**Gemini** /'dʒɛmənaɪ/, *n.* **1.** the Twins, a constellation and sign of the zodiac. **2.** a person born under the sign of Gemini and (according to tradition) exhibiting the typical Gemini personality traits in some degree. *–adj.* **3.** of or pertaining to Gemini. **4.** of or pertaining to such a person or such a personality trait. [L, pl. of *geminus* twin]

**gem iron** /'dʒɛm aɪən/, *n.* a heavy cast iron baking tray with recessed, rounded moulds, each a half sphere, used for cooking gem scones or small round cakes.

**gemma** /'dʒɛmə/, *n., pl.* **gemmae** /'dʒɛmi/. **1.** *Bot.* a cell or cluster of cells, or a leaf- or budlike body, which separates from the parent plant and forms a new plant, as in mosses, liverworts, etc. **2.** a bud, esp. a leaf bud. **3.** *Zool.* a bud of tissues from which a new individual may develop; gemmule. [L: bud, germ. Cf. GEM]

**gemmate** /'dʒɛmeɪt/, *adj., v.,* **-mated, -mating.** *Bot. –adj.* **1.** having buds; increasing by budding. *–v.i.* **2.** to put forth buds; increase by budding. [L *gemmātus,* pp., increased by budding, set with gems]

**gemmation** /dʒɛ'meɪʃən/, *n.* the process of reproduction by gemmae.

**gemmule** /'dʒɛmjul/, *n.* **1.** *Bot.* →**gemma. 2.** *Zool.* an asexually produced mass of cells that will develop into an animal. **3.** *Biol.* one of the hypothetical living units conceived by Darwin as the bearers of the hereditary attributes. [L *gemmula,* diminutive of *gemma* bud]

**gemology** /dʒɛm'ɒlədʒi/, *n.* the study of precious gems. Also, **gemmology.** – **gemologist, gemmologist,** *n.* – **gemological** /dʒɛmə'lɒdʒɪkəl/, **gemmological** /dʒɛmə'lɒdʒɪkəl/, *adj.*

**gemot** /gə'moʊt/, *n. Old Eng. Hist.* a meeting or an assembly, as for judicial or legislative purposes. Also, **gemote.** [OE *gemōt,* from *ge-* together + *mōt* meeting. Cf. MOOT]

**gemsbok** /'gɛmzbɒk/, *n.* a large antelope, *Oryx beisa,* of southern Africa, having long, straight horns and a long, tufted tail. [Afrikaans: chamois buck]

**gem scone** /'dʒɛm skɒn/, *n.* a light, sweet, round scone made by adding flour to creamed butter and sugar, then baking the mixture in a gem iron.

**gemstone** /'dʒɛmstoʊn/, *n.* a precious stone; gem; jewel.

**gen** /dʒɛn/, *n., v.,* **genned, genning.** *Colloq. –n.* **1.** general information. **2.** all the necessary information about a subject. *–v.i.* **3.** to become informed (about), to learn or read up (about) (fol. by *up*). [shortened form of *general information*]

**-gen,** a suffix meaning: **1.** something produced, or growing: *acrogen, endogen, exogen.* **2.** something that produces: *hydrogen, oxygen.* [F *-gène,* from Gk *-genēs* born, produced, from *gen-* bear, produce]

**gen.,** **1.** gender. **2.** general. **3.** genitive. **4.** genus.

**Gen.,** **1.** *Mil.* General. **2.** *Bible.* Genesis.

**gendarme** /ʒɒn'dam/, *n., pl.* **-darmes** /-'damz/. **1.** one of a corps of military policemen who in peacetime engage in civil police work. **2.** *Colloq.* any policeman. [F, formed as sing. from *gens d'armes* men at arms]

**gendarmerie** /ʒɒn'daməri/, *n.* **1.** gendarmes collectively. **2.** *Colloq.* a police station. Also, **gendarmery.**

**gender**[1] /'dʒɛndə/, *n.* **1.** *Gram.* **a.** (in many languages) a set of classes, such as masculine, feminine and neuter, which together include all nouns. Membership in a particular class is shown by the form of the noun itself or by the form or choice of words that modify, replace, or otherwise refer to the noun; e.g., in English, the choice of *he* to replace *the man,* of *she* to replace *the woman,* of *it* to replace *the table,* of *it* or *she* to replace *the ship.* Often the classification correlates in part with sex (**natural gender**) or animateness. **b.** one class of such a set. **c.** such classes or sets collectively or in general. **2.** *Colloq.* sex. **3.** *Obs.* kind, sort, or class. [ME *gendre,* from OF, from L *genus* race, kind, sort, gender. Cf. GENUS, GENRE] – **genderless,** *adj.*

**gender**[2] /gɛn'dɛə/, *n.* an Indonesian percussion instrument, similar to a xylophone.

**gene** /dʒin/, *n.* the unit of inheritance, associated with deoxyribonucleic acid, which is situated on and transmitted by the chromosome, and which develops into a hereditary character as it reacts with the environment and with the other genes. [Gk *geneá* breed, kind]

**genealogical tree** /ˌdʒiniəlɒdʒɪkəl 'tri/, *n.* →**family tree.**

**genealogy** /dʒini'ælədʒi/, *n., pl.* **-gies. 1.** an account of the descent of a person or family through an ancestral line. **2.** the investigation of pedigrees as a department of knowledge. [ME, from LL *geneālogia,* from Gk: tracing of descent] – **genealogical** /dʒiniə'lɒdʒɪkəl/, **genealogic** /dʒiniə'lɒdʒɪk/, *adj.* – **genealogically** /dʒiniə'lɒdʒɪkli/, *adv.* – **genealogist** *n.*

**genecology** /dʒinə'kɒlədʒi/, *n.* study of genetical composition of plant populations in relation to their habitats.

**genera** /'dʒɛnərə/, *n.* plural of **genus.**

**generable** /'dʒɛnərəbəl/, *adj.* that may be created or produced. [L *generābilis*]

**general** /'dʒɛnrəl/, *adj.* **1.** pertaining to, affecting, including, or participated in by all members of a class or group; not partial or particular: *a general election.* **2.** common to many or most of a community; prevalent; usual: *the general practice.* **3.** not restricted to one class or field; miscellaneous: *the general public, general knowledge.* **4.** not limited to a detail of application; not specific or special: *general instructions.* **5.** indefinite or vague: *to refer to a matter in a general way.* **6.** having extended command, or superior or chief rank (often follows noun): *a general officer, governor-general.* –*n.* **7.** *Mil.* **a.** an officer next in rank above a lieutenant general and below a field marshal. **b.** a general officer. **c.** one who fulfils the function of a general officer; a military commander: *Julius Caesar was a great general.* **8.** *Eccles.* the chief of certain religious orders. **9.** a general statement or principle. **10.** *Archaic.* the general public. **11.** *Obs.* a servant, esp. a maid doing general housework. **12. in general, a.** with respect to the whole class referred to. **b.** as a general rule; commonly. [ME, from L *generālis,* of or belonging to a (whole) race, kind, the opposite of *speciālis* special, particular. See GENUS] – **generalness,** *n.*

**general anaesthetic** /– ænəs'θɛtɪk/, *n.* an anaesthetic which anaesthetises the entire body and is accompanied by loss of consciousness.

**General Assembly** /dʒɛnrəl ə'sɛmbli/, *n.* **1.** one of the principal bodies within the United Nations, and the only one in which all members are represented. **2.** the highest court or authority of the Presbyterian Church of each country.

**General Australian** /– ɒs'treɪljən/, *n.* that pronunciation of Australian English adopted by the majority of Australians.

**general election** /dʒɛnrəl ə'lɛkʃən/, *n.* a parliamentary election, not a by-election, in which all seats in the house are thrown open, as a Federal or State election for the Lower House.

**general hospital** /'– hɒspɪtl/, *n.* a hospital which treats many, different types of ailments, which does not specialise in one type of disease or diseases.

**generalisation** /ˌdʒɛnrəlaɪ'zeɪʃən/, *n.* **1.** the act or process of generalising. **2.** a result of this process; general statement, idea, or principle. Also, **generalization.**

**generalise** /'dʒɛnrəlaɪz/, *v.,* **-lised, -lising.** –*v.t.* **1.** to give a general (rather than specific or special) character to. **2.** to infer (a general principle, etc.) from facts, etc. **3.** to make general; bring into general use or knowledge. –*v.i.* **4.** to form general notions. **5.** to deal in generalities. **6.** to make general inferences. Also, **generalize.**

**generalissimo** /ˌdʒɛnrəlɪsɪmoʊ/, *n., pl.* **-mos. 1.** the supreme commander of several armies acting together. **2.** the supreme commander of all the forces of a country. [It., superl. of *generale* general, from L *generālis.* See GENERAL]

**generalist** /'dʒɛnrələst/, *n.* a person with a broad education and ability to grasp basic concepts in various fields (opposed to *specialist*).

**generality** /dʒɛnə'rælәti/, *n., pl.* **-ties. 1.** a general or vague statement: *to speak in vague generalities.* **2.** general principle; general rule or law. **3.** the greater part or majority: *the generality of people.* **4.** state or quality of being general.

**generally** /'dʒɛnrəli/, *adv.* **1.** with respect to the larger part, or for the most part: *a claim generally recognised.* **2.** usually; commonly; ordinarily: *he generally comes at noon.* **3.** without reference to particular persons or things: *generally speaking.*

**general officer** /dʒɛnrəl 'ɒfəsə/, *n.* an officer above the rank of brigadier, holding the rank of either major general, lieutenant general, or general, having command of military formations larger than a brigade or having the duties of a staff officer at a higher headquarters.

**general paralysis of the insane,** *n.* a syphilitic brain disorder characterised by chronic inflammation and degeneration of cerebral tissue, resulting in mental and physical deterioration. *Abbrev.:* G.P.I. Also, **general paresis.**

**general practice** /dʒɛnrəl 'præktəs/, *n.* medical practice involving responsibility for the general health of a number of people in a district.

**general practitioner** /– præk'tɪʃənə/, *n.* a doctor who does not specialise in any particular branch of medicine; a doctor in general practice. *Abbrev.:* G.P.

**general-purpose** /dʒɛnrəl-'pɜpəs/, *adj.* of broad usage; not restricted in function.

**general-purpose outlet** /– 'aʊtlɛt/, *n.* →**power point.**

**general register** /dʒɛnrəl 'rɛdʒəstə/, *n.* one of a specified number of internal addressable registers in a CPU which can be used for temporary storage, as an accumulator, or for any other general purpose.

**general semantics** /– sə'mæntɪks/, *n.* the study of semantics with emphasis on the arbitrary nature of meaning and the difficulties which arise in coping with this arbitrariness.

**generalship** /'dʒɛnrəlʃɪp/, *n.* **1.** skill as commander of a large military force or unit. **2.** management or tactics. **3.** the rank or functions of a general.

**general staff** /dʒɛnrəl 'staf/, *n.* **1.** that section of military staff which is concerned with operations rather than logistics. **2.** non-professional staff in such institutions as hospitals, universities, etc.

**general store** /– 'stɔ/, *n.* a shop at some distance from a major shopping centre, stocking a wide range of goods, as the main store in a small country town.

**general strike** /– 'straɪk/, *n.* a mass strike in all or many trades and industries in a section or in all parts of a country.

**general theory of relativity,** *n. Physics.* See **relativity.**

**generate** /'dʒɛnəreɪt/, *v.t.,* **-rated, -rating. 1.** to bring into existence; give rise to; produce; cause to be: *to generate electricity.* **2.** to beget, to procreate. **3.** *Maths.* **a.** to specify (a set) by applying rules or operations to given quantities. **b.** to trace out (a figure) by the motion of another figure. **4.** *Linguistics.* to produce (sentences, etc.) from a limited inventory of linguistic items by applying a series of grammatical rules. [L *generātus,* pp., begotten]

**generating station** /'dʒɛnəreɪtɪŋ ˌsteɪʃən/, *n. Elect.* →**power station.**

**generation** /dʒɛnə'reɪʃən/, *n.* **1.** the whole body of individuals born about the same time: *the rising generation.* **2.** the age or average lifetime of a generation; term of years (commonly thirty) accepted as the average difference of age between one generation of a family and the next. **3.** a single step in natural descent, as of human beings, animals, or plants. **4.** the act or process of generating; procreation. **5.** the fact of being generated. **6.** production by natural or artificial processes; evolution, as of heat or sound. **7.** the offspring of a given parent or parents, considered as a single step in descent. **8.** *Maths.* the production of a geometrical figure by the motion of another figure. **9.** a period of technological development marked by features non-existent in the previous period. **10.** a subsequent dubbing of an audio or video track, film, etc.: *quality has declined substantially by the fifth* *generation.* **11.** *Linguistics.* the specification of the grammatical sequences of a language by applying a series of formal rules to a limited inventory of linguistic items. [ME, from L *generātio*]

**generation gap** /'– gæp/, *n.* the differences in viewpoint and understanding, esp. of each other's world picture, which exist between members of different generations.

**generation time** /'– taɪm/, *n.* the average time between the creation of a neutron by nuclear fission and a subsequent fission produced by that neutron.

**generative** /'dʒɛnərətɪv/, *adj.* **1.** pertaining to the production of offspring. **2.** capable of producing. **3.** *Linguistics.* **a.** capable of generating. **b.** pertaining to a generative grammar.

**generative grammar** /– 'græmə/, *n.* a grammar consisting of formal rules operating on a limited inventory of linguistic items, which accounts for all the permissible sentences of a language and which defines the characteristics of their internal structure.

**generativist** /'dʒɛnrətəvəst/, *n.* a linguist who espouses the theory of generative grammar.

**generator** /'dʒɛnəreɪtə/, *n.* **1.** a machine which converts mechanical energy into electrical energy; dynamo. **2.** *Chem.* an apparatus for producing a gas or vapour. **3.** one who or that which generates. [L]

**generic** /dʒə'nɛrɪk/, *adj.* **1.** pertaining to a genus. **2.** applicable or referring to all the members of a genus or class. **3.** identified by the name of the product itself, not by a particular brand name. Also, **generical.** [L *genus* kind + -IC. Cf. F *générique*] –**generically,** *adv.*

**generosity** /dʒɛnə'rɒsəti/, *n., pl.* **-ties.** **1.** readiness or liberality in giving. **2.** freedom from meanness or smallness of mind or character. **3.** a generous act. [L *generōsitas* nobility, excellence]

**generous** /'dʒɛnərəs, 'dʒɛnrəs/, *adj.* **1.** munificent or bountiful; unselfish: *a generous giver or gift.* **2.** free from meanness or smallness of mind or character. **3.** furnished liberally; abundant: *a generous portion.* **4.** rich or strong, as wine. **5.** fertile, as soil. [L *generōsus* of noble birth] –**generously,** *adv.* –**generousness,** *n.*

**genesis** /'dʒɛnəsəs/, *n., pl.* **-ses** /-siz/. origin; production; creation. [ME, from L, from Gk: origin, creation]

**genet** /'dʒɛnət/, *n.* **1.** any of several carnivorous mammals of the genus *Genetta* of Europe and Africa related to and resembling the civets, but having a longer tail and less developed scent glands. **2.** the fur of such an animal. Also, **genette** /dʒə'nɛt/. [ME *genete,* from OF, from Sp. *gineta,* from Ar. *jarnait*]

genet

**genetic** /dʒə'nɛtɪk/, *adj.* **1.** *Biol.* pertaining or according to genetics. **2.** pertaining to genesis or origin. Also, **genetical.** [Gk *genetikós* generative] –**genetically,** *adv.*

**genetic code** /– 'koʊd/, *n.* the code whereby codons are translated into amino acids for protein synthesis.

**genetic engineering** /– ɛndʒə'nɪərɪŋ/, *n.* the alteration of the chromosome structure of cells from which breeding takes place in an attempt to control the characteristics of the offspring.

**geneticist** /dʒə'nɛtəsəst/, *n.* one versed in genetics or a student of genetics.

**genetics** /dʒə'nɛtɪks/, *n.* the science of heredity, dealing with resemblances and differences of related organisms flowing from the interaction of their genes and the environment. [pl. of GENETIC (def. 2). See -ICS]

**Geneva bands** /dʒə'nivə bændz/, *n.pl.* two bands, or pendant strips, worn at the throat as part of a clerical garb, worn originally by the Swiss Calvinist clergy.

**Geneva Convention** /– kən'vɛnʃən/, *n.* an international agreement establishing rules for the treatment during war of the sick, the wounded, and prisoners of war. [orig. formulated in 1864 at *Geneva,* Switzerland]

**Geneva cross** /– 'krɒs/, *n.* a red Greek cross on a white ground, displayed in war, etc., to distinguish ambulances, hospitals, and persons serving them; Red Cross.

Geneva cross

**Geneva gown** /– gaʊn/, *n.* a loose, large-sleeved, black preaching gown worn by Protestant clergymen, so-named from its use by the Genevan Calvinist clergy.

**Geneva System** /– sɪstəm/, *n.* a system of nomenclature for organic compounds recommended in 1892.

**genial**[1] /'dʒiniəl/, *adj.* **1.** sympathetically cheerful; cordial: *a genial disposition, a genial host.* **2.** enlivening; supporting life; pleasantly warm, or mild. [L *geniālis* festive, jovial, pleasant, lit., pertaining to generation or to marriage] –**genially,** *adv.* –**genialness,** *n.*

**genial**[2] /dʒə'naɪəl/, *adj.* of or pertaining to the chin. [Gk *géneion* chin + -AL[1]]

**geniality** /dʒini'æləti/, *n.* genial quality; sympathetic cheerfulness or kindliness.

**genic** /'dʒɛnɪk/, *adj.* of, relating to, resembling, or arising from a gene or genes.

**geniculate** /dʒə'nɪkjələt, -leɪt/, *adj.* **1.** having kneelike joints or bends. **2.** bent at a joint like a knee. [L *geniculātus* knotted]

**geniculation** /dʒənɪkjə'leɪʃən/, *n.* **1.** geniculate state. **2.** a geniculate formation. [LL *geniculātio* a bending of the knee]

**genie** /'dʒini/, *n.* a jinnee or spirit of Arabian mythology. [F, from L *genius.* See GENIUS]

**genii** /'dʒiniaɪ/, *n.* plural of **genius** (defs. 5, 6, 8).

**genipap** /'dʒɛnəpæp/, *n.* **1.** the edible fruit of a tropical American tree, *Genipa americana,* about the size of an orange. **2.** the plant. [Pg. *genipapo;* of Tupi orig.]

**genista** /gə'nɪstə, dʒə-/, *n.* any shrub or small tree belonging to the genus *Genista,* many of which are cultivated for their pea-shaped, often yellow flowers.

**genital** /'dʒɛnətl/, *adj.* pertaining to generation or the organs of generation. [L *genitālis*]

**genitalia** /dʒɛnə'teɪliə/, *n. pl.* the genitals. [L]

**genitals** /'dʒɛnətlz/, *n.pl.* the reproductive organs, esp. the external organs.

**genitive** /'dʒɛnətɪv/, *Gram.* –*adj.* **1.** (in some inflected languages) denoting the case of nouns generally used to modify other nouns, often indicating possession, but used also in expressions of measure, origin, characteristic, as *John's* hat, *man's* fate, *week's* holiday, *duty's* call. **2.** denoting the affix or other element characteristic of this case, or a word containing such an element. **3.** similar to such a case form in function or meaning. –*n.* **4.** the genitive case. **5.** a word in that case. **6.** a construction of similar meaning. [ME, from L *genitīvus,* lit., pertaining to generation] –**genitival** /dʒɛnə'taɪvəl/, *adj.* –**genitivally** /dʒɛnə'taɪvəli/, *adv.*

**genitor** /'dʒɛnətə, -tɔ/, *n.* a father in the biological sense, sometimes distinguished from a legal or acting father. [ME, from L]

**genito-urinary** /ˌdʒɛnətoʊ-'jurənri/, *adj.* denoting or pertaining to the genital and urinary organs; urogenital. [*genito-* (combining form of GENITAL) + URINARY]

**genius** /'dʒiniəs/, *n., pl.* **geniuses** *for defs 1-4, 7,* **genii** /'dʒiniaɪ/ *for defs 5, 6, 8.* **1.** exceptional natural capacity for creative and original conceptions; the highest level of mental ability. **2.** a person having such capacity. **3.** natural ability or capacity: *a task suited to one's genius.* **4.** distinctive character or spirit, as of a nation, period, language, etc. **5.** the guardian spirit of a place, institution, etc. **6.** either of two mutually opposed spirits, one good and the other evil, supposed to attend a person throughout his life. **7.** a person who strongly influences the character, conduct, or destiny of another: *an evil genius.* **8.** (*pl.*) any demon or spirit, esp. a genie or jinnee. [L: tutelary spirit, any spiritual being, disposition, orig. a male generative or creative principle. Cf. GENIAL[1], GENITAL, GENUS, GENESIS, KIN]

**genius loci** /– 'loʊsaɪ/, *n.* **1.** guardian of a place. **2.** the peculiar character of a place with reference to the impression that it makes on the mind. [L]

**geno** /ˈdʒinoʊ/, *n.* a man who plots the odds for a bookmaker so that he will make a profit. [GEN(IUS) + -O]

**genoa** /ˈdʒɛnəwə/, *n.* a large balloon jib set in a yacht in light winds.

**Genoa cake** /dʒəˈnoʊə keɪk/, *n.* a rich fruit cake, generally decorated with almonds.

**genocide** /ˈdʒɛnəsaɪd/, *n.* extermination of a national or racial group as a planned move. [Gk *géno(s)* race + -CIDE; coined by Dr Raphael Lemkin, 1944] – **genocidal** /dʒɛnəˈsaɪdl/, *adj.*

**genome** /ˈdʒinoʊm/, *n.* the complete genetic material for any cell.

**genotype** /ˈdʒɛnətaɪp/, *n.* **1.** the fundamental hereditary constitution of an organism. **2.** its breeding formula of genes. **3.** a group of organisms with a common heredity. *–v.t.* **4.** to study the genotype of. [Gk *géno(s)* origin, race + -TYPE] – **genotypic** /dʒɛnəˈtɪpɪk/, *adj.* – **genotypically** /dʒɛnəˈtɪpɪkli/, *adv.*

**-genous,** an adjective suffix derived from nouns in **-gen** and **-geny.** [-GEN + -OUS]

**genre** /ˈʒɒnrə/, *n.* **1.** genus; kind; sort; style. **2.** *Painting, etc.* the category in which scenes from ordinary life are represented (as distinguished from landscapes, etc.). *–adj.* **3.** of or pertaining to genre (def. 2). [F: kind. See GENDER[1]]

**gens** /dʒɛnz/, *n., pl.* **gentes** /ˈdʒɛntiz/. **1.** a group of families in ancient Rome, claiming descent from a common ancestor and united by a common name and common religious rites. **2.** *Anthrop.* a group tracing descent in the male line. [L; also race, people]

**gent** /dʒɛnt/, *n.* (*oft. joc.*) gentleman.

**genteel** /dʒɛnˈtil/, *adj.* **1.** belonging or suited to polite society. **2.** well-bred or refined; polite; elegant; stylish. **3.** affectedly proper in manners and speech. [F *gentil.* See GENTLE] – **genteelly,** *adv.* – **genteelness,** *n.*

**genteelism** /dʒɛnˈtilɪzəm/, *n.* a self-consciously polite synonym for a forthright or crude word.

**gentian** /ˈdʒɛnʃən/, *n.* **1.** any plant of the large genus *Gentiana* comprising herbs with blue, or less frequently white, yellow or red, flowers. **2.** any of various plants related to or resembling *Gentiana.* **3.** the root of *G. lutea,* or a preparation of it, used as a tonic. [ME *gencian,* from L *gentiana;* said to be named after *Gentius,* an Illyrian king]

**gentian blue** /– ˈblu/, *n.* a purplish-blue colour.

**gentian violet** /– ˈvaɪələt/, *n.* →**crystal violet.**

**gentile** /ˈdʒɛntaɪl/, *adj.* **1.** of or pertaining to any people not Jewish. **2.** Christian as distinguished from Jewish. **3.** (among Mormons) of or pertaining to any people not Mormon. **4.** *Obs.* heathen or pagan. *–n.* **5.** a person who is not Jewish, esp. a Christian. **6.** (among Mormons) one not a Mormon. **7.** *Rare.* a heathen or pagan. Also, **Gentile.** [ME *gentil,* from L *gentīlis* belonging to a people, national, LL foreign]

**gentility** /dʒɛnˈtɪləti/, *n., pl.* **-ties. 1.** superior refinement or elegance, possessed or affected. **2.** gentle birth.

**gentle** /ˈdʒɛntl/, *adj.,* **-tler, -tlest,** *v.,* **-tled, -tling.** *–adj.* **1.** mild, kindly, or amiable: *gentle words.* **2.** not severe, rough, or violent: *a gentle wind, a gentle lap.* **3.** moderate; gradual: *gentle heat, a gentle slope.* **4.** of good birth or family; well-born. **5.** characteristic of good birth; honourable; respectable. **6.** easily handled or managed: *a gentle animal.* **7.** soft or low: *a gentle sound.* **8.** *Archaic.* polite; refined. **9.** *Archaic.* noble; chivalrous: *a gentle knight.* *–v.t.* **10.** to tame; render tractable. **11.** *Rare.* to mollify (a person). [ME *gentil,* from OF: of good family, noble, excellent, from L *gentīlis.* See GENTILE] – **gentleness,** *n.* – **gently,** *adv.*

**gentle Annie** /– ˈæni/, *n. N.Z.* a gently sloping hill. [orig. a coachman's term]

**gentle breeze** /– ˈbriz/, *n.* a wind of Beaufort scale force 3, i.e. one with an average wind speed of 7 to 10 knots, or 12 to 19 km/h.

**gentlefolk** /ˈdʒɛntlfoʊk/, *n.pl.* persons of good family and breeding. Also, **gentlefolks.**

**gentleman** /ˈdʒɛntlmən/, *n., pl.* **-men. 1.** a man of good breeding, education, and manners. **2.** (as a polite form of speech) any man. **3.** a male personal servant, or valet, esp. of a man of social position: *a gentleman's gentleman.* **4.** a man of good social standing by birth, esp. one who does not work for a living. **5.** *Hist.* a man above the rank of yeoman. – **gentlemanlike,** *adj.*

**gentleman-at-arms** /ˌdʒɛntlmən-ət-ˈamz/, *n., pl.* **gentlemen-at-arms.** one of a guard of forty gentlemen with their officers who attend the British sovereign on state occasions.

**gentlemanly** /ˈdʒɛntlmənli/, *adj.* like or befitting a gentleman; well-bred. – **gentlemanliness,** *n.*

**gentlemen's agreement** /ˌdʒɛntlmənz əˈgrimənt/, *n.* an agreement binding as a matter of honour alone, not enforceable at law.

**gentle sex** /ˈdʒɛntl sɛks/, *n.* women.

**gentlewoman** /ˈdʒɛntlwʊmən/, *n., pl.* **-women. 1.** a woman of good family or breeding; a lady. **2.** *Hist.* a woman who attends upon a lady of rank. – **gentlewomanly,** *adj.* – **gentlewomanliness,** *n.*

**gentrification** /dʒɛntrəfəˈkeɪʃən/, *n.* the renewal of inner urban areas by young professional people, artists, etc., who find it convenient to live in them.

**gentry** /ˈdʒɛntri/, *n.* **1.** well-born and well-bred people. **2.** the class below the nobility. [ME, from *gent* noble + -RY]

**gents** /dʒɛnts/, *n. Colloq.* a public lavatory for men. Also, **gentlemen's, gents'.**

**genu** /ˈdʒɛnju/, *n., pl.* **genua** /ˈdʒɛnjuə/. **1.** the knee. **2.** a kneelike part or bend. [L]

**genuflect** /ˈdʒɛnjəflɛkt/, *v.i.* to bend the knee or knees, esp. in reverence. [ML *genūflectere,* from L *genū* knee + *flectere* bend] – **genuflector,** *n.*

**genuflection** /dʒɛnjəˈflɛkʃən/, *n.* the act of bending the knee or knees, esp. in worship. Also, **genuflexion.** [ML *genūflexio,* from ML *genūflectere* bend the knee]

**genuine** /ˈdʒɛnjuən/, *adj.* **1.** being truly such; real; authentic: *genuine regret, genuine worth.* **2.** properly so called: *genuine leprosy.* **3.** sincere; free from pretence or affectation: *a genuine person.* [L *genuīnus* native, natural, authentic, genuine] – **genuinely,** *adv.* – **genuineness,** *n.*

**genus** /ˈdʒinəs/, *n., pl.* **genera** /ˈdʒɛnərə/. **1.** a kind; sort; class. **2.** *Biol.* the usual major subdivision of a family or subfamily, usu. consisting of more than one species, essentially very similar to one another and regarded as phylogenetically very closely related. The genus designation is the first part of the scientific name of a species, as in *Lynx canadensis,* the Canadian lynx. **3.** *Logic.* a class or group of individuals including subordinate groups called *species.* [L: race, stock, kind, sort, gender (c. Gk *génos*)]

**-geny,** a suffix meaning 'origin', as in *phylogeny.* [Gk *-geneia,* from *-genēs* born, produced. See -GEN]

**geo-,** a word element meaning 'the earth', as in *geocentric.* [Gk, combining form of *gê*]

**geocentric** /dʒioʊˈsɛntrɪk/, *adj.* **1.** *Astron.* as viewed or measured from the centre of the earth: *the geocentric altitude of a star.* **2.** having or representing the earth as a centre: *a geocentric theory of the universe.* Also, **geocentrical.** – **geocentrically,** *adv.*

**geocentric parallax** /– ˈpærəlæks/, *n.* See **parallax** (def. 2).

**geochemistry** /dʒioʊˈkɛməstri/, *n.* the science dealing with the chemical changes in, and the composition of, the earth, particularly the crust. – **geochemical,** *adj.* – **geochemist,** *n.*

**geochronology** /ˌdʒioʊkrəˈnɒlədʒi/, *n.* the study of the earth's chronology based on geological information. – **geochronological** /ˌdʒioʊkrɒnəˈlɒdʒɪkəl/, *adj.*

**geoclinal valley** /ˌdʒioʊklaɪnəl ˈvæli/, *n.* a wide depression lying between distant ranges and produced by a gentle bending of the earth's crust.

**geod.,** **1.** geodesy. **2.** geodetic.

**geode** /ˈdʒioʊd/, *n.* **1.** a rounded hollow in a rock coated with crystals which have grown freely inwards. **2.** a hollow concretion so formed. [F, from L *geōdēs* jewel, from Gk: adj., earthlike] – **geodic** /dʒiˈɒdɪk/, *adj.*

**geodesic** /dʒioʊˈdɛsɪk, -ˈdisɪk/, *adj.* **1.** Also, **geodesical.** pertaining to the geometry of curved surfaces, in which geodesic lines take the place of the straight lines of plane geometry. *–n.* **2.** a geodesic line.

**geodesic dome** /– ˈdoʊm/, *n.* a dome constructed from a latticework of polygons so that the pressure load is shared evenly throughout the structure, having the advantage that the larger the dome, the stronger it is.

**geodesic line** /– 'laɪn/, *n.* the shortest line lying on a given surface and connecting two given points.

**geodesy** /dʒi'ɒdəsi/, *n.* that branch of applied mathematics which determines the shape and area of large tracts of country, the exact position of geographical points, and the curvature, shape, and dimensions of the earth. Also, **geodetics** /dʒioʊ'dɛtɪks/. [NL *geōdaesia,* from Gk *geōdaisía* art of mensuration] – **geodesist,** *n.*

**geodetic** /dʒioʊ'dɛtɪk/, *adj.* **1.** pertaining to geodesy. **2.** geodesic. Also, **geodetical.** – **geodetically,** *adv.*

**geodynamics** /ˌdʒioʊdaɪ'næmɪks/, *n.* the study of the dynamics of the forces inside the earth. – **geodynamic, geodynamical,** *adj.* – **geodynamicist,** *n.*

**geog.,** **1.** geographer. **2.** geographic; geographical. **3.** geography.

**geognosy** /dʒi'ɒgnəsi/, *n.* that branch of geology which treats of the constituent parts of the earth, its envelope of air and water, its crust, and the condition of its interior. [GEO- + Gk *-gnōsía* knowledge]

**geographer** /dʒi'ɒgrəfə/, *n.* one who specialises in the study and writing of geography.

**geographical** /dʒiə'græfɪkəl/, *adj.* **1.** of or pertaining to geography. **2.** referring to or characteristic of a certain locality, esp. in reference to its location in relation to other places. Also, **geographic.** – **geographically,** *adv.*

**geographic determinism** /dʒiəˌgræfɪk də'tɜmənɪzəm/, *n.* the doctrine which regards geographical conditions as the determining or moulding agency of group life.

**geographic environment** /– ɛn'vaɪrənmənt/, *n.* the entire natural surroundings of man, independent of his activity but underlying and conditioning it.

**geography** /dʒi'ɒgrəfi/, *n., pl.* **-phies. 1.** the study of the areal differentiation of the earth's surface, as shown in the character, arrangement, and interrelations over the world of elements such as climate, relief, soil, vegetation, population, land use, industries, or states, and of the unit areas formed by the complex of these individual elements. **2.** the topographical features of a region, usu. of the earth, but sometimes of Mars, the moon, etc. **3.** a book, esp. a textbook, on this subject. [L *geōgraphia,* from Gk]

**geoid** /'dʒiɔɪd/, *n.* **1.** an imaginary surface which coincides with the mean sea-level over the ocean and its extension under the continents. **2.** the geometrical figure formed by this surface, an ellipsoid flattened at the poles. [Gk *geoeidḗs* earthlike]

**geol.,** **1.** geologic; geological. **2.** geologist. **3.** geology.

**geological** /dʒiə'lɒdʒɪkəl/, *adj.* of or pertaining to geology. Also, **geologic.** – **geologically,** *adv.*

**geological time** /– 'taɪm/, *n.* the time covering the development of the planet earth to the present; about 5000 million years.

**geologise** /dʒi'ɒlədʒaɪz/, *v.,* **-gised, -gising.** *–v.i.* **1.** to study geology. *–v.t.* **2.** to examine geologically. Also, **geologize.**

**geology** /dʒi'ɒlədʒi/, *n., pl.* **-gies. 1.** the science which treats of the earth, the rocks of which it is composed, and the changes which it has undergone or is undergoing. **2.** the geological features of a locality. [NL *geōlogia.* See GEO-, -LOGY] – **geologist,** *n.*

**geom.,** **1.** geometric. **2.** geometrical. **3.** geometry.

**geomagnetic** /ˌdʒioʊmæg'nɛtɪk/, *adj.* of or pertaining to terrestrial magnetism.

**geomancer** /'dʒioʊmænsə/, *n.* one versed in or practising geomancy.

**geomancy** /'dʒioʊmænsi/, *n.* divination by means of the figure made by a handful of earth thrown down at random, or, by figures or lines formed by a number of dots made at random. [ME *geomancie,* from ML *geōmantia,* from Gk (see GEO-, -MANCY)] – **geomantic** /dʒioʊ'mæntɪk/, *adj.*

**geometer** /dʒi'ɒmətə/, *n.* an expert in geometry. [L *geōmetra, geōmetrēs,* from Gk *geōmétrēs* land-measurer, geometer]

**geometric** /dʒiə'mɛtrɪk/, *adj.* **1.** of or pertaining to geometry; according to the principles of geometry. **2.** resembling or employing the lines or figures in geometry. **3.** of or pertaining to painting, sculpture, or ornamentation of predominantly geometrical characteristics or figures. Also, **geometrical.** – **geometrically,** *adv.*

**geometrical optics** /dʒiəˌmɛtrɪkəl 'ɒptɪks/, *n.* the study of optical problems in terms of light rays and their geometry.

**geometrician** /dʒiˌɒmə'trɪʃən, ˌdʒiəmə-/, *n.* an expert in geometry.

**geometric isomerism** /dʒiəˌmɛtrɪk aɪ'sɒmərɪzəm/, *n. Chem.* →**cis-trans isomerism.**

**geometric mean** /– 'min/, *n.* the mean of n positive numbers obtained by taking the nth root of the product of the numbers: *the geometric mean of 6 and 24 is 12.*

**geometric progression** /– prə'grɛʃən/, *n.* a sequence of terms in which the ratio of any term to its predecessor is a constant, as 1, 3, 9, 27, 81 and 243, and 144, 12, 1 and $\frac{1}{12}$.

**geometric ratio** /– 'reɪʃioʊ/, *n.* the ratio of consecutive terms in a geometric progression.

**geometric series** /– 'sɪəriz/, *n.* an infinite series of the form $c + cx + cx^2 + cx^3 \ldots$ where both $c$ and $x$ are real or complex numbers.

**geometrid** /dʒi'ɒmətrɪd/, *adj.* **1.** of or relating to the moths of the family Geometridae, the larvae of which are called measuring worms or loopers. *–n.* **2.** a geometrid moth. [NL *Geōmetridae,* from L *geōmetra* GEOMETER]

**geometrise** /dʒi'ɒmətraɪz/, *v.,* **-trised, -trising.** *–v.i.* **1.** to work by geometrical methods. *–v.t.* **2.** to put into geometric form. Also, **geometrize.**

**geometry** /dʒi'ɒmətri/, *n.* **1.** that branch of mathematics which deduces the properties of figures in space. **2.** the shape of a surface or solid. **3.** the spatial configuration of the elements of a system: *the geometry of the apparatus.* [ME *geometrie,* from L *geōmetria,* from Gk]

**geometry set** /'– sɛt/, *n.* a set of instruments for use in geometry.

**geomorphic** /dʒioʊ'mɔfɪk/, *adj.* **1.** of or pertaining to the figure of the earth, or the forms of its surface. **2.** resembling the earth in form.

**geomorphology** /ˌdʒioʊmɔ'fɒlədʒi/, *n.* the study of the characteristics, origin, and development of land forms.

**geophagism** /dʒi'ɒfədʒɪzəm/, *n.* the practice, usu. found in primitive societies, of eating earth or substances found in the earth, as clay, chalk, etc. Also, **geophagy.** [see GEO-, -PHAGY, -ISM] – **geophagous** /dʒi'ɒfəgəs/, *adj.* – **geophagist** /dʒi'ɒfədʒəst/, *n.*

**geophagy** /dʒi'ɒfədʒi/, *n.* the practice of eating earthy matter, esp. clay or chalk. [GEO- + -PHAGY]

**geophilous** /dʒi'ɒfələs/, *adj.* terrestrial, as certain snails, or any plant fruiting underground.

**geophone** /'dʒiəfoʊn/, *n.* an instrument used to pick up vibrations passing through soil, rocks or ice. [Trademark]

**geophysics** /dʒioʊ'fɪzɪks/, *n.* the physics of the earth, dealing esp. with the study of inaccessible portions of the earth by instruments and apparatus such as the torsion balance, seismograph, and magnetometer. – **geophysical,** *adj.* – **geophysicist,** *n.*

**geophyte** /'dʒioʊfaɪt/, *n.* a plant with underground buds.

**geopolitics** /dʒioʊ'pɒlətɪks/, *n.* the application of political and economic geography to the external political problems of states, notably problems of national power, frontiers, and possibilities for expansion.

**geoponic** /dʒioʊ'pɒnɪk/, *adj.* of or pertaining to tillage or agriculture; agricultural. [Gk *geōponikós*]

**geoponics** /dʒioʊ'pɒnɪks/, *n.* the art or science of agriculture.

**georama** /dʒiə'ramə/, *n.* a large hollow globe on the inside of which is depicted a map of the earth's surface, to be viewed by a spectator within the globe. [F, from Gk *gê* earth + *(h)órama* view]

**Geordie** /'dʒɔdi/, *n. Colloq.* **1.** a Scotsman. **2.** *Brit.* a miner, esp. one from the region around the river Tyne. **3.** a person who works or lives near the river Tyne. [diminutive of *George,* proper name]

**georef** /'dʒiərɛf/, *n.* a worldwide position reference system that may be applied to any map or chart graduated in latitude and longitude regardless of projection. [a shortened form of *world geo(graphic) ref(erence) system*]

**George** /dʒɔdʒ/, *n.* **1.** (formerly) a coin, esp. a guinea, showing the image of St George. *–interj.* **2. by George!** (an exclamation or mild oath.)

**George Cross** /– 'krɒs/, *n.* a medal for outstanding heroism, awarded mainly to civilians.

**George Medal** /– 'mɛdl/, *n.* a medal for heroism, awarded mainly to civilians.

**georgette** /dʒɔ'dʒɛt/, *n.* sheer silk or rayon crepe of dull texture. Also, **georgette crepe.**

**Georgian** /'dʒɔdʒiən, -dʒən/, *adj., n.* **1.** pertaining to the four Georges, kings of England (1714-1830), or the period of their reigns. **2.** pertaining to George V, 1910-36, or George VI, 1936-52, or the period of their reign. *–n.* **3.** a person of either of the Georgian periods in England, esp. a writer of the early period of the reign of George V. **4.** the styles or character of a Georgian period.

**Georgian glass** /– 'glas/, *n.* a common type of opaque glass, often used in roof lights, and frequently wired to prevent accidents when broken. Also, **Georgian wire glass, Georgina glass.**

**georgic** /'dʒɔdʒɪk/, *adj.* **1.** agricultural. *–n.* **2.** a poem on agricultural matters. [L *geōrgicus* agricultural, from Gk *geōrgikós*]

**geoscience** /'dʒioʊsaɪəns/, *n.* the systematic study of the earth; the knowledge gained from such study.

**geoscientist** /dʒioʊ'saɪəntəst/, *n.* a scientist who studies the earth or some aspect of its history, composition, behaviour, etc., as a geologist, geophysicist, geochemist, palaeontologist, etc.

**geostatic** /dʒioʊ'stætɪk/, *adj.* of or pertaining to the pressure exerted by a mass of earth or other similar substance.

**geostationary orbit** /dʒioʊˌsteɪʃənri 'ɔbət/, *n.* →**synchronous equatorial orbit.**

**geostrophic wind speed,** *n.* the speed of the wind calculated from the pressure gradient, the air density, the rotational velocity of the earth, and the latitude, but neglecting the curvature of the path of the air.

**geosynclinal** /ˌdʒioʊsɪn'klaɪnəl/, *adj.* **1.** pertaining to a synclinal fold which involves a relatively large part of the earth's surface. *–n.* **2.** a geosyncline.

**geosyncline** /dʒioʊ'sɪnklaɪn/, *n.* a portion of the earth's crust subsiding for a long time, prevalently linear and usu. containing great thicknesses of sedimentary and volcanic rocks.

**geotaxis** /dʒioʊ'tæksəs/, *n.* a movement of an organism towards or away from a gravitional force. **–geotactic** /dʒioʊ'tæktɪk/, *adj.*

**geotectonic** /ˌdʒioʊtɛk'tɒnɪk/, *adj.* pertaining to the structure of the earth's crust or to the arrangement and form of its constituents.

**geothermic** /dʒioʊ'θɜmɪk/, *adj.* of or pertaining to the internal heat of the earth. Also, **geothermal** /dʒioʊ'θɜməl/.

**geotropic** /dʒioʊ'trɒpɪk/, *adj.* taking a particular direction with reference to the earth: **a. positively geotropic,** directed downwards. **b. negatively geotropic,** directed upwards. **c. transversely geotropic,** directed horizontally. **–geotropically,** *adv.*

**geotropism** /dʒi'ɒtrəpɪzəm/, *n.* a tropism occurring in response to gravitation, as the direction of growth of plants or the ability of some animals to avoid an upside down position in the air. See **negative geotropism, positive geotropism.**

**ger.,** **1.** gerund. **2.** gerundive.

**Ger.,** **1.** German. **2.** Germany.

**Geraldton waxflower** /dʒɛrəltən 'wæksflaʊə/, *n.* an evergreen shrub of western Australia, *Chamelaucium uncinatum,* frequently cultivated elsewhere for its delicate, often pale pink flowers. Also,**Geraldton wax.**

**geranial** /dʒə'reɪniəl/, *n. Chem.* →**citral.**

**geranium** /dʒə'reɪniəm/, *n.* **1.** any of the plants of the genus *Geranium,* most of which have pink or purple flowers, and some of which, as *G. maculatum,* have an astringent root used in medicine; cranesbill. **2.** a plant of the allied genus *Pelargonium,* of which many species are well known in cultivation for their showy flowers (as the **scarlet geraniums**) or their fragrant leaves (as the **rose geraniums**). [L, from Gk *gerántion* crane's-bill]

**geratology** /dʒɛrə'tɒlədʒi/, *n.* the study of the decline of life, as in old age or in animals approaching extinction. [Gk *gēras* old age + -O- + -LOGY]

**gerbera** /'dʒɜbərə/, *n.* any herb of the genus *Gerbera,* of Africa and Asia, esp. *G. jamesonii* widely cultivated for its showy yellow to red, daisy-like flowers.

**gerbil** /'dʒɜbəl/, *n.* any of numerous small, mouselike rodents of the genus *Gerbillus* and related genera, of desert regions of Asia, Africa and southern Russia, having long hind legs, adapted for leaping, and a long tail. Also, **gerbille.** [F *gerbille,* from NL *gerbillus,* diminutive of *gerbo* JERBOA]

gerbil

**gerent** /'dʒɛrənt/, *n.* a ruling power; manager. [L *gerens,* ppr., bearing, conducting, managing]

**gerenuk** /'gɛrənʊk/, *n.* a gazelle, *Litocranius walleri,* of eastern Africa, having long legs and a long slender neck. [Somali *garanug*]

**gerfalcon** /'dʒɜfælkən, -fɔl-/, *n.* →**gyrfalcon.**

**geri** /'dʒɛri/, *n. Colloq.* an old person. [short for GERIATRIC]

**geriatric** /dʒɛri'ætrɪk/, *adj.* **1.** of or pertaining to geriatrics or to aged persons. *–n.* **2.** an aged person, esp. one incapacitated or invalided by old age. [Gk *gêras* old age + *iātrikós* of medicine]

**geriatrician** /dʒɛriə'trɪʃən/, *n.* a doctor who specialises in the study of geriatrics.

**geriatrics** /dʒɛri'ætrɪks/, *n.* the science of the medical and hygienic care of, or the diseases of, aged persons. **–geriatrician** /dʒɛriə'trɪʃən/, **geriatrist,** *n.* **–geriatric,** *adj.*

**germ** /dʒɜm/, *n.* **1.** a micro-organism, esp. when disease-producing; microbe. **2.** that from which anything springs as if from a seed. **3.** *Embryol.* **a.** a bud, offshoot, or seed. **b.** the rudiment of a living organism; an embryo in its early stages. **4.** *Biol.* the initial stage in development or evolution, as a germ cell or ancestral form. [F *germe.* See GERMEN] **–germless,** *adj.*

**german** /'dʒɜmən/, *adj.* **1.** sprung from the same father and mother (always placed after the noun): *a brother-german.* **2.** sprung from the brother or sister of one's father or mother, or from brothers or sisters: *a cousin-german.* **3.** *Obs.* →**germane.** [L *germānus* having the same father (and mother); replacing ME *germain,* from OF]

**German** /'dʒɜmən/, *adj.* **1.** of or pertaining to Germany, its inhabitants, or their language. *–n.* **2.** a native or inhabitant of Germany. **3.** a Germanic language, the language of Germany and Austria and an official language of Switzerland. **4.** High German. [L *Germānus;* orig. uncert.]

**German Democratic Republic,** *n.* official name of **East Germany.**

**germander** /dʒɜ'mændə/, *n.* any of the herbs or shrubs belonging to the genus *Teucrium,* family Labiatae. [ML *germandra,* from LGk *chamándra,* alteration of Gk *chamaídrys,* lit., ground oak]

**germane** /dʒɜ'meɪn/, *adj.* closely related; pertinent: *a remark germane to the question.* [var. of GERMAN]

**germanic** /dʒɜ'mænɪk/, *adj. Chem.* of or containing germanium, esp. in the tetravalent state. [GERMAN(IUM) + -IC]

**Germanic** /dʒɜ'mænɪk/, *adj.* **1.** of the Teutonic race, the peoples belonging to it, or the group of languages spoken by these peoples; Teutonic. **2.** of the Germans; German. *–n.* **3.** a group of Indo-European languages, including English, German, Dutch, Gothic, and the Scandinavian languages. [L *Germānicus*]

**germanium** /dʒɜ'meɪniəm/, *n.* a rare metallic element, normally tetravalent, with a greyish white colour. *Symbol:* Ge; *at. wt:* 72·59; *at. no.:* 32; *sp. gr.:* 5·36 at 20°C. [NL, from L *Germānia* country of the Germans]

**German measles** /dʒɜmən 'mizəlz/, *n.* a contagious disease, usu. mild, accompanied by fever, often some sore throat, and a rash resembling that of scarlet fever, teratogenic in the first trimester of pregnancy; rubella.

**germanous** /dʒɜ'mænəs/, *adj.* containing divalent germanium.

**German sausage** /dʒɜmən 'sɒsɪdʒ/, *n.* →**devon** (def. 3).

**German shepherd dog,** *n.* →**Alsatian.**

**German silver** /dʒɜmən 'sɪlvə/, *n.* →**nickel silver.**

**Germany** /'dʒɜməni/, *n.* a country in central Europe, divided into West Germany and East Germany. German name, **Deutschland.**

**germ cell** /ˈdʒɜm sɛl/, *n.* the sexual reproductive cell at any stage from the primordial cell to the mature gamete.

**germen** /ˈdʒɜmən/, *n.* any of the cells found in the early stages of the embryonic development of an animal, from which gametes are ultimately formed. [L: sprout]

**germicide** /ˈdʒɜməsaɪd/, *n.* an agent that kills germs or micro-organisms. [GERM + -I- + -CIDE] – **germicidal** /dʒɛməˈsaidl/, *adj.*

**germinal** /ˈdʒɜmənəl/, *adj.* **1.** pertaining to a germ or germs. **2.** of the nature of a germ or germ cell. **3.** in the earliest stage of development: *germinal ideas.*

**germinal disc** /– ˈdɪsk/, *n.* →**blastoderm.**

**germinal vesicle** /– ˈvɛsɪkəl/, *n.* the large, vesicular nucleus of an ovum before the polar bodies are formed.

**germinant** /ˈdʒɜmənənt/, *adj.* germinating.

**germinate** /ˈdʒɜməneɪt/, *v.*, **-nated, -nating.** *–v.i.* **1.** to begin to grow or develop. **2.** *Bot.* **a.** to develop into a plant or individual, as a seed, or as a spore, bulb, or the like. **b.** to sprout; put forth shoots. *–v.t.* **3.** to cause to develop; produce. [L *germinātus*, pp.] – **germination** /dʒɜməˈneɪʃən/, *n.* – **germinator,** *n.*

**germinative** /ˈdʒɜmənətɪv/, *adj.* capable of germinating or developing; pertaining to germination.

**germ layer** /ˈdʒɜm leɪə/, *n.* one of the three primary embryonic cell layers, i.e., ectoderm, endoderm, and mesoderm.

**germ plasm** /ˈ– plæzəm/, *n.* the protoplasm of the germ cells containing the units of heredity (chromosomes and genes).

**germ theory** /ˈ– θɪəri/, *n.* **1.** *Biol.* the theory that living matter cannot be produced by evolution or development from non-living matter, but is necessarily produced from germs or seeds; the doctrine of biogenesis. **2.** *Pathol.* the theory that infectious diseases, etc., are due to the agency of germs or micro-organisms.

**germ warfare** /– ˈwɔfɛə/, *n.* →**biological warfare.**

**gerontocracy** /dʒɛrənˈtɒkrəsi/, *n., pl.* **-cies.** **1.** government by old men. **2.** a governing body consisting of old men. [Gk *gérōn* old man + -O- + -CRACY]

**gerontology** /dʒɛrənˈtɒlədʒi/, *n.* the study of old age, its diseases and phenomena. – **gerontologist,** *n.*

**-gerous,** a combining form meaning 'bearing' or 'producing', as in *setigerous.* [L *-ger* bearing + -OUS]

**gerrymander** /ˈdʒɛrimændə/, *v.t.* **1.** *Politics.* to subject (a constituency, etc.) to a gerrymander. **2.** to manipulate unfairly. *–n.* **3.** *Politics.* an arbitrary arrangement of the political divisions of a constituency, etc., made so as to give one party an unfair advantage in elections. [*Gerry* (governor of Massachusetts, U.S.A., whose party in 1812 redistributed the electoral boundaries of Massachusetts) + (SALA)MANDER (from a fancied resemblance to this animal of the gerrymandered map of Massachusetts)]

**gerund** /ˈdʒɛrənd/, *n. Gram.* **1.** (in Latin and some other languages) a derived noun form of verbs, having (in Latin) all case forms but the nominative. For example, Latin *dicendī* gen., *dicendō*, dat., abl., *dicendum*, acc., 'saying'. No nominative form occurs. **2.** (sometimes, from similarity of meaning) the English *-ing* form of a verb (*loving*) when in nominal function. *Hunting* and *writing* are gerunds in the sentences 'Hunting is good exercise' and 'writing is easy'. **3.** (sometimes, in other languages) a form similar to the Latin gerund in meaning or function. [LL *gerundium*, from L *gerundum*, var. of *gerendum*, ger. of L *gerere* bear, conduct] – **gerundial** /dʒəˈrʌndiəl/, *adj.*

**gerundive** /dʒəˈrʌndɪv/, *n. Gram.* **1.** (in Latin) the future passive particle, similar to the gerund in formation. For example, *Haec dicenda est* 'This must be said'. **2.** (sometimes) the English *-ing* form of a verb when used with a mixture of nominal and adjectival function. *Being fixed* is a gerundive in the sentence 'I depend on the car being fixed'. *–adj.* **3.** resembling a gerund. [LL *gerundīvus*, from *gerundium* GERUND] – **gerundival** /dʒɛrənˈdaɪvəl/, *adj.* – **gerundively,** *adv.*

**gesso** /ˈdʒɛsoʊ/, *n.* **1.** gypsum, or plaster of Paris, prepared with size, for use as a ground for painting. **2.** any plaster-like coating, as chalk and glue, to coat a surface for painting, gilding, etc. **3.** a prepared surface of plaster or a plaster-like material for painting, etc. [It., from L *gypsum* GYPSUM]

**gest** /dʒɛst/, *n. Archaic.* **1.** a metrical romance or history. **2.** a story or tale. **3.** a deed or exploit. Also, **geste.** [ME *geste*, from OF, from L *gesta* deeds, properly pp. neut. pl.]

**Gestalt** /gəˈʃtælt/, *n., pl.* **-stalten** /-ˈʃtæltən/. (in psychology) an organised configuration or pattern of experiences or of acts: *the Gestalt of a melody is distinct from the separate notes.* [G: form]

**Gestalt psychology** /– saɪˈkɒlədʒi/, *n.* a school of psychology which believes that experiences and conduct do not occur through the summation of reflexes or other individual elements but through configurations called *Gestalten,* which operate individually or interact mutually.

**gestate** /ˈdʒɛsteɪt/, *v.t.*, **-tated, -tating.** to carry in the womb during the period from conception to delivery. [L *gestātus*, pp., carried]

**gestation** /dʒɛsˈteɪʃən/, *n.* the act or period of gestating. [L *gestātio* a carrying]

**gestetner** /gəˈstɛtnə/, *n.* **1.** a duplicator, in which a stencil cut on a typewriter is wound round two ink-covered cylinders, operating in the same fashion as a silk screen. *–v.t.* **2.** to make a copy on such a machine. [Trademark]

**gesticulate** /dʒɛsˈtɪkjəleɪt/, *v.i.*, **-lated, -lating.** **1.** to make or use gestures, esp. in an animated or excited manner with or instead of speech. *–v.t.* **2.** to express by gesturing. [L *gesticulātus*, pp., having made mimic gestures] – **gesticulator,** *n.*

**gesticulation** /dʒɛsˌtɪkjəˈleɪʃən/, *n.* **1.** the act of gesticulating. **2.** an animated or excited gesture.

**gesticulatory** /dʒɛsˈtɪkjələtri, -təri/, *adj.* characterised by or making gesticulations. Also, **gesticulative.**

**gesture** /ˈdʒɛstʃə/, *n., v.*, **-tured, -turing.** *–n.* **1.** movement of the body, head, arms, hands, or face expressive of an idea or an emotion: *the gestures of an orator, a gesture of impatience.* **2.** any action or proceeding intended for effect or as a formality; demonstration: *a gesture of friendship.* *–v.i.* **3.** to make or use gestures. *–v.t.* **4.** to express by gestures. [ME, from ML *gestūra*, from L *gerere* bear, conduct] – **gesturer,** *n.*

**Gesundheit** /gəˈzʊnthaɪt/, *n.* soundness; health (used after a person has sneezed, or as a toast). [G]

**get** /gɛt/, *v.*, **got** or (*Archaic*) **gat; got; getting;** *n.* *–v.t.* **1.** to obtain, gain, or acquire by any means: *to get favour by service, get a good price.* **2.** to fetch or bring: *I will go and get it.* **3.** to receive or be awarded: *I got a present, he got five years for theft.* **4.** to obtain by labour; earn: *to get one's living.* **5.** to acquire a mental grasp or command of; learn: *to get a lesson by heart.* **6.** to hear or understand: *I didn't get the last word.* **7.** to be afflicted with (an illness, etc.): *have you got a cold?* **8.** to reach or communicate with (someone): *to get him on the phone.* **9.** to cause to be or do: *to get a friend appointed, get one's hair cut, get the fire to burn.* **10.** *Obs.* to capture; seize upon. **11.** *Colloq.* to be under an obligation to; be obliged to: *you have got to go.* **12.** to prevail on: *to get him to speak.* **13.** to prepare; make ready: *to get dinner.* **14.** to beget (now usu. of animals). **15.** *Colloq.* to hit: *the bullet got him in the leg.* **16.** *Colloq.* to make a physical assault on, esp. in vengeance: *I'll get you for that.* **17.** *Colloq.* to grasp or understand the meaning or intention of (a person). **18.** to baffle; reveal the ignorance of: *you've got me there, mate!* **19.** *Colloq.* to have an unspecified effect upon, as irritation, anger, amusement. **20.** *Colloq.* to kill. *–v.i.* **21.** to come to or arrive: *to get home.* **22.** to become; grow: *to get tired.* **23.** to succeed in coming or going (fol. by *away, in, into, out, over, through,* etc.). *–v.* **24.** Some special verb phrases are:

**get about, 1.** to move about. **2.** (of rumours, etc.) to become known.

**get across, 1.** to make understood. **2.** *Colloq.* to irritate or annoy; hinder. **3.** *Theat.* to communicate successfully (to an audience).

**get ahead,** to be successful; make progress.

**get along, 1.** to go; go off. **2.** nonsense! (an exclamation of disbelief). **3.** See **get on.**

**get any,** *Colloq.* have sexual intercourse: *are you getting any?*

**get around, 1.** to move about. **2.** (of rumours, etc.) to become known.

**get at, 1.** to reach; make contact with: *I can't get at it.* **2.** *Colloq.* to hint at or imply: *what's she getting at?* **3.** *Colloq.*

to tamper with, as by corruption or bribery.
**get away,** 1. to escape. 2. to depart. 3. to start in a race: *the horses got away.* 4. to go away, esp. on holiday: *we shall get away this evening.*
**get away from,** 1. to escape. 2. to avoid.
**get away from it all,** to leave business, work, worries, etc., for a holiday.
**get away with,** to avoid punishment or blame for.
**get away (with you),** (an exclamation indicating good-humoured disbelief or dismissal).
**get back,** 1. to return. 2. to recover or make as a profit on. 3. to take vengeance on (fol. by *on* or *at*).
**get by,** to manage; carry on in spite of difficulties.
**get cracking,** *Colloq.* to begin vigorously; hurry.
**get down,** 1. to bring or come down. 2. to concentrate or attend to (fol. by *to*). 3. *Colloq.* to steal (fol. by *on*).
**get even with,** to square accounts with.
**get going,** to begin; make haste.
**get his, hers, etc.** 1. to get a just reward. 2. to be killed.
**get in,** to order or stock up (provisions, etc.).
**get in for one's chop,** to attempt to obtain a fair share.
**get in good with,** to ingratiate oneself with.
**get inside,** 1. to make a way into. 2. to achieve deep understanding of.
**get into,** to become involved or immersed in (an activity): *I was just getting into reading and the phone rang.*
**get in touch with,** 1. to contact; exchange words with (a person). 2. to become familiar with; come to grips with.
**get it in the neck,** to be rebuked or punished.
**get it together,** to achieve harmony or success.
**get lost,** to go away; desist: *get lost, will you!*
**get off,** 1. to escape; evade consequences. 2. to start a journey; leave. 3. to dismount from (a horse or train). 4. *Colloq.* to cease to interfere.
**get off one's bike,** *Colloq.* to become angry.
**get off with,** 1. to behave flirtatiously with. 2. to have sexual intercourse with.
**get on,** 1. to age. 2. to advance one's cause; prosper. 3. to make progress; proceed; advance. 4. to agree or be friendly (with).
**get (on) one's goat,** to annoy; irritate.
**get on one's nerves,** to annoy; irritate.
**get one's own back,** to be revenged.
**get on to,** 1. to discover. 2. to contact; get in touch with (a person).
**get out,** 1. (of information) to become publically known. 2. to succeed in solving.
**get out from under,** to escape from a difficult or threatening situation; abandon one's responsibilities.
**get outside (of),** *Colloq.* to eat.
**get over,** 1. to overcome (a difficulty, etc.) 2. to recover from: *to get over a shock or illness.*
**get round,** 1. to outwit. 2. to cajole or ingratiate oneself with (someone). 3. to overcome (difficulties, etc.).
**get round to,** to come at length to (doing something).
**get set,** 1. (as a command at the start of a running race) be ready. 2. to place a bet (in two-up).
**get (someone) down,** to depress, discourage (someone).
**get (someone) wrong,** to misunderstand: *don't get me wrong!*
**get (stuck) into,** *Colloq.* 1. to attack (a person) vigorously either physically or verbally. 2. to set about a task vigorously. 3. to eat hungrily.
**get through to,** 1. to make a telephone connection with. 2. *Colloq.* to make understand.
**get to (someone),** 1. to arouse deep feeling in (someone). 2. to annoy or irritate (someone).
**get together,** to confer.
**get under one's skin,** to arouse one's irritation or embarrassment.
**get up,** 1. to arise; sit up or stand. 2. to rise from bed. 3. to ascend or mount. 4. to increase in force or violence (of wind, sea, etc.). 5. to dress elaborately. 6. to prepare, arrange, or organise. 7. to acquire a knowledge of: *to get up a subject.* 8. to produce in a specified style, as a book. 9. to work up (a feeling, etc.). 10. to be involved in (esp. mischief, etc.) (fol. by *to*). 11. to be acquitted. 12. to win as an election, courtcase, contest, etc.
**get with,** to have intercourse with.
**get with child,** to make pregnant.
*–n.* 25. (in tennis, etc.) a return of a stroke which would normally be a point for the opponent. 26. an offspring, now only of animals. 27. *Colloq.* a getaway. 28. **do a get,** *Colloq.* to escape; run away. [ME *geten,* from Scand.; cf. Icel. *geta,* c. OE *gietan* (G *-gessen* in *vergessen* forget); akin to L *-hendere* in *prehendere* seize, take, and to Gk *chandánein* hold, contain] – **gettable,** *adj.*

**get-at-able** /gɛt-'æt-əbəl/, *adj. Colloq.* that may be reached or attained; accessible.

**getaway** /'gɛtəweɪ/, *Colloq.* *–n.* 1. a getting away; an escape. 2. the start of a race. 3. **do a getaway,** to escape; leave quickly. *–adj.* 4. pertaining to a getaway: *the getaway car was found.*

**gethsemane** /gɛθ'sɛməni/, *n.* a scene or occasion of suffering. [*Gethsemane,* a garden east of Jerusalem, the scene of Christ's agony and betrayal. See Matt. 26:36, etc.]

**get-out** /'gɛt-aʊt/, *n.* 1. a style of clothing, esp. one which appears artificial. 2. **as all get-out,** *Colloq.* in the extreme: *he's as silly as all get-out.*

**get-rich-quick** /gɛt-ˌrɪtʃ-'kwɪk/, *adj.* of or pertaining to a scheme, business, enterprise, etc., designed to make a lot of money in a short time, sometimes by shady means.

**getter** /'gɛtə/, *n.* 1. a substance used for removing the last traces of gas from such devices as radio valves; if the gas is air, magnesium is often used because, when vaporised, it combines chemically with both oxygen and nitrogen. 2. one who or that which gets.

**get-together** /'gɛt-təgɛðə/, *n. Colloq.* 1. a meeting. 2. a small and informal social gathering.

**get-up** /'gɛt-ʌp/, *n. Colloq.* 1. style of production; appearance: *get-up of a book.* 2. style of dress; costume.

**get-up-and-go** /ˌgɛt-ʌp-ən-'goʊ/, *n.* enthusiasm; energy; enterprise.

**geum** /'dʒiəm/, *n.* any plant of the genus *Geum,* of the rose family.

**GeV,** *Physics.* giga-electron volt.

**gewgaw** /'gigɔ, 'gjugɔ/, *n.* 1. a bit of gaudy or useless finery. *–adj.* 2. showy, but paltry.

**gewurztraminer** /gə'vɜtsˌtræmənə, -trəˌminə/, *n.* a spicy white table wine of the Traminer type. [G]

**geyser** /'gizə, 'gaɪzə/ *for def. 1;* /'gizə/ *for def. 2,* *n.* 1. a hot spring which intermittently sends up fountain-like jets of water and steam into the air. 2. a hot-water heater. [Icel. *Geysir,* i.e. gusher, name of a hot spring in Iceland, from *geysa* rush furiously, gush]

**geyserite** /'gizəraɪt, 'gaɪ-/, *n.* a variety of opaline silica deposited about the orifices of geysers and hot springs; sinter.

**G.G.** /dʒi 'dʒi/; (*joc.*) /'dʒi dʒi/, Governor-General.

**g.gr,** great gross.

**Ghan** /gæn/, *n. Colloq.* 1. an Afghan camel driver among those who came to Australia between 1860 and the 1920s. 2. an Afghan pedlar in the outback. *–adj.* 3. of or pertaining to the Afghan camel drivers. [from *(Af)ghan(istan)*]

**Ghana** /'ganə/, *n.* a republic in West Africa. – **Ghanian,** *adj., n.*

**gharry** /'gæri/, *n.* (in India) a horse-drawn cart or carriage. [Hind. *gari*]

**ghastly** /'gastli/, *adj.,* **-lier, -liest,** *adv.* *–adj.* 1. frightful; dreadful; horrible: *a ghastly murder.* 2. deathly pale: *a ghastly look.* 3. *Colloq.* bad; unpleasant; shocking: *a ghastly failure.* *–adv.* 4. *Archaic.* in a ghastly manner; horribly. 5. *Archaic.* with a deathlike aspect: *ghastly pale.* [ME *gastly,* OE *gāstlic* spectral, from *gāst* spirit + *-lic* -LY] – **ghastliness,** *n.*

**ghat** /gɔt, gat/, *n.* (in India) 1. a passage or stairway descending to a river. 2. a mountain pass. 3. (*pl.*) a range of mountains. Also, **ghaut.** [Hind.]

**ghazi** /'gazi/, *n., pl.* **-zis.** 1. a Muslim warrior fighting against non-Muslims. 2. (*cap.*) a title given in Turkey to a victorious high-ranking warrior, sultan, etc. [Ar., ppr. of *ghazā* fight]

**ghee** /gi/, *n.* a kind of liquid butter, clarified by boiling, made from the milk of cows and buffaloes. [Hind. *ghī*]

**gherkin** /'gɜkən/, *n.* 1. the small, immature fruit of some common varieties of cucumber, used in pickling. 2. the small, spiny fruit of a cucurbitaceous vine, *Cucumis anguria,* of the West Indies, the southern U.S., etc., used in pickling. **3.** the plant yielding it. [var. of *gurchen* (from G), with substitution of -KIN for G diminutive *-chen.* Cf. D *gurkje,* Pol. *ogurek,* etc., from LGk *angoúrion* watermelon]

**ghetto** /ˈgɛtoʊ/, *n., pl.* **ghettos, ghettoes.** a quarter in a city in which any minority group lives. [It. (Venetian), b. Heb. *ghēt* separation and It. *ge(t)to* foundry (from *getar* cast, from L *jacere* throw), as name of Jewish quarter in Venice in the 16th cent.]

**ghilgai** /ˈgɪlgaɪ/, *n.* →**gilgai.**

**ghost** /goʊst/, *n.* **1.** the disembodied spirit of a dead person imagined as wandering among or haunting living persons. **2.** a mere shadow or semblance: *ghost of a chance.* **3.** (*cap.*) a spiritual being: *Holy Ghost.* **4.** *Obs.* spirit; principle of life. **5. give up the ghost, a.** to die. **b.** to despair. **c.** (of a piece of machinery) to break down completely. **6.** *Colloq.* ghost writer. **7.** *Optics, Television.* a bright spot or secondary image, from a defect of the instrument. **8.** a red blood corpuscle with no haemoglobin, rendering it colourless. *–v.t.* **9.** to write for someone else who is publicly known as the author. **10.** to haunt. [ME *goost,* OE *gāst,* c. G *Geist* spirit. Cf. GHASTLY] **– ghostlike,** *adj.*

**ghost bat** /ˈ– bæt/, *n.* a large, cave-dwelling, Australian bat, *Macroderma gigas,* which feeds on birds and small mammals; false vampire.

**ghost gum** /ˈ– gʌm/, *n.* an inland Australian species of *Eucalyptus, E. papuana,* with a smooth white trunk.

**ghostly** /ˈgoʊstli/, *adj.,* **-lier, -liest. 1.** of or pertaining to a ghost; spectral. **2.** *Archaic or Literary.* spiritual. **– ghostliness,** *n.*

**ghost moth** /ˈgoʊst mɒθ/, *n.* →**swift moth.**

**ghost nipper** /ˈ– nɪpə/, *n.* a small, pinkish-white, yabby-like, estuarine, anomuran crustacean, *Trypaea australiensis,* which burrows in soft, muddy sands. [named for its pale colour and habit of nipping]

**ghost shark** /ˈ– ʃak/, *n.* →**rabbit-fish** (def. 2).

**ghost town** /ˈ– taʊn/, *n.* a deserted or semi-deserted town, as a formerly prosperous goldmining town.

**ghost word** /ˈ– wɜd/, *n.* a word with no etymological basis, created through the misunderstanding of an editor, or the mistake of a scribe or printer.

**ghost writer** /ˈ– raɪtə/, *n.* one who does literary work for someone else who takes the credit.

**ghoul** /gul/, *n.* **1.** an evil demon of oriental legend, supposed to feed on human beings, and esp. to rob graves, prey on corpses, etc. **2.** grave robber. **3.** one who revels in what is revolting. [Ar. *ghūl*] **– ghoulish,** *adj.* **– ghoulishly,** *adv.* **– ghoulishness,** *n.*

**G.H.Q.,** General Headquarters.

**Ghurkha** /ˈgɜkə/, *n.* one of a Hindu people whose homeland is now Nepal and whose men have frequently served in the British Army. Also, **gurkha.**

**G.I.**[1] /dʒi ˈaɪ/, *n. Colloq.* **1.** a soldier, usu. other than an officer, in any of the U.S. armed forces. **2.** *U.S. Army.* government issue. *–adj.* **3.** of or standardised by the army: *G.I. shoes.* [abbrev. orig. of *galvanised iron,* used in U.S. Army book-keeping entries of articles made of it; then, by association with *government issue,* of the full range of articles issued and, finally, of the soldiers themselves]

**G.I.**[2] /dʒi ˈaɪ/, *adj. Colloq.* (of a person or place) inconveniently located; inaccessible. [*G(eographically) I(mpossible)*]

**giant** /ˈdʒaɪənt/, *n.* **1.** one of a race of beings in Greek mythology, of more than human size and strength, who were subdued by the Olympian gods. **2.** an imaginary being of human form but superhuman size, strength, etc. **3.** a person or thing of unusually great size, endowments, importance, etc.: *an intellectual giant.* **4.** →**monitor** (def. 5). *–adj.* **5.** gigantic; huge: *the giant cactus.* **6.** great or eminent above others. [ME *geant,* from OF; replacing OE *gīgant,* from L *gigās,* from Gk] **– giantess** /ˈdʒaɪəntɛs/, *n. fem.*

**giant anteater** /– ˈæntitə/, *n.* →**anteater** (def. 3).

**giant beachworm** /– ˈbitʃwɜm/, *n.* a scavenger worm, *Onuphis teres,* which can grow up to two metres in length, and which lives in the sand between high and low tide levels.

**giantism** /ˈdʒaɪəntɪzəm/, *n.* **1.** the quality or character of a giant. **2.** *Pathol.* →**gigantism.**

**giant-killer** /ˈdʒaɪənt-kɪlə/, *n.* an individual, esp. a sportsman or a sporting team, which unexpectedly overcomes an apparently much more powerful rival.

**giant kingfisher** /dʒaɪənt ˈkɪŋfɪʃə/, *n.* →**kookaburra** (def. 1).

**giant lily** /– ˈlɪli/, *n.* →**Gymea lily.**

**giant panic** /– ˈpænɪk/, *n.* a perennial summer-growing drought-resistant grass, *Panicum antidotale,* with strong cane-like stems and large crown development, widely grown as a pasture grass.

**giant perch** /– ˈpɜtʃ/, *n.* a large, silvery-grey, food fish of excellent quality, *Lates calcarifer,* found in coastal rivers and estuaries of tropical northern Australia and the Indo-Pacific; barramundi.

**giant saltbush** /– ˈsɒltbʊʃ/, *n.* →**old-man saltbush.**

**giant skink** /– ˈskɪŋk/, *n.* →**land mullet.**

**giant star** /– ˈsta/, *n.* a star of great luminosity and mass.

**giant wood moth,** *n.* a large, Australian, cossid moth, *Xyleutes durvillei,* having a wingspan of about 17 cm. Its larvae bore into the roots of *Acacia* trees.

**gibber**[1] /ˈdʒɪbə/, *v.i.* **1.** to speak inarticulately; chatter. *–n.* **2.** gibbering utterance. [? frequentative of obs. *gib,* v., caterwaul, behave like a cat; sense development and pronunciation influenced by association with *jabber*]

**gibber**[2] /ˈgɪbə/, *n.* a stone; boulder. [Aboriginal]

**gibber bird** /ˈgɪbə bɜd/, *n.* →**desert chat.**

**gibberellic acid** /dʒɪbəˌrɛlɪk ˈæsəd/, *n.* a metabolic product of the fungus *Gibberella fujikuroa,* $C_{18}H_{21}O_4 \cdot COOH$; stimulates plant growth.

**gibberish** /ˈdʒɪbərɪʃ/, *n.* rapid, unintelligible talk. [GIBBER[1] + -ISH[1] (modelled on *English*)]

**gibber plain** /ˈgɪbə pleɪn/, *n.* a flat tract of desert land in arid regions of Australia on which numerous large boulders occur.

**gibbet** /ˈdʒɪbət/, *n., v.,* **-beted, -beting.** *–n.* **1.** gallows with a projecting arm at the top, from which formerly the bodies of criminals were hung in chains and left suspended after execution. *–v.t.* **2.** to hang on a gibbet. **3.** to put to death by hanging on a gibbet. **4.** to hold up to public scorn. [ME *gibet,* from OF, apparently diminutive of *gibe* staff]

**gibbon** /ˈgɪbən/, *n.* any of the small, slender, long-armed anthropoid apes, genus *Hylobates,* of arboreal habits, found in the East Indies and southern Asia. [F, apparently from a dialect of India]

gibbon

**gibbosity** /gɪˈbɒsəti/, *n., pl.* **-ties. 1.** the state of being gibbous. **2.** a protuberance or swelling.

**gibbous** /ˈgɪbəs/, *adj.* **1.** humpbacked. **2.** (of a heavenly body) so viewed as to appear convex on both margins, as the moon when more than half-full but less than full. Also, **gibbose** /ˈgɪboʊs/. [L *gibbōsus* humped] **– gibbously,** *adv.* **– gibbousness,** *n.*

**gibbsite** /ˈgɪbzaɪt/, *n.* a mineral, hydrated aluminium oxide, $Al_2O_3 \cdot 3H_2O$, occurring in whitish or greyish crystals and masses, an important constituent of bauxite ore. [named after G. *Gibbs,* died 1833, U.S. mineralogist. See -ITE[1]]

**gibe** /dʒaɪb/, *v.,* **gibed, gibing,** *n. –v.i.* **1.** to utter mocking words; scoff; jeer. *–v.t.* **2.** to taunt; deride; flout. *–n.* **3.** a taunting or sarcastic remark. Also, **jibe.** [? from OF *giber* handle roughly, shake, from *gibe* staff, billhook] **– giber,** *n.* **– gibingly,** *adj.*

**giblet** /ˈdʒɪblət/, *n.* (*usu. pl.*) the heart, liver, or gizzard from a fowl, often cooked separately. [ME *gibelet,* from OF: dish of game]

**Gibraltar** /dʒəˈbrɔltə/, *n.* a British crown colony comprising a fortress and seaport situated on a narrow promontory near the southern tip of Spain.

**Gibraltar board** /ˈ– bɔd/, *n. N.Z.* →**plasterboard.**

**gibson girl** /ˈgɪbsən gɜl/, *n.* an emergency radio transceiver. [so called because of its curved shape; after an illustration of an idealised American girl of the 1890s done by C.D. *Gibson,* American illustrator]

**gid** /gɪd/, *n.* a disease in sheep, etc., due to infestation of the brain with larvae of the tapeworm, *Multiceps multiceps;* sturdy. [backformation from GIDDY, *adj.*]

**giddy** /ˈgɪdi/, *adj.*, **-dier, -diest,** *v.*, **-died, -dying.** *–adj.* **1.** frivolously light; impulsive; flighty: *a giddy mind, a giddy girl.* **2.** affected with vertigo; dizzy. **3.** attended with or causing dizziness: *a giddy climb.* *–v.t.* **4.** to make giddy. *–v.i.* **5.** to become giddy. [ME *gidy,* OE *gydig* mad, from *god;* orig. sense presumably god-possessed, in a state of divine frenzy] – **giddily,** *adv.* – **giddiness,** *n.*

**giddy-up** /ˌgɪdi-ˈʌp/, *interj.* (a command to a horse to make it start moving or go faster). Also, **giddup** /gɪdˈʌp/. [var. of *get up*]

**gidgee** /ˈgɪdʒi/, *n.* **1.** a small gregarious Australian tree, *Acacia cambagei,* which gives off an unpleasant odour at the approach of rain; stinking wattle. **2.** any of certain other species of wattle as the poisonous **georgina gidgee,** *Acacia georginae.* **3.** a long spear made from gidgee wood. Also, **gidya** /ˈgɪdiə/, **gidyea** /ˈgɪdiə/. [Aboriginal]

**giegie** /ˈgigi/, *n. N.Z.* →**kiekie.**

**gift** /gɪft/, *n.* **1.** something given; a present. **2.** the act of giving. **3.** the power or right of giving. **4.** a quality, or special ability; natural endowment; talent. **5.** *Colloq.* anything very easily obtained or understood. *–v.t.* **6.** to present with as a gift; bestow gifts upon; endow with. [ME, from Scand.; cf. Icel. *gift,* c. OE *gift* husband's gift to wife at marriage; akin to GIVE *v.*]

**gifted** /ˈgɪftəd/, *adj.* endowed with natural gifts; talented: *a gifted artist.*

**gift-horse** /ˈgɪft-hɔs/, *n. in the phrase* **look a gift-horse in the mouth,** to criticise a gift; accept a gift ungratefully.

**gift of tongues,** *n.* ecstatic utterance used as part of worship by some religious groups. Also, **tongues.**

**gift tax** /ˈgɪft tæks/, *n.* tax paid at the time of making a gift of more than a government-nominated value. Also, **capital transfer tax.**

**gift token** /ˈgɪft toʊkən/, *n.* a voucher given as a present allowing the recipient to choose goods worth a specified amount, usu. from a specified shop. Also, **gift voucher.**

**gift-wrap** /ˈgɪft-ræp/, *v.t.*, **-wrapped, -wrapping.** to wrap (an article) with ornate paper, ribbon, etc., as for a gift. – **gift-wrapping,** *n.*

**gig**[1] /gɪg/, *n.*, *v.*, **gigged, gigging.** *–n.* **1.** *Naut.* **a.** a long, fast-pulling boat used esp. for racing. **b.** the boat reserved for a ship's captain. **2.** a light, two-wheeled one-horse carriage. *–v.i.* **3.** to ride in a gig. [orig. uncert.]

gig[1] (def. 2)

**gig**[2] /gɪg/, *n.*, *v.*, **gigged, gigging.** *–n.* **1.** a spear used in fishing. **2.** a device, commonly four hooks secured back to back, for dragging through a school of fish to hook them through the body. *–v.t.* **3.** to catch (fish) with a gig. *–v.i.* **4.** to fish with a gig. [short for *fizgig,* from Sp. *fisga* harpoon]

**gig**[3] /gɪg/, *v.*, **gigged, gigging,** *n.* *Colloq.* *–v.t.* **1.** to taunt; provoke. *–n.* **2.** a fool; meddler. [Brit. d.]

**gig**[4] /gɪg/, *Colloq.* *–n.* **1.** a booking for a jazzman or pop star to perform at a concert. **2.** a concert of jazz or pop music. **3.** any job or occupation. *–v.i.* **4.** to attend a gig. [orig. unknown]

**gig**[5] /gɪg/, *v.*, **gigged, gigging,** *n.* *Colloq.* *–v.i.* **1.** to watch; stare. *–n.* **2.** an observer; eye witness. **3.** a stickybeak. **4.** →**geek.**

**giga-** /ˈgɪgə-/, a prefix denoting $10^9$ of a given unit, as in *gigametre. Symbol:* G [Gk *gígas* giant]

**giga-electron volt** /ˌgɪgər-əˌlɛktrɒn ˈvoʊlt/, *n.* $10^9$ electron volts. *Abbrev:* GeV; *U.S.,* BeV

**gigantean** /dʒaɪˈgæntiən/, *adj.* gigantic. [L *gigantēus* + -AN. See GIANT]

**gigantesque** /ˌdʒaɪgænˈtɛsk/, *adj.* of a gigantic kind; suited to a giant. [F, from It. *gigantesco,* from *gigante,* from L *gigās* GIANT]

**gigantic** /dʒaɪˈgæntɪk/, *adj.* **1.** of, like, or befitting a giant. **2.** very large; huge. [L *gigās* GIANT + -IC] – **gigantically,** *adv.* – **giganticness,** *n.*

**gigantism** /ˈdʒaɪgæntɪzəm, dʒaɪˈgæntɪzəm/, *n.* abnormally great development in size or stature of the whole body, or of parts of the body, most often due to dysfunction of the pituitary gland. Also, **giantism.**

**gigantomachia** /dʒaɪˌgæntoʊˈmeɪkiə/, *n.* **1.** a war of giants, esp. the war of the giants of Greek mythology against the Olympian gods. **2.** a representation of this, as in sculpture. Also, **gigantomachy** /ˌdʒaɪgænˈtɒməki/. [LL, from Gk: the battle of the giants]

**giggle** /ˈgɪgəl/, *v.*, **-gled, -gling,** *n.* *–v.i.* **1.** to laugh in a silly, undignified way, as from youthful spirits or ill-controlled amusement; titter. *–n.* **2.** a silly, spasmodic laugh; a titter. **3.** *Colloq.* an amusing occasion: *a bit of a giggle.* [apparently backformation from obs. *giglet* giddy, laughing girl, from obs. *gig* flighty, giddy girl. Cf. D *gigelen,* G *gickeln* giggle] – **giggler,** *n.*

**giggle factory** /ˈ– fæktri/, *n.* *Colloq.* a lunatic asylum. Also, **gigglehouse.**

**gigglehat** /ˈgɪgəlhæt/, *n.* *Mil.* a soft hat worn with fatigue dress.

**gigglesuit** /ˈgɪgəlsut/, *n.* **1.** *Mil. Colloq.* →**fatigue dress. 2.** *Prison Colloq. Obs.* prison clothes.

**giggly** /ˈgɪgli/, *adj.*, **-glier, -gliest.** inclined to giggle.

**GIGO** /ˈgigoʊ/, *n.* a situation in which a computer has, usu. inadvertantly, been fed misinformation, resulting in an incorrect output. [*G*(*arbage*) *I*(*n*), *G*(*arbage*) *O*(*ut*)]

**gigolo** /ˈʒɪgəloʊ/, *n.*, *pl.* **-los. 1.** a man supported by a woman, esp. a young man supported by an older woman in return for companionship. **2.** a male professional dancing partner. [F]

**gigot** /ˈdʒɪgət/, *n.* **1.** a leg-of-mutton sleeve. **2.** a leg of mutton. [F, diminutive of d. F *gigue* leg, from *giguer* hop, dance, from OF *gigue* fiddle, from Gmc; cf. G *Geige*]

**gigue** /ʒig/, *n.* **1.** →**jig**[2] (def. 1). **2.** lively music for this dance. **3.** such a piece of music, often forming the concluding movement in the classical suite. [F. See JIG[2]]

**Gila monster** /ˈhilə mɒnstə/, *n.* a large, venomous lizard, *Heloderma suspectum,* of the south-western United States, having the skin studded with yellow or orange and black headlike tubercles. [named after the *Gila* river, in Arizona]

**gilbert** /ˈgɪlbət/, *n.* the c.g.s. unit of magnetomotive force, equal to 0.7958 ampere turns. [named after W. *Gilbert,* 1540-1603, English scientist]

**Gilbertian** /gɪlˈbɜʃən/, *adj.* whimsically or paradoxically humorous in the style of Sir William Schwenk *Gilbert,* 1836-1911, dramatist, humorist and poet; collaborator with Sir Arthur Sullivan in comic operas.

**gild**[1] /gɪld/, *v.t.*, **gilded** or **gilt, gilding. 1.** to coat with gold, gold leaf, or gold-coloured substance. **2.** to give a bright, pleasing, or specious aspect to. **3. gild the lily,** to spoil beauty by overembellishment. **4.** *Obs.* to make red, as with blood. [ME *gilden,* OE *gyldan,* from GOLD. Def. 3 is a misquotation from Shakespeare's *King John,* IV ii 11, 'To gild refined gold, to paint the lily.']

**gild**[2] /gɪld/, *n.* →**guild.** – **gildsman** /ˈgɪldzmən/, *n.*

**gilded** /ˈgɪldəd/, *adj.* **1.** covered or enhanced with gold, or something coloured gold. **2.** having a superficially showy and attractive exterior, covering something of little worth. **3. gilded youth,** a young man of wealth and fashion, usu. idle.

**gilder**[1] /ˈgɪldə/, *n.* one who or that which gilds. [GILD[1] + -ER[1]]

**gilder**[2] /ˈgɪldə/, *n.* →**gulden.**

**gilding** /ˈgɪldɪŋ/, *n.* **1.** the application of gilt. **2.** the gold leaf or other material with which anything is gilded. **3.** the golden surface produced. **4.** any deceptive coating or aspect used to give a fine appearance.

**gilgai** /ˈgɪlgaɪ/, *n.* a natural soil formation occurring extensively in inland Australia, characterised by a markedly undulating surface sometimes with mounds and depressions; probably caused by swelling and cracking of clays during alternating wet and dry seasons; crab-hole country. Also, **ghilgai.** [Aboriginal]

**gilgie** /ˈdʒɪlgi/, *n.* *W.A.* →**yabby** (def. 1). Also, **jilgie.** [Aboriginal]

**gill**[1] /gɪl/, *n.* **1.** an aquatic respiratory organ, either external or internal, usu. feathery, platelike, or filamentous. **2.** one of the radiating vertical plates on the underside of the cap of an agaric. **3.** the ground ivy. **4. fed up to the gills,** *Colloq.*

thoroughly exasperated. **5. white (green) at the gills,** *Colloq.* white-faced through fear, exhaustion, nausea, etc. *–v.t.* **6.** to catch (fish) by the gills in a gill net. **7.** to gut or clean (fish). [ME *gile,* from Scand.; cf. Swed. *gäl,* Dan. *gælle*] – **gilled,** *adj.* – **gill-like,** *adj.*

A

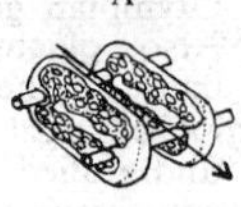

B

gill: A, gill of fish with operculum removed; B, enlarged portion showing capillaries; arrow indicates flow of water

**gill²** /dʒɪl, gɪl/, *n.* a unit of liquid measure in the imperial system, equal to ¼ pint, or 0.142 065 312 5 × $10^{-3}$ $m^3$ (approx. ⅐ litre). [ME *gille,* from OF: wine measure. Cf. GALLON]

**gill fungus** /ˈgɪl fʌŋgəs/, *n.* →**agaric.**

**gillie** /ˈgɪli/, *n., v.,* **-lied, -lying.** *Scot.* *–n.* **1.** a sportsman's attendant, esp. a guide for hunting or fishing. **2.** a male attendant or personal servant of a Highland chieftain. **3.** a low cut shoe with fancy lacing. *–v.t.* **4.** to act as a gillie. Also, **gilly.** [Gaelic *gille* lad, servant]

**gill net** /ˈgɪl nɛt/, *n.* a curtain-like net, suspended vertically in the water, with meshes of such a size as to catch by the gills a fish that has thrust its head through.

**Gill sans** /gɪl ˈsænz/, *n.* (in printing) the first sans-serif type, designed by Eric Gill; cut in 1928.

**gillyflower** /ˈdʒɪliflaʊə/, *n.* **1.** the name for various flowers, as for example, the wallflower, *Cheiranthus cheiri,* the common stock gillyflower, *Matthiola incana,* etc. **2.** *Archaic.* the clove pink. Also, **gilliflower.** [alteration of ME *gilofre,* from OF: clove, from L *caryophyllon,* from Gk *karyóphyllon* clove tree]

**gilt¹** /gɪlt/, *v.* **1.** a past tense and past participle of **gild¹**. *–adj.* **2.** gilded; golden in colour. *–n.* **3.** the gold or other material applied in gilding; gilding. **4. take the gilt of the gingerbread,** *Colloq.* to make a proposition less attractive or desirable.

**gilt²** /gɪlt/, *n.* a sow that has not produced piglets and that has not reached an evident stage of pregnancy. [ME *gilte,* from Scand.; cf. Icel. *gylta*]

**gilt-edged** /ˈgɪlt-ɛdʒd/, *adj.* **1.** having the edges gilded: *gilt-edged paper.* **2.** of the highest order or quality: *gilt-edged securities.*

**gilthead** /ˈgɪlthɛd/, *n.* any of several marine fishes of the family Sparidae having a crescent-shaped golden band across the eyes, especially *Sparus auratus* of the Mediterranean.

**gimbals** /ˈdʒɪmbəlz/, *n.pl.* a contrivance for keeping a suspended object, as a ship's compass, horizontal. [pl. of *gimbal* (now used only attributively and in compounds), var. of *gimmal,* ME *gemel,* from OF: twin]

**gimcrack** /ˈdʒɪmkræk/, *n.* **1.** a showy, useless trifle; gewgaw. *–adj.* **2.** showy but useless. [orig. uncert.]

**gimlet** /ˈgɪmlət/, *n.* **1.** a small tool for boring holes, consisting of a shaft with a pointed screw at one end and a handle at the other. **2.** a tree, *Eucalyptus saluleris,* of western Australia, the bole of which is characteristically twisted and furrowed. *–v.t.* **3.** to pierce with or as with a gimlet. *–adj.* **4.** able to bore through, or penetrate. **5.** deeply penetrating, or thought to be deeply penetrating: *gimlet eyes.* [ME *gymlet,* from OF *guimbelet,* diminutive of **guimbel* WIMBLE]

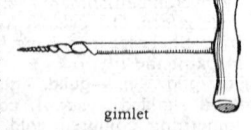

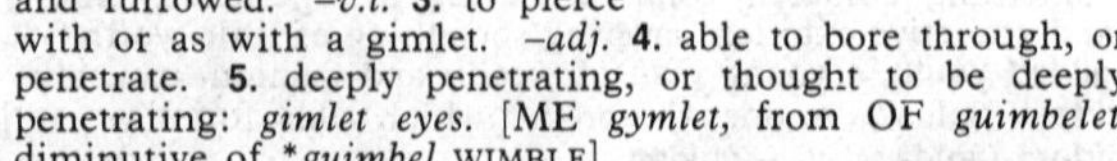

gimlet

**gimme** /ˈgɪmi/, *Colloq.* *–interj.* **1.** give me. *–adj.* **2.** *Golf.* of or pertaining to a putt in which the ball lies so close to the hole that one's opponent concedes that the putt need not be made. **3. gimme girl,** a girl or woman who goes out with or marries a man purely for mercenary motives. *–n.* **4.** *Golf.* a gimme putt.

**gimmick** /ˈgɪmɪk/, *n.* **1.** *Colloq.* a pronounced eccentricity of dress, manner, voice, etc., or an eccentric action or device, esp. one exploited to gain publicity. **2.** any tricky device or means. **3.** *U.S. Colloq.* a device by which a magician works a trick. [? b. *gimmer* trick finger-ring and MAGIC] – **gimmicky,** *adj.*

**gimmickry** /ˈgɪmɪkri/, *n.* gimmicks collectively.

**gimp** /gɪmp/, *n.* a flat trimming of silk, wool, or other cord, sometimes stiffened with wire, for garments, curtains, etc. [apparently from D; ult. orig. unknown]

**gin¹** /dʒɪn/, *n.* **1.** an alcoholic beverage obtained by redistilling spirits with flavouring agents, esp. juniper berries, orange peel, angelica root, etc. **2.** Also, **Hollands gin.** gin flavoured with juniper berries, or similar artificial flavouring. [short for *geneva,* from D *genever,* from OF *genevre,* from L *jūniperus* juniper]

**gin²** /dʒɪn/, *n., v.,* **ginned, ginning.** *–n.* **1.** a machine for separating cotton from its seeds, as a cotton gin. **2.** a trap or snare for game, etc. *–v.t.* **3.** to clear (cotton) of seeds with a gin. **4.** to catch (game, etc.) in a gin. [ME; aphetic var. of OF *engin* ENGINE] – **ginner,** *n.*

**gin³** /gɪn/, *v.i., v.t.,* **gan, gun, ginning.** *Archaic or Poetic.* begin. [ME *ginnen,* OE *ginnan,* aphetic var. of *onginnan.* Cf. OE *beginnan* BEGIN]

**gin⁴** /dʒɪn/, *n.* a card game similar to rummy in which a player with a total of 10 unmatched points or less may end the game. Also, **gin rummy.** [? a pun: *gin* = *rum*]

**gin⁵** /dʒɪn/, *n.* an Aboriginal woman. [Aboriginal]

**gin burglar** /ˈ– bɜglə/, *n.* a white man who has sex with Aboriginal women on a casual basis.

**ging** /gɪŋ/, *n.* a child's catapult.

**gingeli** /ˈdʒɪndʒɪli/, *n.* →**gingili.** Also, **gingelly.**

**ginger** /ˈdʒɪndʒə/, *n.* **1.** the pungent, spicy rhizome of any of the reedlike plants of the genus *Zingiber,* esp. of *Z. officinale,* variously used in cookery and medicine. **2.** any of these plants, native to the East Indies, but now cultivated in most tropical countries. **3.** a reddish brown or tawny colour. **4.** (of hair) red. **5.** *Colloq.* piquancy; animation. *–v.t.* **6.** to treat or flavour with ginger. **7.** *Colloq.* to impart spiciness or piquancy to; make lively. **8.** to steal, esp. as of a prostitute stealing from a man's clothing. [ME *gingivere,* OE *gingifere* from LL *gingiber,* L *zingiberi,* from Gk *zingíberis* ginger, apparently from Prakrit *singabēra*] – **gingerer,** *n.*

**ginger ale** /dʒɪndʒər ˈeɪl/, *n.* a soft drink, flavoured with ginger, used for mixing with spirits, esp. brandy.

**ginger beer** /dʒɪndʒə ˈbɪə/, *n.* a non-alcoholic carbonated drink of water, sugar, yeast, etc., flavoured with ginger.

**ginger beer plant,** *n.* a mixture of yeast and a bacterium used to ferment sugar solution in making ginger beer.

**ginger biscuit** /ˈdʒɪndʒə bɪskət/, *n.* a small, flat, often round biscuit flavoured with ginger.

**gingerbread** /ˈdʒɪndʒəbrɛd/, *n.* **1.** a kind of cake flavoured with ginger and treacle or golden syrup. **2.** something showy but unsubstantial and inartistic. *–adj.* **3.** showy but unsubstantial and inartistic. [alteration of ME *gingimbrat* preserved ginger, from ML **gingimbratum,* from *gingiber* GINGER]

**gingerbread tree** /ˈ– tri/, *n.* a tree, *Parinari macrophyllum,* of western Africa, with a large, edible, farinaceous fruit (**gingerbread plum**).

**ginger group** /ˈdʒɪndʒə grup/, *n.* a splinter group of members of an association, who join together to modernise, activate, or enliven their association and its other members.

**gingerly** /ˈdʒɪndʒəli/, *adv.* **1.** with extreme care or caution; warily. **2.** *Obs.* mincingly; daintily. *–adj.* **3.** cautious or wary. – **gingerliness,** *n.*

**ginger nut** /ˈdʒɪndʒə nʌt/, *n.* →**ginger biscuit.**

**gingerroot** /ˈdʒɪndʒərut/, *n.* →**ginger** (def. 1).

**gingersnap** /ˈdʒɪndʒəsnæp/, *n.* a brittle, wafer-like biscuit flavoured with ginger.

**ginger up** /dʒɪndʒər ˈʌp/, *v.t.* **1.** to increase the energy, gaiety, etc. (of a party or activity). **2.** to make (a group of people) more energetic and efficient.

**gingery** /ˈdʒɪndʒəri/, *adj.* **1.** ginger-like; pungent; spicy. **2.** of the colour of ginger.

**gingham** /ˈgɪŋəm/, *n.* yarn-dyed, plain-weave cotton fabric, usu. striped or checked. [F *guingan,* from Malay *ginggang,* lit., striped]

**gingili** /ˈdʒɪndʒɪli/, *n., pl.* **-lis.** **1.** the sesame (plant). **2.** its oil. Also, **gingeli, gingelly.** [Hind. *jinjalī,* from Ar. *juljulān*]

**gingiva** /dʒɪnˈdʒaɪvə/, *n. Med.* →**gum²**. [L]

**gingival** /dʒɪnˈdʒaɪvəl, ˈdʒɪndʒəvəl/, *adj.* **1.** of or pertaining to the gums. **2.** *Phonet.* made at the gums; alveolar. [L *gingīva* gum + -AL¹]

**gingivitis** /dʒɪndʒəˈvaɪtəs/, *n.* inflammation of the gums.

**ginglymus** /ˈgɪŋgləməs, ˈdʒɪŋ-/, *n.* a joint that permits hinge-like movement in one plane only, as the elbow. [NL, from Gk *ginglymos* hinge] – **ginglymoid,** *adj.*

**gin jockey** /ˈdʒɪn dʒɒki/, *n. Colloq.* a white man who seeks sexual partners among Aboriginal women.

**gink**[1] /gɪŋk/, *n. Colloq.* a look: *have a gink at this.* [var. of GEEK]

**gink**[2] /gɪŋk/, *n. Colloq.* a fellow: *a silly gink.* [Brit. d. *geck, geke,* a fool, simpleton]

**ginkgo** /ˈgɪŋkoʊ/, *n., pl.* **-goes.** a large, ornamental, gymnospermous tree, *Ginkgo biloba,* native to China, with fan-shaped leaves, fleshy fruit, and edible nuts; maidenhair tree. Also, **gingko.** [Jap.]

**ginnery** /ˈdʒɪnəri/, *n., pl.* **-neries.** a mill for ginning cotton.

**gin palace** /ˈdʒɪn pæləs/, *n.* (formerly) a low public house which sold cheap spirits, as gin.

**gin rummy** /dʒɪn ˈrʌmi/, *n.* →**gin**[4].

**ginseng** /ˈdʒɪnsɛŋ/, *n.* **1.** either of two plants, *Panax ginseng* of China, Korea, etc., and *P. quinquefolium* of North America, yielding an aromatic root which is extensively used in medicine by the Chinese. **2.** the root itself. **3.** a preparation made from it. [Chinese (Mandarin) *jên shên,* from *jên* man + *shên,* of obscure meaning]

**gin-sling** /dʒɪn-ˈslɪŋ/, *n.* a long drink made from gin and soda water flavoured with grenadine and lemon juice.

**giocoso** /dʒiəˈkoʊsoʊ/, *adv.* (a musical direction) gaily. [It.] – **giocoso,** *adj.*

**gip**[1] /dʒɪp/, *v.t.,* **gipped, gipping,** *n.* →**gyp**[1]. – **gipper,** *n.*

**gip**[2] /dʒɪp/, *n. Colloq.* **1.** severe pain: *my leg is giving me gip.* **2. give (someone) gip,** to admonish; upbraid. Also, **gyp, jip.**

**gippo** /ˈdʒɪpoʊ/, *n. Colloq.* **1.** an Egyptian. **2.** a gipsy. *–adj.* **3.** Egyptian. **4.** gipsy.

**gipsy** /ˈdʒɪpsi/, *n., pl.* **-sies.** **1.** (*oft. cap.*) one of a nomadic Caucasian minority race of Hindu origin. **2.** (*oft. cap.*) Romany; the language of the gipsies. **3.** a person who resembles or lives like a gipsy. **4.** a wide wheel on a ship's windlass having pockets to grip an anchor cable. *–adj.* **5.** of or pertaining to the gipsies. Also, **gypsy.** [backformation from *gipcyan,* aphetic var. of EGYPTIAN] – **gipsy-like,** *adj.*

**gipsy moth** /– ˈmɒθ/, *n.* a moth, *Lymantria dispar,* whose caterpillar is destructive to trees.

**gipsywort** /ˈdʒɪpsiwɜt/, *n.* an erect perennial herb with small white flowers, *Lycopus europaeus,* family Labiatae, common on the banks of rivers and lakes in Europe and western Asia.

**giraffe** /dʒəˈraf/, *n.* a tall, long-necked, spotted ruminant, *Giraffa camelopardalis,* of Africa, the tallest of existing quadrupeds. [F (now *girafe*), from Ar. *zarāfah,* probably of African orig.]

giraffe

**girandole** /ˈdʒɪrəndoʊl/, *n.* **1.** a rotating and radiating firework. **2.** *Fort.* a group of connected mines. **3.** an ornate branched support for candles or other lights. **4.** a pendant jewel surrounded by smaller jewels. Also, **girandola** /dʒɪˈrændələ/. [F, from It. *girandola,* from *girare* turn, from L *gȳrāre.* See GYRATE]

**girasol** /ˈdʒɪrəsɒl/, *n.* a variety of opal which reflects a floating luminous glow. Also, **girasole, girosol.** [F, from It. *girasole,* from *gira(re)* turn + *sole* sun, in imitation of Gk *hēliotrópion*]

**gird**[1] /gɜd/, *v.t.,* **girt** or **girded, girding.** **1.** to encircle with a belt or girdle. **2.** to surround; hem in. **3.** to prepare (oneself) mentally for action (oft. fol. by *up*). **4.** to endue. [ME *girde(n),* OE *gyrdan,* c. G *gürten*]

**gird**[2] /gɜd/, *v.i.* **1.** to gibe; jeer (fol. by *at*). *–v.t.* **2.** *Obs.* to gibe or jeer at; taunt. *–n.* **3.** *Archaic.* a gibe. [ME; orig. obscure]

**girder** /ˈgɜdə/, *n.* **1.** (in structural work) any main horizontal supporting member or beam, as of steel, reinforced concrete or wood. **2.** one of the principal horizontal timbers which support the joists in certain floors. [GIRD[1] + -ER[1]]

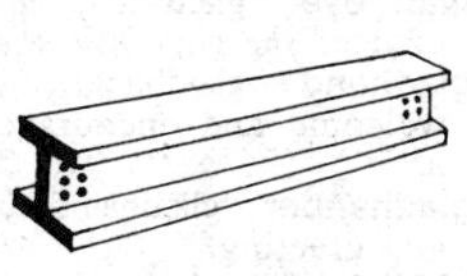

steel girder

**girdle**[1] /ˈgɜdl/, *n., v.,* **-dled, -dling.** *–n.* **1.** a belt, cord, or the like, worn about the waist. **2.** a lightweight undergarment which supports the abdominal region of the body. **3.** any encircling band; compass; limit. **4.** *Gems.* the edge about a brilliant or other cut stone at the junction of the upper and lower faces. **5.** *Anat.* the bony framework which unites the upper or lower extremities to the axial skeleton. **6.** a ring made about a tree trunk, etc., by cutting the bark. *–v.t.* **7.** to encircle with a belt; gird. **8.** to encompass; enclose; encircle. **9.** to cut away the bark in a ring about (a tree, branch, etc.), thus causing death. [ME; OE *gyrdel,* from *gyrdan* GIRD[1]] – **girdle-like,** *adj.* – **girdler,** *n.*

**girdle**[2] /ˈgɜdl/, *n.*→**griddle.**

**girdlecake** /ˈgɜdlkeɪk/, *n.* →**griddlecake.**

**girl** /gɜl/, *n.* **1.** a female child or young person. **2.** a young woman. **3.** a female servant, esp. (in India, Africa, and elsewhere) a native female servant. **4.** *Colloq.* a sweetheart. **5.** *Colloq.* a woman. **6.** See **old girl.** [ME *gurle, girle* child, young person, OE *gyrl-* in *gyrlgyden* virgin goddess. Cf. LG *gör(e)* young person]

**girl Friday** /– ˈfraɪdeɪ/, *n. Colloq.* a female secretary and general assistant in an office.

**girlfriend** /ˈgɜlfrɛnd/, *n.* **1.** a female friend. **2.** a young woman in whom a man or boy has a special interest or to whom he is attracted; a sweetheart.

**girl guide** /gɜl ˈgaɪd/, *n.* a member of an organisation of girls founded in England in 1910 by Lady Agnes Baden-Powell, or an associate organisation in any of several other countries, which aims at developing health, citizenship, character, and home-making ability.

**girlhood** /ˈgɜlhʊd/, *n.* **1.** the state or time of being a girl. **2.** girls collectively.

**girlie** /ˈgɜli/, *Colloq. –n.* **1.** a girl. *–adj.* **2.** illustrating or featuring nude or nearly nude women: *a girlie magazine.*

**girlish** /ˈgɜlɪʃ/, *adj.* of, like, or befitting a girl: *girlish laughter.* – **girlishly,** *adv.* – **girlishness,** *n.*

**girl scout** /gɜl ˈskaʊt/, *n.* a member of any of several sister organisations of the Girl Guides, in the United States and elsewhere.

**girls' night out,** *n. Colloq.* an evening on which a group of women have a night out together.

**girl's week** /ˈgɜlz wik/, *n. Colloq.* the menstrual period.

**girly-girly** /ˈgɜli-ˌgɜli/, *adj.* effusively effeminate in the manner of a small girl.

**girt** /gɜt/, *v.* **1.** a past tense and past participle of **gird**[1]. *–adj.* **2.** *Naut.* (of a vessel) moored so tightly as to prevent swinging.

**girth** /gɜθ/, *n.* **1.** the measure around anything; circumference. **2.** a band passed under the belly of a horse, etc., to secure a saddle or pack on its back. **3.** a band or girdle. *–v.t.* **4.** to bind or fasten with a girth. **5.** to girdle; encircle. [ME *girth, gerth,* from Scand.; cf. Icel. *gjördh* girdle, hoop; akin to GIRD[1]]

**gisarme** /gəˈzam/, *n.* a medieval shafted weapon with a scythelike cutting blade from the back edge of which emerges a long slender blade with a sharp point. [ME *gisharme(e),* from OF *g(u)isarme;* orig. uncert.]

**gismo** /ˈgɪzmoʊ/, *n. Colloq.* a gadget. Also, **gizmo.**

**gist** /dʒɪst/, *n.* **1.** the substance or pith of a matter; essential part: *the gist of an argument.* **2.** the ground on which a legal action rests. [OF, 3rd pers. sing. pres. ind. of *gesir* lie, rest, from L *jacēre*]

**git** /gɪt/, *n. Brit. Colloq.* **1.** a fool. **2.** a bastard.

**gittern** /ˈgɪtɜn/, *n.* →**cittern.** [ME *gitern(e),* from OF *guiterne.* Cf. GUITAR]

**giusto** /ˈdʒʊstoʊ/, *adv.* (in music) a direction that the tempo should be either strictly in accord with that which is marked, as in *allegro giusto,* or appropriate to the piece, as in *tempo giusto.* [It.: just, proper]

**give** /gɪv/, *v.,* **gave, given, giving,** *n.* *–v.t.* **1.** to deliver freely; bestow; hand over: *give someone a present.* **2.** to deliver to another in exchange for something; pay. **3.** to grant permission or opportunity to; enable; assign; award. **4.** to set forth or show; present; offer. **5.** to present to, or as to an audience: *Ladies and Gentleman, I give you the Lord Mayor of Sydney.* **6.** to propose as the subject of a toast: *I give you* *the bride.* **7.** to assign as a basis of calculation or reasoning; suppose; assume: *given these facts.* **8.** to assign to someone as his right, lot, etc.: *to give a child a name, to give him the benefit of the doubt.* **9.** *Orig. U.S. Colloq.* tell; offer as explanation: *don't give me that.* **10.** to be prepared to assign: *I don't give a damn for your views.* **11.** to set aside for a specified purpose: *he gives great attention to detail.* **12.** concede to (someone); admit: *I'll give you that.* **13.** to furnish or provide: *give aid, evidence, etc.* **14.** to afford or yield; produce: *give satisfaction, good results, etc.* **15.** to make, do or perform: *give a start, a lurch, etc.* **16.** to issue; put forth, emit, or utter: *to give a cry, a command, etc.* **17.** to cause: *I was given to understand.* **18.** to impart or communicate: *give advice, give someone a cold.* **19.** to deal or administer: *give one a blow, a medicine, the sacrament, etc.* **20.** to relinquish or surrender: *to give ground, place, etc.* **21.** to put forth; emit (fol. by *off* or *out*). **22.** to produce; present: *to give a play.* **23.** to act as host at (a social function etc.): *to give a party.* **24.** to pledge: *to give one's word of honour.* *–v.i.* **25.** to make a gift or gifts. **26.** to yield, as to pressure or strain; draw back; relax. **27.** to break down; fail. **28.** to be situated facing a specified direction: *the house gives on to the seafront.* **29.** to happen; occur: *what gives in Sydney?* **30.** Some special verb phrases are:

**give away, 1.** to give as a present. **2.** to hand over (the bride) to the bridegroom at a wedding. **3.** to let (a secret) be known. **4.** to betray (a person).

**give (oneself) away,** to reveal something about (oneself) accidentally.

**give birth to, 1.** to bear. **2.** to be the origin of.

**give in, 1.** to yield; acknowledge defeat. **2.** to hand in.

**give (it) away,** to cease to do (something), usu. in exasperation.

**give (it) best,** to acknowledge one's inability to complete an undertaking.

**give of,** to devote; contribute largely.

**give (one) a go,** to allow (one) fair play.

**give out, 1.** to become worn out or used up. **2.** to send out; emit. **3.** to distribute; issue. **4.** to announce publicly. **5.** *Cricket.* (of an umpire) to declare a batsman out.

**give or take,** with an allowance made on either side.

**give over, 1.** to transfer. **2.** to assign for a specific purpose: *the evening was given over to feasting.* **3.** *Colloq.* to desist.

**give rise to,** to be the origin of; cause; result in.

**give up, 1.** to lose all hope. **2.** to abandon as hopeless. **3.** to desist from; forsake: *give up a task.* **4.** to surrender. **5.** to devote entirely. **6.** to inform against.

*–n.* **31.** the act or fact of yielding to pressure; elasticity. [ME, from Scand. (cf. Dan. *give*); replacing ME *yeve(n), yive(n),* OE *gefan, gi(e)fan,* c. D *geven,* G *geben,* Goth. *giban.* Cf. GIFT] **– givable,** *adj.* **– giver,** *n.*

**give-and-take** /gɪv-ən-'teɪk/, *n.* **1.** a method of dealing by compromise or mutual concession; cooperation. **2.** good-humoured exchange of talk, ideas, etc.

**give-away** /'gɪv-əweɪ/, *Colloq.* *–n.* **1.** a betrayal, usu. unintentional: *a dead give-away.* **2.** a premium given with various articles to promote sales, etc. *–adj.* **3.** (of a television program, etc.) characterised by the awarding of prizes, money, etc., to recipients chosen, usu. through a question-and-answer contest.

**given** /'gɪvən/, *v.* **1.** past participle of **give.** *–adj.* **2.** stated, fixed, or specified: *at a given time.* **3.** addicted or disposed (fol. by *to*): *given to drink.* **4.** bestowed as a gift; conferred. **5.** assigned as a basis of calculation, reasoning, etc.: *given A and B, C follows.* **6.** *Maths.* known or determined: *a given magnitude.* **7.** (on official documents) executed and delivered as of the date specified.

**given name** /'– neɪm/, *n.* →**forename.**

**give-way sign** /gɪv-'weɪ saɪn/, *n.* a traffice sign instructing a driver to yield the right of way to traffic from any direction on the road he is joining.

**givor** /'gaɪvə/, *n.* →**guyver.** Also, **givo** /'gaɪvoʊ/.

**gizmo** /'gɪzmoʊ/, *n. Colloq.* →**gismo.**

**gizzard** /'gɪzəd/, *n.* **1.** the grinding or muscular stomach of birds, the organ in which food is triturated after leaving the glandular stomach; ventriculus. **2.** *Colloq.* the heart. [ME *giser,* from OF, from L *gigēria* cooked entrails of poultry]

**Gk,** Greek.

**gl., 1.** gill. **2.** glass. **3.** gloss.

**Gl,** *Chem.* glucinum.

**glabella** /glə'bɛlə/, *n.* the flat area of bone between the eyebrows, used as a craniometric point. [NL, properly fem. of L *glabellus* smooth, hairless, diminutive of *glaber.* See GLABROUS]

**glabellum** /glə'bɛləm/, *n., pl.* **-bella** /-'bɛlə/. →**glabella.**

**glabrate** /'gleɪbreɪt, -brət/, *adj.* **1.** *Zool.* smooth; glabrous. **2.** *Bot.* becoming glabrous; somewhat glabrous.

**glabrous** /'gleɪbrəs/, *adj.* smooth; having a surface devoid of hair or pubescence. [L *glaber* smooth, hairless + -OUS]

**glacé** /'glæseɪ, 'gla-/, *adj.* **1.** iced or sugared, as cake. **2.** crystallised, as fruits. **3.** finished with a gloss, as kid or silk. **4.** *U.S.* frozen. [F, pp. of *glacer,* from *glace* ice, from L *glacies*]

**glacial** /'gleɪʃəl, 'gleɪsiəl/, *adj.* **1.** characterised by the presence of ice in extensive masses or glaciers. **2.** due to or associated with the action of ice or glaciers. **3.** of or pertaining to glaciers or ice sheets. **4.** cold as ice; icy. **5.** *Chem.* of or tending to assume an icelike form, as certain acids. [L *glaciālis* icy] **– glacially,** *adv.*

**glacial acetic acid,** *n.* a 99.5 per cent concentration of acetic acid.

**glacial epoch** /gleɪʃəl 'ipɒk/, *n.* **1.** the geologically recent Pleistocene epoch, during which much of the Northern Hemisphere was covered by great ice sheets; ice age. **2.** any of the glaciations or ice ages of past geological periods as during the Permian and late Pre-Cambrian in Australia.

**glacial meal** /'– mil/, *n.* →**rock-flour.**

**glaciate** /'gleɪsieɪt, 'gleɪʃieɪt/, *v.t.,* **-ated, -ating. 1.** to cover with ice or glaciers. **2.** to affect by glacial action. **– glaciation** /gleɪsi'eɪʃən/, *n.*

**glacier** /'gleɪsiə, 'glæsiə/, *n.* an extended mass of ice formed from snow falling and accumulating over the years and moving very slowly, either descending from high mountains, as in valley glaciers, or moving outwards from centres of accumulation, as in continental glaciers. [F, from *glace* ice, from L *glacies*] **– glaciered,** *adj.*

**glaciology** /gleɪsi'ɒlədʒi/, *n.* the study of ice and geological phenomena involving the action of ice. **– glaciologist,** *n.* **– glaciological** /gleɪsiə'lɒdʒɪkəl/, *adj.*

**glacis** /'glæsəs, 'glæsi/, *n.* **1.** a gentle slope. **2.** a bank of earth in front of the counterscarp or covered way of a fort, having an easy slope towards the field or open country. [F: orig., icy or slippery place, from OF *glacier* slip. See GLACÉ]

**glad**[1] /glæd/, *adj.,* **gladder, gladdest. 1.** delighted or pleased (fol. by *of, at,* etc., or an infinitive or clause): *to be glad at the news, glad to go, glad that one has come.* **2.** characterised by or showing cheerfulness, joy, or pleasure, as looks, utterances, etc. **3.** attended with or causing joy or pleasure: *a glad occasion, glad tidings.* **4.** willing. **5. the glad eye,** an inviting or flirtatious look: *she gave him the glad eye.* **6. the glad hand,** (*usu. ironic*) a welcome; greeting: *give someone the glad hand.* *–v.t.* **7.** *Archaic.* to make glad. [ME; OE *glæd,* c. Icel. *gladhr* bright, glad, D *glad* and G *glatt* smooth; akin to L *glaber* smooth] **– gladly,** *adv.* **– gladness,** *n.*

**glad**[2] /glæd/, *n. Colloq.* →**gladiolus.**

**gladbag** /'glædbæg/, *n.* a plastic bag with flap, suitable for packaging food, etc. [Trademark]

**gladden** /'glædn/, *v.t.* to make glad. **– gladdener,** *n.*

**gladdie** /'glædi/, *n. Colloq.* →**gladiolus.**

**gladdon** /'glædn/, *n.* a dark green perennial herb, *Iris foetidissima,* widespread in western Europe and northern Africa, usu. on calcareous soils.

**glade** /gleɪd/, *n.* an open space in a forest. [akin to GLAD[1] (in obs. sense 'bright')]

**glad eye** /'glæd aɪ/, *n. Colloq.* an inviting or provocative glance: *she gave him the glad eye.*

**gladhand** /'glædhænd/, *v.t.* (*usu. ironic*) to extend effusive welcome and encouragement, often publicly. **– gladhanding,** *n.*

**gladhander** /'glædhændə/, *n.* one who is effusive in welcome and greeting.

**gladiate** /'glædiət, -eɪt, 'gleɪd-/, *adj.* sword-shaped. [L *gladius* sword + -ATE[1]]

**gladiator** /ˈglædieɪtə/, *n.* **1.** *Rom. Hist.* a person, often a slave or captive, who fought in public with a sword or other weapon to entertain the people. **2.** one who takes up a cause or right; a controversialist. [L]

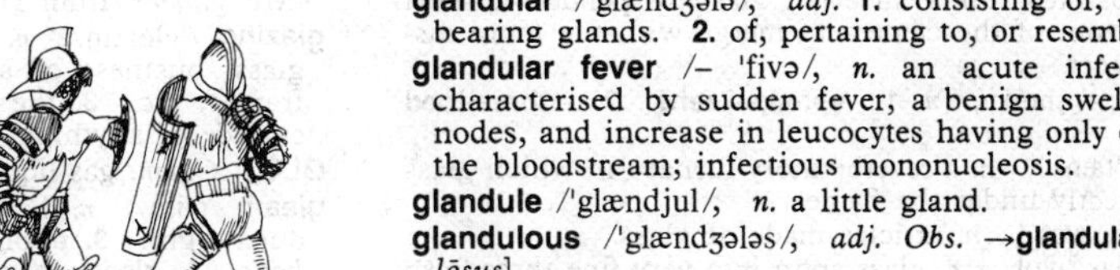
gladiator

**gladiatorial** /ˌglædiəˈtɔriəl/, *adj.* pertaining to gladiators or to their combats.

**gladiola** /glædiˈoʊlə/, *n.* a gladiolus. [L, neut. pl. treated as if fem. sing. See GLADIOLUS]

**gladiolus** /glædiˈoʊləs/, *n., pl.* **-lus, -li** /laɪ/, **-luses.** any plant of the genus *Gladiolus,* native mainly to South Africa, with erect leaves, and spikes of variously coloured flowers; sword lily. [L, diminutive of *gladius* sword]

**glad rags** /ˈglæd rægz/, *n.pl. Colloq.* best clothes donned for special occasions.

**gladsome** /ˈglædsəm/, *adj.* **1.** making joyful; delightful. **2.** glad. – **gladsomely,** *adv.* – **gladsomeness,** *n.*

**Gladstone bag** /glædstən ˈbæg/, *n.* a light travelling bag or small portmanteau hinged to open into two compartments. [named after William Ewart *Gladstone,* 1809-98, British statesman]

**gladwrap** /ˈglædræp/, *n.* thin, clear plastic wrapping, usu. for packaging food, etc. [Trademark]

**glair** /glɛə/, *n.* **1.** the white of an egg. **2.** a glaze or size made of it. **3.** any viscous substance like eggwhite. *–v.t.* **4.** to coat with glair. [ME *glaire,* from OF, from L *clārus* clear]

**glairy** /ˈglɛəri/, *adj.* **1.** of the nature of glair; viscous. **2.** covered with glair. Also, **glaireous** /ˈglɛəriəs/. – **glairiness,** *n.*

**glaive** /gleɪv/, *n. Archaic.* a sword or broadsword. [ME *gleyve,* from OF *glaive* lance, sword, from L *gladius* sword]

**glam** /glæm/, *Colloq. –adj.* **1.** →**glamorous.** *–n.* **2.** →**glamour.**

**glamorise** /ˈglæməraɪz/, *v.t.,* **-rised, -rising.** to make glamorous or give an appearance of glamour to. Also, **glamorize.**

**glamorous** /ˈglæmərəs/, *adj.* full of glamour or charm. Also, **glamourous.** – **glamorously,** *adv.*

**glamour** /ˈglæmə/, *n.* **1.** alluring and often illusory charm; fascination. **2.** magic or enchantment; spell; witchery. Also, *U.S.,* **glamor.** [earlier *glammar,* dissimilated var. of GRAMMAR in sense of 'occult learning', 'magic']

**glance**[1] /glæns, glans/, *v.,* **glanced, glancing,** *n. –v.i.* **1.** to look quickly or briefly. **2.** to gleam or flash. **3.** to go off in an oblique direction from an object struck: *a missile glances away.* **4.** to allude briefly in passing. *–v.t.* **5.** *Obs.* to cast a glance or brief look at; catch a glimpse of. **6.** to cast or reflect, as a gleam. *–n.* **7.** a quick or brief look. **8.** a gleam or flash of light. **9.** a glancing off, as of a missile after striking. **10.** a reference in passing. **11.** *Cricket.* a stroke in which the ball is allowed to glance off the bat. [late ME; nasalised var. of ME *glacen* strike a glancing blow, from OF *glacer* slip]

**glance**[2] /glans/, *n.* any of various minerals having a lustre which indicates their metallic nature. [G *Glanz,* lit., brightness, lustre]

**gland**[1] /glænd/, *n.* **1.** *Anat.* **a.** an organ or tissue which elaborates and discharges a substance which is used elsewhere in the body (*secretion*), or eliminated (*excretion*). **b.** any of various organs or structures likened to true glands. **2.** *Bot.* a secreting organ or structure, esp. one on or near a surface. [F *glande,* from OF *glandre,* from L *glandula,* diminutive of *glans* acorn] – **glandless,** *adj.* – **glandlike,** *adj.*

**gland**[2] /glænd/, *n.* a device for preventing a fluid from leaking from any container or vessel where a rotating or reciprocating shaft emerges from it. [? special use of GLAND[1]]

**glandered** /ˈglændəd/, *adj.* affected with glanders.

**glanders** /ˈglændəz/, *n.* a contagious disease of horses, mules, etc., communicable to man, due to a micro-organism (*Bacillus mallei*), and characterised by swellings beneath the jaw and a profuse mucous discharge from the nostrils. [late ME, from OF *glandres,* from L *glandulae* (swollen) glands] – **glanderous,** *adj.*

**glandular** /ˈglændʒələ/, *adj.* **1.** consisting of, containing, or bearing glands. **2.** of, pertaining to, or resembling a gland.

**glandular fever** /– ˈfivə/, *n.* an acute infectious disease characterised by sudden fever, a benign swelling of lymph nodes, and increase in leucocytes having only one nucleus in the bloodstream; infectious mononucleosis.

**glandule** /ˈglændjul/, *n.* a little gland.

**glandulous** /ˈglændʒələs/, *adj. Obs.* →**glandular.** [L *glandulōsus*]

**glans** /glænz/, *n., pl.* **glandes** /ˈglændiz/. the head of the penis (**glans penis**) or of the clitoris (**glans clitoridis**). [L: lit., acorn]

**glare**[1] /glɛə/, *n., v.,* **glared, glaring.** *–n.* **1.** a strong, dazzling light; brilliant lustre. **2.** dazzling or showy appearance; showiness. **3.** a fierce or piercing look. *–v.i.* **4.** to shine with a strong, dazzling light. **5.** to be too brilliantly ornamented. **6.** to be intensely bright in colour. **7.** to be conspicuous. **8.** to look with a fierce or piercing stare. *–v.t.* **9.** to express with a glare. [ME *glaren,* c. MD and MLG *glaren;* akin to GLASS (cf. OE *glæren* glassy)]

**glare**[2] /glɛə/, *n.* **1.** a bright, smooth surface, as of ice. *–adj.* **2.** bright and smooth; glassy: *glare ice.* [special uses of GLARE[1]]

**glaring** /ˈglɛərɪŋ/, *adj.* **1.** that glares; brilliant; dazzling. **2.** excessively bright; garish. **3.** very conspicuous: *glaring defects.* **4.** staring fiercely. – **glaringly,** *adv.* – **glaringness,** *n.*

**glary** /ˈglɛəri/, *adj.* brilliant; glaring. [GLARE[1] + -Y[1]]

**glass** /glas/, *n.* **1.** a hard, brittle, more or less transparent substance produced by fusion, usu. consisting of mutually dissolved silica and silicates (the ordinary variety used for windows, bottles, and the like, containing silica, soda, and lime). See **crown glass** and **flint glass. 2.** any artificial or natural substance having similar properties and composition, as fused borax, obsidian, etc. **3.** something made of glass, as a window, mirror, lens, barometer, etc. **4.** (*pl.*) a device to aid defective vision, consisting usu. of two glass lenses set in a frame which rests on the nose and is held in place by pieces passing over the ears. **5.** things made of glass collectively; glassware. **6.** a glass container for drinking water, beer, etc. **7.** quantity or contents of a drinking glass; glassful. **8.** →**volcanic glass.** *–adj.* **9.** made of glass. **10.** furnished or fitted with panes of glass; glazed. *–v.t.* **11.** to fit with panes of glass; cover with or encase in glass. **12.** *Poetic.* to reflect: *trees glass themselves in the lake.* [ME *glas,* OE *glæs,* c. D *glas* and G *Glas*] – **glassless,** *adj.* – **glasslike,** *adj.*

**glass-blowing** /ˈglas-bloʊɪŋ/, *n.* **1.** the art or process of forming glass into ware by blowing by mouth or mechanically. **2.** the operation of working glass in a flame, starting with tubing, rod, or cane, and forming laboratory apparatus, ornaments, or knick-knacks. – **glass-blower,** *n.*

**glass brick** /glas ˈbrɪk/, *n.* a hollow block of translucent glass, usu. with one surface patterned, used in constructing partitions, etc.

**glass can** /– ˈkæn/, *n. Colloq.* →**stubby** (def. 6).

**glass-cutter** /ˈglas-kʌtə/, *n.* **1.** a person who cuts or etches the surface of glass. **2.** a tool for cutting glass.

**glass fibre** /ˈglas faɪbə/, *n.* →**fibreglass.**

**glassful** /ˈglasfʊl/, *n., pl.* **-fuls.** as much as a glass holds.

**glass harmonica** /ˌglas haˈmɒnɪkə/, *n.* an instrument consisting of a series of glass bowls graduated in size which can be played by the friction of the moistened finger.

**glasshouse** /ˈglashaʊs/, *n.* **1.** →**greenhouse. 2.** *Brit. Mil. Colloq.* a military prison.

**glassine** /glæˈsin/, *n.* a glazed, semitransparent paper, used for book jackets, etc.

**glass jaw** /glas ˈdʒɔ/, *n. Boxing.* a jaw which is more than commonly susceptible to injury.

**glassmaking** /ˈglasmeɪkɪŋ/, *n.* the art of making glass or glassware. – **glassmaker,** *n.*

**glassman** /ˈglasmən/, *n., pl.* **-men. 1.** one who makes or sells glass. **2.** →**glazier.**

**glasspaper** /ˈglaspeɪpə/, *n.* **1.** a strong paper coated with a layer of glass particles, resembling sandpaper. *–v.t.* **2.** to smooth or polish with glasspaper.

**glass shot** /ˈglas ʃɒt/, *n.* a film shot involving a setting, only part of which is constructed full-size, the remainder being fixed, usu. painted, on a sheet of glass suspended a short distance in front of the camera to merge with the more distant full-size set.

**glass snake** /'– sneɪk/, *n.* **1.** →**snake-lizard.** **2.** →**three-toed skink.**

**glass tank** /– 'tæŋk/, *n.* a reverberatory furnace in which glass is melted directly under the flames.

**glassware** /'glaswɛə/, *n.* articles made of glass.

**glass wool** /glas 'wʊl/, *n.* glass spun into very fine threads so that it resembles cottonwool; used in filtering corrosive liquids, for insulation, etc.

**glasswork** /'glaswɜk/, *n.* **1.** the manufacture of glass and glassware. **2.** the fitting of glass; glazing. **3.** articles of glass collectively; glassware. – **glassworker,** *n.*

**glassworks** /'glaswɜks/, *n.pl. or sing.* a factory in which glass is manufactured.

**glasswort** /'glaswɜt/, *n.* **1.** any of the herbs with succulent leafless stems constituting the genus *Salicornia* and related plants, and formerly much used (when burnt to ashes) as a source of soda for glass-making. **2.** the saltwort, *Salsola kali* (**prickly glasswort**).

**glassy** /'glasi/, *adj.*, **glassier, glassiest,** *n.* –*adj.* **1.** resembling glass, as in transparency, smoothness, etc. **2.** having a fixed, unintelligent stare. **3.** of the nature of glass; vitreous. **4. the glassy eye,** *Colloq.* a glance of cold disdain. –*n.* **5.** *Colloq.* a much-prized, clear-glass marble. **6. the glassy,** *Colloq.* the best; the most superior. – **glassily,** *adv.* – **glassiness,** *n.*

**glauberite** /'glɔbəraɪt, 'glaʊ-/, *n.* a mineral sulphate of calcium and sodium, $Na_2Ca(SO_4)_2$, usu. occurring with rock salt in saline deposits. [named after J. R. *Glauber.* See GLAUBER SALT]

**Glauber salt** /'glɔbə sɒlt, 'glaʊ-/, *n.* sodium sulphate, used as a cathartic, etc. Also, **Glauber's salt.** [named after J. R. *Glauber,* 1604-68, German chemist]

**glaucoma** /glɔ'koʊmə/, *n.* a disease of the eye, characterised by increased pressure within the eyeball with progressive loss of vision. [Gk *glaúkōma* opacity of the crystalline lens. See GLAUCOUS] – **glaucomatous** /glɔ'koʊmətəs, -'kɒmə-/, *adj.*

**glauconite** /'glɔkənaɪt/, *n.* a greenish micaceous mineral, essentially a hydrous silicate of potassium, aluminium and iron and occurring in greensand, clay, etc., of marine origin. [Gk *glaukon,* neut. adj., bluish green + -ITE[1]] – **glauconitic** /glɔkə'nɪtɪk/, *adj.*

**glaucous** /'glɔkəs/, *adj.* **1.** light bluish green or greenish blue. **2.** *Bot.* covered with a whitish bloom, as a plum. [L *glaucus,* from Gk *glaukós* gleaming, silvery, grey, bluish green]

**glaucous gull** /'– gʌl/, *n.* a large white and pale grey gull, *Latus hyperboreus,* of arctic regions.

**Glavert's land snail,** *n.* a nocturnal snail, *Bothriembryon glaverti,* with a cream-coloured shell, found in leaf litter and around tree roots.

**glaze** /gleɪz/, *v.*, **glazed, glazing,** *n.* –*v.t.* **1.** to furnish or fit with glass; cover with glass. **2.** to produce a vitreous or glossy surface on (pottery, pastry, etc.). **3.** to cover with glaze. **4.** *Painting.* to cover (a painted surface or parts of it) with a thin layer of transparent colour in order to modify the tone. **5.** to cover with a smooth lustrous coating; give a glassy surface to, as by polishing. –*v.i.* **6.** to become glazed or glassy. –*n.* **7.** a smooth, glossy surface or coating. **8.** the substance for producing it. **9.** *Ceramics.* **a.** the vitreous or glossy surface or coating on glazed pottery. **b.** the substance or material used to produce such a surface. **10.** *Painting.* a thin layer of transparent colour, spread over a painted surface. **11.** a smooth glossy surface on certain fabrics, produced by means of a friction calender. **12.** *Cookery.* **a.** something used to coat a food, as egg-white on pastry before cooking, or as a syrup applied to a cooked tart. **b.** stock cooked down to a thin paste, for applying to the surface of meats. **13.** *U.S.* glaze ice. [ME *glasen,* from *glas* GLASS] – **glazer,** *n.* – **glazy,** *adj.*

**glaze ice** /'– aɪs/, *n.* a smooth layer of ice which is sometimes formed on terrestrial objects or aircraft when rain is falling and the ground or air temperatures are below freezing point; silver frost. Also, **glazed frost.**

**glazier** /'gleɪziə/, *n.* one who fits windows, etc., with glass. [ME *glasier,* from *glas* GLASS + -IER]

**glazing** /'gleɪzɪŋ/, *n.* **1.** the act of furnishing or fitting with glass; business of a glazier. **2.** glass set, or to be set, in frames, etc. **3.** the act of applying a glaze. **4.** the glassy surface of anything glazed.

**GLC,** *Chem.* gas-liquid chromatography.

**gleam** /glim/, *n.* **1.** a flash or beam of light. **2.** dim or subdued light. **3.** a brief or slight manifestation: *a gleam of hope.* **4. gleam in one's eye,** a look betokening humour or unstated intentions. –*v.i.* **5.** to send forth a gleam or gleams. **6.** to appear suddenly and clearly, like a flash of light. [ME *glem(e),* OE *glæm,* c. OHG *gleimo* glow-worm; akin to OS *glīmo* brightness, etc. See GLIMMER, GLIMPSE]

**gleaming** /'glimɪŋ/, *adj.* beaming; cheerful, as a smile which discloses one's teeth.

**glean** /glin/, *v.t.* **1.** to gather slowly and laboriously in bits. **2.** to gather (grain, etc.) after the reapers or regular gatherers. **3.** to discover or find out. –*v.i.* **4.** to collect or gather anything little by little or slowly. **5.** to gather what is left by reapers. [ME *glene(n),* from OF *glener,* from LL *glenāre,* of Celtic orig.] – **gleaner,** *n.*

**gleaning** /'glinɪŋ/, *n.* **1.** the act of one who gleans. **2.** (*usu. pl.*) that which is gleaned.

**glebe** /glib/, *n.* **1.** →**glebe land.** **2.** *Poetic.* soil; field. [ME, from L *glēba, glaeba* clod, soil, land]

**glebe house** /'– haʊs/, *n.* a dwelling whose rental is available to augment the stipend of the incumbent of the parish or cure specified.

**glebe land** /'– lænd/, *n.* land bequeathed to a specified parish or benefice so that its rental or crops may be employed to augment the income of their incumbent.

**glee** /gli/, *n.* **1.** demonstrative joy; exultation. **2.** a kind of unaccompanied part-song, grave or joyful, for three or more voices. [ME; OE *glēo,* c. Icel. *glȳ*]

**glee club** /'– klʌb/, *n.* a club or group for singing choral music.

**gleeful** /'glifəl/, *adj.* full of glee; merry; exultant. – **gleefully,** *adv.* – **gleefulness,** *n.*

**gleeman** /'glimæn/, *n.*, *pl.* **-men.** *Archaic.* a strolling professional singer or minstrel. [OE *glēomann*]

**gleesome** /'glisəm/, *adj.* →**gleeful.** – **gleesomely,** *adv.* – **gleesomeness,** *n.*

**gleet** /glit/, *n.* **1.** a thin, morbid discharge, as from a wound. **2.** a persistent or chronic gonorrhoea. [ME *glette,* from OF: slime, mucus, pus, foul matter]

**gleisoil** /'gleɪsɔɪl/, *n.* a greyish soil of poor quality, the result of impeded drainage. Also, **gley soil.**

**glen** /glɛn/, *n.* a small, narrow, secluded valley. [ME, from Gaelic *gle(a)nn,* c. Welsh *glyn*]

**glengarry** /glɛn'gæri/, *n.*, *pl.* **-ries.** a Scottish Highlander's cap, with straight sides, a crease along the top, and sometimes short ribbon streamers at the back, worn by Highlanders as part of military dress. [named after *Glengarry,* valley in Inverness-shire, Scotland]

**glenoid** /'glinɔɪd/, *adj.* **1.** shallow or slightly cupped, as the articular cavities of the scapula. **2.** pertaining to such a cavity. [Gk *glēnoeidḗs* like a shallow joint socket. See -OID]

**gliadin** /'glaɪədən/, *n.* a prolamine obtained from wheat and rye. Also, **gliadine** /'glaɪədin, -daɪn/.

**glib** /glɪb/, *adj.*, **glibber, glibbest.** **1.** ready and fluent, often thoughtlessly or insincerely so: *glib speakers, a glib tongue.* **2.** easy, as action or manner. [backformation from obs. *glibbery* slippery, from D *glibberig*] – **glibly,** *adv.* – **glibness,** *n.*

**glide** /glaɪd/, *v.*, **glided, gliding,** *n.* –*v.i.* **1.** to move smoothly along, as if without effort or difficulty, as a flying bird, a boat, a skater, etc. **2.** to pass by gradual or insensible change (oft. fol. by *along, away, by,* etc.). **3.** to go quietly or unperceived; slip (fol. by *in, out,* etc.). **4.** *Aeron.* to move in the air, esp. at an easy angle downwards, by the action of gravity or by virtue of momentum already acquired. **5.** *Music.* to pass from note to note without a break; slur. –*v.t.* **6.** to cause to glide. –*n.* **7.** a gliding movement, as in dancing. **8.** a dance in which such movements are employed. **9.** *Music.* →**slur** (def. 8a). **10.** *Phonet.* **a.** a transitional sound produced while passing from the articulation required by one speech sound to that required by the next, such as the 'y' sound often heard between the *i* and *e* of *quiet.* **b.** →**semivowel. 11.** *Cricket.* the deflection of a ball by the batsman to the leg side. [ME *glide(n),* OE *glīdan,* c. G *gleiten*] – **glidingly,** *adv.*

**glide path** /'– paθ/, *n.* the path followed by an aeroplane as it glides towards a landing.

**glider** /'glaɪdə/, *n.* **1.** one who or that which glides. **2.** a small cup-shaped mould in which the legs of chairs, etc., are stood to prevent them marking the floor. **3.** *Aeron.* a motorless aeroplane for gliding from a higher to a lower level by the action of gravity, or from a lower to a higher level by the action of air currents.

**glider-tug** /'glaɪdə-tʌg/, *n.* a powered aircraft which tows gliders.

**gliding** /'glaɪdɪŋ/, *n.* the sport of flying in a glider.

**gliding possum** /'– pɒsəm/, *n.* any of the arboreal marsupials of Australia and the island of New Guinea, having a parachute-like membrane along the side of the body by which they are able to glide. They range from the pigmy glider, *Acrobates pygmaeus,* the size of a mouse, to the large greater glider, *Schoinobates volans;* flying phalanger. Also, **flying possum.**

**gliding time** /'– taɪm/, *n.* →**flexitime.**

**glimmer** /'glɪmə/, *n.* **1.** a faint or unsteady light; gleam. **2.** a dim perception; inkling. *–v.i.* **3.** to shine faintly or unsteadily; twinkle; flicker. **4.** to appear faintly or dimly. [ME *glemer(en)* gleam, c. G *glimmern.* Cf. OE *gleomu* splendour]

**glimmering** /'glɪmərɪŋ/, *n.* **1.** a faint or unsteady light; a glimmer. **2.** a faint glimpse; inkling. – **glimmeringly,** *adv.*

**glimpse** /glɪmps/, *n., v.,* **glimpsed, glimpsing.** *–n.* **1.** a momentary sight or view. **2.** a momentary or slight appearance. **3.** a vague idea; inkling. **4.** *Archaic.* a gleam, as of light. *–v.t.* **5.** to catch a glimpse of. *–v.i.* **6.** to look briefly, or glance (fol. by *at*). **7.** *Poetic.* to come into view; appear faintly. [ME *glymsen,* c. MHG *glimsen* glow; akin to GLIMMER] – **glimpser,** *n.*

**glint** /glɪnt/, *n.* **1.** a gleam or glimmer; flash. **2.** glinting brightness; lustre. *–v.i.* **3.** to gleam or flash. **4.** to move suddenly; dart. *–v.t.* **5.** to cause to glint; reflect. [ME *glynt,* var. of obs. *glent,* from Scand.; cf. d. Swed. *glänta, glinta* slip, shine]

**glioma** /glaɪ'oʊmə/, *n., pl.* **-mata** /mətə/, **-mas.** a tumour arising from and consisting of neuroglia. [NL, from Gk *glía* glue + *-ōma* -OMA] – **gliomatous** /glaɪ'oʊmətəs/, *adj.*

**glissade** /glɪ'sad, -'seɪd/, *n., v.,* **-saded, -sading.** *–n.* **1.** *Skiing.* a skilful glide over snow or ice in descending a mountain. **2.** *Dancing.* a sliding or gliding step. *–v.i.* **3.** to perform a glissade. [F, from *glisser* slip, slide, b. OF *glacier* slip and *glier* slide (from Gmc; cf. GLIDE)]

**glissando** /glɪ'sændoʊ/, *adj., n., pl.* **-di** /-di/. *–adj.* **1.** performed with a gliding effect as by sliding one finger rapidly over the keys of a piano or strings of a harp. *–n.* **2.** any sliding effect performed on a musical instrument. **3.** (in string playing) →**slide.** [pseudo-It., from F *glissant,* ppr. of *glisser* slide]

**glisten** /'glɪsən/, *v.i.* **1.** to shine with a sparkling light or a faint intermittent glow. *–n.* **2.** a glistening; sparkle. [ME *glis(t)nen,* OE *glisnian,* from *glisian* glitter. See -EN[1]] – **glisteningly,** *adv.*

**glister** /'glɪstə/, *Archaic.* *–v.i.* **1.** to glisten; glitter. *–n.* **2.** a glistening; glitter. [ME; frequentative of obs. v. *glist* glitter, var. of GLISTEN (? backformation)]

**glitch** /glɪtʃ/, *n. Colloq.* **1.** an extraneous electric current or signal, esp. one that interferes in some way with the functioning of a system. **2.** a hitch; snag; malfunction.

**glitter** /'glɪtə/, *v.i.* **1.** to shine with a brilliant, sparkling light or lustre. **2.** to make a brilliant show: *glittering scenes of a court.* *–n.* **3.** glittering light or lustre; splendour. [ME, from Scand.; cf. Icel. *glitra,* frequentative of *glita* shine; cf. OE *glitenian,* G *gleissen* shine, glitter] – **glitteringly,** *adv.*

**glittery** /'glɪtəri/, *adj.* glittering; sparkling.

**gloaming** /'gloʊmɪŋ/, *n. Poetic.* twilight; dusk. [ME *gloming,* OE *glōmung,* from *glōm* twilight]

**gloat** /gloʊt/, *v.i.* **1.** to gaze with exultation; dwell mentally upon something with intense (and often evil) satisfaction: *to gloat over another's misfortunes.* **2.** to smile smugly or scornfully; to display self-complacency. *–n.* **3.** the act of gloating. [cf. Icel. *glotta* grin, smile scornfully, d. Swed. *glotta* peep, G *glotzen* stare] – **gloater,** *n.* – **gloatingly,** *adv.*

**glob** /glɒb/, *n. Colloq.* a rounded lump of some soft but pliable substance: *a glob of cream.* [? b. GLOBE and BLOB]

**global** /'gloʊbəl/, *adj.* **1.** spherical; globe-shaped. **2.** pertaining to or covering the whole world. **3.** all-embracing; comprehensive. – **globally,** *adv.*

**globate** /'gloʊbeɪt/, *adj.* shaped like a globe. Also, **globated.** [L *globātus,* pp., formed into a ball]

**globe** /gloʊb/, *n., v.,* **globed, globing.** *–n.* **1.** the earth (usu. prec. by *the*). **2.** a planet or other celestial body. **3.** a sphere on which is depicted a map of the earth (terrestrial globe) or of the heavens (celestial globe). **4.** a spherical body; sphere. **5.** anything more or less spherical, as a lampshade or a glass fishbowl. **6.** *Hist.* a golden ball borne as an emblem of sovereignty. **7.** →**bulb** (def. 3). *–v.t.* **8.** to form into a globe. *–v.i.* **9.** to take the form of a globe. [F, from L *globus* round body or mass, ball, globe] – **globelike,** *adj.*

**globe amaranth** /– 'æmərænθ/, *n.* →**bachelor's button** (def. 3).

**globe artichoke** /– 'atətʃoʊk/, *n.* a type of artichoke, *Cynara scolymus,* widely cultivated for food.

**globefish** /'gloʊbfɪʃ/, *n., pl.* **-fishes,** (*esp. collectively*) **-fish.** →**puffer** (def. 2).

**globeflower** /'gloʊbflaʊə/, *n.* a plant, *Trollius europaeus,* of Europe, having pale yellow globelike flowers.

**globe-pea** /gloʊb-'pi/, *n.* any shrub of the small Australian genus *Sphaerolobium,* as *S. vimineum,* widespread in the southern half of the continent.

**globe thistle** /gloʊb 'θɪsəl/, *n.* **1.** a coarse perennial herb, *Echinops sphaerocephalus,* family Compositae, with spherical heads of blue, one-flowered capitula; native to central and southern Europe and western Asia. **2.** a related species, *E. ritro,* frequently grown in gardens.

**globetrotter** /'gloʊbtrɒtə/, *n. Colloq.* one who travels widely, esp. for sightseeing. – **globetrotting,** *n., adj.*

**globigerina** /gloʊˌbɪdʒə'raɪnə/, *n., pl.* **-nae** /-ni/. a marine protozoan belonging to the Foraminifera, the shell of which, falling to the ocean floor upon death, forms a mud known as the **globigerina ooze.**

**globin** /'gloʊbən/, *n.* the protein contained in haemoglobin; several types have been identified. [L *globus* GLOBE + -IN[2]]

**globoid** /'gloʊbɔɪd/, *adj.* **1.** approximately globe-shaped. *–n.* **2.** a globoid figure or body.

**globose** /'gloʊboʊs, gloʊ'boʊs/, *adj.* globelike; globe-shaped, or nearly so. Also, **globous** /'gloʊbəs/. [L *globōsus* round as a ball] – **globosely,** *adv.* – **globosity** /gloʊ'bɒsəti/, *n.*

**globular** /'glɒbjələ/, *adj.* **1.** global. **2.** composed of globules. – **globularity** /glɒbjə'lærəti/, *n.* – **globularly,** *adv.*

**globular cluster** /– 'klʌstə/, *n.* one of many self-contained, approximately spherical clusters of about a hundred thousand stars which are gravitationally associated with the Milky Way although they appear to be outside it.

**globule** /'glɒbjul/, *n.* a small spherical body. [F, from L *globulus,* diminutive of *globus* GLOBE]

**globulin** /'glɒbjələn/, *n.* any of a group of plasma proteins. [GLOBULE + -IN[2]]

**glockenspiel** /'glɒkənspil, -kənʃpil/, *n.* **1.** a set of steel bars mounted in a frame and struck with hammers, used in military bands. **2.** a small key-board instrument, imitating the sound of bells. **3.** a set of bells; carillon. [G, from *glocken-,* combining form of *Glocke* bell + *Spiel* play]

glockenspiel

**glomerate** /'glɒmərət/, *adj.* compactly clustered. [L *glomerātus,* pp., wound or formed into a ball]

**glomeration** /glɒmə'reɪʃən/, *n.* **1.** glomerate condition; conglomeration. **2.** a glomerate mass.

**glomerule** /'glɒmərul/, *n.* **1.** *Bot.* a cyme condensed into a headlike cluster. **2.** →**glomerulus.** [F, from NL *glomerulus,* diminutive of L *glomus* ball (of yarn, thread, etc.)]

**glomerulonephritis** /ˌglɒməˌruloʊnə'fraɪtəs/, *n.* a diffuse, non-infective inflammation of the kidneys mainly affecting the glomeruli.

**glomerulus** /glɒ'mɛrələs/, *n., pl.* **-li** /laɪ/. a compact cluster of capillaries, esp. a cluster of vascular tufts in the kidney. [NL. See GLOMERULE] – **glomerular,** *adj.*

**glonoine** /'glɒnouin, -aɪn/, *n. Med.* →**nitroglycerine. Also, glonoin** /'glɒnouən/. [said to be from GL(YCERINE) + chemical symbols *O* (oxygen) and $NO_3$ (nitric anhydride) + -INE[2]]

**gloom**[1] /glum/, *n.* **1.** darkness; dimness. *–v.i.* **2.** to appear or become dark or gloomy. *–v.t.* **3.** to make dark or sombre. [OE *glōm* twilight. See GLOAMING, GLOW]

**gloom**[2] /glum/, *n.* **1.** a state of melancholy or depression; low spirits. **2.** a despondent look or expression. *–v.i.* **3.** to look dismal or dejected; frown. *–v.t.* **4.** to fill with gloom; make gloomy or sad. [ME *gloum(b)e, glomme* frown, lower. See GLUM]

**gloomy**[1] /'glumi/, *adj.,* **gloomier, gloomiest.** dark; deeply shaded. [GLOOM[1] + -Y[1]]

**gloomy**[2] /'glumi/, *adj.,* **gloomier, gloomiest. 1.** causing gloom; depressing: *a gloomy prospect.* **2.** affected with or expressive of gloom; melancholy. [GLOOM[2] + -Y[1]] – **gloomily,** *adv.* – **gloominess,** *n.*

**Gloria** /'glɔriə/, *n.* **1.** (in Christian liturgical worship) the great, or greater, doxology beginning 'Gloria in excelsis Deo' (Glory be to God on high), the lesser doxology beginning 'Gloria Patri' (Glory be to the Father), or the response 'Gloria tibi, Domine' (Glory be to thee, O Lord). **2.** (*l.c.*) a repetition of one of these. **3.** (*l.c.*) a musical setting for one of these, esp. the first. **4.** (*l.c.*) a halo, nimbus, or aureole, or an ornament in imitation of one. [L: glory]

**glorification** /glɔrəfə'keɪʃən/, *n.* **1.** the act of glorifying; exaltation to the glory of heaven. **2.** the state of being glorified. **3.** *Colloq.* a glorified or more splendid form of something.

**glorify** /'glɔrəfaɪ/, *v.t.,* **-fied, -fying. 1.** to magnify with praise; extol. **2.** to transform into something more splendid. **3.** to make glorious; invest with glory. **4.** to promote the glory of (God); ascribe glory and praise in adoration to (God). [ME *glorify(en),* from OF *glorifier,* from LL *glōrificāre.* See GLORY, -FY] – **glorifiable,** *adj.* – **glorifier,** *n.*

**gloriole** /'glɔrioul/, *n.* a halo, nimbus, or aureole. [F, from L *glōriola,* diminutive of *glōria* GLORY, *n.*]

**glorious** /'glɔriəs/, *adj.* **1.** admirable; delightful: *to have a glorious time.* **2.** conferring glory: *a glorious victory.* **3.** full of glory; entitled to great renown: *England is glorious in her poetry.* **4.** brilliantly beautiful: *the glorious heavens.* [ME, from AF, from L *glōriōsus* full of glory] – **gloriously,** *adv.* – **gloriousness,** *n.*

**glory** /'glɔri/, *n., pl.* **glories,** *v.,* **gloried, glorying.** *–n.* **1.** exalted praise, honour, or distinction, accorded by common consent: *paths of glory.* **2.** something that makes honoured or illustrious; a distinguished ornament; an object of pride. **3.** adoring praise or thanksgiving: *give glory to God.* **4.** resplendent beauty or magnificence: *the glory of God.* **5.** a state of splendour, magnificence, or greatest prosperity. **6.** a state of contentment, as one resulting from a triumphant achievement. **7.** the splendour and bliss of heaven; heaven. **8.** a ring, circle, or surrounding radiance of light represented about the head or the whole figure of a sacred person, as Christ, a saint, etc.; a halo, nimbus, or aureole. *–v.i.* **9.** to exult with triumph; rejoice proudly. **10.** to be boastful; exult arrogantly (fol. by *in*). *–interj.* **11.** (*cap.*) Also, **Glory be!** (a mild expression of surprise, elation, or exultation.) [ME, from OF *glorie,* from L *glōria* glory, fame, vainglory, boasting]

**glory box** /'– bɒks/, *n.* a chest in which young women store clothes, linen, etc., in expectation of being married; bottom drawer; hope chest.

**glory hole** /'– houl/, *n.* **1.** a cupboard, small room, etc., where odds and ends can be stored with no regard to order. **2.** *Naut.* the accommodation for stewards in the old passenger liners; usu. well down in the bow where a large number slept in bunks in one compartment.

**glory pea** /– 'pi/, *n.* →**kaka beak.**

**gloss**[1] /glɒs/, *n.* **1.** a superficial lustre: *gloss of satin.* **2.** an external show; specious appearance. *–v.t.* **3.** to put a gloss upon. **4.** to give a specious appearance to (oft. fol. by *over*). [Scand.; cf. Icel. *glossi* spark] – **glosser,** *n.* – **glossless,** *adj.*

**gloss**[2] /glɒs/, *n.* **1.** an explanation by means of a marginal or interlinear note, of a technical or unusual expression in a manuscript text. **2.** a series of verbal interpretations of a text. **3.** a glossary. **4.** an artfully misleading interpretation. *–v.t.* **5.** to insert glosses on; annotate. **6.** to give a specious interpretation of; explain away (oft. fol. by *over*): *to gloss over a mistake.* *–v.i.* **7.** to make glosses. [L *glossa* (explanation of) hard word, from Gk: lit., tongue. Cf. GLOZE] – **glosser,** *n.*

**gloss.,** glossary.

**glossa** /'glɒsə/, *n.* →**tongue.** [see GLOSS[2]] – **glossal,** *adj.*

**glossary** /'glɒsəri/, *n., pl.* **-ries.** a list of basic technical, dialectal, and difficult terms in a subject or field, with definitions. [L *glossārium,* from *glossa* GLOSS[2]] – **glossarial** /glɒ'sɛəriəl/, *adj.* – **glossarist,** *n.*

**glossator** /glɒ'seɪtə/, *n.* **1.** a writer of glosses. **2.** one of the early medieval interpreters (not later than 1250) of the Roman and canon laws. [ML, from L *glossa* GLOSS[2]]

**glossectomy** /glɒ'sɛktəmi/, *n., pl.* **-mies.** the removal of the tongue by surgery.

**glossitis** /glɒ'saɪtəs/, *n.* inflammation of the tongue. [*glosso-* (see GLOSSOLOGY) + -ITIS]

**glossolalia** /glɒsə'leɪliə/, *n.* **1.** non-meaningful speech, often associated with schizophrenic disorders. **2.** →**gift of tongues.** [NL, from Gk *glôssa* tongue + *laleîn* talk, babble]

**glossology** /glɒ'sɒlədʒi/, *n. Obs.* →**linguistics.** [*glosso-* (from Gk, combining form of *glôssa* tongue) + -LOGY]

**glossopteris** /glə'sɒptərəs/, *n.* a genus of extinct plants the fossil remains of which are found widely in Permian rocks of the Southern Hemisphere. They constituted an important element of the vegetation of the ancient continent of Gondwana.

**glossy** /'glɒsi/, *adj.,* **glossier, glossiest. 1.** having a gloss; lustrous. *–n.* **2.** a photograph printed on glossy paper. **3.** an expensively produced magazine, printed on glossy paper, and stylish and sophisticated in content. [GLOSS[1], *n.* + -Y[1]] – **glossily,** *adv.* – **glossiness,** *n.*

**glost** /glɒst/, *n. Ceramics.*→**glaze.**

**-glot,** a suffix indicating proficiency in language, as in *polyglot.* [Gk *glôtta* tongue]

**glottal** /'glɒtl/, *adj.* **1.** pertaining to the glottis or tongue. **2.** *Phonet.* articulated in the glottis.

**glottal stop** /– 'stɒp/, *n.* a stop consonant made by closing the glottis so tightly that no breath can pass through.

**glottic** /'glɒtɪk/, *adj.* **1.** pertaining to the glottis and tongue; glottal. **2.** *Obs.* →**linguistic.**

**glottis** /'glɒtəs/, *n.* the opening at the upper part of the larynx, between the vocal cords. [NL, from Gk: the mouth of the windpipe]

**glottology** /glɒ'tɒlədʒi/, *n. Obs.* →**linguistics.** [*glotto-* (from Gk, combining form of *glôtta* tongue) + -LOGY] – **glottologic** /glɒtə'lɒdʒɪk/, **glottological** /glɒtə'lɒdʒɪkəl/, *adj.* – **glottologist,** *n.*

**glove** /glʌv/, *n., v.,* **gloved, gloving.** *–n.* **1.** a covering for the hand, now made with a separate sheath for each finger and for the thumb. **2.** →**boxing glove. 3. take up** or **throw down the glove.** See **gauntlet**[1] (defs 4, 5). *–v.t.* **4.** to cover with or as with a glove; provide with gloves. **5.** to serve as a glove for. [ME; OE *glōf,* c. Icel. *glōfi*] – **gloveless,** *adj.*

**glove box** /– bɒks/, *n.* **1.** Also, **glove compartment.** a small compartment in a motor vehicle, usu. set into the dashboard, for the storage of small articles, as gloves, etc. **2.** a metal box used by workers who need to manipulate radioactive materials, or materials requiring a dust-free, sterile, or inert atmosphere; manipulation is carried out by means of gloves attached to ports in the walls of the box.

**glove compartment** /'– kəmpatmənt/, *n.* →**glove box.**

**gloveman** /'glʌvmən/, *n.* →**wicket-keeper.**

**glove puppet** /'– pʌpət/, *n.* a puppet with a head, dress and hands, designed so that it fits on the puppeteer's hand like a glove or mitten.

**glover** /'glʌvə/, *n.* one who makes or sells gloves.

**glover's needle** /'glʌvəz nidl/, *n.* a three-sided needle for glove making.

**glow** /glou/, *n.* **1.** light emitted by a substance heated to luminosity; incandescence. **2.** brightness of colour. **3.** a state of bodily heat. **4.** warmth of emotion or passion;

ardour. *–v.i.* **5.** to emit bright light and heat without flame; be incandescent. **6.** to shine like something intensely heated. **7.** to exhibit a strong, bright colour; be lustrously red or brilliant. **8.** to be excessively hot. **9.** to be animated with emotion. [ME *glowe(n)*, OE *glōwan*, akin to G *glühen*, Icel. *glōa*]

**glow discharge** /– ˈdɪstʃadʒ/, *n.* a discharge of electricity through a low-pressure gas which is usu. luminous.

**glower** /ˈgloʊə, ˈglaʊə/, *v.i.* **1.** to look angrily; stare with sullen dislike or discontent. *–n.* **2.** a glowering look; frown. [frequentative of obs. *glow* stare, of uncert. orig.] **– gloweringly,** *adv.*

**glowing** /ˈgloʊɪŋ/, *adj.* **1.** incandescent. **2.** rich and warm in colouring: *glowing colours.* **3.** exhibiting the glow of health, excitement, etc. **4.** ardent or impassioned; enthusiastic: *a glowing account.* **– glowingly,** *adv.*

**glow lamp** /ˈgloʊ læmp/, *n.* a lamp which produces light by means of a flow of electricity through a gas.

**glow-worm** /ˈgloʊ-wɜm/, *n.* **1.** a firefly, esp. the wingless female or the luminous larva. **2.** the larva of certain fungus flies as, in New Zealand, *Bolitophila luminosa.*

**gloxinia** /glɒkˈsɪniə/, *n.* the garden name of tuberous-rooted plants of the genus *Sinningia,* esp. a widely cultivated species, *S. speciosa,* having large white, red, or purple bell-shaped flowers. [NL; named after B. P. *Gloxin,* 18th-cent. German botanist]

**gloze** /gloʊz/, *v.,* **glozed, glozing,** *n.* *–v.t.* **1.** to explain away; extenuate; gloss over (usu. fol. by *over*). **2.** to palliate with specious talk. *–v.i.* **3.** *Obs.* to make glosses; comment. *–n.* **4.** *Rare.* flattery or deceit. **5.** *Obs.* a specious show. [ME *glose,* from OF. See GLOSS[2]]

**glucagon** /ˈglukəgɒn, -gən/, *n.* a hormone produced by the pancreas that increases the blood glucose concentration.

**glucinum** /gluˈsaɪnəm/, *n.* →**beryllium.** *Symbol:* Gl. Also, **glucinium** /gluˈsɪniəm/. [NL, from Gk *glykýs* sweet (some of the salts having a sweet taste)]

**gluco-** /ˈglukoʊ/, a prefix indicating the presence of glucose.

**gluconeogenesis** /ˌglukoʊˌnioʊˈdʒɛnəsəs/, *n.* the formation of glucose by the liver from non-carbohydrate molecules. Also, **glyconeogenesis.** **– gluconeogenetic** /ˌglukoʊˌnioʊdʒəˈnɛtɪk/, *adj.*

**glucoprotein** /ˌglukoʊˈproʊtin/, *n.* a glycoprotein containing glucose.

**glucose** /ˈglukoʊz, -oʊs/, *n.* **1.** *Chem.* a sugar $C_6H_{12}O_6$, having several optically different forms, the dextrorotatory form, dextroglucose, occurring in many fruits, animal tissues and fluids, etc., and having a sweetness about one half that of ordinary sugar. Dextroglucose is the major source of energy for most cells. The laevorotatory form of dextroglucose is rare and not naturally occurring. **2.** a syrup containing dextrose, maltose, and dextrine, obtained by the incomplete hydrolysis of starch. [F, from Gk *glykýs* sweet + *-ose* -OSE[2]]

**glucosidase** /glukəˈsaɪdeɪz/, *n.* an enzyme capable of hydrolysing a glucoside, particularly beta-glucosidase.

**glucoside** /ˈglukəsaɪd/, *n.* one of an extensive group of compounds which yield glucose and some other substance or substances when treated with a dilute acid or glucosidase. [GLUCOS(E) + -IDE] **– glucosidal** /ˌglukəˈsaɪdl/, *adj.*

**glucosuria** /glukəˈsjuriə/, *n. Obs.* →**glycosuria.**

**glucuronic acid** /glukjuˌrɒnɪk ˈæsəd/, *n.* an acid formed from dextroglucose, $C_5H_9O_5$ COOH, which combines with compounds foreign to the body, such as drugs, to make them soluble for excretory purposes.

**glue** /glu/, *n., v.,* **glued, gluing.** *–n.* **1.** an impure gelatine obtained by boiling skins, hoofs, and other animal substances in water, and used for various purposes, as an adhesive medium in uniting substances. **2.** any of various preparations of this substance. **3.** any adhesive substance made from any natural or synthetic resin or material. *–v.t.* **4.** to join or fasten with glue. **5.** to fix or attach firmly, as if with glue; make adhere closely. [ME, from OF *glu,* from LL *glus.* Cf. GLUTEN] **– gluer,** *n.*

**glue ear** /ˈglu ɪə/, *n.* a long-term obstruction of the flow of fluid behind the eardrum, occurring mostly in children and causing difficulty in hearing, earaches, and a discharge from the middle ear.

**gluepot** /ˈglupɒt/, *n.* **1.** a vessel in which glue is melted. **2.** a container for glue. **3.** a muddy or sticky patch of ground.

**glue-sniffer** /ˈglu-snɪfə/, *n.* one who inhales the fumes from plastic cement or glue, for their narcotic effects.

**gluey** /ˈglui/, *adj.,* **gluier, gluiest.** **1.** like glue; viscid; sticky. **2.** full of or smeared with glue. **– glueyness,** *n.*

**gluggy** /ˈglʌgi/, *adj. Colloq.* sticky.

**gluhwein** /ˈgluwaɪn/, *n.* mulled wine. [G: glow-wine]

**glum** /glʌm/, *adj.,* **glummer, glummest.** gloomily sullen or silent; dejected. [cf. LG *glum* turbid, muddy; akin to GLOOM[2]] **– glumly,** *adv.* **– glumness,** *n.*

**glumaceous** /gluˈmeɪʃəs/, *adj.* **1.** glumelike. **2.** consisting of or having glumes.

**glume** /glum/, *n.* one of the characteristic bracts of the inflorescence of grasses, sedges, etc., esp. one of the pair of bracts at the base of a spikelet. [L *glūma* hull or husk (of grain)] **– glumelike,** *adj.*

**glut** /glʌt/, *v.,* **glutted, glutting,** *n.* *–v.t.* **1.** to feed or fill to satiety; sate: *to glut the appetite.* **2.** to feed or fill to excess; cloy. **3. glut the market,** to overstock the market; furnish a supply of any article largely in excess of the demand, so that the price is unusually low. **4.** to choke up: *glut a channel.* *–v.i.* **5.** to eat to satiety. *–n.* **6.** a full supply. **7.** a surfeit. **8.** the act of glutting. **9.** the state of being glutted. [ME *glotye(n),* apparently from obs. *glut,* n., glutton, from OF: adj., greedy. See GLUTTON[1]]

**glutaeal** /gluˈtiəl, ˈglutiəl/, *adj.* →**gluteal.**

**glutamate** /ˈglutəmeɪt/, *n.* a salt or ester of glutamic acid, as monosodium glutamate.

**glutamate dehydrogenase** /– dihaɪˈdrɒdʒəneɪz/, *n.* a key enzyme in the assimilation and removal of ammonia, which catalyses the oxidation of glutamic acid to ammonia and alpha-ketoglutaric acid.

**glutamic acid** /gluˌtæmɪk ˈæsəd/, *n.* an amino acid occurring in proteins, $HOOC \cdot CH_2 \cdot CH_2 \cdot CH(NH_3^+)COO^-$, which plays an important part in the nitrogen metabolism of plants and animals.

**glutamine** /ˈglutəmin/, *n.* an amino acid occurring in proteins, $NH_2COCH_2CH_2CH(NH_3^+)COO^-$, which is an important source of ammonia and nitrogen for many biosynthetic reactions. [GLUT(EN) + AMINE]

**glutathione** /glutəˈθaɪoʊn/, *n.* a peptide widely distributed in nature, important in metabolic reactions and as an electron carrier.

**gluteal** /gluˈtiəl, ˈglutiəl/, *adj.* pertaining to buttock muscles or the buttocks. Also, **glutaeal.** [GLUTE(US) + -AL[1]]

**glutelin** /ˈglutələn/, *n.* any of a group of simple proteins of vegetable origin, esp. from wheat.

**gluten** /ˈglutn/, *n.* **1.** the tough, viscid nitrogenous substance remaining when the flour of wheat or other grain is washed to remove the starch. **2.** glue, or some gluey substance. [L: glue, akin to LL *glus* GLUE]

**gluten bread** /ˈ– brɛd/, *n.* bread made from gluten flour.

**gluten flour** /ˈ– flaʊə/, *n.* wheat flour from which a large part of the starch has been removed, thus increasing the proportion of gluten.

**glutenous** /ˈglutənəs/, *adj.* **1.** like gluten. **2.** containing gluten, esp. in large amounts.

**gluteus** /gluˈtiəs/, *n., pl.* **-tei** /-ˈtiaɪ/. any one of three specific muscles of the buttocks. Also, **glutaeus.** [NL, from Gk *gloutós* rump, pl. buttocks]

**glutinous** /ˈglutənəs/, *adj.* of the nature of glue; gluey; viscid; sticky. [L *glūtinōsus* gluey, viscous] **– glutinously,** *adv.* **– glutinousness, glutinosity** /glutəˈnɒsəti/, *n.*

**glutose** /ˈglutoʊz/, *n.* an ingredient of the syrupy mixture obtained by the action of alkali on laevulose, or in the unfermentable reducing portion of cane molasses.

**glutton**[1] /ˈglʌtn/, *n.* **1.** one who eats to excess; a gormandiser. **2.** one who indulges in something excessively. **3.** one who accepts an inordinate amount of unpleasantness or difficulty (fol. by *for*): *a glutton for punishment, a glutton for work.* [ME *glutun,* from OF *glouton,* from L *glūto, glutto*]

**glutton**[2] /ˈglʌtn/, *n.* a thickset, voracious mammal, *Gulo gulo,* of the weasel family, measuring from 60 to 90 cm in length, and inhabiting northern regions. The kind found in America is usu. called the **wolverine,** and is practically identical with that of Europe and Asia. [translation of Swed. *fjällfräs* (through G *Vielfrass*), whence also NL name of animal, *gulo*]

**gluttonise** /ˈglʌtənaɪz/, *v.*, **-nised, -nising.** *–v.i.* **1.** to eat like a glutton. *–v.t.* **2.** to feast gluttonously on. Also, **gluttonize.**

**gluttonous** /ˈglʌtənəs/, *adj.* **1.** given to excessive eating; voracious. **2.** greedy; insatiable. – **gluttonously,** *adv.* – **gluttonousness,** *n.*

**gluttony** /ˈglʌtəni/, *n., pl.* **-tonies.** excess in eating.

**glycaemia** /glaɪˈkimiə/, *n.* the presence of sugar in the blood. Also, **glycemia.**

**glyceraldehyde** /glɪsəˈrældəhaɪd/, *n.* a crystalline aldose, $C_3H_6O_3$, from which simple sugars are derived, having two enantiomers, dextrorotatory (D-glyceraldehyde and laevorotatory (L-glyceraldehyde), which are the basis for classifying the chirality of other molecules of similar structure, as alpha-amino acids.

**glyceric** /glɪˈsɛrɪk/, *adj.* pertaining to or derived from glycerol.

**glyceric acid** /– ˈæsəd/, *n.* a colourless, syrupy fluid, $CH_2OHCHOHCOOH$, produced during the fermentation of alcohol.

**glyceride** /ˈglɪsəraɪd/, *n.* one of a group of esters obtained from glycerol in combination with acids. [from GLYCER(INE) + -IDE]

**glycerine** /glɪsəˈrin, ˈglɪsərən/, *n. Chem.* →**glycerol.** Also, **glycerin** /ˈglɪsərən/. [F *glycérine,* from Gk *glykerós* sweet + -INE[2]]

**glycerol** /ˈglɪsərɒl/, *n.* a colourless, odourless, liquid alcohol, $HOCH_2CHOHCH_2OH$, of syrupy consistency and sweet taste, obtained by the saponification of natural fats and oils, and used as a solvent, plasticiser, or sweetener.

**glyceryl** /ˈglɪsərəl/, *adj.* denoting or pertaining to the trivalent radical ($-CH_2(CH-)CH_2-$) derived from glycerine. [GLYCER(INE) + -YL]

**glyceryl trinitrate** /– traɪˈnaɪtreɪt/, *n.* →**nitroglycerine.**

**glycine** /ˈglaɪsin/, *n.* a sweet-tasting, colourless, crystalline compound, $NH_3^+CH_2COO^-$, the simplest amino acid occurring in proteins. [Gk *glyk(ýs)* sweet + -INE[2]]

**glycocholic acid** /ˌglaɪkəkɒlɪk ˈæsəd/, *n.* a bile acid, $C_{26}H_{43}NO_6$, which on hydrolysis yields glycine and cholic acid.

**glycogen** /ˈglaɪkədʒən/, *n.* a white, tasteless, polysaccharide $(C_6H_{10}O_5)_n$, found in liver and muscle, which serves as a store of glucose. [Gk *glykýs* sweet + -GEN] – **glycogenic** /glaɪkəˈdʒɛnɪk/, *adj.*

**glycogenesis** /ˌglaɪkoʊˈdʒɛnəsəs/, *n.* the formation of glycogen from glucose.

**glycogenic amino acids,** *n.pl.* those amino acids whose carbon skeletons are metabolised to intermediates in glucose and glycogen synthesis.

**glycogenolysis** /ˌglaɪkoʊdʒəˈnɒləsəs/, *n.* the hydrolysis of glycogen to glucose.

**glycol** /ˈglaɪkɒl/, *n.* **1.** a colourless, sweet-tasting liquid, $CH_2OHCH_2OH$, used as an antifreeze in motor vehicles. **2.** any of a group of alcohols containing two hydroxyl groups. [b. GLYC(ERINE) and (ALCOH)OL]

**glycolic** /glaɪˈkɒlɪk/, *adj.* pertaining to or derived from glycol, as **glycolic acid,** $HOCH_2COOH$.

**glycolysis** /glaɪˈkɒləsəs/, *n.* the catabolism of sugars and starch by enzymes accompanied by the release of energy and the production of lactic or pyruvic acid.

**glyconeogenesis** /ˌglaɪkoʊˌnioʊˈdʒɛnəsəs/, *n.* →**gluconeogenesis.**

**glycoprotein** /ˌglaɪkoʊˈproʊtin/, *n.* any of a group of complex proteins containing a carbohydrate combined with a simple protein, as mucin, etc. Also, **glycopeptide** /ˈglaɪkoʊˈpɛptaɪd/. [Gk *glykýs* sweet + PROTEIN]

**glycosidase** /glaɪkəˈsaɪdeɪz, -deɪs/, *n.* any enzyme which will hydrolyse a glycoside to an aglycone and a sugar.

**glycoside** /ˈglaɪkəsaɪd/, *n.* a derivative formed from a monosaccharide and another molecule, which may be a sugar, by the elimination of water.

**glycosuria** /glaɪkoʊˈsjuriə/, *n.* excretion of glucose in the urine, as in diabetes. Also, **glucosuria.** [NL, from F *glycose* GLUCOSE + *-uria* -URIA] – **glycosuric,** *adj.*

**glycyrrhizin** /glɪsəˈraɪzən, glaɪ-/, *n.* a sweet principle from the roots of licorice, soluble in water; probable formula $C_{44}H_{64}O_{19}$.

**glyoxalin** /glaɪˈɒksələn/, *n. Chem.* →**imidazole.**

**glyph** /glɪf/, *n.* **1.** *Archit.* an ornamental channel or groove, usu. vertical, as in a Doric frieze. **2.** a sculptured figure. **3.** *Archaeol.* a pictograph or hieroglyph. [Gk *glyphḗ* carving] – **glyphic,** *adj.*

**glyptal resin** /glɪptl ˈrɛzən/, *n.* any of a group of adhesive resins formed by reacting polyhydric alcohols (esp. glycerol) with polybasic acids or their anhydrides (as phthalic anhydride). Also, **glyptal, glyptol.**

**glyptic** /ˈglɪptɪk/, *adj.* of or pertaining to carving or engraving, esp. on precious stones. [Gk *glyptikós* of engraving]

**glyptodont** /ˈglɪptədɒnt/, *n.* any extinct mammal, etc., of the genus *Glyptodon,* having the body covered with a horny armour.

**glyptography** /glɪpˈtɒgrəfi/, *n.* **1.** the description or study of engraved gems, etc. **2.** the art or process of engraving on gems or the like. [Gk *glyptó(s)* carved + -GRAPHY]

**gm**[1], gram; grams.

**gm**[2], →**gsm.**

**G.M.,** **1.** General Manager. **2.** George Medal.

**G-man** /ˈdʒi-mæn/, *n. U.S.* an agent for the FBI.

**Gmc,** Germanic.

**G.M.T.,** Greenwich Mean Time.

**gnamma hole** /ˈnæmə hoʊl/, *n.* →**namma hole.**

**gnarl** /nal/, *n.* **1.** a knotty protuberance on a tree; knot. *–v.t.* **2.** to twist. [backformation from GNARLED]

**gnarled** /nald/, *adj.* **1.** (of trees) full of or covered with gnarls. **2.** (of persons) **a.** having a rugged, weatherbeaten appearance. **b.** cross-grained; perverse; cantankerous. Also, **gnarly.** [var. of KNURLED]

**gnash** /næʃ/, *v.t.* **1.** to grind (the teeth) together, esp. in rage or pain. **2.** to bite with grinding teeth. *–v.i.* **3.** to gnash the teeth. *–n.* **4.** the act of gnashing. [unexplained var. of obs. *gnast,* from Scand.; cf. Icel. *gnastan* gnashing]

**gnat** /næt/, *n.* any of various small dipterous insects as **1.** a non-biting midge of the family Chironomidae. **2.** *Chiefly Brit.* a mosquito. [ME; OE *gnæt(t),* c. d. G *Grnatze*]

**gnathion** /ˈneɪθiɒn, ˈnæθ-/, *n.* the lowest point on the anterior margin of the lower jaw in the midsagittal plane. [NL, diminutive of Gk *gnáthos* jaw] – **gnathic,** *adj.*

**-gnathous,** an adjectival word element referring to the jaw, as in *prognathous.* [Gk *gnáthos* jaw + -OUS]

**gnaw** /nɔ/, *v.,* **gnawed, gnawed** or **gnawn, gnawing.** *–v.t.* **1.** to wear away or remove by persistent biting. **2.** to make by gnawing. **3.** to corrode; consume. **4.** to consume with passion; torment. *–v.i.* **5.** to bite persistently. **6.** to cause corrosion. **7.** to act as if by corrosion. [ME *gnawe(n),* OE *gnagan,* c. G *nagen*] – **gnawer,** *n.*

**gnawing** /ˈnɔ-ɪŋ, ˈnɔrɪŋ/, *n.* **1.** the act of one who or that which gnaws. **2.** a persistent pain suggesting gnawing: *the gnawings of hunger.* – **gnawingly,** *adv.*

**gneiss** /ˈnaɪs/, *n.* a metamorphic rock, generally made up of bands which differ in colour and composition, some bands being rich in felspar and quartz, others rich in hornblende or mica. [G] – **gneissic,** *adj.*

**gneissoid** /ˈnaɪsɔɪd/, *adj.* resembling gneiss.

**gnocchi** /ˈnɒki, ˈnjɒki/, *n.* an Italian dish of square or round shapes of semolina paste, used to garnish soup and the like, or served as a savoury dish with cheese sauce. [It.]

**gnome**[1] /noʊm/, *n.* **1.** one of a species of diminutive beings fabled to inhabit the interior of the earth and to act as guardians of its treasures, usu. thought of as shrivelled little old men; a troll. **2.** →**garden gnome.** **3.** a banker, involved in international currency and loan dealings, usu. operating from Zurich, and thought to exercise a mysterious and sinister effect on world economic affairs. [F, from NL (Paracelsus) *gnomus*] – **gnomish,** *adj.*

**gnome**[2] /noʊm/, *n.* a short, pithy expression of a general truth; aphorism. [Gk: judgment, opinion, maxim]

**gnomic** /ˈnoʊmɪk, ˈnɒm-/, *adj.* **1.** like or containing gnomes or aphorisms. **2.** of, pertaining to, or denoting a writer of aphorisms, esp. certain Greek poets. Also, **gnomical.** [Gk *gnōmikós*] – **gnomically,** *adv.*

**gnomist** /ˈnoʊməst/, *n.* a writer of aphorisms.

**gnomon** /ˈnoʊmɒn/, *n.* **1.** a vertical shaft, column, obelisk, or the like, used (esp. by the ancients) as an astronomical instrument for determining the altitude of the sun, the position of a place, etc., by noting the length of the shadow cast at noon. **2.** the vertical triangular plate of a sundial. [L, from Gk: one who knows, an indicator] – **gnomonic** /nɒˈmɒnɪk/, **gnomonical** /nɒˈmɒnɪkəl/, *adj.* – **gnomonically** /nɒˈmɒnɪkli/, *adv.*

**gnosis** /ˈnoʊsəs/, *n.* a knowledge of spiritual things; mystical knowledge. [NL, from Gk: knowledge]

**-gnosis,** a suffix referring to recognition, esp. of a morbid condition, as in *prognosis.* [Gk: knowledge]

**gnostic** /ˈnɒstɪk/, *adj.* Also, **gnostical.** **1.** pertaining to knowledge. **2.** possessing knowledge, esp. esoteric knowledge of spiritual things. **3.** (*cap.*) pertaining to or characteristic of the Gnostics. –*n.* **4.** (*cap.*) a member of any of certain sects among, or religiously akin to, the early Christians, who claimed to have superior knowledge of spiritual things, and explained the world as created by powers or agencies arising as emanations from the Godhead. [LL *Gnosticus,* from Gk *gnōstikós* pertaining to knowledge] – **Gnosticism,** *n.*

**Gnosticise** /ˈnɒstəsaɪz/, *v.,* **-cised, -cising.** –*v.i.* **1.** to adopt or maintain Gnostic views. –*v.t.* **2.** to explain on Gnostic principles; give a Gnostic colouring to. Also, **Gnosticize.**

**G.N.P.** /dʒi ɛn ˈpi/, gross national product.

**gnu** /nu/, *n., pl.* **gnus,** (*esp. collectively*) **gnu.** any of several African antelopes constituting the genus *Connochaetes,* characterised by an oxlike head, curved horns, and a long, flowing tail; a wildebeest. [Xhosa *nqu*]

gnu

**go** /goʊ/, *v.,* **went, gone, going,** *n., pl.* **goes.** –*v.i.* **1.** to move or pass along; proceed. **2.** to move away or out; depart (opposed to *come* or *arrive*). **3.** *Cricket.* to be dismissed. **4.** to keep or be in motion; act, work, or run. **5.** to become; assume another state or condition: *to go mad.* **6.** to continue; be habitually in a specified condition: *to go hungry.* **7.** to act or perform so as to achieve a specified state or condition. **8.** to move towards a point or a given result or in a given manner; proceed; advance. **9.** to be known: *to go by a name.* **10.** to reach or extend: *this road goes to the city.* **11.** (of time) to pass; elapse. **12.** to be awarded, transferred, or applied to a particular recipient or purpose. **13.** to be sold: *the property went for a song.* **14.** *Colloq.* to compare; to be normally: *she's quite young as grandmothers go.* **15.** to conduce or tend: *this only goes to prove the point.* **16.** to turn out: *how did the game go?* **17.** to belong; have a place: *this book goes on the top shelf.* **18.** (of colours, etc.) to harmonise; be compatible; be suited. **19.** to fit into, round, etc. **20.** to be used up, finished or consumed. **21.** to develop, esp. with reference to success, or failure. **22.** to be phrased: *how do the words go?* **23.** to resort; have recourse: *to go to court.* **24.** to be given up; be worn out; be lost or ended. **25.** to die. **26.** to fail; give way. **27.** to begin; come into action: *here goes!* **28.** to be acceptable: *anything goes.* **29.** to carry final authority: *what I say goes.* **30.** to be contained (fol. by *into: 4 goes into 12*). **31.** to contribute to a result: *the items which go to make up a total.* **32.** to be about, intending, or destined (used in the pres. part. fol. by an infinitive): *he is going to write.* **33.** *Colloq.* to copulate. –*v.t.* **34.** to proceed on: *he went his way.* **35.** to share equally (fol. by a complementary substantive): *to go halves.* **36.** to make (a sound, effect, etc.) when operated (fol. by a complementary substantive): *the gun went bang.* **37.** *Cards.* to bid. –*v.* **38.** Some special verb phrases are:

**be going places,** to be likely to achieve notable success.

**go about,** *Naut.* to change course.

**go ahead, 1.** to proceed with permission. **2.** to take the lead; to be in the forefront: *the big horse went ahead soon after the start.*

**go all out,** *Colloq.* to expend the utmost energy.

**go all the way, 1.** to support wholeheartedly; to agree absolutely (fol. by *with*): *Harold Holt went all the way with LBJ.* **2.** *Colloq.* to have sexual intercourse. **3.** to equal; match (fol. by *with*).

**go along with,** to agree; accept.

**go a meal (drink, etc.),** *Colloq.* to need a meal (drink, etc.).

**go around, 1.** to move about; circulate. **2.** to be enough for all: *enough food to go around.*

**go around with,** *Colloq.* **1.** to keep the company of (a member of the opposite sex). **2.** to maintain a friendship with (a person or group of people).

**go at, 1.** to undertake with vigour. **2.** to attack.

**go back on,** *Colloq.* **1.** to fail (someone); let (someone) down. **2.** to fail to keep (one's word, promise, etc.).

**go bush,** *Colloq.* go to the bush or to some place where friends, associates, etc. cannot contact one.

**go by, 1.** to pass. **2.** to be guided by.

**go down, 1.** to descend; slope down. **2.** to be defeated. **3.** to be remembered by posterity. **4.** to fall ill: *he has gone down with the mumps.* **5.** *Colloq.* to be sent to prison. **6.** *Brit.* to leave university at the end of the term or permanently (according to context). **7.** *Bridge.* to fail to make one's contract. **8.** *Mining.* to sink a shaft on a claim. **9.** *Boxing.* to be knocked to the canvas or to slip to the canvas.

**go for, 1.** to attack; set upon. **2.** to be attracted to: *I go for music in a big way.* **3.** to aim for: *he's going for the chairmanship.* **4.** to apply to: *that goes for all of us.*

**go for broke,** *Colloq.* **1.** (gambling, investment, etc.) to risk all one's capital in the hope of very large gain. **2.** to take a major risk in pursuing an activity, objective, etc. to its extreme.

**go in for,** to make (a thing) one's particular interest.

**go into,** to investigate or study thoroughly.

**go in with,** to enter a partnership or other agreement with.

**go it alone,** to act alone.

**go missing, 1.** to get lost. **2.** to absent oneself.

**not go much on,** not to be attracted to or enthused by: *I don't go much on him.*

**go native,** *Colloq.* to turn one's back on the comforts of civilisation and adopt a native style of life.

**go off, 1.** to discharge; explode. **2.** (of food, etc.) to become bad; deteriorate: *the meat's gone off.* **3.** to take place (in a specified manner): *the rehearsal went off well.* **4.** *Colloq.* to come to dislike. **5.** to go away. **6.** Also, **go off pop.** *Colloq.* to reprimand; to scold, become angry with (fol. by *at*). **7.** to get married.

**go on, 1.** to go ahead; proceed; continue. **2.** to manage; do. **3.** to behave; act. **4.** to take place. **5.** to chatter continually. **6.** nonsense! (an exclamation of disbelief). **7.** to use as evidence. **8.** *Colloq.* to get near (an age or a time): *he's going on seventy, it's going on midnight.*

**go out, 1.** to come to a stop; end: *the light went out.* **2.** to attend social functions, etc. **3.** *Cards.* to dispose of the last card in one's hand. **4.** to be broadcast. **5.** *Colloq.* to lose consciousness: *he went out like a light.*

**go out with,** to frequent the society of; date regularly.

**go over, 1.** to read or reread. **2.** to repeat. **3.** to examine. **4.** to have an effect (as specified): *my proposal went over very badly.* **5** *Rugby Football.* to score a try. **6.** to change sides, political allegiance, etc.

**go soft, 1.** to deteriorate intellectually, morally or physically. **2.** to become less severe.

**go through, 1.** to undergo; endure. **2.** to examine in order. **3.** to be accepted.

**go through with,** to complete; bring to a finish.

**go to it,** to undertake any activity with gusto.

**go to show,** to serve as evidence; to help to prove.

**go under,** to be overwhelmed; be ruined.

**go up, 1.** to rise or ascend; advance. **2.** to go to university at the beginning of term

**go wild, 1.** to revert to an untamed or savage state. **2.** to respond (very demonstratively) with extreme emotion, usu. pleasure: *the crowd went wild when the home team won.*

**go with,** *Colloq.* **1.** to harmonise with. **2.** to frequent the society of.

**go without saying,** to be self-evident.

**let go, 1.** to release. **2.** to give free reign to (one's emotion, etc.), esp. in making an attack.

**let oneself go, 1.** to cease to care for one's appearance. **2.** to

become uninhibited.
**that's the way it (she) goes,** *Colloq.* that's how things are.
*–n.* **39.** the act of going: *the come and go of the seasons.* **40.** *Colloq.* energy, spirit, or animation: *to be full of go.* **41.** one's turn to play or to make an attempt at something. **42.** *Colloq.* something that goes well; a success: *to make a go of something.* **43.** *U.S. Colloq.* a bargain. **44.** Some special noun phrases are:
**all the go,** *Colloq.* in the current fashion.
**a rum go,** *Colloq.* a strange or inexplicable situation.
**fair go,** *Colloq.* adequate opportunity: *fair go, spinner*.
**from go to whoa,** from beginning to end.
**from the word go,** from the beginning.
**give (someone) a (fair) go,** *Colloq.* to give (someone) a (fair) chance.
**have (give it) a go,** *Colloq.* **1.** to make an attempt; try: *to have a go at swimming.* **2.** *Cricket.* to hit out recklessly.
**it's a go,** *Colloq.* all's clear
**no go,** not possible; futile; vain.
**on the go,** *Colloq.* constantly going; very active.
**open go, 1.** a situation in which fair play prevails and no unfair restraints or limiting conditions apply: *the election was an open go.* **2.** a situation in which normal restraints do not apply: *it was open go at the bar that night.*
*–adj.* **45.** ready; functioning properly: *all instruments are go.* [ME *go(n),* OE *gān;* akin to D *gaan,* MLG *gān,* OHG *gān, gēn,* G *gehen.* Cf. GANG[2], *v.*]
**goa** /ˈgoʊə/, *n.* the black-tailed gazelle, *Procapra picticaudata,* of the Tibetan plateau. [Tibetan *dgoba*]

goa

**goad** /goʊd/, *n.* **1.** a stick with a pointed end, for driving cattle, etc. **2.** anything that pricks or wounds like such a stick; a stimulus. *–v.t.* **3.** to prick or drive with or as with a goad; incite. [ME *gode,* OE *gād,* c. Langobardic *gaida* arrowhead] **– goadlike,** *adj.*
**goaf** /ˈgoʊf/, *n.* the space left in a mine after the extraction of coal; sometimes packed with waste; gob.
**go-ahead** /ˈgoʊ-əhɛd/, *adj.* **1.** going forward; advancing. **2.** progressive; active; enterprising. *–n.* **3.** permission to proceed.
**goal** /ˈgoʊl/, *n.* **1.** that towards which effort is directed; aim or end. **2.** the terminal point in a race. **3.** a pole or other object by which this is marked. **4.** an area, basket, cage or object or structure towards which the players strive to advance the ball, etc. **5.** the act of throwing or kicking the ball through or over the goal. **6.** the score made by accomplishing this. *–v.i.* **7.** to score a goal. [ME *gol* boundary, limit. Cf. OE *gælan* hinder, impede] **– goalless,** *adj.*
**goal area** /ˈ– ɛəriə/, *n.* **1.** *Soccer.* a rectangular space in front of each goal. **2.** *Hockey.* a semicircular space in front of each goal. A goal is discounted unless the shot is made within the goal area.
**goalie** /ˈgoʊli/, *n. Colloq.* →**goalkeeper.**
**goalkeeper** /ˈgoʊlkipə/, *n.* (in soccer, hockey, etc.) a player whose special duty it is to prevent the ball from going through, into, or over the goal.
**goal kick** /ˈgoʊl kɪk/, *n.* (in soccer) a free kick from a corner of the pitch taken by the defending side if the ball has crossed the goal line after last being touched by a member of the attacking side. **– goal kicker,** *n.*
**goal line** /ˈ– laɪn/, *n.* (in various games) a line, on which the goal stands, marking each end of the field of play.
**goal mouth** /ˈ– maʊθ/, *n.* (in soccer) the area immediately in front of the goal.
**goalpost** /ˈgoʊlpoʊst/, *n.* (in football, etc.) either of the two posts marking the goal.
**goal sneak** /ˈgoʊl snik/, *n. Aus. Rules Colloq.* **1.** a player who catches the opposition unawares and scores a goal. **2.** →**full-forward.**
**goal square** /ˈ– skwɛə/, *n.* (in Australian Rules) the rectangular area in front of the goal, formed by the kick-off line and the goal line; kick-off area.
**goal umpire** /ˈ– ˌʌmpaɪə/, *n.* (in Australian Rules) either of two umpires, one at each goal whose duties are to decide if a goal or behind has been scored, and to signal the score after the 'all clear' signal from the field umpire.
**goanna**[1] /goʊˈænə/, *n.* any of various large Australian varanid (monitor) lizards as the common lace monitor, *Varanus varius,* which occurs generally throughout mainland Australia. [from IGUANA]
**goanna**[2] /goʊˈænə/, *n. Colloq.* a piano. [rhyming slang, *goanna pianna*]

goanna[1]

**goashore** /ˈgoʊəʃɔ/, *n. N.Z.* (formerly) a three-legged iron cooking-pot. [Maori *kohua*]
**goat** /ˈgoʊt/, *n.* **1.** any bovid animal of the genus *Capra,* comprising various agile hollow-horned ruminants closely related to the sheep, found native in rocky and mountainous regions of the Old World, and including domesticated forms common throughout the world. **2.** any of various allied animals, as *Oraemnos montanus* (Rocky Mountain goat), a ruminant of western North America. **3.** (*cap.*) the zodiacal constellation or sign Capricorn. **4.** *Colloq.* a scapegoat; one who is the butt of a joke. **5.** *Colloq.* a fool: *to make a goat of oneself.* **6.** *Colloq.* a lecher; a licentious man. **7.** (*pl.*) (in collocations with *sheep*) evil, bad, or inferior people or things. **8. get (on) one's goat,** *Colloq.* to annoy; enrage; infuriate. **9. a hairy goat,** *Colloq.* a racehorse which does not perform well. **10. run like a hairy goat,** *Colloq.* **a.** to run very slowly. **b.** to run very fast. [ME *gote, goot,* OE *gāt,* c. G *Geiss;* akin to L *haedus* kid] **– goatlike,** *adj.*

goat

**goat antelope** /– ˈæntəloʊp/, *n.* **1.** a goatlike antelope of the genus *Naemorhedus,* as the goral, *N. goral,* or *N. crispus* of Japan. **2.** any antelope of the tribe Rupicaprini, a subdivision of the sheep and goat family, and including the chamois, goral, serow, and Rocky Mountain goat.
**goat country** /ˈ– kʌntri/, *n.* remote areas, esp. infertile or difficult terrain.
**goatee** /goʊˈti/, *n.* a man's beard trimmed to a tuft or a point on the chin.
**goatfish** /ˈgoʊtfɪʃ/, *n., pl.* **-fishes,** (*esp. collectively*) **-fish.** any fish of the tropical and subtropical marine family Mullidae, having a pair of long barbels below the mouth, and including species highly esteemed as a delicacy by the ancient Romans; surmullet; red mullet.
**goatherd** /ˈgoʊthɜd/, *n.* one who tends goats.
**goatish** /ˈgoʊtɪʃ/, *adj.* like a goat; lustful. **– goatishly,** *adv.* **– goatishness,** *n.*
**goatskin** /ˈgoʊtskɪn/, *n.* **1.** the skin or hide of a goat. **2.** leather made from it.
**goat's-rue** /ˈgoʊts-ru/, *n.* **1.** a European herb, *Galega officinalis,* formerly used in medicine. **2.** an American herb, *Tephrosia virginiana.*
**goatsucker** /ˈgoʊtsʌkə/, *n.* **1.** a non-passerine nocturnal bird, *Caprimulgus europaeus,* of Europe, with flat head and wide mouth, formerly supposed to suck the milk of goats. **2.** any of the group of chiefly nocturnal or crepuscular birds to which this species belongs usu. regarded as including two families, the Caprimulgidae (**true goatsuckers** or nightjars) and the Podargidae (frogmouths).
**gob**[1] /gɒb/, *n.* a mass or lump. [ME *gobbe* lump, mass, apparently from OF *go(u)be,* of Gallic derivation]
**gob**[2] /gɒb/, *Colloq. –n.* **1.** the mouth. *–v.i.* **2.** to spit or expectorate. [Gaelic or Irish. Cf. GAB]
**gob**[3] /gɒb/, *n.* →**goaf.**
**gobbet** /ˈgɒbət/, *n.* **1.** a fragment or hunk, esp. of raw flesh. **2.** an extract from a text, selected for a particular reason as for a translation exercise. [ME *gobet,* from OF, diminutive of *gobe* GOB[1]]

**gobble**[1] /'gɒbəl/, *v.*, **-bled, -bling.** *–v.t.* **1.** to swallow hastily in large pieces; gulp. **2.** *Colloq.* to seize upon greedily or eagerly. *–v.i.* **3.** to eat hastily. [from GOB[1]] – **gobbler,** *n.*

**gobble**[2] /'gɒbəl/, *v.*, **-bled, -bling,** *n.* *–v.i.* **1.** to make the characteristic throaty cry of a turkey cock. *–n.* **2.** this sound. [var. of GABBLE taken as imitative of the cry]

**gobbledegook** /'gɒbldi,gʊk, -,guk/, *n. Colloq.* language characterised by circumlocution and jargon: *the gobbledegook of government reports.* Also, **gobbledy-gook.** [grotesque coinage modelled on HOBBLEDEHOY. Final element *gook* may be slang word for tramp, var. of d. *gowk* simpleton, from Scand. Cf. GOBBLE[2], GOO]

**gobbler** /'gɒblə/, *n.* →**turkey cock.**

**go-between** /'goʊ-bətwin/, *n.* one who acts as agent between persons or parties.

**gobiid** /'goʊbiɪd/, *adj.* **1.** of or pertaining to the Gobiidae, a family of marine (mainly coastal) and freshwater fishes. *–n.* **2.** any gobiid fish. Also, **gobioid.**

**gobioid** /'goʊbiɔɪd/, *adj., n.* →**gobiid.**

**goblet** /'gɒblət/, *n.* **1.** a drinking glass with a foot and stem. **2.** *Archaic.* a bowl-shaped drinking vessel. [ME *gobelet,* from OF, diminutive of *gobel* cup; of Celtic orig.]

**goblin** /'gɒblən/, *n.* a grotesque mischievous sprite or elf. [ME *gobelin,* from F (obs.), from MHG *kobold* goblin]

**gobo** /'goʊboʊ/, *n.* (in television, film) any shape, pattern or effect put directly in front of a camera so that the camera must shoot through it to the scene.

**gobstopper** /'gɒbstɒpə/, *n.* a large, round, hard sweet that lasts a long time.

**go-by** /'goʊ-baɪ/, *n. Colloq.* going by without notice; intentional passing by: *to give the go-by.*

**goby** /'goʊbi/, *n., pl.* **-bies,** (*esp. collectively*) **-by. 1.** member of the Gobiidae, a family of marine and freshwater fishes, mostly small and having the pelvic fins united to form a suctorial disc that enables them to cling to rocks, as the **flathead goby,** *Glossogobius giurus,* of eastern Australia and elsewhere. **2.** any member of the closely related family, Eleotridae, in which the pelvic fins are separate. [L *gōbius, cōbius,* from Gk *kōbiós* kind of fish]

**G.O.C.,** General Officer Commanding.

**go-cart** /'goʊ-kat/, *n.* **1.** a small, wheeled vehicle for small children to ride in. **2.** a small framework with castors, in which children learn to walk. **3.** a handcart. **4.** →**go-kart.**

**God** /gɒd/, *n.* **1.** the one Supreme Being, the creator and ruler of the universe. **2.** the Supreme Being considered with reference to a particular attribute: *the God of justice.* **3.** (*l.c.*) a deity, esp. a male deity, presiding over some portion of worldly affairs. **4.** (*cap. or l.c.*) a supreme being according to some particular conception: *the God of pantheism.* **5.** (*l.c.*) an image of a deity; an idol. **6.** (*l.c.*) any deified person or object. **7.** (*l.c., pl.*) the highest gallery in a theatre. **8. God's own country, a.** the United States of America. **b.** (*usu. ironic*) one's own country viewed as the ideal. *–interj.* **9.** (an oath or exclamation used to express weariness, annoyance, disappointment, etc.) [ME and OE, c. D *god,* G *Gott,* Icel. *godh,* Goth. *guth*]

**God almighty** /gɒd ɔl'maɪti/, *interj.* (an expression of surprise or anger).

**God-almighty** /gɒd-ɔl'maɪti/, *adv. Colloq.* extremely; with absurd exaggeration: *don't be so God-almighty pleased with yourself.*

**God-awful** /'gɒd-ɔfəl/, *adj. Colloq.* terrible.

**godchild** /'gɒdtʃaɪld/, *n., pl.* **-children.** one for whom a person (godparent) stands sponsor at baptism.

**goddamn** /gɒd'dæm, 'gɒdæm/, *U.S. –interj.* **1.** (an oath expressing irritation, fury, etc.) *–adj., adv.* **2.** Also, **goddamned.** damned.

**goddaughter** /'gɒddɔtə/, *n.* a female godchild.

**goddess** /'gɒdəs, 'gɒdɛs/, *n.* **1.** a female god or deity. **2.** a woman of extraordinary beauty. **3.** an adored woman. – **goddess-hood, goddess-ship,** *n.*

**Gödel's theorem** /'gɜdəlz θɪərəm/, *n.* the proposition that in a formal axiomatic system, such as logic or mathematics, it is impossible to prove consistency without using methods beyond those of the system itself. [named after Kurt *Gödel,* 1906-78, U.S. logician and mathematician]

**godet** /'goʊdeɪ, -dɛt/, *n.* **1.** a triangular piece of material inserted into a seam to give fullness. **2.** a wheel or roller used in spinning rayon yarn.

**godetia** /gə'diʃə/, *n.* any of the commonly cultivated annuals with colourful flowers, of North America, belonging to the genus *Oenothera.* [named after C. H. *Godet,* 1797-1879, Swiss botanist]

**godfather** /'gɒdfaðə/, *n.* **1.** a man who stands sponsor for a child at baptism or confirmation. *–v.t.* **2.** to act as godfather to; be sponsor for.

**god-fearing** /'gɒd-fɪərɪŋ/, *adj.* pious; deeply religious.

**godforsaken** /'gɒdfəseɪkən/, *adj. Colloq.* desolate; remote.

**Godhead** /'gɒdhɛd/, *n.* **1.** the essential being of God; the Supreme Being. **2.** (*l.c.*) godhood or godship. **3.** (*l.c.*) a deity; god or goddess.

**godhood** /'gɒdhʊd/, *n.* divine character; godship.

**godless** /'gɒdləs/, *adj.* **1.** having or acknowledging no God. **2.** wicked. – **godlessly,** *adv.* – **godlessness,** *n.*

**godlike** /'gɒdlaɪk/, *adj.* like or befitting a god, or God. – **godlikeness,** *n.*

**godly** /'gɒdli/, *adj.,* **-lier, -liest. 1.** conforming to God's laws; pious. **2.** *Archaic.* coming from God; divine. – **godlily,** *adv.* – **godliness,** *n.*

**godmother** /'gɒdmʌðə/, *n.* **1.** a woman who sponsors a child at baptism. **2.** a female sponsor. *–v.t.* **3.** to act as godmother to; sponsor.

**godown** /'goʊdaʊn/, *n.* (in India and eastern Asia) a warehouse. [Malay *godong*]

**godparent** /'gɒdpɛərənt/, *n.* a godfather or godmother.

**godroon** /gə'drun/, *n.* →**gadroon.**

**God's acre** /gɒdz 'eɪkə/, *n.* a burial ground; cemetery.

**godsend** /'gɒdsɛnd/, *n.* something unexpected but particularly welcome and timely, as if sent by God. [earlier *God's send,* var. (under influence of *send,* v.) of *God's sond* or *sand,* OE *sond, sand* message, service]

**godship** /'gɒdʃɪp/, *n.* the rank or character of a god.

**godson** /'gɒdsʌn/, *n.* a male godchild.

**godspeed** /gɒd'spid/, *interj.* **1.** God speed you. *–n.* **2.** a wish of success to one setting out on a journey or undertaking.

**god squad** /'gɒd skwɒd/, *n. Colloq.* (*joc.*) a company of convinced Christians: *he was a member of the god squad.*

**godwit** /'gɒdwɪt/, *n.* any of several large shorebirds of the genus *Limosa,* all with long, slightly up-curved bills, two species of which, the bar-tailed godwit, *Limosa lapponica,* and the black-tailed godwit, *Limosa limosa,* regularly migrate to coastal areas of Australia.

**Godzone** /'gɒdzoʊn/, *n.* (*ironic*) Australia, as the ideal country. Also, **godzone.** [from *God's own country*]

**goer** /'goʊə/, *n.* **1.** a person who attends regularly (usu. used in combination): *a cinemagoer.* **2.** *Colloq.* one who or that which moves fast. **3.** *Colloq.* any activity, project, etc., having evident prospects of success. **4.** *Racing, etc.* an entrant, as a horse or dog, in a race for which there is a money prize and on which bets are placed, which is considered to have good prospects of winning, and whose connections have not made an agreement that it should not win.

**goes** /'goʊz/, *v.* **1.** 3rd person singular present of **go.** *–n.* **2.** plural of **go.**

**goethite** /'goʊθaɪt, 'gɜtaɪt/, *n.* a very common mineral, iron hydroxide, FeO(OH), occurring in crystals, but more commonly in yellow or brown earthy masses, an ore of iron. Also, **göthite.** [named after J. W. von *Goethe,* 1749-1832, German writer and philosopher. See -ITE[1]]

**gofer** /'goʊfə/, *n.* →**gopher**[1].

**goffer** /'goʊfə/, *n.* **1.** an ornamental plaiting used for the frills and borders of women's caps, etc. *–v.t.* **2.** to flute (a frill, etc.), as with a heated iron. **3.** to impress (book edges, etc.) with an ornamental pattern. Also, **gauffer.** [F *gauffer* stamp cloth, paper, etc., from *gaufre* honeycomb, waffle, from D *wafel.* See WAFER]

**go-getter** /'goʊ-gɛtə/, *n. Colloq.* an enterprising, aggressive person, esp. one who will stop at nothing to get what he wants.

**goggle** /'gɒgəl/, *n., v.,* **-gled, -gling.** *–n.* **1.** (*pl.*) spectacles often with special rims, lenses, or sidepieces, so devised as to protect the eyes from wind, dust, or glare. **2.** a goggling look. *–v.i.* **3.** to stare with bulging eyes. **4.** (of the eyes) to roll; bulge and stare. **5.** to roll the eyes. *–v.t.* **6.** to roll (the eyes). [ME *gogelen* look aside; orig. uncert.]

**goggle-eyed** /ˈgɒgəl-aɪd/, *adv.* with prominent, rolling eyes, esp. as a mark of astonishment: *she stared goggle-eyed at the apparition.*

**go-go girl** /ˈgoʊ-goʊ gɜl/, *n.* a girl who performs an individualised, often erotic, dance as an accompaniment to music played in a club or discotheque.

**Goidelic** /gɔɪˈdɛlɪk/, *adj.* **1.** of or pertaining to the Gaels or their language. *–n.* **2.** *Linguistics.* the Gaelic subgroup of Celtic. Also, **Gadhelic.** [OIrish *Goideal* a Gael + -IC]

**go-in** /ˈgoʊ-ɪn/, *n. Colloq.* a fight.

**going** /ˈgoʊɪŋ/, *n.* **1.** a going away; departure: *a safe going and return.* **2.** the condition of something, as of the ground on a racecourse: *the going was bad.* **3.** (of a stair) the horizontal distance between two successive nosings. **4.** (*usu. pl.*) way; deportment. *–adj.* **5.** moving or working, as machinery. **6.** that goes; in existence. **7.** flourishing in business: *a going concern.* **8.** having to do with a going business: *the going value of a company.* **9.** departing. **10. going on,** nearly: *it is going on four o'clock.* **11. the going thing,** the current fad.

**going-away outfit** /ˌgoʊɪŋ-əˈweɪ ˌaʊtfɪt/, *n.* clothing customarily worn by a bride when leaving on her honeymoon.

**going-over** /goʊɪŋ-ˈoʊvə/, *n., pl.* **goings-over.** *Colloq.* **1.** a thorough examination. **2.** a severe beating or thrashing.

**goings-on** /ˌgoʊɪŋz-ˈɒn/, *n.pl. Colloq.* **1.** actions; conduct; behaviour (used chiefly with depreciative force): *we were shocked by the goings-on at the office party.* **2.** current events: *she only kept in touch with the goings-on at home through newspapers.*

**goitre** /ˈgɔɪtə/, *n.* an enlargement of the thyroid gland, on the front and sides of the neck. Also, *U.S.,* **goiter.** [F, from L *guttur* throat]

**goitrous** /ˈgɔɪtrəs/, *adj.* pertaining to or affected with goitre.

**go-kart** /ˈgoʊ-kat/, *n.* a small light vehicle, esp. one without bodywork, having a low-powered engine, used for relatively safe racing. Also, **go-cart, kart.**

**Golconda** /gɒlˈkɒndə/, *n.* (*oft. l.c.*) a mine or source of wealth. [from *Golconda,* a ruined city of India, once renowned for its wealth]

**gold** /goʊld/, *n.* **1.** a precious yellow metal, highly malleable and ductile, and free from liability to rust. *Symbol.:* Au; *at. wt:* 196.967; *at. no.:* 79; *sp. gr.:* 19.3 at 20°C. **2.** coin made of it. **3.** money; wealth. **4.** something likened to this metal in brightness, preciousness, etc.: *a heart of gold.* **5.** bright metallic yellow, sometimes tending towards brown. **6.** a recording which has won, or is likely to win, a gold record; a popular recording. *–adj.* **7.** consisting of gold. **8.** pertaining to gold. **9.** like gold. **10.** of the colour of gold. [ME and OE, c. G *Gold;* akin to Russ. *zoloto*]

**gold-beater's skin** /ˈgoʊld-bitəz skɪn/, *n.* the prepared outside membrane of the large intestine of the ox, used by gold-beaters to lay between the leaves of the metal while they beat it.

**gold-beating** /ˈgoʊld-bitɪŋ/, *n.* the art or process of beating out gold into gold leaf. – **gold-beater,** *n.*

**gold bullion standard,** *n.* a monetary system permitting the movement of gold bullion into and out of the country for international payments, in which the central authority buys and sells gold at the current market rate, and token money (not gold coins) forms the money in circulation.

**gold cap** /ˈgoʊld kæp/, *n.* →**gold top.**

**goldcrest** /ˈgoʊldkrɛst/, *n.* a tiny bird, *Regulus regulus,* with a bright yellow patch on the crown of its head and black bands above the eyes.

**gold-digger** /ˈgoʊld-dɪgə/, *n.* **1.** one who digs or seeks for gold in a goldfield. **2.** *Colloq.* a woman who exploits personal attractiveness for financial gain.

**gold-digging** /ˈgoʊld-dɪgɪŋ/, *n.* **1.** the work of digging for gold. **2.** (*pl.*) a region where digging or seeking for gold, esp. by placer mining, is carried on.

**gold dust** /ˈgoʊld dʌst/, *n.* gold in fine particles.

**golden** /ˈgoʊldən/, *adj.* **1.** of the colour of gold; yellow; bright, metallic, or lustrous like gold. **2.** made or consisting of gold: *golden keys.* **3.** resembling gold in value; most excellent: *a golden opportunity.* **4.** flourishing; joyous: *the golden hours.* **5.** gifted; fortunate and destined for success: *golden boy, golden girl.* **6.** indicating the 50th event of a series, as a wedding anniversary. – **goldenly,** *adv.* – **goldenness,** *n.*

**golden age** /– ˈeɪdʒ/, *n.* **1.** (in Greek and Roman mythology) the first and best age of the world, when mankind lived in innocence and happiness. **2.** the most flourishing period in the history of a nation, literature, etc.

**golden aster** /– ˈæstə/, *n.* any plant of a North American genus, *Chrysopsis,* of aster-like species with bright golden-yellow flowers, esp. a wild flower species, *C. mariana,* abundant in the eastern U.S.

**golden bandicoot** /– ˈbændikut/, *n.* →**wintarro.**

**golden cat** /– ˈkæt/, *n.* either of two medium-sized felines with golden-brown fur, *Felis aurata* of western Africa, and *F. temirincki* of South-East Asia.

**golden chain** /– ˈtʃeɪn/, *n.* →**laburnum.**

**Golden Delicious** /goʊldən dəˈlɪʃəs/, *n.* a variety of yellow apple.

**golden eagle** /goʊldən ˈigəl/, *n.* a large eagle, *Aquila chrysaëtos,* of mountainous regions of the Northern Hemisphere (so called because of the golden-brown feathers on the back of the neck).

**golden hamster** /– ˈhæmstə/, *n.* a short-tailed burrowing rodent, *Mesocricetus auratus,* with a golden coat, native to Asia Minor but kept as a pet in other parts of the world.

**golden handshake** /– ˈhændʃeɪk/, *n. Colloq.* a gratuity or benefit, given to employees as a recognition of their services on the occasion of their retirement or resignation, or as a sop when they are dismissed.

**golden-headed cisticola** /ˌgoʊldən-hɛdəd sɪstəˈkoʊlə/, *n.* a small bird, *Cisticola exilis,* golden buff in colour streaked with grey-brown, which stitches living leaves into its nest in order to conceal it; tailorbird.

**golden mean** /goʊldən ˈmin/, *n.* the happy medium between extremes; moderate course of action. [translation of L *aurea mediocritas* (Horace)]

**golden moths** /– ˈmɒθs/, *n., pl.* **moths.** a terrestrial orchid, *Diuris pedunculata,* with canary-yellow flowers, widespread in south-eastern Australia.

**golden perch** /– ˈpɜtʃ/, *n.* a native Australian freshwater fish, *Plectroplites ambiguus,* often pale yellow or golden in colour; ranked second to Murray Cod as a table fish; callop; yellow-belly; freshwater bream; Murray perch.

**golden pheasant** /– ˈfɛzənt/, *n.* an Asiatic pheasant, *Chrysolophus pictus,* with rich yellow and orange tones in the head and neck plumage of the male.

**golden rain** /– ˈreɪn/, *n.* **1.** →**laburnum.** **2.** the cassia, *Cassia fistula,* an ornamental tropical tree.

**golden retriever** /– rəˈtrivə/, *n.* one of a breed of retrievers with thick, wavy, golden coat.

**goldenrod** /ˈgoʊldənrɒd/, *n.* any plant of the genus *Solidago,* most species of which bear numerous small yellow flowers.

**golden rule** /goʊldən ˈrul/, *n.* **1.** the rule of conduct, *Whatsoever ye would that men should do to you, do ye even so to them.* Matt. 7:12. **2.** rule of three. **3.** any very important rule, esp. of conduct.

**golden saxifrage** /– ˈsæksəfrɪdʒ, -freɪdʒ/, *n.* any of several small perennial herbs of wet places, as the **opposite-leaved golden saxifrage,** *Chrysosplenium oppositifolium,* of western and central Europe.

**goldenseal** /goʊldənˈsil/, *n.* **1.** a herb, *Hydrastis canadensis,* with a thick yellow rootstock. **2.** the rhizomes and roots of this plant, formerly much used in medicine.

**golden section** /goʊldən ˈsɛkʃən/, *n.* the division of a line so that the shorter segment is to the longer as the longer is to the whole, roughly a ratio of three to five; regarded as an ideal division.

**golden syrup** /– ˈsɪrəp/, *n.* a supersaturated solution of sucrose and invert sugars, derived from sugar processing; used in cooking and as a sauce for porridge, desserts, etc.

**golden-tip** /ˈgoʊldən-tɪp/, *n.* any shrub of the small genus *Goodia,* as *G. lotifolia* of south-eastern Australia, with yellow, pea-shaped flowers.

**golden wattle** /goʊldən ˈwɒtl/, *n.* **1.** a broad-leafed Australian acacia, *Acacia pycnantha,* yielding useful gum and tanbark; floral emblem of the Commonwealth of Australia. **2.** any similar acacia, esp. the Sydney golden wattle, *A. longifolia.*

**golden wedding** /– 'wɛdɪŋ/, *n.* the fiftieth anniversary of a wedding.

**gold-exchange standard** /'gould-əkstʃeɪndʒ ˌstændəd/, *n.* a monetary system whose monetary unit is kept at a fixed relation with that of a country on the gold standard by dealings in foreign exchange by the central authority, the money in circulation being token money.

**goldfield** /'gouldfild/, *n.* a district in which gold is mined.

**goldfielder** /'gouldfildə/, *n.* an inhabitant of or worker on a goldfield; goldminer.

**goldfields** /'gouldfildz/, *adj.* of or pertaining to a goldfield.

**gold-filled** /'gould-fɪld/, *adj.* containing a filling of cheaper metal within a layer of gold.

**goldfinch** /'gouldfɪntʃ/, *n.* **1.** a European fringilline songbird, *Carduelis carduelis,* having a crimson face and wings marked with yellow, introduced into Australia where it is now common. **2.** any of certain small American finches, esp. *Spinus tristis,* the male of which has yellow body plumage in summer. [ME; OE *goldfinc.* See GOLD, FINCH]

**goldfish** /'gouldfɪʃ/, *n., pl.* **-fishes,** (*esp. collectively*) **-fish.** a small fish, *Carassius auratus,* of the carp family and originally native to China, prized for aquariums and pools because of its golden colouring and odd form (produced by artificial selection); introduced and now quite widespread in the southern half of Australia.

**goldfish-bowl** /'gouldfɪʃ-boul/, *n.* **1.** a fishbowl. **2.** *Colloq.* a state of helpless exposure to public curiosity; lack of privacy.

**gold foil** /gould 'fɔɪl/, *n.* gold beaten into thin sheets (many times thicker than gold leaf).

**goldfussia** /gould'fʌsiə/, *n.* a small shrub, *Strobilanthes isophyllus,* native to India, with metallic-purple leaves and tubular pale blue flowers.

**goldilocks** /'gouldilɒks/, *n. construed as sing. or pl.* (*sometimes cap.*). **1.** a person with golden hair. **2.** a perennial herb, *Ranunculus auricomus,* common in woods of Europe and northern Asia. **3.** a perennial herb, *Aster linosyris,* found mostly on limestone in central and southern Europe. [from the story *Goldilocks and the Three Bears*]

**gold leaf** /gould 'lif/, *n.* gold beaten into a very thin sheet, used for gilding, etc.

**gold medal** /– 'mɛdl/, *n.* a prize awarded for first place in a race or other competition, esp. the Olympics. See **silver medal, bronze medal.**

**goldmine** /'gouldmaɪn/, *n.* **1.** a mine yielding gold. **2.** a source of great wealth. **3.** a source of anything required: *a goldmine of information.* – **goldminer, goldmining,** *n.*

**gold-of-pleasure** /gould-əv-'plɛʒə/, *n.* a herb, *Camelina sativa,* with small yellowish flowers.

**gold plate** /gould 'pleɪt/, *n.* **1.** a plating, esp. electroplating, of gold. **2.** articles and utensils collectively, esp. tableware, of gold plate or, formerly, solid gold.

**gold point** /'– pɔɪnt/, *n.* the point at which it is equally expensive to buy (or sell), exchange, or export (or import) gold in adjustment of foreign claims (or counterclaims).

**gold record** /– 'rɛkɔd/, *n.* a gold-plated record made by a recording company when a certain number of copies of the record (in Australia 20 000) have been sold, and presented by the company to the artists or other people involved in its production and promotion.

**gold reserve** /'– rəzɜv/, *n.* the total gold coin and bullion held by a central authority either national or international. It is used to make international payments, and nationally to maintain the value of the token notes and coinage issued on behalf of the government.

**gold rush** /'– rʌʃ/, *n.* a large-scale and rapid movement of people to a region where gold has been discovered, as that to Bendigo and Ballarat, Victoria, in the mid-19th century.

**goldsmith** /'gouldsmɪθ/, *n.* one who makes or sells articles of gold (down to the 18th century, often acting also as a banker). [ME and OE]

**goldsmith beetle** /'– bitl/, *n.* either of two scarabaeid beetles of a metallic golden colour, *Cetonia aurata* of Europe or *Cotalpa lanigera* of North America.

**gold standard** /'gould stændəd/, *n.* a monetary system in which there is a free mintage of gold into standard legal coins, free movement of gold into and out of the country, and in which the currency unit is based on gold of a fixed weight and fineness.

**goldstone** /'gouldstoun/, *n.* →**aventurine** (def. 1).

**goldthread** /'gouldθrɛd/, *n.* **1.** a white-flowered herb, *Coptis groenlandica,* with a slender yellow root. **2.** the root itself, used in medicine.

**gold top** /'gould tɒp/, *n.* a mushroom, *Psilocybe cubensis,* with grey-black gills, which often has a yellow staining of the cap, and which can cause hallucinations; a similar species was the basis for a sacred mushroom cult in Mexico and Central and South America. Also, **gold cap**

**golem** /'goulɛm/, *n.* **1.** (in Jewish legend) a figure constructed to represent a human being, and endowed with life, by human agency. **2.** →**automaton.** [Heb.]

**golf** /gɒlf/, *n.* **1.** an outdoor game, in which a small resilient ball is driven with special clubs into a series of holes, distributed at various distances over a course having natural or artificial obstacles, the object being to get the ball into each hole in as few strokes as possible. *–v.i.* **2.** to play golf. [ME (Scot.); orig. uncert.] – **golfer,** *n.*

**golf bag** /'– bæg/, *n.* a bag used for carrying golf clubs, balls, etc.

**golf ball** /'– bɔl/, *n.* **1.** a small white ball with a resilient core of rubber used in playing golf. **2.** *Colloq.* the movable metal ball bearing the type in an electric typewriter.

**golf buggy** /'– bʌgi/, *n.* **1.** a trolley on which a golf bag can be wheeled around a golf course. **2.** a small motorised vehicle used for travelling around a golf course.

**golf club** /'– klʌb/, *n.* **1.** any of the various implements for striking the ball in golf. **2.** an organisation of golf players. **3.** a club with grounds for members to play golf on, often combined with various social amenities.

**golf course** /'– kɔs/, *n.* the ground or course over which golf is played. Also, **golf links.**

**Golgotha** /gɒl'gɒθə, 'gɒlgəθə/, *n.* **1.** →**Calvary.** **2.** a place of suffering or sacrifice. [L (Vulgate), from Gk (N.T.), from Aram. *goghaltā,* Heb. *gulgolĕth* skull; see John 19:17]

**goliard** /'gɒliad/, *n.* one of a number of wandering scholars, clerics, or students in Germany, France, and England, chiefly in the 12th and 13th centuries, noted for their rioting and intemperance, and as the authors of satirical Latin verse. [late ME, from OF: lit., glutton, from *gole,* from L *gula* throat, palate, gluttony] – **goliardic** /gɒli'adɪk/, *adj.*

**goliardery** /gɒli'adəri/, *n.* the poems of the goliards.

**Goliath** /gə'laɪəθ/, *n.* a person of great strength or size; giant. [from *Goliath,* the champion of the Philistines slain by the youthful David (I Sam. 17:4); from L (Vulgate), from Gk (Septuagint), representing Heb. *Golyath*]

**goliath crane** /gəlaɪəθ 'kreɪn/, *n.* a type of powerful travelling crane mounted on a movable gantry.

**goliath frog** /'– frɒg/, *n.* the largest known frog, *Rana goliath,* almost 30 cm long, native to the Congo region of Africa.

**goliath heron** /– 'hɛrən/, *n.* the African giant heron, *Ardea goliath.*

**golliwog**[1] /'gɒliwɒg/, *n.* a soft, black-faced doll. Also, **golly-wog.** [var. of *Golliwogg,* name of a doll coined *c.* 1910 by Florence and Bertha Upton, U.S. writers for children]

**golliwog**[2] /'gɒliwɒg/, *n. Prison Colloq.* an informer. [rhyming slang, *golliwog* dog (def. 11)]

**gollop** /'gɒləp/, *v.t.* to eat quickly and noisily. [b. GULP + GALLOP]

**golly**[1] /'gɒli/, *interj. Colloq.* (a mild expletive expressing surprise, etc.) [a euphemistic var. of *God!*]

**golly**[2] /'gɒli/, *n.* →**golliwog**[1].

**golly**[3] /'gɒli/, *v.,* **-lied, -lying,** *n., pl.* **-lies.** *–v.i. Colloq.* **1.** to spit. *–n.* **2.** spittle.

**golosh** /gə'lɒʃ/, *n.* →**galosh.**

**goloshes** /gə'lɒʃəz/, *n. pl.* →**galoshes.**

**goluptious** /gə'lʌpʃəs/, *adj.* delicious. Also, **galumptious, goloptious.**

**G.O.M.,** grand old man. [orig. applied to W.E. *Gladstone,* 1809-98, British statesman and prime minister]

**gombo** /'gʌmbou/, *n.* →**gumbo.**

**Gomorrah** /gə'mɒrə/, *n.* any very wicked place. Also, **Gomorrha.** [from *Gomorrah,* the ancient city destroyed (with Sodom) for the wickedness of its inhabitants (Genesis 18-19)]

**gompholobium** /gɒmfə'loubiəm/, *n.* any shrub of the endemic Australian genus *Gompholobium,* family Papilionaceae, with yellow, or occasionally reddish, pea-shaped flowers.

**gomphosis** /gɒm'fousəs/, *n.* an immovable articulation in which one bone or part is received in a cavity in another, as a tooth in its socket. [NL, from Gk: a bolting together]

**gomuti** /gə'muti/, *n., pl.* **-tis. 1.** Also, **gomuti palm.** a sago palm, *Arenga pinnata,* of the East Indies; source of palm sugar. **2.** a black, horsehair-like fibre obtained from it, used for making rope, etc. [Malay]

**-gon,** a suffix denoting geometrical figures having a certain number or kind of angles, as in *polygon, pentagon.* [Gk *-gōnos* (neut. *-gōnon*) -angled, -angular]

**gonad** /'gounæd/, *n.* the sex gland, male or female, in which gametes develop and appropriate sex hormones are produced. [NL *gonas,* from Gk *gónos* offspring, seed] – **gonadal** /gou'nædəl/. – **gonadial** /gou'neɪdiəl/. – **gonadic** /gou'nædɪk/, *adj.*

**gonadectomy** /gounə'dɛktəmi/, *n.* the surgical excision of a gonad.

**gonadotrophic** /gɒnədə'troufɪk/, *adj.* pertaining to hormones (gonadotropins) formed in the hypophysis or the placenta which affect the activity of the ovary or testis. Also, **gonadotropic.**

**gonadotropin** /gɒnədə'troupən/, *n.* a hormone having affinity for or a stimulating effect on the gonads.

**gondola** /'gɒndələ/, *n.* **1.** a long, narrow boat with a high peak at each end and often a small cabin near the middle, used on the Venetian canals and usu. propelled at the stern by a single oar or pole. **2.** the car of a dirigible. **3.** the basket suspended beneath a balloon, for carrying passengers, instruments, etc. **4.** a free-standing tray on legs for displaying goods on a shop floor. **5.** *U.S.* →**lighter**[2] (def. 1). [It. (Venetian), from *gondolar, gongolarsi,* from Rom. root *dond-* to rock]

gondola (def. 1)

**gondolier** /gɒndə'lɪə/, *n.* a man who rows or poles a gondola. [F, from It. *gondoliere,* from *gondola*]

**Gondwana** /gɒnd'wanə/, *n.* an ancient continent including India, Australia, Antarctica, parts of Africa and South America in Palaeozoic and Mesozoic times. Also, **Gondwanaland.** [region in India, from Skt]

**gone** /gɒn/, *v.* **1.** past participle of **go.** *–adj.* **2.** departed; left. **3.** lost or hopeless. **4.** used up. **5.** that has departed or passed away; dead. **6.** weak and faint: *a gone feeling.* **7.** pregnant. **8.** *Colloq.* exhilarated; in a state of excitement (as by the influence of drugs, jazz, etc.). **9. far gone,** *Colloq.* **a.** much advanced; deeply involved. **b.** extremely mad. **c.** extremely drunk. **d.** almost exhausted. **e.** dying. **10. gone on,** *Colloq.* infatuated with.

**goner** /'gɒnə/, *n. Colloq.* a person or thing that is dead, lost, or past recovery or rescue.

**gonfalon** /'gɒnfələn/, *n.* **1.** a banner suspended from a crossbar, often with several streamers or tails. **2.** the standard used esp. by the medieval Italian republics. [It. *gonfalone,* from OHG *gundfano,* lit., war flag]

**gong** /gɒŋ/, *n.* **1.** *Music.* an oriental bronze disc with the rim turned up, to be struck with a soft-headed stick. **2.** any saucer-shaped bell, esp. one sounded by a hammer. **3.** *Colloq.* a medal. *–v.t.* **4.** to warn or summon with the striking of a gong. [Malay] – **gonglike,** *adj.*

**gong culture** /'– kʌltʃə/, *n.* the culture of South-East Asia, of which a unifying feature is that the music is based on gongs.

**gonidium** /gə'nɪdiəm/, *n., pl.* **-nidia** /-'nɪdiə/. **1.** an algal one-celled asexual reproductive body, as a tetraspore or zoospore. **2.** an algal cell, or a filament of an alga, growing within the thallus of a lichen. [NL, from Gk *gónos* offspring, seed + *-idion,* diminutive suffix] – **gonidial,** *adj.*

**goniometer** /ˌgouni'ɒmətə/, *n.* an instrument for measuring solid angles, as of crystals. [F *goniomètre,* from Gk *gōnio-* angle + *-mètre* -METER[1]] – **goniometric** /ˌgouniə'mɛtrɪk/, **goniometrical** /ˌgouniə'mɛtrɪkəl/, *adj.* – **goniometry,** *n.*

**gonion** /'gouniən/, *n., pl.* **-nia** /-niə/. the tip of the angle of the lower jaw. [NL, from Gk *gōnía* angle]

**gonium** /'gouniəm/, *n., pl.* **-nia** /-niə/. the germ cell during the phase marked by mitosis. [NL]

**-gonium** /-'gouniəm/, a word element referring to reproductive cells. [NL, from Gk *-gonia,* combining form representing *goneía* generation]

**gonk** /gɒŋk/, *n.* long-haired rag or felt doll popular in the 1960s.

**gono-,** a word element meaning 'sexual' or 'reproductive', as in *gonococcus.* [Gk, combining form of *gónos, gonḗ* seed, generation, etc.]

**gonococcus** /gɒnou'kɒkəs/, *n., pl.* **-cocci** /-'kɒksaɪ/. the causative organism of gonorrhoea. [NL. See GONO-, COCCUS] – **gonococcal,** *adj.*

**gonocyte** /'gɒnousaɪt/, *n.* a germ cell, esp. during the maturation phase; oocyte; spermatocyte.

**gonophore** /'gɒnoufɔ/, *n.* **1.** an asexually produced bud in hydrozoans that gives rise to a medusa or its equivalent. **2.** a prolongation of the axis of a flower above the perianth, bearing the stamens and pistil.

**gonorrhoea** /gɒnə'riə/, *n.* a contagious disease causing purulent inflammation mainly of the urethra and cervix, but occasionally causing proctitis, ophthalmitis, pharyngitis. Also, *Chiefly U.S.,* **gonorrhea.** [LL, from Gk *gonórrhoia,* from *gono-* GONO- + *rhoía* a flow] – **gonorrhoeal,** *adj.*

**gonotocont** /gə'nɒtəkɒnt/, *n.* **1.** a cell that is capable of undergoing meiosis. **2.** any organ containing such a cell. Also, **gonotokont.**

**-gony,** a word element meaning 'production', 'genesis', 'origination', as in *cosmogony, theogony.* [L *-gonia,* from Gk. See -GONIUM and cf. -GENY]

**gonzo** /'gɒnzou/, *adj. Colloq.* eccentric; crazy. [It. *gonzo* simpleton, perhaps from L *Burgundiō* Burgundian]

**gonzo journalism** /– 'dʒɜnəlɪzəm/, *n.* a style of journalism which specialises in the bizarre.

**goo** /gu/, *n. Colloq.* sticky matter. [short for BURGOO]

**goober** /'gubə/, *n. U.S.* →**peanut.** Also, **goober pea.** [Angolan *nguba*]

**Gooch crucible** /gutʃ 'krusəbəl/, *n.* a laboratory filter consisting of a shallow porcelain cup the flat bottom of which contains small holes over which a layer of asbestos fibres are placed. [named after F.A. *Gooch,* d. 1929, U.S. chemist]

**good** /gʊd/, *adj.,* **better, best,** *n., interj. –adj.* **1.** morally excellent; righteous; pious: *a good man.* **2.** satisfactory in quality, quantity, or degree; excellent: *good food, good health.* **3.** right; proper; qualified; fit: *to whatever seems good to you, his credit is good.* **4.** well-behaved: *a good child.* **5.** kind, beneficent (oft. fol. by *for*): *this medicine is good for you.* **6.** fresh and palatable; not tainted. **7.** honourable or worthy; in good standing: *a good name, Mr. Hood and his good lady.* **8.** refined; well-bred; educated. **9.** reliable; safe: *good securities.* **10.** genuine; sound or valid: *good judgment, good reasons.* **11.** loyal; close: *a good friend.* **12.** attractive; fine; beautiful: *she has a good figure.* **13.** (of the complexion) without blemish or flaw. **14.** agreeable; pleasant; genial: *have a good time.* **15.** pleasurable; exciting. **16.** satisfactory for the purpose; advantageous: *a good day for fishing.* **17.** sufficient or ample: *a good supply.* **18.** (of clothes) best or newest. **19.** full: *a good day's journey.* **20.** competent or skilful; clever: *a good manager, good at arithmetic.* **21.** fairly great: *a good deal.* **22. a.** valid (oft. fol. by *for*): *that ticket is good for six months.* **b.** entitling (a person) to (fol. by *for*): *that is good for a beer or two.* **c.** (of a person) willing to provide (fol. by *for*): *he is always good for a loan.* **23. a good press,** *Colloq.* a favourable reaction by newspapers and journals. **24. a good question,** *Colloq.* a difficult or demanding question. **25. a good way,** *Colloq.* a considerable extent. **26. as good as,** in effect; practically: *he as good as said it.* **27. as good as gold,** *Colloq.* well behaved, usu. of children. **28. feel good,** *Colloq.* to be happy or in good health. **29. good and,** (as an intensive): *you can wait until we're good and ready.* **30. good enough,** *Colloq.* satisfactory. **31. good grief,** *Colloq.* (an expression of surprise, vexation, etc.). **32. good iron,** *Colloq.* **a.** (an exclamation of approval). **b.** a likeable person. **33. good luck,** *Colloq.* (an expression wishing a person well). **34. good show,** *Colloq.* (an expression of approval). **35. no good to gundy,** *Colloq.* worthless. **36. that's a good one,** *Colloq.* (an ironic expression of disbelief). **37. too good to be true,** *Colloq.* to be so satisfactory as to be unbelievable. **38. too much of a good thing,** *Colloq.* **a.** excessive. **b.** an excessive amount. *–n.* **39.** profit; worth; advantage; benefit: *what good will that do? to work for the common good.* **40.** excellence or merit; righteousness; kindness; virtue: *to be a power for good, do good.* **41.** (*sometimes cap.*) the force which governs and brings about righteousness and virtue. **42.** a good, commendable, or desirable thing. **43.** (*pl.*) possessions, esp. movable effects or personal chattels. **44.** (*pl.*) articles of trade; wares; merchandise, esp. that which is transported by land. **45.** (*pl.*) *Colloq.* what has been promised or is expected: *to deliver the goods.* **46.** (*pl.*) *Colloq.* the genuine article. **47.** (*pl.*) *Colloq.* evidence of guilt, as stolen articles: *to catch with the goods.* **48. goods and chattels, a.** all moveable properties. **b.** *Colloq.* all (one's) possessions. **49. for good** or **for good and all,** finally and permanently; for ever: *to leave a place for good (and all).* **50. all to the good,** *Colloq.* generally advantageous, often used to justify an unpleasant event. **51. be up to no good,** *Colloq.* to do wrong; break the law in some undisclosed way; behave in a suspicious manner. **52. make good, a.** to make recompense for; pay for. **b.** to keep to an agreement; fulfil. **c.** to be successful. **d.** to prove the truth of; substantiate. *–interj.* **53.** (an expression of approval or satisfaction). **54. good on** or **for you,** *Colloq.* (an expression of approval, encouragement, etc.) [ME; OE *gōd*, c. D *goed*, G *gut*, Icel. *gōdhr*, Goth. *gōths* good; ? orig. meaning fitting, suitable, and akin to GATHER]

**good afternoon** /– aftə'nun/, *interj.* (a conventional expression used at a meeting or parting in the afternoon).

**good behaviour** /gʊd bə'heɪvjə/, *n.* in lieu of imprisonment an offender may be ordered to enter into a recognisance to be of good behaviour for a specified period.

**Good Book** /'gʊd bʊk/, *n.* the Bible.

**goodbye** /gʊd'baɪ/, *interj., n., pl.* **-byes.** *–interj.* **1.** farewell (a conventional expression used at parting). *–n.* **2.** a farewell. Also, *Chiefly U.S.,* **goodby.** [contraction of *God be with you (ye)*]

**good cheer** /gʊd 'tʃɪə/, *n.* **1.** cheerful spirits; courage: *to be of good cheer.* **2.** feasting and merrymaking: *to make good cheer.* **3.** good fare or food; feasting: *to be fond of good cheer.*

**good conduct** /– 'kɒndʌkt/, *n.* orderly behaviour, esp. in conformity with the law.

**good day** /gə 'deɪ/, *interj.* (a conventional expression used at a meeting or a parting during the day.)

**good egg** /gʊd 'ɛg/, *Colloq. –n.* **1.** a pleasant, agreeable, trustworthy person. *–interj.* **2.** (an exclamation of pleasurable surprise.)

**goodenia** /gə'diniə/, *n.* any herb or undershrub of the large, mostly Australian genus *Goodenia* characterised by zygomorphic flowers and a prominent stigma.

**good-enough** /'gʊd-ənʌf/, *adj.* satisfactory: *it's a good-enough idea.*

**good evening** /gʊd 'ivnɪŋ/, *interj.* (a conventional expression used at a meeting or a parting during the evening.).

**good faith** /– 'feɪθ/, *n.* **1.** honesty of purpose or sincerity of declaration: *to act in good faith.* **2.** expectation of such qualities in others: *to take a job in good faith.*

**good fellowship** /– 'fɛləʃɪp/, *n.* a pleasant or genial spirit; conviviality.

**good form** /– 'fɔm/, *n.* conduct that satisfies current commonly accepted standards.

**good-for-nothing** /'gʊd-fə-nʌθɪŋ/, *adj.* **1.** worthless. *–n.* **2.** a worthless person.

**Good Friday** /gʊd 'fraɪdeɪ/, *n.* the Friday before Easter, a holy day of the Christian Church, observed as the anniversary of the crucifixion of Jesus.

**good guts** /'gʊd gʌts/, *n. Colloq.* **1.** accurate information. **2.** such information designed to be used to bring about someone's downfall (fol. by *on*).

**good-hearted** /'gʊd-hatəd/, *adj.* kind; considerate. **–good-heartedly,** *adv.* **–good-heartedness,** *n.*

**good humour** /gʊd 'hjumə/, *n.* a cheerful or amiable mood.

**good-humoured** /'gʊd-hjuməd/, *adj.* having or showing a pleasant, amiable mood: *good-humoured man.* **–good-humouredly,** *adv.* **–good-humouredness,** *n.*

**goodie** /'gʊdi/, *n. Colloq.* **1.** (*pl.*) sweets or cakes. **2.** (*pl.*) attractive foodstuffs, clothes, possessions, etc. **3.** a good person, esp. a hero in a story, play or film. Also, **goody.**

**goodish** /'gʊdɪʃ/, *adj.* rather good; fairly good.

**Good-King-Henry** /ˌgʊd-kɪŋ-'hɛnri/, *n.* an erect, perennial herb, *Chenopodium bonus-henricus,* a widespread weed.

**good life** /gʊd 'laɪf/, *for def. 1;* /'gʊd laɪf/, *for def. 2.* *–n.* **1.** a life led according to religious laws and moral conventions. **2. the good life,** a life filled with material luxuries and comfort. **– good liver,** *n.*

**good-looker** /gʊd-'lʊkə/, *n. Colloq.* a person who has good looks.

**good-looking** /'gʊd-lʊkɪŋ/, *adj.* of good appearance; handsome.

**good looks** /gʊd 'lʊks/, *n.pl.* handsome personal appearance.

**goodly** /'gʊdli/, *adj.,* **-lier, -liest.** **1.** of a good quality: *a goodly gift.* **2.** of good or fine apparance. **3.** of good size or amount: *a goodly sum.* **– goodliness,** *n.*

**goodman** /'gʊdmən/, *n., pl.* **-men.** *Archaic.* **1.** title of respect used for those below the rank of gentleman, esp. a farmer or yeoman. **2.** the master of a household; husband.

**good-mannered** /'gʊd-mænəd/, *adj.* well-behaved; polite.

**good morning** /gəd 'mɔnɪŋ/, *interj.* (a conventional expression used at a meeting or a parting during the morning).

**good nature** /gʊd 'neɪtʃə/, *n.* pleasant disposition; cheerful nature.

**good-natured** /'gʊd-neɪtʃəd/, *adj.* having or showing good nature or a pleasant or complaisant disposition or mood; good-humoured. **– good-naturedly,** *adv.* **– good-naturedness,** *n.*

**goodness** /'gʊdnəs/, *n.* **1.** moral excellence; virtue. **2.** kindly feeling; kindness; generosity. **3.** excellence of quality: *goodness of workmanship.* **4.** the best part of anything; essence; strength. **5.** (used in various exclamatory or emphatic expressions): *thank goodness!* *–interj.* **6.** (an exclamation expressing mild surprise).

**goodness of fit,** *n.* (in statistics) the measure of how closely a set of observed values approximate those derived from a theoretical model.

**good night** /gəd 'naɪt/, *interj.* (a conventional expression used at a meeting or, more usu., a parting during the evening or night).

**goodnight** /gəd'naɪt/, *n.;* /'gʊdnaɪt/, *adj.* *–n.* **1.** a farewell; a leave-taking. *–adj.* **2.** of or pertaining to a parting, esp. final or at night: *a goodnight kiss.*

**goodo** /'gʊdoʊ/, *interj. Colloq.* (an exclamation indicating pleasure, agreement, etc.). Also, **good-oh.**

**good offices** /gʊd 'ɒfəsəz/, *n.pl.* **1.** mediating services in a dispute. **2.** influence esp. with someone in power.

**good Samaritan** /– sə'mærətn/, *n.* a person who is compassionate and helpful to one in distress. [Luke 10: 30-37.]

**Good Shepherd** /gʊd 'ʃɛpəd/, *n.* Jesus Christ.

**good-sized** /'gʊd-saɪzd/, *adj.* of ample size; largish.

**goods lift** /'gʊdz lɪft/, *n.* a lift for the carriage of goods (as against people), as in a block of flats or offices; service lift.

**good speed** /gʊd 'spid/, *n.* good fortune, or success: *to wish a person good speed.*

**goods train** /'gʊdz treɪn/, *n.* a train of goods wagons.

**goods truck** /'– trʌk/, *n.* →**goods wagon.**

**goods wagon** /'– wægən/, *n.* a railway wagon for carrying goods, merchandise, etc. Also, **goods truck.**

**goods yard** /'– jad/, *n.* a railway yard where goods are delivered and collected; freight terminal.

**good-tempered** /'gʊd-tɛmpəd/, *adj.* good-natured; amiable. **– good-temperedly,** *adv.*

**goodtime** /'gʊdtaɪm/, *adj.* **1.** of or pertaining to a relaxed style of rock music which, although it may be rehearsed, has an essentially unrehearsed feeling. **2. goodtime girl,** *Colloq.* a young woman, esp. one of easy virtue.

**good timer** /gʊd 'taɪmə/, *n.* a person who devotes himself to entertainments and amusements while neglecting more serious pursuits.

**good turn** /– 'tɜn/, *n.* →**turn** (def. 82).

**goodwife** /'gʊdwaɪf/, *n., pl.* **-wives** /-waɪvz/. *Archaic.* **1.** the mistress of a household. **2.** a title of respect for a woman.

**goodwill** /gʊd'wɪl/, *n.* **1.** friendly disposition; benevolence; favour. **2.** cheerful acquiescence. **3.** *Comm.* an intangible, saleable asset arising from the reputation of a business and its relations with its customers, distinct from the value of its stock, etc. *–adj.* **4.** exhibiting or attempting to foster goodwill: *a goodwill mission.* Also, **good will.**

**goody**[1] /'gʊdi/, *Colloq. –interj.* **1.** wonderful! how nice! *–n.* **2.** →**goodie.** [GOOD, *adj.* + -Y[1]]

**goody**[2] /'gʊdi/, *n., pl.* **goodies.** a polite term formerly applied to a woman in humble life. [var. of GOODWIFE]

**goody-goody** /'gʊdi-gʊdi/, *n., pl.* **-goodies,** *adj. Colloq. –n.* **1.** a sentimentally or priggishly good person. *–adj.* **2.** affecting goodness.

**gooey** /'gui/, *adj.,* **gooier, gooiest.** *Colloq.* **1.** like goo; sticky; viscoid. **2.** overemotional; sentimental. – **gooiness,** *n.*

**goof** /guf, gʊf/, *Colloq. –n.* **1.** a foolish or stupid person. *–v.i.* **2.** to blunder; slip up. **3. goof off,** to daydream; fritter away time. *–v.t.* **4.** to bungle (something); botch (oft. fol. by *up*). **5.** to swallow (a drug, as amphetamine). [apparently var. of obs. *goff* dolt, from F *goffe*] – **goofy,** *adj.* – **goofily,** *adv.* – **goofiness,** *n.*

**goof ball** /'– bɔl/, *n. Colloq.* an amphetamine pill.

**goofy-foot** /'gufi-fʊt/, *n. Colloq.* a surfboard rider who surfs with his right foot as the lead foot. Also, **goofy-footer.**

**goog** /gʊg/, *n. Colloq.* **1.** an egg. **2. full as a goog, a.** extremely drunk. **b.** well-fed.

**googly** /'gugli/, *n.* (in cricket) a delivery bowled by a wrist-spinner which looks as if it will break one way but in fact goes the other (the right-hander's googly will act as an off-break to the right-handed batsman, the left-hander's will act as a leg-break); bosie; wrong 'un. [orig. unknown]

**googy-egg** /'gʊgi-ɛg/, *n.* (*in children's speech*) an egg.

**gook** /guk, gʊk/, *n. Chiefly U.S. Colloq.* (*derog.*) a foreigner; an Asian, esp. a national of a country in which Western soldiers are fighting, as a Japanese, a Korean, a Vietnamese.

**goolie** /'guli/, *n. Colloq.* **1.** a stone. **2.** a testicle. Also, **gooly.**

**gooligum** /'guligʌm/, *n. Colloq.* (an indefinite name for a thing which a speaker cannot or does not designate more precisely).

**goon** /gun/, *n. Colloq.* **1.** a stupid person. **2.** a hired thug: *goon squad.* **3.** a hooligan or tough.

**goondie** /'gundi/, *n.* an Aboriginal hut or gunyah. [Aboriginal]

**goony bird** /'guni bɜd/, *n.* **1.** *U.S.* →**albatross.** **2.** *Colloq.* a Dakota aeroplane; DC3. Also, **gooney bird.**

**goori** /'guri/, *n. N.Z. Colloq.* →**kuri**[1]. Also, **goorie, goory.**

**goosander** /gu'sændə/, *n.* **1.** a saw-billed fish-eating duck, *Mergus merganser,* of Europe and North America. **2.** any merganser.

**goose**[1] /gus/, *n., pl.* **geese** *for defs 1-4, 7;* **gooses** *for defs 5 and 6.* **1.** any of numerous wild or domesticated web-footed birds of the family Anatidae, most of them larger and with a longer neck than the ducks, as the pied goose; the principal genera are *Anser, Branta,* and *Chen.* **2.** the female of this bird, as distinguished from the male (or gander). **3.** the flesh of the goose. **4.** a silly or foolish person; simpleton. **5.** *Music.* a harsh break in the tone of a clarinet, oboe or bassoon. **6.** a tailor's smoothing-iron with a curved handle. **7.** *Obs.* a game played with counters. **8. cook someone's goose,** *Colloq.* to frustrate or ruin a person's hopes or plans. [ME *gos(e), goos,* OE *gōs* (pl. *gēs*), c. D and G *Gans,* Icel. *gās* goose; akin to L *anser,* Gk *chḗn*] – **gooselike,** *adj.*

**goose**[2] /gus/, *v.,* **goosed, goosing,** *n., pl.* **-ses.** *–v.t.* **1.** to poke someone between the buttocks, usu. in fun and unexpectedly. *–n.* **2.** an unexpected poke between the buttocks.

**gooseberry** /'gʊzbəri, -bri/, *n., pl.* **-ries.** **1.** the small, edible, acid, globular fruit or berry of certain prevailingly prickly shrubs of the genus *Ribes,* esp. *R. grossularia.* **2.** the shrub itself. **3. play gooseberry,** to embarrass or restrict two people who might like to be alone by accompanying them.

gooseberry

**goose bumps** /'gus bʌmps/, *n.*→**goose pimples.**

**goose flesh** /'– flɛʃ/, *n.*→**goose pimples.**

**goosefoot** /'gusfʊt/, *n., pl.* **-foots.** **1.** any plant of the genus *Chenopodium,* containing many widely distributed herbs and shrubs with minute green flowers. **2.** any member of the family Chenopodiaceae.

**goosegrass** /'gusgras/, *n.*→**cleavers.**

**gooseherd** /'gushɜd/, *n.* one who tends geese.

**gooseman** /'gusmæn/, *n. Timber Industry.* one who operates a goose saw.

**gooseneck** /'gusnɛk/, *n.* something curved like the neck of a goose, as an iron hook for attaching a boom to a mast, or a flexible stand for a desk lamp.

**goose pimples** /'gus pɪmpəlz/, *n.pl.* a rough condition of the skin resembling that of a plucked goose caused by erection of the papillae and induced by cold or fear. Also, **goose bumps, goose flesh.** – **goosepimply,** *adj.*

**goose saw** /'– sɔ/, *n. Timber Industry.* a swinging saw used for the trimming, cross-cut trimming, etc. of boards.

**goosestep** /'gusstɛp/, *n., v.,* **-stepped, -stepping.** *–n.* **1.** a military exercise in which the body is balanced on one foot (without advancing) while the other foot is swung forwards and back. **2.** an exaggerated marching step in which the legs are swung high with straight, stiff knees. *–v.i.* **3.** to walk or march in a goosestep.

**goosewing** /'guswɪŋ/, *v.t.* when sailing before the wind, to hold (the jib) on the side opposite to the mainsail.

**goosewinged** /'guswɪŋd/, *adj.* **1.** (of a square sail, usu. a lower, topsail) having the leeside hauled up and made fast and the weather side set, as in strong winds. **2.** (of a fore-and-aft rigged ship) sailing before the wind with the jib to one side and the mainsail to the other.

**goosy** /'gusi/, *adj.* having goose pimples. Also, **goosey.**

**gopak** /'goʊpæk/, *n.* a traditional male Russian dance characterised by high leaps. [Russ., from Ukrainian *hopak,* from *hop!* cry used in dance, from G *hopp!*]

**gopher**[1] /'goʊfə/, *n.* **1.** any of various ground squirrels of western North America, as *Citellus* (or *Spermophilus*) *tridecemlineatus.* **2.** Also, **pocket gopher.** any of various burrowing rodents of the genera *Geomys, Thomomys,* etc. (family Geomyidae), of western and southern North America and Central America, with large external fur-lined cheek pouches. **3.** an edible, burrowing land tortoise, *Gopherus* (or *Testudo*) *polyphemus,* of the south-eastern U.S. **4.** Also, **gopher snake.** a burrowing snake, *Compsosoma corais,* of the southern U.S. [? F *gaufre* honeycomb. See GOFFER]

gopher[1]

**gopher**[2] /'goʊfə/, *n. Colloq.* a person employed to run errands, give general assistance, etc. Also, **gofer.** [from *go for,* by association with GOPHER[1]]

**gopherwood** /'goʊfəwʊd/, *n.* **1.** *U.S.* →**yellowwood.** **2.** an unidentified wood used in building Noah's ark. [*gopher* a tree (from Heb.) + WOOD[1]]

**goral** /'gɔrəl/, *n.* a goat antelope of the genus *Naemorhedus,* of mountainous areas of eastern Asia, having short, backward-curving horns.

**gorblimey** /gɔ'blaɪmi/, *Colloq. –interj.* **1.** (an expression of surprise or amazement.) *–adj.* **2.** vulgar; of or pertaining to the poor or working classes: *he wears gorblimey trousers.* Also, **gorblimy.** [alteration of *God blind me*]

**Gordian** /'gɔdiən/, *adj.* **1.** intricate; resembling the Gordian knot. **2. cut the Gordian knot,** to devise and use instantly a drastic solution to a problem. [from *Gordius,* ancient king of Phrygia, in Asia Minor, who tied a knot which was to be undone only by the one who should rule Asia. It was summarily cut by Alexander the Great in 333 B.C.]

**Gordon setter** /gɔdn 'sɛtə/, *n.* a black, long-haired variety of setter dog with red or tan marks on the muzzle, neck, and legs. Also, **Gordon.**

**gore**[1] /gɔ/, *n.* blood that is shed, esp. when clotted. [ME; OE *gor* dung, dirt, c. D *goor,* OHG *gor* filth]

**gore**[2] /gɔ/, *v.t.*, **gored, goring.** (of an animal) to pierce with the horns or tusks. [ME *goren.* Cf. GORE[3]]

**gore**[3] /gɔ/, *n., v.*, **gored, goring.** *–n.* **1.** a triangular piece of cloth, etc., inserted in a garment, a sail, etc., to give greater width or secure the desired shape or adjustment. **2.** one of the breadths (mostly tapering, or shaped) of a woman's skirt. *–v.t.* **3.** to make or furnish with a gore or gores. [ME; OE *gāra* corner (c. G *Gehre* gusset), from *gār* spear]

**gorge** /gɔdʒ/, *n., v.*, **gorged, gorging.** *–n.* **1.** a narrow cleft with steep, rocky walls, esp. one through which a stream runs. **2.** a gorging or gluttonous meal. **3.** that which is swallowed; contents of the stomach. **4.** a choking mass. **5.** *Fort.* the rear entrance or part of a bastion or similar outwork. **6.** the throat; gullet. *–v.t.* **7.** to stuff with food (mainly reflexive and passive): *gorged with food, he gorged himself.* **8.** to swallow, esp. greedily. **9.** to choke up (mainly passive). *–v.i.* **10.** to eat greedily. [ME, from OF: throat, from LL *gurga,* b. L *gurges* stream, abyss and *gula* throat] **– gorger,** *n.*

**gorgeous** /ˈgɔdʒəs/, *adj.* **1.** sumptuous; magnificent; splendid in appearance or colouring: *she was wearing a gorgeous necklace.* **2.** *Colloq.* very good, pleasing, or enjoyable: *I had a gorgeous weekend.* [late ME, from OF *gorgias* fashionable, gay; orig. uncert.] **– gorgeously,** *adv.* **– gorgeousness,** *n.*

**gorgeous gussies** /– ˈgʌsiz/, *n.pl. Colloq.* frilly panties. [named after *Gussy* Moran, U.S. tennis player *c.* 1954]

**gorgerin** /ˈgɔdʒərən/, *n.* the necklike portion of a capital of a column, a feature forming the junction between a shaft and its capital. [F, from *gorge* throat]

**gorget** /ˈgɔdʒət/, *n.* **1.** a piece of armour for the throat. **2.** a form of wimple, or neck and chest covering, worn by women in the Middle Ages. **3.** a crescent-shaped badge, worn round the neck by officers in the 17th and 18th centuries as a sign of rank. **4.** a patch on the throat of a bird or other animal, distinguished by its colour or otherwise. [late ME, from OF *gorgete,* diminutive of *gorge* throat]

**gorgon** /ˈgɔgən/, *n.* a terrible or repulsive woman. [from the *Gorgons,* in Greek mythology three sisters, Stheno, Euryale, and Medusa, whose heads were covered with snakes instead of hair, and whose glance turned the beholder to stone]

**gorgoneion** /gɔgəˈniən/, *n., pl.* **-neia** /-ˈniə/. a representation of the head of a Gorgon, esp. that of Medusa. [Gk]

**gorgonian**[1] /gɔˈgouniən/, *adj.* (of a woman) having a personality that petrifies and emasculates.

**gorgonian**[2] /gɔˈgouniən/, *n.* **1.** any member of the Gorgonacea, the sea-fans or horny corals of deeper marine waters. *–adj.* **2.** belonging or pertaining to the order Gorgonacea.

**gorgonzola** /gɔgənˈzoulə/, *n.* an Italian variety of semi-soft ripened milk cheese veined with blue-green veins of penicillin mould culture.

**gorgy** /ˈgɔdʒi/, *adj.* precipitous and broken.

**gorilla** /gəˈrɪlə/, *n.* **1.** the largest of the anthropoid apes, *Gorilla gorilla,* ground-living and vegetarian, of western equatorial Africa. **2.** an ugly, brutal fellow. **3.** *Chiefly U.S.* a smash-hit recording. [NL, from Gk; said to be of African orig.]

gorilla

**gormand** /gɔˈmɒnd, ˈgɔmənd/, *n.* →**gourmand.**

**gormandise** /ˈgɔməndaɪz/, *v.*, **-dised, -dising,** *n.* *–v.i., v.t.* **1.** to eat like a glutton. *–n.* **2.** *Rare.* the habits of a glutton. Also, **gormandize.** [F *gourmandise* gluttony] **– gormandiser,** *n.*

**gormless** /ˈgɔmləs/, *adj. Colloq.* (of a person) dull; stupid; senseless. [var. of d. *gaumless,* from *gaum* attention, heed (from Scand.; cf. Icel. *gaumr*) + -LESS] **– gormlessness,** *n.*

**gorse** /gɔs/, *n.* any plant of the genus *Ulex,* esp. *U. europaeus,* a low, much-branched, spiny shrub with yellow flowers, native to Europe and introduced into many countries; furze. [ME *gorst,* OE *gors(t)*; akin to G *Gerste,* L *hordeum* barley] **– gorsy,** *adj.*

**gory** /ˈgɔri/, *adj.*, **gorier, goriest.** **1.** covered or stained with gore; bloody. **2.** resembling gore. **3.** *Colloq.* distasteful or unpleasant: *he read the gory details of the accident.* **– gorily,** *adv.* **– goriness,** *n.*

**gosh** /gɒʃ/, *interj.* (an exclamation or mild oath). [a euphemistic var. of *God!*]

**goshawk** /ˈgɒshɔk/, *n.* any of various powerful, short-winged hawks, formerly much used in falconry, widely dispersed throughout the world, as the Australian goshawk. [ME *goshawke,* OE *gōshafoc* goosehawk]

goshawk

**gosling** /ˈgɒzlɪŋ/, *n.* a young goose. [ME *goselyng,* var. (by association with GOOSE[1]) of *geslyng,* from Scand.; cf. Icel. *gæslingr,* from *gās* goose + *-lingr,* diminutive suffix (see -LING[1])]

**go-slow** /ˈgou-slou/, *Colloq. –n.* **1.** a deliberate curtailment of output by workers as an industrial sanction; work-to-rule. **2.** *Prison.* a punishment cell. *–adj.* **3.** of or pertaining to a go-slow.

**gospel** /ˈgɒspəl/, *n.* **1.** (*oft. cap.*) the body of doctrine taught by Christ and the apostles; Christian revelation. **2.** glad tidings, esp. concerning salvation and the kingdom of God as announced to the world by Christ. **3.** the story of Christ's life and teachings, esp. as contained in the first four books of the New Testament. **4.** (*usu. cap.*) one of these books. **5.** (*oft. cap.*) *Eccles.* an extract from one of the four Gospels, forming part of the Eucharist service in certain Churches. **6.** something regarded as true and implicitly believed: *to take as gospel.* **7.** a doctrine regarded as of prime importance: *political gospel.* *–adj.* **8.** pertaining to the gospel. **9.** in accordance with the gospel; evangelical. [ME *go(d)spel,* OE *gōdspel,* from *gōd* GOOD + *spell* tidings (SPELL[2]), translation of L *ēvangelium.* See EVANGEL[1]]

**gospeller** /ˈgɒspələ/, *n.* **1.** one whose beliefs and teachings are based on a literal acceptance of the four Gospels, and, more generally, of the Bible. **2.** →**hot-gospeller.** Also, *U.S.,* **gospeler.**

**gospel music** /ˈgɒspəl mjuzɪk/, *n.* a primarily vocal music, a precursor of the blues, but based on hymns.

**gospel side** /ˈ– saɪd/, *n.* the left-hand side of a church facing the altar. Cf. **epistle side.**

**gossamer** /ˈgɒsəmə/, *n.* **1.** a fine filmy cobweb, seen on grass and bushes, or floating in the air in calm weather, esp. in autumn. **2.** a thread or a web of this substance. **3.** an extremely delicate variety of gauze. **4.** any finely spun, silken fabric. *–adj.* **5.** Also, **gossamery** /ˈgɒsəməri/. of or like gossamer; thin and light. [ME *gos(e)-somer.* See GOOSE[1], SUMMER[1]; possibly first used as name for late mild autumn (Indian summer), time when goose was a favourite dish (cf. G *Gänsemonat* November), then transferred to the filmy matter also found in that season]

**gossan** /ˈgɒsən/, *n.* a ferruginous deposit filling the upper parts of mineral veins or forming a superficial cover on masses of pyrite. It consists principally of hydrated oxide of iron. [Cornish d.] **– gossanous,** *adj.*

**gossip** /ˈgɒsəp/, *n., v.*, **-siped** or **-sipped, -siping** or **-sipping.** *–n.* **1.** idle talk, esp. about the affairs of others. **2.** light, familiar talk or writing. **3.** a person, esp. a woman, given to tattling or idle talk. **4.** *Archaic.* a friend, esp. a woman. **5.** *Archaic.* a godparent. *–v.i.* **6.** to talk idly, esp. about the affairs of others; go about tattling. *–v.t.* **7.** to repeat like a gossip. **8.** *Archaic.* to stand godparent to. [ME *gossib,* OE *godsibb,* orig., godparent, from *god* GOD + *sibb* related (see SIB[1], adj.)] **– gossiper,** *n.* **– gossiping,** *n.* **– gossipingly,** *adv.*

**gossip column** /ˈ– kɒləm/, *n.* a column or segment of a newspaper, magazine, etc., in which gossip about notable people and events is printed. **– gossip columnist,** *n.*

**gossipmonger** /ˈgɒsəpmʌŋgə/, *n.* one who delights in inventing and spreading gossip.

**gossipy** /ˈgɒsəpi/, *adj.* **1.** given to or fond of gossip. **2.** full of gossip.

**gossypol** /ˈgɒsipɒl/, *n.* undecorticated cotton seed cake or meal which causes loss of appetite in pigs when given in small quantities, or in larger quantities may cause convulsions and death.

**got** /gɒt/, *v.* **1.** past tense and past participle of **get.** **2. have got 'em bad, a.** to be in a nervous condition. **b.** to be suffering from withdrawal symptoms, esp. from alcohol. **3. have got into (someone),** *Colloq.* to be causing (someone) to display anger, irritation, etc.: *what has got into that man.* **4. have got it bad,** to be infatuated (fol. by *for*).

**gotcher** /'gɒtʃə/, *interj. Colloq.* **1.** (an exclamation accompanying the capture of a person). **2.** (an exclamation indicating comprehension and agreement). Also, **gotcha.** [contraction of (*I have*) *got you*]

**Goth** /gɒθ/, *n.* a barbarian; rude person. [orig. one of a Teutonic people who invaded the Roman Empire; ME *Gothe,* from LL *Gothi,* pl.; replacing OE *Gotan,* pl. (*Gota,* sing.), c. Goth. *Gut-* in *Gut-thiuda* Goth people]

**Goth.,** Gothic.

**Gothic** /'gɒθɪk/, *adj.* **1.** *Archit.* denoting or pertaining to a style originating in France and spreading over western Europe from the 12th to the 16th century, characterised by a design emphasing skeleton construction, the elimination of wall planes, the comparatively great height of the buildings, the pointed arch, rib vaulting, and the flying buttress. **2.** of or pertaining to the Gothic Revival. **3.** (*orig. derog.*) denoting all European art of the 12th to the 16th century. **4.** (*sometimes derog.*) pertaining to the Middle Ages; barbarous; rude. **5.** (esp. in literature) stressing irregularity and details, usu. of a grotesque or horrible nature: *a Gothic novel.* **6.** *Print.* (of a typeface) having elaborate pointed characters. *–n.* **7.** Gothic architecture, sculpture, or decoration. **8.** an extinct Germanic language, preserved esp. in Ulfilas's Bible (4th century). **9.** blackletter. [LL *Gothicus*] **– Gothically,** *adv.*

**Gothicise** /'gɒθəsaɪz/, *v.t.,* **-cised, -cising. 1.** to make Gothic, as in style. **2.** to make pseudo-medieval. Also, **Gothicize.**

**Gothicism** /'gɒθəsɪzəm/, *n.* **1.** conformity or devotion to the Gothic style of architecture. **2.** a mixture of the elevated and the bizarre, often with many details, as distinct from the unity and simplicity of classicism. **3.** adherence to aspects of Gothic culture. **4.** (*also l.c.*) barbarism; rudeness. **5.** a Gothic idiom.

**gotta** /'gɒtə/, *v.* contracted form of (*have*) *got to,* or (*have*) *got a.*

**gotten** /'gɒtn/, *v. Chiefly U.S.* a past participle of **get.**

**Götterdämmerung** /gɒtə'dæmərʊŋ, gɜtə'demərʊŋ/, *n.* (in German mythology) the twilight of the gods; the final destruction of the world by the forces of evil.

**gouache** /gu'aʃ, -'æʃ/, *n.* **1.** a method of painting with opaque watercolours. **2.** an opaque colour used in painting a gouache; body colour. **3.** a work executed in this medium. [F, from It. *guazzo* puddle, spray of water, from L *aquātio* a watering, from *aqua* water]

**gouda** /'gaʊdə, 'gu-/, *n.* a semi-soft to hard, sweet-curd cheese, with a smooth, mellow taste, made in a traditional flat wheel shape with rounded edges and a yellow rind. [named after *Gouda,* Holland, where this cheese was orig. made]

**gouge** /gaʊdʒ/, *n., v.,* **gouged, gouging.** *–n.* **1.** a chisel whose blade has a concavo-convex cross-section, the bevel being ground on either the inside or the outside of the cutting end of the tool. **2.** a groove or hole made by gouging. *–v.t.* **3.** to scoop out or turn with or as with a gouge: *gouge a channel, gouge holes.* **4.** to dig or force out with or as with a gouge: *to gouge out an eye.* [F, from LL *gu(l)bia;* of Celtic orig.]

gouge (def. 1)

**gouger** /'gaʊdʒə/, *n.* **1.** one who or that which gouges. **2.** an opal miner, usu. one who works in soft ground. **3.** any miner.

**goulash** /'gulæʃ/, *n.* **1.** *Cookery.* a stew made of meat, usu. beef or veal, flavoured with chopped onions and paprika. **2.** *Bridge.* a deal of unshuffled cards distributed in rounds of five, five, and three. [Hung. *gulyás*]

**Gouldian finch** /ˌguldiən 'fɪntʃ/, *n.* a strikingly multicoloured finch, *Chloebia gouldiae,* of tropical northern Australia. Also, **painted finch, purple-breasted finch.** [named after Elizabeth *Gould,* 1804-1841, natural-history artist, wife of John Gould, ornithologist]

**Gould's goanna** /ˌguldz goʊ'ænə/, *n.* a large, varanid lizard, *Varanus gouldii,* of brownish colour and of slighter build than the common goanna or lace monitor. Also, **sand goanna, ground goanna.** [named after John *Gould,* 1804-1881, English ornithologist and zoologist]

**gouramy** /'gʊərəmi/, *n., pl.* **-mis. 1.** a large, air-breathing nest-building, freshwater, Asiatic fish, *Osphronemus goramy,* highly prized for food. **2.** any of a number of smaller, air-breathing, nest-building, Asiatic fishes (genera *Trichogaster, Colisa,* and *Trichopsis*) widely cultivated in home aquariums, as the **dwarf gouramy,** *Colisa lalia.* Also, **gourami.** [Malay]

**gourd** /gʊəd, gɔd/, *n.* **1.** the fruit of any of various plants of the family Cucurbitaceae, esp. that of *Lagenaria siceraria* (**bottle gourd**), whose dried shell is used for bottles, bowls, etc., or that of certain forms of *Cucurbita pepo* sometimes cultivated for ornament. **2.** a plant bearing such a fruit. **3.** a dried and excavated gourd shell used as a bottle, ladle, flask, etc. **4.** a gourd-shaped, small-necked bottle or flask. [ME, from F *gourde,* from L *cucurbita*] **– gourd-like,** *adj.* **– gourd-shaped,** *adj.*

**gourmand** /gɔ'mɒnd, 'gɔmənd/, *n.* one fond of good eating. Also, **gormand.** [late ME, from F: gluttonous, from *gourmet* GOURMET]

**gourmet** /'gʊəmeɪ, 'gɔ-/, *n.* a connoisseur in the delicacies of the table; an epicure. [F, from OF *gromet* wine-taster, wine merchant's man. Cf. GROOM]

**gout** /gaʊt/, *n.* **1.** a constitutional disease characterised by painful inflammation of the joints (chiefly those in the feet and hands, and esp. in the big toe), and by excess of uric acid in the blood. **2.** *Archaic.* a drop, splash, or spot, esp. of blood. [ME *goute,* from OF, from L *gutta* a drop, ML gout]

**gouty** /'gaʊti/, *adj.,* **goutier, goutiest. 1.** pertaining to or having the nature of gout. **2.** causing gout. **3.** diseased with or subject to gout. **4.** swollen as if from gout. **– goutily,** *adv.* **– goutiness,** *n.*

**Gov** /gʌv/, *n. Chiefly Brit. Colloq.* **1.** a form of address to a male member of a superior social class. **2.** a boss; employer. Also, **gov, Guv, guv.** [abbrev. for *Governor*]

**Gov.,** governor. Also, **gov.**

**govern** /'gʌvən/, *v.t.* **1.** to rule by right of authority, as a sovereign does: *to govern a state.* **2.** to exercise a directing or restraining influence over; guide: *the motives governing a decision.* **3.** to hold in check: *to govern one's temper.* **4.** to serve as or constitute a law for: *the principles governing a case.* **5.** *Gram.* to be accompanied by (a particular form) as in *'they helped us',* not *'they helped we';* the verb *'helped'* is said to govern the objective case of the pronoun. **6.** to regulate (an engine speed) with a governor. *–v.i.* **7.** to exercise the function of government. **8.** to have predominating influence. [ME *governe(n),* from OF *governer,* from L *gubernāre,* from Gk *kybernân* steer, guide, govern] **– governable,** *adj.*

**governance** /'gʌvənəns/, *n.* **1.** government; exercise of authority; control. **2.** method or system of government or management.

**governess** /'gʌvənɛs/, *n.* a woman who directs the education of children, generally in their own homes.

**government** /'gʌvənmənt/, *n.* **1.** the authoritative direction and restraint exercised over the actions of men in communities, societies, and states; direction of the affairs of a state, etc.; political rule and administration: *government is necessary to the existence of society.* **2.** the form or system of rule by which a state, community, etc., is governed: *monarchical government, episcopal government.* **3.** (*sometimes construed as pl.*) the governing body of persons in a state, community, etc.; the executive power; the administration: *the government was defeated in the last election.* **4.** direction; control; rule: *the government of one's conduct.* **5.** the district governed; a province. **6.** *Gram.* the established usage which requires that one word in a sentence should cause another to be of a particular form. **– governmental** /gʌvən'mɛntl/, *adj.* **– governmentally** /gʌvən'mɛntəli/, *adv.*

**government dollar** /– 'dɒlə/, *n.* →**holey dollar.**

**Government house** /gʌvənmənt 'haʊs/, *n.* **1.** the residence of the governor-general. **2.** *Colloq.* (*joc.*) the main homestead on a sheep or cattle station.

**government man** /'gʌvənmənt mæn/, *n.* (formerly) a euphemistic term for a convict.

**government stroke** /– ˈstroʊk/, *n.* the easy pace at which work is done supposed to be typical of those working for the government, originally used specifically of convict road labourers.

**government work** /ˈ– wɜk/, *n.* (formerly) the employment of convicts on public works.

**governor** /ˈgʌvənə, ˈgʌvnə/, *n.* **1.** one charged with the direction or control of an institution, society, etc.: *governors of a bank, governor of a prison.* **2. a.** the representative of the sovereign with statutory powers in a British dependent territory. **b.** the principal representative of the sovereign in a state of the Commonwealth of Australia. **3.** a ruler or chief magistrate appointed to govern a province, town, fort, or the like. **4.** the executive head of a state in the U.S. **5.** *Mach.* a device for regulating a supply of fuel in an engine for ensuring uniform speed regardless of the load. **6.** *Colloq.* **a.** one's employer. **b.** any person of superior status. **c.** one's father. [ME *governour,* from OF *governeor,* from L *gubernātor* steersman, director]

**governor-general** /gʌvənə-ˈdʒɛnrəl/, *n., pl.* **governor-generals, governors-general.** the principal representative of the sovereign in certain independent Commonwealth countries.

**Governor-General's speech** /gʌvənə-ˈdʒɛnrəlz ˌspitʃ/, *n.* a speech read by the Governor-General in his capacity as representative of the Queen, at the opening of Federal parliament.

**governorship** /ˈgʌvənəʃɪp/, *n.* a governor's duties, term in office, etc.

**Governor's speech** /ˈgʌvənəz spitʃ/, *n.* a speech read by the Governor in his capacity as representative of the Queen at the opening of a State parliament.

**Govt,** government. Also, **govt.**

**Gowings** /ˈgaʊɪŋz/, *n. in the phrase* **gone to Gowings,** *Colloq.* **1.** deteriorating financially. **2.** ill, esp. with a hangover. **3.** failing dismally, as of a horse in a race, a football team, etc. [from *Gowing* Bros. Ltd., a Sydney retail firm]

**gown** /gaʊn/, *n.* **1.** a woman's dress, usu. formal, comprising bodice and skirt, usu. joined. **2.** a loose, flowing, outer garment in various forms, worn by men or women as distinctive of office, profession, or status: *a judge's gown, an academic gown.* **3.** members of the university collectively, as opposed to townspeople in a University town: *town and gown.* *–v.t., v.i.* **4.** to dress in, or put on, a gown. [ME *goune,* from OF, from LL *gunna;* orig. uncert.]

**goy** /ˈgɔɪ/, *n., pl.* **goyim** /ˈgɔɪjɪm/. a non-Jew; gentile. [Heb.]

**gozunder** /gəˈzʌndə/, *n.* →**chamber-pot.**

**Gp,** Group.

**G.P.** /dʒi ˈpi/, **1.** *Music.* general pause. **2.** general practitioner.

**G.P.I.** /dʒi pi ˈaɪ/, general paralysis of the insane.

**G.P.O.** /dʒi pi ˈoʊ/, **1.** General Post Office. **2.** general purpose outlet.

**G.P.S.** /dʒi pi ˈɛs/, Greater Public Schools. Also, **GPS.**

**gr.,** **1.** grade. **2.** grain; grains. **3.** gross.

**Gr.,** **1.** Grecian. **2.** Greece. **3.** Greek.

**Graafian follicle** /ˌgrafiən ˈfɒlɪkəl/, *n.* one of many small vesicles within the ovary which, at the time of ovulation, discharge an ovum. Also, **Graafian vesicle.** [named after R. de *Graaf,* 1641-73, Dutch anatomist]

**grab** /græb/, *v.,* **grabbed, grabbing,** *n.* *–v.t.* **1.** to seize suddenly and eagerly; snatch. **2.** to take illegal possession of; seize forcibly or unscrupulously: *to grab land.* **3.** *Colloq.* to affect; impress: *how does that grab you?* **4. grab by the balls,** *Colloq.* to impress very favourably. *–n.* **5.** a sudden, eager grasp or snatch. **6.** seizure or acquisition by violent or unscrupulous means. **7.** that which is grabbed. **8.** a mechanical device for gripping objects. **9.** a card game, usu. played by children. Cf. **snap** (def. 33). [c. MD and MLG *grabben,* Swed. *grabba*] **– grabber,** *n.*

**grab-all** /ˈgræb-ɔl/, *n.* a set net used for fishing near the shore.

**grab bag** /ˈgræb bæg/, *n.* **1.** a lucky dip. **2.** any miscellany of articles.

**grabble** /ˈgræbəl/, *v.i.,* **-bled, -bling. 1.** to feel or search with the hands; grope. **2.** to sprawl; scramble. [frequentative of GRAB. Cf. D *grabbelen*]

**graben** /ˈgrabən/, *n.* →**rift valley.** [G: ditch]

**grabrope** /ˈgræbroʊp/, *n. Naut.* **1.** any of certain lines or ropes on a ship for boatmen to take hold of when coming alongside. **2.** lines attached to lifeboats, etc., to provide support for people in the water. Also, **grabline** /ˈgræblaɪn/.

**grace** /greɪs/, *n., v.,* **graced, gracing.** *–n.* **1.** elegance or beauty of form, manner, motion, or act. **2.** a pleasing or attractive quality or endowment. **3.** favour or goodwill. **4.** manifestation of favour, esp. as by a superior. **5.** mercy; clemency; pardon. **6.** favour shown in granting a delay or temporary immunity: *an act of grace.* **7.** (*pl.*) affected manner; manifestation of pride or vanity: *to put on airs and graces.* **8.** *Law.* an allowance of time to a debtor before suit can be brought against him after his debt has by its terms become payable: *days of grace.* **9.** *Theol.* **a.** the free, unmerited favour and love of God. **b.** the influence or spirit of God operating in man to regenerate or strengthen. **c.** a virtue or excellence of divine origin: *the Christian graces.* **10. fall from grace, a.** *Theol.* to descend into sin or disfavour with God. **b.** to lose favour, esp. with someone in authority. **11. state of grace,** *Theol.* **a.** condition of being in God's favour. **b.** condition of being one of the elect. **12.** spiritual strength: *the grace to perform a duty.* **13.** a short prayer before or after a meal, in which a blessing is asked and thanks are given. **14.** *Music.* an embellishment consisting of a note or notes not essential to the harmony or melody, as an appoggiatura, an inverted mordent, etc. **15.** (*usu. cap.*) a formal title used in addressing or mentioning a duke, duchess, or archbishop, and formerly also a sovereign (prec. by *your, his,* etc.). **16.** (*cap.*) *Class. Myth.* one of three sister goddesses, commonly given as **Aglaia** (brilliance), **Euphrosyne** (joy), and **Thalia** (bloom), presiding over all beauty and charm in nature and humanity. **17.** (*pl.*) the accomplishments and refinements expected of a person, esp. a young woman, who belongs to or wishes to enter the upper levels of society. **18. have the grace to,** to be so kind as to (do something). **19. with (a) bad grace,** unwillingly; reluctantly: *he conceded defeat with bad grace.* **20. with (a) good grace,** willingly; ungrudgingly: *the team lost the match with good grace.* *–v.t.* **21.** to lend or add grace to; adorn. **22.** to favour or honour: *to grace an occasion with one's presence.* **23.** *Music.* to add grace-notes, cadenzas, etc., to. [ME, from OF, from L *grātia* favour, gratitude, agreeableness]

**grace-and-favour** /ˈgreɪs-ən-ˌfeɪvə/, *adj. Brit.* granted by the sovereign as a mark of gratitude: *a grace-and-favour flat.*

**grace-cup** /ˈgreɪs-kʌp/, *n.* **1.** a cup, as of wine, passed round at the end of the meal for the final toast. **2.** the drink.

**graceful** /ˈgreɪsfəl/, *adj.* characterised by grace of form, manner, movement, or speech; elegant; easy or effective. **– gracefully,** *adv.* **– gracefulness,** *n.*

**graceless** /ˈgreɪsləs/, *adj.* **1.** wanting grace, pleasing elegance, charm, or sensitivity. **2.** without any sense of right or propriety. **– gracelessly,** *adv.* **– gracelessness,** *n.*

**grace-note** /ˈgreɪs-noʊt/, *n.* a note not essential to the harmony or melody, added as an embellishment, esp. an appoggiatura.

**gracile** /ˈgræsaɪl/, *adj.* **1.** gracefully slender. **2.** slender; thin. [L *gracilis* slender] **– gracility** /græˈsɪləti/, *n.*

**gracing** /ˈgreɪsɪŋ/, *n.* the act or fact of a person or thing that graces.

**gracious** /ˈgreɪʃəs/, *adj.* **1.** disposed to show grace or favour; kind; benevolent; courteous. **2.** indulgent or beneficent in a condescending or patronising way, esp. to inferiors. **3.** merciful or compassionate. **4.** *Obs.* fortunate or happy. *–interj.* **5.** (an exclamation of surprise, etc.) [ME, from OF, from L *grātiōsus* enjoying or showing favour] **– graciously,** *adv.* **– graciousness, graciosity** /greɪʃiˈɒsəti/, *n.*

**grad.,** **1.** graduate. **2.** graduated.

**gradate** /grəˈdeɪt/, *v.,* **-dated, -dating.** *–v.i.* **1.** to pass by insensible degrees, as one colour into another. *–v.t.* **2.** to cause to gradate. **3.** to arrange in grades.

**gradation** /grəˈdeɪʃən/, *n.* **1.** any process or change taking place through a series of stages, by degrees, or gradually. **2.** (*usu. pl.*) a stage, degree, or grade in such a series. **3.** the passing of one tint or shade of colour to another, or one surface to another, by very small degrees, as in painting, sculpture etc. **4.** the act of grading. **5.** →**ablaut** (def. 2). **– gradational,** *adj.* **– gradationally,** *adv.*

**grade** /greɪd/, *n., v.,* **graded, grading,** *adj.* *–n.* **1.** a degree in a scale, as of rank, advancement, quality, value, intensity, etc. **2.** a class of persons or things of the same relative rank, quality, etc. **3.** a step or stage in a course or process. **4.** a non-SI unit of plane angle, equal to the angle between two radii of a circle which cut off an arc equal to $\frac{1}{400}$ of that circumference (approx. $15.7 \times 10^{-3}$ radians). **5.** a division of a school in terms of pupils' age or academic level. **6.** a number, letter, etc., indicating the relative quality of a student's work in a course, examination, or special subject. **7.** inclination with the horizontal of a road, railway, etc., usu. expressed by stating the vertical rise or fall as a percentage of the horizontal distance. **8.** *Bldg Trades.* the ground level around a building. **9.** an animal resulting from a cross between a parent of common stock and one of a pure breed. **10. make the grade,** to reach a desired minimum level of achievement, qualification. *–v.t.* **11.** to arrange in a series of grades; class; sort. **12.** to determine the grade of. **13.** to cause to pass by degrees, as from one colour or shade to another. **14.** to reduce to a level or to practicable degrees of inclination: *to grade a road.* **15.** to cross (a nondescript animal or a low-grade one) with one of a pure breed. *–v.i.* **16.** to be graded. **17.** to be of a particular grade or quality. *–adj.* **18.** *Sport.* that which is played in grades: *grade cricket; grade football.* [F, from L *gradus* step, stage, degree]

**-grade,** a word element meaning 'walking', 'moving', 'going', as in *retrograde.* [combining form representing L *gradus* step, or *gradī,* v., walk. See GRADE, GRADIENT]

**grader** /'greɪdə/, *n.* **1.** one who or that which grades. **2.** a motor-driven vehicle, with a blade for pushing earth, used for grading roads and for shallow excavation.

**grade school** /'greɪd skul/, *n. U.S.* a primary school.

**grade separation** /'– sɛpə,reɪʃən/, *n.* the separation of the levels at which roads, railways, paths, etc., intersect in order to prevent traffic conflicts or accidents.

**gradient** /'greɪdiənt/, *n.* **1.** the degree of inclination, or the rate of ascent or descent, in a railway, etc. **2.** an inclined surface; grade; ramp. **3.** *Physics.* **a.** change in a variable quantity, as temperature or pressure, per unit distance. **b.** a curve representing such a rate of change. *–adj.* **4.** rising or descending by regular degrees of inclination. **5.** progressing by walking as an animal; gressorial. **6.** of a type suitable for walking, as some birds' feet. [L *gradiens,* ppr., walking, going]

**gradient post** /'– poʊst/, *n.* a short post beside a railway track indicating a change of gradient.

**gradient wind speed,** *n.* the speed of the wind calculated as for geostrophic wind speed, but taking into account the curvature of the path of the air.

**gradin** /'greɪdn/, *n.* **1.** one of a series of steps or seats raised one above another. **2.** *Eccles.* a shelf or one of a series of shelves behind and above an altar. Also, **gradine** /grə'din/. [F, from It. *gradino,* from *grado* GRADE]

**gradiograph** /'greɪdiəgræf, -graf/, *n.* a straightedge with a horizontal upper edge and a lower edge sloping at a required gradient, used for measuring slope, laying pipes, etc.

**gradiometer** /,greɪdi'ɒmətə/, *n.* a surveyor's telescopic instrument for setting out gradients.

**gradual** /'grædʒuəl/, *adj.* **1.** taking place, changing, moving, etc., by degrees or little by little: *gradual improvement in health.* **2.** rising or descending at an even, moderate inclination: *a gradual slope.* *–n.* **3.** *Eccles.* **a.** an antiphon sung between the epistle and the gospel in the Eucharistic service. **b.** a book containing the words and music of the parts of the liturgy which are sung by the choir. [ML *graduālis* (as n., *graduāle*), from L *gradus* step, grade] – **gradually,** *adv.* – **gradualness,** *n.*

**gradualism** /'grædʒuəlɪzəm/, *n.* the principle of achieving an end step by step instead of in one movement or action. [GRADUAL + -ISM] – **gradualist,** *n., adj.*

**graduand** /'grædʒuænd/, *n.* one who has qualified for a degree, but has not yet had it conferred. [ML *graduandus,* ger. of *graduāre;* see GRADUATE]

**graduate** /'grædʒuət/, *n., adj.;* /'grædʒueɪt/, *v.,* **-ated, -ating.** *–n.* **1.** one who has received a degree on completing a course of study, as at a university or college. **2.** a student who holds the first or bachelor's degree and is studying for an advanced degree. **3.** *Prison Colloq.* a criminal who has been in child welfare institutions. **4.** *Rare.* a cylindrical or tapering graduated vessel of glass, for measuring. *–adj.* **5.** that has graduated: *a graduate student.* **6.** of or pertaining to graduates: *a graduate course.* *–v.i.* **7.** to receive a degree or diploma on completing a course of study. **8.** to pass by degrees; change gradually. *–v.t.* **9.** to arrange in grades or gradations; establish gradation in. **10.** to divide into or mark with degrees or other divisions, as the scale of a thermometer. [ML *graduātus,* pp. of *graduāre* admit to an academic degree, from L *gradus* step, grade] – **graduator,** *n.*

**graduation** /grædʒu'eɪʃən/, *n.* **1.** the act of graduating. **2.** the state of having graduated. **3.** the ceremony of conferring a university degree.

**graduation stakes** /'– steɪks/, *n.* a set-weight race for specified restricted class horses run at different set weights in accordance with their class.

**gradus** /'greɪdəs/, *n.* **1.** *Music.* a work consisting wholly or in part, of exercises of increasing difficulty. **2.** a simple dictionary of Latin prosody. [L, short for *gradus ad Parnassum* steps to Parnassus]

**Graecise** /'grisaɪz/, *v.* **-cised, -cising.** *–v.t.* **1.** to impart Greek characteristics to. **2.** to translate into Greek. *–v.i.* **3.** to conform to what is Greek; adopt Greek speech, customs, etc. Also, **Graecize,** *Chiefly U.S.,* **Grecise.** [L *Graecizāre,* from *Graecus* Greek. See -ISE]

**Graecism** /'grisɪzəm/, *n.* **1.** the spirit of Greek thought, etc. **2.** adoption or imitation of this. **3.** an idiom or peculiarity of Greek. Also, *Chiefly U.S.,* **Grecism.**

**Graeco-,** a word element meaning 'Greek'. Also, *Chiefly U.S.,* **Greco-.** [L, combining form of *Graecus*]

**graffiti** /grə'fiti/, *n.pl., sing.* **graffito** /grə'fitoʊ/. **1.** *Archaeol.* an ancient drawing or writing scratched on a wall or other surface. **2.** drawings or words, sometimes obscene, sometimes political, etc., written on the walls of public toilets but often elsewhere, as on bill boards, walls of buildings, etc. [It., from *graffio* a scratch, from Gk *gráphein* mark, draw, write]

**graft**[1] /graft/, *n.* **1.** *Hort.* **a.** a shoot or part of a plant (the scion) inserted in a groove, slit, or the like in another plant or tree (the stock) so as to become nourished by and united with it. **b.** the plant or tree (the united stock and scion) resulting from such an operation. **c.** the place where the scion is inserted. **2.** *Surg.* a portion of living tissue surgically transplanted from one part of an individual to another, or from one individual to another, with a view to its adhesion and growth. **3.** the act of grafting. *–v.t.* **4.** to insert (a graft) into a plant or tree; insert a scion of (one plant) into another plant. **5.** to cause (a plant) to reproduce through grafting. **6.** *Surg.* to transplant (a portion of living tissue) as a graft. **7.** to insert as if by grafting: *to graft a pagan custom upon Christian institutions.* **8.** *Naut.* **a.** to finish off (an eye splice) by tapering the ends of the strands of rope. **b.** to taper (a rope's end) and wrap it round with yarns, usu. marline. *–v.i.* **9.** to insert scions from one tree, or kind of tree, into another. **10.** to become grafted. [earlier *graff,* ME *grafe,* from OF: orig., stylus, pencil, from LL *graphium,* from Gk *grapheíon* stylus] – **grafter,** *n.* – **grafting,** *n.*

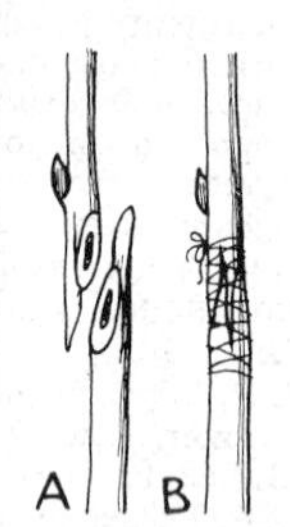

graft[1]: A, splice; B, whip or tongue

**graft**[2] /graft/, *n.* **1.** work, esp. hard work. **2.** the acquisition of gain or advantage by dishonest, unfair, or shady means, esp. through the abuse of one's position or influence in politics, business, etc. **3.** a particular instance, method, or means of thus acquiring gain. **4.** the gain or advantage acquired. *–v.t.* **5.** to obtain by graft. *–v.i.* **6.** to work hard, toil (esp. at physical tasks). **7.** to practise graft. [? identical with GRAFT[1] in expression *spade(s) graft,* var. of *spade(s)-graff,* lit., spade's digging (depth of earth thrown up at a single spading), OE *græf* trench. See GRAVE[1]]

**grafter** /'graftə/, *n.* **1.** a very hard worker; an industrious person. **2.** *Chiefly U.S.* an extortionist.

**graft hybrid** /graft 'haɪbrəd/, *n.* a plant chimera produced as a result of natural or artificial grafting.

**Graham's law** /ˈgreɪəmz lɔ/, *n.* (of gaseous diffusion) the principle that at a given temperature and pressure, the rate of diffusion of a gas is inversely proportional to the square root of its density. [named after Thomas *Graham,* 1805-69, Scottish chemist]

**grail** /greɪl/, *n.* a cup (also taken as a chalice) which according to medieval legend was used by Jesus at the Last Supper, and in which Joseph of Arimathaea received the last drops of Jesus's blood at the cross, used often as a symbol for a lost, pure kind of Christianity; Holy Grail. [ME *grayle,* from OF *graal,* from ML *gradāle* plate, or from L *crātēr* bowl, from Gk *krātēr*]

**grain** /greɪn/, *n.* **1.** a small hard seed, esp. a seed of one of the cereal plants: wheat, rye, oats, barley, maize, or millet. **2.** the gathered seeds of cereal plants in the mass. **3.** the plants themselves, whether standing or gathered. **4.** any small, hard particle, as of sand, gold, pepper, gunpowder, etc. **5.** the smallest unit of weight in most imperial systems, originally determined by the weight of a plump grain of wheat. In the British and U.S. systems –avoirdupois, troy, and apothecaries' –the grain is identical and equal to 64.798 918 × $10^{-6}$ kg. In an avoirdupois ounce there are 437.5 grains; in the troy and apothecaries' ounces there are 480 grains. *Symbol:* gr **6.** the smallest possible amount of anything: *a grain of truth.* **7. with a grain of salt,** with some reserve; without wholly believing. **8.** the arrangement or direction of fibres in wood, or the resulting appearance or markings. **9.** the side of leather from which the hair has been removed. **10.** a stamped pattern to imitate natural grain of leather. **11.** the fibres or yarn in a piece of fabric as differentiated from the fabric itself. **12.** lamination or cleavage of stone, coal, etc. **13.** *Gems.* a unit of weight for pearls equal to 50 mg or ¼ carat. **14.** (in diamond polishing) the cleavage directions. **15.** the size of constituent particles of any substance; texture: *sugar of fine grain.* **16.** granular texture or appearance: *a stone of coarse grain.* **17.** *Metall.* an individual crystal forming part of a pure metal, esp. one which has not attained its regular shape. **18.** *Geol.* the particles or discrete crystals which comprise a rock or sediment. **19.** *Geol.* a direction of splitting in rock, less pronounced than the rift and generally at right angles to it. **20.** *Photog.* one of the particles which constitute a photographic emulsion of a film or plate, the size of which limits the possible magnification of the projected image. **21.** temper or natural character: *to go against the grain.* **22.** *Aerospace.* the solid propellant in a rocket, specially shaped to give the required combustion characteristics. **23.** *Obs.* colour or hue. *–v.t.* **24.** to form into grains, granulate. **25.** to give a granular appearance to. **26.** to paint in imitation of the grain of wood, stone, etc. **27.** *Tanning.* to remove the hair from (skins); soften and raise the grain of (leather). [coalescence of two ME words: ME *greyn,* from OF *grain,* from L *grānum* grain, seed, and ME *grayne* red dye, from OF *graine,* from L *grāna,* pl. of *grānum* grain] **–grainer,** *n.*

**grain alcohol** /ˈ– ˌælkəhɒl/, *n.* alcohol made from grain; ethyl alcohol.

**grain elevator** /ˈ– ˌɛləveɪtə/, *n.* a lift or machine which raises grain to another floor.

**grain growth** /ˈ– grouθ/, *n.* a coarsening of crystal structure under certain conditions of heating, due to some crystals absorbing adjacent ones.

**graining** /ˈgreɪnɪŋ/, *n.* **1.** the pattern of the grain in wood, leather, etc. **2.** the process of simulating such a grain by painting, etc. **3.** the surface thus produced.

**grains** /greɪnz/, *n.pl.* (*oft. construed as sing.*) an iron instrument with barbed prongs, for spearing or harpooning fish. [earlier also *grainse,* from Icel. *grein* division, branch; cf. Swed. *gren*]

**grainsize** /ˈgreɪnsaɪz/, *n.* the size of mineral particles making up a rock or sediment.

**grains of paradise,** *n.* an African plant, *Aframomum melegueta* of the ginger family Zingiberaceae, the pungent, peppery seeds of which are used in liqueurs, veterinary medicines and household remedies. Also, **guinea grains.**

**grainy** /ˈgreɪni/, *adj.,* **grainier, grainiest. 1.** grain-like or granular. **2.** full of grains or grain. **3.** resembling the grain of wood, etc. **4.** (of a voice) rasping; gritty. **–graininess,** *n.*

**grallatorial** /grælәˈtɔriәl/, *adj.* belonging or pertaining to the wading birds, as the snipe, cranes, storks, herons, etc., many species of which have very long legs. [L *grallātor* one who goes on stilts + -IAL]

**gram**[1] /græm/, *n.* a metric unit of mass, one thousandth of a kilogram. *Symbol:* g [F *gramme,* from LL *gramma,* from Gk: a small weight, orig. something drawn]

**gram**[2] /græm/, *n.* **1.** (in some Asian countries) the chickpea, there used as a food for man and cattle. **2.** any of various other plants, as *Phaseolus aureus* (**green gram**) and *P. mungo* (**black gram**), beans cultivated in India as a food crop. [Pg. *grão,* from L *grānum* GRAIN]

**-gram**[1], a word element meaning something drawn or written, as in *diagram, epigram, telegram, monogram.* [Gk *-gramma* something drawn or written, or *-grammon* pertaining to a stroke or line]

**-gram**[2], a word element meaning grams; of or pertaining to a gram, as in *kilogram.* [Gk *grámma* small weight]

**gram.,** **1.** grammar. **2.** grammatical.

**grama grass** /ˈgramә gras/, *n.* any range grass of the western and south-western U.S. of the genus *Bouteloua,* as *B. gracilis,* the commonest species. [*grama,* from Sp.: kind of grass, from L *grāmen* grass]

**gram atom** /ˈgræm ætәm/, *n.* that quantity of an element whose weight in grams is numerically equal to the atomic weight of the element; now replaced by the mole. Also, **gram atomic weight.**

**gram calorie** /– ˈkælәri/, *n.* →**calorie** (def. 1a).

**gram equivalent** /– әˈkwɪvәlәnt/, *n.* the equivalent weight of a substance or radical expressed in grams.

**gramercy** /grәˈmɜsi/, *interj. Archaic.* **1.** many thanks. **2.** (an exclamation of surprise or sudden feeling). [ME, from OF *grant merci.* See GRAND, MERCY]

**gramicidin** /græmәˈsaɪdәn/, *n.* an antibiotic which destroys Gram-positive bacteria. See **Gram's method.** [*Gram-(positive)* + -I- + -CIDE + -IN[2]]

**gramineous** /grәˈmɪniәs/, *adj.* **1.** resembling grass. **2.** pertaining or belonging to the Gramineae (or Poaceae) family, the grass family of plants. [L *grāmineus* pertaining to grass]

**graminivorous** /græmәˈnɪvәrәs/, *adj.* **1.** feeding on seeds or like food. **2.** adapted for feeding on grain, as the jaws, teeth, etc., of squirrels and other rodents.

**gramma** /ˈgræmә/, *n.* a type of pumpkin, *Cucurbita moschata,* the fruit of which is elongated and has an orange flesh and skin.

**grammalogue** /ˈgræmәlɒg/, *n.* **1.** a word represented by a single letter sign as & for *and.* **2.** a word represented in shorthand script by a single stroke.

**grammar** /ˈgræmә/, *n.* **1.** the features of a language (sounds, words, formation and arrangement of words, etc.) considered systematically as a whole, esp. with reference to their mutual contrasts and relations: *English grammar.* **2.** an account of the preceding. **3.** a similar account comparing two or more languages, or different stages of the same language. **4.** speech or writing in accordance with standard usage: *he knows his grammar.* **5.** the elements of any science, art, or subject. **6.** a book treating them. [ME *grammer,* from OF *grammaire,* from L *grammatica,* from Gk *grammatikḗ* grammar, properly fem. of *grammatikós* pertaining to letters or literature] **–grammarless,** *adj.*

**grammarian** /grәˈmɛәriәn/, *n.* **1.** a specialist in the study of grammar. **2.** a person who claims, or is reputed to establish, standards of usage in a language.

**grammar school** /ˈgræmә skul/, *n.* **1.** *Brit.* a secondary school, providing academic education. **2.** (formerly) a school in which Latin and Greek grammar were the principal subjects taught. **3.** *U.S.* a school intermediate between a primary school and a high school.

**grammatical** /grәˈmætɪkәl/, *adj.* **1.** of or pertaining to grammar: *grammatical analysis.* **2.** conforming to standard usage: *grammatical speech.* **–grammatically,** *adv.* **–grammaticalness,** *n.*

**grammaticism** /grәˈmætәsɪzәm/, *n.* a point of grammar.

**grammatology** /græmәˈtɒlәdʒi/, *n.* the study of writing systems. **–grammatologist,** *n.*

**gramme** /græm/, *n.* →**gram**[1].

**gram molecule** /græm 'mɒləkjul/, *n.* that quantity of a substance whose weight in grams is numerically equal to the number which expresses the molecular weight of the substance; now replaced by the mole. Also, **gram-molecular weight.**

**gramophone** /'græməfoun/, *n.* →**record-player.** Also, *Chiefly U.S.,* **phonograph.** [*gramo-,* representing -GRAM[1], + -PHONE; replacing earlier Brit. and modern U.S. PHONOGRAPH] – **gramophonic,** *adj.*

**gramophone record** /'– rɛkɔd/, *n.* →**record** (def. 17).

**grampers** /'græmpəz/, *n. Colloq.* →**grandfather.**

**gramps** /græmps/, *n. Colloq.* →**grandfather.**

**grampus** /'græmpəs/, *n.* **1.** a cetacean, *Grampus griseus,* of the dolphin family, widely distributed in northern seas. **2.** any of various related cetaceans, as the killer, *Orca orca.* **3.** →**grandfather.** [earlier *graundepose,* alteration of *grapays,* from OF *graspeis,* from ML *crassus piscis* fat fish]

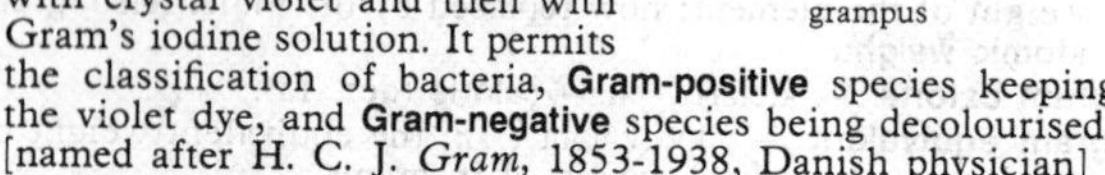

grampus

**Gram's method** /'græmz mɛθəd/, *n.* a method of bacterial staining in which the film is first stained with crystal violet and then with Gram's iodine solution. It permits the classification of bacteria, **Gram-positive** species keeping the violet dye, and **Gram-negative** species being decolourised. [named after H. C. J. *Gram,* 1853-1938, Danish physician]

**grams per square metre,** *n.* →**gsm.**

**gran** /græn/, *n. Colloq.* →**grandmother.**

**granadilla** /grænə'dɪlə/, *n.* **1.** the edible fruit of certain species of passionflower, esp. *Passiflora edulis,* passionfruit. **2.** any of the plants yielding these fruits. Also **grenadilla.** [Sp., diminutive of *granada* pomegranate. See GRENADE]

**granary** /'grænəri/, *n., pl.* **-ries.** **1.** a storehouse or repository for grain, esp. after it has been threshed or husked. **2.** a region abounding in grain. [L *grānārium*]

**gran cassa** /gran 'kasa/, *n.* →**bass drum.** [It.: big drum]

**grand** /grænd/, *adj.* **1.** imposing in size or appearance or general effect: *grand mountain scenery.* **2.** stately, majestic, or dignified. **3.** lofty: *grand ideas.* **4.** magnificent or splendid: *a grand palace, display, etc.* **5.** noble or fine: *a grand old man.* **6.** highest, or very high, in rank or official dignity: *a grand potentate.* **7.** main or principal; chief: *the grand staircase.* **8.** of great importance, distinction, or pretension: *grand personages.* **9.** complete or comprehensive: *a grand total.* **10.** *Colloq.* first-rate; very good; splendid: *to have a grand time, grand weather.* **11.** *Music.* written on a large scale or for a large ensemble: *a grand fugue.* **12.** *Genealogy.* one degree more remote in ascent or descent (used in compounds), as in *grand-aunt, grandchild, etc.* *–n.* **13.** →**piano**[1] (def. 2). **14.** *Colloq.* a thousand dollars. [ME *graunt,* from OF, from L *grandis* large, full-grown, great, grand] – **grandly,** *adv.* – **grandness,** *n.*

**grandad** /'grændæd/, *n. Colloq.* →**grandfather.** Also, **granddad.**

**grandam** /'grændæm/, *n.* **1.** a grandmother. **2.** an old woman. [ME, from AF *graund dame,* from OF *grand* GRAND + *dame* lady, mother, DAME]

**grand-aunt** /'grænd-ant/, *n.* →**great-aunt.**

**grandchild** /'græntʃaɪld/, *n., pl.* **-children.** a child of one's son or daughter.

**grand-daughter** /'græn-dɔtə/, *n.* a daughter of one's son or daughter.

**grand duchess** /græn 'dʌtʃəs/, *n.* **1.** the wife or widow of a grand duke. **2.** a woman who rules a grand duchy in her own right. **3.** a daughter of a tsar or of a tsar's son.

**grand duchy** /– 'dʌtʃi/, *n.* a territory ruled by a grand duke or grand duchess.

**grand duke** /– 'djuk/, *n.* **1.** the sovereign of a territory called a grand duchy, ranking next below a king. **2.** a son of a tsar or of a tsar's son.

**grande dame** /grɒn 'dam/, *n.* a great lady. [F]

**grandee** /græn'di/, *n.* a Spanish nobleman of the highest rank. [Sp., Pg. *grande* great (person). See GRAND]

**grandeur** /'grændʒə/, *n.* the state or quality of being grand; imposing greatness; exalted rank, dignity, or importance. [F, from *grand* GRAND]

**grandfather** /'grænfaðə, 'grænd-/, *n.* the father of one's father or mother.

**grandfather clock** /– 'klɒk/, *n.* a clock with a pendulum, in a tall wooden case.

**grandfatherly** /'grænfaðəli, 'grænd-/, *adj.* **1.** of, or in the manner of, a grandfather. **2.** indulgent; kindly.

**grand final** /græn 'faɪnəl, grænd/, *n.* (in a sporting competition, etc., where the winner is not decided on a simple knockout basis) the final game of a competition, between the two remaining teams or contestants, to determine who shall win the premiership.

**Grand Guignol** /grɒ̃ gi'njɒl/, *n.* **1.** a short horrific drama. **2.** of or pertaining to dramas of this kind. [name of a theatre in Paris]

**grandiloquence** /græn'dɪləkwəns/, *n.* lofty speech; bombast. [L *grandiloquus* speaking loftily + -ENCE]

**grandiloquent** /græn'dɪləkwənt/, *adj.* speaking or expressed in a lofty or pompous style; bombastic. – **grandiloquently,** *adv.*

**grandiose** /'grændious/, *adj.* **1.** grand in an imposing or impressive way. **2.** affectedly grand or stately; pompous. [F, from It. GRANDIOSO. See -OSE[1]] – **grandiosely,** *adv.* – **grandiosity** /grændi'ɒsəti/, *n.*

**grandioso** /,grændi'ousou/, *adj.* **1.** (of music) majestic; broad. *adv.* **2.** (a musical direction) in a majestic style. [It., from L *grandis* GRAND]

**grand jury** /græn 'dʒuri, grænd/, *n. U.S.* a jury of (usu.) 12 to 23 persons designated to inquire into alleged violations of the law in order to ascertain whether the evidence is sufficient to warrant trial by a petty jury.

**grand larceny** /grænd 'lasəni/, *n.* →**larceny.**

**grandma** /'grænma/, *n. Colloq.* →**grandmother.**

**grand mal** /grɒ̃ 'mæl/, *n.* a major epileptic attack with a loss of consciousness. [F: great illness, epilepsy]

**grandmamma** /'grænməma/, *n.* →**grandmother.**

**Grand Master** /grænd 'mastə/, *n.* **1.** the head of a lodge of freemasons, a friendly society, a religious order of knighthood, or the like. **2.** *Chess, Bridge, etc.* an outstandingly expert player, and winner of numerous competitions, tournaments, etc.

**grand monde** /grɒ̃ 'mɒnd/, *n.* the fashionable world; high society. [F: lit., the great world]

**grandmother** /'grænmʌðə, 'grænd-/, *n.* **1.** the mother of one's father or mother. **2. tell that to your grandmother!,** (an expression of disbelief).

**grandmother clock** /– 'klɒk/, *n.* a pendulum clock, similar to but slightly smaller than a grandfather clock.

**grandmotherly** /'grænmʌðəli, 'grænd-/, *adj.* of or in the manner of a grandmother.

**grand-nephew** /'græn-nɛfju, 'grænd-, -nɛvju/, *n.* →**great-nephew.**

**grand-niece** /'græn-nis, 'grænd-/, *n.* →**great-niece.**

**grand opera** /grænd 'ɒprə/, *n.* a serious drama interpreted by music, the text being sung throughout. Cf. **comic opera.**

**grandpa** /'grænpa/, *n. Colloq.* →**grandfather.**

**grandpapa** /'grænpəpa/, *n.* →**grandfather.**

**grandparent** /'grænpɛərənt/, *n.* a parent of a parent.

**grand piano** /,græn pi'ænou, ,grænd/, *n.* →**piano**[1] (def. 2).

**Grand Prix** /grɒ̃ 'pri/, *n.* **1.** an international horse race for three-year olds, run annually in Paris. **2.** any of various motor races, etc., held annually and governed by international rules. **3.** the highest award for a product at an exhibition, as wine, literary publications, etc. [F; lit. great prize, from *Grand Prix de Paris,* the horserace established in 1863]

**grandsire** /'grænsaɪə, 'grænd-/, *n. Archaic.* **1.** →**grandfather.** **2.** →**forefather.** **3.** an old man.

**grand slam** /græn 'slæm, grænd/, *n.* →**slam**[2] (def. 1).

**grandson** /'grænsʌn, 'grænd-/, *n.* a son of one's son or daughter.

**grandstand** /'grænstænd, 'grænd-/, *n.* **1.** the principal stand for spectators at a racecourse, athletic field, etc. **2.** the people sitting in the grandstand. *–v.i.* **3.** to behave ostentatiously in order to impress or win approval. *–adj.* **4.** of or pertaining to a grandstand or the spectators in it. **5.** from a good vantage point, as a grandstand: *a grandstand view of the incident.*

**grandstand finish** /– 'fɪnɪʃ/, *n.* a closely contested finish to a race.

**grand tour** /græn 'tʊə, grænd/, *n.* (formerly) an extended tour on the continent of Europe, esp. as the finishing course in the education of young people of good family.

**grand-uncle** /'grænd-ʌŋkəl/, *n.* →**great-uncle.**

**grand vizier** /grænd vɪ'zɪə/, *n.* the chief officer of state of various Muslim countries, as in the former Ottoman Empire.

**grange** /greɪndʒ/, *n.* **1.** a farm. **2.** a country dwelling house with its various farm buildings; dwelling of a yeoman or gentleman farmer. **3.** (formerly) an outlying farmhouse with barns, etc., belonging to a feudal manor or a religious establishment, where crops and tithes in kind were stored. [ME *graunge,* from AF, var. of OF *grange,* from LL *grānica,* from L *grānum* grain]

**grangerise** /'greɪndʒəraɪz/, *v.t.,* **-rised, -rising. 1.** to augment the illustrative content of (a book) by inserting additional prints, drawings, engravings, etc., not included in the original volume. **2.** to mutilate (books) in order to get illustrative material for such a purpose. Also, **grangerize.** [after J. *Granger,* whose 'Biographical History of England' (1769) was arranged for such illustration]

**granita** /grə'nitə/, *n.* a coarse grained sherbet.

**granite** /'grænət/, *n.* **1.** a granular igneous rock composed chiefly of felspar (orthoclase) and quartz, usu. with one or more other minerals, as mica, hornblende, etc., much used in building, and for monuments, etc. **2.** great hardness or firmness. [It. *granito,* orig. pp. (grained) of *granire,* from *grano,* from L *grānum* grain] – **granitelike,** *adj.* – **granitic** /grə'nɪtɪk/, *adj.*

**graniteware** /'grænətwɛə/, *n.* **1.** a kind of ironware with a grey, stonelike enamel. **2.** pottery with a speckled appearance like granite. **3.** a semivitreous white pottery somewhat harder than earthenware.

**granitite** /'grænətaɪt/, *n.* a granite rich in biotite.

**granivorous** /grə'nɪvərəs/, *adj.* feeding on grain and seeds.

**granny** /'græni/, *n., pl.* **-nies.** *Colloq.* **1.** →**grandmother. 2.** an old woman. **3.** a fussy person. **4.** →**granny knot.** Also, **grannie. 5.** →**Granny Smith.**

**granny flat** /'– flæt/, *n.* a self-contained extension to or section of a house, designed either for a relative of the family, as a grandmother, to live in, or to be rented.

**granny knot** /'– nɒt/, *n.* a reef or square knot in which the second part is crossed the wrong way, making it liable to slip or jam. [orig. a sailor's derog. term for such a knot]

granny knot

**granny's bonnet** /ˌgræniz 'bɒnət/, *n.* **1.** →**columbine**[1]. **2.** a shrub of eastern Australia, *Pimelea linifolia,* with heads of flowers surrounded by greenish bracts.

**Granny Smith** /'græni smɪθ/, *n.* a variety of apple with a green skin and crisp juicy flesh, suitable for eating raw or cooking. [from Maria Ann *Smith,* d. 1870, who first produced them at Eastwood, Sydney]

**granolith** /'grænəlɪθ/, *n.* a paving stone of crushed granite and cement. – **granolithic** /grænə'lɪθɪk/, *adj.*

**granophyre** /'grænəfaɪə/, *n.* a fine-grained or porphyritic granitic rock with a micrographic intergrowth of the minerals of the groundmass. [G *Granophyr,* from *grano-* (combining form of *Granit* GRANITE) + (*Por*)*phyr* porphyry] – **granophyric** /grænə'fɪrɪk/, *adj.*

**grant** /grænt, grant/, *v.t.* **1.** to bestow or confer, esp. by a formal act: *to grant a right.* **2.** to give or accord: *to grant permission.* **3.** to agree or accede to: *to grant a request.* **4.** to admit or concede; accept for the sake of argument: *I grant that point.* **5.** to transfer or convey, esp. by deed or writing: *to grant property.* **6. granted,** *Colloq.* (a reply acceding to a request for permission or pardon). **7. take for granted,** to accept without appreciation. *–n.* **8.** that which is granted, as a privilege or right, a sum of money, as for a student's maintenance, or a tract of land. **9.** the act of granting. **10.** *Law.* an instrument which conveys property. [ME *grant(en),*

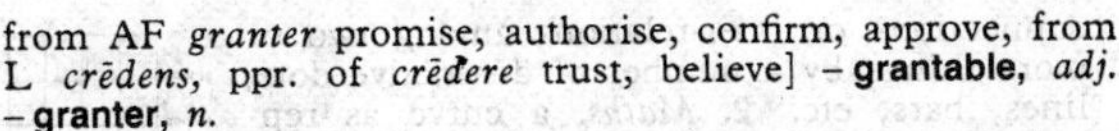

from AF *granter* promise, authorise, confirm, approve, from L *crēdens,* ppr. of *crēdere* trust, believe] – **grantable,** *adj.* – **granter,** *n.*

**grantee** /græn'ti, gran'ti/, *n.* one to whom a grant is made.

**grant of probate,** *n.* an instrument issued by a court or public official authorising an executor to take control of and dispose of the estate of a deceased person, where the deceased made a will.

**grantor** /græn'tɔ, gran'tɔ/, *n.* one who makes a grant.

**grants commission** /'grænts kəmɪʃən, 'grants/, *n.* the body which investigates and reports upon claims by States for grants by the Australian Parliament to meet special needs in those States.

**gran turismo** /græn tu'rɪzmoʊ/, *n.* **1.** a touring car. *–adj.* **2.** of or pertaining to a fast sporty car. Also, **GT.** [It.: grand touring]

**granular** /'grænjələ/, *adj.* **1.** of the nature of granules. **2.** composed of or bearing granules. **3.** showing a granulated structure. – **granularity** /grænjə'lærəti/, *n.* – **granularly,** *adv.*

**granulate** /'grænjəleɪt/, *v.,* **-lated, -lating.** *–v.t.* **1.** to form into granules or grains. **2.** to raise in granules; make rough on the surface. *–v.i.* **3.** to become granular. **4.** *Pathol.* to form granulation tissue. [GRANUL(E) + -ATE[1]] – **granulator,** *n.*

**granulated sugar** /ˌgrænjəleɪtəd 'ʃʊgə/, *n.* a coarsely ground, white sugar, used for sweetening.

**granulation** /grænjə'leɪʃən/, *n.* **1.** the act or process of granulating. **2.** granulated condition. **3.** one of the grains of a granulated surface. **4.** *Pathol.* **a.** the formation of granulation tissue, esp. in healing. **b.** →**granulation tissue. 5.** *Astron.* one of the small short-lived features of the solar surface which in the aggregate give it a mottled appearance when viewed with a telescope.

**granulation tissue** /'– tɪʃu/, *n.* tissue formed in ulcers and in early wounds healing and repair, composed largely of newly growing capillaries and so called from its irregular surface in open wounds; proud flesh.

**granule** /'grænjul/, *n.* a little grain, pellet, or particle. [LL *grānulum,* diminutive of L *grānum* GRAIN]

**granulite** /'grænjəlaɪt/, *n.* a metamorphic rock composed of even-sized interlocking granular minerals, such as quartz, felspar, mica or hornblende, and showing a definite banding. – **granulitic** /grænjə'lɪtɪk/, *adj.*

**granulocyte** /'grænjələsaɪt/, *n.* any blood cell containing specific granules.

**granuloma** /grænjə'loʊmə/, *n.* a tumour of granulation tissue. [L *granul(um)* small grain + -OMA]

**grape** /greɪp/, *n.* **1.** the edible, pulpy, smooth-skinned berry or fruit which grows in clusters on vines of the genus *Vitis* and related plants, esp. *V. vinifera* from which wine is made. **2.** any vine bearing this fruit. **3. the grape,** *Colloq.* wine. **4.** dull, dark purplish red. **5.** (*pl.*) *Vet. Sci.* a morbid growth on the fetlock of a horse, resembling a bunch of grapes. **6.** (*pl.*) *Colloq.* →**haemorrhoids. 7.** *Archaic.* →**grapeshot. 8. a grape on the business,** an interloper; an unwelcome person. **9. in the grip of the grape,** *Colloq.* addicted to drink, esp. wine. [ME, from OF, var. of *crape* cluster of fruit or flowers, orig. hook; of Gmc orig. (cf. G *Krapf* hook). Cf. GRAPNEL, GRAPPLE]

**grapefruit** /'greɪpfrut/, *n.* **1.** a large roundish, yellow-skinned edible citrus fruit with a juicy, acid pulp. **2.** the tropical or semitropical tree, *Citrus paradisi,* from which the fruit is obtained.

**grape hyacinth** /greɪp 'haɪəsɪnθ/, *n.* any plant of the genus *Muscari,* as *M. botryoides,* a species whose globular blue flowers resemble tiny grapes.

**grapery** /'greɪpəri/, *n., pl.* **-ries. 1.** a building where grapes are grown. **2.** a plantation of grapevines.

**grapeshot** /'greɪpʃɒt/, *n. Archaic.* a cluster of small cast-iron balls used as a charge for a cannon.

**grape sugar** /'greɪp ʃʊgə/, *n.* →**dextrose.**

**grapevine** /'greɪpvaɪn/, *n.* **1.** a vine that bears grapes. **2.** *Colloq.* the means by which any form of information is passed, esp. word of mouth. **3.** *Wrestling.* a hold in which a wrestler twists his own leg round his opponent's leg.

**graph** /græf, graf/, *n.* **1.** a diagram representing a system of connections or inter-relations among two or more things by a number of distinctive dots, lines, bars, etc. **2.** *Maths.* a curve as representing a given function. *–v.t.* **3.** to draw a graph of. **4.** to draw (a curve) as representing a given function. [short for *graphic formula* See GRAPHIC]

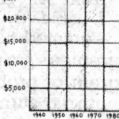

bar graph

**graph-,** variant of **grapho-** before vowels.

**-graph,** a,word,element,meaning:,**1.** drawn or written, as in *autograph.* **2.** something drawn or written, as in *lithograph, monograph.* **3.** an apparatus for drawing, writing, recording, etc., as in *barograph.* [Gk *-graphos* (something) drawn or written, also one who draws or writes. See GRAPHIC]

**grapheme** /ˈgræfim/, *n.* the smallest unit of writing or printing that distinguishes one meaning from another, as, in English, any of the letters of the alphabet.

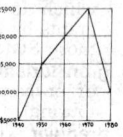

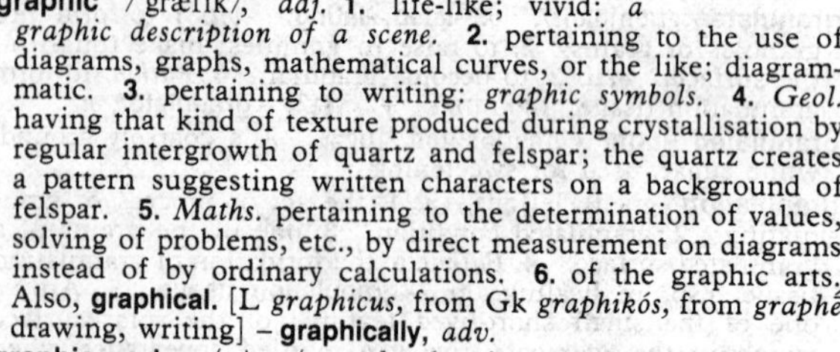

line graph

**graphic** /ˈgræfɪk/, *adj.* **1.** life-like; vivid: *a graphic description of a scene.* **2.** pertaining to the use of diagrams, graphs, mathematical curves, or the like; diagrammatic. **3.** pertaining to writing: *graphic symbols.* **4.** *Geol.* having that kind of texture produced during crystallisation by regular intergrowth of quartz and felspar; the quartz creates a pattern suggesting written characters on a background of felspar. **5.** *Maths.* pertaining to the determination of values, solving of problems, etc., by direct measurement on diagrams instead of by ordinary calculations. **6.** of the graphic arts. Also, **graphical.** [L *graphicus,* from Gk *graphikós,* from *graphḗ* drawing, writing] **– graphically,** *adv.*

**graphic arts** /– ˈats/, *n.pl.* drawing, engraving, etching, painting, and other arts involving the use of lines, strokes, colour, etc., to express or convey ideas.

**graphic equaliser** /– ˈikwəlaɪzə/, *n.* a device which alters the timbre of an instrument, used in sound recording.

**graphics** /ˈgræfɪks/, *n.* **1.** the art of drawing, esp. as concerned with mathematics, engineering, etc. **2.** the science of calculating by diagrams. **3.** the production of patterns and diagrams by computer. **4.** design that incorporates typographical elements; the production of diagrams or pictures in conjunction with text. [GRAPH + -ICS]

**graphite** /ˈgræfaɪt/, *n.* a very common mineral, soft native carbon, occurring in black to dark grey foliated masses with metallic lustre and greasy feel, used in so-called lead pencils, as a lubricant, for making crucibles and other refractories, etc.; plumbago; black lead. [G *Graphit,* from Gk *gráphein* mark, draw, write + *-it* -ITE[1]] **– graphitic** /grəˈfɪtɪk/, *adj.*

**graphitise** /ˈgræfətaɪz/, *v.t.,* **-tised, -tising. 1.** to convert into graphite. **2.** to cover (the surface of an object) with graphite. Also, **graphitize. – graphitisation** /græfətaɪˈzeɪʃən/, *n.*

**grapho-,** a word element meaning 'writing', as in *graphology.* Also, **graph-.** [Gk, combining form of *graphḗ*]

**graphology** /græˈfɒlədʒi/, *n.* the study of handwriting, esp. as regarded as an expression of the writer's character. **– graphologist,** *n.*

**graphos** /ˈgræfɒs/, *n.* a pen used in graphic artwork, which is similar in principle to a fountain pen but designed to be fitted with a variety of nibs. [Trademark]

**graphospasm** /ˈgræfoʊˌspæzəm/, *n.* **→writer's cramp.**

**graph paper** /ˈgræf peɪpə/, *n.* paper on which lines or squares have been printed in order to make it suitable for plotting graphs.

**-graphy,** a combining form denoting some process or form of drawing, representing, writing, recording, describing, etc., or an art or science concerned with some such thing, as in *biography, choreography, geography, orthography, photography.* [Gk *graphía,* from *gráphos.* See -GRAPH, -Y[3]]

grapnel (def. 2)

**grapnel** /ˈgræpnəl/, *n.* **1.** a device consisting essentially of one or more hooks or clamps, for grasping or holding something; a grapple; grappling iron. **2.** a small anchor with three or more flukes. Also, *Naut.,* **grappling iron.** [ME *grapenel,* diminutive of OF *grapin* kind of hook, diminutive of *grape* hook. See GRAPE]

**grappa** /ˈgræpə/, *n.* a coarse spirit distilled from the skins, pips and stalks of grapes after they have been pressed for wine-making. [It.: grape stalk]

**grapple** /ˈgræpəl/, *n., v.,* **-pled, -pling.** *–n.* **1.** a hook or an iron instrument by which one thing, as a ship, fastens on another; a grapnel. **2.** a seizing or gripping. **3.** a grip or close hold in wrestling or hand-to-hand fighting. *–v.t.* **4.** to seize, hold, or fasten with or as with a grapple. **5.** to engage in a struggle or close encounter with. *–v.i.* **6.** to hold or make fast to something as with a grapple. **7.** to use a grapple. **8.** to seize another, or each other, in a firm grip, as in wrestling; clinch. **9.** to try to overcome or deal (fol. by *with*): *to grapple with a problem.* [apparently a frequentative of OE *gegræppian* seize, associated with GRAPNEL] **– grappler,** *n.*

**grappler** /ˈgræplə/, *n. Colloq.* a professional wrestler.

**grappling** /ˈgræplɪŋ/, *n.* **1.** that by which anything is seized and held. **2. →grapnel.**

**grappling iron** /ˈ– aɪən/, *n.* **→grapnel.** Also, **grappling hook.**

**graptolite** /ˈgræptəlaɪt/, *n.* any of the Graptolithina, an order of extinct coelenterates commonly found as fossils. **– graptolitic** /græptəˈlɪtɪk/, *adj.*

**grapy** /ˈgreɪpi/, *adj.* of, like, or composed of grapes.

**grasp** /græsp, grasp/, *v.t.* **1.** to seize and hold by or as by clasping with the fingers. **2.** to seize upon; hold firmly. **3.** to lay hold of with the mind; comprehend; understand. *–v.i.* **4.** to make the motion of seizing; seize something firmly or eagerly. **5.** to catch at; try to seize (fol. by *at*): *a drowning man grasps at a straw.* *–n.* **6.** a grasping or gripping; grip of the hand. **7.** power of seizing and holding; reach: *to have a thing within one's grasp.* **8.** hold, possession, or mastery: *to wrest power from the grasp of a usurper.* **9.** mental hold or comprehension: *a subject beyond one's grasp.* **10.** broad or thorough comprehension: *a good grasp of a subject.* [ME *graspen, grapsen,* c. LG *grapsen;* akin to OE *gegræppian* seize] **– graspable,** *adj.* **– grasper,** *n.*

**grasping** /ˈgræspɪŋ, ˈgrasp-/, *adj.* **1.** that grasps. **2.** greedy. **– graspingly,** *adv.* **– graspingness,** *n.*

**grass** /gras/, *n.* **1.** any plant of the family Gramineae (or Poaceae), characterised by jointed stems, sheathing leaves, flower spikelets, and fruit consisting of a seed-like grain or caryopsis (true grasses). **2.** herbage in general, or the plants on which grazing animals pasture, or which are cut and dried as hay. **3.** *Colloq.* **→marijuana. 4.** grass-covered ground; lawn. **5.** pasture: *half of the farm is grass, to put the animals to grass.* **6.** (*pl.*) stalks or sprays of grass: *filled with dried grasses.* **7.** *Mining.* the surface over a mine. **8. at grass,** *Mining.* (of ore) stacked ready for shipment. **9. let the grass grow under one's feet,** to be lax in one's efforts; miss an opportunity. **10. put out to grass, a.** to withdraw (a racehorse) from racing, etc., due to old age. **b.** *Colloq.* to retire (a person). *–v.t.* **11.** to cover with grass or turf. **12.** to feed with growing grass; pasture. **13.** *Football.* to bring down (an opposing player). **14.** to lay on the grass, as for the purpose of bleaching. **15. grass a catch,** *Cricket.* to drop a catch. *–v.i.* **16.** to feed on growing grass; graze. **17.** to produce grass. **18.** *Colloq.* to inform (*on*). [ME *gras,* OE *græs,* c. D, G, Icel. and Goth. *gras;* akin to GROW and GREEN]

**grassbird** /ˈgrasbɜd/, *n.* any of a number of small birds of the family Sylviidae, which live in swamps and grasslands.

**grass captain** /ˈgras kæptn/, *n.* the foreman at the surface of a mine.

**grass-catcher** /ˈgras-kætʃə/, *n.* a container which can be fitted to a lawn-mower, to catch the grass clippings from the blades.

**grass-clipper** /ˈgras-klɪpə/, *n.* a small manual or electric tool for cutting the grass at the side of paths, fences, etc.

**grass clippings** /ˈgras klɪpɪŋz/, *n.pl.* the cut grass collected after mowing the lawn or clipping the edges.

**grass cloth** /ˈ– klɒθ/, *n.* a cloth made from the fibres of grass, jute, etc.

**grass court** /ˈ– kɔt/, *n.* a tennis court whose playing surface consists of closely mown grass.

**grasser** /ˈgrasə/, *n. Colloq.* **→informer.**

**grass-finch** /ˈgras-fɪntʃ/, *n.* any of numerous species of small, colourful weaverbirds of the family Estrildidae, living and moving in flocks, widely distributed in Australia, Asia and Africa.

**grassfire** /ˈgrasfaɪə/, *n.* a fire, usu. spontaneous, in open grass country, in which the fuel is the standing grass.

**grass-green** /gras-ˈgrin/, *n.* a yellowish-green colour.

**grasshopper** /ˈgrashɒpə/, *n.* **1.** any of numerous orthopterous insects which are terrestrial, herbivorous and have hind legs for leaping, and many of which are destructive to vegetation, as the locusts, certain katydids, etc. **2. knee-high to a grasshopper,** small; young.

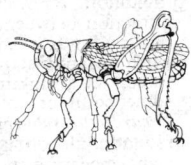

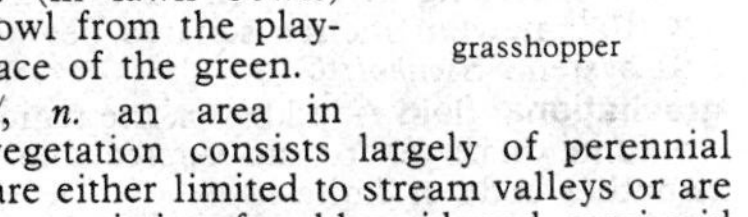

grasshopper

**grassing** /ˈgrasɪŋ/, *n.* (in lawn bowls) the passing of the bowl from the player's hand to the surface of the green.

**grassland** /ˈgraslænd/, *n.* an area in which the natural vegetation consists largely of perennial grasses, where trees are either limited to stream valleys or are widely scattered, characteristic of subhumid and semi-arid climates.

**grass of Parnassus,** *n.* any of the genus Parnassia, family Saxifragaceae or Parnassiaceae, perennials of marshy areas, having broad, smooth leaves and single pale flowers.

**grass parrot** /gras ˈpærət/, *n.* any of various parrots, esp. the budgerigar, which feed on grass seeds.

**grasspay** /grasˈpeɪ/, *adj.* (of a type of sandstone), being a likely source of oil.

**grassroots** /grasˈruts, ˈgrasruts/, *Orig. U.S. Colloq.* –*n.pl.* **1.** the basic essentials or foundation. –*adj.* **2.** pertaining to, close to, or emerging spontaneously from the people.

**grass sickness** /ˈgras sɪknəs/, *n.* an often fatal disease of horses, which can occur when a horse is put out to certain pastures.

**grass snake** /ˈ– sneɪk/, *n.* a non-venomous, dark green snake, *Natrix natrix,* having two yellow patches behind the head, the largest British snake.

**grass tetany** /– ˈtɛtəni/, *n.* a disease of cattle and sheep marked by staggering, convulsions and coma, caused by reduction of blood calcium and magnesium when overeating on lush pastures. Also, **grass staggers.**

**grasstree** /ˈgrasˌtri/, *n.* **1.** any of the woody-stemmed perennials constituting the Australian genus *Xanthorrhoea,* having a tuft of long more or less grass-like leaves, bearing a long dense flower spike, and yielding acaroid gum; black boy; yakka. **2.** any of various other plants or trees, having leaves thought to resemble grass, as the giant grasstree, *Richea pandanifolia,* a small Tasmanian tree.

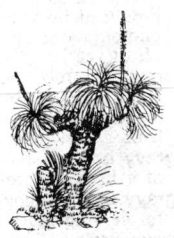

grasstree (def. 1)

**grass widow** /gras ˈwɪdoʊ/, *n.* **1.** a woman whose husband is temporarily absent. **2.** *Colloq.* a woman neglected by her husband. **3.** *U.S.* a woman who is separated, divorced, or lives apart from her husband.

**grass widower** /– ˈwɪdoʊə/, *n.* **1.** a man whose wife is temporarily absent. **2.** *U.S.* a man who is separated, divorced, or lives apart from his wife.

**grass-wrack** /ˈgras-ræk/, *n.* any species of the genus *Zostera,* a grass-like marine flowering plant.

**grass wren** /ˈgras rɛn/, *n.* any of a number of small, ground-dwelling birds of genus *Amytornis,* inhabiting low scrub, grass or rocky areas of inland Australia.

**grassy** /ˈgrasi/, *adj.,* **-sier, -siest. 1.** covered with grass. **2.** pertaining to or consisting of grass; grass-like. **3.** smelling like grass. – **grassiness,** *n.*

**grate**[1] /greɪt/, *n., v.,* **grated, grating.** –*n.* **1.** a frame of metal bars for holding fuel when burning, as in a fireplace or furnace. **2.** a framework of parallel or crossed bars used as a partition, guard, cover, or the like. **3.** a fireplace. –*v.t.* **4.** to furnish with a grate or grates. [ME, from It., from L *crātis* wickerwork, hurdle. Cf. CRATE]

**grate**[2] /greɪt/, *v.,* **grated, grating.** –*v.i.* **1.** to have an irritating or unpleasant effect on the feelings. **2.** to make a sound as of rough scraping. **3.** to sound harshly; jar: *to grate on the ear.* **4.** to scrape or rub with rough or noisy friction, as one thing on or against another. –*v.t.* **5.** to rub together with a harsh, jarring sound: *to grate the teeth.* **6.** to reduce to small particles by rubbing against a rough surface or a surface with many sharp-edged openings: *to grate a nutmeg.* **7.** *Archaic.* to wear down or away by rough friction. [ME, from OF *grater;* of Gmc orig. (cf. G *kratzen* scratch)] – **grater,** *n.* – **grating,** *adj.* – **gratingly,** *adv.*

**grateful** /ˈgreɪtfəl/, *adj.* **1.** warmly or deeply appreciative of kindness or benefits received; thankful: *I am grateful to you for your kindness.* **2.** actuated by or expressing gratitude: *a grateful letter.* **3.** pleasing to the mind or senses; agreeable or welcome; refreshing: *grateful slumber.* [obs. *grate* pleasing, thankful (from L *grātus*) + -FUL] – **gratefully,** *adv.* – **gratefulness,** *n.*

**graticule** /ˈgrætəkjul/, *n.* **1.** a grid of meridians of longitude and parallels of latitude drawn on a particular map projection; the basis on which a map or chart is plotted. **2.** *Physics.* →**reticle.**

**gratification** /grætəfəˈkeɪʃən/, *n.* **1.** the state of being gratified; great satisfaction. **2.** something that gratifies; source of pleasure or satisfaction. **3.** the act of gratifying. **4.** *Archaic.* a reward, recompense, or gratuity.

**gratify** /ˈgrætəfaɪ/, *v.t.,* **-fied, -fying. 1.** to give pleasure to (persons) by satisfying desires or humouring inclinations or feelings. **2.** to satisfy; indulge; humour: *to gratify desires or appetites.* **3.** *Obs.* to reward; remunerate. [F *gratifier,* from L *grātificāri* do a favour to, oblige, gratify] – **gratifier,** *n.*

**gratifying** /ˈgrætəˌfaɪɪŋ/, *adj.* that gratifies; pleasing; satisfying. – **gratifyingly,** *adv.*

**gratin** /ˈgrætn, grəˈtæn/, *n.* →**au gratin.** [F, from *gratter,* earlier *grater* scrape. See GRATE[2]]

**grating** /ˈgreɪtɪŋ/, *n.* **1.** a partition or frame of parallel or crossing bars; open latticework of wood or metal serving as a cover or guard, but admitting light, air, etc. **2.** *Physics.* →**diffraction grating.**

**gratis** /ˈgratəs/, *adv.* **1.** for nothing; gratuitously. –*adj.* **2.** free of cost; gratuitous. [L]

**gratitude** /ˈgrætətʃud/, *n.* the quality or feeling of being grateful or thankful. [LL *grātitūdo,* from L *grātus* pleasing, thankful]

**grattoir** /ˈgrætwa/, *n.* a chipped stone implement used for working wood or leather; scraper. [F, from *gratter* scrape]

**gratuitous** /grəˈtjuətəs/, *adj.* **1.** freely bestowed or obtained; free. **2.** being without reason, cause, or justification: *a gratuitous insult.* **3.** *Law.* given without receiving any return value. [L *grātuītus* free, spontaneous] – **gratuitously,** *adv.* – **gratuitousness,** *n.*

**gratuity** /grəˈtjuəti/, *n., pl.* **-ties. 1.** a gift, usu. of money, over and above payment due for service; tip. **2.** that which is given without claim or demand. **3.** a bounty given to soldiers.

**gratulate** /ˈgrætʃəleɪt/, *v.,* **-lated, -lating.** *Archaic.* –*v.t.* **1.** to hail with joy; express joy at. **2.** to congratulate. –*v.i.* **3.** to express joy. [L *grātulātus,* pp., having expressed joy, congratulated, or thanked] – **gratulatory** /ˈgrætʃələtri, -təri/, *adj.*

**gratulation** /grætʃəˈleɪʃən/, *n. Archaic.* **1.** a feeling of joy. **2.** the expression of joy.

**graunch** /grɔntʃ/, *Chiefly N.Z.* –*v.i.* **1.** to make a grinding or grating sound: *the ship graunched over the rocks.* –*v.t.* **2.** to ruin or damage (usu. with a graunching sound). [Brit. d. *granch, cranch,* var. of *crunch,* or echoic]

**graunchy** /ˈgrɔntʃi/, *adj. N.Z.* difficult; testing.

**graupel** /ˈgraʊpəl/, *n.* →**soft hail.**

**gravamen** /grəˈveɪmən/, *n., pl.* **-vamina** /-ˈvæmənə/. **1.** that part of an accusation which weighs most heavily against the accused; the burden or substantial part of a charge or complaint. **2.** a grievance. [LL, from L *gravāre* load, weigh down. Cf. GRIEVE]

**grave**[1] /greɪv/, *n.* **1.** an excavation made in the earth to receive a dead body in burial. **2.** any place of interment; a tomb or sepulchre. **3.** any place that becomes the receptacle of what is dead, lost or past: *the grave of dead reputations.* **4.** death: *O grave, where is thy victory?* **5. have one foot in the grave,** to be infirm, old, or near death. **6. dig one's own grave,** to cause one's own downfall or ruin. **7. to turn in one's grave,** (of a dead person), to be thought likely to have

i = peat ɪ = pit ɛ = pet æ = pat a = part ɒ = pot ʌ = putt ɔ = port ʊ = put u = pool ɜ = pert ə = apart aɪ = buy eɪ = bay ɔɪ = boy aʊ = how oʊ = hoe ɪə = here ɛə = hair ʊə = tour g = give θ = thin ð = then ʃ = show ʒ = measure tʃ = choke dʒ = joke ŋ = sing j = you õ = Fr. bon

been offended or horrified by a modern event or events. [ME; OE *græf,* c. G *Grab.* See GRAVE[3]]

**grave**[2] /greɪv/; /grav/ *for defs 4 and 6, adj.,* **graver, gravest,** *n.* *–adj.* **1.** dignified; sedate; serious; earnest; solemn: *a grave person, grave thoughts, grave ceremonies.* **2.** weighty, momentous, or important: *grave responsibilities.* **3.** important or critical; involving serious issues: *a grave situation.* **4.** *Phonet.* **a.** spoken on a low pitch or falling pitch because of musical accent. **b.** denoting or having a particular accent (`) indicating originally a comparatively low pitch (as in ancient Greek); later, quality of sound (as in the French *père*), distinct syllabic value (as in *belovèd*), etc. **5.** *Rare.* (of colours) dull; sombre. *–n.* **6.** the grave accent. [F, from L *gravis* heavy] – **gravely,** *adv.* – **graveness,** *n.*

**grave**[3] /greɪv/, *v.t.,* **graved, graved** or **graven, graving.** *Archaic.* **1.** to incise or engrave. **2.** to impress deeply: *graven on the mind.* [ME *grave(n),* OE *grafan,* c. G *graben.* Cf. GRAVE[1], GROOVE, and GRAVURE]

**grave**[4] /greɪv/, *v.t.,* **graved, graving.** to clean (a ship's hull or a ship) by burning or scraping off accretions and paving it over with pitch. [orig. obscure]

**grave**[5] /'graveɪ/, *adv.* (a musical direction) slowly; solemnly. [It., from L *gravis* GRAVE[2]] – **grave,** *adj.*

**graveclothes** /'greɪvklouðz/, *n.pl.* the clothes in which a dead body is interred; cerements.

**grave-digger** /'greɪv-dɪgə/, *n.* **1.** the cause of ruin or downfall. **2.** *Cricket.* the last batsman in the batting order of a team. **3.** *Brit. Mil. Colloq.* strong drink.

**gravel** /'grævəl/, *n., v.,* **-elled, -elling** or (*U.S.*) **-eled, -eling.** *–n.* **1.** small stones and pebbles, or a mixture of these with sand. **2.** *Pathol.* **a.** a collection of small calculi formed in the kidneys. **b.** the disease characterised by such concretions. *–v.t.* **3.** to cover with gravel. [ME, from OF *gravele,* diminutive of *grave* sandy shore; of Celtic orig.]

**gravel-blind** /'grævəl-blaɪnd/, *adj.* more blind or dim-sighted than sand-blind and less than stone-blind.

**gravelly** /'grævəli/, *adj.* **1.** abounding in gravel. **2.** consisting of or resembling gravel. **3.** (of a voice) harsh.

**gravel rash** /'grævəl ræʃ/, *n.* a surface skin rash caused by a fall on gravel, etc.

**gravel road** /'grævəl roud/, *n.* a road with a loose gravel surface.

**gravemente** /gravə'mɛnteɪ/, *adv.* (a musical direction) gravely.

**graven** /'greɪvən/, *v.* **1.** past participle of **grave**[3]. *–adj.* **2.** deeply impressed; firmly fixed. **3.** *Archaic.* carved; engraved.

**graven image** /– 'ɪmɪdʒ/, *n.* →**idol.**

**graver** /'greɪvə/, *n.* **1.** any of various tools for chasing, engraving, etc., as a burin. **2.** *Archaic.* →**engraver.**

**Graves' disease** /'greɪvz dəziz/, *n.* a disease characterised by an enlarged thyroid, rapid pulse, and increased basal metabolism due to excessive thyroid secretion. [named after R. J. *Graves,* 1796-1853, Irish physician]

**gravestone** /'greɪvstoun/, *n.* a stone marking a grave.

**Gravettian** /grə'vɛtiən/, *adj.* of, pertaining to, or characteristic of an Upper Palaeolithic culture of Europe. [after *La Gravette* on the Dordogne, France; see -IAN]

**graveyard** /'greɪvjad/, *n.* cemetery; burial ground.

**graveyard bark** /'– bak/, *n. Colloq.* a loud and distressing cough. Also, **graveyard cough.**

**graveyard humour** /– 'hjumə/, *n.* macabre humour dealing with a gruesome subject, as corpses, skeletons, etc.

**graveyard shift** /'– ʃɪft/, *n. Colloq.* (in mining) the night shift; dogwatch.

**gravid** /'grævəd/, *adj.* →**pregnant.** [L *gravidus*] – **gravidity** /grə'vɪdəti/, *n.*

**gravimeter** /'grævəmitə/, *n.* any apparatus used to determine specific gravity.

**gravimetric** /grævə'mɛtrɪk/, *adj.* **1.** of or pertaining to measurement by weight. **2.** *Chem.* denoting a method of analysing compound bodies by finding the weight of their elements (opposed to *volumetric*). Also, **gravimetrical.** – **gravimetrically,** *adv.*

**gravimetry** /grə'vɪmətri/, *n.* the measurement of weight or density. [L *gravi(s)* heavy + -METRY]

**graving dock** /'greɪvɪŋ dɒk/, *n.* →**dry dock.** [GRAVE[4] + DOCK[1]]

**gravitate** /'grævəteɪt/, *v.i.,* **-tated, -tating.** **1.** to move or tend to move under the influence of gravitational force. **2.** to tend towards the lowest level; sink; fall. **3.** to have a natural tendency or be strongly attracted (fol. by *to* or *towards*). [NL *gravitātus,* pp., from L *gravis* heavy]

**gravitation** /grævə'teɪʃən/, *n.* **1.** *Physics.* **a.** that force of attraction between all particles or bodies, or that acceleration of one towards another, of which the fall of bodies to the earth is an instance. **b.** an act or process caused by this force. **2.** a sinking or falling. **3.** natural tendency towards some point or object of influence: *the gravitation of people towards the suburbs.* – **gravitational,** *adj.* – **gravitationally,** *adv.*

**gravitational constant** /,grævəteɪʃənəl 'kɒnstənt/, *n.* the constant appearing in Newton's law of gravitation, equal to 6.67 $\times$ $10^{-11}$ newton metres squared per kilogram squared in the SI system. *Symbol:* G

**gravitational field** /– 'fild/, *n.* the region in which a body with a finite mass exerts an appreciable force of attraction on another body of finite mass.

**gravitational water** /– 'wɔtə/, *n.* water in the large pores of soil, which the force of gravity will remove from the soil when conditions of free drainage exist.

**gravitative** /'grævə,teɪtɪv/, *adj.* **1.** of or pertaining to gravitation. **2.** tending or causing to gravitate.

**graviton** /'grævətɒn/, *n.* the hypothetical sub-atomic particle associated with the gravitational field.

**gravity** /'grævəti/, *n., pl.* **-ties.** **1.** the force of attraction by which terrestrial bodies tend to fall towards the centre of the earth. **2.** heaviness or weight: *the centre of gravity, specific gravity.* **3.** gravitation in general. **4.** seriousness; dignity; solemnity: *to preserve one's gravity.* **5.** serious or critical character: *the gravity of the situation.* **6.** lowness in pitch, as of sounds. [L *gravitas* heaviness]

**gravity cell** /'– sɛl/, *n.* an electric cell with horizontal electrodes in which the two electrolytes lie in separate layers as a result of their difference in specific gravity.

**gravity dam** /'– dæm/, *n.* a dam which retains the water and resists its pressure by the weight of the retaining wall.

**gravity feed** /'– fid/, *n.* **1.** the supplying of materials, fuels, etc., by the force of gravity alone. **2.** any system designed for this purpose.

**gravure** /grə'vjʊə/, *n.* **1.** a process of photomechanical printing, such as photogravure or rotogravure. **2.** a plate or print produced by gravure. **3.** the metal or wooden plate used in photogravure. [F: engraving, from *graver* engrave, from Gmc; cf. GRAVE[3]]

**gravy** /'greɪvi/, *n., pl.* **-vies.** **1.** the fat and juices that drip from meat during cooking, often made into a dressing for meat, etc. **2.** *Colloq.* any perquisite; money easily acquired. [ME *grave,* from OF: kind of dressing]

**gravy beef** /'– bif/, *n.* a cut of beef from the shin or shank of a hind or foreleg, used to make soup, broth, and brawn.

**gravy boat** /'– bout/, *n.* a small boat-shaped (or other) vessel for serving gravy or sauce.

**gravy train** /'– treɪn/, *n. Colloq.* any course of action which results in the receipt of perquisites: *on the parliamentary gravy train.*

**gray**[1] /greɪ/, *adj., n., v. U.S.* →**grey.**

**gray**[2] /greɪ/, *n.* the SI unit of measurement of absorbed dose of ionising radiation, equal to 1 J/$kg^{-1}$. The gray may also be used as a unit of measurement of other physical quantities related to ionising radiations. *Symbol:* Gy

**grayling** /'greɪlɪŋ/, *n.* **1.** a small freshwater fish, *Prototroctes maraena* of south-eastern Australia, having a narrow grey band along the sides and a distinctively marked yellow fin. **2.** elsewhere, any of the freshwater fishes constituting the genus *Thymallus,* allied to the trout, but having a longer and higher dorsal fin of resplendent colour. **3.** any of certain sombre grey moths of the family Satyridae.

grayling

**graze**[1] /greɪz/, *v.,* **grazed, grazing.** *–v.i.* **1.** to feed on growing herbage, as cattle, sheep etc. *–v.t.* **2.** to feed on (growing grass). **3.** to put cattle, sheep, etc., to feed on (grass, pasture, etc.). 4. to crop growth on a paddock by putting cattle, etc. to graze on it (oft. fol. by *back* or *down*). 5. to tend (cattle, sheep, etc.) while at pasture. [ME *grase(n)*, OE *grasian*, from *græs* GRASS]

**graze²** /greɪz/, *v.*, **grazed, grazing,** *n.* –*v.t.* 1. to touch or rub lightly in passing. 2. to scrape the skin from (the leg, arm, etc.); abrade. –*v.i.* 3. to touch or rub something lightly, or so as to produce slight abrasion, in passing. –*n.* 4. a grazing; a touching or rubbing lightly in passing. 5. a slight scratch in passing; abrasion. [orig. uncert.]

**grazier** /'greɪziə/, *n.* a farmer, usu. a substantial landowner, who grazes sheep or cattle.

**grazioso** /gratsi'oʊsoʊ/, *adv.* (a musical direction) gracefully. [It.] – **grazioso,** *adj.*

**grease** /gris/, *n.*; /griz, gris/, *v.* **greased, greasing.** –*n.* 1. the melted or rendered fat of animals, esp. when in a soft state. 2. fatty or oily matter in general; lubricant. 3. *Colloq.* butter. 4. Also, **grease wool.** wool, as shorn, before being cleansed of the oily matter. 5. *Vet. Sci.* inflammation of a horse's skin in the fetlock region, attended with an oily secretion. –*v.t.* 6. to put grease on; lubricate: *he greased the axle but it did no good.* 7. to smear with grease. 8. to cause to run easily. 9. **grease (someone's) palm,** *Colloq.* to bribe (a person). [ME *grese*, from OF *graisse*, from L *crassus* fat] – **greaseless,** *adj.* – **greaser,** *n.*

**greasebush** /'grisbʊʃ/, *n.* →**greasewood.**

**grease gun** /'gris gʌn/, *n.* a hand-operated device for forcing grease into bearings under pressure.

**grease monkey** /'– mʌŋki/, *n.* →**mechanic.**

**greasepaint** /'grispeɪnt/, *n.* 1. a mixture of tallow or hard grease and a pigment, used by actors for painting their faces. 2. any theatrical make-up.

**greaseproof** /'grispruf/, *adj.* impervious to grease: *greaseproof paper.*

**greaser** /'grizə/, *n. Colloq.* (*derog.*) 1. a member of a Latin-American race, esp. a Mexican. 2. a toadying, sycophantic person.

**greasespot** /'grisspɒt/, *n.* 1. a greasy spot or mark. 2. *Colloq.* →**greaser.** 3. **feel like a greasespot,** *Colloq.* to be in a state of sweatiness; to experience lassitude induced by great heat.

**grease trap** /'gris træp/, *n.* a type of intercepter trap positioned outside a building to collect kitchen grease or waste.

**greasewood** /'griswʊd/, *n.* a shrub, *Sarcobatus vermiculatus*, of the alkaline regions of the western U.S., containing a small amount of oil and used for fuel. Also, **greasebush.**

**greasies** /'griziz/, *n.pl. Colloq.* fish and chips.

**greasy** /'grizi, -si/, *adj.*, **-sier, -siest.** 1. smeared or soiled with grease. 2. composed of or containing grease; oily: *greasy food.* 3. greaselike in appearance or to the touch; slippery. 4. *Vet. Sci.* affected with grease. –*n.* 5. *Colloq.* one who, in a camp, attends to the chores of cooking, cleaning, etc. 6. *Colloq.* a shearer. 7. *Colloq.* (*derog.*) a Greek or Italian immigrant. – **greasily,** *adv.* – **greasiness,** *n.*

**greasyback** /'grizibæk/, *n.* the roof of a mine which may fall in, usu. as a result of water penetrating it.

**greasy spoon** /'– spun/, *n. Colloq.* a cheap restaurant with very plain, often unclean, decor.

**great** /greɪt/, *adj.* 1. unusually or comparatively large in size or dimensions: *a great house, lake, or fire.* 2. large in number; numerous: *a great many, in great detail.* 3. unusual or considerable in degree: *great pain.* 4. notable or remarkable: *a great occasion.* 5. distinguished; famous: *Alexander the Great.* 6. of much consequence; important: *great issues.* 7. chief or principal: *the great seal.* 8. of high rank, official position, or social standing: *a great noble.* 9. of noble or lofty character: *great thoughts.* 10. much in use or favour: *'humour' was a great word with the old physiologists.* 11. being such in an extreme degree: *great friends, a great talker.* 12. of extraordinary powers; having unusual merit; very admirable: *a great statesman.* 13. *Colloq.* skilful or expert (usu. fol. by *at*). 14. *Colloq.* first-rate; very good; fine: *we had a great time.* 15. one degree more remote in direct ascent or descent than a specified relationship: *great-grandfather.* 16. **go great guns,** *Colloq.* to be successful. 17. **great one for,** *Colloq.* enthusiastic about: *he's a great one for reading.* –*n.* 18. *Colloq.* a great person; a person who has accomplished great achievements. 19. →**great organ.** –*adv.* 20. very; extremely. 21. successfully; well: *he's going great in that race.* [ME *greet*, OE *grēat*, c. D *groot*, G *gross*] – **greatness,** *n.*

**great ape** /– 'eɪp/, *n.* 1. one of the larger apes such as the gorilla, chimpanzee, etc. 2. *Colloq.* a fool; clumsy person.

**great auk** /– 'ɔk/, *n.* a large, flightless seabird, *Pinguinus impennis*, formerly abundant on the coasts of the northern Atlantic, but now extinct.

**great-aunt** /'greɪt-ant/, *n.* an aunt of one's father or mother.

**Great Britain** /greɪt 'brɪtn/, *n.* an island in north-western Europe, separated from the mainland by the English Channel and the North Sea, since 1707 the name has applied politically to England, Scotland, and Wales. See **United Kingdom.**

**great circle** /greɪt 'sɜkəl/, *n.* 1. a circle on a sphere the plane of which passes through the centre of the sphere. Cf. **small circle.** 2. the line of shortest distance between two points on the surface of the earth.

great crested grebe

**great circle route,** *n.* the air route which follows the great circle between two points, i.e., the shortest route.

**greatcoat** /'greɪtkoʊt/, *n.* a heavy overcoat.

**great crested grebe,** *n.* a large waterbird, *Podiceps cristanus*, dark brown above and silky white below with a double-horned crest and chestnut frills, which nests on a raft of water plants moored to reeds, and is found mostly in south-eastern Australia; loon.

**Great Dane** /greɪt 'deɪn/, *n.* one of a breed of large, powerful, short-haired dogs, somewhat resembling the mastiff.

**great divide** /greɪt də'vaɪd/, *n.* 1. separation between life and death: **across the great divide.** 2. a crucial stage; crisis.

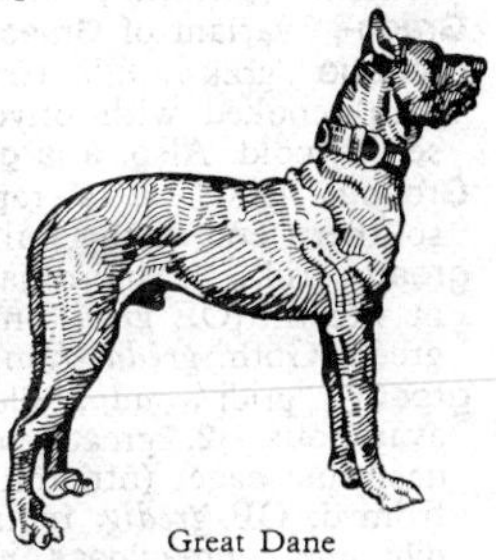

**greater glider** /greɪtə 'glaɪdə/, *n.* the largest of the gliding possums, *Schoinobates volans.*

**greatest** /'greɪtəst/, *adj.* 1. superlative of **great.** 2. **the greatest,** *Colloq.* a. exceptional in one's field of expertise. b. appealing; very nice.

**greatest common factor,** *n.*→**common factor.**

**great-grandchild** /greɪt-'græntʃaɪld/, *n.*, *pl.* **-children.** a grandchild of one's son or daughter.

Great Dane

**great-granddaughter** /greɪt-'grændɔtə/, *n.* a granddaughter of one's son or daughter.

**great-grandfather** /greɪt-'grænfaðə/, *n.* a parent's grandfather.

**great-grandmother** /greɪt-'grænmʌðə/, *n.* a parent's grandmother.

**great-grandparent** /greɪt-'grænpɛərənt/, *n.* a grandfather or grandmother of one's father or mother.

**great-grandson** /greɪt-'grænsʌn/, *n.* a son's or daughter's grandson.

**great grey kangaroo,** *n.* a large, greyish kangaroo with rather woolly fur, *Marcropus giganteus*, which inhabits forest and woodland areas of eastern Australia and Tasmania. The males may reach 1.80 metres in height and measure 2.5 metres from muzzle to tail tip; forester.

**great gross** /greɪt 'groʊs/, *n.* a unit of quantity in the imperial system equal to 12 gross. *Abbrev.*: g.gr.

**great-hearted** /'greɪt-hatəd/, *adj.* 1. having or showing a generous heart; magnanimous. 2. high-spirited; courageous; fearless. – **great-heartedness,** *n.*

**greatly** /'greɪtli/, *adv.* 1. in or to a great degree; much. 2. in a great manner.

**great-nephew** /'greɪt-nɛfju, -nɛvju/, *n.* a son of one's nephew or niece.

**great-niece** /'greɪt-nis/, *n.* a daughter of one's nephew or niece.

**great organ** /'greɪt ɔgən/, *n.* 1. the main section of an organ. 2. the manual controlling this.

**great pox** /– ˈpɒks/, *n.* →**pox** (def. 2).

**Great Russian** /greɪt ˈrʌʃən/, *n.* a member of the main stock of the Russian people, dwelling chiefly in the northern and central parts of the Soviet Union in Europe.

**Great Scott** /– ˈskɒt/, *interj.* (a euphemistic variant of *Great God.*) Also, **Great Scot.**

**great seal** /greɪt ˈsil/, *n.* the principal seal of a government or state.

**great-uncle** /ˈgreɪt-ʌŋkəl/, *n.* an uncle of one's father or mother.

**Great Vowel Shift,** *n.* a sound change which altered the pronunciations of the long vowels of English over the centuries between the Middle English and Modern English periods; it is responsible for the difference between the English and Continental pronunciations of many vowels, the latter having remained in general more constant, e.g., English *fine* /faɪn/, and French *fine* /fin/.

**great white heron,** *n.* a large white egret, *Casmerodius albus,* of south-eastern Europe, tropical Africa, Asia, New Zealand, and America.

**greave** /griv/, *n.* armour for the leg from knee to ankle, usu. of front and back plates. [ME *greves* (pl.), from OF; orig. obscure]

**grebe** /grib/, *n.* any of a number of waterbirds with lobed toes, vestigial tail and weak legs, as the **Australian little grebe,** *Podiceps novaehollandiae,* or the **pied-billed grebe,** *Podilymbus podiceps* of America. [F, orig. uncert.]

**Grecian** /ˈgriʃən/, *adj.* **1.** Greek. *–n.* **2.** a Greek. **3.** an expert in, or student of the Greek language or literature.

**Grecian delight** /– dəˈlaɪt/, *n.* →**Turkish delight.**

**Grecian nose** /– ˈnoʊz/, *n.* a straight nose continuing the line of the forehead without a dip.

**Grecise** /ˈgrisaɪz/, *v.t., v.i.,* **-cised, -cising.** *Chiefly U.S.* →**Graecise.** Also, **Grecize.**

**Grecism** /ˈgrisɪzəm/, *n. Chiefly U.S.* →**Graecism.**

**Greco-,** variant of **Graeco-.**

**grecque** /grɛk/, *adj. Cookery.* **1.** of Greek origin. **2.** (of a dish) cooked with olive oil, lemon juice and spices, usu. served cold. Also, **à la grecque.** [F]

**Greece** /gris/, *n.* a republic in southern Europe at the southern end of the Balkan peninsula.

**greed** /grid/, *n.* inordinate or rapacious desire, esp. for food or wealth. [OE *grǣd* (only in dat. pl.), c. Icel. *grādhr* hunger, greed, Goth. *grēdus* hunger] – **greedless,** *adj.*

**greedy** /ˈgridi/, *adj.,* **-dier, -diest.** **1.** very eager for wealth; avaricious. **2.** greatly desiring food or drink. **3.** keenly desirous; eager (oft. fol. by *of*): *greedy of praise.* [ME *gredy,* from d. OE *grēdig,* replacing OE *grǣdig.* See GREED] – **greedily,** *adv.* – **greediness,** *n.*

**greedy-guts** /ˈgridi-gʌts/, *n. Colloq.* a glutton; one who is prepared to take more than his share of a dish.

**Greek** /grik/, *adj.* **1.** of or pertaining to Greece, the Greeks, or their language. **2.** pertaining to the Greek Church. **3. go Greek,** *Colloq.* to commit buggery. *–n.* **4.** a native or inhabitant of Greece. **5.** the language of the ancient Greeks and any of the languages which have developed from it, such as Hellenistic Greek, Biblical Greek, the Koine, and Modern Greek. **6.** anything unintelligible, as speech, etc.: *it's Greek to me.* **7.** a member of the Greek Orthodox Church. **8.** the group of Indo-European languages to which Greek belongs; Hellenic. [ME *Grekes* (pl.), OE *Grēcas,* learned var. of *Crēcas* (pl.), from L *Graecī,* pl. of *Graecus* a Greek, from Gk *Graikós,* orig. adj.]

**Greek Catholic** /– ˈkæθlɪk/, *n.* **1.** a communicant of any Greek Orthodox Church. **2.** a Greek or Byzantine acknowledging allegiance to the Pope and to the faith of the Western Church but disagreeing in forms of liturgy and ritual; Uniat.

**Greek cross** /– ˈkrɒs/, *n.* a cross consisting of an upright crossed in the middle by a horizontal piece of the same length.

**Greek fire** /– ˈfaɪə/, *n.* an inflammable mixture used by the Byzantine Greeks to set fire to enemy ships, etc.

**Greek Orthodox Church,** *n.* **1.** →**Orthodox Church.** **2.** Also, **Greek Church.** that part of the Orthodox Church which constitutes the established Church in Greece.

**green** /grin/, *adj.* **1.** of the colour of growing foliage, between yellow and blue in the spectrum. **2.** covered with herbage or foliage; verdant: *green fields.* **3.** characterised by the presence of verdure. **4.** consisting of green vegetables: *a green salad.* **5.** full of life and vigour. **6.** unseasoned; not dried or cured: *green timber.* **7.** newborn (of calves and lambs). **8.** not fully developed or perfected in growth or condition; unripe; not properly aged. **9.** immature in age or judgment; untrained; inexperienced: *a green hand.* **10.** simple; gullible; easily fooled. **11.** fresh, recent, or new: *a green wound.* **12.** pale; sickly; wan: *green with fear.* **13.** freshly killed: *green meat.* **14.** uncooked, raw: *green prawns.* **15.** not fired, as bricks or pottery. **16.** *Metall.* **a.** in powder metallurgy, unsintered. **b.** not fully processed or treated. **17.** (of concrete, cement or mortar) freshly poured and not completely set. *–n.* **18.** green colour. **19.** green colouring matter, paint, etc. **20.** grassy land; a plot of grassy ground. **21.** green material or clothing. **22.** *Golf.* **a.** the whole course or links on which golf is played. **b.** a putting green alone. **23.** a bowling green. **24.** (*pl.*) **a.** the leaves and stems of plants, as cabbage, used for food. **b.** fresh leaves or branches of trees, shrubs, etc., used for decoration. *–v.i.* **25.** to become green. **26.** to make green. [ME and OE *grēne,* c. G *grün;* akin to GROW]

**green acid** /– ˈæsəd/, *n.* one of a number of mixtures of sulphonic acids used in the manufacture of detergents.

**green algae** /– ˈældʒi/, *n.* algae belonging to the class Chlorophyceae, grass-green in colour.

**greenback** /ˈgrinbæk/, *n.* **1.** *U.S. Colloq.* a U.S. legal-tender note, usu. printed in green on the back, originally issued against the credit of the country and not against gold or silver on deposit. **2.** *Surfing Colloq.* an unbroken wave.

**green ban** /ˈgrin bæn/, *n.* **1.** a refusal by employees to work or to allow work to proceed on a building site that is situated in a green belt. **2.** a similar refusal with respect to any construction work which would necessitate destroying something of natural, historical or social significance.

**green bean** /– ˈbin/, *n.* the narrow, green, edible seedpod of any of various varieties of bean (plant), as the young pod of the French bean, *Phaseolus vulgaris,* or the runner bean, *P. multiflorus.*

**green belt** /ˈ– bɛlt/, *n.* an area of parkland, rural or uncultivated land, or native bush, near a town or a city on which building is either strictly controlled or not permitted.

**green bird orchid,** *n.* →**bird orchid.**

**greenbone** /ˈgrinboʊn/, *n. N.Z.* →**butterfish** (def. 2).

**green cart** /ˈgrin kat/, *n.* a van which, in popular fancy, takes people to a lunatic asylum.

**green catbird** /– ˈkætbɜd/, *n.* a green bird spotted on the head and underparts, *Ailuroedus crassirostris,* living in rainforests of the central and southern east coast of Australia, and distinguished by its strange wailing cry.

**green corn** /– ˈkɔn/, *n.* →**sweet corn** (def. 2).

**green dragon** /– ˈdrægən/, *n.* an American herb, *Arisaema dracontium,* with a greenish or whitish spathe.

**green duck** /– ˈdʌk/, *n.* a young duckling about ten weeks old and weighing about two kilograms.

**green earth** /– ˈɜθ/, *n.* a green pigment consisting of ferrous hydroxide and silicic acid.

**greenery** /ˈgrinəri/, *n., pl.* **-eries.** **1.** green foliage or vegetation; verdure. **2.** a place where green plants are reared or kept.

**greenery-yallery** /ˌgrinəri-ˈjæləri/, *adj.* pertaining or appropriate to Art Nouveau or the aesthetic movement associated with it. [GREEN + *yaller,* var. of YELLOW: these two colours were particularly associated with the aesthetes of the late nineteenth century]

**green-eyed** /ˈgrin-aɪd/, *adj.* jealous.

**greenfeed** /ˈgrinfid/, *n.* forage grown to be fed fresh to livestock.

**greenfinch** /ˈgrinfɪntʃ/, *n.* a European finch, *Chloris chloris,* with green and yellow plumage, introduced into Australia.

**green fingers** /grin ˈfɪŋgəz/, *n.pl.* skill in gardening and plant-growing.

**green flash** /– ˈflæʃ/, *n.* a phenomenon sometimes observed in a clear atmosphere at sunset when the last part of the sun to remain above the horizon appears as a bright green light.

**greenfly** /ˈgrinflaɪ/, *n.* any of certain greenish insects, esp., a green aphid.

**greengage** /ˈgringeɪdʒ/, *n.* one of several varieties of light green plums. [GREEN + *Gage,* named after Sir William *Gage,* who introduced it into England *c.* 1725]

**green ginger** /grin ˈdʒɪndʒə/, *n.* undried ginger.

**green gland** /– ˈglænd/, *n.* one of the pair of excretory organs in the head region of decapod crustaceans.

**green gram** /– ˈgræm/, *n.* →**mung bean.**

**greengrocer** /ˈgringroʊsə/, *n.* **1.** a retailer of fresh vegetables and fruit. **2.** *Colloq.* a drug pusher specialising in marijuana. **3.** Also, **green Monday.** a large, common cicada, *Cyclochila australasiae,* bright green, usu. with slightly darker green markings on head and thorax.

**greenhead** /ˈgrinhɛd/, *n.* **1.** an aggressive ant, *Ectatomma metallicum,* which gives a painful sting. **2.** a male mallard.

**greenheart** /ˈgrinhat/, *n.* **1.** a South American tree, *Ocotea rodiei,* of the family Lauraceae, whose hard, durable wood is often used for wharves, bridges, and in shipbuilding, and whose bark yields bebeerine; bebeeru. **2.** any of certain other timber trees of tropical America. **3.** their valuable greenish wood.

**greenhide** /ˈgrinhaɪd/, *n.* **1.** untanned skin of animals, usu. cattle. *–adj.* **2.** made of or pertaining to greenhide.

**greenhood** /ˈgrinhʊd/, *n.* any species of the terrestrial orchid genus *Pterostylis,* widespread in Australasia and characterised by a green, occasionally reddish-brown, galea.

**greenhorn** /ˈgrinhɔn/, *n. Colloq.* **1.** a raw, inexperienced person. **2.** a person easily imposed upon or deceived. [orig. applied to an ox with green or young horns]

**greenhouse** /ˈgrinhaʊs/, *n.* a building, chiefly of glass, for the cultivation or protection of plants.

**greenhouse effect** /ˈ– əfɛkt/, *n.* **1.** the increase in temperature in a greenhouse caused by the radiant heat from the sun passing through the glass, while heat within the greenhouse is trapped there by the glass. **2.** the same effect on the temperature of the earth caused by its atmosphere acting as the glass of a greenhouse does, possibly to be increased as man's pollution adds more and more carbon dioxide to the atmosphere.

**greenie** /ˈgrini/, *n. Colloq.* **1.** a conservationist. **2.** *Surfing.* a large green unbroken wave. *–adj.* **3.** sympathetic with moves to conserve the environment, produce whole foods organically, and live more simply: *plastic food is not for greenie households.*

**greening** /ˈgrinɪŋ/, *n.* **1.** any variety of apple the skin of which is green when ripe. **2.** a virus disease which causes floral plant parts to develop a green colour. **3.** the process or stage of becoming green. [GREEN, *adj.* + -ING[1]]

**greenish** /ˈgrinɪʃ/, *adj.* somewhat green; having a tinge of green.

**greenkeeper** /ˈgrinkipə/, *n.* one who maintains greens at a bowls club or on a golf course. – **greenkeep,** *v.*

**Greenland spar** /grinlənd ˈspa/, *n.* **cryolite.**

**green light** /grin ˈlaɪt/, *n.* **1.** a green lamp, used as a signal to mean 'go'. **2.** *Colloq.* permission; authorisation.

**greenling** /ˈgrinlɪŋ/, *n.* any of the spiny-finned fishes constituting the genus *Hexagrammos,* found about rocks and kelp in the northern Pacific Ocean.

**greenly** /ˈgrinli/, *adv. Racing.* erratically: *a young horse running greenly.*

**green manure** /grin məˈnjuə/, *n.* **1.** a green crop, esp. clover and other nitrogen-fixing plants, ploughed into the soil for fertiliser. **2.** manure which has not undergone decay.

**green Monday** /– ˈmʌndeɪ/, *n.* →**greengrocer.** (def. 3).

**green monkey** /– ˈmʌŋki/, *n.* a monkey, *Cercopithecus aethiops sabaeus,* of western Africa, with a greenish grey back and yellow tail.

**greenness** /ˈgrinnəs/, *n.* **1.** the state or quality of being green. **2.** verdure; green vegetation. **3.** lack of experience; immaturity. **4.** naivety; gullibility; innocence.

**green paper** /ˈgrin peɪpə/, *n. Chiefly Brit.* a paper which proposes policy in a given area, issued by government not as a declaration of intent but as a basis for public discussion. Cf. **white paper.**

**green pepper** /– ˈpɛpə/, *n.* **1.** the fruit of the bell or sweet pepper, *Capsicum frutescens* var. *grossum.* **2.** the mild, unripe fruit of any of the garden peppers, *Capsicum frutescens,* used as a green vegetable.

**green plover** /– ˈplʌvə/, *n.* →**lapwing.**

**green prawn** /– ˈprɔn/, *n.* any prawn before it is cooked.

**green revolution** /– rɛvəˈluʃən/, *n.* the great increase in the production of grain in developing countries brought about by the introduction of new techniques and high-yielding crop varieties.

**green ringtail possum,** *n.* a possum, *Pseudocheirus archeri,* of the rainforests of north-eastern Queensland; toolah.

**green room** /ˈ– rum/, *n.* a room set aside for use of artists in a theatre, opera house, television studio, etc., in which they can relax and entertain when they are not performing.

**greens** /grinz/, *n.pl. Colloq.* green vegetables, as lettuce, peas, etc.

**greensand** /ˈgrinsænd/, *n.* **1.** a sandstone containing much glauconite, which gives it a greenish hue. **2.** moulding sand, rich in organic matter, as used in a foundry.

**greenshank** /ˈgrinʃæŋk/, *n.* **1.** a sandpiper with greenish legs, *Tringa nebularia,* which breeds in Eurasia and appears in Australia as a migrant. **2.** a similar, but smaller bird, the **little greenshank,** *T. stagnatilis.*

**green soap** /grin ˈsoʊp/, *n.* a soap made chiefly from potassium hydroxide and linseed oil, used in treating skin diseases.

**greenstick fracture** /ˌgrinstɪk ˈfræktʃə/, *n.* a partial fracture of a bone of a young person or animal, in which only one side of a bone is broken.

**greenstone** /ˈgrinstoʊn/, *n.* **1.** altered basic igneous rocks which owe their colour to the presence of chlorite, hornblende and epidote. **2.** a hard, green nephrite gemstone, found in the western South Island of New Zealand, highly prized by the Maori for working into implements and ornaments.

**greenstuff** /ˈgrinstʌf/, *n.* green vegetables, as cabbage, etc.

**greensward** /ˈgrinswɔd/, *n.* turf green with grass.

**green tea** /grin ˈti/, *n.* a tea subjected to a heating process without previous special withering and fermenting.

**green thumb** /– ˈθʌm/, *n. U.S.* →**green fingers.**

**green turtle** /– ˈtɜtl/, *n.* a sea turtle, *Chelonid mydos,* of tropical waters, having flesh esteemed as food.

**green vegetable** /– ˈvɛdʒtəbəl/, *n.* a vegetable useful for its edible green leaf, seed pod, etc.

**green vitriol** /– ˈvɪtriɒl/, *n.* ferrous sulphate, $FeSO_4 \cdot 7H_2O$, in the form of bluish-green crystals; copperas.

**green water** /– ˈwɔtə/, *n.* water coming aboard a vessel in a solid mass, as opposed to spray.

**green wattle** /ˈ– wɒtl/, *n.* any of a number of species of *Acacia* with finely divided leaves, esp. *A. decurrens.*

**green weed** /– ˈwid/, *n.* a green algae in the form of cylindrical tubes, *Enteromorpha intestinalis,* growing in seawater or in fresh water with fairly high levels of dissolved salt; used as fish bait.

**Greenwich Mean Time,** *n.* mean solar time of the meridian through Greenwich, England, widely used throughout the world as a basis for calculating local time.

**greenwood** /ˈgrinwʊd/, *n.* a wood or forest when green, as in summer.

**greet** /grit/, *v.t.* **1.** to address with some form of salutation; welcome. **2.** to receive with demonstrations of feeling. **3.** to manifest itself to: *music greets the ear.* *–v.i.* **4.** to give salutations on meeting. [ME *grete(n),* OE *grētan,* c. G *grüssen*] – **greeter,** *n.*

**greeting** /ˈgritɪŋ/, *n.* **1.** the act or words of one who greets. **2.** (*usu. pl.*) a friendly message: *send greetings.*

**gregale** /grəˈgali/, *n.* a north-eastern wind in the Mediterranean area. [It., from LL *Grecāl(is)* Greek]

**gregarine** /ˈgrɛgəraɪn, -rin/, *n.* **1.** a type of sporozoan parasite that inhabits the digestive and other cavities of various invertebrates and produces cysts filled with spores. *–adj.* **2.** having the characteristics of or pertaining to a gregarine or gregarines. [NL *Gregarīna,* from L *gregārius* GREGARIOUS]

**gregarious** /grəˈgɛəriəs/, *adj.* **1.** living in flocks or herds, as animals. **2.** *Bot.* growing in open clusters; not matted together. **3.** fond of company; sociable. **4.** pertaining to a flock or crowd. [L *gregārius*] – **gregariously**, *adv.* – **gregariousness**, *n.*

**Gregorian** /grəˈgɔriən/, *adj.* of or pertaining to any of the popes named Gregory.

**Gregorian calendar** /– ˈkæləndə/, *n.* the reformed Julian calendar now in use, according to which the ordinary year consists of 365 days, and a leap year of 366 days occurs in every year whose number is exactly divisible by 4 except centenary years whose numbers are not exactly divisible by 400, as 1700, 1800, and 1900.

**Gregorian chant** /– ˈtʃænt/, *n.* →**plainsong.**

**Gregorian telescope** /– ˈtɛləskoup/, *n.* a telescope similar to the Cassegrainian telescope, but less common.

**Gregorian tones** /– ˈtounz/, *n.pl.* →**tone** (def. 8b).

**greisen** /ˈgraɪzən/, *n.* an altered rock of granitic texture composed chiefly of quartz and topaz; commonly tin-bearing. [G]

**gremial** /ˈgrimiəl/, *n.* a cloth placed on a bishop's lap when he sits in celebrating mass or in conferring orders. [LL *gremiālis* (as n., ML *gremiāle*), from L *gremium* lap, bosom]

**gremlin** /ˈgrɛmlən/, *n.* **1.** a mischievous invisible being, said by airmen in World War II to cause engine trouble and mechanical difficulties. **2.** any source of mischief. [orig. uncert.]

**gremmie** /ˈgrɛmi/, *n. Colloq.* a surfboard rider whose behaviour in the surf is objectionable. Also, **gremmy.**

**gremmy** /ˈgrɛmi/, *n., pl.* **-mies.** →**gremmie.**

**Grenache** /grəˈnæʃ/, *n.* a red grape variety used for making rosé wines and sweet red wine.

**Grenada** /grəˈnadə/, *n.* a country in the Windward Islands, in the West Indies.

**grenade** /grəˈneɪd/, *n.* **1.** a small explosive shell thrown by hand or fired from a rifle. **2.** a glass missile for scattering chemicals in order to put out fires, spread tear gas, etc. [F, from Sp. *granada* pomegranate, from *granado* having grains, from L *grānātus*]

**grenadier** /grɛnəˈdɪə/, *n.* **1.** (in the British Army) a member of the first regiment of household infantry (**Grenadier Guards**). **2.** (formerly) a soldier in an elite unit of men specially chosen for their height and strength. **3.** (formerly) a soldier who threw grenades. **4.** any of several fish of the family Macuoridae, deep-sea fish with sharp, pointed tails. [F, from *grenade* GRENADE]

**grenadilla** /grɛnəˈdɪlə/, *n.* →**granadilla.**

**grenadin** /ˈgrɛnədɪn/, *n.* a small slice of fillet of veal, larded, braised, and served with a vegetable garnish.

**grenadine**[1] /grɛnəˈdin/, *n.* a thin dress fabric of leno weave in silk, nylon, rayon, or wool. [F, ? named after *Granada,* in Spain]

**grenadine**[2] /grɛnəˈdin, ˈgrɛnədin/, *n.* a syrup made from pomegranate juice, used as a sweetening and colouring agent. [F, diminutive of *grenade* pomegranate. See GRENADE]

**grenouilles** /grəˈnui/, *n.pl.* frogs' legs. [F]

**Gresham's law** /ˈgrɛʃəmz lɔ/, *n.* the tendency of the inferior of two forms of currency to circulate more freely than, or to the exclusion of, the superior, because of the hoarding of the latter. [named after Sir Thomas *Gresham,* 1519?-1579, English merchant and financier]

**gressorial** /grɛˈsɔriəl/, *adj.* adapted for walking, as the feet of some birds. [NL *gressōrius* + -AL[1]]

**grevillea** /grəˈvɪliə/, *n.* any shrub or tree of the very large, mainly Australian, genus *Grevillea,* family Proteaceae, many of which are attractive ornamentals and a number, as *G. robusta,* silky oak, useful timber trees.

**grew** /gru/, *v.* past tense of **grow.**

**grey** /greɪ/, *adj.* **1.** of a colour between white and black, having no definite hue; ash-coloured; technically of an achromatic colour. **2.** dark, overcast, dismal, gloomy. **3.** grey-haired. **4.** pertaining to old age. **5.** old or ancient. *–n.* **6.** any achromatic colour; any colour with zero chroma from white to black. **7.** something of this colour. **8.** grey material or clothing: *to dress in grey.* **9.** an unbleached and undyed condition. **10.** a grey horse. **11.** a penny which has two tails. *–v.t.* **12.** to make grey. *–v.i.* **13.** to become grey. Also, *Chiefly U.S.,* **gray.** [ME; OE *grǣg,* c. G *grau*] – **greyly,** *adv.* – **greyness,** *n.*

**grey area** /ˈ– ɛəriə/, *n.* **1.** an issue which is not clear-cut; a subject which is vague and ill-defined. **2.** the area midway between two extremes.

**greybeard** /ˈgreɪbɪəd/, *n.* **1.** a man whose beard is grey; old man; sage. **2.** a kind of earthenware or stoneware jug.

**grey box** /greɪ ˈbɒks/, *n.* an Australian gum tree, *Eucalyptus moluccana,* with fibrous bark and a close-grained yellowish timber.

**grey cast iron,** *n.* a form of cast iron which gives a grey fracture due to the presence of carbon in the form of flake graphite. Also, **grey iron.** See **white cast iron.**

**grey-crowned babbler** /ˌgreɪ-kraund ˈbæblə/, *n.* See **babbler**[1] (def. 2).

**grey duck** /ˈgreɪ dʌk/, *n.* any of several ducks in which certain immature or female plumages are predominantly grey, as the gadwall, *Anas strepera,* and the pintail, *A. acuta.*

**grey eminence** /– ˈɛmənəns/, *n.* one who exercises power through another while keeping in the background. [translation of F ÉMINENCE GRISE]

**grey forester** /– ˈfɒrəstə/, *n.* →**great grey kangaroo.**

**grey ghost** /– ˈgoust/, *n. Colloq.* a parking meter inspector. [from their grey uniforms]

**grey goods** /ˈ– gʊdz/, *n. pl.* undyed woven or knitted fabrics.

**grey gum** /ˈ– gʌm/, *n.* any of several species of *Eucalyptus,* esp. *E. punctata,* of eastern New South Wales, with dull grey bark often with patches of a pinkish or cream colour.

**grey-headed** /ˈgreɪ-hɛdəd/, *adj.* **1.** having grey hair. **2.** of or pertaining to old men. **3.** of long duration; timeworn.

**greyhound** /ˈgreɪhaund/, *n.* **1.** one of a breed of tall, slender dogs, notable for keen sight and for fleetness. **2.** *Colloq.* a swift ship, esp. a fast ocean liner. **3.** *Colloq.* a thinly rolled cigarette. [ME *gre(i)hound,* apparently from Scand.; cf. Icel. *greyhundr,* from *grey* dog, bitch + *hundr* HOUND[1]; replacing OE *grīghund*]

greyhound

**greyhound racing** /ˈ– reɪsɪŋ/, *n.* a sport in which greyhounds racing against each other pursue a mechanically moving dummy hare around a racing track.

**grey iron** /greɪ ˈaɪən/, *n.* →**grey cast iron.**

**greyish** /ˈgreɪɪʃ/, *adj.* having a tinge of grey; similar to grey.

**grey market** /ˈgreɪ makət/, *n.* the non-official section of the money market which includes the buy-back market, the inter-company market and the commercial bill market.

**grey matter** /ˈ– mætə/, *n.* **1.** nervous tissue, esp. of the brain and spinal cord, containing both fibres and nerve cells, and of a dark reddish grey colour. **2.** *Colloq.* brains or intellect.

**grey mould** /– ˈmould/, *n.* **1.** a plant disease, caused by any of several fungi, characterised by a grey, furry growth on the diseased parts. **2.** any of several fungi causing this, as *Botrytis cinerea.*

**grey nurse shark,** *n.* a common shark, *Odontaspis arenarius,* of Australian waters growing to 160 kg with long, thin, ripping teeth, erroneously thought to be dangerous to man, but having a sluggish disposition.

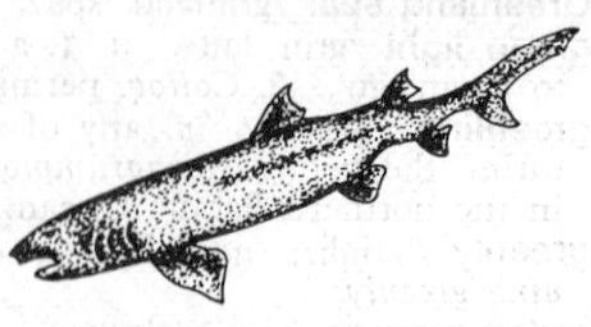

grey nurse shark

**grey parrot** /greɪ ˈpærət/, *n.* an excellent talking bird, *Psittacus erithacus,* of Africa, very commonly kept as a pet.

**grey plover** /– ˈplʌvə/, *n.* a large plover, *Pluvialis squatarola,* of the New and the Old World seen in the Southern Hemisphere as a non-breeding migrant; known as 'black-bellied plover' in North America because of the strikingly black underparts of the breeding plumage.

**grey power** /ˈ– pauə/, *n.* the influence, esp. political, exerted by the elderly.

**grey saltbush** /–ˈsɒltbʊʃ/, *n.* →**coastal saltbush** (def. 2).

**Grey's brush wallaby,** *n.* →**toolache.**

**grey squirrel** /greɪ ˈskwɪrəl/, *n.* a greyish-coloured American squirrel, *Sciurus carolinensis,* of eastern North America; now common in Southern England.

**grey tin** /ˈ– tɪn/, *n.* a crumbly grey cubic form of tin which forms from white tin at temperatures below 13°C.

**greywacke** /ˈgreɪwækə/, *n.* a dark-coloured sandstone or grit, containing fragments of various rocks, such as slate or schist. [half translation, half adoption of G *Grauwache.* See WACKE]

**grey wolf** /ˈgreɪ wʊlf/, *n.* →**timber wolf.**

**gribble** /ˈgrɪbəl/, *n.* a small marine isopod crustacean, *Limnoria,* which destroys submerged timber by boring into it. [? akin to GRUB]

**grid** /grɪd/, *n.* **1.** a grating of crossed bars; gridiron. **2.** *Elect.* a metallic framework employed in a storage cell or battery for conducting the electric current and supporting the active material. **3.** a network of cables, pipes, etc., for the distribution and supply of electricity, gas, water, etc. **4.** *Electronics.* the electrode in a radio valve, usu. made of parallel wires, a helix or coil of wire, or a screen, and controlling the electron flow between the other electrodes. **5.** a network of horizontal and vertical lines designed to give fixed points of reference, as those superimposed on a map, on a printer's layout or on an architect's plan. **6.** *Mining.* a systematic array of points or lines at or along which field observations are made and samples taken during mineral exploration. **7.** *Motor Racing.* starting grid. **8.** *Colloq.* a bicycle. **9.** →**cattlegrid.** [backformation from GRIDIRON]

**grid bias** /ˈ– baɪəs/, *n.* a fixed voltage applied between the cathode and the grid of a radio valve.

**grid circuit** /ˈ– sɜkət/, *n.* that part of a circuit which contains the cathode and the grid of a radio valve.

**grid condenser** /– kənˈdɛnsə/, *n.* a condenser arranged in series with the grid circuit.

**grid convergence** /– kənˈvɜdʒəns/, *n.* the angular difference in direction between grid north and true north, measured east or west from true north.

**grid current** /– ˈkʌrənt/, *n.* the current which moves within a radio valve from the grid to the cathode.

**griddle** /ˈgrɪdl/, *n., v.,* **-dled, -dling.** *–n.* **1.** a flat, heated surface on top of a stove for cooking oatcakes, biscuits, etc. *–v.t.* **2.** to cook on a griddle. Also, **girdle.** [ME *gredil,* from OF: gridiron. See GRILL[1]]

**griddlecake** /ˈgrɪdlkeɪk/, *n.* a quick bread, usu. triangular in shape, made with a scone dough and cooked on both sides on a griddle or frypan. Also, **girdlecake.**

**gride** /graɪd/, *v.,* **grided, griding,** *n.* *–v.i.* **1.** to grate; grind; scrape harshly; make a grating sound. *–v.t.* **2.** to pierce or cut. *–n.* **3.** a griding or grating sound. [metathetic var. of GIRD[2]]

**gridiron** /ˈgrɪdaɪən/, *n.* **1.** a utensil consisting of parallel metal bars on which to grill meat, etc. **2.** any framework or network resembling a gridiron. **3.** →**American football. 4.** *American Football.* the field of play, so called on account of the transverse white lines crossing it every five yards. **5.** a structure above the stage of a theatre, from which hung scenery, etc., is manipulated. *–v.i.* **6.** to buy up land in strips so that the intervening strips fall below a specified area, thus creating difficulties in the scale of land and discouraging other buyers. [ME *gredirne,* etc., replacing ME *gredire,* assimilated var. of *gredile* GRIDDLE; variants in *-irne, -iron* show popular etymological association with ME *iren, irne* iron]

**grid leak** /ˈgrɪd lik/, *n.* a high-resistance device which permits excessive charges on the grid to leak off or escape.

**grid magnetic angle,** *n.* the angular difference in direction between grid north and magnetic north, measured east or west from grid north. Also, **grivation, grid variation.**

**grid north** /grɪd ˈnɔθ/, *n.* the northerly or zero direction indicated by a grid (def. 5).

**grief** /grif/, *n.* **1.** keen mental suffering or distress over affliction or loss; sharp sorrow; painful regret. **2.** a cause or occasion of keen distress or sorrow. **3. come to grief,** to come to a bad end; turn out badly. [ME, from OF, from *grever* GRIEVE] **– griefless,** *adj.*

**grief-stricken** /ˈgrif-strɪkən/, *adj.* stricken or smitten with grief or sorrow; afflicted.

**grievance** /ˈgrivəns/, *n.* **1.** a wrong, real or fancied, considered as grounds for complaint: *a popular grievance.* **2.** resentment or complaint, or the grounds for complaint, against an unjust act: *to have a grievance against someone.*

**grievance day** /ˈ– deɪ/, *n.* (in parliamentary procedure) a day set aside regularly for the discussion of constitutents' problems.

**grievance debate** /ˈ– dəbeɪt/, *n.* (in parliamentary procedure) debate on grievance day.

**grieve** /griv/, *v.,* **grieved, grieving.** *–v.i.* **1.** to feel grief or sorrow. *–v.t.* **2.** to distress mentally; cause to feel grief or sorrow. **3.** *Obs.* to oppress or wrong. [ME *greve(n),* from OF *grever,* from L *gravāre* weigh down] **– griever,** *n.* **– grievingly,** *adv.*

**grievous** /ˈgrivəs/, *adj.* **1.** causing grief or sorrow: *grievous news.* **2.** flagrant; atrocious: *a grievous fault.* **3.** full of or expressing grief; sorrowful: *a grievous cry.* **4.** *Archaic.* burdensome or oppressive. [ME *grevous,* from OF *grever* GRIEVE] **– grievously,** *adv.* **– grievousness,** *n.*

**grievous bodily harm,** *n.* the crime of directly causing some grievous injury to the body of a person with or without a weapon.

**griff[1]** /grɪf/, *n.* an ornament at the base of a column, projecting from the torus towards a corner of the plinth. Also, **griffe.** [F: claw; of Gmc orig.]

**griff[2]** /grɪf/, *n. N.Z. Colloq.* →**griffin[3].**

**griffin[1]** /ˈgrɪfən/, *n.* a mythical monster, usu. having the head and wings of an eagle and the body of a lion. Also, **griffon, gryphon.** [ME *griffon,* from OF *grifon,* from L *grȳphus,* var. of *gryps,* from Gk]

griffin[1]

**griffin[2]** /ˈgrɪfən/, *n.* (in India and the East) a newcomer. [orig. uncert.]

**griffin[3]** /ˈgrɪfən/, *n. N.Z. Colloq.* genuine information; the facts.

**griffon[1]** /ˈgrɪfən/, *n.* a vulture of the genus *Gyps,* esp. *G. fulvus* of southern Europe. [F. See GRIFFIN[1]]

**griffon[2]** /ˈgrɪfən/, *n.* **1.** a small, wiry-haired pet dog of Belgian origin. **2.** one of a breed of coarse-haired hunting dogs combining the qualities of the pointer and the setter. [F; akin to GRIFFIN[1]]

**griffon[3]** /ˈgrɪfən/, *n.* →**griffin[1].**

**Grignard reagent** /ˌgrinja riˈeɪdʒənt/, *n.* any of a group of alkyl magnesium halides which are used in organic synthesis. [named after F. A. V. *Grignard,* 1871-1935, French organic chemist]

**grigri** /ˈgrigri/, *n., pl.* **-gris.** an African charm, amulet, or fetish. Also, **greegree.** [? Wolof (W African language)]

**grike** /graɪk/, *n.* a vertical fissure developed, usu. in a limestone, by solution along a joint. Also, **gryke.**

**grill[1]** /grɪl/, *n.* **1.** a griller. **2.** a meal in which the meat component is grilled. **3.** a grillroom. **4.** *Philately.* a series of small pyramidal impressions in parallel rows impressed or embossed on a stamp. **5. mixed grill,** a dish where a variety of meats (chops, steak, kidneys, bacon, etc.) is grilled and served together. *–v.t.* **6.** to cook under a griller. **7.** to torment with heat. **8.** to mark with a series of parallel bars like those of a grill. **9.** *Colloq.* to subject to severe and persistent cross-examination or questioning. *–v.i.* **10.** to undergo broiling. [F *gril* gridiron, from L *crāticulum,* diminutive of *crātis* wickerwork, hurdle. Cf. GRILLE]

**grill[2]** /grɪl/, *n.* →**grille.**

**grillage** /ˈgrɪlɪdʒ/, *n.* a framework of crossbeams used as a foundation on treacherous ground. [F, from *grille.* See GRILL[1]]

**grille** /grɪl/, *n.* **1.** a lattice or openwork screen, as a window or gate, usu. of metal and often of decorative design. **2.** a grating or screen in a ventilation system. **3.** an ornamental metal screen at the front of a motor car. **4.** *Royal Tennis.* a square-shaped opening in the far corner of the court, on the side of the hazard. [F: grating. See GRILL[1]] **– grilled,** *adj.*

**griller** /ˈgrɪlə/, *n.* **1.** a cooking device, or that part of a stove, in which meat, etc., is cooked by exposure to direct radiant heat. **2.** →**broiler.**

**grillroom** /ˈgrɪlrum/, *n.* a room in a hotel or restaurant where meats, etc., are grilled and served.

**grilse** /grɪls/, *n., pl.* **grilse.** a salmon returning from the sea to the river for the first time. [ME; orig. unknown]

**grim** /grɪm/, *adj.,* **grimmer, grimmest.** **1.** stern; unrelenting; uncompromising: *grim necessity.* **2.** of a sinister or ghastly character; repellent: *a grim joke.* **3.** of a fierce or forbidding aspect: *a grim countenance.* **4.** fierce, savage, or cruel: *grim warrior.* **5.** *Colloq.* disagreeable; unpleasant. [ME and OE, c. OS, OHG *grim,* Icel. *grimmr*] – **grimly,** *adv.* – **grimness,** *n.*

**grimace** /ˈgrɪməs, grəˈmeɪs/, *n., v.,* **-maced, -macing.** *–n.* **1.** a wry face; facial contortion; ugly facial expression. *–v.i.* **2.** to make grimaces. [F, from Sp. *grimazo* panic, fear, from *grima* fright, from Goth.] – **grimacer,** *n.*

**grimalkin** /grɪˈmælkən/, *n.* **1.** a cat. **2.** an old cat. **3.** an ill-tempered old woman. [apparently from GREY + *malkin,* diminutive of *Maud,* proper name]

**grime** /graɪm/, *n., v.,* **grimed, griming.** *–n.* **1.** dirt or foul matter, esp. on or ingrained in a surface. *–v.t.* **2.** to cover with dirt; soil; make very dirty. [apparently special use of OE *grīma* mask, to denote layer of dust, etc., that forms on the face and elsewhere. Cf. Flem. *grym*]

**Grimm's law** /ˈgrɪmz lɔ/, *n.* (in linguistics) the statement of a system of consonant changes from primitive Indo-European into the Germanic languages, esp. as differently reflected in Low and High German, formulated by Jakob Grimm during 1820-22 and independently recognised by Rasmus Rask (1818).

**grimy** /ˈgraɪmi/, *adj.,* **grimier, grimiest.** covered with grime; dirty. – **grimily,** *adv.* – **griminess,** *n.*

**grin** /grɪn/, *v.,* **grinned, grinning,** *n.* *–v.i.* **1.** to smile broadly, or with a wide distension of the mouth. **2.** to draw back the lips so as to show the teeth, as a snarling dog or a person in pain. **3. grin and bear it,** *Colloq.* to endure without complaint. **4. grin through,** (of paint) to show through a top coat because of poor opacity of the top layer. *–v.t.* **5.** to express or produce by grinning. *–n.* **6.** the act of grinning; a broad smile. **7.** the act of withdrawing the lips and showing the teeth. [ME *grinn(en),* OE *grennian*] – **grinner,** *n.* – **grinningly,** *adv.*

**grind** /graɪnd/, *v.,* **ground** or (*Rare*) **grinded, grinding,** *n.* *–v.t.* **1.** to wear, smooth, or sharpen by friction; whet: *to grind a lens, an axe, etc.* **2.** to reduce to fine particles as by pounding or crushing; bray, triturate, or pulverise. **3.** to oppress or torment. **4.** to rub harshly or gratingly; grate together; grit: *to grind one's teeth.* **5.** to operate by turning a crank: *to grind a barrel organ.* **6.** to produce by pulverising, turning a crank, etc.: *to grind flour.* *–v.i.* **7.** to perform the operation of reducing to fine particles. **8.** to rub harshly; grate. **9.** to be or become ground. **10.** to be polished or sharpened by friction. **11.** *Colloq.* to work or study laboriously. **12.** *Colloq.* to rotate the pelvis during or as during sexual intercourse or erotic dancing: *the old bump and grind.* *–n.* **13.** the act of grinding. **14.** a grinding sound. **15.** *Colloq.* laborious or monotonous work; close or laborious study. **16.** *Colloq.* a diligent or laborious student. **17.** *N.Z.* a hard, tiring hike. **18.** *Colloq.* act of sexual intercourse. **19. daily grind,** the daily routine of work. [ME *grind(en),* OE *grindan.* Cf. L *frendere* gnash the teeth, grind to pieces] – **grindingly,** *adv.*

**grindelia** /grɪnˈdiliə/, *n.* **1.** any of the coarse, yellow-flowered herbs constituting the genus *Grindelia.* **2.** the dried leaves and tops of certain species of this plant, used in medicine. [NL; named after D. H. *Grindel,* 1777-1836, Russian scientist]

**grinder** /ˈgraɪndə/, *n.* **1.** one who or that which grinds. **2.** a sharpener of tools. **3.** a molar tooth.

**grindery** /ˈgraɪndəri/, *n.* **1.** materials and tools used by shoemakers. **2.** a place where tools, knives, etc., are ground. **3.** a shop which sells all tools and accessories for the leather and footwear trades.

**grinding wheel** /ˈgraɪndɪŋ wil/, *n.* an abrasive wheel used for cutting and finishing metal.

**grindstone** /ˈgraɪndstoʊn/, *n.* **1.** a rotating solid stone wheel used for sharpening, shaping, etc. **2.** →**millstone.**

**gringo** /ˈgrɪŋgoʊ/, *n., pl.* **-gos.** (among Spanish Americans) a foreigner, esp. an Anglo-Saxon. [Mex. Sp. use of Sp. *gringo* gibberish]

**grip** /grɪp/, *n., v.,* **gripped** or **gript, gripping.** *–n.* **1.** the act of grasping; a seizing and holding fast; firm grasp: *the grip of a vice.* **2.** the power of gripping. **3.** a grasp, hold or control. **4.** a travelling bag; holdall. **5.** mental or intellectual hold; competence. **6.** occupation; regular employment. **7.** a special mode of clasping hands. **8.** something which seizes and holds, as a clutching device on a cable car. **9.** a handle or hilt. **10.** a sudden, sharp pain; spasm of pain. **11.** →**grippe.** **12.** *Films, T.V.* a person employed to carry equipment, shift scenery, props, etc. **13. come (get) to grips with,** to deal with, tackle (an enemy, a problem, etc.) *–v.t.* **14.** to grasp or seize firmly; hold fast. **15.** to take hold on; hold the interest of: *to grip the mind.* **16.** to attach by a grip or clutch. *–v.i.* **17.** to take firm hold; hold fast. **18.** to take hold on the mind. [ME and OE *gripe* grasp, c. G *Griff,* OE *gripa* handful, sheaf. See GRIPE, *v.*] – **gripper,** *n.* – **grippingly,** *adv.*

**gripe** /graɪp/, *v.,* **griped, griping,** *n.* *–v.t.* **1.** to seize and hold firmly; grip; grasp; clutch. **2.** to distress or oppress. **3.** to produce pain in (the bowels) as if by constriction. **4.** *Naut.* to secure (a ship's boat) on the deck or on the davits in order to prevent movement at sea. *–v.i.* **5.** to grasp or clutch, as a miser at gain. **6.** to suffer pain in the bowels. **7.** *Colloq.* to complain constantly; grumble. **8.** *Naut.* to tend to come up into the wind. *–n.* **9.** the act of griping, grasping, or clutching. **10.** a firm hold; clutch. **11.** a grasp; hold; control. **12.** an objection; complaint. **13.** that which grips or clutches; a claw or grip. **14.** *Naut.* (*usu. pl.*) lashing or fittings by which a boat is secured on the deck or on the davits of a ship. **15.** a handle, hilt, etc. **16.** (*usu. pl.*) an intermittent spasmodic pain in the bowels. [ME *gripe(n),* OE *grīpan,* c. D *grijpen,* G *greifen* gripe, seize. Cf. GRIP, GROPE] – **griper,** *n.* – **griping,** *adj.*

**gripman** /ˈgrɪpmæn/, *n.* the person who operates the grip (def. 8) on a cable tram.

**grippe** /grɪp/, *n.* →**influenza.** [F, from *gripper* seize, b. with Russ. *khrip* hoarseness] – **grippelike,** *adj.*

**grisaille** /grəˈzeɪl/, *n.* **1.** monochromatic painting in shades of grey, usu. representing objects in relief. **2.** a painting, a stained-glass window, etc., in this style. [F, from *gris* grey. See GRIZZLE[1]]

**Griselda** /grəˈzeldə/, *n.* a woman of exemplary meekness and patience. [a character in Boccaccio, Chaucer, and elsewhere]

**griseous** /ˈgrɪsiəs, ˈgrɪz-/, *adj.* bluish or pearl grey. [ML *griseus*]

**grisly** /ˈgrɪzli/, *adj.,* **-lier, -liest.** **1.** such as to cause a shuddering horror; gruesome: *a grisly monster.* **2.** formidable; grim: *a grisly countenance.* [ME; late OE *grislic* horrible. Cf. OE *āgrīsan* shudder] – **grisliness,** *n.*

**grison** /ˈgraɪsən, ˈgrɪzən/, *n.* a musteline carnivore, *Grison vittata,* of South and Central America, having the upper surface of the body greyish-white and the lower dark brown. [F, from *gris* grey]

**grissini** /grəˈsini/, *n.pl., sing.* **grissino.** long slender crusty bread sticks. [It. *grissino,* from d. *ghersa* strip]

**grist** /grɪst/, *n.* **1.** corn to be ground. **2.** ground corn; meal produced from grinding. **3.** a quantity of malt for one brewing; the amount of meal from one grinding. **4. it's all grist to the mill,** everything available can be used. [ME; OE *grīst,* from *grindan* GRIND]

**gristle** /ˈgrɪsəl/, *n.* →**cartilage.** [ME and OE; c. OFris. and MLG *gristel.* Cf. OE *grost* cartilage]

**gristly** /ˈgrɪsli/, *adj.* of the nature of, containing, or pertaining to gristle; cartilaginous.

**gristmill** /ˈgrɪstmɪl/, *n.* a mill for grinding grain.

**grit** /grɪt/, *n., v.,* **gritted, gritting.** *–n.* **1.** fine, stony, or hard particles such as are deposited like dust from the air or occur as impurities in food, etc. **2.** *Geol.* a sandstone composed of coarse angular grains and very small pebbles. **3.** firmness of character; indomitable spirit; pluck. *–v.t.* **4.** to grate or grind: *to grit the teeth.* *–v.i.* **5.** to give forth a grating sound, as of sand under the feet; grate. [ME *gre(e)t,* OE *grēot,* c. G *Griess.* Cf. GRITS] – **gritless,** *adj.*

**grits** /grɪts/, *n.pl.* **1.** a grain, esp. oats, hulled and often coarsely ground. **2.** *U.S.* coarsely ground hominy. [ME *gryttes,* OE *gryttan* (pl.), c. G *Grütze*]

**gritty** /ˈgrɪti/, *adj.,* **-tier, -tiest.** **1.** consisting of, containing, or resembling grit; sandy. **2.** resolute and courageous; plucky. – **grittily,** *adv.* – **grittiness,** *n.*

**grivation** /grəˈveɪʃən/, *n.* →**grid magnetic angle.**

**grivet** /ˈgrɪvət/, *n.* a small Abyssinian monkey, *Cercopithecus aethiops,* with a greyish back, grey tail, black face, and dark extremities. [orig. unknown]

**grizzle**[1] /ˈgrɪzəl/, *v.,* **-zled, -zling,** *adj., n.* –*v.i.* **1.** to become grey. –*v.t.* **2.** to make grey. –*adj.* **3.** grey; devoid of hue. –*n.* **4.** grey hair. **5.** a grey wig. [ME *grisel,* from OF, from *gris* grey; of Gmc orig. (cf. G *greis* grey, hoary)]

**grizzle**[2] /ˈgrɪzəl/, *v.i.,* **-zled, -zling.** to whimper; whine; complain fretfully.

**grizzled** /ˈgrɪzəld/, *adj.* **1.** grey-haired, or partly grey-haired. **2.** grey.

**grizzleguts** /ˈgrɪzəlgʌts/, *n. Colloq.* a person given to complaining.

**grizzly** /ˈgrɪzli/, *adj.,* **-zlier, -zliest,** *n., pl.* **-zlies.** –*adj.* **1.** somewhat grey; greyish. **2.** grey-haired. –*n.* **3.** →**grizzly bear.**

**grizzly bear** /ˈ– bɛə/, *n.* a large, ferocious bear, *Ursus horribilis,* of western North America, varying in colour from greyish to brownish.

grizzly bear

**groan** /groʊn/, *n.* **1.** a low, mournful sound uttered in pain or grief. **2.** a deep murmur uttered in derision, disapproval, etc. **3.** a deep grating or creaking noise, as of wood, etc. –*v.i.* **4.** to utter a deep inarticulate sound expressive of grief or pain; moan. **5.** to make a sound similar to a groan; creak; resound harshly. **6.** to be overburdened or overloaded. **7.** to suffer lamentably (fol. by *beneath, under, with*) –*v.t.* **8.** to utter or salute with groans. [ME *grone(n),* OE *grānian,* akin to G *greinen* whine] – **groaner,** *n.* – **groaning,** *n., adj.* – **groaningly,** *adv.*

**groat** /groʊt/, *n.* an English silver coin, issued 1351-1662, worth fourpence. [ME *groot,* from MD: lit., thick (coin)]

**groats** /groʊts/, *n.pl.* **1.** hulled and crushed (or whole) grain, as oats. **2.** the parts of oat kernels used as food. [ME *grotes,* OE *grotan* coarse meal. Cf. OE *grot* particle]

**grocer** /ˈgroʊsə/, *n.* a dealer in general supplies for the table, as flour, sugar, coffee, etc., and in other articles of household use. [ME *grosser,* from OF *grossier,* from LL *grossus* gross]

**grocery** /ˈgroʊsəri/, *n., pl.* **-ceries. 1.** a grocer's store. **2.** (*usu. pl.*) a commodity sold by grocers. **3.** the business of a grocer.

**grocessor** /ˈgroʊsɛsə/, *n. Colloq.* a turkey or other poultry producer who both grows the birds and processes them for market.

**grog** /grɒg/, *n.* **1.** *Colloq.* alcohol, particularly cheap alcohol. **2.** (formerly) an alcoholic mixture, esp. of rum and water. –*v.i.* **3. grog on,** *Colloq.* to indulge in a long session of drinking. [from *grogram* the material of the cloak of Admiral Vernon ('Old Grog'), who in 1740 ordered water to be issued with sailors' pure spirits]

**grog artist** /ˈ– atəst/, *n. Colloq.* a heavy drinker.

**grog blossom** /ˈ– blɒsəm/, *n.* a pattern of mulberry-coloured markings, as a result of telangiectasis, which often develops in the cheek of habitual, excessive drinkers.

**groggery** /ˈgrɒgəri/, *n., pl.* **-geries.** *Colloq.* →**saloon.**

**groggy** /ˈgrɒgi/, *adj.,* **-gier, -giest.** *Colloq.* **1.** staggering, as from exhaustion or blows. **2.** drunk; intoxicated. – **groggily,** *adv.* – **grogginess,** *n.*

**grog-on** /ˈgrɒg-ɒn/, *n. Colloq.* a drinking party.

**grogram** /ˈgrɒgrəm/, *n.* a coarse fabric of silk, of silk and mohair or wool, or of wool, formerly in use. [F *gros grain.* See GROSGRAIN]

**grog shop** /ˈgrɒg ʃɒp/, *n.* **1.** *Colloq.* a shop selling alcohol. **2.** (formerly) a cheap tavern.

G, G, groins (def. 2)

**groin** /grɔɪn/, *n.* **1.** *Anat.* the fold or hollow on either side of the body where the thigh joins the abdomen. **2.** *Archit.* the curved line or edge formed by the intersection of two vaults. **3.** **groyne.** –*v.t.* **4.** *Archit.* to form with groins. [earlier *gryne,* ME *grynde.* Cf. OE *grynde* abyss, akin to *grund* bottom, GROUND[1]]

**grommet** /ˈgrɒmət/, *n.* **1.** →**grummet. 2.** *Surfing Colloq.* a young surfer, usu. in his or her early teens.

**gromwell** /ˈgrɒmwəl/, *n.* any boraginaceous plant of the genus *Lithospermum,* comprising hairy herbs with varicoloured flowers and smooth, stony nutlets, as *Lithospermum arvense,* **corn gromwell.** [ME *gromyl,* from OF *gromil,* from L *grūnum milium* crane millet]

**groom** /grum/, *n.* **1.** a man or boy in charge of horses or the stable. **2.** a man newly married, or about to be married; bridegroom. **3.** any of several officers of a royal household. **4.** *Archaic.* a manservant. –*v.t.* **5.** to tend carefully as to person and dress; make neat or tidy. **6.** to tend (horses). **7.** to prepare for a position, election, etc.: *groom a political candidate.* **8.** to prepare (a ski slope, golf-course, etc.). [ME *grom(e)* boy, groom; cf. D *grom* offspring; apparently akin to GROW]

**groomsman** /ˈgrumzmən/, *n., pl.* **-men.** a man who attends the bridegroom at a wedding.

**groove** /gruv/, *n., v.,* **grooved, grooving.** –*n.* **1.** a furrow or channel cut by a tool. **2.** a rut, furrow, or channel formed by any agency. **3.** a fixed routine: *to get into a groove.* **4.** the track of a gramophone record in which the needle or stylus rides. **5. in the groove,** *Colloq.* in an excited or satisfied emotional state, as through listening to jazz. –*v.t.* **6.** to cut a groove in; furrow. **7.** to fix in a groove. –*v.i.* **8.** *Colloq.* **a.** to be in a state of euphoria. **b.** to be delighted or pleased with (fol. by *on*). [ME *grofe, groof* mining shaft, OE *grōf* ditch, sewer, c. G *Grube* ditch, pit; akin to GRAVE[1], GRAVE[3]]

**groovy** /ˈgruvi/, *adj. Colloq.* **1.** exciting, satisfying, or pleasurable. **2.** appreciative: *a groovy audience.*

**grope** /groʊp/, *v.,* **groped, groping,** *n.* –*v.i.* **1.** to feel about with the hands; feel one's way. **2.** to search blindly or uncertainly. –*v.t.* **3.** to seek by or as by feeling. **4.** *Colloq.* to fondle, embrace clumsily and with sexual intent. –*n.* **5.** a clumsy movement; the action of groping. **6. go the grope,** *Colloq.* grope (def. 4). [ME *grop(i)en,* OE *grāpian,* from *grāp,* n., grasp; akin to GRIPE, *v.*] – **groper,** *n.* – **gropingly,** *adv.*

**groper**[1] /ˈgroʊpə/, *n. Colloq.* →**sandgroper.**

**groper**[2] /ˈgroʊpə/, *n., pl.* **-pers,** (*esp. collectively*) **-per.** any of several species of large Australian or New Zealand marine fish, typically with enormous gape, as the **Queensland groper,** *Promicrops lanceolatus,* the **Bass groper,** *Polyprion moeone,* the New Zealand groper, *Polyprion oxygeneios.*

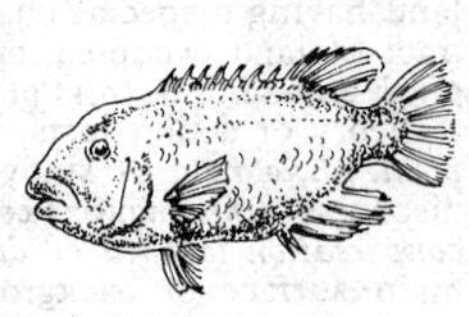
groper[2]

**grosbeak** /ˈgroʊsbik/, *n.* any of various finches having a large, stout conical bill, as the pine grosbeak, *Pinicola enucleator.* [F *grosbec* large beak]

**grosgrain** /ˈgroʊgreɪn/, *n.* heavy, corded, silk or rayon ribbon or fabric. [F *gros grain* large grain. Cf. GROGRAM]

**gros point** /ˈgroʊ pɔɪnt/, *n., pl.* **gros points.** a stitch in embroidery worked over a double-thread canvas; tent stitch. [F: large point]

**gross** /groʊs/, *adj., n., pl.* **grosses** *for def. 7,* **gross** *for def. 8; v.* –*adj.* **1.** whole, entire, or total, esp. without having been subjected to deduction, as for charges, loss, etc.: *gross profits.* **2.** glaring or flagrant: *gross injustice.* **3.** morally coarse; lacking refinement; indelicate or indecent: *gross tastes.* **4.** large, big, or bulky. **5.** thick; dense; heavy: *gross vegetation.* **6.** *Colloq.* repulsive; objectionable. –*n.* **7.** the main body, bulk or mass. **8.** a unit consisting of twelve dozen, or 144. **9. right in gross,** *Law.* a right belonging to someone personally and not in his capacity as the owner or occupier of land. –*v.t.* **10.** to make a gross profit of; earn a total of. [ME, from OF *gros* large (as n., *grosse* twelve dozen), from LL *grossus* thick] – **grossly,** *adv.* – **grossness,** *n.*

**gross national product,** *n.* the total annual value of all legal goods and services produced in a country. Also, **G.N.P.**

**gross ton** /groʊs 'tʌn/, *n.* →**ton**[1] (def. 4).

**gross tonnage** /– 'tʌnɪdʒ/, *n.* a measure of the enclosed internal volume of a ship and its superstructure, with certain spaces exempted.

**grossularite** /'grɒsjələraɪt/, *n.* a mineral, calcium aluminium garnet, $Ca_3Al_2Si_3O_{12}$, occurring often as crystals. [NL *grossulāria* gooseberry + -ITE[1]]

**gross weight** /groʊs 'weɪt/, *n.* total weight without any deduction (opposed to *net weight*).

**grot**[1] /grɒt/, *n. Poetic.* a grotto. [F *grotte,* from It. *grotta.* See GROTTO]

**grot**[2] /grɒt/, *n. Colloq.* filth. [backformation from GROTTY]

**grotesque** /groʊ'tɛsk/, *adj.* **1.** fantastic in the shaping and combination of forms, as in decorative work combining incongruous human and animal figures with scrolls, foliage, etc. **2.** odd or unnatural in shape, appearance, or character; fantastically ugly or absurd; bizarre. *–n.* **3.** any grotesque object or thing. [F, from It. *grottesco* (as n., *grottesca* grotesque decoration, such apparently as was found in ancient excavated dwellings), from *grotta.* See GROTTO] **–grotesquely,** *adv.* **–grotesqueness,** *n.*

16th century grotesque work

**grotesquerie** /groʊ'tɛskəri/, *n., pl.* **-queries. 1.** grotesque character. **2.** something grotesque. **3.** grotesque work. Also, **grotesquery.**

**grotto** /'grɒtoʊ/, *n., pl.* **-toes, -tos. 1.** a cave or cavern. **2.** an artificial cavern-like recess or structure. [It. *grotta,* from VL *crupta,* in L *crypta* subterranean passage or chamber, crypt, from Gk *krýptē* vault]

**grotty** /'grɒti/, *adj. Colloq.* **1.** dirty; filthy. **2.** useless; rubbishy. [alteration of GROTESQUE]

**grouch** /graʊtʃ/, *Colloq. –v.i.* **1.** to be sulky or morose; show discontent; complain. *–n.* **2.** a sulky or morose person. **3.** a sulky or morose mood. [var. of obs. *grutch,* from OF *groucher* grumble]

**grouchy** /'graʊtʃi/, *adj.,* **-chier, -chiest.** *Colloq.* sullenly discontented; sulky; morose; ill-tempered. **–grouchily,** *adv.* **–grouchiness,** *n.*

**ground**[1] /graʊnd/, *n.* **1.** the earth's solid surface; firm or dry land: *fall to the ground.* **2.** earth or soil: *stony ground.* **3.** land having a special character: *rising ground.* **4.** (*oft. pl.*) a tract of land occupied, or appropriated to a special use: *hospital grounds.* **5.** (*oft. pl.*) the foundation or basis on which a theory or action rests; motive; reason: *grounds for a statement.* **6.** a field of study; topic for discussion; subject of a discourse: *the inquiry covered a great deal of ground; the conversation touched on delicate ground.* **7.** the underlying or main surface or background, in painting, decorative work, lace, etc. **8.** (*pl.*) dregs or sediment: *coffee grounds.* **9.** →**earth** (def. 10). **10.** *Music.* →**ground bass. 11.** *Comm.* →**groundage. 12.** Some special noun phrases are:
**break new ground,** to begin a fresh operation.
**common ground,** matters on which agreement exists.
**cut the ground from under one's feet, cut the ground from under someone,** to anticipate the arguments, plans, etc., of another to his disconcertion.
**down to the ground,** *Colloq.* completely, entirely.
**gain ground,** to advance; make progress.
**give ground,** to give way.
**go to ground,** to withdraw from public attention and live quietly.
**have one's feet on the ground,** to be sensible and level-headed.
**hold** or **stand one's ground,** to maintain one's position.
**lose ground, 1.** to lose what one has gained; retreat; give way. **2.** to become less well known or accepted.
**run to ground, 1.** to hunt down; track down. **2.** to pursue (an animal) to its burrow or hole.
**shift one's ground,** to take another position or defence in an argument or situation.
*–adj.* **13.** situated on or at, or adjacent to, the surface of the earth: *the ground floor.* **14.** pertaining to the ground. **15.** *Mil.* operating on land; ground forces. *–v.t.* **16.** to lay or set on the ground. **17.** to place on a foundation; found; fix firmly; settle or establish. **18.** to instruct in elements or first principles. **19.** to furnish with a ground or background on decorative work, etc. **20.** *Elect.* to establish an earth for (a circuit, device, etc.). **21.** *Naut.* to run aground. **22.** to prevent (an aircraft or a pilot) from flying. **23.** to restrict, or withdraw privileges from. *–v.i.* **24.** to come to or strike the ground. [ME and OE *grund,* c. D *grond,* G *Grund* bottom, ground]

**ground**[2] /graʊnd/, *v.* **1.** past tense and past participle of **grind.** *–adj.* **2.** reduced to fine particles or dust by grinding. **3.** having the surface abraded or roughened by or as by grinding: *ground glass.* **4.** minced, as of meat. [see GRIND]

**groundage** /'graʊndɪdʒ/, *n.* a tax levied on vessels stopping at a port.

**ground bait** /'graʊnd beɪt/, *n.* bait dropped to the bottom of the water.

**ground bass** /– 'beɪs/, *n.* a short repeated bass line over which varying melodies or rhythmic patterns are used.

**ground beef** /– 'bif/, *n. U.S.* minced beef.

**ground beetle** /'– bitl/, *n.* any of the numerous beetles of the family Carabidae, most of which are terrestrial.

**groundbreaking** /'graʊndbreɪkɪŋ/, *adj. Colloq.* innovative.

**ground cherry** /'graʊnd tʃɛri/, *n.* any of several species of the American genus *Physalis* grown for their edible yellow berries.

**ground colour** /'– kʌlə/, *n.* **1.** a primary coat of paint. **2.** the background or main colour of a painting, etc.

**ground control** /'– kəntroʊl/, *n.* a system of controlling by means of radiotelephone and light installations the movements of aircraft taxiing and manoeuvring on the ground. See **air traffic control.**

**ground cover** /'– kʌvə/, *n.* **1.** a low spreading plant which covers the earth and retards the growth of weeds. **2.** *Mil.* air support for ground troops.

**ground crew** /'– kru/, *n.* →**ground staff.**

**ground elder** /– 'ɛldə/, *n.* a creeping plant, *Aegopodium podagraria* of the family Umbelliferae, often a troublesome garden weed.

**grounder** /'graʊndə/, *n. Cricket, Baseball, etc.* a ball knocked or thrown along the ground and not rising into the air.

**ground floor** /graʊnd 'flɔ/, *n.* **1.** the floor at or near ground level. Cf. **first floor. 2.** *Colloq.* the most advantageous position or relationship in a business matter or deal.

**ground glass** /– 'glas/, *n.* **1.** glass whose polished surface has been removed by grinding, to diffuse light. **2.** glass ground into fine particles for use as an abrasive, etc.

**ground goanna** /– goʊ'ænə/, *n.* →**Gould's goanna.**

**ground hog** /'– hɒg/, *n.* →**woodchuck.**

**ground ice** /'– aɪs/, *n.* ice which forms below the surface of a body of water, as a lake, etc., and attaches itself to the bottom or to submerged objects; anchor-ice.

**grounding** /'graʊndɪŋ/, *n.* fundamental knowledge of a subject: *a good grounding in mathematics.*

**ground ivy** /graʊnd 'aɪvi/, *n.* a trailing herb, *Glechoma hederacea,* bearing blue flowers.

**groundlark** /'graʊndlak/, *n.* →**Australian pipit.**

**groundless** /'graʊndləs/, *adj.* without basis or reason: *groundless fears.* **–groundlessly,** *adv.* **–groundlessness,** *n.*

**groundling** /'graʊndlɪŋ/, *n.* **1.** a plant or animal that lives on or close to the ground. **2.** any of various fishes that live at the bottom of the water. **3.** a spectator, reader, or other person of inferior tastes; an uncritical or uncultured person. **4.** *Obs.* a spectator in the pit of a theatre which formerly was literally on the ground.

**ground loop** /'graʊnd lup/, *n.* a sharp uncontrollable turn made by a plane when landing, taking off or taxiing.

**groundmass** /'graʊndmæs/, *n.* the crystalline, granular, or glassy base or matrix of a porphyry, in which the larger crystals are enclosed.

**groundnut** /'graʊndnʌt/, *n.* →**peanut.**

**ground owl** /'graʊnd aʊl/, *n.* →**burrowing owl.**

**ground plan** /'– plæn/, *n.* **1.** the plan of a ground floor of a building. **2.** first or fundamental plan.

**ground plate** /'– pleɪt/, *n.* **1.** *Elect.* a metal plate used for making a ground connection to earth. **2.** →**groundsel**[2].

**ground plum** /– 'plʌm/, *n.* **1.** a leguminous plant, *Astragalus crassicarpus,* of the American prairie regions. **2.** its plum-shaped fruit.

**ground rent** /'– rɛnt/, *n.* the rent at which land is leased to a tenant for a specified term, usu. ninety-nine years.

**ground rule** /'– rul/, *n.* a basic rule of a game, meeting, procedure, etc.

**groundsel**[1] /'graʊnsəl/, *n.* any plant of the composite genus *Senecio,* as *S. vulgaris,* a weed bearing small yellow flowers. [ME *grundeswilie,* etc., OE *g(r)undeswelge,* etc., apparently from *gund* pus + *swelgan* swallow (from its use in medicine); or from *grund* ground + *swelgan* (from its speed in spreading)]

**groundsel**[2] /'graʊnsəl/, *n. Obs.* the lowest horizontal timber of a frame or building lying next to the ground. Also, **groundsill, groundsell.**

**groundsel bush** /'– bʊʃ/, *n.* a tall deciduous composite shrub, *Baccharis halimifolia,* native to North America but naturalised elsewhere.

**groundsheet** /'graʊndʃit/, *n.* a waterproof sheet spread on the ground to give protection against dampness.

**ground-shock effect** /'graʊnd-ʃɒk əˌfɛkt/, *n.* the destruction or damage of buildings, etc., as a result of shock waves transmitted through the ground (opposed to **blast effect**).

**groundsman** /'graʊndzmən/, *n., pl.* **-men.** a man responsible for the care and maintenance of a cricket ground, sports field, etc.

**ground speed** /'graʊnd spid/, *n.* the speed of an aircraft in reference to the ground. Cf. **airspeed.**

**ground squirrel** /'– skwɪrəl/, *n.* any of various terrestrial rodents of the squirrel family, as of the genus *Tamias* (chipmunks) and of the genus *Citellus* (or *Spermophilus*).

**ground staff** /'– staf/, *n.* mechanics on an airfield responsible for the maintenance of aircraft; non-flying personnel on an airfield.

**ground state** /'– steɪt/, *n.* the most stable energy state of a particle, nucleus, atom, or molecule.

**ground stroke** /'– stroʊk/, *n.* a tennis stroke played close to the ground immediately after the ball has bounced. Also, **ground shot.**

**ground swell** /'– swɛl/, *n.* **1.** a broad, deep swell or rolling of the sea, due to a distant storm or gale. **2.** (*fig.*) a strong movement of public opinion.

**ground water** /'– wɔtə/, *n.* the water beneath the surface of the ground, consisting largely of surface water that has seeped down.

**ground wave** /'– weɪv/, *n.* that portion of a transmitted radio wave that travels near the surface of the earth.

**groundwork** /'graʊndwɜk/, *n.* the foundation, base, or basis of anything.

**ground zero** /'graʊnd zɪəroʊ/, *n.* the point on the surface of the earth directly below the point at which a nuclear weapon explodes, or the centre of the crater if the weapon is exploded on the ground. Also, **surface zero.**

**group** /grup/, *n.* **1.** any assemblage of persons or things; cluster; aggregation. **2.** a number of persons or things ranged or considered together as being related in some way. **3.** *Ethnol.* a classification more limited than a branch. **4.** a number of businesses, companies, etc., administratively and financially connected. **5.** *Chem.* **a.** number of atoms in a molecule connected or arranged together in some manner; a radical: *the hydroxyl group,* =*OH.* **b.** a vertical column of the periodic table containing elements with similar properties. **6.** *Linguistics.* **a.** a subdivision of a family, usu. the greatest. **b.** any grouping of languages, whether geographically, on the basis of relationship, or otherwise. **7.** *Geol.* a division of stratified rocks comprising two or more formations. **8.** *Mil.* **a.** an ad hoc military force of mixed arms and services, based on a standard combat unit or sub-unit. **b.** (in the Royal Australian Air Force) an operational or administrative subdivision of a command. **9.** *Music.* a section of an orchestra, comprising the instruments of the same class. **10.** a collection of musicians who generally play pop music: *pop group, rock group.* **11.** →**blood group.** **12.** a grouping of plants or animals which have similar characteristics but which are not related under a taxonomic classification. *–v.t.* **13.** to place in a group, as with others. **14.** to arrange in or form into a group or groups. *–v.i.* **15.** to form a group. **16.** to be part of a group. [F *groupe,* from It. *gruppo;* of Gmc orig.]

**group captain** /'– kæptn/, *n.* a commissioned rank in the Royal Australian Air Force above that of wing-commander and below air commodore; equivalent to colonel, in the army and captain in the navy.

**grouper**[1] /'grupə/, *n., pl.* **-pers,** (*esp. collectively*) **-per.** any of various often large fishes, of *Epinephelus* and related genera, found in warm seas. [Pg. *garupa,* apparently representing some South Amer. name]

**grouper**[2] /'grupə/, *n.* **1.** one who supports or belongs to the Industrial Groups, which were formed within trade unions for the purpose of containing or removing communist influence within them. **2.** (*derog.*) any member of a right-wing faction in the Australian Labor Party, or a member of the Democratic Labour Party.

**group grope** /grup 'groʊp/, *n. Colloq.* sexual intercourse mutually undertaken at the same time by three or more people.

**groupie** /'grupi/, *n. Colloq.* a girl who travels with and makes herself available sexually to the male members of a pop or rock group.

**grouping** /'grupɪŋ/, *n.* **1.** the act of forming a group. **2.** an arrangement in a group.

**group marriage** /grup 'mærɪdʒ/, *n.* a form of marriage in which a group of males are united with a group of females to form a single conjugal unit.

**group practice** /'– præktəs/, *n.* a medical practice run by a group of doctors in partnership.

**group stoop** /– 'stup/, *n.* →**gang bang.**

**group therapy** /– 'θɛrəpi/, *n.* the treatment of a group of psychiatric patients in sessions which all attend and in which problems are shared and discussed.

**group velocity** /– və'lɒsəti/, *n.* the velocity with which the energy of a wave is propagated.

**grouse**[1] /graʊs/, *n., pl.* **grouse.** any of various gallinacious birds of the family Tetraonidae, of the Northern Hemisphere, including important game species as the **red grouse,** *Lagopus scoticus,* of Britain, the **ruffed grouse,** *Bonasa umbellus* of North America, and the capercailzie. [orig. uncert.]

**grouse**[2] /graʊs/, *v.,* **groused, grousing,** *n. Colloq.* *–v.i.* **1.** to grumble; complain. *–n.* **2.** a complaint. [orig. unknown. Cf. GROUCH] **– grouser,** *n.*

**grouse**[3] /graʊs/, *adj. Colloq.* **1.** very good. **2. extra grouse,** excellent.

**grout** /graʊt/, *n.* **1.** a thin coarse mortar poured into the joints of masonry and brickwork. **2.** a fine finishing plaster for walls and ceilings. *–v.t.* **3.** to fill up, form or finish the spaces between (stones, etc.) with grout. [OE *grūt;* akin to GRITS, GROATS, and GRIT]

**grouter** /'graʊtə/, *n. Colloq.* **1.** an unfair advantage. **2. come in** or **be on the grouter, a.** to take an unfair advantage of a situation. **b.** (in two-up) to bet on a change in the fall of the coins.

**grove** /groʊv/, *n.* a small wood or plantation of trees. [ME; OE *grāf*]

**grovel** /'grɒvəl/, *v.i.,* **-elled, -elling** or (*U.S.*) **-eled, -eling. 1.** to humble oneself or act in an abject manner, as in fear or in mean servility. **2.** to lie or move with the face downwards and the body prostrate, esp. in abject humility, fear, etc. [backformation from *grovelling,* adv. (from obs. *grufe* face down (from Scand.) + -LING[2]), taken for ppr.]

**grow** /groʊ/, *v.,* **grew, grown, growing.** *–v.i.* **1.** to increase by natural development, as any living organism or part by assimilation of nutriment; increase in size or substance. **2.** to arise or issue as from a germ, stock, or originating source. **3.** to increase gradually; become greater. **4.** to become gradually attached or united by or as by growth. **5.** to come to be, or become, by degrees: *to grow old.* **6. grow up, a.** to increase in growth; attain maturity. **b.** to spring up; arise. *–v.t.* **7.** to cause to grow: *he grows corn.* **8.** to allow to grow: *to grow a beard.* **9.** to cover with a growth (used in the passive): *a field grown with corn.* **10. grow on, a.** to obtain an increasing influence, effect, etc. **b.** to win the affection or admiration of by degrees. **11. grow out of, a.** to become too big or too mature for; outgrow. **b.** to develop from; originate in. **12.** **grow like Topsy,** *Colloq.* to grow in an unplanned, random way. [ME *growe(n),* OE *grōwan,* akin to D *groeien,* OHG *gruwan,* Icel. *grōa.* Cf. GRASS, GREEN]

**grower** /ˈgroʊə/, *n.* **1.** one who grows anything. **2.** a plant that grows in a certain way: *a quick grower.*

**growing pains** /ˈgroʊɪŋ peɪnz/, *n.pl.* **1.** dull, indefinite pains in the limbs during childhood and adolescence, often popularly associated with the process of growing. **2.** difficulties attending any new project.

**growl** /graʊl/, *v.i.* **1.** to utter a deep guttural sound of anger or hostility: *a dog growls.* **2.** to murmur or complain angrily; grumble. **3.** to rumble. *–v.t.* **4.** to express by growling. *–n.* **5.** the act or sound of growling. **6.** *Colloq.* female pudendum. [ME *groule* rumble (said of the bowels), c. G *grollen* rumble] **–growlingly,** *adv.* **–growler,** *n.*

**grown** /groʊn/, *adj.* **1.** advanced in growth: *a grown boy.* **2.** arrived at full growth or maturity; adult: *a grown man.* *–v.* **3.** past participle of **grow.**

**grown-up** /ˈgroʊn-ʌp/, *adj.* **1.** having reached the age of maturity. **2.** characteristic of or suitable for adults. *–n.* **3.** a grown-up person; an adult.

**growth** /groʊθ/, *n.* **1.** the act, process, or manner of growing; development; gradual increase. **2.** stage of development. **3.** something that has grown or developed by or as by a natural process; a product: *a growth of weeds.* **4.** *Pathol.* a morbid mass of tissue, as a tumour. **5.** a source; origin: *vegetables of English growth.*

**growth-centre** /ˈgroʊθ-sɛntə/, *n.* a town and its environs, remote from the capital cities and the subject of development plans drawn up by a government in the interests of decentralisation.

**growth hormone** /ˈ– hɔmoʊn/, *n.* a hormone produced by the pancreas and acting throughout the body affecting growth.

**groyne** /grɔɪn/, *n.* a small jetty built out into the sea or a river in order to prevent erosion of the beach or bank. Also, **groin.**

**grub** /grʌb/, *n., v.,* **grubbed, grubbing.** *–n.* **1.** the bulky larva of certain insects, esp. of scarabaeid and other beetles. **2.** a dull, plodding person; drudge. **3.** *Colloq.* food or victuals. *–v.t.* **4.** to dig; clear of roots, etc. **5.** to dig up by the roots; uproot (oft. fol. by *up* or *out*). **6.** *Colloq.* to supply with food. *–v.i.* **7.** to dig; search by or as by digging. **8.** to lead a laborious or grovelling life; drudge. **9.** to make laborious research; study closely. **10.** *Colloq.* to take 'grub' or food. [ME *grubbe(n)* dig. Cf. G *grübeln* grub, rake, rack (the brains), Icel. *gryfja* hole, pit; probably akin to GRAVE[1]] **–grubber,** *n.*

**grubber** /ˈgrʌbə/, *n.* **1.** →**mullygrubber.** **2.** Also, **grubber kick.** *Rugby Football.* a kick which sends the ball along the ground.

**grubby** /ˈgrʌbi/, *adj.,* **-bier, -biest.** **1.** dirty; slovenly. **2.** infested with or affected by grubs or larvae. [GRUB, *n.* + -Y[1]] **–grubbily,** *adv.* **–grubbiness,** *n.*

**grub hoe** /ˈgrʌb hoʊ/, *n.* a heavy hoe for grubbing up roots, etc.

**grubsaw** /ˈgrʌbsɔ/, *n.* a saw for cutting stone by hand.

**grubscrew** /ˈgrʌbskru/, *n.* →**setscrew.**

**grubstake** /ˈgrʌbsteɪk/, *n., v.,* **-staked, -staking.** *–n.* **1.** provisions, outfit, etc., furnished to a prospector or the like, on condition of participating in the profits of his discoveries. *–v.t.* **2.** to furnish with a grubstake.

**grubstreet** /ˈgrʌbstrit/, *adj. Brit.* (of literary works) produced by a hack; of poor quality: *grubstreet books.* [from *Grub Street,* London (now Milton Street), formerly inhabited by impoverished and hack writers]

**grudge** /grʌdʒ/, *n., v.,* **grudged, grudging.** *–n.* **1.** a feeling of ill will or resentment excited by some special cause, as a personal injury or insult, etc. *–v.t.* **2.** to give or permit with reluctance; submit to unwillingly. **3.** to be dissatisfied at seeing the good fortune of (another). *–v.i.* **4.** to feel dissatisfaction or ill will. [earlier *grutch,* ME *gruche(n),* from OF *gruchier, groucier* murmur, grumble; orig. uncert. Cf. GROUCH] **–grudgeless,** *adj.* **–grudger,** *n.* **–grudgingly,** *adv.*

**grudge match** /ˈ– mætʃ/, *n.* a contest or fight in which there is ill will or personal antipathy between the opponents.

**gruel** /ˈgruəl/, *n., v.,* **-elled, -elling** or (*U.S.*) **-eled, -eling.** *–n.* **1.** a light, usu. thin, cooked cereal made by boiling meal, esp. oatmeal, in water or milk. **2.** any similar substance. *–v.t.* **3.** to punish or use severely; exhaust; disable. [ME, from OF: meal, from diminutive of ML *grūtum,* from Gmc. Cf. GROUT]

**gruelling** /ˈgruəlɪŋ/, *adj.* **1.** exhausting; very tiring; severe. *–n.* **2.** any trying or exhausting procedure or experience. Also, *U.S.* **grueling.**

**gruesome** /ˈgrusəm/, *adj.* such as to make one shudder; inspiring horror; revolting. Also, **grewsome.** [*grue,* v., shudder (c. G *grauen,* Dan. *grue*) + -SOME[1]. Cf. G *grausam* horrible] **–gruesomely,** *adv.* **–gruesomeness,** *n.*

**gruff** /grʌf/, *adj.* **1.** low and harsh; hoarse: *a gruff voice.* **2.** rough; surly: *a gruff manner.* [earlier *grof,* from D, from *ge-* prefix (c. OE *ge-*) + *rof,* akin to OE *hrēof* rough] **–gruffly,** *adv.* **–gruffness,** *n.*

**grugru** /ˈgrugru/, *n.* any of several spiny palms of tropical America, esp. *Acrocomia sclerocarpa.*

**gruie** /ˈgrui/, *n.* →**colane.**

**grumble** /ˈgrʌmbəl/, *v.,* **-bled, -bling,** *n.* *–v.i.* **1.** to murmur in discontent; complain ill-humouredly. **2.** to utter low, indistinct sounds; growl. **3.** to rumble: *the thunder grumbled.* *–v.t.* **4.** to express or utter with murmuring or complaining. *–n.* **5.** an ill-humoured complaining; murmur; growl. **6.** (*pl.*) a grumbling, discontented mood. **7.** a rumble. [? frequentative of OE *grymman* wail, mourn. Cf. OE *grymettan* grunt, roar, rage, G *grummeln* rumble, F *grommeter* mutter] **–grumbler,** *n.* **–grumblingly,** *adv.*

**grume** /grum/, *n.* **1.** a thick, viscous fluid. **2.** *Med.* a clot of blood. [LL *grūmus* little heap]

**grummet** /ˈgrʌmət/, *n.* **1.** *Mach.* a ring or eyelet of metal, rubber, etc. **2.** *Naut.* an eyelet of rope, metal, or the like, as on the edge of a sail. Also, **grommet.** [F *grommette* (obs.) curb of bridle, from LL *grumus* throat]

**grumous** /ˈgruməs/, *adj.* formed of clustered grains, granules, etc., as certain roots. Also, **grumose** /ˈgrumoʊs/. [*grume* (from L *grūmus* little heap, hillock) + -OUS]

**grump** /grʌmp/, *n.* →**grouch.**

**grumpy** /ˈgrʌmpi/, *adj.,* **-pier, -piest.** surly; ill-tempered. [*grump* the sulks (b. GRUNT and DUMP) + -Y[1]] **–grumpily,** *adj.* **–grumpiness,** *n.*

**Grundyism** /ˈgrʌndiɪzəm/, *n.* prudery; narrow-mindedness; excessive attachment to conventional behaviour. [after Mrs *Grundy,* a person mentioned in Thomas Morton's play *Speed the Plough* (1798)]

**grunt** /grʌnt/, *v.i.* **1.** to utter the deep guttural sound characteristic of a pig. **2.** to utter a similar sound. **3.** to grumble, as in discontent. *–v.t.* **4.** to express with a grunt. *–n.* **5.** the sound of grunting. **6.** →**grunter** (def. 3). [ME *grunten,* OE *grunnettan,* frequentative of *grunian* grunt. Cf. G *grunzen,* L *grunnīre*] **–gruntingly,** *adv.*

**grunter** /ˈgrʌntə/, *n.* **1.** a pig. **2.** any animal or person that grunts. **3.** any Australian freshwater fish that emits grunting noises as it respires, as the indigenous **silver perch,** *Bidyanus bidyanus,* or **spangled perch,** *Madigania unicolor.*

**gruyère** /ˈgrujə, gruˈjɛə/, *n.* a firm pale yellow variety of Swiss cheese with some surface growth which gives added flavour. [named after *Gruyère,* district in Switzerland]

**gr. wt,** gross weight.

**gryke** /graɪk/, *n.* →**grike.**

**gryphon** /ˈgrɪfən/, *n.* →**griffin**[1].

**grysbok** /ˈgreɪzbɒk, ˈgraɪz-/, *n.* a small hardy antelope, *Raphicerus melanotis,* of southern Africa. [Afrikaans: grey buck]

**Gs,** gauss.

**gsm** /dʒi ɛs ˈɛm/, grams per square metre, a measure of the density, and hence quality of paper.

**G-string** /ˈdʒi-strɪŋ/, *n.* **1.** a loincloth or breechcloth. **2.** a similar covering, usu. decorated, worn by women entertainers for striptease dancing, etc. [orig. uncert.]

**G-suit** /ˈdʒi-sut/, *n.* a garment which under high positive acceleration exerts pressure on the abdomen and lower parts of the body to retard the flow of blood away from the upper part.

**G.T.** /dʒi ˈti/, gran turismo.

**Gt Br.,** Great Britain. Also, **Gt Brit.**

**gtd,** guaranteed.

**G.T. stripes** /dʒi ti ˈstraɪps/, *n. pl.* **1.** two coloured stripes running along the body of a gran turismo car and indicating its class. **2.** similar decorative stripes on cars, clothes, etc., suggestive of quality or expense.

**G.U.,** genito-urinary.

**guacharo** /ˈgwatʃəroʊ/, *n., pl.* **-ros.** a nocturnal fruit-eating South American bird, *Steatornis caripensis,* valued for the oil produced from the fat of the young. [Sp., from Araucanian *uachar* cave]

**guaco** /ˈgwakoʊ/, *n., pl.* **-cos. 1.** a climbing plant, *Mikania guaco,* of tropical America. **2.** its medicinal leaves, or a substance obtained from them, used as an antidote for snakebites. **3.** a tropical American plant, of the genus *Aristolochia,* also used for snakebites. [Sp., from native name]

**guaiacol** /ˈgwaɪəkɒl/, *n.* a colourless liquid, $CH_3OC_6H_4OH$, resembling creosote, obtained by distillation from guaiacum resin, and in other ways; used to treat phthisis, bronchitis, etc. [GUAIAC(UM) + -OL[2]]

**guaiacum** /ˈgwaɪəkəm/, *n.* **1.** any of the hard-wooded tropical American trees and shrubs constituting the genus *Guaiacum,* esp. *G. officinale* of the West Indies and South America, and *G. sanctum* of the West Indies and Florida. **2.** the hard, heavy wood of such a tree. See **lignum vitae** (def. 1). **3.** a greenish brown resin obtained from such a tree, used as a remedy for rheumatism, cutaneous eruptions, etc. Also, **guaiac** /ˈgwaɪæk/. [NL, from Sp. *guayaco;* from Haitian]

**guan** /gwan/, *n.* any of various large gallinaceous birds constituting the subfamily Penelopinae (family Cracidae), chiefly of Central and South America, allied to the curassows. [? of W Ind. orig.]

**guana** /ˈgwanə/, *n. Obs.* →**goanna**[1].

**guanabana** /gwəˈnabənə/, *n.* →**soursop.** [Sp. *guanábana* fruit of the soursop, from Taino]

**guanaco** /gwaˈnakoʊ/, *n., pl.* **-cos.** a wild South American ruminant, *Lama guanicoe,* of which the llama and alpaca are thought to be domesticated varieties, related to the camels. [Sp., from Quechua *huanacu*]

guanaco

**guanase** /ˈgwaneɪz/, *n.* an enzyme found in thymus, adrenals and pancreas which converts guanine into xanthine. [GUAN(INE) + -ASE]

**guanidine** /ˈgwanədən, -din/, *n.* a strongly caustic substance, $HN{:}C(NH_2)_2$, forming crystalline salts and a wide variety of organic derivatives, used in the manufacture of plastics, resins, rubber accelerators, explosives, etc. Also, **guanidin** /ˈgwanədən/. [from GUANINE with infixed -ID[3]]

**guanine** /ˈgwanin/, *n.* a purine base, $C_5H_5N_5O$, present in all living cells, mainly in combined form, as in nucleic acids; it is also found in guano. [GUANO + -INE[2]]

**guano** /ˈgwanoʊ/, *n., pl.* **-nos. 1.** a natural manure composed chiefly of the excrement of seabirds, found esp. on islands near the Peruvian coast. **2.** any similar substance, as an artificial fertiliser made from fish. [Sp., from Quechua *huanu* dung]

**guanosine** /ˈgwanəsən, -sin/, *n.* a nucleoside of guanine and ribose, present in all living cells, mainly in combined form, as in ribonucleic acids.

**guanylic acid** /gwaˌnɪlɪk ˈæsəd/, *n.* the monophosphate of guanosine, present in all living cells, mainly in combined form, as in ribonucleic acids.

**guarana** /gwəˈranə/, *n.* **1.** a dried paste made from the seeds of a Brazilian shrub, *Paullinia cupana.* **2.** a drink made from this. [Sp. or Pg., from Tupi]

**Guaraní** /gwarəˈni/, *n., pl.* **nís, -níes,** (*esp. collectively*) **-ní. 1.** an important central South American tribe of Tupian family and affiliation. **2.** a member of this tribe. **3.** the Tupian language of the Guaraní tribe.

**guarantee** /gærənˈti/, *n., v.,* **-teed, -teeing.** *–n.* **1.** →**guaranty** (def. 1). **2.** a promise or assurance, esp. one given in writing by a manufacturer, that something is of a specified quality, and generally including an undertaking to make good any defects under certain conditions. **3.** one who gives a guarantee or guaranty; guarantor. **4.** one to whom a guarantee is made. **5.** →**guaranty** (def. 2). **6.** something that has the force or effect of a guaranty: *wealth is no guarantee of happiness.* *–v.t.* **7.** to secure, as by giving or taking security. **8.** to make oneself answerable for on behalf of one primarily responsible: *to guarantee the carrying out of a contract.* **9.** to undertake to secure to another, as rights or possessions. **10.** to serve as a warrant or guarantee for. **11.** to engage (to do something). **12.** to engage to protect or indemnify (fol. by *from, against,* or *in*): *to guarantee one against loss.* **13.** to promise. [apparently for GUARANTY]

**guarantor** /gærənˈtɔ/, *n.* one who makes or gives a guarantee or guaranty.

**guaranty** /ˈgærənti/, *n., pl.* **-ties,** *v.,* **-tied, -tying.** *–n.* **1.** a warrant, pledge, or promise accepting responsibility for the discharging of another's liabilities, as the payment of a debt. **2.** that which is taken or presented as security. **3.** the act of giving security. **4.** one who acts as a guarantor. *–v.t.* **5.** to guarantee. [AF *guarantie,* from *guarant, warant* WARRANT]

**guard** /gad/, *v.t.* **1.** to keep safe from harm; protect; watch over. **2.** to keep under close watch in order to prevent escape, outbreaks, etc.: *to guard a prisoner.* **3.** to keep in check, from caution or prudence: *to guard the tongue.* **4.** to provide with some safeguard or protective appliance, etc. *–v.i.* **5.** to take precautions (fol. by *against*): *to guard against errors.* **6.** to give protection; keep watch; be watchful. *–n.* **7.** one who guards, protects, or keeps a protecting or restraining watch. **8.** one who keeps watch over prisoners or others under restraint. **9.** a body of men, esp. soldiers, charged with guarding a place from disturbance, theft, fire, etc. **10.** restraining watch, as over a prisoner or other person under restraint: *to be kept under close guard.* **11.** a contrivance, appliance, or attachment designed for guarding against injury, loss, etc. **12.** something intended or serving to guard or protect; a safeguard. **13.** a posture of defence or readiness, as in fencing, boxing, bayonet drill, etc. **14.** *American Football.* either of two players holding a position of defence at the right and left of the centre, in the forward line. **15.** *Basketball.* one of the defensive players in a team. **16.** an official in general charge of a railway train. **17.** *Print.* a narrow strip of paper or other material sewn into a book to hold an extra sheet, as a throw-out map. **18. off one's guard.** Also, **off guard.** unprepared to meet a sudden attack; unwary. **19. on one's guard.** Also, **on guard.** watchful or vigilant against attack; cautious; wary. **20. to take guard,** *Cricket.* to position the bat on the wicket in relation to one of the stumps immediately prior to batting. [ME *garde,* from F, of Gmc orig.; see WARD] **–guardable,** *adj.* **–guarder,** *n.*

**guardant** /ˈgadnt/, *adj. Her.* (of an animal) shown full face, with the body seen from the side. Also, **gardant.** [F *gardant,* ppr. of *garder*]

guardant: lions guardant on the coat of arms of England

**guard cell** /ˈgad sɛl/, *n.* either of two specialised epidermal cells which flank the pore of a stoma and usually cause it to open and close.

**guard commander** /ˈ– kəmændə/, *n.* a non-commissioned officer in charge of a guard (def. 9).

**guarded** /ˈgadəd/, *adj.* **1.** cautious; careful: *to be guarded in one's speech.* **2.** protected or watched, as by a guard. **–guardedly,** *adv.* **–guardedness,** *n.*

**guardian** /ˈgadiən/, *n.* **1.** one who guards, protects, or preserves. **2.** *Law.* one who is entrusted by law with the care of the person or property, or both, of another, as of a minor or of some other person legally incapable of managing his own affairs. *–adj.* **3.** guarding; protecting: *a guardian angel.* [ME *gardein,* from AF, from *g(u)arde* GUARD, *n.*] **–guardianship,** *n.*

**guardrail** /ˈgadreɪl/, *n.* **1.** a protective railing; banister; handrail.

**guard ring** /ˈgad rɪŋ/, *n.* a ring placed on a finger to prevent another ring from slipping off.

**guardroom** /ˈgadrum/, *n.* a room or building used for

accommodating military personnel performing guard duties and also for the detention of defaulters. Also, **guardhouse.**

**guardsman** /ˈgadzmən/, *n., pl.* **-men. 1.** a man who acts as a guard. **2.** *Brit.* a soldier in a Guards regiment.

**guard's van** /ˈgadz væn/, *n.* a railway wagon for the guard, usu. attached to the rear of a train; brake van.

**Guat.,** Guatemala.

**Guatemala** /gwʌtəˈmalə/, *n.* a republic in central America. – **Guatemalan,** *adj., n.*

**guava** /ˈgwavə/, *n.* **1.** any of various trees and shrubs of the genus *Psidium,* esp. *P. guajava* and *P. cattleianum,* native to tropical and subtropical America, with a fruit used for jelly, etc. **2.** the fruit, used for making jam, jelly, etc. [Sp. *guayaba;* from South Amer. name]

**guayule** /gwəˈjuli/, *n.* **1.** a rubber-yielding plant, *Parthenium argentatum,* family Compositae, of northern Mexico, etc. **2.** the rubber obtained from this plant. [Mex. Sp., from Nahuatl *cuauhuli*]

**gub** /gʌb/, *n. Colloq. (derog.)* an Aboriginal term for a white man. Also, **gubber, gubba, gubbah.** [Aboriginal: white demon]

**gubba** /ˈgʌbə/, *n. Colloq. (derog.)* **1.** a white man. **2.** a peeping tom. [Aboriginal: white demon]

**gubernaculum** /gjubəˈnækjələm/, *n.* a guiding structure, esp. **gubernaculum dentis,** a connective tissue band joining the sac of an unerupted tooth with the gum, and **gubernaculum testis,** a cord in the foetus between the epididymis and the bottom of the scrotum. [L: helm]

**gubernatorial** /gjubənəˈtɔriəl/, *adj.* of or pertaining to a governor. [L *gubernātor* steersman, governor + -IAL]

**guck** /gʌk/, *n. Colloq.* slimy, objectionable matter: *guck and goo.* [? b. GOO + MUCK]

**guddle** /ˈgʌdl/, *v.,* **-dled, -dling.** *–v.t.* **1.** to fish with the hands by groping under rocks or stones on the banks of a river, etc. *–v.i.* **2.** to catch fish in this manner. [Scot.]

**gudgeon**[1] /ˈgʌdʒən/, *n.* **1.** any of various species of small marine and freshwater fish of the family Gobiidae as the **snakehead gudgeon,** *Ophiocara aporos,* of northern Australia. **2.** a small European freshwater fish, *Gobio gobio,* of the minnow family, which has a thread-like barbel at the corner of the mouth, is easily caught, and is much used for bait. **3.** one who is easily duped or cheated. **4.** a bait or allurement. *–v.t.* **5.** to dupe; cheat. [ME *gogen,* from OF *goujon,* from L *gōbio,* var. of *gōbius* GOBY]

**gudgeon**[2] /ˈgʌdʒən/, *n.* the ring portion of a hinge which fits on to and turns on a pin or hook. [ME *gudyon,* from OF *goujon,* ? from LL *gubia* chisel]

**gudgeon pin** /ˈ– pɪn/, *n.* the pin which connects the piston of an internal-combustion engine to the little end bearing of the connecting rod. Also, **gudgeon wrist pin.**

**guelder-rose** /ˈgɛldə-roʊz/, *n.* the European snowball, *Viburnum opulus* var. *roseum.* [named after *Geldern,* German town, or *Gelder(land),* Dutch province of which Geldern was formerly capital]

**guenon** /ˈginən/, *n.* any of the agile, long-tailed African monkeys, of the genus *Cercopithecus,* with their hairs many-banded, giving a speckled coloration. [F]

**guerdon** /ˈgɜdn/, *Poetic. –n.* **1.** a reward, recompense, or requital. *–v.t.* **2.** to give a guerdon to; reward. [ME, from OF, var. of *werdoun,* from ML *widerdonum,* alteration (probably by association with L *dōnum* gift) of OHG *widarlōn,* from *widar* again, back + *lōn* reward, c. OE *witherlēan*]

**guereza** /ˈgɛrɪzə/, *n.* any of several African monkeys of the genus *Colubus,* having a coat of silky hair, usu. black and white. [Ethiopian native name]

**guerilla** /gəˈrɪlə/, *n.* **1.** a member of a small, independent band of soldiers which harasses the enemy by surprise raids, attacks on communication and supply lines, etc. *–adj.* **2.** pertaining to such fighters or their method of warfare. Also, **guerrilla.** [Sp., diminutive of *guerra* WAR]

**Guernsey** /ˈgɜnzi/, *n., pl.* **-seys. 1.** one of a breed of dairy cattle. **2.** (*l.c.*) a close-fitting knitted jumper, much worn by seamen, footballers, etc. **3. get a guernsey,** *Colloq.* to succeed, win approval (originally to be selected for a football team). [from the Isle of *Guernsey,* in the English Channel]

**guess** /gɛs/, *v.t.* **1.** to form an opinion of at random or from evidence admittedly uncertain: *to guess the age of a woman.* **2.** to estimate or conjecture correctly: *to guess a riddle.* **3.** to think, believe, or suppose: *I guess I can get there in time.* *–v.i.* **4.** to form an estimate or conjecture (oft. fol. by *at*): *to guess at the height of a building.* **5.** to estimate or conjecture correctly. *–n.* **6.** a notion, judgment, or conclusion gathered from mere probability or imperfect information; conjecture; surmise. **7.** the act of forming an opinion in this manner. [ME *gessen,* probably from Scand.: cf. MDan. *getze, gitse* (Dan. *gisse*), from *get-* guess + *-s* suffix, c. MD *gessen,* MLG *gissen*] – **guessable,** *adj.* – **guesser,** *n.* – **guessingly,** *adv.*

**guesstimate** /ˈgɛstəmət/, *n.;* /ˈgɛstəmeɪt/ *v.,* **-mated, -mating.** *Colloq. –n.* **1.** an estimate made chiefly by guessing. *–v.t.* **2.** to estimate in this way.

**guesswork** /ˈgɛswɜk/, *n.* work or procedure based on guessing; conjecture.

**guest** /gɛst/, *n.* **1.** a person entertained at the house or table of another. **2.** one who receives the hospitality of a club, a city, or the like. **3.** a person who pays for lodging, and sometimes food, at a hotel, etc. **4.** *Zool.* a commensal (chiefly of insects living in other insects' nests). *–v.t.* **5.** *Rare.* to entertain as a guest. *–v.i.* **6.** *Rare.* to be a guest. [ME *gest(e),* from Scand. (cf. Icel. *gestr*); replacing OE *g(i)est,* c. D *gast,* G *Gast;* akin to L *hostis* stranger, enemy] – **guestless,** *adj.*

**guesthouse** /ˈgɛsthaʊs/, *n., pl.* **-houses** /-haʊzəz/. a house for the accommodation of paying guests; boarding house; hotel.

**guest night** /ˈgɛst naɪt/, *n.* an evening on which members of a society, club, etc., entertain guests to dinner.

**guestroom** /ˈgɛstrum/, *n.* a room for the accommodation of guests.

**guestrope** /ˈgɛstroʊp/, *n.* **1.** a line along a ship's side or from a boom for boats to make fast alongside. **2.** a line, in addition to the towrope, to steady a boat in tow.

**guff** /gʌf/, *n. Colloq.* empty or foolish talk; humbug; nonsense.

**guffaw** /gʌˈfɔ, gə-/, *n.* **1.** a loud, coarse burst of laughter. *–v.i.* **2.** to laugh loudly and boisterously.

**guidance** /ˈgaɪdns/, *n.* **1.** the act of guiding; leadership; direction. **2.** that which guides. **3.** advice; instruction.

**guide** /gaɪd/, *v.,* **guided, guiding,** *n.* *–v.t.* **1.** to lead or conduct on the way, as to a place or through a region; show the way to. **2.** to direct the movement or course of: *to guide a horse.* **3.** to lead, direct or advise in any course or action. *–n.* **4.** one who guides, esp. one employed to guide travellers, tourists, mountaineers, etc. **5.** a mark or the like to direct the eye. **6.** a guidebook. **7.** a guidepost. **8.** a contrivance for regulating progressive motion or action in a machine. **9.** a spirit believed to direct the utterances of a medium. **10.** →**girl guide.** [ME *guide(n),* from OF *guider,* from Gmc; cf. OE *wītan* look after] – **guidable,** *adj.* – **guideless,** *adj.* – **guider,** *n.*

**guide bars** /ˈ– baz/, *n. pl.* bars which guide the crosshead of a steam engine to avoid lateral thrust on the piston rod. Also, **slide bars.**

**guidebook** /ˈgaɪdbʊk/, *n.* a book of directions and information for travellers, tourists, etc.

**guided** /ˈgaɪdəd/, *adj.* (of weapons) controlled remotely from an external source or by equipment within the weapon itself.

**guided missile** /– ˈmɪsaɪl/, *n.* a missile whose flight path can be controlled throughout its flight either by radio signals from an external source or by internal homing devices. Cf. **ballistic missile.**

**guide-dog** /ˈgaɪd-dɒg/, *n.* a dog specially trained to lead or guide a blind person.

**guided wave** /gaɪdəd ˈweɪv/, *n.* electromagnetic radiation which is guided along a conductor or an insulating surface as opposed to travelling through space.

**guideline** /ˈgaɪdlaɪn/, *n.* **1.** a line drawn as a guide for further writing, drawing, etc. **2.** (*usu. pl.*) a statement which defines policy or the area in which a policy is operative.

**guidepost** /ˈgaɪdpoʊst/, *n.* →**signpost.**

**guider** /ˈgaɪdə/, *n.* **1.** one who guides. **2.** an officer in a company of Girl Guides or Brownies.

**guide rope** /ˈgaɪd roʊp/, *n.* **1.** *Aeron.* a long rope trailing along the ground from a balloon and used to regulate altitude and act as a brake. **2.** a rope fastened to a hoisting or towing line, to guide the object being moved.

**guidon** /ˈgaɪdn/, *n. Mil.* **1.** a swallow-tailed pennant, used as a military standard. **2.** the officer carrying it. [F, from It. *guidone,* b. *guidare* GUIDE and *gonfalone* GONFALON]

**guild** /gɪld/, *n.* **1.** an organisation of persons with common professional or cultural interests formed for mutual aid and protection. **2.** one of the associations, numerous in the Middle Ages, formed for mutual aid and protection or for a common purpose, most frequently by persons associated in trade or industry. Also, **gild.** [ME *gild(e),* from Scand. (cf. Icel. *gildi* guild, payment); replacing OE *gegyld* guild; akin to G *Geld* money, Goth. *gild* tribute]

**guilder** /ˈgɪldə/, *n.* →**gulden.** Also, **gilder.** [early mod. E *gildren,* var. of ME *guldren,* both from D (with intrusive *-r-*) *gulden*]

**guildhall** /ˈgɪldhɔl/, *n.* **1.** the hall of a guild or corporation; town hall. **2.** a guild assembly hall. Also, **gildhall.**

**guildsman** /ˈgɪldzmən/, *n., pl.* **-men.** a member of a guild. Also, **gildsman.**

**guild socialism** /gɪld ˈsoʊʃəlɪzəm/, *n.* a form of socialism by which workers' guilds manage and control government-owned industry.

**guile** /gaɪl/, *n.* insidious cunning; deceitfulness; treachery. [ME, from OF; of Gmc orig., and akin to WILE]

**guileful** /ˈgaɪlfəl/, *adj.* full of guile; wily; deceitful; treacherous. – **guilefully,** *adv.* – **guilefulness,** *n.*

**guileless** /ˈgaɪlləs/, *adj.* free from guile; sincere; honest; frank. – **guilelessly,** *adv.* – **guilelessness,** *n.*

**guillemot** /ˈgɪləmɒt/, *n.* any of several relatively narrow-billed northern oceanic birds of the genera *Cepphus* and *Uria,* as the **black guillemot,** *Cepphus grylle,* and **common guillemot,** *Uria aalge.* [F, apparently diminutive of *Guillaume* William]

guilloche

**guilloche** /gəˈlɒʃ/, *n.* an ornamental band or field with paired ribbons or lines flowing in interlaced curves. [F: graining tool, from MF *goie* a kind of sickle, d. var. of F *gouge* GOUGE, *n.*]

**guillotine** /ˈgɪlətin/, *n.;* /gɪləˈtin/, *v.* **-tined, -tining.** –*n.* **1.** a machine for beheading persons by means of a heavy blade falling in two grooved posts. **2.** a surgical instrument for cutting the tonsils. **3.** a device incorporating a long blade for trimming paper. **4.** a time restriction imposed by resolution on a parliamentary debate. **5. impose the guillotine,** to apply the guillotine to a parliamentary debate. –*v.t.* **6.** to restrict, by resolution, time allowed for a parliamentary debate of a bill or parts of it. **7.** to behead by the guillotine. [F; named after J. I. *Guillotin,* 1738-1814, French physician, who urged its use] – **guillotiner,** *n.*

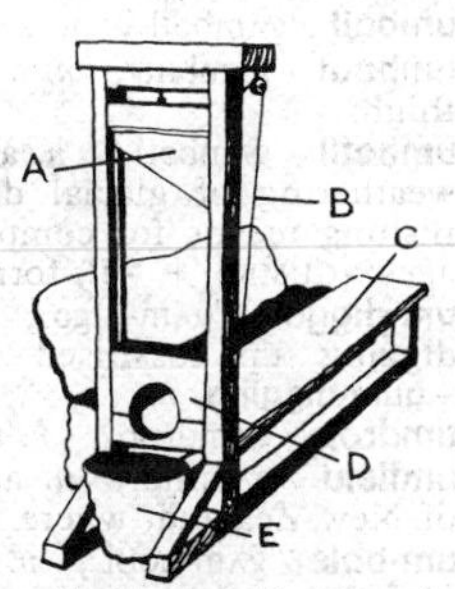


guillotine: A, knife; B, cord which releases knife; C, board to which victim is tied; D, hole for head of victim; E, basket

**guilt** /gɪlt/, *n.* **1.** the fact or state of having committed an offence or crime; grave culpability, as for some conscious violation of moral or penal law. **2.** a feeling of responsibility or remorse for some crime, wrong, etc., either real or imagined. **3. guilt by association,** guilt attached to a person because of his connection with others who are guilty. [ME *gilt,* OE *gylt* offence]

**guilt-complex** /ˈgɪlt-ˌkɒmplɛks/, *n.* an obsessive sense of responsibility or remorse for some crime, wrong, etc., either real or imagined.

**guiltless** /ˈgɪltləs/, *adj.* **1.** free from guilt; innocent. **2.** having no knowledge or experience (fol. by *of*). **3.** destitute or devoid (fol. by *of*). – **guiltlessly,** *adv.* – **guiltlessness,** *n.*

**guilty** /ˈgɪlti/, *adj.,* **-tier, -tiest. 1.** having incurred guilt or grave culpability, as by committing an offence or crime; justly chargeable with guilt (oft. fol. by *of*): *guilty of murder.* **2.** characterised by, connected with, or involving guilt: *guilty intent.* **3.** affected with or showing a sense of guilt: *a guilty conscience.* [ME *gilti,* OE *gyltig*] – **guiltily,** *adv.* – **guiltiness,** *n.*

**guimpe** /gɪmp/, *n.* a kind of chemisette or yoke of lace, embroidery, or other material, worn with a dress cut low at the neck. [earlier *gimp,* c. D *gimp*]

**Guinea** /ˈgɪni/, *n.* **1.** a republic in western Africa, on the Atlantic coast. **2.** (*l.c.*) a British coin issued from 1663 to 1813, at first of a nominal value of 20 shillings, but having since 1717 a fixed value of 21 shillings. **3.** until decimal currency, the sum of 21 shillings. **4.** (*l.c.*) *Colloq.* →**guineafowl.**

**Guinea-Bissau** /gɪni-bɪˈsaʊ/, *n.* a country on the west coast of Africa between Guinea and Senegal.

**guinea corn** /gɪni ˈkɔn/, *n.* →**durra.**

**guinea flower** /ˈgɪni flaʊə/, *n.* any plant of the Australian genus *Hibbertia,* esp. *H. scandens* with large yellow flowers, often found near beaches.

**guineafowl** /ˈgɪnifaʊl/, *n.* any member of an African gallinaceous bird family, the Numididae, which has (usu.) dark grey plumage with small white spots, one species of which is now domesticated throughout the world and valued for its flesh and eggs.

guineafowl

**guinea grass** /ˈgɪni gras/, *n.* a native of tropical Africa, *Panicum maximum,* now naturalised in tropical Australia and planted as a pasture species.

**guinea hen** /ˈ– hɛn/, *n.* **1.** the female of the guineafowl. **2.** any guineafowl.

**guinea pepper** /– ˈpɛpə/, *n.* pepper pods, esp. of *Capsicum frutescens* var. *longum,* from which cayenne is ground.

**guineapig** /ˈgɪnipɪg/, *n.* **1.** a short-eared, short-tailed rodent of the genus *Cavia,* usu. white, black, and tawny, much used in scientific experiments, commonly regarded as the domesticated form of one of the South American wild species of cavy. **2.** *Colloq.* a person used as the subject of any sort of experiment. [GUINEA + PIG[1]; reason for associating animal with Guinea unknown]

guineapig

**guinea worm** /ˈgɪni wɜm/, *n.* a long, slender, nematode worm, *Dracunculus medinensis,* parasitic under the skin of man and other animals, common in parts of India and Africa.

**guipure** /gəˈpjʊə/, *n.* **1.** any of various laces, often heavy, made of linen, silk, etc., with the pattern connected by brides (rather than by a net ground). **2.** any of various laces or trimmings formerly in use, made with cords or heavy threads, metal, etc. [F, from *guiper* cover or whip with silk, etc., from Gmc; cf. WIPE, WHIP]

**guiro** /ˈgwɪəroʊ/, *n.* a percussion instrument consisting of a dried empty gourd, which has parallel notches across which a stick is drawn.

**guise** /gaɪz/, *n., v.,* **guised, guising.** –*n.* **1.** external appearance in general; aspect or semblance: *an old principle in a new guise.* **2.** assumed appearance or mere semblance: *under the guise of friendship.* **3.** style of dress: *in the guise of a shepherdess.* –*v.i.* **4.** *Scot.* to go in disguise. [ME, from OF, from Gmc; cf. WISE[2]]

**guitar** /gəˈta/, *n.* a musical stringed instrument with a long fretted neck and a flat, somewhat violin-like body. The strings, usu. six in number, are plucked or twanged with the fingers or a plectrum. [Sp. *guitarra,* from Gk *kithára* cithara] – **guitarist,** *n.* – **guitarlike,** *adj.*

**guiver** /ˈgaɪvə/, *n. Colloq.* →**guyver.**

**guivo** /ˈgaɪvoʊ/, *n. Colloq.* →**guyver.**

**Gujarati** /gudʒəˈrati/, *n.* **1.** an Indic language of western India. **2.** a native or inhabitant of Gujarat, a state and region in western India.

**guk** /gʌk/, *n.* →**gunk.**

**gulch** /gʌltʃ/, *n. U.S.* a deep, narrow ravine, esp. one marking the course of a stream or torrent. [orig. uncert.]

**gulden** /ˈgʊldən/, *n.* **1.** the monetary unit of the Netherlands. **2.** any of several silver or gold coins formerly current in Germany, Austria, and the Low Countries. Also, **guilder, gilder.** [D: lit., golden]

**gules** /gjulz/, *n.* red. [ME *goules,* from OF *gueules* red fur neckpiece, from *gole* throat, from L *gula*]

**gulf** /gʌlf/, *n.* **1.** a portion of an ocean or sea partly enclosed by land. **2.** a deep hollow; chasm or abyss. **3.** any wide separation, as in social class, education, etc. **4.** something that engulfs or swallows up. *–v.t.* **5.** to swallow like a gulf, or as in a gulf; engulf. [ME *goulf,* from OF *golfe,* from It. *golfo,* from LGk *kólphos,* Gk *kólpos* bosom, gulf] – **gulflike,** *adj.*

**gulfweed** /ˈgʌlfwid/, *n.* **1.** a coarse, olive brown seaweed, *Sargassum bacciferum,* found in the Gulf Stream and elsewhere, characterised by numerous berry-like air vesicles. **2.** any seaweed related to it.

**gulgie** /ˈdʒʊlgi/, *n. W.A.* →**gilgie.**

**gull**[1] /gʌl/, *n.* any of numerous long-winged, web-footed, aquatic birds constituting the sub-family Larinae (family Laridae), esp. of the genus *Larus,* usu. white with grey back and wings, as the silver gull. [ME *gull(e),* ? representing OE word (unrecorded) akin to OE *giellan* yell]

**gull**[2] /gʌl/, *v.t.* **1.** to deceive; trick; cheat. *–n.* **2.** one easily deceived or cheated; a dupe. [? akin to obs. *gull,* v., swallow]

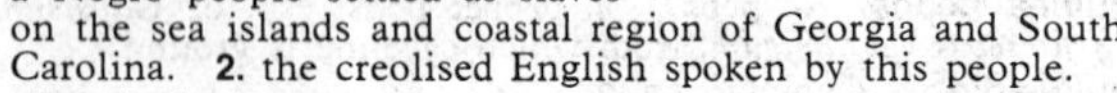

gull[1]

**Gullah** /ˈgʌlə/, *n.* **1.** a member of a Negro people settled as slaves on the sea islands and coastal region of Georgia and South Carolina. **2.** the creolised English spoken by this people.

**gullet** /ˈgʌlət/, *n.* **1.** the oesophagus, or tube by which food and drink swallowed pass to the stomach. **2.** the throat or pharynx. **3.** something like the oesophagus. **4.** a channel for water. **5.** a gully or ravine. **6.** a preparatory cut in excavations. [ME *golet,* from OF *goulet,* from L *gula* throat]

**gullible** /ˈgʌləbəl/, *adj.* easily deceived or cheated. – **gullibility** /gʌləˈbɪləti/, *n.* – **gullibly,** *adv.*

**gulli-gulli man** /ˈgʌli-gʌli mæn/, *n.* a conjuror, esp. in Egypt, who works with live chickens. [from *gulli-gulli* the conjuror's catchword]

**gull plugger** /ˈgʌl plʌgə/, *n. Colloq.* one who shoots indiscriminately at any bird, for sport.

**gull-wing** /ˈgʌl-wɪŋ/, *adj.* **1.** (of an aeroplane wing) with its short inner section sloping up from the fuselage and its outer section horizontal. **2.** (of a car door) opening upwards so as to make a gull-wing shape when open.

**gully** /ˈgʌli/, *n., pl.* **-lies,** *v.,* **-lied, -lying.** *–n.* **1.** a small valley or canyon cut by running water. **2.** a ditch or gutter. **3.** *Cricket.* **a.** a fielding position between the slips and point. **b.** the fielder in this position. *–v.t.* **4.** to make gullies in. **5.** to form (channels) by the action of water. Also, **gulley.** [apparently var. of GULLET, with substitution of -Y[3] for F *-et*]

**gully erosion** /ˈ– əroʊʒən/, *n.* soil erosion caused by run-off, and appearing as deep cracks in the ground.

**gully fern** /ˈ– fɜn/, *n.* a graceful treefern, *Cyathea cunninghamii,* of New Zealand.

**gully-rake** /ˈgʌli-reɪk/, *v.i.,* **-raked, -raking.** *Colloq.* to steal stock.

**gully-raker** /ˈgʌli-reɪkə/, *n. Colloq.* **1.** a person who steals stock. **2.** a stock-whip.

**gully trap** /ˈgʌli træp/, *n.* a water-sealed trap through which the house drainage is connected to the external drains. Also, **gulley trap.**

**gulp** /gʌlp/, *v.i.* **1.** to gasp or choke as when taking large draughts of liquids. *–v.t.* **2.** to swallow eagerly, or in large draughts or pieces (usu. fol. by *down*). **3.** to take in, as by swallowing eagerly; choke back: *to gulp down a sob.* *–n.* **4.** the act of gulping. **5.** the amount swallowed at one time; mouthful. [ME *gulpe(n).* Cf. D *gulpen* gulp, Norw. *glupa* swallow] – **gulper,** *n.*

**gum**[1] /gʌm/, *n., v.,* **gummed, gumming.** *–n.* **1.** any of various viscid, amorphous exudations from plants, hardening on exposure to air, and soluble in, or forming a viscid mass with, water. **2.** any of various similar exudations, as resin, kino, etc. **3.** a preparation of such a substance, as for use in the arts, etc. **4.** Also, **gumtree.** any tree or shrub of the myrtaceous genus *Eucalyptus,* almost entirely Australian but for very few tropical species in New Guinea and other nearby islands, some yielding eucalyptus oil and some hardwood timber, and bearing gumnuts as fruits; eucalyptus. **5.** Also, **gumwood.** the wood of any such tree or shrub. **6.** mucilage; glue. **7.** →**chewing gum. 8.** →**gumdrop.** *–v.t.* **9.** to smear, stiffen, or stick together with gum. **10.** to clog with or as with some gummy substance (oft. fol. by *up*). **11. gum up the works,** to interfere with or spoil something. *–v.i.* **12.** to exude or form gum. **13.** to become gummy; become clogged with a substance. [ME *gomme,* from OF, from var. of L *gummi,* from Gk *kómmi*]

**gum**[2] /gʌm/, *n.* (*oft. pl.*) the firm, fleshy tissue covering the alveolar parts of either jaw and enveloping the bases of the teeth. [ME *gome,* OE *gōma* palate, inside of the mouth; akin to Icel. *gōmr,* G *Gaumen* palate]

**gum**[3] /gʌm/, *interj. Brit.* (a mild oath; a euphemism for *God*): *by gum.*

**gum**[4] /gʌm/, *n.* (in mining) coal dust that is produced by a coal-cutting machine. – **gummer,** *n.* – **gumming,** *n.*

**gum ammoniac** /– əˈmoʊniæk/, *n.* a medicinal gum resin from the umbelliferous plant, *Dorema ammoniacum,* of Persia, etc.

**gum arabic** /– ˈærəbɪk/, *n.* a gum obtained from *Acacia senegal* and other species of acacia, used in calico printing in making mucilage, ink, and the like, in medicine, etc.

**Gumatj** /ˈgʊmʌtʃ/, *n.* an Australian Aboriginal language still in tribal use in the Yirrkala district of the Northern Territory.

**gum benzoin** /gʌm ˈbɛnzoɪn/, *n.* →**benzoin** (def. 1). Also, **gum benjamin.**

**gumbo** /ˈgʌmboʊ/, *n., pl.* **-bos.** *Chiefly U.S.* **1.** →**okra. 2.** soup or stew, usu. containing chicken, thickened with okra pods. **3.** a silty soil, chiefly in the southern and western U.S., becoming very sticky when wet. Also, **gombo.** [from Angolan name]

**gumboil** /ˈgʌmbɔɪl/, *n.* a small abscess on the gum.

**gumboot** /ˈgʌmbut/, *n.* a rubber boot reaching to the knee or thigh.

**gumbotil** /ˈgʌmbətl/, *n.* a sticky clay formed by the thorough weathering of glacial drift, the thickness of the clay furnishing means for comparing relative lengths of interglacial ages. [GUMBO + *-til,* form of TILL[4]]

**gum-digger** /ˈgʌm-dɪgə/, *n.* **1.** *N.Z.* one who is employed digging up fossilised kauri gum. **2.** *Colloq.* a dentist. – **gum-digging,** *n.*

**gumdrop** /ˈgʌmdrɒp/, *n.* a hard gelatinous sweet.

**gumfield** /ˈgʌmfild/, *n.* an area of land on the North Island of New Zealand, where fossilised kauri gum is found.

**gum-hole** /ˈgʌm-hoʊl/, *n. N.Z.* the hole sunk by a gum-digger (def. 1).

**gumland** /ˈgʌmlænd/, *n. N.Z.* poor quality land in which kauri gum may be found.

**gum leaf** /ˈgʌm lif/, *n.* the leaf of the eucalyptus.

**gumleaf band** /ˈgʌmlif bænd/, *n.* a band in which each player uses a gumleaf held against the lips as a resonator, in a fashion similar to the playing of a kazoo.

**gumma** /ˈgʌmə/, *n., pl.* **gummas, gummata** /ˈgʌmətə/. the rubbery, tumour-like lesion of tertiary syphilis. [NL, from L *gummi* GUM[1]]

**gummatous** /ˈgʌmətəs/, *adj.* **1.** of the nature of or resembling a gumma. **2.** pertaining to a gumma.

**gummite** /ˈgʌmaɪt/, *n.* a yellow to red alteration product of pitchblende, having a greasy lustre, and occurring in gumlike masses; a minor ore of uranium.

**gummosis** /gʌˈmoʊsəs/, *n.* an abnormal condition of certain plants such as the cherry, plum, sugar cane, cotton, etc., which causes the excessive formation of gum. [NL, from L *gumm(i)* + -OSIS. See GUM[1]]

**gummous** /ˈgʌməs/, *adj.* consisting of or resembling gum; gummy.

**gummy**[1] /ˈgʌmi/, *adj.,* **-mier, -miest,** *n., pl.* **-mies.** *–adj.* **1.** of the nature of gum; viscid. **2.** covered with or clogged by

i = peat ɪ = pit ɛ = pet æ = pat a = part ɒ = pot ʌ = putt ɔ = port ʊ = put u = pool ɜ = pert ə = apart aɪ = buy eɪ = bay ɔɪ = boy aʊ = how oʊ = hoe ɪə = here ɛə = hair ʊə = tour g = give θ = thin ð = then ʃ = show ʒ = measure tʃ = choke dʒ = joke ŋ = sing j = you õ = Fr. bon

gum or sticky matter. **3.** exuding gum. *–n.* **4.** *(pl.) Colloq.* gumboots.

**gummy**[2] /ˈgʌmi/, *adj.*, **-mier, -miest,** *n., pl.* **-mies.** *–adj.* **1.** showing the gums (**gum**[2]): *a gummy smile.* *–n.* **2.** *Colloq.* an old toothless sheep.

**gummy shark** /ˈ– ʃak/, *n.* a slender, harmless, Australian shark, *Mustelus antarcticus.*

**gumnut** /ˈgʌmnʌt/, *n.* the woody, inedible, ripe capsule of the eucalyptus.

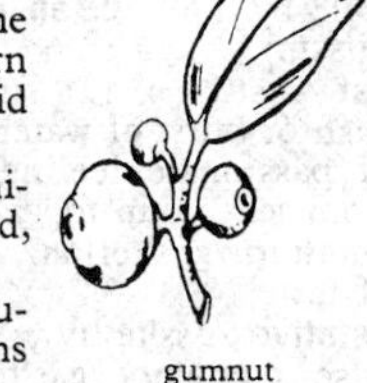
gumnut

**gum plant** /ˈgʌm plænt/, *n.* a plant of the genus *Grindelia* native to the western United States, covered with a viscid secretion.

**gumption** /ˈgʌmpʃən/, *n. Colloq.* **1.** initiative; resourcefulness. **2.** shrewd, practical common sense. [orig. Scot.]

**gum resin** /gʌm ˈrɛzən/, *n.* a plant exudation consisting of a mixture of gums and resins, as bdellium, gamboge, etc.

**gum-shield** /ˈgʌm-ʃild/, *n.* a soft pad which a boxer places in his mouth to protect the gums and teeth.

**gumshoe** /ˈgʌmʃu/, *n., v.,* **-shoed, -shoeing.** *–n.* **1.** one of a pair of galoshes, rubber overshoe. **2.** *U.S. Colloq.* **a.** one who goes about softly, as if wearing rubber shoes. **b.** a policeman or detective. *–v.i.* **3.** *U.S. Colloq.* to go softly as if wearing rubber shoes; move or act stealthily.

**gum silk** /ˈgʌm sɪlk/, *n.* silk which still retains its natural gum.

**gum-spear** /ˈgʌm-spɪə/, *n. N.Z.* long metal spear for probing ground for kauri gum.

**gumsucker** /ˈgʌmsʌkə/, *n. Colloq.* a native of or resident in Victoria.

**gum tips** /ˈgʌm tɪps/, *n. pl.* the colourful new growth of the eucalyptus.

**gum tree** /ˈ– tri/, *n.* **1.** →**gum**[1] (def. 4). **2.** any of various other gum-yielding trees, as the sweet gum and the sapodilla. **3. up a gum tree,** *Colloq.* **a.** in difficulties; in a predicament. **b.** completely baffled.

**gumwood** /ˈgʌmwʊd/, *n.* **1.** →**gum**[1] (def. 5). **2.** the wood of any of the gum trees of western US, as sweet gum.

**gun** /gʌn/, *n., v.,* **gunned, gunning,** *adj.* *–n.* **1.** a metallic tube, with its stock or carriage and attachments, from which heavy missiles are thrown by the force of an explosive; a piece of ordnance. **2.** any portable firearm, as a rifle, revolver, etc. **3.** a long-barrelled cannon, having a flat trajectory. **4.** any similar device for projecting something: *an airgun, cement gun.* **5.** a member of a shooting party. **6.** *Colloq.* a champion, esp. in shearing. **7.** *Colloq.* a large surfboat for riding big waves. **8. beat (jump) the gun, a.** in a race, to begin before the starting gun has fired. **b.** to begin prematurely. **9. carry** or **hold (big) guns,** to be in a powerful or strong position. **10. go great guns,** to have a period of success at something. **11. have the guns for,** to have the ability to do something. **12. jump the gun, a.** to make a false start in a race. **b.** to begin prematurely; be overeager. **13. stick to one's guns,** to maintain one's position in an argument, etc., against opposition. *–v.i.* **14.** to hunt with a gun. **15.** to shoot with a gun. *–v.t.* **16.** to shoot with a gun (oft. fol. by *down*). **17.** *Aeron. Colloq.* to cause to increase in speed very quickly. **18.** to feed fuel to, suddenly and quickly: *to gun an engine.* **19. gun for,** *Colloq.* to seek (a person) with the intention to harm or kill. *–adj.* **20.** *Colloq.* of or pertaining to one who is expert, esp. in shearing: *a gun shearer.* [ME *gunne, gonne,* apparently short for *Gunilda* (L), *gonnyld* (ME), name for engine of war, from Scand.; cf. Icel. *Gunna,* short for *Gunnhildr,* woman's name]

**gunboat** /ˈgʌnboʊt/, *n.* a small vessel of light draught, carrying mounted guns.

**gunboat diplomacy** /– dəˈploʊməsi/, *n.* diplomacy or foreign affairs in conjunction with the use or threat of military force.

**guncarriage** /ˈgʌnkærɪdʒ/, *n.* the carriage or structure on which a gun is mounted, and from which it is fired.

**gun-chain** /ˈgʌn-tʃeɪn/, *n.* the most expert gang working on the chain (def. 12a) in a meatworks.

**guncotton** /ˈgʌnkɒtn/, *n.* a highly explosive cellulose nitrate, made by digesting clean cotton in a mixture of one part nitric acid and three parts sulphuric acid.

**gundabluey** /gʌndəˈblui/, *n.* a species of wattle, *Acacia victoriae,* of inland Australia.

**gun dog** /ˈgʌn dɒg/, *n.* a trained dog which accompanies hunters when they shoot game, esp. game birds.

**gundy** /ˈgʌndi/, *n.* →**gunyah.** Also, **goondie.** [Aboriginal]

**Gundy** /ˈgʌndi/, *n. in the phrases* **gone to Gundy** and **no good to Gundy,** *Colloq.* unsatisfactory; broken; beyond repair; ruined. [? from Aboriginal *gundy, goondie* GUNYAH]

**gunfight** /ˈgʌnfaɪt/, *n. Orig. U.S.* a duel or fight between men armed with guns.

**gunfighter** /ˈgʌnfaɪtə/, *n. U.S.* a person, esp in the U.S. frontier days, who was noted for his prowess in gunfights.

**gunfire** /ˈgʌnfaɪə/, *n.* the firing of a gun or guns.

**gunflint** /ˈgʌnflɪnt/, *n.* the flint in a flintlock.

**gung ho** /gʌŋ ˈhoʊ/, *adj.* intemperately and naively enthusiastic. [pidgin English, from Mandarin Chinese *kung* work + *ho* together]

**gunk** /gʌŋk/, *n. Colloq.* **1.** *(derog.)* a food judged to be bad or inappropriate, esp. oversweet and cloying. **2.** rubbish. **3.** nonsense. Also, **guk.**

**gunlock** /ˈgʌnlɒk/, *n.* the mechanism of a firearm by which the charge is exploded.

**gunman** /ˈgʌnmən/, *n., pl.* **-men. 1.** a man armed with, or expert with, a gun, esp. one ready to use a gun unlawfully. **2.** one who makes guns.

**gunmetal** /ˈgʌnmɛtl/, *n.* **1.** any of various alloys or metallic substances with a dark grey or blackish colour or finish, used for chains, belt buckles, etc. **2.** a dark grey with bluish or purplish tinge. **3.** a bronze formerly much employed for making cannons.

**gun-moll** /ˈgʌn-mɒl/, *n.* →**moll**[1].

**gunnel**[1] /ˈgʌnəl/, *n.* any of certain elongate blennies (fishes) of the family Pholidae, esp. the butterfish, *Pholis gunnellus,* of the northern Atlantic. [orig. uncert.]

**gunnel**[2] /ˈgʌnəl/, *n.* →**gunwale.**

**gunner** /ˈgʌnə/, *n.* **1.** one who works a gun or cannon. **2.** *Mil.* **a.** a private in the artillery. **b.** any artilleryman. **3.** *Navy.* a warrant officer esp. one with responsibilities in gunnery and gunnery training.

**gunnery** /ˈgʌnəri/, *n.* **1.** the art and science of constructing and managing guns, esp. large guns. **2.** the firing of guns. **3.** guns collectively.

**gunnie**[1] /ˈgʌni/, *n. Prison Colloq.* an armed criminal.

**gunnie**[2] /ˈgʌni/, *n.* a girl who is free with sexual favours. [short for GUN-MOLL]

**gunning** /ˈgʌnɪŋ/, *n.* **1.** the act, practice, or art of shooting with guns. **2.** hunting of game with guns.

**Gunn's bandicoot** /ˌgʌnz ˈbændikut/, *n.* a long-nosed bandicoot, *Perameles gunnii,* found in Tasmania and south-eastern Victoria. Also, **Tasmanian barred bandicoot.** [named after Ronald *Gunn,* 1805-1881, naturalist]

**gunny** /ˈgʌni/, *n., pl.* **-nies. 1.** a strong, coarse material made commonly from jute, used for sacking, etc. **2.** Also, **gunnybag, gunnysack.** a bag or sack made of this material. **3.** *Mining.* mine cavity from which ore has been removed. [Hind. *gōni* sack]

**gunpaper** /ˈgʌnpeɪpə/, *n. Mil.* a type of paper treated with nitric acid so that it has a composition similar to that of guncotton.

**gunplay** /ˈgʌnpleɪ/, *n.* gunfire, esp. when occurring in a shoot-out.

**gunport** /ˈgʌnpɔt/, *n.* an aperture in a ship, aircraft, armoured vehicle, fortification, etc., through which a gun can be fired.

**gunpowder** /ˈgʌnpaʊdə/, *n.* **1.** an explosive mixture of saltpetre (potassium nitrate), sulphur, and charcoal, used esp. in gunnery. **2.** a fine variety of green China tea, each leaf of which is rolled into a little ball.

**gunroom** /ˈgʌnrum/, *n.* **1.** a room in which guns are kept. **2.** *Navy.* a mess, for the use of junior naval officers.

**gun-running** /ˈgʌn-rʌnɪŋ/, *n.* the smuggling of guns, etc., into a country. – **gun-runner,** *n.*

**gun shearer** /gʌn ˈʃɪərə/, *n.* an expert shearer, often the best in the shed.

**gunshot** /ˈgʌnʃɒt/, *n.* **1.** a shot fired from a gun. **2.** the range of a gun: *out of gunshot.* **3.** the shooting of a gun. *–adj.* **4.**

made by a gunshot.

**gun-shy** /ˈgʌn-ʃaɪ/, *adj.* **1.** frightened by the use of guns. **2.** nervous of conflict; timid.

**gunslinger** /ˈgʌnslɪŋə/, *n. U.S.* →**gunfighter.**

**gunsmith** /ˈgʌnsmɪθ/, *n.* one who makes or repairs firearms.

**gunstock** /ˈgʌnstɒk/, *n.* **1.** the rear wooden or metal handle or support of a gun, to which the barrel and mechanism are fixed. **2.** a support for a cannon on board a ship.

**Gunter's chain** /ˌgʌntəz ˈtʃeɪn/, *n.* See **chain** (def. 9). [named after Edmund *Gunter,* 1581-1626, English mathematician]

**gunwale** /ˈgʌnəl/, *n.* **1.** the upper edge of a vessel's or boat's side. **2.** the uppermost wale of a ship, next below the bulwarks. Also, **gunnel.** [GUN + *wale* a plank; so called because guns were set upon it]

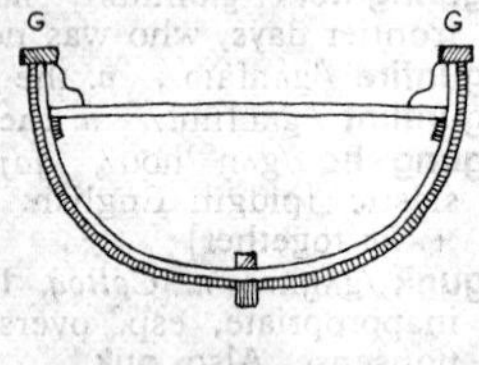

G, gunwale;

**Gunwinggu** /gʊnˈwɪŋgu/, *n.* an Australian Aboriginal language used by about 200 speakers, mainly at Oenpelli, Northern Territory.

**gunyah** /ˈgʌnjə/, *n.* **1.** an Aborigine's hut made of boughs and bark; humpy; mia-mia; wurley. Also, **gunya.** **2.** a small rough hut or shelter in the bush. [Aboriginal]

gunyah

**gunyang** /ˈgʌnjæŋ/, *n.*→**kangaroo apple.** [Aboriginal]

**gup** /gʌp/, *n.* (usu. a derogatory term used by Aborigines to refer to whites) fool; idiot.

**guppy** /ˈgʌpi/, *n., pl.* **-pies.** a viviparous top minnow, *Lebistes reticulatus,* of the family Poeciliidae, common in home aquariums.

**gurgitation** /gɜdʒəˈteɪʃən/, *n.* surging rise and fall; ebullient motion, as of water. [LL *gurgitātus,* pp., engulfed + -ION]

**gurgle** /ˈgɜgəl/, *v.,* **-gled, -gling,** *n.* *–v.i.* **1.** to flow in a broken, irregular, noisy current: *water gurgles from a bottle.* **2.** to make a sound as of water doing this (often used of birds or of human beings). *–v.t.* **3.** to utter with a gurgling sound. *–n.* **4.** the act or noise of gurgling. [? imitative. Cf. G *gurgeln* GARGLE] – **gurglingly,** *adv.*

**gurgler** /ˈgɜglə/, *n. Colloq.* **1.** a plughole. **2. down the gurgler,** ruined; irretrievably lost or destroyed.

**Gurindji** /gʊˈrɪndʒi/, *n.* an Australian Aboriginal language of the Victoria River area near Wave Hill, Northern Territory.

**gurnard** /ˈgɜnəd/, *n., pl.* **-nards,** (*esp. collectively*) **-nard. 1.** any of various marine acanthopterygian fishes of the family Triglidae, as the **red gurnard,** *Currupiscus kumu,* having a spiny head with mailed cheeks, and three pairs of free, finger-like pectoral rays. **2.** any of various similar fishes. See **flying gurnard.** [ME, from OF *gornard,* probably lit., grunter, from Pr. *gourgna* grunt, from L *grunnire* grunt]

**guru** /ˈgʊru, ˈguru/, *n.* **1.** (in Hinduism) a preceptor and spiritual guide. **2.** *Colloq.* an influential teacher or mentor. [Hindi]

**gush** /gʌʃ/, *v.i.* **1.** to issue with force, as a fluid escaping from confinement; flow suddenly and copiously. **2.** *Colloq.* to express oneself extravagantly or emotionally; talk effusively. **3.** to have a copious flow of something, as of blood, tears, etc. *–v.t.* **4.** to emit suddenly, forcibly, or copiously. *–n.* **5.** a sudden and copious emission of a fluid. **6.** the fluid emitted. **7.** gushing or effusive language. [ME *gusche,* ? from *gus-* (see GUST) + *-k* suffix. Cf. Icel. *gusa*] – **gushingly,** *adv.*

**gusher** /ˈgʌʃə/, *n.* **1.** *Colloq.* a person who gushes. **2.** a flowing oilwell, usu. of large capacity.

**gushy** /ˈgʌʃi/, *adj.,* **gushier, gushiest.** *Colloq.* given to or marked by gush or effusiveness. – **gushiness,** *n.*

**gusset** /ˈgʌsət/, *n.* **1.** an angular piece of material inserted in a garment to strengthen, enlarge or give freedom of movement to some part of it. **2.** a metal bracket for strengthening a structure at a joint or angle. **3.** *Armour.* **a.** a mail strip in the armpit region sewn to cloth sleeves. **b.** a narrow articulated plate of the breastplate adjacent to the arm. *–v.t.* **4.** to provide with a gusset. [ME, from OF *gousset,* from *gousse* pod, husk]

**gussie** /ˈgʌsi/, *n. Colloq.* an effeminate man. [diminutive of *Augustus*]

**gussies** /ˈgʌsiz/, *n.pl. Colloq.* frilly pants for women. Also, **gorgeous gussies.** [from *Gussy* Moran, American tennis player c. 1954]

**gussy** /ˈgʌsi/, *v.,* **gussied, gussying.** *–v.i.* **1.** to dress smartly (fol. by *up*). **2. all gussied up,** smartly dressed. [? var. of GUSSIE]

**gust** /gʌst/, *n.* **1.** a sudden, strong blast of wind. **2.** a sudden rush or burst of water, fire, smoke, sound, etc. **3.** an outburst of passionate feeling. [Scand.; cf. Icel. *gustr* a gust, blast, from *gus-,* akin to *gjōsa, gusa* gush]

**gustation** /gʌsˈteɪʃən/, *n.* **1.** the act of tasting. **2.** the faculty of taste.

**gustative** /gʌsˈteɪtɪv/, *adj.* of or pertaining to taste or tasting. Also, **gustatory** /gʌsˈteɪtəri, -tri/.

**gusto** /ˈgʌstoʊ/, *n.* **1.** keen relish or hearty enjoyment, as in eating, drinking, or in action or speech generally: *to tell a story with gusto.* **2.** individual taste or liking. [It., from L *gustus* taste, relish]

**gusty** /ˈgʌsti/, *adj.,* **gustier, gustiest. 1.** blowing or coming in gusts, as wind, rain, storms, etc. **2.** affected or marked by gusts of wind, etc.: *gusty day.* **3.** occurring or characterised by sudden bursts or outbursts, as sound, laughter, etc. – **gustily,** *adv.* – **gustiness,** *n.*

**gut** /gʌt/, *n., v.,* **gutted, gutting.** *–n.* **1.** the alimentary canal between the pylorus and the anus, or some portion of it. **2.** (*pl.*) the bowels or entrails. **3.** (*pl.*) *Colloq.* the stomach or abdomen. **4.** (*pl.*) *Colloq.* courage; stamina; endurance: *to have guts.* **5.** (*pl.*) *Colloq.* essential information: *the guts of the matter.* **6.** (*pl.*) *Colloq.* (in two-up) wagered money in the centre of the ring. **7.** the substance forming the case of the intestine; intestinal tissue or fibre: *sheep's gut.* **8.** a preparation of the intestines of an animal used for various purposes, as for violin strings, tennis rackets, fishing lines, etc. **9.** the silken substance taken from a silkworm killed when about to spin its cocoon, used in making snells for fishhooks. **10.** a narrow passage, as a channel of water or a defile between hills. **11.** a flexible driving shaft to relay power to a tool for machine shearing. **12.** (*pl.*) *Colloq.* the essential parts or contents: *let me get to the guts of the motor.* **13.** (*pl.*) **hate (someone's) guts,** *Colloq.* to loath or detest (someone). **14.** (*pl.*) **have someone's guts for garters,** *Colloq.* to exact revenge on someone. **15.** (*pl.*) **good guts,** *Colloq.* the news; correct information. **16.** (*pl.*) **work one's guts out,** *Colloq.* to work excessively hard. *–v.t.* **17.** to take out the guts or entrails of; disembowel. **18.** to plunder of contents. **19.** to destroy the interior of: *fire gutted the building.* *–adj.* **20.** of or pertaining to feelings, emotion, intuition: *a gut response.* **21.** of or pertaining to that which may engender feeling, emotion, etc.: *a gut issue.* [ME; OE *guttas,* pl., akin to *gēotan* pour]

**gutbucket** /ˈgʌtbʌkət/, *n.* a primitive style of jazz. – **gutbucket,** *adj.*

**gutful** /ˈgʌtfʊl/, *n. Colloq.* (*derog.*) more than enough: *I've had a gutful of this.* Also, (*esp. N.Z.*) **gutsful.**

**Guthrie test** /ˈgʌθri test/, *n.* a blood test in newborn babies to detect phenylketonuria; PKU test.

**gutless** /ˈgʌtləs/, *adj.* **1.** cowardly. **2.** lacking in power, esp. of a car, motor etc. **3. a gutless wonder,** *Colloq.* a person or thing whose performance does not live up to expectation.

**gutrot** /ˈgʌtrɒt/, *n. Colloq.* unhealthy food or drink, esp. any cheap alcoholic drink.

**guts** /gʌts/, *Colloq.* *–n.* **1.** one greedy for food; a glutton. *–v.i.* **2.** to cram (oneself) with food. [pl. GUT]

**gutser** /ˈgʌtsə/, *n. Colloq.* **1.** a person who eats too much. Also, **gutzer. 2. come a gutser, a.** to fall over. **b.** to fail as a result of an error of judgment.

**gutsy** /ˈgʌtsi/, *adj. Colloq.* **1.** full of courage; full of guts. **2.** warmly wholehearted; unreserved. **3.** strong, full-bodied: *a gutsy wine.* **4.** greedy; gluttonous.

**gutta** /ˈgʌtə/, *n., pl.* **guttae** /ˈgʌti/. **1.** a drop, or something resembling one. **2.** *Archit.* one of a series of pendent ornaments, generally in the form of a frustum of a cone, attached to the underside of the mutules, etc., of the Doric entablature. [L: a drop]

**gutta balata** /– bəˈlatə/, *n.* →**balata** (def. 1).

**gutta-percha** /gʌtə-ˈpɜtʃə/, *n.* the coagulated milky juice, nearly white when pure, of various Malaysian trees of the family Sapotaceae, esp. *Palaquium gutta,* variously used in the arts, medicine, and manufacturing, as for insulating electric wires. [Malay *getah* gum, balsam + *percha* kind of tree producing the substance]

**gutter** /ˈgʌtə/, *n.* **1.** a channel at the side (or in the middle) of a road or street, for leading off surface water. **2.** any channel, trough, or the like for carrying off fluid. **3.** Also, **guttering.** a channel at the eaves or on the roof of a building, for carrying off rainwater. **4.** a furrow or channel made by running water. **5.** the abode or resort of the lowest class of persons in the community: *the language of the gutter.* **6.** *Print.* the inner margin of a page. *–v.i.* **7.** to flow in streams. **8.** to form gutters, as water does. **9.** (of a lighted candle) to melt away rapidly and irregularly. *–v.t.* **10.** to make gutters in; channel. **11.** to furnish with a gutter or gutters: *to gutter a house or shed.* [ME *goter,* from OF *goutiere,* from L *gutta* a drop] – **gutterlike,** *adj.* – **guttery,** *adj.*

**guttercrawl** /ˈgʌtəkrɔl/, *v.i.* to drive a car slowly along the kerb or gutter, in order to pick up a prostitute, or a young girl for the purposes of sex.

**guttering** /ˈgʌtərɪŋ/, *n.* →**gutter** (def. 3).

**guttersnipe** /ˈgʌtəsnaɪp/, *n.* a street urchin; gamin.

**guttural** /ˈgʌtərəl/, *adj.* **1.** pertaining to the throat. **2.** harsh; throaty. **3.** pertaining to sounds articulated in the back of the mouth, esp. the velars. *–n.* **4.** a guttural sound. [NL *gutturālis,* from L *guttur* throat] – **gutturally,** *adv.* – **gutturalness,** *n.*

**Guv** /gʌv/, *n.* →**Gov.** Also, **guv.**

**guy**[1] /gaɪ/, *n., v.,* **guyed, guying.** *–n.* **1.** *Colloq.* a fellow or man: *guys and dolls.* **2.** *Colloq.* →**boyfriend.** **3.** a person of grotesque appearance; a person wearing ridiculous clothes. **4.** *Brit.* a grotesque effigy of Guy Fawkes, carried about and burnt on Guy Fawkes Day. **5. the good (bad) guys,** *Colloq.* the heroes (villains). *–v.t.* **6.** *Colloq.* to jeer at or make fun of; ridicule. [from *Guy* Fawkes, the leader of the Gunpowder Plot to assassinate the King in Parliament, London, 5 Nov., 1605]

**guy**[2] /gaɪ/, *n., v.,* **guyed, guying.** *–n.* **1.** a rope or appliance used to guide and steady a thing being hoisted or lowered, or to secure anything liable to shift its position. *–v.t.* **2.** to guide, steady, or secure with a guy or guys. [ME *gye,* from OF *guie* a guide, from *guier* GUIDE]

**Guyana** /giˈanə/, *n.* a country on the north-eastern coast of South America.

**guyver** /ˈgaɪvə/, *n. Colloq.* affected talk and manner; foolish talk or nonsense; ingratiating behaviour. Also, **gyver, guiver, givor, givo, gyvo, guivo.**

**guzinter** /gəˈzɪntə/, *n. Colloq.* a school-teacher. [from the tables learnt by rote, 'one *guzinter* two, two *guzinter* four', etc.]

**guzzle** /ˈgʌzəl/, *v.,* **-zled, -zling.** *–v.t.* **1.** to drink (or sometimes eat) frequently and greedily: *they sat there all evening guzzling their beer.* *–v.i.* **2.** to drink (or eat) in such a manner. – **guzzler,** *n.*

**guzzle-guts** /ˈgʌzəl-gʌts/, *n. Colloq.* a person who eats and drinks to excess, or in a disgusting and noisy manner.

**gwardar** /ˈgwadə/, *n.* a venomous snake, *Pseudonaja nuchalis,* of western and central Australia, related to the common brown snake.

**gy,** grey.

**gybe** /dʒaɪb/, *v.,* **gybed, gybing,** *n.* →**jibe**[1].

**gym** /dʒɪm/, *n.* **1.** →**gymnasium.** **2.** →**gymnastics.**

**Gymea lily** /ˌgaɪmiə ˈlɪli/, *n.* a plant of eastern Australia, *Doryanthes excelsa,* with a tall flower stem bearing a head of red flowers. Also, **giant lily.**

**gymkhana** /dʒɪmˈkanə/, *n.* **1.** a horseriding event featuring games and novelty contests. **2.** a festival featuring gymnastics and athletic showmanship. **3.** Also, **motorkhana.** a series of motoring events designed to test skill and judgment of drivers. [Hind. *gendkhāna,* lit., ball house, raquet-court]

**gymnasia** /dʒɪmˈneɪziə/, *n.* a plural form of **gymnasium.**

**gymnasiarch** /dʒɪmˈneɪziak/, *n.* a magistrate who superintended the gymnasia and certain public games in ancient Athens. [L *gymnasiarchus,* from Gk *gymnasíarchos*]

**gymnasium** /dʒɪmˈneɪziəm/, *n., pl.,* **-siums, -sia** /-ziə/. **1.** a building or room equipped with facilities for gymnastics and sport. **2.** a place where Greek youths met for exercise and discussion. [L, from Gk *gymnásion*]

**gymnast** /ˈdʒɪmnæst, -nəst/, *n.* one trained and skilled in, or a teacher of, gymnastics. [Gk *gymnastḗs* trainer of athletes]

**gymnastic** /dʒɪmˈnæstɪk/, *adj.* pertaining to exercises which develop flexibility, strength, and agility. – **gymnastically,** *adv.*

**gymnastics** /dʒɪmˈnæstɪks/, *n.* **1.** (*construed as pl.*) gymnastic exercises. **2.** (*construed as sing.*) the practice or art of gymnastic exercises.

**gymnosperm** /ˈdʒɪmnoʊˌspɜm/, *n.* a plant having its seeds exposed or naked, not enclosed in an ovary (opposed to *angiosperm*). [NL *gymnospermus,* from Gk *gymnóspermos*]

**gymnospermous** /dʒɪmnoʊˈspɜməs/, *adj.* of the gymnosperm class; having naked seeds.

**gympie nettle** /ˈgɪmpi nɛtl/, *n.* a small tree, *Dendrocnide moroides,* of tropical eastern Australia, bearing stinging hairs and irritant pollen.

**gym-shoe** /ˈdʒɪm-ʃu/, *n.* →**sandshoe.**

**gym-tunic** /ˈdʒɪm-tjunɪk/, *n.* →**sports uniform.**

**gyn-,** variant of **gyno-,** occurring before vowels, as in *gynarchy.*

**gynaecium** /dʒaɪˈnisiəm/, *n., pl.* **-cia** /-siə/. →**gynoecium.** Also, **gynaeceum.**

**gynaecocracy** /dʒaɪnəˈkɒkrəsi/, *n., pl.* **-cies.** political and social leadership by women. Also, *U.S.,* **gynecocracy.** [Gk *gynaikokratía*]

**gynaecologist** /gaɪnəˈkɒlədʒəst/, *n.* a doctor who specialises in women's diseases. Also, *U.S.,* **gynecologist.**

**gynaecology** /gaɪnəˈkɒlədʒi/, *n.* that department of medical science which deals with the functions and diseases peculiar to women. Also, *U.S.* **gynecology.** [Gk *gynaiko-* (combining form of *gynḗ* woman) + -LOGY] – **gynaecological** /gaɪnəkəˈlɒdʒɪkəl/, *adj.*

**gynaecomorphous** /gaɪnəkoʊˈmɔfəs/, *adj.* having the form, appearance, or attributes of a female. Also, *U.S.,* **gynecomorphous.** [Gk *gynaikómorphos* in the shape of a woman]

**gynandromorph** /dʒaɪˈnændrəmɔf/, *n.* an organism with characteristics of both sexes. [Gk *gýnandros* of doubtful sex + -MORPH] – **gynandromorphic** /dʒaɪˌnændrəˈmɔfɪk/, **gynandromorphous** /dʒaɪˌnændrəˈmɔfəs/, *adj.* – **gynandromorphism** /dʒaɪˌnændrəˈmɔfɪzəm/, **gynandromorphy,** *n.*

**gynandrous** /dʒaɪˈnændrəs, dʒə-/, *adj.* having the stamens borne on the pistil and united in a column, as in orchids. [Gk *gýnandros* of doubtful sex]

**gynarchy** /ˈdʒaɪnaki/, *n., pl.* **-chies.** government by a woman or women.

**gynecium** /dʒaɪˈnisiəm/, *n., pl.* **-cia** /-siə/. *Chiefly U.S.* →**gynoecium.**

**gyniatrics** /dʒaɪniˈætrɪks/, *n.* the treatment of diseases peculiar to women. [Gk *gynḗ* woman + *iātrikós* of medicine; see -ICS]

**gyno-,** a word element meaning 'woman', 'female', as in *gynogenic.* Also, **gyn-.** [Gk, combining form of *gynḗ* woman]

**gynobasic** /dʒaɪnoʊˈbeɪsɪk/, *adj.* of a style in a flower which extends to the base of a gynoecium between the carpels.

**gynoecium** /dʒaɪˈnisiəm/, *n., pl.* **-cia** /-siə/. the pistil, or the pistils collectively, of a flower. Also, **gynaeceum, gynaecium, gynecium.** [NL, from *gyn-* GYN- + Gk *oikíon* house]

**gynogenic** /dʒaɪnəˈdʒɛnɪk/, *adj.* female-producing or feminising (opposed to *androgenic*).

**gynophobia** /gaɪnəˈfoʊbiə/, *n.* the fear of women.

**gynophore** /ˈdʒaɪnəfɔ/, *n.* the elongated pedicel or stalk bearing the pistil in some flowers.

**-gynous,** **1.** an adjective combining form referring to the female sex, as in *androgynous.* **2.** a suffix meaning 'woman'. [Gk *-gynos,* from *gynḗ* woman]

**gyp**[1] /dʒɪp/, *v.,* **gypped, gypping,** *n. Colloq.* *–v.t.* **1.** to swindle; cheat; defraud or rob by some sharp practice. **2.** to obtain by swindling or cheating; steal. *–n.* **3.** a swindle. **4.** a swindler or cheat. Also, **gip.** [orig. uncert.] – **gypper,** *n.*

**gyp**[2] /dʒɪp/, *n.* →**gip**[2].

**gyppo** /ˈdʒɪpoʊ/, *n., adj. Colloq.* →**Egyptian.** Also, **gippo.**

**gypsophila** /dʒɪpˈsɒfələ/, *n.* any of the genus *Gypsophila* of slender, graceful herbs, chiefly Mediterranean, allied to the pinks and having small panicled flowers. [NL, from Gk *gýpso(s)* chalk + *phíla,* neut. pl. of *phílos,* adj., fond of]

**gypster** /ˈdʒɪpstə/, *n. Colloq.* a con man. Also, **gipster.**

**gypsum** /ˈdʒɪpsəm/, *n.* a very common mineral, hydrated calcium sulphate, $CaSO_4.2H_2O$, occurring in crystals and in masses, soft enough to be scratched by the fingernail, used to make plaster of Paris, as an ornamental material, as a fertiliser, etc. [L, from Gk *gýpsos* chalk, gypsum]

**gypsy** /ˈdʒɪpsi/, *n., pl.* **-sies,** *adj.* →**gipsy.**

**gypsy moth** /ˈ– mɒθ/, *n.* →**gipsy moth.**

**gypsy sauce** /– ˈsɔs/, *n.* →**zingara sauce.**

**gypsywort** /ˈdʒɪpsiwɜt/, *n.* →**gipsywort.**

**gyrate** /dʒaɪˈreɪt/, *v.,* **-rated, -rating;** /ˈdʒaɪrət/, *adj.* –*v.i.* **1.** to move in a circle or spiral, or round a fixed point; whirl. –*adj.* **2.** *Zool.* having convolutions. [L *gyrātus,* pp., wheeled round, turned]

**gyration** /dʒaɪˈreɪʃən/, *n.* the act of gyrating; circular or spiral motion; revolution; rotation; whirling.

**gyratory** /dʒaɪˈreɪtəri, ˈdʒaɪrətri/, *adj.* moving in a circle or spiral; gyrating.

**gyratory crusher** /– ˈkrʌʃə/, *n.* →**cone crusher.**

**gyre** /ˈdʒaɪə/, *n.* **1.** a ring or circle. **2.** a circular course or motion.

**gyrfalcon** /ˈdʒɜfælkən, -fɔl-/, *n.* any of various large arctic and subarctic falcons, as the **white gyrfalcon,** *Falco rusticolus.* Also, **gerfalcon.** [ME, from OF *gerfaucon;* of Gmc orig.]

**gyro** /ˈdʒaɪroʊ/, *n., pl.* **-ros. 1.** →**gyrocompass. 2.** →**gyroscope.** [short for GYROCOMPASS, GYROSCOPE]

**gyro-,** a word element meaning: **1.** 'ring'; 'circle'. **2.** 'spiral'. [Gk, combining form of *gŷros* ring, circle]

**gyrocompass** /ˈdʒaɪroʊˌkʌmpəs/, *n.* a device used like the ordinary compass for determining directions, but employing a continuously driven gyroscope instead of a magnetised needle or bar, the gyroscope being so mounted that its axis constantly maintains its position with reference to the geographical north, thus dealing with true geographical meridians used in navigation instead of magnetic meridians. Also, **gyroscopic compass.**

**gyrocopter** /ˈdʒaɪroʊˌkɒptə/, *n.* a kind of helicopter, esp. a small, light one-seater.

**gyrofrequency** /dʒaɪroʊˈfrikwənsi/, *n.* →**cyclotron frequency.**

**gyromagnetic ratio** /dʒaɪroʊmægˌnɛtɪk ˈreɪʃioʊ/, *n.* the ratio of the magnetic moment of an atom, nucleus, or particle to its angular momentum.

**gyroplane** /ˈdʒaɪrəpleɪn/, *n.* →**autogyro.**

**gyroscope** /ˈdʒaɪrəskoʊp/, *n.* an apparatus consisting of a rotating wheel so mounted that its axis can turn freely in certain or all directions, and capable of maintaining the same absolute direction in space in spite of movements of the mountings and surrounding parts. It is based on the principle that a body rotating steadily about an axis will tend to resist changes in the direction of the axis, and is used to maintain equilibrium, as in an aeroplane or ship, to determine direction, etc. [F. See GYRO-, -SCOPE] – **gyroscopic** /dʒaɪrəˈskɒpɪk/, *adj.*

gyroscope

**gyroscopic compass** /dʒaɪrəˌskɒpɪk ˈkʌmpəs/, *n.* →**gyrocompass.** Also, **gyrostatic compass.**

**gyrose** /ˈdʒaɪroʊz/, *adj.* marked with wavy lines.

**gyrostabiliser** /dʒaɪroʊˈsteɪbəˌlaɪzə/, *n.* a device for stabilising a seagoing vessel by counteracting its rolling motion from side to side, consisting essentially of a rotating gyroscope weighing about 1 per cent of the displacement of the vessel. Also, **gyrostabilizer.**

**gyrostat** /ˈdʒaɪrəstæt/, *n.* a modification of the gyroscope, consisting of a rotating wheel pivoted within a rigid case.

**gyrostatic** /dʒaɪrəˈstætɪk/, *adj.* pertaining to the gyrostat or to gyrostatics. – **gyrostatically,** *adv.*

**gyrostatics** /dʒaɪrəˈstætɪks/, *n.* the science which deals with the laws of rotating bodies.

**gyrus** /ˈdʒaɪrəs/, *n., pl.* **gyri** /ˈdʒaɪraɪ/. a convolution, esp. of the brain. [L, from Gk *gŷros* ring, circle]

**gyve** /dʒaɪv/, *n., v.,* **gyved, gyving.** –*n.* **1.** (*usu. pl.*) a shackle, esp. for the leg; fetter. –*v.t.* **2.** to shackle. [ME *gives, gyves* (pl.); orig. uncert.]

**gyver** /ˈgaɪvə/, *n.* →**guyver.**

**gyvo** /ˈgaɪvoʊ/, *n.* →**guyver.**

Hh Roman CITY **Hh** Sans Serif MICROGRAMMA *Hh* Script DOVER Hh Decorative VISA

*Although there are numerous typefaces in the world they can be divided into four main classifications. These are:*

*ROMAN or SERIF. This typeface came into being from the technique of the Roman masons who, working in stone, finished off each letter with a serif or small stroke projecting from the top or bottom. This was done to correct any feeling of unevenness or imbalance they may have created in cutting the characters in stone.*

*SANS SERIF (without serif). This typeface is geometric in design and has straight-edged characters and lines of a regular thickness.*

*SCRIPT. Based on the movement of the hand, this typeface is often italicised or slanted, as if drawn by a brush or quill pen.*

*DECORATIVE. Any typeface that exaggerates the characteristics of any of the other three classifications to a degree that places it outside of them.*

*The dictionary entries in this book use a SANS SERIF typeface called Helvetica (set in a bold face for the head words) and a SERIF typeface Plantin (used throughout the body of the entries).*

**H, h** /eɪtʃ/, *n., pl.* **H's** or **Hs, h's** or **hs. 1.** a consonant, the 8th letter of the English alphabet. **2.** (as a symbol) the eighth in a series.

**h, 1.** hour. **2.** *Physics.* Planck's constant.

**h., 1.** harbour. **2.** hard. **3.** hardness. **4.** height. **5.** high. **6.** hour. **7.** hundred. **8.** husband.

**H, 1.** (of pencils) hard. **2.** *Elect.* henry. **3.** hot. **4.** *Chem.* hydrogen. **5.** *Physics.* **a.** intensity of magnetic field. **b.** enthalpy. **6.** heroin. **7.** harbour.

**ha,** hectare.

**ha** /ha/, *interj.* →**hey**[1]. Also, **hah.**

**h.a.,** in the year. [L *hōc annō*]

**Hab.,** *Bible.* Habakkuk.

**habanera** /hæbə'njɛərə/, *n.* a Cuban dance based on two measures in 6/8 time. Also, **havanaise.** [Sp.]

**habeas corpus** /ˌheɪbiəs 'kɔpəs/, *n.* a prerogative writ directed to a person who detains another in custody, commanding him to produce the other person before the court. It is mainly used to test the legality of an imprisonment. [L: you may have the body (the first words of the writ)]

**habendum** /hə'bɛndəm/, *n.* that part of a deed of conveyance which sets out the nature of the estate granted.

**haberdasher** /'hæbədæʃə/, *n.* **1.** a seller of small wares, as buttons, needles, ribbons, etc. **2.** *U.S.* a men's outfitters. [orig. obscure. Cf. AF *hapertas* kind of fabric]

**haberdashery** /'hæbədæʃəri/, *n., pl.* **-ries. 1.** a haberdasher's shop, counter, or section of a department store. **2.** the goods sold there.

**habergeon** /'hæbədʒən/, *n.* **1.** a short hauberk. **2.** any hauberk. Also, **haubergeon.** [ME *haubergeon,* from OF, diminutive of *hauberc* HAUBERK]

**Haber process** /'habə ˌprousɛs/, *n.* an industrial process for preparing ammonia from atmospheric nitrogen, whereby nitrogen is heated with hydrogen under high pressure in the presence of a catalyst; gaseous ammonia being formed according to the equation $N_2 + 3H_2 = 2NH_3$. [named after Fritz *Haber,* 1868-1934, German chemist]

**habile** /'hæbil/, *adj.* skilful; dexterous. [F, from L *habilis* fit, apt]

**habiliment** /hə'bɪləmənt/, *n.* **1.** (*pl.*) clothes or garments, esp. those suited to a particular occasion. **2.** dress; attire. [ME *habylement,* from OF *habillement,* from *habiller* dress, from *habile* (see HABILE)] – **habilimented,** *adj.*

**habit** /'hæbət/, *n.* **1.** a disposition or tendency, constantly shown, to act in a certain way. **2.** such a disposition acquired by frequent repetition of an act. **3.** a particular practice, custom, or usage. **4.** an addiction to, or compulsive need of, esp. narcotics. **5.** customary practice or use: *to act from force of habit.* **6.** mental character or disposition: *habit of mind.* **7.** characteristic bodily or physical condition: *habit of body.* **8.** the characteristic form, aspect mode of growth, etc., of an animal or plant: *a twining habit.* **9.** *Chem.* the characteristic crystalline form of a mineral. **10.** garb of a particular rank, profession, religious order, etc.: *monk's habit.* **11.** a woman's riding dress. *–v.t.* **12.** to clothe; array. **13.** *Obs.* to dwell in. *–v.i.* **14.** *Obs.* to dwell. [L *habitus* condition, appearance, dress; replacing ME *abit,* from OF]

**habitable** /'hæbɪtəbəl/, *adj.* capable of being inhabited. – **habitability** /hæbətə'bɪləti/, **habitableness,** *n.* – **habitably,** *adv.*

**habitant** /'hæbətənt/, *n.* an inhabitant. [late ME, from F, from L *habitans,* ppr., dwelling]

**habitat** /'hæbətæt/, *n.* **1.** the native environment or kind of place where a given animal or plant naturally lives or grows, as warm seas, mountain tops, fresh waters, etc. **2.** place of abode; habitation. [L: it inhabits]

**habitation** /hæbə'teɪʃən/, *n.* **1.** a place of abode; dwelling. **2.** the act of inhabiting; occupancy by inhabitants.

**habited** /'hæbətəd/, *adj.* **1.** dressed in the habit of a religious order. **2.** *Archaic.* clothed.

**habit-forming** /'hæbət-fɔmɪŋ/, *adj.* tending to produce addiction.

**habitual** /hə'bɪtʃuəl/, *adj.* **1.** of the nature of a habit, or fixed by or resulting from habit: *habitual courtesy.* **2.** being such by habit: *a habitual drunkard.* **3.** commonly used (by a given person): *she took her habitual place at the table.* [LL *habituālis*] – **habitually,** *adv.* – **habitualness,** *n.*

**habitual criminal** /– 'krɪmənəl/, *n.* a person aged twenty-five years or over, who has been convicted on indictment and who, on two previous occasions, has served separate terms following conviction for indictable offences.

**habituate** /hə'bɪtʃueɪt/, *v.t.,* **-ated, -ating. 1.** to accustom (a person, the mind, etc.) as to something; make used (*to*). **2.** *Colloq.* to frequent. [LL *habituātus,* pp. of *habituāre* bring into a condition, from L *habitus* HABIT] – **habituation** /həbɪtʃu'eɪʃən/, *n.*

**habitude** /'hæbətiud/, *n.* **1.** customary condition, character, or habit. **2.** a habit or custom. **3.** *Obs.* relationship. [F, from L *habitūdo* condition] – **habitudinal** /hæbə'tjudənəl/, *adj.*

**habitué** /hə'bɪtʃueɪ, hə'bɪtjueɪ/, *n.* a habitual frequenter of a place. [F, pp. of *habituer* HABITUATE]

**hachure** /hæ'ʃjʊə/, *n., v.,* **-chured, -churing.** *–n.* **1.** (in drawing, engraving, etc.) hatching. **2.** (on a map) shading used to indicate relief features, consisting of lines drawn parallel to the slopes and varying in width with the degree of slope. *–v.t.* **3.** to mark or shade with, or indicate by, hachures. [F, from *hacher* HATCH[3]]

**hacienda** /hæsi'ɛndə/, *n.* **1.** a landed estate, ranch, or farm. **2.** the main house on such an estate; a country house. **3.** a stock-raising, mining, or manufacturing establishment in the country. [Sp.: landed property, estate, from L *facienda* things to be done, neut. pl. ger. of *facere* do]

**hack**[1] /hæk/, *v.t.* **1.** to cut, notch, or chop irregularly, as with heavy blows. **2.** to break up the surface of (the ground). **3.** to clear (a path, etc.) by cutting down brush, etc. **4.** to damage by cutting harshly or ruthlessly: *the subeditor hacked the article to bits.* **5.** to kick the shins of intentionally, as in Rugby football. *–v.i.* **6.** to make rough cuts or notches; deal cutting blows. **7.** to kick an opponent's shins intentionally, as in Rugby football. *–n.* **8.** a cut, gash, or notch. **9.** a tool, as an axe, hoe, pick, etc., for hacking. **10.** an act of hacking; a cutting blow. **11.** a short, broken cough. **12.** a gash in the skin produced by a kick, as in Rugby football. **13.** a kick. [ME *hacke(n)*, OE (*tō*)*haccian* hack to pieces, c. D *hakken,* G *hacken*] – **hacker,** *n.*

**hack**[2] /hæk/, *n.* **1.** a horse kept for common hire, or adapted for general work, esp. ordinary riding. **2.** a saddle-horse for the road. **3.** an old or worn-out horse; a jade. **4.** a person who for a living undertakes literary or other work of little or no originality and permanent value; one who does hackwork. **5.** *Colloq.* a taxi. *–v.t.* **6.** to make a hack of; let out for hire. **7.** to make trite or stale by frequent use; hackney. **8.** *Colloq.* to put up with; endure: *I can't hack it.* *–v.i.* **9.** to ride on the road at an ordinary pace, as distinguished from cross-country or military riding. **10.** *Colloq.* to drive a taxi. *–adj.* **11.** hired; of a hired sort: *hack work.* **12.** hackneyed; trite. [short for HACKNEY]

**hack**[3] /hæk/, *n.* **1.** a rack for holding cattle fodder. **2.** a solid foundation or low platform on which newly formed bricks are stacked to dry before burning. *–v.t.* **3.** to place (bricks) on a hack, as for drying.

**hackamore** /'hækəmɔ/, *n. U.S.* **1.** a coil of rope which passes through the horse's mouth and about his neck, used to break a horse. **2.** any of several forms of halter used esp. for breaking horses.

**hackberry** /'hækbɛri/, *n., pl.* **-ries.** **1.** the small, edible, cherry-like fruit of American trees of the genus *Celtis.* **2.** a tree bearing this fruit. **3.** its wood. [var. of *hagberry,* from Scand.; cf. Dan. *haeggebrær*]

**hackbut** /'hækbʌt/, *n.* →**arquebus.** [MF *haquebute,* b. *buter* to butt and MF *haquebusche* (from MD from *hakebus,* lit., a hook gun)]

**hack hammer** /'hæk hæmə/, *n.* an adzelike tool for dressing stone.

**hackie** /'hæki/, *n. Colloq.* a taxidriver. [HACK[2] (def. 5) + *-ie*]

**hacking** /'hækɪŋ/, *n.* **1.** (of a horse) use for general work, esp. ordinary riding. **2.** (of a motor vehicle) use for routine requirements as travelling to and from work, etc.

**hacking cough** /– 'kɒf/, *n.* a deep, harsh, frequently repeated cough.

**hacking jacket** /'– dʒækət/, *n.* a riding jacket, with tight waist, slanted pockets with flaps, and vents at the sides or back.

**hackle**[1] /'hækəl/, *n., v.,* **-led, -ling.** *–n.* **1.** one of the long, slender feathers on the neck or saddle of certain birds, as the domestic cock, much used in making artificial flies for anglers. **2.** the whole neck plumage of the domestic cock, etc. **3.** (*pl.*) the hair on a dog's neck. **4. with one's hackles up,** very angry; on the point of fighting. **5.** *Angling.* **a.** an artificial fly's legs made with hackles (def. 1). **b.** a hackle fly. **6.** a comb for dressing flax or hemp. *–v.t.* **7.** *Angling.* to supply with a hackle. **8.** to comb, as flax or hemp. [ME *hakell.* See HECKLE] – **hackler,** *n.*

**hackle**[2] /'hækəl/, *v.t.,* **-led, -ling.** to cut roughly; hack; mangle. [frequentative of HACK[1], c. MD *hakkelen*]

**hackle fly** /'– flaɪ/, *n.* an artificial fly made with hackles.

**hackly** /'hækli/, *adj.* rough or jagged. [HACKLE[2] + -Y[1]]

**hackney** /'hækni/, *n., pl.* **-neys,** *adj., v.,* **-neyed, -neying.** *–n.* **1.** a horse for ordinary riding or driving. **2.** *Obs.* a horse kept for hire. **3.** a carriage kept for hire. *–adj.* **4.** let out, employed, or done for hire. *–v.t.* **5.** to make common, stale, or trite by frequent use. **6.** to use as a hackney. [ME *hakeney;* orig. uncert.]

**hackney-carriage** /'hækni-kærɪdʒ/, *n.* any carriage or vehicle which plies for hire, originally horse-drawn.

**hackney-coach** /'hækni-koutʃ/, *n.* a four-wheeled carriage, drawn by two horses, having six seats and kept for hire.

**hackneyed** /'hæknid/, *adj.* **1.** made commonplace or trite; stale. **2.** habituated.

**hacksaw** /'hæksɔ/, *n.* a saw used for cutting metal, consisting typically of a narrow, fine-toothed blade fixed in a frame.

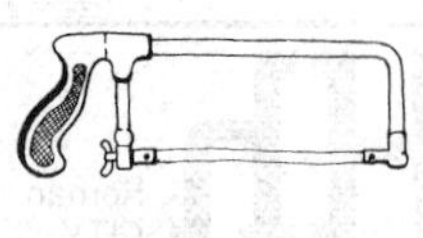
hacksaw

**hackwork** /'hækwɜk/, *n.* the routine aspects of a creative or artistic occupation, considered as mundane, or of an inferior quality, esp. in the literary field.

**had** /hæd/; *weak forms,* /həd, əd, d/ *v.* **1.** past tense and past participle of **have.** **2. have had,** to be utterly exasperated with: *I have had this government.* **3. have had it,** *Colloq.* **a.** to be utterly exasperated. **b.** to be exhausted. **4. be had,** to be cheated or duped.

**hadada** /'hædədə/, *n.* a big brown-green ibis, *Hagedashia hagedash.*

**haddock** /'hædək/, *n., pl.* **-docks,** (*esp. collectively*) **-dock.** a food fish, *Melanogrammus aeglefinus,* of the northern Atlantic, related to but smaller than the cod. [ME *haddoc;* orig. unknown]

**hade** /heɪd/, *n., v.,* **haded, hading.** *Geol.* *–n.* **1.** the angle between a fault plane and a vertical plane striking parallel to the fault. *–v.i.* **2.** to incline from a vertical position. [orig. uncert.]

**hades** /'heɪdiz/, *n. Colloq.* hell. Also, **Hades.** [Gk *Haïdēs* (orig. *aídēs*); in Greek mythology, the subterranean abode of departed spirits or shades]

**hadj** /hædʒ/, *n.* →**hajj.**

**hadji** /'hædʒi/, *n., pl.* **hadjis.** →**hajji.**

**hadn't** /'hædnt/, *v.* a contraction of *had not.*

**hadron** /'hædrɒn/, *n.* any of the elementary sub-atomic particles which exhibit strong nuclear interaction.

**haem** /him/, *n.* a porphyrin containing iron, the precursor of the non-protein portion of haemoglobin.

**haem-,** variant of **haemo-,** before vowels, as in *haemal.* Also, *Chiefly U.S.,* **hem-.** Cf. **haemat-.**

**haema-,** variant of **haemo-.** Also, *Chiefly U.S.,* **hema-.**

**haemachrome** /'himəkroum, 'hɛm-/, *n.* the red colouring matter of the blood.

**haemal** /'himəl/, *adj.* **1.** of or pertaining to the blood or blood vessels. **2.** *Zool.* denoting, pertaining to, or on the side of the body ventral to the spinal axis, containing the heart and great blood vessels.

**haemangioma** /hi,mændʒi'oumə/, *n.* a tumour composed of small blood vessels.

**haemat-,** a prefix equivalent to **haemo-,** as in *haematin.* Also, **haemato-;** *Chiefly U.S.,* **hemat-, hemato-.**

**haematic** /hi'mætɪk/, *adj.* **1.** of or pertaining to blood; haemic. **2.** acting on the blood, as a medicine. *–n.* **3.** a haematic medicine. [Gk *haimatikós* of the blood]

**haematin** /'himətɪn, 'hɛm-/, *n.* a pigment containing iron, produced in the decomposition of haemoglobin as the result of oxidisation of the haem component.

**haematinic** /himə'tɪnɪk, hɛm-/, *n.* **1.** a medicine, as a compound of iron, which tends to increase the amount of haematin or haemoglobin in the blood. *–adj.* **2.** of or obtained from haematin.

**haematite** /'himətaɪt/, *n.* a very common mineral, iron oxide, $Fe_2O_3$, occurring in steel-grey to black crystals and in red earthy masses; the principal ore of iron. Also, **hematite.** [L *haematītes* haematite, from Gk *haimatítēs* bloodlike] – **haematitic** /himə'tɪtɪk/, *adj.*

**haemato-,** a prefix equivalent to **haemo-,** as in *haematogenesis.*

Also, *Chiefly U.S.*, **hemato-**.

**haematocele** /'himatoʊˌsil, 'hɛm-/, *n.* (usu.) a haemorrhage imprisoned in membranous tissue.

**haematocryal** /himə'toʊkriəl, hɛm-/, *adj.* cold-blooded.

**haematogenesis** /himatoʊ'dʒɛnəsəs/, *n.* formation of blood.

**haematogenous** /himə'tɒdʒənəs, hɛm-/, *adj.* **1.** originating in the blood. **2.** blood-producing.

**haematoid** /'himətɔɪd, 'hɛm-/, *adj.* bloodlike. [Gk *haimatoeidēs* bloodlike]

**haematology** /himə'tɒlədʒi, hɛm-/, *n.* the study of the nature, function, and diseases of the blood. [HAEMATO- + -LOGY] – **haematological** /himətə'lɒdʒɪkəl/, *adj.* – **haematologically** /himətə'lɒdʒɪkli/, *adv.* – **haematologist**, *n.*

**haematoma** /himə'toʊmə, hɛm-/, *n., pl.* **-mata** /-mətə/, **-mas.** a bruise or collection of blood in a tissue.

**haematopoiesis** /himətoʊpɔɪ'isəs, hɛm-/, *n.* the formation of blood. [NL, from Gk *haimato-* HAEMATO- + *poíēsis* a making] – **haematopoietic** /himətoʊpɔɪ'ɛtɪk, hɛm-/, *adj.*

**haematosis** /himə'toʊsəs, hɛm-/, *n.* **1.** the formation of blood. **2.** *Physiol.* the conversion of venous into arterial blood; oxygenation in the lungs. [Gk *haimátōsis*, from *haimatoûn* make into blood]

**haematothermal** /himətoʊ'θɜməl, hɛm-/, *adj.* warm-blooded.

**haematoxylin** /himə'tɒksələn/, *n.* **1.** a leguminous plant of a genus *Haematoxylon*, of which only one species, *H. campechianum*, the logwood tree, is known. **2.** the wood of the logwood. **3.** *Chem.* a colourless or pale yellow crystalline compound, $C_{16}H_{14}O_6 \cdot 3H_2O$, the colouring matter of logwood, used as a mordant dye and as an indicator. [NL *haematoxylum* logwood (from Gk *haimato-* HAEMATO- + *xýlon* wood) + -IN[2]]

**-haemia**, variant of **-aemia**. Also, *Chiefly U.S.*, **-hemia**.

**haemic** /'himɪk, 'hɛmɪk/, *adj.* →**haematic.**

**haemin** /'himən/, *n.* the microscopic reddish brown crystals, resulting when a sodium chloride crystal, a drop of glacial acetic acid, and some blood are heated on a slide; used to show the presence of blood. [HAEM- + -IN[2]]

**haemo-**, a word element meaning 'blood' as in *haemolysis*. Also, **haem-**; *Chiefly U.S.*, **hemo-**. Cf. **haema-**, **haemat-**, **haemato-**. [Gk *haimo-*, combining form of *haîma*]

**haemocyte** /'himəsaɪt/, *n.* **1.** a red blood corpuscle. **2.** any blood cell.

**haemocytometer** /himoʊsaɪ'tɒmətə/, *n.* an instrument for counting blood cells. Also, **haemacytometer.**

**haemodialysis** /ˌhimoʊdaɪ'æləsəs/, *n.* →**dialysis** (def. 2).

**haemoglobin** /himə'gloʊbən/, *n.* a haem protein responsible for the red colour of blood which carries oxygen to the tissues; occurring in reduced form **(reduced haemoglobin)** in venous blood, and in combination with oxygen **(oxyhaemoglobin)** in arterial blood.

**haemoid** /'himɔɪd/, *adj.* bloodlike.

**haemoleucocyte** /himoʊ'lukəsaɪt, hɛm-/, *n.* any white blood cell that circulates in the blood. Also, **haemoleukocyte.**

**haemolyse** /'himəlaɪz/, *v.*, **-lysed, -lysing.** *–v.t.* **1.** to cause the haemolysis of (blood). *–v.i.* **2.** to undergo haemolysis. Also, **haemolyze.**

**haemolysin** /himoʊ'laɪsən, hɛm-, hə'mɒləsən/, *n.* an antibody which, in cooperation with a material in fresh blood, causes dissolution of the red blood corpuscles.

**haemolysis** /hi'mɒləsəs/, *n.* the breaking down of the red blood cells with liberation of haemoglobin. – **haemolytic** /himoʊ'lɪtɪk, hɛm-/, *adj.*

**haemophilia** /himə'fɪliə/, *n.* a sex-linked hereditary disease characterised by a tendency to bleed immoderately as from an insignificant wound, due to impaired blood coagulation. [NL, from Gk *haimo-* HAEMO- + *philía* affection, fondness]

**haemophiliac** /himə'fɪliæk/, *n.* a person or organism which has haemophilia.

**haemophilic** /himə'fɪlɪk, hɛm-/, *adj.* **1.** affected by haemophilia. **2.** *Biol.* (of bacteria) developing best in a culture containing blood, or in blood itself.

**haemoptysis** /hə'mɒptəsəs/, *n.* the expectoration of blood or bloody mucus. [NL, from Gk *haimo-* HAEMO- + *ptýsis* spitting]

**haemorrhage** /'hɛmərɪdʒ/, *n.* a discharge of blood, as from a ruptured blood vessel. [L *haemorrhagia*, from Gk *haimorrhagía* a violent bleeding] – **haemorrhagic** /hɛmə'rædʒɪk/, *adj.*

**haemorrhagic septicaemia** /hɛməˌrædʒɪk sɛptə'simiə/, *n.* an acute infectious disease of animals, marked by fever, catarrhal symptoms, pneumonia, and general blood infection; shipping fever; pasteurellosis.

**haemorrhoid** /'hɛmərɔɪd/, *n.* a dilatation of a superficial vein of the canal or margin of the anus; pile. [L *haemorrhoida* piles, from Gk *haemorrhoís*] – **haemorrhoidal** /hɛmə'rɔɪdl/, *adj.*

**haemorrhoidectomy** /hɛmərɔɪ'dɛktəmi/, *n., pl.* **-mies.** the operation for removal of haemorrhoids.

**haemostasis** /himoʊ'steɪsəs, hɛm-/, *n.* the arrest of haemorrhage.

**haemostat** /'himəstæt, 'hɛm-/, *n.* an instrument or agent used to compress or treat bleeding vessels in order to arrest haemorrhage.

**haemostatic** /himoʊ'stætɪk, hɛm-/, *adj.* **1.** arresting haemorrhage, as a drug, styptic. **2.** pertaining to stagnation of the blood. *–n.* **3.** a haemostatic agent or substance.

**haeremai** /'haɪrəmaɪ, hɛ-/, *interj. N.Z.* (an expression of welcome.) [Maori]

**haeres** /'hɪəriz/, *n., pl.* **haeredes** /hə'ridiz/. →**heres.**

**hafiz** /'hʌfɪz, 'hæf-, 'haf-/, *n.* a title of a Muslim who knows the Koran by heart. [Ar. *hāfiz* a guard, one who keeps (in memory)]

**hafnium** /'hæfniəm/, *n.* a metallic element with a valency of four, found in zirconium ores. *Symbol:* Hf; *at. wt:* 178.49; *at. no.:* 72; *sp. gr.:* 13.1. [*Hafn(ia)*, L name of Copenhagen + -IUM]

**haft** /'haft/, *n.* **1.** a handle, esp. of a knife, sword, dagger, etc. *–v.t.* **2.** to furnish with a haft or handle; set in a haft. [ME; OE *hæft*, c. D and G *Heft*]

**hag** /hæg/, *n.* **1.** a repulsive often vicious or malicious, old woman. **2.** a witch. **3.** →**hagfish.** [ME *hagge, hegge;* apparently a familiar short form (with hypocoristic gemination) of OE *hægtesse* fury, witch; akin to G *Hexe* witch] – **haggy,** *adj.*

**Hag.**, *Bible.* Haggai.

**hagfish** /'hægfɪʃ/, *n., pl.* **-fishes,** (*esp. collectively*) **-fish.** any of the eel-like marine cyclostomes constituting the group or order Hyperotreta, notable esp. for their circular suctorial mouth and their habit of boring into the bodies of fishes. Also, **hag.**

**Haggadah** /hə'gadə/, *n., pl.* **-doth** /-doʊθ/. **1.** that part of Jewish traditional literature not concerned with the Law. **2.** the free exposition or homiletic illustration of the Scripture. **3.** the ritual used on the first two nights of Passover. **4.** a book containing it. Also, **Haggada.** [Heb. *haggādāh* narrative, from *higgīd* tell] – **haggadic** /hə'gædɪk, -'gadɪk/, **haggadical** /hə'gædɪkəl, -'gadɪk-/, *adj.*

**haggadist** /hə'gadəst/, *n.* **1.** a writer of Haggadoth. **2.** a student of the Haggadah. – **haggadistic** /hægə'dɪstɪk/, *adj.*

**haggard** /'hægəd/, *adj.* **1.** wild-looking, as from prolonged suffering, anxiety, exertion, want, etc.; careworn; gaunt. **2.** *Falconry.* wild or untamed, esp. of a hawk caught after it has assumed adult plumage. [orig. uncert. Cf. F *hagard* (? from E)] – **haggardly,** *adv.* – **haggardness,** *n.*

**haggis** /'hægəs/, *n.* a dish, originally Scottish, made of the heart, liver, etc., of a sheep, etc., minced with suet and oatmeal, seasoned, and boiled in the stomach of the animal. [? from *hag* chop + *es*, OE *æs* food, meat]

**haggish** /'hægɪʃ/, *adj.* of or like a hag; old and ugly. – **haggishly,** *adv.* – **haggishness,** *n.*

**haggle** /'hægəl/, *v.*, **-gled, -gling,** *n.* *–v.i.* **1.** to bargain in a petty and tedious manner. **2.** to wrangle, dispute, or cavil. *–v.t.* **3.** *Archaic.* to harass with wrangling or haggling. **4.** to mangle in cutting; hack. *–n.* **5.** the act of haggling; wrangle or dispute over terms. [frequentative of d. *hag*, v., cut, hew, hack, from Scand.; cf. Icel. *höggva* strike, hack, c. OE *hēawan* hew] – **haggler,** *n.*

**hagiarchy** /'hægiaki, 'heɪdʒi-/, *n., pl.* **-chies.** →**hagiocracy.**

**hagio-**, a word element meaning 'saint'. Also, **hagi-**. [Gk, combining form of *hágios* sacred, holy]

**hagiocracy** /hægi'ɒkrəsi, heɪdʒi-/, *n., pl.* **-cies.** government by a body of persons esteemed as holy.

**hagiographer** /hægi'ɒgrəfə, heɪdʒi-/, *n.* a writer of lives of the saints; a hagiologist. Also, **hagiographist.**

**hagiography** /hægi'ɒgrəfi, heɪdʒi-/, *n., pl.* **-phies.** the writing and critical study of the lives of the saints; hagiology. – **hagiographic** /hægiəˈgræfɪk, heɪdʒi-/, **hagiographical** /hægiəˈgræfɪkəl, heɪdʒi-/, *adj.*

**hagiolatry** /hægiˈɒlətri, heɪdʒi-/, *n.* the veneration of saints. [HAGIO- + *-latry* (see LATRIA)] – **hagiolater,** *n.* – **hagiolatrous,** *adj.*

**hagiology** /hægiˈɒlədʒi, heɪdʒi-/, *n., pl.* **-gies.** **1.** that branch of literature which deals with the lives and legends of the saints. **2.** a work on these. **3.** a collection of such lives or legends. – **hagiologic** /hægiəˈlɒdʒɪk, heɪdʒi-/, **hagiological** /hægiəˈlɒdʒɪkəl, heɪdʒi-/, *adj.* – **hagiologist,** *n.*

**hagioscope** /ˈhægiəskoup, heɪdʒi-/, *n.* a small opening in a church wall, giving worshippers a view of the high altar; a squint. – **hagioscopic** /hægiəˈskɒpɪk, heɪdʒi-/, *adj.*

**hag-ridden** /ˈhæg-rɪdn/, *adj.* worried or tormented, as by a witch.

**hah** /ha/, *interj.* →**ha.**

**ha-ha**[1] /ha-ˈha/, *interj.* (an imitation of the sound of laughter used as an exclamation of amusement, surprise, derision, etc.)

**ha-ha**[2] /ˈha-ha/, *n.* a wall or other barrier, set in a ditch or depression to divide land without marring the landscape; a sunk fence. [F *haha*]

**ha-ha duck** /ˈha-ha ˌdʌk/, *n. Colloq.* →**kookaburra.**

**hahnium** /ˈhaniəm/, *n. Chem.* a synthetic, radioactive element; (formerly) eka-tantalum. *Symbol;* Ha; at. no.: 105. [named after Otto *Hahn,* 1879-1968, German physicist]

**Haidinger's brush** /ˌhaɪdɪŋəz ˈbrʌʃ/, *n.* an elongated faintly yellowish region seen in the blue sky due to the polarisation of light from the sky. [named after W. K. *Haidinger,* 1795-1871, Austrian mineralogist and physicist]

**haik** /haɪk, heɪk/, *n.* an oblong cloth used as an outer garment by the Arabs. Also, **haick.** [Ar. *hayk,* from *hāk* weave]

**haiku** /ˈhaɪku/, *n.* **1.** a Japanese verse form, developed in the 16th century, usu. containing seventeen syllables, and originally jesting in tone. **2.** an English poem modelled on this Japanese form.

**hail**[1] /heɪl/, *v.t.* **1.** to salute or greet; welcome. **2.** to salute or name as: *to hail (someone as) victor.* **3.** to acclaim; to approve with enthusiasm. **4.** to call out to, in order to attract attention: *to hail a person, to hail a taxi.* –*v.i.* **5.** to call out in order to greet, attract attention, etc. **6. hail from,** to belong to as the place of residence, point of departure, etc. –*n.* **7.** a shout or call to attract attention. **8.** the act of hailing. **9.** a salutation or greeting. **10. within hail,** within reach of the voice. –*interj.* **11.** *Poetic.* (an exclamation of salutation or greeting.) [ME *haile(n),* from obs. *hail,* n. and adj., health(y), from Scand.; cf. Icel. *heill* health, healthy, c. OE *hǣl* (n.), *hāl* (adj.). Cf. WASSAIL] – **hailer,** *n.*

**hail**[2] /heɪl/, *n.* **1.** pellets or small, usu. rounded, balls of ice falling from the clouds in a shower. **2.** a shower or storm of such pellets. **3.** a shower of anything: *a hail of bullets.* –*v.i.* **4.** to pour down hail. **5.** to fall as hail. –*v.t.* **6.** to pour down as or like hail. [ME *hail(e),* OE *hægl,* c. D and G *Hagel*]

**hail-fellow-well-met** /ˌheɪl-fɛlou-wɛl-ˈmɛt/, *adj. Colloq.* **1.** on familiar terms. **2.** social, genial. Also, **hail-fellow.**

**Hail Mary** /ˌheɪl ˈmɛəri/, *n.* →**Ave Maria.**

**hailstone** /ˈheɪlstoun/, *n.* a pellet of hail. [ME, from HAIL[2] + STONE; replacing ME *hawelstone,* OE *hagolstān*]

**hailstorm** /ˈheɪlstɔm/, *n.* a storm with hail; a heavy fall of hail.

**hair** /hɛə/, *n.* **1.** the natural covering of the human head. **2.** the aggregate of hairs which grow on an animal. **3.** one of the numerous fine, usu. cylindrical filaments growing from the skin and forming the coat of most mammals. **4.** a similar fine, filamentous outgrowth from the body of insects, etc. **5.** *Bot.* a filamentous outgrowth of the epidermis. **6.** cloth made of hair from such animals as camel and alpaca. **7.** a very small magnitude, measure, degree, etc.: *he lost the race by a hair.* **8. get in someone's hair,** *Colloq.* to irritate or annoy someone. **9. keep your hair on,** *Colloq.* keep calm; do not get angry. **10. let one's hair down,** to behave in an informal, relaxed, or uninhibited manner. **11. make one's hair stand on end,** to fill with terror; terrify. **12. split hairs,** to make fine or unnecessary distinctions. **13. tear one's hair out,** to show extreme emotion, as anger, anxiety, etc. **14. without turning a hair,** showing no emotion; keeping placid and unmoved. **15. hair of the dog (that bit you),** *Colloq.* an alcoholic drink taken to relieve a hangover. **16. have by the short hairs** or **by the short and curlies,** *Colloq.* to have a person in one's power. [ME *ha(i)re,* from Scand. (cf. Icel. *hār*); replacing ME *her(e),* OE *hǣr,* c. D *haar,* G *Haar*] – **hairlike,** *adj.*

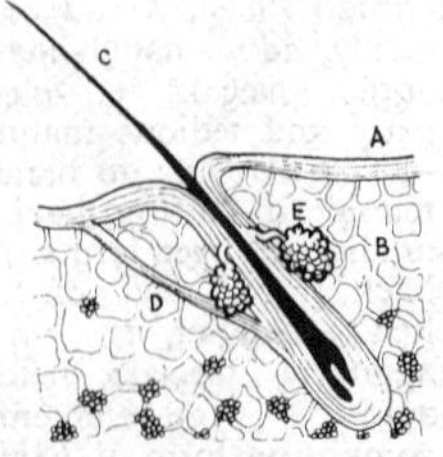

section of skin showing hair root highly magnified: A, cuticle; B, deeper root parts of skin; C, single hair; D, erecting muscle; E, sebaceous glands

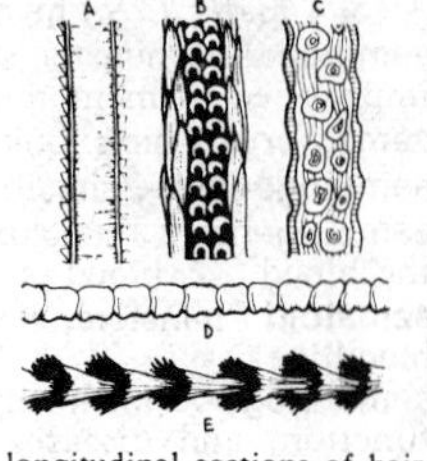

longitudinal sections of hair (enlarged): A, man; B, sable; C, mouse
external view: D, mouse; E, Indian bat

**hair ball** /ˈ– bɔl/, *n.* a ball of hair, in the stomach of a cat, horse, cow, etc., formed as a result of the animal licking its coat.

**hairbreadth** /ˈhɛəbrɛdθ, -brɛtθ/, *n., adj.* →**hair's-breadth.**

**hairbrush** /ˈhɛəbrʌʃ/, *n.* a brush for grooming the hair.

**hairclip** /ˈhɛəklɪp/, *n.* a metal clasp for fastening hair in position.

**haircloth** /ˈhɛəklɒθ/, *n.* stiff cloth woven of hair from horses' tails and manes with cotton warp, for interlinings of clothes, etc.

**hair conditioner** /ˈhɛə kəndɪʃənə/, *n.* a cosmetic applied to the hair so as to improve its general condition.

**hair cream** /ˈ– krim/, *n.* a cosmetic cream to be rubbed into the hair.

**haircut** /ˈhɛəkʌt/, *n.* **1.** a cutting of the hair. **2.** the style in which the hair is cut and worn.

**hairdo** /ˈhɛədu/, *n., pl.* **-dos.** **1.** the style in which a person's hair is arranged, cut, tinted, etc. **2.** the hair so arranged.

**hairdresser** /ˈhɛədrɛsə/, *n.* one who arranges or cuts hair, esp. women's hair.

**hairdressing** /ˈhɛədrɛsɪŋ/, *n.* **1.** the cutting, styling, tinting, and arranging of hair, esp. women's hair. **2.** the occupation of a hairdresser. **3.** a tonic or preparation for the hair.

**hair dryer** /ˈhɛə draɪə/, *n.* a machine for drying hair.

**hair follicle** /ˈ– fɒlɪkəl/, *n.* a small cavity from which a hair develops.

**hairgrass** /ˈhɛəgras/, *n.* **1.** any of several species of grasses belonging to the genus *Deschampsia,* as tufted hairgrass, *D. caespitosa.* **2.** any of several other grasses, as early hairgrass, *Aira praecox.*

**hairgrip** /ˈhɛəgrɪp/, *n.* →**bobby pin.**

**hair lacquer** /ˈhɛə lækə/, *n.* →**hair spray.**

**hairless** /ˈhɛələs/, *adj.* without hair; bald. – **hairlessness,** *n.*

**hairline** /ˈhɛəlaɪn/, *n.* **1.** the line formed at the junction of the hair with the forehead. **2.** a very slender line. **3.** worsted fabric woven with very fine lines or stripes. **4.** *Print.* **a.** a very thin line on the face of a type. **b.** a style of type consisting entirely of such lines. **c.** a thin rule used for printing fine lines. **d.** unwanted lines between letters, caused by worn matrices. – **hairline,** *adj.*

**hairline fracture** /– ˈfræktʃə/, *n.* a break or fault in a bone, metal casting, etc., which reveals itself as a very thin line on the surface.

**hairnet** /ˈhɛənɛt/, *n.* a loosely woven net of hair, nylon, silk, etc., used to cover the hair and hold it in place.

**hair oil** /ˈhɛər ɔɪl/, *n.* a cosmetic oil to be rubbed into the hair, used usu. by men to make the hair stay in place.

**hair pie** /hɛə ˈpaɪ/, *n. Colloq.* cunnilingus.

**hairpiece** /ˈhɛəpis/, *n.* false or substitute hair, usu. mounted on a canvas and wire frame attached to the real hair to enhance or glamorise a style, or to conceal baldness.

**hairpin** /ˈhɛəpɪn/, *n.* a slender U-shaped piece of wire, shell, etc., used by women to fasten up the hair or hold a headdress.

**hairpin bend** /– ˈbɛnd/, *n.* a bend in a road, track, etc., which doubles back in a U-shape.

**hair-raiser** /ˈhɛə-reɪzə/, *n.* anything, as a story, that arouses fear or terror.

**hair-raising** /ˈhɛə-reɪzɪŋ/, *adj.* terrifying.

**hair salt** /ˈhɛə sɒlt/, *n.* natural aluminium sulphate.

**hair's-breadth** /ˈhɛəz-brɛdθ, -brɛtθ, hɛəz-ˈbrɛdθ/, *n.* **1.** a very small space or distance. *–adj.* **2.** extremely narrow or close. Also, **hairsbreadth, hairbreadth.**

**hair seal** /ˈhɛə sil/, *n.* any of various seals with coarse hair and no soft underlying fur (distinguished from *fur seal*).

**hairshirt** /hɛəˈʃɜt/, *n.* a garment of coarse haircloth, worn next to the skin by ascetics and penitents.

**hair slide** /ˈhɛə slaɪd/, *n.* a decorative fastening for the hair.

**hairspace** /ˈhɛəspeɪs/, *n.* (in printing) the thinnest metal space used to separate words, etc.

**hairsplitter** /ˈhɛəsplɪtə/, *n.* one who makes fine or unnecessary distinctions. – **hairsplitting,** *n., adj.*

**hair spray** /ˈhɛə spreɪ/, *n.* a dressing sprayed on the hair, often from a pressure pack, to keep the hairdo in place. Also, **hair lacquer.**

**hairspring** /ˈhɛəsprɪŋ/, *n.* a fine, spiralled spring in a watch or clock for regulating the balance wheel.

**hairstreak** /ˈhɛəstrik/, *n.* any of certain small dark butterflies of the family Lycaenidae, distinguished by one or two thin tails on each of the hind wings.

**hairstroke** /ˈhɛəstroʊk/, *n.* a fine line in writing or printing.

**hairstyle** /ˈhɛəstaɪl/, *n.* the style in which hair is arranged. – **hairstylist,** *n.*

hairspring

**hair-trigger** /ˈhɛə-trɪgə/, *n.* a trigger that allows the firing mechanism of a firearm to be operated by very slight pressure.

**hairworm** /ˈhɛəwɜm/, *n.* any of a number of small, slender worms of the family Trichostrongylidae, parasitic in the alimentary canals of various animals.

**hairy** /ˈhɛəri/, *adj.*, **-rier, -riest. 1.** covered with hair; having much hair. **2.** consisting of or resembling hair. **3.** *Colloq.* difficult: *that's a hairy problem.* **4.** *Colloq.* frightening: *a hairy drive.* **5.** *N.Z. Colloq.* rough; ramshackle; dilapidated. **6.** *Colloq.* angry; excited. **7.** *Colloq.* exciting; stimulating: *a hairy party.*

**hairy bittercress** /– ˈbɪtəkrɛs/, *n.* See **bittercress** (def. 1).

**hairy jew's ear,** *n.* a fungus, *Auricularia polytricha,* which grows in convex ears or brackets on decaying wood, the upper surface being velvety with a dense grey coating of pale hairs, and the lower surface being smooth and purple-brown, often with a pale bloom of spores; used extensively in Chinese cooking.

**hairy-legs** /ˈhɛəri-lɛgz/, *n. Colloq.* **1.** a person who has exceptionally hairy legs. **2.** →**fettler. 3. rack off, hairy-legs!,** (an exclamation of dismissal, contempt, etc.)

**hairy Mary** /hɛəri ˈmɛəri/, *n. Colloq.* →**wiry** (def. 6).

**hairy-nosed wombat** /hɛəri-noʊzd ˈwɒmbæt/, *n.* a wombat of the genus *Lasiorhinus,* having a broad, hairy muzzle, soft silky fur and tapered ears.

**Haiti** /ˈheɪti, haˈiti/, *n.* a republic in the West Indies, occupying the western part of the island of Hispaniola. – **Haitian** /ˈheɪʃən, haˈiʃən/, *adj., n.*

**hajj** /hædʒ/, *n.* the pilgrimage to Mecca, which every good Muslim is supposed to make at least once in his lifetime. Also, **hadj.** [Ar.: pilgrimage]

**hajji** /ˈhædʒi/, *n., pl.* **-jis. 1.** a Muslim who has performed his hajj to Mecca. **2.** a Greek or Armenian who has visited the Holy Sepulchre at Jerusalem. Also, **hadji.** [Turk., from Ar. *hājji* pilgrim]

**haka** /ˈhakə/, *n. N.Z.* **1.** a Maori ceremonial posture dance with vocal accompaniment. **2.** similar debased forms used by schools, sports teams, etc., as aggressive showpieces, or rallies at contests. [Maori]

**hake** /heɪk/, *n., pl.* **hakes,** (*esp. collectively*) **hake. 1.** any of several marine gadoid fishes of the genus *Merluccius,* related to the cod, as *M. merluccius* of European coasts. **2.** any of various related marine fishes, esp. of the genus *Urophycis,* or

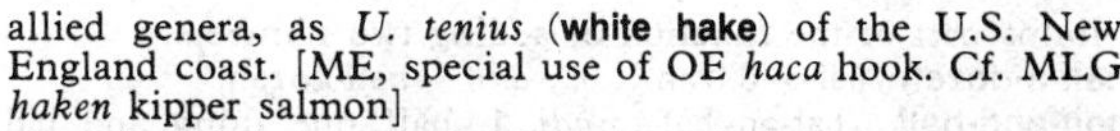

allied genera, as *U. tenius* (**white hake**) of the U.S. New England coast. [ME, special use of OE *haca* hook. Cf. MLG *haken* kipper salmon]

**hakea** /ˈheɪkiə/, *n.* any shrub or tree of the Australian genus *Hakea,* family Proteaceae, characterised by hard woody fruit with winged seeds.

**hakim**[1] /hæˈkim/, *n.* (in Muslim countries) **1.** a wise or learned man. **2.** a physician. Also, **hakeem.** [Ar. *hakīm* wise, wise man]

**hakim**[2] /ˈhækim/, *n.* (in Muslim countries) a ruler; governor; judge. [Ar. *hākim* governor]

**hal-,** variant of **halo-** before vowels, as in *halite.*

**Halafian** /həˈlafiən/, *adj.* of or belonging to the Neolithic culture widespread from Iran to the Mediterranean, characterised by decorated pottery and an abundance of figurines. [named after *Tell Halaf,* a site in N Syria]

**Halakah** /həˈlakə/, *n.* that part of Jewish traditional literature concerned with the Law. Also, **Halacha.** [Heb. *halākāh* rule to go by]

**halation** /həˈleɪʃən/, *n.* the blurring in a photographic negative or print of very light areas (as a window in an interior view) caused by the reflection of light from the back of the support on which the emulsion is coated. [HAL(O) + -ATION]

**halberd** /ˈhælbəd/, *n.* a shafted weapon with an axelike cutting blade, beak, and apical spike, used esp. in the 15th and 16th centuries. Also, **halbert** /ˈhælbət/, **haubert** /ˈhoʊbət/. [late ME *haubert,* from MF *hallebarde,* from MHG *helmbarde*]

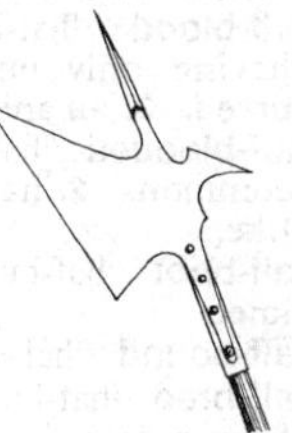

head of halberd

**halberdier** /hælbəˈdɪə/, *n.* a soldier, guard, or attendant armed with a halberd.

**halcyon** /ˈhælsiən/, *n.* **1.** a bird, usu. identified with the kingfisher, fabled by the ancients to breed about the time of the winter solstice in a nest floating on the sea, and to have the power of charming winds and waves into calmness. **2.** any of various kingfishers, esp. of the genus *Halcyon.* *–adj.* **3.** calm, tranquil, or peaceful. **4.** carefree; joyous. **5.** of or pertaining to the halcyon or kingfisher. [L, pseudoetymological var. of *alcyon,* from Gk *alkyṓn* kingfisher]

**halcyon days** /–ˈdeɪz/, *n. pl.* **1.** days of fine and calm weather about the winter solstice, when the halcyon was anciently believed to brood; esp. the seven days before and as many after the winter solstice. **2.** days of peace and tranquillity.

**hale**[1] /heɪl/, *adj.*, **haler, halest.** free from disease or infirmity; robust; vigorous. [ME; OE *hāl,* c. Icel. *heill* hale, whole] – **haleness,** *n.*

**hale**[2] /heɪl/, *v.t.*, **haled, haling. 1.** to haul, pull, or draw with force. **2.** to drag, or bring as by dragging: *to hale a man into court.* [ME *hale(n),* from OF *haler* hale, haul, from Gmc; cf. OHG *halōn,* G *holen* fetch] – **haler,** *n.*

**half** /haf/, *n., pl.* **halves** /havz/, *adj., adv., interj.* *–n.* **1.** one of the two equal (or approximately equal) parts into which anything is or may be divided. **2.** *Sport.* either of the two periods of a game. **3.** *Rugby Football.* **a.** →**half-back. b.** →**five-eighth** (def. 1). **4.** *Golf.* an equal score (with the opponent) either on a hole or a round. **5.** one of a pair. **6.** *Colloq.* a half-pint, esp. of beer. **7. the half of it,** a more significant part of something (usu. used in a negative context): *you think we're in trouble, but that's not the half of it.* **8. go halves,** to share equally. *–adj.* **9.** being one of the two equal (or approximately equal) parts into which anything is or may be divided. **10.** being equal to only about half of the full measure: *half speed.* **11.** partial or incomplete. *–adv.* **12.** to the extent or measure of half: *a bucket half full of water.* **13.** in part; partly. **14.** to some extent. **15. and a half,** of an exceptional nature: *he's a man and a half.* **16. by half,** by a great deal; by too much: *too clever by half.* **17. not half,** *Colloq.* **a.** not really; not at all: *his first poems were not half bad.* **b.** very; surprisingly: *his paintings are not half good.* *–interj.* **18. not half!** *Colloq.* certainly; indeed. [ME and OE, c. MD and MLG *halve* side, half]

**half-adder** /ˈhaf-ædə/, *n.* a circuit in a computer which performs part of the function of adding two numbers.

**half-a-dozen** /haf-ə-ˈdʌzən/, *n., adj.* →**half-dozen.**

**half-and-half** /haf-ən-ˈhaf/, *adj.* **1.** half one thing and half another. *–adv.* **2.** in two equal portions. *–n.* **3.** a mixture of two things.

**half-axe** /ˈhaf-æks/, *n.* one who is foolish or eccentric.

**half-back** /ˈhaf-bæk/, *n.* **1.** *Rugby Football.* **a.** the player who puts the ball in the scrum, and tries to catch it as it emerges. **b.** one of two players, either half-back (def. 1a) or five-eighth (def. 1). **c.** the position in which such a player plays. **2.** *Aus. Rules.* **a.** any of the three positions on the line between the centreline and the full-back line. **b.** a player occupying one of these three positions. **3.** *Soccer.* one of the three players in the next line behind the forward line.

**half-back flanker** /– ˈflæŋkə/, *n.* (in Australian Rules) a player occupying either flank on the half-back line.

**half-baked** /ˈhaf-beɪkt/, *adj.* **1.** insufficiently cooked. **2.** *Colloq.* not completed: *a half-baked scheme.* **3.** *Colloq.* lacking mature judgment or experience: *half-baked theorists.*

**halfbeak** /ˈhafbik/, *n.* any of certain marine fishes constituting the genus *Hemirhamphus* and allied genera, having a long protruding lower jaw.

**half-binding** /ˈhaf-baɪndɪŋ/, *n.* a book having a leather binding on the back and corners, and paper or cloth sides.

**half-blood** /ˈhaf-blʌd/, *n.* **1.** the relation between persons having only one of their parents in common. **2.** →**half-breed. 3.** an animal which has only one parent of pure blood.

**half-blooded** /ˈhaf-blʌdəd/, *adj.* **1.** having only one parent in common. **2.** having parents of different breeds, races, or the like.

**half-boot** /ˈhaf-but/, *n.* a boot reaching about halfway to the knee.

**half-bound** /ˈhaf-baʊnd/, *adj.* bound in half-binding.

**half-bred** /ˈhaf-brɛd/, *adj.* (of a sheep) originally one resulting from a cross between a longwool ram and a merino ewe; now applied more generally.

**half-breed** /ˈhaf-brid/, *n.* **1.** the offspring of parents of different races; one who is half-blooded. *–adj.* **2.** Also, **half-bred.** of or pertaining to the offspring of parents of different races.

**half-brother** /ˈhaf-brʌðə/, *n.* a brother by one parent only.

**half-cadence** /ˈhaf-keɪdəns/, *n.* a musical cadence ending with dominant harmony.

**half-caste** /ˈhaf-kast/, *n.* **1.** a person of mixed race, esp. where the races are of different colours. *–adj.* **2.** of or pertaining to such a person.

**half-cock** /haf-ˈkɒk/, *n.* **1.** the position of the hammer of a firearm when held halfway by mechanism so that it will not operate. **2. go off at half-cock,** to act prematurely.

**half-cocked** /haf-ˈkɒkt/, *adj.* **1.** of a firearm at half-cock. **2. go off half-cocked,** to act prematurely.

**half-crown** /haf-ˈkraʊn/, *n.* (formerly) a silver-nickel coin worth two shillings and sixpence. Also, **half-a-crown.**

**half-day** /haf-ˈdeɪ/, *n.* →**half-holiday.**

**half-dead** /ˈhaf-dɛd/, *adj. Colloq.* very tired; exhausted. Also, (*esp. in predicative use*), **half dead** /haf ˈdɛd/.

**half-dozen** /haf-ˈdʌzən/, *n., adj.* six. Also, **half-a-dozen.**

**half-face** /ˈhaf-feɪs/, *n.* **1.** a profile. *–adj., adv.* **2.** in profile.

**half-forward** /haf-ˈfɔwəd/, *n.* (in Australian Rules) **1.** any of the three positions on the line between the centreline and the full-forward line. **2.** a player occupying one of these positions.

**half-forward flanker** /– ˈflæŋkə/, *n.* (in Australian Rules) a player occupying one of the two positions on either side of the centre half-forward.

**half-frames** /ˈhaf-freɪmz/, *n. pl.* spectacles, used chiefly for reading, which have lenses and lens frames of roughly semi-circular shape, allowing direct vision above the upper straight edge of the lens frames.

**half-hardy** /ˈhaf-hadi/, *adj.* (of plants) growing out of doors, except during winter.

**half-hearted** /ˈhaf-hatəd/, *adj.* having or showing little enthusiasm. – **half-heartedly,** *adv.* – **half-heartedness,** *n.*

**half-hitch** /ˈhaf-hɪtʃ/, *n.* a hitch formed by passing the end of a rope round its standing part and bringing it up through the bight.

**half-holiday** /haf-ˈhɒlədeɪ/, *n.* part, usu. the afternoon, of a working day given for recreation.

**half-hour** /haf-ˈaʊə/, *n.;* /ˈhaf-aʊə/, *adj.* *–n.* **1.** a period of thirty minutes. **2.** the midpoint between the hours. *–adj.* **3.** of or pertaining to a period of thirty minutes.

**half-hourly** /ˈhaf-aʊəli/, *adj.;* /haf-ˈaʊəli/, *adv.* *–adj.* **1.** of or lasting a half-hour. **2.** occurring once every half-hour. *–adv.* **3.** during a half-hour.

**half-inch** /haf-ˈɪntʃ/, *v.t. Colloq.* to pinch; steal. [rhyming slang]

**half-integer** /haf-ˈɪntədʒə/, *n.* any member of the set of numbers that is obtained by dividing the odd integers by two. – **half-integral,** *adj.*

**half-leather** /ˈhaf-lɛðə/, *n.* →**half-binding.**

**half-length** /ˈhaf-lɛŋθ/, *n.* **1.** a portrait showing only the upper part of the body, including the hands. *–adj.* **2.** of or denoting such a portrait. **3.** of or pertaining to a coat, dress, etc., which is not full length.

**half lever** /haf ˈlivə/, *n.* a gymnastic exercise in which the body is positioned with the legs held together at right angles to the trunk.

**half-life** /ˈhaf-laɪf/, *n.* the time required for one half of a sample of unstable material to undergo chemical change, as the disintegration of radioactive material, the chemical change of free radicals, etc.

**half-light** /ˈhaf-laɪt/, *n.* light of much less than normal intensity; twilight.

**half-mast** /haf-ˈmast/, *n.* **1.** a position approximately halfway below the top of a mast, staff, etc. **2. at half-mast,** (of trousers) not extending to the ankles. *–v.t.* **3.** to place (a flag) at half-mast (as a mark of respect for the dead, or as a signal of distress).

**half-measure** /ˈhaf-mɛʒə/, *n.* an inadequate measure, esp. one taken as a compromise.

**halfmens** /ˈhalfmɛnts/, *n.* a plant, *Pachypodium namaquanum,* of the family Apocynaceae, native to southern Africa, having a thick upright stem surmounted by a crown of leaves, supposed to resemble a human being. [Afrikaans: half person]

**half-moon** /haf-ˈmun/, *n.* **1.** →**moon** (def. 2b). **2.** something of the shape of a half-moon or crescent.

**half-mourning** /haf-ˈmɔnɪŋ/, *n.* **1.** a mourning garb less sombre than full mourning. **2.** the period during which it is worn.

**half-nelson** /haf-ˈnɛlsən/, *n.* a wrestling hold, usu. from behind, in which a wrestler pushes one arm under his opponent's arm and places his hand on the nape of his opponent's neck.

**half-pay** /haf-ˈpeɪ/, *n.* **1.** half the full wages or salary. **2.** of or pertaining to a person on half-pay.

**halfpenny** /ˈheɪpni/, *n., pl.* **halfpennies** /ˈheɪpniz/, *for def. 1;* **halfpence** /ˈheɪpəns/ *for def. 2; adj.* *–n.* **1.** a bronze coin of half the value of a penny. **2.** the sum of half a penny. *–adj.* **3.** of the price or value of a halfpenny. **4.** of trifling value.

**halfpennyworth** /ˈheɪpəθ/, *n.* **1.** as much as may be bought for a halfpenny, a former unit of currency. **2.** a trifling amount.

**half-pie** /haf-ˈpaɪ/, *adj. Colloq.* half-hearted; mediocre.

**half-pint** /haf-ˈpaɪnt/, *n.* **1.** half of one pint. **2.** a small person, esp. a small woman. *–adj.* **3.** of or containing a half-pint. **4.** of or pertaining to a small person.

**half-price** /ˈhaf-praɪs/, *adj.* at half the normal price: *half-price bargains.*

**half rhyme** /ˈhaf raɪm/, *n.* (in poetry) a rhyme between words with differing vowels, as *bees* and *buzz.*

**half-seas-over** /haf-siz-ˈoʊvə/, *adj. Colloq.* intoxicated. Also (*esp. in predicative use*), **half seas over.**

**half-sister** /ˈhaf-sɪstə/, *n.* a sister by one parent only.

**half-size** /haf-ˈsaɪz/, *n.* any size, esp. of clothing or the like, which is halfway between two sizes.

**half-slip** /ˈhaf-slɪp/, *n.* a petticoat or slip that hangs from the waist.

**half-sole** /ˈhaf-soʊl/, *n., v.,* **-soled, -soling.** *–n.* **1.** that part of the sole of a boot or shoe which extends from the shank to the end of the toe. *–v.t.* **2.** to repair by putting on a new half-sole.

**half spot** /ˈhaf spɒt/, *n. Colloq.* fifty dollars.

**half-term** /haf-ˈtɜm/, *n. Chiefly Brit.* a period usu. half-way through a school or other term, often made the occasion for a holiday.

**half-thickness** /'haf-θɪknəs/, *n.* the thickness of a specified material which, when introduced into the path of a beam of radiation, reduces its intensity to half its original value. Also, **half-value layer.**

**half-tide** /haf-'taɪd/, *n.* the state of the tide when halfway between high water and low water.

**half-timbered** /'haf-tɪmbəd/, *adj.* (of a house or building) having the frame and principal supports of timber, but with the interstices filled in with masonry, plaster, or the like. – **half-timbering,** *n.*

**half-time** /haf-'taɪm/, *n.* a rest period or interval between the two halves of a game, match, etc.

**half-title** /'haf-taɪtl/, *n.* **1.** the short title of a book printed on the page preceding the titlepage. **2.** the title of any subdivision of a book when printed on a separate page. **3.** the page on which the half-title is printed. Also, **bastard title.**

**half-tone** /'haf-toun/, *n. U.S.* →**semitone.**

**halftone** /'haftoun/, *n.* **1.** *Painting, Photog., etc.* a value intermediate between high light and deep shade. **2.** *Photoengraving.* **a.** a process in which gradation of tone is obtained by a system of minute dots produced by a screen, placed in the camera a short distance in front of the sensitised plate. **b.** the metal plate made by photo-engraving for reproduction by letterpress printing. **c.** a print from it. *–adj.* **3.** pertaining to, using, or used in, the halftone process.

**halftrack** /'haftræk/, *n.* a motor vehicle with its driving wheels on caterpillar tracks.

**half-truth** /'haf-truθ/, *n.* a proposition or statement only partly true, esp. a statement intended to mislead or deceive.

**half-value layer** /haf-vælju 'leɪə/, *n.* →**half-thickness.**

**half-volley** /haf-'vɒli/, *n., v.,* **-leyed, -leying.** *–n.* **1.** a delivered ball or its return, hit or kicked the moment after it bounces from the ground. *–v.t., v.i.* **2.** to hit or play (a half-volley).

**half-wave rectifier** /ˌhaf-weɪv 'rɛktəfaɪə/, *n.* a rectifier which allows current to flow only during half of a cycle of an alternating current.

**halfway** /haf'weɪ/, *adv.;* /'hafweɪ/, *adj.* *–adv.* **1.** half over the way: *to go halfway to a place.* **2.** to or at half the distance: *the rope reaches only halfway.* **3. meet halfway,** to compromise. *–adj.* **4.** midway, as between two places or points. **5.** going to or covering only half the full extent; partial: *halfway measures.*

**halfway house** /'– haus/, *n.* **1.** (formerly) an inn or coaching station half the distance to one's destination. **2.** a position midway between two extremes, as in an argument, debate, etc. **3.** a house, usu. run by an organisation, in which former prisoners, drug addicts, etc, can live until capable of organising their own affairs.

**half-white** /'haf-waɪt/, *n.* a person who has one white and one non-white parent.

**halfwit** /'hafwɪt/, *n.* one who is feeble-minded.

**half-witted** /'haf-wɪtəd/, *adj.* feeble-minded. – **half-wittedly,** *adv.* – **half-wittedness,** *n.*

**half-yearly** /'haf-jɪəli/, *adj.* occurring twice a year; midyear: *half-yearly examinations.*

**halibut** /'hæləbət/, *n., pl.* **-buts,** (*esp. collectively*) **-but. 1.** →**Queensland halibut. 2.** either of two species of large flatfishes, *Hippoglossus hippoglossus* of the North Atlantic and *H. stenolepis* of the North Pacific; the largest of the flatfishes and widely used for food. **3.** any of various other similar flatfishes. Also, **holibut.** [ME *halybutte,* apparently from *haly* (OE *hālig* holy) + *butte* kind of fish; so called because eaten on holy days. Cf. G *Heilbutt*]

**halide** /'heɪlaɪd, 'hæl-/, *n.* **1.** a compound, usu. of two elements only, one of which is a halogen. *–adj.* **2.** of the nature of, or pertaining to, a halide; haloid. Also, **halid** /'heɪləd, 'hæl-/. [HAL(OGEN) + -IDE]

**halite** /'heɪlaɪt, 'hæl-/, *n.* →**rock-salt.** [HAL- + -ITE[1]]

**halitosis** /hælə'tousəs/, *n.* bad or offensive breath. [NL, from L *hālitus* breath + *-ōsis* -OSIS]

**halitus** /'hælətəs/, *n.* an expired breath.

**hall** /hɔl/, *n.* **1.** the entrance room or vestibule of a house or building. **2.** a corridor or passageway in a building. **3.** a large building or room for public assembly and other community uses. **4.** a large building for residence, instruction, or other purposes, as in a university or college. **5.** the proprietor's residence on a large landed estate. **6.** the chief room in a medieval castle or similar structure, used for eating, sleeping, and entertaining. **7.** the house of a medieval chieftain or noble. [ME and OE, c. OHG *halla,* akin to OE *helan* cover, hide, L *cēlāre* hide, Gk *kalýptein* cover]

**Hall effect** /'hɔl əfɛkt/, *n.* the potential difference which develops across a strip of metal which is longitudinally conducting an electric current and which is subjected to a transverse magnetic field. The potential difference is in a plane at right angles to both the current and the magnetic field. [named after Edwin Herbert *Hall,* 1855-1938, U.S. physicist]

**hallelujah** /hælə'lujə/, *interj.* **1.** Praise ye the Lord! *–n.* **2.** an exclamation of 'hallelujah!'. **3.** a musical composition wholly or principally based upon the word *hallelujah.* Also, **halleluiah, alleluia.** [Heb. *hallelūyah* praise ye Jehovah]

**Halley's comet** /ˌhæliz 'kɒmət/, *n.* a comet which appears every 75 or 76 years, its last appearance being in 1910. [named after Edmund *Halley,* 1656-1742, British astronomer who first predicted its return]

**halliard** /'hæliəd/, *n.* →**halyard.**

**hallmark** /'hɔlmak/, *n.* **1.** an official mark or stamp indicating a standard of purity, used in marking gold and silver articles. **2.** any mark or special indication of genuineness, good quality, etc. **3.** any outstanding feature or characteristic. *–v.t.* **4.** to stamp with such a mark. Also, **plate-mark.** [from Goldsmiths' *Hall,* London, the seat of the Goldsmiths' Company which assayed and marked gold and silver articles]

**hallo** /hʌ'lou, hə-/, *interj., n., v.* →**hello.** Also, **halloa** /hə'lou/.

**hall of fame,** *n.* (*oft. cap.*) **1.** *Chiefly U.S.* a building containing statues, busts, etc., commemorating or honouring famous or worthy people. **2.** a group of famous people considered worthy of acclaim.

**hall of residence,** *n.* →**hall** (def. 4).

**halloo** /hə'lu/, *interj., n., pl.* **-loos,** *v.* *–interj.* **1.** (an exclamation used to attract attention, to incite the dogs to the chase, etc.). *–n.* **2.** the cry 'halloo!'. *–v.i.* **3.** to call with a loud voice; shout; cry, as after dogs. *–v.t.* **4.** to incite or chase with shouts and cries of 'halloo!'. **5.** to cry aloud to. **6.** to hunt with shouts. [var. of HOLLO]

**hallow**[1] /'hælou/, *v.t.* **1.** to make holy; sanctify; consecrate. **2.** to honour as holy. [ME *hal(o)we(n),* OE *hālgian,* from *hālig* HOLY]

**hallow**[2] /hə'lou/, *interj., n., v.* →**halloo.** [var. of HALLOO]

**hallowed** /'hæloud/, *in liturgical use often* /'hælouəd/ *adj.* **1.** made holy; sacred; consecrated. **2.** honoured or observed as holy. – **hallowedness,** *n.*

**Halloween** /hælou'in, hælə'win/, *n.* the evening of 31 October, the eve of All Saints' Day. Also, **Hallowe'en.** [*hallow* saint + *een,* var. of *even* EVE]

**Hallowmas** /'hælouˌmæs/, *n. Archaic.* the feast of Allhallows or All Saints' Day, on 1 November.

**hallstand** /'hɔlstænd/, *n.* a piece of furniture, usu. placed in an entrance hall, and designed to hold hats, coats and umbrellas, etc.

**Hallstattian** /hæl'stætiən/, *adj.* pertaining to a variously dated pre-Christian stage of culture in central Europe, characterised by the use of bronze, the introduction of iron, artistic work in pottery, jewellery, etc. [named after *Hallstatt,* village in central Austria, near which a burial ground of the period was found]

**hallucal** /'hæljukəl/, *adj.* referring to the big toe. [NL *hallux* (see HALLUX) + -AL[1]]

**hallucinate** /hə'lusəneɪt/, *v.,* **-nated, -nating.** *–v.t.* **1.** to affect with hallucinations. *–v.i.* **2.** to experience hallucinations. [L *hallūcinātus,* pp. of *(h)allūcinārī* wander in mind, dream]

**hallucination** /həlusə'neɪʃən/, *n.* **1.** subjective sense perceptions for which there is no appropriate external source, as 'hearing voices'. When persistent it is characteristic of severe psychiatric disorder. Cf. **delusion** (def. 4) and **illusion** (def. 4). **2.** a suffering from illusion or false notions.

**hallucinatory** /həlusə'neɪtəri, hə'lusənətri/, *adj.* pertaining to or characterised by hallucination.

**hallucinogen** /hə'lusənədʒən/, *n.* a drug or chemical capable of producing hallucinations. [HALLUCIN(ATION) + -GEN] – **hallucinogenic** /həlusənə'dʒɛnɪk/, *adj.*

**hallucinosis** /həlusə'noʊsəs/, *n.* a psychotic state characterised by hallucinations, typically toxic (esp. alcoholic) in origin. [HALLUCIN(ATION) + -OSIS]

**hallux** /'hæləks/, *n., pl.* **-luces** /-ljusiz/. the innermost of the five digits normally present in the hind foot of air-breathing vertebrates, as: **a.** (in man) the big toe. **b.** (in birds) the hind toe. [NL, from L *(h)allex* big toe, with *-u-* by association with *(h)allus* thumb]

**hallway** /'hɔlweɪ/, *n.* **1.** a corridor, as in a building. **2.** an entrance hall.

**halma** /'hælmə/, *n.* a game played on a chequered board by two, three, or four players, the object being to move one's pieces from one corner of the board to the opposite corner by leaping over other pieces. [Gk: leap]

**halo** /'heɪloʊ/, *n., pl.* **-loes, -los,** *v.,* **-loed, -loing.** *–n.* **1.** a radiance surrounding the head in the representation of a sacred personage. **2.** an ideal glory investing an object viewed with feeling or sentiment: *the halo around Shakespeare's plays.* **3.** *Meteorol.* a circle of light, appearing round the sun or moon, caused by the refraction of light in suspended ice crystals. *–v.t.* **4.** to surround with a halo. *–v.i.* **5.** *Rare.* to form a halo. [L *halōs,* from Gk: disc, halo, threshing floor (on which the oxen trod out a circular path)] – **halo-like,** *adj.*

halo: stylised representation

**halo-,** a word element meaning 'salt', as in *halogen.* [Gk, combining form of *háls*]

**halogen** /'heɪlədʒən, 'hæl-/, *n.* any of the electronegative elements fluorine, chlorine, iodine, bromine, and astatine, which form binary salts by direct union with metals.

**halogenation** /heɪlədʒə'neɪʃən, hæl-/, *n.* the introduction of a halogen into an organic compound.

**haloid** /'heɪlɔɪd, 'hæl-/, *adj.* **1.** denoting any halogen derivative. *–n.* **2.** a haloid salt or derivative.

**halophilous** /hə'lɒfələs/, *adj.* (of an animal or plant) capable of living in salt water.

**halophyte** /'heɪləfaɪt, 'hæl-/, *n.* a plant which grows in salty or alkaline soil. – **halophytic** /heɪlə'fɪtɪk, hæl-/, *adj.*

**halothane** /'heɪləθeɪn, 'hæl-/, *n.* a volatile, sweetish liquid, $CF_3CHBrCl$, used as an anaesthetic inhalant.

**halourni** /hæ'lʊəni/, *n.* a soft cheese, common in Greece and Cyprus, with a firm putty-like texture, and slightly mint flavour, matured in brine.

**halt**[1] /hɔlt, hɒlt/, *v.i.* **1.** to make a temporary stop, as in marching, etc. *–v.t.* **2.** to cause to halt. *–n.* **3.** a temporary stop. **4.** a stopping-place on a railway line, smaller than a station, where a train stops only briefly. *–interj.* **5.** (a command to stop and stand motionless, esp. as to troops.) [G: stoppage]

**halt**[2] /hɔlt, hɒlt/, *v.i.* **1.** to falter as in speech, reasoning, etc. **2.** to be in doubt; waver; hesitate. *–adj.* **3.** *Archaic.* lame; limping: *the halt and the lame.* *–n.* **4.** *Archaic.* lameness; a limp. [ME; OE *h(e)alt,* c. OHG *halz*] – **halting,** *adj.* – **haltingly,** *adv.* – **haltingness,** *n.*

**halter**[1] /'hɔltə, 'hɒltə/, *n.* **1.** a rope or strap with a noose or headstall, for leading or fastening horses or cattle. **2.** a rope with a noose for hanging criminals. **3.** death by hanging. **4.** **halter-neck.** *–v.t.* **5.** to put a halter on; restrain as by a halter. **6.** to hang (a person). [ME; OE *hælftre,* c. G *Halfter*] – **halter-like,** *adj.*

halter[1]

**halter**[2] /'hɔltə, 'hɒltə/, *n.* one who halts or hesitates. [HALT[2] + -ER[1]]

**halter**[3] /'hɔltə, 'hɒltə/, *n.* one who halts or stops. [HALT[1] + -ER[1]]

**haltere** /'hæltɪə/, *n., pl.* **halteres** /hæl'tɪəriz/. one of a pair of modified hind wings of a fly (order Diptera) reduced to slender, club-shaped appendages, used for balancing in flight; balancer. Also, *Chiefly U.S.,* **halter.** [L, from Gk: leaping weight (usu. pl., *haltêres*)]

**halter-neck** /'hɔltə-nɛk, 'hɒl-/, *n.* **1.** a neckline of a woman's dress, blouse, etc., which, fastened by thin straps behind the neck, leaves the back and arms bare. **2.** the garment itself. *–adj.* **3.** of or pertaining to a garment with such a neckline.

**halva** /'hælvə/, *n.* a sweet confection of Middle Eastern origin, containing honey and sesame seeds. Also, **halvah, halwa.** [Yiddish, from Ar. *halwa* sweetmeat]

**halve** /hav/, *v.t.,* **halved, halving.** **1.** to divide in halves; share equally. **2.** to reduce to half. **3.** *Golf.* to play (a hole, match, etc.) in the same number of strokes, as two opponents. [ME *halven,* from HALF]

**halves** /havz/, *n.* **1.** plural of **half.** **2.** **by halves, a.** incompletely. **b.** half-heartedly. **3.** **go halves,** divide equally; share.

**halyard** /'hæljəd/, *n.* a rope or tackle used to hoist or lower a sail, yard, flag, etc. Also, **halliard.** [ME *halier, hallyer* that which hales or hauls (from HALE[2] + -IER); influenced by YARD[1]]

**ham** /hæm/, *n., v.,* **hammed, hamming.** *–n.* **1.** one of the rear quarters of a pig, esp. the heavy-muscled part, between hip and hock. **2.** the meat of this part. **3.** the part of the leg behind the knee. **4.** *(oft. pl.)* the back of the thigh or the thigh and the buttock together. **5.** *Colloq.* **a.** an actor who overacts. **b.** overacting. **6.** *Colloq.* an amateur: *a radio ham.* *–v.i.* **7.** *Colloq.* to act with exaggerated expression of emotion; overact: *to ham it up.* [ME *hamme,* OE *hamm,* c. OHG *hamma* angle of the knee. Cf. LL *camba* bend of leg]

**hamada** /hə'madə/, *n.* a tract of upland stony desert, stripped of sand and dust, in the Sahara. Also, **hammada.**

**hamadryad** /hæmə'draɪəd/, *n., pl.* **-ads, -ades** /-ədiz/. **1.** *Class. Myth.* one of a class of wood nymphs fabled to live and die with the tree which she inhabited. **2.** →**king cobra.** [L *Hamādryas,* from Gk, from *háma* together + *dryás* wood nymph]

**ham-and-beef shop** /hæm-ən-'bif ʃɒp/, *n.* →**delicatessen.**

**hamate** /'heɪmeɪt/, *adj.* **1.** hook-shaped. **2.** *Anat.* having a hooklike process. *–n.* **3.** the medial of the four bones of the distal row of the carpus. [L *hāmātus*]

**hambone** /'hæmboʊn/, *n.* *Colloq.* a male striptease. Also, **bone.**

**hamburger** /'hæmbɜgə/, *n.* **1.** a flat round cake of minced beef, seasoned and fried. **2.** a bread roll, or soft bun containing such meat, cooked and served often with onion, etc.

**ham-de-luxe** /hæm-də-'lʌks/, *n.* prosciutto, neatly tied in a sausage shape.

**hame** /heɪm/, *n.* either of two curved pieces lying upon the collar in the harness of an animal, to which the traces are fastened. [ME, from MD; akin to G *Hamen* fishhook, dragnet, OE *hamele* rowlock]

**hamerkop** /'hæməkɒp, 'heɪm-/, *n.* a heron-like bird, *Scopus umbretta,* the sole member of the family Scopidae, of Africa, Madagascar, and Arabia, coloured brown and having a broad, flat bill and a crest projecting backwards from its head. Also, **hammerhead.** [Afrikaans: hammerhead]

**ham-fisted** /'hæm-fɪstəd/, *adj.* clumsy. Also, **ham-handed.**

**Hamitic** /hæ'mɪtɪk/, *adj.* **1.** of or pertaining to the Hamites or their speech. *–n.* **2.** a family of languages related to the Semitic, spoken in North Africa, including ancient Egyptian and modern Berber.

**hamlet** /'hæmlət/, *n.* **1.** a small village. **2.** a little cluster of houses in the country. **3.** a village without a church of its own, but belonging to the parish of another village or a town. [ME *hamelet,* from OF, diminutive of *hamel* hamlet, diminutive of *ham,* from Gmc; cf. OE *hamm* enclosed land]

**hamlet development** /'– dəvɛləpmənt/, *n.* the development of a number of dwellings around a communal centre for such activities as cooking, eating, recreation, etc.

**hammada** /hə'madə/, *n.* →**hamada.**

**hammer**[1] /'hæmə/, *n.* **1.** an instrument consisting of a solid head, usu. of metal, set crosswise on a handle, used for beating metals, driving in nails, etc. **2.** any of various instruments or devices resembling a hammer in form, action, or use. **3.** *Firearms.* that part of the lock which by its fall or action causes the discharge, as by exploding the percussion cap; the cock. **4.** one of the padded levers by which the strings of a piano are struck. **5.** a keyboard acciaccatura in rock music. **6.** *Athletics.* a metal ball attached to a long, flexible handle, used in certain throwing contests. **7.** *Anat.* **malleus. 8. come** or **go under the hammer,** to be sold by auction. *–v.t.* **9.** to beat or drive with or as with a hammer. **10.** to form with a hammer (oft. fol. by *out*). **11.** to fasten by or as by using a hammer. **12.** to put together or build with a hammer and nails. **13.** to hit with some force; pound. **14.** to contrive or work out laboriously (oft. fol. by *out*). **15.** to state forcefully; present (facts, etc.) aggressively. **16.** to subject forcibly and relentlessly to interrogation, pressure, etc.: *the Minister was hammered by the opposition at question time.* **17.** *Stock Exchange.* **a.** to announce a defaulter on the Stock Exchange. **b.** to depress or beat down (the price of a stock). *–v.i.* **18.** to strike blows with or as with a hammer. **19.** to make persistent or laborious attempts. [ME *hamer,* OE *hamor,* c. G *Hammer*] **– hammerer,** *n.* **– hammerless,** *adj.* **– hammer-like,** *adj.*

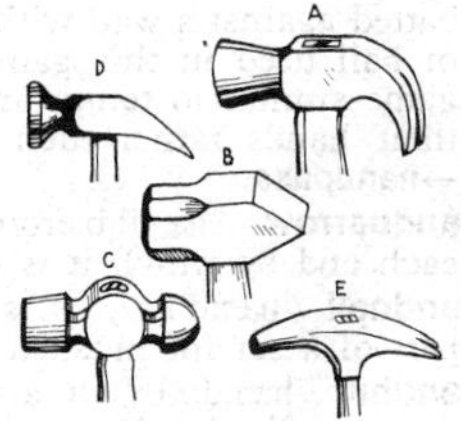

hammers (def. 1): A, nail hammer; B, engineer's hammer; C, machinist's hammer; D, shoemaker's hammer; E, carpetlayer's hammer

**hammer**[2] /ˈhæmə/, *n., Colloq.* **1.** back. **2. be on someone's hammer,** to watch closely; badger. [rhyming slang, *hammer and tack* back]

**hammer and sickle,** *n.* **1.** the emblem of the Soviet Union, adopted in 1923. **2.** any similar emblem of communism outside the Soviet Union.

**hammer and tongs,** *adv. Colloq.* with great noise, vigour, or violence.

**hammerbeam** /ˈhæməbim/, *n.* a horizontal timber beam, which supports a wooden arch in a roof truss.

**hammered work** /hæməd ˈwɜk/, *n.* metalwork formed by the hammers, anvils, punches, etc., of craftsmen.

**hammerhead** /ˈhæməhɛd/, *n.* **1.** the head of a hammer. **2.** any of the sharks constituting the genus *Sphyrna,* characterised by a head expanded laterally so as to resemble a double-headed hammer, esp. *S. zygaena,* a widely distributed species. **3.** →**hamerkop.**

hammerhead

**hammering** /ˈhæmərɪŋ/, *n. Colloq.* **1.** a beating; hiding. **2. take a hammering, a.** to be beaten up. **b.** to be subjected to intense cross-examination or criticism.

**hammer lock** /ˈhæmə lɒk/, *n.* a hold, banned in amateur wrestling, whereby the opponent's arm is twisted and pushed behind his back.

**hammermill** /ˈhæməmɪl/, *n.* a mill through which various stock feeds are passed and crushed to make up a palatable supplement for stock.

**hammer sedge** /hæmə ˈsɛdʒ/, *n.* a small perennial sedge, *Carex hirta,* widespread in damp woods and meadows throughout Europe and temperate Asia.

**hammertoe** /hæməˈtoʊ/, *n.* a clawlike deformity of the toe, caused by permanent bending of the joints.

**hammock** /ˈhæmək/, *n.* a kind of hanging bed or couch made of canvas, netting, or the like. [Sp. *hamaca;* of W Ind. orig.]

**hammy** /ˈhæmi/, *adj.* of one who overacts or that which is overacted.

**hamper**[1] /ˈhæmpə/, *v.t.* **1.** to impede; hinder; hold back. *–n.* **2.** *Naut.* articles which, while necessary to a ship's equipment, are often in the way. [ME *hampren,* orig. uncert.]

**hamper**[2] /ˈhæmpə/, *n.* **1.** a large basket or receptacle made from cane, wickerwork, etc., usu. with a cover. **2. Christmas hamper,** a package of foods traditionally eaten at Christmas festivities, as ham, fruit cake, etc., often given as a present. [ME *hampere;* syncopated var. of HANAPER]

**hamster** /ˈhæmstə/, *n.* **1.** any of a number of short-tailed, stout-bodied, burrowing rodents, having large cheek pouches, and inhabiting parts of Europe and Asia, as *Cricetus cricetus.* **2.** the fur of such an animal. [G]

hamster

**hamstring** /ˈhæmstrɪŋ/, *n., v.,* **-strung** or (*Rare*) **-stringed; -stringing.** *–n.* **1.** (in man) any of the tendons bounding the ham, or hollow of the knee. **2.** (in quadrupeds) the great tendon at the back of the hock. *–v.t.* **3.** to cut the hamstring or hamstrings of and thus disable. **4.** to cripple; render useless; thwart.

**hamulus** /ˈhæmjələs/, *n., pl.* **-li** /-laɪ/. a small hook or hooklike process, as at the end of a bone. [L, diminutive of *hāmus* a hook]

**hanaper** /ˈhænəpə/, *n.* a wicker receptacle for documents. [ME *hanypere,* from OF *hanapier* case for holding a cup, from *hanap* cup, from Gmc; cf. OS *hnapp* cup]

**hance** /hæns/, *n.* **1.** *Naut.* a curved rise to a higher part, as of the bulwarks from the waist to the quarterdeck. **2.** *Archit.* **a.** the sharply curving portion nearest the impost at either side of an elliptical or similar arch. **b.** the haunch of an arch. [n. use of *hance,* v., raise (now obs.), aphetic var. of ENHANCE]

**hand** /hænd/, *n.* **1.** (in man) the terminal, prehensile part of the arm, consisting of the palm and five digits. **2.** the corresponding part of the forelimb in any of the higher vertebrates. **3.** the terminal part of any limb when prehensile, as the hind foot of a monkey, the chela of a crustacean, or (in falconry) the foot of a hawk. **4.** something resembling a hand in shape or function: *the hands of a clock.* **5.** a symbol used in writing or printing to draw attention to something. **6.** a person employed in manual labour; worker; labourer: *a factory hand.* **7.** a person who does a specified thing: *a book by several hands.* **8.** the persons of any company or number: *all hands gave assistance, all hands on deck.* **9.** (*oft. pl.*) possession or power; control, custody, or care: *to have someone's fate in one's hands.* **10.** agency; active cooperation in doing something: *a helping hand.* **11.** side: *on every hand.* **12.** a side of a subject, question, etc.: *on the other hand.* **13.** a source, as of information or of supply: *at first hand.* **14.** style of handwriting. **15.** a person's signature. **16.** skill; execution; touch: *a painting that shows a master's hand.* **17.** a person, with reference to action, ability, or skill: *a poor hand at writing letters.* **18.** a pledge of marriage. **19.** a linear measure in the imperial system, used in giving the height of horses, etc., equal to four inches or 0.1016 m (approx. 10 cm). **20.** *Cards.* **a.** the cards dealt to or held by each player at one time. **b.** the person holding the cards. **c.** a single part of a game, in which all the cards dealt at one time are played. **21.** *Squash.* the time for which a player is hand-in. **22.** skill or knack at manipulating the reins. **23.** a bundle or bunch of various fruit, leaves, etc., as a cluster of bananas or tobacco leaves tied together. **24.** a round or outburst of applause for a performer: *to get a hand.* **25.** what is left from a pork forequarter after the removal of the foreloin: *pork hand.* **26.** Some special noun phrases are:

**a firm hand,** strict control.

**a heavy hand,** severity or oppression.

**a high hand,** dictatorial manner or arbitrary conduct.

**at hand, 1.** within reach; nearby. **2.** near in time. **3.** ready for use.

**at the hand** or **hands of,** from the action or agency of.

**by hand,** by the use of the hands (as opposed to any other means): *to make pottery by hand.*

**change hands,** to pass from one owner to another.

**come to hand,** to be received; come within one's reach.

**declare one's hand,** to reveal one's intentions or circumstances.

**eat out of one's hand,** to be entirely subservient to.

**force someone's hand,** to compel someone to act prematurely or against his better judgment.

**free hand,** freedom to act as desired.

**from hand to hand,** from one person to another.

**from hand to mouth, 1.** by eating at once whatever one

gets. **2.** with attention to immediate wants only.
**give a hand,** to help; assist.
**give one's hand on,** to vouch for.
**hand and glove** or **hand in glove,** on very intimate terms; in league with.
**hand in hand, 1.** with hands mutually clasped. **2.** conjointly or concurrently.
**hand over fist, 1.** easily. **2.** in large quantities: *to make money hand over fist.*
**hands and heels,** *Horseracing.* without the use of a whip.
**hands down,** totally; completely; easily.
**hands off,** keep off; refrain from blows or touching.
**hands up!,** raise the hands (as a sign of surrender).
**hand to hand,** in close combat; at close quarters.
**have a hand in,** to have a part or concern in doing.
**have one's hands full,** to be fully occupied.
**hold the hand out,** *Colloq.* **1.** to exploit the benefits given out by the government and other welfare organisations. **2.** to demand bribe money.
**in good hands,** in the care of someone trustworthy.
**in hand, 1.** under control. **2.** in immediate possession: *cash in hand.* **3.** in process: *keep to the matter in hand.* **4.** *Croquet.* (of a ball) after roquet has been made until croquet has been taken.
**keep one's hand in,** to keep in practice.
**lay hands on, 1.** to assault; to beat up. **2.** to lay one's hands on the head of (a person) as part of a ritual.
**lay one's hands on,** *Colloq.* to obtain.
**off one's hands,** out of one's responsible charge or care.
**old hand, 1.** an experienced person; veteran. **2.** *Obs.* a former convict.
**on hand, 1.** in immediate possession: *cash on hand.* **2.** before one for attention. **3.** present.
**on** or **upon one's hands,** under one's care, management, or responsibility.
**out of hand, 1.** beyond control: *to let one's temper get out of hand.* **2.** at once; without delay.
**out of one's hands,** not one's responsibility; out of one's control.
**play into the hands of,** to act, without full realisation, against one's best interest and in the interest of (an enemy or potential opponent).
**shake hands,** to clasp another's right hand as a salutation, in closing a bargain, etc.
**show of hands,** a voting procedure by which a motion is passed or lost on the basis of an estimate of the number of hands raised.
**take a hand in,** to have a part or concern in doing.
**take in hand, 1.** to assume responsibility for. **2.** to subject to vigorous discipline.
**throw in one's hand,** to give up; stop doing something; surrender.
**to hand, 1.** within reach; at hand. **2.** into one's immediate possession.
**try one's hand,** to attempt, esp. for the first time. (usu. fol. by *at*).
**turn one's hand to,** to turn one's energies to; set to work at.
**upper hand,** a position of marked superiority; whip hand.
**wait on hand and foot,** attend to every need; shower attention upon.
**wash one's hands of,** to have nothing more to do with.
*–v.t.* **27.** to deliver or pass with the hand. **28.** to help or conduct with the hand. **29.** *Naut.* to furl, as a sail. **30.** to pass on; transmit (fol. by *on*). **31. hand down, a.** to deliver the decision of a court. **b.** to transmit from the higher to the lower, in space or time: *to hand down to posterity.* **32. hand in,** to present for acceptance. **33. hand it to,** to give due credit to. **34. hand out,** to distribute. **35. hand off,** *Rugby Football.* to thrust off an opponent who is tackling. **36. hand over, a.** to deliver into another's keeping. **b.** to give up or yield control of. *–adj.* **37.** of or belonging to the hand. **38.** done or made by hand. **39.** that may be carried in, or worn on, the hand. **40.** operated by hand. [ME and OE, c. G *Hand*]

**hand and spring,** *n.* the front trotter, shoulder and belly of pork. Cf. **spring of pork.**

**handbag** /ˈhændbæg/, *n.* a small pouch or bag for carrying in the hand, to contain money and personal articles, etc.

**handball** /ˈhændbɔl/, *n.* **1.** a game in which a small ball is batted against a wall with the (usu. gloved) hand. **2.** the kind of ball used in this game. **3.** *Aus. Rules.* →**handpass. 4.** a game similar to tennis in which the players hit the ball with their hands rather than with racquets. *–v.i.* **5.** *Aus. Rules.* →**handpass.**

**handbarrow** /ˈhændˌbæroʊ/, *n.* **1.** a frame with handles at each end by which it is carried. **2.** →**handcart.**

**handbell** /ˈhændbɛl/, *n.* a bell rung by hand, esp. one that is part of a set for musical performance.

**handbill** /ˈhændbɪl/, *n.* a small printed bill or announcement, usu. for distribution by hand.

**handbook** /ˈhændbʊk/, *n.* a small book or treatise serving for guidance, as in an occupation or study: *handbook of car maintenance.*

**handbrake** /ˈhændbreɪk/, *n.* a brake operated by a hand lever.

**handbreadth** /ˈhændbrɛdθ, -brɛtθ/, *n.* a unit of linear measure from 6 to 10 cm. Also, **hand's-breadth.**

**handcart** /ˈhændkat/, *n.* a small cart drawn or pushed by hand.

**handclap** /ˈhændklæp/, *n., v.,* **-clapped, -clapping.** *–n.* **1.** Also, **clap.** the striking of one palm against the other, usu. repeatedly to indicate appreciation. **2.** →**slow handclap.** *–v.t.* **3.** to give a slow handclap.

**h. & c.,** hot and cold (water).

**handcrafted** /ˈhændkraftəd/, *adj.* →**handmade.**

**hand cream** /ˈhænd krim/, *n.* a preparation to prevent the skin of the hands from becoming dry and scaly.

**handcuff** /ˈhændkʌf/, *n.* **1.** a ring-shaped shackle for the wrist, usu. one of a pair connected by a short chain or linked bar. *–v.t.* **2.** to put handcuffs on.

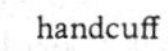
handcuff

**handed** /ˈhændəd/, *adj.* **1.** having a hand or hands. **2.** of or pertaining to preference or necessity in the use of hands, specified in combination: *right-handed, one-handed.* **3.** done by a specified number of hands: *a double-handed game.*

**handfeed** /ˈhændfid/, *v.t.,* **-fed, -feeding.** to raise animals, etc., by feeding by hand.

**handful** /ˈhændfʊl/, *n., pl.* **-fuls. 1.** as much or as many as the hand can grasp or contain. **2.** a small quantity or number: *a handful of men.* **3.** *Colloq.* a thing or a person that is as much as one can manage.

**hand glass** /ˈhænd glas/, *n.* **1.** a small mirror with a handle. **2.** a magnifying glass for holding in the hand.

**hand grenade** /ˈ– grəneɪd/, *n.* a grenade or explosive shell which is thrown by hand and exploded either by impact or by means of a fuse.

**handgrip** /ˈhændgrɪp/, *n.* **1.** a grasping with the hand; a grip, as in greeting. **2.** (*pl.*) hand-to-hand combat. **3.** a handle. [ME; OE *handgripe*]

**hand gun** /ˈhænd gʌn/, *n. Colloq.* →**pistol.**

**hand-held** /ˈhænd-hɛld/, *adj.* held in the hand; supported only by the unaided hand.

**handhold** /ˈhændhoʊld/, *n.* **1.** a grip with the hand. **2.** a thing that can be taken hold of by the hand, as for support.

**hand-horn** /ˈhænd-hɒn/, *n.* the natural horn, producing only the harmonic series; changing this is effected by inserting crooks of different lengths.

**handicap** /ˈhændikæp/, *n., v.,* **-capped, -capping.** *–n.* **1.** a race or other contest in which certain disadvantages or advantages of weight, distance, time, past records, etc., are placed upon competitors to equalise their chances of winning. **2.** the disadvantage or advantage itself. **3.** any encumbrance or disadvantage that makes success more difficult. **4.** a physical disability. *–v.t.* **5.** to serve as a handicap or disadvantage to: *his age handicaps him.* **6.** to subject to a disadvantageous handicap, as a competitor of recognised superiority. **7.** to assign handicaps to (competitors). [orig. *hand i' cap* (with *i'* for *in* before a consonant), referring to the deposit of stakes or forfeits in a cap or hat] – **handicapper,** *n.*

**handicapped** /ˈhændikæpt/, *adj.* **1.** disabled; crippled. **2.** mentally retarded. **3.** (of a player, competitor, etc.) having a handicap.

**handicraft** /ˈhændikraft/, *n.* **1.** manual skill. **2.** a manual art or occupation. [alteration of earlier *handcraft,* OE *handcræft,* modelled on HANDIWORK]

**handicraftsman** /ˈhændikraftsmən/, *n., pl.* **-men.** a person skilled in a handicraft; craftsman.

**handily** /ˈhændəli/, *adv.* **1.** dexterously; expertly. **2.** conveniently.

**hand-in** /ˈhænd-ɪn/, *n.* (in squash) the player who serves the ball.

**handiness** /ˈhændinəs/, *n.* **1.** the state or character of being handy or expert. **2.** the quality of being easily handled; convenience.

**hand-in-glove** /hænd-ɪn-ˈglʌv/, *adv.* in close collaboration (with). – **hand-in-glove,** *adj.*

**handiwork** /ˈhændiwɜk/, *n.* **1.** work done or a thing or things made by the hands. **2.** the labour or action of a particular doer or maker: *the handiwork of man.* **3.** the result of one's action or agency. [ME *handiwerk,* OE *handgeweorc*]

**handkerchief** /ˈhæŋkətʃif/, *n.* a small piece of linen, silk, soft paper, or other fabric, usu. square, carried about the person for wiping the face, nose, etc. [HAND + KERCHIEF]

**handle** /ˈhændl/, *n., v.,* **-dled, -dling.** *–n.* **1.** a part of a thing which is intended to be grasped by the hand in using or moving it. **2.** that by which anything may be held. **3.** something that may be taken advantage of in effecting a purpose. **4.** the feel or touch, as of textiles. **5.** *Colloq.* a title in front of a name. **6.** *Colloq.* a person's name. **7.** *Colloq.* **a.** a beer glass with a handle. **b.** the contents of such a glass. *–v.t.* **8.** to touch or feel with the hand; use the hands on, as in picking up. **9.** to manage in use with the hands; manipulate. **10.** to wield, employ, or use: *to handle one's fists well in a fight.* **11.** to manage, direct, or control: *to handle troops.* **12.** to deal with or treat, as a matter or subject. **13.** to deal with or treat in a particular way: *to handle a person with tact.* **14.** to deal or trade in (goods, etc.). **15.** *Colloq.* to con; deceive. *–v.i.* **16.** to respond to handling. [ME *handlen,* OE *handlian* (c. G *handeln*), from *hand* HAND] – **handled,** *adj.*

**handlebar** /ˈhændlba/, *n.* (*usu. pl.*) the curved steering bar of a bicycle, motorcycle, etc., in front of the rider.

**handlebar moustache** /– məˈstaʃ/, *n.* a moustache with curved ends.

**handler** /ˈhændlə/, *n.* **1.** a person or thing that handles. **2.** *Boxing.* a person who assists in the training of a fighter or is his second during the fight. **3.** the individual who manages a dog, etc., in a contest, in the police force, army etc. **4.** (in motor cycling, etc.) a person who assists a rider at the start of a race and looks after his machine.

**handline** /ˈhændlaɪn/, *n.* a fishing line designed to be held in the hand. Cf. **fishing rod.**

**handling** /ˈhændlɪŋ/, *n.* **1.** a touching, grasping, or using with the hands. **2.** management; treatment. **3.** the process of packing, moving, carrying or transporting something. *–adj.* **4.** of or pertaining to this process.

**handmade** /ˈhændmeɪd/, *adj.* made by hand, not machine.

**handmaid** /ˈhændmeɪd/, *n.* a female servant or personal attendant. Also, **handmaiden.**

**hand-me-down** /ˈhænd-mi-daʊn/, *n. Colloq.* **1.** an article of clothing handed down or acquired at second hand. **2.** a cheap, ready-made garment. Also, **reach-me-down.**

**hand-off** /ˈhænd-ɒf/, *n.* (in Rugby football) a thrust with the hand open, made by a player carrying the ball, to foil the tackle of an opponent.

**hand organ** /ˈhænd ɔgən/, *n.* a portable barrel organ played by means of a crank turned by hand.

**hand-out** /ˈhænd-aʊt/, *n.* **1.** *Squash.* the player who receives the service. **2.** →**handout.**

**handout** /ˈhændaʊt/, *n.* **1.** a prepared statement issued free of charge, esp. to the press, to members of an institution, to the audience at a lecture or performance. **2.** a free sample given as for advertisement. **3.** a portion of food or the like given to a beggar. **4.** food, money, etc. given as charity. **5. live on handouts,** *Colloq.* to subsist on the social benefits offered by charity, private and public. Also, **hand-out.**

**handpass** /ˈhændpas/, *Aus. Rules. –n.* **1.** a pass in which a player attempts to deliver the ball to a team mate by holding the ball in one hand and hitting it away with the other, usu. clenched as a fist. *–v.i.* **2.** to pass the ball thus. Also, **handball.**

**hand-pick** /hænd-ˈpɪk/, *v.t.* **1.** to pick by hand. **2.** to select carefully. – **hand-picked,** *adj.*

**handpiece** /ˈhændpis/, *n.* **1.** the part of a telephone or intercom held to the ear. **2.** the shearing attachment of a shearing-machine.

**handrail** /ˈhændreɪl/, *n.* a rail serving as a support or guard at the side of a stairway, platform, etc.

**hand-reading** /ˈhænd-ridɪŋ/, *n.* →**palmistry.**

**handrush** /ˈhændrʌʃ/, *v.t.* hurry (someone) into a decision.

**handsaw** /ˈhændsɔ/, *n.* a saw used with one hand.

**hand's-breadth** /ˈhændz-brɛdθ, -brɛtθ/, *n.* →**handbreadth.**

**handsel** /ˈhænsəl/, *n., v.,* **-selled, -selling** or (*U.S.*) **-seled, -seling.** *–n.* **1.** a gift or token for good luck or as an expression of good wishes, as at the beginning of the new year, or at entering upon a new state, situation, or enterprise. **2.** a first instalment of payment. **3.** the first use or experience of anything; foretaste. *–v.t.* **4.** to give a handsel to. **5.** to inaugurate auspiciously. **6.** to use, try, or experience for the first time. Also, **hansel.** [ME *handselne,* OE *handselen,* lit., hand gift; akin to Icel. *handsal* the binding of a bargain by joining hands]

**handset** /ˈhændsɛt/, *n., v.,* **-set, -setting,** *adj. –n.* **1.** a part of a telephone combining both the receiver and the transmitter, one at each end of a handle. *–v.t.* **2.** *Print.* to set (type) by hand. *–adj.* **3.** *Print.* (of type) set by hand.

**handshake** /ˈhænʃeɪk, ˈhænd-/, *n.* **1.** a clasping of another's right hand as in salutation, congratulation, agreement, etc. **2. golden handshake,** (*usu. ironic*), a sum of money given to an executive or the like on loss of employment, or retirement.

**handshake grip** /ˈ– grɪp/, *n.* →**eastern grip.**

**hand shears** /ˈhænd ʃɪəz/, *n.pl.* hand-held shears for shearing sheep.

**hand signal** /ˈ– sɪgnəl/, *n.* a signal made by hand, esp. to indicate intention when driving a car.

**handsome** /ˈhænsəm/, *adj.,* **-somer, -somest. 1.** of fine or admirable appearance; comely; tastefully or elegantly fine: *a handsome person.* **2.** considerable, ample, or liberal in amount: *a handsome fortune.* **3.** gracious; generous: *a handsome gift.* **4.** *U.S. Colloq.* dexterous; graceful: *a handsome speech.* [ME *handsom,* from HAND + -SOME[1]; orig., easy to handle] – **handsomely,** *adv.* – **handsomeness,** *n.*

**handspike** /ˈhændspaɪk/, *n.* a bar used as a lever. [from D *handspeck* hand bar, assimilated to *spike*]

**handspring** /ˈhændsprɪŋ/, *n.* a kind of somersault in which the body is supported upon one or both hands while turning in the air.

**handstand** /ˈhænstænd, ˈhænd-/, *n.* the act, or an instance of balancing upside down on one's hands.

**hand tennis** /ˈhænd tɛnəs/, *n.* →**handball** (def. 4).

**hand-to-hand** /hænd-tə-ˈhænd/, *adj.* in close combat; at close quarters.

**hand-to-mouth** /hænd-tə-ˈmaʊθ/, *adj.* precarious; unsettled.

**handtowel** /ˈhændtaʊl, ˈhæntaʊl/, *n.* a small towel for drying the hands.

**handwork** /ˈhændwɜk/, *n.* work done by hand, as distinguished from that done by machine.

**handwriting** /ˈhændˌraɪtɪŋ/, *n.* **1.** writing done with the hand. **2.** a kind or style of writing.

**handwritten** /ˈhændrɪtn/, *adj.* written by hand.

**handy** /ˈhændi/, *adj.,* **-dier, -diest. 1.** ready to hand; conveniently accessible: *to have aspirins handy.* **2.** ready or skilful with the hands; deft; dexterous. **3.** convenient to handle; easily manipulated or manoeuvred: *a handy ship.* **4.** convenient or useful: *a handy tool.*

**handy billy** /– ˈbɪli/, *n.* a small tackle (def. 4b).

**handyman** /ˈhændimæn/, *n.* a man hired to do odd jobs.

**hanepoot** /ˈhænɪput/, *n.* a full-flavoured southern African variety of grape, originally from the Mediterranean area. [Afrikaans: lit., cock foot]

**hang** /hæŋ/, *v.,* **hung** or (*esp. for capital punishment and suicide*) **hanged, hanging,** *n. –v.t.* **1.** to fasten or attach a thing so that it is supported only from above; suspend. **2.** to suspend so as to allow free movement as on a hinge. **3.** to fasten or suspend (a person) on a gallows or the like, esp. as a method of capital punishment. **4.** to suspend by the neck until dead. **5.** *Archaic.* to crucify. **6.** to let droop or bend downwards: *to hang one's head in shame.* **7.** to furnish or decorate with something suspended: *to hang a room with tapestries.* **8.** to fasten into position; fix at a proper angle: *to hang a scythe.* **9.** to attach (paper, etc.) to walls. **10.** to suspend (game) by the feet until it becomes high (def. 28). **11.** *Arts.* **a.** to exhibit (a picture or pictures). **b.** to exhibit the work of (a painter or the like). **12.** to hinge (a door, window, etc.) to its frame. **13.** (used in maledictions and emphatic expressions): *I'll be hanged if I do.* **14.** to keep (a jury) from rendering a verdict, as one juror by refusing to agree with the others. **15.** to trigger off an adverse emotional reaction (fol. by *up*). *–v.i.* **16.** to be suspended; dangle. **17.** to swing freely, as on a hinge. **18.** to be suspended from a cross or gallows; suffer death in this way as punishment. **19.** to bend forwards or downwards; lean over; incline downwards. **20.** to be conditioned or contingent; be dependent. **21.** to hold fast, cling, or adhere; rest for support (fol. by *on* or *upon*). **22.** to be doubtful or undecided; waver or hesitate; remain unfinished. **23.** to loiter or linger: *to hang about a place.* **24.** to rest, float, or hover in the air. **25.** to impend; be imminent. **26.** to remain in attention or consideration: *to hang upon a person's words.* **27.** *Arts.* **a.** to be exhibited, as in an art gallery. **b.** to have one's works exhibited. **28.** to fail to agree, as a jury. *–v.* **29.** Some special verb phrases are:

**hang about** or **around,** to loiter.

**hang (around) with (someone),** to spend time in (someone's) company.

**hang back,** to resist advancing; be reluctant to proceed.

**hang, draw and quarter, 1.** (formerly) to punish (someone) for treason by hanging, disembowelling, and subsequently cutting him into four pieces for public display. **2.** *Colloq.* to punish severely.

**hang fire,** *Colloq.* to be slow in action or acceptance.

**hang five,** *Colloq.* to ride a surfboard standing on the nose of the board with the toes of one foot over the edge.

**hang in, 1.** *Horseracing.* (of horses) to veer away from the most direct course, toward the fence. **2.** (in surfboard riding) to ride close to the breaking part of the wave. **3.** *Colloq.* to persevere.

**hang in the balance,** to be in doubt or suspense.

**hang loose,** to relax; fill in time.

**hang on, 1.** to persevere, to maintain existing conditions with effort. **2.** to linger: *corruption still hangs on in the city.* **3.** to wait: *hang on! I'm not quite ready.* **4.** *Boxing.* to clinch. **5.** *Aus. Rules.* to hold an opponent when he does not have the ball in his possession.

**hang one on (someone),** *Colloq.* to punch (someone).

**hang out, 1.** to lean through an opening. **2.** *Colloq.* to live at or frequent a particular place. **3.** to suspend in open view; display: *to hang out a banner.* **4.** *Horseracing.* (of horses) to veer away from the most direct course, away from the fence. **5.** *Colloq.* (*used in the present tense*) to be addicted to; crave (fol. by *for*): *he's hanging out for some dope.*

**let it all hang out,** *Colloq.* **a.** to allow oneself to speak one's mind or show emotion freely. **b.** to be uninhibited in manner, dress, etc.

**hang out for,** to remain adamant in expectation of (a goal, reward, etc.): *I'll hang out for a higher price before I'll sell.*

**hang ten,** to ride a surfboard while standing on the nose of the board with all one's toes over the edge.

**hang together, 1.** to hold together; remain united. **2.** to be consistent: *his statements do not hang together.*

**hang up, 1.** to suspend on a hook or peg. **2.** to hold up. **3.** to break off telephonic communication by putting down the receiver. **4.** to tether (a horse). **5.** *Shearing.* to stop work, as by hanging up shears.

*–n.* **30.** *Gymnastics.* a position of the body, extended and hanging from the hands. **31.** the way in which a thing hangs: *the hang of a curtain.* **32.** *Colloq.* the precise manner of doing, using, etc., something: *to get the hang of a tool.* **33.** *Colloq.* meaning or force: *to get the hang of a subject.* **34.** the least degree of care, concern, etc. (in mild expletives): *not to give a hang.* **35. hang of a.** Also, **hanguva.** *Colloq.* in an exceptionally great (hurry, difficulty, etc.). [fusion of three verbs: (1) ME and OE *hōn* (orig., v.t.), now obs.; (2) ME *hang(i)en,* OE *hangian* (orig., v.i.); (3) ME *heng(e), hing,* from Scand. (cf. Icel. *hengja* cause to hang)]

**hangar** /ˈhæŋə/, *n.* **1.** a shed or shelter. **2.** a shed for aeroplanes or airships. [F, ? from Gmc]

**hangbird** /ˈhæŋbɜd/, *n.* a bird that builds a hanging nest, esp. the Baltimore oriole.

**hangdog** /ˈhæŋdɒg/, *adj.* **1.** having a dejected, guilty or pitiful aspect. **2.** of or pertaining to a degraded, contemptible or miserable person. **3.** *Brit., U.S.* a degraded, contemptible, or miserable person.

**hanger** /ˈhæŋə/, *n.* **1.** one who hangs. **2.** that on which anything is hung. **3.** a shaped support for a coat or other garment. **4.** something by which a thing is hung, as a loop on a garment. **5.** *Motor Vehicles, etc.* a double-hinged device linking the chassis with each spring. **6.** a light sabre of the 17th and 18th centuries, often worn at sea.

**hanger-on** /hæŋər-ˈɒn/, *n., pl.* **hangers-on.** one who clings to a service, place, or connection; follower.

**hang-fire** /ˈhæŋ-faɪə/, *n.* a device, as an artillery shell, which has been detonated but which has not yet exploded.

**hang-glide** /ˈhæŋ-glaɪd/, *v.i.,* **-glided, -gliding.** to operate a hang-glider.

**hang-glider** /ˈhæŋ-glaɪdə/, *n.* **1.** a simple kite-like glider without a fuselage but with a framework from which a person hangs feet downwards. **2.** the person operating such a glider.

**hang-gliding** /ˈhæŋ-ˌglaɪdɪŋ/, *n.* the sport of flying a hang-glider.

**hangi** /ˈhʌŋi/, *n. N.Z.* **1.** Maori oven in which food is steamed over hot stones in the ground; umu. **2.** food prepared in this manner. **3.** a feast at which such food is served. [Maori]

**hanging** /ˈhæŋɪŋ/, *n.* **1.** capital punishment by suspension with strangulation on a gallows. **2.** (*oft. pl.*) something that hangs or is hung on the walls of a room, as a drapery, tapestry, etc. **3.** the act of one who or that which hangs; suspension. *–adj.* **4.** deserving punishment by hanging. **5.** inclined to inflict death by hanging: *a hanging judge.* **6.** that hangs; pendent; over-hanging. **7.** situated on a steep slope or at a height: *a hanging garden.* **8.** directed downwards: *a hanging look.* **9.** made for hanging an object on.

**hanging buttress** /– ˈbʌtrəs/, *n.* a decorative buttress usu. supported by a corbel.

**hanging figure** /ˈ– fɪgə/, *n.* a printed numeral with an ascender or a descender.

**hanging indentation** /– ɪndɛnˈteɪʃən/, *n.* an arrangement of printed type in which the first line of the paragraph is of full width but the following lines are indented at the left.

**hanging participle** /– ˈpatəsɪpəl/, *n.* →**misrelated participle.**

**hanging valley** /– ˈvæli/, *n.* a tributary valley in a mountainous area, which joins the main valley by a sudden sharp descent, as a result of glacial erosion.

**hangman** /ˈhæŋmən/, *n., pl.* **-men. 1.** one who hangs persons condemned to death; public executioner. **2.** *N.Z. Colloq.* a character; an eccentric person. **3.** a word game in which one player is required to guess the letters making up a word which the other player has chosen, each incorrect guess being registered by a line in a simple drawing of a hanged man; a winning player guesses the word before the picture is completed.

**hangnail** /ˈhæŋneɪl/, *n.* a small piece of partly detached skin at the side or base of the fingernail. Also, **agnail.** [aspirated var. of *angnail,* OE *angnægl;* the aspirated form became standard by popular etymology (associated with HANG)]

**hang-out** /ˈhæŋ-aʊt/, *n. Colloq.* a place where one lives or frequently visits.

**hangover** /ˈhæŋoʊvə/, *n. Colloq.* **1.** something remaining behind from a former period or state of affairs. **2.** the after-effects of excessive indulgence in alcoholic drink.

**hang-up** /ˈhæŋ-ʌp/, *n. Colloq.* something which occasions unease, inhibition, or conflict in an individual.

**hank** /hæŋk/, *n.* **1.** a skein, as of thread or yarn. **2.** a definite length of thread or yarn. **3.** a coil, knot, or loop: *a hank of hair.* **4.** *Naut.* a ring, as of metal, wood, etc., round a stay, to which a sail is attached. [ME, from Scand.; cf. Icel. *hönk* hank, coil, skein]

**hanker** /ˈhæŋkə/, *v.i.* to have a restless or incessant longing (oft. fol. by *after, for,* or an infinitive). [cf. dialect D *hankeren*] – **hankerer,** *n.*

**hankering** /ˈhæŋkərɪŋ/, *n.* a longing; craving.

**hanky** /ˈhæŋki/, *n. Colloq.* →**handkerchief.** Also, **hankie.**

**hanky-panky** /ˌhæŋki-ˈpæŋki/, *n. Colloq.* **1.** trickery; subterfuge or the like. **2.** jugglery or legerdemain. **3.** sexual play.

**Hansard** /ˈhænsad/, *n.* the official printed reports of the debates and proceedings of parliament, esp. in Australia, New Zealand, Britain and Canada. [so called after the *Hansard* family who printed the *Journals of the House of Commons* in England from 1774]

**Hanse** /hæns/, *n.* **1.** a company or guild of merchants. **2.** a fee paid to a medieval trading guild. Also, **Hansa** /ˈhænsə/. [ME, from OF, from MHG: company (of merchants)]

**hansel** /ˈhænsəl/, *n., v.t.,* **-selled, -selling.** →**handsel.**

**Hansen's disease** /ˈhænsənz dəziz/, *n.* →**leprosy.** [named after Gerhard Henrik Armauer *Hansen,* 1841-1912, Norwegian physician who discovered leprosy-causing *Mycobacterium leprae*]

**hansom** /ˈhænsəm/, *n.* a low-hung, two-wheeled, covered vehicle drawn by one horse, for two passengers, the driver being mounted on an elevated seat behind, and the reins running over the roof. [named after J. A. *Hansom,* 1803-82, English patentee]

hansom

**Hanukkah** /ˈhanuka/, *n.* the Feast of the Dedication, a Jewish festival in commemoration of the victory of the Maccabees, lasting eight days (mostly in December). [Heb. *hanukkāh* dedication]

**hanuman** /ˈhanumən/, *n., pl.* **-mans.** the sacred monkey of India, *Presbytis entellus,* having a long tail and a black face fringed with greyish hairs; entellus. [Hind., from Skt *hanumant,* from *hanumat* large-jawed]

**hap** /hæp/, *n., v.,* **happed, happing.** *Archaic. –n.* **1.** one's luck or lot. **2.** an occurrence, happening, or accident. *–v.i.* **3.** to happen: *if it so hap.* [ME, from Scand.; cf. Icel. *happ* hap, chance, good luck. Cf. OE *gehæp,* adj., fit, convenient]

**hapax legomenon** /ˌhæpæks ləˈgɒmənɒn/, *n.* a word or form for which only one citation has been found. Also, **hapax.** [Gk]

**ha'pence** /ˈheɪpəns/, *n.* →**halfpence.**

**ha'penny** /ˈheɪpni/, *n., pl.* **-nies.** →**halfpenny.**

**haphazard** /hæpˈhæzəd/, *adj.* **1.** determined by or dependent on mere chance: *a haphazard remark. –adv.* **2.** in a haphazard manner; at random; by chance. *–n.* **3.** mere chance; accident: *to proceed at haphazard.* [HAP + HAZARD] **–haphazardly,** *adv.* **–haphazardness,** *n.*

**haphtarah** /hæftəˈra, hæfˈtarə/, *n., pl.* **-roth** /-ˈroʊθ/. a portion of the Prophets read immediately after a portion of the Pentateuch in the Jewish synagogue on sabbaths and festivals. Also, **haftarah.** [Heb.: conclusion]

**hapless** /ˈhæpləs/, *adj.* luckless; unfortunate; unlucky. **–haplessly,** *adv.* **–haplessness,** *n.*

**haplite** /ˈhæplaɪt/, *n.* →**aplite.**

**haplo-,** a word element meaning 'single', 'simple'. [Gk, combining form of *haplóos*]

**haplography** /hæpˈlɒgrəfi/, *n.* the omission of a word, syllable, or letter in writing, where it occurs twice in succession, as in *hippotamus* for *hippopotamus.*

**haploid** /ˈhæplɔɪd/, *adj.* Also, **haploidic. 1.** single; simple. **2.** *Biol.* pertaining to a single set of chromosomes. *–n.* **3.** *Biol.* an organism or cell having only one complete set of chromosomes, ordinarily half the normal diploid number.

**haplology** /hæpˈlɒlədʒi/, *n.* the syncope of a syllable within a word, as *syllabi(fi)cation.* [HAPLO- + -LOGY]

**haplosis** /hæpˈloʊsəs/, *n.* the production of haploid chromosome groups during meiosis.

**haply** /ˈhæpli/, *adv. Archaic.* perhaps; by chance.

**ha'p'orth** /ˈheɪpəθ/, *n.* →**halfpennyworth.**

**happen** /ˈhæpən/, *v.i.* **1.** to come to pass, take place, or occur. **2.** to come to pass by chance; occur without apparent reason or design; chance. **3.** to have the fortune or lot (to do or be as specified): *I happened to see him.* **4.** to befall, as to a person or thing. **5.** to come by chance (fol. by *on* or *upon*). *–adj.* **6.** *Brit. Colloq.* perhaps. [ME *happene(n), happen;* from HAP, *n.* + -EN[1]]

**happening** /ˈhæpənɪŋ, ˈhæpnɪŋ/, *n.* **1.** an occurrence, event. **2.** a dramatic or similar performance consisting chiefly of a series of discontinuous events, often involving audience participation.

**happenstance** /ˈhæpənstæns/, *n.* chance: *by pure happenstance.* Also, **happenchance.** [HAPPEN + (CIRCUM)STANCE]

**happily** /ˈhæpəli/, *adv.* **1.** in a happy manner; with pleasure. **2.** luckily. **3.** with skill; aptly; appropriately.

**happiness** /ˈhæpinəs/, *n.* **1.** the quality or state of being happy. **2.** good fortune; pleasure, content, or gladness. **3.** aptness or felicity, as of expression.

**happy** /ˈhæpi/, *adj.,* **-pier, -piest. 1.** characterised by or indicative of pleasure, content, or gladness: *a happy mood.* **2.** delighted, pleased, or glad, as over a particular thing: *to be happy to see a person.* **3.** favoured by fortune; fortunate or lucky: *a happy event.* **4.** apt or felicitous, as actions, utterances, ideas, etc. **5.** *Colloq.* showing an excessive liking for, or quick to use an item indicated (used in combination): *trigger-happy.* **6. happy as Larry,** *Colloq.* very happy. **7. happy days!** *Colloq.* (*sometimes ironic*) have a good time! [ME; from HAP, *n.* + -Y[1]]

**happy families** /– ˈfæmliz/, *n.pl.* a card game in which the object is to gain the greatest number of matching pairs of cards.

**happy family** /– ˈfæmli/, *n.* **1.** →**grey-crowned babbler. 2.** →**apostle bird.** Also, **happy family bird.**

**happy-go-lucky** /ˌhæpi-goʊ-ˈlʌki/, *adj.* **1.** trusting cheerfully to luck. *–adv.* **2.** haphazard; by mere chance.

**happy hour** /ˈhæpi aʊə/, *n. Colloq.* the time in a hotel, club, etc., when drinks are either free or sold at a reduced price.

**Happy Hunting Grounds,** *n.pl.* **1.** (in North American Indian mythology) the world inhabited by souls after death; the afterlife. **2.** (*usu. sing., l.c.*) *Colloq.* a suitable place for an activity: *abandoned gold-rush towns are happy hunting grounds for amateur prospectors.*

**Happy Jack** /ˈhæpi dʒæk/, *n.* →**grey-crowned babbler.**

**happy pill** /ˈhæpi pɪl/, *n. Colloq.* a tranquillising pill.

**hapten** /ˈhæptən/, *n.* an incomplete antigen.

**haptic** /ˈhæptɪk/, *adj.* **1.** of or pertaining to the sense of touch. **2.** favouring the sense of touch. [Gk, from *háptein* to touch]

**hapu** /ˈhapu/, *n. N.Z.* section of a Maori tribe; a class. [Maori]

**hapuku** /ˈhapəkə, həˈpukə/, *n.* the groper, *Polyprion oxygeneios,* of New Zealand and eastern Australian waters. Also, **hapuka.** [Maori]

**harakiri** /hærəˈkɪri/, *n.* suicide by ripping open the abdomen with a dagger or knife, the national form of honourable suicide in Japan, formerly practised among the higher classes when disgraced or sentenced to death. Also, **harakari** /hærəˈkari/, **harikari.** [Jap.: belly cut]

**harangue** /həˈræŋ/, *n., v.,* **-rangued, -ranguing.** *–n.* **1.** a passionate, vehement speech; noisy and intemperate address. **2.** any long, declamatory or pompous speech. *–v.t.* **3.** to address in a harangue. *–v.i.* **4.** to deliver a harangue. [F, from Gmc; cf. OE and OHG *hring* RING[1]] **–haranguer,** *n.*

**harass** /ˈhærəs, həˈræs/, *v.t.* **1.** to trouble by repeated attacks, incursions, etc., as in war or hostilities; harry; raid. **2.** to disturb persistently; torment, as with troubles, cares, etc. [F *harasser,* from OF *harer* set a dog on] **–harasser,** *n.* **–harassingly,** *adv.* **–harassment** /ˈhærəsmənt, həˈræsmənt/, *n.*

**harbinger** /ˈhabɪŋə, -bɪndʒə/, *n.* **1.** one who goes before and makes known the approach of another. **2.** that which foreshadows a future event; an omen. **3.** *Obs.* one sent in advance of troops, a royal train, etc., to provide or secure lodgings and other accommodations. *–v.t.* **4.** to act as harbinger to; herald the coming of. [ME *herbergere,* from OF *herbergeor,* from *herbergier* provide lodging for, from *herberge* lodging, from Gmc. See HARBOUR]

**harbour** /ˈhabə/, *n.* **1.** a portion of a body of water along the shore deep enough for ships, and so situated with respect to coastal features, whether natural or artificial, as to provide protection from winds, waves, and currents. **2.** any place of shelter or refuge. **3.** *Mil.* a bivouac under cover occupied by troops not in close contact with an enemy in order to carry out essential maintenance and replenishment. *–v.t.* **4.** to give shelter to: *to harbour refugees.* **5.** to conceal; give a place to hide: *to harbour smuggled goods.* **6.** to entertain in the mind; indulge (usu. unfavourable or evil feelings): *to harbour suspicion.* **7.** to shelter (a ship) in a harbour or haven. *–v.i.* **8.** (of a ship, etc.) to take shelter in a harbour. Also, *U.S.,* **harbor.** [ME *herber(we), hereberge,* OE *herebeorg* lodgings, quarters, from *here* army + *(ge)beorg* refuge; c. G *Herberge*] – **harbourer,** *n.* – **harbourless,** *adj.*

**harbourage** /ˈhabərɪdʒ/, *n.* **1.** shelter for ships, as in a harbour. **2.** shelter or lodging. **3.** a place of shelter.

**harbourmaster** /ˈhabəmastə/, *n.* an officer in charge of harbour regulations, such as the mooring of vessels.

**harbour of refuge,** *n.* a harbour on an inhospitable coast, used for shelter in bad weather, but having none of the facilities of a port.

**harbour seal** /ˈhabə sil/, *n.* a small, spotted seal, *Phoca vitulina,* of coastal waters of the Northern Hemisphere.

**hard** /had/, *adj.* **1.** solid and firm to the touch; not soft. **2.** firmly formed; tight: *a hard knot.* **3.** difficult to do or accomplish; fatiguing; troublesome: *a hard task.* **4.** difficult or troublesome with respect to an action specified: *hard to please.* **5.** difficult to deal with, manage, control, overcome, or understand: *a hard problem.* **6.** involving or performed with great exertion, energy, or persistence: *hard work.* **7.** carrying on work in this manner: *a hard worker.* **8.** vigorous or violent; severe: *a hard rain.* **9.** oppressive; harsh; rough: *hard treatment.* **10.** unpleasant; unfair; bad: *hard luck.* **11.** austere; uncomfortable; causing pain, poverty, etc.: *hard times.* **12.** unfeeling; callous: *a hard heart.* **13.** harsh or severe in dealing with others: *a hard master.* **14.** incapable of being denied or explained away: *hard facts.* **15.** harsh or unfriendly; not easily moved: *hard feelings.* **16.** harsh or unpleasant to the eye, ear, or aesthetic sense. **17.** severe or rigorous in terms: *a hard bargain.* **18.** not swayed by sentiment or sophistry; shrewd: *to have a hard head.* **19.** in coin rather than in paper currency, or as distinguished from other property: *hard cash.* **20. a.** alcoholic or intoxicating: *hard liquor.* **b.** dangerously addictive: *hard drugs.* **21.** (of water) containing mineral salts which interfere with the action of the soap. **22.** *Physics.* (of radiation) of short wavelength and high penetrating power. **23.** *Agric.* denoting wheats with high gluten content, milled for a bread flour as contrasted with pastry flour. **24.** *Phonet.* **a.** (of consonants) →**fortis. b.** (of *c* and *g*) pronounced as in *come* and *go.* **c.** (of consonants in Slavic languages) not palatalised. **25.** of or pertaining to hardcore pornography. **26. do (it) the hard way,** to choose a needlessly difficult way of doing (something). **27. hard cheese (cheddar) (luck),** *Colloq.* **a.** bad luck. **b.** (an off-hand expression of sympathy). **c.** (a rebuff to an appeal for sympathy). **28. hard of hearing,** partly deaf. **29. hard up,** *Colloq.* urgently in need of something, esp. money. **30. put the hard word on,** *Colloq.* **a.** to ask a favour of. **b.** to ask another for sexual intercourse. *–adv.* **31.** with great exertion; with vigour or violence: *to work hard.* **32.** earnestly or intently: *to look hard at a thing.* **33.** harshly or severely; badly; gallingly: *it goes hard.* **34.** so as to be solid or firm: *frozen hard.* **35.** *Naut.* closely, fully, or to the extreme limit: *hard aport.* **36. hard by,** close or nearby. **37. hard put (to it),** in great difficulties. *–n.* **38.** *Colloq.* an erect penis. **39. get a hard on,** *Colloq.* to have an erection. **40. on the hard,** *Naut.* of a ship, onshore or aground. [ME; OE *heard,* c. G *hart*]

**hard and fast,** *adj.* **1.** strongly binding; not to be set aside or violated: *hard and fast rules.* *–adv.* **2.** firmly and securely: *bound hard and fast.*

**hardback** /ˈhadbæk/, *n.* **1.** a book bound in stiff covers, usu. of boards covered with cloth, etc. *–adj.* **2.** of, denoting, or pertaining to such books or the publishing of such books; casebound. Cf. **paperback.**

**hard-baked** /ˈhad-beɪkt/, *adj.* (of a person) toughened by experience, esp. outwardly.

**hard base** /ˈhad beɪs/, *n. Mil.* a launching base that is protected against a nuclear explosion.

**hard beech** /ˈ– bitʃ/, *n.* →**clinker beech.**

**hard-bitten** /ˈhad-bɪtn/, *adj.* tough; stubborn.

**hardboard** /ˈhadbɔd/, *n.* a material made from wood fibres compressed into sheets, having many household and industrial uses.

**hard-boil** /ˈhad-bɔɪl/, *v.t.* to boil an egg until it is hard throughout.

**hard-boiled** /ˈhad-bɔɪld/, *adj.* **1.** boiled until hard, as an egg. **2.** *Colloq.* hardened by experience: *a hard-boiled person.* **3.** *Colloq.* rough or tough.

**hard case** /had ˈkeɪs/, *n.* **1.** a tough, cynical person. **2.** a witty, consistently amusing person. Also, **hard doer. 3.** an incorrigible person. **4.** a person suffering from drug addiction, esp. to alcohol. – **hard-case,** *adj.*

**hard coal** /– ˈkoʊl/, *n.* →**anthracite.**

**hard copy** /ˈ– kɒpi/, *n.* (in computing) a permanent record as opposed to a display on a cathode ray tube.

**hard core** /ˈ– kɔ/, *n.* the unyielding or intransigent members forming the nucleus of a group.

**hard-core** /ˈhad-kɔ/, *adj.* **1.** of or belonging to the hard core: *a hard-core Communist.* **2.** of or pertaining to a residual chronic social condition: *hard-core unemployment.* **3.** explicit, blunt, unequivocal: *hard-core pornography.* **4.** physically addictive: *hard-core drugs.* *–n.* **5.** →**hard-core pornography.**

**hardcore** /hadˈkɔ/, *n.* solid pieces of rock, gravel or broken brick which form a foundation base for other building materials.

**hard-core pornography** /ˌhad-kɔ pɔˈnɒgrəfi/, *n.* pornography in which erotic activity is explicitly presented (opposed to *soft-core pornography*).

**hard court** /ˈhad kɔt/, *n.* a tennis court with a surface of cinders, sand, asphalt, or the like. – **hard-court,** *adj.*

**hardcover** /ˈhadkʌvə/, *n., adj.* →**hardback.**

**hard doer** /had ˈduə/, *n.* hard case; character; a sport.

**hard drinker** /– ˈdrɪŋkə/, *n.* one who drinks alcohol persistently and to excess.

**hard-earned** /ˈhad-ɜnd/, *n. Colloq.* money. [short for *hard-earned cash*]

**hard-edge** /ˈhad-ɛdʒ/, *adj.* of or pertaining to a modern school of painting originating in the U.S. which defines abstract areas of colour with clean edges.

**harden**[1] /ˈhadn/, *v.t.* **1.** to make hard or harder. **2.** to make obdurate or unyielding; make unfeeling or pitiless: *to harden one's heart.* **3.** to strengthen or confirm with respect to any element of character; toughen. **4.** to make hardy, robust, or capable of endurance. *–v.i.* **5.** to become hard or harder. **6.** to become obdurate, unfeeling, or pitiless. **7.** to become inured or toughened. **8.** *Comm.* (of prices, the market, etc.) **a.** to become higher; rise. **b.** to cease to fluctuate. [HARD + -EN[1]]

**harden**[2] /ˈhadn/, *n.* a coarse fabric made from hards.

**hardened** /ˈhadnd/, *adj.* **1.** made hard; indurated; inured. **2.** obdurate; unfeeling.

**hardened site** /– ˈsaɪt/, *n. Mil.* a site constructed to withstand the blast and associated effects of a nuclear attack and likely to be protected against a chemical, biological or radiological attack.

**hardener** /ˈhadənə/, *n.* **1.** a person or thing that hardens. **2.** one who hardens a specified thing. **3.** a substance mixed with paint or other protective covering to make the finish harder or more durable.

**hardening** /ˈhadənɪŋ/, *n.* **1.** a material which hardens another, as an alloy added to iron to make steel. **2.** the process of becoming hard or rigid.

**harder** /ˈhadə/, *n.* a sea fish, *Mugil cephalus,* a large, striped, edible member of the mullet family (Mugilidae) of warm seas; springer.

**hard-favoured** /ˈhad-feɪvəd/, *adj.* having a hard, unpleasant countenance.

**hard-featured** /ˈhad-fitʃəd/, *adj.* having hard and forbidding features.

**hard-fisted** /ˈhad-fɪstəd/, *adj.* **1.** niggardly; stingy. **2.** having hard or strong hands, as a labourer.

**hardhack** /ˈhadhæk/, *n.* a woolly-leaved shrub, *Spiraea tomentosa,* of North America, having terminal panicles of rose-coloured or white flowers.

**hard-handed** /ˈhad-hændəd/, *adj.* **1.** having hands hardened by toil. **2.** ruling with a strong or cruel hand.

**hard hat** /'had hæt/, *n.* **1.** →**safety helmet.** **2.** *Colloq.* a construction worker, working in an area in which safety helmets must be worn.
**hard-hat** /'had-hæt/, *adj.* of or pertaining to an area, job, etc., in which a safety helmet must be worn: *caution, this is a hard-hat area.*
**hardhead** /'hadhɛd/, *n.* **1.** an obstinate or stubborn person. **2.** a down-to-earth, practical person not easily moved by emotion or sentiment.
**hard-headed** /'had-hɛdəd/, *adj.* not easily moved or deceived; practical; shrewd. – **hard-headedly,** *adv.* – **hard-headedness,** *n.*
**hardheads** /'hadhɛdz/, *n.pl.* any of several members of the genus *Centaurea,* esp. *C. repens;* knapweed.
**hard-hearted** /'had-hatəd/, *adj.* unfeeling; unmerciful; pitiless. – **hard-heartedly,** *adv.* – **hard-heartedness,** *n.*
**hard-hit** /had-'hɪt/, *adj.* severely and adversely affected: *hard-hit by the drought.*
**hard-hitter** /had-'hɪtə/, *n. N.Z.* →**hard-knocker.**
**hardihood** /'hadihʊd/, *n.* hardy spirit or character; boldness or daring.
**hardily** /'hadəli/, *adv.* in a hardy manner.
**hardiness** /'hadinəs/, *n.* **1.** robustness; capability of endurance; strength. **2.** hardihood; audacity.
**hard-knocker** /had-'nɒkə/, *n.* a (black) bowler hat.
**hard labour** /had 'leɪbə/, *n.* labour imposed on prisoners as a punishment, often as part of the sentence.
**hard landing** /'– lændɪŋ/, *n.* a landing by a spacecraft on the moon or some other celestial body which is so violent that the spacecraft is destroyed. Cf. **soft landing.**
**hard line** /had 'laɪn/, *n.* a policy which is severe and which is not subject to change as a result of plea or argument.
**hardline** /'hadlaɪn/, *adj.* not deviating from a set doctrine, policy, etc.: *a hardline attitude to drugs.*
**hardliner** /had'laɪnə/, *n.* a person, esp. a politician, who takes a tough, stubborn view on an issue: *an abortion hardliner.*
**hard lines** /had 'laɪnz/, *n. pl. Colloq.* bad luck; unfair treatment.
**hard luck story,** *n.* an account of personal misfortune, intended to arouse the sympathy of others.
**hardly** /'hadli/, *adv.* **1.** barely; almost not at all: *hardly any, hardly ever.* **2.** not quite: *that is hardly true.* **3.** with little likelihood: *he will hardly come now.* **4.** with trouble or difficulty. **5.** harshly or severely.
**hard-mouthed** /'had-maʊðd/, *adj.* **1.** (of horses) difficult to control with a bit. **2.** (of a person) given to swearing and coarse language.
**hardness** /'hadnəs/, *n.* **1.** the state or quality of being hard. **2.** an instance of this quality. **3.** that quality in impure water which is imparted by the presence of dissolved salts, esp. calcium sulphate. **4.** *Mineral.* the comparative capacity of a substance to scratch another or be scratched by another. See **Mohs scale.**
**hardnose** /'hadnoʊz/, *n.* **1.** a recidivist. **2.** an intransigent person.
**hard-nosed** /'had-noʊzd/, *adj.* ruthless, esp. in business.
**hardpad** /'hadpæd/, *n.* an infectious disease of dogs, caused by a filterable virus.
**hard palate** /had 'pælət/, *n.* →**palate.**
**hardpan** /'hadpæn/, *n.* **1.** any layer of firm detrital matter, as of clay, underlying soft soil. **2.** hard, unbroken ground. **3.** solid foundation; hard underlying reality.
**hard-pressed** /had-'prɛst/, *adj.* under pressure created by natural conditions, a rival, an enemy, etc. (oft. fol. by *by*): *he was hard-pressed by the lack of time.*
**hard radiation** /ˌhad reɪdi'eɪʃən/, *n.* ionising radiation of relatively short wavelength and high penetrating power.
**hard rock** /– 'rɒk/, *n.* a rock music which emphasises the essential features, as strong simple rhythm and an aggressive, energetic style, and which is usu. greatly amplified.
**hard rubber** /– 'rʌbə/, *n.* rubber vulcanised with a large amount of sulphur, usu. 25-35 per cent, to render it stiff and comparatively inflexible.
**hard-rush** /'had-rʌʃ/, *n.* a glaucous, tufted, perennial, *Juncus inflexus,* widespread in damp places in temperate regions.
**hards** /hadz/, *n. pl.* the refuse or coarser parts of flax or hemp, separated in hackling. Also, **hurds.** [ME *herdes,* OE *heordan*]
**hard sauce** /had 'sɔs/, *n.* a sauce made by creaming butter and brown sugar, flavoured with brandy or rum, served with Christmas and other rich puddings.
**hard sell** /– 'sɛl/, *n.* a method of advertising or selling which is direct, forceful, and insistent; high-pressure salesmanship. See **soft sell.**
**hard-sell** /'had-sɛl/, *v.t.* **1.** to sell by forceful, insistent methods. *–adj.* **2.** of or pertaining to such methods.
**hard-set** /'had-sɛt/, *adj.* **1.** in a difficult position. **2.** firmly or rigidly set. **3.** determined; obstinate.
**hard-shell** /'had-ʃɛl/, *adj.* having a firm, hard shell, as a crab in its normal state, not having recently moulted.
**hardship** /'hadʃɪp/, *n.* **1.** a condition that bears hard upon one; severe toil, trial, oppression, or need. **2.** an instance of this; something hard to bear.
**hard-spun** /'had-spʌn/, *adj.* (of yarn) compactly twisted in spinning.
**hard stuff** /'had stʌf/, *n. Colloq.* **1.** strong alcoholic liquor; spirits. **2.** hard drugs, as heroin, etc.
**hardtack** /'hadtæk/, *n.* a kind of hard biscuit used esp. by sailors. [HARD + *tack* taste]
**hardtop** /'hadtɒp/, *n.* **1.** a motor car, esp. a sports car, which is not convertible. **2.** a cinema with a roof (opposed to *drive-in*). *–adj.* **3.** of or pertaining to such a car or cinema.
**hard-up** /'had-ʌp/, *adj.* in financial difficulties; poor. Also (*esp. in predicative positions*), **hard up.**
**hardware** /'hadwɛə/, *n.* **1.** building materials, tools, etc.; ironmongery. **2.** the mechanical equipment necessary for conducting an activity, usu. distinguished from the theory and design which make the activity possible. **3.** *Mil.* arms and the machinery of war generally. **4.** the physical components of a computer system, as the circuitry, magnetic tape units, etc. (opposed to *software*).
**hardware store** /'– stɔ/, *n.* a shop which sells hardware and often various other goods, as crockery, cutlery, lamps, etc.
**hard-wearing** /'had-wɛərɪŋ/, *adj.* tough and long-lasting.
**hard wheat** /had 'wit/, *n.* a wheat with hard kernels used to produce flour for bread, pasta, etc.
**hardwood** /'hadwʊd/, *n.* **1.** the hard, compact wood or timber of various trees, as the eucalyptus, oak, cherry, maple, mahogany, etc. **2.** a tree yielding such wood.
**hardy**[1] /'hadi/, *adj.,* **-dier, -diest.** **1.** capable of enduring fatigue, hardship, exposure, etc.: *hardy animals.* **2.** (of plants) able to withstand the cold of winter in the open air. **3.** requiring great physical endurance: *the hardiest sports.* **4.** bold or daring; courageous, as persons, actions, etc. **5.** unduly bold; presumptuous; foolhardy. [ME *hardi,* from OF, pp. of *hardir* harden, from Gmc; akin to HARD]
**hardy**[2] /'hadi/, *n., pl.* **-dies.** a chisel or fuller with a square shank for insertion into a square hole (**hardy-hole**) in a blacksmith's anvil. [apparently from HARD]
**hare** /hɛə/, *n., pl.* **hares,** (*esp. collectively*) **hare,** *v.,* **hared, haring.** *–n.* **1.** a rodent-like mammal of the genus *Lepus* (order Lagomorpha), rabbit-like, with long ears, divided upper lip, short tail, and lengthened hind limbs adapted for leaping. **2.** any of the larger solitary members of the genus distinguished from the smaller gregarious social rabbits. **3.** any of various similar animals of the same family. **4.** the person chased or pursued in the game of hare and hounds. **5. start a hare,** to bring an irrelevant point into an argument. *–v.i.* **6.** to run fast. [ME; OE *hara,* c. Dan. *hare;* akin to G *Hase.* Cf. OE *hasu* grey] – **harelike,** *adj.*

hare

**hare and hounds,** *n.* a kind of paperchase.
**harebell** /'hɛəbɛl/, *n.* a low herb, the bluebell of Scotland, *Campanula rotundifolia,* with blue, bell-shaped flowers.
**harebrained** /'hɛəbreɪnd/, *adj.* irrational; reckless.
**Hare electoral system,** *n.* a system of counting votes, used in Tasmanian parliamentary elections, in which each succeeding preference expressed by a voter has less value than his first. Also, **Hare-Clarke system.**
**harelip** /'hɛəlɪp/, *n.* **1.** a congenitally deformed lip, usu. the

upper one, in which there is a vertical fissure causing it to resemble the cleft lip of a hare. **2.** the deformity itself. – **hare-lipped,** *adj.*

**harem** /ˈhɛərəm, haˈrim/, *n.* **1.** that part of an oriental palace or house reserved for the residence of women. **2.** the women in an oriental household, mother, sisters, wives, concubines, daughters, entertainers, servants, etc. [Ar. *harīm,* lit., (something) forbidden]

**hare's-ear** /ˈhɛəz-ɪə/, *n.* any of several species of *Bupleurum,* esp. *B. rotundifolium,* a small annual with yellow flowers, a weed of cultivated land, native to Europe and western Asia but introduced into other temperate regions.

**hare's-foot** /ˈhɛəz-fʊt/, *n.* **1.** a small annual, *Trifolium arvense,* with hairy cylindrical heads of pink flowers, widespread in temperate regions on sandy soils. **2.** plants of other species thought to resemble a hare's foot, as **hare's-foot fern,** *Davallia pyxidata.*

**hare's-tail** /ˈhɛəz-teɪl/, *n.* **1.** a small annual grass, *Lagurus ovatus,* with soft, woolly, ovoid flowering heads, occurring in sandy places in south-western Europe and Mediterranean regions. **2.** any of several other grasses with similar heads as species of the genus *Echinopogon.*

**hare-wallaby** /ˈhɛə-wɒləbi/, *n.* any of several species of small, mostly solitary wallabies, of the genera *Lagorchestes* and *Lagostrophus* found in open grassy areas of Australia and resembling hares in their speed and jumping ability.

**hargan** /ˈhagən/, *n.* a mobile circular saw unit powered by a single cylinder engine. Also, **hargan saw.**

**haricot** /ˈhærəkoʊ/, *n.* **1.** the French bean, *Phaseolus vulgaris.* **2.** its pod, **haricot vert** (green bean). **3.** its seed, when pale, **haricot blanc** (white bean), and when dark, **haricot rouge** (red bean). See **kidney bean.** [F, identical with *haricot* ragout]

**harijan** /ˈharədʒən/, *n.* (esp. used by followers of Ghandi) a member of the lowest caste in India; an untouchable. [Skt *harijana* person belonging to the god Vishnu]

**harikari** /hæriˈkari/, *n.* →**harakiri.**

**hark** /hak/, *v.i.* **1.** (*used chiefly in the imperative*) to listen; hearken. **2.** **hark back, a.** to return to a previous point or subject, as in discourse or thought; revert. **b.** (of hounds) to return along the course in order to regain a lost scent. *–n.* **3.** a hunter's cry to hounds. [ME *herk(i)en,* c. OFris. *herkia.* Cf. HEARKEN]

**harken** /ˈhakən/, *v.i., v.t. Chiefly U.S.* →**hearken.**

**harl** /hal/, *n.* →**herl.**

**Harlequin** /ˈhaləkwɪn/, *n.* **1.** (*sometimes l.c.*) a droll character in comedy (originally the early Italian) and pantomime, usu. masked, dressed in particoloured spangled tights, and bearing a wooden sword or magic wand. **2.** (*l.c.*) a buffoon. **3.** (*l.c.*) any one of various small, handsomely marked snakes. **4.** (*l.c.*) a type of opal having small square prisms within the stone, each reflecting a different colour. *–adj.* **5.** (*l.c.*) fancifully varied in colour, decoration, etc. [F; OF *Harlequin, Herlequin,* from ME *Herle King* King Herla (mythical figure); modern meaning from It. *arlecchino,* from F *Harlequin*]

harlequin

**harlequinade** /haləkwəˈneɪd/, *n.* **1.** a pantomime or similar play in which the harlequin plays the principal part. **2.** →**buffoonery.** See **commedia dell'arte.** [F *arlequinade*]

**harlequin duck** /halɛkwən ˈdʌk/, *n.* a small North American diving duck, *Histrionicus histrionicus,* in which the male is bluish grey, marked with black, white, and chestnut.

**harlequinesque** /haləkwəˈnɛsk/, *adj.* in the style or manner of a harlequin.

**harlot** /ˈhalət/, *n.* **1.** a promiscuous woman; prostitute. *–adj.* **2.** pertaining to or like a harlot; low. [ME, from OF: rogue, knave; orig. uncert.]

**harlotry** /ˈhalətri/, *n., pl.* **-ries.** **1.** the practice or trade of prostitution. **2.** harlots collectively.

**harm** /ham/, *n.* **1.** injury; damage; hurt: *to do him bodily harm.* **2.** moral injury; evil; wrong. *–v.t.* **3.** to do harm to; injure; damage; hurt. [ME; OE *hearm,* c. G *Harm.* Cf. Russ. *sram* shame] – **harmer,** *n.*

**harmful** /ˈhamfəl/, *adj.* fraught with or doing harm. – **harmfully,** *adv.* – **harmfulness,** *n.*

**harmless** /ˈhamləs/, *adj.* **1.** without power or tendency to harm: *harmless play.* **2.** *Rare.* unharmed. – **harmlessly,** *adv.* – **harmlessness,** *n.*

**harmonic** /haˈmɒnɪk/, *adj.* **1.** pertaining to harmony, as distinguished from melody and rhythm. **2.** marked by harmony; in harmony; concordant; consonant. **3.** *Maths.* having relations resembling those of musical concords: *a harmonic progression is a series of numbers the reciprocals of which are in arithmetic progression.* *–n.* **4.** *Physics.* an integral multiple of a given frequency, thus 256, 512, 768, cycles per second are the *first, second,* and *third harmonics* of 256 cycles per second. **5.** →**overtone.** [L *harmonicus,* from Gk *harmonikós* skilled in music] – **harmonically,** *adv.*

**harmonica** /haˈmɒnɪkə/, *n.* **1.** a musical instrument having a set of small metallic reeds mounted in a case and played by the breath; a mouth organ. **2.** any of various percussion instruments which use graduated bars of metal or other hard material as sounding elements. [L, n. use of fem. of *harmonicus* HARMONIC]

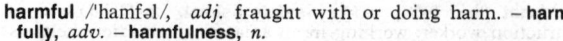

harmonica

**harmonic mean** /haˌmɒnɪk ˈmin/, *n. Maths.* the reciprocal of the average of the reciprocals of a given set of positive numbers.

**harmonic minor** /– ˈmaɪnə/, *n.* the minor musical scale from which chords are formed, having the sixth degree a semitone above the dominant and the seventh degree a semitone below the tonic.

**harmonic motion** /– ˈmoʊʃən/, *n. Physics.* See **simple harmonic motion.**

**harmonicon** /haˈmɒnəkən/, *n.* any of various musical instruments, as a harmonica or an orchestrion. [Gk *harmonikón* (neut.) harmonic]

**harmonics** /haˈmɒnɪks/, *n.* **1.** the science of musical sounds. **2.** (*construed as pl.*) the partials or overtones of a fundamental note. Cf. **harmonic** (def. 3). **3.** (*construed as pl.*) the flageolet-like notes of a string (as a violin string) made to vibrate by touching lightly at a given point and bowing or plucking, so as to bring out an overtone, while suppressing the fundamental. [pl. of HARMONIC. See -ICS]

**harmonic series** /haˌmɒnɪk ˈsɪəriz/, *n.* **1.** *Maths.* any series in which the reciprocals of the terms form an arithmetic progression. **2.** *Music.* the complete range of upper partials produced from and by a fundamental note.

**harmonious** /haˈmoʊniəs/, *adj.* **1.** marked by agreement in feeling or action: *a harmonious group.* **2.** forming a pleasingly consistent whole; congruous. **3.** agreeable to the ear; tuneful; melodious. – **harmoniously,** *adv.* – **harmoniousness,** *n.*

**harmonise** /ˈhamənaɪz/, *v.,* **-nised, -nising.** *–v.t.* **1.** to bring into harmony, accord, or agreement: *to harmonise the views.* **2.** *Music.* to accompany with appropriate harmony. *–v.i.* **3.** to be in agreement in action, sense, or feeling. **4.** to sing in harmony. Also, **harmonize.** – **harmonisation** /hamənaɪˈzeɪʃən/, *n.*

**harmonist** /ˈhamənəst/, *n.* **1.** one who makes a harmony (def. 4). **2.** one skilled in harmony, in music.

**harmonistic** /haməˈnɪstɪk/, *adj.* **1.** pertaining to a harmonist or harmony. **2.** pertaining to the collation and harmonising of parallel passages, as of the Gospels. – **harmonistically,** *adv.*

**harmonium** /haˈmoʊniəm/, *n.* a reed organ, esp. one in which the air is forced outwards through the reeds. [F, from *harmonie,* from L *harmonia* HARMONY]

**harmony** /ˈhaməni/, *n., pl.* **-nies.** **1.** agreement; accord; harmonious relations. **2.** a consistent, orderly, or pleasing arrangement of parts; congruity. **3.** *Music.* **a.** any simultaneous combination of notes. **b.** the simultaneous combination of notes; chordal structure, as distinguished from melody and rhythm. **c.** the science of the structure, relations, and practical combination of chords. **4.** an arrangement of the contents of the Gospels (either of all four or of the first three) designed to show their parallelism, mutual relations, and differences. [ME *harmonie,* from F, from L *harmonia,* from Gk: a joining, concord, music]

**harness** /ˈhanəs/, *n.* **1.** the combination of straps, bands, and other parts forming the working gear of a horse or other draught animal (except the ox). **2.** a similar combination worn by persons for safety, protection, restraint, etc. **3.** *Archaic.* armour for men or horses (or other animals), or a suit of armour. **4. in harness, a.** side by side; together. **b.** working; at one's job. *–v.t.* **5.** to put harness on (a horse, etc.); attach by a harness, as to a vehicle. **6.** to bring under conditions for working: *to harness water-power.* **7.** *Archaic.* to array in armour or equipments of war. [ME, from OF *harnies,* ? from OHG; cf. Icel. *hernest,* from *herr* army (c. OE *here*) + *nest* provisions] **– harnesser,** *n.* **– harnessless,** *adj.* **– harnesslike,** *adj.*

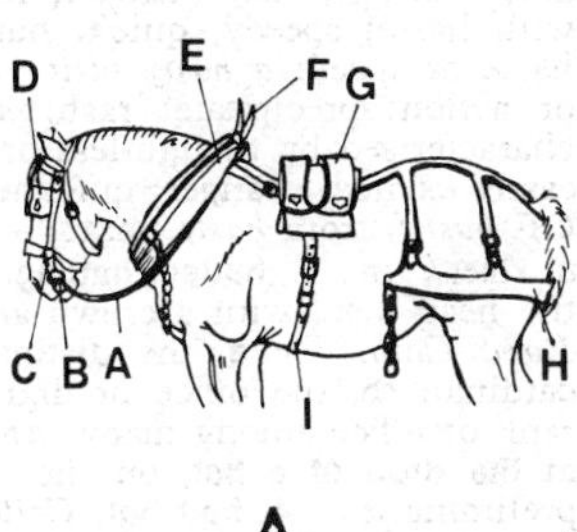


harness: **A,** cart gear; **B,** plough gear

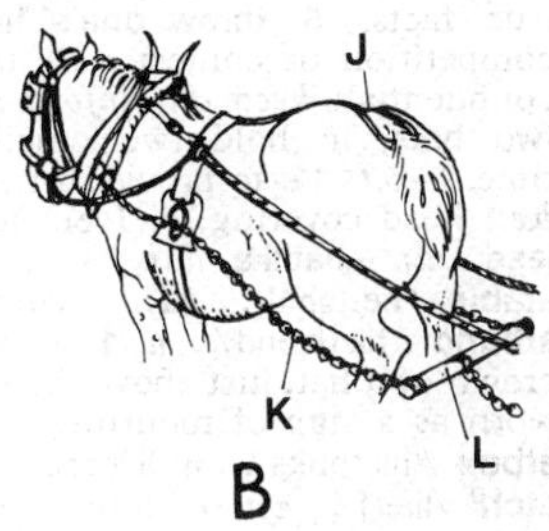


A, reins; B, bit; C, bridle; D, blinkers; E, collar; F, hames; G, saddle; H, breeching; I, girth; J, crupper; K, trace; L, whippletree

**harp** /hap/, *n.* **1.** a musical instrument consisting of a triangular frame (comprising a sounding-board, a pillar, and a curved neck) and strings stretched between sounding-board and neck and plucked with the fingers. **2.** *Music. Colloq.* →**harmonica.** *–v.i.* **3.** to play on a harp. **4.** to dwell persistently or tediously in speaking or writing (fol. by *on* or *upon*). *–v.t.* **5.** *Poetic.* to bring, put, etc., by playing on a harp. **6.** *Archaic.* to give voice or utterance to. [ME *harp(e),* OE *hearpe,* c. D *harp,* G *Harfe,* Icel. *harpa*] **– harper,** *n.*

**harpings** /ˈhapɪŋz/, *n.pl.* the stout wales about the bow of a ship. Also, **harpins** /ˈhapənz/.

**harpist** /ˈhapəst/, *n.* one who plays on the harp, esp. professionally.

**harpoon** /haˈpun/, *n.* **1.** a barbed, spear-like missile attached to a rope, and thrown by hand or shot from a gun, used in catching whales and large fish. **2.** *Colloq.* an additional period taught by a teacher because of the absence of a colleague. *–v.t.* **3.** to strike, catch, or kill with or as with a harpoon. **4.** to require (a teacher) to take an additional period. [D *harpoen,* from F *harpon,* from *harper* grapple, of Gmc orig.] **– harpooner,** *n.* **– harpoonlike,** *adj.*

harp: A, pedestal; B, pedals; C, back; D, sounding-board; E, neck; F, pillar

**harpsichord** /ˈhapsəkɔd/, *n.* a keyboard instrument, precursor of the piano, in common use from the 16th to the 18th century, and revived in the 20th, in which the strings are plucked by leather or quill points connected with the keys. [F (obs.) *harpechorde,* from *harpe* (of Gmc orig.) harp + *chorde* string (see CHORD[1])] **– harpsichordist,** *n.*

**harpy** /ˈhapi/, *n.* **1.** a rapacious, predatory person. **2.** an unattractive, bad-tempered, depraved, old woman. [in Greek mythology, a rapacious, filthy monster with a woman's head and a bird's body; L *harpȳia,* from Gk: lit., snatcher]

**harpy eagle** /ˈ– igəl/, *n.* a large, powerful, crested bird of prey, *Thrasaetus harpyia,* of tropical America.

**harquebus** /ˈhakwəbəs/, *n.* →**arquebus.**

**harquebusier** /hakwəbəˈsɪə/, *n.* a soldier armed with a harquebus.

**harridan** /ˈhærədən/, *n.* a disreputable violent woman; vicious old hag. [cf. F *haridelle* sorry horse, jade]

**harrier**[1] /ˈhæriə/, *n.* **1.** one who or that which harries. **2.** any of several hawks of the genus *Circus* (family Falconidae), all of which course back and forth over pasturelands searching for the small birds and mammals on which they feed. [HARRY, *v.,* + -ER[1]]

**harrier**[2] /ˈhæriə/, *n.* **1.** a breed of small hounds employed in hunting the hare. **2.** a cross-country runner. [special use of HARRIER[1], by association with HARE]

**Harris tweed** /hærəs ˈtwid/, *n.* a loosely woven tweed made and finished by hand in the Outer Hebrides, esp. in the islands of Lewis and Harris, off the W coast of Scotland. [Trademark]

**harrow** /ˈhæroʊ/, *n.* **1.** a wheelless agricultural implement set with teeth, upright discs, etc., usu. of iron, drawn over ploughed land to level it, break clods, etc. *–v.t.* **2.** to draw a harrow over (land, etc.); break or tear with a harrow. **3.** to disturb keenly or painfully; distress the mind, feelings, etc. *–v.i.* **4.** to be broken up by harrowing, as soil, etc. [ME *haru, harwe.* Cf. Icel. *herfi* harrow, MLG *harke* rake] **– harrower,** *n.* **– harrowingly,** *adv.*

**harrowing** /ˈhæroʊɪŋ/, *adj.* disturbing or distressing to the mind, feelings, etc.

**harry** /ˈhæri/, *v.,* **-ried, -rying.** *–v.t.* **1.** to harass by forced exactions, rapacious demands, etc.; torment; worry. **2.** to ravage, as in war; devastate. *–v.i.* **3.** to make harassing incursions. [ME *herien,* OE *her(g)ian* ravage (from *here* army), c.G *(ver)heeren* harry, lay waste]

**harsh** /haʃ/, *adj.* **1.** ungentle and unpleasant in action or effect: *harsh treatment.* **2.** rough to the touch or to any of the senses: *a harsh surface, a harsh voice.* **3.** jarring upon the aesthetic senses; inartistic: *his painting was full of harsh lines and clashing colours.* [unexplained doublet of ME *harsk.* Cf. Dan. *harsk* rancid, G *harsch* harsh, rough, hard] **– harshly,** *adv.* **– harshness,** *n.*

**harslet** /ˈhazlət, ˈhas-/, *n.* →**haslet.**

**hart** /hat/, *n., pl.* **harts,** *(esp. collectively)* **hart.** a male of the deer, commonly the red deer, *Cervus elaphus,* esp. after its fifth year. [ME *hert,* OE *heort,* c. G *Hirsch;* akin to L *cervus* stag]

**hartal** /ˈhatal/, *n.* (in India) **1.** a day of mourning. **2.** a form of passive resistance including the closing of shops. [Hind. *hathtal* market stoppage]

**hartebeest** /ˈhatəbist/, *n.* **1.** a large antelope of southern Africa of the genus *Alcephalus,* as *A. caama,* of a red colour, having a long face with naked muzzle. **2.** any of various allied African antelopes, as some species of the genus *Demaliscus.* [Afrikaans: hart beast]

hartebeest

**hartshorn** /ˈhatshɔn/, *n.* **1.** the antler of the hart, formerly much used as a source of ammonia. **2.** *Old Chem., Pharm.* →**sal volatile.** [var. of *hart's horn*]

**hart's-tongue** /ˈhats-tʌŋ/, *n.* a fern, *Phyllitis scolopendrium,* which has long simple fronds.

**harum-scarum** /hɛərəm-ˈskɛərəm/, *adj.* **1.** reckless; rash. *–adv.* **2.** recklessly; wildly. *–n.* **3.** a reckless person. **4.** reckless conduct. [? var. of *hare 'em scare 'em* (with obs. *hare* harry, scare)]

**harvest** /ˈhavəst/, *n.* **1.** the gathering of crops. **2.** the season of gathering ripened crops, esp. of grain. **3.** a crop or yield, as of grain. **4.** a supply of anything gathered at maturity and stored up: *a harvest of nuts.* **5.** the product or result of any labour or process. *–v.t.* **6.** to gather, as a crop. **7.** to gather the crop from: *to harvest the fields.* *–v.i.* **8.** to gather a crop; reap. [ME; OE *hærfest,* c. G *Herbst* autumn] **– harvesting,** *n.* **– harvestless,** *adj.*

**harvester** /ˈhavəstə/, *n.* **1.** one who harvests; a reaper. **2.** any of various machines for harvesting field crops, such as grain, flax, potatoes, etc. **3.** →**harvestman** (def. 2). **4.** →**combine harvester.**

**harvest festival** /havəst ˈfɛstəvəl/, *n.* a thanksgiving service for harvest.

**harvest home** /–ˈhoʊm/, *n.* **1.** the bringing home of the harvest. **2.** the time of doing it. **3.** a festival celebrated at the close of the harvest.

**harvestman** /ˈhavəstmən/, *n., pl.* **-men. 1.** a man engaged in harvesting. **2.** any of the arachnids of the order Opiliones (or Phalangida), comprising spider-like creatures with small rounded body and usu. very long legs; daddy-long-legs.

**harvest mite** /ˈhavəst maɪt/, *n.* an adult chigger.

**harvest moon** /– ˈmun/, *n.* the moon at and about the period of fullness which is nearest to the autumnal equinox.

**harvest mouse** /–ˈmaʊs/, *n.* a small rodent, *Micromys minutus,* of the family Muridae, inhabiting cornfields and hedgerows of Europe and Asia, and 10 cm long, half of this length consisting of the prehensile tail.

**harvest tick** /– ˈtɪk/, *n.* any of various acarids in an immature stage, common in late summer and autumn, which attach themselves to the skin of man and animals; harvest mite.

**harvey wallbanger** /havi ˈwɔlbæŋə/, *n.* a drink made from vodka, Galliano and orange juice, garnished with a slice of orange and cherries.

**has** /hæz/, *weak forms* /həz, əz/, *v.* 3rd person singular present indicative of **have.**

**has-been** /ˈhæz-bin/, *n. Colloq.* a person or thing that is no longer effective, successful, popular, etc.

**hash**[1] /hæʃ/, *n.* **1.** a dish of chopped, cooked meat, reheated in a highly seasoned sauce. **2.** a mess, jumble, or muddle. **3.** any preparation of old material worked over. **4. make a hash of,** to spoil or make a mess of something. **5.** an unwanted noise in a radio, radar, or television receiver due to set noise, interference, etc. *–v.t.* **6.** to chop into small pieces; mince; make into a hash. [F *hacher,* from *hache* axe. See HATCHET, and cf. HATCH[3]]

**hash**[2] /hæʃ/, *n. Colloq.* →**hashish.**

**Hashemite Kingdom of Jordan,** *n.* official name of Jordan.

**hash house** /ˈhæʃ haʊs/, *n. Colloq.* a cheap restaurant.

**hashish** /hæˈʃiʃ, ˈhæʃɪʃ/, *n.* **1.** the flowering tops, leaves, etc., of Indian hemp, smoked, chewed, or otherwise used as a narcotic and intoxicant. **2.** any of various preparations made from this plant. [Ar. *hashīsh* dry herbage, powdered hemp-leaves]

**hashmagandy** /hæʃməˈgændi/, *n.* a thin and unpalatable stew, made from any available ingredients, as served to shearers, troops, etc.; mulliga stew. Also, **hash magandy, hash-megandy.**

**haslet** /ˈheɪzlət/, *n.* the edible entrails of a pig or other animal, as used for food. Also, **harslet.** [ME *hastelet,* from OF: roasted bit of meat, from *haste* spit, from L *hasta* spear]

**hasn't** /ˈhæzənt/, *v.* contraction of *has not.*

**hasp** /hæsp, hasp/, *n.* **1.** a clasp for a door, lid, etc., esp. one passing over a staple and fastened by a pin or a padlock. *–v.t.* **2.** to fasten with or as with a hasp. [ME *hasp(e),* OE *hæsp, hæpse,* c. G *Haspe;* akin to Icel. *hespa*]

**hassle** /ˈhæsəl/, *n., v.,* **-led, -ling.** *–n.* **1.** a quarrel; squabble. **2.** a struggle; period of unease: *today was a real hassle.* *–v.t.* **3.** worry; harass: *don't hassle me.* – **hassled,** *adj.*

**hassock** /ˈhæsək/, *n.* **1.** a thick, firm cushion used as a footstool or for kneeling. **2.** a rank tuft of coarse grass or sedge, as in a bog. [ME; OE *hassuc* coarse grass]

**hast** /hæst/, *v. Archaic.* 2nd person singular present indicative of **have.**

**hastate** /ˈhæsteɪt/, *adj.* (of a leaf) triangular or shaped like a halberd, with two spreading lobes at the base. [L *hastātus* armed with a spear]

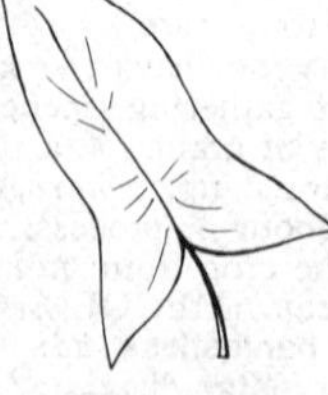

hastate leaf

**haste** /heɪst/, *n., v.,* **hasted, hasting.** *–n.* **1.** energetic speed in motion or action. **2.** speed as a result of urgency. **3.** quickness without due reflection; thoughtless or rash speed: *haste makes waste.* **4. in haste,** with speed, quickly. **5. make haste, a.** to exert oneself to do something quickly. **b.** (with adjunct) to go with haste. *–v.t. v.i.* **6.** *Archaic.* to hasten. [ME, from OF, from Gmc; cf. OE *hæst* violence]

**hasten** /ˈheɪsən/, *v.i.* **1.** to move or act with haste; proceed with haste; hurry: *to hasten to a place.* *–v.t.* **2.** to cause to hasten; accelerate. – **hastener,** *n.*

**hasty** /ˈheɪsti/, *adj.,* **hastier, hastiest. 1.** moving or acting with haste; speedy; quick; hurried. **2.** made or done with haste or speed: *a hasty visit.* **3.** unduly quick in movement or action; precipitate; rash: *hasty reply.* **4.** done with or characterised by thoughtless or angry haste: *hasty words.* **5.** easily excited to anger; quick-tempered; irascible. [ME, from OF *hastif,* from *haste* HASTE] – **hastily,** *adv.* – **hastiness,** *n.*

**hat** /hæt/, *n., v.,* **hatted, hatting.** *–n.* **1.** a shaped covering for the head, usu. with a crown and a brim, worn outdoors. **2.** *Rom. Cath. Ch.* **a.** the distinctive red head covering of a cardinal. **b.** the office or dignity of cardinal. **c.** *Colloq.* a rank or office among many: *which hat is he wearing now?* **3. at the drop of a hat,** on the spur of the moment; without preliminaries. **4. bad hat,** *Colloq.* a bad or immoral person. **5. eat one's hat,** *Colloq.* to be very surprised if a certain event happens: *if he wins this game I'll eat my hat.* **6. my hat!,** (an exclamation of surprise and disbelief.) **7. old hat,** *Colloq.* (of ideas, etc.) old fashioned; out of date. **8. talk through one's hat,** *Colloq.* to talk nonsense; speak without knowledge of the true facts. **9. throw one's hat into the ring,** to join in a competition or contest. **10. under one's hat,** *Colloq.* secret, confidential: *keep this information under your hat.* **11. wear two hats,** to hold two official appointments at the same time. *–v.t.* **12.** to provide with a hat; put a hat on. [ME; OE *hætt* head covering, c. Icel. *höttr* hood; akin to HOOD] – **hatless,** *adj.* – **hatlike,** *adj.*

**hatable** /ˈheɪtəbəl/, *adj.* →**hateable.**

**hatband** /ˈhætbænd/, *n.* **1.** a band or ribbon placed about the crown of a hat, just above the brim. **2.** a black band similarly worn as a sign of mourning.

**hatbox** /ˈhætbɒks/, *n.* a case or box for a hat.

**hatch**[1] /hætʃ/, *v.t.* **1.** to bring forth (young) from the egg. **2.** to cause young to emerge from (the egg). **3.** to contrive; devise; concoct: *to hatch a plot.* *–v.i.* **4.** to be hatched. *–n.* **5.** the act of hatching. **6.** that which is hatched, as a brood. [ME *hacche,* akin to G *hecken*] – **hatcher,** *n.*

**hatch**[2] /hætʃ/, *n.* **1.** a cover for an opening in a ship's deck, a floor, a roof, or the like. **2.** the opening itself. **3.** (*oft. pl.*) a hatchway. **4.** a ship's deck: *under hatches.* **5.** an opening in the floor or roof of a building. **6.** the cover over such an opening. **7.** the lower half of a divided door. **8.** a wicket. **9.** an opening in the wall between a kitchen and dining room, through which food is served. **10. down the hatch,** drink up! [ME *hacche,* OE *hæcc* grating, hatch]

**hatch**[3] /hætʃ/, *v.t.* **1.** to mark with lines, esp. closely set parallel lines, as for shading in drawing or engraving. *–n.* **2.** a shading line in drawing or engraving. [F *hacher* chop, hash, hatch. See HASH[1]]

**hatchabator** /ˈhætʃəbeɪtə/, *n.* →**incubator.**

**hatchability** /hætʃəˈbɪləti/, *n.* **1.** (in poultry farming) that quality of fertilised eggs that makes possible normal embryonic development and the emergence of normal young when incubated. **2.** (in incubation practice) the percentage of fertile eggs which hatch.

**hatchback** /ˈhætʃbæk/, *n.* a type of car fitted with a door at the rear which includes the rear-vision window, and which has hinges at the top.

**hatchel** /ˈhætʃəl/, *n., v.,* **-elled, -elling.** *–n.* **1.** an instrument for cleaning flax; heckle. *–v.t.* **2.** to heckle. [phonetic doublet of HACKLE[1]. Cf. HECKLE] – **hatcheller,** *n.*

**hatchery** /ˈhætʃəri/, *n., pl.* **-eries.** a place for hatching eggs of hens, fish, etc.

**hatchet** /ˈhætʃət/, *n.* **1.** a small, short-handled axe for use with one hand. **2.** a tomahawk. **3. bury the hatchet,** to make peace. **4. dig up** (or **take up) the hatchet,** to prepare for war. [ME, from F *hachette,* diminutive of *hache* axe, from Gmc; cf. HACK[1]] – **hatchet-like,** *adj.*

**hatchet face** /ˈ– feɪs/, *n.* a sharp, narrow face. – **hatchet-faced,** *adj.*

**hatchet man** /ˈ– mæn/, *n.* **1.** a man employed or delegated to perform unpleasant tasks, such as cutting costs, firing personnel, etc., for an employer. **2.** a hired assassin.

**hatching** /ˈhætʃɪŋ/, *n.* a series of lines, generally parallel, used in shading or modelling. [HATCH[3] + -ING[1]]

**hatchment** /ˈhætʃmənt/, *n.* (in heraldry) a square tablet, set diagonally, bearing the arms of a deceased person. [aspirated var. of *atch(e)ment,* syncopated form of ACHIEVEMENT]

**hatchway** /ˈhætʃweɪ/, *n.* **1.** an opening (covered by a hatch) in a ship's deck, for passage to parts below, esp. the hold; hatch. **2.** the opening of any trapdoor, as in a floor, ceiling, or roof.

hatchment

**hate** /heɪt/, *v.*, **hated, hating,** *n.* *–v.t.* **1.** to regard with a strong or passionate dislike; detest. **2.** to dislike; be unwilling: *I hate to do it.* *–v.i.* **3.** to feel hatred. *–n.* **4.** hatred; strong dislike. **5.** the object of hatred. **6. have a hate,** feel strong antipathy or dislike (fol. by *on* or *against*). *–adj.* **7.** devoted to expressing resentment or dislike: *a hate session.* [ME *hat(i)en,* OE *hatian,* c. G *hassen*] – **hater,** *n.*

**hateable** /ˈheɪtəbəl/, *adj.* deserving to be hated. Also, **hatable.**

**hateful** /ˈheɪtfəl/, *adj.* **1.** exciting hate; detestable; odious. **2.** *Archaic.* full of hate; malignant; malevolent. – **hatefully,** *adv.* – **hatefulness,** *n.*

**hatful** /ˈhætfʊl/, *n. Colloq.* a considerable quantity or number: *a hatful of runs.*

**hath** /hæθ/, *v. Archaic.* 3rd person singular present indicative of **have.**

**hatha-yoga** /ˈhatə-joʊgə/, *n.* a school of yoga dealing esp. with the physical exercises beneficial to an aspirant. [Skt *hatha* force, persistence]

**hatpin** /ˈhætpɪn/, *n.* a long, often decorated pin, used by women to secure a hat to the hair.

**hatred** /ˈheɪtrəd/, *n.* the feeling of one who hates; intense dislike; detestation. [ME *hatered(en),* from *hate* hate + *-reden,* OE *-rǣden,* suffix making abstract nouns]

**hatstand** /ˈhætstænd/, *n.* a tall stand with spreading arms or pegs on which hats, coats, etc., are hung.

**hatter** /ˈhætə/, *n.* **1.** a maker or seller of hats. **2.** *Colloq.* **a.** a miner who works alone. **b.** a lonely and eccentric bush dweller. **3. mad as a hatter,** very eccentric; crazy.

**hat-trick** /ˈhæt-trɪk/, *n.* **1.** *Cricket.* the act by a bowler of taking three wickets with three successive balls. **2.** any similar feat in other sports involving a set of three items.

**haubergeon** /ˈhɔbədʒən/, *n.* →**habergeon.**

**hauberk** /ˈhɔbɜk/, *n.* a piece of armour originally intended for the protection of the neck and shoulders, but early developed into a long coat of mail reaching below the knees. [ME, from OF *hauberc,* from Gmc; cf. OHG *halsberg* neck protection]

hauberk

**hauerite** /ˈhaʊəraɪt/, *n.* a rare mineral consisting of manganese sulphide which occurs as small dark crystals in clay, etc.

**haughty** /ˈhɔti/, *adj.*, **-tier, -tiest. 1.** disdainfully proud; arrogant; supercilious. **2.** *Archaic.* exalted, lofty, or noble. [extended form of *haught,* orig. *haut,* from F: high, in OF *halt,* from L *altus,* b. with OG *hauh* (later *hōh*) high] – **haughtily,** *adv.* – **haughtiness,** *n.*

**hauhau** /ˈhaʊhaʊ/, *n. N.Z.* (formerly) a member of a 19th-century Maori religious sect. [Maori] – **hauhauism,** *n.*

**haul** /hɔl/, *v.t.* **1.** to pull or draw with force; move or transport by drawing. **2. haul over the coals,** *Colloq.* to rebuke; scold. **3. haul up,** *Colloq.* **a.** to bring up, as before a superior, for reprimand; call to account. **b.** to change the course of (a ship), esp. so as to sail closer to the wind. *–v.i.* **4.** to pull or tug. **5.** to change one's course of procedure or action; go in a given direction. **6.** *Naut.* to sail, as in a particular direction. **7.** (of the wind) to change direction, shift, or veer (oft. fol. by *round* or *to*). **8. haul off, a.** *Naut.* to change the course of a ship so as to get farther off from an object. **b.** to draw off or away. **c.** *U.S. Colloq.* to draw the arm back preparatory to striking a blow. *–n.* **9.** the act of hauling; a strong pull or tug. **10.** that which is hauled. **11.** the distance over which anything is hauled. **12.** *Fishing.* **a.** the quantity of fish taken at one draught of the net. **b.** the draught of a fishing net. **13.** *Colloq.* the taking or acquisition of anything, or that which is taken. [earlier *hall,* phonetic var. of HALE[2]] – **hauler,** *n.*

**haulage** /ˈhɔlɪdʒ/, *n.* **1.** the act or labour of hauling. **2.** transport, esp. heavy road transport. **3.** charge for hauling.

**haulier** /ˈhɔliə/, *n.* a person or company engaged in haulage (def. 2).

**haulm** /hɔm/, *n.* **1.** stems or stalks collectively, as of grain or of peas, beans, hops, etc., esp. as used for litter or thatching. **2.** a single stem or stalk. Also, **halm.** [ME *halm,* OE *healm,* c. D *halm* and G *Halm*]

**haunch** /hɔntʃ/, *n.* **1.** the hip. **2.** the fleshy part of the body about the hip. **3.** a hindquarter of an animal. **4.** the leg and loin of an animal, as used for food. **5.** *Archit.* **a.** either side of an arch, extending from the vertex or crown to the impost. **b.** the part of a beam projecting below a floor or roof slab. [ME *hanche,* from OF, from Gmc; cf. MD *hancke*]

**haunchbone** /ˈhɔntʃboʊn/, *n.* the ilium or hipbone.

**haunt** /hɔnt/, *v.t.* **1.** to reappear frequently to after death; visit habitually as a supposed spirit or ghost. **2.** to intrude upon continually; recur persistently: *memories that haunt one.* **3.** to worry or disturb: *his guilt haunted him.* **4.** to resort to much; visit frequently. **5.** to frequent the company of; be often with. *–v.i.* **6.** to reappear continually, as a disembodied spirit. **7.** to resort habitually. **8.** to associate, as with a person. *–n.* **9.** (*oft. pl.*) a place of frequent resort: *to revisit one's old haunts.* [ME *haunten,* from OF *hanter* haunt, dwell, from Gmc; cf. OE *hāmettan* shelter, from *hām* home] – **haunter,** *n.* – **hauntingly,** *adv.*

**haunted** /ˈhɔntəd/, *adj.* **1.** frequented or visited by ghosts: *a haunted house.* **2.** preoccupied or worried by something: *haunted by fear.*

**haunting** /ˈhɔntɪŋ/, *adj.* **1.** (of music) fascinating, evoking memories. **2.** (of a memory, etc.) recurring persistently.

**Hausa** /ˈhaʊsə/, *n.* **1.** a prominent Negro stock in northern Nigeria, and in parts of Niger and Cameroun. **2.** their language, used widely in western Africa as a language of commerce.

**hausfrau** /ˈhaʊsfraʊ/, *n.* a woman, usu. plain and dowdy, who occupies herself almost exclusively with household chores. [G]

**haustellum** /hɔsˈtɛləm/, *n., pl.* **haustella** /hɔsˈtɛlə/. (in certain crustaceans and insects) an organ or part of the proboscis adapted for sucking blood or plant juices. [NL, diminutive of L *haustrum* machine for drawing water] – **haustellate,** *adj.*

**haustorium** /hɔsˈtɔriəm/, *n., pl.* **haustoria** /hɔsˈtɔriə/. an intracellular feeding organ of a parasite which does not kill the host cells but lives with them. [NL, from *haustor* drinker]

**hautboy** /ˈoʊbɔɪ/, *n.* →**oboe.** [F *hautbois,* from *haut* high + *bois* wood; named with reference to its high notes]

**haute couture** /oʊt kəˈtjʊə/, *n.* high fashion; the clothes designed and made by the most famous couturiers. [F]

**haute cuisine** /– kwəˈzin/, *n.* cooking to a high standard. [F]

**haute école** /– eɪˈkɒl/, *n.* an elaborate method of training horses for exhibition. [F]

**hauteur** /oʊˈtɜ/, *n.* haughty manner or spirit; haughtiness. [F, from *haut* high. See HAUGHTY]

**haut monde** /oʊt ˈmɒnd/, *n.* high society. [F]

**havanaise** /hævəˈneɪz/, *n.* →**habanera.**

**havarti** /hæˈvati/, *n.* a light coloured, aromatic cheese with a sweet, delicate but slightly sharp flavour. [named after *Havarti,* North Zeeland, Denmark]

**have** /hæv/, *v., pres.* 1 **have,** 2 **have** or **hast,** 3 **has** or **hath,** *pl.* **have;** *pt. and past part.* **had,** *pres. part.* **having.** *–v.t.* **1.** to possess; own; to hold for use: *to have property; to have a car.* **2.** to be made of or to contain: *this volume has an index.* **3.** to hold or possess in some other relation, as of kindred, friendship, association, etc.: *he has two brothers; she has twenty private pupils.* **4.** to hold or possess in a relative position: *to have someone under one's thumb.* **5.** to possess as a characteristic or a feature: *he has blue eyes, I have a shocking temper.* **6.** to get, receive, or take: *I had no news for six months.* **7.** to be required, compelled, or under obligation (fol. by an infinitive): *I have to stop now.* **8.** to experience, enjoy or suffer: *to have a pleasant time.* **9.** to hold or stage (a social occasion, etc.): *to have a party.* **10.** to eat, drink or partake of: *he had a meal.* **11.** to hold in mind, sight, etc.:

*to have doubts.* **12.** to require or cause (to do something, to be done, or as specified): *have it ready at five.* **13.** to arrange, put or keep in a specific place: *why not have the bookshelves in the corner.* **14.** to engage in or perform: *to have a talk.* **15.** to be scheduled for: *I have two appointments tomorrow.* **16.** to show or exhibit in action: *to have a care; have mercy.* **17.** to permit or allow: *I will not have it.* **18.** to buy, accept or take: *I'll have this one, thanks.* **19.** to invite or expect visitors, etc.: *we have twenty people coming for dinner.* **20.** to assert or maintain: *rumour has it so.* **21.** to know or understand, esp. for use: *to have neither Latin nor Greek; to have the necessary technique.* **22.** to give birth to: *to have a baby.* **23.** to wear (fol. by *on*). **24.** to possess sexually; to copulate with. **25.** *Colloq.* to hold at a disadvantage: *he has you there.* **26.** *Colloq.* to outwit, deceive, or cheat: *a person not easily had.* *–v.* **27.** Some special verb phrases are:
**had better,** ought to: *you had better do as you are told.*
**had rather,** to consider as preferable: *I had rather you came early.* Also, **had sooner.**
**have at,** *Archaic.* to attack.
**have done,** to cease or finish (oft. fol. by *with*).
**have had it,** *Colloq.* **1.** to be fated beyond hope of recovery, to die, be defeated, etc. **2.** to have failed to take advantage of a last chance. **3.** to become out of fashion or no longer popular.
**have had (someone** or **something),** *Colloq.* to be annoyed or exasperated with: *I've had you; I've had this job.*
**have it away,** *Brit. Colloq.* to have sexual intercourse.
**have it coming to one,** *Colloq.* to deserve an unpleasant fate.
**have it in for,** *Colloq.* to hold a grudge against.
**have it made,** *Colloq.* to be assured of success.
**have it off,** *Colloq.* to have sexual intercourse.
**have it out,** to have a candid argument; to discuss a matter extensively.
**have on, 1.** to be wearing. **2.** to have arranged or planned: *what appointments do you have on tomorrow?*
**have oneself on,** *Colloq.* to delude oneself, esp. as a result of pandering to one's own ego.
**have someone in** (or **over**), to invite or entertain someone at home.
**have someone on,** *Colloq.* **1.** to tease or deceive a person. **2.** to accept a fight or competition with a person: *I'll have him on anytime.*
**have to do with, 1.** to have dealings with: *she will have nothing to do with him.* **2.** to concern: *that has nothing to do with you.*
**have up,** *Colloq.* to bring before the authorities, esp. in court (fol. by *for*): *he was had up for theft.*
**let someone have it,** *Colloq.* to launch a strong attack upon someone.
**not having any,** *Colloq.* **1.** refusing to accept something. **2.** refusing to join in some activity.
*–v.i.* **28.** to possess money, etc.; be well off. *–aux. v.* **29.** (used with the past participle of a verb to form a compound or perfect tense): *they have gone.* *–n. Colloq.* **30.** a delusion; trick: *it was a bit of a have.* **31. the haves and the have-nots,** *Colloq.* the rich and the poor. [ME *have(n),* OE *habban,* c. D *hebben,* G *haben,* Icel. *hafa,* Goth. *haban;* akin to L *capere* take]

**haven** /ˈheɪvən/, *n.* **1.** a harbour or port. **2.** an inlet of a sea or river mouth where ships can obtain good anchorage. **3.** any place of shelter and safety. *–v.t.* **4.** to shelter as in a haven. [ME; OE *hæfen,* c. G *Hafen*] – **havenless,** *adj.*

**have-not** /ˈhæv-nɒt/, *n. Colloq.* a poor person.

**haven't** /ˈhævənt/, *v.* contraction of *have not.*

**haversack** /ˈhævəsæk/, *n.* **1.** a soldier's bag for rations. **2.** any bag carried on the back or shoulders, used for provisions and the like. [F *havresac,* from LG *habersack,* lit., oat sack]

**havoc** /ˈhævək/, *n., v.,* **-ocked, -ocking.** *–n.* **1.** devastation; ruinous damage. **2. play havoc with,** to ruin; destroy. **3.** *Archaic.* a word used as the signal for pillage in warfare: *to cry havoc.* *–v.t.* **4.** to work havoc upon. *–v.i.* **5.** to work havoc. [ME *havok,* from AF, var. of OF *havot,* used esp. in phrase *crier havot* cry havoc, give the call for pillaging; probably from Gmc] – **havocker,** *n.*

**haw**[1] /hɔ/, *n.* the fruit of the Old World hawthorn, *Crataegus oxyacantha,* or of other species of the same genus. [ME; OE *haga.* Cf. HAWTHORN]

**haw**[2] /hɔ/, *interj.* **1.** (an utterance marking hesitation in speech.) *–n.* **2.** the utterance 'haw'. *–v.i.* **3.** to use 'haw', as in hesitation. [imitative]

**haw**[3] /hɔ/, *n.* the nictitating membrane of a horse, dog, etc., formerly only when inflamed. [orig. uncert.]

**Hawaiian** /həˈwaɪən/, *adj.* **1.** of or pertaining to Hawaii. *–n.* **2.** a native or inhabitant of Hawaii. **3.** the aboriginal language of Hawaii, a Polynesian language.

**Hawaiian flare** /– ˈflɛə/, *n.* an open kerosene torch for illuminating gardens, etc., at night.

**Hawaiian guitar** /– gəˈta/, *n.* a guitar, originally acoustic with a soundbox, now also electric with a flat board, held horizontally on one's lap and played with a metal slide. Also, **steel guitar.**

**Hawaiki** /ˈhawaɪki/, *n.* the legendary Polynesian ancestral homeland of the New Zealand Maori. [Maori]

**haw-haw** /hɔ-ˈhɔ/, *interj.* **1.** (an affected utterance marking hesitation in speech.) *–n.* **2.** the utterance 'haw-haw'. **3.** loud vulgar laughter; a guffaw. *–v.i.* **4.** to guffaw; laugh loudly. *–adj.* **5.** affectedly superior in enunciation.

**hawk**[1] /hɔk/, *n.* **1.** any of numerous diurnal birds of prey of the family Falconidae, as the falcons, buzzards, kites, harriers, etc., esp. the short-winged, long-tailed accipiters, as the goshawk. **2.** any of certain non-falconiform birds, as the nighthawk. **3.** a person who preys on others, as a sharper. **4.** a politician or political adviser who favours aggressive or intransigent military policies (opposed to *dove*). *–v.i.* **5.** to fly, or hunt on the wing, like a hawk. **6.** to hunt with hawks trained to pursue game. [ME *hauk(e),* OE *hafoc,* c. G *Habicht*] – **hawkish,** *adj.* – **hawklike,** *adj.*

hawk[1] (def. 1): chicken hawk

**hawk**[2] /hɔk/, *v.t.* **1.** to offer for sale by outcry in a street or from door to door. *–v.t.* **2. hawk about,** to spread, esp. news and the like. *–v.i.* **3.** to carry wares about; peddle. [backformation from HAWKER[2]]

**hawk**[3] /hɔk/, *v.i.* **1.** to make an effort to raise phlegm from the throat; clear the throat noisily. *–v.t.* **2.** to raise by hawking: *to hawk up phlegm.* *–n.* **3.** a noisy effort to clear the throat. [imitative]

**hawk**[4] /hɔk/, *n.* a small square board with a handle underneath, used by plasterers to hold small quantities of mortar. [orig. uncert.]

**hawkbill** /ˈhɔkbɪl/, *n.* →**hawk's-bill.**

**hawkbit** /ˈhɔkbɪt/, *n.* any of the perennial herbs belonging to the genus *Leontodon,* as *L. hirsutus,* **hairy hawkbit.**

**hawker**[1] /ˈhɔkə/, *n.* →**falconer.** [HAWK[1], *v.* + -ER[1]]

**hawker**[2] /ˈhɔkə/, *n.* one who travels from place to place or house to house selling goods. [apparently from MLG *hoker.* Cf. G *Höker,* D *heuker* retail dealer. See HUCKSTER]

**Hawkesbury clock** /hɔksbri ˈklɒk/, *n. Obs.* a kookaburra.

**hawk-eyed** /ˈhɔk-aɪd/, *adj.* having very keen eyes.

**hawking** /ˈhɔkɪŋ/, *n.* →**falconry.**

**hawkmoth** /ˈhɔkmɒθ/, *n.* any of certain moths of the family Sphingidae, noted for their very swift flight and ability to hover while sipping nectar from flowers.

**hawknose** /ˈhɔknoʊz/, *n.* a nose curved like the beak of a hawk. – **hawknosed,** *adj.*

**hawk-owl** /ˈhɔk-aʊl/, *n.* a strikingly barred grey and white owl, *Surnia ulula,* of northern parts of the Northern Hemisphere, so named because it is diurnal.

**hawk's-beard** /ˈhɔks-bɪəd/, *n.* any species of the genus *Crepis,* family Compositae, having yellow or orange flowers.

**hawk's-bill** /ˈhɔks-bɪl/, *n.* a turtle, *Eretmochelys imbricata,* yielding tortoiseshell and having a mouth shaped like the bill of a hawk. Also, **hawkbill, hawk's-bill turtle.**

**hawk's-eye** /ˈhɔks-aɪ/, *n.* a dark blue chatoyant stone used for ornament; a silicified crocidolite.

**hawkweed** /ˈhɔkwid/, *n.* **1.** any herb of the genus *Hieracium,* with yellow, orange, or red flowers. **2.** any of various related plants, as *Picris hieracioides* and *Tolpis barbata,* **yellow**

hawkweed.

**hawse** /hɔz/, *n.* **1.** the part of a ship's bow having holes for the cables to pass through. **2.** a hawsehole. **3.** the space between the stem of a ship at anchor and the anchors. **4.** the situation of a ship's cables when she is moored with both bow anchors: *a clear hawse.* [ME *halse,* probably from Scand.; cf. Icel. *hāls* part of ship's bow, front sheet of sail, lit. neck, c. OE *hals* neck]

**hawsehole** /ˈhɔzhoʊl/, *n.* a hole in the bow of a ship, through which a cable is passed.

**hawse pipe** /ˈhɔz paɪp/, *n.* the pipe through the bow of a ship to its forecastle in which the anchor is stowed and through which the chain cable passes to the windlass.

**hawser** /ˈhɔzə/, *n.* a small cable or large rope used in warping, mooring, towing, etc. [ME *haucer,* from OF *haucier* raise, from L *altus* high]

**hawser bend** /ˈ– bɛnd/, *n.* a knot uniting the ends of two hawsers.

**hawser-laid** /ˈhɔzə-leɪd/, *adj.* **1.** (of a rope) having its yarns spun right-handed and laid up left-handed into strands; the strands are then laid up right-handed to complete the rope. **2.** →**cable-laid.**

**hawthorn** /ˈhɔθɔn/, *n.* any species of the genus *Crataegus,* usu. small trees with stiff thorns, cultivated in hedges for their white or pink blossoms and bright-coloured fruits; may. [ME; OE *haguthorn,* c. D *haagdoorn.* See HAW[1]]

**hay**[1] /heɪ/, *n.* **1.** grass cut and dried for use as fodder. **2.** grass mowed or intended for mowing. **3.** *Colloq.* money. **4. hit the hay,** to go to bed. **5. make hay, a.** to cut grass for fodder. **b.** to scatter everything in disorder. **6. make hay while the sun shines,** to make the most of opportunity. **7. roll in the hay,** to sport sexually or copulate with another. *–v.t.* **8.** to convert (grass) into hay. **9.** to furnish (horses, etc.) with hay. *–v.i.* **10.** *Agric.* (of hay in the pasture) to ripen, ready for cutting and baling (fol. by *off*). [ME; OE *hēg, hīeg,* c. G *Heu*]

**hay**[2] /heɪ/, *n.* a kind of old country dance with winding movements. Also, **hey.** [F (15thC) *haye* kind of dance]

**haybox** /ˈheɪbɒks/, *n.* a closed box containing moist hay which by natural processes develops enough heat to cook food slowly. Also, **hay oven.**

**hayburner** /ˈheɪbɜnə/, *n.* *Colloq.* a horse.

**haycock** /ˈheɪkɒk/, *n.* a small conical pile of hay thrown up in a hayfield, while the hay is awaiting removal.

**hayfeeder** /ˈheɪfidə/, *n.* a rack in a paddock in which baled hay is placed for the self-feeding of cattle.

**hay fever** /ˈheɪ fivə/, *n.* a catarrhal affection of the mucous membranes of the eyes and respiratory tract, attacking susceptible persons (usu.) during the summer, and due to the action of the pollen of certain plants.

**hayfield** /ˈheɪfild/, *n.* a field in which grass is grown for making into hay, or where haymaking is in progress.

**hayfork** /ˈheɪfɔk/, *n.* a fork used for turning or lifting hay, operated either by hand or machine.

**hayloft** /ˈheɪlɒft/, *n.* a loft in a stable or barn, for the storage of hay.

**haymaker** /ˈheɪmeɪkə/, *n.* **1.** one who makes hay. **2.** one who tosses and spreads hay to dry after it has been mowed. **3.** *Boxing.* a wild, unscientific sideways blow. **–haymaking,** *n.*

**haymow** /ˈheɪmaʊ/, *n.* **1.** a mow or mass of hay stored in a barn. **2.** the place in a barn or shed where hay is stored. **3.** a rick or stack of hay.

**hay oven** /ˈheɪ ʌvən/, *n.* →**haybox.**

**hayrick** /ˈheɪrɪk/, *n.* →**haystack.**

**hayseed** /ˈheɪsid/, *n.* **1.** grass seed, esp. that shaken out of hay. **2.** small bits of the chaff, etc., of hay. **3.** *Colloq.* a countryman or rustic.

**hayshed** /ˈheɪʃɛd/, *n.* a shed, often a framework with a roof but no walls, for storing hay.

**haystack** /ˈheɪstæk/, *n.* **1.** Also, **hayrick.** a stack of hay with a conical or ridged top, built up in the open air for preservation, and sometimes thatched or covered. **2.** *Canoeing Colloq.* a stationary white-headed wave caused by fast-flowing water moving into slow water.

**haywire** /ˈheɪwaɪə/, *n.* **1.** wire used to bind hay. *–adj.* **2.** in disorder; out of order. **3.** out of control; crazy: *to go haywire.*

**hazard** /ˈhæzəd/, *n.* **1.** a risk; exposure to danger or harm. **2.** the cause of such a risk; a potential source of harm, injury, difficulty, etc.: *the motor car has become a major hazard in modern life.* **3.** chance; uncertainty. **4.** the uncertainty of the result in throwing a die. **5.** a game for any number of players played with two dice, complicated by various arbitrary rules, formerly much played. **6.** *Golf.* an obstacle, as a bunker, road, bush, water, or the like, on the course. **7.** *Royal Tennis.* **a.** any of certain openings in the walls of the court, the striking of a ball into which scores the striker a point. **b.** that side of the court into which the ball is served (**hazard side**). **8.** *Billiards.* a stroke made when a ball, other than the striker's ball, is pocketed after contact with another ball (**winning hazard**), or when the striker's ball is pocketed after contact with another ball (**losing hazard**). **9.** *Show-jumping.* a fence or other obstacle on a show-jumping course. **10. at hazard, a.** at risk; staked. **b.** by chance: *we met at hazard.* *–v.t.* **11.** to venture to offer (a statement, conjecture, etc.). **12.** to put to the risk of being lost; to expose to risk. **13.** to take or run the risk of (a misfortune, penalty, etc.). **14.** to venture upon (anything of doubtful issue). [ME *hasard,* from OF, from Ar. *az-zahr* the die] **–hazardable,** *adj.* **–hazarder,** *n.* **–hazardless,** *adj.*

**hazard flasher** /ˈ– flæʃə/, *n.* (in a motor vehicle) a switch which enables all turning-indicator lights to be flashed simultaneously as a warning device.

**hazard lights** /ˈ– laɪts/, *n. pl.* the indicators of a vehicle when flashing simultaneously as a sign that the car is immobilised and a hazard to other traffic.

**hazardous** /ˈhæzədəs/, *adj.* **1.** full of risk; perilous; risky. **2.** dependent on chance: *a hazardous contract.* **–hazardously,** *adv.* **–hazardousness,** *n.*

**haze**[1] /heɪz/, *n.* **1.** an aggregation of minute suspended particles of vapour, dust, etc., near the surface of the earth, causing an appearance of thin mist in the atmosphere. **2.** obscurity or vagueness of the mind, perception, feelings, etc. [orig. obscure]

**haze**[2] /heɪz/, *v.t.,* **hazed, hazing. 1.** (in a rodeo) to assist a bulldogger by riding alongside and guiding a steer. **2.** *U.S.* to subject (freshmen or newcomers) to harassment, abuse and ridiculous tricks. **3.** *Chiefly Naut.* to harass with unnecessary or disagreeable tasks. [cf. MF *haser* irritate, annoy] **–hazer,** *n.*

**hazed-off** /heɪzd-ˈɒf/, *adj.* *Colloq.* sun-dried, as land.

**hazel** /ˈheɪzəl/, *n.* **1.** any shrub or small tree of the genus *Corylus,* which bears edible nuts, as *C. avellana* of Europe or *C. americana* and *C. cornuta* of America. **2.** any of certain other similar shrubs or trees, or their wood. **3.** the hazelnut or filbert. **4.** the wood of a hazel. **5.** light reddish brown of a hazelnut. *–adj.* **6.** of or pertaining to the hazel. **7.** made of the wood of the hazel. **8.** having a hazel colour. [ME *hazel(l),* OE *hæs(e)l,* c. G *Hasel;* akin to L *corylus* hazel shrub]

**hazelnut** /ˈheɪzəlnʌt/, *n.* the nut of the hazel.

**hazy** /ˈheɪzi/, *adj.,* **-zier, -ziest. 1.** characterised by the presence of haze; misty: *hazy weather.* **2.** lacking distinctness; vague; confused: *a hazy proposition.* **–hazily,** *adv.* **–haziness,** *n.*

**hazzan** /həˈzan, ˈhazən/, *n.* →**chazzan.**

**HB** /eɪtʃ ˈbi/, *adj.* **1.** (of pencils) hard and black. *–n.* **2.** such a pencil.

**H-bomb** /ˈeɪtʃ-bɒm/, *n.* hydrogen bomb.

**h'cap,** handicap.

**H.C.F.** /eɪtʃ si ˈɛf/, highest common factor. Also, **h.c.f.**

**hcp,** handicap.

**hdqrs,** headquarters.

**he** /hi/; *weak form* /i/; *Brit. weak forms* /hɪ, ɪ/ *pron., poss.* **his,** *obj.* **him,** *pl.* **they;** *n., pl.* **hes. 1.** the male being in question or last mentioned. **2.** anyone; that person: *he who hesitates is lost.* *–n.* **3.** a man or any male person or animal (correlative to *she*). *–adj.* **4.** male or masculine, esp. of animals. [ME *he,* OE *hē* (gen. *his,* dat. *him,* acc. *hine*), c. OS *he, hi,* OFris. *hi, he.* Cf. SHE, HER, IT, HENCE, HERE, HITHER]

**He,** *Chem.* helium.

**H.E.,** **1.** His Eminence. **2.** His Excellency. **3.** (*sometimes l.c.*) high explosive.

**head** /hɛd/, *n.* **1.** the upper part of the human body, joined to the trunk by the neck. **2.** the corresponding part of an animal's body. **3.** the head considered as the seat of thought, memory, understanding, etc.: *to have a head for mathematics.* **4.** the position of leadership; chief command; greatest authority. **5.** one to whom others are subordinate; a leader or chief. **6.** that part of anything which forms or is regarded as forming the top, summit, or upper end: *head of a page.* **7.** the foremost part or end of anything; a projecting part: *head of a procession, head of a rock.* **8.** Also, **loose head.** *Rugby Football.* in a scrum, the front-row forward who has only one shoulder in contact with an opposite player. **9.** a person considered with reference to his mind, disposition, attributes, etc.: *wise heads, crowned heads.* **10.** a person or animal considered merely as one of a number (with pl. **head**): *ten head of cattle, to charge so much a head.* **11.** a measurement to show the difference in height between two people, or the distance between two horses in a race. **12.** culmination or crisis; conclusion: *to bring matters to a head.* **13.** the hair covering the head: *to comb someone's head.* **14.** something resembling a head in form: *a head of lettuce.* **15.** a rounded or compact part of a plant, usu. at the top of the stem, as of leaves (as in the cabbage or lettuce), leaf-stalks (as in the celery), flower buds (as in the cauliflower), sessile florets, etc. **16.** that part of a cereal plant, as wheat, barley, etc., which contains the flowers and hence the fruit, grains and kernels. **17.** the striking part of an instrument, tool, weapon, or the like, (opposed to the gripping part), as the part of a golf club which includes the face and with which the ball is hit. **18.** the maturated part of an abscess, boil, etc. **19.** a projecting point of a coast, esp. when high, as a cape, headland, or promontory. **20.** the obverse of a coin, as bearing a head or other principal figure (opposed to *tail*). **21.** one of the chief points or divisions of a discourse; topic. **22.** *Archaic.* strength or force gradually attained; progress. **23.** the source of a river or stream. **24.** collar, froth or foam, as that formed on beer when poured. **25.** (in winemaking) the skins and seeds of the grapes, which have risen to the top of the wine during fermentation; cap. **26.** the headline or group of headlines at the top of a newspaper article. **27.** the forepart of a ship, etc. **28.** the upper edge (or corner) of a sail. **29.** *Naut.* the upper end of any spar, derrick, etc. **30.** *Naut.* a shaped vertical timber. **31.** a ship's toilet. **32.** *Gram.* **a.** that member of an endocentric construction which belongs to the same form class and may play the same grammatical role as the construction itself. **b.** the member upon which another depends and to which it is subordinate; for example, in *the first prize, first prize* is head and *the* is attribute, and in *first prize,* the head is *prize* and the attribute is *first.* **33.** the stretched membrane covering the end of a drum or similar instrument. **34.** *Mining.* a level or road driven into the solid coal for proving or working a mine. **35.** *Bowls.* the collection of bowls around the jack at the completion of an end. **36.** the height of the free surface of a liquid above a given level. **37.** *Mach.* a device on turning and boring machines, esp. lathes, holding one or more cutting tools to the work. **38.** the pressure of a confined body of steam, etc., per unit of area. **39.** the height of a column of fluid required for a certain pressure. **40.** *Jazz.* the written melody and chord changes from which the improvisation is derived. **41.** the part or parts of a tape-recorder which come into direct contact with the tape and serve to record, reproduce, or erase electromagnetic impulses on it. **42.** *Colloq.* a person who uses drugs regularly, esp. marijuana and LSD. **43.** Some special noun phrases are:

**by** or **down by the head,** *Naut.* so loaded as to draw more water forward than aft.

**come to a head,** to reach a crisis.

**get a big (swelled) head,** to become conceited.

**give someone** (or **something**) **his (its) head, 1.** to allow greater freedom. **2.** to allow (a horse) greater freedom in running.

**go to one's head, 1.** to make one confused or dizzy. **2.** to make one conceited.

**have a (good) head on one's shoulders,** to have a balanced and sensible outlook.

**have heads over,** *Colloq.* to punish the people responsible for (a blunder).

**have one's head screwed on the right way,** to have a lot of commonsense.

**have (someone's) head,** *Colloq.* to punish (someone) severely.

**head and shoulders (above),** by far superior to.

**head over heels (tail) (turkey), 1.** upside-down; headlong as after a somersault. **2.** completely, utterly.

**keep one's head above water,** to remain in control of a difficult situation, esp. a financial one.

**keep one's head down, 1.** to work hard and consistently. **2.** to stay out of view and hence out of trouble.

**lay** or **put heads together,** to come together to scheme.

**lose one's head,** to panic, become flustered, esp. in an emergency.

**make head or tail of,** to understand; work out: *I can't make head or tail of this question.*

**need one's head read,** (*joc.*) to be insane.

**off one's head,** mad; very excited; delirious.

**off the top of one's head,** extempore; impromptu.

**one's head off,** to an extreme; excessively: *talk one's head off.*

**on one's own head,** as one's own responsibility.

**out of one's head, 1.** from one's mind, memory, imagination, etc.: *that story has come completely out of my head.* **2.** out of one's mind; demented; delirious.

**over one's head, 1.** passing over one having a prior claim or a superior position. **2.** beyond one's comprehension.

**pull one's head in,** to mind one's own business.

**take (it) into one's head,** to conceive an idea, plan, or the like.

**turn its head,** (of a racing dog) to attack another dog during the race.

**turn someone's head,** to make someone vain or conceited.

**win against the head,** *Rugby Football.* to hook the ball despite the opposing team's advantage in having a loose head.

–*adj.* **44.** situated at the top or front: *the head division of a parade.* **45.** being in the position of leadership or superiority. **46.** coming from in front: *a headwind.* –*v.t.* **47.** to go at the head of or in front of; lead, precede: *to head a list.* **48.** to outdo or excel. **49.** to be the head or chief of. **50.** to turn the head or front of in a specified direction: *to head one's boat for the shore.* **51.** to go round the head of (a stream, etc.). **52.** to furnish or fit with a head. **53.** to take the head of (an animal) off. **54.** to poll (a tree). **55.** *Agric.* to harvest, esp. a grain crop, by removing the head. **56.** *Football.* to propel (the ball) by action of the head. **57. head off,** to intercept (something) and force (it) to change course. **58. head them,** (in two-up) to make the coins land with heads upwards. –*v.i.* **59.** to move forwards towards a point specified; direct one's course; go in a certain direction (oft. fol. by *for*). **60.** to come or grow to a head; form a head. [ME *he(v)ed,* OE *hēafod,* c. D *hoofd,* G *Haupt,* Icel. *höfudh,* Goth. *haubith*] –**headlike,** *adj.*

**-head**[1], a suffix denoting state, condition, character, etc., as in *godhead,* and other words, now mostly archaic or obsolete, many being superseded by forms in **-hood.** [ME *-hede, -hed,* from *hede* rank, condition, character; akin to OE *hād,* whence the suffix -HOOD]

**-head**[2], a suffix indicating a person typified by a specified predilection, as *acidhead.*

**headache** /ˈhɛdeɪk/, *n.* **1.** a pain situated in the head. **2.** *Colloq.* a troublesome or worrying problem. –**headachy,** *adj.*

**headband** /ˈhɛdbænd/, *n.* **1.** a band worn round the head; a fillet. **2.** a band sewn to the head and tail of the back of a book, sometimes as decoration but usu. to protect and strengthen the binding.

**headboard** /ˈhɛdbɔd/, *n.* a board forming the head of anything, esp. of a bed.

**head boy** /hɛd ˈbɔɪ/, *n.* **1. a.** (in a boys' school) the head prefect, or captain of the school. **b.** (in a co-educational school) a boy who shares the captaincy with the head girl. **2.** (in a colonial society where colonisers use natives as servants) the native man who has authority over other native domestics and labourers.

**headcount** /ˈhɛdkaʊnt/, *n.* a tally of the number of people in a group.

**headdress** /ˈhɛddrɛs/, *n.* **1.** a covering or decoration for the head. **2.** *Obs.* an arrangement of the hair.

**headed** /ˈhɛdəd/, *adj.* **1.** having a heading. **2.** shaped or grown into a head.

**-headed,** a suffix meaning: **1.** having a specified kind of head: *long-headed, wrong-headed.* **2.** having a specified number of heads: *two-headed.*

**header** /ˈhɛdə/, *n.* **1.** one who or an apparatus which removes or puts a head on something. **2.** a form of reaping machine which cuts off and gathers only the head of the grain. **3.** a chamber to which the ends of a number of tubes are connected so that water or steam may pass freely from one tube to the other. **4.** *Bldg Trades.* a brick or stone laid with its length across the thickness of a wall. Cf. **Flemish bond.** **5.** *Soccer.* a shot made with the head. **6.** *Colloq.* a plunge or dive headfirst, as into water. **7. take a header,** *Colloq.* to dive.

**headfirst** /hɛdˈfɜst/, *adv.* **1.** with the head in front or bent forwards; headlong. **2.** rashly; precipitately. Also, **headforemost** /hɛdˈfɔmoʊst/.

**headframe** /ˈhɛdfreɪm/, *n.* the structure over the top of a mine shaft used for supporting the winding equipment.

**headgate** /ˈhɛdgeɪt/, *n.* **1.** a control gate at the upstream end of a canal or lock. **2.** a floodgate of a race, sluice, etc.

**headgear** /ˈhɛdgɪə/, *n.* **1.** any covering for the head. **2.** the parts of a harness about an animal's head. **3.** *Mining.* **a.** that part of the winding machinery which is attached to the headframe of a mine shaft. **b.** the headframe and its auxiliary fittings.

**head girl** /hɛd ˈgɜl/, *n.* **1.** (in a girl's school) the captain of the school, or head prefect. **2.** (in a co-educational school) the girl who shares the captaincy with the head boy.

**headhigh** /ˈhɛdhaɪ/, *Rugby League.* *–adj.* **1.** (of a tackle) taken about the head. *–n.* **2.** such an illegal tackle.

**head-hunting** /ˈhɛd-hʌntɪŋ/, *n.* **1.** (among certain primitive tribes) the practice of making incursions for procuring human heads as trophies or for use in religious ceremonies. **2.** *Colloq.* the eliminating of political enemies. **3.** *Colloq.* (in a business or other organisation) the seeking out of a scapegoat for a misfortune or setback. **4.** *Colloq.* the search for new executives, usu. senior, through personal contacts rather than advertisements. **5.** *Rugby Football Colloq.* illegal tackling about the head, often in the hope of injuring and incapacitating players of the opposing team.

**heading** /ˈhɛdɪŋ/, *n.* **1.** something that serves as a head, top, or front. **2.** a title or caption of a page, chapter, etc. **3.** a section of a subject of discourse; a topic. **4.** a horizontal passage in the earth, as for an intended tunnel, for working a mine, for ventilation or drainage, etc.; a drift. **5.** the end of such a passage. **6.** (on South Australian opal fields) a section driven off at right angles to the shaft when encouraging traces of potch are met. **7.** *Aeron.* the angle made by the longitudinal axis of an aircraft in flight with a given meridian. **8.** *Naut.* the pocket in a flag, containing the rope. **9.** navigational direction; bearing.

**heading dog** /ˈ– dɒg/, *n.* a dog trained to head off and stop livestock.

**headlamp** /ˈhɛdlæmp/, *n.* →**headlight.**

**headland** /ˈhɛdlənd, -lænd/, *n.* **1.** a promontory extending into a large body of water, such as a sea or lake. **2.** a strip of unploughed land at the ends of furrows or near a fence or border.

**headless** /ˈhɛdləs/, *adj.* **1.** having no head; deprived of the head. **2.** without a leader or chief. **3.** foolish; stupid. [ME *he(ve)dles,* OE *hēafodlēas.* See -LESS]

**headlight** /ˈhɛdlaɪt/, *n.* a light equipped with a reflector, on the front of any vehicle.

**headline** /ˈhɛdlaɪn/, *n., v.,* **-lined, -lining.** *–n.* **1.** a display line over an article, etc., as in a newspaper. **2.** the line at the top of a page, containing the title, pagination, etc. **3.** (*pl.*) the few most important items of news very briefly stated: *here again are the headlines.* **4.** (in palmistry) a line of the head. *–v.t.* **5.** to furnish with a headline.

**headlock** /ˈhɛdlɒk/, *n.* a wrestling hold in which a combatant locks his arm around his opponent's head.

**headlong** /ˈhɛdlɒŋ/, *adv.* **1.** headfirst: *to plunge headlong.* **2.** rashly; without deliberation. **3.** precipitately; with great speed. *–adj.* **4.** done or going with the head foremost. **5.** characterised by haste; precipitate. **6.** rash; impetuous. **7.** *Archaic.* steep; precipitous. [late ME *hedlong,* from *hed* HEAD + *long,* adv. suffix; replacing *headling,* ME *hedlyng.* See -LING[2]]

**headman** /ˈhɛdmən/, *n., pl.* **-men.** a chief man; a chief or leader. [ME *hevedmon,* OE *hēafodman*]

**headmaster** /ˈhɛdmastə, hɛdˈmastə/, *n.* the male principal of a school. – **headmastership,** *n.*

**headmistress** /ˈhɛdmɪstrəs, hɛdˈmɪstrəs/, *n.* the female principal of a school.

**head money** /ˈhɛd mʌni/, *n.* **1.** a tax of so much per head or person. **2.** a reward paid for each person captured or brought in. **3.** a reward for the killing, and sometimes for the actual head, of an outlaw or enemy.

**headmost** /ˈhɛdmoʊst/, *adj.* foremost; most advanced.

**head music** /ˈhɛd mjuzɪk/, *n.* heavy rock or acid rock.

**head note** /ˈ– noʊt/, *n.* a note sung in the head register. Also, *Chiefly U.S.,* **head tone.**

**head of the river,** *n.* **1.** a rowing regatta held on a particular river as the Sydney G.P.S. regatta on the Nepean. **2.** the winners of such a regatta.

**head-on** /hɛd-ˈɒn/, *adv.;* /ˈhɛd-ɒn/, *adj., n.* *–adv.* **1.** with the head or front striking or opposed to something: *the cars came to a halt head-on.* *–adj.* **2.** of or pertaining to what has met head-on: *a head-on collision.* **3.** of or pertaining to a direct confrontation: *a head-on argument.* *–n.* **4.** a head-on collision.

**headphone** /ˈhɛdfoʊn/, *n.* (*oft. pl.*) a device consisting of one or two earphones with attachments for holding them over the ears.

**headpiece** /ˈhɛdpis/, *n.* **1.** armour for the head; a helmet. **2.** any covering for the head. **3.** headphones. **4.** the head as the seat of the intellect; judgment. **5.** the top piece or part of any of various things. **6.** *Print.* a decorative piece at the head of a page, chapter, etc.

**headpin** /ˈhɛdpɪn/, *n.* **1.** *Tenpin Bowling.* the number one pin situated at the apex of the tenpin triangle. **2.** →**kingpin.**

**head-puller** /ˈhɛd-pʊlə/, *n.* *Colloq.* a person who directs a shop assistant's attention elsewhere while an accomplice steals.

**headquarter** /hɛdˈkwɔtə/, *v.t.* to provide with headquarters.

**headquarters** /ˈhɛdkwɔtəz, hɛdˈkwɔtəz/, *n.pl. or sing.* **1.** any centre from which official orders are issued: *police headquarters.* **2.** any centre of operations. **3.** the offices of a military commander; the place where a commander customarily issues his orders. **4.** a military unit consisting of the commander, his staff, and other assistants. **5.** the building occupied by a headquarters.

**headrace** /ˈhɛdreɪs/, *n.* the race, flume, or channel leading to a waterwheel or the like.

**head register** /ˈhɛd rɛdʒəstə/, *n.* the upper register of the singing voice, thought of as striking sympathetic vibrations in the head and face. Also, **head voice.**

**head resistance** /ˈ– rəzɪstəns/, *n.* →**profile drag.**

**headrest** /ˈhɛdrɛst/, *n.* a rest or support of any kind for the head, as on a dentist's chair.

**headroom** /ˈhɛdrum/, *n.* the clear height from floor to ceiling; the clearance of a bridge, between the decks of a ship, etc.

**headsail** /ˈhɛdsəl/, *n.* a triangular sail running on a stay forward of the foremast.

**headscarf** /ˈhɛdskaf/, *n.* a square piece of material worn by women as a covering for the head. Also, **headsquare** /ˈhɛdskwɛə/.

**head sea** /ˈhɛd si/, *n.* a sea in which the waves approach the vessel from the direction steered.

**head serang** /hɛd səˈræŋ/, *n.* *Colloq.* the person in charge; boss. Also, **head sherang** /hɛd ʃəˈræŋ/. [HEAD + Pers. *serang* boatswain]

**headset** /ˈhɛdsɛt/, *n.* →**headphones.**

**headship** /ˈhɛdʃɪp/, *n.* the position of head or chief; chief authority; leadership; supremacy.

**headshrinker** /ˈhɛdʃrɪŋkə/, *n.* **1.** a headhunter who shrinks and preserves the heads of his victims. **2.** Also, **shrink.** *Colloq.* a psychiatrist.

**headsman** /ˈhɛdzmən/, *n., pl.* **-men.** one who beheads condemned persons; a public executioner.

**headspring** /ˈhɛdsprɪŋ/, *n.* **1.** the fountainhead or source of a stream. **2.** the source of anything.

**headstall** /ˈhɛdstɔl/, *n.* that part of a bridle or halter which encompasses the head.

**headstand** /ˈhɛdstænd/, *n.* a position of the body in which it is balanced vertically, the head and hands on the ground.

**head start** /hɛd ˈstat/, *n.* an initial advantage in a race, competition, etc.

**head station** /ˈ– steɪʃən/, *n.* the main buildings or establishment on a large grazing property. Cf. **back-station, out-station.**

**headstock** /ˈhɛdstɒk/, *n.* the part of a machine containing the working members, as the assembly supporting and driving the live spindle in a lathe.

**headstone** /ˈhɛdstoun/, *n.* a stone set at the head of a grave.

**headstream** /ˈhɛdstrim/, *n.* a stream that forms the source, or one of the sources, of a river.

**headstrong** /ˈhɛdstrɒŋ/, *adj.* **1.** bent on having one's own way; wilful. **2.** proceeding from wilfulness: *a headstrong course.* – **headstrongness,** *n.*

**head tone** /ˈhɛd toun/, *n. Chiefly U.S.* →**head note.**

**head voice** /ˈhɛd vɔɪs/, *n.* →**head register.**

**headwaters** /ˈhɛdwɔtəz/, *n. pl.* the upper tributaries of a river.

**headway** /ˈhɛdweɪ/, *n.* **1.** motion forwards or ahead; advance. **2.** progress in general. **3.** rate of progress. **4.** the interval between two trains, etc., travelling in the same direction over the same route.

**headwind** /ˈhɛdwɪnd/, *n.* a wind that blows directly against the course of a ship or the like.

**headword** /ˈhɛdwɜd/, *n.* **1.** a word heading or beginning a chapter, paragraph, or the like. **2.** a word or expression beginning an entry in a dictionary, etc., which the rest of the entry defines and describes.

**headwork** /ˈhɛdwɜk/, *n.* mental labour; thought. – **headworker,** *n.*

**heady** /ˈhɛdi/, *adj.,* **-ier, -iest. 1.** rashly impetuous. **2.** intoxicating. [ME *he(ve)di.* See HEAD, *n.,* -Y[1]] – **headily,** *adv.* – **headiness,** *n.*

**heal** /hil/, *v.t.* **1.** to make whole or sound; restore to health; free from ailment. **2.** to free from anything evil or distressing; amend: *to heal a quarrel.* **3.** to cleanse or purify. *–v.i.* **4.** to effect a cure. **5.** to become whole or sound; get well (oft. fol. by *up* or *over*). [ME *hele(n),* OE *hǣlan,* from *hāl* hale, WHOLE] – **healer,** *n.* – **healing,** *n.* – **healingly,** *adv.*

**healing** /ˈhilɪŋ/, *adj.* **1.** that heals; curing; curative: *healing ointment.* **2.** growing sound; getting well.

**health** /hɛlθ/, *n.* **1.** soundness of body; freedom from disease or ailment. **2.** the general condition of the body or mind with reference to soundness and vigour: *good health.* **3.** a polite or complimentary wish for a person's health, happiness, etc., esp. as a toast. **4. to your health!,** (an expression of goodwill, esp. as a toast). [ME *helthe,* OE *hǣlth,* from *hāl* hale, whole. See WHOLE, -TH[1]]

**health camp** /ˈ– kæmp/, *n. N.Z.* a camp intended to improve children of less than usual physiological or emotional health.

**health centre** /ˈ– sɛntə/, *n.* a welfare centre set up by a state authority for the care of the general health of the residents in that area, esp. mothers and babies. See **baby health centre.**

**health farm** /ˈ– fam/, *n.* a place, usu. in the country, where people go to improve their health.

**health food** /ˈ– fud/, *n.* food that is characterised by its health-giving properties.

**healthful** /ˈhɛlθfʊl/, *adj.* **1.** conducive to health; wholesome, or salutary: *healthful diet.* **2.** healthy. – **healthfully,** *adv.* – **healthfulness,** *n.*

**health inspector** /ˈhɛlθ ɪnspɛktə/, *n.* an officer appointed to inspect working and living conditions, buildings, etc., in the area, to ensure that they conform to health regulations.

**health physics** /ˈ– fɪsɪks/, *n.* the branch of physics dealing with the effects of ionising radiation on living organisms, esp. with the protection of human beings from those effects.

**health salts** /ˈ– sɒlts/, *n. pl.* salts, sometimes flavoured, which dissolve in water with effervescence and which are taken for the relief of flatulence, etc., and for their mildly laxative effect.

**health stamp** /ˈ– stæmp/, *n. N.Z.* one of an annual stamp-issue, part of the sale proceeds of which goes towards supporting health camps.

**health visitor** /ˈ– vɪzətə/, *n. Brit.* a state-registered nurse appointed to visit and look after the health of people in a certain area, esp. mothers and babies, the old and sick.

**healthy** /ˈhɛlθi/, *adj.,* **-thier, -thiest. 1.** possessing or enjoying health: *healthy body or mind.* **2.** pertaining to or characteristic of health: *a healthy appearance.* **3.** conducive to health, or healthful: *healthy recreations.* – **healthily,** *adv.* – **healthiness,** *n.*

**healy** /ˈhili/, *n., v.,* **-lied, -lying.** *–n.* **1.** *Prison Colloq.* an artifice or stratagem, esp. one needed to carry out some illegal act successfully. **2.** an illegal means of earning a living: *what's your latest healy?* *–v.i.* **3.** to catch on; to understand.

**heap** /hip/, *n.* **1.** an assemblage of things, lying one on another; a pile: *a heap of stones.* **2.** *Colloq.* a great quantity or number; a multitude. **3.** *Colloq.* something very old and dilapidated, esp. a motor car. **4. give (someone) heaps,** *Colloq.* **a.** express strong displeasure with (someone); criticise severely. **b.** to tease; provoke to anger, annoyance, etc., by banter or mockery. **5. give it heaps,** to treat with firmness, in order to exact good performance. **6. strike all of a heap,** *Colloq.* to dumbfound; amaze; overwhelm. *–v.t.* **7.** to gather, put, or cast in a heap; pile (oft. fol. by *up, on, together,* etc.). **8.** to accumulate or amass (oft. fol. by *up*): *to heap up riches.* **9.** to cast or bestow in great quantity: *to heap blessings or insults upon a person.* **10.** to load or supply abundantly with something: *to heap a person with favours.* **11. heap coals of fire on (someone's) head,** to mortify or make ashamed (a person who has acted unkindly) by being especially kind to him. *–v.i.* **12.** to become heaped or piled, as sand, snow, etc.; rise in a heap or heaps. [ME *heep,* OE *hēap* heap, multitude, troop, c. LG *hōp;* akin to G *Haufen*] – **heaper,** *n.*

**hear** /hɪə/, *v.,* **heard** /hɜd/, **hearing.** *–v.t.* **1.** to perceive by the ear. **2.** to listen to: *to refuse to hear a person.* **3.** to learn by the ear or by being told; be informed of: *to hear news.* **4.** to be among the audience at or of: *to hear an opera.* **5.** to give a formal, official, or judicial hearing to, as a sovereign, a teacher, an assembly, or a judge does. **6.** to listen to with favour, assent, or compliance. **7. hear things,** to imagine noises; hallucinate. **8. hear out,** to listen to (someone or something) until the end. *–v.i.* **9.** to have perception of sound by the ear; have the sense of hearing. **10.** to listen or take heed (in imperative, 'hear! hear!', used to applaud or show approval of a speaker's words). **11.** to receive information by the ear or otherwise: *to hear from a friend.* **12.** to listen with favour or assent: *he would not hear of it.* [ME *here(n),* OE *hēran,* c. G *hören*] – **hearer,** *n.*

**Heard and McDonald Islands,** *n. pl.* a group of islands in the Antarctic off the south-west coast of Tasmania; a territory of Australia.

**hearing** /ˈhɪərɪŋ/, *n.* **1.** the faculty or sense by which sound is perceived. **2.** the act of perceiving sound. **3.** opportunity to be heard: *to grant a hearing.* **4.** *Law.* the trial of an action. **5.** earshot: *out of hearing.*

**hearing aid** /ˈ– eɪd/, *n.* a compact, inconspicuous amplifier worn to improve one's hearing.

**hearken** /ˈhakən/, *Archaic.* *–v.i.* **1.** to listen; to give heed or attend to what is said. *–v.t.* **2.** to listen to; hear. Also, **harken.** [ME *herken,* OE *he(o)rcnian;* akin to HARK] – **hearkener,** *n.*

**hearsay** /ˈhɪəseɪ/, *n.* gossip; rumour.

**hearse** /hɜs/, *n.* a funeral vehicle for conveying a dead person to the place of burial. [ME *herse,* from OF *herce* harrow, frame, from L *hirpex, irpex* large rake used as harrow]

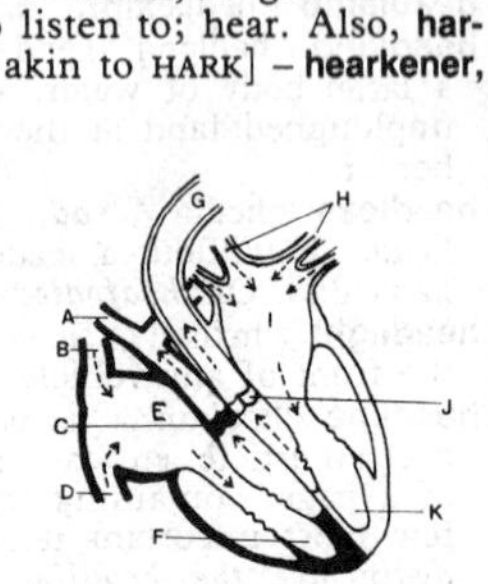

heart (def. 1): A, pulmonary artery; B, superior vena cava; C, pulmonary valve; D, interior vena cava; E, right auricle; F, right ventricle; G, aorta; H, pulmonary veins; I, left auricle; J, aortic valve; K, left ventricle

**heart** /hat/, *n.* **1.** a hollow muscular organ which by rhythmic contraction and dilatation keeps the blood in circulation throughout the body. **2.** this organ considered as the seat of life, or vital powers, or of thought, feeling, or emotion: *to die of a broken heart.* **3.** the seat of emotions and affections (often in contrast to the *head* as the seat of the intellect): *to win a person's heart.* **4.** feeling; sensibility; capacity for sympathy: *to have no heart.* **5.** spirit, courage, or enthusiasm: *to take heart.* **6.** the innermost or middle part of anything. **7.** the vital or essential part; core: *the very heart of the matter.* **8.** the breast or bosom: *to clasp a person to one's heart.* **9.** a person, esp. in expressions of praise or affection: *dear heart.* **10.** a figure or object with rounded sides meeting in an obtuse point at the bottom and curving inwards to a cusp at the top. **11.** *Cards.* **a.** a playing card of a suit marked with heart-shaped figures in red. **b.** (*pl.*) the suit of cards bearing this symbol. **c.** (*pl. construed as sing.*) a game in which the players try to avoid taking tricks containing hearts. **12.** *Bot.* the core of a tree; the solid central part without sap or albumen. **13.** good condition for production, growth, etc., as of land or crops. **14.** Some special noun phrases are:

heart (def. 10)

**after one's own heart,** appealing to one's taste or affection.
**at heart,** in one's heart, thoughts, or feelings; in reality.
**be all heart,** (*usu. ironic*) to be full of consideration and kindness.
**break the heart of,** **1.** to disappoint grievously in love. **2.** to crush with sorrow or grief.
**by heart,** from memory; committing to memory.
**close to one's heart,** deeply affecting one's interests and affections.
**cry one's heart out,** to cry bitterly or violently.
**eat one's heart out,** to pine or fret, esp. with envy.
**from (the bottom of) one's heart,** sincerely.
**have a change of heart,** to reverse a decision or opinion.
**have a heart,** to be reasonable; show mercy.
**have at heart,** to cherish as an object, aim, etc.
**have one's heart in one's mouth,** to be very frightened.
**have the heart,** **1.** to have enough courage. **2.** (in negative sentences) to be unfeeling enough.
**heart and soul,** completely; wholly.
**heart of hearts,** at the depth of one's feelings: *he knew in his heart of hearts that he was wrong.*
**heart of oak,** a courageous and long-suffering spirit.
**lose one's heart,** to fall in love.
**set one's heart at rest,** to ease one's anxieties: *the doctor was able to set her heart at rest.*
**set one's heart on,** to desire greatly; to resolve to obtain (something).
**take heart,** to find new courage or strength; be reassured or encouraged.
**take to heart,** **1.** to think seriously about. **2.** to be deeply affected by; grieve over.
**to one's heart's content,** as much as one wishes.
**wear one's heart upon one's sleeve,** to reveal openly one's feelings, intentions, etc.
**with all one's heart,** with all willingness; heartily.
*–v.t. Archaic.* **15.** to encourage. [ME *herte,* OE *heorte,* c. G *Herz*]

**heartache** /ˈhateɪk/, *n.* mental anguish; painful sorrow.

**heart attack** /ˈhat ətæk/, *n.* **1.** myocardial infarction. **2.** →**coronary thrombosis.**

**heartbeat** /ˈhatbit/, *n.* a pulsation of the heart, including one complete systole and diastole.

**heart block** /ˈhat blɒk/, *n.* a cardiac arrhythmia resulting from a disturbance in the transmission of impulses from the atria to the ventricles.

**heartbreak** /ˈhatbreɪk/, *n.* crushing sorrow or grief.

**heartbreaking** /ˈhatbreɪkɪŋ/, *adj.* causing heartbreak. – **heartbreaker,** *n.*

**heartbroken** /ˈhatbroukən/, *adj.* crushed with sorrow or grief. – **heartbrokenly,** *adv.* – **heartbrokenness,** *n.*

**heartburn** /ˈhatbɜn/, *n.* **1.** a burning sensation in the epigastrium. **2.** envy; bitter jealousy.

**heartburning** /ˈhatbɜnɪŋ/, *n.* rankling discontent, esp. from envy or jealousy; a grudge.

**heart disease** /ˈhat dəziz/, *n.* any condition of the heart which impairs its functioning.

**hearted** /ˈhatəd/, *adj.* having a specified kind of heart: *hard-hearted, tender-hearted.*

**hearten** /ˈhatn/, *v.t.* to give courage to; cheer.

**heart failure** /ˈhat feɪljə/, *n.* **1.** inability of the heart to pump adequate blood for maintenance of the circulation leading to congestion of the tissues, shortness of the breath, etc. **2.** →**heart attack.**

**heartfelt** /ˈhatfɛlt/, *adj.* deeply or sincerely felt; earnest; sincere: *heartfelt joy, heartfelt words.*

**heart-free** /ˈhat-fri/, *adj.* not in love.

**hearth** /haθ/, *n.* **1.** that part of the floor of a room on which the fire is made or above which is a stove, fireplace, furnace, etc. **2.** the fireside; home. **3.** *Metall.* **a.** the lower part of a blast furnace, cupola, etc., in which the molten metal collects and from which it is tapped out. **b.** the part of an open hearth, reverberatory furnace, etc., upon which the charge is placed and melted down or refined. **c.** a brazier, chafing dish, or box for charcoal. [ME *herth(e),* OE *he(o)rth,* c. G *Herd;* akin to L *carbo* charcoal]

**hearthrug** /ˈhaθrʌg/, *n.* a rug laid in front of the fireplace.

**hearthstone** /ˈhaθstoun/, *n.* **1.** a stone forming a hearth. **2.** the fireside; home. **3.** a soft stone, or a preparation of powdered stone and clay, used to whiten or scour hearths, steps, floors, etc.

**heartily** /ˈhatəli/, *adv.* **1.** in a hearty manner; sincerely; cordially. **2.** eagerly; enthusiastically. **3.** with a hearty appetite. **4.** thoroughly; completely.

**heartland** /ˈhatlænd/, *n.* the central area of a continent or land mass, farthest removed from the sea.

**heart-leaf poison** /hat-lif ˈpɔɪzən/, *n.* a shrub, *Gastrolobium bilobum,* native to Australia, which is poisonous to stock.

**heartless** /ˈhatləs/, *adj.* without heart or feeling; unfeeling; cruel: *heartless words.* – **heartlessly,** *adv.* – **heartlessness,** *n.*

**heart-lung machine** /hat-ˈlʌŋ məʃin/, *n.* a machine used at operations to take over the action of the heart and lungs to allow surgery to be performed on them.

**heart murmur** /ˈhat mɜmə/, *n.* a sound caused by turbulent blood flow through the heart.

**heart-rending** /ˈhat-rɛndɪŋ/, *adj.* causing acute mental anguish. – **heart-rendingly,** *adv.*

**hearts** /hats/, *n.* →**heart** (def. 11c).

**hearts-and-flowers** /hats-ən-ˈflauəz/, *n. Chiefly U.S.* excessive sentimentality.

**heart-searching** /ˈhat-sɜtʃɪŋ/, *adj.* involving a close examination of one's deepest feelings.

**heart's-ease** /ˈhats-iz/, *n.* **1.** peace of mind. **2.** the pansy, or some other plant of the genus *Viola.* [ME *hertes ese.* See HEART, EASE]

**heartseed** /ˈhatsid/, *n.* →**balloon vine.**

**heart-shaped** /ˈhat-ʃeɪpt/, *adj.* having the shape of a heart; cordate.

**heartsick** /ˈhatsɪk/, *adj.* **1.** sick at heart; grievously depressed or unhappy. **2.** characterised by or showing grievous depression. – **heartsickness,** *n.*

**heartsore** /ˈhatsɔ/, *adj.* **1.** sore at heart; grieved. **2.** showing grief.

**heart-starter** /ˈhat-statə/, *n. Colloq.* **1.** an alcoholic drink, esp. one taken early in the day, often as a remedy for a hangover. **2.** any drink, as strong coffee, etc., taken before one begins the day's activities.

**heart-stricken** /ˈhat-strɪkən/, *adj.* deeply affected with grief, etc. Also, **heart-struck** /ˈhat-strʌk/.

**heartstrings** /ˈhatstrɪŋz/, *n.pl.* the deepest feelings; the strongest affections: *to pull at one's heartstrings.*

**heart-throb** /ˈhat-θrɒb/, *n.* the object of an infatuation, usu. a member of the opposite sex, as a pop singer, film star, or the like.

**heart-to-heart** /ˈhat-tə-hat/, *adj.;* /hat-tə-ˈhat/, *n.* –*adj.* **1.** frank; sincere. –*n.* **2.** a frank and sincere conversation usu. between two people.

**heart transplant** /ˈhat trænsplænt/, *n.* an operation in which the heart of one person is transplanted into the body of another.

**heart-warming** /ˈhat-wɔmɪŋ/, *adj.* emotionally moving in a way which evokes a pleased and approving response.

**heart-whole** /ˈhat-houl/, *adj.* **1.** having the heart untouched by love. **2.** wholehearted; sincere.

**heartwood** /ˈhatwud/, *n.* the hard central wood of the trunk of an exogenous tree.

**heartworm** /ˈhatwɜm/, *n.* a filarial worm living in the heart and pulmonary arteries of dogs.

**hearty** /'hati/, *adj.*, **-tier, -tiest,** *n., pl.* **-ties.** *–adj.* **1.** warm-hearted; affectionate; cordial; friendly: *a hearty welcome.* **2.** heartfelt; genuine; sincere: *hearty approval or dislike.* **3.** enthusiastic or zealous; vigorous: *a hearty laugh.* **4.** physically vigorous; strong and well: *hale and hearty.* **5.** substantial or satisfying: *a hearty meal.* **6.** enjoying or requiring abundant food: *a hearty appetite.* **7.** (of soil) fertile. *–n.* **8.** *Colloq.* a brave or good fellow. **9.** a sailor. – **heartiness,** *n.*

**heat** /hit/, *n.* **1.** the quality or condition of being hot. **2.** the sensation of hotness or warmth; heated bodily condition. **3.** *Psychol.* a blended sensation, caused by stimulating the warmth and cold receptors on the skin. **4.** *Physics.* a form of energy resident in the random motion of molecules, which will raise the temperature of the body to which it is added. **5.** *Physics.* the amount of heat (def. 4) evolved or absorbed per unit amount of substance in a process as combustion. **6.** hot condition of the atmosphere or physical environment; hot season or weather. **7.** warmth or intensity of feeling: *the heat of an argument.* **8.** a fit of passion. **9.** the height of greatest intensity of any action: *to do a thing at white heat.* **10.** a single intense effort. **11.** *Colloq.* pressure of police, prison or other investigation or activity; *lie low while the heat's on.* **12.** a single course in or division of a race or other contest. **13.** a single operation of heating, as of metal in a furnace, in the heat-treating and melting of metals. **14.** *Zool.* **a.** sexual excitement in animals, esp. females. **b.** the period or duration of such excitement. **15. on heat,** (of female animals) in a state of sexual excitement occurring at oestrus. **16. put the heat on,** *Colloq.* to put pressure on. *–v.t.* **17.** to make hot or warm. **18.** to excite in mind or feeling; inflame with passion. *–v.i.* **19.** to become hot or warm. **20.** to become excited in mind or feeling. [ME *hete,* OE *hǣtu;* akin to G *Hitze*] – **heatless,** *adj.*

**heat balance** /'– bæləns/, *n.* an evaluation of the efficiency of a furnace, steam-engine, or other equipment, by drawing up a balance sheet of the heat input and heat output.

**heat barrier** /'– bærɪə/, *n.* →**thermal barrier.**

**heat capacity** /'– kəpæsəti/, *n.* the heat required to raise the temperature of a unit mass of a substance one kelvin; water equivalent. Also, **thermal capacity.**

**heat-centre** /'hit-sɛntə/, *n.* any one of several areas in the central nervous system which control the regulation of body temperature.

**heat content** /'hit ˌkɒntɛnt/, *n.* →**enthalpy.**

**heat death** /'– dɛθ/, *n.* (of the universe) the proposition that the universe will come to an end when all its components are at the same temperature, the entropy of the universe will then be at a maximum and its available energy nil. This follows from the second law of thermodynamics if the universe is considered a closed system.

**heated** /'hitəd/, *adj.* **1.** warmed; having the temperature raised. **2.** inflamed; vehement; angry.

**heat engine** /'hit ɛndʒən/, *n.* an engine which transforms heat energy into mechanical energy.

**heater** /'hitə/, *n.* **1.** an apparatus for heating, as a furnace. **2.** *Electronics.* that element of a radio valve which carries the current for heating a cathode. **3.** *Colloq. U.S.* a pistol or revolver.

**heat exchanger** /'hit əkstʃeɪndʒə/, *n.* any device for transferring the heat of one fluid to another, without allowing them to mix.

**heat exhaustion** /'– əgzɔstʃən/, *n.* prostration caused by prolonged exposure to intense heat, sometimes accompanied by rapidly rising body temperature.

**heath** /hiθ/, *n.* **1.** a tract of open, uncultivated land covered by low, usu. small-leaved, shrubs. **2.** any of various low evergreen shrubs of the family Ericaceae, common on waste land, as *Calluna vulgaris,* the common heather of England and Scotland with small pinkish purple flowers. **3.** any plant of the genus *Erica,* or of the family Ericaceae. **4.** any other heathlike species, esp. of the family Epacridaceae, as species of the genera *Epacris* and *Leucopogon.* [ME; OE *hǣth,* c. D *heide* and G *Heide*]

**heathen** /'hiðən/, *n., pl.* **-thens, -then,** *adj.* *–n.* **1.** an unconverted individual of a people which does not acknowledge the God of the Bible; one who is neither Christian, Jewish, nor Muslim; pagan. **2.** an irreligious or unenlightened person. *–adj.* **3.** pagan; pertaining to the heathen. **4.** irreligious or unenlightened. [ME *hethen,* OE *hǣthen,* n., adj., c. D *heiden,* n., G *Heide,* n., Icel. *heidhinn,* adj.; commonly explained as meaning orig. heath-dweller. See HEATH, and cf. PAGAN] – **heathenness,** *n.*

**heathendom** /'hiðəndəm/, *n.* **1.** heathenism; heathen worship or customs. **2.** heathen lands or people.

**heathenise** /'hiðənaɪz/, *v.,* **-nised, -nising.** *–v.t.* **1.** to make heathen or heathenish. *–v.i.* **2.** to become heathen or heathenish. **3.** to practise heathenism. Also, **heathenize.**

**heathenish** /'hiðənɪʃ/, *adj.* **1.** pertaining to the heathen. **2.** like or befitting the heathen; barbarous. – **heathenishly,** *adv.* – **heathenishness,** *n.*

**heathenism** /'hiðənɪzəm/, *n.* **1.** the condition, belief, or practice of a heathen. **2.** pagan worship; irreligion. **3.** barbaric morals or behaviour; barbarism.

**heathenry** /'hiðənri/, *n.* **1.** heathenism. **2.** heathen people; the heathen.

**heather** /'hɛðə/, *n.* any of various heaths, esp. *Calluna vulgaris* (**Scotch heather**). See **heath** (def. 2). [b. HEATH and obs. *hadder* heather (orig. uncert.)]

heather

**heather-mixture** /'hɛðə-mɪkstʃə/, *adj.* having the colour and appearance of heather, esp. as certain fabrics or wools of a mixed or speckled hue.

**heathery** /'hɛðəri/, *adj.* **1.** of or like heather. **2.** abounding in heather. Also, **heathy** /'hiθi/.

**heath grass** /'hiθ gras/, *n.* a European grass, *Sieglingia decumbens,* growing in spongy, wet, cold soils. Also, **heather grass.**

**heath-myrtle** /hiθ-'mɜtl/, *n.* a shrub, *Micromyrtus ciliata,* family Myrtaceae, found in sandy soil in south-eastern Australia.

**Heath Robinson** /hiθ 'rɒbənsən/, *adj.* **1.** having a ridiculously complicated, impractical appearance. **2.** impractical and absurdly complex, as a scheme. [after the drawings of William *Heath Robinson,* 1872-1944, English cartoonist]

**heat lightning** /hit 'laɪtnɪŋ/, *n.* flashes of light near the horizon on summer evenings, reflections of more distant lightning.

**heat money** /'– mʌni/, *n.* a special rate paid to employees required to perform work where the temperature is raised considerably above the normal level by artificial means.

**heat pipe** /'– paɪp/, *n.* a device for heat transfer based on vaporisation and capillary action, which is more effective in transporting heat than metallic conductors.

**heat prostration** /'– prɒstreɪʃən/, *n.* exhaustion and bodily distress caused by high temperatures.

**heat pump** /'– pʌmp/, *n.* a device which, by means of a compressible refrigerant, transfers heat from a body (the atmosphere, the earth, a lake, etc.) and then either pumps it back into the body (for heating) or elsewhere (for cooling).

**heat rash** /'– ræʃ/, *n.* an eruption or efflorescence on the skin due to heat.

**heat reservoir** /'– rɛzəvwa/, *n.* →**storage heater.**

**heat-resistant** /'hit-rəzɪstənt/, *adj.* of or pertaining to any material or surface which does not break or crack when moderate heat is applied to it, as cookware, pyrex glass, etc.

**heat-resisting steel** /ˌhit-rəzɪstɪŋ 'stil/, *n.* steel which contains a high percentage of chromium and possibly nickel and/or tungsten; used when high resistance to oxidisation or good mechanical properties are required at high temperatures.

**heat shield** /'hit shild/, *n.* a device which protects men or equipment from heat; esp. a shield in front of a spacecraft to protect it from excessive heat on re-entry into the earth's atmosphere.

**heat sink** /'– sɪŋk/, *n.* anything which is designed to conduct heat away and allow its harmless dissipation, as a metal plate attached to a transistor which is producing heat, the special layers in the skin of supersonic aircraft, etc.

**heatstroke** /'hitstroʊk/, *n.* collapse or fever caused by exposure to excessive heat.

**heat-treat** /'hit-trit/, *v.t.* to subject (a metal) to heat treatment.

**heat treatment** /'hit tritmənt/, *n.* any process in which a metal is subjected to one or more temperature cycles in the solid state, to confer desirable properties on it.

**heatwave** /ˈhitweɪv/, *n.* **1.** an air mass of high temperature, covering an extended area and moving relatively slowly. **2.** a prolonged period of excessively warm weather.

**heave** /hiv/, *v.*, **heaved** or (*Chiefly Naut.*) **hove, heaving,** *n.* *–v.t.* **1.** to raise or lift with effort or force; hoist. **2.** to lift and throw, often with effort or force: *to heave an anchor overboard.* **3.** *Naut.* **a.** to haul, draw, or pull, as by a cable. **b.** to cause (a ship) to move in a certain direction. **4.** to utter laboriously or painfully: *to heave a sigh.* **5.** to cause to rise and fall with or as with a swelling motion. **6.** to raise or force up in a swelling movement; force to bulge. **7.** *Geol.* to cause a horizontal displacement in (a stratum, vein, etc.). See **heave** (def. 19). **8. heave to,** to stop the headway of (a vessel), esp. by bringing the head to the wind and trimming the sails so that they act against one another; to stop (a vessel). *–v.i.* **9.** to rise and fall with or as with a swelling motion. **10.** to breathe with effort; pant. **11.** to vomit; retch. **12.** to rise as if thrust up, as a hill; swell or bulge. **13.** *Naut.* **a.** to haul or pull, as at a cable; to push, as at the bar of a capstan. **b.** to move a ship, or move as a ship does, by such action. **c.** to move or go (fol. by *about, ahead,* etc.). **14. heave in sight,** to rise into view as from below the horizon, as a ship. **15. heave to,** *Naut.* to heave a vessel to. *–interj.* **16. heave ho!,** (an exclamation used by sailors when heaving the anchor up, etc.) *–n.* **17.** the act of heaving. **18.** (of the sea) the force exerted by the swell. **19.** *Geol.* **a.** the horizontal component of the apparent displacement resulting from a fault, measured in a vertical plane perpendicular to its strike. **b.** a displacement of the floor of a mine, caused by the weight of the pillars, or simply by excavation and release of stress. [ME *heve(n),* OE *hebban* (pret. *hōf, hefde,* pp. *hafen*), c. G *heben;* akin to L *capere* take]

**heave-ho** /ˈhiv-hoʊ, hiv-ˈhoʊ/, *n.* **1.** dismissal; rejection. **2.** the sack: *the boss gave me the old heave-ho.*

**heaven** /ˈhɛvən/, *n.* **1.** the abode of God, the angels, and the spirits of the righteous after death; the place or state of existence of the blessed after the mortal life. **2.** (*cap., oft. pl.*) the celestial powers; God. **3.** a euphemistic term for God in various emphatic expressions: *for heaven's sake.* **4.** (*chiefly pl.*) the sky or firmament, or expanse of space surrounding the earth. **5.** a place or state of supreme bliss: *a heaven on earth.* **6. heavens!,** (an interjection to express surprise.) **7. move heaven and earth,** to do all that is possible. **8.** See **seventh heaven.** [ME *heven,* OE *hefen, heofon* (c. MLG *heven*), apparently akin to Goth. *himins,* Icel. *himinn*]

**heaven-born** /ˈhɛvən-bɔn/, *adj.* **1.** of heavenly birth. **2.** very talented; born with a special aptitude.

**heavenly** /ˈhɛvənli/, *adj.* **1.** resembling or befitting heaven; blissful; beautiful: *a heavenly spot.* **2.** of or in the heavens: *the heavenly bodies.* **3.** of, belonging to, or coming from the heaven of God, the angels, etc. **4.** celestial or divine: *heavenly peace.* – **heavenliness,** *n.*

**heaven-sent** /ˈhɛvən-sɛnt/, *adj.* sent by heaven; providential.

**heavenward** /ˈhɛvənwəd/, *adj.* **1.** directed towards heaven. *–adv.* **2.** heavenwards.

**heavenwards** /ˈhɛvənwədz/, *adv.* towards heaven. Also, **heavenward.**

**heaver** /ˈhivə/, *n.* **1.** one who or that which heaves. **2.** *Naut.* a staff, generally slightly less than a metre in length, used for twisting or heaving a tight rope or strap.

**heaves** /hivz/, *n.* a disease of horses, similar to asthma in man, characterised by difficult breathing; broken wind.

**heavier-than-air** /ˌhɛviə-ðən-ˈɛə/, *adj.* **1.** of greater specific gravity than the air, as aeroplanes. **2.** of or pertaining to such aircraft.

**heavily** /ˈhɛvəli/, *adv.* **1.** with great weight or burden: *a heavily loaded wagon.* **2.** in an oppressive manner: *cares weigh heavily upon him.* **3.** with great force; violently. **4.** severely; intensely: *to suffer heavily.* **5.** to a large amount; densely; thickly: *heavily wooded.* **6.** laboriously; sluggishly: *he walked heavily across the room.*

**heaviness** /ˈhɛvinəs/, *n.* the state or quality of being heavy; weight; burden; gravity.

**Heaviside layer** /ˈhɛvisaɪd leɪə/, *n.* the lower region, or regions, of the ionosphere chiefly responsible for the reflection of radio waves of certain frequencies, thus making long-distance radio communication possible. Also, **E-layer, Kenelly-Heaviside layer.** [named after Oliver *Heaviside,* 1850-1925, English physicist]

**heavy** /ˈhɛvi/, *adj.*, **-ier, -iest,** *n., pl.* **-ies.** *–adj.* **1.** of great weight; hard to lift or carry: *a heavy load.* **2.** of great amount, force, intensity, etc: *a heavy vote.* **3.** bearing hard upon; burdensome; harsh; distressing: *heavy taxes.* **4.** having much weight in proportion to bulk; being of high specific gravity: *a heavy metal.* **5.** broad, thick, or coarse; not delicate: *heavy lines.* **6.** of more than the usual, average, or specified weight: *heavy cargo.* **7.** connected or concerned with the manufacture of goods of more than the usual weight: *heavy industry.* **8.** *Mil.* **a.** heavily armed or equipped. **b.** of the larger sizes: *heavy weapons.* **9.** serious; grave: *a heavy offence.* **10.** hard to deal with; trying; difficult: *a heavy task.* **11.** being such in an unusual degree: *a heavy smoker.* **12.** weighted or laden: *air heavy with moisture.* **13.** depressed with trouble or sorrow; showing sorrow: *a heavy heart.* **14.** overcast or cloudy: *heavy sky.* **15.** clumsy; slow in movement or action. **16.** without vivacity or interest; ponderous; dull: *a heavy style.* **17.** loud and deep: *a heavy sound.* **18.** exceptionally dense in substance; insufficiently raised or leavened; thick: *heavy bread.* **19.** not easily digested: *heavy food.* **20.** (of music, literature, etc.) intellectual or deep. **21.** important; serious; meaningful: *a heavy emotion.* **22.** pregnant. **23.** *Theat.* sober, serious, or sombre: *a heavy part.* **24.** coercive; threatening: *the cops were really heavy.* **25.** *Chem.* referring to an isotope of greater atomic weight: *heavy hydrogen.* **26.** *Colloq.* **a.** a person who is eminent and influential in the sphere of his activities, as a senior student, an important business man, etc. **b.** (*derog.*) a person of some status who unpleasantly exercises his authority or seeks to intimidate. **c.** a man who attempts to intimidate a woman into sexual submission. **27.** *Colloq.* a detective. **28.** *Theat.* **a.** a villainous part or character. **b.** an actor who plays villainous parts or characters. **29.** *Mil.* a gun of great weight or heavy calibre. **30. do a heavy,** to exert authority; intimidate. *–v.t.* **31.** to confront, put pressure on. *–adv.* **32.** heavily. [ME *hevi,* OE *hefig,* from *hefe* weight; akin to HEAVE, *v.*]

**heavy-armed** /ˈhɛvi-amd/, *adj.* (formerly) equipped with heavy arms or armour, as troops.

**heavy-duty** /ˈhɛvi-djuti/, *adj.* **1.** sturdy; durable. **2.** having a high import or export tax rate.

**heavy earth** /hɛvi ˈɜθ/, *n.* →**baryta.**

**heavy-footed** /ˈhɛvi-fʊtəd/, *adj.* **1.** having a heavy tread while walking. **2.** insensitive; overbearing.

**heavy-handed** /ˈhɛvi-hændəd/, *adj.* **1.** oppressive; harsh. **2.** clumsy. – **heavy-handedness,** *n.*

**heavy-hearted** /ˈhɛvi-hatəd/, *adj.* sorrowful; melancholy; dejected. – **heavy-heartedness,** *n.*

**heavy hydrogen** /hɛvi ˈhaɪdrədʒən/, *n.* **1.** any of the heavy isotopes of hydrogen. **2.** →**deuterium.**

**heavy-laden** /ˈhɛvi-leɪdn/, *adj.* **1.** laden with a heavy burden. **2.** very weary or troubled.

**heavy metal** /hɛvi ˈmɛtl/, *n.* **1.** a style of rock music dominated by electric guitars played at high levels of amplification and with great timbral distortion. **2.** large military weapons or ammunition. – **heavy-metal,** *adj.*

**heavy mud** /hɛvi ˈmʌd/, *n.* a drilling mud having a high specific gravity, usu. attained by adding powdered heavy minerals such as ground barytes to normal drilling mud.

**heavy rock** /– ˈrɒk/, *n.* a form of rock music, usu. loud and with a strong rhythmic beat, which places an emphasis on lyrics of a serious or intensely personal nature.

**heavy spar** /– ˈspa/, *n.* →**barytes.**

**heavy water** /– ˈwɔtə/, *n.* water in which hydrogen atoms have been replaced by deuterium, used mainly as a source of deuterons for experiments in nuclear physics. *Symbol:* $D_2O$; *sp. gr.:* 1.1056 at 25°C.

**heavyweight** /ˈhɛviweɪt/, *n.* **1.** one of more than average weight. **2.** a boxer in the heaviest group; an amateur fighter exceeding 81 kg in weight or a professional fighter exceeding 79.378 kg in weight. **3.** a professional wrestler exceeding 88.904 kg. **4.** *Colloq.* a person of considerable power, influence, or forcefulness in a certain field, as a writer, philosopher, or statesman.

**Heb.**, **1.** Hebrew. **2.** *Bible.* Hebrews.

**hebdomad** /ˈhɛbdəmæd/, *n.* **1.** the number seven. **2.** seven days; a week. [L *hebdomas,* from Gk]

**hebdomadal** /hɛbˈdɒmədl/, *adj.* weekly. Also, **hebdomadary.** [LL *hebdomadālis*] – **hebdomadally,** *adv.*

**hebephrenia** /hɛbəˈfriniə/, *n.* a form of dementia praecox incident to the age of puberty, characterised by childish behaviour, hallucinations, and emotional deterioration. [Gk *hēbē* youth + *phrēn* mind + *-ia* -IA]

**hebetate** /ˈhɛbəteɪt/, *v.,* **-tated, -tating,** *adj.* –*v.t.* **1.** to make dull or blunt. –*v.i.* **2.** to become blunt or dull. –*adj.* **3.** *Bot.* having a blunt, soft point, as awns. [L *hebetātus,* pp., blunted, dulled] – **hebetation** /hɛbəˈteɪʃən/, *n.*

**hebetic** /həˈbɛtɪk/, *adj.* pertaining to or occurring in puberty. [Gk *hēbētikós* youthful]

**hebetude** /ˈhɛbətʃud/, *n.* the state of being dull; lethargy; mental dullness. [LL *hebetūdo,* from L *hebes* dull]

**Hebraic** /həˈbreɪɪk, hi-/, *adj.* Hebrew. [LL *Hebraicus,* from Gk *Hebraikós;* replacing OE *Ebrēisc*] – **Hebraically,** *adv.*

**Hebraise** /ˈhibreɪˌaɪz/, *v.,* **-ised, -ising.** –*v.t.* **1.** to make Hebrew. –*v.i.* **2.** to become Hebrew. **3.** to conform to the Hebrew usage or type. **4.** to use a Hebrew idiom or manner of speech. Also, **Hebraize.** [Gk *hebraízein* speak Hebrew]

**Hebraism** /ˈhibreɪɪzəm/, *n.* **1.** a Hebrew idiom. **2.** Hebrew character, spirit, thought, or practice.

**Hebraist** /ˈhibreɪəst/, *n.* **1.** one versed in Hebrew language and learning. **2.** one imbued with the Hebrew spirit. – **Hebraistic,** *adj.*

**Hebrew** /ˈhibru/, *n.* **1.** a member of that branch of the Semitic race descended from the line of Abraham; an Israelite; a Jew. **2.** a Semitic language, the language of the ancient Hebrews, which although not a vernacular after 100 B.C. was retained as the scholarly and liturgical language of Jews and now is used as the language of Israeli Jews. –*adj.* **3.** of or pertaining to the Hebrews or their language. [ME *Ebreu,* from OF, from ML *Ebreus,* L *Hebraeus,* from Gk *Hebraîos,* from Aram. *ʻEbhrāyā,* from Heb. *ʻIbhrī,* said to mean 'one from beyond'; replacing OE *Ebrēas* (pl.), from ML *Ebrēi*]

**hecatomb** /ˈhɛkətoum, -tum/, *n.* **1.** a great public sacrifice, originally of a hundred oxen, as to the Greek gods. **2.** any great slaughter. [L *hecatombē,* from Gk *hekatómbē*]

**heck** /hɛk/, *n., interj.* (a euphemism for hell): *what the heck, get the heck out of here.*

**heckelphone** /ˈhɛkəlfoun/, *n.* a bass oboe, sounding an octave lower in pitch than the oboe. [named after the inventor, Wilhelm *Heckel,* 1856-1909, German instrument-maker. See -PHONE]

**heckle** /ˈhɛkəl/, *v.,* **-led, -ling,** *n.* –*v.t.* **1.** Also, **hatchel.** to badger or torment; harass, esp. a public speaker, with questions and gibes. **2.** to cut (flax or hemp) with a hatchel. [from HECKLE, *n.*] –*n.* **3.** →**hatchel.** [late ME *hekele,* n., phonetic var. of ME *hechele;* akin to HACKLE[1], HATCHEL] – **heckler,** *n.* – **heckling,** *n.*

**hectare** /ˈhɛktɛə/, *n.* a surface measure, the common unit of land measure in the metric system, equal to 100 ares, or 10 000 square metres (approx. 2.47 acres). *Symbol:* ha [F. See HECTO-, ARE[2]]

**hectic** /ˈhɛktɪk/, *adj.* **1.** characterised by great excitement, passion, activity, confusion, haste: *hectic meeting, hectic day.* **2.** marking a particular habit or condition of body, as the fever of phthisis (**hectic fever**) when this is attended by flushed cheeks (**hectic flush**), hot skin, and emaciation. **3.** pertaining to or affected with such fever; consumptive. –*n.* **4.** a hectic fever. **5.** a hectic flush. **6.** a consumptive person. [LL *hecticus,* from Gk *hektikós* habitual, hectic] – **hectically,** *adv.*

**hecto-** /ˈhɛktə-/, a prefix denoting $10^2$ of a given unit, as in *hectogram.* Also, *before vowels,* **hect-**[1]. *Symbol:* h [F, from Gk *hekatón* hundred]

**hectocotylus** /hɛktouˈkɒtələs/, *n., pl.* **-li** /-laɪ, -li/. a modified tentacle of the male of certain cephalopods which is used to transfer sperm into the female. [NL, from *hecto-* HECTO- + Gk *kotýlē* cup]

**hectograph** /ˈhɛktəgræf/, *n.* **1.** a process for making copies of a writing, etc., from a prepared gelatine surface to which the original has been transferred. **2.** the apparatus used. –*v.t.* **3.** to copy with the hectograph.

**hector** /ˈhɛktə/, *n.* **1.** a blustering, domineering fellow; swashbuckler; bully. –*v.t.* **2.** to treat with insolence; bully; torment. –*v.i.* **3.** to act in a blustering, domineering way; be a bully. [from *Hector,* in Greek mythology the eldest son of Priam, king of Troy, and the finest warrior on the Trojan side against the Greeks]

**he'd** /hid/, contraction of: **1.** he had. **2.** he would.

**heddle** /ˈhɛdl/, *n.* (in a loom) one of the sets of vertical cords or wires, forming the principal part of the harness which guides the warp threads. [metathetic var. of *heald,* OE *hefeld* thread (for weaving)]

**hedenbergite** /ˈhɛdnˌbɜgaɪt, -bəˌgaɪt/, *n.* a mineral of the pyroxene group, $CaFe(SiO_3)_2$; occurs in limestones in the form of black crystals. [named after L. *Hedenberg,* 19th C Swedish chemist]

**hedge** /hɛdʒ/, *n., v.,* **hedged, hedging.** –*n.* **1.** a row of bushes or small trees planted close together, esp. when forming a fence or boundary. **2.** any barrier or boundary. **3.** an act or a means of hedging a bet or the like. **4.** an investment, fiscal policy, etc., designed to offset losses caused by inflation or other business hazard. –*v.t.* **5.** to enclose with or separate by a hedge (oft. fol. by *in, off, about,* etc.): *to hedge a garden.* **6.** to surround, as with a hedge; hem in (oft. fol. by *in*). **7.** to surround so as to prevent escape or hinder free movement; obstruct (oft. fol. by *in* or *up*): *to be hedged by difficulties.* **8.** to protect (a bet, etc.) by taking some offsetting risk. –*v.i.* **9.** to avoid taking an open or decisive course. **10.** to protect a bet, speculation, etc., by taking some offsetting risk. **11.** *Finance.* to enter transactions that will protect against loss through a compensatory price movement. [ME *hegge,* OE *hegge* (oblique case), c. G *Hecke.* Cf. HAW[1], HAY[1]]

**hedgehog** /ˈhɛdʒhɒg/, *n.* **1.** any of several nocturnal, insectivorous mammals of the family Erinaceidae, of the genus *Erinaceus* of Europe, Africa and Asia having erectile spines on the upper part of the body and able to roll into a ball for protection. **2.** any of several other spine-bearing mammals. **3.** →**hedgehog cake.**

hedgehog

**hedgehog cake** /ˈ– keɪk/, *n.* a heavy chocolate-flavoured uncooked cake made from biscuit crumbs, shortening, nuts and broken pieces of arrowroot biscuit. Also, **hedgehog.**

**hedgehop** /ˈhɛdʒhɒp/, *v.i.,* **-hopped, -hopping.** to fly an aeroplane at a very low altitude, as for spraying crops, bombing in warfare, etc. – **hedgehopper,** *n.* – **hedgehopping,** *n., adj.*

**hedge-hyssop** /ˈhɛdʒ-hɪsəp/, *n.* **1.** any of the low herbs constituting the genus *Gratiola,* as *G. officinalis,* a medicinal species of Europe. **2.** any of certain similar plants, as *Scutellaria minor,* an English skullcap.

**hedgemustard** /ˈhɛdʒmʌstəd/, *n.* any of several species of *Sisymbrium,* as *S. officinale,* with stiff erect stems and yellow flowers, widespread as a weed of cultivation in temperate regions. Also, **hedge-mustard.**

**hedge-parsley** /ˈhɛdʒ-pasli/, *n.* any of several species of annual umbelliferous plants belonging to the genus *Torilis,* widespread in temperate regions.

**hedgepig** /ˈhɛdʒpɪg/, *n.* →**hedgehog.**

**hedger** /ˈhɛdʒə/, *n.* **1.** one who makes or repairs hedges. **2.** one who hedges in betting, etc.

**hedgerow** /ˈhɛdʒrou/, *n.* a row of bushes or trees forming a hedge.

**hedge-sparrow** /ˈhɛdʒ-spærou/, *n.* a small European passerine bird, *Prunella modularis,* which frequents hedges and which is an accentor rather than a true sparrow.

**hedge tear** /ˈhɛdʒ tɛə/, *n.* a two-sided tear in material causing a flap of loose material in the shape of a right-angled triangle.

**hedgy** /ˈhɛdʒi/, *adj.* abounding in hedges.

**hedonic** /hiˈdɒnɪk, hɛ-/, *adj.* **1.** pertaining to or consisting in pleasure. **2.** pertaining to hedonism or hedonics. [Gk *hēdonikós* pleasurable] – **hedonically,** *adv.*

**hedonics** /hiˈdɒnɪks, hɛ-/, *n.* the study of pleasurable and painful states of consciousness.

**hedonism** /ˈhidənɪzəm, ˈhɛ-/, *n.* **1.** the doctrine that pleasure or happiness is the highest good. **2.** devotion to pleasure. – **hedonist,** *n., adj.* – **hedonistic** /hidəˈnɪstɪk, hɛ-/, *adj.* – **hedonistically** /hidəˈnɪstɪkli, hɛ-/, *adv.*

**-hedron,** a combining form denoting geometrical solid figures having a certain number of faces, as in *polyhedron.* [Gk *-edron,* neut. of *-edros,* adj., having bases, -sided, from *hédra* seat, base]

**heebie-jeebies** /ˈhibi-dʒibiz/, *n.pl. Colloq.* **1.** a condition of nervousness or revulsion. **2.** →**delirium tremens.** [coined by W. DeBeck, 1890-1942, U.S. cartoonist]

**heed** /hid/, *v.t.* **1.** to give attention to; regard; notice. *–v.i.* **2.** to give attention; have regard. *–n.* **3.** careful attention; notice; observation (usu. with *give* or *take*). [ME *hede(n),* OE *hēdan,* c. G *hüten* attend to, mind; akin to HOOD, *n.*] – **heeder,** *n.*

**heedful** /ˈhidfəl/, *adj.* attentive; mindful: *heedful of others.* – **heedfully,** *adv.* – **heedfulness,** *n.*

**heedless** /ˈhidləs/, *adj.* careless; thoughtless; unmindful. – **heedlessly,** *adv.* – **heedlessness,** *n.*

**heehaw** /ˈhihɔ/, *n.* **1.** the braying sound made by an ass. **2.** rude laughter. *–v.i.* **3.** to bray. [imitative]

**heel**[1] /hil/, *n.* **1.** (in man) the back part of the foot, below and behind the ankle. **2.** an analogous part in other vertebrates. **3.** either hind foot or hoof of some animals, as the horse. **4.** the part of a stocking, shoe, or the like, covering the heel. **5.** a solid part of wood, rubber, etc., attached to the sole of a shoe, under the heel. **6.** the part of the palm of a hand or glove nearest the wrist. **7.** something resembling the human heel in position, shape, etc.: *heel of bread.* **8.** the latter or concluding part of anything: *heel of a session.* **9.** *Bot.* the older basal part of a shoot removed from a plant which usu. produces roots readily when planted. **10.** *Naut.* **a.** the after end of a ship's keel. **b.** the lower part of a mast, a boom, a sternpost, a rafter, etc. **11.** the crook in the head of a golf club. **12.** *Colloq.* a despicable person; cad. **13.** Some special noun phrases are:

**at one's heels,** close behind one.

**cool** (or **kick**) **one's heels,** *Colloq.* to be kept waiting, esp. as deliberate policy.

**dig one's heels in,** to maintain an immovable position in debate, etc.; be stubborn.

**down at heel, 1.** having the shoe heels worn down. **2.** shabby. **3.** slipshod or slovenly. **4.** in straitened circumstances; impoverished.

**kick up one's heels,** to enjoy oneself.

**lay by the heels,** to capture; seize.

**on the heels of,** closely following.

**show a clean pair of heels,** to escape by outdistancing pursuers.

**take to one's heels,** to run off or away.

**to heel, 1.** (of a dog) following a person with the nose close to his left heel. **2.** under control.

*–v.t.* **14.** to furnish with heels, as shoes. **15.** to perform (a dance) with the heels. **16.** *Golf.* to strike (the ball) with the heel of the club. **17.** *Rugby Football.* to kick (the ball) through or out of the scrum with the heel. **18.** to follow at the heels of. **19.** to arm (a gamecock) with spurs. **20. heel in,** to plant cuttings or plants temporarily before putting them in their permanent growing site. *–v.i.* **21.** to follow at one's heels. **22.** to use the heels, as in dancing. **23.** *Rugby Football.* to heel the ball. [ME; OE *hēl(a),* apparently from *hōh* HOCK[1]. Cf. D *hiel,* Icel. *hæll*] – **heeler,** *n.* – **heelless,** *adj.*

**heel**[2] /hil/, *v.i.* **1.** (of a ship, etc.) to lean to one side; cant; tilt. *–v.t.* **2.** to cause to lean or cant. *–n.* **3.** a heeling movement; a cant. [earlier *heeld,* ME *helde(n),* OE *h(i)eldan* bend, incline, from *heald,* adj., sloping]

**heel-and-toe** /hil-ən-ˈtoʊ/, *adj., v.,* **-toed, -toeing.** *–adj.* **1.** denoting a pace, as in walking contests, in which the heel of the front foot touches ground before the toes of the rear one leave it. *–v.i.* **2.** to operate the accelerator and brake of a motor vehicle with the heel and the toe of the same foot.

**heeler** /ˈhilə/, *n.* **1.** *Colloq.* a dog which follows at one's heel. **2.** (of a cattle or sheep dog) one which rounds up stock by following at their heels.

**heeling dog** /ˈhilɪŋ dɒg/, *n. N.Z.* →**heeler** (def. 2).

**heelpiece** /ˈhilpis/, *n.* **1.** a piece serving as or fitted to a heel of a shoe or stocking. **2.** a terminal part of anything.

**heelpost** /ˈhilpoʊst/, *n.* a post made to withstand strain, forming or fitted to the heel or end of something, as the post on which a gate or door is hinged.

**heeltap** /ˈhiltæp/, *n.* **1.** a layer of leather or the like in a shoe heel; a lift. **2.** a small quantity of a drink left in a glass after drinking. **3.** dregs; residue.

**heft** /hɛft/, *v.t.* **1.** to try the weight of by lifting. **2.** to heave or lift. *–n.* **3.** *Obs.* weight; heaviness. [from HEAVE]

**hefty** /ˈhɛfti/, *adj.,* **-tier, -tiest.** *Colloq.* **1.** heavy; weighty. **2.** big and strong; powerful; muscular. – **heftily,** *adv.* – **heftiness,** *n.*

**Hegelian** /həˈgeɪliən/, *adj.* **1.** of or pertaining to G. W. F. Hegel, German philosopher, 1770-1831, or to Hegelianism. *–n.* **2.** one who accepts the philosophical opinions of Hegel. – **Hegelianism,** *n.*

**Hegelian dialectic** /– daɪəˈlɛktɪk/, *n.* (in Hegelianism) the pattern or mechanism of development by inner conflict, the scheme of which is *thesis, antithesis,* and *synthesis* (i.e., an original tendency, its opposing tendency, and their unification in a new movement).

**hegemony** /ˈhɛgəməni, ˈhɛdʒ-, həˈgɛməni/, *n., pl.* **-nies. 1.** leadership or predominant influence exercised by one state over others, as in a confederation. **2.** leadership; predominance. [Gk *hēgemonía*] – **hegemonic** /hɛgəˈmɒnɪk, hɛdʒ-/, *adj.*

**Hegira** /ˈhɛdʒərə/, *n.* **1.** a flight, similar to that of Mohammed, A.D. 570? - 632, Arab prophet, founder of Islam, from persecutions in Mecca to his successes in Medina. (The date of Mohammed's flight, A.D. 622, is the starting point in the Muslim calender). **2.** the Muslim era itself. Also, **Hejira.** [ML, from Ar. *hijra* departure, migration]

**hegumen** /həˈgjumən/, *n. Greek Orthodox Church.* the head of a monastery. Also, **hegumenos.** [ML *hēgūmenus,* from Gk *hēgoúmenos,* properly ppr. of *hēgeîsthai* lead]

**Heidelberg jaw** /haɪdlbɜg ˈdjɔ/, *n.* a lower jaw supposed to belong to a very early human species, found in 1907 near Heidelberg, Germany.

**Heidelberg man** /– ˈmæn/, *n.* the primitive man, *Homo erectus,* reconstructed from the Heidelberg jaw.

**heifer** /ˈhɛfə/, *n.* **1.** a cow that has not produced a calf and is under three years of age. **2.** *Colloq.* a girl or woman. [ME *hayfre,* OE *hēa(h)f(o)re, hēahfru,* from *hēah* HIGH (i.e. grown) + *-fore,* fem. equivalent of *fearr* bull. Cf. Gk *póris* young cow]

**heifer dust** /ˈ– dʌst/, *n. Colloq.* nonsense; rubbish. Cf. **bulldust.**

**heifer paddock** /ˈ– pædək/, *n. Colloq.* a girl's school.

**heigh** /heɪ/, *interj.* →**hey**[1].

**heigh-ho** /heɪ-ˈhoʊ/, *interj.* (an exclamation of melancholy, weariness, surprise, or exultation.)

**height** /haɪt/, *n.* **1.** the state of being high. **2.** extent upwards; altitude; stature; distance upwards; elevation: *height of an object above the ground.* **3.** a high place or level; a hill or mountain. **4.** the highest part; the top; apex. **5.** the highest or culminating point; utmost degree: *the height of the season.* **6.** high degree, as of a quality. [ME; OE *hiehtho, hē(a)hthu.* See HIGH, -TH[1]]

**heighten** /ˈhaɪtn/, *v.t.* **1.** to increase the height of; make higher. **2.** to increase the intensity of, as in a drawing. *–v.i.* **3.** to become higher. **4.** to increase; augment. – **heightener,** *n.*

**height money** /ˈhaɪt mʌni/, *n.* a special rate paid to employees required to work at specified heights above ground or water level.

**heil** /haɪl/, *interj.* (a German greeting) hail!

**heinous** /ˈheɪnəs, ˈhi-/, *adj.* hateful; odious; gravely reprehensible: *a heinous offence.* [ME *heynous,* from OF *hainos,* from *haine* hatred, from *haïr* hate; of Gmc orig. and akin to HATE] – **heinously,** *adv.* – **heinousness,** *n.*

**Heinz** /haɪnz/, *n. Colloq.* →**bitser.** [from advertisement for *Heinz* soup, emphasising many varieties]

**heir** /ɛə/, *n.* **1.** *Law.* one who inherits the property of a deceased person, testate or intestate and is liable for the payments of the debts of the deceased and of the legacies. **2.** Also, **haeres, heres.** *Law.* one who succeeds by descent, the term applying to the heirs of heirs comprehended in infinitum: *the heirs of the Duchy of Savoy.* **3.** one to whom something falls or is due. **4.** a person, society, etc., considered as the continuer of a tradition, policy, or the like previously established. *–v.t.* **5.** to inherit; succeed to. [ME, from OF, from L *hēres*] – **heirless,** *adj.*

**heir apparent** /ɛər ə'pærənt/, *n., pl.* **heirs apparent.** an heir whose right is indefeasible, provided he survives the ancestor.

**heir-at-law** /ɛər-ət-'lɔ/, *n., pl.* **heirs-at-law.** an heir by legal right.

**heir by custom,** *n.* one whose right as an heir is determined by customary modes of descent, as gavelkind, and the like.

**heir-designate** /ɛə-'dɛzɪgnət/, *n.* a person who has been designated as another's heir.

**heirdom** /'ɛədəm/, *n.* heirship; inheritance.

**heiress** /'ɛərɛs, -əs/, *n.* **1.** a female heir. **2.** a woman inheriting or expected to inherit considerable wealth.

**heirloom** /'ɛəlum/, *n.* **1.** any family possession transmitted from generation to generation. **2.** *Law.* a chattel that descends to the heir, as a portrait of an ancestor, etc. [HEIR + LOOM[1], orig. tool or implement]

**heir presumptive** /ɛə prə'zʌmptɪv/, *n.* an heir whose expectation may be defeated by the birth of a nearer heir.

**heirship** /'ɛəʃɪp/, *n.* the position or rights of an heir; right of inheritance; inheritance.

**heist** /haɪst/, *v.t.* **1.** to rob; steal. *–n.* **2.** a robbery; burglary. Also, **hoist.**

**Hejira** /'hɛdʒərə/, *n.* →**Hegira.**

**hektare** /'hɛktɛə/, *n.* →**hectare.**

**hekto-,** variant of **hecto-.**

**held** /hɛld/, *v.* past tense and past participle of **hold.**

**held ball** /– 'bɔl/, *n. Basketball.* **1.** a ball held by two opposing players neither of which can gain possession. **2.** a ball which a player makes no real attempt to put into play.

**heldentenor** /'hɛldəntenə/, *n.* a tenor with a large, untiring voice suited to the heroic roles of grand opera. [G: lit., hero tenor]

**heli-,** variant of **helio-,** before vowels, as in *helianthus.*

**heliacal** /hə'laɪəkəl/, *adj.* pertaining to or occurring near the sun, esp. applied to such risings and settings of a star as are most nearly coincident with those of the sun while yet being visible. Also, **heliac** /'hiliæk/. [LL *hēliacus* (from Gk *hēliakós* of the sun) + -AL[1]] – **heliacally,** *adv.*

**helianthus** /hili'ænθəs/, *n.* →**sunflower.** [NL, from Gk *hḗlios* sun + *ánthos* flower]

**helical** /'hɛlɪkəl/, *adj.* pertaining to or having the form of a helix. [L *helix* HELIX + -AL[1]] – **helically,** *adv.*

**helical gear** /– 'gɪə/, *n.* a gearwheel in which the teeth are at an angle to the wheel axis and form part of a helix described on the face of the wheel.

**helices** /'hɛləsiz/, *n.* plural of **helix.**

**helichrysum** /hili'krɪsəm/, *n.* any plant of the large genus, *Helichrysum,* as *H. bracteatum* of Australia grown for its flowers which have large yellow, chaffy bracts.

**helicograph** /'hɛlɪkoʊ,græf, -,graf/, *n.* a device for drawing spiral lines.

**helicoid** /'hɛləkɔɪd/, *adj.* **1.** coiled or curving like a helix; spiral. *–n.* **2.** *Geom.* a warped surface generated by a straight line so moving as always to cut or touch a fixed helix. [Gk *helikoeidḗs* of spiral form] – **helicoidal** /hɛlə'kɔɪdl/, *adj.* – **helicoidally** /hɛlə'kɔɪdəli/, *adv.*

**helicon** /'hɛləkən/, *n.* a tuba in coiled form to be carried over the shoulder in cavalry bands. [named after *Helicon,* mountain in Boeotia, S Greece, regarded in ancient Greece as the source of poetic inspiration; associated with HELIX] – **Heliconian** /hɛlə'koʊniən/, *adj.*

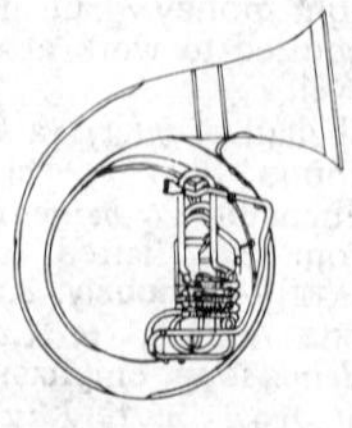
helicon

**helicopter** /'hɛlikɒptə, 'hɛlə-/, *n.* any of a class of heavier-than-air craft which are lifted and sustained in the air by helicoid surfaces or propellers turning on vertical axes by virtue of power supplied from an engine. [F *hélicoptère,* from *hélico-* (combining form. See HELIX) + Gk *pterón* wing]

**helicopter gunship** /– 'gʌnʃɪp/, *n.* a helicopter armed with guns, rockets, etc., enabling it to attack ground forces.

**helio-,** a word element meaning 'sun', as in *heliocentric.* Also, **heli-.** [Gk, combining form of *hḗlios*]

**heliocentric** /,hilioʊ'sɛntrɪk/, *adj.* **1.** as viewed or measured from the centre of the sun. **2.** having or representing the sun as a centre. – **heliocentrically,** *adv.*

**heliocentric parallax** /– 'pærəlæks/, *n.* See **parallax** (def. 3).

**heliodor** /'hɛliədɔ/, *n.* a variety of clear yellow beryl, which occurs in south-western Africa, and which is used in jewellery.

**heliogram** /'hiliəgræm/, *n.* a heliographic message. [HELIO(GRAPH) + (TELE)GRAM]

**heliograph** /'hiliəgræf, -graf/, *n.* **1.** a device for signalling by means of a movable mirror which flashes beams of light to a distant point. **2.** an apparatus for photographing the sun. *–v.t., v.i.* **3.** to communicate by heliograph. – **heliographer** /hili'ɒgrəfə/, *n.* – **heliographic** /hiliə'græfɪk/, *adj.* – **heliography** /hili'ɒgrəfi/, *n.*

**heliolatry** /hili'ɒlətri/, *n.* worship of the sun. – **heliolater,** *n.* – **heliolatrous,** *adj.*

**heliolithic** /,hilioʊ'lɪθɪk/, *adj.* pertaining to a society which is characterised by sun-worship and the erection of megaliths. [HELIO- + -LITH + -IC]

**heliometer** /hili'ɒmətə/, *n.* an instrument for measuring the diameter of the sun and the angular distance between two celestial bodies.

**heliostat** /'hiliəstæt/, *n.* an instrument consisting of a mirror moved by clockwork, for reflecting the sun's rays in a fixed direction.

**heliotaxis** /hilioʊ'tæksəs/, *n.* a phototaxis in response to sunlight. – **heliotactic,** *adj.*

**heliotherapy** /hilioʊ'θɛrəpi/, *n.* treatment of disease by means of sunlight.

**heliotrope** /'hɛliətroʊp, 'hiliə-, 'hɛljə-, 'hiljə-/, *n.* **1.** *Bot.* any plant that turns towards the sun. **2.** any herb or shrub of the boraginaceous genus *Heliotropium,* esp. *H. arborescens,* a garden plant with small, fragrant purple flowers, and caterpillar weed, *H. europaeum,* a common noxious weed. **3.** the medicinal valerian, *Valeriana officinalis.* **4.** light tint of purple; reddish lavender. **5.** →**bloodstone. 6.** a form of heliograph used in surveying in which a mirror is used to reflect the sun's rays and a line of sight enables the operator to transmit the reflected beam in the direction of the observer. [F, from L *hēliotropium,* from Gk *hēliotrópion* sundial, plant, bloodstone]

**heliotropic** /hiliə'trɒpɪk/, *adj.* growing towards the light. – **heliotropically,** *adv.*

**heliotropism** /hili'ɒtrəpɪzəm/, *n.* heliotropic habit of growth.

**heliotype** /'hiliətaɪp/, *n., v.,* **-typed, -typing.** *–n.* **1.** a picture or print produced by a photomechanical process in which the impression in ink is taken directly from a prepared gelatine film which has been exposed under a negative. **2.** Also, **heliotypy** /'hiliətaɪpi/. the process itself. *–v.t.* **3.** to make a heliotype of. – **heliotypic** /hiliə'tɪpɪk/, *adj.*

**heliozoan** /hiliə'zoʊən/, *n.* **1.** one of the Heliozoa, an order of protozoans, distinguished by a spherical body and radiating pseudopodia. *–adj.* **2.** belonging or pertaining to the Heliozoa.

**helipad** /'hɛlipæd/, *n.* an aerodrome or landing place for helicopters.

**heliport** /'hɛlipɔt/, *n.* a landing place for helicopters, often the roof of a building, with facilities for passenger handling.

**helipterum** /hɛ'lɪptərəm/, *n.* any plant of the genus *Helipterum,* family Compositae, usu. with yellow, pink or white flowers, some species of which, as *H. roseum* from western Australia, have flowers which can be picked for dried flower arrangements.

**helium** /'hiliəm/, *n.* an inert gaseous element present in the sun's atmosphere, certain minerals, natural gas, etc., and also occurring as a radioactive decomposition product. *Symbol:* He; *at. wt:* 4.0026; *at. no.:* 2; *density:* 0.1785 at 0°C and 760 mm pressure. [NL, from Gk *hḗlios* sun]

**helix** /'hilɪks, 'hɛl-/, *n., pl.* **helices** /'hɛləsiz, 'hil-/, **helixes. 1.** a spiral. **2.** *Geom.* the curve assumed by a straight line drawn on a plane when that plane is wrapped round a cylindrical surface of any kind, esp. a right circular cylinder, as the curve of a screw thread. **3.** *Anat.* the curved fold forming most of the rim of the external ear. [L, from Gk: anything of spiral shape]

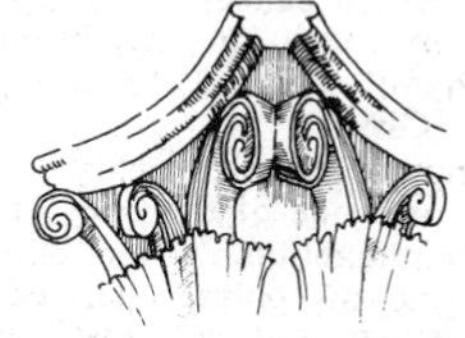
helix in a Corinthian capital

**hell** /hɛl/, *n.* **1.** the place or state of punishment of the wicked after death; the abode of evil and condemned spirits; Gehenna or Tartarus. **2.** any place or state of torment or misery: *a hell on earth.* **3.** the powers of evil. **4.** anything that causes torment; any severe or extremely unpleasant experience, either mental or physical. **5.** the abode of the dead; Sheol or Hades. **6.** *Brit.* a gambling house. **7.** a receptacle into which a tailor throws his shreds or a printer his type. **8.** **come hell or high water,** whatever happens. **9.** Some special noun phrases are:
**beat hell out of** (a person), to physically assault a person in a vindictive manner.
**blast hell out of** (a person), to verbally assault a person; to severely reprimand.
**for the hell of it,** for no specific reason; for its own sake.
**get the hell,** move rapidly or energetically (fol. by *out of, into,* etc.).
**give (someone) hell,** to make things unpleasant for (someone).
**hell for leather,** at top speed; recklessly fast.
**hell of a, 1.** appallingly difficult, unpleasant, etc. **2.** notable; remarkable. Also, **helluva.**
**hell's bells,** (a mild imprecation).
**hell's teeth,** (an exclamation of astonishment, indignation, etc.)
**hell to pay,** serious unwanted consequences.
**like hell, 1.** very much (used as general intensive). **2.** not at all; definitely not.
**merry hell,** an upheaval; a severe reaction; severe pain.
**not a hope in hell,** not the slightest possibility.
**play hell with, 1.** to cause considerable damage, injury or harm to. **2.** *Colloq.* to reprimand severely; scold.
**raise hell,** cause enormous trouble.
**the hell with it,** (an expression of disgust or rejection.)
**what the hell,** (an exclamation of contempt, dismissal, or the like).
*–interj.* **10.** (an exclamation of annoyance, disgust, etc.). [ME *helle,* OE *hel(l),* c. G *Hölle.* Cf. HALL]

**he'll** /hil/, contraction of: **1.** he will. **2.** he shall.

**Helladic** /hɛ'lædɪk/, *adj.* of or pertaining to the Bronze Age culture on the mainland of ancient Greece, about 2900 - 1100 B.C. [L *Helladicus,* from Gk *Helladikós* of or from Greece]

**Hellas** /'hɛlæs/, *n.* ancient and modern Greek name of **Greece.**

**hell-bent** /hɛl-'bɛnt/, *adj.* stubbornly or recklessly determined.

**hellbox** /'hɛlbɒks/, *n.* →**hell** (def. 7).

**hellcat** /'hɛlkæt/, *n.* **1.** an evil-tempered, unmanageable woman. **2.** a hag or witch.

**hellebore** /'hɛləbɔ/, *n.* **1.** any plant of the genus *Helleborus,* esp. *H. niger* **(black hellebore),** a European herb with showy flowers; Christmas rose. **2.** any of the coarse herbs constituting the genus *Veratrum,* as *V. album* **(European white hellebore).** **3.** the powdered root of American white hellebore, used to kill lice and caterpillars. [Gk *helléboros;* replacing earlier *ellebor(e),* ME *el(l)bre,* etc., from L *elleborus*]

**Hellene** /'hɛlin/, *n.* a Greek. [Gk *Héllēn*]

**Hellenic** /hɛ'lɛnɪk, hə-, 'hɛlənɪk/, *adj.* **1.** pertaining to the modern Greeks. **2.** pertaining to the ancient Greeks, or their language, culture, etc., before the time of Alexander the Great (contrasted with *Hellenistic*). *–n.* **3.** a group of Indo-European languages, including Greek. **4.** Greek, esp. Modern Greek.

**Hellenise** /'hɛlənaɪz/, *v.,* **-nised, -nising.** *–v.t.* **1.** to make Greek in character. *–v.i.* **2.** to adopt Greek ideas or customs. Also, **Hellenize.** [Gk *Hellēnízein*] **– Hellenisation** /hɛlənaɪ'zeɪʃən/, *n.* **– Helleniser,** *n.*

**Hellenism** /'hɛlənɪzəm/, *n.* **1.** ancient Greek culture or ideals. **2.** the character or spirit of the Greeks. **3.** adoption of Greek speech, ideas, or customs.

**Hellenist** /'hɛlənəst/, *n.* **1.** one who adopts or adopted Greek speech, ideas, or customs. **2.** one who admires or studies Greek civilisation. [Gk *Hellēnistḗs*]

**Hellenistic** /hɛlə'nɪstɪk/, *adj.* **1.** pertaining to Hellenists. **2.** following or resembling Greek usage. **3.** pertaining to the Greeks or their language, culture, etc., after the time of Alexander the Great when Greek characteristics were modified by foreign elements. **– Hellenistically,** *adv.*

**hellfire** /hɛl'faɪə, 'hɛlfaɪə/, *n.* **1.** the fire of hell. **2.** punishment in hell.

**hellhole** /'hɛlhoʊl/, *n. Colloq.* a highly unpleasant place.

**hellhound** /'hɛlhaʊnd/, *n.* **1.** a hound of hell; a demon. **2.** a fiendish person. [ME *hellehound,* OE *hellehund* hell's hound]

**hellion** /'hɛliən/, *n. Colloq.* a troublesome, mischief-making person. [HELL + *-ion* as in *scullion*]

**hellish** /'hɛlɪʃ/, *adj.* **1.** of, like, or befitting hell; infernal; wicked. **2.** Also **hellishing.** extremely, very: *hellish hot.* **– hellishly,** *adv.* **– hellishness,** *n.*

**hello** /hʌ'loʊ, hə-/, *interj., n., pl.* **-los,** *v.,* **-loed, -loing.** *–interj.* **1.** (an exclamation to attract attention, answer a telephone, or express greeting.) **2.** (an exclamation of surprise, etc.) *–n.* **3.** the call 'hello'. *–v.i.* **4.** to call 'hello'. Also, **hallo, hullo.** [var. of HALLO]

**hell's angel** /hɛlz 'eɪndʒəl/, *n.* originally a member of a group of lawless, usu. leather-jacketed, motor-cyclists known for their disturbance of civil order in the U.S., esp. California, later applied to similar people elsewhere.

**helluva** /'hɛləvə/, *adj. Colloq.* **1.** very good: *he's a helluva fellow.* **2.** very bad: *we had a helluva time.* **3.** (an intensifier): *we had a helluva good time.*

**helm**[1] /hɛlm/, *n.* **1.** the tiller or wheel by which the rudder of a vessel is controlled. **2.** the entire steering apparatus. **3.** a moving of the helm. **4.** the place or post of control: *the helm of affairs.* *–v.t.* **5.** to steer; direct. [ME *helme,* OE *helma;* akin to MHG *helm* handle, Icel. *hjálm* rudder] **– helmless,** *adj.*

**helm**[2] /hɛlm/, *n.* **1.** *Archaic.* a helmet. *–v.t.* **2.** to furnish or cover with a helmet. [ME and OE, c. D *helm* and G *Helm.* See HELMET]

**helmet** /'hɛlmət/, *n.* **1.** a defensive covering for the head: **a.** any of various forms of protective head covering worn by soldiers, firemen, divers, etc. **b.** medieval armour for the head. **c.** *Fencing, Singlestick, etc.* a protective device for the head and face consisting of reinforced wire mesh. **2.** anything resembling a helmet in form or position. [ME, from OF, diminutive of *helme* helm, helmet, from Gmc. See HELM[2]] **– helmeted,** *adj.*

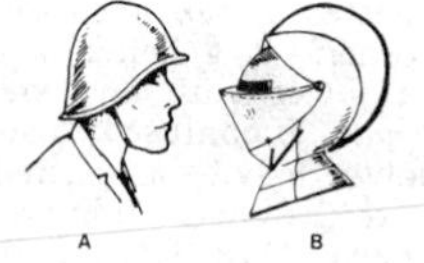

helmets: A, modern; B, medieval

**helmet orchid** /'– ɔkəd/, *n.* any species of the orchid genus *Corybas,* tiny terrestrial herbs found from India to New Zealand.

**helminth** /'hɛlmɪnθ/, *n.* a worm, esp. a parasitic worm. [Gk *hélmins*]

**helminthiasis** /hɛlmɪn'θaɪəsəs/, *n.* a medical condition characterised by worms in the body. [NL, from Gk *helminthiân* suffer from worms + *-(i)āsis* -(I)ASIS]

**helminthic** /hɛl'mɪnθɪk/, *adj.* **1.** pertaining to worms. **2.** expelling intestinal worms. Also, **helminthous.**

**helminthoid** /hɛl'mɪnθɔɪd, 'hɛlmɪnθɔɪd/, *adj.* resembling or shaped like a helminth; vermiform.

**helminthology** /hɛlmɪn'θɒlədʒi/, *n.* the science of worms, esp. of parasitic worms. **– helminthological** /ˌhɛlmɪnθə'lɒdʒəkəl/, *adj.* **– helminthologically** /ˌhɛlmɪnθə'lɒdʒəkli/, *adv.*

**helmsman** /'hɛlmzmən/, *n., pl.* **-men.** the man at the helm who steers a ship; a steersman.

**helophyte** /'hɛləfaɪt/, *n.* a plant growing in mud or marsh. **– helophytic** /hɛlə'fɪtɪk/, *adj.*

**helot** /'hɛlət/, *n.* a serf or slave; a bondman. [name of the serfs in Sparta, ancient city in S Greece, who were owned by the state and under allotment to landowners]

**helotism** /'hɛlətɪzəm/, *n.* →**serfdom.** Also, **helotage.**

**helotry** /'hɛlətri/, *n.* **1.** serfdom; slavery. **2.** helots collectively.

**help** /hɛlp/, *v.,* **helped** or (*Archaic*) **holp; helped** or (*Archaic*)

**holpen; helping;** *n.* *–v.t.* **1.** to cooperate effectively with a person; aid; assist: *to help a man in his work.* **2.** to furnish aid to; contribute strength or means to; assist in doing: *remedies that help digestion.* **3.** to succour; save; rescue. **4.** to relieve (someone) in need, sickness, pain, or distress. **5.** to refrain from; avoid (with *can* or *cannot*): *he can't help doing it.* **6.** to remedy, stop, or prevent: *nothing will help now.* **7.** to contribute an improvement to: *the use of a little make-up would help her appearance.* **8.** to serve food to at table (fol. by *to*): *help her to salad.* **9. help oneself (to),** to take or appropriate at will. *–v.i.* **10.** to give aid; be of service or advantage: *every little helps.* **11. help out,** to be of assistance; assist one in or as in a crisis or difficulty. *–n.* **12.** the act of helping; aid or assistance; relief or succour. **13.** a person or thing that helps. **14.** a hired helper. **15.** a body of such helpers. **16.** a domestic servant or a farm labourer. **17.** means of remedying, stopping, or preventing: *the thing is done, and there is no help for it now.* *–interj.* **18.** (a call for assistance.) **19. so help me,** (an exclamation giving assurance of the speaker's veracity). [ME *helpe(n)*, OE *helpen*, c. G *helfen*] – **helpable,** *adj.*

**helper** /ˈhɛlpə/, *n.* a person or thing that helps.

**helpful** /ˈhɛlpfəl/, *adj.* giving or affording help; useful. – **helpfully,** *adv.* – **helpfulness,** *n.*

**helping** /ˈhɛlpɪŋ/, *n.* **1.** the act of one who or that which helps. **2.** a portion served to a person at one time. *–adj.* **3.** giving assistance, support, etc.: *a helping hand.* – **helpingly,** *adv.*

**helping hand** /– ˈhænd/, *n.* aid; assistance: *the Lions Club gave a helping hand to the bushfire victims.*

**helpless** /ˈhɛlpləs/, *adj.* **1.** unable to help oneself; weak or dependent: *a helpless invalid.* **2.** without help, aid, or succour. **3.** incapable, inefficient, or shiftless. **4.** *Rare.* affording no help. – **helplessly,** *adv.* – **helplessness,** *n.*

**helpmate** /ˈhɛlpmeɪt/, *n.* **1.** a companion and helper. **2.** a wife or husband. [HELP + MATE[1]. Cf. HELPMEET]

**helpmeet** /ˈhɛlpmit/, *n. Archaic.* helpmate. [erroneously from Gen. 2:18, 20, 'an help meet for him']

**helter-skelter** /hɛltə-ˈskɛltə/, *adv.* **1.** in headlong, disorderly haste: *to run helter-skelter.* *–n.* **2.** tumultuous haste or disorder. **3.** a helter-skelter flight, course, or performance. **4.** a tower with an external spiral slide, as at a fairground. *–adj.* **5.** confused; disorderly; carelessly hurried. [imitative]

**helve** /hɛlv/, *n., v.,* **helved, helving.** *–n.* **1.** the handle of an axe, hatchet, hammer, or the like. *–v.t.* **2.** to furnish with a helve. [ME; OE *h(i)elfe*]

**Helvetia** /hɛlˈviʃə/, *n. Poetic.* Switzerland. [an alpine region in Roman times, corresponding to the W and N parts of modern Switzerland, a republic in central Europe]

**Helvetian** /hɛlˈviʃən/, *adj.* **1.** of or pertaining to Helvetia or the Helvetii. **2.** Swiss. *–n.* **3.** one of the Helvetii. **4.** a Swiss. [L *Helvētius* + -AN]

**hem**[1] /hɛm/, *v.,* **hemmed, hemming,** *n.* *–v.t.* **1.** to enclose or confine (fol. by *in, round,* or *about*): *hemmed in by enemies.* **2.** to fold back and sew down the edge of (cloth, a garment, etc.). **3.** to form an edge or border to or about. *–n.* **4.** the edge made by folding back the margin of cloth and sewing it down. **5.** the edge or border of a garment, etc., esp. at the bottom. **6.** the edge, border, or margin of anything. [ME *hemm(e)*, OE *hem*, probably akin to *hamm* enclosure]

**hem**[2] /hɛm/, *interj., n., v.,* **hemmed, hemming.** *–interj.* **1.** (an utterance resembling a slight clearing of the throat, used to attract attention, express doubt, etc.). *–n.* **2.** the utterance or sound of 'hem'. *–v.i.* **3.** to utter the sound 'hem'. **4.** to hesitate in speaking. **5. hem and haw,** to avoid giving a direct answer. [imitative]

**hem-,** *Chiefly U.S.* variant of **haem-**. For words beginning in **hem-, hema-, hemo-,** see preferred spelling under **haem-, haema-, haemo-.**

**he-man** /ˈhi-mæn/, *n. Colloq.* a tough or aggressively masculine man.

**hematite** /ˈhimətaɪt/, *n.* →**haematite.**

**heme** /him/, *n. Chiefly U.S.* →**haem.**

**hemelytron** /həˈmɛlətrən/, *n., pl.* **-tra** /-trə/. one of the fore wings of hemipterous and esp. heteropterous insects, leathery at the base and membranous at the tip. Also, **hemielytron.** [var. of *hemielytron*, from HEMI- + ELYTRON] – **hemelytral,** *adj.*

**hemeralopia** /hɛmərəˈloupiə/, *n.* a condition of the eyes, which causes inability to see as distinctly in a bright light as in a dull one; day blindness.

**hemi-,** a prefix meaning 'half', as in *hemialgia.* Cf. **semi-.** [Gk]

**hemialgia** /hɛmiˈældʒə/, *n.* pain or neuralgia involving only one side of the body or head.

**hemicellulose** /hɛmiˈsɛljulouz, -ous/, *n.* any of a group of gummy polysaccharides, intermediate in complexity between sugar and cellulose, which hydrolyse to monosaccharides more readily than cellulose.

**hemichordate** /hɛmiˈkɔdeɪt/, *adj.* **1.** denoting or pertaining to the Hemichordata, a chordate subphylum that comprises a large number of small, widely distributed marine animals. *–n.* **2.** a hemichordate animal.

**hemicrania** /hɛmiˈkreɪniə/, *n. Obs.* pain in one side of the head; migraine. [LL, from Gk *hēmikrānía* a pain on one side of the head]

**hemicycle** /ˈhɛmisaɪkəl/, *n.* **1.** a semicircle. **2.** a semicircular structure. [F, from L *hēmicyclium,* from Gk *hēmikýklion*] – **hemicyclic** /hɛmiˈsaɪklɪk/, *adj.*

**hemidemisemiquaver** /ˈhɛmidɛmi,sɛmikweɪvə/, *n. Music.* a note one sixty-fourth the duration of a semibreve.

**hemielytron** /hɛmiˈɛlətrɒn/, *n., pl.* **-tra** /-trə/. →**hemelytron.**

**hemi-head** /ˈhɛmi-hɛd/, *n.* (of an internal combustion engine) having hemispherically shaped combustion chambers.

**hemihedral** /hɛmiˈhidrəl/, *adj.* (of a crystal) having only half the planes or faces required by the maximum symmetry of the system to which it belongs. [HEMI- + Gk *hédra* seat, base + -AL[1]] – **hemihedrally,** *adv.* – **hemihedrism, hemihedry,** *n.*

**hemihydrate** /hɛmiˈhaɪdreɪt/, *n.* a hydrate in which there are two molecules of the compound for each molecule of water.

**hemimorphic** /hɛmiˈmɔfɪk/, *adj.* (of a crystal) having the two ends of an axis unlike in their planes or modifications; lacking a centre of symmetry. – **hemimorphism, hemimorphy,** *n.*

**hemimorphite** /hɛmiˈmɔfaɪt/, *n.* a mineral, hydrous zinc silicate, $Zn_4Si_2O_7(OH)_2H_2O$, an ore of zinc.

**hemiplegia** /hɛmiˈplidʒə/, *n.* paralysis of one side of the body, resulting from a disease of the brain or of the spinal cord.

**hemiplegic** /hɛmiˈplidʒɪk/, *adj.* **1.** of or pertaining to hemiplegia. *–n.* **2.** a person who is paralysed from the waist down.

**hemipterous** /həˈmɪptərəs/, *adj.* belonging or pertaining to insects of the order Hemiptera, including the true bugs (Heteroptera), whose forewings are in part thickened and leathery, and the cicadas, leaf-hoppers, aphids, etc., (Homoptera) whose wings are entirely membranous. [HEMI- + Gk *pterón* wing + -OUS]

**hemisphere** /ˈhɛməsfɪə/, *n.* **1.** half of the terrestrial globe or celestial sphere. **2.** a map or projection of either of these. **3.** the half of a sphere. **4.** *Anat.* either of the lateral halves of the cerebrum. [L *hēmisphaerium,* from Gk *hēmisphaírion;* replacing ME *emysperie,* from OF *emispere*]

**hemispherical** /hɛmiˈsfɛrəkəl/, *adj.* **1.** of or pertaining to a hemisphere. **2.** in the form of a hemisphere. Also, **hemispheric.** – **hemispherically,** *adv.*

**hemispheroid** /hɛmiˈsfɪərɔɪd/, *n.* half of a spheroid. – **hemispheroidal** /,hɛmisfɪəˈrɔɪdl/, *adj.*

**hemistich** /ˈhɛmistɪk/, *n.* **1.** the exact or approximate half of a stich, or poetic verse or line, esp. as divided by a caesura or the like. **2.** an incomplete line, or a line of less than the usual length. [L *hēmistichium,* from Gk *hēmistíchion*] – **hemistichal** /ˈhɛmistɪkəl, hɛmiˈstɪkəl/, *adj.*

**hemiterpene** /hɛmiˈtɜpin/, *n.* one of a group of hydrocarbon isomers of the general formula $C_5H_8$, related to, and half the molecular weight of, the terpenes.

**hemitrope** /ˈhɛmitroup/, *adj., n.* →**twin** (def. 5). [F. See HEMI-, -TROPE] – **hemitropic** /hɛmiˈtrɒpɪk/, *adj.*

**hemline** /ˈhɛmlaɪn/, *n.* the bottom edge of a dress, skirt, etc.

**hemlock** /ˈhɛmlɒk/, *n.* **1.** a poisonous umbelliferous herb, *Conium maculatum,* with spotted stems, finely divided leaves, and small white flowers, used medicinally as a powerful sedative. **2.** a poisonous drink made from this herb. **3. a.** →**hemlock spruce. b.** its wood. [ME *hemeluc,* OE *hemlic, hym(e)lic(e),* ? from *hymele* hop plant + *-k* suffix (see -OCK).

i = peat ɪ = pit ɛ = pet æ = pat a = part ɒ = pot ʌ = putt ɔ = port ʊ = put u = pool ɜ = pert ə = apart aɪ = buy eɪ = bay ɔɪ = boy aʊ = how
oʊ = hoe ɪə = here ɛə = hair ʊə = tour g = give θ = thin ð = then ʃ = show ʒ = measure tʃ = choke dʒ = joke ŋ = sing j = you õ = Fr. bon

Note that hemlock and hops agree in having a sedative effect]

**hemlock spruce** /– 'sprus/, *n.* any of the trees of the coniferous genus *Tsuga,* esp. a tree of eastern North America, *T. canadensis,* whose bark is used in tanning.

**hemmer** /'hɛmə/, *n.* **1.** one who or that which hems. **2.** Also, **hemming foot.** a sewing-machine attachment for hemming edges.

**hemo-,** *Chiefly U.S.* variant of **haemo-.** Also, **hem-.** For words beginning in **heme-**, see preferred spelling under **haemo-.**

**hemp** /hɛmp/, *n.* **1.** a tall, annual herb, *Cannabis sativa,* native to Asia, but cultivated in many parts of the world, and yielding hashish, bhang, cannabin, etc. **2.** the tough fibre of this plant used for making coarse fabrics, ropes, etc. **3.** any of various plants resembling hemp. **4.** any of various fibres similar to hemp. **5.** →**marijuana.** **6.** *N.Z.* New Zealand flax, *Phormium tenax.* [ME; OE *henep, hænep,* c. G *Hanf,* Gk *kánnabis* CANNABIS]

**hemp agrimony** /– 'ægrəməni/, *n.* →**crofton weed.**

**hempen** /'hɛmpən/, *adj.* **1.** made of hemp. **2.** of or pertaining to hemp. **3.** resembling hemp.

**hempseed** /'hɛmpsid/, *n.* the seed of hemp, used as a food for cagebirds.

**hemstitch** /'hɛmstɪtʃ/, *v.t.* **1.** to hem along a line from which threads have been drawn out, stitching the crossthreads into a series of little groups. *–n.* **2.** the stitch used or the needlework done in hemstitching. [HEM[1], *n.* + STITCH[1], *v.*]

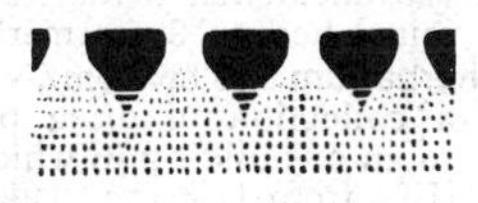

hemstitch

**hen** /hɛn/, *n.* **1.** the female of the domestic fowl. **2.** the female of any bird, esp. of a gallinaceous bird. **3.** *Colloq.* a woman, esp. a fussy or foolish woman. **4. scarce (rare) as hen's teeth,** *Colloq.* extremely rare. [ME and OE *hen(n)* (from OE *hana* cock), c. G *Henne*]

**hen-and-chicken fern** /hɛn-ən-'tʃɪkən fɜn/, *n.* **1.** an attractive fern of eastern Australia, *Asplenium bulbiferum,* so called because the new shoots grow on the parent fern. **2.** any of various similar plants. Also, **hen-and-chickens.**

**hen-and-chickens** /hɛn-ən-'tʃɪkənz/, *n.* **1.** any of several herbs, esp. those having offshoot or runner plants growing around the parent. **2.** a species of houseleek, *Sempervivum tectorum,* native to Europe. **3.** →**ground ivy.**

**henbane** /'hɛnbeɪn/, *n.* a herb, native to the Old World, *Hyoscyamus niger,* bearing sticky, hairy foliage with a disagreeable smell, and yellowish brown flowers, and possessing narcotic and poisonous properties; esp. destructive to domestic fowls. [ME. See HEN, BANE]

**henbit** /'hɛnbɪt/, *n.* a weed, *Lamium amplexicaule,* with small purplish flowers; deadnettle.

**hen-cackle** /'hɛn-kækəl/, *n. N.Z. Colloq.* a mountain considered easy to climb.

**hence** /hɛns/, *adv.* **1.** as an inference from this fact; for this reason; therefore: *of the best quality and hence satisfactory.* **2.** *Archaic.* from this time onwards; henceforth. **3.** *Archaic.* at the end of a given period: *a month hence.* **4.** *Archaic.* from this source or origin. **5.** *Archaic.* from this place; away from here. *–interj.* **6.** *Archaic.* depart! [ME *hen(ne)s,* from *hen* hence (OE *heona, heonan*) + *-(e)s,* adv. suffix]

**henceforth** /hɛns'fɔθ/, *adv.* from this time forth; from now on. Also, **henceforwards** /hɛns'fɔwədz/, **henceforward.**

**henchman** /'hɛntʃmən/, *n., pl.* **-men.** **1.** a trusty attendant or follower. **2.** a ruthless and unscrupulous follower. **3.** *Obs.* a squire or page. [ME *henchemanne, henxtman,* probably orig. meaning groom, and apparently from OE *hengest* stallion + *mann* man]

**hencoop** /'hɛnkup/, *n.* a cage for poultry.

**hendecagon** /hɛn'dɛkəgən/, *n.* a polygon having eleven angles and eleven sides. [Gk *héndeka* eleven + -GON] – **hendecagonal** /hɛndə'kægənəl/, *adj.*

**hendecahedron** /ˌhɛndɛkə'hidrən/, *n.* a solid figure with eleven faces.

**hendecasyllable** /'hɛndɛkəˌsɪləbəl/, *n.* a metrical line of eleven syllables. [L *hendecasyllabus* (conformed to SYLLABLE), from Gk *hendekasýllabos*] – **hendecasyllabic** /ˌhɛndɛkəsə'læbɪk/, *adj., n.*

**hendiadys** /hɛn'daɪədəs/, *n.* a figure of speech in which a complex idea is expressed by two words connected by a copulative conjunction, for example, *to look with eyes and envy* instead of *with envious eyes.* [LL, from Gk phrase *hèn dià dyoîn* one through two]

**henequen** /'hɛnəkɪn/, *n.* the fibre of an agave, *Agave fourcroydes,* of Yucatan, used for making ropes, coarse fabrics, etc. Also, **henequin.** [Sp. *jeniquén;* from native name]

**hen fruit** /'hɛn frut/, *n. Colloq.* hen's eggs.

**henge** /hɛndʒ/, *n.* a type of ritual monument consisting of upright stones arranged in a circle, usu. surrounded by a ditch with a bank, similar to the stone circle of Stonehenge. [backformation from *Stonehenge,* prehistoric monument in S England]

**henhouse** /'hɛnhaʊs/, *n.* **1.** a coop for hens or other fowl. **2.** (*joc.*) a house or establishment inhabited mainly by women.

**henna** /'hɛnə/, *n.* **1.** a shrub or small tree, *Lawsonia inermis,* of Asia and the Levant. **2.** a reddish orange dye or cosmetic made from the leaves of this plant. **3.** reddish or orange-brown. *–v.t.* **4.** to tint or dye with henna. [Ar. *ḥinnā'*]

**hennery** /'hɛnəri/, *n., pl.* **-neries.** a place where domestic fowls are kept.

**henotheism** /'hɛnoʊθiˌɪzəm/, *n.* **1.** the worship of one particular divinity among others existent, in contrast with *monotheism,* which teaches that there exists only one God. **2.** ascription of supreme divine attributes to whichever one of several gods is at the time addressed. [*heno-* (combining form representing Gk neut. *hén* one) + THEISM] – **henotheist,** *n.* – **henotheistic** /hɛnoʊθi'ɪstɪk/, *adj.*

**hen party** /'hɛn pati/, *n.* a party exclusively for women.

**henpeck** /'hɛnpɛk/, *v.t.* (of a wife) to domineer over (her husband). – **henpecked,** *adj.*

**henrun** /'hɛnrʌn/, *n.* an enclosure for domestic fowls.

**henry**[1] /'hɛnri/, *n., pl.* **-rys.** the derived SI unit of inductance, equivalent to the inductance of a circuit in which an electromotive force of one volt is produced by a current in the circuit which varies at the rate of one ampere per second. *Symbol:* H [named after Joseph *Henry,* 1797-1878, U.S. physicist]

**henry**[2] /'hɛnri/, *n. Colloq.* a signature. [short for U.S. colloq. John *Henry,* an autographed signature]

**Henry's law** /hɛnriz 'lɔ/, *n.* the principle that the weight of a gas dissolved by a given volume of liquid at constant temperature is directly proportional to the pressure of the gas. [named after William *Henry,* 1774-1836, English chemist]

**Henry the Third,** *n. Colloq.* a turd. [rhyming slang]

**hens' night** /'hɛnz naɪt/, *n.* →**girls' night out.** Cf. **stag party.**

**he-oak** /'hi-oʊk/, *n.* any of various species of casuarina, esp. *Casuarina stricta.*

**hep**[1] /hɛp/, *adj. Chiefly U.S. Colloq.* having inside knowledge, or being informed of current styles, esp. in jazz (oft. fol. by *to*): *to be hep to swing music.* Also, **hip.**

**hep**[2] /hɛp/, *n. Colloq.* hepatitis. [shortened form]

**heparin** /'hɛpərən/, *n.* a polysaccharide containing sulphate groups produced in the liver which prevents the coagulation of the blood, and is used in the treatment of thrombosis. [Gk *hêpar* liver + -IN[2]]

**hepatic** /hə'pætɪk/, *adj.* **1.** of or pertaining to the liver. **2.** acting on the liver, as a medicine. **3.** liver-coloured; dark reddish brown. **4.** *Bot.* belonging or pertaining to the liverworts. *–n.* **5.** a medicine acting on the liver. **6.** a liverwort. [L *hēpaticus,* from Gk *hēpatikós* of the liver]

**hepatica** /hə'pætɪkə/, *n., pl.* **-ces, -cae** /-si/. any of the herbs, with three-lobed leaves and delicate purplish, pink, or white flowers constituting the genus *Hepatica.* [NL, properly fem. of L *hēpaticus* hepatic]

**hepatise** /'hɛpətaɪz/, *v.t.,* **-tised, -tising.** to convert (a lung, etc.) into liver-like tissue by engorgement. Also, **hepatize.** – **hepatisation** /hɛpətaɪ'zeɪʃən/, *n.*

**hepatitis** /hɛpə'taɪtəs/, *n.* a serious viral disease characterised by inflammation or enlargement of the liver, fever or jaundice. See **infectious hepatitis, serum hepatitis.** [NL, from Gk *hêpar* liver + *-ītis* -ITIS]

**hepcat** /'hɛpkæt/, *n. Colloq.* an expert performer, or a knowing admirer, of jazz.

**hepialid** /hɛpi'æləd/, *adj.* **1.** of or pertaining to the Hepialidae, a family of moths having vestigial mouth parts, short antennae and larvae which tunnel in the soil or in trees. *–n.* **2.** a moth of the family Hepialidae.

**Hepplewhite** /'hɛpəlwaɪt/, *adj.* an 18th-century English style of furniture characterised by oval or shield-shaped open chair backs. [from George *Hepplewhite,* d. 1786, English designer and cabinet-maker]

**hepta-,** a prefix meaning 'seven'. Also, before vowels, **hept-**. [Gk, combining form of *heptá*]

**heptad** /'hɛptæd/, *n.* **1.** the number seven. **2.** a group of seven. **3.** *Chem.* an element, atom, or radical having a valency of seven. [LL *heptas,* from Gk: the number seven]

**heptagon** /'hɛptəgɒn, -gən/, *n.* a polygon having seven angles and seven sides. [Gk *heptágōnos* seven-cornered] – **heptagonal** /hɛp'tægənəl/, *adj.*

A B

heptagons: A, regular; B, irregular

**heptahedron** /hɛptə'hidrən/, *n., pl.* **-drons, -dra** /-drə/. a solid figure having seven faces. – **heptahedral,** *adj.*

**heptamerous** /hɛp'tæmərəs/, *adj.* consisting of or divided into seven parts.

**heptameter** /hɛp'tæmətə/, *n.* a verse of seven metrical feet. [LL *heptametrum,* from Gk *heptámetron*] – **heptametrical** /hɛptə'mɛtrɪkəl/, *adj.*

**heptane** /'hɛpteɪn/, *n.* any of nine isomeric hydrocarbons, $C_7H_{16}$, of the methane series, some of which are obtained from petroleum and which are used in fuels, as solvents, and as chemical intermediates.

**heptangular** /hɛp'tæŋgjələ/, *adj.* having seven angles.

**heptarchy** /'hɛptaki/, *n., pl.* **-chies. 1.** a government by seven persons. **2.** a group of seven states or kingdoms, each under its own ruler. **3.** (*oft. cap.*) the seven principal concurrent early English kingdoms. [HEPT- + -ARCHY] – **heptarch,** *n.* – **heptarchic** /hɛp'takɪk/, *adj.*

**heptastich** /'hɛptəstɪk/, *n.* a strophe, stanza, or poem consisting of seven lines or verses. [HEPTA- + Gk *stíchos* row, line]

**Heptateuch** /'hɛptətjuk/, *n.* the first seven books of the Old Testament. [LL *Heptateuchos,* from Gk: seven-volume (work)]

**heptavalent** /hɛp'tævələnt, hɛptə'veɪlənt/, *adj.* having a valency of seven; septivalent.

**heptode** /'hɛptoud/, *n.* a seven element vacuum tube.

**heptose** /'hɛptouz, -tous/, *n.* any of a group of monosaccharides which contain seven oxygen atoms.

**her** /hɜ/; *weak forms* /hə, ə/ *pron.* **1.** the objective case of *she.* *–adj.* **2.** the possessive form of *she,* used before a noun (cf. **hers**). **3.** of, belonging to, or having to do with a female person or personified thing. [ME *her(e),* OE *hire,* gen. and dat. of *hēo* she (fem. of *hē* he)]

**her.,** heraldry.

**herald** /'hɛrəld/, *n.* **1.** a messenger; forerunner or harbinger. **2.** one who proclaims or announces (often used as the name of a newspaper). **3.** a royal or official proclaimer or messenger. **4.** an officer who arranged tournaments and other medieval functions, announced challenges, marshalled combatants, etc., later employed also to arrange tourneys, processions, funerals, etc., and to regulate the use of armorial bearings. *–v.t.* **5.** to give tidings of; proclaim. **6.** to usher in. [ML *heraldus* (of Gmc orig.); replacing ME *heraud,* from OF *herau(l)t*]

**heraldic** /hə'rældɪk/, *adj.* of or pertaining to heralds or heraldry. – **heraldically,** *adv.*

**heraldry** /'hɛrəldri/, *n., pl.* **-dries. 1.** the science of armorial bearings. **2.** the art of blazoning armorial bearings, of settling the right of persons to bear arms or to use certain bearings, of tracing and recording genealogies, of recording honours, and of deciding questions of precedence. **3.** the office or duty of a herald. **4.** a heraldic device, or a collection of such devices. **5.** a coat of arms; armorial bearings. **6.** heraldic symbolism. **7.** heraldic pomp or ceremony.

**herald snake** /'hɛrəld sneɪk/, *n.* a nocturnal African snake, *Leptodira hotanbaeia,* of the family Colubridae, olive-brown in colour, with a bright red upper lip.

**herb** /hɜb/, *n.* **1.** a flowering plant whose stem above ground does not become woody and persistent. **2.** such a plant when valued for its medicinal properties, flavour, scent, or the like. **3.** *Rare.* herbage. **4.** *Colloq.* (*pl.*) power, esp. of cars: *this car has plenty of herbs.* **5. give it herbs,** *Colloq.* to accelerate a motor vehicle. **6. the herb,** *Colloq.* marijuana. *–v.i.* **7.** *Colloq.* (of a motor vehicle) to travel at speed. *–v.t.* **8.** *Colloq.* to convey at speed. [ME *(h)erbe,* from F, from L *herba* vegetation, grass, herb] – **herbless,** *adj.* – **herblike,** *adj.*

**herbaceous** /hɜ'beɪʃəs/, *adj.* **1.** of, pertaining to, or of the nature of a herb; herblike. **2.** (of plants or plant parts) not woody. **3.** (of flowers, sepals, etc.) having the texture, colour, etc., of an ordinary foliage leaf.

**herbaceous border** /– 'bɔdə/, *n.* a border of herbaceous plants around a garden bed.

**herbage** /'hɜbɪdʒ/, *n.* **1.** non-woody vegetation. **2.** the succulent parts (leaves and stems) of herbaceous plants. **3.** vegetation grazed by animals; pasturage. [ME, from F, from *herbe* grass. See HERB]

**herbal** /'hɜbəl/, *adj.* **1.** of, pertaining to, or consisting of herbs. *–n.* **2.** a treatise on herbs or plants.

**herbalist** /'hɜbələst/, *n.* **1.** one who collects or deals in herbs, esp. medicinal herbs. **2.** one who heals by the use of medicinal herbs. **3.** (formerly) an expert in herbs or plants.

**herbarium** /hɜ'bɛəriəm/, *n., pl.* **-bariums, -baria** /-'bɛəriə/. **1.** a collection of dried plants systematically arranged. **2.** a room or building in which a herbarium is kept. Also, **herbary.** [LL, from L *herba* HERB. Cf. ARBOUR]

**herb bennet** /hɜb 'bɛnət/, *n.* **1.** a perennial herb, *Geum urbanum,* family Rosaceae, of Europe and western Asia, having yellow flowers and an aromatic, tonic astringent root; geum. **2.** any other geum. Also, **bennet.** [ME *herbe beneit,* probably from OF *herbe beneite,* translation of ML *herba benedicta* blessed herb]

**herb Christopher** /– 'krɪstəfə/, *n.* →**baneberry.**

**herb Gerard** /– 'dʒɛrəd/, *n.* →**ground elder.**

**herbicide** /'hɜbəsaɪd/, *n.* a chemical or biological agent which kills plants or inhibits their growth.

**herbivore** /'hɜbəvɔ/, *n.* a herbivorous animal.

**herbivorous** /hɜ'bɪvərəs/, *adj.* feeding on plants. [NL *herbivorus* herb-eating. See HERB, -VOROUS]

**herb Paris** /hɜb 'pærəs/, *n.* a European herb, *Paris quadrifolia,* formerly used in medicine.

**herb Peter** /– 'pitə/, *n.* →**cowslip.**

**herb Robert** /– 'rɒbət/, *n.* a species of geranium, *Geranium robertianum,* with reddish purple flowers.

**herby** /'hɜbi/, *adj.* **1.** abounding in herbs or grass. **2.** pertaining to or like herbs.

**herculean** /hɜkjə'liən, hɜ'kjuliən/, *adj.* **1.** requiring the strength of a Hercules; very hard to perform: *a herculean task.* **2.** prodigious in strength, courage, or size.

**Hercules** /'hɜkjəliz/, *n.* a man of great strength and powerful physique. [from *Hercules,* in classical mythology a celebrated hero; L, from Gk *Hēraklês,* lit., having the glory of Hera]

**Hercules'-club** /hɜkjəliz-'klʌb/, *n.* **1.** a prickly tree of North America, *Zanthoxylum clava-herculis,* with a medicinal bark and berries. **2.** a prickly shrub of North America, *Aralia spinosa,* with medicinal bark and root.

**herd**[1] /hɜd/, *n.* **1.** a number of animals, esp. cattle, kept, feeding, or travelling together; drove; flock. **2.** (*derog.*) a large company of people. **3. the herd,** the common people; the rabble. *–v.i.* **4.** to unite or go in a herd; to assemble or associate as a herd. *–v.t.* **5.** to form into or as if into a herd. [ME; OE *heord,* c. G *Herde*]

**herd**[2] /hɜd/, *n.* **1.** a herdsman (usu. in combination): *cowherd.* *–v.t.* **2.** to tend, drive, or lead a herd of cattle, sheep, etc. [ME; OE *hierde,* c. G *Hirte;* from Gmc stem represented by HERD[1]]

**herd-book** /'hɜd-bʊk/, *n.* a book in which the genealogies of the animals in a herd are recorded.

**herder** /'hɜdə/, *n.* →**herdsman** (def. 1).

**herd instinct** /'hɜd ɪnstɪŋkt/, *n.* the instinct which urges men or animals to cluster or act in a group, to conform, or follow the herd.

**herdsman** /'hɜdzmən/, *n., pl.* **-men.** the keeper of a herd.

**herd tester** /'hɜd tɛstə/, *n.* **1.** a person employed by a State government to monitor the milk production of dairy herds. **2.** *N.Z.* a government officer who tests dairy herds for disease.

**herd testing** /'– tɛstɪŋ/, *n.* an organised system of weighing, testing and recording the milk and butterfat of every cow in a dairy herd.

**here** /hɪə/, *adv.* **1.** in this place; in this spot or locality (opposed to *there*): *put it here.* **2.** to or towards this place; hither: *come here.* **3.** at this point; at this juncture: *here the speaker paused.* **4.** (often used in pointing out or emphasising some person or thing present): *my friend here knows the facts.* **5.** present (used in answer to rollcall, etc.). **6.** in the present life or state. **7.** Some special adverb phrases are:
**here and now,** at this very moment; immediately.
**here and there, 1.** in this place and in that; in various places; at intervals. **2.** hither and thither; to and fro.
**here goes!,** (an exclamation to show one's resolution on beginning some bold or unpleasant act.)
**here's to,** a formula in offering a toast: *here's to you!*
**here to-day and gone to-morrow,** (of someone or something) staying in one place for only a short time.
**here we** (or **you**) **are,** *Colloq.* here is what we (or you) want, or are looking for.
**here we go again!** (an exclamation indicating exasperation or resignation at a course of action about to occur yet once again.)
**neither here nor there,** irrelevant; unimportant.
*–n.* **8.** this place. **9.** this world; this life. **10. here and now, a.** the immediate present. **b.** this world; this life. [ME; OE *hēr,* c. D and G *hier,* Icel. and Goth. *hēr;* from the demonstrative stem represented by HE]

**here-,** a word element meaning 'this (place)', 'this (time)', etc., used in combination with certain adverbs and prepositions. [special use of HERE]

**hereabout** /'hɪərəbaʊt/, *adv.* about this place; in this neighbourhood. Also, **hereabouts.**

**hereafter** /hɪər'aftə/, *adv.* **1.** after this in time or order; at some future time. **2.** in the world to come. *–n.* **3.** a future life; the world to come. **4.** time to come; the future. [ME *hereafter,* OE *hēræfter,* from *hēr* HERE + *æfter* AFTER]

**hereat** /hɪər'æt/, *adv.* **1.** at this time; when this happened. **2.** by reason of this; because of this.

**hereby** /'hɪəbaɪ/, *adv.* **1.** by this; by means of this; as a result of this. **2.** *Archaic.* nearby.

**hereditable** /hə'rɛdɪtəbəl/, *adj.* heritable. [F (obs.), from LL *hērēditāre* inherit, from L *hēres* heir] – **hereditability** /həˌrɛdɪtə'bɪləti/, *n.* – **hereditably,** *adv.*

**hereditament** /hɛrə'dɪtəmənt/, *n.* **1.** *Law.* any inheritable estate or interest in property. **2.** *Law.* chattels such as charters, deeds, tombstones, etc., which descend to all heirs with an inheritance; loosely used of articles such as plate, pictures, furniture, etc., which, as directed by will or settlement, belong absolutely to the first person entitled. [ML *hērēditāmentum,* from LL *hērēditāre.* See HEREDITABLE]

**hereditarianism** /hərɛdɪ'tɛəriənɪzəm/, *n.* the belief that it is a person's heredity which most significantly shapes his personality. Cf. **environmentalism.**

**hereditary** /hə'rɛdətri/, *adj.* **1.** passing, or capable of passing, naturally from parents to offspring: *hereditary traits.* **2.** pertaining to inheritance or heredity: *hereditary descent.* **3.** being such through feelings, etc., derived from predecessors: *a hereditary enemy.* **4.** *Law.* **a.** descending by inheritance. **b.** transmitted or transmissible in the line of descent by force of law. **c.** holding a title, etc., by inheritance: *a hereditary proprietor.* [L *hērēditārius* of an inheritance] – **hereditarily,** *adv.* – **hereditariness,** *n.*

**hereditist** /hə'rɛdətəst/, *n.* one who considers heredity as more important than environment in shaping behaviour.

**heredity** /hə'rɛdəti/, *n., pl.* **-ties. 1.** the transmission of genetic characteristics from parents to progeny; the factor which determines the extent to which an individual resembles his or its progenitors, dependent upon the separation and regrouping of genes during meiosis and fertilisation. **2.** the genetic characteristics transmitted to an individual by its parents. [L *hērēditas* heirship, inheritance]

**Hereford** /'hɛrəfəd/, *n.* one of a highly productive, hardy, early maturing breed of beef cattle, characterised by a red body, white face, and other white markings. [named after *Herefordshire,* county in W England]

**herein** /hɪər'ɪn/, *adv.* **1.** in or into this place. **2.** in this fact, circumstance, etc.; in view of this. [ME and OE *hērinne,* from *hēr* HERE + *inne* IN, *adv.*]

**hereinafter** /hɪərɪn'aftə/, *adv.* afterwards in this document, statement, etc.

**hereinbefore** /hɪərɪnbə'fɔ/, *adv.* before in this document, statement, etc.

**hereinto** /hɪər'ɪntu/, *adv.* **1.** into this place. **2.** into this matter or affair.

**hereof** /hɪər'ɒv/, *adv.* **1.** of this: *upon the receipt hereof.* **2.** concerning this: *more hereof later.*

**hereon** /hɪər'ɒn/, *adv.* →**hereupon.**

**heres** /'hɪəriz/, *n., pl.* **heredes** /hə'ridiz/. →**heir.** Also, **haeres.** [L]

**heresiarch** /hə'riziak/, *n.* a leader in heresy; the chief of a heretical sect. [LL *haeresiarcha,* from Gk *hairesiárchēs* leader of a school or sect]

**heresy** /'hɛrəsi/, *n., pl.* **-sies. 1.** doctrine contrary to the orthodox or accepted doctrine of a church or religious system. **2.** the maintaining of such an opinion or doctrine. [ME *(h)eresie,* from OF, from L *haeresis,* from Gk *haíresis* a taking, choice]

**heretic** /'hɛrətɪk/, *n.* **1.** a professed believer who maintains religious opinions contrary to those accepted by his church or rejects doctrines prescribed by his church. *–adj.* **2.** heretical. [ME *heretyke,* from F *hérétique,* from LL *haereticus,* adj., n., from Gk *hairetikós* able to choose]

**heretical** /hə'rɛtɪkəl/, *adj.* of, pertaining to, or like heretics or heresy. – **heretically,** *adv.*

**hereto** /hɪə'tu/, *adv.* to this place, thing, document, circumstance, proposition, etc.: *attached hereto.*

**heretofore** /hɪətu'fɔ/, *adv.* before this time.

**hereunder** /hɪər'ʌndə/, *adv.* **1.** under this; subsequently set down. **2.** under authority of this.

**hereunto** /hɪərʌn'tu/, *adv.* →**hereto.**

**hereupon** /hɪərə'pɒn/, *adv.* upon this; following immediately upon this.

**herewith** /hɪə'wɪθ/, *adv.* **1.** together with this. **2.** by means of this.

**heritable** /'hɛrətəbəl/, *adj.* **1.** capable of being inherited; inheritable; hereditary. **2.** capable of inheriting. [ME, from OF, from *heriter.* See HERITAGE] – **heritability** /hɛrətə'bɪləti/, *n.* – **heritably,** *adv.*

**heritage** /'hɛrətɪdʒ/, *n.* **1.** that which comes or belongs to one by reason of birth; an inherited lot or portion. **2.** something reserved for one: *the heritage of the righteous.* **3.** *Law.* **a.** that which has been or may be inherited by legal descent or succession. **b.** any property, esp. land, that devolves by right of inheritance. **4.** *Bible.* God's chosen people; the Israelites. [ME *(h)eritage,* from OF, from *heriter* inherit, from LL *hērēditāre*]

**heritance** /'hɛrətəns/, *n. Archaic.* →**inheritance.**

**heritor** /'hɛrətə/, *n. Archaic.* →**inheritor.** [ME *heriter,* from AF, from L *hērēditārius* HEREDITARY] – **heritress** /'hɛrətrəs/, *n. fem.*

**herk** /hɜk/, *v.i. Colloq.* to vomit.

**herl** /hɜl/, *n.* **1.** a barb, or the barbs, of a feather, much used in dressing anglers' flies. **2.** a fly so dressed. Also, **harl.** [ME *herle, harle,* from MLG: fibre]

herm: upper part of a double herm

**herm** /hɜm/, *n.* a kind of monument or statue, common in ancient Athens, consisting of a head, usu. that of the god Hermes, supported on a quadrangular pillar corresponding roughly in mass to the absent body and furnished with genitalia, in the case of the male, and often with projections near the shoulders on which wreaths might be hung.

**herma** /'hɜmə/, *n., pl.* **-mae** /-mi/, **-mai** /-maɪ/. →**herm.** [L, also *Hermēs,* from Gk]

**hermaphrodite** /hɜ'mæfrədaɪt/, *n.* **1.** an animal or a flower having normally both the male and the female organs of generation. **2.** a person with male and female sexual organs and characteristics. **3.** a person or thing in which two opposite qualities are combined. *–adj.* **4.** of or like a hermaphrodite. **5.** combining two opposite qualities. **6.** *Bot.* →**monoclinous.** [ME, from L *hermaphrodītus,* from Gk *hermaphróditos.* As proper name, son of Hermes and Aphrodite (Greek deities), who became united in body with the nymph Salmacis while bathing in her fountain] – **hermaphroditic** /hɜmæfrəˈdɪtɪk/, **hermaphroditical** /hɜmæfrəˈdɪtɪkəl/, *adj.* – **hermaphroditically** /hɜmæfrəˈdɪtɪkli/, *adv.*

hermaphrodite brig

**hermaphrodite brig** /– brɪg/, *n.* (formerly) a brigantine.

**hermaphroditism** /hɜˈmæfrədaɪˌtɪzəm/, *n.* the condition of a hermaphrodite.

**hermeneutic** /hɜməˈnjutɪk/, *adj.* interpretative; explanatory. Also, **hermeneutical.** [Gk *hermēneutikós* of interpreting] – **hermeneutically,** *adv.* – **hermeneutist,** *n.*

**hermeneutics** /hɜməˈnjutɪks/, *n.* **1.** the science of interpretation, esp. of the Scriptures. **2.** that branch of theology which treats of the principles of biblical exegesis.

**hermetic** /hɜˈmɛtɪk/, *adj.* **1.** made airtight by fusion or sealing. **2.** unaffected by external influences. **3.** pertaining to occult sciences. Also, **hermetical.** [ML *hermēticus,* from *Hermes* Trismegistus, said to have invented a seal to make vessels airtight]

**hermetically** /hɜˈmɛtɪkli/, *adv.* so as to be airtight: *hermetically sealed.*

**hermit** /ˈhɜmət/, *n.* **1.** one who has retired to a solitary place for a life of religious seclusion. **2.** any person living in seclusion. **3.** *Zool.* an animal of solitary habits. **4.** *Obs.* →**beadsman.** [ME *(h)ermite,* from OF, from LL *erēmīta,* from Gk *erēmítēs* a hermit, properly adj., of the desert] – **hermitic, hermitical,** *adj.* – **hermitically,** *adv.*

**hermitage** /ˈhɜmətɪdʒ/, *n.* **1.** the abode of a hermit. **2.** any secluded habitation. **3.** *(cap.)* a full-bodied wine produced in south-eastern France. **4.** a similar wine produced elsewhere.

**hermit crab** /ˈhɜmət kræb/, *n.* any of numerous decapod crustaceans of the families Paguridae and Coenobitidae, which protect their exposed soft parts by occupying the cast-off shell of a univalve mollusc.

hermit crab

**hermit sheep** /'– ʃip/, *n. N.Z.* a sheep that leaves the flock and wanders in inaccessible mountain country.

**hernia** /ˈhɜniə/, *n., pl.* **-nias.** the protrusion of an organ or tissue through an opening in its surrounding tissues, esp. in the abdominal region; a rupture. [ME, from L] – **hernial,** *adj.*

**herniate** /ˈhɜnieɪt/, *v.i.,* **-ated, -ating.** to protrude through an abnormal bodily opening. – **herniation** /hɜniˈeɪʃən/, *n.*

**herniorrhaphy** /hɜniˈɒrəfi/, *n., pl.* **-phies.** the surgical operation for repair of a hernia.

**hero** /ˈhɪəroʊ/, *n., pl.* **-roes. 1.** a man of distinguished courage or performance, admired for his noble qualities. **2.** one invested with heroic qualities in the opinion of others. **3.** the principal male character in a story, play, etc. **4.** (in early mythological antiquity) a being of godlike prowess and beneficence, esp. one who came to be honoured as a divinity. **5.** (in the Homeric period) a warrior chieftain of special strength, courage, or ability. **6.** (in later periods of antiquity) an immortal being, intermediate in nature between gods and men. [backformation from ME *heroës,* pl., from L, from Gk]

**heroic** /həˈroʊɪk/, *adj.* Also, **heroical. 1.** of or pertaining to heroes. **2.** suitable to the character of a hero; daring; noble. **3.** having or displaying the character or attributes of a hero; intrepid; determined: *a heroic explorer.* **4.** having or involving recourse to bold, daring, or extreme measures. **5.** dealing with or applicable to heroes, as in literature. **6.** of or pertaining to the heroes of antiquity: *the heroic age.* **7.** used in heroic poetry. See **heroic verse. 8.** resembling heroic poetry in language or style; magniloquent; grand. **9.** (of style or language) high-flown; heightened; extravagant. **10.** *Arts.* of a size larger than life and (usu.) less than colossal. *–n.* **11.** *(usu. pl.)* →**heroic verse. 12.** *(pl.)* extravagant language, behaviour, or sentiment. – **heroically,** *adv.* – **heroicalness, heroicness,** *n.*

**heroic age** /'– eɪdʒ/, *n.* a period of legendary heroic activity, as that of ancient Greece or Rome, when heroes were supposed to have lived, seeking glory in heroic response to the challenges of destiny and the gods.

**heroic couplet** /– ˈkʌplət/, *n.* a pair of rhyming iambic lines of ten syllables, used in heroic verse.

**heroic tenor** /'– tɛnə/, *n.* →**heldentenor.**

**heroic verse** /– ˈvɜs/, *n.* a form of verse adapted to the treatment of heroic or exalted themes; in classical poetry, the hexameter; in English, German, and Italian, the iambic of ten syllables; and in French, the Alexandrine (which see). The following is an example of English heroic verse:
*Achilles' wrath, to Greece the direful spring*
*Of woes unnumbered, heavenly goddess, sing!*

**heroin** /ˈhɛrəwən/, *n.* a derivative of morphine, $C_{21}H_{23}NO_5$, formerly used as a sedative, etc., and constituting a dangerous addictive drug; diamorphine. [Trademark (effect of drug is to make one feel like a 'hero'); G, from Gk *hḗrō(s)* HERO + *-in* -IN[2]]

**heroine** /ˈhɛrəwən/, *n.* **1.** a woman of heroic character; a female hero. **2.** the principal female character in a story, play, etc. [L, from Gk, from *hḗrōs* hero]

**heroism** /ˈhɛroʊɪzəm/, *n.* **1.** the qualities of a hero or heroine. **2.** heroic conduct; valour.

**heron** /ˈhɛrən/, *n.* any of the long-legged, long-necked, long-billed wading birds constituting the family Ardeidae, including the true herons, bitterns, egrets, etc., as the white-faced heron. [ME *heiroun,* from OF *hairon,* from Gmc; cf. OHG *heiger*]

heron

**heronry** /ˈhɛrənri/, *n., pl.* **-ries.** a place where a colony of herons breeds.

**hero-worship** /ˈhɪəroʊ-wɜʃɪp/, *n., v.,* **-shipped, -shipping** or *(U.S.)* **-shiped, -shiping.** *–n.* **1.** profound reverence for great men or their memory. **2.** the worship of deified heroes, as practised by the ancients. **3.** admiration or adulation for another person. *–v.t.* **4.** to feel reverence or adulation for. – **hero-worshipper,** *n.*

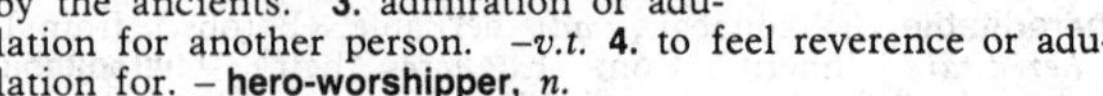

**herp.,** herpetology. Also, **herpet.**

**herpes** /ˈhɜpiz/, *n.* any of certain inflammatory infections of the skin or mucous membrane, characterised by clusters of vesicles which tend to spread. [L, from Gk: lit., a creeping] – **herpetic** /hɜˈpɛtɪk/, *adj.*

**herpes facialis** /– feɪʃiˈeɪləs/, *n.* a cold sore, esp. on the lips. Also, **herpes labialis** /– leɪbiˈeɪləs/. [L]

**herpes simplex** /– ˈsɪmplɛks/, *n.* **1.** →**cold sore. 2.** a similar form of herpes occurring on the genitals.

**herpes zoster** /– ˈzɒstə/, *n.* →**shingles.**

**herpet.,** herpetology.

**herpetology** /hɜpəˈtɒlədʒi/, *n.* the branch of zoology that treats of reptiles and amphibians. [Gk *herpetón* reptile + -o- + -LOGY] – **herpetological** /hɜpətəˈlɒdʒɪkəl/, *adj.* – **herpetologically** /hɜpətəˈlɒdʒəkli/, *adv.* – **herpetologist,** *n.*

**Herr** /hɛə/, *n., pl.* **Herren** /ˈhɛərən/. a conventional German title of respect for a man (equivalent to *Mr).*

**herrenvolk** /ˈhɛrənfɒlk/, *n.* →**master race.** [G]

**herring** /ˈhɛrɪŋ/, *n., pl.* **-rings,** *(esp. collectively)* **-ring. 1.** any of a number of marine and freshwater fishes belonging to various families as the ox-eye herring, freshwater herring, tommy ruff. **2.** any fish of the marine family Clupeidae, including *Clupea harengus,* an important food fish which occurs in enormous shoals in the North Sea and the North Atlantic. [ME *hering,* OE *hǣring,* c. G *Häring*]

herringbone

**herringbone** /ˈhɛrɪŋboʊn/, *n., adj., v.,* **-boned, -boning.** *–n.* **1.** a pattern consisting of adjoining rows of parallel lines so arranged that any two rows have the form of a V or inverted V; used in masonry, textiles, embroidery, etc. **2.** an embroidery stitch resembling cross-stitch. *–adj.* **3.** having or resembling herring-bone. *–v.t.* **4.** to make or pattern in herringbone. **5.** *Skiing.* to climb a steep slope step by step with the skis turned out to form a V and edged into the snow.

**herringbone bond** /'– bɒnd/, *n.* an ornamental form of brickwork peculiar to Anglo-Saxon architecture used to fill panels of half-timbering.

**herringbone dairy** /'– dɛəri/, *n.* a dairy so arranged that the cows stand obliquely on either side of a central passage for milking.

**herringbone gear** /'– gɪə/, *n.* a helical gear with V-shaped teeth, one half of each tooth forming part of a right-handed helix and the other half forming part of a left-handed helix. Also, **double helical gear.**

**herring cale** /hɛrɪŋ 'keɪl/, *n.* an elongate weed-dwelling fish, *Olisthops cyanomelas,* of Australian marine waters; rock whiting; stranger.

**herring gull** /'– gʌl/, *n.* a common large gull, *Larus argentatus,* with grey and white plumage and black wing tips.

**hers** /hɜz/, *pron.* **1.** (form of the possessive *her,* used predicatively or without a noun following): *the fault was hers.* **2.** the person(s) or thing(s) belonging to her: *herself and hers, a friend of hers.*

**herself** /hə'sɛlf/, *pron.* **1.** a reflexive form of *her: she cut herself.* **2.** an emphatic form of *her* or *she* used: **a.** as object: *she used it for herself.* **b.** in apposition to a subject or object: *she herself did it.* **3.** her proper or normal self; her normal state of mind (used after *be, become,* or *come to*): *she is herself again.*

**hertz** /hɜts/, *n.* the derived SI unit of frequency, defined as the frequency of a periodic phenomenon of which the periodic time is one second; one cycle per second. *Symbol:* Hz [named after H. R. *Hertz,* 1857-94, German physicist]

**Hertzian wave** /hɜtsiən 'weɪv/, *n.* an electromagnetic wave, artificially produced as a means of transmission in radiotelegraphy, and first fully investigated by Hertz. [See HERTZ]

**Hertzsprung-Russell diagram** /ˌhɜtsprʌŋ-ˌrʌsəl 'daɪəgræm/, *n.* a graph in which the absolute luminosity of a star is plotted against its spectral type (an indication of its temperature). The theory of stellar evolution has been derived from these diagrams. *Abbrev.:* H-R diagram [named after Ejnar *Hertzsprung,* 1873-1967, Danish astronomer, and Henry Norris *Russell,* 1877-1957, U.S. astronomer]

**he's** /hiz/, contraction of *he is* or *he has.*

**hesitancy** /'hɛzətənsi/, *n., pl.* **-cies.** hesitation; indecision. Also, **hesitance.** [L *haesitantia* stammering]

**hesitant** /'hɛzətənt/, *adj.* **1.** hesitating; undecided. **2.** lacking readiness of speech. – **hesitantly,** *adv.*

**hesitate** /'hɛzəteɪt/, *v.i.,* **-tated, -tating. 1.** to hold back in doubt or indecision: *to hesitate to believe.* **2.** to have scrupulous doubts; be unwilling. **3.** to pause. **4.** to falter in speech; stammer. [L *haesitātus,* pp., stuck fast] – **hesitator,** *n.* – **hesitatingly,** *adv.*

**hesitation** /'hɛzəteɪʃən/, *n.* **1.** the act of hesitating; a delay from uncertainty of mind: *to be lost by hesitation.* **2.** a state of doubt. **3.** a halting or faltering in speech.

**hesitative** /'hɛzəteɪtɪv/, *adj.* characterised by hesitation; hesitating. – **hesitatively,** *adv.*

**Hesperian** /hɛs'pɪəriən/, *adj.* **1.** western, applied to Italy in ancient Greek contexts, and to Spain in Roman contexts. **2.** of or pertaining to the Hesperides. [L *Hesperius* (from Gk *hespérios* at evening, western) + -AN]

**hesperidin** /hɛs'pɛrədən/, *n.* a crystallisable glucoside found in the spongy envelope of oranges and lemons. [Gk *Hesperides,* a class of plants including the orange + -IN[2]]

**hesperidium** /hɛspə'rɪdiəm/, *n., pl.* **-peridia** /-pə'rɪdiə/. the fruit of a citrus plant, as an orange.

**Hesperus** /'hɛsprəs/, *n.* →**vesper** (def. 2).

**hessian** /'hɛʃən/, *n.* a strong fabric made from jute, used for sacks, carpet backing, etc. Also, *U.S.,* **burlap.**

**Hessian fly** /hɛʃən 'flaɪ/, *n.* a small dipterous insect, *Mayetiola destructor,* whose larva is one of the most destructive pests of wheat.

**hessonite** /'hɛsənaɪt/, *n.* a yellowish or brownish variety of garnet, sometimes used in jewellery. Also, **essonite.** [Gk *hḗssōn* less, inferior + -ITE[1]]

**Hess's law** /'hɛsəz lɔ/, *n.* the law which states that if a chemical reaction occurs in stages, the sum of the heat evolved in each state is equal to the total heat evolved when the reaction occurs directly. [named after G. H. *Hess,* 1806-50, Russian chemist]

**hest** /hɛst/, *n. Archaic.* →**behest.** [ME *hest(e),* OE *hǣs,* akin to *hātan* bid]

**hetaera** /hə'tɪərə/, *n., pl.* **-taerae** /-'tɪəri/. a female paramour, or concubine, esp. in ancient Greece. [Gk *hetaíra,* fem. of *hetaîros* companion]

**hetaerism** /hə'tɪərɪzəm/, *n.* female companionship outside marriage, of both a sexual and intellectual nature. Also, **hetairism.** – **hetaerist,** *n.* – **hetaeristic** /hɛtɪə'rɪstɪk/, *adj.* – **hetaeristically** /hɛtɪə'rɪstɪkli/, *adv.*

**hetaira** /hə'taɪərə/, *n., pl.* **-tairai** /-'taɪəraɪ/. →**hetaera.**

**hetero** /'hɛtəroʊ/, *adj., n. Colloq.* →**heterosexual.**

**hetero-,** a word element meaning 'other' or 'different', as in *heterocercal.* Also, before vowels, **heter-.** [Gk, combining form of *héteros*]

**heteroatomic molecule** /ˌhɛtəroʊəˌtɒmɪk 'mɒləkjul/, *n.* a molecule which has more than one type of atom.

**heterocercal** /hɛtəroʊ'sɜkəl/, *adj.* **1.** having an unequally divided tail or caudal fin, the backbone running into a much larger upper lobe, as in sharks. **2.** denoting such a tail or caudal fin (cf. *homocercal*). [HETERO- + Gk *kérkos* tail + -AL[1]]

heterocercal tail

**heterochromatic** /ˌhɛtəroʊkroʊ'mætɪk/, *adj.* **1.** of, having, or pertaining to more than one colour. **2.** having a pattern of mixed colours.

**heterochromatin** /hɛtəroʊ'kroʊmətən/, *n.* chromatin which remains compact during mitosis. Sex chromosomes may consist entirely of heterochromatin.

**heterochromous** /hɛtəroʊ'kroʊməs/, *adj.* of different colours. [Gk *heteróchrōmos*]

**heteroclite** /'hɛtəroʊklaɪt/, *adj.* **1.** exceptional or anomalous. **2.** *Gram.* irregular in inflection. *–n.* **3.** a person or thing that deviates from the ordinary rule or form. **4.** *Gram.* a heteroclite word. [F, from LL *heteroclitus,* from Gk *heteróklitos* irregularly inflected]

**heterocyclic** /hɛtəroʊ'saɪklɪk, -'sɪklɪk/, *adj.* **1.** *Chem.* referring to organic chemistry as dealing with ring compounds with both carbon atoms and atoms of other elements in the ring. **2.** *Chem.* denoting such compounds. **3.** *Bot.* having different numbers of parts in different whorls.

**heterodox** /'hɛtərədɒks, 'hɛtrə-/, *adj.* **1.** not in accordance with established or accepted doctrines or opinions, esp. in theology. **2.** holding unorthodox doctrines or opinions. [Gk *heteródoxos* of another opinion]

**heterodoxy** /'hɛtərədɒksi, 'hɛtrə-/, *n., pl.* **-doxies. 1.** heterodox state or quality. **2.** a heterodox opinion, etc.

**heterodyne** /'hɛtərədaɪn, 'hɛtrə-/, *adj., n., v.,* **-dyned, -dyning.** *–adj.* **1.** denoting or pertaining to a method of receiving continuous-wave radiotelegraph signals by impressing upon the continuous radiofrequency oscillations another set of radiofrequency oscillations of a slightly different frequency, the interference resulting in fluctuations or beats of audio frequency. *–n.* **2.** a heterodyne method. *–v.i.* **3.** to produce a heterodyne effect.

**heteroecious** /hɛtə'riʃəs/, *adj.* pertaining to or characterised by heteroecism. [HETER(O)- + Gk *oikía* house + -OUS]

**heteroecism** /hɛtə'risɪzəm/, *n.* the development of different stages of a parasitic species on different host plants, as in fungi.

**heterogamete** /hɛtəroʊ'gæmit/, *n.* a gamete of different character from one of the opposite sex (opposed to *isogamete*).

**heterogamous** /hɛtə'rɒgəməs/, *adj.* **1.** *Biol.* having unlike gametes, or reproducing by the union of such gametes (opposed to *isogamous*). **2.** *Bot.* having flowers or florets of two sexually different kinds (opposed to *homogamous*).

**heterogamy** /hɛtə'rɒgəmi/, *n.* a heterogamous state.

**heterogeneity** /ˌhɛtəroʊdʒə'niəti/, *n., pl.* **-ties.** the character or state of being heterogeneous; composition from dissimilar parts; disparateness.

**heterogeneous** /hɛtəroʊ'dʒiniəs/, *adj.* **1.** different in kind; unlike; incongruous. **2.** composed of parts of different kinds; having widely unlike elements or constituents; not homogeneous. [ML *heterogeneus,* from Gk *heterogenḗs* of different kinds] – **heterogeneously,** *adv.* – **heterogeneousness,** *n.*

**heterogenous** /hɛtə'rɒdʒənəs/, *adj.* having its source outside the organism; having a foreign origin.

**heterogonous** /hɛtə'rɒgənəs/, *adj.* **1.** *Bot.* noting or pertaining to monoclinous flowers of two or more kinds occurring on different individuals of the same species, the kinds differing in the relative length of stamens and pistils (opposed to *homogonous*). **2.** *Zool.* →**heterogynous.**

**heterogony** /hɛtə'rɒgəni/, *n.* **1.** the alternation of dioecious and hermaphrodite individuals in successive generations, as in certain nematodes. **2.** (in more recent usage) the alternation of parthenogenetic and sexual generations.

**heterograft** /'hɛtəroʊgraft/, *n.* the grafting of skin, tissue, etc., from an individual of one species to an individual of another species.

**heterogynous** /hɛtə'rɒdʒənəs/, *adj.* having females of two different kinds, one sexual and the other abortive or neuter, as ants.

**heterologous** /hɛtə'rɒləgəs/, *adj.* **1.** having a different relation; not corresponding. **2.** *Pathol.* consisting of tissue unlike the normal tissue, as a tumour.

**heterology** /hɛtə'rɒlədʒi/, *n.* **1.** *Biol.* the lack of correspondence of organic structures as the result of unlike origins of constituent parts. **2.** *Pathol.* abnormality; structural difference from a type or normal standard.

**heterolysis** /hɛtə'rɒləsəs/, *n.* dissolution of the cells of one organism by the enzymes of another.

**heteromerous** /hɛtə'rɒmərəs/, *adj.* having or consisting of parts which differ in quality, number of elements, or the like: *a heteromerous flower.*

**heteromorphic** /hɛtəroʊ'mɔfɪk/, *adj.* **1.** *Biol.* dissimilar in shape, structure, or magnitude. **2.** *Entomol.* undergoing complete metamorphosis; possessing varying forms. Also, **heteromorphous.** – **heteromorphism, heteromorphy,** *n.*

**heteronomous** /hɛtə'rɒnəməs/, *adj.* **1.** subject to or involving different laws. **2.** pertaining to, or characterised by, heteronomy. **3.** *Biol.* characterising an organism which is metameric, or segmented, most or all of whose segments are specialised in different ways. [HETERO- + Gk *nómos* law + -OUS]

**heteronomy** /hɛtə'rɒnəmi/, *n.* condition of being under the rule of another (opposed to *autonomy*).

**heteronym** /'hɛtərənɪm/, *n.* a word having a different sound and meaning from another, but the same spelling, as *lead* (to conduct) and *lead* (a metal).

**heteronymous** /hɛtə'rɒnəməs/, *adj.* **1.** pertaining to or of the nature of a heteronym. **2.** having different names, as a pair of correlatives. **3.** *Optics.* denoting or pertaining to the images formed in a kind of double vision in which the image seen by the right eye is on the left side, and vice versa. [Gk *heterṓnymos* having a different name]

**heterophony** /hɛtə'rɒfəni/, *n.* the simultaneous rendition in music of different variations of the one melodic structure.

**heterophyllous** /hɛtəroʊ'fɪləs/, *adj.* having different kinds of leaves on the same plant. [HETERO- + Gk *phýllon* leaf + -OUS] – **heterophylly** /'hɛtəroʊˌfɪli/, *n.*

**heteroplasty** /'hɛtəroʊˌplæsti/, *n.* the surgical repair of lesions with tissue from another individual, either of the same or of another species. – **heteroplastic** /hɛtəroʊ'plæstɪk/, *adj.*

**heteropterous** /hɛtə'rɒptərəs/, *adj.* of or pertaining to the true bugs of the suborder Heteroptera which have forewings thickened at the base and membranous at the apex. [NL *Heteroptera,* class name (from *hetero-* HETERO- + Gk *pterá* wings) + -OUS]

**heterorganic** /hɛtərɔ'gænɪk/, *adj. Phonet.* articulated at a different point in the oral cavity, as /t/ and /k/.

**heterosexual** /hɛtəroʊ'sɛkʃuəl/, *adj.* **1.** *Biol.* pertaining to the other sex or to both sexes. **2.** exhibiting or pertaining to heterosexuality. *–n.* **3.** a heterosexual person.

**heterosexuality** /hɛtəroʊˌsɛkʃu'æləti/, *n.* sexual feeling for a person (or persons) of opposite sex.

**heterosis** /hɛtə'roʊsəs/, *n.* the increase in growth, size, fecundity, function, yield, or other characters in hybrids over those of the parents. [LGk: alteration]

**heterosporous** /hɛtə'rɒspərəs, -roʊ'spɔrəs/, *adj.* having more than one kind of spore.

**heterospory** /hɛtə'rɒspəri/, *n.* the production in plants of both microspores and megaspores.

**heterotaxis** /hɛtəroʊ'tæksəs/, *n.* abnormal or irregular arrangement, as of parts of the body, geological strata, etc. (opposed to *homotaxis*). Also, **heterotaxy.** – **heterotaxic, heterotactic,** *adj.*

**heterothallic** /hɛtəroʊ'θælɪk/, *adj.* (of plants) having mycelia of two unlike types both of which must participate in the sexual process (opposed to *homothallic*). [HETERO- + Gk *thallós* shoot, sprout + -IC] – **heterothallism,** *n.*

**heterotopia** /hɛtəroʊ'toʊpiə/, *n.* **1.** misplacement or displacement, as of an organ. **2.** the formation of tissue in a part where it is abnormal. Also, **heterotopy** /hɛtə'rɒtəpi/. [NL, from Gk *hetero-* HETERO- + *-topia* (from *tópos* place)] – **heterotopic** /hɛtəroʊ'tɒpɪk/, **heterotopous** /hɛtə'rɒtəpəs/, *adj.*

**heterotransplant** /hɛtəroʊ'trænsplænt/, *n.* the surgical transfer of an organ from an individual of one species to an individual of another species.

**heterotrophic** /hɛtəroʊ'trɒfɪk/, *adj.* incapable of synthesising proteins and carbohydrates, as animals and dependent plants (opposed to *autotrophic*).

**heterotypic** /hɛtəroʊ'tɪpɪk/, *adj.* applying meiotic division which reduces the chromosome number during the development of the reproductive cells. Also, **heterotypical.**

**heterozygote** /hɛtəroʊ'zaɪgoʊt/, *n.* a hybrid containing genes for two unlike characteristics; an organism which will not breed true to type. – **heterozygous** /hɛtəroʊ'zaɪgəs/, *adj.*

**hetman** /'hɛtmən/, *n., pl.* **-mans.** a Cossack chief; ataman. [Pol., from G *Hauptmann* captain]

**het-up** /'hɛt-ʌp/, *adj. Colloq.* anxious; worried. Also, **het up.** [alteration of *heated-up*]

**heulandite** /'hjuləndaɪt/, *n.* a mineral of the zeolite group, hydrous calcium aluminium silicate, $CaAl_2 \cdot Si_7O_{18} \cdot 6H_2O$, which occurs as monoclinic crystals in igneous rocks. [named after Henry *Heuland,* 19thC English mineralogist; see -ITE[1]]

**heurism** /'hjurɪzəm/, *n.* the heuristic method or principle in teaching. – **heurist,** *n.*

**heuristic** /hju'rɪstɪk/, *adj.* **1.** serving to find out; furthering investigation. **2.** (of a teaching method) encouraging the student to discover for himself. **3.** *Maths.* (of a method of solving problems) one for which no algorithm exists and which therefore depends on inductive reasoning from past experience of similar problems. [apparently b. Gk *heurís(kein)* find + obs. *(heure)tic* inventive (from Gk *heuretikós*)] – **heuristically,** *adv.*

**hew** /hju/, *v.,* **hewed, hewed** or **hewn, hewing.** *–v.t.* **1.** to strike forcibly with an axe, sword, or the like; chop; hack. **2.** to make or shape with cutting blows: *to hew a passage.* **3.** to sever (a part) from a whole by means of cutting leaves (fol. by *away, off, out, from,* etc.). **4.** to cut down; fell: *to hew down trees.* *–v.i.* **5.** to deal cutting blows; to cut. [ME *hewe(n),* OE *hēawan,* c. G *hauen*] – **hewer,** *n.*

**hex** /hɛks/, *n.* **1.** an evil spell or charm. **2.** an evil, dominating influence over someone or something. **3.** a person who exerts such an influence. *–v.t.* **4.** to curse; practise witchcraft on. **5.** to wish or bring misfortune, as if by an evil spell. [G *Hexe* witch. See HAG]

**hexa-,** a prefix meaning 'six', as in *hexagon.* Also, before vowels **hex-.** [Gk, combining form of *héx*]

**hexachlorophane** /hɛksə'klɔrəfeɪn/, *n.* →**hexachlorophene.**

**hexachlorophene** /hɛksə'klɔrəfin/, *n.* an antiseptic agent, $C_{13}H_6Cl_6O_2$, often used as an ingredient in soaps and creams intended to sterilise the skin. Also, **hexachlorophane.**

**hexachord** /'hɛksəkɔd/, *n.* a diatonic series of six degrees, having (in medieval music) a semitone between the third and fourth notes and whole tones between the others. [LGk *hexáchordos*]

**hexad** /'hɛksæd/, *n.* **1.** the number six. **2.** a group or series of six. [LL *hexas,* from Gk: the number six] – **hexadic** /hɛk'sædɪk/, *adj.*

**hexadecane** /ˈhɛksədəkeɪn, hɛksəˈdɛkeɪn/, *n.* →**cetane.**

**hexadecimal** /hɛksəˈdɛsəməl/, *adj.* pertaining to a number system used in computing having 16 as its base.

**hexagon** /ˈhɛksəgɒn, -gən/, *n.* a polygon having six angles and six sides.

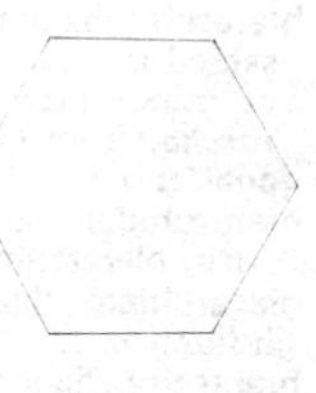
hexagon

**hexagonal** /hɛkˈsægənəl/, *adj.* **1.** of, pertaining to, or having the form of a hexagon. **2.** having a hexagon as a base or cross-section. **3.** divided into hexagons, as a surface. **4.** *Crystall.* denoting or pertaining to the hexagonal system. – **hexagonally,** *adv.*

**hexagonal system** /ˈ– sɪstəm/, *n.* a system of crystallisation characterised by three equal lateral axes intersecting at angles of 60° and a vertical axis of hexagonal symmetry and of different length at right angles to them.

**hexagram** /ˈhɛksəgræm/, *n.* **1.** a six-pointed starlike figure formed of two equilateral triangles placed concentrically with their sides parallel, and on opposite sides of the centre. **2.** *Geom.* a figure of six lines.

hexagram

**hexahedron** /hɛksəˈhidrən/, *n., pl.* **-drons, -dra** /-drə/. a solid figure having six faces. – **hexahedral,** *adj.*

**hexamerous** /hɛkˈsæmərəs/, *adj.* **1.** consisting of or divided into six parts. **2.** *Zool.* having a radially symmetrical arrangement of organs in six groups.

**hexameter** /hɛkˈsæmətə/, *n.* **1.** the dactylic verse of six feet, of Greek and Latin epic and other poetry (**dactylic hexameter**), in which the first four feet are dactyls or spondees, the fifth is ordinarily a dactyl, and the last is a trochee or spondee with a caesura usu. following the long syllable in the third foot. **2.** any hexameter verse. *–adj.* **3.** consisting of six metrical feet. [L, from Gk *hexámetros* of six measures] – **hexametric** /hɛksəˈmɛtrɪk/, **hexametrical** /hɛksəˈmɛtrɪkəl/, *adj.*

**hexamethylenetetramine** /hɛksəˌmɛθəlinˈtɛtrəmin/, *n.* a colourless crystalline compound, $(CH_2)_6N_4$, used as a urinary antiseptic, an accelerator, an absorbent in gasmasks, and in the manufacture of sythetic resins. Also, **hexamethylenetetramin** /-ˈtɛtrəmən/.

**hexamine** /ˈhɛksəmin, hɛkˈsæmin/, *n.* →**hexamethylenetetramine.** [Trademark]

**hexamitiasis** /hɛksəməˈtaɪəsəs/, *n.* infectious catarrhal enteritis, a highly infectious disease of turkeys.

**hexane** /ˈhɛkseɪn/, *n.* any of the five isomeric saturated hydrocarbons, $C_6H_{14}$, derived from the fractional distillation of petroleum. [Gk *héx* six (with reference to the atoms of carbon) + -ANE]

**hexangular** /hɛkˈsæŋgjələ/, *adj.* having six angles.

**hexapod** /ˈhɛksəpɒd/, *n.* **1.** one of the Hexapoda; insect. *–adj.* **2.** having six feet. [Gk *hexápous* six-footed] – **hexapodous** /hɛkˈsæpədəs/, *adj.*

**hexapody** /hɛkˈsæpədi/, *n., pl.* **-dies.** a line or verse consisting of six metrical feet.

**hexarchy** /ˈhɛksaki/, *n., pl.* **-chies.** a group of six states or kingdoms, each under its own ruler.

**hexastich** /ˈhɛksəstɪk/, *n.* a strophe, stanza, or poem consisting of six lines or verses. Also, **hexastichon** /hɛksˈæstəkɒn/. [Gk *hexástichos* of six rows or lines]

**hexatone** /ˈhɛksətoʊn/, *n.* a gapped scale containing only six notes in an octave.

**hexavalent** /hɛkˈsævələnt, hɛksəˈveɪlənt/, *adj.* having a valency of six; sexivalent; sexavalent.

**Hexham grey** /hɛksəm ˈgreɪ/, *n.* an especially large and voracious variety of mosquito found in the locality of Hexham in New South Wales.

**Hexham scent** /– ˈsɛnt/, *n.* a fragrant yellow-flowered herbaceous plant, *Melilotus indica;* King Island melilot.

**hexode** /ˈhɛksoʊd/, *n.* a six element vacuum tube.

**hexogen** /ˈhɛksədʒən/, *n.* →**cyclonite.**

**hexone** /ˈhɛksoʊn/, *n.* any of various organic ketones which contain six atoms of carbon in the molecule. [Gk *héx* six + -ONE, after G *Hexon*]

**hexosan** /ˈhɛksəsæn, -sən/, *n.* any of a group of hemicelluloses which hydrolyse to hexoses. [HEXOS(E) + -AN]

**hexose** /ˈhɛksoʊz, -oʊs/, *n.* any of a class of sugars containing six atoms of carbon, as glucose and fructose.

**hexyl** /ˈhɛksəl/, *n.* the univalent radical, $C_6H_{13}$, derived from hexane.

**hexylresorcinol** /hɛksəlrəˈzɔsənɒl/, *n.* a colourless, crystalline antiseptic, $C_{12}H_{18}O_2$, which is less toxic and more powerful than phenol.

**hey**[1] /heɪ/, *interj.* (an exclamation used to call attention, give encouragement, etc.) Also, **heigh, ha.**

**hey**[2] /heɪ/, *n.* →**hay**[2].

**heyday** /ˈheɪdeɪ/, *n.* **1.** the stage or period of highest vigour or fullest strength. **2.** high spirits. *–interj.* **3.** *Archaic.* (an exclamation of cheerfulness, surprise, wonder, etc.) [alteration of HIGH DAY]

**hey-diddle-diddle**[1] /ˌheɪ-dɪdl-ˈdɪdl/, *n. Colloq.* **1.** the middle. **2. through the hey-diddle-diddle,** *Football, etc.,* between the goalposts; a goal. [rhyming slang]

**hey-diddle-diddle**[2] /ˌheɪ-dɪdl-ˈdɪdl/, *n. Colloq.* a piddle, urination. [rhyming slang]

**hey-presto** /heɪ-ˈprɛstoʊ/, *interj.* (an exclamation of triumph, etc., on the completion of a conjuring trick, feat, etc.)

**h.f.,** (*sometimes cap.*) *Elect.* high frequency.

**Hf,** *Chem.* hafnium.

**Hg,** *Chem.* mercury. [L *hydrargyrus,* from Gk]

**HG,** High German.

**H.H.,** **1.** His, or Her, Highness. **2.** His Holiness.

**hi** /haɪ/, *interj.* (an exclamation, esp. of greeting.)

**hiatus** /haɪˈeɪtəs/, *n., pl.* **-tuses, -tus. 1.** a break, with a part missing; an interruption; lacuna: *a hiatus in a manuscript.* **2.** a gap or opening. **3.** *Gram., Pros.* a break or slight pause due to the coming together without contraction of two vowels in successive words or syllables. **4.** *Anat.* a natural fissure, cleft, or foramen in a bone or other structure. [L: gap] – **hiatal** /haɪˈeɪtl/, *adj.*

**hiatus hernia** /– ˈhɜniə/, *n.* herniation of a part of the stomach through the oesophageal hiatus, often causing heartburn.

**hibachi** /hɪˈbatʃi/, *n.* a portable brazier on which foods are barbecued, consisting of a heavy wire grill over a pot-shaped container for burning charcoal. [Jap.]

hibachi

**hibbertia** /hɪˈbɜʃə/, *n.* any plant of the Australian genus *Hibbertia.* See **guinea flower.**

**hibernaculum** /haɪbəˈnækjələm/, *n., pl.* **-la** /-lə/. **1.** a protective case or covering for winter, as of an animal or a plant bud. **2.** Also, **hibernacle** /ˈhaɪbənækəl/. winter quarters, as of a hibernating animal. [L: winter residence]

**hibernal** /haɪˈbɜnəl/, *adj.* of or pertaining to winter; wintry. [LL *hībernālis* wintry]

**hibernate** /ˈhaɪbəneɪt/, *v.i.,* **-nated, -nating. 1.** to spend the winter in close quarters in a dormant condition, as certain animals. **2.** to withdraw into or remain in seclusion. [L *hībernātus,* pp., wintered] – **hibernation** /haɪbəˈneɪʃən/, *n.*

**Hibernia** /haɪˈbɜniə/, *n.* Latin or literary name of **Ireland.**

**Hibernian** /haɪˈbɜniən/, *adj.* **1.** Irish. *–n.* **2.** a native of Ireland. [L *Hibernia* Ireland + -AN]

**Hibernicise** /haɪˈbɜnəsaɪz/, *v.t.,* **-cised, -cising.** to make Irish in form or character. Also, **Hibernicize.**

**Hibernicism** /haɪˈbɜnəsɪzəm/, *n.* **1.** an idiom peculiar to Irish English. **2.** an Irish characteristic. Also, **Hibernianism** /haɪˈbɜniəˌnɪzəm/.

**hibiscus** /haɪˈbɪskəs/, *n.* any of the herbs, shrubs or trees belonging to the genus *Hibiscus,* esp. *H. rosa-sinensis,* with broad, showy, short-lived flowers. [L, from Gk *hibískos* mallow]

**hiccup** /ˈhɪkʌp/, *n.* **1.** a quick, involuntary inspiration suddenly checked by closure of the glottis, producing a characteristic sound. **2.** (*usu. pl.*) the condition of having such spasms: *to have the hiccups.* *–v.i.* **3.** to make the sound of a hiccup. **4.** to have the hiccups. Also, **hiccough** /ˈhɪkʌp/. [earlier *hickock,* from *hick* (imitative) + -OCK. Cf. LG *hick* hiccup]

**hick**[1] /hɪk/, *Colloq.* *–n.* **1.** an unsophisticated person. **2.** a farmer. *–adj.* **3.** pertaining to or characteristic of hicks. [familiar form of *Richard,* man's name]

**hick**[2] /hɪk/, *n. Orig. U.S. Colloq.* a pimple. Also, **hickey.** [orig. unknown]

**hickory** /'hɪkəri/, *n., pl.* **-ries. 1.** any of the North American trees of the genus *Carya,* certain of which, as the pecan, *C. illinoensis* (*C. pecan*), bear sweet, edible nuts (hickory nuts), and others, as the shagbark, *C. ovata,* yield valuable hard wood and edible nuts. **2.** the wood of such a tree. **3.** a switch, stick, etc. of this wood. **4.** any of many other trees with tough, resilient timbers, as *Acacia implexa* and *Flindersia ifflaiana.* [Amer. Ind. Cf. Algonquian *pawcohiccoro* walnut kernel mush]

**hickory nut** /'– nʌt/, *n.* a nut, usu. sweet and edible, from certain of the hickory trees.

**hid** /hɪd/, *v.* past tense and past participle of **hide**[1].

**hidalgo** /hɪ'dælgoʊ/, *n., pl.* **-gos** /-goʊz/. (in Spain) a man of the lower nobility. [Sp., contraction of *hijo de algo* son of (man of) property]

**hidden** /'hɪdn/, *adj.* **1.** concealed; obscure; latent. *–v.* **2.** past participle of **hide**[1].

**hidden hand** /– 'hænd/, *n.* a secret or occult influence, esp. of a malevolent nature.

**hiddenite** /'hɪdənaɪt/, *n.* a rare, transparent emerald green or yellowish green variety of spodumene, a valuable gem. [discovered by W. E. *Hidden,* 1853-1918, U.S. mineralogist. See -ITE[1]]

**hide**[1] /haɪd/, *v.,* **hid, hidden** or **hid, hiding.** *–v.t.* **1.** to conceal from sight; prevent from being seen or discovered. **2.** to obstruct the view of; cover up: *the sun was hidden by clouds.* **3.** to conceal from knowledge; keep secret: *to hide one's feelings.* **4. hide one's head,** *Colloq.* to be ashamed. *–v.i.* **5.** to conceal oneself; lie concealed. *–n.* **6.** a covered place to hide in while shooting or observing wildlife. [ME *hide(n),* OE *hȳdan,* c. MLG *hüden*] **– hider,** *n.*

**hide**[2] /haɪd/, *n., v.,* **hided, hiding.** *–n.* **1.** the skin of an animal, esp. one of the larger animals, raw or dressed: *the hide of a calf.* **2.** *Colloq.* the human skin. **3.** *Colloq.* impudence: *he's got a hide!* **4. a thick hide,** *Colloq.* insensitivity to criticism. **5. hide nor hair,** not a vestige; no clue. **6. no hide no Christmas box,** *Colloq.* no reward is to be had without impudent initiative. *–v.t.* **7.** *Obs.* to flog or thrash. [ME; OE *hȳd,* c. G *Haut*]

**hide**[3] /haɪd/, *n.* an old English measure of land, usu. 120 acres or approx. 486 square kilometres, considered adequate for one free family and its dependants. [ME; OE *hīd(e), hīg(i)d,* from *hīg(an)* family, household + *-id,* suffix of appurtenance]

**hide-and-seek** /haɪd-n-'sik/, *n.* a children's game in which some hide and others seek them.

**hideaway** /'haɪdəweɪ/, *n. Colloq.* a place of concealment; a refuge.

**hidebound** /'haɪdbaʊnd/, *adj.* **1.** narrow and rigid in opinion: *a hidebound pedant.* **2.** (of a horse, etc.) having the back and ribs bound tightly by the hide. [HIDE[2] + BOUND[1]]

**hideous** /'hɪdiəs/, *adj.* **1.** horrible or frightful to the senses; very ugly: *a hideous monster.* **2.** shocking or revolting to the moral sense: *a hideous crime.* [ME *hidous,* from AF, from *hi(s)de* horror, fear; orig. uncert.] **– hideously,** *adv.* **– hideousness,** *n.*

**hide-out** /'haɪd-aʊt/, *n.* a safe retreat for those who are being pursued, esp. by the law; a hiding-place; refuge.

**hi-diddle-diddle**[1] /ˌhaɪ-dɪdl-'dɪdl/, *n.* →**hey-diddle-diddle**[1].

**hi-diddle-diddle**[2] /ˌhaɪ-dɪdl-'dɪdl/, *n.* →**hey-diddle-diddle**[2].

**hiding** /'haɪdɪŋ/, *n.* **1.** the act of concealing; concealment: *to remain in hiding.* **2.** a place or means of concealment. **3.** (*pl.*) →**hide-and-seek.** [HIDE[1] + -ING[1]]

**hiding**[2] /'haɪdɪŋ/, *n.* **1.** a beating. **2.** a defeat. [HIDE[2] + -ING[1]]

**hidrosis** /hə'droʊsəs/, *n. Pathol.* **1.** excessive perspiration due to drugs, disease. **2.** any of certain diseases characterised by sweating. [NL, special use of Gk *hídrōsis* perspiration] **– hidrotic** /hə'drɒtɪk/, *adj.*

**hidy-hole** /'haɪdi-hoʊl/, *n.* a hiding place. Also, **hidey hole.**

**hie** /haɪ/, *v.i.,* **hied, hieing.** to hasten; speed; go in haste. [ME; OE *hīgian* strive. Cf. D *hijgen* pant]

**hielamon** /'hiləmən/, *n.* a shield made of bark or wood. Also, **hieleman.** [Aboriginal]

**hier-,** variant of **hiero-** before a vowel, as in *hierarchy.*

**hierarch** /'haɪərak/, *n.* **1.** one who rules or has authority in sacred things. **2.** a chief priest. **3.** one of a body of officials or minor priests in some ancient Greek temples. [ML *hierarcha,* from Gk *hierárchēs* steward of sacred rites] **– hierarchal,** *adj.*

**hierarchical** /haɪə'rakɪkəl/, *adj.* of or belonging to a hierarchy. Also, **hierarchic. – hierarchically,** *adv.*

**hierarchism** /'haɪərakɪzəm/, *n.* hierarchical principles, rule, or influence.

**hierarchy** /'haɪəraki/, *n., pl.* **-chies. 1.** any system of persons or things in a graded order, etc. **2.** *Science.* a series of successive terms of different rank. The terms *phylum, class, order, family, genus,* and *species* constitute a hierarchy in zoology. **3.** government by ecclesiastical rulers. **4.** the power or dominion of a hierarch. **5.** an organised body of ecclesiastical officials in successive ranks or orders: *the Roman Catholic hierarchy.* **6.** one of the three divisions of the angels, each made up of three orders, conceived as constituting a graded body. **7.** the collective body of angels (**celestial hierarchy**).

**hieratic** /haɪə'rætɪk/, *adj.* **1.** pertaining to priests or to the priesthood; priestly. **2.** denoting or pertaining to a form of ancient Egyptian writing consisting of abridged forms of hieroglyphics, used by the priests in their records. **3.** denoting or pertaining to certain styles in art whose types or methods are fixed by or as by religious tradition. *–n.* **4.** ancient Egyptian hieratic writing. Also, **hieratical.** [L *hierāticus,* from Gk *hierātikós* priestly, sacerdotal] **– hieratically,** *adv.*

**hiero-,** a word element meaning 'sacred', as in *hierocracy.* Also, before a vowel, **hier-.** [Gk, combining form of *hierós* holy]

**hierocracy** /haɪə'rɒkrəsi/, *n., pl.* **-cies.** rule or government by priests or ecclesiastics. **– hierocrat** /'haɪərəkræt/, *n.* **– hierocratic** /haɪərə'krætɪk/, *adj.*

**hierodule** /'haɪərədjul/, *n.* a slave in an ancient Greek temple, dedicated to the service of a deity. [Gk *hieródoulos* temple slave] **– hierodulic** /haɪərə'djulɪk/, *adj.*

**hieroglyphic** /haɪərə'glɪfɪk/, *adj.,*Also,,**hieroglyphical. 1.** designating or pertaining to a writing system, particularly that of the ancient Egyptians, in which many of the symbols are conventionalised pictures of the thing named by the words for which the symbols stand. **2.** inscribed with hieroglyphic symbols. **3.** hard to decipher; hard to read. *–n.* **4.** Also, **hieroglyph** /'haɪərəglɪf/. a hieroglyphic symbol. **5.** (*usu. pl.*) hieroglyphic writing. **6.** a figure or symbol with a hidden meaning. **7.** (*pl.*) writing difficult to decipher. [LL *hieroglyphicus,* from Gk *hieroglyphikós*] **– hieroglyphically,** *adv.*

hieroglyphics

**hieroglyphist** /haɪərə'glɪfəst, haɪə'rɒgləfəst/, *n.* **1.** a student of hieroglyphics. **2.** a writer of hieroglyphics.

**hierogram** /'haɪərəgræm/, *n.* a sacred, esp. hieroglyphic, symbol.

**hierogrammat** /haɪərə'græmət/, *n.* a writer of sacred records, esp. in hieroglyphics. Also, **hierogrammate. – hierogrammatic** /haɪərəgrə'mætɪk/, **hierogrammatical** /haɪərəgrə'mætɪkəl/, *adj.* **– hierogrammatist,** *n.*

**hierolatry** /haɪə'rɒlətri/, *n.* →**hagiolatry. – hierolater,** *n.* **– hierolatrous,** *adj.*

**hierology** /haɪə'rɒlədʒi/, *n.* literature or learning regarding sacred things. **– hierologic** /haɪərə'lɒdʒɪk/, **hierological** /haɪərə'lɒdʒɪkəl/, *adj.* **– hierologically** /haɪərə'lɒdʒɪkli/, *adv.* **– hierologist,** *n.*

**hierophant** /'haɪərəfænt/, *n.* **1.** (in ancient Greece, etc.) an official expounder of rites of worship and sacrifice. **2.** any interpreter of sacred mysteries or esoteric principles. [LL *hierophantēs,* from Gk] **– hierophantic** /haɪərə'fæntɪk/, *adj.* **– hierophantically** /haɪərə'fæntɪkli/, *adv.*

**hifalutin** /haɪfə'lutn/, *adj. Colloq.* →**highfalutin.**

**hi-fi** /'haɪ-faɪ/, *adj.* **1.** →**high-fidelity.** *–n.* **2.** a high-fidelity record-player, etc.

**hi-fi system** /'haɪ-faɪ ˌsɪstəm/, *n.* a high-quality audio system for the home.

**higgle** /'hɪgəl/, *v.i.*, **-gled, -gling.** to bargain, esp. in a petty way; haggle. [apparently var. of HAGGLE]

**higgledy-piggledy** /hɪgəldi-'pɪgəldi/, *Colloq.* –*adv.* **1.** in a jumbled confusion. –*adj.* **2.** confused; jumbled.

**higgler** /'hɪglə/, *n.* a huckster or pedlar.

**high** /haɪ/, *adj.* **1.** having a great or considerable reach or extent upwards; lofty; tall. **2.** having a specified extent upwards. **3.** situated above the ground or some base; elevated. **4.** far above the horizon, as a heavenly body. **5.** lying or being above the general level: *high ground.* **6.** of more than average or normal height or depth: *the river was high after the rain.* **7.** intensified; exceeding the common degree or measure; strong; intense, energetic: *high speed.* **8.** assigning or attributing a great amount, value, or excellence: *high estimate.* **9.** expensive, costly, or dear. **10.** exalted in rank, station, estimation, etc.; of exalted character or quality: *a high official.* **11.** *Music.* **a.** acute in pitch. **b.** a little sharp, or above the desired pitcn. **12.** produced by relatively rapid vibrations; shrill: *high sounds.* **13.** extending to or from an elevation: *a high dive.* **14.** of great amount, degree, force, etc.: *a high temperature.* **15.** chief; principal; main: *the high altar of a church.* **16.** of great consequence; important; grave; serious: *high treason.* **17.** of a period of time, at its fullest point of development: *the High Renaissance.* **18.** lofty; haughty; arrogant: *he spoke in a high and mighty manner.* **19.** advanced to the utmost extent, or to the culmination: *high tide.* **20.** elated; merry or hilarious: *high spirits.* **21.** *Colloq.* intoxicated or elated with alcohol or drugs. **22.** luxurious; extravagant: *high living.* **23.** remote: *high latitude, high antiquity.* **24.** extreme in opinion or doctrine, esp. religious or political. **25.** designating or pertaining to highland or inland regions. **26.** *Biol.* having a relatively complex structure: *the higher mammals.* **27.** *Phonet.* pronounced with the tongue relatively close to the roof of the mouth: *'feed' and 'food' have high vowels.* **28. a.** (of meat, esp. game) tending towards a desirable amount of decomposition; slightly tainted. **b.** smelly; bad. **29.** having a comparatively large amount of a particular constituent: *high-protein food.* **30.** *Cards.* **a.** having greater value than another card. **b.** capable of taking a trick; being a winning card. **31. high as a kite, a.** under the influence of drugs or alcohol. **b.** in exuberant spirits. **32. high relief.** See **relief** (defs 9 and 10) and **alto-rilievo.** –*adv.* **33.** at or to a high point, place, or level, or a high rank or estimate, a high amount or price, or a high degree. **34.** *Naut.* close to the wind (said of a ship when sailing by the wind, with reference to the smallest angle with the wind at which the sails will remain full and the ship make headway). **35. high and dry, a.** (of a ship) wholly above water-level at low tide. **b.** *Colloq.* abandoned; stranded; deserted. **36. high and low,** everywhere. –*n.* **37.** that which is high; a high level: *share prices reached a new high.* **38.** top gear. **39.** *Meteorol.* a pressure system characterised by relatively high pressure at its centre; an anticyclone. **40.** *Colloq.* high school. **41.** *Cards.* the ace or highest trump out. **42.** *Colloq.* euphoric state induced by drugs. **43. on a high,** experiencing a euphoric state induced by drugs. **44. on high, a.** at or to a height; above. **b.** in heaven. [ME *heigh,* etc., OE *hēah,* c. G *hoch*]

**high altar** /– 'ɔltə/, *n.* the main altar of a large church.

**highball** /'haɪbɔl/, *n.* whisky or other liquor diluted with water, soda, or ginger ale, and served with ice in a tall glass.

**highblocked** /'haɪblɒkt/, *adj.* of a house which stands on very high foundations, as in the northern parts of Australia. Also, **highblock.**

**highborn** /'haɪbɔn/, *adj.* of high rank by birth.

**highbred** /'haɪbrɛd/, *adj.* **1.** of superior breed. **2.** characteristic of superior breeding: *highbred manners.*

**highbrow** /'haɪbraʊ/, *Colloq.* –*n.* **1.** a person who has pretensions to superior taste in artistic matters. –*adj.* **2.** of or pertaining to highbrows. **3.** of or pertaining to that which highbrows approve of: *highbrow music.* Cf. **lowbrow.**

**high-camp** /haɪ-'kæmp/, *adj.* affected; ostentatious, as typical of certain homosexuals.

**highchair** /'haɪtʃɛə/, *n.* a tall chair for use by a young child at mealtimes.

**High Church** /haɪ 'tʃɜtʃ/, *n.* a party in the Anglican Church which lays great stress on church authority and jurisdiction, ritual, etc. (opposed to *Low Church* and *Broad Church*). – **High-Church,** *adj.* – **High-Churchman,** *n.*

**high-class** /'haɪ-klas/, *adj.* of superior quality.

**high-coloured** /'haɪ-kʌləd/, *adj.* **1.** strong or glaring in colour. **2.** florid or red: *a high-coloured complexion.*

**high comedy** /haɪ 'kɒmədi/, *n.* comedy dealing with polite society, depending largely on witty dialogue. Cf. **low comedy.**

**high command** /– kə'mænd/, *n.* those among the most senior officers of a nation's armed forces who act as a group to make the most important decisions of strategy and policy.

**high commissioner** /– kə'mɪʃənə/, *n.* the chief representative of a sovereign member of the Commonwealth of Nations in the country of another sovereign member, usu. equivalent in rank to an ambassador, as the Australian High Commissioner in London.

**high country** /'– kʌntri/, *n.* hilly land on mountain approaches, esp. when used for pastoral purposes. – **high-country,** *adj.*

**high court** /– 'kɔt/, *n.* a supreme court of justice.

**High Court of Australia,** *n.* the Federal court established under the Constitution to determine matters of first instance and appeals from the Supreme Courts of the States.

**High Court of Justice,** *n. Brit.* the lower branch of the Supreme Court of Judicature, nearly equivalent to an Australian Supreme Court.

**high day** /'haɪ deɪ/, *n.* **1.** a holy or festal day. **2.** →**heyday.**

**higher criticism** /haɪə 'krɪtəsɪzəm/, *n.* the study of literature, esp. the Bible, by scientific and historical techniques.

**higher education** /haɪər ɛdʒə'keɪʃən/, *n.* education beyond secondary education.

**higher mathematics** /haɪə mæθə'mætɪks/, *n.* the more scientifically treated and advanced portions of mathematics customarily embracing all beyond ordinary arithmetic, geometry, algebra, and trigonometry.

**higher-up** /haɪər-'ʌp/, *n. Colloq.* one occupying a superior position.

**highest common factor,** *n.* the greatest number which is a factor (def. 2) of all the numbers in the group of numbers in question. *Abbrev.:* **H.C.F., h.c.f.**

**high explosive** /haɪ əks'ploʊzɪv/, *n.* a class of explosive, as TNT, in which the reaction is so rapid as to be practically instantaneous, used for bursting charges in shells and bombs.

**highfalutin** /haɪfə'lutn/, *adj. Colloq.* pompous; haughty; pretentious. Also, **hifalutin, highfaluting.**

**high-fidelity** /haɪ-fə'dɛləti/, *adj.* (of an amplifier, radio receiver, etc.) reproducing the full audio range of the original sounds with relatively little distortion. Also, **hi-fi.**

**high-flier** /'haɪ-flaɪə/, *n.* **1.** one who or that which flies high. **2.** one who is extravagant or goes to extremes in aims, pretensions, opinions, etc. **3.** *Stock Exchange.* a share which rises rapidly in price, well beyond traders' expectations. Also, **high-flyer.**

**high-flown** /'haɪ-floʊn/, *adj.* **1.** extravagant in aims, pretensions, etc. **2.** pretentiously lofty; bombastic.

**high-flying** /'haɪ-flaɪɪŋ/, *adj.* **1.** that flies high, as a bird. **2.** extravagant or extreme in aims, opinions, etc.

**high frequency** /haɪ 'frikwənsi/, *n.* **1.** a radio frequency in the range 3 to 30 megacycles per second. *Abbrev.:* h.f. **2.** any audible frequency which is high in pitch. – **high-frequency,** *adj.*

**high-frequency welding** /ˌhaɪ-frikwənsi 'wɛldɪŋ/, *n.* →**radio frequency welding.**

**High German** /haɪ 'dʒɜmən/, *n.* **1.** any form of the German language of central and southern Germany, Switzerland, and Austria, including Old High German and Middle High German. **2.** standard German.

**high-grade** /'haɪ-greɪd/, *adj.* **1.** of superior quality. **2.** (of ore) with a relatively high yield of the metal for which it is mined.

**high-growth area** /haɪ-'groʊθ ɛəriə/, *n.* an urban or suburban developed area characterised by high growth in population and/or building activity, sometimes including commercial and industrial activity.

**high-handed** /'haɪ-hændəd/, *adj.* overbearing; arbitrary: *a high-handed manner.* – **high-handedly,** *adv.* – **high-handedness,** *n.*

**high hat** /ˈhaɪ hæt/, *n.* **1.** →**top hat.** **2.** Also, **top hat.** *Films, Television, etc.* the lowest tripod used to hold a camera, usu. 15 cm high. **3.** a part of a drum kit consisting of two cymbals which are struck together by the use of a pedal device.

**high-hat** /ˈhaɪ-hæt/, *v.*, **-hatted, -hatting,** *adj. Colloq.* –*v.t.* **1.** to snub or treat condescendingly. –*adj.* **2.** snobbish; affectedly superior.

**high horse** /ˈhaɪ hɔs/, *n.* **1.** a warhorse; charger. **2. on one's high horse,** *Colloq.* assuming an arrogant or superior air. **3. get off one's high horse,** *Colloq.* to stop being arrogant, self-righteous, etc.

**highjack** /ˈhaɪdʒæk/, *v.t., v.i. Colloq.* →**hijack.**

**high jinks** /ˈhaɪ dʒɪŋks/, *n.pl. Colloq.* boisterous, unrestrained merrymaking.

**high jump** /ˈ– dʒʌmp/, *n.* **1.** *Athletics.* a vertical jump in which one attempts to go as high as possible. **2.** *Athletics.* a contest for the highest such jump. **3. for the high jump,** *Colloq.* (to be) about to face an unpleasant experience, esp. a punishment or reprimand. **4.** *Prison Colloq.* →**quarter sessions.**

**highland** /ˈhaɪlənd/, *n.* **1.** an elevated region; a plateau: *a jutting highland.* **2.** (*pl.*) a mountainous region or elevated part of a country. –*adj.* **3.** of, pertaining to, or characteristic of highlands.

**highlander** /ˈhaɪləndə/, *n.* an inhabitant of high land, esp. a member of the Gaelic race of the Scottish Highlands, or an indigenous inhabitant of the Papua New Guinea highlands. Also, **Highlander.**

**Highland fling** /haɪlənd ˈflɪŋ/, *n.* a vigorous Scottish country dance, a form of the reel.

**high-level** /ˈhaɪ-lɛvəl/, *adj.* **1.** carried out at or from a high altitude. **2.** involving or engaged in by persons holding a high position or rank.

**high-level language** /ˈ– læŋgwɪdʒ/, *n.* a language used for writing computer programs which is closer to human language or conventional mathematical notation than to machine language. Cf. **low-level language.**

**high life** /ˈhaɪ laɪf/, *n.* a luxurious style of living.

**highlight** /ˈhaɪlaɪt/, *v.*, **-lighted, -lighting,** *n.* –*v.t.* **1.** to emphasise or make prominent. **2.** (in photography, painting, etc.) to emphasise (the areas of greatest brightness) with paint or by exposing lighter areas. **3.** to treat portions of hair by tinting or bleaching. –*n.* **4.** a conspicuous or striking part: *the highlight of his talk.* **5.** *Art.* the point of most intense light in a picture or form. **6. a.** (*pl.*) flecks of colour in hair which gleam in the light. **b.** an area of hair which has been highlighted.

**highlighter** /ˈhaɪlaɪtə/, *n.* a cosmetic, usu. glossy, used to highlight the cheekbones, or make other features, as eyelids prominent.

**highly** /ˈhaɪli/, *adv.* **1.** in or to a high degree: *highly amusing.* **2.** with high appreciation or praise: *to speak highly of a person.* **3.** at or to a high price.

**highly-geared** /haɪli-ˈgɪəd/, *adj.* See **gearing** (def. 3).

**highly strung** /– ˈstrʌŋ/, *adj.* tense; in a state of (esp. nervous) tension: *highly strung nerves, highly strung people.* Also, **high-strung.**

**highly-wrought** /ˈhaɪli-rɔt/, *adj.* **1.** wrought with a high degree of skill; ornate. **2.** highly agitated. Also, **high-wrought.**

**High Mass** /haɪ ˈmæs/, *n.* a mass celebrated according to the complete rite by a priest or prelate attended by a deacon and subdeacon, parts of the mass being chanted or sung by the ministers and parts by the choir. During a High Mass incense is burnt before the oblations, the altar, the ministers, and the people.

**high-minded** /ˈhaɪ-maɪndəd/, *adj.* **1.** having or showing high, exalted principles or feelings: *a high-minded ruler.* **2.** proud or arrogant. – **high-mindedly,** *adv.* – **high-mindedness,** *n.*

**high-necked** /ˈhaɪ-nɛkt/, *adj.* (of a garment) high at the neck.

**highness** /ˈhaɪnəs/, *n.* **1.** the state of being high; loftiness; dignity. **2.** (*cap.*) a title of honour given to royal or princely personages (prec. by *His, Your,* etc.).

**high-octane** /haɪ-ˈɒkteɪn/, *adj.* (of a petrol) having a relatively high octane number, characterised by high efficiency and good antiknock properties. See **octane number.**

**high-pass filter** /ˈhaɪ-pas fɪltə/, *n.* a filter which allows only signals with frequencies above a certain value, which may be fixed or variable, to pass.

**high-pitched** /ˈhaɪ-pɪtʃt/, *adj.* **1.** *Music.* played or sung at a high pitch. **2.** (of a discussion, argument, etc.) marked by strong feeling; emotionally intense. **3.** (of a roof) nearly perpendicular; steep. **4.** aspiring; lofty; lofty in tone.

**high place** /ˈhaɪ pleɪs/, *n.* **1.** (in Semitic religions) a place of worship, usu. on a hilltop. **2.** (*pl.*) the uppermost levels of government and society: *corruption in high places.*

**high point** /ˈ– pɔɪnt/, *n.* a very rewarding or interesting place, occasion, or point in time: *the Barron Falls were the high point of the tour.*

**high-powered** /ˈhaɪ-paʊəd/, *adj.* **1.** (of an optical instrument) capable of giving a high magnification. **2.** energetic; vigorous; forceful: *a high-powered sales campaign.*

**high-pressure** /ˈhaɪ-prɛʃə/, *adj.* **1.** having or involving a pressure above the normal: *high-pressure steam.* **2.** vigorous; persistent: *high-pressure salesmanship.*

**high-priced** /ˈhaɪ-praɪst/, *adj.* expensive.

**high priest** /haɪ ˈprist/, *n.* **1.** a chief priest. **2.** an influential or powerful person in a high position, or an expert in his field. **3.** *Judaism.* in the priestly hierarchy, the highest-ranking priest who alone may enter the holy of holies.

**high-proof** /ˈhaɪ-pruf/, *adj.* containing a high percentage of alcohol: *high-proof spirits.*

**high relief** /haɪ rəˈlif/, *n.* →**alto-rilievo.**

**high-rise** /ˈhaɪ-raɪz/, *adj.* **1.** →**multistorey.** –*n.* **2.** a multistorey building, esp. a high block of flats.

**high-riser** /haɪ-ˈraɪzə/, *n.* →**dragster** (def. 2).

**highroad** /ˈhaɪroʊd/, *n.* **1.** a main road; a highway. **2.** an easy or certain course: *the highroad to success.*

**high school** /ˈhaɪ skul/, *n.* →**secondary school.** – **high-schooler,** *n.*

**high sea** /– ˈsi/, *n.* **1.** sea or ocean beyond a country's territorial waters. **2.** (*usu. pl.*) the open, unenclosed waters of any sea or ocean; common highway.

**high season** /ˈ– sizən/, *n.* the part of the year in which tourist accommodation, fares, etc., are high because of a seasonal demand.

**highset** /ˈhaɪsɛt/, *adj.* →**highblocked.**

**high society** /haɪ səˈsaɪəti/, *n.* →**society** (def. 9).

**high-sounding** /ˈhaɪ-saʊndɪŋ/, *adj.* having an imposing or pretentious sound: *high-sounding titles.*

**high-speed** /ˈhaɪ-spid/, *adj.* **1.** operating, or capable of operating at a high speed. **2.** *Photog.* (of film) useable with low illumination and short exposures. **3.** (of steel) esp. hard and capable of retaining its hardness even at red heat, so that it can be used for lathe tools.

**high-spirited** /ˈhaɪ-spɪrətəd/, *adj.* having a high, proud, or bold spirit; mettlesome.

**high spot** /ˈhaɪ spɒt/, *n.* an outstanding feature, esp. of a program of entertainment.

**high-stepping** /ˈhaɪ-stɛpɪŋ/, *adj.* **1.** (of a horse) moving with the leg raised high off the ground. **2.** (of a person) fashionably dressed; having fashionable pretensions. **3.** dedicated to the pursuit of pleasure; leading a hectic life. – **high-stepper,** *n.*

**high strikes** /ˈhaɪ straɪks/, *n. Colloq.* outlandish or eccentric behaviour. [corruption of HYSTERICS]

**high-strung** /ˈhaɪ-strʌŋ/, *adj.* →**highly strung.**

**hight** /haɪt/, *adj. Archaic.* called or named: *Childe Harold was he hight.* [ME; OE *heht,* reduplicated preterite of *hātan* name, call, promise, command, c. G *heissen;* current meaning taken from OE *hātte,* passive of *hātan*]

**high table** /ˈhaɪ teɪbəl/, *n.* a table, esp. one on a dais, at which the senior members of a college take their meals.

**hightail** /ˈhaɪteɪl/, *v.i. Colloq.* to move away quickly (oft. fol. by *it*): *he hightailed it out of town.*

**high tea** /haɪ ˈti/, *n. Brit.* a main evening meal with meat, fish, etc., (usu. taking the place of dinner), at which tea is served.

**high-tension** /ˈhaɪ-tɛnʃən/, *adj.* (of a device, circuit, circuit component, etc.) subjected to, or capable of operating under, a relatively high voltage, usu. 1000 volts or more. *Abbrev.:* H.T.

**high tide** /haɪ 'taɪd/, *n.* **1.** the tide at high water. **2.** the time of high water. **3.** the culminating point.

**high time** /– 'taɪm/, *n.* **1.** the right time; the time just before it is too late: *it's high time that was done.* **2.** *Colloq.* an enjoyable and gay time: *a high old time at the party.*

**high-toned** /'haɪ-toʊnd/, *adj.* **1.** high in tone or pitch. **2.** having high principles; dignified. **3.** *U.S. Colloq.* of, or with pretensions to, superior social status.

**high treason** /haɪ 'trizən/, *n.* treason against the sovereign or state.

**highty-tighty** /haɪti-'taɪti/, *interj., adj.* →**hoity-toity.**

**high-up** /'haɪ-ʌp/, *adj., n., pl.* **-ups.** *–adj.* **1.** holding an important position or rank. *–n.* **2.** a person of great importance or high rank.

**high water** /haɪ 'wɔtə/, *n.* water at its greatest elevation, as in a river.

**high-water mark** /haɪ-'wɔtə mak/, *n.* **1.** a mark showing the highest level reached by a body of water. **2.** the highest point of anything.

**highway** /'haɪweɪ/, *n.* **1.** a main road, as one between towns. **2.** any public passage, either a road or waterway. **3.** any main or ordinary route, track, or course.

**highwayman** /'haɪweɪmən/, *n., pl.* **-men.** a robber on the highway, esp. one on horseback.

**highway robbery** /haɪweɪ 'rɒbəri/, *n. Colloq.* →**daylight robbery.**

**high wind** /haɪ 'wɪnd/, *n.* a wind of Beaufort scale force 7, i.e. one with an average wind speed of 28 to 33 knots, or 50 to 61 km/h.

**highwire** /'haɪwaɪə/, *n.* a high tightrope.

**high words** /haz 'wɜdz/, *n.pl. Colloq.* a heated argument; row.

**hijack** /'haɪdʒæk/, *v.t.* **1.** to steal (something) in transit, as a lorry and the goods it carries. **2.** to seize by force or threat of force a vehicle, esp. a passenger-carrying vehicle, as an aircraft. *–v.i.* **3.** to engage in such stealing. Also, **highjack.** [backformation from HIJACKER]

**hijacker** /'haɪdʒækə/, *n.* one who hijacks. [? from HIGH(WAYMAN) + *jacker,* apparently from *jack,* v., hunt by night with aid of a jacklight]

**hike** /haɪk/, *v.,* **hiked, hiking,** *n. –v.i.* **1.** to walk a long distance, esp. through country districts, for pleasure. **2.** to pull or drag (fol. by *up*). *–v.t.* **3.** to increase (a fare, price, etc.) (fol. by *up*). *–n.* **4.** a long walk in the country. **5.** an increase in wages, fares, prices, etc. [? akin to HITCH] – **hiker,** *n.*

**hilarious** /hə'lɛəriəs/, *adj.* **1.** boisterously gay. **2.** cheerful. **3.** funny; provoking mirth. [HILARI(TY) + -OUS] – **hilariously,** *adv.* – **hilariousness,** *n.*

**hilarity** /hə'lærəti/, *n.* **1.** boisterous gaiety. **2.** cheerfulness. [L *hilaritas*]

**hill** /hɪl/, *n.* **1.** a conspicuous natural elevation of the earth's surface, smaller than a mountain. **2.** an artificial heap or pile: *anthill.* **3.** a little heap of earth raised about a cultivated plant or a cluster of such plants. **4. as old as the hills,** *Colloq.* very old. **5.** (*pl.*) **take to the hills,** to run away and hide. **6. over the hill,** past prime efficiency; past the peak of physical or other condition, etc. *–v.t.* **7.** to form into a hill or heap. **8.** to bank up (a plant, etc.) with earth. [ME; OE *hyll,* c. MD *hille;* akin to L *collis* hill, *columen* top, *columna* COLUMN] – **hiller,** *n.*

**hillbilly** /'hɪlbɪli/, *n., pl.* **-lies. 1.** *Orig. U.S.* a rustic or yokel living in the backwoods or mountains. *–adj.* **2.** rustic. [HILL + *Billy,* pet var. of *William,* man's name]

**hill climb** /'hɪl klaɪm/, *n.* a road race over a hilly course, held by a motor car or motorcycle club.

**hillock** /'hɪlək/, *n.* a little hill. – **hillocky,** *adj.*

**hillside** /'hɪlsaɪd/, *n.* the side or slope of a hill.

**hill site** /'hɪl saɪt/, *n.* situation on a hill; an elevated site.

**hill station** /'– steɪʃən/, *n.* any town or resort in southern Asia at a high altitude where relief may be found from the tropical heat.

**hilltop** /'hɪltɒp/, *n.* the top or summit of a hill.

**hilly** /'hɪli/, *adj.,* **hillier, hilliest. 1.** abounding in hills: *hilly country.* **2.** elevated; steep. – **hilliness,** *n.*

**hilt** /hɪlt/, *n.* **1.** the handle of a sword or dagger. **2.** the handle of any weapon or tool. **3. to the hilt,** fully; completely: *armed to the hilt.* *–v.t.* **4.** to furnish with a hilt. [ME *hylt,* OE *hilt, hilte,* c. MD *hilt, hilte;* of obscure orig.] – **hilted,** *adj.*

**hilum** /'haɪləm/, *n., pl.* **-la** /-lə/. **1.** *Bot.* **a.** the mark or scar on a seed produced by separation from its funicle or placenta. **b.** the nucleus of a granule of starch. **2.** *Anat.* the region at which the vessels, nerves, etc., enter or emerge from a part. [L: little thing, trifle]

**him** /hɪm/, *pron.* objective case of *he.* [ME and OE; dat. of *hē* HE]

**himself** /hɪm'sɛlf/, *pron.* **1.** a reflexive form of *him: he cut himself.* **2.** an emphatic form of *him* or *he* used: **a.** as object: *he used it for himself.* **b.** in apposition to a subject or object: *he did it himself.* **3.** his proper or normal self; his usual state of mind (used after such verbs as *be, become,* or *come to*): *he is himself again.* **4.** *Chiefly Brit. Colloq.* a man who is dominant in a house, office, etc., esp. the master of the house: *is himself at home today?*

**hinau** /'hinaʊ/, *n.* an evergreen tree, *Elaeocarpus dentatus,* of New Zealand, with straw-coloured flowers. [Maori]

**hind**[1] /haɪnd/, *adj.,* **hinder, hindmost** or **hindermost.** situated behind or at the back; posterior: *the hind legs of an animal.* [? short for BEHIND, but cf. OE *hindan,* adv., from behind, G *hinten,* adv.]

**hind**[2] /haɪnd/, *n.* the female of the deer, chiefly the red deer, esp. in and after the third year. [ME and OE; c. Icel. *hind.* Cf. D *hinde* and G *Hinde*]

**Hind.,** **1.** Hindustan. **2.** Hindustani.

**hindbrain** /'haɪndbreɪn/, *n.* **1.** the cerebellum, pons, and medulla oblongata or the embryonic nervous tissue from which they develop; the entire rhombencephalon or some part of it. **2.** →**metencephalon.**

**hinder**[1] /'hɪndə/, *v.t.* **1.** to interrupt; check; retard: *to be hindered by storms.* **2.** to prevent from acting or taking place; stop: *to hinder a man from committing a crime.* *–v.i.* **3.** to be an obstacle or impediment. [ME *hindre(n),* OE *hindrian* (c. G *hindern,* etc.), from *hinder* behind, back] – **hinderer,** *n.* – **hinderingly,** *adv.*

**hinder**[2] /'haɪndə/, *adj.* situated at the rear or back; posterior: *the hinder part of the ship.* [ME, apparently representing OE *hinder,* adv., behind, c. G *hinter,* prep.]

**hindgut** /'haɪndgʌt/, *n.* the lower portion of the embryonic digestive canal from which the colon and rectum develop.

**Hindi** /'hɪndi/, *n.* **1.** one of the modern Indic languages of northern India, usu. divided into Eastern and Western Hindi. **2.** a literary language derived from Hindustani, used by Hindus. [Hind., from *Hind* India]

**hindmost** /'haɪndmoʊst/, *adj.* **1.** farthest behind; nearest the rear; last. **2. (the) devil take the hindmost,** *Colloq.* those in the rear must look after themselves. Also, **hindermost** /hɪndəmoʊst/.

**Hindoo** /'hɪndu/, *n., pl.* **-doos,** *adj.* →**Hindu.**

**Hindooism** /'hɪnduɪzəm/, *n.* →**Hinduism.**

**Hindoostani** /hɪndu'stani/, *adj., n.* →**Hindustani.**

**hindquarter** /'haɪndkwɔtə/, *n.* **1.** the posterior end of a halved carcase of beef, lamb, etc., sectioned usu. between the twelfth and thirteenth ribs. **2.** rear part.

**hindrance** /'hɪndrəns/, *n.* **1.** an impeding, stopping, or preventing. **2.** a means or cause of hindering.

**hindsight** /'haɪndsaɪt/, *n.* perception of the nature and exigencies of a case after the event: *hindsight is easier than foresight.*

**Hindu** /'hɪndu, hɪn'du/, *n.* **1.** a native of India who adheres to Hinduism. **2.** any person who adheres to Hinduism. *–adj.* **3.** of or pertaining to Hindus or Hinduism. Also, **Hindoo.** [Hind., Pers., from *Hind* India]

**Hinduism** /'hɪnduɪzəm/, *n.* the dominant religion of India, evolved from the teaching of the Vedas, comprising a complex body of religious, social, cultural, and philosophical beliefs, and characterised by a system of divinely ordained caste. Although it has a general tendency towards pantheism, in its popular form it is polytheistic and is marked by an absence of creed or dogma, an elaborate ritual, and a belief in reincarnation. Also, **Hindooism.**

**Hindustan** /hɪndu'stan/, *n.* **1.** Persian name of India. **2.** the predominantly Hindu areas of the Indian sub-continent.

**Hindustani** /hɪndu'stani/, *n.* **1.** a standard language or lingua franca of northern India based on a dialect of Western Hindi spoken around Delhi. *–adj.* **2.** of or pertaining to Hindustan, its people, or their languages. Also, **Hindoostani.** [Hind., Pers., from HINDUSTAN]

**hindward** /'haɪndwəd/, *adj.* backward. – **hindwards,** *adv.*

**hinge** /hɪndʒ/, *n., v.,* **hinged, hinging.** *–n.* **1.** the movable joint or device on which a door, gate, shutter, lid, etc., turns or moves. **2.** a natural anatomical joint at which motion occurs about a transverse axis, as that of the knee or a bivalve shell. **3.** that on which something turns or depends; principle; central rule. *–v.i.* **4.** to depend or turn on, or as if on, a hinge: *everything hinges on his decision.* *–v.t.* **5.** to furnish with or attach by a hinge or hinges. **6.** to attach as by a hinge. **7.** to cause to depend: *to hinge action upon future sales.* [ME *heng, hing,* OE *hencg.* See HANG, *v.*] – **hinged,** *adj.*

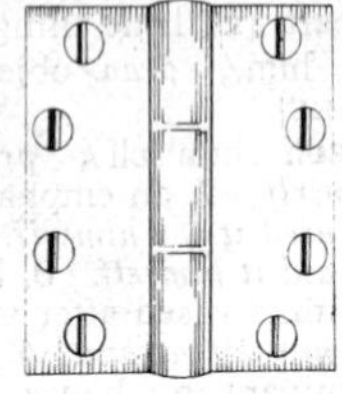
metal hinge

**hinny** /'hɪni/, *n., pl.* **-nies.** the offspring of a stallion and she-donkey. See **mule**[1] (defs 1 and 2). [L *hinnus*]

**hint** /hɪnt/, *n.* **1.** an indirect or covert suggestion or implication; an intimation. **2.** a brief, helpful suggestion; a piece of advice. **3.** a very small or barely perceptible amount. *–v.t.* **4.** to give a hint of. *–v.i.* **5.** to make indirect suggestion or allusion (usu. fol. by *at*). [var. of *hent,* n., from Brit. obs. *hent,* v., seize] – **hinter,** *n.*

**hinterland** /'hɪntəlænd/, *n.* **1.** an inland area supplying goods to a port. **2.** the land lying behind a coastal district. **3.** an area or sphere of influence in the unoccupied interior claimed by the state possessing the coast. **4.** the remote or less developed parts of a country. [G: lit., hinder land, i.e. land behind]

**hip**[1] /hɪp/, *n., v.,* **hipped, hipping.** *–n.* **1.** the projecting part of each side of the body formed by the side of the pelvis and the upper part of the femur, with the flesh covering them; the haunch. **2.** the hip joint. **3. have someone on** (or **upon**) **the hip,** to have someone at a disadvantage. **4.** *Archit.* the inclined projecting angle formed by the junction of a sloping side and a sloping end, or of two adjacent sloping sides, of a roof. *–v.t.* **5.** to injure or dislocate the hip of. **6.** *Archit.* to form (a roof) with a hip or hips. [ME; OE *hype,* c. G *Hüfte*] – **hipless,** *adj.* – **hiplike,** *adj.*

**hip**[2] /hɪp/, *n.* the ripe fruit of a rose, esp. of a wild rose. [ME *hepe,* OE *hēope* hip, brier, c. OHG *hiufo* bramble]

**hip**[3] /hɪp/, *interj.* (an exclamation used in cheers or in signalling for cheers): *hip, hip, hooray!* [orig. unknown]

**hip**[4] /hɪp/, *adj. Chiefly U.S. Colloq.* →**hep**[1].

hip[2]

**hipbath** /'hɪpbaθ/, *n.* a bath in which one can sit, but not lie down.

**hipbone** /'hɪpboun/, *n.* →**innominate bone.**

**hipflask** /'hɪpflask/, *n.* a flask, usu. containing alcoholic liquor, designed to be carried in a hip pocket.

**hip joint** /'hɪp dʒɔɪnt/, *n.* the joint between the hip and the thigh.

**hippeastrum** /hɪpi'æstrəm/, *n.* any bulbous plant of the South American genus *Hippeastrum,* many species of which have been developed as garden plants for their large, brightly coloured, funnel-shaped flowers.

**hipped**[1] /hɪpt/, *adj.* **1.** having hips. **2.** *Archit.* formed with a hip or hips, as a roof. [HIP[1] + -ED[3]]

**hipped**[2] /hɪpt/, *adj.* **1.** *U.S. Colloq.* greatly interested in; having an obsession (usu. fol. by *on*): *he's hipped on playing a tuba.* **2.** Also, **hippish.** melancholy; depressed; bored. [earlier *hypped,* from *hyp,* n., short form of HYPOCHONDRIA]

**hipped roof** /– 'ruf/, *n.* →**hip roof.**

**hippie** /'hɪpi/, *n.* one who rejects conventional social values in favour of new standards of awareness (sometimes drug-induced), universal love or union with nature, etc. Also, **hippy.** [? from HIP[4] + -IE]

**hippie trail** /'– treɪl/, *n.* **1.** a travel route which takes in those places in the world where hippies congregate, as India, Bali, etc. **2.** a similar route within Australia, esp. along the north-eastern coast.

**hippo** /'hɪpoʊ/, *n., pl.* **-pos.** *Colloq.* →**hippopotamus.**

**hippocampus** /hɪpoʊ'kæmpəs/, *n., pl.* **-pi** /-paɪ/. **1.** *Class. Myth.* a seahorse with two forefeet, and a body ending in the tail of a dolphin or fish. **2.** *Anat.* an enfolding of cerebral cortex into the cavity of a cerebral hemisphere having the shape in cross-section of a seahorse. [L: a sea-monster, from Gk *hippokámpos*] – **hippocampal,** *adj.*

**hip-pocket** /hɪp-'pɒkət/, *n.* **1.** a pocket on the back of a man's trousers in which his wallet might be kept. *–adj.* **2.** concerned with money: *a hip-pocket issue.*

**hip-pocket nerve** /– 'nɜv/, *n.* an imaginary nerve which is sensitive to demands for one's money, esp. through government action to increase taxation or weaken one's economic security.

**hippocras** /'hɪpəkræs/, *n.* (formerly) an English cordial made of wine mixed with spices, etc. [ME *ypocras,* from OF, from the name of *Hippocrates.* See HIPPOCRATIC OATH]

**Hippocratic oath** /hɪpə,krætɪk 'oʊθ/, *n.* an oath embodying the duties and obligations of physicians, sometimes taken by those about to enter upon the practice of medicine. [named after *Hippocrates,* 460? - 357 B.C., Greek physician, known as the father of medicine]

**hippodrome** /'hɪpədroum/, *n.* **1.** an arena or structure for equestrian and other spectacles. **2.** (in ancient Greece and Rome) a course or circus for horseraces and chariot races. **3.** a variety theatre; music hall. [L *hippodromos* a racecourse, from Gk]

**hippogriff** /'hɪpəgrɪf/, *n.* a fabulous creature resembling a griffin but having the body and hind parts of a horse. Also, **hippogryph.** [F *hippogriffe,* from It. *ippogrifo,* from *ippo-* (from Gk *híppos* horse) + *grifo* GRIFFIN[1]]

**hippomania** /hɪpə'meɪniə/, *n.* **1.** excessive interest in or fondness for horses. **2.** addiction to gambling on horseraces. – **hippomaniac,** *n.* – **hippomanic** /-'mænɪk/, *adj.*

**hippopotamus** /hɪpə'pɒtəməs/, *n., pl.* **-muses, -mi** /-maɪ/. **1.** a large herbivorous mammal, *Hippopotamus amphibius,* having a thick hairless body, short legs and large head and muzzle, found in and near the rivers and lakes of Africa, and able to remain under water for a considerable time. **2.** a similar but much smaller animal, *Choeropsis liberiensis,* of West Africa. [L, from LGk *hippopótamos,* for earlier *híppos ho potámios* the horse of the river; replacing ME *ypotame,* from OF, from ML *ypotamus*]

hippopotamus

**hippus** /'hɪpəs/, *n.* **1.** rhythmic dilatation and contraction of the pupil of the eye, independent of changes in light intensity; tremor of the iris. **2.** a constant involuntary winking of the eyes.

**hippy**[1] /'hɪpi/, *adj. Colloq.* having large hips.

**hippy**[2] /'hɪpi/, *n.* →**hippie.**

**hip roof** /'hɪp ruf/, *n.* a roof with sloping ends and sides; a hipped roof.

**hipshot** /'hɪpʃɒt/, *adj.* **1.** having the hip dislocated. **2.** lame; awkward. [HIP[1], *n.* + SHOT[2], *pp.*]

**hipster** /'hɪpstə/, *adj.* **1.** (of trousers, skirts, underpants) hanging from the hips, not from the waist. *–n.* **2.** (*pl.*) a pair of trousers or briefs hanging thus. **3.** *Colloq.* →**hippie.**

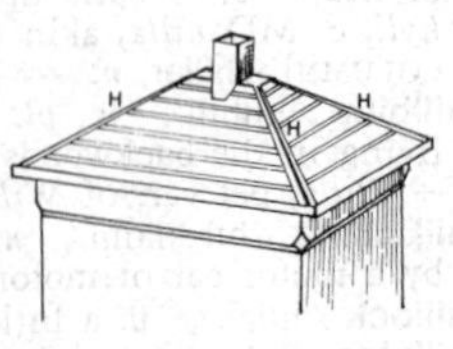

H, hip roof

**hircine** /'hɜsaɪn/, *adj.* **1.** of, pertaining to, or resembling a goat. **2.** having a goatish smell. **3.** lustful. [L *hircīnus* of a goat]

**hire** /'haɪə/, *v.,* **hired, hiring,** *n.* *–v.t.* **1.** to engage the services of for payment: *to hire a clerk.* **2.** to engage the temporary use of for payment: *to hire a car.* **3.** to grant the temporary use of, or the services of, for a payment (oft. fol. by *out*). *–n.* **4.** the price or compensation paid, or contracted to be paid, for the temporary use of something or for personal services or labour; pay. **5.** the act of hiring. [ME; OE *hȳr*, c. G *Heuer*] – **hireable,** *adj.* – **hirer,** *n.*

**hire-car** /'haɪə-ka/, *n.* a car, usu. with driver, available for hire.

**hireling** /'haɪəlɪŋ/, *n.* **1.** (*usu. derog.*) one working only for payment. **2.** a mercenary. *–adj.* **3.** (*usu. derog.*) serving for hire. **4.** venal; mercenary.

**hire-purchase** /haɪə-'pɜtʃəs/, *n.* **1.** a system whereby a person pays for a commodity by regular instalments, while having full use of it after the first payment. *–adj.* **2.** pertaining to or bought with the aid of such a system.

**hirsute** /'hɜsjut/, *adj.* **1.** hairy. **2.** *Bot., Zool.* covered with long, rather stiff hairs. **3.** of, pertaining to, or of the nature of hair. [L *hirsūtus* rough, hairy] – **hirsuteness,** *n.*

**Hirudinea** /hɪrə'dɪniə/, *n.pl.* a class of annelid worms comprising the leeches. [NL, from L *hirūdo* leech]

**hirundine** /hɪ'rʌndaɪn/, *adj.* of, pertaining to, or resembling the swallow. [LL *hirundineus*]

**his** /hɪz/; *weak form* /ɪz/, *pron.* **1.** the possessive form of *he: his house, this book is his.* **2.** the person(s) or thing(s) belonging to him: *himself and his.* **3. of his,** belonging to or associated with him: *a friend of his.* *–adj.* **4.** belonging to, pertaining to, or owned by him; made, done, experienced, etc., by him. [ME and OE; gen. of masc. *hē* HE, also of neut. *hit* IT]

**Hispania** /hɪs'pænjə/, *n. Poetic.* Spain. [L: the Spanish peninsula (with Portugal)]

**Hispanic** /hɪs'pænɪk/, *adj.* **1.** Spanish. **2.** Latin American.

**hispid** /'hɪspəd/, *adj.* rough with stiff hairs, bristles, or minute spines: *hispid stems.* [L *hispidus*] – **hispidity** /hɪs'pɪdəti/, *n.*

**hiss** /hɪs/, *v.i.* **1.** to make or emit a sharp sound like that of the letter *s* prolonged, as a goose or a snake does, or as steam does rushing through a small opening. **2.** to express disapproval or contempt by making this sound. *–v.t.* **3.** to express disapproval of by hissing. **4.** to force or drive by hissing (fol. by *away, down,* etc.). **5.** to utter with a hiss. *–n.* **6.** a hissing sound, esp. in disapproval. [unexplained var. of d. E *hish,* ME *hisshe(n)* hiss, OE *hyscan* jeer at, rail] – **hisser,** *n.*

**hissing** /'hɪsɪŋ/, *n.* **1.** the act of hissing. **2.** the sound of a hiss. **3.** *Archaic.* an occasion or object of scorn.

**hist** /hɪst/, *interj.* **1.** (a sibilant exclamation used to attract attention, command silence, etc.) *–v.t.* **2.** to use the exclamation 'hist' to. [var. of WHIST[1]. Cf. HUSH[1]]

**hist.,** **1.** histology. **2.** historical. **3.** history.

**histaminase** /hɪs'tæməneɪs/, *n.* an enzyme capable of making histamine inactive, used in treating allergies.

**histamine** /'hɪstəmin/, *n.* an amine, $C_3H_3N_2CH_2CH_2NH_2$, produced by the loss of carbon dioxide from histidine. It is released by the tissues in allergic reactions, is a powerful uterine stimulant, and lowers the blood pressure. [HIST(IDINE) + AMINE] – **histaminic** /hɪstə'mɪnɪk/, *adj.*

**histidine** /'hɪstədin/, *n.* an amino acid, $C_3H_3N_2CH_2CH(NH_3^+)COO^-$, occurring in proteins, and converted in most cells into histamine, an essential amino acid in man. [HIST(O)- + -ID[3] + -INE[2]. Cf. G *Histidin*]

**histo-,** a word element meaning 'tissue', as in *histogen.* Also, before vowels, **hist-.** [Gk, combining form of *histós* web, tissue]

**histogen** /'hɪstədʒən/, *n.* the regions in a plant in which tissues undergo differentiation.

**histogenesis** /hɪstoʊ'dʒɛnəsəs/, *n.* the formation and differentiation of a living tissue.

**histogram** /'hɪstəgræm/, *n.* a graph of a frequency distribution in which equal intervals of values are marked on a horizontal axis and the frequency corresponding to each interval is indicated by the height of a rectangle having the interval as its base.

**histoid** /'hɪstɔɪd/, *adj.* denoting a tumour composed of connective tissue or its equivalent.

**histology** /hɪs'tɒlədʒi/, *n.* **1.** the science that treats of organic tissues. **2.** the study of the structure, esp. the microscopic structure, of organic tissues. – **histological** /hɪstə'lɒdʒəkəl/, **histologic** /hɪstə'lɒdʒɪk/, *adj.* – **histologist** /hɪs'tɒlədʒəst/, *n.*

**histolysis** /hɪs'tɒləsəs/, *n.* disintegration or dissolution of organic tissues.

**histone** /'hɪstoʊn/, *n.* any of a class of basic proteins as globin, that can release on hydrolysis a high proportion of basic amino acids. [HIST(O)- + -ONE. Cf. G *Histon*]

**histopathology** /hɪstoʊpə'θɒlədʒi/, *n.* the study of minute changes in diseased tissue.

**historian** /hɪs'tɔriən/, *n.* **1.** a writer of history. **2.** an expert in history; an authority on history. **3.** a student of history.

**historic** /hɪs'tɒrɪk/, *adj.* well-known or important in history: *historic scenes.* Also, **historical.**

**historical** /hɪs'tɒrɪkəl/, *adj.* **1.** relating to or concerned with history or past events. **2.** dealing with or treating of history or past events. **3.** pertaining to or of the nature of history: *historical evidence.* **4.** pertaining to or of the nature of history as opposed to legend or fiction: *the historical King Arthur.* **5.** narrated or mentioned in history; belonging to the past. **6.** →**historic.** [L *historicus* (from Gk *historikós*) + -AL[1]] – **historically,** *adv.* – **historicalness,** *n.*

**historical geography** /– dʒi'ɒgrəfi/, *n.* the study of the geography of a past period or periods.

**historical materialism** /– mə'tɪəriəlɪzəm/, *n.* that part of Marxist theory which maintains that ideas and institutions develop as a superstructure upon an economic base, and that they are altered as a result of class struggles, and that each ruling class produces another which will destroy it, the final stage being the emergence of a classless society.

**historical method** /– 'mɛθəd/, *n.* the development of general principles by the study of the historical facts.

**historical present** /– 'prɛzənt/, *n.* the present tense of a verb when it is used in narrative to indicate past events: *I walk in yesterday and what do I find?*

**historicism** /hɪs'tɒrəsɪzəm/, *n.* the belief that all social and cultural facts are historically determined, that the standards of one age are inapplicable to any other, and that periods in history should only be studied in terms of their own values. – **historicist,** *n., adj.*

**historicity** /hɪstə'rɪsəti/, *n.* historical authenticity.

**historic present** /hɪs,tɒrɪk 'prɛzənt/, *n.* a present tense used in the narration of past events for stylistic effect.

**historic tense** /– 'tɛns/, *n.* →**preterite.**

**historiographer** /hɪstɒri'ɒgrəfə/, *n.* **1.** a historian. **2.** an official historian, as of a court, an institution, etc. [LL *historiographus* (from Gk *historiográphos*) + -ER[1]]

**historiography** /hɪstɒri'ɒgrəfi/, *n.* **1.** the writing of history, esp. as based on the critical examination and evaluation of material taken from primary sources. **2.** the study of the development of historical method.

**history** /'hɪstri, 'hɪstəri/, *n., pl.* **-ries.** **1.** the branch of knowledge dealing with past events. **2.** the record of past events, esp. in connection with the human race. **3.** a continuous, systematic written narrative, in order of time, of past events as relating to a particular people, country, period, person, etc. **4.** the aggregate of past events. **5.** a past worthy of record or out of the ordinary: *a ship with a history.* **6.** a systematic account of any set of natural phenomena, without reference to time. **7.** a drama representing historical events. **8. be history, a.** to be dead. **b.** to be ruined or incapacitated. **c.** to be broken beyond repair. **9. go down in history,** of an event or person, to be sufficiently significant to be always remembered. **10. make history,** to achieve lasting fame. **11. be ancient history,** to be finished or gone irrevocably. [ME, from L *historia,* from Gk: a learning or knowing by inquiry, information, narrative, history]

**histrionic** /hɪstri'ɒnɪk/, *adj.* **1.** of or pertaining to actors or acting. **2.** artificial; theatrical. Also, **histrionical.** [LL *histriōnicus*] – **histrionically,** *adv.*

**histrionics** /hɪstri'ɒnɪks/, *n.pl.* **1.** dramatic representation; theatricals; acting. **2.** artificial or melodramatic behaviour, speech, etc., for effect.

**hit** /hɪt/, *v.,* **hit, hitting,** *n., adj.* *–v.t.* **1.** to deal a blow or stroke; bring forcibly into collision. **2.** to come against with an impact or collision, as a missile, a flying fragment, a falling body, or the like does. **3.** to reach with a missile, a weapon, a blow, or the like (intentionally or otherwise), as

one throwing, shooting or striking; succeed in striking. **4.** to drive or propel by a stroke. **5.** to have a marked effect on; affect severely. **6.** to assail effectively and sharply. **7.** to reach (a specified level or figure). **8.** to be published in or appear in (a newspaper). **9.** to come or light upon; meet; find: *to hit the right road.* **10.** to guess correctly. **11.** to succeed in representing or producing exactly: *to hit a likeness in a portrait.* **12.** to arrive at: *to hit town.* **13.** to begin to travel on: *to hit the trail.* **14.** to demand or obtain money from: *the building company hit me for a thousand dollars.* **15.** *Colloq.* to inject any form of drugs. **16.** Some special verb phrases are:
**hit for six, 1.** *Cricket.* (of a batsman) to strike (the ball) so that it lands outside the playing area, the stroke being worth six runs. **2.** to confuse or disturb greatly: *the bad news hit him for six.*
**hit home,** to make an impact or impression upon.
**hit it off,** *Colloq.* to get on well together; agree.
**hit off,** to make a beginning; commence.
**hit on** or **upon,** to come upon unexpectedly; find by chance.
**hit (one) hard,** to have a severe and distressing effect upon (one).
**hit the bottle** or **booze,** *Colloq.* to drink heavily; become an alcoholic.
**hit the ceiling** or **roof,** *Colloq.* to display extreme anger or astonishment.
**hit the deck, 1.** to prostrate oneself on the ground, usu. in self-protection. **2.** *Colloq.* to get out of bed.
**hit the headlines,** to gain publicity; to achieve notoriety.
**hit the lip,** to ride a surfboard off the extremity of a wave.
**hit the nail on the head, 1.** to sum up with clarity and incisiveness. **2.** to give perfect satisfaction.
**hit the road,** to set out.
**hit the sack** or **hay,** *Colloq.* to go to bed.
**hit the spot,** *Colloq.* to fulfill a need; satisfy.
**not to know what hit one,** to be taken unawares; be thrown into confusion or dismay.
*–v.i.* **17.** to strike with a missile, weapon, or the like; deal a blow or blows (oft. fol. by *out*). **18. hit up, a.** *Tennis.* to warm up by hitting the ball back and forth across the net, disregarding the rules of play. **b.** *Colloq.* to take a drug, as heroin, usu. by injecting it into the bloodstream. *–n.* **19.** an impact or collision, as of one thing against another. **20.** a stroke that reaches an object; blow. **21.** *Fencing.* a point scored by a touch with the tip of the blade of a foil or épée, or the edge of the blade of a sabre, against any part of the opponent's body in the target (def. 5). **22.** *Backgammon.* **a.** a game won by a player after his opponent has thrown off one or more men from the board. **b.** any winning game. **23.** a successful stroke, performance, or production; success: *the play is a hit.* **24.** an effective or telling expression or saying; gibe; taunt. **25.** *Colloq.* a shot of heroin or any drug; a fix. *–adj.* **26.** successful; achieving popularity. [ME *hitte(n)*, OE *hittan*, from Scand.; cf. Icel. *hitta* come upon (by chance), meet] – **hittable,** *adj.* – **hitter,** *n.*

**hit-and-miss** /hɪt-n-ˈmɪs/, *adj.* haphazard; random. Also, **hit-or-miss.**

**hit-and-miss brickwork** /–ˈbrɪkwɜk/, *n.* stretcher bond laid with a gap of approx. 50 mm instead of a perpend, for ventilation.

hit-and-miss brickwork

**hit-and-run** /hɪt-n-ˈrʌn/, *adj.* **1.** denoting or pertaining to the driver of a motor vehicle who leaves the scene of an accident in which he was involved without stopping to give assistance or fulfil any legal obligations. **2.** of or pertaining to such an accident. **3.** (of an air-raid) lasting only a short time and marked by a rapid withdrawal from the area of attack. Also, **hit-run.**

**hit-bound** /ˈhɪt-baʊnd/, *adj.* (of a song) predicted by disc jockeys, etc., to become a hit.

**hitch** /hɪtʃ/, *v.t.* **1.** to make fast, esp. temporarily, by means of a hook, rope, strap, etc.; tether. **2.** to harness (an animal) to a vehicle (oft. fol. by *up*). **3.** to raise with jerks (usu. fol. by *up*): *to hitch up one's trousers.* **4.** to move or draw (something) with a jerk. **5.** *Colloq.* to obtain or seek to obtain (a ride) from a passing vehicle. *–v.i.* **6.** to harness an animal to a vehicle (fol. by *up*). **7.** to become fastened or caught, as on something. **8.** to stick, as when caught. **9.** to fasten oneself or itself to something (oft. fol. by *on*). **10.** *Colloq.* to seek to obtain a ride from passing vehicles. *–n.* **11.** a making fast, as to something, esp. temporarily. **12.** *Naut., etc.* any of various forms of knot or fastening made with rope or the like. **13.** a halt; an obstruction: *a hitch in the proceedings.* **14.** a hitching movement; a jerk or pull. **15.** a fastening that joins a movable tool to the mechanism that pulls it. **16.** *U.S. Colloq.* a period of military service. **17.** *Colloq.* a ride from a passing vehicle. [ME *hytche(n)*; orig. uncert.] – **hitcher,** *n.*

hitch: Cobb and Co hitch, used in erecting or mending fences and stockyards

**hitched** /hɪtʃt/, *adj. Colloq.* married.

**hitchhike** /ˈhɪtʃhaɪk/, *v.i.,* **-hiked, -hiking.** *Colloq.* to travel by obtaining rides in passing vehicles. – **hitchhiker,** *n.*

**hitching post** /ˈhɪtʃɪŋ poʊst/, *n.* a post to which horses, etc., are tied.

**hither** /ˈhɪðə/, *adv.* **1.** to or towards this place; here: *to come hither.* **2. hither and thither,** this way and that; in various directions. *–adj.* **3.** on or towards this side; nearer: *the hither side of the hill.* **4.** earlier; more remote. [ME and OE *hider*, c. Icel. *hedhra*; from demonstrative stem represented by HE]

**hithermost** /ˈhɪðəmoʊst/, *adj.* nearest in this direction.

**hitherto** /hɪðəˈtu/, *adv.* **1.** up to this time; until now: *a fact hitherto unknown.* **2.** *Archaic.* to here.

**hitherwards** /ˈhɪðəwədz/, *adv. Archaic.* hither. Also, **hitherward.**

**hit man** /ˈhɪt mæn/, *n. Colloq.* a hired assassin.

**hit-or-miss** /hɪt-ɔ-ˈmɪs/, *adj.* →**hit-and-miss.**

**hit-out** /ˈhɪt-aʊt/, *n.* **1.** *Aus. Rules.* the punching or palming of the ball by a player at a ball-up or a boundary throw-in, usu. aimed at delivering the ball to a team-mate. **2.** a brisk gallop.

**hit parade** /ˈhɪt pəreɪd/, *n.* a selection of the most popular songs on the radio.

**hit song** /ˈ– sɒŋ/, *n.* song which has achieved considerable popularity, esp. one at the top of the hit parade. Also, **hit time.**

**hit-squad** /ˈhɪt-skwɒd/, *n.* a group of people formed and trained to murder, esp. for political purposes.

**Hittite** /ˈhɪtaɪt/, *n.* **1.** one of a powerful, civilised ancient people who flourished in Asia Minor and adjoining regions (1900-1200 B.C.). **2.** an extinct language of the Indo-European family, preserved in cuneiform inscriptions. **3.** inscriptions, in hieroglyphics, of a language related to the preceding. *–adj.* **4.** having to do with the Hittites or their language. [Heb. *Hitt(īm)* (cf. Hittite *Khatti*) + -ITE[1], replacing earlier *Hethite* (cf. Vulgate *Hethaei*)]

**hive** /haɪv/, *n., v.,* **hived, hiving.** *–n.* **1.** an artificial shelter for honeybees; a beehive. **2.** the bees inhabiting a hive. **3.** something resembling a beehive in structure or use. **4.** a place swarming with busy occupants: *a hive of industry.* **5.** a swarming or teeming multitude. *–v.t.* **6.** to gather into or cause to enter a hive. **7.** to shelter as in a hive. **8.** to store up in a hive. **9.** to lay up for future use or enjoyment. **10. hive off, a.** *Comm.* (of shareholders in a company) to buy (shares) in a new company being formed by the existing one. **b.** (of an organisation, business, etc.) to operate (one group or function) from the rest. *–v.i.* **11.** to enter a hive. **12.** to live together in a hive. **13.** to break away from a group (fol. by *off*). [ME; OE *hȳf*. Cf. Icel. *hūfr* ship's hull] – **hiveless,** *adj.* – **hivelike,** *adj.*

**hive bee** /ˈ– bi/, *n.* →**honeybee.**

**hives** /haɪvz/, *n.* any of various eruptive diseases of the skin, as the weals of urticaria. [orig. Scot.]

**H.M.,** His (or Her) Majesty.

**H.M.A.S.** /ˈeɪtʃ ɛm ˌeɪ ɛs/, His (or Her) Majesty's Australian Ship.

**H.M.S.** /ˈeɪtʃ ɛm ɛs/, **1.** His (or Her) Majesty's Service. **2.** His (or Her) Majesty's Ship.

**ho** /hoʊ/, *interj.* **1.** (an exclamation of surprise, exultation.) **2.** (a call to attract attention, sometimes specially used after a word denoting a destination): *westward ho!* [ME; c. Icel. *hō*]

**Ho,** *Chem.* holmium.

**H.O.,** Head Office.

**hoactzin** /hoʊˈæktsɪn/, *n.* →**hoatzin.**

**hoar** /hɔ/, *adj.* **1.** covered with hoarfrost. **2.** *Archaic.* grey-haired with age; hoary; old. *–n.* **3.** a hoary coating or appearance. **4.** →**frost** (def. 3). [ME *hor,* OE *hār,* c. G *hehr* august, sublime]

**hoard** /hɔd/, *n.* **1.** an accumulation of something for preservation or future use: *a hoard of gold.* *–v.t.* **2.** to accumulate for preservation or future use, esp. in a secluded place. *–v.i.* **3.** to accumulate money, food, or the like, esp. in a secluded place. [ME *hord(e),* OE *hord,* c. OHG *hort* treasure] **– hoarder,** *n.*

**hoarding**[1] /ˈhɔdɪŋ/, *n.* **1.** the act of one who hoards. **2.** (*pl.*) that which is hoarded. [HOARD + -ING[1]]

**hoarding**[2] /ˈhɔdɪŋ/, *n.* **1.** a temporary fence enclosing a building during erection. **2.** a large billboard on which advertisements or notices are displayed. [obs. *hoard,* n., apparently from MD *horde* hurdle. Cf. obs. F hourd scaffolding]

**hoarfrost** /ˈhɔfrɒst/, *n.* →**frost** (def. 3).

**hoarfrost point** /ˈ– pɔɪnt/, *n.* the temperature to which humid air must be cooled, without change of pressure or humidity, for it to become saturated in the presence of ice. Also, **frost point.**

**hoarhound** /ˈhɔhaʊnd/, *n.* →**horehound.**

**hoarse** /hɔs/, *adj.,* **hoarser, hoarsest. 1.** having a vocal tone characterised by weakness of intensity and excessive breathiness; husky. **2.** having a raucous voice. **3.** making a harsh, low sound. [ME *hoors,* apparently from Scand.; cf. Icel. *hāss;* replacing ME *hoos,* OE *hās,* c. LG *hēs*] **– hoarsely,** *adv.* **– hoarseness,** *n.*

**hoarsen** /ˈhɔsən/, *v.t.* **1.** to make hoarse. *–v.i.* **2.** to become hoarse.

**hoary** /ˈhɔri/, *adj.,* **hoarier, hoariest. 1.** grey or white with age. **2.** ancient or venerable. **3.** grey or white. **– hoariness,** *n.*

**hoary cress** /– ˈkrɛs/, *n.* a perennial herb, *Cardaria draba,* a vigorous weed of cultivated land in temperate regions, spreading by means of underground stolons and root buds, and having a hoary appearance because of a thick cover of short, grey hairs. Also, **hoary pepperwort.**

**hoatzin** /hoʊˈætsɪn/, *n.* a South American crested bird, *Opisthocomus hoazin,* remarkable for claws on its wings. Also, **hoactzin.** [Amer. Sp., from Nahuatl *uatzin* pheasant]

**hoax** /hoʊks/, *n.* **1.** a humorous or mischievous deception, esp. a practical joke. *–v.t.* **2.** to deceive by a hoax. [contraction of HOCUS] **– hoaxer,** *n.*

**hob**[1] /hɒb/, *n.* **1.** a projection or shelf around a fireplace, for kettles, saucepans, etc. **2.** a rounded peg or pin used as a target in certain games, as quoits. **3.** any of these games. **4.** the hardened-steel master tool used in hobbing. [var. of obs. *hub* hob (in a fireplace); ? same as HUB]

**hob**[2] /hɒb/, *n.* **1.** a hobgoblin or elf. **2.** *Colloq.* mischief: *to play hob.* [ME *Hob,* for *Robert,* or *Robin,* man's name]

**Hobartian** /hoʊˈbatiən/, *n.* **1.** one who was born in Hobart, the capital city of Tasmania, or who has come to regard it as his home town. *–adj.* **2.** of or pertaining to the city of Hobart.

**hobbing** /ˈhɒbɪŋ/, *n.* a process of forming a mould cavity by forcing a hardened-steel master into a softer cavity blank to form a mould.

**hobble** /ˈhɒbəl/, *v.,* **-bled, -bling,** *n.* *–v.i.* **1.** to walk lamely; limp. **2.** to proceed irregularly and haltingly: *hobbling verse.* *–v.t.* **3.** to cause to limp. **4.** to fasten together the legs of (a horse, etc.) so as to prevent free motion. **5.** to embarrass; impede; perplex. *–n.* **6.** the act of hobbling; an uneven, halting gait; a limp. **7.** Also, **hobble chain.** a rope, strap, etc., used to hobble an animal. **8.** *Colloq.* an awkward or difficult situation. [ME *hobelen;* apparently akin to *hob* protuberance, uneven ground. Cf. d. HG *hoppeln* jolt] **– hobbler,** *n.* **– hobbling,** *adj.* **– hobblingly,** *adv.*

**hobbledehoy** /hɒbəldiˈhɔɪ/, *n.* **1.** an adolescent boy. **2.** an awkward, clumsy boy. [orig. uncert.]

**hobble skirt** /ˈhɒbəl skɜt/, *n.* a woman's ankle-length skirt which is so narrow at the bottom that it restricts her ability to walk.

**hobby**[1] /ˈhɒbi/, *n., pl.* **-bies. 1.** a spare-time activity or pastime, etc., pursued for pleasure or recreation. **2.** *Archaic.* a small horse. **3.** a child's hobbyhorse. [ME *hoby, hobyn,* probably for *Robin,* or *Robert,* man's name. Cf. DOBBIN, HOB[2]. Def. 2 was orig. meaning, whence def. 3 and *hobbyhorse.* Def. 1 is short for *hobbyhorse*] **– hobbyist,** *n.*

**hobby**[2] /ˈhɒbi/, *n., pl.* **-bies.** a small Old World falcon, *Falco subbuteo,* formerly flown at such small game as larks. [ME, from OF *hobet,* diminutive of *hobe* hobby (falcon), probably from L *albus* white (as applied to a special kind of falcon), ? also b. with OF *hober* hop]

**hobby farm** /ˈ– fam/, *n.* a farm maintained for interest's sake, usu. not the owner's chief source of income. **– hobby farmer,** *n.*

**hobbyhorse** /ˈhɒbihɔs/, *n.* **1.** a stick with a horse's head, or a rocking horse, ridden by children. **2.** a figure of a horse, attached at the waist of a performer in a morris dance, pantomime, etc. **3.** a favourite topic; obsessive notion.

**hobgoblin** /ˈhɒbgɒblən/, *n.* **1.** anything causing superstitious fear; a bogy. **2.** a mischievous goblin. [HOB[2] + GOBLIN]

**hobnail** /ˈhɒbneɪl/, *n.* a large-headed nail for protecting the soles of heavy boots and shoes. [HOB[1] + NAIL]

hobnail

**hobnailed** /ˈhɒbneɪld/, *adj.* furnished with hobnails.

**hobnob** /ˈhɒbnɒb/, *v.i.,* **-nobbed, -nobbing.** to associate on very friendly terms: *hobnobbing with the management got him his golden handshake.* [earlier *hab or nab* alternately, lit., have or have not]

**hobo** /ˈhoʊboʊ/, *n., pl.* **-bos, -boes. 1.** a tramp or vagrant. **2.** a migratory worker. [rhyming formation, ? based on *beau* fop, used as (sarcastic) word of greeting, e.g. in *hey, bo!*] **– hoboism,** *n.*

**hobson-jobson** /hɒbsən-ˈdʒɒbsən/, *n.* the assimilation of a word or words from a foreign language to the sound of a familiar word or words in the mother tongue. [Anglo-Indian modification of Ar. *yā Hasan! yā Husain!* O Hasan! O Husain! (a cry repeated at the Muharram festival as an expression of mourning for Hasan and Husain, the grandsons of the prophet Mohammed): *hobson-jobson* itself an example of this]

**Hobson's choice** /ˈhɒbsənz tʃɔɪs/, *n.* the choice of taking either the thing offered or nothing; the absence of real choice. [after Thomas *Hobson,* 1544-1631, of Cambridge, who hired out horses, and obliged each customer to take the horse nearest the stable door or none at all]

**hock**[1] /hɒk/, *n.* **1.** the joint in the hind leg of the horse, etc., above the fetlock joint, corresponding to the ankle in man but raised from the ground and protruding backwards when bent. **2.** a corresponding joint in a fowl. **3.** a cut of pork through the joint of a leg or foreleg. *–v.t.* **4.** →**hamstring.** [ME *hoch, hogh, howh,* OE *hōh* hock, heel. Cf. HEEL[1]]

**hock**[2] /hɒk/, *n.* **1.** a dry white wine, grown along the Rhine river. **2.** any similar wine made elsewhere. [short for *hockamore,* obs. of *Hochheimer,* a Rhine wine produced near Hochheim, Germany]

**hock**[3] /hɒk/, *Colloq.* *–v.i.* **1.** →**pawn. 2.** to sell (esp. illegally). *–n.* **3. in hock,** pawned. [D *hok* hovel, prison, debt]

**hock**[4] /hɒk/, *n. Colloq.* an active male homosexual.

**hocket** /ˈhɒkət/, *n.* a stylistic feature of medieval polyphony whereby two voices, with single notes or small groups of notes, are rapidly alternated, one part resting while the other sounds. [ME, from OF *hocquet* interruption, hiccup]

**hockey** /ˈhɒki/, *n.* a game in which opposing sides seek with sticks curved at one end to drive a ball (in **field hockey**) or puck (in **ice hockey**) into their opponents' goal. [*hock* stick with hook at one end, var. of HOOK]

**hockey stick** /ˈ– stɪk/, *n.* a long stick curved at the base for hitting the ball in hockey.

**hockshop** /ˈhɒkʃɒp/, *n. U.S. Colloq.* →**pawnshop.**

**hocky** /ˈhɒki/, *adj.* (of a sheep or goat) having hocks which incline inwards. – **hockiness,** *n.*

**hocus** /ˈhoʊkəs/, *v.t.,* **-cused, -cusing,** or **-cussed, -cussing. 1.** to play a trick on; hoax; cheat. **2.** to stupefy with a drug or a drugged drink. **3.** to drug (a drink).

**hocus-pocus** /hoʊkəs-ˈpoʊkəs/, *n., v.,* **-cused, -cusing,** or **-cussed, -cussing.** *–n.* **1.** a formula used in conjuring or incantations. **2.** a juggler's trick; sleight of hand. **3.** trickery or deception. **4.** unnecessary mystification or elaboration extended to cover deception or something basically simple. *–v.t.* **5.** to play tricks on or with. *–v.i.* **6.** to perform tricks; practise deception. [orig. jugglers' jargon, simulating Latin]

**hod** /hɒd/, *n.* **1.** a portable trough for carrying mortar, bricks, etc., fixed crosswise on top of a pole and carried on the shoulder. **2.** →**coalscuttle.** [cf. MD *hodde* basket, c. HG *hotte,* OF *hotte* (from G), d. E *hot* (from OF) pannier]

**hodad** /ˈhoʊdæd/, *n. Colloq.* a swimmer who annoys or impedes surfboard riders. Also, **ho-dad.**

**hoddie** /ˈhɒdi/, *n. Colloq.* →**hodman.**

**hodgepodge** /ˈhɒdʒpɒdʒ/, *n.* →**hotchpotch.**

**Hodgkin's disease** /ˈhɒdʒkənz dəziz/, *n.* a malignant disease of lymphatic tissue. [named after Thomas *Hodgkin,* 1798-1866, English physician]

**hodman** /ˈhɒdmən/, *n., pl.* **-men.** a bricklayer's assistant. [HOD + MAN]

**hodograph** /ˈhɒdəgræf, -graf/, *n.* the curve drawn through the ends of the vectors which represent the velocities of a particle at successive instants; used to determine the acceleration of a particle moving along a curved path. [Gk *hodó(s)* way + -GRAPH]

**hodometer** /hɒˈdɒmətə/, *n.* →**odometer.**

**hodoscope** /ˈhɒdəskoʊp/, *n.* an apparatus for tracing the path of a charged particle, esp. a cosmic-ray particle.

**hoe** /hoʊ/, *n., v.,* **hoed, hoeing.** *–n.* **1.** a long-handled implement with a thin, flat blade usu. set transversely, used to break up the surface of the ground, destroy weeds, etc. *–v.t.* **2.** to dig, scrape, weed, cultivate, etc., with a hoe. *–v.i.* **3.** to use a hoe. **4. hoe in,** *Colloq.* **a.** to commence to eat heartily. **b.** to begin something energetically. **5. hoe into,** *Colloq.* **a.** to eat (food) heartily. **b.** to attack (a person) vigorously, usu. verbally. **c.** to undertake (a job) with vigour. [ME *howe,* from OF *houe,* from Gmc; cf. G *Haue*] – **hoer,** *n.*

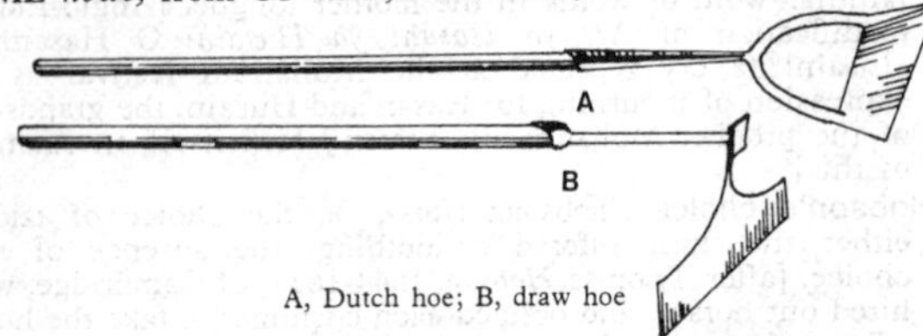

A, Dutch hoe; B, draw hoe

**hoedown** /ˈhoʊdaʊn/, *n. U.S.* **1.** a boisterous square dance. **2.** the music of such a dance. **3.** a party at which such dances are performed.

**hog** /hɒg/, *n., v.,* **hogged, hogging.** *–n.* **1.** a mammal of the family Suidae; a pig (in the U.S., the general word). **2.** a domesticated swine, esp. a castrated boar, bred for slaughter. **3.** →**hogget. 4.** *Colloq.* a selfish, gluttonous, or filthy person. **5.** a ship of which the hull droops at both ends. **6. go the whole hog,** *Colloq.* to do completely and thoroughly; to commit oneself unreservedly to a course of action. **7. live high on the hog,** *Colloq.* to live luxuriously, extravagantly. *–v.t.* **8.** *Colloq.* to appropriate selfishly; take more than one's share of. **9.** to arch (the back) upwards like that of a hog. **10.** to cut (a horse's mane) short. *–v.i.* **11.** (of a ship's hull) to droop at both ends. [ME; OE *hogg,* from OBritish; cf. Welsh *hwch* sow] – **hoglike.**

**hogback** /ˈhɒgbæk/, *n.* a ridge produced by highly tilted strata which resist erosion. Also, **hogsback.**

**hogfish** /ˈhɒgfɪʃ/, *n., pl.* **-fishes,** *(esp. collectively)* **-fish.** any of various fishes, as *Lachnolaemus maximus,* a labroid food fish of the south-eastern U.S. coast and the West Indies, or *Percina caprodes,* found in American lakes and streams, or *Orthopristis chrysopterus,* one of the grunts of the southern coasts of the U.S.

**hogget** /ˈhɒgət/, *n.* **1.** a young sheep of either sex, from the age of ten months to the cutting of its first two adult teeth. **2.** the meat of such a sheep. Also, **hog.**

**hoggish** /ˈhɒgɪʃ/, *adj.* **1.** like or befitting a hog. **2.** selfish; gluttonous; filthy. – **hoggishly,** *adv.* – **hoggishness,** *n.*

**hogmanay** /hɒgməˈneɪ, ˈhɒgməneɪ/, *n. Scot. (oft. cap.)* **1.** New Year's Eve. **2.** the celebrations held on this occasion. [ONF *hoguinané,* OF *aguillanneuf* New Year's Eve; orig. unknown]

**hognose snake** /ˈhɒgnoʊz sneɪk/, *n.* any of the harmless American snakes constituting the genus *Heterodon,* notable for their hoglike snouts and their curious actions and contortions when disturbed.

**hognut** /ˈhɒgnʌt/, *n.* **1.** →**pignut. 2.** →**earthnut.**

**hog peanut** /hɒg ˈpinʌt/, *n.* a twining plant, *Amphicarpa bracteata,* with pods which ripen in or on the ground.

**hogsback** /ˈhɒgzbæk/, *n.* **1.** →**hogback. 2.** *N.Z.* a cloud formation shaped like a hogback.

**hog's-fennel** /ˈhɒgz-fɛnəl/, *n.* any of several species of umbelliferous plants of the genus *Peucedanum,* as *P. palustre,* a biennial occurring in wet places in Europe and western Asia.

**hogshead** /ˈhɒgzhɛd/, *n.* **1.** a unit of measurement of capacity in the imperial system, equal to 52 gallons (approx. 236.4 litres). **2.** a container or cask (esp. of beer or cider) having approximately such a capacity, the value depending on the locality and use. [ME *hoggeshed,* lit., hog's head; unexplained]

**hogtie** /ˈhɒgtaɪ/, *v.t.,* **-tied, -tying.** *Chiefly U.S.* **1.** to tie as a hog is tied, with all four feet together. **2.** to hamper; impede.

**hogwash** /ˈhɒgwɒʃ/, **1.** any worthless stuff. **2.** meaningless or insincere talk, etc.

**hogweed** /ˈhɒgwid/, *n.* any of a number of unrelated coarse weeds.

**ho-hum** /hoʊ-ˈhʌm/, *adj.* boring; plain; lacking vitality or interest.

**hoick**[1] /hɔɪk/, *v.t.* **1.** to hoist abruptly. **2.** to cause to rise sharply or abruptly, as an aeroplane.

**hoick**[2] /hɔɪk/, *v.i. Colloq.* to clear the throat and spit. [imitative]

**hoicks** /hɔɪks/, *interj.* (a cry used to incite hounds in hunting.) Also, **hoick** /hɔɪk/.

**hoiden** /ˈhɔɪdən/, *n., adj.* →**hoyden.**

**hoi polloi** /hɔɪ pəˈlɔɪ/, *n.* the common people; the masses (sometimes prec. pleonastically by *the*). [Gk: the many]

**hoist** /hɔɪst/, *v.t.* **1.** to raise or lift, esp. by some mechanical appliance: *to hoist sail.* **2.** *Colloq.* to steal, esp. to shoplift. **3.** *Colloq.* to throw. *–n.* **4.** an apparatus for hoisting, as a lift. **5.** a lift for heavy goods; goods lift. **6.** the act of hoisting; a lift. **7.** *Naut.* **a.** the vertical length of any sail other than a course. **b.** the perpendicular height of a sail or flag. **c.** a string of flags raised as a signal. **8.** *Colloq.* a theft; housebreaking. [later form of *hoise;* cf. G *hissen*] – **hoister,** *n.*

**hoity-toity** /hɔɪti-ˈtɔɪti/, *adj.* **1.** giddy; flighty. **2.** assuming; haughty. Also, **highty-tighty.** [reduplicative derivative of obs. *hoit,* v., to romp, riot]

**hokey-pokey** /hoʊki-ˈpoʊki/, *n.* **1.** →**hocus-pocus. 2.** a kind of dance. **3.** *N.Z.* a toffee-like sweet.

**hokonui** /hoʊkəˈnui/, *n. N.Z. Colloq.* any illicitly-distilled spirits. [from *Hokonui,* district of Southland Province, N.Z.]

**Hokonui** /hoʊkəˈnui/, *adj.* **1.** pertaining to a geological period or system of rocks in New Zealand which correspond with the Triassic and Jurassic periods or systems. **2.** of or denoting the major mountain-building episode at the close of the Hokonui period and which preceded the Cretaceous period in New Zealand.

**hokum** /ˈhoʊkəm/, *n. U.S. Colloq.* **1.** nonsense; bunk. **2.** elements of low comedy or farce introduced into a play or the like for the laughs they may bring. **3.** sentimental or pathetic matter of an elementary or stereotyped kind introduced into a play or the like. [b. HOCUS-POCUS and BUNKUM]

**Holarctic realm** /hɒˌlaktɪk ˈrɛlm/, *n.* a biogeographical realm comprising the Palaearctic and the Nearctic regions.

**hold**[1] /hoʊld/, *v.,* **held; held** or *(Archaic)* **holden; holding;** *n.* *–v.t.* **1.** to have or keep in the hand; keep fast; grasp. **2.** to reserve; retain; set aside. **3.** to bear, sustain, or support with the hand, arms, etc., or by any means. **4.** to keep in a specified state, relation, etc.: *to hold the enemy in check.* **5.** to keep in custody; detain. **6.** to engage in; preside over; carry on; pursue; observe or celebrate: *to hold a meeting.* **7.** to have the ownership or use of; keep as one's own; occupy: *to hold office.* **8.** to contain or be capable of containing: *this bottle holds two litres.* **9.** to have or keep in the mind; think or believe; entertain: *to hold a belief.* **10.** to regard or consider: *to hold a person responsible.* **11.** *Law.* to decide. **12.** to regard with varying degrees of affection: *to hold one dear, to hold one cheap.* **13.** to keep (territory, etc.) forcibly, as against an adversary. *–v.i.* **14.** to remain or continue in a specified state, relation, etc.: *to hold still.* **15.** to remain fast; adhere; cling: *the anchor holds.* **16.** to keep or maintain a grasp on something. **17.** to maintain one's position against opposition; continue in resistance. **18.** to hold property by some tenure; derive title (fol. by *from* or *of*). **19.** to remain attached, faithful, or steadfast: *to hold to one's purpose.* **20.** to remain valid; be in force: *the rule does not hold.* **21.** to refrain or forbear (usu. in the imperative). **22.** *Colloq.* to have adequate money or assets: *how are you holding?* *–v.* **23.** Some special verb phrases are:

**hold a catch,** *Cricket.* to retain the ball after a catch for the specified time, to prove the catch is valid.

**hold back, 1.** to restrain or check. **2.** to retain possession of; keep back; withhold.

**hold down,** to continue to hold (a position, job, etc.), esp. in spite of difficulties.

**hold forth, 1.** to put forward; propose. **2.** to harangue.

**hold good,** to be true; be valid.

**hold in, 1.** to restrain, check, or curb. **2.** to restrain or contain oneself.

**hold it,** to stop; wait.

**hold off, 1.** to keep aloof or at a distance. **2.** to refrain from action.

**hold on, 1.** to keep fast hold on something. **2.** to continue; persist. **3.** *Colloq.* to stop or halt (chiefly in the imperative).

**hold one's own,** to maintain one's position or condition.

**hold one's tongue** or **one's peace,** to keep silent; cease or refrain from speaking.

**hold out, 1.** to offer or present. **2.** to extend or stretch forth. **3.** to continue to exist; last. **4.** to refuse to yield or submit. **5.** *Orig. U.S. Colloq.* to keep back something expected or due.

**hold over, 1.** to keep for future consideration or action; postpone. **2.** *Music.* to prolong (a note) from one to the next.

**hold the ball,** *Aus. Rules.* to retain possession of the ball when seized by another player thereby incurring a penalty.

**hold the line,** (of a person on the telephone) to wait.

**hold the road,** (of tyres on a car) to grip the road.

**hold someone's hand,** to provide moral support; encourage.

**hold to,** to abide by; keep to.

**hold together, 1.** to cause to remain in one piece: *only one bolt holds it together.* **2.** to cause to remain functioning as a unit: *only the sergeant held the company together.* **3.** to remain whole or in one piece.

**hold up, 1.** to keep in an erect position. **2.** to present to notice; exhibit; display. **3.** to hinder; delay. **4.** to stop by force in order to rob.

**hold water, 1.** to retain water; not let water run through. **2.** to prove sound, tenable, or valid: *Mr Black's claims will not hold water.*

**hold with,** to agree with; approve of.

*–n.* **24.** the act of holding fast by a grasp of the hand or by some other physical means; grasp; grip: *take hold.* **25.** something to hold a thing by, as a handle; something to grasp for support. **26.** a thing that holds fast or supports something else. **27.** a controlling force, or dominating influence: *to have a hold on a person.* **28.** *Archery.* the time during which the archer stands with bow drawn before loosing the arrow. **29.** *Archaic.* a fortified place, or stronghold. **30. get a hold on oneself,** *Colloq.* to get control over oneself. [ME *holden,* OE *h(e)aldan,* c. G *halten*]

**hold**[2] /hoʊld/, *n. Naut.* the interior of a ship below the deck, esp. where the cargo is stowed. [var. of HOLE, c. D *hol* hole, hold]

**holdall** /ˈhoʊldɔl/, *n.* a portable case or bag. Also, **carryall.**

**holdback** /ˈhoʊldbæk/, *n.* **1.** the iron or strap on the shaft of a vehicle to which the breeching of the harness is attached, enabling the horse to hold back or to back the vehicle. **2.** a restraint; check.

**holder** /ˈhoʊldə/, *n.* **1.** something to hold a thing with. **2.** one who has the ownership, possession, or use of something; an owner; a tenant. **3.** the payee or endorsee in possession of a bill of exchange or promissory note. **4.** →**shareholder. 5.** one who wins and keeps a sports cup until the next contest or championship is held.

**holder for value,** *n.* a holder of a bill of exchange or promissory note for which valuable consideration has been given.

**holder in due course,** *n.* a holder who has taken a bill of exchange, cheque, or note, which is complete and regular on the face of it under certain conditions, namely that the bill is not overdue, that it is without notice of previous dishonour, and it is taken in good faith and for value without notice of any defect.

**holdfast** /ˈhoʊldfast/, *n.* **1.** something used to hold or secure a thing in place; a catch, hook, or clamp. **2.** *Bot.* any of several sucker-like organs serving to attach a plant to something.

**holding** /ˈhoʊldɪŋ/, *n.* **1.** (*oft. pl.*) property owned, esp. stocks and shares, and land. *–adj.* **2.** having adequate resources, esp. of money.

**holding company** /ˈ– ˌkʌmpəni/, *n.* **1.** a company controlling, or able to control, other companies by virtue of share ownership in these companies. **2.** a company which owns stocks or securities of other companies, deriving income from them.

**holding over** /– ˈoʊvə/, *n.* the keeping in possession of land by a lessee after his tenancy has terminated; if done with the lessor's consent he becomes a tenant at will or sufferance; if without, he is a trespasser.

**holding paddock** /ˈ– pædək/, *n.* a paddock to hold stock awaiting sale, routine handling, etc.

**holding pattern** /ˈ– pætn/, *n.* the more or less circular flight paths of aircraft being held near a busy airport, waiting their turn to land.

**holding pen** /ˈ– pɛn/, *n.* a pen in which stock are held to await sale, routine handling, etc.

**holdover** /ˈhoʊldoʊvə/, *n. U.S. Colloq.* something which remains behind from a former period.

**hold-up** /ˈhoʊld-ʌp/, *n. Colloq.* **1.** a forcible stopping and robbing of a person, bank, etc. **2.** a delay; stoppage.

**hole** /hoʊl/, *n., v.,* **holed, holing.** *–n.* **1.** an opening through anything; an aperture. **2.** a hollow place in a solid body or mass; a cavity: *a hole in the ground.* **3.** the excavated habitation of an animal; a burrow. **4.** a small, mean abode or town. **5.** a dungeon; place of confinement. **6.** *Colloq.* an embarrassing position or predicament: *to find oneself in a hole.* **7.** *U.S.* a cove or small harbour. **8.** *Colloq.* a fault or flaw: *to pick holes in a plan.* **9.** *Golf.* **a.** the small cavity into which the ball is to be placed. **b.** →**fairway. c.** the score made by playing the ball from the tee to its corresponding hole. **10.** *Electronics.* the absence of an electron in the valency structure of a semiconductor which acts as a mobile vacancy with positive charge and mass. **11.** *Colloq.* any of certain apertures of the body, as the mouth, anus, or female genitals. *–v.t.* **12.** to make a hole or holes in. **13.** to put or drive into a hole. **14.** *Golf.* to drive the ball into (a hole). **15.** to bore (a tunnel, etc.) **16.** *Colloq.* to fire a bullet into. *–v.i.* **17.** to make a hole or holes. **18.** *Golf.* to drive the ball into a hole (oft. fol. by *out.*). **19. hole up, a.** to go into a hole; retire for the winter, as a hibernating animal. **b.** to hide (often from the police). [ME; OE *hol* hole, cave, den, orig. neut. of *hol,* adj., c. G *hohl* hollow] – **holey,** *adj.*

**hole-and-corner** /hoʊl-ən-ˈkɔnə/, *adj.* furtive; secretive; underhand.

**Hole and Corner man,** *n.* (formerly) a person who advocated severity in dealing with transported convicts and was opposed to the emancipists.

**hole conduction** /ˈhoʊl kəndʌkʃən/, *n.* the motion of a gap in the regularity of the electrons in a crystal lattice.

**hole in one,** *n. Golf.* **1.** a score of one stroke only for a hole. See **birdie.** *–v.i.* **2.** to achieve such a score.

**hole-in-one** /hoʊl-ɪn-ˈwʌn/, *n., v.,* **holed-in-one, holing-in-one.** *Golf.* *–n.* **1.** a shot from the tee which lands in the hole. *–v.i.* **2.** to make such a shot.

**hole in the heart,** *n.* a condition, often congenital, in which one of the chambers of the heart has an abnormal opening in its wall.

**hole puncher** /'houl pʌntʃə/, *n.* a device for cutting holes in paper, to enable loose sheets to be collected in folders, files, etc.

**holey dollar** /houli 'dɒlə/, *n.* (formerly) a silver dollar from which the centre had been punched, both pieces remaining in currency as coins. Cf. **dump**[2]. Also, **holy dollar.**

**holibut** /'hɒləbət/, *n., pl.* **-buts,** (*esp. collectively*) **-but.** →**halibut.**

**holiday** /'hɒlədeɪ/, *n.* **1.** a day fixed by law or custom on which ordinary business is suspended in commemoration of some event or in honour of some person, etc. **2.** any day of exemption from labour. **3.** a religious feast; holy day. **4.** (*oft. pl.*) a period of cessation from work, or of recreation; a vacation. *–adj.* **5.** pertaining to a festival; joyous: *a holiday mood.* **6.** suited only to a holiday. *–v.i.* **7.** to take a holiday: *to holiday on the Gold Coast.* [ME; OE *hāligdæg* holy day]

**holiday camp** /'– kæmp/, *n.* an organised camp, usu. for groups of young people or schoolchildren, during holiday periods for the purposes of recreation, sport, hobbies, etc.

**holiday house** /'– haus/, *n.* a house on the beach or at some other holiday centre, and used mainly during annual holidays, sometimes rented out for the remainder of the year. Also, **holiday cottage, holiday home.**

**holiday-maker** /'hɒlədeɪ-meɪkə/, *n.* a person on holiday, esp. at a resort.

**holiday work** /'hɒlədeɪ wɜk/, *n.* **1.** work performed on a public holiday. **2.** Also, **holiday job.** temporary work performed by a student in an annual holiday.

**holier-than-thou** /ˌhouliə-ðən-'ðau/, *adj.* sanctimonious; smug; self-righteous.

**holily** /'houləli/, *adv.* **1.** piously or devoutly. **2.** in a sacred manner. [ME; OE *hāliglīce,* from *hālig* HOLY + *-līce* -LY]

**holiness** /'houlinəs/, *n.* **1.** the state or character of being holy; sanctity. **2.** (*cap.*) a title of the pope, and formerly also of other high ecclesiastical dignitaries, etc. (preceded by *his* or *your*). [ME *holynesse,* OE *hālignes*]

**holism** /'houlɪzəm/, *n.* the philosophical theory that wholes (which are more than the mere sums of their parts) are fundamental aspects of the real. [HOL(O)- + -ISM] – **holist,** *n.* – **holistic** /hou'lɪstɪk/, *adj.*

**holland** /'hɒlənd/, *n.* a kind of coarse linen fabric.

**Holland** /'hɒlənd/, *n.* →**Netherlands, The.**

**hollandaise sauce** /hɒlənˌdeɪz 'sɔs/, *n.* a yellow sauce made of eggs, lemon juice or vinegar, butter, and seasonings.

**holland blind** /hɒlənd 'blaɪnd/, *n.* a window blind of holland or other fabric.

**Hollander** /'hɒləndə/, *n.* a native of the Netherlands; a Dutchman.

**Hollands gin** /'hɒləndz dʒɪn/, *n.* →**gin**[1] (def. 2). [orig. made in *Holland*]

**holler** /'hɒlə/, *v.i.* **1.** to cry aloud; shout. *–v.t.* **2.** to shout (something). *–n.* **3.** a loud cry of pain, surprise, to attract attention, etc. [F *holà* stop]

**hollies** /'hɒliz/, *n. pl. Colloq.* holidays.

**hollow** /'hɒlou/, *adj.* **1.** having a hole or cavity within; not solid; empty: *a hollow ball.* **2.** having a depression or concavity: *a hollow surface.* **3.** sunken, as the cheeks or eyes. **4.** (of sound) not resonant; dull, muffled, or deep: *a hollow voice.* **5.** without substantial or real worth; vain: *a hollow victory.* **6.** insincere or false: *hollow compliments.* **7.** hungry. **8. have hollow legs,** to have a prodigious appetite. *–n.* **9.** an empty space within anything; a hole; a depression or cavity. **10.** a valley: *the hollow of a hill.* *–v.t.* **11.** to make hollow. **12.** to form by making hollow (oft. fol. by *out*). *–v.i.* **13.** to become hollow. *–adv.* **14.** in a hollow manner. **15.** *Colloq.* utterly: *to beat someone hollow.* [ME *hol(o)u, holw(e),* n., adj., OE *holh* hollow (place)] – **hollowly,** *adv.*

**hollow-eyed** /'hɒlou-aɪd/, *adj.* having sunken eyes.

**hollow log** /hɒlou 'lɒg/, *n. Colloq.* a new Australian. [rhyming slang, *hollow log* wog, new Australian]

**hollow way** /– 'weɪ/, *n.* a track cut down, usu. by water erosion, below the level of surrounding fields.

**holly** /'hɒli/, *n., pl.* **-lies. 1.** any of the trees or shrubs of the genus *Ilex,* esp. those species having glossy, spiny-edged leaves and small, whitish flowers succeeded by bright red berries. **2.** the foliage and berries, much used for decoration, esp. during the Christmas season. [ME *holig, holi,* OE *holegn* (with loss of *-n*); akin to D *hulst,* G *Hulst,* F *houx,* Welsh *celyn*]

**holly fern** /'– fɜn/, *n.* a rhizomatous fern with toothed pinnae, *Polystichum lonchitis,* found on non-acid mountain rocks of the northern temperate zone.

**hollyhock** /'hɒlihɒk/, *n.* **1.** a tall plant, *Althea rosea,* common in cultivation, having showy flowers of various colours. **2.** the flower itself. [ME *holihoc,* from *holi* HOLY + *hoc* mallow, OE *hocc*]

**holly oak** /'hɒli ouk/, *n.* →**holm oak.**

**hollywood** /'hɒliwud/, *n. in the phrase* **do a hollywood,** to gain attention by one's dramatic behaviour. [from *Hollywood,* centre of the U.S. film industry]

**holm**[1] /houm/, *n. Brit.* **1.** a low, flat tract of land beside a river or stream. **2.** a small island, esp. one in a river or lake. [ME and OE, from Scand.; cf. Icel. *holmr* islet]

**holm**[2] /houm/, *n.* →**holm oak.** [ME; dissimilated var. of *holn,* OE *holen* holly (dental + dental became dental + labial)]

**holmic** /'hɒlmɪk/, *adj.* of or containing holmium in the trivalent state.

**holmium** /'hɒlmiəm/, *n.* a rare-earth element found in gadolinite. *Symbol:* Ho; *at. wt:* 164.93; *at. no.:* 67. [NL; named after *Stockholm,* Sweden]

**holm oak** /'houm ouk/, *n.* an evergreen oak, *Quercus ilex,* of southern Europe, with foliage resembling that of the holly.

**holo-,** a word element meaning 'whole' or 'entire', as in *holocaust.* [Gk, combining form of *hólos*]

**holoblastic** /hɒlə'blæstɪk/, *adj.* (of eggs which undergo total cleavage) wholly germinal (opposed to *meroblastic*).

**holocaine** /'hɒləkeɪn/, *n.* **1.** *Chem.* a colourless crystalline basic compound, $C_{18}H_{22}N_2O_2$, used as a local anaesthetic. **2.** *Pharm.* a local anaesthetic resembling cocaine in its action, used chiefly for the eye.

**holocaust** /'hɒləkɒst, -kɔst/, *n.* **1.** great or wholesale destruction of life, esp. by fire. **2.** an offering devoted wholly to burning; a burnt offering. [LL *holocaustum,* from Gk *holókauston* a burnt offering, properly neut. of *holókaustos* burnt whole] – **holocaustic** /hɒlə'kɒstɪk/, *adj.*

**Holocene** /'hɒləsin/, *adj.* designating or pertaining to the Recent epoch. [HOLO- + -CENE]

**hologram** /'hɒləgræm/, *n.* a negative produced by holography.

**holograph** /'hɒləgræf/, *adj.* **1.** Also, **holographic** /hɒlə'græfɪk/. wholly written by the person in whose name it appears: *a holograph letter.* *–n.* **2.** a holograph writing. **3.** *Law.* a deed in writing, written entirely by the grantor himself. [LL *holographus,* from Gk *holographos*]

**holography** /hɒ'lɒgrəfi/, *n.* a form of photography in which no lens is used and in which a photographic plate records the interference pattern between two portions of a laser beam.

**holohedral** /hɒlə'hidrəl/, *adj.* (of a crystal) having all the planes or faces required by the maximum symmetry of the system to which it belongs. [HOLO- + Gk *hédra* seat, base + -AL[1]] – **holohedrism,** *n.*

**holophote** /'hɒləfout/, *n.* an apparatus by which practically all the light from a lighthouse lamp, etc., is thrown in the desired direction. [HOLO- + Gk *phôs* light] – **holophotal** /hɒlə'foutl/, *adj.*

**holophrastic** /hɒlə'fræstɪk/, *adj.* expressing a whole meaning or sentence in a single word, as in the language of very young children. For example, the word *wet!* meaning *my pants are wet.* [HOLO- + Gk *phrastikós* expressive]

**holophytic** /hɒlə'fɪtɪk/, *adj.* obtaining nutriment by the synthesisation of inorganic substances, in the manner of green plants.

**holothurian** /hɒlə'θjuriən, '-θjuər-/, *n.* any of the Holothuroidea, a class of echinoderms having a long leathery body and tentacles round the anterior end as the sea-cucumber. [NL *Holothuria* genus name (from L, from Gk *holothoúria*) + -AN]

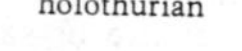
holothurian

**holozoic** /hɒlə'zouɪk/, *adj.* feeding on organisms or on solid matter derived from them, in the manner of most animals.

**holp** /hɒlp/, *v. Archaic.* past tense of **help.**

**holpen** /'hɒlpən/, *v. Archaic.* past participle of **help.**

**hols** /hɒlz/, *n.pl. Colloq.* →**holiday** (def. 4).

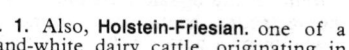

**Holstein** /'houlstaɪn/, *n.* **1.** Also, **Holstein-Friesian.** one of a breed of large, black-and-white dairy cattle, originating in North Holland and Friesland.

**holster** /'hɒlstə/, *n.* a leather case for a pistol, attached to a belt or a saddle. [var. of *hulster,* from Swed. *hölster,* whence also D *holster;* akin to OE *heolstor* cover] – **holstered,** *adj.*

**holt**[1] /hoult/, *n. Chiefly Poetic.* **1.** a wood or grove. **2.** a wooded hill. [ME *holte,* OE *holt,* c. G *Holz* wood]

**holt**[2] /hoult/, *n.* **1.** grip; control: *get a holt on yourself.* **2.** (*pl.*) **come to holts with,** face up to; get a grip on. **3.** (*pl.*) **get into holts with,** *Colloq.* to become involved in an argument with. [Brit. d., var. of HOLD[1]]

**holus-bolus** /ˌhouləs-'bouləs/, *adv. Colloq.* **1.** all at once. **2.** in its entirety.

**holy** /'houli/, *adj.,* **-lier, -liest,** *n., pl.* **-lies.** *–adj.* **1.** specially recognised as or declared sacred by religious use or authority; consecrated: *a holy day.* **2.** dedicated or devoted to the service of God, the Church, or religion: *a holy man.* **3.** saintly or godly; pious or devout. **4.** of religious purity, exaltation, solemnity, etc.: *a holy love.* **5.** entitled to worship or profound religious reverence because of divine character or origin, or connection with God or divinity: *holy Bible.* **6.** religious: *holy rites.* **7. holy terror,** *Colloq.* a person difficult to deal with; an alarming or frightening person. *–n.* **8.** a place of worship; a sacred place. **9.** that which is holy. [ME *holi,* OE *hālig, hāleg,* c. D and G *heilig,* akin to HALE[1] and HEAL]

**Holy Bible** /houli 'baɪbəl/, *n.* →**Bible** (def. 1).

**Holy City** /– 'sɪti/, *n.* a city regarded as particularly sacred by the adherents of a religious faith, as Jerusalem by Jews and Christians, Mecca and Medina by Muslims, and Varanasi by Hindus.

**Holy Communion** /– kə'mjunjən/, *n.* →**communion** (def. 5b).

**holy day** /'houli deɪ/, *n.* a consecrated day or religious festival, esp. one other than Sunday.

**holy-dollar** /houli-'dɒlə/, *n.* →**holey dollar.**

**Holy Father** /houli 'faðə/, *n.* a title of the pope.

**Holy Ghost** /– 'goust/, *n.* the third person of the Trinity.

**Holy Grail** /– 'greɪl/, *n.* →**grail.**

**holy-grass** /'houli-gras/, *n.* any species of the sweet-scented tufted perennial grasses of the genus *Hierochloe,* as *H. redolens.*

**holy Joe** /houli 'dʒou/, *n. Colloq.* **1.** a member of a religious order. **2.** one of unpleasantly rigid religious principle. **3.** a Roman Catholic.

**Holy Land** /'houli lænd/, *n.* Palestine, now divided between Israel and Jordan.

**holy of holies,** *n.* **1.** a place of special sacredness. **2.** the inner and smaller chamber of the Jewish tabernacle and temple entered only by the high priest and but once a year.

**holy orders** /ˌhouli 'ɔdəz/, *n.* **1.** the rite or sacrament of ordination. **2.** the rank or status of an ordained Christian minister. **3.** the major degrees or grades of the Christian ministry.

**holy roller** /– 'roulə/, *n. Colloq.* a member of a particular protestant sect in North America, the meetings of which involve frenzied emotion.

**Holy Roman Empire,** *n.* the empire in western and central Europe which began with the coronation of Otto the Great, king of Germany, as Roman emperor A.D. 962, and ended with the renunciation of the Roman imperial title of Francis II in 1806, regarded theoretically as the continuation of the Western Empire and as the temporal form of a universal dominion whose spiritual head was the pope. It is sometimes regarded as originating with Charlemagne, who was crowned Roman emperor A.D 800.

**Holy Rood** /houli 'rud/, *n.* **1.** the cross on which Jesus died. **2.** (*l.c.*) a crucifix, esp. one above a rood screen.

**Holy Scripture** /– 'skrɪptʃə/, *n.* →**Scripture** (def. 1).

**Holy See** /– 'si/, *n.* **1.** the see of Rome; the office or jurisdiction of the pope. **2.** the papal court.

**Holy Spirit** /– 'spɪrət/, *n.* →**Holy Ghost.**

**holystone** /'houlistoun/, *n., v.,* **-stoned, -stoning.** *–n.* **1.** a soft sandstone used for scrubbing the decks of a ship. *–v.t.* **2.** to scrub with a holystone.

**holytide** /'houlitaɪd/, *n. Archaic.* a holy season.

**holy war** /houli 'wɔ/, *n.* a war waged for an allegedly holy purpose; a crusade.

**holy water** /'– wɔtə/, *n.* water blessed by a priest.

**Holy Week** /'houli wik/, *n.* the week preceding Easter Sunday.

**Holy Writ** /– 'rɪt/, *n.* the Scriptures.

**homage** /'hɒmɪdʒ/, *n.* **1.** respect or reverence paid or rendered. **2.** the formal acknowledgment by which a feudal tenant or vassal declared himself to be the man of his lord, owing him faith and service. **3.** the relation thus established of a vassal to his lord. **4.** something done or given in acknowledgment or consideration of vassalage. [ME, from OF, from LL *homo* vassal, L man]

**hombre** /'ɒmbreɪ/, *n. Chiefly U.S.* a man who is Spanish by descent; by extension, a man.

**homburg** /'hɒmbɜg/, *n.* a felt hat with a soft crown dented lengthways and a narrow brim.

**home** /houm/, *n., adj., adv., v.,* **homed, homing.** *–n.* **1.** a house, or other shelter that is the fixed residence of a person, a family, or a household. **2.** a place of one's domestic affections. **3.** (*oft. cap.*) an institution for the homeless, sick, etc. **4.** the dwelling place or retreat of an animal. **5.** the place or region where something is native or most common. **6.** any place of existence or refuge: *a heavenly home.* **7.** one's native place or own country. **8.** (in games) the goal; finishing post; base. **9.** *Baseball.* the plate at which the batter stands and which he must return to and touch after running round the bases, in order to score a run. **10.** *Obs.* Great Britain, esp. England. **11. a home away from home,** a place having the comforts of home. **12. at home, a.** in one's own house or country. **b.** in a situation familiar to one; at ease. **c.** prepared to receive social visits. **d.** familiar with; accustomed to; well-informed. **e.** (of a football team, etc.) in one's own town or one's own grounds. **13. who is he when he's at home?** (an exclamation, usu. scornful, indicating that the person referred to has an undeservedly high opinion of himself). *–adj.* **14.** of, pertaining to, or connected with one's home, town, centre of operations, or country; domestic. **15.** that strikes home, or to the mark aimed at; to the point: *a home thrust.* **16. home and hosed,** finished successfully. **17. home on the pig's back,** certain to succeed. *–adv.* **18.** to, towards, or at home: *to go home.* **19.** deep; to the heart; effectively and completely. **20.** to the mark or point aimed at: *to strike home.* **21.** *Naut.* all the way; as far as possible: *to heave the anchor home.* **22. bring home to,** to cause (someone) to realise fully. **23. nothing to write home about,** not remarkable; unexciting; inferior. *–v.i.* **24.** to go or return home. **25.** (of guided missiles, aircraft, etc.) to proceed, esp. under control of an automatic aiming mechanism towards an airport, fixed or moving target, etc. (oft. fol. by *in, on* or *on to*). **26.** to have the home where specified. *–v.t.* **27.** to bring or send home. **28.** to provide with a home. **29.** to direct, esp. under control of an automatic aiming device, towards an airport, target, etc. [ME; OE *hām* home, dwelling, c G *Heim*]

**home aid** /– 'eɪd/, *n.* →**domestic help.**

**home base** /– 'beɪs/, *n.* →**home** (def. 9).

**homebody** /'houmbɒdi/, *n. Colloq.* one who likes being at home.

**home-bred** /'houm-brɛd/, *adj.* **1.** bred at home; native; indigenous; domestic. **2.** unpolished; unsophisticated.

**home-brew** /'houm-bru/, *adj.;* /houm-'bru/, *n.* *–adj.* **1.** →**home-brewed.** *–n.* **2.** a home-brewed beverage.

**home-brewed** /'houm-brud/, *adj.* (of beer or other fermented

beverage) brewed at home, as for home consumption.
**homecoming** /ˈhoʊmkʌmɪŋ/, *n.* a return to a home.
**home-cooked** /ˈhoʊm-kʊkt/, *adj.* cooked at home.
**home country** /ˈhoʊm kʌntri/, *n.* **1.** for a person living in an adopted country, or just visiting, that country which he thinks of as home. **2.** (formerly) for Australians, whether they had been there or not, England, or another part of the United Kingdom.
**home-deliver** /hoʊm-dəˈlɪvə/, *v.t.* **1.** to deliver (goods, etc.) to the purchaser's home. *–v.i.* **2.** to offer a service whereby goods are delivered to the purchaser's home. – **home-delivery,** *n.*
**home delivery** /hoʊm dəˈlɪvəri/, *n.* **1.** a service which provides for goods, etc., to be delivered to a customer's home. **2.** the delivery of a child in the home of the mother, rather than in hospital.
**home economics** /hoʊm ɛkəˈnɒmɪks/, *n.* the art and science of home-making, including the purchase, preparation, and service of food, the selection and making of clothing, the choice of furnishings, the care of children, etc. Also, **home science.**
**home-grown** /ˈhoʊm-groʊn/, *adj.* (esp. of fruit and vegetables) produced in one's own country, region, estate, garden, etc.
**home help** /hoʊm ˈhɛlp/, *n.* →**domestic help.**
**home key** /ˈ– ki/, *n.* the basic key in which a musical work is written.
**homeland** /ˈhoʊmlænd/, *n.* one's native land.
**homeless** /ˈhoʊmləs/, *adj.* **1.** having no home. **2.** *Rare.* affording no home: *the homeless sea.* – **homelessly,** *adv.* – **homelessness,** *n.*
**homelike** /ˈhoʊmlaɪk/, *adj.* like or suggestive of home; familiar; comfortable.
**home loan** /hoʊm ˈloʊn/, *n.* a sum of money lent at interest for the purpose of purchasing a home.
**homely** /ˈhoʊmli/, *adj.,* **-lier, -liest. 1.** proper or suited to the home or to ordinary domestic life; plain; unpretentious: *homely fare.* **2.** not good-looking; plain: *a homely girl.* [ME] – **homeliness,** *n.*
**homemade** /ˈhoʊmmeɪd/, *adj.* made at home.
**home-maker** /ˈhoʊm-meɪkə/, *n.* one who creates and maintains a comfortable and welcoming ambience for the members of a household.
**home movie** /hoʊm ˈmuvi/, *n.* a moving film made by amateurs, recording family activities, and usu. shown only to family or friends.
**homeo-,** variant of **homoeo-.**
**homeomorphism** /ˌhoʊmiəˈmɔfɪzəm/, *n.* →**homoeomorphism.** – **homeomorphous,** *adj.*
**homeopathy** /hoʊmiˈɒpəθi/, *n.* →**homoeopathy.** – **homeopathic** /hoʊmiəˈpæθɪk/, *adj.* – **homeopathically** /hoʊmiəˈpæθɪkli/, *adv.* – **homeopathist, homeopath** /ˈhoʊmiəpæθ/, *n.*
**homeostasis** /ˌhoʊmioʊˈsteɪsəs/, *n.* **1.** physiological equilibrium within living creatures involving a balance of functions and chemical composition. **2.** maintenance of social equilibrium. – **homeostatic,** *adj.*
**home paddock** /hoʊm ˈpædək/, *n.* the paddock closest to the house on a station.
**home plate** /ˈ– pleɪt/, *n.* →**home** (def. 9).
**homer** /ˈhoʊmə/, *n. Colloq.* **1.** *Baseball.* a home run. **2.** a homing pigeon. [HOME + -ER[1]]
**home range** /ˈhoʊm reɪndʒ/, *n.* a defined region about which an animal habitually moves in its natural state.
**Homeric** /hoʊˈmɛrɪk/, *adj.* **1.** of, pertaining to, or suggestive of Homer, c. 10th century B.C. epic poet, reputed author of the *Iliad* and *Odyssey,* or his poetry. **2.** heroic or imposing in proportion or character: *Homeric laughter.*
**home rule** /hoʊm ˈrul/, *n.* self-government in internal affairs by the inhabitants of a dependent country.
**home-ruler** /hoʊm-ˈrulə/, *n.* an advocate of home rule.
**home run** /ˈhoʊm rʌn/, *n.* (in baseball, etc.) a run made on a hit which enables the batter, without aid from fielding errors of the opponents, to make a non-stop circuit of the bases.
**home science** /– ˈsaɪəns/, *n.* →**home economics.**
**homesick** /ˈhoʊmsɪk/, *adj.* ill or depressed from a longing for home. – **homesickness,** *n.*
**home signal** /ˈhoʊm sɪgnəl/, *n.* a railway signal for controlling train movements into or through a section or block. Cf. **distant signal.**
**homespun** /ˈhoʊmspʌn/, *adj.* **1.** spun or made at home: *homespun cloth.* **2.** made of such cloth. **3.** plain; unpolished; simple. *–n.* **4.** cloth made at home, or of homespun yarn. **5.** cloth of similar appearance to that hand-spun and hand-woven.
**homestead** /ˈhoʊmstɛd/, *n.* **1.** the main residence on a sheep or cattle station or large farm. **2.** *U.S.* a dwelling with its land and buildings, occupied by the owner as a home, and exempted by law from seizure or sale for debt.

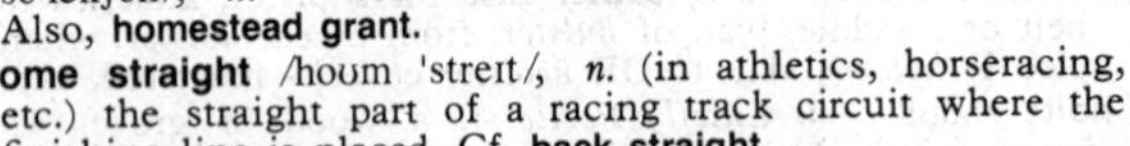
homestead

**homesteader** /ˈhoʊmstɛdə/, *n.* one who owns a homestead.
**homestead selection** /– səˈlɛkʃən/, *n.* →**free selection.** Also, **homestead grant.**
**home straight** /hoʊm ˈstreɪt/, *n.* (in athletics, horseracing, etc.) the straight part of a racing track circuit where the finishing line is placed. Cf. **back straight.**
**home stretch** /– ˈstrɛtʃ/, *n.* **1.** the straight part of a racetrack leading to the finish line, after the last turn. **2.** *Colloq.* the last stages of any project or undertaking.
**homestrip** /ˈhoʊmstrɪp/, *n.* a private landing strip, as that on a cattle station.
**home thrust** /ˈhoʊm θrʌst/, *n.* **1.** a deep thrust with a weapon. **2.** an effective, cutting remark.
**home town** /ˈhoʊm taʊn/, *n.* **1.** the town in which a person spent his early years and which he still thinks of as home. **2.** the town in which a person lives.
**home-town** /ˈhoʊm-taʊn/, *adj.* **1.** of a person, esp. a naive girl, whose experience has been extremely limited. **2.** biased; one-eyed, esp. of a sporting crowd or an umpire, etc.: *home-town decision.*
**home truth** /hoʊm ˈtruθ/, *n.* a disagreeable statement of fact that hurts the sensibilities.
**home turn** /– ˈtɜn/, *n.* the bend in a racecourse just before the home straight.
**home unit** /ˈ– junət/, *n.* **1.** one of a number of dwelling apartments in the same building, each owned under separate title, frequently by the occupier. Cf. **flat**[2] (def. 1). **2.** a block of such units. Also, **unit.**
**homeward** /ˈhoʊmwəd/, *adj.* **1.** directed towards home. *–adv.* **2.** homewards.
**homewards** /ˈhoʊmwədz/, *adv.* towards home. Also, **homeward.**
**homework** /ˈhoʊmwɜk/, *n.* **1.** the part of a lesson or lessons prepared outside school hours. **2. do one's homework,** *Colloq.* to undertake preparatory work for a meeting, interview, discussion, etc.
**homey** /ˈhoʊmi/, *adj.* **-mier, -miest. 1.** *Colloq.* homelike; comfortable; friendly. **2.** English. *–n.* **3.** an Englishman. Also, **homy.**
**homicidal** /hɒməˈsaɪdl/, *adj.* **1.** pertaining to homicide. **2.** having a tendency to homicide. – **homicidally,** *adv.*
**homicide** /ˈhɒməsaɪd/, *n.* **1.** the killing of one human being by another. **2.** a murderer. [ME, from OF, from L *homicīdium* (def. 1), *homicīda* (def. 2). See -CIDE]
**homiletic** /hɒməˈlɛtɪk/, *adj.* **1.** pertaining to preaching or to homilies. **2.** of the nature of a homily. **3.** of homiletics. Also, **homiletical.** [Gk *homilētikós* affable] – **homiletically,** *adv.*
**homiletics** /hɒməˈlɛtɪks/, *n.* the art of preaching; the branch of practical theology that treats of homilies or sermons. [pl. of HOMILETIC. See -ICS]
**homilist** /ˈhɒmələst/, *n.* one who writes or delivers homilies.
**homily** /ˈhɒməli/, *n., pl.* **-lies. 1.** a religious discourse addressed to a congregation; a sermon. **2.** an admonitory or moralising discourse. [ML *homīlia,* from Gk: discourse; replacing ME *omelie,* from OF]
**homing** /ˈhoʊmɪŋ/, *adj.* **1.** directing or guiding towards home; returning home. **2.** having the ability to return home, esp. from a long distance.
**homing device** /ˈ– dəvaɪs/, *n.* a mechanism incorporated into

a guided missile, aeroplane, etc., which aims it towards its objective.

**homing pigeon** /'– pɪdʒən/, *n.* a pigeon trained to fly home from a distance, employed to carry messages.

**hominid** /'hɒmənɪd/, *n.* a member of the Hominidae, a family comprising man and manlike fossils. Also, **hominoid.**

**hominoid** /'hɒmənɔɪd/, *adj.* **1.** manlike. **2.** of or pertaining to the superfamily Hominoidea which includes man and the anthropoid apes. *–n.* **3.** a manlike creature.

**hominy** /'hɒməni/, *n.* **1.** maize hulled and crushed or coarsely ground, and prepared for use as food by boiling in water or milk. **2.** *Prison Colloq.* any similar porridge-like food. [Algonquian; cf. *tackhummin* grind corn (from *ahäm* he beats, he pounds + *min* berry, fruit)]

**hominy gazette** /– gə'zɛt/, *n. Prison Colloq.* news or rumour that circulates within a gaol when the cells are opened and breakfast is distributed.

**hommos** /'hʊməs/, *n.* an hors d'oeuvre made from ground chickpeas and sesame oil flavoured with lemon and garlic. Also, **hoummos, hummus.** [Ar.]

**homo** /'hoʊmoʊ/, *n., adj. Colloq.* →**homosexual.**

**homo-,** a combining form meaning 'the same' (opposed to *hetero-*), as in *homocercal.* [Gk, combining form of *homós* same]

**Homo** /'hoʊmoʊ/, *n., pl.* **Homines** /'hɒməniz/. the primate genus that includes modern man, *Homo sapiens,* and a number of closely related extinct species, as the Neanderthal man. [L: man]

**homocentric** /hoʊmoʊ'sɛntrɪk/, *adj.* **1.** having the same centre; concentric. **2.** diverging from, or converging to, the same centre.

**homocercal** /hoʊmə'sɜkəl, hɒmə-/, *adj.* **1.** having the tail or the caudal fin symmetrical as to its upper and under halves. **2.** denoting such a tail or caudal fin. [HOMO- + Gk *kérkos* tail + -AL[1]]

homocercal tail

**homochromatic** /hoʊmoʊkrə'mætɪk, hɒmoʊ-/, *adj.* of or pertaining to one hue only; monochromatic. – **homochromatism** /hoʊmoʊ'kroʊmətɪzəm, hɒmoʊ-/, *n.*

**homochromous** /hoʊmə'kroʊməs, hɒmə-/, *adj.* being all of one colour, as a composite flower or flower head. [Gk *homóchrōmos*]

**homocyclic** /hoʊmoʊ'saɪklɪk/, *adj.* (of organic compounds) containing a ring structure of atoms of the same element, esp. carbon.

**homodont** /'hoʊmədɒnt/, *adj.* having teeth all of the same kind, as most vertebrates other than mammals.

**homodyne** /'hɒmədaɪn, 'hoʊmoʊ-/, *n.* a radio receiver which demodulates an amplitude-modulated signal by the process of mixing the carrier signal with the sidebands. – **homodynamic** /ˌhɒmədaɪ'næmɪk, ˌhoʊmoʊ-/, *adj.*

**homoeo-,** a word element meaning 'similar' or 'like', as in *homoeomorphism.* Also, **homeo-, homoio-.** [Gk *homoio-,* combining form of *hómoios* like]

**homoeomorphism** /hoʊmioʊ'mɔfɪzəm/, *n.* similarity in crystalline form, but not necessarily in chemical composition. Also, **homeomorphism.** [Gk *homoiómorphos* of like form + -ISM] – **homoeomorphous,** *adj.*

**homoeopathic** /hoʊmioʊ'pæθɪk/, *adj.* **1.** of, pertaining to, or according to the principles of homoeopathy. **2.** practising or advocating homoeopathy. Also, **homeopathic.** – **homoeopathically,** *adv.*

**homoeopathist** /hoʊmi'ɒpəθəst/, *n.* one who practises or favours homoeopathy. Also, **homeopathist, homoeopath** /'hoʊmiəpæθ/.

**homoeopathy** /hoʊmi'ɒpəθi/, *n.* a method of treating disease by drugs, given in minute doses, which produce in a healthy person symptoms similar to those of the disease (opposed to *allopathy*). Also, **homeopathy.**

**homoeostasis** /hoʊmioʊ'steɪsəs/, *n.* a tendency towards the maintenance of internal stability of a system, as by coordinated functioning of brain, heart, liver, etc. [HOMOEO- + STASIS] – **homoeostatic** /hoʊmioʊ'stætɪk/, *adj.*

**homoeothermic** /hoʊmioʊ'θɜmɪk/, *adj.* maintaining a near constant body temperature; warm-blooded. Also, **homothermous.**

**homoeotransplant** /hoʊmioʊ'trænsplænt/, *n.* a piece of tissue taken from one individual and transplanted to another individual of the same species.

**homo erectus** /ˌhoʊmoʊ ə'rɛktəs/, *n.* an extinct genus of apelike men; Pithecanthropus.

**homogamous** /hɒ'mɒgəməs/, *adj.* **1.** having flowers or florets which do not differ sexually (opposed to *heterogamous*). **2.** having the stamens and pistils maturing simultaneously (opposed to *dichogamous*). [Gk *homógamos* married to the same wife]

**homogamy** /hɒ'mɒgəmi/, *n.* **1.** *Bot.* the state of being homogamous. **2.** *Biol.* interbreeding of individuals of like characteristics.

**homogeneity** /hoʊmədʒə'niəti, hɒmə-/, *n.* composition from like parts; congruity of constitution.

**homogeneous** /hoʊmə'dʒiniəs, hɒmə-/, *adj.* **1.** composed of parts all of the same kind; not heterogeneous. **2.** of the same kind or nature; essentially alike. **3.** *Maths.* **a.** having a common property. **b.** denoting a sum of terms all of the same degree. [ML *homogeneus,* from Gk *homogenḗs* of the same kind] – **homogeneously,** *adv.* – **homogeneousness,** *n.*

**homogenise** /hə'mɒdʒənaɪz/, *v.,* **-nised, -nising.** *–v.t.* **1.** to make homogeneous; form by mixing and emulsifying: *homogenised milk.* *–v.i.* **2.** to become homogenous. Also, **homogenize.** – **homogenisation** /həˌmɒdʒənaɪ'zeɪʃən/, *n.* – **homogeniser,** *n.*

**homogenous** /hə'mɒdʒənəs/, *adj.* corresponding in structure because of a common origin.

**homogeny** /hə'mɒdʒəni/, *n.* correspondence of structure and embryological development. [Gk *homogéneia* community of origin]

**homogonous** /hə'mɒgənəs/, *adj.* pertaining to monoclinous flowers which do not differ in the relative length of stamens and pistils. – **homogonously,** *adv.*

**homogony** /hə'mɒgəni/, *n.* the state of being homogonous. [HOMO- + Gk *gónos* offspring + -Y[3]]

**homograph** /'hɒməgræf/, *n.* a word of the same written form as another, but of different origin and meaning, as *fair*[1] and *fair*[2]. – **homographic** /hɒmə'græfɪk/, *adj.*

**homoio-,** variant of **homoeo-.**

**homoiothermic** /həmɔɪə'θɜmɪk/, *adj.* warm-blooded; having a constant body temperature, as most birds and mammals. Also, **homoiothermal, homoiothermous.**

**homologate** /hə'mɒləgeɪt/, *v.t.,* **-gated, -gating.** to approve; ratify. [ML *homologātus,* pp. of *homologāre,* from Gk *homologeîn* agree to, allow] – **homologation** /həmɒlə'geɪʃən/, *n.*

**homologated.** /hə'mɒləgeɪtəd/, *adj.* fulfilling the correct specifications for a particular class of vehicle, as required by a regulating body for motor sports.

**homological** /hɒmə'lɒdʒɪkəl/, *adj.* →**homologous.** Also, **homologic.** – **homologically,** *adv.*

**homologise** /hə'mɒlədʒaɪz/, *v.,* **-gised, -gising.** *–v.t.* **1.** to make or show to be homologous. *–v.i.* **2.** to be homologous; correspond. Also, **homologize.**

**homologous** /hə'mɒləgəs/, *adj.* **1.** having the same or a similar relation; corresponding, as in relative position, structure, etc. **2.** *Biol.* corresponding in type of structure and in origin, but not necessarily in function: *the wing of a bird and the foreleg of a horse are homologous.* **3.** *Chem.* of the same chemical type, but differing by a fixed increment in certain constituents. **4.** *Med., etc.* pertaining to the relation between bacteria and the immune serum prepared from them. [ML *homologus,* or from Gk *homólogos* agreeing, of one mind]

**homologous chromosomes** /– 'kroʊməsoʊmz/, *n.* pairs of similar chromosomes, one of maternal, the other of paternal origin, which carry the Mendelian pairs of alleles or genes.

**homologue** /'hɒməlɒg/, *n.* **1.** something homologous. **2.** *Biol.* a homologous organ or part. **3.** *Chem.* any member of a homologous series of compounds.

**homology** /hə'mɒlədʒi/, *n., pl.* **-gies. 1.** the state of being homologous; homologous relation or correspondence. **2.**

*Biol.* **a.** a fundamental similarity due to community of descent. **b.** a structural similarity of two segments of one animal based on a common developmental origin. **3.** *Chem.* the similarity of organic compounds of a series in which each member differs from its adjacent compounds by a single group. [LL *homologia,* from Gk: agreement, assent, conformity]

**homolysis** /hɒˈmɒləsəs/, *n.* the splitting of a molecule into two neutral atoms.

**homomorphism** /hoʊmoʊˈmɔfɪzəm/, *n.* **1.** *Biol.* correspondence in form or external appearance but not in type of structure and in origin. **2.** *Zool.* resemblance between the young and the adult. Also, **homomorphy.** – **homomorphic, homomorphous,** *adj.*

**homonym** /ˈhɒmənɪm/, *n.* **1.** a word like another in sound and perhaps in spelling, but different in meaning, as *meat* and *meet.* **2.** a homophone. **3.** a homograph. **4.** a namesake. **5.** *Biol.* a name given to a species or genus, which has been used at an earlier date for a different species or genus, and which is therefore rejected. [L *homōnymus* having the same name, from Gk *homṓnymos*] – **homonymic,** *adj.*

**homonymous** /həˈmɒnəməs/, *adj.* **1.** of the nature of homonyms; having the same name. **2.** *Optics.* denoting or pertaining to the images formed in a kind of double vision in which the image seen by the right eye is on the right side and vice versa.

**homonymy** /həˈmɒnəmi/, *n.* homonymous state.

**homophone** /ˈhɒməfoʊn, ˈhoʊmə-/, *n.* **1.** *Phonet.* a word pronounced the same as another, whether spelled the same or not: *heir* and *air* are homophones. **2.** (in writing) an element which represents the same spoken unit as another, as (usu.) English *ks* and *x.*

**homophonic** /hɒməˈfɒnɪk, hoʊmə-/, *adj.* **1.** having the same sound. **2.** having one part or melody predominating (opposed to *polyphonic*). [Gk *homóphōnos* of the same sound + -IC]

**homophonous** /həˈmɒfənəs/, *adj.* identical in pronunciation.

**homophony** /həˈmɒfəni/, *n.* **1.** the quality of being homophonic. **2.** homophonic music.

**homoplastic** /hoʊmoʊˈplæstɪk/, *adj.* **1.** (in transplantation) involving the transfer of tissue from one individual to another of the same species. **2.** (of transplanted tissue) obtained from another individual of the same species as the recipient.

**homopolar** /hoʊmoʊˈpoʊlə/, *adj.* of uniform polarity; not ionised.

**homopolar bond** /– ˈbɒnd/, *n.* a covalent bond.

**homopolar generator** /– ˈdʒɛnəreɪtə/, *n.* a direct current generator consisting of a rotating disc in a steady magnetic field; Faraday disc.

**homopterous** /həˈmɒptərəs/, *adj.* pertaining or belonging to the Homoptera, a suborder of hemipterous insects having wings of the same texture throughout, comprising the aphids, cicadas, etc. [Gk *homópteros* with the same plumage]

**homorganic** /hɒmɔˈgænɪk/, *adj.* *Phonet.* articulated at the same place, as /t/ and /d/.

**Homo sapiens** /ˌhoʊmoʊ ˈsæpiɛnz, -piənz/, *n.* modern man, the single surviving species of the genus *Homo* and of the primate family, Hominidae, to which it belongs. [NL, from L *homo* man + *sapiens* intelligent, wise]

**homosexual** /hoʊmoʊˈsɛkʃuəl, hɒmə-/, *adj.* **1.** pertaining to or exhibiting homosexuality. –*n.* **2.** a homosexual person, esp. a male.

**homosexuality** /ˌhoʊmoʊsɛkʃuˈæləti, ˌhɒmə-/, *n.* sexual feeling for a person of the same sex, esp. between men.

**homosporous** /həˈmɒspərəs, hoʊmoʊˈspɔrəs/, *adj.* having spores of one kind only.

**homospory** /həˈmɒspəri/, *n.* the production of a single kind of spore, neither microspore nor megaspore.

**homostadial** /hoʊmoʊˈsteɪdiəl/, *adj.* (of cultures, etc.) at the same level of technological advance, regardless of actual dates. [HOMO + STAD(IUM) (def. 3) + -AL[1]]

**homotaxis** /hoʊmoʊˈtæksəs/, *n.* similarity of arrangement, as of geological strata, which, though not necessarily contemporaneous, have the same relative position. – **homotaxic,** *adj.*

**homothallic** /hoʊmoʊˈθælɪk/, *adj.* having all mycelia alike, the opposite sexual functions being performed by different cells of single mycelium. [HOMO- + Gk *thallós* sprout + -IC]

**homothermous** /hoʊmoʊˈθɜməs/, *adj.* →**homoeothermic.**

**homothetic** /hoʊməˈθɛtɪk/, *adj.* similarly placed; similar.

**homotransplant** /hoʊmoʊˈtrænsplænt/, *n.* a piece of tissue or an organ taken from one individual to be transplanted to another individual of the same species. – **homotransplantable,** *adj.*

**homotransplantation** /hoʊmoʊˌtrænsplænˈteɪʃən/, *n.* the operation which involves transplanting tissue from one individual to another of the same species.

**homozygosis** /hoʊməzaɪˈgoʊsəs, -zə-, hɒmə-/, *n.* the union of like gametes, resulting in a homozygote. [HOMO- + Gk *zýgōsis* joining]

**homozygote** /hoʊmoʊˈzaɪgoʊt, hɒmə-/, *n.* an organism with identical pairs of genes with respect to any given pair of hereditary characters, and hence breeding true for those characteristics. – **homozygous,** *adj.*

**homunculus** /hɒˈmʌŋkjələs/, *n., pl.* **-li** /-laɪ/. **1.** a diminutive human; dwarf. **2.** a fully formed miniature human being, once believed, according to certain medical theories, to be found in the spermatozoon. Also, **homuncule.** [L, diminutive of *homo* man]

**homy** /ˈhoʊmi/, *adj.* →**homey.**

**hon.,** **1.** honourably. **2.** honorary.

**Hon.,** Honourable.

**Hond.,** Honduras.

**Honduras** /hɒnˈdjurəs/, *n.* a republic in Central America. – **Honduran,** *adj., n.*

**hone** /hoʊn/, *n., v.,* **honed, honing.** –*n.* **1.** a whetstone of fine, compact texture, esp. one for sharpening razors. –*v.t.* **2.** to sharpen on or as on a hone: *to hone a razor.* **3.** to cut back, trim. [ME; OE *hān* stone, rock, c. Icel. *hein* hone]

**honest** /ˈɒnəst/, *adj.* **1.** honourable in principles, intentions, and actions; upright: *an honest person.* **2.** showing uprightness and fairness: *honest methods.* **3.** acquired fairly: *honest money.* **4.** open; sincere: *an honest face.* **5.** genuine or unadulterated: *honest commodities.* **6.** truthful; creditable; candid. **7.** chaste or virtuous; respectable. **8. make an honest woman of,** *Colloq.* to marry. [ME *honeste,* from OF, from L *honestus* honourable, worthy, virtuous]

**honestly** /ˈɒnəstli/, *adv.* **1.** with honesty; in an honest manner. –*interj.* **2.** (an exclamation used to emphasise the honesty or integrity of one's intentions, statements, etc.). **3.** (an expression of exasperation).

**honesty** /ˈɒnəsti/, *n.* **1.** the quality or fact of being honest; uprightness, probity, or integrity. **2.** truthfulness, sincerity, or frankness. **3.** freedom from deceit or fraud. **4.** a herb, *Lunaria annua,* with purple flowers and a persistent satiny septum to the fruit. **5.** *Archaic.* chastity.

**honey** /ˈhʌni/, *n., pl.* **honeys,** *adj., v.,* **honeyed, honeying.** –*n.* **1.** a sweet, viscid fluid produced by bees from the nectar collected from flowers, and stored in their nests or hives as food. **2.** the nectar of flowers. **3.** any of various similar products produced by insects or in other ways. **4.** something sweet, delicious, or delightful: *the honey of flattery.* **5.** *Colloq.* a person or thing which inspires affectionate admiration: *that machine is a honey.* **6.** sweet one; darling (a term of endearment). –*adj.* **7.** of or like honey; sweet; dear. –*v.i.* **8.** *Archaic or U.S.* to talk sweetly; use endearments. [ME *huny,* OE *hunig,* c. D *honig,* G *Honig*] – **honey-like,** *adj.*

**honeybag** /ˈhʌnibæg/, *n.* *Colloq.* honey, esp. that from wild bees; sugarbag.

**honey bear** /ˈhʌni bɛə/, *n.* →**kinkajou.**

**honeybee** /ˈhʌnibi/, *n.* a bee that collects and stores honey, specifically *Apis mellifera.*

**honey bun** /ˈ– bʌn/, *n.* (a term of endearment); darling. Also, **honey bunch.**

**honey buzzard** /ˈhʌni bʌzəd/, *n.* a European hawk, *Pernis apivoris,* which feeds on insects and small reptiles, and which destroys nests of bees and wasps to eat the larvae.

honeycomb

**honey cart** /ˈhʌni kat/, *n.* *Colloq.* **sanitary cart.**

**honeycomb** /ˈhʌnikoʊm/, *n.* **1.** a structure of wax containing rows of hexagonal cells, formed by bees for the reception of honey and pollen and of their eggs. **2.** any substance, as a

i = peat ɪ = pit ɛ = pet æ = pat a = part ɒ = pot ʌ = putt ɔ = port ʊ = put u = pool ɜ = pert ə = apart aɪ = buy eɪ = bay ɔɪ = boy aʊ = how oʊ = hoe ɪə = here ɛə = hair ʊə = tour g = give θ = thin ð = then ʃ = show ʒ = measure tʃ = choke dʒ = joke ŋ = sing j = you õ = Fr. bon

casting of iron, etc., having cells like those of a honeycomb. **3.** the reticulum of a ruminant. *–adj.* **4.** having the structure or appearance of a honeycomb: *honeycomb weave.* *–v.t.* **5.** to reduce to a honeycomb; pierce with many holes or cavities: *a rock honeycombed with passages.* [ME *hunycomb,* OE *hunigcamb*]

**honeydew** /ˈhʌnidju/, *n.* **1.** the sweet material which exudes from the leaves of certain plants in hot weather. **2.** a sugary material secreted by aphids, leaf-hoppers, etc.

**honeydew melon** /–ˈmɛlən/, *n.* a sweet-flavoured, white-fleshed muskmelon with a smooth, pale green rind.

**honeyeater** /ˈhʌniˌitə/, *n.* any of numerous oscine birds constituting the family Meliphagidae, chiefly of Australasia, with a bill and tongue adapted for extracting the nectar from flowers.

**honeyed** /ˈhʌnid/, *adj.* **1.** dulcet or mellifluous; ingratiating: *honeyed words.* **2.** containing, consisting of, or resembling honey: *honeyed drinks.*

**honeyflow** /ˈhʌniflou/, *n.* a supply or period of availability of floral nectar suitable for bees to convert into honey.

**honey flower** /ˈhʌni flauə/, *n.* a woody shrub, *Lambertia formosa,* of sandstone areas of New South Wales.

**honey-guide** /ˈhʌni-gaɪd/, *n.* any of various small, dull-coloured non-passerine birds (genus *Indicator, Prodotiscus, Melichneutes,* etc.), of Africa, Asia, and the East Indies, some of which are said to guide men or animals to places where honey may be found.

**honey-locust** /ˈhʌni-loukəst/, *n.* **1.** Also, **locust.** a tree, *Gleditsia triacanthos,* of North America, having pods with a sweet pulp. **2.** →**mesquite.** **3.** any of various other trees, usu. having either sweet pods or durable timber.

**honeymoon** /ˈhʌnimun/, *n.* **1.** a holiday spent by a newly married couple before settling down to normal domesticity. **2.** the first weeks immediately after marriage. **3.** any period of happy or harmonious relationship. *–v.i.* **4.** to spend one's honeymoon (usu. fol. by *in* or *at*). [traditionally referred to an equation between the changes of love and the phases of the moon] – **honeymooner,** *n.*

**honey plant** /ˈhʌni plænt/, *n.* any plant esp. useful in furnishing nectar to bees, as *Echium lycopsis.*

**honey possum** /ˈ– pɒsəm/, *n.* the small nectar-feeding possum, *Tarsipes spencerae,* of south-western Australia; noolbenger; tait. Also, **honey mouse.**

**honey pot** /ˈ– pɒt/, *n.* **1.** a pot for honey. **2.** *Colloq.* →**honey** (def. 6). **3.** *Colloq.* →**dive-bomb** (def. 3). **4.** *Colloq.* a toilet, esp. a sanitary can. **5.** *Colloq.* the female pudendum. *–v.i.* **6.** *Colloq.* →**dive-bomb.** (def. 2).

**honey-pot ant** /ˌhʌni-pɒt ˈænt/, *n.* an Australian species of ant, *Camponotus inflatus,* characterised by the fact that some workers store excess food in a distended abdomen.

**honey-sucker** /ˈhʌni-sʌkə/, *n.* **1.** a bird that eats the nectar of flowers. **2.** →**honeyeater.**

**honeysuckle** /ˈhʌnisʌkəl/, *n.* **1.** any of the upright or climbing shrubs constituting the genus *Lonicera,* some species of which are cultivated for their fragrant white, yellow, or red tubular flowers. **2.** any of various other fragrant or ornamental plants. **3.** any of several Australian trees or shrubs of the genus *Banksia.* **4.** *N.Z.* a stately, upright tree, *Knightia excelsa,* with masses of dark-red flowers, the wood of which is often used for furniture making; rewarewa. [ME *honiesoukel,* from *honisouke* (OE *hunisūce*) lit., honeysuck + *-el,* diminutive suffix] – **honeysuckled,** *adj.*

**honeysweet** /ˈhʌniswit/, *adj.* sweet as honey.

**hong** /hɒŋ/, *n.* **1.** (in China) a group of rooms or buildings forming a warehouse, factory, etc. **2.** one of the foreign factories formerly maintained at Canton. [Chinese (Cantonese): row, rank (Mandarin *hang*)]

**hongi** /ˈhɒŋi/, *n.* *N.Z.* a Maori greeting, expressed by touching or rubbing noses. [Maori]

**Hong Kong** /hɒŋ ˈkɒŋ/, *n.* a British crown colony in south-eastern China, comprising the island of Hong Kong and an area of the adjacent mainland. Also, **Hongkong.**

**honi soit qui mal y pense** /ɒni ˌswa ki ˌmæl i ˈpɒns/, shamed be he who thinks evil of it (motto of the Order of the Garter). [F]

**honk** /hɒŋk/, *n.* **1.** the cry of the wild goose. **2.** any similar sound, as a motor-car horn. *–v.i.* **3.** to emit a honk. **4.** *Cycling.* to stand on the pedals of a cycle while going uphill. [imitative] – **honker,** *n.*

**honky** /ˈhɒŋki/, *n., pl.* **-kies.** *U.S. Colloq.* (*derog.*) a white man.

**honky-tonk** /ˈhɒŋki-tɒŋk/, *n.* **1.** *Chiefly U.S. Colloq.* a cheap, sordid nightclub, dance hall, etc. *–adj.* **2.** *U.S. Colloq.* of or pertaining to a honky-tonk. **3.** *Music.* of or pertaining to a style of ragtime piano-playing. [orig. uncert.]

**honor** /ˈɒnə/, *n., v.t. U.S.* →**honour.** – **honorable,** *adj.*

**honorarium** /ɒnəˈrɛəriəm/, *n., pl.* **-rariums, -raria** /-ˈrɛəriə/. **1.** an honorary reward, as in recognition of professional services on which no price may be set. **2.** a fee for services rendered by a professional person. [L, properly neut. of *honōrārius* HONORARY]

**honorary** /ˈɒnərəri/, *adj.* **1.** given for honour only, without the usual duties, privileges, emoluments, etc.: *an honorary title.* **2.** holding a title or position conferred for honour only: *an honorary president.* **3.** (of a position, job, etc.) unpaid: *the honorary secretary of the committee.* **4.** (of an obligation) depending on one's honour for fulfilment. **5.** given, made, or serving as a token of honour: *an honorary gift.* **6.** conferring an honour. *–n.* **7.** a specialist working in a public hospital. [L *honōrārius* relating to honour]

**honorific** /ɒnəˈrɪfɪk/, *adj.* Also, **honorifical.** **1.** doing or conferring honour. **2.** having the quality of an honorific. *–n.* **3.** (in certain languages, as Chinese and Japanese) a class of forms used to show respect, esp. in direct address. **4.** a title or term of respect, as *Doctor, Professor, Rt Hon.* [L *honōrificus.* See HONOUR, *n.*, -(I)FIC] – **honorifically,** *adv.*

**honour** /ˈɒnə/, *n.* **1.** high public esteem; fame; glory: *a roll of honour.* **2.** credit or reputation for behaviour that is becoming or worthy. **3.** a source of credit or distinction: *to be an honour to one's family.* **4.** high respect, as for worth, merit, or rank: *to be held in honour.* **5.** such respect manifested: *to be received with honour.* **6.** a special privilege or favour: *I have the honour to acknowledge your letter.* **7.** (*usu. pl.*) high rank, dignity, or distinction: *political honours.* **8.** a deferential title, esp. of certain judges (prec. by *his, your,* etc.). **9.** high-minded character or principles; fine sense of one's obligations: *a man of honour.* **10.** (*pl.*) (in universities) **a.** scholastic or academic achievement in a degree examination higher than that required for a pass degree. **b.** the grade of scholarship achieved: *first-class honours.* **c.** the course of study. **11.** chastity or purity in a woman. **12.** *Bridge.* any one of the five highest ranking cards in each suit; for scoring purposes, any one of the highest cards of the trump suit or any one of the four aces at no trump. **13.** *Whist.* any of the four highest trump cards. **14.** *Golf.* the preference of teeing off before the other players or side, given after the first hole to the player or players who won the previous hole. **15. do honour to, a.** to show respect to. **b.** to be a credit to. **16. do the honours,** to act or preside as host. **17. on** or **upon one's honour, a.** acknowledging personal responsibility for one's actions. **b.** pledging one's reputation as to the truthfulness of a statement, etc. **c.** promising obedience or good behaviour. *–v.t.* **18.** to hold in honour or high respect; revere. **19.** to treat with honour. **20.** to confer honour or distinction upon. **21.** to worship (the Supreme Being). **22.** to show a courteous regard for: *to honour an invitation.* **23.** to accept and pay (a cheque, etc.) when due. **24.** to accept the validity of (a document, etc.). Also, *U.S.,* **honor.** [ME *onor, honour, honor,* from OF *onur,* from L *honor* honour, repute] – **honourer,** *n.* – **honourless,** *adj.*

**honourable** /ˈɒnərəbəl/, *adj.* **1.** in accordance with principles of honour; upright: *an honourable man.* **2.** of high rank, dignity or distinction; noble, illustrious, or distinguished. **3.** (*cap.*) **a.** a title prefixed to the name of certain high officials, including members of parliament, esp. when one member refers to another: *the honourable member, the honourable gentleman.* **b.** *Brit.* a title prefixed to the forename of younger sons of earls and all children of viscounts and barons. *Abbrev.:* Hon. *–n.* **4.** *Brit Colloq.* a person who bears the title *Honourable.*

**honour point** /ˈɒnə pɔɪnt/, *n.* a point midway between the fess point and top of an escutcheon.

**honour roll** /ˈ– roul/, *n.* →**roll of honour.**

**honours degree** /ˈɒnəz dəgri/, *n.* an academic degree obtained with honours.

**honours list** /ˈ– lɪst/, *n.* the civil and military awards of honours and ranks, approved by the Sovereign and published on 1 January (New Year's Honours) and 10 June (Birthday Honours) of each year.

**honours of war,** *n. pl.* privileges granted to a capitulating force, as of marching out of their camp or entrenchments with all their arms and with colours flying.

**honours school** /ˈɒnəz skul/, *n.* (in a university) the courses which lead to a bachelor's degree with honours.

**honour system** /ˈɒnə sɪstəm/, *n.* a system in which exams are completed, services paid for, etc., with little or no supervision.

**Hons,** Honours.

**hooch** /hutʃ/, *n. U.S. Colloq.* **1.** alcoholic beverages. **2.** alcoholic liquor illicitly distilled and distributed. [short for *hoochinoo,* alteration of *Hutanuwu,* name of Alaskan Indian tribe which made alcoholic liquor]

**hood** /hʊd/, *n.* **1.** a soft or flexible covering for the head and neck, either separate or attached to a cloak or the like. **2.** something resembling or suggesting this, as a hood-shaped petal or sepal, etc. **3.** a piece of hood-shaped material, attached to an academic gown, the colour and material of the lining depending on the degree held and the university by which the degree was awarded. **4.** the top of a motor car. **5.** *U.S.* a motor-car bonnet. **6.** *Falconry.* a cover for the entire head of a hawk, used when it is not in pursuit of game. **7.** *Colloq.* a hoodlum. *–v.t.* **8.** to furnish with a hood. **9.** to cover with, or as with, a hood. [ME *hode,* OE *hōd,* c. G *Hut* hat] **– hoodless,** *adj.* **– hoodlike,** *adj.*

**-hood,** a suffix denoting state, condition, character, nature, etc., or a body of persons of a particular character or class: *childhood, likelihood, priesthood, sisterhood.* [ME *-hode, -hod,* OE *-hād,* c. G *-heit;* orig. separate word, OE *hād* condition, state, etc.]

**hooded** /ˈhʊdəd/, *adj.* **1.** having, or covered with, a hood. **2.** hood-shaped. **3.** *Zool.* having on the head a hoodlike formation, crest, arrangement of colours, or the like. **4.** *Bot.* **→cucullate.**

**hooded seal** /– ˈsil/, *n.* **→bladdernose.**

**hoodlum** /ˈhudləm/, *n.* **1.** a petty gangster; ruffian. **2.** a destructive, noisy, or rough child or young person. [orig. uncert.] **– hoodlumism,** *n.*

**hood mould** /ˈhʊd mould/, *n.* (in Gothic and Elizabethan architecture) a projecting moulding over the headstone or arch to a door or window. Also, **label mould.**

**hoodoo** /ˈhudu/, *n., pl.* **-doos,** *v.,* **-dooed, -dooing.** *–n.* **1.** voodoo. **2.** *Colloq.* a person or thing that brings bad luck. **3.** *Colloq.* bad luck. **4.** an earth pillar. *–v.t.* **5.** *Colloq.* to bring or cause bad luck to. [apparently var. of VOODOO]

**hoodwink** /ˈhʊdwɪŋk/, *v.t.* **1.** to deceive; humbug. **2.** to blindfold. **3.** to cover or hide. **– hoodwinker,** *n.*

**hooey** /ˈhui/, *U.S. Colloq.* *–interj.* **1.** (an exclamation of disapproval.) *–n.* **2.** silly or worthless stuff; nonsense.

**hoof** /hʊf/, *n., pl.* **hoofs, hooves,** *v.* *–n.* **1.** the horny covering protecting the ends of the digits or encasing the foot in certain animals, as the ox, horse, etc. **2.** the entire foot of a horse, donkey, etc. **3.** a hoofed animal; one of a herd. **4.** *Colloq.* (*joc.*) the human foot. **5. on the hoof,** (of livestock) alive, not butchered. *–v.i.* **6. hoof it,** *Colloq.* to walk. **7.** *Colloq.* to dance. [ME; OE *hōf,* c. G *Huf*] **– hooflike,** *adj.*

**hoofbound** /ˈhʊfbaʊnd/, *adj.* (of horses) having the heels of the hoofs dry and contracted, causing lameness.

**hoofed** /hʊft/, *adj.* having hoofs; ungulate.

**hoofer** /ˈhʊfə/, *n. U.S. Colloq.* one who makes dancing an occupation, as a chorus girl.

**hoo-ha** /ˈhu-ha/, *n. Colloq.* a fuss; turmoil; argument.

**hook** /hʊk/, *n.* **1.** a curved or angular piece of metal or other firm substance catching, pulling, or sustaining something. **2.** a fishhook. **3.** that which catches; a snare; a trap. **4.** something curved or bent like a hook, as a mark or symbol, etc. **5.** a sharp curve or angle in the length or course of anything. **6.** a curved spit of land. **7.** a recurved and pointed organ or appendage of an animal or plant. **8.** *Golf.* a drive or other stroke which curves to the left of the player striking the ball. **9.** *Cricket.* a curving stroke of the bat, whereby the ball is driven to the on side of the field. **10.** *Boxing.* a curving blow made with the arm bent, and coming in to the opponent from the side: *right hook.* **11.** *Music.* a stroke or line attached to the stem of a quaver, semiquaver, etc. **12.** (*pl.*) *Colloq.* fingers. **13. by hook or by crook,** by any means, fair or foul. **14. hook, line, and sinker,** completely. **15. off the hook, a.** off the peg. **b.** out of a predicament. **c.** (of a telephone) with the receiver lifted. **16. on one's own hook,** *Colloq.* on one's own responsibility. **17. on the hook, a.** waiting; being delayed. **b.** in a difficult predicament. **18. put the hooks into,** *Colloq.* to borrow from; cadge. **19. sling one's hook,** *Colloq.* to depart. *–v.t.* **20.** to seize, fasten, or catch hold of and draw in with or as with a hook. **21.** to catch (fish) with a fish-hook. **22.** *Colloq.* to seize by stealth, pilfer, or steal. **23.** to catch by artifice. **24.** to catch on the horns, or attack with the horns. **25.** to catch hold of and draw (loops of yarn) through cloth with or as with a hook. **26.** to make hook-shaped; crook. **27.** *Hockey.* to hook another player's stick. **28.** *Boxing.* to deliver a hook. **29.** *Cricket, Golf.* to hit (the ball) with a hook. **30.** *Colloq.* to marry: *she's managed to hook a rich man.* **31. hook up, a.** to fasten with a hook or hooks. **b.** to put together (mechanical apparatus) and connect it to the source of power. **32. hook it,** *Colloq.* to depart; clear off. *–v.i.* **33.** to become attached or fastened by or as by a hook; join on. **34.** to curve or bend like a hook. **35.** *Boxing.* to deliver a hook. **36.** *Cricket, Golf.* **a.** (of the player) to make a hooking stroke. **b.** (of the ball) to describe a course to the left or on side of the player after being hooked. **37.** *Colloq.* to depart; clear off. [ME *hoke,* OE *hōc,* c. D *hoek* hook, angle, corner, point of land]

**hookah** /ˈhʊkə/, *n.* a pipe with a long, flexible tube by which the smoke of tobacco, marijuana, etc., is drawn through a vessel of water and thus cooled; narghile. Also, **hooka.** [Ar. *huqqa* box, vase, pipe for smoking]

hookah

**hook and eye,** *n.* a fastening arrangement consisting of a hook on one part, which catches on to a bar or loop on the other part.

**hooked** /hʊkt/, *adj.* **1.** bent like a hook; hookshaped. **2.** having a hook or hooks. **3.** made with a hook. **4.** caught, as a fish. **5.** *Colloq.* addicted; obsessed (usu. fol. by *on*). **6.** *Colloq.* married.

**hooked rug** /– ˈrʌg/, *n.* a rug made by drawing loops of yarn or cloth through a foundation of gunny, or the like, to form a pattern.

**hooker**[1] /ˈhʊkə/, *n.* **1.** one or that which hooks. **2.** *Rugby Football.* **a.** the central forward in the front row of the scrum, whose job it is to pull back the ball with his foot. **b.** the position played by such a forward. **3.** *Colloq.* a prostitute. [HOOK + -ER[1]]

**hooker**[2] /ˈhʊkə/, *n.* a fishing boat with hooks and lines instead of nets. [D *hoeker,* from *hoek* HOOK]

**hooker**[3] /ˈhʊkə/, *n. Chiefly U.S., Canada. Colloq.* a glass of spirits, esp. whisky. [orig. unknown]

**Hooke's law** /ˈhʊks lɔ/, *n.* the principle that, within the elastic limit, the strain on a body is proportional to the stress producing it. [named after R. *Hooke,* 1635-1703, English physicist]

**hook grass** /ˈhʊk gras/, *n.* any of a number of species of the sedge *Uncinia,* which have the rachilla produced into a long hooked bristle.

**hooknose** /ˈhʊknouz/, *n.* an aquiline or beaklike nose.

**hook-nosed** /ˈhʊk-nouzd/, *adj.* having a hooknose.

**hook-up** /ˈhʊk-ʌp/, *n.* **1.** *Radio.* **a.** a diagram of radio apparatus, showing the connection of the different elements. **b** the elements as set up for operation. **2.** combination; connection. **3.** *Radio, Television.* a link-up, often temporary, of different stations for a special broadcast.

**hookworm** /ˈhʊkwɜm/, *n.* **1.** any of certain bloodsucking nematode worms, as *Ancylostoma duodenale* and *Necator americanus,* parasitic in the intestine of man and other animals. **2. →hookworm disease.**

**hookworm disease** /ˈ– dəziz/, *n.* hookworm infestation of the intestine resulting in anaemia.

**hooky**[1] /ˈhʊki/, *adj.* **1.** full of hooks. **2.** hook-shaped. [HOOK + -Y[1]]

**hooky**[2] /ˈhʊki/, *n. Colloq.* unjustifiable absence from school (used in the phrase *play hooky*). Also, **hookey.** [HOOK (def. 37) + -Y[3]]

**hooley** /ˈhuli/, *n. Colloq.* a wild party. [orig. uncert. ? Irish]

**hooligan** /ˈhuləgən/, *Colloq. –n.* **1.** a hoodlum; young street rough. *–adj.* **2.** of or like hooligans. [var. of *Houlihan*, Irish surname which came to be associated with rowdies] **– hooliganism,** *n.*

**hoon** /hun/, *n. Colloq.* **1.** a loutish, aggressive, or surly youth. **2.** a foolish or silly person, esp. one who is a show-off. **3.** one who lives off the proceeds of prostitution.

**hoop** /hup/, *n.* **1.** a circular band or ring of metal, wood, or other stiff material. **2.** such a band to hold together the staves of a cask, barrel, etc. **3.** a large ring of wood or plastic for children's games. **4.** something resembling a hoop. **5.** that part of a finger ring which surrounds the finger. **6.** one of the iron arches used in croquet. **7.** a circular band of stiff material used to expand a woman's skirt. **8.** →**hoop skirt. 9.** a large ring, with paper stretched over it through which circus animals, etc., jump. **10.** *Colloq.* →**jockey** (def. 1). **11. go through the hoop,** go through a bad time; undergo an ordeal. **12. jump through hoops,** to obey without question, in the manner of a trained dog. **13. put through (the) hoops,** subjected to a series of often unreasonable tests or trials. *–v.t.* **14.** to bind or fasten with a hoop or hoops. **15.** to encircle; embrace. [ME *hop(e)*, late OE *hōp*, c. D *hope*] **– hooped,** *adj.*

**hoop iron** /ˈ– aɪən/, *n.* thin strips of iron or steel used for diagonal bracing, for reinforcing masonry and brickwork, and as a connection between building elements.

**hoopla** /ˈhupla/, *n.* a game in which hoops are thrown in an attempt to encircle objects offered as prizes.

**hoopoe** /ˈhupu, ˈhupoʊ/, *n.* any of the non-passerine birds of the family Upupidae of Europe, Asia and Africa, esp. *Upupa epops,* having distinctively patterned plumage, an erectile fanlike crest and a slender down-curved bill. [var. of obs. *hoopoop,* c. LG *huppup* (imitative of its cry); cf. L *upupa*]

**hoop pine** /ˈhup paɪn/, *n.* a valuable softwood timber tree of northern Australia and New Guinea, *Araucaria cunninghamii.*

**hoop skirt** /– ˈskɜt/, *n.* **1.** a woman's skirt, made to stand out from the waist by an undergarment of flexible hoops connected by tapes. **2.** the framework for such a skirt.

**hoop snake** /ˈ– sneɪk/, *n.* a harmless snake, *Abastor erythrogrammus,* formerly believed to take its tail in its mouth and roll along like a hoop.

**hooray**[1] /həˈreɪ, ˈhureɪ/, *interj.* **1.** (an exclamation of joy, applause, or the like). *–v.i.* **2.** to shout 'hooray'. *–n.* **3.** the exclamation 'hooray'. Also, **hoorah, hurray.**

**hooray**[2] /ˈhureɪ/, →**hooroo.**

**hooroo** /ˈhuru/, *interj. Colloq.* goodbye. Also, **hooray, ooray, ooroo.**

**hoosegow** /ˈhusgaʊ/, *n. U.S. Colloq.* a gaol. Also, **hoosgow.** [Sp. *juzga(d)o* court of justice; (in Mex. Sp.) gaol]

**hoot**[1] /hut/, *v.i.* **1.** to cry out or shout, esp. in disapproval or derision. **2.** (of an owl) to utter its cry. **3.** to utter a similar sound. **4.** to blow a horn or factory hooter; honk. **5.** to laugh. *–v.t.* **6.** to assail with shouts of disapproval or derision. **7.** to drive (*out, away, off,* etc.) by hooting. **8.** to express in hoots. *–n.* **9.** the cry of an owl. **10.** any similar sound, as an inarticulate shout. **11.** a cry or shout, esp. of disapproval or derision. **12.** *Colloq.* a thing of no value: *I don't give a hoot.* **13.** an amusing or funny thing. [ME *huten;* probably imitative] **– hooter,** *n.*

**hoot**[2] /hut/, *n. Chiefly N.Z. Colloq.* money, esp. money paid as recompense. Also, **hootoo, hout, hutu.** [Maori *utu*]

**hootch** /hutʃ/, *n.* →**hooch.**

**hootenanny** /ˈhutənæni/, *n. Orig. U.S.* →**festivity.**

**hooter** /ˈhutə/, *n.* **1.** one who hoots. **2.** a factory siren. **3.** a horn on a motor vehicle. **4.** *Colloq.* the nose.

**hoot owl** /ˈhut aʊl/, *n.* an owl that hoots (distinguished from *screech owl*).

**hoover** /ˈhuvə/, *n.* **1.** →**vacuum cleaner.** *–v.t.* **2.** →**vacuum clean.** [Trademark]

**hooves** /huvz/, *n.* a plural of **hoof.**

**hoozle** /ˈhuzəl/, *v.t.,* **-zled, -zling. 1.** (of a dog) to drive (sheep) towards the shepherd. **2.** to cheat; swindle. [? var. of HUSTLE]

**hop**[1] /hɒp/, *v.,* **hopped, hopping,** *n. –v.i.* **1.** to leap; move by leaping with all feet off the ground. **2.** to spring or leap on one foot. **3.** to make a flight or trip. **4.** *U.S. Colloq.* (of an aeroplane, etc.) to leave the ground in beginning a flight (oft. fol. by *off*). **5.** *Colloq.* to dance. **6.** to limp. **7. hop it,** *Colloq.* to go away; leave. *–v.t.* **8.** *Colloq.* to jump off (something elevated), or over (a fence, ditch, etc.) **9.** *Colloq.* to board or alight from a car, train, etc. (fol. by *in, on* or *off*). **10.** *Colloq.* (of an aeroplane, etc.) to cross by a flight. **11. hop into,** *Colloq.* **a.** to set about something energetically: *he hopped into the job at once.* **b.** to put (clothes) on briskly: *he hopped into his cossie.* **12. hop into bed,** to have casual sex (usu. fol. by *with*). **13. hop up and down,** *Colloq.* to express agitation. **14. hop to,** to come or act quickly: *hop to it.* *–n.* **15.** an act of hopping; short leap. **16.** a leap on one foot. **17.** *Colloq.* a flight of an aeroplane. **18.** *Colloq.* a dance, or dancing party **19. on the hop, a.** unprepared. **b.** busy, moving. [ME *hoppen,* OE *hoppian,* c. G *hopfen*]

**hop**[2] /hɒp/, *n., v.,* **hopped, hopping.** *–n.* **1.** one of the twining plants of three species of the genus *Humulus,* the male flowers of which grow in panicled racemes and the female in conelike forms. **2.** (*pl.*) the dried ripe cones of the female flowers of the hop plant, used in brewing, medicine, etc. **3.** (*pl.*) →**beer. 4.** any of several plants thought to resemble the hop, as *Rumex roseus* (common in the Flinders Ranges of South Australia) and species of the genus *Daviesia.* *–v.t.* **5.** to treat or flavour with hops. [ME *hoppe,* from MD, c. G *Hopfen*]

hop[2]

**hopbush** /ˈhɒpbʊʃ/, *n.* any shrub of the genus *Dodonaea,* widespread in Australia, which has papery, often reddish, winged fruits and is thought to resemble the hop.

**hop-clover** /ˈhɒp-kloʊvə/, *n.* a trefoil, *Trifolium procumbens,* whose withered yellow flowers resemble the strobiluses of hop.

**hope** /hoʊp/, *n., v.,* **hoped, hoping.** *–n.* **1.** expectation of something desired; desire accompanied by expectation. **2.** a particular instance of such expectation or desire: *a hope of success.* **3.** confidence in a future event; ground for expecting something: *there is no hope of his recovery.* **4.** a person or thing that expectations are centred in: *the hope of the family.* **5. great white hope,** a person from whom or a thing from which exceptionally great successes or benefits are expected. **6. some hope!** (an expression of pessimism, resignation, or disbelief). *–v.t.* **7.** to look forward to with desire and more or less confidence. **8.** to trust in the truth of a matter (with a clause): *I hope that you are satisfied.* *–v.i.* **9.** to have an expectation of something desired: *we hope to see you, to hope for his pardon.* **10.** *Archaic.* to trust or rely. **11. hope against hope,** to continue to hope, although there are not apparent grounds for such hope. [ME; OE *hopa,* c. G *Hoffe*] **– hopingly,** *adv.*

**hope chest** /ˈ– tʃɛst/, *n. U.S.* →**glory box.**

**hopeful** /ˈhoʊpfəl/, *adj.* **1.** full of hope; expressing hope: *hopeful words.* **2.** exciting hope; promising advantage or success: *a hopeful prospect.* *–n.* **3.** a promising young person. **– hopefully,** *adv.* **– hopefulness,** *n.*

**hopefully** /ˈhoʊpfəli/, *adv.* **1.** in a hopeful fashion. **2.** *Colloq.* it is hoped: *hopefully the drought will soon end.*

**hopeless** /ˈhoʊpləs/, *adj.* **1.** affording no hope; desperate: *a hopeless case.* **2.** without hope; despairing: *hopeless grief.* **3.** not possible to resolve or solve: *a hopeless problem.* **4.** not able to learn, perform, act, etc., incompetent: *a hopeless pupil.* **– hopelessly,** *adv.* **– hopelessness,** *n.*

**hophead** /ˈhɒphɛd/, *n. Colloq.* **1.** one who drinks alcoholic beverages to excess. **2.** one addicted to drugs.

**hop lily** /ˈhɒp lɪli/, *n.* a tufted grasslike perennial, *Johnsonia lupulina,* with large overlapping bracts, native to the south-eastern part of Western Australia.

**hoplite** /ˈhɒplaɪt/, *n.* a heavily armed foot soldier of ancient

Greece. [Gk *hoplī́tēs*]

**hop-o'-my-thumb** /ˌhɒp-ə-maɪ-ˈθʌm/, *n.* a tiny person.

**hopper** /ˈhɒpə/, *n.* **1.** one who or that which hops. **2.** any one of various jumping insects, as grasshoppers, leafhoppers, cheese maggots, etc. **3.** a funnel-shaped chamber in which materials are stored temporarily and later discharged through the bottom. **4.** →**hop-picker.**

**hopper car** /ˈ– ka/, *n.* a railway wagon for coal, sand, etc., with devices by which the contents can be speedily dumped.

**hop-picker** /ˈhɒp-pɪkə/, *n.* one who or a machine which picks hops.

**hopping** /ˈhɒpɪŋ/, *adj.* **1.** moving rapidly. **2.** Also, **hopping mad.** very annoyed; furious. *–n.* **3.** the act of gathering hops.

**hopping-mouse** /ˈhɒpɪŋ-maʊs/, *n.* any of various Australian endemic rodents of the genus *Notomys,* which hop rapidly like a kangaroo.

**hopple** /ˈhɒpəl/, *v.,* **-pled, -pling,** *n.* *–v.t.* **1.** to hobble; tether. *–n.* **2.** (*pl.*) gear used on horses entered in trotting races.

**hopsack** /ˈhɒpsæk/, *n.* **1.** a coarse, jute sacking material. **2.** a fabric with coarse surface, used to make clothing. Also, **hopsacking.**

**hopscotch** /ˈhɒpskɒtʃ/, *n.* a children's game in which the player hops from one compartment to another of a diagram traced on the ground, without touching a line. [HOP[1] + SCOTCH (def. 2)]

**hop, step, and jump,** *n.* **1.** →**triple jump.** **2.** a short distance.

**hopvine** /ˈhɒpvaɪn/, *n.* **1.** the stem of a hop plant. **2.** the plant itself.

**hor.,** **1.** horizon. **2.** horizontal.

**horal** /ˈhɔrəl/, *adj.* pertaining to an hour or hours; hourly. [LL *hōrālis,* from L *hōra* HOUR]

**horary** /ˈhɔrəri/, *adj.* **1.** pertaining to an hour; indicating the hours: *the horary circle.* **2.** occurring every hour; hourly. **3.** lasting an hour. [ML *hōrārius,* from L *hōra* HOUR]

**Horatian ode** /həreɪʃən ˈoʊd/, *n.* →**ode** (def. 5).

**horde** /hɔd/, *n., v.,* **horded, hording.** *–n.* **1.** (*oft. derog.*) a great company or multitude. **2.** a tribe or troop of Asiatic nomads. **3.** any nomadic group. **4.** a moving pack of animals, insects, etc. **5.** an exogamous kinship grouping within an Aboriginal tribe; section. *–v.i.* **6.** to gather in a horde. [Pol. *horda,* from Turkic *ordū* camp; cf. URDU]

**horehound** /ˈhɔhaʊnd/, *n.* **1.** a perennial herb, *Marrubium vulgare,* native to the Old World, with downy leaves and small whitish flowers and containing a bitter medicinal juice. **2.** any of various plants of the mint family. Also, **hoarhound.** [ME *horehune,* OE *hārhūne,* from *hār* grey + *hūne* horehound]

**hori** /ˈhɔri/, *n. N.Z. Colloq.* (*derog.*) a Maori. [Maori: George (Christian name)]

**horizon** /həˈraɪzən/, *n.* **1.** the line or circle which forms the apparent boundary between earth and sky (**apparent** or **visible horizon**). **2.** *Astron.* **a.** the plane which is tangent to the earth at the place of the observer and extends to the celestial sphere (**sensible horizon**). **b.** the great circle of the celestial sphere whose plane is parallel to the sensible horizon of a particular place and passes through the centre of the earth, or the plane itself (**astronomical** or **celestial horizon**). **3.** the limit or range of perception, knowledge, or the like. **4.** *Geol.* a plane in rock strata characterised by particular features, as occurrence of distinctive fossil species. **5.** one of the series of distinctive layers found in a vertical cross-section of any well-developed soil. **6.** *Geol.* the surface separating two beds of rock. [L, from Gk: bounding circle, horizon, properly ppr., bounding; replacing ME *orizonte,* from OF]

**horizontal** /hɒrəˈzɒntl/, *adj.* **1.** at right-angles to the vertical; in a horizontal position. **2.** reclining. **3.** near, on, or parallel to the horizon. **4.** of or pertaining to the horizon. **5.** measured or contained in a plane parallel to the horizon: *a horizontal distance.* *–n.* **6.** a horizontal line, plane, position, etc. **7.** *Tas.* a slender rainforest tree, *Anodopetalum biglandulosum,* which makes almost impenetrable thickets. **– horizontality, horizontalness,** *n.* **– horizontally,** *adv.*

**horizontal bar** /– ˈba/, *n.* a bar for swinging, chinning, and other gymnastic exercises.

**horizontal intensity** /– ɪnˈtɛnsəti/, *n.* the component of the earth's magnetic field which acts in a horizontal direction; equal to the product of the total intensity and the cosine of the angle of dip.

**horizontally-opposed** /hɒrəˌzɒntəli-əˈpoʊzd/, *adj.* of or pertaining to an internal combustion engine in which the cylinders lie paired on either side of the crankcase, each pair in the same plane.

**horizontal mobility** /hɒrəˌzɒntl moʊˈbɪləti/, *n.* the movement of individuals or groups from one position to another without lowering or raising their occupational or social status.

**horizontal stabiliser** /– ˈsteɪbəlaɪzə/, *n.* →**tailplane.**

**hormone** /ˈhɔmoʊn/, *n.* **1.** any of various substances which are formed in endocrine organs and which activate specifically receptive organs when transported to them by the body fluids. The internal secretions of the thyroid gland, pancreas, etc., are hormones. **2.** a synthetic substance having the same effect. **3.** →**plant hormone.** [Gk *hormôn,* ppr., setting in motion] **– hormonal,** *adj.*

**hormone cream** /ˈ– krim/, *n.* a skin cream containing one or more hormones.

**hormone treatment** /ˈ– tritmənt/, *n.* medical treatment involving the use of hormone creams, etc.

**hormonology** /hɔməˈnɒlədʒi/, *n.* →**endocrinology.**

**horn** /hɔn/, *n.* **1.** a hard, projected, often curved and pointed, hollow and permanent growth (usu. one of a pair, a right and a left) on the head of certain mammals, as cattle, sheep, goats, antelopes, etc. (**true horn**). **2.** each of the pair of solid, deciduous, usu. branched bony growths, or antlers, on the head of a deer. **3.** some similar growth, as the tusk of a narwhal. **4.** a process projecting from the head of an animal and suggestive of a horn, as a feeler, tentacle, crest, etc. **5.** the substance of which true horns are composed. **6.** any similar substance, as that of hoofs, nails, corns, etc. **7.** an article made of horn, as a thimble, a spoon, or a shoehorn. **8.** any hornlike projection or extremity. **9.** something formed from or resembling the hollow horn of an animal: *a drinking horn.* **10.** a part like a horn of an animal attributed to deities, demons, etc.: *the devil's horn.* **11.** *Obs.* the imaginary projection on a cuckold's brow. **12.** *Colloq.* →**erection** (def. 4b). **13.** *Music.* a wind instrument, originally formed from the hollow horn of an animal but now usu. made of brass or other metal or material. **14.** *Colloq.* a trumpet. **15.** *Colloq.* a saxophone. **16.** *Colloq.* a French horn. **17.** an instrument for sounding a warning signal: *a motor horn.* **18.** *Aeron.* a local projecting balance on the control surfaces of an aircraft. **19.** *Radio.* a tube of varying cross-section used in some loud-speakers to couple the diaphragm to the sound transmitting space. **20.** →**tweeter.** **21.** the high protuberant part at the front and top of a saddle; the pommel. **22.** one of the extremities of the crescent moon. **23.** a symbol of power, as in the Bible: *a horn of salvation.* **24.** each of the alternatives of a dilemma. **25. draw (pull) one's horns in,** to economise; reduce one's activities; retreat. *–v.t.* **26.** to butt or gore with the horns. **27.** to furnish with horns. *–v.i.* **28. horn in,** *Colloq.* to thrust oneself forward obtrusively. *–adj.* **29.** made of horn. [ME *horn(e),* OE *horn,* c. G *Horn;* akin to L *cornu,* Gk *kéras* horn] **– horned,** *adj.* **– hornless,** *adj.* **– hornlike,** *adj.*

horns (def. 13): A, continental hunting horn; B, military bugle without keys

**hornbeam** /ˈhɔnbim/, *n.* any of the shrubs or small trees constituting the genus *Carpinus,* with a heavy, hard wood, as *C. betulus,* native to Europe and northern Asia, also found in heavy soils of south-eastern England.

**hornbill** /ˈhɔnbɪl/, *n.* any of the large non-passerine, tropical Old World birds constituting the family Bucerotidae, characterised by a very large bill surmounted by a horny protuberance, sometimes of enormous size.

**hornblende** /ˈhɔnblɛnd/, *n.* any of the common black or dark-coloured aluminous varieties of amphibole. [G] **– hornblendic** /hɔnˈblɛndɪk/, *adj.*

**hornblende schist** /ˈ– ʃɪst/, *n.* a variety of schist containing needles of hornblende which lie in parallel planes in the rock.

**hornbook** /ˈhɔnbʊk/, *n.* **1.** a leaf or page containing the alphabet, religious materials, etc., covered with a sheet of transparent horn and fixed in a frame with a handle, formerly used in teaching children to read. **2.** a primer, or book of rudiments.

**horned pondweed** /hɔnd ˈpɒndwid/, *n.* a slender, submerged, perennial plant, *Zanichellia palustris,* of the family Zanichelliaceae, widespread in fresh or brackish water.

**horned poppy** /– ˈpɒpi/, *n.* any of several species of herbs of Europe and western Asia, belonging to the genus *Glaucium,* esp. the **yellow horned poppy,** *G. flavum,* with large flowers and long curved capsules.

**horned toad** /– ˈtoʊd/, *n.* any of various small, harmless lizards, genus *Phrynosoma,* of western North America, with flattened body and hornlike spines on the head and body.

**horned viper** /– ˈvaɪpə/, *n.* →**viper** (def. 3).

**hornet** /ˈhɔnət/, *n.* **1.** any large, strong, social wasp of the family Vespidae having an exceptionally severe sting. **2. mad as a hornet,** *Colloq.* extremely angry. [ME *harnete,* OE *hyrnet(u),* c. G *Hornisse*]

**hornet's nest** /ˈhɔnəts nɛst/, *n.* a great deal of trouble, hostility.

**hornito** /hɔˈnitoʊ/, *n., pl.* **-tos** /-toʊz/. a low oven-shaped mound, common in the volcanic districts of South America, etc., usu. emitting hot smoke and vapours from its sides and summit. [Sp., diminutive of *horno,* from L *furnus* oven]

**horn of plenty,** *n.* →**cornucopia.**

**hornpipe** /ˈhɔnpaɪp/, *n.* **1.** an English folk clarinet with an ox horn to conceal the reed and another one to form the bell. **2.** a lively dance (originally to hornpipe music) usu. by a single person, popular among sailors. **3.** a piece of music for or in the style of such a dance.

**horn-rimmed** /ˈhɔn-rɪmd/, *adj.* (of spectacles) with frames or rims made of horn, tortoiseshell, or a plastic in imitation of horn.

**horn silver** /ˈhɔn sɪlvə/, *n.* →**cerargyrite.**

**hornstone** /ˈhɔnstoʊn/, *n.* **1.** a variety of quartz resembling flint. **2.** an argillaceous rock baked and partly recrystallised by the heat of an igneous intrusion.

**horntail** /ˈhɔnteɪl/, *n.* any of various wasplike insects of the family Siricidae, the females of which have a hornlike spine at the end of the abdomen.

**hornworm** /ˈhɔnwɜm/, *n.* any of various caterpillars of hawkmoths, characterised by a hornlike caudal projection.

**hornwort** /ˈhɔnwɜt/, *n.* any plant of the genus *Ceratophyllum,* comprising aquatic herbs common in ponds and slow streams.

**horny** /ˈhɔni/, *adj.,* **-nier, -niest. 1.** hornlike through hardening; callous: *horny hands.* **2.** consisting of a horn or a hornlike substance; corneous. **3.** more or less translucent, like horn. **4.** having a horn or horns or hornlike projections. **5.** (of a male) randy; sexually excited. – **horniness,** *n.*

**horol.,** horology.

**horologe** /ˈhɒrəlɒdʒ/, *n.* any instrument for indicating the time. [L *hōrologium,* from Gk *hōrológion* an instrument for telling the hour; replacing ME *orloge,* from OF]

**horologic** /hɒrəˈlɒdʒɪk/, *adj.* pertaining to a horologe or to horology. Also, **horological.**

**horologist** /həˈrɒlədʒəst/, *n.* an expert in horology. Also, **horologer.**

**horology** /həˈrɒlədʒi/, *n.* the art or science of making timepieces or of measuring time.

**horomai** /ˈhɒrəmaɪ/, *interj.* →**haeremai.**

**horopito** /hɒrəˈpitoʊ/, *n. N.Z.* →**peppertree** (def. 3).

**horoscope** /ˈhɒrəskoʊp/, *n.* **1.** a diagram of the heavens for use in calculating nativities, etc. **2.** the art or practice of foretelling future events by observation of the stars and planets. [ME and OE *horoscopus,* from L, from Gk *hōroskópos* sign in the ascendant at time of birth]

**horoscopy** /hɒˈrɒskəpi/, *n.* **1.** the casting or taking of horoscopes. **2.** the aspects of the heavens at a given moment, esp. that of a person's birth.

**horrendous** /hɒˈrɛndəs, hə-/, *adj.* dreadful; horrible. [L *horrendus,* ger. of *horrēre* bristle, shudder] – **horrendously,** *adv.*

**horrent** /ˈhɒrənt/, *adj.* bristling; standing erect like bristles. [L *horrens,* ppr., standing on end. Cf. HORRID]

**horrible** /ˈhɒrəbəl/, *adj.* **1.** causing or tending to cause horror; dreadful: *a horrible sight.* **2.** extremely unpleasant; deplorable; excessive: *horrible conditions.* [ME, from OF, from L *horribilis* terrible, fearful] – **horribleness,** *n.*

**horribly** /ˈhɒrəbli/, *adv.* **1.** in a horrible fashion. **2.** *Colloq.* (an intensifier): *I was horribly put out by the rain.*

**horrid** /ˈhɒrəd/, *adj.* **1.** such as to cause horror; dreadful; abominable. **2.** *Colloq.* extremely unpleasant or disagreeable: *horrid weather.* [L *horridus* bristling, rough] – **horridly,** *adv.* – **horridness,** *n.*

**horrific** /hɒˈrɪfɪk, hə-/, *adj.* causing horror. [L *horrificus*]

**horrify** /ˈhɒrəfaɪ/, *v.t.,* **-fied, -fying.** to cause to feel horror; strike with horror; shock intensely. [L *horrificāre* cause horror] – **horrification** /hɒrəfəˈkeɪʃən/, *n.*

**horripilation** /hɒrəpəˈleɪʃən/, *n.* a bristling of the hair on the skin from cold, fear, etc.; goose pimples. [LL *horripilātio,* from L *horripilāre* bristle with hairs]

**horror** /ˈhɒrə/, *n.* **1.** a shuddering fear or abhorrence; a painful emotion excited by something frightful or shocking: *to shrink back in horror.* **2.** anything that excites such a feeling: *the horrors of war.* **3.** a character, look, appearance, etc., such as to excite a shuddering fear: *a scene of horror.* **4.** *Colloq.* something considered atrocious or bad: *that hat is a horror.* **5.** a painful or intense aversion or repugnance: *a horror of publicity.* **6.** (*pl.*) *Colloq.* **a.** great sensation of fear: *heights give me the horrors.* **b.** →**delirium tremens. 7.** *Obs.* a bristling. *–interj.* **8.** (*also pl.*) (an expression of dismay, often jocular). [L; replacing ME *orrour,* from OF]

**horror comic** /ˈ– kɒmɪk/, *n.* a magazine in comic-strip form exploiting horrific themes.

**horror film** /ˈ– fɪlm/, *n.* a film which treats supernatural or horrific subjects in a sensational way.

**horror-struck** /ˈhɒrə-strʌk/, *adj.* filled with horror; shocked. Also, **horror-stricken.**

**hors de combat** /ˌɔ də ˈkɒmbæt/, *adj.* **1.** out of the fight; disabled; no longer able to fight. **2.** unable to act, participate, etc., because of illness; laid low. [F]

**hors d'oeuvre** /ɔ ˈdɜv/, *n.* an appetiser, canapé or savoury, served with cocktails, before a meal, etc. [F: aside from (the main body of the) work]

**horse** /hɔs/, *n., pl.* **horses,** (*esp. collectively*) **horse,** *v.,* **horsed, horsing,** *adj.* *–n.* **1.** a large, solid-hoofed quadruped, *Equus caballus,* domesticated since prehistoric times, and employed as a beast of draught and burden and for carrying a rider. **2.** a male horse, fully-grown and past its fourth birthday. **3.** any animal of the family Equidae (**horse family**), which includes

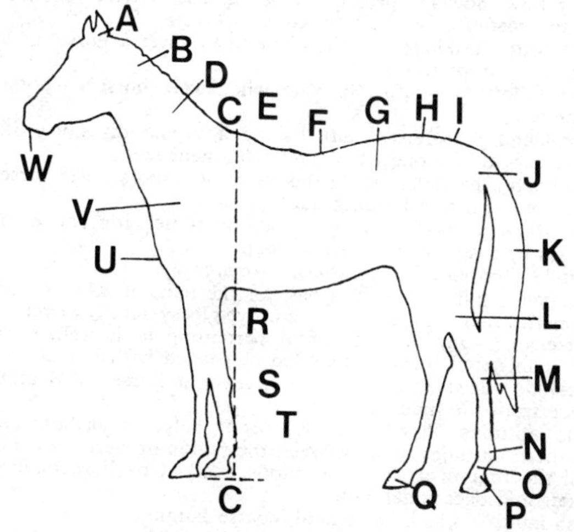


horse: A, poll; B, crest; C, height; D, withers; E, chest; F, loins; G, hip; H, croup; I, dock; J, hindquarters; K, tail; L, gaskin; M, hock; N, fetlock; O, pastern; P, heel, Q, hoof; R, elbow; S, knee; T, splint-bone; U, breast; V, shoulder; W, muzzle

the ass, zebra, etc. **4.** soldiers serving on horseback; cavalry: *a thousand horse.* **5.** something on which a person rides, sits, or exercises as if on a horse's back: *rocking horse.* **6.** a leather-covered block, adjustable in height, used for vaulting and other gymnastic exercises. **7.** a frame, block, etc., with legs on which something is mounted or supported. **8.** *Naut.* a metal rod or the like fitted to the deck of a sailing ship, to which is attached a traveller which retains the main sheet while allowing it to run from side to side. **9.** *Mining.* a mass of rock enclosed within a lode or vein. **10.** *Colloq.* →**heroin.** **11.** Some special noun phrases are:
**a dark horse,** a person of unknown potential.
**back the wrong horse,** to support the wrong or losing contender.
**eat like a horse,** to have a prodigious appetite.
**from the horse's mouth,** from an authoritative source.
**hold one's horses,** to restrain one's impulses; hold back.
**horse of another colour,** a different thing altogether.
**look a gift-horse in the mouth,** →**gift-horse.**
**get on one's high horse,** to stand on one's dignity.
**white horse,** the foamy crest of a wave.
**willing horse,** a willing worker.
*–v.t.* **12.** to provide with a horse or horses. **13.** to set on horseback. **14.** to set or carry on a person's back or one's own back. **15.** *Obs.* **a.** to place (someone) on a person's back or on a wooden horse or the like to be flogged. **b.** to flog. *–v.i.* **16.** to mount or go on a horse. **17. horse about** or **around,** to act or play roughly or boisterously. *–adj.* **18.** unusually large for one of its kind. **19.** of or pertaining to a horse or horses. **20.** mounted on horses. [ME and OE *hors,* c. OS and OHG *hros,* G *Ross,* Icel. *hross*]

**horse-and-buggy age** /hɔs-ən-ˈbʌgi eɪdʒ/, *n.* the past viewed as being totally outmoded and surpassed by present technological achievement.

**horseback** /ˈhɔsbæk/, *n.* **1.** the back of a horse: *on horseback.* **2.** *U.S.* a low ridge of sand, gravel, or rock. Cf. **hogback.**

**horse bean** /ˈhɔs bin/, *n. Colloq.* a small-fruited form of broadbean, *Vicia faba.*

**horseblock** /ˈhɔsblɒk/, *n.* a step or block for mounting and dismounting a horse.

**horsebox** /ˈhɔsbɒks/, *n.* a van or trailer for conveying horses by road, rail, etc.

**horse brass** /ˈhɔs bras/, *n.* a brass ornament, originally as worn on a horse's harness.

**horse chestnut** /– ˈtʃɛsnʌt/, *n.* **1.** the shiny, brown nutlike seed of several species of *Aesculus,* ornamental trees bearing large digitate leaves and upright clusters of showy white, red, or yellow flowers, principally *A. hippocastanum* (**common horse chestnut**). **2.** the tree itself.

**horsecloth** /ˈhɔsklɒθ/, *n.* a cloth used to cover a horse, or as part of its trappings.

**horse-duffer** /ˈhɔs-dʌfə/, *n.* one who steals horses. **– horse-duffing,** *n.*

**horse-faced** /ˈhɔs-feɪst/, *adj.* having a supposedly horse-like face, as with a lantern jaw, and prominent teeth.

**horseflesh** /ˈhɔsflɛʃ/, *n.* **1.** the flesh of a horse. **2.** horses collectively, esp. for riding, racing, etc.

**horse float** /ˈhɔs floʊt/, *n.* a van or trailer for conveying horses by road, rail, etc. Also, **float.**

**horsefly** /ˈhɔsflaɪ/, *n., pl.* **-flies.** →**march fly.**

**horsehair** /ˈhɔshɛə/, *n.* **1.** a hair, or the hair, of a horse, esp. from the mane or tail. **2.** a sturdy, glossy fabric woven of horsehair. *–adj.* **3.** made of or pertaining to horsehair. **4.** (of upholstered furniture) stuffed or padded with horsehair.

**horsehide** /ˈhɔshaɪd/, *n.* **1.** the hide of a horse. **2.** leather made from the hide of a horse.

**horse latitudes** /ˈhɔs lætətjudz/, *n. pl.* belts of northern and southern latitudes lying between the region of westerly winds and the region of the trade winds, marked by light baffling winds and occasional calms.

**horse laugh** /ˈ– laf/, *n.* a loud, coarse laugh.

**horseleech** /ˈhɔslitʃ/, *n.* a large leech, as *Haemopsis sanguisorba,* said to attack the mouths of horses while they are drinking.

**horseless** /ˈhɔsləs/, *adj.* **1.** without a horse. **2.** self-propelled: *a horseless carriage.*

**horse mackerel** /ˈhɔs mækərəl/, *n.* **1.** any of several carangid fishes of the genus *Trachurus* as *T. declivis* and *T. novaezelandiae,* found in Australian waters or *T. symmetricus,* of the Pacific coast of the U.S. **2.** →**bonito.**

**horseman** /ˈhɔsmən/, *n., pl.* **-men.** **1.** a rider on horseback. **2.** one who attends to horses or is skilled in managing them.

**horsemanship** /ˈhɔsmənʃɪp/, *n.* **1.** the management of horses. **2.** equestrian skill.

**horse marine** /ˈhɔs mərin/, *n.* **1.** *U.S.* a member of an imaginary corps of mounted marines. **2.** *U.S.* (formerly) a marine mounted on horseback, or a cavalryman doing duty on board ship. **3.** *U.S.* a person out of his element. **4. tell that (it) to the (horse) marines,** *Orig. U.S.* (an expression of disbelief).

**horsemeat** /ˈhɔsmit/, *n.* the flesh of a horse used as animal food, etc.

**horsemint** /ˈhɔsmɪnt/, *n.* **1.** a wild mint, *Mentha longifolia,* originally native to Europe. **2.** any of various other plants as *Monarda punctata,* an erect odorous herb of America.

**horse mushroom** /hɔs ˈmʌʃrum/, *n.* a large, platelike, coarse mushroom.

**horse nettle** /ˈ– nɛtl/, *n.* one of several prickly species of *Solanum,* as *S. carolinense.*

**horse opera** /ˈ– ɒprə/, *n.* a television, radio, or film drama about the U.S. Wild West, as one featuring cowboys and Indians, gold prospectors, or the like.

**horse pick** /ˈ– pɪk/, *n.* a metal hook used for removing stones, etc., lodged in a horse's hoof.

**horse pistol** /ˈ– pɪstl/, *n.* a kind of large pistol formerly carried by horsemen.

**horseplay** /ˈhɔspleɪ/, *n.* rough or boisterous play.

**horsepower** /ˈhɔspaʊə/, *n.* a unit of measurement of power, or rate of doing work, in the imperial system, defined as 550 pounds-force per second (approx. 745 watts.).

**horserace** /ˈhɔsreɪs/, *n.* a race between horses with jockeys.

**horseracing** /ˈhɔsreɪsɪŋ/, *n.* the practice or sport of racing with horses.

**horseradish** /ˈhɔsrædɪʃ/, *n.* **1.** a cultivated plant, *Armoracia lapathifolia.* **2.** its pungent root, ground and used as a condiment and in medicine.

**horseradish tree** /ˈ– tri/, *n.* a tropical Asian tree, *Moringa pterygosperma,* with a thick trunk and creamy flowers, with edible fruits, leaves and shoots.

**horse sense** /ˈhɔs sɛns/, *n. Colloq.* **1.** plain, practical, common sense. **2.** an ability to judge horseflesh, to ride well, etc.

**horses for courses,** *n.* **1.** a theory that a horse which races well on one track or type of track should not be run on a different track to which it is not suited. **2.** the notion that a person should be matched with a position, task, etc., suited to his or her particular talents.

**horseshit** /ˈhɔsʃɪt/, *n. U.S. Colloq.* nonsense; rubbish; bullshit.

**horseshoe** /ˈhɔsʃu/, *n., v.,* **-shoed, -shoeing.** *–n.* **1.** a U-shaped iron plate nailed to a horse's hoof to protect it. **2.** something shaped like a horseshoe. **3.** *U.S.* (*pl. construed as sing.*) a game using horseshoes or similar pieces, the object being to throw the piece so as to encircle an iron stake 10 to 12 metres away. **4.** a symbol of good luck. *–v.t.* **5.** to put horseshoes on; to shoe. *–adj.* **6.** with the shape of a horseshoe.

**horseshoe crab** /ˈ– kræb/, *n.* any of various marine arthropods, esp. of the genus *Limulus,* with a carapace shaped somewhat like a horseshoe; king crab.

horseshoe crab

**horseshoe fern** /ˈ– fɜn/, *n.* **king-fern** (def. 1).

**horseshoe roll** /– ˈroʊl/, *n.* a horseshoe-shaped bread roll.

**horseshoe vetch** /– ˈvɛtʃ/, *n.* a small, spreading perennial, *Hippocrepis comosa,* with heads of few, long-stalked yellow flowers, found on calcareous soils of western and southern Europe.

**horse's hoof** /hɔsəz ˈhʊf/, *n. Colloq.* a homosexual. [rhyming slang, *horse's hoof* poof, homosexual]

**horseshow** /ˈhɔsʃoʊ/, *n.* a competitive display of the qualities and capabilities of horses and their riders.

**horse-stinger** /ˈhɔs-stɪŋə/, *n. Colloq.* →**dragonfly.** [from the erroneous belief that it stings horses]

**horse tail** /ˈhɔs teɪl/, *n.* →**ponytail.**

**horsetail** /ˈhɔsteɪl/, *n.* any of the perennial, herbaceous, pteridophytic plants constituting the widely distributed genus *Equisetum,* characterised by hollow, jointed stems.

**horse-tailer** /ˈhɔs-teɪlə/, *n.* the man who tends the horses at a stock camp.

**horse-trading** /ˈhɔs-treɪdɪŋ/, *n.* shrewd and close bargaining. – **horse-trader,** *n.*

**horsewhip** /ˈhɔswɪp/, *n., v.,* **-whipped, -whipping.** *–n.* **1.** a whip for controlling horses. *–v.t.* **2.** to beat with a horsewhip.

**horsewoman** /ˈhɔswʊmən/, *n., pl.* **-women. 1.** a woman who rides on horseback. **2.** a woman who is skilful in managing or riding horses.

**Horsfield's bushlark** /hɔsfildz ˈbʊʃlak/, *n.* →**singing bushlark.**

**horst** /hɔst/, *n.* a portion of the earth's crust, bounded on at least two sides by faults, that has been moved upwards in relation to adjacent portions. [G: eyrie, thicket]

**horsy** /ˈhɔsi/, *adj.,* **-sier, -siest. 1.** pertaining to, characteristic of, or of the nature of a horse or horses: *horsy talk.* **2.** dealing with, interested in, or devoted to horses, horseracing, etc. **3.** *Colloq.* large and supposedly horselike in appearance or manner. – **horsiness,** *n.*

**hort., 1.** horticultural. **2.** horticulture.

**hortative** /ˈhɔtətɪv/, *adj.* →**hortatory.** [L *hortātīvus*] – **hortatively,** *adv.*

**hortatory** /hɔˈteɪtəri, ˈhɔtətri/, *adj.* encouraging; inciting, exhorting; urging to some course of conduct or action: *a hortatory address.* [LL *hortātōrius* encouraging]

**horticulture** /ˈhɔtəkʌltʃə/, *n.* **1.** commercial cultivation of fruit, vegetables, and flowers, including berries, grapes, vines and nuts. **2.** the science or art of growing fruit, vegetables, flowers or ornamental plants. **3.** the cultivation of a garden. [*horti-* (combining form of L *hortus* garden) + CULTURE] – **horticultural** /hɔtəˈkʌltʃərəl/, *adj.* – **horticulturist** /hɔtəˈkʌltʃərəst/, **horticulturalist** /hɔtəˈkʌltʃərələst/, *n.*

**hortus siccus** /hɔtəs ˈsɪkəs/, *n.* a collection of dried plants; a herbarium. [L: dry garden]

**Hos.,** *Bible.* Hosea.

**hosanna** /hoʊˈzænə/, *interj.* **1.** (an exclamation, originally an appeal to God for deliverance, used in praise of God or Christ). *–n.* **2.** a cry of 'hosanna'. **3.** a shout of praise or adoration; an acclamation. [LL, from Gk, from Heb. *hōsh(i)ʿāhnnā* save, pray!]

**hose** /hoʊz/, *n., pl.* **hose,** (*Archaic*) **hosen,** *v.,* **hosed, hosing.** *–n.* **1.** an article of clothing for the foot and lower part of the leg; a stocking. **2.** a garment for the legs and thighs, as tights or breeches, formerly worn by men. **3.** a flexible tube for conveying water, etc., to a desired point: *a garden hose.* **4.** a sheath, or sheathing part, as that enclosing the kernel of grain. *–v.t.* **5.** to water, wash, or drench by means of a hose. [ME and OE, c. D *hoos,* G *Hose,* Icel. *hosa*]

**hose cock** /ˈ– kɒk/, *n.* a bib cock fitted with threads for a hose connection.

**hosepipe** /ˈhoʊzpaɪp/, *n.* →**hose** (def. 3).

**hosier** /ˈhoʊziə/, *n.* one who makes or deals in hose or stockings, or goods knitted or woven like hose.

**hosiery** /ˈhoʊzəri/, *n.* **1.** hose or stockings of any kind. **2.** the business of a hosier.

**hosp.,** hospital.

**hospice** /ˈhɒspəs/, *n.* **1.** a house of shelter or rest for pilgrims, strangers, etc., esp. one kept by a religious order. **2.** a hospital for terminally ill patients. [F, from L *hospitium* hospitality]

**hospitable** /hɒsˈpɪtəbəl/, *adj.* **1.** affording a generous welcome to guests or strangers: *a hospitable city.* **2.** inclined to or characterised by hospitality: *a hospitable reception.* **3.** favourably receptive or open (fol. by *to*): *hospitable to new ideas.* [F (obs.), from LL *hospitāre* receive as a guest + *-able* -ABLE] – **hospitableness,** *n.* – **hospitably,** *adv.*

**hospital** /ˈhɒspɪtl/, *n.* **1.** an institution in which sick or injured persons are given medical or surgical treatment. **2.** a similar establishment for the care of animals. **3.** *Archaic.* an old people's home. **4.** a shop for repairing specific things: *a dolls' hospital.* [ME, from OF, from LL *hospitāle* inn, properly neut. of L *hospitālis* pertaining to guests, hospitable]

**hospital brandy** /ˈ– brændi/, *n.* brandy, usu. not of the highest quality, which is nominally reserved for medicinal use.

**hospital corner** /ˈ– kɔnə/, *n.* the corner of a made bed when the sheets and/or blankets have been folded in the manner prescribed in hospitals.

**hospitalise** /ˈhɒspətəlaɪz/, *v.t.,* **-lised, -lising.** to place for medical care, etc., in a hospital. Also, **hospitalize.** – **hospitalisation** /hɒspətəlaɪˈzeɪʃən/, *n.*

**hospitality** /hɒspəˈtæləti/, *n., pl.* **-ties.** the reception and entertainment of guests or strangers with liberality and kindness.

**hospitaller** /ˈhɒspɪtələ/, *n.* a person, esp. a member of a religious order, devoted to the care of the sick or needy in hospitals. Also, *U.S.* **hospitaler.** [ME, from OF *hospitalier,* from *hospital* HOSPITAL]

**hospital orderly** /hɒspɪtl ˈɔdəli/, *n.* a serviceman of any of the three services carrying out medical duties in hospital wards.

**hospital paddock** /ˈ– pædək/, *n.* a paddock in which animals are quarantined because of illness.

**hospital patient** /ˈ– peɪʃənt/, *n.* a patient in a public hospital, who is treated by the hospital with the facilities at its disposal.

**hospital school** /ˈ– skul/, *n.* a classroom, or a system of lessons within wards, for children of school age who are confined to a hospital, usu. for a protracted period of time.

**hospital ship** /ˈ– ʃɪp/, *n.* a ship built or specially converted for use as transport for sick and wounded in wartime.

**hospitium** /hɒsˈpɪtiəm/, *n., pl.* **-pitia** /-ˈpɪtiə/. →**hospice.**

**host**[1] /hoʊst/, *n.* **1.** one who entertains guests in his own home or elsewhere: *the host at a theatre party.* **2.** the landlord of an inn. **3.** an animal or plant from which a parasite obtains nutrition. **4.** an animal or person that receives tissue, an organ, etc., transplanted from another. *–v.t.* **5.** to act as a host (def. 1). **6.** to compere (a television show, etc.). [ME (*h*)*oste,* from OF, from L *hospes* host, guest, stranger. Cf. GUEST, HOST[2]]

**host**[2] /hoʊst/, *n.* **1.** a multitude or great number of persons or things: *a host of details.* **2.** *Archaic.* an army. [ME, from OF, from ML *hostis* army, from L: stranger, enemy. Cf. GUEST, HOST[1]]

**Host** /hoʊst/, *n.* the bread consecrated in the celebration of the Eucharist; a consecrated wafer. [ME *hoste,* from ML *hostia,* in L animal sacrificed]

**hostage** /ˈhɒstɪdʒ/, *n.* **1.** a person given or held as a security for the performance of certain actions as the payment of ransom, etc. **2.** *Obs.* the condition of a hostage. **3.** a security or pledge. **4. give a hostage to fortune,** to hand over one's future happiness, success, etc., into the hands of fate by taking an action that renders one more than normally vulnerable. [ME (*h*)*ostage,* from OF, from *oste* guest, from L *hospes* and ? b. with L *obses* hostage]

**hostel** /ˈhɒstəl, hɒsˈtɛl/, *n.* **1.** a supervised place of accommodation, usu. supplying board and lodging, provided at a comparatively low cost, as one for students, nurses, or the like. **2.** →**youth hostel. 3.** *Archaic.* an inn. [ME (*h*)*ostel,* from OF, from *oste* guest]

**hosteller** /ˈhɒstələ/, *n.* a person who stays at youth hostels.

**hostelling** /ˈhɒstəlɪŋ/, *n.* the practice of staying at youth hostels.

**hostelry** /ˈhɒstəlri/, *n., pl.* **-ries.** *Archaic.* a hostel or inn. [ME (*h*)*ostelerie,* from OF, from *hostel.* See HOSTEL]

**hostess** /ˈhoʊstɛs/, *n.* **1.** a female host; a woman who entertains guests. **2.** an air hostess. **3.** a paid dancing partner. **4.** a female innkeeper.

**hostess gown** /ˈ– gaʊn/, *n.* a full-length semi-formal dress, esp. worn when entertaining at home; an informal evening dress. Also, **hostess dress.**

**hostie** /ˈhoʊsti/, *n. Colloq.* →**air hostess.**

**hostile** /ˈhɒstaɪl/, *adj.* **1.** opposed in feeling, action, or character; unfriendly; antagonistic: *hostile criticism.* **2.** of or characteristic of an enemy: *hostile ground.* **3. go hostile,** *N.Z. Colloq.* become angry (fol. by *at*). *–n.* **4.** *U.S.* **a.** a warring Red Indian. **b.** one of the enemy. [late ME, from L *hostīlis,* from *hostis* enemy. See HOST[2]] – **hostilely,** *adv.*

**hostile witness** /– 'wɪtnəs/, *n.* a witness who is biased against the party examining him.

**hostility** /hɒs'tɪləti/, *n., pl.* **-ties.** **1.** hostile state; enmity; antagonism. **2.** a hostile act. **3.** (*pl.*) acts of warfare.

**hostler** /'ɒslə/, *n. Archaic.* →**ostler.**

**host rock** /'houst rɒk/, *n.* the wall rock of an epigenetic ore deposit.

**hot** /hɒt/, *adj.,* **hotter, hottest,** *adv., v.,* **hotted, hotting,** *n.* –*adj.* **1.** having or communicating heat; having a high temperature: *a hot stove.* **2.** having a sensation of great bodily heat; attended with or producing such a sensation. **3.** having an effect as of burning on the tongue, skin, etc., as pepper, mustard, a blister, etc. **4.** having or showing intense feeling; ardent or fervent; vehement; excited: *hot temper.* **5.** lustful. **6.** violent, furious, or intense: *the hottest battle.* **7.** strong or fresh, as a scent or trail. **8.** new; recent; fresh: *hot off the press.* **9.** following very closely; close: *to be hot on one's heels.* **10.** (of colours) with red predominating. **11.** *Games.* close to the sought-for object or answer. **12.** *Colloq.* fashionable and exciting. **13.** currently popular: *the hot favourite (horse), a hot sales item.* **14.** (of motor cars) tuned or modified for high speeds: *a hot rod.* **15.** *Jazz.* **a.** arousing, or capable of arousing, enthusiasm and admiration; intense; compulsive. **b.** (of a musician) playing such music. **16.** *Colloq.* recently stolen or otherwise illegally obtained; wanted by the police. **17.** radioactive, esp. to a degree injurious to health. **18. a bit hot,** unfair; dishonest; high-priced. **19. blow hot and cold,** change attitudes frequently; vacillate. **20. hot as Hay, Hell and Booligal,** *Colloq.* very hot. **21. hot as Hades,** *Colloq.* very hot. **22. go hot and cold all over** or **go all hot and cold,** to experience, or exhibit signs of, shock or embarrassment. **23. hot and bothered,** upset; flustered; exasperated. **24. hot under the collar,** angry; annoyed. **25. in hot water,** *Colloq.* in trouble. **26. like a cat on a hot tin-roof,** in a state of extreme agitation. **27. like a cat on hot bricks,** in a state of extreme agitation. **28. make it hot for,** *Colloq.* to make life unpleasant for. **29. not so (too) hot,** *Colloq.* **a.** not very good; disappointing. **b.** unwell. **30. sell** or **go like hot cakes,** to sell or be removed quickly, esp. in large quantities. –*adv.* **31.** in a hot manner; hotly. –*v.t.* **32.** to heat (usu. fol. by *up*). **33. hot up, a.** to heat: *to hot up the milk.* **b.** to escalate: *he hotted up his attack.* **c.** to stir up: *to hot things up a bit.* **d.** to tune or modify (a motor vehicle) for high speeds. **e.** to grow excited or wild: *the party began to hot up.* –*n.* **34.** (*pl.*) *Colloq.* a strong sexual attraction (fol. by *for*): *to have the hots for Sadie.* [ME *ho(o)t,* OE *hāt,* c. G *heiss*]

**hot air** /– 'ɛə/, *n. Colloq.* empty, pretentious talk or writing.

**hot-air balloon** /hɒt-ɛə bə'lun/, *n.* a balloon (def. 1) which is kept aloft by heating the air within it, usu. by a controlled flame beneath its opening.

**hot atom** /hɒt 'ætəm/, *n.* an atom that has high kinetic or internal energy as a result of exposure to a nuclear process.

**hotbed** /'hɒtbɛd/, *n.* **1.** a bed of earth, heated by fermenting manure, etc., and usu. covered with glass, for growing plants out of season. **2.** a place favouring rapid growth, esp. of something bad: *a hotbed of vice.*

**hot-blooded** /'hɒt-blʌdəd/, *adj.* virile; adventurous; excitable; impetuous.

**hotbox** /'hɒtbɒks/, *n.* an overheated journal box, on a railway carriage or locomotive, caused by the friction of a rapidly revolving axle.

**hot bread** /'hɒt brɛd/, *n.* →**quick bread.**

**hotchpot** /'hɒtʃpɒt/, *n.* the bringing together of shares or properties in order to divide them equally, esp. when they are to be divided among the children of a parent dying intestate. [ME *hochepot,* from OF: ragout, from *hocher* shake + *pot* pot]

**hotchpotch** /'hɒtʃpɒtʃ/, *n.* **1.** a heterogeneous mixture; a jumble. **2.** *Law.* →**hotchpot.** **3.** a thick soup or stew made from meat and vegetables. Also, **hodgepodge.** [rhyming var. of HOTCHPOT]

**hot cross bun,** *n.* a bun with a cross on it, eaten chiefly on Good Friday.

**hot dog** /'hɒt dɒg, /hɒt 'dɒg/, *n., v.,* **dogged, dogging,** *interj.* –*n.* **1.** a hot frankfurter or sausage, esp. as served in a split roll with mustard. **2.** a short surfboard designed to turn quickly back and forth across the wave. **3.** *U.S.* an expert. –*v.i.* **4.** to ride a surfboard quickly back and forth across the face of a wave. –*interj.* **5.** *U.S.* (an exclamation indicating enthusiasm, admiration, surprise, etc.). Also, **hot-dog.** – **hot-dogger,** *n.*

**hot-dogging** /hɒt-'dɒgɪŋ/, *n.* a type of competition snow skiing, where points are awarded according to the class and degree of difficulty of the jumps, rather than according to time taken; free style.

**hotel** /hou'tɛl/, *n.* a building in which accommodation and food, and usu. alcoholic drinks are available; public house. [F: (earlier *hostel*) HOSTEL]

**hotelier** /hou'tɛliə/, *n.* one who manages a hotel or hotels.

**hot flushes** /hɒt 'flʌʃəz/, *n. pl.* momentary sensations of heat, often accompanied by a heightening of facial colour and perspiration, a common menopausal symptom.

**hotfoot** /'hɒtfʊt/, *v.i.* **1.** Also, **hotfoot it.** to move with great speed. –*adv.* **2.** with great speed. –*n.* **3.** *U.S.* a practical joke in which a match is inserted in the side of a person's shoe and lit.

**hot-galvanise** /hɒt-'gælvənaɪz/, *v.t.,* **-nised, -nising.** to coat another metal with zinc by immersing it in a bath of molten zinc. Also, **hot-galvanize.**

**hot-gospeller** /hɒt-'gɒspələ/, *n. Colloq.* a revivalist preacher. Also, *U.S.,* **hot-gospeler.**

**hothead** /'hɒthɛd/, *n.* a hot-headed person.

**hot-headed** /'hɒt-hɛdəd/, *adj.* hot or fiery in spirit or temper; impetuous; rash. – **hot-headedly,** *adv.* – **hot-headedness,** *n.*

**hothouse** /'hɒthaus/, *n.* **1.** an artificially heated greenhouse for the cultivation of tender plants. –*adj.* **2.** of or pertaining to a delicate plant grown in a hothouse. **3.** *Colloq.* delicate; over-protected.

**hot licks** /hɒt 'lɪks/, *n.pl.* →**licks.**

**hot line** /'– laɪn/, *n.* **1.** a direct telephone connection open to immediate communication in an emergency, as between the heads of state of the Soviet Union and the United States. **2.** any especially important telephone connection.

**hot metal** /– 'mɛtl/, *n.* molten iron.

**hot-metal** /'hɒt-mɛtl/, *adj.* of or pertaining to a mechanical typesetting system which uses molten metal, or to the machinery involved in such a system.

**hot mix** /hɒt 'mɪks/, *n.* a mixture of bituminous binder and aggregate with or without mineral filler, produced hot in a mixing plant and delivered in a hot condition to the purchaser for spreading and compacting.

**hot money** /'– mʌni/, *n.* **1.** a disability allowance paid to a worker for working in especially hot conditions, as near a blast furnace. **2.** *Colloq.* money in a money market or foreign exchange market which is likely to be withdrawn hastily following small changes in market conditions.

**hot pack** /'– pæk/, *n.* a hot compress.

**hotpants** /'hɒtpænts/, *n. pl.* **1.** *Colloq.* **a.** strong sexual desires. **b.** one who has strong sexual desires: *she's a real little hotpants.* **2.** brief, tight shorts, usu. conspicuously coloured, worn by women.

**hot place** /'hɒt pleɪs/, *n.* a working place where the temperature is raised considerably above normal by artificial means. See **heat money.**

**hotplate** /'hɒtpleɪt/, *n.* **1.** a portable appliance for cooking or keeping food warm. **2.** a solid, electrically heated metal plate, usu. on top of an electric stove, upon which food, etc., may be heated or cooked.

**hotpoint** /'hɒtpɔɪnt/, *v.t. Prison Colloq.* to cheat; deceive. Also, **point.** – **hotpointer,** *n.*

**hotpot** /'hɒtpɒt/, *n.* **1.** mutton or beef cooked with potatoes, etc., in a covered pot. **2.** *Horseracing.* the short-priced favourite, usu. odds-on.

**hot potato** /hɒt pə'teɪtou/, *n. Colloq.* a risky situation, difficult person, or any other thing which needs careful handling.

**hot-press** /'hɒt-prɛs/, *n.* **1.** a machine applying heat in conjunction with mechanical pressure, as for producing a smooth surface on paper, for expressing oil, etc. –*v.t.* **2.** to subject to treatment in a hot-press.

**hot rod** /'hɒt rɒd/, *n. Colloq.* a car (usu. an old one) whose engine has been altered for increased speed.

**hot seat** /'– sit/, *n.* **1.** the electric chair. **2.** *Colloq.* a position involving difficulties or danger.

**hot-shot** /ˈhɒt-ʃɒt/, *adj.* **1.** exceptionally proficient. *–n.* **2.** one who is exceptionally proficient, often ostentatiously so.

**hot spot** /ˈhɒt spɒt/, *n.* **1.** an unpleasantly hot locality, town, etc. **2.** *Geol.* a place of high heat concentration near the earth's surface. **3.** a place where a dangerous political situation exists or may develop into revolution, war, etc. **4.** *Mil.* a region in a contaminated area, etc. **5.** a nightclub or similar place of entertainment.

**hot spring** /– ˈsprɪŋ/, *n.* a naturally heated spring, often containing mineral substances in solution.

**hotspur** /ˈhɒtspɜ/, *n.* an impetuous person; a hothead. [from Sir Henry Percy, known as *Hotspur,* 1364-1403, English military leader]

**hot stuff** /ˈhɒt stʌf/, *n. Colloq.* **1.** a woman or girl who is sexually exciting. **2.** something or someone of great excellence or interest.

**hot-tempered** /ˈhɒt-tɛmpəd/, *adj.* short-tempered; having a quick temper.

**Hottentot** /ˈhɒtəntɒt/, *n.* **1.** a member of a native African race of yellowish brown colour and low stature, sometimes said to be of mixed Bushman and Bantu origin. **2.** the language of the Hottentots, having no certain affinity. [D (Afrikaans), imitative of the language]

**Hottentot fig** /– ˈfɪg/, *n.* any of various plants of the family Ficoidaceae, esp. *Carpobrotus edulis,* of southern Africa, having cream or pink flowers and a sour-tasting fruit used for making jam and in the preparation of medicine. Also, **sourfig.**

**hottie** /ˈhɒti/, *n. Colloq.* a hot-water bottle.

**hot-tin** /hɒt-ˈtɪn/, *v.t.,* **-tinned, -tinning.** to coat another metal with tin by immersing it in a bath of molten tin.

**hot tip** /hɒt ˈtɪp/, *n.* information as to the likely winner of a race, etc., on which one is wagering a bet.

**hot-water boat** /hɒt-ˈwɔtə boʊt/, *n. Colloq.* (*joc.*) a small powered pleasure boat as a runabout (opp. to *sailing boat*).

**hot-water bottle** /hɒt-ˈwɔtə bɒtl/, *n.* a container, usu. of rubber, of a flat oblong shape, which is filled with hot water and used to warm parts of the body, or a bed. Also, *U.S.,* **hot-water bag.**

**hot-water service** /ˈ– sɜvəs/, *n.* a household system for providing hot water.

**hot-wire** /ˈhɒt-waɪə/, *adj.* (of an ammeter or voltmeter) depending upon the expansion, or change in resistance, of a wire when it is heated by the passage of a current.

**hot-work** /ˈhɒt-wɜk/, *v.t.* to shape a metal by rolling, forging, etc., at a temperature high enough to permit recrystallisation.

**Houdan** /ˈhudæn/, *n.* a breed of the domestic fowl of French origin, having a heavy, globular crest and evenly mottled black-and-white plumage. [named after *Houdan,* town in France, near Paris]

**houhere** /ˈhoʊhɛri/, *n.* a tree of New Zealand coastal and lowland forests, *Hoheria populnea,* with a layer of reticulate bark fibres; ribbonwood.

**hound**[1] /haʊnd/, *n.* **1.** a dog of any of various breeds used in the chase and commonly hunting by scent. **2.** any dog. **3.** *Colloq.* a mean, despicable fellow. **4.** *U.S. Colloq.* an addict. **5.** a player in hare and hounds. **6. follow the hounds,** to follow a hunt, esp. on foot. **7. ride to hounds,** to fox-hunt. *–v.t.* **8.** to hunt or track with hounds, or as a hound does; pursue. **9.** to harass unceasingly. **10.** to incite (a hound, etc.) to pursuit or attack; urge on. [ME; OE *hund,* c. G *Hund.* Cf. L *canis,* Gk *kýōn* dog]

**hound**[2] /haʊnd/, *n.* **1.** (*pl.*) *Naut.* fittings at a masthead, serving to support rigging or trestletrees. **2.** *Chiefly U.S.* a bar, usu. used in pairs, to strengthen various portions of the running gear of a vehicle. [ME *hūn,* from Scand.; cf. Icel. *húnn* knob at the masthead]

**hound's-tongue** /ˈhaʊndz-tʌŋ/, *n.* any plant of the genus *Cynoglossum,* with prickly fruit and tongue-like leaves. [ME and OE *hundestunge,* translation of L *cynoglōssum,* from Gk *kynóglōsson* dog-tongued]

**hound's-tooth** /ˈhaʊndz-tuθ/, *adj.* **1.** printed, decorated, or woven with a pattern of broken checks. *–n.* **2.** a pattern of contrasting jagged checks.

**hound's tooth check,** *n.* a pattern of jagged checks, often black or brown on a light base.

**hour** /ˈaʊə/, *n.* **1.** a space of time equal to one 24th part of a mean solar day or civil day; 60 minutes. **2.** a short or limited period of time. **3.** a particular or appointed time: *his hour of triumph.* **4.** the present time: *the man of the hour.* **5.** any definite time of day, or the time indicated by a timepiece: *what is the hour?* **6.** (*pl.*) time spent in work, study, etc.: *after hours, office hours.* **7.** (*pl.*) customary time of going to bed and getting up: *to keep late hours.* **8.** distance normally covered in an hour's travelling. **9.** *Astron.* **a.** a unit of measure of right ascension, etc., representing 15 degrees, or the 24th part of a great circle. **b.** See **sidereal hour. 10.** a single period of class instruction. **11.** (*pl.*) *Eccles.* **a.** the seven stated times of the day for prayer and devotion, the canonical hours. **b.** the offices or services prescribed for these times. **c.** a book containing them. **12. one's hour, a.** death; the time to die. **b.** a crucial moment. **13. the small hours,** the hours immediately following midnight. [ME *ure, ore, hore,* from OF, from L *hōra* time, season, hour, from Gk; akin to YEAR]

**hour circle** /ˈ– sɜkəl/, *n.* any great circle in the celestial sphere passing through the celestial poles.

**hourglass** /ˈaʊəglas/, *n.* **1.** an instrument for measuring time, consisting of two bulbs of glass joined by a narrow passage through which a quantity of sand (or mercury) runs in just an hour. *–adj.* **2.** of, or pertaining to a woman's figure which resembles an hourglass; having a narrow waist.

hourglass

**hour hand** /ˈaʊə hænd/, *n.* the hand that indicates the hours on a clock or watch.

**houri** /ˈhʊəri, ˈhuri/, *n., pl.* **-ris. 1.** one of the beautiful virgins provided in paradise to all faithful Muslims. **2.** any alluring woman, esp. of oriental origin. [F, from Pers. *hūrī,* from Ar. *hūr,* pl. of *haurā'* having black eyes like a gazelle]

**hourly** /ˈaʊəli/, *adj.* **1.** of, pertaining to, occurring, or done each successive hour. **2.** frequent; continual. *–adv.* **3.** every hour; hour by hour. **4.** frequently.

**hour show** /ˈaʊə ʃoʊ/, *n.* a series of newsreels, etc., shown in a small cinema and lasting about one hour.

**house** /haʊs/, *n., pl.* **houses** /haʊzəz/; /haʊz/, *v.,* **housed, housing;** /haʊs/, *adj.* *–n.* **1.** a building for human habitation. **2.** a place of lodgment, rest, etc., as of an animal. **3.** a household. **4.** a building for any purpose: *a house of worship.* **5.** a place of entertainment; a theatre. **6.** the audience of a theatre, etc. **7.** an inn; a public house. **8.** a family regarded as consisting of ancestors and descendants: *the house of Habsburg.* **9.** the building in which a legislative or deliberative body meets. **10.** the body itself: *the House of Representatives.* **11.** a quorum of such a body. **12.** the Stock Exchange in London. **13.** a firm or commercial establishment: *the house of Rothschild.* **14.** an advisory or deliberative group, esp. in Church or university affairs. **15.** a residential hall for students as in some universities. **16.** a subdivision of a school, comprising children of all ages and classes. **17.** a boarding-house attached to and forming part of a school. **18.** the members of such a subdivision, or boarding house. **19.** the management of a gambling casino or commercial establishment. **20.** *Astrol.* **a.** one of the twelve divisions of the heavens. **b.** a sign of the zodiac in which a planet exerts its greatest influence. **21. the little house,** *Colloq.* an outside toilet. **22. keep house,** to manage a house; look after a home. **23. keep open house,** to be very hospitable. **24. like a house on fire,** very well; with great rapidity. **25. put** or **set one's house in order,** to put one's affairs into good condition. **26. bring down the house,** to be extraordinarily well received or applauded. **27. on the house,** free; as a gift from the management. **28. safe as houses,** completely safe. **29. the house,** *Colloq.* the main homestead on a sheep or cattle station. *–v.t.* **30.** to put or receive into a house; provide with a house. **31.** to give shelter to; harbour; lodge. **32.** to remove from exposure; put in a safe place. **33.** *Naut.* to place in a secure or protected position. **34.** *Carp.* to fix in a socket or the like. *–v.i.* **35.** to take shelter; dwell. *–adj.* **36.** for, or suitable for a house. **37.** of or pertaining to a house. [ME *hous,* OE *hūs,* c. D *huis,* G *Haus,* Icel. and Goth. *hūs*]

**house agent** /'– eɪdʒənt/, *n.* →**estate agent.**

**house arrest** /'– ərɛst/, *n.* confinement to one's place of residence (by an authority).

**houseboat** /'haʊsboʊt/, *n.* a boat fitted up for use as a floating dwelling but not suited to rough water.

**housebound** /'haʊsbaʊnd/, *adj.* restricted or confined to the house, as through ill health.

**houseboy** /'haʊsbɔɪ/, *n.* a male servant, esp. in a British colonial possession, who helps in the house.

**housebreaker** /'haʊsbreɪkə/, *n.* **1.** one who breaks into and enters a house with felonious intent. **2.** one who demolishes houses. – **housebreaking,** *n.*

**housebreaking** /'haʊsbreɪkɪŋ/, *n.* the unlawful breaking into another person's residence for the purpose of committing a crime, esp. theft.

**housebroken** /'haʊsbroʊkən/, *n.* house-trained and generally able to act in a manner suited to being indoors.

**house call** /'haʊs kɔl/, *n.* a visit made by a doctor to a patient in the patient's home.

**house centipede** /'– sɛntəpid/, *n.* a pale brown centipede with dark markings on the dorsal surface, *Allothereua maculata,* having long antennae and fifteen pairs of long, slender legs.

**housecoat** /'haʊskoʊt/, *n.* a dresslike garment of one piece, fastening down the front, and often long, worn about the house.

**housedog** /'haʊsdɒg/, *n.* a dog trained to guard the house; a watchdog.

**housefather** /'haʊsfaðə/, *n.* a man who is in charge of a group, esp. of children, who live together as in a convention centre, orphanage, etc.

**house flag** /'haʊs flæg/, *n.* a flag, usu. flown by a ship, but also flown on buildings, etc., denoting which company or owner they belong to.

**housefly** /'haʊsflaɪ/, *n., pl.* **-flies. 1.** a common dipterous insect, *Musca domestica,* found in nearly all parts of the world. **2.** any of several other dipterous insects resembling this.

housefly

**houseful** /'haʊsfʊl/, *n.* as much as a house can hold or comfortably accommodate.

**house guest** /'haʊs gɛst/, *n.* a guest who is living at one's home for a short period of time.

**household** /'haʊshoʊld/, *n.* **1.** the people of a house collectively; a family, including servants, etc.; a domestic establishment. *–adj.* **2.** of or pertaining to a household; domestic: *household furniture.* **3.** used for maintaining and keeping a house. **4.** of or pertaining to the royal or imperial household. **5.** very common.

**householder** /'haʊshoʊldə/, *n.* **1.** one who holds or occupies a house. **2.** the head of a family.

**household name** /haʊshoʊld 'neɪm/, *n.* a famous person, as a politician, television personality, etc., known in most homes.

**household word** /haʊshoʊld 'wɜd/, *n.* a byword; a well-known phrase or word.

**house journal** /'haʊs dʒɜnəl/, *n.* an internal journal of a company, presenting its news to its employees. Also, **house magazine.**

**housekeeper** /'haʊskipə/, *n.* **1.** a paid employee who is hired to run a house, direct the domestic work, catering, etc. **2.** a female employee of a hotel responsible for the cleaning staff.

**housekeeping** /'haʊskipɪŋ/, *n.* **1.** the maintaining of a house or domestic establishment. **2.** the management of household affairs. **3.** the money used for this purpose.

**housel** /'haʊzəl/, *n. Archaic.* →**Eucharist.** [ME; OE *hūsl,* c. Goth. *hūnsl* sacrifice]

**houseleek** /'haʊslik/, *n.* **1.** a herb of the family Crassulaceae, *Sempervivum tectorum,* with pink flowers and thick, succulent leaves, found growing on the roofs and walls of houses. **2.** any plant of the genus *Sempervivum.*

**houselights** /'haʊslaɪts/, *n.pl.* the auditorium lights of a theatre, cinema, etc., which are lowered during a performance.

**houseline** /'haʊslaɪn/, *n.* (in sailing) a small line of three strands, used for seizings, etc.

**house magazine** /'haʊs mægəzin/, *n.* →**house journal.**

**housemaid** /'haʊsmeɪd/, *n.* a female servant employed in general work in a household.

**housemaid's knee** /haʊsmeɪdz 'ni/, *n.* inflammation of the bursa over the anterior region of the knee.

**houseman** /'haʊsmən/, *n., pl.* **-men.** *Brit.* a member of the medical staff of a hospital, commonly a recent medical graduate acting as assistant to a physician or surgeon.

**house-manager** /'haʊs-mænədʒə/, *n.* the manager of a theatre, club, concert-hall or other place of entertainment.

**house martin** /haʊs 'matn/, *n.* a bird, *Delichon urbica,* of the family Hirundinidae (swallow family), about 13 cm long, of Europe and Asia, which nests on cliffs and the walls of houses.

**housemaster** /'haʊsmastə/, *n.* a man in charge of a house (def. 16 or def. 17) within a school.

**housemistress** /'haʊsmɪstrəs/, *n.* a woman in charge of a house (def. 16 or def. 17) within a school.

**housemother** /'haʊsmʌðə/, *n.* a woman who is in charge of a group, esp. of children, who live together as in a convention centre, orphanage, etc.

**house mouse** /'haʊs maʊs/, *n.* a rodent, *Mus musculus,* of the family Muridae which originally lived wild on the steppes of Asia, but which has come to live commensally with man in all parts of the world.

**house of cards,** *n.* a flimsy structure or plan, liable to collapse at any minute.

**House of God,** *n.* a building devoted to religious observances; a church; chapel, etc.

**house of ill repute,** *n.* →**brothel.** Also, **house of evil repute, house of ill fame.**

**House of Representatives,** *n.* **1.** the lower legislative branch of the federal parliament of Australia, elected on a population basis and having approximately twice as many members as the Senate. **2.** a similar body elsewhere, as Mexico, Japan, etc.

**houseparent** /'haʊspɛərənt/, *n.* **1.** one of a married couple in charge of a house party which young people attend. **2.** one such in charge of a dormitory or hostel where children or young people reside.

**house party** /'haʊs pati/, *n.* **1.** an entertainment of guests overnight or for some days at a host's house, esp. in the country. **2.** the guests.

**house physician** /'– fəzɪʃən/, *n. Brit.* a resident physician in a hospital, or other public institution.

**house plant** /'– plænt/, *n.* a plant which can be grown indoors.

**houseproud** /'haʊspraʊd/, *adj.* overcareful about the cleaning of a house and the appearance of its contents.

**house red** /haʊs 'rɛd/, *n.* a red house wine.

**houseroom** /'haʊsrum/, *n.* space or accommodation in a house.

**house-seat** /'haʊs-sit/, *n.* a seat in a theatre, concert-hall, etc., reserved by the management for special guests.

**house sparrow** /'haʊs spæroʊ/, *n.* a grey and brown bird, *Passer domesticus,* of the family Ploceidae, about 13 cm long, native to Europe, Asia and North Africa, and, introduced into Australia and America.

**house surgeon** /'– sɜdʒən/, *n. Brit.* a resident surgeon in a hospital.

**house-to-house** /'haʊs-tə-haʊs/, *adj.* carried out systematically through all the buildings in a neighbourhood, etc.: *a house-to-house search by the police.*

**housetop** /'haʊstɒp/, *n.* **1.** the top or roof of a house. **2. from the housetops,** *Colloq.* publicly.

**house-train** /'haʊs-treɪn/, *v.t.* to train (an animal) so that it may be kept inside a house without inconvenience to other occupants; esp. to train it to control its natural excretory functions. – **house-training,** *n.*

**house-trained** /'haʊs-treɪnd/, *adj.* (of a pet) trained to excrete outside the house.

**house union** /'haʊs junjən/, *n.* a union to which all employees, regardless of profession or trade, may belong by virtue of working for the one employer.

**house-warming** /'haʊs-wɔmɪŋ/, *n.* a party to celebrate beginning one's occupancy of a new house.

**house white** /haʊs 'waɪt/, *n.* a white house wine.

**housewife** /'haʊswaɪf/, *n., pl.* **-wives** /-waɪvz/. **1.** the woman in charge of a household, esp. a wife who does no other job. **2.** a small case for needles, thread, etc.

**housewifely** /'haʊswaɪfli/, *adj.* of, like, or befitting a housewife. – **housewifeliness,** *n.*

**housewifery** /'haʊswɪfəri/, *n.* the function or work of a housewife; housekeeping.

**house wine** /'haʊs waɪn/, *n.* a bulk wine served by a club or restaurant, often bearing the establishment's label.

**housework** /'haʊswɜk/, *n.* the work of cleaning, cooking, etc., to be done in housekeeping.

**housie-housie** /'haʊzi-haʊzi/, *n.* a gambling game in which players put markers on a card of numbered squares according to the numbers drawn and announced by a caller; bingo; lotto; tombola; Also, **housey-housey, housie.**

**housing**[1] /'haʊzɪŋ/, *n.* **1.** something serving as a shelter, covering, or the like; a shelter; lodging. **2.** houses collectively. **3.** the act of one who houses or puts under shelter. **4.** the providing of houses for the community: *the housing of immigrants.* **5.** *Mach.* a frame, plate or the like, that supports a part of a machine, etc. **6.** *Carp.* the space made in one piece of wood, or the like, for the insertion of another. **7.** *Naut.* **a.** the inboard end of a bowsprit. **b.** the part of a mast which is below deck. [HOUSE, *v.* + -ING[1]]

**housing**[2] /'haʊzɪŋ/, *n.* **1.** a covering of cloth for the back and flanks of a horse or other animal, for protection or ornament. **2.** a covering of cloth or the like. **3.** (*oft. pl.*) a caparison or trapping. [*house* (ME, from OF *houce*) covering of cloth + -ING[1]]

**housing association** /'– əsoʊsieɪʃən/, *n.* a non-profitmaking society or body for constructing, improving or managing houses.

**housing development** /'– dəvɛləpmənt/, *n.* a group of houses, home units, etc., and their associated services, planned and built in accordance with a single master plan.

**housing estate** /'– əsteɪt/, *n.* →**housing development.**

**houting** /'haʊtɪŋ/, *n.* a seafish, *Coregonus oxyrhynchus,* that spawns in fresh waters; a popular food fish of European waters.

**hove** /hoʊv/, *v.* past tense and past participle of **heave.**

**hovea** /'hoʊviə/, *n.* any plant of the Australian genus *Hovea,* family Papilionaceae, with clusters of small purple pea-shaped flowers.

**hovel** /'hɒvəl/, *n., v.,* **-elled, -elling,** or (*U.S.*) **-eled, -eling.** *–n.* **1.** a small, mean dwelling house; a wretched hut. **2.** an open shed, as for sheltering cattle, tools, etc. *–v.t.* **3.** *Obs.* to shelter or lodge as in a hovel. [ME *hovel, hovyl;* orig. uncert.]

**hoven** /'hoʊvən/, *n.* →**bloat** (def. 5).

**hover** /'hɒvə/, *v.i.* **1.** to hang fluttering or suspended in the air: *a hovering bird.* **2.** to keep lingering about; wait near at hand. **3.** to remain in an uncertain or irresolute state; waver: *hovering between life and death.* *–n.* **4.** the act of hovering. **5.** the state of hovering. **6.** the sheet metal canopy over the heat source in a poultry incubator. [ME *hoveren,* frequentative of *hoven* hover; orig. uncert.] – **hoverer,** *n.* – **hoveringly,** *adv.*

**hoverbed** /'hɒvəbɛd/, *n.* a bed used in the treatment of severe burns, on which the patient is cushioned on a current of warm air.

**hovercraft** /'hɒvəkraft/, *n.* **1.** a vehicle able to travel in close proximity to the ground or water, on a cushion of air created by and contained within a curtain of air formed by one or more streams of air ejected downwards from the periphery of the vehicle.

**hoverfly** /'hɒvəflaɪ/, *n.* a name given to several of the larger flies of the family Syrphidae which have wasplike markings, and the habit of hovering during flight.

**hoverport** /'hɒvəpɔt/, *n.* a port for hovercraft.

**hovertrain** /'hɒvətreɪn/, *n.* a train which is a hovercraft.

**how** /haʊ/, *adv.* **1.** in what way or manner; by what means: *how did it happen?* **2.** to what extent, degree, etc.: *how much?* **3.** at what price: *how do you sell these apples?* **4.** in what state or condition: *how are you?* **5.** for what reason; why. **6.** to what effect or with what meaning: *how do you mean?* **7.** what? **8.** (used to add intensity): *how well I remember.* **9. and how,** *Colloq.* very much indeed; certainly. **10. how about that!** (an exclamation of surprise (sometimes ironic) or of triumph). **11. how come?** *Colloq.* how did this happen; why? **12. how's that? a.** what is the explanation of that? **b.** Also, **howzat?** *Cricket.* an appeal by the fielding side to the umpire to declare a batsman out. **13. how's things,** (a form of greeting). **14. how's tricks,** (a form of greeting). *–conj.* **15.** concerning the condition or state in which: *she wondered how she appeared to a stranger.* **16.** concerning the extent or degree to which: *I don't mind how long you take.* **17.** concerning the means or way in which: *it worried him how she got to work.* **18.** in whatever manner: *come how you like.* *–n.* **19.** a question beginning with 'how'. **20.** *Colloq.* way or manner of doing: *to consider the hows of a problem.* [ME *hou, how,* OE *hū,* c. D *hoe;* akin to WHO]

**howbeit** /haʊ'biət/, *adv.* **1.** nevertheless. *–conj.* **2.** *Obs.* although. [ME *how be hit* however it may be. Cf. ALBEIT]

**howdah** /'haʊdə/, *n.* (in the East Indies) a seat, commonly with a railing and a canopy, placed on the back of an elephant. [Hind. *haudah,* from Ar. *haudaj*]

**how-do-you-do** /haʊ-də-jə-'du/, *interj.* **1.** (a form of greeting). *–n.* **2.** a difficult or embarrassing situation: *a fine how-do-you-do.* Also, **how-de-do.**

**howe'er** /haʊ'ɛə/, *conj., adv.* however.

**however** /haʊ'ɛvə/, *conj.* **1.** nevertheless; yet; in spite of that. *–adv.* **2.** to whatever extent or degree; no matter how (far, much, etc.). **3.** in whatever condition, state, or manner: *go there however you like.* **4.** Also, **how ever.** (interrogatively) how in any circumstances: *however did you manage?* [ME]

**howitzer** /'haʊɪtsə/, *n.* a comparatively short-barrelled cannon, used esp. for shelling at a steep angle, as in reaching troops behind cover. [earlier *hauwitzer,* apparently from D *houwitser,* from *houwits(e)* catapult. Cf. G *Haubitze,* earlier *haufnitz,* from Czech *houfnice* catapult]

**howl** /haʊl/, *v.i.* **1.** to utter a loud, prolonged, mournful cry, as that of a dog or wolf. **2.** to utter a similar cry in distress, pain, rage, etc.; wail. **3.** to make a sound like an animal howling: *the wind is howling.* *–v.t.* **4.** to utter with howls. **5.** to drive or force by howls (oft. fol. by *down*). *–n.* **6.** the cry of a dog, wolf, etc. **7.** a cry or wail, as of pain or rage. **8.** a sound like wailing: *the howl of the wind.* **9.** a loud scornful laugh or yell. [ME *houle.* Cf. G *heulen;* imitative]

**howler** /'haʊlə/, *n.* **1.** one who or that which howls. **2.** Also, **howling monkey.** any of the large, prehensile-tailed tropical American monkeys of the genus *Alouatta,* the males of which make a howling noise. **3.** *Colloq.* an esp. glaring and ludicrous blunder. **4.** *Elect.* a device for testing telephone apparatus which provides a suitable current by using acoustic feedback between the telephone transmitter and receiver.

**howlie** /'haʊli/, *n. Colloq.* →**U-ie.**

**howling** /'haʊlɪŋ/, *adj.* **1.** producing or uttering a howl. **2.** *Colloq.* enormous; very great: *his play was a howling success.* *–n.* **3.** unwanted feedback at audio frequencies in an amplifier.

**howling jackass** /– 'dʒækæs/, *n.* →**kookaburra** (def. 2).

**howsoever** /haʊsoʊ'ɛvə/, *adv.* **1.** to whatsoever extent or degree. **2.** in whatsoever manner.

**howsomever** /haʊsəm'ɛvə/, *adv.* →**however.**

**how-to-vote card** /haʊ-tə-'voʊt ˌkad/, *n.* a card or piece of paper distributed at an election by a party or candidate showing the voter the ranking of preferences recommended by the party or candidate.

**howzat** /haʊ'zæt/, *interj. Cricket Colloq.* →**how** (def. 12b).

**hoy**[1] /hɔɪ/, *n.* **1.** a sloop-rigged boat, single-decked and used for fishing. **2.** a small boat used in harbour, as a ferry between a ship and the shore. [ME, from MD *hoei, hoede*]

**hoy**[2] /hɔɪ/, *interj.* **1.** (an exclamation to attract attention.) *–n.* **2. give a hoy,** call out; attract attention. [ME]

**hoy**[3] /hɔɪ/, *v.t. Colloq.* to throw.

**hoy**[4] /hɔɪ/, *n.* a game of chance, similar to bingo, in which playing cards are used.

**hoyden** /'hɔɪdən/, *n.* **1.** a rude or ill-bred girl; tomboy.

–*adj.* **2.** hoydenish; boisterous. Also, **hoiden.** [orig. uncert.] – **hoydenish,** *adj.* – **hoydenishness,** *n.*

**Hoyle** /hɔɪl/, *n.* **1.** a book of rules for card and other indoor games originally compiled by Edmund Hoyle, 1672-1769. **2. according to Hoyle,** (in any context) in accordance with the recognised rules.

**h.p.,** horsepower. Also, **hp.**

**H.P.,** **1.** hire purchase. **2.** horsepower.

**H.Q.** /eɪtʃ 'kju/, headquarters. Also, **h.q.**

**hr,** hour.

**H.R.,** House of Representatives.

**H-R diagram** /eɪtʃ-a 'daɪəgræm/, *n.* Hertzsprung-Russell diagram.

**H.R.H.,** His, or Her, Royal Highness.

**hrs,** hours.

**H.S.C.** /eɪtʃ ɛs 'si/, Higher School Certificate.

**ht,** height.

**Hts,** Heights.

**ht wkt,** hit wicket.

**hub** /hʌb/, *n.* **1.** the central part of a wheel, as that part into which the spokes are inserted. **2.** the part in central position around which all else revolves: *the hub of the universe.* **3.** the peg or hob used as a target in quoits, etc. **4.** *Coining.* a design of hardened steel in relief used as a punch in making a die. [cf. HOB[1]]

**hubble-bubble** /'hʌbəl-bʌbəl/, *n.* **1.** a crude type of hookah. **2.** a bubbling sound. **3.** confusion; turmoil.

**Hubble's constant** /hʌbəlz 'kɒnstənt/, *n.* the ratio of the distance between the local group of galaxies and a receding cluster of galaxies, to the rate at which the distant cluster recedes. [named after Edwin Powell *Hubble,* 1889-1953, U.S. astronomer]

**hub brake** /'hʌb breɪk/, *n.* a brake which operates on the hub of a wheel.

**hubbub** /'hʌbʌb/, *n.* **1.** a loud, confused noise, as of many voices. **2.** tumult; uproar.

**hubby** /'hʌbi/, *n. Colloq.* husband.

**hub-cap** /'hʌb-kæp/, *n.* a covering for the hub of a wheel of a motor car, etc.

**hubris** /'hjubrəs/, *n.* insolence or wanton violence stemming from excessive pride. Also, **hybris.** [Gk] – **hubristic** /hju'brɪstɪk/, *adj.* – **hubristically** /hju'brɪstɪkli/, *adv.*

**huckaback** /'hʌkəbæk/, *n.* towelling of linen or cotton, of a distinctive weave. Also, **huck.**

**huckleberry** /'hʌkəlbɛri/, *n., pl.* **-ries. 1.** the dark blue or black edible berry of any of various shrubs of the American genus *Gaylussacia.* **2.** a shrub yielding such a berry. **3.** →**blueberry** (def. 1). [var. of *hurtleberry* WHORTLEBERRY]

**hucklebone** /'hʌkəlboʊn/, *n.* **1.** the anklebone, astragalus, or talus. **2.** *Obs.* the hipbone.

**huckster** /'hʌkstə/, *n.* Also, **hucksterer. 1.** a retailer of small articles; a hawker. **2.** a street pedlar of fruit and vegetables. **3.** a cheaply mercenary person. –*v.i.* **4.** to deal in small articles or make petty bargains. [ME *huccster, hokester.* Cf. G *höken* to retail goods]

**huddle** /'hʌdl/, *v.,* **-dled, -dling,** *n.* –*v.t.* **1.** to heap or crowd together confusedly. **2.** to draw (oneself) closely together; nestle (oft. fol. by *up*). **3.** to do hastily and carelessly (oft. fol. by *up, over,* or *together*). **4.** to put on (clothes) with careless haste (oft. fol. by *on*). –*v.i.* **5.** to gather or crowd together in a confused mass. –*n.* **6.** a confused heap, mass, or crowd; a jumble. **7.** confusion or disorder. **8.** *Colloq.* a conference held in secret. [orig. uncert.; cf. ME *hodre* to wrap up, c. LG *hudren*] – **huddler,** *n.*

**Hudibrastic** /hjudə'bræstɪk/, *adj.* **1.** of or pertaining to, or resembling the style of, Samuel Butler's *Hudibras* (published 1663-78), a mock-heroic satirical poem written in tetrameter couplets. **2.** of a playful burlesque style.

**hue**[1] /hju/, *n.* **1.** that property of colour by which the various regions of the spectrum are distinguished, as red, blue, etc. **2.** variety of a colour; a tint: *pale hues.* **3.** colour: *all the hues of the rainbow.* **4.** *Obs.* form or appearance. **5.** *Obs.* complexion. [ME *hewe,* OE *hīw* form, appearance, colour]

**hue**[2] /hju/, *n.* outcry, as of pursuers; clamour. [ME *hu,* from OF, from *heur* cry out, shout; probably imitative]

**hue and cry,** *n.* **1.** the pursuit of a felon or an offender with loud outcries or clamour to give an alarm. **2.** a proclamation for the capture of a criminal. **3.** any public clamour against or over something.

**hued** /hjud/, *adj.* having a hue or colour: *golden-hued.*

**huff** /hʌf/, *n.* **1.** a sudden swell of anger; a fit of resentment: *to leave in a huff.* –*v.t.* **2.** to give offence to; make angry. **3.** to treat with arrogance or contempt; bluster at; hector or bully. **4.** *Draughts.* to remove (a piece) from the board as a penalty for failing to make a compulsory capture. –*v.i.* **5.** to take offence. **6.** *Archaic.* to swell with pride or arrogance; swagger or bluster. **7.** to puff or blow. [imitative]

**huffish** /'hʌfɪʃ/, *adj.* **1.** petulant. **2.** swaggering; hectoring. – **huffishly,** *adv.* – **huffishness,** *n.*

**huffy** /'hʌfi/, *adj.,* **-fier, -fiest. 1.** easily offended or touchy. **2.** offended; sulky: *a huffy mood.* – **huffily,** *adv.* – **huffiness,** *n.*

**hug** /hʌg/, *v.,* **hugged, hugging,** *n.* –*v.t.* **1.** to clasp tightly in the arms, esp. with affection; embrace. **2.** to cling firmly or fondly to: *to hug an opinion.* **3.** to keep close to, as in sailing, horseracing or going along: *to hug the shore, to hug the rails.* **4. hug oneself,** congratulate oneself; be self-satisfied. –*v.i.* **5.** *Archaic.* to cling together; lie close. –*n.* **6.** a tight clasp with the arms; a warm embrace. [cf. Icel. *hugga* console]

**huge** /hjudʒ/, *adj.,* **huger, hugest. 1.** extraordinarily large in bulk, quantity, or extent: *a huge mountain.* **2.** large in scope, character, extent. [ME *huge, hoge;* ? aphetic var. of OF *ahuge* great, large, high; orig. uncert.] – **hugeness,** *n.*

**hugely** /'hjudʒli/, *adv.* **1.** in a huge fashion. **2.** *Colloq.* extremely; immoderately: *he laughed hugely.*

**hugger-mugger** /'hʌgə-mʌgə/, *n.* **1.** disorder or confusion; a muddle. **2.** *Archaic.* secrecy or concealment: *in hugger-mugger.* –*adj.* **3.** secret or clandestine. **4.** disorderly or confused. –*v.t.* **5.** to keep secret or concealed. –*v.i.* **6.** to act secretly; take secret counsel.

**Hughie** /'hjui/, *n. Colloq.* a jocular name for the powers above used when encouraging a heavy rainfall or a good surf: *send her down, Hughie! whip 'em up, Hughie!*

**Huguenot** /'hjugənoʊ, -nɒt/, *n.* a member of the Reformed or Calvinistic communion of France in the 16th and 17th centuries; a French Protestant. [F, earlier *eiguenot,* from Swiss G *Eidgenosse* confederate, from *Eid* oath + *Genoss* companion, associate, influenced by name *Hugues* Hugh]

**huh** /hʌ/, *interj.* (an expression of interrogation or contempt).

**huhu** /'huhu/, *n. N.Z.* **1.** the beetle *Prionoplus reticularis.* **2.** Also, **huhu grub.** its larva, eaten as a delicacy by the Maori. [Maori]

**hui** /'hui/, *n. N.Z.* **1.** a Maori community gathering. **2.** *Colloq.* a boisterous party or gathering. [Maori]

**huia** /'hujə/, *n.* a rare New Zealand bird, *Heteralocha acutirostris,* glossy black with orange wattles, whose white-tipped tailfeathers were valued by Maoris as ornaments. [Maori]

**hula hoop** /'hulə hup/, *n.* a round plastic or cane hoop for rotating about the body, used for physical exercise or in children's play.

**hula-hula** /hulə-'hulə/, *n.* a kind of native Hawaiian dance, with intricate arm movements, which tells a story in mime. Also, **hula.** [Hawaiian]

**hula skirt** /'hulə skɜt/, *n.* **1.** a skirt made of grass blades bound to a waistband and worn by a hula dancer. **2.** any similar skirt made in plastic, etc.

**hulk** /hʌlk/, *n.* **1.** the body of an old or dismantled ship. **2.** a vessel specially built to serve as a storehouse, prison, etc., and not for sea service. **3.** a bulky or unwieldy person or mass of anything. **4.** a burnt-out or stripped vehicle, building, or the like. **5.** *Archaic.* a heavy unwieldy vessel. –*v.i.* **6.** *U.S.* to loom in bulky form; be bulky (oft. fol. by *up*). [ME *hulke,* OE *hulc,* probably from ML *hulcus,* from Gk *holkás* trading vessel]

**hulking** /'hʌlkɪŋ/, *adj.* bulky; heavy and clumsy. Also, **hulky.**

**hull**[1] /hʌl/, *n.* **1.** the husk, shell, or outer covering of a seed or fruit. **2.** the calyx of certain fruits, as the strawberry and raspberry. **3.** any covering or envelope. –*v.t.* **4.** to remove the hull of. [ME; OE *hulu* husk, pod; akin to *helan* cover, hide. Cf. HALL, HELL, HOLE] – **huller,** *n.*

**hull**[2] /hʌl/, *n.* **1.** the frame or body of a ship, exclusive of masts, yards, sails, and rigging. **2.** *Aeron.* the boatlike fuselage of a flying boat on which the plane lands or takes off. *–v.t.* **3.** to strike or pierce the hull of (a ship), as with a torpedo. [orig. uncert. Cf. HULL[1], HOLD[2], HOLE]

**hullabaloo** /hʌləbəˈlu/, *n.* a clamorous noise or disturbance; an uproar.

**hull-down** /ˈhʌl-daʊn/, *adj.* **1.** (of a ship) with its hull hidden by the waves or horizon. **2.** (of a tank) with its body concealed and only its tunnels showing.

**hullo** /ˈhʌloʊ, həˈloʊ/, *interj., n., v.i.* →**hello.**

**hulloo** /hʌˈlu/, *interj., n., v.i.* →**halloo.**

**hull speed** /ˈhʌl spid/, *n.* the maximum speed of a boat which has a hull which cannot plane, determined in part by the vessel's length.

**hum**[1] /hʌm/, *v.,* **hummed, humming,** *n., interj. –v.i.* **1.** to make a low, continuous, droning sound. **2.** to give forth an indistinct sound of mingled voices or noises. **3.** to utter an indistinct sound in hesitation, embarrassment, dissatisfaction, etc.; hem. **4.** to sing with closed lips, without articulating words. **5.** *Colloq.* to be in a state of busy activity: *to make things hum.* **6.** *Colloq.* to smell strongly, esp. disagreeably. *–v.t.* **7.** to sound, sing, or utter by humming. **8.** to bring, put, etc., by humming: *to hum a child to sleep.* *–n.* **9.** the act or sound of humming; an inarticulate or indistinct murmur; a hem. *–interj.* **10.** (an inarticulate sound uttered in hesitation, dissatisfaction, etc.) [ME *humme,* c. G *hummen* hum; imitative. Cf. HUMBLEBEE] – **hummer,** *n.*

**hum**[2] /hʌm/, *n., v.,* **hummed, humming.** *–n.* **1.** a person who persistently cadges or scrounges. *–v.t.* **2.** to cadge. *–v.i.* **3.** to cadge (fol. by *for*). [short for HUMBUG]

**human** /ˈhjumən/, *adj.* **1.** of, pertaining to, or characteristic of man: *human nature.* **2.** having the nature of man; being a man: *the human race.* **3.** of or pertaining to mankind generally: *human affairs.* *–n.* **4.** a human being. [L *hūmānus* of a man; replacing ME *humain,* from OF] – **humanness,** *n.*

**human being** /– ˈbiɪŋ/, *n.* a member of the human race, *Homo sapiens.*

**humane** /hjuˈmeɪn/, *adj.* **1.** characterised by tenderness and compassion for the suffering or distressed: *humane feelings.* **2.** (of branches of learning or literature) tending to refine; civilising: *humane studies.* [var. of HUMAN. Cf. GERMANE, GERMAN] – **humanely,** *adv.* – **humaneness,** *n.*

**human-interest** /hjumən-ˈɪntrəst/, *adj.* (of a news item, story, etc.) detailing the emotions and vicissitudes of people, usu. ordinary people.

**humanise** /ˈhjumənaɪz/, *v.,* **-nised, -nising.** *–v.t.* **1.** to make humane, kind, or gentle. **2.** to make human. *–v.i.* **3.** to become human or humane. Also, **humanize.** – **humanisation** /hjumənaɪˈzeɪʃən/, *n.* – **humaniser,** *n.*

**humanism** /ˈhjumənɪzm/, *n.* **1.** any system or mode of thought or action in which human interests predominate. **2.** devotion to or study of the humanities; polite learning; literary culture. **3.** (*sometimes cap.*) the studies, principles or culture of the Humanists (def. 4).

**humanist** /ˈhjumənəst/, *n.* **1.** a student of human nature or affairs. **2.** one devoted to or versed in the humanities. **3.** a classical scholar. **4.** (*sometimes cap.*) one of the scholars of the Renaissance who pursued and disseminated the study and understanding of the cultures of ancient Rome and Greece. **5.** (*sometimes cap.*) one who favours the thought and practice of a humanist philosophy. – **humanistic,** /hjuməˈnɪstɪk/, *adj.*

**humanitarian** /hjumænəˈtɛəriən/, *adj.* **1.** having regard to the interests of all mankind; broadly philanthropic. **2.** pertaining to ethical or theological humanitarianism. *–n.* **3.** one who professes ethical or theological humanitarianism. **4.** a philanthropist.

**humanitarianism** /hjumænəˈtɛəriənɪzəm/, *n.* **1.** humanitarian principles or practices; comprehensive philanthropy. **2.** *Ethics.* **a.** the doctrine that man's obligations are concerned wholly with the welfare of the human race. **b.** the doctrine that mankind may become perfect without divine aid. **3.** *Theol.* the doctrine that Jesus Christ possessed a human nature only.

**humanity** /hjuˈmænəti/, *n., pl.* **-ties.** **1.** the human race; mankind. **2.** the condition or quality of being human; human nature. **3.** the quality of being humane; kindness; benevolence. **4. the humanities, a.** the study of the Latin and Greek classics. **b.** the study of literature, philosophy, art, etc., as distinguished from the social and physical sciences. [ME *humanitee,* from F *humanité,* from L *hūmānitas*]

**humankind** /hjumənˈkaɪnd/, *n.* the human race.

**humanly** /ˈhjumənli/, *adv.* **1.** in a human manner; by human means. **2.** according to human knowledge, or capability. **3.** from a human point of view.

**human nature** /hjumən ˈneɪtʃə/, *n.* **1.** the quality inherent in all persons by virtue of their common humanity. **2.** the make-up or conduct of human beings that distinguishes them from other animal forms, generally regarded as produced by living in primary groups.

**humanoid** /ˈhjumənɔɪd/, *adj.* **1.** like a human. *–n.* **2.** (in science fiction) a robot made in human form.

**human rights** /hjumən ˈraɪts/, *n.pl.* those rights which are held to be justifiably claimed by any individual.

**humble** /ˈhʌmbəl/, *adj.,* **-bler, -blest,** *v.,* **-bled, -bling.** *–adj.* **1.** low in station, grade of importance, etc.; lowly: *humble origin.* **2.** modest; meek; without pride. **3.** courteously respectful: *in my humble opinion.* **4.** low in height, level, etc. *–v.t.* **5.** to lower in condition, importance, or dignity; abase. **6.** to make meek: *to humble one's heart.* [ME, from OF, from L *humilis* low, humble] – **humbleness,** *n.* – **humbler,** *n.* – **humbling,** *adj.* – **humbly,** *adv.*

**humblebee** /ˈhʌmbəlbi/, *n.* →**bumblebee.**

**humble pie** /hʌmbəl ˈpaɪ/, *n.* **1.** *Obs.* a pie made of the umbles (innards; less delectable parts) of deer, etc. **2. eat humble pie,** to be humiliated; be forced to apologise humbly.

**humbug** /ˈhʌmbʌg/, *n., v.,* **-bugged, -bugging.** *–n.* **1.** *Obs.* a deluding trick; a hoax; a fraud. **2.** *Colloq.* a quality of falseness or deception. **3.** *Colloq.* one who seeks to impose deceitfully upon others; a cheat; an imposter. **4.** a kind of hard, peppermint sweet, usu. having a striped pattern. *–v.t.* **5.** to impose upon by humbug or false pretence; delude. *–v.i.* **6.** to practise humbug. [orig. unknown] – **humbugger,** *n.*

**humbuggery** /ˈhʌmbʌgəri/, *n.* pretence; sham.

**humdinger** /ˈhʌmdɪŋə/, *n.* *Colloq.* a person or thing remarkable of its kind.

**humdrum** /ˈhʌmdrʌm/, *adj.* **1.** lacking variety; dull: *a humdrum existence.* *–n.* **2.** humdrum character or routine; monotony. **3.** monotonous or tedious talk. **4.** a dull boring fellow. [varied reduplication of HUM[1]]

**humectant** /hjuˈmɛktənt/, *adj.* **1.** attracting or retaining moisture. *–n.* **2.** a moistening agent. [L *(h)ūmectāre* to moisten]

**humeral** /ˈhjumərəl/, *adj.* **1.** of the shoulder. **2.** *Anat., Zool.* of or related to the humerus or brachium. [L *humerus* shoulder + -AL[1]]

**humerus** /ˈhjumərəs/, *n., pl.* **-meri** /-məraɪ/. **1.** (in man) the single long bone in the arm which extends from the shoulder to the elbow. **2.** a corresponding bone in the forelimb of other animals or in the wings of birds. [L, var. of *umerus* shoulder]

**humic** /ˈhjumɪk/, *adj.* of or denoting something (as an acid) derived from humus. [L *humus* ground, mould + -IC]

**humid** /ˈhjuməd/, *adj.* moist or damp, with liquid or vapour: *humid air.* [L *(h)ūmidus* moist] – **humidly,** *adv.* – **humidness,** *n.*

**humidifier** /hjuˈmɪdəfaɪə/, *n.* a device for regulating air moisture content and temperature in an air-conditioned room or building.

**humidify** /hjuˈmɪdəfaɪ/, *v.t.,* **-fied, -fying.** to make humid. – **humidification** /hjuˌmɪdəfəˈkeɪʃən/, *n.* – **humidifier,** *n.*

**humidistat** /hjuˈmɪdəstæt/, *n.* →**hygrostat.**

**humidity** /hjuˈmɪdəti/, *n.* **1.** humid condition; dampness. **2.** *Meteorol.* **a.** the condition of the atmosphere with regard to its water-vapour content. **b.** the ratio, expressed as a percentage, of the water-vapour present in the atmosphere to the amount required to saturate it at the same temperature (the **relative humidity**). **c.** the mass of water-vapour present in unit volume of air, esp. per cubic metre (the **absolute humidity,** or **vapour concentration**).

**humidor** /ˈhjumədɔ/, *n.* a container or storage room for cigars or other preparations of tobacco, fitted with means for keeping the tobacco suitably moist.

**humiliate** /hjuˈmɪlieɪt/, *v.t.,* **-ated, -ating.** to lower the pride or self-respect of; cause a painful loss of dignity to; mortify. [LL *humiliātus*, pp., humbled]

**humiliation** /hjumɪli'eɪʃən/, *n.* **1.** the act of humiliating. **2.** the state or feeling of being humiliated; mortification.

**humility** /hju'mɪləti/, *n., pl.* **-ties.** the quality of being humble; modest sense of one's own significance. [ME *humilite,* from F, from L *humilitas*]

**humming** /'hʌmɪŋ/, *adj.* **1.** that hums; buzzing. **2.** *Colloq.* extraordinarily active, intense, great, or big.

**hummingbird** /'hʌmɪŋbɜd/, *n.* any of numerous very small American birds constituting the family Trochilidae, characterised by narrow wings whose rapid vibration produces a hum, by slender bill, and usu. by brilliant plumage.

**hummingbird moth** /'– mɒθ/, *n.* →**hawkmoth.**

**hummock** /'hʌmək/, *n.* **1.** an elevated tract rising above the general level of a marshy region. **2.** a knoll or hillock. **3.** a ridge in an icefield.

**hummocky** /'hʌməki/, *adj.* **1.** abounding in hummocks. **2.** like a hummock.

**hummus** /'hʊməs/, *n.* →**hommos.**

**humor** /'hjumə/, *n., v.t. U.S.* →**humour.**

**humoresque** /hjumə'rɛsk/, *n.* a musical composition of humorous or capricious character. [G *Humoreske,* from L *hūmor* HUMOUR + *-eske* -ESQUE]

**humorist** /'hjumərəst/, *n.* **1.** one who exercises the faculty of humour. **2.** a professional writer, actor, etc., whose work is humorous. – **humoristic** /hjumə'rɪstɪk/, *adj.*

**humorous** /'hjumərəs/, *adj.* **1.** characterised by humour; amusing; funny: *the humorous side of things.* **2.** having or showing the faculty of humour; droll; facetious: *a humorous person.* **3.** *Obs.* pertaining or due to the bodily humours. **4.** *Obs.* moist. – **humorously,** *adv.* – **humorousness,** *n.*

**humour** /'hjumə/, *n.* **1.** the quality of being funny: *the humour of a situation.* **2.** the faculty of perceiving what is amusing or comical: *sense of humour.* **3.** the faculty of expressing the amusing or comical. **4.** speech or writing showing this faculty. **5.** mental disposition or tendency; frame of mind. **6.** capricious or freakish inclination; whim or caprice; odd traits. **7.** *Obs. Physiol.* one of the four chief bodily fluids, blood, choler or yellow bile, phlegm, and melancholy or black bile (**cardinal humours**), regarded as determining, by their relative proportions in the system, a person's physical and mental constitution. **8.** *Biol.* any animal or plant fluid, whether natural or morbid, such as the blood or lymph. **9. out of humour,** displeased or dissatisfied; cross. *–v.t.* **10.** to comply with the humour of; indulge: *to humour a child.* **11.** to accommodate oneself to. Also, *U.S.,* **humor.** [ME *humour,* from AF, from L *(h)ūmor* moisture, liquid] – **humourless,** *adj.*

**hump** /hʌmp/, *n.* **1.** a rounded protuberance, esp. on the back, as that due to abnormal curvature of the spine in man, or that normally present in certain animals such as the camel and bison. **2.** a low, rounded rise of ground; hummock. **3.** *Colloq.* a good surfing wave. **4.** *Railways.* an elevated section of track from which wagons, etc., are allowed to run, under gravity, to be sorted at lower levels. **5.** (*pl.*) transverse ridges spaced at intervals in a road to deter a motorist from speeding; speed bumps. **6. the hump,** *Colloq.* a fit of bad humour: *to get the hump.* **7. over the hump,** over the worst part or period of a difficult, dangerous, etc., time. *–v.t.* **8.** to raise (the back, etc.) in a hump. **9.** *Colloq.* **a.** to place or bear on the back or shoulder. **b.** to carry: *to hump the bluey.* *–v.i.* **10.** to rise in a hump. **11.** *Colloq.* (of men) to have sexual intercourse with a woman. [backformation from HUMPBACKED] – **humped,** *adj.*

hump (def. 9b): hump the bluey

**humpback** /'hʌmpbæk/, *n.* **1.** a back with a hump. **2.** one who has such a back; hunchback. **3.** a whale of the genus *Megaptera,* with a humplike back.

**humpback bridge** /'– brɪdʒ/, *n.* an abrupt, steep road bridge, often narrow.

**humpbacked** /'hʌmpbækt/, *adj.* having a hump on the back. [b. *crumpbacked* and *huckbacked* (or *hunchbacked*)]

**humph** /hʌmf/, *interj.* (an expression indicating disbelief, dissatisfaction, contempt, etc.)

**humpy**[1] /'hʌmpi/, *adj.,* **-pier, -piest. 1.** full of humps. **2.** humplike.

**humpy**[2] /'hʌmpi/, *n.* **1.** a temporary bush shelter used by Aborigines; gunyah. **2.** any rude or temporary dwelling; a bush hut. [Aboriginal]

**humus** /'hjuməs/, *n.* the dark organic material in soils, produced by the decomposition of vegetable or animal matter, essential to fertility and favourable moisture supply. [L: earth, ground]

**Hun** /hʌn/, *n.* **1.** a barbarous, destructive person, originally a member of a warlike Asian people who devastated Europe in the 4th and 5th centuries. **2.** *Colloq.* **a.** a German soldier, unit, aircraft, or the like, in World Wars I and II. **b.** any German. [sing. of *Huns,* OE *Hūnas,* Icel. *Hūnar.* Cf. LL *Hunnī,* Chinese *Han;* all from native name]

**hunch** /hʌntʃ/, *v.t.* **1.** to thrust out or up in a hump: *to hunch one's back.* *–v.i.* **2.** to walk, sit, or stand in a bent position (usu. fol. by *up*). *–n.* **3.** a hump. **4.** *Colloq.* a premonition or suspicion. **5.** a lump or thick piece. [apparently backformation from HUNCHBACKED]

**hunchback** /'hʌntʃbæk/, *n.* →**humpback** (def.2).

**hunchbacked** /'hʌntʃbækt/, *adj.* →**humpbacked.** [b. *huckbacked* and *bunchbacked*]

**hundred** /'hʌndrəd/, *n., pl.* **-dreds,** (*as after a numeral*) **-dred. 1.** a cardinal number, ten times ten. **2.** a symbol for this number, as 100 or C. **3.** a set of a hundred persons or things: *a hundred of the men.* **4.** a historical administrative division of an English county. **5. a hundred to one,** of remote possibility. *–adj.* **6.** amounting to one hundred in number. [ME *hondred,* OE *hundred,* c. G *hundert*]

**hundredfold** /'hʌndrədfoʊld/, *adj.* **1.** comprising a hundred parts or members. **2.** a hundred times as great or as much. *–adv.* **3.** in a hundredfold measure.

**hundred-per-cent** /hʌndrəd-pə-'sɛnt/, *adv.;* /'hʌndrəd-pə-sɛnt/, *adj.* *–adv.* **1.** completely; entirely. *–adj.* **2.** perfect; complete: *a hundred-per-cent success.*

**hundreds and thousands,** *n.pl.* very small, brightly coloured sugary balls, used in decorating cakes, sweets etc.

**hundredth** /'hʌndrədθ/, *adj.* **1.** next after the ninety-ninth. **2.** being one of a hundred equal parts. *–n.* **3.** a hundredth part, esp. of one ($\frac{1}{100}$). **4.** the hundredth member of a series.

**hundredweight** /'hʌndrədweɪt/, *n., pl.* **-weights,** (*as after a numeral*) **-weight.** a unit of weight in the imperial system, equal to 112 lb. (approx. 50.8 kg) and, in the U.S., to 100 lb. (approx. 45.36 kg). *Symbol:* cwt

**hung** /hʌŋ/, *v.* past tense and past participle of **hang.**

**Hung., 1.** Hungarian. **2.** Hungary.

**Hungarian** /hʌŋ'gɛəriən/, *adj.* **1.** of or pertaining to Hungary or its people. *–n.* **2.** a native or inhabitant of Hungary; a Magyar. **3.** the language of Hungary, of the Ugric group; Magyar. [HUNGARY + -AN]

**Hungary** /'hʌngəri/, *n.* a republic in central Europe.

**hunger** /'hʌŋgə/, *n.* **1.** the painful sensation or state of exhaustion caused by need of food: *to collapse from hunger.* **2.** a craving appetite; need for food. **3.** strong or eager desire: *hunger for praise.* *–v.i.* **4.** to feel hunger; be hungry. **5.** to have a strong desire. *–v.t.* **6.** *Obs.* to subject to hunger; starve. [ME; OE *hungor,* c. G *Hunger*]

**hunger-fine** /'hʌŋgə-faɪn/, *adj.* of or pertaining to wool which is unnaturally fine due to undernourishment of the sheep over an extended period.

**hunger march** /'hʌŋgə matʃ/, *n.* a march undertaken by unemployed or hungry workers to draw attention to their troubles. – **hunger-marcher,** *n.*

**hunger pain** /'hʌŋgə peɪn/, *n.* a pain caused by lack of food.

**hunger strike** /'hʌŋgə straɪk/, *n.* a persistent refusal to eat, as a protest against imprisonment, restraint, compulsion, etc.

**hung-over** /hʌŋ-'oʊvə/, *adj.* suffering the after-effects of drinking too much alcohol. [backformation from HANGOVER]

**hungry** /'hʌŋgri/, *adj.,* **-grier, -griest. 1.** craving food; having a keen appetite. **2.** indicating, characteristic of, or characterised by hunger or meanness: *a lean and hungry look.* **3.** strongly or eagerly desirous. **4.** always seeking money; avaricious; mean. **5.** lacking needful or desirable elements;

not fertile; poor: *hungry land.* **6.** marked by scarcity of food. [ME; OE *hungrig.* See -Y[1]] – **hungrily,** *adv.* – **hungriness,** *n.*

**hung-up** /ˈhʌŋ-ʌp/, *adj. Colloq.* (of a person) displaying emotional stress. Also, (*esp. in predicative positions*), **hung up.**

**hunk** /hʌŋk/, *n.* **1.** a large piece or lump; a chunk. **2.** *Colloq.* a sexually attractive male. [probably akin to Flemish *hunke;* cf. D *homp* lump] – **hunky,** *adj.*

**hunker** /ˈhʌŋkə/, *v.i. U.S.* to squat (close to the ground) with the body leaning forward. [? Scand. d., from ON *hokra* to crouch]

**hunkers** /ˈhʌŋkəz/, *n.pl. U.S.* **1.** the haunches. **2. on one's hunkers,** on one's haunches.

**hunky**[1] /ˈhʌŋki/, *adj. Colloq.* →**hunky-dory.**

**hunky**[2] /ˈhʌŋki/, *n., pl.* **-kies.** *U.S. Colloq.* (*derog.*) an unskilled or semiskilled workman of foreign birth, esp. a Hungarian; bohunk. [abbrev. of *Hungarian* + -Y[1]]

**hunky-dory** /hʌŋki-ˈdɔri/, *adj. Colloq.* perfectly all right, satisfactory. [obs. *hunk* goal, home (in games), from D *honk,* from MD *honc* hiding place]

**hunt** /hʌnt/, *v.t.* **1.** to chase (game or other wild animals) for the purpose of catching or killing. **2.** to scour (a region) in pursuit of game. **3.** to use or manage (a horse, etc.) in the chase. **4.** to pursue with force, hostility, etc.: *he was hunted from the village.* **5.** to search for; seek; endeavour to obtain or find. **6.** to search (a place) thoroughly. **7.** *Bellringing.* to alter the place of (a bell) in a hunt. **8.** to drive away; sack; dismiss. **9. hunt along,** to drive (a motor vehicle) at its maximum speed. **10. hunt away,** to drive (sheep) forward during mustering. **11. hunt down,** to pursue with intent to kill or capture. **12. hunt up,** to look for, esp. with success: *hunt up a reference in a book.* –*v.i.* **13.** to engage in the chase. **14.** to make a search or quest (oft. fol. by *for* or *after*). **15.** *Bellringing.* to alter the place of a bell in its set according to certain rules. **16.** *Mach.* to oscillate periodically as the speed of an engine or the position of a needle of a measuring instrument. –*n.* **17.** the act of hunting game or other wild animals; the chase. **18.** a body of persons associated for the purpose of hunting; an association of huntsmen. **19.** a pack of hounds engaged in the chase. **20.** a district hunted with hounds. **21.** pursuit. **22.** a search. **23.** *Bellringing.* a regularly varying order of permutations in the ringing of a group of from five to twelve bells. [ME *hunte(n),* OE *huntian,* from *hunta* hunter. Cf. OE *hentan* pursue]

**huntaway** /ˈhʌntəweɪ/, *n.* a sheepdog trained to drive sheep forward.

**hunter** /ˈhʌntə/, *n.* **1.** a huntsman. **2.** one who searches or seeks for something: *a fortune-hunter.* **3.** a horse used, or trained for use in hunting. **4.** an animal that hunts game or prey, esp. a dog. **5.** a watch with a hinged cover to protect its face.

**hunting** /ˈhʌntɪŋ/, *n.* **1.** the act of one who or that which hunts. **2.** *Elect.* the periodic oscillating of a rotating electromechanical system about a mean space position, as in a synchronous motor. **3.** any periodic variation in the speed of an engine, or in the position of the needle of a measuring instrument. –*adj.* **4.** of, for, or engaged in hunting: *a hunting cap.*

**hunting ground** /ˈ– graʊnd/, *n.* **1.** the area where hunting takes place. **2. happy hunting ground, a.** (*pl.*) (in North American Indian mythology) the world inhabited by souls after death. **b.** any place where what is sought is available in good supply: *the street stalls were a happy hunting ground for small etchings.*

**hunting horn** /ˈ– hɔn/, *n.* **1.** a cylindrical instrument, about 20 cm long, used in foxhunting to give signals. **2.** an early form of orchestral horn, consisting of a conical tube coiled in a circle, used in hunting in some countries for giving the signals.

**hunting knife** /ˈ– naɪf/, *n.* a knife sometimes used to kill game, but more commonly to skin and cut it up.

**Huntington's chorea** /ˌhʌntɪŋtənz kɔˈriə/, *n.* See **chorea** (def. 1). Also, **Huntington's disease.**

**hunting watch** /ˈhʌntɪŋ wɒtʃ/, *n.* →**hunter** (def. 5).

**huntress** /ˈhʌntrəs/, *n.* **1.** a woman who hunts. **2.** *Rare.* a mare employed in hunting.

**huntsman** /ˈhʌntsmən/, *n., pl.* **-men. 1.** the man in charge of hounds during a hunt. **2.** one who hunts game, etc.

**huntsman's-cup** /hʌntsmənz-ˈkʌp/, *n.* a plant of the genus *Sarracenia,* esp. *S. purpurea,* the pitcher plant, which grows in boggy areas.

**huntsman spider** /hʌntsmən ˈspaɪdə/, *n.* any of numerous species of the family Sparassidae, esp. the medium to large spiders of the genus *Isopoda,* with flattened, brown or grey, hairy bodies. See **tarantula, triantelope.**

**huntswoman** /ˈhʌntswʊmən/, *n.* a woman who hunts.

**hunt the slipper,** *n.* a game for children in which an object previously hidden is looked for, called **hunt the thimble** if the object is a thimble.

**hunza pie** /hʌnzə ˈpaɪ/, *n.* a spinach pie with a wholemeal pastry.

**Huon pine** /hjuɒn ˈpaɪn/, *n.* a large coniferous timber tree, *Dacrydium franklinii,* found in Tasmania. [named after the river *Huon* in Tasmania]

Huon pine

**hurdle** /ˈhɜdl/, *n., v.,* **-dled, -dling.** –*n.* **1.** a barrier in a racetrack, to be leapt by the contestants. **2. the hurdles,** a race in which such barriers are leapt. **3.** a difficult problem to be overcome; obstacle. **4.** a movable rectangular frame of interlaced twigs, crossed bars, or the like, as for a temporary fence. **5.** any of various obstacles, as a hedge, low wall, fence, over which horses must jump in steeplechasing, etc. **6.** a frame or sledge on which criminals were formerly drawn to the place of execution. –*v.t.* **7.** to leap over (a hurdle, etc.) as in a race. **8.** to master (a difficulty, problem, etc.). **9.** to construct with hurdles; enclose with hurdles. –*v.i.* **10.** to leap over a hurdle or other barrier. [ME *hirdel, hurdel,* OE *hyrdel,* from *hyrd-* (c. G *Hürde* hurdle) + *-l* suffix; akin to L *crātis* wickerwork, Gk *kýrtos* basket, cage] – **hurdler,** *n.*

**hurdle gate** /ˈ– geɪt/, *n.* a gate usu. made from a rectangular frame and horizontal bars of split wood, or sometimes from some other wooden hurdle (def. 4).

**hurds** /hɜdz/, *n. pl.* →**hards.**

**hurdy-gurdy** /ˈhɜdi-gɜdi/, *n., pl.* **-dies. 1.** a barrel organ or similar instrument played by turning a crank. **2.** a lute or guitar-shaped stringed musical instrument sounded by the revolution, against the strings, of a rosined wheel turned by a crank. **3. on a hurdy-gurdy,** *Colloq.* involved in a mindless and seemingly never-ending round of activities. [apparently imitative]

**hurl** /hɜl/, *v.t.* **1.** to drive or throw with great force. **2.** to throw down; overthrow. **3.** to utter with vehemence. –*v.i.* **4.** to throw a missile. **5.** *Colloq.* to vomit. –*n.* **6.** a forcible or violent throw; a fling. **7.** *Colloq.* the act of vomiting. [ME *hurlen;* early association with HURTLE, but properly frequentative of obs. *hurr* (imitative) make a vibrating sound. Cf. obs. *hurling,* n., roll of thunder, d. G *hurlen* roll, rumble (said of thunder)] – **hurler,** *n.*

**hurly** /hɜli/, *n., pl.* **-lies.** commotion; hurly-burly.

**hurly-burly** /ˈhɜli-bɜli/, *n., pl.* **-burlies,** *adj.* –*n.* **1.** commotion; tumult. –*adj.* **2.** full of commotion; tumultuous. [modified form of *hurling and burling*]

**hurray** /həˈreɪ/, *interj., v.i., n.* →**hooray.** Also, **hurrah.**

**hurricane** /ˈhʌrəkən, -ɪkən/, *n.* **1.** a violent tropical cyclonic storm. **2.** a storm of the most intense severity. **3.** *Meteorol.* a wind of Beaufort scale force 12, i.e. with average windspeed of more than 63 knots, or more than 117 km/h. **4.** anything suggesting a violent storm. **5.** →**hurricane lamp.** [Sp. *huracán,* from Carib]

**hurricane deck** /ˈ– dɛk/, *n.* a light upper deck on passenger steamers, etc.

**hurricane lamp** /ˈ– læmp/, *n.* **1.** a kerosene lamp the flame of which is protected by a glass chimney or other similar device. **2.** a candlestick with a chimney.

**hurried** /ˈhʌrid/, *adj.* **1.** driven or impelled to hurry, as a person. **2.** characterised by or done with hurry; hasty. – **hurriedly,** *adj.* – **hurriedness,** *n.*

**hurry** /ˈhʌri/, *v.,* **-ried, -rying,** *n., pl.* **-ries.** –*v.i.* **1.** to move, proceed, or act with haste, often undue haste. –*v.t.* **2.** to drive or move (someone or something) with speed, often with

i = peat ɪ = pit ɛ = pet æ = pat a = part ɒ = pot ʌ = putt ɔ = port ʊ = put u = pool ɜ = pert ə = apart aɪ = buy eɪ = bay ɔɪ = boy aʊ = how
oʊ = hoe ɪə = here ɛə = hair ʊə = tour g = give θ = thin ð = then ʃ = show ʒ = measure tʃ = choke dʒ = joke ŋ = sing j = you õ = Fr. bon

confused haste. **3.** to hasten; urge forwards (oft. fol. by *up*). **4.** to impel with undue haste to thoughtless action: *to be hurried into a decision.* *–n.* **5.** need or desire for haste: *to be in a hurry to begin.* **6.** hurried movement or action; haste. [orig. obscure; ? imitative] – **hurryingly,** *adv.*

**hurry-scurry** /hʌri-'skʌri/, *n., pl.* **-ries,** *adv., adj., v.,* **-ried, -rying.** *–n.* **1.** headlong, disorderly haste; hurry and confusion. *–adv.* **2.** with hurrying and scurrying. **3.** confusedly; in a bustle. *–adj.* **4.** characterised by headlong, disorderly flight or haste. *–v.i.* **5.** to rush or go hurry-scurry. Also, **hurry-skurry.** [var. reduplication of HURRY]

**hurry-up** /'hʌri-ʌp/, *n.* **1.** a reminder or prompting to action. *–adj.* **2.** prompting; urging: *a hurry-up call.*

**hurst** /hɜst/, *n.* **1.** a copse or wood. **2.** a wooded hill. [ME, OE *hyrst;* c. LG *horst*]

**hurt** /hɜt/, *v.,* **hurt, hurting,** *n.* *–v.t.* **1.** to cause bodily injury to (with or without consequent pain). **2.** to cause bodily pain to or in: *the wound still hurts him.* **3.** to damage (a material object, etc.) by striking, rough use, or otherwise: *to hurt furniture.* **4.** to affect adversely; harm: *to hurt one's reputation.* **5.** to cause mental pain to; grieve: *to hurt one's feelings.* *–v.i.* **6.** to cause pain (bodily or mental): *my finger still hurts.* **7.** to cause injury, damage, or harm. *–n.* **8.** a blow that inflicts a wound; bodily injury. **9.** injury; damage or harm. **10.** an injury that gives mental pain, as an insult. [ME *hurte(n),* probably from OF *hurter* strike against, from *hurt* a blow]

**hurter** /'hɜtə/, *n.* **1.** a supporting or strengthening part. **2.** (in a vehicle) a butting piece on the shoulder of an axle against which the hub strikes. [ME *hurtour,* from HURT, *v.* + *-our* -OR[2]. Cf. F *hurtoir* a knocker]

**hurtful** /'hɜtfəl/, *adj.* such as to cause hurt or injury; injurious; harmful. – **hurtfully,** *adv.* – **hurtfulness,** *n.*

**hurtle** /hɜtl/, *v.,* **-tled, -tling,** *n.* *–v.i.* **1.** to rush violently and noisily. **2.** to resound, as in collision or rapid motion. **3.** *Rare.* to strike together or against something. *–v.t.* **4.** to drive violently; fling; dash. **5.** to dash against; collide with. *–n.* **6.** *Poet.* clash; collision; shock; clatter. [ME; frequentative of HURT]

**husband** /'hʌzbənd/, *n.* **1.** the man of a married pair (correlative of *wife*). *–v.t.* **2.** to manage, esp. with prudent economy; economise: *to husband one's resources.* **3.** *Obs.* to till; cultivate. [ME *husbond(e),* OE *hūsbōnda,* from *hūs* house + *bōnda* householder (from Scand.; cf. Icel. *bōndi*)] – **husbandless,** *adj.*

**husband-beater** /'hʌzbənd-bitə/, *n. Colloq.* a very long, narrow, loaf of bread.

**husbandman** /'hʌzbəndmən/, *n., pl.* **-men.** →**farmer.**

**husbandry** /'hʌzbəndri/, *n.* **1.** the business of a farmer; agriculture; farming. **2.** careful or thrifty management; frugality; thrift. **3.** the management of domestic affairs, or of resources generally.

**hush**[1] /hʌʃ/, *interj.* **1.** (a command to be silent or quiet.) *–v.i.* **2.** to become or be silent or quiet. *–v.t.* **3.** to make silent; silence. **4.** to suppress mention of; keep concealed. **5.** to calm or allay: *to hush someone's fears.* *–n.* **6.** silence or quiet, esp. after noise. *–adj.* **7.** *Archaic.* silent; quiet. [apparently backformation from ME *husst,* also *hust, huyst,* adj. (orig. interj.), taken as pp. Cf. WHIST[1]]

**hush**[2] /hʌʃ/, *v.t.* **1.** to wash away (surface soil) to expose the underlying rock formation for prospecting. **2.** to wash (an ore) in a strong cascade of water so that the earth is carried away. [imitative]

**hushaby** /'hʌʃəbaɪ/, *v.i.* (used imperatively) go to sleep; be still.

**hush-hush** /'hʌʃ-hʌʃ/, *adj. Colloq.* highly confidential.

**hush money** /'hʌʃ mʌni/, *n.* a bribe to keep silent about something.

**husk** /hʌsk/, *n.* **1.** the dry external covering of certain fruits or seeds, esp. of an ear of maize. **2.** the enveloping or outer part of anything, esp. when dry or worthless. *–v.t.* **3.** to remove the husk from. [ME *huske,* from *hus-* (cf. OE *hosu* pod, husk) + *-k* suffix. See -OCK] – **husker,** *n.* – **husklike,** *adj.*

**husking** /'hʌskɪŋ/, *n.* the act of removing husks, esp. those of maize.

**husky**[1] /'hʌski/, *adj.,* **-kier, -kiest,** *n., pl.* **-kies.** *–adj.* **1.** *Colloq.* burly; big and strong. **2.** having a semi-whispered vocal tone; somewhat hoarse. **3.** abounding in husks. **4.** like husks. *–n.* **5.** *U.S. Colloq.* a big and strong person. [HUSK, *n.* + -Y[1]] – **huskily,** *adv.* – **huskiness,** *n.*

**husky**[2] /'hʌski/, *n., pl.* **-kies.** (*also cap.*) an Eskimo dog. [? a shortened var. of ESKIMO]

**hussar** /hə'za/, *n.* **1.** (originally) one of a body of light Hungarian cavalry formed during the 15th century. **2.** one of a class of similar troops, usu. with striking or showy uniforms, in European armies. [Hung. *huszár,* orig. freebooter, from OSerbian *husar,* var. of *kursar,* from It. *corsaro* CORSAIR]

**hussy** /'hʌsi, 'hʌzi/, *n., pl.* **-sies.** **1.** an ill-behaved girl. **2.** a lewd woman. [familiar var. of HOUSEWIFE (ME *huswif*)]

**hustings** /'hʌstɪŋz/, *n.pl.* **1.** an electioneering platform. **2.** election proceedings. [ME *husting,* from Scand.; cf. Icel. *hūsthing* house assembly, council summoned by king or leader]

**hustle** /'hʌsəl/, *v.,* **-tled, -tling,** *n.* *–v.i.* **1.** to proceed or work rapidly or energetically. **2.** to push or force one's way. **3.** to solicit for or as a prostitute. *–v.t.* **4.** to force roughly or hurriedly: *they hustled him out of the city.* **5.** to shake, push, or shove roughly. **6.** to urge to greater efforts; prod; hurry along. **7.** *U.S.* **a.** to obtain (money) by questionable methods. **b.** to pursue sales with aggressive energy. *–n.* **8.** energetic activity, as in work. **9.** discourteous shoving, pushing, or jostling. [var. spelling of *hussell, hus(s)le,* from D *husselen,* assimilated var. of *hutselen,* frequentative of *hutsen* shake, jog]

**hustler** /'hʌslə/, *n.* an energetic person who sweeps aside all obstacles in his path, as a pushy salesman.

**hut** /hʌt/, *n., v.,* **hutted, hutting.** *–n.* **1.** a simple, small house as a beach hut, bushwalker's hut. **2.** (in snow country) a large building for accommodating skiers. **3.** *Mil.* a wooden or metal structure for the temporary housing of troops. **4.** the house in which the employees on a sheep or cattle station live. *–v.t.* **5.** to place in or furnish with a hut. *–v.i.* **6.** to lodge or take shelter in a hut. [F *hutte,* from G *Hütte;* probably akin to HIDE[1]] – **hutlike,** *adj.*

**hutch** /hʌtʃ/, *n.* **1.** a coop for confining small animals: *rabbit hutch.* **2.** a hut or cabin. **3** a shack or shanty. **4.** a chest, box, or trough: *a grain hutch.* **5.** a baker's kneading trough. *–v.t.* **6.** to put away in or as in a hutch; hoard. [ME *huche,* from OF, from ML *hūtica* chest; ? of Gmc orig.]

**hutchie** /'hʊtʃi/, *n.* a waterproof sheet thrown over a tree branch or other stick for temporary shelter.

**hutkeep** /'hʌtkip/, *v.i.* to act as hutkeeper.

**hutkeeper** /'hʌtkipə/, *n.* (formerly) **1.** the cook, caretaker, etc., of a hut used by a convict gang. **2.** an assigned man or stockman's offsider fulfilling such a function.

**Huygens eyepiece** /haɪgənz 'aɪpis/, *n.* an eyepiece which is often used in microscopes, consisting of two plano-convex lenses with their plane sides towards the observer. The lenses are separated by a distance of half the sum of the focal lengths, which are in the ratio 3 to 1 (the lens of shorter focal length being nearer the observer). [from Christian *Huygens,* 1629-95, Dutch physicist]

**huzza** /hʌ'za/, *interj., n., pl.* **-zas,** *v.,* **-zaed, -zaing.** *–interj.* **1.** (an exclamation of exultation, applause, or the like.) *–n.* **2.** the exclamation 'huzza'. *–v.i.* **3.** to shout 'huzza'. *–v.t.* **4.** to salute with huzzas: *crowds huzzaed the triumphant hero.*

**h.w.s.,** hot-water service.

**Hwy,** highway.

**hyacinth** /'haɪəsənθ/, *n.* **1.** any of the bulbous plants constituting the genus *Hyacinthus,* esp. *H. orientalis,* widely cultivated for its spikes of fragrant, white or coloured, bell-shaped flowers. **2.** a hyacinth bulb or flower. **3.** (among the ancients) a plant supposed to spring from the blood of Hyacinthus and variously identified as iris, gladiolus, larkspur, etc. **4.** a reddish- orange zircon; the jacinth. **5.** (among the ancients) an uncertain gem, possibly our amethyst or sapphire. [L *hyacinthus,* from Gk *hyákinthos* kind of flower, also a gem. Cf. JACINTH]

**hyacinthine** /haɪə'sɪnθin, -aɪn/, *adj.* **1.** of or like the hyacinth. **2.** adorned with hyacinths.

**hyacinth orchid** /'haɪəsənθ ɔkəd/, *n.* a terrestrial saprophytic orchid, *Dipodium punctatum,* with numerous pink spotted flowers, found near the base of large trees, esp. eucalypts.

**hyaena** /haɪ'inə/, *n.* →**hyena.**

**hyaline** /'haɪəlin, -laɪn/, *n.* **1.** something glassy or transparent. *–adj.* **2.** glassy; crystalline; transparent. [LL *hyalinus,* from Gk *hyálinos* of glass]

**hyaline cartilage** /– 'katəlɪdʒ/, *n.* the typical translucent form of cartilage, containing little fibrous tissue.

**hyalite** /'haɪəlaɪt/, *n.* a colourless variety of opal, sometimes transparent like glass, and sometimes whitish and translucent occurring in globular or botryoidal forms. [HYAL(O)- + -ITE[1]]

**hyalo-**, a word element meaning 'glass'. Also, before vowels, **hyal-**. [Gk, combining form of *hýalos*]

**hyaloid** /'haɪəlɔɪd/, *n.* **1.** *Anat.* the hyaloid membrane of the eye. *–adj.* **2.** glassy; hyaline. [Gk *hyaloeidḗs* like glass. See HYALO-, -OID]

**hyaloid membrane** /– 'mɛmbreɪn/, *n.* the capsule of the vitreous humour of the eye, a delicate, pellucid, and nearly structureless membrane.

**hyalophane** /haɪ'æləfeɪn/, *n.* a rare form of felspar containing some barium; occurs in colourless crystals in dolomite.

**hyaloplasm** /'haɪələplæzəm/, *n.* the pellucid portion of the protoplasm of a cell, as distinguished from the granular and reticular portions.

**hyaluronic acid** /haɪəlju,rɒnɪk 'æsəd/, *n.* any of a group of complex polysaccharides found in the vitreous humour of the eye, umbilical cord, synovial fluid, and other animal tissues.

**hybrid** /'haɪbrɪd, -brəd/, *n.* **1.** the offspring of two animals or plants of different races, breeds, varieties, species, or genera. **2.** a half-breed; a mongrel. **3.** anything derived from heterogeneous sources, or composed of elements of different or incongruous kind. **4.** a word derived from elements of different languages. *–adj.* **5.** bred from two distinct races, breeds, varieties, species, or genera. **6.** composed of elements of different or incongruous kinds. **7.** (of a word) composed of elements originally drawn from different languages. [L *hybrida,* var. of *hibrida* offspring of a tame sow and wild boar, a mongrel]

**hybridise** /'haɪbrədaɪz/, *v.,* **-dised, -dising.** *–v.t.* **1.** to cause to produce hybrids; cross. **2.** to form in a hybrid manner. *–v.i.* **3.** to cause the production of hybrids by crossing different species, etc. Also, **hybridize.** – **hybridisable,** *adj.* – **hybridisation** /haɪbrədaɪ'zeɪʃən/, *n.* – **hybridiser,** *n.*

**hybridism** /'haɪbrədɪzəm/, *n.* **1.** Also, **hybridity** /haɪ'brɪdəti/. hybrid character. **2.** the production of hybrids. – **hybridist,** *n.*

**hybris** /'haɪbrəs/, *n.* →**hubris.**

**hydantoin** /haɪ'dæntoʊɪn/, *n.* a colourless, needle-like crystalline compound, $C_3H_4N_2O_2$, used in the synthesis of pharmaceutical substances and resins. [irregularly from Gk *hýd(ōr)* water + *(all)antoin* (from ALLANTO(IS) + -IN[2])]

**hydatid** /haɪ'dætəd/, *n.* **1.** a cyst with watery contents, produced in man and animals by a tapeworm in the larval state. **2.** the encysted larva of a tapeworm; a cysticercus. [Gk *hydatís* watery vesicle]

**hydnocarpate** /hɪdnoʊ'kapeɪt/, *n.* a salt or ester of hydnocarpic acid. [NL *hydnocarpus* (from Gk *hýdno(n)* truffle + *karpós* fruit) + -ATE[2]]

**hydnocarpic acid** /hɪdnoʊ,kapɪk 'æsəd/, *n.* a white crystalline acid, $C_5H_7(CH_2)_{10}COOH$, obtained from chaulmoogra oil, used to treat leprosy.

**hydr-[1]**, variant of **hydro-[1]**, before vowels, as in *hydrangea.*

**hydr-[2]**, variant of **hydro-[2]**, before vowels, as in *hydrazine.*

**hydra** /'haɪdrə/, *n., pl.* **-dras, -drae** /-dri/. **1.** (*sometimes l.c.*) any persistent evil arising from many sources or difficult to overcome: *a hydra-headed monster.* **2.** *Zool.* any of the freshwater polyps constituting the genus *Hydra.* [a monstrous serpent of Greek mythology, slain by Hercules, represented as having nine heads, each of which was replaced by two after being cut off, unless the wound was cauterised; L, from Gk: water-serpent; replacing ME *ydre,* from OF]

**hydracid** /haɪ'dræsəd/, *n.* an acid which contains no oxygen.

**hydrangea** /haɪ'dreɪndʒə/, *n.* any shrub of the genus *Hydrangea,* species of which are cultivated for their large showy white, pink, or blue flower clusters. [NL, from *hydr-* HYDR-[1] + Gk *angeîa,* pl. of *angeîon* vessel; so called from cup-shaped seed capsule]

**hydrant** /'haɪdrənt/, *n.* an upright pipe with a spout, nozzle, or other outlet, usu. in the street, for drawing water from a main or service pipe.

**hydranth** /'haɪdrənθ/, *n.* the terminal part of a hydroid polyp that bears the mouth and tentacles and contains the stomach region. [HYDR(A) (def. 2) + Gk *ánthos* flower]

**hydrargyriasis** /,haɪdrədʒə'raɪəsəs/, *n.* mercurial poisoning.

**hydrargyrum** /haɪ'dradʒərəm/, *n.* →**mercury.** [NL, from L *hydrargyrus,* from Gk *hydrárgyros*]

**hydrastine** /haɪ'dræstin, -taɪn/, *n.* an alkaloid found in the root of goldenseal.

**hydrastinine** /haɪ'dræstənin, -naɪn/, *n.* a substance used as a heart stimulant or to control uterine haemorrhage.

**hydrate** /'haɪdreɪt/, *n., v.,* **-drated, -drating.** *–n.* **1.** any of a class of compounds containing chemically combined water, esp. salts containing water of crystallisation. *–v.t.* **2.** to combine chemically with water. – **hydration** /haɪ'dreɪʃən/, *n.* – **hydrator,** *n.*

**hydrated** /'haɪdreɪtəd/, *adj.* chemically combined with water in its molecular form.

**hydraul.,** hydraulics.

**hydraulic** /haɪ'drɒlɪk/, *adj.* **1.** operated by or employing water or other liquid. **2.** pertaining to water or other liquid, or to hydraulics. **3.** hardening under water, as a cement. [L *hydraulicus,* from Gk *hydraulikós* pertaining to the water organ, an ancient musical instrument] – **hydraulically,** *adv.*

**hydraulic accumulator** /– ə'kjumjəleɪtə/, *n.* **1.** a device, consisting of a hydraulic ram loaded with a heavy weight, for storing water under pressure in order to equalise the load on machinery supplied by a pump when the demand is intermittent. **2.** any apparatus for absorbing shock or storing energy in a hydraulic system.

**hydraulic brake** /– 'breɪk/, *n.* a brake operated by fluid pressures in cylinders and connecting tubular lines.

**hydraulic machinery** /– mə'ʃinəri/, *n.* mechanical devices such as pumps, turbines, couplings, etc., in which the flow of a liquid either produces or is produced by their operation.

**hydraulic press** /– 'prɛs/, *n.* a machine permitting a small force applied to a small piston to produce through fluid pressure a large force on a large piston.

**hydraulic ram** /– 'ræm/, *n.* a device by which the energy of descending water is utilised to raise a part of the water to a height greater than that of the source.

**hydraulics** /haɪ'drɒlɪks/, *n.* the science treating of the laws governing water or other liquids in motion and their applications in engineering; practical or applied hydrodynamics. [pl. of HYDRAULIC. See -ICS]

**hydraulic torque converter,** *n.* →**fluid drive.**

**hydrazine** /'haɪdrəzin, -zaɪn/, *n.* **1.** a compound, $N_2H_4$, which is a weak base in solution and forms a large number of salts resembling ammonium salts, used as a reducing agent and as a jet-propulsion fuel. **2.** a class of substances derived by replacing one or more hydrogen atoms in hydrazine by an organic radical. [HYDR-[2] + AZ(O)- + -INE[2]]

**hydrazo group** /haɪ'dreɪzoʊ grup/, *n.* the bivalent group -HN·NH-. Also, **hydrazo radical.**

**hydrazoic** /haɪdrə'zoʊɪk/, *adj.* denoting or pertaining to hydrazoic acid; triazoic.

**hydrazoic acid** /– 'æsəd/, *n.* a highly toxic acid composed of hydrogen and nitrogen, $HN_3$, occurring as a very explosive, colourless liquid with a penetrating smell.

**hydrazone** /'haɪdrəzoʊn/, *n.* any of a class of compounds formed from the condensation of an aldehyde or ketone with hydrazine.

**hydria** /'haɪdriə/, *n.* (in ancient Greece) a large jar or pitcher with two or three handles, for carrying water. [Gk]

**hydric** /'haɪdrɪk/, *adj.* **1.** pertaining to, or containing, hydrogen. **2.** pertaining to an environment containing, or requiring an abundance of moisture (opposed to *xeric, mesic*). **3. a.** containing acid hydrogen. **b.** containing hydroxyl, esp. of alcohols and phenols.

**hydride** /'haɪdraɪd/, *n.* a compound of hydrogen with another element or a radical.

**hydriodic acid** /haɪdri,ɒdɪk 'æsəd/, *n.* an aqueous solution of hydrogen iodide. [HYDR-[2] + IOD(INE) + -IC]

**hydro[1]** /'haɪdroʊ/, *n.* a hotel or resort having facilities for people undergoing hydropathic treatment. [short for HYDROPATHIC]

**hydro**[2] /ˈhaɪdroʊ/, *adj.* hydro-electric: *a hydro system.*

**hydro-**[1], a word element meaning 'water', as in *hydrogen.* Also, **hydr-**. [Gk, combining form of *hýdōr* water]

**hydro-**[2], *Chem.* a word element often indicating combination of hydrogen with a negative element or radical: *hydrobromic.* Also, **hydr-**. [combining form of HYDROGEN]

**hydro-aeroplane** /haɪdroʊ-ˈɛərəpleɪn/, *n.* →**hydroplane.**

**hydrobromic acid** /ˌhaɪdroʊbroʊmɪk ˈæsəd/, *n.* an aqueous solution of hydrogen bromide.

**hydrocarbon** /haɪdroʊˈkabən/, *n.* any of a class of compounds containing only hydrogen and carbon, such as methane, $CH_4$, ethylene, $C_2H_4$, acetylene, $C_2H_2$, and benzene, $C_6H_6$. [HYDRO-[2] + CARBON]

**hydrocele** /ˈhaɪdrəsil/, *n.* an accumulation of serous fluid, usu. about the testis. [L, from Gk *hydrokḗlē*]

**hydrocellulose** /haɪdroʊˈsɛljəloʊz, -oʊs/, *n.* a gelatinous substance obtained by partially hydrolysing cellulose; used in the manufacture of paper and certain textiles.

**hydrocephalus** /haɪdroʊˈsɛfələs/, *n.* an accumulation of serous fluid within the cranium, esp. in infancy, often causing great enlargement of the skull, and compression of the brain. Also, **hydrocephaly** /haɪdroʊˈsɛfəli/. [NL, from Gk *hydroképhalon* water in the head] – **hydrocephalic** /ˌhaɪdroʊsəˈfælɪk/, **hydrocephalous**, *adj.*

**hydrochloric acid** /ˌhaɪdrəklɒrɪk ˈæsəd/, *n.* a colourless, poisonous fuming liquid formed by the solution of hydrogen chloride in water, used extensively in chemical and industrial processes; the commercial form is muriatic acid. [HYDRO-[1] + CHLORIC]

**hydrochloride** /haɪdrəˈklɔraɪd/, *n.* a salt formed by the direct union of hydrochloric acid with an organic base, rendering the latter more soluble.

**hydrocolloid** /haɪdrəˈkɒlɔɪd/, *n.* any substance that will form a gel with the addition of water.

**hydro-cooling** /haɪdroʊ-ˈkulɪŋ/, *n.* a method of preserving fruit or vegetables by immersing them in chilled water, or by spraying.

**hydrocortisone** /haɪdroʊˈkɔtəzoʊn/, *n.* a compound secreted from the adrenal gland, used esp. as an anti-inflammatory agent.

**hydrocyanic acid** /ˌhaɪdroʊsaɪˌænɪk ˈæsəd/, *n.* a colourless, poisonous liquid formed by the solution of hydrogen cyanide, HCN, in water, with a smell like that of bitter almonds; prussic acid. [HYDRO-[2] + CYANIC]

**hydrodesulphurisation** /ˌhaɪdroʊdiˌsʌlfəraɪˈzeɪʃən/, *n.* the treatment of crude oil with hydrogen to remove sulphur and metals.

**hydrodynamic** /ˌhaɪdroʊdaɪˈnæmɪk/, *adj.* **1.** pertaining to forces in or motions of fluids. **2.** pertaining to hydrodynamics.

**hydrodynamics** /ˌhaɪdroʊdaɪˈnæmɪks/, *n.* the science of the mechanics of fluids, generally liquids, including hydrostatics and hydrokinetics.

**hydro-electric** /ˌhaɪdroʊ-əˈlɛktrɪk/, *adj.* pertaining to the generation and distribution of electric energy derived from the energy of falling water or other hydraulic source. – **hydro-electricity** /ˌhaɪdroʊ-əlɛkˈtrɪsəti/, *n.*

**hydrofluoboric acid** /ˌhaɪdroʊfluəˌbɔrɪk ˈæsəd/, *n.* →**fluoroboric acid.**

hydrofoil (def. 2)

**hydrofluoric acid** /haɪdroʊˌflurɪk ˈæsəd/, *n.* a colourless, corrosive, poisonous solution of hydrogen fluoride in water, used to etch glass and in certain industrial processes. [HYDRO-[2] + FLUORIC]

**hydrofoil** /ˈhaɪdrəfɔɪl/, *n.* **1.** one of two or more ski-like members, mounted at the ends of struts beneath a powered boat, supporting the hull above the surface of the water when a certain speed has been attained. **2.** a boat equipped with such members. **3.** ski-like members at the side of a boat, acting as stabilisers.

**hydrogen** /ˈhaɪdrədʒən/, *n.* a colourless, odourless, inflammable gas, which combines chemically with oxygen to form water; the lightest of the known elements. *Symbol:* H; *at. wt:* 1.00797; *at. no.:* 1; *weight of one litre at 760 mm pressure and 0°C:* 0.08987 g. [F *hydrogène*, from *hydro-* HYDRO-[1] + *-gène* -GEN]

**hydrogenate** /haɪˈdrɒdʒəneɪt/, *v.t.*, **-nated, -nating.** to combine or treat with hydrogen: *to hydrogenate vegetable oil to fat.* – **hydrogenation** /haɪˌdrɒdʒəˈneɪʃən/, *n.*

**hydrogen bomb** /ˈhaɪdrədʒən bɒm/, *n.* a bomb whose potency is based on the release of nuclear energy resulting from the fusion of hydrogen isotopes in the formation of helium. It is many times more powerful than the atom bomb. Also, **fusion bomb.**

**hydrogen bond** /ˈ– bɒnd/, *n.* a weak chemical bond of considerable importance which occurs between a hydrogen atom attached to a strongly electronegative atom and a second strongly electronegative atom with a lone pair of electrons, as fluorine, oxygen, nitrogen.

**hydrogen bromide** /– ˈbroʊmaɪd/, *n.* a colourless, poisonous gas, HBr, with a pungent smell.

**hydrogen chloride** /– ˈklɔraɪd/, *n.* a colourless, poisonous gas, HCl, obtained by burning hydrogen in chlorine, or esp. as a result of the chlorination of organic compounds.

**hydrogen cyanide** /– ˈsaɪənaɪd/, *n.* a highly poisonous, volatile gas, HCN, with an odour of bitter almonds.

**hydrogen fluoride** /– ˈfluraɪd/, *n.* a colourless, fuming, corrosive, poisonous gas or volatile liquid, HF, used in the manufacture of hydrofluoric acid and in industry generally.

**hydrogen iodide** /– ˈaɪədaɪd/, *n.* a poisonous, colourless gas, HI, with a suffocating smell.

**hydrogen ion** /ˈ– aɪən/, *n.* ionised hydrogen of the form $H^+$.

**hydrogen ion concentration,** *n.* the number of gram ions (moles) of hydrogen ion in a litre of solution; a measure of the acidity or alkalinity of a solution. See **pH.**

**hydrogenise** /haɪˈdrɒdʒənaɪz/, *v.t.*, **-nised, -nising.** →**hydrogenate.** Also, **hydrogenize.**

**hydrogenous** /haɪˈdrɒdʒənəs/, *adj.* **1.** of or containing hydrogen. **2.** formed or produced by water.

**hydrogen peroxide** /haɪdrədʒən pəˈrɒksaɪd/, *n.* a colourless, unstable, oily liquid, $H_2O_2$, the aqueous solution of which is used as an antiseptic and a bleaching agent.

**hydrogen sulphide** /– ˈsʌlfaɪd/, *n.* a colourless, inflammable, cumulatively poisonous gas, $H_2S$, smelling like rotten eggs; sulphuretted hydrogen.

**hydrograph** /ˈhaɪdrəgræf, -graf/, *n.* a graph showing the seasonal change in the level, flow, or velocity of water in a channel, reservoir, or the like.

**hydrography** /haɪˈdrɒgrəfi/, *n.* **1.** the science of the measurement, description, and mapping of the surface waters of the earth, with special reference to their use for navigation. **2.** those parts of a map, collectively, that represent surface waters. – **hydrographer,** *n.* – **hydrographic** /haɪdrəˈgræfɪk/, **hydrographical** /haɪdrəˈgræfɪkəl/, *adj.* – **hydrographically** /haɪdrəˈgræfɪkli/, *adv.*

**hydroid** /ˈhaɪdrɔɪd/, *adj.* **1.** denoting or pertaining to that form of hydrozoan which is asexual and grows into branching colonies by budding. –*n.* **2.** that phase of a hydrozoan coelenterate that consists of polyp forms usu. growing as an attached colony. [HYDR(A) (def. 2) + -OID]

**hydro-industrialisation** /ˌhaɪdroʊɪnˌdʌstriəlaɪˈzeɪʃən/, *n.* the encouraging of heavy industry by the provision of a cheap supply of hydro-electricity.

**hydrokinetic** /ˌhaɪdroʊkaɪˈnɛtɪk, -kə-/, *adj.* **1.** pertaining to the motion of fluids. **2.** pertaining to hydrokinetics. Also, **hydrokinetical.**

**hydrokinetics** /ˌhaɪdroʊkaɪˈnɛtɪks, -kə-/, *n.* the branch of hydrodynamics that treats of the laws governing liquids or gases in motion.

**hydrolase** /ˈhaɪdrəleɪz/, *n.* any enzyme that catalyses a hydrolytic reaction.

**hydrolith** /ˈhaɪdrəlɪθ/, *n.* calcium hydride, $CaH_2$.

**hydrology** /haɪˈdrɒlədʒi/, *n.* the science dealing with water on the land, or under the earth's surface, its properties, laws, geographical distribution, etc. – **hydrologic** /haɪdrəˈlɒdʒɪk/, **hydrological** /haɪdrəˈlɒdʒɪkəl/, *adj.* – **hydrologist,** *n.*

**hydrolysate** /haɪˈdrɒləseɪt/, *n.* any compound formed by hydrolysis.

**hydrolyse** /ˈhaɪdrəlaɪz/, *v.t., v.i.*, **-lysed, -lysing.** to subject or be subjected to hydrolysis. Also, *U.S.*, **hydrolyze.** – **hydrolysable,** *adj.*

**hydrolysis** /haɪˈdrɒləsəs/, *n., pl.* **-ses** /-siz/. chemical decomposition by which a compound is resolved into other compounds by taking up the elements of water.

**hydrolyte** /ˈhaɪdrəlaɪt/, *n.* a substance subjected to hydrolysis.

**hydrolytic** /haɪdrəˈlɪtɪk/, *adj.* producing hydrolysis, or related to the process or results of hydrolysis. – **hydrolytically,** *adv.*

**hydromancy** /ˈhaɪdrəmænsi/, *n.* divination by means of water. [F *hydromancie,* from LL *hydromantīa,* from Gk, from *hydro-* HYDRO-[1] + *manteía* divination] – **hydromantic** /haɪdrəˈmæntɪk/, *adj.*

**hydromechanics** /ˌhaɪdroʊməˈkænɪks/, *n.* →**hydrodynamics.** – **hydromechanical,** *adj.*

**hydromedusa** /ˌhaɪdroʊməˈdjusə/, *n., pl.* **-sas, -sae** /-si/. the medusa form of a hydrozoan coelenterate. [NL. See HYDRO-[1], MEDUSA] – **hydromedusan,** *adj.*

**hydromel** /ˈhaɪdrəmel/, *n.* a liquid consisting of honey and water, and, when fermented, known also as mead. [L *hydromeli,* from Gk: honey water]

**hydrometallurgy** /haɪdroʊˈmɛtələdʒi/, *n.* the practice of extracting metals from ores by leaching with solutions such as mercury, cyanides, acids, brines, etc. – **hydrometallurgical** /ˌhaɪdroʊmɛtəˈlɜdʒɪkəl/, *adj.*

**hydrometeor** /haɪdroʊˈmitiɔ/, *n.* the state or effect of water, water-vapour, or ice in the atmosphere, as rain, ice crystals, hail, fog, and clouds. – **hydrometeorology** /haɪdroʊ ˌmitiəˈrɒlədʒi/, *n.*

**hydrometer** /haɪˈdrɒmətə/, *n.* a sealed cylinder with weighted bulb and graduated stem for determining the specific gravity of liquids by reading the level of the liquid on the emerging stem when immersed in the liquid. – **hydrometric** /haɪdroʊˈmɛtrɪk/, **hydrometrical** /haɪdroʊˈmɛtrɪkəl/, *adj.* – **hydrometry,** *n.*

**hydronium** /haɪˈdroʊniəm/, *adj.* (of a hydrogen ion) hydrated with a water molecule, forming the unstable group, $H_3O^+$; oxonium. Also, **hydroxonium.**

**hydropathy** /haɪˈdrɒpəθi/, *n.* the treatment of disease by the use of water; hydrotherapy. [HYDRO-[1] + -PATHY] – **hydropathic** /haɪdroʊˈpæθɪk/, **hydropathical** /haɪdroʊˈpæθɪkəl/, *adj.* – **hydropathist, hydropath** /ˈhaɪdrəpæθ/, *n.*

**hydrophane** /ˈhaɪdrəfeɪn/, *n.* a partly translucent variety of opal, which becomes more translucent when immersed in water. – **hydrophanous** /haɪˈdrɒfənəs/, *adj.*

**hydrophilic** /haɪdrəˈfɪlɪk/, *adj.* having an affinity for water.

**hydrophilic contact lenses,** *n. pl.* contact lenses which absorb water, thereby increasing their malleability.

**hydrophilous** /haɪˈdrɒfələs/, *adj.* (of flowers) pollinated by the agency of water currents.

**hydrophobia** /haɪdrəˈfoʊbiə/, *n. Pathol.* **1.** rabies. **2.** a morbid dread of water, resulting from the difficulty in swallowing water, as in rabies; any morbid or unnatural dread of water. [LL, from Gk: horror of water]

**hydrophobic** /haɪdrəˈfoʊbɪk/, *adj.* **1.** *Pathol.* of or pertaining to hydrophobia. **2.** *Chem.* having little or no affinity for water.

**hydrophone** /ˈhaɪdrəfoʊn/, *n.* **1.** an instrument employing the principles of the microphone, used to detect the flow of water through a pipe. **2.** a device for locating sources of sound under water, as for detecting submarines by the noise of their engines, etc. **3.** *Med.* an instrument used in auscultation, whereby sounds are intensified through a column of water.

**hydrophyte** /ˈhaɪdrəfaɪt/, *n.* a plant growing in water or very moist ground. – **hydrophytic** /haɪdrəˈfɪtɪk/, *adj.*

**hydropic** /haɪˈdrɒpɪk/, *adj.* →**dropsical.** Also, **hydropical.** [L *hydrōpicus,* from Gk *hydrōpikós;* replacing ME *ydropik,* from OF]

**hydroplane** /ˈhaɪdrəpleɪn/, *n., v.,* **-planed, -planing.** –*n.* **1.** an aeroplane provided with floats, or with a boatlike underpart, enabling it to light upon or ascend from water. **2.** an attachment to an aeroplane enabling it to glide on the water. **3.** a light, high-powered boat, usu. with one or more steps in the bottom, designed to plane along the surface of the water at very high speeds. **4.** a horizontal rudder for submerging or elevating a submarine boat. –*v.i.* **5.** to skim over water in the manner of a hydroplane. **6.** to travel in a hydroplane (boat).

**hydroponics** /haɪdrəˈpɒnɪks/, *n.* the cultivation of plants by placing the roots in liquid nutrient solutions rather than in soil; soilless growth of plants. [HYDRO-[1] + L *pōnere* place + -ICS] – **hydroponic,** *adj.*

**hydroquinone** /haɪdrəkwɪˈnoʊn/, *n.* **1.** a white, crystalline compound, $C_6H_4(OH)_2$, formed by the reduction of quinone, used to inhibit autoxidation reactions. **2.** *Pharm.* →**antipyretic.** Also, **hydroquinol** /haɪdrəˈkwɪnɒl/.

**hydroscope** /ˈhaɪdrəskoʊp/, *n.* an optical apparatus which enables the observer to view objects below the surface of the sea. – **hydroscopic** /haɪdrəˈskɒpɪk/, *adj.*

**hydrosol** /ˈhaɪdrəsɒl/, *n.* a colloidal suspension in water. [HYDRO-[1] + SOL(UTION)]

**hydrosome** /ˈhaɪdrəsoʊm/, *n.* the entire body of a compound hydrozoan. Also, **hydrosoma** /haɪdrəˈsoʊmə/.

**hydrosphere** /ˈhaɪdrəsfɪə/, *n.* the water on the surface of the globe; the water of the oceans.

**hydrostat** /ˈhaɪdrəstæt/, *n.* **1.** an electrical device for detecting the presence of water, as from overflow or leakage. **2.** any of various devices for preventing injury to a steam-boiler from a low water level.

**hydrostatic** /haɪdrəˈstætɪk/, *adj.* of or pertaining to hydrostatics. Also, **hydrostatical.** – **hydrostatically,** *adv.*

**hydrostatics** /haɪdrəˈstætɪks/, *n.* the statics of fluids, a branch of science usu. confined to the equilibrium and pressure of liquids.

**hydrosulphate** /haɪdroʊˈsʌlfeɪt/, *n.* a compound between sulphuric acid and an organic base, esp. with alkaloids.

**hydrosulphide** /haɪdroʊˈsʌlfaɪd/, *n.* **1.** a compound containing the univalent radical HS-. **2.** (loosely) a sulphide.

**hydrosulphite** /haɪdroʊˈsʌlfaɪt/, *n.* a salt containing $S_2O_4^{2-}$ ions, hyposulphite, dithionite; short for sodium hyposulphite, which is used as a bleach.

**hydrosulphuric acid** /haɪdroʊsʌlˌfjurɪk ˈæsəd/, *n.* an aqueous solution of hydrogen sulphide.

**hydrosulphurous** /haɪdroʊˈsʌlfərəs/, *adj.* →**hyposulphurous (acid).**

**hydrotaxis** /haɪdroʊˈtæksəs/, *n.* a movement of organisms towards or away from water.

**hydrotherapeutics** /ˌhaɪdroʊθɛrəˈpjutɪks/, *n.* that branch of therapeutics which deals with the curative use of water. – **hydrotherapeutic,** *adj.*

**hydrotherapy** /haɪdroʊˈθɛrəpi/, *n.* treatment of disease by means of water. – **hydrotherapic** /ˌhaɪdroʊθəˈræpɪk/, *adj.*

**hydrothermal** /haɪdroʊˈθɜməl/, *adj.* **1.** denoting or pertaining to the action of hot, aqueous solutions or gases within or on the surface of the earth. **2.** designating the results of such action.

**hydrothorax** /haɪdrəˈθɔræks/, *n.* an accumulation of serous fluid in one or both pleural cavities, often associated with kidney or heart failure. – **hydrothoracic** /haɪdrəθɔˈræsɪk/, *adj.*

**hydrotropic** /haɪdrəˈtrɒpɪk/, *adj.* **1.** turning or tending towards moisture, as growing organs. **2.** taking a particular direction with reference to moisture.

**hydrotropism** /haɪˈdrɒtrəpɪzəm/, *n.* **1.** a tropism in response to water. **2.** hydrotropic tendency or growth.

**hydrous** /ˈhaɪdrəs/, *adj.* **1.** containing water. **2.** *Chem.* containing water or its elements in some kind of union, as in hydrates or in hydroxides.

**hydroxide** /haɪˈdrɒksaɪd/, *n.* a compound containing the hydroxyl (OH) group.

**hydroxonium** /haɪdrɒkˈsoʊniəm/, *n.* →**hydronium.**

**hydroxy acid** /haɪˌdrɒksi ˈæsəd/, *n.* **1.** organic acid containing both a carboxyl and a hydroxyl group. **2.** one of a class of organic acids containing a hydroxyl group and showing properties of both an alcohol and acid.

**hydroxyl** /haɪˈdrɒksəl/, *n.* a univalent radical or group, OH, containing hydrogen and oxygen.

**hydroxylamine** /haɪˌdrɒksələˈmin, -ˈlæmən/, *n.* an unstable, weakly basic, crystalline compound, $NH_2OH$, used as a reducing agent, analytical reagent, and chemical intermediate.

**hydrozoan** /haɪdrəˈzoʊən/, *adj.* **1.** pertaining to the Hydrozoa, a class of coelenterates that comprises solitary or colonial polyps and free-swimming medusas. –*n.* **2.** a member of the

Hydrozoa. [NL *Hydrozoōn* (from *hydro-*, combining form of *hydra* (def. 2) + Gk *zôion* animal) + -AN]

**hyena** /haɪˈinə/, *n.* any of the nocturnal carnivores of the family Hyaenidae, feeding chiefly on carrion, as *Hyaena hyaena,* the **striped laughing hyena**, an African and Asiatic species about the size of a large dog, *H. brunnea,* the **brown hyena** of southern Africa, and *Crocuta crocuta,* the **spotted hyena** of Africa south of the Sahara. Also, **hyaena.** [L *hyaena,* from Gk *hýaina,* from *hýs* hog; replacing ME *hiene,* from OF]

striped laughing hyena

**hyeto-**, a word element meaning 'rain'. [combining form of Gk *hyetós*]

**hyetograph** /ˈhaɪətəgræf, -graf/, *n.* **1.** an instrument for collecting, measuring, and recording rainfall. **2.** a map or chart showing average rainfall in a particular locality.

**hygiene** /ˈhaɪdʒin/, *n.* the science which deals with the preservation of health. Also, **hygienics** /haɪˈdʒinɪks/. [F, from Gk *hygieinós* healthful, sanitary]

**hygienic** /haɪˈdʒinɪk/, *adj.* **1.** sanitary; clean. **2.** pertaining to hygiene. – **hygienically,** *adv.*

**hygienist** /ˈhaɪdʒinəst/, *n.* an expert in hygiene. Also, **hygeist** /ˈhaɪdʒiəst/, **hygieist** /ˈhaɪdʒiəst/.

**hygric** /ˈhaɪgrɪk/, *adj.* pertaining to water or moisture.

**hygro-**, a word element meaning 'wet', 'moist'. Also, before vowels, **hygr-**, [Gk, combining form of *hygrós*]

**hygrogram** /ˈhaɪgrəgræm/, *n.* a record of the relative humidity of the atmosphere, as measured by a hygrograph.

**hygrograph** /ˈhaɪgrəgræf, -graf/, *n.* a self-recording hygrometer.

**hygrometer** /haɪˈgrɒmətə/, *n.* an instrument for determing the humidity of the atmosphere.

**hygrometric** /haɪgrəˈmɛtrɪk/, *adj.* pertaining to the hygrometer or hygrometry.

**hygrometry** /haɪˈgrɒmətri/, *n.* the branch of physics that examines the humidity of air and gases.

**hygrophilous** /haɪˈgrɒfɪləs/, *adj.* (of plants), growing in a moist or damp environment.

**hygrophyte** /ˈhaɪgrəfaɪt/, *n.* a plant which grows in a damp or moist habitat.

**hygroscope** /ˈhaɪgrəskoʊp/, *n.* an instrument which indicates the approximate humidity of the air.

**hygroscopic** /haɪgrəˈskɒpɪk/, *adj.* absorbing or attracting moisture from the air.

**hygrostat** /ˈhaɪgrəstæt/, *n.* an apparatus for keeping the humidity constant; a humidistat.

**hylo-**, a word element meaning 'wood', 'matter'. [Gk, combining form of *hýlē*]

**hylozoism** /haɪləˈzoʊɪzəm/, *n.* the doctrine that matter is inseparable from life, which is a property of matter. [HYLO- + Gk *zōḗ* life + -ISM] – **hylozoist,** *n.* – **hylozoistic** /haɪləzoʊˈɪstɪk/, *adj.* – **hylozoistically** /haɪləzoʊˈɪstɪkli/, *adv.*

**hymen** /ˈhaɪmən/, *n.* a fold of mucous membrane partially closing the external orifice of the vagina. [Gk: thin skin, membrane]

**hymeneal** /haɪməˈniəl/, *adj.* **1.** pertaining to marriage. *–n.* **2.** marriage song.

**hymenium** /haɪˈminiəm/, *n., pl.* **-nia** /-niə/. the spore-producing layer in most ascomycete or basidiomycete fungi.

**hymenopter** /ˈhaɪmənɒptə/, *n.* →**hymenopteron.** – **hymenopteran** /haɪməˈnɒptərən/, *adj., n.*

**hymenopteron** /haɪməˈnɒptərən/, *n., pl.* **-tera** /-tərə/. a hymenopterous insect.

**hymenopterous** /haɪməˈnɒptərəs/, *adj.* belonging or pertaining to the Hymenoptera, an order of insects having (when winged) four membranous wings, and including the wasps, bees, ants, ichneumon flies, sawflies, etc. [Gk *hymenópteros* membrane-winged]

**hymn** /hɪm/, *n.* **1.** a song or ode in praise or honour of God, a deity, a nation, etc. *–v.t.* **2.** to praise or celebrate in a hymn; express in a hymn. *–v.i.* **3.** to sing hymns. [LL *hymnus,* from Gk *hýmnos;* replacing ME *ymne* (from OF) and ME *ymyn,* OE *ym(e)n,* from LL (Eccl.) *ymnus*] – **hymnlike,** *adj.*

**hymnal** /ˈhɪmnəl/, *n.* **1.** Also, **hymnbook.** a book of hymns for use in divine worship. *–adj.* **2.** of or pertaining to hymns.

**hymnist** /ˈhɪmnəst/, *n.* a composer of hymns.

**hymnody** /ˈhɪmnədi/, *n.* **1.** the singing or the composition of hymns or sacred songs. **2.** hymns collectively. [ML *hymnōdia,* from Gk *hymnōidía* the singing of a hymn] – **hymnodist,** *n.*

**hymnology** /hɪmˈnɒlədʒi/, *n.* **1.** the study of hymns, their history, classification, etc. **2.** the composition of hymns. **3.** hymns collectively. – **hymnologic** /hɪmnəˈlɒdʒɪk/, **hymnological** /hɪmnəˈlɒdʒɪkəl/, *adj.* – **hymnologist,** *n.*

**hyoid** /ˈhaɪɔɪd/, *adj.* **1.** denoting or pertaining to a U-shaped bone at the root of the tongue in man, or a corresponding bone or collection of bones in animals. *–n.* **2.** the hyoid bone, cartilage, arch, ligament, etc. [NL *hyoïdēs,* from Gk *hyoeidḗs* shaped like the letter upsilon]

**hyoscine** /ˈhaɪəsin/, *n.* **1.** an alkaloid chemically identical with scopolamine, used as a mydriatic, muscle relaxant, cerebral depressant, etc. [Trademark; syncopated var. of HYOSCYAMINE]

**hyoscyamine** /haɪəˈsaɪəmin, -mən/, *n.* a poisonous alkaloid, $C_{17}H_{23}NO_3$, isomeric with atropine, obtained from henbane and other solanaceous plants, used as a sedative, mydriatic, etc. [L *hyoscyamus* (from Gk *hyoskýamos* henbane, lit., hog's bean) + -INE[2]]

**hyp-**, variant of **hypo-**, before most vowels, as in *hypaesthesia.*

**hyp.**, **1.** hypotenuse. **2.** hypothesis. **3.** hypothetical.

**hypabyssal** /haɪpəˈbɪsəl/, *adj.* **1.** of or pertaining to minor intrusions such as sills and dykes, and to the rocks in such intrusions which have crystallised under conditions intermediate between the plutonic and extrusive classes of rocks. **2.** →**intermediate**[2] (def. 2).

**hypaesthesia** /haɪpəsˈθiziə, ˈθiʒə/, *n.* diminished sense of pain, heat, cold, or touch. Also, *Chiefly U.S.,* **hypesthesia.** – **hypaesthesic** /haɪpəsˈθisɪk/, *adj.*

**hypaethral** /haɪˈpiθrəl/, *adj.* open to the sky or having no roof, as a building (used esp. of classical architecture). [L *hypaethrus* (from Gk *hýpaithros* under the sky) + -AL[1]]

**hypallage** /haɪˈpælədʒi/, *n.* a figure of speech in which two elements are reversed.

**hypanthium** /haɪˈpænθiəm/, *n., pl.* **-thia** /-θiə/. a fleshy, cup-shaped part of some flowers situated above or below the ovary and bearing the sepals, petais, and stamens on its rim.

**hype**[1] /haɪp/, *n., v.,* **hyped, hyping.** *U.S. –n.* **1.** fraud; racket; swindle. **2.** hypocrisy; pretentiousness. *–v.t.* **3.** to bluff; con, as by false publicity. [orig. unknown]

**hype**[2] /haɪp/, *n., v.,* **hyped, hyping.** *Colloq. –n.* **1.** a hypodermic needle. **2.** a drug addict. *–v.t.* **3.** to stimulate; make excited (fol. by *up*). **4.** to increase the power, speed, etc. of a car engine, etc. (usu. fol. by *up*): *he hyped up his F.J.* **5.** to persuade, exhort to greater achievement, as of a coach convincing a team that success can be theirs. [shortened form of HYPODERMIC]

**hyped-up** /ˈhaɪpt-ʌp/, *adj.* **1.** improved in performance, esp. of a car which has been modified for some special race or purpose and is no longer a standard model. **2.** stimulated; excited.

**hyper** /ˈhaɪpə/, *adj. Colloq.* nervous; on edge; over-stimulated.

**hyper-**, **1.** a prefix meaning 'over', and usu. implying excess or exaggeration. **2.** *Chem.* the same as **super-**, indicating the highest of a series of compounds: *hyperchloric acid.* The prefix *per-* is now generally used for *hyper-*, as in *perchloric, permanganic,* etc. [Gk, representing *hypér,* prep., over, above, beyond, as adv. overmuch, beyond measure; akin to SUPER, OVER]

**hyperacidity** /haɪpərəˈsɪdəti/, *n.* excessive acidity as of the gastric juice. – **hyperacid** /haɪpərˈæsəd/, *adj.*

**hyperactive** /haɪpərˈæktɪv/, *adj.* overactive.

**hyperacusis** /haɪpərəˈkjusəs/, *n.* excessive acuteness of the sense of hearing. [NL, from Gk *hyper-* HYPER- + *ákousis* hearing]

**hyperaemia** /haɪpəˈrimiə/, *n.* an increase in the blood in any part of the body. Also, *Chiefly U.S.,* **hyperemia.** [NL. See HYPER-, -EMIA] – **hyperaemic,** *adj.*

**hyperaesthesia** /haɪpərəs'θiziə, 'θiʒə/, *n.* a straining or intensification of the normal senses. Also, *Chiefly U.S.*, **hyperesthesia.** – **hyperaesthetic** /haɪpərəs'θɛtɪk/, *adj.*

**hyperalgesia** /ˌhaɪpəræl'dʒiziə/, *n.* an exaggerated feeling or sense of pain. [NL, from Gk *hyper-* HYPER- + *álgēsis* sense of pain + *-ia* -IA] – **hyperalgesic,** *adj.*

**hyperbaric** /haɪpə'bærɪk/, *adj.* of or pertaining to pressures higher than normal atmospheric pressure. [HYPER + BAR(O)- + -IC]

**hyperbola** /haɪ'pɜbələ/, *n., pl.* **-las.** a curve consisting of two distinct and similar branches, formed by the intersection of a plane with a right circular cone when the plane makes a greater angle with the base than does the generator of the cone. [NL, from Gk *hyperbolḗ*, lit., a throwing beyond. See HYPERBOLE]

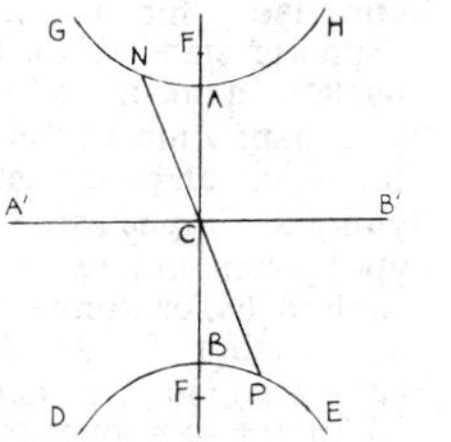

hyperbola: DBE, GAH, opposite branches of a hyperbola; F, F, foci; C, centre; AB, transverse axis; A' B', conjugate axis; NCP, diameter

**hyperbole** /haɪ'pɜbəli/, *n.* obvious exaggeration, for effect; an extravagant statement not intended to be taken literally. [L, from Gk: a throwing beyond, excess, hyperbole, also a hyperbola]

**hyperbolic** /haɪpə'bɒlɪk/, *adj.* **1.** having the nature of hyperbole; exaggerated. **2.** using hyperbole, or exaggerating. **3.** of or pertaining to the hyperbola. Also, **hyperbolical.** – **hyperbolically,** *adv.*

**hyperbolic functions** /– 'fʌŋkʃənz/, *n.* six mathematical functions which express angles in terms of distances between points on a hyperbola; analogous to the trigonometrical rations, they are written *sinh, cosh, tanh, cosech sech, cotanh.* Sinh $x$ is defined as $\frac{1}{2}(e^x - e^{-x})$ and cosh $x$ as $\frac{1}{2}(e^x + e^{-x})$. The remaining four functions are derived from sinh and cosh on the same basis as that by which the trigonometrical ratios are derived from sin and cos.

**hyperbolise** /haɪ'pɜbəlaɪz/, *v.,* **-lised, -lising.** *–v.i.* **1.** to use hyperbole; exaggerate. *–v.t.* **2.** to represent or express with hyperbole or exaggeration. Also, **hyperbolize.**

**hyperbolism** /haɪ'pɜbəlɪzəm/, *n.* the use of hyperbole.

**hyperboloid** /haɪ'pɜbəlɔɪd/, *n.* a quadric surface having a finite centre and some of its plane sections hyperbolas.

**hyperborean** /haɪpə'bɔriən/, *adj.* arctic; frigid. [in Greek mythology, one of a people supposed to live in a land beyond Boreas, the north wind; LL *Hyperboreānus,* in L *Hyperboreus,* from Gk *Hyperbóreos* beyond Boreas, the north wind]

**hypercorrect** /haɪpəkə'rɛkt/, *adj.* excessively correct. – **hypercorrection,** *n.*

**hypercritic** /haɪpə'krɪtɪk/, *n.* one who is excessively or captiously critical.

**hypercritical** /haɪpə'krɪtɪkəl/, *adj.* excessively critical; overcritical. – **hypercritically,** *adv.*

**hyperemesis** /haɪpər'ɛməsəs/, *n.* excessive vomiting, esp. **hyperemesis gravidarum,** excessive vomiting occurring during pregnancy.

**hyperemia** /haɪpər'imiə/, *n. Chiefly U.S.* →**hyperaemia.** – **hyperemic,** *adj.*

**hyperesthesia** /haɪpərəs'θiziə, 'θiʒə/, *n. Chiefly U.S.* →**hyperaesthesia.** – **hyperesthetic** /haɪpərəs'θɛtik/, *adj.*

**hypereutectoid** /ˌhaɪpəju'tɛktɔɪd/, *adj.* **1.** (of steel) containing more carbon than eutectoid steel, i.e. more than 0.9 per cent. **2.** (of any alloy) containing more of the alloying element than the eutectoid element.

**hyperextension** /haɪpərəks'tɛnʃən/, *n.* **1.** the extension of a part beyond the plane of the body, as when the arm is drawn back to its maximum extent. **2.** the state of being so drawn.

**hyperfine structure** /ˌhaɪpəfaɪn 'strʌktʃə/, *n.* **1.** the occurrence of very closely spaced energy levels in an atom, due to coupling between the momentum of the orbital electrons and the spin of the nucleus. **2.** the splitting of certain spectral lines due either to the effect described in def. 1 or to the presence of different isotopes.

**hyperfocal distance** /ˌhaɪpəfoʊkəl 'dɪstəns/, *n.* the distance in front of a camera lens beyond which all objects are in focus, for a given f number.

**hyperglycaemia** /haɪpəglaɪ'simiə/, *n.* an excessive amount of glucose in the blood. Also, *U.S.,* **hyperglycemia.**

**hypergolic** /haɪpə'gɒlɪk/, *adj.* (of a rocket fuel) igniting spontaneously when mixed with an oxidant.

**hyperirritability** /haɪpərˌɪrətə'bɪləti/, *n.* increased irritability.

**hyperkeratosis** /ˌhaɪpəkɛrə'toʊsəs/, *n., pl.* **-ses** /-siz/. **1.** an enlargement, discolouration and roughening of a part of the outer corneal layer of the skin, usu. as a result of exposure to the sun. **2.** any of various conditions involving hyperkeratoses. [NL, from Gk *hyper-* HYPER- + *kéras* horn + *-osis* -OSIS]

**hyperkinesia** /haɪpəkə'niʒə, -kaɪ-/, *n.* abnormal amount of muscular action; spasm. [NL, from Gk *hyper-* HYPER- + *kī́nēsis* movement + *-ia* -IA] – **hyperkinetic** /haɪpəkə'nɛtɪk, -kaɪ-/, *adj.*

**hypermarket** /'haɪpəmakət/, *n. Chiefly U.S., Brit.* an extremely large self-service store, usu. situated outside a town, having an extensive car park and selling a wide range of goods. Also, **hypermart.**

**hypermeter** /haɪ'pɜmətə/, *n.* a verse or line having one or more syllables at the end in addition to those proper to the metre. – **hypermetric** /haɪpə'mɛtrɪk/, **hypermetrical** /haɪpə'mɛtrɪkəl/, *adj.*

**hypermetropia** /haɪpəmə'troʊpiə/, *n.* a condition of the eye in which parallel rays are focused behind the retina, distant objects being seen more distinctly than near ones; long-sightedness. [NL, from Gk *hypérmetros* beyond measure + *-opia* -OPIA]

**hypermetropic** /haɪpəmə'trɒpɪk/, *adj.* pertaining to or affected with hypermetropia; long-sighted.

**hyperon** /'haɪpərɒn/, *n.* any of a group of elementary particles which have short lives and greater mass than a neutron.

**hyperopia** /haɪpə'roʊpiə/, *n.* →**hypermetropia.** – **hyperopic** /haɪpə'rɒpɪk/, *adj.*

**hyperosmia** /haɪpə'roʊzmiə/, *n.* increased acuteness in the sense of smell.

**hyperostosis** /haɪpərəs'toʊsəs/, *n., pl.* **-ses** /-siz/. **1.** an increase or outgrowth of bony tissue. **2.** an overgrowth of bone.

**hyperparasite** /haɪpə'pærəsaɪt/, *n.* an organism which lives parasitically in or on another parasite.

**hyperphysical** /haɪpə'fɪzɪkəl/, *adj.* above or beyond the physical; immaterial; supernatural.

**hyperpiesia** /haɪpəpaɪ'iziə/, *n.* unusually high blood pressure. [NL, from Gk *hyper-* HYPER- + *píesis* pressure + *-ia* -IA]

**hyperpituitarism** /haɪpəpɪ'tjuətərɪzəm/, *n.* **1.** overactivity of the pituitary gland. **2.** the resultant condition, as gigantism or acromegaly.

**hyperplasia** /haɪpə'plæziə/, *n.* **1.** *Pathol., Bot.* abnormal multiplication of cells. **2.** *Pathol.* enlargement of a part due to numerical increase of its cells. – **hyperplasic, hyperplastic** /haɪpə'plæstɪk/, *adj.*

**hyperploid** /'haɪpəplɔɪd/, *adj.* **1.** having or being a chromosome number which is more than an exact multiple of the monoploid number. *–n.* **2.** a cell or organism which is hyperploid. [HYPER- + (DI)PLOID]

**hyperpnoea** /haɪpə'pniə, haɪpə'niə/, *n.* increased intake and depth of respiration. Also, *Chiefly U.S.,* **hyperpnea.** [NL, from Gk *hyper-* HYPER- + *pnoiḗ* breathing]

**hyperpyrexia** /haɪpəpaɪ'rɛksiə/, *n.* an abnormally high fever. – **hyperpyretic** /haɪpəpaɪ'rɛtɪk/, **hyperpyrexial,** *adj.*

**hyperreactive** /haɪpəri'æktɪv/, *adj.* reacting excessively strongly to certain stimuli.

**hypersensitive** /haɪpə'sɛnsətɪv/, *adj.* **1.** excessively sensitive. **2.** *Pathol.* allergic to a substance to which a normal individual does not react. – **hypersensitiveness, hypersensitivity** /ˌhaɪpəsɛnsə'tɪvəti/, *n.*

**hypersonic** /haɪpə'sɒnɪk/, *adj.* describing a velocity in excess of mach 5. See **mach number.**

**hyperspace** /'haɪpəspeɪs/, *n.* a Euclidean space of more than three dimensions.

**hyperstereoscopy** /ˌhaɪpəsteri'ɒskəpi/, *n.* stereoscopic viewing in which the relief effect is noticeably exaggerated, caused by the extension of the camera base; exaggerated stereo.

**hypersthene** /'haɪpəsθin/, *n.* a common mineral of the

pyroxene group, iron magnesium silicate, occurring in green to black masses as an important constituent of basic igneous rocks. [HYPER- + Gk *sthénos* strength (with reference to frangibility)] – **hypersthenic** /haɪpəs'θɛnɪk/, *adj.*

**hypertension** /haɪpə'tɛnʃən/, *n.* **1.** elevation of the blood pressure, esp. the diastolic pressure. **2.** an arterial disease of which this is the outstanding sign.

**hypertensive** /haɪpə'tɛnsɪv/, *adj.* of, exhibiting or pertaining to hypertension, esp. of blood; tending to raise blood pressure.

**hyperthyroidism** /haɪpə'θaɪrɔɪdɪzəm/, *n.* **1.** overactivity of the thyroid gland. **2.** a pathological condition, consisting of a complex of symptoms, produced by this. – **hyperthyroid,** *n.*

**hypertonic** /haɪpə'tɒnɪk/, *adj.* **1.** *Physiol.* possessing too much tone. **2.** *Chem.* denoting a solution of higher osmotic pressure than another solution with which it is compared.

**hypertrophy** /haɪ'pɜtrəfi/, *n., pl.* **-phies,** *v.,* **-phied, -phying.** *–n.* **1.** *Pathol., Bot.* enlargement of a part or organ; excessive growth. **2.** excessive growth or accumulation of any kind. *–v.t., v.i.* **3.** to affect with or undergo hypertrophy. – **hypertrophic** /haɪpə'trɒfɪk/, *adj.*

**hyperventilate** /haɪpə'vɛntəleɪt/, *v.i.,* **-ated, -ating.** to be affected by hyperventilation. [backformation from HYPERVENTILATION]

**hyperventilation** /ˌhaɪpəvɛntə'leɪʃən/, *n.* the excessive exposure of the lungs to oxygen resulting in a rapid loss of carbon dioxide from the blood; abnormally increased respiration.

**hypesthesia** /haɪpəs'θiʒə/, *n. Chiefly U.S.* →**hypaesthesia.** – **hypesthesic,** *adj.*

**hypethral** /haɪ'piθrəl/, *adj. Chiefly U.S.* →**hypaethral.**

**hypha** /'haɪfə/, *n., pl.* **-phae** /-fi/. (in fungi) one of the threadlike elements of the mycelium. [NL, from Gk *hyphḗ* web] – **hyphal,** *adj.*

**hyphen** /'haɪfən/, *n.* **1.** a short stroke (-) used to connect the parts of a compound word or the parts of a word divided for any purpose. *–v.t.* **2.** hyphenate. [LL, from Gk: name of sign, special use of *hyphén,* adv., together, from *hypó* under + *hén,* neut. of *heîs* one]

**hyphenate** /'haɪfəneɪt/, *v.,* **-nated, -nating,** *adj.* *–v.t.* **1.** to join by a hyphen. **2.** to write with a hyphen. *–adj.* **3.** hyphenated. – **hyphenation** /haɪfə'neɪʃən/, *n.*

**hyphenise** /'haɪfənaɪz/, *v.t.,* **-nised, -nising.** →**hyphenate.** Also, **hyphenize.**

**hypnagogic** /hɪpnə'gɒdʒɪk/, *adj.* pertaining to the state of one who is not yet fully asleep during which dream-like images may be experienced. Also, **hypnogogic.** [HYPNO- + *-agogic,* from Gk *-agōgikós* leading]

**hypno-,** a word element meaning 'sleep' or 'hypnosis', as in *hypnology.* Also, before vowels (usu.), **hypn-.** [Gk, combining form of *hýpnos* sleep]

**hypnoanalysis** /ˌhɪpnouə'næləsəs/, *n.* a method employed by some psychoanalysts who attempt to secure analytic data, free associations, and early emotional reactions while the patient is under hypnosis.

**hypnogenesis** /hɪpnou'dʒɛnəsəs/, *n.* the inducing of a hypnotic state.

**hypnogogic** /hɪpnə'goudʒɪk/, *adj.* of or pertaining to the state of mind between sleeping and walking during which images from the subconscious enter the conscious mind.

**hypnoid** /'hɪpnɔɪd/, *adj.* Also, **hypnoidal** /hɪp'nɔɪdl/. relating to a state resembling sleep or hypnosis.

**hypnoidal** /hɪp'nɔɪdl/, *adj.* a mild state of hypnosis; a quasi-hypnotic state. Also, **hypnoid.**

**hypnology** /hɪp'nɒlədʒi/, *n.* the science dealing with the phenomena of sleep or hypnosis. – **hypnologic** /hɪpnə'lɒdʒɪk/, **hypnological** /hɪpnə'lɒdʒɪkəl/, *adj.* – **hypnologist,** *n.*

**hypnopaedia** /hɪpnou'pidiə/, *n.* teaching a person by words uttered while he is asleep. [HYPNO- + Gk *paideía* education]

**hypnopompic** /hɪpnou'pɒmpɪk/, *adj.* pertaining to the state of one who is not yet fully awake during which dream-like images may be experienced. [HYPNO- + Gk *pompḗ* a sending out + -IC]

**hypnosis** /hɪp'nousəs/, *n. pl.* **-ses** /-siz/. **1.** *Psychol.* a trance-like mental state induced in a cooperative subject by suggestion. **2.** a sleepy condition. **3.** →**hypnotism.** [NL, from Gk *hypnoûn* put to sleep]

**hypnotherapy** /hɪpnou'θɛrəpi/, *n.* treatment of disease by means of hypnotism. – **hypnotherapeutic** /ˌhɪpnouθɛrə'pjutɪk/, *adj.*

**hypnotic** /hɪp'nɒtɪk/, *adj.* **1.** pertaining to hypnosis or hypnotism. **2.** susceptible to hypnotism, as a person. **3.** hypnotised. **4.** inducing sleep. *–n.* **5.** an agent or drug that produces sleep; a sedative. **6.** one subject to hypnotic influence. **7.** a person under the influence of hypnotism. [LL *hypnōticus,* from Gk *hypnōtikós* inclined to sleep] – **hypnotically,** *adv.*

**hypnotise** /'hɪpnətaɪz/, *v.t.,* **-tised, -tising.** to put in the hypnotic state. Also, **hypnotize.** – **hypnotisable,** *adj.* – **hypnotisation** /hɪpnətaɪ'zeɪʃən/, *n.* – **hypnotiser,** *n.*

**hypnotism** /'hɪpnətɪzəm/, *n.* **1.** the science dealing with the induction of hypnosis. **2.** the induction of hypnosis.

**hypnotist** /'hɪpnətəst/, *n.* one who hypnotises.

**hypo**[1] /'haɪpou/, *n.* sodium thiosulphate (sometimes called sodium hyposulphite), $Na_2S_2O_3 \cdot 5H_2O$, a photographic fixing agent. [short for HYPOSULPHITE]

**hypo**[2] /'haɪpou/, *n. Colloq.* a hypodermic needle or injection. [short for HYPODERMIC]

**hypo-,** **1.** a prefix meaning 'under', either in place or in degree ('less', 'less than'). **2.** *Chem.* a prefix applied to the inorganic acids (as *hypochlorous acid*) and to their salts (as *potassium hypochlorite*) to indicate a low valency state for the designated element. Also, **hyp-.** [Gk, representing *hypó,* prep. and adv., under; akin to SUB-]

**Hypo-,** a prefix indicating the plagal form of a mode: *the Hypodorian mode.* [Gk *hypó* under (the final of the plagal mode lies a fourth below that of the normal mode)]

**hypoacidity** /ˌhaɪpouə'sɪdəti/, *n.* acidity in a lesser degree than is usual or normal, as of the gastric juice.

**hypoactivity** /ˌhaɪpouæk'tɪvəti/, *n.* diminished activity, esp. applied to the secretory activity of a gland.

**hypoblast** /'haɪpəblæst/, *n.* the inner layer of a gastrula, consisting of endoblast, or endoblast and mesoblast. – **hypoblastic** /haɪpə'blæstɪk/, *adj.*

**hypocalcaemia** /ˌhaɪpoukæl'simiə/, *n.* a deficiency of calcium in the blood.

**hypocaust** /'haɪpəkɔst/, *n.* a hollow space or system of flues in the floor or walls of a Roman building or room, which received and distributed the heat from a furnace. [L *hypocaustum,* from Gk *hypókauston* room heated from below]

**hypocentre** /'haɪpousɛntə/, *n.* the point within the earth where an earthquake originates.

**hypochlorite** /haɪpə'klɔraɪt/, *n.* a salt or ester of hypochlorous acid.

**hypochlorous acid** /haɪpəˌklɔrəs 'æsəd/, *n.* an acid, HOCl whose solutions have strong bleaching properties.

**hypochondria** /haɪpə'kɒndriə/, *n.* **1.** Also, **hypochondriasis** /haɪpəkɒn'draɪəsəs/. *Psychol.* a morbid condition characterised by depressed spirits and fancies of ill health, referable to the physical condition of the body or one of its parts. **2.** (*orig. as pl.*) the parts of the body under the cartilage of the breastbone and above the navel. [LL: pl., the abdomen, from Gk *hypochóndria* (neut. pl.) def. 2; orig. thought to be the seat of melancholy]

**hypochondriac** /haɪpə'kɒndriæk/, *adj.* Also, **hypochondriacal** /haɪpəkɒn'draɪəkəl/. **1.** pertaining to or suffering from hypochondria or morbid depression. **2.** of or pertaining to the hypochondria (def. 2): *the hypochondriac regions.* *–n.* **3.** a person suffering from or subject to hypochondria. – **hypochondriacally,** *adv.*

**hypochondrium** /haɪpə'kɒndriəm/, *n., pl.* **-dria** /-driə/. **1.** either of two regions of the human abdomen, situated on opposite sides (left and right) of the epigastrium, above the lumbar regions. **2.** a corresponding region in lower animals. [NL]

**hypocorism** /haɪ'pɒkərɪzəm/, *n.* **1.** a pet name, esp. a diminutive: *Betty for Elizabeth.* **2.** →**euphemism.** [LL, from Gk *hypokórisma* endearing name]

**hypocoristic** /haɪpəkə'rɪstɪk/, *adj.* endearing, as a pet name; diminutive; euphemistic. [Gk *hypokoristikós*] – **hypocoristically,** *adv.* – **hypocorism** /haɪ'pɒkərɪzəm/, *n.*

**hypocotyl** /haɪpə'kɒtl/, *n.* (in the embryo of a plant) that part of the stem below cotyledons.

[HYPO- + COTYL(EDON)] – **hypocotylous,** *adj.*

**hypocrisy** /hɪ'pɒkrəsi/, *n., pl.* **-sies. 1.** the act of pretending to have a character or beliefs, principles, etc., that one does not possess. **2.** pretence of virtue or piety; false goodness. [ME *ypocrisie,* from OF, from LL *hypocrisis,* from Gk *hypókrisis* acting of a part, pretence]

**hypocrite** /'hɪpəkrɪt/, *n.* one given to hypocrisy; one who feigns virtue or piety; a pretender. [ME *ypocrite,* from OF, from LL *hypocrita,* from Gk *hypokritḗs,* actor, pretender, hypocrite] – **hypocritical** /hɪpə'krɪtɪkəl/, *adj.* – **hypocritically** /hɪpə'krɪtɪkli/, *adv.*

P C H R

diagram of a seedling: H, hypocotyl: C, cotyledons; P, plumule; R, roots

**hypocycloid** /haɪpə'saɪklɔɪd/, *n.* a curve generated by the motion of a point on the circumference of a circle which rolls internally, without slipping, on a given circle. – **hypocycloidal** /haɪpəsaɪ'klɔɪdl/, *adj.*

**hypoderm** /'haɪpədɜm/, *n.* **1.** *Zool.* the epidermis of an arthropod, situated beneath the cuticle. **2.** *Bot.* hypodermis. – **hypodermal** /haɪpə'dɜməl/, *adj.*

**hypodermic** /haɪpə'dɜmɪk/, *adj.* **1.** characterised by the introduction of medical remedies under the skin: *hypodermic injection.* **2.** introduced under the skin: *a hypodermic needle.* **3.** pertaining to parts under the skin. **4.** lying under the skin, as tissue. *–n.* **5.** a hypodermic remedy. **6.** a hypodermic injection. **7.** the administration of drugs into subcutaneous body tissues. **8.** a hypodermic syringe. – **hypodermically,** *adv.*

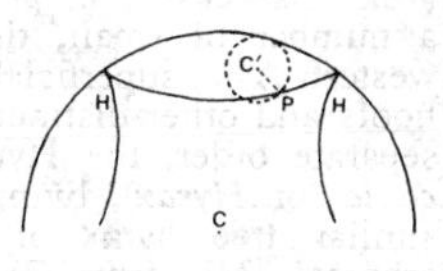

H, hypocycloid traced by a point P; C', centre of moving circle; C, centre of fixed circle

**hypodermic needle** /– 'nidl/, *n.* a hollow needle used to inject solutions subcutaneously.

**hypodermic syringe** /– sə'rɪndʒ/, *n.* a small glass piston or barrel syringe having a detachable hollow needle used to inject solutions subcutaneously; now also made of other materials, as plastics.

**hypodermis** /haɪpə'dɜməs/, *n.* **1.** the surface epithelium of an invertebrate when covered over by the non-cellular secretion that it produces. **2.** *Bot.* a tissue or layer of cells beneath the epidermis. [NL]

**hypo-eutectoid** /haɪpə-ju'tɛktɔɪd/, *adj.* **1.** (of steel) containing less carbon than eutectoid steel, i.e. less than 0.9 percent. **2.** (of any alloy) containing less of the alloying element than the eutectoid element.

**hypogastric** /haɪpə'gæstrɪk/, *adj.* **1.** situated below the stomach. **2.** of or pertaining to the hypogastrium.

**hypogastrium** /haɪpə'gæstriəm/, *n., pl.* **-tria** /-triə/. **1.** the lower part of the abdomen. **2.** the region between the right and left iliac regions. [NL, from Gk *hypogástrion,* properly neut. of *hypogástrios* abdominal]

**hypogeal** /haɪpə'dʒiəl/, *adj.* underground; subterranean. [L *hypogēus* (from Gk *hypógeios* underground) + -AL[1]]

**hypogene** /'haɪpədʒin/, *adj.* **1.** formed beneath the earth's surface as granite (opposed to *epigene*). **2.** (of mineral or ore deposits) formed by ascending waters (opposed to *supergene*). [HYPO- + *-gene* (var. of -GEN)]

**hypogenous** /haɪ'pɒdʒənəs/, *adj.* growing beneath, or on the undersurface, as fungi on leaves.

**hypogeous** /haɪpə'dʒiəs, hɪpə-/, *adj.* **1.** underground; subterranean. **2.** *Bot.* growing or remaining underground. [L *hypogēus,* from Gk *hypógeios*]

**hypogeum** /haɪpə'dʒiəm/, *n., pl.* **-gea** /-'dʒiə/. **1.** the underground part of a building. **2.** an underground structure or burial chamber; an artificial cave. [L, from Gk *hypógeion,* neut. of *hypógeios* underground]

**hypoglossal** /haɪpə'glɒsəl/, *adj.* situated under the tongue wholly or in part. [HYPO- + Gk *glôssa* tongue + -AL[1]]

**hypoglossal nerve** /– 'nɜv/, *n.* either of the last pair of cranial nerves which gives rise to the movements of the tongue; twelfth cranial nerve.

**hypoglycaemia** /ˌhaɪpoʊglaɪ'simiə/, *n.* a decreased sugar level in the blood. Also, *U.S.,* **hypoglycemia.** – **hypoglycaemic,** *adj.*

**hypognathous** /haɪ'pɒgnəθəs/, *adj.* **1.** having a protruding lower jaw. **2.** having downwardly directed mouthparts.

**hypogynous** /haɪ'pɒdʒənəs/, *adj.* **1.** situated on the receptacle beneath the pistil, as stamens, etc. **2.** having stamens, etc., so arranged. – **hypogyny,** *n.*

**hypoid** /'haɪpɔɪd/, *adj.* pertaining to a gear system, the cogs of which have tooth shapes generated by a hypocycloidal curve, and much used in motor car transmissions. [shortened form of HYPOCYCLOID]

**hypokinesia** /ˌhaɪpoʊkaɪ'niziə/, *n.* muscular movement that has decreased abnormally. Also, **hypokinesis.** – **hypokinetic,** *adj.*

**hypomagnesaemia** /ˌhaɪpoʊmægnə'simiə/, *n.* deficiency of magnesium in the blood of cattle constituting a prime factor in grass tetany or milk fever. Also, *U.S.,* **hypomagnesemia.** [NL]

**hyponasty** /'haɪpənæsti/, *n.* increased growth along the lower surface of an organ or part, causing it to bend upwards. [HYPO- + Gk *nastós* pressed close, compact + -Y[3]] – **hyponastic** /haɪpə'næstɪk/, *adj.*

**hyponitrite** /haɪpə'naɪtraɪt/, *n.* a salt or ester of hyponitrous acid.

**hyponitrous acid** /ˌhaɪpənaɪtrəs 'æsəd/, *n.* an unstable crystalline acid, $H_2N_2O_2$.

**hypopharynx** /haɪpoʊ'færɪŋks/, *n.* the part of the pharynx into which the larynx opens extending from the epiglottis to the top of the oesophagus.

**hypophosphate** /haɪpə'fɒsfeɪt/, *n.* a salt or ester of hypophosphoric acid.

**hypophosphite** /haɪpə'fɒsfaɪt/, *n.* a salt of hypophosphorous acid, as $NaH_2PO_2 \cdot 2H_2O$.

**hypophosphoric acid** /ˌhaɪpəfɒsˌfɒrɪk 'æsəd/, *n.* a tetrabasic acid, $H_4P_2O_6$, produced by the slow oxidation of phosphorus in moist air.

**hypophosphorous acid** /haɪpəˌfɒsfərəs 'æsəd/, *n.* a monobasic acid of phosphorus, $H_3PO_2$, having salts which are used in medicine.

**hypophysis** /haɪ'pɒfəsəs/, *n., pl.* **-ses** /-siz/. the pituitary gland of the brain. [NL, from Gk: outgrowth, process]

**hypopituitarism** /haɪpəpə'tjuətərɪzəm/, *n.* **1.** abnormally diminished activity of the pituitary gland. **2.** the pathological condition produced by this, resulting in obesity, retention of adolescent traits, and, in extreme cases, dwarfism.

**hypoplasia** /haɪpə'plæziə/, *n.* **1.** *Pathol., Bot.* abnormal deficiency of cells or structural elements. **2.** *Pathol.* an underdeveloped condition in which an organ or structure remains immature or subnormal in size. [HYPO- + -PLASIA]

**hypopnoea** /haɪ'pɒpniə, haɪpə'niə/, *n.* abnormally shallow breathing, usu. with decreased breathing rate. [NL, from *hypo-* HYPO- + Gk *pnoiá* breath]

**hypopyon** /haɪ'poʊpiɒn/, *n.* an effusion of pus into the anterior chamber of the eye, or that cavity which contains the aqueous humour. [NL, from Gk: ulcer, properly neut. of *hypópyos* tending to suppuration]

**hypostasis** /haɪ'pɒstəsəs/, *n., pl.* **-ses. 1.** *Metaphys.* **a.** that which stands under and supports; foundation. **b.** the underlying or essential part of anything as distinguished from attributes; substance, essence, or essential principle. **2.** *Theol.* **a.** one of the three real and distinct subsistences in the one undivided substance or essence of God. **b.** a person of the Trinity. **c.** the one personality of Christ in which His two natures, human and divine, are united. **3.** *Med.* the accumulation of blood or solids of a fluid by gravity due to poor circulation or standing. [LL, from Gk: substance, nature, essence, also sediment]

**hypostasise** /haɪ'pɒstəsaɪz/, *v.t.,* **-sised, -sising.** →**hypostatise.** Also, **hypostasize.**

**hypostatic** /haɪpə'stætɪk/, *adj.* **1.** of or pertaining to a hypostasis; elementary. **2.** *Theol.* pertaining to or constituting a distinct personal being or subsistence. **3.** *Med.* arising from downward pressure. **4.** *Genetics.* (of non-allelic genes) recessive. Also, **hypostatical.** [Gk *hypostatikós* pertaining to substance] – **hypostatically,** *adv.*

**hypostatise** /haɪ'pɒstətaɪz/, *v.t.,* **-tised, -tising.** to treat or regard as a distinct substance or reality. Also, **hypostatize.** – **hypostatisation** /haɪˌpɒstətaɪˈzeɪʃən/, *n.*

**hypostyle** /ˈhaɪpəstaɪl/, *adj.* **1.** having many columns carrying the roof or ceiling: *a hypostyle hall.* –*n.* **2.** a hypostyle structure. [Gk *hypóstȳlos* resting on pillars]

**hyposulphite** /haɪpəˈsʌlfaɪt/, *n.* **1.** a salt of hyposulphurous acid. **2.** sodium thiosulphate, antichlor, or hypo ($Na_2S_2O_3 \cdot 5H_2O$), a bleach and photographic fixing agent.

**hyposulphuric acid** /ˌhaɪpoʊsʌlˌfjurɪk ˈæsəd/, *n.* former name of dithionic acid.

**hyposulphurous acid** /ˌhaɪpoʊˌsʌlfərəs ˈæsəd/, *n.* →**dithionous acid.**

**hypotaxis** /haɪpəˈtæksəs/, *n.* dependent relation or construction, as of clauses. [NL, from Gk: subjection] – **hypotactic,** *adj.*

**hypotension** /haɪpəˈtɛnʃən/, *n.* abnormally low blood pressure.

**hypotenuse** /haɪˈpɒtənjuz/, *n.* the side of a right-angled triangle opposite the right angle. Also, *Obs.,* **hypothenuse.** [LL *hypotēnūsa,* from Gk *hypoteínousa,* ppr. fem., subtending]

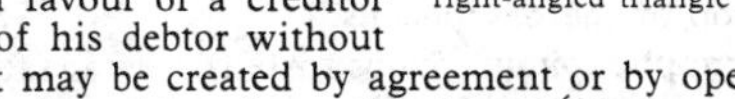

hypotenuse of a right-angled triangle

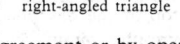

**hypothalamus** /haɪpəˈθæləməs/, *n.* the portion of the diencephalon concerned with emotional expression and visceral responses.

**hypothec** /haɪˈpɒθɪk/, *n. Rom. and Scot. Law.* a security in favour of a creditor over the property of his debtor without possession of it. It may be created by agreement or by operation of law. [LL *hypothēca,* from Gk *hypothḗkē* deposit, pledge]

**hypothecary** /haɪˈpɒθəkəri/, *adj.* **1.** of or pertaining to a hypothec. **2.** created or secured by a hypothec.

**hypothecate** /haɪˈpɒθəkeɪt/, *v.t.,* **-cated, -cating. 1.** to pledge to a creditor as security without delivering over; mortgage. **2.** to put in pledge by delivery, as stocks given as security for a loan. [ML *hypothēcātus,* pp. of *hypothēcāre,* from LL *hypothēca* HYPOTHEC] – **hypothecation** /ˌhaɪpɒθəˈkeɪʃən/, *n.* – **hypothecator,** *n.*

**hypothermia** /haɪpəˈθɜmiə/, *n.* **1.** subnormal body temperature. **2.** the artificial reduction of body temperature to slow metabolic processes, usu. to facilitate heart surgery. [HYPO- + Gk *thérm(ē)* heat + -IA] – **hypothermal,** *adj.*

**hypothesis** /haɪˈpɒθəsəs/, *n., pl.* **-ses** /-siz/. **1.** a proposition (or set of propositions) proposed as an explanation for the occurrence of some specified group of phenomena, either asserted merely as a provisional conjecture to guide investigation (a **working hypothesis**), or accepted as highly probable in the light of established facts. **2.** a proposition assumed as a premise in an argument. **3.** the antecedent of a conditional proposition. **4.** a mere assumption or guess. [NL, from Gk: supposition, basis]

**hypothesise** /haɪˈpɒθəsaɪz/, *v.,* **-sised, -sising.** –*v.i.* **1.** to form a hypothesis. –*v.t.* **2.** to assume by hypothesis. Also, **hypothesize.**

**hypothetical** /haɪpəˈθɛtɪkəl/, *adj.* **1.** assumed by hypothesis; supposed: *a hypothetical case.* **2.** pertaining to, involving, or of the nature of hypothesis: *hypothetical reasoning.* **3.** given to making hypotheses: *a hypothetical person.* **4.** *Logic.* **a.** conditional; characterising propositions having the form *if A, then B.* **b.** (of a syllogism) having a premise which is a hypothetical proposition. **c.** (of a proposition) not well supported by evidence, whose status is therefore highly conjectural. Also, **hypothetic.** [LL *hypotheticus* (from Gk *hypothetikós* supposed) + -AL[1]] – **hypothetically,** *adv.*

**hypothyroidism** /haɪpəˈθaɪrɔɪdɪzəm/, *n.* **1.** abnormally diminished activity of the thyroid gland. **2.** the condition produced by a deficiency of thyroid secretion, resulting in goitre, myxoedema, and, in children, cretinism.

**hypotonic** /haɪpəˈtɒnɪk/, *adj.* **1.** *Physiol.* under the normal tone. **2.** *Chem.* denoting a solution of lower osmotic pressure than one with which it is compared.

**hypoventilation** /ˌhaɪpoʊˌvɛntəˈleɪʃən/, *n.* the insufficient exposure of the lungs to oxygen, resulting in reduced oxygen content of the blood or increased carbon dioxide content (or both).

**hypoxanthine** /haɪpəˈzænθin, -θaɪn/, *n.* a crystalline compound, $C_5H_4N_4O$, related to xanthine and found in animal and vegetable tissues. – **hypoxanthic,** *adj.*

**hypoxia** /haɪˈpɒksiə/, *n.* any state where a physiologically inadequate amount of oxygen is available to or utilised by tissue.

**hypsography** /hɪpˈsɒgrəfi/, *n.* a branch of geography which deals with the measurement and mapping of areas of the earth's surface with reference to sea-level. – **hypsographic** /hɪpsəˈgræfɪk/, **hypsographical** /hɪpsəˈgræfɪkəl/, *adj.*

**hypsometer** /hɪpˈsɒmətə/, *n.* **1.** an instrument for measuring altitude by determining the boiling point of a liquid at the given height. **2.** (sometimes) the boiler of a hypsometer. [Gk *hýpso(s)* height + -METER[1]]

**hypsometry** /hɪpˈsɒmətri/, *n.* vertical control in mapping; the establishment of elevations or altitudes. – **hypsometric** /hɪpsəˈmɛtrɪk/, **hypsometrical** /hɪpsəˈmɛtrɪkəl/, *adj.* – **hypsometrically** /hɪpsəˈmɛtrɪkli/, *adv.*

**hyracoid** /ˈhaɪrəkɔɪd/, *adj.* belonging or pertaining to the order Hyracoidea, that comprises the hyraxes. [NL *hyrax* HYRAX + -OID] – **hyracoidean** /haɪrəˈkɔɪdiən/, *adj., n.*

**hyrax** /ˈhaɪræks/, *n., pl.* **hyraxes, hyraces** /ˈhaɪrəsiz/. any of a number of small, timid mammals of Africa and south-western Asia, superficially resembling rodents but having tiny hoofs and other distinctive characteristics. They constitute a separate order, the Hyracoidea, the **rock hyrax,** genus *Procavia* (or *Hyrax*), living mostly in rocky places, the closely similar **tree hyrax** of Africa, genus *Dendrohyrax,* being arboreal. [NL, from Gk: shrewmouse]

**hyson** /ˈhaɪsən/, *n.* a Chinese green tea, the early crop and the inferior leaves being called **young hyson** and **hyson skin** respectively. [Chinese (Cantonese) *hei-ch'un,* lit., blooming spring (Mandarin *hsi-ch'un*)]

**hyssop** /ˈhɪsəp/, *n.* **1.** an aromatic herb, *Hyssopus officinalis,* with blue flowers. **2.** (in the Bible and derived use) a plant, perhaps, the caper, whose twigs were used in ceremonial sprinkling. [L *hyssōpus,* from Gk *hýssōpos* kind of plant; replacing OE *ysope*]

**hyster-,** variant of **hystero-,** before vowels; as in *hysterectomy.*

**hysterectomy** /hɪstəˈrɛktəmi/, *n., pl.* **-mies.** the excision of the uterus.

**hysteresis** /hɪstəˈrisəs/, *n.* the extent to which the strain in a material reflects the stress to which it has been subjected in the past as well as its present stress; the time-lag exhibited by a material in reacting to the stress to which it is subjected, esp. with reference to magnetic forces applied to a ferromagnetic material. [NL, from Gk: deficiency] – **hysteretic** /hɪstəˈrɛtɪk/, *adj.*

**hysteresis loop** /– ˈlup/, *n.* a graphical representation of the hysteresis of a system. Also, **hysteresis cycle.**

**hysteresis loss** /– ˈlɒs/, *n.* the loss of energy, as heat, by a system exhibiting hysteresis.

**hysteria** /hɪsˈtɪəriə/, *n.* **1.** morbid or senseless emotionalism; emotional frenzy. **2.** a psychoneurotic disorder characterised by violent emotional outbreaks, perversion of sensory and motor functions, and various morbid effects due to autosuggestion. [HYSTER(IC) + -IA]

**hysteric** /hɪsˈtɛrɪk/, *n.* **1.** (*usu. pl.*) a fit of hysteria; hysteria. **2.** a person subject to hysteria. –*adj.* **3.** hysterical.

**hysterical** /hɪsˈtɛrɪkəl/, *adj.* **1.** resembling or suggesting hysteria; emotionally disordered. **2.** of, pertaining to, or characteristic of hysteria: *her hysterical behaviour at the funeral revealed how much she really loved him.* **3.** suffering from or subject to hysteria. [L *hystericus* (from Gk *hysterikós* suffering in the uterus) + -AL[1]] – **hysterically,** *adv.*

**hysterical fever** /– ˈfivə/, *n.* an increase in temperature without obvious cause other than hysteria.

**hysterical pregnancy** /– ˈprɛgnənsi/, *n.* →**phantom pregnancy.**

**hystero-,** a word element meaning 'uterus', as in *hysterotomy.* Also, **hyster-.** [Gk, combining form of *hystéra*]

**hysteroid** /ˈhɪstərɔɪd/, *adj.* resembling hysteria. Also, **hysteroidal.** [HYSTER- + -OID]

**hysteron proteron** /ˌhɪstərɒn ˈproʊtərɒn/, *n.* **1.** *Logic.* an attempted proof of a proposition which is based on premises that can be established only with the help of that proposition. This involves a fallacy, since it inverts the true order of logical dependence. **2.** *Rhet.* a figure of speech in which the logical order of two elements in discourse is reversed. [LL, from Gk *hýsteron* (neut. of *hýsteros* latter), *próteron* (neut. of *próteros* being before, sooner)]

**hysterotomy** /hɪstəˈrɒtəmi/, *n., pl.* **-mies.** the operation of cutting into the uterus, as used in Caesarean section.

**hystricomorphic** /hɪstrəkəˈmɔfɪk/, *adj.* belonging or pertaining to the Hystricomorpha, the suborder of rodents that includes the porcupines, chinchilla, agouti, coypu, guineapig, etc. [*hystrico-* (combining form of L *hystrix* porcupine, from Gk) + -MORPHIC]

**hyzone** /ˈhaɪzoʊn/, *n.* triatomic hydrogen, $H_3$.

**Hz,** *Physics.* hertz.

Ii Roman ROCKWELL

Ii Sans Serif PEIGNOT

Script WINDSOR

Ii Decorative FRIARS

*Although there are numerous typefaces in the world they can be divided into four main classifications. These are:*

*ROMAN or SERIF. This typeface came into being from the technique of the Roman masons who, working in stone, finished off each letter with a serif or small stroke projecting from the top or bottom. This was done to correct any feeling of unevenness or imbalance they may have created in cutting the characters in stone.*

*SANS SERIF (without serif). This typeface is geometric in design and has straight-edged characters and lines of a regular thickness.*

*SCRIPT. Based on the movement of the hand, this typeface is often italicised or slanted, as if drawn by a brush or quill pen.*

*DECORATIVE. Any typeface that exaggerates the characteristics of any of the other three classifications to a degree that places it outside of them.*

*The dictionary entries in this book use a SANS SERIF typeface called Helvetica (set in a bold face for the head words) and a SERIF typeface Plantin (used throughout the body of the entries).*

**I, i** /aɪ/, *n., pl.* **I's** or **Is, i's** or **is. 1.** the ninth letter and third vowel of the English alphabet. **2.** the ninth in any series. **3.** any sound represented by the letter **I. 4.** an I-shaped object. **5.** Roman numeral for one. See **Roman numerals.**

**i,** *Maths.* the imaginary number $\sqrt{-1}$; the square root of minus one.

**-i-,** an ending for the first element of many compounds, originally found in the combining form of many Latin words, but often used in English as a connective irrespective of etymology, as in *cuneiform, Frenchify,* etc.

**i., 1.** intransitive. **2.** island.

**I,** *Chem.* iodine.

**I** /aɪ/, *pron., nom.* **I,** *poss.* **my** or **mine,** *obj.* **me;** *pl. nom.* **we,** *poss.* **ours** or **our,** *obj.* **us;** *n., pl.* **I's.** *–pron.* **1.** the subject form of the singular pronoun of the first person, used by a speaker of himself. *–n.* **2.** the pronoun *I* used as a noun: *the 'I' in this novel is John.* **3.** *Metaphys.* the ego. [ME *ik, ich, i,* OE *ic, ih,* c. G *ich;* akin to L *ego,* Gk *egō*]

**-ia,** a suffix of nouns, esp. having restricted application in various fields, thus, in medicine (disease: *malaria*), in geography (countries: *Rumania*), in botany (genera: *Wisteria*), in names of Roman feasts (*Lupercalia*), in Latin or Latinising plurals (*Reptilia, bacteria*), and in collectives (*insignia, militia*). [L or Gk, both from *-i-,* orig. or connective vowel + *-a* (fem. sing. nom. ending) or *-a* (neut. pl. nom. ending)]

**-ial,** variant of **-al**[1], as in *judicial, imperial.* [L *-iālis, -iāle,* adj. suffix, from *-i-,* orig. or connective vowel + *-ālis, -āle* -AL[1]]

**iamb** /ˈaɪæmb, ˈaɪæm/, *n.* a metrical foot of two syllables, a short followed by a long, or an unaccented by an accented (◡ ˗), as in *Come live with me and be my love.* [L *iambus* an iambic verse or poem, from Gk *íambos*]

**iambic** /aɪˈæmbɪk/, *adj.* **1.** *Pros.* **a.** pertaining to the iamb. **b.** consisting of or employing an iamb or iambs. **2.** *Gk Lit.* of a kind of satirical poetry written in iambs. *–n.* **3.** *Pros.* **a.** an iamb. **b.** (*usu. pl.*) a verse or poem consisting of iambs. **4.** a satirical poem in this metre. – **iambically,** *adv.*

**iambus** /aɪˈæmbəs/, *n., pl.* **-bi** /-baɪ/, **-buses.** →**iamb.**

**-ian,** variant of **-an,** as in *amphibian, Grecian.* [L *-iānus,* from *-i-,* orig. or connective vowel + *-ānus* -AN]

**-iana.** See **-ian, -ana.**

**-iasis,** a suffix of nouns denoting state or condition, esp. a morbid condition or a form of disease, as in *ankylostomiasis.* [NL, from Gk, from *-i-,* orig. or connective vowel (see -I-) + *-āsis* -ASIS]

**IATA** /aɪˈatə/, *n.* International Air Transport Association

**iatric** /aɪˈætrɪk/, *adj.* pertaining to a physician or to medicine. Also, **iatrical.** [Gk *iātrikós*]

**iatrochemistry** /aɪˌætroʊˈkɛməstri/, *n.* medieval medical chemistry.

**iatrogenic** /aɪˌætroʊˈdʒɛnɪk/, *adj.* (of an illness, real or imagined) caused or produced by diagnosis or treatment by a physician.

**-iatry,** a combining form meaning 'medical care', as in *psychiatry.* [Gk *iātreía* healing]

**ib.,** ibidem.

**I-beam** /ˈaɪ-bim/, *n.* a beam in the shape of the capital I.

**Iberian** /aɪˈbɪəriən/, *adj.* **1.** of or pertaining to Iberia, a peninsula in south-western Europe, comprising present-day Spain and Portugal. *–n.* **2.** one of the inhabitants of Iberia, from whom the Basques are supposed to be descended. **3.** the language of the Iberians from which Basque developed.

ibex

**ibex** /ˈaɪbɛks/, *n., pl.* **ibexes, ibices** /ˈaɪbəsiz/, (*esp. collectively*) **ibex.** any of various Old World wild goats with large recurved horns, esp. *Capra ibex,* of the European Alps and Apennines. [L]

**ibid.** /ˈɪbɪd/, ibidem.

**ibidem** /ˈɪbədɛm, ɪˈbaɪdəm/, *adv.* in the same book, chapter, page, etc. [L]

**ibis** /ˈaɪbəs/, *n.* **1.** any of various wading birds of the family Threskiornithidae, of warm regions, allied to the herons and storks and having a long, thin, down-curved bill. **2.** the sacred ibis, *Threskiornis aethiopica* of Egypt and other parts of Africa, with white and black plumage, venerated by the ancient Egyptians. [L, from Gk; of Egyptian orig.]

white ibis of northern and eastern Australia

**-ible,** variant of **-able,** occurring in words taken from the Latin, as in *credible, horrible, legible, visible,* or modelled on the Latin type as *addible* (for *addable*), *reducible.* [ME *-ible,* from OF, from L *-ibilis,* var. of *-bilis* after consonant stems. See -BLE]

sacred ibis

**Ibo** /ˈiboʊ/, *n.* **1.** a Negro people living in the area of the lower Niger river. **2.** a member of this people. **3.** the language of this people, used esp. for trade and education in south-eastern Nigeria.

**-ic,** **1.** a suffix forming adjectives from nouns or stems not used as words themselves, meaning 'pertaining or belonging to' (*poetic, metallic, Homeric*), found extensively in adjective nouns of a similar type (*public, magic*), and in nouns the adjectives of which end in *-ical*, (*music, critic*). **2.** *Chem.* a suffix showing that an element is present in a compound at a high valency; at least higher than when the suffix *-ous* is used. [representing in part Gk *-ikos;* often L *-icus;* sometimes F *-ique*]

**i/c.,** **1.** in charge. **2.** in command.

**IC** /aɪ 'si/, *n.* an integrated circuit.

**-ical,** a compound suffix forming adjectives from nouns (*rhetorical*), providing synonyms to words ending in *-ic* (*poetical*), and providing an adjective with additional meanings to those in the *-ic* form (*economical*). [-IC + -AL[1]; in some cases representing LL *-icālis,* from adj. endings *-ic(us)* -IC + *-ālis* -AL[1]]

**ICBM** /ˌaɪ si bi 'ɛm/, intercontinental ballistic missile. Also, **I.C.B.M.**

**ice** /aɪs/, *n., v.,* **iced, icing,** *adj.* *–n.* **1.** the solid form of water, produced by freezing; frozen water. **2.** the frozen surface of a body of water. **3.** any substance resembling this: *camphor ice.* **4.** ice-cream. **5.** a frozen dessert made of sweetened water and fruit juice. **6.** reserve; formality: *to break the ice.* **7.** *Colloq.* a diamond or diamonds. **8. cut no ice,** *Colloq.* to make no impression; be unconvincing (oft. fol. by *with*): *his excuses cut no ice with me.* **9. on ice,** waiting or in readiness: *he kept the project on ice for some time.* **10. on thin ice,** in a risky or delicate situation. *–v.t.* **11.** to cover with ice. **12.** to change into ice; freeze. **13.** to cool with ice, as a drink. **14.** to refrigerate with ice. **15.** to make cold as if with ice. **16.** to cover (cakes, etc.) with icing. *–v.i.* **17.** to freeze. **18.** to become covered with ice (oft. fol. by *up*). *–adj.* **19.** of ice. [ME *is(e),* OE *īs,* c. G *Eis*] **– iceless,** *adj.* **– icelike,** *adj.*

**-ice,** a suffix used in many nouns to indicate state or quality, as in *service, justice.* [ME *-is(e), -ys(e),* etc., from OF *-ice, -ise,* from L *-itius, -itia, -itium*]

**ice age** /'aɪs eɪdʒ/, *n.* (*sometimes caps*) the glacial epoch.

**ice-axe** /'aɪs-æks/, *n.* an axe used by mountaineers, etc., to cut footholds in ice.

**icebag** /'aɪsbæg/, *n.* a bag containing ice, applied to the head.

**iceberg** /'aɪsbɜg/, *n.* **1.** a large floating mass of ice, detached from a glacier and carried out to sea. **2.** *Colloq.* a regular winter swimmer. **3.** *Colloq.* a cold, reserved person. [half Anglicisation, half adoption of D *ijsberg* ice mountain, c. G *Eisberg,* Swed. *isberg*]

**iceblink** /'aɪsblɪŋk/, *n.* a luminous appearance near the horizon, due to the reflection of light from ice.

**iceblock** /'aɪsblɒk/, *n.* **1.** an ice-cube. **2.** a frozen flavoured confection originally water based, sometimes on a stick.

**ice-blue** /aɪs-'blu/, *adj.* very pale blue.

**iceboat** /'aɪsbout/, *n.* **1.** **→ice-yacht.** **2.** **→icebreaker** (def. 1).

**icebound** /'aɪsbaʊnd/, *adj.* **1.** held fast or hemmed in by ice; frozen in: *an icebound ship.* **2.** obstructed or shut off by ice: *an icebound harbour.*

**icebox** /'aɪsbɒks/, *n.* **1.** a box or chest to hold ice for keeping food, etc., cool. **2.** a compartment in a refrigerator for keeping ice.

**icebreaker** /'aɪsbreɪkə/, *n.* **1.** a strong ship for breaking channels through ice. **2.** a tool or machine for chopping ice into small pieces. **3.** a structure of masonry or timber for protection against moving ice. **4.** *Colloq.* anything which breaks down reserve or reticence.

**ice bucket** /'aɪs bʌkət/, *n.* a small insulated bucket containing cubes of ice for adding to drinks, or crushed ice in which a bottle of wine or the like is immersed to cool.

**icecap** /'aɪskæp/, *n.* a cap of ice over an area (sometimes vast), sloping in all directions from the centre.

**ice chest** /'aɪs tʃɛst/, *n.* an ice-cooled container for food.

**ice-cold** /'aɪs-kould/, *adj.;* /aɪs-'kould/, *n.* *–adj.* **1.** cold as ice. *–n.* **2.** *Colloq.* a can of beer.

**ice-cream** /'aɪs-krim/, *n.* a frozen food made of cream, rich milk, or evaporated milk, sweetened and variously flavoured.

**ice-cream cone** /'– koun/, *n.* **1.** a cone-shaped edible wafer designed to hold ice-cream. **2.** such a wafer holding ice-cream.

**ice-cream soda** /– 'soudə/, *n.* a drink consisting of flavoured aerated water topped up with ice-cream, served in a tall glass.

**ice-cube** /'aɪs-kjub/, *n.* a small cube of ice, made by freezing water in an icetray in a refrigerator.

**iced** /aɪst/, *adj.* **1.** covered with ice. **2.** cooled by means of ice. **3.** *Cookery.* covered with icing.

**icefall** /'aɪsfɔl/, *n.* a sudden steepening in a glacier marked by deep crevasses and perched ice blocks.

**icefield** /'aɪsfild/, *n.* a very large icefloe.

**icefloe** /'aɪsflou/, *n.* a sheet of floating ice.

**icefoot** /'aɪsfʊt/, *n.* a belt of ice along the shore in polar regions, formed where snow on the shore meets the sea water.

**ice-free** /'aɪs-fri/, *adj.* (of a port, river, or the like) free from ice, and therefore navigable, all the year round.

**icefront** /'aɪsfrʌnt/, *n.* the cliff-like edge of a floating icesheet or the end of a glacier which discharges to the sea.

**ice hockey** /'aɪs hɒki/, *n.* a game resembling hockey, played on an ice-rink by two teams of six players each, with a puck in place of a ball.

**icehouse** /'aɪshaʊs/, *n.* a building for storing ice.

**Icel.,** **1.** Iceland. **2.** Icelandic.

**Iceland** /'aɪslənd, -lænd/, *n.* a large island in the northern Atlantic between Greenland and Denmark; an independent republic. **– Icelander** /'aɪsləndə, -læn-/, *adj., n.*

**Icelandic** /aɪs'lændɪk/, *adj.* **1.** pertaining to Iceland, its inhabitants, or their language. *–n.* **2.** the language of Iceland, a Scandinavian language.

**Iceland moss** /aɪslənd 'mɒs/, *n.* an edible lichen, *Cetraria islandica,* of arctic regions, used to some extent in medicine.

**Iceland poppy** /– 'pɒpi/, *n.* a poppy, esp. *Papaver nudicaule,* of arctic regions, used to some extent in medicine, and popular as a garden annual.

**Iceland spar** /– 'spa/, *n.* a transparent variety of calcite that is double-refracting and is used for polarising light.

**ice machine** /'aɪs məʃin/, *n.* a machine which produces ice, usu. as cubes, etc., for use in drinks.

**ice-maker** /'aɪs-meɪkə/, *n.* a machine, mainly in commercial use in hotels, bars, etc., which makes sheets of ice and then cuts or crushes them into party ice.

**ice needles** /'aɪs nidlz/, *n.pl.* a form of precipitation consisting of very small ice crystals that seem to float in the air.

**icepack** /'aɪspæk/, *n.* **1.** a large area of floating ice, as in arctic seas. **2.** a cold compress consisting of a bag filled with crushed ice.

**icepick** /'aɪspɪk/, *n.* a pick or other tool for breaking ice.

**ice plant** /'aɪs plænt/, *n.* **1.** a low succulent plant, *Gasoul crystallinum,* originally of the Old World, with leaves covered by glistening vesicles. **2.** any of certain similar species belonging to other genera.

**ice point** /'– pɔɪnt/, *n.* the temperature of equilibrium between ice and water under normal atmospheric pressure; the melting point of ice.

**icerink** /'aɪsrɪŋk/, *n.* **→rink** (defs 1, 3, 4).

**ice-sailing** /'aɪs-seɪlɪŋ/, *n.* the sport of racing ice-yachts across ice.

**ice-scoured area** /ˌaɪs-skaʊəd 'ɛəriə/, *n.* an area having surface features resulting from scouring by an advancing icesheet during glaciation.

**icesheet** /'aɪsʃit/, *n.* **1.** a broad, thick sheet of ice covering an extensive area for a long period of time. **2.** a glacier covering a large part of a continent.

**iceshelf** /'aɪsʃɛlf/, *n.* a floating icesheet which covers an extensive area of ocean.

**ice show** /'aɪs ʃou/, *n.* an entertainment, often a pantomime, performed on ice.

**ice skate** /'– skeɪt/, *n.* (*usu. pl.*) **1.** a thin metal runner attached to the shoe, for skating on ice. **2.** a shoe fitted with such a runner.

**ice-skate** /'aɪs-skeɪt/, *v.i.,* **-skated, -skating.** to skate on ice. **– ice-skater,** *n.*

**icetray** /'aɪstreɪ/, *n.* a tray for icing water into cubes in the icebox of a refrigerator.

**ice-water** /'aɪs-wɔtə/, *n.* chilled water, often with ice blocks.

**ice-yacht** /'aɪs-jɒt/, *n.* a triangular wooden frame fitted with steel runners and sails, for ice-sailing.

**ichneumon** /ɪk'njumən/, *n.* **1.** a slender carnivorous mammal, *Herpestes ichneumon,* of Egypt, resembling the weasel in form and habits, and said to devour crocodiles' eggs. **2.** →**ichneumon fly.** [L, from Gk: lit., tracker]

ichneumon

**ichneumon fly** /'– flaɪ/, *n.* any insect belonging to the large hymenopterous family Ichneumonidae, whose larvae are parasites and destroy caterpillars and other larvae.

**ichnite** /'ɪknaɪt/, *n.* a fossil footprint. [Gk *íchnos* track + -ITE[1]]

**ichnography** /ɪk'nɒgrəfi/, *n., pl.* **-phies. 1.** the drawing of ground plans. **2.** a ground plan. [L *ichnographia,* from Gk: a tracing out. See -GRAPHY] – **ichnographic** /ɪknə'græfɪk/, **ichnographical** /ɪknə'græfɪkəl/, *adj.* – **ichnographically** /ɪknə'græfɪkli/, *adv.*

**ichor**[1] /'aɪkɔ/, *n.* an ethereal fluid supposed to flow in the veins of the gods. [Gk]

**ichor**[2] /'aɪkɔ/, *n.* an acrid watery discharge, as from an ulcer or wound. [NL, from Gk, special use of *ichṓr* ICHOR[1]] – **ichorous** /'aɪkərəs/, *adj.*

**ichthammol** /'ɪkθəmɒl/, *n.* a mixture of ammonium sulphonates of an oily substance prepared by destructive distillation of bituminous shale or schist; used as a mild antiseptic and in the treatment of certain skin disorders.

**ichthyic** /'ɪkθiɪk/, *adj.* of or pertaining to fishes. [Gk *ichthyikós* fishy]

**ichthyo-,** a word element meaning 'fish', as in *ichthyology.* Also, before vowels, **ichthy-.** [Gk, combining form of *ichthýs*]

**ichthyoid** /'ɪkθiɔɪd/, *adj.* **1.** Also, **ichthyoidal** /ɪkθi'ɔɪdl/. fish-like. –*n.* **2.** any fishlike vertebrate. [Gk *ichthyoeidḗs* fishlike. See -OID]

**ichthyol** /'ɪkθiɒl/, *n.* Also, **ichthammol.** a dark brown to black syrupy compound, $C_{28}H_{36}O_6S_3(NH_3)_2 \cdot 2H_2O$, used as an astringent, antiseptic, and alterant, esp. for skin diseases. [Trademark; from ICHTHY(O)- + -OL[2]; so called because obtained from rocks containing fossilised fishes]

**ichthyol.** ichthyology. Also, **ichth.**

**ichthyology** /ɪkθi'ɒlədʒi/, *n.* the branch of zoology that treats of fishes. – **ichthyologic** /ɪkθiə'lɒdʒɪk/, **ichthyological** /ɪkθiə'lɒdʒɪkəl/, *adj.* – **ichthyologist,** *n.*

**ichthyomancy** /'ɪkθiə,mænsi/, *n.* divination by means of fish.

**ichthyornis** /ɪkθi'ɔnəs/, *n.* any of an extinct genus of toothed birds, *Ichthyornis,* with vertebrae resembling those of fishes. [NL, from Gk *ichthy-* ICHTHY(O)- + *órnis* bird]

**ichthyosaur** /'ɪkθiəsɔ/, *n.* any of an extinct order, Ichthyosauria, of marine reptiles, fishlike in form, ranging from one to twelve metres in length, with a round tapering body, a large head, four paddle-like flippers, and a vertical caudal fin. [NL *ichthyosaurus,* from Gk *ichthyo-* ICHTHYO- + *saûros* lizard]

ichthyosaur

**ichthyosaurus** /ɪkθiə'sɔrəs/, *n., pl.* **-sauri** /-'sɔraɪ/. →**ichthyosaur.**

**ichthyosis** /ɪkθi'oʊsəs/, *n.* a congenital disease in which the epidermis continually flakes off in large scales or plates. – **ichthyotic** /ɪkθi'ɒtɪk/, *adj.*

**-ician,** a compound suffix esp. applied to an expert in a field, as in *geometrician.* [-IC + -IAN; replacing ME *-icien,* from OF]

**icicle** /'aɪsɪkəl/, *n.* a pendent tapering mass of ice formed by the freezing of dripping water. [ME *isykle,* OE *īsgicel,* from *īs* ice + *gicel* icicle. Cf. Icel. *jökull* mass of ice, glacier] – **icicled,** *adj.*

**icily** /'aɪsəli/, *adv.* in an icy manner.

**iciness** /'aɪsinəs/, *n.* the state of being icy or very cold.

**icing** /'aɪsɪŋ/, *n.* **1.** a preparation of sugar, often made with egg whites, for covering cakes, etc. **2.** →**frosting. 3. the icing on the cake,** the most enjoyable or advantageous aspects of a job, situation, etc; the finishing touches.

**icing sugar** /'– ʃʊgə/, *n.* a finely ground powdered sugar.

**ickle** /'ɪkəl/, *adj.* (*joc.*) little; small.

**icky** /'ɪki/, *adj. Colloq.* **1.** sticky; gooey. **2.** difficult to deal with; disagreeable; troublesome. **3.** *Jazz.* sentimental; sickly.

**icon** /'aɪkɒn/, *n., pl.* **icons. 1.** a picture, image, or other representation. **2.** *Eastern Ch.* a representation in painting, enamel, etc., of some sacred personage, as Christ or a saint or angel, itself venerated as sacred. **3.** a sign or representation which stands for its object by virtue of a resemblance or analogy to it. Also, **eikon, ikon.** [L, from Gk *eikṓn* likeness, image]

**iconic** /aɪ'kɒnɪk/, *adj.* **1.** pertaining to or of the nature of an icon, portrait, or image. **2.** *Art.* (of statues, portraits, etc.) executed according to a convention or tradition. Also, **iconical.** [L *īconicus,* from Gk *eikonikós* representing a figure, copied]

**icono-,** a word element meaning 'likeness' or 'image', as in *iconography.* [Gk, combining form of *eikṓn*]

**iconoclasm** /aɪ'kɒnəklæzəm/, *n.* the action or spirit of iconoclasts.

**iconoclast** /aɪ'kɒnəklæst/, *n.* **1.** a breaker or destroyer of images, esp. those set up for religious veneration. **2.** one who attacks cherished beliefs as based on error or superstition. [LL *īconoclastēs,* from LGk *eikonoklástēs,* from *eikono-* ICONO- + *klástēs* breaker] – **iconoclastic** /aɪ,kɒnə'klæstɪk/, *adj.* – **iconoclastically** /aɪ,kɒnə'klæstɪkli/, *adv.*

**iconographic** /aɪ,kɒnə'græfɪk/, *adj.* of or pertaining to icons or iconography. Also, **iconographical.**

**iconography** /aɪkə'nɒgrəfi/, *n., pl.* **-phies. 1.** the making of an icon; representation by means of drawing, painting, or carving figures, etc. **2.** the subject matter of an icon, image, or representation, or of groups of them. **3.** the description or analysis of icons. [ML *īconographia,* from Gk *eikonographía.* See ICONO-, -GRAPHY]

**iconolatry** /aɪkə'nɒlətri/, *n.* the worship or adoration of icons. – **iconolater,** *n.*

**iconology** /aɪkə'nɒlədʒi/, *n.* **1.** the branch of knowledge concerned with pictorial or sculptural representations. **2.** such representations collectively. **3.** a description or interpretation of statues, pictures, etc. **4.** symbolical representation. – **iconological** /aɪkənə'lɒdʒɪkəl/, *adj.* – **iconologist,** *n.*

**iconoscope** /aɪ'kɒnəskoʊp/, *n.* the cathode ray tube which focuses the optical image which the cathode ray beam scans. [Trademark]

**iconostasis** /aɪkə'nɒstəsəs/, *n., pl.* **-ses** /-siz/. (in the Eastern Church) a partition or screen on which icons are placed, separating the sanctuary from the main part of the church. Also, **iconostas** /aɪ'kɒnəstæs/. [NL, from NGk *eikonóstasis,* from Gk *eikono-* ICONO- + *stásis* a standing, station]

**icosahedron** /aɪkəsə'hidrən/, *n., pl.* **-drons, -dra** /-drə/. a solid figure having twenty faces. [Gk *eikosáedron*] – **icosahedral,** *adj.*

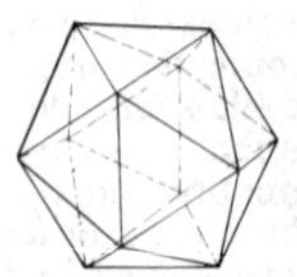
icosahedron (regular)

**-ics,** a suffix of nouns, originally plural as denoting things pertaining to a particular subject, but now mostly used as singular as denoting the body of matters, facts, knowledge, principles, etc., pertaining to a subject, and hence a science or art, as in *ethics, physics, politics, tactics.* [pl. of -IC; orig. representing Gk *-iká* (in L *-ica*), neut. pl. adj., suffix meaning (things) pertaining to]

**ictal** /'ɪktəl/, *adj.* pertaining to or caused by an ictus.

**icteric** /ɪk'tɛrɪk/, *adj.* pertaining to or affected with icterus; jaundiced. Also. **icterical.** [L *ictericus,* from Gk *ikterikós*]

**icterus** /'ɪktərəs/, *n.* →**jaundice.** [NL, from Gk *íkteros*]

**ictus** /'ɪktəs/, *n., pl.* **-tuses, -tus. 1.** *Pros.* rhythmical or metrical stress. **2.** *Pathol.* **a.** a fit. **b.** a stroke, as sunstroke. [L: blow, stroke]

**I.C.U.,** intensive care unit.

**icy** /'aɪsi/, *adj.,* **icier, iciest. 1.** made of or covered with ice. **2.** resembling ice. **3.** cold: *icy wind.* **4.** slippery: *icy road.* **5.** without warmth of feeling; frigid: *an icy stare.* [late ME *isy,* OE *īsig.* See ICE, -Y[1]]

**icy pole** /'– poʊl/, *n.* an ice block on a stick.

**id** /ɪd/, *n.* the part of the psyche residing in the unconscious which is the source of instinctive energy. Its impulses, which seek satifaction in accordance with the pleasure principle, are modified by the ego and the superego before they are given overt expression. [special use of L *id* it, as translation of G *Es*]

**-id**[1], **1.** a noun suffix meaning 'daughter of', as in *Nereid,* and used also in astronomy to form names of meteors appearing to radiate in showers from particular constellations, etc., as in *Andromedid.* **2.** a suffix used in naming epics, as in *Aeneid.* [L *-id-* (nom. *-is*), fem. patronymic suffix, from Gk]

**-id**[2], a suffix of nouns and adjectives indicating members of a zoological family, as in *cichlid,* or of some other group or division, as in *acarid, arachnid.* [NL *-idae,* in zoological family names pl. of L *-idēs* (masc. patronymic suffix), from Gk; sometimes from NL *-ida,* in group names, taken as neut. pl. of L *-idēs.* Cf. F *-ide*]

**-id**[3], variant of **-ide**, as in *parotid.*

**-id**[4], a quasi-suffix common in adjectives, esp. of states which appeal to the senses, as in *torrid, acid.* [L *-idus*]

**id.**, idem.

**I'd** /aɪd/, contraction of *I would, I should,* or *I had.*

**ID** /aɪ 'di/, *n.* identification.

**-idae**, a suffix of the taxonomic names of families in zoology, as in *Canidae.* [NL, from Gk *-idai,* pl. of *-idēs,* patronymic suffix]

**ID card** /aɪ 'di ˌkad/, *n.* a card which identifies the bearer and usu. has some personal details as address, age, affiliation, etc.

**-ide**, a noun suffix in names of chemical compounds, as in *bromide.* Also, **-id**[3]. [abstracted from OXIDE]

**idea** /aɪ'dɪə/, *n.* **1.** any conception existing in the mind as the result of mental apprehension or activity. **2.** a thought, conception, or notion: *what an idea!* **3.** an impression: *a general idea of what it's like.* **4.** an opinion, view, or belief. **5.** a plan of action; an intention: *the idea of becoming an engineer.* **6.** a fantasy. **7.** *Philos.* **a.** a concept developed by the mind (if empirical, in close connection with sense perception). **b.** a conception of what is desirable, or what ought to be; a governing conception or principle; ideal. **c.** (in Platonic philosophy) an archetype or pattern of which the individual objects in any natural class are imperfect copies and from which they derive their being. **d.** (in Kantian philosophy) a concept formed from notions and transcending the possibility of experience. **8.** *Music.* a theme, phrase, or figure. **9.** *Obs.* a likeness. **10.** *Obs.* a mental image. [L, from Gk, from *ideîn* see; orig. in def. 7c] – **idealess,** *adj.*

**ideal** /aɪ'dɪəl/, *n.* **1.** a conception of something in its highest perfection. **2.** a standard of perfection or excellence. **3.** a person or thing regarded as realising such a conception or conforming to such a standard, and taken as a model for imitation. **4.** an ultimate object or aim of endeavour, esp. one of high or noble character. **5.** that which exists only in idea. *–adj.* **6.** conceived as constituting a standard of perfection or excellence: *ideal beauty.* **7.** regarded as perfect of its kind; best: *an ideal spot for a home.* **8.** existing only in idea. **9.** not real or practical; visionary. **10.** based upon an ideal or ideals: *the ideal school in art.* **11.** *Philos.* **a.** existing as an archetype or Platonic idea. **b.** pertaining to a possible state of affairs considered as highly desirable. **c.** pertaining to or of the nature of idealism. [LL *ideālis,* from L *idea* IDEA] – **idealness,** *n.*

**ideal gas** /– 'gæs/, *n.* the theoretical concept of a gas consisting of perfectly elastic molecules between which no forces of attraction exist; a gas which obeys the ideal gas law; perfect gas.

**ideal gas law,** *n.* →**gas laws.**

**idealise** /aɪ'dɪəlaɪz/, *v.,* **-lised, -lising.** *–v.t.* **1.** to make ideal; represent in an ideal form or character; exalt to an ideal perfection or excellence. *–v.i.* **2.** to represent something in an ideal form; imagine or form an ideal or ideals. Also, **idealize.** – **idealisation** /aɪˌdɪəlaɪ'zeɪʃən/, *n.* – **idealiser,** *n.*

**idealism** /aɪ'dɪəlɪzəm/, *n.* **1.** the cherishing or pursuit of ideals, as for attainment. **2.** the practice of idealising. **3.** something idealised; an ideal representation. **4.** the imaginative treatment of subjects in art or literature, usu. on a high ethical plane and devoid of accidental details (opposed to *realism*). **5.** *Philos.* **a.** any system or theory which maintains that the real is of the nature of thought, or that the object of external perception consists of ideas. **b.** the tendency to represent things in an ideal form, or as they ought to be rather than as they are, with emphasis on values.

**idealist** /aɪ'dɪələst/, *n.* **1.** one who cherishes or pursues ideals, as for attainment. **2.** a visionary or unpractical person. **3.** one who represents things as they might be rather than as they are. **4.** a writer or artist who treats subjects imaginatively. **5.** one who accepts the doctrines of idealism. *–adj.* **6.** idealistic.

**idealistic** /aɪdɪə'lɪstɪk/, *adj.* pertaining to idealism or to idealists. – **idealistically,** *adv.*

**ideality** /aɪdi'æləti/, *n., pl.* **-ties.** **1.** ideal quality or character. **2.** capacity to idealise.

**ideally** /aɪ'dɪəli/, *adv.* **1.** in accordance with an ideal; perfectly. **2.** in idea, thought, or imagination.

**ideal type** /aɪdɪəl 'taɪp/, *n.* an imaginary construction of what an object would be if it were allowed to develop without any interference from accidental or irrelevant factors.

**idea-monger** /aɪ'dɪə-mʌŋgə/, *n. Colloq.* an inventive, creative person.

**ideate** /aɪ'dieɪt/, *v.,* **-ated, -ating;** /aɪ'diət, -eɪt/, *n., adj.* *–v.t.* **1.** to form in idea, thought, or imagination. *–v.i.* **2.** to form ideas; think. *–n.* **3.** *Philos.* the object of which an idea is formed. *–adj.* **4.** concerned with ideas. – **ideation** /aɪdi'eɪʃən/, *n.* – **ideational** /aɪdi'eɪʃənəl/, *adj.* – **ideationally** /aɪdi'eɪʃənli/, *adv.*

**idée fixe** /ˌideɪ 'fiks/, *n.* a fixed idea; obsession. [F]

**idem** /'ɪdɛm, 'aɪdɛm/, *pron., adj.* the same as previously given or mentioned. [L]

**identic** /aɪ'dɛntɪk/, *adj.* **1.** *Obs.* identical. **2.** *Diplomacy.* (of action, notes, etc.) identical in form, as when two or more governments deal simultaneously with another government. [ML *identicus*]

**identical** /aɪ'dɛntɪkəl/, *adj.* **1.** agreeing exactly. **2.** same, or being the same one. [IDENTIC + -AL[1]. See IDENTITY] – **identically,** *adv.* – **identicalness,** *n.*

**identical proposition** /– prɒpə'zɪʃən/, *n.* a proposition expressed by a sentence in which the subject and predicate have the same meaning.

**identical twin** /– 'twɪn/, *n.* one of twins of the same sex which develop from one fertilised ovum.

**identification** /aɪˌdɛntəfə'keɪʃən/, *n.* **1.** the act of identifying. **2.** the state of being identified. **3.** something that identifies one, as a driver's licence, passport, etc.

**identification parade** /'– pəreɪd/, *n.* a line-up of persons which contains one suspected of a crime and which is inspected by a victim, witness, etc. in order to identify the suspect.

**identify** /aɪ'dɛntəfaɪ/, *v.,* **-fied, -fying.** *–v.t.* **1.** to recognise or establish as being a particular person or thing; attest or prove to be as purported or asserted: *to identify handwriting, identify the bearer of a cheque.* **2.** to make, represent to be, or regard or treat as the same or identical. **3.** to associate in feeling, interest, action, etc. (fol. by *with*). **4.** *Biol.* to determine to what group (a given specimen) belongs. **5.** *Psychol.* to make (oneself) one with another person by putting oneself in his place. **6.** *Psychol.* to adapt one's ideas and behaviour, usu. unconsciously, to fit in with those of a person or group regarded as a model. **7.** to serve as a means of identification for. *–v.i.* **8.** to make oneself one with another or others. – **identifiable,** *adj.* – **identifier,** *n.*

**identikit** /aɪ'dɛntikɪt/, *n.* **1.** a number of alternative, typical facial characteristics which can be superimposed upon a frame to form a likeness; used by police as a system of criminal identification. **2.** any picture so composed. [Trademark]

**identity** /aɪ'dɛntəti/, *n., pl.* **-ties.** **1.** the state or fact of remaining the same one, as under varying aspects or conditions. **2.** the condition of being oneself or itself, and not another: *he doubted his own identity.* **3.** *Colloq.* an odd, interesting or famous, person; character: *a local identity.* **4.** condition, character, or distinguishing features of person or things: *a case of mistaken identity.* **5.** the state or fact of being the same one. **6.** exact likeness in nature or qualities. **7.** an instance or point of sameness or likeness. **8.** *Maths.* an equation which is true for all values of its variables. *–adj.* **9.** effective as a means of identification: *an*

*identity card.* [LL *identitas,* apparently from L *identi-* (as in *identidem* repeatedly), for *īdem* the same + *-tas* -TY[2]]
**identity crisis** /'– kraɪsəs/, *n.* a phase of crisis in the attempt of an individual to establish his identity in relation to society.
**identity disc** /'– dɪsk/, *n.* one of a pair of small discs, worn at all times by Australian soldiers for identification, esp. in the event of death or injury in battle. Also, **identity tag.**
**ideo-,** a word element meaning 'idea', as in *ideograph.* [Gk, combining form of *idéa* idea]
**ideograph** /'ɪdiougræf, -graf/, *n.* a written symbol representing the idea of something directly, and not its name or sound. Also, **ideogram** /'ɪdiougræm/. **– ideographic** /ɪdiou'græfɪk/, **ideographical** /ɪdiou'græfɪkəl/, *adj.* **– ideographically** /ɪdiou'græfɪkli/, *adv.*

ideograph: Chinese characters for 'tree'

**ideography** /ɪdi'ɒgrəfi/, *n.* the use of ideographs.
**ideological** /ˌaɪdiə'lɒdʒɪkəl/, *adj.* **1.** pertaining to ideology. **2.** speculative; visionary. Also, **ideologic. – ideologically,** *adv.*
**ideologist** /aɪdi'ɒlədʒəst/, *n.* **1.** an expert in ideology. **2.** one who deals with systems of ideas. **3.** one who advocates or is preoccupied by a specific ideology. **4.** →**visionary.**
**ideology** /aɪdi'ɒlədʒi/, *n., pl.* **-gies. 1.** the body of doctrine, myth, and symbols of a social movement, institution, class, or large group. **2.** such a body of doctrine, etc., with reference to some political and cultural plan, as that of fascism, together with the devices for putting it into operation. **3.** *Philos.* **a.** the science of ideas. **b.** a system which derives ideas exclusively from sensation. **4.** theorising of a visionary or unpractical nature.
**ides** /aɪdz/, *n.pl.* (in the ancient Roman calendar) the 15th day of March, May, July, or October, and the 13th day of the other months. [F, from L *īdūs,* pl.]
**id est** /ɪd 'ɛst/, that is. [L]
**idio-,** a word element meaning 'peculiar' or 'proper to one', as in *idiosyncrasy.* [Gk, combining form of *ídios* own, private, peculiar]
**idioblast** /'ɪdioublæst/, *n.* a cell which differs greatly from the surrounding cells or tissue.
**idiocy** /'ɪdiəsi/, *n., pl.* **-cies. 1.** the condition of being an idiot; extreme degree of mental deficiency. **2.** senseless folly. [? Gk *idiōteía* uncouthness, defenceless condition; or from IDIOT, on model of *prophecy* from *prophet*]
**idiographic** /ɪdiou'græfɪk/, *adj.* pertaining to the intensive psychological study of an individual case, as a personality or social situation (opposed to *nomothetic*).
**idiolect** /'ɪdioulɛkt/, *n.* an individual's personal variety of a particular language system. [IDIO- + Gk *légein* to speak]
**idiom** /'ɪdiəm/, *n.* **1.** a form of expression peculiar to a language, esp. one having a significance other than its literal one. **2.** a variety or form of a language; a dialect. **3.** the language peculiar to a people. **4.** the peculiar character or genius of a language. **5.** a distinct style or character, as in music, art, etc.: *the idiom of Bach.* [LL *idiōma,* from Gk: a peculiarity]
**idiomatic** /ˌɪdiə'mætɪk/, *adj.* **1.** peculiar to or characteristic of a particular language. **2.** exhibiting the characteristic modes of expression of a speaker, group, dialect, etc. Also, **idiomatical.** [Gk *idiōmatikós*] **– idiomatically,** *adv.* **– idiomaticalness,** *n.*
**idiomorphic** /ˌɪdiou'mɔfɪk/, *adj.* **1.** denoting or pertaining to a mineral constituent of a rock, which has its own characteristic outward crystalline form, and not one forced upon it by the other constituents of the rock. **2.** having its own form. **– idiomorphically,** *adv.*
**idiopathic** /ˌɪdiou'pæθɪk/, *adj.* of unknown cause, as a disease.
**idiopathy** /ɪdi'ɒpəθi/, *n., pl.* **-thies.** a disease not preceded or occasioned by any other. [Gk *idiopátheia.* See IDIO-, -PATHY]
**idiophone** /'ɪdiəfoun/, *n.* a musical instrument made of some solid, naturally sonorous material, as cymbals, xylophones, glass harmonicas, etc.
**idioplasm** /'ɪdiouplæzəm/, *n.* →**germ plasm. – idioplasmic** /ˌɪdiou'plæzmɪk/, **idioplasmatic** /ˌɪdiouplæz'mætɪk/, *adj.*
**idiosyncrasy** /ˌɪdiou'sɪŋkrəsi/, *n., pl.* **-sies. 1.** any tendency, characteristic, mode of expression, or the like, peculiar to an individual. **2.** the physical constitution peculiar to an individual. **3.** a peculiarity of the physical or the mental constitution, esp. susceptibility towards drugs, food, etc. See **allergy** (def. 1). [Gk *idiosynkrāsía*] **– idiosyncratic** /ˌɪdiousɪŋ'krætɪk/, *adj.* **– idiosyncratically** /ˌɪdiousɪŋ'krætɪkli/, *adv.*
**idiot** /'ɪdiət/, *n.* **1.** an utterly foolish or senseless person. **2.** one hopelessly deficient, esp. from birth, in the ordinary mental powers. [ME, from L *idiōta,* from Gk *idiṓtēs* a private, non-professional, or ignorant person]
**idiot board** /'– bɔd/, *n.* a prompting device held before television speakers but not projected on to the film. Also, **idiot card.**
**idiot box** /'– bɒks/, *n. Colloq.* a television set.
**idiotic** /ɪdi'ɒtɪk/, *adj.* of or like an idiot; senselessly foolish. Also, **idiotical.** [LL *idiōticus,* from Gk *idiōtikós* private, unskilful] **– idiotically,** *adv.*
**idiotism** /'ɪdiətɪzəm/, *n.* **1.** idiotic conduct or action. **2.** *Rare.* idiocy. **3.** *Obs.* an idiom. [IDIOT + -ISM; in def. 3, from F *idiotisme,* from LL *idiōtismus* a common way of speaking, from Gk *idiōtismós* common manners]
**idiot tape** /'ɪdiət teɪp/, *n.* an unjustified tape used for computer typesetting.
**-idium,** a diminutive suffix (Latinisation of Greek *-idion*) used in zoological, biological, botanical, anatomical, and chemical terms.
**idle** /'aɪdl/, *adj.,* **idler, idlest,** *v.,* **idled, idling.** *–adj.* **1.** unemployed, or doing nothing: *idle workmen.* **2.** unoccupied, as time: *idle hours.* **3.** not kept busy or in use or operation: *idle machinery.* **4.** habitually doing nothing or avoiding work. **5.** of no real worth, importance, or significance: *idle talk.* **6.** baseless or groundless: *idle fears.* **7.** frivolous or vain: *idle pleasures.* **8.** futile or ineffective: *idle threats.* **9.** useless: *idle rage.* **10. the idle rich,** those whose wealth, usu. inherited, is such that they have no need to work for a living. *–v.i.* **11.** to pass time in idleness. **12.** to move, loiter, or saunter idly. **13.** *Mach.* to operate, usu. at minimum speed, while the transmission is disengaged. *–v.t.* **14.** to pass (time) in idleness. **15.** to cause (a person) to be idle. [ME and OE *īdel,* c. G *eitel*] **– idleness,** *n.* **– idly,** *adv.*
**idler** /'aɪdlə/, *n.* **1.** one who idles. **2.** *Mach.* an idle pulley or wheel.
**idler pulley** /'– puli/, *n.* a loose pulley made to press or rest on a belt in order to tighten or guide it.
**idler wheel** /'– wil/, *n.* **1.** a cogwheel placed between two other cogwheels in order to transfer the motion of one to the other without changing the direction of rotation. **2.** an idle pulley.

I, idle wheel; C, cogwheel

**idocrase** /'aɪdəkreɪz, 'ɪdə-, -eɪs/, *n.* →**vesuvianite.** [F, from Gk *eîdos* form + *krâsis* mixture]
**idol** /'aɪdl/, *n.* **1.** an image or other material object representing a deity to which religious worship is addressed. **2.** *Bible.* a false god, as of a heathen people. **3.** any person or thing blindly adored or revered. **4.** a mere image or semblance of something, visible but without substance, as a phantom. **5.** a figment of the mind. **6.** a false conception or notion; fallacy. [ME, from OF *idole,* from L *īdōlum,* from Gk *eídōlon* image, phantom, idol]
**idolater** /aɪ'dɒlətə/, *n.* **1.** a worshipper of idols. **2.** an adorer or devotee. Also, **idolist** /'aɪdələst/. [ME *idolatrer,* from OF *idolatre,* from LL *īdōlolatrēs,* from Gk *eidōlolátrēs* idol worshipper] **– idolatress,** *n. fem.*
**idolatrise** /aɪ'dɒlətraɪz/, *v.,* **-trised, -trising.** *–v.t.* **1.** →**idolise.** *–v.i.* **2.** to worship idols. Also, **idolatrize.**
**idolatrous** /aɪ'dɒlətrəs/, *adj.* **1.** pertaining to or of the nature of idolatry. **2.** worshipping idols. **3.** blindly adoring. **4.** *Obs.* used in or designed for idolatry. **– idolatrously,** *adv.* **– idolatrousness,** *n.*
**idolatry** /aɪ'dɒlətri/, *n., pl.* **-tries. 1.** the worship of idols. **2.**

blind adoration, reverence, or devotion. [ME *idolatrie,* from OF, from LL *īdōlolatrīa,* from Gk *eidōlolatreía*]

**idolise** /ˈaɪdəlaɪz/, *v.t.,* **-lised, -lising.** to regard with blind adoration or devotion. Also, **idolize.** – **idolisation** /aɪdəlaɪˈzeɪʃən/, *n.* – **idoliser,** *n.*

**idolism** /ˈaɪdəlɪzəm/, *n.* **1.** →**idolatry. 2.** idolising.

**idyll** /ˈaɪdəl, ˈɪdəl/, *n.* **1.** a poem or prose composition consisting of a 'little picture', usu. describing pastoral scenes or events or any charmingly simple episode, appealing incident, or the like. **2.** a simple descriptive or narrative piece in verse or prose. **3.** material suitable for an idyll. **4.** an episode or scene of idyllic charm. **5.** *Music.* a composition, usu. instrumental, of a pastoral or sentimental character. Also, *U.S.,* **idyl.** [L *īdyllium,* from Gk *eidýllion,* diminutive of *eîdos* form]

**idyllic** /aɪˈdɪlɪk, ɪˈdɪlɪk/, *adj.* **1.** suitable for or suggestive of an idyll; charmingly simple or poetic. **2.** of, pertaining to, or of the nature of an idyll. – **idyllically,** *adv.*

**idyllist** /ˈaɪdələst, ˈɪdələst/, *n.* a writer of idylls. Also, *U.S.,* **idylist.**

**-ie,** a hypocoristic suffix of nouns, the same as **-y**², used colloquially: **1.** as an endearment, or affectionately, esp. with and among children: *doggie,* a dog; *littlie,* a child. **2.** as a familiar abbreviation: *budgie,* a budgerigar; *conchie,* conscientious, or a conscientious objector; *mossie,* a mosquito; *postie,* a postman. **3.** as a nominalisation: *greenie,* a conservationist; *stubbie,* a small, squat beer bottle.

**i.e.,** id est.

**IE,** Indo-European.

**-ier,** variant of **-eer,** as in *brigadier, halberdier,* etc. [F, from L *-ārius*]

**-ies,** a word element representing the plural formation of nouns and third person singular of verbs for words ending in *-y, -ie,* and sometimes *-ey.* See **-s**² and **-s**³; **-es.**

**if** /ɪf/, *conj.* **1.** in case that; granting or supposing that; on condition that. **2.** even though. **3.** whether. **4. if only,** (used to introduce a phrase expressing a wish, esp. one that cannot now be fulfilled or is thought unlikely to be fulfilled): *If only I had known! If only he would come!* –*n.* **5.** a condition; a supposition. [ME; OE *gif,* c. Icel. *if,* later *ef* (also used as n., *ef* doubt)]

**iff,** a written form of abbreviation of the phrase 'if and only if', used in mathematics and logic to introduce a condition which is necessary as well as sufficient, or a statement that is implied by and implies the preceding one.

**iffy** /ˈɪfi/, *adj. Colloq.* dubious; odd.

**-ify,** variant of **-fy,** used when the preceding stem or word element ends in a consonant, as in *intensify.* [-I- + -FY]

**IG,** Indo-Germanic.

**igloo** /ˈɪglu/, *n., pl.* **-loos. 1.** a dome-shaped Eskimo hut, built of blocks of hard snow. **2.** an excavation made by a seal in the snow over its breathing hole in the ice. [Eskimo: house]

**igneous** /ˈɪgniəs/, *adj.* pertaining to or of the nature of fire. [L *igneus* of fire]

**igneous rock** /– ˈrɒk/, *n.* rock formed from magma which has cooled and solidified either at the earth's surface (volcanic rock) or deep within the earth's crust (plutonic rock).

**ignescent** /ɪgˈnɛsənt/, *adj.* **1.** emitting sparks of fire, as certain stones when struck with steel. **2.** bursting into flame. –*n.* **3.** an ignescent substance. [L *ignescens,* ppr., taking fire]

**ignimbrite** /ˈɪgnəmbraɪt/, *n.* a fine-grained rhyoletic tuff produced by eruptions of dense clouds of incandescent volcanic glass in a semi-molten or viscous state.

**ignis fatuus** /ˌɪgnɪs ˈfætʃuəs/, *n., pl.* **ignes fatui** /ˌɪgniz ˈfætʃuaɪ/. **1.** a flitting phosphorescent light seen at night, chiefly over marshy ground, and supposed to be due to spontaneous combustion of gas from decomposed organic matter; will-o'-the-wisp; marsh light. **2.** something deluding or misleading. [L: foolish fire]

**ignite** /ɪgˈnaɪt/, *v.,* **-nited, -niting.** –*v.t.* **1.** to set on fire; kindle. **2.** *Chem.* to heat intensely; roast. –*v.i.* **3.** to take fire; begin to burn. [L *ignītus,* pp.] – **ignitable, ignitible,** *adj.* – **ignitability** /ɪgˌnaɪtəˈbɪləti/, **ignitibility** /ɪgˌnaɪtəˈbɪləti/, *n.*

**igniter** /ɪgˈnaɪtə/, *n.* **1.** one who or that which ignites. **2.** *Electronics.* the carborundum rod used to initiate the discharge in an ignitron tube.

**ignition** /ɪgˈnɪʃən/, *n.* **1.** the act of igniting. **2.** the state of being ignited. **3.** (in an internal-combustion engine) the process which ignites the fuel in the cylinder. **4.** a means or device for igniting.

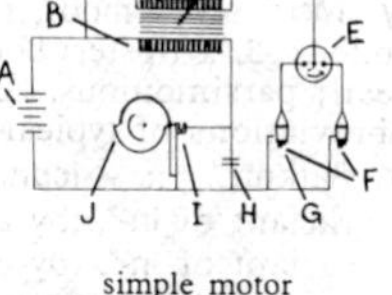

simple motor vehicle ignition: A, battery; B, primary; C, secondary; D, soft iron core; E, distributor; F, spark plugs; G, spark gap; H, capacitor; I, contact points; J, cam

**ignition coil** /ˈ– kɔɪl/, *n.* an induction coil used in an internal-combustion engine for converting the battery voltage to the high tension required by the sparking plugs.

**ignition key** /ˈ– ki/, *n.* a key for operating an ignition switch.

**ignition temperature** /ˈ– tɛmprətʃə/, *n.* the lowest temperature at which a combustible substance in air will ignite and continue burning.

**ignitron** /ɪgˈnaɪtrɒn, ˈɪgnətrɒn/, *n.* a mercury-pool cathode-arc rectifier with a carborundum rod projecting into the mercury pool. The tube conducts current when the anode is positive. [IGNI(TION) + (ELEC)TRON]

**ignoble** /ɪgˈnoʊbəl/, *adj.* **1.** of low character, aims, etc.; mean; base. **2.** of low grade or quality; inferior. **3.** not noble; of humble birth or station. [L *ignōbilis* unknown, lowborn] – **ignobility** /ɪgnoʊˈbɪləti/, **ignobleness,** *n.* – **ignobly,** *adv.*

**ignominious** /ɪgnəˈmɪniəs/, *adj.* **1.** marked by or attended with ignominy; discreditable; humiliating: *an ignominious retreat.* **2.** covered with or deserving ignominy; contemptible. [L *ignōminiōsus*] – **ignominiously,** *adv.* – **ignominiousness,** *n.*

**ignominy** /ˈɪgnəməni/, *n., pl.* **-minies. 1.** disgrace; dishonour; public contempt. **2.** base quality or conduct; a cause of disgrace. [L *ignōminia* disgrace, dishonour]

**ignoramus** /ɪgnəˈreɪməs/, *n., pl.* **-muses.** an ignorant person. [L: we do not know, we disregard]

**ignorance** /ˈɪgnərəns/, *n.* the state or fact of being ignorant; lack of knowledge, learning, or information.

**ignorant** /ˈɪgnərənt/, *adj.* **1.** destitute of knowledge; unlearned. **2.** lacking knowledge or information as to a particular subject or fact. **3.** uninformed; unaware. **4.** due to or showing lack of knowledge: *an ignorant statement.* **5.** *Colloq.* ignorant of polite ways, etc.; ill-mannered; boorish. [ME, from L *ignōrans,* ppr., not knowing] – **ignorantly,** *adv.*

**ignore** /ɪgˈnɔ/, *v.,* **-nored, -noring,** *n.* –*v.t.* **1.** to refrain from noticing or recognising: *ignore his remarks.* **2.** *U.S. Law* (of the grand jury) to reject (a bill of indictment) as without sufficient evidence. –*n.* **3. treat with ignore,** to disregard entirely. [L *ignōrāre* not to know, disregard] – **ignorable,** *adj.* – **ignorer,** *n.*

**iguana** /ɪˈgwanə/, *n.* any of various large lizards of the family Iguanidae, esp. *I. iguana,* of tropical America, often having spiny projections on the head and back. [Sp., from Arawak *iwana*]

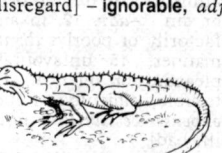

iguana

**iguanid** /ɪˈgwanɪd, ɪgjuˈanɪd/, *n.* any lizard of the family Iguanidae, having widespread distribution among tropical islands of the Southern Hemisphere, most of which are arboreal to a certain extent, a few species being semi-aquatic.

**iguanodon** /ɪˈgwanədɒn, ɪgjuˈan-/, *n.* any member of the extinct bipedal dinosaurian genus *Iguanodon,* found as a fossil in Europe, comprising reptiles from 5 to 9 metres long, with denticulate teeth like those of the iguana. [IGUAN(A) + Gk *odoús* tooth]

**ihram** /əˈram/, *n.* the dress worn by Muslim pilgrims to Mecca, consisting of two white cotton cloths, one round the waist, the other over the left shoulder. [Ar., from *harama* forbid]

**IHS,** a shortening of Greek ΙΗΣΟΥΣ Jesus, sometimes taken as representing: **1.** (L *Iesus Hominum Salvator*) Jesus, Saviour of Men. **2.** (L *In Hoc Signo Vinces*) in this sign (the cross) shalt thou conquer. **3.** (L *In Hoc Salus*) in this (cross) is salvation.

**ikebana** /ɪki'banə/, *n.* the art of Japanese flower arrangement in which flowers are displayed according to strict rules.

**Ikey Mo** /aɪki 'moʊ/, *Colloq.* –*n.* **1.** a Jew. **2.** a money-lender. **3.** a tipster; bookmaker. –*adj.* **4.** cunning; nifty. **5.** mean; parsimonious. Also, **ikeymo** /aɪki'moʊ/. [from familiar abbreviations of typical Jewish names *Isaac* and *Moses*]

**ikon** /'aɪkɒn/, *n.* →**icon.**

**il-**[1], variant of **in-**[2], (by assimilation) before *l*, as in *illation.*

**il-**[2], variant of **in-**[3], (by assimilation) before *l*, as in *illogical.*

**-il,** variant of **-ile,** as in *civil.*

**ilang-ilang** /ˌilæŋ-'ilæŋ/, *n.* →**ylang-ylang.**

**-ile,** a suffix of adjectives expressing capability, susceptibility, liability, aptitude, etc., as in *agile, docile, ductile, fragile, prehensile, tensile, volatile.* Also, **-il.** [L *-ilis;* also used to represent L *-īlis*]

**ileac** /'ɪliæk/, *adj.* of or pertaining to the ileum.

**ileitis** /ɪli'aɪtəs/, *n.* inflammation of the ileum.

**ileo-,** a word element meaning 'ileum', as in *ileostomy.* [L, combining form of *īleum* groin, flank]

**ileostomy** /ɪli'ɒstəmi/, *n., pl.* **-mies.** the formation of an artificial opening into the ileum.

**ileum** /'ɪliəm/, *n.* **1.** *Anat.* the third and lowest division of the small intestine, continuous with the jejunum and ending at the caecum. **2.** *Entomol.* a narrower part of the intestine of an insect, following the stomach. [NL, from LL: groin, flank, in L (usually pl.) *īlia* flanks, entrails]

**ileus** /'ɪliəs/, *n.* intestinal obstruction. [L, from Gk *ileós,* var. of *eileós* colic]

**ilex** /'aɪlɛks/, *n.* **1.** the holm oak. **2.** any tree or shrub of the genus *Ilex.* **3.** holly. [NL: the holly genus, L: the holm oak]

**iliac** /'ɪliæk/, *adj.* of or pertaining to the ilium. [LL *īliacus* pertaining to the flank, from L *īlium*]

**-ility,** a compound suffix making abstract nouns from adjectives by replacing the adj. suffixes: *-il(e), -le,* as in *civility, sterility, ability.* [F *-ilité, from* L *-ilitas*]

**ilium** /'ɪliəm/, *n., pl.* **ilia** /'ɪliə/. the broad upper portion of either innominate bone. [NL, special use of L *īlium* flank]

**ilk** /ɪlk/, *adj.* **1.** same. **2.** *Scot.* each; every. –*n.* **3.** family, class, or kind: *he and all his ilk.* [ME *ilk,* OE *elc, ylc,* var. of *ælc* EACH]

**ilka** /'ɪlkə/, *adj. Scot.* →**ilk.** [ILK + A[1] (indef. art.)]

**ill** /ɪl/, *adj.,* **worse, worst,** *n., adv.* –*adj.* **1.** physically disordered, as the health; unwell, sick, or indisposed. **2.** evil, wicked, or bad: *ill repute.* **3.** objectionable, unsatisfactory, poor, or faulty: *ill manners.* **4.** hostile or unkindly: *ill feeling.* **5.** unfavourable or adverse: *ill luck.* **6.** unskilful; inexpert. –*n.* **7.** evil. **8.** harm or injury. **9.** a disease or ailment. **10.** trouble or misfortune. **11.** *Archaic.* wickedness or sin. –*adv.* **12.** in an ill manner; wickedly. **13.** unsatisfactorily or poorly: *ill at ease.* **14.** in a hostile or unfriendly manner. **15.** unfavourably or unfortunately. **16.** with displeasure or offence. **17.** faultily or improperly. **18.** with trouble, difficulty, or inconvenience: *buying a new car is an expense we can ill afford.* [ME *ill,* from Scand.; cf. Icel. *illr* ill, bad]

**I'll** /aɪl/, contraction of *I will* or *I shall.*

**ill-advised** /'ɪl-ədvaɪzd/, *adj.* acting or done without due consideration; imprudent. – **ill-advisedly** /ɪl-əd'vaɪzədli/, *adv.*

**ill-assorted** /'ɪl-əsɔtəd/, *adj.* badly matched.

**ill-at-ease** /ɪl-ət-'iz/, *adj.* uncomfortable; uneasy. Also, (*in predicative use*) **ill at ease.**

**illation** /ɪ'leɪʃən/, *n.* **1.** the act of inferring. **2.** an inference or conclusion. [LL *illātio* a carrying in]

**illative** /ɪ'leɪtɪv/, *adj.* pertaining to or expressing illation; inferential: *an illative word such as 'therefore'.* [L *illātīvus*] – **illatively,** *adv.*

**illaudable** /ɪ'lɔdəbəl/, *adj.* not laudable. – **illaudably,** *adv.*

**Illawarra flame-tree** /ˌɪləwɒrə 'fleɪm-tri/, *n.* →**flame-tree.**

**Illawarra shorthorn** /– 'ʃɔthɔn/, *n.* one of a breed of dairy cattle developed in the Illawarra district of New South Wales.

Illawarra shorthorn

**ill-behaved** /'ɪl-bəheɪvd/, *adj.* badly behaved.

**ill-boding** /'ɪl-boʊdɪŋ/, *adj.* foreboding evil; inauspicious; unlucky: *ill-boding stars.*

**ill-bred** /'ɪl-brɛd/, *adj.* showing or due to lack of proper breeding; unmannerly; rude: *he remained serene in a houseful of ill-bred children.* – **ill-breeding** /ɪl-'bridɪŋ/, *n.*

**illchiljera** /ɪl'tʃɪldʒərə/, *n.* →**knob-tailed gecko.** [Aboriginal]

**ill-conditioned** /'ɪl-kəndɪʃənd/, *adj.* churlish; surly.

**ill-defined** /'ɪl-dəfaɪnd/, *adj.* badly or weakly defined; unclear.

**ill-disposed** /'ɪl-dɪspoʊzd/, *adj.* unsympathetic; unfriendly.

**ill effect** /ɪl ə'fɛkt/, *n.* a harmful or unpleasant consequence. Also, **ill-effect.**

**illegal** /ɪ'ligəl/, *adj.* not legal; unauthorised. [ML *illēgālis,* from L *il-* IL-[2] + *lēgālis* LEGAL] – **illegally,** *adv.* – **illegalness,** *n.*

**illegalise** /ɪ'ligəlaɪz/, *v.t.,* **-lised, -lising.** to make illegal: *they even wanted to illegalise smoking.* Also, **illegalize.**

**illegality** /ɪli'gæləti/, *n., pl.* **-ties. 1.** illegal condition or quality; unlawfulness. **2.** an illegal act.

**illegible** /ɪ'lɛdʒəbəl/, *adj.* not legible; impossible or hard to read or decipher: *this letter is completely illegible.* – **illegibility** /ɪˌlɛdʒə'bɪləti/, **illegibleness,** *n.* – **illegibly,** *adv.*

**illegitimacy** /ɪlə'dʒɪtəməsi/, *n., pl.* **-cies.** the state or quality of being illegitimate.

**illegitimate** /ɪlə'dʒɪtəmət/, *adj., v.,* **-mated, -mating,** *n.* –*adj.* **1.** not legitimate; unlawful: *an illegitimate act.* **2.** born out of wedlock: *an illegitimate child.* **3.** irregular; not in good usage. **4.** *Logic.* not in accordance with the principle of inference. –*v.t.* **5.** to pronounce illegitimate. –*n.* **6.** a bastard; an illegitimate person. **7.** (formerly) a free settler (as opposed to a *legitimate*). – **illegitimately,** *adv.*

**ill fame** /ɪl 'feɪm/, *n.* **1.** bad repute or name. **2. house of ill fame,** a brothel. – **ill-famed,** *adj.*

**ill-fated** /'ɪl-feɪtəd/, *adj.* **1.** destined to an unhappy fate: *an ill-fated person.* **2.** bringing bad fortune.

**ill-favoured** /'ɪl-feɪvəd/, *adj.* **1.** not pleasant in appearance; ugly: *an ill-favoured child.* **2.** offensive; unpleasant; objectionable. – **ill-favouredly,** *adv.* – **ill-favouredness,** *n.*

**ill feeling** /ɪl 'filɪŋ/, *n.* enmity or resentment.

**ill-founded** /'ɪl-faʊndəd/, *adj.* on a weak or illogical basis: *an ill-founded plea for mercy.*

**ill-gotten** /'ɪl-gɒtn/, *adj.* acquired by evil means: *ill-gotten gains.*

**ill health** /ɪl 'hɛlθ/, *n.* an unsound or disordered condition of health. Also, **ill-health.**

**ill humour** /– 'hjumə/, *n.* a disagreeable mood. – **ill-humoured,** *adj.* – **ill-humouredly,** *adv.*

**illiberal** /ɪ'lɪbərəl, -lɪbrəl/, *adj.* **1.** narrow-minded; bigoted. **2.** without culture; unscholarly; vulgar. **3.** *Rare.* not generous in giving; niggardly. [L *illīberālis* mean, sordid] – **illiberality** /ɪˌlɪbə'ræləti/, **illiberalness,** *n.* – **illiberally,** *adv.*

**illicit** /ɪ'lɪsət/, *adj.* not permitted or authorised; unlicensed; unlawful. [L *illicitus* forbidden] – **illicitly,** *adv.* – **illicitness,** *n.*

**illimitable** /ɪ'lɪmətəbəl/, *adj.* not limitable; limitless; boundless. – **illimitability** /ɪˌlɪmətə'bɪləti/, **illimitabless,** *n.* – **illimitably,** *adv.*

**illinium** /ɪ'lɪniəm/, *n.* →**promethium.** [*Illin(ois),* a U.S. State, + -IUM]

**illit.,** illiterate.

**illiteracy** /ɪ'lɪtərəsi, ɪ'lɪtrəsi/, *n., pl.* **-cies. 1.** lack of ability to read and write. **2.** the state of being illiterate; lack of education. **3.** *Rare.* a literal or a literary error.

**illiterate** /ɪ'lɪtərət, ɪ'lɪtrət/, *adj.* **1.** unable to read and write: *an illiterate tribe.* **2.** lacking education. **3.** showing lack of culture. –*n.* **4.** an illiterate person. [L *illiterātus* unlettered] – **illiterately,** *adv.* – **illiterateness,** *n.*

**ill-judged** /'ɪl-dʒʌdʒd/, *adj.* injudicious; unwise.

**ill-looking** /'ɪl-lʊkɪŋ/, *adj.* **1.** ugly. **2.** sinister.

**ill-mannered** /'ɪl-mænəd/, *adj.* having bad manners; impolite; rude. – **ill-manneredly,** *adv.*

**ill nature** /ɪl 'neɪtʃə/, *n.* unkindly or unpleasant disposition.

**ill-natured** /'ɪl-neɪtʃəd/, *adj.* **1.** having or showing an unkindly or unpleasant disposition. **2.** cross; peevish. – **ill-naturedly,** *adv.* – **ill-naturedness,** *n.*

**illness** /'ɪlnəs/, *n.* **1.** a state of bad health; sickness. **2.** an attack of sickness. **3.** *Obs.* wickedness.

**illogical** /ɪˈlɒdʒɪkəl/, *adj.* not logical; contrary to or disregardful of the rules of logic; unreasonable. – **illogicality** /ɪˌlɒdʒɪˈkæləti/, **illogicalness**, *n.* – **illogically**, *adv.*

**ill-omened** /ˈɪl-oʊmənd/, *adj.* having or attended by bad omens; ill-starred.

**ill-starred** /ˈɪl-stad/, *adj.* **1.** under the influence of an evil star; ill-fated; unlucky. **2.** disastrous.

**ill temper** /ɪl ˈtɛmpə/, *n.* bad disposition.

**ill-tempered** /ˈɪl-tɛmpəd/, *adj.* irritable; morose; bad-tempered. – **ill-temperedly**, *adv.* – **ill-temperedness**, *n.*

**ill-timed** /ˈɪl-taɪmd/, *adj.* badly timed; inopportune.

**ill-treat** /ɪl-ˈtrit/, *v.t.* to treat badly; maltreat. – **ill-treatment**, *n.*

**ill turn** /ɪl ˈtɜn/, *n.* an unkind and vicious act.

**illume** /ɪˈljum/, *v.t.*, **-lumed, -luming.** *Poetic.* →**illuminate.**

**illuminance** /ɪˈljumənəns/, *n.* illumination (def. 5) at a point of a surface, measured in lux.

**illuminant** /ɪˈljumənənt/, *n.* an illuminating agent or material.

**illuminate** /ɪˈljuməneɪt/, *v.*, **-nated, -nating,** *adj., n.* –*v.t.* **1.** to supply with light; light up. **2.** to throw light on (a subject); make lucid or clear. **3.** to decorate with lights, as in celebration. **4.** to enlighten, as with knowledge. **5.** to make resplendent or illustrious. **6.** to decorate (a letter, a page, a manuscript, etc.) with colour, gold, or the like. –*v.i.* **7.** to display lights, as in celebration. **8.** to become illuminated. –*adj.* **9.** *Archaic.* illuminated. **10.** *Obs.* enlightened. –*n.* **11.** *Archaic.* one who is or affects to be specially enlightened. [L *illūminātus,* pp.] – **illuminating,** *adj.* – **illuminatingly,** *adv.*

**illuminati** /ɪlumәˈnati/, *n.pl., sing.* **-to** /-toʊ/. **1.** persons possessing or claiming to possess superior enlightenment. **2.** (*cap.*) a name given to different religious societies or sects because of their claim to enlightenment. [L, pl. of *illūminātus* enlightened]

**illumination** /ɪljuməˈneɪʃən/, *n.* **1.** the act of illuminating. **2.** the fact or condition of being illuminated. **3.** a decoration consisting of lights. **4.** intellectual or spiritual enlightenment. **5.** the amount of light falling on unit area of the surface per second; the derived SI unit of illumination is the lux (lumen per square metre). **6.** a supply of light. **7.** decoration, as of a letter, page, or manuscript, with a painted design in colour, gold, etc.

**illuminative** /ɪˈljumənətɪv/, *adj.* illuminating.

**illuminator** /ɪˈljuməneɪtə/, *n.* **1.** one who or that which illuminates. **2.** a device for illuminating, such as a light source with lens or a mirror for concentrating light. **3.** one who paints manuscripts, books, etc., with designs in colour, gold, or the like.

**illumine** /ɪˈljumən/, *v.*, **-mined, -mining.** –*v.t.* **1.** to illuminate. –*v.i.* **2.** to be illuminated. [ME *illumyne(n)*, from F *illuminer,* from L *illūmināre* light up] – **illuminable,** *adj.*

**illuminism** /ɪˈljumənɪzəm/, *n.* **1.** the doctrines or claims of illuminati. **2.** a doctrine advocating enlightenment. – **illuminist,** *n.*

**illuminometer** /ɪˌljuməˈnɒmətə/, *n.* a type of photometer.

**illus.,** **1.** illustrated. **2.** illustration.

**ill use** /ɪl ˈjus/, *n.* bad, unjust, or cruel treatment. Also, **ill usage.**

**ill-use** /ɪl-ˈjuz/, *v.t.*, **-used, -using.** to treat badly, unjustly, or cruelly.

**illusion** /ɪˈluʒən/, *n.* **1.** something that deceives by producing a false impression. **2.** the act of deceiving; deception; delusion; mockery. **3.** the state of being deceived, or an instance of this; a false impression or belief. **4.** *Psychol.* normal mis-perception of some object or situation (e.g. optical illusions). Cf. **delusion** (def. 4), **hallucination.** **5.** a very thin, delicate kind of tulle. [ME, from L *illūsio* mocking, illusion]

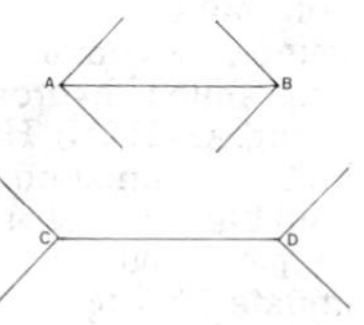

optical illusion: line AB equals line CD

**illusionary** /ɪˈluʒənəri, -ʒənri/, *adj.* pertaining to or characterised by illusions. Also, **illusional.**

**illusionism** /ɪˈluʒənɪzəm/, *n.* **1.** a theory or doctrine that the material world is an illusion. **2.** *Painting.* the effect of deceiving the eye into believing that a painted surface is an actual scene. Cf. **trompe l'oeil.**

**illusionist** /ɪˈluʒənəst/, *n.* **1.** one subject to illusions. **2.** a conjurer or magician. **3.** an adherent of illusionism.

**illusive** /ɪˈlusɪv/, *adj.* →**illusory.** – **illusively,** *adv.* – **illusiveness,** *n.*

**illusory** /ɪˈluzəri/, *adj.* **1.** causing illusion; deceptive. **2.** of the nature of an illusion; unreal. – **illusorily,** *adv.* – **illusoriness,** *n.*

**illust.,** **1.** illustrated. **2.** illustration.

**illustrate** /ˈɪləstreɪt/, *v.t.*, **-strated, -strating.** **1.** to make clear or intelligible, as by examples; exemplify. **2.** to furnish (a book, etc.) with drawings or pictorial representations intended for elucidation or adornment. **3.** *Archaic.* to enlighten. [L *illustrātus,* pp., illuminated]

**illustrated** /ˈɪləstreɪtəd/, *adj.* **1.** bearing illustrations; pictorially decorated. –*n.* **2.** an illustrated magazine.

**illustration** /ɪləsˈtreɪʃən/, *n.* **1.** that which illustrates, as a picture in a book, etc. **2.** a comparison or an example intended for explanation or corroboration. **3.** the act of rendering clear; explanation; elucidation. **4.** *Rare.* illustriousness; distinction. – **illustrational,** *adj.*

**illustrative** /ˈɪləstreɪtɪv, ɪˈlʌstrətɪv/, *adj.* serving to illustrate. – **illustratively** /ˈɪləˌstreɪtɪvli/, *adv.*

**illustrator** /ˈɪləstreɪtə/, *n.* **1.** an artist who makes illustrations. **2.** one who or that which illustrates.

**illustrious** /ɪˈlʌstriəs/, *adj.* **1.** highly distinguished; renowned; famous. **2.** glorious, as deeds, etc. **3.** *Obs.* luminous; bright. [L *illustri(s)* lit up, bright + -OUS] – **illustriously,** *adv.* – **illustriousness,** *n.*

**ill will** /ɪl ˈwɪl/, *n.* hostile or unfriendly feeling. – **ill-willed,** *adj.*

**ill-wisher** /ˈɪl-wɪʃə, ɪl-ˈwɪʃə/, *n.* one who wishes ill fortune to another.

**Illyrian** /ɪˈlɪriən/, *adj.* **1.** pertaining to Illyria an ancient country along the east coast of the Adriatic. –*n.* **2.** a native or inhabitant of Illyria. **3.** an extinct Indo-European language probably allied with Albanian. **4.** a group of Indo-European languages including Albanian.

**illywhacker** /ˈɪliwækə/, *n.* a confidence man; trickster.

**ilmenite** /ˈɪlmənaɪt/, *n.* a very common black mineral, iron titanate, $FeTiO_3$, occurring in crystals but more commonly massive; the principal ore of titanium. [from *Ilmen* (name of mountain range in the Urals) + -ITE[1]]

**im-**[1], variant of **in-**[2] used before *b, m,* and *p,* as in *imbrute, immingle.*

**im-**[2], variant of **in-**[3] used before *b, m,* and *p,* as in *immoral, imparity, imperishable.*

**im-**[3], variant of **in-**[1], before *b, m,* and *p,* as in *imbed, impearl.* Also, **em-**[1].

**I'm** /aɪm/, contraction of *I am.*

**image** /ˈɪmɪdʒ/, *n., v.*, **-aged, -aging.** –*n.* **1.** a likeness or similitude of a person, animal, or thing. **2.** an optical counterpart or appearance of an object, such as is produced by reflection from a mirror, refraction by a lens, or the passage of luminous rays through a small aperture. **3.** a mental picture or representation; an idea or conception. **4.** the impression a public figure, esp. a politician, strives to create for the public. **5.** *Psychol.* the reliving of a sensation in the absence of the original stimulus. **6.** form, appearance, or semblance. **7.** Also, **spitting image.** a counterpart or copy: *the child is the image of its mother.* **8.** a symbol or emblem. **9.** a type or embodiment. **10.** a description of something in speech or writing. **11.** *Rhet.* a figure of speech, esp. a metaphor or a simile. **12.** *Archaic.* an illusion or apparition. –*v.t.* **13.** to picture or represent in the mind; imagine; conceive. **14.** to make an image of. **15.** to set forth in speech or writing; describe. **16.** to reflect the likeness of; mirror. **17.** to symbolise or typify. **18.** *Rare.* to resemble. [ME, from F, from L *imāgo* copy, image]

**image converter** /ˈ– kənvɜtə/, *n.* Also, **image tube.** a device for converting electromagnetic radiation, as X-rays, into a visible image.

**image orthicon** /– ˈɔθəkɒn/, *n.* →**orthicon.**

**imagery** /ˈɪmɪdʒri, -dʒəri/, *n., pl.* **-ries.** **1.** the formation of images, figures, or likenesses of things, or such images collectively: *a dream's dim imagery.* **2.** *Psychol.* a person's tendencies to form images. **3.** images or statues. **4.** the use of rhetorical images. **5.** figurative description or illustration; rhetorical images collectively.

**imaginable** /ɪˈmædʒənəbəl/, *adj.* capable of being imagined or conceived. – **imaginableness,** *n.* – **imaginably,** *adv.*

**imaginal** /ɪˈmædʒənəl/, *adj.* **1.** of or pertaining to an insect imago. **2.** in the form of an insect imago.

**imaginary** /ɪˈmædʒənəri, -ənri/, *adj., n., pl.* **-ries.** *–adj.* **1.** existing only in the imagination or fancy; not real; fancied: *an imaginary illness.* **2.** *Maths.* denoting or pertaining to a quantity or expression involving the square root of a negative quantity. *–n.* **3.** *Maths.* an imaginary expression or quantity. – **imaginarily,** *adv.* – **imaginariness,** *n.*

**imaginary number** /– ˈnʌmbə/, *n.* the square root of a negative number; thus $\sqrt{-1}$ is an imaginary number, denoted by i; $i^2 = -1$.

**imagination** /ɪmædʒəˈneɪʃən/, *n.* **1.** the action of imagining, or of forming mental images or concepts of what is not actually present to the senses. **2.** the faculty of forming such images or concepts. **3.** the power of reproducing images stored in the memory under the suggestion of associated images **(reproductive imagination),** or of recombining former experiences in the creation of new images different from any known by experience **(productive** or **creative imagination).** **4.** the faculty of producing ideal creations consistent with reality, as in literature (distinguished from *fancy*). **5.** the product of imagining; a conception or mental creation, often a baseless or fanciful one. **6.** *Archaic.* a plan, scheme, or plot. [ME, from L *imāginātio*] – **imaginational,** *adj.*

**imaginative** /ɪˈmædʒənətɪv/, *adj.* **1.** characterised by or bearing evidence of imagination: *an imaginative tale.* **2.** pertaining to or concerned with imagination: *the imaginative faculty.* **3.** given to imagining, as persons. **4.** having exceptional powers of imagination. **5.** fanciful. – **imaginatively,** *adv.* – **imaginativeness,** *n.*

**imagine** /ɪˈmædʒən/, *v.,* **-ined, -ining.** *–v.t.* **1.** to form a mental image of (something not actually present to the senses). **2.** to think, believe, or fancy. **3.** to assume or suppose. **4.** to conjecture or guess: *I cannot imagine what you mean.* **5.** *Archaic.* to plan, scheme, or plot. *–v.i.* **6.** to form mental images of things not present to the senses; use the imagination. **7.** to suppose; think; conjecture. [ME *imagine(n),* from F *imaginer,* from L *imāginārī* picture to oneself, fancy] – **imaginer,** *n.*

**imagism** /ˈɪmədʒɪzəm/, *n.* a method or movement in poetic composition, originating about 1912, which aimed particularly at 'images' or clear pictures of what the poet has in mind, and used rhythm or cadence rather than the conventional metrical forms. See **free verse.** – **imagist,** *n., adj.* – **imagistic** /ɪməˈdʒɪstɪk/, *adj.*

**imago** /ɪˈmeɪgoʊ/, *n., pl.* **imagos, imagines** /ɪˈmeɪdʒəniz/. **1.** *Entomol.* an adult insect. **2.** *Psychoanal.* an idealised concept of a loved one, formed in childhood and retained uncorrected in adult life. [NL, special use of L *imāgo* image]

**imam** /ɪˈmam/, *n.* **1.** the officiating priest of a mosque. **2.** the title for a Muslim religious leader or chief. **3.** one of a succession of seven or twelve religious leaders, believed to be divinely inspired, of the Shiites. Also, **imaum** /ɪˈmam, ɪˈmɔm/. [Ar. *imām* leader, guide]

**imamate** /ɪˈmameɪt/, *n.* **1.** the office of an imam. **2.** the region or territory governed by an imam.

**imaret** /ɪˈmarət/, *n.* (among the Turks) a hospice for pilgrims, etc. [Turk., from Ar. *'imāra(t)* building, dwelling place]

**imbalance** /ɪmˈbæləns/, *n.* **1.** the state or condition of lacking balance. **2.** faulty muscular or glandular co-ordination.

**imbecile** /ˈɪmbəsil, -saɪl/, *n.* **1.** a person of defective mentality above the grade of idiocy. **2.** *Colloq.* a silly person; fool. *–adj.* **3.** mentally feeble. **4.** showing mental feebleness or incapacity. **5.** silly; absurd. **6.** *Rare.* weak or feeble. [F, from L *imbēcillus* weak, feeble] – **imbecilely,** *adv.* – **imbecilic** /ɪmbəˈsɪlɪk/, *adj.*

**imbecility** /ɪmbəˈsɪləti/, *n., pl.* **-ties.** **1.** feebleness of mind; mental weakness that falls short of absolute idiocy. **2.** an instance or point of weakness or feebleness. **3.** silliness or absurdity. **4.** an instance of this.

**imbed** /ɪmˈbɛd/, *v.t.,* **-bedded, -bedding.** →**embed.**

**imbibe** /ɪmˈbaɪb/, *v.,* **-bibed, -bibing.** *–v.t.* **1.** to drink in, or drink. **2.** to absorb or take in as if by drinking. **3.** to take or receive into the mind, as knowledge, ideas, etc. *–v.i.* **4.** to drink; absorb liquid or moisture. **5.** *Obs.* to soak or saturate; imbue. [ME, from L *imbibere* drink in] – **imbiber,** *n.*

**imbibition** /ɪmbɪˈbɪʃən/, *n.* **1.** the act of imbibing. **2.** *Chem.* the absorption or adsorption of a liquid by a solid or gel causing swelling. **3.** *Photog.* the absorption of a dye by gelatine in colour printing.

**imbo** /ˈɪmboʊ/, *n. Colloq.* a simpleton; fool. [shortened form of IMBECILE]

**imbricate** /ˈɪmbrəkeɪt/, *adj., v.,* **-cated, -cating.** *–adj.*,Also,,**imbricated.** **1.** bent and hollowed like a roof tile. **2.** of, like, or decorated with lines or curves resembling overlapping tiles. **3.** *Biol.* overlapping like tiles, as scales, leaves, etc. **4.** characterised by, or as by, overlapping scales. *–v.t.* **5.** to overlap like tiles or shingles. *–v.i.* **6.** to be arranged in an overlapping manner. [L *imbricātus,* pp., covered with gutter tiles] – **imbricately,** *adv.* – **imbricative,** *adj.*

A, imbricate flower; B, imbricate scale of cone

**imbrication** /ɪmbrəˈkeɪʃən/, *n.* **1.** an overlapping, as of tiles or shingles. **2.** a decorative pattern imitating this.

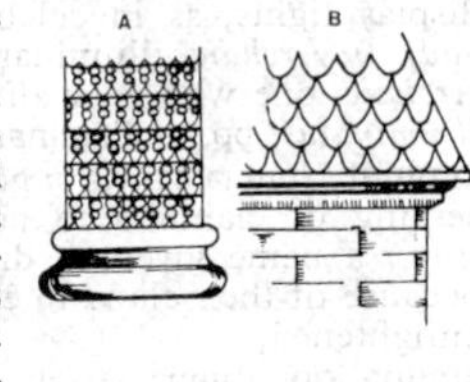

A, ornamental imbrication on a column; B, imbrication on roof tiles

**imbroglio** /ɪmˈbroʊlioʊ/, *n., pl.* **-os.** **1.** an intricate and perplexing state of affairs; a complicated or difficult situation. **2.** a misunderstanding or disagreement of a complicated nature, as between persons or nations. **3.** a confused heap. [It.: confusion, from *imbrogliare* confuse, embroil]

**imbrue** /ɪmˈbru/, *v.t.,* **-brued, -bruing.** **1.** to wet in or with something that stains, now esp. blood; stain with blood. **2.** to permeate; impregnate (usu. fol. by *with*). [ME *enbrewe(n),* from OF *embreuver* give to drink, from L *bibere* drink] – **imbruement,** *n.*

**imbrute** /ɪmˈbrut/, *v.,* **-bruted, -bruting.** *–v.t.* **1.** to degrade to the level of a brute. *–v.i.* **2.** to sink to the level of a brute. Also, **embrute.** [IM-[1] + BRUTE, *n.*] – **imbrutement,** *n.*

**imbue** /ɪmˈbju/, *v.t.,* **-bued, -buing.** **1.** to impregnate or inspire, as with feelings, opinions, etc. **2.** to saturate with moisture, impregnate with colour, etc. **3.** to imbrue. [L *imbuere*] – **imbuement,** *n.*

**I.M.F.** /aɪ ɛm ˈɛf/, International Monetary Fund.

**imidazole** /ɪməˈdæzoʊl, ɪmədəˈzoʊl/, *n.* an organic heterocyclic compound, $C_3H_4N_2$; glyoxalin. [IMID(E) + AZ(O)- + -OLE]

**imide** /ˈɪmaɪd/, *n.* a compound derived from ammonia by replacement of two hydrogen atoms by acidic radicals, characterised by the -NH group. Also, **imid** /ˈɪməd/. [arbitrary alteration of AMIDE]

**imido-,** a combining form indicating an imide.

**imine** /ɪˈmin, ˈɪmin/, *n.* a compound containing the NH group united with a non-acid radical. [alteration of AMINE modelled on IMIDE]

**imino-,** a combining form indicating an imine.

**imipramine hydrochloride** /ɪˌmɪprəmin haɪdrəˈklɔraɪd/, *n.* a drug, $C_{19}H_{24}N_2$ HCl, used to treat endogenous depression.

**imit.,** **1.** imitation. **2.** imitative.

**imitable** /ˈɪmətəbəl/, *adj.* that may be imitated. – **imitability** /ɪmətəˈbɪləti/, *n.*

**imitate** /ˈɪməteɪt/, *v.t.,* **-tated, -tating.** **1.** to follow or endeavour to follow in action or manner. **2.** to mimic or counterfeit. **3.** to make a copy of; reproduce closely. **4.** to have or assume the appearance of; simulate. [L *imitātus,* pp., having copied] – **imitator,** *n.*

**imitation** /ɪməˈteɪʃən/, *n.* **1.** a result or product of imitating. **2.** the act of imitating. **3.** *Biol.* close external resemblance of an organism to some other organism or to objects in its environment. **4.** *Psychol.* a response or state of mind brought about by observation and copying in some respects the act of another. **5.** a counterfeit. **6.** a literary composition that imitates the manner or subject of another author or work. **7.** mimesis. **8.** *Music.* the repetition of a melodic phrase at a different pitch or key from the original, or in a different voice part. *–adj.* **9.** made to imitate a genuine or superior article or thing: *imitation pearls.* [L *imitātio*] – **imitational,** *adj.*

**imitative** /ˈɪmətətɪv/, *adj.* **1.** imitating or copying, or given to imitating. **2.** characterised by or involving imitation or copying. **3.** *Biol.* →**mimetic.** **4.** made in imitation of something. **5.** →**onomatopoeic.** – **imitatively,** *adv.* – **imitativeness,** *n.*

**immaculate** /ɪˈmækjulət, -kjə-/, *adj.* **1.** free from spot or stain; spotlessly clean, as linen. **2.** free from moral blemish or impurity; pure, or undefiled. **3.** free from fault or flaw; free from errors, as a text. **4.** *Zool., Bot.* without spots or coloured marks; unicolour. [late ME, from L *immaculātus* unspotted] – **immaculacy, immaculateness,** *n.* – **immaculately,** *adv.*

**Immaculate Conception** /ɪˌmækjələt kənˈsɛpʃən/, *n.* the Roman Catholic doctrine that the Virgin Mary was without the stain of original sin.

**immanent** /ˈɪmənənt/, *adj.* **1.** remaining within; indwelling; inherent. **2.** (of a mental act) taking place within the mind of the subject, and having no effect outside it. **3.** *Theol.* **a.** of or pertaining to the continuing presence of God among His people and in each individual believer. **b.** (of the deity) seen as indwelling in the Church. [LL *immanens,* ppr., remaining in] – **immanence, immanency,** *n.* – **immanently,** *adv.*

**immaterial** /ɪməˈtɪəriəl/, *adj.* **1.** of no essential consequence; unimportant. **2.** not material; incorporeal; spiritual. [ML *immātēriālis,* from LL, from *im-* IM-² + *mātēriālis* MATERIAL; replacing ME *immaterielle,* from F] – **immaterially,** *adv.* – **immaterialness,** *n.*

**immaterialise** /ɪməˈtɪəriəlaɪz/, *v.t.,* **-lised, -lising.** to make immaterial. Also, **immaterialize.**

**immaterialism** /ɪməˈtɪəriəlɪzəm/, *n.* the doctrine that there is no material world, but that only immaterial substances or spiritual beings exist (opposed to *materialism*). – **immaterialist,** *n.*

**immateriality** /ˌɪmətɪəriˈæləti/, *n., pl.* **-ties. 1.** the state or character of being immaterial. **2.** something immaterial.

**immature** /ɪməˈtjuə, -tjɔ/, *adj.* **1.** not mature, ripe, developed, or perfected. **2.** *Phys. Geog.* youthful. **3.** *Archaic.* premature. [L *immātūrus* unripe] – **immaturely,** *adv.* – **immaturity, immatureness,** *n.*

**immeasurable** /ɪˈmɛʒərəbəl/, *adj.* incapable of being measured; limitless. – **immeasurability** /ˌɪmɛʒərəˈbɪləti/, **immeasurableness,** *n.* – **immeasurably,** *adv.*

**immediacy** /ɪˈmidiəsi/, *n.* **1.** the character of being immediate. **2.** *Philos.* **a.** that nature of a thing in virtue of which it exists, acts, or appears, directly and not through any intervening object, operation, or representation. **b.** that which the mind experiences when anything exists, acts, or appears thus.

**immediate** /ɪˈmidiət/, *adj.* **1.** occurring or accomplished without delay; instant: *an immediate reply.* **2.** pertaining to the present time or moment: *our immediate plans.* **3.** having no time intervening; present or next adjacent: *the immediate future.* **4.** having no object or space intervening; nearest or next: *in the immediate vicinity.* **5.** without intervening medium or agent; direct: *an immediate cause.* **6.** having a direct bearing: *immediate consideration.* **7.** *Metaphys.* indemonstrable; intuitive. [ML *immediātus* not mediate] – **immediateness,** *n.*

**immediate constituent** /– kənˈstɪtʃuənt/, *n. Linguistics.* the parts into which any fragment of language can most immediately be divided, as the subject and predicate of a sentence, or the verb and object of a predicate. *Abbrev.:* i.c.

**immediately** /ɪˈmidiətli/, *adv.* **1.** without lapse of time, or without delay; instantly; at once. **2.** without intervening medium or agent; concerning or affecting directly. **3.** with no object or space intervening. **4.** closely: *immediately in the vicinity.* *–conj.* **5.** immediately that; the moment that; as soon as.

**immedicable** /ɪˈmɛdəkəbəl/, *adj.* →**incurable.**

**immemorial** /ɪməˈmɔriəl/, *adj.* extending back beyond memory, record, or knowledge: *from time immemorial.* [ML *immemoriālis,* from L *im-* IM-² + *memoriālis* MEMORIAL] – **immemorially,** *adv.*

**immense** /ɪˈmɛns/, *adj.* **1.** vast; huge; very great: *an immense territory.* **2.** immeasurable; boundless. **3.** *Colloq.* very good or fine. [L *immensus* boundless, unmeasured] – **immensely,** *adv.* – **immenseness,** *n.*

**immensity** /ɪˈmɛnsəti/, *n., pl.* **-ties. 1.** vastness; hugeness; enormous extent: *the immensity of the Roman empire.* **2.** the state of being immense; boundless extent; infinity. **3.** a vast expanse; an immense quantity.

**immensurable** /ɪˈmɛnʃərəbəl, -ʃrəbəl/, *adj.* →**immeasurable.** [LL *immensurābilis*] – **immensurability** /ɪˌmɛnʃərəˈbɪləti/, *n.*

**immerge** /ɪˈmɜdʒ/, *v.,* **-merged, -merging.** *Rare.* *–v.t.* **1.** to immerse. *–v.i.* **2.** to plunge, as into a fluid. **3.** to disappear as by plunging. [L *immergere*] – **immergence,** *n.*

**immerse** /ɪˈmɜs/, *v.t.,* **-mersed, -mersing. 1.** to plunge into or place under a liquid; dip; sink. **2.** to baptise by immersion. **3.** to embed; bury. **4.** to involve deeply; absorb. [L *immersus,* pp., dipped]

**immersed** /ɪˈmɜst/, *adj.* **1.** plunged or sunk in or as in a liquid. **2.** *Biol.* somewhat or wholly sunk in the surrounding parts, as an organ. **3.** *Rare.* baptised.

**immersion** /ɪˈmɜʃən, -ʒən/, *n.* **1.** the act of immersing. **2.** the state of being immersed. **3.** baptism by plunging the whole person into water. **4.** the state of being deeply engaged; absorption. **5.** *Astron.* the disappearance of a celestial body by passing either behind another or into its shadow. Cf. **emersion.**

**immersion heater** /ˈ– hitə/, *n.* an electrical heater, usu. thermostatically controlled, immersed in a liquid to heat it.

**immersionism** /ɪˈmɜʃənɪzəm/, *n.* **1.** the doctrine that immersion is essential to Christian baptism. **2.** the practice of baptism by immersion. – **immersionist,** *n.*

**immersion objective** /ɪˌmɜʃən əbˈdʒɛktɪv/, *n.* a type of lens used in microscopes in which the lowest lens of the objective system is immersed in a drop of cedar-wood oil placed on the slide to be examined.

**immesh** /ɪˈmɛʃ/, *v.t.* →**enmesh.**

**immethodical** /ɪməˈθɒdɪkəl/, *adj.* not methodical; without method. – **immethodically,** *adv.*

**immigrant** /ˈɪməgrənt/, *n.* **1.** one who or that which immigrates. **2.** a person who migrates into a country for permanent residence. *–adj.* **3.** immigrating.

**immigrate** /ˈɪməgreɪt/, *v.,* **-grated, -grating.** *–v.i.* **1.** to pass or come into a new habitat or place of residence. **2.** to come into a country of which one is not a native for the purpose of permanent residence. *–v.t.* **3.** to introduce as settlers. [L *immigrātus,* pp.]

**immigration** /ɪməˈgreɪʃən/, *n.* **1.** the act of immigrating. **2.** immigrants collectively.

**imminence** /ˈɪmənəns/, *n.* **1.** the state or fact of being imminent or impending: *imminence of war.* **2.** that which is imminent; impending evil or danger.

**imminent** /ˈɪmənənt/, *adj.* **1.** likely to occur at any moment; impending: *war is imminent.* **2.** projecting or leaning forward; overhanging. [L *imminens,* ppr., projecting over] – **imminently,** *adv.*

**immingle** /ɪˈmɪŋgəl/, *v.t., v.i.,* **-gled, -gling.** →**intermingle.**

**immiscible** /ɪˈmɪsəbəl/, *adj.* not miscible; incapable of being mixed. – **immiscibility** /ɪˌmɪsəˈbɪləti/, *n.* – **immiscibly,** *adv.*

**immitigable** /ɪˈmɪtəgəbəl/, *adj.* not mitigable; not to be mitigated. [LL *immitigābilis*] – **immitigability** /ɪˌmɪtəgəˈbɪləti/, *n.* – **immitigably,** *adv.*

**immix** /ɪˈmɪks/, *v.t.* to mix in; mingle. [backformation from ME *immixt,* pp. (from L *immixtus,* pp., intermingled), apparently taken as pp. of E formation]

**immixture** /ɪˈmɪkstʃə/, *n.* **1.** the act of immixing. **2.** the state of being immixed; involvement.

**immobile** /ɪˈmoubaɪl/, *adj.* **1.** not mobile; immovable. **2.** that does not move; motionless. [L *immōbilis;* replacing ME *inmobill,* from IN-³ + MOBIL(E)]

**immobilise** /ɪˈmoubəlaɪz/, *v.t.,* **-lised, -lising. 1.** to make immobile; fix so as to be or become immovable. **2.** *Finance.* to establish a monetary reserve by withdrawing (specie) from circulation; create fixed capital in place of (circulating capital). **3.** to deprive of the capacity for mobilisation. Also, **immobilize.** – **immobilisation** /ɪˌmoubəlaɪˈzeɪʃən/, *n.*

**immobility** /ɪməˈbɪləti/, *n.* the character or condition of being immobile or irremovable.

**immoderate** /ɪ'mɒdərət, -drət/, *adj.* **1.** not moderate; exceeding just or reasonable limits; excessive; extreme. **2.** *Obs.* intemperate. **3.** *Obs.* without bounds. [L *immoderātus* without measure] – **immoderately,** *adv.* – **immoderateness,** *n.*

**immoderation** /ɪˌmɒdə'reɪʃən/, *n.* lack of moderation.

**immodest** /ɪ'mɒdəst/, *adj.* **1.** not modest in conduct, utterance, etc.; indecent; shameless. **2.** not modest in assertion or pretension; forward; impudent. – **immodestly,** *adv.* – **immodesty,** *n.*

**immolate** /'ɪməleɪt/, *v.t.*, **-lated, -lating. 1.** to sacrifice. **2.** to kill as a sacrificial victim; offer in sacrifice. [L *immolātus*, pp., sacrificed, orig., sprinkled with sacrificial meal] – **immolator,** *n.*

**immolation** /ɪmə'leɪʃən/, *n.* **1.** the act of immolating. **2.** the state of being immolated. **3.** a sacrifice.

**immoral** /ɪ'mɒrəl/, *adj.* not moral; not conforming to the moral law; not conforming to accepted patterns of conduct. – **immorally,** *adv.*

**immoral contract** /– 'kɒntrækt/, *n.* a legal contract which is void because it is based on a sexually immoral consideration, as a contract for future illicit cohabitation.

**immorality** /ɪmə'ræləti/, *n.*, *pl.* **-ties. 1.** immoral quality, character, or conduct; wickedness; vice. **2.** sexual impurity; unchastity. **3.** an immoral act.

**immortal** /ɪ'mɔtl/, *adj.* **1.** not mortal; not liable or subject to death; undying. **2.** remembered or celebrated through all time. **3.** not liable to perish or decay; imperishable; everlasting. **4.** perpetual, lasting, or constant: *an immortal enemy.* **5.** pertaining to immortal beings or immortality. *–n.* **6.** an immortal being. **7.** a person, esp. an author, of enduring fame. **8.** (*usu. pl.*) one of the gods of classical mythology. [ME, from L *immortālis* undying] – **immortally,** *adv.*

**immortalise** /ɪ'mɔtəlaɪz/, *v.t.*, **-lised, -lising. 1.** to make immortal; endow with immortality. **2.** to bestow unending fame upon; perpetuate. Also, **immortalize.** – **immortalisation** /ɪˌmɔtəlaɪ'zeɪʃən/, *n.* – **immortaliser,** *n.*

**immortality** /ɪmɔ'tæləti/, *n.* **1.** immortal condition or quality; unending life. **2.** enduring fame.

**immortelle** /ɪmɔ'tɛl/, *n.* an everlasting plant or flower, esp. *Xeranthemum annuum.* [F, properly fem. of *immortel,* from L *immortālis* IMMORTAL]

**immotile** /ɪ'moʊtaɪl/, *adj.* not motile.

**immovable** /ɪ'muvəbəl/, *adj.* **1.** incapable of being moved; fixed; stationary. **2.** not moving; motionless. **3.** not subject to change; unalterable. **4.** incapable of being affected with feeling; emotionless: *an immovable heart or face.* **5.** incapable of being moved from one's purpose, opinion, etc.; steadfast; unyielding. **6.** not changing from one date to another in different years: *an immovable feast.* **7.** *Law.* **a.** not liable to be removed, or permanent in place. **b.** (of property) real, as distinguished from personal. *–n.* **8.** something immovable. **9.** (*pl.*) *Law.* lands and the appurtenances thereof, as trees, buildings, etc. Also (esp. defs 7 and 9), **immoveable.** – **immovability** /ɪˌmuvə'bɪləti/, **immovableness,** *n.* – **immovably,** *adv.*

**immun.,** immunology. Also, **immunol.**

**immune** /ə'mjun, ɪ-/, *adj.* **1.** protected from a disease or the like, as by inoculation. **2.** exempt. *–n.* **3.** one who is immune. [ME, from L *immūnis* exempt]

**immunise** /'ɪmjunaɪz, -jə-/, *v.t.*, **-nised, -nising.** to make immune. Also, **immunize.** – **immunisation** /ˌɪmjənaɪ'zeɪʃən/, *n.*

**immunity** /ə'mjunəti, ɪ-/, *n.*, *pl.* **-ties. 1.** the state of being immune from, or insusceptible to, a particular disease or the like. **2.** exemption from any natural or usual liability. **3.** exemption from obligation, service, duty, or liability to taxation, jurisdiction, etc. **4.** special privilege. **5.** *Eccles.* **a.** the exemption of ecclesiastical persons and things from secular or civil liabilities, duties, and burdens. **b.** a particular exemption of this kind. [ME, from L *immūnitas* exemption, ML sanctuary]

**immunochemistry** /ˌɪmjənoʊ'kɛməstri/, *n.* the chemistry of immunology. –**immunochemical,** *adj.* –**immunochemically,** *adv.*

**immunogenic** /ɪˌmjunoʊ'dʒɛnɪk, 'ɪmjun-/, *adj.* causing immunity.

**immunol.,** immunology.

**immunology** /ɪmju'nɒlədʒi/, *n.* that branch of medical science which deals with immunity from disease and the production of such immunity. – **immunologic** /ɪmjunə'lɒdʒɪk/, **immunological** /ɪˌmjunə'lɒdʒɪkəl/, *adj.* – **immunologist,** *n.*

**immunotherapy** /ˌɪmjunoʊ'θɛrəpi/, *n.* the treating of disease by stimulating the body to produce more antibodies.

**immure** /ɪ'mjuə/, *v.t.*, **-mured, -muring. 1.** to enclose within walls. **2.** to shut in; confine. **3.** to imprison. **4.** to build into or entomb in a wall. **5.** *Obs.* to surround with walls; fortify. [ML *immūrāre,* from L *im-* IM-[1] + *mūrus* wall] – **immurement,** *n.*

**immutable** /ɪ'mjutəbəl/, *adj.* not mutable; unchangeable; unalterable; changeless. – **immutability** /ɪˌmjutə'bɪləti/, **immutableness,** *n.* – **immutably,** *adv.*

**imp** /ɪmp/, *n.* **1.** a little devil or demon; an evil spirit. **2.** a mischievous child. [ME and OE *impe* a shoot, a graft]

**imp.,** **1.** imperative. **2.** imperfect. **3.** imperial.

**Imp.,** **1.** (L *Imperator*) Emperor. **2.** (L *Imperatrix*) Empress.

**impact** /'ɪmpækt/ *n;* /ɪm'pækt/, *v., –n.* **1.** the striking of one body against another. **2.** an impinging: *the impact of light on the eye.* **3.** forcible contact or impinging: *the tremendous impact of the shot.* **4.** influence or effect exerted by a new idea, concept, ideology, etc. **5. make an impact on,** to impress. *–v.t.* **6.** to drive or press closely or firmly into something; pack in. *–v.i.* **7.** *Colloq.* to collide. [L *impactus,* pp., driven in]

**impact-absorbing** /'ɪmpækt-əbzɔbɪŋ/, *adj.* of or pertaining to parts of a motor car, as the instrument panel, which are designed to minimise the effects of a collision, either because they give way or because they are made of resilient material.

**impact driver** /'ɪmpækt draɪvə/, *n.* a screwdriver so designed that a sharp tap on its handle rotates the blade, used to dislodge very tight screws.

**impacted** /ɪm'pæktəd/, *adj.* **1.** wedged in. **2.** *Dentistry.* denoting a tooth incapable of growing out or erupting, and remaining within the jawbone. **3.** driven together; tightly packed.

**impaction** /ɪm'pækʃən/, *n.* **1.** the act of impacting. **2.** the state of being impacted; close fixation. **3.** *Dentistry.* a tooth which has not erupted that is embedded in the jawbone.

**impact-telescoping** /'ɪmpækt-tɛləskoupɪŋ/, *adj.* of or pertaining to a steering column, or other parts of a motor car, which are designed to telescope upon impact, thus minimising the effects of the collision.

**impact test** /'ɪmpækt tɛst/, *n.* a test applied to a metal, or other material, to determine its resistance to a suddenly applied stress.

**impact zone** /'– zoun/, *n.* (in surfing) the point at which the breaking wave hits land and exerts maximum force.

**impair** /ɪm'pɛə/, *v.t.* **1.** to make worse; diminish in value, excellence, etc. *–v.i.* **2.** to become worse. *–n.* **3.** *Archaic.* impairment. [ME *empeire(n),* from OF *empeirer,* from L *im-* IM-[1] + *pējor* worse] – **impairer,** *n.* – **impairment,** *n.*

**impala** /ɪm'palə/, *n.* an antelope, *Aepyceros melampus,* from southern and eastern Africa, which can leap up to 9 metres. [Zulu]

**impale** /ɪm'peɪl/, *v.t.*, **-paled, -paling. 1.** to fix upon a sharpened stake or the like. **2.** to pierce with a sharpened stake thrust up through the body, as for torture or punishment. **3.** to fix upon, or pierce through with, anything pointed. **4.** to make helpless as if pierced through. **5.** *Rare.* to enclose with or as with pales or stakes; fence in; hem in. **6.** to combine (two coats of arms) on one shield by putting them side by side with a vertical line between. Also, **empale.** [ML *impālāre,* from L *im-* IM-[1] + *pālus* stake] – **impalement,** *n.*

**impalpable** /ɪm'pælpəbəl/, *adj.* **1.** not palpable; incapable of being perceived by the sense of touch; intangible. **2.** incapable of being readily grasped by the mind: *impalpable distinctions.* **3.** (of powder) so fine that when rubbed between the fingers no grit is felt. – **impalpability** /ɪmˌpælpə'bɪləti/, *n.* – **impalpably,** *adv.*

**impanation** /ɪmpæ'neɪʃən/, *n.* the doctrine that the body and blood of Christ are in the bread and wine after consecration. [ML *impānātio,* from *impānāre* embody in bread, from L *im-*

IM-[1] + *pānis* bread]

**impanel** /ɪm'pænəl/, *v.t.*, **-elled, -elling** or (*U.S.*) **-eled, -eling.** →**empanel.**

**imparadise** /ɪm'pærədaɪs/, *v.t.*, **-dised, -dising. 1.** to put in or as in paradise; make supremely happy. **2.** to make a paradise of.

**imparipinnate** /ˌɪmpærə'pɪneɪt, -'pɪnət/, *adj.* pinnate with a terminal leaflet.

**imparity** /ɪm'pærəti/, *n.*, *pl.* **-ties.** lack of parity or equality; disparity; an inequality.

**impark** /ɪm'pak/, *v.t.* **1.** to shut up as in a park. **2.** to enclose as a park. [AF *enparker.* See IM-[1], PARK] – **imparkation** /ɪmpa'keɪʃən/, *n.*

**impart** /ɪm'pat/, *v.t.* **1.** to make known, tell, or relate: *to impart a secret.* **2.** to give, bestow, or communicate. **3.** to grant a part or share of. *–v.i.* **4.** *Archaic.* to grant a part or share; give. [ME, from L *impartīre* share] – **impartation** /ɪmpa'teɪʃən/, **impartment,** *n.* – **imparter,** *n.*

**impartial** /ɪm'paʃəl/, *adj.* not partial; unbiased; just. – **impartiality** /ˌɪmpaʃi'æləti/, **impartialness,** *n.* – **impartially,** *adv.*

**impartible** /ɪm'patəbəl/, *adj.* not partible; indivisible. [LL *impartībilis*] – **impartibility** /ɪmˌpatə'bɪləti/, *n.* – **impartibly,** *adv.*

**impassable** /ɪm'pasəbəl/, *adj.* not passable; that cannot be passed over, through, or along: *muddy, impassable roads.* – **impassability** /ɪmˌpasə'bɪləti/, **impassableness,** *n.* – **impassably,** *adv.*

**impasse** /'ɪmpas/, *n.* **1.** a position from which there is no escape. **2.** a road or way that has no outlet. [F]

**impassible** /ɪm'pasəbəl/, *adj.* **1.** incapable of suffering pain. **2.** incapable of suffering harm. **3.** incapable of emotion; impassive. [LL *impassibilis.* See IM-[2], PASSIBLE] – **impassibility** /ɪmˌpasə'bɪləti/, **impassibleness,** *n.* – **impassibly,** *adv.*

**impassion** /ɪm'pæʃən/, *v.t.* to fill, or affect strongly, with passion. [It. *impassionare,* from *im-* IM-[1] + *passione* PASSION]

**impassionate** /ɪm'pæʃənət/, *adj. Rare.* **1.** free from passion; dispassionate. **2.** impassioned. [It. *impassionato,* pp., from *im-* IM-[2] + *passione* PASSION]

**impassioned** /ɪm'pæʃənd/, *adj.* filled with passion; passionate; ardent. – **impassionedly,** *adv.* – **impassionedness,** *n.*

**impassive** /ɪm'pæsɪv/, *adj.* **1.** without emotion; apathetic; unmoved. **2.** calm; serene. **3.** unconscious. **4.** not subject to suffering. – **impassively,** *adv.* – **impassiveness, impassivity** /ɪmpæ'sɪvəti/, *n.*

**impaste** /ɪm'peɪst/, *v.t.*, **-pasted, -pasting. 1.** to cover with or enclose in a paste. **2.** to form into a paste. **3.** to lay on thickly, as paste. [It. *impastare,* from *im-* IM-[1] + *pasta* (from LL *pasta* PASTE)] – **impastation** /ɪmpæs'teɪʃən/, *n.*

**impasto** /ɪm'pæstoʊ/, *n.* **1.** the laying on of colours thickly. **2.** colour so laid on. [It., from *impastare.* See IMPASTE]

**impatience** /ɪm'peɪʃəns/, *n.* **1.** lack of patience. **2.** eager desire for relief or change; restlessness. **3.** intolerance of anything that thwarts or hinders.

**impatiens** /ɪm'peɪʃiɛnz/, *n.* any of a genus, *Impatiens,* of annual plants having irregular flowers, in which the calyx and corolla are not clearly distinguishable. [NL, n. use of L adj. See IMPATIENT]

**impatient** /ɪm'peɪʃənt/, *adj.* **1.** not patient; not bearing pain, opposition, etc., with composure. **2.** indicating lack of patience: *an impatient answer.* **3.** intolerant (fol. by *of*): *impatient of any interruptions.* **4.** restless in desire or expectation; eagerly desirous (to do something). [ME *impacient,* from L *impatiens* not bearing or enduring] – **impatiently,** *adv.*

**impawn** /ɪm'pɔn/, *v.t.* to put in pawn; pledge.

**impeach** /ɪm'pitʃ/, *v.t.* **1.** to challenge the credibility of: *to impeach a witness.* **2.** to bring an accusation against a person in respect of treason or some other grave criminal offence. **3.** to call in question; cast an imputation upon: *to impeach one's motives.* [ME *empeche(n),* from OF *empechier* hinder, from LL *impedicāre* catch, entangle, from L *in-* IN-[2] + *pedica* fetter] – **impeacher,** *n.*

**impeachable** /ɪm'pitʃəbəl/, *adj.* **1.** liable to be impeached. **2.** making one liable to impeachment, as an offence. – **impeachability** /ɪmˌpitʃə'bɪləti/, *n.*

**impeachment** /ɪm'pitʃmənt/, *n.* **1.** the act of impeaching. **2.** *U.S.* (in Congress, or a state legislature) the presentation of formal charges against a public official by the lower house, as a preliminary to a trial before the upper house.

**impearl** /ɪm'pɜl/, *v.t.* **1.** to form into pearl-like drops. **2.** to make pearl-like or pearly. **3.** *Poetic.* to adorn with pearls or pearl-like drops.

**impeccable** /ɪm'pɛkəbəl/, *adj.* **1.** faultless or irreproachable: *impeccable manners.* **2.** not liable to sin; exempt from the possibility of doing wrong. *–n.* **3.** an impeccable person. [LL *impeccābilis.* Cf. PECCABLE] – **impeccability** /ɪmˌpɛkə'bɪləti/, *n.* – **impeccably,** *adv.*

**impeccant** /ɪm'pɛkənt/, *adj.* not sinning; sinless. – **impeccancy,** *n.*

**impecunious** /ɪmpə'kjuniəs/, *adj.* having no money; penniless; poor. – **impecuniously,** *adv.* – **impecuniousness, impecuniosity** /ˌɪmpəkjuni'ɒsəti/, *n.*

**impedance** /ɪm'pidns/, *n.* **1.** *Elect.* the apparent resistance, or total opposition to current of an alternating current circuit, consisting of two components, reactance and true or ohmic resistance. **2.** *Physics.* the ratio of pressure to particle velocity at a given point in a soundwave. [IMPEDE + -ANCE]

**impede** /ɪm'pid/, *v.t.*, **-peded, -peding.** to retard in movement or progress by means of obstacles or hindrances; obstruct; hinder. [L *impedīre* entangle, hamper (orig., as to the feet)] – **impeder,** *n.* – **impedingly,** *adv.*

**impedient** /ɪm'pidiənt/, *adj.* **1.** impeding. *–n.* **2.** that which impedes. [L *impediens,* ppr.]

**impediment** /ɪm'pɛdəmənt/, *n.* **1.** some physical defect, esp. a speech disorder: *an impediment in speech.* **2.** obstruction or hindrance; obstacle. **3.** (*usu. pl.*) impedimenta. **4.** *Law.* (esp. *Eccles.*) **a.** a bar, usu. of blood or affinity, to marriage: *a diriment impediment.* **b.** a restraint on marriage, preventing a completely lawful union: *a minor impediment.* [ME, from L *impedīmentum* hindrance] – **impedimental** /ɪmˌpɛdə'mɛntl/, **impedimentary** /ɪmˌpɛdə'mɛntəri/, *adj.*

**impedimenta** /ɪmˌpɛdə'mɛntə/, *n.pl.* **1.** baggage, etc., which impedes progress, as supplies carried with an army. **2.** *Law.* impediments. [L]

**impeditive** /ɪm'pɛdətɪv/, *adj.* tending to impede.

**impel** /ɪm'pɛl/, *v.t.*, **-pelled, -pelling. 1.** to drive or urge forward; press on; incite or constrain to action in any way. **2.** to drive, or cause to move, onwards; propel; impart motion to. [L *impellere*]

**impellent** /ɪm'pɛlənt/, *adj.* **1.** impelling. *–n.* **2.** an impelling agency or force.

**impeller** /ɪm'pɛlə/, *n.* **1.** one who or that which impels. **2.** the rotating member of a centrifugal pump, turbine, fluid coupling, etc. Also, **impellor.**

**impend** /ɪm'pɛnd/, *v.i.* **1.** to be imminent; be near at hand. **2.** to threaten. **3.** to hang or be suspended; overhang (fol. by *over*). [L *impendēre* hang over]

**impendent** /ɪm'pɛndənt/, *adj.* →**impending.** – **impendence, impendency,** *n.*

**impending** /ɪm'pɛndɪŋ/, *adj.* **1.** about to happen; imminent. **2.** overhanging.

**impenetrability** /ɪmˌpɛnətrə'bɪləti/, *n.* **1.** impenetrable quality. **2.** *Physics.* that property of matter in virtue of which two bodies cannot occupy the same space simultaneously.

**impenetrable** /ɪm'pɛnətrəbəl/, *adj.* **1.** not penetrable; that cannot be penetrated, pierced, or entered. **2.** inaccessible to ideas, influences, etc. **3.** incapable of being comprehended; unfathomable: *an impenetrable mystery.* **4.** *Physics.* excluding all other bodies from the space occupied. – **impenetrableness,** *n.* – **impenetrably,** *adv.*

**impenitent** /ɪm'pɛnətənt/, *adj.* not penitent; obdurate. – **impenitence, impenitency, impenitentness,** *n.* – **impenitently,** *adv.*

**impennate** /ɪm'pɛneɪt/, *adj.* featherless or wingless.

**imper.,** imperative.

**imperative** /ɪm'pɛrətɪv/, *adj.* **1.** not to be avoided or evaded: *an imperative duty.* **2.** of the nature of or expressing a command; commanding. **3.** *Gram.* designating or pertaining to the verb mood specialised for use in command, requests, and the like, or a verb inflected for this mode, as *listen! go! run!* etc. *–n.* **4.** a command. **5.** *Gram.* **a.** the imperative mood. **b.** a verb therein. [L *imperātīvus* of a command] – **imperatival** /ɪmˌpɛrə'taɪvəl/, *adj.* – **imperatively,** *adv.* – **imperativeness,** *n.*

**imperator** /ɪmpə'ratɔ, -'reɪtɔ/, *n.* **1.** an absolute or supreme ruler. **2.** a title of the Roman emperors. **3.** a temporary title accorded a victorious Roman general. [L. Cf. EMPEROR] – **imperatorial** /ɪm,pɛrəˈtɔriəl/, *adj.* – **imperatorially** /ɪm,pɛrəˈtɔriəli/, *adv.*

**imperceptible** /ɪmpəˈsɛptəbəl/, *adj.* **1.** very slight, gradual, or subtle: *imperceptible gradations.* **2.** not perceptible; not affecting the perceptive faculties. *–n.* **3.** that which is imperceptible. – **imperceptibility** /,ɪmpəsɛptəˈbɪləti/, **imperceptibleness,** *n.* – **imperceptibly,** *adv.*

**imperception** /ɪmpəˈsɛpʃən/, *n.* lack of perception.

**imperceptive** /ɪmpəˈsɛptɪv/, *adj.* not perceptive; lacking perception. – **imperceptivity** /ɪmpəsɛpˈtɪvəti/, **imperceptiveness,** *n.*

**impercipient** /ɪmpəˈsɪpiənt/, *adj.* lacking perception; not able to perceive. – **impercipience,** *n.*

**imperf.,** imperfect.

**imperfect** /ɪmˈpɜfəkt/, *adj.* **1.** characterised by or subject to defects. **2.** not perfect; lacking completeness: *imperfect vision.* **3.** *Bot.* (of a flower) lacking certain parts. **4.** *Gram.* designating a tense which denotes action going on but not completed, esp. in the past. For example, in the sentence *He was building the wall when it happened, was building* is in the imperfect tense. Cf. **perfect, pluperfect.** **5.** *Law.* without legal effect or support; unenforceable. **6.** *Music.* denoting the consonances of third and sixth. Cf. **perfect** (def. 13a.) *–n.* **7. a.** the imperfect tense. **b.** a form therein. [L *imperfectus* unfinished; replacing ME *imparfit,* from F *imparfait*] – **imperfectly,** *adv.* – **imperfectness,** *n.*

**imperfect cadence** /– ˈkeɪdəns/, *n.* a cadence in which there is a progression from a tonic chord, or a chord other than dominant or tonic, to the dominant chord.

**imperfection** /ɪmpəˈfɛkʃən/, *n.* **1.** an imperfect detail: *a law of imperfections.* **2.** the character or condition of being imperfect.

**imperfective** /ɪmpəˈfɛktɪv/, *adj.* **1.** denoting an aspect of the verb, as in Russian, which indicates incompleteness of the action or state at a temporal point of reference. *–n.* **2.** the imperfective aspect. **3.** a verb in this aspect.

**imperforate** /ɪmˈpɜfəreɪt, -rət/, *adj.* **1.** Also, **imperforated.** not perforate; having no perforation. **2.** *Philately.* having no perforations or cuts to separate the individual stamps readily. *–n.* **3.** an imperforate stamp. – **imperforation** /ɪm,pɛfəˈreɪʃən/, *n.*

**imperial** /ɪmˈpɪəriəl/, *adj.* **1.** of or pertaining to an empire. **2.** of or pertaining to an emperor or empress. **3.** characterising the rule or authority of a sovereign state over its dependencies. **4.** of the nature or rank of an emperor or supreme ruler. **5.** of a commanding quality, manner, or aspect. **6.** domineering; imperious. **7.** befitting an emperor or empress; very fine or grand; magnificent. **8.** of special size or quality, as various products, commodities, etc. **9.** (of weights and measures) conforming to the standards legally established in Britain. **10.** (*oft. cap.*) of or pertaining to the British Empire. *–n.* **11.** a small pointed beard growing beneath the lower lip. **12.** the top of a carriage, esp. of a diligence. **13.** a case for luggage carried there. **14.** a member of an imperial party or of imperial troops. **15.** an emperor or empress. **16.** any of various articles of special size or quality. [ME, from L *imperiālis* of the empire or emperor] – **imperially,** *adv.* – **imperialness,** *n.*

**imperial bushel** /– ˈbʊʃəl/, *n.* →**bushel** (def. 1).

**imperial gallon** /– ˈgælən/, *n.* →**gallon** (def. 1).

**imperialise** /ɪmˈpɪəriəlaɪz/, *v.t.,* **-lised, -lising.** **1.** to cause to belong to an empire; rule according to imperial government. **2.** to render imperial. Also, **imperialize.**

**imperialism** /ɪmˈpɪəriəlɪzəm/, *n.* **1.** the policy of extending the rule or authority of an empire or nation over foreign countries, or of acquiring and holding colonies and dependencies. **2.** advocacy of imperial interests. **3.** the policy of so uniting the separate parts of an empire with separate governments as to secure for certain purposes a single state. **4.** imperial government. **5.** an imperial system of government. – **imperialist,** *n., adj.* – **imperialistic** /ɪm,pɪəriəˈlɪstɪk/, *adj.* – **imperialistically** /ɪm,pɪəriəˈlɪstɪkli/, *adv.*

**imperil** /ɪmˈpɛrəl/, *v.t.,* **-rilled, -rilling,** or (*U.S.*) **-riled, -riling.** to put in peril; endanger. – **imperilment,** *n.*

**imperious** /ɪmˈpɪəriəs/, *adj.* **1.** domineering, dictatorial, or overbearing: *an imperious tyrant, imperious temper.* **2.** urgent; imperative: *imperious need.* [L *imperiōsus* commanding] – **imperiously,** *adv.* – **imperiousness,** *n.*

**imperishable** /ɪmˈpɛrɪʃəbəl/, *adj.* not perishable; indestructible; enduring. – **imperishability** /ɪm,pɛrɪʃəˈbɪləti/, **imperishableness,** *n.* – **imperishably,** *adv.*

**imperium** /ɪmˈpɪəriəm/, *n., pl.* **-peria** /-ˈpɪəriə/. command; supreme power. [L. Cf. EMPIRE]

**impermanent** /ɪmˈpɜmənənt/, *adj.* not permanent. – **impermanence, impermanency,** *n.*

**impermeable** /ɪmˈpɜmiəbəl/, *adj.* **1.** not permeable; impassable. **2.** (of substances) not permitting the passage of a fluid through the pores, interstices, etc. – **impermeability** /ɪm,pɜmiəˈbɪləti/, **impermeableness,** *n.* – **impermeably,** *adv.*

**impermissible** /ɪmpəˈmɪsəbəl/, *adj.* not permitted. – **impermissibility** /,ɪmpəmɪsəˈbɪləti/, *n.*

**impers.,** impersonal.

**impersonal** /ɪmˈpɜsənəl/, *adj.* **1.** not personal; without personal reference or connection: *an impersonal remark.* **2.** having no personality: *an impersonal deity.* **3.** *Gram.* **a.** (of a verb) having only third person singular forms, rarely if ever accompanied by an expressed subject, as Latin *pluit* (it is raining), or accompanied regularly by a non-significant subject word, as English *it is raining.* **b.** (of a pronoun) indefinite, as French *on* (one). *–n.* **4.** *Gram.* an impersonal verb or pronoun. – **impersonally,** *adv.*

**impersonalise** /ɪmˈpɜsənəlaɪz/, *v.t.,* **-lised, -lising.** to make impersonal. Also, **impersonalize.**

**impersonality** /ɪm,pɜsəˈnæləti/, *n.* the quality of being impersonal.

**impersonate** /ɪmˈpɜsəneɪt/, *v.,* **-nated, -nating,** *adj.* *–v.t.* **1.** to assume the character of; pretend to be. **2.** to represent in personal or bodily form; personify; typify. **3.** to personate, esp. on the stage. *–adj.* **4.** embodied in a person; invested with personality. – **impersonation** /ɪm,pɜsəˈneɪʃən/, *n.* – **impersonator,** *n.*

**impertinence** /ɪmˈpɜtənəns/, *n.* **1.** unmannerly intrusion or presumption; insolence. **2.** impertinent quality or action; irrelevance. **3.** inappropriateness or incongruity. **4.** triviality or absurdity. **5.** something impertinent.

**impertinency** /ɪmˈpɜtənənsi/, *n., pl.* **-cies.** →**impertinence.**

**impertinent** /ɪmˈpɜtənənt/, *adj.* **1.** intrusive or presumptuous, as persons or their actions: *an impertinent boy.* **2.** not pertinent or relevant; irrelevant: *any impertinent detail.* **3.** inappropriate or incongruous. **4.** trivial, silly, or absurd. [ME, from LL *impertinens* not belonging] – **impertinently,** *adv.*

**imperturbable** /ɪmpəˈtɜbəbəl/, *adj.* incapable of being perturbed or agitated; not easily excited; calm: *imperturbable composure.* – **imperturbability** /,ɪmpətɜbəˈbɪləti/, **imperturbableness,** *n.* – **imperturbably,** *adv.*

**imperturbation** /,ɪmpɜtəˈbeɪʃən/, *n.* freedom from perturbation; tranquillity; calmness.

**impervious** /ɪmˈpɜviəs/, *adj.* **1.** not pervious; impermeable: *impervious to water.* **2.** impenetrable: *impervious to reason.* Also, **imperviable.** – **imperviously,** *adv.* – **imperviousness,** *n.*

**impetigo** /ɪmpəˈtaɪgoʊ/, *n.* a contagious skin disease, esp. of children, marked by a superficial pustular eruption, particularly on the face. [L, from *impetere* attack] – **impetiginous** /ɪmpəˈtɪdʒənəs/, *adj.*

**impetrate** /ˈɪmpətreɪt/, *v.t.,* **-trated, -trating.** **1.** to obtain by entreaty. **2.** *Rare.* to entreat, or ask urgently for. [L *impetrātus,* pp., obtained by request] – **impetration** /ɪmpəˈtreɪʃən/, *n.* – **impetrative,** *adj.* – **impetrator,** *n.*

**impetuosity** /ɪm,pɛtʃuˈɒsəti/, *n., pl.* **-ties.** **1.** impetuous quality. **2.** an impetuous action.

**impetuous** /ɪmˈpɛtʃuəs/, *adj.* **1.** acting with or characterised by a sudden or rash energy: *an impetuous girl.* **2.** having great impetus; moving with great force; violent: *the impetuous winds.* [ME, from LL *impetuōsus,* from L *impetus* an attack] – **impetuously,** *adv.* – **impetuousness,** *n.*

**impetus** /ˈɪmpətəs/, *n., pl.* **-tuses.** **1.** moving force; impulse; stimulus: *a fresh impetus.* **2.** the force with which a moving body tends to maintain its velocity and overcome resistance; energy of motion. [L: onset]

**impf.,** imperfect.

**impiety** /ɪm'paɪəti/, *n., pl.* **-ties.** **1.** lack of piety; lack of reverence for God; ungodliness. **2.** lack of dutifulness or respect. **3.** an impious act, practice, etc.

**impinge** /ɪm'pɪndʒ/, *v.,* **-pinged, -pinging.** *–v.i.* **1.** to strike or dash; collide (fol. by *on, upon,* or *against*): *rays of light impinging on the eye.* **2.** to encroach or infringe (fol. by *on* or *upon*). **3.** to make an impression (*on*). *–v.t.* **4.** *Obs.* to come into violent contact with. [L *impingere* drive in or at, strike against] – **impingent,** *adj.* – **impingement,** *n.*

**impious** /'ɪmpiəs, ɪm'paɪəs/, *adj.* **1.** not pious; lacking reverence for God; ungodly. **2.** not reverent towards parents; undutiful. [L *impius*] – **impiously,** *adv.* – **impiousness,** *n.*

**impish** /'ɪmpɪʃ/, *adj.* of or like an imp; mischievous. – **impishly,** *adv.* – **impishness,** *n.*

**implacable** /ɪm'plækəbəl/, *adj.* not placable; not to be appeased or pacified; inexorable: *an implacable enemy.* – **implacability** /ɪm,plækə'bɪləti/, **implacableness,** *n.* – **implacably,** *adv.*

**implacental** /ɪmplə'sɛntəl/, *adj.* having no placenta, as a monotreme or marsupial.

**implant** /ɪm'plænt, -'plant/, *v.;* /'ɪmplænt, -plant/, *n.* *–v.t.* **1.** to instil or inculcate: *implant sound principles.* **2.** to plant in something; infix: *implant living tissue.* **3.** to plant: *implant the seeds.* *–n.* **4.** *Med.* **a.** tissue implanted into the body by grafting. **b.** a small tube containing a radioactive substance, as radium, surgically implanted in tissue for the treatment of tumours, cancer, etc. [IM-[1] + PLANT, *v.*] – **implanter,** *n.*

**implantation** /ɪmplæn'teɪʃən/, *n.* **1.** the act of implanting. **2.** the state of being implanted. **3.** *Pathol.* **a.** the movement of cells to a new region. **b.** metastasis, when spontaneous. **4.** *Med.* the application of solid medicine underneath the skin.

**implausible** /ɪm'plɔzəbəl/, *adj.* not plausible; not having the appearance of truth or credibility. – **implausibility** /ɪm,plɔzə'bɪləti/, *n.* – **implausibly,** *adv.*

**implead** /ɪm'plid/, *v.t.* to prosecute or take proceedings against a person in a court of justice. [ME *emplede(n),* from AF *empleder,* var. of OF *emplaidier,* from *em-* IM-[1] + *plaidier* PLEAD]

**implement** /'ɪmpləmənt/, *n.;* /'ɪmpləmɛnt/, *v.* *–n.* **1.** an instrument, tool, or utensil: *agricultural implements.* **2.** an article of equipment or outfit, as household furniture or utensils, ecclesiastical vessels or vestments, etc. **3.** a means; agent. *–v.t.* **4.** to provide with implements. **5.** to put (a plan, proposal, etc.) into effect. **6.** to satisfy, as requirements or conditions. **7.** to fill up or supplement. [late ME, from LL *implementum* a filling up (hence, probably, a thing that completes a want), from L *implēre* fill up] – **implemental** /ɪmplə'mɛntl/, *adj.* – **implementation** /ɪmpləmɛn'teɪʃən/, *n.*

**impletion** /ɪm'pliʃən/, *n.* **1.** the act of filling. **2.** the state of being filled. **3.** that which fills up; a filling. [LL *implētio,* from L *implēre* fill up]

**implicate** /'ɪmpləkeɪt/, *v.t.,* **-cated, -cating.** **1.** to involve as being concerned in a matter, affair, condition, etc.: *to be implicated in a crime.* **2.** to imply as a necessary circumstance, or as something to be inferred or understood. **3.** to affect, or cause to be affected. **4.** to fold or twist together; intertwine; interlace: *implicated leaves.* [L *implicātus,* pp., entangled, involved]

**implication** /ɪmplə'keɪʃən/, *n.* **1.** the act of implying. **2.** the state of being implied. **3.** something implied or suggested as naturally to be inferred without being expressly stated. **4.** *Logic.* the relation which holds between two propositions (or classes of propositions) in virtue of which one is logically deducible from the other. **5.** the act of involving. **6.** the state of being involved in some matter: *implication in a conspiracy.* **7.** the act of intertwining or entangling. **8.** the resulting condition. – **implicational,** *adj.* – **implicationally,** *adv.*

**implicative** /'ɪmpləkeɪtɪv, ɪm'plɪkətɪv/, *adj.* tending to implicate or imply; characterised by or involving implication. – **implicatively,** *adv.*

**implicit** /ɪm'plɪsət/, *adj.* **1.** (of belief, confidence, obedience, etc.) unquestioning, unreserved, or absolute. **2.** implied, rather than expressly stated: *an implicit consent.* **3.** virtually contained (fol. by *in*). **4.** *Maths.* (of a function) having the dependent variable not explicitly expressed in terms of the independent variables. **5.** *Obs.* entangled. [L *implicitus,* var. of *implicātus,* pp., entangled, involved] – **implicitly,** *adv.*

**implied** /ɪm'plaɪd/, *adj.* involved, indicated, or suggested by implying; tacitly understood: *an implied rebuke.*

**implied contract** /'– kɒntrækt/, *n.* a contract not based on express words but arising from other circumstances. Also, **implied promise, implied term.**

**impliedly** /ɪm'plaɪədli/, *adv.* by implication.

**implode** /ɪm'ploud/, *v.,* **-ploded, -ploding.** *–v.i.* **1.** to burst inwards (opposed to *explode*). *–v.t.* **2.** *Phonet.* to pronounce by implosion. [IM-[1] + *-plode,* modelled on EXPLODE]

**implore** /ɪm'plɔ/, *v.,* **-plored, -ploring.** *–v.t.* **1.** to call upon in urgent or piteous supplication, as for aid or mercy; beseech; entreat: *they implored him to go.* **2.** to make urgent supplication for (aid, mercy, pardon, etc.): *implore forgiveness.* *–v.i.* **3.** to make urgent or piteous supplication. [L *implōrāre* invoke with tears] – **imploration** /ɪmplɔ'reɪʃən/, *n.* – **imploratory,** *adj.* – **implorer,** *n.* – **imploringly,** *adv.* – **imploringness,** *n.*

**implosion** /ɪm'plouʒən/, *n.* **1.** a bursting inwards (opposed to *explosion*). **2.** *Phonet.* (of stops) **a.** a beginning marked by abrupt interruption of the breath stream, as for *p, t, k.* **b.** an ending marked by abrupt intake of air. [IM-[1] + *-plosion,* modelled on EXPLOSION]

**implosive** /ɪm'plousɪv/, *Phonet.* *–adj.* **1.** characterised by a partial vacuum behind the point of closure. *–n.* **2.** an implosive stop.

**imply** /ɪm'plaɪ/, *v.t.,* **-plied, -plying.** **1.** to involve as a necessary circumstance: *speech implies a speaker.* **2.** (of words) to signify or mean. **3.** to indicate or suggest, as something naturally to be inferred, without express statement. **4.** *Obs.* to enfold. [ME *implie(n),* from OF *emplier,* from L *implicāre* enfold, entangle, involve]

**impolite** /ɪmpə'laɪt/, *adj.* not polite or courteous; uncivil; rude. – **impolitely,** *adv.* – **impoliteness,** *n.*

**impolitic** /ɪm'pɒlətɪk/, *adj.* inexpedient; injudicious. – **impoliticly,** *adv.* – **impoliticness,** *n.*

**imponderable** /ɪm'pɒndərəbəl, -drəbəl/, *adj.* **1.** not ponderable; that cannot be weighed. *–n.* **2.** an imponderable thing, force, or agency. – **imponderability** /ɪm,pɒndərə'bɪləti/, **imponderableness,** *n.* – **imponderably,** *adv.*

**import** /ɪm'pɔt, 'ɪmpɔt/, *v.;* /'ɪmpɔt/, *n.* *–v.t.* **1.** to bring in from a foreign country, as merchandise or commodities, for sale, use, processing, or re-export. **2.** to bring or introduce from one use, connection, or relation into another. **3.** to convey as a meaning or implication, as words, statements, actions, etc., do; to make known or express. **4.** to be of consequence or importance to; concern. **5.** to be incumbent on; be the duty of. *–v.i.* **6.** to be of consequence or importance; matter. *–n.* **7.** that which is imported from abroad; an imported commodity or article. **8.** the act of importing or bringing in; importation, as of goods from abroad. **9.** meaning; implication; purport. **10.** consequence or importance. **11.** *Colloq.* a person who has been brought into a business, team, etc., from outside. [ME, from L *importāre* bring in, bring about] – **importable,** *adj.* – **importability** /ɪm,pɔtə'bɪləti/, *n.* – **importer,** *n.*

**importance** /ɪm'pɔtns/, *n.* **1.** the quality or fact of being important. **2.** important position or standing; personal or social consequence. **3.** consequential air or manner. **4.** *Obs.* an important matter. **5.** *Obs.* importunity. **6.** *Obs.* import or meaning.

**important** /ɪm'pɔtnt/, *adj.* **1.** of much significance or consequence: *an important event.* **2.** mattering much (fol. by *to*): *details important to a fair decision.* **3.** of more than ordinary title to consideration or notice: *an important example.* **4.** prominent: *an important part.* **5.** of considerable influence or authority, as a person, position, etc. **6.** of social consequence or distinction, as a person, family, etc. **7.** pompous. **8.** *Obs.* importunate. [F, from ML *importans,* ppr. of *importāre* be of consequence, L bring in, cause] – **importantly,** *adv.*

**importation** /ɪmpɔ'teɪʃən/, *n.* **1.** the bringing in of merchandise from foreign countries, for sale, use, processing, or re-export. **2.** something imported; an import.

**importee** /ɪmpɔ'ti/, *n.* a person imported from abroad.

**importunacy** /ɪm'pɔtʃənəsi/, *n.* the quality of being importunate.

**importunate** /ɪm'pɔtʃənət/, *adj.* **1.** urgent or persistent in solicitation. 2. pertinacious, as solicitations or demands. 3. troublesome. – **importunately,** *adv.* – **importunateness,** *n.*

**importune** /ɪm'pɔtʃun, ɪmpɔ'tjun/, *v.,* **-tuned, -tuning,** *adj.* –*v.t.* 1. to beset with solicitations; beg urgently or persistently. 2. to beg for (something) urgently or persistently. 3. *Obs.* to annoy. 4. *Obs.* to press; impel. –*v.i.* 5. to make urgent or persistent solicitations. –*adj.* 6. importunate. [ME, from MF *importun,* from L *importūnus* unfit, inconvenient, troublesome] – **importunely,** *adv.* – **importuner,** *n.*

**importunity** /ɪmpɔ'tjunəti/, *n., pl.* **-ties.** 1. the state of being importunate; persistence in solicitation. 2. (*pl.*) importunate solicitations or demands.

**impose** /ɪm'poʊz/, *v.,* **-posed, -posing.** –*v.t.* 1. to lay on or set as something to be borne, endured, obeyed, fulfilled, etc.: *to impose taxes.* 2. to put or set by, or as by, authority: *to impose an arbitrary meaning upon words.* 3. to obtrude or thrust (oneself, one's company, etc.) upon others. 4. to pass or palm off fraudulently or deceptively. 5. to lay (the hands) ceremonially on the head of a candidate for confirmation or ordination, or on the sick or those in distress. 6. *Print.* to lay (type pages, etc.) in proper order on an imposing stone or the like and secure in a chase for printing. 7. to subject to some penalty, etc. –*v.i.* 8. to make an impression on the mind; impose one's or its authority or influence. 9. to obtrude oneself or one's requirements, as upon others. 10. to presume, as upon patience, good nature, etc. 11. (of something fraudulent) to produce a false impression or act with a delusive effect (fol. by *upon* or *on*). [F *imposer,* from *im-* IM-[1] + *poser* put (see POSE[1])] – **imposable,** *adj.* – **imposer,** *n.*

**imposing** /ɪm'poʊzɪŋ/, *adj.* making an impression on the mind, as by great size, stately appearance, etc. – **imposingly,** *adv.* – **imposingness,** *n.*

**imposing stone** /'– stoʊn/, *n.* a slab resting upon a frame, on which pages of type or plates are imposed and corrected.

**imposition** /ɪmpə'zɪʃən/, *n.* 1. the laying on of something as a burden, obligation, etc. 2. something imposed, as a burden, levy, tax, etc.; an unusual or extraordinarily burdensome requirement or task. 3. a literary exercise imposed as at school as a punishment. 4. the act of imposing by or as by authority. 5. an imposing upon a person as by taking undue advantage of his good nature, or something that has the effect of doing this. 6. the act of imposing fraudulently or deceptively on others; imposture. 7. the ceremonial laying on of hands, as in confirmation. 8. *Print.* the arrangement of pages in proper order in a chase for printing.

**impossibility** /ɪm,pɒsə'bɪləti/, *n., pl.* **-ties.** 1. the quality of being impossible. 2. something impossible.

**impossible** /ɪm'pɒsəbəl/, *adj.* 1. not possible; that cannot be, exist, or happen. 2. that cannot be done or effected. 3. that cannot be true, as a rumour. 4. not to be done, endured, etc., with any degree of reason or propriety: *an impossible situation.* 5. utterly impracticable. 6. hopelessly unsuitable, undesirable, or objectionable: *an impossible person.* [ME, from L *impossibilis*] – **impossibly,** *adv.*

**impost**[1] /'ɪmpɒst/, *n.* 1. a tax, tribute, or duty. 2. imposition. 3. a customs duty. [ML *impostus* a tax, L *impositus* laid on]

**impost**[2] /'ɪmpoʊst/, *n. Archit.* 1. the point where an arch rests on a wall or column. 2. a horizontal block supported by upright stones. [F *imposte,* from It. *imposta* architectural impost, from *impostare* set upon, from L *impositus,* pp., placed upon]

**impostor** /ɪm'pɒstə/, *n.* 1. one who imposes fraudulently upon others. 2. one who practises deception under an assumed character or name. [LL, from L *impōnere* impose]

**imposture** /ɪm'pɒstʃə/, *n.* 1. the action or practice of imposing fraudulently upon others. 2. deception practised under an assumed character or name, as by an impostor. 3. an instance or piece of fraudulent imposition. [LL *impostūra,* from L *impōnere* impose] – **imposturous,** *adj.*

**impotence** /'ɪmpətəns/, *n.* the condition or quality of being impotent. Also, **impotency.**

**impotent** /'ɪmpətənt/, *adj.* 1. not potent; lacking power or ability. 2. utterly unable (to do something). 3. without force or effectiveness. 4. lacking bodily strength, or physically helpless, as an aged person or a cripple. 5. (of a male) wholly lacking in sexual power. Cf. **frigid.** – **impotently,** *adv.*

**impound** /ɪm'paʊnd/, *v.t.* 1. to shut up in a pound, as a stray animal. 2. to confine within an enclosure or within limits: *water impounded in a reservoir.* 3. to seize, take, or appropriate summarily. 4. to seize and retain in custody of the law, as a document for evidence. – **impoundable,** *adj.* – **impoundment, impoundage,** *n.* – **impounder,** *n.*

**impoverish** /ɪm'pɒvərɪʃ, -vrɪʃ/, *v.t.* 1. to reduce to poverty: *a country impoverished by war.* 2. to make poor in quality, productiveness, etc.; exhaust the strength or richness of: *to impoverish the soil.* Also, *Obs.,* **empoverish.** [ME *empoveris(en),* from OF *empoveriss-,* stem of *empoverir,* from *em-* EM-[1] + *povre* POOR] – **impoverisher,** *n.* – **impoverishment,** *n.*

**impoverished** /ɪm'pɒvərɪʃt, -vrɪʃt/, *adj.* 1. reduced to poverty. 2. poor in quality.

**impracticable** /ɪm'præktɪkəbəl/, *adj.* 1. not practicable; that cannot be put into practice with the available means: *an impracticable plan.* 2. unsuitable for practical use or purposes, as a device, material, etc. 3. (of ground, places, etc.) impassable. 4. (of persons, etc.) hard to deal with because of stubbornness, lack of flexibility, etc. – **impracticability** /ɪm,præktɪkə'bɪləti/, **impracticableness,** *n.* – **impracticably,** *adv.*

**impractical** /ɪm'præktɪkəl/, *adj.* not practical. – **impracticality** /ɪm,præktə'kæləti/, **impracticalness,** *n.* – **impractically,** *adv.*

**imprecate** /'ɪmprəkeɪt/, *v.,* **-cated, -cating.** –*v.t.* 1. call down or invoke (esp. evil or curses), as upon a person. –*v.i.* 2. to curse; swear. [L *imprecātus,* pp., having invoked] – **imprecator,** *n.* – **imprecatory** /'ɪmprəkeɪtəri, ɪmprə'keɪtəri/, *adj.*

**imprecation** /ɪmprə'keɪʃən/, *n.* 1. the act of imprecating; cursing. 2. a curse or malediction.

**imprecise** /ɪmprə'saɪs/, *adj.* not precise; ill-defined. – **imprecisely,** *adv.* – **impreciseness,** *n.*

**imprecision** /ɪmprə'sɪʒən/, *n.* lack of precision; inexactness.

**impregnable** /ɪm'prɛgnəbəl/, *adj.* 1. strong enough to resist attack; not to be taken by force: *an impregnable fort.* 2. not to be overcome or overthrown: *an impregnable argument.* [ME *imprenable,* from F, from *im-* IM-[2] + *prenable* PREGNABLE] – **impregnability** /ɪm,prɛgnə'bɪləti/, *n.* – **impregnably,** *adv.*

**impregnate** /'ɪmprɛgneɪt/, *v.* **-nated, -nating;** /ɪm'prɛgnət, -neɪt/, *adj.* –*v.t.* 1. to make pregnant; get with child or young. 2. to fertilise. 3. to charge with something infused or permeating throughout; saturate. 4. to fill interstices with a substance. 5. to furnish with some actuating or modifying element infused or introduced; imbue, infect, or tincture. –*adj.* 6. impregnated. [LL *impraegnātus,* pp., made pregnant] – **impregnation** /ɪmprɛg'neɪʃən/, *n.* – **impregnator,** *n.*

**impresario** /ɪmprə'sarioʊ/, *n., pl.* **-os.** 1. the organiser or manager of an opera, ballet, or theatre company or orchestra. 2. a personal manager, teacher, or trainer of concert artists. [It., from *impresa* enterprise]

**imprescriptible** /ɪmprə'skrɪptəbəl/, *adj.* not subject to prescription. – **imprescriptibly,** *adv.*

**impress**[1] /ɪm'prɛs/, *v.,* **-pressed** or (*Archaic*) **-prest; -pressing;** /'ɪmprɛs/, *n.* –*v.t.* 1. to affect deeply or strongly in mind or feelings, esp. favourably; influence in opinion. 2. (*used negatively*) to produce an unfavourable reaction in: *I wasn't impressed by his scruffy appearance.* 3. to fix deeply or firmly in the mind or memory, as ideas, facts, etc. 4. to urge, as something to be remembered or done. 5. to press (a thing) into or on something. 6. to produce (a mark, figure, etc.) by pressure; stamp; imprint. 7. to apply with pressure, so as to leave a mark. 8. to subject to, or mark by, pressure with something. 9. to furnish with a mark, figure, etc., by or as by stamping. –*n.* 10. the act of impressing. 11. a mark made by or as by pressure; stamp; imprint. 12. a distinctive character or effect imparted. [ME *impresse(n),* from L *impressus,* pp., pressed upon] – **impresser,** *n.*

**impress**[2] /ɪm'prɛs/, *v.,* **-pressed** or (*Archaic*) **-prest; -pressing;** /'ɪmprɛs/, *n.* –*v.t.* 1. to press or force into public service, as seamen. 2. to seize or take for public use. 3. to enlist or persuade (to aid). –*n.* 4. *Obs.* impressment. [IM-[1] + PRESS[2]]

**impressible** /ɪm'prɛsəbəl/, *adj.* capable of being impressed; impressionable. – **impressibility** /ɪm,prɛsə'bɪləti/, *n.*

**impression** /ɪm'prɛʃən/, *n.* 1. a strong effect produced on the intellect, feelings, or conscience. 2. the first and immediate effect upon the mind in outward or inward perception; sensation. **3.** the effect produced by an agency or influence. **4.** a notion, remembrance, or belief, often one that is vague or indistinct. **5.** a mark, indentation, figure, etc., produced by pressure. **6.** *Print, etc.* **a.** the process or result of printing from type, plates, etc. **b.** a printed copy from type, a plate, an engraved block, etc. **c.** one of a number of printings made at different times from the same set of type, without alteration (as distinguished from an *edition*). **d.** the total number of copies of a book, etc., printed at one time from the one setting of type. **7.** *Dentistry.* a mould taken in plastic materials or plaster of Paris of teeth and the surrounding tissues. **8.** an image in the mind caused by something external to it. **9.** the act of impressing. **10.** the state of being impressed. **11.** an imitation, esp. one given for entertainment, of the idiosyncrasies of some well-known person or type. [ME, from L *impressio.* See IMPRESS[1]]

**impressionable** /ɪm'prɛʃənəbəl, -prɛʃnəbəl/, *adj.* **1.** easily impressed or influenced; susceptible. **2.** capable of being impressed. – **impressionability** /ɪm,prɛʃənə'bɪləti/, **impressionableness,** *n.*

**impressionism** /ɪm'prɛʃənɪzəm/, *n.* **1.** a style of painting, developed esp. by French artists 1865-1880, which was concerned with the analysis of tone and colour and with the effects of light on surfaces, and whose adherents painted landscapes from life, catching the impression of light by applying paint in small, bright dabs of colour. **2.** a musical or literary style intended to convey an effect or overall impression of a subject. **3.** the building up of a general impression in a film by joining together a series of shots of subjects which are in actuality disconnected in space or time or both. – **impressionist,** *n., adj.* – **impressionistic** /ɪm,prɛʃə'nɪstɪk/, *adj.*

**impressive** /ɪm'prɛsɪv/, *adj.* such as to impress the mind; arousing solemn feelings: *an impressive ceremony.* – **impressively,** *adv.* – **impressiveness,** *n.*

**impressment** /ɪm'prɛsmənt/, *n.* the impressing of men, property, etc., as for public service or use. [IMPRESS[2] + -MENT]

**imprest**[1] /'ɪmprɛst/, *n.* **1.** an advance of money, esp. for some public business. **2.** (formerly) an advance payment made to a soldier or sailor at enlistment. [IM-[1] + *prest* (from OF *prester* lend, from L *praestāre* stand for). Cf. It. *imprestare* lend]

**imprest**[2] /ɪm'prɛst/, *v. Archaic.* past tense and past participle of **impress.**

**imprimatur** /ɪmprə'matə, -'meɪtə/, *n.* **1.** an official licence to print or publish a book, etc. **2.** licence; sanction; approval. [NL: let it be printed]

**imprint** /'ɪmprɪnt/, *n.;* /ɪm'prɪnt/, *v.* –*n.* **1.** a mark made by pressure; a figure impressed or printed on something. **2.** any impression or impressed effect. **3.** *Bibliog.* information printed at the foot or back of the titlepage of a book indicating the name of the publisher, usu. supplemented with the place and date of publication. **4.** the printer's name and address as indicated on any printed matter. –*v.t.* **5.** to impress (a quality, character, or distinguishing mark). **6.** to produce (a mark, etc.) on something by pressure. **7.** to fix firmly on the mind, memory, etc. **8.** to make an imprint upon. –*v.i.* **9.** to learn to identify, as a voice, smell, etc. (fol. by *on*): *ducklings imprint on the mother's voice.* [ME *empreynte(n),* from OF *empreinter,* from *empreinte* a stamp, from L *imprimere* impress, imprint] – **imprinter,** *n.*

**imprison** /ɪm'prɪzən/, *v.t.* **1.** to put into or confine in a prison; detain in custody. **2.** to shut up as if in a prison; hold in restraint. – **imprisonment,** *n.*

**improbability** /ɪm,prɒbə'bɪləti/, *n., pl.* **-ties.** **1.** the quality or fact of being improbable; unlikelihood. **2.** something improbable or unlikely.

**improbable** /ɪm'prɒbəbəl/, *adj.* not probable; unlikely to be true or to happen. – **improbably,** *adv.*

**improbity** /ɪm'proʊbəti/, *n.* the reverse of probity; dishonesty; wickedness. [ME *improbite,* from L *improbitas* wickedness]

**impromptu** /ɪm'prɒmptʃu/, *adj.* **1.** made or done without previous preparation: *an impromptu address.* **2.** suddenly or hastily prepared, made, etc.: *an impromptu dinner.* **3.** improvised, or having the character of an improvisation. –*adv.* **4.** without preparation: *verses written impromptu.* –*n.* **5.** something impromptu; an impromptu speech, musical composition, performance, etc. **6.** a short musical composition, popular in the 19th century, suggesting improvisation by its casual mood. [F, from L *in promptū* in readiness]

**improper** /ɪm'prɒpə/, *adj.* **1.** not proper; not strictly belonging, applicable, or right: *an improper use for a thing.* **2.** not in accordance with propriety of behaviour, manners, etc.: *improper conduct.* **3.** unsuitable or inappropriate, as for the purpose or occasion: *improper tools.* **4.** abnormal or irregular. – **improperly,** *adv.* – **improperness,** *n.*

**improper fraction** /– 'frækʃən/, *n.* a fraction having the numerator greater than the denominator.

**impropriate** /ɪm'proʊpriət, -prieɪt/, *adj;* /ɪm'proʊprieɪt/, *v.,* **-ated, -ating.** –*adj.* **1.** *Eccles. Law.* devolved into the hands of a layman. –*v.t.* **2.** *Eccles. Law.* to place (ecclesiastical property) in lay hands. [ML *impropriātus,* pp. of *impropriāre,* from L *im-* IM-[1] + *proprius* one's own, PROPER] – **impropriation** /ɪm,proʊpri'eɪʃən/, *n.*

**impropriator** /ɪm'proʊprieɪtə/, *n.* a layman in possession of church property or revenues.

**impropriety** /ɪmprə'praɪəti/, *n., pl.* **-ties.** **1.** the quality of being improper; incorrectness. **2.** inappropriateness. **3.** unseemliness. **4.** an erroneous or unsuitable expression, act, etc. **5.** an improper use of a word.

**improve** /ɪm'pruv/, *v.,* **-proved, -proving;** /'ɪmpruv/, *n.* –*v.t.* **1.** to bring into a more desirable or excellent condition: *to improve one's health.* **2.** to make (land) more profitable or valuable by enclosure, cultivation, etc.; increase the value of (property) by betterments, as buildings. **3.** to turn to account; make good use of: *to improve an opportunity.* –*v.i.* **4.** to increase in value, excellence, etc.; become better: *the situation is improving.* **5.** to make improvements (fol. by *on* or *upon*): *to improve on one's earlier work.* –*n.* **6. on the improve,** *Colloq.* getting better. [AF *emprower,* from OF *em-* IM-[1] + *prou* profit] – **improvable,** *adj.* – **improvability** /ɪm,pruvə'bɪləti/, **improvableness,** *n.* – **improvably,** *adv.* – **improvingly,** *adv.*

**improved pasture** /ɪmpruvd 'pastʃə/, *n.* **1.** an improved species of forage plant, grown as pasture. **2.** the area of land on which such pasture is grown. **3.** natural pasture which has been top-dressed.

**improvement** /ɪm'pruvmənt/, *n.* **1.** the act of improving. **2.** the state of being improved. **3.** a change or addition whereby a thing is improved. **4.** some thing or person that represents an advance on another in excellence or achievement. **5.** a bringing into a more valuable or desirable condition, as of land; a making or becoming better; a betterment. **6.** something done or added to land which increases its value. **7.** profitable use: *the improvement of one's time.*

**improver** /ɪm'pruvə/, *n.* **1.** one who or that which improves. **2.** an unapprenticed junior in a trade or industry who is undergoing instruction in his calling. **3.** →**improver handicap.** **4.** →**improver horse.**

**improver handicap** /– 'hændikæp/, *n.* a restricted race for horses which are specified as being in the improver class in accordance with the rules operating in each State in Australia.

**improver horse** /– 'hɔs/, *n.* a horse eligible to run in an improver handicap. Also, **improver-class horse.**

**improvident** /ɪm'prɒvədənt/, *adj.* **1.** not provident; lacking foresight; incautious or unwary. **2.** neglecting to provide for future needs. – **improvidence,** *n.* – **improvidently,** *adv.*

**improvisation** /ɪmprəvaɪ'zeɪʃən/, *n.* **1.** the act of improvising. **2.** something improvised.

**improvisator** /'ɪmprəvaɪzeɪtə, ɪm'prɒvəzeɪtə/, *n.* one who improvises.

**improvisatory** /ɪmprəvaɪ'zeɪtəri/, *adj.* of or pertaining to an improvisator or improvisation. – **improvisatorial** /,ɪmprəvaɪzə'tɔriəl/, *adj.* – **improvisatorially,** *adv.*

**improvise** /'ɪmprəvaɪz/, *v.,* **-vised, -vising.** –*v.t.* **1.** to prepare or provide offhand or hastily; extemporise. **2.** to compose (verse, music, etc.) on the spur of the moment. **3.** to recite, sing, etc., extemporaneously. –*v.i.* **4.** to compose, utter, or execute anything extemporaneously: *he improvised in rhyme.* [F *improviser,* from It. *improvvisare,* from *improvviso* extempore, from L *imprōvīsus* unforeseen, unexpected] – **improviser,** *n.*

**improvised** /'ɪmprəvaɪzd/, *adj.* made or said without previous preparation.

**imprudent** /ɪm'prudnt/, *adj.* not prudent; lacking prudence or discretion. [L *imprūdens*] – **imprudence,** *n.* – **imprudently,** *adv.*

**impudence** /'ɪmpjudəns, -pjə-/, *n.* **1.** the quality or fact of being impudent; effrontery; insolence. **2.** impudent conduct or language. Also, **impudency.**

**impudent** /'ɪmpjudənt, -pjə-/, *adj.* characterised by a shameless boldness, assurance, or effrontery: *impudent behaviour.* [L *impudens* shameless] – **impudently,** *adv.*

**impudicity** /ɪmpju'dɪsəti/, *n.* immodesty.

**impugn** /ɪm'pjun/, *v.t.* to assail by words or arguments, as statements, motives, veracity, etc.; call in question; challenge as false. [ME *impugne(n),* from OF *impugner,* from L *impugnāre* attack] – **impugnable,** *adj.* – **impugnation** /ɪmpʌg'neɪʃən/, **impugnment,** *n.* – **impugner,** *n.*

**impuissant** /ɪm'pwisənt/, *adj.* impotent; feeble; weak. [F. See IM-², PUISSANT] – **impuissance,** *n.*

**impulse** /'ɪmpʌls/, *n.* **1.** the inciting influence of a particular feeling, mental state, etc.: *to act under the impulse of pity.* **2.** sudden, involuntary inclination prompting to action, or a particular instance of it: *to be swayed by impulse.* **3.** an impelling action or force, driving onwards or inducing motion. **4.** the effect of an impelling force; motion induced; impetus given. **5.** *Physiol.* a stimulus conveyed by the nervous system, muscle fibres, etc., either exciting or limiting organic functioning. **6.** *Mech.* the product of a force and the time during which it acts (sometimes restricted to cases in which the force is great and the time short, as in the blows of a hammer). **7.** *Elect.* a single, usu. sudden, flow of current in one direction. [L *impulsus* a push against]

**impulse buyer** /'– baɪə/, *n.* one who buys on impulse what strikes the eye in a shop, etc., rather than what has been planned and budgeted for.

**impulse turbine** /'– tɜbaɪn/, *n.* See **turbine.**

**impulsion** /ɪm'pʌlʃən/, *n.* **1.** the act of impelling, driving onwards, or pushing. **2.** the resulting state or effect; impulse; impetus. **3.** the inciting influence of some feeling or motive; mental impulse. **4.** constraining or inciting action on the mind or conduct: *divine impulsion.* [ME, from L *impulsio* influence, instigation]

**impulsive** /ɪm'pʌlsɪv/, *adj.* **1.** actuated or swayed by emotional or involuntary impulses: *an impulsive child.* **2.** having the power or effect of impelling; characterised by impulsion: *impulsive forces.* **3.** inciting to action: *an impulsive influence on humanity.* **4.** *Mech.* (of forces) acting momentarily; not continuous. – **impulsively,** *adv.* – **impulsiveness,** *n.*

**impunity** /ɪm'pjunəti/, *n.* exemption from punishment or ill consequences. [L *impūnitas* omission of punishment]

**impure** /ɪm'pjuə/, *adj.* **1.** not pure; mixed with extraneous matter, esp. of an inferior or contaminating kind: *impure water.* **2.** modified by admixture, as colour. **3.** mixed or combined with something else: *an impure style of architecture.* **4.** ceremonially unclean, as things, animals, etc. **5.** not morally pure; unchaste: *impure language.* **6.** marked by foreign and unsuitable or objectionable elements or characteristics, as a style of art or of literary expression. [L *impūrus* not pure] – **impurely,** *adv.* – **impureness,** *n.*

**impurity** /ɪm'pjʊərəti/, *n., pl.* **-ties. 1.** the quality or state of being impure. **2.** (*oft. pl.*) that which is or makes impure: *impurities in drinking water.*

**imputable** /ɪm'pjutəbəl/, *adj.* that may be imputed; attributable. – **imputability** /ɪm,pjutə'bɪləti/, **imputableness,** *n.* – **imputably,** *adv.*

**imputation** /ɪmpju'teɪʃən/, *n.* **1.** the act of imputing. **2.** an attribution, esp. of fault, crime, etc.

**impute** /ɪm'pjut/, *v.t.,* **-puted, -puting. 1.** to attribute (something discreditable) to a person. **2.** to attribute or ascribe. **3.** *Law.* to charge. **4.** *Theol.* to attribute (righteousness, guilt, etc.) vicariously; ascribe as derived from another. [ME, from L *imputāre* bring into the reckoning] – **imputative,** *adj.* – **imputatively,** *adv.* – **imputativeness,** *n.* – **imputer,** *n.*

**impv.,** imperative.

**in** /ɪn/, *prep.* a particle expressing: **1.** inclusion within space or limits, a whole, material or immaterial surroundings, etc.: *in the city, in the army, dressed in white, in politics.* **2.** inclusion within, or occurrence during the course of or at the expiry of, a period or limit of time: *in ancient times, to do a task in an hour, return in ten minutes.* **3.** situation, condition, occupation, action, manner, relation, means, etc.: *in darkness, in sickness, in service, in crossing the street, in confidence, in French.* **4.** object or purpose: *in honour of the event.* **5.** motion or direction from without to a point within (now usu. into), or transition from one state to another: *to put in operation, break in two.* **6.** pregnancy with: *the mare's in foal again.* **7. be in it,** to be part of a project or venture. **8. have it in (one),** to have the ability. **9. in it,** of advantage; profitable: *what's in it for me.* **10. in that,** for the reason that. **11. nothing in it,** (in a competitive situation) no difference in performance, abilities, etc., between the contestants. *–adv.* **12.** in or into some place, position, state, relation, etc. **13.** on the inside, or within. **14.** in one's house or office. **15.** in office or power. **16.** in possession or occupancy. **17.** having the turn to play, in a game. **18. count in,** to include in a projected enterprise. *–adj.* **19.** that is or gets in; internal; inward; incoming; inbound. **20.** in favour; on friendly terms: *he's in with the managing director.* **21.** in fashion: *Mexican jewellery is in this year.* **22.** in season: *strawberries are in now.* **23.** alight: *leave the fire in overnight.* **24. in for, a.** about to undergo (esp. something boring or disagreeable). **b.** entered for. **c.** involved to the limit of. **25. in for it,** about to be reprimanded or punished. **26. in like Flynn,** successful in a particular enterprise, esp. sexually. **27. in on,** having a share in or a part of, esp. something secret, or known to just a few people. **28. well in, a.** *Horseracing.* (of a horse) given a light handicap. **b.** comfortably off. **29. well in with,** on good terms with. *–n.* **30.** (*pl.*) those who are in, as the political party in power. **31.** influence; pull; connection: *she has an in with the management – she married a director.* **32. ins and outs, a.** nooks or recesses; windings and turnings. **b.** intricacies. [ME and OE, c. D and G *in,* Icel. *í,* Goth. *in;* akin to L *in,* Gk *en*]

**in-**¹, a prefix representing English *in,* as in *income, indwelling, inland,* but used also as a verb-formative with transitive, intensive, or sometimes little apparent force, as in *intrust, inweave,* etc. It often assumes the same phases as **in-**², as **en-**¹, **em-**¹, and **im-**³. [ME and OE; representing IN, *adv.*]

**in-**², a prefix of Latin origin meaning primarily 'in', but used also as a verb-formative with the same force as **in-**¹, as in *incarcerate, incantation.* Also, **il-**¹, **im-**¹, **ir-**². Cf. **em-**¹, **en-**¹. [L, representing *in,* prep. (in F *en*), c. IN, *prep.*]

**in-**³, a prefix of Latin origin corresponding to English *un-,* having a negative or privative force, freely used as an English formative, esp. of adjectives and their derivatives and of nouns, as in *inattention, indefensible, inexpensive, inorganic, invariable.* This prefix assumes the same phonetic phases as **in-**², as in *impartial, immeasurable, illiterate, irregular,* etc. In French it became *en-* and thus occurs unfelt in such words as *enemy* (French *ennemi,* Latin *inimicus,* lit., not friendly). Also, **il-**², **im-**², **ir-**². [L; akin to Gk *an-, a-* A-⁶, and UN-¹]

**-in**¹, a suffix used in adjectives of Greek or Latin origin meaning 'pertaining to' and (in nouns thence derived) also imitated in English, as in *coffin, cousin, lupin,* etc.; and occurring unfelt in abstract nouns formed as nouns in Latin, as *ruin.* [ME *-in, -ine,* from OF, from L *-inus, -ina, -inum,* from Gk *-inos, -inē, -inon*]

**-in**², a noun suffix used in chemical and mineralogical nomenclature without any formal significance, though it is usu. restricted to certain neutral compounds, glycerides, glucosides, and proteins as *albumin, butyrin.* In some compounds, as *glycerine,* the spelling *-ine* is also used, although an attempt is made to restrict *-ine* to basic compounds. [NL *-ina.* See -INE²]

**-in**³, the second part of a compound, indicating a communal session of the activity named, as *sit-in, sleep-in, slim-in, teach-in.*

**in.,** inch; inches.

**In,** *Chem.* indium.

**inability** /ɪnə'bɪləti/, *n.* lack of ability; lack of power, capacity, or means.

**in absentia** /ɪn æb'sɛntiə, -ʃiə/, *adv.* in or during (one's) absence. [L]

**inaccessible** /ɪnək'sɛsəbəl/, *adj.* not accessible; unapproachable. – **inaccessibility** /,ɪnəksɛsə'bɪləti/, **inaccessibleness,** *n.* – **inaccessibly,** *adv.*

**inaccuracy** /ɪn'ækjurəsi/, *n., pl.* **-cies. 1.** the quality of being inaccurate. **2.** that which is inaccurate.

**inaccurate** /ɪn'ækjurət/, *adj.* not accurate. – **inaccurately,** *adv.* – **inaccurateness,** *n.*

**inaction** /ɪn'ækʃən/, *n.* absence of action; idleness.

**inactivate** /ɪn'æktəveɪt/, *v.t.*, **-vated, -vating.** **1.** to make inactive. **2.** *Med.* to stop the activity of (certain biological substances).

**inactive** /ɪn'æktɪv/, *adj.* **1.** not active; inert. **2.** indolent; sluggish; passive. **3.** *Chiefly U.S. Mil.* not on active duty or status. **4.** *Phys. Chem.* denoting a compound which does not rotate the plane of vibration of polarised light. – **inactivation** /ˌɪnæktə'veɪʃən/, *n.* – **inactively,** *adv.* – **inactivity** /ɪnæk'tɪvəti/, **inactiveness,** *n.*

**inadaptable** /ɪnə'dæptəbəl/, *adj.* not adaptable; incapable of being adapted. – **inadaptability** /ɪnəˌdæptə'bɪləti/, *n.*

**inadequate** /ɪn'ædəkwət/, *adj.* not adequate. – **inadequacy, inadequateness,** *n.* – **inadequately,** *adv.*

**inadmissible** /ɪnəd'mɪsəbəl/, *adj.* not admissible: *inadmissible evidence.* – **inadmissibility** /ɪnədˌmɪsə'bɪləti/, *n.* – **inadmissibly,** *adv.*

**inadvertence** /ɪnəd'vɜtns/, *n.* **1.** the quality of being inadvertent; heedlessness. **2.** an act or effect of inattention; an oversight. [ML *inadvertentia*]

**inadvertency** /ɪnəd'vɜtnsi/, *n., pl.* **-cies.** →**inadvertence.**

**inadvertent** /ɪnəd'vɜtnt/, *adj.* **1.** not attentive; heedless. **2.** characterised by lack of attention, as actions, etc. **3.** unintentional: *an inadvertent insult.* – **inadvertently,** *adv.*

**inadvisable** /ɪnəd'vaɪzəbəl/, *adj.* not advisable; inexpedient. – **inadvisability** /ɪnədˌvaɪzə'bɪləti/, *n.* – **inadvisably,** *adv.*

**-inae,** a suffix of the taxonomic names of zoological subfamilies. [L, fem. pl. of adjectives ending in *-īnus.* See -INE[1]]

**inalienable** /ɪn'eɪliənəbəl/, *adj.* not alienable; that cannot be transferred to another: *inalienable rights.* – **inalienability** /ɪnˌeɪliənə'bɪləti/, *n.* – **inalienably,** *adv.*

**inalterable** /ɪn'ɔltərəbəl, -trəbəl/, *adj.* not alterable. – **inalterability** /ɪnˌɔltərə'bɪləti/, *n.* – **inalterably,** *adv.*

**inamorata** /ɪnˌæmə'ratə/, *n., pl.* **-tas.** a female lover; a woman who loves or is loved. [It. *innamorata* sweetheart (fem.), from *amore* love, from L *amor*]

**inamorato** /ɪnæmə'ratoʊ/, *n., pl.* **-tos.** a male lover. [see INAMORATA]

**in-and-in** /ɪn-ənd-'ɪn/, *adv.* repeatedly within the same family, strain, etc.: *to breed stock in-and-in.*

**inane** /ɪn'eɪn/, *adj.* **1.** lacking sense or ideas; silly: *inane questions.* **2.** empty; void. *–n.* **3.** that which is inane or void; the void of infinite space. [L *inānis* empty, vain] – **inanely,** *adv.*

**inanga** /'inʌŋə/, *n. N.Z.* a small fish, *Galaxias attenuatus;* whitebait. [Maori]

**inanimate** /ɪn'ænəmət/, *adj.* **1.** not animate; lifeless. **2.** spiritless; sluggish; dull. – **inanimately,** *adv.* – **inanimateness,** *n.*

**inanition** /ɪnə'nɪʃən/, *n.* **1.** exhaustion from lack of nourishment; starvation. **2.** emptiness. [ME, from LL *inānītio,* from L *inānīre* make empty]

**inanity** /ɪn'ænəti/, *n., pl.* **-ties.** **1.** lack of sense or ideas; silliness. **2.** an inane remark, etc. **3.** emptiness.

**inappeasable** /ɪnə'pizəbəl/, *adj.* not appeasable; not to be appeased: *inappeasable anger.*

**inappetence** /ɪn'æpətəns/, *n.* lack of appetence or appetite. Also, **inappetency.**

**inapplicable** /ɪn'æplɪkəbəl, ɪnə'plɪkəbəl/, *adj.* not applicable; unsuitable. – **inapplicability** /ɪnəˌplɪkə'bɪləti/, **inapplicableness,** *n.* – **inapplicably,** *adv.*

**inapposite** /ɪn'æpəzət/, *adj.* not apposite; not pertinent. – **inappositely,** *adv.* – **inappositeness,** *n.*

**inappreciable** /ɪnə'priʃəbəl/, *adj.* imperceptible; insignificant: *an inappreciable difference.* – **inappreciably,** *adv.*

**inappreciative** /ɪnə'priʃətɪv/, *adj.* →**unappreciative.** – **inappreciatively,** *adv.* – **inappreciativeness,** *n.*

**inapprehensible** /ˌɪnæprə'hɛnsəbəl/, *adj.* not to be grasped by the senses or intellect.

**inapprehension** /ˌɪnæprə'hɛnʃən/, *n.* lack of apprehension.

**inapprehensive** /ˌɪnæprə'hɛnsɪv/, *adj.* **1.** not apprehensive (oft. fol. by *of*). **2.** without apprehension.

**inapproachable** /ɪnə'proʊtʃəbəl/, *adj.* **1.** not approachable. **2.** without rival. – **inapproachability** /ɪnəˌproʊtʃə'bɪləti/, *n.* – **inapproachably,** *adv.*

**inappropriate** /ɪnə'proʊpriət/, *adj.* not appropriate. – **inappropriately,** *adv.* – **inappropriateness,** *n.*

**inapt** /ɪn'æpt/, *adj.* **1.** not apt or fitted. **2.** without aptitude or capacity. – **inaptly,** *adv.* – **inaptness,** *n.*

**inaptitude** /ɪn'æptətʃud/, *n.* **1.** lack of aptitude; unfitness. **2.** unskilfulness.

**inarch** /ɪn'atʃ/, *v.t.* to graft by uniting a growing branch to a stock without separating the branch from its parent stock. [IN-[2] + ARCH[1]]

inarching

**inarm** /ɪn'am/, *v.t.* to hold in, or as in, the arms.

**inarticulacy** /ɪna'tɪkjuləsi/, *n.* inarticulateness.

**inarticulate** /ɪna'tɪkjələt/, *adj.* **1.** not articulate; not uttered or emitted with expressive or intelligible modulations: *inarticulate sounds.* **2.** unable to use articulate speech: *inarticulate with rage.* **3.** unable to express oneself clearly and fluently in speech. **4.** *Anat., Zool.* not jointed; having no articulation or joint. [LL *inarticulātus* not distinct. See IN-[3], ARTICULATE] – **inarticulately,** *adv.* – **inarticulateness,** *n.*

**inartificial** /ˌɪnatə'fɪʃəl/, *adj.* **1.** not artificial; natural; artless; plain or simple. **2.** inartistic. – **inartificiality** /ˌɪnatəfɪʃi'æləti/, *n.* – **inartificially,** *adv.*

**inartistic** /ɪna'tɪstɪk/, *adj.* **1.** not artistic; aesthetically poor. **2.** lacking in artistic sense. Also, **inartistical.** – **inartistically,** *adv.*

**inasmuch as** /ɪnəz'mʌtʃ əz/, *conj.* **1.** in view of the fact that; seeing that; since. **2.** in so far as; to such a degree as.

**inattention** /ɪnə'tɛnʃən/, *n.* **1.** lack of attention; negligence. **2.** an act of neglect.

**inattentive** /ɪnə'tɛntɪv/, *adj.* not attentive. – **inattentively,** *adv.* – **inattentiveness,** *n.*

**inaudible** /ɪn'ɔdəbəl/, *adj.* incapable of being heard. – **inaudibility** /ˌɪnɔdə'bɪləti/, *n.* – **inaudibly,** *adv.*

**inaugural** /ɪn'ɔgjərəl/, *adj.* **1.** of or pertaining to an inauguration. *–n.* **2.** an address, as by a president, at the beginning of a term of office. [F, from *inaugurer,* from L *inaugurāre* INAUGURATE]

**inaugurate** /ɪn'ɔgjəreɪt/, *v.t.*, **-rated, -rating.** **1.** to make a formal beginning of; initiate; commence; begin. **2.** to induct into office with formal ceremonies; install. **3.** to introduce into public use by some formal ceremony. [L *inaugurātus,* pp., consecrated or installed with augural ceremonies] – **inauguration** /ɪnˌɔgjə'reɪʃən/, *n.* – **inaugurator,** *n.*

**inauspicious** /ɪnɔ'spɪʃəs/, *adj.* not auspicious; ill-omened; unfavourable; unlucky. – **inauspiciously,** *adv.* – **inauspiciousness,** *n.*

**inbeing** /'ɪnbiɪŋ/, *n.* **1.** the condition of existing in something else; immanence. **2.** inward nature.

**inboard** /'ɪnbɔd/, *adj.* **1.** (of the engine of a motor boat) located within the boat usu. about amidships, driving a propeller by a shaft passing through a gland at the stern. Cf. **outboard, inboard-outboard.** **2.** within the hull or interior, or towards the centre, of a ship. *–n.* **3.** a motor so located. – **inboard,** *adv.*

**inboard-outboard** /ˌɪnbɔd-'aʊtbɔd/, *adj.* (of the engine of a motor boat) located within the boat but driving the propeller by shafting and gearing within metal arms pivoted to the stern of the boat. Cf. **inboard, outboard.**

**inborn** /'ɪnbɔn/, *adj.* implanted by nature; innate.

**inbound** /'ɪnbaʊnd/, *adj.* inward bound: *inbound ships.*

**inbreathe** /ɪn'brið/, *v.t.*, **-breathed, -breathing.** **1.** to breathe in; infuse. **2.** to inspire.

**inbred** /'ɪnbrɛd/, *adj.* **1.** bred within; innate; native. **2.** resulting from or involved in inbreeding.

**inbreed** /ɪn'brid/, *v.t.*, **-bred, -breeding.** **1.** to breed (animals) in-and-in. **2.** to breed within; engender.

**inbreeding** /'ɪnbridɪŋ/, *n.* the mating of related individuals such as cousins, sire-daughter, brother-sister, or self-fertilised plants. Inbreeding automatically fixes the genes, making them homozygous.

**in-built** /ˈɪn-bɪlt/, *adj.* **1.** inherent. **2.** →**built-in.**

**inburst** /ˈɪnbɜst/, *n. Rare.* a bursting in; irruption.

**inc.,** **1.** included. **2.** including. **3.** inclusive. **4.** (*also cap.*) incorporated. **5.** increase.

**incalculable** /ɪnˈkælkjuləbəl, -kjə-/, *adj.* **1.** that cannot be calculated; beyond calculation. **2.** that cannot be forecast. **3.** uncertain. – **incalculability** /ɪnˌkælkjuləˈbɪləti, -kjə-/, **incalculableness,** *n.* – **incalculably,** *adv.*

**incalescent** /ɪnkəˈlɛsənt/, *adj.* increasing in heat. [L *incalescens,* ppr.] – **incalescence,** *n.*

**in camera** /ɪn ˈkæmərə/, *adj.* **1.** (of a case) heard by a judge in his private room or in court with the public excluded. **2.** in private; in secret: *the meeting was held in camera.* [L: in the chamber]

**incandesce** /ɪnkænˈdɛs/, *v.,* **-desced, -descing.** *–v.i.* **1.** to glow with heat. *–v.t.* **2.** to cause to glow. [L *incandescere* grow hot, glow]

**incandescence** /ɪnkænˈdɛsəns/, *n.* the state of a body caused by approximately white heat, when it may be used as a source of artificial light.

**incandescent** /ɪnkænˈdɛsənt/, *adj.* **1.** (of light, etc.) produced by incandescence. **2.** glowing or white with heat. **3.** intensely bright; brilliant. [L *incandescens,* ppr., growing hot] – **incandescently,** *adv.*

**incandescent lamp** /– ˈlæmp/, *n.* a lamp whose light is due to the glowing of some material, as the common electric lamp which contains a filament rendered luminous by the passage of current through it.

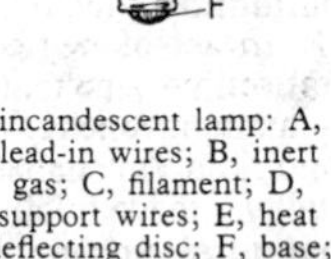


incandescent lamp: A, lead-in wires; B, inert gas; C, filament; D, support wires; E, heat deflecting disc; F, base; G, exhaust tube

**incantation** /ɪnkænˈteɪʃən/, *n.* **1.** the chanting or uttering of words purporting to have magical power. **2.** the formula employed; a spell or charm. **3.** magical ceremonies. **4.** magic; sorcery. [ME *incantacion,* from LL *incantātio* enchantment]

**incapable** /ɪnˈkeɪpəbəl/, *adj.* **1.** not capable. **2.** not having the capacity or power for a specified act or function (fol. by *of*). **3.** not open to the influence; not susceptible or admitting (fol. by *of*): *incapable of exact measurement.* **4.** without ordinary capability or ability; incompetent: *incapable workers.* **5.** without qualification, esp. legal qualification (oft. fol. by *of*): *incapable of holding public office. –n.* **6.** a thoroughly incompetent person. [LL *incapābilis.* See IN-[3], CAPABLE] – **incapability** /ɪnˌkeɪpəˈbɪləti/, **incapableness,** *n.* – **incapably,** *adv.*

**incapacitate** /ɪnkəˈpæsəteɪt/, *v.t.,* **-tated, -tating.** **1.** to deprive of capacity; make incapable or unfit; disqualify. **2.** *Law.* to deprive of power to perform acts with legal consequences. – **incapacitation** /ɪnkəˌpæsəˈteɪʃən/, *n.*

**incapacity** /ɪnkəˈpæsəti/, *n., pl.* **-ties.** **1.** lack of capacity; incapability. **2.** legal disqualification. [ML *incapācitas*]

**incapsulate** /ɪnˈkæpsjuleɪt, -sjə-/, *v.t., v.i.,* **-lated, -lating.** →**encapsulate.** – **incapsulation** /ɪnˌkæpsjuˈleɪʃən, -sjə-/, *n.*

**incarcerate** /ɪnˈkasəreɪt/, *v.,* **-rated, -rating;** /ɪnˈkasərət, -səreɪt/, *adj. –v.t.* **1.** to imprison; confine. **2.** to enclose; constrict closely. *–adj.* **3.** imprisoned. [ML *incarcerātus,* pp. of *incarcerāre,* from L *in-* IN-[2] + *carcer* prison] – **incarceration** /ɪnˌkasəˈreɪʃən/, *n.* – **incarcerator,** *n.*

**incardinate** /ɪnˈkadəneɪt/, *v.t.,* **-nated, -nating.** **1.** to institute as a cardinal. **2.** to institute as chief presbyter, priest, etc., in a particular church or place. [ML *incardinātus,* pp. See CARDINAL] – **incardination** /ɪnˌkadəˈneɪʃən/, *n.*

**incarnadine** /ɪnˈkanədaɪn/, *adj., n., v.,* **-dined, -dining.** *–adj.* **1.** flesh-coloured; pale red. **2.** crimson. *–n.* **3.** an incarnadine colour. *–v.t.* **4.** to make incarnadine. [F *incarnadin,* from d. It. *incarnadino,* from LL *incarnātus.* See INCARNATE]

**incarnate** /ɪnˈkanət, -neɪt/, *adj.;* /ˈɪnkaneɪt/ *v.,* **-nated, -nating.** *–adj.* **1.** embodied in flesh; invested with a bodily, esp. a human, form: *a devil incarnate.* **2.** personified or typified, as a quality or idea: *chivalry incarnate.* **3.** flesh-coloured or crimson. *–v.t.* **4.** to put into or represent in a concrete form, as an idea. **5.** to be the embodiment or type of. **6.** to embody in flesh; invest with a bodily, esp. a human, form. [ME, from LL *incarnātus,* pp., made flesh]

**incarnation** /ɪnkaˈneɪʃən/, *n.* **1.** an incarnate being or form. **2.** a living being embodying a deity or spirit. **3.** assumption of human form or nature, as by a divine being: *the incarnation of God in Christ.* **4.** a person or thing representing or exhibiting some quality, idea, etc., in typical form. **5.** the act of incarnating. **6.** the state of being incarnated. [ME, from LL *incarnātio*]

**incaution** /ɪnˈkɔʃən/, *n.* lack of caution; heedlessness; carelessness. [IN-[3] + CAUTION]

**incautious** /ɪnˈkɔʃəs/, *adj.* not cautious; careless; rash; heedless. – **incautiously,** *adv.* – **incautiousness,** *n.*

**incendiarism** /ɪnˈsɛndʒərɪzəm/, *n.* **1.** the act or practice of an incendiary; malicious burning. **2.** inflammatory agitation; the arousing of passions or violence.

**incendiary** /ɪnˈsɛndʒəri/, *adj., n., pl.* **-aries.** *–adj.* **1.** used or adapted for setting property on fire: *incendiary bombs.* **2.** of or pertaining to the criminal setting on fire of property. **3.** tending to arouse strife, sedition, etc.; inflammatory: *incendiary speeches. –n.* **4.** one who maliciously sets fire to buildings or other property. **5.** *Mil.* a shell, bomb, etc., containing phosphorus or similar material producing great heat. **6.** one who stirs up strife, sedition, etc.; an agitator. [L *incendiārius* causing fire]

**incense**[1] /ˈɪnsɛns/, *n., v.,* **-censed, -censing.** *–n.* **1.** an aromatic gum or other substance producing a sweet smell when burnt, used esp. in religious ceremonies. **2.** the perfume or smoke arising from such a substance when burnt. **3.** any pleasant perfume or fragrance. **4.** homage or adulation. *–v.t.* **5.** to perfume with incense. **6.** to burn incense for. *–v.i.* **7.** to burn or offer incense. [LL *incensum* incense, properly pp. neut. of L *incendere* set on fire; replacing ME *encens,* from OF]

**incense**[2] /ɪnˈsɛns/, *v.t.,* **-censed, -censing.** to inflame with wrath; make angry; enrage. [ME *incence(n),* from L *incensus,* pp., set on fire, kindled] – **incensement,** *n.*

**incense plant** /ˈɪnsɛns plænt/, *n.* a tall herb, *Calomeria amaranthoides,* common in forests in south-eastern Australia, having a large conspicuous panicle of reddish flowers and a musty perfume.

**incensory** /ˈɪnsɛnsəri/, *n.* a vessel for burning incense.

**incentive** /ɪnˈsɛntɪv/, *n.* **1.** that which incites to action, etc. *–adj.* **2.** inciting, as to action; stimulating; provocative. **3.** of or pertaining to extra money, benefits, etc., given to employees, to encourage greater output, or output of higher quality.

**inception** /ɪnˈsɛpʃən/, *n.* beginning; start.

**inceptive** /ɪnˈsɛptɪv/, *adj.* **1.** *Gram.* (of a derived verb, or of an aspect in verb inflection) expressing the beginning of the action indicated by the underlying verb. For example: Latin verbs in *-sco* generally have inceptive force, as *calescō* 'become or begin to be hot' from *caleō* 'be hot'. **2.** beginning; initial. *–n.* **3.** *Gram.* **a.** the inceptive aspect. **b.** a verb in the inceptive aspect. – **inceptively,** *adv.*

**incertitude** /ɪnˈsɜtətʃud/, *n.* **1.** uncertainty; doubtfulness. **2.** insecurity. [IN-[3] + CERTITUDE]

**incessant** /ɪnˈsɛsənt/, *adj.* continuing without interruption: *an incessant noise.* [LL *incessans* unceasing] – **incessancy, incessantness,** *n.* – **incessantly,** *adv.*

**incest** /ˈɪnsɛst/, *n.* **1.** sexual intercourse between persons closely related by blood. **2.** the crime of sexual intercourse between persons within the degrees of consanguinity in which marriage is forbidden. [ME, from L *incestus* or *incestum* (neut.) unchaste]

**incestuous** /ɪnˈsɛstʃuəs/, *adj.* **1.** guilty of incest. **2.** involving incest. **3.** (*derog.*) of or pertaining to a close-knit group of people, not genealogically related, but interacting exclusively within the group for the advancement and mutual support of the members.

**inch**[1] /ɪntʃ/, *n.* **1.** a unit of length in the imperial system, $\frac{1}{12}$ of a foot or 25.4 × $10^{-3}$ m (25.4 mm). **2.** See **inch of mercury.** **3.** See **inch of water.** **4.** a very small amount of anything. **5.** **by inches, a.** by a narrow margin: *he escaped death by inches.* **b.** Also, **inch by inch.** by degrees; very gradually. **6.** **every inch,** in every respect: *every inch a king.* **7. within an**

**inch of,** almost; very near: *she came within an inch of being knocked down by a car.* –*v.t., v.i.* **8.** to move by inches or small degrees. [ME; OE *ynce,* from L *uncia* twelfth part, inch, ounce. Cf. OUNCE[1]]

**inch**[2] /ɪntʃ/, *n. Scot.* a small island. [ME, from Gaelic *innse,* gen. of *innis* island]

**inchmeal** /'ɪntʃmil/, *adv.* by inches; inch by inch; little by little (often prec. by *by*).

**inchoate** /'ɪnkoʊeɪt/, *adj.* **1.** just begun; incipient. **2.** immature; rudimentary. **3.** lacking organisation; unformed. [L *inchoātus, incohātus,* pp., begun] – **inchoately,** *adv.* – **inchoateness,** *n.*

**inchoation** /ɪnkoʊ'eɪʃən/, *n.* beginning; origin.

**inchoative** /ɪn'koʊətɪv/, *adj.* **1.** *Gram.* inceptive. **2.** *Rare.* inchoate. –*n.* **3.** *Gram.* an inceptive.

**inch of mercury,** *n.* a unit of pressure in the imperial system equal to approx. 3386.38 pascals (approx. 33.9 millibars).

**inch of water,** *n.* a unit of pressure in the imperial system equal to approx. 248.64 pascals.

**inchworm** /'ɪntʃwɜm/, *n.* →**measuring worm.**

**incidence** /'ɪnsədəns/, *n.* **1.** the range of occurrence or influence of a thing, or the extent of its effects: *the incidence of a disease.* **2.** the falling, or direction or manner of falling, of a ray of light, etc., on a surface. **3.** a falling upon, affecting, or befalling. **4.** the fact or the manner of being incident. **5.** *Geom.* partial coincidence of two figures, as of a line and a plane containing it.

**incident** /'ɪnsədənt/, *n.* **1.** an occurrence or event. **2.** a distinct piece of action, or an episode, as in a story or play. **3.** something that occurs casually in connection with something else. **4.** something appertaining or attaching to something else. **5. a.** an occurrence, such as a clash between troops of countries whose relations are already strained, which is liable to have grave consequences. **b.** a disturbance, esp. one of a serious nature such as a riot or rebellion, about which precise information is lacking. –*adj.* **6.** likely or apt to happen (fol. by *to*). **7.** naturally appertaining: *hardships incident to the life of an explorer.* **8.** conjoined or attaching, esp. as subordinate to a principal thing. **9.** falling or striking on something. [ME, from L *incidens,* ppr., befalling]

**incidental** /ɪnsə'dɛntl/, *adj.* **1.** happening or likely to happen in fortuitous or subordinate conjunction with something else. **2.** liable to happen or naturally appertaining (fol. by *to*). **3.** incurred casually and in addition to the regular or main amount: *incidental expenses.* –*n.* **4.** something incidental, as a circumstance. **5.** (*pl.*) minor expenses.

**incidentally** /ɪnsə'dɛntəli, -'dɛntli/, *adv.* **1.** in an incidental manner. **2.** by the way.

**incidental music** /ɪnsə'dɛntl ˌmjuzɪk/, *n.* music played during the action of a film, play, etc., but not forming an essential part of the performance.

**incinerate** /ɪn'sɪnəreɪt/, *v.,* **-rated, -rating.** –*v.t.* **1.** to reduce to ashes; cremate. –*v.i.* **2.** to burn to ashes. [ML *incinerātus,* pp. of *incinerāre,* from L *in-* IN-[2] + *cinis* ashes] – **incineration,** /ɪnˌsɪnə'reɪʃn/ *n.*

**incinerator** /ɪn'sɪnəreɪtə/, *n.* a furnace or apparatus for incinerating.

**incipient** /ɪn'sɪpiənt/, *adj.* beginning to exist or appear; in an initial stage. [L *incipiens,* ppr.] – **incipience, incipiency,** *n.* – **incipiently,** *adv.*

**incipit** /ɪn'kɪpət/, here begins. [L]

**incise** /ɪn'saɪz/, *v.t.,* **-cised, -cising. 1.** to cut into; cut marks, etc. upon. **2.** to make (marks, etc.) by cutting; engrave; carve. [F *inciser,* from L *incīsus,* pp., cut into]

**incised** /ɪn'saɪzd/, *adj.* **1.** cut into: *the incised gums.* **2.** made by cutting: *an incised wound.*

**incision** /ɪn'sɪʒən/, *n.* **1.** a cut, gash, or notch. **2.** the act of incising. **3.** a cutting into, esp. for surgical purposes. **4.** incisiveness; keenness. [ME, from L *incīsio*]

**incisive** /ɪn'saɪsɪv/, *adj.* **1.** penetrating, trenchant, or biting: *an incisive tone of voice.* **2.** sharp; keen; acute. **3.** adapted for cutting: *the incisive teeth.* – **incisively,** *adv.* – **incisiveness,** *n.*

**incisor** /ɪn'saɪzə/, *n.* a tooth in the anterior part of the jaw adapted for cutting. [NL]

**incisory** /ɪn'saɪzəri/, *adj.* adapted for cutting, as the incisor teeth.

**incisure** /ɪn'sɪʒə/, *n.* a notch, as in a bone or other structure. – **incisural,** *adj.*

**incite** /ɪn'saɪt/, *v.t.,* **-cited, -citing.** to urge on; stimulate or prompt to action. [late ME, from L *incitāre* set in motion] – **incitation** /ɪnsaɪ'teɪʃən/, *n.* – **inciter,** *n.* – **incitingly,** *adv.*

**incitement** /ɪn'saɪtmənt/, *n.* **1.** the act of inciting. **2.** the state of being incited. **3.** that which incites; motive; incentive.

**incivility** /ɪnsə'vɪləti/, *n., pl.* **-ties. 1.** the quality or fact of being uncivil; uncivil behaviour or treatment. **2.** an uncivil act.

**incl.,** **1.** including. **2.** inclusive.

**in-clearing** /'ɪn-klɪərɪŋ/, *n.* the total of cheques, etc., drawn on a member bank of a clearing house, and received by that bank for settlement from the clearing house.

**inclement** /ɪn'klɛmənt/, *adj.* (of the weather, etc.) not clement; severe or harsh. [L *inclēmens* harsh] – **inclemency,** *n.* – **inclemently,** *adv.*

**inclinable** /ɪn'klaɪnəbəl/, *adj.* **1.** having a mental bent or tendency in a certain direction; inclined. **2.** favourable. **3.** capable of being inclined.

**inclination** /ɪnklə'neɪʃən/, *n.* **1.** a set or bent (esp. of the mind or will); a liking or preference: *much against his inclination.* **2.** that to which one is inclined. **3.** the act of inclining. **4.** the state of being inclined. **5.** deviation or amount of deviation from a normal, esp. horizontal or vertical, direction or position. **6.** an inclined surface. **7.** *Maths.* the difference in direction of two lines or two planes as measured by the angle. **8.** *Astron.* **a.** one of the elements of an orbit of a planet, etc. **b.** the angle between the orbital plane and the ecliptic or other suitably chosen plane. **9.** →**dip** (def. 30). [late ME, from L *inclīnātio* a leaning] – **inclinational,** *adj.*

**inclinator** /'ɪnkləneɪtə/, *n.* a trolley set on rails installed to carry goods or people up or down a steep slope to a house, etc.

**inclinatory** /ɪnklə'neɪtəri, ɪn'klaɪnətri/, *adj.* related to or characterised by inclination.

**incline** /ɪn'klaɪn/, *v.,* **-clined, -clining;** /'ɪnklaɪn, ɪn'klaɪn/, *n.* –*v.i.* **1.** to have a mental tendency; be disposed. **2.** to deviate from the vertical or horizontal; slant. **3.** to tend, in a physical sense; approximate: *the leaves incline to a blue.* **4.** to tend in course or character. **5.** to lean; bend. –*v.t.* **6.** to dispose (a person) in mind, habit, etc. (fol. by *to*). **7.** to bow (the head, etc.). **8.** to cause to lean or bend in a particular direction. **9.** to turn towards (to listen favourably): *incline one's ear.* –*n.* **10.** an inclined surface; a slope. [L *inclīnāre* incline; replacing ME *enclyne,* from OF *encliner*] – **incliner,** *n.*

**inclined** /ɪn'klaɪnd/, *adj.* **1.** disposed, esp. favourably (fol. by *to*): *inclined to stay.* **2.** having a (physical) tendency. **3.** deviating in direction from the horizontal or vertical; sloping. **4.** in a direction making an angle with anything else.

**inclined plane** /– 'pleɪn/, *n.* a plane surface inclined to the horizon, or forming with a horizontal plane any angle but a right angle.

AC, inclined plane; CB, height of AC; BA, base; BAC, angle of inclination

**inclinometer** /ɪnklə'nɒmətə/, *n.* **1.** *Aeron.* an instrument for measuring the angle an aircraft makes with the horizontal. **2.** an instrument for determining the inclination or dip of the earth's magnetic force using a magnetic needle. [INCLINE + -O- + METER[1]]

**inclose** /ɪn'kloʊz/, *v.t.,* **-closed, -closing.** *Law or Archaic.* →**enclose.** – **incloser,** *n.*

**inclosure** /ɪn'kloʊʒə/, *n.* →**enclosure.**

**include** /ɪn'klud/, *v.t.,* **-cluded, -cluding. 1.** to contain, embrace, or comprise, as a whole does parts or any part or element. **2.** to place in an aggregate, class, category, or the like. **3.** to contain as a subordinate element; involve as a factor. **4. include out,** *Colloq.* to count as not participating: *you can include me out in this match.* [ME *include(n),* from L *inclūdere* shut in] – **includible, includable,** *adj.*

**included** /ɪn'kludəd/, *adj.* **1.** enclosed; embraced; comprised.

2. *Bot.* not projecting beyond the mouth of the corolla, as stamens or a style.

**incluse** /ɪn'klus/, *n.* →**recluse** (def. 2).

**inclusion** /ɪn'kluʒən/, *n.* **1.** the act of including. **2.** the state of being included. **3.** that which is included. **4.** *Biol.* a body suspended in the cytoplasm, as a granule, etc. **5.** *Mineral.* a solid body or a body of gas or liquid enclosed within the mass of a mineral. **6.** *Geol.* a fragment of another substance enclosed in a crystal. **7.** *Geol.* a fragment of older rock enclosed in an igneous rock. [L *inclūsio*]

**inclusion body** /'– bɒdi/, *n.* a particle which takes a characteristic stain, found in a virus-infected cell nucleus or cytoplasm.

**inclusive** /ɪn'klusɪv/, *adj.* **1.** including in consideration or account, as the stated limit or extremes: *from six to ten inclusive.* **2.** including a great deal, or including everything concerned; comprehensive. **3.** that includes; enclosing; embracing. **4.** **inclusive of,** including. – **inclusively,** *adv.* – **inclusiveness,** *n.*

**incoercible** /ɪnkoʊ'ɜsəbəl/, *adj.* **1.** not coercible. **2.** *Physics.* incapable of being reduced to a liquid form by any amount of pressure.

**incog** /ɪn'kɒg/, *adj., adv., n. Colloq.* →**incognito.**

**incogitable** /ɪn'kɒdʒətəbəl/, *adj.* unthinkable. [LL *incogitābilis*] – **incogitability** /ɪnˌkɒdʒətə'bɪləti/, *n.*

**incogitant** /ɪn'kɒdʒətənt/, *adj.* **1.** thoughtless; inconsiderate. **2.** not having the faculty of thinking.

**incognita** /ɪnkɒg'nitə/, *adj., n., pl.* **-tas, -te** /-teɪ/. *–adj.* **1.** (of a woman or girl) having the real name or identity concealed. *–n.* **2.** a woman or girl who is incognita. [fem. of INCOGNITO]

**incognito** /ɪnkɒg'nitoʊ/, *adj., adv., n., pl.* **-tos, -ti** /-ti/. *–adj.* **1.** having one's identity concealed, as under an assumed name (esp. to avoid notice or formal attentions). *–adv.* **2.** with the real identity concealed: *to travel incognito.* *–n.* **3.** one who is incognito. **4.** the state of being incognito. **5.** the character or disguise assumed by an incognito or incognita. [It., from L *incognitus* unknown]

**incognizant** /ɪn'kɒgnəzənt/, *adj.* not cognizant; without knowledge; unaware (fol. by *of*). – **incognizance,** *n.*

**incoherence** /ɪnkoʊ'hɪərəns/, *n.* **1.** the state of being incoherent. **2.** something incoherent; an incoherent statement, etc.

**incoherency** /ɪnkoʊ'hɪərənsi/, *n., pl.* **-cies.** →**incoherence.**

**incoherent** /ɪnkoʊ'hɪərənt/, *adj.* **1.** without logical connection; disjointed; rambling: *an incoherent sentence.* **2.** characterised by such thought or language, as a person: *incoherent with rage.* **3.** not coherent or cohering: *an incoherent mixture.* **4.** without physical cohesion; loose: *incoherent dust.* **5.** without unity or harmony of elements: *an incoherent public.* **6.** without congruity of parts; uncoordinated. **7.** naturally different, or incompatible, as things. – **incoherently,** *adv.*

**incombustible** /ɪnkəm'bʌstəbəl/, *adj.* **1.** not combustible; incapable of being burnt. *–n.* **2.** an incombustible substance. – **incombustibility** /ˌɪnkəmbʌstə'bɪləti/, **incombustibleness,** *n.* – **incombustibly,** *adv.*

**income** /'ɪnkʌm, 'ɪŋ-/, *n.* **1.** the returns that come in periodically, esp. annually, from one's work, property, business, etc.; revenue; receipts. **2.** something that comes in.

**income group** /'– grup/, *n.* a group of people having similar incomes.

**incomer** /'ɪnkʌmə/, *n.* **1.** one who comes in. **2.** an immigrant. **3.** an intruder. **4.** a successor.

**income tax** /'ɪnkʌm tæks/, *n.* **1.** a tax levied on incomes. **2.** an annual government tax on personal incomes, usu. graduated and with certain deductions and exemptions.

**incoming** /'ɪnkʌmɪŋ/, *adj.* **1.** coming in: *the incoming tide.* **2.** succeeding, as an office-holder. **3.** accruing as profit. **4.** entering; beginning. *–n.* **5.** a coming in; arrival: *the incoming of spring.* **6.** (*usu. pl.*) that which comes in, esp. revenue.

**incommensurable** /ɪnkə'mɛnʃərəbəl/, *adj.* **1.** not commensurable; having no common measure or standard of comparison. **2.** utterly disproportionate. **3.** *Maths.* (of two or more quantities) **a.** having no common measure. **b.** having no common factor other than 1. *–n.* **4.** that which is incommensurable. – **incommensurability** /ˌɪnkəmɛnʃərə'bɪləti/, **incommensurableness,** *n.* – **incommensurably,** *adv.*

**incommensurate** /ɪnkə'mɛnʃərət/, *adj.* **1.** not commensurate; disproportionate; inadequate: *means incommensurate to our wants.* **2.** incommensurable. – **incommensurately,** *adv.* – **incommensurateness,** *n.*

**incommode** /ɪnkə'moʊd/, *v.t.,* **-moded, -moding.** **1.** to inconvenience or discomfort. **2.** to impede; hinder. [L *incommodāre*]

**incommodious** /ɪnkə'moʊdiəs/, *adj.* **1.** not affording sufficient room. **2.** inconvenient. – **incommodiously,** *adv.* – **incommodiousness,** *n.*

**incommodity** /ɪnkə'mɒdəti/, *n., pl.* **-ties.** **1.** inconvenience. **2.** something inconvenient.

**incommunicable** /ɪnkə'mjunɪkəbəl/, *adj.* **1.** incapable of being communicated, imparted, or told to others. **2.** incommunicative. – **incommunicability** /ˌɪnkəmjunɪkə'bɪləti/, **incommunicableness,** *n.* – **incommunicably,** *adv.*

**incommunicado** /ˌɪnkəmjunə'kadoʊ/, *adj.* (esp. of a prisoner) deprived of communication with others. [Sp. *incomunicado,* from *comunicar* COMMUNICATE]

**incommunicative** /ɪnkə'mjunəkətɪv/, *adj.* not communicative; reserved. – **incommunicatively,** *adv.* – **incommunicativeness,** *n.*

**incommutable** /ɪnkə'mjutəbəl/, *adj.* **1.** not exchangeable. **2.** unchangeable. – **incommutability** /ˌɪnkəmjutə'bɪləti/, **incommutableness,** *n.* – **incommutably,** *adv.*

**incompact** /ɪnkəm'pækt/, *adj.* not compact; loose. – **incompactly,** *adv.* – **incompactness,** *n.*

**incomparable** /ɪn'kɒmpərəbəl, -prəbəl/, *adj.* **1.** matchless or unequalled: *incomparable beauty.* **2.** not comparable. – **incomparability** /ɪnˌkɒmpərə'bɪləti, -prə-/, **incomparableness,** *n.* – **incomparably,** *adv.*

**incompatible** /ɪnkəm'pætəbəl/, *adj.* **1.** not compatible; incapable of existing together in harmony. **2.** contrary or opposed in character; discordant. **3.** that cannot coexist or be conjoined. **4.** *Logic.* (of two or more propositions) that cannot be true simultaneously. **5.** (of positions, ranks, etc.) unable to be held simultaneously by one person. **6.** *Pharm., Med.* pertaining to drugs or the like which interfere with one another chemically or physiologically and therefore cannot be prescribed together. **7.** *Biol.* of or pertaining to the incapacity of cells or tissue from one individual to tolerate those of another when an organic union of some description is formed between them, as by transplantation, grafting, parasitism or the transfusion of blood. *–n.* **8.** (*usu. pl.*) an incompatible person or thing. **9.** an incompatible drug or the like. **10.** (*pl.*) *Logic.* **a.** two or more propositions which cannot be true simultaneously. **b.** two or more attributes which cannot simultaneously belong to the same object. – **incompatibleness,** *n.* – **incompatibly,** *adv.*

**incompetence** /ɪn'kɒmpətəns/, *n.* **1.** the character or condition of being incompetent; inability. **2.** *Law.* the condition of lacking the power to act with legal effectiveness. Also, **incompetency.**

**incompetent** /ɪn'kɒmpətənt/, *adj.* **1.** not competent; lacking qualification or ability: *an incompetent candidate.* **2.** characterised by or showing incompetence. **3.** *Law.* not legally qualified; inadmissible, as evidence. *–n.* **4.** an incompetent person. **5.** *Law.* a person lacking power to act with legal effectiveness. [LL *incompetens* insufficient] – **incompetently,** *adv.*

**incomplete** /ɪnkəm'plit/, *adj.* not complete; lacking some part. [ME, from LL *incomplētus*] – **incompletely,** *adv.* – **incompleteness, incompletion,** *n.*

**incompliant** /ɪnkəm'plaɪənt/, *adj.* **1.** not compliant; unyielding. **2.** not pliant. – **incompliance, incompliancy,** *n.* – **incompliantly,** *adv.*

**incomprehensible** /ˌɪnkɒmprə'hɛnsəbəl/, *adj.* not comprehensible; not understandable; unintelligible. – **incomprehensibility** /ˌɪnkɒmprəˌhɛnsə'bɪləti/, **incomprehensibleness,** *n.* – **incomprehensibly,** *adv.*

**incomprehension** /ˌɪnkɒmprə'hɛnʃən/, *n.* failure to understand; lack of comprehension: *he greeted my explanation with a blank look of incomprehension.*

**incomprehensive** /ˌɪnkɒmprə'hɛnsɪv/, *adj.* not comprehensive. – **incomprehensively,** *adv.* – **incomprehensiveness,** *n.*

**incompressible** /ɪnkəm'prɛsəbəl/, *adj.* not compressible. – **incompressibility** /ɪnkəmˌprɛsə'bɪləti/, *n.*

**incomputable** /ɪnkəm'pjutəbəl/, *adj.* →**incalculable.**
**inconceivable** /ɪnkən'sivəbəl/, *adj.* unimaginable; unthinkable; incredible. – **inconceivability** /ˌɪnkənsivə'bɪləti/, **inconceivableness,** *n.* – **inconceivably,** *adv.*
**inconclusive** /ɪnkən'klusɪv/, *adj.* **1.** not conclusive; not such as to settle a question: *inconclusive evidence.* **2.** without final results: *inconclusive experiments.* – **inconclusively,** *adv.* – **inconclusiveness,** *n.*
**incondensable** /ɪnkən'dɛnsəbəl/, *adj.* incapable of being condensed. – **incondensability** /ˌɪnkəndɛnsə'bɪləti/, *n.*
**incondite** /ɪn'kɒndaɪt/, *adj.* **1.** ill-constructed. **2.** crude; rough. [L *inconditus* disordered]
**inconformity** /ɪnkən'fɔməti/, *n.* lack of conformity; failure or refusal to conform.
**incongruent** /ɪn'kɒŋgruənt/, *adj.* not congruent; incongruous. – **incongruence,** *n.* – **incongruently,** *adv.*
**incongruity** /ɪnkɒŋ'gruəti/, *n., pl.* **-ties. 1.** the quality of being incongruous. **2.** something incongruous.
**incongruous** /ɪn'kɒŋgruəs/, *adj.* **1.** out of keeping or place; inappropriate; unbecoming; absurd: *an incongruous effect.* **2.** not harmonious in character; inconsonant; lacking harmony of parts: *incongruous mixtures.* **3.** inconsistent: *acts incongruous with their principles.* [L *incongruus*] – **incongruously,** *adv.* – **incongruousness,** *n.*
**inconsecutive** /ɪnkən'sɛkjətɪv/, *adj.* not consecutive. – **inconsecutively,** *adj.* – **inconsecutiveness,** *n.*
**inconsequent** /ɪn'kɒnsəkwənt/, *adj.* **1.** characterised by lack of sequence in thought, speech, or action. **2.** not following from the premises: *an inconsequent deduction.* **3.** characterised by lack of logical sequence: *inconsequent reasoning.* **4.** irrelevant: *an inconsequent remark.* **5.** not in keeping with the general character or design: *inconsequent ornamentation.* [L *inconsequens* without connection] – **inconsequence,** *n.* – **inconsequently,** *adv.*
**inconsequential** /ˌɪnkɒnsə'kwɛnʃəl/, *adj.* **1.** of no consequence; trivial. **2.** inconsequent; illogical; irrelevant. – **inconsequentiality** /ˌɪnkɒnsəˌkwɛnʃi'æləti/, *n.* – **inconsequentially,** *adv.*
**inconsiderable** /ɪnkən'sɪdrəbəl/, *adj.* **1.** small as in value, amount, size, etc. **2.** not worthy of consideration or notice; trivial. – **inconsiderableness,** *n.* – **inconsiderably,** *adv.*
**inconsiderate** /ɪnkən'sɪdərət, -drət/, *adj.* **1.** without due regard for the rights or feelings of others: *it was inconsiderate of him to forget.* **2.** done or acting without consideration; thoughtless. – **inconsiderately,** *adv.* – **inconsiderateness, inconsideration** /ˌɪnkənsɪdə'reɪʃən/, *n.*
**inconsistency** /ɪnkən'sɪstənsi/, *n., pl.* **-cies. 1.** the quality of being inconsistent. **2.** something inconsistent. Also, **inconsistence.**
**inconsistent** /ɪnkən'sɪstənt/, *adj.* **1.** lacking in harmony between the different parts or elements; self-contradictory. **2.** lacking agreement, as one thing with another, or two or more things in relation to each other; at variance. **3.** not consistent in principles, conduct, etc. **4.** acting at variance with professed principles. **5.** *Logic.* incompatible. – **inconsistently,** *adv.*
**inconsolable** /ɪnkən'soʊləbəl/, *adj.* not consolable: *inconsolable grief.* – **inconsolability** /ˌɪnkənsoʊlə'bɪləti/, **inconsolableness,** *n.* – **inconsolably,** *adv.*
**inconsonant** /ɪn'kɒnsənənt/, *adj.* not consonant or in accord. – **inconsonance,** *n.* – **inconsonantly,** *adv.*
**inconspicuous** /ɪnkən'spɪkjuəs/, *adj.* not conspicuous, noticeable, or prominent. – **inconspicuously,** *adv.* – **inconspicuousness,** *n.*
**inconstant** /ɪn'kɒnstənt/, *adj.* not constant; changeable; fickle; variable: *inconstant winds.* – **inconstancy,** *n.* – **inconstantly,** *adv.*
**inconsumable** /ɪnkən'sjuməbəl/, *adj.* not consumable; incapable of being consumed.
**incontestable** /ɪnkən'tɛstəbəl/, *adj.* not contestable; not admitting of dispute; incontrovertible: *incontestable proof.* – **incontestability** /ˌɪnkəntɛstə'bɪləti/, **incontestableness,** *n.* – **incontestably,** *adv.*
**incontinent** /ɪn'kɒntənənt/, *adj.* **1.** not continent; not holding or held in; unceasing or unrestrained: *an incontinent flow of talk.* **2.** lacking in restraint, esp. over the sexual appetite. **3.** unable to contain or retain (usu. fol. by *of*). **4.** *Pathol.* unable to restrain natural discharges or evacuations. [ME, from L *incontinens* not holding back] – **incontinence, incontinency,** *n.* – **incontinently,** *adv.*
**incontrollable** /ɪnkən'troʊləbəl/, *adj.* not controllable; uncontrollable: *an incontrollable desire.*
**incontrovertible** /ˌɪnkɒntrə'vɜtəbəl/, *adj.* not controvertible; indisputable. – **incontrovertibility** /ˌɪnkɒntrəˌvɜtə'bɪləti/, **incontrovertibleness,** *n.* – **incontrovertibly,** *adv.*
**inconvenience** /ɪnkən'viniəns/, *n., v.,* **-ienced, -iencing.** *–n.* **1.** the quality or state of being inconvenient. **2.** an inconvenient circumstance or thing; something that causes discomfort, trouble, etc. *–v.t.* **3.** to put to inconvenience; incommode.
**inconveniency** /ɪnkən'viniənsi/, *n., pl.* **-cies.** →**inconvenience.**
**inconvenient** /ɪnkən'viniənt/, *adj.* arranged or happening in such a way as to be awkward, inopportune, disadvantageous, or troublesome: *an inconvenient time for a visit.* [ME, from L *inconveniens* not consonant] – **inconveniently,** *adv.*
**inconvertible** /ɪnkən'vɜtəbəl/, *adj.* **1.** (of paper money) not capable of being converted into specie. **2.** not interchangeable. – **inconvertibility** /ˌɪnkənvɜtə'bɪləti/, **inconvertibleness,** *n.* – **inconvertibly,** *adv.*
**inconvincible** /ɪnkən'vɪnsəbəl/, *adj.* not convincible; incapable of being convinced. – **inconvincibility** /ˌɪnkənvɪnsə'bɪləti/, *n.* – **inconvincibly,** *adv.*
**incoordinate** /ɪnkoʊ'ɔdənət/, *adj.* not coordinate; not coordinated.
**incoordination** /ɪnkoʊˌɔdə'neɪʃən/, *n.* lack of coordination.
**incorp.,** incorporated.
**incorporable** /ɪn'kɔpərəbəl/, *adj.* of that which it is possible to incorporate or include.
**incorporate**[1] /ɪn'kɔpəreɪt/, *v.,* **-rated, -rating;** /ɪn'kɔpərət, -prət/, *adj.* *–v.t.* **1.** to create or form a legal corporation. **2.** to form into a society or organisation. **3.** to put or introduce into a body or mass as an integral part or parts. **4.** to take in or include as a part or parts, as the body or mass does. **5.** to form or combine into one body or uniform substance, as ingredients. **6.** to embody. *–v.i.* **7.** to unite or combine so as to form one body. **8.** to form a corporation. *–adj.* **9.** incorporated, as a company. **10.** combined into one body, mass, or substance. **11.** *Obs.* embodied. [ME, from LL *incorporātus,* pp., embodied. See IN-[2]] – **incorporative** /ɪn'kɔpərətɪv/, *adj.*
**incorporate**[2] /ɪn'kɔpərət, -prət/, *adj.* not embodied; incorporeal. [LL *incorporātus.* See IN-[3]]
**incorporated** /ɪn'kɔpəreɪtəd/, *adj.* **1.** formed or constituted as a company. **2.** combined in one body; made part of.
**incorporation** /ɪnˌkɔpə'reɪʃən/, *n.* **1.** the act of incorporating. **2.** the state of being incorporated.
**incorporator** /ɪn'kɔpəreɪtə/, *n.* **1.** *U.S.* one of the signers of the articles or certificate of incorporation. **2.** *U.S.* one of the persons to whom the charter is granted in a corporation created by special act of the legislature. **3.** one who incorporates.
**incorporeal** /ɪnkɔ'pɔriəl/, *adj.* **1.** not corporeal or material; spiritual. **2.** pertaining to non-material beings. **3.** *Law.* without material existence, but existing in contemplation of law, as a franchise. – **incorporeally,** *adv.*
**incorporeity** /ɪnˌkɔpə'riəti/, *n., pl.* **-ties.** the quality of being incorporeal; disembodied existence or entity. Also, **incorporeality.**
**incorrect** /ɪnkə'rɛkt/, *adj.* **1.** not correct as to fact: *an incorrect statement.* **2.** improper: *incorrect behaviour.* **3.** not correct in form or manner: *an incorrect copy.* – **incorrectly,** *adv.* – **incorrectness,** *n.*
**incorrigible** /ɪn'kɒrədʒəbəl/, *adj.* **1.** not corrigible; bad beyond correction or reform: *an incorrigible liar.* **2.** impervious to punishment; wilful; uncontrollable: *an incorrigible child.* **3.** firmly fixed; not easily changed: *an incorrigible habit.* *–n.* **4.** one who is incorrigible. **5.** *Obs.* a convict, esp. one thought of as being beyond redemption. – **incorrigibility** /ɪnˌkɒrədʒə'bɪləti/, **incorrigibleness,** *n.* – **incorrigibly,** *adv.*
**incorrupt** /ɪnkə'rʌpt/, *adj.* **1.** not corrupt; not debased or perverted; morally upright. **2.** not to be bribed. **3.** *Obs.* free

from decomposition or putrefaction. **4.** not vitiated by errors or alterations. Also, **incorrupted.** – **incorruptly,** *adv.* – **incorruptness,** *n.*

**incorruptible** /ɪnkəˈrʌptəbəl/, *adj.* **1.** incapable of physical corruption; everlasting; eternal. **2.** that cannot be perverted or bribed: *incorruptible by money.* – **incorruptibility** /ˌɪnkərʌptəˈbɪləti/, **incorruptibleness,** *n.* – **incorruptibly,** *adv.*

**incr.,** **1.** increase. **2.** increment.

**incrassate** /ɪnˈkræseɪt/, *v.,* **-sated, -sating;** /ɪnˈkræsət, -seɪt/, *adj.* –*v.t.* **1.** *Obs.* to thicken. **2.** *Pharm.* to make (a liquid) thicker by addition of another substance or by evaporation. –*v.i.* **3.** *Obs.* to become thick or thicker. –*adj.* **4.** Also, **incrassated.** *Bot., Entomol.* thickened or swollen. [LL *incrassātus,* pp.] – **incrassation** /ɪnkræsˈeɪʃən/, *n.*

**increase** /ɪnˈkris/, *v.,* **-creased, -creasing;** /ˈɪnkris/, *n.* –*v.t.* **1.** to make greater in any respect; augment; add to. **2.** to make more numerous. –*v.i.* **3.** to become greater or more numerous: *sales increased.* **4.** to multiply by propagation. –*n.* **5.** growth or augmentation in numbers: *the increase of crime.* **6.** multiplication by propagation; production of offspring. **7.** offspring or progeny. **8.** the act or process of increasing. **9.** that by which something is increased. **10.** the result of increasing. **11.** produce of the earth. **12.** product; profit; interest. [ME *encrese(n),* from AF *encres(s)-,* var. of OF *encreis(s)-,* stem of *encreistre,* from L *increscere*] – **increasable,** *adj.* – **increaser,** *n.* – **increasingly,** *adv.*

**increate** /ɪnkriˈeɪt, ˈɪnkrieɪt/, *adj.* **1.** not created; uncreated. **2.** existing without having been created.

**incredible** /ɪnˈkrɛdəbəl/, *adj.* **1.** seeming too extraordinary to be possible: *an incredible act of heroism.* **2.** not credible; that cannot be believed. – **incredibility** /ɪnˌkrɛdəˈbɪləti/, **incredibleness,** *n.* – **incredibly,** *adv.*

**incredulity** /ɪnkrəˈdjuləti/, *n.* the quality of being incredulous; a refusal of belief.

**incredulous** /ɪnˈkrɛdʒələs/, *adj.* **1.** not credulous; indisposed to believe; sceptical. **2.** indicating unbelief: *an incredulous smile.* – **incredulously,** *adv.* – **incredulousness,** *n.*

**increment** /ˈɪnkrəmənt, ˈɪŋ-/, *n.* **1.** something added or gained; an addition or increase. **2.** profit. **3.** the act or process of increasing; growth. **4.** an increase in salary resulting from progression within a graduated scale of salaries, designed to reward an employee for increases in skill or experience. **5.** *Maths.* **a.** the difference between two values of a variable; an increase (positive, negative, or zero) in an independent variable. **b.** the increase of a function due to this. –*v.t.* **6.** *Computers.* to increase the numerical contents of (a counter). [ME, from L *incrēmentum* an increase] – **incremental** /ɪnkrəˈmɛntl, ɪŋ-/, *adj.*

**increscent** /ɪnˈkrɛsənt/, *adj.* increasing or waxing, as the moon. [L *increscens,* ppr.]

**incretion** /ɪnˈkriʃən/, *n.* **1.** a substance, as an autacoid, secreted internally. **2.** the process of such secretion. [backformation from *incretionary,* from IN-[2] + *-cretionary,* modelled on CONCRETIONARY]

**incriminate** /ɪnˈkrɪməneɪt/, *v.t.,* **-nated, -nating.** **1.** to charge with a crime or fault. **2.** to involve in an accusation. [ML *incrīminātus,* pp., accused of a crime. See IN-[2], CRIMINATE] – **incrimination** /ɪnkrɪməˈneɪʃən/, *n.* – **incriminator,** *n.* – **incriminatory** /ɪnˈkrɪmənətri/, *adj.*

**incrust** /ɪnˈkrʌst/, *v.t.* →**encrust.**

**incrustation** /ɪnkrʌsˈteɪʃən/, *n.* →**encrustation.**

**incubate** /ˈɪnkjubeɪt, ˈɪŋ-/, *v.,* **-bated, -bating.** –*v.t.* **1.** to sit upon (eggs) for the purpose of hatching. **2.** to hatch (eggs), as by sitting upon them or by artificial heat. **3.** to maintain (bacterial cultures, etc.) at the most favourable temperature for development. **4.** to keep at even temperature, as prematurely born infants. **5.** to produce as if by hatching; formulate; develop; give shape to. –*v.i.* **6.** to sit upon eggs. **7.** to undergo incubation. **8.** to grow; take shape. [L *incubātus,* pp., hatched, sat on] – **incubative, incubatory,** *adj.*

**incubation** /ɪnkjuˈbeɪʃən, ɪŋ-/, *n.* **1.** the act or process of incubating. **2.** the condition or quality of being incubated. – **incubational,** *adj.*

**incubation period** /ˈ– pɪəriəd/, *n.* the period between infection and the appearance of signs of a disease.

**incubator** /ˈɪnkjubeɪtə, ˈɪŋ-/, *n.* **1.** an apparatus for hatching eggs artificially, consisting essentially of a case heated by a lamp or the like. **2.** a boxlike apparatus in which prematurely born infants are kept at a constant and suitable temperature. **3.** a device in which bacterial cultures, etc., are developed at a constant suitable temperature. **4.** one who or that which incubates. [L]

**incubus** /ˈɪnkjubəs, ˈɪŋ-/, *n., pl.* **-bi** /-baɪ/, **-buses.** **1.** an imaginary demon or evil spirit supposed to descend upon sleeping persons, esp. one reputed to have sexual intercourse with sleeping women. **2.** something that weighs upon or oppresses one like a nightmare. **3.** a nightmare. [ME, from LL: nightmare, ML: a demon, from L *incubāre* lie on]

**incudes** /ɪnˈkjudiz/, *n.* plural of **incus.**

**inculcate** /ˈɪnkʌlkeɪt/, *v.t.,* **-cated, -cating.** to impress by repeated statement or admonition; teach persistently and earnestly; instil (usu. fol. by *upon* or *in*). [L *inculcātus,* pp., stamped in, impressed upon] – **inculcation** /ɪnkʌlˈkeɪʃən/, *n.* – **inculcator,** *n.*

**inculpable** /ɪnˈkʌlpəbəl/, *adj.* not culpable; blameless. – **inculpably,** *adv.*

**inculpate** /ˈɪnkʌlpeɪt/, *v.t.,* **-pated, -pating.** **1.** to charge with fault; blame; accuse. **2.** to involve in a charge; incriminate. [ML *inculpātus,* pp. of *inculpāre,* from *in-* IN-[2] + *culpāre* blame] – **inculpation** /ɪnkʌlˈpeɪʃən/, *n.*

**inculpatory** /ɪnˈkʌlpətəri, -tri/, *adj.* tending to inculpate; imputing blame; incriminating.

**incumbency** /ɪnˈkʌmbənsi/, *n., pl.* **-cies.** **1.** that which is incumbent. **2.** an incumbent weight or mass. **3.** the position or office of the holder of an ecclesiastical benefice. **4.** *Rare.* the state of being incumbent. **5.** *Rare.* a duty or obligation.

**incumbent** /ɪnˈkʌmbənt/, *adj.* **1.** resting on one; obligatory: *a duty incumbent upon me.* **2.** lying, leaning, or pressing on something: *incumbent posture.* –*n.* **3.** the holder of an office. **4.** one who holds an ecclesiastical benefice. **5.** *Bot.* of cotyledons, with the back of one lying against the radicle. [ME, from L *incumbens,* ppr., leaning upon] – **incumbently,** *adv.*

**incumber** /ɪnˈkʌmbə/, *v.t.* →**encumber.**

**incumbrance** /ɪnˈkʌmbrəns/, *n.* →**encumbrance.**

**incunabula** /ɪnkjuˈnæbjulə/, *n.pl., sing.* **-lum.** **1.** books produced in the infancy of printing (before 1500) from movable type. **2.** the earliest stages or first traces of anything. [L: cradle, beginning, swaddling clothes] – **incunabular,** *adj.*

**incur** /ɪnˈkɜ/, *v.t.,* **-curred, -curring.** **1.** to run or fall into (some consequence, usu. undesirable or injurious). **2.** to become liable or subject to through one's own action; bring upon oneself: *to incur his displeasure.* [ME, from L *incurrere* run into, or against] – **incurrable,** *adj.*

**incurable** /ɪnˈkjurəbəl/, *adj.* **1.** not curable. –*n.* **2.** one suffering from an incurable disease. – **incurability** /ɪnˌkjurəˈbɪləti/, **incurableness,** *n.* – **incurably,** *adv.*

**incurious** /ɪnˈkjuriəs/, *adj.* **1.** not curious; inattentive or unobservant. **2.** indifferent. **3.** deficient in interest or novelty. – **incuriosity** /ˌɪnkjuriˈɒsəti/, **incuriousness,** *n.* – **incuriously,** *adv.*

**incurrence** /ɪnˈkʌrəns/, *n.* the act of incurring, bringing on, or subjecting oneself to something.

**incurrent** /ɪnˈkʌrənt/, *adj.* carrying, or relating to, an inward current. [L *incurrens,* ppr., running into]

**incursion** /ɪnˈkɜʒən/, *n.* **1.** a hostile entrance into or invasion of a place or territory, esp. one of sudden character; raid; attack. **2.** a harmful inroad. **3.** a running in: *the incursion of sea-water.* [ME, from L *incursio* onset]

**incursive** /ɪnˈkɜsɪv/, *adj.* making incursions.

**incurvate** /ɪnˈkɜvət, -veɪt/, *adj.;* /ˈɪnkɜveɪt/, *v.* **-vated, -vating.** –*adj.* **1.** curved, esp. inwards. –*v.t.* **2.** to make curved; turn from a straight line or course; curve, esp. inwards. [L *incurvātus,* pp., bent in] – **incurvation** /ɪnkɜˈveɪʃən/, **incurvature,** *n.*

**incurve** /ɪnˈkɜv/, *v.,* **-curved, -curving;** /ˈɪnkɜv/, *n.* –*v.t.* **1.** to curve inwards. –*n.* **2.** *Baseball.* an inward-curving ball, i.e. towards the batter. [L *incurvāre* bend in]

**incus** /ˈɪŋkəs/, *n., pl.* **incudes** /ɪnˈkjudiz/. the middle one of a chain of three small bones in the middle ear of man and other mammals. See **malleus** and **stapes.** [L: anvil] – **incudal,** *adj.*

**incuse** /ɪn'kjuz/, *adj., n., v.,* **-cused, -cusing.** *–adj.* **1.** hammered or stamped in, as a figure on a coin. *–n.* **2.** an incuse figure or impression. *–v.t.* **3.** to hammer or stamp, as a figure on a coin. [L *incūsus,* pp., forged with a hammer]

**ind-,** variant of **indo-** before vowels, as in *indene.*

**ind.,** **1.** independent. **2.** indicative.

**Ind** /ɪnd/, *n.* **1.** *Poetic.* India. **2.** *Obs.* the Indies.

**Ind.,** **1.** India. **2.** Indian. **3.** Indies.

**indaba** /ɪn'dabə/, *n.* **1.** a meeting with or between natives, esp. native councillors in South Africa; a conference or consultation. **2.** *Colloq.* concern; affair. [Zulu: affair, business, topic]

**indamine** /'ɪndəmin/, *n.* any of a certain series of basic organic compounds which form bluish and greenish salts, used in the manufacture of dyes. [IND(IGO) + AMINE]

**indanthrene** /ɪn'dænθrin/, *n.* (*also cap.*) a blue, insoluble, anthraquinone dyestuff, $C_{28}H_{14}O_4N_2$. [Trademark]

**indebt** /ɪn'dɛt/, *v.t.* to place under obligation for benefits, favours, assistance, etc., received. [first used in pp., ME *endetted,* after OF *endetter,* from *en-* EN-[1] + *dette* DEBT]

**indebted** /ɪn'dɛtəd/, *adj.* **1.** owing money. **2.** being under an obligation for benefits, favours, assistance etc., received.

**indebtedness** /ɪn'dɛtədnəs/, *n.* **1.** the state of being indebted. **2.** an amount owed. **3.** debts collectively.

**indecency** /ɪn'disənsi/, *n., pl.* **-cies.** **1.** the quality of being indecent. **2.** impropriety; indelicacy or immodesty. **3.** obscenity. **4.** an indecent act, remark, etc.

**indecent** /ɪn'disənt/, *adj.* **1.** offending against recognised standards of propriety or good taste; vulgar: *indecent language.* **2.** not decent; unbecoming or unseemly: *indecent conduct.* – **indecently,** *adv.*

**indecent assault** /– ə'sɒlt/, *n.* an assault in which an individual is subjected to some form of sexual activity, esp. against his or her will.

**indecent exposure** /– ɛks'poʊʒə/, *n.* the revealing to view of those parts of the body, esp. the genitals, which by law and convention should be covered by clothing under the given circumstances.

**indeciduate** /ɪndə'sɪdʒuət, -eɪt/, *adj.* not deciduate.

**indeciduous** /ɪndə'sɪdʒuəs/, *adj.* **1.** not deciduous, as leaves. **2.** (of trees) evergreen.

**indecipherable** /ɪndə'saɪfrəbəl/, *adj.* not decipherable. – **indecipherability** /ˌɪndəsaɪfrə'bɪləti/, *n.*

**indecision** /ɪndə'sɪʒən/, *n.* inability to decide.

**indecisive** /ɪndə'saɪsɪv, -'sɪzɪv/, *adj.* **1.** not decisive or conclusive: *a severe but indecisive battle.* **2.** characterised by indecision, as persons; irresolute; undecided. – **indecisively,** *adv.* – **indecisiveness,** *n.*

**indecl.,** indeclinable.

**indeclinable** /ɪndə'klaɪnəbəl/, *adj.* not declined, esp. of a word belonging to a form class most of whose members are declined, as the Latin adjective *decem* (ten). – **indeclinably,** *adv.*

**indecomposable** /ɪnˌdikəm'poʊzəbəl/, *adj.* not decomposable.

**indecorous** /ɪn'dɛkərəs/, *adj.* not decorous; violating propriety; unseemly. [L *indecōrus*] – **indecorously,** *adv.* – **indecorousness,** *n.*

**indecorum** /ɪndə'kɔrəm/, *n.* **1.** indecorous behaviour or character. **2.** something indecorous. [L, properly neut. of *indecōrus* indecorous]

**indeed** /ɪn'did/, *adv.* **1.** in fact; in reality; in truth; truly (used for emphasis, to confirm and amplify a previous statement, to intensify, to indicate a concession or admission, or, interrogatively, to obtain confirmation). *–interj.* **2.** (an expression of surprise, incredulity, irony, etc.) [ME *in dede.* See IN, *prep.,* DEED, *n.*]

**indef.,** indefinite.

**indefatigable** /ɪndə'fætɪgəbəl/, *adj.* incapable of being tired out; not yielding to fatigue. [L *indēfatīgābilis*] – **indefatigability** /ˌɪndəfætɪgə'bɪləti/, **indefatigableness,** *n.* – **indefatigably,** *adv.*

**indefeasibility of title,** *n.* the means whereby, under the Torrens System of land registration, a registered proprietor (except in certain cases such as fraud) has paramount title over his land, estate or interest in land, and holds the same free from any unregistered interests.

**indefeasible** /ɪndə'fizəbəl/, *adj.* not defeasible; not to be annulled or made void; not forfeitable. – **indefeasibility** /ˌɪndəfizə'bɪləti/, *n.* – **indefeasibly,** *adv.*

**indefectible** /ɪndə'fɛktəbəl/, *adj.* **1.** not defectible; not liable to defect or failure; unfailing. **2.** not liable to fault or imperfection; faultless. – **indefectibility** /ˌɪndəfɛktə'bɪləti/, *n.* – **indefectibly,** *adv.*

**indefensible** /ɪndə'fɛnsəbəl/, *adj.* **1.** that cannot be justified; inexcusable: *an indefensible remark.* **2.** that cannot be defended by force of arms: *an indefensible frontier.* – **indefensibility** /ˌɪndəfɛnsə'bɪləti/, **indefensibleness,** *n.* – **indefensibly,** *adv.*

**indefinable** /ɪndə'faɪnəbəl/, *adj.* not definable; indescribable. – **indefinableness,** *n.* – **indefinably,** *adv.*

**indefinite** /ɪn'dɛfənət/, *adj.* **1.** not definite; without fixed or specified limit; unlimited: *an indefinite number.* **2.** not clearly defined or determined; not precise. **3.** *Gram.* not specifying precisely, as the indefinite pronoun *some.* **4.** *Bot.* **a.** very numerous or not easily counted, as stamens. **b.** (of an inflorescence) indeterminate. [L *indēfīnītus*] – **indefinitely,** *adv.* – **indefiniteness,** *n.*

**indefinite article** /– 'atɪkəl/, *n.* the article (as *a, an*) which classes as 'single and unidentified' the noun it modifies.

**indehiscent** /ɪndə'hɪsənt/, *adj.* not dehiscent; not opening at maturity. – **indehiscence,** *n.*

**indelible** /ɪn'dɛləbəl/, *adj.* **1.** incapable of being deleted or obliterated: *an indelible impression.* **2.** making indelible marks: *an indelible pencil.* [L *indēlēbilis* that cannot be destroyed] – **indelibility** /ɪnˌdɛlə'bɪləti/, **indelibleness,** *n.* – **indelibly,** *adv.*

**indelicacy** /ɪn'dɛləkəsi/, *n., pl.* **-cies.** **1.** the quality of being indelicate. **2.** something indelicate.

**indelicate** /ɪn'dɛləkət/, *adj.* **1.** not delicate; lacking delicacy. **2.** offensive to a sense of propriety, or modesty; unrefined. – **indelicately,** *adv.*

**indemnification** /ɪnˌdɛmnəfə'keɪʃən/, *n.* **1.** the act of indemnifying. **2.** the state of being indemnified. **3.** that which serves to indemnify; compensation.

**indemnify** /ɪn'dɛmnəfaɪ/, *v.t.,* **-fied, -fying.** **1.** to compensate for damage or loss sustained, expense incurred, etc. **2.** to engage to make good or secure against anticipated loss; give security against (future damage or liability). – **indemnifier,** *n.*

**indemnity** /ɪn'dɛmnəti/, *n., pl.* **-ties.** **1.** protection or security against damage or loss. **2.** compensation for damage or loss sustained. **3.** something paid by way of such compensation. **4.** legal protection, as by insurance, from liabilities or penalties incurred by one's actions. **5.** legal exemption from penalties attaching to unconstitutional or illegal actions, granted to public officers and other persons. [late ME, from LL *indemnitas,* from L *indemnis* unharmed]

**indemonstrable** /ɪndə'mɒnstrəbəl/, *adj.* not demonstrable; incapable of being demonstrated or proved. – **indemonstrability** /ˌɪndəmɒnstrə'bɪləti/, *n.* – **indemonstrably,** *adv.*

**indene** /'ɪndin/, *n.* a colourless liquid hydrocarbon, $C_9H_8$, obtained from coal tar by fractional distillation. [IND- + -ENE]

**indent**[1] /ɪn'dɛnt/ *v.;* /'ɪndɛnt/ *n.* *–v.t.* **1.** to form deep recesses in: *the sea indents the coast.* **2.** to set in or back from the margin, as the first line of a paragraph. **3.** to sever (a document drawn up in duplicate) along an irregular line as a means of identification. **4.** to cut or tear the edge of (copies of a document) in an irregular way. **5.** to make toothlike notches in; notch. **6.** to indenture, as an apprentice. **7.** to draw an order upon. **8.** to order, as commodities. *–v.i.* **9.** to form a recess. **10.** to enter into an agreement by indenture. **11.** to make out an order or requisition in duplicate. **12.** *Mil.* to make a requisition. *–n.* **13.** a toothlike notch or deep recess; an indentation. **14.** an indention. **15.** an official requisition for stores. **16.** an order for goods. **17.** an indenture. [ME *endente(n),* from OF *endenter,* from *en-* EN-[1] + *dent* tooth] – **indenter,** *n.*

indented moulding

**indent**[2] /ɪn'dɛnt/, *v.;* /'ɪndɛnt/ *n.* *–v.t.* **1.** to dent or press in so as to form a dent. **2.** to make a dent in. *–n.* **3.** a dent. [ME, from IN-[2] + DENT[1]]

**indentation** /ındɛn'teıʃən/, *n.* **1.** a cut, notch, or deep recess: *various bays and indentations.* **2.** a series of incisions or notches. **3.** a notching or being notched. **4.** an indention. [INDENT[1] + -ATION]

**indenting** /ın'dɛntıŋ/, *n.* →**toothing.**

**indention** /ın'dɛnʃən/, *n.* **1.** an indenting. **2.** an indentation. **3.** an indenting of a line or lines, and leaving of blank space. **4.** the blank space so left.

**indentor** /ın'dɛntə/, *n.* an instrument, usu. made of an extremely hard substance as diamond, used to assess the hardness of a metal and its resistance to indentation.

**indenture** /ın'dɛntʃə/, *n., v.,* **-tured, -turing.** *–n.* **1.** a deed or agreement executed in two or more copies with edges correspondingly indented as a means of identification. **2.** any deed, contract, or sealed agreement between two or more parties. **3.** a contract by which a person, as an apprentice, is bound to service. **4.** any official or formal list, certificate, etc., authenticated for use as a voucher or the like. **5.** the formal agreement between a group of bondholders and the debtor as to the terms of the debt. **6.** indentation. *–v.t.* **7.** to bind by indenture, as an apprentice. [ME *endenture,* from OF *endenteure* indentation]

**independence** /ındə'pɛndəns/, *n.* **1.** the state or quality of being independent. **2.** freedom from subjection, or from the influence of others. **3.** exemption from external control or support. **4.** a competency.

**independency** /ındə'pɛndənsi/, *n., pl.* **-cies.** **1.** independence. **2.** a territory not under the control of any other power. **3.** (*cap.*) *Eccles.* **a.** the principle that the individual congregation or church is an autonomous and equalitarian society free from any external ecclesiastical control. **b.** the polity based on this principle.

**independent** /ındə'pɛndənt/, *adj.* **1.** not influenced by others in matters of opinion, conduct, etc.; thinking or acting for oneself: *an independent person.* **2.** not subject to another's authority or jurisdiction; autonomous; free. **3.** not influenced by the thought or action of others: *independent research.* **4.** not dependent; not depending or contingent on something else for existence, operation, etc. **5.** not relying on another or others for aid or support. **6.** declining others' aid or support; refusing to be under obligation to others. **7.** possessing a competency. **8.** sufficient to support a person so that he does not have to look for a living. **9.** expressive of a spirit of independence; self-confident; unconstrained. **10.** free from party commitments in voting. **11.** (of a school), non-government. **12.** *Maths.* (of a quantity or variable), not depending upon another for value. *–n.* **13.** an independent person or thing. **14.** *Politics.* one who votes without blind loyalty to any organised party. **– independently,** *adv.*

**independent clause** /'– klɔz/, *n.* →**main clause.**

**independent contractor** /– 'kɒntræktə/, *n.* a person who undertakes to perform work for another for a consideration and who, in the performance of it is his own master, subject only to the conditions of the contract, written or oral.

**independent front suspension,** *n.* a method of suspending the front wheels of a motor vehicle to the chassis by individual spindle and coil-spring mountings for each wheel.

**independent means** /ındə,pɛndənt 'minz/, *n.* private income.

**independent school** /'– skul/, *n.* a non-government school.

**in-depth** /'ın-dɛpθ/, *adj.* with thorough coverage: *an in-depth discussion.*

**indescribable** /ındə'skraıbəbəl/, *adj.* not describable. **– indescribability** /,ındəskraıbə'bıləti/, *n.* **– indescribably,** *adv.*

**indestructible** /ındə'strʌktəbəl/, *adj.* not destructible. **– indestructibility** /,ındəstrʌktə'bıləti/, **indestructibleness,** *n.* **– indestructibly,** *adv.*

**indeterminable** /ındə'tɜmənəbəl/, *adj.* **1.** not determinable; incapable of being ascertained. **2.** incapable of being decided or settled. **– indeterminably,** *adv.*

**indeterminacy principle** /ındə'tɜmınəsi prınsəpəl/, *n.* →**uncertainty principle.**

**indeterminate** /ındə'tɜmənət/, *adj.* **1.** not determinate; not fixed in extent; indefinite; uncertain. **2.** not clear; vague: *a cloudy and indeterminate meaning.* **3.** not established. **4.** not settled or decided. **5.** *Maths.* (of a quantity) having no fixed value. **6.** *Bot.* (of an inflorescence) having the axis or axes not ending in a flower or bud, thus allowing further elongation. **7.** *Engineering.* (of a framework, etc.) such that its forces cannot be determined by simple vector analysis. **– indeterminately,** *adv.* **– indeterminancy, indeterminateness,** *n.*

**indeterminate music** /– 'mjuzık/, *n.* music in which the composer leaves great scope for the performer to vary the composition during performance and which often involves sounds from sources other than traditional musical instruments.

**indeterminate sentence** /– 'sɛntəns/, *n.* a penalty imposed by a court which has relatively wide limits or no limits, as imprisonment for one to ten years.

**indetermination** /,ındətɜmə'neıʃən/, *n.* **1.** the condition or quality of being indeterminate. **2.** an unsettled state, as of the mind.

**indeterminism** /ındə'tɜmənızəm/, *n.* **1.** the doctrine that human actions, though somewhat influenced by pre-existing psychological and other conditions, are not entirely governed by them, but contain a certain freedom and spontaneity. **2.** the theory that the will is to some extent independent of the strength of motives, or may itself modify their strength in choice. **– indeterminist,** *n., adj.*

**index** /'ındɛks/, *n., pl.* **-dexes, -dices** /-dəsız/, *v.* *–n.* **1.** a detailed alphabetical key to names, places, and topics in a book with reference to their page number, etc., in the book. **2.** something used or serving to point out; a sign, token, or indication: *a true index of his character.* **3.** something that serves to direct attention to some fact, condition, etc.; a guiding principle. **4.** a pointer or indicator in a scientific instrument. **5.** a piece of wood, metal, or the like, serving as a pointer or indicator. **6.** *Print., etc.* a sign (as ☛, etc.) used to point out a particular note, paragraph, etc. **7.** the index finger; the forefinger. **8.** *Science.* a number or formula expressing some property, ratio, etc., of a thing indicated. **9.** *Alg.* **a.** an exponent. **b.** the integer n in a radical $\sqrt[n]{-}$ defining the n-th root: $\sqrt[3]{7}$ *is a radical having index three.* **10.** (*cap.*) a list of books which Roman Catholics are forbidden by Church authority to read without special permission, or which are not to be read unless expurgated or corrected (L *Index Librorum Prohibitorum,* **Index of Prohibited Books**), or a list of books of the latter class only, with specification of objectionable passages (L *Index Expurgatorius,* **Expurgatory Index**). **11.** *Obs.* a table of contents. **12.** *Obs.* a preface. *–v.t.* **13.** to provide with an index, as a book. **14.** to enter in an index, as a word. **15.** to serve to indicate. **16.** to adjust wages, taxes, etc., regularly in accordance with changes in commodity and other prices. [ME, from L: index, forefinger, sign] **– indexer,** *n.* **– indexical** /ın'dɛksıkəl/, *adj.* **– indexless,** *adj.*

**indexation** /ındɛk'seıʃən/, *n.* the adjustment of one variable in the light of changes in another variable, esp. the adjustment of wages to compensate for rises in the cost of living.

**index finger** /'ındɛks fıŋgə/, *n.* →**forefinger.**

**index number** /'– nʌmbə/, *n.* a number indicating change in magnitude, as of price, wage, employment, or production shifts, relative to the magnitude at some specified point usu. taken to be 100.

**index of refraction,** *n.* →**refractive index.**

**India** /'ındiə/, *n.* a republic in southern Asia. [OE, from L, from Gk, from *Indós* river Indus (from Pers. *Hind,* c. Skt *Sindhu* river Indus, orig. river)]

**Indiaman** /'ındiəmən/, *n., pl.* **-men.** (formerly) a large merchant ship in the India trade.

**Indian** /'ındiən/, *n.* **1.** a member of any of the races native to India or the East Indies (East Indian). **2.** →**Amerindian** (def. 1). **3.** *Colloq.* →**Amerindian** (def. 2). **4.** (formerly) an Aborigine or Maori. *–adj.* **5.** of or pertaining to India or the East Indies (often East Indian). **6.** →**Amerindian** (defs 3 and 4). [ME, from INDIA + -AN]

**Indian club** /– 'klʌb/, *n.* a bottle-shaped wooden club, one of a pair swung by the hands in gymnastics.

**Indian corn** /– 'kɔn/, *n.* →**maize.**

**Indian file** /'– faıl/, *n.* single file, as of persons walking.

**Indian giver** /'– gıvə/, *n. Colloq.* a person who gives something as a gift to another and later takes or demands it back.

**Indian hemp** /– 'hɛmp/, *n.* **1.** a tall, annual herb, *Cannabis sativa,* native to Asia but cultivated in many parts of the world and yielding hashish, bhang, cannabin, etc. **2.** any of several plants of the genus *Apocynum,* native to America, whose roots have laxative and emetic properties.

**Indian ink** /– 'ɪŋk/, *n.* **1.** a black pigment consisting of lampblack mixed with glue. **2.** a liquid ink from this. Also, *U.S.,* **India ink.**

**indianite** /'ɪndiənaɪt/, *n.* →**anorthite.**

**Indian liquorice** /ɪndiən 'lɪkərɪʃ, 'lɪkərɪs/, *n.* a woody shrub, *Abrus precatorius,* of India, etc., whose seeds are used for beads, and whose root is employed as a substitute for liquorice; crab's eyes; jequirity beans.

**Indian meal** /– 'mil/, *n.* →**corn meal** (def. 2).

**Indian millet** /– 'mɪlət/, *n.* →**durra.**

**Indian myna** /– 'maɪnə/, *n.* →**myna.**

**Indian Ocean** /– 'oʊʃən/, *n.* an ocean west of Australia, south of Asia and east of Africa.

**Indian pipe** /– 'paɪp/, *n.* a leafless saprophytic plant, *Monotropa uniflora,* of North America and Asia, having a solitary flower, and resembling a tobacco pipe.

**Indian red** /– 'rɛd/, *n.* **1.** earth of a yellowish-red colour, found esp. in the Persian Gulf, which serves as a pigment and as a polish for gold and silver objects. **2.** a pigment of that colour prepared by oxidising the salts of iron.

**Indian reservation** /– rɛzə'veɪʃən/, *n.* a tract of land set apart by the government for the use of an American Indian people or tribe.

**Indian rice** /– 'raɪs/, *n.* a grass of marshes of the central and south-eastern U.S., *Zizania aquatica.*

**Indian runner duck,** *n.* one of a breed of small, domestic ducks, variously coloured white and fawn.

**Indian shot** /ɪndiən 'ʃɒt/, *n.* →**canna.**

**Indian summer** /– 'sʌmə/, *n.* **1.** a period of summer weather occurring after the summer season. **2.** a peaceful and quiet old age.

**Indian tobacco** /– tə'bækoʊ/, *n.* a common American herb, *Lobelia inflata,* with small blue flowers and inflated capsules.

**India paper** /'ɪndiə peɪpə/, *n.* **1.** a thin, soft, absorbent paper made in the Orient, used for impressions of engravings. **2.** a thin, tough, opaque paper used in printing Bibles, prayerbooks, large reference works, etc.

**India print** /– 'prɪnt/, *n.* a cotton fabric block-printed in India.

**indiarubber** /ɪndiə'rʌbə/, *n.* **1.** a highly elastic substance obtained from the milky juice of numerous tropical plants, used for rubbing out pencil marks, and variously in the arts and manufactures; caoutchouc; gum elastic; rubber. *–adj.* **2.** of, made of, or pertaining to indiarubber. Also, **india rubber.**

**indic.,** indicative. Also, **ind.**

**Indic** /'ɪndɪk/, *adj.* **1.** of or pertaining to India; Indian. **2.** of or pertaining to a subgroup of the Indo-Iranian languages including Sanskrit and many modern languages of India, Pakistan and Ceylon. [L *Indicus,* from Gk *Indikós*]

**indican** /'ɪndɪkən/, *n.* **1.** *Chem.* a glucoside, $C_{14}H_{17}NO_6$, which occurs in plants yielding indigo, and from which indigo is obtained. **2.** *Biochem.* a component of urine, indoxyl potassium sulphate, $C_8H_6NO_4SK$. [L *indicum* indigo + -AN]

**indicant** /'ɪndɪkənt/, *adj.* **1.** indicating; indicative. *–n.* **2.** that which indicates.

**indicate** /'ɪndəkeɪt, -dɪkeɪt/, *v.t.,* **-cated, -cating. 1.** to be a sign of; betoken; imply: *his hesitation indicates unwillingness.* **2.** to point out or point to; direct attention to: *to indicate a place on a map.* **3.** to show, or make known: *the thermometer indicates temperature.* **4.** to state or express, esp. briefly or in a general way: *to indicate one's intentions.* **5.** *Med.* **a.** (of symptoms, etc.) to point out (a particular remedy, treatment, etc.) as suitable or necessary. **b.** to show the presence of (a disease, etc.). [L *indicātus,* pp.]

**indicated airspeed** /ˌɪndəkeɪtəd 'ɛəspid/, *n.* the reading of an airspeed indicator which, at high altitudes, will be lower than the true airspeed owing to the lower air density.

**indicated horsepower** /– 'hɔspaʊə/, *n.* the horsepower developed by a reciprocating engine as calculated from the indicator diagram, it exceeds the brake horsepower by the power lost in the engine by friction, pumping etc.

**indication** /ɪndə'keɪʃən, ɪndɪ-/, *n.* **1.** anything serving to indicate or point out, as a sign, token, etc. **2.** *Med.* a special symptom or the like which points out a suitable remedy or treatment or shows the presence of a disease. **3.** the act of indicating. **4.** the degree marked by an instrument.

**indicative** /ɪn'dɪkətɪv/, *adj.* **1.** that indicates; pointing out; suggestive (fol. by *of*). **2.** *Gram.* designating or pertaining to the mood of the verb used in ordinary statements, questions, etc., in contrast to hypothetical statements or those made without reference to a specific actor or time of action. For example: in the sentence *John plays football,* the verb *plays* is in the indicative mood. *–n.* **3.** *Gram.* **a.** the indicative mood. **b.** a verb in the indicative. [late ME, from L *indicātīvus*] – **indicatively,** *adv.*

**indicator** /'ɪndəkeɪtə, 'ɪndɪ-/, *n.* **1.** one who or that which indicates. **2.** a pointing or directing device, as a pointer on an instrument or a flashing light on a motor car. **3.** an instrument which indicates the condition of a machine, etc. **4.** a pressure gauge; an apparatus for recording the variations of pressure or vacuum in the cylinder of an engine. **5.** *Chem.* a substance used (esp. in volumetric analysis) to indicate (as by a change in colour) the condition of a solution, the point at which a certain reaction ends and another begins, etc.

**indicator diagram** /– 'daɪəgræm/, *n.* a graphical representation of the pressure and volume changes of the working fluid within the cylinder of a reciprocating engine or pump as obtained with an indicator.

**indicator light** /'–ˌlaɪt/, *n.* →**indicator** (def. 2).

**indicatory** /ɪn'dɪkətri/, *adj.* serving to indicate.

**indices** /'ɪndəsiz/, *n.* plural of **index.**

**indicia** /ɪn'dɪʃiə/, *n. pl., sing.* **-dicium** /-'dɪʃiəm/. signs; markings; indications. [L, pl. of *indicium* sign, mark] – **indicial,** *adj.*

**indict** /ɪn'daɪt/, *v.t.* **1.** to charge with an offence or crime; accuse. **2.** *U.S.* (of a grand jury) to bring a formal accusation against, as a means of bringing to trial. [ME *endite(n),* from AF *enditer* accuse, indict. Cf. OF *enditer* INDITE] – **indicter,** *n.*

**indictable** /ɪn'daɪtəbəl/, *adj.* **1.** liable to be indicted, as a person. **2.** making one liable to be indicted, as an offence.

**indictment** /ɪn'daɪtmənt/, *n.* **1.** the act of indicting. **2.** *Law.* a formal written accusation (formerly presented by a grand jury) for the purpose of trial by jury. **3.** an accusation. **4.** the state of being indicted.

**indifference** /ɪn'dɪfrəns/, *n.* **1.** lack of interest or concern. **2.** unimportance. **3.** the quality or fact of being indifferent. **4.** mediocre quality.

**indifference curve** /'– kɜv/, *n.* a graph, whose co-ordinates represent the quantities of alternative goods and services that tend to leave the consumer indifferent in his choice because he judges them of equal value.

**indifference point** /'– pɔɪnt/, *n.* a position or value at a point between two opposites of experience, such as a temperature experienced as neither warm nor cold, or a feeling value that is neither pleasant nor unpleasant.

**indifferent** /ɪn'dɪfrənt/, *adj.* **1.** without interest or concern; not caring; apathetic. **2.** having neither favourable nor unfavourable feelings towards some thing or person; impartial. **3.** neutral in character or quality; neither good nor bad: *an indifferent specimen.* **4.** falling short of any standard of excellence; not very good: *an indifferent play; indifferent health.* **5.** of only moderate amount, extent, etc. **6.** not making a difference, or mattering, either way, as to a person. **7.** immaterial or unimportant. **8.** not essential or obligatory, as an observance. **9.** making no difference or distinction, as between persons or things: *indifferent justice.* **10.** neutral in chemical, electrical, or magnetic quality. **11.** *Biol.* not differentiated or specialised, as cells or tissues. [ME, from L *indifferens* (def. 3)] – **indifferently,** *adv.*

**indifferentism** /ɪn'dɪfrəntɪzəm/, *n.* **1.** systematic indifference. **2.** the principle that differences of religious belief are essentially unimportant. – **indifferentist,** *n.*

**indigence** /'ɪndɪdʒəns/, *n.* indigent state; poverty.

**indigene** /'ɪndədʒin/, *n.* one who or that which is indigenous or native; a native; an autochthon; an aboriginal inhabitant. [F, from L *indigena*]

**indigenise** /ɪn'dɪdʒənaɪz/, *v.t.,* **-nised, -nising.** to make more marked the national or racial character of (a group of people, or some activity or organisation associated with them): *she* *indigenised music education in Australian schools.* – **indigenisation** /ɪnˌdɪdʒənaɪˈzeɪʃən/, *n.*

**indigenous** /ɪnˈdɪdʒənəs/, *adj.* **1.** originating in and characterising a particular region or country; native (usu. fol. by *to*): *the plants indigenous to Canada.* **2.** innate; inherent; natural (usu. fol. by *to*). [LL *indigenus,* from L *indigena* native] – **indigenously,** *adv.* – **indigenousness,** *n.*

**indigent** /ˈɪndədʒənt/, *adj.* lacking the necessities of life; needy; poor. [ME, from L *indigens,* ppr.] – **indigently,** *adv.*

**indigested** /ɪndəˈdʒɛstəd, ɪndaɪ-/, *adj.* **1.** without arrangement or order. **2.** unformed or shapeless. **3.** not digested; undigested. **4.** not duly considered.

**indigestible** /ɪndəˈdʒɛstəbəl, ɪndaɪ-/, *adj.* not digestible; not easily digested. – **indigestibility** /ˌɪndədʒɛstəˈbɪləti/, **indigestibleness,** *n.* – **indigestibly,** *adv.*

**indigestion** /ɪndəˈdʒɛstʃən, ɪndaɪ-/, *n.* incapability of, or difficulty in, digesting food; dyspepsia.

**indigestive** /ɪndəˈdʒɛstɪv, ɪndaɪ-/, *adj.* attended with or suffering from indigestion; dyspeptic.

**indignant** /ɪnˈdɪgnənt/, *adj.* affected with or characterised by indignation. [L *indignans,* ppr., deeming unworthy] – **indignantly,** *adv.*

**indignation** /ɪndɪgˈneɪʃən/, *n.* strong displeasure at something deemed unworthy, unjust, or base; righteous anger.

**indignity** /ɪnˈdɪgnəti/, *n., pl.* **-ties. 1.** injury to dignity; slighting or contemptuous treatment; a humiliating affront, insult, or injury. **2.** *Obs.* unworthiness. **3.** *Obs.* disgrace or disgraceful action. [L *indignitas* unworthiness]

**indigo** /ˈɪndɪgoʊ/, *n., pl.* **-gos,** *adj.* –*n.* **1.** a blue dye obtained from various plants, esp. of the genus *Indigofera.* **2.** indigo blue or indigotin, the colouring principle of this dye. **3.** a plant of the leguminous genus *Indigofera.* **4.** a deep violet blue between violet and blue in the spectrum. –*adj.* **5.** of the colour indigo. [Sp. or Pg., from L *indicum* indigo, lit., Indian (dye), from Gk *indikón*] – **indigotic** /ɪndɪˈgɒtɪk/, *adj.*

**indigo blue** /– ˈblu/, *n.* **1.** the colour indigo. **2.** the essential colouring principle (a chemical compound, $C_{16}H_{10}N_2O_2$), which is contained, together with other substances, in the dye indigo, and which can also be prepared artificially. Also, **indigotin.**

**indigo bunting** /– ˈbʌntɪŋ/, *n.* a small fringilline bird, *Passerina cyared,* of North and Central America, the male of which is indigo blue. Also, **indigo bird, indigo finch.**

**indigoid** /ˈɪndɪgɔɪd/, *adj.* **1.** of or pertaining to that group of vat dyes which have a molecular structure like that of indigo. –*n.* **2.** an indigoid substance. [INDIG(O) + -OID]

**indirect** /ɪndəˈrɛkt, ɪndaɪˈrɛkt/, *adj.* **1.** not direct in space; deviating from a straight line: *an indirect course in sailing.* **2.** coming or resulting otherwise than directly or immediately, as effects, consequences, etc.: *an indirect advantage.* **3.** not direct in action or procedure; not straightforward; crooked: *indirect methods.* **4.** not descending in a direct line of succession, as a title or inheritance. **5.** not direct in bearing, application, force, etc.: *indirect evidence.* **6.** *Gram.* not consisting exactly of the words originally used, as in *He said he was hungry* instead of the direct *He said, 'I am hungry'.* – **indirectly,** *adv.* – **indirectness,** *n.*

**indirect election** /– əˈlɛkʃən/, *n.* an election for an office by means of a college which has already been chosen by voters, as the American Presidential elections.

**indirect evidence** /– ˈɛvədəns/, *n.* →**circumstantial evidence.**

**indirect free kick,** *n.* (in soccer) a kick awarded after an infringement, from which a goal cannot be scored unless the ball first touches another player after being kicked.

**indirection** /ɪndəˈrɛkʃən/, *n.* **1.** indirect action or procedure. **2.** a roundabout course or method. **3.** deceitful or crooked dealing.

**indirect lighting** /ˌɪndərɛkt ˈlaɪtɪŋ/, *n.* reflected or diffused light, used in interiors to avoid glare, shadows, etc.

**indirect object** /– ˈɒbdʒɛkt/, *n.* (in English and some other languages) the object with reference to which (for whose benefit, in whose interest, etc.) the action of a verb is performed, in English distinguished from the direct object by its position in the sentence or by the use of a preposition (*to* or *for*), for example *the boy* in *he gave the boy a book* or *he gave a book to the boy.*

**indirect rule** /– ˈrul/, *n.* a system of government whereby the people governed are allowed certain powers, such as administrative, legal etc.

**indirect speech** /– ˈspitʃ/, *n.* →**reported speech.**

**indirect tax** /– ˈtæks/, *n.* a tax levied on persons who reimburse themselves by passing the cost on to others, as sales tax which is levied on commodities before they reach the consumer and ultimately paid as part of their market price.

**indiscernible** /ɪndəˈsɜnəbəl/, *adj.* not discernible; imperceptible. – **indiscernibleness,** *n.* – **indiscernibly,** *adv.*

**indiscipline** /ɪnˈdɪsəplən/, *n.* lack of discipline.

**indiscoverable** /ɪndəsˈkʌvərəbəl/, *adj.* not discoverable; undiscoverable.

**indiscreet** /ɪndəsˈkrit/, *adj.* not discreet; lacking prudence; lacking sound judgment: *indiscreet praise.* – **indiscreetly,** *adv.* – **indiscreetness,** *n.*

**indiscrete** /ɪndəsˈkrit/, *adj.* not discrete. [L *indiscrētus* not separated]

**indiscretion** /ɪndəsˈkrɛʃən/, *n.* **1.** lack of discretion; imprudence. **2.** an indiscreet act or step.

**indiscriminate** /ɪndəsˈkrɪmənət/, *adj.* **1.** not discriminating; making no distinction: *indiscriminate in one's friendships.* **2.** not discriminate; confused: *indiscriminate slaughter.* – **indiscriminately,** *adv.* – **indiscriminateness,** *n.*

**indiscriminating** /ɪndəsˈkrɪməneɪtɪŋ/, *adj.* not discriminating. – **indiscriminatingly,** *adv.*

**indiscrimination** /ˌɪndəskrɪməˈneɪʃən/, *n.* **1.** the fact of not discriminating. **2.** the condition of not being discriminated. **3.** lack of discernment or discrimination. – **indiscriminative** /ɪndəsˈkrɪmənətɪv/, *adj.*

**indispensable** /ɪndəsˈpɛnsəbəl/, *adj.* **1.** not dispensable; absolutely necessary or requisite: *an indispensable man.* **2.** that cannot be disregarded or neglected: *an indispensable obligation.* –*n.* **3.** one who or that which is indispensable. – **indispensability** /ˌɪndəspɛnsəˈbɪləti/, **indispensableness,** *n.* – **indispensably,** *adv.*

**indispose** /ɪndəsˈpoʊz/, *v.t.,* **-posed, -posing. 1.** to put out of the proper condition (for something); make unfit; disqualify. **2.** to make ill, esp. slightly. **3.** to disincline; render averse or unwilling.

**indisposed** /ɪndəsˈpoʊzd/, *adj.* **1.** sick or ill, esp. slightly: *indisposed with a cold.* **2.** disinclined or unwilling.

**indisposition** /ˌɪndɪspəˈzɪʃən/, *n.* **1.** the state of being indisposed; a slight illness. **2.** disinclination; unwillingness.

**indisputable** /ɪndəsˈpjutəbəl/, *adj.* not disputable; not open to question. – **indisputability** /ˌɪndəspjutəˈbɪləti/, **indisputableness,** *n.* – **indisputably,** *adv.*

**indissoluble** /ɪndəˈsɒljubəl/, *adj.* **1.** not dissoluble; incapable of being dissolved, decomposed, undone, or destroyed. **2.** firm or stable. **3.** perpetually binding or obligatory. – **indissolubility** /ˌɪndəsɒljuˈbɪləti/, **indissolubleness,** *n.* – **indissolubly,** *adv.*

**indistinct** /ɪndəsˈtɪŋkt/, *adj.* **1.** not distinct; not clearly marked off or defined. **2.** not clearly distinguishable or perceptible, as to the eye, ear, or mind. **3.** not distinguishing clearly. [L *indistinctus*] – **indistinctly,** *adv.* – **indistinctness,** *n.*

**indistinctive** /ɪndəsˈtɪŋktɪv/, *adj.* **1.** without distinctive characteristics. **2.** not capable of making distinction. – **indistinctively,** *adv.* – **indistinctiveness,** *n.*

**indistinguishable** /ɪndəsˈtɪŋgwɪʃəbəl/, *adj.* **1.** not distinguishable. **2.** indiscernible. – **indistinguishableness,** *n.* – **indistinguishably,** *adv.*

**indite** /ɪnˈdaɪt/, *v.t.,* **-dited, -diting. 1.** to compose or write, as a speech, poem, etc. **2.** *Archaic.* to treat in a literary composition. [ME *endite(n),* from OF *enditer* dictate, write, from L *in-* IN-[2] + *dictāre* pronounce. Cf. INDICT] – **inditement,** *n.* – **inditer,** *n.*

**indium** /ˈɪndiəm/, *n.* a rare metallic element, soft, white, malleable and easily fusible, found combined in various ores, esp. sphalerite, so called from the two indigo-blue lines in its spectrum. *Symbol:* In; *at. wt:* 114.82; *at. no.:* 49; *sp. gr.:* 7.3 at 20°C. [IND(O)- + -IUM]

**indiv.,** individual.

**indivertible** /ɪndəˈvɜtəbəl, ɪndaɪ-/, *adj.* not divertible; not to be turned aside. – **indivertibly,** *adv.*

**individual** /ɪndəˈvɪdʒuəl/, *adj.* **1.** single; particular; separate.

2. existing as a distinct, indivisible entity, or considered as such: *individual members.* 3. pertaining or peculiar to a single person or thing: *individual tastes.* 4. intended for the use of one person only: *individual portions.* 5. distinguished by peculiar and marked characteristics; exhibiting individuality: *a highly individual style.* 6. of which each is different or of a different design from the others: *a set of individual coffee cups.* *–n.* 7. a single human being, as distinguished from a group. 8. a person: *a strange individual.* 9. a distinct, indivisible entity; a single thing, being, instance, or item. 10. a group considered as a unit. 11. *Biol.* **a.** a single or simple organism capable of independent existence. **b.** a member of a compound organism or colony, as one of the distinct elements or zooids which make up a compound hydrozoan, or sometimes (when a whole plant or tree is regarded as a colony or compound organism) a single shoot or bud. [ME, from ML *indīviduālis,* from L *indīviduus* indivisible]

**individualise** /ɪndə'vɪdʒuəlaɪz/, *v.t.,* **-lised, -lising.** 1. to make individual; give an individual or distinctive character to. 2. to mention, indicate, or consider individually; specify; particularise. Also, **individualize.** – **individualisation** /ˌɪndəvɪdʒuəlaɪ'zeɪʃən/, *n.* – **individualiser,** *n.*

**individualism** /ɪndə'vɪdʒuəlɪzəm/, *n.* 1. a social theory advocating the liberty, rights, or independent action of the individual. 2. the principle or habit of independent thought or action. 3. the pursuit of individual rather than common or collective interests; egoism. 4. individual character; individuality. 5. an individual peculiarity. 6. *Philos.* **a.** the doctrine of pure egoism, or that nothing exists but the individual self. **b.** the doctrine that nothing is real but individual things. **c.** the principle that all actions are determined by, or at least exist for, the benefit of the individual.

**individualist** /ɪndə'vɪdʒuələst/, *n.* 1. one characterised by individualism in thought or action. 2. an advocate of individualism. – **individualistic** /ˌɪndəvɪdʒuə'lɪstɪk/, *adj.*

**individuality** /ˌɪndəvɪdʒu'æləti/, *n., pl.* **-ties.** 1. the particular character, or aggregate of qualities, which distinguishes one person or thing from others: *a person of marked individuality.* 2. (*pl.*) individual characteristics. 3. a person or thing of individual or distinctive character. 4. the state or quality of being individual; existence as a distinct individual. 5. the interests of the individual as distinguished from the interests of the community.

**individually** /ɪndə'vɪdʒuəli/, *adv.* 1. in an individual manner. 2. separately. 3. personally.

**individuate** /ɪndə'vɪdʒueɪt/, *v.t.,* **-ated, -ating.** 1. to form an individual or distinct entity. 2. to give an individual or distinctive character to; individualise. [ML *indīviduātus,* pp. of *indīviduāre,* from L *indīviduus.* See INDIVIDUAL]

**individuation** /ˌɪndəvɪdʒu'eɪʃən/, *n.* 1. the act of individuating. 2. the state of being individuated; individual existence; individuality. 3. *Philos.* the determination or contraction of a general nature to an individual mode of existence; development of the individual from the general.

**indivisible** /ɪndə'vɪzəbəl/, *adj.* 1. not divisible; incapable of being divided: *one nation indivisible.* *–n.* 2. something indivisible. – **indivisibility** /ˌɪndəvɪzə'bɪləti/, **indivisibleness,** *n.* – **indivisibly,** *adv.*

**indo-,** a combining form of **indigo.** Also, **ind-.**

**Indo-,** a word element meaning 'of or in India' as in *Indo-African* (of India and Africa), or 'Indian' as in *Indo-British* (British in India). [L, from Gk, combining form of L *Indus,* Gk *Indós*]

**Indo-Aryan** /ɪndoʊ-'ɛəriən/, *n.* 1. a member of one of the peoples of India and Pakistan who are Indo-European in speech and Caucasian in physical characteristics. *–adj.* 2. →**Indic** (def. 2). 3. of or pertaining to the Indo-Aryans.

**indocile** /ɪn'doʊsaɪl/, *adj.* not docile; not amenable to teaching. – **indocility** /ɪndoʊ'sɪləti/, *n.*

**indoctrinate** /ɪn'dɒktrəneɪt/, *v.t.,* **-nated, -nating.** 1. to instruct (in a doctrine, etc.). 2. to teach or inculcate. 3. to imbue (a person, etc.) with learning. [IN-[2] + L *doctrīna* teaching, DOCTRINE + -ATE[1]] – **indoctrination** /ɪnˌdɒktrə'neɪʃən/, *n.* – **indoctrinator,** *n.* – **indoctrinatory,** *adj.*

**Indo-European** /ˌɪndoʊ-jurə'piən/, *n.* 1. a major family of languages that includes most of the languages of Europe (now spread to other parts of the world), many of those of Asia, and a few scattered others. 2. the prehistoric parent language of this family. 3. a member of any of the peoples speaking an Indo-European language. *–adj.* 4. of or pertaining to Indo-European. 5. speaking an Indo-European language.

**Indo-Germanic** /ˌɪndoʊ-dʒə'mænɪk/, *n., adj.* (formerly in use) Indo-European.

**Indo-Hittite** /ˌɪndoʊ-'hɪtaɪt/, *n.* a linguistic stock comprising Indo-European and the Anatolian languages.

**Indo-Iranian** /ˌɪndoʊ-ɪ'reɪniən/, *n.* one of the principal groups within the Indo-European family of languages, including Persian and the Indo-European languages of India and Pakistan.

**indole** /'ɪndoʊl/, *n.* a colourless, low-melting solid, $C_8H_7N$, with a faecal smell, found in the oil of jasmine and clove and as a putrefaction product from animals' intestines, used in perfumery and as a reagent. Also, **indol** /'ɪndoʊl, -dɒl/. [IND- + -OLE]

**indole acetic acid,** *n.* an important plant growth hormone.

**indolence** /'ɪndələns/, *n.* the state of being indolent. [L *indolentia* freedom from pain]

**indolent** /'ɪndələnt/, *adj.* 1. having or showing a disposition to avoid exertion: *an indolent person.* 2. *Pathol.* sluggish. [LL *indolens* not suffering] – **indolently,** *adv.*

**indomitable** /ɪn'dɒmətəbəl/, *adj.* that cannot be subdued or overcome, as persons, pride, courage, etc. [LL *indomitābilis,* from L *in-* IN-[3] + *domitāre* (frequentative of *domāre* tame)] – **indomitableness,** *n.* – **indomitably,** *adv.*

**Indonesia** /ɪndə'niʒə/, *n.* a republic in the Malay Archipelago.

**Indonesian** /ɪndə'niʒən/, *n.* 1. a member of the ethnic group consisting of the native peoples of Indonesia, the Filipinos, and the Malays of Malaya. 2. a member of a light-coloured race supposed to have been dominant in the Malay Archipelago before the Malays, and believed to constitute one element of the present mixed population of Malaysia and perhaps Polynesia. 3. →**Bahasa Indonesia.** 4. a group of Austronesian languages, including those of the Philippines, the Malagasy Republic, Taiwan, and Indonesia, as well as Malay. *–adj.* 5. of or pertaining to the Malay Archipelago. 6. of or pertaining to Indonesia, the Indonesians, or their languages. [INDO- + Gk *nêsos* island + -IAN]

**indoor** /'ɪndɔ/, *adj.* occurring, used, etc., in a house or building, rather than out of doors: *indoor games.*

**indoors** /ɪn'dɔz/, *adv.* in or into a house or building.

**Indo-Pacific** /ˌɪndoʊ-pə'sɪfɪk/, *adj.* 1. of or pertaining to a geographical area extending from the western Pacific to the eastern Indian Ocean, and including the land masses which border these oceans. 2. of or pertaining to the flora and fauna which are common to this area.

**indophenol** /ɪndoʊ'finɒl/, *n.* 1. a coal-tar dye resembling indigo and giving indigo-blue shades. 2. any of various related dyes. [INDO- + PHENOL]

**indorse** /ɪn'dɔs/, *v.t.,* **-dorsed, -dorsing.** →**endorse.** [var. of ENDORSE, conformed to ML *indorsāre* put on the back. See IN-[2], DORSUM] – **indorsable,** *adj.* – **indorsee** /ɪndɔ'si/, *n.* – **indorsement,** *n.* – **indorser,** *n.*

**indoxyl** /ɪn'dɒksəl/, *n.* a crystalline compound, $C_8H_7NO$, which is formed by the hydrolysis of indican and is readily oxidised to furnish indigo.

**in-draught** /'ɪn-draft/, *n.* 1. a draught or drawing inward. 2. an inward flow or current.

**indrawn** /'ɪndrɔn/, *adj.* drawn in; introspective.

**indri** /'ɪndri/, *n., pl.* **-dris.** a short-tailed lemur, *Indri indri,* of Madagascar, about 60 cm in length. [Malagasy, said to be an exclamation, 'lo! see!', erroneously taken as the name of the animal]

**indubitable** /ɪn'djubətəbəl/, *adj.* that cannot be doubted; unquestionable; certain. – **indubitableness,** *n.* – **indubitably,** *adv.*

**induce** /ɪn'djus/, *v.t.,* **-duced, -ducing.** 1. to lead or move by persuasion or influence, as to some action, state of mind, etc.: *to induce a person to go.* 2. to bring about, produce, or cause: *opium induces sleep.* 3. *Physics.* to produce (an electric current, etc.) by induction. 4. *Logic.* to assert or establish (a proposition about a class of phenomena) on the basis of observations on a number of particular facts. **5.** to inititiate (labour) artificially in pregnancy. [ME *induce(n)*, from L *indūcere* lead in, bring in, persuade] – **inducer,** *n.* – **inducible,** *adj.*

**induced drag** /ɪnˌdjust 'dræg/, *n.* (in aerodynamics) that part of drag which is caused by lift.

**induced radioactivity** /– ˌreɪdioʊæk'tɪvəti/, *n.* radioactivity which has been induced in stable elements by bombarding them with high-energy particles (e.g. neutrons). Also, **artificial radioactivity.**

**inducement** /ɪn'djusmənt/, *n.* **1.** the act of inducing. **2.** something that induces or persuades; an incentive. **3.** *Law.* matters of inducement which are explanatory or introductory statements in pleadings.

**inducement allowance** /'– əlaʊəns/, *n.* an allowance paid to employees to encourage them to work on a particular project or in a particular, remote, or otherwise unfavourable area.

**induct** /ɪn'dʌkt/, *v.t.* **1.** to lead or bring in; introduce, esp. formally, as into a place, office, etc. **2.** to introduce in knowledge or experience (fol. by *to*). **3.** *U.S.* to call up for military service. [ME, from L *inductus*, pp.]

**inductance** /ɪn'dʌktəns/, *n.* **1.** that property of a circuit by virtue of which electromagnetic induction takes place. See **mutual inductance** and **self-inductance.** **2.** a piece of equipment providing inductance in a circuit or other system; inductor.

**inductile** /ɪn'dʌktaɪl/, *adj.* not ductile; not pliable. – **inductility** /ɪndʌk'tɪləti/, *n.*

**induction** /ɪn'dʌkʃən/, *n.* **1.** *Elect.* **a.** the process by which a body having electrical or magnetic properties calls forth similar properties in a neighbouring body without direct contact. **b.** a tendency of electric currents to resist change. **2.** *Electronics.* a process by which an electrical conductor may be charged. **3.** *Logic.* **a.** the process of discovering explanations for a set of particular facts, by estimating the weight of observational evidence in favour of a proposition which (usu.) asserts something about that entire class of facts. **b.** a conclusion reached by this process. **4.** a bringing forward or adducing, as of facts, evidence, etc. **5.** the act of inducing, bringing about, or causing: *induction by the hypnotic state.* **6.** *Physiol.* the process whereby a tissue stimulates or alters other adjacent tissues. **7.** the act of inducing; introduction or initiation. **8.** the artificial initiation of labour in pregnancy. **9.** formal introduction into an office or benefice; installation. **10.** an introductory unit in a literary work; a prelude or scene, independent of the main performance but related to it. **11.** *Archaic.* a preface. [ME, from L *inductio*]

**induction coil** /'– kɔɪl/, *n.* a transformer designed as two concentric coils with a common soft iron core, with the inner coil (primary) of few turns and the outer coil (secondary) of a great number of turns. When the primary is excited by rapidly interrupted or variable current, high voltage is induced in the secondary.

induction coil: A, oil; B, primary terminal; C, high-voltage terminal; D, primary lead; E, secondary lead; F, primary winding; G, secondary winding; H, centre core

**induction heating** /– 'hitɪŋ/, *n.* a form of heating of electrically conducting materials by the currents induced in them by an alternating magnetic field. Also, **eddy current heating.**

**induction motor** /'– moʊtə/, *n.* a type of electric motor in which an alternating current fed to the primary winding causes an induced current to flow through the secondary winding of the rotor; the interaction between these currents causes the rotation of the rotor.

**induction stroke** /'– stroʊk/, *n.* the downward movement of the piston in a reciprocating engine which draws the explosive charge into the cylinder.

**induction valve** /'– vælv/, *n.* the valve through which the explosive charge is drawn into the cylinder of a reciprocating engine. Also, **induction port, inlet valve.**

**inductive** /ɪn'dʌktɪv/, *adj.* **1.** pertaining to or involving electrical or magnetic induction. **2.** operating by induction: *an inductive machine.* **3.** pertaining to or employing logical induction. **4.** *Physiol.* eliciting some reaction within an organism. **5.** serving to induce; leading or influencing (fol. by *to*). **6.** introductory. – **inductively,** *adv.* – **inductiveness,** *n.*

**inductivity** /ɪndʌk'tɪvəti/, *n., pl.* **-ties.** **1.** an inductive property. **2.** capacity of producing induction. **3.** inductance.

**inductor** /ɪn'dʌktə/, *n.* **1.** a device, the primary purpose of which is to introduce inductance into an electric circuit. **2.** one who inducts, as into office.

**indue** /ɪn'dju/, *v.t.*, **-dued, -duing.** →**endue.**

**indulge** /ɪn'dʌldʒ/, *v.*, **-dulged, -dulging.** *–v.i.* **1.** to indulge oneself; yield to an inclination (oft. fol. by *in*): *to indulge in apple pie.* **2.** *Colloq.* to drink alcohol in excessive amounts. *–v.t.* **3.** to yield to, satisfy, or gratify (desires, feelings, etc.). **4.** to yield to the wishes or whims of: *to indulge a child.* **5.** to allow (oneself) to follow one's own will (fol. by *in*). **6.** *Comm.* to grant an extension of time, for payment or performance, to (a person, etc.) or on (a bill, etc.). **7.** *Rare.* to grant (something) by favour. [L *indulgēre* be kind, yield, grant] – **indulger,** *n.* – **indulgingly,** *adv.*

**indulgence** /ɪn'dʌldʒəns/, *n., v.*, **-genced, -gencing.** *–n.* **1.** the act or practice of indulging; gratification of desire. **2.** indulgent allowance or tolerance. **3.** humouring. **4.** something granted or taken in gratification of desire. **5.** *Rom. Cath. Ch.* a remission of the temporal punishment still due to sin after it has been forgiven. **6.** *Comm.* an extension, through favour, of time for payment or performance. *–v.t.* **7.** *Rom. Cath. Ch.* to furnish with an indulgence.

**indulgency** /ɪn'dʌldʒənsi/, *n., pl.* **-cies.** →**indulgence.**

**indulgent** /ɪn'dʌldʒənt/, *adj.* characterised by or showing indulgence: *an indulgent parent.* [L *indulgens*, ppr.] – **indulgently,** *adv.*

**induline** /'ɪndjulaɪn, -lin/, *n.* any of a large class of dyes yielding colours similar to indigo. [IND- + *-ul* (from L *-ulum*, diminutive suffix) + -INE[2]]

**indult** /ɪn'dʌlt/, *n.* a general faculty granted for a specific time or a specific number of cases by the Holy See to bishops and others, of doing something not permitted by the common law of the Church; a grant, privilege, favour. [LL *indultum* indulgence, properly pp. neut.]

**indumentum** /ɪndju'mɛntəm/, *n.* a covering of hair, feathers, or the like. [L]

**induplicate** /ɪn'djuplɪkət, -keɪt/, *adj.* folded or rolled inwards (said of the parts of the calyx or corolla in aestivation when the edges are bent abruptly towards the axis, or of leaves in vernation when the edges are rolled inwards and then arranged about the axis without overlapping). Also, **induplicative.** [IN-[2] + DUPLICATE (def. 2)] – **induplication** /ɪnˌdjuplə'keɪʃən/, *n.*

**indurate** /'ɪndʒureɪt/, *v.*, **-rated, -rating;** /'ɪndʒurət/, *adj.* *–v.t.* **1.** to make hard; inure. *–v.i.* **2.** to become hard; harden. *–adj.* **3.** hardened; callous; inured. [ME, from L *indūrātus*, pp.] – **induration** /ɪndʒu'reɪʃən/, *n.* – **indurative,** *adj.*

**indusium** /ɪn'djuziəm/, *n., pl.* **-sia.** **1. a.** *Bot.* a membranous outgrowth covering the sori in ferns. **b.** the pollen cup of the goodenia. **2.** *Anat., Zool.* an enveloping layer or membrane. **3.** *Embryol.* →**amnion.** [L: tunic] – **indusial,** *adj.*

**indust.,** **1.** industry. **2.** industrial.

**industrial** /ɪn'dʌstriəl/, *adj.* **1.** of or pertaining to, of the nature of, or resulting from industry or productive labour: *the industrial arts.* **2.** having highly developed industries: *an industrial nation.* **3.** engaged in an industry or industries: *industrial workers.* **4.** pertaining to the workers in industries: *industrial training.* **5.** designed for use in industry: *industrial diamonds.* *–n.* **6.** a worker in some industry, esp. a manufacturing industry. **7.** one who conducts or owns an industrial enterprise. **8.** (*pl.*) stocks and shares in industrial enterprises. [INDUSTRY + -AL[1]. Cf. F *industriel*] – **industrially,** *adv.*

**industrial action** /– 'ækʃən/, *n.* organised disruptive action, as a strike or go-slow, taken by a group of workers, to promote what they conceive to be either their own interests or the general public good.

**industrial court** /– 'kɔt/, *n.* a court set up to hear trade and industrial disputes.

**industrial design** /– də'zaɪn/, *n.* the designing of objects for manufacture. – **industrial designer,** *n.*

**industrial estate** /– əˈsteɪt/, *n.* a tract of land specially allocated for the building of factories, etc.

**industrialise** /ɪnˈdʌstriəlaɪz/, *v.t.*, **-lised, -lising.** to introduce industry into (an area) on a large scale. Also, **industrialize.** – **industrialisation** /ɪnˌdʌstriəlaɪˈzeɪʃən/, *n.*

**industrialism** /ɪnˈdʌstriəlɪzəm/, *n.* an economic organisation of society built largely on mechanised industry rather than agriculture, craftsmanship, or commerce.

**industrialist** /ɪnˈdʌstriələst/, *n.* one who conducts or owns an industrial enterprise.

**industrial park** /ɪndʌstriəl ˈpak/, *n.* an area of land planned for industry and business. Also, **industrial estate.**

**industrial relations** /– rəˈleɪʃənz/, *n. pl.* **1.** the management or study of the relations between employers and employees. **2.** the relationship itself usu. in a given industry, locality, etc.

**industrial revolution** /– rɛvəˈluʃən/, *n.* **1.** the radical social, economic and physical transformation of a country by the general introduction of mechanical means of manufacture. **2.** (*oft. caps*) the period in history when such a development took place in England, the first country to experience such a revolution, in the late 18th and early 19th centuries.

**industrials** /ɪnˈdʌstriəlz/, *n. pl.* shares, stocks, etc., in industrial concerns.

**industrial union** /– ˈjunjən/, *n.* **1.** a union having the right to enrol as members all of the people employed in a particular industry. **2.** a trade union, or organisation of employers, registered under the appropriate industrial legislation to give it access to industrial tribunals, etc.

**industrious** /ɪnˈdʌstriəs/, *adj.* **1.** hard-working; diligent: *an industrious person.* [L *industriōsus* diligent] – **industriously,** *adv.* – **industriousness,** *n.*

**industry** /ˈɪndəstri/, *n., pl.* **-tries. 1.** a particular branch of trade or manufacture: *the steel industry.* **2.** any large-scale business activity: *the tourist industry.* **3.** manufacture or trade as a whole: *the growth of industry in underdeveloped countries.* **4.** the ownership and management of companies, factories, etc.: *friction between labour and industry.* **5.** systematic work or labour. **6.** assiduous activity at any work or task. [ME *industrie,* from L *industria* diligence]

**industry allowance** /ˈ– əlaʊəns/, *n.* an allowance paid to employees in a particular industry or section of an industry, to compensate them for the existence of certain unfavourable features (as intermittency of work) characteristic of the industry.

**industry award** /ˈ– əwɔd/, *n.* an award covering all employees, whatever their classification, in a particular industry or branch of industry.

**indwell** /ɪnˈdwɛl/, *v.*, **-dwelt, -dwelling.** *–v.t.* **1.** to inhabit. *–v.i.* **2.** to dwell (fol. by *in*). – **indweller** /ˈɪndwɛlə/, *n.*

**indwelling** /ˈɪndwɛlɪŋ/, *adj.* **1.** inhabiting, dwelling within. **2.** *Med.* of or pertaining to an object left in a part of the body after introduction, as a catheter, needle, etc.

**-ine**[1], an adjective suffix meaning 'of or pertaining to', 'of the nature of', 'made of', 'like', as in *asinine, crystalline, equine, marine.* [L *-īnus;* also *-inus,* from Gk *-inos*]

**-ine**[2], **1.** a noun suffix denoting some action, procedure, art, place, etc., as in *discipline, doctrine, medicine, latrine.* **2.** a suffix occurring in many nouns of later formation and various meanings, as in *famine, routine, grenadine, vaseline.* **3.** a noun suffix used particularly in chemical terms, as *bromine, chlorine,* and esp. names of basic substances, as *amine, aniline, caffeine, quinine, quinoline.* Cf. **-in**[2]. [F, from L *-ina,* orig. fem. of *-inus;* also used to represent Gk *-inē,* fem. n. suffix, as in *heroine*]

**inebriant** /ɪnˈibriənt/, *adj.* **1.** inebriating; intoxicating. *–n.* **2.** an intoxicant. [L *inēbrians,* ppr.]

**inebriate** /ɪnˈibrieɪt/, *v.*, **-ated, -ating;** /ɪnˈibriət/, *n., adj.* *–v.t.* **1.** to make drunk; intoxicate. **2.** to intoxicate mentally or emotionally; exhilarate. *–n.* **3.** an intoxicated person. **4.** a habitual drunkard. *–adj.* **5.** Also, **inebriated.** drunk; intoxicated. [L *inēbriātus,* pp.] – **inebriation** /ɪnˌibriˈeɪʃən/, *n.*

**inebriety** /ɪnəˈbraɪəti, ɪni-/, *n.* drunkenness.

**inedible** /ɪnˈɛdəbəl/, *adj.* not edible; unfit to be eaten. – **inedibility** /ɪnˌɛdəˈbɪləti/, *n.*

**inedita** /ɪnˈɛdətə/, *n. pl.* unpublished works of an author. [neut. pl. of L *inēditus,* from IN-[3] + *ēditus,* pp. of *ēdere* give out, publish]

**inedited** /ɪnˈɛdətəd/, *adj.* **1.** unpublished. **2.** not edited.

**ineducable** /ɪnˈɛdʒəkəbəl/, *adj.* incapable of being educated, esp. as a result of mental retardation.

**ineffable** /ɪnˈɛfəbəl/, *adj.* **1.** that cannot be uttered or expressed; inexpressible; unspeakable: *ineffable joy.* **2.** that must not be uttered: *the ineffable name.* [ME, from L *ineffābilis*] – **ineffability** /ɪnˌɛfəˈbɪləti/, **ineffableness,** *n.* – **ineffably,** *adv.*

**ineffaceable** /ɪnəˈfeɪsəbəl/, *adj.* not effaceable; indelible: *an ineffaceable impression.* – **ineffaceability** /ɪnəˌfeɪsəˈbɪləti/, *n.* – **ineffaceably,** *adv.*

**ineffective** /ɪnəˈfɛktɪv/, *adj.* **1.** not effective; ineffectual, as efforts. **2.** inefficient, as a person. **3.** lacking in artistic effect, as a design or work. – **ineffectively,** *adv.* – **ineffectiveness,** *n.*

**ineffectual** /ɪnəˈfɛktʃuəl/, *adj.* **1.** not effectual; without satisfactory or decisive effect: *an ineffectual remedy.* **2.** unavailing; futile: *his efforts were ineffectual.* **3.** powerless or impotent. – **ineffectuality** /ɪnəˌfɛktʃuˈæləti/, **ineffectualness,** *n.* – **ineffectually,** *adv.*

**inefficacious** /ˌɪnɛfəˈkeɪʃəs/, *adj.* not able to produce the desired effect. – **inefficaciously,** *adv.* – **inefficaciousness, inefficacity** /ˌɪnɛfəˈkæsəti/, *n.*

**inefficacy** /ɪnˈɛfəkəsi/, *n.* lack of efficacy or power to produce the desired effect.

**inefficiency** /ɪnəˈfɪʃənsi/, *n.* the condition or quality of being inefficient; lack of efficiency.

**inefficient** /ɪnəˈfɪʃənt/, *adj.* not efficient; unable to effect or accomplish in a capable, economical way. – **inefficiently,** *adv.*

**inelastic** /ɪnəˈlæstɪk/, *adj.* not elastic; lacking elasticity; unyielding. – **inelasticity** /ɪnəlæsˈtɪsəti, ɪnˌi-/, *n.*

**inelegance** /ɪnˈɛləgəns/, *n.* **1.** the state or character of being inelegant; lack of elegance. **2.** that which is inelegant or ungraceful.

**inelegancy** /ɪnˈɛləgənsi/, *n., pl.* **-cies.** →**inelegance.**

**inelegant** /ɪnˈɛləgənt/, *adj.* not elegant; not nice or refined; vulgar. – **inelegantly,** *adv.*

**ineligible** /ɪnˈɛlədʒəbəl/, *adj.* **1.** not eligible; not proper or suitable for choice. **2.** legally disqualified to hold an office. **3.** legally disqualified to function as a juror, voter, witness, or to become the recipient of a privilege. *–n.* **4.** one who is ineligible, esp. as a suitor, husband, or member of an athletic team. – **ineligibility** /ɪnˌɛlədʒəˈbɪləti/, *n.* – **ineligibly,** *adv.*

**ineloquent** /ɪnˈɛləkwənt/, *adj.* not eloquent. – **ineloquence,** *n.* – **ineloquently,** *adv.*

**ineluctable** /ɪnəˈlʌktəbəl/, *adj.* that cannot be escaped from, as a fate. [L *inēluctābilis*] – **ineluctability** /ɪnəˌlʌktəˈbɪləti/, *n.* – **ineluctably,** *adv.*

**ineludible** /ɪnəˈludəbəl/, *adj.* not eludible; inescapable. – **ineludibly,** *adv.*

**inenarrable** /ɪnəˈnærəbəl/, *adj.* incapable of being explained or told; indescribable; ineffable. [ME, from MF, from L *inēnarrābilis,* from IN-[3] + *ēnarrāre* explain in detail + -ABLE]

**inept** /ɪnˈɛpt/, *adj.* **1.** not apt, fitted, or suitable; unsuitable. **2.** inappropriate; out of place. **3.** absurd or foolish, as a proceeding, remark, etc. [L *ineptus*] – **ineptly,** *adv.* – **ineptness,** *n.*

**ineptitude** /ɪnˈɛptətjud/, *n.* **1.** the quality of being inept. **2.** an inept act or remark.

**inequality** /ɪnəˈkwɒləti/, *n., pl.* **-ties. 1.** the condition of being unequal; lack of equality; disparity: *inequality of treatment.* **2.** social disparity: *the inequality between the rich and the poor.* **3.** inadequacy. **4.** injustice; partiality. **5.** unevenness, as of surface. **6.** an instance of unevenness. **7.** variableness, as of climate. **8.** *Astron.* **a.** any component part of the departure from uniformity in astronomical phenomena, esp. in orbital motion. **b.** the amount of such a departure. **9.** *Maths.* an expression of two unequal quantities connected by the sign $>$ or $<$, as, $a > b$, '*a* is greater than *b*'; $a < b$, '*a* is less than *b*'. [late ME, from ML *inaequālitas* unevenness]

**inequi-,** a word element meaning 'unequal' or 'unequally', as in *inequidistant.* [IN-[3] + EQUI-]

**inequilateral** /ɪnˌikwəˈlætrəl/, *adj.* not equilateral. – **inequilaterally,** *adv.*

**inequitable** /ɪn'ɛkwətəbəl/, *adj.* not equitable; unfair. – **inequitably,** *adv.*

**inequity** /ɪn'ɛkwəti/, *n., pl.* **-ties.** **1.** lack of equity; unfairness. **2.** an unfair circumstance or proceeding.

**ineradicable** /ɪnə'rædəkəbəl/, *adj.* not eradicable; that cannot be eradicated, rooted out, or removed utterly. – **ineradicably,** *adv.*

**inerasable** /ɪnə'reɪzəbəl/, *adj.* not erasable; not to be erased or effaced. – **inerasably,** *adv.*

**inerrable** /ɪn'ɛrəbəl/, *adj.* incapable of erring; infallible. [LL *inerrābilis*] – **inerrability** /ɪn,ɛrə'bɪləti/, **inerrableness,** *n.* – **inerrably,** *adv.*

**inerrant** /ɪn'ɛrənt/, *adj.* free from error. [L *inerrans,* ppr., not wandering] – **inerrancy,** *n.*

**inerratic** /ɪnə'rætɪk/, *adj.* not erratic or wandering; fixed, as a so-called 'fixed' star.

**inert** /ɪn'ɜt/, *adj.* **1.** having no inherent power of action, motion, or resistance: *inert matter.* **2.** without active properties, as a drug. **3.** of an inactive or sluggish habit or nature. [L *iners* unskilled, idle] – **inertly,** *adv.* – **inertness,** *n.*

**inert gas** /– 'gæs/, *n.* See **rare gas.**

**inertia** /ɪn'ɜʃə/, *n.* **1.** inert condition; inactivity; sluggishness. **2.** *Physics.* **a.** that tendency of matter to retain its state of rest or of uniform motion in a straight line. **b.** an analogous property of a force: *electric inertia.* [L: lack of skill, inactivity] – **inertial,** *adj.*

**inertial guidance** /ɪn,ɜʃəl 'gaɪdns/, *n.* a system of missile guidance in which velocities or distances, deduced from accelerations measured within the missile, are compared with data stored before launching.

**inertial navigation** /– nævə'geɪʃən/, *n.* a system of aircraft navigation in which accurate position information is computed from measurement of accelerations relative to a fixed starting point.

**inertial system** /'– sɪstəm/, *n.* a frame of reference in which a body only changes velocity if acted upon by a force; a frame of reference in which Newtonian mechanics apply.

**inertia reel seat belt,** *n.* a recoiling seat belt which extends when pulled gently but will not extend when pulled suddenly. Also, **inertial reel seat belt.**

**inertia selling** /ɪn'ɜʃə sɛlɪŋ/, *n.* the provision of articles to people who have not asked for them, in the hope that these people, rather than refusing or returning them, will accept and pay for them.

**inescapable** /ɪnəs'keɪpəbəl/, *adj.* that cannot be escaped or ignored.

**inessential** /ɪnə'sɛnʃəl/, *adj.* **1.** not essential; not necessary. **2.** without essence; insubstantial. *–n.* **3.** that which is not essential. – **inessentiality** /,ɪnəsɛnʃi'æləti/, *n.*

**inestimable** /ɪn'ɛstəməbəl/, *adj.* **1.** that cannot be estimated, or too great to be estimated. **2.** of incalculable value. [ME, from F, from L *inaestimābilis.* See IN-[3], ESTIMABLE] – **inestimably,** *adv.*

**inevitable** /ɪn'ɛvətəbəl/, *adj.* **1.** that cannot be avoided, evaded, or escaped; certain or necessary: *an inevitable conclusion.* **2.** sure to befall, happen, or come, by the very nature of things. *–n.* **3.** that which is unavoidable. [ME, from L *inēvitābilis.* See IN-[3], EVITABLE] – **inevitability** /ɪn,ɛvətə'bɪləti/, **inevitableness,** *n.* – **inevitably,***adv.*

**inexact** /ɪnəg'zækt, ɪnɛg-/, *adj.* not exact; not strictly accurate. – **inexactly,** *adv.* – **inexactness,** *n.*

**inexactitude** /ɪnəg'zæktətjud, ɪnɛg-/, *n.* the state or character of being inexact or inaccurate; inexactness. [IN-[3] + EXACTITUDE]

**inexcusable** /ɪnək'skjuzəbəl, ɪnɛk-/, *adj.* not excusable; incapable of being explained away or justified. – **inexcusability** /ɪnək,skjuzə'bɪləti/, **inexcusableness,** *n.* – **inexcusably,** *adv.*

**inexecutable** /ɪn,ɛksə'kjutəbəl/, *adj.* something which cannot be put into practice.

**inexertion** /ɪnəg'zɜʃən, ɪnɛg-/, *n.* lack of exertion.

**inexhaustible** /ɪnəg'zɔstəbəl, ɪnɛg-/, *adj.* **1.** not exhaustible; incapable of being exhausted: *an inexhaustible supply.* **2.** unfailing; tireless. – **inexhaustibility** /ɪnəg,zɔstə'bɪləti/, **inexhaustibleness,** *n.* – **inexhaustibly,** *adv.*

**inexistent** /ɪnəg'zɪstənt, ɪnɛg-/, *adj.* not existent; having no existence. – **inexistence, inexistency,** *n.*

**inexorable** /ɪn'ɛksərəbəl, ɪn'ɛgz-/, *adj.* **1.** unyielding or unalterable: *inexorable facts.* **2.** not to be persuaded, moved, or affected by prayers or entreaties. [L *inexōrābilis.* See IN-[3], EXORABLE] – **inexorability** /ɪn,ɛksərə'bɪləti, ɪn,ɛgz-/, **inexorableness,** *n.* – **inexorably,** *adv.*

**inexpedient** /ɪnək'spidiənt, ɪnɛk-/, *adj.* not expedient; not suitable, judicious, or advisable. – **inexpedience, inexpediency,** *n.* – **inexpediently,** *adv.*

**inexpensive** /ɪnək'spɛnsɪv, ɪnɛk-/, *adj.* not expensive; costing little. – **inexpensively,** *adv.* – **inexpensiveness,** *n.*

**inexperience** /ɪnək'spɪəriəns, ɪnɛk-/, *n.* lack of experience, or of knowledge or skill gained from experience.

**inexperienced** /ɪnək'spɪəriənst, ɪnɛk-/, *adj.* not experienced; without knowledge or skill gained from experience.

**inexpert** /ɪn'ɛkspɜt/, *adj.* not expert; unskilled. – **inexpertly,** *adv.* – **inexpertness,** *n.*

**inexpiable** /ɪn'ɛkspiəbəl/, *adj.* **1.** not to be expiated; admitting of no expiation or atonement: *an inexpiable crime.* **2.** not to be appeased by expiation; implacable: *inexpiable hate.* [L *inexpiābilis*] – **inexpiableness,** *n.* – **inexpiably,** *adv.*

**inexplicable** /ɪnək'splɪkəbəl, ɪnɛk-/, *adj.* not explicable; incapable of being explained. [late ME, from L *inexplicābilis* that cannot be unfolded] – **inexplicability** /,ɪnəksplɪkə'bɪləti/, **inexplicableness,** *n.* – **inexplicably,** *adv.*

**inexplicit** /ɪnək'splɪsət, ɪnɛk-/, *adj.* not explicit or clear; not clearly stated. [L *inexplicitus*] – **inexplicitly,** *adv.* – **inexplicitness,** *n.*

**inexpressible** /ɪnək'sprɛsəbəl, ɪnɛk-/, *adj.* not expressible; that cannot be uttered or represented in words: *inexpressible grief.* – **inexpressibility** /,ɪnəksprɛsə'bɪləti/, **inexpressibleness,** *n.* – **inexpressibly,** *adv.*

**inexpressive** /ɪnək'sprɛsɪv, ɪnɛk-/, *adj.* not expressive; lacking in expression. – **inexpressively,** *adv.* – **inexpressiveness,** *n.*

**inexpugnable** /ɪnəks'pʌgnəbəl, ɪnɛks-/, *adj.* that cannot be taken by force; impregnable; unconquerable: *an inexpugnable fort.* [L *inexpugnābilis*] – **inexpugnability** /,ɪnəkspʌgnə'bɪləti/, **inexpugnableness,** *n.* – **inexpugnably,** *adv.*

**inextensible** /ɪnək'stɛnsəbəl, ɪnɛk-/, *adj.* not extensible. – **inextensibility** /ɪnəkstɛnsə'bɪləti/, *n.*

**in extenso** /ɪn ɛk'stɛnsoʊ/, *adv.* at full length. [L]

**inextinguishable** /ɪnək'stɪŋgwɪʃəbəl, ɪnɛk-/, *adj.* not extinguishable; not to be extinguished, quenched, suppressed, or brought to an end: *inextinguishable fire, inextinguishable rage.* – **inextinguishably,** *adv.*

**inextirpable** /ɪnək'stɜpəbəl, ɪnɛk-/, *adj.* incapable of being extirpated: *an inextirpable disease.*

**in extremis** /ɪn ɛk'striməs/, *adv.* **1.** in extremity. **2.** near death. [L: in the extremes]

**inextricable** /ɪn'ɛkstrɪkəbəl/, *adj.* **1.** from which one cannot extricate oneself: *an inextricable maze.* **2.** that cannot be disentangled, undone, or loosed, as a tangle, knot, grasp, etc. **3.** hopelessly intricate, involved, or perplexing: *inextricable confusion.* [late ME, from L *inextrīcābilis*] – **inextricability** /,ɪnəkstrɪkə'bɪləti, ,ɪnɛk-/, **inextricableness,** *n.* – **inextricably,** *adv.*

**inf.,** infinitive.

**infallible** /ɪn'fæləbəl/, *adj.* **1.** not fallible; exempt from liability to error, as persons, their judgment, pronouncements, etc. **2.** absolutely trustworthy or sure: *an infallible rule.* **3.** unfailing in operation; certain: *an infallible remedy.* **4.** *Rom. Cath. Ch.* immune from fallacy or liability to error in expounding matters of faith or morals in virtue of the promise made by Christ to the Church. *–n.* **5.** an infallible person or thing. [late ME, from ML *infallibilis.* See IN-[3], FALLIBLE] – **infallibility** /ɪn,fælə'bɪləti/, **infallibleness,** *n.* – **infallibly,** *adv.*

**infamous** /'ɪnfəməs/, *adj.* **1.** of ill fame; having an extremely bad reputation: *an infamous city.* **2.** such as to deserve or to cause evil repute; detestable; shamefully bad: *infamous conduct.* **3.** *Law.* **a.** deprived of credit and of certain rights as a citizen, in consequence of conviction of certain offences. **b.** (of offences, etc.) involving such deprivation. [ME, from ML *infāmōsus* (in L *infāmis*)] – **infamously,** *adv.* – **infamousness,** *n.*

**infamous conduct** /– 'kɒndʌkt/, *n.* professional conduct by medical and dental practitioners, etc., which competent practitioners of good repute would reasonably regard as disgraceful or dishonourable.

**infamy** /ˈɪnfəmi/, *n., pl.* **-mies.** **1.** ill fame, shameful notoriety, or public reproach. **2.** infamous character or conduct. **3.** an infamous act or circumstance. **4.** *Law.* the loss of credit incurred by conviction of an infamous offence, affecting a witness's credibility but not his right to give evidence. [late ME, from L *infāmia*]

**infancy** /ˈɪnfənsi/, *n., pl.* **-cies.** **1.** the state or period of being an infant; babyhood; early childhood. **2.** the corresponding period in the existence of anything: *the infancy of the world.* **3.** infants collectively. **4.** *Law.* the period of life to the age of majority (in the common law, to the end of the eighteenth year); minority; nonage. [L *infantia,* lit., inability to speak]

**infant** /ˈɪnfənt/, *n.* **1.** a child during the earliest period of its life, or a baby. **2.** *Law.* a person who is not of full age, esp. one who has not attained the age of eighteen years. **3.** a beginner, as in learning. **4.** anything in the first period of existence or the first stage of progress. *–adj.* **5.** of or pertaining to infants or infancy: *infant years.* **6.** being in infancy: *an infant child.* **7.** being in the earliest stage: *an infant industry.* **8.** of or pertaining to the legal state of infancy; minor. [L *infans* young child, properly adj., not speaking; replacing ME *enfaunt,* from OF] – **infanthood,** *n.*

**infanta** /ɪnˈfæntə/, *n.* **1.** a daughter of the king of Spain or of Portugal. **2.** an infante's wife. [Sp. and Pg. See INFANTE]

**infante** /ɪnˈfænti/, *n.* a son of the king of Spain or of Portugal, not heir to the throne. [Sp. and Pg., from L *infans* INFANT]

**infanticide** /ɪnˈfæntəsaɪd/, *n.* **1.** the killing of an infant. **2.** the practice of killing newborn children. **3.** one who kills an infant. [LL *infanticīdium* (defs 1 and 2), *infanticīda* (def. 3). See -CIDE]

**infantile** /ˈɪnfəntaɪl/, *adj.* **1.** characteristic of or befitting an infant; babyish; childish: *infantile behaviour.* **2.** of or pertaining to infants: *infantile disease.* **3.** being in the earliest stage. Also, **infantine.** [LL *infantilis*]

**infantile paralysis** /– pəˈræləsəs/, *n.* →**poliomyelitis.**

**infantilise** /ɪnˈfæntəlaɪz/, *v.t.,* **-ised, -ising.** to keep (a person) at the level of a child; to nurture an inappropriate image of (a person) as a child. Also, **infantilize.**

**infantilism** /ɪnˈfæntəlɪzəm/, *n.* **1.** a pattern of speech characterised by those deviations from normal articulation or voice that are typical of very young children. **2.** *Psychol.* the persistence in an adult of markedly childish anatomical, physiological, or psychological characteristics.

**infantine** /ˈɪnfəntaɪn/, *adj.* →**infantile.**

**infantry** /ˈɪnfəntri/, *n.* soldiers or military units that fight on foot, with bayonets, rifles, machine guns, grenades, mortars, etc. [F *infanterie,* from It. *infanteria,* from *infante* youth, foot soldier. See INFANT]

**infantryman** /ˈɪnfəntrimən/, *n., pl.* **-men.** a soldier of the infantry.

**infants' school** /ˈɪnfənts skul/, *n.* a school, or classes attached to a primary school, for children from about five to eight years of age. Also, **infant school.**

**infarct** /ɪnˈfakt/, *n.* a circumscribed portion of tissue which has been suddenly deprived of its blood supply by embolism or thrombosis and which, as a result, is undergoing death (necrosis), to be replaced by scar tissue. [L *infar(c)tus,* pp., stuffed in]

**infarction** /ɪnˈfakʃən/, *n.* **1.** the formation of an infarct. **2.** an infarct.

**infatuate** /ɪnˈfætʃueɪt/, *v.t.,* **-ated, -ating;** /ɪnˈfætʃuət, -eɪt/, *adj., n.* *–v.t.* **1.** to affect with folly; make fatuous. **2.** to inspire or possess with a foolish or unreasoning passion, as of love. *–adj.* **3.** infatuated. *–n.* **4.** a person who is infatuated. [L *infatuātus,* pp., made foolish]

**infatuated** /ɪnˈfætʃueɪtəd/, *adj.* made foolish by love; blindly in love. – **infatuatedly,** *adv.*

**infatuation** /ɪnfætʃuˈeɪʃən/, *n.* **1.** the act of infatuating. **2.** the state of being infatuated. **3.** foolish or all-absorbing passion. **4.** the object of one's infatuation.

**infeasible** /ɪnˈfizəbəl/, *adj.* not feasible; impracticable. – **infeasibility** /ɪnˌfizəˈbɪləti/, *n.*

**infect** /ɪnˈfɛkt/, *v.t.* **1.** to impregnate (a person, organ, wound, etc.) with disease-producing germs. **2.** to affect with disease. **3.** to impregnate with something that affects quality, character, or condition, esp. unfavourably: *to infect the air with poison gas.* **4.** to taint, contaminate, or affect morally: *infected with greed.* **5.** to imbue with some pernicious belief, opinion, etc. **6.** to affect so as to influence feeling or action: *his courage infected the others.* **7.** *Law.* to taint with illegality, or expose to penalty, forfeiture, etc. *–adj.* **8.** *Archaic.* infected. [ME *infect(en),* from L *infectus,* pp., put in, dyed, imbued, infected] – **infector,** *n.*

**infection** /ɪnˈfɛkʃən/, *n.* **1.** the action of infecting. **2.** an infecting with germs of disease, as through the medium of infected insects, air, water, clothing, etc. **3.** an infecting agency or influence. **4.** the state of being infected. **5.** an infectious disease. **6.** the condition of suffering an infection. **7.** an influence or impulse passing from one to another and affecting feeling or action.

**infectious** /ɪnˈfɛkʃəs/, *adj.* **1.** communicable by infection, as diseases. **2.** causing or communicating infection. **3.** tending to spread from one to another: *laughter is infectious.* **4.** *Law.* capable of contaminating with illegality; exposing to seizure or forfeiture. – **infectiously,** *adv.* – **infectiousness,** *n.*

**infectious disease** /– dəˈziz/, *n.* **1.** a disease caused by germs, as bacteria or filterable viruses. **2.** any disease, produced by the action of a micro-organism in the body, which may or may not be contagious.

**infectious hepatitis** /– hɛpəˈtaɪtəs/, *n.* a form of hepatitis transmitted by contaminated food or drink.

**infectious mononucleosis** /– ˌmɒnoʊnjukliˈoʊsəs/, *n.* →**glandular fever.**

**infective** /ɪnˈfɛktɪv/, *adj.* →**infectious.** – **infectively,** *adv.* – **infectiveness, infectivity** /ɪnfɛkˈtɪvəti/, *n.*

**infelicitous** /ɪnfəˈlɪsətəs/, *adj.* **1.** not felicitous, happy, or fortunate; unhappy. **2.** inapt or inappropriate: *an infelicitous remark.* – **infelicitously,** *adv.*

**infelicity** /ɪnfəˈlɪsəti/, *n., pl.* **-ties.** **1.** the state of being unhappy; unhappiness. **2.** ill fortune. **3.** an unfortunate circumstance; a misfortune. **4.** inaptness or inappropriateness as of action or expression. **5.** something inapt or infelicitous: *infelicities of style.* **6.** a tactless remark or act.

**infelt** /ˈɪnfɛlt/, *adj.* felt within; heartfelt.

**infer** /ɪnˈfɜ/, *v.,* **-ferred, -ferring.** *–v.t.* **1.** to derive by reasoning; conclude or judge from premises or evidence. **2.** *Colloq.* (of facts, circumstances, statements, etc.) to indicate or involve as a conclusion; imply. **3.** *Colloq.* to imply or hint. *–v.i.* **4.** to draw a conclusion, as by reasoning. [L *inferre* bring in or on, infer] – **inferable,** *adj.* – **inferably,** *adv.*

**inference** /ˈɪnfərəns/, *n.* **1.** the act or process of inferring. **2.** that which is inferred. **3.** *Colloq.* implication. **4.** *Logic.* **a.** the process of deriving the strict logical consequences of assumed premises. **b.** the process of arriving at some conclusion which, though it is not logically derivable from the assumed premises, possesses some degree of probability relative to the premises. **c.** a proposition reached by a process of inference.

**inferential** /ɪnfəˈrɛnʃəl/, *adj.* pertaining to or depending on inference. – **inferentially,** *adv.*

**inferior** /ɪnˈfɪəriə/, *adj.* **1.** lower in station, rank, or degree (fol. by *to*). **2.** of comparatively low grade; poor in quality: *an inferior brand.* **3.** less important, valuable, or excellent: *an inferior workman.* **4.** lower in place or position (now chiefly in scientific or technical use). **5.** *Bot.* **a.** situated below some other organ. **b.** (of a calyx) inserted below the ovary. **c.** (of an ovary) having a superior calyx. **6.** *Astron.* **a.** (of a planet) having an orbit within that of the earth; applied to the planets Mercury and Venus. **b.** (of a conjunction of an inferior planet) taking place between the sun and the earth. **c.** lying below the horizon: *the inferior part of a meridian.* **7.** *Print.* lower than the main line of type, as the figures in chemical formulae; subscript. *–n.* **8.** one inferior to another or others, as in rank or merit. **9.** *Print.* an inferior letter or figure; a subscript. [ME, from L, comparative of *inferus* being below, under, nether. Cf. UNDER] – **inferiority** /ɪnˌfɪəriˈɒrəti, ˌɪnfɪə-/, *n.* – **inferiorly,** *adv.*

**inferior court** /– ˈkɔt/, *n.* any court from which an appeal can be made a superior court.

**inferiority complex** /ɪnfɪəriˈɒrəti ˌkɒmplɛks/, *n.* **1.** *Psychiatry.*

a complex arising from intense feelings of inferiority, and resulting in either extreme reticence or aggressiveness due to overcompensation. **2.** *Colloq.* a feeling of inferiority or inadequacy.

**infernal** /ɪnˈfɜnəl/, *adj.* **1.** of or pertaining to the lower world of classical mythology: *the infernal regions.* **2.** of, inhabiting, or befitting hell. **3.** hellish; fiendish; diabolical: *an infernal plot.* **4.** *Colloq.* abominable; confounded: *an infernal nuisance.* [ME, from LL *infernālis* of the lower regions] – **infernality** /ɪnfɜˈnæləti/, *n.* – **infernally,** *adv.*

**infernal machine** /– məˈʃin/, *n.* an explosive mechanical apparatus intended to destroy life or property, esp. one disguised as something harmless.

**inferno** /ɪnˈfɜnoʊ/, *n., pl.* **-nos. 1.** hell; the infernal regions. **2.** an infernal or hell-like region. [It.: hell, from L *infernus* underground]

**infertile** /ɪnˈfɜtaɪl/, *adj.* not fertile; unfruitful; unproductive; barren: *infertile soil.* – **infertility** /ɪnfəˈtɪləti/, *n.*

**infest** /ɪnˈfɛst/, *v.t.* **1.** to haunt or overrun in a troublesome manner, as predatory bands, destructive animals, vermin, etc., do. **2.** to be numerous in, as anything troublesome: *the cares that infest the day.* [late ME, from L *infestāre* assail, molest] – **infester,** *n.*

**infestation** /ɪnfɛsˈteɪʃən/, *n.* **1.** the act of infesting. **2.** the state of being infested. **3.** a harassing or troublesome invasion.

**infeudation** /ɪnfjuˈdeɪʃən/, *n. Old Eng. Law.* **1.** the grant of an estate in fee. **2.** the relation of lord and vassal established by the grant and acceptance of such an estate. **3.** the granting of tithes to a mere layman. [ML *infeudātio,* from *infeudāre* enfeoff]

**infibulate** /ɪnˈfɪbjuleɪt, -jə-/, *v.t.,* **-ated, -ating.** to enclose with a clasp, esp. the genitals to prevent sexual intercourse. [L *infibulāre,* from *in-* IN-[2] + *fībula* clasp] – **infibulation** /ɪnfɪbjuˈleɪʃən, -jə-/, *n.*

**infidel** /ˈɪnfədɛl/, *n.* **1.** an unbeliever. **2.** one who does not accept a particular faith, esp. Christianity (formerly applied by Christians esp. to a Muslim). **3.** (in Muslim use) one who does not accept the Muslim faith. *–adj.* **4.** without religious faith. **5.** due to or manifesting unbelief. **6.** not accepting a particular faith, esp. Christianity or Islam; heathen. **7.** rejecting the Christian religion while accepting no other; not believing in the Bible or any divine revelation. **8.** of or pertaining to unbelievers or infidels. [late ME, from L *infidēlis* unfaithful, LL unbelieving]

**infidelity** /ɪnfəˈdɛləti/, *n., pl.* **-ties. 1.** unfaithfulness. **2.** adultery. **3.** lack of religious faith, esp. Christian. **4.** a breach of trust.

**infield** /ˈɪnfild/, *n.* **1.** *Cricket.* the part of the field near the wickets. **2.** *Baseball.* the diamond. **3.** that part of farmlands nearest to the main farm buildings.

**infielder** /ˈɪnfildə/, *n.* (in cricket, baseball, etc.) a player stationed in the infield.

**infighter** /ˈɪnfaɪtə/, *n.* one who practises or is adept at infighting.

**infighting** /ˈɪnfaɪtɪŋ/, *n.* **1.** *Boxing.* fighting at close quarters, so that blows using the full reach of the arm cannot be delivered. **2.** the secret and often ruthless struggle that takes place among members of the same organisation competing for power within it.

**infilling** /ˈɪnfɪlɪŋ/, *n.* brickwork fitted inside a timber frame as in half-timbered buildings, for fire or thermal insulation. Also, **infill.**

**infiltrate** /ˈɪnfəltreɪt/, *v.,* **-trated, -trating,** *n. –v.t.* **1.** to filter into or through; permeate. **2.** to cause to pass in by, or as by, filtering: *the troops infiltrated the enemy lines.* **3.** to join (an organisation) for the unstated purpose of influencing it; to subvert. *–v.i.* **4.** to pass in or through a substance, etc., by or as by filtering. *–n.* **5.** that which infiltrates. **6.** *Pathol.* cells or a substance which pass into the tissues and form a morbid accumulation. – **infiltrative,** *adj.* – **infiltrator,** *n.*

**infiltration** /ɪnfəlˈtreɪʃən/, *n.* **1.** the act or process of infiltrating. **2.** the state of being infiltrated. **3.** that which infiltrates; an infiltrate. **4.** *Mil.* a method of attack in which small bodies of soldiers or individual soldiers penetrate into the enemy's line at weak or unguarded points, in order to bring fire eventually upon the enemy's flanks or rear.

**infin.,** infinitive.

**infinite** /ˈɪnfənət/, *adj.* **1.** immeasurably great: *a truth of infinite importance.* **2.** indefinitely or exceedingly great: *infinite sums of money.* **3.** unbounded or unlimited; perfect: *the infinite wisdom of God.* **4.** endless or innumerable; inexhaustible. **5.** *Maths.* **a.** not finite. **b.** (of a set) having the same number of elements as some proper part of itself. *–n.* **6.** that which is infinite. **7. the Infinite** or **the Infinite Being,** God. **8.** *Maths.* an infinite quantity or magnitude. **9.** the boundless regions of space. [ME, from L *infīnītus*] – **infinitely,** *adv.* – **infiniteness,** *n.*

**infinitesimal** /ˌɪnfɪnəˈtɛzməl, -ˈtɛsəməl/, *adj.* **1.** indefinitely or exceedingly small: *the infinitesimal vessels of the nervous system.* **2.** immeasurably small; less than an assignable quantity: *to an infinitesimal degree.* **3.** pertaining to or involving infinitesimals. *–n.* **4.** an infinitesimal quantity. **5.** *Maths.* a variable having zero as a limit. – **infinitesimally,** *adv.*

**infinitesimal calculus** /– ˈkælkjələs/, *n.* the differential calculus and the integral calculus, considered together.

**infinitival** /ɪnˌfɪnəˈtaɪvəl/, *adj. Gram.* of or pertaining to the infinitive mode. – **infinitivally,** *adv.*

**infinitive** /ɪnˈfɪnətɪv/, *Gram. –n.* **1.** (in many languages) a noun form derived from verbs, which names the action or state without specifying the subject, as Latin *esse* to be, *fuisse* to have been. **2.** (in English) the simple form of the verb (*come, take, eat*) used after certain other verbs (I didn't *eat*), or this simple form preceded by *to* (the **marked infinitive,** I wanted *to come*). *–adj.* **3.** of or pertaining to the infinitive or its meaning. [late ME, from LL *infīnītīvus* unlimited, indefinite] – **infinitively,** *adv.*

**infinitude** /ɪnˈfɪnətʃud/, *n.* **1.** infinity: *divine infinitude.* **2.** an infinite extent, amount, or number.

**infinity** /ɪnˈfɪnəti/, *n., pl.* **-ties. 1.** the state of being infinite: *the infinity of God.* **2.** that which is infinite. **3.** infinite space, time, or quantity: *any time short of infinity.* **4.** an infinite extent, amount, or number. **5.** an indefinitely great amount or number. **6.** *Maths.* **a.** the concept of increasing without bound. **b.** infinite distance, or an infinitely distant part of space. **7.** *Photog.* a distance between the subject and the camera lens sufficiently large for all the light rays reflected by the subject to be regarded as parallel. [ME *infinite,* from L *infinitas*]

**infirm** /ɪnˈfɜm/, *adj.* **1.** feeble in body or health. **2.** not steadfast, unfaltering, or resolute, as persons, the mind, etc.: *infirm of purpose.* **3.** not firm, solid, or strong: *an infirm support.* **4.** unsound or invalid, as an argument, a title, etc. *–v.t.* **5.** *Archaic.* to invalidate. [ME, from L *infirmus*] – **infirmly,** *adv.* – **infirmness,** *n.*

**infirmary** /ɪnˈfɜməri/, *n., pl.* **-ries.** a place for the care of the infirm, sick, or injured; a hospital. [ML *infirmāria,* from L *infirmus* infirm]

**infirmity** /ɪnˈfɜməti/, *n., pl.* **-ties. 1.** a physical weakness or ailment: *the infirmities of age.* **2.** the state of being infirm; lack of strength. **3.** a moral weakness or failing. [ME *infirmyte,* from L *infirmitas*]

**infirm worker** /ˌɪnfɜm ˈwɜkə/, *n.* a worker who is certified as infirm and therefore entitled to earn less than the normal minimum rate prescribed for his classification.

**infix** /ɪnˈfɪks/, *v.;* /ˈɪnfɪks/, *n. –v.t.* **1.** to fix, fasten, or drive in: *he infixed the fatal spear.* **2.** to implant: *the habits they infixed.* **3.** to fix in the mind or memory, as a fact or idea; impress. **4.** *Gram.* to add as an infix. *–v.i.* **5.** *Gram.* (of a linguistic form) to admit an infix. *–n.* **6.** *Gram.* an affix which is inserted within the body of the element to which it is added, as Latin *m* in *accumbō* I lie down, as compared with *accubuī* I lay down. [L *infixus,* pp., fastened in] – **infixion,** *n.*

**in flagrante delicto** /ɪn fləˌgrænti dəˈlɪktoʊ/, *adv.* in the very act of committing the offence. [L]

**inflame** /ɪnˈfleɪm/, *v.,* **-flamed, -flaming.** *–v.t.* **1.** to set aflame or afire. **2.** to light or redden with or as with flames: *the setting sun inflames the sky.* **3.** to kindle or excite (passions, desires, etc.). **4.** to arouse to a high degree of passion or feeling. **5.** to cause to redden through anger, rage, or some other emotion. **6.** to make more violent. **7.** to excite inflammation in: *her eyes were inflamed with crying.* **8.** to raise (the blood, bodily tissue, etc.) to a morbid or feverish heat. *–v.i.* **9.** to burst into flame; take fire. **10.** to be kindled, as passion. **11.** to become hot with passion, as the heart. **12.** to become morbidly affected with inflammation. [ME *enflame(n)*, from OF *enflamer*, from L *inflammāre* set on fire] – **inflamer,** *n.* – **inflamingly,** *adv.*

**inflammable** /ɪnˈflæməbəl/, *adj.* **1.** capable of being set on fire; combustible. **2.** easily roused to passion; excitable. *–n.* **3.** something which is inflammable. – **inflammability,** /ɪnˌflæməˈbɪləti/, **inflammableness,** *n.* – **inflammably,** *adv.*

**inflammation** /ɪnfləˈmeɪʃən/, *n.* **1.** the act of inflaming. **2.** the state of being inflamed. **3.** *Pathol.* a reaction of the body to injurious agents, commonly characterised by heat, redness, swelling, pain, etc., and disturbed function.

**inflammatory** /ɪnˈflæmətəri, -tri/, *adj.* **1.** tending to inflame; kindling passion, anger, etc.: *inflammatory speeches.* **2.** *Pathol.* pertaining to or attended with inflammation. – **inflammatorily,** *adv.*

**inflate** /ɪnˈfleɪt/, *v.*, **-flated, -flating.** *–v.t.* **1.** to distend; swell or puff out; dilate. **2.** to distend with gas: *inflate a balloon.* **3.** to puff up with pride, satisfaction, etc. **4.** to elate. **5.** to expand (currency, prices, etc.) unduly; raise above the previous or proper amount or value. *–v.i.* **6.** to cause inflation. **7.** to become inflated. [L *inflātus*, pp., puffed up] – **inflatable,** *adj.* – **inflator,** *n.*

**inflated** /ɪnˈfleɪtəd/, *adj.* **1.** distended with air or gas; swollen. **2.** puffed up, as with pride. **3.** turgid or bombastic, as language. **4.** resulting from inflation: *inflated values of land.* **5.** unduly expanded, as currency. **6.** *Bot.* hollow or swelled out with air: *inflated perianth.* – **inflatedness,** *n.*

**inflation** /ɪnˈfleɪʃən/, *n.* **1** undue expansion or increase of the currency of a country, esp. by the issuing of paper money not redeemable in specie. **2.** a substantial rise of prices caused by an undue expansion in paper money or bank credit. **3.** the act of inflating. **4.** the state of being inflated.

**inflationary** /ɪnˈfleɪʃənəri, -ʃənri/, *adj.* of or causing inflation: *inflationary legislation.*

**inflationary spiral** /– ˈspaɪrəl/, *n.* the situation in which increasing prices lead to increasing wages which lead to increasing prices, and so on.

**inflationism** /ɪnˈfleɪʃənɪzəm/, *n.* the policy or practice of inflation through expansion of currency or bank deposits.

**inflationist** /ɪnˈfleɪʃənəst/, *n.* an advocate of inflation through expansion of currency or bank deposits.

**inflect** /ɪnˈflɛkt/, *v.t.* **1.** to bend; turn from a direct line or course. **2.** to modulate (the voice). **3.** *Gram.* **a.** to apply inflection to (a word). **b.** to recite or display all, or a distinct set of, the inflections of (a word), in a fixed order: *to inflect Latin 'amō' as 'amō, amās, amat', etc., or 'nauta' as 'nauta, nautam, nautae, nautae, nautā'*, etc. *–v.i.* **4.** *Gram.* to be characterised by inflection. [ME *inflecte(n)*, from L *inflectere* bend] – **inflective,** *adj.* – **inflector,** *n.*

**inflection** /ɪnˈflɛkʃən/, *n.* **1.** modulation of the voice; change in pitch or tone of voice. **2.** *Gram.* **a.** the existence in a language of sets of forms built normally on a single stem, having different syntactic functions and meanings, but all those of a single stem being members of the same fundamental part of speech and constituting forms of the same 'word'. **b.** the set of forms of a single word, or a recital or display thereof in a fixed order. **c.** a single pattern of formation of such sets, as *noun inflection, verb inflection.* **d.** a change in the form of a word, generally by affixation, by means of which a change of meaning or relationship to some other word or group of words is indicated. **e.** the affix added to the stem to produce this change. For example: the *-s* in *dogs* and *-ed* in *played* are inflections. **3.** a bend or angle. **4.** *Maths.* a change of curvature from convex to concave or vice versa. Also, **inflexion.** – **inflectional,** *adj.* – **inflectionally,** *adv.* – **inflectionless,** *adj.*

**inflection point** /ˈ– pɔɪnt/, *n.* a point of inflection on a curve.

**inflexed** /ɪnˈflɛkst/, *adj.* inflected; bent or folded downwards or inwards: *an inflexed leaf.*

**inflexible** /ɪnˈflɛksəbəl/, *adj.* **1.** not flexible; rigid: *an inflexible rod.* **2.** unyielding in temper or purpose: *inflexible to threats.* **3.** unalterable; not permitting variation. [ME, from L *inflexibilis.* See IN-[3], FLEXIBLE] – **inflexibility** /ɪnˌflɛksəˈbɪləti/, **inflexibleness,** *n.* – **inflexibly,** *adv.*

**inflexion** /ɪnˈflɛkʃən/, *n.* →**inflection.** – **inflexional,** *adj.* – **inflexionally,** *adv.* – **inflexionless,** *adj.*

**inflict** /ɪnˈflɪkt/, *v.t.* **1.** to lay on: *to inflict a dozen lashes.* **2.** to impose as something that must be borne or suffered: *to inflict punishment.* **3.** to impose (anything unwelcome). [L *inflictus*, pp., struck against] – **inflictor,** *n.* – **inflictive,** *adj.*

**infliction** /ɪnˈflɪkʃən/, *n.* **1.** the act of inflicting. **2.** something inflicted, as punishment, suffering, etc.

**in-flight** /ˈɪn-flaɪt/, *adj.* during an aeroplane flight: *in-flight service.*

**inflorescence** /ɪnfləˈrɛsəns/, *n.* **1.** a flowering or blossoming. **2.** *Bot.* **a.** the arrangement of flowers on the axis. **b.** the flowering part of a plant. **c.** a flower cluster. **d.** flowers collectively. **e.** a single flower. [NL *inflōrescentia*, from LL *inflōrescens*, ppr., coming into flower] – **inflorescent,** *adj.*

forms of inflorescence: A, capitulum of daisy; B, spadix within the spathe of calla

**inflow** /ˈɪnfloʊ/, *n.* that which flows in; influx.

**influence** /ˈɪnfluəns/, *n.*, *v.*, **-enced, -encing.** *–n.* **1.** invisible or insensible action exerted by one thing or person on another. **2.** power of producing effects by invisible or insensible means: *spheres of influence.* **3.** a thing or person that exerts action by invisible or insensible means: *beneficial influences.* **4.** *Astrol.* **a.** the supposed radiation of an ethereal fluid from the stars, regarded in astrology as affecting human actions and destinies, etc. **b.** the exercise of occult power by the stars, or such power as exercised. **5.** *Poetic.* the exercise of similar power by human beings. *–v.t.* **6.** to exercise influence on; modify, affect, or sway: *to influence a person by bribery.* **7.** to move or impel to, or to do, something. [ME, from ML *influentia*, lit., a flowing in, from L *influens* influent] – **influencer,** *n.*

**influence mine** /ˈ– maɪn/, *n. Mil.* a mine actuated by the effect of a ship on some physical condition in the vicinity of the mine, or on radiations emanating from the mine.

**influence sweep** /ˈ– swip/, *n. Mil.* a sweep (def. 31) designed to produce an influence similar to that produced by a ship and thus actuate mines.

**influent** /ˈɪnfluənt/, *adj.* **1.** flowing in. *–n.* **2.** →**tributary.** [ME, from L *influens*, ppr., flowing in]

**influential** /ɪnfluˈɛnʃəl/, *adj.* having or exerting influence, esp. great influence. [ML *influentia* INFLUENCE + -AL[1]] – **influentially,** *adv.*

**influenza** /ɪnfluˈɛnzə/, *n.* **1.** *Pathol.* an acute, extremely contagious, commonly epidemic disease characterised by general prostration, and occurring in several forms with varying symptoms, usu. with nasal catarrh and bronchial inflammation, and due to a specific virus; grippe. **2.** *Vet. Sci.* an acute, contagious disease occurring in horses and swine, manifested by fever and catarrhal inflammations of the eyes, nasal passages, and bronchi. [It.: influx of disease, epidemic, influenza. See INFLUENCE] – **influenzal,** *adj.* – **influenza-like,** *adj.*

**influx** /ˈɪnflʌks/, *n.* **1.** the act of flowing in; an inflow. **2.** the place or point at which one stream flows into another or into the sea. **3.** the mouth of a stream. **4.** the arrival of people or things in large numbers or great quantity. [LL *influxus*, from L *influere* flow in]

**info** /ˈɪnfoʊ/, *n. Colloq.* information.

**infold** /ɪnˈfoʊld/, *v.t. Chiefly U.S.* **1.** →**enfold. 2.** to fold in. – **infolder,** *n.* – **infoldment,** *n.*

**inform** /ɪnˈfɔm/, *v.t.* **1.** to impart knowledge of a fact or circumstance to: *I informed him of my arrival.* **2.** to supply (oneself) with knowledge of a matter or subject: *he informed himself of all the pertinent facts.* **3.** to give character to; pervade with determining effect on the character. **4.** to animate or inspire. *–v.i.* **5.** to give information, esp. to furnish incriminating evidence to a prosecuting officer. [L *informāre*; replacing ME *enforme*, from OF] – **informingly,** *adv.*

**informal** /ɪnˈfɔməl/, *adj.* **1.** not according to prescribed or customary forms; irregular: *informal proceedings.* **2.** without formality; unceremonious: *an informal visit.* **3.** not requiring formal dress: *an informal dinner.* **4.** denoting speech characterised by colloquial usage, having the flexibility of grammar, syntax, and pronunciation allowable in conversation. **5.** characterising the second singular pronominal or verbal form, or its use, in certain languages: *the informal 'tu' in French.* **6.** (of a vote) invalid. *–adv.* **7. vote informal,** to mark a ballot-paper incorrectly thereby invalidating one's vote. – **informally,** *adv.*

**informal art** /'– at/, *n.* a style of art developed in the 1950s which depends on the abandonment of all objective forms in favour of creation through spontaneity and improvisation of new and unknown forms.

**informality** /ɪnfɔ'mæləti/, *n., pl.* **-ties. 1.** the state of being informal; absence of formality. **2.** an informal act.

**informal vote** /ɪnfɔməl 'voʊt/, *n.* (in an election) a ballot paper which is invalid because, either by accident or design, it has been incorrectly completed or not completed.

**informant** /ɪn'fɔmənt/, *n.* one who informs or gives information.

**in forma pauperis** /ɪn fɔmə 'pɒpərəs, 'paʊ-/, *n.* the legal practice of allowing a poor person to bring or defend an action without payment of court or professional fees. [L: in the character of a pauper]

**informatics** /ɪnfə'mætɪks/, *n.* a discipline of science which investigates the structure and properties of scientific information as opposed to the content.

**information** /ɪnfə'meɪʃən/, *n.* **1.** knowledge communicated or received concerning some fact or circumstance; news. **2.** knowledge on various subjects, however acquired. **3.** the act of informing. **4.** the state of being informed. **5.** *Law.* a statement of facts made before a justice or magistrate by the person prosecuting or his representative. **6.** (in communication theory) a quantitative measure of the contents of a message. [L *informātio;* replacing ME *enformacion,* from OF] – **informational,** *adj.*

**information retrieval** /'– rətrivəl/, *n.* the recovering of specific information from data stored in a computer.

**information science** /'– saɪəns/, *n.* the study of the collection, organisation and communication of data, usu. with computers.

**information theory** /'– θɪəri/, *n.* the theory of coding and transmitting messages over communication channels subject to interference.

**informative** /ɪn'fɔmətɪv/, *adj.* affording information; instructive: *an informative book.* Also, **informatory** /ɪn'fɔmətəri, -tri/.

**informed** /ɪn'fɔmd/, *adj.* knowledgeable; learned: *informed opinion was always kind to Chifley.*

**informer** /ɪn'fɔmə/, *n.* **1.** one who furnishes incriminating evidence to a prosecuting officer. **2.** an informant.

**infortune** /ɪn'fɔtʃun/, *n.* **1.** *Astrol.* a planet or aspect of evil influence. **2.** *Obs.* misfortune. [ME, from F. See IN-[3], FORTUNE]

**infra** /'ɪnfrə/, *adv.* (in a text) below. Cf. **supra.** [L]

**infra-,** a prefix meaning 'below' or 'beneath', as in *infra-axillary* (below the axilla). [L, representing *infrā,* adv. and prep., below, beneath]

**infracostal** /ɪnfrə'kɒstl/, *adj.* below the ribs.

**infract** /ɪn'frækt/, *v.t.* to break; violate or infringe. [L *infractus,* pp., broken off] – **infractor,** *n.*

**infraction** /ɪn'frækʃən/, *n.* breach; violation; infringement: *an infraction of a treaty or law.*

**infra dig** /ɪnfrə 'dɪg/, *adj. Colloq.* beneath one's dignity. [abbrev. L *infrā dignitātem*]

**infralapsarian** /ɪnfrəlæp'sɛəriən/, *n.* **1.** one who believes in infralapsarianism. *–adj.* **2.** pertaining to infralapsarianism or those who hold it. [INFRA- + L *lapsus* a fall + -ARIAN]

**infralapsarianism** /ɪnfrəlæp'sɛəriənɪzəm/, *n.* a doctrine adopted by Calvinists from St Augustine, that God decreed the creation, permitted the fall as logically subordinate, planned the redemption of a chosen number and the eternal punishment of the remainder, all as part of a preconceived plan for the universe. Also, **sublapsarianism.**

**infrangible** /ɪn'frændʒəbəl/, *adj.* **1.** unbreakable. **2.** inviolable. – **infrangibility** /ɪn,frændʒə'bɪləti/, **infrangibleness,** *n.* – **infrangibly,** *adv.*

**infra-red** /ɪnfrə-'rɛd/, *n.;* /'ɪnfrə-rɛd/ *adj.* *–n.* **1.** the part of the invisible spectrum contiguous to the red end of the visible spectrum, comprising radiation of greater wavelength than that of red light. *–adj.* **2.** denoting or pertaining to the infra-red or its component rays: *infra-red radiation.*

**infra-red film** /– 'fɪlm/, *n.* film sensitive to near infra-red wave length. Cf. **far infra-red.**

**infra-red photography** /– fə'tɒgrəfi/, *n.* photography employing infra-red film. Cf. **far infra-red.**

**infrasonic** /'ɪnfrəsɒnɪk/, *adj.* of or pertaining to sounds with frequencies below the audible range.

**infrastructure** /'ɪnfrəstrʌktʃə/, *n.* **1.** the basic framework or underlying foundation (as of an organisation or a system). **2.** the buildings or permanent installations associated with an organisation, operation, etc.

**infrequency** /ɪn'frikwənsi/, *n.* the state of being infrequent. Also, **infrequence.**

**infrequent** /ɪn'frikwənt/, *adj.* **1.** happening or occurring at long intervals or not often: *infrequent visits.* **2.** not constant, habitual, or regular: *an infrequent visitor.* **3.** not plentiful. – **infrequently,** *adv.*

**infringe** /ɪn'frɪndʒ/, *v.,* **-fringed, -fringing.** *–v.t.* **1.** to commit a breach or infraction of; violate or transgress. *–v.i.* **2.** to encroach or trespass (fol. by *on* or *upon*): *don't infringe on his privacy.* [L *infringere* break off] – **infringer,** *n.*

**infringement** /ɪn'frɪndʒmənt/, *n.* **1.** a breach or infraction, as of a law, right, or obligation; violation; transgression. **2.** the act of infringing.

**infundibuliform** /ɪnfʌn'dɪbjələfɔm/, *adj.* funnel-shaped.

**infundibulum** /ɪnfʌn'dɪbjələm/, *n., pl.* **-la** /-lə/. **1.** a funnel-shaped organ or part. **2.** *Anat.* **a.** a funnel-shaped extension of the cerebrum connecting the pituitary body to the base of the brain. **b.** a space in the right auricle at the root of the pulmonary artery. [L: funnel] – **infundibular** /ɪnfʌn'dɪbjələ/, **infundibulate** /ɪnfʌn'dɪbjələt, -leɪt/, *adj.*

infundibuliform corolla of morning glory

**infuriate** /ɪn'fjurieɪt/, *v.,* **-ated, -ating.** *–v.t.* **1.** to make furious; enrage. **2.** to annoy intensely. [ML *infuriātus,* pp., enraged] – **infuriately,** *adv.* – **infuriatingly,** *adv.* – **infuriation** /ɪn,fjuri'eɪʃən/, *n.*

**infuscate** /ɪn'fʌskeɪt/, *adj.* (of insects) darkened with a fuscous or brownish shade. Also, **infuscated.** [L *infuscātus,* pp., darkened]

**infuse** /ɪn'fjuz/, *v.t.,* **-fused, -fusing. 1.** to introduce as by pouring; cause to penetrate; instil (fol. by *into*). **2.** to imbue or inspire (*with*). **3.** to pour in. **4.** to steep or soak (a plant, etc.) in a liquid so as to extract its soluble properties or ingredients. **5.** *Cookery.* to boil slowly in a solution. [ME, from L *infūsus,* pp., poured in or on] – **infuser,** *n.* – **infusive** /ɪn'fjusɪv/, *adj.*

**infusible**[1] /ɪn'fjuzəbəl/, *adj.* not fusible; incapable of being fused or melted. [IN-[3] + FUSIBLE] – **infusibility** /ɪn,fjuzə'bɪləti/, **infusibleness,** *n.*

**infusible**[2] /ɪn'fjuzəbəl/, *adj.* capable of being infused. [INFUSE, *v.* + -IBLE]

**infusion** /ɪn'fjuʒən/, *n.* **1.** the act of infusing. **2.** that which is infused. **3.** a liquid extract obtained from a substance by steeping or soaking it in water. **4.** *Med.* **a.** the introduction of a saline or other solution into a vein, artery, or tissue. **b.** the solution used.

**infusionism** /ɪn'fjuʒənɪzəm/, *n.* the doctrine that at birth a pre-existent soul is planted in the human body for its earthly lifetime. – **infusionist,** *n.*

**infusorial** /ɪnfju'zɔriəl/, *adj.* containing or consisting of infusorians: *infusorial earth.*

**infusorian** /ɪnfju'zɔriən/, *n.* **1.** any protozoan of the class Infusoria, mostly microscopic and aquatic, having vibratile cilia. **2.** *Obs.* any of a miscellaneous variety of minute or microscopic animal and vegetable organisms (constituting the old group Infusoria) frequently developed in infusions of decaying organic matter. *–adj.* **3.** of, denoting, or pertaining to the Infusoria. [NL *Infusori(a)* (from L *infūsus,* pp., poured in) + -AN]

**-ing**[1], a suffix of nouns formed from verbs, expressing the action of the verb or its result, product, material, etc., as in *the art of building, a new building, cotton wadding.* It is also used to form nouns from words other than verbs, as in *offing, shirting.* Verbal nouns ending in *-ing* are often used attributively, as in *the printing trade,* and in composition, as in *drinking song.* In some compounds, as *sewing machine,* the first element might reasonably be regarded as the participial adjective (see **-ing**²), the compound thus meaning 'a machine that sews', but it is commonly taken as a verbal noun, the compound being explained as 'a machine for sewing'. [ME *-ing,* OE *-ing, -ung*]

**-ing**², a suffix forming the present participle of verbs, such participles often being used as adjectives (participial adjectives), as in *warring factions.* Cf **-ing**¹. [ME *-ing, -inge;* replacing ME *-inde, -ende,* OE *-ende*]

**ingather** /ɪn'gæðə/, *v.t.* to gather in; collect; bring in, as a harvest. – **ingatherer,** *n.*

**ingeminate** /ɪn'dʒɛməneɪt/, *v.t.,* **-nated, -nating.** to repeat; reiterate. [L *ingeminātus,* pp., redoubled] – **ingemination** /ɪndʒɛmə'neɪʃən/, *n.*

**ingenerate**¹ /ɪn'dʒɛnərət/, *adj.* not generated; self-existent. [LL *ingenerātus.* See IN-³]

**ingenerate**² /ɪn'dʒɛnəreɪt/, *v.,* **-rated, -rating;** /ɪn'dʒɛnərət/, *adj. Archaic.* –*v.t.* **1.** to engender. –*adj.* **2.** inborn; innate. [L *ingenerātus,* pp., generated within. See IN-²] – **ingeneration** /ɪn,dʒɛnər'eɪʃən/, *n.*

**ingenious** /ɪn'dʒiniəs/, *adj.* **1.** (of things, actions, etc.) showing cleverness of invention or construction: *an ingenious machine.* **2.** having inventive faculty; skilful in contriving or constructing: *an ingenious mechanic.* [ME, from L *ingeniōsus* of good natural talents] – **ingeniously,** *adv.* – **ingeniousness,** *n.*

**ingenue** /'õʒənu, -'nju/, *n.* **1.** the part of an ingenuous girl, esp. as represented on the stage. **2.** the actress who plays such a part. [F, fem. of *ingénu* ingenuous, from L *ingenuus*]

**ingenuity** /ɪndʒə'njuəti/, *n., pl.* **-ties. 1.** the quality of being ingenious; inventive talent. **2.** skilfulness of contrivance or design, as of things, actions, etc. **3.** an ingenious contrivance. **4.** *Obs.* ingenuousness. [L *ingenuitas* frankness. Cf. INGENUOUS]

**ingenuous** /ɪn'dʒɛnjuəs/, *adj.* **1.** free from reserve, restraint, or dissimulation. **2.** artless; innocent. [L *ingenuus* native, innate, freeborn, noble, frank] – **ingenuously,** *adv.* – **ingenuousness,** *n.*

**ingest** /ɪn'dʒɛst/, *v.t.* **1.** *Physiol.* to put or take (food, etc.) into the body. **2.** *Aeron.* (of a jet engine) to draw in (foreign matter). [L *ingestus,* pp., carried, or poured in] – **ingestion,** *n.* – **ingestive,** *adj.*

**ingle** /'ɪŋgl/, *n.* a household fire or fireplace. [orig. uncert. Cf. Gaelic *aingeal* fire]

**inglenook** /'ɪŋglnʊk/, *n.* a corner by the fire.

**ingleside** /'ɪŋglsaɪd/, *n.* a fireside.

**inglorious** /ɪn'glɔriəs/, *adj.* shameful; disgraceful: *inglorious flight.* – **ingloriously,** *adv.* – **ingloriousness,** *n.*

**in-goal** /'ɪn-goʊl/, *n.* (in Rugby football) an area between the goal line and dead-ball line in which tries are scored by placing the ball on the ground.

**ingoing** /'ɪngoʊɪŋ/, *adj.* **1.** going in; entering. –*n.* **2.** *Law.* expense incurred in the purchase of fixtures, etc., left by a previous tenant.

**ingot** /'ɪŋgət/, *n.* **1.** the casting obtained when melted metal is poured into a mould (**ingot mould**) with the expectation that it be further processed. **2.** a cast metal mass, formed by rolling, etc., or by smelting and casting to shape. –*v.t.* **3.** to make ingots of; shape into ingots. [ME: mould for metal. Cf. OE *ingyte* pouring in]

**ingot iron** /'– aɪən/, *n.* a very low carbon steel, usu. made in an open hearth furnace, containing only very small quantities of other elements.

**ingot steel** /'– stil/, *n.* steel which, while molten, is poured into moulds giving it a temporary massive shape suitable for further working by rolling or forging.

**ingraft** /ɪn'graft/, *v.t.* →**engraft.**

**ingrain** /ɪn'greɪn/, *v.;* /'ɪngreɪn/, *adj., n.* –*v.t.* **1.** to fix deeply and firmly, as in the nature or mind. –*adj.* **2.** ingrained. **3.** (of carpets) made of yarn dyed before weaving, and so woven as to show the pattern on both sides. **4.** dyed in grain, or through the fibre. **5.** dyed in the yarn, or in a raw state, before manufacture. –*n.* **6.** yarn, wool, etc., dyed before manufacture. **7.** an ingrain carpet. Also, **engrain** for defs 1, and 2.

**ingrained** /'ɪngreɪnd/, *adj.* **1.** fixed firmly: *ingrained dirt.* **2.** deep-rooted: *ingrained habits.* **3.** inveterate; thorough.

**ingrate** /'ɪngreɪt/, *n.* **1.** an ungrateful person. –*adj.* **2.** ungrateful. [ME, from L *ingrātus* unpleasing, not grateful]

**ingratiate** /ɪn'greɪʃieɪt/, *v.t.,* **-ated, -ating.** to establish (oneself) in the favour or good graces of others. [IN-² + L *grātia* favour, grace + -ATE¹] – **ingratiatingly,** *adv.* – **ingratiation** /ɪn,greɪʃi'eɪʃən/, *n.*

**ingratiatory** /ɪn'greɪʃiətri/, *adj.* serving or intended to ingratiate.

**ingratitude** /ɪn'grætətʃud/, *n.* the state of being ungrateful; unthankfulness.

**ingravescent** /ɪngrə'vɛsənt/, *adj.* increasing in severity, as a disease. [L *ingravescens,* ppr., growing heavier] – **ingravescence,** *n.*

**ingredient** /ɪn'gridiənt/, *n.* **1.** something that enters as an element into a mixture: *the ingredients of a cake.* **2.** a constituent element of anything. [late ME, from L *ingrediens,* ppr., entering]

**ingress** /'ɪngrɛs/, *n.* **1.** the act of going in or entering. **2.** the right of going in. **3.** a means or place of going in; an entrance. [ME, from L *ingressus* entrance] – **ingression** /ɪn'grɛʃən/, *n.* – **ingressive** /ɪn'grɛsɪv/, *adj.* – **ingressiveness** /ɪn'grɛsɪvnəs/, *n.*

**ingressive** /ɪn'grɛsɪv/, *adj.* **1.** pertaining to that which goes or comes in: *the ingressive air we breathe in.* **2.** pertaining to a speech sound made by ingressive air as a vocal click. –*n.* **3.** such a sound. – **ingressiveness,** *n.*

**in-ground** /'ɪn-graʊnd/, *adj.* of or pertaining to a swimming pool, etc., which is in an excavated hole in the ground: *in-ground pool.*

**in-group** /'ɪn-grup/, *n.* a group reserving favourable treatment and acceptance to its own members and denying them to outsiders or members of other groups.

**ingrowing** /'ɪngroʊɪŋ/, *adj.* **1.** growing into the flesh: *an ingrowing toenail.* **2.** growing within or inwards.

**ingrown** /'ɪngroʊn/, *adj.* **1.** having grown into the flesh. **2.** grown within or inwards.

**ingrowth** /'ɪngroʊθ/, *n.* **1.** growth inwards. **2.** something formed by growth inwards.

**inguinal** /'ɪŋgwənəl/, *adj.* of, pertaining to, or situated in the groin. [L *inguinālis*]

**ingulf** /ɪn'gʌlf/, *v.t.* →**engulf.**

**ingurgitate** /ɪn'gɜdʒəteɪt/, *v.,* **-tated, -tating.** –*v.t.* **1.** to swallow greedily or in great quantity, as food. **2.** →**engulf.** –*v.i.* **3.** to drink largely; swill. [L *ingurgitātus,* pp., poured in] – **ingurgitation** /ɪn,gɜdʒə'teɪʃən/, *n.*

**inhabit** /ɪn'hæbət/, *v.t.* **1.** to live or dwell in (a place), as persons or animals. **2.** to have its seat, or exist, in. –*v.i.* **3.** *Archaic.* to live or dwell, as in a place. [L *inhabitāre;* replacing ME *enhabite,* from F] – **inhabitable,** *adj.* – **inhabitability** /ɪn,hæbətə'bɪləti/, *n.* – **inhabitation** /ɪn,hæbə'teɪʃən/, *n.*

**inhabitancy** /ɪn'hæbətənsi/, *n., pl.* **-cies.** residence as an inhabitant. Also, **inhabitance.**

**inhabitant** /ɪn'hæbətənt/, *n.* a person or an animal that inhabits a place; a permanent resident. Also, *Obs.,* **inhabiter.** [late ME, from L *inhabitans,* ppr., dwelling in]

**inhalant** /ɪn'heɪlənt/, *adj.* **1.** serving for inhalation. –*n.* **2.** an apparatus or medicine used for inhaling.

**inhalation** /ɪnhə'leɪʃən/, *n.* **1.** the act of inhaling. **2.** a medicinal preparation to be inhaled.

**inhalator** /'ɪnhəleɪtə/, *n.* an apparatus to help one inhale air, anaesthetic, medicinal vapours, etc.

**inhale** /ɪn'heɪl/, *v.,* **-haled, -haling.** –*v.t.* **1.** to breathe in; draw in by, or as by, breathing: *to inhale air.* –*v.i.* **2.** to draw into the lungs, esp. smoke of cigarettes, cigars, etc.: *do you inhale?* [L *inhālāre*]

**inhaler** /ɪn'heɪlə/, *n.* **1.** an apparatus used in inhaling medicinal vapours, anaesthetics, etc. **2.** one who inhales.

**inharmonic** /ɪnha'mɒnɪk/, *adj.* not harmonic.

**inharmonious** /ɪnha'moʊniəs/, *adj.* **1.** not harmonious; discordant. **2.** not congenial; disagreeable. [IN-³ + HARMONIOUS] – **inharmoniously,** *adv.* – **inharmoniousness,** *n.*

**inhaul** /'ɪnhɔl/, *n.* a rope for hauling in a sail or spar. Also, **inhauler.**

**inhere** /ɪn'hɪə/, *v.i.*, **-hered, -hering.** to exist permanently and inseparably (in), as a quality, attribute, or element; belong intrinsically; be inherent. [L *inhaerēre* stick in or to]

**inherence** /ɪn'hɪərəns/, *n.* **1.** the state or fact of inhering or being inherent. **2.** *Philos.* the relation of an attribute to its subject.

**inherency** /ɪn'hɪərənsi/, *n., pl.* **-cies. 1.** →**inherence. 2.** something inherent.

**inherent** /ɪn'hɛrənt, ɪn'hɪərənt/, *adj.* existing in something as a permanent and inseparable element, quality, or attribute. [L *inhaerens,* ppr., sticking in or to] – **inherently,** *adv.*

**inherit** /ɪn'hɛrət/, *v.t.* **1.** to take or receive (property, a right, a title, etc.) as the heir of the former owner. **2.** to succeed (a person) as heir. **3.** to receive (anything) as by succession from predecessors. **4.** to possess as a hereditary characteristic. **5.** to receive as one's portion. **6.** *Obs.* to make (one) heir (fol. by *of*). *–v.i.* **7.** to take or receive property, etc., as being heir to it. **8.** to have succession as heir. **9.** to receive qualities, powers, duties, etc., as by inheritance (fol. by *from*). [ME *enherite(n),* from OF *enheriter,* from *en-* EN-[1] + *heriter* (from L *hērēditāre* inherit)]

**inheritable** /ɪn'hɛrətəbəl/, *adj.* **1.** capable of being inherited. **2.** capable of inheriting; qualified to inherit. – **inheritability** /ɪn,hɛrətə'bɪləti/, **inheritableness,** *n.* – **inheritably,** *adv.*

**inheritance** /ɪn'hɛrətəns/, *n.* **1.** that which is or may be inherited; any property passing at the owner's death to the heir or those entitled to succeed. **2.** a hereditary characteristic or characteristics collectively. **3.** anything received from progenitors or predecessors as if by succession: *an inheritance of family pride.* **4.** portion, peculiar possession, or heritage: *the inheritance of the saints.* **5.** the act or fact of inheriting: *to receive property by inheritance.* **6.** *Obs.* the right of inheriting.

**inherited** /ɪn'hɛrətəd/, *adj.* received by inheritance.

**inheritor** /ɪn'hɛrətə/, *n.* one who inherits; heir. – **inheritress** /ɪn'hɛrətrəs/, *n. fem.*

**inheritrix** /ɪn'hɛrətrɪks/, *n., pl.* **inheritrices** /ɪn,hɛrə'traɪsiz/. a female inheritor.

**inhesion** /ɪn'hiʒən/, *n.* the state or fact of inhering; inherence. [LL *inhaesio*]

**in. Hg,** inch of mercury.

**inhibit** /ɪn'hɪbət/, *v.t.* **1.** to restrain, hinder, arrest, or check (an action, impulse, etc.). **2.** to prohibit; forbid. **3.** *Chem.* to decrease the rate of a chemical reaction or to stop it completely. [late ME, from L *inhibitus,* pp., held back, restrained] – **inhibiter,** *n.*

**inhibition** /ɪnə'bɪʃən, ɪnhɪ-/, *n.* **1.** the act of inhibiting. **2.** the state of being inhibited. **3.** *Psychol.* the blocking of any psychological process by another psychological process. **4.** *Physiol.* a restraining, arresting, or checking, as of action: **a.** the reduction of a reflex or other activity as the result of an antagonistic stimulation. **b.** a state created at synapses making them less excitable to other sources of stimulation. **5.** *Eccles. Law.* the order by a bishop that a clergyman should cease from performing any duty.

**inhibitor** /ɪn'hɪbətə/, *n.* **1.** *Chem.* a substance that retards or prevents a chemical reaction. **2.** an inhibiter.

**inhibitory** /ɪn'hɪbətri, -təri/, *adj.* serving or tending to inhibit. Also, **inhibitive.**

**in. $H_2O$,** inch of water.

**inhospitable** /ɪnhɒs'pɪtəbəl/, *adj.* **1.** not inclined to or characterised by hospitality, as persons, actions, etc. **2.** (of a region, climate, etc.) not offering shelter, favourable conditions, etc. – **inhospitableness,** *n.* – **inhospitably,** *adv.* – **inhospitality** /ɪn,hɒspə'tæləti/, *n.*

**in-house** /'ɪn-haʊs/, *adj.* of or pertaining to a publication, regulation, lecture-program, etc., which is relevant only to the people within a particular organisation as a business house, university, etc.

**inhuman** /ɪn'hjumən/, *adj.* **1.** lacking natural human feeling or sympathy for others; brutal. **2.** not human. [late ME *unhumayn,* from L *inhūmānus.* See IN-[3]] – **inhumanly,** *adv.* – **inhumanness,** *n.*

**inhumane** /ɪnhju'meɪn/, *adj.* not humane; lacking humanity or kindness. – **inhumanely,** *adv.*

**inhumanity** /ɪnhju'mænəti/, *n., pl.* **-ties. 1.** the state or quality of being inhuman or inhumane; cruelty: *man's inhumanity to man.* **2.** an inhuman or inhumane act.

**inhumation** /ɪnhju'meɪʃən/, *n.* the act of inhuming, esp. as opposed to cremation; burial.

**inhume** /ɪn'hjum/, *v.t.,* **-humed, -huming.** to bury; inter. [L *inhumāre* bury in the ground]

**inimical** /ɪ'nɪmɪkəl/, *adj.* **1.** adverse in tendency or effect: *a climate inimical to health.* **2.** unfriendly or hostile. [LL *inimīcālis,* from L *inimīcus* unfriendly, an enemy] – **inimicality** /ɪ,nɪmɪ'kæləti/, *n.* – **inimically,** *adv.*

**inimitable** /ɪ'nɪmɪtəbəl/, *adj.* incapable of being imitated; surpassing imitation. – **inimitability** /ɪ,nɪmɪtə'bɪləti/, **inimitableness,** *n.* – **inimitably,** *adv.*

**inion** /'ɪniən/, *n.* a point at the external occipital protuberance of the skull. [NL, from Gk: back of the head]

**iniquitous** /ɪ'nɪkwətəs/, *adj.* characterised by iniquity. – **iniquitously,** *adv.* – **iniquitousness,** *n.*

**iniquity** /ɪ'nɪkwəti/, *n., pl.* **-ties. 1.** gross injustice; wickedness. **2.** a violation of right or duty; wicked action; sin. [ME *iniquite,* from L *inīquitas* injustice]

**init.,** initial.

**initial** /ɪ'nɪʃəl/, *adj., n., v.,* **-ialled, -ialling** or (*U.S.*) **-ialed, -ialing.** *–adj.* **1.** of or pertaining to the beginning; incipient: *the initial step in a process.* **2.** at the beginning of a word or syllable. *–n.* **3.** an initial letter, as of a word. **4.** the first letter of a proper name. **5.** a letter of extra size or ornamental character used at the beginning of a chapter or other division of a book, etc. *–v.t.* **6.** to mark or sign with an initial or initials, esp. as an indication of responsibility for or approval of the contents. [L *initiālis* of the beginning] – **initially,** *adv.*

**initiate** /ɪ'nɪʃieɪt/, *v.,* **-ated, -ating;** /ɪ'nɪʃiət, -eɪt/, *adj., n.* *–v.t.* **1.** to begin, set going, or originate: *to initiate reforms.* **2.** to introduce into the knowledge of some art or subject. **3.** to admit with formal rites into secret knowledge, a society, etc. **4.** to propose (a measure) by initiative procedure: *to initiate a constitutional amendment.* *–adj. Obs.* **5.** initiated; begun. **6.** admitted into a society, etc., or into the knowledge of a subject. *–n.* **7.** one who has been initiated. [L *initiātus,* pp., begun, initiated] – **initiator,** *n.* – **initiatress** /ɪ'nɪʃiətrəs/, **initiatrix** /ɪ'nɪʃiətrɪks/, *n. fem.*

**initiation** /ɪnɪʃi'eɪʃən/, *n.* **1.** formal admission into a society, etc. **2.** the ceremony of admission. **3.** the act of initiating. **4.** the fact of being initiated. **5.** *Theosophy.* development of consciousness surpassing the average human level. **6.** the starting of a chain reaction in fissile material, as in an atomic bomb.

**initiation ceremony** /'– sɛrəməni/, *n.* a religious ceremony in a tribe or clan to signify the coming of age or puberty of its members, esp. the young men.

**initiative** /ɪ'nɪʃiətɪv/, *n.* **1.** an introductory act or step; leading action: *to take the initiative.* **2.** readiness and ability in initiating action; enterprise: *to lack initiative.* **3.** *Govt.* **a.** a procedure by which a specified number of voters may propose a statute, constitutional amendment, or ordinance, and compel a popular vote on its adoption. **b.** the general right or ability to present a new bill or measure, as in a legislature. *–adj.* **4.** serving to initiate; pertaining to initiation. – **initiatively,** *adv.*

**initiatory** /ɪ'nɪʃiətri, -təri/, *adj.* **1.** introductory; initial: *an initiatory step.* **2.** serving to initiate or admit into a society, etc. – **initiatorily,** *adv.*

**inject** /ɪn'dʒɛkt/, *v.t.* **1.** to force (a fluid) into a passage, cavity, or tissue. **2.** to force a fluid into (a person, tissue, etc.) esp. for medical purposes. **3.** to introduce (something new or different) into a thing: *to inject comedy into a situation.* **4.** to introduce arbitrarily or inappropriately. **5.** to interject (a remark, suggestion, etc.), as into conversation. **6.** *Geol.* to intrude; to force or thrust (lava) into cavities, rock, etc. [L *injectus,* pp., thrown or put in]

**injected** /ɪn'dʒɛktəd/, *adj.* inflamed; reddened; hyperaemic; bloodshot.

**injection** /ɪn'dʒɛkʃən/, *n.* **1.** the act of injecting. **2.** that which is injected. **3.** a liquid injected into the body, esp. for medical purposes, as a hypodermic or an enema. **4.** the state of being hyperaemic or bloodshot. **5.** →**fuel-injection.**

**injection moulding** /'– moʊldɪŋ/, *n.* a process for moulding thermoplastic materials by heating them and then injecting them under pressure into a cool closed mould.

**injector** /ɪn'dʒɛktə/, *n.* **1.** one who or that which injects. **2.** a device for forcing water into a steam boiler. **3.** a device for spraying fuel into a combustion chamber.

**in-joke** /'ɪn-dʒoʊk/, *n.* a joke or allusion understood only by a select group, to the bewilderment and exclusion of outsiders.

**injudicious** /ɪndʒu'dɪʃəs/, *adj.* not judicious; showing lack of judgment; unwise; imprudent. – **injudiciously,** *adv.* – **injudiciousness,** *n.*

**Injun** /'ɪndʒən/, *n. Colloq.* a North American Indian.

**injunction** /ɪn'dʒʌŋkʃən/, *n.* **1.** *Law.* a judicial process or order requiring the person or persons to whom it is directed to do or (more commonly) not to do a particular thing. **2.** the act of enjoining. **3.** that which is enjoined; a command, order or admonition. [LL *injunctio* command] – **injunctive,** *adj.*

**injure** /'ɪndʒə/, *v.t.*, **-jured, -juring.** **1.** to do or cause harm of any kind to; damage; hurt; impair: *to injure the hand.* **2.** to do wrong or injustice to. [backformation from INJURY, *n.*, replacing earlier *injury,* v.] – **injurer,** *n.*

**injured** /'ɪndʒəd/, *adj.* **1.** harmed, damaged, or hurt. **2.** offended; wronged: *an injured look.*

**injurious** /ɪn'dʒuriəs/, *adj.* **1.** harmful, hurtful, or detrimental, as in effect: *injurious habits.* **2.** doing or involving injury or wrong, as to another. **3.** insulting or abusive. [late ME, from L *injūriōsus,* wrongful] – **injuriously,** *adv.* – **injuriousness,** *n.*

**injury** /'ɪndʒəri/, *n., pl.* **-ries.** **1.** harm of any kind done or sustained: *to escape without injury.* **2.** a particular form or instance of harm: *severe bodily injuries.* **3.** wrong or injustice done or suffered. **4.** *Law.* the infringement of a right (opposed to *damage).* [ME *injurie,* from L *injūria* wrong, harm, insult]

**injury time** /'– taɪm/, *n.* extension of the playing time of a sporting match to compensate for any time lost through injury.

**injustice** /ɪn'dʒʌstəs/, *n.* **1.** the quality or fact of being unjust. **2.** unjust action or treatment; violation of another's rights. **3.** an unjust act or circumstance. [ME, from F, from L *injustitia*]

**ink** /ɪŋk/, *n.* **1.** a fluid or viscous substance used for writing or printing. **2.** a dark, protective fluid ejected by the cuttlefish and other cephalopods. **3.** *Colloq.* cheap wine. –*v.t.* **4.** to mark, stain, cover, or smear with ink. [ME *inke, enke,* from OF *enque,* from LL *encaustum,* from Gk *énkauston* kind of ink] – **inker,** *n.* – **inkless,** *adj.* – **inklike,** *adj.*

**ink-cap** /'ɪŋk-kæp/, *n.* any of various mushrooms of the genus *Coprinus,* whose gills disintegrate into blackish liquid after the spores mature, esp. *C. atramentarius.* Also, **inky cap.**

**inked** /ɪŋkt/, *adj. Colloq.* drunk; intoxicated.

**inkhorn** /'ɪŋkhɔn/, *n.* a small container of horn or other material, formerly used to hold writing ink.

**inkhorn term** /'– tɜm/, *n.* a pedantic or affectedly erudite term taken from another language, esp. Latin or Greek; common in the 16th century in English.

**inkle** /'ɪŋkəl/, *n.* **1.** a kind of linen tape. **2.** the linen thread or yarn from which this tape is made.

**inkling** /'ɪŋklɪŋ/, *n.* **1.** a hint, intimation, or slight suggestion. **2.** a vague idea or notion. [ME *inclen* to hint at + -ING[1]. Cf. OE *inca* suspicion]

**inkstand** /'ɪŋkstænd/, *n.* a stand for holding ink, pens, etc.

**ink table** /'ɪŋk teɪbəl/, *n.* (in printing) a flat metal surface over which the ink is distributed at a desired consistency. Also, **ink slab, inking table, inking slab.**

**inkweed** /'ɪŋkwid/, *n.* a tall herbaceous shrub, *Phytolacca octandra,* native to tropical America but a weed of waste ground elsewhere.

**inkwell** /'ɪŋkwɛl/, *n.* a container for ink, esp. one let into the surface of a desk.

**inky** /'ɪŋki/, *adj.*, **-ier, -iest.** **1.** black as ink: *inky shadows.* **2.** resembling ink. **3.** stained with ink: *inky fingers.* **4.** of or pertaining to ink. **5.** consisting of or containing ink. **6.** written with ink. – **inkiness,** *n.*

**inlaid** /'ɪnleɪd/, *adj.* **1.** set in the surface of a thing: *an inlaid design in wood.* **2.** decorated or made with a design set in the surface: *an inlaid table.*

**inland** /'ɪnlænd/, *adj.* **1.** pertaining to or situated in the interior part of a country or region: *inland cities.* **2.** carried on within a country; domestic; not foreign: *inland trade.* **3.** confined to a country. –*adv.* **4.** in or towards the interior of a country. –*n.* **5.** the interior part of a country, away from the border. [ME and OE; from IN-[1] + LAND]

**inlander** /'ɪnlændə, -ləndə/, *n.* a person living inland.

**in-law** /'ɪn-lɔ/, *n.* a relative by marriage.

**inlay** /ɪn'leɪ/, *v.*, **-laid, -laying;** /'ɪnleɪ/, *n.* –*v.t.* **1.** to decorate (an object) with veneers of fine materials set in its surface. **2.** to insert, or apply (layers of fine materials) in a surface of an object. **3.** *Hort.* to place (a fitted scion) into a prepared stock, as in an inlay graft. –*n.* **4.** inlaid work. **5.** veneer of fine material inserted in something else, esp. for ornament. **6.** a design or decoration made by inlaying. **7.** *Dentistry.* a filling of metal, porcelain, or plastic which is fitted and fastened into a tooth as a solid mass. **8.** *Hort.* an inlay graft. **9.** the act or process of inlaying. – **inlayer,** *n.*

**inlay graft** /'ɪnleɪ graft/, *n.* (in horticulture) a graft in which the scion is matched into a place in the stock from which a piece of corresponding bark has been removed.

**inlet** /'ɪnlət/, *n.;* /ɪn'lɛt/, *v.*, **-let, -letting.** –*n.* **1.** an indentation of a shore line, usu. long and narrow, or a narrow passage between islands. **2.** a place of admission; an entrance. **3.** something put in or inserted. –*v.t.* **4.** to put in; insert.

**inlet valve** /'– vælv/, *n.* →**induction valve.**

**inlier** /'ɪnlaɪə/, *n.* (in geology) an outcrop of a formation completely surrounded by younger strata.

**in limine** /ɪn 'lɪməni/, *adv. Law.* at the outset. [L]

**in-line** /'ɪn-laɪn/, *adj.* of or pertaining to an internal combustion engine in which the cylinders are arranged in one straight line rather than in horizontally-opposed or other configurations.

**in loc. cit.** /ɪn lɒk 'sɪt/, *adv.* in the place cited. [L *in locō citātō*]

**in loco** /ɪn 'loʊkoʊ/, *adv.* in place; in the proper place. [L]

**in loco parentis** /ɪn ˌloʊkoʊ pə'rɛntəs/, *adv.* in the place of a parent; replacing a parent. [L]

**inly** /'ɪnli/, *adv. Archaic.* **1.** inwardly. **2.** intimately; deeply; sincerely. [ME *inliche,* OE *inlīce,* from *inlic* inward]

**inlying** /'ɪnlaɪɪŋ/, *adj.* **1.** lying within. **2.** lying towards or close to a point regarded as central: *inlying suburbs.* **3.** (of ships, islands, etc.) near the coast.

**inmate** /'ɪnmeɪt/, *n.* **1.** one of those confined in a hospital, prison, etc. **2.** *Archaic.* one who dwells with another or others in the same house. [IN-[1] + MATE[1]]

**in medias res** /ɪn ˌmidiəs 'reɪs/, *adv.* in the middle of things: *Homer began his story in medias res.* [L]

**in mem.,** in memoriam.

**in memoriam** /ɪn mə'mɔriəm/, *adv.* in memory (of); to the memory (of); as a memorial (to). [L]

**inmesh** /ɪn'mɛʃ/, *v.t.* →**enmesh.**

**inmost** /'ɪnmoʊst/, *adj.* **1.** situated farthest within: *the inmost recesses of the forest.* **2.** most intimate: *one's inmost thoughts.* [ME; OE *innemest,* a double superl., from *inne* within + *-m-* + *-est* (superl. suffix). See IN-[1], -MOST]

**inn** /ɪn/, *n.* **1.** a small hotel that provides lodging, food, etc., for travellers and others: *a country inn.* **2.** *Brit.* a tavern. **3.** **a.** a house or place of residence for students (now only in names of buildings derived from such use): *the Inns of Court.* **b.** a legal society occupying such a house. [ME *inne,* OE *inn* house] – **innless,** *adj.*

**innards** /'ɪnədz/, *n.* the inward parts of the body; entrails; viscera. [alteration of INWARDS[1]]

**innate** /ɪn'eɪt/, *adj.* **1.** inborn; existing or as if existing in one from birth: *innate modesty.* **2.** inherent in the essential character of something. **3.** arising from the constitution of the mind, rather than acquired from experience: *innate ideas.* [late ME *innat,* from L *innātus,* pp., inborn] – **innately,** *adv.* – **innateness,** *n.*

**inner** /'ɪnə/, *adj.* **1.** situated farther within; interior: *an inner door.* **2.** more intimate, private, or secret: *the inner circle of his friends.* **3.** mental or spiritual: *the inner life.* **4.** not obvious; esoteric: *an inner meaning.* –*n.* **5.** the ring next surrounding the bull's-eye of a target. **6.** a shot that strikes this; the second highest score. [ME; OE *innera,* compar. of *inne* within. Cf. INMOST] – **innerness,** *n.*

**inner bar** /– 'ba/, *n. Law.* Queen's Counsel collectively.

**inner city** /– 'sɪti/, *n.* the central area of a city, esp. in the context of problems of overcrowding, poverty, etc.

**inner-directed** /'ɪnə-dərɛktəd/, *adj.* guided by one's own set of values rather than external pressures. – **inner-direction,** *n.*

**inner ear** /'ɪnər ɪə/, *n.* the section of the ear made up of the cochlea, the vestibule and the semicircular canals. Also, **internal ear.**

**inner man** /ɪnə 'mæn/, *n.* **1.** the soul; spiritual and intellectual aspect of a person. **2.** *Colloq.* the stomach or appetite.

**Inner Mongolia** /ɪnə mɒŋ'goʊliə/, *n.* the Inner Mongolian Autonomous Region of China. See **Mongolia.**

**innermost** /'ɪnəmoʊst/, *adj.* **1.** farthest inwards; inmost. –*n.* **2.** innermost part. [ME, from INNER + -MOST]

**innersole** /'ɪnəsoʊl/, *n.* →**insole.**

**inner space** /ɪnə 'speɪs/, *n.* **1.** the regions between the earth and outer space. **2.** the part of the mind or personality that is not normally perceived consciously.

**inner tube** /– 'tjub/, *n.* an inflatable, airtight rubber tube which fits inside the outer cover of a pneumatic tyre.

**innervate** /'ɪnəveɪt/, *v.t.*, **-vated, -vating. 1.** to communicate nervous energy to; stimulate through nerves. **2.** to grow nerves into. [IN-[2] + NERVE + -ATE[1]]

**innervation** /ɪnə'veɪʃən/, *n.* **1.** the act of innervating. **2.** the state of being innervated. **3.** *Anat.* the disposition of nerves in a body or some part of it.

**innerve** /ɪ'nɜv/, *v.t.*, **-nerved, -nerving.** to supply with nervous energy; invigorate; animate.

**inning** /'ɪnɪŋ/, *n.* **1.** reclaiming, as of marsh or flooded land. **2.** (*usu. pl.*) land reclaimed from the sea, etc. **3.** enclosure, as of waste land. **4.** harvesting, as of crops. **5.** *Baseball.* a round in which both teams bat, with each side getting three outs. **6.** *U.S.* →**innings** (defs 2, 3). [ME *inninge,* OE *innung* a putting in]

**innings** /'ɪnɪŋz/, *n.pl.* (*construed as sing.*) **1.** *Cricket.* **a.** the turn of any one member of the batting team to bat. **b.** one of the major divisions of a match, consisting of the turns at batting of all the members of one team until they are all out or until the team declares. **c.** the runs scored during such a turn or such a division. **2.** a similar opportunity to score in certain other games. **3.** any opportunity for some activity; a turn. **4.** land reclaimed from the sea, etc.; inning. **5. have had a good innings,** *Colloq.* to have had a long life or long and successful career.

**innkeeper** /'ɪnkipə/, *n.* the keeper of an inn. Also, *Rare,* **innholder** /'ɪnhoʊldə/.

**innocence** /'ɪnəsəns/, *n.* **1.** the state or fact of being innocent; freedom from sin or moral wrong. **2.** freedom from legal or specific wrong; guiltlessness: *the prisoner proved his innocence.* **3.** simplicity or guilelessness. **4.** chastity. **5.** lack of knowledge or sense. **6.** harmlessness or innocuousness. **7.** an innocent person or thing. Also, *Obs.,* **innocency.**

**innocent** /'ɪnəsənt/, *adj.* **1.** free from any moral wrong; not tainted with sin; pure: *innocent children.* **2.** free from legal or specific wrong; guiltless: *to be innocent of crime.* **3.** not involving evil intent or motive: *an innocent misrepresentation.* **4.** free from any quality that can cause physical or moral injury; harmless: *innocent fun.* **5.** devoid (fol. by *of*): *a law innocent of merit.* **6.** having or showing the simplicity or naivety of an unworldly person: *she looks so innocent.* –*n.* **7.** an innocent person. **8.** a young child. **9.** a guileless person. **10.** a simpleton or idiot. [ME, from L *innocens* harmless] – **innocently,** *adv.*

**innocuous** /ɪn'ɒkjuəs/, *adj.* not harmful or injurious; harmless. [L *innocuus*] – **innocuously,** *adv.* – **innocuousness,** *n.*

**innominate** /ɪ'nɒmənət/, *adj.* having no name; anonymous. [LL *innominātus* unnamed]

**innominate bone** /'– boʊn/, *n.* either of the two bones forming the sides of the pelvis, each consisting of three consolidated bones, known as ilium, ischium, and pubis.

**innovate** /'ɪnəveɪt/, *v.*, **-vated, -vating.** –*v.i.* **1.** to bring in something new; make changes in anything established (fol. by *on* or *in*). –*v.t.* **2.** to bring in (something new) for the first time. [L *innovātus,* pp., renewed, altered] – **innovative, innovatory,** *adj.* – **innovator,** *n.*

**innovation** /ɪnə'veɪʃən/, *n.* **1.** something new or different introduced. **2.** the act of innovating; introducing of new things or methods. – **innovational,** *adj.* – **innovationist,** *n.*

**innoxious** /ɪ'nɒkʃəs/, *adj.* harmless; innocuous. – **innoxiously,** *adv.* – **innoxiousness,** *n.*

**innuendo** /ɪnju'ɛndoʊ/, *n., pl.* **-dos, -does. 1.** an indirect intimation about a person or thing, esp. of a derogatory nature. **2.** *Law.* **a.** a parenthetic explanation or specification in a pleading. **b.** (in an action for slander or libel) the explanation and elucidation of the words alleged to be defamatory. **c.** the word or expression thus explained. [L: intimation, abl. gerund of *innuere* give a nod, intimate]

**innumerable** /ɪ'njumərəbəl, ɪ'njumrəbəl/, *adj.* **1.** very numerous. **2.** incapable of being numbered or definitely counted. Also, **innumerous.** – **innumerableness, innumerability** /ɪˌnjumərə'bɪləti/, *n.* – **innumerably,** *adv.*

**innumerate** /ɪ'njumərət/, *adj.* **1.** unacquainted with the basic principles of mathematics. **2.** displaying mathematical incapacity or ineptitude. – **innumeracy,** *n.*

**innutrition** /ɪnju'trɪʃən/, *n.* lack of nutrition. – **innutritious,** *adj.*

**inobservance** /ɪnəb'zɜvəns/, *n.* **1.** lack of observance or noticing; inattention: *drowsy inobservance.* **2.** non-observance. – **inobservant,** *adj.*

**inoccupation** /ˌɪnɒkju'peɪʃən/, *n.* lack of occupation.

**inoculable** /ɪ'nɒkjuləbəl/, *adj.* capable of being inoculated. – **inoculability** /ɪnɒkjulə'bɪləti/, *n.*

**inoculant** /ɪn'ɒkjulənt/, *n.* an inoculating substance.

**inoculate** /ɪ'nɒkjuleɪt/, *v.*, **-lated, -lating,** *n.* –*v.t.* **1.** to implant (a disease) in a person or animal by the introduction of germs or virus, as through a puncture, in order to produce a mild form of the disease and thus secure immunity. **2.** to impregnate (a person or animal) thus. **3.** to introduce (micro-organisms) into surroundings suited to their growth, esp. into the body. **4.** to imbue (a person, etc.), as with ideas. **5.** *Agric.* to introduce rhizobium bacteria to a seed before sowing, to promote germination and growth. –*v.i.* **6.** to perform inoculation. –*n.* **7.** a substance to be inoculated. [late ME, from L *inoculātus,* pp., grafted, implanted] – **inoculative,** *adj.* – **inoculator,** *n.*

**inoculation** /ɪˌnɒkju'leɪʃən/, *n.* **1.** the act of inoculating. **2.** the substance inoculated.

**inoculum** /ɪ'nɒkjuləm/, *n.* the substance used to make an inoculation. [NL]

**inodorous** /ɪn'oʊdərəs/, *adj.* not odorous; odourless; having no smell. – **inodorously,** *adj.* – **inodorousness,** *n.*

**in-off** /'ɪn-ɒf/, *n.* (in billiards) a ball that strikes another ball and then goes into a pocket.

**inoffensive** /ɪnə'fɛnsɪv/, *adj.* **1.** doing no harm; harmless; unoffending: *a mild, inoffensive man.* **2.** not objectionable, or not being a cause of offence. – **inoffensively,** *adv.* – **inoffensiveness,** *n.*

**inofficious** /ɪnə'fɪʃəs/, *adj. Law.* not in accordance with moral duty: *an inofficious testament or will* (one disposing of property contrary to the dictates of natural affection or to just expectations). [L *inofficiōsus.* See IN-[3], OFFICIOUS] – **inofficiously,** *adv.* – **inofficiousness,** *n.*

**inoperable** /ɪn'ɒpərəbəl, -'ɒprə-/, *adj.* **1.** not operable. **2.** not admitting of a surgical operation without risk.

**inoperative** /ɪn'ɒpərətɪv, -'ɒprə-/, *adj.* **1.** not operative; not in operation. **2.** without effect: *inoperative remedies.* – **inoperativeness,** *n.*

**inopportune** /ɪn'ɒpətʃun/, *adj.* not opportune; inappropriate; (with regard to time) unseasonable: *an inopportune visit.* – **inopportunely,** *adv.* – **inopportuneness, inopportunity** /ˌɪnɒpə'tjunəti/, *n.*

**inordinate** /ɪn'ɔdənət/, *adj.* **1.** not within proper limits; excessive: *inordinate demands.* **2.** disorderly. **3.** unrestrained in conduct, etc. **4.** irregular: *inordinate hours.* [ME *inordinat,* from L *inordinātus* disordered] – **inordinacy, inordinateness,** *n.* – **inordinately,** *adv.*

**inorganic** /'ɪnɔgænɪk/, *adj.* **1.** not having the organisation which characterises living bodies. **2.** not characterised by vital processes. **3.** *Chem.* denoting or pertaining to compounds not containing carbon, excepting cyanides and carbonates. Cf. **organic** (def. 1). **4.** not fundamental; extraneous. – **inorganically,** *adv.*

**inorganic chemistry** /– 'kɛməstri/, *n.* the branch of chemistry which makes a study of inorganic substances.

**inosculate** /ɪn'ɒskjuleɪt/, *v.*, **-lated, -lating.** *–v.t.* **1.** to unite by openings, as arteries in anastomosis. **2.** to connect or join so as to make continuous, as fibres. *–v.i.* **3.** to open into one another. **4.** to unite intimately. [IN-[2] + LL *osculātus,* pp., supplied with a mouth or outlet] – **inosculation** /ɪˌnɒskju'leɪʃən/, *n.*

**inositol** /ɪn'oʊsətɒl/, *n.* a sweet crystalline substance, $C_6H_6(OH)_6$, first found in heart muscle, but widely distributed in plants and seeds as phytin, and also occurring in animal tissue and in urine. [*in-,* combining form representing Gk *ís* fibre, + -OS(E)[2] + -IT(E)[1] + -OL[1]]

**in-patient** /'ɪn-peɪʃənt/, *n.* a patient who is lodged and fed as well as treated in a hospital.

**in perpetuum** /ɪn pɜ'pɛtʃuəm/, *adv.* for ever. [L]

**in personam** /ɪn pɜ'soʊnəm/, *adv.* against a person, as a legal proceeding (contrasted with *in rem*). [L]

**input** /'ɪnpʊt/, *n.* **1.** that which is put in. **2.** the current or voltage fed to an electrical machine, circuit, or device. **3.** *Computers.* information which is fed into a computer before it performs a computation.

**input/output** /ɪnpʊt/'aʊtpʊt/, *n.* the section of the system which controls the passage of information into and out of a computer. *Abbrev.:* I/O

**input-output analysis** /ɪnpʊt-'aʊtpʊt əˌnæləsəs/, *n.* the analysis of the results of electronic data processing.

**inquest** /'ɪnkwɛst/, *n.* **1.** a legal or judicial inquiry, esp. before a jury. **2.** one made by a coroner (**coroner's inquest**). **3.** the body of men appointed to hold such an inquiry, esp. a coroner's jury. **4.** their decision or finding. **5.** *Colloq.* an inquiry into the reasons for the failure of a project, etc. [ME *enqueste,* from OF, from L *inquīsīta* (*rēs*) (a thing) inquired into, properly pp. fem.]

**inquietude** /ɪn'kwaɪətjud/, *n.* **1.** restlessness; uneasiness. **2.** (*pl.*) disquieting thoughts.

**inquiline** /'ɪnkwəlaɪn/, *n.* **1.** *Zool.* an animal that lives in an abode properly belonging to another; a guest. *–adj.* **2.** of the nature of an inquiline. [L *inquilīnus*] – **inquilinity** /ɪnkwə'lɪnəti/, *n.* – **inquilinous** /ɪnkwə'laɪnəs/, *adj.*

**inquire** /ɪn'kwaɪə/, *v.*, **-quired, -quiring.** *–v.i.* **1.** to make investigation (fol. by *into*). **2.** *Chiefly U.S.* →**enquire.** *–v.t.* **3.** →**enquire.** [L *inquīrere,* replacing ME *enquere,* from OF] – **inquirer,** *n.*

**inquiring** /ɪn'kwaɪərɪŋ/, *adj.* **1.** given to inquiry or research; seeking information or knowledge: *an inquiring mind.* **2.** questioning; curious: *an inquiring look.*

**inquiry** /ɪn'kwaɪəri/, *n., pl.* **-ries. 1.** an investigation, as into a matter. **2.** the act of inquiring, or seeking information by questioning; interrogation. **3.** →**enquiry.** Also, **enquiry.**

**inquisition** /ɪnkwə'zɪʃən/, *n.* **1.** the act of inquiring; inquiry; research. **2.** an investigation, or process of inquiry. **3.** an inquiry conducted by judicial officers or such non-judicial officers as coroners. **4.** the finding of such an inquiry. **5.** the document embodying the result of such inquiry. **6.** (*cap.*) *Rom. Cath. Ch.* a special tribunal for the defence of Catholic teaching in faith and morals, the judgment of heresy, the application of canonical punishment, and the judgment of mixed marriages and the Pauline privileges. [ME *inquisicion,* from L *inquīsītio* a searching into] – **inquisitional,** *adj.*

**inquisitionist** /ɪnkwə'zɪʃənəst/, *n.* →**inquisitor.**

**inquisitive** /ɪn'kwɪzətɪv/, *adj.* **1.** unduly curious; prying. **2.** inquiring; desirous of or eager for knowledge. *–n.* **3.** an inquisitive person. – **inquisitively,** *adv.* – **inquisitiveness,** *n.*

**inquisitor** /ɪn'kwɪzətə/, *n.* **1.** one who makes inquisition. **2.** a questioner, esp. an inquisitive one. **3.** one who investigates by virtue of his office. **4.** a member of the Inquisition. – **inquisitress,** *n. fem.*

**inquisitorial** /ɪnˌkwɪzə'tɔriəl/, *adj.* **1.** pertaining to an inquisitor or inquisitors, or to inquisition. **2.** exercising the office of an inquisitor. **3.** *Law.* pertaining to a trial with one person or group acting as prosecutor and judge, or to secret criminal prosecutions. **4.** resembling an inquisitor. **5.** inquisitive. – **inquisitorially,** *adv.* – **inquisitorialness,** *n.*

**in rem** /ɪn 'rɛm/, *adv.* against a thing, as a legal proceeding for its recovery (contrasted with *in personam*). [L]

**in rerum natura** /ɪn ˌrɛərəm næ'tjurə/, *adv.* in the nature of things. [L]

**inroad** /'ɪnroʊd/, *n.* **1.** forcible or serious encroachment: *inroads on our savings.* **2.** a hostile or predatory incursion; a raid; a foray.

**inrush** /'ɪnrʌʃ/, *n.* a rushing in; an influx. – **inrushing,** *n., adj.*

**ins,** inches.

**insalivate** /ɪn'sæləveɪt/, *v.t.*, **-vated, -vating.** to mix with saliva, as food. – **insalivation** /ɪnˌsælə'veɪʃən/, *n.*

**insalubrious** /ɪnsə'lubriəs/, *adj.* **1.** unfavourable to health. **2.** unsavoury; squalid: *the more insalubrious suburbs of Melbourne.* – **insalubriously,** *adv.* – **insalubrity,** *n.*

**insane** /ɪn'seɪn/, *adj.* **1.** not sane; not of sound mind; mentally deranged. **2.** characteristic of one mentally deranged. **3.** set apart for the care and confinement of mentally deranged persons: *an insane asylum.* **4.** utterly senseless: *an insane attempt.* **5.** *Colloq.* fantastic; wonderful. – **insaneness,** *n.*

**insanitary** /ɪn'sænətəri, -tri/, *adj.* not sanitary; unclean and likely to carry infection: *insanitary houses.* – **insanitariness,** *n.*

**insanitation** /ɪnˌsænə'teɪʃən/, *n.* lack of sanitation or sanitary regulation; insanitary condition.

**insanity** /ɪn'sænəti/, *n., pl.* **-ties. 1.** the condition of being insane; more or less permanent derangement of one or more psychical functions, due to disease of the mind. **2.** *Law.* such unsoundness of mind as affects legal responsibility or capacity. **3.** extreme folly.

**insatiable** /ɪn'seɪʃəbəl/, *adj.* not satiable; incapable of being satisfied: *insatiable desire.* – **insatiability** /ɪnˌseɪʃə'bɪləti/, **insatiableness,** *n.* – **insatiably,** *adv.*

**insatiate** /ɪn'seɪʃiət/, *adj.* insatiable: *insatiate greed.* – **insatiately,** *adv.* – **insatiateness,** *n.*

**inscape** /'ɪnskeɪp/, *n.* the essential inner nature of a thing, person, emotion, etc. [IN-[1] + (LAND)SCAPE, coined by Gerard Manley Hopkins, 1844-89, English poet]

**inscribe** /ɪn'skraɪb/, *v.t.*, **-scribed, -scribing. 1.** to write or engrave (words, characters, etc.). **2.** to mark (a surface) with words, characters, etc., esp. in a durable or conspicuous way. **3.** to address or dedicate (a book, photograph, etc.) informally, esp. by a handwritten note. **4.** to enrol, as on an official list. **5.** *Obs.* **a.** to record or register the names of purchasers of (stocks, etc.). **b.** to issue (stock) without certificates, the names of the stockholders being written in a register. **6.** *Geom.* to draw or delineate (one figure) within another figure so that the inner lies in the boundary of the outer at as many points as possible. [L *inscrībere* write in or upon] – **inscribable,** *adj.* – **inscriber,** *n.*

**inscription** /ɪn'skrɪpʃən/, *n.* **1.** something inscribed. **2.** a brief, more or less informal dedication, as of a book or a work of art. **3.** a note inscribed in a book, usu. signed. **4.** *Archaeol.* a historical, religious, or other record cut, impressed, painted, or written on stone, brick, metal, or other hard surface. **5.** the act of inscribing. **6.** *Obs.* an inscribing of issued securities. [ME, from L *inscriptio*] – **inscriptional,** *adj.* – **inscriptionless,** *adj.*

**inscriptive** /ɪns'krɪptɪv/, *adj.* pertaining to or of the nature of an inscription. – **inscriptively,** *adv.*

**inscroll** /ɪn'skroʊl/, *v.t.* to write on a scroll.

**inscrutable** /ɪn'skrutəbəl/, *adj.* **1.** incapable of being searched into or scrutinised; impenetrable to investigation. **2.** not easily understood; mysterious; enigmatic. **3.** impenetrable or unfathomable physically. [late ME, from LL *inscrūtābilis*] – **inscrutability** /ɪnˌskrutə'bɪləti/, **inscrutableness,** *n.* – **inscrutably,** *adv.*

**insect** /'ɪnsɛkt/, *n.* **1.** *Zool.* any animal of the subphylum or class Insecta, a group of small, air-breathing arthropods characterised by a body clearly divided into three parts, head, thorax, and abdomen, and by having only three pairs of legs, and usu. hav-

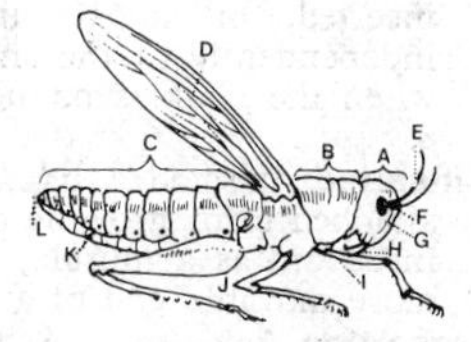

insect (grasshopper): A, head; B, thorax; C, abdomen; D, wings; E, antenna; F, simple eye; G, compound eye; H, palpus; I, leg; J, ear; K, spiracle; L, ovipositor

ing two pairs of wings. **2.** any small, air-breathing arthropod, such as a spider, tick, or centipede, having superficial, general similarity to the Insecta. **3.** *Colloq.* a contemptible person. *–adj.* **4.** of, pertaining to, or like an insect. **5.** *Colloq.* contemptible. [L *insectum* (so-called from the segmented form), properly neut. of *insectus,* pp., cut in or up] – **insect-like,** *adj.*

**insectarium** /ɪnsɛk'tɛəriəm/, *n., pl.* **-tariums, -taria.** a place in which a collection of living insects is kept, as in a zoo. [NL]

**insectary** /ɪn'sɛktəri/, *n., pl.* **-ries.** a laboratory for the study of live insects, their life histories, effects on plants, reaction to insecticides, etc.

**insecticide** /ɪn'sɛktəsaɪd/, *n.* **1.** a substance or preparation used for killing insects. **2.** the killing of insects. [L *insectum* + -I- + -CIDE] – **insecticidal** /ɪn,sɛktə'saɪdl/, *adj.*

**insectivore** /ɪn'sɛktəvɔ/, *n.* **1.** an insectivorous animal. **2.** any of the Insectivora, the mammalian order that includes the moles, the shrews, and the hedgehogs. [NL *insectivorus,* from L *insectum* insect + *-i-* -I- + *-vorus* devouring]

**insectivorous** /ɪnsɛk'tɪvərəs/, *adj.* adapted to feeding on insects, as shrews, moles, hedgehogs, etc.

**insecure** /ɪnsə'kjuə/, *adj.* **1.** exposed to danger; unsafe. **2.** not firm or safe: *insecure foundations.* **3.** not free from fear, doubt, etc. – **insecurely,** *adv.*

**insecurity** /ɪnsə'kjurəti/, *n., pl.* **-ties. 1.** unsafe condition; lack of assurance or sureness; uncertainty; instability. **2.** something insecure.

**inseminate** /ɪn'sɛməneɪt/, *v.t.,* **-nated, -nating. 1.** to sow; inject seed into. **2.** to introduce semen into (a female) to cause fertilisation; impregnate. **3.** to sow as seed in something; implant. [L *insēminātus,* pp., sown, planted in] – **insemination** /ɪn,sɛmə'neɪʃən/, *n.*

**insensate** /ɪn'sɛnseɪt, -sət/, *adj.* **1.** not endowed with sensation: *insensate stone.* **2.** without feeling; unfeeling. **3.** without sense, understanding, or judgment. – **insensately,** *adv.* – **insensateness,** *n.*

**insensibility** /ɪn,sɛnsə'bɪləti/, *n., pl.* **-ties. 1.** lack of physical sensibility; absence of feeling or sensation. **2.** lack of moral sensibility or susceptibility of emotion.

**insensible** /ɪn'sɛnsəbəl/, *adj.* **1.** incapable of feeling or perceiving; deprived of sensation; unconscious, as a person after a violent blow. **2.** without, or not subject to, a particular feeling: *insensible to shame.* **3.** unconscious, unaware, or unappreciative: *we are not insensible of your kindness.* **4.** not perceptible by the senses: *insensible transitions.* **5.** unresponsive in feeling. **6.** not susceptible of emotion or passion; void of any feeling. **7.** *Rare.* not endowed with feeling or sensation, as matter. – **insensibly,** *adv.*

**insensitive** /ɪn'sɛnsətɪv/, *adj.* **1.** not sensitive: *an insensitive skin.* **2.** not susceptible to agencies or influences: *insensitive to light.* **3.** deficient in sensibility or acuteness of feeling: *an insensitive nature.* – **insensitiveness, insensitivity** /ɪn,sɛnsə'tɪvəti/, *n.*

**insentient** /ɪn'sɛnʃiənt/, *adj.* without sensation or feeling; inanimate. – **insentience,** *n.*

**inseparable** /ɪn'sɛpərəbəl, -prə-/, *adj.* **1.** incapable of being separated, parted, or disjoined: *inseparable companions.* *–n.* (*usu. pl.*) **2.** something inseparable. **3.** an inseparable companion or friend. – **inseparability** /ɪn,sɛpərə'bɪləti/, **inseparableness,** *n.* – **inseparably,** *adv.*

**insert** /ɪn'sɜt/, *v.;* /'ɪnsɜt/, *n.* *–v.t.* **1.** to put or set in: *to insert a key in a lock.* **2.** to introduce into the body of something: *to insert an advertisement in a newspaper.* *–n.* **3.** something inserted, or to be inserted. **4.** an extra leaf printed independently of the sheets comprising a book but included when the book is bound. [L *insertus,* pp., put in] – **inserter,** *n.*

**inserted** /ɪn'sɜtəd/, *adj.* **1.** *Bot.* (esp. of the parts of a flower) attached to or growing out of some part. **2.** *Anat.* having an insertion, as a muscle, tendon, or ligament; attached, as the more movable end of a muscle.

**insertion** /ɪn'sɜʃən/, *n.* **1.** the act of inserting: *each insertion of an advertisement.* **2.** something inserted: *an insertion into a text.* **3.** *Bot., Zool., etc.* **a.** the manner or place of attachment, as of an organ. **b.** attachment of a part or organ, with special reference to the site or manner of such attachment. **4.** lace, embroidery, or the like, to be sewn at each edge between parts of other material.

**in-service** /'ɪn-sɜvəs/, *adj.* of or pertaining to any training undertaken in conjunction with the actual performance of the work involved, as courses in remedial reading techniques, creative drama, etc. for teachers.

**insessorial** /ɪnsɛ'sɔriəl/, *adj.* **1.** adapted for perching, as a bird's foot. **2.** habitually perching, as a bird. **3.** of or pertaining to birds that perch. [NL *Insessorēs* the perching birds (considered as an order), pl. of *insessor* (from *in* on + *sessor* sitter) + -IAL]

**inset** /'ɪnsɛt/, *n.;* /ɪn'sɛt/, *v.* **-set, -setting.** *–n.* **1.** something inserted; an insert. **2.** a smaller picture, map, etc., inserted within the border of a larger one. **3.** *Theat.* a small scene played within another for rapid scene-shifting. **4.** →**influx. 5.** the act of setting in. *–v.t.* **6.** to set in; insert. **7.** to insert as an inset. **8.** to insert an inset in.

**insheathe** /ɪn'ʃið/, *v.t.,* **-sheathed, -sheathing.** to enclose in or as in a sheath; sheathe.

**inshore** /'ɪnʃɔ, ɪn'ʃɔ/, *adj.;* /ɪn'ʃɔ/, *adv.* *–adj.* **1.** lying near the shore; operating close to the shore: *inshore fishing.* *–adv.* **2.** towards the shore: *they went closer inshore.*

**inshrine** /ɪn'ʃraɪn/, *v.t.,* **-shrined, -shrining.** →**enshrine.**

**inside** /ɪn'saɪd/, *prep., adv.;* /'ɪnsaɪd/, *n., adj.* *–prep.* **1.** on the inner side of; within: *inside the circle.* **2.** before the elapse of: *inside an hour.* *–adv.* **3.** in or into the inner part: *to go inside.* **4.** indoors: *he is working inside.* **5.** by nature; fundamentally: *inside, he's very kind.* **6.** *Colloq.* to or in prison. *–n.* **7.** the inner part; interior: *the inside of the house.* **8.** the inner side or surface: *the inside of the hand.* **9.** (*oft. pl.*) *Colloq.* the inward parts of the body, esp. the stomach and intestines. **10.** the inward nature. **11.** an inside passenger or place in a coach, etc. **12.** (*pl.*) internal thoughts or feelings, etc. **13.** the part of a curved track or course nearer to the centre of the curves; the inside lane: *a horse coming up fast on the inside; the inside of the bend.* **14.** an inner group of persons having private knowledge about a circumstance or case. **15.** *Soccer, etc.* Also, **inside forward.** an inside left or inside right. **16.** *Surfing.* the inner part of a breaking wave closest to the white water. **17. inside out, a.** with the inner side reversed to face outwards. **b.** thoroughly; completely: *he knows his job inside out.* *–adj.* **18.** situated or being on or in the inside; interior. **19.** acting, employed, done, or originating within a building or place: *the robbery was an inside job.* **20.** derived from the inner circle of those concerned in and having private knowledge of a case: *inside information.* **21.** running nearer to the centre and therefore shorter: *the inside lane of a track.*

**inside centre** /– 'sɛntə/, *n.* (in Rugby football) the player positioned between the five-eighth (def. 1a) and the outside centre; second five-eighth.

**inside job** /– 'dʒɒb/, *n. Colloq.* a crime committed by or with the assistance of someone who is a member of the group or organisation against which the crime is directed.

**inside left** /– 'lɛft/, *n.* (in soccer, hockey, etc.) a player in the forward line between centre-forward and outside left.

**insider** /ɪn'saɪdə/, *n.* **1.** one who is inside some place, society, etc. **2.** *Colloq.* one who is within a limited circle of persons who understand the actual facts of a case. **3.** *Colloq.* one who has some special advantage.

**inside right** /ɪnsaɪd 'raɪt/, *n.* (in soccer, hockey, etc.) a player in the forward line between centre-forward and outside right.

**insidious** /ɪn'sɪdiəs/, *adj.* **1.** intended to entrap or beguile: *an insidious design.* **2.** stealthily treacherous or deceitful: *an insidious enemy.* **3.** operating or proceeding inconspicuously but with grave effect: *an insidious disease.* [L *insidiōsus* cunning, artful] – **insidiously,** *adv.* – **insidiousness,** *n.*

**insight** /'ɪnsaɪt/, *n.* **1.** an understanding gained or given of something: *this little insight into the life of the village.* **2.** penetrating mental vision or discernment; faculty of seeing into inner character or underlying truth: *a man of great insight.* **3.** *Psychol.* **a.** the sudden grasping of a solution; configurational learning. **b.** the ability to see oneself as others see one; self-knowledge. **c.** *Psychiatry.* the capacity of a mental patient to know that he is suffering from mental disorder. [ME; from IN-[1] + SIGHT]

**insignia** /ɪn'sɪgniə/, *n.pl., sing.* **insigne** /-ni/. **1.** badges or distinguishing marks of office or honour: *military insignia.*

2. distinguishing marks or signs of anything: *insignia of mourning.* [L, pl. of *insigne* mark, badge, properly neut. of *insignis* distinguished by a mark]

**insignificance** /ɪnsɪgˈnɪfɪkəns/, *n.* the quality or condition of being insignificant; lack of significance.

**insignificancy** /ɪnsɪgˈnɪfɪkənsi/, *n., pl.* **-cies.** **1.** insignificance. **2.** an insignificant person or thing.

**insignificant** /ɪnsɪgˈnɪfɪkənt/, *adj.* **1.** unimportant, trifling, or petty, as things, matters, details, etc. **2.** too small to be important: *an insignificant sum.* **3.** of no consequence, influence, or distinction, as persons. **4.** without weight of character; contemptible: *an insignificant fellow.* **5.** without meaning; meaningless, as terms. *–n.* **6.** a word, thing, or person without significance. – **insignificantly,** *adv.*

**insignis pine** /ɪnˈsɪgnɪs paɪn/, *n.* →**radiata pine.**

**insincere** /ɪnsənˈsɪə, -sɪn-/, *adj.* not sincere; not honest in the expression of actual feeling. – **insincerely,** *adv.*

**insincerity** /ɪnsənˈsɛrəti, -sɪn-/, *n., pl.* **-ties.** the quality of being insincere; lack of sincerity; deceitfulness.

**insinuate** /ɪnˈsɪnjueɪt/, *v.,* **-ated, -ating.** *–v.t.* **1.** to suggest or hint slyly. **2.** instil or infuse subtly or artfully into the mind: *to insinuate doubt.* **3.** to bring or introduce into a position or relation by indirect or artful methods: *to insinuate oneself into the favour of another.* *–v.i.* **4.** to make insinuations. [L *insinuātus,* pp., brought in by windings or turnings] – **insinuatingly,** *adv.* – **insinuative,** *adj.* – **insinuator,** *n.*

**insinuation** /ɪnˌsɪnjuˈeɪʃən/, *n.* **1.** covert or artful suggestion or hinting, as of something not plainly stated. **2.** a suggestion or hint of this kind. **3.** subtle or artful instilment into the mind. **4.** the act of insinuating. **5.** ingratiation: *he made his way by flattery and insinuation.* **6.** the art or power of stealing into the affections and pleasing. **7.** an ingratiating act or speech.

**insipid** /ɪnˈsɪpəd/, *adj.* **1.** without distinctive, interesting, or attractive qualities: *an insipid tale.* **2.** without sufficient taste to be pleasing, as food or drink: *a rather insipid fruit.* [LL *insipidus* tasteless] – **insipidity** /ɪnsɪˈpɪdəti/, **insipidness,** *n.* – **insipidly,** *adv.*

**insipience** /ɪnˈsɪpiəns/, *n.* lack of wisdom; folly. [late ME, from L *insipientia*] – **insipient,** *adj.* – **insipiently,** *adv.*

**insist** /ɪnˈsɪst/, *v.i.* **1.** to be emphatic, firm, or pertinacious on some matter of desire, demand, intention, etc.: *he insisted on that privilege.* **2.** to lay emphasis in assertion: *to insist on the justice of a claim.* **3.** to assert or maintain positively. **4.** to dwell with earnestness or emphasis (fol. by *on* or *upon*): *to insist on a point in a discourse.* [L *insistere* insist, stand or press upon] – **insister,** *n.*

**insistence** /ɪnˈsɪstəns/, *n.* **1.** the act or fact of insisting. **2.** the quality of being insistent.

**insistency** /ɪnˈsɪstənsi/, *n., pl.* **-cies.** **1.** the quality of being insistent; insistence. **2.** that which is insistent.

**insistent** /ɪnˈsɪstənt/, *adj.* **1.** insisting; earnest or emphatic in dwelling upon, maintaining, or demanding something; persistent. **2.** compelling attention or notice: *an insistent tone.* – **insistently,** *adv.*

**in situ** /ɪn ˈsɪtʃu/, *adv.* in its original place. [L]

**insnare** /ɪnˈsnɛə/, *v.t.,* **-snared, -snaring.** →**ensnare.**

**insobriety** /ɪnsəˈbraɪəti/, *n.* lack of sobriety.

**insociable** /ɪnˈsoʊʃəbəl/, *adj.* →**unsociable.** – **insociability** /ɪnˌsoʊʃəˈbɪləti/, *n.* – **insociably,** *adv.*

**in so far,** *conj.* to such an extent (usu. fol. by *as*). Also, *Chiefly U.S.,* **insofar,** *adv.*

**insolate** /ˈɪnsəleɪt/, *v.t.,* **-lated, -lating.** to expose to the sun's rays; treat by exposure to the sun's rays. [L *insōlātus,* pp., placed in the sun]

**insolation** /ɪnsəˈleɪʃən/, *n.* **1.** exposure to the sun's rays, specifically as a process of treatment. **2.** *Pathol.* sunstroke. **3.** *Meteorol.* solar radiation received on a given body or over a given area. [LL *insōlātio*]

**insole** /ˈɪnsoʊl/, *n.* **1.** the inner sole of a shoe or boot. **2.** a thickness of warm or waterproof material laid as an inner sole within a shoe. Also, **innersole.**

**insolence** /ˈɪnsələns/, *n.* **1.** insolent behaviour or speech. **2.** the quality of being insolent.

**insolent** /ˈɪnsələnt/, *adj.* **1.** boldly rude or disrespectful; contemptuously impertinent; insulting: *an insolent reply.* *–n.* **2.** an insolent person. [ME, from L *insolens* unaccustomed, unusual, excessive, arrogant] – **insolently,** *adv.*

**insoluble** /ɪnˈsɒljubəl/, *adj.* **1.** incapable of being dissolved: *insoluble salts.* **2.** that cannot be solved: *an insoluble problem.* [ME, from L *insolūbilis*] – **insolubility** /ɪnˌsɒljuˈbɪləti/, **insolubleness,** *n.* – **insolubly,** *adv.*

**insolvable** /ɪnˈsɒlvəbəl/, *adj.* incapable of being solved or explained: *an insolvable problem.* – **insolvability** /ɪnˌsɒlvəˈbɪləti/, *n.* – **insolvably,** *adv.*

**insolvency** /ɪnˈsɒlvənsi/, *n.* the condition of being insolvent; bankruptcy.

**insolvent** /ɪnˈsɒlvənt/, *Law.* *–adj.* **1.** not solvent; unable to satisfy creditors or discharge liabilities, either because liabilities exceed assets or because of inability to pay debts as they mature. **2.** pertaining to bankrupt persons or bankruptcy. *–n.* **3.** one who is insolvent.

**insomnia** /ɪnˈsɒmniə/, *n.* inability to sleep, esp. when chronic; sleeplessness. [L] – **insomnious,** *adj.*

**insomniac** /ɪnˈsɒmniæk/, *n.* **1.** one who suffers from insomnia. *–adj.* **2.** suffering from insomnia. **3.** of, pertaining to, or causing insomnia.

**in so much,** *conj.* **1.** to such an extent or degree (*that*); so (*that*). **2.** →**inasmuch** (*as*). Also, *Chiefly U.S.,* **insomuch,** *adv.*

**insouciance** /ɪnˈsusiəns, -sjəns/, *n.* the quality of being insouciant. [F, from *insouciant* INSOUCIANT]

**insouciant** /ɪnˈsusiənt, -sjənt/, *adj.* free from concern; without anxiety; carefree. [F, from *soucier* care, from L *sollicitāre*] – **insouciantly,** *adv.*

**Insp.,** Inspector.

**inspect** /ɪnˈspɛkt/, *v.t.* **1.** to look carefully at or over; view closely and critically: *to inspect every part.* **2.** to view or examine formally or officially: *to inspect troops.* [L *inspectus,* pp.]

**inspection** /ɪnˈspɛkʃən/, *n.* **1.** inspecting, esp. careful or critical inspecting or viewing. **2.** formal or official viewing or examination: *an inspection of the troops.* [ME, from L *inspectio*] – **inspectional,** *adj.*

**inspective** /ɪnˈspɛktɪv/, *adj.* **1.** given to making inspection. **2.** pertaining to inspection.

**inspector** /ɪnˈspɛktə/, *n.* **1.** one who inspects. **2.** an officer appointed to inspect. **3.** one who makes assessments for taxation purposes: *an inspector of taxes.* **4.** a police officer ranking above sergeant and below chief inspector. **5.** the rank of any of these. [L] – **inspectoral, inspectorial** /ɪnspɛkˈtɔriəl/, *adj.* – **inspectorship,** *n.*

**inspectorate** /ɪnˈspɛktərət/, *n.* **1.** the office or function of an inspector. **2.** a body of inspectors. **3.** a district under an inspector.

**inspirable** /ɪnˈspaɪərəbəl/, *adj.* capable of being inspired.

**inspiration** /ɪnspəˈreɪʃən/, *n.* **1.** an inspiring or animating action or influence: *I cannot write without inspiration.* **2.** something inspired, as a thought. **3.** a result of inspired activity. **4.** a thing or person that inspires. **5.** *Theol.* **a.** a divine influence directly and immediately exerted upon the mind or soul of a man. **b.** the divine quality of the writings or words of men so influenced. **6.** the drawing of air into the lungs; inhalation. **7.** the act of inspiring. **8.** the state of being inspired.

**inspirational** /ɪnspəˈreɪʃənəl/, *adj.* **1.** imparting inspiration. **2.** under the influence of inspiration; inspired. **3.** of or pertaining to inspiration. – **inspirationally,** *adv.*

**inspiratory** /ɪnˈspɪrətri/, *adj.* pertaining to inspiration or inhalation.

**inspire** /ɪnˈspaɪə/, *v.,* **-spired, -spiring.** *–v.t.* **1.** to infuse an animating, quickening, or exalting influence into: *his courage inspired his followers.* **2.** to produce or arouse (a feeling, thought, etc.): *to inspire confidence in others.* **3.** to affect with a specified feeling, thought, etc.: *inspire a person with distrust.* **4.** to influence or impel: *opposition inspired him to a greater effort.* **5.** to animate, as an influence, feeling, thought, or the like does: *inspired by a belief in a better future.* **6.** to communicate or suggest by a divine or supernatural influence: *writings inspired by God.* **7.** to guide or control by divine influence. **8.** to prompt or instigate (utterances, etc.) by influence without avowal of responsibility. **9.** to give rise to, occasion, or cause. **10.** to take (air, gases, etc.) into the lungs in breathing; inhale. **11.** *Archaic.* to infuse (breath, life, etc. *into*) by breathing. **12.** *Archaic.* to breathe into or upon. *–v.i.* **13.** to give inspiration. **14.** to inhale. [ME *inspire(n)*, from L *inspīrāre* breathe into] **– inspirer,** *n.* **– inspiringly,** *adv.*

**inspirit** /ɪn'spɪrət/, *v.t.* to infuse (new) spirit or life into. **– inspiritingly,** *adv.*

**inspissate** /ɪn'spɪseɪt/, *v.* **-sated, -sating.** *–v.t.* **1.** to thicken, as by evaporation; make dense. *–v.i.* **2.** to become dense. [LL *inspissātus*, pp.] **– inspissation** /ɪnspɪs'eɪʃən/, *n.*

**inst.,** **1.** instant (def. 5). **2.** (*also cap.*) institute. **3.** (*also cap.*) institution. **4.** instrumental.

**instability** /ɪnstə'bɪləti/, *n.* the state of being instable; lack of stability or firmness.

**instable** /ɪn'steɪbəl/, *adj.* not stable; unstable.

**install** /ɪn'stɔl/, *v.t.* **1.** to place in position for service or use, as a system of electric lighting, etc. **2.** to establish in any office, position, or place. **3.** to induct into an office, etc., with ceremonies or formalities, as by seating in a stall or official seat. [ML *installāre.* See IN-[2], STALL[1]] **– installer,** *n.*

**installation** /ɪnstə'leɪʃən/, *n.* **1.** something installed. **2.** a system of machinery or apparatus placed in position for use. **3.** the act of installing. **4.** the fact of being installed. **5.** *Mil.* a military facility comprising an area or a number of buildings, containing soldiers or equipment. [ML *installātio*]

**instalment**[1] /ɪn'stɔlmənt/, *n.* **1.** any of several parts into which a debt or other sum payable is divided for payment at successive fixed times: *to pay for furniture by instalments.* **2.** a single portion of something furnished or issued by parts at successive times: *a serial in six instalments.* Also, *U.S.,* **installment.** [IN-[2] + obs. *stalment* instalment (from *stall*, v., arrange payment)]

**instalment**[2] /ɪn'stɔlmənt/, *n.* **1.** the act of installing. **2.** the fact of being installed; installation. Also, *U.S.,* **installment.** [INSTALL + -MENT]

**instamatic** /ɪnstə'mætɪk/, *n.* a small, simple camera with a cartridge loading system.

**instance** /'ɪnstəns/, *n., v.,* **-stanced, -stancing.** *–n.* **1.** a case of anything: *fresh instances of oppression.* **2.** an example put forth in proof or illustration: *an instance of carelessness.* **3.** legal process (now chiefly in certain expressions): *a court of first instance.* **4.** *Archaic.* urgency. **5. at the instance of,** at the urgency, solicitation, instigation, or suggestion of. **6. for instance,** for example; as an example. **7. give (someone) a for instance,** *Colloq.* to give (someone) an example. *–v.t.* **8.** to cite as an instance or example. **9.** *Rare.* to exemplify by an instance. *–v.i.* **10.** *Rare.* to cite an instance. [ME *instaunce*, from AF, from L *instantia* presence, urgency]

**instancy** /'ɪnstənsi/, *n.* **1.** the quality of being instant; urgency; pressing nature. **2.** *Rare.* immediateness.

**instant** /'ɪnstənt/, *n.* **1.** an infinitesimal or very short space of time; a moment: *not an instant too soon.* **2.** the point of time now present, or present with reference to some action or event. **3.** a particular moment: *at the instant of contact.* *–adj.* **4.** succeeding without any interval of time; immediate: *instant relief.* **5.** present; current (now used elliptically): *the 10th instant* (the tenth day of the present month). **6.** pressing or urgent: *instant need.* **7.** (of a foodstuff) processed for immediate and simple preparation, as by adding water: *instant coffee.* [late ME, from L *instans*, ppr., standing upon, insisting, being at hand]

**instantaneity** /ɪn,stæntə'niəti/, *n.* the quality or fact of being instantaneous; instantaneousness.

**instantaneous** /ɪnstən'teɪniəs/, *adj.* **1.** occurring, done, or completed in an instant: *an instantaneous explosion.* **2.** existing at or pertaining to a particular instant: *the instantaneous position of something.* **– instantaneously,** *adv.*

**instantaneous frequency** /– 'frikwənsi/, *n.* the rate of change of phase of an oscillation, expressed in radians per second divided by $2\pi$.

**instanter** /ɪn'stæntə/, *adv.* →**instantly.** [L: urgently]

**instantly** /'ɪnstəntli/, *adv.* **1.** immediately; at once. **2.** *Archaic.* urgently.

**instant replay** /ɪnstənt 'ripleɪ/, *n.* a replay shown on television immediately after a sporting event or highlight, often in slow motion.

**instar** /'ɪnsta/, *n.* an insect in any one of its periods of post-embryonic growth between moults. [L: form, likeness]

**instate** /ɪn'steɪt/, *v.t.,* **-stated, -stating.** to put into a certain state, condition, or position; install. **– instatement,** *n.*

**in statu quo** /ɪn ,stætʃu 'kwoʊ/, in the state in which (anything was or is). [L]

**instauration** /ɪnstɔ'reɪʃən/, *n.* renewal; restoration; renovation; repair. [L *instaurātio*]

**instead** /ɪn'stɛd/, *adv.* **1.** in the stead or place; in lieu (fol. by *of*): *come by plane instead of by train.* **2.** in one's (its, their, etc.) stead: *she sent the boy instead.* [orig. two words, *in stead* in place]

**instep** /'ɪnstɛp/, *n.* **1.** the arched upper surface of the human foot between the toes and the ankle. **2.** the part of a shoe, stocking, etc., over the instep. **3.** the front of the hind leg of a horse, etc., between the hock and the pastern joint; cannon. [apparently from IN-[1] + STEP]

**instigate** /'ɪnstəgeɪt/, *v.t.,* **-gated, -gating.** **1.** to spur on, set on, or incite to some action or course: *to instigate someone to commit a crime.* **2.** to bring about by incitement; foment: *to instigate a quarrel.* [L *instīgātus*, pp.] **– instigative,** *adj.* **– instigator,** *n.*

**instigation** /ɪnstə'geɪʃən/, *n.* **1.** the act of instigating. **2.** an incentive. [late ME, from L *instīgātio*]

**instil** /ɪn'stɪl/, *v.t.,* **-stilled, -stilling.** **1.** to infuse slowly or by degrees into the mind or feelings; insinuate; inject: *courtesy must be instilled in childhood.* **2.** to put in drop by drop. Also, *Chiefly U.S.,* **instill.** [L *instillāre* pour in by drops] **– instiller,** *n.* **– instilment,** *n.*

**instillation** /ɪnstɪ'leɪʃən/, *n.* **1.** the act of instilling. **2.** something instilled.

**instinct**[1] /'ɪnstɪŋkt/, *n.* **1.** *Sociol., Psychol., etc.* an inborn pattern of activity and response common to a given biological stock. **2.** innate impulse or natural inclination, or a particular natural inclination or tendency. **3.** a natural aptitude or gift for something: *an instinct for art.* **4.** natural intuitive power. [late ME, from L *instinctus*, n., instigation, impulse]

**instinct**[2] /ɪn'stɪŋkt/, *adj.* urged or animated from within; infused or filled with some active principle (fol. by *with*). [L *instinctus*, pp., instigated, impelled]

**instinctive** /ɪn'stɪŋktɪv/, *adj.* **1.** pertaining to or of the nature of instinct. **2.** prompted by or resulting from instinct. Also, **instinctual.** **– instinctively,** *adv.*

**institute** /'ɪnstətʃut/, *v.,* **-tuted, -tuting,** *n.* *–v.t.* **1.** to set up or establish: *institute a government.* **2.** to set on foot; inaugurate; initiate: *institute a new course.* **3.** to set in operation: *institute a suit.* **4.** to bring into use or practice: *to institute laws.* **5.** to establish in an office or position. **6.** *Eccles.* to assign to or invest with a spiritual charge. *–n.* **7.** a society or organisation for carrying on a particular work, as of literary, scientific, or educational character. **8.** the building occupied by such a society. **9.** *Educ.* **a.** an institution, generally beyond the secondary school level, devoted to instruction in technical subjects, usu. separate but sometimes organised as a part of a university. **b.** a unit within a university organised for advanced instruction and research in a relatively narrow field of subject matter. **c.** a short instructional program set up for a particular group interested in some specialised type of activity. **10.** an established principle, law, custom, or organisation. **11.** (*pl.*) an elementary textbook of law designed for beginners. **12.** something instituted. [ME *institut*, pp., set up, established, from L *institūtus*]

**instituter** /'ɪnstətʃutə/, *n.* →**institutor.**

**institution** /ɪnstə'tjuʃən/, *n.* **1.** an organisation or establishment for the promotion of a particular object, usu. one for some public, educational, charitable, or similar purpose. **2** a building used for such work, as a college, school, hospital mental hospital, or the like. **3.** a concern engaged in some activity, as an insurance company. **4.** *Sociol.* an organised pattern of group behaviour, well-established and accepted as a fundamental part of a culture, such as slavery. **5.** any established law, custom, etc. **6.** any familiar practice or object. **7.** the act of instituting or setting up; establishment *the institution of laws.* **8.** *Eccles.* **a.** the origination of the Eucharist, and enactment of its observance, by Christ. **b.** the investment of a clergyman with a spiritual charge.

**institutional** /ɪnstə'tjuʃənəl/, *adj.* **1.** of, pertaining to, or established by institution. **2.** pertaining to organised societies or to the buildings used for their work. **3.** of the nature of an institution. **4.** characterised by uniformity and dullness. **5.** pertaining to institutes or principles, esp. of jurisprudence. – **institutionally,** *adv.*

**institutionalise** /ɪnstə'tjuʃənəlaɪz/, *v.t.,* **-lised, -lising. 1.** to make institutional. **2.** to make into or treat as an institution. **3.** to put (a person) into an institution. **4.** to make (a person) dependent on an institution, as a prison, mental hospital, etc., to the point where he cannot live successfully outside it. Also, **institutionalize.** – **institutionalisation** /ˌɪnstəˌtjuʃənəlaɪ'zeɪʃən/, *n.*

**institutionalised** /ɪnstə'tjuʃənəlaɪzd/, *adj.* dependent upon an institution, as a prison, hospital, etc.

**institutionalism** /ɪnstə'tjuʃənəlɪzəm/, *n.* **1.** the system of institutions or organised societies for public, charitable, or similar purposes. **2.** strong attachment to established institutions, as of religion.

**institutionary** /ɪnstə'tjuʃənri, -nəri/, *adj.* **1.** of or relating to an institution or to institutions; institutional. **2.** of or pertaining to institution, esp. ecclesiastical institution.

**institutive** /'ɪnstətjutɪv/, *adj.* tending or intended to institute or establish. – **institutively,** *adv.*

**institutor** /'ɪnstətjutə/, *n.* one who institutes or founds. Also, **instituter.**

**instr.,** **1.** instructor. **2.** instrument. **3.** instrumental.

**instruct** /ɪn'strʌkt/, *v.t.* **1.** to direct or command; furnish with orders or directions: *the doctor instructed me to diet.* **2.** to furnish with knowledge, esp. by a systematic method; teach; train; educate. **3.** to furnish with information; inform or apprise. **4.** *Law.* **a.** to give instructions, as a client to a solicitor, or a solicitor to a barrister. **b.** (of a judge) to outline or explain the legal principles involved in a case, for the guidance of (the jury). [late ME *instructe,* from L *instructus,* pp., built, prepared, furnished, instructed]

**instruction** /ɪn'strʌkʃən/, *n.* **1.** the act or practice of instructing or teaching; education. **2.** knowledge or information imparted. **3.** an item of such knowledge or information. **4.** (*usu. pl.*) an order or direction. **5.** the act of furnishing with authoritative directions. **6.** *Computers.* a number or symbol which causes a computer to perform some specified action. **7.** (*pl.*) *Law.* the factual information and directives given by a client to a solicitor, or by a solicitor to a barrister. [late ME *instruccion,* from L *instructio*] – **instructional,** *adj.*

**instructive** /ɪn'strʌktɪv/, *adj.* serving to instruct or inform; conveying instruction, knowledge, or information. – **instructively,** *adv.* – **instructiveness,** *n.*

**instructor** /ɪn'strʌktə/, *n.* one who instructs; a teacher. [late ME, from ML: teacher, L: preparer] – **instructorless,** *adj.* – **instructorship,** *n.* – **instructress,** *n. fem.*

**instrument** /'ɪnstrəmənt/, *n.* **1.** a mechanical device or contrivance; a tool; an implement: *a surgeon's instruments.* **2.** a contrivance for producing musical sounds: *a stringed instrument.* **3.** a thing with or by which something is effected; a means; an agency: *an instrument of government.* **4.** a formal legal document, as a contract, promissory note, deed, grant, etc. **5.** one who is used by another. **6.** a device for measuring the present value of a quantity under observation. **7.** *Elect.* an electrical device which displays information about the state of some part of an aircraft, motor car, etc. [ME, from L *instrūmentum*]

**instrumental** /ɪnstrə'mentl/, *adj.* **1.** serving as an instrument or means. **2.** of or pertaining to an instrument. **3.** performed on or written for a musical instrument or musical instruments: *instrumental music.* **4.** *Gram.* **a.** (in some inflected languages) denoting a case having as its chief function the indication of means or agency. **b.** denoting the affix or other element characteristic of this case, or a word containing such an element. **c.** similar to such a case form in function or meaning, as the Latin *instrumental ablative.* –*n.* **5.** a piece of music performed without a vocal part. **6.** *Gram.* **a.** the instrumental case. **b.** a word in that case. **c.** a construction of similar meaning. [ME, from ML *instrūmentālis*]

**instrumentalism** /ɪnstrə'mentəlɪzəm/, *n.* a form of pragmatism which maintains that the function of thought is to be instrumental to control of the environment and that ideas have value according to their function in human experience or progress.

**instrumentalist** /ɪnstrə'mentələst/, *n.* **1.** one who performs on a musical instrument. **2.** an advocate of instrumentalism. –*adj.* **3.** of or pertaining to instrumentalism.

**instrumentality** /ˌɪnstrəmen'tæləti/, *n., pl.* **-ties. 1.** the quality of being instrumental. **2.** the fact or function of serving some purpose. **3.** a means or agency.

**instrumentally** /ɪnstrə'mentəli/, *adv.* **1.** by the use of an instrument. **2.** with or on an instrument.

**instrumentation** /ˌɪnstrəmen'teɪʃən/, *n.* **1.** the arranging of music for instruments, esp. for an orchestra; orchestration. **2.** the use of, or work done by, instruments. **3.** instrumental agency; instrumentality.

**instrument board** /'ɪnstrəmənt bɔd/, *n.* a surface on which instruments are mounted in a small boat, plane, etc. Also, **instrument panel.**

**instrument flight rules,** *n.pl.* the aviation code of regulations for flying using instruments for navigation, etc.

**instrument flying** /'ɪnstrəmənt flaɪɪŋ/, *n.* the navigation of an aircraft by instruments alone, with no visual cues.

**instrument landing** /'– lændɪŋ/, *n.* the landing of an aircraft with the use of instruments alone and no visual cues, as in dense fog.

**instrument landing system,** *n.* a radio-navigation landing aid which provides an approaching aircraft with lateral and vertical guidance and with marker-beacon indications at specified points.

**instrument panel** /'ɪnstrəmənt pænəl/, *n.* a panel on the dashboard of a motor vehicle or above the controls of an aircraft, etc., which contains the instruments measuring velocity, power, and other relevant data.

**insubordinate** /ɪnsə'bɔdənət/, *adj.* **1.** not submitting to authority; disobedient: *insubordinate crew.* **2.** not in a subordinate position. –*n.* **3.** one who is insubordinate. – **insubordinately,** *adv.* – **insubordination** /ˌɪnsəbɔdə'neɪʃən/, *n.*

**insubstantial** /ɪnsəb'stænʃəl/, *adj.* **1.** not substantial; slight. **2.** without reality; unreal: *the insubstantial stuff of dreams.* – **insubstantiality** /ˌɪnsəbstænʃi'æləti/, *n.*

**insufferable** /ɪn'sʌfərəbəl, -frəbəl/, *adj.* not to be endured; intolerable; unbearable: *insufferable insolence.* – **insufferableness,** *n.* – **insufferably,** *adv.*

**insufficiency** /ɪnsə'fɪʃənsi/, *n.* deficiency in amount, force, or fitness; inadequateness. Also, **insufficience.**

**insufficient** /ɪnsə'fɪʃənt/, *adj.* **1.** not sufficient; lacking in what is necessary or required: *an insufficient answer.* **2.** deficient in force, quality, or amount; inadequate: *insufficient protection.* – **insufficiently,** *adv.*

**insufflate** /'ɪnsəfleɪt/, *v.t.,* **-flated, -flating. 1.** to blow or breathe (something) in. **2.** *Med.* to blow (air or a medicinal substance) into some opening or upon some part of the body. **3.** *Eccles.* to breathe upon, esp. upon one being baptised or the water of baptism. [LL *insufflātus,* pp., breathed into] – **insufflation** /ɪnsə'fleɪʃən/, *n.* – **insufflator,** *n.*

**insular** /'ɪnsjulə, 'ɪnʃulə/, *adj.* **1.** of or pertaining to an island or islands: *insular possessions.* **2.** dwelling or situated on an island. **3.** forming an island: *insular rocks.* **4.** detached; standing alone. **5.** characteristic or suggestive of inhabitants of an island. **6.** narrow or illiberal: *insular prejudices.* **7.** *Anat.* pertaining to existing tissue, as an island (def. 6), esp. to the islets of Langerhans. –*n.* **8.** an inhabitant of an island. [LL *insulāris* of an island] – **insularity** /ɪnsju'lærəti/, *n.* – **insularism,** *n.* – **insularly,** *adv.*

**insular climate** /– 'klaɪmət/, *n.* a type of climate characterised by little seasonal temperature change and associated with coastal areas and islands in temperate latitudes.

**insulate** /'ɪnʃuleɪt/, *v.t.,* **-lated, -lating. 1.** to cover or surround (an electric wire, etc.) with non-conducting material. **2.** *Physics, etc.* to separate by the interposition of a non-conductor, in order to prevent or reduce the transfer of electricity, heat, or sound. **3.** to place in an isolated situation or condition; segregate. **4.** to install an insulating material in the roof of (a house), to retain warmth in winter and keep out heat in summer. [L *insulātus* made into an island]

**insulating tape** /ˈɪnʃuleɪtɪŋ teɪp/, *n.* tape which has been impregnated with an adhesive insulating compound; used for covering joints in electrical wires, etc.

**insulation** /ɪnʃuˈleɪʃən/, *n.* **1.** material used for insulating. **2.** the act of insulating. **3.** the resulting state.

**insulator** /ˈɪnʃuleɪtə/, *n.* **1.** *Elect.* **a.** a material of such low conductivity that the flow of current through it is usually negligible. **b.** insulating material, often glass or porcelain, in a unit form so designed as to support a charged conductor and electrically isolate it. **2.** one who or that which insulates. **3.** a source of protection from normal social and/or economic consequences: *money is a great insulator.*

**insulin** /ˈɪnʃələn, -sjələn, -sələn/, *n.* a hormone produced by the beta cells of the islets of Langerhans in the pancreas and secreted in response to high blood glucose levels; it allows the transport of glucose across cell membranes. A deficiency of insulin results in inability to utilise glucose and produces diabetes. [Trademark; L *insula* island (with reference to the islands of the pancreas) + -IN²]

**insult** /ɪnˈsʌlt/, *v.*; /ˈɪnsʌlt/, *n.* –*v.t.* **1.** to treat insolently or with contemptuous rudeness; affront. –*n.* **2.** an insolent or contemptuously rude action or speech; affront. **3.** something having the effect of an affront. **4. add insult to injury,** to compound a grievance. [L *insultāre* leap on or at, insult] – **insulter,** *n.* – **insulting,** *adj.* – **insultingly,** *adv.*

**insuperable** /ɪnˈsupərəbəl, -prəbəl, -ˈsju-/, *adj.* incapable of being passed over, overcome, or surmounted: *an insuperable barrier.* – **insuperability** /ɪnˌsupərəˈbɪləti/, **insuperableness,** *n.* – **insuperably,** *adv.*

**insupportable** /ɪnsəˈpɔtəbəl/, *adj.* not endurable; insufferable. – **insupportableness,** *n.* – **insupportably,** *adv.*

**insuppressible** /ɪnsəˈprɛsəbəl/, *adj.* that cannot be suppressed. – **insuppressibly,** *adv.*

**insurable** /ɪnˈʃɔrəbəl, -ˈʃʊə-/, *adj.* **1.** capable of being insured, as against risk of loss or harm. **2.** proper to be insured. – **insurability** /ɪnˌʃɔrəˈbɪləti/, *n.*

**insurance** /ɪnˈʃɔrəns, -ˈʃʊə-/, *n.* **1.** the act, system, or business of insuring property, life, the person, etc., against loss or harm arising in specified contingencies, as fire, accident, death, disablement, or the like, in consideration of a payment proportionate to the risk involved. **2.** the contract thus made, set forth in a written or printed agreement (policy). **3.** the amount for which anything is insured. **4.** the premium paid for insuring a thing. **5.** *Colloq.* an alternative to fall back on if one's main objective is lost: *she already has a boyfriend–so this bloke is just insurance.* **6.** *Colloq.* protection money. **7. buy insurance,** to protect oneself against a possible future setback. –*adj.* **8.** often pertaining to a company, agent, etc., dealing with insurance.

**insurant** /ɪnˈʃɔrənt, -ˈʃʊə-/, *n.* the person who takes out an insurance policy.

**insure** /ɪnˈʃɔ, ˈ-ʃʊə/, *v.*, **-sured, -suring.** –*v.t.* **1.** to guarantee against risk of loss or harm. **2.** to secure indemnity to or on, in case of loss, damage, or death. **3.** to issue or procure an insurance policy on. **4.** *Chiefly U.S.* to ensure. –*v.i.* **5.** to issue or procure an insurance policy. [var. of ENSURE]

**insured** /ɪnˈʃɔd, ɪnˈʃʊəd/, *n.* a person covered by an insurance policy.

**insurer** /ɪnˈʃɔrə, -ˈʃʊə-/, *n.* **1.** one who contracts to indemnify against losses, etc. **2.** one who insures.

**insurgence** /ɪnˈsɜdʒəns/, *n.* an act of insurgency.

**insurgency** /ɪnˈsɜdʒənsi/, *n.* **1.** the state of being insurgent. **2.** a condition of insurrection against an existing government by a group not recognised as a belligerent.

**insurgent** /ɪnˈsɜdʒənt/, *n.* **1.** one who rises in forcible opposition to lawful authority; one who engages in armed resistance to a government or to the execution of laws. –*adj.* **2.** rising in revolt; rebellious. **3.** (of the sea, etc.) rising or surging up. [L *insurgens*, ppr., rising on or up]

**insurmountable** /ɪnsəˈmaʊntəbəl/, *adj.* incapable of being surmounted, passed over, or overcome: *an insurmountable obstacle.* – **insurmountably,** *adv.*

**insurrection** /ɪnsəˈrɛkʃən/, *n.* the act of rising in arms or open resistance against civil or established authority. [late ME, from LL *insurrectio*, from L *insurgere* rise up] – **insurrectional,** *adj.* – **insurrectionally,** *adv.* – **insurrectionary,** *adj.*, *n.* – **insurrectionism,** *n.* – **insurrectionist,** *n.*

**insusceptible** /ɪnsəˈsɛptəbəl/, *adj.* **1.** not liable to be affected or influenced by (fol. by *of*): *insusceptible of flattery.* **2.** not accessible or sensitive (fol. by *to*): *insusceptible to infection.* – **insusceptibility** /ˌɪnsəsɛptəˈbɪləti/, *n.*

**inswathe** /ɪnˈsweɪð/, *v.t.*, **-swathed, -swathing.** →**enswathe.**

**inswept** /ˈɪnswɛpt/, *adj.* tapering at the end, as an aeroplane wing, or the body of a motor vehicle.

**inswing** /ˈɪnswɪŋ/, *n.* (in cricket) the movement from off to leg of a bowled ball. Cf. **outswing.** – **inswinger,** *n.*

**inswinger** /ˈɪnswɪŋə/, *n.* **1.** *Cricket.* a ball bowled so as to swerve from off to leg. **2.** *Soccer.* a pass or kick, esp. a corner (def. 12), which curves towards the goal.

**int.,** **1.** interest. **2.** interior. **3.** interjection. **4.** international. **5.** intransitive.

**intact** /ɪnˈtækt/, *adj.* remaining uninjured, unaltered, sound, or whole; unimpaired. [late ME, from L *intactus*] – **intactness,** *n.*

**intaglio** /ɪnˈtaliou/, *n.*, *pl.* **intaglios, intagli** /ɪnˈtalji/. **1.** a gem, seal, piece of jewellery, or the like, cut with an incised or sunken design. **2.** incised carving, as opposed to carving in relief. **3.** ornamentation with a figure or design sunk below the surface. **4.** an incised or countersunk die. **5.** a figure or design so produced. **6.** *Print.* the method of printing from plates on which the image has been incised or etched (opposed to *letterpress*). [It., from *intagliare* cut in, engrave] – **intagliated** /ɪnˈtalieɪtəd/, *adj.*

**intake** /ˈɪnteɪk/, *n.* **1.** the point at which a fluid is taken into a channel, pipe, etc. **2.** the act of taking in. **3.** that which is taken in. **4.** the quantity taken in: *the intake of oxygen.* **5.** a narrowing or contraction.

**intal** /ˈɪntæl/, *n.* (*also cap.*) a synthetic drug, disodium cromoglycate, which is inhaled as a fine powder to prevent asthma attacks. [Trademark]

**intangible** /ɪnˈtændʒəbəl/, *adj.* **1.** incapable of being perceived by the sense of touch, as incorporeal or immaterial things. **2.** not definite or clear to the mind: *intangible arguments.* **3.** (of an asset) existing only in connection with something else, as the goodwill of a business. –*n.* **4.** something intangible. – **intangibility** /ɪnˌtændʒəˈbɪləti/, **intangibleness,** *n.* – **intangibly,** *adv.*

**intarsia** /ɪnˈtasiə/, *n.* a highly developed form of inlay or marquetry in wood, originally as produced in Italy during the Renaissance. [It., from *intarsiare* inlay]

**integer** /ˈɪntədʒə/, *n.* **1. a.** Also, **positive integer.** any of the numbers 1, 2, 3, etc. **b.** any of the numbers 0, 1, -1, 2, -2, etc. **c.** a whole number as distinguished from a fraction, or a mixed number. **2.** a complete entity. [L: untouched, whole, entire]

**integrable** /ˈɪntəgrəbəl/, *adj.* capable of being integrated, as a mathematical function or differential equation.

**integral** /ˈɪntəgrəl/, *adj.* **1.** of or pertaining to a whole; belonging as a part of the whole; constituent or component: *the integral parts of the human body.* **2.** necessary to the completeness of the whole. **3.** made up of parts which together constitute a whole. **4.** *Rare.* entire or complete: *his integral love.* **5.** *Arith.* pertaining to or being an integer; not fractional. **6.** *Maths.* pertaining to or involving integrals. –*n.* **7.** an integral whole. **8.** *Maths.* the result of the operation inverse to differentiation (see **integration,** def. 4); an expression from which a given function, equation, or system of equations is derived by differentiation. [LL *integrālis*] – **integrality** /ɪntəˈgræləti/, *n.* – **integrally,** *adv.*

**integral calculus** /– ˈkælkjələs/, *n.* the branch of mathematics dealing with the finding and properties of integrals.

**integrand** /ˈɪntəgrænd/, *n.* the expression which is to be integrated. [L *integrandus*, ger. of *integrāre* make whole]

**integrant** /ˈɪntəgrənt/, *adj.* **1.** making up, or belonging as a part to, a whole; constituent. –*n.* **2.** an integrant part. [L *integrans*, ppr., making whole]

**integrate** /ˈɪntəgreɪt/, *v.*, **-grated, -grating.** –*v.t.* **1.** to bring together (parts) into a whole. **2.** to make up or complete as a whole, as parts do. **3.** to indicate the total amount or the mean value of. **4.** *Maths.* to find the integral of. **5.** to combine (educational facilities, student bodies, and other systems, previously segregated by race), into one unified system. **6.** to amalgamate (a racial or religious minority group) with the rest of the community. *–v.i.* **7.** *Chiefly U.S.* (of educational and other public systems) to become unified. [L *integrātus,* pp., made whole] – **integrative,** *adj.*

**integrated** /'ɪntəgreɪtəd/, *adj.* of or pertaining to a balanced personality; whole; harmonious.

**integrated circuit** /– 'sɜkət/, *n.* an assembly of miniature electronic components simultaneously produced in batch processing. Also, **IC**

**integration** /ɪntə'greɪʃən/, *n.* **1.** the act of integrating; combination into an integral whole. **2.** behaviour, as of the individual, in harmony with the environment. **3.** *Psychol.* the organisation of personality traits into a hierarchy of functions. **4.** *Maths.* the operation of finding the integral of a function or equation (the inverse of *differentiation*). **5.** the combination of educational and other public facilities, previously segregated by race, into one unified system. **6.** the amalgamation of a racial or religious minority group with the rest of the community. [L *integrātio* renewal, restoration]

**integrationist** /ɪntə'greɪʃənəst/, *n.* one who favours integration in dealing with racial sub-cultures.

**integrator** /'ɪntəgreɪtə/, *n.* **1.** one who or that which integrates. **2.** an instrument for performing numerical integrations.

**integrity** /ɪn'tɛgrəti/, *n.* **1.** soundness of moral principle and character; uprightness; honesty. **2.** the state of being whole, entire, or undiminished: *to preserve the integrity of the empire.* **3.** sound, unimpaired, or perfect condition: *the integrity of the text.* [late ME, from L *integritas*]

**integument** /ɪn'tɛgjumənt/, *n.* **1.** a skin, shell, rind, or the like. **2.** a covering. [L *integumentum*]

**integumentary** /ɪn,tɛgju'mɛntəri/, *adj.* of, pertaining to, or like an integument.

**intellect** /'ɪntəlɛkt/, *n.* **1.** the power or faculty of the mind by which one knows, understands, or reasons, as distinct from that by which one feels and that by which one wills; the understanding. **2.** understanding or mental capacity, esp. of a high order. **3.** a particular mind or intelligence, esp. of a high order. **4.** the person possessing it. **5.** minds collectively, as of a number of persons, or the persons themselves. [ME, from L *intellectus* a discerning, perceiving]

**intellection** /ɪntə'lɛkʃən/, *n.* **1.** the action or process of understanding; the exercise of the intellect. **2.** a particular act of the intellect. **3.** a conception or idea as the result of such an act.

**intellective** /ɪntə'lɛktɪv/, *adj.* **1.** having power to understand; intelligent. **2.** of or pertaining to the intellect. – **intellectively,** *adv.*

**intellectual** /ɪntə'lɛktʃuəl/, *adj.* **1.** appealing to or engaging the intellect: *intellectual pursuits.* **2.** of or pertaining to the intellect: *intellectual powers.* **3.** directed or inclined towards things that involve the intellect: *intellectual tastes.* **4.** possessing or showing intellect or mental capacity, esp. to a high degree: *an intellectual writer.* **5.** characterised by or suggesting a predominance of intellect: *an intellectual face.* *–n.* **6.** an intellectual being or person. **7.** a member of a class or group professing, or supposed to possess, enlightened judgment and opinions with respect to public or political questions. [ME, from L *intellectuālis*] – **intellectually,** *adv.* – **intellectualness,** *n.*

**intellectualise** /ɪntə'lɛktʃuəlaɪz/, *v.,* **-lised, -lising.** *–v.t.* **1.** to make intellectual; consider or treat in intellectual terms. *–v.i.* **2.** to avoid the emotional aspect of a problem; to reduce by rationalising. Also, **intellectualize.** – **intellectualisation** /ɪntə,lɛktʃuəlaɪ'zeɪʃən/, *n.*

**intellectualism** /ɪntə'lɛktʃuəlɪzəm/, *n.* **1.** the exercise of the intellect; devotion to intellectual pursuits. **2.** *Philos.* **a.** the doctrine that knowledge is wholly or chiefly derived from pure reason. **b.** the belief that reason is the ultimate principle of reality. – **intellectualist,** *n.* – **intellectualistic** /ɪntə,lɛktʃuə'lɪstɪk/, *adj.*

**intellectuality** /,ɪntə,lɛktʃu'æləti/, *n., pl.* **-ties.** **1.** the quality of being intellectual. **2.** intellectual character or power.

**intellectual property,** /ɪntə,lɛktʃuəl 'prɒpəti/, *n.* the rights of creative workers in literary, artistic, industrial and scientific fields which can be protected either by copyright or trademarks, patents, etc.

**intelligence** /ɪn'tɛlədʒəns/, *n.* **1.** capacity for understanding and for other forms of adaptive behaviour; aptitude in grasping truths, facts, meaning, etc. **2.** good mental capacity: *a task requiring intelligence.* **3.** the faculty of understanding. **4.** (*oft. cap.*) an intelligent being, esp. an incorporeal one. **5.** knowledge of an event, circumstance, etc., received or imparted; news; information. **6.** the gathering or distribution of information, esp. secret information which might prove detrimental to an enemy. **7.** a staff of persons engaged in obtaining such information; secret service. **8.** the capacity which a computerised machine derives from programs built into it to recognise specified conditions and perform nonconstant functions independently of an operator. **9.** *Obs.* interchange of information, thoughts, etc., or communication.

**intelligence quotient** /'– kwoʊʃənt/, *n.* a ratio of mental age to chronological age. A child with a mental age of 12 years and an actual age of 10 years has an intelligence quotient, or IQ, of 1.2 (usu. expressed as 120).

**intelligencer** /ɪn'tɛlədʒənsə/, *n.* **1.** an informer; a spy. **2.** *Archaic.* one who or that which conveys information.

**intelligence test** /ɪn'tɛlədʒəns tɛst/, *n.* any of several psychological tests, either verbal or non-verbal, which attempt to measure the mental development, as distinct from the educational achievement, of an individual.

**intelligent** /ɪn'tɛlədʒənt/, *adj.* **1.** having a good understanding or mental capacity; quick to understand, as persons or animals: *intelligent pupils.* **2.** showing quickness of understanding, as actions, utterances, etc.: *an intelligent answer.* **3.** having the faculty of understanding: *an intelligent being.* **4.** *Rare.* having understanding or knowledge (fol. by *of*). **5.** of or pertaining to a computerised piece of machinery which is programmed to recognise specific sets of conditions and to carry out nonconstant functions independently of an operator. [L *intelligens,* var. of *intellegens,* ppr.] – **intelligently,** *adv.*

**intelligential** /ɪn,tɛlə'dʒɛnʃəl/, *adj.* **1.** of or pertaining to the intelligence or understanding. **2.** endowed with intelligence. **3.** conveying information.

**intelligentsia** /ɪn,tɛlə'dʒɛntsiə/, *n.pl.* a class or group of persons having or claiming special enlightenment in views or principles; the intellectuals. [Russ., from L *intelligentia* intelligence]

**intelligibility** /ɪn,tɛlədʒə'bɪləti/, *n., pl.* **-ties.** the quality or character of being intelligible; capability of being understood.

**intelligible** /ɪn'tɛlədʒəbəl/, *adj.* **1.** capable of being understood; comprehensible. **2.** *Philos.* apprehensible by the mind. [ME, from L *intelligibilis,* var. of *intellegibilis*] – **intelligibleness,** *n.* – **intelligibly,** *adv.*

**intemperance** /ɪn'tɛmpərəns, -prəns/, *n.* **1.** immoderate indulgence in alcoholic drink. **2.** excessive indulgence of a natural appetite or passion. **3.** lack of moderation or due restraint, as in action or speech.

**intemperate** /ɪn'tɛmpərət, -prət/, *adj.* **1.** given to or characterised by immoderate indulgence in intoxicating drink. **2.** immoderate as regards indulgence of appetite or passion. **3.** not temperate; unrestrained or unbridled. **4.** extreme in temperature, as climate, etc. – **intemperately,** *adv.* – **intemperateness,** *n.*

**intend** /ɪn'tɛnd/, *v.t.* **1.** to have in mind as something to be done or brought about: *he intends to enlist.* **2.** to design or mean for a particular purpose, use, recipient, etc.: *a book intended for reference.* **3.** to design to express or indicate. *–v.i.* **4.** to have a purpose or design: *he may intend otherwise.* [ME *intende(n),* from L *intendere* extend, intend; replacing ME *entenden,* from OF *entendre*] – **intender,** *n.*

**intendance** /ɪn'tɛndəns/, *n.* the function of an intendant; superintendence; intendancy.

**intendancy** /ɪn'tɛndənsi/, *n., pl.* **-cies.** **1.** the office or function of an intendant. **2.** a body of intendants. **3.** a district under the charge of an intendant.

**intendant** /ɪn'tɛndənt/, *n.* **1.** one who has the direction or management of some public business, the affairs of an establishment, etc.; a superintendent. **2.** the administrator of an opera house or theatre. [F, from L *intendens,* ppr., extending, attending]

**intended** /ɪn'tɛndəd/, *adj.* **1.** purposed or designed: *to produce the intended effect.* **2.** prospective: *one's intended wife.* *–n.* **3.** *Colloq.* an intended husband or wife.

**intendment** /ɪn'tɛndmənt/, *n.* the manner of understanding, construing, or viewing something; the true meaning as fixed by law.

**intens.**, intensive.

**intense** /ɪn'tɛns/, *adj.* **1.** existing or occurring in a high or extreme degree: *intense heat.* **2.** acute, strong, or vehement, as sensations, feelings, or emotions: *intense anxiety.* **3.** of an extreme kind; very great, strong, keen, severe, etc.: *an intense gale.* **4.** *Photog.* **a.** strong: *intense light.* **b.** →**dense** (def. 4). **5.** having or exhibiting some characteristic quality in a high degree. **6.** strenuous or earnest, as activity, exertion, diligence, thought, etc.: *an intense life.* **7.** having or showing great strength or vehemence of feeling, as a person, the face, language, etc. **8.** susceptible to strong emotion; emotional: *an intense person.* [ME, from L *intensus,* pp., stretched tight, intense] – **intensely,** *adv.* – **intenseness,** *n.*

**intensifier** /ɪn'tɛnsəfaɪə/, *n.* **1.** one who or that which intensifies. **2.** *Gram.* a linguistic element or word which increases the semantic effect of a word or phrase but has itself minimal semantic content, as *very.*

**intensify** /ɪn'tɛnsəfaɪ/, *v.,* **-fied, -fying.** *–v.t.* **1.** to make intense or more intense. **2.** *Photog.* to increase the contrast or density of (an image) on a negative or print. *–v.i.* **3.** to become intense or more intense. – **intensification.** *n.* – **intensifier,** *n.*

**intension** /ɪn'tɛnʃən/, *n.* **1.** intensification; increase in degree. **2.** intensity; high degree. **3.** relative intensity; degree. **4.** exertion of the mind; determination. **5.** *Logic.* the sum of the attributes contained in a concept or connoted by a term. Cf. **extension** (def. 10). [L *intensio*]

**intensitometer** /ɪnˌtɛnsə'tɒmətə/, *n.* a device for measuring the intensity of X-rays during an exposure in radiography.

**intensity** /ɪn'tɛnsəti/, *n., pl.* **-ties.** **1.** the quality or condition of being intense. **2.** great energy, strength, vehemence, etc., as of activity, thought, or feeling. **3.** high or extreme degree, as of cold. **4.** the degree or extent to which something is intense. **5. a.** loudness or softness of vocal tone. **b.** carrying power of voice. **6.** the strength or sharpness of a colour due especially to its degree of freedom from admixture with its complementary colour. **7.** *Photog.* **a.** strength, as of light. **b.** →**density** (def. 4). **8.** *Physics.* **a.** the strength of an electric current in amperes. **b.** potential difference; voltage. **c.** the strength of an electrical or magnetic field. **d.** the magnitude, as of a force, per unit of area, volume, etc.

**intensive** /ɪn'tɛnsɪv/, *adj.* **1.** of, pertaining to, or characterised by intensity: *intensive fire from machine guns.* **2.** intensifying. **3.** *Med.* **a.** increasing in intensity or degree. **b.** instituting treatment to the limit of safety. **4.** *Econ.* of or denoting methods designed to increase effectiveness, as, in agriculture, a more thorough tillage, the application of fertilisers, etc., to secure the most from each acre (opposed to *extensive*). **5.** *Gram.* indicating increased emphasis or force. For example: *certainly, tremendously* are intensive adverbs. *–n.* **6.** something that intensifies. **7.** *Gram.* →**intensifier.** [ML *intensīvus*] – **intensively,** *adv.* – **intensiveness,** *n.*

**intensive care** /– 'kɛə/, *n.* medical therapy for the critically ill, usu. given under hospital supervision and for a short period of time.

**intensive care unit,** *n.* that section of a hospital in which intensive care is given. *Abbrev.:* I.C.U.

**intensive stocking** /ɪnˌtɛnsɪv 'stɒkɪŋ/, *n.* a technique of stocking land on a long term basis above what is normally considered to be the carrying capacity of the land, for example, by implementing strategic or rotational grazing.

**intent**[1] /ɪn'tɛnt/, *n.* **1.** an intending or purposing, as to commit some act: *criminal intent.* **2.** that which is intended; purpose; aim; design; intention: *my intent was to buy.* **3.** *Law.* the state of a person's mind which directs his actions towards a specific object. **4. to all intents and purposes, a.** for all practical purposes; practically. **b.** for all the ends and purposes in view. **5.** the end or object intended. [partly ME *intent,* var. of *entent,* from OF: intention, from L *intentus* a stretching out; partly ME *intente,* var. of *entente,* from OF: purpose, from L *intendere* stretch out]

**intent**[2] /ɪn'tɛnt/, *adj.* **1.** firmly or steadfastly fixed or directed (upon something): *an intent gaze.* **2.** having the gaze or thoughts earnestly fixed on something: *intent on one's job.* **3.** bent, as on some purpose: *intent on revenge.* **4.** earnest: *an intent person.* [L *intentus,* pp., stretched, intent] – **intently,** *adv.* – **intentness,** *n.*

**intention** /ɪn'tɛnʃən/, *n.* **1.** the act of determining mentally upon some action or result; a purpose or design. **2.** the end or object intended. **3.** (*pl.*) *Colloq.* purposes with respect to a proposal of marriage. **4.** the act or fact of intending or purposing. **5.** *Logic.* **a.** the mental act of initially directing attention to something. **b. first intention,** direct cognition of an object viewed or thought of through its general concept rather than subsumed under it. **c. second intention,** cognition of an object viewed or thought of as an embodiment of one or more general concepts, the attention being directed to the concepts as well as to the object. **6.** *Surg., Med.* a manner or process of healing, as in the healing of a lesion or fracture without granulation (**healing by first intention**) or the healing of a wound by granulation after suppuration (**healing by second intention**). **7.** meaning. **8.** *Obs.* intentness. [L *intentio;* replacing ME *entencion,* from OF]

**intentional** /ɪn'tɛnʃənəl/, *adj.* **1.** done with intention or on purpose: *an intentional insult.* **2.** of or pertaining to intention or purpose. **3.** *Metaphys.* **a.** pertaining to an appearance, phenomenon, or representation in the mind; phenomenal; representational. **b.** pertaining to the capacity of mind to refer to objects of all sorts. – **intentionally,** *adv.*

**intentional fallacy** /– 'fæləsi/, *n.* in literary criticism, the notion, now usu. seen as unsupportable, that literature may be understood only in forms of the intention and purpose of the writer.

**inter** /ɪn'tɜ/, *v.t.,* **-terred, -terring.** **1.** to deposit (a dead body, etc.) in a grave or tomb; bury, esp. with ceremonies. **2.** *Obs.* to put into the earth. [ME *entere(n),* from OF *enterrer,* from *en-* EN-[1] + *terre* earth (from L *terra*)]

**inter-**, a prefix meaning 'between', 'among', 'mutually', 'reciprocally', 'together', as in *intercellular, intercity, intermarry, interweave.* [L, combining form of *inter,* adv. and prep., between, among, during]

**inter.**, intermediate.

**interact** /ɪntər'ækt/, *v.i.* to act on each other.

**interaction** /ɪntər'ækʃən/, *n.* action on each other; reciprocal action.

**interactive** /ɪntər'æktɪv/, *adj.* **1.** of or pertaining to things or persons which act on each other. **2.** *Computers.* (of systems, etc.) immediately responsive to commands, data, etc., as opposed to systems arranged for batch processing.

**inter alia** /ɪntər 'eɪliə/, *adv.* among other things. [L]

**inter alios** /– 'eɪliɒs/, *adv.* among others. [L]

**interatomic** /ɪntərə'tɒmɪk/, *adj.* between atoms.

**interblend** /ɪntə'blɛnd/, *v.,* **-blended** or **-blent, -blending.** *–v.t.* **1.** to blend (two or more substances) with each other. *–v.i.* **2.** to blend, one with another.

**interbrain** /'ɪntəbreɪn/, *n.* →**diencephalon.**

**interbreed** /ɪntə'brid/, *v.,* **-bred, -breeding.** *–v.i.* **1.** to breed by the crossing of different animal or plant species, breeds, varieties, or individuals. *–v.t.* **2.** to cause to interbreed.

**intercalary** /ɪn'tɜkələri, ɪntə'keɪləri/, *adj.* **1.** interpolated; interposed; intervening. **2.** inserted or interpolated in the calendar, as an extra day, month, etc., to make the calendar year equal to the solar year. **3.** having such an inserted day, month, etc., as a year. [L *intercalārius*]

**intercalate** /ɪn'tɜkəleɪt/, *v.t.,* **-lated, -lating.** **1.** to interpolate; interpose. **2.** to insert (an extra day, month, etc.) in the calendar, to make the calendar year equal to the solar year. [L *intercalātus,* pp.] – **intercalative,** *adj.*

**intercalation** /ɪnˌtɜkə'leɪʃən/, *n.* **1.** the act of intercalating; insertion or interpolation, as in a series. **2.** that which is intercalated; an interpolation.

**intercede** /ɪntə'sid/, *v.i.,* **-ceded, -ceding.** to interpose on behalf of one in difficulty or trouble, as by pleading or petition: *to intercede with the governor for a condemned man.* [L *intercēdere* intervene] – **interceder,** *n.*

**intercellular** /ɪntə'sɛljələ/, *adj.* situated between or among cells or cellules.

**intercept** /ɪntə'sɛpt/, *v.;* /'ɪntəsɛpt/, *n.* *–v.t.* **1.** to take or seize on the way from one place to another; cut off from the intended destination: *to intercept a messenger.* **2.** to stop the natural course of (light, water, etc.). **3.** to stop or check (passage, etc.). **4.** to take possession of (a ball, etc.) passed or thrown to an opponent, as in a football game. **5.** to prevent or cut off the operation or effect of: *to intercept the view.* **6.** to cut off from access, sight, etc. **7.** *Chiefly Maths.* to mark off or include, as between two points or lines. *–n.* **8.** an interception. **9.** the taking possession of the ball from one's opposition, as in a football game. **10.** *Maths.* an intercepted part of a line. [L *interceptus,* pp.] – **interceptive,** *adj.*

arc of circle intercepted by line between points X and Y

**interception** /ɪntəˈsɛpʃən/, *n.* **1.** the act of intercepting. **2.** the state or fact of being intercepted. **3.** *Mil.* the engaging of an enemy force in an attempt to hinder or prevent it from carrying out its mission.

**interceptor** /ɪntəˈsɛptə, ˈɪntə-/, *n.* **1.** one who or that which intercepts. **2.** *Mil.* a type of fighter aircraft with a high rate of climb and speed, used chiefly for the interception of enemy aircraft. Also, **intercepter.**

**interceptor trap** /ˈ– træp/, *n.* a trap which collects grease and other kinds of waste in a drainage system.

**intercession** /ɪntəˈsɛʃən/, *n.* **1.** the act of interceding. **2.** an interposing or pleading on behalf of one in difficulty or trouble. **3.** *Eccles.* **a.** an interposing or pleading with God on behalf of another or others, as that of Christ or that of the saints on behalf of men. **b.** a pleading against others. [L *intercessio*] – **intercessional,** *adj.*

**intercessor** /ɪntəˈsɛsə, ˈɪntəsɛsə/, *n.* one who intercedes.

**intercessory** /ɪntəˈsɛsəri/, *adj.* making intercession: *the Lord's Prayer has an intercessory petition.*

**interchange** /ɪntəˈtʃeɪndʒ/, *v.,* **-changed, -changing;** /ˈɪntətʃeɪndʒ/, *n.* *–v.t.* **1.** to put each of (two things) in the place of the other. **2.** to cause (one thing) to change places with another; transpose. **3.** to give and receive (things) reciprocally; exchange: *they interchanged gifts.* **4.** to cause to follow one another alternately: *to interchange cares with pleasures.* *–v.i.* **5.** to occur by turns or in succession; alternate. **6.** to change places, as two persons or things, or as one with another. *–n.* **7.** the act of interchanging; reciprocal exchange: *the interchange of commodities.* **8.** a changing of places, as between two persons or things, or of one with another. **9.** alternation; alternate succession. **10.** any major road junction, esp. where motorways converge. **11.** a point, in a public transport system, at which passengers can change from one vehicle to another. **12.** *Aus. Rules.* one of two players kept in reserve, who may replace any player in his team at any time; the replaced player may himself subsequently interchange with another player in his team. [INTER- + CHANGE; replacing ME *enterchaunge,* from OF *entrechangier* (v.), *entrechange* (n.)] – **interchanger,** *n.*

**interchangeable** /ɪntəˈtʃeɪndʒəbəl/, *adj.* **1.** capable of being put or used in the place of each other, as two things: *interchangeable words.* **2.** (of one thing) that may be put in the place of, or may change places with, something else. – **interchangeability** /ˌɪntətʃeɪndʒəˈbɪləti/, **interchangeableness,** *n.* – **interchangeably,** *adv.*

**intercity** /ɪntəˈsɪti/, *adj.* between cities.

**interclavicle** /ɪntəˈklævɪkəl/, *n.* a median membrane bone developed between the collarbones, or in front of the breastbone, in many vertebrates. – **interclavicular** /ɪntəkləˈvɪkjələ/, *adj.*

**interclub** /ɪntəˈklʌb/, *adj.* of activities in which two or more clubs compete or take part.

**intercollegiate** /ɪntəkəˈlidʒət/, *adj.* between colleges, or representative of different colleges.

**intercolumniation** /ɪntəkəˌlʌmniˈeɪʃən/, *n.* **1.** the space between two adjacent columns of a building, usu. the clear space between the lower parts of the shafts. **2.** the system of spacing between columns. [L *intercolumnium* space between columns + -ATION]

**intercom** /ˈɪntəkɒm/, *n. Colloq.* →**intercommunication system.**

**intercommon** /ɪntəˈkɒmən/, *v.i. Eng. Law.* to allow the pasturing of the cattle of two manors in the commons of each where these commons lie together. [ME *entercomen,* from AF *entrecomuner,* from *entre-* INTER- + *comuner* share] – **intercommoning,** *n.*

**intercommunicate** /ɪntəkəˈmjunəkeɪt/, *v.i.* **-cated, -cating.** **1.** to communicate with each other. **2.** to be adjoined or connected, as rooms. – **intercommunication** /ˌɪntəkəmjunəˈkeɪʃən/, *n.* – **intercommunicative,** *adj.*

**intercommunication system** /ˌɪntəkəmjunəˈkeɪʃən sɪstəm/, *n.* an internal or closed audio system, as within an office complex, school, ship, etc.

**intercommunion** /ɪntəkəˈmjunjən/, *n.* **1.** mutual communion, association, or relations. **2.** communion taken together by members of different religious denominations.

**intercommunity** /ɪntəkəˈmjunəti/, *adj.* of or pertaining to common ownership, use, participation, etc.

**inter-company market** /ˌɪntə-kʌmpəni ˈmakət/, *n.* the section of the money market which deals with loans between companies.

**interconnect** /ɪntəkəˈnɛkt/, *v.t.* **1.** to connect (one with another). *–v.i.* **2.** to become connected, one with another. – **interconnection,** *n.*

**intercontinental** /ˌɪntəkɒntəˈnɛntl/, *adj.* between continents.

**intercontinental ballistic missile,** *n.* a ballistic missile with a range which permits it to travel from one continent to another. *Abbrev.:* ICBM

**intercooler** /ˈɪntəkulə/, *n.* an intermediate heat exchanger, acting between two stages of a heating or cooling process.

**intercostal** /ɪntəˈkɒstl/, *adj.* **1.** pertaining to muscles, parts, or intervals between the ribs. **2.** situated between the ribs. *–n.* **3.** an intercostal muscle, part, or space. [NL *intercostālis.* See INTER-, COSTA, -AL[1]] – **intercostally,** *adv.*

**intercourse** /ˈɪntəkɔs/, *n.* **1.** dealings or communication between individuals. **2.** interchange of thoughts, feelings, etc. **3.** sexual intercourse. [INTER- + COURSE; replacing late ME *entercourse,* from OF *entrecors,* from L *intercursus* a running between]

**intercrop** /ɪntəˈkrɒp/, *v.,* **-cropped, -cropping.** *–v.i.* **1.** to use (the space) between the rows of an orchard, vineyard, or field for the simultaneous production of a different cultivated crop. *–v.t.* **2.** to plant such a crop. *–n.* **3.** the secondary crop itself.

**intercross** /ɪntəˈkrɒs/, *v.;* /ˈɪntəkrɒs/, *n.* *–v.t.* **1.** to cross (things), one with another. **2.** to cross (each other), as streets do. **3.** to cross in interbreeding. *–v.i.* **4.** to cross each other. **5.** →**interbreed.** *–n.* **6.** an instance of cross-fertilisation.

**intercrystalline fracture** /ɪntəˌkrɪstəlaɪn ˈfræktʃə/, *n.* the fracture of a metal in which the line of failure passes round the boundaries of the crystals rather than through the crystals themselves. Cf. **transcrystalline fracture.**

**intercurrent** /ɪntəˈkʌrənt/, *adj.* **1.** intervening, as of time or events. **2.** *Pathol.* (of a disease) occurring while another disease is in progress. [L *intercurrens,* ppr., running between, intervening] – **intercurrence,** *n.*

**interdenominational** /ˌɪntədənɒməˈnæʃənəl, -ˈneɪ-/, *adj.* between or involving two or more (religious) denominations.

**interdental** /ɪntəˈdɛntl/, *adj.* **1.** between teeth. **2.** *Phonet.* with the tip of the tongue between the upper and lower front teeth. – **interdentally,** *adv.*

**interdepartmental** /ɪntəˌdipatˈmɛntl, ˌɪntədəpat-/, *adj.* between or involving two or more departments. – **interdepartmentally,** *adv.*

**interdependent** /ɪntədəˈpɛndənt/, *adj.* mutually dependent; dependent on each other. – **interdependence, interdependency,** *n.* – **interpedently,** *adv.*

**interdict** /ˈɪntədɪkt, -daɪt/ *n.;* /ɪntəˈdɪkt, -ˈdaɪt/, *v.* *–n.* **1.** *Rom. Law.* a general or special order of the Roman praetor forbidding or commanding an act; the procedure by which an interdict was sought. **2.** *Civil Law.* any prohibitory act or decree of a court or an administrative officer. **3.** *Scot. Law.* an injunction. **4.** *Rom. Cath. Ch.* a punishment by which the faithful, remaining in communion with the Church, are prohibited from participation in certain sacred acts. *–v.t.* **5.** *Rom. Cath. Ch.* to prohibit the exercise of (stated privileges and functions within the Church). **6.** to forbid; prohibit. **7.** *Mil.* **a.** to isolate, or seal off an area by any means; to deny the use of a route or approach. **b.** to impede by steady bombardment: *constant air attacks interdicted the enemy's advance.* [L *interdictus,* pp.; replacing ME *entredite(n),* from OF *entredit,* pp. of *entredire*]

**interdiction** /ɪntəˈdɪkʃən/, *n.* **1.** the act of interdicting. **2.** the state of being interdicted. **3.** an interdict. **4.** *Mil.* planned operations aimed at destroying or neutralising the enemy's military potential and disrupting the movement of his forces into, out of and within the battle area.

**interdictory** /ɪntəˈdɪktəri/, *adj.* interdicting.

**interdisciplinary** /ɪntəˈdɪsəplənəri, -nri/, *adj.* of or pertaining to education courses, committees, etc., in which two or more disciplines co-operate.

**inter-dominion** /ɪntə-dəˈmɪnjən/, *adj.* (of diplomatic relations, sporting contests, etc.) involving different countries in the Commonwealth (def. 3), esp. Australia and New Zealand.

**interest** /ˈɪntrəst, -tərəst/, *n.* **1.** the feeling of one whose attention or curiosity is particularly engaged by something: *to have great interest in a subject.* **2.** a particular feeling of this kind: *a man of varied intellectual interests.* **3.** the power of exciting such feeling; interesting quality: *questions of great interest.* **4.** concernment, importance, or moment: *a matter of primary interest.* **5.** a business, cause, or the like, in which a number of persons are interested. **6.** a share in the ownership of property, in a commercial or financial undertaking, or the like. **7.** any right of ownership in property, commercial undertakings, etc. **8.** a number or group of persons, or a party, having a common interest: *the banking interest.* **9.** something in which one has an interest, as of ownership, advantage, attention, etc. **10.** the relation of being affected by something in respect of advantage or detriment: *an arbitrator having no interest in the outcome.* **11.** benefit or advantage: *to have one's own interest in mind.* **12.** regard for one's own advantage or profit; self-interest: *rival interests.* **13.** *Comm.* **a.** payment, or a sum paid, for the use of money borrowed (the principal), or for the forbearance of a debt. **b.** the rate per cent per unit of time represented by such payment. **14.** something added or thrown in above an exact equivalent. **15.** *Obs.* influence from personal importance or capability; power of influencing the action of others. **16. in the interest** (or **interests**) **of,** on the side of what is advantageous to; on behalf of: *in the interest of good government.* –*v.t.* **17.** to engage or excite the attention or curiosity of: *a story which interested him greatly.* **18.** to concern (a person, etc.) in something; involve: *every citizen is interested in this law.* **19.** to cause to take a personal concern or share; induce to participate: *to interest a person in an enterprise.* [late ME, n. use of L *interest* it concerns; replacing ME *interesse,* from ML: compensation for loss (n. use of L inf.)]

**interested** /ˈɪntrəstəd/, *adj.* **1.** having an interest in something; concerned: *those interested should apply in person.* **2.** participating; having an interest or share; having money involved: *one interested in the funds.* **3.** having the attention or curiosity engaged: *an interested spectator.* **4.** characterised by a feeling of interest. **5.** influenced by personal or selfish motives: *an interested witness.* – **interestedly,** *adv.* – **interestedness,** *n.*

**interest-free** /ˈɪntrəst-fri/, *adj.* of loans which are made without any charging of interest.

**interest group** /ˈɪntrəst grup/, *n.* a group of people organised to promote some social, political or economic interest which they have in common.

**interesting** /ˈɪntrəstɪŋ/, *adj.* **1.** arousing a feeling of interest: *an interesting face.* **2.** engaging or exciting and holding the attention or curiosity: *an interesting book.* **3. interesting condition,** pregnancy. – **interestingly,** *adv.* – **interestingness,** *n.*

**interface** /ˈɪntəfeɪs/, *n.;* /ɪntəˈfeɪs/, *v.,* **-faced, -facing.** –*n.* **1.** a surface regarded as the common boundary to two bodies or spaces. **2.** *Chem.* the surface which separates two phases. **3.** the point or area at which any two systems or disciplines interact: *the interface between a computer and a typesetting machine.* –*v.t.* **4.** to cause (two systems) to interact: *to interface the computer and the teletype.* **5.** to insert an interfacing into. –*v.i.* **6.** (of systems) to interact. **7.** to communicate; exchange ideas with (fol. by *with*).

**interfacial** /ɪntəˈfeɪʃəl/, *adj.* **1.** included between two faces. **2.** pertaining to an interface.

**interfacial surface tension,** *n.* the surface tension at the interface between two immiscible liquids. Also, **interfacial tension.**

**interfacing** /ˈɪntəfeɪsɪŋ/, *n.* fabric placed between outer material and facing to give body.

**interfere** /ɪntəˈfɪə/, *v.i.,* **-fered, -fering.** **1.** to clash; come into collision; be in opposition: *the claims of two nations may interfere.* **2.** to come into opposition, as one thing with another, esp. with the effect of hampering action or procedure: *these interruptions interfere with the work.* **3.** to interpose or intervene for a particular purpose. **4.** to take a part in the affairs of others; meddle: *to interfere in others' disputes.* **5.** (of things) to strike against each other, or one against another, so as to hamper or hinder action; come into physical collision. **6.** to strike one foot or leg against the opposite foot or leg in going, as a horse. **7.** *Physics.* to cause interference. **8.** to molest sexually (fol. by *with*). [OF *entreferir* strike each other, from *entre-* INTER- + *ferir* (from L *ferīre* strike)] – **interferer,** *n.* – **interferingly,** *adv.*

**interference** /ɪntəˈfɪərəns/, *n.* **1.** the act or fact of interfering. **2.** *Physics.* the action of waves (as of light, sound, etc.), when meeting, by which they reinforce or cancel each other. **3.** *Radio.* **a.** the jumbling of radio signals by receiving signals other than the desired ones. **b.** the signals which produce the incoherence. **4.** sexual molestation.

**interference drag** /ˈ– dræg/, *n.* additional drag due to interaction of two aerodynamic bodies.

**interference pattern** /ˈ– pætn/, *n. Physics.* the alternating dark and light bands produced by interference. Also, **interference fringes.**

**interferential** /ɪntəfəˈrɛnʃəl/, *adj.* of or pertaining to interference.

**interferometer** /ɪntəfəˈrɒmətə/, *n.* any instrument which divides a beam of light or other electromagnetic radiation into a number of beams and re-unites them to produce interference; used to measure small distances, compare lengths, and measure diameters of stars.

**interferon** /ɪntəˈfɪərɒn/, *n.* a protein produced by animal cells in response to virus infection, that inhibits replication of virus particles.

**interfile** /ɪntəˈfaɪl/, *v.t.,* **-filed, -filing.** to combine into a single arrangement (two or more similarly arranged sets of items, as cards, documents, etc.).

**interflow** /ɪntəˈfloʊ/, *v.;* /ˈɪntəfloʊ/, *n.* –*v.i.* **1.** to flow into each other; intermingle. –*n.* **2.** an interflowing.

**interfluent** /ɪntəˈfluənt/, *adj.* interflowing.

**interfluve** /ˈɪntəfluv/, *n.* the ridge between two adjacent river valleys.

**interfold** /ɪntəˈfoʊld/, *v.t.* to fold, one within another; fold together.

**interfuse** /ɪntəˈfjuz/, *v.,* **-fused, -fusing.** –*v.t.* **1.** to pour (something) between or through; diffuse throughout. **2.** to intersperse, intermingle, or permeate with something. **3.** to blend or fuse, one with another. –*v.i.* **4.** to become blended or fused, one with another. [L *interfūsus,* pp.] – **interfusion,** *n.*

**intergalactic** /ɪntəgəˈlæktɪk/, *adj.* existing or occurring between galaxies.

**interglacial** /ɪntəˈgleɪʃəl, -ˈgleɪsiəl/, *adj.* occurring or formed between times of glacial action.

**intergrade** /ˈɪntəgreɪd/, *n.;* /ɪntəˈgreɪd/, *v.,* **-graded, -grading.** –*n.* **1.** an intermediate grade. –*v.i.* **2.** to pass gradually, one into another, as different species. – **intergradation** /ɪntəgrəˈdeɪʃən/, *n.* – **intergradient** /ɪntəˈgreɪdiənt/, *adj.*

**intergranular** /ɪntəˈgrænjələ/, *adj.* between grains (of a rock).

**intergrowth** /ˈɪntəgroʊθ/, *n.* growth or growing together, as of one thing with another.

**inter-house deadlock** /ˌɪntə-haʊs ˈdɛdlɒk/, *n.* the cessation of legislative proceedings when agreement cannot be reached between the two houses in a bicameral parliament.

**interim** /ˈɪntərəm/, *n.* **1.** an intervening time; the meantime: *in the interim.* **2.** a temporary or provisional arrangement. –*adj.* **3.** belonging to or connected with an intervening period of time: *an interim dividend.* **4.** temporary; provisional: *an interim order.* [L: in the meantime]

**interim award** /– əˈwɔd/, *n.* an award made by an arbitration court pending the full and complete hearing of an application to it.

**interior** /ɪnˈtɪəriə/, *adj.* **1.** being within; inside of anything; internal; farther towards a centre: *the interior parts of a* house. **2.** of or pertaining to that which is within; inside: *an interior view.* **3.** situated inside and at a distance from the coast or border: *the interior parts of a country.* **4.** pertaining to the inland. **5.** domestic: *the interior trade.* **6.** inner, private, or secret: *an interior cabinet.* **7.** mental or spiritual. **8.** *Geom.* (of an angle) inner, as an angle formed between two parallel lines when cut by a third line, or an angle formed by two adjacent sides of a closed polygon. *–n.* **9.** the internal part; the inside. **10.** *Art.* **a.** the inside part of a building, considered as a whole from the point of view of artistic design or general effect, convenience, etc., or a single room or apartment so considered. **b.** a pictorial representation of the inside of a building, room, etc. **11.** a film sequence shot indoors. **12.** the inland parts of a region, country, etc.: *the interior of Africa.* **13.** the domestic affairs of a country as distinguished from its foreign affairs: *the Department of the Interior.* **14.** the inner or inward nature or character of anything. [L: inner] – **interiority** /ɪnˌtɪəriˈɒrəti/, *n.* – **interiorly,** *adv.*

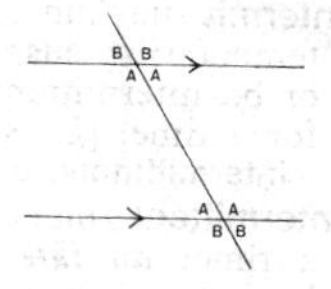

A, interior angle; B, exterior angle

**interior decorator** /– ˈdɛkəreɪtə/, *n.* a person whose occupation is planning the decoration, furnishings, draperies, etc., of homes, rooms, or offices. – **interior decoration,** *n.*

**interior designer** /– dəˈzaɪnə/, *n.* →**interior decorator.**

**interior drainage** /– ˈdreɪnɪdʒ/, *n.* a drainage system whose waters do not flow to the sea either above or below ground, but evaporate within the land area. Also, **internal drainage.**

**interiorise** /ɪnˈtɪəriəraɪz/, *v.t.*, **-rised, -rising.** →**internalise.**

**interior monologue** /– ˈmɒnəlɒg/, *n.* literary attempts to reproduce the thoughts and mental processes as they present themselves to the consciousness without restructuring for verbal acceptability or logic.

**inter-island** /ˈɪntər-aɪlənd/, *adj.* **1.** between islands. **2.** *N.Z.* between the North and South Islands of New Zealand: *inter-island ferry.*

**interj.,** interjection.

**interjacent** /ɪntəˈdʒeɪsənt/, *adj.* lying between; intervening; intermediate.

**interject** /ɪntəˈdʒɛkt/, *v.t.* **1.** to throw in abruptly between other things. **2.** to interpolate; interpose: *to interject a careless remark.* **3.** to interrupt a conversation or speech; heckle. [L *interjectus,* pp.] – **interjector,** *n.*

**interjection** /ɪntəˈdʒɛkʃən/, *n.* **1.** the act of throwing between; an interjecting. **2.** the utterance of ejaculations expressive of emotion; an ejaculation or exclamation. **3.** something, as a remark, interjected. **4.** *Gram.* **a.** (in many languages) a form class, or 'part of speech', comprising words which constitute utterances or clauses in themselves, without grammatical connection. **b.** such a word, as English *tut-tut!* Such words often include speech sounds not otherwise found in the language. **c.** any word or construction similarly used, as English *goodness me!* – **interjectional,** *adj.* – **interjectionally,** *adv.*

**interjectory** /ɪntəˈdʒɛktəri/, *adj.* **1.** interjectional. **2.** interjected. – **interjectorily,** *adv.*

**interknit** /ɪntəˈnɪt/, *v.t.*, **-knitted** or **-knit, -knitting.** to knit together, one with another; intertwine.

**interlace** /ɪntəˈleɪs/, *v.*, **-laced, -lacing.** *–v.i.* **1.** to cross one another as if woven together; intertwine; blend intricately: *interlacing boughs.* *–v.t.* **2.** to dispose (threads, strips, parts, branches, etc.) so as to intercross one another, passing alternately over and under. **3.** to mingle; blend. **4.** to diversify as with threads woven in. **5.** to intersperse or intermingle. **6.** *Railways, etc.* to lay (two railway tracks) so that the inner rails overlap, as in a section passing through a tunnel or over a bridge, in order to narrow the roadbed without switching to a single track. – **interlacement,** *n.*

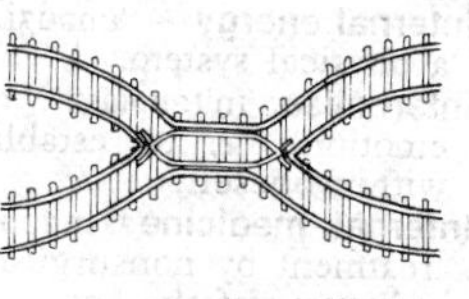
interlace (def. 6): interlaced track

**interlaminate** /ɪntəˈlæməneɪt/, *v.t.*, **-nated, -nating.** to interlay or lay between laminae; interstratify. – **interlamination** /ˌɪntəlæməˈneɪʃən/, *n.*

**interlard** /ɪntəˈlad/, *v.t.* **1.** to diversify with something intermixed or interjected; intersperse (fol. by *with*): *to interlard one's speech with oaths.* **2.** (of things) to be intermixed in. [F *entrelarder,* from *entre-* INTER- + *larder* LARD, *v.*]

**interlay** /ɪntəˈleɪ/, *v.t.*, **-laid, -laying.** **1.** to lay between; interpose. **2.** to diversify with something laid between or inserted: *silver interlaid with gold.*

**interleaf** /ˈɪntəlif/, *n., pl.* **-leaves** /-livz/; /ɪntəˈlif/, *v.* *–n.* **1.** an additional leaf, usu. blank, inserted between or bound with the regular printed leaves of a book. *–v.t., v.i.* **2.** →**interleave.**

**interleave** /ɪntəˈliv/, *v.*, **-leaved, -leaving.** *–v.t.* **1.** to provide blank leaves in (a book) for notes or written comments. **2.** to insert blank leaves between (the regular printed leaves), as to protect the illustrations, etc. **3.** to insert (blank leaves) between printed leaves. *–v.i.* **4.** to insert blank leaves or sheets between printed leaves or sheets after printing or during binding. Also, **interleaf.**

**interlibrary loan** /ɪntəlaɪbri ˈloʊn, -brəri-/, *n.* **1.** a system by which one library borrows a publication from another library. **2.** a loan made in this way.

**interline**[1] /ɪntəˈlaɪn/, *v.t.*, **-lined, -lining.** **1.** to write or insert (words, etc.) between the lines of writing or print. **2.** to mark or inscribe (a document, book, etc.) between the lines. [late ME, from ML *interlineāre*]

**interline**[2] /ɪntəˈlaɪn/, *v.t.*, **-lined, -lining.** to provide (a garment) with an inner lining, between the ordinary lining and the outer fabric. [INTER- + LINE[2]]

**interlineal** /ɪntəˈlɪniəl/, *adj.* →**interlinear.** – **interlineally,** *adv.*

**interlinear** /ɪntəˈlɪniə/, *adj.* **1.** situated between the lines; inserted between lines. **2.** having interpolated lines; interlined: *an interlinear translation.* **3.** *Obs.* having the same text in various languages set in alternate lines: *the interlinear Bible.*

**interlineate** /ɪntəˈlɪnieɪt/, *v.t.*, **-ated, -ating.** →**interline**[1].

**interlineation** /ˌɪntəlɪniˈeɪʃən/, *n.* an insertion between the lines of written or printed text. Also, **interlining.**

**interlining**[1] /ˈɪntəlaɪnɪŋ/, *n.* **1.** an inner lining placed between the ordinary lining and the outer fabric of a garment. **2.** material used for this purpose. [INTERLINE[2] + -ING[1]]

**interlining**[2] /ˈɪntəlaɪnɪŋ/, *n.* →**interlineation.**

**interlink** /ɪntəˈlɪŋk/, *v.t., v.i.* **1.** to link, one with another. *–n.* **2.** a connecting link.

**interlock** /ɪntəˈlɒk/, *v.*; /ˈɪntəlɒk/, *n.* *–v.i.* **1.** to engage with each other: *interlocking branches.* **2.** to fit into each other, as parts of machinery, so that all action is simultaneous. **3.** (of railway points, signals, etc.) to arrange and operate in an interlocking system. *–v.t.* **4.** to lock one with another. **5.** to fit the parts of (something) together so that all must move together, or in the same way. **6.** *Railways.* to arrange (points, etc.) so that their positions are not independent of one another and their movements succeed each other in prearranged order. *–n.* **7.** *Textiles.* a smooth knitted fabric, esp. one made of cotton yarn. – **interlocker,** *n.*

**interlocution** /ɪntələˈkjuʃən/, *n.* conversation; dialogue. [L *interlocūtio* a speaking between]

**interlocutor** /ɪntəˈlɒkjətə/, *n.* **1.** one who takes part in a conversation or dialogue. **2.** one who enters into conversation with another. **3.** the man in the middle of the line of performers of a minstrel troupe, who carries on a conversation with the end men. – **interlocutress** /ɪntəˈlɒkjətrəs/, **interlocutrice, interlocutrix** /ɪntəˈlɒkjətrɪks/, *n. fem.*

**interlocutory** /ɪntəˈlɒkjətri/, *adj.* **1.** of the nature of, pertaining to, or occurring in conversation: *interlocutory instruction.* **2.** interjected into the main course of speech. **3.** *Law.* **a.** incidental to the final judgment in an action; not finally decisive of a case. **b.** pertaining to a provisional decision.

**interlope** /ˈɪntəloʊp/, *v.i.*, **-loped, -loping.** **1.** to intrude into some region or field of trade without a proper licence. **2.** to thrust oneself into the affairs of others. [INTER- + LOPE, *v.*] – **interloper,** *n.*

**interlotting** /ˈɪntəlɒtɪŋ/, *n.* the grouping together by a wool broker of small lines of wool of similar type to form a single lot of reasonable size.

**interlude** /ˈɪntəlud/, *n.* **1.** an intervening episode, period, space, etc. **2.** a form of short dramatic piece, esp. of a light or farcical character, formerly introduced between the parts of miracle plays and moralities or given as part of other entertainments. **3.** one of the early English farces or comedies (such as those by John Heywood) which grew out of such pieces. **4.** an intermediate performance or entertainment, as between the acts of a play. **5.** an instrumental passage or a piece of music rendered between the parts of a song, church service, drama, etc. **6.** a period of inactivity; lull. [ME, from ML *interlūdium,* from *inter-* INTER- + *-lūdium,* from L *lūdus* play]

**interlunar** /ɪntəˈlunə/, *adj.* pertaining to the moon's monthly period of invisibility between the old moon and the new.

**interlunation** /ɪntəluˈneɪʃən/, *n.* the interlunar period.

**intermarry** /ɪntəˈmæri/, *v.i.,* **-ried, -rying.** **1.** to become connected by marriage, as two families, tribes, castes, or races. **2.** to marry within the limits of the family or of near relationship. **3.** to marry, one with another. – **intermarriage,** *n.*

**intermaxillary** /ɪntəmækˈsɪləri/, *adj.* **1.** situated between the maxillary or upper jawbones. **2.** of or pertaining to the back and middle of the upper jaw: *intermaxillary teeth.* **3.** (in Crustacea) situated between those somites of the head which bear the maxillae.

**intermeddle** /ɪntəˈmɛdl/, *v.i.,* **-dled, -dling.** to take part in a matter, esp. officiously; interfere; meddle. – **intermeddler,** *n.*

**intermediacy** /ɪntəˈmidiəsi, -dʒəsi/, *n.* the state of being intermediate, or of acting intermediately.

**intermediary** /ɪntəˈmidiəri, -dʒəri/, *adj., n., pl.* **-aries.** *–adj.* **1.** being between; intermediate. **2.** acting between persons, parties, etc.; serving as an intermediate agent or agency: *an intermediary power.* *–n.* **3.** an intermediate agent or agency; a go-between. **4.** a medium or means. **5.** an intermediate form or stage.

**intermediate**[1] /ɪntəˈmidiət, -dʒət/, *adj.* **1.** being, situated, or acting between two points, stages, things, persons, etc.: *the intermediate links.* **2.** *Geol.* (of igneous rocks) having between 52 and 65 per cent silica. *–n.* **3.** something intermediate. **4.** *Chem.* a derivative of the initial material formed before the desired product of a chemical process. **5.** →**intermediate handicap.** **6.** →**intermediate horse.** **7.** *Rare.* an intermediary. [ML *intermediātus,* from L *intermedius* between] – **intermediately,** *adv.* – **intermediateness,** *n.*

**intermediate**[2] /ɪntəˈmidieɪt/, *v.i.* **-ated, -ating.** to act as an intermediary; intervene; mediate. [INTER- + MEDIATE, *v.*] – **intermediation** /ˌɪntəmidiˈeɪʃən/, *n.* – **intermediator,** *n.*

**intermediate frequency** /ɪntəˌmidiət ˈfrikwənsi/, *n. Radio.* the middle frequency in a superheterodyne receiver, at which most of the amplification takes place.

**intermediate handicap** /– ˈhændikæp/, *n.* a race for horses which are specified as being in the intermediate class, in accordance with the rules operating in each State in Australia.

**intermediate horse** /ˈ– hɔs/, *n.* a horse eligible to run in an intermediate handicap. Also, **intermediate-class horse.**

**intermediate patient** /ˈ– peɪʃənt/, *n.* a patient in a ward of a public hospital but having private medical treatment.

**intermediate range ballistic missile,** *n.* a ballistic missile with a range of 1500 to 2800 km. *Abbrev.:* IRBM

**interment** /ɪnˈtɜmənt/, *n.* the act of interring; burial.

**intermesh** /ɪntəˈmɛʃ/, *v.i.* to interlock; fit well together.

**intermezzo** /ɪntəˈmɛtsoʊ/, *n., pl.* **-zos, -zi** /-tsi/. **1.** a short dramatic, musical, or other entertainment of light character introduced between the acts of a drama or opera. **2.** a short musical composition between main divisions of an extended musical work. **3.** an independent musical composition of similar character. [It., from L *intermedius* between]

**intermigration** /ɪntəmaɪˈgreɪʃən/, *n.* reciprocal migration; interchange of habitat by migrating bodies.

**interminable** /ɪnˈtɜmənəbəl/, *adj.* **1.** that cannot be terminated; unending: *interminable talk.* **2.** endless; having no limits: *interminable sufferings.* [ME, from LL *interminābilis*] – **interminably,** *adv.*

**interminable debt** /– ˈdɛt/, *n.* a debt without maturity date.

**intermingle** /ɪntəˈmɪŋgl/, *v.t., v.i.,* **-gled, -gling.** to mingle, one with another. – **interminglement,** *n.*

**intermission** /ɪntəˈmɪʃən/, *n.* **1.** an interval, esp. in the cinema. **2.** the act of intermitting. **3.** the state of being intermitted. [L *intermissio*]

**intermissive** /ɪntəˈmɪsɪv/, *adj.* **1.** characterised by intermission. **2.** intermittent.

**intermit** /ɪntəˈmɪt/, *v.,* **-mitted, -mitting.** *–v.t.* **1.** to discontinue temporarily; suspend. *–v.i.* **2.** to stop or pause at intervals, or be intermittent. **3.** to cease, stop, or break off operations for a time. [L *intermittere* leave off, omit, leave an interval] – **intermittingly,** *adv.*

**intermittent** /ɪntəˈmɪtənt/, *adj.* **1.** that intermits, or ceases for a time: *an intermittent process.* **2.** alternately ceasing and beginning again: *an intermittent fever.* **3.** (of streams, lakes, or springs) recurrent; showing water only part of the time. – **intermittence, intermittency,** *n.* – **intermittently,** *adv.*

**intermittent fever** /– ˈfivə/, *n.* a fever in which feverish periods lasting a few hours alternate with periods in which the temperature is normal.

**intermix** /ɪntəˈmɪks/, *v.t., v.i.* →**intermingle.**

**intermixture** /ɪntəˈmɪkstʃə/, *n.* **1.** the act of intermixing. **2.** a mass of ingredients mixed together. **3.** something added by intermixing.

**intermolecular** /ɪntəməˈlɛkjələ/, *adj.* between molecules.

**intermundane** /ɪntəˈmʌndeɪn/, *adj.* between worlds.

**intern**[1] /ɪnˈtɜn/, *v.;* /ˈɪntɜn/, *n.* *–v.t.* **1.** to oblige to reside within prescribed limits under prohibition to leave them, as prisoners of war or enemy aliens, or as combatant troops who take refuge in a neutral country. **2.** to hold within a country until the termination of a war, as a vessel of a belligerent which has put into a neutral port and remained beyond a limited period allowed. *–n.* **3.** *Chiefly U.S.* an internee. [F *interner,* from L *internus* internal]

**intern**[2] /ˈɪntɜn/, *U.S.* *–n.* **1.** Also, **interne.** a resident member of the medical staff of a hospital, usu. a recent graduate of a university still in partial training. *–v.i.* **2.** to be or perform the duties of an intern. [F *interne,* from L *internus* internal] – **internship,** *n.*

**intern**[3] /ɪnˈtɜn/, *adj., n. Archaic.* internal. [L *internus*]

**internal** /ɪnˈtɜnəl/, *adj.* **1.** situated or existing in the interior of something; interior: *internal organs.* **2.** of or pertaining to the inside or inner part. **3.** to be taken inwardly: *internal stimulants.* **4.** existing, occurring, or found within the limits or scope of something. **5.** existing or occurring within a country; domestic: *internal affairs.* **6.** pertaining to the domestic affairs of a country. **7.** studying or studied within the confines of a university or similar institution, and subject to its discipline, etc. **8.** of the mind or soul; mental or spiritual; subjective. **9.** *Anat., Zool.* inner; not superficial; away from the surface or next to the axis of the body or of a part: *the internal carotid artery.* *–n.* **10.** (*pl.*) entrails. **11.** (*pl.*) inner or intrinsic attributes. [ML *internālis,* from L *internus* inward] – **internality** /ɪntɜˈnæləti/, *n.* – **internally,** *adv.*

**internal-combustion engine** /ɪnˌtɜnəl-kəmˈbʌstʃən ɛndʒən/, *n.* an engine of one or more working cylinders in which the process of combustion takes place within the cylinder.

**internal drainage** /ɪnˌtɜnəl ˈdreɪnɪdʒ/, *n.* →**interior drainage.**

**internal ear** /ˈ– ɪə/, *n.* →**inner ear.**

**internal energy** /– ˈɛnədʒi/, *n.* the total energy associated with a physical system.

**internalise** /ɪnˈtɜnəlaɪz/, *v.t.,* **-lised, -lising.** **1.** to suppress (an emotion). **2.** to establish (information, values, attitudes) within oneself.

**internal medicine** /ɪnˌtɜnəl ˈmɛdəsən/, *n.* the diagnosis and treatment by nonsurgical means of the diseases of the inner structures of the body.

**internal rhyme** /– ˈraɪm/, *n.* rhyme between syllables in the same line of verse.

**internal secretion** /– səˈkriʃən/, *n.* the secretion directly into the bloodstream of a substance manufactured within the body, esp. a hormone.

**internat.,** international.

**international** /ɪntəˈnæʃnəl/, *adj.* **1.** between or among nations: *an international armament race.* **2.** of or pertaining to different nations or their citizens: *a matter of international concern.* **3.** pertaining to the relations between nations: *international law.* *–n.* **4.** (*oft. cap.*) Also, **Internationale.** socialist association intended to unite the working classes o all countries in promoting their own interests and social and industrial reforms, by political means. **5.** a sporting fixture between two countries: *rugby international.* **6.** a sportsman chosen to represent his country in international sporting events. – **internationality** /ɪntəˌnæʃə'næləti/, *n.* – **internationally,** *adv.*

**international candle** /– 'kændl/, *n. Obs.* See **candle** (def. 3).

**International Date Line,** *n.* →**date line** (def. 2).

**Internationale** /ɪntəˌnæʃə'nal/, *n.* **1.** →**international** (def. 4). **2.** a revolutionary socialist hymn.

**internationalise** /ɪntə'næʃnəlaɪz/, *v.t.*, **-lised, -lising.** to make international; bring under international control. Also, **internationalize.** – **internationalisation** /ɪntəˌnæʃnəlaɪ'zeɪʃən/, *n.*

**internationalism** /ɪntə'næʃnəlɪzəm/, *n.* **1.** the principle of cooperation among nations, to promote their common good, sometimes as contrasted with nationalism, or devotion to the interests of a particular nation. **2.** international character, relations, cooperation, or control. **3.** (*cap.*) the principles or methods advocated by any association known as an International.

**internationalist** /ɪntə'næʃnələst/, *n.* **1.** an advocate of internationalism. **2.** one versed in international law and relations. **3.** (*cap.*) a member or adherent of an International.

**international knot** /ɪntəˌnæʃnəl 'nɒt/, *n.* See **knot** (def. 9b).

**international law** /– 'lɔ/, *n.* the body of rules which civilised nations recognise as binding them in their conduct towards one another.

**international nautical mile,** *n.* See **mile** (def. 2). Also, **nautical mile.**

**International Phonetic Alphabet,** *n.* an alphabet designed to provide a consistent and universally understood system of letters and other symbols for writing the speech sounds of all languages. *Abbrev.:* IPA

**international practical temperature scale,** *n.* a scale of temperature defined to conform closely with the thermodynamic scale and expressed in kelvins (K) or Celsius degrees (°C).

**international sea and swell scale,** *n.* a combined scale for recording the sea from calm to phenomenal, by figures 0 to 9 read horizontally, and the swell from no swell to confused swell, by figures 00 to 99 read vertically; direction is indicated by a number from one to nine, where each number represents a cardinal point.

**International System of Units,** *n.* an internationally recognised system of metric units, now adopted as the basis of Australia's metric system, in which the seven base units are the metre, kilogram, second, ampere, kelvin, mole and candela. *Abbrev.:* SI Also, **Système Internationale d'Unités.** See **metric system.**

**interne** /'ɪntɜn/, *n.* →**intern**[2].

**internecine** /ɪntə'nisaɪn/, *adj.* **1.** mutually destructive. **2.** characterised by great slaughter. [L *internecīnus,* from *internecio* slaughter]

**internee** /ˌɪntɜ'ni/, *n.* one interned as a prisoner of war, or as a citizen of a hostile country in time of war.

**internment** /ɪn'tɜnmənt/, *n.* **1.** the act of interning. **2.** the state or condition of being interned; confinement.

**internment camp** /'– kæmp/, *n.* (during wartime) a military camp for the confinement of enemy aliens, prisoners of war, etc.

**internode** /'ɪntənoʊd/, *n.* a part or space between two nodes, knots, or joints, as the portion of a plant stem between two nodes. – **internodal** /ɪntə'noʊdl/, *adj.*

**internuncial** /ɪntə'nʌnsiəl, -ʃəl/, *adj.* (of a nerve cell or a chain of nerve cells) linking the incoming and outgoing nerve fibres of the nervous system.

**internuncio** /ɪntə'nʊnsioʊ/, *n., pl.* **-cios.** a papal ambassador ranking next below a nuncio. [It., from L *internuntius*]

**interoceanic** /ˌɪntəroʊʃi'ænɪk/, *adj.* between oceans.

**interoceptive** /ɪntəroʊ'sɛptɪv/, *adj.* pertaining to interoceptors, the stimuli impinging upon them, and the nerve impulses initiated by them.

**interoceptor** /ɪntəroʊ'sɛptə/, *n.* a nerve ending or sense organ responding to stimuli originating from within the body. [*intero-* inside (NL combining form modelled on *extero-* outside) + *-ceptor.* See RECEPTOR]

**interpellant** /ɪntə'pɛlənt/, *n.* one who interpellates. [F, ppr. of *interpeller,* from L *interpellāre* interrupt in speaking]

**interpellate** /ɪn'tɜpəleɪt, ɪntə'pɛleɪt/, *v.t.*, **-lated, -lating.** to call formally upon (a minister or member of the government) in interpellation. [L *interpellātus,* pp., interrupted in speaking] – **interpellator** /ɪn'tɜpəleɪtə, ɪntəpə'leɪtə/, *n.*

**interpellation** /ɪnˌtɜpə'leɪʃən, ɪntəpə'leɪʃən/, *n.* a procedure in some legislative bodies of asking a government official to explain an act or policy, usu. leading in parliamentary government to a vote of confidence. [L *interpellātio* interruption]

**interpenetrate** /ɪntə'pɛnətreɪt/, *v.*, **-trated, -trating.** *–v.t.* **1.** to penetrate thoroughly; permeate. **2.** to penetrate reciprocally. *–v.i.* **3.** to penetrate between things or parts. **4.** to penetrate each other. – **interpenetration** /ˌɪntəpɛnə'treɪʃən/, *n.* – **interpenetrative,** *adj.*

**interpersonal** /ɪntə'pɜsənəl/, *adj.* of or pertaining to relations between persons. – **interpersonally,** *adv.*

**interpetiolar** /ɪntə'pɛtiələ/, *adj.* (of stipules) between the petioles of opposite leaves.

**interphone** /'ɪntəfoʊn/, *n.* a telephone connecting offices, stations, etc., as in a building or ship; an intercom.

**interplanetary** /ɪntə'plænətri/, *adj.* situated within the solar system, but not within the atmosphere of the sun or any planet.

**interplay** /'ɪntəpleɪ/, *n.*; /ɪntə'pleɪ/, *v.* *–n.* **1.** reciprocal play, action, or influence: *the interplay of plot and character.* *–v.i.* **2.** to exert influence on each other.

**interplead** /ɪntə'plid/, *v.i.* to litigate with each other in order to determine which is the rightful claimant against a third party.

**interpleader** /ɪntə'plidə/, *n.* **1.** a proceeding by which two parties making the same claim against a third party determine judicially which is the rightful claimant. **2.** a party who interpleads.

**Interpol** /'ɪntəpɒl/, *n.* the International Criminal Police Commission.

**interpolate** /ɪn'tɜpəleɪt/, *v.*, **-lated, -lating.** *–v.t.* **1.** to alter (a text, etc.) by the insertion of new matter, esp. deceptively or without authorisation. **2.** to insert (new or spurious matter) thus. **3.** to introduce (something additional or extraneous) between other things or parts; interject; interpose; intercalate. **4.** *Maths.* to insert or find intermediate terms in (a sequence). *–v.i.* **5.** to make interpolations. [L *interpolātus,* pp., furbished, altered, falsified] – **interpolator,** *n.* – **interpolative** /ɪn'tɜpəleɪtɪv/, *adj.*

**interpolation** /ɪnˌtɜpə'leɪʃən/, *n.* **1.** the act of interpolating. **2.** the fact of being interpolated. **3.** something interpolated, as a passage introduced into a text.

**interpose** /ɪntə'poʊz/, *v.*, **-posed, -posing.** *–v.t.* **1.** to place between; cause to intervene: *to interpose an opaque body between a light and the eye.* **2.** to put (a barrier, obstacle, etc.) between, or in the way. **3.** to bring (influence, action, etc.) to bear between parties, or on behalf of a party or person. **4.** to put in (a remark, etc.) in the midst of a conversation, discourse, or the like. *–v.i.* **5.** to come between other things; assume an intervening position or relation. **6.** to step in between parties at variance; mediate. **7.** to put in or make a remark by way of interruption. [F *interposer.* See INTER-, POSE[1]] – **interposal,** *n.* – **interposer,** *n.* – **interposingly,** *adv.*

**interposition** /ɪntəpə'zɪʃən/, *n.* **1.** the act or fact of interposing or of being interposed. **2.** something interposed.

**interpret** /ɪn'tɜprət/, *v.t.* **1.** to set forth the meaning of; explain or elucidate: *to interpret omens.* **2.** to explain, construe, or understand in a particular way: *to interpret a reply as favourable.* **3.** to bring out the meaning of (a dramatic work, music, etc.) by performance or execution. **4.** to translate. *–v.i.* **5.** to translate what is said in a foreign language. **6.** to give an explanation. [ME *interprete(n),* from L *interpretārī* explain] – **interpretable,** *adj.* – **interpretability** /ɪnˌtɜprətə'bɪləti/, *n.* – **interpretive,** *adj.* – **interpretively,** *adv.*

**interpretation** /ɪnˌtɜprə'teɪʃən/, *n.* **1.** the act of interpreting; elucidation: *the interpretation of nature.* **2.** an explanation given: *to put a wrong interpretation on a passage.* **3.** a construction placed upon something: *a charitable interpretation.* **4.** a way of interpreting. **5.** the rendering of a dramatic part, music, etc., so as to bring out the meaning, or to indicate one's particular conception of it. **6.** translation. [ME, from L *interpretātio*] – **interpretational,** *adj.*

**interpretation section** /'– sɛkʃən/, *n.* a section in a legal statute or clause in a deed setting out the meanings attached to particular words used in the instrument.

**interpretative** /ɪn'tɜprətətɪv, -tətɪv/, *adj.* **1.** serving to interpret; explanatory. **2.** deduced by interpretation. – **interpretatively,** *adv.*

**interpreter** /ɪn'tɜprətə/, *n.* **1.** one who interprets. **2.** *Computers.* **a.** a program which causes a computer to obey instructions in some code different from the basic code of the computer. **b.** a machine which interprets the holes on a punched card.

**interracial** /ɪntə'reɪʃəl/, *adj.* **1.** existing between races, or members of different races. **2.** of or for persons of different races: *interracial camps for children.*

**interradial** /ɪntə'reɪdiəl/, *adj.* situated between the radii or rays: *the interradial petals in an echinoderm.*

**interregnum** /ɪntə'rɛgnəm/, *n., pl.* **-nums, -na** /nə/. **1.** an interval of time between the close of a sovereign's reign and the accession of his normal or legitimate successor. **2.** any period during which a state has no ruler or only a temporary executive. **3.** any pause or interruption in continuity. [L, from *inter-* INTER- + *regnum* REIGN] – **interregnal,** *adj.*

**interrelate** /ɪntərə'leɪt/, *v.t.,* **-lated, -lating.** to bring into reciprocal relation.

**interrelated** /ɪntərə'leɪtəd/, *adj.* reciprocally related.

**interrelation** /ɪntərə'leɪʃən/, *n.* reciprocal relation. – **interrelationship,** *n.*

**interrex** /ɪntə'rɛks/, *n., pl.* **interreges** /ɪntə'ridʒiz/. a person holding supreme authority in a state during an interregnum. [L, from *inter-* INTER- + *rex* king]

**interrog.,** **1.** interrogation. **2.** interrogative.

**interrogate** /ɪn'tɛrəgeɪt/, *v.,* **-gated, -gating.** *–v.t.* **1.** to ask a question or a series of questions of (a person), esp. closely or formally. **2.** to examine by questions; question: *they were interrogated by the police.* *–v.i.* **3.** to ask questions. **4.** *Elect.* to send a signal to a transponder. [late ME, from L *interrogātus,* pp.] – **interrogatingly,** *adv.* – **interrogator,** *n.*

**interrogation** /ɪn,tɛrə'geɪʃən/, *n.* **1.** the act of interrogating; questioning. **2.** an instance of being interrogated or questioned. **3.** a question. **4.** an interrogation mark. – **interrogational,** *adj.*

**interrogation mark** /'– mak/, *n.* →**question mark.**

**interrogative** /ɪntə'rɒgətɪv/, *adj.* **1.** pertaining to or conveying a question. **2.** *Gram.* (of an element or construction) forming or constituting a question: *an interrogative pronoun, an interrogative sentence.* *–n.* **3.** *Gram.* an interrogative word, element, or construction, as *'who?'* and *'what?'* – **interrogatively,** *adv.*

**interrogatory** /ɪntə'rɒgətri/, *adj., n., pl.* **-tories.** *–adj.* **1.** interrogative; questioning. *–n.* **2.** a question or inquiry. **3.** *Law.* a formal or written question. – **interrogatorily,** *adv.*

**in terrorem clause** /ɪn tə'rɔrəm klɔz/, *n.* a clause in a will which makes a gift of personalty subject to a condition. [L *in terrorem* in fear, for a threat]

**interrupt** /ɪntə'rʌpt/ *v.;* /'ɪntərʌpt/, *n., adj.* *–v.t.* **1.** to make a break in (an otherwise continuous extent, course, process, condition, etc.). **2.** to break off or cause to cease, as in the midst or course: *he interrupted his work to answer the bell.* **3.** to stop (a person) in the midst of doing or saying something, esp. as by an interjected remark: *I don't want to be interrupted.* *–v.i.* **4.** to cause a break or discontinuance; interrupt action or speech: *please don't interrupt.* *–n.* **5.** *Computers.* a command causing the computer to transfer from one program, usu. the background, to another, usu. to perform a short task, after which it resumes where it left off. **6.** *Computers.* such a suspension of program. *–adj.* **7.** *Computers.* of or pertaining to a system of interrupt. [ME *interrupte(n),* from L *interruptus,* pp., broken apart] – **interruptive,** *adj.*

**interrupted cadence** /ɪntə,rʌptəd 'keɪdəns/, *n.* a musical cadence in which there is a progression from a dominant chord to a submediant one or to one other than dominant or tonic, which implies by its partial completeness an expected tonic chord.

**interrupted screw** /– 'skru/, *n.* a screw with a discontinuous helix, as in a cannon breech, formed by cutting away part or parts of the thread, sometimes with part of the shaft beneath, used with a corresponding locknut.

**interrupter** /ɪntə'rʌptə/, *n.* **1.** one who or that which interrupts. **2.** *Elect.* a device for interrupting or periodically making and breaking a circuit. Also, **interruptor.**

**interruption** /ɪntə'rʌpʃən/, *n.* **1.** the act of interrupting. **2.** the state of being interrupted. **3.** something that interrupts. **4.** cessation; intermission.

**interscapular** /ɪntə'skæpjələ/, *adj.* between the scapulae or shoulder blades.

**inter se** /ɪntə 'seɪ/, *adv.* **1.** among or between themselves. *–adj.* **2.** of or pertaining to livestock breeding in which animals similarly bred are mated to each other. [L]

**intersect** /ɪntə'sɛkt/, *v.t.* **1.** to cut or divide by passing through or lying across: *one road intersects another.* *–v.i.* **2.** to cross, as lines. **3.** *Geom.* to have one or more points in common: *intersecting lines.* [L *intersectus,* pp., cut off]

**intersection** /ɪntə'sɛkʃən, 'ɪntəsɛkʃən/, *n.* **1.** the act, fact, or place of intersecting. **2.** a place where two or more roads meet. – **intersectional,** *adj.*

**interseptal** /ɪntə'sɛptl/, *adj.* between septa.

**intersex** /'ɪntəsɛks/, *n.* an individual displaying characteristics of both the male and female sexes of the species.

**intersexual** /ɪntə'sɛkʃuəl/, *adj.* **1.** *Biol.* of or pertaining to an intersex. **2.** existing between the sexes.

**intersidereal** /,ɪntəsaɪ'dɪəriəl/, *adj.* →**interstellar.**

**interspace** /'ɪntəspeɪs, ɪntə'speɪs/, *n.;* /ɪntə'speɪs/, *v.,* **-spaced, -spacing.** *–n.* **1.** a space between things. **2.** an intervening interval of time. *–v.t.* **3.** to put a space between. **4.** to occupy or fill the space between. – **interspatial,** *adj.*

**intersperse** /ɪntə'spɜs/, *v.t.,* **-spersed, -spersing.** **1.** to scatter here and there among other things: *to intersperse flowers among shrubs.* **2.** to diversify with something scattered or introduced here and there: *his speech was interspersed with long and boring quotations from the poets.* [L *interspersus* strewn] – **interspersion** /ɪntə'spɜʒən/, *n.*

**interstate** /'ɪntəsteɪt/, *adj.;* /ɪntə'steɪt/, *adv.* *–adj.* **1.** between or jointly involving states: *interstate trade.* *–adv.* **2.** temporarily in a state (def. 9) of which one is not a resident: *he's interstate, travelling interstate.* **3.** from another state: *he gets his raw materials interstate.* Cf. **intrastate.** – **interstater,** *n.*

**interstellar** /'ɪntəstɛlə/, *adj.* between the stars; intersidereal: *interstellar matter.*

**interstice** /ɪn'tɜstəs/, *n.* **1.** an intervening space. **2.** a small or narrow space between things or parts; small chink, crevice, or opening. [L *interstitium* space between]

**interstitial** /ɪntə'stɪʃəl/, *adj.* **1.** pertaining to, situated in, or forming interstices. **2.** *Anat.* situated between the cellular elements of a structure or part: *interstitial tissue.* *–n.* **3.** *Crystall.* a defect in a crystal caused by an extra atom or ion between normal sites in the lattice. – **interstitially,** *adv.*

**interstitial compound** /– 'kɒmpaʊnd/, *n.* a compound of a metal and certain metalloids in which the metalloid atoms occupy interstices between the atoms of the metal lattice.

**interstratify** /ɪntə'strætəfaɪ/, *v.,* **-fied, -fying.** *–v.i.* **1.** to lie in interposed or alternate strata. *–v.t.* **2.** to interlay with or interpose between other strata. **3.** to arrange in alternate strata. – **interstratification** /,ɪntəstrætəfə'keɪʃən/, *n.*

**intertexture** /ɪntə'tɛkstʃə/, *n.* **1.** the act of interweaving. **2.** the condition of being interwoven. **3.** something formed by interweaving.

**intertribal** /'ɪntətraɪbəl/, *adj.* between tribes: *intertribal warfare.*

**intertropical** /'ɪntətrɒpɪkəl/, *adj.* between the tropics (of Cancer and Capricorn).

**intertwine** /ɪntə'twaɪn/, *v.,* **-twined, -twining.** *–v.i.* **1.** to twine together. *–v.t.* **2.** to interweave with one another. – **intertwinement,** *n.* – **intertwiningly,** *adv.*

**intertype** /'ɪntətaɪp/, *n.* a slug-setting, hot-metal composing machine, similar to the linotype.

**interurban** /'ɪntərɜbən/, *adj.* between cities or towns.

**interval** /'ɪntəvəl/, *n.* **1.** an intervening period of time: *an interval of fifty years.* **2.** a period of cessation; a pause: *intervals between attacks.* **3.** a period during which action temporarily ceases; a break, as between acts of a play in a theatre. **4.** a space intervening between things, points, limits, qualities, etc.: *an interval of three metres between columns.* **5.** **at intervals,** at particular times or places with gaps in between. **6.** the space between soldiers or units in military formation. **7.** *Music.* the difference in pitch between two notes as, **a. harmonic interval,** an interval between two notes sounded simultaneously. **b. melodic interval,** an interval between two notes sounded successively. [ME *intervall,* from L *intervallum*]

**intervene** /ɪntə'vin/, *v.i.,* **-vened, -vening.** **1.** to come between in action; intercede: *to intervene in a dispute.* **2.** to come or be between, as in place, time, or a series. **3.** to fall or happen between other events or periods: *nothing interesting has intervened.* **4.** (of things) to occur incidentally so as to modify a result. **5.** to come in, as something not belonging. **6.** *Law.* to interpose and become a party to a suit pending between other parties. [L *intervenīre* come between] – **intervener,** *n.*

**intervenient** /ɪntə'viniənt/, *adj.* **1.** intervening, as in place, time, order, or action. **2.** incidental.

**intervention** /ɪntə'vɛnʃən/, *n.* **1.** the act or fact of intervening. **2.** the interposition or interference of one state in the affairs of another: *intervention in the domestic policies of smaller nations.* – **interventional,** *adj.*

**interventionist** /ɪntə'vɛnʃənəst/, *n.* one who favours intervention, as in the affairs of another state.

**interview** /'ɪntəvju/, *n.* **1.** a meeting of persons face to face, esp. for formal conference in business, etc., or for radio and television entertainment, etc. **2.** the conversation of a writer or reporter with a person or persons from whom material for a news or feature story or other writing is sought. **3.** the report of such conversation. *–v.t.* **4.** to have an interview with: *to interview the president.* [F *entrevue,* from *entrevoir,* reflexive, see (each other), from *entre-* INTER- + *voir* (from L *vidēre*) see] – **interviewer,** *n.*

**interviewee** /ɪntəvju'i/, *n.* one who is being interviewed.

**inter vivos** /ɪntə 'vivous/, *adv. Law.* between living persons. [L]

**intervocalic** /ɪntəvoʊ'kælɪk/, *adj. Phonet.* occurring between vowels.

**intervolve** /ɪntə'vɒlv/, *v.,* **-volved, -volving.** *–v.t.* **1.** to roll, wind, or involve, one within another. *–v.i.* **2.** to intertwine. [INTER- + L *volvere* roll]

**interweave** /ɪntə'wiv/, *v.,* **-wove** or **-weaved; -woven** or **-wove** or **-weaved; -weaving.** *–v.t.* **1.** to weave together, one with another, as threads, strands, branches, roots, etc. **2.** to intermingle or combine as if by weaving: *to interweave truth with fiction.* *–v.i.* **3.** to become woven together, interlaced, or intermingled. – **interweavement,** *n.* – **interweaver,** *n.*

**intestacy** /ɪn'tɛstəsi/, *n.* the state or fact of being intestate at death.

**intestate** /ɪn'tɛsteɪt, -tət/, *adj.* **1.** (of a person) dying without having made a will. **2.** (of things) not disposed of by will; not legally devised or bequeathed. *–n.* **3.** one who dies intestate. [ME, from L *intestātus* having made no will]

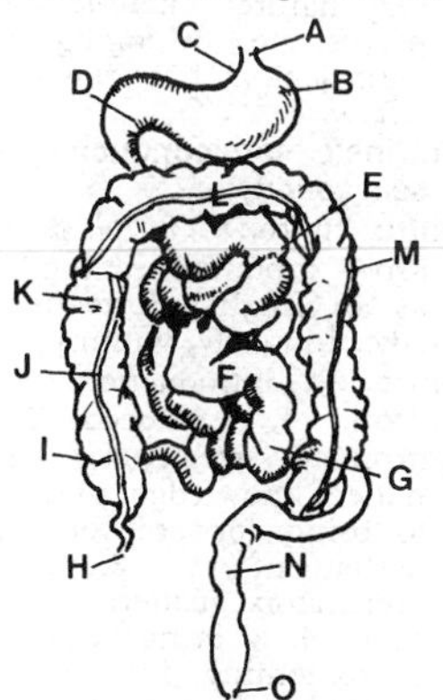


human intestines: A, end of oesophagus; B, cardiac end of stomach; C, stomach; D, duodenum; E, jejunum; F, small intestine; G, ileum; H, vermiform appendix; I, caecum; J, large intestine; K, ascending colon; L, transverse colon; M, descending colon; N, rectum; O, anus

**intestinal** /ɪn'tɛstənəl, ɪntɛs'taɪnəl/, *adj.* **1.** of or pertaining to the intestine. **2.** occurring or found in the intestine. [ML *intestīnālis*] – **intestinally,** *adv.*

**intestinal flora** /ɪn'tɛstənəl ˌflɔrə/, *n.* harmless bacteria, etc., which live in the intestinal tract.

**intestine** /ɪn'tɛstən/, *n.* **1.** (*oft. pl.*) the lower part of the alimentary canal, extending from the pylorus to the anus. **2.** a definite portion of this part. The **small intestine** comprises the duodenum, jejunum, and ileum; the **large intestine** comprises the caecum, colon, and rectum. *–adj.* **3.** internal; domestic; civil: *intestine strife.* [L *intestīna,* pl., entrails]

**inthrone** /ɪn'θroun/, *v.t.,* **-throned, -throning.** → **enthrone.**

**intima** /'ɪntəmə/, *n., pl.* **-mae** /-mi/. the innermost membrane or lining of some organ or part, esp. that of an artery, vein, or lymphatic. [NL, properly fem. of L *intimus* inmost]

**intimacy** /'ɪntəməsi/, *n., pl.* **-cies.** **1.** the state of being intimate; intimate association or friendship. **2.** an instance of this. **3.** sexual intercourse.

**intimate**[1] /'ɪntəmət/, *adj.* **1.** associated in close personal relations: *an intimate friend.* **2.** characterised by or involving personally close or familiar association: *an intimate gathering.* **3.** private; closely personal: *one's intimate affairs.* **4.** maintaining sexual relations. **5.** aimed at establishing an atmosphere of friendliness and informality, as in a small theatre, restaurant, etc. **6.** (of acquaintance, knowledge, etc.) arising from close personal connection or familiar experience. **7.** detailed; deep: *a more intimate analysis.* **8.** close union or combination of particles or elements: *an intimate mixture.* **9.** inmost; deep within. **10.** pertaining to the inmost or essential nature; intrinsic: *the intimate structure of an organism.* **11.** pertaining to or existing in the inmost mind: *intimate beliefs.* *–n.* **12.** an intimate friend or associate. [in form from LL *intimātus,* pp., put or pressed into, but with sense of L *intimus* inmost] – **intimately,** *adv.* – **intimateness,** *n.*

**intimate**[2] /'ɪntəmeɪt/, *v.t.,* **-mated, -mating.** **1.** to make known indirectly; hint; suggest. **2.** to make known, esp. formally; announce. [LL *intimātus,* pp., put or pressed into, announced] – **intimation** /ɪntə'meɪʃən/, *n.*

**intimidate** /ɪn'tɪmədeɪt/, *v.t.,* **-dated, -dating.** **1.** to make timid, or inspire with fear; overawe; cow. **2.** to force into or deter from some action by inducing fear: *to intimidate a voter.* [ML *intimidātus,* pp., made afraid. See TIMID] – **intimidation** /ɪnˌtɪmə'deɪʃən/, *n.* – **intimidator,** *n.*

**intituled** /ɪn'tɪtʃuld/, *adj.* (usu. in memoranda relating to an Act of Parliament and passing between the two Houses of Parliament) entitled. [properly pp. of ME *intitule,* from OF *intituler,* from LL *intitulāre*]

**into** /'ɪntu/; *before consonants* /'ɪntə/, *prep.* **1.** in to; in and to (expressing motion or direction towards the inner part of a place or thing, and hence entrance or inclusion within limits, or change to new circumstances, relations, condition, form, etc.). **2.** *Maths.* being the divisor of: *2 into 10 equals 5.* **3.** *Colloq.* devoted to the use or practice of; having an enthusiasm for: *I am into health foods.* [ME *in to*]

**intoed** /'ɪntoud/, *adj.* having inwardly turned toes.

**intolerable** /ɪn'tɒlrəbəl/, *adj.* not tolerable; unendurable; insufferable: *intolerable agony.* – **intolerability** /ɪnˌtɒlrə'bɪləti/, **intolerableness,** *n.* – **intolerably,** *adv.*

**intolerance** /ɪn'tɒlərəns/, *n.* **1.** lack of toleration; indisposition to tolerate contrary opinions or beliefs. **2.** incapacity or indisposition to bear or endure: *intolerance of heat.* **3.** an intolerant act.

**intolerant** /ɪn'tɒlərənt/, *adj.* **1.** not tolerating contrary opinions, esp. in religious matters; bigoted: *an intolerant zealot.* **2.** unable or indisposed to tolerate or endure (fol. by *of*): *intolerant of excesses.* *–n.* **3.** an intolerant person. – **intolerantly,** *adv.*

**intomb** /ɪn'tum/, *v.t.* →**entomb.** – **intombment,** *n.*

**intonate** /'ɪntəneɪt/, *v.t.,* **-nated, -nating.** **1.** to utter with a particular tone or modulation of voice. **2.** to intone or chant. [ML *intonātus,* pp.]

**intonation** /ɪntə'neɪʃən/, *n.* **1.** the pattern or melody of pitch changes revealed in connected speech; esp. the pitch pattern of a sentence, which distinguishes kinds of sentences and speakers of different nationalities. **2.** the act of intonating. **3.** the manner of producing musical notes, specifically the relation in pitch of notes to their key or harmony. **4.** the opening phrase in a Gregorian chant, usu. sung by only one or two voices.

**intone** /ɪn'toun/, *v.,* **-toned, -toning.** *–v.t.* **1.** to utter with a particular tone; intonate. **2.** to give tone or variety of tone to; vocalise. **3.** to utter in a singing voice (the first notes of a section in a liturgical service). **4.** to recite in monotone. *–v.i.* **5.** to speak or recite in a singing voice, esp. in monotone. **6.** *Music.* to produce a note, or a particular series of notes, like a scale, esp. with the voice; sing or chant. [late

ME, from ML *intonāre.* Cf. INTONATE] – **intoner,** *n.*

**intorsion** /ɪn'tɔʃən/, *n.* a twisting or winding, as of the stem of a plant.

**intort** /ɪn'tɔt/, *v.t.* to twist inwards, curl, or wind: *intorted horns.* [L *intortus,* pp.]

**in toto** /ɪn 'toʊtoʊ/, *adv.* in all; in the whole; wholly. [L]

**intoxicant** /ɪn'tɒksəkənt/, *adj.* **1.** intoxicating. *–n.* **2.** an intoxicating agent, as liquor or certain drugs.

**intoxicate** /ɪn'tɒksəkeɪt/, *v.,* **-cated, -cating;** /ɪn'tɒksəkət, -keɪt/, *adj.* *–v.t.* **1.** to affect temporarily with loss of control over the physical and mental powers, by means of alcoholic liquor, a drug, or other substance. **2.** to excite mentally beyond self-control or reason. *–v.i.* **3.** to cause or produce intoxication: *an intoxicating liquor.* [ME, from ML *intoxicātus,* pp., poisoned. See TOXIC] – **intoxicatingly,** *adv.* – **intoxicative,** *adj.*

**intoxicated** /ɪn'tɒksəkeɪtəd/, *adj.* **1.** drunk. **2.** excited mentally beyond reason or self-control.

**intoxication** /ɪn,tɒksə'keɪʃən/, *n.* **1.** inebriation; drunkenness. **2.** *Pathol.* poisoning. **3.** the act of intoxicating. **4.** overpowering action or effect upon the mind.

**intr.,** intransitive.

**intra-,** a prefix meaning 'within', freely used as an English formative, esp. in scientific terms, sometimes in opposition to *extra-.* Cf. **intro-.** [L, representing *intrā,* adv. and prep., within, akin to *interior* inner, and *inter* between]

**intra-atomic** /'ɪntrə-ətɒmɪk/, *adj.* within an atom or atoms.

**intracardiac** /'ɪntrə,kadiæk/, *adj.* within the heart.

**intracellular** /'ɪntrəsɛljələ/, *adj.* within a cell or cells.

**intracranial** /'ɪntrə,kreɪniəl/, *adj.* within the cranium or skull.

**intractable** /ɪn'træktəbəl/, *adj.* **1.** not docile; stubborn: *an intractable disposition.* **2.** (of things) hard to deal with; unmanageable. – **intractability** /ɪn,træktə'bɪləti/, **intractableness,** *n.* – **intractably,** *adv.*

**intrados** /ɪn'treɪdɒs/, *n.* the interior curve or surface of an arch or vault; soffit. Cf. **extrados.** [F, from L *intra-* INTRA- + F *dos* (from L *dorsum* back)]

**intramolecular** /ɪntrəmə'lɛkjələ/, *adj.* within the molecule or molecules.

**intramural** /ɪntrə'mjurəl/, *adj.* **1.** within the walls or enclosing limits, as of a city or a building. **2.** *Anat.* within the substance of a wall, as of an organ. **3.** *Chiefly U.S.* engaged in or pertaining to a single college, or its students.

**intramuscular** /'ɪntrəmʌskjələ/, *adj.* situated or occurring within a muscle.

**intrans.,** intransitive.

**intransigent** /ɪn'trænsədʒənt/, *adj.* **1.** uncompromising, esp. in politics; irreconcilable. *–n.* **2.** one who is irreconcilable, esp. in politics. [F *intransigeant,* from Sp., from (*los*) *intransigentes* revolutionary party refusing compromise, from L *in-* IN-[3] + *transigentēs,* ppr. pl., coming to an agreement] – **intransigence, intransigency,** *n.* – **intransigently,** *adv.*

**intransitive** /ɪn'trænsətɪv/, *adj.* **1.** having the quality of an intransitive verb. *–n.* **2.** an intransitive verb. – **intransitively,** *adv.*

**intransitive verb** /– 'vɜb/, *n.* a verb that is never accompanied by a direct object, as *come, sit, lie,* etc.

**intrant** /'ɪntrənt/, *n.* one who enters (esp. a college, association, etc.); entrant. [L *intrans,* ppr., entering]

**intranuclear** /'ɪntrə,njukliə/, *adj.* within a nucleus or nuclei.

**intra-ocular** /'ɪntrə-ɒkjələ/, *adj.* situated or occurring within the eyeball.

**intrastate** /'ɪntrəsteɪt/, *adj.* within a state: *intrastate commerce.*

**intratelluric** /,ɪntrətɛl'jurɪk, -tə'lu-/, *adj.* **1.** situated in, taking place in, or resulting from action, within the earth itself, usu. within the earth's crust. **2.** designating the period of crystallisation of an eruptive rock which precedes its extrusion on the surface or the crystals in a porphyritic lava formed prior to its extrusion.

**intra-uterine** /ɪntrə-'jutəraɪn, -rin/, *adj.* within the uterus.

**intra-uterine device** /– də'vaɪs/, *n.* a contraceptive device, usu. made of metal, inserted into the uterus. *Abbrev.:* I.U.D.

**intravenous** /ɪntrə'vinəs/, *adj.* **1.** within a vein or the veins. **2.** denoting or pertaining to an injection into a vein. – **intravenously,** *adv.*

**intra vires** /ɪntrə 'vaɪriz/, *adv.* within the powers (of a company, the constitution, etc.). [L]

**in-tray** /'ɪn-treɪ/, *n.* a tray or other receptacle for incoming letters, files, job assignments, etc., awaiting attention.

**intrazonal soil** /,ɪntrəzoʊnəl 'sɔɪl/, *n.* one of a group of mature soils which have been more affected by some local factor or relief or rock type than by climate and vegetation.

**intreat** /ɪn'trit/, *v.t., v.i. Archaic.* →**entreat.**

**intrench** /ɪn'trɛntʃ/, *v.t., v.i.* →**entrench.** – **intrencher,** *n.* – **intrenchment,** *n.*

**intrepid** /ɪn'trɛpəd/, *adj.* fearless; dauntless: *intrepid courage.* [L *intrepidus* not alarmed] – **intrepidity** /ɪntrə'pɪdəti/, *n.* – **intrepidly,** *adv.*

**intricacy** /'ɪntrəkəsi/, *n., pl.* **-cies. 1.** intricate character or state. **2.** an intricate part, action, etc.

**intricate** /'ɪntrəkət/, *adj.* **1.** perplexingly entangled or involved: *a maze of intricate paths.* **2.** confusingly complex; complicated; hard to understand: *an intricate machine.* [late ME, from L *intrīcātus,* pp., entangled] – **intricately,** *adv.* – **intricateness,** *n.*

**intrigant** /'ɪntrəgənt/, *n.* one who carries on intrigue. Also, **intriguant.** [F, from It. *intrigante,* ppr. of *intrigare.* See INTRIGUE, *v.*]

**intrigante** /ɪntrə'gænt, -'gɒnt/, *n.* a woman intrigant. Also, **intriguante.**

**intrigue** /ɪn'trig/, *v.,* **-trigued, -triguing;** /ɪn'trig, 'ɪntrig/, *n.* *–v.t.* **1.** to excite the curiosity or interest of by puzzling, novel, or otherwise arresting qualities. **2.** to take the fancy of: *her hat intrigued me.* **3.** to beguile by appeal to the curiosity, interest, or fancy (fol. by *into*). **4.** to puzzle: *I am intrigued by this event.* **5.** to bring or force by underhand machinations. **6.** *Rare.* to entangle. **7.** *Obs.* to plot for. *–v.i.* **8.** to use underhand machinations; plot craftily. **9.** to carry on a clandestine or illicit love affair. *–n.* **10.** the use of underhand machinations to accomplish designs. **11.** a plot or crafty dealing: *political intrigues.* **12.** a clandestine or illicit love affair. **13.** the series of complications forming the plot of a play. [F *intriguer,* from It. *intrigare,* from L *intrīcāre* entangle, perplex] – **intriguer,** *n.* – **intriguingly,** *adv.*

**intrinsic** /ɪn'trɪnzɪk, -sɪk/, *adj.* **1.** belonging to a thing by its very nature: *intrinsic merit.* **2.** *Anat.* (of certain muscles, nerves, etc.) belonging to or lying within a given part. Also, **intrinsical.** [ML *intrinsecus* inward (L inwardly)] – **intrinsically,** *adv.*

**intrinsic semiconductor** /– ,sɛmikən'dʌktə/, *n.* See **extrinsic semiconductor.**

**intro** /'ɪntroʊ/, *n., pl.* **-tros.** *Colloq.* →**introduction.**

**intro-,** a prefix meaning 'inwardly', 'within', occasionally used as an English formative. Cf. **intra-.** [L, representing *intrō,* adv., inwardly, within]

**intro.,** **1.** introduction. **2.** introductory. Also, **introd.**

**introd.,** **1.** introduced. **2.** introduction.

**introduce** /ɪntrə'djus/, *v.t.,* **-duced, -ducing. 1.** to bring into notice, knowledge, use, vogue, etc.: *to introduce a fashion.* **2.** to bring forward for consideration, as a proposed bill in parliament, etc. **3.** to bring forward with preliminary or preparatory matter: *to introduce a subject with a long preface.* **4.** to bring (a person) to the knowledge or experience of something (fol. by *to*): *to introduce a person to chess.* **5.** to lead, bring, or put into a place, position, surroundings, relations, etc.: *to introduce a figure into a design.* **6.** to bring (a person) into the acquaintance of another: *he introduced his sister to us.* **7.** to present formally, as to a person, an audience, or society. [late ME, from L *intrōdūcere* lead in] – **introducer,** *n.* – **introducible,** *adj.*

**introduction** /ɪntrə'dʌkʃən/, *n.* **1.** the act of introducing. **2.** a formal presentation of one person to another or others. **3.** something introduced. **4.** a preliminary part, as of a book, musical composition, or the like, leading up to the main part. **5.** an elementary treatise: *an introduction to botany.* [ME, from L *intrōductio*]

**introductory** /ɪntrə'dʌktri, -təri/, *adj.* serving to introduce; preliminary; prefatory. Also, **introductive.** – **introductorily,** *adv.*

**introit** /'ɪntrɔɪt/, *n.* **1.** *Rom. Cath. Ch.* a shortened psalm preceded and followed by an antiphon at the beginning of the Mass. **2.** *Anglican Ch.* a psalm or anthem sung as the celebrant of the holy communion enters the sanctuary. **3.** any psalm or anthem sung at the beginning of divine service

in a Christian church. [late ME, from L *introitus* entrance]
**introitus** /ɪn'troʊətəs/, *n.* the entrance to a body cavity or space, esp. the vagina. [L]
**introjection** /ɪntrə'dʒɛkʃən/, *n.* a primitive and early unconscious psychic process by which an external object or individual is represented by an image which in turn is incorporated into the psychic apparatus of someone else. [INTRO- + L *-jectio* a throwing]
**intropunitive** /ɪntroʊ'pjunətɪv/, *adj.* blaming oneself rather than other people or circumstances.
**introrse** /ɪn'trɔs/, *adj.* turned or facing inwards, as anthers which open towards the gynoecium. [L *introrsus*] – **introrsely,** *adv.*
**introspect** /ɪntrə'spɛkt/, *v.i.* **1.** to practise introspection; consider one's own internal state or feelings. *–v.t.* **2.** to look into; examine. [L *intrōspectus,* pp., looked into] – **introspective,** *adj.* – **introspectively,** *adv.* – **introspectiveness,** *n.*
**introspection** /ɪntrə'spɛkʃən/, *n.* observation or examination of one's own mental states or processes.
**introversion** /ɪntrə'vɜʒən/, *n.* **1.** the act of introverting. **2.** introverted state. **3.** *Psychol.* interest directed inwards or upon the self. Cf. **extroversion.** – **introversive** /ɪntrə'vɜsɪv/, *adj.*
**introvert** /'ɪntrəvɜt/, *n., adj.;* /ɪntrə'vɜt/, *v.* *–n.* **1.** *Psychol.* one characterised by introversion; a person concerned chiefly with his own thoughts. Cf. **extrovert.** **2.** *Zool., etc.* a part that is or can be introverted. *–adj.* **3.** marked by introversion. *–v.t.* **4.** to turn inwards. **5.** to direct (the mind, etc.) inwards or upon the self. **6.** *Zool., etc.* to sheathe a part of, within another part; invaginate. [INTRO- + L *vertere* turn]
**intrude** /ɪn'trud/, *v.,* **-truded, -truding.** *–v.t.* **1.** to thrust or bring in without reason, permission, or welcome. **2.** *Geol.* to thrust or force in. *–v.i.* **3.** to thrust oneself in; come uninvited: *to intrude upon his privacy.* [L *intrūdere* thrust in] – **intruder,** *n.* – **intrudingly,** *adv.*
**intrusion** /ɪn'truʒən/, *n.* **1.** the act of intruding: *an unwarranted intrusion.* **2.** *Law.* a wrongful entry after the determination of a particular estate, made before the remainderman or reversioner has entered. **3.** *Geol.* **a.** the forcing of extraneous matter, as molten rock, into some other formation. **b.** the matter forced in.
**intrusive** /ɪn'trusɪv, -zɪv/, *adj.* **1.** intruding. **2.** characterised by or involving intrusion. **3.** apt to intrude; coming unbidden or without welcome. **4.** *Geol.* **a.** (of rocks) having been forced, while molten or plastic, into fissures or other openings or between layers of other rocks. **b.** denoting or pertaining to plutonic rocks. **5.** *Phonet.* inserted without grammatical or historical justification. – **intrusively,** *adv.* – **intrusiveness,** *n.*
**intrust** /ɪn'trʌst/, *v.t.* →**entrust.**
**intubate** /'ɪntʃəbeɪt/, *v.t.,* **-bated, -bating.** **1.** to insert a tube into. **2.** to treat by inserting a tube, as into the larynx. – **intubation** /ɪntʃə'beɪʃən/, *n.*
**intuit** /ɪn'tjuət/, *v.,* **-ited, -iting.** *–v.t.* **1.** to know by intuition. *–v.i.* **2.** to receive knowledge by intuition. [L *intuitus,* pp.]
**intuition** /ɪntʃu'ɪʃən/, *n.* **1.** direct perception of truths, facts, etc., independently of any reasoning process. **2.** a truth or fact thus perceived. **3.** the ability to perceive in this way. **4.** *Philos.* **a.** an immediate cognition of an object not inferred or determined by a previous cognition of the same object. **b.** any object or truth so discerned. **c.** pure, untaught, non-inferential knowledge. [ML *intuitio,* from L *intuērī* look at, consider]
**intuitional** /ɪntʃu'ɪʃənəl/, *adj.* **1.** pertaining to or of the nature of intuition. **2.** characterised by intuition; having intuition. **3.** based on intuition as a principle. – **intuitionally,** *adv.*
**intuitionalism** /ɪntʃu'ɪʃənəlɪzəm/, *n.* →**intuitionism.** – **intuitionalist,** *n.*
**intuitionism** /ɪntʃu'ɪʃənɪzəm/, *n.* **1.** *Ethics.* the doctrine that moral values and duties can be discerned directly. **2.** *Metaphys.* **a.** the doctrine that in perception external objects are given immediately, without the intervention of a representative idea. **b.** the doctrine that knowledge rests upon axiomatic truths discerned directly. – **intuitionist,** *n., adj.*
**intuitive** /ɪn'tjuətɪv/, *adj.* **1.** perceiving by intuition, as a person, the mind, etc. **2.** perceived by, resulting from, or involving intuition: *intuitive knowledge.* **3.** of the nature of intuition. – **intuitively,** *adv.* – **intuitiveness,** *n.*
**intuitivism** /ɪn'tjuətəvɪzəm/, *n.* **1.** ethical intuitionism. **2.** intuitive perception; insight. – **intuitivist,** *n.*
**intumesce** /ɪntʃu'mɛs/, *v.i.,* **-mesced, -mescing.** **1.** to swell up, as with heat; become tumid. **2.** to bubble up. [L *intumescere* swell up]
**intumescence** /ɪntʃu'mɛsəns/, *n.* **1.** a swelling up as with congestion. **2.** swollen state. **3.** a swollen mass. – **intumescent,** *adj.*
**inturn** /'ɪntɜn/, *n.* an inward turn, as of the toes.
**intussuscept** /ɪntəsə'sɛpt/, *v.t.* to take within, as one part of the intestine into an adjacent part; invaginate. [backformation from INTUSSUSCEPTION] – **intussusceptive,** *adj.*
**intussusception** /ɪntəsə'sɛpʃən/, *n.* **1.** a taking within. **2.** *Pathol.* the slipping of one part within another; invagination. [L *intus* within + *susceptio* a taking up]
**intwine** /ɪn'twaɪn/, *v.t., v.i.,* **-twined, -twining.** →**entwine.**
**intwist** /ɪn'twɪst/, *v.t.* →**entwist.**
**inulin** /'ɪnjələn/, *n.* a polysaccharide which undergoes hydrolysis, and is obtained from the roots of certain plants, esp. elecampane, dahlia, and Jerusalem artichoke. [L *inula* elecampane + -IN[2]]
**inunction** /ɪn'ʌŋkʃən/, *n.* **1.** the act of anointing. **2.** *Med.* the rubbing in of an oil or ointment. [late ME, from L *inunctio* an anointing]
**inundatal** /ɪnʌn'deɪtl/, *adj.* (of plants) growing in an area subject to flooding.
**inundate** /'ɪnʌndeɪt/, *v.t.,* **-dated, -dating.** **1.** to overspread with a flood; overflow; flood; deluge. **2.** to overspread as with or in a flood; overwhelm. [L *inundātus,* pp., overflowed] – **inundation** /ɪnʌn'deɪʃən/, *n.* – **inundator,** *n.*
**inurbane** /ɪnɜ'beɪn/, *adj.* not urbane; lacking in courtesy or suavity. – **inurbanity** /ɪnɜ'bænəti/, *n.* – **inurbanely,** *adv.*
**inure** /ən'juə, ɪn-/, *v.,* **inured, inuring.** *–v.t.* **1.** to toughen or harden by exercise; accustom; habituate (fol. by *to*): *to inure a person to danger.* *–v.i.* **2.** to come into use; take or have effect. Also, **enure.** [late ME, v. use of obs. phrase *in ure* in use, from IN, prep., + obs. *ure* use, work (from AF, from L *opera*)] – **inurement,** *n.*
**inurn** /ɪn'ɜn/, *v.t.* **1.** to put into an urn, esp. a funeral urn. **2.** to bury; inter. – **inurnment,** *n.*
**inutile** /ɪn'jutaɪl/, *adj.* useless; of no use or service; unprofitable. [late ME, from L *inūtilis*]
**inutility** /ɪnju'tɪləti/, *n., pl.* **-ties.** **1.** uselessness. **2.** a useless thing or person.
**inv.,** invoice.
**in vacuo** /ɪn 'vækjuoʊ/, *adv.* in a vacuum. [L]
**invade** /ɪn'veɪd/, *v.,* **-vaded, -vading.** *–v.t.* **1.** to enter as an enemy; go into with hostile intent: *Caesar invaded Britain.* **2.** to enter like an enemy: *locusts invaded the fields.* **3.** (of a disease, etc.) to enter, as to cause disease, injury, etc.: *the poison invaded his system.* **4.** to enter as if to take possession: *to invade a friend's quarters.* **5.** to intrude upon: *to invade the privacy of a family.* **6.** to encroach or infringe upon: *to invade the rights of citizens.* **7.** to penetrate: *the smell of cooking invaded the bedrooms.* *–v.i.* **8.** to make an invasion. [late ME, from L *invādere* go into, attack] – **invader,** *n.*
**invaginable** /ɪn'vædʒənəbəl/, *adj. Rare.* capable of being invaginated; susceptible of invagination.
**invaginate** /ɪn'vædʒəneɪt/, *v.,* **-nated, -nating;** /ɪn'vædʒənət, -neɪt/, *adj.* *–v.t.* **1.** to insert or receive as into a sheath; sheathe. **2.** to fold or draw (a tubular organ, etc.) back within itself; introvert; intussuscept. *–v.i.* **3.** to become invaginated; undergo invagination. **4.** to form a pocket by turning in. *–adj.* **5.** invaginated. [IN-[2] + L *vāgina* sheath + -ATE[1]]
**invagination** /ɪn,vædʒə'neɪʃən/, *n.* **1.** the act or process of invaginating. **2.** *Embryol.* the inward movement of a portion of the wall of a blastula in the formation of a gastrula. **3.** *Pathol.* →**intussusception.**
**invalid**[1] /'ɪnvəlɪd, -lid/, *n.* **1.** an infirm or sickly person: *a hopeless invalid.* **2.** a serviceman disabled for active service. *–adj.* **3.** deficient in health; weak; sick: *his invalid sister.* **4.** of or for invalids: *invalid diets.* *–v.t.* **5.** to affect with disease; make an invalid: *invalided for life.* **6.** to class, or remove from active service, as an invalid. *–v.i.* **7.** to be-

come an invalid. **8.** (of a serviceman) to retire from active service because of illness or injury. [L *invalidus* infirm, not strong]

**invalid**[2] /ɪn'væləd/, *adj.* **1.** not valid; of no force, weight, or cogency; weak: *invalid arguments.* **2.** without legal force, or void, as a contract. [IN-[3] + VALID] – **invalidly,** *adv.*

**invalidate** /ɪn'vælədeɪt/, *v.t.*, **-dated, -dating. 1.** to render invalid. **2.** to deprive of legal force or efficacy. – **invalidation** /ɪnˌvælə'deɪʃən/, *n.* – **invalidator,** *n.*

**invalid chair** /'ɪnvəlɪd tʃɛə/, *n.* a chair, usu. collapsible, and always mobile, used for the transport of invalids unable to walk.

**invalidism** /'ɪnvəlɪdɪzəm/, *n.* prolonged ill health.

**invalidity** /ɪnvə'lɪdəti/, *n.* lack of validity.

**invaluable** /ɪn'væljəbəl/, *adj.* that cannot be valued or appraised; of inestimable value. – **invaluableness,** *n.* – **invaluably,** *adv.*

**invar** /ɪn'va, 'ɪnvə/, *n.* **1.** an iron alloy, containing 35.5 per cent nickel, having a very low coefficient of expansion at atmospheric temperatures. **2.** (*cap.*) a trademark for this alloy. [short for INVARIABLE]

**invariable** /ɪn'vɛəriəbəl/, *adj.* **1.** not variable or not capable of being varied; not changing or not capable of being changed; always the same. *–n.* **2.** an invariable quantity; a constant. – **invariability**/ɪnˌvɛəriə'bɪləti/, **invariableness,** *n.* – **invariably,** *adv.*

**invariant** /ɪn'vɛəriənt/, *adj.* **1.** unvarying; invariable; constant. *–n.* **2.** *Maths.* a fixed quantity.

**invasion** /ɪn'veɪʒən/, *n.* **1.** the act of invading or entering as an enemy. **2.** the entrance or advent of anything troublesome or harmful, as disease. **3.** entrance as if to take possession or overrun. **4.** infringement by intrusion: *invasion of privacy.* [LL *invāsio* an attack]

**invasive** /ɪn'veɪsɪv, -zɪv/, *adj.* **1.** characterised by or involving invasion; offensive: *invasive war.* **2.** invading, or tending to invade; intrusive.

**invective** /ɪn'vɛktɪv/, *n.* **1.** vehement denunciation; an utterance of violent censure or reproach. **2.** a railing accusation; vituperation. *–adj.* **3.** censoriously abusive; vituperative; denunciatory. [ME, from LL *invectīvus* abusive] – **invectively,** *adv.* – **invectiveness,** *n.*

**inveigh** /ɪn'veɪ/, *v.i.* to attack vehemently in words; rail: *to inveigh against democracy.* [ME *inveh*, from L *invehere* carry or bear into, assail] – **inveigher,** *n.*

**inveigle** /ɪn'veɪgəl/, *v.t.*, **-gled, -gling. 1.** to draw by beguiling or artful inducements (fol. by *into,* sometimes *from, away,* etc.): *to inveigle a person into playing bridge.* **2.** to allure, win, or seduce by beguiling. [late ME *enve(u)gle,* from F *aveugler* blind, delude] – **inveiglement,** *n.* – **inveigler,** *n.*

**invent** /ɪn'vɛnt/, *v.t.* **1.** to originate as a product of one's own contrivance: *to invent a machine.* **2.** to produce or create with the imagination: *to invent a story.* **3.** to make up or fabricate as something merely fictitious or false: *to invent excuses. –v.i.* **4.** to devise something new, as by ingenuity. [late ME, from L *inventus,* pp., discovered, found out] – **inventible,** *adj.*

**inventer** /ɪn'vɛntə/, *n.* →**inventor.**

**invention** /ɪn'vɛnʃən/, *n.* **1.** the act of inventing. **2.** *Patent Law.* the conception of an idea and the means or apparatus by which the result is obtained. **3.** anything invented or devised. **4.** the exercise of imaginative or creative power in literature or art. **5.** the act of producing or creating by exercise of the imagination. **6.** the power or faculty of inventing, devising, or originating. **7.** something fabricated, as a false statement. **8.** *Sociol.* the creation of a new culture trait, pattern, etc. **9.** *Music.* a short piece, contrapuntal in nature, generally based on one subject. **10.** *Speech.* (classically) one of the five steps in speech preparation, the process of choosing ideas appropriate to the subject, audience, and occasion. [ME, from L *inventio*]

**inventive** /ɪn'vɛntɪv/, *adj.* **1.** apt at inventing, devising, or contriving. **2.** having the function of inventing. **3.** pertaining to, involving, or showing invention. – **inventively,** *adv.* – **inventiveness,** *n.*

**inventor** /ɪn'vɛntə/, *n.* one who invents, esp. one who devises some new process, appliance, machine, or article; one who makes inventions. Also, **inventer.**

**inventory** /'ɪnvəntri, ɪn'vɛntəri/, *n., pl.* **-tories,** *v.,* **-toried, -torying.** *–n.* **1.** a detailed descriptive list of articles, with number, quantity, and value of each. **2.** a formal list of movables, as of a merchant's stock of goods. **3.** a complete listing of work in progress, raw materials, finished goods on hand, etc., made each year by a business concern. **4.** items in such a list. **5.** the value of a stock of goods. *–v.t.* **6.** to make an inventory of; enter in an inventory. [late ME, from ML *inventōrium,* L *inventārium* list] – **inventorial** /ɪnvən'tɔriəl/, *adj.* – **inventorially** /ɪnvən'tɔriəli/, *adv.*

**inveracity** /ɪnvə'ræsəti/, *n., pl.* **-ties. 1.** untruthfulness. **2.** an untruth.

**inverse** /ɪn'vɜs, 'ɪnvɜs/, *adj., n.;* /ɪn'vɜs/ *v.,* **-versed, -versing.** *–adj.* **1.** reversed in position, direction, or tendency: *inverse order.* **2.** opposite to in nature or effect, as a mathematical relation or operation: *subtraction is the inverse operation to addition.* **3.** inverted, or turned upside down. *–n.* **4.** an inverted state or condition. **5.** that which is inverse; the direct opposite. *–v.t.* **6.** *Rare.* to invert. [L *inversus,* pp., turned about] – **inversely,** *adv.*

**inverse function** /– 'fʌŋkʃən/, *n.* the mathematical function which replaces another function when the dependent and independent variables of the first function are interchanged, as log $x$ is the inverse function of $e^x$. If $y$ is a trigonometrical ratio of the angle $x$, as $y = \sin x$, then $x$ is the inverse function of $y$, i.e. $x = \text{arc} \sin y$ or $\sin^{-1} y$.

**inverse sine** /'– saɪn/, *n.* →**arc sine.**

**inverse square law,** *n.* any mathematical relation which states that the intensity of an effect at a point B, due to a source A, varies inversely as the square of the distance AB.

**inverse tangent** /'ɪnvɜs tændʒənt/, *n.* →**arc tangent.**

**inversion** /ɪn'vɜʒən/, *n.* **1.** the act of inverting. **2.** an inverted state. **3.** anything inverted. **4.** any change from the normal word order or syntactic construction of a language, esp. for literary effect, as 'came the dawn'. **5.** *Anat.* the turning inwards of a part, as the foot (opposed to *eversion*). **6.** *Chem.* a hydrolysis of certain carbohydrates, as cane sugar, which results in a reversal of direction of the rotary power of the carbohydrate solution, the plane of polarised light being bent from right to left or vice versa. **7.** *Music.* **a.** the process, or result, of transposing the notes of an interval or chord so that the original bass becomes an upper voice. **b.** (in counterpoint) the transposition of the upper voice part below the lower, and vice versa. **c.** presentation of a melody in contrary motion to its original form. **d.** (in twelve-tone composition) the presentation of a tone row in a form in which each interval is the complement of the corresponding interval in the original row, where the total number of tones is twelve; e.g. an interval of five tones becomes an interval of seven tones. **8.** *Psychiatry.* assumption of the sexual role of the opposite sex; homosexuality. **9.** *Phonet.* →**retroflexion. 10.** *Meteorol.* a reversal in the normal temperature lapse rate, in which the temperature rises with increased elevation, instead of falling. **11.** something inverted. **12.** *Rhet.* reversal of the usual or natural order of words; anastrophe. [L *inversio*]

**inversion layers** /'– leɪəz/, *n. pl.* layers of warm air persisting above cold air which trap dust, smoke, etc., above large cities, causing smog to persist.

**inversive** /ɪn'vɜsɪv/, *adj.* characterised by inversion.

**invert** /ɪn'vɜt/, *v.;* /'ɪnvɜt/, *adj., n.* *–v.t.* **1.** to turn upside down, inside out, or inwards. **2.** to reverse in position, direction, or order. **3.** to turn or change to the opposite or contrary, as in nature, bearing, or effect: *to invert a process.* **4.** *Chem.* to subject to inversion. See **inversion** (def. 6). **5.** *Phonet.* to articulate, as a retroflex vowel. *–adj.* **6.** *Chem.* inverted. **7.** *Music.* to make an inversion. See **inversion** (def. 7). **8.** →**homosexual. 9. a.** the lowest visible surface. **b.** the floor of a culvert, drain, or sewer. [L *invertere* turn about, upset] – **invertible,** *adj.*

**invertase** /ɪn'vɜteɪz/, *n.* an enzyme which causes the inversion of cane sugar, thus changing it into invert sugar. It is found in yeast and in the digestive juices of animals; sucrase. [INVERT + -ASE]

**invertebrate** /ɪn'vɜtəbrət, -breɪt/, *adj.* **1.** *Zool.* not vertebrate; without a backbone. **2.** of or pertaining to animals without backbones. *–n.* **3.** an invertebrate animal. **4.** one who lacks strength of character. – **invertebracy** /ɪn'vɜtəbrəsi/, **invertebrateness,** *n.*

**inverted comma** /ɪnˌvɜtəd 'kɒmə/, *n.* →**quotation mark.**

**inverted mordent** /– 'mɔdənt/, *n.* (in music) a melodic embellishment consisting of a rapid alternation of a principal note with a note one degree above it; pralltriller.

**inverted snob** /– 'snɒb/, *n.* one whose snobbery takes the form of shunning the more elevated members of society and ostentatiously professing an allegiance with the poor and lowly. – **inverted snobbery,** *n.*

**inverter** /ɪn'vɜtə/, *n.* **1.** one who or that which inverts. **2.** *Elect.* →**converter. 3.** *Electronics.* an amplifier which inverts its input signal. Also, **invertor.**

**invert soap** /'ɪnvɜt soʊp/, *n.* an emulsifiable salt whose action is responsible for soapy qualities.

**invert sugar** /– 'ʃʊgə/, *n.* a mixture of glucose and fructose formed naturally in fruits and produced artificially in syrups or fondants by treating cane sugar with acids.

**invest** /ɪn'vɛst/, *v.t.* **1.** to put (money) to use, by purchase or expenditure, in something offering profitable returns, esp. interest or income. **2.** to spend: *to invest large sums in books.* **3.** to clothe. **4.** to cover or adorn as an article of attire does. **5.** *Rare.* to put on (a garment, etc.). **6.** to cover or surround as if with a garment, or like a garment: *spring invests the trees with leaves.* **7.** to surround (a place) with military forces or works so as to prevent approach or escape; besiege. **8.** to endue or endow: *to invest a friend with every virtue.* **9.** to belong to, as a quality or character does. **10.** to settle or vest (a power, right, etc.), as in a person. **11.** to clothe in or with the insignia of office. **12.** to install in an office or position; furnish with power, authority, rank, etc. *–v.i.* **13.** to invest money; make an investment. **14. invest in,** *Colloq.* to buy; spend money on. [late ME, from L *investīre* clothe] – **investor,** *n.*

**investigate** /ɪn'vɛstəgeɪt/, *v.,* **-gated, -gating.** *–v.t.* **1.** to search or inquire into; search or examine into the particulars of; examine in detail. **2.** to examine in order to obtain the true facts: *to investigate a murder.* *–v.i.* **3.** to make inquiry, examination, or investigation. [L *investīgātus,* pp., tracked, traced out] – **investigable** /ɪn'vɛstəgəbəl/, *adj.* – **investigative, investigatory** /ɪn'vɛstəgeɪtəri/, *adj.*

**investigation** /ɪnˌvɛstə'geɪʃən/, *n.* **1.** the act or process of investigating. **2.** a searching inquiry in order to ascertain facts; a detailed or careful examination.

**investigator** /ɪn'vɛstəgeɪtə/, *n.* **1.** one who investigates. **2.** a private investigator.

**investitive** /ɪn'vɛstətɪv/, *adj.* **1.** serving to invest: *an investitive act.* **2.** pertaining to investiture.

**investiture** /ɪn'vɛstɪtʃə/, *n.* **1.** the act of investing. **2.** the formal bestowal or presentation of a possessory or prescriptive right, as to a fief, usu. involving the giving of insignia. **3.** the state of being invested, as with a garment, quality, etc. [ME, from ML *investītūra*]

**investment** /ɪn'vɛstmənt/, *n.* **1.** the investing of money or capital in order to secure profitable returns, esp. interest or income. **2.** a particular instance or mode of investing. **3.** a thing invested in. **4.** that which is invested. **5.** the act of investing or state of being invested, as with a garment. **6.** *Biol.* any covering, coating, outer layer, or integument, as of an animal or vegetable body. **7.** an investing with a quality, attribute, etc. **8.** the investiture with an office, dignity, or right. **9.** the surrounding of a place with military forces or works, as in a siege.

**investment bank** /'– bæŋk/, *n.* a private banking firm which moves or issues securities; an underwriter.

**investment trust** /'– trʌst/, *n.* a trust whose function is the judicious buying and selling of shares of companies at the discretion of its board of management.

**inveteracy** /ɪn'vɛtərəsi/, *n.* the state of being inveterate: *the inveteracy of people's prejudices.*

**inveterate** /ɪn'vɛtərət/, *adj.* **1.** confirmed in a habit, practice, feeling, or the like: *an inveterate gambler.* **2.** firmly established by long continuance, as a disease or sore, a habit or practice (often bad), or a feeling (often hostile); chronic. [ME *inveterat,* from L *inveterātus,* pp., rendered old] – **inveterately,** *adv.* – **inveterateness,** *n.*

**invidious** /ɪn'vɪdiəs/, *adj.* **1.** such as to bring odium, unpopularity, or envious dislike: *an invidious honour.* **2.** calculated to excite ill will or resentment or give offence: *invidious remarks.* **3.** offensively or unfairly discriminating: *invidious comparisons.* [L *invidiōsus* envious] – **invidiously,** *adv.* – **invidiousness,** *n.*

**invigilate** /ɪn'vɪdʒəleɪt/, *v.i.,* **-lated, -lating. 1.** to keep watch over students at an examination. **2.** *Obs.* to keep watch. [L *invigilātus,* pp., watched over] – **invigilation** /ɪnˌvɪdʒə'leɪʃən/, *n.* – **invigilator,** *n.*

**invigorant** /ɪn'vɪgərənt/, *n.* →**tonic.**

**invigorate** /ɪn'vɪgəreɪt/, *v.t.,* **-rated, -rating.** to give vigour to; fill with life and energy: *to invigorate the body.* [IN-[2] + VIGO(U)R + -ATE[1]] – **invigoratingly,** *adv.* – **invigoration** /ɪnˌvɪgə'reɪʃən/, *n.* – **invigorative** /ɪn'vɪgərətɪv/, *adj.* – **invigoratively,** *adv.* – **invigorator,** *n.*

**invincible** /ɪn'vɪnsəbəl/, *adj.* **1.** that cannot be conquered or vanquished: *an invincible force.* **2.** insuperable; insurmountable: *invincible difficulties.* [ME, from L *invincibilis.* See IN-[3], VINCIBLE] – **invincibility** /ɪnˌvɪnsə'bɪləti/, **invincibleness,** *n.* – **invincibly,** *adv.*

**in vino veritas** /ɪn ˌvinoʊ 'vɛrətæs/, (people speak the truth when they are drunk). [L]

**inviolable** /ɪn'vaɪələbəl/, *adj.* **1.** that must not be violated; that is to be kept free from violence or violation of any kind, or treated as if sacred: *an inviolable sanctuary.* **2.** that cannot be violated, subjected to violence, or injured. – **inviolability** /ɪnˌvaɪələ'bɪləti/, **inviolableness,** *n.* – **inviolably,** *adv.*

**inviolate** /ɪn'vaɪələt, -leɪt/, *adj.* **1.** free from violation, injury, desecration, or outrage. **2.** undisturbed. **3.** unbroken. **4.** not infringed. – **inviolacy** /ɪn'vaɪələsi/, **inviolateness,** *n.* – **inviolately,** *adv.*

**invisible** /ɪn'vɪzəbəl/, *adj.* **1.** not visible; not perceptible by the eye: *invisible agents of the Devil.* **2.** withdrawn from or out of sight. **3.** not perceptible or discernible by the mind: *invisible differences.* **4.** (of colours) of a very deep shade, or a scarcely distinguishable hue: *invisible green.* **5.** not ordinarily found in financial statements: *goodwill is an invisible asset.* **6.** concealed from public knowledge. *–n.* **7.** an invisible thing or being. **8. the invisible, a.** the unseen or spiritual world. **b.** (*cap.*) God. – **invisibility** /ɪnˌvɪzə'bɪləti/, **invisibleness,** *n.* – **invisibly,** *adv.*

**invisible exports** /– 'ɛkspɔts/, *n. pl.* services, as banking commissions, insurance premiums, freight charges, etc., which earn foreign currency for the country providing them.

**invisible imports** /– 'ɪmpɔts/, *n. pl.* activities, services incurred, etc., as holidays abroad, which spend currency in foreign countries.

**invisible ink** /– 'ɪŋk/, *n.* a fluid used for writing or drawing that is invisible until the surface is processed in some way, as by heating or chemical treatment.

**invisible mending** /– 'mɛndɪŋ/, *n.* a process of mending in which the torn threads are joined individually, so that the mend is almost invisible.

**invitation** /ɪnvə'teɪʃən/, *n.* **1.** the act of inviting. **2.** the written or spoken form with which a person is invited. **3.** attraction or allurement. *–adj.* **4.** restricted to invited individuals or teams: *an invitation golf match.* [L *invītātio*]

**invitatory** /ɪn'vaɪtətri/, *adj.* serving to invite; conveying an invitation.

**invite** /ɪn'vaɪt/, *v.,* **-vited, -viting,** *n.* *–v.t.* **1.** to ask in a kindly, courteous, or complimentary way, to come or go to some place, gathering, entertainment, etc., or to do something: *to invite friends to dinner.* **2.** to request politely or formally: *to invite donations.* **3.** to act so as to bring on or render probable: *to invite danger.* **4.** to give occasion for. **5.** to attract, allure, or tempt. *–n.* **6.** *Colloq.* an invitation. [L *invītāre*] – **inviter,** *n.*

**invitee** /ɪnvaɪ'ti/, *n.* a person entering another's premises by invitation.

**inviting** /ɪn'vaɪtɪŋ/, *adj.* that invites; especially attractive, alluring, or tempting: *an inviting offer.* – **invitingly,** *adv.* – **invitingness,** *n.*

**invito domino** /ɪnˌvitoʊ 'dɒmənoʊ/, *adv. Law.* without the consent of the owner. [L]

**in vitro** /ɪn 'vɪtroʊ/, *adv., adj.* in an artificial environment, as a test tube. [NL: lit., in glass]

**in vivo** /ɪn 'vivoʊ/, *adv., adj.* within a living organism. [L:

lit., within the living body]

**invocate** /ˈɪnvəkeɪt/, *v.t.*, **-cated, -cating.** *Rare.* →**invoke.** [L *invocātus,* pp.] – **invocative** /ɪnˈvɒkətɪv/, *adj.* – **invocator,** *n.*

**invocation** /ɪnvəˈkeɪʃən/, *n.* **1.** the act of invoking; calling upon a deity, etc., for aid, protection, inspiration, etc. **2.** a form of words used in invoking, esp. as part of a public religious service. **3.** an entreaty for aid and guidance from a Muse, deity, etc., at the beginning of an epic or epic-like poem. **4.** a calling upon a spirit by incantation, or the incantation or magical formula used.

**invocatory** /ɪnˈvɒkətri/, *adj.* pertaining to or of the nature of invocation.

**invoice** /ˈɪnvɔɪs/, *n., v.,* **-voiced, -voicing.** *–n.* **1.** a written list of merchandise, with prices, delivered or sent to a buyer. **2.** an itemised bill containing the prices which comprise the total charge. *–v.t.* **3.** to present an invoice to (a customer, or the like). **4.** to make an invoice of. **5.** to enter in an invoice. [*invoyes,* pl. of (obs.) *invoy* invoice, from F *envoy* sending, thing sent. See ENVOY[1]]

**invoke** /ɪnˈvoʊk/, *v.t.,* **-voked, -voking. 1.** to call for with earnest desire; make supplication or prayer for: *to invoke God's mercy.* **2.** to call on (a divine being, etc.), as in prayer. **3.** to appeal to, as for confirmation. **4.** to call on to come or to do something. **5.** to call forth or upon (a spirit) by incantation; conjure. [late ME, from L *invocāre*] – **invoker,** *n.*

**involucel** /ɪnˈvɒljəsɛl/, *n.* a secondary involucre, as in a compound cluster of flowers. [NL *involucellum,* diminutive of L *involūcrum* cover] – **involucellate** /ɪnˌvɒljəˈsɛleɪt/, *adj.*

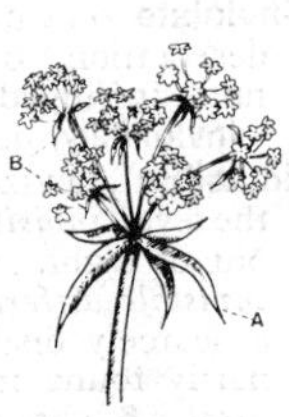

A, involucre; B, involucel

**involucrate** /ɪnvəˈlukrət, -kreɪt/, *adj.* having an involucre.

**involucre** /ɪnvəˈlukə/, *n.* **1.** *Bot.* a collection or rosette of bracts subtending a flower cluster, umbel, or the like. **2.** a covering, esp. a membranous one. [F, from L *involūcrum* wrapper, covering] – **involucral,** *adj.*

**involuntary** /ɪnˈvɒləntri/, *adj.* **1.** not voluntary; acting, or done or made without one's own volition, or otherwise than by one's own will or choice: *an involuntary listener.* **2.** unintentional. **3.** *Physiol.* acting independently of, or done or occurring without, conscious control: *involuntary muscles.* – **involuntarily,** *adv.* – **involuntariness,** *n.*

**involute** /ˈɪnvəlut/, *adj.* **1.** involved or intricate. **2.** *Bot.* rolled inwards from the edge, as a leaf. **3.** *Zool.* (of shells) having the whorls closely wound. *–n.* **4.** *Geom.* any curve of which a given curve is the evolute. [L *involūtus,* pp., rolled up] – **involutedly,** *adv.*

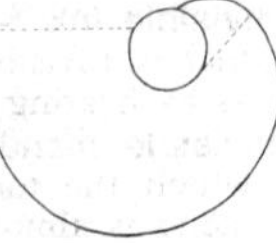
involute of a circle

**involution** /ɪnvəˈluʃən/, *n.* **1.** the act of involving. **2.** the state of being involved. **3.** something complicated. **4.** *Bot., etc.* **a.** a rolling up or folding in on itself. **b.** a part so formed. **5.** *Biol.* retrograde development; degeneration. **6.** *Physiol.* bodily changes involving a lessening of activity, esp. of the sex organs, occurring in late middle age. **7.** *Gram.* complicated construction; the separation of the subject from its predicate by the interjection of matter that should follow the verb or be placed in another sentence. **8.** *Maths.* **a.** the raising of a quantity or expression to any given power. **b.** a function that is its own inverse. [LL *involūtio* a rolling up] – **involutional,** *adj.*

involute leaves of poplar

**involve** /ɪnˈvɒlv/, *v.t.,* **-volved, -volving. 1.** to include as a necessary circumstance, condition, or consequence; imply; entail. **2.** to affect, as something within the scope of operation. **3.** to include, contain, or comprehend within itself or its scope. **4.** to bring into an intricate or complicated form or condition. **5.** to bring into difficulties (fol. by *with*): *a plot to involve one government with another.* **6.** to cause to be inextricably associated or concerned, as in something embarrassing or unfavourable. **7.** to combine inextricably (fol. by *with*). **8.** to implicate, as in guilt or crime, or in any matter or affair. **9.** to be highly or excessively interested in. **10.** to roll, wrap, or shroud, as in something that surrounds. **11.** to envelop or enfold, as the surrounding thing does. **12.** to swallow up, engulf, or overwhelm. **13.** to roll up on itself; wind spirally, coil, or wreathe. [ME, from L *involvere* roll in or on, enwrap, involve] – **involver,** *n.*

**involved** /ɪnˈvɒlvd/, *adj.* **1.** complicated; difficult to follow: *his statistical procedures were very involved.* **2.** sincerely concerned: *she is a caring and involved social worker.* **3.** (often placed after its noun) implicated (in a crime): *one of the soldiers involved shot himself.* **4.** having close personal, esp. sexual, relations (fol. by *with*): *she had been involved with Harry years before.*

**involvement** /ɪnˈvɒlvmənt/, *n.* **1.** the state of being involved. **2.** (*euph.*) an affair or romantic entanglement.

**invulnerable** /ɪnˈvʌlnərəbəl/, *adj.* **1.** incapable of being wounded, hurt, or damaged. **2.** proof against attack: *invulnerable arguments.* – **invulnerability** /ɪnˌvʌlnərəˈbɪləti/, **invulnerableness,** *n.* – **invulnerably,** *adv.*

**inwale** /ˈɪnweɪl/, *n.* a wale in a boat running along the inside of the top of the upper fore and aft plating.

**inwall** /ɪnˈwɔl/, *v.t.* →**enwall.**

**inward** /ˈɪnwəd/, *adj.* **1.** proceeding or directed towards the inside or interior. **2.** situated within; interior, internal: *an inward room.* **3.** pertaining to the inside or inner part. **4.** situated within the body: *the inward parts.* **5.** pertaining to the inside of the body: *inward convulsions.* **6.** inland: *inward passage.* **7.** intrinsic; inherent; essential: *the inward nature of a thing.* **8.** inner, mental, or spiritual: *inward peace.* **9.** muffled or indistinct, as the voice. *–adv.* **10.** inwards. *–n.* **11.** the inward or internal part; the inside. **12.** (*pl.*) →**innards.** [ME *in(ne)ward,* OE *in(ne)weard,* from *in(ne)* IN, *adv.* + *-weard* -WARD]

**inwardly** /ˈɪnwədli/, *adv.* **1.** in or on, or with reference to, the inside or inner part. **2.** privately; secretly: *laughing inwardly.* **3.** in low tones; not aloud. **4.** *Archaic.* towards the inside, interior, or centre.

**inwardness** /ˈɪnwədnəs/, *n.* **1.** the state of being inward or internal. **2.** depth of thought or feeling; earnestness. **3.** occupation with what concerns man's inner nature; spirituality. **4.** the inward or intrinsic character of a thing. **5.** inward meaning.

**inwards[1]** /ˈɪnədz/, *n.pl.* →**innards.**

**inwards[2]** /ˈɪnwədz/, *adv.* **1.** towards the inside or interior, as of a place, a space, or a body. **2.** into the mind or soul. **3.** in the mind or soul, or mentally or spiritually; inwardly. Also, **inward.** [INWARD + adv. genitive *-s*]

**inweave** /ɪnˈwiv/, *v.t.,* **-wove** or **-weaved; -woven** or **-weaved; -weaving.** →**enweave.**

**inwind** /ɪnˈwaɪnd/, *v.t.,* **-wound, -winding.** →**enwind.**

**inwrap** /ɪnˈræp/, *v.t.,* **-wrapped, -wrapping.** →**enwrap.**

**inwreathe** /ɪnˈrið/, *v.t.,* **-wreathed, -wreathing.** →**enwreathe.**

**inwrought** /ɪnˈrɔt/, *adj.* **1.** wrought or worked with something by way of decoration. **2.** wrought or worked in, as a decorative pattern. **3.** worked in or closely combined with something.

**inyala** /ɪnˈjalə/, *n.* a small antelope, *Tragelaphus angasi,* of southern Africa, having a white stripe down the back; bastard kudu. Also, **nyala.** [Zulu]

**Io,** *Chem.* ionium.

**io** /ˈaɪoʊ/, *n., pl.* **ios.** →**io moth.**

**I/O,** input/output.

**I/O** /aɪˈoʊ/, input/output.

**iod-,** variant of **iodo-,** usu. before vowels, as in *iodic.*

**iodate** /ˈaɪədeɪt/, *n., v.,* **-dated, -dating.** *–n.* **1.** *Chem.* a salt of iodic acid, as *sodium iodate,* $NaIO_3$. *–v.t.* **2.** to iodise. – **iodation** /aɪəˈdeɪʃən/, *n.*

**iodeosin** /ˌaɪoʊdiˈoʊsən/, *n. Chem.* a red powder, $C_{20}H_8I_4O_5$, used as an indicator in analytical chemistry; tetraiodofluorescein.

**iodic** /aɪˈɒdɪk/, *adj.* containing iodine, esp. in the pentavalent state. [IOD- + -IC]

**iodic acid** /– ˈæsəd/, *n.* a white crystalline water-soluble solid, $HIO_3$, which forms iodates.

**iodide** /ˈaɪədaɪd/, *n.* a compound, usu. of two elements only, one of which is iodine; a salt of hydriodic acid. Also, **iodid** /ˈaɪədɪd/.

**iodimetry** /aɪəˈdɪmətri/, *n. Chem.* →**iodometry.**

**iodine** /ˈaɪədin, ˈaɪədaɪn/, *n.* a non-metallic element occurring, at ordinary temperatures, as a greyish black crystalline solid, which sublimes to a dense violet vapour when heated, used in medicine as an antiseptic; the radioactive isotope, iodine-131, is used in the diagnosis and treatment of disorders of the thyroid gland. *Symbol:* I; *at. wt:* 126.9044; *at. no.:* 53; *sp. gr.:* (solid) 4.93 at 20°C. Also, **iodin** /ˈaɪədən/. [F *iode* iodine (from Gk *iṓdēs*, properly, rust-coloured, but taken to mean violet-like) + -INE[2]]

**iodine value** /ˈ– væljuː/, *n.* a measure of the amount of unsaturated fatty acid present in a fat, oil, resin or other natural product; the weight of iodine absorbed by 100 grams of the substance.

**iodise** /ˈaɪədaɪz/, *v.t.*, **-dised, -dising.** to treat, impregnate, or affect with iodine. Also, **iodize.** – **iodiser,** *n.*

**iodism** /ˈaɪədɪzəm/, *n.* a morbid condition due to the use of iodine or its compounds.

**iodo-,** a word element meaning 'iodine', as in *iodometry.* Also, **iod-.** [combining form representing NL *iōdum*]

**iodoform** /aɪˈɒdəfɔm, aɪˈoʊ-/, *n.* a yellowish crystalline compound, $CHI_3$, analogous to chloroform, used as an antiseptic. [IODO- + FORM(YL)]

**iodole** /ˈaɪədoʊl/, *n.* a greyish yellow crystalline powder, $C_4I_4NH$, which is odourless, colourless and tasteless, and which is used medically; tetraiodopyrrole.

**iodometry** /aɪəˈdɒmətri/, *n.* a volumetric analytical procedure for determining iodine, or materials which will liberate iodine or react with iodine. Also, **iodimetry.** – **iodometric** /aɪədoʊˈmɛtrɪk/, *adj.*

**iodous** /aɪˈɒdəs/, *adj.* **1.** *Chem.* containing iodine, esp. in the divalent state. **2.** like iodine.

**Io moth** /ˈaɪoʊ mɒθ/, *n.* a showy and beautiful moth of North America, *Automeris io*, of yellow colouration, with prominent pink and bluish eyespots on the hind wings.

**ion** /ˈaɪən/, *n.* **1.** an electrically charged atom, radical, or molecule, formed by the loss or gain of one or more electrons. **Positive ions,** created by electron loss, are called *cations* and are attracted to the cathode in electrolysis. **Negative ions,** created by electron gain, are called *anions* and are attracted to the anode. The valency of an ion is equal to the number of electrons lost or gained and is indicated by a plus sign for cations and minus for anions, thus: $Na^+$, $Cl^-$, $Ca^{++}$, $S^=$. **2.** one of the electrically charged particles formed in a gas by the action of an electric discharge, etc. [Gk, ppr. neut. of *iénai* go] – **ionic** /aɪˈɒnɪk/, *adj.*

**-ion,** a suffix of nouns denoting action or process, state or condition, or sometimes things or persons, as in *allusion, communion, flexion, fusion, legion, opinion, suspicion, union.* Also, **-tion** and **-ation.** Cf. **-cion, -xion.** [L *-io*, suffix forming nouns, esp. from verbs]

**ion engine** /ˈaɪən ɛndʒən/, *n.* a rocket engine the propelling force of which is obtained by the discharge at the rear of electrostatically-accelerated charged positive ions. Cf. **plasma engine.**

**ion exchange** /aɪən əksˈtʃeɪndʒ/, *n.* the process of reciprocal transfer of ions between a solution and a resin.

**ion exchange chromatography,** *n.* a method of separating ions, as in water softening processes based on this method.

**Ionian** /aɪˈoʊniən/, *adj.* **1.** pertaining to Ionia (an ancient region in Asia Minor). **2.** pertaining to a branch of the Greek race named after Ion, the legendary founder. *–n.* **3.** an Ionian Greek.

**Ionian mode** /– ˈmoʊd/, *n.* a musical scale, represented by the white keys of a keyboard instrument, beginning on C.

**Ionic** /aɪˈɒnɪk/, *adj.* **1.** *Archit.* denoting or pertaining to one of the three Greek orders (def. 33), distinguished by its slender proportions, the volutes on the capitals, and the continuous (often figured) frieze. **2.** *Pros.* denoting or employing one of two feet consisting of two long and two short syllables: **the greater Ionic,** two long and two short syllables, ¯ ¯ ˘ ˘; **the lesser Ionic,** two short and two long syllables, ˘ ˘ ¯ ¯. **3.** pertaining to the Ionians. **4.** (*l.c.*) *Chem.* of, or pertaining to, ions. *–n.* **5.** *Pros.* an Ionic foot, verse, or metre. **6.** (*also l.c.*) *Print.* a style of typeface without strong distinction between thick and thin strokes, often used as a newspaper typeface. **7.** a dialect of ancient Greek, including Attic and the language of Homer. [L *Iōnicus*, from Gk *Iōnikós*]

**ionic bond** /aɪɒnɪk ˈbɒnd/, *n. Chem.* →**electrovalent bond.**

**ionic hypothesis** /– haɪˈpɒθəsəs/, *n.* the hypothesis that those compounds which render water conductive when dissolved in it, do so by splitting up into charged atoms, or groups of atoms, called ions; the passage of these ions through the solution constitutes an electric current.

**ionic mobility** /– moʊˈbɪləti/, *n.* the velocity of an ion in an electric field of one volt per centimetre.

**ionisation chamber** /aɪənaɪˈzeɪʃən tʃeɪmbə/, *n.* a device for measuring the strength of ionising radiation, consisting of a gas-filled chamber containing two electrodes between which a potential difference is maintained. The radiation ionises the gas, and the current flowing between the electrodes is a measure of its strength.

**ionisation potential** /– pəˈtɛnʃəl/, *n.* the energy required to remove an electron from an atom.

**ionise** /ˈaɪənaɪz/, *v.*, **-nised, -nising.** *–v.t.* **1.** to separate or change into ions. **2.** to produce ions in. *–v.i.* **3.** to become changed into ions, as by dissolving. Also, **ionize.** – **ionisation** /aɪənaɪˈzeɪʃən/, *n.* – **ioniser,** *n.*

**ionising radiation** /ˌaɪənaɪzɪŋ reɪdiˈeɪʃən/, *n.* any radiation (either electromagnetic or corpuscular) which causes ionisation in the matter through which it passes.

**ionium** /aɪˈoʊniəm/, *n.* a naturally occurring radioactive isotope of thorium. *Symbol:* Io; *at. wt:* 230; *at. no.:* 90.

**ionone** /ˈaɪənoʊn/, *n.* either one or a mixture of two unsaturated ketones, $C_{13}H_{20}O$, used in perfumery.

**ionosphere** /aɪˈɒnəsfɪə/, *n.* **1.** the succession of ionised layers that constitute the outer regions of the earth's atmosphere beyond the stratosphere, considered as beginning with the Heaviside layer at about 100 kilometres and extending upwards several hundred kilometres. **2.** *Obs.* the Heaviside layer.

**I.O.O.F.** /ˌaɪ dʌbl oʊ ˈɛf/, *n.* Independent Order of Oddfellows.

**Iora** /ˈjɔrə, iˈɔrə/, *n.* the Australian Aboriginal language formerly spoken in the region of present-day Sydney and probably limited to the southern side of Port Jackson.

**iota** /aɪˈoʊtə/, *n.* **1.** the ninth letter (Ι, ι, = English I, i) of the Greek alphabet (the smallest letter). **2.** a very small quantity; a tittle; a jot.

**iotacism** /aɪˈoʊtəsɪzəm/, *n.* conversion of other vowel sounds into that of iota (English ē). [L *iōtacismus*, from Gk *iōtakismós*]

**IOU** /aɪ oʊ ˈju/, *n.* a written acknowledgment of a debt, containing the expression IOU (I owe you). Also, **I.O.U.**

**-ious,** a termination consisting of the suffix **-ous** with a preceding original or euphonic vowel **i.** Cf. **-eous.**

**I.P.** /aɪ ˈpi/, *n. Colloq.* (usu. among school teachers) an irate parent.

**IPA** /aɪ pi ˈeɪ/, International Phonetic Alphabet.

**ipecacuanha** /ˌɪpəkækjuˈænə/, *n.* **1.** the dried root of two small shrubby South American plants, *Cephaelis ipecacuanha*, and *C. acuminata*, used as an emetic, purgative, etc. **2.** a drug consisting of the roots of these plants. **3.** the plants themselves. Also, **ipecac** /ˈɪpəkæk/. [Pg., from Tupi *ipekaa-guéne*, from *ipeh* low + *kaâ* leaves + *guéne* vomit]

**ipomoea** /ɪpəˈmiə, aɪpə-/, *n.* **1.** any plant of the genus *Ipomoea*, of the morning-glory family, containing many species with ornamental flowers. **2.** the dried root of the plant, *Ipomoea orizabensis*, yielding a resin which is a cathartic. [NL, from Gk *íps* kind of worm + *hómoios* like]

**ipse dixit** /ɪpseɪ ˈdɪksət/, *n.* an assertion without proof. [L: he himself said it]

**ipso facto** /ɪpsoʊ ˈfæktoʊ/, *adv.* by the fact itself; by that very fact: *it is condemned ipso facto.* [L]

**i.q.,** the same as. [L *idem quod*]

**IQ** /aɪ ˈkju/, intelligence quotient. Also, **I.Q.**

**ir-**[1], variant of **in-**[2], before *r*, as in *irradiate.*

**ir-**[2], variant of **in-**[3], before *r*, as in *irreducible.*

**Ir,** *Chem.* iridium.

**Ir.,** **1.** Ireland. **2.** Irish.

**I.R.A.** /aɪ ar ˈeɪ/, Irish Republican Army.

**Iran** /ɪˈræn, -ˈran/, *n.* an Islamic republic in south-western Asia.

**Iranian** /ɪˈreɪniən, -ˈran-/, *adj.* **1.** pertaining to Iran (or Persia). **2.** pertaining to Iranian (def. 3). *–n.* **3.** a subgroup of Indo-European languages including Persian and Pushtu. **4.** Persian (the language). **5.** an inhabitant of Iran; a Persian.

**Iraq** /ɪˈrak/, *n.* a republic in south-western Asia, north of Saudi Arabia and west of Iran, centring in the Tigris-Euphrates basin of Mesopotamia.

**Iraqi** /ɪˈraki/, *n., pl.* **-qis,** *adj.* *–n.* **1.** a native of Iraq. **2.** Also, **Iraqi Arabic.** the dialect of Arabic spoken in Iraq. *–adj.* **3.** of or pertaining to Iraq or its inhabitants.

**irascible** /ɪˈræsəbəl/, *adj.* **1.** easily provoked to anger: *an irascible old man.* **2.** characterised by, excited by, or arising from anger: *an irascible nature.* [ME, from LL *īrascibilis*] **– irascibility** /ɪˌræsəˈbɪləti/, **irascibleness,** *n.* **– irascibly,** *adv.*

**irate** /aɪˈreɪt/, *adj.* angry; enraged: *the irate colonel.* [L *īrātus,* pp.] **– irately,** *adv.*

**IRBM** /ˌaɪ a bi ˈɛm/, intermediate range ballistic missile.

**ire** /ˈaɪə/, *n.* anger; wrath. [ME, from OF, from L *īra*] **– ireless,** *adj.*

**ireful** /ˈaɪəfəl/, *adj.* **1.** full of ire; wrathful: *an ireful look.* **2.** irascible. **– irefully,** *adv.* **– irefulness,** *n.*

**Ireland** /ˈaɪələnd/, *n.* **1.** one of the British Isles in the Atlantic west of Britain, divided into the Republic of Ireland and Northern Ireland. **2.** a republic occupying most of the southern part of the island of Ireland. Official name: **Republic of Ireland. 3.** See **Northern Ireland.**

**irenic** /aɪˈrinɪk/, *adj.* peaceful; tending to promote or encourage peace or peaceful arts. Also, **irenical.** [Gk *eirēnikós*]

**irenics** /aɪˈrinɪks/, *n.* irenic theology, promoting Christian unity.

**iridaceous** /ɪrəˈdeɪʃəs/, *adj.* **1.** belonging to the Iridaceae, or iris family of plants, which includes, besides various flags, the crocus, gladiolus, and freesia. **2.** resembling or pertaining to plants of the genus *Iris.* [NL *Iris* the iris genus (see IRIS) + -ACEOUS]

**iridescence** /ɪrəˈdɛsəns/, *n.* iridescent quality; a play of lustrous, changing colours.

**iridescent** /ɪrəˈdɛsənt/, *adj.* displaying colours like those of the rainbow. [L *īris* rainbow + -ESCENT] **– iridescently,** *adv.*

**iridic** /aɪˈrɪdɪk, əˈrɪdɪk/, *adj.* of or containing iridium, esp. in the tetravalent state.

**iridise** /ˈɪrədaɪz, ˈaɪ-/, *v.t.,* **-dised, -dising.** to cover with iridium. Also, **iridize. – iridisation** /ˌɪrədaɪˈzeɪʃən, ˌaɪ-/, *n.*

**iridium** /aɪˈrɪdiəm, əˈrɪdiəm/, *n.* a precious metallic element resembling platinum, used in platinum alloys and for the points of gold pens. *Symbol:* Ir; *at. wt:* 192.2; *at. no.* 77; *sp. gr.:* 22.4 at 20°C. [NL, from L *īris* rainbow; named from its iridescence in solution]

**iridosmine** /ɪrəˈdɒzmən, aɪrə-/, *n.* a native alloy of iridium and osmium, usu. containing some rhodium, ruthenium, platinum, etc., used esp. for the points of gold pens; osmiridium. Also, **iridosmium.** [IRID(IUM) + OSM(IUM) + -INE[2]]

**iridous** /ˈɪrədəs, ˈaɪ-/, *adj.* containing trivalent iridium.

**iris** /ˈaɪrəs/, *n., pl.* **irises, irides** /ˈaɪrədiz/. **1.** *Anat.* the contractile circular diaphragm forming the coloured portion of the eye and containing a circular opening (the pupil) in its centre. **2.** *Bot.* **a.** a family of plants, Iridaceae. **b.** any plant of the genus *Iris,* including various perennial herbs with handsome flowers and sword-shaped leaves; the fleur-de-lis or flag. **c.** the flower of any such plant. **d.** →**orrisroot. 3.** an iris diaphragm. [ME, from L, from Gk]

**iris diaphragm** /– ˈdaɪəfræm/, *n.* a composite diaphragm with a central aperture readily adjustable for size, used to regulate the amount of light admitted to a lens or optical system.

**Irish** /ˈaɪrɪʃ/, *adj., n., pl.* **Irish.** *–adj.* **1.** of or characteristic of Ireland or its people. **2.** containing an inherent contradiction. *–n.* **3.** the inhabitants of Ireland and their descendants elsewhere. **4.** the aboriginal Celtic-speaking people of Ireland. **5.** the Celtic language of Ireland in its historical (Old Irish, Middle Irish) or modern form. **6.** Irish English. **7. get one's Irish up,** *Colloq.* to become angry. [ME *Irisc, Iris(c)h,* from OE *Iras,* pl., people of Ireland (c. Icel. *Irar*)]

**Irish coffee** /– ˈkɒfi/, *n.* a mixture of hot coffee and whisky served with a whipped cream topping.

**Irishman** /ˈaɪrɪʃmən/, *n., pl.* **-men. 1.** a man born in Ireland or of Irish ancestry. **2.** *N.Z.* →**matagouri. – Irishwoman,** *n. fem.*

**Irishman's hurricane** /ˌaɪrɪʃmənz ˈhʌrəkən/, *n. Naut. Colloq.* a dead calm.

Irish setter

**Irish moss** /aɪrɪʃ ˈmɒs/, *n.* **1.** a purplish brown, cartilaginous seaweed, *Chondrus crispus,* of the Atlantic coasts of Europe and North America; carrageen. **2.** this seaweed, dried and bleached, used as a substitute for gelatine, and commercially as a thickening agent.

**Irish setter** /– ˈsɛtə/, *n.* a rich chestnut coloured variety of setter.

**Irish stew** /– ˈstju/, *n.* a stew usu. made of mutton, lamb, or beef, with potatoes, onions, etc.

**Irish terrier** /– ˈtɛriə/, *n.* one of a breed of small, active, intelligent dogs with wiry hair, usu. of a reddish tinge.

Irish terrier

**Irish water-spaniel** /– ˈwɔtə-spænjəl/, *n.* one of an ancient breed of spaniels, notable for its coat of dense crisp ringlets, usu. liver-coloured.

**Irish wolfhound** /– ˈwʊlfhaʊnd/, *n.* a shaggy-coated breed of wolfhound, at almost one metre high at shoulder, the tallest known dog, developed in Ireland as early as the 3rd century A.D.

**Irish yew** /– ˈju/, *n.* a widely cultivated columnar form of the common yew, *Taxus baccata* var. *stricta.*

Irish wolfhound

**iritis** /aɪˈraɪtəs/, *n.* inflammation of the iris of the eye. [NL, from IR(IS) + -ITIS] **– iritic** /aɪˈrɪtɪk/, *adj.*

**irk** /ɜk/, *v.t.* to weary, annoy, or trouble: *it irked him to wait.* [ME *irke, yrk(e)* tire, from Scand.; cf. Icel. *yrkja* work, c. OE *wyrcan;* see WORK]

**irksome** /ˈɜksəm/, *adj.* causing weariness, disgust, or annoyance: *irksome restrictions.* **– irksomely,** *adv.* **– irksomeness,** *n.*

**iron** /ˈaɪən/, *n.* **1.** *Chem.* a ductile, malleable, silver-white metallic element, scarcely known in a pure condition, but abundantly used in its crude or impure forms containing carbon (see **pig-iron, cast iron, steel,** and **wrought iron**) for making tools, implements, machinery, etc. Symbol: Fe (L *ferrum*); *at. wt:* 55.847; *at. no.:* 26; *sp. gr.:* 7.86 at 20°C. **2.** something hard, strong, rigid, unyielding, or the like: *hearts of iron.* **3.** an instrument, utensil, weapon, etc., made of iron. **4.** an iron or steel implement used heated for smoothing or pressing cloth, etc. **5.** an iron-headed golf club intermediate between a cleek and a mashie: *a driving iron.* **6.** a branding iron. **7.** *Brit. Colloq.* →**pistol. 8.** →**harpoon. 9.** (*pl.*) **a.** an iron shackle or fetter: *body irons, leg irons.* **b.** iron supports to correct leg malformations, etc. **10.** →**stirrup** (def. 1). **11. good iron!** (an exclamation of approval, agreement, etc.). **12. in irons,** *Naut.* **a.** lying head to the wind and having no headway, unable to fall off on either tack. **b.** imprisoned in iron chains. **13. strike while the iron is hot,** to take immediate action while the opportunity is still available. **14. too many irons in the fire,** too many undertakings. *–adj.* **15.** made of iron. **16.** resembling iron in colour, firmness, etc.: *an iron will.* **17.** stern, harsh, or cruel. **18.** not to be broken. **19.** degenerate, debased, or wicked. **20.** capable of great endurance; extremely robust or hardy. **21.** firmly binding or clasping. *–v.t.* **22.** to smooth or press with a heated iron, as clothes, etc. **23.** to furnish, mount, or arm with iron. **24.** to shackle or fetter with irons. **25.** to flatten; knock down (fol. by *out*). **26. iron out, a.** to press (a garment, etc.) **b.** to smooth and remove (problems and difficulties, etc.). **27. iron (oneself) out,** to get drunk. *–v.i.* **28.** to press clothes, etc., with a heated iron. [ME *iren, ysen,* OE *iren, īsen, īsern,* c. G *Eisen*] – **ironless,** *adj.* – **iron-like,** *adj.* – **ironer,** *n.*

**Iron Age** /ˈaɪən eɪdʒ/, *n.* **1.** *Archaeol.* the time during which early man lived and made implements of iron, and which followed the Stone and Bronze Ages. **2.** (*l.c.*) *Class. Myth.* the last and worst age of the world. **3.** (*l.c.*) any age or period of degeneracy or wickedness.

**ironbark** /ˈaɪənbak/, *n.* any of a group of species of *Eucalyptus,* with a characteristic dark deeply fissured bark, as *E. paniculata,* **grey ironbark.**

**ironbark orchid** /ˈ– ɔkəd/, *n.* →**white feather orchid.**

**ironbound** /ˈaɪənbaʊnd/, *adj.* **1.** bound with iron. **2.** rock-bound; rugged. **3.** hard, rigid, or unyielding.

**ironclad** /ˈaɪənklæd/, *adj.* **1.** covered or cased with iron plates, as a vessel for naval warfare; armour-plated. **2.** very rigid or strict: *an ironclad agreement.* *–n.* **3.** a warship of the middle and late 19th century fitted with armour plating.

**Iron Curtain** /aɪən ˈkɜtn/, *n.* **1.** a rigid division of Europe, formed by ideological differences between those European countries partly or wholly within the Soviet sphere of influence and those partly or wholly within the U.S. sphere of influence; physically formed by the frontiers between West Germany, Austria, and Italy on the one side, and East Germany, Czechoslovakia, Hungary, and Yugoslavia on the other. **2.** the state of censorship, control of movement, etc., pertaining in the countries of Eastern Europe.

**irone** /ˈaɪroʊn, aɪˈroʊn/, *n.* a colourless liquid, $C_{13}H_{20}O$, obtained from the orrisroot, and used in perfumery.

**iron-fisted** /ˈaɪən-fɪstəd/, *adj.* **1.** ruthless. **2.** close-fisted; niggardly.

**iron gang** /ˈaɪən gæŋ/, *n.* (formerly), a party of convicts kept in iron chains, usu. employed in road-building. Also, **ironed gang.**

**iron glance** /ˈ– glæns/, *n. Mineral.* →**hematite.**

**iron-grey** /aɪən-ˈgreɪ/, *adj.* of a grey colour like that of freshly broken iron.

**iron gum** /ˈaɪən gʌm/, *n.* one of several species of *Eucalyptus* which have particularly strong wood.

**iron hand** /– ˈhænd/, *n.* severe control; strictness.

**iron-handed** /ˈaɪən-hændəd/, *adj.* controlling with severity or strictness; iron-fisted.

**iron horse** /aɪən ˈhɔs/, *n. Archaic.* **1.** a locomotive. **2.** a bicycle or tricycle.

**ironic** /aɪˈrɒnɪk/, *adj.* **1.** pertaining to, of the nature of, or characterised by irony: *an ironic compliment.* **2.** using, or addicted to irony: *an ironic speaker.* **3.** of the nature of or containing irony. Also, **ironical** /aɪˈrɒnɪkəl/. [L *īrōnicus,* from Gk *eirōnikós* dissembling, feigning ignorance] – **ironically,** *adv.* – **ironicalness,** *n.*

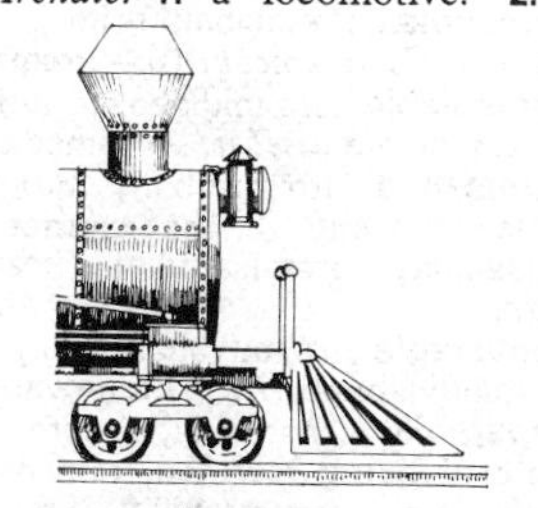
iron horse

**ironing** /ˈaɪənɪŋ/, *n.* **1.** the act or process of pressing clothes, sheets, etc., with a heated iron. **2.** clothes, linen, etc., that have been ironed, or are to be ironed.

**ironing-board** /ˈaɪənɪŋ-bɔd/, *n.* a flat narrow board, usu. cloth-covered, often mounted on legs which can be folded to lie flat, and used for pressing clothes, linen, etc.

**ironist** /ˈaɪrənəst/, *n.* one who makes much use of irony.

**iron lace** /aɪən ˈleɪs/, *n.* cast-iron ornamentation often of an intricate kind associated particularly with 19th century terrace houses.

iron lace

**iron lung** /– ˈlʌŋ/, *n.* a chamber in which alternate pulsations of high and low pressure can be used to force normal lung movements, used esp. in some cases of poliomyelitis.

**iron maiden** /– ˈmeɪdn/, *n.* **1.** a medieval instrument of torture consisting of a hollow metal box in the shape of a female body, hinged and lined with spikes, into which the victim was locked. **2.** *Colloq.* a particularly difficult and cantankerous woman.

**iron man** /ˈ– mæn/, *n. Colloq.* **1.** a man of exceptional physical strength. **2.** (formerly) a pound note.

**iron-man** /ˈaɪən-mæn/, *adj.* of or pertaining to an endurance race in a surf carnival.

**ironmaster** /ˈaɪənmastə/, *n.* a manufacturer of iron; the master of ironworks.

**ironmonger** /ˈaɪənmʌŋgə/, *n.* a dealer in metal ware, tools, cutlery, locks, etc.

**ironmongery** /ˈaɪənmʌŋgəri/, *n., pl.* **-ries. 1.** the goods, shop, or business of an ironmonger. **2.** firearms.

**iron mould** /ˈaɪən moʊld/, *n.* **1.** a stain on cloth, etc., made by rusty iron or ink. **2.** damp mould developing in clothing waiting to be ironed.

**iron olivine** /– ˈɒləvin/, *n.* →**fayalite.**

**iron-on** /ˈaɪən-ɒn/, *adj.* **1.** of or pertaining to an item which is designed to be affixed to an article of clothing with the pressure of a heated iron: *an iron-on transfer.* *–n.* **2.** such an item.

**iron pyrites** /aɪən paɪˈraɪtiz/, *n.* **1.** pyrite, or ordinary pyrites; fool's gold. **2.** →**marcasite. 3.** →**pyrrhotite.**

**iron rations** /ˈ– ræʃənz/, n.pl. emergency reserve rations, esp. those of troops in wartime.

**irons** /ˈaɪənz/, *n.pl.* **1.** fetters and chains: *clap him in irons!* **2. irons in the fire:** separate interests, projects, etc.: *I have many irons in the fire.*

**ironside** /ˈaɪənsaɪd/, *n.* **1.** a person with great power of endurance or resistance. **2.** (*pl.*) →**ironclad.** [orig. a trooper of the army of Oliver Cromwell, 1599-1658, general, statesman, and Lord Protector of the British Commonwealth 1653-58]

**ironsmith** /ˈaɪənsmɪθ/, *n.* a worker in iron; a blacksmith.

**ironstone** /ˈaɪənstoʊn/, *n.* **1.** any ore of iron (commonly a carbonate of iron) with clayey or siliceous impurities. **2.** *Geol.* a sandstone containing 20 to 30 per cent of iron oxide, usu. limonite. **3.** a hard white stoneware pottery.

**iron sulphate** /aɪən ˈsʌlfeɪt/, *n.* →**ferrous sulphate.**

**ironware** /ˈaɪənwɛə/, *n.* articles of iron, as pots, kettles, tools, etc.; hardware.

**ironwood** /ˈaɪənwʊd/, *n.* **1.** any of various trees with hard heavy wood, as *Acacia excelsa* and *Erythrophloem chlorostachys* of Australia, species of the genus *Metrosideros* of New Zealand, and *Carpinus caroliniana* of America. **2.** the wood of such a tree.

**ironwork** /ˈaɪənwɜk/, *n.* **1.** work in iron. **2.** parts or articles made of iron: *ornamental ironwork.*

**ironworker** /ˈaɪənwɜkə/, *n.* a worker in iron.

**ironworks** /ˈaɪənwɜks/, *n.pl. or sing.* an establishment where iron is smelted or where it is cast or wrought.

**irony**[1] /ˈaɪrəni/, *n., pl.* **-nies. 1.** a figure of speech or literary device in which the literal meaning is the opposite of that intended, esp., as in the Greek sense, when the locution understates the effect intended, employed in ridicule or merely playfully. **2.** an ironical utterance or expression. **3.** simulated ignorance in discussion **(Socratic irony). 4.** the quality or effect, or implication of a speech or situation in a play or the like understood by the audience but not grasped by the characters of the piece **(dramatic irony). 5.** an outcome of events contrary to what was, or might have been, expected. **6.** an ironical quality. [L *īrōnīa,* from Gk *eirōneía* dissimulation, understatement]

**irony**[2] /ˈaɪəni/, *adj.* consisting of, containing, or resembling iron. [ME *yrony,* from IRON + -Y[1]]

**Iroquoian** /ɪrəˈkwɔɪən/, *adj.* belonging to or constituting a linguistic family of the Iroquoian-Caddoan stock of North American Indians, of Canada and the eastern U.S., including the Iroquois confederacy, the Cherokees, Wyandots or Hurons, Erie, and others.

**irradiant** /ɪ'reɪdiənt/, *adj.* irradiating; radiant; shining. – **irradiance, irradiancy,** *n.*

**irradiate** /ɪ'reɪdieɪt/, *v.,* **-ated, -ating;** /ɪ'reɪdiət, -eɪt/, *adj.* –*v.t.* **1.** to shed rays of light upon; illuminate. **2.** to illumine intellectually or spiritually. **3.** to brighten as if with light. **4.** to radiate (light, etc.). **5.** to heat with radiant energy. **6.** to cure or treat by exposure to radiation, as of ultraviolet light. **7.** to expose to radiation. –*v.i.* **8.** to emit rays; shine. **9.** to become radiant. –*adj.* **10.** irradiated; bright. [L *irradiātus,* pp., illumined] – **irradiative** /ɪ'reɪdiətɪv/, *adj.* – **irradiator,** *n.*

**irradiation** /ɪ,reɪdi'eɪʃən/, *n.* **1.** the act of irradiating. **2.** the state of being irradiated. **3.** intellectual or spiritual enlightenment. **4.** a ray of light; a beam. **5.** *Optics.* the apparent enlargement of a bright object when seen against a dark ground. **6.** the use of X-rays or other radiations for the treatment of disease, etc. **7.** the process of exposure to radiation. **8.** the intensity of radiation falling on a given point; radiant energy received per unit of time per unit area of irradiated surface.

**irrational** /ɪ'ræʃənəl/, *adj.* **1.** without the faculty of, or not endowed with, reason: *irrational animals.* **2.** without, or deprived of, sound judgment. **3.** not in accordance with reason; utterly illogical: *irrational fear.* **4.** *Maths.* **a.** (of numbers) not expressible as a ratio of two integers. **b.** (of functions) not expressible as a ratio of two polynomials. **5.** *Gk and Lat. Pros.* **a.** of or pertaining to a substitution in the normal metrical pattern, esp. a long syllable for a short syllable. **b.** denoting a foot containing such a substitution. –*n.* **6.** an irrational number or quantity. [late ME, from L *irratiōnālis*] – **irrationally,** *adv.* – **irrationalness,** *n.*

**irrationalise** /ɪ'ræʃənəlaɪz/, *v.t.,* **-lised, -lising.** to render irrational. Also, **irrationalize.**

**irrationalism** /ɪ'ræʃənəlɪzəm/, *n.* →**irrationality.**

**irrationality** /ɪ,ræʃə'nælәti/, *n., pl.* **-ties. 1.** the quality of being irrational. **2.** an irrational, illogical, or absurd action, thought, etc.

**irreclaimable** /ɪrə'kleɪməbəl/, *adj.* not reclaimable; incapable of being reclaimed. – **irreclaimability** /ɪrə,kleɪmə'bɪləti/, **irreclaimableness,** *n.* – **irreclaimably,** *adv.*

**irreconcilable** /ɪ'rɛkənsaɪləbəl/, *adj.* **1.** that cannot be harmonised or adjusted; incompatible: *two irreconcilable statements.* **2.** that cannot be brought to acquiescence or content; implacably opposed: *irreconcilable enemies.* –*n.* **3.** one who or that which is irreconcilable. **4.** one who remains opposed to agreement or compromise. – **irreconcilability** /ɪ,rɛkənsaɪlə'bɪləti/, **irreconcilableness,** *n.* – **irreconcilably,** *adv.*

**irrecoverable** /ɪrə'kʌvərəbəl, -'kʌvrə-/, *adj.* **1.** that cannot be regained: *an irrecoverable debt.* **2.** that cannot be remedied or rectified: *irrecoverable sorrow.* – **irrecoverableness,** *n.* – **irrecoverably,** *adv.*

**irrecusable** /ɪrə'kjuzəbəl/, *adj.* not to be objected to or rejected. [LL *irrecūsābilis* not to be refused] – **irrecusably,** *adv.*

**irredeemable** /ɪrə'dimәbəl/, *adj.* **1.** not redeemable; incapable of being bought back or paid off. **2.** not convertible into specie, as paper money. **3.** beyond redemption; irreclaimable. **4.** irremediable, irreparable, or hopeless. – **irredeemableness,** *n.* – **irredeemably,** *adv.*

**irredentist** /ɪrə'dɛntəst/, *n.* **1.** a member of a party in any country advocating the acquiring of some region, actually included in another country, but claimed as properly belonging to the former country by reason of racial, cultural, ethnic, historical or other ties. –*adj.* **2.** pertaining to or advocating irredentism. [from *Irridentist,* a member of an Italian patriotic association, prominent in 1878; It. *irredentista,* from (*Italia*) *irredenta* (Italy) unredeemed, fem. of *irredento,* from L *in-* IN-[3] + *redemptus,* pp., redeemed] – **irredentism,** *n.*

**irreducible** /ɪrə'djusəbəl/, *adj.* **1.** not reducible; incapable of being reduced or diminished: *the irreducible minimum.* **2.** incapable of being brought into a different condition or form. – **irreducibility** /,ɪrədʒusə'bɪləti/, **irreducibleness,** *n.* – **irreducibly,** *adv.*

**irredundant** /ɪrə'dʌndənt/, *adj. Maths.* containing no redundant elements.

**irrefragable** /ɪ'rɛfrəgəbəl/, *adj.* not to be refuted; undeniable. [LL *irrefragābilis*] – **irrefragability** /ɪ,rɛfrəgə'bɪləti/, **irrefragableness,** *n.* – **irrefragably,** *adv.*

**irrefrangible** /ɪrə'frændʒəbəl/, *adj.* **1.** not to be broken or violated; inviolable: *an irrefrangible rule of etiquette.* **2.** incapable of being refracted: *X-rays are irrefrangible.* – **irrefrangibly,** *adv.*

**irrefutable** /ɪ'rɛfjətəbəl, ɪrə'fjutəbəl/, *adj.* not refutable; incontrovertible: *irrefutable logic.* – **irrefutability** /ɪrəfjutə'bɪləti/, *n.* – **irrefutably,** *adv.*

**irreg., 1.** irregular. **2.** irregularly.

**irregardless** /ɪrə'gadləs/, *adj. Colloq.* regardless; unmindful; not withstanding.

**irregular** /ɪ'rɛgjələ/, *adj.* **1.** without symmetry, even shape, formal arrangement, etc.: *an irregular pattern.* **2.** not characterised by any fixed principle, method, or rate: *irregular intervals.* **3.** not according to rule, or to the accepted principle, method, course, order, etc. **4.** not conformed or conforming to rules of justice or morality, as conduct, transactions, mode of life, etc., or persons. **5.** *Bot.* not uniform; (of a flower) having the members of some or all of its floral circles or whorls differing from one another in size or shape, or extent of union. **6.** *Gram.* not conforming to the most prevalent pattern of formation, inflection, construction, etc.: *the verbs 'keep' and 'see' are irregular in their inflection.* **7.** *Mil.* (formerly, of troops) not belonging to the established forces. –*n.* **8.** one who or that which is irregular. **9.** *Mil.* a soldier not of a regular military force. [ML *irregulāris;* replacing ME *irreguler,* from OF. See IR-[2], REGULAR] – **irregularly,** *adv.*

**irregularity** /ɪ,rɛgjə'lærəti/, *n., pl.* **-ties. 1.** the state or fact of being irregular. **2.** something irregular. **3.** a breach of rules, etiquette, or principle.

**irrelative** /ɪ'rɛlətɪv/, *adj.* **1.** not relative; without relation (fol. by *to*). **2.** →**irrelevant.** – **irrelatively,** *adv.* – **irrelativeness,** *n.*

**irrelevance** /ɪ'rɛləvəns/, *n.* **1.** the quality of being irrelevant. **2.** an irrelevant thing, act, etc.

**irrelevancy** /ɪ'rɛləvənsi/, *n., pl.* **-cies.** →**irrelevance.**

**irrelevant** /ɪ'rɛləvənt/, *adj.* **1.** not relevant; not applicable or pertinent: *irrelevant remarks.* **2.** *Law.* (of evidence) having no probative value upon any issue in the case. – **irrelevantly,** *adv.*

**irreligion** /ɪrə'lɪdʒən/, *n.* **1.** lack of religion. **2.** hostility to or disregard of religion; impiety. – **irreligionist,** *n.*

**irreligious** /ɪrə'lɪdʒəs/, *adj.* **1.** not religious; impious; ungodly. **2.** showing disregard for or hostility to religion. [LL *irreligiōsus*] – **irreligiously,** *adv.* – **irreligiousness,** *n.*

**irremeable** /ɪ'rɛmiəbəl, ɪ'rim-/, *adj.* from which one cannot return. [L *irremeābilis*] – **irremeably,** *adv.*

**irremediable** /ɪrə'midiəbəl/, *adj.* not remediable; irreparable: *irremediable disease.* – **irremediableness,** *n.* – **irremediably,** *adv.*

**irremissible** /ɪrə'mɪsəbəl/, *adj.* **1.** not remissible; unpardonable, as a sin. **2.** that cannot be remitted, as a duty. – **irremissibility** /,ɪrəmɪsə'bɪləti/, **irremissibleness,** *n.* – **irremissibly,** *adv.*

**irremovable** /ɪrə'muvəbəl/, *adj.* not removable. – **irremovability** /,ɪrəmuvə'bɪləti/, *n.* – **irremovably,** *adv.*

**irreparable** /ɪ'rɛpərəbəl, ɪ'rɛprəbəl/, *adj.* not reparable; incapable of being rectified, remedied, or made good: *an irreparable loss.* – **irreparability** /ɪ,rɛpərə'bɪləti, -rɛprə-/, **irreparableness,** *n.* – **irreparably,** *adv.*

**irrepealable** /ɪrə'piləbəl/, *adj.* not repealable. – **irrepealably,** *adv.*

**irreplaceable** /ɪrə'pleɪsəbəl/, *adj.* that cannot be replaced: *an irreplaceable souvenir.*

**irrepressible** /ɪrə'prɛsəbəl/, *adj.* not repressible. – **irrepressibility** /,ɪrəprɛsə'bɪləti/, **irrepressibleness,** *n.* – **irrepressibly,** *adv.*

**irreproachable** /ɪrə'proutʃəbəl/, *adj.* not reproachable; free from blame. – **irreproachability** /,ɪrəproutʃə'bɪləti/, **irreproachableness,** *n.* – **irreproachably,** *adv.*

**irresistible** /ɪrə'zɪstəbəl/, *adj.* not resistible; that cannot be resisted or withstood; tempting: *an irresistible impulse.* – **irresistibility** /,ɪrəzɪstə'bɪləti/, **irresistibleness,** *n.* – **irresistibly,** *adv.*

**irresolute** /ɪ'rɛzəlut/, *adj.* not resolute; doubtful or undecided; infirm of purpose; vacillating. – **irresolutely,** *adv.* – **irresoluteness,** *n.*

**irresolvable** /ɪrə'zɒlvəbəl/, *adj.* not resolvable; incapable of being resolved; not analysable; not solvable.

**irrespective** /ɪrə'spɛktɪv/, *adj.* without regard to something else, esp. something specified; independent (fol. by *of*): *irrespective of all rights.* – **irrespectively,** *adv.*

**irrespirable** /ɪ'rɛspərəbəl, ɪrəs'paɪrəbəl/, *adj.* not respirable; unfit for respiration.

**irresponsible** /ɪrə'spɒnsəbəl/, *adj.* **1.** not responsible; not answerable or accountable: *an irresponsible ruler.* **2.** not capable of responsibility; done without a sense of responsibility: *mentally irresponsible.* –*n.* **3.** an irresponsible person. – **irresponsibility** /ˌɪrəspɒnsə'bɪləti/, **irresponsibleness,** *n.* – **irresponsibility,** *adv.*

**irresponsive** /ɪrə'spɒnsɪv/, *adj.* not responsive; not responding, or not responding readily, as in speech, action, or feeling. – **irresponsiveness,** *n.*

**irretentive** /ɪrə'tɛntɪv/, *adj.* not retentive; lacking power to retain, esp. mentally. – **irretentiveness,** *n.*

**irretraceable** /ɪrə'treɪsəbəl/, *adj.* not retraceable; that cannot be retraced: *an irretraceable step.*

**irretrievable** /ɪrə'trivəbəl/, *adj.* not retrievable; irrecoverable; irreparable. – **irretrievability** /ˌɪrətrivə'bɪləti/, **irretrievableness,** *n.* – **irretrievably,** *adv.*

**irreverence** /ɪ'rɛvrəns, ɪ'rɛvərəns/, *n.* **1.** the quality of being irreverent; lack of reverence or respect. **2.** the condition of not being reverenced: *to be held in irreverence.*

**irreverent** /ɪ'rɛvrənt, ɪ'rɛvərənt/, *adj.* not reverent; manifesting or characterised by irreverence; deficient in veneration or respect: *an irreverent reply.* [L *irreverens*] – **irreverently,** *adv.*

**irreversible** /ɪrə'vɜsəbəl/, *adj.* not reversible; that cannot be reversed. – **irreversibility** /ˌɪrəvɜsə'bɪləti/, **irreversibleness,** *n.* – **irreversibly,** *adv.*

**irrevocable** /ɪ'rɛvəkəbəl/, *adj.* not to be revoked or recalled; that cannot be repealed or annulled: *an irrevocable decree.* – **irrevocability** /ɪˌrɛvəkə'bɪləti/, **irrevocableness,** *n.* – **irrevocably,** *adv.*

**irrigable** /'ɪrəgəbəl/, *adj.* that may be irrigated.

**irrigate** /'ɪrəgeɪt/, *v.t.,* **-gated, -gating. 1.** to supply (land) with water and thereby promote vegetation by means of canals, esp. artificially made, passing through it. **2.** *Med.* to supply (a wound, etc.) with a constant flow of some liquid. [L *irrigātus,* pp.] – **irrigator,** *n.*

**irrigation** /ɪrə'geɪʃən/, *n.* **1.** the supplying of land with water from artificial channels to promote vegetation. **2.** *Med.* the covering or washing out of anything with water or other liquid for the purpose of making or keeping it moist, as in local medical treatment. **3.** the state of being irrigated. – **irrigational,** *adj.*

**irrigation block** /'– blɒk/, *n.* a block of land watered by an irrigation scheme.

**irrigative** /'ɪrəgeɪtɪv/, *adj.* serving for or pertaining to irrigation.

**irritability** /ɪrətə'bɪləti/, *n., pl.* **-ties. 1.** the quality of being irritable. **2.** an irritable state or condition. **3.** *Physiol., Biol.* the ability to be excited to a characteristic action or function by the application of some stimulus, as heat, etc. [L *irrītābilitas*]

**irritable** /'ɪrətəbəl/, *adj.* **1.** easily irritated; readily excited to impatience or anger. **2.** *Physiol., Biol.* displaying irritability (def. 3). **3.** *Pathol.* susceptible to physical irritation; liable to shrink, become inflamed, etc., when stimulated: *an irritable wound.* [L *irrītābilis*] – **irritableness,** *n.* – **irritably,** *adv.*

**irritant** /'ɪrətənt/, *adj.* **1.** irritating. –*n.* **2.** anything that irritates. **3.** *Pathol., Med.* something, as a poison or a therapeutic agent, producing irritation. [L *irrītans,* ppr.] – **irritancy,** *n.*

**irritate** /'ɪrəteɪt/, *v.t.,* **-tated, -tating. 1.** to excite to impatience or anger. **2.** *Physiol., Biol.* to excite (a living system) to some characteristic action or function. **3.** *Pathol.* to bring (a bodily part, etc.) to an abnormally excited or sensitive condition. [L *irrītātus,* pp.] – **irritator,** *n.*

**irritating** /'ɪrəteɪtɪŋ/, *adj.* causing irritation; provoking: *an irritating reply.* – **irritatingly,** *adv.*

**irritation** /ɪrə'teɪʃən/, *n.* **1.** the act of irritating. **2.** the state of being irritated. **3.** *Physiol., Pathol.* **a.** the bringing of a bodily part or organ to an abnormally excited or sensitive condition. **b.** the condition itself.

**irritative** /'ɪrəteɪtɪv/, *adj.* **1.** serving or tending to irritate. **2.** *Pathol.* characterised or produced by irritation of some bodily part, etc.: *an irritative fever.*

**irrupt** /ɪ'rʌpt/, *v.i.* to burst or intrude suddenly.

**irruption** /ɪ'rʌpʃən/, *n.* a breaking or bursting in; a violent incursion or invasion. [L *irruptio*]

**irruptive** /ɪ'rʌptɪv/, *adj.* **1.** characterised by or pertaining to irruption. **2.** *Geol.* →**intrusive.**

**is** /ɪz/; *weak forms* /z, s/ *v.* 3rd person singular present indicative of **be.** [OE *is,* c. Icel. *es, er;* akin to G *ist,* Goth. *ist,* L *est,* Gk *estí,* Skt *astí.* See BE]

**is-,** variant of **iso-,** before some vowels, as in *isallobar.*

**Is., 1.** *Bible.* Also, **Isa.** Isaiah. **2.** Also, **is.** Island. **3.** Isle.

**isabel** /'ɪzəbɛl/, *n.* **1.** a dingy yellowish grey colour. –*adj.* **2.** of the colour of isabel. Also, **isabella** /ɪzə'bɛlə/, **isabelline** /ɪzə'bɛlaɪn, -ən/.

**isagogic** /aɪsə'gɒdʒɪk/, *adj.* **1.** introductory, esp. to the interpretation of the Bible. –*n.* **2.** (*usu. pl.*) **a.** introductory studies. **b.** the department of theology which is introductory to exegesis and the literary history of the Bible. [L *īsagōgicus* introductory, from Gk *eisagōgikós,* lit., leading into]

**isallobar** /aɪ'sæləba/, *n.* a line on a weather map connecting places having equal pressure changes. [IS- + ALLO- + *-bar.* See ISOBAR]

**isallotherm** /aɪ'sæləθɜm/, *n.* a line on a weather map connecting points having equal temperature variations over a given period.

**isarithm** /'aɪsərɪðəm/, *n.* →**isopleth.**

**-isation,** a noun suffix, combination of **-ise** with **-ation.**

**I.S.B.N.,** International Standard Book Number.

**Iscariot** /ɪs'kæriət/, *n.* one who betrays another; a traitor. [from Judas *Iscariot,* the betrayer of Jesus (Mark 3:19, 14:10-11); L *Iscariōta,* from Gk *Iskariṓtēs,* from Heb. *ish-qerīyōth* man of *Kerioth* (a place in Palestine)]

**ischaemia** /ɪs'kimiə/, *n.* local anaemia produced by local obstacles to the arterial flow. Also, **ischemia.** [NL, from Gk *íschein* check + *-aemia* -AEMIA] – **ischaemic** /ɪs'kimɪk/, *adj.*

**ischiadic** /ɪski'ædɪk/, *adj.* pertaining to the ischium; sciatic. Also, **ischiatic** /ɪski'ætɪk/.

**ischium** /'ɪskiəm/, *n., pl.* **-chia** /-kiə/. **1.** the lowermost of the three parts composing either innominate bone. **2.** either of the bones on which the body rests when sitting. [NL, from Gk *ischíon* hip joint, haunch, ischium] – **ischial,** *adj.*

**-ise**[1], a suffix of verbs having the following senses: **a.** intransitively, of following some line of action, practice, policy, etc., as in *Atticise, apologise, economise, theorise, tyrannise,* or of becoming (as indicated), as *crystallise* and *oxidise* (intr.), and **b.** transitively, of acting towards or upon, treating, or affecting in a particular way, as in *baptise, colonise,* or of making or rendering (as indicated), as in *civilise, legalise.* Also, **-ize.** Cf. **-ism** and **-ist.** [from (often directly) Gk *-izein.* Cf. F *-iser,* G *-isieren,* etc.]

**-ise**[2], a noun suffix indicating quality, condition, or function, as in *merchandise, franchise.*

**isenthalpic** /aɪsən'θælpɪk/, *adj.* (in thermodynamics) of equal or constant enthalpy.

**isentropic** /aɪsən'trɒpɪk/, *adj.* (in thermodymics) of equal or constant entropy.

**-ish**[1], **1.** a suffix used to form adjectives from nouns, with the sense of: **a.** 'belonging to' (a people, country, etc.), as in *British, Danish, English, Spanish.* **b.** 'after the manner of', 'having the characteristics of', 'like', as in *babyish, girlish, mulish* (such words being now often depreciatory). **c.** 'addicted to', 'inclined or tending to', as in *bookish, freakish.* **2.** a suffix used to form adjectives from other adjectives, with the sense of 'somewhat', 'rather', as in *oldish, reddish, sweetish.* [ME; OE *-isc,* c. G *-isch,* Gk *-iskos;* akin to -ESQUE]

**-ish**[2], a suffix forming simple verbs. [F *-iss-,* extended stem of verbs in *-ir,* from L *-isc-,* in inceptive verbs]

**Ishmael** /'ɪʃmeɪl/, *n.* an outcast. Also, **Ishmaelite** /'ɪʃməlaɪt/. [from *Ishmael,* the outcast son of the patriarch Abraham (Gen. 16:11, 12); Heb. *Yishmāʿēl,* lit., God will hear]

**isinglass** /'aɪzɪŋglas/, *n.* a pure, transparent or translucent form of gelatine, esp. that derived from the air bladders of certain fishes. [MD; popular modification (by association with

GLASS) of *hysenblas,* c. G *Hausenblase* isinglass, lit., sturgeon bladder]

**isl.,** **1.** (*pl.* **isls**) island. **2.** isle.

**Islam** /ˈɪzlæm, -lam/, *n.* **1.** the religion of the Muslims, based on the teachings of the prophet Mohammed as set down in the Koran, the fundamental principle being absolute submission to a unique and personal god, Allah. **2.** the whole body of Muslim believers, their civilisation, and their lands. [Ar.: submission (to the will of God)] – **Islamic** /ɪzˈlæmɪk/, **Islamitic** /ɪzləˈmɪtɪk/, *adj.*

**Islamise** /ˈɪzləmaɪz/, *v.t.,* **-mised, -mising.** to convert to or bring under the influence or control of Islam. Also, **Islamize.**

**Islamism** /ˈɪzləmɪzəm/, *n.* the religion of Islam.

**Islamite** /ˈɪzləmaɪt/, *n.* →**Muslim.**

**island** /ˈaɪlənd/, *n.* **1.** a tract of land completely surrounded by water, and not large enough to be called a continent. **2.** a clump of woodland in a prairie. **3.** an isolated hill. **4.** something resembling an island. **5.** a platform in the middle of a street, at a crossing, for the safety of pedestrians. **6.** *Physiol., Anat.* an isolated portion of tissue or aggregation of cells. **7.** *Naut.* the superstructure of a ship. **8. the Islands,** the Pacific Islands; Polynesia. *–adj.* **9.** (*cap.*) of the Islands (def. 8): *Island oranges.* *–v.t.* **10.** to make into an island. **11.** to dot with islands. **12.** to place on an island; isolate. [ME *iland, yland,* OE *īland, īgland,* from *īg, īeg* island + *land* land; *-s-* inserted through erroneous association with ISLE] – **island-like,** *adj.*

**islander** /ˈaɪləndə/, *n.* **1.** a native or inhabitant of an island. **2.** (*cap.*) a native or inhabitant of the Pacific Islands. **3.** (*cap.*) native or inhabitant (or one of their descendants) of the Torres Strait Islands. **4.** (*cap.*) a native or inhabitant of the Bass Strait Islands.

**island universe** /aɪlənd ˈjunəvɜs/, *n.* →**galaxy.**

**isle** /aɪl/, *n., v.,* **isled, isling.** *–n.* **1.** a small island: *the Scilly Isles.* **2.** *Chiefly Poetic.* an island. *–v.t.* **3.** to make into or as into an isle. **4.** to place on or as on an isle. *–v.i.* **5.** to dwell or remain on an isle. [ME *isle, ile,* from OF, from L *insula*]

**islet** /ˈaɪlət/, *n.* a small island. [F *islette* (now *îlette*), diminutive of *isle* ISLE]

**islets of Langerhans,** /ˌaɪləts əv ˈlæŋəhæns/, *n.pl.* See **pancreas.** Also, **islands of Langerhans.** [named after Paul *Langerhans,* 1847-88, German physician]

**ism** /ˈɪzəm/, *n.* a distinctive doctrine, theory, system, or practice: *this is the age of isms.* [n. use of -ISM]

**-ism,** a suffix of nouns denoting action or practice, state or condition, principles, doctrines, a usage or characteristic, etc., as in *baptism, barbarism, criticism, Darwinism, plagiarism, realism.* Cf. **-ist** and **-ise**[1]. [from (often directly) Gk *-ismos, -isma,* noun suffix. See -ISE[1]]

**isn't** /ˈɪzənt/, *v.* contraction of *is not.*

**iso-,** **1.** a prefix meaning 'equal'. **2.** *Chem.* a prefix added to the name of one compound to denote another isomeric with it. Also, **is-.** [Gk, combining form of *ísos* equal]

**isoagglutination** /ˌaɪsoʊəˌglutəˈneɪʃən/, *n.* the clumping of the red blood cells of an animal by a transfusion from another animal of the same species.

**isoagglutinin** /ˌaɪsoʊəˈglutənən/, *n.* an agglutinin which can effect isoagglutination.

**isobar** /ˈaɪsəba/, *n.* **1.** *Meteorol., etc.* a line drawn on a weather map, etc., connecting all points having the same barometric pressure (reduced to sea-level), measured in millibars, at a specified time or over a certain period. **2.** *Physics, Chem.* Also, **isobare** /ˈaɪsəbɛə/. one of two or more atoms of different atomic number, but having the same atomic weight. [Gk *isobarḗs* of equal weight]

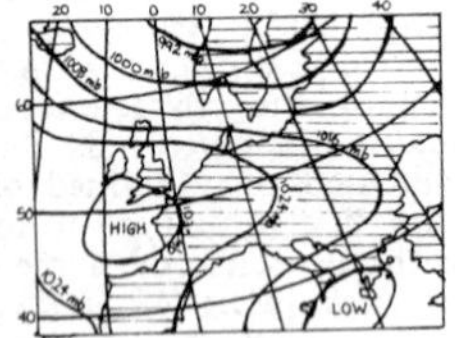

isobars (def. 1): mb, millibars

**isobaric** /aɪsəˈbærɪk/, *adj.* **1.** having or showing equal barometric pressure. **2.** of or pertaining to isobars. **3.** *Med.* of or pertaining to a solution for spinal anaesthesia having the same density as the cerebro-spinal fluid.

**isobath** /ˈaɪsəbæθ/, *n.* a line drawn on a chart of the oceans, connecting all points having the same depth. – **isobathic** /aɪsəˈbæθɪk/, *adj.*

**isobilateral** /ˌaɪsoʊbaɪˈlætərəl, -ˈlætrəl/, *adj.* of or pertaining to leaves which are more or less vertical and with both sides having the same structure, as those of the genus *Iris.*

**isobutane** /aɪsoʊˈbjuteɪn/, *n.* an isomeric form of butane, $(CH_3)_2CHCH_3$, used as a fuel and refrigerant.

**isobutylene** /aɪsoʊˈbjutəlin/, *n.* a colourless inflammable gas, $(CH_3)_2C{=}CH_2$, used in the manufacture of butyl rubber. Also, **isobutene.**

**isocarpic** /aɪsoʊˈkapɪk/, *adj.* (of a flower) having carpels equal in number to the other floral parts.

**isocheim** /ˈaɪsoʊkaɪm/, *n.* a line on a map connecting places which have the same mean winter temperature. Also, **isochime.** [ISO- + Gk *cheîma* winter] – **isocheimal** /aɪsoʊˈkaɪməl/, *adj.*

**isochor** /ˈaɪsəkɔ/, *n.* a line representing the variation in pressure with temperature, under a constant volume. Also, **isochore.** [ISO- + Gk *chṓra* place] – **isochoric** /aɪsəˈkɒrɪk/, *adj.*

**isochromatic** /ˌaɪsoʊkroʊˈmætɪk/, *adj.* **1.** *Optics.* having the same colour or tint. **2.** *Physics.* involving radiation of constant wavelength or frequency. **3.** →**orthochromatic.**

**isochronal** /aɪˈsɒkrənəl/, *adj.* **1.** equal or uniform in time. **2.** performed in equal intervals of time. **3.** characterised by motions or vibrations of equal duration. [Gk *isóchronos* equal in age or time + -AL[1]] – **isochronally,** *adv.*

**isochrone** /ˈaɪsəkroʊn/, *n.* a line on a map or chart joining points associated with the same time difference or the same time, or connecting points at which an event occurs simultaneously.

**isochronise** /aɪˈsɒkrənaɪz/, *v.t.,* **-nised, -nising.** to make isochronal. Also, **isochronize.**

**isochronism** /aɪˈsɒkrənɪzəm/, *n.* isochronal character or action.

**isochronous** /aɪˈsɒkrənəs/, *adj.* →**isochronal.** – **isochronously,** *adv.*

**isochroous** /aɪˈsɒkroʊəs/, *adj.* having the same colour throughout.

**isoclinal** /aɪsoʊˈklaɪnəl/, *adj.* **1.** of or pertaining to equal inclination; inclining or dipping in the same direction. **2.** denoting or pertaining to a line on the earth's surface connecting points of equal dip or inclination of the earth's magnetic field. **3.** *Geol.* denoting or pertaining to a fold of strata which is of the nature of an isocline. *–n.* **4.** an isoclinal line. Also, **isoclinic** /aɪsoʊˈklɪnɪk/. [Gk *isoklinḗs* equally balanced + -AL[1]]

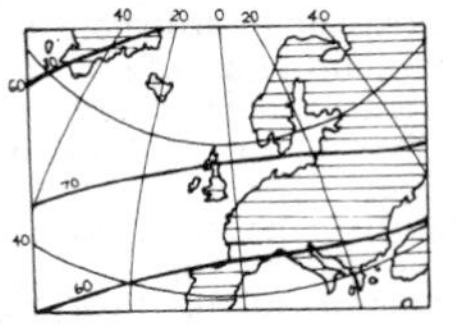
isoclinal lines (def. 2)

**isocline** /ˈaɪsəklaɪn/, *n.* a fold of strata so tightly compressed that the parts on each side dip in the same direction. [Gk *isoklinḗs* equally balanced]

**isocracy** /aɪˈsɒkrəsi/, *n., pl.* **-cies.** a government in which all have equal political power. [Gk *isokratía.* See ISO-, -CRACY] – **isocratic** /aɪsəˈkrætɪk/, *adj.*

**isocyanide** /aɪsoʊˈsaɪənaɪd/, *n.* a compound containing the group – NC; carbylamine.

**isocyanine** /aɪsoʊˈsaɪənin, -naɪn/, *n.* a member of the cyanines. See **cyanine.**

**isodiametric** /ˌaɪsoʊdaɪəˈmɛtrɪk/, *adj.* **1.** having equal diameters or axes. **2.** *Bot.* having the diameter similar throughout, as a cell. **3.** (of crystals) having two, or three, equal horizontal axes and a third, or fourth, unequal axis at right angles thereto.

**isodiaphere** /aɪsoʊˈdaɪəfɪə/, *n.* one of two or more nuclides in which the difference between the number of neutrons and protons is the same, as a nuclide and its decay product after it has emitted an alpha particle. [ISO- + Gk *diaphérein* differ]

**isodimorphism** /ˌaɪsoʊdaɪˈmɔfɪzəm/, *n.* isomorphism between the forms of two dimorphous substances. – **isodimorphous,** *adj.*

**isodynamic** /ˌaɪsoʊdaɪˈnæmɪk, -də-/, *adj.* **1.** pertaining to or

i = peat ɪ = pit ɛ = pet æ = pat a = part ɒ = pot ʌ = putt ɔ = port ʊ = put u = pool ɜ = pert ə = apart aɪ = buy eɪ = bay ɔɪ = boy aʊ = how oʊ = hoe ɪə = here ɛə = hair ʊə = tour g = give θ = thin ð = then ʃ = show ʒ = measure tʃ = choke dʒ = joke ŋ = sing j = you õ = Fr. bon

characterised by equality of force, intensity, or the like. **2.** denoting or pertaining to a line on the earth's surface connecting points of equal horizontal intensity of the earth's magnetic field. Also, **isodynamical.**

**isoelectric** /ˌaɪsoʊə'lɛktrɪk/, *adj.* equal in electric potential.

**isoelectric point** /'– pɔɪnt/, *n.* the pH at which a substance is electrically neutral or least ionised.

**isoelectronic** /ˌaɪsoʊəlɛk'trɒnɪk/, *adj.* signifying a set of elements having similar chemical properties by virtue of their atomic structure.

**isoenzyme** /aɪsoʊ'ɛnzaɪm/, *n.* any of two or more forms of an enzyme, which catalyse the same reaction.

**isogamete** /ˌaɪsoʊgæ'mit/, *n.* one of a pair of conjugating gametes, exhibiting no sexual or morphological differentiation.

**isogamous** /aɪ'sɒgəməs/, *adj.* having two similar gametes in which no differentiation can be distinguished, or reproducing by the union of such gametes (opposed to *heterogamous*).

**isogamy** /aɪ'sɒgəmi/, *n.* the fusion of two gametes of similar form, as in certain algae.

**isogenous** /aɪ'sɒdʒənəs/, *adj.* of the same or similar origin, as parts derived from the same or corresponding tissues of the embryo. [ISO- + -GENOUS] – **isogeny,** *n.*

**isogeotherm** /aɪsoʊ'dʒiəθɜm/, *n.* an imaginary line or surface passing through points in the interior of the earth which have the same mean temperature. [ISO- + GEO- + Gk *thérmē* heat] – **isogeothermal** /ˌaɪsoʊdʒiə'θɜməl/, **isogeothermic** /ˌaɪsoʊdʒiə'θɜmɪk/, *adj.*

**isogloss** /'aɪsəglɒs/, *n.* an imaginary line separating two localities which differ in some feature of their speech. [ISO- + Gk *glôssa* word, speech, tongue]

**isogon** /'aɪsəgɒn/, *n.* **1.** a line on a map of the earth's surface connecting points of equal declination of the earth's magnetic field; an isogonic or isogonal line. **2.** *Geom.* an equiangular polygon. [Gk *isogṓnios* having equal angles]

**isogonic** /aɪsə'gɒnɪk/, *adj.* **1.** having or pertaining to equal angles. **2.** denoting or pertaining to an isogon. *–n.* **3.** →**isogon.** Also, **isogonal** /aɪ'sɒgənəl/.

**isogram** /'aɪsəgræm/, *n.* →**isopleth.**

**isograph** /'aɪsəgræf, -graf/, *n.* a line drawn on a map to indicate areas having common linguistic characteristics. – **isographic** /aɪsə'græfɪk/, *adj.*

**isogriv** /'aɪsəgrɪv/, *n.* a line drawn on a map or chart joining points of equal grivation.

**isohaline** /aɪsə'heɪlin, -laɪn/, *n.* a line drawn on a map of the sea or ocean, connecting points where salinity is equal.

**isohel** /'aɪsəhɛl/, *n.* a line drawn on a map, etc., connecting places which receive equal amounts of sunshine.

**isohyet** /aɪsoʊ'haɪət/, *n.* a line drawn on a map connecting points having equal rainfall at a certain time or for a stated period. [ISO- + Gk *hyetós* rain]

**isolable** /'aɪsələbəl/, *adj.* that can be isolated.

**isolate** /'aɪsəleɪt/, *v.t.,* **-lated, -lating.** **1.** to set or place apart; detach or separate so as to be alone. **2.** *Med.* to keep (an infected person) from contact with non-infected ones. **3.** *Chem.* to obtain (a substance) in an uncombined or pure state. **4.** *Elect.* to insulate. [backformation from *isolated,* ppl. adj., from It. *isolato* (from L *insulātus;* see INSULATE) + -ED[2]] – **isolator,** *n.*

**isolated children's allowance,** *n.* an allowance made to assist students who are geographically restricted, disabled or handicapped, or in need of special instruction, or from an itinerant family.

**isolating** /'aɪsəleɪtɪŋ/, *adj.* (in linguistics) analytic.

**isolating language** /ˌaɪsəleɪtɪŋ 'læŋgwɪdʒ/, *n.* a language which uses few or no bound forms.

**isolating transformer** /– træns'fɔmə/, *n.* a transformer placed between the source of electrical power and a portable appliance for reasons of safety.

**isolation** /aɪsə'leɪʃən/, *n.* **1.** the act of isolating. **2.** the state of being isolated. **3.** the complete separation from others of a person suffering from a contagious or infectious disease. **4.** the separation of a nation from other nations by a policy of non-participation in international affairs. **5.** *Sociol.* See **social isolation.**

**isolation allowance** /'– əlaʊəns/, *n.* an allowance paid to employees to compensate them for working in areas which are relatively deprived of, and far from, various social amenities.

**isolationism** /aɪsə'leɪʃənɪzəm/, *n.* the policy of seeking political or national isolation.

**isolationist** /aɪsə'leɪʃənəst/, *n.* one who favours a policy of non-participation in international affairs.

**isolative** /'aɪsəleɪtɪv/, *adj.* **1.** *Phonology.* (of a sound-change) occurring independently of neighbouring sounds. **2.** tending to isolate.

**isoleucine** /aɪsə'lusin/, *n.* an amino acid, $C_2H_5CH(CH_3)CH(NH_3^+)COO^-$, occurring in proteins, and essential in man.

**isologue** /'aɪsəlɒg/, *n.* one of two or more compounds with a similar molecular structure but which contain different numbers of atoms of the same valency. – **isologous** /aɪ'sɒləgəs/, *adj.*

**isomagnetic** /ˌaɪsoʊmæg'nɛtɪk/, *adj.* **1.** denoting or pertaining to an imaginary line on the earth's surface, or a corresponding line on a map or the like, connecting places which have the same magnetic elements. *–n.* **2.** an isomagnetic line.

**isomer** /'aɪsəmə/, *n.* **1.** *Chem.* a compound which is isomeric with one or more other compounds. **2.** *Physics.* a nuclide which is isomeric with one or more other nuclides.

**isomerase** /aɪ'sɒməreɪz, -eɪs/, *n.* any enzyme that catalyses the conversion of one chemical isomer into another.

**isomeric** /aɪsoʊ'mɛrɪk/, *adj.* **1.** *Chem.* (of compounds) composed of the same kinds and numbers of atoms which differ from each other in the arrangement of the atoms and, therefore, in one or more properties. **2.** *Physics.* (of nuclides) having the same atomic number and mass but a different energy state. [Gk *isomerḗs* having equal parts + -IC]

**isomerise** /aɪ'sɒməraɪz/, *v.t.* **-rised, -rising.** to convert from one isomeric form to another. Also, **isomerize.**

**isomerism** /aɪ'sɒmərɪzəm/, *n.* the state or condition of being isomeric.

**isomerous** /aɪ'sɒmərəs/, *adj.* **1.** having an equal number of parts, markings, etc. **2.** *Bot.* (of a flower) having the same number of members in each whorl.

**isometric** /aɪsə'mɛtrɪk/, *adj.* Also, **isometrical.** **1.** pertaining to or having equality of measure. **2. a.** pertaining to increased muscle activity which does not involve shortening of the muscle. **b.** pertaining to exercises involving such activity. **3.** *Crystall.* denoting or pertaining to that system of crystallisation which is characterised by three equal axes at right angles to one another. **4.** *Pros.* of equal measure; made up of regular feet. **5.** (of a projection, drawing, etc., representing a solid object) having three mutually perpendicular axes represented as being equally inclined to the plane of projection, all lines being drawn to scale. *–n.* **6.** (*pl.*) a system of physical exercises in which muscles are pitted against each other or against a fixed object. [Gk *isómetros* of equal measure + -IC] – **isometrically,** *adv.*

**isometropia** /aɪsəmə'troʊpiə/, *n.* a condition in which the refraction is the same in the two eyes. [ISO- + Gk *métron* measure + -OPIA]

**isometry** /aɪ'sɒmətri/, *n.* **1.** equality of measure. **2.** *Geog.* equality with respect to height above sea-level.

**isomorph** /'aɪsəmɔf/, *n.* **1.** an organism which is isomorphic with another or others. **2.** an isomorphous substance.

**isomorphic** /aɪsə'mɔfɪk/, *adj.* **1.** *Biol.* being of the same or of like form; different in ancestry, but alike in appearance. **2.** *Crystall.* →**isomorphous.** **3.** *Linguistics.* having similar morphological forms.

**isomorphism** /aɪsə'mɔfɪzəm/, *n.* the state or property of being isomorphous or isomorphic.

**isomorphous** /aɪsə'mɔfəs/, *adj.* (of a substance) undergoing a more or less extended, continuous variation in chemical composition, with accompanying variations in physical and chemical properties, but maintaining the same crystal structure.

**isoneph** /'aɪsənɛf/, *n.* a line on a map, etc., connecting places which have the same amounts of cloud cover.

**isoniazid** /aɪsoʊ'naɪəzɪd/, *n.* a soluble colourless, crystalline compound, $C_6H_7N_3O$, used in the treatment of tuberculosis. [*isoni(cotinic acid hydr)azid(e)*]

**isonomy** /aɪˈsɒnəmi/, *n.* equality of political rights. [Gk *isonomía*] – **isonomic** /aɪsəˈnɒmɪk/, *adj.*
**iso-octane** /aɪsoʊ-ˈɒkteɪn/, *n.* an isomer of octane used to determine the knocking qualities of a fuel.
**isoperimetric** /ˌaɪsoʊpɛrəˈmɛtrɪk/, *adj.* having perimeters of equal length.
**isopiestic** /ˌaɪsoʊpiˈɛstɪk/, *adj.* **1.** isobaric; denoting equal pressure. *–n.* **2.** →**isobar** (def. 1). [ISO- + Gk *piestós*, vbl. adj. of *piézein* press + -IC]
**isopleth** /ˈaɪsəplɛθ/, *n.* a line drawn on a map or chart through all points having the same numerical value of any element, or of the ratio of values of two elements. Also, **isogram.** [Gk *isoplēthḗs* equal in number]
**isopod** /ˈaɪsəpɒd/, *n.* **1.** any of the Isopoda, an order or suborder of crustaceans (freshwater, marine, and terrestrial) with seven pairs of legs, and body flattened dorsoventrally. *–adj.* **2.** pertaining to the Isopoda. **3.** having the feet all alike, or similar in character. [NL *Isopoda*, pl., genus type. See ISO-, -POD] – **isopodan** /aɪˈsɒpədən/, *adj., n.* – **isopodous** /aɪˈsɒpədəs/, *adj.*
**isoprene** /ˈaɪsəprin/, *n.* a colourless liquid hydrocarbon, $C_5H_8$, of the terpene class, produced from rubber or from oil of turpentine by pyrolysis and convertible into rubber by polymerisation. [? ISO- + PR(OPYL) + -ENE]
**isopropyl** /aɪsoʊˈproʊpəl/, *n.* the univalent radical, $(CH_3)_2CH$.
**isopropyl alcohol** /– ˈælkəhɒl/, *n.* a colourless liquid, $(CH_3)_2CHOH$, used in the manufacture of antifreeze and as a solvent.
**isopropyl ether** /– ˈiθə/, *n.* a colourless liquid, $(C_3H_7)_2O$, used as a solvent for waxes, fats, etc.
**isopteran** /aɪˈsɒptərən/, *adj.* **1.** belonging to the insect order Isoptera, which contains the termites or white ants. *–n.* **2.** an isopteran insect.
**isopterous** /aɪˈsɒptərəs/, *adj.* belonging to the order Isoptera, which contains the social insects, termites or white ants.
**isosceles** /aɪˈsɒsəliz/, *adj.* (of a triangle) having two sides equal. [LL, from Gk *isoskelḗs* with equal legs]
**isoseismic** /aɪsoʊˈsaɪzmɪk/, *adj.* **1.** pertaining to equal intensity of earthquake shock. **2.** denoting or pertaining to an imaginary line on the earth's surface connecting points characterised by such intensity. *–n.* **3.** an isoseismic line. Also, **isoseismal.**
**isostasy** /aɪˈsɒstəsi/, *n.* **1.** *Geol.* the equilibrium of the earth's crust, a condition in which the forces tending to elevate balance those tending to depress. **2.** equilibrium when there is pressure from all sides; hydrostatic equilibrium. [ISO- + Gk *stásis* a standing]
**isostatic** /aɪsoʊˈstætɪk/, *adj.* pertaining to or characterised by isostasy. – **isostatically,** *adv.*
**isosteric** /aɪsoʊˈstɛrɪk/, *adj.* pertaining to compounds which have similar physical properties owing to a similarity in the molecular configuration of the atoms, even though the atom may be of different elements.
**isosterism** /aɪˈsɒstərɪzəm/, *n.* the quality or state of being isosteric.
**isosyllabic** /ˌaɪsoʊsəˈlæbɪk/, *adj.* of a metrical structure in which all the syllables have the same duration.
**isotactic** /aɪsəˈtæktɪk/, *adj.* of a polymer, having substituent groups or atoms located all on the same side of the backbone of a polymer chain.
**isothere** /ˈaɪsəθɪə/, *n.* a line connecting places on the earth's surface which have the same mean summer temperature. [ISO- + Gk *théros* summer] – **isotheral** /aɪˈsɒθərəl/, *adj.*
**isotherm** /ˈaɪsəθɜm/, *n.* **1.** *Meteorol.* a line connecting points on the earth's surface having the same (mean) temperature. **2.** *Physics, Chem.* an isothermal line. [ISO- + Gk *thérmē* heat]
**isothermal** /aɪsəˈθɜməl/, *adj.* **1.** *Physics, Chem.* pertaining to or indicating equality of temperature. **2.** *Meteorol.* of or pertaining to an isotherm. *–n.* **3.** *Meteorol.* →**isotherm.** – **isothermally,** *adv.*
**isothermal line** /'– laɪn/, *n.* a line or graph showing relations of variables under conditions of uniform temperature.
**isothermal process** /– ˈproʊsɛs/, *n.* a process which takes place without change in temperature.
**isotone** /ˈaɪsətoʊn/, *n.* one of two or more atoms whose nuclei contain the same number of neutrons although they have different atomic numbers.
**isotonic** /aɪsəˈtɒnɪk/, *adj.* **1.** pertaining to solutions characterised by equal osmotic pressure. **2.** *Physiol.* **a.** denoting or pertaining to a solution containing just enough salt to prevent the destruction of the red blood corpuscles when added to the blood. **b.** denoting or pertaining to a contraction of a muscle when under a constant tension. **3.** *Music.* of or characterised by equal tones. [Gk *isótonos* having equal accent or tone + -IC]
**isotope** /ˈaɪsətoʊp/, *n.* any of two or more forms of a chemical element, having the same number of protons in the nucleus and, hence, the same atomic number, but having different numbers of neutrons in the nucleus and, hence, different atomic weights. There are 275 isotopes of the 81 stable elements in addition to over 800 radioactive isotopes, so that isotopic forms of every element are known. Isotopes of a single element possess almost identical properties. [ISO- + Gk *tópos* place] – **isotopic** /aɪsəˈtɒpɪk/, *adj.*
**isotopic number** /ˌaɪsətɒpɪk ˈnʌmbə/, *n.* the difference between the number of neutrons and the number of protons in an isotope; neutron excess.
**isotopic spin** /– ˈspɪn/, *n.* a quantum number used to work out the properties of groups of elementary particles when the members of the group are identical except in respect of charge; no rotation is implied but the concept bears a formal resemblance to angular momentum.
**isotopy** /aɪˈsɒtəpi/, *n.* isotopic character.
**isotransplant** /aɪsoʊˈtrænsplænt/, *n.* tissue transplanted from one individual to another of the same inbred strain.
**isotropic** /aɪsəˈtrɒpɪk/, *adj.* **1.** *Physics.* having one or more properties that are the same in all directions. **2.** *Zool.* lacking axes which are predetermined, as in some eggs. Also, **isotropous** /aɪˈsɒtrəpəs/. [ISO- + Gk *trópos* turn, way + -IC]
**isotropy** /aɪˈsɒtrəpi/, *n.* the state or property of being isotropic.
**I-spy** /aɪ-ˈspaɪ/, *n.* a game in which one player tells the others the initial letter of the name of something visible to them all, and they then guess its name. [after the first words of the rhyme *I spy, with my little eye, something beginning with ...*]
**Israel** /ˈɪzreɪl/, *n.* **1.** the people traditionally descended from Jacob, the father of the twelve Hebrew patriachs; the Hebrew or Jewish people. **2.** God's chosen people; the elect. **3.** a republic in south-west Asia, on the Mediterranean. **4.** the Christian Church. [Heb. *Yisrā'ēl* he who striveth with God; the name given to Jacob after he wrestled with the angel (Gen. 32:28)]
**Israeli** /ɪzˈreɪli/, *n., pl.* **-lis,** *adj. –n.* **1.** a native or inhabitant of Israel. *–adj.* **2.** of Israel.
**Israelite** /ˈɪzrəlaɪt/, *n.* **1.** a descendant of Israel or Jacob, the father of the twelve Hebrew patriarchs; a Hebrew; a Jew. **2.** one of God's chosen people. *–adj.* **3.** pertaining to Israel; Jewish.
**I.S.S.N.,** International Standard Serial Number.
**issuable** /ˈɪʃuəbəl/, *adj.* **1.** that may be issued or may issue. **2.** forthcoming. **3.** *Law.* that admits of issue being taken. [ISSU(E) + -ABLE] – **issuably,** *adv.*
**issuance** /ˈɪʃuəns/, *n.* **1.** the act of issuing. **2.** →**issue.**
**issuant** /ˈɪʃuənt/, *adj.* **1.** *Rare.* emerging. **2.** *Her.* (of a beast) having only the upper half seen.
**issue** /ˈɪʃu, ˈɪʃju, ˈɪsju/, *n., v.,* **issued, issuing.** *–n.* **1.** the act of sending, or promulgation; delivery; emission. **2.** that which is issued. **3.** a quantity issued at one time: *the latest issue of a periodical.* **4.** *Bibliog.* the printing of copies of a work from the original setting of type, but with some slight changes in the preliminary or appended matter. **5.** a point in question or dispute, as between contending parties in an action at law. **6.** a point or matter the decision of which is of special or public importance: *the political issues.* **7.** a point the decision of which determines a matter: *the real issue.* **8.** a point at which a matter is ready for decision: *to bring a case to an issue.* **9.** something proceeding from any source, as a product, effect, result, or consequence. **10.** the ultimate result, event, or outcome of a proceeding, affair, etc.: *the issue of a contest.* **11.** a distribution of food (rations), clothing, equipment, or ammunition to a number of officers or servicemen, or to a military unit. **12.** offspring or progeny: *to die without issue.* **13.** a going, coming, passing, or flowing

out: *free issue and entry.* **14.** a place or means of egress; an outlet or vent. **15.** that which comes out, as an outflowing stream. **16.** *Pathol.* **a.** a discharge of blood, pus, or the like. **b.** an incision, ulcer, or the like emitting such a discharge. **17.** *Chiefly Law.* the yield or profit from land or other property. **18. at issue, a.** in controversy: *a point at issue.* **b.** in disagreement. **c.** inconsistent; inharmonious (fol. by *with*). **19. the (whole) issue,** everything, the lot. **20. join issue, a.** to join in controversy. **b.** to submit an issue jointly for legal decision. **21. take issue,** to disagree. *–v.t.* **22.** to put out; deliver for use, sale, etc.; put into circulation. **23.** to print (a publication) for sale or distribution. **24.** to distribute (food, clothing, etc.) to one or more officers or servicemen or to a military unit. **25.** to send out; discharge; emit. *–v.i.* **26.** to go, pass, or flow out; come forth; emerge: *to issue forth to battle.* **27.** to be sent or put forth authoritatively or publicly, as a writ, money, etc. **28.** to be published, as a book. **29.** to come or proceed from any source. **30.** to arise as a result or consequence; result. **31.** *Chiefly Law.* to proceed as offspring, or be born or descended. **32.** *Chiefly Law.* to come as a yield or profit, as from land. **33.** to have the specified outcome. **34.** to result (oft. fol. by *in*). **35.** to end. [ME, from OF, from pp. of *issir, eissir,* from L *exīre* go out] – **issueless,** *adj.* – **issuer,** *n.*

**issued capital** /ɪʃud 'kæpətl/, *n.* →**paid-up capital.**

**-ist,** a suffix of nouns, often accompanying verbs ending in *-ise* or nouns ending in *-ism,* denoting one who does, practises, or is concerned with something, or holds certain principles, doctrines, etc., as in *apologist, dramatist, machinist, plagiarist, realist, socialist, theorist.* [from (often directly) Gk *-istēs* noun suffix. See -ISE[1], -ISM]

**Isth.,** isthmus. Also, **isth.**

**isthmian** /'ɪsθmiən/, *adj.* **1.** of or pertaining to an isthmus. **2.** (*cap.*) of the Isthmus of Corinth or of Panama. *–n.* **3.** a native or inhabitant of an isthmus.

**isthmus** /'ɪsməs/, *n., pl.* **-muses. 1.** a narrow strip of land, bordered on both sides by water, connecting two larger bodies of land. **2.** *Anat., etc.* a connecting part, organ, or passage, esp. when narrow or joining structures or cavities larger than itself. [L, from Gk *isthmós* narrow passage, neck, isthmus]

**-istic,** a suffix of adjectives (and in the plural of nouns from adjectives) formed from nouns in *-ist,* and having reference to such nouns, or to associated nouns in *-ism,* as in *deistic, euphuistic, puristic,* etc. In nouns it has usu. a plural form, as in *linguistics.* [-IST + -IC]

**-istical,** See **-istic, -al**[1].

**-istics,** See **-istic, -ics.**

**istle** /'ɪstli/, *n.* a fibre from various tropical American trees of the species *Agave* or *Yucca,* used in making carpets, etc. Also, **ixtle.** [Amer. Sp., from Nahuatl *ixtli*]

**it** /ɪt/; *weak form* /ət/, *pron., poss.* **its** or (*Obs.*) **it,** *obj.* **it,** *pl.* **they;** *n. –pron.* a personal pronoun of the third person and neuter gender, which corresponds to *he* and *she,* and which is used: **1.** as a substitute for a neuter noun or a noun representing something possessing sex when sex is not particularised or considered: *the baby lost its rattle.* **2.** to refer to some matter expressed or understood, or some thing or notion not definitely conceived: *how goes it?* **3.** to refer to the subject of inquiry or attention, whether impersonal or personal, in sentences asking or stating what or who this is: *who is it? it is I.* **4.** as the grammatical subject of a clause of which the logical subject is a phrase or clause, generally following, regarded as in apposition to it: *it is hard to believe that.* **5.** in impersonal constructions: *it snows.* **6.** without definite force after an intransitive verb: *to foot it* (go on foot). *–n.* **7.** (in children's games) the player called upon to perform some task, as in tag the one who must catch the other players. **8.** *Colloq.* sex appeal. **9. with it, a.** in accordance with current trends and fashions; fashionable. **b.** well-informed and quick-witted. [ME and OE *hit* (gen. *his,* dat. *him,* acc. *hit*), neut. of *he* HE]

**ITA** /aɪ ti 'eɪ/, Initial Teaching Alphabet.

**itacolumite** /ɪtə'kɒljəmaɪt/, *n.* a sandstone consisting of interlocking quartz grains and mica scales, found in Brazil, North Carolina, etc., and remarkable for its flexibility when in thin slabs. [*Itacolumi,* mountain in Brazil + -ITE[1]]

**ital.,** italic (type).

**Ital., 1.** Italian. **2.** Italy. Also, **It.**

**Italian** /ɪ'tæljən, ə'tæl-/, *adj.* **1.** of or pertaining to Italy, its people, or their language. *–n.* **2.** a native or inhabitant of Italy. **3.** a Romance language, the language of Italy, official also in some cantons of Switzerland. [ME, from L *Italiānus*]

**Italianate** /ɪ'tæljəneɪt/, *adj., v.,* **-nated, -nating.** *–adj.* **1.** Italianised; conforming to the Italian type or style. *–v.t.* **2.** to Italianise.

**Italianise** /ɪ'tæljənaɪz/, *v.,* **-nised, -nising.** *–v.i.* **1.** to become Italian in manner, etc.; speak Italian. *–v.t.* **2.** to make Italian. Also, **Italianize.** – **Italianisation** /ɪˌtæljənaɪ'zeɪʃən/, *n.*

**Italianism** /ɪ'tæljənɪzəm/, *n.* **1.** an Italian practice, trait, or idiom. **2.** Italian quality or spirit.

**Italian rye** /ɪtæljən 'raɪ/, *n.* a widely cultivated and naturalised annual or biennial grass from western and southern Europe, *Lolium multiflorum.*

**italic** /ɪ'tælɪk/, *adj.* **1.** designating or pertaining to a style of printing types in which the letters usu. slope to the right (thus, *italic*), patterned upon a compact manuscript hand, and used for emphasis, etc. **2.** (*cap.*) of or pertaining to Italy, esp. ancient Italy or its tribes. *–n.* **3.** (*oft. pl.*) italic type. **4.** (*cap.*) a principal group of Indo-European languages, including Latin and other languages of ancient Italy, notably Oscan and Umbrian, and closely related to Celtic. [L *Italicus*]

**italicise** /ɪ'tæləsaɪz/, *v.,* **-cised, -cising.** *–v.t.* **1.** to print in italic type. **2.** to underscore with a single line, as in indicating italics. *–v.i.* **3.** to use italics. Also, **italicize.**

**Italicism** /ɪ'tæləsɪzəm/, *n.* →**Italianism.**

**Italy** /'ɪtəli/, *n.* a republic in southern Europe.

**itch** /ɪtʃ/, *v.i.* **1.** to have or feel a peculiar irritation of the skin which causes a desire to scratch the part affected. **2.** to have a desire to do or to get something: *itch after fame.* **3. an itching palm,** a grasping disposition; greed. *–n.* **4.** the sensation of itching. **5. the itch,** a contagious disease caused by the itch mite which burrows into the skin; scabies. **6.** an uneasy or restless desire or longing: *an itch for authorship.* [ME *(y)icchen,* OE *gicc(e)an,* c. D *jeuken,* G *jucken*]

**itch mite** /'– maɪt/, *n.* a parasitic mite, *Sarcoptes scabiei,* causing itch or scabies in man and a form of mange in animals.

**itchy** /'ɪtʃi/, *adj.,* **-ier, -iest. 1.** having an itching sensation. **2.** of the nature of itching. – **itchiness,** *n.*

**-ite**[1], a suffix of nouns denoting esp. **1.** persons associated with a place, tribe, leader, doctrine, system, etc., as in *Campbellite, Israelite, labourite.* **2.** minerals and fossils, as in *ammonite, anthracite.* **3.** explosives, as in *cordite, dynamite.* **4.** chemical compounds, esp. salts of acids whose names end in *-ous,* as in *phosphite, sulphites.* **5.** pharmaceutical and commercial products, as in *vulcanite.* **6.** a member or component of a part of the body, as in *somite.* [from (often directly) Gk *-ītēs* (fem. *-itis*), noun and adj. suffix. Cf. -ITIS]

**-ite**[2], a suffix forming adjectives and nouns from adjectives, and some verbs, as in *composite, opposite, requisite, erudite,* etc. [L *-itus, -ītus,* pp. ending]

**item** /'aɪtəm/, *n.* **1.** a separate article or particular: *fifty items on the list.* **2.** a separate piece of information or news, as in a newspaper. *–v.t.* **3.** to set down or enter as an item, or by or in items. **4.** to make a note or memorandum of. *–adv.* **5.** *Obs.* likewise. [ME, from L: (adv.) just so, likewise]

**itemise** /'aɪtəmaɪz/, *v.t.,* **-mised, -mising.** to state by items; give the particulars of: *to itemise an account.* Also, **itemize.** – **itemisation** /aɪtəmaɪ'zeɪʃən/, *n.* – **itemiser,** *n.*

**iterance** /'ɪtərəns/, *n.* →**iteration.**

**iterant** /'ɪtərənt/, *adj.* repeating.

**iterate** /'ɪtəreɪt/, *v.t.,* **-rated, -rating. 1.** to utter again or repeatedly. **2.** to do (something) over again or repeatedly. [L *iterātus,* pp.]

**iteration** /ɪtə'reɪʃən/, *n.* **1.** repetition. **2.** *Computers.* the repetition of a sequence of steps under the control of a conditional.

**iterative** /'ɪtərətɪv/, *adj.* **1.** repeating; making repetition; repetitious. **2.** *Gram.* →**frequentative.**

**ithyphallic** /ɪθi'fælɪk/, *adj.* **1.** pertaining to the phallus, as carried in ancient festivals of Bacchus. **2.** grossly indecent; obscene. **3.** *Class. Pros.* denoting or pertaining to any of several metres employed in hymns sung in Bacchic processions. *–n.* **4.** a poem in ithyphallic metre. **5.** an indecent poem. [L *īthyphallicus,* from Gk *īthyphallikós,* from *īthýphallos* erect phallus]

**Itie** /ˈaɪtaɪ/, *n. Colloq.* an Italian. Also, **eyetie, eytie.**

**itinerancy** /aɪˈtɪnərənsi/, *n.* **1.** the act of travelling from place to place. **2.** a going about from place to place in the discharge of duty or the prosecution of business. **3.** a body of itinerants. **4.** the state of being itinerant. **5.** the system of rotation governing the ministry of the Methodist Church. Also, **itineracy.**

**itinerant** /aɪˈtɪnərənt/, *adj.* **1.** itinerating; journeying; travelling from place to place, or on a circuit, as a preacher, judge, or pedlar. *–n.* **2.** one who travels from place to place, esp. for duty or business. [LL *itinerans,* ppr.] – **itinerantly,** *adv.*

**itinerary** /aɪˈtɪnəri/, *n., pl.* **-ries,** *adj. –n.* **1.** a line of travel; a route. **2.** an account of a journey; a record of travel. **3.** a book describing a route or routes of travel, with information for travellers. **4.** a plan of travel. *–adj.* **5.** pertaining to travelling or travel routes. **6.** *Rare.* itinerant.

**itinerate** /aɪˈtɪnəreɪt/, *v.i.,* **-rated, -rating.** to go from place to place, esp. in a regular circuit, as to preach. [LL *itinerātus,* pp.] – **itineration** /ˌaɪtɪnəˈreɪʃən/, *n.*

**-ition,** a noun suffix, as in *expedition, extradition,* etc., being *-tion* with a preceding original or formative vowel, or, in other words, **-ite**[1] + **-ion.** [L *-itio, -ītio.* Cf. F *-ition,* G *-ition*]

**-itious,** an adjective suffix occurring in adjectives associated with nouns in *-ition,* as *expeditious,* etc. [L *-icius, -īcius*]

**-itis,** a noun suffix used in pathological terms denoting inflammation of some part or organ, as in *bronchitis, gastritis, neuritis.* [Gk. See -ITE[1]]

**-itive,** a suffix of adjectives and nouns of adjectival origin, as in *definitive, fugitive.* [L *-itīvus, -ītīvus*]

**it'll** /ˈɪtl/, *v.* **1.** a contraction of *it will.* **2.** a contraction of *it shall.*

**-itol,** a suffix used in names of alcohols containing more than one hydroxyl group. [-ITE[1] + -OL[1]]

**its** /ɪts/, *adj., pron.* possessive form of *it.* [poss. case of IT, formerly written *it's*]

**it's** /ɪts/, contraction of *it is.*

**itself** /ɪtˈsɛlf/, *pron.* **1.** the reflexive form of *it: a thermostatically controlled electric fire switches itself off.* **2.** an emphatic form of *it* used: **a.** as object: *the earth gathers its fruits to itself.* **b.** in opposition to a subject or object: *the moon itself is dead.* **3.** in its normal or usual state: *the child is itself again.*

**itsy-bitsy** /ˈɪtsi-ˌbɪtsi/, *adj. Colloq.* (*joc.*) small; insubstantial. Also, **itty-bitty.**

**-ity,** a suffix forming abstract nouns of condition, characteristics, etc., as in *jollity, civility, Latinity.* [ME *-ite,* from F *-ité,* from L *-itāt-,* stem of *-itas*]

**I.U.C.D.** /ˌaɪ ju si ˈdi/, *n.* →**intra-uterine device.** [(*I*)*ntra-* (*U*)*terine* (*C*)*ontraceptive* (*D*)*evice*]

**I.U.D.** /aɪ ju ˈdi/, *n.* →**intra-uterine device.**

**-ium,** a suffix representing Latin neuter suffix, used esp. to form names of metallic elements.

**-ive,** a suffix of adjectives (and nouns of adjectival origin) expressing tendency, disposition, function, connection, etc., as in *active, corrective, destructive, detective, passive, sportive.* Cf. **-ative.** [L *-īvus;* also representing F *-if* (masc.), *-ive* (fem.), from L]

**I've** /aɪv/, *v.* contraction of *I have.*

**ivied** /ˈaɪvid/, *adj.* covered or overgrown with ivy.

**ivory** /ˈaɪvəri, ˈaɪvri/, *n., pl.* **-ries,** *adj. –n.* **1.** the hard white substance, a variety of dentine, composing the main part of the tusks of the elephant, walrus, etc., used for carvings, billiard balls, etc. **2.** a tusk, as of an elephant. **3.** dentine of any kind. **4.** some substance resembling ivory. **5.** *Colloq.* tooth, or the teeth. **6.** an article made of ivory, as a carving or a billiard ball. **7.** (*pl.*) *Colloq.* **a.** the keys of a piano, accordion, etc. **b.** dice. **8.** the hard endosperm (**vegetable ivory**) of the ivory nut, used for ornamental purposes, buttons, etc. **9.** creamy white. **10. tickle the ivories,** to play the piano. *–adj.* **11.** consisting or made of ivory. **12.** of the colour ivory. [ME *yvory,* etc., from OF *yvoire,* from L *eboreus* made of ivory] – **ivory-like,** *adj.*

**ivory black** /– ˈblæk/, *n.* a fine black pigment made by calcining ivory.

**Ivory Coast** /aɪvəri ˈkoʊst/, *n.* a republic in western Africa.

**ivory gull** /aɪvəri ˈgʌl/, *n.* a white arctic gull, *Pagophila eburnea.*

**ivory nut** /ˈ– nʌt/, *n.* **1.** the seed of a low-growing South American palm, *Phytelephas macrocarpa,* forming the source of vegetable ivory. **2.** a similar seed from other palms.

**ivory palm** /ˈ– pam/, *n.* the palm yielding the common ivory nut.

**ivory tower** /– ˈtaʊə/, *n.* **1.** a place withdrawn from the world and worldly acts and attitudes. **2.** an attitude of aloofness from or contempt for worldly matters or behaviour. [translation of F *tour d'ivoire,* first used by Sainte-Beuve, 1804-69, French critic]

**ivy** /ˈaɪvi/, *n., pl.* **ivies.** **1.** a climbing vine, *Hedera helix,* with smooth, shiny, evergreen leaves, yellowish inconspicuous flowers, and black berries, widely grown as an ornamental. **2.** any of various other climbing or trailing plants, as *Parthenocissus tricuspidata* (**Japanese ivy**), *Glechoma hederacea* (**ground ivy**), etc. [ME; OE *īfig;* akin to G *Efeu*] – **ivy-like,** *adj.*

**Ivy League** /aɪvi ˈlig/, *n. U.S.* **1.** a group of highly regarded universities and colleges, esp. Yale, Harvard, Princeton, Columbia, Dartmouth, Cornell, Pennsylvania, and Brown, with high social and scholastic reputations. **2.** of, or pertaining to these universities, colleges, their students or graduates.

**iwis** /iˈwɪs/, *adv. Obs.* certainly. Also, **ywis.** [ME adv. use of neut. of OE adj. *gewis* certain, c. D *gewis,* G *gewiss* certain, certainly; akin to WIT[2], *v.,* know]

**ixia** /ˈɪksiə/, *n.* any plant of the genus *Ixia,* comprising southern African plants with sword-shaped leaves and showy ornamental flowers. [NL (named with reference to the juice), from Gk: birdlime]

**ixtle** /ˈɪkstli, ˈɪs-/, *n.* →**istle.**

**izard** /ˈɪzəd/, *n.* the chamois which inhabits the Pyrenees. [F *isard*]

**-ization,** →**-isation.**

**-ize,** variant of **-ise**[1], as in *realize.*

**izzard** /ˈɪzəd/, *n. Archaic.* the letter Z. [unexplained var. of ZED]

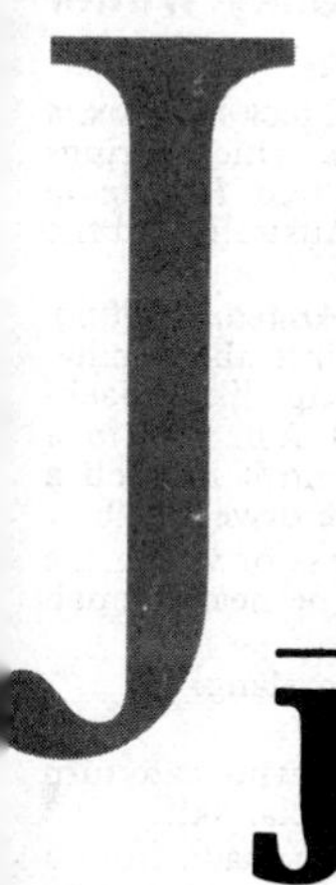

Jj Roman ASTER   Jj Sans Serif ANTIQUE OLIVE   Jj Script PATRICIAN   Jj Decorative RUBENS

*Although there are numerous typefaces in the world they can be divided into four main classifications. These are:*

*ROMAN or SERIF. This typeface came into being from the technique of the Roman masons who, working in stone, finished off each letter with a serif or small stroke projecting from the top or bottom. This was done to correct any feeling of unevenness or imbalance they may have created in cutting the characters in stone.*

*SANS SERIF (without serif). This typeface is geometric in design and has straight-edged characters and lines of a regular thickness.*

*SCRIPT. Based on the movement of the hand, this typeface is often italicised or slanted, as if drawn by a brush or quill pen.*

*DECORATIVE. Any typeface that exaggerates the characteristics of any of the other three classifications to a degree that places it outside of them.*

*The dictionary entries in this book use a SANS SERIF typeface called Helvetica (set in a bold face for the head words) and a SERIF typeface Plantin (used throughout the body of the entries).*

**J, j** /dʒeɪ/, *n., pl.* **J's** or **Js, j's** or **js.** **1.** a consonant, the 10th letter of the English alphabet. **2.** Roman numeral for 1.

**j,** the imaginary number, $\sqrt{-1}$.

**J,** joule.

**J.,** **1.** journal. **2.** Judge. **3.** Justice.

**Ja.,** January.

**J.A.,** Judge Advocate.

**jab** /dʒæb/, *v.,* **jabbed, jabbing,** *n.* *–v.i.* **1.** to thrust smartly or sharply, as with the end or point of something. *–v.t.* **2.** to poke (something) smartly or sharply. *–n.* **3.** a poke with the end or point of something; a smart or sharp thrust. **4.** *Colloq.* an injection with a hypodermic needle. Also, **job.** [var. (orig. Scot.) of JOB[2]]

**jabber** /ˈdʒæbə/, *v.i.* **1.** to utter rapidly, indistinctly, imperfectly, or nonsensically; chatter. *–v.t.* **2.** to utter (words) in a confused, indistinct fashion. *–n.* **3.** rapid or nonsensical talk or utterance; gibberish. [apparently imitative] **– jabberer,** *n.* **– jabberingly,** *adv.*

**jabberwocky** /ˈdʒæbəwɒki/, *n.* **1.** incoherent or meaningless speech, esp. invented language. **2.** *Colloq.* nonsense. [coined by Lewis Carroll in *Through the Looking Glass* (1871)]

**jabiru** /dʒæbəˈru/, *n.* **1.** Australia's only stork, *Xenorhynchus asiaticus,* white with glossy green-black head, neck, tail, and a black band across upper and lower wing surfaces, found along the north and east coast; policeman bird. **2.** a similar bird, *Jabiru mycteria,* inhabiting the warmer parts of America. [Tupi-Guarani]

jabiru (def. 1)

**jaborandi** /dʒæbəˈrændi/, *n., pl.* **-dis.** **1.** any of certain South American shrubs of the genus *Pilocarpus.* **2.** the dried leaflets of *Pilocarpus jaborandi* and other species containing the alkaloid pilocarpine, used as a sudorific and sialagogue and in ophthalmology. [Tupi-Guarani]

**jabot** /ˈʒæboʊ/, *n.* a falling ruffle, cascade, or other arrangement of lace, embroidery, or the like, worn at the neck or the front of a dress by women and formerly by men. [F: lit., bird's crop]

**jaboticaba** /dʒəbɒtiˈkabə/, *n.* a small tree, *Myticaria cauliflora,* originating in Brazil, which sets its large, round purple fruit directly onto its trunk.

**jacamar** /ˈdʒækəmə/, *n.* any bird of the tropical American family Galbulidae, usu. bright green above, with long bills. [Tupi *jacamáciri*]

**jacana** /dʒəˈkanə/, *n.* any of various birds of the family Jacanidae, as the lotus bird, *Irediparra gallinacea,* of northern and eastern Australia, which has enormously lengthened toes and a long, sharp hind claw, adapted for running on floating vegetation; lily trotter. [Pg., from Tupi *jasaná*]

jacaranda

**jacaranda** /dʒækəˈrændə/, *n.* **1.** any of the tall tropical American trees constituting the genus *Jacaranda,* esp. *J. mimosifolia* cultivated in many warm countries for its lavender-blue flowers. **2.** their fragrant ornamental wood. **3.** any of various related or similar trees. **4.** their wood. [Tupi-Guarani]

**jacinth** /ˈdʒæsɪnθ/, *n.* →**hyacinth** (def. 4). [ME *iacynt,* from OF *jacinte,* from L *hyacinthus* HYACINTH]

**jack**[1] /dʒæk/, *n.* **1.** a man or fellow. **2.** (*cap.* or *l.c.*) a sailor. **3.** any of various mechanical contrivances or devices, as a contrivance for raising heavy weights short distances. **4.** a device for turning a spit, etc. **5.** any of the four knaves in playing cards. **6. a.** a knucklebone or plastic imitation, a set of which is used in a children's game where they are thrown into the air and caught on the back of the hand. **b.** (*pl.*) the game itself. **7.** a small bowl used as a mark for the players to aim at, in the game of bowls. **8.** a small union or ensign used by a ship or vessel as a signal, etc., and flown from the jackstaff as an indication of nationality. **9.** →**jackass.** **10.** →**jack rabbit.** **11.** *Elect.* a connecting device to which the wires of a circuit may be attached and which is arranged for the insertion of a plug. **12.** *Naut.* a horizontal bar or crosstree of iron at the topgallant masthead. **13.** *Music.* the moving part of the mechanism of early keyboard instruments that holds the quill or plectrum. **14.** any of several carangoid fishes, esp. of the genus *Caranx.* **15.** *N.Z.* young male fish. **16.** *Colloq.* a police-

jack[1] (def. 3)

man. **17.** *Colloq.* a double-headed coin. **18.** *Colloq.* venereal disease. **19. the house that Jack built,** *Colloq.* the V.D. clinic. **20. every man jack,** everyone without exception. **21. I'm all right Jack,** (an expression of selfish complacency on the part of the speaker). *–v.t.* **22.** to lift or move with or as with a jack, or contrivance for raising (usu. fol. by *up*). **23.** *N.Z. Colloq.* **a.** to arrange, organise, prepare. **b.** fix up, renovate (fol. by *up*). **24.** *Colloq.* to raise (prices, wages, etc.) (usu. fol. by *up*). *–v.i.* **25. jack up,** *Colloq.* to refuse; be obstinate; resist. *–adj.* **26. jack of,** fed up with. **27.** weary, tired. [orig. proper name *Jack,* earlier *Jacken,* dissimilated var. of *Jankin,* from *Jan* John + -KIN]

**jack**[2] /dʒæk/, *n.* **1.** a defensive coat, usu. of leather, formerly worn by foot soldiers and others. **2.** a container for alcoholic drink, originally of waxed leather coated with tar. [ME *iacke,* from OF *jaque, jaques,* from Sp. *jaco,* ? from Ar. *shakk*]

**jack-a-dandy** /dʒæk-ə-'dændi/, *n., pl.* **-dies.** →**dandy**[1] (def. 1).

**jackal** /'dʒækəl/, *n.* **1.** any of several races of wild dog of the genus *Canis,* esp. *Canis aureus,* of Asia and Africa, which hunt in packs at night and which were formerly supposed to hunt prey for the lion. **2.** one who does drudgery for another, or who serves the purpose of another. [Turk. *chakāl,* from Pers. *shag-(h)āl*]

jackal

**jackanapes** /'dʒækəneɪps/, *n.* **1.** a pert, presuming young man; whippersnapper. **2.** a mischievous child. **3.** a conceited person; coxcomb. **4.** *Archaic.* an ape or monkey. [var. of ME *Jack Napes,* nickname of William, Duke of Suffolk, 1396-1450, whose badge was an ape's clog and chain; probably orig. used as name for tame ape or monkey]

**jackaroo** /dʒækə'ru/, *n.* →**jackeroo.**

**jackass** /'dʒækæs/, *n.* **1.** a male donkey. **2.** a very stupid or foolish person. **3.** *Naut.* a bag or plug for stopping a hawse pipe to prevent water from entering. **4.** a kookaburra. **5.** the grey butcher bird, *Cracticus torquatus.*

**jackass fish** /'– fɪʃ/, *n.* a marine food fish of the morwong group, *Nemadactylus macropterus,* found in southern Australian and New Zealand waters.

**jack bean** /'dʒæk bin/, *n.* a trailing leguminous plant, *Canavalia ensiformis,* grown as a vegetable in the tropics and subtropics.

**jack boot** /'– but/, *n.* a large leather boot reaching up to and sometimes over the knee, orig. one serving as armour, now frequently associated with the exercise of force or oppression.

**jackdaw** /'dʒækdɔ/, *n.* **1.** a glossy black European bird, *Corvus monedula,* of the crow family, frequenting steeples, ruins, etc. **2.** the great-tailed grackle, *Cassidix mexicanus,* a large glossy blackbird of the southern U.S. and Mexico. [JACK[1] + DAW, *n.*]

**jacked-up** /dʒækt-'ʌp/, *adj. Colloq.* infected with venereal disease. Also (*esp. in predicative positions*), **jacked up.**

**jacker** /'dʒækə/, *n.* one who uses a jack[1] (def. 3), as a sawmill worker who handles logs.

**jackeroo** /dʒækə'ru/, *n.* **1.** an apprentice station hand on a sheep or cattle station. *–v.i.* **2.** to work as a trainee on such a station: *he's jackerooing in Queensland this year.* Also, **jackaroo.** [b. *Jack* Christian name + KANGAROO[1]]

**jacket** /'dʒækət/, *n.* **1.** a short coat, in various forms, worn by both men and women. **2.** something designed to be fastened about the body for other purpose than clothing: *a straitjacket.* **3.** Also, **dust jacket, dustcover.** a detachable paper cover, usu. illustrated in colour, for protecting the binding of a book. **4.** the skin of a potato. **5.** the outer casing or covering of a boiler, pipe, tank, etc. **6.** the natural coat of certain animals. *–v.t.* **7.** to cover with a jacket. [ME *iaquet,* from OF *jaquete,* diminutive of *jaque* JACK[2]] **–jacketed,** *adj.* **–jacketless,** *adj.* **–jacketlike,** *adj.*

**jackfish** /'dʒækfɪʃ/, *n.* →**pike**[1] (def. 2).

**Jack Frost** /dʒæk 'frɒst/, *n.* frost or freezing cold personified.

**jackfruit** /'dʒækfrut/, *n.* **1.** a Polynesian tree, *Artocarpus heterophyllus,* with a fruit resembling breadfruit. **2.** the fruit itself, one of the largest known (up to more than 30 kg).

**jackhammer** /'dʒækhæmə/, *n.* a hand-held hammerdrill operated by compressed air; used for drilling rocks.

**jack-in-the-box** /'dʒæk-ɪn-ðə-bɒks/, *n.* **1.** Also, **jack-in-a-box.** a toy consisting of a figure, enclosed in a box, which springs out when the lid is unfastened. **2.** a seashore tree, *Hernandia peltata,* widely spread from Asia to northern Australia and the western Pacific.

**jackknife** /'dʒæknaɪf/, *n., pl.* **-knives,** *v.,* **-knifed, -knifing.** *–n.* **1.** a large knife with a blade that folds into the handle. **2.** →**jackknife dive.** *–v.i.* **3.** to bend or fold up, like a jackknife. **4.** (of a horse) to buck bringing all four feet to a point. **5.** (of a semi-trailer) to go out of control in such a way that the trailer swings round towards the driver's cab.

**jackknife dive** /'– daɪv/, *n.* a dive in the process of which the body bends so that the hands briefly touch or nearly touch the toes; pike dive.

**Jack-'n'-Jill** /dʒæk-ən-'dʒɪl/, *n.* →**bill.** [rhyming slang]

**Jacko** /'dʒækoʊ/, *n. Colloq.* →**kookaburra.**

**jack-of-all-trades** /ˌdʒæk-əv-'ɔl-treɪdz/, *n.* one who can turn his hand to anything but who has no one special skill.

**jack-o'-lantern** /'dʒæk-ə-læntən/, *n.* **1.** a lantern made from a hollowed-out pumpkin, with holes cut to represent human eyes, nose, mouth, etc. **2.** →**ignis fatuus.**

**jack pine** /'dʒæk paɪn/, *n.* a slender pine, *Pinus banksiana,* covering tracts of barren land in Canada and the northern U.S.

**jack plane** /'– pleɪn/, *n.* (in carpentry) a plane used for rough work.

**jackpot** /'dʒækpɒt/, *n.* **1.** *Poker.* a pool that accumulates until a player opens the betting with a pair of jacks or better. **2.** the chief prize to be won on a gambling machine, as a poker machine, or in a lottery, a game or contest such as bingo, a quiz, etc. **3. hit the jackpot,** to win chief prize on a gambling machine; achieve great success; be very lucky.

**jackpot tote** /'– toʊt/, *n.* a series of horse races, generally more than four, on which the winnings of each preceding race are placed on the next, and the prize thus accumulates.

**jack rabbit** /'dʒæk ræbət/, *n.* any of various large hares of western North America, having very long limbs and ears.

**jackscrew** /'dʒækskru/, *n.* →**screw-jack.**

**jackshaft** /'dʒækʃaft/, *n.* a short shaft, usu. intermediate between the motor or engine and the machine to be driven.

**jackshay** /'dʒækʃeɪ/, *n. Colloq.* a tin quart pot used by bushmen for boiling water. Also, **jackshea.**

**jacksnipe** /'dʒæksnaɪp/, *n.* **1.** a small, relatively short-billed snipe, *Limnocryptes minima,* of Europe and Asia. **2.** any of several related snipes. [JACK[1] + SNIPE]

**jackstaff** /'dʒækstaf/, *n.* a flagstaff at the bow of a vessel on which the jack is flown.

**jackstay** /'dʒæksteɪ/, *n.* a rope, rod, or the like, on a yard, used for tying the head of a square sail to the yard, and as a handrail.

**jackstraw** /'dʒækstrɔ/, *n.* **1.** a straw-stuffed figure of a man. **2.** an insignificant person. **3.** one of a number of straws, or strips of wood, bone, etc., used in a game in which they are thrown on a table in confusion and are to be picked up singly without disturbing the others. **4.** (*pl. construed as sing.*) the game itself; fiddlesticks.

**jacksy** /'dʒæksi/, *n. N.Z. Colloq.* the posterior; the buttocks.

**Jack Tar** /dʒæk 'ta/, *n. Brit.* a sailor. Also, **jack tar.**

**Jack the Painter,** *n.* a strong green bush tea, which discolours utensils.

**Jacky** /'dʒæki/, *n. Colloq. in the phrases* **1. sit (up) like Jacky,** to behave with full confidence; to be on one's best behaviour. **2. work like Jacky,** to work very hard.

**jackyard** /'dʒækjad/, *n.* a small boom used to extend a topsail in a yacht.

**Jacky Howe** /dʒæki 'haʊ/, *n. Colloq.* **1.** a navy or black woollen singlet worn by labourers, bushmen, etc. **2.** any similar singlet. Also, **Jimmy Howe.** [? from name of Australian world champion shearer of 1892]

**jacky lizard** /'dʒæki lɪzəd/, *n.* a small long-tailed arboreal agamid lizard, *Amphibolurus muricatus,* which inhabits the western districts of Queensland and New South Wales. Also, **blood sucker, tree dragon.**

**Jacky Winter** /dʒæki 'wɪntə/, *n.* a small grey-brown flycatcher, *Microeca leucophaea,* found in many parts of Australia and

New Guinea.

**Jacobean** /dʒækəˈbiən/, *adj.* **1.** of or pertaining to the reign of James I of England or his times: *Jacobean drama.* **2.** of or pertaining to the late English Gothic style of architecture and furnishings, showing Italian influence, which flourished in the first half of the 17th century. *–n.* **3.** a Jacobean writer, personage, etc. [NL *Jacōbaeus,* from LL *Jacōbus* James + -AN]

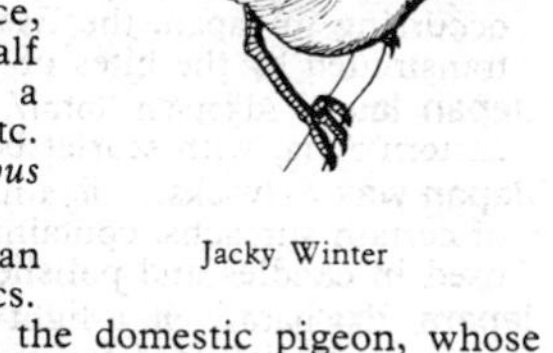
Jacky Winter

**Jacobin** /ˈdʒækəbən/, *n.* **1.** an extreme radical, esp. in politics. **2.** (*l.c.*). an artificial variety of the domestic pigeon, whose neck feathers form a hood. [from *Jacobin,* a member of a club or society of French revolutionaries organised in 1789; ME, from ML *Jacōbīnus,* from LL *Jacōbus* James] **–Jacobinic** /dʒækəˈbɪnɪk/, **Jacobinical** /dʒækəˈbɪnɪkəl/, *adj.* **–Jacobinically** /dʒækəˈbɪnɪkli/, *adv.*

**Jacobinism** /ˈdʒækəbənɪzəm/, *n.* referring to the principles of the Jacobins.

**Jacob's-ladder** /dʒeɪkəbz-ˈlædə/, *n.* **1.** a garden plant, *Polemonium caeruleum,* whose leaves have a ladder-like arrangement. **2.** any of certain related species.

**jaconet** /ˈdʒækənət/, *n.* a lightweight cotton fabric, used in the manufacture of surgical dressings. [Urdu *jagannāthī,* after *Jagannāthpūrī* in Orissa, India, where this fabric was originally made]

**Jacquard loom** /ˈdʒækad lum/, *n.* a pattern loom for weaving elaborate designs. [named after J. M. *Jacquard,* 1752-1834, French inventor]

**Jacquard weave** /ˈ– wiv/, *n.* a fabric woven on a Jacquard loom.

**jac shirt** /ˈdʒæk ʃɜt/, *n.* a man's casual shirt, fitted with a band at the waist, worn outside the trousers and similar to a jacket.

**jactation** /dʒækˈteɪʃən/, *n.* **1.** boasting. **2.** *Pathol.* a restless tossing of the body. [L *jactātio* a throwing]

**jactitation** /dʒæktəˈteɪʃən/, *n.* **1.** *Law.* the assertion of a false claim, to the injury of another. **2.** *Pathol.* →**jactation** (def. 2). [ML *jactitātio,* from L *jactitāre* bring forward in public, utter]

**jade**[1] /dʒeɪd/, *n.* **1.** either of two minerals, jadeite or nephrite, sometimes green, highly esteemed as an ornamental stone for carvings, jewellery, etc. **2.** Also, **jade green.** green; varying from bluish green to yellowish green. [F, from Sp. (*piedra de*) *ijada,* lit., (stone of) colic (Sp. *ijada* pain in the side, colic, from L *ilia* flanks. See ILIUM)] **–jadelike,** *adj.*

**jade**[2] /dʒeɪd/, *n., v.,* **jaded, jading.** *–n.* **1.** a horse, esp. one of inferior breed, or worn out, or vicious. **2.** (*derog.*) a woman. *–v.t.* **3.** to make exhausted by working hard; to weary or fatigue; tire. *–v.i.* **4.** to become exhausted by working hard. [ME, orig. uncert. Cf. Icel. *jalda* mare] **–jadish,** *adj.* **–jadishly,** *adv.* **–jadishness,** *n.*

**jaded** /ˈdʒeɪdəd/, *adj.* **1.** worn out. **2.** sated: *a jaded appetite.* **–jadedly,** *adv.* **–jadedness,** *n.*

**jade green** /dʒeɪd ˈgrin/, *n.* the colour of jade.

**jadeite** /ˈdʒeɪdaɪt/, *n.* a mineral, essentially sodium aluminium silicate, $NaAlSi_2O_6$, occurring in tough masses, whitish to dark green. See **jade**[1] (def. 1).

**jaeger** /ˈjeɪgə/, *n.* **1.** any of the rapacious seabirds constituting the family Stercorariidae which pursue weaker birds in order to make them disgorge their prey; a skua. **2.** a hunter. Also, **jäger, yager.** [G: hunter, from *jagen* hunt]

**jaffle** /ˈdʒæfəl/, *n.* a toasted pie with a bread crust, savoury or sweet filling, cooked in a buttered jaffle iron.

**jaffle iron** /ˈ– aɪən/, *n.* a double-sided hinged pie-shaped mould with a long handle for cooking jaffles.

**jag**[1] /dʒæg/, *n., v.,* **jagged, jagging.** *–n.* **1.** a sharp projection on an edge or surface. *–v.t.* **2.** to cut or slash, esp. in points or pendants along the edge; form notches, teeth, or ragged points in. [ME *jaggen;* ? imitative]

**jag**[2] /dʒæg/, *n.* **1.** a drinking bout. **2.** any sustained single activity, often carried to excess: *an eating jag, a fishing jag.* [U.S. d. *jag* a load carried on the back; thus as much drink as a man can carry]

**jäger** /ˈjeɪgə/, *n.* →**jaeger.**

**jagged**[1] /ˈdʒægəd/, *adj.* having notches, teeth, or ragged edges. **–jaggedly,** *adv.* **–jaggedness,** *n.*

**jagged**[2] /ˈdʒægd/, *adj. Colloq.* intoxicated, drunk.

**jaggy** /ˈdʒægi/, *adj.,* **-gier, -giest.** jagged; notched.

**jaguar** /ˈdʒægjuə/, *n.* a large, ferocious, spotted feline, *Panthera onca,* of tropical America. [Tupi-Guarani *jaguara*]

jaguar

**jaguarondi** /dʒægwəˈrɒndi/, *n., pl.* **-dis.** a short-legged long-bodied wild cat, *Felis yagouaroundi,* of tropical America. Also, **jaguarundi** /dʒægwəˈrʌndi/. [Tupi-Guarani]

**Jahveh** /ˈjaveɪ/, *n.* →**Yahweh.** Also, **Jahve, Jah** /ja/.

**jail** /dʒeɪl/, *n.* →**gaol.** [ME *jaiole,* from OF: prison, cage, from L *cavea* cavity, enclosure, cage. See GAOL]

**jail-bait** /ˈdʒeɪl-beɪt/, *n. Colloq.* →**gaol-bait.**

**jailbird** /ˈdʒeɪlbɜd/, *n.* →**gaolbird.**

**jailbreak** /ˈdʒeɪlbreɪk/, *n.* →**gaolbreak.**

**jail delivery** /ˈdʒeɪl dəlɪvəri/, *n.* →**gaol delivery.**

**jailer** /ˈdʒeɪlə/, *n.* →**gaoler.**

**jail fever** /ˈdʒeɪl fivə/, *n.* →**gaol fever.**

**jail gang** /ˈ– gæŋ/, *n.* →**gaol gang.**

**jailhouse** /ˈdʒeɪlhaʊs/, *n., pl.* **-houses** /-haʊzəz/. *Chiefly U.S.* →**gaol.** Also, **gaolhouse.**

**jailie** /ˈdʒeɪli/, *n. Colloq.* →**gaolie.**

**jake** /dʒeɪk/, *adj. Colloq.* all right: *she'll be jake.* Also, **jakerloo.**

**jakes** /dʒeɪks/, *n. Archaic.* →**toilet.**

**jalap** /ˈdʒɒləp, ˈdʒæl-/, *n.* **1.** a purgative drug from the tuberous root of a plant, *Ipomoea purga* of Mexico, or of some other plants of the family Convolvulaceae. **2.** any of these plants from which this drug is obtained. **3.** →**madeira vine.** [Sp. *jalapa;* named after *Jalapa,* a city in E Mexico] **–jalapic** /dʒəˈlæpɪk/, *adj.*

**jalapin** /ˈdʒæləpən/, *n.* a resin which is one of the purgative principles of jalap. [JALAP + -IN[2]]

**jalopy** /dʒəˈlɒpi/, *n., pl.* **-lopies.** *Colloq.* an old, decrepit, or unpretentious motor car.

**jalousie** /ˈʒæluzi, dʒəˈlusi/, *n.* a kind of blind or shutter made with slats fixed at an angle. [F: lit., jealousy]

**jam**[1] /dʒæm/, *v.,* **jammed, jamming,** *n.* *–v.t.* **1.** to press or squeeze tightly between bodies or surfaces, so that motion or extrication is made difficult or impossible. **2.** to bruise or crush by squeezing. **3.** to press, push, or thrust violently, as into a confined space or against some object. **4.** to fill or block up by crowding: *crowds jam the doors.* **5.** to cause to become wedged, caught, or displaced, so that it cannot work, as a machine, part, etc. **6.** *Radio.* **a.** to interfere with (signals, etc.) by sending out others of approximately the same frequency. **b.** (of signals, etc.) to interfere with (other signals, etc.). **7.** to apply (brakes) forcibly (fol. by *on*). *–v.i.* **8.** to become wedged or fixed; stick fast. **9.** to press or push violently, as into a confined space or against one another. **10.** (of a machine, etc.) to become unworkable as through the wedging or displacement of a part. **11.** *Music.* to take part in a jam (def. 15). *–n.* **12.** the act of jamming. **13.** the state of being jammed. **14.** a mass of vehicles, people, or objects jammed together: *a traffic jam.* **15.** Also, **jam session.** a meeting of musicians for the spontaneous and improvisatory performance of music, esp. jazz, usu. for their own enjoyment. **16.** →**jamwood.** **17.** *Colloq.* a difficult or awkward situation; a fix. **18.** **put on jam,** to affect a self-important manner. [apparently imitative Cf. CHAMP[1]]

**jam**[2] /dʒæm/, *n.* a preserve of whole fruit, slightly crushed, boiled with sugar. [? same as JAM[1]] **–jam-like,** *adj.* **–jammy,** *adj.*

**Jamaica** /dʒəˈmeɪkə/, *n.* an island country in the West Indies, south of Cuba.

**Jamaican** /dʒəˈmeɪkən/, *adj.* **1.** of, pertaining to, or obtained from the island of Jamaica. *–n.* **2.** a native or an inhabitant of Jamaica.

i = peat ɪ = pit ɛ = pet æ = pat a = part ɒ = pot ʌ = putt ɔ = port ʊ = put u = pool ɜ = pert ə = apart aɪ = buy eɪ = bay ɔɪ = boy aʊ = how
oʊ = hoe ɪə = here ɛə = hair ʊə = tour g = give θ = thin ð = then ʃ = show ʒ = measure tʃ = choke dʒ = joke ŋ = sing j = you õ = Fr. bon

**jamas** /ˈdʒaməz/, *n.pl. Colloq.* →**pyjamas.** Also, **jamies.**

**jamb** /dʒæm/, *n.* **1.** the side of an opening; a vertical piece forming the side of a doorway, window, or the like. **2.** →**jambeau.** Also, **jambe.** [ME *jambe,* from F: leg, jamb, from LL *gamba* hoof]

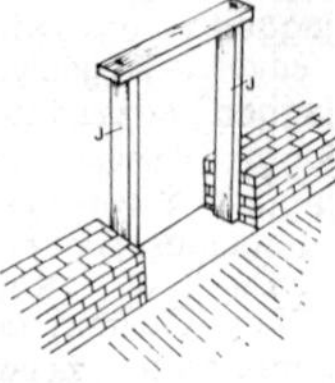


J, jamb

**jambeau** /ˈdʒæmboʊ/, *n., pl.* **-beaux** /-boʊz/. armour for the leg; a greave.

**jamboree** /dʒæmbəˈri/, *n.* **1.** a large gathering or rally of boy scouts, usu. national or international. **2.** *Colloq.* a carousal; any noisy merrymaking. [apparently b. JABBER and F *soirée,* with *-m-* from JAM[1] crowd]

**jam-jar** /ˈdʒæm-dʒa/, *n.* a jar, usu. of glass, for holding jam.

**jam melon** /ˈdʒæm mɛlən/, *n.* **1.** a large melon with a dark green striped rind, not palatable in its fresh state but used in making jams. **2.** the vine producing this fruit, *Citrullus lanatus,* var. *Citroides,* thought to be originally from Africa.

**jammy** /ˈdʒæmi/, *adj.* **1.** of or pertaining to jam. **2.** smeared or covered with jam. **3.** *Colloq.* easy; requiring no effort.

**jam-packed** /dʒæm-ˈpækt/, *adj. Colloq.* crowded.

**jam session** /ˈdʒæm sɛʃən/, *n.* →**jam**[1] (def. 15).

**jam tarts** /– ˈtats/, *n.pl.* a procumbent shrub, *Melichrus procumbens,* family Epacridaceae, found in coastal and mountain heath of New South Wales.

**jam tree** /ˈ– tri/, *n.* →**raspberry-jam tree.**

**jamwood** /ˈdʒæmwʊd/, *n.* the wood of the raspberry-jam tree. Also, **jam.**

**Jan.,** January.

**jane** /dʒeɪn/, *n. Colloq.* a woman.

**jangle** /ˈdʒæŋgəl/, *v.,* **-gled, -gling,** *n.* *–v.i.* **1.** to sound harshly or discordantly: *a jangling noise.* **2.** *Archaic.* to speak angrily; wrangle. *–v.t.* **3.** to cause to sound harshly or discordantly. **4.** to cause to become upset or irritated. *–n.* **5.** a harsh or discordant sound. **6.** an altercation; quarrel. [ME *jangle(n),* from OF *jangler* chatter, tattle; ? of Gmc orig.] **– jangler,** *n.*

**janissary** /ˈdʒænəsəri/, *n., pl.* **-saries. 1.** an infantryman in the Turkish sovereign's personal standing army from the 14th century until 1826. **2.** any Turkish soldier. Also, **janizary** /ˈdʒænəzəri/. [F *janissaire,* from Turk. *yeñicheri* new soldiery]

**janitor** /ˈdʒænətə/, *n.* **1.** a doorkeeper or porter. **2.** *U.S.* a caretaker. [L: doorkeeper. See JANUS-FACED] **– janitorial** /dʒænəˈtɔriəl/, *adj.* **– janitress** /ˈdʒænətrəs/, *n. fem.*

**Jansenism** /ˈdʒænsənɪzəm/, *n.* a doctrinal system which maintained the radical corruption of human nature and the inability of the will to do good, and that Christ died for the predestined and not for all men. [orig. referring to Cornelis *Jansen,* 1585-1638, Dutch Roman Catholic theologian, and his followers]

**January** /ˈdʒænjuəri/, *n., pl.* **-ries.** the first month of the year, containing 31 days. [L *Jānuārius* the month of *Janus* (see JANUS-FACED); replacing ME *Jenever,* from ONF, and OE *Ianuarius,* from L]

**Janus-faced** /ˈdʒeɪnəs-feɪst/, *adj.* two-faced; deceitful. [referring to *Janus,* an ancient Roman (perhaps solar) deity, regarded as presiding over doors and gates and over beginnings and endings, commonly represented with two faces looking in opposite directions. Cf. *January,* first month of the year]

**Jap** /dʒæp/, *adj., n. Colloq.* →**Japanese.**

**Jap.,** Japanese.

**japan** /dʒəˈpæn/, *n., adj., v.,* **-panned, -panning.** *–n.* **1.** any of various hard, durable, black varnishes (orig. from Japan) for coating wood, metal, etc. **2.** work varnished and figured in the Japanese manner. *–adj.* **3.** of or pertaining to japan. *–v.t.* **4.** to varnish with japan; lacquer. **5.** to coat with any material which gives a hard, black gloss. [special use of JAPAN]

**Japan** /dʒəˈpæn/, *n.* a constitutional monarchy on a chain of islands off the east coast of Asia.

**Japanese** /dʒæpəˈniz/, *adj., n., pl.* **-nese.** *–adj.* **1.** of or pertaining to Japan, its people, or their language. *–n.* **2.** a native of Japan, or a descendant of one. **3.** the language of Japan (no known congeners). **4. have a Japanese bladder,** *Colloq.* to suffer from frequency (def. 7).

**Japanese cedar** /– ˈsidə/, *n.* a tall evergreen coniferous tree, *Cryptomeria japonica,* of China and Japan.

**Japanese ivy** /– ˈaɪvi/, *n.* a woody, oriental, climbing shrub, *Parthenocissus tricuspidata.*

**Japanese lantern** /– ˈlæntn/, *n.* →**Chinese lantern** (def. 1).

**Japanese river fever,** *n.* a group of infectious diseases occurring in Japan, the East Indies, and probably elsewhere, transmitted by the bites of mites; tsutsugamushi fever.

**Japan laurel** /dʒəpæn ˈlɒrəl/, *n.* a shrub, *Aucuba japonica,* of eastern Asia, with scarlet berries.

**Japan wax** /– ˈwæks/, *n.* a natural wax obtained from the fruit of certain sumachs, containing a high proportion of palmitin; used in candles and polishes.

**japara** /dʒəˈparə/, *n.* a light-weight, tightly-woven, waterproof cotton material used for making tents, oilskins, etc.

**jape** /dʒeɪp/, *v.,* **japed, japing,** *n.* *–v.i.* **1.** *Archaic.* to jest; joke; gibe. *–n.* **2.** a joke; jest; gibe. [ME; orig. uncert.] **– japer,** *n.*

**Japhetic** /dʒəˈfɛtɪk/, *adj.* **1.** of or pertaining to a hypothetical linguistic family of Europe and western Asia, which was considered by some to have developed before Indo-European and Semitic. *–n.* **2.** the Japhetic linguistic family. [from *Japheth,* the third son of Noah; from Heb. *Yepheth*]

**japonica** /dʒəˈpɒnɪkə/, *n.* any of several garden shrubs with white, pink or red flowers belonging to the genus *Chaenomeles,* as *C. speciosa* and *C. japonica.* [NL, fem. of *Japonicus* of Japan]

**jar**[1] /dʒa/, *n.* **1.** a broad-mouthed earthen or glass vessel, commonly cylindrical in form. **2.** the quantity contained in it. **3.** *Colloq.* a glass of beer. [F *jarre,* from Pr. *jarro,* or Sp. *jarra,* from Ar. *jarrah* earthen vessel]

**jar**[2] /dʒa/, *v.,* **jarred, jarring,** *n.* *–v.i.* **1.** to produce a harsh, grating sound; sound discordantly. **2.** to have a harshly unpleasant effect upon the nerves, feelings, etc. **3.** to vibrate audibly; rattle. **4.** to vibrate or shake (without reference to sound). **5.** to be at variance; conflict; clash. *–v.t.* **6.** to cause to sound harshly or discordantly. **7.** to cause to rattle or shake. **8.** to have a harshly unpleasant effect upon (the feelings, nerves, etc.) (oft. fol. by *on*). *–n.* **9.** a harsh, grating sound. **10.** a discordant sound or combination of sounds. **11.** a vibrating movement, as from concussion. **12.** a harshly unpleasant effect upon the mind or feelings due to physical or other shock. **13.** a quarrel; conflict, as of opinions, etc. [cf. OE *cearcian* creak]

**jardinière** /ʒadɪniˈɛə/, *n.* **1.** an ornamental receptacle or stand for holding plants, flowers, etc. **2.** a variety of glazed, diced, or boiled vegetables, each type cooked separately, and arranged around the main dish in separate groups. [F, fem. of *jardinier* gardener, from *jardin* GARDEN]

**jargon**[1] /ˈdʒagən/, *n.* **1.** the language peculiar to a trade, profession, or other group: *medical jargon.* **2.** speech abounding in uncommon or unfamiliar words. **3.** (*derog.*) any talk or writing which one does not understand. **4.** unintelligible or meaningless talk or writing; gibberish. **5.** debased, outlandish or barbarous language. *–v.i.* **6.** to utter or talk jargon or a jargon. [ME from OF; orig. uncert.]

**jargon**[2] /ˈdʒagən/, *n.* a colourless-to-smoky semiprecious variety of the mineral zircon. [F, from It. *giargone,* ? from Pers. *zargūn* gold-coloured. Cf. ZIRCON]

**jargonise** /ˈdʒagənaɪz/, *v.,* **-nised, -nising.** *–v.i.* **1.** to talk jargon or a jargon. *–v.t.* **2.** to translate into jargon. Also, **jargonize.**

**jarl** /jal/, *n. Scand. Hist.* a chieftain; an earl. [Scand.; cf. Icel. *jarl.* See EARL]

**jarosite** /ˈdʒærəsaɪt/, *n.* a yellowish or brownish mineral, $K_2Fe_6(SO_4)_4(OH)_{12}$, occurring in crystals or large masses. [named after Barranco *Jaroso,* in Almeria, south-eastern Spain. See -ITE[1]]

**jarrah** /ˈdʒærə/, *n.* a large tree of western Australia, *Eucalyptus marginata,* with durable dark red timber. [Aboriginal]

**Jas,** *Bible.* James.

**jasmine** /ˈdʒæzmən/, *n.* **1.** any of the shrubs or climbing plants of the genus *Jasminum,* often cultivated for their fragrant flowers. **2.** any of various plants of other genera as Carolina jasmine. Also, **jessamine.** [F *jasmin,* from Ar.

*yāsmīn,* from Pers.]

**jasper** /'dʒæspə/, *n.* a compact, opaque, often highly coloured, cryptocrystalline variety of quartz commonly used in decorative carvings. [ME *jaspre,* from OF, var. of *jaspe,* from L *iaspis,* from Gk; of Eastern orig.]

**jaundice** /'dʒɔndəs/, *n., v.,* **-diced, -dicing.** *–n.* **1.** *Pathol.* a morbid bodily condition due to the presence of increased amounts of bile pigments in the blood, characterised by yellowness of the skin, the whites of the eyes, etc., by lassitude, and by loss of appetite. **2.** the state of feeling in which views are coloured or judgment is distorted. *–v.t.* **3.** to affect with jaundice. **4.** to distort or prejudice, as with pessimism, jealousy, resentment, etc. [ME *jaunes, jaundis,* from OF *jaunisse,* from *jaune* yellow, from L *galbinus* greenish yellow]

**jaunt** /dʒɔnt/, *v.i.* **1.** to make a short journey, esp. for pleasure. *–n.* **2.** such a journey. [? nasalised var. of *jot* jog, jolt]

**jaunting car** /'dʒɔntɪŋ ka/, *n.* a light, two-wheeled, horse-drawn vehicle, popular in Ireland, having seats on each side set back to back, with a perch in front for the driver.

**jaunty** /'dʒɔnti/, *adj.,* **-tier, -tiest. 1.** easy and sprightly in manner or bearing. **2.** smartly trim or effective, as clothing. **3.** Also, **jaundy, jonty.** *Naut. Colloq.* →**master-at-arms.** [earlier *janty,* from F *gentil.* See GENTLE, GENTEEL] – **jauntily,** *adv.* – **jauntiness,** *n.*

**Jav.,** Javanese.

**Java man** /'dʒavə mæn/, *n.* →**Pithecanthropus.**

**Javanese** /dʒavə'niz/, *adj., n., pl.* **-nese.** *–adj.* **1.** of or pertaining to the island of Java, its people, or their language. *–n.* **2.** a member of the native Malayan race of Java, esp. of that branch of it in the central part of the island. **3.** the language of central Java, of the Austronesian family.

**Javan rusa deer,** *n.* a type of red deer, *Cervus elaphus* (or *Cervus rusa*), widely distributed throughout the Pacific region, and now common in those parts of Australia into which it has been introduced.

**Java sparrow** /'dʒavə spærou/, *n.* a small greyish bird, *Padda oryzivora,* of tropical Asia, commonly kept as a cagebird.

**javelin** /'dʒævələn/, *n.* **1.** a spear to be thrown by hand. **2.** *Sport.* a metal or wooden shaft, with a metal point, thrown for distance. *–v.t.* **3.** to strike or pierce with or as with a javelin. [F *javeline;* probably from Celtic]

**javelin fish** /'– fɪʃ/, *n.* an Australian semitropical marine fish of genus *Pomadasys,* having a well developed long spine on the anal fin; Queensland trumpeter.

**Javel water** /'dʒavəl wɔtə, dʒə'vel/, *n.* sodium hypochlorite, NaOCl, dissolved in water, used as a bleach, antiseptic, etc. Also, **Javelle water.** [named after *Javel,* district of Paris]

**jaw** /dʒɔ/, *n.* **1.** one of the two bones or structures (upper and lower) which form the framework of the mouth. **2.** *Dentistry.* either jawbone containing its complement of teeth and covered by the soft tissues. **3.** the mouth parts collectively, or the mouth. **4.** anything likened to this: *the jaws of a gorge, of death, etc.* **5.** one of two or more parts, as of a machine, which grasp or hold something: *the jaws of a vice.* **6.** *Colloq.* **a.** talkativeness; continual talk. **b.** moralising or reproving talk. *–v.i.* **7.** *Colloq.* to talk at length; gossip. *–v.t.* **8.** *Colloq.* to talk reprovingly; lecture; admonish. [ME *jawe, jowe,* from OF *jo(u)e* cheek, jaw] – **jawless,** *adj.*

**jawbone** /'dʒɔboun/, *n., v.,* **-boned, -boning.** *–n.* **1.** any bone of the jaws; a maxilla or mandible. **2.** the bone of the lower jaw. *–v.i.* **3.** *Colloq.* to talk, esp. at length, as in expounding an idea, presenting an argument, etc.

**jaw-breaker** /'dʒɔ-breɪkə/, *n.* **1.** *Colloq.* a word hard to pronounce. **2.** *Colloq.* a large, hard or sticky sweet. **3.** Also, **jaw-crusher.** a machine to break up ore, consisting of a fixed plate and a hinged jaw moved by a toggle joint. – **jaw-breaking,** *adj.*

**jaw harp** /'dʒɔ hap/, *n.* →**jew's-harp.**

**jay**[1] /dʒeɪ/, *n.* **1.** any of a number of Australian birds as certain currawongs, cuckoo-shrikes, or the white-winged clough. **2.** any of several crested or uncrested birds of the corvine subfamily Garrulinae, all of them robust, noisy, and mischievous, as the **common jay,** *Garrulus glandarius,* of Europe, and the **bluejay,** *Cyanocitta cristata,* of America. **3.** a simple-minded or gullible person; a simpleton. [ME, from OF. Cf. ML *gaius,* special use of proper name *Gaius*]

**jay**[2] /dʒeɪ/, *n.* a marijuana cigarette. [from *j(oint)* marijuana cigarette]

**jaybird** /'dʒeɪbɜd/, *Colloq. –v.i.* **1.** to do housework in the nude. *–n.* **2.** a person who does this.

**jaywalk** /'dʒeɪwɔk/, *v.i. Colloq.* to cross a street otherwise than by a pedestrian crossing or in a heedless manner, as against traffic lights. [JAY[1] (see def. 3) + WALK] – **jaywalker,** *n.* – **jaywalking,** *n.*

**jazz** /dʒæz/, *n.* **1.** a type of popular music of American Negro origin, which sprang up in and around New Orleans and is marked by frequent improvisation and syncopated rhythms. **2.** a piece of such music. **3.** dancing or a dance performed to such music, as with violent bodily motions and gestures. **4.** *Colloq.* liveliness; noisiness; spirit. **5.** *Colloq.* pretentious or insincere talk. **6. and all that jazz,** *Colloq.* and all that sort of thing; et cetera. *–adj.* **7.** of the nature of or pertaining to jazz. *–v.t.* **8.** to play (music) in the manner of jazz. **9.** *Colloq.* to put vigour or liveliness into (oft. fol. by *up*). *–v.i.* **10.** to dance to jazz music. **11.** *Colloq.* to play or perform jazz music. **12.** *Colloq.* to act or proceed with great energy oı liveliness. [orig. obscure; said to have been long used by Negroes of the southern U.S., esp. those of Louisiana]

**jazz band** /'– bænd/, *n.* a band adapted for or devoted to the playing of jazz.

**jazz/rock** /dʒæz/'rɒk/, *n.* a style of modern music which employs both jazz and rock idiom. Also, **jazz-rock, jazz rock.**

**jazzy** /'dʒæzi/, *adj.,* **-zier, -ziest. 1.** *Colloq.* pertaining to or suggestive of jazz music; wildly active or lively. **2.** having very bright or glaring colours; vividly patterned.

**J.C.,** Jesus Christ.

**jealous** /'dʒɛləs/, *adj.* **1.** feeling resentment against a successful rival or at success, advantages, etc. (fol. by *of*). **2.** characterised by or proceeding from suspicious fears or envious resentment: *jealous intrigues.* **3.** inclined to or troubled by suspicions or fears of rivalry, as in love or aims: *a jealous husband.* **4.** solicitous or vigilant in maintaining or guarding something. **5.** (in biblical use) intolerant of unfaithfulness or rivalry: *the Lord is a jealous God.* [ME *gelos, jalous,* from OF, from LL *zēlōsus,* from L *zēlus,* from Gk *zêlos* ZEAL] – **jealously,** *adv.* – **jealousness,** *n.*

**jealousy** /'dʒɛləsi/, *n., pl.* **-ousies. 1.** resentment against a successful rival or the possessor of any coveted advantage. **2.** mental uneasiness from suspicion or fear of rivalry, as in love or aims. **3.** the state or feeling of being jealous. **4.** an instance of jealous feeling.

**jean** /dʒin/, *n.* **1.** a stout twilled cotton fabric. **2.** (*pl.*) clothes of this material, esp. close-fitting trousers. [probably from F *Gênes* Genoa]

**jeanery** /'dʒinəri/, *n.* a shop which sells nothing but jeans.

**jeep** /dʒip/, *n.* a small (usu. $\frac{1}{4}$ tonne capacity) military motor vehicle. [? special use of *jeep,* name of fabulous animal in comic strip 'Popeye', or alteration of *G.P.* (for General Purpose Vehicle)]

**jeepers creepers** /dʒipəz 'kripəz/, *interj. Orig. U.S. Colloq.* (an expression of surprise). [euph. for *Jesus Christ*]

**jeer**[1] /dʒɪə/, *v.i.* **1.** to speak or shout derisively; gibe or scoff rudely. *–v.t.* **2.** to treat with scoffs or derision; make a mock of (oft. fol. by *at*). **3.** to drive (*out, off,* etc.) by jeers. *–n.* **4.** a jeering utterance; a derisive or rude gibe. [? OE *cēir* clamour, from *cēgan* call out] – **jeerer,** *n.* – **jeeringly,** *adv.*

**jeer**[2] /dʒɪə/, *n.* (*usu. pl.*) *Naut.* tackle for hoisting or lowering heavy yards. [? lit., mover, from GEE[1]]

**jehad** /dʒə'hæd/, *n.* →**jihad.**

**jehovah** /dʒə'houvə/, *n.* **1.** a name of God in the Old Testament, an erroneous rendering of the ineffable name, JHVH, in the Hebrew Scriptures. **2.** (in modern Christian use) God.

**Jehovah's Witness** /dʒəhouvəz 'wɪtnəs/, *n.* a member of a sect of Christians who are pacifists, believe in the imminent establishment of God's rule on earth, and do not recognise the authority of the state when it conflicts with religious principles.

**jejune** /dʒə'dʒun/, *adj.* **1.** deficient in nourishing or substantial qualities. **2.** unsatisfying to the mind; dull; boring. [L *jējūnus* fasting, empty, dry, poor] – **jejunely,** *adv.* – **jejuneness,** **jejunity** /dʒə'dʒunəti/, *n.*

**jejunum** /dʒəˈdʒunəm/, *n.* the middle portion of the small intestine, between the duodenum and the ileum. [NL, properly neut. of L *jējūnus* empty]

**Jekyll-and-Hyde** /dʒɛkəl-ən-ˈhaɪd/, *adj.* (of a person) having sharply contrasted good and bad qualities. [named after *Dr Jekyll and Mr Hyde* (1886), a novel by R. L. Stevenson]

**jell** /dʒɛl/, *v.i. Colloq.* **1.** to form a jelly. **2.** to take shape; crystallise; become definite.

**jellied** /ˈdʒɛlid/, *adj.* **1.** brought to the consistency of jelly. **2.** containing or spread over with jelly.

**jellify** /ˈdʒɛləfaɪ/, *v.*, **-fied, -fying.** *–v.t.* **1.** to make into a jelly; reduce to a gelatinous state. *–v.i.* **2.** to become gelatinous; turn into jelly. – **jellification** /dʒɛləfəˈkeɪʃən/, *n.*

**jelly** /ˈdʒɛli/, *n., pl.* **-lies,** *v.,* **-lied, -lying.** *–n.* **1.** a food preparation of a soft, elastic consistency due to the presence of gelatine, pectin, etc., as fruit juice boiled down with sugar. **2.** anything of the consistency of jelly. **3.** *Colloq.* →**gelignite. 4. turn to jelly,** *Colloq.* to become weak with fear. *–v.t.* **5.** to bring to the consistency of jelly. *–v.i.* **6.** to come to the consistency of jelly. [ME *gele,* from OF *gelee* frost, jelly, from L *gelāta,* properly pp. fem., frozen] – **jelly-like,** *adj.*

**jelly baby** /ˈ– beɪbi/, *n.* a soft gelatinous sweet moulded into the shape of a baby.

**jelly bean** /ˈ– bin/, *n.* a small, bean-shaped lolly with a hardened sugar coating over a chewy gelatinous centre.

**jelly blubber** /ˈ– blʌbə/, *n.* →**jellyfish.**

**jelly cake** /ˈ– keɪk/, *n.* a small rounded cake filled with cream, rolled first in jelly which is about to set, and then in dessicated coconut.

**jellyfish** /ˈdʒɛlifɪʃ/, *n., pl.* **-fishes,** (*esp. collectively*) **-fish.** any of various marine coelenterates of a soft, gelatinous structure, esp. one with an umbrella-like body and long, trailing tentacles; a medusa.

jellyfish

**jelly-leaf** /ˈdʒɛli-lif/, *n.* →**Paddy's lucerne.**

**jelly plant** /ˈdʒɛli plænt/, *n.* any of various seaweeds from which colloidal jellies are extracted for commercial use, esp. in bacteriological preparations and in ice cream.

**jemenfoutisme** /ʒəmɒ̃fuˈtɪzmə/, *n.* nonchalance; indifference. [F *je m'en fous*]

**jemmy** /ˈdʒɛmi/, *n., pl.* **-mies,** *v.,* **-mied, -mying.** *–n.* **1.** a short crowbar. *–v.t.* **2.** to force open (a door, etc.) with a jemmy. Also, *U.S.,* **jimmy.** [apparently a form of *James*]

**je ne sais quoi** /ʒə nə seɪ ˈkwa/, I know not what; an indefinable something. [F]

**jennet** /ˈdʒɛnət/, *n.* **1.** a small Spanish horse. **2.** a female donkey; jenny ass. Also, **genet, gennet.** [ME *genett,* from OF *genet,* from Sp. *jinete* mounted soldier, horse, from Ar. *Zenāta,* name of Berber tribe noted for cavalry]

**jenny** /ˈdʒɛni/, *n., pl.* **-nies. 1.** →**spinning jenny. 2.** female of some animals: *jenny wren.* **3.** the offspring of a male horse and female donkey; reciprocal of mule. [properly, a woman's name]

**jeopardise** /ˈdʒɛpədaɪz/, *v.t.,* **-dised, -dising.** to put in jeopardy; risk. Also, **jeopardize;** *U.S.,* **jeopard.**

**jeopardy** /ˈdʒɛpədi/, *n.* **1.** hazard or risk of loss or harm. **2.** peril or danger: *for a moment his life was in jeopardy.* **3.** *Law.* the hazard of being found guilty, and of consequent punishment, undergone by criminal defendants on trial. [ME *iuparti,* etc., from OF *jeu parti,* lit., divided game, even game or chance]

jerboa

**jequirity** /dʒəˈkwɪrəti/, *n., pl.* **-ties. 1.** the Indian liquorice plant, *Abrus precatorius,* of India and Brazil, whose seed (**jequirity bean**) is used in medicine. **2.** the seeds collectively. [F *jéquirity,* from Tupi-Guarani *jekiriti*]

**jequirity beans** /ˈ– binz/, *n.pl.* →**Indian liquorice.**

**Jer.,** *Bible.* Jeremiah.

**jerboa** /dʒɜˈbouə/, *n.* **1.** any of several small carnivorous leaping marsupials of the genus *Antechinomys,* which inhabit the central desert of Australia and resemble the jerboa (def. 2). **2.** any of various mouselike rodents of the family Dipodidae of North Africa and Asia, with long hind legs used for jumping, and a long tail. [NL, from ML *jerbōa,* from Ar. *yerbōʻ, yarbūʻ* flesh of the loins (from the highly developed thighs)]

**jerboa pouched mouse,** *n.* →**jerboa** (def. 1). Also, **jerboa kangaroo.**

**jerboa rat** /dʒɜˌbouə ˈræt/, *n.* any of several indigenous large rats of the genus *Notomys,* with hind legs adapted for leaping, and resembling the North American jerboa.

**jeremiad** /dʒɛrəˈmaɪəd/, *n.* a lamentation; a lugubrious complaint. [F *jérémiade,* from *Jérémie* Jeremiah; with ref. to the biblical 'Lamentations'. See JEREMIAH]

**jeremiah** /dʒɛrəˈmaɪə/, *n.* one who denounces wrongdoing and prophesies calamities. [from *Jeremiah, c.* 650-585 B.C., a Hebrew prophet of the Old Testament]

**jerk**[1] /dʒɜk/, *n.* **1.** a quick, sharp thrust, pull, throw, or the like; a sudden start. **2.** *Physiol.* a sudden movement of an organ or a part. **3.** *Weightlifting.* a lift in which the barbell is raised first to the shoulders, then jerked above the head with the arms held straight. **4.** *Colloq.* a stupid or naive person. **5.** (*pl.*) *U.S.* paroxysms or violent spasmodic muscular movements as resulting from excitement caused by certain religious services. **6.** (*pl.*) See **physical jerks.** *–v.t.* **7.** to give a sudden thrust, pull, or twist to; move or throw with a quick, suddenly arrested motion. **8.** to utter in a broken, spasmodic way (usu. fol. by *out*). *–v.i.* **9.** to give a jerk or jerks. **10.** to move with a quick, sharp motion; move spasmodically. **11. jerk off,** *Colloq.* to masturbate. [apparently imitative]

**jerk**[2] /dʒɜk/, *v.t.* **1.** to preserve meat, esp. beef (**jerked beef**) by cutting in strips and curing by drying in the sun. *–n.* **2.** jerked meat, esp. beef. [Amer. Sp. *charquear,* from *charque, charqui* jerked meat, charqui, from Quechua]

**jerker** /ˈdʒɜkə/, *n.* →**boundary rider.**

**jerkin** /ˈdʒɜkən/, *n.* a close-fitting jacket or short coat, as one of leather worn in the 16th and 17th centuries. [orig. unknown]

jerkin

**jerk-off** /ˈdʒɜk-ɒf/, *n. Colloq.* **1.** an act of male masturbation. **2.** a male masturbator. **3.** a very foolish person; an idiot.

**jerky** /ˈdʒɜki/, *adj.,* **-kier, -kiest.** characterised by jerks or sudden starts; spasmodic. – **jerkily,** *adv.* – **jerkiness,** *n.*

**jeroboam** /dʒɛrəˈbouəm/, *n.* a wine bottle with the capacity of 6 normal bottles. [from *Jeroboam,* first king of the northern kingdom of Israel, described as 'a mighty man' who 'made Israel to sin']

**jerquer** /ˈdʒɜkə/, *n.* (formerly) an internal check officer in the Department of Customs and Excise concerned mainly with accounting for and checking manifested goods. [orig. uncert.]

**jerry**[1] /ˈdʒɛri/, *n., pl.* **-ries.** *Colloq.* **1.** →**chamber-pot. 2.** lavatory. [apparently from JEROBOAM]

**jerry**[2] /ˈdʒɛri/, *v.i.,* **-ried, -rying.** to understand, realise (usu. fol. by *to*): *he jerries to what's going on.*

**Jerry** /ˈdʒɛri/, *n., pl.* **-ries.** *Colloq.* **1.** a German, esp. a German soldier. **2.** (collectively) Germans.

**jerry-build** /ˈdʒɛri-bɪld/, *v.t.,* **-built, -building.** to build cheaply, shoddily, and flimsily. – **jerry-built,** *adj.* – **jerry-builder,** *n.*

**jerry can** /ˈdʒɛri kæn/, *n.* a flat can for transporting fluids, esp. motor fuel, and containing between 20 and 23 litres. [see JERRY[1]]

**jerry-jerry** /ˈdʒɛri-dʒɛri/, *n.* a small shrub, *Ammannia multiflora,* family Lythraceae, widespread in Australia.

**jersey** /ˈdʒɜzi/, *n.* **1.** (*cap.*) one of a breed of dairy cattle whose milk contains a high proportion of butterfat. **2.** a close-fitting, usu. woollen, outer garment for the upper part of the body; jumper[2] (def. 1). **3.** a similar garment worn by members of a sporting team as a uniform. **4.** →**jersey cloth. 5.** (originally) a close-fitting, heavy woollen garment as worn by seamen. [from the Island of *Jersey,* in the English Channel]

**jersey cloth** /'– klɒθ/, *n.* a machine-knitted fabric of wool, silk, or artificial fibre, used for making garments, etc.

**Jerusalem artichoke** /dʒəˌrusələm 'atətʃoʊk/, *n.* **1.** a species of sunflower, *Helianthus tuberosus,* having edible tuberous underground stems or rootstocks. **2.** the tuber itself. [*Jerusalem,* alteration (by popular etymology) of It. *girasole* sunflower, from *girare* turn + *sole* sun]

**Jerusalem cherry** /– 'tʃɛri/, *n.* a South American shrub with white flowers and red fruits, *Solanum pseudocapsicum,* often grown and sometimes escaping from cultivation.

**Jerusalem cross** /– 'krɒs/, *n.* a cross whose four arms are each capped with a crossbar.

**Jerusalem sage** /–'seɪdʒ/, *n.* a hairy shrub with yellow flowers from the Mediterranean region, *Phlomis fruticosa,* often cultivated and sometimes naturalised.

**jess** /dʒɛs/, *Falconry.* *–n.* **1.** a short strap fastened round the leg of a hawk and attached to the leash. *–v.t.* **2.** to put jesses on (a hawk). [ME *ges,* from OF, from *jeter* throw, from LL *jectāre,* replacing L *jactāre*] – **jessed** /dʒɛst/, *adj.*

**jessamine** /'dʒɛsəmən/, *n.* →**jasmine.**

**jessant** /'dʒɛsənt/, *adj. Her.* **1.** shooting up, as a plant. **2.** coming forth; issuant. **3.** lying across.

**Jesse window** /'dʒɛsi wɪndoʊ/, *n.* a church window with a genealogical tree showing the descent of Christ from Jesse.

**jest** /dʒɛst/, *n.* **1.** a witticism, joke, or pleasantry. **2.** a piece of raillery or banter. **3.** sport or fun: *to speak half in jest, half in earnest.* **4.** the object of laughter, sport, or mockery; a laughing-stock. **5.** *Obs.* an exploit. See **gest.** *–v.i.* **6.** to speak in a playful, humorous, or facetious way; joke. **7.** to speak or act in mere sport, rather than in earnest; trifle (*with*). **8.** to utter derisive speeches; gibe or scoff. *–v.t.* **9.** to jest at; deride; banter. [var. of GEST]

**jester** /'dʒɛstə/, *n.* **1.** one who is given to witticisms, jokes, and pranks. **2.** a professional fool or clown, kept by a prince or noble, esp. during the Middle Ages.

**jesting** /'dʒɛstɪŋ/, *adj.* **1.** given to jesting; playful. **2.** fit for joking; unimportant; trivial: *no jesting matter.* *–n.* **3.** pleasantry; triviality. – **jestingly,** *adv.*

**Jesu** /'jeɪzu, 'dʒizju/, *n. Poetic.* Jesus. [L, oblique (usu. voc.) case form of *Jesus* Jesus]

**Jesuit** /'dʒɛʒjuət/, *n.* **1.** a crafty, intriguing, or equivocating person (in allusion to the methods ascribed to the order by its opponents). *–adj.* **2.** of or pertaining to a Jesuit or Jesuitism. [named after a Roman Catholic religious order (Society of *Jesus*) founded by Ignatius Loyola in 1534. NL *Jēsuīta,* see JESU, -IT(E)[1]]

**Jesuitical** /dʒɛʒju'ɪtəkəl/, *adj.* (*sometimes l.c.*) sly; crafty; casuistic. Also, **Jesuitic.** – **Jesuitically,** *adv.*

**Jesuitism** /'dʒɛʒjuətɪzəm/, *n.* a principle or practice such as casuistry ascribed to the Jesuits by their opponents. Also, **Jesuitry.**

**Jesus** /'dʒizəs/, *n.* **1.** Also, **Jesus Christ.** See **Christian.** *–interj. Colloq.* **2.** (an exclamation indicating surprise, indignation, etc.). [ME and OE, from LL, from Gk *Iēsoûs,* from Heb. *Yeshūaʻ,* earlier *Yehōshūaʻ,* lit., Jehovah is salvation]

**Jesus-freak** /'dʒizəs-frik/, *n. Colloq.* one, often outside the established churches, whose involvement in his religious experiences is the dominating factor in his personality.

**jet**[1] /dʒɛt/, *n., v.,* **jetted, jetting.** *–n* **1.** a free or submerged stream of fluid produced by efflux from a nozzle, orifice, etc. **2.** that which so issues, as water or gas. **3.** the spout used: *gas jet.* **4.** a jet plane. *–v.i.* **5.** to spout. **6.** to travel. *–v.t.* **7.** to shoot forth in a stream. **8.** *Agric.* to apply fluid or powder under pressure (to the breech or body of an animal) to destroy parasites. [F, from *jeter,* v.]

**jet**[2] /dʒɛt/, *n.* **1.** a compact black coal, susceptible of a high polish, used for making beads, jewellery, buttons, etc. **2.** a deep, glossy black. **3.** *Obs.* black marble. *–adj.* **4.** consisting or made of jet. **5.** of the colour jet; black as jet. [ME *gete, iete,* from OF *jaiet,* from L *gagātēs,* from Gk, from *Gágai,* town in Lycia, Asia Minor]

**jet black** /– 'blæk/, *n.* a deep black colour.

**jet engine** /– 'ɛndʒən/, *n.* any engine in which a jet, esp. of gaseous combustion prod :cts, provides the propulsive force.

**jet lag** /'– læg/, *n.* bodily discomfort caused by the disturbance of normal patterns of eating and sleeping, as on a journey by aeroplane.

**jetliner** /'dʒɛtlaɪnə/, *n. Colloq.* a commercial jet plane.

**jet plane** /'dʒɛt pleɪn/, *n.* an aeroplane operated by jet propulsion.

**jet-propelled** /'dʒɛt-prəpɛld/, *adj.* **1.** of or pertaining to a vehicle, esp. an aircraft which is propelled by jet engines. **2.** very fast, as of a jet aeroplane.

**jet propulsion** /dʒɛt prə'pʌlʃən/, *n.* a method of producing a propelling force upon an air or water craft through the reaction of a high-velocity jet, usu. of heated gases, discharged towards the rear. Also, **reaction propulsion.**

**jetsam** /'dʒɛtsəm/, *n.* goods thrown overboard to lighten a vessel in distress, which sink or are washed ashore. See **flotsam.** [var. of *jetson,* syncopated form of JETTISON; assimilated to FLOTSAM]

**jet set** /'dʒɛt sɛt/, *n.* **1.** a rich and fashionable social set whose means enable them to travel from resort to resort by jet plane in the pursuit of pleasure. *–v.i.* **2.** to associate with or imitate the lifestyle of the jetset. – **jetsetter,** *n.*

**jet stream** /'– strim/, *n.* **1.** *Meteorol.* a horizontal cone of air, at altitudes of between about 4 575 m and 12 200 m, extending for great distances along the track of a wind and moving at very high speeds. **2.** *Aeron.* the exhaust of a jet engine or a rocket engine.

**jettison** /'dʒɛtəsən, -zən/, *n.* **1.** the act of casting cargo, etc., overboard to lighten a vessel or aircraft. **2.** →**jetsam.** *–v.t.* **3.** to throw (cargo, etc.) overboard, esp. to lighten a vessel or aircraft in distress. **4.** to throw off, as an obstacle or burden. [AF *getteson,* var. of OF *getaison,* from *geter* throw]

**jetton** /'dʒɛtn/, *n. Brit.* →**token** (def. 5). [F *jeton,* from *jeter* throw, cast, cast up (accounts, etc.)]

**jetty**[1] /'dʒɛti/, *n., pl.* **-ties.** **1.** a pier or structure of stones, piles, or the like, projecting into the sea or other body of water so as to protect a harbour, deflect the current, etc. **2.** a wharf or landing pier. **3.** the piles or wooden structure protecting a pier. [ME *gette,* from OF *jetee,* n. use of fem. pp. of *jeter* throw]

**jetty**[2] /'dʒɛti/, *adj.* **1.** made of jet. **2.** resembling jet; black as jet, or of the colour jet. [JET[2] + -Y[1]]

**jeu d'esprit** /ʒɜ də'spri/, *n.* a witticism. [F]

**Jew** /dʒu/, *n.* **1.** one of the Hebrew or Jewish people; a Hebrew; an Israelite. **2.** one whose religion is Judaism. **3.** *Colloq.* (*derog.*) a usurer; miser; one who drives a hard bargain. *–adj.* **4.** (*derog.*) of Jews; Jewish. [ME *Jeu, Giu,* from OF *Juieu,* from L *Jūdaeus,* from Gk *Ioudaîos,* properly one of the tribe of Judah, from Heb. *Yehūdāh* Judah]

**Jew-baiting** /'dʒu-beɪtɪŋ/, *n.* active anti-Semitism. – **Jew-baiter,** *n.*

**jewel** /'dʒuəl/, *n., v.,* **-elled, -elling** or (*U.S.*) **-eled, -eling.** *–n.* **1.** a cut and polished precious or semiprecious stone; a gem. **2.** a fashioned ornament for personal adornment, usu. set with gems. **3.** a precious possession. **4.** a thing or person of great worth or rare excellence. **5.** a precious stone (or some substitute) used as a bearing of great durability in a watch or delicate instrument. **6.** an ornamental boss of glass, sometimes cut with facets, in stained-glass work. **7.** something resembling a gem in appearance, ornamental effect, etc., as a star, a berry, etc. *–v.t.* **8.** to set or adorn with jewels. [ME *iuel,* from AF, from L *jocus* jest, sport] – **jewel-like,** *adj.*

**jewel beetle** /'– bitl/, *n.* any of various brilliantly coloured, Australian wood-boring beetles of the family Buprestidae.

**jewelfish** /'dʒuəlfɪʃ/, *n., pl.* **-fishes,** (*esp. collectively*) **-fish.** a brilliantly coloured aquarium fish, *Hemichromis binaculatus.*

**jeweller** /'dʒuələ/, *n.* one who makes, or deals in, jewels or jewellery. Also, *U.S.,* **jeweler.**

**jeweller's shop** /'dʒuələz ʃɒp/, *n. Colloq.* a rich find of gold, opal, etc.

**jewellery** /'dʒuəlri/, *n.* jewels; articles made of gold, silver, precious stones, etc., for personal adornment. Also, *Chiefly U.S.,* **jewelry.**

**Jewess** /'dʒuɛs/, *n.* a Jewish girl or woman.

**jewfish** /'dʒufɪʃ/, *n., pl.* **-fishes,** (*esp. collectively*) **-fish.** **1.** in Australia, **a.** any of several species of large, marine fishes of the family Sciaenidae, valued as food and for sport, as the mulloway, *Sciaena antarctica.* **b.** a large foodfish, *Glaucosoma hebraicum,* found in coastal waters of western Australia. **2.** elsewhere, any of various large, marine fishes of the family Serranidae as the **spotted jewfish,** *Promicropsi taiara,* and the **California jewfish,** *Stereolepsi gigas.* [apparently from JEW + FISH]

**jewie** /ˈdʒui/, *n. Colloq.* →**jewfish.**

**Jewish** /ˈdʒuɪʃ/, *adj.* **1.** of, pertaining to, or characteristic of the Jews; Hebrew. *–n.* **2.** Yiddish. – **Jewishness,** *n.*

**Jewish calendar** /– ˈkæləndə/, *n.* the lunisolar calendar in use among the Jews, reckoning from the Creation (dated traditionally during the year 3761 B.C.), the year containing 12 or (intercalary years) 13 months, of 29 or 30 days each, which, beginning during September or October, are as follows: Tishri, Heshvan, Kislev, Tebet, Shebat, Adar, Nissan, Iyyar, Sivan, Tammuz, Ab, and Elul.

**jewish lightning** /– ˈlaɪtnɪŋ/, *n.* the putative cause of fire when a building has been burned down for insurance money.

**jew lizard** /ˈdʒu lɪzəd/, *n.* →**bearded lizard.**

**Jewry** /ˈdʒuri/, *n., pl.* **-ries. 1.** the Jewish people collectively. **2.** a district inhabited by Jews; a ghetto. **3.** *Archaic.* Judea. [ME *Jewerie,* from AF *juerie,* var. of OF *juierie*]

**jew's ear** /ˈdjuz ɪə/, *n.* **1.** an edible tropical fungus, *Auricularia delicata,* often found on rotting logs where it grows in glistening brown or tan coloured ears. **2.** any of various other related species, as the hairy jew's ear.

**jew's-harp** /ˈdʒuz-hap/, *n.* a musical instrument consisting of a circular metal frame with a metal tongue which is plucked while the frame is held between the teeth, the varying position of the mouth changing the tone. Also, **jaw harp.** [apparently jocular in orig., as it is not a harp and has no connection with the Jews]

jew's-harp

**jezebel** /ˈdʒɛzəbɛl/, *n.* a shameless, abandoned woman. [from *Jezebel,* the wife of Ahab, king of Israel, notorious for her conduct (see I Kings 16:31, 21:25, II Kings, 9:30-37)]

**jib[1]** /dʒɪb/, *n.* **1.** a triangular sail (or either of two triangular sails, **inner jib** and **outer jib**) set in front of the forward (or single) mast. **2.** any of certain similar sails set beyond the jib proper, as a **flying jib. 3. cut of one's jib,** *Colloq.* one's general appearance. [? akin to GIBBET]

J, jib[1]

**jib[2]** /dʒɪb/, *v.i., v.t.,* **jibbed, jibbing.** →**jibe[1].**

**jib[3]** /dʒɪb/, *v.,* **jibbed, jibbing,** *n. –v.t.* **1.** to move restively sideways or backwards instead of forwards, as an animal in harness; balk. **2.** to hold back or balk at doing something. **3. jib at,** be reluctant; show unwillingness. *–n.* **4.** an animal that jibs. [orig. uncert.] – **jibber,** *n.*

**jib[4]** /dʒɪb/, *n.* the projecting arm of a crane; the boom of a derrick. [apparently short for GIBBET]

**jibbong** /ˈdʒɪbɒŋ/, *n. Obs.* →**geebung.**

**jib boom** /ˈdʒɪb bum/, *n.* a spar forming a continuation of a bowsprit.

**jib door** /ˈ– dɔ/, *n.* a door built flush with the wall in order to be as inconspicuous as possible.

**jibe[1]** /dʒaɪb/, *v.,* **jibed, jibing,** *n. –v.i.* **1.** to shift from one side to the other when running before the wind, as a fore-and-aft sail or its boom. **2.** to alter the course so that the sail shifts in this manner. *–v.t.* **3.** to cause (a sail, etc.) to jibe. *–n.* **4.** the act of jibing. Also, **gybe.** [D *gijben*]

**jibe[2]** /dʒaɪb/, *v.t., v.i.,* **jibed, jibing,** *n.* →**gibe.** – **jiber,** *n.*

**jiffy** /ˈdʒɪfi/, *n., pl.* **-fies.** *Colloq.* a very short time: *to do something in a jiffy.* Also, **jiff.** [orig. unknown]

**jiffy bag** /ˈ– bæg/, *n.* a strong, padded paper bag sold by post offices for sending objects by mail. [Trademark]

**jig[1]** /dʒɪg/, *n., v.,* **jigged, jigging.** *–n.* **1.** a device for holding the work in a machine tool, esp. one for accurately guiding a drill or group of drills so as to ensure uniformity in successive pieces machined. **2.** a device used in fishing, esp. a hook or collection of hooks loaded with metal or having a spoon-shaped piece of bone or other material attached, for drawing through the water. **3.** an apparatus for separating ore from gangue, etc., by shaking in or treating with water. *–v.t.* **4.** to treat, cut, or produce by using any of the mechanical contrivances called jigs. *–v.i.* **5.** to use a jig (mechanical contrivance). [var. of GAUGE. Cf. E *jeg* kind of gauge]

**jig[2]** /dʒɪg/, *n., v.,* **jigged, jigging.** *–n.* **1.** a rapid, lively, springy, irregular dance for one or more persons, usu. in triple time. **2.** a piece of music for, or in the time of, such a dance. **3.** *Obs.* a jest, prank, or a trick. **4. the jig is up,** the game is up; there is no further chance. *–v.t.* **5.** to dance (a jig or any lively dance). **6.** to sing or play in the time or rhythm of a jig. **7.** to move with a jerky or bobbing motion; jerk up and down or to and fro. *–v.i.* **8.** to dance or play a jig. **9.** to move with a quick, jerky motion; hop; bob. [apparently var. of JOG, *v.*] – **jiglike,** *adj.*

**jig[3]** /dʒɪg/, *v.,* **jigged, jigging.** *Colloq. –v.i.* **1.** to play truant. *–v.t.* **2. jig it,** to play truant. **3. jig school,** to stay away from school without permission.

**jigger[1]** /ˈdʒɪgə/, *n.* **1.** one who or that which jigs. **2.** *Naut.* **a.** the lowest square sail on a jiggermast. **b.** a jiggermast. **c.** light tackle used about the deck of a ship. **3.** any of various mechanical devices, many of which have a jerky or jolting motion. **4.** a name for any mechanical device, the correct name of which one does not know. **5.** a jig for separating ore. **6.** a jig for fishing. **7.** *Golf.* a club (No. 4 iron). **8.** *Billiards.* →**bridge[1]** (def. 10). **9. a.** a measure for alcohol used in cocktails. **b.** a small measure of whisky. [JIG[1] + -ER[1]]

**jigger[2]** /dʒɪgə/, *n.* →**chigoe.**

**jigger[3]** /ˈdʒɪgə/, *v.t.* to break or destroy.

**jiggerboard** /ˈdʒɪgəbɔd/, *n.* →**springboard** (def. 4).

**jiggered** /ˈdʒɪgəd/, *v.* **1.** past participle of **jigger.** *–adj. Colloq.* **2.** a word used as a vague substitute for a taboo word: *I'm jiggered if I know; the machine is jiggered.* **3. jiggered up, a.** exhausted; tired. **b.** broken; destroyed.

**jiggermast** /ˈdʒɪgəmast/, *n.* the fourth mast of a sailing ship. Also, **jigger.**

**jiggery-pokery** /dʒɪgəri-ˈpoʊkəri/, *n. Colloq.* dishonest dealing; trickery.

**jiggle** /ˈdʒɪgəl/, *v.,* **-gled, -gling,** *n. –v.t., v.i.* **1.** to move up and down or to and fro with short, quick jerks. *–n.* **2.** a jiggling movement. [frequentative of JIG[2]]

**jigjig** /ˈdʒɪgdʒɪg/, *n. Colloq.* sexual intercourse.

**jigsaw** /ˈdʒɪgsɔ/, *n.* **1.** a narrow saw mounted vertically in a frame, used for cutting curves, etc. **2.** a jigsaw puzzle.

**jigsaw puzzle** /ˈ– pʌzəl/, *n.* small, irregularly shaped pieces of wood or cardboard, which, when correctly fitted together, form a picture.

**jihad** /dʒəˈhæd/, *n.* **1.** a holy war waged by Muslims against unbelievers as a religious duty. **2.** any vigorous campaign on behalf of a principle, etc. Also, **jehad.** [Ar.: effort, strife

**jilgie** /ˈdʒɪlgi/, *n.* →**gilgie.**

**jillaroo** /dʒɪləˈru/, *n.* a female jackeroo.

**jilt** /dʒɪlt/, *v.t.* **1.** to cast off (a lover or sweetheart) after encouragement or engagement. *–n.* **2.** a woman who jilts a lover. [orig. uncert.] – **jilter,** *n.*

**jim** /dʒɪm/, *n. Colloq.* a £1 note, or that amount. [abbrev. Brit. obs. *Jimmy* O'Goblin, a sovereign]

**Jim Crow** /dʒɪm ˈkroʊ/, *n. U.S.* **1.** (*derog.*) Negro. **2.** practice or policy of segregating Negroes, as in public places, public transport, etc. **3.** (*l.c.*) a tool for bending or straightening railway lines. – **Jim-Crow, jim-crow,** *adj.*

**Jim Crowism** /dʒɪm ˈkroʊɪzəm/, *n.* racial discrimination.

**jiminy** /ˈdʒɪməni/, *interj.* (a mild exclamation of surprise.) Also, **jiminy cricket.** [alteration of L *Jesu, Domine!* Jesus, Lord!]

**jimjams** /ˈdʒɪmdʒæmz/, *n.pl. Colloq.* **1.** extreme nervousness. **2.** →**delirium tremens.**

**jimmy** /ˈdʒɪmi/, *n., pl.* **-mies,** *v.,* **-mied, -mying.** *U.S.* →**jemmy.**

**Jimmy Brits** /dʒɪmi ˈbrɪts/, *n. Colloq.* the shits. [rhyming slang]

**Jimmy Grant** /– ˈgrænt/, *n.* immigrant or emigrant. [rhyming slang]

**Jimmy Woodser** /– ˈwʊdzə/, *n. Colloq.* **1.** one who drinks alone in a bar. **2.** an alcoholic drink consumed alone. [from the name of a fictitious drinking companion *Jimmy Woods*]

**jimson weed** /ˈdʒɪmsən wid/, *n.* one of the thorn-apples, *Datura stramonium,* a coarse herb with white flowers and very poisonous leaves, widespread in the Northern Hemisphere. Also, **Jimson weed.** [alteration of *Jamestown weed;* named after *Jamestown,* in Virginia, U.S.A.]

jimson weed

**Jindyworobaks** /dʒɪndiˈwɒrəbæks/, *n.* an Australian cultural movement which aimed at establishing distinctly Australian literary, esp. verse, forms conscious of the natural environment and Australia's history and traditions, primeval, colonial and modern; influential through annual literary anthologies published 1938-53. [Aboriginal: to annex, join]

**jingaloes** /ˈdʒɪŋəloʊz/, *interj.* (an expression of surprise).

**jingle** /ˈdʒɪŋgəl/, *v.,* **-gled, -gling,** *n.* *–v.i.* **1.** to make clinking or tinkling sounds, as coins, keys, etc., when struck together repeatedly. **2.** to move or proceed with such sounds. **3.** to sound in a manner suggestive of this, as verse or any sequence of words: *a jingling ballad.* **4.** to make rhymes. *–v.t.* **5.** to cause to jingle. *–n.* **6.** a clinking or tinkling sound, as of small bells or of small pieces of metal struck together repeatedly. **7.** something that makes such a sound, as a small bell or a metal pendant. **8.** a musical succession of like sounds, as in rhyme or alliteration, without particular regard for sense; jingling verse. **9.** a piece of such verse. **10.** a simple, repetitious, catchy rhyme set to music, used esp. for advertising. **11.** (in Ireland and Australia) a covered two wheeled carriage. [ME *gynglen,* apparently imitative; but cf. D *jengelen*] – **jinglingly,** *adv.* – **jingly,** *adj.*

**jingling Johnny** /dʒɪŋglɪŋ ˈdʒɒni/, *n., pl.* **jingling Johnnies. 1.** a person who shears sheep by hand. **2.** (*pl.*) hand shears.

**jingo** /ˈdʒɪŋgoʊ/, *n.* *Colloq.* a word used in vehement asseveration in the phrase 'by jingo'. [orig. uncert.; first used in conjurer's jargon]

**jingoism** /ˈdʒɪŋgoʊɪzəm/, *n.* fervent and excessive patriotism. [JINGO (used in chauvinist song advocating belligerent British policy against Russia in 1878) + -ISM] – **jingoist,** *n., adj.* – **jingoistic** /dʒɪŋgoʊˈɪstɪk/, *adj.*

**jink** /dʒɪŋk/, *v.i.* *Rugby Football.* to swerve when running with the ball so as to deceive an opponent.

**jinker** /ˈdʒɪŋkə/, *n.* *Colloq.* **1.** a wheeled conveyance for logs. **2.** (formerly) a light, two-wheeled, horsedrawn conveyance for two or three passengers. Also, **junker. 3.** a trotting or pacing gig.

jinker

**jinks** /dʒɪŋks/, *n.pl.* *Colloq.* romping games or play; boisterous, unrestrained merrymaking, esp. in the phrase *high jinks.* [cf. Brit. d. *chink* to gasp, from OE *cincung* hearty laughter]

**jinn** /dʒɪn/, *n.pl., sing.* **jinee. 1.** (in Islamic mythology) a class of spirits lower than the angels, capable of appearing in human and animal forms, and influencing mankind for good and evil. **2.** (*construed as sing. with pl.* **jinns**) a spirit of this class. Also, **djinn.** [Ar., pl. of *jinnī* a demon. Cf. GENIE]

**jinrikisha** /dʒɪnˈrɪkʃə/, *n.* →**rickshaw.**

**jinx** /dʒɪŋks/, *Colloq.* *–n.* **1.** a person, thing, or influence supposed to bring bad luck. *–v.t.* **2.** to bring bad luck to someone; hex. [var. of *jynx,* from L *iynx,* from Gk: bird (wryneck) used in witchcraft, hence, a spell]

**jip** /dʒɪp/, *n.* →**gip**[2].

**jitney** /ˈdʒɪtni/, *n., pl.* **-neys,** *v.,* **-neyed, -neying.** *Orig. U.S.* *–n.* **1.** *Colloq.* a motor car which carries passengers, originally each for a fare of five cents. **2.** *Obs. Colloq.* a five-cent piece. *–v.t.* **3.** to carry in a jitney. *–v.i.* **4.** to ride in a jitney.

**jitter** /ˈdʒɪtə/, *Colloq.* *–n.* **1.** (*pl.*) nervousness; nerves (usu. prec. by *the*). **2.** *Electronics.* the rapid fluctuation of a signal caused by instability in a circuit. *–v.i.* **3.** to behave nervously. [var. of *chitter* shiver. Cf. CHATTER]

**jitterbug** /ˈdʒɪtəbʌg/, *n., v.,* **-bugged, -bugging.** *–n.* **1.** a vigorous dance, popular in the 1940s, performed mainly to boogie-woogie and swing music. **2.** one who dances the jitterbug. **3.** one who is nervous or easily flustered. *–v.i.* **4.** to dance the jitterbug.

**jittery** /ˈdʒɪtəri/, *adj.* nervous; jumpy.

**jiujitsu** /dʒuˈdʒɪtsu/, *n.* →**jujitsu.** Also, **jiujutsu.**

**jive** /dʒaɪv/, *n., v.,* **jived, jiving.** *–n.* **1.** jargon used by jazz musicians. **2.** a dance performed to beat music. *–v.i.* **3.** to dance to beat music. [orig. uncert.]

**JJ.,** **1.** Judges. **2.** Justices.

**Jn,** *Bible.* John.

**jnana-yoga** /dʒəˈnanə-joʊgə/, *n.* spiritual discipline attained through philosophical knowledge. [Skt *jñāna,* from *jñā,* to know]

**JND,** just noticeable difference.

**jnl,** journal.

**Jno.,** John.

**jnr,** junior.

**Joan of Arc,** *n.* *Colloq.* a shark. [rhyming slang]

**job**[1] /dʒɒb/, *n., v.,* **jobbed, jobbing,** *adj.* *–n.* **1.** a piece of work; an individual piece of work done in the routine of one's occupation or trade. **2.** a piece of work of defined character undertaken for a fixed price. **3.** the unit or material being worked upon. **4.** the product or result. **5.** anything one has to do. **6.** a post of employment. **7.** enterprise; occupation; industry: *the cattle job.* **8.** *Colloq.* an affair, matter, occurrence, or state of affairs: *to make the best of a bad job.* **9.** a piece of public or official business carried through with a view to improper private gain; an instance of jobbery. **10.** *Colloq.* a difficult task. **11.** *Colloq.* a theft or robbery, or any criminal deed. **12. a good job,** *Colloq.* a lucky state of affairs. **13. get on with the job,** to pursue a specific task with vigour and determination. **14. give up as a bad job,** to abandon as unprofitable an undertaking already begun. **15. just the job,** *Colloq.* exactly what is required. **16. make a good job of,** to complete satisfactorily. **17. on the job,** *Colloq.* busy; occupied. **18. the devil's own job,** an extremely difficult or frustrating experience. *–v.i.* **19.** to work at jobs, or odd pieces of work; do piecework. **20.** to do business as a jobber (def. 2). **21.** to turn public business, etc., improperly to private gain. *–v.t.* **22.** to buy in large quantities and sell to dealers in small lots. **23.** to let out (work) in separate portions, as among different contractors or workmen. *–adj.* **24.** of or for a particular job or transaction. **25.** bought or sold together; lumped together: *job lot.* [orig. uncert.] – **jobless,** *adj.* – **joblessness,** *n.*

**job**[2] /dʒɒb/, *v.t., v.i.,* **jobbed, jobbing,** *n.* *Colloq.* jab; hit; punch: *shut up or I'll job you.* [ME *jobbe(n)*; ? imitative. Cf. JAB]

**Job** /dʒoʊb/, *n.* a person who shows exemplary fortitude, piety, etc., in the face of undeserved suffering. [from *Job,* the much afflicted hero of a book of the Old Testament; from Heb. *Iyyōbh*]

**jobber** /ˈdʒɒbə/, *n.* **1.** a wholesale merchant, esp. one selling to retailers. **2.** a dealer in stock exchange securities. Cf. **broker. 3.** a pieceworker. **4.** one who practises jobbery.

**jobbery** /ˈdʒɒbəri/, *n.* the practice of making improper private gains from public or official business.

**jobbies** /ˈdʒɒbiz/, *n.pl.* (*in children's speech*) defecation.

**jobbing** /ˈdʒɒbɪŋ/, *n.* **1.** piecework. **2.** the practice of dealing in stock exchange securities. **3.** →**jobbery.**

**job costing** /ˈdʒɒb kɒstɪŋ/, *n.* a type of costing in which costs are recorded against each individual job or order.

**jobless** /ˈdʒɒbləs/, *adj.* **1.** without a job; unemployed. *–n.* **2. the jobless,** unemployed people as a group. – **joblessness,** *n.*

**job lot** /dʒɒb ˈlɒt/, *n.* **1.** any large lot of goods handled by a jobber. **2.** a miscellaneous quantity of goods.

**Job's comforter** /dʒoʊbz ˈkʌmfətə/, *n.* one who professes to give comfort but who achieves the opposite result.

**job-sharing** /ˈdʒɒb-ʃɛərɪŋ/, *n.* the sharing of one job between two or more employees. See **wage-sharing.**

**Job's-tears** /dʒoʊbz-ˈtɪəz/, *n.pl.* **1.** the hard, nearly globular involucres which surround the female flowers in a species of grass, *Coix lacryma-jobi,* and which when ripe are used as beads. **2.** (*construed as sing., l.c.*) the grass itself, native to Asia but cultivated elsewhere.

**joc.,** jocular.

**jock** /dʒɒk/, *n. Colloq.* **1.** a jockstrap. **2.** *Chiefly U.S.* a male athlete, esp. one in college or university.

**Jock** /dʒɒk/, *n.* nickname for a Scot.

**jockey** /ˈdʒɒki/, *n., pl.* **-eys,** *v.,* **-eyed, -eying.** *–n.* **1.** one who professionally rides horses in races. **2.** a person accompanying a taxidriver who, if a potential passenger gives a destination which does not suit the driver, pretends that he has already hired the taxi to take him to another destination, thus providing the driver with an excuse for not accepting the passenger. *–v.t.* **3.** to ride (a horse) as a jockey. **4.** to bring, put, etc., by skilful manoeuvring. **5.** to trick or cheat. **6.** to manipulate trickily. *–v.i.* **7.** to aim at an advantage by skilful manoeuvring (oft. fol. by *for*). **8.** to act trickily; seek an advantage by trickery. **9. jockey for position,** to attempt to gain an advantageous position (in a race, contest, etc.). [diminutive of *Jock,* Scot. var. of *Jack*] **– jockeyship,** *n.*

**jockey cap** /ˈ– kæp/, *n.* a cap having a close-fitting head-piece and a long peak sloping upwards, as worn by a jockey.

**jockey club** /ˈ– klʌb/, *n.* an association for the regulation and promotion of thoroughbred horseracing.

**jockey pole** /ˈ– poʊl/, *n.* a small pole on a sailing ship, used to hold out a jib on a square run when sails are wing-and-wing, or to bear out a line controlling the spinnaker boom.

**jockeys** /ˈdʒɒkiz/, *n.pl.* close fitting brief underpants for men. Also, **jockey shorts.**

**jockey scales** /ˈdʒɒki skeɪlz/, *n.pl.* a large set of scales, similar to the scales on which jockeys are weighed.

**jockey spider** /ˈ– spaɪdə/, *n.* →**red-back spider.**

**jocko** /ˈdʒɒkoʊ/, *n., pl.* **-os. 1.** the chimpanzee. **2.** (*cap.*) a familiar name for any monkey. [F, from W Afr. name of the chimpanzee, recorded as *engeco, ncheko*]

**jocks** /dʒɒks/, *n.pl.* →**jockeys.**

**jockstrap** /ˈdʒɒkstræp/, *n. Colloq.* a support for the genitals; usu. of elastic cotton webbing, and worn by male athletes, dancers, etc. [obs. Brit. colloq. *jock* penis (? short for earlier *jockum, jockam,* of unknown orig.) + STRAP]

**jocose** /dʒəˈkoʊs/, *adj.* given to or characterised by joking; jesting; humorous; playful. [L *jocōsus*] **– jocosely,** *adv.* **– jocoseness,** *n.*

**jocosity** /dʒəˈkɒsəti/, *n., pl.* **-ties. 1.** the state or quality of being jocose. **2.** joking or jesting. **3.** a joke or jest.

**jocular** /ˈdʒɒkjələ/, *adj.* given to, characterised by, intended for, or suited to joking or jesting; waggish; facetious. [L *joculāris*] **– jocularly,** *adv.*

**jocularism** /ˈdʒɒkjələrɪzəm/, *n.* a joke; amusing remark.

**jocularity** /dʒɒkjəˈlærəti/, *n., pl.* **-ties. 1.** the state or quality of being jocular. **2.** jocular speech or behaviour. **3.** a jocular remark or act.

**jocund** /ˈdʒɒkənd/, *adj.* cheerful; merry; gay; blithe; glad. [ME, from LL *jocundus* pleasant] **– jocundly,** *adv.*

**jocundity** /dʒəˈkʌndəti/, *n., pl.* **-ties. 1.** the state of being jocund; gaiety. **2.** a jocund remark or act.

**jodhpurs** /ˈdʒɒdpəz/, *n.pl.* riding breeches reaching to the ankle, and fitting closely from the knee down, worn also in sports, etc. [named after *Jodhpur,* a town in W Rajasthan, India]

**joe**[1] /dʒoʊ/, *n. Colloq.* ewe: *a bare-bellied joe.* [palatalised form of YEO]

**joe**[2] /dʒoʊ/, *v.,* **joed, joeing,** *n. –v.t.* **1.** to jeer at; abuse. *–n.* **2.** a fool. **3. make a joe of oneself,** to behave in a foolish manner. [from the practice in the gold diggings of yelling *Joe* at the troopers. See JOE[1]]

**joe**[3] /dʒoʊ/, *n.* →**Joe**[2].

**Joe**[1] /dʒoʊ/, *n. Colloq.* (formerly) a trooper; a military policeman. [from C. *Joseph* La Trobe, whose regulation the troopers were enforcing, esp. in the gold diggings]

**Joe**[2] /dʒoʊ/, *n. U.S. Colloq.* **1.** a man; an average fellow: *he's a good Joe.* **2.** an enlisted man in the U.S. army: *a G. I. Joe.* Also, **joe.**

**Joe Blake** /– ˈbleɪk/, *n. Colloq.* a snake. [rhyming slang]

**Joe Blakes** /–ˈbleɪks/, *n.pl. Colloq.* →**delirium tremens.** [rhyming slang, *Joe Blakes* the shakes]

**Joe Bloggs** /– ˈblɒgz/, *n.* the average citizen.

**Joe Blow** /– ˈbloʊ/, *n. Colloq.* the man in the street; the average citizen. Also, **Joe Bloggs.** [from JOE[2] (def. 1) + *Blow,* probably just for the rhyme]

**joes** /dʒoʊz/, *n.pl. Colloq.* **1.** →**delirium tremens.** Also, **Joes. 2.** a mood of depression; blues. [short for JOE BLAKES]

**joey** /ˈdʒoʊi/, *n., pl.* **-eys. 1** any young animal, esp. a kangaroo. **2.** *N.Z.* an opossum. **3.** a young child. [Aboriginal]

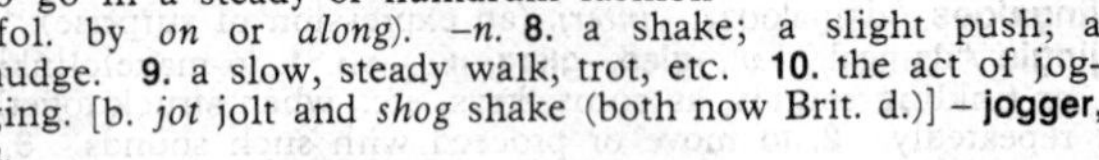

joey

**Joey** /ˈdʒoʊi/, *n. Colloq.* →**Joe**[1]. Also, **joey.**

**jog** /dʒɒg/, *v.,* **jogged, jogging,** *n. –v.t.* **1.** to move or shake with a push or jerk. **2.** to give a slight push to, as to arouse the attention; nudge. **3.** to stir up by hint or reminder: *to jog a person's memory.* *–v.i.* **4.** to move with a jolt or jerk. **5.** to run at a jogtrot. **6.** to go or travel with a jolting pace or motion. **7.** to go in a steady or humdrum fashion (fol. by *on* or *along*). *–n.* **8.** a shake; a slight push; a nudge. **9.** a slow, steady walk, trot, etc. **10.** the act of jogging. [b. *jot* jolt and *shog* shake (both now Brit. d.)] **– jogger,** *n.*

**jogging** /ˈdʒɒgɪŋ/, *n.* a form of physical exercise in which one runs at a jogtrot, usu. as a regular practice and for some distance.

**jogging suit** /ˈ– sut/, *n.* →**tracksuit.**

**joggle** /ˈdʒɒgəl/, *v.,* **-gled, -gling,** *n. –v.t.* **1.** to shake slightly; move to and fro as by repeated jerks. **2.** to join or fasten by a joggle or joggles. *–v.i.* **3.** to move irregularly; have a jogging or jolting motion; shake. *–n.* **4.** the act of joggling. **5.** a slight shake; a jolt. **6.** a moving with jolts or jerks. **7.** a projection on one of two joining surfaces, or a notch on the other, to prevent slipping. [frequentative of JOG]

**jogtrot** /ˈdʒɒgtrɒt/, *n., v.,* **-trotted, -trotting.** *–n.* **1.** a slow, regular, bouncing pace, as of a horse. **2.** a routine or humdrum mode of procedure. *–v.i.* **3.** to move at a jogtrot.

**john**[1] /dʒɒn/, *n. Colloq.* (*oft. cap.*) a policeman. [rhyming slang, *John* Hop, COP[1]]

**john**[2] /dʒɒn/, *n. Colloq.* a toilet.

**john**[3] /dʒɒn/, *n. Colloq.* a Chinese. [from popular name *John* Chinaman]

**John** /dʒɒn/, *n.* →**John Thomas.**

**John Barleycorn** /– ˈbalikɔn/, *n.* a facetious personification of barley as used in the brewing of beer.

**John Bull** /– ˈbʊl/, *n.* the typical Englishman. [after *John Bull,* the chief character in *The History of John Bull* (1712) by John Arbuthnot]

**John Citizen** /– ˈsɪtəzən/, *n.* the man in the street.

**John Doe** /– ˈdoʊ/, *n.* a fictitious character in legal proceedings.

**John Dory** /–ˈdɔri/, *n.* **1.** a thin, deep-bodied, highly esteemed food fish of Australian waters, *Zeus australis.* **2.** a similar fish, *Zeus faber,* found elsewhere. [*John* + DORY[2] the name of the fish]

**Johne's disease** /ˈjoʊnəz dəziz/, *n.* a chronic diarrhoeal disease of cattle and sheep caused by infection with an organism related to the tubercle bacillus. [named after H. A. *Johne,* 1839-1910, German scientist]

**johnny** /ˈdʒɒni/, *n. Colloq.* fellow; man.

**Johnny Bliss** /dʒɒni ˈblɪs/, *n. Colloq.* an act of urination. [rhyming slang, *Johnny Bliss* piss]

**johnnycake** /ˈdʒɒnikeɪk/, *n.* **1.** a small flat damper of wheatmeal or flour about as big as the palm of the hand, cooked on both sides often on top of the embers of a campfire or in a camp oven. **2.** *U.S.* a similar cake or bread made of corn meal and water or milk. [orig. obscure. The first element may be from obs. *jonakin, jonikin* (apparently of Indian origin) a form of thin griddlecake]

**Johnny-come-lately** /ˌdʒɒni-kʌm-ˈleɪtli/, *n.* a late arrival.

**Johnny Raw** /dʒɒni ˈrɔ/, *n.* an inexperienced person; new chum. Also, **Jacky Raw.**

**Johnny Woodser** /– ˈwʊdzə/, *n. N.Z. Colloq.* →**Jimmy Woodser.**

**Johnson grass** /ˈdʒɒnsən gras/, *n.* a species of *Sorghum, S. halepense,* a native of the Mediterranean region but now widespread in many temperate and tropical countries, and

i = peat ɪ = pit ɛ = pet æ = pat a = part ɒ = pot ʌ = putt ɔ = port ʊ = put u = pool ɜ = pert ə = apart aɪ = buy eɪ = bay ɔɪ = boy aʊ = how
oʊ = hoe ɪə = here ɛə = hair ʊə = tour g = give θ = thin ð = then ʃ = show ʒ = measure tʃ = choke dʒ = joke ŋ = sing j = you õ = Fr. bon

poisonous to stock.

**Johnsonian** /dʒɒn'souniən/, *adj.* of a style of writing which is measured and dignified with many Latinate words and much parentheses. [after Dr. Samuel *Johnson,* 1709-84, English writer]

**John Thomas** /dʒɒn 'tɒməs/, *n. Colloq.* the penis. Also, **John.**

**joie de vivre** /ʒwa də 'vivrə/, *n.* joy of living. [F]

**join** /dʒɔɪn/, *v.t.* **1.** to bring or put together, in contact or connection (sometimes fol. by *up*). **2.** to come into contact, connection, or union with: *the brook joins the river.* **3.** to bring together in relation, purpose, action, coexistence, etc.: *to join forces.* **4.** to become a member of (a society, party, etc.); enlist in (one of the armed forces). **5.** to come into the company of: *I'll join you later.* **6.** to unite in marriage. **7.** to meet or engage in (battle, conflict, etc.). **8.** to adjoin: *his land joins mine.* **9.** *Geom.* to draw a curve or straight line between. **10.** (of animals) to mate. *–v.i.* **11.** to come into or be in contact or connection, or form a junction. **12.** to become united, associated, or combined; associate or ally oneself (fol. by *with*). **13.** to take part with others (oft. fol. by *in*). **14.** to be contiguous or close; lie or come together; form a junction. **15.** *Obs.* to meet in battle or conflict. **16.** **join up, a.** to enlist in one of the armed forces. **b.** to become a member; fall in (*with*): *I joined up with the stragglers.* *–n.* **17.** joining. **18.** a place or line of joining; a seam. [ME *join(en),* from OF *joindre,* from L *jungere* join, yoke] – **joinable,** *adj.*

**joinder** /'dʒɔɪndə/, *n.* **1.** the act of joining. **2.** *Law.* **a.** the joining of causes of action in a suit. **b.** the joining of parties in a suit. **c.** the acceptance by a party to an action of an issue tendered. [F *joindre* JOIN]

**joiner** /'dʒɔɪnə/, *n.* **1.** one who or that which joins. **2.** a craftsman who works in wood already cut and shaped; a worker in wood who constructs the fittings of a house, furniture, etc.

**joinery** /'dʒɔɪnəri/, *n.* **1.** the art or trade of a joiner. **2.** a joiner's work or his product.

**joint** /dʒɔɪnt/, *n.* **1.** the place or part in which two things, or parts of one thing, are joined or united, either rigidly or so as to admit of motion; an articulation. **2.** (in an animal body) **a.** the movable place or part where two bones or two segments join. **b.** the hingelike or other arrangement of such a part. **3.** *Biol.* **a.** a portion, esp. of an animal or plant body, connected with another portion by an articulation, node, or the like. **b.** a portion between two articulations, nodes, or the like. **4.** *Bot.* the part of a stem from which a branch or a leaf grows; a node. **5.** one of the portions into which a carcass is divided by a butcher, esp. one ready for cooking. **6.** *Geol.* a fracture or parting which interrupts abruptly the physical continuity of a rock mass. **7.** *Colloq.* the house, unit, office, etc., regarded as in some sense one's own: *come round to my joint.* **8.** a disreputable bar, restaurant, or nightclub; a dive. **9.** a concealable firearm. **10.** **out of joint, a.** dislocated. **b.** out of order; in a bad state. **11.** *Colloq.* a marihuana cigarette. *–adj.* **12.** shared by or common to two or more. **13.** sharing or acting in common. **14.** joined or associated, as in relation, interest, or action: *joint owners.* **15.** held, done, etc., by two or more in conjunction or in common: *a joint effort.* **16.** *Law.* joined together in obligation or ownership. **17.** *Parl. Proc.* of or pertaining to both branches of a bicameral legislature. **18.** (of a diplomatic action) in which two or more governments are formally united. *–v.t.* **19.** to unite by a joint or joints. **20.** to form or provide with a joint or joints. **21.** to divide at a joint, or separate into pieces. **22.** to prepare (a board, etc.) for fitting in a joint. **23.** to fill up (the joints of stone, interstices in brickwork, etc.) with mortar. [ME *iointe,* from OF *joint, jointe* (n. use of pp. of *joindre* JOIN), from L *junctus, juncta,* properly pp. of *jungere*]

**joint account** /'– əkaʊnt/, *n.* a bank account kept in the names of two or more persons or parties and subject to withdrawals by any one of them.

**joint committee** /– kə'mɪti/, *n.* a committee comprising members of both houses of parliament.

**joint custody** /– 'kʌstədi/, *n.* custody of the children of a marriage shared by their divorced parents.

**jointed** /'dʒɔɪntəd/, *adj.* **1.** provided with joints. **2.** formed with knots or nodes.

**jointer** /'dʒɔɪntə/, *n.* **1.** one who or that which joints. **2.** a bricklayer's tool used for putting a surface finish on a mortar joint; a tool for pointing. **3.** *Carp.* a plane for smoothing edges to be joined.

**joint ill** /'dʒɔɪnt ɪl/, *n.* a disease of young foals (horses) characterised by swollen inflamed joints, high fever, and, usu. by death a few days after birth.

**jointing** /'dʒɔɪntɪŋ/, *n.* **1.** the operation of making joints. **2.** any material used for making a joint between two surfaces pressure-tight, as asbestos, rubber, etc.

**jointly** /'dʒɔɪntli/, *adv.* together; in common.

**jointress** /'dʒɔɪntrəs/, *n.* a woman entitled to a jointure.

**joint sitting** /dʒɔɪnt 'sɪtɪŋ/, *n.* both the houses of parliament sitting together, as the House of Representatives and the Senate in Federal Parliament, to resolve a deadlock after a double dissolution.

**joint stock** /'– stɒk/, *n.* stock or capital divided into a number of shares.

**joint-stock company** /dʒɔɪnt-'stɒk ˌkʌmpəni/, *n.* a company whose ownership is divided into transferable shares, the object usu. being the division of profits among the members in proportion to the number of shares held by each.

**joint tenant** /dʒɔɪnt 'tɛnənt/, *n.* one who holds property in common with another person or persons so that each owns an undivided moiety of the whole; on death, interest in this moiety passes to the surviving co-owner or co-owners.

**jointure** /'dʒɔɪntʃə/, *n. Law.* **1.** an estate or property settled on a woman in consideration of marriage, and to be enjoyed by her after her husband's decease. **2.** *Obs.* a joint tenancy limited in favour of a man and his wife. [ME, from F, from L *junctūra* a joining]

**joist** /dʒɔɪst/, *n.* **1.** any of the parallel lengths of timber, steel, etc., used for supporting floors, ceilings, etc. *–v.t.* **2.** to furnish with or fix on joists. [ME *giste,* from OF, from *gesir* lie, rest, from L *jacēre* lie; akin to GIST] – **joistless,** *adj.*

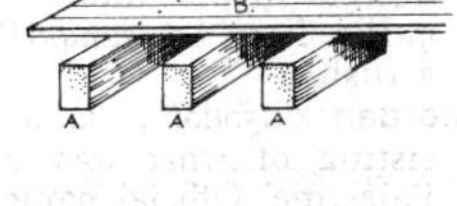

A, joist; B, floorboards

**jo-jo** /'dʒoʊ-dʒoʊ/, *n.* any prostrate herb of the genus *Soliva,* esp. *Soliva pterosperma* which has fruit-bearing sharp-pointed styles; native to America but commonly a lawn weed; bindi-eye.

**joke** /dʒoʊk/, *n., v.,* **joked, joking.** *–n.* **1.** something said or done to excite laughter or amusement; a playful or mischievous trick or remark. **2.** an amusing or ridiculous circumstance. **3.** an object of joking or jesting; a thing or person laughed at rather than taken seriously. **4.** a matter for joking about; trifling matter: *the loss was no joke.* **5.** **the joke is on (someone),** *Colloq.* (said of a person who has become the object of laughter or ridicule, usu. after a reversal of fortune). *–v.i.* **6.** to speak or act in a playful or merry way. **7.** to say something in mere sport, rather than in earnest. [L *jocus* jest, sport] – **jokeless,** *adj.* – **jokingly,** *adv.*

**joker** /'dʒoʊkə/, *n.* **1.** one who jokes. **2.** an extra playing card in a pack, used in some games, often counting as the highest card or to represent a card of any denomination or suit the holder wishes. **3.** *Colloq.* a fellow or bloke: *a funny sort of joker.* **4.** *Colloq.* a hidden clause in any paper, document, etc., which largely changes its apparent nature. **5.** **the joker in the pack,** a person whose behaviour is unpredictable.

**jollification** /dʒɒləfə'keɪʃən/, *n.* jolly merrymaking; a jolly festivity. [JOLLY, *adj.* + -FICATION]

**jollify** /'dʒɒləfaɪ/, *v.,* **-fied, -fying.** *Colloq.* *–v.t.* **1.** to make jolly or merry. *–v.i.* **2.** to be merry.

**jollity** /'dʒɒləti/, *n., pl.* **-ties. 1.** jolly state, mood, or proceedings. **2.** (*pl.*) jolly festivities.

**jolly** /'dʒɒli/, *adj.,* **-lier, -liest,** *v.,* **-lied, -lying,** *n., pl.* **-lies,** *adv.* *–adj.* **1.** in good spirits, gay: *in a moment he was as jolly as ever.* **2.** cheerfully festive or convivial. **3.** *Colloq.* amusing; pleasant. **4.** joyous, glad. *–v.t.* **5.** *Colloq.* to talk or act agreeably to (a person) in order to keep him in good humour, esp. with the purpose of gaining something (oft. fol. by *along*); cajole; flatter. *–n.* **6.** *Colloq.* a bit of agreeable talk or action to put a person in good humour. *–adv.* **7.** *Colloq.*

extremely; very: *jolly well.* [ME *joli(f)*, from OF, ? of Gmc orig.; cf. Icel. *jōl* YULE] –**jollily,** *adv.* –**jolliness,** *n.*

**jolly-boat** /ˈdʒɒli-bout/, *n.* a ship's work boat, smaller than a cutter, hoisted at the stern of a sailing vessel for handy use.

**Jolly Roger** /dʒɒli ˈrɒdʒə/, *n.* the pirates' flag.

**jollytail** /ˈdʒɒliteɪl/, *n.* a small fish, *Galaxias attenuatus,* of New Zealand and Tasmanian waters; whitebait.

**jolt** /dʒoult/, *v.t.* **1.** to jar or shake as by a sudden rough thrust. –*v.i.* **2.** to proceed in an irregular or bumpy manner. –*n.* **3.** a jolting shock or movement. [b. Brit. d. *jot* jolt and obs. *joll* knock about] –**jolter,** *n.*

**jolty** /ˈdʒoulti/, *adj.* full of jolts; uneven; bumpy.

**jonah** /ˈdʒounə/, *n.* **1.** a person regarded as bringing bad luck. –*v.t.* **2.** to jinx. Also, **Jonas.** [from *Jonah,* a Hebrew prophet of a book of the Old Testament who for his impiety was thrown overboard from his ship to allay a tempest; he was swallowed by a large fish and lived in its belly three days before he was vomited up]

**jonathan** /ˈdʒɒnəθən/, *n.* a variety of red apple that matures in early autumn.

**jongleur** /ʒɒŋˈglɜ/, *n.* (in medieval France and Norman England) an itinerant minstrel or entertainer who sang songs (sometimes of his own composition), and told stories. [F, b. OF *jogleor* and *jangler* JANGLE. See JUGGLER]

**jonick** /ˈdʒɒnɪk/, *adj.* fair; straightforward; reliable; honest. Also, **jonnick, junnick.** [Brit. d. *jannock* fair, straightforward]

**jonnie** /ˈdʒɒni/, *n. Colloq.* a jonathan apple.

**jonnop** /dʒɒnˈɒp/, *n. Colloq.* a policeman. [contraction of rhyming slang *John Hop,* cop[1]]

**jonquil** /ˈdʒɒŋkwɪl/, *n.* **1.** a species of narcissus, *Narcissus jonquilla,* with long, narrow rushlike leaves and fragrant yellow or white flowers. **2.** any of certain species of *Narcissus* other than *N. jonquilla* which have a number of small flowers in the inflorescence and strap-shaped leaves. [F *jonquille,* from Sp. *junquillo,* diminutive of *junco,* from L *juncus* a rush]

**Jordan** /ˈdʒɔdən/, *n.* a country in south-western Asia, consisting of what was formerly Trans-Jordan and a part of Palestine. Official name: **Hashemite Kingdom of Jordan.**

**Jordan almond** /– ˈamənd/, *n.* a large, hard-shelled type of Spanish almond. [ME *jardyne* (from F *jardin* garden) *almaunde,* i.e. garden almond. See ALMOND]

**jorum** /ˈdʒɔrəm/, *n.* a large bowl or vessel for holding drink, or its contents: *a jorum of punch.* [said to be named after *Joram,* who brought to David vessels of silver, gold, and brass. See 2 Sam. 8:10]

**joseph** /ˈdʒouzəf/, *n.* a long cloak with a cape, worn chiefly in the 18th century, esp. by women. [from *Joseph,* a Hebrew patriarch, the first son by Rachel of Jacob, who made him a coat of many colours. See Gen. 37]

**josh** /dʒɒʃ/, *U.S. Colloq.* –*v.t.* **1.** to chaff; tease. –*v.i.* **2.** to banter in a teasing way. –*n.* **3.** a chaffing remark; a piece of banter. [? var. of Brit. d. *joss* jostle] –**josher,** *n.*

**Josh.,** *Bible.* Joshua.

**Joshua tree** /ˈdʒɒʃjuə tri/, *n.* a tree, *Yucca brevifolia,* growing in arid or desert regions of the south-western United States. See **yucca.**

**joss**[1] /dʒɒs/, *v.t. N.Z.* →**josh** (def. 1).

**joss**[2] /dʒɒs/, *n. Colloq.* boss.

**Joss** /dʒɒs/, *n.* a Chinese deity or idol. [pidgin English, from Pg. *deos,* from L *deus* god]

**josser**[1] /ˈdʒɒsə/, *n. N.Z.* a person who josses.

**josser**[2] /ˈdʒɒsə/, *n. Colloq.* a parson. [Joss + -ER[1]]

**joss house** /ˈdʒɒs haus/, *n.* a Chinese temple.

**joss stick** /ˈ– stɪk/, *n.* a slender stick of a dried fragrant paste, burnt by the Chinese as incense, etc.

**jostle** /ˈdʒɒsəl/, *v.,* **-tled, -tling,** *n.* –*v.t.* **1.** to strike or push roughly or rudely against; elbow roughly; hustle. **2.** to drive or force by or as by pushing or shoving. –*v.i.* **3.** to collide (fol. by *with*) or strike or push (fol. by *against*) as in passing or in a crowd; push or elbow one's way rudely. **4.** to strive as with collisions, rough pushing, etc., for room, place, or any advantage. –*n.* **5.** a collision, shock, or push. Also, **justle.** [ME *justil,* frequentative of *just* JOUST] –**jostlement,** *n.* –**jostler,** *n.*

**jot** /dʒɒt/, *n., v.,* **jotted, jotting.** –*n.* **1.** the least part of something; a little bit: *I don't care a jot.* –*v.t.* **2.** to write or mark down briefly (usu. fol. by *down*). [L *iōta* IOTA]

**jota** /ˈhoutə/, *n., pl.* **-tas.** a fast and lively Spanish dance in triple time, usu. performed with castanets.

**jotter** /ˈdʒɒtə/, *n.* **1.** one who jots things down. **2.** a small notebook.

**jotting** /ˈdʒɒtɪŋ/, *n.* **1.** the act of one who jots. **2.** something jotted down; a brief note or memorandum.

**joule** /dʒul/, *n.* the derived SI unit of work or energy, defined as the work done when the point of application of a force of one newton is displaced through a distance of one metre in the direction of the force. *Symbol:* J [named after J.P. *Joule.* See JOULE'S LAW]

**Joule's law** /ˈdʒulz lɔ/, *n.* **1.** the principle that internal energy of a given mass of gas is independent of its volume or pressure and depends only on its temperature. **2.** the principle that the heat produced by an electric current is equal to the product of the resistance of the circuit through which it is passing, the square of the current, and the time for which it flows. [named after J. P. *Joule,* 1818-89, British physicist]

**Joule-Thomson effect** /dʒul-ˈtɒmsən əfɛkt/, *n.* the change of temperature exhibited by a gas when it is expanded through a small hole or a porous plug. Also, **Joule-Kelvin effect.** [named after J.P. *Joule* (see JOULE'S LAW) and Sir William *Thomson,* First Baron Kelvin, 1824-1907, British physicist and mathematician]

**jounce** /dʒauns/, *v.,* **jounced, jouncing,** *n.* –*v.i.* **1.** to move violently up and down; bounce. –*v.t.* **2.** to cause to jounce. –*n.* **3.** a jouncing movement. [? b. obs. *joll* knock about and BOUNCE]

**journ.,** journalism.

**journal** /ˈdʒɜnəl/, *n.* **1.** a daily record, as of occurrences, experiences, or observations; diary. **2.** a register of the daily transactions of a public or legislative body. **3.** a newspaper, esp. a daily one. **4.** any periodical or magazine, esp. one published by a learned society. **5.** *Bookkeeping.* **a.** a daybook. **b.** (in double entry) a book in which all transactions are entered (from the daybook or blotter) in systematic form, to facilitate posting into the ledger. **6.** *Naut.* a log or logbook. **7.** *Mach.* that part of a shaft or axle in actual contact with a bearing. [ME, from OF, from LL *diurnālis* DIURNAL]

**journalese** /dʒɜnəˈliz/, *n.* the style of writing or expression (considered inferior to that of conventional literary work) supposed to characterise newspapers.

**journalise** /ˈdʒɜnəlaɪz/, *v.,* **-lised, -lising.** –*v.t.* **1.** to enter or record in a journal. **2.** to tell or relate, as done in a journal. **3.** (in double-entry bookkeeping) to systematise and enter in a journal, preparatory to posting to the ledger. –*v.i.* **4.** to keep or make entries in a journal. Also, **journalize.**

**journalism** /ˈdʒɜnəlɪzəm/, *n.* **1.** the occupation of writing for, editing, and conducting newspapers and other periodicals. **2.** newspapers collectively.

**journalist** /ˈdʒɜnələst/, *n.* one engaged in journalism.

**journalistic** /dʒɜnəˈlɪstɪk/, *adj.* of, pertaining to, or characteristic of journalists or journalism. –**journalistically,** *adv.*

**journey** /ˈdʒɜni/, *n., pl.* **-neys,** *v.,* **-neyed, -neying.** –*n.* **1.** a course of travel from one place to another, esp. by land. **2.** a distance travelled, or suitable for travelling, in a specified time: *a day's journey.* –*v.i.* **3.** to make a journey; travel. [ME *jorney,* from OF *jornee* a day's time, from L *diurnus* of the day, daily] –**journeyer,** *n.*

**journeyman** /ˈdʒɜnimən/, *n., pl.* **-men. 1.** one who has served his apprenticeship at a trade or handicraft, and who works at it for another. **2.** *Obs.* one hired to do work for another, usu. for a day. [obs. *journey* a day's work + MAN]

**journeywork** /ˈdʒɜniwɜk/, *n.* **1.** the work of a journeyman. **2.** routine work; hackwork.

**journo** /ˈdʒɜnou/, *n. Colloq.* →**journalist.**

**joust** /dʒaust/, *n.* **1.** a combat in which two armoured knights or men-at-arms on horseback opposed each other with lances. **2.** (*pl.*) a tournament. –*v.i.* **3.** to contend in a joust or tournament. Also, **just.** [ME *j(o)uste(n),* from OF *j(o)uster,* from L *juxtā* near] –**jouster,** *n.*

**Jove** /dʒouv/, *n.* **1.** (in Roman mythology) the greatest of the gods. –*interj.* **2. by Jove,** (a mild oath). [L *Jovis* Jupiter]

**jovial** /'dʒoʊviəl/, *adj.* **1.** endowed with or characterised by a hearty, joyous humour or a spirit of good fellowship. **2.** (*cap.*) of or pertaining to the god Jove or Jupiter. [L *Joviālis* of Jupiter (in astrology the planet is regarded as exerting a happy influence)] – **jovially,** *adv.* – **jovialness,** *n.*

**joviality** /dʒoʊvi'æləti/, *n.* the state or quality of being jovial; merriment; jollity.

**jowl**[1] /dʒaʊl/, *n.* **1.** a jaw, esp. the underjaw. **2.** the cheek. [ME *chawl, chavel,* OE *ceafl* jaw; akin to D *kevel* gum, d. G *Kiefer* jaw, chap, Icel. *kjaptr* mouth, jaw]

**jowl**[2] /dʒaʊl/, *n.* **1.** a fold of flesh hanging from the jaw, as of a fat person. **2.** the dewlap of cattle. **3.** the wattle of fowls. [ME *cholle,* apparently from OE *ceole* throat]

**joy** /dʒɔɪ/, *n.* **1.** an emotion of keen or lively pleasure arising from present or expected good; exultant satisfaction; great gladness; delight. **2.** a source or cause of gladness or delight: *a thing of beauty is a joy for ever.* **3.** a state of happiness or felicity. **4.** the manifestation of glad feeling; outward rejoicing; festive gaiety. **5. not to have any joy,** to be unsuccessful (oft. fol. by *of*). *–v.i.* **6.** to feel joy; be glad; rejoice. *–v.t.* **7.** *Obs.* to gladden. [ME *joie,* from OF, from L *gaudia,* pl. of *gaudium* joy, gladness]

**joy-flight** /'dʒɔɪ-flaɪt/, *n.* a joy-ride in an aeroplane, etc.

**joyful** /'dʒɔɪfəl/, *adj.* **1.** full of joy, as a person, the heart, etc.; glad; delighted. **2.** showing or expressing joy, as looks, actions, speech, etc. **3.** causing or bringing joy, as an event, a sight, news, etc.; delightful. – **joyfully,** *adv.* – **joyfulness,** *n.*

**joyless** /'dʒɔɪləs/, *adj.* **1.** destitute of joy or gladness. **2.** causing no joy or pleasure. – **joylessly,** *adv.* – **joylessness,** *n.*

**joyous** /'dʒɔɪəs/, *adj.* joyful. – **joyously,** *adv.* – **joyousness,** *n.*

**joy-ride** /'dʒɔɪ-raɪd/, *n., v.,* **-rode, -riding.** *Colloq. –n.* **1.** a pleasure ride, as in a motor car, esp. when the car is driven recklessly or used without the owner's permission. **2.** a junket (def. 3). *–v.i.* **3.** to take such a ride. – **joy-rider,** *n.* – **joy-riding,** *n., adj.*

**joystick** /'dʒɔɪstɪk/, *n.* the control stick of an aeroplane. [from jocular comparison with a penis]

**joy-weed** /'dʒɔɪ-wid/, *n.* the small Australian plants of the genus *Alternanthera,* family Amaranthaceae, common esp. in inland areas.

**J.P.** /dʒeɪ 'pi/, Justice of the Peace.

**Jr,** Junior. Also, **jr.**

**juba** /'dʒubə/, *n.* a lively dance developed by plantation Negroes of the United States.

**jubbah** /'dʒʊbə/, *n.* a kind of long outer garment with sleeves, worn in Muslim countries. [Ar.]

**jube**[1] /'dʒubi/, *n.* **1.** a screen with an upper platform, separating the choir of a church from the nave and often supporting a rood. **2.** a rood loft. [L: bid thou, the first word of a formula spoken from the gallery above the rood screen]

**jube**[2] /dʒub/, *n.* a fruit flavoured, chewy lolly made of gelatine or gum arabic, sugar and flavourings. Also, **jujube.**

**jubilant** /'dʒubələnt/, *adj.* **1.** jubilating; rejoicing; exultant. **2.** expressing or exciting joy; manifesting or denoting exultation or gladness. [L *jūbilans,* ppr.] – **jubilance, jubilancy,** *n.* – **jubilantly,** *adv.*

**jubilate** /'dʒubəleɪt/, *v.i.,* **-lated, -lating.** **1.** to manifest or feel great joy; rejoice; exult. **2.** to celebrate a jubilee or joyful occasion. [L *jūbilātus,* pp. of *jūbilāre* shout for joy] – **jubilatory** /'dʒubəleɪtəri/, *adj.*

**Jubilate** /dʒubɪ'lati/, *n.* **1.** the 100th Psalm (99th in the Vulgate), used as a canticle in the Anglican liturgy. **2.** the third Sunday (**Jubilate Sunday**) after Easter (when the 66th psalm, 65th in the Vulgate, is used as the introit). **3.** a musical setting of this psalm. [L: shout ye, the first word of both psalms in the Vulgate]

**jubilation** /dʒubə'leɪʃən/, *n.* **1.** the act of jubilating; rejoicing; exultation. **2.** a joyful or festive celebration.

**jubilee** /dʒubə'li/, *n.* **1.** the celebration of any of certain anniversaries, as the 25th (**silver jubilee**), 50th (**golden jubilee**), or 60th or 75th (**diamond jubilee**). **2.** the completion of the 50th year of any continuous course or period, as of existence or activity, or its celebration. **3.** *Rom. Cath. Ch.* an appointed year (or other period) now ordinarily every 25th year, in which remission from the penal consequences of sin is granted upon repentance and the performance of certain religious acts. **4.** (among the ancient Hebrews) a year to be observed every 50th year (see Lev. 25), and to be announced by the blowing of trumpets, during which the fields were to be left untilled, alienated lands to be restored, and Hebrew bondmen to be set free. **5.** any season or occasion of rejoicing or festivity. **6.** rejoicing or jubilation. [ME *jubile,* from F, from LL *jūbilaeus,* from Gk *iōbēlaîos,* from Heb. *yōbēl* ram, ram's horn (used as a trumpet; cf. Lev. 25: 9)]

**Jud.,** *Bible.* **1.** Judges. **2.** Judith (Apocrypha).

**Judaic** /dʒu'deɪɪk/, *adj.* **1.** of or pertaining to Judaism. **2.** of or pertaining to the Jews; Jewish. [L *Jūdaicus,* from Gk *Ioudaïkós*]

**Judaism** /'dʒudeɪ,ɪzəm/, *n.* the religion of the Jews, deriving its authority from the precepts of the Old Testament and the teaching of the rabbis as expounded in the Talmud. It is founded on belief in the one and only God, who is transcendent, the creator of all things, and the source of all righteousness, and in the duty of all Jews to bear witness to this belief.

**Judaist** /'dʒudeɪəst/, *n.* **1.** an adherent of Judaism. **2.** a Jewish Christian in the early Christian Church who followed or advocated Jewish rules or practices. – **Judaistic** /dʒudeɪ'ɪstɪk/, *adj.*

**judas** /'dʒudəs/, *n.* **1.** one treacherous enough to betray a friend; traitor. **2.** Also, **judas hole.** a peephole in a door. [orig. from *Judas* Iscariot, the betrayer of Jesus (Mark 3:19)]

**Judas sheep** /'dʒudəs ʃip/, *n.* a sheep kept at an abattoirs because of its ability to lead a flock and used to lead others in to slaughter.

**Judas tree** /'– tri/, *n.* **1.** a purple-flowered leguminous European and Asiatic tree, *Cercis siliquastrum,* supposed to be the kind upon which Judas hanged himself. **2.** any of various other trees of the same genus, as the redbud.

**judder** /'dʒʌdə/, *v.i.* **1.** to vibrate; shake. *–n.* **2.** a shaking; vibration. [b. JUMP and SHUDDER]

**Judg.,** *Bible.* Judges.

**judge** /dʒʌdʒ/, *n., v.,* **judged, judging.** *–n.* **1.** a public officer authorised to hear and determine causes in a court of law; a magistrate charged with the administering of justice. **2.** a person appointed to decide in any competition or contest; an authorised arbiter. **3.** one qualified to pass a critical judgment: *a judge of horses.* **4.** an administrative head of Israel in the period between Joshua's death and Saul's accession. *–v.t.* **5.** to try (a person or a case) as a judge does; pass sentence on or in. **6.** to form a judgment or opinion of or upon; decide upon critically; estimate. **7.** to decide or decree judicially or authoritatively. **8.** to infer, think, or hold as an opinion. **9.** (of the Hebrew judges) to govern. *–v.i.* **10.** to act as a judge; pass judgment. **11.** to form an opinion or estimate. **12.** to make a mental judgment. [ME *juge,* from OF, from L *jūdex*] – **judger,** *n.* – **judgeless,** *adj.* – **judgelike,** *adj.* – **judgeship,** *n.*

**judge advocate** /– 'ædvəkət/, *n.* a legal officer appointed to sum up the evidence at a court martial and to direct the court on questions of law.

**judge advocate general,** *n.* a senior legal official appointed to advise the governor-general, ministers and senior military commanders in matters of law.

**judgment** /'dʒʌdʒmənt/, *n.* **1.** the act of judging. **2.** *Law.* **a.** the judicial decision of a cause in court. **b.** the obligation, esp. a debt, arising from a judicial decision. **c.** the certificate embodying such a decision. **3.** ability to judge justly or wisely, esp. in matters affecting action; good sense; discretion. **4.** the forming of an opinion, estimate, notion, or conclusion, as from circumstances presented to the mind. **5.** the opinion formed. **6.** a misfortune regarded as inflicted by divine sentence, as for sin. **7.** (*oft. cap.*) the final trial of all mankind, both the living and the dead, at the end of the world (often, **Last Judgment**). Also, **judgement.**

**Judgment Day** /'dʒʌdʒmənt deɪ/, *n.* (*sometimes l.c.*) the day of God's final judgment of mankind at the end of the world; doomsday.

**judicable** /'dʒudəkəbəl/, *adj.* **1.** capable of being judged or tried. **2.** liable to be judged or tried.

**judicative** /'dʒudəkətɪv/, *adj.* having ability to judge; judging: *the judicative faculty.*

**judicator** /'dʒudəkeɪtə/, *n.* one who acts as judge or sits in judgment. [LL]

**judicatory** /ˈdʒudəkeɪtəri/, *adj., n., pl.* **-tories.** *–adj.* **1.** of or pertaining to judgment or the administration of justice: *judicatory power.* *–n.* **2.** a court of justice; a tribunal. **3.** the administration of justice. [LL *jūdicātōrius*]

**judicature** /ˈdʒudəkətʃə/, *n.* **1.** the administration of justice, as by judges or courts. **2.** the office, function, or authority of a judge. **3.** the extent of jurisdiction of a judge or court. **4.** a body of judges. **5.** the power of administering justice by legal trial and determination. [ML *jūdicātūra,* from *jūdicātus,* pp., judged]

**judicature system** /ˈ– sɪstəm/, *n.* the system established in England in 1873-5 and largely adopted in Australia and New Zealand, reorganising the courts of law and simplifying procedure.

**judiciable** /dʒuˈdɪʃiəbəl/, *adj.* capable of being judged or tried.

**judicial** /dʒuˈdɪʃəl/, *adj.* **1.** pertaining to judgment in courts of justice or to the administration of justice: *judicial proceedings.* **2.** pertaining to courts of law or to judges: *judicial functions.* **3.** of or pertaining to a judge; proper to the character of a judge; judgelike. **4.** inclined to make or give judgments; critical; discriminating. **5.** decreed, sanctioned, or enforced by a court: *a judicial separation.* **6.** pertaining to judgment or decision in a dispute or contest: *a judicial duel.* **7.** inflicted by God as a judgment or punishment. [ME, from L *jūdiciālis* of a court of justice] – **judicially,** *adv.*

**Judicial Committee of the Privy Council,** *n.* the tribunal of Privy Councillors who are or have been superior court judges in Britain, the Dominions, or British possession; it is the final court of appeal from the courts of certain Commonwealth countries.

**judiciary** /dʒuˈdɪʃəri/, *adj., n., pl.* **-aries.** *–adj.* **1.** pertaining to judgment in courts of justice, or to courts or judges; judicial. *–n.* **2.** the judicial branch of government. **3.** the system of courts of justice in a country. **4.** the judges collectively.

**judicious** /dʒuˈdɪʃəs/, *adj.* **1.** using or showing judgment as to action or practical expediency; discreet, prudent, or politic. **2.** having, exercising, or showing good judgment; wise, sensible, or well-advised: *a judicious selection.* [F *judicieux,* from L *jūdicium* judgment] – **judiciously,** *adv.* – **judiciousness,** *n.*

**judo** /ˈdʒudoʊ/, *n.* a style of self-defence derived from jujitsu, employing less violent methods and emphasising the sporting element. [Jap.: lit., soft art]

**judoka** /ˈdʒudoʊka/, *n.* a competitor in a judo contest. [Jap.]

**judy** /ˈdʒudi/, *n. Colloq.* a woman, or girl. [familiar var. of *Judith,* woman's name]

**jug** /dʒʌg/, *n., v.,* **jugged, jugging.** *–n.* **1.** a vessel in various forms for holding liquids, commonly having a handle, often a spout or lip, and sometimes a lid. **2.** the contents of any such vessel. **3.** *U.S.* a deep vessel, usu. of earthenware, with a handle and a narrow neck stopped by a cork. **4.** *Colloq.* prison or gaol. **5.** *Colloq.* the music of a jug band. *–v.t.* **6.** to put into a jug. **7.** to stew or boil (meat) in a jug or jar. **8.** *Colloq.* to commit to gaol, or imprison. [? special use of *Jug,* hypocoristic var. of *Joan* or *Joanna,* woman's name]

**jugal** /ˈdʒugəl/, *adj.* of or pertaining to the cheek or the cheekbone. [L *jugālis,* from *jugum* a yoke]

**jugal bone** /ˈ– boʊn/, *n.* **1.** (in man) the cheekbone. **2.** a corresponding bone in animals.

**jugate** /ˈdʒugeɪt, -gət/, *adj.* having the leaflets in pairs, as a pinnate leaf. [L *jugātus,* pp., joined]

**jug band** /ˈdʒʌg bænd/, *n.* a light offshoot of jazz characterised by zany out-of-time singing and home-made instruments such as washing boards, jugs and other kitchen ware.

**jugged hare** /dʒʌgd ˈhɛə/, *n.* hare stewed, as in a stone pot.

**juggernaut** /ˈdʒʌgənɔt/, *n.* **1.** anything to which a person blindly devotes himself, or is cruelly sacrificed. **2.** any large, relentless, destructive force. *–v.i.* **3.** to proceed relentlessly. [from an idol of India, annually drawn on an enormous vehicle under whose wheels devotees are said to have thrown themselves to be crushed; Hind. *Jagannāth,* from Skt *Jagannātha* lord of the world]

**juggins** /ˈdʒʌgənz/, *n. Colloq.* a simpleton; naive person; fool. [orig. surname]

**juggle** /ˈdʒʌgəl/, *v.,* **-gled, -gling,** *n.* *–v.t.* **1.** to keep (several objects, as balls, plates, knives) in continuous motion in the air at the same time by tossing and catching. **2.** to manipulate or alter by artifice or trickery: *to juggle accounts.* *–v.i.* **3.** to perform feats of manual or bodily dexterity, such as tossing up and keeping in continuous motion a number of balls, plates, knives, etc. **4.** to use artifice or trickery. *–n.* **5.** the act of juggling; a trick; a deception. [ME *jogel(en),* from OF *jogler,* from L *joculārī* jest]

**juggler** /ˈdʒʌglə/, *n.* **1.** one who performs juggling feats, as with balls, knives, etc. **2.** one who deceives by trickery; a trickster. [ME *jugelour, jogeler,* from OF *jogleor,* from L *joculātor* jester]

**jugglery** /ˈdʒʌgləri/, *n., pl.* **-gleries.** **1.** the art or practice of a juggler. **2.** the performance of juggling feats. **3.** any trickery or deception.

**Jugoslav** /ˈjugəslav/, *n., adj.* →**Yugoslav.** – **Jugoslavic** /jugəˈslavɪk/, *adj.*

**Jugoslavia** /jugəˈslaviə/, *n.* →**Yugoslavia.** – **Jugoslavian,** *adj., n.*

**jugular** /ˈdʒʌgjulə/, *adj.* **1.** *Anat.* **a.** of or pertaining to the throat or neck. **b.** denoting or pertaining to any of certain large veins of the neck, esp. one (**external jugular vein**) collecting blood from the superficial parts of the head, or one (**internal jugular vein**) receiving blood from within the skull. **2.** (of a fish) having the pelvic fins at the throat, before the pectoral fins. *–n.* **3.** *Anat.* a jugular vein. [NL *jugulāris,* from L *jugulum* collarbone, throat, diminutive of *jugum* a yoke]

**jugulate** /ˈdʒʌgjuleɪt/, *v.t.,* **-lated, -lating.** **1.** to check or suppress (disease, etc.) by extreme measures. **2.** to cut the throat of; kill. **3.** to strangle. [L *jugulātus,* pp., slain] – **jugulation** /dʒʌgjuˈleɪʃən/, *n.*

**juice** /dʒus/, *n.* **1.** the liquid part of plant or animal substance. **2.** any natural fluid secreted by an animal body. **3.** any extracted liquid, esp. from a fruit. **4.** essence; strength. **5.** *Colloq.* **a.** electric power. **b.** petrol, fuel oil, etc., used to run an engine. **6.** *Colloq.* any alcoholic beverage. [ME *jus,* from OF, from L: broth] – **juiceless,** *adj.*

**juice-freak** /ˈdʒus-frɪk/, *n. Colloq.* one who seeks stimulation from alcohol rather than drugs.

**juicer** /ˈdʒusə/, *n.* appliance used to extract juice from fruit and vegetables.

**juicy** /ˈdʒusi/, *adj.,* **-cier, -ciest.** **1.** full of juice; succulent. **2.** interesting; vivacious; colourful; spicy. – **juicily,** *adv.* – **juiciness,** *n.*

**jujitsu** /dʒuˈdʒɪtsu/, *n.* a Japanese method of defending oneself without weapons in personal encounter, which employs the strength and weight of the opponent to overcome him. Also, **jiujitsu, jiujutsu, jujutsu.** [Jap.: soft (or pliant) art]

**juju** /ˈdʒudʒu/, *n.* (among native tribes of western Africa) **1.** some object venerated superstitiously and used as a fetish or amulet. **2.** the magical power attributed to such an object. **3.** a ban or interdiction effected by it. [Hausa]

**jujube** /ˈdʒudʒub/, *n.* **1.** the edible plumlike fruit of any of certain Old World trees of the genus *Zizyphus.* **2.** any tree producing this fruit. **3.** →**jube**[2]. [F, from ML *jujuba,* from LL *zīzyphum,* from Gk *zízyphon*]

**jukebox** /ˈdʒukbɒks/, *n.* a coin-operated record-player permitting selection of the record to be played. [Gullah *juke* wicked, bawdy (as in *juke house* brothel) + BOX[1]]

**Jul.,** July.

**julep** /ˈdʒuləp/, *n.* **1.** a sweet drink, variously prepared and sometimes medicated. **2.** *U.S.* mint julep. [ME, from OF, from Ar. *julāb,* from Pers. *gulāb* rosewater, julep]

**Julian calendar** /ˌdʒuliən ˈkæləndə/, *n.* the calendar established by Julius Caesar in 46 B.C. which fixed the length of the year at 365 days, with 366 days in every fourth year (leap year), and months similar to today's. Cf. **Gregorian calendar.**

**julienne** /dʒuliˈɛn/, *adj.* **1.** of vegetables, fruit, etc. prepared as a garnish by cutting in very thin strips about the length of a match stick. *–n.* **2.** a clear soup containing vegetables cut into thin strips or small pieces. [F, special use of *Julienne,* woman's name]

**July** /dʒəˈlaɪ/, *n., pl.* **-lies.** the seventh month of the year, containing 31 days. [ME *Julie,* OE *Julius,* from L; named after *Julius* Caesar, who was born in this month]

**jumble** /'dʒʌmbəl/, *v.*, **-bled, -bling,** *n.* *–v.t.* **1.** to mix in a confused mass; put or throw together without order. **2.** to muddle or confuse mentally. *–v.i.* **3.** to meet or come together confusedly; be mixed up. *–n.* **4.** a confused mixture; a medley. **5.** a state of confusion or disorder. **6.** Also, **jumbal.** a small, flat, sweet cake, usu. round, with a hole in the middle. [? b. JOIN and TUMBLE] – **jumbler,** *n.*

**jumble sale** /'– seɪl/, *n.* a sale of cheap miscellaneous articles, generally second-hand, in aid of charity.

**jumbo** /'dʒʌmboʊ/, *n., pl.* **-bos,** *adj. Colloq.* *–n.* **1.** an elephant. **2.** *Mining.* a drill carriage on which several drills for horizontal drilling are placed. **3.** *Mining.* a mobile scaffold to assist drilling in large headings. **4.** *Mining.* a drilling platform used in tunnelling. **5.** any very large intercontinental jet plane, esp. the Boeing 747. **6.** anything bigger than usual. *–adj.* **7.** very large: *a jumbo sale.* [named after *Jumbo,* an elephant at the London Zoo, subsequently sold to Phineas T. Barnum]

**jumbuck** /'dʒʌmbʌk/, *n. Colloq.* a sheep. [Aboriginal corruption of *jump up*]

**jump** /dʒʌmp/, *v.i.* **1.** to spring clear of the ground or other support by a sudden muscular effort; propel oneself forwards, backwards, upwards or downwards; leap. **2.** to move or go quickly: *she jumped into a taxi.* **3.** to rise suddenly or quickly: *he jumped from his chair.* **4.** to move suddenly or abruptly, as from surprise or shock; start: *the sudden noise made him jump.* **5.** *Draughts.* to capture an opponent's man by moving over it to an unoccupied square. **6.** to rise suddenly in amount, price, etc. **7.** to pass abruptly, ignoring intervening stages: *to jump to a conclusion.* **8.** to change suddenly: *the traffic lights jumped from green to red.* **9.** to move or change suddenly, haphazardly, or aimlessly: *she kept jumping from one thing to another without being able to concentrate.* **10.** (of a typewriter) to omit letters, etc., because of a defect. **11.** *Colloq.* (of a wound, etc.) to hurt; throb. **12.** *Contract Bridge.* to bid exceptionally and unnecessarily high in order to indicate additional strength. **13.** (of a computer) to leave the sequence of instructions in a program and start obeying a different sequence elsewhere in the program. **14.** **go jump (in the lake),** (an expression of annoyance or dismissal). **15.** **jump at,** accept eagerly; seize: *he jumped at the chance of a new job.* **16.** **jump down one's throat,** to speak suddenly and sharply to someone. **17.** **jump on or upon,** to scold; rebuke; reprimand. **18.** **jump out of one's skin,** to be frightened suddenly. **19.** **jump to it,** *Colloq.* to move quickly; hurry. *–v.t.* **20.** to leap or spring over: *to jump a stream.* **21.** to cause to jump or leap. **22.** to skip or pass over; bypass. **23.** (of a motor vehicle) to ignore or anticipate (a traffic light). **24.** *Chess.* to capture (an opponent's man) by moving over it to an unoccupied square. **25.** *U.S. Colloq.* to attack suddenly without warning. **26.** *Bridge.* to raise (the bid) by more than the necessary overcall. **27.** to abscond from or evade by absconding. **28.** **a.** to seize or occupy (a mining claim, etc.) on the ground of some flaw in the holder's title. **b.** to encroach on another's rights. **29.** (of a train) to spring off or leave (the track). **30.** **jump bail,** to abscond when at liberty following the payment of bail money. **31.** **jump the box,** to give evidence in the witness box. **32.** **jump the gun,** *Colloq.* to start prematurely; obtain an unfair advantage. **33.** **jump the point,** *Colloq.* to assume command of an establishment, situation, place of business etc. **34.** **jump the queue,** to overtake a queue; obtain something out of one's proper turn. **35.** **jump the rattler,** *Colloq.* to ride illegally on a freight train. *–n.* **36.** the act of jumping; a leap. **37.** a space or obstacle or apparatus cleared in a leap. **38.** a descent by parachute from an aeroplane. **39.** a sudden rise in amount, price, etc. **40.** a sudden upward or other movement of an inanimate object. **41.** an abrupt transition from one point or thing to another, with omission of what intervenes. **42.** *Colloq.* a head start in time or space; advantageous beginning. **43.** *Sport.* any of several athletic games which feature a leap or jump. **44.** *Films.* a break in the continuity of action due to a failure to match action between a long shot and a closer shot of the same scene. **45.** a sudden start, as from nervous excitement. **46.** (*pl.*) a physical condition characterised by such starts; restlessness; anxiety. **47.** *Colloq.* an act of coitus. **48.** **get the jump on,** take by surprise; get an advantage over. **49.** **for (or on) the (high) jump(s),** up for trial. **50.** **high jump,** execution by hanging. **51.** **one jump ahead,** in a position of advantage. **52.** **take a (running) jump at yourself,** *Colloq.* **a.** (an impolite dismissal indicating the speaker's wish to end the conversation). **b.** (an impolite instruction to a person to reconsider his attitude or performance). [apparently imitative]

**jump ball** /'– bɔl/, *n.* (in basketball, netball, etc.) a ball tossed between two opposing players by the referee.

**jump bid** /'– bɪd/, *n.* (in bridge) any bid which is higher than that needed to increase the bid made previously.

**jump cut** /'– kʌt/, *n.* (in films) a sudden change from one scene to another designed to produce a startling effect.

**jumped-up** /'dʒʌmpt-ʌp/, *adj. Colloq.* upstart; parvenu; conceited.

**jumper**[1] /'dʒʌmpə/, *n.* **1.** one who or that which jumps. **2.** a boring tool or device worked with a jumping motion. **3.** *Elect.* **a.** Also, **jumper lead.** a short length of conductor used to make a connection usu. temporary, between terminals, around a break in a circuit, or around an instrument. **b.** a section of conductor linking the coaches of an electric train. **4.** a kind of sled. **5.** *Mining Colloq.* one who usurps another miner's claim. [JUMP, *v.* + -ER[1]]

**jumper**[2] /'dʒʌmpə/, *n.* **1.** an outer garment, usu. of wool, for the upper part of the body; pullover, sweater, jersey. **2.** *Orig. U.S.* a pinafore frock. **3.** a loose, outer jacket, worn esp. by sailors. [F *juppe,* var. of *jupe* (cf. JUPON) + -ER[2]]

**jumper ant** /'dʒʌmpər ænt/, *n.* a reddish-black ant of the genus *Promyrmecia,* which has a painful bite.

**jumper leads** /'dʒʌmpə lidz/, *n.pl.* a pair of heavy jumpers used in starting a motor vehicle with a flat battery, by connecting this battery to a charged one. Also, **jump leads.**

**jumping bean** /'dʒʌmpɪŋ bin/, *n.* the seed of any of certain Mexican plants of the family Euphorbiaceae, which is inhabited by the larva of a small moth whose movements cause the seed to move about or jump.

**jumping jack** /'– dʒæk/, *n.* **1.** a small firework which is propelled as it explodes several times. **2.** a toy consisting of a jointed figure of a man which is made to jump, or go through various contortions, as by pulling a string attached to its limbs.

**jumping-off place** /dʒʌmpɪŋ-'ɒf pleɪs/, *n.* **1.** a place used as a starting point. **2.** *U.S.* an out-of-the-way place; the farthest limit of anything settled or civilised.

**jumping plant louse,** *n.* any of various psyllids.

**jumping spider** /'dʒʌmpɪŋ spaɪdə/, *n.* a small spider, *Cosmophasis micarioides,* found in Queensland and the islands of New Guinea, which pounces on its prey.

**jump-jet** /'dʒʌmp-dʒɛt/, *n.* →**STOL.**

**jumpmaster** /'dʒʌmpmastə/, *n.* one who controls parachutists from the time they enter the aircraft until they exit; stick commander.

**jump seat** /'dʒʌmp sit/, *n.* a small seat, often folding, as one placed near the exit door of an aircraft.

**jump shot** /'– ʃɒt/, *n.* (in basketball) a shot at the basket made by a player releasing the ball when he is at the top of a leap.

**jump-start** /'dʒʌmp-stat/, *v.t.* **1.** →**clutch-start** (def. 1). **2.** to start (a motor vehicle) by connecting its battery by means of jumper leads to the battery of another vehicle. *–n.* **3.** an instance of jump-starting.

**jumpsuit** /'dʒʌmpsut/, *n.* **1.** a close-fitting outer garment covering all of the body and the legs. **2.** a one-piece loose outer garment for a small child, combining a sleeved top and short or long trousers; all-in-one.

**jump turn** /'dʒʌmp tɜn/, *n.* a turn made in deep snow at low speeds, from a standstill position, when a skier jumps around the stocks placed together near the tip of the skis.

**jump-up** /'dʒʌmp-ʌp/, *n. Colloq.* →**escarpment.**

**jumpy** /'dʒʌmpi/, *adj.,* **jumpier, jumpiest.** **1.** characterised by or inclined to sudden, involuntary starts, esp. from nervousness, fear, excitement, etc. **2.** causing to jump or start. – **jumpiness,** *n.*

**Jun.,** **1.** June. **2.** junior.

**Junc.,** Junction.

**juncaceous** /dʒʌŋ'keɪʃəs/, *adj.* pertaining or belonging to, or resembling, the Juncaceae, or rush family of plants. [L *juncus* a rush + -ACEOUS]

**junction** /'dʒʌŋkʃən/, *n.* **1.** the act of joining; combination. **2.** the state of being joined; union. **3.** a place or station where railway lines meet or cross. **4.** a place of joining or meeting. **5.** *Electronics.* (in a transistor or other semiconductor device) a point or surface where two materials having different electrical properties are in contact. **6.** a cable linking two telephone exchanges. [L *junctio* a joining]

**junction box** /'– bɒks/, *n.* a box in which a connection is made between several electric circuits.

**junction rectifier** /– 'rɛktəfaɪə/, *n.* a rectifier consisting of two different semiconductors in contact.

**junction transistor** /– træn'zɪstə/, *n.* a transistor consisting of several different types of semiconductor material in contact with one another.

**juncture** /'dʒʌŋktʃə/, *n.* **1.** a point of time, esp. one made critical or important by a concurrence of circumstances. **2.** a critical state of affairs; a crisis; a critical moment. **3.** the line or point at which two bodies are joined; a joint or articulation; a seam. **4.** *Phonetics.* the transition between phonemes, especially as it applies to word and morpheme boundaries. The distinction between *an aim* and *a name* is maintained in English by different types of juncture. **5.** the act of joining. **6.** the state of being joined; junction. **7.** something by which two things are joined. [ME, from L *junctūra* joining, joint]

**June** /dʒun/, *n.* the sixth month of the year, containing 30 days. [ME; OE *Iuni*, from L *Jūnius;* named after the *Jūnius* gens of Rome]

**Juneberry** /'dʒunbɛri/, *n., pl.* **-ries.** →**serviceberry.**

**June bug** /'dʒun bʌg/, *n.* **1.** (in the northern United States) any of the large brown scarabaeid beetles of the genus *Phyllophaga* (*Lachnosterna*), which appear about June. **2.** (in the southern United States) a large, greenish scarabaeid beetle, *Cotinis nitida.* Also, **June beetle.**

**Jungian** /'jʊŋiən/, *adj.* **1.** of or pertaining to the theories of C. G. Jung, 1875-1961, psychiatrist and psychologist. *–n.* **2.** a follower of Jung or an advocate of his theories.

**jungle** /'dʒʌŋgəl/, *n.* **1.** wild land overgrown with dense, rank vegetation, often nearly impenetrable, as in tropical countries. **2.** a tract of such land. **3.** a tropical rainforest with thick, impenetrable undergrowth. **4.** anything confusing, perplexing, or in disorder. **5.** any place or situation characterised by a struggle for survival, ruthless competition, etc. [Hind. *jangal* desert, forest, from Skt *jangala* dry, desert]

**jungle bunny** /'– bʌni/, *n. Colloq.* (*derog.*) a name used by some white people to describe Aboriginals, Melanesians, Negroes, etc.

**jungle fever** /'– fivə/, *n.* a severe variety of malarial fever occurring in the East Indies and other tropical regions.

**jungle fowl** /'– faʊl/, *n.* **1.** →**scrub fowl. 2.** any of various East Indian gallinaceous birds of the genus *Gallus,* certain species of which are supposed to have given rise to the domestic fowl.

**jungle green** /– 'grin/, *n.* a dark, drab green colour, esp. as used for military uniforms

**jungle gym** /'– dʒɪm/, *n.* a three-dimensional structure of vertical and horizontal bars for children to play on; monkey bars. [Trademark]

**jungle juice** /'– dʒus/, *n. Colloq.* **1.** a rough alcoholic drink originally made by soldiers in New Guinea. **2.** any drink considered to be as rough.

**jungle kangaroo** /'– kæŋgə,ru/, *n.* →**agile wallaby.**

**jungle law** /– 'lɔ/, *n.* →**law of the jungle.**

**junior** /'dʒunjə/, *adj.* **1.** younger (often used, esp. as abbreviated *Jr* or *Jun.,* after the name of a person who is the younger of two persons of the same name, as a son having the same name as his father). **2.** of something designed for young people: *a junior text-book.* **3.** of more recent appointment or admission, as to an office or status; of lower rank or standing. **4.** *Law.* subordinate to preferred creditors, mortgagees, and the like. **5.** of later date; subsequent to. *–n.* **6.** a person who is younger than another. **7.** any minor or child, esp. a male. **8.** one who is of more recent entrance into, or of lower standing in, an office, class, profession, etc.; one employed as the subordinate of another. **9.** *Law.* any barrister who is not a Queen's Counsel. **10.** *Rowing.* an oarsman who has won an open rowing event in a clinker boat but not in a shell. **11.** an amateur wrestler not exceeding 48 kg in weight. [L, contraction of *juvenior,* compar. of *juvenis* young]

**junior college** /– 'kɒlɪdʒ/, *n. U.S.* a school taking pupils for their final two years of secondary schooling, in preparation for university courses, etc.

**junior heavyweight** /– 'hɛviweɪt/, *n.* a professional wrestler weighing between 83.461 and 88.904 kg.

**junior high school,** *n.* a secondary school providing courses for less than the full six years of secondary education.

**junior middleweight** /dʒunjə 'mɪdəlweɪt/, *n.* a professional boxer weighing between 66.678 and 69.853 kg.

**junior school** /'– skul/, *n.* **1.** →**junior high school. 2.** →**primary school.**

**junior welterweight** /– 'wɛltəweɪt/, *n.* a professional boxer weighing between 61.235 and 63.503 kg.

**juniper** /'dʒunəpə/, *n.* any of the coniferous evergreen shrubs or trees constituting the genus *Juniperus,* esp. *J. communis,* whose cones form purple berries used in making gin and in medicine as a diuretic, or *J. virginiana,* a North American species. [ME *junipere,* from L *jūniperus.* See GIN[1]]

**junk**[1] /dʒʌŋk/, *n.* **1.** any old or discarded material, as metal, paper, rags, etc. **2.** *Colloq.* anything that is regarded as worthless or mere trash. **3.** old cable or cordage used when untwisted for making gaskets, swabs, oakum, etc. **4.** hard salt meat used for food on shipboard. **5.** tissue in the sperm whale containing spermaceti. **6.** *Colloq.* any narcotic drug. *–v.t.* **7.** *Colloq.* to cast aside as junk, discard as no longer of use. [orig. uncert.]

**junk**[2] /dʒʌŋk/, *n.* a kind of sea-going ship used in Chinese and other waters, having square sails spread by battens, a high stern, and usu. a flat bottom. [Pg. *junco,* from Malay *jong, ajong,* apparently from Javanese *jong*]

junk[2]: Chinese junk

**junk art** /– 'at/, *n.* a style of art, consisting principally of assemblages and constructions made from urban debris, as scrapped metal, wood and rubber.

**junker** /'dʒʌŋkə/, *n.* →**jinker** (defs 1 and 2).

**Junker** /'jʊŋkə/, *n.* **1.** a member of a class of aristocratic landholders, esp. in East Prussia, strongly devoted to maintaining the social and political privileges of their group. **2.** a narrow-minded, haughty, overbearing member of the aristocracy of Prussia, etc. [G; in MHG *junc herre* young gentleman]

**junket** /'dʒʌŋkət/, *n.* **1.** a sweet custard-like food of flavoured milk curded with rennet. **2.** a feast or merrymaking; a picnic; a pleasure excursion. **3.** a trip, as by a legislative committee, official body, or an individual politician at public expense and ostensibly to obtain information. *–v.i.* **4.** to feast; picnic; go on a junket or pleasure excursion. **5.** to go on a junket (def. 3). [ME *jonket* basket made of rushes, *joncate* curded food made in a vessel of rushes, from OF *jonquette,* from *jonc* a rush, from L *juncus*] **– junketer,** *n.*

**junk food** /'dʒʌŋk fud/, *n.* food thought to be of little nutritional value, as hamburgers, chips, etc.

**junk-heap** /'dʒʌŋk-hip/, *n.* **1.** a rubbish tip; place where discarded objects are put. **2.** (*fig.*) the place to which unwanted or superannuated people are consigned.

**junkie** /'dʒʌŋki/, *n. Colloq.* a drug addict. Also, **junky.**

**junk shop** /'dʒʌŋk ʃɒp/, *n.* **1.** a shop selling second-hand goods, esp. of inferior quality. **2.** →**ship chandler.**

**junkyard** /'dʒʌŋkjad/, *n.* an open-air place where junk is stored.

**junnick** /'dʒʌnɪk/, *adj.* →**jonick.**

**Juno** /'dʒunoʊ/, *n.* a woman of imposing figure or appearance. [from *Juno,* an ancient Roman goddess, wife of Jupiter, presiding over marriage and women]

**junoesque** /dʒunoʊ'ɛsk/, *adj.* (of a woman) stately.

**junr,** junior.

**junta** /'dʒʌntə/, *n.* **1.** a small ruling group in a country, either elected or self-chosen, esp. one which has come to power after a revolution. **2.** a council. **3.** a deliberative or administrative council, esp. in Spain and Latin America. [Sp., from L *juncta,* fem. pp., joined]

**Jupiter** /'djupətə/, *n.* **1.** the supreme deity of the ancient Romans, the god of the heavens, manifesting himself esp. in atmospheric phenomena; Jove. **2.** the largest planet, fifth in order from the sun. [L, var. of *Jūppiter,* contraction of *Jovis pater* father Jove]

**jupon** /'ʒupɒn/, *n.* a close-fitting tunic, usu. padded and bearing heraldic arms, worn over armour. [ME *jupone,* from F *jupon,* from *jupe* jacket, from Ar. *jubbah*]

**jural** /'dʒʊərəl, dʒurəl/, *adj.* **1.** pertaining to law; legal. **2.** pertaining to rights and obligations. [L *jūs* right, law + -AL[1]] – **jurally,** *adv.*

**Jurassic** /dʒu'ræsɪk/, *adj.* **1.** pertaining to a period of the Mesozoic era, following the Cretaceous and preceding the Triassic. –*n.* **2.** the Jurassic period. [F *jurassique*]

**jurat** /'dʒurət/, *n.* **1.** *Law.* a certificate on an affidavit, by the officer, showing by whom, when, and before whom it was sworn to. **2.** a sworn officer; a magistrate; a member of a permanent jury. [ML *jūrātus,* lit., one sworn, *jūrātum,* neut., that which is sworn, properly pp. of L *jūrāre* swear]

**juridical** /dʒu'rɪdɪkəl/, *adj.* **1.** of or pertaining to the administration of justice. **2.** of or pertaining to law or jurisprudence; legal. Also, **juridic.** [L *jūridicus* relating to justice + -AL[1]] – **juridically,** *adv.*

**juridical days** /– 'deɪz/, *n. pl.* the days in court on which law is administered; days on which the court can lawfully sit.

**jurimetrics** /dʒurə'mɛtrɪks/, *n.* the practice of adopting scientific method in the study of legal matters. [L *juri(s)* of the law + *-metrics*] – **jurimetrician** /dʒurəmə'trɪʃən/, **jurimetricist,** *n.*

**juris.,** jurisprudence.

**jurisconsult** /'dʒurəskənsʌlt, 'dʒʊər-/, *n.* **1.** *Rom. and Civil Law.* one authorised to give legal advice. **2.** *Civil Law.* a master of the civil law. [L *jūrisconsultus* one skilled in the law]

**jurisdiction** /dʒurəs'dɪkʃən/, *n.* **1.** the right, power, or authority to administer justice by hearing and determining controversies. **2.** power; authority; control. **3.** the extent or range of judicial or other authority. **4.** the territory over which authority is exercised. [ME, from L *jūrisdictio* administration of the law, authority] – **jurisdictional,** *adj.* – **jurisdictionally,** *adv.*

**jurisprudence** /dʒurəs'prudns/, *n.* **1.** the science or philosophy of law. **2.** a body or system of laws. **3.** a department of law: *medical jurisprudence.* **4.** *Civil Law.* decisions of courts of appeal or other higher tribunals. [L *jūrisprūdentia* the science of the law] – **jurisprudential** /ˌdʒurəspru'dɛnʃəl/, *adj.*

**jurisprudent** /dʒurəs'prudnt/, *adj.* **1.** versed in jurisprudence. –*n.* **2.** one versed in jurisprudence.

**jurist** /'dʒurəst, 'dʒʊə-/, *n.* **1.** one who professes the science of law. **2.** one versed in the law. **3.** one who writes on the subject of law. [ML *jūrista,* from L *jūs* right, law]

**juristic** /dʒu'rɪstɪk/, *adj.* of or pertaining to a jurist or to jurisprudence; relating to law; juridical; legal. Also, **juristical.** – **juristically,** *adv.*

**juror** /'dʒʊərə, 'dʒurə/, *n.* **1.** one of a body of persons sworn to deliver a verdict in a case submitted to them; a member of any jury. **2.** one of the panel from which a jury is selected. **3.** *Obs.* one who has taken an oath or sworn allegiance. [ME *jurour,* from AF, from L *jūrātor* swearer]

**jury**[1] /'dʒʊəri, 'dʒuri/, *n., pl.* **-ries.** **1.** a body of persons sworn to render a verdict or true answer on a question or questions officially submitted to them. **2.** such a body selected according to law and sworn to inquire into or determine the facts concerning a cause or an accusation submitted to them and to render a verdict. **3.** a body of persons chosen to adjudge prizes, etc., as in a competition. [ME *juree,* from AF, from *jure* one sworn, from L *jūrāre* swear] – **juryless,** *adj.*

**jury**[2] /'dʒʊəri, 'dʒuri/, *adj. Naut.* makeshift, temporary, as for an emergency. [first found in *jury mast,* probably from OF *ajurie* relief, help, from L *adjūtāre* help]

**jury-box** /'dʒʊəri-bɒks, 'dʒuri-/, *n.* an enclosed space in a court of law where members of a jury sit.

**juryman** /'dʒʊərimən, 'dʒuri-/, *n., pl.* **-men** /-mən/. a member of a jury.

**jury mast** /'dʒʊəri mast, 'dʒuri/, *n.* a temporary mast replacing one that has been broken or carried away. [see JURY[2]]

**jury-rigged** /'dʒʊəri-rɪgd, 'dʒuri-/, *adj. Naut.* temporarily rigged. [see JURY[2]]

**jus**[1] /ʒus/, *n.* juice; gravy. [F, from L]

**jus**[2] /dʒʊs/, *n., pl.* **jura** /'dʒʊərə, 'dʒurə/. *Law.* **1.** a right. **2.** law as a system or in the abstract. [L: law, right]

**jus'** /dʒʌs, dʒəs/, *adj., adv.* contraction of **just.**

**jussive** /'dʒʌsɪv/, *adj. Gram.* **1.** expressing a mild command. The jussive mood occurs in the Semitic languages. –*n. Gram.* **2.** a jussive form or grammatical construction. [L *jussus,* pp., commanded + -IVE]

**just**[1] /dʒʌst/, *adj.* **1.** actuated by truth, justice, and lack of bias: *to be just in one's dealings.* **2.** in accordance with true principles; equitable; even-handed: *a just award.* **3.** based on right; rightful; lawful: *a just claim.* **4.** agreeable to truth or fact; true; correct: *a just statement.* **5.** given or awarded rightly, or deserved, as a sentence, punishment, reward, etc. **6.** in accordance with standards, or requirements; proper, or right: *just proportions.* **7.** (esp. in biblical use) righteous. **8.** actual, real, or genuine. –*adv.* **9.** within a brief preceding time, or but a moment before: *they have just gone.* **10.** exactly or precisely: *that is just the point.* **11.** by a narrow margin; barely: *it just missed the mark.* **12.** only or merely: *he is just an ordinary man.* **13.** *Colloq.* actually; truly; positively: *the weather is just glorious.* [ME, from L *justus* righteous]

**just**[2] /dʒʌst/, *n., v.i.* →**joust.** – **juster,** *n.*

**justice** /'dʒʌstəs/, *n.* **1.** the quality of being just; righteousness, equitableness, or moral rightness: *to uphold the justice of a cause.* **2.** rightfulness or lawfulness, as of a claim or title; justness of ground or reason: *to complain with justice.* **3.** the moral principle determining just conduct. **4.** conformity to this principle as manifested in conduct; just conduct, dealing, or treatment. **5.** the requital of desert as by punishment or reward. **6.** the maintenance or administration of law, as by judicial or other proceedings: *a court of justice.* **7.** judgment of persons or causes by judicial process: *to administer justice in a community.* **8.** a judicial officer; a judge or magistrate. **9. do justice to, a.** to render or concede what is due to (a person or thing, merits, intentions, etc.); treat or judge fairly. **b.** to exhibit (oneself) in a just light, as in doing something. **c.** to show just appreciation of (something) by action. **10.** (*cap.*) **a.** the title of certain judges, as judges of the High Court and Supreme Courts in Australia. **b.** the courtesy title of some other judges, as judges of the Federal courts in Australia. [ME *justise,* from OF, from L *justitia*]

**justice of the peace,** *n.* a person who by Crown appointment is a justice within a certain district for the conservation of the peace and for the execution of prescribed duties; he may act ministerially as by issuing a warrant, or in a preliminary investigation of indictable offences or judicially as in courts of petty sessions, and in civil summary proceedings. *Abbrev.:* J.P.

**justiceship** /'dʒʌstəsʃɪp/, *n.* the office of a justice.

**justiciable** /dʒʌs'tɪʃiəbəl/, *adj.* **1.** capable of being settled by a court of law. **2.** subject to the action of a court of law.

**justiciary** /dʒʌs'tɪʃəri/, *adj., pl.* **-ries.** of or pertaining to the administration of justice. [ML *justitiārius* judge, from L *justitia* justice]

**justifiable** /'dʒʌstəfaɪəbəl/, *adj.* capable of being justified; that can be shown to be, or can be defended as being, just or right; defensible. – **justifiability** /ˌdʒʌstəfaɪə'bɪləti/, **justifiableness,** *n.* – **justifiably,** *adv.*

**justification** /dʒʌstəfə'keɪʃən/, *n.* **1.** something that justifies; a defensive plea; an excuse; a justifying fact or circumstance. **2.** the act of justifying. **3.** the state of being justified. **4.** *Theol.* the act of God whereby man is made just, or free from the guilt of sin. **5.** *Print.* the equal spacing of words and lines to a given measure.

**justificatory** /'dʒʌstəfəkeɪtəri/, *adj.* serving to justify; affording justification. Also, **justificative.**

**justifier** /'dʒʌstəfaɪə/, *n.* one who or that which justifies.

**justify** /'dʒʌstəfaɪ/, *v.,* **-fied, -fying.** –*v.t.* **1.** to show (an act, claim, statement, etc.) to be just, right, or warranted: *the end justifies the means.* **2.** to defend or uphold as blameless, just, or right. **3.** declare guiltless; absolve; acquit. **4.** *Theol.* to declare (a person) free from the penalty of sin. **5.** *Print.* to adjust exactly; make (lines) of the proper length by spacing. *–v.i.* **6.** *Law.* **a.** to show a satisfactory reason or excuse for something done. **b.** to qualify as bail or surety. **7.** *Print.* to conform or fit exactly, as lines of type. [ME *justifie(n)*, from OF *justifier,* from LL *justificāre* act justly towards]

**justly** /ˈdʒʌstli/, *adv.* **1.** in a just manner; honestly; fairly. **2.** in conformity to fact or rule; accurately.

**justness** /ˈdʒʌstnəs/, *n.* **1.** the quality or state of being just, equitable, or right; lawfulness. **2.** conformity to fact or rule; correctness; exactness; accuracy.

**jut** /dʒʌt/, *v.,* **jutted, jutting,** *n.* *–v.i.* **1.** to extend beyond the main body or line; project; protrude (oft. fol. by *out*). *–n.* **2.** something that juts out; a projection or protruding point. [var. of JET[1], *v.*]

**jute** /dʒut/, *n.* **1.** a strong fibre used for making fabrics, cordage, etc., obtained from two East Indian plants of the family Tiliaceae, *Corchorus capsularis* and *C. olitorius.* **2.** either of these plants. **3.** any plant of the same genus. **4.** the coarse fabric woven from jute fibres; gunny. [Bengali *jhōto,* from Skt *jūta* braid of hair] **– jutelike,** *adj.*

**juvenal** /ˈdʒuvənəl/, *n.* the plumage stage of an altricial bird when it leaves the nest. [L *juvenālis,* var. of *juvenīlis* young, pertaining to youth]

**juvenescent** /dʒuvəˈnɛsənt/, *adj.* becoming youthful; growing young again; youthful. [L *juvenescens,* ppr., reaching the age of youth] **– juvenescence,** *n.*

**juvenile** /ˈdʒuvənaɪl/, *adj.* **1.** pertaining to, suitable for, characteristic of, or intended for young persons: *juvenile behaviour, juvenile books, a juvenile court.* **2.** young. **3.** inappropriately suggestive of the behaviour or sentiments of a young person; frivolous; idiotic. *–n.* **4.** a young person; a youth. **5.** *Theat.* **a.** a youthful male role. **b.** an actor who plays such parts. **6.** *Ornith.* a young bird in the stage when it has fledged, if altricial, or has replaced down of hatching, if precocial. **7.** a book for young people. **8.** a two-year old horse. **9.** →**juvenile handicap.** [L *juvenīlis* of youth] **– juvenilely,** *adv.* **– juvenileness,** *n.*

**juvenile court** /ˈ– kɔt/, *n.* a special court for the trial of children and young persons under a statutory age (commonly 18 years in Australia).

**juvenile delinquent** /– dəˈlɪŋkwənt/, *n.* a child or young adolescent given to antisocial behaviour, as vandalism, arson, etc., and beyond parental control. **– juvenile delinquency,** *n.*

**juvenile handicap** /– ˈhændikæp/, *n.* a restricted horserace for juveniles.

**juvenilia** /dʒuvəˈnɪliə/, *n.pl.* works, esp. writings, produced in youth. [L, neut. pl. of *juvenīlis* young]

**juvenility** /dʒuvəˈnɪləti/, *n., pl.* **-ties. 1.** juvenile state, character, or manner. **2.** *(pl.)* youthful qualities or performances. **3.** young persons collectively.

**juxta-,** a word element meaning 'near', 'close to', 'beside'. [combining form representing L *juxtā,* prep. and adv.]

**juxtapose** /dʒʌkstəˈpoʊz, ˈdʒʌkstəpoʊz/, *v.t.,* **-posed, -posing.** to place in close proximity or side by side.

**juxtaposition** /dʒʌkstəpəˈzɪʃən/, *n.* **1.** a placing close together. **2.** position side by side. [F, from L *juxtā* JUXTA- + *positio* a placing, position]

**Jy,** July.

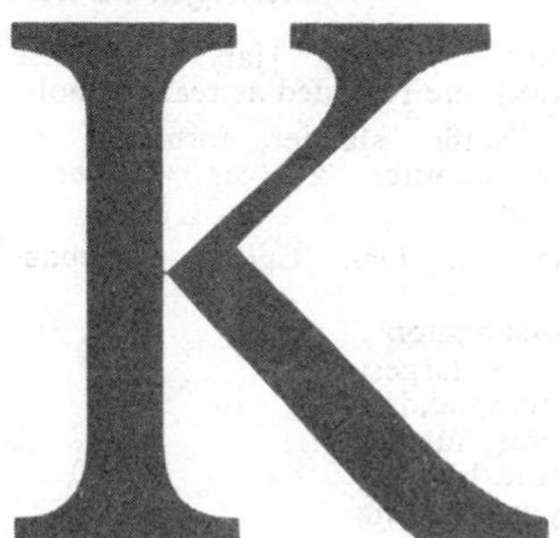

Kk Roman LECTURA **Kk** Sans Serif FOLIO 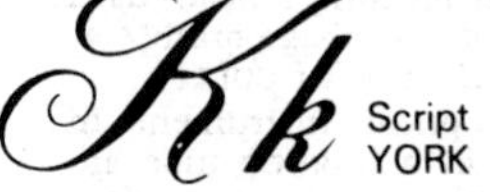 Script YORK  Decorative KOSTER

*Although there are numerous typefaces in the world they can be divided into four main classifications. These are:*

*ROMAN or SERIF. This typeface came into being from the technique of the Roman masons who, working in stone, finished off each letter with a serif or small stroke projecting from the top or bottom. This was done to correct any feeling of unevenness or imbalance they may have created in cutting the characters in stone.*

*SANS SERIF (without serif). This typeface is geometric in design and has straight-edged characters and lines of a regular thickness.*

*SCRIPT. Based on the movement of the hand, this typeface is often italicised or slanted, as if drawn by a brush or quill pen.*

*DECORATIVE. Any typeface that exaggerates the characteristics of any of the other three classifications to a degree that places it outside of them.*

*The dictionary entries in this book use a SANS SERIF typeface called Helvetica (set in a bold face for the head words) and a SERIF typeface Plantin (used throughout the body of the entries).*

**K, k** /keɪ/, *n., pl.* **K's** or **Ks, k's** or **ks.** a consonant, the 11th letter of the English alphabet.

**k,** **1.** kilo-. **2.** Boltzmann's constant.

**k.,** **1.** *Elect.* capacity. **2.** karat or carat. **3.** *Chess.* king. **4.** knit. **5.** killed. **6.** knot.

**K,** **1.** *Chem.* potassium. [L *kalium*] **2.** *Physics.* kelvin. **3.** *Chess.* king. **4.** Knight. **5.** equilibrium constant. **6.** Köchel. **7.** *Computers.* $2^{10}$ words, bytes or bits.

**K.,** *Bible.* Kings.

**ka** /ka/, *n.* the name given by ancient Egyptians to a presiding or second spirit supposed to be present in a man or statue. [Egypt]

**kA,** kiloamperes.

**Ka,** equilibrium constant of an acid and water mixture containing ions and un-ionised molecules.

**kabab** /kə'bæb/, *n.* →**kebab.**

**kabala** /kə'balə/, *n.* →**cabbala.** Also, **kabbala.**

**kabana** /kə'bænə, -'banə/, *n.* a smoked sausage, usu. long and thin.

**kabanossi** /kæbə'nɒsi/, *n.* →**cabanossi.**

**kabeljou** /'kabəljaʊ, 'kɒ-, -joʊ/, *n.* a large southern African marine food fish, *Otolinthus ruber*; salmon-bass. [Afrikaans, from D *kabeljauw* cod]

**kabob** /kə'bɒb/, *n.* →**kebab.**

**kabuki** /kə'buki/, *n.* a form of Japanese popular theatre, with stylised acting, music, and dancing, in which male actors play all dramatic roles.

**kadaicha magic** /kə'daɪtʃə mædʒɪk/, *n.* magic carried out by the kadaicha man; pointing the bone. [Aboriginal]

**kadaicha man** /'– mæn/, *n.* among tribal Aborigines, the man empowered to avenge a grievance held by a tribal member, by pointing the bone at the wrongdoer. Also, **kadaitja man, kurdaitcha man.**

**kadaicha shoes** /'– ʃuz/, *n.pl.* in certain central Australian Aboriginal tribes, shoes made of human hair, string and emu feathers, matted with human blood, worn by a man who has been chosen to avenge the death of someone (every death being supposedly due to the magic influence of some enemy) so that his footsteps may not be traced. Also, **kadaitja shoes, kurdaitcha shoes.**

kadaicha shoes

**kadi** /'kadi, 'keɪ-/, *n., pl.* **-dis.** →**cadi.**

**Kaffir** /'kæfə/, *n.* **1.** (*derog.*) a member of a South African Negroid race inhabiting parts of the Cape of Good Hope, Natal, etc. **2.** (*derog.*) any South African negro. **3.** a Bantu language. **4.** (*l.c.*) Also, **kaffir corn.** any of certain grain sorghums, varieties of *Sorghum bicolor,* with stout, short-jointed, leafy stalks, cultivated in South Africa. Also, **Kafir.** [Ar. *kāfir* unbeliever]

**Kaffir orange** /kæfər 'ɒrɪndʒ/, *n.* the fruit of a Portuguese East African tree with hard shell-like rind and brown glistening pulp, resembling but not related to the orange.

**Kafkaesque** /kæfkə'ɛsk/, *adj.* of, relating to, or similar to the writings of Franz Kafka, 1883-1924, Austrian novelist.

**kaftan** /'kæftæn/, *n.* →**caftan.**

**kafuffle** /kə'fʌfəl, -'fʊfəl/, *n. Colloq.* argument; commotion; rumpus. Also, **kafoofle, kerfuffle, kerfoofle.**

**kahawai** /'kahəwaɪ/, *n. N.Z.* →**Australian salmon.** [Maori]

**kahikatea** /kaɪkə'tiə/, *n.* a tall gymnospermous tree with evergreen, brownish green foliage, *Podocarpus dacrydiodes,* native to New Zealand, where it provides a valuable source of timber; white pine. [Maori]

**kahikatoa** /kaɪkə'toʊə/, *n. N.Z.* a tea-tree, *Leptospermum scoparium;* manuka. [Maori]

**kai** /kaɪ/, *n.* food; a meal. [Melanesian Pidgin *kaikai* food]

**Kaikoura** /kaɪ'kʊərə/, *adj.* of or pertaining to the major mountain-building episode in New Zealand, which reached its height at the end of the Tertiary period.

**kainga** /'kaɪŋə/, *n. N.Z.* a Maori village. [Maori]

**kainite** /'kaɪnaɪt, 'keɪ-/, *n.* a mineral double salt of magnesium sulphate and potassium chloride, $MgSO_4 \cdot KCl \cdot 3H_2O$; a source of potassium salts. [G *Kainit.* See CAINO-, -ITE[1]]

**kainogenesis** /kaɪnoʊ'dʒɛnəsəs/, *n.* →**cainogenesis.** –**kainogenetic** /,kaɪnoʊdʒə'nɛtɪk/, *adj.* –**kainogenetically** /,kaɪnoʊdʒə'nɛtɪkli/, *adv.*

**Kainozoic** /kaɪnoʊ'zoʊɪk, keɪ-/, *adj., n.* →**Cainozoic.**

**Kaiser** /'kaɪzə/, *n.* **1.** a German emperor. **2.** an Austrian emperor. **3.** *Hist.* a ruler of the Holy Roman Empire. **4.** (*l.c.*) an emperor; a Caesar. [G, replacing ME *caiser(e), keiser(e),* from Scand. (cf. Icel. *keisari*); replacing ME and OE *cāsere,* from L *Caesar*] –**kaisership,** *n.*

**kaka** /'kaka/, *n.* a New Zealand parrot, *Nestor meridionalis,* chiefly greenish or olive brown in colour. [Maori]

**kaka beak** /'– bik/, *n.* an evergreen shrub, *Clianthus puniceus,* with pinnate leaves and clusters of bright red, pointed flowers, native to New Zealand, but extensively cultivated; parrot's beak; glory pea.

**kakapo** /'kakəpoʊ/, *n.* a large, almost flightless, and now rare, nocturnal parrot, *Strigops habroptilus,* of New Zealand. [Maori *kaka* parrot + *po* night]

**kakemono** /kakə'moʊnoʊ/, *n., pl.* **-nos.** an upright Japanese wall picture, usu. long and narrow, painted on silk, paper or other material, and mounted on a roller. [Jap. *kake* hang + *mono* thing]

**kaki** /'kaki/, *n., pl.* **-kis. 1.** the Japanese persimmon tree. **2.** its fruit. [Jap.]

**kalamazoo** /'kæləməzu/, *n.* a four wheeled rail trolley pumped along by hand. [from *Kalamazoo,* a town in Michigan, U.S.]

**kale** /keɪl/, *n.* **1.** a plant of the family Cruciferae, *Brassica oleracea,* var. *acephala,* with leaves not forming a head, used as a potherb. **2.** *Scot.* cabbage. **3.** *Scot.* a cabbage broth. **4.** *U.S. Colloq.* money. Also, **kail.** [ME *cale,* var. of COLE]

**kaleidoscope** /kə'laɪdəskoʊp/, *n.* an optical instrument in which pieces of coloured glass, etc., in a rotating tube are shown by reflection in continually changing symmetrical forms. [Gk *kalós* beautiful + *eîdo(s)* form + -SCOPE]

**kaleidoscopic** /kəlaɪdə'skɒpɪk/, *adj.* **1.** of, pertaining to, or resembling a kaleidoscope. **2.** continually changing, in colour, pattern, relationship, etc. **3.** extremely complex; admitting of many and varied interpretations. Also, **kaleidoscopical.** – **kaleidoscopically,** *adv.*

**kalends** /'kæləndz/, *n.pl.* →**calends.**

**kali** /'kæli, 'keɪli/, *n., pl.* **kalis.** →**glasswort.** [Ar. *qalī* (*qilā*). See ALKALI]

**kalian** /kæli'an/, *n.* an Eastern pipe in which the smoke is drawn through water; hookah. [Pers.]

**kaliph** /'keɪləf, 'kæl-/, *n.* →**caliph.**

**kalmia** /'kælmiə/, *n.* any plant of the North American genus *Kalmia,* comprising evergreen shrubs with showy flowers, as *K. latifolia,* the mountain laurel. [NL, after P. *Kalm,* 1715-79, Swedish botanist]

**kalong** /'kalɒŋ/, *n.* any of the large fruit-bats or flying foxes, belonging to the genus *Pteropus.* [Malay]

**kalpak** /'kælpæk/, *n.* a large black cap of sheepskin or other heavy material, worn by Armenians, Turks, etc. Also, **calpac.** [Turk. *qālpāq*]

**kalsomine** /'kælsəmaɪn/, *n., v.,* **-mined, -mining.** *–n.* **1.** a white or tinted wash for walls, ceilings, etc. *–v.t.* **2.** to wash or cover with kalsomine. Also, **calcimine.** [orig. uncert.]

**kamacite** /'kæməsaɪt/, *n.* an iron-nickel alloy found in meteorites.

**kamahi** /'kaməhi/, *n.* a New Zealand forest tree, *Weinmannia racemosa.* [Maori]

**kamala** /kə'malə, 'kæmələ/, *n.* a powder from the capsules of an East Indian tree, *Mallotus philippinensis,* used as a yellow dye and in medicine as an anthelmintic. [Skt]

**kame** /keɪm/, *n.* **1.** a lead rod for framing a pane in a lattice or stained-glass window. **2.** *Phys. Geog.* a ridge or mound of detrital material, esp. of stratified sand and gravel left by a retreating icesheet. [var. of COMB[1]]

**Kameraigal** /'kæməraɪgʌl/, *n.* an Australian Aboriginal language formerly spoken in the Sydney region; related dialects probably covered an area from the north side of Port Jackson up as far as the Hunter. Also, **Cammeraygal.**

**Kamikaze** /kæmə'kazi/, *n.* **1.** a member of a corps in the Japanese airforce in World War II whose mission was to crash their aircraft, loaded with explosives, into an enemy target, as a ship. **2.** (*l.c.*) *Colloq.* (in surf-riding) a deliberate wipe-out. *–adj.* **3.** of or pertaining to a Kamikaze. **4.** (*l.c.*) *Colloq.* (*joc.*) dangerous; suicidal: *his kamikaze driving.* [Jap.: divine wind]

**Kamilaroi** /'kæmələrɔɪ/, *n.* an Australian Aboriginal language of the central north-west of New South Wales, formerly stretching from the Liverpool Ranges to the Queensland border.

**kampong** /'kæmpɒŋ, kæm'pɒŋ/, *n.* a village or settlement in Malaysia. [Malay]

**Kampuchea** /kæmpə'tʃiə/, *n.* a country in south-east Asia. Official name: **Democratic Kampuchea.** Formerly, **Cambodia.**

**kana** /'kanə/, *n.* the Japanese syllabary. [Jap.: lit., false symbols, so called because KANJI are regarded as real symbols]

**kanaka** /kə'nækə/, *n.* **1.** a Pacific islander, formerly one brought to Australia as a labourer. **2.** (*cap.*) a native Hawaiian. [Hawaiian: lit., man]

**Kanakalander** /kə'nækəlændə/, *n. Obs. Colloq.* →**Queenslander.**

**kanga** /'kæŋgə/, *n. Colloq.* →**kangaroo**[2].

**kangaroo**[1] /kæŋgə'ru/, *n.* **1.** the largest members of the family Macropodidae, herbivorous marsupials of the Australian region, with powerful hind legs developed for leaping, a sturdy tail serving as a support and balance, a small head, and very short forelimbs. The recognised kangaroo types are: **a.** the great grey or forester, *Macropus giganteus.* **b.** the western grey or western forester, *M. fulginosus.* **c.** the wallaroo or euro, *M. robustus.* **d.** the antelope kangaroo, *M. antilopinus.* **e.** the red or plains kangaroo, *Megaleia rufa.* **2.** (*cap.*) a member of an Australian representative Rugby League team. **3.** (*pl.*) *Brit. Stock Exchange. Colloq.* Australian mining and other shares. *–v.t.* **4.** *Colloq.* to release the clutch of a car unevenly so that the car moves forward in a series of jerks. *–v.i.* **5.** *Colloq.* (of a car) to move forward in a jerky manner. **6.** *Colloq.* to squat over a toilet seat, while avoiding contact with it. [Aboriginal]

kangaroo[1]

**kangaroo**[2] /kæŋgə'ru/, *n. Prison Colloq.* a warder. Also, **kanga.** [rhyming slang, *kangaroo* SCREW (def. 12)]

**kangaroo apple** /'– æpəl/, *n.* either of two shrubs, *Solanum aviculare* and *S. laciniatum,* which have berries which are edible when completely ripe, but contain the toxic alkaloid solanine when immature.

**kangaroo bar** /'– ba/, *n.* a heavy metal bar in front of the radiator of a motor vehicle which protects the vehicle if it strikes kangaroos or stock.

**kangaroo closure** /– 'kloʊʒə/, *n.* a means of closing parliamentary debate in which the speaker restricts discussion to only those amendments which he selects.

**kangaroo court** /– 'kɔt/, *n. Chiefly Brit., U.S. Colloq.* an unauthorised or irregular court conducted with disregard for or perversion of legal procedure, as a mock court by prisoners in a gaol, or by trade unionists in judging workers who do not follow union decisions.

**kangaroo dog** /'– dɒg/, *n.* a dog bred for kangaroo-hunting.

**kangaroo drive** /'– draɪv/, *n.* an organised expedition to hunt for and shoot kangaroos, usu. conducted at night, with the aid of spotlights.

kangaroo grass

**kangaroo fence** /kæŋgə'ru fɛns/, *n.* a high fence, about 2.5 metres in height, built to keep out kangaroos from a rural property. Also, **marsupial fence.**

**kangaroo grass** /'– gras/, *n.* **1.** a tall grass, *Themeda australis,* widespread in forest and grassland in Australia and providing useful fodder. **2.** any of several other similar Australian grasses.

**kangaroo-paw** /kæŋgə'ru-pɔ/, *n.* any of several plants of the western Australia genus, *Anigozanthos,* having an inflorescence bearing a resemblance to the paw of a kangaroo, esp. *A. manglesii,* red and green kangaroo-paw, the floral emblem of Western Australia.

kangaroo-paw

**kangaroo rat** /kæŋgə'ru ræt/, *n.* any of various small jumping rodents of the family Heteromyidae, of Mexico and the western United States, such as those of the genus *Dipodomys.*

**kangaroo route** /'– rut/, *n.* the Qantas air-route between Sydney and London. [orig. because of the long hop necessitated by the capture of Singapore during World War II]

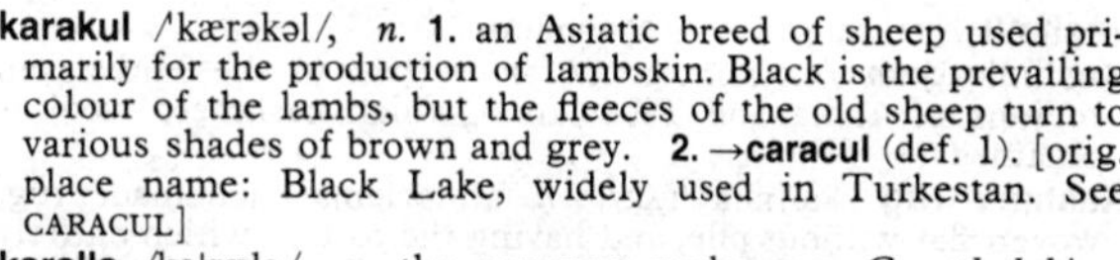

kangaroo rat

**kangaroo-tail soup** /ˌkæŋgəru-teɪl 'sup/, *n.* a soup made from kangaroo-tail meat, regarded as a delicacy.

**kangaroo-thorn** /kæŋgə'ru-θɔn/, *n.* an Australian species of wattle, *Acacia armata,* which forms a prickly hedge.

**kanji** /'kændʒi/, *n.* a system of Japanese writing using Chinese-derived characters. [Jap. from *kan* Chinese + *ji* ideograph]

**kanooka** /kæ'nukə/, *n.* a tree of moist coastal forests of eastern Australia, *Tristania laurina*; water-gum.

**kantar** /kæn'ta/, *n.* (in Muslim countries) a unit of weight corresponding to the hundredweight, but varying in different localities. [Ar. *quintār,* from L *centenārium* one hundred (lbs) weight. See QUINTAL]

**Kantian** /'kæntiən/, *adj.* **1.** of or pertaining to Immanuel Kant or Kantianism. *–n.* **2.** a follower of Kant. [from Immanuel *Kant,* 1724-1804, German philosopher]

**Kantianism** /'kæntiənɪzəm/, *n.* the doctrine of Immanuel Kant that every attribute is merely a mode in which the mind is affected, and has no application to a thing in itself. A thing in itself is unthinkable, and ideas are of two kinds only, those presented in sensation, and those introduced in the process of thinking. Religious and strict moral ideas are, however, admitted as regulative principles.

**kanuka** /kə'nukə/, *n. N.Z.* a tea-tree, *Leptospermum ericoides;* manuka.

**kaoliang** /keɪoʊli'æŋ/, *n.* one of the varieties of grain sorghum, *Sorghum bicolor.* [Chinese (Mandarin) from *kao* tall + *liang* millet]

**kaolin** /'keɪələn/, *n.* **1.** a rock composed essentially of clay minerals of the kaolinite group. **2.** a fine white clay used in the manufacture of porcelain and used medically as an absorbent; china clay. [F, from Chinese *Kao-ling* high hill, name of a mountain in China which yielded the first kaolin sent to Europe]

**kaolinite** /'keɪələnaɪt/, *n.* hydrated aluminium disilicate, $Al_2Si_2O_5(OH)_4$, a very common mineral, the commonest constituent of kaolin.

**kaomagma** /keɪoʊ'mægmə/, *n.* (*also cap.*) an intestinal adsorbent preparation containing kaolin and aluminium hydroxide for controlling diarrhoea. [Trademark]

**Kaomycin** /keɪoʊ'maɪsən/, *n.* a flavoured suspension containing neomycin and kaolin to control bacterial diarrhoea. [Trademark]

**kaon** /'keɪɒn/, *n. Physics.* a K-meson. [*ka* name of letter K + (MES)ON]

**kapai** /'kæpaɪ/, *interj. N.Z. Colloq.* **1.** (an exclamation of pleasure, approval, etc.) *–adj.* **2.** good, agreeable. [Maori]

**Kapellmeister** /kæ'pɛlmaɪstə/, *n., pl.* **-ter. 1.** choirmaster. **2.** a conductor of an orchestra. **3.** bandmaster. [G, from *Kapelle* chapel (choir) + *Meister* master]

**kapok** /'keɪpɒk/, *n.* **1.** the silky down which invests the seeds of several trees in the family Bombacaceae, as *Ceiba pentandra* of the East Indies, Africa, and tropical America, which is used for stuffing pillows, etc., and for sound insulation. **2.** a tree bearing this or similar down. [Malay *kāpoq*]

**kappa** /'kæpə/, *n.* the tenth letter of the Greek alphabet (K, ϰ).

**kaput** /kæ'pʊt, kə-/, *adj. Colloq.* **1.** smashed; ruined. **2.** broken, not working. [G]

**karabiner** /kærə'binə/, *n.* (in mountaineering) a springloaded metal clip designed for joining ropes together.

**karaka** /kə'rækə/, *n.* a small evergreen coastal tree of New Zealand, *Corynocarpus laevigata,* family Anacardiaceae, having very poisonous seeds and bright orange fruits. Also, **karaka-berry.** [Maori]

**karakul** /'kærəkəl/, *n.* **1.** an Asiatic breed of sheep used primarily for the production of lambskin. Black is the prevailing colour of the lambs, but the fleeces of the old sheep turn to various shades of brown and grey. **2.** →**caracul** (def. 1). [orig. place name: Black Lake, widely used in Turkestan. See CARACUL]

**karalla** /kə'rælə/, *n.* the common wedge-pea, *Gompholobium huegelii,* of south-eastern Australia.

**karamu** /'karəmu/, *n.* any of the New Zealand shrubs of the genus *Coprosma,* esp. *C. robusta.* [Maori]

**karat** /'kærət/, *n.* →**carat.**

**karate** /kə'rati/, *n.* a method of defensive fighting in which hands, elbows, feet, and knees are the only weapons used. [Jap.: lit., empty hand]

**karee** /kə'ri/, *n.* a small tree, *Rhus gueinzii,* of the family Anacardiaceae, found in southern Africa. [Afrikaans]

**Karitane** /'kærətani/, *adj.* **1.** of or pertaining to a nurse trained in the care of mothers and newborn children according to the principles of the Plunket Society. **2.** of or pertaining to a nursery home or hospital run on those principles. [from *Karitane,* a town in the South Island of N.Z., headquarters of the Plunket Society]

**karkalla** /ka'kælə/, *n.* a prostrate succulent plant, *Carpobrotus rossii,* of southern Australia.

**karma** /'kamə/, *n.* **1.** *Hinduism, Buddhism, etc.* the cosmic operation of retributive justice, according to which a person's status in life is determined by his own deeds in a previous incarnation. **2.** *Theosophy.* the doctrine of inevitable consequence. **3.** fate; destiny. [Skt: deed, action] – **karmic,** *adj.*

**karma-yoga** /'kamə-joʊgə/, *n.* yoga through actions performed unselfishly, for the welfare of others. [Skt *karman* work, office + YOGA]

**karo** /'karoʊ/, *n., pl.* **-ros.** an evergreen shrub or small tree of New Zealand, *Pittosporum crassifolium,* family Pittosporaceae, having red flowers and hairy fruit and leaves. [Maori]

**kaross** /kə'rɒs/, *n.* a mantle or blanket of animal skin worn by tribesmen in southern Africa. [Afrikaans *karos,* ? from Hottentot]

**karrabul** /'kærəbʊl/, *n.* the northern nail-tailed wallaby of northern Australia, *Onychogalea unguifera.*

**karri** /'kæri/, *n., pl.* **-ris.** a rapidly growing western Australian tree, *Eucalyptus diversicolor,* family Myrtaceae, valuable for its hard, durable timber. [Aboriginal]

**karst** /kast/, *n.* a barren region composed of limestone or dolomite and characterised by underground drainage systems, sinkholes, gorges, etc. [named after the *Karst* region in NW Yugoslavia]

**kart** /kat/, *n.* →**go-kart.**

**karyo-,** a word element meaning 'nucleus of a cell'. [Gk, combining form of *káryon* nut, kernel]

**karyogamy** /kæri'ɒgəmi/, *n.* the fusion of the nuclei of cells, as in fertilisation. – **karyogamic** /kæriə'gæmɪk/, *adj.*

**karyokinesis** /ˌkærioʊkə'nisəs, -kaɪ-/, *n.* **1.** →**mitosis. 2.** the series of active changes which take place in the nucleus of a living cell in the process of division. [KARYO- + Gk *kī́nēsis* movement] – **karyokinetic** /ˌkærioʊkə'nɛtɪk, -kaɪ-/, *adj.*

**karyolymph** /'kærioʊlɪmf/, *n.* the transparent or translucent fluid in a nucleus.

**karyolysis** /kæri'ɒləsəs/, *n.* the dissolution of a cell nucleus. – **karyolitic** /kæriə'lɪtɪk/, *adj.*

**karyomitome** /kæri'ɒmətoʊm/, *n.* the network or reticulum in the nucleus of a cell. [KARYO- + Gk *mítos* thread + *-ome,* var. of -OMA]

**karyoplasm** /'kærioʊplæzəm/, *n.* the substance of the nucleus of a cell. – **karyoplasmic** /kærioʊ'plæzmɪk/, *adj.*

**karyosome** /'kæriəsoʊm/, *n.* any of certain irregular or spherical bodies observed in and supposed to be in a portion of the netlike structure in the nucleus of a cell. [KARYO- + -SOME[3]]

**karyotin** /kæri'oʊtən/, *n.* nuclear material; chromatin. [Gk *karyōtós* nutlike + -IN[2]]

**karyotype** /'kæriətaɪp/, *n.* the appearance (size, shape, and number) of the chromosomes in a cell.

**kasbah** /'kæzba/, *n.* the older, native quarter of a North African town. Also, **casbah.**

**kasher** /'kaʃə/, *adj., n.* →**kosher.**

i = peat ɪ = pit ɛ = pet æ = pat a = part ɒ = pot ʌ = putt ɔ = port ʊ = put u = pool ɜ = pert ə = apart aɪ = buy eɪ = bay ɔɪ = boy aʊ = how oʊ = hoe ɪə = here ɛə = hair ʊə = tour g = give θ = thin ð = then ʃ = show ʒ = measure tʃ = choke dʒ = joke ŋ = sing j = you õ = Fr. bon

**kashmir** /kæʃ'mɪə/, *n.* →**cashmere.**

**Kashmir goat** /kæʃmɪə 'goʊt/, *n.* a goat of the Himalayan regions of India and Tibet from which cashmere wool is obtained.

**Kashmir rug** /kæʃmɪə 'rʌg/, *n.* an oriental handmade rug, woven flat without pile, and having the pattern which entirely covers its surface embroidered with coloured yarns. [from *Kashmir,* an area in NW India and NE Pakistan]

**kashrus** /'kæʃrus/, *n.* **1.** the body of dietary laws prescribed for Jews. *–adj.* **2.** fitness for use according to these laws. Also, **kashrut** /'kæʃrut/.

**kasseri** /'kæsəri/, *n.* a cheese suitable for grating and cooking, which can be eaten fresh or matured, sold in waxen loaves.

**kat** /kæt, kat/, *n.* an evergreen shrub, *Catha edulis,* of North Africa and Arabia, the leaves of which are chewed or prepared into a drink as a narcotic. Also, **khat, qat.** [Ar. *qat*]

**kata-,** variant of **cata-.** Also, **kat-, kath-.**

**katabatic** /kætə'bætɪk/, *adj.* (of winds and air currents) blowing downhill, as during the night when air in the upper slopes is cooled by radiation and so becomes denser.

**katabolism** /kə'tæbəlɪzəm/, *n.* →**catabolism.**

**Kath** /kæθ/, *n. Colloq.* a long period of time, esp. a long gaol sentence. Also, **Kathleen Mavourneen.** [from the song *Kathleen Mavourneen,* the refrain of which is *It may be for years, it may be forever*]

**kathode** /'kæθoʊd/, *n.* →**cathode.**

**kation** /'kætaɪən/, *n.* →**cation.**

**katipo** /'kætɪpoʊ/, *n.* a venomous New Zealand spider, *Latrodectus katipo,* closely related to the red-back spider. [Maori]

**katunga** /kə'tʌŋgə/, *n.* →**quandong.**

**katydid** /'keɪtidɪd/, *n.* any of the large, usu. green, long-horned American grasshoppers of the family Tettigoniidae, known for the loud note of the males of some species, notably *Platyphyllum concavum.* [imitative of the sound made]

**kauri** /'kaʊri/, *n., pl.* **-ris. 1.** a tall coniferous tree, *Agathis australis,* of New Zealand, yielding a valuable timber and a resin. **2.** its wood. **3.** →**kauri gum. 4.** any of various other trees of the genus *Agathis,* as Queensland kauri, *A. robusta.* [Maori]

**kauri gum** /'– gʌm/, *n.* the resin, used in making varnish, which exudes from the thick bark of the kauri. Masses weighing as much as 45 kg are found in soil where the trees have grown. Also, **kauri copal, kauri resin.**

**kava** /'kavə/, *n.* **1.** a Polynesian shrub, *Piper methysticum,* of the pepper family. Its root has aromatic and pungent qualities. **2.** a fermented, intoxicating beverage made from the roots of the kava. [Polynesian]

**kawaka** /'kawaka/, *n. N.Z.* →**arbor vitae** (def. 2). [Maori]

**kawakawa** /'kawəkawə/, *n. N.Z.* →**peppertree** (def. 2). [Maori]

**kayak** /'kaɪæk/, *n.* **1.** an Eskimo hunting craft with a skin cover on a light framework, made watertight by flexible closure round the waist of the occupant. **2.** any of various light canoes in imitation of this. Also, **kaiak.** [Eskimo]

Eskimo kayak

**kayo** /'keɪoʊ/, *n., pl.* **-os,** *v.,* **-oed, -oing.** *Colloq. –n.* **1.** →**knockout.** *–v.t.* **2.** to knock (someone) out. [pronunciation of the initial letters in *knock-out*]

**kazak** /kʌ'zʌk/, *n.* a Caucasian rug, usu. rich and striking in colour, featuring large geometric designs, with a thick pile, and very durable. [Turk. *Kazakh,* a member of a Turkic race in central Asia]

**kazoo** /kə'zu/, *n.* a short plastic or metal tube with a membrane-covered side hole, into which a person sings or hums; mirliton; Tommy talker. Also, **gazoo.** [imitative]

**Kb,** equilibrium constant of a base and water mixture containing ions and un-ionised molecules.

**K.B.** /keɪ 'bi/, **1.** *Chess.* king's bishop. **2.** Knight Bachelor.

**K.B.E.** /keɪ bi 'i/, Knight (Commander of the Order) of the British Empire.

**kc.,** kilocycle; kilocycles.

**K.C.** /keɪ 'si/, **1.** King's Counsel. **2.** Knight Commander.

**K.C.B.** /keɪ si 'bi/, Knight Commander of the Bath.

**K.C.M.G.** /keɪ si ɛm 'dʒi/, Knight Commander of the Order of St Michael and St George.

**K.C.V.O.** /keɪ si vi 'oʊ/, Knight Commander of the (Royal) Victorian Order.

**kd,** killed.

**kea** /'kiə/, *n.* a large, greenish New Zealand parrot, *Nestor notabilis.* [Maori]

**kebab** /kə'bæb/, *n.* →**shish kebab.** Also, **kabob, cabob, kabab, kebob.** [Ar. *kabāb*]

**Kechua** /'kɛtʃwə/, *n.* →**Quechua.**

**keck**[1] /kɛk/, *v.i.* **1.** to retch; be nauseated. **2.** to feel or show disgust or strong dislike. [akin to CHOKE]

**keck**[2] /kɛk/, *n.* any of several white-flowered, coarse, perennial, umbelliferous herbs, esp. cow-parsley and hogweed. [backformation from *kecks,* var. of Brit. d. *kex,* taken as pl.]

**keckle** /'kɛkəl/, *v.t.,* **-led, -ling.** *Naut.* to wind old rope round (a cable or hawser) as a protection against chafing. [orig. unknown] – **keckling,** *n.*

**ked** /kɛd/, *n.* the sheep tick.

**kedge** /kɛdʒ/, *v.,* **kedged, kedging,** *n. –v.t.* **1.** to warp or pull (a ship, etc.) along by means of a rope attached to an anchor. *–v.i.* **2.** to move by being pulled along with the aid of an anchor. *–n.* **3.** Also, **kedge anchor.** a small anchor used in kedging. [ME *cagge(n)* warp, fasten]

**kedgeree** /kɛdʒə'ri/, *n.* a dish of rice, cooked with white or smoked fish. [Hindi *khicari*]

**keef** /ki'ɛf/, *n.* →**kef** (def. 2).

**keel**[1] /kil/, *n.* **1.** a longitudinal timber, or combination of timbers, iron plates, or the like, extending along the middle of the bottom of a vessel from stem to stem and supporting the whole frame. **2.** a ship. **3.** a part corresponding to a ship's keel in some other structure, as in an aircraft fuselage. **4.** *Bot., Zool.* a longitudinal ridge, as on a leaf or bone; a carina. **5.** the prominent breast-bone of poultry and other birds, and of certain dogs, as the dachshund. **6. on an even keel,** in a steady or balanced state or manner. *–v.t.* **7.** to upset (a boat) so as to bring the wrong side or part uppermost. *–v.i.* **8.** (of a boat) to turn or roll on the keel (fol. by *over*). **9. keel over,** *Colloq.* to collapse suddenly. [ME *kele,* from Scand.; cf. Icel. *kjölr*]

**keel**[2] /kil/, *n.* **1.** →**keelboat. 2.** a quantity of coal, etc., sufficient to fill a keel. [ME *kele,* from MD *kiel;* c. OE *cēol* ship]

**keel**[3] /kil/, *n.* a fatal disease of domestic ducks. [special use of KEEL[1]]

**keel**[4] /kil/, *n. Brit.* **1.** a variety of red ochre used for marking sheep, etc.; ruddle. *–v.t.* **2.** to mark (sheep) with keel. [ME *keyle;* cf. Gael. *cīl*]

**keelage** /'kilɪdʒ/, *n.* formerly, dues paid by a vessel to a port owner for occupying a berth or anchorage.

**keelboat** /'kilboʊt/, *n.* a sailing yacht having an external heavy keel, the weight being provided to hold up the sails against the wind. Also **keeler, keel.**

**keelhaul** /'kilhɔl/, *v.t.* **1.** *Naut.* to haul (a person) under the keel of a vessel, as for punishment. **2.** *Colloq.* to reprimand severely. [D *kielhalen,* from *kiel* keel + *halen* haul]

**Keeling Islands** /,kilɪŋ 'aɪləndz/, *n.* →**Cocos Islands.**

**keelson** /'kɛlsən, 'kil-/, *n.* a strengthening line of timbers or iron plates in a ship, above and parallel with the keel. Also, **kelson.** [KEEL[1]; orig. obscure]

**keen**[1] /kin/, *adj.* **1.** sharp, or so shaped as to cut or pierce substances readily: *a keen blade.* **2.** sharp, piercing, or biting: *a keen wind, keen satire.* **3.** characterised by strength and distinctness of perception, as the ear or hearing, the eye, sight, etc. **4.** having or showing great mental penetration or acumen: *keen reasoning.* **5.** animated by or showing competitiveness: *keen prices.* **6.** intense, as feeling, desire, etc. **7.** ardent; eager (oft. fol. by *about, for,* etc., or an infinitive). **8.** having a fondness or devotion (for) (fol. by *on*). [ME *kene,* OE *cēne,* c. G *kühn* bold] – **keenly,** *adv.* – **keenness,** *n.*

**keen**[2] /kin/, *n.* **1.** a wailing lament for the dead. *–v.i.* **2.** to wail in lamentation for the dead. [Irish *caoine,* from *caoinim* I lament] – **keener,** *n.*

**keep** /kip/, *v.,* **kept, keeping,** *n. –v.t.* **1.** to maintain in one's action or conduct: *to keep watch, step, or silence.* **2.** to cause to continue in some place, position, state, course, or action specified: *to keep a light burning.* **3.** to maintain in condition or order, as by care and labour. **4.** to hold in custody or under guard, as a prisoner; detain; prevent from coming or going. **5.** to have habitually in stock or for sale. **6.** to maintain in one's service or for one's use or enjoyment. **7.** to associate with: *to keep bad company.* **8.** to have the charge or custody of. **9.** to withhold from the knowledge of others: *to keep a secret.* **10.** to withhold from use; reserve. **11.** to restrain: *for heaven's sake keep him from laughing.* **12.** to maintain by writing, as entries, etc.: *to keep a diary.* **13.** to record (business transactions, etc.) regularly: *to keep records.* **14.** to observe; pay obedient regard to (a law, rule, promise, etc.). **15.** to conform to; follow; fulfil: *to keep one's word.* **16.** to observe (a season, festival, etc.) with formalities or rites: *to keep Christmas.* **17.** to maintain or carry on, as an establishment, business, etc.; manage: *to keep house.* **18.** to guard, protect. **19.** to maintain or support (a person, etc.). **20.** to take care of; tend: *to keep sheep.* **21.** to maintain in active existence, or hold, as an assembly, court, fair, etc. **22.** to maintain one's position in or on. **23.** to continue to hold or have: *to keep a thing in mind.* **24.** to save, hold, or retain in possession. *–v.i.* **25.** to continue in an action, course, position, state, etc.: *to keep in sight.* **26.** to remain, or continue to be as specified: *to keep cool.* **27.** to remain or stay in a place: *to keep indoors.* **28.** to continue unimpaired or without spoiling: *the milk will keep on ice.* **29.** to admit of being reserved for a future occasion. **30.** to keep oneself or itself (fol. by *away, back, off, out,* etc.): *keep off the grass.* **31.** to restrain oneself: *try to keep from smiling.* **32.** to admit of being reserved for a future occasion, often in a context of threat: *I won't deal with him now. He will keep.* *–v.* **33.** Some special verb phrases are:

**keep at, 1.** to persist in. **2.** to badger, hector or bully.

**keep back, 1.** to withhold. **2.** to restrain; hold in check. **3.** to stay away; not advance.

**keep down, 1.** to restrain; prevent from rising. **2.** to retain or continue in, as a job. **3.** to consume (food) without regurgitating it.

**keep in, 1.** to retract: *he kept his stomach in.* **2.** to remain indoors. **3.** to provide with: *he kept her in clothes.* **4.** to detain a child after school.

**keep in with,** *Colloq.* to keep oneself in favour with.

**keep nit,** *Colloq.* to keep watch (usu. while an illegal activity is afoot).

**keep on,** to persist.

**keep time, 1.** to record time, as a watch or clock does. **2.** to beat, mark, or observe the rhythmic accents of music, etc. **3.** to perform rhythmic movements in unison.

**keep to, 1.** to adhere to (an agreement, plan, facts, etc.). **2.** to confine oneself to: *to keep to one's bed.*

**keep to oneself,** to hold aloof from the society of others.

**keep track of, tabs on,** to keep account of.

**keep under, 1.** to dominate. **2.** to maintain in an anaesthetised state.

**keep up, 1.** to maintain an equal rate of speed, activity, or progress, as with another. **2.** to bear up; continue without breaking down, as under strain.

**keep up with the Joneses,** to compete with one's neighbours in the accumulation of material possessions, esp. as status symbols.

**keep wicket,** *Cricket.* to act as wicket-keeper.

*–n.* **34.** subsistence; board and lodging: *to work for one's keep.* **35.** the innermost and strongest structure or central tower of a medieval castle. **36. for keeps,** *Colloq.* **a.** for keeping as one's own permanently: *to play for keeps.* **b.** permanently; altogether. [ME *kepen,* OE *cēpan,* observe, heed, regard, await, take; akin to Icel. *kōpa* stare]

**keeper** /ˈkipə/, *n.* **1.** one who keeps, guards, or watches. **2.** gamekeeper. **3.** wicket-keeper. **4.** shopkeeper. **5.** goalkeeper. **6.** a person in charge of something valuable, as the custodian of a museum, zoo, or any section thereof. **7.** something that keeps, or serves to guard, hold in place, retain, etc. **8.** →**guard ring. 9.** a belt loop. **10.** *Elect.* a soft iron bar placed across the poles of a permanent magnet in order to prevent loss of magnetism during storage. – **keeperless,** *adj.*

**keeping** /ˈkipɪŋ/, *n.* **1.** just conformity in things or elements associated together: *his deeds are not in keeping with his words.* **2.** the act of one who or that which keeps; observance, custody, or care. **3.** *Mech.* any of various devices for holding something in position. **4.** maintenance or keep. **5.** holding, reserving, or retaining. – **keepership,** *n.*

**keepings off** /ˈkipɪŋz ɒf/, *n.* a children's game in which each of two teams seeks to gain and retain possession of an object, usu. a ball.

**keepsake** /ˈkipseɪk/, *n.* anything kept, or given to be kept, for the sake of the giver, as a token of remembrance, friendship, etc.

**keeshond** /ˈkeɪshɒnd, ˈkis-/, *n., pl.* **-honds** or **-honden** /-hɒndən/. one of a breed of small dogs, originating in Holland, with ash-grey coat, and a ruff around the neck. [D, equivalent to *Kees* (familiar form of proper name *Cornelius*) + *hond* dog]

**'keet** /kit/, *n. Colloq.* **1.** →**lorikeet. 2.** →**parakeet.**

**keeve** /kiv/, *n.* a kind of large vat, esp. one used for washing tin or copper ores.

**kef** /keɪf/, *n.* (among the Arabs) **1.** a state of drowsy contentment, as from the use of a narcotic. **2.** Also, **keef.** a substance, esp. a smoking preparation of hemp leaves, used to produce this state. Also, **kief, kaif.** [Ar.: pleasure]

**keg** /kɛg/, *n.* **1.** (in the imperial system) a barrel or container, usu. holding 9 gallons (40.9 litres) or 18 gallons (81.8 litres). **2.** a barrel of beer. *–adj.* **3.** of or pertaining to or accompanied by a beer keg: *a keg party; keg cricket.* [late ME *cag,* from Scand.; cf. Icel. *kaggi*]

**keir** /kɪə/, *n.* →**kier.**

**kellick** /ˈkɛlɪk/, *n.* **1.** a small anchor or weight for mooring a boat, sometimes consisting of a stone secured by pieces of wood. **2.** any anchor. Also, **killick.** [Brit. d. *kelk* a large detached stone]

**kelly**[1] /ˈkɛli/, *n. Colloq.* **1.** a crow. **2.** a prostitute. **3.** a ticket-inspector. [? Brit. d. *kelp;* ult. orig. uncert.]

**kelly**[2] /ˈkɛli/, *n.* **1.** an axe. **2. swing kelly,** to work with an axe. [Trademark]

**kelly**[3] /ˈkɛli/, *n.* (in rotary drilling) the square or hexagonal shaft which is driven by the rotary table and which in turn rotates the drill pipe and bit. [? from *Kelly* common Irish surname]

**keloid** /ˈkilɔɪd/, *n.* a kind of fibrous tumour forming hard, irregular clawlike excrescences on the skin, usu. at the site of a scar. Also, **cheloid.** [*k-* var., from Gk *kēl(ís)* stain + -OID; *ch-* var., from Gk *chēl(ḗ)* claw + -OID]

**kelp** /kɛlp/, *n.* **1.** any of the large brown seaweeds, as *Macrocystis* or *Sarcophycus.* **2.** the ash of such seaweeds. [ME *culp;* ult. orig. unknown]

**kelpfish** /ˈkɛlpfɪʃ/, *n.* a small, common, shallow marine fish of New Zealand waters, *Chironemus marmoratus;* wirra.

**kelpie**[1] /ˈkɛlpi/, *n.* one of a breed of Australian sheepdogs developed from imported Scottish collies, having a smooth coat of variable colour and pricked ears. [probably from the name of an early specimen of the breed]

kelpie[1]

**kelpie**[2] /ˈkɛlpi/, *n. Colloq.* a kelpfish.

**kelson** /ˈkɛlsən/, *n.* →**keelson.**

**kelt** /kɛlt/, *n.* a salmon that has recently spawned. [ME (N d.)]

**Kelt** /kɛlt/, *n.* →**Celt.** – **Keltic,** *n., adj.*

**kelter** /ˈkɛltə/, *n.* →**kilter.**

**kelvin** /ˈkɛlvən/, *n.* the base SI unit of thermodynamic temperature, equal to the fraction 1/273.16 of the temperature of the triple point of water; as a unit of temperature interval, one kelvin is equivalent to one degree Celsius. See **Celsius.** Symbol: K [named after Lord *Kelvin,* 1824-1907, British physicist and mathematician]

**Kelvin scale** /ˈkɛlvən skeɪl/, *n.* a scale of temperature (**Kelvin temperature**), based on thermodynamic principles, in which zero is equivalent to −273.16°C or −459.69°F.

**Kembla** /ˈkɛmblə/, *n.* →**change** (def. 25). [rhyming slang, *Kembla Grange*]

**kemp** /kɛmp/, *n.* a coarse, brittle, dead fibre of wool, usu. short, wavy and white or opaque, used in mixed wools, as for carpets. [ME *kempe* coarse hair]

**kempt** /kɛmpt/, *adj. Colloq.* combed; well-groomed;

personally clean. [pp. of Brit. d. *kemb* COMB[1]]

**ken** /kɛn/, *n., v.,* **kenned** or **kent, kenning.** *–n.* **1.** range of sight or vision. **2.** knowledge or cognisance; mental perception. *–v.t.* **3.** *Archaic.* to see; descry; recognise. **4.** *Scot.* to have acquaintance with. *–v.i.* **5.** *Archaic.* to have knowledge of something. [ME *kennen,* OE *cennan,* c. Icel. *kenna* make known, know (cf. later E senses), G *kennen* know; orig. a causative of the verb represented by CAN[1]]

**kendo** /ˈkɛndoʊ/, *n.* a Japanese style of fencing with bamboo staves.

**kennel** /ˈkɛnəl/, *n., v.,* **-nelled, -nelling** or (*U.S.*) **-neled, -neling.** *–n.* **1.** a house for a dog or dogs. **2.** (*usu. pl., construed as sing.*) an establishment where dogs are bred or boarded. **3.** (*derog.*) a wretched abode. *–v.t.* **4.** to put into or keep in a kennel. *–v.i.* **5.** to take shelter or lodge in a kennel. [ME *kenel,* from AF, from VL *canīle,* from L *canis* dog]

**kennel cough** /ˈkɛnəl kɒf/, *n.* a cough resulting from a throat infection which dogs often contract from other dogs in a veterinary hospital, boarding kennels, etc.

**kennelmate** /ˈkɛnəlmeɪt/, *n.* a dog which is housed in the same kennel as another.

**kenogenesis** /kinoʊˈdʒɛnəsəs/, *n. Chiefly U.S.* →**cainogenesis.**

**kenosis** /kəˈnoʊsəs/, *n.* Christ's renunciation of divine privilege at the incarnation in order that He might become entirely man while remaining truly God (based on Phil. 2:6, 7, R.V.). [NL, from Gk: an emptying] – **kenotic** /kəˈnɒtɪk/, *adj.*

**kentia palm** /ˈkɛntiə pam/, *n.* a palm, *Howea forsteriana,* native to Lord Howe Island but widely cultivated as an ornamental.

**kentledge** /ˈkɛntlɪdʒ/, *n.* pig-iron used as permanent ballast in a ship. [orig. uncert.]

**Kenya** /ˈkɛnjə/, *n.* a republic in eastern Africa. – **Kenyan,** *adj., n.*

**kephalin** /ˈkɛfəlɪn/, *n.* →**cephalin.**

**kepi** /ˈkeɪpi, kɛˈpi/, *n., pl.* **-pis.** a French military cap with a flat circular top and a horizontal visor. [F *képi,* from d. G *Käppi,* diminutive of G *Kappe* cap]

**Kepler's laws** /ˈkɛpləz lɔz/, *n.pl.* three laws of planetary motion stating: **1.** that the planets move in elliptical orbits about the sun, which is situated at one focus of the ellipses. **2.** that the radius vectors joining each planet to the sun describe equal areas in equal times. **3.** that the ratio of the square of the planet's year to the cube of the planet's mean distance from the sun is the same for each planet. [named after Johann *Kepler,* 1571-1630, German astronomer]

kepi

**kept** /kɛpt/, *v.* past tense and past participle of **keep.**

**keramic** /kəˈræmɪk/, *adj.* →**ceramic.**

**keratin** /ˈkɛrətən/, *n.* a widespread animal protein found in horn, feathers, hair, hoofs. Also, **ceratin.** [Gk *kéras* horn + -IN[2]]

**keratinise** /kəˈrætənaɪz, ˈkɛrə-/, *v.,* **-nised, -nising.** *–v.t.* **1.** to make keratinous. *–v.i.* **2.** to become keratinous. Also, **keratinize.** – **keratinisation** /kəˌrætənaɪˈzeɪʃən/, *n.*

**keratinous** /kəˈrætənəs/, *adj.* composed of or resembling keratin.

**keratogenous** /kɛrəˈtɒdʒənəs/, *adj.* producing horn or a horny substance. [*kerato-* (combining form representing Gk *kéras* horn) + -GENOUS]

**keratoid** /ˈkɛrətɔɪd/, *adj.* resembling a horn; horny. [Gk *keratoeidḗs*]

**keratosis** /kɛrəˈtoʊsəs/, *n.* a pathological condition of the skin characterised by a horny or scaly growth, as a wart. [KERATIN + -OSIS]

**kerb** /kɜb/, *n.* **1.** a line of joined stones, concrete, or the like at the edge of a street, wall, etc. **2.** *Stock Exchange.* **a.** the pavement or street as a market for the sale of securities. **b.** (*pl.*) dealings conducted after normal hours, originally in the street. **3.** the fender of a hearth. **4.** the framework round the top of a well. *–v.t.* **5.** to furnish with, or protect by a kerb. Cf. **curb.** [var. spelling of CURB]

**kerb broker** /ˈ– broʊkə/, *n.* a broker who is not a member of a stock exchange.

**kerbing** /ˈkɜbɪŋ/, *n.* the material forming a kerb. Also, *U.S.,* **curbing.**

**kerb market** /ˈkɜb makət/, *n.* →**kerb** (def. 2).

**kerbstone** /ˈkɜbstoʊn/, *n.* one of the stones, or a range of stones, forming a kerb, as along the outer edge of a pavement, etc. Also, *U.S.,* **curbstone.**

**kerchief** /ˈkɜtʃəf, kəˈtʃɪf/, *n.* **1.** a cloth worn as a head covering, esp. by women. **2.** a cloth worn or carried on the person. [ME *curchef,* contraction of *coverchef,* from OF *couvrechief,* from *couvrir* COVER + *chief* head. Cf. CHIEF]

**kereru** /ˈkɛrəru/, *n. N.Z.* →**kuku.**

**kerf** /kɜf/, *n.* **1.** the cut or incision made by a saw or other instrument. **2.** that which is cut. [ME *kerf, kyrf,* OE *cyrf* a cutting, akin to *ceorfan,* v., cut, CARVE]

**kerfuffle** /kəˈfʌfəl, -ˈfʊfəl/, *n. Colloq.* →**kafuffle.** Also, **kerfoofle.**

**kermes** /ˈkɜmiz/, *n.* **1.** a red dye formerly prepared from the dried bodies of the females of a scale insect, *Kermes ilices,* which lives on certain oaks of the Mediterranean region. **2.** the small evergreen oak, *Quercus coccifera,* on which the insect is found. **3.** amorphous antimony trisulphide. [Ar., Pers. *qirmiz.* Cf. CARMINE, CRIMSON]

**kermis** /ˈkɜməs/, *n.* an annual fair or festival attended with sports and merrymaking, sometimes for charitable purposes. Also, **kermess, kirmess.** [D, var. of *kermisse, kerkmisse* church mass (on the anniversary of the dedication of a church)]

**kern**[1] /kɜn/, *n.* **1.** a part of the face of a type projecting beyond the body or shank, as in certain italic letters. *–v.t.* **2.** to form or furnish with a kern, as a type or letter. [F *carne* point, from L *cardo* hinge]

**kern**[2] /kɜn/, *n.* (in engineering) the central part of an area, through which all compressive forces must pass. [G *Kern* core]

**kernel** /ˈkɜnəl/, *n., v.,* **-nelled, -nelling,** or (*U.S.*) **-neled, -neling.** *–n.* **1.** the softer, usu. edible, part contained in the shell of a nut or the stone of a fruit. **2.** the body of a seed within its husk or integuments. **3.** a grain, as of wheat. **4.** the central part of anything; the nucleus; the core. *–v.t.* **5.** to enclose as a kernel. [ME *kirnel, curnel,* OE *cyrnel,* diminutive of *corn* seed, grain. See CORN[1]] – **kernelless,** *adj.*

**kernicterus** /kəˈnɪktərəs/, *n.* a severe form of jaundice in the newborn, usu. causing death or permanent brain damage. [G, from *Kern* core (see KERN[2]) + *Icterus* ICTERUS]

**kernite** /ˈkɜnaɪt/, *n.* a mineral, hydrated sodium borate, ($Na_2B_4O_7 \cdot 4H_2O$), occurring in transparent colourless crystals. [named after *Kern* County, in California + -ITE[1]]

**kero** /ˈkɛroʊ/, *n. Colloq.* →**kerosene.**

**kerosene** /kɛrəˈsin, ˈkɛrəsin/, *n.* a mixture of liquid hydrocarbons, obtained in the distillation of petroleum, with boiling points in the range 150°-300°C, used for lamps, engines, heaters. Also, **kerosine.** [Gk *kērós* wax + -ENE]

**kerosene grass** /ˈ– gras/, *n.* any of various short-lived native perennials of the genus, *Aristida,* esp. bunched kerosene grass, *A. contorta,* having coarse, wiry stems, three awns and sparse leaf growth; plentiful on sandy soils in low rainfall areas of Australia.

**kerosene tin** /ˈ– tɪn/, *n.* a 16-litre container used originally as a container for kerosene, but then for many other purposes.

**kerrawang** /ˈkɛrəwæŋ/, *n.* any shrub of the genus *Rulingia,* family Sterculiaceae, found in south-eastern Australia. [Aboriginal]

**Kerr cell** /ˈkɜ sɛl/, *n.* a cell, based on the Kerr effect, which is used as a high-speed camera shutter.

**Kerr effect** /ˈkɜr əfɛkt/, *n.* the rotation of the plane of polarisation of light when it is passed through certain liquids or solids to which a potential difference is applied. [named after John *Kerr,* 1824-1907, Scottish physicist]

**Kerry blue** /kɛri ˈblu/, *n.* one of a breed of large Irish terrier, having a soft, wavy, bluish coat.

**kersey** /ˈkɜzi/, *n., pl.* **-seys.** **1.** a compact, well-fulled woollen cloth with a fine nap and smooth face. **2.** a coarse twilled woollen cloth with a cotton warp. [ME; ? named after *Kersey,* in Suffolk, England]

**kerseymere** /ˈkɜzimɪə/, *n.* a twilled fine woollen cloth of a fancy weave. [KERSEY + (CASSI)MERE]

**kerugma** /kəˈrʊgmə/, *n., pl.* **-mata** /-mətə/. **1.** preaching or proclamation of religious truths. **2.** the essence of the Gospel teaching as distinct from the myth or narrative; distinguished also from the Church's doctrinal and ethical teaching. Also, **kerygma.** [Gk *kérugma* a proclamation] – **kerugmatik** /kɛrəgˈmætɪk/, *adj.*

**kestrel** /ˈkɛstrəl/, *n.* **1.** →**nankeen kestrel.** **2.** a common small falcon, *Falco tinnunculus,* of northern parts of the Eastern Hemisphere, notable for hovering in the air with its head to the wind. [var. of earlier *castrel.* Cf. F *crécerelle*]

**ketch** /kɛtʃ/, *n.* a fore-and-aft rigged vessel with a large mainmast and a smaller mast aft, but forward of the rudder post. [earlier *catch,* apparently from CATCH, *v.*]

**ketchup** /ˈkɛtʃəp/, *n.* any of several sauces or condiments for meat, fish, etc.: *tomato ketchup; mushroom ketchup.* Also, **catsup, catchup.** [apparently from Chinese (Amoy d.) *kê-tsiap* brine of pickled fish. Cf. Malay *kechop* sauce (? from Chinese)]

**ketene** /ˈkitin/, *n.* **1.** a gas, $H_2C{=}C{=}O$, with a penetrating smell, obtained from acetic anhydride or acetone. **2.** a class of compounds having the type formulas, $RHC{=}C{=}O$ and $R_2C{=}C{=}O$. [KET(ONE) + -ENE]

**keto acid** /kitoʊ ˈæsəd/, *n.* a compound that is both a ketone and an acid, as acetoacetic acid.

**keto-enol tautomerism** /ˌkitoʊ-ˌinɒl tɔˈtɒmərɪzəm/, *n.* a type of tautomerism involving migration of a proton, in which the individual tautomers may be isolated as a keto form and an enol.

**keto form** /ˈkitoʊ fɔm/, *n.* (in a keto-enol tautomeric substance) the form with the characteristics of a ketone.

**ketohexose** /kɛtoʊˈhɛksoʊz, -oʊs/, *n.* any of a group of carbohydrates containing six carbon atoms and a ketone group.

**ketone** /ˈkitoʊn/, *n.* any of a class of organic compounds, having the general formula, RCOR', containing the carbonyl group, CO, attached to two organic radicals, as acetone, $CH_3COCH_3$. [G *Keton*(aphetically derived from *A Keton*) + *-e* from *acetone*] – **ketonic** /kəˈtɒnɪk/, *adj.*

**ketone bodies** /ˈ– bodiz/, *n.pl.* beta-hydroxybutyric acid and acetoacetic acid produced in the liver, alternatives to glucose as an energy-source for many cells. The excretion of these compounds, plus acetone, is associated with diabetes; acetone bodies.

**ketonuria** /kitəˈnjuriə/, *n.* the excretion of ketones in the urine.

**ketose** /ˈkitoʊz, -oʊs/, *n.* any of the sugars which have a ketone group or its equivalent.

**ketosis** /kiˈtoʊsəs/, *n.* the condition of having elevated levels of ketone bodies in the blood and urine, as in diabetes, acidosis, etc. [KET(ONE) + -OSIS]

**kettle** /ˈkɛtl/, *n.* **1.** a portable container with a cover, a spout, and a handle, in which to boil water for making tea and other uses; teakettle. **2.** any of various containers for cooking foods, melting glue, etc. **3.** a fish kettle. **4.** an open vessel for heating metals of low melting point. **5.** a kettleful. **6.** a kettledrum. **7.** a kettle hole. **8. kettle of fish, a.** a mess, muddle, or awkward state of affairs (often preceded ironically by *pretty, fine,* etc.). **b.** any situation or state of affairs: *this is a different kettle of fish altogether.* [ME *ketel,* from Scand. (cf. Icel. *ketill,* c. OE *cetel,* G *Kessel*), from L *catillus,* diminutive of *catīnus* bowl, pot]

kettledrum

**kettledrum** /ˈkɛtldrʌm/, *n.* a drum consisting of a hollow hemisphere of brass or copper with a skin stretched over it, which can be accurately tuned. – **kettledrummer,** *n.*

**kettleful** /ˈkɛtlfʊl/, *n.* as much as a kettle will hold: *a kettleful of water.*

**kettle hole** /ˈkɛtl hoʊl/, *n.* a kettle-shaped cavity in rock or detrital material, esp. in glacial drift.

**keV** /keɪ i ˈvi/, *Physics.* kilo-electron-volt(s).

**kevel** /ˈkɛvəl/, *n.* a sturdy bit, bollard, etc., on which the heavier hawsers of a ship may be secured. [ME *kevile,* from ONF *keville* pin, from L *clāvicula* little key]

**kewpie**[1] /ˈkjupi/, *n.* a small, very plump doll, usu. made of plaster or celluloid. [Trademark]

**kewpie**[2] /ˈkjupi/, *n. Colloq.* a prostitute. [rhyming slang, *kewpie doll* MOLL[1]]

**key**[1] /ki/, *n., pl.* **keys,** *adj., v.,* **keyed, keying.** *–n.* **1.** an instrument for fastening or opening a lock by moving its bolt. **2.** a means of attaining, understanding, solving, etc.: *the key to a problem.* **3.** a book or the like containing the solutions or translations of material given elsewhere as exercises. **4.** the system or pattern used to decode a cryptogram, etc. **5.** a systematic explanation of abbreviations, symbols, etc., used in a dictionary, map, etc. **6.** something that secures or controls entrance to a place. **7.** a pin, bolt, wedge, or other piece inserted in a hole or space to lock or hold parts of a mechanism or structure together; a cotter. **8.** *Carp., etc.* a small piece of wood, etc., set across the grain to prevent warping. **9.** a contrivance for grasping and turning a bolt, nut, etc., as for winding a clockwork mechanism, for turning a valve or stopcock. **10.** one of a set of levers or parts pressed in operating a telegraph, typewriter, etc. **11.** *Music.* **a.** that part of the lever mechanism of a piano, organ, or woodwind instrument, which a finger operates. **b.** the keynote or tonic of a scale. **c.** the relationship perceived between all notes in a given unit of music to a single note or a keynote; tonality. **d.** the principal tonality of a composition: *symphony in the key of C minor.* **12.** tone or pitch, as of voice: *to speak in a high key.* **13.** strain, or characteristic style, as of expression or thought. **14.** degree of intensity, as of feeling or action. **15.** *Elect.* **a.** a device for opening and closing electrical contacts. **b.** a hand-operated switching device ordinarily formed of concealed spring contacts with an exposed handle or push-button, capable of switching one or more parts of a circuit. **16.** *Bot., Zool.* a systematic tabular classification of the significant characteristics of the members of a group of organisms to facilitate identification and comparison. **17.** *Masonry.* a keystone. **18.** *Bldg Trades.* any grooving or roughness on a surface to improve bond. **19.** the average of the tone and colour values of a painting, being high if the tones are kept near white and the colours pale and bright, and low if the tones are kept near black and the colours dark and dull. **20.** →**samara.** **21. given the key,** *Prison Colloq.* declared an habitual criminal. *–adj.* **22.** chief; major; fundamental; indispensable: *the key industries of a nation.* **23.** *Photog.* predominant; determining tonal value: *the key tone of a photograph.* **24.** *Advertising, Journalism, etc.* identifying: *a key line, a key number.* *–v.t.* **25.** to bring to a particular degree of intensity of feeling, excitement, energy, etc. (oft. fol. by *up*). **26.** to adjust (one's speech, actions, etc.) as if to a particular key, in order to come into harmony with external factors, as the level of understanding of one's hearers. **27.** *Music.* to regulate the key or pitch of. **28.** to fasten, secure, or adjust with a key, wedge, or the like, as parts of a mechanism. **29.** to provide with a key or keys. **30.** (in the layout of publications) to identify by symbols the position on the layout (of artwork, copy, etc.) (oft. fol. by *up*). **31.** to give (an advertisement) a letter or number to enable replies to it to be identified. **32.** to lock with, or as with, a key. **33.** *Masonry.* to provide (an arch, etc.) with a keystone. **34.** *Bldg Trades.* **a.** to prepare (a surface) by grooving, roughening, etc., to receive paint. **b.** to cause (paint, etc.) to adhere to a surface. *–v.i.* **35.** *Bldg Trades.* (of paint, etc.) to adhere to a surface. [ME *key(e), kay(e),* OE *cǣg,* c. OFris. *kei, kai*]

**key**[2] /ki/, *n., pl.* **keys.** (in the Caribbean area) a reef or low island; cay. [Sp. *cayo*]

**keyboard** /ˈkibɔd/, *n.* **1.** the row or set of keys on a piano, typewriter, etc. **2.** any of two or more sets of keys, as on large organs, or harpsichords.

**keyboardist** /ˈkibɔdəst/, *n.* a musician in a group who plays any of various keyboard instruments, as a piano, organ, etc., as required.

**keyboard operator** /ˈkibɔd ɒpəreɪtə/, *n.* a person who operates a device with a keyboard as a typewriter, computer terminal, etc.

**key fruit** /ˈki frut/, *n.* →**samara.**

**keyhole** /ˈkihoʊl/, *n.* a hole for a key to a lock.

**keyhole limpet** /ˈ– lɪmpət/, *n.* a gastropod mollusc of the genus *Fissurela,* which has a hole at the apex of its shell.

**keyless** /'kiləs/, *adj.* **1.** without a key. **2.** not requiring a key.

**keylock closure** /'kilɒk kloʊʒə/, *n.* a strong notched plastic strip used for fastening the top of large disposable plastic bags.

**keyman** /'kimæn/, *n. Prison Colloq.* an habitual prisoner.

**key money** /'ki mʌni/, *n.* a sum of money paid by a prospective tenant for the opportunity of obtaining an interest in a property.

**Keynesian** /'kinziən/, *adj.* **1.** of, pertaining to, or denoting the economic theories, policies, etc., of J. M. Keynes and his followers, esp. the systematic explanation of the determinants of effective demand and the policy of maintaining high employment and of controlling inflation by capital and public investment and by varying taxation and interest rates. *–n.* **2.** one who supports the theories, policies, etc., of Keynes. [from John Maynard *Keynes,* 1st Baron, 1883-1946, English economist]

**keynote** /'kinoʊt/, *n., adj., v.,* **-noted, -noting.** *–n.* **1.** *Music.* the note on which a key (system of notes) is founded; the tonic. **2.** the main interest or determining principle of a conference, political campaign, advertising campaign etc. *–adj.* **3.** that which pertains to or defines the main interest or determining principle: *keynote address, keynote speaker.* *–v.t.* **4.** *U.S.* to announce the policy, determining principle etc. of a political party etc. Also, **key-note.**

**key plate** /'ki pleɪt/, *n.* (in the offset lithography process where colour separation is not photomechanical) a plate used in multicolour printing to prepare other plates to print each colour.

**key position** /– pə'zɪʃən/, *n.* (in Australian Rules) any of the central positions on the five lines: full-back, centre half-back, centre, centre half-forward, full-forward.

**key punch** /'– pʌntʃ/, *n.* a keyboard by means of which holes are punched into tape or cards which can then be read by a computer. Also, **card punch.**

**key-punch** /'ki-pʌntʃ/, *v.i.* **1.** to use a key punch. *–v.t.* **2.** to input (data) using a key punch. **– key-puncher,** *n.*

**key punch operator,** *n.* one who uses a key punch. Also, **K.P.O.**

**key ring** /'ki rɪŋ/, *n.* a ring, usu. of metal, for holding keys, etc.

**key signature** /'– sɪgnətʃə/, *n.* (in notation) the group of sharps or flats placed after the clef to indicate the tonality of the music following.

**keystone** /'kistoʊn/, *n.* **1.** the wedge-shaped piece at the summit of an arch, regarded as holding the other pieces in place. **2.** something on which associated things depend.

keystone

**keyway** /'kiweɪ/, *n.* a slot or chase cut in a surface of contact to receive a key to prevent relative movement.

**key word** /'ki wɜd/, *n.* **1.** a significant word: *courage is the key word in this situation.* **2.** the word on which the understanding of a code rests.

**kg,** **1.** keg; kegs. **2.** kilogram; kilograms.

**K.G.** /keɪ 'dʒi/, Knight of the Garter.

**K.G.B.** /keɪ dʒi 'bi/, *n.* the secret police of the Soviet Union. [Russ. *K(omitet) G(osudarstrennoi) B(ezopasnosti),* lit., Committee of State Security]

**K.G.C.B.,** Knight Grand Cross of the order of the Bath.

**kgf,** kilogram-force.

**khaddar** /'kadə/, *n.* hand-spun, hand-woven cloth produced in India. Also, **khadi.** [Hind.]

**khaki** /ka'ki, 'kaki/, *n., pl.* **-kis,** *adj.* *–n.* **1.** dull yellowish brown. **2.** stout twilled cotton uniform cloth of this colour, worn esp. by soldiers. **3.** a similar fabric of wool. *–adj.* **4.** of the colour of khaki. **5.** made of khaki. [Hind.: dusty, from *khāk* dust]

**khaki weed** /'– wid/, *n.* any of several species of *Alternanthera,* native to South America but introduced to other countries, having yellowish-green leaves and prickly seeds which attach themselves to grazing animals.

**khalif** /ka'lif/, *n.* →**caliph.** Also, **khalifa.**

**khan** /kan/, *n.* **1.** (in the Altaic group of languages) the title borne by hereditary rulers, as: **a.** a hereditary chief of a tribal following. **b.** a hereditary lord of a territorial domain. **2.** the supreme ruler of the Tartar tribes, as well as emperor of China, during the Middle Ages, being a descendant of Genghis Khan. **3.** a title of respect in Iran, Afghanistan, Pakistan, etc. [ME, from Turk. (whence Pers. and Ar.): lord, prince]

**khanate** /'kaneɪt/, *n.* the dominion of a khan.

**khat** /kæt, kat/, *n.* →**kat.**

**khedive** /kə'div/, *n.* title of the Turkish viceroys in Egypt, 1867-1914. [Turk. *khedīv,* from Pers. *khidīv* lord, sovereign] **– khedival, khedivial** /kə'diviəl/, *adj.* **– khedivate, khediviate,** *n.*

**Khmer** /kmɛə, kmɜ/, *n.* **1.** a member of the Khmer Republic. **2.** a language of Kampuchea, of the Mon-Khmer family. *–adj.* **3.** denoting a richly figurative style of architecture developed in the Khmer Republic between the 7th and 13th centuries.

**Khmer Republic** /– rə'pʌblɪk/, *n.* a republic in south-east Asia, formerly the kingdom of Cambodia, currently known as Kampuchea.

**Khyber** /'kaɪbə/, *n. Colloq.* arse. [rhyming slang, *Khyber Pass* arse]

**kHz,** kilohertz.

**kiang** /ki'æŋ/, *n.* a wild ass, *Equus hemionus kiang,* of certain mountainous regions of eastern Asia.

**kia-ora** /kɪə-'ɔrə/, *interj. N.Z.* good luck. [Maori]

**kiap** /'kiæp/, *n.* **1.** the government. **2.** a government official. [Papuan]

**kibble**[1] /'kɪbəl/, *v.,* **-bled, -bling,** *adj.* *–v.t.* **1.** to grind into small particles. *–adj.* **2.** of or pertaining to wheat, grain, etc., which has been kibbled. [orig. unknown]

**kibble**[2] /'kɪbəl/, *n.* **1.** a large iron bucket used in mining. **2.** a large cement container. [G Kübel]

**kibbutz** /kɪ'bʊts/, *n., pl.* **kibbutzim** /kɪ'bʊtsɪm, kɪbʊt'sim/. (in Israel) a communal agricultural settlement. [Modern Heb. *qibbūsh* gathering]

**kibitz** /'kɪbɪts/, *v.i. U.S. Colloq.* to act as a kibitzer.

**kibitzer** /'kɪbɪtsə/, *n. U.S. Colloq.* **1.** a spectator at a card game who looks at the players' cards over their shoulders. **2.** a giver of unwanted advice. [Yiddish, from colloq. G *Kiebitz* kibitzer (properly, lapwing) + *-er* -ER[1]]

**kiblah** /'kɪbla/, *n.* **1.** the point (the Kaaba at Mecca) towards which Muslims turn at prayer. **2.** the facing towards Mecca, wherever orthodox Muslims pray. [Ar. *qibla*]

**kibosh** /'kaɪbɒʃ/, *n. Colloq.* →**kybosh.**

**kick** /kɪk/, *v.t.* **1.** to strike with the foot. **2.** to drive, force, make, etc., by or as by kicks. **3.** to strike in recoiling. **4.** *Football.* to score (a goal) by a kick. **5. kick about** or **around,** *Colloq.* **a.** to maltreat: *the way they kick that dog about is disgusting.* **b.** to discuss or consider at length or in some detail (an idea, proposal, or the like). **6. kick in,** *Colloq.* to contribute, as to a collection for a presentation. **7. kick oneself,** to reproach oneself. **8. kick out,** *Colloq.* to dismiss; get rid of. **9. kick the bucket,** *Colloq.* to die. **10. kick the habit,** *Colloq.* **a.** to give up cigarettes, alcohol, etc., to which one has become addicted. **b.** to forego any pleasure. **11. kick the tin,** to give money; contribute. **12. kick up,** *Colloq.* to stir up; to cause (disturbance, trouble, noise, etc.): *to kick up a fuss.* **13. kick up one's heels,** *Colloq.* to enjoy oneself in an exuberant manner. **14. kick upstairs,** to promote someone to a position which has status but no real power; to remove someone from a particular office by promotion. *–v.i.* **15.** to strike out with the foot. **16.** to have the habit of thus striking out, as a horse. **17.** *Colloq.* to resist, object, or complain. **18.** to recoil, as a firearm when fired. **19.** to rise sharply, as a ball after bouncing (oft. fol. by *up*). **20. kick against the pricks,** *Colloq.* to indulge in futile struggles against the harsh realities of life. **21. kick off, a.** *Rugby, Soccer.* to kick the ball from the half-way line at the start of the game and of the second half, and after each score has been made. **b.** *Colloq.* to start, commence. **c.** *U.S. Colloq.* to die. **d.** *Surfing.* to get off a wave by kicking the surfboard out of the wave. **e.** Also, **kick in, kick out.** *Aus. Rules.* to kick the ball back into play after a behind has been scored. **22. kick on,** *Colloq.* **a.** to carry on or continue, esp. with just adequate resources: *we'll kick on until the fresh supplies get here.* **b.** to continue a party or other festivity: *we kicked on* *until the early hours.* –*n.* **23.** the act of kicking; a blow or thrust with the foot. **24.** *Football.* **a.** the act of kicking a football. **b.** the kicked ball: *his fist kick hit the cross-bar.* **c.** the distance covered by a kicked ball: *a long kick for touch.* **25.** power or disposition to kick. **26.** the right of or a turn at kicking. **27.** a recoil, as of a gun. **28.** *Colloq.* an objection or complaint. **29.** *Colloq.* any thrill or excitement that gives pleasure; any act, sensation, etc., that gives satisfaction. **30.** *Colloq.* a stimulating or intoxicating quality in alcoholic drink. **31.** *Colloq.* vigour, energy, or vim. **32.** *Colloq.* →**shout** (def. 8). **33.** *Colloq.* the start of a race. **34.** *Colloq.* trouser pocket. **35.** *Brit. Colloq.* sixpence. **36. a kick in the arse,** *Colloq.* **a.** a setback. **b.** retribution. **37. a kick in the pants,** a sharp reprimand. **38. a kick in the teeth,** a grave set-back. **39. for kicks,** *Colloq.* for the sake of gaining some excitement or entertainment. [ME *kike.* Cf. Icel. *kikna* sink at the knees] – **kickable,** *adj.* – **kicker,** *n.*

**kickback** /ˈkɪkbæk/, *n. Colloq.* **1.** a response, usu. vigorous. **2.** any sum paid for favours received or hoped for.

**kicking** /ˈkɪkɪŋ/, *v.* **1.** present participle of **kick. 2. be alive and kicking,** *Colloq.* to be in good health and spirits. **3. be kicking along,** *Colloq.* to be coping adequately with one's life. **4. be kicking around,** *Colloq.* **a.** to lie scattered around. **b.** to be freely available.

**kick-off** /ˈkɪk-ɒf/, *n.* **1.** *Aus. Rules.* Also, **kick-in, kick-out.** a kick from the kick-off line, usu. by the defending full-back, to put the ball back into play after a behind. **2.** *Rugby Football.* a kick from a spot in the centre of the field which starts a game or the second half of the game. **3.** *Soccer.* a kick which starts the game or the second half of a game, or which restarts the game after a goal. **4.** *Colloq.* the beginning or initial stage of something.

**kick-off area** /ˈ– ɛəriə/, *n.* →**goal square.**

**kick-off lines** /ˈ– laɪnz/, *n.pl. Aus. Rules.* two lines, 9 metres long, running forward from the goal posts and a third line joining their forward extremities.

**kick pleat** /ˈkɪk plit/, *n.* a short flat pleat, about 8 to 12 cm from the hem at the back of a straight skirt, dress, etc., enabling the wearer to walk freely.

**kickshaw** /ˈkɪkʃɔ/, *n.* **1.** any fancy dish in cookery. **2.** any dainty, unsubstantial, or paltry trifle. [F; ? alteration of *quelque chose* something]

**kick-sorter** /kɪk-ˈsɔtə/, *n.* an apparatus for detecting pulses of electrical energy in a specified intensity range.

**kick-start** /ˈkɪk-stat/, *v.t.* **1.** to start (a motor) with a kick-starter. –*n.* **2.** →**kick-starter.**

**kick-starter** /ˈkɪk-statə/, *n.* a starter for an engine, esp. on a motorcycle or lawn-mower, which is operated by the foot. Also, **kick-start.**

**kick turn** /ˈkɪk tɜn/, *n.* a 90° turn made from a stationary position, when a skier using his stocks for balance, lifts the downhill ski clear of the snow and reverses the direction of it.

**kid**[1] /kɪd/, *n., v.,* **kidded, kidding.** –*n.* **1.** a young goat. **2.** kidskin. **3.** *Colloq.* a child or young person. **4.** *Horseracing Colloq.* an apprentice jockey. –*v.i.* **5.** (of a goat) to give birth to (young). –*adj.* **6.** young; younger: *my kid brother.* [ME, apparently from Scand.; cf. Icel. *kidh,* Swed. and Dan. *kid*]

**kid**[2] /kɪd/, *v.,* **kidded, kidding,** *n. Colloq.* –*v.t.* **1.** to tease; banter; jest with. **2.** to humbug or fool. –*v.i.* **3.** to speak or act deceptively, in jest; jest. –*n.* **4.** kidding; humbug; chaffing. [? special use of KID[1] (def. 3)] – **kidder,** *n.*

**kiddie** /ˈkɪdi/, *n., pl.* **-dies.** *Colloq.* →**child.** Also, **kiddy.** [KID[1] + -IE]

**kiddo** /ˈkɪdoʊ/, *n., pl.* **-dos, -does.** *Colloq.* (a familiar form of address.) [KID[1] + (*d*) + -O]

**Kiddush** /kɪˈdʊʃ/, *n.* (in Judaism) a traditional blessing of wine on the Sabbath eve and of wine and bread on the Sabbath, both after a religious service.

**kid gloves** /kɪd ˈglʌvz/, *n.pl.* **1.** gloves made of kidskin. **2. handle with kid gloves,** to handle very gently or tactfully.

**kidnap** /ˈkɪdnæp/, *v.t.,* **-napped, -napping,** or (*U.S.*) **-naped, -naping.** to steal or abduct (a child or other person); carry off (a person) against his will by unlawful force or by fraud, often with a demand for ransom. [KID[1] (def. 3) + obs. *nap,* v., seize] – **kidnapper,** *n.*

**kidney** /ˈkɪdni/, *n., pl.* **-neys. 1.** (in man) either of a pair of bean-shaped glandular organs, about 10 cm in length, in the back part of the abdominal cavity, which excrete urine. **2.** a corresponding organ in other vertebrate animals, or an organ of like function in invertebrates. **3.** the meat of an animal's kidney used as a food. **4.** constitution or temperament. **5.** kind, sort, or class. [ME *kidenei,* from *kiden-* (orig. and meaning uncert.) + *ey* egg] – **kidney-like,** *adj.*

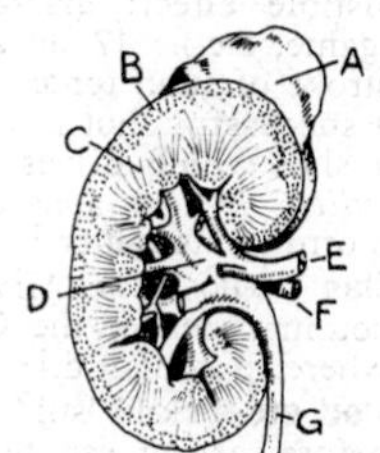

human kidney (section): A, suprarenal gland; B, cortex; C, tubular portion, consisting of cones; D, renal pelvis; E, renal artery; F, renal vein; G, ureter

**kidney bean** /ˈ– bin/, *n.* **1.** →**French bean. 2.** the dried, somewhat kidney-shaped seed of the French bean, esp. if dark in colour.

**kidney fern** /ˈ– fɜn/, *n. N.Z.* a fern, *Cardiomanes reniforme,* characterised by kidney-shaped leaves.

**kidney machine** /ˈ– məʃin/, *n.* a machine for carrying out haemodialysis.

**kidney-shaped** /ˈkɪdni-ʃeɪpt/, *adj.* having the general shape of a long oval indented at one side.

**kidney stone** /ˈkɪdni stoʊn/, *n.* a renal calculus.

**kidney transplant** /ˈ– trænsplænt/, *n.* an operation involving the transplantation of a kidney from one person to another.

**kidney vetch** /ˈ– vɛtʃ/, *n.* an Old World leguminous herb, *Anthyllis vulneraria,* formerly used as a remedy for kidney diseases.

**kidney weed** /ˈ– wid/, *n.* a prostrate herb *Dichondra repens,* often forming dense mats and occasionally used as a lawn.

**kidney worm** /ˈ– wɜm/, *n.* **1.** a parasitic nematode, *Stephanurus dentatus,* which attacks pigs. **2.** a parasitic nematode, *Dioctophyma renale,* which attacks men, dogs, and other mammals.

**kidskin** /ˈkɪdskɪn/, *n.* **1.** leather made from the skin of a kid or goat. **2.** a synthetic material in imitation of this.

**kid-stakes** /ˈkɪd-steɪks/, *n.pl. Colloq.* **1.** nonsense; joking pretence: *the pre-season competition is just kid-stakes compared to the premiership.* **2.** a small amount, esp. of money, small stakes.

**kidult** /ˈkɪdʌlt/, *adj.* of or pertaining to books, films, etc., suitable for both children and adults. [b. KID[1] (def. 3) + ADULT]

**kiekie** /ˈkiki/, *n. N.Z.* a forest climber, *Freycinetia banksii,* with fleshy edible flower bracts. Also, **gigi, giegie.** [Maori]

**kier** /kɪə/, *n.* **1.** a large boiler or vat used in bleaching, etc. –*v.t.* **2.** to remove impurities from a fabric by boiling in such a vessel. Also, **keir.** [Scand.; cf. Icel. *ker* tub]

**kieselguhr** /ˈkizəlgʊə/, *n.* diatomaceous earth. [G, from *Kiesel* flint + *Guhr* earthy deposit]

**kieserite** /ˈkizəraɪt/, *n.* a mineral, hydrated magnesium sulphate, found in salt deposits in Germany, used for making Epsom salts. [named after D. G. *Kieser,* d. 1862, German physician. See -ITE[1]]

**kikuyu** /kaɪˈkuju/, *n.* a perennial grass, *Pennisetum clandestinum,* suitable to a wide variety of soil types and producing a thick growth of runners; widely used as a lawn grass.

**kilderkin** /ˈkɪldəkɪn/, *n.* **1.** a unit of measurement of capacity in the imperial system equal to 17 gallons (approx. 77.28 litres). **2.** a container or barrel (esp. of beer) having approx. such a capacity.

**kiley** /ˈkaɪli/, *n.* →**kylie.**

**kill** /kɪl/, *v.t.* **1.** to deprive (any living creature or thing) of life in any manner; cause the death of; slay. **2.** to destroy; to do away with; extinguish: *kill hope.* **3.** to destroy or neutralise the active qualities of. **4.** to spoil the effect of. **5.** to pass (the time) idly while waiting for something to come, happen, or the like: *he killed time waiting for the bus to come.* **6.** to overcome completely or with irresistible effect. **7.** to cancel (a word, paragraph, item, etc.). **8.** to defeat or veto (a legislative bill, etc.). **9.** *Elect.* to render (a circuit) dead. **10.** *Tennis.* to hit (a ball) with such force that its return is impossible. **11. kill off,** to destroy completely and often indiscriminately. **12. kill two birds with one stone,** to achieve two (or more) objectives by one action. *–v.i.* **13.** to inflict or cause death. **14.** to commit murder. **15.** to have an irresistible effect: *dressed to kill.* *–n.* **16.** the act of killing (game, etc.). **17.** an animal or animals killed. **18.** *Tennis.* a stroke of such force that it cannot be returned. **19.** *Shooting.* a successful shot in clay-pigeon shooting. **20. the kill,** *Bowls.* a shot which drives the jack out of the playing area. [ME *cullen, kyllen;* apparently from OE *-colla* (in *morgen-colla* morning slaughter)]

**killas** /ˈkɪləs/, *n. Mining.* **1.** slates or schists forming the country rock of the Cornish tin veins. **2.** similar rock elsewhere. [Cornish d.]

**killed steel** /kɪld ˈstil/, *n.* steel that has been fully deoxidised before casting, esp. by the addition of manganese, silicon, and aluminium.

**killer** /ˈkɪlə/, *n.* **1.** one who or that which kills. **2.** something particularly effective: *that joke is a killer.* **3.** an animal selected as meat.

**killer instinct** /ˈkɪlər ɪnstɪŋkt/, *n.* in competitive sport, etc., a fierce determination to win.

**killer whale** /kɪlə ˈweɪl/, *n.* a swift, predacious, toothed whale, *Orcinus orca,* of worldwide distribution; grampus.

**killick** /ˈkɪlɪk/, *n.* →**kellick.** Also, **killock.**

**killifish** /ˈkɪlifɪʃ/, *n., pl.* **-fish,** (*esp. collectively*) **-fish.** any of numerous small fishes of the family Cyprinodontidae found chiefly in fresh or brackish waters of warm regions.

**killing** /ˈkɪlɪŋ/, *n.* **1.** the act of one who or that which kills. **2.** *Colloq.* a stroke of extraordinary success, as in a successful speculation in stocks. *–adj.* **3.** that kills. **4.** exhausting. **5.** *Colloq.* irresistibly funny. – **killingly,** *adv.*

**killjoy** /ˈkɪldʒɔɪ/, *n.* a person or thing that spoils the joy or enjoyment of others.

**kiln** /kɪln/, *n.* **1.** a furnace or oven for burning, baking, or drying something, esp. one for calcining limestone or one for baking bricks. *–v.t.* **2.** to burn, bake, or treat in a kiln. [ME *kylne,* OE *cyl(e)n,* from L *culīna* kitchen]

**kiln-dry** /ˈkɪln-draɪ/, *v.t.,* **-dried, -drying.** to dry in a kiln.

**kilo** /ˈkiloʊ/, *n. Colloq.* →**kilogram.**

**kilo-** /ˈkɪlə-/, a prefix denoting $10^3$ of a given unit, as in *kilogram. Symbol:* k [F, representing Gk *chílioi* thousand]

**kilogram** /ˈkɪləgræm/, *n.* **1.** a unit of mass equal to 1000 grams. **2.** *Physics.* the SI unit of mass, based on the international prototype kept at Sèvres, France. *Symbol:* kg [F *kilogramme.* See KILO-, -GRAM[2]]

**kilogram-force** /kɪləgræm-ˈfɔs/, *n.* a non-SI unit of force, equal to 9.806 65 newtons. *Symbol:* kgf

**kilojoule** /ˈkɪlədʒul/, *n.* one thousand joules; the unit used to express the fuel or energy value of food; the quantity of a food capable of producing such a unit of energy. *Symbol:* kJ [KILO- + JOULE]

**kilometre** /ˈkɪləmitə/; *deprecated* /kəˈlɒmətə/, *n.* a unit of length, the common measure of distances equal to 1000 metres. *Symbol:* km Also, *U.S.,* **kilometer.** [F *kilomètre.* See KILO-, -METRE] – **kilometric** /kɪləˈmɛtrɪk/, **kilometrical** /kɪləˈmɛtrɪkəl/, *adj.*

**kilopond** /ˈkɪləpɒnd/, *n.* →**kilogram-force.** *Symbol:* kp

**kiloton** /ˈkɪlətʌn/, *n.* **1.** 1000 tons. **2.** an explosive force equal to that of 1000 tons of TNT.

**kiloton weapon** /ˈ– wɛpən/, *n.* a nuclear weapon, the yield of which is measured in terms of thousands of tons of trinitrotoluene explosive equivalents.

**kilowatt** /ˈkɪləwɒt/, *n.* one thousand watts. *Symbol:* kW [KILO- + WATT]

**kilowatt-hour** /kɪləwɒt-ˈaʊə/, *n.* a unit of energy equivalent to that transferred or expended in one hour by one kilowatt of power, 3.6 x $10^6$ joules. *Symbol:* kW.h

**kilpatrick** /kɪlˈpætrɪk/, *adj.* (of oysters) served grilled on the shell, under a layer of chopped bacon and worcestershire sauce.

**kilt** /kɪlt/, *n.* **1.** any short, pleated skirt, esp. one worn by men in the Scottish Highlands. *–v.t.* **2.** to draw or tuck up (the skirt, etc.) about one. **3.** to pleat (cloth, a skirt, etc.) in deep vertical folds. [ME *kylte,* probably from Scand.; cf. Dan. *kilte* tuck up] – **kiltlike,** *adj.*

**kilted** /ˈkɪltəd/, *adj.* **1.** wearing a kilt. **2.** pleated.

**kilter** /ˈkɪltə/, *n.* good condition; order: *the engine was out of kilter.* Also, **kelter.**

**kiltie** /ˈkɪlti/, *n. Colloq.* one who wears a kilt, esp. a member of a Scottish Highland regiment. Also, **kilty.**

**kilting** /ˈkɪltɪŋ/, *n.* (in a skirt, etc.) an arrangement of flat pleats set close together, each overlapping half of the last.

**kimberlite** /ˈkɪmbəlaɪt/, *n.* a variety of mica peridotite which occurs in narrow pipe-like bodies and which often contains diamonds. – **kimberlitic** /kɪmbəˈlɪtɪk/, *adj.*

**kimono** /ˈkɪmənoʊ, kəˈmoʊnoʊ/, *n., pl.* **-nos.** **1.** a wide-sleeved robe characteristic of Japanese costume. **2.** a woman's loose dressing-gown. [Jap.]

kimono

**kin** /kɪn/, *n.* **1.** one's relatives collectively, or kinsfolk. **2.** family relationship or kinship. **3.** a group of persons descended from a common ancestor, or constituting a family, clan, tribe, or race. **4.** a relative or kinsman. **5.** someone or something of the same kind or nature. **6. of kin,** of the same family; related; akin. *–adj.* **7.** of kin; related; akin. **8.** of the same kind or nature; having affinity. [ME; OE *cynn,* c. OHG *chunni,* Icel. *kyn,* Goth. *kuni;* from Gmc root equivalent to L *gen-,* Gk *gen-,* Skt *jan-* beget, produce] – **kinless,** *adj.*

**-kin,** a diminutive suffix, attached to nouns to signify a little object of the kind mentioned: *lambkin, catkin.* [ME; akin to D and LG *-ken,* G *-chen*]

**kina** /ˈkinə/, *n.* **1.** the larger unit of currency in Papua New Guinea. See **toea.** **2.** a sea urchin of the genus *Evechinus.* [Papuan]

**kinaesthesia** /kaɪnəsˈθiziə, kɪn-, -ˈθiʒə/, *n.* the sensation of movement or strain in muscles, tendons, joints. Also, **kinaesthesis;** *Chiefly U.S.,* **kinesthesia, kinesthesis.** [NL, from Gk, *kīneîn* move + *-aisthēsía* perception] – **kinaesthetic** /kaɪnəsˈθɛtɪk, kɪn-/, *adj.*

**kinaki** /ˈkinaki/, *n. N.Z.* a relish. [Maori]

**kinase** /ˈkaɪneɪz/, *n.* an enzyme which catalyses any reaction involving the hydrolysis of ATP.

**kinchella** /kɪnˈtʃɛlə/, *n. Colloq. in the phrase,* **put kinchella on (shears),** to sharpen (hand shears). Also, **kinchela.** [from *Kinchella,* the author of a pamphlet on caring for and sharpening shears]

**kind**[1] /kaɪnd/, *adj.* **1.** of a good or benevolent nature or disposition, as a person. **2.** having, showing, or proceeding from benevolence: *kind words.* **3.** cordial; well-meant: *kind regards.* **4.** indulgent, considerate, or helpful (oft. fol. by *to*): *to be kind to animals.* **5.** *Archaic.* loving. [ME *kinde,* OE *gecynde,* from *gecynd* nature. See KIND[2]]

**kind**[2] /kaɪnd/, *n.* **1.** a class or group of individuals of the same nature or character, esp. a natural group of animals or plants. **2.** nature or character as determining likeness or difference between things: *things differing in degree rather than in kind.* **3.** a person or thing as being of a particular character or class: *he is a strange kind of hero.* **4.** a more or less adequate or inadequate example, or a sort, of something: *the vines formed a kind of roof.* **5.** *Archaic.* the nature, or natural disposition or character: *after one's kind.* **6. in kind, a.** in something of the same kind in the same way: *to retaliate in kind.* **b.** in goods or natural produce, instead of money. **7. kind of** (used adverbially), *Colloq.* after a fashion; to some extent; somewhat; rather: *the room was kind of dark.* [ME *kinde,* OE *gecynd.* See KIN]

**kinder** /ˈkɪndə/, *n. Colloq.* →**kindergarten.** Also, **kindy.**

**kindergarten** /ˈkɪndəgatn/, *n.* **1.** a school for furthering the mental, social, and physical development of young children, usu. children under the age of five, by means of games, occupations, etc., that make use of their natural tendency to express themselves in action. **2.** any nursery school. **3.** *N.S.W., A.C.T.,* the first grade in the infants' school. [G: lit., children's garden, coined by Friedrich Froebel, 1782-1852, German educational reformer]

**kindergartener** /ˈkɪndəgatnə/, *n.* **1.** a kindergarten teacher. **2.** a child who attends a kindergarten. Also, **kindergartner.**

**kind-hearted** /ˈkaɪnd-hatəd/, *adj.* having or showing a kind heart; kindly. – **kind-heartedly,** *adv.* – **kind-heartedness,** *n.*

**kindle** /ˈkɪndəl/, *v.,* **-dled, -dling.** *–v.t.* **1.** to set (a fire, flame, etc.) burning or blazing. **2.** to set fire to, or ignite (fuel or any combustible matter). **3.** to excite; stir up or set going; to animate, rouse, or inflame. **4.** to light up, illuminate, or make bright. *–v.i.* **5.** to begin to burn, as combustible matter, a light, or a fire or flame. **6.** to become roused, ardent, or inflamed. **7.** to become lit up, bright, or glowing, as the sky at dawn or the eyes with ardour. [ME *kindlen,* probably from Scand.; cf. Icel. *kynda* kindle, *kyndill* candle, torch] – **kindler,** *n.*

**kindliness** /ˈkaɪndlinəs/, *n.* **1.** the state or quality of being kindly; benevolence. **2.** a kindly deed.

**kindling** /ˈkɪndlɪŋ/, *n.* **1.** material for starting a fire. **2.** the act of one who kindles.

**kindly** /ˈkaɪndli/, *adj.*, **-lier, -liest,** *adv.* *–adj.* **1.** having, showing, or proceeding from a benevolent disposition or spirit; kind-hearted; good-natured; sympathetic: *kindly people.* **2.** gentle or mild, as rule or laws. **3.** pleasant, genial, or benign. **4.** favourable, as soil for crops. **5.** *Mining.* of a rock congenial or likely to carry ore. *–adv.* **6.** in a kind manner; with sympathetic or helpful kindness. **7.** cordially or heartily: *we thank you kindly.* **8.** with liking; favourably: *to take kindly to an idea.* **9.** obligingly; please: *kindly go away.* [ME *kyndly,* OE *gecyndelīc* natural, from *gecynde* KIND[1] + *-līc* -LY]

**kindly ground** /ˈ– graʊnd/, *n.* those rocks in which lodes become productive of mineral of value.

**kindness** /ˈkaɪndnəs/, *n.* **1.** the state or quality of being kind. **2.** a kind act: *his many kindnesses to me.* **3.** kind behaviour: *I will never forget your kindness.* **4.** friendly feeling, or liking.

**kindred** /ˈkɪndrəd/, *n.* **1.** a body of persons related to another, or a family, tribe, or race. **2.** one's relatives collectively; kinsfolk; kin. **3.** relationship by birth or descent or sometimes by marriage; kinship. **4.** natural relationship, or affinity. *–adj.* **5.** associated by origin, nature, qualities, etc.: *kindred languages.* **6.** related by birth or descent, or having kinship: *kindred tribes.* **7.** belonging to kin or relatives: *kindred blood.* [ME *kindrede(n).* See KIN, -RED]

**kindy** /ˈkɪndi/, *n.* →**kindergarten.**

**kine** /kaɪn/, *n.pl. Archaic.* plural of **cow.**

**kinematics** /kaɪnəˈmætɪks, kɪn-/, *n.* **1.** that branch of mechanics which treats of pure motion, without reference to mass or cause. **2.** the theory of mechanical contrivance for converting one kind of motion into another (**applied kinematics**). [Gk *kínēma* motion + -ICS] – **kinematic, kinematical,** *adj.*

**kinematic viscosity** /ˌkaɪnəmætɪk vɪsˈkɒsəti/, *n.* the absolute viscosity of a fluid divided by its density, usu. measured in stokes.

**kinematograph** /kaɪnəˈmætəgræf, kɪn-/, *n., v.t., v.i.* →**cinematograph.**

**kineme** /ˈkaɪnim/, *n.* a meaningful unit of body movement or gesture made in non-verbal communication.

**kinemics** /kaɪˈnimɪks/, *n.* the study of units of gestural expression.

**kinesic** /kaɪˈnisɪk/, *adj.* of, or pertaining to non-vocal communication accomplished by movement or gesture.

**kinesics** /kaɪˈnisɪks/, *n.* the study of non-linguistic body motion in its relation to communication.

**kinesiology** /kaɪˌnisiˈɒlədʒi/, *n.* the field of study concerned with the mechanics of movements of the human body.

**kinesthesia** /kaɪnəsˈθiziə, kɪn-, -ˈθiʒə/, *n. Chiefly. U.S.* →**kinaesthesia.** Also, **kinesthesis.** – **kinesthetic** /kaɪnəsˈθɛtɪk, kɪn-/, *adj.*

**kinetic** /kəˈnɛtɪk, kaɪ-/, *adj.* **1.** pertaining to motion. **2.** caused by motion. [Gk *kīnētikós*]

**kinetic art** /– ˈat/, *n.* artistic constructions which have one or more moving elements, whether activated by motor, by hand, or by air currents, etc.

**kinetic energy** /– ˈɛnədʒi/, *n.* the energy which a body possesses by virtue of its motion; the energy which any system possesses by virtue of the motion of its components.

**kinetics** /kəˈnɛtɪks, kaɪ-/, *n.* the branch of mechanics which treats of the action of forces in producing or changing the motion of masses.

**kinetic theory of gases,** *n.* a theory that the particles in a gas move freely and rapidly along straight lines but often collide, resulting in variations in their velocity and direction. Pressure is thus interpreted as the force due to the impacts of these particles, and temperature as the average kinetic energy.

**kinfolks** /ˈkɪnfoʊks/, *n.pl.* →**kinsfolk.** Also, **kinfolk.**

**king** /kɪŋ/, *n.* **1.** a male sovereign or monarch; a man who holds by life tenure (and usu. by hereditary right) the chief authority over a country and people. **2.** (*cap*) God or Christ: *King of Kings, King of Heaven.* **3.** a person or thing preeminent in its class: *the lion is the king of beasts.* **4.** a playing card bearing the formalised picture of a king, in most games counting as next highest below the ace, or highest, in its suit. **5.** the chief piece in a game of chess, moving one square at a time in any direction. **6.** a piece that has moved entirely across the board in the game of draughts and has been crowned. **7.** *Colloq.* one who displays the greatest expertise in some field. **8.** a man who has grown wealthy and powerful from a specified industry: *cattle king; wool king.* *–adj.* **9.** the largest: *king size, king prawn, king bed.* [ME; OE *cyng, cyning,* c. D *koning,* G *König,* Icel. *konungr,* Swed. *konung,* Dan. *konge*] – **kingless,** *adj.* – **kinglike,** *adj.*

**king barracouta** /– bærəˈkutə/, *n.* a heavy and thick-set barracouta of New Zealand and southern Australian waters, *Rexea solandri;* Tasmanian kingfish.

**King Billy pine,** *n.* →**King William pine.**

**kingbolt** /ˈkɪŋboʊlt/, *n.* **1.** a vertical bolt connecting the body of a horse-drawn vehicle with the fore axle, the body of a railway carriage with a truck, etc. **2.** →**kingrod.**

**king brown snake,** *n.* →**mulga snake.**

**King Charles spaniel,** *n.* a small black-and-tan toy spaniel with a rounded head, short muzzle, full eyes, and well-fringed ears and feet.

**king cobra** /kɪŋ ˈkɒbrə/, *n.* a large, venomous, elapid snake, *Naja hannah,* of India and South-East Asia; hamadryad.

**king crab** /ˈ– kræb/, *n.* **1.** →**horseshoe crab.** **2.** a large crab, *Paralithodes camtschatica,* widely distributed in coastal waters of the northern Pacific.

**kingcraft** /ˈkɪŋkraft/, *n.* the art of ruling as king; royal statesmanship.

**kingcup** /ˈkɪŋkʌp/, *n.* a widespread northern temperate ranunculaceous plant of marshes and fens, *Caltha palustris,* which has smooth heart-shaped leaves and large, bright yellow flowers.

**kingdom** /ˈkɪŋdəm/, *n.* **1.** a state or government having a king or queen as its head. **2.** anything conceived as constituting a realm or sphere of independent action or control: *the kingdom of thought.* **3.** a realm or province of nature, esp. one of the three great divisions of natural objects: *the animal, vegetable, and mineral kingdoms.* **4.** the spiritual sovereignty of God or Christ. **5.** the domain over which this extends, whether in heaven or on earth. [ME; OE *cyningdōm*]

**kingdom come** /– ˈkʌm/, *n.* the kingdom of Christ to come; the next world.

**king-fern** /ˈkɪŋ-fɜn/, *n.* **1.** the widespread fern *Marattia salicina.* **2.** *N.Z.* →**mamaku.**

**kingfish** /ˈkɪŋfɪʃ/, *n., pl.* **-fishes,** (*esp. collectively*) **-fish.** **1.** any of various fishes conspicuous for size or some other quality. **2.** →**opah.** **3.** the Spanish mackerel.

**kingfisher** /ˈkɪŋfɪʃə/, *n.* any of numerous fish- or insect-eating birds of the almost cosmopolitan family Alcedinidae, all of which are stout-billed and small-footed, and many of which are crested or brilliantly coloured. Those which eat fish capture them by diving.

**king hit** /ˈkɪŋ hɪt/, *n. Colloq.* **1.** a knock-out blow. **2.** any sudden misfortune.

**king-hit** /ˈkɪŋ-hɪt/, *v.t.,* **-hit, -hitting.** *Colloq.* to punch forcibly and without warning.

**kinghood** /ˈkɪŋhʊd/, *n.* →**kingship.**

**kingie** /ˈkɪŋi/, *n.* **1.** the giant beachworm at that stage in its development when it is found at the lowest tide level, where it can grow up to about 60cm in length and become very thick. **2.** →**king prawn.**

**king-in-his-carriage** /ˌkɪŋ-ɪn-ɪz-ˈkærɪdʒ/, *n.* a terrestrial orchid, *Drakaea glyptodon,* endemic in south-western Australia.

**King Island melilot,** *n.* →**Hexham scent.**

**kinglet** /ˈkɪŋlət/, *n.* **1.** a king ruling over a small country or territory. **2.** any of several small birds of the genus *Regulus,* as the firecrest or the goldcrest of Europe or the **golden-crowned kinglet**, *R. Satrapa* of North America.

**kingly** /ˈkɪŋli/, *adj.*, **-lier, -liest**, *adv.* *–adj.* **1.** having the rank of a king. **2.** consisting of kings or of royal rank. **3.** resembling, suggesting, or befitting a king; kinglike: *he strode into the room with a kingly air.* **4.** pertaining or proper to a king or kings. *–adv.* **5.** in a kingly manner. – **kingliness,** *n.*

**king-maker** /ˈkɪŋ-meɪkə/, *n.* one who has sufficient power to influence decisively the appointment or choice made for some important office.

**king mutton-bird** /kɪŋ ˈmʌtn-bɜd/, *n.* →**sooty shearwater.**

**king of the herrings,** *n.* **1.** the shad, genus *Clupea,* said to resemble a large herring. **2.** any of several other fish, as the oarfish, opah, rabbit-fish.

**kingpin** /ˈkɪŋpɪn/, *n.* **1.** the pin by which a stub axle is articulated to an axle beam or steering head in a motor car; a swivel pin. **2.** *Bowling.* **a.** the pin in the centre when the pins are in place. **b.** the pin at the front apex. **3.** *Colloq.* the principal person in a company, etc. **4.** *Colloq.* the chief element of any system or the like. **5.** →**kingbolt.** **6.** a child's game, similar to hand-tennis, but in which the ball must bounce first on the hitter's side of the centre line.

**kingpost** /ˈkɪŋpoʊst/, *n.* **1.** a vertical post between the apex of a triangular roof truss and the tie beam in order to support the tie beam when it bears a heavy ceiling load. **2.** →**samson post.** Also, **kingbolt.**

A, kingpost; B, tie beam; C, strut or brace

**king prawn** /kɪŋ ˈprɔn/, *n.* a large, edible prawn of eastern Australian waters, *Penaeus plebejus,* brownish in colour with a blue tail; red when cooked.

**kingrod** /ˈkɪŋrɒd/, *n.* a vertical steel rod connecting the apex of a triangular roof truss and the tie beam in order to support the tie beam when it bears a heavy ceiling load. Also, **kingbolt.**

**King's Counsel** /kɪŋz ˈkaʊnsəl/, *n.* (when the reigning monarch is a man) →**Queen's Counsel.**

**king's English** /kɪŋz ˈɪŋglɪʃ/, *n.* standard Southern British English, esp. considered as correct or desirable usage. Also, **queen's English.**

**king's evidence** /– ˈɛvədəns/, *n.* (when the reigning monarch is a man) →**queen's evidence.**

**king's evil** /– ˈivəl/, *n.* scrofula, originally so-called because it was supposed to be curable by the touch of the sovereign.

**king's highway** /– ˈhaɪweɪ/, *n.* (when the reigning monarch is a man) →**queen's highway.**

**kingship** /ˈkɪŋʃɪp/, *n.* **1.** kingly state, office, or dignity. **2.** kingly rule. **3.** aptitude for kingly duties. **4.** *Rare.* a title used in referring to a king (prec. by *his, your,* etc.).

**king-size** /ˈkɪŋ-saɪz/, *adj. Colloq.* larger than the usual size. Also, **king-sized.**

**king snake** /ˈkɪŋ sneɪk/, *n.* any of certain large harmless American snakes, esp. *Lampropeltis getulus,* which feed on other snakes, including rattlesnakes.

**king's scout** /kɪŋz ˈskaʊt/, *n.* (when the reigning monarch is a man) →**queen's scout.**

**king's shilling** /– ˈʃɪlɪŋ/, *n.* **1.** a shilling given to a new recruit to the British army, acceptance of which constituted, until 1879, a binding enlistment. **2. take the king's shilling,** to enlist in the army.

**King's speech** /kɪŋz ˈspitʃ/, *n.* (when the reigning monarch is a man) →**Queen's speech.**

**king tide** /ˈkɪŋ taɪd/, *n.* →**spring tide.**

**king-truss** /ˈkɪŋ-trʌs/, *n.* a truss framed with a kingpost.

**King William pine,** *n.* a valuable softwood timber tree, *Athrotaxis selaginoides,* found in moist forests in Tasmania. Also, **King Billy pine.**

**kingwood** /ˈkɪŋwʊd/, *n.* **1.** a Brazilian wood streaked with violet tints, used esp. in cabinetwork. **2.** the tree *Dalbergia cearensis,* which yields it. Also, **violet wood.**

**kingworm** /ˈkɪŋwɜm/, *n.* a beachworm, *Australonuphis teres,* growing up to a maximum of 100 cm with a width of 2.5 cm, greenish to brownish in colour with darker brown bands on the dorsal side and which is distributed along the east coast of Australia as far north as Fraser Island.

**kink** /kɪŋk/, *n.* **1.** a twist or curl, as in a thread, rope, or hair, caused by its doubling or bending upon itself. **2.** a crick, as in the neck or back. **3.** a mental twist; an odd notion; a whim. **4.** a deviation, esp. sexual. *–v.i., v.t.* **5.** to form or cause to form a kink or kinks, as a rope. [orig. nautical term, probably from D: twirl. Cf. Icel. *kinka* nod archly]

**kinkajou** /ˈkɪŋkədʒu/, *n.* a brownish, soft-furred, arboreal, prehensile-tailed mammal, *Potos flavus,* of Central and South America, related to the raccoon. [Canadian F; orig. the same word as CARCAJOU, from Tupi]

**kinky** /ˈkɪŋki/, *adj.*, **-kier, -kiest.** **1.** full of kinks. **2.** *Colloq.* appealing in an individual way. **3.** *Colloq.* having unusual tastes; perverted. **4.** *Colloq.* eccentric; mad. – **kinkiness,** *n.*

**kino gum** /ˈkinoʊ gʌm/, *n.* the reddish or black catechu-like inspissated juice or gum of certain trees, as that from *Pterocarpus marsupium* of India and Ceylon and *Eucalyptus camaldulensis* of Australia, used in medicine and tanning. [*kino* apparently from Mandingo *keno*]

**kinsfolk** /ˈkɪnzfoʊk/, *n.pl.* relatives or kindred. Also, **kinfolks, kinfolk.**

**kinship** /ˈkɪnʃɪp/, *n.* **1.** the state or fact of being of kin; family relationship. **2.** relationship by nature, qualities, etc.; affinity.

**kinship system** /ˈ– sɪstəm/, *n.* the system of relationships traditionally accepted by a particular culture and the rights and obligations which they involve.

**kinsman** /ˈkɪnzmən/, *n., pl.* **-men. 1.** a male blood relative. **2.** (sometimes) a relative by marriage. **3.** a person of the same race. – **kinswoman,** *n. fem.*

**kiore** /kiˈɔri/, *n.* →**Maori rat.** [Maori]

**kiosk** /ˈkiɒsk/, *n.* **1.** a small, light structure for the sale of newspapers, cigarettes, etc. **2.** a building, or part of a building, for the sale of light refreshments as at a hospital, railway station, park, etc. **3.** *Brit.* →**telephone box. 4.** a kind of open pavilion or summerhouse common in Turkey and Iran. [Turk. *kiūsk* pavilion]

**kip**[1] /kɪp/, *n., v.,* **kipped, kipping.** *Colloq. –n.* **1.** *Chiefly Brit.* sleep. *–v.i.* **2. kip down,** to go to bed; sleep. [cf. OE *cip* brothel]

**kip**[2] /kɪp/, *n.* a small thin piece of wood used for spinning coins in two-up; bat; kylie. [? var. of CHIP]

**kip**[3] /kɪp/, *n.* a unit of force in the imperial system, equal to 1000 lbf or approx. 4448 newtons. [KI(LO)- + P(OUND)]

**kip**[4] /kɪp/, *n.* **1.** the hide of a young or small beast. **2.** a bundle or set of such hides, containing a definite number. [ME *kipp* MLG, from *kip* pack (of hides), akin to Icel. *kippi* bundle]

**kipper**[1] /ˈkɪpə/, *n.* **1.** a kippered fish, esp. a herring. **2.** a method of curing fish by splitting, salting, drying, and smoking. **3.** *Colloq.* an Englishman. *–v.t.* **4.** to cure (herring, salmon, etc.) by cleaning, salting, etc., and drying in the air or in smoke. [? special use of *kipper,* OE *cypera* spawning salmon]

**kipper**[2] /ˈkɪpə/, *n.* an Aboriginal youth who has completed the initiation rite. [Aboriginal]

**Kipp's apparatus** /ˈkɪps æpəˌratəs/, *n.* an apparatus used in laboratories for the production of a gas which can be made by the action of a liquid on a solid; used esp. for the production of hydrogen sulphide.

**kipsie** /ˈkɪpsi/, *n. Colloq.* a house; the home. [diminutive of KIP[1] (a place to sleep)]

**Kirchhoff's laws** /ˈkɜkɒfs lɔz/, *n.pl. Physics.* two laws relating to electrical circuits which state: **1.** that in any network of wires the algebraic sum of the currents which meet at a point is zero. **2.** that the algebraic sum of the electromotive forces in any closed circuit is equal to the algebraic sum of the products of the resistances of each portion of the circuit and the currents flowing through them. [named after G. R. *Kirchhoff,* 1824-87, German physicist]

**kirk** /kɜk/, *n.* **1.** *Scot.* a church. **2. the Kirk,** the Established Church of Scotland, as distinguished from the Scottish Episcopal Church. [ME, from Scand.; cf. Icel. *kirkja,* c. CHURCH]

**kirkman** /ˈkɜkmən/, *n., pl.* **-men.** *Scot.* **1.** a member or follower of the Kirk. **2.** a churchman; ecclesiastic.

**Kirman** /kɜˈman/, *n.* a Persian rug marked by ornate flowing designs and light, muted colours. [var. of *Kerman,* a town and province in Iran]

**kirmess** /ˈkɜməs/, *n.* →**kermis.**

**kirsch** /kɪəʃ, kɜʃ/, *n.* a colourless brandy distilled in Germany, Alsace, and Switzerland from wild black cherries. Also, **kirshwasser** /ˈkɪəʃvasə, ˈkɜʃ-/. [G: cherry water]

**kirtle** /ˈkɜtl/, *n.* **1.** a woman's gown or skirt. **2.** *Archaic.* a man's tunic or coat. [ME *kurtel,* OE *cyrtel,* c. Icel. *kyrtill* tunic, from L *curtus* cut short] – **kirtled,** *adj.*

**kish** /kɪʃ/, *n.* a variety of graphite which sometimes forms on the surface of a molten bath of iron which has a high carbon content.

**kismet** /ˈkɪzmət, ˈkɪs-/, *n.* fate; destiny. [Turk. from Pers. *qismat,* from Ar., from *qasama* divide]

**kiss** /kɪs/, *v.t.* **1.** to touch or press with the lips, while compressing and then separating them, in token of greeting, affection, etc. **2.** to touch gently or lightly. **3.** to put, bring, take, etc., by, or as if by, kissing: *kiss your dreams goodbye.* **4. kiss the dust, a.** to be killed. **b.** to be humiliated. –*v.i.* **5.** to kiss someone, something, or each other. –*n.* **6.** the act of kissing. **7.** a slight touch or contact. [ME *kysse(n),* OE *cyssan* (c. G *küssen*), from *coss* a kiss, c. G *Küss*] – **kissable,** *adj.*

**kiss-curl** /ˈkɪs-kɜl/, *n.* a small curl, esp. on the forehead.

**kisser** /ˈkɪsə/, *n.* **1.** one who kisses. **2.** *Colloq.* the mouth.

**kiss of death,** *n.* any act, fact, influence, relationship, etc., which proves disastrous.

**kiss of life,** *n.* artificial respiration performed by the mouth-to-mouth or mouth-to-nose method.

**kit**[1] /kɪt/, *n., v.,* **kitted, kitting.** –*n.* **1.** a set or collection of tools, supplies, etc., for a specific purpose: *a first-aid kit.* **2.** a set or collection of parts to be assembled: *a model aircraft kit.* **3.** a case containing tools, parts, etc., or the case with its contents. **4.** *Chiefly Mil.* a set of clothing or personal equipment for a specific purpose: *the soldiers were issued with a complete kit.* **5. the (whole) kit and caboodle,** *Colloq.* **a.** the whole thing; an item with all its parts. **b.** the whole group. –*v.t.* **6.** *Mil.* to provide with kit. [ME *kyt, kitt,* apparently from MD *kitte* kind of tub. Cf. Norw. *kitte* bin]

**kit**[2] /kɪt/, *n.* a kind of small violin, used by dancing masters from the 16th to the 18th century. [orig. uncert.]

**kit**[3] /kɪt/, *n. N.Z.* a woven flax basket. [Maori *kete* flax basket]

**kit.,** kitchen.

**kitbag** /ˈkɪtbæg/, *n.* a long canvas bag in which soldiers, etc., carry their personal belongings.

**kitchen** /ˈkɪtʃən/, *n.* **1.** a room or place equipped for or appropriated to cooking. **2.** the culinary department; cuisine. **3. the rounds of the kitchen,** *Colloq.* a severe scolding. [ME *kitchene,* OE *cycene,* from L *coquīna*]

**kitchener** /ˈkɪtʃənə/, *n.* **1.** one employed in, or in charge of, a kitchen. **2.** an elaborate cooking stove.

**kitchenette** /kɪtʃəˈnɛt/, *n.* a small kitchen.

**kitchen garden** /kɪtʃən ˈgadn/, *n.* →**vegetable garden.** – **kitchen gardener.**

**kitchenman** /ˈkɪtʃənmæn/, *n.* a man employed as an assistant in the kitchen of a hotel, restaurant, etc.

**kitchen midden** /kɪtʃən ˈmɪdn/, *n.* →**midden** (def. 2). [translation of Dan. *kökkenmödding*]

**kitchen section** /ˈ– sɛkʃən/, *n. Colloq.* the percussion section of the conventional orchestra.

**kitchen sink** /– ˈsɪŋk/, *n.* **1.** a sink in a kitchen. **2. everything but the kitchen sink,** *Colloq.* a large number of miscellaneous items.

**kitchen-sink** /kɪtʃən-ˈsɪŋk/, *adj.* (of plays, etc.) dealing realistically with the sordid aspects of contemporary domestic life.

**kitchen tea** /kɪtʃən ˈti/, *n.* →**shower tea.**

**kitchen tidy** /– ˈtaɪdi/, *n.* small garbage bin kept in the kitchen.

**kitchenware** /ˈkɪtʃənwɛə/, *n.* cooking equipment or utensils.

**kite** /kaɪt/, *n., v.,* **kited, kiting.** –*n.* **1.** a light frame covered with some thin material, to be flown in the wind at the end of a long string. **2.** any of various medium-sized hawks of the family Accipitridae with long wings and tail as the black kite, *Milvus migrans* of Eurasia, Africa and Australia. **3.** a person who preys on others; a sharper. **4.** *Naut.* **a.** any light sail that is usu. spread in light winds, and furled in a strong breeze. **b.** *Colloq.* a spinnaker. **5.** *Comm.* a fictitious negotiable instrument, not representing any actual transaction, used for raising money or sustaining credit. **6.** *Colloq.* an aeroplane. **7.** *Colloq.* a hang-glider. **8.** *Colloq.* a cheque, esp. one forged or stolen. **9.** *Prison Colloq.* a newspaper. **10. fly a kite,** *Colloq.* **a.** to pass off a forged cheque. **b.** to test public opinion by spreading rumours, etc. –*v.i.* **11.** *Colloq.* to fly or move with a rapid or easy motion like that of a kite. **12.** *Comm.* to obtain money or credit through kites. –*v.t.* **13.** *Comm.* to employ as a kite. [ME *kyte,* OE *cȳta;* akin to G *Kauz* kind of owl]

**kite balloon** /ˈ– bəlun/, *n.* a captive balloon, used for observation.

**kith** /kɪθ/, *n.* **1.** one's acquaintances or friends (now chiefly Scot. except in *kith and kin* and often confused in meaning with *kin*). **2. kith and kin,** friends and relatives. [ME *kitthe,* OE *cȳth, cȳththu* knowledge, acquaintance, native land, from *cūth* known, pp. of *cunnan* CAN[1]]

**kithara** /ˈkɪθərə/, *n.* a musical instrument of ancient Greece; cithara. [Gk]

**kitsch** /kɪtʃ/, *n.* pretentious or worthless art, literature, etc. [G]

**kitset** /ˈkɪtsɛt/, *n.* the component parts needed to assemble an article as a radio or a piece of furniture, or model as an aeroplane.

**kitten** /ˈkɪtn/, *n.* **1.** a young cat. **2.** a playful or skittish girl. **3. have kittens,** *Colloq.* to be anxious or alarmed. –*v.i.* **4.** (of cats) to give birth to; bear. [ME *kitoun, kyton,* from d. OF; cf. OF *chitoun, chaton,* diminutive of *chat* cat] – **kitten-like,** *adj.*

**kittenish** /ˈkɪtənɪʃ/, *adj.* **1.** kitten-like; artlessly playful. **2.** of a woman affecting naive, sexually enticing behaviour. – **kittenishly,** *adv.* – **kittenishness,** *n.*

**kittiwake** /ˈkɪtiweɪk/, *n.* either of two gulls of the genus *Rissa,* having the hind toe very short or rudimentary. [imitative of its cry]

**kittle** /ˈkɪtl/, *v.,* **-tled, -tling,** *adj.,* **-tler, -tlest.** *Brit.* –*v.t.* **1.** to tickle. **2.** to excite or arouse. –*adj.* **3.** difficult to deal with; risky; ticklish. [Scand.; cf. Icel. *kitla* tickle]

**kitty**[1] /ˈkɪti/, *n., pl.* **-ties.** **1.** a kitten. **2.** a pet name for a cat. [KITT(EN) + -Y[2]]

**kitty**[2] /ˈkɪti/, *n., pl.* **-ties.** **1.** a jointly held fund or collection, usu. of small amounts of money; savings; accumulation. **2.** a pool into which each player in a card game places a certain sum of money as a stake. **3.** *Bowling.* the jack. [apparently familiar derivation of *kitcot,* phonetic var. of *kidcot* prison, from KID[1] (in sense of slave or criminal) + COT[2]]

**kitty litter** /ˈ– lɪtə/, *n.* a granular, absorbent and deodorised preparation designed for cat excreta. [Trademark]

**kiwi** /ˈkiwi/, *n.* **1.** any of several flightless birds of New Zealand, constituting the genus *Apteryx,* having vestigial wings, stout legs and a long slender bill. **2.** (*cap.*) *Colloq.* a New Zealand soldier or representative sportsman, esp. a Rugby League representative. **3.** (*cap.*) *Colloq.* any New Zealander. –*adj.* **4.** (*cap.*) of or pertaining to New Zealand. [Maori]

kiwi

**Kiwi fruit** /ˈ– frut/, *n.* →**Chinese gooseberry.**

**Kiwiland** /ˈkiwilænd/, *n. Colloq.* →**New Zealand.**

**K Kt,** *Chess.* king's knight.

**kL,** kilolitre

**klangfarbenmelodie** /klæŋˈfabənˌmɛlədi/, *n.* a succession of different timbres, as from different orchestral instruments, linked together in a discernible form, as pitches are linked together to make a melody. [G]

**Klansman** /ˈklænzmən/, *n., pl.* **-men.** a member of the Ku Klux Klan.

**klaxon** /ˈklæksən/, *n.* a type of warning hooter with a strident tone, originally used in motor vehicles. [Trademark]

**Klebs-Löffler bacillus** /klɛbz-ˈlɜflə bəˌsɪləs/, *n.* the bacillus *Corynebacterium diphtheriae,* which causes diptheria. [named after Edwin *Klebs,* 1834-1913, and F. A. J. *Löffler,* 1852-1915, German bacteriologists]

**kleenex** /ˈklinɛks/, *n.* →**tissue** (def. 5). [Trademark]

**kleptomania** /klɛptəˈmeɪniə/, *n.* an irresistible desire to steal, without regard to personal needs. Also, **cleptomania.** [NL, from Gk *kléptēs* thief + *-mania* -MANIA]

**kleptomaniac** /klɛptəˈmeɪniæk/, *n.* one affected with kleptomania. Also, **cleptomaniac.**

**klieg eyes** /ˈklig aɪz/, *n.pl.* inflammation and oedema of the eyes as a result of prolonged exposure to arc lights, as the klieg lights of the film industry.

**klieg light** /ˈ– laɪt/, *n.* a floodlight with an arc-light source used in film studios to project a beam of high actinic power. [named after J. H. *Kliegl,* 1869-1959, and his brother, Anton T. *Kliegl,* 1872-1927, German-born U.S. inventors]

**klinki pine** /ˈklɪŋki paɪn/, *n.* a valuable softwood timber tree, *Araucaria klinkii,* found in forests in New Guinea.

**klipspringer** /ˈklɪpsprɪŋə/, *n.* a small, active African antelope, *Oreotragus oreotragus,* of mountainous regions from the Cape of Good Hope to Ethiopia. [Afrikaans: lit., rock-springer]

klipspringer

**klystron** /ˈklaɪstrɒn/, *n.* an electron tube used to generate or amplify electromagnetic radiation in the microwave regions. [apparently from Gk *klystḗr* syringe]

**km,** kilometre; kilometres.

**K-meson** /ˈkeɪ-mizɒn/, *n.* one of a group of mesons all of which have a mass approximately equal to half of that of a proton; they exist in positive, negative, and neutral charged states. Also, **kaon.**

**km/s,** kilometres per second.

**kn,** international knot.

**knack** /næk/, *n.* a faculty or power of doing something with ease as from special skill; aptitude. [ME *knak;* ? akin to *knack,* v., strike (imitative)]

**knacker** /ˈnækə/, *n.* **1.** one who buys old or useless horses for slaughter. **2.** one who buys old houses, ships, etc., to break them up for scrap. **3.** (*pl.*) *Colloq.* testicles. [obs. *knack,* v. (from Scand.; cf. Icel. *hnakkr* nape of neck, saddle) + -ER[1]; orig. sense, saddler] – **knackery,** *n.*

**knackered** /ˈnækəd/, *adj. Colloq.* exhausted; worn out.

**knackwurst** /ˈnækwɜst/, *n.* a short, thick, highly seasoned sausage like a frankfurter. [G, from *knacken* to crack (as the skin does when bitten) + *Wurst* sausage]

**knag** /næg/, *n.* **1.** a knot in wood. **2.** the base of a branch. [ME, c. G *Knagge* knot, peg]

**knaggy** /ˈnægi/, *adj.* knotty; rough with knots.

**knap** /næp/, *v.t.,* **knapped, knapping.** to break up (ore) into small pieces with a hard, short blow; chip. [late ME; c. D *knappen* to crack]

**knapsack** /ˈnæpsæk/, *n.* a leather or canvas case for clothes and the like, carried on the back, esp. by soldiers. [LG, from *knappen* bite, eat + *sack* SACK[1]]

**knapweed** /ˈnæpwid/, *n.* any of a number of old world plants of the genus *Centaurea;* hardheads.

**knar** /na/, *n.* a knot on a tree or in wood. [ME *knarre,* c. D *knar*] – **knarred,** *adj.*

**knave** /neɪv/, *n.* **1.** an unprincipled or dishonest fellow. **2.** *Cards.* a playing card bearing the formalised picture of a prince, in most games counting as next below the queen in its suit; jack. **3.** *Archaic.* a male servant or man of humble position. [ME; OE *cnafa,* c. G *Knabe* boy]

**knavery** /ˈneɪvəri/, *n., pl.* **-ries. 1.** action or practice characteristic of a knave. **2.** unprincipled or dishonest dealing; trickery. **3.** a knavish act or practice.

**knavish** /ˈneɪvɪʃ/, *adj.* **1.** like or befitting a knave; dishonest. **2.** waggish; mischievous. – **knavishly,** *adv.* – **knavishness,** *n.*

**knawel** /ˈnɔəl/, *n.* any of several small plants of the genus *Scleranthus,* as *S. annuus,* **annual knawel,** widespread in sandy places. [G *Knäuel,* lit., ball of yarn]

**knead** /nid/, *v.t.* **1.** to work (dough, etc.) into a uniform mixture by pressing, folding and stretching. **2.** to manipulate by similar movements, as the body in massage. **3.** to make by kneading. **4.** to make kneading motions with. [ME *kneden,* OE *cnedan,* c. G *kneten*] – **kneader,** *n.*

**knee** /ni/, *n., v.,* **kneed, kneeing.** –*n.* **1.** the joint or region in man between the thigh and the lower part of the leg. **2.** the joint or region of other vertebrates corresponding or homologous to the human knee, as in the leg of a bird, the hind limb of a horse, etc. **3.** a joint or region likened to this but not homologous with it, as the tarsal joint of a bird, or the carpal joint in the forelimb of a horse, cow, etc. **4.** the part of a garment covering the knee. **5.** something resembling a knee joint, esp. when bent, as a fabricated support or brace with a leg running at an angle to the main member. **6.** a piece of wood or metal with an angular bend. **7. bring someone to his knees,** to compel someone to submit. –*v.t.* **8.** to strike or touch with the knee. –*v.i.* **9.** *Obs. or Poetic.* to go down on the knees; kneel. [ME *know(e), kne(w),* OE *cnēo(w),* c. D *knie,* G *Knie.* Cf. KNEEL]

**knee-bend** /ˈni-bɛnd/, *n.* a physical exercise which involves bending both knees so as to lower the body with the trunk still vertical, then straightening them to restore the body to its original position, all without the assistance of the hands.

**kneeboard** /ˈnibɔd/, *n.* a short surfboard ridden in a kneeling position.

**knee breeches** /ˈni brɪtʃəz/, *n. pl.* breeches reaching to or just below the knee.

**kneecap** /ˈnikæp/, *n.* **1.** the patella, the flat, movable bone at the front of the knee. **2.** a protective covering, usu. knitted, for the knee.

**knee-deep** /ˈni-dip/, *adj.* **1.** so deep as to reach the knees: *the snow lay knee-deep.* **2.** submerged or covered by something having such depth.

**knee drop** /ˈni drɒp/, *n.* (in wrestling) lifting an opponent and dropping him onto one's own bent knee.

**knee-high** /ˈni-haɪ/, *adj.* **1.** as high as the knees. **2. knee-high to a grasshopper,** *Colloq.* very small in height.

**knee-hole** /ˈni-houl/, *n.* a space into which to fit the knees, as under a desk.

**knee jerk** /ˈni dʒɜk/, *n.* a brisk reflex lifting of the leg induced by tapping the tendon below the kneecap; patellar reflex.

**knee-jerk reaction,** *n.* automatic aversion or predictable opposition to a person or idea.

**kneel** /nil/, *v.,* **knelt** or **kneeled, kneeling,** *n.* –*v.i.* **1.** to fall or rest on the knees or a knee. **2. kneel on,** *Colloq.* to oppress; force into submission. –*n.* **3.** the action or position of kneeling. [ME *knele(n), knewlen,* OE *cnēowlian* (c. D *knielen,* LG *knelen*), from *cnēow* KNEE] – **kneeler,** *n.*

**knee-length** /ˈni-lɛŋθ/, *adj.* (of a garment) coming down as far as the knees.

**kneepad** /ˈnipæd/, *n.* a pad to protect the knee.

**kneepan** /ˈnipæn/, *n.* the kneecap or patella.

**kneepiece** /ˈnipis/, *n.* armour for the knee, of hardened leather or of steel.

**knee-sprung** /ˈni-sprʌŋ/, *adj.* (of a horse, mule, etc.) having a forward bowing of the knee caused by inflammatory shortening of the flexor tendons.

**kneetrembler** /ˈnitrɛmblə/, *n. Colloq.* the act of sexual intercourse when both parties are standing.

**knell** /nɛl/, *n.* **1.** the sound made by a bell rung slowly for a death or a funeral. **2.** any sound announcing the death of a person or the extinction, failure, etc., of something. **3.** any mournful sound. –*v.i.* **4.** to sound, as a bell, esp. as a funeral bell. **5.** to give forth a mournful, ominous, or warning sound. –*v.t.* **6.** to proclaim or summon by, or as by, a bell. [ME *knelle, knylle,* OE *cnyllan* strike, ring (a bell), c. Icel. *knylla* beat, strike]

**knelt** /nɛlt/, *v.* past tense and past participle of **kneel.**

**knew** /nju/, *v.* past tense of **know.**

**knickerbockers** /ˈnɪkəbɒkəz/, *n.pl.* **1.** loosely fitting short breeches gathered in at the knee. **2.** a similar garment worn as decorative underpants. [from *Knickerbocker,* a descendant of the Dutch settlers of New York]

**knickers** /ˈnɪkəz/, *n. pl.* **1.** →**panties. 2.** →**knickerbockers.** Also, **knicks.** [shortened form of KNICKERBOCKERS]

**knick-knack** /ˈnɪk-næk/, *n.* **1.** a pleasing trifle; a trinket or gimcrack. **2.** a bit of bric-a-brac. Also, **nick-nack.** [dissimilated reduplication of KNACK]

**knife** /naɪf/, *n., pl.* **knives,** *v.,* **knifed, knifing.** *–n.* **1.** a cutting instrument consisting essentially of a thin blade (usu. of steel and with a sharp edge) attached to a handle. **2.** a knifelike weapon; a dagger; a short sword. **3.** any blade for cutting, as in a tool or machine. **4. get one's knife into,** to bear a grudge against; desire to hurt. **5. put the knife into,** to destroy a reputation or person maliciously. **6. war to the knife,** war without mercy; relentless hostility. *–v.t.* **7.** to apply a knife to; cut, stab, etc., with a knife. **8.** to endeavour to defeat in a secret or underhand way. **9. knife in the back,** to betray, esp. to destroy a person's reputation or career in his or her absence. [ME *knif,* OE *cnīf,* c. Icel. *knīfr*] **– knifeless,** *adj.* **– knifelike,** *adj.*

**knifeboard** /ˈnaɪfbɔd/, *n.* (formerly) **1.** a board on which knives were cleaned. **2.** a long double bench on the top deck of an open-top bus or tram. *–adj.* **3.** of or pertaining to such benches: *knifeboard seating.*

**knife edge** /ˈnaɪf ɛdʒ/, *n.* **1.** the edge of a knife. **2.** anything very sharp. **3.** a wedge, on the fine edge of which a scale beam, pendulum, or the like, oscillates.

**knife-edged** /ˈnaɪf-ɛdʒd/, *adj.* having a thin, sharp edge.

**knife pleat** /ˈnaɪf plit/, *n.* one of a series of very fine pleats.

**knife switch** /ˈ– swɪtʃ/, *n.* a form of air-switch in which the moving element, usu. a hinged blade, enters or embraces the contact clips.

**knight** /naɪt/, *n.* **1.** *Medieval Hist.* **a.** a mounted soldier serving under a feudal superior. **b.** a man, usu. of noble birth, who, after an apprenticeship as page and squire, was raised to honourable military rank and bound to chivalrous conduct. **2.** any person of a rank similar to that of the medieval knight. **3.** a man upon whom a certain dignity, corresponding to that of the medieval knight, and with it the honorific *Sir,* is conferred by a sovereign for life, because of personal merit or for services rendered to the country. **4.** *Chess.* a piece shaped like a horse's head, moving two squares horizontally or vertically, and then one square obliquely or vice versa. **5.** a member of any order or association of men bearing the name of *Knights.* *–v.t.* **6.** to dub or create (a man) a knight. [ME; OE *cniht* boy, manservant; c. D *knecht,* G *Knecht*]

**knight bachelor** /– ˈbætʃələ/, *n.* the lowest in rank among British knights, not belonging to any special order.

**knight banneret** /– ˈbænərət/, *n.* →**banneret** (def. 2).

**knight-errant** /naɪt-ˈɛrənt/, *n., pl.* **knights-errant.** a wandering knight; a knight in medieval times, who travelled in search of adventures, to exhibit military skill, etc.

**knight-errantry** /naɪt-ˈɛrəntri/, *n., pl.* **knight-errantries. 1.** conduct or a performance like that of a knight-errant. **2.** quixotic conduct or action.

**knightheads** /ˈnaɪthɛdz/, *n.pl.* the top of two heavy timbers built up one on each side of the stem of a sailing ship, to support the bowsprit.

**knighthood** /ˈnaɪthʊd/, *n.* **1.** the rank or dignity of a knight. **2.** the profession or vocation of a knight. **3.** knightly character or qualities. **4.** the body of knights.

**knightly** /ˈnaɪtli/, *adj.* **1.** of or belonging to a knight: *knightly deeds.* **2.** characteristic of a knight. **3.** being or resembling a knight. **4.** composed of knights. *–adv.* **5.** in a manner befitting a knight. **– knightliness,** *n.*

**knit** /nɪt/, *v.,* **knitted** or **knit, knitting,** *n.* *–v.t.* **1.** to make (a garment, fabric, etc.) by interlacing loops of yarn either by hand with knitting needles or by machine. **2.** to join closely and firmly together, as members or parts. **3.** to contract into folds or wrinkles: *to knit the brow.* *–v.i.* **4.** to become closely and firmly joined together; grow together, as broken bones do. **5.** to contract, as the brow does. **6.** to become closely or intimately united. *–n.* **7.** fabric produced by interlooping of a yarn or yarns. [ME *knitte,* OE *cynttan* tie, from *cnotta* KNOT[1]] **– knitter,** *n.*

**knitting** /ˈnɪtɪŋ/, *n.* **1.** the act of a person or thing that knits. **2.** the act of forming a fabric by looping a continuous yarn. **3.** knitted work.

**knitting machine** /ˈ– məʃin/, *n.* a machine which produces knitted goods.

**knitting needle** /ˈ– nidl/, *n.* an instrument for knitting; a straight, slender rod of steel, plastic, etc., with rounded ends.

**knitwear** /ˈnɪtwɛə/, *n.* clothing made of knitted fabric.

**knives** /naɪvz/, *n.* plural of **knife.**

**knob** /nɒb/, *n., v.,* **knobbed, knobbing.** *–n.* **1.** a projecting part, usu. rounded, forming the handle of a door, drawer, or the like. **2.** a rounded lump or protuberance on the surface or at the end of something, as a knot on a tree trunk, a pimple on the skin, etc. **3.** *Archit.* an ornamental boss, as of carved work. **4.** a rounded hill or mountain, esp. an isolated one. **5.** *Colloq.* the penis. *–v.t.* **6.** to furnish with knobs; produce knobs on. *–v.i.* **7.** to form a knob or knobs. [ME. Cf. G *Knobbe*] **– knobbed,** *adj.* **– knoblike,** *adj.*

**knobble** /ˈnɒbəl/, *n.* a small knob.

**knobbly** /ˈnɒbli/, *adj.* full or covered with knobbles; knobby; knotty.

**knobby**[1] /ˈnɒbi/, *adj.,* **-bier, -biest. 1.** abounding in knobs. **2.** knoblike. **– knobbiness,** *n.*

**knobby**[2] /ˈnɒbi/, *n.* →**nobby**[2].

**knobkerrie** /ˈnɒbkɛri/, *n.* a short, heavy stick or club with a knob on one end, used for both striking and throwing by South African natives. [Afrikaans *knopkiri,* from *knop* knob + Hottentot *kiri* stick, club]

**knob-tailed gecko** /nɒb-teɪld ˈgɛkoʊ/, *n.* a small, Northern Territory gecko, *Nephrurus asper,* having curious rugosities on its body and a terminal knob on its tail; illchiljera.

**knock** /nɒk/, *v.i.* **1.** to strike a sounding blow with the fist, knuckles, or anything hard, esp. on a door, window, or the like, as in seeking admittance, calling attention, giving a signal, etc. **2.** (of an internal-combustion engine) to make a metallic noise as a result of faulty combustion. **3.** to collide (usu. followed by *against* or *into*). *–v.t.* **4.** to give a sounding or forcible blow to; hit; strike; beat. **5.** to drive, force, or render by a blow or blows: *to knock a man senseless.* **6.** to strike (a thing) against something else. **7.** *Colloq.* to criticise; find fault with. *–v.* **8.** Some special verb phrases are:

**knock about,** or **around, 1.** to wander in an aimless way; lead an irregular existence. **2.** to treat roughly; maltreat.

**knock around with,** *Colloq.* to keep company with.

**knock back, 1.** *Colloq.* to consume, esp. rapidly: *he knocked back two cans of beer.* **2.** *Colloq.* to refuse. **3.** to set back; impede.

**knock down, 1.** to strike to the ground with a blow. **2.** *N.Z.* to fell (a tree). **3.** (in auctions) to signify the sale of (the thing bid for) by a blow with a hammer or mallet; assign as sold to the highest bidder. **4.** to reduce the price of. **5.** to take apart (a motor vehicle, machine, etc.) to facilitate handling. **6.** to spend freely: *to knock down one's cheque.* **7.** *N.Z.* to swallow (a drink).

**knock end wise (endways),** to lay flat with a blow.

**knock into a cocked hat,** *Colloq.* to defeat; get the better of.

**knock it off,** *Colloq.* stop it (usu. used to put an end to an argument, fight, criticism, etc.).

**knock off,** *Colloq.* **1.** to stop an activity, esp. work. **2.** to deduct. **3.** to steal. **4.** to compose (an article, poem, or the like) hurriedly. **5.** to defeat, put out of a competition. **6.** to kill. **7.** (of a man) to have sexual intercourse with. **8.** to eat up; consume. **9.** (of police) to arrest (a person) or raid (a place).

**knock on,** *Rugby Football.* to knock (the ball) forwards in catching it (an infringement of the rules).

**knock oneself out,** to exhaust oneself by excessive mental or physical work.

**knock one's eye out,** to cause one to feel excessive admiration.

**knock on the head,** to put an end to.

**knock out, 1.** to defeat (an opponent) in a boxing match by striking him down with a blow after which he does not rise within a prescribed time. **2.** to render senseless. **3.** to destroy; damage severely. **4.** to earn.

**knock spots off,** *Colloq.* to defeat; get the better of.

**knock the bottom out of,** to refute (an argument); render invalid.

**knock together,** to assemble (something) hastily; put together roughly.

**knock up, 1.** to arouse; awaken. **2.** to construct (something) hastily or roughly. **3.** *Sport.* to score runs, tries, etc. **4.** *Tennis.* to practise. **5.** to exhaust; wear out. **6.** to become exhausted. **7.** *Colloq.* to make pregnant.

*–n.* **9.** the act or sound of knocking. **10.** a rap, as at a

door. **11.** a blow or thump. **12.** the noise resulting from faulty combustion or from incorrect functioning of some part of an internal-combustion engine. **13.** *Cricket.* an innings. **14.** *Colloq.* adverse criticism. **15. take a knock,** to suffer a reverse, esp. a finanical one. **16. take the knock,** *Horseracing, etc. Colloq.* (of a punter) to admit that one is unable to settle one's debts with one's bookmaker. **17. take the knock on (someone),** *Colloq.* to cheat (someone) of his share in part or whole; to welsh on. [ME *knokke,* unexplained var. of *knoke,* OE *cnocian,* c. Icel. *knoka;* ? imitative in orig.]

**knockabout** /ˈnɒkəbaʊt/, *n.* **1.** *Naut.* a small handy yacht with a jib and mainsail but no bowsprit. **2.** *Colloq.* a station hand; odd-job man. *–adj.* **3.** suitable for rough use, as a garment. **4.** characterised by knocking about; rough; boisterous: *knockabout comedy.* Also, **knock-around.**

**knock-back** /ˈnɒk-bæk/, *n. Colloq.* a refusal; rejection.

**knockdown** /ˈnɒkdaʊn/, *adj.* **1.** such as to knock something down; overwhelming; irresistible: *a knockdown blow.* **2.** constructed in separate parts, so as to be readily knocked down or taken apart, as a boat, a piece of furniture, etc. **3. knockdown price,** the reserve price of an article at an auction, below which it cannot be knocked down. *–n.* **4.** a knockdown object. **5.** the act of knocking down, esp. by a blow. **6.** that which falls or overwhelms. **7.** *Naut.* a sudden heeling over of a sailing boat to a large angle usu. caused by a gust of wind. **8.** *Colloq.* a formal introduction.

**knocked-up** /nɒkt-ˈʌp/, *adj.* **1.** exhausted; fatigued. Also, esp. in predicative use, **knocked up.** **2.** *Chiefly U.S.* pregnant.

**knocker** /ˈnɒkə/, *n.* **1.** one who or that which knocks. **2.** a hinged knob, bar, etc., on a door, for use in knocking. **3.** *Colloq.* a persistently hostile critic or carping detractor. **4. on the knocker,** *Colloq.* at the right time, punctual: *he was there on the knocker.*

**knockers** /ˈnɒkəz/, *n. pl. Colloq.* breasts.

**knock-for-knock agreement** /nɒk-fə-nɒk əgˈrimənt/, *n.* an agreement between insurance companies, whereby each company bears the loss to its own policy holder without requiring him to bring an action against the other party involved, as in a motor car collision.

**knocking shop** /ˈnɒkɪŋ ʃɒp/, *n. Colloq.* a brothel.

**knock-knee** /ˈnɒk-ni/, *n.* **1.** inward curvature of the legs, causing the knees to knock together in walking. **2.** (*pl.*) such knees. – **knock-kneed,** *adj.*

**knock-on** /nɒk-ˈɒn/, *n.* (in Rugby Football) the act or infringement of knocking on.

**knockout** /ˈnɒkaʊt/, *n.* **1.** the act of knocking out. **2.** state or fact of being knocked out. **3.** a knockout blow. **4.** *Colloq.* a person or thing of overwhelming success or attractiveness. **5.** *Aus. Rules.* →**hit-out** (def. 1). *–adj.* **6.** that knocks out. **7.** (of a competition) eliminating competitors at each round until only the winner remains. **8.** (of card games) eliminating players under certain circumstances, as on the failure to win a trick.

**knockout drop** /ˈ– drɒp/, *n. Colloq.* a sedative pill, often added to a drink. Also, **knock-drop.**

**knocktaker** /ˈnɒkteɪkə/, *n. Colloq.* something which is a certainty to win, as a racehorse.

**knock-up** /ˈnɒk-ʌp/, *n.* practice before a game commences, as in tennis, squash, etc.

**knoll**[1] /nɒl/, *n.* a small, rounded hill or eminence; a hillock. [ME *knol,* OE *cnol(l),* c. Norw. *knoll* hillock]

**knoll**[2] /nɒl/, *v.t. Archaic.* **1.** to ring a knell for; announce by strokes of a bell or the like. **2.** to ring or toll (a bell). *–v.i.* **3.** to sound, as a bell; ring. **4.** to sound a knell. *–n.* **5.** a stroke of a bell in ringing or tolling. [ME; akin to KNELL]

**Knoop hardness** /nup ˈhadnəs/, *n.* microhardness of metal measured by resistance to indentation by a pyramidal diamond indentor. [named after F. *Knoop,* 20th-cent. U.S. chemist]

**knop** /nɒp/, *n.* a small, rounded protuberance; a knob; a boss, stud, or the like, as for ornament. [ME and OE, c. G *Knopf*]

**knot**[1] /nɒt/, *n., v.,* **knotted, knotting.** *–n.* **1.** an interlacement of a cord, rope, or the like, drawn tight into a lump or knob, as for fastening two cords, etc., together or to something else. **2.** a piece of ribbon or similar material tied or folded upon itself and used or worn as an ornament. **3.** a cluster of persons or things. **4.** *Bot.* a protuberance in the tissue of a plant; an excrescence on a stem, branch, or root; a node or joint in a stem, esp. when of swollen form. **5.** *Zool.* a hard lump in an animal body as a swelling or the like in a muscle, gland, etc. **6.** the hard, cross-grained mass of wood at the place where a branch joins the trunk of a tree. **7.** a part of this mass showing in a piece of timber, etc. **8.** any of various diseases of trees characterised by the formation of an excrescence, knob, or gnarl. **9.** *Naut.* **a.** originally one of a series of equal divisions on a log line, marked off by strings knotted through the strands and made of such a length that the number running out in a certain time indicated the ship's speed in nautical miles per hour. **b.** a unit of speed, used in marine and aerial navigation, and in meteorology, of one international nautical mile per hour or 0.514 444 44 m/s (approx. 1.85 km/h). **10. at a rate of knots,** very fast. **11.** something involved or intricate; a difficulty; a knotty problem. **12.** a bond or tie. *–v.t.* **13.** to tie in a knot or knots; form a knot or knots in. **14.** to secure by a knot. **15.** to form protuberances, bosses, or knobs in; make knotty. *–v.i.* **16.** to become tied or tangled in a knot or knots. **17.** to form knots or joints. [ME *knot(te),* OE *cnotta,* c. D *knot*] – **knotless,** *adj.*

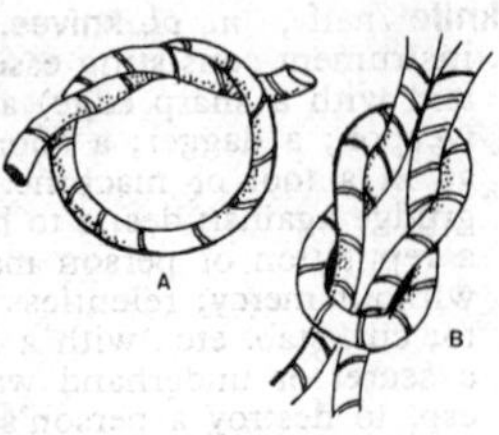

knot: A, overhand; B, reef knot

**knot**[2] /nɒt/, *n.* either of two grey shorebirds of the genus *Calidris,* which migrate to Australia, among other countries, from breeding grounds in the Arctic Circle. [? imitative of its call]

**knot garden** /ˈ– gadn/, *n.* a formal garden with the beds arranged so as to make complicated, usu. geometrical, patterns.

**knothole** /ˈnɒthoʊl/, *n.* a hole in a board or plank formed by the falling out of a knot or a portion of a knot.

**knotted** /ˈnɒtəd/, *adj.* **1.** knotty. **2.** *Bot.* having many nodes or nodelike swellings; gnarled. **3.** *Zool.* having one or more swellings; nodose. **4. get knotted,** *Colloq.* go away, leave me alone.

**knotting** /ˈnɒtɪŋ/, *n.* a solution of shellac in industrial methylated spirits, used in the preparation of wood for covering knots and other resinous areas which might stain or soften a coat of paint.

**knotty** /ˈnɒti/, *adj.,* **-tier, -tiest.** **1.** characterised by knots; full of knots. **2.** involved, intricate, or difficult: *a knotty problem.* – **knottiness,** *n.*

**knotweed** /ˈnɒtwid/, *n.* →**wireweed.** Also, **knotgrass.**

**knout** /naʊt/, *n.* **1.** a kind of whip or scourge formerly used in Russia for flogging criminals. *–v.t.* **2.** to flog with the knout. [F, from Russ. *knut*]

**know** /noʊ/, *v.,* **knew, known, knowing,** *n.* *–v.t.* **1.** to perceive or understand as fact or truth, or apprehend with clearness and certainty. **2.** to have fixed in the mind or memory: *to know a poem by heart.* **3.** to be cognisant or aware of; to be acquainted with (a thing, place, person etc.), as by sight, experience, or report. **4.** to understand from experience or attainment (fol. by *how* before an infinitive): *to know how to make something.* **5.** to be able to distinguish, as one from another. **6. not to know from Adam,** not to know or recognise (someone). **7. know chalk from cheese,** to be able to note differences. **8. know the ropes, a.** to know the various ropes about a vessel, as a sailor does. **b.** *Colloq.* to understand the details or methods of any business or the like. **9. know which side one's bread is buttered,** to know where the advantage lies. *–v.i.* **10.** to have knowledge, or clear and certain perception, as of fact or truth. **11.** to be cognisant or aware, as of some fact, circumstances, or occurrence; have information, as about something. *–n.* **12. in the know,** having inside knowledge. [ME *know(e), knawe(n),* OE *(ge)cnāwan,* c. OHG *-cnāan* know, Icel. *knā* (pres. ind.) know how, can; akin to L *(g)nōscere,* Gk *gignṓskein*] – **knower,** *n.*

**knowable** /ˈnoʊəbəl/, *adj.* that may be known. – **knowableness,** *n.*

**know-all** /ˈnoʊ-ɔl/, *n. Colloq.* **1.** one who claims to know everything, or everything about a particular subject. **2.** one who appears to know everything.

**know-how** /ˈnoʊ-haʊ/, *n.* knowledge of how to do something; faculty or skill for a particular thing.

**knowing** /ˈnoʊɪŋ/, *adj.* **1.** shrewd, sharp, or astute; often affecting or suggesting shrewd or secret understanding of matters: *a knowing glance.* **2.** having knowledge or information; intelligent; wise. **3.** conscious; intentional; deliberate. **–knowingly,** *adv.* **–knowingness,** *n.*

**knowledge** /ˈnɒlɪdʒ/, *n.* **1.** acquaintance with facts, truths, or principles, as from study or investigation; general erudition. **2.** familiarity or conversance, as with a particular subject, branch of learning, etc. **3.** acquaintance; familiarity gained by sight, experience, or report: *a knowledge of human nature.* **4.** the fact or state of knowing; perception of fact or truth; clear and certain mental apprehension. **5.** the state of being cognisant or aware, as of a fact or circumstance. **6.** that which is known, or may be known. **7.** the body of truths or facts accumulated by mankind in the course of time. **8.** the sum of what is known. **9.** cognisance of facts, or range of cognisance: *this has happened twice within my knowledge.* **10.** *Law or Archaic.* sexual intercourse: *carnal knowledge.* **11. to one's knowledge, a.** according to one's certain knowledge. **b.** (with a negative) so far as one knows: *I never saw him, to my knowledge.* [ME *knowleche,* from KNOW]

**knowledgeable** /ˈnɒlədʒəbəl/, *adj.* possessing knowledge or understanding; intelligent.

**known** /noʊn, ˈnoʊən/, *v.* past participle of **know.**

**known quantity** /– ˈkwɒntəti/, *n.* a quantity whose value is given, in algebra, etc., frequently represented by a letter from the first part of the alphabet, as *a, b,* or *c.*

**knuckle** /ˈnʌkəl/, *n., v.,* **-led, -ling.** *–n.* **1.** a joint of a finger, esp. one of the joints at the roots of the fingers. **2.** the rounded prominence of such a joint when the finger is bent. **3.** a joint of meat, consisting of the parts about the carpal or tarsal joint of a quadruped. **4.** an angle between two members or surfaces of a vessel. **5.** a cylindrical projecting part on a hinge, through which an axis or pin passes; the joint of a hinge. **6. go the knuckle,** to fight; punch. **7. near (close to) the knuckle,** (of a remark, joke, etc.) near the limit of what is permitted or acceptable. *–v.i.* **8.** to hold the knuckles close to the ground in playing marbles (oft. fol. by *down*). **9.** to apply oneself vigorously or earnestly, as to a task (fol. by *down*). **10.** to yield or submit (oft. fol. by *down* or *under*). **11.** (of a horse, etc.) to stumble (oft. fol. by *over*). *–v.t.* **12.** to assault, with fists or knuckle-dusters. **13.** to press or touch with the knuckles: *to knuckle one's brow in respect.* [ME *knokel;* akin to D *kneukel,* G *Knöckel,* diminutive of a word represented by D *knok,* G *Knochen* bone]

**knucklebone** /ˈnʌkəlboʊn/, *n.* **1.** (in man) a bone forming a knuckle of a finger. **2.** (in quadrupeds) a bone homologous with a wrist, ankle, or fingerbone of man, or its knobbed end. **3.** →**jack**[1] (def. 6a)

**knuckle-duster** /ˈnʌkəl-dʌstə/, *n.* a piece of metal fitted across the knuckles, used as a weapon.

**knucklehead** /ˈnʌkəlhɛd/, *n.* a fool.

**knuckle joint** /ˈnʌkəl dʒɔɪnt/, *n.* **1.** a joint forming a knuckle. **2.** *Mach.* a flexible hinged joint formed by two abutting links.

**knuckle sandwich** /– ˈsænwɪtʃ/, *n. Colloq.* a punch in the mouth.

**knur** /nɜ/, *n.* an excrescence, esp. on a tree. [ME *knorre,* c. MD, MHG *knorre*]

**knurl** /nɜl/, *n.* **1.** a small ridge or the like, esp. one of a series, as on the edge of a thumbscrew to assist in obtaining a firm grip. *–v.t.* **2.** to make knurls or ridges on. [apparently from *knur* lump, knot, ME *knurre*]

**knurled** /nɜld/, *adj.* **1.** having small ridges on the edge or surface; milled. **2.** having knurls or knots; gnarled.

**knurly** /ˈnɜli/, *adj.,* **-lier, -liest.** having knurls or knots; gnarled.

**K.O.** /keɪ ˈoʊ/, knockout. Also, **k.o.**

**koala** /koʊˈalə/, *n.* a sluggish, tailless, grey, furry, arboreal marsupial, *Phascolarctos cinereus,* of Australia, about 75 cm long. Also, **koala bear.** [Aboriginal]

**kobold** /ˈkɒboʊld/, *n.,*(in,German,folklore). **1.** a kind of spirit or goblin, often mischievous, that haunts houses. **2.** a spirit that haunts mines or other underground places. [G]

koala

**Köchel** /ˈkɜʃəl, ˈkɜkəl/, *n.* indicating the serial number in the catalogue of Mozart's work made in 1862 by Ludwig von Köchel, 1800-77, musician and scholar.

**Koch's bacillus** /kɒks bəˈsɪləs/, *n.* a bacillus, *Mycobacterium tuberculosis,* that causes tuberculosis. Also, **Koch bacillus.** [named after Robert *Koch,* 1843-1910, German bacteriologist who discovered it]

**koel** /ˈkoʊəl/, *n.* **1.** a migratory cuckoo, *Eudynamys scolopacea,* of northern and eastern Australian coastal areas and islands to the north, glossy blue-black (male) with a conspicuously long tail and a distinctive 'cooee' call; cooee bird; black cuckoo. **2.** any of several closely related and very similar birds found elsewhere. [Hind. *kōīl,* from Skt *kokila*]

**kohekohe** /ˈkoʊiˌkoʊi/, *n.* a tree of New Zealand coastal and lowland forests, *Dysoxylum spectabile,* with tough freely-splitting wood. [Maori]

**kohl** /koʊl/, *n.* a powder, as finely powdered sulphide of antimony, used in the East to darken the eyelids, make eyebrows, etc. [Ar. Cf. ALCOHOL]

**kohlrabi** /koʊlˈrabi/, *n., pl.* **-bies.** a cultivated variety of *Brassica oleracea,* variety *gongylodes,* whose stem above ground swells into an edible bulblike formation. [G, b. G *Kohl* cabbage and It. *cauli* (or *cavoli*) *rape,* pl. of *cavolo rapa* cabbage turnip. Cf. COLE, RAPE[2]]

**koilonychia** /kɔɪloʊˈnɪkiə/, *n.* a spoon-shaped depression in the nails. [Gk, from *koilo-* (combining form of *koîlos* hollow) + stem of *ónyx* nail + *-ia* -IA]

**Koine** /ˈkɔɪni/, *n.* the standard Attic Greek which replaced other dialects and flourished under the Roman Empire. [Gk, short for *koinḕ diálektos* common dialect]

**kokako** /ˈkoʊˌkakoʊ/, *n.* a dark grey, long-tailed bird of New Zealand, *Callaeas cinerea,* with brightly coloured wattles; wattled crew.

**kokum** /ˈkoʊkəm/, *n. Obs.* feigned concern or kindness. [orig. uncert.]

**kola** /ˈkoʊlə/, *n.* →**cola**[1].

**kola nut** /ˈ– nʌt/, *n.* →**cola nut.**

**kolinsky** /kəˈlɪnski/, *n., pl.* **-skies.** **1.** a mink, *Mustela sibirica,* of Siberia and northern Asia having fur uniformly buff or tawny, somewhat paler below, varied with black and white on the head. **2.** the fur of such an animal. [Russ. *Kolinski,* adj., pertaining to *Kola,* a peninsula in the NW Soviet Union]

**kolkhoz** /kɒlˈkɔz/, *n.* (in the U.S.S.R.) a collective farm, the holding being common property of all. [Russ., from *kol*(*lektivnoe*) COLLECTIVE + *khoz*(*yaistvo*) farm]

**Kol Nidre** /kɒl ˈnɪdri, -rə/, *n. Judaism.* a prayer recited on the eve of Yom Kippur asking for the annulment of vows to God and forgiveness for transgressions.

**Kolrausch's law** /ˈkɒlraʊʃəz lɔ/, *n.* the law which states that when ionisation is complete the conductivity of an electrolyte is equal to the sum of the conductivities of the ions into which the solute dissociates. [named after F.W. *Kolrausch,* 1840-1910, German physicist]

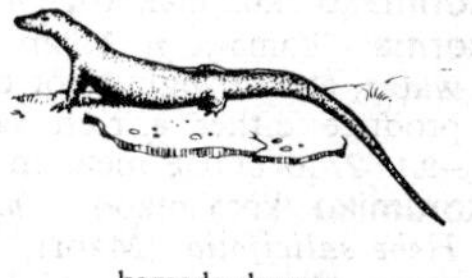
komodo dragon

**komijne kaas** /kəˈminə kas/, *n.* a cheese of Dutch origin, with a distinctive, spicy taste, made by mixing cheddar cheese with cumin seeds.

**komodo dragon** /kəˌmoʊdoʊ ˈdrægən/, *n.* a giant monitor, *Varanus komodoensis,* of the island of Komodo in Indonesia: up to 3.5m long.

**koneke** /ˈkɒnɛki/, *n. N.Z.* a sledge (formerly one with runners in front and wheels at the back). Also, **konaki.** [Maori]

**Kongo** /ˈkɒŋgoʊ/, *n., pl.* **-gos, -go.** **1.** a Bantu people centred around the lower river Congo. **2.** a member of this people. **3.** the Bantu language of this people.

**konini** /kəˈnini, ˈkoʊnɪni/, *n.* the dark purple berry of the New Zealand forest tree *Fuchsia excorticata.* [Maori]

**konk** /kɒŋk/, *n. Colloq.* →**conk.**

**konometer** /kəˈnɒmətə/, *n.* an apparatus for measuring the amount of dust in the air (esp. in a mine). Also, **konimeter.**

**kon-tiki** /kɒn-ˈtɪki/, *n. N.Z.* a small raft used to float fishing lines off-shore.

**koodoo** /ˈkudu/, *n., pl.* **-doos.** →**kudu.**

**kook** /kuk/, *n. Colloq.* **1.** a strange or eccentric person. **2.** *Surfing.* a beginner, esp. one who imitates others badly.

**kookaburra** /ˈkʊkəbʌrə/, *n.* either of two Australian kingfishers renowned for their harsh voices and call resembling human laughter: **1.** Also, **laughing kookaburra.** the large, dark brown and white **common kookaburra,** *Dacelo gigas,* native to eastern Australia and introduced into western Australia and Tasmania; giant kingfisher; ha-ha duck; laughing jackass; settler's clock. **2.** a slightly smaller bird with a paler head, the **blue-winged kookaburra,** *D. leachii,* of tropical northern Australia and New Guinea; barking jackass; howling jackass. [Aboriginal]

kookaburra

**kooky** /ˈkuki/, *adj. Colloq.* eccentric; odd. – **kookily,** *adv.*

**koori** /ˈkʊəri/, *Colloq.* –*n.* **1.** an Aborigine. –*adj.* **2.** Aboriginal. Also, **koorie.** [orig. uncert.]

**kootchar** /ˈkutʃə/, *n.* a small sweat bee which has no sting, *Trigona australis.*

**kop** /kɒp/, *n. S. African.* an isolated hill; a residual rock mass, the result of desert denudation. [Afrikaans, from D: head]

**kopeck** /ˈkoʊpɛk/, *n.* a Russian monetary unit and copper coin, the hundredth part of a rouble. Also, **kopek, copeck.** [Russ. *kopeika*]

**kopi** /ˈkoʊpi/, *n.* gypsum which sometimes contains good opal.

**kopje** /ˈkɒpi/, *n. S. African.* a small kop. Also, **koppie.** [Afrikaans, diminutive of KOP]

**koradji** /kɒˈradʒi/, *n.* →**sorcerer.** [Aboriginal]

**Koran** /kɔˈran, kə-/, *n.* the sacred scripture of Islam, believed by orthodox Muslims to contain revelations made in Arabic by Allah directly to Mohammed. [Ar. *qurʼān* reading, recitation, from *qaraʼa* read] – **Koranic** /kɔˈrænɪk/, *adj.*

**korari** /koʊˈrari/, *n.* **1.** the flower stalks belonging to the New Zealand flax, *Phormium tenax.* **2.** the plant itself. [Maori]

**Korea** /kəˈriə/, *n.* a country in East Asia, on a peninsula between the Sea of Japan and the Yellow Sea; currently divided in the vicinity of 38°N into **South Korea** and **North Korea.**

**Korean** /kəˈriən/, *adj.* **1.** of Korea, its people, or language. –*n.* **2.** a native or inhabitant of Korea. **3.** the language of Korea, of no known linguistic affinity.

**korero** /kəˈriroʊ/, *n. N.Z.* **1.** a discussion, talk. –*v.i.* **2.** to discuss. [Maori]

**korimako** /kɒriˈmakoʊ/, *n. N.Z.* →**bellbird.** (def. 2).

**korma** /ˈkɔmə/, *n.* **1.** an Indian dish of meat braised with water, stock, yoghurt or cream, and spices which combine to produce either a rich sauce or a dry crust on the meat. –*v.t.* **2.** to braise meat in this way.

**koromiko** /kɒrəˈmikoʊ/, *n.* a flowering shrub of New Zealand, *Hebe salicifolia.* [Maori]

**korora** /ˈkoʊrərə/, *n. N.Z.* →**little penguin.** [Maori]

**korowai** /ˈkɒroʊwaɪ/, *n. N.Z.* a cloak or mantle worn by Maoris and made of woven scraped flax with black fringing.

**koru** /ˈkɒru/, *n. N.Z.* a spiral design occurring frequently in Maori carving and tattooing, leading to a loop motif like the top of an uncurling fern frond.

**kosh** /kɒʃ/, *n., v.t.* →**cosh**[2].

**kosher** /ˈkɒʃə, ˈkoʊʃə/, *adj.* **1.** fit, lawful, or ritually permitted, according to the Jewish law, used of food and vessels for food ritually proper for use, esp. of meat slaughtered in accordance with the law of Moses. **2.** (of shops, houses, etc.) selling or using food prepared according to the Jewish law. –*n.* **3.** *Colloq.* kosher food. –*v.t.* **4.** to prepare (food) according to the Jewish law. Also, **kasher.** [Heb. *kāshēr* fit, proper, lawful]

**kotare** /ˈkoʊtəri/, *n. N.Z.* →**sacred kingfisher.** [Maori]

**koto** /ˈkoʊtoʊ/, *n., pl.* **-tos.** a Japanese musical instrument having numerous strings, stretched over a vaulted, wooden sounding-board: plucked with the fingers. [Jap.]

koto

**kotow** /koʊˈtaʊ/, *v.i., n.* →**kowtow.** – **kotower,** *n.*

**kotuku** /ˈkoʊtʊku/, *n. N.Z.* the white heron, *Egretta alba.* [Maori]

**kotukutuku** /koʊˈtuku,tuku/, *n.* a forest tree of New Zealand, *Fuchsia excorticata,* which bears dark purple fruit called konini.

**koumis** /ˈkumɪs/, *n.* →**kumis.** Also, **koumiss, koumyss, kumiss.**

**koura** /ˈkoʊrə/, *n. N.Z.* →**crayfish.** [Maori]

**kowari** /kəˈwari/, *n.* a small carnivorous, brush-tailed marsupial mouse, *Dasyuroides byrnei,* living in burrows in the arid region at the junction of the Northern Territory, South Australia and Queensland.

**Koweit** /koʊˈweɪt/, *n.* →**Kuwait.**

**kowhai** /ˈkoʊwaɪ, ˈkoʊfaɪ/, *n.* a tree of New Zealand, *Sophora microphylla,* noted for its golden, bell-shaped flowers. [Maori]

**kowtow** /kaʊˈtaʊ/, *v.i.* **1.** to knock the forehead on the ground while kneeling, as an act of reverence, worship, apology, etc. **2.** to act in an obsequious manner; show servile deference. –*n.* **3.** the act of kowtowing. Also, **kotow.** [Chinese (Mandarin) *kʻo-tʻou,* lit., knock-head] – **kowtower,** *n.*

**kp,** kilopond.

**KP,** king's pawn.

**K.P.O.** /keɪ pi ˈoʊ/, *n.* →**key punch operator.**

**Kr,** *Chem.* krypton.

**Kr.,** **1.** Krona. **2.** Krone. **3.** Króna.

**KR,** *Chess.* king's rook.

**kraal** /kral/, *n.* **1.** a village of natives in southern or central Africa, usu. surrounded by a stockade or the like and often having a central space for cattle, etc. **2.** the kraal as a social unit. **3.** *S. African.* an enclosure for cattle, etc. –*v.t.* **4.** to shut up in a kraal, as cattle. [Afrikaans, from Pg. *curral* enclosure. Cf. CORRAL]

**kraft paper** /ˈkraft peɪpə/, *n.* a strong paper, usu. brown, processed from wood pulp, used in bags and as wrapping paper. [G *Kraft* strength]

**krait** /kraɪt/, *n.* any of the extremely venomous snakes of the genus *Bungarus* of south-eastern Asia, esp. *B. coeruleus* of India. [Hind. *karait*]

**kraken** /ˈkrakən/, *n.* a mythical sea-monster said to appear at times off Norway. [Norw.]

**kraut** /kraʊt/, *n. Colloq.* (*usu. derog.*) a German.

**Krebs cycle** /ˈkrɛbz saɪkəl/, *n.* →**citric acid cycle.** [named after Sir H. A. *Krebs,* b. 1900, British biochemist]

**kremlin** /ˈkrɛmlən/, *n.* **1.** the citadel of a Russian town or city. **2.** (*cap.*) the citadel of Moscow, including within its walls the chief office of the Soviet government. [Russ. *kreml* citadel]

**krimmer** /ˈkrɪmə/, *n.* a lambskin from the Crimean region, dressed as a fur, with wool in loose soft curls and usu. whitish or pale grey. Also, **crimmer.** [G, from *Krim* Crimea]

**kris** /kris/, *n.* a short sword or heavy dagger with a wavy blade, used by the Malays. Also, **crease, creese.** [Malay]

**Krishna** /ˈkrɪʃnə/, *n.* the most popular Hindu deity, as an incarnation of Vishnu; the famous teacher in the Bhagavad-gita. [Skt, special use of *krishna* black]

**krona** /ˈkroʊnə/, *n., pl.* **-nor** /-nə/. the monetary unit of Sweden. *Abbrev.:* Kr. [Swed.: crown]

**króna** /ˈkroʊnə/, *n., pl.* **krónur** /-nə/. the monetary unit of Iceland. *Abbrev.:* Kr. [Icel.: crown]

**krone** /ˈkroʊnə/, *n., pl.* **-ner** /-nə/. **1.** the monetary unit of Denmark. **2.** the monetary unit of Norway. *Abbrev.:* Kr. [Dan.: crown]

**krummhorn** /ˈkrʌmhɔn/, *n.* →**crumhorn.**

**krupuk** /ˈkrupʊk/, *n.* an Indonesian cracker made from flour and seasoning, dried, and deep fried in oil before serving. [Bahasa Indonesia]

**krypton** /ˈkrɪptɒn/, *n.* an inert monatomic gaseous element present in very small amounts in the atmosphere, of some use in high-power, tungsten-filament light bulbs. *Symbol:* Kr; *at. wt:* 83·80; *at. no.:* 36; *weight of one litre at 0° C, and 760 mm. pressure:* 3·708 g. [NL, from Gk, neut. of *kryptós* hidden. See CRYPT]

**kryptonite** /ˈkrɪptənaɪt/, *n.* an imaginary substance, supposedly the only thing which can destroy the superhuman powers of the fictional character Superman.

**kt,** **1.** karat; carat. **2.** knot.

**Kt,** knight.

**K.T.** /keɪ ˈti/, **1.** Knight of the (Order of the) Thistle. **2.** Knight Templar.

**kuaka** /kuˈakə/, *n. N.Z.* the godwit, *Limosa lapponica.* [Maori]

**kudos** /ˈkjudɒs/, *n.* glory; renown. [Gk *kŷdos*]

**kudu** /ˈkudu/, *n.* either of two African antelopes, *Tragelaphus Stepsiceroo* or T. *imberbis* having vertical white strips on the body and long corkscrew-like horns in the male. Also, **koodoo.** [Hottentot]

**kukri** /ˈkʊkri/, *n.* a knife with a curved blade, used by the Gurkhas. [Hind.]

**kuku** /ˈkuku/, *n.* a large, richly coloured, fruit-eating native pigeon, *Hemiphaga novaeseelandiae,* of New Zealand forest areas; woodpigeon. Also, **kukupa.**

**kulak** /ˈkulæk/, *n.* (in Russia) **1.** (before the revolution) a hard-fisted merchant or a village usurer. **2.** any peasant who employed hired labour or possessed any machinery. [Russ.: fist, tight-fisted person]

**kulich** /ˈkulɪtʃ/, *n.* a traditional Russian Easter yeast cake, with dried fruit, made in a long cylindrical shape, iced and decorated, served with paskha. [Russ.]

**kultarr** /ˈkʊlta/, *n.* a small, dark grey marsupial mouse, *Antechinomys laniger,* of eastern Australia.

**Kultur** /kʊlˈtʊə/, *n.* **1.** culture as a social force causing evolutionary development to higher forms of civilisation. **2.** a civilisation characteristic of a time or a people. [G, from L *cultūra* CULTURE]

**kumara** /ˈkumərə/, *n. N.Z.* →**sweet potato.** [Maori]

**kumis** /ˈkuməs/, *n.* **1.** a slightly alcoholic beverage made from fermented mare's or camel's milk, drunk by Asiatic nomads, etc. **2.** a similar drink prepared from other milk, esp. that of the cow, and used for dietetic and medicinal purposes. Also, **Koumis, Koumiss, Koumyos, Kumiss.** [Russ. *kumys, from* Tartar *kumiz.* Cf. F, *koumis.* G *Kumyss*]

**kümmel** /ˈkʊməl/, *n.* a colourless cordial or liqueur flavoured with cumin, caraway seeds, etc., made esp. in the Baltic area. [G *Kümmel* cumin]

**kumquat** /ˈkʌmkwɒt/, *n.* **1.** a small, round, or oblong citrus fruit with a sweet rind and acid pulp, used chiefly for preserves, being the fruit of *Fortunella japonica* and related species, shrubs native to China and cultivated in many other countries. **2.** the plant itself. Also, **cumquat.** [Chinese, Cantonese pronunciation of Mandarin *kin ku,* lit., gold orange]

**kunai** /ˈkunaɪ/, *n.* →**blady grass.**

**kung-fu** /kʊŋ-ˈfu, kʌŋ-ˈfu/, *n.* karate in the form developed in China.

**kunzite** /ˈkʊntsaɪt/, *n.* a transparent lilac variety of spodumene, used as a gem. [named after G.F. *Kunz,* 1856-1932, U.S. expert in precious stones. See -ITE[1]]

kurrajong: flower and leaf

**kurdaitcha shoes** /kɜˈdaɪtʃə ʃuz/, *n.pl.* →**kadaicha shoes.**

**kurgan** /ˈkɜgən/, *n.* a mound or barrow covering a burial in a pit grave. [Russ.]

**kuri**[1] /ˈkuri/, *n.* **1.** *N.Z.* a Maori-bred dog; a mongrel. **2.** (*derog.*) a Maori. Also, **goori, goorie.** [Maori]

**kuri**[2] /ˈkuri/, *n., adj.* →**koori.**

**kurrajong** /ˈkʌrədʒɒŋ/, *n.* **1.** a tree, *Brachychiton populneum,* wide-spread in eastern Australia where it is valued as fodder. **2.** any of a number of species, mostly in the families Sterculiaceae and Malvaceae, as *Hibiscus heterophyllus,* **green kurrajong.** [Aboriginal]

**kurrajong-pod beetle** /ˌkʌrədʒɒŋ-ˈpɒd bitl/, *n.* a highly specialised, Australian fruit beetle, *Circopes pilistriatus,* which passes the whole of its life cycle in the seed pod of the kurrajong tree.

**kurtosis** /kɜˈtoʊsəs/, *n.* the shape, or a measure indicating the shape, of the curve of a frequency distribution graph near its mean. [Gk *kýrtōsis* convexity, curvature]

**Kuwait** /kuˈweɪt/, *n.* an independent state in north-east Arabia, on the north-west coast of the Persian Gulf.

**Kuwaiti** /kuˈweɪti/, *n.* **1.** a native of Kuwait. *–adj.* **2.** of or pertaining to Kuwait or its inhabitants.

**kV,** kilovolt.

**kvass** /kvas/, *n.* a Russian beer made from barley, malt, and rye. Also, **kvas, quass.** [Russ. *kvas*]

**kW,** kilowatt.

**kwashiorkor** /kwæʃiˈɔkə/, *n.* a nutritional disease chiefly of children in Africa, associated with a corn diet with its lack of protein, and marked by oedema, potbelly, and changes in skin pigmentation. [native name in Ghana]

**kway** /kweɪ/, *n. Colloq.* a thief who does not specialise in any one line of activity; an allrounder. [? mispronunciation of *quay* in Circular Quay, Sydney]

**kwela** /ˈkweɪlə/, *n.* a type of music resembling jazz, popular in South Africa among Bantu and Cape Coloured communities, chiefly using simple instruments, as the penny whistle. [from Bantu: climb up]

**kWh,** kilowatt hour.

**kyanite** /ˈkaɪənaɪt/, *n.* a mineral aluminium silicate, $Al_2SiO_5$, occurring in blue or greenish bladed crystals, used as a refractory. Also, **cyanite.** [CYAN(O)-[1] + -ITE[1]]

**kybosh** /ˈkaɪbɒʃ/, *Colloq. n.* **1.** nonsense. **2. put the kybosh on,** to put a stop to. *–v.t.* **3.** to put an end to; stop. Also, **kibosh.** [orig. uncert.]

**kylie** /ˈkaɪli/, *n.* **1.** a boomerang having one side flat and the other convex. **2.** →**kip**[2]. Also, **kiley.** [Aboriginal]

**kymograph** /ˈkaɪməgræf/, *n.* **1.** an instrument by which variations of fluid pressure, as the waves of the pulse, can be measured and graphically recorded. **2.** an instrument measuring the angular oscillations of an aeroplane in flight with respect to axes fixed in space. Also, **cymograph.** [*kymo-* (combining form of Gk *kŷma* wave) + -GRAPH] – **kymographic** /kaɪməˈgræfɪk/, *adj.*

**Kymric** /ˈkɪmrɪk/, *adj., n.* →**Cymric.**

**Kymry** /ˈkɪmri/, *n.pl.* →**Cymry.** Also, **Kymrie.**

**kyphosis** /kaɪˈfoʊsəs/, *n.* a curvature of the spine, convex backwards. [NL, from Gk: bunched state]

**Kyrie eleison** /ˌkɪərieɪ əˈleɪsɒn, -sən/, *n.* **1.** 'Lord, have mercy', a petition used: **a.** in various offices of the Eastern and Roman churches. **b.** as a response in Anglican services. **2.** a musical setting of this. [Gk *Kýrie eléēson*]

**Kyu** /kju/, *n.* **1.** one of the six grades into which inexperienced judo contestants are divided. **2.** a contestant placed in one of such grades. Cf. **Dan**[2].

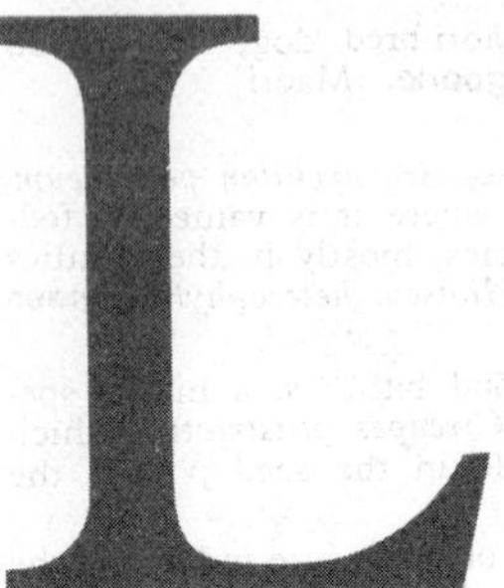

Ll Roman ALBERTUS

Ll Sans Serif METRO

Ll Script MAGNOLIA

Ll Decorative LAFAYETTE

*Although there are numerous typefaces in the world they can be divided into four main classifications. These are:*

*ROMAN or SERIF. This typeface came into being from the technique of the Roman masons who, working in stone, finished off each letter with a serif or small stroke projecting from the top or bottom. This was done to correct any feeling of unevenness or imbalance they may have created in cutting the characters in stone.*

*SANS SERIF (without serif). This typeface is geometric in design and has straight-edged characters and lines of a regular thickness.*

*SCRIPT. Based on the movement of the hand, this typeface is often italicised or slanted, as if drawn by a brush or quill pen.*

*DECORATIVE. Any typeface that exaggerates the characteristics of any of the other three classifications to a degree that places it outside of them.*

*The dictionary entries in this book use a SANS SERIF typeface called Helvetica (set in a bold face for the head words) and a SERIF typeface Plantin (used throughout the body of the entries).*

**L, l** /ɛl/, *n., pl.* **L's** or **Ls, l's** or **ls. 1.** a consonant, the 12th letter of the English alphabet. **2.** the Roman numeral for 50. See **Roman numerals.**

**l,** litre.

**l-,** former abbreviation for **laevo-.**

**l., 1.** latitude. **2.** law. **3.** left. **4.** length. **5.** (*pl.* **ll.**) line; lines. **6.** link.

**L,** *pl.* **L's. 1.** something having a shape like that of the letter L. **2.** Also, **l.** *Elect.* coefficient of inductance. **3.** Latin. **4.** learner (driver). **5.** *Physics.* length. **6.** litre. **7.** lambert. **8.** *Geog.* (terrestrial) longitude.

**L-,** a prefix used to describe the configurations of chemical compounds that have the same chirality as L-glyceraldehyde. See **glyceraldehyde.**

**L., 1.** Lake. **2.** large. **3.** Latin. **4.** latitude. **5.** law. **6.** left.

**la**[1] /la/, *n.* **1.** the syllable used for the sixth note of the scale in solfège. See **solfège. 2.** →**lah.**

**la**[2] /la, lɔ/, *interj. Archaic.* (an exclamation of wonder, surprise, etc.). [ME and OE; weak var. of OE *lā* LO]

**la**[3] /la/, *n. Colloq.* →**toilet.** Also, **lala** /ˈlala/.

**La, 1.** *Chem.* lanthanum. **2.** lambert.

**LA,** Legislative Assembly.

**laager** /ˈlagə/, *S. African.* –*n.* **1.** a camp or encampment, esp. within a circle of wagons. –*v.t.* **2.** to arrange as a laager. –*v.i.* **3.** to encamp in a laager. Also, **lager.** [Afrikaans, var. of *lager,* c. G *Lager* camp. Cf. LAIR[1]]

**lab** /læb/, *n. Colloq.* laboratory.

**labarum** /ˈlæbərəm/, *n., pl.* **-ra** /-rə/. **1.** an ecclesiastical standard or banner, as for carrying in procession. **2.** the military standard of Constantine the Great and later Christian emperors of Rome, bearing Christian symbols. [L, corresponding to Gk *lábaron;* ult. orig. unknown]

**labdanum** /ˈlæbdənəm/, *n.* a resinous juice that exudes from various rockroses of the genus *Cistus,* used in perfumery, fumigating substances, medicinal plasters, etc. Also, **ladanum.** [ML, from L *lādanum,* from Gk *lā́danon* mastic. Cf. Pers. *lādan* shrub]

**labefaction** /læbəˈfækʃən/, *n.* a shaking or weakening; overthrow; downfall. Also, **labefactation** /læbəfækˈteɪʃən/. [L *labefactus,* pp., weakened + -ION]

**label** /ˈleɪbəl/, *n., v.,* **-belled, -belling,** or (*U.S.*) **-beled, -beling.** –*n.* **1.** a slip of paper or other material for affixing to something to indicate its nature, ownership, destination, etc. **2.** a short word or phrase of description for a person, group, movement, etc. **3.** a strip or narrow piece of anything. **4.** *Archit.* a moulding or dripstone over a door or window, esp. one which extends horizontally across the top of the opening and vertically downwards for a certain distance at the sides. **5.** *Colloq.* the trade name, esp. of a gramophone record company. –*v.t.* **6.** to affix a label to; mark with a label. **7.** to designate or describe by or on a label: *the bottle was labelled poison.* **8.** to put in a certain class; to describe by a verbal label. **9.** *Physics.* to replace (a stable atom) in a compound by a radioactive isotope of that atom so that its path through a mechanical or biological system can be traced. [ME, from OF, ? from Gmc; cf. LAP[1]] –**labeller,** *n.*

**labellum** /ləˈbɛləm/, *n., pl.* **-bella.** that division of the corolla, as in orchids, which differs more or less markedly from the other divisions, often forming the most conspicuous part. [L, diminutive of *labrum* lip] –**labelloid,** *adj.*

L, labellum

**label mould** /ˈleɪbəl mould/, *n.* →**hood mould.**

**labia** /ˈleɪbiə/, *n.* plural of **labium.**

**labial** /ˈleɪbiəl/, *adj.* **1.** pertaining to or of the nature of a labium. **2.** *Music.* giving forth sounds produced by the impact of a stream of air upon the sharp edge of a lip, as a flute or pipe organ. **3.** of or pertaining to lips. **4.** *Phonet.* involving lip articulation, as *p, v, m, w,* or a rounded vowel. –*n.* **5.** a labial consonant. [ML *labiālis,* from L *labium* lip] –**labiality** /leɪbiˈæləti/, *n.* –**labially,** *adv.*

**labialise** /ˈleɪbiəlaɪz/, *v.t.,* **-lised, -lising.** *Phonet.* to give a labial character to (a sound), e.g. to round (a vowel). Also, **labialize.** –**labialisation** /ˌleɪbiəlaɪˈzeɪʃən/, *n.*

**labiate** /ˈlæbieɪt, ˈleɪbiət/, *adj.* **1.** lipped; having parts which are shaped or arranged like lips. **2.** *Bot.* (of a gamopetalous corolla or gamosepalous calyx) (usu.) two-lipped; bilabiate. –*n.* **3.** a plant belonging to the family Labiatae, the mint family.

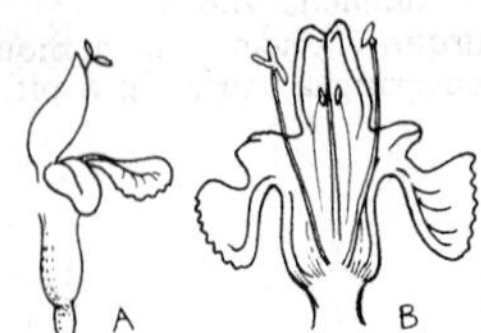


labiate corolla: A, seen from the side; B, laid open, front view

**labile** /ˈleɪbaɪl/, *adj.* **1.** apt to lapse or change; unstable;

lapsable. **2.** *Med.* denoting or pertaining to a mode of application of electricity in which the active electrode is moved over the part to be acted upon. [late ME *labyl,* from LL *lābilis,* from L *lābī* fall, slide. Cf. LAPSE] – **lability** /lə'bɪləti/, *n.*

**labiodental** /ˌleɪbioʊ'dɛntl/, *Phonet.* –*adj.* **1.** with the lower lip close to the upper front teeth, as in *f* or *v.* –*n.* **2.** a labiodental sound.

**labionasal** /ˌleɪbioʊ'neɪzəl/, *Phonet.* –*adj.* **1.** articulated with the lips and given resonance in the nasal passage, as *m.* –*n.* **2.** a labionasal sound.

**labiovelar** /ˌleɪbioʊ'vilə/, *Phonet.* –*adj.* **1.** with simultaneous bilabial and velar articulations. –*n.* **2.** a labiovelar sound, as *w.*

**labium** /'leɪbiəm/, *n., pl.* **-bia** /-biə/. **1.** a lip or lip-like part. **2.** *Anat.* **a.** either lip, upper or under, of the mouth, respectively called **labium superiore** and **labium inferiore.** **b.** one of the four 'lips' guarding the orifice of the vulva, including the two outer cutaneous folds (**labia majora**) and the two inner membranous folds (**labia minora**). **3.** *Bot.* the lower lip of a bilabiate corolla. **4.** *Entomol.* the posterior unpaired member of the mouthparts of an insect, formed by the united second maxillae. [L: lip]

**lablab** /'læblæb/, *n.* a perennial twining herb, *Lablab purpureus,* with flattened pods and white or purple flowers, widely used as a stock feed because of its high protein content; dolichos.

**labor** /'leɪbə/, *n. Chiefly U.S.* →**labour.**

**laboratory** /lə'bɒrətri/, *n., pl.* **-ries,** *adj.* –*n.* **1.** a building or part of a building fitted with apparatus for conducting scientific investigations, experiments, tests, etc., or for manufacturing chemicals, medicines, etc. **2.** any place where or in which similar processes are carried on by natural forces. –*adj.* **3.** serving a function in a laboratory. **4.** relating to techniques of work in a laboratory. [ML *labōrātōrium* workshop] – **laboratorial** /læbɒrə'tɔriəl/, *adj.*

**laborious** /lə'bɔriəs/, *adj.* **1.** requiring much labour, exertion, or perseverance: *a laborious undertaking.* **2.** requiring labour in construction or execution. **3.** given to or diligent in labour. [ME, from L *labōriōsus*] – **laboriously,** *adv.* – **laboriousness,** *n.*

**Laborite** /'leɪbəraɪt/, *n. Colloq.* a supporter of a Labor Party. Also, *Chiefly Brit.,* **Labourite.**

**labour** /'leɪbə/, *n.* **1.** bodily toil for the sake of gain or economic production. **2.** those engaged in such toil considered as a class; the labouring people organised in trade unions and political parties. **3.** work, esp. of a hard or fatiguing kind. **4.** a work or task done or to be done: *the twelve labours of Hercules.* **5.** the pangs and efforts of childbirth; travail. **6.** the time during which the pangs and efforts of childbirth take place. –*v.i.* **7.** to perform labour; exert one's powers of body or mind; work; toil. **8.** to work (*for*); strive, as towards a goal. **9.** to be burdened, troubled, or distressed: *you are labouring under a misapprehension.* **10.** to be in travail or childbirth. **11.** to roll or pitch heavily, as a ship. –*v.t.* **12.** to work hard and long at; elaborate: *don't labour the point.* **13.** *Archaic or Poetic.* to work or till (soil, etc.). Also, *Chiefly U.S.,* **labor.** [ME, from OF, from L *labor* toil, distress] – **labouringly,** *adv.*

**labour camp** /'– kæmp/, *n.* a camp where convicts do manual labour.

**laboured** /'leɪbəd/, *adj.* **1.** laboriously formed; made or done with laborious pains or care. **2.** not easy or natural. Also, *U.S.,* **labored.**

**labourer** /'leɪbərə/, *n.* **1.** one engaged in work which requires physical effort rather than skill or training: *a farm labourer.* **2.** one who labours. Also, *U.S.,* **laborer.**

**labour exchange** /'leɪbər əkstʃeɪndʒ/, *n. Brit.* →**unemployment office.**

**labour-intensive** /'leɪbər-ɪnˌtɛnsɪv/, *adj.* of or pertaining to an industry which, while not needing a very large capital investment in plant, etc., requires a comparatively large labour force (opposed to *capital-intensive*).

**Labourite** /'leɪbəraɪt/, *n. Chiefly Brit. Colloq.* →**Laborite.**

**labour market** /'leɪbə makət/, *n.* the available supply of labour considered with reference to the demand for it.

**labour relations** /'– rəleɪʃənz/, *n.pl.* relations between management and labour, esp. in industry.

**labour-saving** /'leɪbə-seɪvɪŋ/, *adj.* saving, or effecting economy in, labour: *labour-saving device.*

**labour ward** /'leɪbə wɔd/, *n.* a hospital ward set aside for childbirth.

**Labrador** /'læbrədɔ/, *n.* **1.** a peninsula in north-eastern North America between Hudson Bay, the Atlantic, and the Gulf of St Lawrence, containing the Canadian provinces of Newfoundland and Quebec. **2.** the portion of Newfoundland in the eastern part of this peninsula. **3.** (l.c.) one of a breed of dogs with black or golden coats, originating in Newfoundland.

**labradorite** /læbrə'dɔraɪt/, *n.* a mineral of the plagioclase felspar group, often characterised by a brilliant change of colours with blue and green most common. [from *Labrador,* a Canadian peninsula, where it was discovered + -ITE[1]]

**labret** /'leɪbrət/, *n.* a lip ornament worn by primitive tribes, in a pierced hole. [L *labrum* lip + -ET]

**labroid** /'læbrɔɪd, 'leɪbrɔɪd/, *adj.* **1.** belonging to or resembling the Labridae, a family of thick-lipped marine fishes including the tautog, etc. –*n.* **2.** a labroid fish. Also, **labrid** /'læbrəd/. [L *lābrus* kind of fish + -OID]

**labrum** /'leɪbrəm, 'læbrəm/, *n., pl.* **labra** /'leɪbrə, 'læbrə/. **1.** a lip or liplike part. **2.** *Zool.* **a.** the anterior unpaired member of the mouthparts of an arthropod, projecting in front of the mouth. **b.** the outer margin of the aperture of a gastropod's shell. **3.** *Anat.* a ring of cartilage about the edge of a joint surface of a bone. [L: lip]

**laburnum** /lə'bɜnəm/, *n.* any of several small leguminous trees, having pendulous racemes of yellow flowers, somewhat similar to those of wisteria. *Laburnum anagyroides* of Europe is most common. [L]

**labyrinth** /'læbərɪnθ/, *n.* **1.** an intricate combination of passages in which it is difficult to find one's way or to reach the exit. **2.** a maze of paths bordered by high hedges, as in a park or garden. **3.** a complicated or tortuous arrangement, as of streets, buildings, etc. **4.** any confusingly intricate state of things or events; an entanglement. **5.** *Anat.* **a.** the internal ear, a complex structure including a bony portion (**osseous labyrinth**) and a membranous portion (**membranous labyrinth**) contained in it. **b.** the aggregate of air-chambers in the ethmoid bone, between the eye and the upper part of the nose. **6.** an enclosure for a high-performance loudspeaker which is designed to eliminate unwanted standing waves by means of air chambers. [L *labyrinthus,* from Gk *labýrinthos;* in Greek mythology, the Cretan maze constructed by Daedalus]

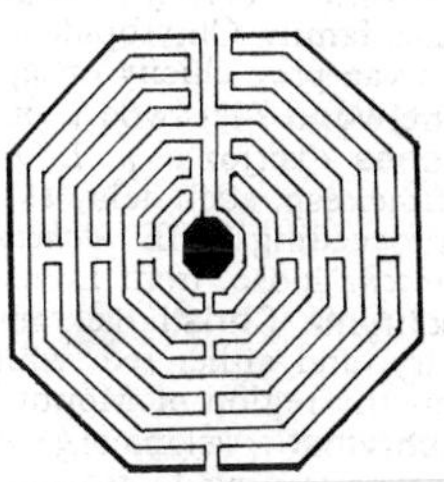
labyrinth

**labyrinthine** /læbə'rɪnθaɪn/, *adj.* **1.** pertaining to or forming a labyrinth. **2.** mazy; intricate. Also, **labyrinthian** /læbə'rɪnθiən/, **labyrinthic.**

**labyrinthitis** /læbrən'θaɪtəs/, *n.* inflammation of the labyrinth of the inner ear, which may cause dizziness, vertigo and nausea.

**lac** /læk/, *n.* a resinous substance deposited on the twigs of various trees in southern Asia by the lac insect, and used in the manufacture of varnishes, sealing wax, etc., and in the production of a red colouring matter. See **shellac.** [Hind. *lākh,* from Skt *lākshā*]

**laccolith** /'lækəlɪθ/, *n.* a mass of igneous rock formed from magma which when rising from below did not find its way to the surface, but spread out laterally into a lenticular body, thereby causing the overlying strata to bulge upwards. Also, **laccolite** /'lækəlaɪt/. [Gk *lákko(s)* pond + -LITH] – **laccolithic** /lækə'lɪθɪk/, **laccolitic** /lækə'lɪtɪk/, *adj.*

**lace** /leɪs/, *n., v.,* **laced, lacing.** –*n.* **1.** a netlike ornamental fabric made of threads by hand or machine. **2.** a cord or string for holding or drawing together, as when passed through holes in opposite edges: *shoelaces.* **3.** ornamental cord or braid, as on uniforms. **4.** spirits added to coffee or other beverage. –*v.t.* **5.** to fasten, draw together, or compress by means of a lace. **6.** to pass (a cord, etc.) as a lace, as through holes. **7.** to adorn or trim with lace. **8.** to compress the waist of (a person) by drawing tight the laces of a corset, etc. **9.** to interlace or intertwine. **10.** *Brit. Colloq.* to lash, beat, or thrash. **11.** to mark or streak, as with colour. **12.** to intermix, as coffee with spirits. *–v.i.* **13.** to be fastened with a lace. **14. lace into,** *Brit.* to attack (someone) verbally or physically. [ME *las,* from OF *laz* noose, string, from L *laqueus* noose, snare. Cf. LASSO]

**lacebark** /ˈleɪsbak/, *n.* **1.** →**houhere.** **2.** Also, **lace-wood.** a tree of eastern Australian brush forests, *Brachychiton discolor,* with pink bell-shaped flowers.

**lace-fern** /ˈleɪs-fɜn/, *n.* any fern of the genus *Cheilanthes,* esp. *C. gracillima* cultivated for its delicate foliage.

**lace monitor** /leɪs ˈmɒnətə/, *n.* a large, common, tree-climbing goanna, *Varanus varius,* black with bands of yellow spots, widely distributed throughout mainland Australia; tree goanna.

**lacerate** /ˈlæsəreɪt/, *v.,* **-rated, -rating;** /ˈlæsəreɪt, -rət/, *adj.* *–v.t.* **1.** to tear roughly; mangle: *to lacerate the flesh.* **2.** to hurt: *to lacerate a person's feelings.* *–adj.* **3.** lacerated. [L *lacerātus,* pp.] – **lacerable,** *adj.* – **lacerative,** *adj.*

**lacerated** /ˈlæsəreɪtəd/, *adj.* **1.** mangled; jagged. **2.** *Bot., Zool.* having the edge variously cut as if torn into irregular segments, as a leaf.

**laceration** /læsəˈreɪʃən/, *n.* **1.** the act of lacerating. **2.** the result of lacerating; rough, jagged tear.

**lacertilian** /læsəˈtɪliən/, *adj.* **1.** of or pertaining to the Lacertilia, a suborder of reptiles comprising the common lizards and their allies. See **saurian** (def. 1). *–n.* **2.** a lacertilian reptile. Also, **lacertian** /ləˈsɜʃən/. [NL *Lacertilia,* pl. (from L *lacerta* lizard) + -AN]

**lacewing** /ˈleɪswɪŋ/, *n.* any of various neuropterous insects of the family Chrysopidae, with delicate lacelike wings, whose larvae prey chiefly on aphids.

**lace-wood** /ˈleɪs-wʊd/, *n.* →**lacebark.**

**laches** /ˈlætʃəz/, *n. Law.* neglect to do a thing at the proper time, esp. such delay as will bar a party from bringing a legal proceeding. [ME *lachesse,* from AF, var. of *laschesse,* from *lasche* loose, from L *laxus* lax]

**lachryma Christi** /lækrəmə ˈkrɪsti/, *n.* a still wine, sweet or dry, and either red, white, or rosé, made from grapes grown in the region of Mount Vesuvius, Italy. [L: tear of Christ]

**lachrymal** /ˈlækrəməl/, *adj.* **1.** of or pertaining to tears; producing tears. **2.** characterised by tears; indicative of weeping. **3.** *Anat., etc.* denoting, pertaining to, or situated near the glands, ducts, or the like, concerned in the secretion or conveyance of tears. *–n.* **4.** (*pl.*) *Anat.* tear-secreting glands. **5.** a lachrymatory. Also, **lacrimal, lacrymal.** [ML *lachrymālis, lacrimālis,* from L *lacrima* tear]

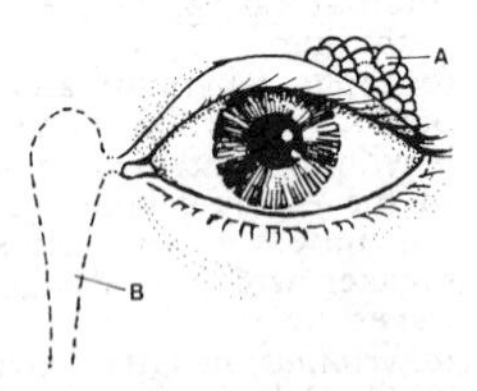

human eye (section): A, lachrymal gland; B, lachrymal sac

**lachrymal duct** /ˈ– dʌkt/, *n.* →**tear duct.**

**lachrymator** /ˈlækrəmeɪtə/, *n.* a substance which causes tears to be shed; a tear gas.

**lachrymatory** /ˈlækrəˌmeɪtəri, -tri/, *adj., n., pl.* **-ries.** *–adj.* **1.** of, pertaining to, or causing the shedding of tears. *–n.* **2.** Also, **lachrymal.** a small, narrow-necked vase found in ancient Roman tombs, formerly thought to have been used to hold the tears of bereaved friends.

**lachrymose** /ˈlækrəmoʊs/, *adj.* **1.** given to shedding tears; tearful. **2.** suggestive of or tending to cause tears; mournful. [L *lac(h)rimōsus,* from *lac(h)rima* tear] – **lachrymosely,** *adv.*

**lacing** /ˈleɪsɪŋ/, *n.* **1.** the act of one who or that which laces. **2.** a laced fastening, or a lace for such use. **3.** a trimming of lace or braid. **4.** *Brit.* a thrashing. **5.** spirits added to strengthen or flavour coffee, tea, etc. **6.** *Bldg Trades.* Also, **lacing course.** a course of brickwork in a flint or rubble wall.

**laciniate** /ləˈsɪnieɪt, -ət/, *adj. Bot., Zool.* cut into narrow, irregular lobes; slashed; jagged. [L *lacinia* lappet + -ATE[1]]

**lac insect** /ˈlæk ɪnsɛkt/, *n.* a homopterous insect, *Laccifer lacca,* of India, the females of which produce lac.

**lack** /læk/, *n.* **1.** deficiency or absence of something requisite, desirable, or customary: *lack of money or skill.* **2.** something lacking or wanting: *skilled labour was the chief lack.* *–v.t.* **3.** to be deficient in, destitute of, or without: *to lack strength.* **4.** to fall short in respect of: *the vote lacks three to be a majority.* *–v.i.* **5.** to be absent, as something requisite or desirable. [ME *lak,* from MLG or MD: deficiency. Cf. Icel. *lakr* deficient]

laciniate leaf

**lackadaisical** /lækəˈdeɪzɪkəl/, *adj.* sentimentally or affectedly languishing; weakly sentimental; listless. [*lackadaisy,* var. of LACKADAY (see ALACK) + -ICAL] – **lackadaisically,** *adv.* – **lackadaisicalness,** *n.*

**lackaday** /ˈlækədeɪ/, *interj. Archaic.* →**alack.**

**lacker** /ˈlækə/, *n., v.t.* →**lacquer.** – **lackerer,** *n.*

**lacker band** /– ˈbænd/, *n. Vic. Colloq.* →**rubber band.** [modification of ELASTIC + BAND[2]]

**lackey** /ˈlæki/, *n., pl.* **-eys,** *v.,* **-eyed, -eying.** *–n.* **1.** a footman or liveried manservant. **2.** a servile follower. *–v.t.* **3.** to attend as a lackey does. Also, **lacquey.** [F *laquais,* from Sp. *lacayo* foot soldier]

**lacklustre** /ˈlæklʌstə, lækˈlʌstə/, *adj.* **1.** lacking lustre or brightness; dull. *–n.* **2.** a lack of lustre; that which lacks brightness. Also, *U.S.,* **lackluster.**

**laconic** /ləˈkɒnɪk/, *adj.* using few words; expressing much in few words; concise. Also, **laconical.** [L *lacōnicus,* from Gk *lakōnikós* 'Laconian. See LACONISM] – **laconically,** *adv.*

**laconism** /ˈlækənɪzəm/, *n.* **1.** laconic brevity. **2.** a laconic utterance or sentence. Also, **laconicism** /ləˈkɒnəsɪzəm/. [Gk *lakōnismós* imitation of Laconians (Spartans), who were noted for brief, pithy speech]

**lacquer** /ˈlækə/, *n.* **1.** a protective coating consisting of a resin and/or a cellulose ester dissolved in a volatile solvent, sometimes with pigment added. **2.** any of various resinous varnishes, esp. a natural varnish obtained from a Japanese tree, *Rhus verniciflua,* used to produce a highly polished, lustrous surface on wood, etc. **3.** ware coated with such a varnish, and often inlaid. **4.** hair spray. *–v.t.* **5.** to coat with or as with lacquer. Also, **lacker.** [F (obs.) *lacre* sealing wax, from Ar. *lakk,* from Pers. *lāk;* akin to LAC] – **lacquerer,** *n.*

**lacquey** /ˈlæki/, *n., pl.* **-eys,** *v.t.,* **-eyed, -eying.** →**lackey.**

**lacrimal** /ˈlækrəməl/, *adj., n.* →**lachrymal.** Also, **lacrymal.**

**lacrosse** /ləˈkrɒs/, *n.* a ball game of Amerindian origin played by two teams of ten players each, who strive to send a ball through a goal by means of long-handled racquets. [F *la crosse* the crook (the racquet used in the game). See CROSSE]

**lact-,** a word element meaning 'milk'. Also, **lacto-.** [L *lacti-,* combining form of *lac*]

**lactalbumin** /lækˈtælbjəmən/, *n.* a milk protein.

**lactam** /ˈlæktæm/, *n.* an organic compound formed from an amino acid by elimination of water from the amino and carboxyl groups. [LACT(ONE) + AM(IDE)]

**lactase** /ˈlækteɪz, -eɪs/, *n.* an enzyme capable of hydrolysing lactose into glucose and galactose.

**lactate** /ˈlækteɪt/, *n.;* /lækˈteɪt/, *v.,* **-tated, -tating.** *–n.* **1.** *Chem.* an ester or salt of lactic acid. *–v.i.* **2.** to produce milk.

**lactate dehydrogenase** /– dihaɪˈdrɒdʒəneɪz/, *n.* an enzyme existing in multiple forms which catalyses the oxidation of lactate to pyruvic acid used in diagnosis of myocardial infarction.

**lactation** /lækˈteɪʃən/, *n.* **1.** the secretion or formation of milk. **2.** the period of milk production.

**lacteal** /ˈlæktiəl/, *adj.* **1.** pertaining to, consisting of, or resembling milk; milky. **2.** *Anat.* conveying or containing chyle. *–n.* **3.** *Anat.* any of the minute lymphatic vessels which convey chyle from the small intestine to the thoracic duct. [L *lacteus* milky + -AL[1]] – **lacteally,** *adv.*

**lacteous** /ˈlæktiəs/, *adj.* milky; of the colour of milk.

**lactescent** /lækˈtɛsənt/, *adj.* **1.** becoming or being milky. **2.** *Bot.* forming a milky juice. **3.** *Entomol.* secreting a milky fluid. [L *lactescens,* ppr.] – **lactescence,** *n.*

**lactic** /ˈlæktɪk/, *adj.* pertaining to or obtained from milk.

**lactic acid** /– 'æsəd/, *n.* **1.** *Chem.* an acid, $CH_3CHOHCOOH$, found in sour milk. **2.** *Biochem.* the end product of anaerobic glycolysis.

**lactiferous** /læk'tɪfərəs/, *adj.* **1.** producing milk; concerned with the secretion of milk. **2.** conveying milk or a milky fluid. [LL *lactifer* milk-bearing + -OUS]

**lacto-**, variant of **lact-**, before consonants.

**lactobacillus** /ˌlæktoʊbə'sɪləs/, *n., pl.* **-cilli** /-'sɪlaɪ/. any bacterium of the genus *Lactobacillus,* a group of aerobic, long, slender rods which produce large amounts of lactic acid in the fermentation of carbohydrates, esp. in milk. The species most important to man is *Lactobacillus acidophilus.* See **acidophilus milk.**

**lactoflavin** /læktoʊ'fleɪvən/, *n.* →**riboflavin.** Also, **lactoflavine.**

**lactometer** /læk'tɒmətə/, *n.* an instrument for determining the specific gravity of milk.

**lactone** /'læktoun/, *n.* one of a class of internal esters derived from hydroxy acids. – **lactonic** /læk'tɒnɪk/, *adj.*

**lactoprotein** /læktoʊ'proutin/, *n.* any protein in milk.

**lactose** /'læktouz, -ous/, *n.* a crystalline disaccharide, $C_{12}H_{22}O_{11}$, present in milk, used as a food and in medicine; milk sugar. [LACT- + -OSE[2]]

**lacuna** /lə'kjunə, -'ku-/, *n., pl.* **-nae** /-ni/, **-nas.** **1.** a pit or cavity; an interstitial or intercellular space as in plant or animal tissue. **2.** *Anat.* one of the numerous minute cavities in the substance of bone, supposed to contain nucleate cells. **3.** *Bot.* an airspace lying in the midst of the cellular tissue of plants. **4.** a gap or hiatus, as in a manuscript. [L: gap]

**lacunal** /lə'kjunəl, -'ku-/, *adj.* **1.** of or pertaining to a lacuna. **2.** having lacunae. Also, **lacunary** /lə'kjunəri/.

**lacunar** /lə'kjunə, -'ku-/, *adj., n., pl.* **lacunars, lacunaria** /lækjə'nɛəriə/. *–adj.* **1.** lacunal. *–n.* **2.** *Archit.* **a.** a ceiling, or an undersurface, as of a cornice formed of sunken compartments. **b.** one of the compartments. [L, from *lacūna* pit, hollow]

**lacunose** /lə'kjunous, -'ku-/, *adj.* full of or having lacunae.

**lacustrine** /lə'kʌstraɪn/, *adj.* **1.** of or pertaining to a lake. **2.** living or occurring on or in lakes, as various animals and plants. **3.** formed at the bottom or along the shore of lakes, as geological strata. [L **lacustris* (from *lacus* lake, modelled on *palustris* of a swamp) + -INE[1]]

**lacy** /'leɪsi/, *adj.,* **-cier, -ciest.** resembling lace; lacelike. – **lacily,** *adv.* – **laciness,** *n.*

**lad** /læd/, *n.* **1.** a boy or youth. **2.** *Colloq.* (in familiar use) any male. **3.** *Colloq.* a devil-may-care, dashing man; a libertine. [ME *ladde* attendant, OE *Ladda* (nickname), of obscure orig. Cf. Norw. *askeladd* male Cinderella]

**ladanum** /'lædənəm/, *n.* →**labdanum.**

**ladder** /'lædə/, *n.* **1.** a structure of wood, metal, or rope, commonly consisting of two sidepieces between which a series of bars or rungs are set at suitable distances, forming a means of ascent or descent. **2.** something like a ladder. **3.** a line or a place in a stocking, etc., where a series of stitches have slipped out or come undone. **4.** a means of rising, as to eminence: *ladder of success.* **5.** a hierarchical order or rank: *low in the social ladder.* *–v.t.* **6.** to cause a ladder (in a stocking). *–v.i.* **7.** (of a stocking) to develop a ladder. [ME; OE *hlǣder,* c. G *Leiter*]

**ladder back** /'– bæk/, *n.* a chair back having a number of horizontal slats between uprights.

**ladder-proof** /'lædə-pruf/, *adj.* (of textiles, esp. for stockings, etc.) not liable to ladder.

**ladder stitch** /'lædə stɪtʃ/, *n.* an embroidery stitch in which crossbars at equal distances are produced between two solid ridges of raised work.

**laddie** /'lædi/, *n. Chiefly Scot.* a young lad; a boy. Also, **laddy.**

**lade** /leɪd/, *v.,* **laded, laden** or **laded, lading.** *–v.t.* **1.** to put (something) on or in as a burden, load, or cargo; load. **2.** to load oppressively; burden: *laden with responsibilities.* **3.** to fill abundantly: *trees laden with fruit.* **4.** to lift or throw in or out, as a fluid, with a ladle or other utensil. *–v.i.* **5.** to take on a load. **6.** to lade a liquid. [ME *lade(n),* OE *hladan* load, draw (water), c. D *laden;* akin to G *laden* load. Cf. LADLE]

**la-di-da** /la-di-'da/, *Colloq. –adj.* **1.** affectedly pretentious, esp. in manner, speech, or bearing. *–n.* **2.** (*euph.*) the toilet. Also, **lah-di-day.** – **la-di-dady,** *adj.*

**ladies** /'leɪdiz/, *n. Colloq.* a toilet for women. Also, **ladies'.**

**ladies' fingers** /'leɪdiz fɪŋgəz/, *n.* **1.** plural of **lady's finger.** **2.** →**kidney vetch.**

**ladies' lounge** /'– laʊndʒ/, *n.* a hotel bar where ladies may drink. Also, **ladies' parlour.**

**ladies' man** /'– mæn/, *n.* a man noted for his attentions to women.

**ladies' parlour** /'– palə/, *n.* →**ladies' lounge.**

**Ladin** /læ'din/, *n.* **1.** a Rhaeto-Romanic language of the southern Tyrol. **2.** →**Romansh.** **3.** a person who speaks Ladin. [Romansh, from L *Latīnus* Latin]

**lading** /'leɪdɪŋ/, *n.* **1.** the act of lading. **2.** load; freight; cargo: *a bill of lading.*

**ladino** /lə'dinoʊ/, *n.* **1.** (*cap.*) a mixed Spanish and Hebrew dialect spoken by Jews of Spanish extraction now living in Turkey and elsewhere. **2.** (in Spanish America) a mestizo. **3.** an uncontrollable horse, steer etc.; a stray. *–adj.* **4.** wild; vicious; cunning. [Sp., from L *Latīnus* Latin]

**ladle** /'leɪdl/, *n., v.,* **-dled, -dling.** *–n.* **1.** a long-handled utensil with a dish-shaped or cup-shaped bowl for dipping or conveying liquids. **2.** *Metall.* a bucket-like container for transferring molten metal. *–v.t.* **3.** to dip or convey with or as with a ladle. [ME *ladel,* OE *hlædel,* from *hladan* LADE] – **ladleful,** *n.* – **ladler,** *n.*

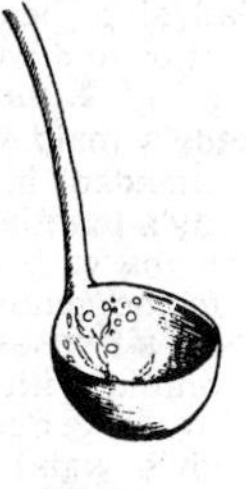

ladle

**lad's-love** /'lædz-lʌv/, *n.* an evergreen shrub from southern Europe, *Artemisia abrotanum,* often cultivated for its fragrant leaves and yellow capitula.

**lady** /'leɪdi/, *n., pl.* **-dies,** *adj.* *–n.* **1.** a woman of good family or social position, or of good breeding, refinement, etc. (correlative of *gentleman*). **2.** a polite term for any woman. **3.** (*cap.*) **a.** a less formal substitute, often used conversationally, for the specific title and rank of a countess, marchioness, viscountess or baroness, which title she may hold by marriage, by courtesy, or in her own right. **b.** the title, prefixed to the Christian name of daughters of a duke, marquess or earl. **c.** the courtesy title of the wife of a knight or a baronet. **d.** a prefix to a title of honour or respect: *Lady Mayoress.* **4.** a woman: *the tea lady.* **5.** a wife. **6.** a woman who has proprietary rights or authority, as over a manor (correlative of *lord*). **7.** (*cap.*) the Virgin Mary (usu., **Our Lady**). **8.** the mistress of a household: *the lady of the house.* **9.** a woman who is the object of chivalrous devotion. *–adj.* **10.** (*usu. cap.*) **a.** a prefix to the names of allegorical personages: *Lady Luck.* **b.** a prefix to the name of a goddess. **11.** being a lady: *a lady reporter.* **12.** of a lady; ladylike. [ME *lavedi, levedi,* OE *hlǣfdige,* ? orig. meaning loaf-kneader, from *hlāf* LOAF[1] + *-dige,* akin to *dāh* DOUGH. Cf. LORD]

**ladybird** /'leɪdibɜd/, *n.* a beetle of the family Coccinellidae, of graceful form and delicate coloration. The larvae feed upon plant-lice and small insects. Also, **lady beetle,** *U.S.,* **ladybug.** [LADY (uninflected poss. case) Virgin Mary + BIRD[1]; i.e., (our) Lady's bird]

**Lady Blamey** /leɪdi 'bleɪmi/, *n. Colloq.* a beer glass made by cutting the top off an empty beer bottle. [from *Lady Blamey,* wife of General Blamey, 1884-1951]

ladybird

**lady bountiful** /leɪdi 'baʊntəfəl/, *n.* a woman noted for her generosity, which is often slightly ostentatious.

**ladybug** /'leɪdibʌg/, *n. U.S.* →**ladybird.**

**Lady Chapel** /'leɪdi tʃæpəl/, *n.* a chapel dedicated to the Virgin Mary, attached to a church, and generally behind the high altar at the extremity of the apse.

**Lady Day** /'– deɪ/, *n.* **1.** the feast of the Annunciation, 25 March. **2.** one of various days celebrated in honour of the Virgin Mary.

**lady-fern** /ˈleɪdi-fɜn/, *n.* any of several species of ferns belonging to the genus *Athyrium,* esp. *A. filixfemina,* common in woods in the Northern Hemisphere.

**ladyfinger** /ˈleɪdifɪŋgə/, *n.* **1.** any of various cakes, biscuits, etc., fancifully thought to resemble a finger, as a kind of small, crisp sponge cake. **2.** a thin, baked roll of filo pastry with various fillings, usu. heavily spiced. **3.** any of several small-fruited bananas. **4.** a large, elongated dessert grape. Also, **lady's finger.**

**lady-in-waiting** /ˌleɪdi-ɪn-ˈweɪtɪŋ/, *n., pl.* **ladies-in-waiting.** a lady who is in attendance upon a queen or princess.

**lady-killer** /ˈleɪdi-kɪlə/, *n. Colloq.* a man supposed to be dangerously fascinating to women. – **lady-killing,** *n., adj.*

**ladylike** /ˈleɪdilaɪk/, *adj.* **1.** like a lady. **2.** befitting a lady: *ladylike manners.* – **ladylikeness,** *n.*

**ladylove** /ˈleɪdilʌv/, *n.* a beloved lady; sweetheart.

**Lady Muck** /leɪdi ˈmʌk/, *n.* a woman who affects the manner of a grand lady, usu. in an overbearing and unconvincing manner.

**lady's finger** /leɪdiz ˈfɪŋgə/, *n., pl.* **ladies' fingers.** →**ladyfinger.**

**ladyship** /ˈleɪdiʃɪp/, *n.* **1.** (*oft. cap.*) the form used in speaking of or to a woman having the title of *Lady* (prec. by *her, your,* etc.). **2.** the rank of a lady.

**lady's maid** /ˈleɪdiz meɪd/, *n.* a maid who is a lady's personal attendant in dressing, etc.

**lady's-mantle** /leɪdiz-ˈmæntl/, *n.* any of a number of perennial herbs with dense clusters of small green flowers belonging to the genus *Alchemilla.*

**lady's-tresses** /leɪdiz-ˈtrɛsəz/, *n.* any of several species of orchid with erect twisted spikes of small flowers belonging to the genus *Spiranthes,* as *S. sinensis.*

**lady's waist** /leɪdiz ˈweɪst/, *n. Colloq.* **1.** a small thin beer glass. **2.** the contents of such a glass.

**laevo-,** denoting a substance that rotates the plane of plane-polarised light to the left. *Symbol:* π. Also, *U.S.,* **levo-.**

**laevoglucose** /livoʊˈglukoʊz, -oʊs/, *n.* See **glucose.**

**laevoglycerol** /livoʊˈglɪsərɒl/, *n.* the laevorotatory form of glycerol.

**laevogyrate** /livoʊˈdʒaɪrət/, *adj. Optics, Crystall., etc.* →**laevorotatory.** Also, *U.S.,* **levogyrate.**

**laevorotation** /ˌlivoʊroʊˈteɪʃən/, *n. Optics, Chem., etc.* the rotation of the plane of polarisation to the left. Also, *U.S.,* **levorotation.**

**laevorotatory** /ˌlivoʊroʊˈteɪtəri/, *adj.* turning the plane of polarisation of light to the left, as certain crystals, etc. Also, **laevogyrate,** *U.S.,* **levorotatory.**

**laevulic acid** /liˌvjulɪk ˈæsəd/, *n.* a hygroscopic acid, $CH_3COCH_2CH_2COOH$, obtained industrially from sugar by reaction with hydrochloric acid, and used to clean metals, such as milk cans, to guard against bacterial infection. Also, **laevulinic acid,** *U.S.,* **levulic acid, levulinic acid.**

**laevulin** /ˈlɛvjulən/, *n.* a polysaccharide from which laevulose can be formed, occurring in the tubers of certain species of helianthus, etc. Also, *U.S.,* **levulin.**

**laevulose** /ˈlɛvjəloʊz, -oʊs/, *n.* fructose; fruit sugar. Also, *U.S.,* **levulose.** [L *laevus* left + -ULE + -OSE[2]]

**lag**[1] /læg/, *v.,* **lagged, lagging,** *n.* –*v.i.* **1.** to move slowly; fall behind; hang back (oft. fol. by *behind*). **2.** to decrease, wane, or flag: *his interest in the project is lagging.* **3.** *Marbles.* to throw one's shooting marble towards a line on the ground in order to decide on the order of play. **4.** *Billiards.* (in deciding the order of play) to drive the cue ball to the end cushion and return, the winner being the one who comes nearest to the head rail. –*n.* **5.** a lagging or falling behind; retardation. **6.** *Mech.* the amount of retardation of some movement. **7.** *Engineering.* the interval by which a periodic signal follows another signal with the same period. **8.** *Marbles, Billiards.* the act of lagging. [Scand.; cf. Norw. *lagga* go slowly]

**lag**[2] /læg/, *v.,* **lagged, lagging,** *n. Colloq.* –*v.t.* **1.** to send to prison. **2.** to arrest. **3.** to report the misdemeanours of (someone). –*n.* **4.** a convict, esp. an habitual criminal: *an old lag.* **5.** a term of penal servitude. [orig. unknown]

**lag**[3] /læg/, *n., v.,* **lagged, lagging.** –*n.* **1.** one of the staves or strips which form the periphery of a wooden drum, the casing of a boiler, etc. –*v.t.* **2.** to cover, as pipes, to prevent heat loss. [Scand.; cf. Swed. *lagg* stave]

**lagan** /ˈlægən/, *n. Law.* anything sunk in the sea, but attached to a buoy, etc., so that it may be recovered. Also, **ligan.** [OF; of Scand. orig. and akin to LIE[2], LAY[1]]

**lager**[1] /ˈlagə/, *n.* a German type of beer brewed by the bottom-fermentation method and stored for up to several months. Also, **lager beer.** [G *Lagerbier,* from *Lager* store + *Bier* beer]

**lager**[2] /ˈlagə/, *n., v.t., v.i. S. African.* →**laager.**

**lagerphone** /ˈlagəfoʊn/, *n.* a homemade musical instrument consisting of beer bottle tops loosely nailed to a broom-handle which is struck by a small piece of hard-wood.

lagerphone

**lagerstroemia** /lægəˈstrimiə/, *n.* an Old World genus of shrubs and trees which provides a number of garden shrubs with colourful red, pink, mauve or white flowers.

**laggard** /ˈlægəd/, *adj.* **1.** lagging; backward; slow. –*n.* **2.** one who lags; lingerer. – **laggardly,** *adv.* – **laggardness,** *n.*

**lagger** /ˈlægə/, *n.* one who lags; a laggard.

**lagging**[1] /ˈlægɪŋ/, *n.* the act of lagging behind. [LAG[1] + -ING[1]]

**lagging**[2] /ˈlægɪŋ/, *n.* **1.** the act of covering a boiler, etc. with heat-insulating material. **2.** the covering formed. **3.** the material used. **4.** (*pl.*) the coverings to the centre of an arch or to the supports in a tunnel, to form a continuous surface. [LAG[3] + -ING[1]]

**lagging**[3] /ˈlægɪŋ/, *n. Colloq.* a term of imprisonment. [LAG[2] + -ING[1]]

**lagomorph** /ˈlægəmɔf/, *n.* any of the Lagomorpha, an order of mammals resembling the rodents but having two pairs of upper incisors, and including the hares, rabbits, and pikas, formerly classified as a suborder of rodents. [Gk *lagṓ(s)* hare + -MORPH]

**lagoon** /ləˈgun/, *n.* **1.** an area of shallow water separated from the sea by low banks. **2.** any small, pondlike body of water, esp. one communicating with a larger body of water, as the expanse of water inside a coral atoll. **3.** a stretch of open water, sometimes appearing only seasonally, too small to be called a lake. Also, **lagune.** [It., Sp. *laguna,* from L *lacūna* pool, pond] – **lagoonal,** *adj.*

**lah** /la/, *n.* the syllable used for the sixth note of the scale in solfa. Also, **la.** See **solfa.**

**lahar** /ˈlaha/, *n.* a mudflow containing a great amount of volcanic matter. [Javanese]

**lah-di-dah** /la-di-ˈda/, *adj. Colloq.* →**la-di-da.**

**laic** /ˈleɪˌɪk/, *adj.* **1.** Also, **laical.** lay; secular. –*n.* **2.** layman. [LL *lāicus,* from Gk *lāïkós,* from *lāós* people] – **laically,** *adv.*

**laicise** /ˈleɪəsaɪz/, *v.t.,* **-cised, -cising.** to deprive of clerical character. Also, **laicize.** – **laicisation** /leɪəsaɪˈzeɪʃən/, *n.*

**laid** /leɪd/, *v.* past tense and past participle of **lay**[1].

**laid-back** /ˈleɪd-bæk/, *adj.* relaxed; nonchalant; at ease. Also, **laidback.**

**laid paper** /ˈleɪd peɪpə/, *n.* paper with fine parallel and cross lines produced in manufacturing. Cf. **wove paper.**

**lain** /leɪn/, *v.* past participle of **lie**[2].

**lair**[1] /lɛə/, *n.* **1.** the den or resting place of a wild beast. **2.** a place in which to lie or rest; a bed. –*v.t.* **3.** to place in a lair. **4.** to serve as a lair for. –*v.i.* **5.** to go to, lie in, or have a lair. [ME *leir,* OE *leger,* c. D and OHG *leger* bed, camp; akin to LIE[2]]

**lair**[2] /lɛə/, *n. Colloq.* **1.** a flashily dressed young man of brash and vulgar behaviour. –*v.i.* **2.** to dress up in flashy clothes (oft. fol. by *up*). –*v.t.* **3.** to renovate or dress up something in bad taste (fol. by *up*). **4. lair it up,** to behave in a brash and vulgar manner. Also, **lare.** [backformation from LAIRY]

**laird** /lɛəd/, *n.* in Scotland, a landed proprietor. [var. of LORD] – **lairdship,** *n.*

**lairise** /ˈlɛəraɪz/, *v.i.,* **-ised, -ising.** *Colloq.* to behave like a lair; to indulge in brash, vulgar exhibitionism. [LAIR[2] + -ISE[1]]

**lairy** /ˈlɛəri/, *adj. Colloq.* **1.** exhibitionistic; flashy. **2.** vulgar. Also, **leary, leery.** [var. of LEERY]

**laissez faire** /ˌleɪseɪ 'fɛə/, *n.* **1.** the theory or system of government that upholds the autonomous character of the economic order, believing that government should intervene as little as possible in the direction of economic affairs. **2.** the doctrine of non-interference, esp. in the conduct of others. Also, **laisser faire.** [F: lit., allow to act]

**laissez-faire** /ˌleɪseɪ-'fɛə/, *adj.* of or pertaining to the principle of laissez faire. Also, **laisser-faire.**

**laitance** /'leɪtns/, *n.* the scum or whitish deposit that rises to the surface of newly placed concrete.

**laity** /'leɪəti/, *n.* **1.** laymen, as distinguished from clergymen. **2.** the people outside a particular profession, as distinguished from those belonging to it. [LAY[3] + -TY[2]]

**lake**[1] /leɪk/, *n.* **1.** a body of water (fresh or salt) of considerable size, surrounded by land. **2.** some similar body of water or other liquid. [ME; OE *lacu* stream, pool, pond; replacing ME *lac,* from OF, from L *lacus* lake, tank]

**lake**[2] /leɪk/, *n.* **1.** any of various pigments prepared from animal, vegetable, or coal-tar colouring matters by union (chemical or other) with metallic compounds. **2.** a red pigment prepared from lac or cochineal by combination with a metallic compound. [F *laque,* from Pers. *lāk.* See LAC]

**lake-dweller** /'leɪk-dwɛlə/, *n.* an inhabitant of a lake-dwelling.

**lake-dwelling** /'leɪk-dwɛlɪŋ/, *n.* a dwelling, esp. of prehistoric times, built on piles or other support over the water of a lake.

**lakefront** /'leɪkfrʌnt/, *n.* the land along the shore of a lake.

**lake herring** /'leɪk hɛrɪŋ/, *n.* →**freshwater herring** (defs 3 and 4).

**lakeland terrier** /leɪklənd 'tɛriə/, *n.* one of a breed of small terriers, with harsh, dense coat; tan, black, or white in colour.

**laky**[1] /'leɪki/, *adj.* of or like a lake. [LAKE[1] + -Y[1]]

**laky**[2] /'leɪki/, *adj.* of the colour of a lake pigment. [LAKE[2] + -Y[1]]

**lallation** /læ'leɪʃən/, *n.* a speech defect consisting in pronouncing an *l* sound instead of *r.* [L *lallāre* sing lullaby + -ATION]

**lam**[1] /læm/, *v.,* **lammed, lamming.** *Colloq –v.t.* **1.** to beat; strike. *–v.i.* **2. lam into,** to thrash; rain down a succession of blows on. [Scand.; cf. Icel. *lamdhi,* p.t. of *lemja* beat; akin to LAME[1]]

**lam**[2] /læm/, *n., v.,* **lammed, lamming.** *U.S. Colloq. –n.* **1.** precipitate escape. **2. on the lam,** escaping or fleeing. **3. take it on the lam,** to flee or escape in great haste. *–v.i.* **4.** to run quickly; run off or away. [special use of LAM[1]. Cf. *beat it* be off]

**Lam.,** *Bible.* Lamentations.

**lama** /'lamə/, *n.* a priest or monk of the form of Buddhism prevailing in Tibet, Mongolia, etc. [Tibetan *blama* (*b-* is silent)]

**Lamaism** /'lamaˌɪzəm/, *n.* the form of Buddhism in Tibet and Mongolia which has developed an organised hierarchy and a host of deities and saints. **– Lamaist,** *n.*

**Lamarckism** /lə'makɪzəm/, *n.* the theory that characters acquired by habits, use, disuse, or adaptations to changes in environment may be inherited. [named after Jean Baptiste de *Lamarck,* 1744-1829, French biologist who first systematically propounded the theory]

**lamasery** /'lamasəri/, *n., pl.* **-series.** (in Tibet, Mongolia, etc.) a monastery of lamas.

**lamb** /læm/, *n.* **1.** a young sheep. **2.** the meat of a young sheep with no permanent teeth, about 12 months old. **3.** one who is young, gentle, meek, innocent, etc. **4. the Lamb (of God),** Christ. **5.** one who is easily cheated, esp. an inexperienced speculator. *–v.i.* **6.** to give birth to a lamb. *–v.t.* **7. lamb down, a.** to tend (ewes) at lambing time. **b.** *Colloq.* to spend (money) in a reckless or lavish fashion. **c.** *Colloq.* to induce (someone) to spend in a reckless fashion. **d.** *Colloq.* to swindle; cheat; fleece. [ME and OE, c. G *Lamm*]

**lambaste** /læm'beɪst/, *v.t.,* **-basted, -basting. 1.** to beat severely. **2.** (in sailors' use) to beat with a rope's end. Also, **lambast** /læm'bæst/. [apparently from LAM[1] + BASTE[3]]

**lambda** /'læmdə/, *n.* the eleventh letter of the Greek alphabet (Λ, λ).

**lambdacism** /'læmdəsɪzəm/, *n.* excessive use of the sound *l,* its misarticulation, or its substitution for *r.*

**lambdoid** /'læmdɔɪd/, *adj.* having the shape of the Greek capital lambda (Λ). Also, **lambdoidal** /læm'dɔɪdl/. [NL *lambdoīdēs,* from Gk *lambdoeidḗs.* See LAMBDA, -OID]

**lambdoidal suture** /læmˌdɔɪdl 'sutʃə/, *n.* the suture between the occipital and the two parietal bones of the skull, continued forward between the parietal bones.

**lambency** /'læmbənsi/, *n., pl.* **-cies. 1.** the quality of being lambent. **2.** that which is lambent.

**lambent** /'læmbənt/, *adj.* **1.** running or moving lightly over a surface: *lambent tongues of flame.* **2.** playing lightly and brilliantly over a subject: *lambent wit.* **3.** softly bright: *a steady, lambent light.* [L *lambens,* ppr., licking] **– lambently,** *adv.*

**lamber-down** /læmə-'daʊn/, *n.* →**shanty-keeper.**

**lambert** /'læmbət/, *n.* an imperial unit of measurement of luminance equal to $1/\pi \times 10^4$ candela per square metre (approx. 3183 cd/m$^2$). *Symbol:* L, La [named after J. H *Lambert,* 1728-77, German physicist and astronomer]

**Lambert's law** /'læmbəts lɔ/, *n.* the law which states that the illumination of a surface from a point source of light is inversely proportional to the square of the distance between the surface and the source. [named after J.H. *Lambert.* See LAMBERT]

**lambkin** /'læmkən/, *n.* **1.** a little lamb. **2.** any young and tender creature. [ME *lambkyn.* See LAMB, -KIN]]

**lamblike** /'læmlaɪk/, *adj.* like a lamb; gentle; meek.

**lambrequin** /'læmbrəkən, -bəkən/, *n.* **1.** a textile fabric worn over a helmet in medieval times to protect it from heat, rust, and sword blows. **2.** a hanging or drapery covering the upper part of an opening, as a door or window, or suspended from a shelf. [F, from Flemish *lamperkin,* diminutive of *lamper* veil]

**lamb's ear** /'læmz ɪə/, *n.* a woolly-leaved perennial with crimson flowers, *Stachys lanata,* native to the Caucasus and Iran, often used as an edging plant because of its decorative foliage. Also, **lamb's tongue.**

**lamb's fry** /'– fraɪ/, *n.* lamb's liver, when used for food.

**lambskin** /'læmskɪn/, *n.* **1.** the skin of a lamb, esp. when dressed with the wool on. **2.** leather made from such skin. **3.** parchment made from such skin. **4.** a kind of cotton cloth having a raised surface and deep nap.

**lamb's-tail** /'læmz-teɪl/, *n.* a rampant American climber, *Anredera cordifolia,* with long cream-coloured inflorescences.

**lamb's tongue** /'læmz tʌŋ/, *n.* **1.** a perennial weed, *Plantago lanceolata,* native to Europe and Asia, having a strong taproot and lanceolate leaves; rib grass. **2.** →**lamb's ear.**

**lamb's wool** /'– wʊl/, *n.* a soft, fluffy wool, with superior spinning qualities, shorn from a lamb of seven months.

**lame**[1] /leɪm/, *adj.,* **lamer, lamest,** *v.,* **lamed, laming.** *–adj.* **1.** crippled or physically disabled, as a person or animal, esp. in the foot or leg so as to limp or walk with difficulty. **2.** impaired or disabled through defect or injury, as a limb. **3.** defective in quality or quantity; insufficient: *a lame excuse.* *–v.t.* **4.** to make lame or defective. [ME; OE *lama,* c. G *lahm*] **– lamely,** *adv.* **– lameness,** *n.*

**lame**[2] /leɪm/, *n.* one of numerous overlapping plates used in building elements of flexible armour. [F, from L *lāmina* thin piece or plate]

**lamé** /'lameɪ/, *n.* an ornamental fabric in which metallic threads are woven with silk, wool, artificial fibres, or cotton. [F: lit., laminated, from OF *lame* gold or silver thread or wire]

**lamebrain** /'leɪmbreɪn/, *n. U.S. Colloq.* a foolish, unintelligent person.

**lame duck** /leɪm 'dʌk/, *n. Colloq.* a person or thing that is disabled, helpless, ineffective, or inefficient.

**lamella** /lə'mɛlə/, *n., pl.* **-mellae** /-'mɛli/, **-mellas. 1.** a thin plate, scale, membrane, or layer, as of bone, tissue, cell walls, etc. **2.** *Bot.* **a.** an erect scale or blade inserted at the junction of the claw and limb in some corollas, and forming a part of their corona or crown. **b.** a gill, one of the radiating vertical plates on the underside of the pileus of an agaric. **c.** (in mosses) a thin sheet of cells standing up along the midrib of a leaf. [L, diminutive of *lāmina* LAMINA]

**lamellar** /lə'mɛlə/, *adj.* **1.** referring to a lamella or lamellae. **2.** →**lamellate.**

**lamellate** /'læməleɪt, lə'mɛleɪt/, *adj.* **1.** composed of or having lamellae. 2. flat; platelike. Also, **lamellated** /ˈlæməleɪtəd/.

**lamellibranch** /ləˈmɛləbræŋk/, *n.* any of the Lamellibranchiata, a class of molluscs comprising the oysters, clams, mussels, scallops, etc., characterised by a bivalve shell enclosing the headless body and lamellate gills. [NL *Lāmellibranchia,* pl., from L *lāmelli-* thin plate + Gk *brán-chia* gills] – **lamellibranchiate** /ləmɛləˈbræŋkiət, -eɪt/, *adj., n.*

**lamellicorn** /ləˈmɛləkɔn/, *Entomol.* –*adj.* **1.** having antennae with lamellate and leaf-like terminal segments, as beetles of the group Lamellicornia, which includes the scarabaeids and stag-beetles. **2.** (of antennae) having leaf-like terminal segments. –*n.* **3.** a lamellicorn beetle. [NL *lāmellicornis,* from L *lāmelli-* thin plate + *-cornis* horned]

**lamellirostral** /ləmɛliˈrɒstrəl/, *adj.* having a beak equipped with thin plates or lamellae for straining water and mud from food, as ducks, geese, swans, and flamingos. Also, **lamellirostrate.** [L *lāmelli-* thin plate + ROSTRAL]

**lamellose** /ləˈmɛloʊs, ˈlæməloʊs/, *adj.* →**lamellate.**

**lament** /ləˈmɛnt/, *v.t.* **1.** to feel or express sorrow or regret for; mourn for or over: *lament his absence, one's folly.* –*v.i.* **2.** to feel, show, or express grief, sorrow, or sad regret (oft. fol. by *over*). –*n.* **3.** an expression of grief or sorrow. **4.** a formal expression of sorrow or mourning, esp. in verse or song; an elegy or dirge, often played on the bagpipes. [L *lāmentārī* wail, weep] – **lamenter,** *n.*

**lamentable** /ˈlæməntəbəl, ləˈmɛntəbəl/, *adj.* **1.** that is to be lamented: *a lamentable occurrence.* **2.** *Rare.* mournful. – **lamentableness,** *n.* – **lamentably,** *adv.*

**lamentation** /læmənˈteɪʃən/, *n.* **1.** the act of lamenting. **2.** a lament.

**lamented** /ləˈmɛntəd/, *adj.* **1.** mourned for, as one who is dead: *the late lamented Grady.* **2.** regretted.

**lamia** /ˈleɪmiə/, *n., pl.* **-mias, -miae** /-mii/. **1.** *Class. Myth.* one of a class of mythical monsters, commonly represented with the head and breast of a woman and the body of a serpent, said to allure youths and children in order to suck their blood. **2.** a vampire; a female demon. [ME, from L, from Gk]

**lamina** /ˈlæmənə/, *n., pl.* **-nae** /-ni/, **-nas. 1.** a thin plate, scale, or layer. **2.** a layer or coat lying over another, applied to the plates of minerals, bones, etc. **3.** *Bot.* the blade or expanded portion of a leaf. [L: thin plate, leaf, layer. Cf. LAMELLA]

**laminable** /ˈlæmənəbəl/, *adj.* capable of being laminated.

**laminal** /ˈlæmənəl/, *adj. Phonet.* pronounced with the blade of the tongue as articulator.

**laminar** /ˈlæmənə/, *adj.* composed of, or arranged in, laminae. Also, **laminary** /ˈlæmənəri, -nri/.

**laminar flow** /– ˈfloʊ/, *n.* a flow of a viscous fluid in which neighbouring layers are not mixed.

**laminate** /ˈlæməneɪt/, *v.,* **-nated, -nating;** /ˈlæməneɪt, -nət/, *adj.* –*v.t.* **1.** to separate or split into thin layers. **2.** to form (metal) into a lamina, as by beating or rolling. **3.** to construct by placing layer upon layer. **4.** to cover or overlay with laminae. –*v.i.* **5.** to split into thin layers. –*adj.* **6.** composed of, or having, a lamina or laminae. [LAMIN(A) + -ATE[1]]

**laminated** /ˈlæməneɪtəd/, *adj.* formed of, or set in, thin layers or laminae.

**laminated glass** /– ˈglas/, *n.* glass made by joining two plates or panes with a layer of plastic or artificial resin between them which retains the fragments if the glass is broken.

**laminated plastic** /– ˈplæstɪk/, *n.* a stiff board, or glossy surface covering, made from compressed sheets of paper or textile impregnated with a synthetic resin.

**lamination** /læməˈneɪʃən/, *n.* **1.** the act or process of laminating. **2.** the state of being laminated. **3.** laminated structure; arrangement in thin layers. **4.** a lamina.

**lamington** /ˈlæmɪŋtən/, *n.* a cake confection made by covering a cube of sponge cake in chocolate icing and shredded coconut. [apparently named after Lord *Lamington,* Governor of Queensland, 1895-1901]

**laminitis** /læməˈnaɪtəs/, *n.* inflammation of sensitive laminae in the hoof of a horse, or other hoofed animals, caused by overwork, overfeeding, etc. [NL]

**laminose** /ˈlæmənoʊs/, *adj.* laminate; laminar.

**lammergeyer** /ˈlæməgaɪə/, *n.* the bearded vulture, *Gypaëtus barbatus,* the largest European bird of prey, ranging in the mountains from southern Europe to China. Also, **lammergeier.** [G *Lämmergeier,* lit., lambs' vulture (from its preying on lambs)]

**lamp** /læmp/, *n.* **1.** any of various devices for using an illuminant, as gas or electricity, or for heating, as by burning alcohol. **2.** a vessel for containing an inflammable liquid, as oil, which is burnt at a wick as a means of illumination. **3.** any source as of intellectual or spiritual light. **4.** *Poetic.* a torch. **5.** *Poetic.* a celestial body, as the moon. **6.** (*pl.*) *Colloq.* the eyes. –*v.t.* **7.** *Colloq.* to observe; look at. [ME *lampe,* from OF, from L *lampas,* from Gk: torch, light, lamp]

**lampas** /ˈlæmpəs/, *n.* a type of brocaded fabric of silk and cotton, or cotton only, used in upholstery, etc. [ME, from OFlem. *lampers*]

**lampblack** /ˈlæmpblæk/, *n.* a fine black pigment consisting of almost pure carbon collected as soot from the smoke of burning oil, gas, etc.

**lamper eel** /ˈlæmpər il/, *n.* →**lamprey.**

**lampion** /ˈlæmpiən/, *n.* a kind of lamp, often of coloured glass. [F, from It. *lampione* carriage or street lamp, from *lampa* LAMP]

**lamplight** /ˈlæmplaɪt/, *n.* the light shed by a lamp.

**lamplighter** /ˈlæmplaɪtə/, *n.* **1.** one who lights street lamps, esp. (formerly) gas lamps. **2.** *U.S.* a contrivance for lighting lamps.

**lampoon** /læmˈpun/, *n.* **1.** a malicious or virulent satire upon a person, institution, government, etc., in either prose or verse. –*v.t.* **2.** to assail in a lampoon. [F *lampon,* said to be a modification of *lampons* let us drink (used in songs or verses), imper. of *lamper*] – **lampooner, lampoonist,** *n.* – **lampoonery,** *n.*

**lamppost** /ˈlæmppoʊst/, *n.* a post, of concrete, steel, or iron, used to support a lamp which lights a street, park, etc.

**lamprey** /ˈlæmpri/, *n., pl.* **-preys.** any of the eel-like cyclostome fishes constituting the group Hypercoartia. Some species attach themselves to fishes and rasp a hole in the flesh with their horny teeth so that they can suck the blood of the victim. [ME, from OF *lampreie,* from LL *lamprēda*]

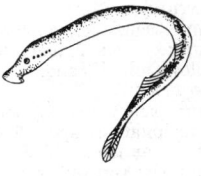

lamprey

**lamprophyre** /ˈlæmprəfaɪə/, *n.* a group of dark dyke rocks in which dark minerals occur both as phenocrysts and in the groundmass, and light-coloured minerals occur in the groundmass; the essential constituents are biotite, hornblende, pyroxene or a combination of these together with felspars or felspathoids. [*lampro-* (combining form representing Gk *lamprós* clear) + -PHYRE]

**lampshade** /ˈlæmpʃeɪd/, *n.* a covering, often decorative, to diffuse or concentrate the light of a lamp.

**lamp-shell** /ˈlæmp-ʃɛl/, *n.* →**brachiopod.**

**lamp standard** /ˈlæmp stændəd/, *n.*→**lamppost.**

**lanate** /ˈleɪneɪt/, *adj.* woolly; covered with something resembling wool. [L *lānātus*]

**lance** /læns, lans/, *n., v.,* **lanced, lancing.** –*n.* **1.** a long, shafted weapon with a metal head, used by mounted soldiers in charging. **2.** a soldier armed with this weapon. **3.** an implement resembling the weapon, as a spear for killing a harpooned whale. **4.** a lancet. –*v.t.* **5.** to open with, or as if with, a lancet: *to lance an abscess.* **6.** to pierce with a lance. [ME, from F, from L *lancea*]

**lance bombardier** /– bɒmbəˈdɪə/, *n.* a non-commissioned officer in the Royal Regiment of Australian Artillery, corresponding in rank to a lance corporal.

**lance corporal** /– ˈkɔprəl/, *n.* the lowest non-commissioned officer rank in the Australian Army, below corporal.

**lance-head lizard** /ˈlæns-hɛd lɪzəd/, *n.* →**Burton's legless lizard.**

**lance jack** /læns ˈdʒæk/, *n. Colloq.* →**lance corporal.**

**lancelet** /ˈlænslət, ˈlans-/, *n.* any of various small, flattened, fish-like animals of the subphylum Cephalochordata, of tropical and temperate seacoasts, showing vertebrate characteristics but having a notochord rather than a vertebral column; amphioxus. [LANCE, *n.* + -LET]

**lanceolate** /'lænsiəleɪt, 'lans-, -lət/, *adj.* **1.** shaped like the head of a lance. **2.** (of leaves, etc.) narrow, and tapering towards the apex or (sometimes) each end. [L *lanceolātus,* from *lanceola,* diminutive of *lancea* lance]

**lancer** /'lænsə, 'lan-/, *n.* **1.** a soldier belonging to one of certain regiments officially called Lancers. **2.** (formerly) a mounted soldier armed with a lance.

**lance rest** /'læns rɛst/, *n.* (in medieval armour) a support, bolted to the breastplate, upon which the lance rested when couched for use.

lancelet

**lancers** /'lænsəz, 'lan-/, *n.pl.* **1.** a form of quadrille (dance). **2.** music for such a set of dances.

**lance sergeant** /læns 'sadʒənt/, *n.* a corporal appointed to act as sergeant, without increase in pay; an acting sergeant.

**lancet** /'lænsət, 'lans-/, *n.* **1.** a small surgical instrument, usu. sharp-pointed and two-edged, for opening abscesses, etc. **2.** *Archit.* **a.** a lancet arch. **b.** a lancet window. [late ME *lawnset,* from OF *lancette,* diminutive of *lance* LANCE]

**lancet arch** /'– atʃ/, *n.* an arch the head of which is acutely pointed.

**lanceted** /'lænsətəd, 'lans-/, *adj.* having a lancet arch or lancet windows.

lanceolate leaf

**lancet fish** /'lænsət fɪʃ/, *n.* a large marine fish of the genus *Alepisaurus,* with enormous dagger-like teeth. Also, **wolf-fish.**

**lancet window** /'– wɪndoʊ/, *n.* a high, narrow window terminating in a lancet arch.

**lancewood** /'lænswʊd, 'lans-/, *n.* **1.** the tough, elastic wood of any of various trees, as *Harpullia pendula* and *Albizia basaltica.* **2.** a tree which yields it. **3.** *N.Z.* a tree, *Pseudopanax crassifolium,* an immature form of which has distinctive lanceolate leaves.

**lancinate** /'lænsəneɪt, 'lans-/, *v.t.,* **-nated, -nating.** to tear or rend; stab or pierce. [L *lancinātus,* pp.] – **lancination** /lænsə'neɪʃən, lans-/, *n.*

**land** /lænd/, *n.* **1.** the solid substance of the earth's surface. **2.** the exposed part of the earth's surface, as distinguished from the submerged part: *to travel by land.* **3.** ground, esp. with reference to quality, character, or use: *forest land.* **4.** agricultural areas as opposed to urban. **5.** *Law.* **a.** any part of the earth's surface which can be owned as property, and everything annexed to it, whether by nature or by the hand of man. **b.** any hereditament, tenement, or other interest held in land. **6.** *Econ.* natural resources as a factor of production. **7.** a part of the earth's surface marked off by natural or political boundaries or the like; a region or country. **8.** a realm or domain. **9.** a surface between furrows, as on a millstone or on the interior of a rifle barrel. **10. see how the land lies,** to investigate a situation, circumstances, etc. **11. be on the land,** to own, manage or work on a farm, etc. **12.** *Chiefly U.S. Colloq.* (*euph.*) Lord: *land's sake, my land.* *–v.t.* **13.** to bring to or put on land or shore: *to land passengers or goods from a vessel.* **14.** to bring into, or cause to arrive in, any place, position, or condition. **15.** *Colloq.* to secure; make certain of; gain or obtain: *to land a job.* **16.** *Angling.* to bring (a fish) to land, or into a boat, etc., as with a hook or a net. **17.** to give (someone) a task which they may be unwilling to perform (fol. by *with*): *the headmaster landed him with the task of reorganisation.* *–v.i.* **18.** to come to land or shore: *the boat lands at Devonport.* **19.** to go or come ashore from a ship or boat. **20.** to alight upon the ground as from an aeroplane, a train, or after a jump or the like. **21.** to come to rest or arrive in any place, position, or condition. **22.** to hit or strike and come to rest on the surface of something: *the plane landed in water.* **23. land on one's feet. a.** to have good luck. **b.** to emerge successfully from an adverse situation. [ME and OE, c. G *Land*]

**land agent** /'– eɪdʒənt/, *n.* **1.** →**estate agent. 2.** *Brit.* the steward or manager of a landed estate.

**land art** /'– at/, *n.* an art movement in the U.S. since the late 1960s which rejects the sophistication of contemporary professional art and of urban life in general, and seeks elemental experience by the digging of trenches, building of mounds, etc., in deserted and remote places; earthworks.

**landau** /'lændoʊ, -dɔ, -daʊ/, *n.* **1.** a four-wheeled, two-seated vehicle with a top made in two parts, which may be let down or folded back. **2.** *Archaic.* a sedan type motor vehicle with a short convertible back. [named after *Landau,* a town in Germany]

**landaulet** /lændə'lɛt, -doʊ-/, *n.* *Obs.* a motor vehicle having a convertible top for the back seat, with the front seat either roofed or open. Also, **landaulette.**

landau

**land breeze** /'lænd briz/, *n.* a thermally produced wind blowing during the night from the cool land on to the adjoining warmer sea.

**land certificate** /'– səˌtɪfɪkət/, *n.* a certificate under the seal of a land registry, containing a copy of the registered particulars of a piece of land.

**land crab** /'– kræb/, *n.* any of several crabs, esp. of the family Gecarcinidae, which are partially adapted to terrestrial life. Land crabs of varied species occur in many tropical regions.

**land cress** /'– krɛs/, *n.* a biennial cruciferous herb with yellow flowers, *Brassica verna,* native to the Mediterranean region but widely naturalised in temperate zones.

**landed** /'lændəd/, *adj.* **1.** owning land: *a landed proprietor.* **2.** consisting of land: *landed property.*

**landfall** /'lændfɔl/, *n.* **1.** an approach to or sighting of land. **2.** the land sighted or reached.

**landform** /'lændfɔm/, *n.* any of the numerous features which make up the surface of the earth, as plain, plateau, canyon.

**land grant** /'lænd grænt/, *n.* the grant of Crown land, as to an individual, government body, organisation, etc.

**landgrave** /'lændgreɪv/, *n.* **1.** the title of certain princes. **2.** *Hist.* a German count having jurisdiction over a considerable territory. [G *Landgraf*]

**landgraviate** /lænd'greɪviət, -eɪt/, *n.* the office, jurisdiction, or territory of a landgrave.

**landgravine** /'lændgrəvin/, *n.* **1.** the wife of a landgrave. **2.** a woman of the rank of a landgrave. [G *Landgräfin*]

**land-holder** /'lænd-hoʊldə/, *n.* a holder, owner, or occupant of land. – **land-holding,** *adj.*

**landing** /'lændɪŋ/, *n.* **1.** the act of one who or that which lands. **2.** a place where persons or goods are landed, as from a ship. **3.** *Archit.* **a.** the floor at the head or foot of a flight of stairs. **b.** a platform between flights of stairs.

**landing beam** /'– bim/, *n.* a radio beam transmitted from an airfield to indicate to a pilot the height and position of his aircraft when approaching to land.

**landing card** /'– kad/, *n.* a card issued to passengers to regulate landing from a boat, aeroplane, etc.

**landing craft** /'– kraft/, *n.* a low, flat-bottomed boat, used for landing troops and equipment on a beach.

**landing field** /'– fild/, *n.* an area of land, cleared to allow aircraft to take off and land.

**landing gear** /'– gɪə/, *n.* the undercarriage of an aircraft.

**landing net** /'– nɛt/, *n.* a scoop-shaped net, used for lifting a hooked fish out of the water and on to the land or boat.

**landing party** /'– pati/, *n.* a detachment of a ship's crew, sent ashore for exploratory or hostile action.

**landing stage** /'– steɪdʒ/, *n.* a fixed or floating wharf.

**landing strip** /'– strɪp/, *n.* an area of flat land used by aeroplanes for landing and taking off and having only rudimentary facilities, or none at all, for servicing and passenger handling.

**landjobber** /'lænddʒɒbə/, *n.* →**land shark.**

**landlady** /'lændleɪdi/, *n., pl.* **-dies. 1.** a woman who owns and leases land, buildings, etc. **2.** a woman who owns or runs an inn, lodging house, or boarding house.

**ländler** /'lɛntlə/, *n.* **1.** a country dance for couples in triple time. **2.** the music for this dance. [G, from d. *Landl* Upper Austria, where this dance originated]

**landless** /ˈlændləs/, *adj.* without land; owning no land.

**landline** /ˈlændlaɪn/, *n.* a telecommunications line, running under or along the ground.

**landlocked** /ˈlændlɒkt/, *adj.* **1.** shut in more or less completely by land. **2.** living in waters shut off from the sea as some fish: *a landlocked salmon.*

**landlord** /ˈlændlɔd/, *n.* **1.** one who owns and leases land, buildings, etc., to another. **2.** the master of an inn, lodging house, etc. **3.** a landowner.

**landlordism** /ˈlændlɔdɪzəm/, *n.* the practice under which property or land which is owned by one person is leased to another for his occupancy or use.

**landlubber** /ˈlændlʌbə/, *n. Naut.* a landsman or raw seaman. [LAND + LUBBER] – **landlubberly,** *adj.*

**landmark** /ˈlændmak/, *n.* **1.** a conspicuous object on land that serves as a guide, as to vessels at sea. **2.** a prominent or distinguishing feature, part, event, etc.: *the Eureka rebellion was a landmark in Australian history.* **3.** something used to mark the boundary of land.

**landmass** /ˈlændmæs/, *n.* a body of land, usu. extensive, as a large island or continent, surrounded by water.

**landmine** /ˈlændmaɪn/, *n.* **1.** a bomb dropped by parachute, causing widespread damage. **2.** →**mine**² (def. 7).

**land mullet** /ˈlænd mʌlət/, *n.* the largest Australian skink, of genus *Egernia,* having shiny, dark brown or black scales; found in the coastal border region of Queensland and New South Wales; black skink; giant skink.

**land of milk and honey,** *n.* a land of great fertility and promise.

**landowner** /ˈlændounə/, *n.* an owner or proprietor of land. – **landownership,** *n.* – **landowning,** *n., adj.*

**landplane** /ˈlændpleɪn/, *n., v.,* **-planed, -planing.** *–n.* **1.** a machine for smoothing out irregularities in the surface of an area of land. *–v.i.* **2.** to make the surface even by means of a landplane, esp. for flood irrigation.

**land power** /ˈlænd pauə/, *n.* **1.** a nation having an important and powerful army. **2.** military power on land.

**landrace** /ˈlændreɪs/, *n.* a smallish lop-eared breed of pig, having a coat of short white hairs.

**landrail** /ˈlændreɪl/, *n.* →**corncrake.**

**land reclamation** /ˈlænd rɛkləˌmeɪʃən/, *n.* the improvement or the draining of land, so that it may be used for farming, building, etc.

**land reform** /ˈ– rəfɔm/, *n.* a redistribution of land holdings, usu. effected by government, with the aim of dividing very large properties, belonging to a few wealthy owners, into smaller parcels of land, so that people who own no land have an opportunity to acquire some.

**land registry** /ˈ– rɛdʒəstri/, *n.* a registry for officially recording the title to, dealings with, and charges on land.

**land rights** /ˈ– raɪts/, *n.pl.* the rights of the original inhabitants of a country to possess land, esp. sacred tribal grounds.

**land sailer** /ˈ– seɪlə/, *n.* →**land yacht.**

**Landsborough grass** /ˈlændzbərə gras/, *n.* a small variety of Flinders grass, *Iseilema membranaceum,* widespread in Australia. [named after *Landsborough,* a town in SE queensland]

**landscape** /ˈlændskeɪp/, *n., v.,* **-scaped, -scaping.** *–n.* **1.** a view or prospect of rural scenery, more or less extensive, such as is comprehended within the scope or range of vision from a single point of view. **2.** a piece of such scenery. **3.** a picture representing natural inland or coastal scenery. **4.** such pictures as a category. **5.** *Print.* a page or illustration larger in width than depth. *–v.t.* **6.** to improve the landscape. *–v.i.* **7.** to do landscape gardening as a profession. [earlier *landskip, landskap,* from D *landschap,* c. OE *landsceap, landscipe,* G *Landschaft* region. See LAND, -SHIP]

**landscape architect** /– ˈakətɛkt/, *n.* one whose profession is to adapt an area of land to give a particular visual effect. – **landscape architecture,** *n.*

**landscape gardening** /– ˈgadənɪŋ/, *n.* the art of arranging trees, shrubbery, paths, fountains, etc., to produce picturesque effects. – **landscape gardener,** *n.*

**land shark** /ˈlænd ʃak/, *n.* one who makes excessive profits from speculating in land.

**landsknecht** /ˈlæntskənɛkt/, *n.* →**lansquenet.**

**landslide** /ˈlændslaɪd/, *n.* **1.** the sliding down of a mass of soil, detritus, or rock on a steep slope. **2.** the mass itself. **3.** an election in which a particular candidate or party receives an overwhelming mass or majority of votes. **4.** any overwhelming victory.

**landslip** /ˈlændslɪp/, *n.* →**landslide** (defs 1 and 2).

**Landsmål** /ˈlʌntsmoul/, *n.* →**Nynorsk.** [Norw.: country's speech]

**landsman** /ˈlændzmən/, *n., pl.* **-men.** **1.** one who lives, or engages in an occupation, on land (opposed to *seaman*). **2.** *Naut.* **a.** a sailor on his first voyage. **b.** an inexperienced seaman, rated below an ordinary seaman.

**land tax** /ˈlænd tæks/, *n.* a tax on land, the unimproved value of which exceeds a specified sum.

**landward** /ˈlændwəd/, *adj.* **1.** lying, facing, or tending towards the land or away from the coast: *a landward breeze.* **2.** being in the direction of the land. *–adv.* **3.** →**landwards.**

**landwards** /ˈlændwədz/, *adv.* towards the land or interior. Also, **landward.**

**land yacht** /ˈlænd jɒt/, *n.* a wind-propelled land vehicle, usu. resembling a marine yacht.

**lane** /leɪn/, *n.* **1.** a narrow way or passage between hedges, fences, walls, or houses. **2.** any narrow or well-defined passage, track, channel, or course. **3.** a stock route which has fences on both sides. **4.** a fixed route pursued by ocean-going ships or aircraft. **5.** →**laneway.** **6.** (in racing) each of the spaces between the cords or chalked lines which mark the courses of the competitors. **7.** *Tenpin Bowling.* a narrow alley, usu. with a polished wooden floor, on which the ball is bowled. [ME and OE, c. D *laan*]

**laneway** /ˈleɪnweɪ/, *n.* a lane marked out on a road outside of which a vehicle should not move except when road signs allow him to do so and when he has given proper indication. Also, **lane.**

**lang** /læŋ/, *adj., n., adv. Scot.* →**long**¹.

**lang.,** language.

**Langerhans** /ˈlæŋəhænz/, *n.* **islets of.** See **pancreas.**

**langlauf** /ˈlæŋlauf/, *adj.* of or pertaining to cross-country skiing on narrow skis with only the toes secured and ankles free. [G, from *lang* long + *lauf* run] – **langlaufer,** *n.*

**langley** /ˈlæŋli/, *n.* a non SI unit of measurement of solar radiation in energy per unit area of irradiated surface equivalent to 41 868 joules per square metre.

**Langobardic** /læŋgəˈbadɪk/, *adj.* **1.** pertaining to the Langobards (or Lombards), an ancient Germanic tribe which settled in north Italy. *–n.* **2.** the language of the Langobards, a dialect of High German.

**langouste** /ˈlɒŋgust, lɒŋˈgust/, *n.* the French gastronomic name for the spiny lobster; prepared and cooked like lobster.

**langrage** /ˈlæŋgrɪdʒ/, *n.* a kind of shot consisting of bolts, nails, etc., fastened together or enclosed in a case, formerly used for damaging sails and rigging in battles at sea. Also, **langridge.** [orig. unknown]

**langsyne** /læŋˈsaɪn/, *Scot. –adv.* **1.** long since; long ago. *–n.* **2.** time long past. [*lang* long + *syne,* contraction of ME *sithen,* OE *siththan* SINCE]

**language** /ˈlæŋgwɪdʒ, ˈlæŋwɪdʒ/, *n.* **1.** communication by voice in the distinctively human manner, using arbitrary auditory symbols in conventional ways with conventional meanings. **2.** any set or system of such symbols as used in a more or less uniform fashion by a number of people, who are thus enabled to communicate intelligibly with one another. **3.** the non-linguistic means of communication of animals: *the language of birds.* **4.** any basis of communication and understanding: *the language of flowers; corporal punishment is the only language children understand.* **5.** linguistics. **6.** strong language: *his language shocked us.* **7.** the speech or phraseology peculiar to a class, profession, etc. **8.** form or manner of expression: *in his own language.* **9.** speech or expression of a particular character: *flowery language.* **10.** diction or style of writing. **11. speak (someone's) language,** to be in sympathy with; have the same mode of thinking; share the same jargon. **12. speak the same (a different) language,** to be in (out of) sympathy or accord, esp. as a result of shared (different) background, education, etc. [ME, from OF *langage,* from *langue* tongue, from L *lingua*]

**language laboratory** /ˈ– ləˌbɒrətri/, *n.* a place where languages are taught by the use of tape-recorders and other devices.

**langue** /lɒŋg/, *n. Linguistics.* the abstract, underlying system of language possessed by all members of a speech community. Cf. **parole** (def. 5).

**langue d'oc** /lɒŋgə 'dɒk/, *n.* **1.** the Romance language of medieval southern France. **2.** →**Provencal.** [OF: '*oc*' language, i.e. the language in which *oc* yes was used. See LANGUE D'OÏL]

**langue d'oïl** /lɒŋgə dɒ'il/, *n.* the French of medieval northern France. [OF: '*oïl*' language (OF *oïl* yes). See LANGUE D'OC]

**languet** /'læŋgwət/, *n.* any of various small tongue-shaped parts, processes, or projections. [ME, from F *languette,* diminutive of *langue,* from L *lingua* tongue]

**languette** /'læŋgwɛt/, *n.* a thin plate fastened to the mouth of certain organ pipes. [F]

**languid** /'læŋgwəd/, *adj.* **1.** drooping or flagging from weakness or fatigue; faint. **2.** lacking in spirit or interest; indifferent. **3.** lacking in vigour or activity; slack; dull: *a languid market.* **4.** slow and graceful in movement; luxuriating or voluptuous in idleness. [L *languidus*] – **languidly,** *adv.* – **languidness,** *n.*

**languish** /'læŋgwɪʃ/, *v.i.* **1.** to become or be weak or feeble; droop or fade. **2.** to lose activity and vigour. **3.** to pine or suffer under any unfavourable conditions: *to languish ten years in a dungeon.* **4.** to pine with desire or longing for. **5.** to assume an expression of tender, sentimental melancholy. –*n.* **6.** the act of languishing. **7.** *Obs.* a languishing expression. [ME *languish(en),* from F *languiss-,* stem of *languir,* from L *languēre*] – **languisher,** *n.*

**languishing** /'læŋgwɪʃɪŋ/, *adj.* **1.** becoming languid, in any way. **2.** lingering: *a languishing death.* **3.** expressive of languor; indicating tender, sentimental melancholy: *a languishing sigh.* – **languishingly,** *adv.*

**languishment** /'læŋgwɪʃmənt/, *n.* **1.** the act of languishing. **2.** languishing condition. **3.** a languishing expression.

**languor** /'læŋgə/, *n.* **1.** physical weakness or faintness. **2.** lack of energy; indolence. **3.** emotional softness or tenderness. **4.** lack of spirit. **5.** soothing or oppressive stillness. [L; replacing ME *langur,* from OF]

**languorous** /'læŋgərəs/, *adj.* **1.** characterised by languor; languid. **2.** inducing languor. – **languorously,** *adv.*

**langur** /lʌŋ'gʊə/, *n.* any of certain large, slender, long-limbed, long-tailed Asiatic monkeys of the sub-family Colobinae, as the haruman (the sacred monkey of India). [Hind. Cf. Skt *lāngūlin* having a tail]

**laniard** /'lænjəd/, *n.* →**lanyard.**

**laniary** /'lænjəri/, *adj.* **1.** (of teeth) adapted for tearing. –*n.* **2.** a laniary or canine tooth. [L *laniārius* of a butcher, from *lanius* butcher]

**lank** /læŋk/, *adj.* **1.** meagrely slim; lean; gaunt: *a tall, lank man.* **2.** (of plants, etc.) unduly long and slender. **3.** (of hair) straight and limp; not resilient or wiry. [OE *hlanc,* akin to OHG *hlanca* loin, side. Cf. FLANK] – **lankly,** *adv.* – **lankness,** *n.*

**lanky** /'læŋki/, *adj.,* **-kier, -kiest.** somewhat lank; ungracefully tall and thin; rangy. – **lankily,** *adv.* – **lankiness,** *n.*

**lanner** /'lænə/, *n.* **1.** a falcon, *Falco biarmicus,* of southern Europe, northern Africa, and southern Asia. **2.** the female of this bird, used in falconry. Cf. **lanneret.** [ME *lanere,* from OF *lanier* cowardly (bird)]

**lanneret** /'lænərɛt/, *n. Falconry.* the male lanner, which is smaller than the female. [ME *lanret,* from OF *laneret,* from *lanier* LANNER]

**lanolin** /'lænələn/, *n.* a fatty substance, extracted from wool, used in ointments. Also, **lanoline** /'lænəlin/. [L *lāna* wool + -OL[2] + -IN[2]]

**lansquenet** /'lænskənɛt/, *n.* mercenary foot soldier, formerly used in the German and other Continental armies. Also, **landsknecht.** [F, from G *Landsknecht,* from *Lands* land's + *Knecht* manservant. See KNIGHT]

**lantana** /læn'tanə/, *n.* any plant of the mostly tropical genus *Lantana,* including species much cultivated for their aromatic yellow or orange flowers, as *L. camara,* which has become a troublesome weed in tropical and subtropical regions. [NL: viburnum, from It. d.]

**lantern** /'læntən/, *n.* **1.** a transparent or translucent case for enclosing a light and protecting it from the wind, rain, etc. **2.** a magic lantern. **3.** the chamber at the top of a lighthouse, surrounding the light. **4.** *Archit.* **a.** a more or less open construction on the top of a tower or crowning a dome. **b.** any light decorative structure of relatively small size crowning a roof. **c.** a raised construction on the roof of a building, designed to admit light. **d.** an open-sided structure on a roof to let out smoke or to assist ventilation. [ME *lanterne,* from F, from L *lanterna,* from Gk *lamptḗr* a light torch, b. with L *lucerna* a lamp]

**lanterne rouge** /læntən 'ruʒ/, *n.* the last man to finish a stage of a cycling race. [F: red lantern]

**lantern-fish** /'læntən-fɪʃ/, *n.* any small marine fish of the family Myctophidae, with rows of luminescent spots, living in the open sea and coming to the surface at night.

**lantern-fly** /'læntən-flaɪ/, *n.* any of certain tropical homopterous insects of the family Fulgoridae, formerly supposed to emit light.

**lantern jaws** /læntən dʒɔz/, *n.pl.* long thin jaws (with sunken cheeks). – **lantern-jawed,** *adj.*

**lantern pinion** /– 'pɪnjən/, *n.* a wheel used like a pinion consisting essentially of two parallel discs or heads whose peripheries are connected by a series of bars which engage with the teeth of another wheel. Also, **lantern wheel.**

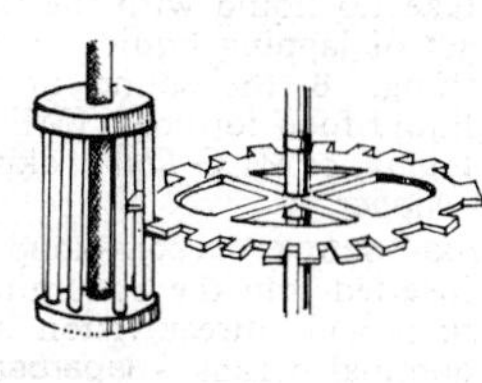
lantern pinion

**lantern slide** /'– slaɪd/, *n.* →**slide** (def. 12).

**lanthanide** /'lænθənaɪd/, *n.* any of the closely related metallic elements with atomic numbers 57-71 (see **rare-earth elements,** def. 1). Also, **lanthanon.**

**lanthanum** /'lænθənəm/, *n.* a rare-earth, trivalent, metallic element, allied to aluminium, found in certain rare minerals, as monazite. *Symbol:* La; *at. wt:* 138.91; *at. no.:* 57; *sp. gr.:* 6.17-6.19 at 20°C. [NL, from Gk *lanthánein* escape notice]

**lanuginose** /lə'nudʒənoʊs, -'nju-/, *adj.* **1.** covered with lanugo, or soft, downy hairs. **2.** of the nature of down; downy. Also, **lanuginous.** [L *lānūginōsus* woolly]

**lanugo** /lə'nugoʊ, -'nju-/, *n.* a coat of delicate, downy hairs, esp. that with which the human foetus or a newborn infant is covered. [L: woolly substance]

**lanyard** /'lænjəd/, *n.* **1.** *Naut.* **a.** a short rope or cord for securing or holding something, esp. a rope rove through deadeyes to secure and tighten rigging. **b. knife lanyard,** a cord to which a knife is attached, worn by seamen around the neck. **2.** a woven coloured cord worn around the shoulder of military (or some other) uniforms. Colours denote the Regiment, Corps, etc. Also, **laniard.** [b. ME *lanyer* (from F *lanière* rope) and YARD[1]]

**Lao People's Democratic Republic,** *n.* official name of **Laos.**

**laos** /'leɪɒs, laʊs/, *n.* →**galangal.**

**Laos** /laʊs/, *n.* a country in South East Asia. – **Laotian** /leɪ'oʊʃən/, *adj., n.*

**lap**[1] /læp/, *n.* **1.** the part of the clothing that lies on the front portion of the body from the waist to the knees when one sits. **2.** this portion of the body, esp. as the place in or on which something is held or a child is nursed, cherished, etc. **3.** that in which anything rests or reposes, or is nurtured or fostered. **4.** an area of control, charge, or responsibility: *the future is in the lap of Fortune.* **5.** a laplike or hollow place, as a hollow among hills. **6.** the front part of a skirt, esp. as held up to contain something. **7.** a loose border or fold. **8.** a part of a garment which projects or extends over another. **9. in the lap of luxury,** in affluent circumstances. [ME *lappe,* OE *læppa,* c. D *lap;* akin to G *Lappen* lap]

**lap**[2] /læp/, *v.,* **lapped, lapping,** *n.* –*v.t.* **1.** to fold over or about something; wrap or wind round something. **2.** to enwrap in something; wrap up; clothe. **3.** to enfold or hold in or as in the lap; nurse, fondle, or cherish. **4.** to lay (something) partly over something underneath; lay (things) together, one partly over another. **5.** to lie partly over (something underneath). **6.** to get a lap or more ahead of (a competitor) in racing. **7.** to cut or polish (a gem, etc.) with a lap. **8.** to join, as by scarfing, to form a single piece with the same dimensions throughout. *–v.i.* **9.** to be folded over; fold or wind round something. **10.** *Obs.* to lie partly over or alongside something else; lie together, one partly over or beside another. **11.** to lie upon and extend beyond a thing. **12.** to extend beyond a limit. *–n.* **13.** the act of lapping. **14.** the amount of a material required to go round a thing once. **15.** a single round or circuit of the course in racing. **16.** the act of overlapping. **17.** the state of overlapping. **18.** the point or place of overlapping. **19.** an overlapping part. **20.** the extent or amount of overlapping. **21.** a rotating wheel or disc holding an abrasive or polishing powder on its surface, used for gems, cutlery, etc. [ME *lappe(n)*; apparently from LAP[1]] – **lapper,** *n.*

**lap**[3] /læp/, *v.,* **lapped, lapping,** *n.* *–v.t.* **1.** (of water) to wash against or beat upon (something) with a lapping sound. **2.** to take up (liquid) with the tongue; lick up (oft. fol. by *up*). **3.** to receive and accept avidly (fol. by *up*). *–v.i.* **4.** (of water) to wash with a sound as of licking up a liquid. **5.** to take up liquid with the tongue; lick up a liquid. *–n.* **6.** the act of lapping liquid. **7.** the lapping of water against something. **8.** the sound of this. **9.** something lapped up, as liquid food for dogs. [ME *lappe,* unexplained var. of *lape,* OE *lapian,* c. MLG *lapen;* akin to L *lambere,* Gk *láptein* lick, lap] – **lapper,** *n.*

**laparoscope** /ˈlæpərəskoup/, *n.* an instrument which can be inserted into the abdominal cavity through a small incision, to provide direct vision or enable minor surgery to the abdominal organs. – **laparoscopic** /læpərəˈskɒpɪk/, *adj.*

**laparoscopy** /læpəˈrɒskəpi/, *n.* the insertion into the abdominal cavity of a laparoscope.

**laparotomy** /læpəˈrɒtəmi/, *n.* **1.** a surgical incision through the flank or loin. **2.** any incision into any part of the abdominal wall, usu. to establish the diagnosis. [*laparo-* (combining form representing Gk *lapárā* flank) + -TOMY]

**lapboard** /ˈlæpbɔd/, *n.* a thin, flat board to be held on the lap for use as a table.

**lap-dog** /ˈlæp-dɒg/, *n.* a small pet dog.

**lapel** /ləˈpɛl/, *n.* part of a garment folded back on the breast, esp. a continuation of a coat collar. [diminutive of LAP[1]] – **lapelled,** *adj.*

**La Perouse** /la pəˈruz/, *n. Colloq.* alcoholic beverage. Also, **larper.** [rhyming slang, *La Perouse* (a promontory at Botany Bay, N.S.W.) booze]

**lapful** /ˈlæpfʊl/, *n., pl.* **-fuls.** as much as the lap can hold.

**lapidary** /ˈlæpədəri/, *n., pl.* **-ries,** *adj.* *–n.* **1.** a workman who cuts, polishes, and engraves stones, esp. precious stones. **2.** an old book on the lore of gems. **3.** an expert on gems. *–adj.* **4.** pertaining to the cutting or engraving of stones. **5.** of or pertaining to inscriptions cut in stone, or to any formal inscriptions. **6.** characteristic of or suitable for monumental inscriptions. [ME *lapidarie,* from L *lapidārius* of stones or stone (as n., a stonecutter)]

**lapidate** /ˈlæpədeɪt/, *v.t.,* **-dated, -dating.** *Rare.* **1.** to pelt with stones. **2.** to stone to death. [L *lapidātus,* pp.] – **lapidation** /læpəˈdeɪʃən/, *n.*

**lapilli** /ləˈpɪlaɪ/, *n.pl., sing.* **-pillus** /-ˈpɪləs/. stony particles or fragments ejected from volcanoes, technically those of rounded shape and less than 25 mm in diameter. [L, diminutive of *lapis* a stone]

**lapis lazuli** /læpəs ˈlæzjəli, -laɪ/, *n.* **1.** a deep blue stone containing sodium, aluminium, calcium, sulphur, and silicon, and consisting of a mixture of several minerals, used chiefly for ornamental purposes. **2.** sky blue; azure. [ML, from L *lapis* stone + ML *lazulī,* gen. of *lazulum* lapis lazuli (see AZURE)]

**lap joint** /ˈlæp dʒɔɪnt/, *n.* a joint used where two boards intersect and one or both are cut out to allow for the intersection.

**Lapland** /ˈlæplənd/, *n.* a region inhabited by Lapps in northern Norway, northern Sweden, northern Finland, and the Kola peninsula of the north-western Soviet Union.

**lap-lap** /ˈlæp-læp/, *n.* a waistcloth or loincloth worn in Papua New Guinea and the South Pacific.

**Lapp** /læp/, *n.* **1.** Also, **Laplander.** one of a Finnic people of northern Norway, Sweden, and Finland, and adjacent regions, characterised by small stature and short, broad heads. **2.** Also, **Lappish.** any of the languages of the Lapps, closely related to Finnish. [Swed.]

**lappet** /ˈlæpət/, *n.* **1.** a small lap, flap, or loosely hanging part, esp. of a garment or headdress. **2.** a loose fold of flesh or the like. **3.** a lobe of the ear, etc. **4.** *Ornith.* a wattle or other fleshy process on a bird's head. [diminutive of LAP[1]]

**lapsable** /ˈlæpsəbəl/, *adj.* liable to lapse.

**lapse** /læps/, *n., v.,* **lapsed, lapsing.** *–n.* **1.** a slip or slight error: *a lapse of memory.* **2.** a failure or miscarriage through some fault, slip, or negligence: *a lapse of justice.* **3.** a gliding or passing away, as of time. **4.** the act of falling, slipping, sliding, etc., slowly or as by degrees. **5.** *Law.* the termination of a right or privilege through neglect to exercise it or through failure of some contingency. **6.** a falling, or sinking to a lower grade, condition, or degree: *a lapse into savagery.* **7.** a moral fall, as from rectitude. **8.** a falling into disuse. *–v.i.* **9.** to pass slowly, silently, or by degrees. **10.** *Law.* **a.** to pass from one to another by lapse. **b.** to become void, as a legacy to one who predeceases the testator. **11.** (of insurance) to cease to be in force. **12.** to fall or sink to a lower grade or condition. **13.** to fall into disuse. **14.** to fall, slip, or glide, esp. downwards. **15.** to deviate from principles, accuracy, etc.; make a slip or error. **16.** to pass away, as time. [late ME, from L *lapsus,* n., a fall, slip] – **lapser,** *n.*

**lapse rate** /ˈ– reɪt/, *n.* the rate of decrease of atmospheric temperature with increase of elevation vertically above a given location.

**lapstreak** /ˈlæpstrik/, *adj.* **1.** (of a boat) built with each plank overlapping the one below it; clinker-built. *–n.* **2.** a lapstreak boat. [LAP[2], *n.* + STREAK]

**lapwing** /ˈlæpwɪŋ/, *n.* a large Old World plover, *Vanellus vanellus,* with strikingly upcurved slender crest, erratic courtship flight and shrill cries; pewit; green plover. [ME *lapwinge,* OE *hlēapewince,* from *hlēapan* leap + *-wince* (akin to OHG *winkan* waver, totter, and OE *wincian* wink)]

**Larakia** /lærəˈkiə/, *n.* the Australian Aboriginal language formerly spoken in the region of present-day Darwin. Also, **Larrakeah.**

**Laramide** /ˈlærəmaɪd/, *adj.* of or pertaining to the major mountain-building episode of late Cretaceous and early Tertiary times in North America.

**larapinta** /lærəˈpɪntə/, *n.* a dunnart, *Sminthopsis froggatti,* of Australian central areas, having a long tail and a prominent facial stripe. [Aboriginal]

**larboard** /ˈlabəd/, *Naut. Obs.* *–n.* **1.** →**port**[2] (def. 1). *–adj.* **2.** →**port**[2] (defs 2 and 3). [early mod. E *larborde* (assimilated to STARBOARD); replacing ME *laddeborde,* from *ladde* (orig. uncert.) + *borde,* OE *bord* ship's side]

**larcenous** /ˈlasənəs/, *adj.* **1.** of, like, or of the nature of larceny. **2.** guilty of larceny. – **larcenously,** *adv.*

**larceny** /ˈlasəni/, *n., pl.* **-nies.** *Law.* the wrongful taking and carrying away of the personal goods of another with intent permanently to deprive him thereof. [late ME, apparently from AF *larcin* (from L *latrōcinium* robbery) + -Y[3]]

**larch** /latʃ/, *n.* **1.** any of the coniferous trees constituting the genus *Larix,* characterised by a tough, durable wood. **2.** the wood of such a tree. [G *Lärche,* from L *larix*]

**lard** /lad/, *n.* **1.** rendered pig fat, esp. the internal fat of the abdomen. *–v.t.* **2.** to apply lard or grease to. **3.** to prepare or enrich (lean meat, etc.) with pork or bacon, esp. with lardoons. **4.** to intersperse with something for improvement or ornamentation. [ME, from OF: fat of pork, bacon, from L *lār(i)dum* fat of pork] – **lardlike,** *adj.* – **lardy,** *adj.*

**lardaceous** /laˈdeɪʃəs/, *adj.* lardlike; fatty.

**larder** /ˈladə/, *n.* a room or place where food is kept; a pantry. [ME, from OF *lardier,* from *lard* LARD]

**lardoons** /laˈdunz/, *n. pl.* strips of larding fat (pork or bacon) of varying lengths and thickness, threaded into meat, poultry and game. Also, **lardons** /ˈladnz/.

**lardy cake** /ˈladi keɪk/, *n.* a rich, sweet, breadlike cake made with bread dough, lard, sugar, and dried fruit.

**lare** /lɛə/, *n., v.,* **lared, laring.** →**lair**[2].

**lares and penates** /ˌlarɛz ənd pəˈnatɛz/, *n.pl.* **1.** *Roman Myth.* **a.** household gods. **b.** the tutelary deities of the state. **2.** the cherished possessions of a family or household.

**largamente** /lagəˈmɛnteɪ/, *adv.* (a musical direction) broadly. [It.]

**large** /ladʒ/, *adj.*, **larger, largest,** *n., adv.* *–adj.* **1.** being of more than common size, amount, or number. **2.** of great scope or range; extensive or broad: *large powers.* **3.** on a great scale: *a large producer.* **4.** grand or pompous. **5.** *Obs.* generous. **6.** *Obs.* (of the wind) free; fair. *–n.* **7.** *Music.* the longest note in medieval music; equal to eight semibreves: ⟼. **8. at large, a.** at liberty; free from restraint or confinement: *the murderer is at large.* **b.** at length; to a considerable length: *to discourse at large on a subject.* **c.** as a whole; in general: *the country at large.* **9. in large,** or **in the large,** on a large scale: *viewed in the large.* *–adv.* **10.** *Naut.* before the wind; with the wind free or on the quarter, or in such a direction that all sails will draw. [ME, from OF, from L *larga,* fem. of *largus* abundant, liberal] – **largeness,** *n.*

**large calorie** /'– kæləri/, *n.* See **calorie** (def. 1b).

**large-hearted** /'ladʒ-hatəd/, *adj.* having or showing generosity. – **large-heartedness,** *n.*

**large intestine** /ladʒ ɪn'tɛstən/, *n.* See **intestine.**

**largely** /'ladʒli/, *adv.* **1.** to a great extent; in great part. **2.** in great quantity; much.

**large-minded** /'ladʒ-maɪndəd/, *adj.* having or showing tolerant views or liberal ideas. – **large-mindedness,** *n.*

**large-scale** /'ladʒ-skeɪl/, *adj.* **1.** very extensive; of great scope. **2.** made to a large scale: *a large-scale map.*

**large-scale integration** /– ɪntə'greɪʃən/, *n.* an electronic manufacturing process which creates memories and complex circuits for computers with storage densities of millions of words per cubic centimetre.

**largess** /la'dʒɛs/, *n.* **1.** generous bestowal of gifts. **2.** the gifts or a gift (as of money) so bestowed. **3.** *Archaic.* generosity. Also, **largesse.** [ME *larges,* from OF *largesse,* from *large* LARGE]

**larghetto** /la'gɛtoʊ/, *adj., n., pl.* **-ghettos.** *–adj.* **1.** (a musical direction) somewhat slow; not so slow as largo, but usu. slower than andante. *–n.* **2.** a larghetto movement. [It., diminutive of *largo* LARGO]

**largish** /'ladʒɪʃ/, *adj.* rather large.

**largo** /'lagoʊ/, *adv., adj., n., pl.* **-gos.** *–adv.* **1.** (a musical direction) in a slow and solemn manner. *–adj.* **2.** slow; in a broad, dignified style. *–n.* **3.** a largo movement. [It., from L *largus* large]

**lariat** /'læriət/, *n. U.S.* **1.** a long, noosed rope for catching horses, cattle, etc.; a lasso. **2.** a rope or cord for picketing animals while grazing. [Sp. *la reata* the rope]

**larine** /'læraɪn, -rin/, *adj.* **1.** of the nature of or resembling a gull. **2.** of or pertaining to the suborder Lari, family Laridae, or subfamily Larinae, containing the gulls. [NL *Larinae,* from LL *larus,* from Gk *láros* kind of seabird]

**lark**[1] /lak/, *n.* **1.** any of numerous oscinine singing birds, mostly of the Old World, of the family Alaudidae, characterised by an unusually long, straight hind claw, esp. the skylark, *Alauda arvensis.* **2.** any of various similar birds of other families, as the titlark (family Motacillidae) of America and Europe. [ME *larke,* OE *lāwerce,* c. G *Lerche*]

**lark**[2] /lak/, *Colloq.* *–n.* **1.** a merry or hilarious adventure; prank. **2.** a frolic. *–v.i.* **3.** to play pranks; have fun. Also, **skylark.** [orig. uncert.] – **larker,** *n.* – **larksome,** *adj.*

**larkspur** /'lakspɜ/, *n.* any plant of the genus *Delphinium,* so called from the spur-shaped formation of the calyx and petals. [LARK[1] + SPUR]

**Larmor precession** /lamə prə'sɛʃən/, *n.* the precession of a charged particle in a magnetic field. [named after Sir Joseph *Larmor,* 1857-1947, English physicist]

**Larrakeah** /lærə'kiə/, *n.* →**Larakia.**

**larrikin** /'lærəkən/, *n. Colloq.* **1.** (formerly) a lout, a hoodlum. **2.** a mischievous young person. [? Brit. (Warwickshire and Worcestershire) d. *larrikin* mischievous youth] – **larrikinism,** *n.* – **larrikinish,** *adj.*

**larrup** /'lærəp/, *v.t.,* **-ruped, -ruping.** *Colloq.* to beat; thrash. [cf. D *larpen* thrash] – **larruper,** *n.*

**larry** /'læri/, *n.* a hoe with a hole in the centre used for mixing cement.

**larva** /'lavə/, *n., pl.* **-vae** /-vi/. **1.** *Entomol.* the young of any insect which undergoes metamorphosis. **2.** any animal in an analogous immature form. **3.** the young of any invertebrate animal. [NL, special use of L *larva* ghost, spectre, skeleton, mask]

**larval** /'lavəl/, *adj.* of or in the form of a larva.

**larvicide** /'lavəsaɪd/, *n.* an agent for killing larvae.

**laryngeal** /lærən'dʒiəl/, *adj.* of or pertaining to the larynx. Also, **laryngal** /lə'rɪŋgəl/. [NL *laryngeus* (from *larynges,* pl. of *larynx* LARYNX) + -AL[1]]

**laryngectomy** /lærɪŋ'dʒɛktəmi/, *n.* the surgical removal of the larynx.

**laryngitis** /lærən'dʒaɪtəs/, *n.* inflammation of the larynx. [NL, from LARYNG(O)- + -ITIS] – **laryngitic** /lærən'dʒɪtɪk/, *adj.*

**laryngo-,** a combining form of **larynx.** Also, before vowels, **laryng-.**

**laryngol.,** laryngology.

**laryngology** /lærɪŋ'gɒlədʒi/, *n.* the study of the larynx and its diseases. – **laryngological** /lərɪŋgə'lɒdʒɪkəl/, *adj.* – **laryngologist,** *n.*

**laryngoscope** /lə'rɪŋgəskoʊp/, *n.* an apparatus for examining the larynx. – **laryngoscopic** /lərɪŋgə'skɒpɪk/, *adj.*

**laryngotomy** /lærɪŋ'gɒtəmi/, *n.* the cutting into the larynx by a surgeon.

**larynx** /'lærɪŋks/, *n., pl.* **larynges** /lə'rɪndʒiz/, **larynxes. 1.** *Anat.* the cavity at the upper end of the human trachea or windpipe containing the vocal cords and acting as the organ of voice. **2.** *Zool.* **a.** a similar vocal organ in other mammals, etc. **b.** a corresponding structure in other animals. [NL, from Gk]

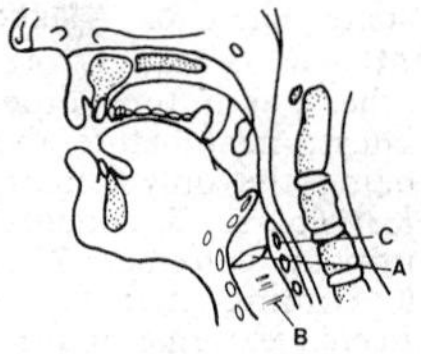

human larynx (section): A, larynx; B, trachea; C, oesophagus

**lasagne** /lə'sanjə/, *n.* **1.** a form of pasta cut into long ribbons. **2.** any of several dishes made with this, esp. with minced meat, tomato, and cheese. [It., from L *lasanum* cooking-pot]

**lascar** /'læskə/, *n.* an East Indian sailor. [Pg. *laschar,* short for *lasquarin* soldier, from Hind. (Pers.) *lashkarī,* adj., military (as n., soldier), from *lashkar* army, camp]

**lascivious** /lə'sɪviəs/, *adj.* **1.** inclined to lust; wanton or lewd. **2.** inciting to lust or wantonness. [LL *lascīviōsus,* from L *lascīvia* wantonness] – **lasciviously,** *adv.* – **lasciviousness,** *n.*

**lase** /leɪz/, *v.i.,* **lased, lasing. 1.** (of a substance) to undergo the physical processes (of excitation and stimulated emission) employed in the laser. **2.** (of a device) to operate as a laser.

**laser** /'leɪzə/, *n.* **1.** a device for producing a coherent, monochromatic, high-intensity beam of radiation of a frequency within, or near to, the range of visible light; an optical maser. [*l(ight) a(mplification by) s(timulated) e(mission of) r(adiation)*]

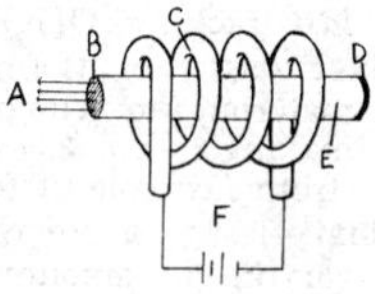

crystal laser (simplified diagram): A, output beam; B, partially reflecting coating; C, flash lamp; D, totally reflecting coating; E, laser crystal; F, power source

**lash**[1] /læʃ/, *n.* **1.** the flexible part of a whip; the piece of cord or the like forming the extremity of a whip. **2.** a swift stroke or blow, with a whip, etc., as a punishment: *sentenced to fifty lashes.* **3.** a sharp stroke given to the feelings, etc., as of censure or satire. **4.** a swift dashing or sweeping movement; a switch: *a lash of an animal's tail.* **5.** a violent beating or impact, as of waves, rain, etc., against something. **6.** an eyelash. **7.** *Colloq.* **a.** →**coitus. b.** anything which thrills or pleases. **8.** *Obs. Colloq.* brawling; fighting. **9. have a lash at,** *Colloq.* to attempt. *–v.t.* **10.** to strike or beat, now usu. with a whip or something slender and flexible. **11.** to beat violently or sharply against. **12.** to drive by strokes of a whip or the like. **13.** to dash, fling, or switch suddenly and swiftly. **14.** to assail severely with words, as by censure or satire. *–v.i.* **15.** to strike vigorously at, as with a weapon, whip, or the like (oft. fol. by *out*). **16.** to move suddenly and swiftly; rush, dash, or flash. **17.** to burst into violent action or speech (fol. by *out*). **18.** to spend money freely (fol. by *out*). [ME *lassh:* orig. obscure] – **lasher,** *n.*

**lash**[2] /læʃ/, *v.t.* to bind or fasten with a rope, cord, or the like. [special use of LASH[1]] – **lasher,** *n.*

**LASH** /læʃ/, *n.* a ship which is unloaded using lighters carried on board. Also, **lash.** [*L(ighter) A(board) Sh(ip)*]

**lashed** /læʃt/, *adj.* having lashes, or eyelashes.

**lashing**[1] /ˈlæʃɪŋ/, *n.* **1.** the act of one who or that which lashes. **2.** a whipping. **3.** a severe scolding. **4.** (*pl.*) *Colloq.* large quantities; plenty (usu. fol. by *of*). [LASH[1] + -ING[1]; for def. 4 cf. LASH[1] (def. 18)]

**lashing**[2] /ˈlæʃɪŋ/, *n.* **1.** a binding or fastening with a rope or the like. **2.** the rope or the like used. [LASH[2] + -ING[1]]

**lasiandra** /læsiˈændrə/, *n.* the former generic name of the large tropical American genus *Tibouchina,* many species of which, as *T. urvilleana,* a shrub with large violet to reddish-purple flowers, are cultivated as ornamentals.

**lass** /læs/, *n.* **1.** a girl or young woman. **2.** any woman. **3.** a female sweetheart. [ME *lasse;* orig. uncert.]

**lassie** /ˈlæsi/, *n.* a girl; lass.

**lassitude** /ˈlæsətʃud/, *n.* weariness of body or mind from strain, oppressive climate, etc.; languor. [L *lassitūdo* weariness]

**lasso** /læˈsu/, *n., pl.* **-sos, -soes,** *v.,* **-soed, -soing.** *–n.* **1.** a long rope or line of hide or other material, with a running noose at one end, used for catching horses, cattle, etc. *–v.t.* **2.** to catch with a lasso. [Sp. *lazo,* from L *laqueus* noose, snare. Cf. LACE] – **lassoer,** *n.*

**last**[1] /last/, *adj.* **1.** occurring or coming latest, or after all others, as in time, order, or place: *the last line on the page.* **2.** latest; next before the present; most recent: *last week.* **3.** being the only remaining: *one's last penny.* **4.** final: *in his last hours.* **5.** conclusive: *the last word in an argument.* **6.** utmost; extreme. **7.** coming after all others in importance. **8.** coming after all others in suitability or likelihood. **9.** *Eccles.* extreme or final, as to a dying person (applied to the sacraments of penance, viaticum, and extreme unction collectively). **10. on one's last legs,** on the verge of collapse. *–adv.* **11.** after all others. **12.** on the most recent occasion. **13.** in the end; finally; in conclusion. *n.* **14.** that which is last. **15.** *Colloq.* the final mention or appearance: *to see the last of that woman.* **16.** the end or conclusion. **17. at (long) last,** after much has intervened. **18. breathe one's last,** to die. [ME *last, latst,* syncopated var. of *latest,* OE *latost, lætest,* super. of *læt* late]

**last**[2] /last/, *v.i.* **1.** to go on, or continue in progress, existence or life; endure: *so long as the world lasts.* **2.** to continue unexpended or unexhausted; be enough (*for*): *while our money lasts.* **3.** to continue in force, vigour, effectiveness, etc.: *to last in a race.* **4.** to continue to remain in a good condition. [ME *lasten,* OE *lǣstan* follow, perform, continue, last (from *lāst* track), c. OHG *leisten* follow. See LAST[3]] – **laster,** *n.*

**last**[3] /last/, *n.* **1.** a model of the human foot, of wood or other material, on which boots or shoes are shaped, as in the making. *–v.t.* **2.** to shape on or fit to a last. [ME; OE *læste* (from *lāst* sole of foot, track), c. G *Leisten* last] – **laster,** *n.*

**last**[4] /last/, *n.* any of various large units of weight or capacity, varying in amount in different localities and for different commodities. [ME; OE *hlæst,* c. G *Last* load; akin to LADE]

**last day** /– ˈdeɪ/, *n.* **1.** the final day spent at a place, institution, school, etc. **2.** (*also cap.*) the day on which the world ends.

**last-ditch** /ˈlast-dɪtʃ/, *adj.* **1.** made in or as a final and desperate effort. **2.** fought with desperate and uncompromising spirit.

**lasting** /ˈlastɪŋ/, *adj.* **1.** that lasts; enduring; permanent; durable. *–n.* **2.** (*pl.*) a strong, durable, closely woven fabric, used for the uppers of shoes, for covering buttons, etc. – **lastingly,** *adv.* – **lastingness,** *n.*

**Last Judgment** /last ˈdʒʌdʒmənt/, *n.* →**judgment** (def. 7).

**lastly** /ˈlastli/, *adv.* finally, in conclusion, or in the last place.

**last-minute** /ˈlast-mɪnət/, *adj.* made or occurring at the last possible opportunity.

**last post** /last ˈpoʊst/, *n.* **1.** a signal on a bugle giving notice to retire for the night. **2.** a similar bugle call sounded at military funerals.

**last sacraments** /– ˈsækrəmənts/, *n.pl.* the sacraments of penance, viaticum and extreme unction, when administered to a dying person. Also, **last rites.**

**last straw** /– ˈstrɔ/, *n. Colloq.* the culminating irritation, mishap, etc., which is followed by a strong outburst or reaction. [from the saying 'the last straw breaks the camel's back']

**last trump** /– ˈtrʌmp/, *n.* the angelic trumpet call which wakens the dead before the Last Judgment.

**last word** /– ˈwɜd/, *n.* **1.** ultimate authority. **2.** (*pl.*) the final words of a dying person.

**lat.,** latitude.

**Lat.,** Latin.

**latch** /lætʃ/, *n.* **1.** a device for holding a door, gate, or the like closed, consisting basically of a bar falling or sliding into a catch, groove, hole, etc. *–v.t.* **2.** to close or fasten with a latch. *–v.i.* **3.** to fasten tightly so that the latch is in position. **4. latch on to,** *Colloq.* **a.** to fasten or attach (oneself) to. **b.** to understand; comprehend. [ME *lacche,* OE *læccan* take hold of, catch, take]

**latchet**[1] /ˈlætʃət/, *n. Archaic.* a strap or lace for fastening a shoe. [ME *lachet,* from OF, d. var. of *lacet,* diminutive of *laz* LACE]

**latchet**[2] /ˈlætʃət/, *n.* a red or pinkish gurnard, *Pterygotrigla polyommata,* of the southern Australian coast.

**latchkey** /ˈlætʃki/, *n.* a key for drawing back or releasing a latch, esp. on an outer door.

**latchkey child** /ˈ– tʃaɪld/, *n.* a child whose parents are absent from home before or after school hours and for whom inadequate childminding arrangements have been made.

**latchstring** /ˈlætʃstrɪŋ/, *n.* a string passed through a hole in a door, for raising the latch from the outside.

**late** /leɪt/, *adj.,* **later** or **latter, latest** or **last,** *adv.,* **later, latest.** *–adj.* **1.** occurring, coming, or being after the usual or proper time: *late frosts.* **2.** continued until after the usual time or hour; protracted: *a late session.* **3.** far advanced in time: *a late hour.* **4.** belonging to time just before the present: *the latest fashions.* **5.** immediately preceding that which now exists: *his late residence.* **6.** recently deceased: *the late president.* **7.** occurring at an advanced stage in life: *a late marriage.* **8.** belonging to an advanced period or stage in the history or development of something: *Late Latin.* **9. of late,** recently. *–adv.* **10.** after the usual or proper time, or after delay: *to come late.* **11.** until after the usual time or hour; until a late hour at night: *to work late.* **12.** at or to an advanced time, period, or stage. **13.** recently but no longer. [ME; OE *læt* slow, late, c. G *lass* slothful] – **lateness,** *n.*

**late blight** /– ˈblaɪt/, *n.* a serious disease of potatoes caused by the fungus *Phytophthora infestans.*

**latecomer** /ˈleɪtkʌmə/, *n.* one who arrives late: *latecomers will be excluded from the first act.*

**late cut** /leɪt ˈkʌt/, *n.* (in cricket) a stroke that sends the ball well behind point, in the direction of the slips.

**lateen** /ləˈtin/, *adj.* pertaining to or having a lateen sail or sails. [F (*voile*) *latine* Latin (sail)]

**lateen-rigged** /ləˈtin-rɪgd/, *adj.* having lateen sails.

**lateen sail** /ləˈtin seɪl/, *n.* a triangular sail extended by a long tapering yard, slung at about one quarter the distance from the lower end, which is brought down at the tack, used in xebecs, feluccas, etc., on the Mediterranean.

lateen sail

**Late Greek** /leɪt ˈgrik/, *n.* the Greek of the early Byzantine Empire and of patristic literature, from about A.D. 300 to 700.

**Late Latin** /– ˈlætn/, *n.* the Latin of the late Western Roman Empire and of patristic literature, from about A.D. 300 to 700.

**lately** /ˈleɪtli/, *adv.* of late; recently; not long since.

**latency** /ˈleɪtnsi/, *n.* **1.** the state of being latent or concealed. **2.** *Computers.* a delay encountered when waiting for a specific response, often caused by queueing of discs or tapes.

**latency period** /ˈ– pɪəriəd/, *n.* the stage of personality development, extending from about four to five years of age to the beginning of puberty, during which sexual urges often appear to lie dormant.

**latent** /ˈleɪtnt/, *adj.* **1.** hidden; concealed; present, but not visible or apparent: *latent ability.* **2.** *Pathol.* (of an infectious agent) remaining in a resting or hidden phase; dormant. **3.** *Psychol.* below the surface, but potentially able to achieve expression. **4.** *Bot.* (of buds which are not externally manifest) dormant or undeveloped. [L *latens,* ppr., lying hid] – **latently,** *adv.*

**latent defect** /– 'difɛkt/, *n.* a hidden defect which could not have been discovered by reasonable examination.

**latent function** /– 'fʌŋkʃən/, *n.* a function which exists unrecognised within a social attitude or action and which will produce results not previously foreseen.

**latent heat** /– 'hit/, *n.* **1.** (of fusion) the heat required to effect the change of state from solid to liquid. **2.** (of vaporisation) the heat required to effect the change of state from liquid to gas.

**latent learning** /– 'lɜnɪŋ/, *n.* learning which has taken place without conscious aim and which is not evident until the person is presented with a specific task.

**latent period** /'– pɪəriəd/, *n.* **1.** the period that elapses before the presence of a disease is manifested by symptoms. **2.** *Physiol.* the lag between stimulus and reaction.

**lateral** /'lætərəl, 'lætrəl/, *adj.* **1.** of or pertaining to the side; situated at, proceeding from, or directed to a side: *a lateral view.* **2.** *Phonet.* with the airstream escaping from the mouth on one or both sides of an obstruction formed by the tongue. *–n.* **3.** a lateral part or extension, as a branch or shoot. **4.** *Mining.* a small drift off to the side of a principal one. **5.** *Phonet.* a lateral sound. **6.** a small irrigation channel distributing water from the main canal. [L *laterālis,* from *latus* side] – **laterally,** *adv.*

**laterality** /lætə'rælәti/, *n.* the dominance of the right-hand or the left-hand member of a pair of bodily organs, as the hands, in relation to a particular function, as writing.

**lateral line** /'lætərəl laɪn/, *n.* the line of mucous pores, with sensory function, along the sides of fishes.

**lateral thinking** /– 'θɪŋkɪŋ/, *n.* a way of thinking which seeks the solution to a problem by making associations with other apparently unrelated areas, rather than by pursuing one logical train of thought.

**laterite** /'lætəraɪt/, *n.* a reddish ferruginous soil formed in tropical regions by the decomposition of the underlying rock; characterised by a porous red concretionary crust, an underlying mottled zone, and a leached white zone below. [L *later* brick + -ITE[1]]

**lateritious** /lætə'rɪʃəs/, *adj.* of the colour of laterite; brick red. Also, **latericeous.**

**latescent** /lə'tɛsənt/, *adj.* becoming latent. [L *latescens,* ppr., hiding oneself] – **latescence,** *n.*

**latest** /'leɪtəst/, *adj.* (*superlative of* **late**). **1.** after all others. **2.** current; most up to date. **3. at the latest,** not any later than (a particular time). **4. the latest,** the most recent disclosure, gossip, fashion, advance, development, etc.

**latewood** /'leɪtwʊd/, *n.* →**summerwood.**

**latex** /'leɪtɛks/, *n., pl.* **latices** /'lætəsiz/, **latexes** /'leɪtɛksəz/. **1.** *Bot.* a milky liquid in certain plants, as milkweeds, euphorbias, poppies, the plants yielding indiarubber, etc., which coagulates on exposure to the air. **2.** any emulsion of particles of synthetic rubber or plastic in water. [L: liquid]

**lath** /laθ/, *n., pl.* **laths** /laðz, laθs/, *v.* *–n.* **1.** a thin, narrow strip of wood used with others like it to form a groundwork for supporting the slates or other covering of a roof or the plastering of a wall or ceiling, to construct latticework, and for other purposes. **2.** such strips collectively. **3.** work consisting of such strips. **4.** any material used as a substitute for laths, such as metal lathing or patent lathing. **5.** a thin, narrow, flat piece of wood used for any purpose. *–v.t.* **6.** to cover or line with laths. [ME *la(th)the,* replacing ME *latt,* OE *lætt,* c. D *lat*] – **lathlike,** *adj.*

**lathe** /leɪð/, *n., v.,* **lathed, lathing.** *–n.* **1.** a machine for use in working metal, wood, etc., which holds the material and rotates it about a horizontal axis against a tool that shapes it. *–v.t.* **2.** to cut, shape, or otherwise treat on a lathe. [ME *lath* stand, from Scand.; cf. Dan. *-lad* stand, lathe, c. OE *hlæd* heap, mound]

**lather**[1] /'læðə/, *n.* **1.** foam or froth made from soap moistened with water, as by a brush for shaving. **2.** foam or froth formed in profuse sweating, as of a horse. *–v.i.* **3.** to form a lather, as soap. **4.** to become covered with lather, as a horse. *–v.t.* **5.** to apply lather to; cover with lather. **6.** *Colloq.* to beat or flog. [ME, OE *lēathor,* c. Icel. *laudhr* washing soda, foam] – **latherer,** *n.*

**lather**[2] /'laθə/, *n.* a workman who puts up laths. [LATH, *v.* + -ER[1]]

**lathery** /'læðəri/, *adj.* consisting of, covered with, or capable of producing lather.

**lathing** /'laθɪŋ/, *n.* **1.** the act or process of applying laths to a wall or the like. **2.** work consisting of laths; laths collectively. Also, **lathwork.**

**lathy** /'laθi/, *adj.* lathlike; long and thin.

**latices** /'lætəsiz/, *n.* a plural of **latex.**

**laticiferous** /lætə'sɪfərəs/, *adj.* bearing or containing latex. [L *latex* a liquid + -I- + -FEROUS]

**Latin** /'lætn/, *n.* **1.** the Italic language spoken in ancient Rome, fixed in 2nd-1st century B.C., becoming the official language of the Empire. **2.** one of the forms of literary Latin, as Medieval Latin, Late Latin, Biblical Latin, Liturgical Latin, or of non-classical Latin, as Vulgar Latin. **3.** a native or inhabitant of Latium; an ancient Roman. **4.** a member of any Latin race. **5.** a Roman Catholic. *–adj.* **6.** denoting or pertaining to those peoples (the Italians, French, Spanish, Portuguese, Rumanians, etc.) using languages derived from that of ancient Rome. **7.** denoting or pertaining to the Western Church (which from early times down to the Reformation everywhere used Latin as its official language) or the Roman Catholic Church. **8.** of or pertaining to Latium or its inhabitants. **9.** →**Roman** (def. 4). **10.** Latin-American. [ME and OE, from L *Latīnus*]

**Latin America** /– ə'mɛrɪkə/, *n.* part of the American continents south of the United States, in which Romance languages are officially spoken. – **Latin-American,** *adj.*

**Latin Church** /– 'tʃɜtʃ/, *n.* →**Roman Catholic Church.**

**Latin cross** /– 'krɒs/, *n.* an upright bar crossed near the top by a shorter transverse piece.

**Latinise** /'lætənaɪz/, *v.,* **-nised, -nising.** *–v.t.* **1.** to cause to conform to the customs, etc., of the Latins or Latin Church. **2.** to intermix with Latin elements. **3.** to translate into Latin. *–v.i.* **4.** to use words and phrases from Latin: *he Latinises frequently in his poetry.* Also, **Latinize.** – **Latinisation** /lætənaɪ'zeɪʃən/, *n.*

**Latinism** /'lætənɪzəm/, *n.* a mode of expression imitating Latin.

**Latinist** /'lætənəst/, *n.* a specialist in Latin.

**Latinity** /lə'tɪnəti/, *n.* **1.** use of the Latin language. **2.** Latin style or idiom.

**latish** /'leɪtɪʃ/, *adj.* somewhat late.

**latitude** /'lætətʃud/, *n.* **1.** *Geog.* **a.** the angular distance north or south from the equator of a point on the earth's surface, measured on the meridian of the point. **b.** a place or region as marked by this distance. **2.** freedom from narrow restrictions; permitted freedom of action, opinion, etc. **3.** *Astron.* **a.** Also, **celestial latitude.** the angular distance of a heavenly body from the ecliptic. **b.** Also, **galactic latitude.** the angular distance of a heavenly body from the galactic plane. **4.** *Photog.* the range of exposures over which proportional representation of subject brightness is obtained. [ME, from L *lātitūdo* breadth]

A, latitude and parallel; B, longitude and meridian

**latitudinal** /lætə'tjudənəl/, *adj.* pertaining to latitude. – **latitudinally,** *adv.*

**latitudinarian** /,lætətjudə'nɛəriən/, *adj.* **1.** allowing, or characterised by, latitude in opinion or conduct, esp. in religious views. *–n.* **2.** one who is latitudinarian in opinion or conduct. **3.** *Anglican Ch.* one of those divines in the 17th century who maintained the wisdom of the episcopal form of government and ritual, but denied that they possess divine origin and authority. – **latitudinarianism,** *n.*

**latitudinous** /lætə'tjudənəs/, *adj.* broad or wide in interpretation, ideas or interests.

**latria** /lə'traɪə/, *n.* (in Roman Catholic theology) that supreme worship which may be offered to God only. Cf. **dulia.** [LL, from Gk *latreía* service, worship]

**latrine** /lə'trin/, *n.* a toilet, esp. in a camp, barracks, factory, or the like. [F, from L *lātrina*]

**latten** /'lætn/, *n.* **1.** a brasslike alloy, commonly made in thin sheets, formerly much used for church utensils. **2.** →**tin plate.** **3.** any metal in thin sheets. [ME *latoun,* from OF *laton,* from *latte.* See LATTICE]

**latter** /'lætə/, *adj.* **1.** being the second mentioned of two (opposed to *former*): *I prefer the latter proposition to the former.* **2.** more advanced in time; later: *in these latter days of human progress.* **3.** nearer, or comparatively near, to the end or close: *the latter years of one's life.* **4.** *Poetic.* being the concluding part of. [ME *latt(e)re,* OE *lætra,* compar. of *læt* late]

**latter-day** /'lætə-deɪ/, *adj.* **1.** of a latter or more advanced day or period, or modern: *latter-day problems.* **2.** of the concluding or final days of the world.

**Latter-day Saint** /lætə-deɪ 'seɪnt/, *n.* →**Mormon.**

**latterly** /'lætəli/, *adv.* **1.** of late; lately. **2.** in the latter or concluding part of a period.

**lattermost** /'lætəmoust/, *adj.* latest; last.

**lattice** /'lætəs/, *n., v.,* **-ticed, -ticing.** –*n.* **1.** a structure of crossed wooden or metal strips with open spaces between, used as a screen, etc. **2.** a window, gate, or the like, so constructed. **3.** Also, **crystal lattice, space lattice.** *Crystall.* the regular network of fixed points about which molecules, atoms, or ions vibrate in a crystal structure. **4.** *Physics.* a structure within a nuclear reactor consisting of discrete bodies of fissile and non-fissile material, the latter usually being the moderator. –*v.t.* **5.** to furnish with a lattice or latticework. **6.** to form into or arrange like latticework. [ME *latis,* from OF *lattis,* from *latte* lath, from Gmc; cf. OE *lætt* lath]

**latticework** /'lætəswɜk/, *n.* **1.** work consisting of crossed strips with openings between. **2.** →**lattice** (def. 1).

**latticing** /'lætəsɪŋ/, *n.* **1.** the act or process of furnishing with or making latticework. **2.** →**latticework.**

**laud** /lɔd/, *v.t.* **1.** to praise; extol. –*n.* **2.** music or a song in praise or honour of anyone. **3. lauds, laudes.** *Eccles.* a canonical hour, characterised esp. by psalms of praise which follows, and is usu. recited with, matins. [ME *laude,* back-formation from *laudes,* pl., from L: praises] – **lauder,** *n.*

**laudable** /'lɔdəbəl/, *adj.* praiseworthy or commendable. – **laudability** /lɔdə'bɪləti/, **laudableness,** *n.* – **laudably,** *adv.*

**laudanum** /'lɔdnəm/, *n.* **1.** tincture of opium. **2.** (formerly) any preparation in which opium was the chief ingredient. [orig. ML var. of LADANUM; arbitrarily used by Paracelsus to name a remedy based on opium]

**laudation** /lɔ'deɪʃən/, *n.* the act of lauding; praise.

**laudatory** /'lɔdətri/, *adj.* containing or expressing praise. Also, **laudative.**

**laugh** /laf/, *v.i.* **1.** to express mirth, amusement, derision, etc., by an explosive, inarticulate sound of the voice, facial expressions, etc. **2.** to experience the emotion so expressed. **3.** to utter a cry or sound resembling the laughing of human beings, as some animals do. **4. don't make me laugh!** (an exclamation indicating disbelief). **5. laugh at, a.** to make fun of; deride; ridicule. **b.** to be sympathetically amused by: *she laughed at his fear of air travel.* **6. laugh fit to kill,** to laugh extremely heartily. **7. laugh in** or **up one's sleeve,** to laugh inwardly at something. **8. laugh on the other** or **wrong side of one's face** or **mouth,** to evince disappointment, chagrin, displeasure, etc. –*v.t.* **9.** to drive, put, bring, etc., by or with laughter. **10.** to utter with laughter. **11. laugh like a drain,** to laugh loudly. **12. laugh off** or **away,** to dismiss (a situation, criticism, or the like) by treating lightly or with ridicule. **13. laugh out of court,** to dismiss by means of ridicule. –*n.* **14.** the act or sound of laughing, or laughter. **15.** an expression of mirth, derision, etc. **16.** (*oft. ironic*) a cause for laughter: *that's a laugh.* **17. have the (last) laugh,** to prove ultimately successful; win after an earlier defeat. [ME *laugh(en),* d. OE *hlæhhan,* OE *hliehhan,* c. Icel. *hlæja,* Goth. *hlahjan;* akin to G *lachen*] – **laugher,** *n.*

**laughable** /'lafəbəl/, *adj.* such as to excite laughter; funny; amusing; ludicrous. – **laughableness,** *n.* – **laughably,** *adv.*

**laughing** /'lafɪŋ/, *n.* **1.** laughter. –*adj.* **2.** that laughs; giving vent to laughter, as persons. **3. no laughing matter,** a serious matter. **4.** uttering sounds like human laughter, as some birds. **5.** suggesting laughter by brightness, etc. – **laughingly,** *adv.*

**laughing gas** /'– gæs/, *n.* nitrous oxide, $N_2O$, which when inhaled sometimes produces exhilarating effects, used as an anaesthetic in dentistry, etc.

**laughing hyena** /– haɪ'inə/, *n.* any member of the family Hyaenidae; any hyena.

**laughing jackass** /– 'dʒækæs/, *n.* →**kookaburra.**

**laughing kookaburra** /– 'kukəbʌrə/, *n.* →**kookaburra** (def. 1).

**laughing-stock** /'lafɪŋ-stɒk/, *n.* a butt for laughter; an object of ridicule.

**laugh-line** /'laf-laɪn/, *n.* →**laughter-line.**

**laughter** /'laftə/, *n.* **1.** the action or sound of laughing. **2.** an experiencing of the emotion expressed by laughing: *inward laughter.* **3.** an expression or appearance of merriment or amusement. [ME; OE *hleahtor*]

**laughter-line** /'laftə-laɪn/, *n.* one of the wrinkles found at the corners of the eyes or mouth supposedly formed by a well-established habit of laughter. Also, **laugh-line.**

**launce** /lans/, *n.* →**sand-eel.**

**launch**[1] /lɔntʃ/, *n.* **1.** a heavy open or half-decked boat. **2.** the largest boat carried by a warship. [Sp., Pg. *lancha*]

**launch**[2] /lɔntʃ/, *v.t.* **1.** to set (a boat) afloat; lower into the water. **2.** to cause (a newly built ship) to move or slide from the stocks into the water. **3.** to start on a course, career, etc. **4.** to set going: *to launch a scheme.* **5.** to send forth; start off (forcefully): *the plane was launched from the deck of the carrier.* **6.** to throw or hurl: *to launch a spear.* –*v.i.* **7.** to burst out or plunge boldly into action, speech, etc. **8.** to start out or forth; push out or put forth on the water. –*n.* **9.** the sliding or movement of a boat or vessel from the land or dock into the water. **10.** the act of launching a glider, etc., into the air. [ME *launche(n),* from ONF *lancher,* var. of central OF *lancier* LANCE, *v.*] – **launcher,** *n.*

**launch complex** /'– ˌkɒmplɛks/, *n.* the buildings and ancillary equipment required for launching a rocket.

**launcher** /'lɔntʃə/, *n.* a structure which supports a ballistic or guided missile at the appropriate elevation and bearing before launching.

**launching pad** /'lɔntʃɪŋ pæd/, *n.* a base from which a rocket is launched. Also, **launch pad.**

**launch shoe** /'lɔntʃ ʃu/, *n.* a launcher which carries a missile in its launching position on an aircraft and provides electrical and other services prior to launching. Also, **launching shoe.**

**launch vehicle** /'– viɪkəl/, *n.* →**booster** (def. 4b).

**launder** /'lɔndə/, *v.t.* **1.** to wash and iron (clothes, etc.). **2.** to transfer (funds of suspect or illegal origin) usu. to a foreign country, and then later to recover them from sources which give them the appearance of being legitimate. –*v.i.* **3.** to do or wash laundry. –*n.* **4.** (in ore dressing) a passage carrying products of intermediate grade, and residue, which are in water suspension. **5.** a trough in which ore, gravel, etc., are washed; a strake (def. 5). [ME *lander* one who washes, contraction of *lavender,* from OF *lavandier* a washer, from LL *lavandārius,* from L *lavandus,* ger. of *lavāre* wash] – **launderer,** *n.*

**laundress** /'lɔndrəs/, *n.* a woman whose occupation is the washing and ironing of clothes, etc.

**laundrette** /lɔn'drɛt/, *n.* →**laundromat.**

**laundromat** /'lɔndrəmæt/, *n.* a commercial premises with coin-operated washing machines, spin-dryers, hot-air dryers and often dry-cleaning machines. Also, **laundrette.** [Trademark]

**laundry** /'lɔndri/, *n., pl.* **-dries.** **1.** articles of clothing, etc., to be washed. **2.** the room in a house set aside for the washing of clothes. **3.** the act of laundering.

**laundryman** /'lɔndrimən/, *n., pl.* **-men.** **1.** a man who works in or conducts a laundry. **2.** a man who collects and delivers laundry or works in a laundry.

**laundry tub** /'lɔndri tʌb/, *n.* a tub, formerly often one of a pair, in a laundry.

**laundrywoman** /'lɔndriwumən/, *n., pl.* **-women.** →**laundress.**

**lauraceous** /lɒ'reɪʃəs/, *adj.* belonging to the Lauraceae, or laurel family of plants. [L *laurus* laurel + -ACEOUS]

**laureate** /ˈlɒriət/, *adj.* **1.** crowned or decked with laurel as a mark of honour. **2.** specially recognised or distinguished, or deserving of distinction, esp. for poetic merit: *poet laureate.* **3.** consisting of laurel. *–n.* **4.** one crowned with laurel. **5.** a poet laureate. [ME *laureat,* from L *laureātus* (def. 1)] **– laureateship,** *n.*

**laurel** /ˈlɒrəl/, *n., v.t.,* **-relled, -relling.** *–n.* **1.** a small evergreen tree, *Laurus nobilis,* of Europe (the **true laurel**), having aromatic leaves used in cookery; sweet bay. **2.** any tree of the same genus (*Laurus*). **3.** Also, **mountain laurel.** any of various trees or shrubs similar to the true laurel belonging to the genus *Kalmia.* **4.** an evergreen tree, *Prunus laurocerasus,* the **cherry laurel.** **5.** other trees as *Cinnamomum camphora,* **camphor laurel** and *Aucuba japonica,* **spotted laurel.** **6.** the foliage of the true laurel as an emblem of victory or distinction. **7.** a branch or wreath of it. **8.** (*usu. pl.*) honour won, as by achievement. **9. look to one's laurels,** to be aware of the possibility of being excelled by one's rivals. **10. rest on one's laurels,** to be content with present achievements. *–v.t.* **11.** to adorn or wreathe with laurel. **12.** to honour with marks of distinction. [ME *laurer, laureal,* from F *laurier, lorier,* from OF *lor,* from L *laurus* laurel]

**Laurentian** /lɒˈrɛnʃən/, *adj.* denoting or pertaining to a series of rocks of the Archaean system, occurring in Canada near the St Lawrence river and the Great Lakes, or the major mountain-building episode to which these rocks were subject in Archaean times.

**lauric acid** /lɔrɪk ˈæsəd, lɒ-/, *n.* a white crystalline insoluble solid, $CH_3(CH_2)_{10}COOH$, occurring as glycerides in milk, palm oil, laurel oil, etc.; used in the manufacture of detergents and cosmetics.

**laurite** /ˈlɔraɪt, ˈlɒ-/, *n.* a mineral sulphide of ruthenium and osmium, which occurs as small cubic crystals often associated with platinum.

**laurustinus** /lɒrəsˈtaɪnəs/, *n.* an evergreen garden shrub, *Viburnum tinus,* native to southern Europe, with white or pinkish flowers. [NL, from obs. Bot. name *Laurus tinus,* from L *laurus* laurel + *tinus* kind of plant]

**lauryl alcohol** /lɒrəl ˈælkəhɒl/, *n.* a crystalline solid, $CH_3(CH_2)_{10}CH_2OH$, used in the manufacture of detergents.

**lauter tun** /ˈlaʊtə tʌn, ˈlɔɪ-/, *n.* a large tank or vat used in brewing, with a perforated base, used for draining the clear wort from the boiled malt mash residue. [G *lauter* pure, clear + TUN]

**lav** /læv/, *n. Colloq.* →**lavatory.**

**lava** /ˈlavə/, *n.* **1.** the molten or fluid rock (magma), which issues from a volcanic vent. **2.** the igneous rock formed when this solidifies and loses its volatile constituents, occurring in many varieties differing greatly in structure and constitution. [It. (Neapolitan): orig., stream, from *lavare* wash, from L]

**lavabo** /ləˈveɪboʊ, ləˈvaboʊ/, *n., pl.* **-boes, -bos.** *Eccles.* **1.** the ritual washing of the celebrant's hands after the offertory in the mass, accompanied in the Roman rite by the recitation of Psalms 26:6-12, or, in the Douay Version, Psalms 25:6-12 (so called from the first word of this passage in the Latin version). **2.** the passage recited. **3.** the small towel or the basin used. **4.** (in many medieval monasteries) a large stone basin from which the water issued by a number of small orifices around the edge, for the performance of ablutions. [L: I will wash]

**lavage** /ˈlævɪdʒ/, *n.* **1.** a washing. **2.** *Med.* **a.** cleansing by injection or the like. **b.** the washing out of the stomach. [F, from *laver* LAVE]

**lava-lava** /ˈlavə-lavə/, *n.* a rectangular cloth worn like a kilt or skirt by Polynesians, esp. Samoans. [Samoan]

**lavation** /læˈveɪʃən/, *n.* the process of washing. **– lavational,** *adj.*

**lavatory** /ˈlævətri/, *n., pl.* **-ries.** **1.** a room fitted with a toilet, often with means for washing the hands and face, and often with other toilet conveniences. **2.** a water-closet or urinal; a toilet. **3.** a bowl or basin for washing or bathing purposes. **4.** any place where washing is done. [ME *lavatorie,* from LL *lavātōrium*]

**lavatory paper** /ˈ– peɪpə/, *n.* →**toilet paper.**

**lave** /leɪv/, *v.,* **laved, laving.** *Poetic.* *–v.t.* **1.** to wash; bathe. **2.** (of a river, the sea, etc.) to wash or flow against. *–v.i.* **3.** to bathe. [ME; OE *lafian* pour water on, wash. Cf. F *laver,* L *lavāre*]

**lavender** /ˈlævəndə/, *n.* **1.** a pale, bluish purple colour. **2.** a plant of the genus *Lavandula,* esp. *L. officinalis,* a small Old World shrub with spikes of fragrant pale purple flowers, yielding an oil (**oil of lavender**) used in medicine and perfumery. **3.** the dried flowers or other parts of this plant placed among linen, etc., for scent or as a preservative. *–adj.* **4.** pale bluish-purple. [ME *lavendre,* from AF, from ML *lavendula, livendula;* ? from L *lavāre* wash or L *līvēre* be livid or bluish]

**lavender bag** /ˈ– bæg/, *n.* a small bag usu. of muslin, filled with dried lavender, used to perfume linen, etc.

**lavender water** /ˈ– wɔtə/, *n.* a perfume made from distilled lavender, alcohol, and ambergris.

**laver**[1] /ˈleɪvə/, *n.* **1.** *Old Testament.* a large basin upon a foot or pedestal in the court of the Jewish tabernacle, and subsequently in the temple, containing water for the ablutions of the priests, and for the washing of the sacrifices in the temple service. **2.** *Eccles.* the font or the water of baptism. **3.** any spiritually cleansing agency. **4.** *Archaic.* a basin, bowl, or cistern to wash in. **5.** *Archaic.* any bowl or pan for water. [ME, from OF *laveoir,* from LL *lavātōrium* lavatory]

**laver**[2] /ˈleɪvə/, *n.* any of several edible seaweeds, esp. of the genus *Porphyra.* [L: kind of water plant]

**lavish** /ˈlævɪʃ/, *adj.* **1.** using or bestowing in great abundance or without stint (oft. fol. by *of*): *lavish of time.* **2.** expended, bestowed, or occurring in profusion: *lavish gifts, lavish spending.* *–v.t.* **3.** to expend or bestow in great abundance or without stint: *to lavish favours on a person.* [late ME, adj. use of obs. *lavish* profusion, from OF *lavasse* deluge, from *laver* LAVE] **– lavisher,** *n.* **– lavishness,** *n.* **– lavishly,** *adv.*

**lavolta** /ləˈvɒltə/, *n.* an early French dance in which the dancer pivots and makes a high leap or spring into the air. [It. *la volta* the turn]

**lavvy** /ˈlævi/, *n. Colloq.* →**lavatory.**

**law** /lɔ/, *n.* **1.** the principles and regulations emanating from a government and applicable to a people, whether in the form of legislation or of custom and policies recognised and enforced by judicial decision. **2.** any written or positive rule, or collection of rules, prescribed under the authority of the state or nation, whether by the people in its constitution, as the **organic law,** or by the legislature in its **statute law,** or by the treaty-making power, or by municipalities in their ordinances or **bylaws.** **3.** the controlling influence of such rules; the condition of society brought about by their observance: *to maintain law and order.* **4.** an agent that helps to maintain these rules. **5.** a system or collection of such rules. **6.** the department of knowledge concerned with these rules; jurisprudence: *to study law.* **7.** the body of such rules concerned with a particular subject or derived from a particular source: *commercial law.* **8.** an act of the supreme legislative body of a state or nation, as distinguished from the constitution. **9.** the principles applied in the courts of common law, as distinguished from equity. **10.** the profession which deals with law and legal procedure: *to practise law.* **11.** legal action; litigation. **12.** any rule or principle of proper conduct or collection of such rules. **13.** (in philosophical and scientific use) **a.** a statement of a relation or sequence of phenomena invariable under the same conditions. **b.** a mathematical rule. **14.** a commandment or a revelation from God. **15.** (*oft. cap.*) a divinely appointed order or system. **16. the Law,** the Mosaic Law (often in contrast to *the Gospel*). **17.** the five books of Moses (the Pentateuch) containing this system and forming the first of the three Jewish divisions of the Old Testament. **18.** the preceptive part of the Bible, esp. of the New Testament, in contradistinction to its promises: *the law of Christ.* **19.** *Sport.* a start given to an animal that is to be hunted, or to a weaker competitor in a race. **20. be a law unto oneself,** to do what one wishes, without regard for established rules and modes of behaviour. **21. lay down the law,** to tell people authoritatively what to do, or state one's opinions authoritatively. **22. take the law into one's own hands,** to seek justice by one's own means, disregarding usual judicial procedures. [ME *law, lagh,* OE *lagu,* from Scand.; cf. Icel. *lag* layer, pl. *lög* law, lit., that which is laid down;

akin to LAY[1], LIE[2]]

**law-abiding** /ˈlɔr-əbaɪdɪŋ/, *adj.* abiding by or keeping the law; obedient to law: *law-abiding citizens.*

**law-breaker** /ˈlɔ-breɪkə/, *n.* one who breaks or violates the law. – **law-breaking,** *n., adj.*

**law court** /ˈlɔ kɔt/, *n.* See **court** (def. 13a).

**lawful** /ˈlɔfəl/, *adj.* **1.** allowed or permitted by law; not contrary to law. **2.** legally qualified or entitled: *lawful king.* **3.** recognised or sanctioned by law. **4.** valid; legitimate: *a lawful marriage.* – **lawfully,** *adv.* – **lawfulness,** *n.*

**lawgiver** /ˈlɔgɪvə/, *n.* one who gives or promulgates a law or a code of laws. – **lawgiving,** *n., adj.*

**lawks** /lɔks/, *interj. Archaic.* (an exclamation of surprise). [mincing alteration of LORD]

**lawless** /ˈlɔləs/, *adj.* **1.** regardless of or contrary to law: *lawless violence.* **2.** uncontrolled by law; unbridled: *lawless passions.* **3.** without law; not regulated by law. – **lawlessly,** *adv.* – **lawlessness,** *n.*

**law list** /ˈlɔ lɪst/, *n.* an annual publication containing lists of barristers and solicitors.

**law-maker** /ˈlɔ-meɪkə/, *n.* one who makes or enacts law; a legislator. – **law-making,** *n., adj.*

**lawman** /ˈlɔmæn/, *n. U.S.* an officer of the law.

**law merchant** /lɔ ˈmɜtʃənt/, *n.* →**commercial law.**

**lawn**[1] /lɔn/, *n.* **1.** a stretch of grass-covered land, esp. one closely mowed, as near a house, etc. **2.** *Archaic.* →**glade.** [earlier *laund,* from OF *la(u)nde* wooded ground; of Celtic orig.] – **lawny,** *adj.*

**lawn**[2] /lɔn/, *n.* a thin or sheer linen or cotton fabric, either plain or printed. [ME *laun(e), laund(e)*; probably named after *Laon,* a town in N France, where much linen was made] – **lawny,** *adj.*

**lawn bowls** /– ˈboʊlz/, *n.* a game in which the players roll biased or weighted balls along a green in an effort to bring them as near as possible to a stationary ball called the jack.

**lawn-mower** /ˈlɔn-moʊə/, *n.* a machine for cutting grass.

**lawn sleeves** /ˈlɔn slivz/, *n.pl.* **1.** the sleeves of lawn of an Anglican bishop. **2.** the office of an Anglican bishop. **3.** an Anglican bishop or bishops.

**lawn tennis** /– ˈtɛnəs/, *n.* tennis (def. 1) played on a grass court.

**law of contradiction,** *n.* the law which asserts that a proposition cannot at the same time be both true and false, or alternatively that a thing cannot at the same time both have and not have a given property.

**law of diminishing returns,** *n.* the principle that the returns on total output decrease as labour and capital are expanded beyond a certain point.

**law of increasing returns,** *n.* the observed fact that in some industries expenditure of labour or capital up to a certain point has the capacity to decrease the cost per unit of a commodity and thereby increase the corresponding returns.

**law of nations,** *n.* →**international law.**

**law of the jungle,** *n.* **1.** the principle that might is right; allowing superior strength, viciousness and cunning to be the arbiters of who shall survive, as animals do in the jungle. **2.** the same principle applied to the activities of mankind as among a group of unprincipled mercenaries, of unscrupulous businessmen operating under laissez-faire capitalism, etc. Also, **jungle law.**

**lawrencium** /lɒˈrɛnsiəm, lɔ-/, *n.* a transuranic element produced synthetically. *Symbol:* lw; *at. no.:* 103. [named after Ernest O. *Lawrence,* 1901-58, U.S. physicist, inventor of cyclotron]

**law report** /ˈlɔ rəpɔt/, *n.* the published account of a legal proceeding, stating the facts of the case, the principles of law involved, and the reasons given by the court for its decision.

**law sitting** /ˈ– sɪtɪŋ/, *n.* the period of the year during which judicial business is conducted.

**lawsuit** /ˈlɔsut/, *n.* a suit at law; a prosecution of a claim in a law court.

**lawyer** /ˈlɔɪjə/, *n.* **1.** one whose profession it is to conduct suits in court or to give legal advice and aid. **2.** *New Testament.* an interpreter of the Mosaic law. **3.** →**bush-lawyer** (def. 1).

**lawyer-cane** /ˈlɔɪjə-keɪn/, *n.* any of certain species of the genus *Calamus,* family Palmae, and the genus *Flagellaria,* family Flagellariaceae, tropical climbers whose spines cling to flesh and clothing. Also, **lawyer-palm, lawyer-vine.**

**lax**[1] /læks/, *adj.* **1.** lacking in strictness or severity; careless or negligent: *lax morals.* **2.** not rigidly exact or precise; vague: *lax ideas on a subject.* **3.** loose or slack; not tense, rigid, or firm: *a lax cord.* **4.** open or not retentive, as the bowels. **5.** (of a person) having the bowels unduly open. **6.** loosely cohering; open or not compact, as a panicle of a plant. **7.** *Phonet.* pronounced with relatively relaxed muscles. [ME, from L *laxus* loose, slack] – **laxly,** *adv.* – **laxness,** *n.*

**lax**[2] /læks/, *n.* →**salmon.** [Swed. or G *Lachs;* replacing OE *leax*]

**laxation** /lækˈseɪʃən/, *n.* **1.** a loosening or relaxing. **2.** the state of being loosened or relaxed. **3.** →**laxative.** [ME *laxacion,* from L *laxātio* a widening]

**laxative** /ˈlæksətɪv/, *n.* **1.** *Med.* a laxative medicine or agent. –*adj.* **2.** *Med.* mildly purgative. **3.** *Pathol.* **a.** (of the bowels) subject to looseness. **b.** (of a disease) characterised by looseness of the bowels. [L *laxātīvus* loosening; replacing ME *laxatif,* from F]

**laxity** /ˈlæksəti/, *n.* the state or quality of being lax or loose. [L *laxitas*]

**lay**[1] /leɪ/, *v.,* **laid, laying,** *n.* –*v.t.* **1.** to put or place in a position of rest or recumbency: *to lay a book on a desk.* **2.** to bring, throw, or beat down, as from an erect position: *to lay a person low.* **3.** to cause to subside: *to lay the dust.* **4.** to allay, appease, or suppress. **5.** to smooth down or make even: *to lay the nap of cloth.* **6.** to bury. **7.** to bring forth and deposit (an egg or eggs). **8.** to deposit as a wager; stake; bet: *I'll lay you ten to one.* **9.** to put away for future use (fol. by *by*). **10.** to place, set, or cause to be in a particular situation, state, or condition: *to lay hands on a thing.* **11.** to place before a person, or bring to a person's notice or consideration: *he laid his case before the commission.* **12.** to put to; place in contiguity; apply: *to lay a hand on a child.* **13.** to set (a trap, etc.). **14.** to place or locate (a scene): *the scene is laid in France.* **15.** to present, bring forward, or prefer, as a claim, charge, etc. **16.** to impute, attribute, or ascribe. **17.** to impose as a burden, duty, penalty, or the like: *to lay an embargo on shipments of oil.* **18.** to bring down (a stick, etc.), as on a person, in inflicting punishment. **19.** to dispose or place in proper position or in an orderly fashion: *to lay bricks.* **20.** to set (a table). **21.** to form by twisting strands together, as a rope. **22.** to place on or over a surface, as paint; cover or spread with something else. **23.** to devise or arrange, as a plan. **24.** *Naut.* to head a ship towards (an object or compass point), esp. on the closest course she will make to the wind. **25.** to adjust a gun for direction and elevation before firing. **26.** to put (dogs) on a scent. **27.** *Colloq.* to have sexual intercourse with. –*v.* **28.** Some special verb phrases are:

**lay aboard,** *Naut.* (of a boat) to come alongside a ship.

**lay an egg,** *Colloq.* **1.** to drop a bomb. **2.** to defecate. **3.** to blunder; flop, as in the theatre.

**lay down, 1.** to put (something) down on the ground, to relinquish. **2.** to record (speech, a track of music, etc.) on a tape or disc.

**lay down one's arms,** to surrender.

**lay hold of** or **on,** to grasp; seize; catch.

**lay in, 1.** to build up a store of (provisions, etc.). **2.** *Naut.* to move along a yard, towards the mast.

**lay in (there),** *Colloq.* to maintain a course of action despite opposition, setbacks, etc.

**lay it on, 1.** to exaggerate. **2.** to chastise severely.

**lay off, 1.** to put aside. **2.** to dismiss, esp. temporarily, as a workman. **3.** to mark or plot off. **4.** *Colloq.* to desist. **5.** *Colloq.* to cease to annoy (someone). **6.** *Horseracing, etc.* (of a bookmaker) to make a bet with another bookmaker to cover projected losses on a race. **7.** to protect a bet or speculation by taking some off-setting risk.

**lay on,** to provide or supply.

**lay oneself open,** to expose oneself (to adverse criticism or the like).

**lay out, 1.** to extend at length. **2.** to spread out to the sight, air, etc.; spread out in order. **3.** to stretch out and prepare (a body) for burial. **4.** *Colloq.* to expend (money) for a particular purpose. **5.** to exert (oneself) for some purpose, effect, etc. **6.** to plot or plan out. **7.** *Naut.* to move along a yard, away from the mast. **8.** to strike down, esp. to knock unconscious.

**lay siege to,** to besiege.

**lay to,** *Naut.* **1.** to check the motion of (a ship). **2.** to put (a ship, etc.) in a dock or other place of safety.

**lay up, 1.** to put away, as for future use; store up. **2.** to cause to remain in bed or indoors through illness.

**lay waste,** to devastate.

*–v.i.* **29.** to lay eggs. **30.** to wager or bet. **31.** to deal or aim blows (fol. by *on, at, about, into,* etc.). **32.** to apply oneself vigorously. **33.** *Naut.* to take a specified position. *–n.* **34.** the way or position in which a thing is laid or lies. **35.** *Ropemaking.* the quality of a fibre rope characterised by the degree of twist, the angles formed by the strands and by the fibres in the strands. **36.** a share of the profits or the catch of a whaling or fishing voyage, distributed to officers and crew. **37.** *Colloq.* **a.** a person considered as a sex object: *a good lay, an easy lay.* **b.** the sexual act. [ME *lay(en), legge(n),* OE *lecgan* (causative of *licgan* LIE[2]), c. D *leggen,* G *legen,* Icel. *leggja,* Goth. *lagjan*]

**lay**[2] /leɪ/, *v.* past tense of **lie**[2].

**lay**[3] /leɪ/, *adj.* **1.** belonging to, pertaining to, or performed by the people or laity, as distinguished from the clergy: *a lay sermon.* **2.** not belonging to, connected with, or proceeding from a profession, esp. the law or medicine. [ME *laye,* from OF *lai,* from LL *lāicus* LAIC]

**lay**[4] /leɪ/, *n.* **1.** a short narrative or other poem, esp. one to be sung. **2.** a song. [ME *lai,* from OF, ? from Gmc; cf. OHG *leich* song]

**layabout** /'leɪəbaʊt/, *n.* one who does not work; a loafer; an idler.

**lay-away** /'leɪ-əweɪ/, *n. U.S.* →**lay-by** (defs 1 and 2).

**layback** /'leɪbæk/, *n.* a method of rockclimbing in which the body is held in a nearly horizontal position by pulling with the hands on the near edge of a crack and pushing with the feet on the far side.

**lay brother** /'leɪ brʌðə/, *n.* a man who has taken religious vows and habit, but is employed chiefly in manual work.

**lay-by** /'leɪ-baɪ/, *n.* **1.** the reservation of an article by payment of a cash deposit. **2.** an item so reserved or so purchased. **3.** *Brit.* a part of a road or railway where vehicles may draw up out of the stream of traffic. *–v.t.* **4.** to put (something) on lay-by (def. 1).

**lay day** /'leɪ deɪ/, *n.* **1.** one of a certain number of days allowed by a charter party for loading or unloading a vessel without demurrage. **2.** a rest day, as in cricket, sailing, etc.

**layer** /'leɪə/, *n.* **1.** a thickness of some material laid on or spread over a surface; a stratum. **2.** something which is laid. **3.** one who or that which lays. **4.** *Hort.* **a.** a shoot or twig placed partly under the ground while still attached to the living stock, for the purpose of propagation. **b.** a plant which has been propagated by layering. *–v.t.* **5.** to make a layer of. **6.** *Hort.* to propagate by layers. [ME, from LAY[1] + -ER[1]]

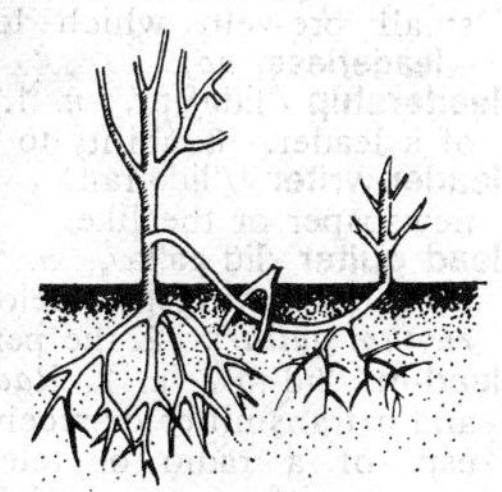
layer (def. 4)

**layer cake** /'– keɪk/, *n.* a cake made in layers with a cream or other filling between the layers.

**layering** /'leɪərɪŋ/, *n.* a method of propagating plants by causing their shoots to take root while still attached to the mother plant. Also, *Chiefly U.S.,* **layerage** /'leɪərɪdʒ/.

**layette** /leɪ'ɛt/, *n.* a complete outfit of clothing, toilet articles, etc., for a newborn child. [F: box, drawer, layette, diminutive of *laie* chest, trough, from Flemish *laeye*]

**lay figure** /'leɪ fɪgə/, *n.* **1.** a jointed model of the human body, usu. of wood, from which artists work in the absence of a living model. **2.** a mere puppet or nonentity; a person of no importance. [replacing obs. *layman* (from D *leeman,* from *lee* joint, limb (c. E *lith,* now d.) + *man* MAN), with *figure* substituted for *man,* to avoid confusion with eccles. term]

**laying-off season** /leɪɪŋ-'ɒf sizən/, *n.* that period of the year during which seasonal workers, as cane-cutters, fruit-pickers, etc., are laid off.

**layman** /'leɪmən/, *n., pl.* **-men.** one of the laity; one not a clergyman or not a member of some particular profession. [LAY[3] + MAN]

**lay-off** /'leɪ-ɒf/, *n.* **1.** the act of laying off. **2.** an interval of enforced unemployment.

**layout** /'leɪaʊt/, *n.* **1.** a laying or spreading out. **2.** an arrangement or plan. **3.** the plan or sketch of a page, magazine, book, advertisement, or the like, indicating the arrangement of materials.

**lay preacher** /leɪ 'pritʃə/, *n.* a layman, esp. in the nonconformist churches, who may preach and take services. Also, **local preacher.**

**lay reader** /– 'ridə/, *n.* **1.** *C. of E.* a layman who may conduct morning and evening prayer, and preach for a particular parish, but who is not permitted to hold communion. **2.** *Rom. Cath. Ch.* a layman who represents the congregation in the sanctuary at mass, and reads certain parts of the liturgy, as the epistle and the gospel.

**lay shaft** /'– ʃaft/, *n.* a secondary, geared shaft in a gearbox to and from which the drive is transferred.

**laywoman** /'leɪwʊmən/, *n., pl.* **-women.** a female member of the laity.

**lazar** /'læzə/, *n. Archaic.* **1.** a person, esp. a beggar or poor person, infected with a loathsome disease. **2.** →**leper.** [ME, from ML *lazarus,* special use of *Lazarus,* the beggar 'full of sores', of the parable in Luke 16] – **lazar-like,** *adj.*

**lazaretto** /læzə'rɛtoʊ/, *n., pl.* **-tos. 1.** a hospital for those affected with contagious or loathsome diseases. **2.** a building or a ship set apart for quarantine purposes. **3.** *Naut.* a place in some merchant ships, usu. near the stern, in which provisions and stores are kept. Also, **lazaret** /læzə'rɛt/, **lazarette.** [It. *lazzaretto,* var. of Venetian *lazareto,* b. *nazareto* (abbrev. of name of leper hospital *Santa Maria di Nazaret*) and *lazaro* lazar, leper]

**laze** /leɪz/, *v.,* **lazed, lazing.** *–v.i.* **1.** to be lazy; idle or lounge lazily. *–v.t.* **2.** to pass (time) lazily (fol. by *away*). *–n.* **3.** the act of lazing. [backformation from LAZY]

**lazulite** /'læʒjəlaɪt/, *n.* an azure blue mineral, hydrous magnesium iron aluminium phosphate, (FeMg)- $Al_2P_2O_8(OH)_2$. [ML *lāzulum* lapis lazuli + -ITE[1]]

**lazurite** /'læʒjəraɪt/, *n.* a mineral, sodium aluminium silicate and sulphide, $Na_5Al_3Si_3O_{12}S_3$, occurring in deep blue crystals and used for ornamental purposes. [ML *lāzur* AZURE + -ITE[1]]

**lazy** /'leɪzi/, *adj.,* **-zier, -ziest. 1.** disinclined to exertion or work; idle. **2.** slow-moving; sluggish: *a lazy stream.* [orig. uncert.; of. LG *lasich* languid, feeble] – **lazily,** *adv.* – **laziness,** *n.*

**lazybones** /'leɪziboʊnz/, *n. Colloq.* a lazy person.

**lazy ration** /'leɪzi ræʃən/, *n.* (formerly) a subsistence ration supplied to recalcitrant convicts.

**lazy Susan** /– 'suzən/, *n.* **1.** a revolving tray for serving condiments or food. **2.** a corner cupboard in a kitchen, etc. containing several shelves which revolve for easy access to stored goods.

**lazy tongs** /'– tɒŋz/, *n. pl.* a kind of extensible tongs for grasping objects at a distance, consisting of a series of pairs of crossing pieces, each pair pivoted together in the middle and connected with the next pair at the extremities.

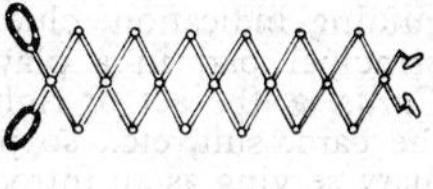
lazy tongs

**lb.,** *pl.* **lbs, lb.** pound (weight). [L *libra,* the ancient Roman pound (weight)]

**l.b.** /ɛl 'bi/, (in cricket) leg bye.

**lbf,** pound-force.

**l.b.w.** /ɛl bi 'dʌbəlju/, (in cricket) leg before wicket.

**l.c.,** (in printing) lower case.

**L.C.,** Legislative Council.

**l.c.d.** /ɛl si 'di/, lowest common denominator.

**l.c.f.** /ɛl si 'ɛf/, lowest common factor.

**LCL,** Liberal and Country League.

**l.c.m.** /ɛl si 'ɛm/, least or lowest common multiple. Also, **L.C.M.**

**LCP,** Liberal-Country Party.

**LD,** **1.** lethal dose. **2.** Low Dutch. Also, **L.D.**

**LD-50,** median lethal dose.

**L-dopa** /ɛl-ˈdoʊpə/, *n.* a synthetically-produced substance, similar to dopa, used in the treatment of Parkinson's disease. [see DOPA]

**lea**[1] /li/, *n. Archaic.* a tract of open ground, esp. grassland; a meadow. [ME *ley,* OE *lēa(h),* c. OHG *lōh,* L *lūcus* grove]

**lea**[2] /li/, *n.* a measure of yarn of varying quantity, for wool usu. 73.15 metres, cotton and silk 109.73 metres, linen 274.32 metres. [ME, ? akin to F *lier* tie]

**leach** /litʃ/, *v.t.* **1.** to cause (water, etc.) to percolate through something. **2.** to remove soluble constituents from (ashes, soil, etc.) by percolation. *–v.i.* **3.** (of ashes, soil, etc.) to undergo the action of percolating water. **4.** to percolate, as water. *–n.* **5.** a leaching. **6.** the material leached. **7.** a vessel for use in leaching. [unexplained var. of *letch,* v. (whence d. *letch,* n., bog, etc.), OE *leccan* moisten, wet, causative of LEAK]

**leachate** /ˈlitʃeɪt/, *n.* water carrying impurities which has percolated through the earth, a rubbish tip, mine waste, etc.; liquid sullage.

**leachy** /ˈlitʃi/, *adj.* →**porous.**

**lead**[1] /lid/, *v.,* **led, leading,** *n.* *–v.t.* **1.** to take or conduct on the way; go before or with to show the way. **2.** to conduct by holding and guiding: *to lead a horse by a rope.* **3.** to guide in direction, course, action, opinion, etc.; to influence or induce: *too easily led.* **4.** to conduct or bring (water, wire, etc.) in a particular course. **5.** (of a road, passage, etc.) to serve to bring (a person, etc.) to a place through a region, etc. **6.** to take or bring: *the prisoners were led in.* **7.** to be at the head of, command, or direct (an army, organisation, etc.). **8.** to go at the head of or in advance of (a procession, list, body, etc.); to be first in or go before. **9.** to have the directing or principal part in (a movement, proceedings, etc.). **10.** to begin or open, as a dance, discussion, etc. **11.** to act as leader of (an orchestra, etc.). **12.** to go through or pass (life, etc.): *to lead a dreary existence.* **13.** *Cards.* to begin a round, etc., with (a card or suit specified). **14.** to aim and fire a firearm or gun ahead of (a moving target) in order to allow for the travel of the target and time of flight of the bullet or shell in reaching it. **15. lead (someone) a chase** or **dance,** to cause (someone) unnecessary difficulty or trouble. **16. lead (someone) by the nose,** to enforce one's will on (someone), esp. unpleasantly. **17. lead (someone) on,** to induce or encourage (someone) to a detrimental or undesirable course of action. **18. lead the way,** to go in advance of others, esp. as a guide. *–v.i.* **19.** to act as a guide; show the way. **20.** to be led, or submit to being led, as an animal. **21.** to afford passage to a place, etc., as a road, stairway, or the like. **22.** to go first; be in advance. **23.** to take the directing or principal part. **24.** to take the initiative (oft. fol. by *off*). **25.** *Boxing.* to take the offensive by striking at an opponent. **26.** *Cards.* to make the first play (oft. fol. by *off*). **27. lead up to,** to prepare gradually for. *–n.* **28.** the first or foremost place; position in advance of others. **29.** the extent of advance. **30.** something that leads. **31.** a thong or line for holding a dog or other animal in check. **32.** a guiding indication; clue. **33.** precedence. **34.** *Theat.* **a.** the principal part in a play. **b.** the person who plays it. **35.** *Cards.* **a.** the act or right of playing first, as in a round. **b.** the card, suit, etc., so played. **36.** *Journalism.* a short summary serving as an introduction to a news story or article. **37.** *Elect.* a single conductor, often flexible and insulated, used in connections between pieces of electrical apparatus. **38.** *Engineering.* the interval by which a periodic signal precedes another signal of the same phase. **39.** *Boxing.* the act of taking the offensive by striking at an opponent. **40.** *Naut.* the course of a rope. **41.** →**leadblock.** **42.** (*pl.*) *Naut.* beacons or lights set in line for sighting, to enable a ship to steer through a narrow channel. **43.** an open channel through a field of ice. **44.** *Mining.* **a.** →**lode.** **b.** an auriferous deposit in an old river-bed. **45.** the act of aiming a firearm or gun ahead of a target moving across the line of fire. *–adj.* **46.** solo or dominating as in a musical structure: *lead singer, lead guitar, lead break.* [ME *leden,* OE *lǣdan* (causative of *līthan* go, travel), c. D *leiden,* G *leiten,* Icel. *leidha*]

**lead**[2] /lɛd/, *n.* **1.** *Chem.* a heavy, comparatively soft, malleable bluish-grey metal, sometimes found native, but usu. combined as sulphide, in galena. *Symbol:* Pb; *at. wt:* 207.19; *at. no.:* 82; *sp. gr.:* 11.34 at 20°C. **2.** something made of this metal or one of its alloys. **3.** a plummet or mass of lead suspended by a line, as for taking soundings. **4. heave the lead,** *Naut.* to take a sounding with a lead. **5. swing the lead,** to be idle when there is work to be done. **6. put lead in one's pencil,** (of a male) to increase sexual capacity. **7.** bullets; shot. **8.** black lead or graphite. **9.** a small stick of it as used in pencils. **10.** Also, **leading.** *Print.* a thin strip of type metal or brass, less than type high, for increasing the space between lines of type. **11.** frames of lead in which panes are fixed, as in windows of stained glass. **12.** (*pl.*) sheets or strips of lead used for covering roofs. **13.** See **red lead, white lead.** *–v.t.* **14.** to cover, line, weight, treat, or impregnate with lead or one of its compounds. **15.** *Print.* to insert leads between the lines of. **16.** to fix (window glass) in position with leads. *–adj.* **17.** containing or made of lead. **18. go down like a lead balloon,** to fail dismally; fail to elicit the desired response. [ME *lede,* OE *lēad,* c. D *lood,* G *Lot* plummet]

**lead acetate** /– ˈæsəteɪt/, *n.* a white soluble crystalline salt, $(CH_3COO)_2Pb \cdot 3H_2O$, with a sweet taste, used as a mordant and as a drier in paints; sugar of lead.

**lead arsenate** /– ˈasəneɪt/, *n.* plumbous arsenate, $Pb_3$- $(AsO_4)_2$, a very poisonous crystalline compound, used as an insecticide.

**Leadbeater's cockatoo** /ˌlɛdbitəz kɒkəˈtu/, *n.* →**Major Mitchell.**

**leadblock** /ˈlidblɒk/, *n.* a fixed block on a sailing boat, used in altering the direction of pull on a line. Also, **lead.**

**leaden** /ˈlɛdn/, *adj.* **1.** consisting or made of lead. **2.** inertly heavy, or hard to lift or move, as weight, the limbs, etc. **3.** oppressive; burdensome. **4.** sluggish, as the pace. **5.** dull, spiritless, or gloomy, as the mood, thoughts, etc. **6.** of a dull grey: *leaden skies.* – **leadenly,** *adv.* – **leadenness,** *n.*

**leader** /ˈlidə/, *n.* **1.** one who or that which leads. **2.** a guiding or directing head, as of any army, movement, etc. **3.** *Music.* **a.** the principal violinist, cornet-player, or singer in an orchestra, band, or chorus, to whom solos are usu. assigned. **b.** →**concertmaster.** **4.** a horse harnessed in front of a team. **5.** a principal or important editorial article, as in a newspaper. **6.** a featured article of trade, esp. one offered at a low price to attract customers. **7.** *Naut.* a piece of metal or wood having apertures for lines to lead them to their proper places. **8.** (*pl.*) *Print.* a row of dots or short lines to lead the eye across a space. **9.** the net used to direct fish into a weir, pound, etc. **10.** *Films.* a blank strip at the beginning of a reel of film, used to ease threading, and for identification purposes. **11.** *Hort.* the long slender extension shoots of trees, esp. of fruit trees, which are cut back in pruning. **12.** *Law.* a Queen's Counsel in charge of a case. **13.** *Mining.* a small ore-vein which leads or points to a richer lode. – **leaderless,** *adj.*

**leadership** /ˈlidəʃɪp/, *n.* **1.** the position, function, or guidance of a leader. **2.** ability to lead.

**leader-writer** /ˈlidə-raɪtə/, *n.* one who writes leaders in a newspaper or the like.

**lead guitar** /lid gəˈta/, *n.* **1.** an electric guitar in a rock group used for playing the melodic line and solo parts (opposed to *rhythm guitar*). **2.** the person who plays lead guitar.

**lead-in** /ˈlid-ɪn/, *n.* **1.** *Radio.* connection between the aerial and a transmitter or receiving set. **2.** a general introduction, esp. of a radio or television broadcast. **3.** an opening; opportunity.

**leading**[1] /ˈlidɪŋ/, *n.* **1.** the act of one who or that which leads; guidance, direction; lead. *–adj.* **2.** directing; guiding. **3.** chief; principal; most important; foremost. [LEAD[1] + -ING[1]]

**leading**[2] /ˈlɛdɪŋ/, *n.* **1.** a covering or framing of lead. **2.** *Print.* →**lead**[2] (def. 10). [LEAD[2] + -ING[1]]

**leading article** /lidɪŋ ˈatɪkəl/, *n.* a principal editorial article in a newspaper; a leader.

**leading dog** /ˈ– dɒg/, *n.* a dog trained to run at the head of a mob of sheep and keep them steady.

**leading edge** /ˈ– ɛdʒ/, *n.* the edge of an aerofoil or propeller blade facing the direction of motion.

**leading hand** /– ˈhænd/, *n.* a senior tradesman; the grade above tradesman and below charge hand.

**leading lady** /– ˈleɪdi/, *n.* the principal actress in a play, film, etc.

i = peat ɪ = pit ɛ = pet æ = pat a = part ɒ = pot ʌ = putt ɔ = port ʊ = put u = pool ɜ = pert ə = apart aɪ = buy eɪ = bay ɔɪ = boy aʊ = how oʊ = hoe ɪə = here ɛə = hair ʊə = tour g = give θ = thin ð = then ʃ = show ʒ = measure tʃ = choke dʒ = joke ŋ = sing j = you õ = Fr. bon

**leading light** /– 'laɪt/, *n. Colloq.* a person outstanding in a particular sphere.

**leading man** /– 'mæn/, *n.* the principal male actor in a play, film, etc.

**leading note** /'– noʊt/, *n. Music.* the seventh degree of a diatonic scale.

**leading question** /– 'kwɛstʃən/, *n.* a question so worded as to suggest the proper or desired answer.

**leading rein** /'– reɪn/, *n.* a long rein clipped onto the bridle or halter for leading a horse. Also, **leading string.**

**leadlight window** /lɛdlaɪt 'wɪndoʊ/, *n.* a window made from various pieces of glass, sometimes coloured or frosted, set in a lead frame.

**lead line** /'lɛd laɪn/, *n. Naut.* a line used in taking soundings.

**lead monoxide** /– mə'nɒksaɪd/, *n.* →**litharge.**

**lead-off** /'lid-ɒf/, *n.* an act which starts something; start; beginning.

**lead oxide** /lɛd 'ɒksaɪd/, *n.* →**litharge.**

**lead paint** /– 'peɪnt/, *n.* paint containing lead pigment, esp. white lead.

**lead pencil** /– 'pɛnsəl/, *n.* an implement for writing or drawing made of graphite in a wooden or metal holder.

**lead poisoning** /– 'pɔɪzənɪŋ/, *n.* a diseased condition due to the introduction of lead into the system, common among workers in lead or its compounds; plumbism.

**lead screw** /'lid skru/, *n.* the device by which traversing is effected on a lathe.

**leadsman** /'lɛdzmən/, *n., pl.* **-men.** *Naut.* a man who heaves the lead in taking soundings.

**lead tetraethyl** /ˌlɛd tɛtrə'ɛθəl/, *n.* a colourless liquid, $Pb(C_2H_5)_4$, used in petrol for internal-combustion engines because of its antiknock properties.

**lead time** /'lid taɪm/, *n.* the time required for preparation before a project can begin.

**lead-up** /'lid-ʌp/, *n.* preparatory speech or action; introduction (oft. fol. by *to*).

**leady** /'lɛdi/, *adj.* like lead; leaden.

**leaf** /lif/, *n., pl.* **leaves** /livz/, *v.* *–n.* **1.** one of the expanded, usu. green, organs borne by the stem of a plant. **2.** any similar or corresponding lateral outgrowth of a stem. **3.** a petal: *a rose leaf.* **4.** foliage or leafage. **5. in leaf,** covered with foliage or leaves. **6.** *Bibliog.* a unit generally comprising two printed pages of a book, one on each side, but also applied to blank or illustrated pages. **7.** a thin sheet of metal, etc. **8.** a lamina or layer. **9.** a sliding, hinged, or detachable flat part, as of a door, tabletop, etc. **10.** a single strip of metal in a composite, or leaf, spring. **11.** *Bldg Trades.* one of the two solid outer parts of a cavity wall. **12.** a layer of fat, esp. that about the kidneys of a pig. **13. take a leaf out of someone's book,** to follow someone's example. **14. turn over a new leaf,** to begin a new and better course of conduct or action. *–v.i.* **15.** to put forth leaves. *–v.t.* **16. leaf through,** to turn the pages of quickly. [ME *leef,* OE *lēaf,* c. G *Laub*] – **leaf-like,** *adj.*

**leafage** /'lifɪdʒ/, *n.* →**foliage.**

**leaf curl** /'lif kɜl/, *n.* →**curl** (def. 16).

**leaf-hopper** /'lif-hɒpə/, *n.* any of the leaping homopterous insects of the family Cicadellidae, including many crop pests.

**leaf-lard** /'lif-lad/, *n.* lard prepared from the leaf (def. 12) of the pig.

**leafless** /'lifləs/, *adj.* without leaves. – **leaflessness,** *n.*

**leaflet** /'liflət/, *n.* **1.** one of the separate blades or divisions of a compound leaf. **2.** a small leaf-like part or structure. **3.** a small or young leaf. **4.** a small flat or folded sheet of printed matter, as for distribution. *–v.i.* **5.** to distribute leaflets, esp. as part of a campaign.

**leaf mould** /'lif moʊld/, *n.* **1.** *Hort.* a mass of semi-decayed leaves used as a constituent of potting composts. **2.** *Bot.* any of a number of fungi which attack the foliage of cultivated plants.

**leaf spring** /'– sprɪŋ/, *n.* a long, narrow, multiple spring composed of several layers of spring metal bracketed together.

**leafstalk** /'lifstɔk/, *n.* →**petiole** (def. 1).

**leafy** /'lifi/, *adj.,* **-fier, -fiest.** **1.** abounding in, covered with, or consisting of leaves or foliage: *the leafy woods.* **2.** leaf-like; foliaceous. – **leafiness,** *n.*

**league**[1] /lig/, *n., v.,* **leagued, leaguing,** *adj.* *–n.* **1.** a covenant or compact made between persons, parties, states, etc., for the maintenance or promotion of common interests or for mutual assistance or service. **2.** the aggregation of persons, parties, states, etc., associated in such a covenant; a confederacy. **3. in league,** united by or having a compact or agreement; allied (oft. fol. by *with*). **4.** category or class: *they are not in the same league.* **5.** an association of sporting clubs which arranges matches between teams of approximately similar standard. **6.** (*cap.*) →**Rugby League.** *–v.t.* **7.** to unite in a league; combine. *–v.i.* **8.** to join in a league. *–adj.* **9.** of or belonging to a league. **10.** of or pertaining to Rugby League. [ME *ligg,* from OF *ligue,* from It. *liga, lega,* from *legare,* from L *ligāre* bind]

**league**[2] /lig/, *n.* a former unit of distance, varying at different periods and in different countries, usu. estimated roughly at 3 miles or 5 kilometres. [ME *le(u)ge,* from LL *leuga, leuca,* said to be of Gallic orig.]

**leaguer**[1] /ligə/, *n.* **1.** a siege. **2.** a military camp, esp. of a besieging army. **3.** a defensive military formation adopted for collective protection of a force by night when the force must be in immediate readiness. *–v.t.* **4.** to besiege. [D *leger* bed, camp. See LAIR[1], LAAGER]

**leaguer**[2] /'ligə/, *n.* a member of a league. [LEAGUE[1] + -ER[1]]

**leak** /lik/, *n.* **1.** an unintended hole, crack, or the like by which fluid, gas, etc., enters or escapes. **2.** any avenue or means of unintended entrance or escape, or the entrance or escape itself. **3.** *Elect.* a point where current escapes from a conductor, as because of poor insulation. **4.** the act of leaking. **5.** an accidental or apparently accidental disclosure of information, etc. **6.** *Colloq.* an act of passing water; urination. *–v.i.* **7.** to let fluid, gas, etc. enter or escape, as through an unintended hole, crack, permeable material, or the like: *the roof is leaking.* **8.** to pass in or out in this manner, as water, etc.: *gas leaking from a pipe.* **9.** to transpire or become known undesignedly (fol. by *out*). **10.** *Colloq.* to pass water; urinate. *–v.t.* **11.** to let (fluid, etc.) leak in or out. **12.** to disclose (information, esp. of a confidential nature), esp. to the media. [ME *leke,* from Scand.; cf. Icel. *leka* drip, leak, c. MD *leken*]

**leakage** /'likɪdʒ/, *n.* **1.** the act of leaking; leak. **2.** that which leaks in or out. **3.** the amount that leaks in or out. **4.** *Comm.* an allowance for loss by leaking. **5.** *Physics.* the escape of any radiation through a shield round a nuclear reactor.

**leakage current** /'– kʌrənt/, *n.* a relatively small current flowing through or across the surface of an insulator when a voltage is impressed upon it.

**leaky** /'liki/, *adj.,* **-kier, -kiest.** **1.** allowing fluid, gas, etc., to leak in or out. **2.** *Colloq.* allowing confidential information to be made public: *that department is very leaky.* – **leakiness,** *n.*

**leal** /lil/, *adj. Archaic or Scot.* loyal. [ME *lele,* from OF *leial.* See LOYAL] – **leally,** *adv.*

**lean**[1] /lin/, *v.,* **leant** or **leaned, leaning,** *n.* *–v.i.* **1.** to incline or bend from a vertical position or in a particular direction. **2.** to incline in feeling, opinion, action, etc.: *to lean towards socialism.* **3.** to rest against or on something for support: *lean against a wall.* **4.** to depend or rely: *to lean on empty promises.* **5. lean on,** to intimidate; apply pressure on. **6. lean over backwards.** See **backwards** (def. 7). *–v.t.* **7.** to incline or bend: *he leant his head forward.* **8.** to cause to lean or rest (fol. by *against, on, upon,* etc.): *lean your arm against the railing.* *–n.* **9.** the act of leaning; inclination. [ME *lene(n),* OE *hleonian,* c. G *lehnen;* akin to L *-clīnāre* incline]

**lean**[2] /lin/, *adj.* **1.** (of persons or animals) scant of flesh; thin; not plump or fat: *lean cattle.* **2.** (of meat) containing little or no fat. **3.** lacking in richness, fullness, quantity, etc.: *a lean diet, lean years.* **4.** deficient in a particular ingredient, as of clay which is not very plastic, or of one which contains little valuable material. **5.** *Print.* (of letters or strokes) thin; narrow. *–n.* **6.** that part of flesh which consists of muscular tissue rather than fat. **7.** the lean part of anything. [ME *lene,* OE *hlǣne*] – **leanly,** *adv.* – **leanness,** *n.*

**lean-face** /'lin-feɪs/, *adj.* (of printing type) not having the full breadth; thin; narrow. Also, **thin-face.**

**leangle** /ˈliˈæŋgəl/, *n.* a heavy aboriginal weapon; club. [Aboriginal]

**leaning** /ˈlinɪŋ/, *n.* inclination; tendency: *strong literary leanings.*

**leant** /lɛnt/, *v.* a past tense and past participle of **lean**[1].

**lean-to** /ˈlin-tu/, *n., pl.* **-tos.** a shelter made of wood, galvanised iron, etc., propped against a building, wall, etc.

**leap** /lip/, *v.,* **leapt** or **leaped, leaping,** *n.* *–v.i.* **1.** to spring through the air from one point or position to another: *to leap over a ditch.* **2.** to move quickly and lightly: *to leap aside.* **3.** to pass, come, rise, etc., as if with a bound: *to leap to a conclusion.* *–v.t.* **4.** to jump over: *to leap a wall.* **5.** to pass over as if by a leap. **6.** to cause to leap. *–n.* **7.** a spring, jump, or bound; a light springing movement. **8.** the space cleared in a leap. **9.** a place leapt, or to be leapt, over or from. **10.** an abrupt transition, esp. a rise. **11.** *Music.* a melodic interval greater than a second. **12. a leap forward,** a sudden progressive development. **13. by leaps and bounds,** very rapidly. **14. leap in the dark,** an action taken without knowledge of the possible outcomes. [ME *lepe(n),* OE *hlēapan* leap, run, c. G *laufen* run. Cf. LOPE] – **leaper,** *n.*

**leapfrog** /ˈlipfrɒg/, *n., v.,* **-frogged, -frogging.** *–n.* **1.** a game in which one player leaps over another who is in a stooping posture. *–v.t.* **2.** *Mil.* to advance (two military units) by engaging one with the enemy while moving the other forward. **3.** to jump over (a person or thing) in, or as in, leapfrog. **4.** to move or advance (something) by leaping in this manner over obstacles. *–v.i.* **5.** to progress by, or as if by leapfrog.

**leapt** /lɛpt/, *v.* a past tense and past participle of **leap.**

**leap year** /ˈlip jɪə/, *n.* a year containing 366 days, or one day (29 February) more than the ordinary year, to offset the difference in length between the ordinary year and the astronomical year (being, in practice, every year whose number is exactly divisible by 4, as 1948, except centenary years not exactly divisible by 400, as 1900).

**lear** /lɪə/, *n.* →**lehr.**

**learn** /lɜn/, *v.,* **learnt** or **learned** /lɜnd/, **learning.** *–v.t.* **1.** to acquire knowledge of or skill in by study, instruction, or experience: *to learn French.* **2.** to memorise. **3.** to become informed of or acquainted with; ascertain: *to learn the truth.* **4.** to acquire (a habit or the like). **5.** (*in non-standard speech*) to teach (someone) a lesson: *I'll learn you.* *–v.i.* **6.** to acquire knowledge or skill: *to learn rapidly.* **7.** to become informed (fol. by *of*): *to learn of an accident.* [ME *lernen,* OE *leornian,* c. G *lernen;* akin to OE *gelǣran* teach]

**learned** /ˈlɜnəd/, *adj.* **1.** having much knowledge gained by study; scholarly: *a group of learned men.* **2.** of or showing learning. **3.** applied as a term of courtesy to a member of the legal profession: *my learned friend.* – **learnedly,** *adv.* – **learnedness,** *n.*

**learner** /ˈlɜnə/, *n.* **1.** an employee under twenty-two years of age who is not an apprentice but is serving in a particular industry or section of an industry in order to be considered a qualified worker. **2.** one who is learning to drive a motor vehicle.

**learners' chain** /ˈlɜnəz tʃeɪn/, *n.* the least expert gang working on a chain (def. 12a) in a meatworks.

**learner's permit** /ˈ– pɜmɪt/, *n.* a restricted licence to drive a motor vehicle, issued to a learner on the condition that he is accompanied when driving by a fully licensed driver.

**learning** /ˈlɜnɪŋ/, *n.* **1.** knowledge acquired by systematic study in any field or fields of scholarly application. **2.** the act or process of acquiring knowledge or skill. **3.** *Psychol.* the modification of behaviour through interaction with the environment.

**learnt** /lɜnt/, *v.* a past tense and past participle of **learn.**

**leary**[1] /ˈlɪəri/, *adj.* →**leery**[1].

**leary**[2] /ˈlɪəri/, *adj. Colloq.* →**lairy.**

**lease** /lis/, *n., v.,* **leased, leasing.** *–n.* **1.** an instrument conveying property to another for a definite period, or at will, usu. in consideration of rent or other periodical compensation. **2.** the period of time for which it is made. **3. a new lease of life,** a renewed zest for life. *–v.t.* **4.** to grant the temporary possession or use of (lands, tenements, etc.) to another, usu. for compensation at a fixed rate; let. **5.** to take or to hold by a lease, as lands. [ME *lese,* from AF *les* a letting, from OF *laissier* let, from L *laxāre* loosen] – **leaser,** *n.*

**lease-back** /ˈlis-bæk/, *n.* a financial arrangement in which the owner of a property sells it to an investor who at the same time grants the seller a long-term lease of the property.

**leasehold** /ˈlishoʊld/, *n.* **1.** a land interest acquired under a lease. *–adj.* **2.** held by lease. **3.** of or pertaining to land owned by the Crown and which is leased out, usu. for a specified time period.

**leaseholder** /ˈlishoʊldə/, *n.* a tenant under a lease.

**leash** /liʃ/, *n.* **1.** a strong lead for a dog. **2.** *Sport.* a set of three, as of hounds. *–v.t.* **3.** to secure or hold in or as in a leash. [ME *lees, lese,* from OF *laisse,* from L *laxa,* fem. of L *laxus* loose, lax]

**least** /list/, *adj.* **1.** little beyond all others in size, amount, degree, etc.; smallest; slightest: *the least distance.* **2.** *Archaic.* lowest in consideration or dignity. *–n.* **3.** that which is least; the least amount, quantity, degree, etc. **4. at least, a.** at the least or lowest estimate. **b.** at any rate; in any case. **5. in the least,** in the smallest degree. *–adv.* **6.** to the least extent, amount, or degree. [ME *leest(e),* OE *lǣst,* superl. of *lǣs(sa)* LESS]

**least common multiple,** *n.* →**common multiple.**

**least squares** /list ˈskwɛəz/, *n. pl.* a statistical method of determining constants from observations, by minimising squares of residuals between observations and their theoretical expected values.

**leastways** /ˈlistweɪz/, *adv. Colloq.* at least; at any rate. Also, **leastwise** /ˈlistwaɪz/.

**leat** /lit/, *n.* a conduit by which water is conducted on to a waterwheel. [ME, OE *gelǣt,* from *lǣtan* LET[1]]

**leather** /ˈlɛðə/, *n.* **1.** the skin of animals prepared for use by tanning or a similar process. **2.** some article or appliance made of this material. *–v.t.* **3.** to cover or furnish with leather. **4.** *Colloq.* to beat with a leather strap. [ME *lether,* OE *lether* (in compounds), c. D *leder* and G *Leder,* Icel. *ledhr*]

**leatherback** /ˈlɛðəbæk/, *n.* a large marine turtle, *Dermochelys coriacea,* with a longitudinally ridged flexible carapace formed of a mosaic of small bony plates embedded in a leathery skin; luth. Also, **leathery turtle.**

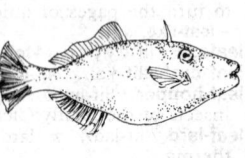

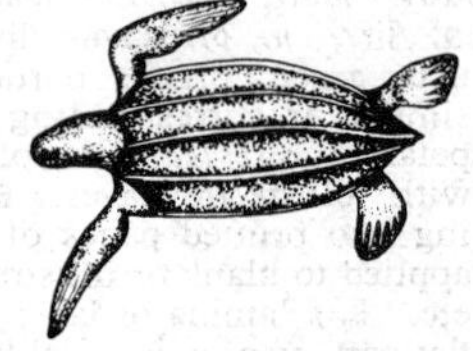

leatherback

**leatherette** /lɛðəˈrɛt/, *n.* a substitute for leather, used in making bags, suitcases, etc., consisting mostly of vegetable fibre, as paper stock, variously treated. Also, **leatheroid.**

**leatherhead** /ˈlɛðəhɛd/, *n.* →**noisy friar-bird.**

**leatherjacket** /ˈlɛðədʒækət/, *n.* **1.** any of numerous species of fish, esp. of the family Aleuteridae, having a roughened skin which can be removed in one piece like a jacket, and a prominent, erectable dorsal spine; triggerfish. **2.** a mixture of flour and water, fried and cooked on red-hot embers.

leatherjacket (def. 1)

**leathern** /ˈlɛðən/, *adj. Archaic.* **1.** made of leather. **2.** resembling leather. [ME and OE *lether(e)n.* See -EN[2]]

**leatherneck** /ˈlɛðənɛk/, *n. Colloq.* **1.** *U.S.* →**marine** (def. 3). **2.** a handyman on a station; rouseabout.

**leatherwood** /ˈlɛðəwʊd/, *n.* **1.** an Australian tree, *Eucryphia lucida,* which is a valuable honey tree. **2.** any of certain other trees with tough bark as *Acradenia franklinii* of Tasmania and *Dirca palustris* of America.

**leatherwork** /ˈlɛðəwɜk/, *n.* hand-made leather goods.

**leathery** /ˈlɛðəri/, *adj.* like leather; tough and flexible.

**leathery turtle** /– ˈtɜtl/, *n.* →**leatherback.**

**leave**[1] /liv/, *v.,* **left, leaving.** *–v.t.* **1.** to go away from, depart from, or quit, as a place, a person, or a thing. **2.** to let stay or be as specified: *to leave a door unlocked.* **3.** to desist from, stop, or abandon (fol. by *off*). **4.** to let (a person, etc.) remain in a position to do something without interference: *leave him alone.* **5.** to let (a thing) remain for action or decision. **6.** to omit or exclude (fol. by *out*). **7.** to allow to remain in the same place, condition, etc. **8.** to let remain, or have remaining behind, after going, disappearing, ceasing, etc.: *the wound left a scar.* **9.** to have remaining after death: *he leaves a widow.* **10.** to give in charge; give for use after one's death or departure. **11.** to have as a remainder after subtraction: *2 from 4 leaves 2.* **12.** *Cricket.* (of the ball) to move away from (the batsman) towards the off, as a leg break or outswinger. **13. leave (someone) be,** to cease interfering or taking an active interest in someone's affairs. **14. leave (someone) cold,** to make little or no impression. **15. leave (someone) for dead,** to outclass or outstrip (someone) in a competition. **16. leave it at that,** to go no further; do or say nothing more. **17. leave off, a.** not to put on (an item of clothing): *he left off his hat.* **b.** to exclude from: *they left her name off the list.* **c.** *Colloq.* to cease doing (something) *leave off crying now.* **18. leave (someone) to it,** to leave (someone) alone to get on with something. *–v.i.* **19.** to go away, depart, or set out: *we leave for Tasmania tomorrow.* **20. leave be,** to cease to remonstrate; to allow a situation to take its own course. [ME *leve(n)*, OE *lǣfan* (from *lāf* remainder), c. OHG *leiban,* Icel. *leifa,* Goth. *-laibjan*] – **leaver,** *n.*

**leave**[2] /liv/, *n.* **1.** permission to do something. **2.** permission to be absent, as from duty: *to be on leave.* **3.** the time this permission lasts: *30 days' leave.* **4.** a farewell: *to take leave of someone.* [ME *leve,* OE *lēaf.* Cf. D *(oor)lof,* G *(Ur)laub,* *(Ver)laub* FURLOUGH]

**leave**[3] /liv/, *v.i.,* **leaved, leaving.** to put forth leaves; leaf. [var. of LEAF, *v.i.*]

**leaved** /livd/, *adj.* having leaves; leafed.

**leaven** /ˈlɛvən/, *n.* **1.** a mass of fermenting dough reserved for producing fermentation in a new batch of dough. **2.** any substance which produces fermentation. **3.** an agency which works in a thing to produce a gradual change or modification. *–v.t.* **4.** to produce bubbles of gas in (dough or batter) by means of any of a variety of leavening agents. **5.** to permeate with an altering or transforming influence. [ME *levain,* from OF, from L *levāmen* that which raises] – **leavening,** *n.*

**leave of absence,** *n.* permission to be absent.

**leaves** /livz/, *n.* plural of **leaf.**

**leave-taking** /ˈliv-teɪkɪŋ/, *n.* the saying of farewell.

**leaving** /ˈlivɪŋ/, *n.* **1.** that which is left; residue. **2.** (*pl.*) remains; refuse.

**Lebanese** /lɛbəˈniz/, *adj.* **1.** of or pertaining to Lebanon. *–n.* **2.** a native of Lebanon.

**Lebanon** /ˈlɛbənɒn/, *n.* a republic at the eastern end of the Mediterranean, north of Israel.

**lebensraum** /ˈleɪbənzraʊm/, *n.* additional territory desired by a nation for expansion of trade, etc. [G: room for living]

**Leboyer** /ləˈbɔɪə/, *adj.* denoting a practice which aims to ease the trauma of childbirth for a baby, by providing a quiet, softly-lit atmosphere, and immediate physical contact with the parents. [named after Frédérick *Leboyer,* b. 1918, French doctor who initiated this practice]

**Le Châtelier's principle** /lə ʃəˈtɛljəz prɪnsəpəl/, *n.* the principle which states that if a system is in equilibrium a change in one of the conditions will shift the equilibrium so that the system tends to return to its original condition. [named after H. L. *Le Châtelier,* 1850-1936, French chemist]

**lecher** /ˈlɛtʃə/, *n.* a man immoderately given to sexual indulgence; a lewd man. [ME *lechur,* from OF *lecheor* gourmand, sensualist, from *lechier* lick, live in sensuality, from Gmc; cf. LICK]

**lecherous** /ˈlɛtʃərəs/, *adj.* **1.** given to or characterised by lechery. **2.** inciting to lechery. – **lecherously,** *adv.* – **lecherousness,** *n.*

**lecher wires** /ˈlɛkə waɪəz/, *n. pl.* parallel wires of such length and terminations that the system will resonate (i.e., standing waves will appear) if the frequency of the excitation is correct. [named after Ernst *Lecher,* b. 1926, Austrian physicist]

**lechery** /ˈlɛtʃəri/, *n.* free indulgence of lust.

**lecithin** /ˈlɛsəθən/, *n.* →**phosphatidyl choline.** [Gk *lékithos* egg yolk + -IN[2]]

**Leclanché cell** /ləˈklɒnʃeɪ sɛl/, *n.* a primary cell with a carbon cathode surrounded by manganese dioxide in a porous pot, and a zinc anode dipping into a solution of ammonium chloride, which produces 1.5 volts. [named after Georges *Leclanché,* d. 1882, French chemist]

**lect.,** **1.** lecture. **2.** lecturer.

**lectern** /ˈlɛktən/, *n.* a reading desk in a church, esp. that from which the lessons are read. [earlier *lecturn,* Latinised and metathetic var. of ME *lettrun,* from OF, from ML *lectrum,* from L *legere* read]

**lection** /ˈlɛkʃən/, *n.* **1.** a reading or version of a passage in a particular copy of a text. **2.** a lesson, or portion of sacred writing, read in divine service. [ME, from L *lectio* a reading]

**lectionary** /ˈlɛkʃənəri/, *n., pl.* **-ries.** a book, or a list, of lections for reading in divine service.

**lector** /ˈlɛktɔ/, *n.* a reader, as of lectures in a college or university or of scriptural lessons. [late ME, from L]

**lecture** /ˈlɛktʃə/, *n., v.,* **-tured, -turing.** *–n.* **1.** a discourse read or delivered before an audience, esp. for instruction or to set forth some subject: *a lecture on Picasso.* **2.** a speech of warning or reproof as to conduct; a long, tedious reprimand. *–v.i.* **3.** to give a lecture. *–v.t.* **4.** to deliver a lecture to or before; instruct by lectures. **5.** to rebuke or reprimand at some length. [ME, from LL *lectura,* from L *legere* read]

**lecturer** /ˈlɛktʃərə/, *n.* **1.** one who lectures. **2.** a regular member of the teaching staff of a college or university, employed to deliver lectures.

**lectureship** /ˈlɛktʃəʃɪp/, *n.* the office of lecturer.

**lecture theatre** /ˈlɛktʃə θɪətə/, *n.* a theatre specially designed to be used for lectures.

**lecture tour** /ˈ– tʊə/, *n.* an organised visit to several different places for the purpose of giving lectures, usu. by invitation.

**led** /lɛd/, *v.* past tense and past participle of **lead**[1].

**LED** /lɛd/, *n.* light-emitting diode.

**lederhosen** /ˈleɪdəhoʊzən/, *n.pl.* shorts of leather with thick, distinctive H-shaped braces, worn by men in German-speaking regions, as Bavaria, the Tyrol, etc. [G: leather trousers]

**ledge** /lɛdʒ/, *n.* **1.** any relatively narrow, horizontal projecting part, or any part affording a horizontal shelf-like surface. **2.** a more or less flat shelf of rock protruding from a cliff or slope. **3.** a reef, ridge, or line of rocks in the sea or other water bodies. **4.** *Mining.* a lode or vein. **5.** the horizontal part of a fence, rail, gate, etc. [ME *legge* transverse bar, OE *lecg* (exact meaning not clear), from *lecgan* LAY[1]] – **ledged,** *adj.*

**ledger** /ˈlɛdʒə/, *n.* **1.** *Bookkeeping.* an account book of final entry, containing all the accounts. **2.** a horizontal timber fastened to the vertical uprights of a scaffold, to support the putlogs. **3.** a flat slab of stone laid over a grave or tomb. [ME *legger* (book), from *leggen* LAY[1] (see LEDGE)]

**ledger-baiting** /ˈlɛdʒə-beɪtɪŋ/, *n.* →**ledgering.**

**ledger board** /ˈlɛdʒə bɔd/, *n.* the horizontal part of a fence, rail, etc.

**ledgering** /ˈlɛdʒərɪŋ/, *n.* any of several fishing methods in which the tackle lies on the bottom so that the fish does not feel the weight of lead when it bites. Also, **legering.**

**ledger line** /ˈlɛdʒə laɪn/, *n.* →**leger line.**

**ledger tackle** /ˈ– tækəl/, *n.* fishing apparatus set up so that the lead lies on the bottom. Also, **leger tackle.**

L, leger line

**lee**[1] /li/, *n.* **1.** →**shelter** (def. 2). **2.** the side or part that is sheltered or turned away from the wind. **3.** *Chiefly Naut.* the quarter or region towards which the wind blows. *–adj.* **4.** *Chiefly Naut.* pertaining to, situated in, or moving towards the quarter or region towards which the wind blows (opposed to *weather*). [ME; OE *hlēo* shelter]

**lee**[2] /li/, *n.* (*usu. pl.*) that which settles from a liquid, esp. from wine; sediment; dregs. [ME *lie,* from OF, from LL *lia,* of Gallic orig.]

**leeboard** /ˈlibɔd/, *n.* a flat board let down vertically into the water on the leeside of a ship or boat to prevent leeward motion.

sailing vessel with leeboard

**leech**[1] /litʃ/, *n.* **1.** any of the bloodsucking or carnivorous, usu. aquatic, worms constituting the class Hirudinea, certain freshwater species of which were formerly much used by physicians for blood-letting. **2.** an instrument used for drawing blood. **3.** a person who clings to another with a view to gain. **4.** *Archaic.* a physician. *–v.t.* **5.** to apply leeches to so as to bleed. **6.** *Archaic.* to cure; heal. [ME *leche,* OE *lǣce* (by confusion with *lǣce* physician); replacing ME *liche,* OE *lȳce,* from *lūcan* draw out, burst out] – **leechlike,** *adj.*

**leech**[2] /litʃ/, *n. Naut.* **1.** either of the perpendicular or sloping edges of a square sail. **2.** the after edge of a fore-and-aft sail. [ME *lek, leche,* apparently c. G *Liek* bolt rope, leech rope; akin to Icel. *līk* leech line]

**leek** /lik/, *n.* **1.** a plant of the lily family, *Allium porrum,* allied to the onion but having a cylindrical bulb, and used in cookery. **2.** any of various allied species. **3.** the national emblem of Wales. [ME; OE *lēac,* c. G *Lauch*]

**leek orchid** /ˈ– ɔkəd/, *n.* any species of the terrestrial orchid genus *Prasophyllum,* of Australia and New Zealand, comprising herbs with one leaf and usu. numerous, small, reversed flowers.

**leer**[1] /lɪə/, *n.* **1.** a side glance, esp. of sly or insulting suggestion or significance. *–v.i.* **2.** to look with a leer. [special use of obs. *leer* cheek, OE *hlēor*] – **leeringly,** *adv.*

**leer**[2] /lɪə/, *n.* →**lehr.**

**leery**[1] /ˈlɪəri/, *adj. Colloq.* **1.** doubtful; suspicious. **2.** knowing; sly. **3. leery of the brush,** *Colloq.* (of a man) nervous about getting married. [? obs. sense of LEER[1]]

**leery**[2] /ˈlɪəri/, *adj. Colloq.* →**lairy.**

**lees** /liz/, *n.* plural of **lee**[2].

**lee shore** /ˈli ʃɔ/, *n.* a shore towards which the wind blows.

**leeside** /ˈlisaɪd/, *n.* the side of any object which is turned away from the wind.

**leet** /lit/, *n. Obs.* **1.** a special type of manorial court or its jurisdiction. **2.** the jurisdiction of such a court, and the area over which this extended. Also, **court leet.** [ME *lete,* from AF, ? from OE *lǣth* landed property]

**lee tide** /ˈli taɪd/, *n.* a tidal current running in the direction towards which the wind is blowing. Also, **leeward tide.**

**leeway** /ˈliweɪ/, *n.* **1.** the lateral movement of a ship to leeward, or the resulting deviation from her true course. **2.** *Aeron.* the amount an aeroplane is blown off its normal course by cross-winds. **3.** *Naut.* the distance a ship is forced sideways from her course by the wind. **4.** *Colloq.* extra space, time, money, etc.

**leeward** /ˈliwəd/; *Naut.* /ˈluəd/, *adj.* **1.** pertaining to, situated in, or moving towards the quarter towards which the wind blows (opposed to *windward*). *–n.* **2.** the leeside; the point or quarter towards which the wind blows. *–adv.* **3.** towards the lee.

**left**[1] /lɛft/, *adj.* **1.** belonging or pertaining to the side of a person or thing which is turned towards the west when facing north (opposed to *right*). **2.** belonging or pertaining to the political left. **3. have two left feet,** *Colloq.* to be clumsy. *–n.* **4.** the left side, or what is on the left side. **5.** (in continental Europe) that part of a legislative assembly which sits on the left side of the chamber as viewed by the president, a position customarily assigned to representatives holding socialist or radical views. **6.** (*oft. cap.*) a party or group holding such views. **7.** a punch with the left hand, as in boxing. [ME; special use of d. OE *left* (OE *lyft*) weak, infirm. Cf. MD and MLG *lucht*]

**left**[2] /lɛft/, *v.* past tense and past participle of **leave**[1].

**left back** /– ˈbæk/, *n.* (in soccer, hockey, etc.) the full-back on the left side of the field of play.

**left-branching** /ˈlɛft-bræntʃɪŋ/, *adj.* (of a grammatical construction) having most of its constituents on the left of its node on a tree diagram (def. 2).

**left foot** /lɛft ˈfʊt/, *v.t.* **1.** (in football) to kick (the ball) with the left foot. *–n.* **2. kick with the left foot,** *Colloq.* to be a Roman Catholic.

**left-footer** /lɛft-ˈfʊtə/, *n. Colloq.* a Roman Catholic. – **left-footed,** *adj.*

**left half** /lɛft ˈhaf/, *n.* (in soccer, hockey, etc.) the left of the three players in the half-back line.

**left-hand** /ˈlɛft-hænd/, *adj.* **1.** on or to the left: *left-hand drive.* **2.** of, for, or with the left hand.

**left-hand drive** /– ˈdraɪv/, *n.* **1.** a system where the steering wheel and other controls are fitted on the left side of a motor car. **2.** a vehicle with a left-hand drive steering system.

**left-handed** /ˈlɛft-hændəd/, *adj.* **1.** having the left hand more serviceable than the right; preferring to use the left hand. **2.** adapted to or performed by the left hand. **3.** situated on the side of the left hand. **4.** moving or rotating from right to left. **5.** ambiguous or doubtful: *a left-handed compliment.* **6.** clumsy or awkward. **7.** morganatic (from the bridegroom's giving the bride his left hand instead of his right as was customary at morganatic weddings). – **left-handedly,** *adv.* – **left-handedness,** *n.*

**leftie** /ˈlɛfti/, *n. Colloq.* **1.** a left-handed person. **2.** →**leftist.** Also, **lefty.**

**left inner** /lɛft ˈɪnə/, *n. Hockey.* →**inside left.**

**leftist** /ˈlɛftəst/, *n.* **1.** a member of a socialist or radical party or a person sympathising with their views. *–adj.* **2.** having socialist or radical political ideas. [LEFT[1] (def. 5) + -IST]

**leftover** /ˈlɛftoʊvə/, *n.* **1.** something left over or remaining. **2.** a remnant of food, as from a meal.

**leftward** /ˈlɛftwəd/, *adj.* **1.** situated on the left. **2.** directed towards the left. *–adv.* **3.** leftwards.

**leftwards** /ˈlɛftwədz/, *adv.* towards or on the left. Also, **leftward.**

**left wing** /lɛft ˈwɪŋ/, *n.* **1.** members of a socialist, progressive, or radical political party or section of a party, generally those favouring extensive political reform. **2.** such a group, party, or a group of such parties. **3.** *Sport.* that part of the field of play which forms the left flank of the area being attacked by either team. **4.** *Sport.* a player positioned on the left flank, as the outside left in soccer, the left or the wing three-quarters in Rugby football, etc. – **left-wing,** *adj.* – **left-winger,** *n.*

**leg** /lɛg/, *n., v.,* **legged, legging,** *adj.* *–n.* **1.** one of the members or limbs which support and move the human or animal body. **2.** this part of an animal, esp. lamb or veal, used as meat to roast, bake, etc. **3.** that part of the limb between the knee and the ankle. **4.** something resembling or suggesting a leg in use, position, or appearance. **5.** that part of a garment, such as a stocking, trousers, or the like, which covers the leg. **6.** one of the supports of a piece of furniture. **7.** one of the sides of a pair of dividers or compasses. **8.** one of the sides of a triangle other than the base or hypotenuse. **9.** a timber, bar, etc., serving to prop or shore up a structure. **10.** one of the distinct portions of any course: *the last leg of a trip.* **11.** *Naut.* **a.** one of the series of straight runs which make up the zigzag course of a sailing ship. **b.** one straight or nearly straight part of a multiple-sided course in a sailing race. **12.** *Sport.* **a.** one of a number of parts of a contest, each of which must be completed in order to determine the winner. **b.** a stage or given distance in a relay race. **13.** *Cricket.* the leg side. **14. a leg up,** assistance in climbing or mounting; any assistance. **15. have not a leg to stand on,** not to have any good reason at all. **16. pull (someone's) leg,** to make fun of; to tease. **17. shake a leg,** *Colloq.* to hurry up. **18. show a leg,** to make an appearance. *–v.t.* **19.** *Obs.* to propel (a boat) through a canal tunnel by means of pressing two feet against the top and sides of the tunnel. *–v.t.* **20. leg it,** *Colloq.* to walk or run. *–adj.* **21.** *Cricket.* of or pertaining to the leg side: *leg slip; leg stump.* [ME, from Scand.; cf. Icel. *leggr*] – **legless,** *adj.*

**leg.,** **1.** legal. **2.** legate. **3.** legato. **4.** legislative. **5.** legislature.

**legacy** /ˈlɛgəsi/, *n., pl.* **-cies.** **1.** *Law.* a gift of property, esp. personal property, as money, by will; a bequest. **2.** anything handed down by an ancestor or predecessor. **3.** a consequence: *this is a legacy of the war in Vietnam.* [ME *legacie,* from OF: legateship, from ML *lēgātia,* from L *lēgātus* LEGATE]

**legal** /'ligəl/, *adj.* **1.** appointed, established, or authorised by law; deriving authority from law. **2.** of or pertaining to law: connected with the law or its administration: *the legal profession.* **3.** permitted by law, or lawful: *such acts are not legal.* **4.** recognised by law rather than by equity. **5.** characteristic of the profession of the law: *a legal mind.* **6.** *Theol.* **a.** of or pertaining to the Mosaic Law. **b.** of or pertaining to the doctrine of salvation by good works rather than through free grace. [L *lēgālis* pertaining to law] – **legally,** *adv.*

**legal aid** /– 'eɪd/, *n.* financial assistance given to persons according to a scale based on income and capital for the purpose of legal proceedings in practically all courts.

**legal centre** /'– sɛntə/, *n.* a centre which makes available legal advice and assistance to those who are unable or unwilling to seek them from traditional legal sources as solicitors, chamber magistrates, etc.

**legal eagle** /'– igəl/, *n. Colloq.* a lawyer.

**legalese** /'ligəliz/, *n.* (*sometimes pejor.*) the specialist and often obscure language in which legal documents are expressed; legal language.

**legal fiction** /ligəl 'fɪkʃən/, *n.* See **fiction** (def. 4).

**legalise** /'ligəlaɪz/, *v.t.,* **-lised, -lising.** to make legal; authorise; sanction. Also, **legalize.** – **legalisation** /ligəlaɪ'zeɪʃən/, *n.*

**legalism** /'ligəlɪzəm/, *n.* **1.** strict adherence, or the principle of strict adherence, to law or formulated rules. **2.** *Theol.* the doctrine of salvation by good works. – **legalist,** *n.* – **legalistic** /ligə'lɪstɪk/, *adj.*

**legality** /lə'gæləti, li-/, *n., pl.* **-ties. 1.** the state or quality of being in conformity with the law; lawfulness. **2.** attachment to or observance of law. **3.** *Theol.* reliance on good works for salvation, rather than on free grace.

**legal separation** /ligəl sɛpə'reɪʃən/, *n.* judicial separation.

**legal tender** /– 'tɛndə/, *n.* currency which may be lawfully tendered or offered in payment of money debts and which may not be refused by creditors.

**legate** /'lɛgət/, *n.* **1.** an ecclesiastic delegated by the pope as his representative. **2.** *Rom. Hist.* **a.** an assistant to a general or to a consul or magistrate, in the government of any army or a province; a commander of a legion. **b.** a provincial governor of senatorial rank appointed by the emperor. **3.** →**envoy**[1]. [ME *legat,* from L *lēgātus* deputy, properly pp. of *lēgāre* depute, delegate] – **legateship,** *n.* – **legatine,** *adj.*

**legatee** /lɛgə'ti/, *n.* one to whom a legacy is bequeathed.

**legation** /lə'geɪʃən/, *n.* **1.** a diplomatic minister and his staff when the minister is not of the highest (or ambassadorial) rank. **2.** the official residence or place of business of a minister. **3.** the office or position of a legate. [late ME, from L *lēgātio* embassy] – **legationary,** *adj.*

**legato** /lə'gatoʊ/, *adv.* **1.** (usu. a musical direction) in a smooth, even style, without breaks between the successive notes. *–adj.* **2.** (of music, dance, etc.) performed legato. Cf. **staccato.** [It., pp. of *legare,* from L *ligāre* bind]

**legator** /lɛgə'tɔ/, *n.* one who bequeaths; a testator. – **legatorial,** *adj.*

**leg before wicket,** *n.* (in cricket) the act of stopping with the leg or some other part of the body, a pitched ball which would otherwise have hit the wicket, for which a batsman may be declared out. *Abbrev.:* l.b.w.

**leg break** /'lɛg breɪk/, *n.* (in cricket) a ball bowled so as to change direction from leg to off when it pitches.

**leg bye** /'– baɪ/, *n.* (in cricket) a run scored after the ball has struck part of the batsman's body other than his hand. *Abbrev.:* l.b.

**legend** /'lɛdʒənd/, *n.* **1.** a non-historical or unverifiable story handed down by tradition from earlier times and popularly accepted as historical. **2.** matter of this kind. **3.** an inscription, esp. on a coin, a coat of arms, a monument, or under a picture, or the like. **4.** explanatory matter in a table or the like forming part of an illustration. **5.** a story of the life of a saint. **6.** a collection of stories of any admirable person. **7.** Also, **legende.** a vocal or instrumental composition depicting a short legend or event from a legend; loosely used for short romantic compositions. [ME *legende,* from OF, from ML *legenda,* lit., things to be read, orig. neut. pl. gerundive of L *legere* read]

**legendary** /'lɛdʒəndəri, -dri/, *adj., n., pl.* **-ries.** *–adj.* **1.** pertaining to or of the nature of a legend or legends. **2.** celebrated or described in legend. *–n.* **3.** a collection of legends.

**legendry** /'lɛdʒəndri/, *n.* legends collectively.

**leger** /'lɛdʒə/, *n.* an area or a stand in a racecourse some distance away from the winning post. Also, **leger enclosure.** [from the St *Leger,* an annual horserace first run in 1776 at Doncaster, England]

**legerdemain** /lɛdʒədə'meɪn/, *n.* **1.** sleight of hand. **2.** trickery; deception. **3.** any artful trick. [ME, from F *léger de main* light(ness) of hand]

**legering** /'lɛdʒərɪŋ/, *n.* →**ledgering.**

**leger line** /'lɛdʒə laɪn/, *n.* **1.** *Music.* a short line added when necessary above or below the lines of a stave to increase the range of the stave. **2.** *Angling.* a line used in ledgering. Also, **ledger line.** [LEDGER (special use) + LINE[1]]

**leger tackle** /'– tækəl/, *n.* →**ledger tackle.**

**leges** /'leɪdʒeɪz/, *n.* plural of **lex.**

**legged** /'lɛgəd, lɛgd/, *adj.* having a specified number or kind of legs: *one-legged, long-legged.*

**leggie** /'lɛgi/, *n. Cricket. Colloq.* **1.** →**leg break. 2.** →**leg spinner.**

**leggiero** /lə'dʒɛəroʊ/, *adv.* (a musical direction) lightly. [It.]

**legging** /'lɛgɪŋ/, *n.* (*usu. pl.*) an extra outer covering for the leg, usu. extending from the ankle to the knee, but sometimes higher.

**leg glance** /'lɛg glæns/, *n.* (in cricket) a glancing stroke by the batsman directing the ball down fine on the leg side of the wicket.

**leggy** /'lɛgi/, *adj.* having long legs.

**leghorn** /'lɛghɔn/, *for defs 1 and 2;* /lɛ'gɔn/, *for def. 3, n.* **1.** a fine, smooth, plaited straw. **2.** a hat, etc., made of this. **3.** one of a Mediterranean breed of the domestic fowl, characterised by prolific laying of white-shelled eggs.

**legible** /'lɛdʒəbəl/, *adj.* **1.** that may be read or deciphered, esp. with ease, as writing or printing. **2.** that may be discerned or distinguished. [ME, from LL *legibilis,* from L *legere* read] – **legibility** /lɛdʒə'bɪləti/, **legibleness,** *n.* – **legibly,** *adv.*

**legion** /'lidʒən/, *n.* **1.** an infantry brigade in the army of ancient Rome, numbering from 3000 to 6000 men, and usu. combined with from 300 to 700 cavalry. **2.** one of certain military bodies of modern times, as the Foreign Legion. **3.** a military or semi-military unit. **4.** any large body of armed men. **5.** any great host or multitude, whether of persons or of things. *–adj.* **6.** containing or amounting to a great number. [ME, from OF, from L *legio*]

**legionary** /'lidʒənəri, 'lidʒənri/, *adj., n., pl.* **-ries.** *–adj.* **1.** pertaining or belonging to a legion. **2.** constituting a legion or legions. *–n.* **3.** *Hist.* a soldier of a legion.

**legionnaire** /lidʒə'nɛə/, *n.* a member of a legion, esp. the French Foreign Legion. [F]

**legionnaire's disease** /lidʒə'nɛəz dəziz/, *n.* a disease, thought to be a form of pneumonia, caused by a ground-occurring organism which sometimes circulates in air-conditioning systems. [so named because the organism was first isolated, in 1978, after a group of U.S. ex-servicemen contracted the disease at a conference]

**Legis.,** Legislature.

**legislate** /'lɛdʒəsleɪt/, *v.,* **-lated, -lating.** *–v.i.* **1.** to exercise the function of legislation; make or enact laws. *–v.t.* **2.** to effect, bring (*into*), put (*out*) etc., by legislation. [backformation from LEGISLATION or LEGISLATOR]

**legislation** /lɛdʒəs'leɪʃən/, *n.* **1.** the act of making or enacting laws. **2.** a law or a body of laws enacted. [LL *lēgislātio,* L *lēgis lātio* the proposing of a law]

**legislative** /'lɛdʒəslətɪv/, *adj.* **1.** having the function of making laws: *a legislative body.* **2.** of or pertaining to legislation: *legislative proceedings.* **3.** ordained by legislation: *a legislative penalty.* **4.** pertaining to a legislature: *a legislative recess.* *–n.* **5.** *Rare.* the legislature. – **legislatively,** *adv.*

**Legislative Assembly** /– ə'sɛmbli/, *n.* the lower chamber of certain bicameral parliaments.

**Legislative Council** /– 'kaʊnsəl/, *n.* the upper chamber of certain bicameral parliaments.

**legislator** /ˈlɛdʒəsleɪtə/, *n.* **1.** one who gives or makes laws. **2.** a member of a legislative body. [L *legis lātor* bringer of a law] – **legislatress,** *n. fem.*

**legislatorial** /lɛdʒəsləˈtɔriəl/, *adj.* of or pertaining to legislators or legislations.

**legislature** /ˈlɛdʒəsleɪtʃə, -lətʃə/, *n.* the legislative body of a country or state.

**legist** /ˈlidʒəst/, *n.* one versed in law.

**legit** /ləˈdʒɪt/, *adj. Colloq.* legitimate, truthful.

**legitimacy** /ləˈdʒɪtəməsi/, *n.* the state or fact of being legitimate.

**legitimate** /ləˈdʒɪtəmət/, *adj.;* /ləˈdʒɪtəmeɪt/, *v.,* **-mated, -mating;** /ləˈdʒɪtəmət/, *n.* –*adj.* **1.** according to law; lawful. **2.** in accordance with established rules, principles, or standards. **3.** of the normal or regular type or kind. **4.** in accordance with the laws of reasoning; logically inferable; logical: *a legitimate conclusion.* **5.** born in wedlock, or of parents legally married. **6.** resting on or ruling by the principle of hereditary right: *a legitimate sovereign.* **7.** genuine; not spurious. **8.** *Theat.* pertaining to or denoting plays or acting with a serious and literary purpose. –*v.t.* **9.** to make or pronounce lawful. **10.** to establish as lawfully born. **11.** to show or declare to be legitimate or proper. **12.** to authorise; justify. –*n.* **13.** (formerly) a convict. [late ME, from ML *lēgitimātus,* pp. of *lēgitimāre* make lawful, from L *lēgitimus* lawful] – **legitimately,** *adv.* – **legitimateness,** *n.* – **legitimation** /lədʒɪtəˈmeɪʃən/, *n.*

**legitimatise** /ləˈdʒɪtəmətaɪz/, *v.t.,* **-tised, -tising.** →**legitimate.** Also, **legitimatize.**

**legitimise** /ləˈdʒɪtəmaɪz/, *v.t.,* **-mised, -mising.** →**legitimate.** Also, **legitimize.** – **legitimisation** /lədʒɪtəmaɪˈzeɪʃən/, *n.*

**legitimist** /ləˈdʒɪtəməst/, *n.* a supporter of legitimate authority, esp. of a claim to a throne based on direct descent. – **legitimism,** *n.* – **legitimistic** /lədʒɪtəˈmɪstɪk/, *adj.*

**legless lizard** /lɛgləs ˈlɪzəd/, *n.* any of a number of species of the Australasian family, Pygopodidae, snake-like in appearance and having only rudimentary limbs. Also, **snake lizard.**

**leg-of-mutton** /lɛg-ə-ˈmʌtn/, *adj.* **1.** having the triangular shape of a leg of mutton, as a sail, etc. **2.** (of a sleeve) very full at the shoulder then narrowing so as to be closely fitting at the wrist.

leg-of-mutton sleeves

**leg opener** /ˈlɛg oʊpənə/, *n. Colloq.* an alcoholic drink calculated to facilitate the seduction of a woman.

**leg-pull** /ˈlɛg-pʊl/, *n.* **1.** a minor act of deceit; a hoax. **2.** a teasing. – **leg-puller,** *n.*

**leg room** /ˈlɛg rum/, *n.* **1.** space in which to accommodate one's legs: *there was very little leg room in the back of the car.* **2.** freedom to operate as one pleases.

**leg rope** /ˈ– roʊp/, *n.* **1.** a rope used for securing an animal, as a cow in the bails, by tying up a back leg. **2.** a rope used by surfers to tie themselves by the leg to the surfboard.

**leg-rope** /ˈlɛg-roʊp/, *v.,* **-roped, -roping,** *n.* –*v.t.* **1.** to catch and rope (an animal) by the hind leg, esp. a cow in a bail. **2.** *Colloq.* to delay; halt: *measures designed to leg-rope inflation.* –*n.* **3.** the rope used in leg-roping.

**leg side** /ˈlɛg saɪd/, *n.* (in cricket) that half of the field which is behind the batsman as he stands ready to receive the bowling; opposed to **off side.**

**leg-side** /ˈlɛg-saɪd/, *adj.* (in cricket) of or pertaining to the leg side. Also, **legside.**

**leg slip** /ˈlɛg slɪp/, *n.* **1.** (in cricket) the position of a fielder who stands close behind and to the leg side of the batsman. **2.** a fielder in this position.

**leg spin** /ˈ– spɪn/, *n.* (in cricket) the spin which a bowler imparts to a ball to achieve a leg break.

**leg spinner** /ˈ– spɪnə/, *n. Cricket.* **1.** →**leg break.** **2.** a bowler who specialises in such deliveries.

**leg stump** /ˈ– stʌmp/, *n.* (in cricket) the stump on the leg side.

**legume** /ˈlɛgjum/, *n.* **1.** any plant of the family Leguminosae, (including the Papilionaceae, Caesalpiniaceae and Mimosaceae), esp. those used for feed, food, or soil-improving crop. **2.** the pod or seed vessel of such a plant, which is usually dehiscent by both sutures, thus dividing into two parts or valves. **3.** any table vegetable of the family Leguminosae. [F, from L *legūmen* legume, pulse, lit., something gathered (or picked)]

**legumin** /ˈlɛgjumən/, *n.* a protein resembling casein, obtained from the seeds of leguminous and other plants. [LEGUME + -IN[2]]

**leguminous** /ləˈgjumənəs/, *adj.* pertaining to, of the nature of, or bearing legumes. [L *legūmen* LEGUME + -OUS]

**leg-up** /ˈlɛg-ʌp/, *n.* assistance in climbing or mounting something, as a wall or a horse, given by joining one's hands to provide a step for the person climbing.

**legwork** /ˈlɛgwɜk/, *n.* work involving travel, esp. on foot, as running errands, seeking out information in different places, etc.

**lehr** /lɪə/, *n.* a long tunnel-shaped oven for annealing glass. Also, **leer, lier, lear.** [G: pattern]

**lei** /leɪ/, *n., pl.* **leis.** (in the Hawaiian Islands) a wreath of flowers, leaves, etc., for the neck or head. [Hawaiian]

leis

**Leicester** /ˈlɛstə/, *n.* **1.** one of an English variety of large early-maturing sheep with coarse, long wool and a heavy mutton yield. **2.** a type of mild, whole-milk cheese, dark orange in colour and similar to cheddar. [from *Leicester,* a town in England]

**Leichhardt bean** /ˈlaɪkat bin/, *n.* a Queensland cassia, *Cassia brewsteri,* the seed-pods of which act as a purgative when eaten; Queensland bean. [named after the German-born Australian explorer F.W.L. *Leichhardt,* 1813-48, who recorded eating them]

**Leichhardt tree** /ˈ– tri/, *n.* a large handsome tree of northern Australia, *Sarcocephalus coadunatus,* with large glossy leaves and dense clusters of yellow flowers.

**leilira** /laɪˈlɪərə/, *n.* a multipurpose stone knife with a resin hand grip or a resin-hafted wooden handle.

leilira

**leiomyoma** /ˌlaɪoʊmaɪˈoʊmə/, *n., pl.* **-omata** /-ˈoʊmətə/, **-omas.** a tumour made up of non-striated muscular tissue. Cf. **rhabdomyoma.** [*leio-* (from Gk, combining form of *leîos* smooth) + MYOMA]

**leister** /ˈlistə/, *n.* **1.** a spear having three or more prongs, used to spear fish, esp. salmon. –*v.t.* **2.** to strike (a fish) with a leister. [Scand.; cf. Icel. *ljōstr,* from *ljōsta* strike]

**leisure** /ˈlɛʒə/, *n.* **1.** the condition of having one's time free from the demands of work or duty; ease: *enjoying a life of leisure.* **2.** free or unoccupied time. **3. at leisure, a.** with free or unrestricted time. **b.** without haste. **4. at one's leisure,** when one has leisure. **5. lady of leisure,** a woman who has no regular employment, esp. a married woman. –*adj.* **6.** free or unoccupied: *leisure hours.* **7.** having leisure. [ME *leiser,* from OF *leisir* (inf.), from L *licēre* be permitted]

**leisure centre** /ˈ– sɛntə/, *n.* →**creative leisure centre.**

**leisured** /ˈlɛʒəd/, *adj.* **1.** having leisure: *the leisured classes.* **2.** leisurely.

**leisurely** /ˈlɛʒəli/, *adj.* **1.** acting, proceeding, or done without haste; deliberate: *a leisurely stroll.* **2.** showing or suggesting ample leisure; unhurried: *a leisurely manner.* –*adv.* **3.** in a leisurely manner; without haste. – **leisureliness,** *n.*

**leitmotiv** /ˈlaɪtmoʊˌtif/, *n.* (in a music drama) a theme associated throughout the work with a particular person, situation, or idea. Also, **leitmotif.** [G *Leitmotiv* leading motive]

**leman** /ˈlimən/, *n. Archaic.* **1.** a sweetheart. **2.** a mistress. [ME *lemman,* earlier *leofmon,* from *leof* dear (see LIEF) + *mon* MAN]

**Le Mans start** /lə mɒnz ˈstat/, *n.* a method of starting a race in which the drivers run to their cars from the opposite side of the track and drive off from a standing start. [named after *Le Mans,* a racing circuit in France]

**lemma**[1] /ˈlɛmə/, *n., pl.* **lemmas, lemmata** /ˈlɛmətə/. **1.** a subsidiary proposition introduced in proving some other proposition; a helping theorem. **2.** an argument, theme or subject. **3.** the heading of a gloss, annotation, etc. [L, from Gk *lêmma* premise]

**lemma**[2] /ˈlɛmə/, *n., pl.* **lemmas, lemmata** /ˈlɛmətə/. a bract in a grass spikelet just below the pistil and stamens. [Gk *lémma* shell, husk]

**lemmatise** /ˈlɛmətaɪz/, *v.t.,* **-tised, -tising.** *Linguistics.* **1.** to mark with a classificatory label, as headwords in a dictionary. **2.** to identify the underlying morphemic forms of words in (a corpus of language data).

**lemming** /ˈlɛmɪŋ/, *n.* any of various small, mouselike rodents of the genera *Lemmus, Myopus,* and *Dicrostonyx,* of far northern regions, as *L. lemmus,* of Norway, Sweden, and elsewhere, noted for its mass migrations in periods of population increase. [Norw.]

lemming

**lemniscate** /ˈlɛmnəskət/, *n.* a plane curve in the shape of the figure 8. [L *lemniscātus* having ribbons, from Gk *lemnískos* ribbon]

**lemniscus** /lɛmˈnɪskəs/, *n.* a secondary sensory pathway of the central nervous system which usu. crosses over and terminates in the thalamus. [NL, from L: ribbon]

**lemon** /ˈlɛmən/, *n.* **1.** the yellowish acid fruit of the tree *Citrus limon.* **2.** the tree itself. **3.** clear, light yellow colour. **4.** *Colloq.* something distasteful, disappointing, or unpleasant. **5.** *Colloq.* a foolish, sour, or ugly person. **6.** *Colloq. (pl.)* **a.** *Aus. Rules.* →**three-quarter time. b.** *Rugby, Soccer.* →**half-time.** *–adj.* **7.** having a lemon colour. **8.** consisting of, made or flavoured with lemons. [ME *lymon,* from OF *limon,* from Ar., Pers. *līmūn*]

**lemonade** /lɛməˈneɪd/, *n.* **1.** a carbonated soft drink made of lemons, sugar, etc. **2.** lemon squash. [F *limonade,* from *limon* LEMON]

**lemon balm** /ˈlɛmən bam/, *n.* →**balm** (def. 5).

**lemon cheese** /– ˈtʃiz/, *n.* a viscous mixture of lemon rind and juice, egg yolks, butter and sugar, thickened with flour; used mostly for cake, tart and pie fillings. Also, **lemon butter, lemon curd, lemon spread.**

**lemon geranium** /– dʒəˈreɪniəm/, *n.* a hybrid plant, *Pelargonium limoneum,* whose leaves give off a lemon fragrance.

**lemon grass** /ˈ– gras/, *n.* a tufted perennial grass, *Cymbopogon citratus,* cultivated in the tropics as the source of lemon grass oil.

**lemonhead** /ˈlɛmənhɛd/, *n. Colloq.* a surfie with bleached hair.

**lemon-scented gum** /lɛmən-sɛntəd ˈgʌm/, *n.* a tall slender tree, *Eucalyptus citriodora,* of Queensland, bearing foliage with a strong lemon perfume esp. when crushed.

**lemon sole** /lɛmən ˈsoʊl/, *n.* a fine food fish of northern European waters, *Pleuronectes microcephalus,* a flat sea fish which rarely grows more than 40 cm long.

**lemon squash** /– ˈskwɒʃ/, *n.* a soft drink made of crushed lemons sweetened and diluted with water.

**lemon squeezer** /ˈ– skwizə/, *n.* **1.** a kitchen juice-extractor comprising a serrated peak rising from a saucer-shaped base on which halved lemons, etc. may be squeezed down to extract the juice. **2.** *N.Z. Colloq.* the former brimmed and peaked infantry dress hat of similar shape.

**lemon verbena** /– vɜˈbinə/, *n.* a small garden shrub, *Aloysia triphylla,* with long, slender leaves that have a lemon-like fragrance.

**lemonwood** /ˈlɛmənwʊd/, *n.* the New Zealand tree *Pittosporum eugenioides* whose leaves when bruised have a lemon-like fragrance.

**lemony** /ˈlɛməni/, *adj. Colloq.* angry; irritable.

**Lempert operation** /ˈlɛmpət ɒpəˌreɪʃən/, *n.* →**fenestration.** [named after Julius *Lempert,* b. 1890, U.S. otologist who devised it]

**lemur** /ˈlimə/, *n.* any of various small, arboreal, chiefly nocturnal mammals, esp. of the genus *Lemur,* allied to the monkeys, usu. having a foxlike face and woolly fur, and found chiefly in Madagascar. [NL, from L *lemures,* pl., ghosts, spectres; so called because of nocturnal habits]

lemur

**lemuroid** /ˈlimərɔɪd/, *adj.* **1.** lemur-like; of the lemur kind. *–n.* **2.** →**lemur.**

**lend** /lɛnd/, *v.,* **lent, lending.** *–v.t.* **1.** to give the temporary use of (money, etc.) for a consideration. **2.** to grant the use of (something) with the understanding that it (or its equivalent in kind) shall be returned. **3.** to furnish or impart: *distance lends enchantment to the view.* **4.** to give or contribute obligingly or helpfully: *to lend one's aid to a cause.* **5.** to adapt (oneself or itself) to something. **6. lend a hand,** to assist. **7. lend an ear,** *Archaic.* to listen. *–v.i.* **8.** to make a loan or loans. [ME *lende;* replacing ME *lene(n),* OE *lǣnan,* from *lǣn* loan] – **lender,** *n.*

**lending library** /ˈlɛndɪŋ laɪbri/, *n.* a library which lends books, records, etc., as a public library or a commercial establishment charging a small fee.

**lend-lease** /lɛnd-ˈlis/, *n., v.,* **-leased, -leasing.** *–n.* **1.** an arrangement, orig. between the U.S. and Britain, where British land was leased to the U.S. in return for the use of U.S. destroyers. **2.** any similar arrangement, or reciprocal loan of goods, personnel, livestock, etc. *–v.t.* **3.** to exchange (goods, etc.) in such an arrangement. Also, **lease-lend.**

**length** /lɛŋθ/, *n.* **1.** the linear magnitude of anything as measured from end to end: *the length of a river.* **2.** extent from beginning to end of a series, enumeration, account, book, etc. **3.** extent in time; duration: *the length of a battle.* **4.** a distance determined by the length of something specified: *to hold a thing at arm's length.* **5.** a piece or portion of a certain or a known length: *a length of rope.* **6.** a stretch or extent of something, esp. a long stretch. **7.** the extent, or an extent, of going, proceeding, etc. **8.** the quality or fact of being long rather than short: *a journey remarkable for its length.* **9.** the measure from end to end of a horse, boat, etc., as a unit of distance in racing: *a horse wins by two lengths.* **10.** *Pros. and Phonet.* **a.** (of a vowel or syllable) quantity (whether long or short). **b.** the quality of vowels. **11.** *Cricket.* **a.** the distance travelled by the ball before it pitches on to the wicket, after delivery by the bowler. **b.** a desirable length, making it difficult for the batsman to know how to play the ball: *he bowls short of a length.* **12. at length, a.** to or in the full extent. **b.** after a time; in the end. **13. go to any length(s),** to do whatever is necessary, no matter how difficult, dangerous, etc., to achieve something. **14. slip (someone) a length,** (of a man) to have sexual intercourse with (someone). [ME and OE, from *lang* LONG[1]. See -TH[1]]

**lengthen** /ˈlɛŋθən/, *v.t.* **1.** to make greater in length. *–v.i.* **2.** to become greater in length. **3.** (of odds) to increase.

**lengthways** /ˈlɛŋθweɪz/, *adv.* in the direction of the length.

**lengthwise** /ˈlɛŋθwaɪz/, *adv.* **1.** lengthways. *–adj.* **2.** longitudinal; running lengthways.

**lengthy** /ˈlɛŋθi/, *adj.,* **-thier, -thiest.** having or being of great length, esp. speeches, writings, etc. – **lengthily,** *adv.* – **lengthiness,** *n.*

**leniency** /ˈliniənsi/, *n.* the quality of being lenient. Also, **lenience.**

**lenient** /ˈliniənt/, *adj.* **1.** mild, clement, or merciful, as in treatment, spirit, or tendency; gentle. **2.** *Archaic.* softening, soothing, or alleviative. [L *lēniens,* ppr., softening] – **leniently,** *adv.*

**lenis** /ˈlinəs, ˈleɪ-/, *adj., n., pl.* **lenes** /ˈliniz, ˈleɪ-/. *Phonet.* *–adj.* **1.** pronounced with relatively weak muscular tension and breath pressure, resulting in weak fricative or explosive sound: *v* and *b* are lenis, as compared to fortis *f* and *p.* *–n.* **2.** a lenis consonant. [L: gentle]

**lenition** /ləˈnɪʃən/, *n.* a weakening of the articulation of a consonant, often leading, in the historical development of a language, to radical sound changes and even to loss of the sound. [LENI(S) + -TION]

**lenitive** /ˈlɛnətɪv/, *adj.* **1.** softening, soothing, or mitigating, as medicines or applications. **2.** mildly laxative. *–n.* **3.** a lenitive medicine or application; a mild laxative. **4.** *Rare.* anything that softens or soothes.

**lenity** /ˈlɛnəti/, *n., pl.* **-ties. 1.** the quality or fact of being mild or gentle, as towards others. **2.** a lenient act. [L *lēnitas*]

**leno** /ˈlinoʊ/, *adj.* (of a weave) having the warp yarns woven in twisted pairs between the filling yarns, usu. in a light, gauzy fabric. [F *linon,* from *lin* LINEN, from L *līnum* flax]

**lens** /lɛnz/, *n., pl.* **lenses. 1.** a piece of transparent substance, usu. glass, having two (or two main) opposite surfaces, either both curved or one curved and one plane, used for changing the convergence of light rays, as in magnifying, or in correcting errors of vision. **2.** a combination of such pieces. **3.** some analogous device, as for affecting soundwaves, electromagnetic radiation, or streams of electrons. **4.** *Anat.* a part of the eye, a crystalline lens. **5.** *Geol.* a body of ore or rock thick in the middle and thin at the edges, similar to a double convex lens. [L: a lentil (which is shaped like a biconvex lens)]

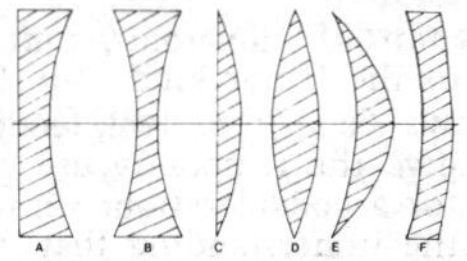

lenses: A, plano-concave; B, bi-concave (concavo-concave); C, plano-convex; D, bi-convex (convexo-convex); E, the meniscus (converging concavo-convex);F, concavo-convex

**lens flare** /ˈ- flɛə/, *n.* a condition which occurs when a camera is pointed directly at a strong light source, causing the image of the object being photographed to be diffused.

**lens turret** /ˈ- tʌrət/, *n.* a revolving device on a camera bearing two or more lenses, any one of which can quickly be turned into position for shooting.

**lent** /lɛnt/, *v.* past tense and past participle of **lend.**

**Lent** /lɛnt/, *n.* **1.** an annual season of fasting and penitence in preparation for Easter, beginning on Ash Wednesday and including the forty weekdays next before Easter, observed by the Roman Catholic, Anglican, and other Churches. **2.** (in the Middle Ages) a period from Martinmas (11 Nov.) to Christmas, known as St Martin's Lent. **3.** Lent term. [ME *lente(n),* OE *len(c)ten* spring, Lent; akin to D *lente* spring, G *Lenz*]

**lentamente** /lɛntəˈmɛnti/, *adv.* (a musical direction) slowly. [It., from *lento* LENTO]

**lentando** /lɛnˈtændoʊ/, *adv.* (a musical direction) gradually more slowly. [It., ger. of *lentare* slacken, from L *lentus* slow]

**Lenten** /ˈlɛntən/, *adj.* (*oft. l.c.*) of, pertaining to, or suitable for Lent. [LENT + -EN[2]]

**lenticel** /ˈlɛntəsɛl/, *n.* a body of cells formed in the periderm of a stem, appearing on the surface of the plant as a lens-shaped spot, and serving as a pore. [NL *lenticella,* var. of L *lenticula* LENTIL]

**lenticular** /lɛnˈtɪkjələ/, *adj.* **1.** of or pertaining to a lens. **2.** →**biconvex. 3.** resembling a lentil (seed) in form. [L *lenticulāris* lentil-shaped]

**lentigo** /lɛnˈtaɪgoʊ/, *n., pl.* **-tigines** /-ˈtɪdʒəniz/. **1.** →**freckle. 2.** →**naevus.** [L, from *lens* a lentil]

**lentil** /ˈlɛntəl/, *n.* **1.** an annual plant, *Lens culinaris,* having flattened, biconvex seeds which constitute a food similar to peas and beans. **2.** the seed. [ME *lentille,* from F, from L *lenticula,* diminutive of *lens* a lentil]

**lentissimo** /lɛnˈtɪsɪmoʊ/, *adv.* **1.** (a musical direction) very slowly. *–adj.* **2.** very slow. [It., from *lento* LENTO]

**lento** /ˈlɛntoʊ/, *adv.* **1.** (a musical direction) slowly. *–adj.* **2.** slow. [It., from L *lentus*]

**lentoid** /ˈlɛntɔɪd/, *adj.* having the shape of a biconvex lens.

**Lent term** /ˈlɛnt tɜm/, *n.* the first term of the academic year at some universities.

**Lenz's law** /ˈlɛnzəz lɔ/, *n.* the law which states that when an electric circuit and a magnetic field move relative to each other, the current induced in the circuit will have a magnetic field opposing the motion. [named after H. *Lenz,* 1804-65, German physicist]

**Leo** /ˈlioʊ/, *n.* **1.** a constellation and sign of the zodiac, represented by a lion. **2.** a person born under the sign of Leo, and (according to tradition) exhibiting the typical Leo personality traits in some degree. *–adj.* **3.** of or pertaining to such a person or such a personality trait. [L. See LION]

**leonine** /ˈliənaɪn/, *adj.* **1.** of or pertaining to the lion. **2.** lionlike. [ME *leonyne,* from L *leōnīnus*]

**leopard** /ˈlɛpəd/, *n.* **1.** a large, ferocious, spotted Asiatic or African carnivore, *Panthera pardus,* of the cat family, usu. tawny, with black markings; the Old World panther. **2.** any of various related animals, as the jaguar (**American leopard**), the cheetah (**hunting leopard**), and the ounce (**snow leopard**). **3.** *Her.* a lion pictured as walking with his head turned towards the spectator, one front paw usu. raised. [ME, from OF, from LL *leopardus,* from LGk *leópardos.* See LION, PARD[1]] – **leopardess,** *n. fem.*

leopard

**leopard seal** /ˈ- sil/, *n.* →**sea leopard.**

**leopard shark** /ˈ- ʃak/, *n.* →**zebra shark.**

**leopard tree** /ˈ- tri/, *n.* either of two species of *Flindersia* with spotted bark. Also, **leopardwood tree.**

**leotard** /ˈliətad/, *n.* a close-fitting one-piece garment with a low neck and tights, worn by acrobats, dancers, etc. [named after Jules *Léotard,* 19th-cent. French acrobat]

**Lepcha** /ˈlɛptʃə/, *n., pl.* **-cha, -chas. 1.** a member of a Mongoloid people living in Sikkim, India. **2.** the Sino-Tibetan language of this people.

**leper** /ˈlɛpə/, *n.* **1.** a person affected with leprosy. **2. social leper,** a person ostracised by society. [ME *lepre,* from OF: leprosy, from L *lepra,* from Gk, properly fem. of *leprós* scaly]

**lepido-,** a word element meaning 'scale', used esp. in scientific terms. [Gk, combining form of *lepís* scale]

**lepidolite** /ləˈpɪdəlaɪt, ˈlɛpədəlaɪt/, *n.* a mineral of the mica group, potassium lithium aluminium silicate, commonly occurring in lilac, rose-coloured, or greyish white scaly masses. [LEPIDO- + -LITE]

**lepidopteron** /lɛpəˈdɒptərən/, *n., pl.* **-tera** /-tərə/. any lepidopterous insect.

**lepidopterous** /lɛpəˈdɒptərəs/, *adj.* belonging or pertaining to the Lepidoptera, an order of insects comprising the butterflies and moths, which in the adult state have four membranous wings more or less covered with small scales. Also, **lepidopteral.** [NL *Lepidoptera,* pl., having scaly wings + -OUS. See LEPIDO-, -PTEROUS] – **lepidopteran,** *adj., n.*

**lepidote** /ˈlɛpədoʊt/, *adj.* covered with scurfy scales or scaly spots. [Gk *lepidōtós* scaly]

**leporine** /ˈlɛpəraɪn/, *adj.* of, pertaining to, or resembling the hare. [L *leporīnus*]

**leprechaun** /ˈlɛprəkɔn/, *n.* **1.** in Irish folklore, a little sprite, or goblin. **2.** *Colloq.* an Irishman. [earlier *lubrican,* from Irish *lupracān,* metathetic var. of *luchorpān* a little sprite, from *lu* little + *corpān,* diminutive of *corp* body (from L *corpus*)]

**leprosarium** /lɛprəˈsɛəriəm/, *n., pl.* **-saria** /-ˈsɛəriə/. a centre for the treatment of leprosy.

**leprosy** /ˈlɛprəsi/, *n.* a mildly infectious disease due to a micro-organism, *Bacillus leprae,* and variously characterised by ulcerations, tubercular nodules, spots of pigmentary excess or deficit, loss of fingers and toes, anaesthesia in certain nerve regions, etc; Hansen's disease. [LL *leprōsus* leprous + -Y[3]]

**leprous** /ˈlɛprəs/, *adj.* **1.** affected with leprosy. **2.** of or like leprosy. [ME, from LL *leprōsus,* from L *lepra* leprosy. See LEPER] – **leprously,** *adv.*

**lepto-,** a combining form meaning 'fine', 'small', 'thin', often occurring in terms of zoology and botany. [Gk, combining form of *leptós*]

**leptokurtosis** /ˌlɛptoʊkəˈtoʊsəs/, *n.* a distribution curve which has a sharper peak than normal. [LEPTO- + Gk *kúrtōsis* bulge, convexity] – **leptokurtic** /lɛptoʊˈkɜtɪk/, *adj.*

**lepton** /ˈlɛptɒn/, *n., pl.* **-ta** /-tə/. **1.** an ancient Greek coin. **2.** a minor modern Greek coin equal to one hundredth of a drachma. **3.** *Physics.* any one of a group of elementary particles which includes electrons, neutrinos, and muons. [Gk, properly neut. of *leptós* small]

**lepton**[1] /ˈlɛptən/, *n.* **1.** an ancient Greek coin. **2.** a minor modern Greek coin equal to one hundredth of a drachma. [Gk, prop. neut. of *leptós* small]

**lepton**[2] /ˈlɛptɒn/, *n. Physics.* any of a group of elementary particles which includes electrons, neutrinos, and muons. [LEPTO- + -(I)ON]

**leptophyllous** /lɛptoʊ'fɪləs/, *adj.* having long, slender leaves. [LEPTO- + -PHYLLOUS]

**leptorrhine** /'lɛptərin, -raɪn/, *adj.* having a narrow high-bridged nose. [LEPTO- + Gk *rhís* nose]

**leptosome** /'lɛptəsoʊm/, *n.* a person with a small slender body. [G *Leptosom,* from *lepto-* LEPTO- + *-som* -SOME[3]] – **leptosomic** /lɛptə'soʊmɪk/, *adj.* – **leptosomatic** /ˌlɛptoʊsə'mætɪk/, *adj.*

**leptospermum** /lɛptoʊ'spɜməm/, *n.* any shrub or small tree of the genus *Leptospermum,* family Myrtaceae, mostly native to Australia and New Zealand, as *L. scoparium,* in Australia called *tea-tree,* in New Zealand *manuka.*

**leptospira** /lɛp'tɒspərə/, *n.* a genus of extremely slender aerobic spirochaetes, free-living or parasitic in mammals. [NL, from LEPTO- + L *spira* coil, twist]

**leptospirosis** /ˌlɛptoʊspə'roʊsəs/, *n., pl.* **-ses.** any of several diseases of man and domestic animals caused by infection with spirochaetes of the genus *Leptospira.*

**lerp** /lɜp/, *n.* a sweet, edible, waxy secretion found on the leaves of eucalypts, and produced by the young of psyllids as a protection. [Aboriginal]

**les** /lɛz/, *n., adj. Colloq.* →**lesbian.**

**lesbian** /'lɛzbiən/, *n.* **1.** a female homosexual. *–adj.* **2.** of or pertaining to female homosexuals. [from the reputed sexual practices of the ancient inhabitants of the Greek island of *Lesbos* (Lesvos), birthplace of Sappho, a homosexual poetess of the 6th cent. B.C.]

**lesbianism** /'lɛzbiənɪzəm/, *n.* sexual relations between women.

**leschenaultia** /lɛʃə'nɔltiə/, *n.* any member of the Australian plant genus *Leschenaultia* comprising small shrubs or herbs, many with bright-coloured flowers, as *L. biloba* of western Australia with blue flowers and *L. formosa* with red.

**lese-majesty** /lɪz-'mædʒəsti/, *n.* **1.** any of various crimes or offences against the sovereign power in a state. **2.** (*joc.*) any presumptuous conduct. [F *lèse-majesté,* from L *laesa mājestas* injured sovereignty]

**lesion** /'liʒən/, *n.* **1.** an injury; a hurt; a wound. **2.** *Pathol.* any localised, morbid structural change in the body. [late ME, from ML *lēsio,* L *laesio* an injury]

**leslie** /'lɛzli/, *n.* a speaker or amplifier in which two horns (def. 16) connected to the diaphragm revolve rapidly to produce a tremolo effect. [Trademark]

**Lesotho** /lə'soʊtoʊ/, *n.* a kingdom entirely surrounded by the Republic of South Africa.

**lespedeza** /lɛspə'dizə/, *n.* any plant of the genus *Lespedeza,* esp. *L. stipulacea,* used in higher rainfall areas as pasture legumes. [NL; named after Vincente Manuel de *Céspedes,* misspelled *Léspedes,* 18th-cent. Spanish governor of E Florida]

**less** /lɛs/, *adv.* **1.** to a smaller extent, amount, or degree: *less exact.* *–adj.* **2.** smaller in size, amount, degree, etc.; not so large, great, or much: *less speed.* **3.** lower in consideration, dignity, or importance: *no less a person than the manager.* *–n.* **4.** a smaller amount or quantity. *–prep.* **5.** minus; without: *a year less two days.* [ME; OE *lǣs*(*sa*), c. OFris. *lēs*(*sa*) less; a compar. form (positive lacking, superl. *least*)]

**-less,** a suffix of adjectives meaning 'without', as in *childless, peerless.* In adjectives derived from verbs, it indicates failure or inability to perform or be performed, as in *resistless, countless.* [ME *-les,* OE *-lēas,* representing *lēas,* adj., free from, without, c. Icel. *lauss* free, LOOSE]

**lessee** /lɛ'si/, *n.* one to whom a lease is granted. – **lessee-ship,** *n.*

**lessen** /'lɛsən/, *v.i.* **1.** to become less. *–v.t.* **2.** to make less. **3.** to represent as less; depreciate; disparage.

**lesser** /'lɛsə/, *adj.* **1.** less; smaller, as in size, amount, importance, etc.: *a lesser evil.* **2.** being the smaller or less important of two. [late ME, from LESS + -ER[4]]

**lesson** /'lɛsən/, *n.* **1.** something to be learned or studied. **2.** a part of a book or the like assigned to a pupil for study: *the lesson for today is on page 22.* **3.** a length of time during which a pupil or class studies one subject. **4.** a useful or salutary piece of practical wisdom imparted or learned: *this experience taught me a lesson.* **5.** something from which one learns or should learn, as an instructive or warning example: *this experience was a lesson to me.* **6.** a reproof or punishment intended to teach one better ways. **7.** a portion of Scripture or other sacred writing read, or appointed to be read, at divine service. *–v.t.* **8.** to admonish or reprove. [ME, from OF *leçon,* from L *lectio* a reading]

**lessor** /lɛ'sɔ, 'lɛsɔ/, *n.* one who grants a lease.

**lest** /lɛst/, *conj.* **1.** for fear that; that ... not; so that ... not. **2.** (after words expressing fear, danger, etc.) that: *there was danger lest the plan become known.* [ME *leste,* late OE *the lǣste,* earlier *thȳ lǣs the* the lest (lit., whereby less that; *the* is the relative particle)]

**Lesueur's rat-kangaroo** /ləˌsɜz ræt-kæŋgə'ru/, *n.* →**boodie rat.** [named after C.A. *Lesueur,* 1778-1846, French artist and naturalist]

**let**[1] /lɛt/, *v.,* **let, letting,** *n.* *–v.t.* **1.** to allow or permit. **2.** to allow to pass, go, or come. **3.** to cause or allow to escape. **4.** to grant the occupancy or use of (land, buildings, rooms, space, etc., or movable property) for rent or hire (occasionally fol. by *out*). **5.** to contract for performance: *to let work to a carpenter.* **6.** to cause or make: *to let one know.* **7.** (as an auxiliary used to propose or order): *let me see.* *–v.* **8.** Some special verb phrases are:

**let alone** or **be,** to cease to remonstrate with or harass.

**let it be,** to allow a situation to take its own course.

**let down,** to lower.

**let (someone) down,** to disappoint (someone); fail.

**let fly,** to throw.

**let go,** *Colloq.* **1.** to break wind; fart. **2.** to express one's anger without restraint. **3.** to cease to make claims which are no longer appropriate on people with whom one has had a close relationship.

**let in on,** to share secret information with.

**let off, 1.** to excuse; to exempt from (something arduous, as a punishment, or the like). **2.** to explode (a firework, or other explosive device). **3.** *Colloq.* to fart.

**let off steam,** to express one's anger and frustration, often by indirect and harmless means.

**let on,** *Colloq.* **1.** to divulge information, esp. indiscreetly. **2.** to pretend: *he let on that he was a detective.*

**let oneself go,** to neglect onself.

**let one's hair down,** to abandon oneself to pleasure.

**let out, 1.** to divulge. **2.** to make (a garment, etc.) larger. **3.** to emit: *he let out a laugh.* **4.** to free from imputation of guilt: *that lets him out.*

**let in for,** to oblige to do something without prior consent or knowledge.

**let up,** *Colloq.* to slacken or stop.

*–v.i.* **9.** to be rented or leased. *–n.* **10.** a lease. [ME *leten,* OE *lǣtan,* c. D *laten,* G *lassen;* akin to LATE]

**let**[2] /lɛt/, *n., v.,* **letted** or **let, letting.** *–n.* **1.** *Archaic.* hindrance or obstruction; an impediment or obstacle: *without let or hindrance.* **2.** *Tennis, etc.* an interference with the course of the ball (of some kind specified in the rules) on account of which the stroke or point must be played over again. **3.** *Squash.* a bodily movement of one player which impedes that of the other player as he attempts to play the ball, as a result of which the point must be replayed. *–v.t.* **4.** *Archaic.* to hinder; stand in the way of. [ME *letten,* OE *lettan* (from *læt* slow, tardy, LATE), c. Icel. *letja* hinder]

**-let,** a diminutive suffix, used often for little objects, as in *frontlet, bracelet, kinglet.* [OF *-elet,* from *-el* (sometimes from L *-ellus,* diminutive suffix, sometimes from L *-āle,* neut.; see -AL[1]) + *-et* -ET]

**letdown** /'lɛtdaʊn/, *n.* disillusionment or disappointment.

**lethal** /'liθəl/, *adj.* of, pertaining to, or such as to cause death; deadly. [L *lēt*(*h*)*ālis*]

**lethargic** /lə'θadʒɪk/, *adj.* **1.** pertaining to or affected with lethargy; drowsy; sluggish. **2.** producing lethargy. Also, **lethargical.** – **lethargically,** *adv.*

**lethargy** /'lɛθədʒi/, *n., pl.* **-gies. 1.** a state of drowsy dullness or suspension of the faculties and energies; apathetic or sluggish inactivity. **2.** *Pathol.* a morbid state or a disorder characterised by overpowering drowsiness or sleep. [LL *lēthargia,* from Gk: drowsiness; replacing ME *litargie,* from ML *litargia*]

**Lethe** /ˈliθi/, *n.* forgetfulness; oblivion. [L, from Gk *Lḗthē* forgetting; in later classical mythology applied as proper name to a river in Hades whose water caused forgetfulness of the past for those who drank it]

**let-out** /ˈlɛt-aʊt/, *n.* an escape from an obligation.

**Letraset** /ˈlɛtrəsɛt/, *n.* lettering printed on a special backing sheet, which is transferred to another surface through the application of pressure to the backing sheet, and which is used particularly in the preparation of artwork for printing. [Trademark]

**letter** /ˈlɛtə/, *n.* **1.** a communication in writing or printing addressed to a person or a number of persons. **2.** one of the marks or signs conventionally used in writing and printing to represent speech sounds; an alphabetic character. **3.** a printing type bearing such a mark or character. **4.** a particular style of type. **5.** such types collectively. **6.** actual terms or wording, as distinct from general meaning or intent. **7.** (*pl.*) literature in general; belles-lettres. **8.** (*pl.*) the profession of literature, or authorship: *a man of letters.* **9. to the letter, a.** with close adherence to the actual wording or the literal meaning. **b.** to the fullest extent. *–v.t.* **10.** to mark or write with letters. [ME, from OF *lettre,* from L *littera, lītera* alphabetic character, pl. epistle, literature] **– letterer,** *n.*

**letter bomb** /ˈ– bɒm/, *n.* a small bomb sealed into an envelope to look like a letter, which explodes when opened.

**letterbox** /ˈlɛtəbɒks/, *n.* **1.** a receptacle with a slot for posting mail. **2.** a box or other shaped receptacle for incoming mail at the front gate of a house or on the inside of the front door. *–v.i.* **3.** to distribute pamphlets, etc., through suburban letterboxes: *I'm letterboxing the northern suburbs this election.*

**lettercard** /ˈlɛtəkad/, *n.* a card sold by the post office with a stamp already printed on it, which can usu. be posted at a lower rate than letters in envelopes.

**lettered** /ˈlɛtəd/, *adj.* **1.** educated or learned. **2.** pertaining to or characterised by polite learning or literary culture. **3.** marked with or as with letters.

**letterhead** /ˈlɛtəhɛd/, *n.* **1.** a printed heading on writing paper, esp. one giving the name and address of a business concern, an institution, etc. **2.** such writing paper.

**lettering** /ˈlɛtərɪŋ/, *n.* **1.** the act or process of inscribing with or making letters. **2.** the letters themselves.

**letter of advice,** *n.* **1.** a document, esp. in commercial shipments, giving specific information as to the consignor's agent in the consignee's territory, his bank, warehouse, etc. **2.** *Comm.* a drawer's document, usu. forwarded ahead of the bill of lading and other papers giving title to goods shipped by the drawer, stating that a bill has been issued against the drawee.

**letter of credit,** *n.* **1.** an order issued by a banker, allowing a person named to draw money to a specified amount from correspondents of the issuer. **2.** an instrument issued by a banker, authorising a person named to make drafts upon the issuer up to an amount specified.

**letter of identification,** *n.* a letter signed by a banker issued together with a letter of credit, also signed by the person in whose favour the credit is issued, thus enabling him to identify himself to the paying agent when cashing drafts drawn under the letter of credit. Also, **letter of indication.**

**letter of marque,** *n.* licence or commission granted by a state to a private citizen to capture and confiscate merchant ships of another nation. Also, **letter of marque and reprisal.**

**letter-perfect** /lɛtə-ˈpɜfəkt/, *adj.* **1.** knowing one's part, lesson, or the like, perfectly. **2.** accurate; exact.

**letterpress** /ˈlɛtəprɛs/, *n.* **1.** a method of relief printing in which the type or illustrations to be printed stand above the areas of the printing forme which are not to be printed. **2.** the matter thus printed. **3.** printed text or reading matter, as distinguished from illustrations, etc.

**letters of administration,** *n.pl.* an instrument issued by a court or public official authorising an administrator to take control of and dispose of the estate of the deceased, where the deceased died intestate.

**letters of credence,** *n.pl.* papers formally authorising a nation's diplomatic agents, issued by the appointing state.

**letters patent** /lɛtəz ˈpeɪtnt/, *n.pl.* a written or printed instrument issued by the sovereign power, conferring upon a patentee for a limited time the exclusive right to make, use, and sell his invention.

**Lettish** /ˈlɛtɪʃ/, *adj.* **1.** pertaining to the Letts or their language. *–n.* **2.** the language of Latvia.

**lettuce**[1] /ˈlɛtəs/, *n.* **1.** a biennial plant, *Lactuca sativa,* with large succulent leaves which are much used for salad. **2.** any other species of *Lactuca* as *L. saligna,* wild lettuce. [ME *letuse,* from OF *laitues,* pl., from L *lactūca*]

**lettuce**[2] /ˈlɛtəs/, *n. Colloq.* →**paper money.** [? from the colour green, frequently used for bank notes]

**let-up** /ˈlɛt-ʌp/, *n. Colloq.* a slackening; cessation; pause.

**leucaemia** /luˈkimiə/, *n.* →**leukaemia.**

**leucine** /ˈlusin/, *n.* an amino acid essential to man, $(CH_3)_2CHCH_2CH(NH_3^+)COO^-$, a constituent of proteins. Also, **leucin** /ˈlusən/. [LEUC(O)- + -INE[2]]

**leucite** /ˈlusaɪt/, *n.* a whitish or greyish mineral, potassium aluminium silicate, $KAlSi_2O_6$, found in certain volcanic rocks. [G *Leucit,* from *leuc-* LEUC(O)- + *-it* -ITE[1]] **– leucitic** /luˈsɪtɪk/, *adj.*

**leuco-,** a word element meaning 'white'. Also, before vowels, **leuc-.** [Gk *leuko-,* combining form of *leukós*]

**leuco base** /lukoʊ ˈbeɪs/, *n.* a colourless or slightly coloured compound made by reducing a dye and which is readily oxidised to regenerate the dye.

**leucocratic** /lukəˈkrætɪk/, *adj.* composed predominantly of light-coloured minerals. [LEUCO- + -CRAT + -IC]

**leucocyte** /ˈlukəsaɪt/, *n.* one of the white or colourless corpuscles of the blood, concerned in the destruction of disease-producing micro-organisms, etc.; white blood cell.

**leucocytic** /lukəˈsɪtɪk/, *adj.* **1.** pertaining to leucocytes. **2.** characterised by an excess of leucocytes.

**leucocytosis** /ˌlukoʊsaɪˈtoʊsəs/, *n.* the presence of an increased number of leucocytes in the blood, esp. when temporary, as in infection, and not due to leukaemia. [NL. See LEUCOCYTE, -OSIS] **– leucocytotic** /ˌlukoʊsaɪˈtɒtɪk/, *adj.*

**leucoplast** /ˈlukəplæst/, *n.* one of the colourless bodies found within the protoplasm of vegetable cells, and serving as points around which starch forms.

**leucopoenia** /lukəˈpiniə/, *n.* a decrease in the number of white cells in the blood. Also, *U.S.,* **leucopenia.**

**leucopoiesis** /ˌlukoʊpɔɪˈisəs/, *n.* the formation and development of the white blood cells.

**leucorrhoea** /lukəˈriə/, *n.* a whitish discharge from the female genital organs. Also, *Chiefly U.S.,* **leucorrhea.** [NL. See LEUCO-, -RHOEA]

**leucosis** /luˈkoʊsəs/, *n.* a progressively fatal disease of cattle and calves characterised by enlargement of the lymph nodes.

**leucosticte** /lukoʊˈstɪkti/, *n.* any of several montane finches of the genus *Leucosticte,* commonly called rosy finches.

**leucotomy** /luˈkɒtəmi/, *n.* →**lobotomy.**

**leucoxene** /luˈkɒksin/, *n.* a mineral, an amorphous hydrated titanium dioxide, formed by the alteration of ilmenite and other titanium-bearing minerals.

**leukaemia** /luˈkimiə/, *n.* a disease, usu. fatal, characterised by excessive production of white blood cells, which are usu. found in greatly increased numbers in the blood. There is an accompanying anaemia, often severe, and the spleen and lymph glands are usu. enlarged and in a state of great activity. Also, **leucaemia, leukemia.** [NL, from Gk *leukós* white + *-aemia* -AEMIA]

**Lev.,** *Bible.* Leviticus.

**Levalloisian** /lɛvəˈlɔɪziən/, *adj.* of, pertaining to, or characteristic of a tradition of the Middle Palaeolithic era notable for a method of producing stone tools. [from *Levallois-(Perret),* a town in N France + -IAN]

**Levant** /ləˈvænt/, *n.* **1.** lands bordering the eastern shore of the Mediterranean and the Aegean, esp. Syria, Lebanon, and Israel. **2.** (*l.c.*) a superior grade of morocco having a large and prominent grain, orig. made in the Levant, and used for bookbinding; Levant morocco. [F, properly ppr. of *(se) lever* rise (with reference to the rising sun). See LEVER]

**levanter** /ləˈvæntə/, *n.* an easterly wind which sometimes blows in the Strait of Gibraltar and in southern Spain.

**Levantine** /ˈlɛvəntaɪn/, *adj.* **1.** of or pertaining to the Levant. *–n.* **2.** a native or a vessel of the Levant. [LEVANT + -INE[1]. Cf. F *levantin*]

**levator** /lə'veɪtə, -tɔ/, *n., pl.* **levatores** /lɛvə'tɔriz/. **1.** *Anat.* a muscle that raises some part of the body. **2.** *Surg.* an instrument used to raise a depressed part of the skull. [L: a lifter]

**levee**[1] /'lɛvi/, *n.* **1.** a raised riverside built up naturally by the river by deposition of silt during flooding. **2.** a man-made embankment for preventing the overflowing of a river. **3.** *Agric.* one of the small continuous ridges surrounding fields that are to be irrigated. **4.** *Hist.* a landing place for vessels; a quay. [F *levée,* from *lever* raise. See LEVER]

**levee**[2] /'lɛvi, 'lɛveɪ/, *n.* **1.** *Hist.* a reception of visitors held on rising from bed, as formerly by a royal or other personage. **2.** a reception held at any time of day. [F *levé, lever* a rising. See LEVER]

**level** /–'lɛvəl/, *adj., n., v.,* **-elled, -elling** or (*U.S.*) **-eled, -eling,** *adv.* *–adj.* **1.** having no part higher than another; having an even surface. **2.** being in a plane parallel to the plane of the horizon; horizontal. **3.** on an equality, as one thing with another, or two or more things with one another. **4.** even, equable, or uniform. **5.** mentally well-balanced: *a level head.* **6. one's level best,** *Colloq.* one's very best; one's utmost. *–n.* **7.** a device used for determining, or adjusting something to, a horizontal surface. **8.** such a device consisting of a glass tube containing alcohol or ether with a movable bubble which when in the centre indicates horizontalness. **9.** a surveying instrument combining such a device with a mounted telescope. **10.** a measuring of differences in elevation with such an instrument. **11.** an imaginary line or surface everywhere perpendicular to the plumb-line. **12.** the horizontal line or plane in which anything is situated, with regard to its elevation. **13.** level position or condition. **14.** a level tract of land, or an extent of country approximately horizontal and unbroken by irregularities. **15.** a level or flat surface. **16.** one of various positions with respect to height; a height: *the water rose to a level of ten metres.* **17.** *Mining.* a depth at which tunnelling for gold, opal, etc., might take place. **18.** a position or plane, high or low: *acting on the level of amateurs.* **19. find one's level,** to find the most suitable place for oneself, esp. with regard to the people around: *he found his level among the older students.* **20. on the level,** sincere; honest. *–v.t.* **21.** to make (a surface) level or even: *to level ground before building.* **22.** to raise or lower to a particular level, or position. **23.** to bring (something) to the level of the ground: *the city was levelled by one atomic bomb.* **24.** to knock down, as a person. **25.** to bring (two or more things) to an equality of status, condition, etc. **26.** to make even or uniform, as colouring. **27.** to aim or point at a mark, as a weapon, criticism, etc. **28.** to turn (looks, etc.) in a particular direction. **29.** *Survey.* to find the relative elevation of different points in (land) as with a level. *–v.i.* **30.** to arrive at a common level; stabilise (oft. fol. by *out*): *food prices levelled last quarter.* **31.** to aim a weapon, etc. **32.** *Survey.* to take levels; use a level. **33.** *Aeron.* to fly at a constant height. *–adv.* **34.** in a level, direct or even way or line. [ME *livel,* from OF, from L *lībella,* diminutive of *lībra* a balance, level] – **levelly,** *adv.* – **levelness,** *n.*

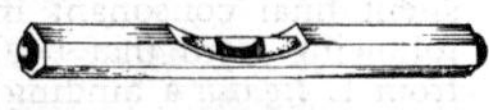

level (def. 8)

**level crossing** /– 'krɒsɪŋ/, *n.* a place where a road and railway intersect at the same level.

**level-head** /'lɛvəl-hɛd/, *n.* a person having common sense, sound judgment, etc.

**level-headed** /'lɛvəl-hɛdəd/, *adj.* **1.** having common sense and sound judgment. **2.** down-to-earth; practical. **3.** calm; not easily flustered. – **level-headedness,** *n.*

**leveller** /'lɛvələ/, *n.* one who or that which levels. Also, *U.S.,* **leveler.**

**levelling rod** /'lɛvəlɪŋ rɒd/, *n.* a graduated rod used for measuring heights in connection with a surveyor's level. Also, **levelling staff;** *U.S.,* **leveling rod.**

**level-pegging** /lɛvəl-'pɛgɪŋ/, *adj.* on equal terms. [from cribbage, in which the score is kept with rows of pegs]

**lever** /'livə/, *n.* **1.** a bar or rigid piece acted upon at different points by two forces, as a voluntarily applied force (the *power*) and a resisting force (the *weight*), which generally tend to rotate it in opposite directions about a fixed axis or support (the *fulcrum*). **2.** any of various mechanical devices operating on this principle, as a crowbar. *–v.t.* **3.** to move with a lever. *–v.i.* **4.** to apply a lever. [ME *levere,* from OF *leveor,* lit., raiser, from *lever* raise, (refl.) rise, from L *levāre* lighten, lift, raise] – **lever-like,** *adj.*

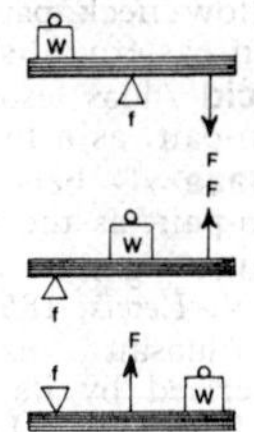


three basic types of lever: f, fulcrum; F, force needed to raise weight; W, weight

**leverage** /'livərɪdʒ/, *n.* **1.** the action of a lever. **2.** the mechanical mechanical advantage or power gained by using a lever. **3.** power of action; means of influence.

**leveret** /'lɛvərət/, *n.* a young hare. [ME, from OF *levrete,* diminutive of *levre,* from L *lepus* hare]

**leviable** /'lɛviəbəl/, *adj.* **1.** that may be levied. **2.** liable or subject to a levy.

**leviathan** /lə'vaɪəθən/, *n.* **1.** a sea-monster mentioned in the Old Testament. **2.** any huge marine animal, as the whale. **3.** anything, esp. a ship, of huge size. [ME, from LL, from Heb. *liwyāthān,* probably meaning the coiling up (snake)]

**levigate** /'lɛvəgeɪt/, *v.t.,* **-gated, -gating.** **1.** to rub, grind, or reduce to a fine powder, as in a mortar, with or without the addition of a liquid. **2.** *Chem.* to make a homogeneous mixture of, as gels. [L *lēvigātus,* pp., made smooth] – **levigation** /lɛvə'geɪʃən/, *n.*

**levirate** /'lɛvərət/, *n.* a custom of the ancient Hebrews, requiring a man under certain circumstances to marry the widow of his brother or nearest kinsman. [L *lēvir* husband's brother + -ATE[1]] – **leviratic** /lɛvə'rætɪk/, **leviratical** /lɛvə'rætɪkəl/, *adj.*

**levis** /'livaɪz/, *n.pl.* (*also cap.*) jeans. [Trademark]

**levitate** /'lɛvəteɪt/, *v.,* **-tated, -tating.** *–v.i.* **1.** to rise or float in the air, esp. through some allegedly supernatural power that overcomes gravity. *–v.t.* **2.** to cause to rise or float in the air. **3.** *Med.* to support (a patient) by levitation. [LEVIT(Y) + -ATE[1]; modelled on GRAVITATE] – **levitator,** *n.*

**levitation** /lɛvə'teɪʃən/, *n.* **1.** the act or phenomenon of levitating. **2.** (among spiritualists) the alleged phenomenon of bodies heavier than air being by spiritual means rendered buoyant in the atmosphere. **3.** *Med.* support of a patient on a bed of air by application of the hovercraft principle, used in the treatment of severe burns.

**levity** /'lɛvəti/, *n., pl.* **-ties.** **1.** lightness of mind, character, or behaviour; lack of proper seriousness or earnestness: *she accused him of levity in his discussion of the divorce law.* **2.** an instance or exhibition of this. **3.** fickleness. **4.** lightness in weight. [L *levitas*]

**levo-,** *U.S.* variant of **laevo-.**

**levoglucose** /livoʊ'glukoʊz, -koʊs/, *n. U.S.* →**laevoglucose.**

**levogyrate** /livoʊ'dʒaɪrət/, *adj. U.S. Optics, Crystall., etc.* →**laevorotatory.**

**levorotation** /ˌlivoʊroʊ'teɪʃən/, *n. U.S.* →**laevorotation.**

**levorotatory** /ˌlivoʊroʊ'teɪtəri/, *adj. U.S.* →**laevorotatory.**

**levulin** /'lɛvjəlɪn/, *n. U.S.* →**laevulin.**

**levulinic acid** /ˌlɛvjəlɪnɪk 'æsəd/, *n. U.S.* →**laevulic acid.** Also, **levulic acid.**

**levulose** /'lɛvəloʊz, -oʊs/, *n. U.S.* →**laevulose.**

**levy** /'lɛvi/, *n., pl.* **-ies,** *v.,* **-ied, -ying.** *–n.* **1.** a raising or collecting, as of money or troops, by authority or force. **2.** that which is raised, as a tax assessment or a body of troops. *–v.t.* **3.** to make a levy of; collect (taxes, contributions, etc.). **4.** to impose (a tax): *to levy a duty on imported wines.* **5.** to raise or enlist (troops, etc.) for service. **6.** to start, or make (war, etc.). *–v.i.* **7.** to make a levy. **8.** *Law.* to seize or attach property by judicial order. [ME, from F *levée,* from *lever* raise. See LEVER] – **levier** /'lɛviə/, *n.*

**lewd** /lud, ljud/, *adj.* **1.** inclined to, characterised by, or inciting to lust or lechery. **2.** obscene or indecent, as language, songs, etc. [ME *leud, lewede,* OE *lǣw(e)de* LAY[3]; orig. uncert.] – **lewdly,** *adv.* – **lewdness,** *n.*

**Lewin honeyeater** /luən 'hʌniˌitə/, *n.* an insectivorous and fruit-eating bird, *Meliphaga lewini,* olive-green with prominent yellow neck patches, found in areas of rainforest and scrub in eastern Australia; banana-bird.

**Lewis acid** /ˈluəs æsəd/, *n.* any substance which accepts an electron-pair, as a hydrogen ion or boron trifluoride.

**Lewis base** /ˈ– beɪs/, *n.* any substance which donates an electron-pair, as the hydroxide ion or ammonia.

**Lewis gun** /ˈ– gʌn/, *n.* a light air-cooled machine gun. [named after I.N. *Lewis,* 1858-1931, U.S. army officer]

**lewisite** /ˈluəsaɪt/, *n.* a chemical warfare agent, $C_2H_2AsCl_3$, characterised by its vesicant action. [named after W. Lee *Lewis,* 1878 -1943, U.S. chemist. See -ITE[1]]

**lex** /lɛks/, *n., pl.* **leges** /ˈleɪgeɪz/. law. [L: the law]

**lexeme** /ˈlɛksim/, *n.* a minimal unit of the vocabulary of a language. – **lexemic** /lɛkˈsimɪk/, *adj.*

**lexical** /ˈlɛksɪkəl/, *adj.* **1.** pertaining to words or to a vocabulary, as that of an author or a language. **2.** pertaining to or of the nature of a lexicon. [LEXIC(ON) + -AL[1]] – **lexically,** *adv.*

**lexical meaning** /– ˈminɪŋ/, *n.* that part of the meaning of a linguistic form which does not depend on its membership of a particular form class, esp. (of inflected words) the meaning common to all the members of an inflectional paradigm, e.g., the meaning common to *eat, eats, ate, eaten, eating,* despite their differences in form.

**lexicog.,** **1.** lexicographical. **2.** lexicography.

**lexicographer** /lɛksəˈkɒgrəfə/, *n.* a writer or compiler of a dictionary. [LGk *lexikográphos* (from *lexikó(n)* wordbook + *-gráphos* writer) + -ER[1]]

**lexicography** /lɛksəˈkɒgrəfi/, *n.* the writing or compiling of dictionaries. – **lexicographic** /lɛksəkəˈgræfɪk/, **lexicographical** /lɛksəkəˈgræfɪkəl/, *adj.* – **lexicographically** /lɛksəkəˈgræfɪkli/, *adv.*

**lexicology** /lɛksəˈkɒlədʒi/, *n.* the study of the history, form, and meaning of words. – **lexicological** /lɛksəkəˈlɒdʒɪkəl/, *adj.* – **lexicologist,** *n.*

**lexicon** /ˈlɛksəkən/, *n.* **1.** a wordbook or dictionary, esp. of Greek, Latin, or Hebrew. **2.** the list or vocabulary of words belonging to a particular subject, field, or class. **3.** the total stock of words in a given language. [ML (much used in Latin titles of dictionaries), from Gk *lexikón,* neut. of *lexikós* of or for words]

**lexicostatistics** /ˌlɛksɪkoustəˈtɪstɪks/, *n.pl.* (*construed as sing.*) the comparison and classification of dialects and languages on the basis of their percentage of shared vocabulary. – **lexicostatistic,** *adj.* – **lexicostatistical,** *adj.*

**lexis** /ˈlɛksəs/, *n.* the whole body of words in a language. [Gk: speech; word]

**lex talionis** /ˌlɛks tæliˈounəs/, *n.* the law of retaliation, as an eye for an eye, a tooth for a tooth. [NL]

**ley** /li, leɪ/, *n.* arable land temporarily sown with grass. [var. of LEA[1]]

**Leyden** /ˈleɪdən/, *n.* a semi-hard cheese, with a rich, dark yellow texture spiced with caraway, cloves and cumin. Also, **Leiden.** [named after *Leyden* (*Leiden*), a town in the Netherlands]

**Leyden jar** /ˈ– dʒa/, *n.* a device for storing electric charge, consisting essentially of a glass jar lined inside and outside, for about two-thirds of its height, with tinfoil. [see LEYDEN]

**ley farming** /ˈli famɪŋ/, *n.* the growing of grass or legumes in rotation with other crops as part of a soil conservation program. [var. of LEA[1]]

**lezzy** /lɛzi/, *n. Colloq.* →**lesbian.** Also, **lezz, lez.**

**l.f.,** *Radio.* low frequency.

**LG,** Low German. Also, **L.G.**

**lge,** large.

**LGk,** Late Greek. Also, **L.Gk.**

**LGS ratio** /ɛl dʒi ˌɛs ˈreɪʃiou/, *n.* the ratio of a trading bank's liquid assets and government securities to its deposits. [L(*iquid Assets and*) G(*overnment*) S(*ecurities*)]

**l.h.,** *Music.* left hand.

**Lhasa apso** /lasə ˈæpsou/, *n.* a small dog of Tibetan breed having an upward curving tail and long, straight, usu. brownish hair, which falls heavily over the eyes.

**LHeb.,** Late Hebrew.

**Li,** *Chem.* lithium.

**liability** /laɪəˈbɪləti/, *n., pl.* **-ties.** **1.** an obligation, esp. for payment; debt or pecuniary obligations (opposed to *asset*). **2.** something disadvantageous. **3.** the state or fact of being liable: *liability to jury duty, liability to disease.*

**liable** /ˈlaɪəbəl/, *adj.* **1.** subject, exposed, or open to something possible or likely, esp. something undesirable. **2.** under legal obligation; responsible or answerable. [late ME, from F *lier* bind (from L *ligāre*) + -ABLE] – **liableness,** *n.*

**liaise** /liˈeɪz/, *v.i.,* **-aised, -aising.** to maintain contact and act in concert (usu. fol. by *with*). [backformation from LIAISON]

**liaison** /liˈeɪzən/, *n.* **1.** *Mil., etc.* the contact maintained between units, in order to ensure concerted action. **2.** a similar connection or relation maintained between non-military units, bodies, etc. **3.** an illicit sexual relationship. **4.** *Cookery.* a thickening, as of beaten eggs and cream, for sauces, soups, etc. **5.** *Phonet.* (*esp. in French*) the articulation of a normally silent final consonant in a word as the initial sound of a following word that begins with a vowel or a silent *h.* [F, from L *ligātio* a binding]

**liana** /liˈanə/, *n.* a climbing plant or vine. Also, **liane** /liˈan/. [F *liane,* earlier *liorne,* b. *viorne* (from L *viburnum* viburnum) and *lier* bind (from L *ligāre*)]

**liar** /ˈlaɪə/, *n.* **1.** one who lies, or tells lies. **2. make a liar of,** *Colloq.* to prove wrong.

**lias** /ˈlaɪəs/, *n.* a series of marine sediments, the Lower Jurassic rocks of north-western Europe. [ME, from OF *liois* kind of limestone, of Gmc orig.] – **liassic** /laɪˈæsɪk/, *adj.*

**lib.,** **1.** book. [L *liber*] **2.** librarian. **3.** library.

**Lib** /lɪb/, *n. Colloq.* a member of a Liberal party.

**libanomancy** /ləˈbænəmænsi/, *n.* the use of incense as a means of interpreting omens.

**libation** /laɪˈbeɪʃən/, *n.* **1.** a pouring out of wine or other liquid in honour of a deity. **2.** the liquid poured out. [ME, from L *lībātio*]

**libber** /ˈlɪbə/, *n.* a liberationist, esp. one involved in women's liberation.

**libel** /ˈlaɪbəl/, *n., v.,* **-belled, -belling** or (*U.S.*) **-beled, -beling.** *–n.* **1.** *Law.* **a.** defamation by written or printed words, pictures, or in any form other than by spoken words or gestures. **b.** the crime of publishing it. **2.** anything defamatory, or that maliciously or damagingly misrepresents. **3.** *Law.* a formal written declaration or statement, as one containing the allegations of a plaintiff or the grounds of a charge. *–v.t.* **4.** to publish a malicious libel against. **5.** to misrepresent damagingly. **6.** to institute suit against by a libel, as in an admiralty court. [ME, from L *libellus,* diminutive of *liber* book]

**libellant** /ˈlaɪbələnt/, *n.* one who libels, or institutes suit. Also, *U.S.,* **libelant.**

**libellee** /laɪbəˈli/, *n.* one against whom a libel instituting a suit has been filed; the respondent. Also, *U.S.,* **libelee.**

**libeller** /ˈlaɪbələ/, *n.* one who libels; one who publishes a libel assailing another. Also, *U.S.,* **libeler.**

**libellous** /ˈlaɪbələs/, *adj.* containing, constituting, or involving a libel; maliciously defamatory. Also, *U.S.,* **libelous.** – **libellously,** *adv.*

**liber** /ˈlaɪbə/, *n.* →**phloem.** [L]

**liberal** /ˈlɪbrəl, ˈlɪbərəl/, *adj.* **1.** favourable to progress or reform, as in religious or political affairs. **2.** (*cap.*) of or pertaining to the Liberal political party. **3.** favourable to or in accord with the policy of leaving the individual as unrestricted as possible in the opportunities for self-expression or self-fulfilment. **4.** of representational forms of government rather than aristocracies and monarchies. **5.** free from prejudice or bigotry; tolerant. **6.** giving freely or in ample measure: *a liberal donor.* **7.** given freely or abundantly: *a liberal donation.* **8.** not strict or rigorous: *a liberal interpretation of a rule.* **9.** befitting a freeman, a gentleman, or a non-professional person. *–n.* **10.** a person of liberal principles or views, esp. in religion or politics. **11.** (*oft. cap.*) a member of the Liberal party in politics. **12. small-l liberal,** a person with conservative tendencies, but who prides himself on an independent, progressive point of view. [ME, from L *līberālis* pertaining to a free man] – **liberally,** *adv.* – **liberalness,** *n.*

**liberal arts** /– ˈats/, *n. pl.* the course of instruction at a university, comprising the arts, natural sciences, social sciences, and humanities. [anglicisation of L *artēs līberālēs* arts of free men]

**liberalise** /ˈlɪbrəlaɪz, -bərəl-/, *v.*, **-lised, -lising.** *–v.t.* **1.** to make liberal. *–v.i.* **2.** to become liberal. Also, **liberalize.** – **liberaliser,** *n.*

**liberalism** /ˈlɪbrəlɪzəm, -bərəl-/, *n.* **1.** liberal principles, as in religion or politics. **2.** (*sometimes cap.*) the principles and practices of a liberal party in politics. **3.** a movement in modern Protestantism which emphasises freedom from tradition and authority, the adjustment of religious beliefs to scientific conceptions, and the spiritual capacities of men. – **liberalist,** *n., adj.* – **liberalistic** /lɪbrəˈlɪstɪk/, *adj.*

**liberality** /lɪbəˈrælәti/, *n., pl.* **-ties. 1.** the quality of being liberal in giving; generosity; bounty. **2.** a liberal gift. **3.** breadth of mind. **4.** liberalism.

**liberal-minded** /ˈlɪbrəl-maɪndəd/, *adj.* tolerant; generous in outlook (opposed to *narrow-minded*).

**liberate** /ˈlɪbəreɪt/, *v.t.*, **-rated, -rating. 1.** to set free, as a prisoner, occupied territory, etc.; release. **2.** to disengage; set free from combination, as a gas. **3.** to free from convention or from a repressive social order. **4.** *Colloq.* to shoplift; steal. [L *līberātus,* pp.] – **liberator,** *n.*

**liberation** /lɪbəˈreɪʃən/, *n.* **1.** the state of freedom from bondage. **2.** the freeing of oppressed or minority groups: *women's liberation.* – **liberationist,** *n.*

**Liberia** /laɪˈbɪəriə/, *n.* a republic in western Africa; founded by freed American slaves. – **Liberian,** *adj., n.*

**libertarian** /lɪbəˈtɛəriən/, *n.* **1.** one who advocates liberty, esp. with regard to thought or conduct. **2.** one who maintains the doctrine of free will. *–adj.* **3.** advocating liberty. **4.** maintaining the doctrine of free will. [LIBERT(Y) + -ARIAN] – **libertarianism,** *n.*

**liberticide** /lɪˈbɜtəsaɪd/, *n.* **1.** a destroyer of liberty. **2.** destruction of liberty. [LIBERTY + -CIDE] – **liberticidal** /lɪbɜtəˈsaɪdl/, *adj.*

**libertinage** /ˈlɪbətənɪdʒ/, *n.* libertine conduct, esp. in sexual or religious matters.

**libertine** /ˈlɪbətin/, *n.* **1.** one free from restraint or control, esp. in moral or sexual matters; a dissolute or licentious man. **2.** a freethinker in religious matters. *–adj.* **3.** free from moral or sexual restraint; dissolute; licentious. **4.** freethinking in religious matters. [ME, from L *lībertīnus* freedman]

**libertinism** /ˈlɪbətənɪzəm/, *n.* libertine practices or habits of life; licentiousness.

**liberty** /ˈlɪbəti/, *n., pl.* **-ties. 1.** freedom from arbitrary or despotic government. **2.** freedom from external or foreign rule; independence. **3.** freedom from control, interference, obligation, restriction, hampering conditions, etc.; power or right of doing, thinking, speaking, etc., according to choice. **4.** freedom from captivity, confinement, or physical restraint: *the prisoner soon regained his liberty.* **5.** leave granted to a sailor, esp. in the navy, to go ashore. **6.** the freedom of, or right of frequenting or using a place, etc. **7.** unwarranted or impertinent freedom in action or speech, or a form or instance of it: *to take liberties.* **8. apply liberty to,** *Law.* (of a judge) to permit (a party) to come to court again without taking out another summons. **9. at liberty, a.** free from bondage, captivity, confinement, or restraint. **b.** unoccupied or disengaged. **c.** free, permitted, or privileged to do or be as specified. [ME *libertie,* from OF *liberte,* from L *lībertas*]

**libidinous** /ləˈbɪdənəs/, *adj.* full of lust; lustful; lewd. [ME *lybydynous,* from L *libīdinōsus*] – **libidinously,** *adv.* – **libidinousness,** *n.*

**libido** /ləˈbidoʊ/, *n.* **1.** *Psychol.* all of the instinctive energies and desires which are derived from the id. **2.** the innate actuating or impelling force in living beings; the vital impulse or urge. **3.** the sexual instinct. [L: pleasure, longing] – **libidinal** /ləˈbɪdənəl/, *adj.*

**Libra** /ˈlɪbrə, ˈlibrə/, *n.* **1.** a constellation and sign of the zodiac, represented by a balance. **2.** →**Libran.** [L: pound, balance, level]

**Libran** /ˈlɪbrən, li-/, *n.* **1.** a person born under the sign of Libra, and (according to tradition) exhibiting the typical Libran personality traits in some degree. *–adj.* **2.** of or pertaining to Libra. **3.** of or pertaining to such a person or such a personality trait.

**librarian** /laɪˈbrɛəriən/, *n.* **1.** a person trained in librarianship. **2.** a person in charge of a library.

**librarianship** /laɪˈbrɛəriənʃɪp/, *n.* **1.** a profession concerned with organising collections of books and related materials in libraries and of making these resources available to readers and others. **2.** the position or duties of a librarian.

**library** /ˈlaɪbri, -brəri/, *n., pl.* **-ries. 1.** a place set apart to contain books and other literary material for reading, study, or reference, as a room, set of rooms, or building where books may be read or borrowed. **2.** a lending library or a public library. **3.** a collection of manuscripts, publications, and other materials for reading, study, or reference. **4.** a series of books of similar character, or alike in size, binding, etc., issued by a single publishing house. **5.** a collection of films, records, music, etc. **6.** *Computers.* an organised collection of programs or routines suitable for a particular model of computer. [ME *librarie,* from L *librārium* place to keep books]

**library binding** /ˈ– baɪndɪŋ/, *n.* **1.** the process of specialised binding of books, etc., for public and private libraries. **2.** a superior, durable binding used on books for libraries.

**library book** /ˈ– bʊk/, *n.* a book belonging to a library, esp. a lending library.

**library edition** /ˈ– ədɪʃən/, *n.* **1.** a strongly-bound edition of good size and print, esp. a uniform edition of a writer's works, suitable for library use. **2.** an edition of a newspaper for reference in certain libraries.

**librate** /ˈlaɪbreɪt/, *v.i.*, **-brated, -brating. 1.** to oscillate; sway. **2.** to be poised or balanced.

**libration** /laɪˈbreɪʃən/, *n.* a real or apparent oscillatory motion, esp. of the moon. [L *lībrātio* balance, a moving from side to side]

**libratory** /ˈlaɪbrətəri, -tri/, *adj.* →**oscillatory.**

**librettist** /ləˈbrɛtəst/, *n.* the writer of a libretto.

**libretto** /ləˈbrɛtoʊ/, *n., pl.* **-tos, -ti** /-ti/. **1.** the text or words of an opera or other extended musical composition. **2.** a book or booklet containing such a text. [It., diminutive of *libro* book, from L *liber*]

**libriform** /ˈlaɪbrəfɔm/, *adj.* (in botany) having the form of or resembling liber or phloem. [LIB(E)R + -I- + -FORM]

**librium** /ˈlɪbriəm/, *n.* a mild tranquillising drug used to treat conditions of neurosis; chlordiazepoxide. [Trademark]

**Libya** /ˈlɪbjə/, *n.* a republic in northern Africa between Tunisia and Egypt.

**Libyan** /ˈlɪbjən/, *adj.* **1.** of or pertaining to Libya. *–n.* **2.** a native or inhabitant of Libya. **3.** Berber (def. 2), esp. in its ancient form.

**Libyan Arab Jamahiriya,** *n.* official name of **Libya.**

**lic'd,** licensed.

**lice** /laɪs/, *n.* plural of **louse.**

**lice ladders** /ˈ– lædəz/, *n.pl. Colloq.* →**sidelevers.**

**licence** /ˈlaɪsəns/, *n.* **1.** formal permission or leave to do or not to do something. **2.** formal permission from a constituted authority to do something, as to carry on some business or profession, to be released from gaol for part of one's sentence under specific restrictions, etc. **3.** a certificate of such permission; an official permit. **4.** freedom of action, speech, thought, etc., permitted or conceded. **5.** intentional deviation from rule, convention, or fact, as for the sake of literary or artistic effect: *poetic licence.* **6.** excessive or undue freedom or liberty. **7.** licentiousness. Also, *U.S.,* **license.** [ME, from OF, from L *licentia*]

**licence number** /ˈ– nʌmbə/, *n.* the official number on a driver's or other licence.

**license** /ˈlaɪsəns/, *v.*, **-censed, -censing,** *n.* *–v.t.* **1.** to grant authoritative permission or licence to; authorise. *–n.* **2.** *U.S.* licence.

**licensed** /ˈlaɪsənst/, *adj.* (of a club, restaurant, etc.) authorised to sell alcoholic beverages for consumption on the premises.

**licensed victualler** /– ˈvɪtlə/, *n.* a publican or landlord licensed to sell wines and spirits, etc. Also, **victualler.**

**licensee** /laɪsənˈsi/, *n.* one to whom a licence is granted, esp. to sell alcoholic drinks, as the licensee of a hotel.

**licenser** /ˈlaɪsənsə/, *n.* one who grants licences. Also, **licensor.**

**licentiate** /laɪˈsɛnʃiət/, *n.* **1.** one who has received a licence, as from a university or college, to practise an art or profession. **2.** the holder of a certain university degree intermediate between that of bachelor and that of doctor, now confined chiefly to certain continental European universities. – **licentiateship,** *n.*

**licentious** /laɪˈsɛnʃəs/, *adj.* **1.** sensually unbridled; libertine; lewd. **2.** unrestrained by law or morality; lawless; immoral. **3.** going beyond customary or proper bounds or limits. [ML *licentiōsus*] – **licentiously,** *adv.* – **licentiousness,** *n.*

**lichee** /laɪˈtʃi/, *n.* →**lychee.**

**lichen** /ˈlaɪkən/, *n.* **1.** any one of the group, Lichenes, of the Thallophyta, compound plants (fungi in symbiotic union with algae) having a vegetative body (thallus) growing in greenish, grey, yellow, brown, or blackish crustlike patches or bushlike forms on rocks, trees, etc. **2.** *Pathol.* any of various eruptive skin diseases. [L, from Gk *leichḗn*] – **lichen-like,** *adj.* – **lichenous,** *adj.*

**lichenin** /ˈlaɪkənɪn/, *n.* a polysaccharide starch, $(C_6H_{10}O_5)_n$, a white gelatinous substance derived from certain mosses. [LICHEN + -IN[2]]

**lichenoid** /ˈlaɪkənɔɪd/, *adj.* lichen-like.

**lichenology** /laɪkəˈnɒlədʒi/, *n.* the branch of botany that treats of lichens. – **lichenological** /laɪkənəˈlɒdʒɪkəl/, *adj.* – **lichenologist,** *n.*

**lichgate** /ˈlɪtʃgeɪt/, *n.* a roofed gate to a churchyard, under which a bier is set down to await the coming of the clergyman. Also, **lychgate.** [*lich* (OE *līc,* c. D *lijk*) body, corpse + GATE[1]]

**lichi** /laɪˈtʃi/, *n., pl.* **-chis.** →**lychee.**

**licit** /ˈlɪsət/, *adj.* permitted; lawful. [late ME, from L *licitus,* pp.] – **licitly,** *adv.*

**lick** /lɪk/, *v.t.* **1.** to pass the tongue over the surface of (oft. fol. by *off, from,* etc.) **2.** to affect by strokes of the tongue: *to lick the plate clean.* **3.** to pass or play lightly over, as flames do. **4.** *Colloq.* to overcome in a fight, etc.; defeat. **5.** *Colloq.* to outdo; surpass. **6. lick into shape,** to bring to a state of completion or perfection; make efficient. **7. lick one's chops** or **lips,** to anticipate greedily. **8. lick one's wounds,** to retire and recover after a defeat. **9. lick someone's boots,** to act in a subservient manner; fawn upon. **10. lick the dust, a.** to be killed or wounded. **b.** to grovel; humble oneself abjectly. *–n.* **11.** a stroke of the tongue over something. **12.** a small quantity. **13. a.** a place to which wild animals resort to lick salt occurring naturally there. **b.** an artificial food or salt block for livestock. **14.** *Jazz.* a short instrumental decoration usu. about one bar long which is played between the phrases of a song or melodic line: *he played hot licks on the trumpet.* **15. for the lick of one's life,** at great speed. **16. lick and a promise, a.** a feeble, perfunctory, or superficial attempt at doing something. **b.** a hasty tidy-up. [ME *licke(n),* OE *liccian,* c. D. *likken,* G *lecken;* akin to L *lingere*] – **licker,** *n.*

**lickerish** /ˈlɪkərɪʃ/, *adj. Archaic.* **1.** eager for choice food. **2.** greedy. **3.** lustful. Also, **liquorish.** [earlier *lickerous* (influenced by *lick* and *liquor,* with substitution of suffix -ISH[1] for -OUS), ME *likerous,* representing an AF var. of OF *lecheros,* from *lecheor* gourmand, sensualist. See LECHER]

**lick-hole** /ˈlɪk-hoʊl/, *n.* **1.** a place where wild animals or livestock go to lick naturally occurring salt. **2.** a place where an artificial food block or rock salt is placed for livestock to lick.

**licking** /ˈlɪkɪŋ/, *n.* **1.** *Colloq.* **a.** a beating or thrashing. **b.** a defeat; setback. **2.** the act of one who or that which licks.

**lickspittle** /ˈlɪkspɪtl/, *n. Brit.* an abject toady.

**licorice** /ˈlɪkərɪʃ, ˈlɪkrɪʃ, -rəs/, *n.* →**liquorice**[1].

**lid** /lɪd/, *n.* **1.** a movable piece, whether separate or hinged, for closing the opening of a vessel, box, etc.; a movable cover. **2.** an eyelid. **3.** *Bot.* (in mosses) **a.** the cover of the capsule; operculum. **b.** the upper section of a pyxidium. **4.** *Colloq.* a hat. **5. dip one's lid, a.** to lift one's hat as a mark of respect. **b.** to respect someone (fol. by *to*). **6. put the lid on, a.** to clamp down on or put an end to: *to put the lid on prostitution.* **b.** to remove as a possibility: *that puts the lid on our holiday.* [ME; OE *hlid,* c. D *lid,* G *Lid*] – **lidded,** *adj.*

**lidless** /ˈlɪdləs/, *adj.* **1.** having no lid. **2.** (of eyes) having no eyelids.

**lido** /ˈlidoʊ/, *n. Brit.* an open-air public swimming pool. [from the *Lido,* a famous beach resort near Venice; It., from L *lītus* shore]

**lie**[1] /laɪ/, *n., v.,* **lied, lying.** *–n.* **1.** a false statement made with intent to deceive; an intentional untruth; a falsehood. **2.** something intended or serving to convey a false impression. **3.** the charge or accusation of lying; a flat contradiction. **4. give the lie (to), a.** to charge with lying; contradict flatly. **b.** to imply or show to be false; belie. [ME; OE *lyge,* c. Icel. *lygi*] *–v.i.* **5.** to speak falsely or utter untruth knowingly, as with intent to deceive. **6.** to express what is false, or convey a false impression. *–v.t.* **7.** to bring to a specific state or effect by lying: *to lie oneself out of a difficulty.* [ME *lien,* OE *lēogan,* c. Goth. *liugan*]

**lie**[2] /laɪ/, *v.,* **lay, lain, lying,** *n.* *–v.i.* **1.** to be in a recumbent or prostrate position, as on a bed or the ground; recline. **2.** to assume such a position (fol. by *down*): *to lie down on the ground.* **3.** to be buried (in a particular spot). **4.** to rest in a horizontal position; be stretched out or extended: *a book lying on the table.* **5.** to be or remain in a position or state of inactivity, subjection, restraint, concealment, etc.: *to lie in ambush.* **6.** to rest, press, or weigh (fol. by *on* or *upon*): *these things lie upon my mind.* **7.** to depend (fol. by *on* or *upon*). **8.** to be found, occur, or be (where specified): *the fault lies here.* **9.** to be placed or situated: *land lying along the coast.* **10.** to consist or be grounded (fol. by *in*): *the real remedy lies in education.* **11.** to be in or have a specified direction: *the trail from here lies to the west.* **12.** *Law.* to be sustainable or admissible, as an action or appeal. **13.** *Archaic.* to lodge; sojourn. **14. as far as in me lies,** to the best of my ability. **15. let sleeping dogs lie,** to avoid any disturbance, or a controversial topic or action. **16. lie down under,** to accept (abuse, etc.) without protest. **17. lie in, a.** to be confined in childbed. **b.** to stay late in bed. **18. lie in state,** (of a corpse) to be honourably displayed, as in a church, etc. **19. lie low,** to be in hiding. **20. lie off,** (of a ship) to stand some distance away from the shore. **21. lie over,** to be postponed or deferred. **22. lie to,** *Naut.* (of a ship) to lie comparatively stationary, usu. with the head as near the wind as possible. **23. lie up, a.** to stay in bed. **b.** (of a ship) to go into dock. **24. lie with, a.** to be the function or responsibility of: *it lies with you to resolve the problem.* **b.** to have sexual intercourse with. **25. take lying down,** to submit without resistance or protest. *–n.* **26.** manner of lying; the relative position or direction in which something lies: *lie of the land.* **27.** the place where a bird, beast, or fish is accustomed to lie or lurk. **28.** *Golf.* the ground position of the golf ball. [ME *lie(n),* *liggen,* OE *licgan,* c. D *liggen,* G *liegen,* Icel. *liggja,* Goth. *ligan*]

**Liechtenstein** /ˈlɪktənstaɪn/, *n.* a small principality in central Europe between Austria and Switzerland.

**lied** /lid/, *n., pl.* **lieder** /ˈlidə/. a song, lyric, or ballad, esp. one characteristic of the German Romantic period. [G]

**liedertafel** /ˈlidətæfəl/, *n.* a group formed for the pleasure of singing in chorus. [G]

**lie detector** /ˈlaɪ dətɛktə/, *n.* an instrument, as a polygraph, for recording a person's involuntary physiological responses while under interrogation as an indication of the veracity of any statements he makes.

**lie-down** /laɪ-ˈdaʊn/, *n.* a rest taken while lying down.

**lief** /lif/, *adv.* **1.** Also, **lieve.** gladly; willingly. *–adj. Archaic.* **2.** willing. **3.** beloved; dear. [ME *leef,* OE *lēof,* c. G *lieb*]

**liege** /lidʒ, liʒ/, *n.* **1.** a lord entitled to allegiance and service. **2.** a vassal or subject, as of a ruler. *–adj.* **3.** entitled to, or owing, allegiance and service. **4.** pertaining to the relation between vassal and lord. **5.** loyal; faithful. [ME *lige,* from OF: liege, free, exempt, from LL *lēticus,* from *lētus* free man, of Gmc orig.]

**liegeman** /ˈlidʒmən/, *n., pl.* **-men.** **1.** a vassal; a subject. **2.** a faithful follower.

**lie-in** /ˈlaɪ-ɪn/, *n.* a period of rest or sleep taken by remaining in bed till some time after one's normal hour of rising.

**lien**[1] /ˈliən/, *n.* (in law) the right to hold property or to have it sold or applied for payment of a claim. [F, from L *ligāmen* band, tie]

**lien**[2] /ˈliən/, *n.* →**spleen.**

**lientery** /ˈlaɪəntəri/, *n.* a form of diarrhoea in which the food is discharged undigested or only partly digested. [ML *līenteria,* from Gk *leienteria*] – **lienteric** /laɪənˈtɛrɪk/, *adj.*

i = peat ɪ = pit ɛ = pet æ = pat a = part ɒ = pot ʌ = putt ɔ = port ʊ = put u = pool ɜ = pert ə = apart aɪ = buy eɪ = bay ɔɪ = boy aʊ = how oʊ = hoe ɪə = here ɛə = hair ʊə = tour g = give θ = thin ð = then ʃ = show ʒ = measure tʃ = choke dʒ = joke ŋ = sing j = you õ = Fr. bon

**lier** /lɪə/, *n.* →**lehr.**

**lierne** /li'ɜn/, *n.* a short connecting rib used in Gothic vaulting. [late ME, from F, var. of *liorne.* See LIANA]

**lieu** /lu, lju/, *n.* **1.** place; stead. **2. in lieu of,** instead of. [ME *liue,* from F *lieu,* from L *locus* place]

**Lieut.,** Lieutenant.

**Lieut. Col.,** Lieutenant Colonel.

**lieutenancy** /lɛf'tɛnənsi/, *n., pl.* **-cies. 1.** the office, authority, incumbency, or jurisdiction of a lieutenant. **2.** lieutenants collectively.

**lieutenant** /lɛf'tɛnənt/; *U.S.* /lu'tɛnənt/ *n.* **1.** *Mil.* a commissioned officer ranking below a captain and above a second lieutenant. **2.** *Navy.* a commissioned officer ranking below a lieutenant commander and above a sublieutenant. **3.** the rank of either of these. **4.** one who holds an office, civil or military, in subordination to a superior, for whom he acts. [ME *levetenant,* from F *lieutenant,* from *lieu* (from L *locus*) place + *tenant,* ppr. of *tenir* (from L *tenēre*) hold]

**lieutenant colonel** /– 'kɜnəl/, *n.* **1.** a commissioned army officer ranking below a colonel and above a major, equivalent to commander in the navy, and wing-commander in the air force. **2.** the rank itself.

**lieutenant commander** /– kə'mændə/, *n.* **1.** a naval officer ranking below a commander and above a lieutenant. **2.** the rank itself.

**lieutenant general** /– 'dʒɛnrəl/, *n.* **1.** an army officer ranking below a general and above a major general, equal to vice-admiral in the navy, and air marshal in the air force. **2.** the rank itself.

**lieutenant governor** /– 'gʌvənə/, *n.* a deputy governor.

**Lieut. Gen.,** Lieutenant General.

**Lieut. Gov.,** Lieutenant Governor.

**lieve** /liv/, *adv.* →**lief.**

**life** /laɪf/, *n., pl.* **lives. 1.** the condition which distinguishes animals and plants from inorganic objects and dead organisms. The distinguishing manifestations of life are: growth through metabolism, reproduction, and the power of adaptation to environment through changes originating internally. **2.** (*collectively*) the distinguishing phenomena (esp. metabolism, growth, reproduction, and spontaneous adaptation to environment) of plants and animals, arising out of the energy relationships with protoplasm. **3.** the animate existence, or the term of animate existence, of an individual: *to risk one's life.* **4.** a corresponding state, existence, or principle of existence conceived as belonging to the soul: *eternal life.* **5.** state or condition of existence as a human being: *life is not a bed of roses.* **6.** period of existence from birth to death: *in later life she became more placid.* **7. a.** the term of existence, activity, or effectiveness of something inanimate, as a machine or a lease. **b.** *Physics.* Also, **lifetime.** the average period between the appearance and disappearance of a particle. **8.** a living being: *several lives were lost.* **9.** living things collectively, whether animals or plants: *insect life.* **10.** course or mode of existence: *married life.* **11.** a biography: *a life of Menzies.* **12.** animation, liveliness: *a speech full of life.* **13.** that which makes or keeps alive; the vivifying or quickening principle. **14.** existence in the world of affairs, society, etc. **15.** one who or that which enlivens: *the life of the party.* **16.** effervescence or sparkle, as of wines. **17.** pungency or strong, sharp flavour, as of substances when fresh or in good condition. **18.** *Cricket.* the quality in the pitch which causes the ball to rise abruptly or unevenly after leaving the ground. **19.** the living form or model as the subject or representation in art. **20. a.** a prison sentence covering the rest of the convicted person's natural life. **b.** the maximum possible term of imprisonment that can be awarded by the laws of a state. **21. (a matter of) life and death,** a critical situation. **22. as large as life,** *Colloq.* actually; in person. **23. come to life, a.** to recover consciousness. **b.** to display liveliness or vigour. **c.** to appear lifelike; be convincing or realistic. **24. for dear life,** urgently; desperately. **25. for the life of one,** with the greatest effort: *for the life of me I can't understand him.* **26. from the life** (of a drawing, painting, etc.) drawn from a living model. **27. have the time of one's life,** to enjoy oneself enormously. **28. not on your life,** *Colloq.* absolutely not. **29. such is life!** (an exclamation indicating resignation or tolerance). **30. take one's life in one's hands,** to risk death. **31. that's life,** (an exclamation indicating resignation or tolerance). **32. to the life,** being an exact imitation or copy. [ME; OE *līf,* c. D *lijf* body, G *Leib,* Icel. *līf* life, body]

**life assurance** /'– əʃɔrəns/, *n.* insurance providing payment of a specific sum of money to a named beneficiary upon the death of the assured, or to the assured or to a named beneficiary should the assured reach a specified age. Also, **life insurance.**

**lifebelt** /'laɪfbɛlt/, *n.* a belt of buoyant material to keep a person afloat in the water.

**lifeblood** /'laɪfblʌd/, *n.* **1.** the blood necessary to life. **2.** the element that vivifies, animates or supports anything. Also, **life's blood.**

**lifeboat** /'laɪfboʊt/, *n.* **1.** a shore-based boat esp. built for rescuing the occupants of ships in distress along the coast. **2.** a boat, provisioned and equipped for abandoning ship, carried in davits so that it may be lowered quickly.

**lifebuoy** /'laɪfbɔɪ/, *n.* a buoyant device (in various forms) for throwing, as from a vessel, to persons in the water, to enable them to keep afloat until rescued.

**life cycle** /'laɪf saɪkəl/, *n.* the course of development from the fertilisation of the egg to the production of a new generation of germ cells.

**life expectancy** /'– əkspɛktənsi/, *n.* the probable life span of an individual or class of persons, determined statistically, and affected by such factors as heredity, physical condition, nutrition, occupation, etc.

**life form** /'– fɔm/, *n.* the generic category to which anything which is alive belongs.

**life-giving** /'laɪf-gɪvɪŋ/, *adj.* imparting life or vitality; invigorating.

**lifeguard** /'laɪfgad/, *n.* **1.** a person employed at a place where people bathe to rescue and give first aid to those in distress. **2.** one of a bodyguard of soldiers.

**life history** /laɪf 'hɪstri/, *n.* **1.** the series of living phenomena exhibited by an organism in the course of its development from the egg to its adult state. **2.** a life cycle.

**life insurance** /'– ɪnʃɔrəns/, *n.* →**life assurance.**

**life interest** /– 'ɪntrəst/, *n.* an entitlement, lasting for one's life time only, to benefits, dividends or interest from an investment, property, etc.

**life jacket** /'– dʒækət/, *n.* an inflatable or buoyant sleeveless jacket for keeping a person afloat in water. Also, **life vest.**

**lifeless** /'laɪfləs/, *adj.* **1.** not endowed with life: *lifeless matter.* **2.** destitute of living things: *a lifeless planet.* **3.** deprived of life, or dead: *lifeless bodies.* **4.** without animation, liveliness, or spirit: *lifeless performance.* **5.** insensible, as one in a faint. **– lifelessly,** *adv.* **– lifelessness,** *n.*

**lifelike** /'laɪflaɪk/, *adj.* resembling or simulating real life: *a lifelike picture.* **– lifelikeness,** *n.*

**lifeline** /'laɪflaɪn/, *n.* **1.** a line fired across a vessel by which a hawser for a breeches buoy may be hauled aboard. **2.** a line or rope for saving life, as one attached to a lifeboat. **3.** the line by which a deep-sea diver is lowered and raised. **4.** any of several lines, which are anchored and used by bathers for support. **5.** a route over which supplies can be sent to an area otherwise isolated. **6.** any vital line of communication. **7.** a telephone link with a counsellor for people in mental or emotional distress. **8.** *Palmistry.* a line on the palm of the hand supposed to indicate the length and significant events of one's life.

**lifelong** /'laɪflɒŋ/, *adj.* lasting or continuing throughout life: *lifelong regret.*

**life-model** /laɪf-'mɒdl/, *v.i.,* **-modelled, -modelling.** to pose as a model for an artist or art class.

**life peer** /'laɪf pɪə/, *n.* a peer holding a title which lapses at his death. **– life peeress,** *n. fem.*

**life-preserver** /'laɪf-prəzɜvə/, *n.* **1.** *Brit.* a short stick with a weighted head, used for self-defence; bludgeon. **2.** *U.S.* a life jacket, lifebelt, or other device for saving persons in the water from sinking and drowning.

**lifer** /'laɪfə/, *n. Colloq.* one sentenced to imprisonment for life.

**life raft** /'laɪf raft/, *n.* a raft carried by a ship for use in emergencies at sea.

**lifesaver** /ˈlaɪfseɪvə/, *n.* **1.** one of a group of volunteers who patrol surfing beaches, etc., making sure that bathers swim in designated safe areas, and who are trained in rescue and resuscitation methods. **2.** any person who restores another to good spirits with comfort, help, etc. **3.** anything restorative or beneficially rectifying: *that bank loan was a real lifesaver.*

**lifesaving** /ˈlaɪfseɪvɪŋ/, *n.* the activities of life-savers often regarded as an organised sport: *my son is doing lifesaving at school.* Also, **surf-lifesaving.**

**life's blood** /laɪfs ˈblʌd/, *n.* →**lifeblood.**

**life sciences** /ˈlaɪf saɪənsəz/, *n.pl.* biology, botany, physiology, or any other science concerned with living things.

**life-size** /ˈlaɪf-saɪz/, *adj.* of the size of life or the living original: *life-size picture or statue.* Also, **life-sized.**

**life span** /ˈlaɪf spæn/, *n.* the longest period over which the life of any plant or animal organism or species may extend, according to the available biological knowledge concerning it. Cf. **life expectancy.**

**lifestyle** /ˈlaɪfstaɪl/, *n.* a mode of life chosen by a person or group. Also, **life-style.**

**life support system,** *n.* all the equipment which makes human life possible in a system in which it would normally die, as for astronauts, brain-damaged patients, etc.

**life's work** /laɪfs ˈwɜk/, *n.* →**lifework.**

**lifetime** /ˈlaɪftaɪm/, *n.* **1.** the time that one's life continues; one's term of life: *peace within our lifetime.* **2.** →**life** (def. 7b). *–adj.* **3.** lasting a lifetime.

**lifework** /laɪfˈwɜk/, *n.* the work or labour of a lifetime. Also, **life's work.**

**lift** /lɪft/, *v.t.* **1.** to move or bring (something) upwards from the ground or other support to some higher position; hoist. **2.** to raise or direct upwards: *to lift the hand, head, or eyes.* **3.** to hold up or display on high. **4.** to raise in rank, condition, estimation, etc.; elevate or exalt. **5.** to make louder or more audible: *to lift the voice.* **6.** to rescind or remove; bring to an end: *to lift the ban on the import of drugs.* **7.** to carry: *this ship can lift 3 000 tonnes of cargo.* **8.** to move (cattle, goods, etc.) from one place to another. **9.** *Colloq.* to steal or plagiarise. **10.** to dig up (root crops). **11.** to perform a facelift on. **12.** *U.S.* to pay off a mortgage, etc. **13.** *Golf.* to pick or take up. **14.** *Agric.* to transport cattle or goods from one place to another. *–v.i.* **15.** to go up; give to upward pressure: *the lid won't lift.* **16.** to pull or strain in the effort to lift something: *to lift at a heavy weight.* **17.** to move upwards or rise; rise and disperse, as clouds, fog, etc. **18.** to rise to view above the horizon when approached, as land seen from the sea. *–n.* **19.** the act of lifting, raising, or rising: *the lift of a hand.* **20.** extent of rise, or distance through which anything is raised. **21.** lifting or raising force. **22.** the weight or load lifted. **23.** a moving platform or cage for conveying goods, people, etc., from one level to another, as in a building. **24.** any device or apparatus for lifting. **25.** a helping upwards or onwards. **26.** a ride in a vehicle, esp. one given free of charge to a traveller on foot. **27.** exaltation or uplift, as in feeling. **28.** a rise or elevation of ground. **29.** *Aeron.* a force exerted by the air on an aerofoil and acting perpendicularly to the flight path. **30.** one of the layers of leather forming the heel of a boot or shoe. **31.** *Mining.* a thickness (of ore) mined in one operation. **32.** the direction in which a wave breaks or a surfer travels. **33.** the establishment of a sheepdog's control over a flock, before they are rounded up. [ME *lifte(n)*, from Scand.; cf. Icel. *lypta* lift, from *lopt* air, sky] – **lifter,** *n.*

**liftboy** /ˈlɪftbɔɪ/, *n.* a boy who operates a lift in a hotel, department store, etc.

**lifter** /ˈlɪftə/, *n.* (in cricket) a ball which rises quickly and sharply after bouncing.

**lifting body** /ˈlɪftɪŋ bɒdi/, *n.* a wingless aircraft which derives aerodynamic lift from its shape alone.

**liftman** /ˈlɪftmæn/, *n.* a man who operates a lift in a hotel, department store, etc.

**lift-off** /ˈlɪft-ɒf/, *n.* **1.** Also, **blast-off.** the start of a rocket's flight from its launching pad. *–adj.* **2.** removable by lifting: *a lift-off lid.*

**lift-on, lift-off** /lɪft-ˌɒn, lɪft-ˈɒf/, *adj.* of or pertaining to a method of transportation of goods in which they are packed in containers which can be easily moved from ship to wharf by fork-lifts: *lift-on, lift-off shipping.*

**lift-out** /ˈlɪft-aʊt/, *n.* a special supplement in a newspaper, magazine, etc., designed to be lifted out in one piece.

**lift-pump** /ˈlɪft-pʌmp/, *n.* any pump which merely lifts or raises a liquid (distinguished from *force-pump*).

**liftslab** /ˈlɪftslæb/, *n.* a system of erecting multistorey buildings, in which the floor slabs, cast at ground level, are lifted up one by one.

**ligament** /ˈlɪgəmənt/, *n., pl.* **ligaments, ligamenta** /lɪgəˈmɛntə/. **1.** *Anat.* a band of tissue, usu. white and fibrous, serving to connect bones, hold organs in place, etc. **2.** a connecting tie; bond. [ME, from L *ligāmentum* a tie, band]

**ligamentous** /lɪgəˈmɛntəs/, *adj.* pertaining to, of the nature of, or forming a ligament. Also, **ligamentary** /lɪgəˈmɛntəri/.

**ligan** /ˈlaɪgən/, *n. Law.* →**lagan.**

**ligancy** /ˈlɪgənsi, ˈlaɪ-/, *n.* →**coordination number.**

**ligand** /ˈlɪgənd, ˈlaɪ-/, *n.* a molecule, atom or ion bonded to the central metal atom or ion in a coordination compound.

**ligate** /ˈlaɪgeɪt/, *v.t.,* **-gated, -gating.** to bind, as with a ligature; tie up, as a bleeding artery. [L *ligātus,* pp.] – **ligation** /laɪˈgeɪʃən/, *n.*

**ligature** /ˈlɪgətʃə/, *n., v.,* **-tured, -turing.** *–n.* **1.** the act of binding or tying up. **2.** anything that serves for binding or tying up, as a band, bandage, or cord. **3.** a tie or bond. **4.** *Print., Writing.* a stroke or bar connecting two letters. **5.** *Print.* a character or type combining two or more letters, as fi, ffl. **6.** *Music.* **a.** a slur. **b.** a group of notes connected by a slur. **c.** a metal band for adjusting the position of the reed on clarinets and saxophones. **7.** *Surg.* a thread or wire for constriction of blood vessels, etc., or for removing tumours by strangulation. *–v.t.* **8.** to bind with a ligature; tie up; ligate. [ME, from LL *ligātūra,* from L *ligāre* bind]

**liger** /ˈlaɪgə/, *n.* the offspring of a male lion and a female tiger. Cf. **tigon.**

**light**[1] /laɪt/, *n., adj., v.,* **lit** or **lighted, lighting.** *–n.* **1.** that which makes things visible, or affords illumination: *all colours depend on light.* **2.** *Physics.* **a.** Also, **luminous energy, radiant energy.** electromagnetic radiation to which the organs of sight react, ranging in wavelength from about $4 \times 10^{-7}$ to $7.7 \times 10^{-7}$ metres and propagated at a speed of $2.9979 \times 10^{8}$ metres per second. It is considered variously as a wave, corpuscular, or quantum phenomenon. **b.** the sensation produced by it on the organs of sight. **c.** a similar form of radiant energy which does not affect the retina, as ultraviolet or infra-red rays. **3.** an illuminating agent or source, as the sun, a lamp, or a beacon. **4.** the light, radiance, or illumination from a particular source: *the light of a candle.* **5.** the illumination from the sun, or daylight. **6.** daybreak or dawn. **7.** daytime. **8.** measure or supply of light; illumination: *the wall cuts off our light.* **9.** a particular light or illumination in which an object seen takes on a certain appearance: *viewing the portrait in various lights.* **10.** *Art.* **a.** the effect of light falling on an object or scene as represented in a picture. **b.** one of the brightest parts of a picture. **11.** (*pl.*) →**highlight** (def. 6). **12.** the aspect in which a thing appears or is regarded: *this shows up in a favourable light.* **13.** a gleam or sparkle, as in the eyes. **14.** a means of igniting, as a spark, flame, match, or the like: *could you give me a light?* **15.** state of being visible, exposed to view, or revealed to public notice or knowledge: *to come to light.* **16.** a window, or a pane or compartment of a window. **17.** mental or spiritual illumination or enlightenment: *to throw light on a mystery.* **18.** (*pl.*) information, ideas, or mental capacities possessed: *to act according to one's lights.* **19.** a person who is an illuminating or shining example; a luminary. **20.** a light-house. **21.** a traffic light. **22.** *Archaic.* the eyesight. **23. bring to light,** to discover; reveal. **24. come to light,** to be discovered; become known. **25. in a good (bad) light,** under favourable (unfavourable) circumstances. **26. in the light of,** taking into account; considering. **27. out like a light,** unconscious, esp. after being struck, or receiving an anaesthetic. **28. see the light, a.** to come into existence. **b.** to be made public, or published, as a book. **c.** to accept or understand an idea; realise the truth of something. **d.** to be converted, esp. to Christianity. **29. shed** or **throw light on,** to make clear; explain. *–adj.* **30.** having light or illumination, rather than dark: *the lightest room in the entire house.* **31.** pale, whitish, or not deep or dark in colour: *a light red.* *–v.t.* **32.** to set burning (a candle, lamp, pipe for smoking, etc.); kindle (a fire); ignite (fuel, a match, etc.). **33.** to switch on (an electric light). **34.** to give light to; illuminate; to furnish with light or illumination. **35.** to make bright as with light or colour (usu. with *up*): *a huge room lit up with candles.* **36.** to cause (the face, etc.) to brighten or become animated (oft. fol. by *up*): *a smile lit up her face.* **37.** to conduct with a light: *a candle to light you to bed.* *–v.i.* **38.** to take fire or become kindled. **39.** to become bright as with light or colour: *the sky lights up at sunset.* **40.** to brighten with animation or joy, as the face, eyes, etc. (oft. fol. by *up*). [ME; OE *lēoht*, c. D *licht*, G *Licht;* akin to Icel. *ljōs*, Goth. *liuhath*, also to L *lux* light, Gk *leukós* light, bright]

**light**[2] /laɪt/, *adj.* **1.** of little weight; not heavy: *a light load.* **2.** of little weight in proportion to bulk; of low specific gravity: *a light metal.* **3.** of less than the usual or average weight: *light clothing.* **4.** of small amount, force, intensity, etc.: *a light rain, light sleep.* **5.** gentle; delicate; exerting only slight pressure. **6.** easy to endure, deal with, or perform: *light duties.* **7.** not profound, serious, or heavy: *light reading.* **8.** of little moment or importance; trivial: *the loss was no light matter.* **9.** easily digested. **10.** not heavy or strong, as wine, etc. **11.** spongy or well leavened, as bread. **12.** porous or friable, as soil. **13.** slender or delicate in form or appearance: *a light, graceful figure.* **14.** airy or buoyant in movement: *light as air.* **15.** nimble or agile: *light on one's feet.* **16.** free from any burden of sorrow or care: *a light heart.* **17.** cheerful; gay: *a light laugh.* **18.** characterised by lack of proper seriousness; frivolous: *light conduct.* **19.** wanton; immoral. **20.** easily swayed or changing; volatile: *to be light of love.* **21.** dizzy; slightly delirious: *his head is light.* **22.** *Mil.* lightly armed or equipped: *light infantry.* **23.** adapted by small weight or slight build for small loads or swift movement: *light vessels.* **24.** *Phonet.* **a.** having a less than normally strong pronunciation, as of a vowel or syllable. **b.** (of *l* sounds) resembling a front vowel in quality: *French l is lighter than English l.* **25. light on,** *Colloq.* in short supply; scarce. **26. make light of,** treat as of little importance. *–adv.* **27.** lightly. **28.** *Colloq.* with little or no luggage: *to travel light.* **29.** with little or no cargo: *a ship sailing light.* [ME; OE *lēoht, līht*, c. D *licht*, G *leicht*]

**light**[3] /laɪt/, *v.i.*, **lighted** or **lit, lighting. 1.** to get down or descend, as from a horse or a vehicle. **2.** to come to rest, as on a spot or thing; land. **3.** to come by chance, happen, or hit (fol. by *on* or *upon*): *to light on a clue.* **4.** to fall, as a stroke, weapon, vengeance, choice, etc., on a place or person. **5. light out,** *Colloq.* to depart hastily. [ME *liht(en)*, *light(en)*, OE *līhtan* alight, orig. make light, relieve of a weight, from *līht* LIGHT[2], *adj.*]

**light air** /– 'ɛə/, *n.* a wind of Beaufort scale force 1, i.e. one with average wind speed of 1 to 3 knots, or 1 to 5 km/h.

**light ale** /– 'eɪl/, *n.* **1.** *Chiefly Brit.* a pale malt beer of low alcoholic strength, usu. bottled; pale ale. **2.** a low alcohol beer.

**light barrier** /'– bæriə/, *n.* the speed of light as the limiting speed attainable by any object.

**light breeze** /– 'briz/, *n.* a wind of Beaufort scale force 2, i.e. one with average wind speed of 4 to 6 knots, or 6 to 11 km/h.

**light bulb** /'– bʌlb/, *n.* →**bulb** (def. 3).

**light container load,** *n.* a shipping container loaded and unloaded at a container depot with the contents consigned to two or more consignees.

**light displacement mass,** *n.* the mass of a ship when it is empty, measured in tonnes.

**light displacement tonnage,** *n.* the mass of a ship when it is empty, measured in tons. Also, **light ship weight.**

**light-emitting diode** /ˌlaɪt-əmɪtɪŋ 'daɪoʊd/, *n.* a semiconductor diode that emits light when a current flows through it. *Abbrev.:* **LED**

**lighten**[1] /'laɪtn/, *v.i.* **1.** to become lighter or less dark; brighten. **2.** to shine, gleam, or be bright. **3.** to flash as or like lightning. **4.** to brighten or light up, as the face, eyes, etc. *–v.t.* **5.** to illuminate. **6.** to brighten (the eyes, features, etc.). **7.** to make lighter; make less dark. [ME, from LIGHT[1], *adj.* + -EN[1]] – **lightener,** *n.*

**lighten**[2] /'laɪtn/, *v.t.* **1.** to make lighter; lessen the weight of (a load, etc.); reduce the load of (a ship, etc.). **2.** to make less burdensome; mitigate: *to lighten taxes.* **3.** to cheer or gladden. *–v.i.* **4.** to become less burdensome, oppressive, etc. **5.** to become more cheerful or lively. [ME, from LIGHT[2], *adj.* + -EN[1]]

**lighter**[1] /'laɪtə/, *n.* **1.** one who or that which lights. **2.** a mechanical device for lighting cigarettes, cigars, etc. [ME; from LIGHT[1], *v.* + -ER[1]]

**lighter**[2] /'laɪtə/, *n.* **1.** a vessel, commonly a flat-bottomed unpowered barge, used in lightening or unloading and also in loading ships, or in transporting goods for short distances. *–v.t.* **2.** to convey in or as in a lighter. [ME, from LIGHT[2], *v.* + -ER[1]]

**lighterage** /'laɪtərɪdʒ/, *n.* **1.** the use of lighters. **2.** a fee paid for lighter service. [LIGHTER[2] + -AGE]

**lighterman** /'laɪtəmən/, *n.* one who navigates a lighter.

**lighter-than-air** /laɪtə-ðən-'ɛə/, *adj.* **1.** of less specific gravity than the air. **2.** of or pertaining to such aircraft.

**lightface** /'laɪtfeɪs/, *n.* a type characterised by thin lines.

**light fantastic** /laɪt fæn'tæstɪk/, *n.* the motions of dancing; dancing: *trip the light fantastic.*

**lightfast** /'laɪtfast/, *adj.* (of a pigment, dye, or dyed fabric) not affected by light, esp. not bleached by sunlight.

**light-fingered** /'laɪt-fɪŋgəd/, *adj.* having nimble fingers, esp. in picking pockets; thievish.

**light fingers** /'laɪt fɪŋgəz/, *n.* *Colloq.* a petty thief; pickpocket.

**light flyweight** /– 'flaɪweɪt/, *n.* an amateur boxer weighing no more than 48 kg.

**light-footed** /'laɪt-fʊtəd/, *adj.* stepping lightly or nimbly. Also, *Poetic,* **light-foot** /'laɪt-fʊt/. – **light-footedly,** *adv.* – **light-footedness,** *n.*

**light-handed** /'laɪt-hændəd/, *adj.* **1.** having a light, skilful, or delicate touch. **2.** carrying little in the hands. **3.** understaffed.

**light-headed** /'laɪt-hɛdəd/, *adj.* **1.** having or showing a frivolous or volatile disposition: *light-headed persons.* **2.** giddy, dizzy, drunk, or delirious. – **light-headedly,** *adv.* – **light-headedness,** *n.*

**light-hearted** /'laɪt-hatəd/, *adj.* carefree; cheerful; gay: *a light-hearted laugh.* – **light-heartedly,** *adv.* – **light-heartedness,** *n.*

**light heavyweight** /laɪt 'hɛviweɪt/, *n.* **1.** a boxer weighing between 75 and 81 kg (in the amateur ranks) or between 72.574 and 79.378 kg (in the professional ranks). **2.** a professional wrestler weighing between 78.925 and 83.461 kg.

**light-horseman** /laɪt-'hɔsmən/, *n., pl.* **-men.** a light-armed cavalry soldier.

**lighthouse** /'laɪthaʊs/, *n.* a tower or other structure displaying a light or lights for the guidance of mariners.

Macquarie lighthouse

**lighting** /'laɪtɪŋ/, *n.* **1.** the act of igniting or illuminating. **2.** arrangement or method of lights. **3.** the way light falls upon a face, object, etc., esp. in a picture.

**lighting rigger** /'– rɪgə/, *n.* one who sets and arranges stage lighting.

**lightless** /'laɪtləs/, *adj.* **1.** without light; receiving no light; dark. **2.** giving no light.

**lightly** /'laɪtli/, *adv.* **1.** with little weight, force, intensity, etc.: *to press lightly on a bell.* **2.** to only a small amount or degree. **3.** easily; without trouble or effort: *lightly come, lightly go.* **4.** cheerfully: *to take the news lightly.* **5.** frivolously: *to behave lightly.* **6.** without due consideration or reason (often with a negative): *an offer not lightly to be refused.* **7.** nimbly: *to leap lightly aside.* **8.** indifferently or slightingly: *to think lightly of one's achievements.* **9.** airily; buoyantly: *flags floating lightly.*

**light meter** /'laɪt mitə/, *n.* (in photography) an instrument which measures the light intensity and indicates the proper exposure for a given scene. Also, **exposure meter.**

**light middleweight** /– 'mɪdəlweɪt/, *n.* an amateur boxer weighing between 67 and 71 kg.

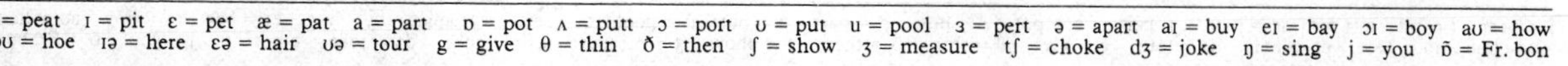

**light-minded** /ˈlaɪt-maɪndəd/, *adj.* having or showing a light mind; characterised by levity; frivolous. – **light-mindedly,** *adv.* – **light-mindedness,** *n.*

**light music** /laɪt ˈmjuzɪk/, *n.* music produced for popular entertainment, esp. that played by a conventional orchestra.

**lightness**[1] /ˈlaɪtnəs/, *n.* **1.** the state of being light, illuminated, or whitish. **2.** thin or pale coloration. [ME *lightnesse,* OE *lihtnes,* from *līht* LIGHT[1], bright + *-nes* -NESS]

**lightness**[2] /ˈlaɪtnəs/, *n.* **1.** the state or quality of being light in weight. **2.** the state or quality of being light as to specific gravity: *the lightness of cork.* **3.** the quality of being agile, nimble, or graceful. **4.** lack of pressure or burdensomeness. **5.** gayness; cheerfulness. **6.** levity in actions, thought, or speech. [LIGHT[2], *adj.* + -NESS]

**lightning** /ˈlaɪtnɪŋ/, *n.* a flashing of light, or a sudden illumination of the sky, caused by the discharge of atmospheric electricity. [var. of *lightening,* from LIGHTEN[1], *v.* + -ING[1]]

**lightning arrester** /ˈ– ərɛstə/, *n.* a device preventing damage to radio, telephonic, or other electrical equipment from lightning or other high-voltage currents, reducing the voltage of a surge applied to its terminals and restoring itself to its original operating condition.

**lightning bug** /ˈ– bʌg/, *n.* →**firefly** (def. 1).

**lightning conductor** /ˈ– kəndʌktə/, *n.* a rodlike conductor installed to divert atmospheric electricity away from a structure and protect the structure from lightning by providing a path to earth. Also, **lightning rod.**

**lightning strike** /– ˈstraɪk/, *n.* a stoppage of work by employees with little or no warning to employers.

**light-o'-love** /laɪt-ə-ˈlʌv/, *n.* **1.** a person with whom one is in love. **2.** *Brit., U.S.* a wanton coquette; prostitute.

**light opera** /laɪt ˈɒprə/, *n.* →**operetta.**

**light-pen** /ˈlaɪt-pɛn/, *n.* a light sensitive device, made to look like a pen, which by moving the position of a point of light on a display screen, can interact with a computer.

**light quantum** /ˈlaɪt kwɒntəm/, *n.* →**photon.**

**lights** /laɪts/, *n.pl.* the lungs, esp. of sheep, pigs, etc.

**lightship** /ˈlaɪtˌʃɪp/, *n.* a ship anchored in a specific location and displaying a light or lights for the guidance of mariners.

**lightshow** /ˈlaɪtˌʃoʊ/, *n.* a visual extravaganza of coloured, bright and flashing lights and various kinds of film which dominates the room space, and which is usu. used to accompany heavy rock music or acid rock.

**lightsome**[1] /ˈlaɪtsəm/, *adj.* **1.** light, esp. in form, appearance, or movement; airy; buoyant; agile; nimble. **2.** cheerful; gay. **3.** frivolous. [LIGHT[2] + -SOME[1]] – **lightsomely,** *adv.* – **lightsomeness,** *n.*

**lightsome**[2] /ˈlaɪtsəm/, *adj.* **1.** luminous. **2.** well-lighted or illuminated. [LIGHT[1] + -SOME[1]] – **lightsomeness,** *n.*

**lights out** /ˈlaɪts aʊt/, *n.* a signal that all or certain lights in a barracks, camp, school boarding house, etc., are to be extinguished.

**light-struck** /ˈlaɪt-strʌk/, *adj.* (of film, etc.) injured or fogged by accidental exposure to light.

**light-switch** /ˈlaɪt-swɪtʃ/, *n.* a switch for turning a light on and off.

**lightweight** /ˈlaɪtweɪt/, *adj.* **1.** light in weight. **2.** unimportant, not serious; trivial. *–n.* **3.** one of less than average weight. **4.** *Colloq.* a person of little mental force or of slight influence or importance. **5.** a boxer who weighs between 57 and 60 kg (in amateur ranks), or between 58.967 and 61.235 kg (in professional ranks).

**light well** /ˈlaɪt wɛl/, *n.* a well[2] (def. 5) designed to allow light into the inner rooms of a building.

**light welterweight** /– ˈwɛltəweɪt/, *n.* an amateur boxer weighing between 60 and 63.5 kg.

**light-year** /ˈlaɪt-jɪə/, *n.* the distance traversed by light in one year (9.460 55 × $10^{15}$ metres), used as a unit in measuring stellar distances. *Symbol:* l.y.

**lign-aloes** /laɪn-ˈæloʊz/, *n.* the drug aloes; aloes-wood.

**ligneous** /ˈlɪgniəs/, *adj.* of the nature of or resembling wood; woody. [L *ligneus* wooden]

**ligni-,** variant of **ligno-.**

**ligniform** /ˈlɪgnəfɔm/, *adj.* having the form of wood; resembling wood, as a variety of asbestos.

**lignify** /ˈlɪgnəfaɪ/, *v.,* **-fied, -fying.** *–v.t.* **1.** to convert into wood. *–v.i.* **2.** to become woody. – **lignification** /lɪgnəfəˈkeɪʃən/, *n.*

**lignin** /ˈlɪgnən/, *n.* an organic substance which, with cellulose, forms the chief part of woody tissue.

**lignite** /ˈlɪgnaɪt/, *n.* an imperfectly formed coal, usu. dark brown, and often having a distinct woody texture; brown coal; wood coal. [F, from L *lignum* wood. See -ITE[1]] – **lignitic** /lɪgˈnɪtɪk/, *adj.*

**lignite wax** /ˈ– wæks/, *n.* →**montan wax.**

**ligno-,** a word element meaning 'wood'. [combining form representing L *lignum*]

**lignocaine** /ˈlɪgnəkeɪn/, *n.* a drug used: **a.** as a local anaesthetic, topically or by infiltration. **b.** as an anti-arrhythmic drug by intravenous injection. [LIGNO-, L equivalent of XYLO- + *-caine,* after COCAINE (compound's orig. name *xylocaine*)]

**lignocellulose** /lɪgnoʊˈsɛljəloʊz, -oʊs/, *n.* any of various compounds of lignin and cellulose found in wood and other fibres.

**lignose** /ˈlɪgnoʊz, -oʊs/, *n.* one of the constituents of lignin. [L *lignōsus* woody]

**lignotuber** /ˈlɪgnoʊˌtjubə/, *n.* a woody swelling, partly or wholly underground, at the base of the stem of certain plants and containing numerous cortical buds.

**lignum** /ˈlɪgnəm/, *n.* a tall, almost leafless shrub, *Muehlenbeckia cunninghamii,* common on low lying ground in the interior of Australia.

**lignum vitae** /– ˈvaɪti, ˈvitaɪ/, *n.* **1.** the hard, extremely heavy wood of either of two species of guaiacum, *Guaiacum officinale* and *G. sanctum,* used for making pulleys, rulers, etc., and formerly thought to have great medicinal powers. **2.** either tree. **3.** any of various other trees with a similar hard wood. [NL: wood of life]

**ligroin** /ˈlɪgroʊən/, *n.* a mixture of hydrocarbons of the paraffin series; usu. applied to a mixture with a boiling point in the range 70-120°C.

**ligula** /ˈlɪgjələ/, *n., pl.* **-lae** /-li/, **-las. 1.** *Bot., Zool.* a tongue-like or strap-shaped part or organ. **2.** *Bot.* →**ligule.** [L: strap, var. of *lingula,* diminutive of *lingua* tongue] – **ligular,** *adj.*

**ligulate** /ˈlɪgjələt, -leɪt/, *adj.* **1.** having or forming a ligula. **2.** strap-shaped.

**ligule** /ˈlɪgjul/, *n.* **1.** a thin, membranous outgrowth from the base of the blade of most grasses. **2.** a strap-shaped corolla, as in the ray flowers of various members of the Compositae. [L *lingula;* see LIGULA]

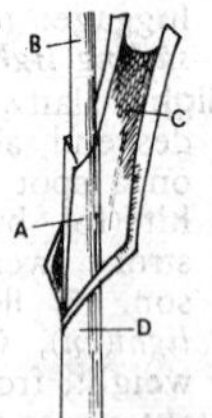

A, ligule; B, stem; C, leaf blade; D, leaf sheath

**likable** /ˈlaɪkəbəl/, *adj.* →**likeable.**

**like**[1] /laɪk/, *prep., adj.* (*Archaic* **liker, likest**), *adv., conj., n. –prep.* **1.** similarly to; in a manner characteristic of: *they lived like kings.* **2.** typical or characteristic of: *an act of kindness just like him.* **3.** bearing resemblance to: *he is like his father.* **4.** for example; as; such as: *the basic necessities of life, like food and drink.* **5.** indicating a probability of: *it looks like being a fine day, that seems like a good idea.* **6.** desirous of; disposed to (after *feel*): *I feel like a double whisky.* **7.** introducing an intensive, sometimes facetious, comparison: *like hell, like anything. –adj.* **8.** of the same form, appearance, kind, character, amount, etc.: *a like instance.* **9.** corresponding or agreeing in general or in some noticeable respect; similar; analogous: *drawing, painting, and like arts.* **10.** bearing resemblance. **11.** *Archaic.* likely. *–adv.* **12.** *Colloq.* as it were: *it's a bit tough, like. –conj.* **13.** *Colloq.* just as, or as: *he did it like he wanted.* **14.** *Colloq.* as if: *he acted like he was afraid. –n.* **15.** something of a similar nature (prec. by *the*): *oranges, lemons, and the like.* **16.** a like person or thing, or like persons or things; a counterpart, match, or equal: *no one has seen his like in a long time.* [ME; OE *gelīc,* c. D *gelijk,* G *gleich,* Icel. *glīkr,* Goth. *galeiks* like, lit., of the same body, or form]

**like**[2] /laɪk/, *v.,* **liked, liking,** *n. –v.t.* **1.** to take pleasure in; find agreeable to one's taste. **2.** to regard with favour, or have a kindly or friendly feeling for (a person, etc.). *–v.i.* **3.** to feel inclined, or wish: *come whenever you like. –n.* **4.** (*usu. pl.*) a favourable feeling; preference: *likes and dislikes.* [ME *like(n),* OE *līcian,* c. D *lijken,* Icel. *līka*]

**-like,** a suffix of adjectives, use of **like**[1], as in *childlike, lifelike, horselike,* sometimes hyphenated.

**likeable** /ˈlaɪkəbəl/, *adj.* readily or easily liked; pleasing. Also, **likable.** – **likeableness,** *n.*

**likelihood** /ˈlaɪklihʊd/, *n.* **1.** the state of being likely or probable; probability. **2.** a probability or chance of something: *there is a strong likelihood of his succeeding.* **3.** *Archaic.* promising character, or promise. Also, **likeliness.**

**likely** /ˈlaɪkli/, *adj.,* **-lier, -liest,** *adv.* –*adj.* **1.** probably or apparently going or destined (to do, be, etc.): *likely to happen.* **2.** seeming like truth, fact, or certainty, or reasonably to be believed or expected; probable: *a likely story.* **3.** apparently suitable: *a likely spot to build on.* **4.** promising: *a fine likely boy.* –*adv.* **5.** probably. [ME, from Scand.; cf. Icel. *líkligr,* from *líkr* LIKE[1], *adj.* + *-ligr* -LY]

**like-minded** /ˈlaɪk-maɪndəd/, *adj.* having a like opinion or interest. – **like-mindedness,** *n.*

**liken** /ˈlaɪkən/, *v.t.* to represent as like; compare.

**likeness** /ˈlaɪknəs/, *n.* **1.** a representation, picture, or image, esp. a portrait. **2.** the semblance or appearance of something: *to assume the likeness of a swan.* **3.** the state or fact of being like.

**likewise** /ˈlaɪkwaɪz/, *adv.* **1.** moreover; also; too. **2.** in like manner. [abbrev. of *in like wise.* See LIKE[1], -WISE, *n.*]

**liking** /ˈlaɪkɪŋ/, *n.* **1.** preference, inclination, or favour. **2.** pleasure or taste: *much to his liking.* **3.** the state or feeling of one who likes. [ME; OE *līcung,* from *līcian* please]

**lilac** /ˈlaɪlək/, *n.* **1.** any of the shrubs constituting the genus *Syringa,* as *S. vulgaris,* the common garden lilac, with large clusters of fragrant purple or white flowers. **2.** pale reddish purple. **3.** the scent of lilac, esp. in perfumes, etc. –*adj.* **4.** having the colour lilac. [F (obs.), or from Sp., from Ar. *līlak,* from Pers., var. of *nīlak* bluish, from *nīl* blue, indigo (c. Skt *nīla* dark blue). Cf. ANIL]

**lilaceous** /laɪˈleɪʃəs/, *adj.* of or approaching the colour lilac.

**liliaceous** /lɪliˈeɪʃəs/, *adj.* **1.** of or like the lily. **2.** belonging to the Liliaceae, or lily family of plants. [LL *līliāceus,* from L *līlium* LILY]

**lilied** /ˈlɪlid/, *adj.* **1.** lily-like; white. **2.** abounding in lilies.

**Lilliputian** /lɪləˈpjuʃən/, *adj.* **1.** tiny; diminutive. **2.** narrow-minded; petty. –*n.* **3.** a tiny being. **4.** a person of narrow outlook; a petty-minded person. [from *Lilliput,* an imaginary island inhabited by tiny people, in *Gulliver's Travels* (1726) by Jonathan Swift]

**lilly pilly** /ˈlɪli pɪli/, *n.* a tree, *Aemena smithii,* with purplish white fruits, common along streams and in rainforests of eastern Australia. Also, **lilli-pilli.** [orig. uncert.]

**li-lo** /ˈlaɪ-loʊ/, *n.* an inflatable rubber mattress. Also, **Li-Lo.** [Trademark]

**lilt** /lɪlt/, *n.* **1.** rhythmic swing or cadence. **2.** a lilting song or tune. –*v.i. v.t.* **3.** to sing or play in a light, tripping, or rhythmic manner. [ME *lulte;* cf. D *lul* pipe]

**lily** /ˈlɪli/, *n., pl.* **-ies,** *adj.* –*n.* **1.** any plant of the genus *Lilium,* comprising scaly-bulbed herbs with showy funnel-shaped or bell-shaped flowers of various colours, as *L. tigrinum,* tiger lily and *L. longiflorum,* november lily. **2.** the flower or the bulb of such a plant. **3.** any plant with similar flowers as *Amaryllis belladonna,* belladonna lily. **4.** →**fleur-de-lis.** **5.** (*derog.*) a man who does not conform to some conventional notion of masculinity, as an artist, a homosexual, etc. –*adj.* **6.** white as a lily. **7.** delicately fair. **8.** pure; unsullied. **9.** pale. [ME and OE *lilie,* from L *līlium;* cf. Gk *leírion*]

lily

**lily iron** /ˈ– aɪən/, *n.* a harpoon whose head may be detached.

**lily-livered** /ˈlɪli-lɪvəd/, *adj.* weak; cowardly.

**lily-of-the-valley** /lɪli-əv-ðə-ˈvæli/, *n., pl.* **lilies-of-the-valley.** a stemless herb, *Convallaria majalis,* with a raceme of drooping, bell-shaped, fragrant white flowers.

**lily pad** /ˈlɪli pæd/, *n.* the large, floating leaf of a waterlily.

**lily trotter** /ˈ– trɒtə/, *n.* →**jacana.**

**lilywhite** /ˈlɪliwaɪt/, *n.* **1.** *Sport.* an amateur. –*adj.* **2.** as white as a lily. **3.** beyond reproach; innocent. **4.** *Chiefly U.S.* advocating racial segregation and discrimination in favour of whites. Also, **lily-white.**

**lima bean** /laɪmə ˈbin/, *n.* **1.** a kind of bean, including several varieties of *Phaseolus lunatus,* with a broad, flat, edible seed. **2.** the seed, much used for food.

**limacine** /ˈlɪməsaɪn, -sən, ˈlaɪmə-/, *adj.* pertaining to, or having the characteristics of, slugs. [L *līmax* slug, snail + -INE[1]]

**limb**[1] /lɪm/, *n.* **1.** a part or member of an animal body distinct from the head and trunk, as a leg, arm, or wing. **2.** a large or main branch of a tree. **3.** a projecting part or member: *the four limbs of a cross.* **4.** a person or thing regarded as a part, member, branch, offshoot, or scion of something. **5. out on a limb,** in a dangerous or exposed position. [ME and OE *lim,* c. Icel. *limr*] – **limbed** /lɪmd/, *adj.* – **limbless,** *adj.*

**limb**[2] /lɪm/, *n.* **1.** the edge of the disc of the sun, moon, or planet. **2.** the graduated edge of a quadrant or similar instrument. **3.** *Bot.* the upper spreading part of a gamopetalous corolla; the expanded portion of a petal, sepal, or leaf. **4.** *Archery.* the upper or lower portion of a bow. [L *limbus* border. Cf. LIMBUS and LIMBO]

**limbate** /ˈlɪmbeɪt/, *adj.* bordered, as a flower in which one colour is surrounded by an edging of another. [LL *limbātus,* from L *limbus* LIMB[2]]

**limber**[1] /ˈlɪmbə/, *adj.* **1.** bending readily; flexible; pliant. **2.** characterised by ease in bending the body; supple; lithe. –*v.i.* **3.** to make oneself limber (fol. by *up*). –*v.t.* **4.** to make limber. [? akin to LIMB[1]] – **limberly,** *adv.* – **limberness,** *n.*

**limber**[2] /ˈlɪmbə/, *n.* **1.** the detachable forepart of a guncarriage, consisting of two wheels, an axle, a pole, etc. –*v.t.* **2.** to attach the limber to (a gun), in preparation for moving away (usu. fol. by *up*). [late ME, ? from F *limonière*]

**limber**[3] /ˈlɪmbə/, *n.* one of a series of holes or channels in the lower structure of a ship which allows liquids to flow to the pumps. [? alteration of F *lumière* hole, lit., light]

**limbic** /ˈlɪmbɪk/, *adj.* pertaining to or of the nature of a limbus or border; marginal.

**limbo**[1] /ˈlɪmboʊ/, *n., pl.* **-bos.** **1.** (*oft. cap.*) a supposed region on the border of hell or heaven, the abode after death of unbaptised infants (**limbo of infants**), or one serving as the temporary abode of the righteous who died before the coming of Christ (**limbo of the fathers** or **patriarchs**). **2.** a place to which persons or things are regarded as being relegated when cast aside, forgotten, past, or out of date. **3.** prison, gaol, or confinement. **4. in limbo,** →**no-man's-land** (defs 4, 5, 6). [ME, from ML *in limbo* on the border (of hell). See LIMB[2], LIMBUS]

**limbo**[2] /ˈlɪmboʊ/, *n.* a type of dance where each dancer in turn bends backwards in order to pass underneath a horizontal bar which is gradually lowered. [West Indian native name]

**Limburger** /ˈlɪmbɜgə/, *n.* a semi-soft, surface ripened cheese with a strong aroma and flavour. Also, **Limburg cheese.** [named after *Limburg,* Belgium]

**limbus** /ˈlɪmbəs/, *n., pl.* **-bi** /-baɪ/. **1.** →**limbo**[1]. **2.** (in scientific or technical use) a border, edge, or limb. [L]

**lime**[1] /laɪm/, *n., v.,* **limed, liming.** –*n.* **1.** the oxide of calcium, CaO, a white caustic solid (**quicklime** or **unslaked lime**) prepared by calcining limestone, etc., used in making mortar and cement. When treated with water it produces calcium hydroxide, $Ca(OH)_2$, or **slaked lime.** **2.** any calcium compounds for improving crops on lime-deficient soils. **3.** →**birdlime.** –*v.t.* **4.** to treat (soil, etc.) with lime or compounds of calcium. **5.** to smear (twigs, etc.) with birdlime. **6.** to catch with, or as with, birdlime. [ME; OE *līm,* c. D *lijm,* G *Leim,* L *līmus* slime; akin to LOAM]

**lime**[2] /laɪm/, *n.* **1.** the small, greenish yellow, acid fruit of a tropical tree, *Citrus aurantifolia,* allied to the lemon. **2.** the tree itself. **3.** a related tree as the desert lemon. [F, from Sp. *lima;* akin to LEMON]

**lime**[3] /laɪm/, *n.* →**linden.** [unexplained var. of obs. *line, lind,* ME and OE *lind.* See LINDEN]

**lime-burner** /ˈlaɪm-bɜnə/, *n.* one who makes lime by burning or calcining limestone, etc.

**lime-green** /laɪm-ˈgrin/, *n.* the yellow-green colour of the lime fruit.

**lime-juicer** /ˈlaɪm-dʒusə/, *n. Colloq.* (formerly) **1.** an Englishman, esp. a recent immigrant. **2. a.** a British ship. **b.** a British sailor.

**limekiln** /ˈlaɪmkɪln/, *n.* a kiln or furnace for making lime by calcining limestone or shells.

**limelight** /ˈlaɪmlaɪt/, *n.* **1.** (formerly) a strong light, made by heating a cylinder of lime in a flame of mixed gases, thrown upon the stage to illuminate particular persons or objects. **2.** the glare of public interest or notoriety. **3. steal the limelight,** to make oneself the centre of attention.

**limelighter** /ˈlaɪmlaɪtə/, *n.* one who seeks the limelight.

**limen** /ˈlaɪmən/, *n., pl.* **limens, limina** /ˈlɪmənə/. →**threshold** (def. 5). [L]

**limerick** /ˈlɪmərɪk/, *n.* a type of humorous verse of five lines, in which the first and second lines rhyme with the fifth line, and the shorter third line rhymes with the shorter fourth. [named after *Limerick,* Ireland; orig., a song with refrain, 'Will you come up to Limerick?']

**lime-soda** /ˈlaɪm-soʊdə/, *adj.* of a process for softening water by treating it with lime and sodium carbonate.

**limestone** /ˈlaɪmstoʊn/, *n.* a rock consisting wholly or chiefly of calcium carbonate, originating principally from the calcareous remains of organisms, and when heated yielding quicklime.

**lime sulphur** /laɪm ˈsʌlfə/, *n.* a compound of lime and sulphur, forming polysulphides, used to dip sheep to prevent infestation by itch mites and in orchards to control fungus diseases and sucking insects.

**lime tree** /ˈ– tri/, *n.* **1.** →**lime**[2]. **2.** →**linden.**

**lime twig** /ˈ– twɪg/, *n.* **1.** a twig smeared with birdlime to catch birds. **2.** a snare.

**limewater** /ˈlaɪmwɔtə/, *n.* **1.** an aqueous solution of slaked lime, used medicinally and otherwise. **2.** water containing naturally an unusual amount of calcium carbonate or calcium sulphate.

**limey** /ˈlaɪmi/, *n., pl.* **-meys,** *adj. Colloq. –n.* **1.** a British sailor or ship. **2.** an Englishman. *–adj.* **3.** British. [from the prescribed used of lime juice against scurvy in British ships in the 18th century]

**limicoline** /laɪˈmɪkəlaɪn, -lin/, *adj.* shore-inhabiting; of or pertaining to numerous birds of the families Charadriidae (plovers) and Scolopacidae (sandpipers). [LL *līmicola* dweller in mud + -INE[1]]

**limicolous** /laɪˈmɪkələs/, *adj.* living in mud or muddy regions.

**liminal** /ˈlɪmənəl/, *adj.* of or pertaining to the limen or threshold (def. 5). [L *līmen* threshold + -AL[1]]

**limit** /ˈlɪmət/, *n.* **1.** the final or furthest bound or point as to extent, amount, continuance, procedure, etc.: *the limit of vision.* **2.** a boundary or bound, as of a country, tract, district, etc. **3.** *Obs.* an area or region within boundaries. **4.** *Maths.* **a.** (of a function at a point) a number such that the value of the function can be made arbitrarily close to this number by restricting its argument to be sufficiently near the point. **b.** (of a sequence to infinity) a number such that the elements of the sequence eventually approach it in value. **5.** *Games.* the maximum sum by which a bet may be raised at any one time. **6. the (dizzy) limit,** someone or something that exasperates to an intolerable degree. *–v.t.* **7.** to restrict by or as by fixing limits (fol. by *to*): *to limit questions to twenty-five words.* **8.** to confine or keep within limits: *to limit expenditures.* **9.** *Law.* to fix or assign definitely or specifically. [ME *lymyte,* from OF *limite,* from L *līmes* boundary] – **limitable,** *adj.*

**limitary** /ˈlɪmətəri, -tri/, *adj.* **1.** of, pertaining to, or serving as a limit. **2.** subject to limits; limited.

**limitation** /lɪməˈteɪʃən/, *n.* **1.** that which limits; a limit or bound; a limited condition or circumstance; restriction. **2.** a limiting condition: *one should know one's limitations.* **3.** act of limiting. **4.** state of being limited. **5.** *Law.* the assignment, as by statute, of a period of time within which an action must be brought, or the period of time assigned: *a statute of limitations.*

**limitative** /ˈlɪmətətɪv/, *adj.* limiting; restrictive.

**limited** /ˈlɪmətəd/, *adj.* **1.** confined within limits; restricted, circumscribed, or narrow: *a limited space.* **2.** restricted with reference to governing powers by limitations prescribed in a constitution: *a limited monarchy.* **3.** restricted as to amount of liability. **4.** (of a train) restricted as to places at which it stops, class of tickets available, number of passengers, etc. *–n.* **5.** a limited train: *the Brisbane Limited.* – **limitedly,** *adv.* – **limitedness,** *n.*

**limited company** /ˈ– kʌmpəni/, *n.* a company which can issue subscription and which may be listed on the stock exchange; there is a minimum number of shareholders but no maximum; on liquidation the liability of the shareholders for the companies debts is limited to any amounts unpaid on their shares. Also, **limited-liability company.**

**limited edition** /– əˈdɪʃən/, *n.* **1.** an edition of a book; lithographic print, etc., of which there is a limited number of copies available.

**limited liability** /– laɪəˈbɪləti/, *n.* the liability, either by law or contract, only to a limited amount for debts of a trading company or limited partnership.

**limited partnership** /– ˈpatnəʃɪp/, *n.* a partnership in which at least one partner must be a general or unlimited partner liable for all the debts and obligations of the partnership, the others being liable only to the extent of the amount of capital each has put into the partnership. – **limited partner,** *n.*

**limiter** /ˈlɪmətə/, *n.* **1.** one who or that which limits. **2.** an electronic device which restricts output to a certain range of values irrespective of the size of the input.

**limiting** /ˈlɪmətɪŋ/, *adj.* of the nature of a limiting adjective or a restrictive clause.

**limiting adjective** /ˈ– ˌædʒəktɪv/, *n.* (in English and some other languages) one of a small group of adjectives which modify the nouns to which they are applied by restricting rather than describing or qualifying. *This, some,* and *certain* are limiting adjectives.

**limitless** /ˈlɪmətləs/, *adj.* without limit; boundless.

**limit of location,** *n.* (formerly) a boundary set by colonial governors in Australia within which settlers could select land.

**limmo** /ˈlɪmoʊ/, *n. Colloq.* →**limousine.**

**limn** /lɪm/, *v.t.* **1.** to represent in drawing or painting. **2.** *Archaic.* to portray in words. [ME *lymne(n),* var. of *lumine* illuminate, from OF *luminer,* from L *lūmen* light]

**limnology** /lɪmˈnɒlədʒi/, *n.* the scientific study of bodies of fresh water, as lakes and ponds, with reference to their physical, geographical, biological, and other features. [Gk *límnē* lake + -O- + -LOGY] – **limnological** /lɪmnəˈlɒdʒɪkəl/, *adj.* – **limnologist,** *n.*

**limonene** /ˈlɪmənin/, *n.* a liquid terpene, $C_{10}H_{16}$, occurring in two optically different forms, the dextrorotatory form being present in the essential oils of lemon, orange, etc., and the laevorotatory in Douglas fir needle oil. [NL *limonum* lemon + -ENE]

**limonite** /ˈlaɪmənaɪt/, *n.* an important iron ore, a hydrated ferric oxide, $2Fe_2O_3 \cdot 3H_2O$, varying in colour from dark brown to yellow. [Gk *leimṓn* meadow + -ITE[1]] – **limonitic** /laɪməˈnɪtɪk/, *adj.*

**Limousin** /lɪməˈzin/, *n.* one of a breed of large-framed beef cattle, of European origin, with a slow growth rate and red-gold to wheat in colour. [from *Limousin,* a former province in central France]

**limousine** /ˈlɪməzin, lɪməˈzin/, *n.* **1.** any large, luxurious car, esp. a chauffeur-driven one. **2.** an airline bus carrying passengers between the city terminal and the airport. [F: orig., cloak, from *Limousin,* a former province in central France]

**limp**[1] /lɪmp/, *v.i.* **1.** to walk with a laboured, jerky movement, as when lame; progress with great difficulty. **2.** to proceed in a lame or faltering manner: *his verse limps.* *–n.* **3.** a lame movement or gait. [ME; cf. MHG *limpfen* limp and OE *lempheal*t lame] – **limper,** *n.*

**limp**[2] /lɪmp/, *adj.* **1.** lacking stiffness or firmness, as of substance, fibre, structure, or bodily frame: *a limp body.* **2.** tired; lacking vitality. **3.** without proper firmness, force, energy, etc., as of character. [akin to Icel. *limpa* indisposition] – **limply,** *adv.* – **limpness,** *n.*

**limpet** /ˈlɪmpət/, *n.* **1.** *Zool.* any of various marine gastropods with a low conical shell open beneath, found adhering to rocks, used for bait and sometimes for food. **2.** one who is reluctant to give up a position or office. **3.** *Engineering.* an open caisson shaped so as to fit a dock wall. [ME *lempet,* OE *lempedu,* from LL *lamprēda* limpet, LAMPREY]

**limpet mine** /'– maɪn/, *n.* an adhesive mine to be placed against the hull of a ship.

**limpid** /'lɪmpəd/, *adj.* **1.** clear, transparent, or pellucid, as water, crystal, air, etc. **2.** free from obscurity; lucid: *a limpid style.* [L *limpidus*] – **limpidity** /lɪm'pɪdəti/, **limpidness,** *n.* – **limpidly,** *adv.*

**limping** /'lɪmpɪŋ/, *adj.* of or pertaining to the legal status of some relationships, as marriage, adoption of children, etc., which, contracted in one country, may not conform to the laws of and therefore may not be recognised in another country.

**limpkin** /'lɪmpkən/, *n.* a large, loud-voiced, wading bird, *Aramus guarauna,* intermediate in size and character between the cranes and the rails, which inhabits Florida, Central America, and the West Indies.

**limuloid** /'lɪmjəlɔɪd/, *adj.* **1.** resembling or pertaining to the horseshoe crabs, esp. to *Limulus.* –*n.* **2.** →**horseshoe crab.** [LIMUL(US) + -OID]

**limulus** /'lɪmjələs/, *n., pl.* **-li** /-laɪ/. a crab of the genus *Limulus;* a horseshoe crab. [NL, from L: somewhat askew, diminutive of *līmus* sidelong]

**limy** /'laɪmi/, *adj.,* **-mier, -miest. 1.** consisting of, containing, or like lime. **2.** smeared with birdlime.

**lin.,** **1.** lineal. **2.** linear.

**linac** /'lɪnæk, 'laɪ-/, *n.* →**linear accelerator.**

**linage** /'laɪnɪdʒ/, *n.* **1.** alignment. **2.** number of lines of written or printed matter covered. Also, **lineage.**

**linalool** /lə'næloʊ,ɒl, lɪnə'lul/, *n.* a colourless liquid, unsaturated alcohol, $C_{10}H_{17}OH$, related to the terpenes, found in several essential oils. [Sp. *linalo(e)* fragrant Mexican wood + -OL[1]]

**linarite** /'laɪnəraɪt/, *n.* a mineral, hydrous sulphate of lead and copper, consisting of deep blue crystals resembling azurite.

**linchpin** /'lɪntʃpɪn/, *n.* **1.** a pin inserted through the end of an axle to keep the wheel on. **2.** the key point of a plan, argument, etc. Also, **lynchpin. 3.** a key person or event, as in a play, etc. [*linch-,* OE *lynis* linchpin (c. G *Lünse*) + PIN]

**Lincoln** /'lɪŋkən/, *n.* one of a large English variety of mutton sheep, with a heavy fleece of long, coarse wool.

**linctus** /'lɪŋktəs/, *n.* a medicine for soothing the throat and chest. [L, pp. of *lingere* lick]

**lindane** /'lɪndeɪn/, *n.* gamma-benzene hexachloride, $C_6H_6Cl_6$, a highly toxic white powder or flakes, having a musty odour and used as a systemic insecticide. [Trademark]

**linden** /'lɪndən/, *n.* any of the trees of the genus *Tilia,* which have yellowish or cream-coloured flowers and more or less heart-shaped leaves, as *T. europaea,* a common European species, and *T. americana,* a large American species often cultivated as a shade tree. [n. use of obs. ME and OE adj. *linden* pertaining to a lime tree, from *lind* lime tree (c. G *Linde*) + -EN[2]]

**line**[1] /laɪn/, *n., v.,* **lined, lining.** –*n.* **1.** a mark or stroke long in proportion to its breadth, made with a pen, pencil, tool, etc., on a surface. **2.** something resembling a traced line, as a band of colour, a seam, a furrow, etc.: *lines of stratification in rock.* **3.** a furrow or wrinkle on the face, etc. **4.** something arranged along a line, esp. a straight line; a row or series: *a line of trees.* **5.** a row of people standing side by side or one behind another. **6.** a row of written or printed letters, words, etc.: *a page of thirty lines.* **7.** a verse of poetry. **8.** (*pl.*) the spoken words of a drama, etc., or of an actor's part: *the hero forgot his lines.* **9.** a ploy; deceit: *he gave me the old line about working late.* **10.** a short written message: *a line from a friend.* **11.** an indication of demarcation; boundary; limit: *to draw a line between right and wrong.* **12.** a course of action, procedure, thought, etc.: *the Communist Party line.* **13.** a piece of useful or pertinent information: *get a line on his activities during the war.* **14.** a course of direction; route: *the line of march.* **15.** *Colloq.* a bush road. **16.** a continuous series of persons or animals in chronological succession, esp. in family descent: *a line of great kings.* **17.** (*pl.*) outline or contour: *a ship of fine lines.* **18.** (*pl.*) plan of construction, action, or procedure: *two books written on the same lines.* **19.** (*pl.*) *Brit. Colloq.* a certificate of marriage. **20.** a department of activity; a kind of occupation or business: *what line is your father in?* **21. a.** any transport company or system. **b.** a system of public conveyances, as buses, steamers, etc., plying regularly between places. **22.** a strip of railway track, a railway, or a railway system. **23.** *Elect.* a wire circuit connecting two or more pieces of electrical apparatus. **24.** *Television.* one scanning line. **25.** *Fine Arts.* a mark from a crayon, pencil, brush, etc., in a work of graphic art, which defines the limits of the forms employed and is used either independently or in combination with modelling by means of shading. **26.** *Maths.* a continuous extent of length, straight or curved, without breadth or thickness; the trace of a moving point. **27.** a straight line drawn from an observed object to the fovea of the eye: *line of sight.* **28.** *Cricket.* the direction of the ball after it leaves the bowler's hand, usu. considered in relation to the stumps: *the bowler's line varied too much.* **29.** a circle of the terrestrial or of the celestial sphere: *the equinoctial line.* **30.** a supply of commercial goods of the same general class. **31.** *Bridge.* the line drawn between points counting towards game (**below the line**) and bonus, sometimes known as honour points (**above the line**). **32.** *Music.* one of the straight, horizontal, parallel strokes of the stave, or one above or below it. **33.** *Music.* one of the parts, usu. melodic, of a composition for many instruments or voices: *the vocal line; the violin line.* **34.** *Mil.* **a.** a defensive position. **b.** a series of fortifications: *the Maginot line.* **35.** (*pl.*) *Mil.* one of the rows of huts, tents, etc., within a camp. **36.** the line of arrangement of an army or of the ships of a fleet as drawn up ready for battle: *line of battle.* **37.** a body or formation of troops or ships drawn up abreast. **38.** a thread, string, or the like. **39.** →**clothes line. 40.** a strong cord or slender rope. **41.** a cord, wire, or the like used for measuring or as a guide. **42.** *Naut.* **a.** a length of rope for any purpose. **b.** a pipe or hose: *a steam line.* **43.** a length of cord, nylon, silk, or the like, bearing a hook or hooks, used in fishing. **44.** a wire or cable for a telephone or telegraph. **45.** a telephonic channel to a particular party: *I'm sorry, sir, that line is busy.* **46.** telephonic access to external channels from an internal system: *Get me a line please, Miss Jones.* **47.** *Sport.* a mark indicating the boundaries or divisions of a field or court. **48.** *Fencing.* one of the eight imaginary lines forming the target on the fencer's body. **49.** (*pl.*) a school punishment, usu. consisting of writing out a phrase or sentence a specified number of times. **50.** a former unit of length equivalent to $\frac{1}{12}$ inch. **51. bring into line,** to cause or persuade to agree or conform. **52. come (fall) into line,** to agree; conform. **53. do a line for,** to flirt with. **54. do a line with,** to enter into an amorous relationship with. **55. draw the line at,** to impose a limit; refuse to do. **56. get a line on,** to obtain information about. **57. get one's lines crossed,** to misunderstand. **58. hard lines,** *Colloq.* bad luck. **59. in line, a.** straight; in alignment. **b.** in conformity or agreement. **c.** well-placed; with a good chance: *in line for promotion.* **60. lay it on the line,** to state the case openly and honestly. **61. line of least resistance,** course of action requiring the minimum of effort or presenting the fewest difficulties. **62. out of line,** not in accord with standard practice, agreement, etc.; deviant. **63. pay on the line,** to pay promptly. **64. read between the lines,** to find in something spoken or written more meaning than the words appear to express. **65. shoot a line,** *Colloq.* to boast. **66. the line,** the equator. **67. toe the line,** to conform; obey. –*v.i.* **68.** to take a position in a line; range or queue (oft. fol. by *up*). –*v.t.* **69.** to bring into a line, or into line with others (oft. fol. by *up*). **70.** to trace by or as by a line or lines; delineate. **71.** to mark with a line or lines: *to line paper for writing.* **72.** to cover with lines or wrinkles: *a face lined with worry.* **73.** to sketch verbally or in writing; outline. **74.** to arrange a line along. **75.** to form a line along: *people lined the streets.* **76.** to measure or test with a line. **77. line up,** to get hold of; make available: *we must line up a chairman for the conference.* [ME, partly from OF *ligne,* from VL **linja,* from L *līnea* thread, line, from *līnum* flax, and partly from OE *līne* rope, line, series, rule, representing a Gmc borrowing of L *līnea*] – **line-like,** *adj.*

**line**[2] /laɪn/, *v.t.,* **lined, lining. 1.** to cover or fit on the inner side with something: *to line drawers with paper.* **2.** to provide with a layer of material applied to the inner side: *to line a coat with silk.* **3.** to cover: *walls lined with bookcases.* **4.** to furnish or fill: *to line one's pockets with money.* **5.** to reinforce the back of a book with glued fabric, paper, vellum, etc. [ME *lyne(n)*, from *line*, n., flax, linen (as used for lining), OE *līn*, from L *līnum*]

**lineage**[1] /ˈlɪniɪdʒ/, *n.* **1.** lineal descent from an ancestor; ancestry or extraction. **2.** the line of descendants of a particular ancestor; family; race. [LINE(AL) + -AGE; replacing ME *linage*, from OF *lignage*, from *ligne* LINE[1]]

**lineage**[2] /ˈlaɪnɪdʒ/, *n.* →**linage.**

**lineal** /ˈlɪniəl/, *adj.* **1.** being in the direct line, as a descendant, ancestor, etc., or descent, etc. **2.** of or transmitted by lineal descent. **3.** linear. [ME, from LL *līneālis*, from L *līnea* LINE[1]] – **lineally,** *adv.*

**lineament** /ˈlɪniəmənt/, *n.* **1.** a feature or detail of a face, body, or figure, considered with respect to its outline or contour. **2.** a distinctive characteristic. [ME, from L *līneāmentum*]

**linear** /ˈlɪniə/, *adj.* **1.** extended in a line: *a linear series.* **2.** involving measurement in one dimension only; pertaining to length: *linear measure.* **3.** of or pertaining to a line or lines: *linear perspective.* **4.** of or pertaining to a work of art in which emphasis is placed on the outlines and edges of the forms represented. **5.** consisting of or involving lines: *linear design.* **6.** looking like a line: *linear nebulae.* **7.** *Maths.* of the first degree, as an equation. **8.** resembling a thread; narrow and elongated: *a linear leaf.* **9.** *Elect.* having an output directly proportional to the input. [L *līneāris*, from *līnea* LINE[1]] – **linearly,** *adv.* – **linearity** /lɪniˈærəti/, *n.*

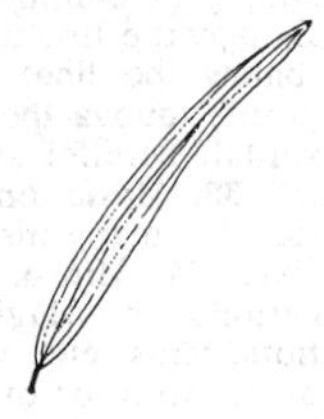

linear (def. 8): linear leaf

**linear accelerator** /lɪniər əkˈseləreɪtə/, *n.* an apparatus for accelerating ions to high energies.

**linear equation** /lɪniər əˈkweɪʒən/, *n.* an equation, all of whose variables are in the first degree.

**linearism** /ˈlɪniərɪzəm/, *n.* emphasis on line or contour as opposed to mass and colour.

**linear momentum** /lɪniə məˈmɛntəm/, *n.* →**momentum.**

**linear motor** /ˈ– moʊtə/, *n.* a form of induction motor in which the stator and rotor are linear instead of cylindrical, and parallel instead of coaxial.

**linear perspective** /– pəˈspɛktɪv/, *n.* that branch of perspective which regards only the apparent positions, magnitudes, and forms of objects delineated.

**lineate** /ˈlɪniət, -ieɪt/, *adj.* marked with lines, esp. longitudinal and more or less parallel lines. Also, **lineated.** [L *līneātus*, pp., lined]

**lineation** /lɪniˈeɪʃən/, *n.* **1.** a marking with or tracing by lines. **2.** a division into lines. **3.** a line; an outline. **4.** an arrangement or group of lines.

**lineball** /ˈlaɪnbɔl/, *n.* **1.** a ball which lands on the line, and is not definitely in or out of the playing area. **2.** an issue, as an election, which is not definitely decided either way. *–adj.* **3.** of or pertaining to such an issue.

**line breeding** /ˈlaɪn bridɪŋ/, *n.* a form of mild inbreeding directed towards keeping the offspring closely related to a highly admired ancestor.

**line drawing** /ˈ– drɔ-ɪŋ/, *n.* a drawing made using only lines to provide both outline and gradations in tone.

**line engraving** /– ɛnˈgreɪvɪŋ/, *n.* **1.** a style of engraving in which the burin makes curved regular furrows that markedly swell and taper. **2.** a plate so engraved. **3.** a print or picture made from it.

**line honours** /ˈ– ɒnəz/, *n.pl.* credit won by a competitor for crossing the finishing line ahead of the others in the race, determined without reference to handicaps, etc.

**line-kick** /ˈlaɪn-kɪk/, *n. Rugby Football.* a kick aimed at putting the ball into touch.

**lineman** /ˈlaɪnmən/, *n.* →**linesman.**

**linen** /ˈlɪnən/, *n.* **1.** fabric woven from flax yarns. **2.** clothes or other articles made of linen cloth or some substitute, as cotton. **3.** yarn made of flax fibre. **4.** thread made of flax yarns. **5. wash one's dirty linen in public,** to discuss disagreeable personal affairs in public. *–adj.* **6.** made of linen. [ME *lin(n)en*, n. and adj., OE *linnen, līnen*, adj., from *līn* linen + -EN[2]]

**linen basket** /ˈ– baskət/, *n.* →**clothes basket.**

**linen cupboard** /ˈ– kʌbəd/, *n.* a cupboard where linen, towels, etc., are stored. Also, **linen closet.**

**linen paper** /ˈ– peɪpə/, *n.* paper made from pure linen or from substitutes which produce a similar paper finish.

**line of battle,** *n.* the formations taken up by ground or sea forces immediately before engaging in battle: *the lines of battle were being drawn up.*

**line of fire,** *n.* the area directly in the path of missiles, firearms, etc.

**line of force,** *n.* a line in a field of force esp. a magnetic or electrical field of force, whose direction at any point is that of the force in the field at that point.

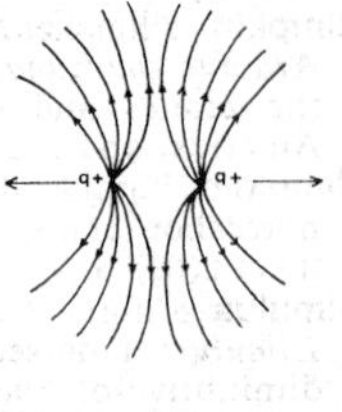

**line of sight,** *n.* an imaginary line between an observer and a celestial body which is coincident with light rays from that body.

**line-of-sight velocity** /laɪn-əv-saɪt vəˈlɒsəti/, *n.* the velocity of a celestial body in a direction which directly approaches, or recedes from the earth. Also, **radial velocity.**

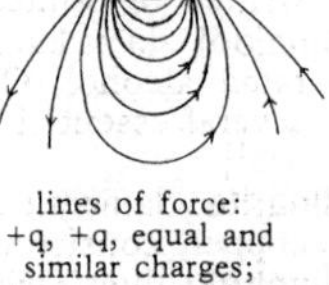

lines of force: +q, +q, equal and similar charges; +q, −q, equal but but opposite charges

**lineolate** /ˈlɪniəleɪt/, *adj.* marked with minute lines; finely lineate. Also, **lineolated.** [L *līneola* (diminutive of *līnea* LINE[1]) + -ATE[1]]

**line-out** /ˈlaɪn-aʊt/, *n.* (in Rugby Union football) the throw-in of the ball from touch, the forwards of each team forming up in parallel lines at right angles to the touchlines.

**line printer** /ˈlaɪn prɪntə/, *n.* a machine which prints the output of a computer a line at a time at rates which may be thousands of lines a minute; distinguished from machines which print a character at a time, as a teleprinter.

**liner**[1] /ˈlaɪnə/, *n.* **1.** one of a commercial line of steamships or aeroplanes. **2.** one who or that which traces by or marks with lines. **3.** a cosmetic used to outline and highlight the eyes. [LINE[1] + -ER[1]]

**liner**[2] /ˈlaɪnə/, *n.* **1.** one who fits or provides linings. **2.** something serving as a lining. **3.** a sleeve, usu. plastic, which protects a record cover. [LINE[2] + -ER[1]]

**liner note** /ˈ– noʊt/, *n.* the blurb on a record cover.

**linesman** /ˈlaɪnzmən/, *n., pl.* **-men. 1.** *Sport.* an official on the sidelines who assists the referee or umpire in determining whether the ball is still in play. **2.** one who erects or repairs telephone, electric power, or other overhead wires. **3.** the member of a surf-lifesaving team who handles the surf-line. Also, **lineman.**

**line spectrum** /laɪn ˈspɛktrəm/, *n.* an emission or absorption spectrum consisting of a number of sharply defined lines, as produced by an element in the atomic state. Each line corresponds to a particular wavelength.

**line-up** /ˈlaɪn-ʌp/, *n.* **1.** a particular order or disposition of persons or things as lined up or drawn up for action, inspection, participation, as in a sporting team, a music band, etc. **2.** the persons or things themselves: *two suspects were included in the police line-up.* **3.** an organisation of people, companies, etc., for some common purpose. **4.** a sequence of programs or events: *tonight's T.V. line-up is a knockout.* **5.** *Surfing.* the point where the waves are consistently starting to break.

**liney** /ˈlaɪni/, *adj.,* **-nier, -niest.** →**liny.**

**ling**[1] /lɪŋ/, *n., pl.* **lings,** (*esp. collectively*) **ling. 1.** a common fish, *Lotella calaria*, belonging to the family Gadidae, reddish-brown in colour with a small barbel on the chin, found around the southern coast of Australia; beardie. **2.** an elongated marine gadoid food fish, *Molva molva*, of Greenland and northern Europe. **3.** any of certain other fishes, as the burbot. [ME *ling, lenge;* akin to LONG[1]]

**ling**[2] /lɪŋ/, *n.* the common heather, *Calluna vulgaris.* [ME *lyng*, from Scand.; cf. Icel. *lyng*, Dan. *lyng*, Swed. *ljung*]

**-ling**[1], suffix found in some nouns, often pejorative, denoting one concerned with (*hireling, underling*); also diminutive (*princeling, duckling*). [ME and OE]

**-ling**[2], an adverbial suffix expressing direction, position, state, etc., as in *darkling, sideling.* [ME and OE]

**ling.**, linguistics.

**linga** /ˈlɪŋɡə/, *n.* **1.** *Sanskrit Gram.* the masculine gender. **2.** (in popular Hindu mythology) a phallus, symbol of Shiva. **3.** the male genitals. Also, **lingam** /ˈlɪŋɡəm/. [Skt *linga* (stem), neut. nom. *lingam*]

**linger** /ˈlɪŋɡə/, *v.i.* **1.** to remain or stay on in a place longer than is usual or expected, as if from reluctance to leave it. **2.** to remain alive; continue or persist, although tending to cease or disappear: *hope lingers.* **3.** to dwell in contemplation, thought, or enjoyment. **4.** to be tardy in action; delay; dawdle. **5.** to walk slowly; to saunter along. *–v.t.* **6.** to drag out or protract. **7.** to pass (time, life, etc.) in a leisurely or a tedious manner (fol. by *away* or *out*). **8.** *Hort.* to delay the blooming of (flowers) by artificial means. [ME *lenger,* frequentative of *lenge,* OE *lengan* delay, from *lang* LONG[1]] **– lingerer,** *n.*

**lingerie** /ˈlɒnʒəreɪ/, *n.* **1.** underwear or other garments of cotton, silk, nylon, lace, etc., worn by women. **2.** *Archaic.* linen goods in general. [F, from *linge* linen, from L *līnum* flax]

**lingo** /ˈlɪŋɡoʊ/, *n., pl.* **-goes.** *Colloq.* **1.** language. **2.** peculiar or unintelligible language. **3.** language or terminology peculiar to a particular field, group, etc.; jargon. [Lingua Franca, from Pr. *lengo,* b. with It. *lingua,* both from L *lingua* tongue; cf. also Pg. *lingoa*]

**lingua** /ˈlɪŋɡwə/, *n., pl.* **-guae** /-ɡwi/. the tongue or a part like a tongue. [L]

**lingua franca** /– ˈfræŋkə/, *n.* **1.** any language widely used as a medium among speakers of other languages. **2.** (*cap.*) the Italian-Provençal jargon formerly widely used in eastern Mediterranean ports. [It.: Frankish tongue]

**lingual** /ˈlɪŋɡwəl/, *adj.* **1.** of or pertaining to the tongue or some tongue-like part. **2.** pertaining to languages. **3.** *Phonet.* articulated with the tongue, esp. with the tip of the tongue. [ML *linguālis,* from L *lingua* tongue, language] **– lingually,** *adv.*

**linguiform** /ˈlɪŋɡwəfɔm/, *adj.* tongue-shaped. [L *lingua* tongue + -I- + -FORM]

**linguist** /ˈlɪŋɡwəst/, *n.* **1.** a person who is skilled in foreign languages; polyglot. **2.** a person who specialises in linguistics. [L *lingua* language + -IST]

**linguistic** /lɪŋˈɡwɪstɪk/, *adj.* **1.** of or belonging to language: *linguistic change.* **2.** of or pertaining to linguistics. Also, **linguistical. – linguistically,** *adv.*

**linguistic atlas** /ˈ– ætləs/, *n.* →**dialect atlas.**

**linguistic form** /– ˈfɔm/, *n.* any meaningful unit of speech, as a sentence, phrase, word, suffix, etc.

**linguistic geography** /– dʒiˈɒɡrəfi/, *n.* →**dialect geography.**

**linguistics** /lɪŋˈɡwɪstɪks/, *n.* the science of language, including among its fields phonetics, phonemics, morphology, and syntax, and having as principal divisions **descriptive linguistics,** which seeks to describe and to develop explanatory models for languages as they exist, and **comparative** (or **historical**) **linguistics,** which treats linguistic change, esp. by the study of data taken from various languages.

**linguistic stock** /lɪŋɡwɪstɪk ˈstɒk/, *n.* **1.** a parent language and all its derived dialects and languages. **2.** the people speaking any of these dialects or languages.

**lingulate** /ˈlɪŋɡjəleɪt/, *adj.* formed like a tongue; ligulate. [L *lingulātus*]

**liniment** /ˈlɪnəmənt/, *n.* a liquid preparation, usu. oily, for rubbing on or applying to the skin, as for sprains, bruises, etc. [ME, from LL *linīmentum*]

**linin** /ˈlaɪnən/, *n.* the substance forming the netlike structure which connects the chromatin granules in the nucleus of a cell. [L *līnum* flax + -IN[2]]

**lining** /ˈlaɪnɪŋ/, *n.* **1.** that with which something is lined; a layer of material on the inner side of something. **2.** *Bookbinding.* the material used to strengthen the back of a book after the sheets have been folded, backed, and sewn. **3.** the act of one who or that which lines something. [ME, from LINE[2] + -ING[1]]

**lining figure** /ˈ– fɪɡə/, *n.* (in printing) a numeral which is the same height as a capital letter. Also, **modern figure.**

**link**[1] /lɪŋk/, *n.* **1.** one of the rings or separate pieces of which a chain is composed. **2.** anything serving to connect one part or thing with another; a bond or tie. **3.** a ring, loop, lock of hair, or the like. **4.** one of a number of sausages in a chain. **5.** →**cufflink. 6.** one of the 100 wire rods forming the divisions of a surveyor's chain of 66 ft (20.12 m). **7.** the set or effective length of one of these rods used as a measuring unit in the imperial system, equal to $\frac{1}{100}$ of a chain, 7.92 in. or 0.201 168 m. **8.** *Chem.* →**bond. 9.** *Elect.* →**fuse link. 10.** *Mach.* a rigid movable piece or rod connected with other parts by means of pivots or the like, for the purpose of transmitting motion. *–v.t.* **11.** to join by or as by a link or links. *–v.i.* **12.** to join; unite. **13. link up,** to make contact; communicate (fol. by *with*). [ME *link(e),* from Scand.; cf. Swed. *länk,* c. OE *hlence* corselet]

**link**[2] /lɪŋk/, *n.* a torch of tow and pitch or the like. [? ML *linchinus,* var. of *lichinus* match, wick, from Gk *lýchnos* lamp]

**linkage** /ˈlɪŋkɪdʒ/, *n.* **1.** the act of linking. **2.** the state or manner of being linked. **3.** a system of links. **4.** *Genetics.* the association of two or more genes located on the same chromosome so that they tend to be passed from generation to generation as an inseparable unit. **5.** *Mech.* any of various mathematical or drawing devices consisting of a combination of bars or pieces pivoted together so as to turn about one another, usu. in parallel planes. **6.** *Elect.* the product of the magnetic flux passing through an electric circuit by the number of turns in the circuit.

**linkage group** /ˈ– ɡrup/, *n.* a group of genes in one chromosome that tend to be inherited as an inseparable unit.

**linkboy** /ˈlɪŋkbɔɪ/, *n.* (formerly) a boy hired to carry a torch for a pedestrian on dark streets. Also, **linkman.**

**linked** /lɪŋkt/, *adj.* exhibiting linkage.

**linking verb** /ˈlɪŋkɪŋ vɜb/, *n.* →**copula** (def. 2).

**linkman** /ˈlɪŋkmæn/, *n.* (in television, radio, etc.) a compere who links various sections of a program.

**links** /lɪŋks/, *n.pl.* →**golf course.** [ME *lynkys* slopes, OE *hlincas,* pl. of *hlinc* rising ground, from *hlin* (cf. *hlinian* lean, recline)]

**link-up** /ˈlɪŋk-ʌp/, *n.* a means of contact or communication.

**linkwork** /ˈlɪŋkwɜk/, *n.* **1.** a thing composed of links, as a chain. **2.** a linkage. **3.** *Mach.* a mechanism or device in which motion is transmitted by links.

**Linnean** /ləˈniən/, *adj.* **1.** of or pertaining to Carolus Linnaeus, (Carl von Linné), 1707-78, a Swedish botanist, who established the binomial system of scientific nomenclature. **2.** denoting, or pertaining to, a system of botanical classification introduced by him and formerly used (based mainly on the number or characteristics of the stamens and pistils). Also, **Linnaean.**

**linnet** /ˈlɪnət/, *n.* **1.** a small Old World fringilline song bird, *Carduelis cannabina.* **2.** any of various related birds, as the house finch. [ME *linet,* from OF *linette,* from *lin* flax (because the bird feeds on flaxseeds)]

**lino** /ˈlaɪnoʊ/, *n.* →**linoleum.**

**linocut** /ˈlaɪnoʊkʌt/, *n.* **1.** a design cut in relief on a block of linoleum. **2.** a print made from such a cut.

**linoleic acid** /lɪnoʊˌliɪk ˈæsəd/, *n.* a polyunsaturated fatty acid, $C_{17}H_{31}COOH$, occurring as a glyceride in fats and drying oils such as linseed oil; an essential part of mammalian diets.

**linolenic acid** /lɪnoʊˌlinɪk ˈæsəd, -ˌlɛnɪk/, *n.* a polyunsaturated fatty acid $C_{17}H_{29}COOH$, occurring as a glyceride in linseed oil; used as a drying agent in paints; an essential part of mammalian diets.

**linoleum** /laɪˈnoʊliəm/, *n.* a floor covering formed by coating hessian or canvas with linseed oil, powdered cork, and rosin, and adding pigments of the desired colour. Also, **lino** /ˈlaɪnoʊ/. [L *līnum* flax + *oleum* oil]

**linotile** /ˈlaɪnoʊtaɪl/, *n.* a tile of linoleum.

**linotype** /ˈlaɪnətaɪp/, *n.* **1.** a keyboard-operated composing machine which casts solid lines of type. **2.** printing produced by such a machine. *–v.i.* **3.** to use a linotype machine. *–v.t.* **4.** to set type using a linotype machine. [Trademark; orig. phrase *'line o' type'* line of type]

**linsang** /ˈlɪnsæŋ/, *n.* a catlike, viverrine carnivore with retractile claws and a long tail, of the genus *Prionodon* (or *Linsang*) of the East Indies, or *Poina* of Africa. [Malay]

**linseed** /ˈlɪnsid/, *n.* the seed of flax. [ME *linsed,* OE *līnsǣd,* from *līn* flax + *sǣd* seed]

**linseed cake** /ˈ– keɪk/, *n.* crushed linseed, from which the oil has been extracted, used as cattle food.

**linseed oil** /– ˈɔɪl/, *n.* a drying oil obtained by pressing linseed, used in making paints, printing inks, linoleum, etc.

**lint** /lɪnt/, *n.* **1.** a soft material for dressing wounds, etc., procured by scraping or otherwise treating linen cloth. **2.** bits of thread or fluff. [ME *lyn(e)t* flax, ? OE *linwyrt,* from *līn* flax + *wyrt* WORT[2]] – **linty,** *adj.*

**lint cotton** /– ˈkɒtn/, *n.* a fibrous coat of thickened convoluted hairs borne by the seeds of cotton plants, which makes up the staple of cotton fibre after ginning.

**lintel** /ˈlɪntl/, *n.* a horizontal supporting member above an opening such as a window or a door. Also, **lintol.** [ME *lyntel,* from OF *lintel, linter,* from VL *līmitāle,* diminutive of L *līmes* boundary, LIMIT]

**linter** /ˈlɪntə/, *n.* **1.** (*pl.*) short cotton fibres which stick to seeds after a first ginning. **2.** a machine which removes lint from cloth.

**lintwhite** /ˈlɪntwaɪt/, *n. Chiefly Scot.* →**linnet.** [ME (northern d.) *lynkwhyte,* replacing OE *līnetwīge,* equivalent to *līn(e)* flax + *-twīge* plucker]

**liny** /ˈlaɪni/, *adj.,* **-nier, -niest. 1.** full of or marked with lines. **2.** linelike. Also, **liney.**

**lion** /ˈlaɪən/, *n.* **1.** a large, greyish tan cat, *Panthera leo,* native to Africa and southern Asia, the male of which usu. has a mane. **2.** this animal as the national emblem of Britain. **3.** (*pl. cap.*) the British representative Rugby Union team. **4.** a man of great strength, courage, etc. **5.** a person of note or celebrity who is much sought after. **6.** (*cap.*) *Astron.* Leo. **7. the lion's share,** the largest portion of anything. [ME, from OF, from L *leo,* from Gk *léōn.* Cf. LEO]

lion

**lioncel** /ˈlaɪənsel/, *n. Her.* a small or young lion.

**lioness** /ˈlaɪənɛs/, *n.* a female lion.

**lion-hearted** /ˈlaɪən-hatəd/, *adj.* courageous; brave.

**lionise** /ˈlaɪənaɪz/, *v.t.,* **-nised, -nising.** to treat (a person) as a celebrity. Also, **lionize.** – **lionisation** /laɪənaɪˈzeɪʃən/, *n.*

**lip** /lɪp/, *n., adj., v.,* **lipped, lipping.** *–n.* **1.** either of the two fleshy parts or folds forming the margins of the mouth and performing an important function in speech. **2.** (*pl.*) these parts as organs of speech. **3.** *Colloq.* impudent talk. **4.** a liplike part or structure. **5.** *Bot.* either of the two parts **(upper** and **lower)** into which the corolla or calyx of certain plants (esp. the mint family) is divided. **6.** *Zool.* **a.** →**labium. b.** the outer or the inner margin of the aperture of a gastropod's shell. **7.** *Music.* the position and arrangement of lips and tongue in playing a wind instrument. **8.** any edge or rim. **9.** a projecting edge, as of a jug. **10.** the crest of a wave which is starting to break, but is not yet curling. **11.** the edge of an opening or cavity, as of a canyon or wound. **12.** *Carp.* the blade at the end of an auger which cuts the chip after it has been circumscribed by the spur. **13. bite one's lip, a.** to show vexation. **b.** to stifle one's feelings, esp. anger or irritability. **14. button the lip,** to be silent. **15. curl one's lip,** to show scorn. **16. give (someone) lip,** to talk, esp. to a superior, in a cheeky or insolent manner. **17. hang on the lips of,** to listen very attentively or eagerly. **18. keep a stiff upper lip,** to face misfortune bravely, esp. without outward show of perturbation. **19. smack one's lips,** to show enjoyment or anticipation of something enjoyable, esp. food. *–adj.* **20.** of or pertaining to the lips or a lip. **21.** pertaining to, characterised by, or made with the lips. *–v.t.* **22.** to touch with the lips. **23.** *Golf.* to hit the ball over the rim of (the hole). **24.** to utter, esp. softly. **25.** *Obs.* to kiss. **26.** to affix lipping to the edge of (a door, board, etc.). *–v.i.* **27.** to use the lips in playing a musical wind instrument. [ME *lip(pe),* OE *lippa,* c. D *lip,* G *Lippe;* akin to L *labium, labrum*]

**lip-,** variant of **lipo-,** before vowels, as in *lipectomy.*

**lipase** /ˈlɪpeɪz, ˈlaɪ-/, *n.* one of the enzymes produced by the liver, pancreas, and other organs of the digestive system which convert oils or fats into fatty acids and glycerol. [LIP- + -ASE]

**lipectomy** /lɪˈpɛktəmi, laɪ-/, *n., pl.* **-mies.** an operation for removal of superficial fat, usu. a pendulous abdominal apron of fat, in obese persons.

**lipid** /ˈlɪpɪd, ˈlaɪ-/, *n.* any of a group of organic compounds which make up the fats and other esters which have analogous solubility properties. They have a greasy feeling and are insoluble in water, but soluble in alcohols, ethers, and other fat solvents. Also, **lipide** /ˈlɪpaɪd, ˈlaɪ-/. [LIP- + -ID[3]]

**lipo-,** in chemistry a word element meaning 'fat', as in *lipochrome.* Also, **lip-.** [Gk, combining form of *lípos* fat]

**lipochrome** /ˈlɪpəkroʊm/, *n.* any natural pigment containing a lipid, esp. the pigments of butterfat.

**lipoclastic** /lɪpəˈklæstɪk/, *adj.* capable of splitting fats, esp. applied to enzymes which are capable of hydrolysing fats; lipolytic.

**lipogenesis** /lɪpoʊˈdʒɛnəsəs/, *n.* the process of fatty acid synthesis.

**lipoid** /ˈlɪpɔɪd, ˈlaɪpɔɪd/, *adj.* **1.** fatty; resembling fat. *–n.* **2.** one of a group of fats or fatlike substances such as lecithins, waxes, etc. [LIP- + -OID] – **lipoidal** /lɪˈpɔɪdl/, *adj.*

**lipolysis** /lɪˈpɒləsəs/, *n.* the resolution of fats into fatty acids and glycerol, as by lipase. [LIPO- + -LYSIS] – **lipolytic** /lɪpəˈlɪtɪk/, *adj.*

**lipoma** /lɪˈpoʊmə/, *n., pl.* **-mata** /-mətə/, **-mas.** a tumour made up of fat tissue; a fatty tumour. [LIP- + -OMA]

**lipophilic** /lɪpəˈfɪlɪk/, *adj.* having an affinity for lipids.

**lipoprotein** /lɪpəˈproʊtin/, *n.* any of a group of complex compounds of lipids and proteins.

**lipped** /lɪpt/, *adj.* **1.** having lips or a lip. **2.** *Bot.* →**labiate.**

**lippie** /ˈlɪpi/, *n. Colloq.* →**lipstick.** Also, **lippy.** [abbrev. of LIPSTICK + -IE]

**lipping** /ˈlɪpɪŋ/, *n.* a strip, usu. wooden, fixed to the edge of a door, board etc.

**lippy** /ˈlɪpi/, *n., pl.* **-pies.** *Colloq.* →**lippie.**

**lip-read** /ˈlɪp-rid/, *v.,* **-read** /-rɛd/, **-reading.** *–v.t.* **1.** to understand spoken words by watching the movement of a speaker's lips. *–v.i.* **2.** to read lips.

**lip-reading** /ˈlɪp-ridɪŋ/, *n.* the reading or understanding, as by a deaf person, of the movements of another's lips when forming words. – **lip-reader,** *n.*

**lip-service** /ˈlɪp-sɜvəs/, *n.* service with words only; insincere profession of devotion or goodwill.

**lipstick** /ˈlɪpstɪk/, *n.* a stick or elongated piece of cosmetic preparation for colouring the lips. Also, **lippie.**

**liq.,** **1.** liquid. **2.** liquor.

**liquate** /ˈlaɪkweɪt/, *v.t.,* **-quated, -quating. 1.** to heat (a metal, etc.) sufficiently to melt the more fusible portion and so separate a metal from impurities or other metals. **2.** to separate by such a fusion (oft. fol. by *out*). [L *liquātus,* pp., made liquid, melted] – **liquation** /laɪˈkweɪʃən/, *n.*

**liquefacient** /lɪkwəˈfeɪʃənt/, *n.* that which liquefies or promotes liquefaction.

**liquefaction** /lɪkwəˈfækʃən/, *n.* the process of liquefying or making liquid.

**liquefied petroleum gas,** *n.* light hydrocarbons as butane and propanes, liquefied under pressure. Also, **bottled gas.** *Abbrev.* L.P.G.

**liquefy** /ˈlɪkwəfaɪ/, *v.,* **-fied, -fying.** *–v.t.* **1.** to make liquid. *–v.i.* **2.** to become liquid. Also, **liquify.** [late ME, from L *liquefacere* make liquid] – **liquefiable,** *adj.* – **liquefier,** *n.*

**liquescent** /lɪˈkwɛsənt/, *adj.* **1.** becoming liquid; melting. **2.** tending towards a liquid state. [L *liquescens,* ppr.] – **liquescence, liquescency,** *n.*

**liqueur** /ləˈkjuə, ləˈkɜ/, *n.* any of a class of alcoholic liquors, usu. strong, sweet, and highly flavoured, as chartreuse, curacao, etc.; a cordial. [F. See LIQUOR]

**liqueur brandy** /– ˈbrændi/, *n.* a brandy of age and mellow flavour, reminiscent of a liqueur.

**liquid** /ˈlɪkwəd/, *adj.* **1.** composed of molecules which move freely among themselves but do not tend to separate like those of gases; neither gaseous nor solid. **2.** of or pertaining to liquids: *liquid measure.* **3.** such as to flow like water; fluid. **4.** clear, transparent, or bright: *liquid eyes.* **5.** sounding smoothly or agreeably: *liquid tones.* **6.** *Phonet.* identified with or being either *r* or *l.* **7.** in cash or readily convertible into cash: *liquid assets.* **8. to go liquid,** to realise assets for cash. *–n.* **9.** a liquid substance. **10.** *Phonet.* either *r* or *l.* [ME, from L *liquidus*] – **liquidly,** *adv.* – **liquidness,** *n.*

**liquid air** /– 'ɛə/, *n.* air in its liquid state; an intensely cold, transparent liquid.

**liquidambar** /lɪkwəd'æmbə/, *n.* **1.** any tree of the genus *Liquidambar,* as *L. styraciflua,* a large American tree, having star-shaped leaves and, in warm regions, exuding a fragrant yellowish balsamic liquid used in medicine. **2.** this liquid. See **storax** (def. 2). [NL, from L *liquidus* LIQUID + ML *ambar* AMBER]

**liquid assets** /lɪkwəd 'æsɛts/, *n. pl.* **1.** that part of a trading bank's assets which consist of its notes and coins, its cash with the Reserve Bank of Australia, and its Commonwealth Treasury bills. **2.** the cash and readily realisable assets of a company.

**liquidate** /'lɪkwədeɪt/, *v.,* **-dated, -dating.** *–v.t.* **1.** to settle or pay (a debt, etc.): *to liquidate a claim.* **2.** to reduce (accounts) to order; determine the amount of (indebtedness or damages). **3.** to convert into cash. **4.** to get rid of, esp. by killing or other violent means. **5.** to break up, abolish, or do away with. *–v.i.* **6.** to liquidate debts or accounts; go into liquidation. [ML *liquidātus,* pp., from L *liquidus*]

**liquidation** /lɪkwə'deɪʃən/, *n.* **1.** the process of realising upon assets and of discharging liabilities in winding up the affairs of a business, estate, etc. **2.** the process of converting securities or commodities into cash for the purpose of taking profits or preventing losses. **3.** liquidated state. **4.** destruction.

**liquidator** /'lɪkwədeɪtə/, *n.* a person appointed to carry out the winding up of a company.

**liquid crystal** /lɪkwəd 'krɪstl/, *n.* a liquid having different optical properties in different directions and other crystalline characteristics.

**liquid crystal display,** *n.* an array of numbers on an electronic calculator, meter, etc., made up of liquid-crystal cells which display different number patterns as different electric fields are applied to them.

**liquid fire** /– 'faɪə/, *n.* flaming petroleum or the like as employed against the enemy in warfare.

**liquid glass** /– 'glas/, *n.* →**waterglass** (def. 5).

**liquidise** /'lɪkwədaɪz/, *v.t.,* **-dised, -dising.** to make liquid; liquefy. Also, **liquidize.**

**liquidiser** /'lɪkwədaɪzə/, *n.* →**blender.**

**liquidity** /lə'kwɪdəti/, *n.* **1.** liquid state or quality. **2.** the state of having assets either in cash or readily convertible into cash.

**liquidity preference** /– 'prɛfrəns/, *n.* the choice between holding wealth as idle money or in the form of income-earning assets.

**liquid laugh** /lɪkwɪd 'laf/, *n. Colloq.* vomit.

**liquid lunch** /– 'lʌntʃ/, *n. Colloq.* alcoholic drink, usu. beer, consumed instead of food at the normal lunchtime.

**liquid measure** /'– mɛʒə/, *n.* an imperial system of units of capacity formerly used in measuring liquid commodities, in which 4 gills = 1 pint, 2 pints = 1 quart, 4 quarts = 1 gallon.

**liquid oxygen** /– 'ɒksədʒən/, *n.* oxygen in its liquid state; a pale blue liquid which boils at −182.9°C; used as an oxidant in rockets. *Abbrev.:* lox.

**liquid paper** /– 'peɪpə/, *n.* a white substance in a solvent, painted on paper to cover errors, etc; white-out. [Trademark]

**liquid paraffin** /– 'pærəfən/, *n.* →**paraffin oil** (def. 1).

**liquid ratio** /– 'reɪʃioʊ/, *n.* the ratio of a company's liquid assets to its current liabilities. Also, **liquidity ratio.**

**liquify** /'lɪkwəfaɪ/, *v.t., v.i.,* **-fied, -fying.** →**liquefy.**

**liquor** /'lɪkə/, *n.* **1.** spirits (as brandy or whisky) as distinguished from fermented beverages (as wine or beer). **2.** *Chiefly U.S.* any alcoholic drink, esp. spirits. **3.** any liquid substance. **4.** *Pharm.* a solution of a medicinal substance in water. **5.** Also, **liquor amnii** /laɪkwɔr 'æmniˌaɪ/. *Embryol.* liquid contained in the amnion which surrounds the foetus; the waters. **6.** a solution of a substance, esp. a concentrated one used in an industrial process. **7.** *Brewing.* water, when added in brewing processes. *–v.t.* **8.** *Colloq.* to furnish with liquor or drink (oft. fol. by *up*). [L: liquid (state), liquid; replacing ME *licur, licour,* from OF]

**liquorice**[1] /'lɪkərɪʃ, 'lɪkrɪʃ, -rəs/, *n.* **1.** a leguminous plant, *Glycyrrhiza glabra,* of Europe and Asia. **2.** the sweet-tasting dried root of this plant, or an extract made from it, used in medicine, confectionery, etc. **3.** any of various related or similar plants, as *G. acanthocarpa.* Also, **licorice, liquorish.** [ME *lycorys,* from AF, from LL *liquiritia,* L *glycyrrhīza,* from Gk *glykýrrhīza,* from *glykús* sweet + *rhízā* root; influenced by L *liquor* liquor]

**liquorice**[2] /'lɪkərɪʃ/, *adj. Archaic.* →**lickerish.**

**liquorice allsorts** /– 'ɔlsɔts/, *n.pl.* variously shaped sweets, liquorice flavoured or having liquorice sections.

**liquor store** /'lɪkə stɔ/, *n.* a shop licensed to sell bottled or canned alcoholic liquor; bottle shop; cellars.

**lira** /'lɪərə/, *n., pl.* **lire** /'lɪəreɪ/, **liras. 1.** the monetary unit of Italy. **2.** a Turkish unit of currency. [It., d. var. of *lib(b)ra,* from L *lībra* pound]

**liriodendron** /ˌlɪrioʊ'dɛndrən/, *n., pl.* **-drons, -dra.** a tree of the genus *Liriodendron,* of which the tulip tree, *L. tulipifera,* native to eastern North America, is the chief representative. See **tulip tree.** [NL, from Gk *leírion* lily + *-dendron* -DENDRON]

**lisle** /laɪl/, *n.* **1.** knitted goods, as hose, made of lisle thread. *–adj.* **2.** made of lisle thread.

**lisle thread** /'– θrɛd/, *n.* a smooth, hard-twisted cotton thread. [named after *Lisle* (now Lille), town in N France where it was first made]

**lis mota** /lɪs 'moʊtə/, *n. Law.* existing or anticipated litigation. [L]

**lisp** /lɪsp/, *n.* **1.** a speech defect consisting in pronouncing *s* and *z* like or nearly like the *th* sounds of *thin* and *this,* respectively. **2.** the act, habit, or sound of lisping. *–v.t.* **3.** to pronounce with a lisp. *–v.i.* **4.** to speak with a lisp. [ME *wlispe, lipse,* OE *-wlispian* (in *āwlyspian*), from *wlisp* lisping. Cf. D *lispen,* G *lispeln*] – **lisper,** *n.* – **lispingly,** *adv.*

**lis pendens** /lɪs 'pɛndɛnz/, *n.* **1.** a pending suit. **2.** the rule allowing for registration of land subject to a pending action. **3.** the rule placing property involved in litigation under the court's jurisdiction. [L]

**Lissajous figure** /'lisəʒu ˌfɪgə/, *n.* the locus of the resultant displacement of two or more simple periodic motions usu. at right angles. [named after Jules *Lissajous,* 1822-80, French physicist]

**lissom** /'lɪsəm/, *adj.* **1.** lithe, esp. of body; limber or supple. **2.** agile or active. Also, *Chiefly U.S.,* **lissome.** [var. of LITHESOME] – **lissomness,** *n.*

**lissotrichous** /lə'sɒtrəkəs/, *adj.* having straight hair. [Gk *lissó(s)* smooth + *thríx* hair + -OUS]

**list**[1] /lɪst/, *n.* **1.** a record consisting of a series of names, words, or the like; a number of names of persons or things set down one after another. *–v.t.* **2.** to set down together in a list; to make a list of. **3.** to enter in a list with others. **4.** *Archaic.* to enlist. **5.** to register a security on a stock exchange so that it may be traded there. *–v.i. Archaic.* **6.** to enlist. [special use of LIST[2]. Cf. F *liste* (from G) in same sense]

**list**[2] /lɪst/, *n.* **1.** a border or bordering strip of anything (now chiefly of cloth). **2.** a division of the hair or beard. **3.** *U.S.* one of the ridges or furrows of earth thrown up by a lister. *–v.t.* **4.** to border or edge. **5.** *U.S.* to produce furrows and ridges in (land) by means of a lister. **6.** *U.S.* (in cotton culture) to prepare (land) for the crop by making alternating ridges and furrows. [ME *lyst(e),* OE *līste* border, edging, strip, c. D *lijst,* G *Leiste*]

**list**[3] /lɪst/, *n.* **1.** a careening, or leaning to one side, as of a ship. *–v.i.* **2.** (of a ship) to careen; incline to one side: *the ship listed to starboard.* *–v.t.* **3.** to cause (a ship) to lean to one side: *the weight of the misplaced cargo listed the ship to starboard.* [orig. obscure]

**list**[4] /lɪst/, *Archaic. –v.t.* **1.** to be pleasing to; please. **2.** to like or desire. *–v.i.* **3.** to like; wish; choose. [ME *luste(n)* OE *lystan,* c. G *lüsten,* Icel. *lysta*]

**list**[5] /lɪst/, *Archaic or Poetic. –v.i.* **1.** to listen. *–v.t.* **2.** to listen to. [ME *list(e),* OE *hlystan,* from *hlyst* hearing (c. Icel.

*hlust* ear); akin to LISTEN]

**listen** /ˈlɪsən/, *v.i.* **1.** to give attention with the ear; attend closely for the purpose of hearing; give ear. **2.** to give heed; yield to advice. **3.** to wait attentively (fol. by *for*). **4. listen in, a.** to eavesdrop. **b.** to listen to a radio program. *–v.t.* **5.** *Poetic.* to hear; give ear to. [ME *lis(t)ne(n)*, OE *hlysnan*, c. MHG *lüsenen;* akin to LIST[5]] – **listener,** *n.*

**listening post** /ˈlɪsnɪŋ poʊst/, *n.* **1.** *Mil.* a post or position, as in advance of a defensive line, established for the purpose of listening to detect the enemy's movements. **2.** any position maintained to obtain information.

**lister** /ˈlɪstə/, *n. U.S.* a plough with a double mouldboard used to prepare the soil for planting by producing furrows and ridges, and often fitted with attachments for dropping and covering the seeds. Also, **lister plow, lister plough.** [see LIST[2] (def. 3)]

**l'istesso tempo** /lɪsˌtɛsoʊ ˈtɛmpoʊ/, *adv.* (a musical direction) at the same speed. [It.]

**listing** /ˈlɪstɪŋ/, *n.* an entry in a list as in a catalogue, telephone directory, etc.

**listless** /ˈlɪstləs/, *adj.* **1.** feeling no inclination towards or interest in anything. **2.** characterised by or indicating such feeling: *a listless mood.* [late ME, from LIST[4] + -LESS] – **listlessly,** *adv.*

**listlessness** /ˈlɪstləsnəs/, *n.* **1.** the state of being listless. **2.** languid inattention.

**list price** /ˈlɪst praɪs/, *n.* price given in a catalogue; an advertised price.

**lists** /lɪsts/, *n.pl.* **1.** the barriers enclosing the field of combat at a tournament. **2.** the enclosed field. **3.** any place or scene of combat. **4. enter the lists,** to take part in a contest or competition. [ME *liste* boundary, limit (same word as LIST[2])]

**lit** /lɪt/, *v.* **1.** past tense and past participle of **light**[1] and **light**[3]. *–adj.* **2.** *Colloq.* drunk; intoxicated (oft. fol. by *up*).

**lit.,** **1.** litre. **2.** literal. **3.** literally. **4.** literary. **5.** literature.

**litany** /ˈlɪtəni/, *n., pl.* **-nies.** **1.** a ceremonial or liturgical form of prayer consisting of a series of invocations or supplications with responses which are the same for a number in succession. **2.** Also, **the Litany.** the general supplication in this form in the Book of Common Prayer. **3.** a prolonged recitation; monotonous account. [LL *litanīa,* from Gk *litaneía* litany, an entreating; replacing ME *letanie,* from OF]

**litchi** /laɪˈtʃi, ˈlɪtʃi/, *n., pl.* **-chis.** →**lychee.**

**-lite,** a word element used in names of minerals, or fossils: *chrysolite, aerolite.*Cf. **-lith.** [F, from Gk *líthos* stone. Cf. G *-lit(h)*]

**liter** /ˈlitə/, *n. U.S.* →**litre.**

**literacy** /ˈlɪtərəsi/, *n.* the state of being literate; possession of education.

**literacy test** /ˈ– tɛst/, *n.* an examination to determine whether a person meets the literacy requirement for voting, etc.

**literal** /ˈlɪtrəl, ˈlɪtərəl/, *adj.* **1.** following the letter, or exact words, of the original, as a translation. **2.** (of persons) tending to construe words in the strict sense or in an unimaginative way; matter-of-fact; prosaic. **3.** in accordance with, involving, or being the natural or strict meaning of the words or word; not figurative or metaphorical: *the literal meaning of a word.* **4.** true to fact; not exaggerated: *a literal statement of conditions.* **5.** being actually such, without exaggeration or inaccuracy: *the literal extermination of a city.* **6.** of or pertaining to the letters of the alphabet. **7.** of the nature of letters. **8.** expressed by letters. **9.** affecting a letter or letters: *a literal error.* *–n.* **10.** *Print.* a misprint in printed matter, esp. of one letter only. [ME, from LL *litterālis,* from *littera* LETTER] – **literalness,** *n.*

**literalise** /ˈlɪtrəlaɪz/, *v.t.,* **-lised, -lising.** to make literal, interpret literally. Also, **literalize.** – **literaliser,** *n.*

**literalism** /ˈlɪtrəlɪzəm, ˈlɪtərəlɪzəm/, *n.* **1.** adherence to the exact letter or the literal sense, as in translation or interpretation. **2.** a peculiarity of expression resulting from this. **3.** exact representation or portrayal, without idealisation, as in art or literature. – **literalist,** *n., adj.* – **literalistic** /ˈlɪtrəlɪstɪk, -tər-/, *adj.*

**literality** /lɪtəˈræləti/, *n., pl.* **-ties.** **1.** the quality of being literal. **2.** a literal interpretation.

**literally** /ˈlɪtrəli, ˈlɪtərəli/, *adv.* **1.** in a literal manner; word for word: *to translate literally.* **2.** in the literal sense. **3.** actually; without exaggeration or inaccuracy.

**literary** /ˈlɪtərəri, ˈlɪtrəri/, *adj.* **1.** pertaining to or of the nature of books and writings, esp. those classed as literature: *literary history.* **2.** versed in or acquainted with literature. **3.** engaged in writing books, etc., or in literature as a profession: *a literary man.* **4.** pedantic; excessively affected in displaying learning. – **literarily,** *adv.* – **literariness,** *n.*

**literate** /ˈlɪtərət/, *adj.* **1.** able to read and write. **2.** having an education; educated. **3.** literary. *–n.* **4.** one who can read and write. **5. a learned person.** [ME *litterate,* from L *litterātus, līterātus* lettered]

**literati** /lɪtəˈrati/, *n.pl.* men of learning; men of letters; scholarly or literary people. [L]

**literatim** /lɪtəˈratɪm/, *adv.* letter for letter; literally. [ML, from L *littera* LETTER]

**literature** /ˈlɪtrətʃə, ˈlɪtərətʃə/, *n.* **1.** writings in which expression and form, in connection with ideas of permanent and universal interest, are characteristic or essential features, as poetry, romance, history, biography, essays, etc.; belles-lettres. **2.** the entire body of writings of a specific language, period, people, subject, etc.: *the literature of Australia.* **3.** the writings dealing with a particular subject. **4.** the profession of a writer or author. **5.** literary work or production. **6.** *Colloq.* printed matter of any kind, as circulars or advertising matter. **7.** *Rare.* polite learning or literary culture. [ME *litterature,* from F, from L *litterātūra* learning]

**lith-,** a combining form meaning 'stone'. Also, **litho-.** [Gk, combining form of *líthos*]

**-lith,** a noun termination meaning 'stone', as in *acrolith, megalith, nephrolith, palaeolith,* sometimes occurring in words, as *batholith, laccolith,* that are variants of forms in *-lite.* Cf. **-lite.** [see LITH-]

**lith.,** **1.** lithograph. **2.** lithography. Also, **litho., lithog.**

**Lith.,** **1.** Lithuania. **2.** Lithuanian.

**litharge** /ˈlɪθadʒ/, *n.* lead monoxide, a yellow earthy substance used in compounding glazes and glasses. [ME *litarge,* from OF, from L *lithargyrus,* from Gk *lithárgyros* spume of silver]

**lithe** /laɪð/, *adj.* bending readily; pliant; limber; supple. Also, **lithesome** /ˈlaɪðsəm/. [ME *lith(e),* OE *līthe,* c. G *lind* mild] – **lithely,** *adv.* – **litheness,** *n.*

**lithia** /ˈlɪθiə/, *n.* a white oxide of lithium, $Li_2O$. [NL, from Gk *líthos* stone]

**lithia water** /ˈ– wɔtə/, *n.* a mineral water, natural or artificial, containing lithium salts.

**lithic** /ˈlɪθɪk/, *adj.* **1.** pertaining to or consisting of stone. **2.** *Pathol.* pertaining to stony concretions, or calculi, formed within the body, esp. in the bladder. **3.** *Chem.* of, pertaining to, or containing lithium. [Gk *lithikós* of stones]

**-lithic,** an adjective suffix identical with **lithic,** used esp. in archaeology, e.g., *palaeolithic.*

**lithium** /ˈlɪθiəm/, *n.* a soft silver-white metallic element (the lightest of all metals) occurring combined in certain minerals. *Symbol:* Li; *at. wt:* 6·939; *at. no.:* 3; *sp. gr.:* 0·53 at 20°C. [NL, from Gk *líthos* stone + *-ium* -IUM; so named because found in minerals]

**litho-,** variant of **lith-,** before consonants, as in *lithography.*

**litho.,** **1.** lithograph. **2.** lithography.

**lithog.,** **1.** lithograph. **2.** lithography.

**lithograph** /ˈlɪθəgræf/, *n.* **1.** a print produced by lithography. *–v.t.* **2.** to produce or copy by lithography.

**lithographer** /lɪˈθɒgrəfə/, *n.* a person who works at lithography.

**lithography** /lɪˈθɒgrəfi/, *n.* the art or process of printing a picture, writing, or the like, from a flat surface of aluminium, zinc or stone, with some greasy or oily substance. – **lithographic** /lɪθəˈgræfɪk/, **lithographical** /lɪθəˈgræfɪkəl/, *adj.* – **lithographically** /lɪθəˈgræfɪkli/, *adv.*

**lithoid** /ˈlɪθɔɪd/, *adj.* stonelike; stony. Also, **lithoidal** /lɪˈθɔɪdl/. [Gk *lithoeidḗs.* See LITH-, -OID]

**lithology** /lɪˈθɒlədʒi/, *n.* **1.** the science dealing with the minute mineral characters of rock specimens. **2.** *Med. Rare.* the science treating of calculi in the human body. – **lithologic** /lɪθəˈlɒdʒɪk/, **lithological** /lɪθəˈlɒdʒɪkəl/, *adj.*

**litholopaxy** /ˈlɪθələpæksi, lɪˈθɒlə-/, *n.* the crushing of a bladder stone by a lithotrite, followed by washing out the fragments so produced.

**lithomancy** /ˈlɪθəmænsi/, *n.* divination by means of stones, usu. precious.

**lithomarge** /ˈlɪθəmadʒ/, *n.* kaolin (clay) in compact, massive, usu. impure form. [NL *lithomarga,* from *litho-* LITHO- + L *marga* marl]

**lithophyte** /ˈlɪθəfaɪt/, *n.* **1.** *Zool.* a polyp with a hard or stony structure, as a coral. **2.** *Bot.* any plant growing on the surface of rocks. – **lithophytic** /lɪθəˈfɪtɪk/, *adj.*

**lithopone** /ˈlɪθəpoʊn/, *n.* a white pigment consisting of zinc sulphide and barium sulphate, used in the manufacture of linoleum and rubber articles. [LITHO- + Gk *pónos* task]

**lithosphere** /ˈlɪθəsfɪə/, *n.* the crust of the earth.

**lithotomy** /lɪˈθɒtəmi/, *n., pl.* **-mies.** the operation or art of cutting for stone in the urinary bladder. [LL *lithotomia,* from Gk. See LITHO-, -TOMY] – **lithotomic** /lɪθəˈtɒmɪk/, **lithotomical** /lɪθəˈtɒmɪkəl/, *adj.* – **lithotomist** /lɪˈθɒtəməst/, *n.*

**lithotrite** /ˈlɪθətraɪt/, *n.* an instrument for performing lithotrity.

**lithotrity** /lɪˈθɒtrəti/, *n., pl.* **-ties.** the operation of crushing stone in the urinary bladder into particles that may be voided. [LITHO- + L *trītus,* pp., rubbed + -Y[3]]

**Lithuania** /lɪθjuˈeɪniə/, *n.* a constituent republic of the Soviet Union in the western part of Europe on the Baltic. – **Lithuanian,** *adj., n.*

**litigable** /ˈlɪtɪgəbəl/, *adj.* subject to litigation.

**litigant** /ˈlɪtəgənt/, *n.* **1.** one engaged in a lawsuit. *–adj.* **2.** litigating; engaged in a lawsuit. [L *lītigans,* ppr.]

**litigate** /ˈlɪtəgeɪt/, *v.,* **-gated, -gating.** *–v.t.* **1.** to make the subject of a lawsuit; to contest at law. **2.** to dispute (a point, etc). *–v.i.* **3.** to carry on a lawsuit. [L *lītigātus,* pp.] – **litigator,** *n.*

**litigation** /lɪtəˈgeɪʃən/, *n.* **1.** the process of litigating. **2.** **→lawsuit.**

**litigious** /ləˈtɪdʒəs/, *adj.* **1.** of or pertaining to litigation. **2.** excessively prone to litigate: *a litigious person.* [ME, from L *lītigiōsus* disputatious] – **litigiously,** *adv.* – **litigiousness,** *n.*

**litmus** /ˈlɪtməs/, *n.* a blue colouring matter obtained from certain lichens, esp. *Roccella tinctoria.* In alkaline solution litmus turns blue, in acid solution red; hence it is widely used as an indicator, esp. in the form of strips of paper impregnated with a solution of the colouring matter (**litmus paper**). [ME *litmose,* from Scand.; cf. Icel. *litmosi* dyeing-moss]

**litotes** /ˈlaɪtətiz/, *n., pl.* **-tes.** a figure of speech in which an affirmative is expressed by the negative of its contrary, as in *not bad at all.* [NL, from Gk: diminution]

**litre** /ˈlitə/, *n.* a unit of capacity in the metric system, formerly equal to the volume of one kilogram of water at its maximum density or approx. equal to 1.00028 × $10^{-3}$ $m^3$, now exactly equal to $10^{-3}$ $m^3$. It is commonly used to express volumes of liquids. *Symbol:* L, l. Also, U.S., **liter.** [F, from *litron* old measure of capacity, from LL *lītra* measure for liquids, from Gk: pound]

**-litre,** a word element meaning litres; of or pertaining to litres, as in *centilitre.* Also, *U.S.,* **-liter.**

**litter** /ˈlɪtə/, *n.* **1.** things scattered about; scattered rubbish. **2.** a condition of disorder or untidiness. **3.** a number of young brought forth at one birth. **4.** a framework of canvas stretched between two parallel bars, for the transportation of the sick and the wounded. **5.** a vehicle carried by men or animals, consisting of a bed or couch, often covered and curtained, suspended between shafts. **6.** *Agric.* **a.** a bed or stratum of various materials, esp. a deep layer of straw and dung in an animal shed. **b.** straw, hay, etc., used as a protection for plants. **7.** the rubbish of dead leaves and twigs scattered upon the floor of the forest. **8.** **→kitty litter.** *–v.t.* **9.** to strew (a place) with scattered objects. **10.** to scatter (objects) in disorder. **11.** to be strewn about (a place) in disorder (fol. by *up*). **12.** to give birth to (young), said chiefly of animals. **13.** to supply (an animal) with litter for a bed. **14.** to use (straw, hay, etc.) for litter. **15.** to cover (a floor, etc.) with litter, or straw, hay, etc. *–v.i.* **16.** to give birth to a litter. [ME *litere,* from AF, from *lit* bed, from L *lectus*]

**littérateur** /lɪtərəˈtɜ/, *n.* a writer of literary works. Also, **litterateur.** [F, from L *litterātor*]

**litter-bin** /ˈlɪtə-bɪn/, *n.* a large container, esp. one in a public place, used as a receptacle for litter. Also, **litter-basket** /ˈlɪtə-baskət/.

**litterbug** /ˈlɪtəbʌg/, *n.* one who drops rubbish, esp. in public places.

**littermate** /ˈlɪtəmeɪt/, *n.* a dog which is from the same litter as another.

**little** /ˈlɪtl/, *adj.,* **less** or **lesser, least;** or **littler, littlest;** *adv.,* **less, least;** *n.* *–adj.* **1.** small in size; not big or large: *a little child.* **2.** small in extent or duration; short; brief: *a little while.* **3.** small in number: *a little army.* **4.** small in amount or degree; not much: *little hope.* **5.** (by litotes) sufficient to have an effect; appreciable: *having a little trouble.* **6.** being such on a small scale: *little farmers.* **7.** small in force; weak: *a little voice.* **8.** small in consideration, dignity, consequence, etc.: *little discomforts.* **9.** mean, narrow, or illiberal: *a little mind.* **10.** endearingly small or considered as such: *Bless your little heart!* **11.** amusingly small or so considered: *I understand his little ways.* **12. little green man,** an imaginary person from outer space. *–adv.* **13.** not at all (before a verb): *he little knows what awaits him.* **14.** in only a small amount or degree; not much: *a zeal little tempered by humanity.* **15.** rarely; infrequently: *I see my mother very little.* *–n.* **16.** that which is little; a small amount, quantity, or degree. **17.** a short distance: *please step back a little.* **18.** a short time: *stay here a little.* **19. little by little,** by degrees; gradually. **20. make little of, a.** to belittle; disparage. **b.** to understand only partially; grasp inadequately: *I can make little of your writing.* **21. not a little,** (by litotes) a very great deal; considerable. [ME and OE *lytel,* c. D *luttel,* d. G *lützel*] – **littleness,** *n.*

**little auk** /– ˈɔk/, *n.* a small, short-billed seabird, *Plautus alle,* of Greenland and Arctic areas; dovekie.

**little finger** /– ˈfɪŋgə/, *n.* the finger on the outer edge of a hand, farthest from the thumb; usu. the smallest of the fingers.

**little hours** /ˈ– aʊəz/, *n.pl. Rom. Cath. Ch.* the hours of prime, tierce, sext, and nones, and sometimes also vespers and complin.

**little house** /ˈ– haʊs/, *n. Colloq.* a toilet.

**Little Johnny** /– ˈdʒɒni/, *n.* an imaginary person regarded as the archetypal child.

**little lunch** /ˈ– lʌntʃ/, *n.* **→playlunch.**

**little man** /ˈ– mæn/, *n.* a businessman, manufacturer, farmer, etc., operating on a small scale.

**little office** /ˈ– ɒfəs/, *n. Rom. Cath. Ch.* a service, resembling the breviary but shorter, in honour of the Virgin Mary.

**little penguin** /– ˈpɛŋgwən/, *n.* a small penguin, *Eudyptula minor,* steely blue on top and white underneath, with silver-grey eyes and a black bill, found in the southern coastal regions of Australia and in New Zealand. Also, **fairy penguin.**

little penguin

**little people** /ˈ– pipəl/, *n.* small legendary beings as elves, pixies, or leprechauns. Also, **little folk.**

**Little Russian** /lɪtl ˈrʌʃən/, *n.* a member of a division of the Russian people dwelling in southern and south-western Soviet Union in Europe and in adjoining regions.

**little slam** /ˈlɪtl slæm/, *n.* **→slam**[2] (def. 1).

**little tern** /ˈ– tɜn/, *n.* the smallest Australian tern, *Sterna albifrons,* grey, with white underparts, black-tipped flight feathers, black crown, and white on the forehead extending in thin lines over the eyes, found on the north and east coasts of Australia, and also in North America, Africa, Europe, central Asia and Japan.

**little theatre** /– ˈθɪətə/, *n.* **1.** a small theatre, producing plays whose effectiveness would be lost in larger houses. **2.** plays that would not draw audiences sufficient to fill the ordinary theatre, esp. as produced by a movement in the early 20th century, identified with various theatrical experiments and innovations. **3.** amateur theatricals.

**little toe** /– ˈtoʊ/, *n.* the toe on the outer edge of the foot, farthest from the hallux; usu. the smallest of the toes.

**little woman** /– 'wʊmən/, *n. Colloq.* one's wife (oft. prec. by *the*).

**littlie** /'lɪtəli/, *n.* a child.

**littoral** /'lɪtərəl/, *adj.* **1.** pertaining to the shore of a lake, sea, or ocean. *–n.* **2.** a littoral region. [L *littorālis*]

**liturgical** /lɪ'tɜdʒɪkəl/, *adj.* **1.** of or pertaining to public worship. **2.** having to do with liturgies or forms of public worship. **3.** of or pertaining to the liturgy or Eucharistic service. **4.** of or pertaining to liturgics. Also, **liturgic.** [Gk *leitourgikós* ministering + -AL[1]] – **liturgically,** *adv.*

**Liturgical Latin** /lɪˌtɜdʒɪkəl 'lætn/, *n.* the Latin characteristic of the liturgies of the Western Church.

**liturgics** /lɪ'tɜdʒɪks/, *n.* **1.** the science or art of conducting public worship. **2.** the study of liturgies.

**liturgist** /'lɪtədʒəst/, *n.* **1.** an authority on liturgies. **2.** a compiler of a liturgy or liturgies. **3.** one who uses, or favours the use of, a liturgy.

**liturgy** /'lɪtədʒi/, *n., pl.* **-gies. 1.** a form of public worship; a ritual. **2.** a collection of formularies for public worship. **3.** a particular arrangement of services. **4.** a particular form or type of the Eucharistic service. **5.** the service of the Eucharist, esp. in the Eastern Church. [ML *līturgia,* from Gk *leitourgía* public duty, public worship]

**livable** /'lɪvəbəl/, *adj.* **1.** suitable for living in; habitable. **2.** that can be lived with; companionable. **3.** worth living; endurable. Also, **liveable.** – **livableness,** *n.*

**live**[1] /lɪv/, *v.,* **lived** /lɪvd/, **living.** *–v.i.* **1.** to have life, as an animal or plant; be alive; be capable of vital functions. **2.** to continue to live; remain alive: *to live long.* **3.** to continue in existence, operation, memory, etc.; last: *looks which lived in my memory.* **4.** to escape destruction or remain afloat, as at sea. **5.** to maintain life; rely for maintenance: *to live on one's income.* **6.** to feed or subsist (fol. by *on* or *upon*): *to live on rice.* **7.** to dwell or reside: *to live in a cottage.* **8.** to pass life (as specified): *they lived happily ever after.* **9.** to direct or regulate one's life: *to live by the golden rule.* **10.** to experience or enjoy life to the full. **11. live and learn,** to acquire new knowledge; to learn through experience. **12. live dangerously,** to take risks; live with little regard to one's personal safety. **13. live high,** to live at a high standard; live luxuriously. **14. live in** (or **out**), to reside at (or away from) the place of one's work. **15. live together,** *Colloq.* to dwell together as lovers; cohabit. **16. live with,** *Colloq.* to dwell together with, as a husband or wife or lover; to cohabit with. **17. live with oneself,** to come to terms with one's conscience; to retain one's self-respect. *–v.t.* **18.** to pass (life): *to live a life of ease.* **19.** to carry out or exhibit in one's life. **20. live down,** to live so as to cause (something) to lose force or be forgotten: *to live down a mistake.* **21. live it up,** *Colloq.* to live wildly and exuberantly; go on a spree. **22. live up to,** to accord with or maintain (expectations or standards). [ME *liv(i)en,* OE *lifian, libban,* c. D *leven,* G *leben*]

**live**[2] /laɪv/, *adj.* **1.** being in life, living, or alive: *live animals.* **2.** of or pertaining to life of living beings: *live weight* (the weight of an animal while living). **3.** characterised by or indicating the presence of living creatures. **4.** full of life, energy, or activity. **5.** *Colloq.* of present interest, as a question or issue. **6.** burning or glowing, as a coal. **7.** vivid or bright, as colour. **8.** flowing freely, as water. **9.** fresh, as air. **10.** loaded or unexploded, as a cartridge or shell. **11.** *Elect.* electrically connected to a source of potential difference, or electrically charged so as to have a potential different from that of earth: *a live wire.* **12.** moving, or imparting motion or power: *the live centre of a lathe.* **13.** still in use, or to be used, as type set up or copy for printing. **14.** (of a radio or television program) broadcast or televised at the moment it is being presented at the studio. **15.** denoting or pertaining to an actual public performance in the theatre or the like, opposed to a filmed or broadcast performance. **16.** *Acoustics.* (of a room, etc.) having a relatively long reverberation period. **17.** (of a betting ticket, wager, etc.) still dependent on the results of a race yet to be run, esp. where the wager involves more than one race. *–adv.* **18.** (of a radio or television program) not taped; at the time of its happening: *this race is brought to you live from the Olympic swimming pool.* [aphetic var. of ALIVE, used attributively]

**liveable** /'lɪvəbəl/, *adj.* →**livable.**

**liveableness** /'lɪvəbəlnəs/, *n.* the quality of being comfortable and convenient to live in.

**live axle** /laɪv 'æksəl/, *n.* an axle cast in one piece so that the wheels on that axle do not move independently of each other.

**livebearer** /'laɪvbɛərə/, *n.* any fish of the viviparous family Poeciliidae, esp. those kept in home aquariums.

**live-bearing** /'laɪv-bɛərɪŋ/, *adj.* →**viviparous.**

**live centre** /laɪv 'sɛntə/, *n.* →**centre** (def. 10a).

**live-cross** /'laɪv-krɒs/, *n.* a live interview on television, made by an outside-broadcast team, and featured in a program done in the studio, as in the news presentation.

**lived** /lɪvd/, *adj.* having life or a life (as specified): *long-lived.*

**lived-in** /'lɪvd-ɪn/, *adj.* (of a house, room, etc.) frequently occupied, inhabited.

**livelihood** /'laɪvlihʊd/, *n.* means of maintaining life; maintenance: *to gain a livelihood.* [earlier *liveliod,* metathetic var. of ME *livilod,* OE *līf(ge)lād* life-support (cf. LIFE, LODE, LOAD); current form influenced by obs. *livelihood* liveliness]

**live load** /laɪv 'loʊd/, *n.* a load that is applied temporarily, as the weight of a train passing over a bridge.

**livelong** /'lɪvlɒŋ/, *adj.* **1.** long to the full extent (used of time): *the livelong day.* **2.** whole or entire. *–n.* **3.** a perennial crassulaceous herb with fleshy leaves and clusters of reddish purple flowers, *Sedum telephium,* widespread in woods and hedgerows in northern temperate regions. [alteration (by association with LIVE[1]) of *leeve long,* ME *leve longe* dear long. Cf. LIEF, LONG[1]]

**lively** /'laɪvli/, *adj.,* **-lier, -liest,** *adv. –adj.* **1.** full or suggestive of life or vital energy; active, vigorous, or brisk: *a lively discussion.* **2.** animated, spirited, vivacious, or sprightly: *a lively tune.* **3.** eventful, stirring, or exciting: *a lively time.* **4.** strong, keen, or distinct: *a lively recollection.* **5.** striking, telling, or effective, as an expression or instance. **6.** vivid or bright, as colour or light. **7.** sparkling, as wines. **8.** fresh, as air. **9.** riding the sea buoyantly, as a ship. *–adv.* **10.** with activity, vigour, or animation; briskly. [ME; OE *līflīc*] – **livelily,** *adv.* – **liveliness,** *n.*

**liven** /'laɪvən/, *v.t.* **1.** to put life into; rouse; cheer (oft. fol. by *up*). *–v.i.* **2.** to become more lively; brighten (usu. fol. by *up*). – **livener,** *n.*

**live oak** /laɪv 'oʊk/, *n.* **1.** an evergreen species of oak, *Quercus virginiana,* of the southern U.S., with a hard wood used in shipbuilding, etc. **2.** any of various related trees.

**liver**[1] /'lɪvə/, *n.* **1.** (in man) a large, reddish brown glandular organ (divided by fissures into five lobes) in the upper right-hand side of the abdominal cavity, secreting bile and performing various metabolic functions, and formerly supposed to be the seat of love, desire, courage, etc. **2.** an organ in other animals similar to the human liver, often used as food. **3.** a disordered state of the liver. **4.** a reddish brown colour. *–adj.* **5.** of the colour of liver. [ME; OE *lifer,* c. D *lever,* G *Leber,* Icel. *lifr*]

**liver**[2] /'lɪvə/, *n.* **1.** one who lives. **2.** one who leads a life (as specified): *an evil liver.* **3.** a dweller. [LIVE[1] + -ER[1]]

**liver extract** /'lɪvər ˌɛkstrækt/, *n.* an extract of mammalian liver, used to treat anaemia.

**liver fluke** /'lɪvə fluk/, *n.* a cestode platyhelminth parasitic worm, *Fasciola hepatica,* which lives in the bile ducts of sheep.

**liveried** /'lɪvərid/, *adj.* clad in livery, as servants.

**liverish** /'lɪvərɪʃ/, *adj.* **1.** having one's liver out of order. **2.** disagreeable as to disposition. Also, **livery.**

**liver of sulphur,** *n. Obs.* a red-brown mixture of sulphides obtained by fusing potassium carbonate with sulphur; used as an insecticide, fungicide, and in treating skin diseases. [translation of L *hepar sulphuris*]

**liver salts** /'lɪvə sɒlts/, *n.pl.* →**health salts.**

**liver sausage** /lɪvə 'sɒsɪdʒ/, *n.* →**liverwurst.**

**liverwort** /'lɪvəwɜt/, *n.* any of the cryptogamic plants which belong to the class Hepaticae, comprising mosslike or thalloid plants which grow mostly on damp ground, in water, or on tree trunks.

**liverwurst** /'lɪvəwɜst/, *n.* a sausage made with a large percentage of liver. Also, **liver sausage.** [LIVER[1] + WURST]

**livery**[1] /'lɪvəri/, *n., pl.* **-ries. 1.** a distinctive dress, badge, or device provided for retainers, as of a feudal lord. **2.** a kind of uniform worn by servants, now only menservants, of a person or household. **3.** a distinctive dress worn by an official, a member of a company or guild, etc. **4.** *Brit.* **livery company.** the entire guild company entitled to wear such livery. **5.** characteristic dress, garb, or outward appearance: *the green livery of summer.* **6.** the keep, or feeding, stabling, etc., of horses for pay. [ME *livere, levere,* from AF *liveré,* pp. of *livrer* deliver, from L *līberāre* liberate]

**livery**[2] /ˈlɪvəri/, *adj.* →**liverish.**

**liveryman** /ˈlɪvərimən/, *n., pl.* **-men. 1.** a keeper of or an employee in a livery stable. **2.** *Brit.* a member of a livery company.

**livery stable** /ˈlɪvəri steɪbəl/, *n.* a stable where horses and vehicles are cared for or let out for hire.

**lives** /laɪvz/, *n.* plural of **life.**

**live steam** /laɪv ˈstim/, *n.* **1.** steam fresh from the boiler and at full pressure. **2.** steam which has performed no work or only part of its work.

**livestock** /ˈlaɪvstɒk/, *n.* the horses, cattle, sheep, and other useful animals kept or bred on a farm or ranch.

**liveware** /ˈlaɪvwɛə/, *n.* the personnel involved with the use of a computer, as programmers, key punch operators, etc. See **software, hardware.**

**livewire** /ˈlaɪvwaɪə/, *n.* an energetic, alert person.

**livid** /ˈlɪvəd/, *adj.* **1.** having a discoloured bluish appearance due to a bruise, to congestion of blood vessels, etc., as the flesh, face, hands, or nails. **2.** dull blue; dark greyish blue. **3.** angry; enraged. [L *līvidus*] – **lividly,** *adv.* – **lividness, lividity** /lɪˈvɪdəti/ *n.*

**living** /ˈlɪvɪŋ/, *adj.* **1.** that lives; alive, or not dead. **2.** in actual existence or use: *living languages.* **3.** active; strong: *a living faith.* **4.** burning or glowing, as a coal. **5.** flowing freely, as water. **6.** (of rock or stone, etc.) in its natural state and place; native, as part of the earth's crust. **7.** lifelike, as a picture. **8.** of or pertaining to living beings: *within living memory.* **9.** pertaining to or sufficient for living: *living conditions.* **10.** absolute; entire (used as an intensifier): *to scare the living daylights out of someone.* *–n.* **11.** the act or condition of one who or that which lives: *living is very expensive these days.* **12.** manner or course of life: *holy living.* **13.** means of maintaining life; livelihood: *to earn one's living.* **14.** an ecclesiastical benefice. **15. the living,** (*collectively*) those alive at any one given time. **16. for a living,** as a livelihood. **17. good living,** a style of life which is typified by a high standard of material goods. – **livingly,** *adv.* – **livingness,** *n.*

**living allowance** /ˈ– əlaʊəns/, *n.* an allowance paid to a person to compensate him for additional expense or inconvenience incurred as a result of having to live away from home to pursue a course of study or work at a particular place.

**living death** /– ˈdɛθ/, *n.* a life without any hope of happiness; an utterly wretched existence.

**living room** /ˈ– rum/, *n.* a room in a house, flat, etc., used both for entertaining and for relaxing, recreation, etc.; drawing room; sitting room; lounge; parlour.

**Livingstone daisy** /lɪvɪŋstən ˈdeɪzi/, *n.* a prostrate annual plant, *Dorotheanthus bellidiformis,* with somewhat crystalline stems and brightly coloured daisy-like flowers which open only in bright sunshine.

**living wage** /ˈlɪvɪŋ weɪdʒ/, *n.* a wage on which it is possible for a wage-earner to live according to minimum customary standards.

**lixiviate** /lɪkˈsɪvieɪt/, *v.t.,* **-ated, -ating.** to treat with a solvent; leach. [LIXIVI(UM) + -ATE[1]] – **lixiviation** /lɪkˌsɪviˈeɪʃən/, *n.*

**lixivium** /lɪkˈsɪviəm/, *n., pl.* **lixiviums, lixivia** /lɪkˈsɪviə/. **1.** the solution, containing alkaline salts, obtained by leaching wood ashes with water; lye. **2.** any solution obtained by leaching. [L, properly neut. of *lixīvius* made into lye]

lizard

**lizard** /ˈlɪzəd/, *n.* **1.** any of the typical lizards of the Old World family Lacertidae, esp. of the genus *Lacerta.* **2.** any reptile of the order Sauria, including also larger forms, the monitors, geckos, chameleons, and various limbless forms. **3.** leather made from the skin of any of various lizards, used for making shoes, etc. **4.** *Colloq.* an idler or lounger in places of social enjoyment, public resort, etc., esp. one who associates with women; a lounge lizard. **5.** a sheep musterer; a property employee who maintains boundary fences. **6.** a shearing handpiece. [ME *lesard,* from OF (masc.), also *lesarde,* fem., from L *lacertus,* masc., *lacerta,* fem.]

**lizard fish** /ˈ– fɪʃ/, *n.* any of various large-mouthed fishes (family Synodontidae) with lizard-like heads, as *Trachinocephalus myops* of tropical Australian waters.

**lk,** link.

**Lk,** *Bible.* Luke.

**'ll,** a contraction of *will* or *shall.*

**ll.,** lines.

**LL,** **1.** Late Latin. **2.** Low Latin. Also, **L.L.**

**llama** /ˈlamə/, *n.* **1.** a woolly-haired South American ruminant of the genus *Lama* (or *Auchenia*), probably a domesticated variety of the guanaco, used as a beast of burden. **2.** the fine, soft fleece of the llama, combined with the wool for coating. [Sp., from Quechua]

llama

**llano** /ˈlanoʊ, ˈljanoʊ/, *n., pl.* **-nos** /-noʊz/. (in Spanish America) an extensive grassy plain with few trees. [Sp.: a plain, as adj., flat, level, from L *plānus* PLAIN[1]]

**LLB** /ɛl ɛl ˈbi/, Bachelor of Laws. [L *Lēgum Baccalaureus*]

**LLD** /ɛl ɛl ˈdi/, Doctor of Laws. [L *Lēgum Doctor*]

**LLM** /ɛl ɛl ˈɛm/, Master of Laws. [L *Lēgum Magister*]

**lm,** lumen.

**LMP,** *Med.* last menstrual period.

**LNG,** *Chem.* liquified natural gas.

**lnge,** lounge.

**lo** /loʊ/, *interj.* look! see! behold! [ME; OE *lā!* lo! behold! c. Goth. *laian* revile, Icel. *lā* scold]

**loach** /loʊtʃ/, *n.* any of various slender European and Asiatic freshwater fishes of the family Cobitidae, with several barbels about a small mouth: related to the minnows. [ME *loch,* from OF *loche;* ? of Celtic orig.]

**load** /loʊd/, *n.* **1.** that which is laid on or placed in anything for conveyance. **2.** the quantity that can be or usu. is carried, as in a cart; this quantity taken as a unit of measure or weight. **3.** anything upborne or sustained: *the load of fruit on a tree.* **4.** something that weighs down or oppresses like a burden. **5.** the amount of work required of a person, machine, organisation, etc. **6.** the charge of a firearm. **7.** (*pl.*) *Colloq.* a great quantity or number: *loads of people.* **8.** the weight supported by a structure or part. **9.** *Elect.* the power delivered by a generator, motor, power station, or transformer (oft. fol. by *on*). **10.** *Elect., Physics.* the resistance or impedance connected to a network containing a source or sources of electromotive force. **11.** *Mech.* the external resistance overcome by an engine, dynamo, or the like, under a given condition, measured by the power required. **12.** *Colloq.* an infection of venereal disease, usu. gonorrhoea. **13.** *Colloq.* a sufficient quantity of liquor drunk to intoxicate. **14. get a load of,** *Colloq.* **a.** to look at; observe. **b.** to listen; to hear. *–v.t.* **15.** to put a load on or in: *to load a cart.* **16.** to supply abundantly or excessively with something: *to load a person with gifts.* **17.** to give bias to, esp. by fraudulent means. **18.** to weigh down, burden, or oppress. **19.** to add to the weight of, often fraudulently, as metals. **20.** to make (dice) heavier on one side than on the others by fraudulent means so as to cause them to fall with a particular face upwards. **21.** *Insurance.* to increase (a net premium, etc.). See **loading** (def. 6). **22.** to take on as a load: *a vessel loading coal.* **23.** to charge (a firearm, camera, etc.) **24.** to add additional material to (concrete) containing elements of high atomic number, esp. iron or lead, for use in shielding a nuclear reactor. **25.** to improve the surface of paper by adding china clay, titanium dioxide or barium sulphate. **26. load the dice,** to place in an especially favourable or unfavourable position. *–v.i.* **27.** to put on or take on a load. **28.** to load a firearm, camera, etc. **29.** to become loaded. **30.** to enter a means of conveyance: *the football fans loaded into* *special buses.* [ME *lode;* orig. the same word as LODE (OE *lād* way, source, carrying), but now differential in spelling and sense, and associated with LADE] – **loader,** *n.*

**load displacement** /'– dɪsˌpleɪsmənt/, *n.* the amount of water displaced by a ship when it is fully loaded.

**loaded** /'loʊdəd/, *adj.* **1.** carrying or bearing a load. **2.** charged with ammunition. **3.** (of a question, statement, etc.) unfair; weighted so as to produce a prejudicial effect. **4.** (of dice) fraudulently weighted so as to produce certain combinations. **5.** *Colloq.* unjustly incriminated; framed. **6.** *Colloq.* very wealthy. **7.** *Colloq.* incapacitated through excess alcohol or drugs.

**loaded displacement mass,** *n.* the mass of a ship when it is loaded, measured in tonnes.

**loaded displacement tonnage,** *n.* the mass of a ship when it is loaded, measured in tons.

**loader** /'loʊdə/, *n.* **1.** one who or that which loads. **2.** a mechanism for loading earth or granular material, as a ship-loader. **3.** a machine which is designed to move earth, etc., by means of a powered scoop, as a front-end loader.

**load factor** /'loʊd fæktə/, *n.* **1.** the ratio of the average load of electricity over a designated period of time to the peak load occurring in that period. **2.** the ratio of the load carried by an aircraft to the weight of the aircraft.

**loading** /'loʊdɪŋ/, *n.* **1.** the act of one who or that which loads. **2.** that with which something is loaded; a load; a burden; a charge. **3.** an extra rate paid to employees in recognition of a particular aspect of their employment, as shift work. **4.** *Elect.* the process of adding inductances to a telephone circuit, radio aerial, etc. **5.** the ratio of the gross weight of an aeroplane to engine power (**power-loading**), wing span (**span-loading**), or wing area (**wing-loading**). **6.** *Insurance.* an addition to the normal premium on the policy of a person whose life expectancy is considered to be less than the mortality tables would indicate.

**loading bay** /'– beɪ/, *n.* an entrance in a building designed to facilitate the loading and unloading of trucks.

**loading coil** /'– kɔɪl/, *n.* an electrical inductance coil used to improve the characteristics of a transmission line.

**load line** /'loʊd laɪn/, *n.* **1.** *Naut.* one of several lines on the side of a ship, as the Plimsoll line, established by statute and indicating the maximum legal draught for a certain set of conditions. **2.** *Electronics.* a line drawn on a graph of the characteristics of a semiconductor or vacuum tube in order to determine its behaviour in a particular circuit.

**loadstar** /'loʊdsta/, *n.* →**lodestar.**

**loadstone** /'loʊdstoʊn/, *n.* →**lodestone.**

**loaf**[1] /loʊf/, *n., pl.* **loaves** /loʊvz/. **1.** a portion of bread or cake baked in a mass of definite form. **2.** a shaped or moulded mass of food, as of sugar, chopped meat, etc.: *a veal loaf.* [ME *lo(o)f,* OE *hlāf* loaf, bread, c. G *Laib*]

**loaf**[2] /loʊf/, *v.i.* **1.** to lounge or saunter lazily and idly. **2.** to idle away time. *–v.t.* **3.** to idle (usu. fol. by *away*): *to loaf one's life away.* *–n.* **4.** an idle or relaxing time; rest. **5.** an easy job; sinecure. [backformation from LOAFER]

**loaf**[3] /loʊf/, *n. Colloq.* **1.** head; intelligence; brains. **2. use one's loaf,** to think; apply one's intelligence. [probably rhyming slang, *loaf of bread* head]

**loafer** /'loʊfə/, *n.* **1.** an idler; one who does no work. **2.** *Brit.* a type of jacket for casual wear. [probably from G (*Land*)-*läufer* tramp, vagabond]

**loafers** /'loʊfəz/, *n.pl.* a pair of casual shoes.

**loaf sugar** /loʊf 'ʃʊgə/, *n.* a small rectangular block of sugar.

**loam** /loʊm/, *n.* **1.** a loose soil composed of clay and sand, esp. a kind containing organic matter and of great fertility. **2.** a mixture of clay, sand, straw, etc., used in making moulds for founding, and in plastering walls, stopping holes, etc. **3.** *Archaic.* earth. *–v.t.* **4.** to cover or stop with loam. **5.** *Mining.* to sort through a section or container of dirt and separate out opal, gold, etc. *–v.i.* **6.** to search for a mineral, usu. gold, by washing loam from the base of a hill to isolate the required mineral. [ME *lome, lam(e),* OE *lām,* c. D *leem,* G *Lehm* loam, clay] – **loamly,** *adj.*

**loan** /loʊn/, *n.* **1.** the act of lending; a grant of the use of something temporarily: *the loan of a book.* **2.** something lent or furnished on condition of being returned, esp. a sum of money lent at interest. *–v.t.* **3.** to make a loan of; lend. **4.** to lend (money) at interest. *–v.i.* **5.** to make a loan or loans. [ME *lon(e), lan(e),* OE *lān,* apparently from Scand.; cf. Icel. *lān,* c. OE *lǣn* loan, grant] – **loaner,** *n.*

**loan collection** /'– kəlɛkʃən/, *n.* a number of works of art, lent by their owners for a single or long-term exhibition.

**loan shark** /'– ʃak/, *n. Colloq.* one who loans money at an excessive rate of interest.

**loan word** /'– wɜd/, *n.* a word of one language adopted into another at any period in history, for example: *wine* (into Old English from Latin), *blitz* (into Modern English from German). [translation of G *Lehnwort*]

**loath** /loʊθ/, *adj.* **1.** reluctant, averse, or unwilling. **2. nothing loath,** very willingly. Also, **loth.** [ME *lothe,* OE *lāth* hostile, hateful, c. Icel. *leidhr* loathed, D *leed,* G *Leid* sorrow]

**loathe** /loʊð/, *v.t.,* **loathed, loathing. 1.** to feel hatred, disgust, or intense aversion for. **2.** to feel a physical disgust for (food, etc.). [ME *lothien,* OE *lāthian* be hateful, from *lāth* LOATH] – **loather,** *n.*

**loathing** /'loʊðɪŋ/, *n.* **1.** strong dislike mingled with disgust; intense aversion. **2.** physical disgust, as for food. – **loathingly,** *adv.*

**loathly**[1] /'loʊθli/, *adv.* reluctantly; unwillingly. [LOATH + -LY]

**loathly**[2] /'loʊðli/, *adj. Archaic.* →**loathsome.** [LOATHE + -LY]

**loathsome** /'loʊðsəm/, *adj.* such as to excite loathing; hateful; disgusting. – **loathsomely,** *adv.* – **loathsomeness,** *n.*

**loaves** /loʊvz/, *n.* plural of **loaf**[1].

**lob**[1] /lɒb/, *n., v.,* **lobbed, lobbing.** *–n.* **1.** *Tennis.* a ball struck high into the opponent's court. **2.** *Cricket.* a slow underhand ball. *–v.t.* **3.** *Tennis.* to strike (a ball) high into the air. **4.** *Cricket.* to bowl with a slow movement. **5.** to throw, fling in a careless or untidy fashion. *–v.i.* **6.** *Tennis.* to lob a ball. **7.** *Cricket.* to bowl a lob. **8.** *Colloq.* to move or go: *where are you lobbing?* **9.** *Colloq.* to arrive (usu. fol. by *at*). **10.** *Colloq.* to find by chance (fol. by *onto*). **11. lob in,** *Colloq.* to arrive unannounced or unexpectedly. **12. lob off,** *Colloq.* to depart; go away. [ME *lobbe* pollack; later, bumpkin; as v., move clumsily. See LUBBER]

**lob**[2] /lɒb/, *n.* →**lugworm.**

**lobar** /'loʊbə/, *adj.* of or pertaining to a lobe, as of the lungs: *lobar pneumonia.*

**lobate** /'loʊbeɪt/, *adj.* **1.** having a lobe or lobes; lobed. **2.** having the form of a lobe. **3.** *Ornith.* denoting or pertaining to a foot in which the individual toes have membranous flaps along the sides. Also, **lobated.** [NL *lobātus,* from LL *lobus* LOBE] – **lobately,** *adv.*

**lobation** /loʊ'beɪʃən/, *n.* **1.** lobate formation. **2.** →**lobe.**

**lobby**[1] /'lɒbi/, *n., pl.* **-bies,** *v.,* **-bied, -bying.** *–n.* **1.** a corridor, vestibule, or entrance hall, as in a public building, often serving as an anteroom. **2.** a group of persons who attempt to enlist popular and political support for some particular cause, originally those who frequented legislative lobbies or chambers. **3.** a sectional interest, cause, etc., supported by a group of people. *–v.i.* **4.** to frequent the lobby of a legislative chamber to influence the members. **5.** to solicit the votes of members of a legislative body in the lobby or elsewhere. *–v.t.* **6.** to influence (legislators), or urge or procure the passage of (a bill), by lobbying. [ML *lobia, lobium* covered walk; of Gmc origin (cf. G *Laube* an arbour). See LODGE]

**lobby**[2] /'lɒbi/, *n. Qld.* →**yabby.** [shortened form of LOBSTER + -Y[2]]

**lobbyism** /'lɒbiˌɪzəm/, *n.* **1.** the system of lobbying. **2.** the practices of those who lobby. – **lobbyist,** *n.*

**lobe** /loʊb/, *n.* **1.** a roundish projection or division, as of an organ, a leaf, etc. **2.** *Anat.* the soft pendulous lower part of the external ear. **3.** *Electronics.* a part of the energy radiated from a directional aerial. [F, from LL *lobus,* from Gk *lobós*]

**lobectomy** /lə'bɛktəmi/, *n.* excision of a lobe of an organ as the brain, lung, etc.

**lobed** /loʊbd/, *adj.* **1.** having a lobe or lobes; lobate. **2.** *Bot.* (of a leaf) having lobes or divisions extending less than halfway to the middle of the base.

**lobelia** /lə'biljə/, *n.* any of the herbaceous plants constituting the genus *Lobelia,* comprising many species, both wild and cultivated, with blue, red, yellow, or white flowers. [NL, named after M. de *Lobel,* 1538-1616, Flemish botanist, physician to James I of England]

**loblolly** /ˈlɒbˌlɒli/, *n., pl.* **-ies. 1.** *Naut.* a thick gruel. **2.** a pine, *Pinus taeda,* of the southern U.S. **3.** the wood of this tree. Also, **loblolly pine** (for defs 2, 3). [probably from d. *lob* sup noisily + *lolly* gruel]

**loblolly boy** /ˈ– bɔɪ/, *n. Obs.* the attendant of a ship's surgeon.

**lobo** /ˈloʊboʊ/, *n., pl.* **-bos.** a large grey wolf of the western U.S. [Sp., from L *lupus* wolf]

**lobotomy** /ləˈbɒtəmi/, *n.* the cutting into or across a lobe of the brain, usu. of the cerebrum, to alter brain function, esp. in the treatment of mental disorders. Also, **leucotomy.**

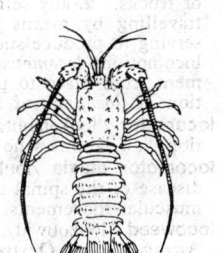

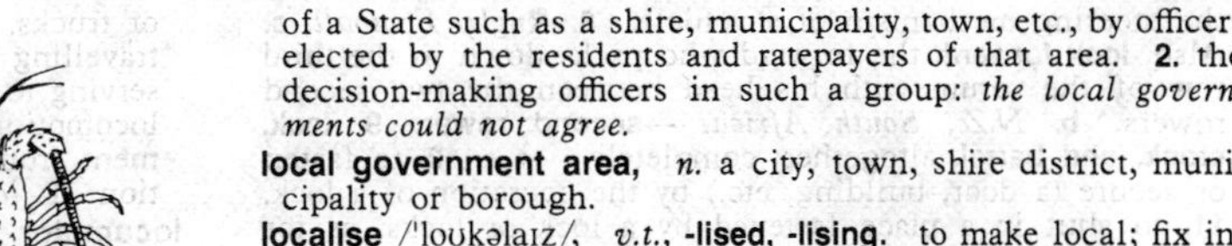

lobster (def. 1)

**lobscouse** /ˈlɒbskaʊs/, *n. Naut.* a stew of meat, potatoes, onions, ship biscuit, etc. [cf. Dan. *lapscous,* D *lapskous.* See LOBLOLLY]

**lobster** /ˈlɒbstə/, *n.* **1.** Also, **spiny lobster,** any of various large, edible, marine, stalk-eyed, decapod crustaceans of the family Palinuridae, having a long tail, spiny carapace and elongated, whip-like antennae, found in Australia and New Zealand waters and widely distributed elsewhere; crayfish. **2.** any of various crustaceans of the family Homaridae of the northern Atlantic, somewhat similar in appearance but having the first pair of legs modified into large, pincer-tipped claws. [ME *lobster, lop(i)ster,* OE *loppestre,* from *loppe* spider (both creatures having many projecting parts). See LOP[1], -STER]

**lobster Newburg** /– ˈnjubɜg/, *n.* sliced lobster, sautéed in butter, cooked in thick cream and sherry.

**lobster pot** /ˈ– pɒt/, *n.* a trap in which lobsters are caught.

**lobster thermidor** /– ˈθɜmədɔ/, *n.* lobster, removed from the shell and sauteed in a rich creamy white sauce, and served returned to the shell, topped with grated cheese.

lobster (def. 2)

**lobulate** /ˈlɒbjələt/, *adj.* having or consisting of lobules.

**lobule** /ˈlɒbjul/, *n.* **1.** a small lobe. **2.** a subdivision of a lobe. [NL *lobulus,* diminutive of LL *lobus* LOBE] – **lobular,** *adj.*

**lobworm** /ˈlɒbwɜm/, *n.* →**lugworm.** Also, **lob.**

**local** /ˈloʊkəl/, *adj.* **1.** pertaining to or characterised by place, or position in space: *local situation.* **2.** pertaining to, characteristic of, or restricted to a particular place or particular places: *a local custom.* **3.** pertaining to a town or a small district rather than the entire state or country. **4.** pertaining to or affecting a particular part or particular parts, as of a system or object: *a local disease.* **5.** (of an aesthesia or an anaesthetic) acting on only a section of the body, without loss of consciousness. **6.** *Brit.* stopping at all stations: *a local train.* *–n.* **7.** a local train, bus, etc. **8.** a newspaper item of local interest. **9.** a suburban newspaper. **10.** *U.S.* a local branch of a union, fraternity, etc. **11.** the closest or preferred hotel in the neighbourhood of one's home or place of work. **12.** a local inhabitant. **13.** →**local anaesthetic.** [ME, from LL *locālis,* from L *locus* place]

**local anaesthetic** /– ænəsˈθɛtɪk/, *n.* a drug, usu. injected, which anaesthetises only part of the body.

**local authority** /– ɔˈθɒrəti, əˈθɒr-/, *n. Chiefly Brit.* the body of people, both elected and paid workers, responsible for the administration of local government. Also, **local body.**

**local colour** /– ˈkʌlə/, *n.* **1.** distinctive characteristics or peculiarities of a place or period as represented in literature, drama, etc., or observed in reality. **2.** the true colour of any particular object or part in a picture.

**locale** /loʊˈkal/, *n.* a place or locality, esp. with reference to events or circumstances connected with it. [F *local,* n. use of adj. See LOCAL, *adj.*]

**local government** /loʊkəl ˈgʌvənmənt/, *n.* **1.** the administration of the affairs of some nominated area smaller than that of a State such as a shire, municipality, town, etc., by officers elected by the residents and ratepayers of that area. **2.** the decision-making officers in such a group: *the local governments could not agree.*

**local government area,** *n.* a city, town, shire district, municipality or borough.

**localise** /ˈloʊkəlaɪz/, *v.t.,* **-lised, -lising.** to make local; fix in, or assign or restrict to, a particular place or locality. Also, **localize.** – **localisable,** *adj.* – **localisation** /loʊkəlaɪˈzeɪʃən/, *n.*

**localiser** /ˈloʊkəlaɪzə/, *n.* a directional radio beacon which provides an aircraft with an indication of its lateral position while landing. Also, **localiser beacon.**

**localism** /ˈloʊkəlɪzəm/, *n.* **1.** a manner of speaking, pronunciation, usage, or inflection that is peculiar to one locality. **2.** a local custom. **3.** attachment to a particular locality.

**locality** /loʊˈkæləti/, *n., pl.* **-ties. 1.** a place, spot, or district, with or without reference to things or persons in it. **2.** the place in which a thing is or occurs. **3.** state or condition of being local or having place.

**locality allowance** /ˈ– əlaʊəns/, *n.* an allowance paid above the usual rate of pay as compensation for working under difficult conditions peculiar to a particular locality.

**locally** /ˈloʊkəli/, *adv.* **1.** in a particular place, or places. **2.** with regard to place. **3.** in a local respect.

**local oscillator** /loʊkəl ˈɒsəleɪtə/, *n.* an oscillator in a receiver, whose output is mixed with a signal borne by a carrier wave in order to alter the frequency of the carrier.

**local time** /ˈ– taɪm/, *n.* the time at any given place on earth as determined from the position of the sun only; it is **local noon** when the sun crosses the meridian and shadows are at their shortest.

**locate** /loʊˈkeɪt/, *v.,* **-cated, -cating.** *–v.t.* **1.** to discover the place or location of: *to locate a leak in a pipe.* **2.** to set, fix, or establish in a place, situation, or locality; place; settle: *to locate one's headquarters in Norfolk Island.* **3.** (formerly) to grant land. **4.** to refer (something), as by opinion or statement, to a particular place: *locate the garden of Eden in Babylonia.* *–v.i.* **5.** to find a suitable location: *the new Sydney airport must locate somewhere.* [L *locātus,* pp., placed]

**location** /loʊˈkeɪʃən/, *n.* **1.** a place of settlement or residence: *a good location for a doctor.* **2.** a place or situation occupied: *a house in a fine location.* **3.** a tract of land located, or of designated situation or limits: *a mining location.* **4.** (in South Africa and elsewhere) an area set aside for the native population. **5.** *Films.* a place, outside the studio, affording suitable environment for photographing particular plays, incidents, etc. hence, *on location.* **6.** the act of locating; state of being located. **7.** *Civil Law.* a letting or lease (from the point of view of the lessor). **8.** *Computers.* a specific register in the high-speed memory of a computer. **9.** *Law.* a contract for the temporary use of a chattel, or the service of a person for an ascertained hire.

**locative** /ˈlɒkətɪv/, *adj.* **1.** (in some inflected languages) denoting a case, having as chief function indication of place in or at which, as Latin *domī* 'at home'. *–n.* **2.** the locative case. **3.** a word in that case. [ML *locātīvus.* See LOCATE, -IVE]

**loc. cit.** /lɒk ˈsɪt/, *adv.* in the place or passage already mentioned. [L *locō citātō*]

**loch** /lɒk/, *n. Scot.* **1.** a lake. **2.** Also, **sea loch.** an arm of the sea, esp. when partially landlocked. [Gaelic. Cf. LOUGH]

**lochia** /ˈlɒkiə/, *n.pl.* the liquid discharge from the uterus after childbirth. [NL, from Gk, neut. pl. of *lóchios* pertaining to childbirth] – **lochial** /ˈlɒkiəl/, *adj.*

**loci**[1] /ˈlɒki, ˈloʊki/, *n.* plural of **locus.**

**loci**[2] /ˈloʊki/, *n. N.Z.* →**locomotive.**

**lock**[1] /lɒk/, *n.* **1.** a device for securing a door, gate, lid, drawer, or the like, in position when closed, consisting of a bolt or system of bolts propelled and withdrawn by a mechanism operated by a key, dial, etc. **2. a.** a device to keep a wheel from rotating. **b.** steering lock. **3.** a contrivance for fastening or securing something. **4.** the mechanism in a firearm by means of which it can be kept from operating. **5.** an enclosed portion of a canal, river, etc., with gates at each end, for raising or lowering vessels from one level to another. **6.** any of various grapples or holds in wrestling, esp. any hold in which an arm or leg of one wrestler is held about the body of his opponent. **7.** the radius of turning in the steering mechanism of a vehicle. **8.** *Rugby Football.* **a.** Also, **lock forward.** the forward who packs down in the third row of the scrum with his head between the two second rowers. **b.** *N.Z., South Africa.* →**second rower. 9. lock, stock, and barrel,** altogether; completely. *–v.t.* **10.** to fasten or secure (a door, building, etc.) by the operation of a lock. **11.** to shut in a place fastened by a lock or locks, as for security or restraining (fol. by *up, in,* etc.): *to lock a prisoner in a cell.* **12.** to exclude by or as by a lock (usu. fol. by *out*). **13.** to make fast or immovable by or as by a lock: *to lock a wheel.* **14.** to fasten or fix firmly, as by engaging parts (oft. fol. by *up*). **15.** *Print.* to make (type, etc.) immovable in a chase by securing the quoins (fol. by *up*). **16.** to join or unite firmly by interlinking or intertwining: *to lock arms.* **17.** of a limb, to straighten fully, esp. when bearing great loads, as in weightlifting. **18.** to move (a ship) by means of a lock or locks, as in a canal. **19.** to furnish with locks, as a canal. **20.** to enclose (a waterway) with a lock (fol. by *off*). *–v.i.* **21.** to become locked: *this door locks with a key.* **22.** to become fastened, fixed, or interlocked. **23.** to go or pass by means of a lock or locks, as a vessel. **24.** to construct locks in waterways. [ME; OE *loc* fastening; akin to OE *lūcan,* D *luiken,* Icel. *lūka,* Goth. *galūkan* shut, close]

**lock**[2] /lɒk/, *n.* **1.** a tress or portion of hair. **2.** (*pl.*) the hair of the head. **3.** a flock or small portion of cotton, flax, etc. **4.** (usu. pl.) a second cut or small portion of wool from the lower parts of the legs and edges of the fleece. [ME *locke,* OE *locc* lock of hair, c. Icel. *lokkr,* D *lok* curl, G *Locke*]

**lockage** /ˈlɒkɪdʒ/, *n.* **1.** the construction, use, or operation of locks, as in a canal or stream. **2.** passage through a lock or locks. **3.** toll paid for such passage.

**locker** /ˈlɒkə/, *n.* **1.** a chest, drawer, compartment, closet, or the like, that may be locked. **2.** *Naut.* a chest or compartment in which to stow things. **3.** one who or that which locks. **4.** →**Davy Jones's Locker.**

**locket** /ˈlɒkət/, *n.* a small case for a miniature portrait, a lock of hair, or other keepsake, usu. worn on a chain hung round the neck. [ME, from F *loquet* latch, catch, diminutive of OF *loc* lock, from Gmc; cf. LOCK[1]]

**lock-gate** /ˈlɒk-geɪt/, *n.* a gate at each end of a lock[1] (def. 5).

**lock-in amplifier** /lɒk-in ˈæmpləfaɪə/, *n.* an amplifier which is sensitive to a very narrow band of frequencies; used to extract a faint signal from background noise.

**lockjaw** /ˈlɒkdʒɔ/, *n.* tetanus in which the jaws become firmly locked together.

**locknit** /ˈlɒknɪt/, *n.* **1.** a type of close-knitted fabric designed so that it will not run. *–adj.* **2.** of or pertaining to a locknit fabric. Also, **lock-knit.**

**locknut** /ˈlɒknʌt/, *n.* **1.** a supplementary nut screwed down upon another to prevent it from shaking loose. **2.** a nut in which spontaneous motion is prevented by springs fitting between the threads, or by interlocking parts.

**lockout** /ˈlɒkaʊt/, *n.* the closing of a business, or wholesale dismissal of employees by the employer because the employees refuse to accept his terms or because the employer refuses to operate on terms set by a union.

**locksmith** /ˈlɒksmɪθ/, *n.* one who makes or mends locks.

**lockstitch** /ˈlɒkstɪtʃ/, *n.* a sewing-machine stitch in which two threads are locked together at small intervals.

**lockup** /ˈlɒkʌp/, *n.* **1.** a gaol, esp. a local gaol to which offenders are taken before their first court hearing. **2.** the act of locking up. **3.** a garage or other storage space, usu. rented, capable of being locked up. *–adj.* **4.** (of a room, garage, etc.) able to be locked up.

**loco**[1] /ˈloʊkoʊ/, *n.* →**locomotive.**

**loco**[2] /ˈloʊkoʊ/, *n., pl.* **-cos,** *v.,* **-coed, -coing,** *adj. U.S. –n.* **1.** →**locoweed. 2.** *Colloq.* a mad or crazy person. *–v.t.* **3.** to poison with locoweed. **4.** to make crazy. *–adj.* **5.** *Colloq* insane; crazy. [Sp.: insane, from L *glaucus* sparkling]

**loco disease** /ˈ– dəziz/, *n.* **1.** *U.S.* a disease affecting the brain of animals, caused by eating locoweed. **2.** a similar disease suffered by sheep which have eaten any of several toxic species of the Darling Pea.

**locomotion** /loʊkəˈmoʊʃən/, *n.* the act or power of moving from place to place. [L *locō,* abl. of *locus* place + MOTION]

**locomotive** /loʊkəˈmoʊtɪv/, *n.* **1.** a self-propelled vehicle running on a railway track, designed to pull railway carriages or trucks. **2.** any self-propelled vehicle. *–adj.* **3.** moving or travelling by means of its own mechanism or powers. **4.** serving to produce such movement, or adapted for or used in locomotion: *locomotive organs.* **5.** of or pertaining to movement from place to place. **6.** having the power of locomotion. [L *locō,* abl. of *locus* place + MOTIVE, *adj.*]

**locomotor** /ˈloʊkəmoʊtə/, *adj.* **1.** of or pertaining to locomotion. *–n.* **2.** one who or that which has locomotive power.

**locomotor ataxia** /loʊkə,moʊtər əˈtæksiə/, *n.* a degenerative disease of the spinal cord, marked by loss of control over the muscular movements, mainly in walking; tabes dorsalis.

**locoweed** /ˈloʊkoʊwid/, *n.* any of various plants of the genera *Astragalus* and *Oxytropis* of the south-western U.S., producing loco disease in sheep, horses, etc. [LOCO[2] + WEED[1]]

**locular** /ˈlɒkjələ/, *adj.* having one or more loculi, chambers, or cells. [LL *loculāris* kept in boxes, from L *loculus* box, cell]

**loculate** /ˈlɒkjəleɪt, -lət/, *adj.* having one or more loculi. Also, **loculated.** [L *loculātus* furnished with compartments]

**loculus** /ˈlɒkjələs/, *n., pl.* **-li** /-laɪ/. **1.** *Bot., Zool., Anat.* a small compartment or chamber; a cell. **2.** *Bot.* **a.** the cell of a carpel in which the seed is contained. **b.** the cell of an anther in which the pollen is contained. [L: a little place, box, diminutive of *locus* place]

**locum** /ˈloʊkəm/, *n.* a temporary substitute for a doctor, lawyer, etc. Also, **locum tenens** /– ˈtɛnənz/. [ML: one holding the office (of another)]

**locus** /ˈlɒkəs, ˈloʊkəs/, *n., pl.* **loci** /ˈlɒki, ˈloʊki/. **1.** a place; a locality. **2.** *Maths.* a curve or other figure considered as generated by a point, line, or surface, which moves or is placed according to a definite law. **3.** *Genetics.* the chromosomal position of a gene as determined by its linear order relative to the other genes on that chromosome. [L: place]

**locus classicus** /– ˈklæsɪkəs/, *n.* a commonly cited or authoritative passage illustrating or explaining a subject. [L]

**locus standi** /– ˈstændi/, *n.* recognition by a court of a party's right to appear in a proceeding. [L: place to stand on]

**locust** /ˈloʊkəst/, *n.* **1.** any of the grasshoppers with short antennae which constitute the family Acrididae, including the notorious migratory species, such as *Locusta migratoria* of the Old World, which swarm in immense numbers and strip the vegetation from large areas. **2.** *Colloq.* →**cicada. 3.** Also, **black locust.** a thorny-branched, white-flowered American fabaceous tree, *Robinia pseudoacacia;* acacia. **4.** its durable wood. **5.** any of various other trees, as the carob and the honey-locust. [ME, from L *locusta* locust, lobster]

locust

**locusta** /loʊˈkʌstə/, *n., pl.* **-tae** /-ti/. the spikelet of grasses. [NL, special use of L *locusta* LOCUST]

**locution** /ləˈkjuʃən/, *n.* **1.** a particular form of expression; a phrase or expression. **2.** style of speech or verbal expression; phraseology. [ME, from L *locūtio*]

**lode** /loʊd/, *n.* **1.** a veinlike deposit, usu. metalliferous. **2.** any body of ore set off from adjacent rock formations. [ME; OE *lād* way, course, carrying (see LOAD), c. OHG *leita* procession, Icel. *leidh* way, course]

**lodestar** /ˈloʊdsta/, *n.* **1.** a star that shows the way. **2.** something that serves as a guide or on which the attention is fixed. Also, **loadstar.** [ME *loode sterre.* See LOAD, LODE, STAR, *n.*]

**lodestone** /ˈloʊdstoʊn/, *n.* **1.** a variety of magnetite which possesses magnetic polarity and attracts iron. **2.** a piece of this serving as a magnet. **3.** something that attracts. Also, **loadstone.** [LOAD + STONE]

**lodge** /lɒdʒ/, *n., v.,* **lodged, lodging.** *–n.* **1.** a small, slight, or rude shelter or habitation, as of boughs, poles, skins, earth, rough boards, or the like; cabin or hut. **2.** a building used for temporary, usu. holiday, accommodation: *fishing lodge, ski lodge.* **3.** a house or cottage, as in a park or on an estate, occupied by a gatekeeper, caretaker, gardener, or the like. **4.** the residence of a school or college head or master. **5.** a place of abode or sojourn. **6.** the meeting place of a branch of a secret society. **7.** the members composing the branch. **8.** den or habitation of an animal or animals, esp. beavers. *–v.i.* **9.** to have a habitation or quarters, esp. temporarily, as in a place or house. **10.** to be fixed or implanted, or be caught in a place or position. *–v.t.* **11.** to furnish with a habitation or quarters, esp. temporarily. **12.** to furnish with a room or rooms in one's house for payment, or have as a lodger. **13.** to serve as a habitation or shelter for, as a house does; shelter; harbour. **14.** to put or deposit, as in a place, for storage or keeping. **15.** to bring or send into a particular place or position: *to lodge a bullet in one's heart.* **16.** to vest (power, etc.). **17.** to lay (information, a complaint, etc.) before a court or the like. **18.** to track (a deer) to its lair. [ME *loge,* from OF: hut, orig. leafy shelter, from Gmc (cf. OHG *lauba* arbour)]

**lodger** /ˈlɒdʒə/, *n.* one who lives in hired quarters in another's house. Cf. **boarder.**

**lodging** /ˈlɒdʒɪŋ/, *n.* **1.** accommodation in a house, esp. in rooms for hire: *to furnish board and lodging.* **2.** a place of abode, esp. a temporary one. **3.** (*pl.*) a room or rooms hired for residence in another's house.

**lodging house** /ˈ– haʊs/, *n.* a house in which lodgings are let, esp. a house other than an inn, hotel, or hostel.

**lodgment** /ˈlɒdʒmənt/, *n.* **1.** act of lodging. **2.** state of being lodged. **3.** something lodged or deposited. **4.** *Mil.* a position or foothold gained from an enemy, or an entrenchment made upon it. **5.** *Rare.* a lodging place; lodgings. Also, **lodgement.**

**lodicule** /ˈlɒdɪkjul/, *n.* a small turgid scale found in some grass flowers. [L *lōdīcula,* diminutive of *lōdix* blanket]

**loess** /ˈloʊəs/, *n.* a loamy deposit formed by wind, usu. yellowish and calcareous, common in Europe and Asia, and in the Mississippi valley in the U.S. [G]

**loft** /lɒft/, *n.* **1.** the space between the underside of a roof and the ceiling of a room beneath it. **2.** a gallery or upper level in a church, hall, etc., designed for a special purpose: *a choirloft.* **3.** →**hayloft. 4.** *U.S.* any upper storey of a warehouse, mercantile building, or factory, esp. of buildings designed for small, light industries. **5.** *Golf.* **a.** the slope of the face of a club backwards from the vertical, tending to drive the ball upwards. **b.** the act of lofting. **c.** a lofting stroke. **6.** *Golf.* to slant the face of (a club). *–v.t.* **7.** *Golf, Cricket, etc.* to hit (a ball) into the air or over an obstacle. **8.** to clear (an obstacle) thus. **9.** *U.S.* to provide (a house, etc.) with a loft. *–v.i.* **10.** *Golf, Cricket, etc.* to loft the ball. [ME *lofte,* late OE *loft,* from Scand.; cf. Icel. *lopt* the air, sky, an upper room; akin to LIFT]

**lofting iron** /ˈlɒftɪŋ aɪən/, *n.* an iron-headed golf club used in lofting the ball. Also, **lofter.**

**lofty** /ˈlɒfti/, *adj.*, **-tier, -tiest. 1.** extending high in the air; of imposing height: *lofty mountains.* **2.** exalted in rank, dignity, or character. **3.** elevated in style or sentiment, as writings, etc. **4.** haughty; proud. **5.** *Colloq.* a term of address for a tall person. **– loftily,** *adv.* **– loftiness,** *n.*

**log** /lɒg/, *n., v.,* **logged, logging.** *–n.* **1.** an unhewn portion or length of the trunk or a large limb of a felled tree. **2.** something inert or heavy. **3.** *Naut.* **a.** a device for determining the speed of and distance covered by a ship. **b.** Also, **chip log,** a device consisting of a chip (**logchip**) attached to the end of a line (**logline**) thrown over the stern to measure the speed of a ship. **c.** Also, **patent log,** an instrument indicating speed and distance which is secured to a ship's railing, and usu. operated by a propeller-like implement on the end of a line trailing astern. **4. a.** the official record which a ship's master is obliged by law to keep, of particulars of a ship's voyage, as weather, crew, cargo, etc. **b.** the record which the engine-room and bridge officers keep of the particulars of each watch. **5.** Also, **flightlog,** a listing of navigational, meteorological, and other significant data concerning an air journey. **6.** the register of the operation of a machine. **7.** a record kept of development during the drilling of a well, esp. of the geological formations penetrated. **8.** a submission or listing: *the trade union's log of claims.* **9.** *Naut. Colloq.* a slow boat. **10.** *Colloq.* a marijuana cigarette. **11.** Also, **log of wood.** *Colloq.* a fool; a lazy person. **12. the logs,** *Convict Obs. Colloq.* a gaol; prison. *–v.t.* **13.** to cut (trees) into logs. **14.** to cut down trees or timber on (land). **15. a.** to enter in a ship's log. **b.** to record in a ship's log a punishment given to (a seaman). **16.** *Chiefly Naut.* to travel (a distance) according to the indication of a log. **17.** to record in an aeroplane's log (the number of hours spent in the air). *–v.i.* **18.** to cut down trees and get out logs from the forest for timber. [ME *logge;* apparently var. of *lug* pole (see LUGSAIL)]

**log.** /lɒg/, logarithm.

**loganberry** /ˈloʊgənbəri, -bri/, *n., pl.* **-ries. 1.** the large, dark red, acid fruit of the plant *Rubus loganobaccus,* with long prostrate canes. **2.** the plant itself. [named after J. H. *Logan,* 1841-1928, of California, U.S., by whom first grown]

**loganiaceous** /loʊˌgeɪniˈeɪʃəs/, *adj.* belonging to the Loganiaceae, a family of herbs, shrubs, and trees of tropical and subtropical regions, including the nux vomica tree and other plants with poisonous properties. [NL *Logania,* the typical genus (named after James *Logan,* 1674-1751, of Philadelphia, U.S.) + -ACEOUS]

**logaoedic** /lɒgəˈidɪk/, *adj.* **1.** composed of dactyls and trochees or of anapaests and iambs, producing a movement somewhat suggestive of prose. *–n.* **2.** a logaoedic verse. [LL *logaoedicus,* from Gk *logaoidikós,* from *lógos* prose + *aoidḗ* song + *-ikos* -IC]

**logarithm** /ˈlɒgərɪðəm/, *n.* the exponent of that power to which a fixed number (called the *base*) must be raised in order to produce a given number (called the *antilogarithm*): *3 is the logarithm of 8 to the base 2.* [NL *logarithmus,* from Gk *lógos* proportion + *arithmós* number]

**logarithmic** /lɒgəˈrɪðmɪk/, *adj.* pertaining to a logarithm or logarithms. Also, **logarithmical. – logarithmically,** *adv.*

**logarithmic scale** /– ˈskeɪl/, *n.* a scale of measurement in which an increase of one unit represents a logarithmic increase (usu. tenfold) in the quantity measured.

**logbook** /ˈlɒgbʊk/, *n.* **1.** *Naut.* **a.** a book in which are officially recorded the indications of the log. **b.** the record itself. **2.** any similar book or record pertaining to an aircraft.

**logchip** /ˈlɒgtʃɪp/, *n.* See **log** (def. 3b). Also, **logship.**

**loge** /loʊʒ/, *n.* a box in a theatre or opera house. [F. See LODGE]

**logger** /ˈlɒgə/, *n.* the person who cuts trees into suitable lengths after the trees have been felled.

**loggerhead** /ˈlɒgəhɛd/, *n.* **1.** →**loghead. 2.** Also, **loggerhead turtle.** a large-headed marine turtle, *Caretta caretta,* of all oceans. **3.** Also, **loggerhead shrike,** a common North American butcher-bird, *Lanius ludovicianus,* grey above, white below, with black and white wings and tail and black facial mask. **4.** a ball or bulb of iron with a long handle, used, after being heated, to melt tar, heat liquids, etc. **5.** a rounded post in the stern of a whaleboat, around which the harpoon line is passed. **6. at loggerheads,** engaged in dispute. [backformation from *loggerheaded,* var. of obs. *logheaded* stupid]

**loggia** /ˈloʊdʒiə, ˈlɒdʒiə/, *n.* **1.** a gallery or arcade open to the air on at least one side. **2.** a space within the body of a building but open to the air on one side, serving as an open-air room or as an entrance porch. [It. See LODGE, *n.*]

**logging** /ˈlɒgɪŋ/, *n.* the process, work, or business of cutting down trees and getting out logs from the forest for timber.

**loghead** /ˈlɒghɛd/, *n. Colloq.* a thick-headed or stupid person; a blockhead.

**logia** /ˈlɒgiə/, *n.* plural of **logion.**

**logic** /ˈlɒdʒɪk/, *n.* **1.** the science which investigates the principles governing correct or reliable inference. **2.** reasoning or argumentation, or an instance of it. **3.** the system or principles of reasoning applicable to any branch of knowledge or study. **4.** reasons or sound sense, as in utterances or actions. **5.** convincing force: *the irresistible logic of facts.* [ME *logik,* from ML *logica,* from Gk *logikḗ,* properly fem. of *logikós* pertaining to reason]

**logical** /ˈlɒdʒɪkəl/, *adj.* **1.** according to the principles of logic: *a logical inference.* **2.** reasoning in accordance with the principles of logic, as a person, the mind, etc. **3.** reasonable; reasonably to be expected: *war was the logical consequence of such threats.* **4.** of or pertaining to logic. **– logicality** /lɒdʒəˈkæləti/, **logicalness,** *n.* **– logically,** *adv.*

**logical design** /– dəˈzaɪn/, *n.* the design of a digital computer or other digital equipment out of logical elements. **– logic designer, logical designer,** *n.*

**logical element** /– ˈɛləmənt/, *n.* the basic unit from which computers and other digital equipment are built, which operates on signals represented by ones and zeros and acts as a gate, passing or stopping one signal according to whether other signals have certain required values or not.

**logical positivism** /– 'pɒzətəvɪzəm/, *n.* a philosophy deriving from Auguste Comte and developed by the Vienna Circle in the early twentieth century which stresses linguistic analysis and teaches that, apart from tautology, only that is meaningful that can, in principle, be verified by observation.

**logician** /lə'dʒɪʃən/, *n.* one skilled in logic.

**logion** /'lɒgiɒn/, *n., pl.* **logia** /'lɒgiə/. **1.** a traditional saying or maxim, as of a religious teacher. **2.** (*oft. cap.*) a saying of Jesus (used esp. with reference to sayings of Jesus contained in collections supposed to have been among the sources of the present Gospels, or to sayings ascribed to Jesus but not recorded in the Gospels). [Gk: announcement, oracle]

**logistic** /lə'dʒɪstɪk/, *adj.* **1.** pertaining to military logistics. **2.** of or pertaining to symbolic or mathematical logic. Also, **logistical.** [see LOGISTICS]

**logistics** /lə'dʒɪstɪks/, *n.* the branch of military science concerned with the mathematics of transportation and supply, and the movement of bodies of troops. [F *logistique,* from *loger* lodge, or *logis* lodging. See -ICS]

**logistics branch** /'– bræntʃ/, *n.* that section of a military staff which is concerned with the procurement, maintenance, movement and distribution of material.

**logline** /'lɒglaɪn/, *n.* See **log** (def. 3b).

**logo** /'loʊgoʊ/, *n.* →**logotype.**

**logo-**, a word element denoting speech. [Gk, combining form of *lógos* word, speech]

**logogram** /'lɒgəgræm/, *n.* **1.** Also, **logograph.** a conventional abbreviated symbol for a frequently recurring word or phrase. **2.** →**logogriph.** – **logogrammatic** /lɒgəgrə'mætɪk/, *adj.*

**logographic** /lɒgə'græfɪk/, *adj.* **1.** consisting of logograms: *logographic writing.* **2.** of or pertaining to logography. Also, **logographical.**

**logography** /lɒ'gɒgrəfi/, *n.* **1.** printing with logotypes. **2.** a method of longhand reporting, each of several reporters in succession taking down a few words. [Gk *logographía* a writing of speeches]

**logogriph** /'lɒgəgrɪf/, *n.* **1.** an anagram, or a puzzle involving anagrams. **2.** a puzzle in which a certain word, and other words formed from any or all of its letters, must be guessed from indications given in a set of verses. [F *logogriphe,* from Gk *logo-* LOGO- + *grîphos* fishing basket, riddle] – **logogriphic** /lɒgə'grɪfɪk/ *adj.*

**logomachy** /lə'gɒməki/, *n., pl.* **-chies.** contention about words, or in which words are used as verbiage, regardless of their true meaning. [Gk *logomachía.* See LOGO-, -MACHY] – **logomachist,** *n.*

**logopaedics** /lɒgə'pidɪks/, *n.* scientific study and treatment of speech defects. Also, *U.S.,* **logopedics.** – **logopaedist,** *n.*

**logopedics** /lɒgəpidɪks/, *n. U.S.* →**logopaedics.**

**logorrhea** /lɒgə'riə/, *n.* a mental disorder characterised by excessive, and sometimes incoherent, talking.

**logos** /'lɒgɒs/, *n.* **1.** (*oft. cap.*) *Philos.* the rational principle that governs and develops the universe. **2.** (*cap.*) *Theol.* Jesus Christ, the Divine Word (see John, 1:1, 14), the second person of the Trinity. [Gk: word, speech, reason, account, reckoning, proportion]

**logotype** /'lɒgoʊtaɪp/, *n.* **1.** a single printing type bearing two or more distinct (not combined) letters, or a syllable or word. Cf. **ligature. 2.** Also, **logo.** a trademark or symbol designed to identify a company, organisation, etc. – **logotypy,** *n.*

**logrolling** /'lɒgroʊlɪŋ/, *n.* burling.

**logrunner** /'lɒgrʌnə/, *n.* →**chowcilla.**

**logway** /'lɒgweɪ/, *n.* →**gangway** (def. 7).

**logwood** /'lɒgwʊd/, *n.* **1.** the heavy brownish red heartwood of a West Indian and Central American tree, *Haematoxylon campechianum,* much used in dyeing. **2.** the tree itself.

**-logy,** **1.** a combining form naming sciences or bodies of knowledge, as in *palaeontology, theology.* **2.** a termination of many nouns referring to writing, collections, as in *trilogy, martyrology.* [Gk *-logia,* from *log-* speak, *lógos* discourse; replacing earlier *-logie,* from F. Cf. G *-logie*]

**loin** /lɔɪn/, *n.* **1.** (*usu. pl.*) the part or parts of the body of man or of a quadruped animal on either side of the vertebral column, between the false ribs and hipbone. **2.** a standard cut of lamb, veal, or pork from the upper flank including the lower eight ribs. **3.** *Bible and Poetic.* the part of the body which should be clothed and girded, or which is regarded as the seat of physical strength and generative power. **4. gird up one's loins,** to make ready or prepare oneself for action of some kind. [ME *loyne,* from OF *loigne,* from L *lumbus*]

**loincloth** /'lɔɪnklɒθ/, *n.* a piece of cloth worn about the loins or hips.

**loin-clout** /'lɔɪn-klaʊt/, *n.* a strip of cloth tied round the loins.

**loiter** /'lɔɪtə/, *v.i.* **1.** to linger idly or aimlessly in or about a place. **2.** to move or go in a slow or lagging manner: *to loiter along.* **3.** to waste time or dawdle over work, etc. *–v.t.* **4.** to pass (time, etc.) in an idle or aimless manner (fol. by *away*). [ME *lotere,* apparently frequentative of obs. *lote* lurk, ME *lotie(n), lutie(n), loyt.* Cf. OE *lūtian* lurk] – **loiterer,** *n.* – **loiteringly,** *adv.*

**l.o.l.** /ɛl oʊ 'ɛl/, *n. Colloq.* little old lady.

**loll** /lɒl/, *v.i.* **1.** to recline or lean in a relaxed or indolent manner; lounge: *to loll on a sofa.* **2.** to hang loosely or droopingly. *–v.t.* **3.** to allow to hang or droop. *n.* **4.** *Archaic.* act of lolling. **5.** one who or that which lolls. [ME *lolle, lulle.* Cf. MD *lollen* sleep] – **loller,** *n.*

**lollipop** /'lɒlipɒp/, *n.* **1.** a kind of boiled sweet or toffee, often a piece on the end of a stick. **2.** an item in a series more trivial and more superficially enjoyable than the others (of music, films etc.).

**lollop** /'lɒləp/, *v.i.* to move with bounding, ungainly leaps. [extension of LOLL, in this sense perhaps influenced by GALLOP]

**lolly** /'lɒli/, *n.* **1.** any sweet, esp. a boiled one. **2.** *Brit.* a flavoured frozen confection on a stick. **3.** *Cricket.* an easy catch. **4.** *Colloq.* **a.** the head. **b.** the temper. **5.** *Colloq.* money. **6. do one's lolly,** *Colloq.* to lose one's temper.

**lolly legs** /'– lɛgz/, *n. Colloq.* a tall, ungainly person with skinny legs.

**lolly water** /'– wɔtə/, *n.* a sweet soft drink.

**Lombardy poplar** /lɒmbədi 'pɒplə/, *n.* See **poplar** (def. 1).

**loment** /'loʊmɛnt/, *n.* a legume which is contracted in the spaces between the seeds, and breaks at maturity into one-seeded indehiscent joints. [ME *lomente,* from L *lōmentum* bean meal] – **loment-like,** *adj.*

**lomentaceous** /loʊmɛn'teɪʃəs/, *adj.* of the nature of a loment; loment-like.

**lomentum** /loʊ'mɛntəm/, *n., pl.* **-ta** /-tə/. *n.* a dry fruit derived from one carpel which breaks up transversely into one-seeded segments at maturity. [L]

**lon.,** longitude.

**London pride** /lʌndən 'praɪd/, *n.* a perennial herb, *Saxifraga umbrosa,* with sprays of pale pink flowers, commonly cultivated.

**London rocket** /– 'rɒkət/, *n.* an Old World plant, *Sisymbrium irio,* which has become a widespread weed.

**lone** /loʊn/, *adj.* **1.** being alone; unaccompanied; solitary: *a lone traveller.* **2.** standing apart, or isolated, as a house. **3.** *Poetic.* lonely. **4.** unmarried or widowed. [aphetic var. of ALONE, used attributively]

**lone hand** /– 'hænd/, *n.* **1.** *Cards.* **a.** a hand which is so strong that it is played without the hand of a partner. **b.** one who plays such a hand. **2.** independent action, often unpopular, taken without outside assistance. **3.** one who takes such action.

**lonely** /'loʊnli/, *adj.,* **-lier, -liest. 1.** lone; solitary; without company. **2.** destitute of sympathetic or friendly companionship or relationships: *a lonely exile.* **3.** remote from men or from places of human habitation or resort: *a lonely road.* **4.** standing apart; isolated: *a lonely tower.* **5.** affected with, characterised by, or causing a depressing feeling of being alone; lonesome: *a lonely heart.* – **lonelily,** *adv.* – **loneliness,** *n.*

**lonely heart** /– 'hat/, *n.* a person who is unhappy because he or she lives alone.

**loner** /'loʊnə/, *n.* **1.** one who dislikes company. **2.** →**lone hand** (def. 3).

**lonesome** /'loʊnsəm/, *adj.* **1.** lonely in feeling; depressed by solitude or by a sense of being alone: *to feel lonesome.* **2.**

attended with or causing such a state of feeling: *a lonesome journey.* **3.** depressingly lonely in situation: *a lonesome road.* – **lonesomely,** *adv.* – **lonesomeness,** *n.*

**lone wolf** /loʊn 'wʊlf/, *n.* See **wolf** (def. 11).

**long**[1] /lɒŋ/, *adj.,* **longer** /'lɒŋgə/, **longest** /'lɒŋgəst/, *n., adv.* –*adj.* **1.** having considerable or great extent from end to end; not short: *a long distance.* **2.** having considerable or great extent in duration: *a long visit.* **3.** having many items; of more than average number: *a long list.* **4.** having considerable or great extension from beginning to end, as a series, enumeration, account, book, etc.; not brief. **5.** having a specified extension in space, duration, etc.: *ten metres long.* **6.** continuing too long: *a long speech.* **7.** beyond the normal extension in space, duration, quantity, etc.: *a long match.* **8.** extending to a great distance in space or time: *a long memory.* **9.** broad; taking in all aspects: *a long look at his future.* **10.** having a long time to run, as a promissory note. **11.** not likely: *a long chance.* **12.** the longest of several or the longer of two. **13.** concentrated; intense: *taking a long look at his faults.* **14.** (of drinks) of considerable or great quantity; thirst-quenching rather than intoxicating, as a diluted alcoholic drink. **15.** *Chiefly Law.* distant or remote in time: *a long date.* **16.** relatively much extended: *a long reach.* **17.** tall. **18.** (of the head or skull) of more than ordinary length from front to back. **19.** *Phonet.* **a.** lasting a relatively long time: *'feed' has a longer vowel than 'feet' or 'fit'.* **b.** belonging to a class of sounds considered as usu. longer in duration than another class. **20.** *Comm.* **a.** owning some commodity or stock. **b.** depending for profit on a rise in prices. **21.** (in gambling) **a.** of an exceptionally large difference in proportional amounts on an event: *long odds.* **b.** of or pertaining to the larger number in the odds in betting. **22.** *Cricket.* in the field, near the boundary; deep. **23.** **in the long run,** after a long course of experience; in the final result. **24.** **long in the tooth,** *Colloq.* elderly. –*n.* **25.** something that is long. **26.** **before long,** in the near future; soon. **27.** **the long and the short of,** the kernel; substance of; gist. –*adv.* **28.** for or through a great extent of space or, esp., time: *a reform long advocated.* **29.** for or throughout a specified extent, esp. of time: *how long did he stay?* **30.** (in elliptical expressions) gone, occupying, delaying, etc., a long or a specified time: *don't be long.* **31.** (for emphasis, after nouns denoting a period of time) throughout the whole length: *all summer long.* **32.** at a point of time far distant from the time indicated: *long before.* **33.** **so** (or **as**) **long as,** provided that. **34.** **so long,** *Colloq.* goodbye. [ME *longe,* OE *lang, long,* c. D and G *lang*]

**long**[2] /lɒŋ/, *v.i.* **1.** to have a prolonged or unceasing desire, as for something not immediately (if ever) attainable. **2.** to have an earnest or strong desire. [ME *longen,* OE *langian* lengthen, (impersonal) arouse desire in, from *lang* LONG[1]]

**long.,** longitude.

**longa** /'lɒŋgə/, *n.* a note in medieval music, ꟼ equal to two minims or half the length of a large (def. 7).

**longan** /'lɒŋgən/, *n.* **1.** the small, one-seeded, greenish brown, pleasant-tasting fruit of the large, evergreen, tree, *Euphoria longan,* native to China and allied to the lychee. **2.** the tree. Also, **lungan.** [NL *longanum,* from Chinese *lung-yen* dragon's eye]

**long black** /lɒŋ 'blæk/, *n. Colloq.* a large cup of black coffee.

**long blow** /'– bloʊ/, *n.* a shearing stroke along a sheep's back.

**longboat** /'lɒŋboʊt/, *n.* the largest and strongest boat belonging to a sailing ship.

**longbow** /'lɒŋboʊ/, *n.* **1.** the bow drawn by hand and discharging a long feathered arrow. **2.** **draw** (**pull**) **the longbow,** to tell exaggerated stories.

**longcloth** /'lɒŋklɒθ/, *n.* a fine soft cotton cloth of softly twisted yarns, so named because it was originally wound on long rolls, used mainly for underwear and linings.

**long-distance** /'lɒŋ-dɪstəns/, *adj.* **1.** extending or travelling over an extensive area of time or space. **2.** (of telephone calls) between distant points; trunk.

**long division** /'lɒŋ dəvɪʒən/, *n.* an algorithm for dividing one number by a second, in which the first step consists of obtaining the first digit of the quotient and the partial remainder by repeated trials. At each step the next digit of the quotient and the partial remainder are derived.

**long-drawn** /'lɒŋ-drɔn/, *adj.* **1.** drawn out; prolonged: *a long-drawn narrative.* **2.** *Rare.* long.

**long-eared bandicoot** /lɒŋ-ɪəd 'bændikut/, *n.* a bandicoot of the genera *Macrotis* or *Chaeropus,* having long ears and silky hair, found in arid areas of Australia; rabbit-eared bandicoot; bilby.

**longee** /lɒŋ'gi/, *n.* →**lungi.**

**longeron** /'lɒndʒərən/, *n.* a main longitudinal brace or support on an aeroplane. [F, from *long* LONG[1]]

**longeval** /lɒn'dʒivəl/, *adj.* long-lived; living to a great age. Also, **longaeval.** [L *longaevus* aged + -AL[1]]

**longevity** /lɒn'dʒɛvəti/, *n.* **1.** length or duration of life. **2.** long life; great duration of life.

**longevous** /lɒn'dʒivəs/, *adj.* →**longeval.** [L *longaevus* aged]

**long face** /lɒŋ 'feɪs/, *n.* a dismal or unhappy expression.

**long game** /'– geɪm/, *n.* the part of a game of golf played from the tee up the fairway where shots of maximum distance are desired.

**long-grain** /'lɒŋ-greɪn/, *adj.* **1.** (of rice, etc.) with a long grain. **2.** (of paper) cut so that the grain imparted by the manufacturing process runs parallel to the longer side.

**long-hair** /'lɒŋ-hɛə/, *n. Colloq.* (*usu. derog.*) **1.** a long-haired man. **2.** an intellectual. **3.** a hippie.

**long-haired** /'lɒŋ-hɛəd/, *adj.* **1.** with long hair. **2.** (*sometimes derog.*) highbrow; intellectual.

**longhand** /'lɒŋhænd/, *n.* writing of the ordinary kind, in which the words are written out in full (distinguished from *shorthand*).

**long haul** /lɒŋ 'hɔl/, *n.* **1.** anything which is very long-lasting and arduous: *training to be a doctor is a long haul.* **2.** a long distance: *it's a long haul to Darwin from Alice.*

**longhead** /'lɒŋhɛd/, *n.* a dolichocephalic person.

**longheaded** /'lɒŋhɛdəd/, *adj.* **1.** →**dolichocephalic.** **2.** of great discernment or foresight; far-seeing or shrewd. – **longheadedness,** *n.*

**long hop** /'lɒŋ hɒp/, *n.* (in cricket) a ball pitched so short that it is easy for the batsman to hit.

**longhorn** /'lɒŋhɔn/, *n.* **1.** (*usu. cap.*) one of a kind of cattle predominating on the ranges of northern Mexico and the Great Plains of the U.S. in the early 19th century, developed from Spanish cattle introduced at Vera Cruz about 1521, characterised by long horns and rangy conformation. **2.** (*cap.*) a breed of English cattle characterised by excessive horn growth.

**long house** /'lɒŋ haʊs/, *n.* a house of great length, particularly a communal dwelling as with certain tribes in New Guinea and North America.

**longicorn** /'lɒndʒəkɔn/, *adj.* **1.** having long antennae, as beetles of the group Longicornia (family Cerambycidae). **2.** belonging to this group. –*n.* **3.** a longicorn or longhorned beetle. [NL *longicornis,* from L *longi-* long + *-cornis* horned]

**longing** /'lɒŋɪŋ/, *n.* **1.** prolonged, unceasing, or earnest desire. **2.** an instance of it. –*adj.* **3.** having a prolonged or earnest desire. **4.** characterised or showing such desire: *a longing look.* – **longingly,** *adv.*

**longish** /'lɒŋɪʃ/, *adj.* somewhat long.

**longitude** /'lɒŋgətʃud/, *n.* **1.** *Geog.* angular distance east or west on the earth's surface, measured along the equator by the angle contained between the meridian of a particular place and some prime meridian, as that of Greenwich, or by the corresponding difference in time. **2.** *Astron.* **a.** the arc of the ecliptic measured eastwards from the vernal equinox to the foot of the great circle passing through the poles of the ecliptic and the point on the celestial sphere in question (**celestial longitude**). **b.** the arc on the galactic circle measured from its intersection with the celestial equator (**galactic longitude**). [ME, from L *longitūdo* length]

**longitudinal** /lɒŋgə'tjudənəl/, *adj.* **1.** of or pertaining to longitude or length: *longitudinal distance.* **2.** *Zool.* pertaining to or extending along the long axis of the body, or the direction from front to back, or head to tail. **3.** extending in the direction of the length of a thing; running lengthways. – **longitudinally,** *adv.*

**longitudinal wave** /– 'weɪv/, *n. Physics.* a wave in which the vibration or displacement is in the direction of propagation, as a sound wave.

**long john** /ˈlɒŋ dʒɒn/, *n. N.Z. Colloq.* an oblong loaf of bread.

**long johns** /ˈ– dʒɒns/, *n.pl. Colloq.* a pair of long warm underpants.

**long jump** /ˈ– dʒʌmp/, *n.* **1.** a jump in which athletes aim to cover the greatest distance from a given mark. **2.** the athletic contest for the longest such jump.

**longleaf pine** /lɒŋlif ˈpaɪn/, *n.* **1.** an important American pine, *Pinus palustris,* valued as a source of turpentine and for its timber. **2.** the wood of this tree.

**long leg** /lɒŋ ˈlɛg/, *n. Cricket.* **1.** a leg side fielding position behind the batsman and close to the boundary. **2.** a fielder in this position.

**long-limbed** /ˈlɒŋ-lɪmd/, *adj.* **1.** having long limbs. **2.** agile; athletic.

**long-line** /ˈlɒŋ-laɪn/, *n.* a fishing line with a large number of hooks attached to it.

**long-lived** /ˈlɒŋ-lɪvd/, *adj.* having a long life or existence; functioning for a long time.

**long measure** /ˈlɒŋ mɛʒə/, *n.* linear measure.

**long-necked tortoise** /ˌlɒŋ-nɛkt ˈtɔtəs/, *n.* the common water tortoise, *Chelodina longicollis,* of eastern and southern Australia which, like all Australian tortoises, retracts its head to one side of the body and possesses clawed and webbed feet. Also, **snake-necked tortoise.**

**long-nosed bandicoot** /ˌlɒŋ-noʊzd ˈbændikut/, *n.* **1.** the common bandicoot *Perameles nasuta,* of eastern Australian rainforests. **2.** any bandicoot of the genera *Perameles* and *Echymipera.*

**long-off** /lɒŋ-ˈɒf/, *n.* **1.** (in cricket) an offside fielding position behind the bowler. **2.** a fielder in this position.

**long-on** /lɒŋ-ˈɒn/, *n.* **1.** (in cricket) a legside fielding position behind the bowler; deep mid-on. **2.** a fielder in this position.

**long paddock** /ˈlɒŋ pædək/, *n.* a stock route or open road, esp. regarded as a place where people, too poor to own their own paddocks or pay for agistment, can graze their horses, cattle, etc.

**long pig** /– ˈpɪg/, *n.* human flesh, as eaten by cannibals, esp. in certain Pacific Islands. [translation from native language]

**long-playing** /ˈlɒŋ-pleɪɪŋ/, *adj.* (of a gramophone record) having microgrooves, being made of plastic rather than shellac, and being designed to revolve at $33\frac{1}{3}$ r.p.m. *Abbrev.:* LP

**long-range** /ˈlɒŋ-reɪndʒ/, *adj.* **1.** extending into the future: *long-range weather forecasts.* **2.** designed for great distances: *a long-range gun, bomber, etc.*

**long service leave,** *n.* an extended period of leave from employment, earned through long service.

**longshanks** /ˈlɒŋʃæŋks/, *n. Colloq.* a tall man.

**longship** /ˈlɒŋʃɪp/, *n.* an ancient ship, having a long, narrow, open hull, propelled by a sail and a number of oars, esp. ships of war and other ships, as of the Vikings in northern Europe.

**longshore** /ˈlɒŋʃɔ/, *adj.* existing, found, or employed along the shore: *longshore fisheries.*

**longshoreman** /lɒŋˈʃɔmən/, *n., pl.* **-men.** *U.S.* a wharf labourer; waterside worker. [*longshore,* aphetic var. of *alongshore* + MAN]

**long shot** /ˈlɒŋ ʃɒt/, *n.* **1.** an attempt which has little hope of success, but which if successful may offer great rewards. **2.** a photograph or a film or television shot taken from some distance.

**long-sighted** /ˈlɒŋ-saɪtəd/, *adj.* **1.** far-sighted; hypermetropic. **2.** having great foresight; foreseeing remote results. Cf. **far-sighted.** – **long-sightedness,** *n.*

**long-sleever** /lɒŋ-ˈslivə/, *n. Colloq.* **1.** a tall glass. **2.** a long drink. **3.** a pint glass of beer.

**long soup** /ˈlɒŋ sup/, *n.* a Chinese soup consisting largely of chicken stock and long flat noodles.

**longstanding** /ˈlɒŋstændɪŋ/, *adj.* existing or occurring for a long time: *a longstanding feud.*

**long-stop** /ˈlɒŋ-stɒp/, *n.* **1.** *Cricket.* **a.** a fielding position directly behind the wicket-keeper. **b.** a fielder in this position. **2.** (in similar games) one who stands behind the back-stop.

**long-suffering** /ˈlɒŋ-sʌfərɪŋ/, *adj.* **1.** enduring injury or provocation long and patiently. *–n.* **2.** long and patient endurance of injury or provocation.

**long suit** /ˈlɒŋ sut/, *n.* **1.** *Cards.* the suit in a hand which has the most cards. **2.** one's strongest point; that field in which one most excels.

**long-tail finch** /lɒŋ-teɪl ˈfɪntʃ/, *n.* a handsome multi-hued Australian finch, *Poëphila acuticauda.*

**long-term** /ˈlɒŋ-tɜm/, *adj.* **1.** extending over a period of time of considerable length. **2.** maturing over several years or more.

**long-term bond** /– ˈbɒnd/, *n.* a bond not maturing for many years.

**long-term memory** /– ˈmɛməri/, *n.* the part of the memory which stores experience on a long-term basis. Cf. **short-term memory.**

**long-time** /ˈlɒŋ-taɪm/, *adj.* old: *my long-time friend.*

**long title** /ˈlɒŋ taɪtl/, *n.* the full title of an act of parliament (or bill).

**long tom** /ˈ– tɒm/, *n.* any of various elongate Australian marine and estuarine fishes of the family Belonidae resembling garfish but with both jaws produced as a long pointed snout; needlefish.

**long ton** /ˈlɒŋ tʌn/, *n.* See **ton**[1] (def. 1).

**long'uns** /ˈlɒŋənz/, *n.pl. Colloq.* long trousers.

**long vacation** /lɒŋ vəˈkeɪʃən/, *n.* the long summer holiday at universities, etc. Also, **long vac.**

**long-waisted** /ˈlɒŋ-weɪstəd/, *adj.* of more than average length from the shoulders to the waist.

**longwall mining** /lɒŋwɔl ˈmaɪnɪŋ/, *n.* the system by which coal is extracted from a long continuous face.

**long wave** /ˈlɒŋ weɪv/, *n.* an electromagnetic wave with a wavelength of over 1 kilometre. – **long-wave,** *adj.*

**longways** /ˈlɒŋweɪz/, *adv.* →**lengthways.** Also, **longwise.**

**long weekend** /lɒŋ wikˈɛnd/, *n.* a weekend of three days, the Friday or Monday being either a public or self-awarded holiday.

**longwinded** /ˈlɒŋwɪndəd/, *adj.* **1.** tediously wordy in speech or writing. **2.** writing or talking tediously and continuously. **3.** able to breathe deeply. – **longwindedly,** *adv.* – **longwindedness,** *n.*

**long wool breed,** *n.* one of several British breeds of sheep distinguished by a long and comparatively gaunt frame, which produces a great weight of fleece in proportion to that of body.

**loo**[1] /lu/, *n., pl.* **loos,** *v.,* **looed, looing.** *–n.* **1.** a game of cards in which forfeits are paid into a pool. **2.** the forfeit or sum paid into the pool. **3.** the fact of being looed. *–v.t.* **4.** to subject to a forfeit at loo. [shortened form of *lanterloo,* from F, meaningless refrain of a song]

**loo**[2] /lu/, *n. Colloq.* a toilet. [mincing var. of LAVATORY, but cf. d. *lew,* OE *hlēow* shelter]

**loofah** /ˈlufə/, *n.* **1.** a tropical, annual, climbing herb, *Luffa cylindrica.* **2.** the fibrous network of its fruit, used as a bath sponge. [Ar.]

**look** /lʊk/, *v.i.* **1.** to fix the eyes upon something or in some direction in order to see. **2.** to glance or gaze, in a manner specified: *to look questioningly at a person.* **3.** to use the sight in seeking, searching, examining, watching, etc.: *to look through the papers.* **4.** to tend, as in bearing or significance: *conditions look towards war.* **5.** to appear or seem (as specified) to the eye: *to look pale.* **6.** to seem to the mind: *the case looks promising.* **7.** to direct the mental regard or attention: *to look at the facts.* **8.** to have an outlook or afford a view: *the window looks upon the street.* **9.** to face or front: *the house looks east.* *–v.* **10.** Some special verb phrases are:

**it looks like it,** it seems likely.

**look after, 1.** to follow with the eye, as a person or thing moving away. **2.** to seek, as something desired. **3.** to take care of: *to look after a child.*

**look alive,** (an expression used to urge speed).

**look down on,** to have contempt for; regard with disdain.

**look down one's nose,** to regard with barely concealed contempt.

**look for, 1.** to seek, as a person or thing. **2.** to anticipate; expect.

**look forward to,** to anticipate with pleasure.

**look here,** (an expression used to attract attention, for emphasis, or the like).

**look in,** **1.** to take a look into a place. **2.** to come in for a brief visit.
**look into,** to investigate; examine.
**look like,** to seem likely to; appear probable: *the horse looks like falling down.*
**look lively** or **sharp,** to make haste; be alert.
**look on,** to be a mere spectator.
**look on the bright (the worst) side,** to consider something with optimism (with pessimism).
**look out,** **1.** to look forth, as from a window or a place of observation. **2.** to be on guard. **3.** to take watchful care (fol. by *for*): *to look out for oneself.*
**look to,** **1.** to direct the glance or gaze to. **2.** to give attention to. **3.** to direct the expectations or hopes to, as for something desired. **4.** to look forward expectantly to.
**look up,** **1.** to direct the eyes upwards. **2.** *Colloq.* to rise in amount or value; improve: *things are looking up.*
**look up to,** to regard with admiration, or esteem.
**not to know which way to look,** to feel embarrassed.
*–v.t.* **11.** to try to find; seek (fol. by *up, out,* etc.): *to look a name up in a directory.* **12.** to express or suggest by looks: *she looked compassion.* **13.** to view, inspect or examine (fol. by *over*). **14.** to direct a look towards: *she looked him full in the face.* **15.** to have the aspect or appearance appropriate to: *look one's age, look an idiot.* **16.** to visit or make contact with (fol. by *up*). **17. look daggers at,** to scowl at; to express anger with a look. *–n.* **18.** the act of looking: *a look of enquiry.* **19.** a visual search or examination. **20.** way of looking or appearing to the eye or mind; aspect: *the look of an honest man.* **21.** (*pl.*) general aspect; appearance: *to like the looks of a place, good looks.* **22. for the look of the thing,** for the sake of appearances. **23. have a good look (around),** *Colloq.* to inspect inquisitively. [ME *lōke(n)*, OE *lōcian.* Cf. d. G *lugen* look out, spy]

**look-a-like** /ˈlʊk-ə-laɪk/, *n.* **1.** something or someone that bears a striking similarity to another in appearance. *–adj.* **2.** bearing a striking similarity to another.

**looker** /ˈlʊkə/, *n.* **1.** one who looks. **2.** Also, **good looker.** *Colloq.* an unusually good-looking person.

**looker-on** /lʊkər-ˈɒn/, *n., pl.* **lookers-on.** one who looks on; a spectator.

**look-in** /ˈlʊk-ɪn/, *n. Colloq.* a chance of participating: *she was such a good player that he didn't get a look-in.*

**looking glass** /ˈlʊkɪŋ glas/, *n.* **1.** a mirror made of glass with a metallic or amalgam backing. **2.** such glass as a material.

**lookout** /ˈlʊkaʊt/, *n.* **1.** the act of looking out. **2.** a watch kept, as for something that may come or happen. **3.** a person or group stationed or employed to keep such a watch. **4.** a station or place from which a watch is kept. **5.** view; prospect; outlook. **6.** a place on a high vantage point, esp. a mountain, from which one can admire the view. **7.** *Colloq.* the proper object of one's watchful care or concern: *that's his lookout.*

**look-over** /ˈlʊk-oʊvə/, *n.* a survey; inspection.

**looksee** /ˈlʊksi/, *n.* →**look** (def. 19).

**loom**[1] /lum/, *n.* **1.** a machine or apparatus for weaving yarn or thread into a fabric. **2.** the art or the process of weaving. **3.** the part of an oar between the blade and the handle. *–v.t.* **4.** *Rare.* to weave on a loom. [ME *lome*, OE *gelōma* tool, implement. Cf. HEIRLOOM]

**loom**[2] /lum/, *v.i.* **1.** to appear indistinctly, or come into view in indistinct and enlarged form. **2.** to rise before the vision with an appearance of great or portentous size. *–n.* **3.** a looming appearance, as of something seen indistinctly at a distance or through a fog. [cf. d. Swed. *loma* move slowly]

**loom**[3] /lum/, *n.* **1.** →**loon**[1]. **2.** a guillemot or murre. [Scand; cf. Icel. *lōmr*, Swed. *lom.* See LOON[1]]

**loon**[1] /lun/, *n.* **1.** →**great crested grebe.** **2.** any of several large, short-tailed web-footed, fish-eating diving birds of the Northern Hemisphere, constituting the genus *Gavia,* as the common loon or great northern diver, *Gavia immer,* of the Old and New Worlds. [var. of LOOM[3]]

**loon**[2] /lun/, *n.* a simple-minded or stupid person. [ME *lowen, loun.* Cf. Icel. *lūinn* exhausted]

**loony** /ˈluni/, *adj.,* **loonier, looniest,** *n., pl.* **loonies.** *Colloq.* *–adj.* **1.** lunatic; crazy. **2.** extremely or senselessly foolish. *–n.* **3.** →**lunatic.** Also, **looney, luny.** [var. of *luny,* familiar shortening of LUNATIC] – **looniness,** *n.*

**loony bin** /ˈ– bɪn/, *n. Colloq.* →**lunatic asylum.**

**loop**[1] /lup/, *n.* **1.** a folding or doubling of a portion of a cord, lace, ribbon, etc., upon itself, so as to leave an opening between the parts. **2.** anything shaped more or less like a loop, as a line drawn on paper, a part of a letter, a part of a path, a line of motion, etc. **3.** a curved piece or a ring of metal, wood, etc., used for the insertion of something, or as a handle, or otherwise. **4.** one of the principal ridge-shapes of a fingerprint, consisting of at least one set of ridges crossing themselves at the base of a curve (distinguished from *arch* and *whorl*). **5.** *Railways, etc.* a branch or line that returns to the main line. **6.** *Aeron.* a manoeuvre executed in such a manner that the aeroplane performs a closed curve in a vertical plane. **7.** *Physics.* the part of a vibrating string, column of air, or the like, between two adjacent nodes; antinode. **8.** *Elect.* **a.** a closed electric or magnetic circuit. **9.** *Med.* an intra-uterine contraceptive device, formerly made in metal, now in plastic. *–v.t.* **10.** to form into a loop or loops. **11.** to make a loop or loops in. **12.** to enfold or encircle in or with something arranged in a loop. **13.** to fasten by forming into a loop, or by means of something formed into a loop. **14.** to fly (an aeroplane) in a loop or series of loops. **15.** to construct a closed electric or magnetic circuit. *–v.i.* **16.** to make or form a loop or loops. **17.** to move by forming loops, as a measuring worm. **18.** (of a canoe) to turn end over end in rough water. **19. loop the loop,** *Aeron.* to perform a loop (def. 6). [ME *loupe.* Cf. Gaelic and Irish *lub* loop, bend]

**loop**[2] /lup/, *n. Archaic.* a small or narrow opening, as in a wall; a loophole. [ME *loupe.* Cf. MD *lūpen* peer]

**looper** /ˈlupə/, *n.* **1.** one who or that which loops something or forms loops. **2.** Also, **looper caterpillar, inch worm.** a measuring worm. **3.** the thread-holder in a sewing machine using two threads.

**loophole** /ˈluphoʊl/, *n., v.,* **-holed, -holing.** *–n.* **1.** a small or narrow opening, as in a wall, for looking through, or for admitting light and air, or particularly, in a fortification, for the discharge of missiles against an enemy outside. **2.** an opening or aperture. **3.** an outlet, or means of escape or evasion. *–v.t.* **4.** to furnish with loopholes. [LOOP[2] + HOLE, *n.*]

**loop-the-loop** /lup-ðə-ˈlup/, *n. Colloq.* soup. [rhyming slang]

**loopy** /ˈlupi/, *adj.* **1.** full of loops. **2.** *Colloq.* slightly mad or eccentric.

**loose** /lus/, *adj.,* **looser, loosest,** *adv., v.,* **loosed, loosing.** *–adj.* **1.** free from bonds, fetters, or restraint: *to get one's hand loose.* **2.** free or released from fastening or attachment: *a loose end.* **3.** uncombined, as a chemical element. **4.** not bound together, as papers or flowers. **5.** not put in a package or other container: *loose mushrooms.* **6.** unemployed or unappropriated: *loose funds.* **7.** wanting in retentiveness or power of restraint: *a loose tongue.* **8.** lax, as the bowels. **9.** free from moral restraint, or lax in principle or conduct. **10.** wanton or unchaste: *a loose woman.* **11.** not firm or rigid: *a loose tooth, a loose rein.* **12.** not fitting closely, as garments. **13.** not close or compact in structure or arrangement; having spaces between the parts, or open: *a loose weave.* **14.** (of earth, soil, etc.) not cohering: *loose sand.* **15.** not strict, exact, or precise: *loose thinking.* **16.** free from restraining conditions or factors: *the Commonwealth of Nations is a loose association of sovereign states.* **17.** *Cricket.* (of a ball) inaccurate and easily hit by the batsman. **18. the loose head,** *Rugby Football.* →**loosehead.** **19. at a loose end, a.** in an unsettled or disorderly condition. **b.** unoccupied; having nothing to do. *–n.* **20.** *Rugby Football.* a loose scrummage: *pick the ball up in the loose.* **21. on the loose, a.** free from restraint. **b.** on a spree. **c.** (of women) living by prostitution. *–adv.* **22.** in a loose manner; loosely. **23.** so as to become free from restraint, independent, etc.: *he cut loose from his family.* *–v.t.* **24.** to let loose, or free from bonds or restraint. **25.** to release, as from constraint, obligation, penalty, etc. **26.** *Chiefly Naut.* to set free from fastening or attachment: *loose a boat from its moorings.* **27.** to unfasten, undo, or untie, as a bond, fetter, or knot. **28.** to shoot, or let fly. **29.** to make less tight; slacken or relax. **30.** to render less firmly fixed, or loosen. *–v.i.* **31.** to let go a hold. **32.** to weigh anchor. **33.** to shoot or let fly an arrow, etc. [ME *los, loos,* from Scand.; cf. Icel. *lauss* loose, free, empty, c. D and G *los* loose, free] – **loosely,** *adv.* – **looseness,** *n.*

**loosebox** /ˈlusbɒks/, *n.* a stall for a horse or other large animal, usu. in a stable.

**loose change** /lus ˈtʃeɪndʒ/, *n.* a small amount of money in coins, usu. the change from a note.

**loose container load,** *n.* a shipping container full of miscellaneous consignments. Cf. **full container load.**

**loose cover** /lus ˈkʌvə/, *n.* a cloth cover for a piece of furniture, made so as to be easily removable. Also, *U.S.,* **slip cover.**

**loose end** /– ˈɛnd/, *n.* **1.** something left unsettled or incomplete. **2. at a loose end,** without a specific task to do or pastime to follow.

**loose forward** /– ˈfɔwəd/, *n.* (in rugby union) a breakaway or lock.

**loosehead** /lusˈhɛd/, *n. Rugby Union.* **1.** that side of the scrum on which a team's prop forward has his head outside or loose (by convention the left-hand side, from which the ball is served into the scrum). **2.** Also, **loosehead prop.** the prop-forward who plays on the loosehead. **3. have the loosehead,** to have the advantage of serving the scrum (usu. done on the loosehead). Cf. **tighthead.**

**loose-jointed** /ˈlus-dʒɔɪntəd/, *adj.* **1.** having loose joints. **2.** loosely built or framed.

**loose-knit** /ˈlus-nɪt/, *adj.* **1.** loosely-interwoven. **2.** linked in a tenuous way.

**loose-leaf** /ˈlus-lif/, *adj.* (of a book, etc.) having individual leaves that may be inserted or removed without tearing.

**loose-leaf folder** /– ˈfoʊldə/, *n.* a folder designed to take a loose-leaf book, etc.

**loose man** /lus ˈmæn/, *n.* (in Australian Rules) a player who remains unmarked by an opponent.

**loosen** /ˈlusən/, *v.t.* **1.** to unfasten or undo, as a bond or fetter. **2.** to make less tight; slacken or relax: *to loosen one's grasp.* **3.** to make less firmly fixed in place: *to loosen a clamp.* **4.** to let loose or set free from bonds, restraint, or constraint. **5.** to make less close or compact in structure or arrangement. **6.** to make less dense or coherent: *to loosen the soil.* **7.** to open, or relieve the costiveness of, (the bowels). **8.** to relax in strictness or severity, as restraint or discipline. *–v.i.* **9.** to become loose or looser. – **loosener,** *n.*

**loosestrife** /ˈlusstraɪf/, *n.* **1.** any of various leafy-stemmed herbs of the genus *Lysimachia,* as yellow loosestrife *L. vulgaris,* a common yellow-flowered species. **2.** any of various herbaceous plants of the genus *Lythrum,* as purple loosestrife *L. salicaria,* a purple-flowered species. [LOOSE, *v.,* + STRIFE, erroneous translation of L *lysimachia* (actually from Gk proper name *Lysímachos,* lit., the one loosing (i.e. ending) strife)]

**loot** /lut/, *n.* **1.** spoils or plunder taken by pillaging, as in war. **2.** anything dishonestly and ruthlessly appropriated: *a burglar's loot.* **3.** the act of looting or plundering: *the loot of a conquered city.* **4.** *Colloq.* money. *–v.t.* **5.** to take or carry off, as loot. **6.** to despoil by taking loot; plunder or pillage (a city, house, etc.), as in war. **7.** to rob, as by burglary, corrupt practice in public office, etc. *–v.i.* **8.** to take loot; plunder. [Hind. *lūt*] – **looter,** *n.*

**lop**[1] /lɒp/, *v.,* **lopped, lopping,** *n.* *–v.t.* **1.** to cut off the branches, twigs, etc., of (a tree or other plant). **2.** to cut off the head, limbs, etc., of (a person) or parts of (a thing). **3.** to cut off (branches, twigs, etc.) from a tree or other plant. **4.** to cut off (the head, limbs, etc.) from a person. *–v.i.* **5.** to cut off branches, twigs, etc., as of a tree. **6.** to remove parts by or as by cutting. *–n.* **7.** parts or a part lopped off. **8.** the smaller branches and twigs of trees. [ME (def. 8), etymologically identical with obs. *lop* spider, both objects being marked by many projecting parts] – **lopper,** *n.*

**lop**[2] /lɒp/, *v.,* **lopped, lopping.** *–v.i.* **1.** to hang loosely or limply; droop. **2.** to sway, move, or go in a drooping or heavy, awkward way. *–v.t.* **3.** to let hang or droop. [from obs. *lop,* n., lobe (var. of LAP[1] lobe); lit., to behave like a *lop,* i.e., to dangle, hang loosely]

**lope** /loʊp/, *v.,* **loped, loping,** *n.* *–v.i.* **1.** to move or run with bounding steps, as a quadruped, or with a long, easy stride, as a person. **2.** to canter leisurely with a rather long, easy stride, as a horse. *–v.t.* **3.** to cause to lope, as a horse. *–n.* **4.** the act or the gait of loping. **5.** a long, easy stride. [late ME, var. of obs. *loup* leap, from Scand.; cf. Icel. *hlaupa*] – **loper,** *n.*

**lop-eared** /ˈlɒp-ɪəd/, *adj.* having ears that lop or hang down.

**lophobranch** /ˈloʊfəbræŋk/, *n.* **1.** any of the Lophobranchii, an order or group of teleostean fishes having gills in tufts, as the seahorses, pipefishes, etc. *–adj.* **2.** belonging or pertaining to the Lophobranchii. [Gk *lópho(s)* crest + *bránchia* gills] – **lophobranchiate** /loʊfəˈbræŋkiət, -eɪt/, *adj., n.*

**lophophore** /ˈloʊfəfɔ/, *n.* a ridged or elongated structure bearing ciliate tentacles, in the invertebrate phyla Bryozoa, Brachiopoda, and Phoronidea, which aids in feeding.

**loppy** /ˈlɒpi/, *adj.* **1.** lopping; limp. *–n.* **2.** a handyman on a station; rouseabout; leatherneck. [LOP[2] + -Y[1]]

**lopsided** /ˈlɒpsaɪdəd/, *adj.* **1.** lopping or inclining to one side. **2.** heavier, larger, or more developed on one side than on the other; asymmetrical. – **lopsidedly,** *adv.* – **lopsidedness,** *n.*

**loq.,** (formerly, a stage direction) he (she) speaks. [L *loquitur*]

**loquacious** /ləˈkweɪʃəs/, *adj.* **1.** talking or disposed to talk much or freely; talkative. **2.** characterised by or showing a disposition to talk much: *a loquacious mood.* [LOQUACI(TY) + -OUS] – **loquaciously,** *adv.*

**loquacity** /ləˈkwæsəti/, *n.* **1.** the state of being loquacious. **2.** loquacious flow of talk. Also, **loquaciousness.** [L *loquācitas*]

**loquat** /ˈloʊkwɒt, -kwət/, *n.* **1.** a small, evergreen tree, *Eriobotrya japonica,* native to China and Japan, but cultivated elsewhere for ornament and for its yellow plumlike fruit. **2.** the fruit. [Chinese (Cantonese) *luh kwat* rush orange]

**loran** /ˈlɔrən, ˈlɒ-/, *n.* a long-range radionavigation position fixing system using the time difference of reception of pulse type transmissions from two or more fixed stations. [*lo(ng) ra(nge) (electronic) n(avigation)*]

**lord** /lɔd/, *n.* **1.** one who has dominion over others; a master, chief, or ruler. **2.** one who exercises authority from property rights; an owner or possessor of land, houses, etc. **3.** a feudal superior; the proprietor of a manor. **4.** *Mining.* the owner of land on which a mine is situated to whom rent or royalty is paid. **5.** *Archaic.* a husband. **6.** a dominant person; one who is a leader in his own sphere. **7.** a titled nobleman, or peer. **8.** (*cap.*) the title (in collocation with some other word or words) of certain high officials: *Lord Mayor of Sydney.* **9.** (*cap.*) (in ceremonial use) the title of a bishop or archbishop. **10.** (*cap.*) the title substituted in less formal use for marquess, earl, viscount, or baron: *Lord Kitchener* for *Earl Kitchener.* **11.** (*cap.*) the courtesy title of younger sons of a duke or marquess (used as a prefix before the Christian name): *Lord John Russell.* **12.** (*cap.*) an honorary title of a judge of the Supreme Court. **13. Lords,** the temporal and spiritual members of the British House of Lords. **14.** (*cap.*) the Supreme Being, Jehovah, or God. **15.** (*cap.*) the Saviour, Jesus Christ. **16.** *Astrol.* a planet having dominating influence. *–interj.* **17.** (*oft. cap.*) (the noun Lord (God) used as an exclamation of surprise, etc.). *–v.i.* **18.** to play the lord; behave in a lordly manner; domineer (oft. with indefinite *it*): *to lord it over someone.* [ME *lord, loverd,* OE *hlāford,* from *hlāf* LOAF[1] + *weard* keeper. Cf. LADY, WARD]

**Lord Chamberlain** /lɔd ˈtʃeɪmbələn/, *n.* the chief officer in the British royal household, responsible for arrangements at state occasions, in charge of many royal staff and formerly licenser of plays and public theatres.

**Lord High Chancellor,** *n.* (in Britain) the head of the judiciary who is also usu. a cabinet minister, Speaker of the House of Lords, keeper of the great seal, etc. Also, **Lord Chancellor.**

**Lord Howe Island,** *n.* an island in the south Pacific Ocean, east of Australia, a dependency of New South Wales.

**Lord Lieutenant** /lɔd lɛfˈtɛnənt/, *n.* **1.** *Brit.* the title of various high officials holding authority deputed from a sovereign. **2.** (formerly) the viceroy in Ireland.

**lordling** /ˈlɔdlɪŋ/, *n.* a little or petty lord.

**lordly** /ˈlɔdli/, *adj.,* **-lier, -liest,** *adv.* *–adj.* **1.** suitable for a lord, as things; grand or magnificent. **2.** insolently imperious: *lordly contempt.* **3.** of or pertaining to a lord or lords. **4.** having the character or attributes of a lord, as a person. **5.** befitting a lord, as actions. *–adv.* **6.** in the manner of a lord. – **lordliness,** *n.*

**lord mayor** /lɔd 'mɛə/, *n.* (in some cities as Sydney, Melbourne, etc.) →**mayor.**

**Lord Muck** /lɔd 'mʌk/, *n.* a man who affects the manner of a grand gentleman, usu. in an overbearing and unconvincing manner.

**Lord of Hosts,** *n.* Jehovah, the Supreme Ruler.

**lordosis** /lɔ'dousəs/, *n.* forward curvature of the spine. [NL, from Gk: a bending back] – **lordotic** /lɔ'dɒtɪk/, *adj.*

**Lord Privy Seal,** *n.* (in Britain) the officer who formerly affixed the privy seal to charters, etc. He is now usu. a member of the cabinet but has no official duties.

**lordship** /'lɔdʃɪp/, *n.* **1.** (*oft. cap.*) the form used in speaking of or to a judge or certain nobleman (usu. prec. by *his, your,* etc.). **2.** the state or dignity of a lord. **3.** *Hist.* **a.** the authority or power of a lord. **b.** the domain of a lord. **4. his lordship, a.** an arrogant, overbearing man. **b.** (*joc.*) one's husband.

**lord spiritual** /lɔd 'spɪrətʃəl/, *n., pl.* **lords spiritual.** *Brit.* a bishop or archbishop, considered in his capacity of a member of the House of Lords.

**Lord's Prayer, the,** *n.* the prayer given by Jesus to His disciples.

**Lord's Supper, the,** *n.* **1.** the Last Supper of Jesus and His disciples. **2.** the sacrament in commemoration of this; the Eucharist; the communion; the mass.

**Lord's table, the,** *n.* the communion table or the altar.

**lord temporal** /lɔd 'tɛmpərəl/, *n., pl.* **lords temporal.** (in Britain) one who, by right of birth or elevation is entitled to sit in the House of Lords.

**lore**[1] /lɔ/, *n.* **1.** the body of knowledge, esp. of a traditional, anecdotal, or popular nature, on a particular subject: *the lore of herbs.* **2.** learning, knowledge, or erudition. **3.** *Archaic.* **a.** teaching or instruction. **b.** that which is taught. [ME; OE *lār,* c. D *leer,* G *Lehre* teaching. Cf. LEARN]

**lore**[2] /lɔ/, *n.* the space between the eye and the bill of a bird, or a corresponding space in other animals, as snakes. [L *lōrum* thong]

**Lorentz force** /'lɒrənts fɔs/, *n.* the sum of the electric and magnetic forces on a moving electric charge.

**Lorentz transformation** /– trænsfə'meɪʃən/, *n.* the mathematical relationship between space and time coordinates in two frames of reference, esp. at relativistic velocities. [named after H. *Lorentz,* 1853-1928, Dutch physicist]

**lorgnette** /lɔ'njɛt/, *n.* **1.** a pair of eyeglasses mounted on a long handle. **2.** →**opera glasses.** [F, from *lorgner* look sidelong at, eye, from OF *lorgne* squinting]

**lorgnon** /lɔ'njɒn/, *n.* **1.** an eyeglass, or a pair of eyeglasses. **2.** →**opera glasses.** [F, from *lorgner.* See LORGNETTE]

**lorica** /lɒ'raɪkə/, *n., pl.* **-cae** /-si/. **1.** a hard protective case or sheath, as the protective coverings secreted by certain infusorians. **2.** a cuirass or corselet, originally of leather. [L: a corselet, a defence]

**loricate** /'lɒrəkeɪt/, *adj.* covered with a lorica. Also, **loricated.**

**lorikeet** /'lɒrəkit, lɒrə'kit/, *n.* any of various small, brightly-coloured, arboreal parrots found mainly in Australasia, esp. of the genera *Trichoglossus* and *Glossopsitta,* having brush-like tongues specialised for feeding on nectar. [LORY + (PARA)KEET]

rainbow lorikeet

**lorilet** /lɒrə'lɛt/, *n.* →**Marshall's fig-parrot.**

**loris** /'lɔrəs/, *n.* any of several slow-moving, nocturnal, arboreal primates of the genera *Loris* and *Nycticebus* of tropical Asia, having large eyes, woolly fur and no tail. [NL, from D *loeris* booby]

**lorn** /lɔn/, *adj. Archaic.* forsaken, desolate, wretched, or forlorn. [ME *lorn,* OE *loren,* pp. of *-lēosan* LOSE (recorded in compounds)]

**lorry** /'lɒri/, *n.* →**truck**[1] (def. 3). [cf. Brit. d. *lurry* pull, drag, lug]

**lory** /'lɔri/, *n., pl.* **-ries.** any of various lorikeets and parrots of the Malay Archipelago, Australasia, etc. [Malay *lūrī*]

**losable** /'luzəbəl/, *adj.* that may be lost.

**Loschmidt's number** /'lɒʃmɪts nʌmbə/, *n.* the number of molecules in a cubic metre of a perfect gas at normal temperature and pressure; approximately equal to $2.7 \times 10^{25}$. [named after Joseph *Loschmidt,* 1821-95, German physicist]

**lose** /luz/, *v.,* **lost, losing.** *–v.t.* **1.** to come to be without, by some chance, and not know the whereabouts of: *to lose a ring.* **2.** to suffer the loss or deprivation of: *to lose one's life.* **3.** to be bereaved of by death: *to lose a child.* **4.** to fail to keep, preserve, or maintain control of: *to lose one's balance.* **5.** to cease to have: *to lose all fear.* **6.** to bring to destruction or ruin (now chiefly in the passive): *ship and crew were lost.* **7.** to have slip from sight, hearing, attention, etc.: *to lose a face in a crowd.* **8.** to become separated from and ignorant of (the way, etc.). **9.** to leave far behind in a pursuit, race, etc. **10.** to use to no purpose, or waste: *to lose time in waiting.* **11.** to fail to have, get, catch, etc.; miss: *to lose an opportunity.* **12.** to fail to win (a prize, stake, etc.). **13.** to be defeated in (a game, lawsuit, battle, etc.). **14.** to cause the loss of: *the delay lost the battle for them.* **15.** to let (oneself) go astray; become bewildered: *to be lost in a wood.* **16.** to absorb or engross in something to the exclusion of knowledge or consciousness of all else (usu. used reflexively or in the passive): *to be lost in thought.* **17. lose face,** to lose prestige or dignity by having an error or foolish action made public. **18. lose one's head,** to behave irrationally or out of character. **19. lose one's heart,** to form a deep emotional attachment (fol. by *to*). **20. lose one's nerve,** to become afraid to do something. **21. lose sleep over,** to worry about excessively. **22.** to suffer loss: *to lose on a contract.* **23.** to lose ground, fall behind, or fail to hold one's own, as in a race or other contest. **24.** to fail to win, as in a contest; be defeated. **25. lose out,** *Colloq.* to be defeated or bettered (fol. by *to*): *I lost out to my rival.* **26. lose out on,** *Colloq.* to fail to achieve (a goal, etc.): *I lost out on that deal.* [ME *lose(n),* OE *-leōsan;* replacing ME *lese(n),* OE *-lēosan* (cf. *choose,* replacing *chese*), c. G (*ver*)*lieren.* See LOSS] – **loser,** *n.*

**losel** /'louzəl/, *Archaic.* *–n.* **1.** a worthless person. *–adj.* **2.** worthless; good-for-nothing. [akin to LOSE]

**loser** /'luzə/, *n.* **1.** an unsuccessful person; someone who is a failure: *a born loser.* **2. a good (bad) loser,** someone who loses with good (bad) grace.

**losing** /'luzɪŋ/, *adj.* **1.** that loses. *–n.* **2.** (*pl.*) losses. – **losingly,** *adv.*

**loss** /lɒs/, *n.* **1.** detriment or disadvantage from failure to keep, have, or get: *to bear the loss of a robbery.* **2.** that which is lost. **3.** amount or number lost. **4.** a being deprived of or coming to be without something that one has had: *loss of friends.* **5.** a bereavement. **6.** the accidental or inadvertent losing of something dropped, misplaced, or of unknown whereabouts: *to discover the loss of a document.* **7.** a losing by defeat, or failure to win: *the loss of a bet.* **8.** failure to make good use of something, as time; waste. **9.** failure to preserve or maintain: *loss of speed.* **10.** destruction or ruin. **11.** *Comm.* failure to recover the costs of a transaction or the like, in the form of benefits derived. **12.** *Mil.* **a.** the losing of soldiers by death, capture, etc. **b.** (*oft. pl.*) the number of soldiers so lost. **13.** *Insurance.* **a.** occurrence of a risk covered by a contract of insurance so as to result in insurer liability. **b.** that which causes such a loss. **c.** an example of such a loss. **14. at a loss, a.** in a state of bewilderment or uncertainty. **b.** in a state of embarrassment for lack of something: *to be at a loss for words.* **15. a dead loss, a.** a complete failure. **b.** an utterly useless person or thing. [ME; OE *los* destruction, c. Icel. *los* breaking up; akin to LOSE]

**loss leader** /'– lidə/, *n.* a popular article which is sold at a loss for the purpose of attracting trade to a shop or store.

**loss ratio** /'– reɪʃiou/, *n.* the ratio of paid-in premiums to losses sustained during a certain period.

**lossy** /'lɒsi/, *adj.* of or pertaining to that which induces energy losses in associated oscillations: *the vocal tract is lossy because speech sound energy is dissipated by its absorption in the tissues lining the tract.*

**lost** /lɒst/, *adj.* **1.** no longer possessed or retained: *lost friends.* **2.** no longer to be found: *lost articles.* **3.** having gone astray or lost the way; bewildered as to place, direction, etc. **4.** not used to good purpose, as opportunities, time, labour, etc.; wasted. **5.** that one has failed to win: *a lost prize.* **6.** attended with defeat: *a lost battle.* **7.** destroyed or ruined: *lost ships.* **8. lost to, a.** no longer belonging to. **b.** no longer possible or open to: *the opportunity was lost to him.* **c.** insensible to: *to be lost to all sense of duty.* *–v.* **9.** past tense of **lose.**

**lost cause** /– 'kɔs/, *n.* a cause for which defeat has occurred or is inevitable.

**lost generation** /– dʒɛnə'reɪʃən/, *n.* any generation considered to have lost its values or spiritual direction because of some cataclysmic event as a war.

**lost soul** /– 'soʊl/, *n.* **1.** a person who persists in his wickedness and whose soul is therefore damned. **2.** a person who has set himself outside his social peer group through his attitudes or behaviour; an outsider.

**lost time allowance,** *n.* an allowance paid to casual employees to compensate them for time lost in finding new employment.

**lost wax process,** *n.* a process of casting used esp. for statuary in which the figure is modelled in wax and then covered in plaster; when the plaster has set the wax is melted out and replaced by metal.

**lost weekend** /– wik'ɛnd/, *n. Colloq.* **1.** a weekend spent secretly with one's lover. **2.** a weekend spent in drunken oblivion. **3.** a weekend spent in prison as part of a sentence.

**lost woman** /– 'wʊmən/, *n.* a woman who has lost her status in society, usu. as the result of a sexual episode.

**lot** /lɒt/, *n., v.,* **lotted, lotting,** *adv.* *–n.* **1.** one of a set of objects drawn from a receptacle, etc., to decide a question or choice by chance. **2.** the casting or drawing of such objects as a method of deciding something: *to choose a person by lot.* **3.** the decision or choice so made. **4.** allotted share or portion. **5.** the portion in life assigned by fate or providence, or one's fate, fortune, or destiny. **6.** a distinct portion or piece of land; plot: *a parking lot.* **7.** *Chiefly U.S.* a piece of land forming a part of a district, city, or other community. **8.** *Films.* the site used for film-making, as the studios, locations, etc. **9.** a distinct portion or parcel of anything, as of merchandise. **10.** a number of things or persons collectively. **11.** *Colloq.* a person of a specified sort: *a bad lot.* **12.** *Colloq.* a great many or a great deal: *a lot of books.* **13. the lot, a.** the entire amount or quantity. **b.** *Prison Colloq.* a life sentence. **14. throw in one's lot with,** to give one's entire support to. *–v.t.* **15.** to divide or distribute by lot. **16.** to assign to one as his lot; allot. **17.** to divide into lots, as land. *–adv.* **18. a lot,** to a considerable degree; much: *that is a lot better.* [ME; OE *hlot,* akin to G *Los,* Icel. *hlutr,* Goth. *hlauts*]

**loth** /loʊθ/, *adj.* →**loath.**

**Lothario** /lə'θarioʊ, -'θɛə-/, *n., pl.* **-tharios.** a jaunty libertine; a rake. [named after a character in *The Fair Penitent* (1703) by Nicholas Rowe]

**lotion** /'loʊʃən/, *n.* a watery liquid containing insoluble medicinal matter applied externally to the skin. [ME, from L *lōtio* a washing]

**lots** /lɒts/, *n. pl. Colloq.* **1.** a large quantity or number: *lots of money, lots of dollars.* *–adv.* **2.** (an intensifier): *it's lots faster to travel by plane. See* **lot** (defs 12, 18).

**lottery** /'lɒtəri, 'lɒtri/, *n., pl.* **-teries.** **1.** a scheme or arrangement for raising money, as for some public, charitable, or private purpose, by the sale of a large number of tickets, certain among which, as determined by chance after the sale, entitle the holders to prizes. **2.** any scheme for the distribution of prizes by chance. **3.** any affair of chance. [It. *lotteria,* from *lotto* lot, from F *lot,* from Gmc; cf. LOT]

**lotto** /'lɒtoʊ/, *n.* **1.** →**housie-housie.** **2.** any of various similar games in which items have to be matched. [It. See LOTTERY]

**lotus** /'loʊtəs/, *n.* **1.** a plant, commonly identified with a species of jujube or of elm tree, referred to in Greek legend as yielding a fruit which induced a state of dreamy and contented forgetfulness in those who ate it. **2.** the fruit itself. **3.** any species of *Nelumbium,* including the sacred lotus of India which is similar to the water-lily. **4.** any of various water-lilies of the genus *Nymphaea* including *N. lotus* of Egypt. **5.** a representation of such a plant, common in Egyptian and Hindu decorative art. **6.** any of the papilionaceous herbs of the genus *Lotus,* certain of which are valued as pasture plants. Also, **lotos.** [L, from Gk *lōtós*]

**lotus bird** /'– bɜd/, *n.* the Australian jacana, *Jacana gallinacea.*

**lotus-eater** /'loʊtəs-itə/, *n.* **1.** an eater of the fruit which induced languor and forgetfulness of home. **2.** one who leads a life of indolent ease, indifferent to the busy world.

**lotus land** /'loʊtəs lænd/, *n.* **1.** land of the lotus-eaters. **2. live in lotus land, a.** to live without giving thought to the future. **b.** to consume unnecessarily large quantities of natural resources without consideration of future needs.

**lotus position** /'loʊtəs pəzɪʃən/, *n.* a seated yogic pose where the legs are crossed symmetrically so that the feet are resting on the opposite thighs.

**louche** /luʃ/, *adj.* sinister; disreputable; devious. [F: cross-eyed]

**loud** /laʊd/, *adj.* **1.** striking strongly upon the organs of hearing, as sound, noise, the voice, etc.; strongly audible. **2.** making, emitting, or uttering strongly audible sounds: *loud knocking.* **3.** full of sound or noise, or resounding. **4.** clamorous, vociferous, or blatant. **5.** emphatic or insistent: *to be loud in one's praises.* **6.** excessively striking to the eye, or offensively showy, as colours, dress or the wearer, etc.; garish. **7.** obtrusively vulgar, as manners, persons, etc. *–adv.* **8.** loudly. [ME; OE *hlūd,* c. G *laut*] – **loudly,** *adv.* – **loudness,** *n.*

**louden** /'laʊdn/, *v.i.* **1.** to become louder. *–v.t.* **2.** to make louder.

**loudhailer** /laʊd'heɪlə/, *n.* a megaphone with a built-in amplifier.

**loudish** /'laʊdɪʃ/, *adj.* somewhat loud.

**loudmouth** /'laʊdmaʊθ/, *n.* **1.** a person who speaks loudly and self-assertively. *–v.i.* **2.** to speak in this manner.

**loudmouthed** /'laʊdmaʊðd/, *adj.* loud of voice or utterance; vociferous; blatant.

**loud pedal** /'laʊd pɛdl/, *n.* →**sustaining pedal.**

**loudspeaker** /laʊd'spikə, 'laʊdspikə/, *n.* any of various devices by which speech, music, etc., can be made audible throughout a room, hall, or the like.

**lough** /lɒk/, *n.* **1.** →**lake**[1]. **2.** an arm of the sea. [ME, from Irish *loch.* Cf. LOCH]

**Louis Quatorze** /,lui kæ'tɔz/, *n.* of the period of Louis XIV of France or the styles of architecture, decoration, etc., prevailing about that time (1650-1700), relying more upon classical models than those of the Louis Treize period, and richly ornamented.

**Louis Quinze** /– 'kænz, 'kanz/, *adj.* of the period of Louis XV of France or the styles of architecture, decoration, etc., (known as *rococo*) prevailing about that time (1700-1750), smaller in scale and more delicate in ornament than those of the Louis Quatorze period.

**Louis Seize** /– 'seɪz, 'sɛz/, *adj.* of the period of Louis XVI of France or the styles of architecture, decoration, etc. prevailing about that time (1750-1790), characterised by a recurrence of classical models.

**Louis Treize** /– 'treɪz, 'trɛz/, *adj.* of the period of Louis XIII of France or the styles of architecture, decoration, etc., prevailing about that time (1600-1650), less light and elegant than those of the earlier Renaissance, and employing forms and features based on the classical.

**lounge** /laʊndʒ/, *v.,* **lounged, lounging,** *n.* *–v.i.* **1.** to pass time idly and indolently. **2.** to recline indolently; loll. **3.** to move or go (*about, along, off,* etc.) in a leisurely, indolent manner. *–v.t.* **4.** to pass (time, etc.) in lounging (fol. by *away* or *out*). *–n.* **5.** →**lounge room.** **6.** a large room in a hotel, etc., used by guests for relaxation purposes. **7.** Also, **lounge bar.** in a hotel, a bar providing tables and chairs where, in some parts of the country a man may drink only if accompanied by a woman. Cf. **public bar, saloon bar.** **8.** in a cinema, the most expensive and most comfortably furnished section of seats. **9.** →**couch**[1] (def. 1). **10.** the act or a spell of lounging. [? akin to obs. *lungis* laggard, from OF *longis* one who is long (i.e. slow)] – **lounger,** *n.*

**lounge lizard** /'– lɪzəd/, *n.* See **lizard** (def. 4).

**lounge room** /'– rum/, *n.* the living room of a private residence.

**lounge suit** /'– sut/, *n.* a suit worn by men as informal day wear.

**lounge suite** /'– swit/, *n.* a set of matched furniture, usu. consisting of a couch and two armchairs, for use in the lounge room.

**loup** /lu/, *n.* a cloth mask, often of silk, which covers only half the face. [F: lit., wolf, from L *lupus*]

**loup-garou** /lu-ga'ru/, *n., pl.* **loups-garous.** →**werewolf.** [F, from *loup* wolf (from L *lupus*) + *garou* werewolf, of Gmc orig.]

**lour** /'laʊə/, *v.i.* **1.** to be dark and threatening, as the sky or the weather. **2.** to frown, scowl, or look sullen. *–n.* **3.** a dark, threatening appearance, as of the sky, weather, etc. **4.** a frown or scowl. Also, *Chiefly U.S.,* **lower.** [ME *loure(n)* frown, lurk; cf. G *lauern* lurk]

**lourie** /'lʊəri/, *n.* any bird of the African family Musophagidae; touraco. [Malay *lūrī* LORY]

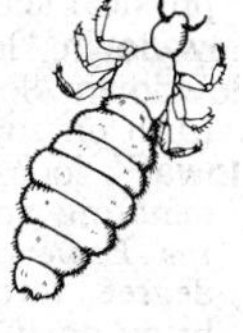

head louse

**louse** /laʊs/, *n., pl.* **lice** /laɪs/ *or* (*def. 3*) **louses;** *v.,* **loused, lousing.** *–n.* **1.** any of the small, wingless, blood-sucking insects of the order Anoplura, including several species associated with man, as the **human louse,** *Pediculus humanus* (including the races known as **head louse,** *P. capitis,* and **body louse,** *P. corporis*), and the **crablouse,** *Phthirius pubis.* **2.** any of various other insects parasitic on animals or plants, as those of the order Mallophaga (**biting bird lice**) or the homopterous family Aphididae (**plant lice**). **3.** *Colloq.* a despicable person. *–v.t.* **4.** *Colloq.* to spoil (fol. by *up*). [ME *lows(e), lous(e),* OE *lūs* (pl. *lȳs*), c. G *Laus*]

**lousewort** /'laʊswɜt/, *n.* any of the herbs constituting the large genus *Pedicularis,* as *P. sylvatica* (**pasture lousewort**), an English species formerly supposed to breed lice in sheep, and *P. canadensis* (**wood betony**).

**lousy** /'laʊzi/, *adj.,* **lousier, lousiest,** *n., pl.* **-sies.** *–adj.* **1.** infested with lice. **2.** *Colloq.* mean, contemptible or unpleasant. **3.** *Colloq.* inferior, no good. **4.** *Colloq.* well supplied: *he's lousy with money.* **5.** *Colloq.* trifling; mere: *he was fined a lousy $100.* **6.** *Colloq.* unwell. *–n.* **7.** *Colloq.* a bad mood; fit of depression. **– lousily,** *adv.* **– lousiness,** *n.*

**lout** /laʊt/, *n.* **1.** *Colloq.* a rough, uncouth and sometimes violent young man. **2.** an awkward, stupid person; a boor. [perhaps from obs. *lout* stoop, bow low] **– loutish,** *adj.* **– loutishly,** *adv.* **– loutishness,** *n.*

**louvre** /'luvə/, *n.* **1.** a turret or lantern on the roof of a medieval building, to supply ventilation or light. **2.** an arrangement of louvre-boards or the like closing a window or other opening, or a single louvre-board. **3.** one of a number of slitlike openings in the bonnet or body of a motor vehicle for the escape of heated air from within. Also, **louver.** [ME *lover,* from OF; orig. uncert.]

**louvre-board** /'luvə-bɔd/, *n.* one of a series of overlapping, sloping boards, slats, or the like, in an opening, so arranged as to admit air but exclude rain. Also, **louver-board.**

**louvre van** /'luvə væn/, *n.* a freight carriage with open louvre doors, designed for the ventilation of perishable transportable goods.

**lovable** /'lʌvəbəl/, *adj.* of such a nature as to attract love. Also, **loveable. – lovability** /lʌvə'bɪləti/, **lovableness,** *n.* **– lovably,** *adv.*

**lovage** /'lʌvɪdʒ/, *n.* a European herb, *Levisticum officinale,* cultivated in gardens. [ME *loveache,* from OF *levesche,* from LL *levisticum,* apparently alteration of L *ligusticum,* properly neut. of *Ligusticus* Ligurian]

**love** /lʌv/, *n., v.,* **loved, loving.** *–n.* **1.** a strong or passionate affection for another person. **2.** sexual passion or desire, or its gratification. **3.** an object of love or affection; a sweetheart. **4.** a feeling of warm personal attachment or deep affection, as for a friend (or between friends), parent, child, etc. **5.** strong predilection or liking for anything: *love of books.* **6.** the benevolent affection of God for His creatures, or the reverent affection due from them to God. **7.** *Tennis, etc.* nothing; no score. **8. for love, a.** out of affection. **b.** for nothing; without compensation. **9. for the love of,** for the sake of. **10. in love,** feeling deep affection or passion (oft. fol. by *with*). **11. make love, a.** to court. **b.** to have sexual intercourse. **12. love at first sight,** an overwhelming experience of falling in love with someone or something not previously encountered. *–v.t.* **13.** to have love or affection for. **14.** to have a strong or passionate affection for another person. **15.** to have a strong liking for; take great pleasure in: *to love music.* *–v.i.* **16.** to have love or affection, esp. to be or fall in love with one of the opposite sex. [ME; OE *lufu,* c. OHG *luba*]

**loveable** /'lʌvəbəl/, *adj.* →**lovable.**

**love affair** /'lʌv əfɛə/, *n.* **1.** a particular experience of being in love. **2.** a sexual relationship between two people.

**love apple** /'– æpəl/, *n.* →**tomato.**

**lovebird** /'lʌvbɜd/, *n.* **1.** any of various small parrots, esp. of the genera *Agapornis,* of Africa, and *Psittacula,* of South America, remarkable for the fact that the members of each pair keep close together when perching. **2.** *Colloq.* →**budgerigar.** **3.** *Colloq.* a man or a woman acting lovingly towards a member of the opposite sex.

**love child** /'lʌv tʃaɪld/, *n.* an illegitimate child.

**love feast** /'– fist/, *n.* **1.** (among the early Christians) a meal eaten in token of brotherly love and charity. **2.** *Chiefly U.S.* a rite practised by a few denominations such as Mennonites and Dunkers; a fellowship meal. **3.** a banquet or gathering of persons to promote good feeling.

**love game** /– 'geɪm/, *n.* (in tennis) a game in which one player scores no more than love (zero).

**lovegrass** /'lʌvgras/, *n.* any of various grasses of the genus *Eragrostis,* many of the perennial native Australian species having hairy leaves and sometimes a woolly covering on the roots as protection against dry conditions; found in inland areas of Australia. Also, **love grass.**

**love-hate** /'lʌv-heɪt/, *adj.* pertaining to an ambivalent state of mind in which one experiences feelings of love and hate for the same object.

**love-in** /'lʌv-ɪn/, *n.* a gathering for the display of communal goodwill and love.

**love-in-a-mist** /lʌv-ɪn-ə-'mɪst/, *n.* a herbaceous plant, *Nigella damascena,* with feathery dissected leaves and whitish or blue flowers.

**love-in-idleness** /lʌv-ɪn-'aɪdlnəs/, *n.* the wild pansy, *Viola tricolor.*

**love-interest** /'lʌv-ɪntrəst/, *n.* a theme in a novel, play, film, etc., which deals with the love between two characters.

**love-juice** /'lʌv-dʒus/, *n. Colloq.* **1.** →**aphrodisiac.** **2.** a sexual secretion.

**love knot** /'lʌv nɒt/, *n.* a knot of ribbon as a token of love.

**loveless** /'lʌvləs/, *adj.* **1.** devoid of or unattended with love. **2.** feeling no love. **3.** receiving no love. **– lovelessly,** *adv.* **– lovelessness,** *n.*

**love letter** /'lʌv lɛtə/, *n.* a letter expressing amorous sentiments.

**love-lies-bleeding** /ˌlʌv-laɪz-'blidɪŋ/, *n.* any of several species of amaranth, esp. *Amaranthus caudatus,* with spikes of crimson flowers.

**love-life** /'lʌv-laɪf/, *n.* the aspect of a person's life which has to do with sexual relations.

**lovelock** /'lʌvlɒk/, *n.* **1.** any conspicuous lock of hair. **2.** (formerly) a long, flowing lock or curl, dressed separately from the rest of the hair, worn by courtiers.

**lovelorn** /'lʌvlɔn/, *adj.* forsaken by one's love; forlorn or pining from love. **– lovelornness,** *n.*

**lovely** /'lʌvli/, *adj.,* **-lier, -liest.** **1.** charmingly or exquisitely beautiful: *a lovely flower.* **2.** having a beauty that appeals to the heart as well as to the eye, as a person, a face, etc. **3.** *Colloq.* delightful, or highly pleasing: *to have a lovely time.* **4.** of a great moral or spiritual beauty: *lovely character.* [ME *lovelich,* OE *luflic* amiable] **– loveliness,** *n.*

**lovemaking** /'lʌvmeɪkɪŋ/, *n.* **1.** sexual play and intercourse. **2.** (formerly) courtship.

**love match** /'lʌv mætʃ/, *n.* a linking of two people esp. in marriage for reasons of love alone, as opposed to pecuniary or other considerations.

**love-nest** /'lʌv-nɛst/, *n.* a retreat for lovers, esp. illicit.

**love-object** /'lʌv-ɒbdʒɛkt/, *n.* the object towards which love is directed.

**love-play** /'lʌv-pleɪ/, *n.* →**foreplay.**

**love potion** /'lʌv poʊʃən/, *n.* a drink which is supposed to make the drinker fall in love, often with the first person seen after drinking.

**lover** /ˈlʌvə/, *n.* **1.** someone who loves another; esp. a man in love with a woman. **2.** a sexual partner, esp. one distinguished by attentiveness or sexual powers: *he's quite a lover.* **3.** (*pl.*) a couple in love with each other or having a love affair. **4.** one who has a strong predilection or liking for something: *a lover of music.*

**love-scene** /ˈlʌv-sin/, *n.* a scene in a novel, play, film, etc., which portrays a sexual relationship of some kind.

**love seat** /ˈlʌv sit/, *n.* a seat for two persons, often S-shaped.

**love set** /– ˈsɛt/, *n.* (in tennis) a set in which one player does not score more than love (zero).

**lovesick** /ˈlʌvsɪk/, *adj.* **1.** languishing with love. **2.** expressive of such languishing. – **lovesickness,** *n.*

**loving** /ˈlʌvɪŋ/, *adj.* feeling or showing love; affectionate; fond: *loving glances.* – **lovingly,** *adv.* – **lovingness,** *n.*

**loving-cup** /ˈlʌvɪŋ-kʌp/, *n.* **1.** a large cup, as of silver, commonly with several handles, given as a prize, award, etc.; cup (def. 2). **2.** a similar cup which is filled with wine and passed around an assembly, at a banquet or the like.

**loving-kindness** /ˌlʌvɪŋ-ˈkaɪndnəs/, *n.* kindness arising from love (used primarily of the Deity).

**low**[1] /loʊ/, *adj.* **1.** situated or occurring not far above the ground, floor, or base: *a low shelf.* **2.** not far above the horizon, as a heavenly body. **3.** lying or being below the general level: *low ground.* **4.** *Print.* (of type or blocks) below the level of the forme surface. **5.** designating or pertaining to regions near the sea-level or sea as opposed to highland or inland regions: *Low Countries.* **6.** prostrate or dead: *to lay one low.* **7.** profound or deep, as a bow. **8.** (of a garment) low-necked. **9.** of small extent upwards, or not high or tall: *low walls.* **10.** rising but slightly from a surface: *low relief.* **11.** of less than average or normal height or depth, as a liquid, stream, etc. **12.** reduced to the least height, depth, or the like: *low tide.* **13.** lacking in strength or vigour; feeble; weak. **14.** affording little strength or nourishment, as diet. **15.** small in amount, degree, force, etc.: *a low number.* **16.** having a small amount of a particular constituent: *low-calorie diet.* **17.** *Cards.* having smaller value than another card. **18.** denoted by a low number: *a low latitude* (one near the equator). **19.** assigning or attributing no great amount, value, or excellence: *a low estimate of something.* **20.** depressed or dejected: *low spirits.* **21.** far down in the scale of rank or estimation; humble: *low birth.* **22.** of inferior quality or character: *a low type of intellect.* **23.** lacking in dignity or elevation, as of thought or expression. **24.** concealed; unnoticeable: *lie low.* **25.** grovelling or abject; mean or base: *a low trick.* **26.** coarse or vulgar: *low company.* **27.** *Biol.* having a relatively simple structure; not complex in organisation. **28.** *Music.* produced by relatively low vibrations, as sounds; grave in pitch. **29.** not loud: *a low murmur.* **30.** relatively late or recent, as a date. **31.** holding to Low-Church principles and practices. **32.** *Phonet.* pronounced with the tongue held relatively low in the mouth: *'hot' has a low vowel.* **33.** *Motor Vehicles.* of or pertaining to low-transmission gear ratio. *–adv.* **34.** in or to a low position, point, degree, etc. **35.** near the ground, floor, or base; not aloft. **36.** humbly. **37.** at or to a low pitch. **38.** in a low tone; softly; quietly. **39.** far down in time, or late. *–n.* **40.** that which is low; a low level. **41.** *Motor Vehicles.* a transmission gear ratio providing the least forward speed, usu. used to start a motor vehicle, or for extra power; first. **42.** *Meteorol.* a pressure system characterised by relatively low pressure at the centre. **43.** *Cards.* **a.** the lowest trump card. **b.** a card of small value. **44.** a point of least value, amount, etc.; nadir: *prices reached an all-time low.* [ME *lowe, lohe,* earlier *lah,* from Scand.; cf. Icel. *lāgr,* akin to LIE[2]] – **lowness,** *n.*

**low**[2] /loʊ/, *v.i.* **1.** to utter the sound characteristic of cattle; moo. *–v.t.* **2.** to utter by or as by lowing. *–n.* **3.** the act or the sound of lowing. [ME *low(en),* OE *hlōwan,* c. D *loeien*]

**lowan** /ˈloʊən/, *n.* →**mallee fowl.** [Aboriginal]

**low area** /ˈloʊ ɛəriə/, *n.* a region where the atmospheric or barometric pressure is lower than that of the surrounding regions: *the low area in the central part of a cyclone.*

**lowborn** /ˈloʊbɔn/, *adj.* of humble birth.

**lowboy** /ˈloʊbɔɪ/, *n.* **1.** a piece of furniture for holding clothes, similar to a wardrobe, but not so tall. **2.** *U.S.* a low chest of drawers supported on short legs.

**lowbred** /ˈloʊbrɛd/, *adj.* characterised by or characteristic of low or vulgar breeding.

**lowbrow** /ˈloʊbraʊ/, *Colloq.* *–n.* **1.** a person of low intellectual calibre or culture. *–adj.* **2.** being a lowbrow. **3.** pertaining or proper to lowbrows.

**Low Church** /loʊ ˈtʃɜtʃ/, *n.* a party in the Anglican Church which lays little stress on sacraments and church authority, etc., and holds evangelical views (opposed to *High Church*). – **Low-Church,** *adj.* – **Low-Churchman,** *n.*

**low cloud** /loʊ ˈklaʊd/, *n.* cloud with an average height of less than 2800 metres above the ground.

**low comedy** /– ˈkɒmədi/, *n.* comedy which depends on physical action and situation rather than on wit and dialogue.

**low-down** /ˈloʊ-daʊn/, *adj.* low; dishonourable; mean.

**lowdown** /ˈloʊdaʊn/, *n.* *Colloq.* the actual unadorned facts or truth on some subject.

**lower**[1] /ˈloʊə/, *adj.* **1.** comparative of **low**[1]. **2.** (*oft. cap.*) *Geol.* denoting an earlier division of a period, system, or the like: *the Lower Devonian.* *–v.t.* **3.** to reduce in amount, price, degree, force, etc. **4.** to make less loud, as the voice. **5.** to bring down in rank or estimation, degrade, or humble; abase (oneself), as by some sacrifice of dignity. **6.** to cause to descend, or let down: *to lower a flag.* **7.** to make lower in height or level: *to lower the water in a canal.* **8.** *Music.* to make lower in pitch; flatten. *–v.t.* **9.** to become lower or less. **10.** to descend; sink.

**lower**[2] /ˈlaʊə/, *v.i., n.* *Chiefly U.S.* →**lour.**

**lower case** /loʊə ˈkeɪs/, *n.* (in printing) the lower half of a pair of cases which contains the small letters of the alphabet. *Abbrev.:* l.c.

**lower-case** /ˈloʊə-keɪs/, *adj., v.,* **-cased, -casing.** *–adj.* **1.** (of a letter) small; minuscule (as opposed to *capital*). **2.** *Print.* pertaining to or belonging in the lower case. See **case**[2] (def. 8). *–v.t.* **3.** to print or write with a lower-case letter or letters.

**lower chamber** /ˈloʊə tʃeɪmbə/, *n.* →**lower house.**

**lower class** /loʊə ˈklas/, *n.* the class of people socially and conventionally regarded as being lower or lowest in the social hierarchy, commonly identified with the working class.

**lower-class** /ˈloʊə-klas/, *adj.* belonging or pertaining to the lower class.

**lower deck** /loʊə ˈdɛk/, *n.* **1.** *Naut.* the deck below a main deck. **2.** (in the Royal Australian Navy) junior sailors collectively.

**lower house** /ˈloʊə haʊs/, *n.* in a bicameral parliament, the lower legislative body, usu. more numerous and more directly representative of the electorate than the upper house. Also, **lower chamber.**

**lowering** /ˈlaʊərɪŋ/, *adj.* **1.** dark and threatening, as the sky, clouds, weather, etc. **2.** frowning or sullen, as the face, gaze, etc. – **loweringly,** *adv.*

**lowermost** /ˈloʊəmoʊst/, *adj.* lowest.

**lower world** /ˈloʊə wɜld/, *n.* **1.** the regions of the dead, conceived by the ancients as lying beneath the earth's surface; hades. **2.** the earth as distinguished from the heavenly bodies or from heaven.

**lowest common denominator,** *n.* **1.** →**common denominator.** **2.** (*usu. derog.*) the least worthy of the goals, values, opinions, etc., which are held in common by a group of people. **3.** the group of people who hold the least worthy of goals, values, opinions, etc., in a society.

**lowest common multiple,** *n.* See **common multiple.**

**low explosive** /loʊ əksˈploʊsɪv/, *n.* a relatively slow-burning explosive, usu. set off by heat or friction, and used for propelling charges in guns or for ordinary blasting.

**low frequency** /– ˈfrikwənsi/, *n.* a radio frequency in the range 30 to 300 kilohertz. – **low-frequency,** *adj.*

**low-geared** /ˈloʊ-gɪəd/, *adj.* See **gearing** (def. 3).

**Low German** /loʊ ˈdʒɜmən/, *n.* the Germanic speech of northern Germany and the Low Countries; Plattdeutsch.

**low-grade** /ˈloʊ-greɪd/, *adj.* of inferior quality.

**lowheel** /ˈloʊhil/, *n.* *Colloq.* →**prostitute.**

**low-key** /ˈloʊ-ki/, *adj.* **1.** underplayed; restrained. **2.** (of a person) not given to emotional display; quiet; unobtrusive.

**lowland** /ˈlouland/, *n.* **1.** land low with respect to neighbouring country. *–adj.* **2.** of, pertaining to, or characteristic of lowland or lowlands.

**lowlander** /ˈloulanda/, *n.* an inhabitant of lowlands.

**Low Latin** /lou ˈlætn/, *n.* any form of non-classical Latin, as Late Latin, Vulgar Latin, or Medieval Latin.

**low-level language** /ˈlou-lɛvəl ˌlæŋgwɪdʒ/, *n.* a language used for writing computer programs which is closer to machine language than human language. See **high-level language.**

**low-life** /ˈlou-laɪf/, *n.* the vulgar or more seamy elements of society.

**low-loader** /ˈlou-louda/, *n.* a road or rail vehicle in which the carrying platform is kept low for ease in loading and to give clearance under bridges, etc., for large objects.

**lowly** /ˈlouli/, *adj.*, **-lier, -liest,** *adv.* *–adj.* **1.** humble in station, condition, or nature: *a lowly cottage.* **2.** low in growth or position. **3.** humble in spirit; meek. *–adv.* **4.** in a low position, manner, or degree. **5.** in a lowly manner; humbly. **– lowliness,** *n.*

**low mass** /lou ˈmæs/, *n.* a mass said, and not sung, by a priest, assisted by a server only.

**low-minded** /ˈlou-maɪndəd/, *adj.* having or showing a low, coarse, or vulgar mind; mean. **– low-mindedly,** *adv.* **– low-mindedness,** *n.*

**low-necked** /ˈlou-nɛkt/, *adj.* (of a garment) cut low so as to leave the neck and shoulders exposed; décolleté.

**low-pass filter** /ˈlou-pas fɪltə/, *n.* a filter which allows only signals with frequencies below a certain value, which may be fixed or variable, to pass.

**low-pitched** /ˈlou-pɪtʃt/, *adj.* **1.** pitched in a low register or key. **2.** produced by slow vibrations; relatively grave in pitch or soft in sound. **3.** (of a roof) having a low proportion of vertical to lateral dimension.

**low-pressure** /ˈlou-prɛʃə/, *adj.* having or involving a low or below-normal pressure (as of steam, etc.).

**low profile** /lou ˈproufaɪl/, *n.* a low-keyed, uncommitted policy or reticent style of behaviour. **– low-profile,** *adj.*

**low relief** /– rəˈlif/, *n.* →**bas-relief.**

**low-rise** /ˈlou-raɪz/, *adj.* (of a building) having one or two storeys.

**lowry** /ˈlauri/, *n.* any of various rosellas. [var. of LORY]

**low season** /lou sizən/, *n.* the part of the year in which tourist accommodation, fares, etc., are low because of a seasonal demand.

**low-spirited** /ˈlou-spɪrətəd/, *adj.* depressed; dejected. **– low-spiritedly,** *adv.* **– low-spiritedness,** *n.*

**Low Sunday** /lou ˈsʌndeɪ/, *n.* the Sunday next after Easter.

**low-tension** /ˈlou-tɛnʃən/, *adj. Elect.* **1.** having or designed for use at low voltage, usu. less than 750 volts. **2.** the winding of a transformer designed to operate at the lower voltage. *Abbrev.:* L.T. Cf. **high-tension.**

**low tide** /lou ˈtaɪd/, *n.* **1.** the tide at low water. **2.** the time of low water. **3.** the lowest point of decline of anything.

**low-voltage** /ˈlou-voultɪdʒ/, *adj.* denoting an electric system with an operating voltage under 250 volts.

**low water** /lou ˈwɔtə/, *n.* water at its lowest level, as in a river.

**low-water mark** /lou-ˈwɔtə mak/, *n.* **1.** the level reached by water, usu. tidal water, when at its lowest depth. **2.** the least distinguished event in a series of events; the nadir.

**Low Week** /ˈlou wik/, *n.* the week after Easter Week.

**low wine** /ˈlou waɪn/, *n.* brandy or whisky after first distillation, and before second distillation.

**lox** /lɒks/, *n. Colloq.* →**liquid oxygen.** [L(IQUID) OX(YGEN)]

**loxodromic** /lɒksəˈdrɒmɪk/, *adj.* pertaining to oblique sailing or sailing on rhumb lines (loxodromic lines). Also, **loxodromical.** [Gk *loxó(s)* oblique + *drómos* a running course + -IC]

**loxodromics** /lɒksəˈdrɒmɪks/, *n.* the art of oblique sailing. Also, **loxodromy** /lɒkˈsɒdrəmi/.

**loyal** /ˈlɔɪəl/, *adj.* **1.** faithful to one's allegiance, as to the sovereign, government, or state: *a loyal subject.* **2.** faithful to one's oath, engagements or obligations: *to be loyal to a vow.* **3.** faithful to any leader, party, or cause, or to any person or thing conceived as imposing obligations: *a loyal friend.* **4.** characterised by or showing faithfulness to engagements, allegiance, obligations, etc.: *loyal conduct.* [F, from L *lēgālis* LEGAL] **– loyally,** *adv.*

**loyalist** /ˈlɔɪələst/, *n.* one who is loyal; a supporter of the sovereign of the existing government, esp. in time of revolt. **– loyalism,** *n.*

**loyalty** /ˈlɔɪəlti/, *n., pl.* **-ties. 1.** the state or quality of being loyal; faithfulness to engagements or obligations. **2.** faithful adherence to a sovereign or government, or to a leader, cause, or the like.

**lozenge** /ˈlɒzəndʒ/, *n.* **1.** a small flavoured cake or confection of sugar, often medicated, originally diamond-shaped. **2.** *Geom.* →**diamond. 3.** *Her.* a shield of this shape. [ME *losenge,* from OF, apparently from Pr. *lausa* stone slab]

**LP** /ɛl ˈpi/, *adj.* **1.** →**long-playing.** *–n.* **2.** such a record. [L(ONG)-P(LAYING)]

**L.P.G.** /ɛl pi ˈdʒi/, liquid petroleum gas.

**L-plate** /ˈɛl-pleɪt/, *n.* the usu. small square placard, on which appears the letter L, which is displayed on a vehicle being driven by one who is learning to drive. [L (def. 4) + PLATE[1]]

**LRTI** /ˈlɜti/, *n.* a lower respiratory tract infection.

**l.s.d.** /ɛl ɛs ˈdi/, *n.* **1.** pounds, shillings, and pence. **2.** *Colloq.* money. [L *librae, solidi, denarii* (Roman coinage)]

**LSD** /ɛl ɛs ˈdi/, *n.* lysergic acid diethylamide, a crystalline solid, $C_{15}H_{15}N_2CON\ (C_2H_5)_2$, which produces temporary hallucinations and a schizophrenia-like psychotic state.

**lt,** light.

**l.t.,** long ton.

**Lt,** Lieutenant.

**L.T.,** low-tension.

**Ltd,** limited. See **limited** (def. 3).

**L.Th.** /ɛl ti ˈeɪtʃ/, Licentiate in Theology.

**l.u.,** lock-up. Also, **L.U.**

**Lu,** *Chem.* lutetium.

**luau** /ˈluau/, *n.* a Hawaiian feast. [Hawaiian *lu'au*]

**luau light** /ˈ– laɪt/, *n.* →**Hawaiian flare.**

**lubber** /ˈlʌbə/, *n.* **1.** a big, clumsy, stupid person. **2.** (among sailors) an awkward or unskilled seaman; land-lubber. [ME *lober.* See LOB[1]]

**lubber line** /ˈ– laɪn/, *n.* a datum line on an instrument, as a compass, radar screen, etc., which represents the fore-and-aft axis of the aircraft, ship, etc., and from which navigational bearings are taken.

**lubberly** /ˈlʌbəli/, *adj.* **1.** like or of a lubber. *–adv.* **2.** in a lubberly manner. **– lubberliness,** *n.*

**lubber's hole** /ˈlʌbəz houl/, *n. Naut.* an open space in the platform at the head of a lower mast, through which a sailor may mount and descend without going outside the rim.

**lube** /lub/, *n. Colloq.* a lubrication, esp. of a motor vehicle.

**lubra** /ˈlubrə/, *n.* (*sometimes derog.*) an Aboriginal woman. [Aboriginal]

**lubricant** /ˈlubrəkənt/, *n.* **1.** a lubricating material. *–adj.* **2.** lubricating.

**lubricate** /ˈlubrəkeɪt/, *v.t.,* **-cated, -cating. 1.** to apply some oily, greasy, or other substance to, in order to diminish friction; oil or grease, as parts of a mechanism. **2.** to make slippery or smooth. [L *lūbricātus,* pp., made slippery] **– lubrication** /lubrəˈkeɪʃən/, *n.* **– lubricative,** *adj.*

**lubricator** /ˈlubrəkeɪtə/, *n.* a person or a device that lubricates or furnishes lubricant.

**lubricious** /luˈbrɪʃəs/, *adj.* →**lubricous.**

**lubricity** /luˈbrɪsəti/, *n., pl.* **-ties. 1.** slipperiness or oily smoothness of surface. **2.** capacity for lubrication. **3.** shiftiness. **4.** lewdness. [LL *lūbricitas,* from L *lūbricus* lubricous]

**lubricous** /ˈlubrəkəs/, *adj.* **1.** slippery, as of surface; of an oily smoothness. **2.** unstable; uncertain; shifty. **3.** →**lewd.** Also, **lubricious** /lubˈrɪʃəs/. [L *lūbricus*]

**luce** /lus/, *n.* **1.** a freshwater fish, the pike, esp. when full-grown. **2.** *Her.* a device representing a pike.

**lucent** /ˈlusənt/, *adj. Archaic.* **1.** shining. **2.** transparent. [L *lūcens,* ppr., shining] **– lucence, lucency,** *n.*

**lucerne** /ˈlusən/, *n.* **1.** a forage plant of the family Papilionaceae with bluish purple flowers, *Medicago sativa;* alfalfa. **2.** any of various other fodder legumes, as Townsville lucerne, *Stylosanthes sundaica,* and tree lucerne, *Chaemacytisus prolifer.* [F *luzerne,* from Pr. *luzerno,* from L *lux* light]

**luces** /ˈlusiz/, *n.* plural of **lux.**

**lucid** /ˈlusəd/, *adj.* **1.** shining or bright. **2.** clear or transparent. **3.** easily understood: *a lucid explanation.* **4.** characterised by clear perception or understanding; rational or sane: *a lucid interval.* [L *lūcidus*] – **lucidity** /luˈsɪdəti/, **lucidness,** *n.* – **lucidly,** *adv.*

**Lucifer** /ˈlusəfə/, *n.* **1.** a proud, rebellious archangel, identified with Satan, who fell from heaven. **2.** the planet Venus when appearing as the morning star. **3.** (*l.c.*) →**friction match.** [L: the morning star, properly adj., light-bringing]

**luciferase** /luˈsɪfəreɪz/, *n.* an enzyme which is present in the luminous organs of fireflies, etc., and which, acting upon luciferin, produces luminosity. [L *lūcifer* light-bringing + -ASE]

**luciferin** /luˈsɪfərən/, *n.* a protein occurring in fireflies, etc., luminous when acted upon by luciferase. [L *lūcifer* light-bringing + -IN[2]]

**lucifer match** /ˈlusəfə mætʃ/, *n.* →**friction match.** Also, **lucifer.**

**luciferous** /luˈsɪfərəs/, *adj.* bringing or giving light. [L *lūcifer* light-bringing + -OUS]

**luck** /lʌk/, *n.* **1.** that which happens to a person, either good or bad, as if by chance, in the course of events: *to have good luck.* **2.** good fortune; advantage or success considered as the result of chance: *to wish one luck.* **3. bad luck!,** (an exclamation of sympathy to someone in misfortune). **4. be in luck,** to experience good fortune. **5. be out of luck,** to experience a frustration of one's wishes, expectations or needs. **6. devil's own luck,** *Chiefly Brit. Colloq.* unusually good fortune, thought to be from the devil. **7. down on one's luck,** in poor or unfortunate circumstances. **8. good luck!,** (an exclamation conveying the good wishes of the speaker). **9. half your luck,** (an expression indicating envy at someone else's good luck). **10. here's luck!,** (an expression of goodwill, esp. as a toast). **11. just one's luck,** typical of one's luck, regarded as invariably bad. **12. no such luck,** (*usu. ironic*) unfortunately not. **13. (one's) luck is in,** one is experiencing a continued run of good fortune. **14. push one's luck,** to try to stretch one's luck too far. **15. the luck of the draw,** the outcome of chance. [ME *lucke,* from LG or D *luk,* also *Geluk,* c. G *Glück*]

**luckily** /ˈlʌkəli/, *adv.* by good luck; fortunately: *luckily he had enough money to pay the bill.*

**luckless** /ˈlʌkləs/, *adj.* having no luck. – **lucklessly,** *adv.* – **lucklessness,** *n.*

**lucky** /ˈlʌki/, *adj.,* **-ier, -iest.** **1.** having or attended with good luck; fortunate. **2.** happening fortunately: *a lucky accident.* **3.** bringing or presaging good luck, or supposed to do so: *a lucky penny.* – **luckiness,** *n.*

**lucky dip** /ˈ– dɪp/, *n.* **1.** (at a fair, party etc.,) a large barrel or the like in which prizes are hidden in sawdust, etc. from which participants select one article. **2.** the act of dipping into such a barrel and selecting an article. **3.** *Colloq.* a chance; an undertaking of uncertain outcome.

**lucrative** /ˈlukrətɪv/, *adj.* profitable; remunerative: *a lucrative business.* [ME, from L *lucrātīvus*] – **lucratively,** *adv.* – **lucrativeness,** *n.*

**lucre** /ˈlukə/, *n.* gain or money as the object of sordid desire: *filthy lucre.* [ME, from L *lucrum* gain]

**lucubrate** /ˈlukjəbreɪt/, *v.i.,* **-brated, -brating.** **1.** to work, write, study, etc., laboriously, esp. at night. **2.** to write learnedly. [L *lūcubrātus,* pp.] – **lucubrator,** *n.*

**lucubration** /lukjəˈbreɪʃən/, *n.* **1.** laborious work, study, etc., esp. at night. **2.** a learned or carefully written production. **3.** (*oft. pl.*) any literary effort.

**luculent** /ˈlukjələnt/, *adj.* **1.** clear or lucid, as explanations, etc. **2.** convincing. [ME, from L *lūculentus*] – **luculently,** *adv.*

**luculia** /ləˈkuliə/, *n.* any shrub or small tree of the small East Asian genus *Luculia,* as *L. gratissima* from the Himalayas with large fragrant clusters of tubular rosy-pink flowers.

**luderick** /ˈludərɪk/, *n.* a highly prized Australian estuarine and rock fish, *Girella tricuspidata,* usu. black or dark brown above and having dark bars down back and sides; nigger; darkie; black bream. [Aboriginal]

**ludicrous** /ˈludəkrəs/, *adj.* such as to cause laughter or derision; ridiculous; amusingly absurd: *a ludicrous incident.* [L *lūdicrus* sportive] – **ludicrously,** *adv.* – **ludicrousness,** *n.*

**ludo** /ˈludoʊ/, *n.* a children's game played on a board with counters and dice, for up to four players.

**lues** /ˈluiz/, *n.* →**syphilis.** [L: plague]

**luff** /lʌf/, *Naut.* –*n.* **1.** the forward edge of a fore-and-aft sail. –*v.i.* **2.** Also, **luff up.** to bring the head of a sailing vessel closer to or directly into the wind, with sails shaking. **3.** to alter the angle of the jib of a crane, and thus alter the radius of lifting. –*v.t.* **4.** to force an opponent in a sailing race to alter course to windward. **5.** to alter the angle of (the jib of a crane). [early ME *lof, loof,* apparently from OF *lof* a contrivance for altering a ship's course (later, as also D *loef,* the weather side), of Gmc orig.]

**luffing crane** /ˈlʌfɪŋ kreɪn/, *n.* a crane with a jib whose angle, and hence the radius of lifting, can be altered.

**luff tackle** /ˈlʌf tækəl/, *n. Naut.* a purchase or tackle with a double block at the top and a single one at the bottom.

**luff wire** /ˈ– waɪə/, *n.* a wire rope in the forward edge of a sail.

**lug**[1] /lʌg/, *v.,* **lugged, lugging,** *n.* –*v.t.* **1.** to pull along or carry with force or effort. –*v.i.* **2.** to pull; tug. **3.** (of a horse) to race erratically, hanging in to the rails. –*n.* **4.** an act of lugging; a forcible pull; a haul. [ME *lugg(e),* from Scand.; cf. Swed. *lugga* pull by the hair]

**lug**[2] /lʌg/, *n.* **1.** *Colloq.* an ear. **2.** one of the earflaps of a cap. **3.** a projecting piece by which anything is held or supported. **4.** a leather loop hanging down from a saddle, through which a shaft is passed for support. **5. blow down someone's lug,** *Colloq.* to harangue someone. [? special use of LUG[1]]

**lug**[3] /lʌg/, *n.* →**lugsail.** [see LUGSAIL]

**lug**[4] /lʌg/, *n.* →**lugworm.** [orig. uncert.; ? from Irish Gaelic. Cf. Irish *lurg*]

**luggage** /ˈlʌgɪdʒ/, *n.* trunks, suitcases, etc., used in travelling; baggage. [LUG[1] + -AGE]

**luggage-rack** /ˈlʌgɪdʒ-ræk/, *n.* **1.** a device (usu. a shelf made out of a metal frame and wire mesh, attached to a wall) installed in train compartments, hotel rooms, etc., in which luggage may be conveniently and safely placed. **2.** →**roof-rack.**

**luggage van** /ˈlʌgɪdʒ væn/, *n.* a railway van, or part of a van, used for transporting passengers' luggage.

**lugger**[1] /ˈlʌgə/, *n.* a vessel with lugsails; a small sailing vessel, frequently two masted, often associated with island trading, pearl or trepang fishing, etc. [from LUGSAIL]

**lugger**[2] /ˈlʌgə/, *n. Colloq.* a person who subjects others to long, unwelcome monologues. [LUG[2] + -ER[2]]

**lugsail** /ˈlʌgsəl/, *n.* a quadrilateral sail bent upon a yard that crosses the mast obliquely. Also, **lug.** [*lug* pole (now d.) + SAIL]

**lugubrious** /ləˈgubriəs/, *adj.* mournful; doleful; dismal: *lugubrious tones.* [L *lūgubri(s)* mournful + -OUS] – **lugubriously,** *adv.* – **lugubriousness,** *n.*

**lugworm** /ˈlʌgwɜm/, *n.* any annelid of the genus *Arenicola,* comprising marine worms with tufted gills, which burrow in the sand of the seashore and are much used for bait. Also, **lug.** [LUG[4] + WORM]

**lukewarm** /ˈlukwɔm/, *adj.* **1.** moderately warm; tepid. **2.** having or showing little ardour or zeal; indifferent: *lukewarm applause.* [ME *lukewarme,* from *luke* tepid (apparently from *lew* tepid, OE *-hlēow*) + *warme* WARM] – **lukewarmly,** *adv.* – **lukewarmness,** *n.*

**lull** /lʌl/, *v.t.* **1.** to put to sleep or rest by soothing means: *to lull a child by singing.* **2.** to soothe or quiet. **3.** to lead into a false sense of security. –*v.i.* **4.** to become lulled, quieted, or stilled. –*n.* **5.** a lulled condition; a temporary quiet or stillness: *a lull in a storm.* **6.** a soothing sound: *the lull of falling waters.* [ME *lulle(n).* Cf. Swed. *lulla,* G *lullen,* also L *lallāre* sing lullaby]

**lullaby** /ˈlʌləbaɪ/, *n., pl.* **-bies,** *v.,* **-bied, -bying.** –*n.* **1.** the utterance 'lullaby' or a song containing it; a cradlesong. **2.** any lulling song. –*v.t.* **3.** to lull with or as with a lullaby. [ME interj. *lulla!* (from LULL) + *-by* (from BYE-BYE)]

**lulu** /ˈlulu/, *n. Colloq.* **1.** an amazing person, event, or thing. **2.** a tall story. [orig. uncert.]

**lumbago** /lʌmˈbeɪgoʊ/, *n.* myalgia in the lumbar region; rheumatic pain in the muscles of the small of the back. [LL, from L *lumbus* loin]

**lumbar** /ˈlʌmbə/, *adj.* **1.** of or pertaining to the loin or loins. *–n.* **2.** a lumbar vertebra, artery, or the like. [NL *lumbāris,* from L *lumbus* loin]

**lumbar puncture** /ˈ– pʌŋktʃə/, *n.* the insertion of a hollow needle between the lumbar vertebrae into the spinal cord to draw off some of the cerebrospinal fluid, to inject drugs, etc.

**lumber**[1] /ˈlʌmbə/, *n.* **1.** timber sawn or split into planks, boards, etc. **2.** miscellaneous useless articles that are stored away. *–v.i.* **3.** to cut timber and prepare it for market. *–v.t.* **4.** to heap together in disorder. **5.** to fill up or obstruct with miscellaneous useless articles; encumber. **6.** *Colloq.* to foist off on or leave with, as with something or someone unwelcome or unpleasant. **7.** *Colloq.* to arrest (def. 1). [orig. uncert.] – **lumberer,** *n.*

**lumber**[2] /ˈlʌmbə/, *v.i.* to move clumsily or heavily, esp. from great or ponderous bulk. [ME *lomere(n).* Cf. d. Swed. *lomra* resound, *loma* walk heavily]

**lumbering**[1] /ˈlʌmbərɪŋ/, *n. Chiefly U.S. and Canada.* the trade or business of cutting and preparing timber. [LUMBER[1] + -ING[1]]

**lumbering**[2] /ˈlʌmbərɪŋ/, *adj.* moving clumsily or heavily; awkward. [LUMBER[2] + -ING[2]] – **lumberingly,** *adv.*

**lumberjack** /ˈlʌmbədʒæk/, *Chiefly U.S. and Canada n.* one who works at lumbering.

**lumber-jacket** /ˈlʌmbə-dʒækət/, *n.* a man's or woman's casual heavy woollen jacket, usu. having bold colours and patterns, fastened up to the neck by a zip or the like, as worn originally by lumberjacks.

**lumberman** /ˈlʌmbəmæn/, *n., pl.* **-men.** **1.** one who cuts and prepares timber. **2.** one who deals in lumber.

**lumber-room** /ˈlʌmbə-rum/, *n.* a room in a house used for storing furniture or the like which is not in use; boxroom.

**lumberyard** /ˈlʌmbəjad/, *n.* →**timber yard.**

**lumbrical** /ˈlʌmbrɪkəl/, *n.* one of four wormlike muscles in the palm of the hand and in the sole of the foot. Also, **lumbricalis** /lʌmbrəˈkeɪləs/. [NL *lumbrīcālis,* from L *lumbrīcus* earthworm]

**lumbricoid** /ˈlʌmbrɪkɔɪd/, *adj.* resembling an earthworm. [L *lumbrīcus* earthworm + -OID]

**lumen** /ˈlumən/, *n., pl.* **-mens, -mina** /-mənə/. **1.** *Optics.* the derived SI unit of luminous flux; the light emitted in a unit solid angle of one steradian by a point source having a uniform intensity of one candela. *Symbol:* lm **2.** *Anat.* the canal, duct, or cavity of a tubular organ. **3.** *Bot.* (of a cell) the cavity which the cell walls enclose. [L: light, window]

**Lumholtz's tree-kangaroo** /ˌlʌmhɒltsəz ˈtri-kæŋgəru/, *n.* a stocky, greyish marsupial, *Dendrolagus lumholtzi,* found in mountainous forest areas of north-eastern Queensland, having long, powerful, forelegs, a long, cylindrical, non-prehensile tail, and a distinctive white band above the eyes; boongary. [named after Dr. Carl *Lumholtz,* 1851-1922, Norwegian naturalist]

**luminance** /ˈlumənəns/, *n.* **1.** the state or quality of being luminous. **2.** *Photom.* (in a given direction, at a point on the surface of the source or the receptor, or at a point on the path of the beam) the luminous flux leaving, arriving at, or passing through an element of surface at the point, and within an element of solid angle divided by the product of the solid angle and the area of orthogonal projection, measured in candela per square metre. [L *lūmen* light + -ANCE]

**luminary** /ˈlumənəri, -mənri/, *n., pl.* **-naries.** **1.** a celestial body, as the sun or moon. **2.** a body or thing that gives light. **3.** a person who enlightens mankind or makes some subject clear. **4.** a famous person; celebrity. [late ME, from ML *lūminārium* a light, lamp, heavenly body]

**luminesce** /luməˈnɛs/, *v.i.* **-nesced, -nescing.** to exhibit luminescence.

**luminescence** /luməˈnɛsəns/, *n.* an emission of light not due directly to incandescence and occurring at a temperature below that of incandescent bodies; a term including phosphorescence, fluorescence, etc.

**luminescent** /luməˈnɛsənt/, *adj.* characterised by or pertaining to luminescence. [L *lūmen* light + -ESCENT]

**luminiferous** /luməˈnɪfərəs/, *adj.* producing light. [L *lūmen* light + -I- + -FEROUS]

**luminosity** /luməˈnɒsəti/, *n., pl.* **-ties.** **1.** the quality of being luminous. **2.** something luminous. **3.** *Astron.* the amount of light emitted by a star, usu. expressed as a magnitude.

**luminous** /ˈlumənəs/, *adj.* **1.** radiating or reflecting light; shining. **2.** lighted up or illuminated; well lighted. **3.** brilliant intellectually; enlightening, as a writer or his writings. **4.** clear; readily intelligible. [ME *luminose,* from L *lūminōsus*] – **luminously,** *adv.* – **luminousness,** *n.*

**luminous efficiency** /– əˈfɪʃənsi/, *n.* **1.** (of a source) the ratio of the light emitted to the energy input, esp. when expressed as lumens per watt for electric lamps. **2.** (of a radiation) the ratio of the luminous flux to the radiant flux.

**luminous energy** /– ˈɛnədʒi/, *n.* **1.** light. **2.** *Optics.* the time integral of luminous flux.

**luminous flux** /– ˈflʌks/, *n.* the rate of transmission of luminous energy; luminous power. Its unit is the lumen.

**luminous intensity** /– ɪnˈtɛnsəti/, *n.* (of a point source of light) the luminous flux emitted per unit solid angle, measured in candela.

**luminous paint** /– ˈpeɪnt/, *n.* paint which contains a phosphorescent compound and therefore glows after exposure to light.

**lumisterol** /luməˈstɪərɒl, luˈmɪstərɒl/, *n.* a water-soluble compound present in vitamin $D_1$, produced when ergosterol is irradiated by ultraviolet light.

**lummox** /ˈlʌməks/, *n. Colloq.* a clumsy, stupid person.

**lump**[1] /lʌmp/, *n.* **1.** a piece or mass of solid matter without regular shape, or of no particular shape. **2.** a protuberance or swelling: *a lump on the head.* **3.** an aggregation, collection, or mass: *in the lump.* **4.** *Colloq.* a stupid, clumsy person. **5.** **have a lump in the throat,** *Colloq.* to feel very emotional. *–adj.* **6.** in the form of a lump or lumps: *lump sugar.* **7.** including a number of items taken together or in the lump: *a lump sum.* *–v.t.* **8.** to unite into one aggregation, collection, or mass. **9.** to deal with in the lump or mass. **10.** to make into a lump or lumps. **11.** to raise into or cover with lumps. *–v.i.* **12.** to form or raise a lump or lumps. **13.** to move heavily. [ME *lumpe, lomp(e).* Cf. Dan. *lump(e)* lump, d. Norw. *lump* block]

**lump**[2] /lʌmp/, *v.t. Colloq.* **1.** to endure or put up with (a disagreeable necessity): *if you don't like it, you can lump it.* **2.** to carry (usu. something heavy or cumbersome). [orig. uncert.]

**lumpen** /ˈlʌmpən, ˈlʊm-/, *adj. Colloq.* wretched; purposeless; unprincipled. [backformation from LUMPENPROLETARIAT]

**lumpenproletariat** /ˌlʌmpənproʊləˈtɛəriət, ˌlʊmpən-/, *n.* the most degraded and miserable members of the proletariat, who do not participate in the workers' attempts to improve their conditions and change society. [G, coinage of Karl Marx, from *Lumpen* rag + PROLETARIAT] – **lumpenproletarian,** *adj.*

**lumper** /ˈlʌmpə/, *n. Colloq.* a wharf labourer.

**lumpfish** /ˈlʌmpfɪʃ/, *n., pl.* **-fishes,** (*esp. collectively*) **-fish.** →**lumpsucker.**

**lump hammer** /ˈlʌmp hæmə/, *n.* a hammer similar to but smaller than a sledge-hammer.

**lumpish** /ˈlʌmpɪʃ/, *adj.* **1.** like a lump. **2.** clumsy or stupid: *she called him a lumpish boor.* – **lumpishly,** *adv.* – **lumpishness,** *n.*

**lumpsucker** /ˈlʌmpsʌkə/, *n.* a clumsy-looking fish, *Cyclopterus lumpus,* with a high, ridged back, of the North Atlantic Ocean.

**lumpy** /ˈlʌmpi/, *adj.,* **lumpier, lumpiest.** **1.** full of lumps: *lumpy gravy.* **2.** covered with lumps, as a surface. **3** like a lump, as in being heavy or clumsy. **4.** (of water) rough or choppy. – **lumpily,** *adv.* – **lumpiness,** *n.*

**lumpy jaw** /ˈ– dʒɔ/, *n.* actinomycosis of the head in cattle. Also, **lump jaw.**

**lumpy wool** /– ˈwʊl/, *n.* an infectious skin disease of sheep causing wool fibres to bind into a hard mass; mycotic dermatitis.

**lunacy** /ˈlunəsi/, *n., pl.* **-cies.** **1.** intermittent insanity. **2.** any form of insanity (usu. except idiocy). **3.** extreme foolishness or an instance of it: *her decision to resign was sheer lunacy.* **4.** *Law.* unsoundness of mind sufficient to incapacitate one for civil transactions. [LUN(ATIC) + -ACY]

**luna moth** /ˈlunə mɒθ/, *n.* a large American moth, *Tropaea luna,* with light green colouration, purple-brown markings, lunate spots, and long tails. Also, **Luna moth.**

**lunar** /'lunə/, *adj.* **1.** of or pertaining to the moon: *the lunar orbit.* **2.** measured by the moon's revolutions: *a lunar month.* **3.** resembling the moon; round or crescent-shaped. **4.** of or pertaining to silver. [L *lūnāris* of the moon, crescent]

**lunar caustic** /– 'kɒstɪk/, *n.* silver nitrate, $AgNO_3$, esp. in a sticklike mould, used to cauterise tissues.

**lunarian** /lu'nɛəriən/, *n.* **1.** a supposed inhabitant of the moon. **2.** a selenographer. *–adj.* **3.** →**lunar.**

**lunar module** /lunə 'mɒdʒul/, *n.* the section of a space vehicle which detaches in lunar orbit and descends to the surface of the moon.

**lunar month** /– 'mʌnθ/, *n.* See **month** (def. 5).

**lunar year** /– 'jɪə/, *n.* See **year** (def. 4).

**lunate** /'luneɪt/, *adj.* crescent-shaped. Also, **lunated.** [L *lūnātus*]

**lunatic** /'lunətɪk/, *n.* **1.** an insane person. *–adj.* **2.** insane or mad; crazy. **3.** indicating lunacy; characteristic of a lunatic. **4.** designated for or used by the insane: *a lunatic asylum.* Also (*for defs 2 and 3*), **lunatical** /lu'nætɪkəl/. [ME *lunatik,* from LL *lūnāticus* mad, from L *lūna* moon] – **lunatically,** *adv.*

**lunatic asylum** /'– əsaɪləm/, *n.* →**psychiatric hospital.**

**lunatic fringe** /– 'frɪndʒ/, *n.* the more extreme members of a community or group.

**lunatic soup** /– 'sup/, *n. Colloq.* any alcoholic drink, esp. a strong drink, as brandy.

**lunation** /lu'neɪʃən/, *n.* the time from one new moon to the next (about 29½ days); a lunar month.

**lunch** /lʌntʃ/, *n.* **1.** a meal taken at midday or shortly after; luncheon. **2.** a snack or light meal taken at any time of day. *–adj.* **3.** of or pertaining to lunch. *–v.i.* **4.** to eat lunch. **5.** *Colloq.* to fart. *–v.t.* **6.** to entertain (someone) to lunch. [short for LUNCHEON]

**lunch box** /'lʌntʃ bɒks/, *n.* a container for a packed lunch.

**lunchbreak** /'lʌntʃbreɪk/, *n.* →**lunch hour.**

**luncheon** /'lʌntʃən/, *n.* →**lunch.** [b. LUMP[1] and d. *nuncheon* (ME *nonshench,* from *non* noon + *shench* (OE *scenc*) a drink)]

**luncheonette** /lʌntʃə'nɛt/, *n.* a cafe or restaurant serving quick snacks and light meals.

**luncheon meat** /'lʌntʃən mit/, *n.* a pulverised mixture of meat, usu. pork, and cereal, in loaf form.

**luncheon sausage** /'– sɒsɪdʒ/, *n.* luncheon meat in sausage form.

**lunch hour** /'lʌntʃ aʊə/, *n.* lunchtime, not necessarily an hour long: *lunch hour is from 12.30 to 1.10.* Also, **lunchbreak.**

**lunchtime** /'lʌntʃtaɪm/, *n.* **1.** the time, usu. around or soon after midday, when lunch is eaten. *–adj.* **2.** denoting, pertaining to, or taking place at this time.

**lune**[1] /lun/, *n.* **1.** anything shaped like a crescent or a half-moon. **2.** a crescent-shaped plane figure bounded by two arcs of circles, either on a plane or a spherical surface. **3.** *Rom. Cath. Ch.* →**lunette** (def. 6). [F, from L *lūna* moon]

**lune**[2] /lun/, *n. Falconry.* a line for holding a hawk. [ME; var. of *loigne,* from OF, from LL *longia,* from L *longus* long]

**lunette** /lu'nɛt/, *n.* **1.** any of various objects or spaces of crescent-like or semicircular outline or section. **2.** an arched or rounded aperture or window, as in a vault. **3.** a painting, etc., filling an arched space, usu. a semicircle or a flatter chord of a circle. **4.** *Fort.* a work consisting of a salient angle with two flanks and an open gorge. **5.** *Ordn.* a towing ring in the trail-plate of a towed vehicle, as a guncarriage. **6.** Also, **lune.** *Rom. Cath. Ch.* a crescent-shaped fitting to hold the consecrated Host within a monstrance for adoration and benediction. **7.** a crescent or half-moon shaped billabong. **8.** a crescent or half-moon shaped sand dune. [F, diminutive of *lune* moon. See LUNE[1]]

**lung** /lʌŋ/, *n.* **1.** either of the two saclike respiratory organs in the thorax of man and the higher vertebrates. **2.** an analogous organ in certain invertebrates, as arachnids, terrestrial gastropods, etc. [ME *lunge(n),* OE *lungen,* c. G *Lunge;* akin to LIGHT[2]]

**lungan** /'lʌŋgən/, *n.* →**longan.**

**lunge**[1] /lʌndʒ/, *n., v.,* **lunged, lunging.** *–n.* **1.** a thrust, as in fencing. **2.** any sudden forward movement; plunge. *–v.i.* **3.** to make a lunge or thrust; move with a lunge. *–v.t.* **4.** to thrust; cause to move with a lunge. [aphetic var. of *allonge* (obs.), from F, from *allonger* lengthen, extend, lunge, from *à* to (from L *ad*) + *long* long (from L *longus*)]

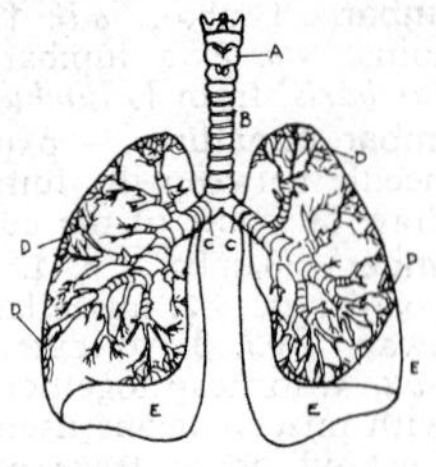

human lung (section): A, larynx; B, trachea; C, bronchi; D, ramifications of bronchial tubes; E, uncut surface

**lunge**[2] /lʌndʒ/, *n., v.,* **lunged, lunging.** *–n.* **1.** a long rope used to guide a horse during training or exercise. **2.** a ring or circular track for such training or exercise. *–v.t.* **3.** to train or exercise (a horse) by the use of a lunge or rope, or on a lunge or track. [F *longe* halter, lunge, var. of OF *loigne.* See LUNE[2]]

**lunger belt** /'lʌndʒə bɛlt/, *n. Gymnastics.* a safety belt attached by pulleys to the ceiling.

**lungfish** /'lʌŋfɪʃ/, *n., pl.* **-fishes,** (*esp. collectively*) **-fish.** any of several elongated tropical freshwater fishes of the order Dipnoi, as the Queensland lungfish, that breathes by means of modified lung-like structures as well as gills. Cf. **Queensland lungfish.**

lungfish

**lungi** /lʊŋ'gi/, *n.* a loincloth. Also, **lungee.**

**lunging rein** /'lʌndʒɪŋ reɪn/, *n.* →**lunge**[2] (def. 1).

**lungworm** /'lʌŋwɜm/, *n.* **1.** any nematode worm of the superfamily Metastrongylidae, parasitic in lungs of various mammals. **2.** a nematode worm of the genus *Rhabdias,* parasitic in the lungs of reptiles and amphibians.

**lungwort** /'lʌŋwɜt/, *n.* a small perennial herb with spotted leaves and blue flowers, *Pulmonaria officinalis,* native to central and southern Europe, frequently cultivated and naturalised elsewhere.

**luni-,** a word element meaning 'moon'. [combining form representing L *lūna*]

**lunisolar** /luni'soʊlə/, *adj.* pertaining to or based upon the relations or joint action of the moon and sun: *the lunisolar cycle.*

**lunitidal** /luni'taɪdl/, *adj.* pertaining to that part of the tidal movement dependent on the moon.

**lunitidal interval** /– 'ɪntəvəl/, *n.* the period of time between the moon's transit and the next high lunar tide.

**lunkhead** /'lʌŋkhɛd/, *n. U.S. Colloq.* a stupid fellow; blockhead. Also, **lunk.**

**lunula** /'lunjələ/, *n., pl.* **-lae** /-li/. something shaped like a narrow crescent, as the small white area at the base of the human fingernail. Also, **lunule** /'lunjul/. [L, diminutive of *lūna* moon]

**lunular** /'lunjələ/, *adj.* crescent-shaped: *lunular markings.*

**lunulate** /'lunjəleɪt/, *adj.* **1.** having lunular markings. **2.** crescent-shaped. Also, **lunulated.**

**luny** /'luni/, *adj.,* **-nier, -niest,** *n., pl.* **-nies.** →**loony.**

**lupin** /'lupən/, *n.* any plant of the leguminous genus *Lupinus,* as *L. albus* (**white lupin**), a European herb with edible seeds cultivated from ancient times, or *L. polyphyllus,* a native of North America often cultivated, with a wide range of flower colours. Also, *Chiefly U.S.,* **lupine.** [ME, from L *lupīnus, lupīnum.* See LUPINE]

**lupine** /'lupaɪn/, *adj.* **1.** pertaining to or resembling the wolf. **2.** allied to the wolf. **3.** savage; ravenous. [L *lupīnus* of a wolf]

**lupinosis** /lupə'noʊsəs/, *n.* a disease of the liver in cattle, caused by a toxin associated with the fungus *Phomopsis* which develops on the stems of sweet lupins in wet summer weather.

**lupulin** /'lupjələn/, *n.* the glandular hairs of the hop, *Humulus lupulus,* used in medicine. [NL *lupulus* (diminutive of L *lupus* hop) + -IN[2]]

**lupus** /'lupəs/, *n.* a cutaneous disease due to the tubercle bacillus. [L: wolf]

**lurch**[1] /lɜtʃ/, *n.* **1.** sudden leaning or roll to one side, as of a ship or a staggering person. **2.** a sudden swaying or staggering movement. *–v.i.* **3.** to make a lurch; move with lurches; stagger: *the wounded man lurched across the room at his assailant.* [orig. uncert.; first in nautical use]

**lurch**[2] /ˈlɜtʃ/, *n.* **1.** the position of one discomfited or in a helpless plight: *to leave someone in the lurch.* **2.** a situation at the close of various games in which the loser scores nothing or is far behind his opponent. [F (obs.) *lourche* (n.) a game, (adj.) discomfited; ? of Gmc orig.]

**lurcher** /ˈlɜtʃə/, *n.* **1.** one who lurks or prowls; a petty thief; a poacher. **2.** a crossbred hunting dog. [Brit. d. *lurch* loiter about suspiciously (? var. of LURK) + -ER[1]]

**lure** /ˈluə, ˈljuə/, *n., v.,* **lured, luring.** *–n.* **1.** anything that attracts, entices, or allures. **2.** a decoy; a bait, esp. an artificial one, used in angling. **3.** a feathered decoy, sometimes baited, on a long thong, used in falconry to recall the hawk. **4.** Also, **metal hare, tin hare.** an imitation hare, mechanically driven, which greyhounds pursue in a race. **5.** a flap or tassel dangling from the dorsal fin of pediculate fish. *–v.t.* **6.** to decoy; entice; allure. **7.** to draw as by a lure. [ME, from OF *leurre,* from Gmc; cf. G *Luder* bait] **– lurer,** *n.*

**lurex** /ˈlurɛks, ˈluə-/, *n.* **1.** a yarn incorporating metallic thread. **2.** the fabric made from this yarn. [Trademark]

**lurgy** /ˈlɜgi/, *n. Colloq.* **1.** a fictitious, very infectious disease. **2.** any illness. Also, **lurgi.** [coined by Spike Milligan, b. 1918, British comedian]

**lurid** /ˈlurəd/, *adj.* **1.** lit up or shining with an unnatural or wild (esp. red or fiery) glare: *a lurid sky.* **2.** glaringly vivid or sensational: *lurid tales.* **3.** terrible in fiery intensity, fierce passion, or wild unrestraint: *lurid crimes.* **4.** wan, pallid, or ghastly in hue. [L *lūridus* pale yellow, wan] **– luridly,** *adv.* **– luridness,** *n.*

**lurk** /lɜk/, *v.i.* **1.** to lie in concealment, as men in ambush; remain in or about a place secretly or furtively. **2.** to go furtively; slink; steal. **3.** to exist unperceived or unsuspected. *–n. Colloq.* **4.** a place of resort; hide-out. **5.** a dodge; a slightly underhand scheme. **6.** a convenient, often unethical, method of performing a task, earning a living, etc. **7.** a job. [ME, frequentative of LOUR. Cf. Norw. *lurka* sneak away] **– lurky,** *adj.*

**lurk man** /ˈ– mæn/, *n.* **1.** one who lives by his wits, as a confidence man, or an inventive layabout. **2.** one who is adept at exploiting an institutional system for his own benefit. [LURK, *n.,* + MAN]

**luscious** /ˈlʌʃəs/, *adj.* **1.** highly pleasing to the taste or smell: *luscious peaches.* **2.** sweet to the senses or the mind. **3.** very luxurious; extremely attractive. **4.** sweet to excess; cloying. [late ME; ? aphetic var. of DELICIOUS] **– lusciously,** *adv.* **– lusciousness,** *n.*

**lusec** /ˈlusɛk/, *n.* a non-SI unit of measurement of pumping speed equal to a speed of 1 litre per second at a pressure of 0.001 mmHg (133.322 37 × $10^{-6}$ watts).

**lush**[1] /lʌʃ/, *adj.* **1.** tender and juicy, as plants or vegetation; succulent; luxuriant. **2.** characterised by luxuriant vegetation. **3.** *Colloq.* characterised by luxury and comfort. **4.** sexually attractive. [ME *lusch,* probably var. of *lasch,* from OF *lasche* loose, slack] **– lushly,** *adv.* **– lushness,** *n.*

**lush**[2] /lʌʃ/, *Colloq. –n.* **1.** intoxicating liquor. **2.** a drunken person. **3.** a drinking bout. **4.** one who takes alcoholic drinks, esp. regularly. *–v.i.* **5.** to drink liquor. *–v.t.* **6.** to drink (liquor). [orig. uncert.]

**lushington** /ˈlʌʃɪŋtən/, *n. Colloq.* a drunkard. Also, **Alderman Lushington.**

**lushy** /ˈlʌʃi/, *adj. Colloq.* drunk; tipsy.

**Lusitanian** /lusəˈteɪniən/, *adj.* **1.** →**Portuguese.** **2.** *Biol.* of or pertaining to south-western Europe.

**lust** /lʌst/, *n.* **1.** passionate or overmastering desire (fol. by *for* or *of*): *lust for power.* **2.** sexual desire or appetite. **3.** unbridled or lawless sexual desire or appetite. **4.** sensuous desire or appetite considered as sinful. **5.** *Obs.* pleasure or delight. *–v.i.* **6.** to have strong or inordinate desire, esp. sexual desire (oft. fol. by *for* or *after*). [ME *luste,* OE *lust,* c. D *lust,* G *Lust* pleasure, desire]

**luster** /ˈlʌstə/, *n., v.t., v.i. U.S.* →**lustre.**

**lustered** /ˈlʌstəd/, *adj. U.S.* →**lustred.**

**lustful** /ˈlʌstfəl/, *adj.* **1.** full of or imbued with lust; libidinous. **2.** *Archaic.* lusty. **– lustfully,** *adv.* **– lustfulness,** *n.*

**lustral** /ˈlʌstrəl/, *adj.* **1.** of, pertaining to, or employed in the lustrum or rite of purification. **2.** occurring every five years. [L *lustrālis*]

**lustrate** /ˈlʌstreɪt/, *v.t.,* **-trated, -trating.** to purify by a propitiatory offering or other ceremonial method. [L *lustrātus,* pp.] **– lustration** /lʌsˈtreɪʃən/, *n.*

**lustre**[1] /ˈlʌstə/, *n.* **1.** the state or quality of shining by reflecting light; glitter, glisten, sheen, or gloss: *the lustre of satin.* **2.** some substance used to impart sheen or gloss. **3.** radiant or luminous brightness; radiance. **4.** radiance of beauty, excellence, merit distinction, or glory: *achievements that add lustre to one's name.* **5.** a shining object. **6.** a chandelier or candle holder, usu. ornamented with cut-glass pendants. **7.** a fabric of wool and cotton with a lustrous surface. **8.** *Ceramics.* a shiny, metallic, sometimes iridescent film produced on the surface of pottery or porcelain. **9.** *Mineral.* the nature of the surface of a mineral with respect to its reflecting qualities: *greasy lustre.* *–v.t.* **10.** to finish with a lustre or gloss. *–v.i.* **11.** *Rare.* to shine with lustre. Also, *U.S.,* **luster.** [F, from It. *lustro,* from *lustrare* to shine, from L: illuminate]

**lustre**[2] /ˈlʌstə/, *n.* →**lustrum.** Also, *U.S.,* **luster.**

**lustred** /ˈlʌstəd/, *adj.* having a lustre. Also, *U.S.,* **lustered.**

**lustrous** /ˈlʌstrəs/, *adj.* **1.** having lustre; shining; glossy, as silk; bright, as eyes. **2.** brilliant or splendid. **– lustrously,** *adv.* **– lustrousness,** *n.*

**lustrum** /ˈlʌstrəm/, *n., pl.* **-tra** /-trə/, **-trums.** **1.** a period of five years. **2.** a lustration or ceremonial purification of the ancient Roman people performed every five years, after the taking of the census. [L]

**lusty** /ˈlʌsti/, *adj.,* **-tier, -tiest.** **1.** full of or characterised by healthy vigour. **2.** hearty, as a meal or the like. [ME, from LUST, *n.* + -Y[1]] **– lustily,** *adv.* **– lustiness,** *n.*

**lutanist** /ˈlutənəst/, *n.* →**lutenist.**

**lute**[1] /lut/, *n., v.,* **luted, luting.** *–n.* **1.** a stringed musical instrument formerly much used, having a long, fretted neck and a hollow, typically pear-shaped body with a vaulted back, the strings being plucked with the fingers of one hand (or struck with a plectrum) and stopped on the frets with those of the other. *–v.i.* **2.** to play on a lute. [ME, from OF *lut,* from Pr. *laüt,* from Ar. *al-ʿūd* the lute]

lute[1]

**lute**[2] /lut/, *n., v.,* **luted, luting.** *–n.* **1.** →**luting.** *–v.t.* **2.** (in building) to seal or cement with luting. [ME, n., from ML *lutum* adhesive mud or clay]

**lutecium** /luˈtiʃəm/, *n.* →**lutetium.**

**lutenist** /ˈlutənəst/, *n.* a player on the lute. Also, **lutanist.** [ML *lūtānista,* from *lūtāna* lute]

**luteolin** /luˈtiələn/, *n.* a yellow colouring matter, $C_{15}H_{10}O_6$, obtained from the weed *Reseda luteolar,* used in dyeing silk, etc., and formerly in medicine. [F *lutéoline,* from L *lūteolus* yellowish]

**luteous** /ˈlutiəs/, *adj.* yellow, generally with a tinge of orange or red. [L *lūteus* golden yellow]

**lutetium** /luˈtiʃəm/, *n.* a lanthanide, or rare-earth, trivalent, metallic element. *Symbol:* Lu; *at. wt:* 174.97; *at. no.:* 71. Also, **lutecium.** Formerly, **cassiopeium.** [NL, from L *Lutetia* Paris]

**luth** /luθ/, *n.* →**leatherback.**

**Lutheran** /ˈluθərən/, *adj.* **1.** of or pertaining to Luther, adhering to his doctrines, or belonging to one of the Protestant churches which bears his name. *–n.* **2.** a follower of Luther, or an adherent of his doctrines; a member of the Lutheran Church. [from Martin *Luther,* 1483-1546, German leader of the Protestant Reformation] **– Lutheranism,** *n.*

**luthern** /ˈluθən/, *n.* a dormer window. [unexplained var. of obs. *lucerne,* from L *lucerna* window, light]

**luthier** /ˈlutiə/, *n.* originally a maker of lutes, but later of stringed instruments, as viols, violins, etc. [F]

**luting** /ˈlutɪŋ/, *n.* any viscous substance, as clay, concrete or mortar, used in building to fill gaps or joints. [see LUTE[2]]

**luv** /lʌv/, *n. Colloq.* variant of **love.**

**lux** /lʌks/, *n., pl.* **lux.** the derived SI unit of illumination, defined as an illumination of one lumen per square metre. *Symbol:* lx [L: light]

**luxate** /'lʌkseɪt/, *v.t.,* **-ated, -ating.** to put out of joint; dislocate. [L *luxātus,* pp.] – **luxation** /lʌk'seɪʃən/, *n.*

**Luxembourg** /'lʌksəmbɜg/, *n.* a constitutional monarchy and grand duchy between Germany, France, and Belgium.

**luxuriance** /lʌg'ʒuriəns/, *n.* the condition of being luxuriant; luxuriant growth or productiveness; rich abundance. Also, **luxuriancy.**

**luxuriant** /lʌg'ʒuriənt/, *adj.* **1.** abundant or exuberant in growth, as vegetation. **2.** producing abundantly, as soil. **3.** richly abundant, profuse, or superabundant. **4.** florid, as imagery or ornamentation. [L *luxurians,* ppr., growing rank] – **luxuriantly,** *adv.*

**luxuriate** /lʌg'ʒurieɪt/, *v.t.,* **-ated, -ating. 1.** to indulge in luxury; revel; enjoy oneself without stint. **2.** to take great delight. [L *luxuriātus,* pp., grown exuberantly, indulged to excess] – **luxuriation** /lʌg,ʒuri'eɪʃən/, *n.*

**luxurious** /lʌg'ʒuriəs/, *adj.* **1.** characterised by luxury; ministering or conducing to luxury: *a luxurious hotel.* **2.** given or inclined to luxury. – **luxuriously,** *adv.* – **luxuriousness,** *n.*

**luxury** /'lʌkʃəri/, *n., pl.* **-ries,** *adj.* *–n.* **1.** anything conducive to sumptuous living, usu. a delicacy, elegance, or refinement of living rather than a necessity. **2.** any form or means of enjoyment. **3.** free indulgence in sumptuous living, costly food, clothing, comforts, etc. **4.** the means of luxurious enjoyment or sumptuous living. *–adj.* **5.** pertaining or conducive to luxury. [ME *luxvrie* lust, from L *luxuria*]

**lw,** *Chem.* lawrencium.

**l.w.b.,** long wheel base.

**l.w.m.,** low-water mark.

**lx,** lux.

**-ly,** **1.** the normal adverbial suffix, added to almost any descriptive adjective, as in *gladly, gradually.* **2.** the adverbial suffix applied to units of time, meaning 'per', as in *hourly.* **3.** adjective suffix meaning 'like', as in *saintly, manly.* [ME *-li, -ly, lich(e),* OE *-līc,* c. G *-lich,* representing a Gmc noun (OE *līc,* etc.) meaning body. See LIKE[1]]

**l.y.,** light year.

**lycanthrope** /'laɪkənθroʊp, laɪ'kænθroʊp/, *n.* **1.** a person affected with lycanthropy. **2.** a werewolf or alien spirit in the physical form of a bloodthirsty wolf. [Gk *lykánthrōpos,* lit., wolf-man]

**lycanthropy** /laɪ'kænθrəpi/, *n.* **1.** a kind of insanity in which the patient imagines himself to be a wolf or other wild beast. **2.** the supposed or fabled assumption of the form of a wolf by a human being. – **lycanthropic** /laɪkən'θrɒpɪk/, *adj.*

**lycée** /'liseɪ/, *n.* (in France) a secondary school maintained by the state. [F, from L *Lycēum* LYCEUM]

**lyceum** /laɪ'siəm/, *n.* a building, hall, or the like, devoted to instruction by lectures; a library, etc. [L, from Gk *Lýkeion* the Lyceum at Athens (so named from the neighbouring temple of Apollo), properly neut. of *Lýkeios,* an epithet of Apollo]

**lychee** /laɪ'tʃi/, *n.* **1.** the fruit of a Chinese tree, *Litchi chinensis,* consisting of a thin brittle shell, enclosing a sweet jelly-like pulp and a single seed. **2.** the tree. Also, **lichee, lichi, litchi.** [Chinese *li-tchi*]

**lychee nut** /– 'nʌt/, *n.* the brownish, dried lychee fruit.

**lychgate** /'lɪtʃgeɪt/, *n.* →**lichgate.**

**lychnis** /'lɪknɪs/, *n.* any of the showy-flowered species of the genus *Lychnis* or related genera, as *Lychnis coronaria,* rose campion. [L, from Gk]

**lycopodium** /laɪkə'poʊdiəm/, *n.* **1.** Also, **lycopod** /'laɪkəpɒd/. any plant of the genus *Lycopodium,* which comprises erect or creeping usu. mosslike, evergreen-leaved pteridophytes, as *L. deuterodensum,* mountain moss; club moss. **2.** Also, **lycopodium powder.** a highly inflammable powder made from the spores of such a plant, used in making fireworks. [NL, from Gk *lýko(s)* wolf + *-podium* -PODIUM]

lychee

**lyddite** /'lɪdaɪt/, *n.* a high explosive consisting chiefly of picric acid. [named after *Lydd,* in Kent, England. See -ITE[1]]

**Lydian** /'lɪdiən/, *adj.* **1.** (of music) softly or sensuously sweet; voluptuous. *–n.* **2.** the language of Lydia, an ancient kingdom in western Asia Minor, probably Anatolian.

**Lydian mode** /– 'moʊd/, *n.* a scale, represented by the white keys of a keyboard instrument, beginning on F.

**lye** /laɪ/, *n.* any solution resulting from leaching, percolation, or the like. [ME *lie, ley,* OE *lēag,* c. G *Lauge*]

**lying**[1] /'laɪɪŋ/, *n.* **1.** the telling of lies; untruthfulness. *–adj.* **2.** that lies; untruthful; false. [from LIE[1]. See -ING[1], -ING[2]]

**lying**[2] /'laɪɪŋ/, *v.* present participle of **lie.**

**lying-in** /laɪɪŋ-'ɪn/, *n.* **1.** confinement in childbirth. *–adj.* **2.** pertaining to childbirth: *a lying-in hospital.*

**lyme grass** /'laɪm gras/, *n.* **1.** a large, glaucous, perennial grass, *Elymus arenarius,* widely distributed on coastal dunes in northern temperate regions. **2.** any other species of *Elymus.*

**lymph** /lɪmf/, *n.* a clear, yellowish, slightly alkaline fluid derived from the tissues of the body and conveyed to the bloodstream by the lymphatic vessels. [L *lympha* water]

**lymph-,** a combining form of **lymph,** as in *lymphoid.*

**lymphadenitis** /lɪm,fædə'naɪtəs, ,lɪmfædə-/, *n.* inflammation of a lymph gland. [LYMPH- + ADEN(O) + -ITIS]

**lymphangial** /lɪm'fændʒiəl/, *adj.* relating to the lymphatic vessels.

**lymphangitis** /lɪmfæn'dʒaɪtəs/, *n.* inflammation of the lymphatic vessels. Also, **lymphangiitis** /lɪm,fændʒi'aɪtəs/. [NL *lymphangiitis,* from *lymph-* LYMPH- + Gk *angeî(on)* vessel + *-ītis* -ITIS]

**lymphatic** /lɪm'fætɪk/, *adj.* **1.** pertaining to, containing, or conveying lymph: *a lymphatic vessel.* **2.** denoting, pertaining to, or having a temperament characterised by sluggishness of thought and action, formerly supposed to be due to an excess of lymph in the system. *–n.* **3.** a lymphatic vessel. [NL *lymphāticus* pertaining to lymph. Cf. L *lymphāticus* mad]

**lymph cell** /'lɪmf sɛl/, *n.* →**lymphocyte.**

**lymph gland** /– glænd/, *n.* any of the glandlike bodies occurring in the lymphatic vessels. Also, **lymph node, lymphatic gland.**

**lympho-,** variant of **lymph-,** before consonants.

**lymphocyte** /'lɪmfəsaɪt/, *n.* a leucocyte formed in lymphoid tissues, with little cytoplasm and no cytoplasmic granules. Their numbers are increased in certain diseases such as tuberculosis and typhoid fever. Also, **lymph cell.**

**lymphoid** /'lɪmfɔɪd/, *adj.* **1.** resembling, of the nature of, or pertaining to, lymph. **2.** denoting or pertaining to a tissue **(lymphoid tissue)** forming the greater part of the lymph glands. **3.** pertaining to a lymphocyte.

**lyncean** /lɪn'siən/, *adj.* **1.** lynxlike. **2.** sharp-sighted.

**lynch** /lɪntʃ/, *v.t.* to put (a person) to death (by hanging, burning, or otherwise) by some concerted action without authority or process of law, for some offence known or imputed. [see LYNCH LAW] – **lyncher,** *n.* – **lynching,** *n.*

**lynch law** /– lɔ/, *n.* the administration of summary punishment, esp. death, upon an offender (actual or reputed) by private persons acting in concert without authority of law. [orig. *Lynch's law;* named after Captain William *Lynch,* 1742-1820, of Virginia, U.S., who introduced the practice]

**lynch mob** /– mɒb/, *n.* **1.** a mob which lynches, or intends to lynch, a person. **2.** any group which acts, or attempts to act, in a harsh, arbitrary manner.

**lynx** /lɪŋks/, *n., pl.* **lynxes,** (*esp. collectively*) **lynx.** any of various wildcats of the genus *Lynx,* having long limbs and short tail, and usu. with tufted ears, as *L. rufus,* the **bay lynx,** a common North American species, and *L. canadensis,* a large, densely furred species of Canada and the northern U.S. [ME, from L, from Gk] – **lynxlike,** *adj.*

**lynx-eyed** /'lɪŋks-aɪd/, *adj.* →**sharp-sighted.**

**lyo-,** a word element meaning 'dispersion', 'solution', 'dissolved', as in *lyophilic.* [combining form representing Gk *lýein* dissolve]

**lyonnaise** /liə'neɪz/, *adj.* (of food, esp. fried potatoes) cooked with pieces of onion. [F]

**lyophilic** /laɪə'fɪlɪk/, *adj.* (of a colloid) having dispersed particles with an affinity for the liquid in which they are dispersed.

**lyophilise** /laɪ'ɒfəlaɪz/, *v.t.*, **-lised, -lising.** →**freeze-dry.** Also, **lyophilize.**

**lyophobic** /laɪə'foʊbɪk/, *adj.* (of a colloid) having dispersed particles with little or no affinity for the liquid in which they are dispersed.

lyrate leaf

**lyrate** /'laɪəreɪt, -rət/, *adj.* **1.** *Bot.* (of a pinnate leaf) divided transversely into several lobes, the smallest at the base. **2.** *Zool.* lyre-shaped, as the tail of certain birds. Also, **lyrated.**

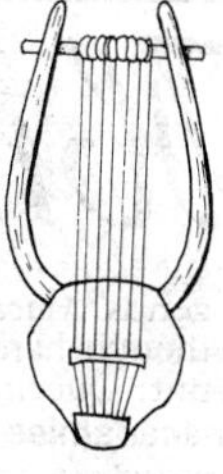
lyre

**lyre** /'laɪə/, *n.* a musical instrument of ancient Greece, consisting of a soundbox, with two curving arms carrying a crossbar (yoke) from which strings are stretched to the body, used to accompany the voice in singing and recitation. [ME *lire,* from OF, from L *lyra,* from Gk]

**lyrebird** /'laɪəbɜd/, *n.* either of two ground-dwelling birds of south-east Australia, the superb lyrebird, *Menura novaehollandiae,* and the Albert lyrebird, *M. alberti,* noted for their fine loud voices, powers of mimicry and the spectacular displays of the males during which they spread their long, lyre-shaped tails.

**lyric** /'lɪrɪk/, *adj.* Also, **lyrical** (for defs 1-6). **1.** (of poetry) having the form and musical quality of a song, and esp. the character of a songlike outpouring of the poet's own thoughts and feelings (as distinguished from *epic* and *dramatic* poetry, with their more extended and set forms and their presentation of external subjects). **2.** pertaining to or writing such poetry: *a lyric poet.* **3.** characterised by or indulging in a spontaneous, ardent expression of feeling. **4.** pertaining to, rendered by, or employing singing. **5.** pertaining, adapted, or sung to the lyre, or composing poems to be sung to the lyre: *ancient Greek lyric odes.* **6.** (of a voice) relatively light of volume and modest in range (most suited for graceful, cantabile melody). *–n.* **7.** a lyric poem. **8.** (*oft. pl.*) the words of a song. [L *lyricus,* from Gk *lyrikós* of a lyre] **– lyrically,** *adv.* **– lyricalness,** *n.*

**lyricism** /'lɪrəsɪzəm/, *n.* **1.** lyric character or style, as in poetry. **2.** lyric outpouring of feeling; emotionally expressed enthusiasm. Also, **lyrism.**

**lyricist** /'lɪrəsəst/, *n.* **1.** a lyric poet. **2.** one who writes the words for songs.

**lyrist** /'laɪərəst/ *for def. 1;* /'lɪrəst/ *for def. 2, n.* **1.** one who plays on the lyre. **2.** a lyric poet.

**lys-,** variant of **lyso-,** before vowels.

**lyse** /laɪs, laɪz/, *v.,* **lysed, lysing.** *–v.t.* **1.** to cause dissolution or destruction of cells by lysins. *–v.i.* **2.** to undergo lysis. [backformation from LYSIN]

lyrebird

**-lyse,** a word element making verbs of processes represented by nouns in *-lysis,* as in *catalyse.* Also, Chiefly *U.S.,* **-lyze.** [backformation from -LYSIS, influenced by -ISE[1]]

**lysergic acid** /laɪˌsɜdʒɪk 'æsəd/, *n.* **1.** a crystalline tetracyclic acid which can be produced from ergot. **2.** *Colloq.* →**LSD.**

**lysergic acid diethylamide,** *n.* See **LSD.**

**lysin** /'laɪsən/, *n.* an antibody or other agent which disintegrates the bacterial cell (bacteriolysis) or the red blood cell (haemolysis). [var. of LYSINE with arbitrary sense-distinction. See -IN[2]]

**lysine** /'laɪsin/, *n.* an essential amino acid, $NH_2(CH_2)_4CH(NH_3^+)COO^-$, occurring in proteins. [Gk *lýsis* a loosing + -INE[2]]

**lysis** /'laɪsəs/, *n.* **1.** *Med., Biochem.* the dissolution or destruction of cells by lysins or other agents. **2.** *Med.* the gradual recession of a disease, as distinguished from the crisis, in which the change is abrupt. [NL, from Gk: a loosing]

**-lysis,** a word element, esp. in scientific terminology, meaning breaking down, decomposition, as in *analysis, electrolysis.* [Gk. See LYSIS]

**lyso-,** a word element meaning 'decomposition'. Also, **lys-.** [Gk. See LYSIS]

**lysol** /'laɪsɒl/, *n.* (*sometimes cap.*) a clear, brown, oily liquid, a solution of cresols in soap, used as a disinfectant and antiseptic. [Trademark; from Gk *lýsis* solution + -OL[2]]

**lysosome** /'laɪsəsoʊm/, *n.* one of the minute granules, smaller than mitochondria but larger than microsomes, present in living cells, and containing many lytic enzymes. **– lysosomal** /laɪsə'soʊməl/, *adj.*

**lysozyme** /'laɪsəzaɪm/, *n.* an enzyme present in eggwhite, that acts as a bacteriocide by hydrolising polysaccharides of bacterial cell walls.

**lyssophobia** /lɪsə'foʊbiə/, *n.* **1.** morbid fear of insanity. **2.** morbid fear of rabies. [Gk *lýssa* rage, rabies + -O- + -PHOBIA]

**-lyte,** a word element denoting something subjected to a certain process (indicated by a noun ending in *-lysis*), as in *electrolyte.* [Gk *-lytos* that may be or is loosed]

**lythraceous** /lɪθ'reɪʃəs, laɪθ'reɪ-/, *adj.* belonging to the Lythraceae, or loosestrife family of plants.

**lytic** /'lɪtɪk/, *adj.* pertaining to *-lyte* or *-lysis,* esp. adapted in biochemistry to hydrolytic enzyme action. [independent use of -LYTIC]

**-lytic,** a termination of adjectives corresponding to nouns in *-lysis,* as in *analytic* (*analysis*), *paralytic* (*paralysis*). [Gk *-lytikós*]

**lytta** /'lɪtə/, *n., pl.* **lyttas, lyttae** /'lɪti/. a long, wormlike cartilage in the tongue of the dog and other carnivorous animals. [NL, from Gk, var. of *lýssa* rabies. See LYSSOPHOBIA]

**-lyze,** →**-lyse.**

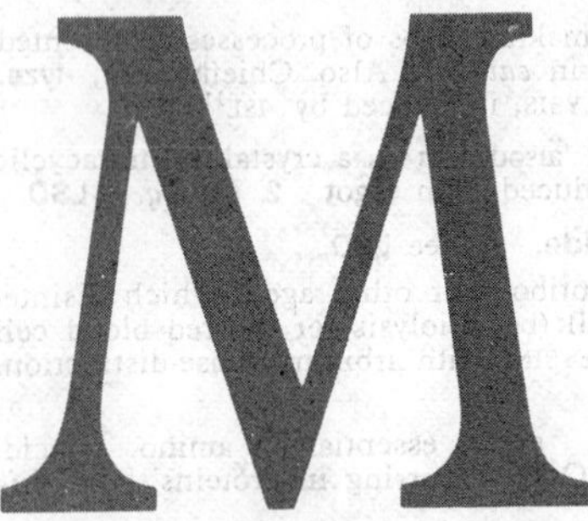

Mm Roman CHELTENHAM  Mm Sans Serif HARRY  Mm Script ARTSCRIPT  Mm Decorative TANNEN ERAS

*Although there are numerous typefaces in the world they can be divided into four main classifications. These are:*

*ROMAN or SERIF. This typeface came into being from the technique of the Roman masons who, working in stone, finished off each letter with a serif or small stroke projecting from the top or bottom. This was done to correct any feeling of unevenness or imbalance they may have created in cutting the characters in stone.*

*SANS SERIF (without serif). This typeface is geometric in design and has straight-edged characters and lines of a regular thickness.*

*SCRIPT. Based on the movement of the hand, this typeface is often italicised or slanted, as if drawn by a brush or quill pen.*

*DECORATIVE. Any typeface that exaggerates the characteristics of any of the other three classifications to a degree that places it outside of them.*

*The dictionary entries in this book use a SANS SERIF typeface called Helvetica (set in a bold face for the head words) and a SERIF typeface Plantin (used throughout the body of the entries).*

**M, m** /ɛm/, *n., pl.* **M's** or **Ms, m's** or **ms.** **1.** a consonant, the 13th letter of the English alphabet. **2.** the Roman numeral for 1000. **3.** *Print.* em.

**m,** **1.** metre. **2.** milli-.

**m-,** abridgment of **meta-** (def. 2).

**m.,** **1.** maiden over. **2.** male. **3.** mark. **4.** married. **5.** masculine. **6.** *Mech.* mass. **7.** medium. **8.** noon. [L *meridies*] **9.** mile. **10.** million. **11.** minim. **12.** minute. **13.** modification of. **14.** month. **15.** morning.

**M,** **1.** Middle. **2.** Medieval. **3.** mega-.

**M** /ɛm/, *adj.* denoting a film which parents are advised not to let their children see; a film for mature audiences.

**M.,** **1.** Majesty. **2.** medicine. **3.** meridian. **4.** noon. [L *meridies*] **5.** Monday. **6.** (*pl.* **MM**) Monsieur.

**ma** /ma/, *n. Colloq.* mamma; mother.

**mA,** milliampere.

**Ma,** *Chem.* masurium.

**M.A.** /ɛm 'eɪ/, Master of Arts. [L *Magister Artium*]

**ma'am** /mæm, mam/; *if unstressed* /məm/ *n.* **1.** madam. **2.** the term of address for a female royal person.

**Mabuiag** /'mɒbwiʌg/, *n.* an Australian Aboriginal language used by several thousand speakers in the Torres Strait Islands.

**mac** /mæk/, *n. Colloq.* mackintosh.

**Mac** /mæk/, *n. Chiefly U.S. Colloq.* →**Mack.**

**Mac-** /mæk, mək/, a prefix found in many family names of Irish or Scottish Gaelic origin. Also, written **Mc-, Mc,** and **M'-**. [Irish and Gaelic: son]

**macabre** /mə'kabə, -brə/, *adj.* **1.** gruesome; horrible; grim; ghastly. **2.** of or suggestive of the allegorical dance of death. [ME, from F, ? from Ar. *maqbara* graveyard]

**macadam** /mə'kædəm/, *n.* **1.** a macadamised road or pavement. **2.** the broken stone used in making such a road. [named after J. L. *McAdam,* 1756-1836, Scottish inventor]

**macadamia nut** /mækə'deɪmiə nʌt/, *n.* any small tree of the genus *Macadamia,* of eastern Australia, which bears edible though hard-shelled nuts and is grown commercially; bopple nut; Queensland nut.

**macadamise** /mə'kædəmaɪz/, *v.t.,* **-mised, -mising.** to construct (a road) by laying and rolling successive layers of broken stone. Also, **macadamize.** – **macadamisation** /mə,kædəmaɪ'zeɪʃən/, *n.*

**macaque** /mə'kak/, *n.* any monkey of the genus *Macaca,* chiefly found in Asia, characterised by cheek pouches and, generally, a short tail. [F, from Pg. *macaco,* from Fiot, a Congolese language]

stump-tailed macaque

**macaroni** /mækə'roʊni/, *n., pl.* **-nis, -nies.** **1.** a kind of pasta of Italian origin, prepared from wheat flour, in the form of dried, hollow tubes, to be cooked for food. **2.** an English dandy of the 18th century who affected foreign ways. **3.** *Colloq.* nonsense. Also, **maccaroni.** [It. *maccaroni, now maccheroni,* pl. of *maccarone,* now *maccherone,* from LGk *makaría* food of broth and pearl barley, orig. happiness]

**macaronic** /mækə'rɒnɪk/, *adj.* Also, **macaronical.** **1.** characterised by a mixture of Latin words with words from another language, or with non-Latin words provided with Latin terminations, as a kind of burlesque verse. **2.** involving a mixture of languages. **3.** *Obs.* mixed; jumbled. *–n.* **4.** (*pl.*) macaronic verses. [ML *macarōnicus,* from It. *maccaroni* MACARONI] – **macaronically,** *adv.*

**macaroni cheese** /,mækəroʊni 'tʃiz/, *n.* a dish of macaroni, usu. baked in a cheese sauce.

**macaroon** /mækə'run/, *n.* a sweet cake or biscuit made of eggwhites, sugar, little or no flour, and frequently almond paste, coconut, etc. [F *macaron,* from It. *maccarone,* sing., MACARONI]

**Macassar oil** /mə,kæsər 'ɔɪl/, *n.* **1.** (originally) an oil for the hair made from materials obtained from Macassar, a seaport in Indonesia. **2.** a similar oil or preparation for the hair.

**macaw** /mə'kɔ/, *n.* any of various large, long-tailed parrots, chiefly of the genus *Ara,* of tropical and subtropical America, noted for their brilliant plumage and harsh voice. [Pg. *macao;* of Brazilian orig.]

**maccaboy** /'mækəbɔɪ/, *n.* a kind of snuff, usu. rose-scented. Also, **maccoboy.** [from *Macouba,* name of district in Martinique, an island in the E Indies]

**maccaroni** /mækə'roʊni/, *n., pl.* **-nis, -nies.** →**macaroni.**

**mace**[1] /meɪs/, *n.* **1.** *Hist.* a clublike weapon of war often with a flanged or spiked metal head. **2.** a staff borne before or by certain officials as a symbol of office. **3.** the bearer of such a staff. **4.** *Billiards.* a light stick with a flat head, formerly used instead of a cue. [ME, from OF. Cf. L *mateola* mallet]

**mace**[2] /meɪs/, *n.* a spice ground from the layer between a nutmeg shell and its outer husk, resembling nutmeg in flavour. [ME *macis,* from OF, from L *mac(c)is* a spice]

**mace-bearer** /'meɪs-bɛərə/, *n.* one who carries the mace, as in a procession, before dignitaries.

**macedoine** /mæsə'dwan/, *n.* **1.** a mixture of vegetables or fruit diced and served as a salad or otherwise. **2.** a jellied mixture of fruits. **3.** →**medley** (def. 1). Also, **macédoine.** [F: lit., Macedonian]

**macer** /'meɪsə/, *n.* →**mace-bearer.** [ME *masere,* from OF *maissier,* from *masse* MACE[1]]

mace[1]

**macerate** /'mæsəreɪt/, *v.,* **-rated, -rating.** *–v.t.* **1.** to soften, or separate the parts of (a substance) by steeping in a liquid, with or without heat. **2.** to soften or break up (food) by action of a solvent. **3.** to cause to grow thin. *–v.i.* **4.** to undergo maceration. **5.** to become thin; waste away. [L *mācerātus,* pp.] **– macerater, macerator,** *n.* **– maceration** /mæsə'reɪʃən/, *n.*

**mach** /mæk/, *n.* the ratio of the speed of an object to the speed of sound in the medium, usu. air; mach 1 in air is about 380 metres per second at sea level. See **mach number.** [named after Ernst *Mach,* 1838-1916, Austrian physicist]

**mach.,** **1.** machine. **2.** machinery. **3.** machinist.

**machete** /mə'ʃɛti/, *n.* a large, heavy knife used esp. in Latin-American countries as both a tool and a weapon. [Sp., from L *mactāre* slaughter]

**Machiavellian** /mækiə'vɛliən/, *adj.* **1.** of, like, or befitting Machiavelli. **2.** being or acting in accordance with Machiavelli's political doctrines, which placed expediency above political morality, and countenanced the use of craft and deceit in order to maintain the authority and effect the purposes of the ruler. **3.** characterised by subtle or unscrupulous cunning; wily; astute. *–n.* **4.** a follower of Machiavelli or his doctrines. Also, **Machiavelian.** [from Niccolò di Bernardo *Machiavelli,* 1469-1527, Italian statesman and writer] **– Machiavellianism, Machiavellism,** *n.*

**machicolated** /mə'tʃɪkəleɪtəd/, *adj.* furnished with machicolations. [ML *machicolātus,* pp. + -ED[2]]

**machicolation** /mətʃɪkə'leɪʃən/, *n.* **1.** an opening in the floor between the corbels of a projecting gallery or parapet, as on a wall or in the vault of a passage, through which missiles, molten lead, etc., might be cast upon an enemy beneath. **2.** a projecting gallery or parapet with such openings.

machicolation

**machinate** /'mæʃəneɪt, 'mækəneɪt/, *v.,* **-nated, -nating.** to contrive or devise, esp. artfully or with evil purpose. [L *māchinātus,* pp.] **– machinator,** *n.*

**machination** /mæʃə'neɪʃən, mækə'neɪʃən/, *n.* **1.** the act or process of machinating. **2.** (*usu. pl.*) a crafty scheme; evil design; plot.

**machine** /mə'ʃin/, *n., v.,* **-chined, -chining.** *–n.* **1.** an apparatus consisting of interrelated parts with separate functions, which is used in the performance of some kind of work: *a sewing machine.* **2.** a mechanical apparatus or contrivance; a mechanism. **3.** something operated by a mechanical apparatus, as a motor vehicle, a bicycle, or an aeroplane. **4.** *Mech.* **a.** a device which transmits and modifies force or motion. **b. simple machines,** the six (sometimes more) elementary mechanisms, i.e., the lever, wheel and axle, pulley, screw, wedge, and inclined plane. **5.** a contrivance, esp. in the ancient theatre, for producing stage effects. **6.** some agency, personage, incident, or other feature introduced for effect into a literary composition. **7.** any complex agency or operating system: *the machine of government.* **8.** the body of persons conducting and controlling the activities of a political party or other organisation. **9.** a person or agency acting like a mere mechanical apparatus. **10. the machine,** *N.Z.* →**totalisator.** *–v.t.* **11.** to make, prepare, or finish with a machine. [F, from L *māchina,* from Doric Gk *māchanā́,* Attic Gk *mēchanḗ*]

**machine-finished** /mə'ʃin-fɪnɪʃt/, *adj.* of or pertaining to paper which has received no additional finishing process after leaving the paper-making machine.

**machine-gun** /mə'ʃin-gʌn/, *n., v.,* **-gunned, -gunning.** *–n.* **1.** a small arm operated by a mechanism, able to deliver a rapid and continuous fire of bullets as long as the firer keeps pressure on the trigger. *–v.t.* **2.** to shoot at, using a machine-gun.

**machine language** /mə'ʃin læŋgwɪdʒ/, *n.* a low-level and therefore complex binary code which is a precise set of operating instructions for a computer, as opposed to a more symbolic, generalised code. Also, **machine code.**

**machinery** /mə'ʃinəri/, *n., pl.* **-ries.** **1.** machines or mechanical apparatus. **2.** the parts of a machine, collectively: *the machinery of a watch.* **3.** contrivances for producing stage effects. **4.** personages, incidents, etc., introduced into a literary composition, as in developing a story or plot. **5.** any system by which action is maintained: *the machinery of government.*

**machine shop** /mə'ʃin ʃɒp/, *n.* a workshop in which metal and other substances are cut, shaped, etc., by machine tools.

**machine tool** /'– tul/, *n.* a power-operated machine, as a lathe, etc., used for general cutting and shaping operations.

**machinist** /mə'ʃinəst/, *n.* **1.** a person who operates machinery, esp. a highly trained and skilled operator of machine tools. **2.** a person, esp. a girl, employed to operate a sewing machine. **3.** one who makes and repairs machines. **4.** *Rare.* a person who builds or operates machinery in a theatre.

**machismo** /mə'tʃɪzmoʊ, mə'kɪzmoʊ/, *n.* flamboyant virility; masculine display emphasising strength.

**machmeter** /'mækmitə/, *n.* an instrument which indicates the mach number of an aircraft when it is in flight.

**mach number** /'mæk nʌmbə/, *n.* a number indicating the ratio between the airspeed of an object and the speed of sound at a given altitude, etc.

**macho** /'mætʃoʊ, 'mækoʊ/, *n.* **1.** a man who displays machismo. *–adj.* **2.** showily virile. [Mex. Sp.]

**-machy,** a combining form meaning combat, as in *logomachy.* [Gk *-machia,* from *-machos* fighting]

**Mack** /mæk/, *n. Chiefly U.S. Colloq.* (an informal term of address to a man.)

**mackerel** /'mækərəl/, *n.* **1.** a common iridescent greenish fish with irregular darker markings on the back, *Scomber australasicus,* widely distributed in Australian and New Zealand waters and in various parts of the Pacific. **2.** →**Spanish mackerel.** **3.** an abundant food fish of the North Atlantic, *Scomber scombrus,* with wavy cross markings on the back and streamlined for swift swimming. [ME *makerel,* from OF *maquerel;* orig. unknown]

mackerel (def. 3)

**mackerel shark** /'– ʃak/, *n.* **1.** →**porbeagle.** **2.** a shark belonging to the family Lamnidae, esp. of the genus *Isurus.*

**mackerel sky** /– 'skaɪ/, *n.* **1.** sky nearly covered with high, small, white, fleecy clouds arranged in bands. **2.** an extensive group of altocumulus clouds arranged in regular waves with blue sky showing in the gaps.

**mackintosh** /'mækəntɒʃ/, *n.* **1.** a raincoat made of cloth rendered waterproof by indiarubber. **2.** such cloth. **3.** any raincoat. Also, **macintosh.** [named after Charles *Macintosh,* 1766-1843, the inventor]

**mackle** /'mækəl/, *n., v.,* **-led, -ling.** *–n.* **1.** a blur in printing, as from a double impression. *–v.t.* **2.** to blur, as from a double impression in printing. *–v.i.* **3.** to become blurred. Also, **macule.** [F *macule,* from L *macula* spot]

**macle** /'mækəl/, *n.* →**twin** (def. 5). [F, from L *macula* spot]

**Macquarie Island** /mə,kwɒri 'aɪlənd/, *n.* an island south east of Tasmania, which is a dependency of Tasmania.

**macramé** /mə'krami/, *n.* a kind of lace or ornamental work made by knotting thread or cord in patterns. [cf. Turk. *magrama* towel, handkerchief, etc.]

**macro-**, a prefix meaning 'long', 'large', 'great', 'excessive', used esp. in scientific terminology, contrasting with *micro-,* as in *macrocosm, macropod.* Also, before vowels, **macr-**. [Gk *makro-,* combining form of *makrós*]

**macrobiotic** /ˌmækroubaɪˈɒtɪk/, *adj.* **1.** relating to the prolongation of life; tending to prolong life. **2.** of or pertaining to a largely vegetarian dietary system formulated as part of Zen Buddhism and intended to prolong life.

**macrocarpa** /mækrouˈkapə/, *n.* the evergreen conifer, *Cupressus macrocarpa,* often planted for ornament and for windbreaks and shelter-belts.

**macrocosm** /ˈmækrəkɒzəm/, *n.* the great world, or universe (opposed to *microcosm*). [F *macrocosme,* from ML *macrocosmus,* from *macro-* MACRO- + Gk *kósmos* world] – **macrocosmic** /mækrəˈkɒzmɪk/, *adj.*

**macrocyst** /ˈmækrousɪst/, *n.* **1.** a cyst of large size, esp. the archicarp of certain fungi of the group Discomycetes. **2.** a multinuclear mass of protoplasm enclosed in a cyst.

**macrocyte** /ˈmækrousaɪt/, *n.* an abnormally large red blood cell. – **macrocytic** /mækrouˈsɪtɪk/, *adj.*

**macrocytic anaemia** /ˌmækrousɪtɪk əˈnimiə/, *n.* an anaemia characterised by predominance of macrocytes.

**macrodont** /ˈmækrədɒnt/, *adj.* **1.** having large teeth. *–n.* **2.** a large tooth. – **macrodontous** /mækrəˈdɒntəs/, *adj.*

**macro-economic** /ˌmækrou-ɛkəˈnɒmɪk, -ikə-/, *adj.* of or pertaining to the economy as a whole.

**macro-economics** /ˌmækrou-ɛkəˈnɒmɪks, -ikə-/, *n.* study of the economic system as a whole, as opposed to micro-economics. [MACRO - + ECONOMICS]

**macrogamete** /mækrouˈgæmit/, *n.* the female (and larger) of two conjugating gametes. Also, **megagamete.**

**macrograph** /ˈmækrougræf/, *n.* a photograph or other image equal to or larger than the original.

**macromolecule** /mækrouˈmɒləkjul/, *n.* a molecule of very large size, as of a synthetic polymer, protein or nucleic acid.

**macron** /ˈmækrɒn/, *n.* a short horizontal line used as a diacritic over a vowel to indicate that it is a 'long' sound, as in *fāte.* [Gk *makrón,* neut., long]

**macronutrient** /mækrouˈnjutriənt/, *n.* a substance, as oxygen, hydrogen, etc., required in large amounts, for good health. Cf. **micronutrient.**

**macrophysics** /ˈmækrouˌfɪzɪks, ˌmækrouˈfɪzɪks/, *n.* the part of physics that deals with physical objects large enough to be observed and treated directly.

**macropod** /ˈmækrəpɒd/, *adj.* **1.** of or related to the Macropodidae, a family of herbivorous marsupials comprising the kangaroos, wallabies, rat-kangaroos and tree-kangaroos, having short forelimbs, long hind limbs adapted for hopping, and long, muscular tails. *–n.* **2.** a macropod marsupial. Also, **macropodid.** [MACRO- + -POD]

macropod: kangaroo

**macroscopic** /mækrəˈskɒpɪk/, *adj.* **1.** visible to the naked eye (opposed to *microscopic*). **2.** comprehensive; concerned with large units or issues.

**macrosporangium** /ˌmækrouspəˈrændʒiəm/, *n.* →**megasporangium.**

**macrospore** /ˈmækrouspɔ/, *n.* →**megaspore.**

**macrosporophyll** /mækrouˈspɒrəfɪl/, *n.* →**megasporophyll.**

**macrostructure** /ˈmækroustrʌktʃə/, *n.* **1.** *Metall.* the general crystalline structure of metals and alloys as revealed on an etched surface examined by the naked eye or at low magnification. **2.** *Geol.* a structural feature of rocks that can be discerned by the unaided eye or with the aid of a simple magnifier.

**macrozamia** /mækrouˈzeɪmiə/, *n.* any species of the Australian genus *Macrozamia,* a group of plants with stiff, palm-like pinnate leaves and nut-like fruit, as the *M. spiralis,* or burrawang, of the eastern coast.

**macruran** /məˈkrurən/, *adj.* **1.** belonging or pertaining to the Macrura, a group of stalk-eyed decapod crustaceans with long tails, including lobsters, shrimps, etc. *–n.* **2.** a macruran crustacean. [NL *macrūra,* pl. (from Gk *makrós* long + *ourá* tail) + -AN]

**macrurous** /məˈkrurəs/, *adj.* long-tailed, as the lobster (opposed to *brachyurous*).

**macula** /ˈmækjələ/, *n., pl.* **-lae** /-li/. a spot as on the sun, in the skin, or the like. [ME, from L] – **macular,** *adj.*

**maculate** /ˈmækjəleɪt/, *v.,* **-lated, -lating;** /ˈmækjələt/, *adj.* *–v.t.* **1.** to mark with a spot or spots; stain. **2.** to sully or pollute. *–adj.* **3.** spotted; stained. **4.** defiled or impure. [late ME, from L *maculātus,* pp.]

**maculation** /mækjəˈleɪʃən/, *n.* **1.** the act of spotting. **2.** a spotted condition. **3.** a marking of spots, as on an animal. **4.** a disfiguring spot or stain.

**macule** /ˈmækjul/, *n., v.t., v.i.,* **-uled, -uling.** →**mackle.**

**mad** /mæd/, *adj.,* **madder, maddest,** *v.,* **madded, madding.** *–adj.* **1.** disordered in intellect; insane. **2.** *Colloq.* moved by anger. **3.** (of wind, etc.) furious in violence. **4.** (of animals) **a.** abnormally furious: *a mad bull.* **b.** affected with rabies; rabid: *a mad dog.* **5.** wildly excited; frantic: *mad haste.* **6.** senselessly foolish or imprudent: *a mad scheme.* **7.** wild with eagerness or desire; infatuated: *to be mad about someone.* **8.** wildly gay or merry: *to have a mad time.* **9. like mad, a.** in the manner of a madman. **b.** with great haste, impetuosity, or enthusiasm. **10. mad as a cut snake,** *Colloq.* insane; crazy. [ME *mad, madd(e),* OE *gemǣd(d), gemǣded,* pp. of a verb derived from OE *gemād* mad, c. OHG *gameit* foolish]

**Madagascan realm** /mædəˌgæskən ˈrɛlm/, *n.* a biogeographical realm comprising the islands of **Madagascar, Mauritius, Reunion, Rodriguez** and the **Seychelles,** the mammal and bird assemblies of which differ significantly from those of neighbouring Africa. Distinctive birds were the dodo and solitaire, now extinct.

**Madagascar** /mædəˈgæskə/, *n.* an island republic in the Indian Ocean, off the south-east coast of Africa. Official name: **Democratic Republic of Madagascar.** – **Madagascan,** *adj., n.*

**madam** /ˈmædəm/, *n., pl.* **madams** /ˈmædəmz/, **mesdames** /meɪˈdæm, -ˈdam/. **1.** a polite term of address used originally to a woman of rank or authority, but now used to any woman. **2.** the woman in charge of a brothel. [ME *madame,* from OF, orig. *ma dame* my lady. See DAME]

**Madame** /məˈdam, ˈmædəm/, *n., pl.* **mesdames** /meɪˈdæm, -ˈdam/. a conventional French title of respect for a married woman (equivalent to *Mrs*) or for a woman whose marital status is unknown; also sometimes applied by English speakers to a married woman who is not English-speaking: *Madame Chiang Kai-shek. Abbrev.:* Mme, *pl.* Mmes. [F. See MADAM]

**madcap** /ˈmædkæp/, *adj.* **1.** wildly impulsive; lively: *a madcap girl.* *–n.* **2.** a madcap person, esp. a girl.

**madden** /ˈmædn/, *v.t.* **1.** to make mad or insane. **2.** to infuriate. *–v.i.* **3.** to become mad; act as if mad; rage.

**maddening** /ˈmædənɪŋ/, *adj.* **1.** driving to madness or frenzy. **2.** infuriating; exasperating. – **maddeningly,** *adv.*

**madder** /ˈmædə/, *n.* **1.** a plant of the rubiaceous genus *Rubia,* esp. *R. tinctorum,* a European herbaceous climbing plant with panicles of small yellowish flowers. **2.** the root of this plant, used to some extent (esp. formerly) in medicine, and particularly for making dyes which give red and other colours. **3.** the dye or colouring matter itself. **4.** a colour produced by such a dye. [ME *mad(d)er,* OE *mæd(e)re,* c. Icel. *madhra*]

**madding** /ˈmædɪŋ/, *adj.* **1.** mad; acting as if mad: *the madding crowd.* **2.** making mad.

**made** /meɪd/, *v.* **1.** past tense and past participle of **make.** *–adj.* **2.** produced by making, preparing, etc. **3.** artificially produced. **4.** assured of success or fortune: *a made man.* **5. have (got) it made,** to be assured of success.

**madeira** /məˈdɪərə/, *n.* a rich, strong, white wine resembling sherry. [from *Madeira,* an island off the coast of Africa, where it was orig. made; from Pg.: lit., wood, timber, from L *māteria;* so called because island was once thickly forested]

**Madeira cake** /məˈdɪərə keɪk/, *n.* a rich, yellow cake, containing no fruit, and flavoured only with lemon.

**Madeira vine** /ˈ– vaɪn/, *n.* a rapidly growing, twining plant, *Anredera cordifolia,* with a tuberous root, long leaves and fragrant white flowers. Also, **mignonette vine.**

**madeleine** /ˈmædəleɪn/, *n.* a small, fancy sponge cake baked in a dariole, coated with jam and desiccated coconut.

**mademoiselle** /ˌmædəmwəˈzɛl, ˌmæmwəˈzɛl, mæmˈzɛl/, *n., pl.* **mesdemoiselles** /ˌmeɪdəmwəˈzɛl/. **1.** (*cap.*) the conventional

French title of respect and term of address for a girl or unmarried woman (equivalent to *Miss*). *Abbrev.*: Mlle, *pl.* Mlles. **2.** a young, unmarried girl or woman. [F, orig. *ma demoiselle* my demoiselle. See DEMOISELLE, DAMSEL]

**made-money** /'meɪd-mʌni/, *adj.* of or pertaining to a money-market borrow-and-lend operation which results in a sure profit.

**maderise** /'mædəraɪz/, *v.i.*, **-rised, -rising.** (of wine) to become old and woody. [Sp. *madera* MADEIRA] – **maderisation** /mædəraɪ'zeɪʃən/, *n.*

**made-to-measure** /'meɪd-tə-mɛʒə/, *adj.* (of clothes, etc.) made to fit an individual; made to fit individual requirements; made-to-order.

**made-to-order** /'meɪd-tu-ɔdə/, *adj.* →**made-to-measure.**

**made-up** /'meɪd-ʌp/, *adj.* **1.** concocted; invented: *a made-up story.* **2.** wearing facial cosmetics. **3.** put together; finished.

**madhouse** /'mædhaʊs/, *n.* **1.** an asylum for the insane. **2.** a place of commotion and confusion.

**madison** /'mædəsən/, *n.* (in cycling) a long-distance track race between teams of riders in which each team must have at least one of its riders on the track at any one stage of the race. [from races held in the 1890s in *Madison* Square Gardens, U.S.]

**madly** /'mædli/, *adv.* **1.** insanely. **2.** wildly; furiously: *they worked madly to fix the bridge.* **3.** foolishly.

**madman** /'mædmən/, *n.*, *pl.* **-men.** an insane person.

**mad mullah** /mæd 'mʌlə/, *n. Colloq.* one whose behaviour is wild and unrestrained. [see MULLAH]

**madness** /'mædnəs/, *n.* **1.** the state of being mad; insanity. **2.** →**rabies. 3.** senseless folly. **4.** frenzy; rage.

**mado** /'meɪdoʊ/, *n.* a small sea fish, *Atypichthys mado* or *A. strigatus*, found in southern Australian and northern New Zealand waters. [Aboriginal]

**Madonna** /mə'dɒnə/, *n.* **1.** the Virgin Mary (usu. prec. by *the*). **2.** a picture or statue representing the Virgin Mary. **3.** *Obs.* (*l.c.*) an Italian title of respect for a woman. [It.: my lady. See DONNA]

**Madonna lily** /– 'lɪli/, *n.* a perennial herb with long stems bearing pure white flowers, *Lilium candidum,* native to the eastern Mediterranean region, but cultivated since early times.

**madras** /mə'dræs/, *n.* **1.** a light cotton fabric with cords set at intervals or with woven stripes or figures, often of another colour, used for shirts, etc. **2.** Also, **madras muslin.** a thin curtain fabric of a light, gauzelike weave with figures of heavier yarns. **3.** a large brightly coloured kerchief, of either silk or cotton, often used for turbans. [named after *Madras,* state in India]

**Madras** /mə'dræs/, *adj.* **1.** of or pertaining to an Indian dish flavoured with fragrant spices, esp. chilli: *beef Madras.* *–n.* **2.** such a dish. [from *Madras,* India, where the dish originated]

**madrepore** /'mædrəpɔ/, *n.* any of various corals (**madreporarians**) of the genus *Madrepora,* noted for reef-building in tropical seas. [F, from It. *madrepora,* apparently from *madre* mother (from L *māter*) + *poro* (from Gk *pôros* kind of stone)] – **madreporic** /mædrə'pɒrɪk/, *adj.*

madrepore

**madrigal** /'mædrɪgəl/, *n.* **1.** a lyric poem suitable for musical setting, usu. short and often of amatory character (esp. in vogue in the 16th century and later in Italy, France, England, and elsewhere). **2.** a part-song without instrumental accompaniment, usu. for five or six voices, and making abundant use of contrapuntal imitation. **3.** any part-song. **4.** any song. [It. *madrigale,* from ML *mātricālis* simple, naive, from L *mātrix* womb]

**madrigalist** /'mædrɪgələst/, *n.* a composer or a singer of madrigals.

**madrilène** /mædrə'lɛn/, *n.* a clear thin soup made with a chicken stock and strongly flavoured with tomato. [F]

**madroña** /mə'droʊnjə/, *n.* an evergreen tree or shrub, *Arbutus menziesii,* of western North America, having a hard wood and a smooth bark, and bearing a yellow, scarcely edible berry. Also, **madroño.** [Sp.: the arbutus or strawberry tree, from L *mātūrus* ripe]

**maduro** /mə'djʊəroʊ/, *adj.* (of cigars) strong and darkly coloured. [Sp.: mature, from L *mātūrus*]

**madwoman** /'mædwʊmən/, *n.* **1.** a woman who is insane. **2.** *Colloq.* a woman whose behaviour is considered to be outrageous or eccentric. **3. be all over the place** or **look like a madwoman's breakfast** (**washing**) (**custard**) (**knitting**) (**lunch box**), *Colloq.* to be in complete confusion and disarray.

**maelstrom** /'meɪlstrəm/, *n.* **1.** any great or violent whirlpool. **2.** a restless confusion of affairs, influence, etc. [from *Maelstrom,* famous whirlpool off the coast of Norway; early mod. D, from *malen* grind, whirl + *stroom* stream]

**maemae** /'maɪmaɪ/, *n.* →**mai mai.**

**maenad** /'minæd/, *n.* frenzied or raging woman. Also, **menad.** [in Greek mythology, a female attendant of Dionysus; L *Maenas,* from Gk *mainás* a mad woman] – **maenadic** /mi'nædɪk/, *adj.*

**maestoso** /maɪs'toʊsoʊ/, *adv.* **1.** (a musical direction) in a majestic or stately manner. *–adj.* **2.** majestic; stately. [It., from *maesta* majesty, from L *mājestas*]

**maestro** /'maɪstroʊ/, *n.*, *pl.* **-tri** /-tri/. **1.** an eminent musical composer, teacher, or conductor. **2.** (*cap.*) a title of respect for addressing such a person. **3.** a master of any art. [It.: master]

**Mae West** /meɪ 'wɛst/, *n.* an inflatable life-preserving jacket for airmen or sailors who fall in the sea. [named after *Mae West,* 1892-1980, U.S. actress]

**maffick** /'mæfɪk/, *v.i. Chiefly Brit.* to celebrate with extravagant public demonstrations. [backformation from *Mafeking,* a town in N part of the Republic of South Africa which was besieged for 217 days by the Boers 1899-1900; the relief of the town was celebrated in London with extravagant joy] – **mafficker,** *n.*

**Mafia** /'mafiə, 'mæfiə/, *n.* **1.** (in Sicily) **a.** (*l.c.*) a popular spirit of hostility to legal restraint and to the law, often manifesting itself in criminal acts. **b.** a 19th-century secret society (similar to the Camorra in Naples) acting in this spirit. **2.** a criminal secret society of Sicilians or other Italians, at home or in foreign countries. Also, **Maffia.** [It. (Sicilian): boldness, bravery, from *Màffio,* var. of *Maffèo,* from L *Matthaeus* Matthew]

**mafic** /'mæfɪk/, *adj.* of some igneous rocks and their constituent minerals, composed dominantly of the magnesium rock-forming silicates. Cf. **felsic.**

**mag** /mæg/, *v.i.* to chatter; to talk rapidly and to little purpose. – **magger,** *n.*

**mag.** /mæg/, **1.** magazine. **2.** magnetism. **3.** magnitude.

**magazine** /mægə'zin/, *n.* **1.** a periodical publication, usu. bound and with a paper cover, containing miscellaneous articles or pieces, in prose or verse, often with illustrations. **2.** a program on radio or television, usu. documentary, on a number of miscellaneous topics. **3.** a room or place for keeping gunpowder and other explosives, as in a fort or on a warship. **4.** a building or place for keeping military stores, as arms, ammunition, provisions, etc. **5.** a collection of war munitions. **6.** a metal receptacle for a number of cartridges which is inserted into certain types of automatic weapons and which must be removed when empty and replaced by a full receptacle in order to continue firing. **7.** a supply chamber as in a stove, etc. **8.** *Photog.* a light-proof enclosure containing film which enables a camera to be loaded or unloaded in daylight. **9.** a storehouse; warehouse. *–adj.* **10.** of or pertaining to a magazine. [F *magasin,* from It. *magazzino* storehouse, from Ar. *makhāzin,* pl. of *makhzan* storehouse]

**Magdalenian** /mægdə'liniən/, *adj.* denoting the period or culture stage in the Old World Stone Age (Upper Palaeolithic) in which Cro-Magnon man reached his highest level of industry and art. [Latinised form of (La) *Madeleine,* France, where implements and art of this period were found. See -IAN]

**mage** /meɪdʒ/, *n. Archaic.* →**magician.** [ME, from F, from L *magus*]

**Magellanic cloud** /ˌmædʒəlænɪk 'klaʊd/, *n.* either of two bright cloud-like patches of stars in the southern heavens. [named after Ferdinand *Magellan,* c. 1480-1521,

Portuguese navigator]

**magenta** /məˈdʒɛntə/, *n.* **1.** →**fuchsine.** **2.** reddish purple. –*adj.* **3.** of reddish purple colour. [named after *Magenta,* town in N Italy, west of Milan]

**maggie** /ˈmægi/, *n. Colloq.* a magpie.

**maggot** /ˈmægət/, *n.* **1.** the legless larva of a fly, as of the housefly. **2.** a fly larva living in decaying matter. **3.** an odd fancy; whim. **4. mad as a maggot,** *Colloq.* very angry. [ME *magot;* orig. uncert.]

**maggoty** /ˈmægəti/, *adj.* **1.** infested with maggots, as food. **2.** having queer notions; full of whims. **3.** *Colloq.* angry.

**Magi** /ˈmeɪdʒaɪ/, *n.pl., sing.* **-gus** /-gəs/. **1.** (*also l.c.*) the three wise men who came from the east to Jerusalem to do homage to the infant Jesus. **2.** the Zoroastrian priests of ancient Media and Persia, reputed to possess supernatural powers. [see MAGUS] – **Magian,** *adj.* – **Magianism,** *n.*

**magic** /ˈmædʒɪk/, *n.* **1.** the art of producing effects claimed to be beyond the natural human power and arrived at by means of supernatural agencies or through command of occult forces in nature. **2.** the exercise of this art. **3.** the effects produced. **4.** power or influence exerted through this art. **5.** any extraordinary or irresistible influence: *the magic in a great name.* **6.** legerdemain; conjuring. –*adj.* Also, **magical. 7.** employed in magic: *magic spells.* **8.** mysteriously enchanting: *magic beauty.* **9.** of, pertaining to, or due to magic: *magic rites.* **10.** producing the effects of magic; like magic. [ME *magike,* from LL *magica,* in L *magicē,* from Gk *magikḗ,* properly fem. of *magikós* Magian, magic] – **magically,** *adv.*

**magic carpet** /– ˈkapət/, *n.* a legendary carpet on which a person may travel wherever he wants to.

**magic eye** /– ˈaɪ/, *n.* **1.** *Electronics.* a triode valve with a special fluorescent coating, used to tune radio receivers; as the tuning dial is moved the fluorescence varies in proportion to the carrier intensity. **2.** a photo-mechanism used to distinguish winners of races where the contests are close.

**magician** /məˈdʒɪʃən/, *n.* **1.** one skilled in magic arts. **2.** a juggler; conjurer. [ME *magicien,* from OF, from L *magicus* MAGIC]

**magic lantern** /mædʒɪk ˈlæntən/, *n.* a lantern-slide projector.

**magic mushroom** /– ˈmʌʃrum/, *n.* →**gold top.**

**magic number** /– ˈnʌmbə/, *n.* any one of the numbers 2, 8, 20, 28, 50, 82, or 126; atomic nuclei containing these numbers of neutrons or protons have exceptional stability.

**magic square** /– ˈskwɛə/, *n.* a square array of integers such that the sums of the numbers in each row and each column are all the same.

**maginnis** /məˈgɪnəs/, *n.* **1.** Also **crooked maginnis.** a wrestling hold from which there is no escape. **2. put the maginnis on (someone),** to have (someone) completely in one's power. [? from a wrestler named *McGinnis*]

**magisterial** /mædʒəsˈtɪəriəl/, *adj.* **1.** of, pertaining to, or befitting a master; authoritative: *a magisterial pronouncement.* **2.** imperious; domineering. **3.** of or befitting a magistrate or his office. **4.** of the rank of a magistrate. [ML *magisteriālis,* from LL *magisterius,* from L *magister* MASTER] – **magisterially,** *adv.*

**magistracy** /ˈmædʒəstrəsi/, *n., pl.* **-cies. 1.** the office or function of a magistrate. **2.** a body of magistrates. **3.** the district under a magistrate. Also, **magistrature.**

**magistral** /ˈmædʒəstrəl/, *adj.* **1.** *Pharm.* prescribed or prepared for a particular occasion, as a remedy (opposed to *officinal*). **2.** *Fort.* principal. **3.** *Rare.* magisterial. –*n.* **4.** →**magistral line.** [L *magistrālis* of a master]

**magistral line** /ˈ– laɪn/, *n.* the line from which the position of the other lines of fieldworks is determined.

**magistrate** /ˈmædʒəstreɪt, -trət/, *n.* **1.** a person charged with executive functions. **2.** a justice of the peace, paid or unpaid, who officiates in a magistrate's court. [ME *magistrat,* from L *magistrātus* the office of a chief, a magistrate]

**Magistrate's Court** /ˈmædʒəstreɪts kɔt/, *n.* →**Court of Petty Sessions.**

**magma** /ˈmægmə/, *n., pl.* **-mata** /-mətə/, **-mas. 1.** any crude mixture of finely divided mineral or organic matters. **2.** *Geol.* molten material under conditions of intense heat and great pressure occurring beneath the solid crust of the earth, and from which igneous rocks are formed. **3.** *Chem., Pharm.* a paste composed of solid and liquid matter. [L, from Gk: a salve] – **magmatic** /mægˈmætɪk/, *adj.*

**magmatic stoping** /mægmætɪk ˈstoupɪŋ/, *n.* →**stoping.**

**magna cum laude** /ˌmægna kum ˈlaudeɪ/, *adv.* with great praise (used chiefly in American universities to grant the middle of three special honours for above-average academic performance). [L]

**magnalium** /mægˈneɪliəm/, *n.* a light alloy of aluminium, containing magnesium and sometimes copper, nickel, tin, or lead.

**magnanimity** /mægnəˈnɪməti/, *n., pl.* **-ties. 1.** quality of being magnanimous. **2.** a magnanimous act.

**magnanimous** /mægˈnænəməs/, *adj.* **1.** generous in forgiving an insult or injury; free from petty resentfulness or vindictiveness. **2.** high-minded; noble. **3.** proceeding from or revealing nobility of mind, etc. [L *magnanimus* great-souled] – **magnanimously,** *adv.* – **magnanimousness,** *n.*

**magnate** /ˈmægneɪt, ˈmægnət/, *n.* **1.** a great or dominant person in a district or, esp. in some field of business: *a property magnate.* **2.** a person of eminence or distinction in any field. **3.** a member of the upper house of certain European parliaments, as formerly in Hungary and Poland. [late ME, from LL *magnas,* from L *magnus* great]

**magnesia** /mægˈniʃə, -ˈniʒə, -ˈniziə/, *n.* a magnesium oxide, MgO, a white tasteless substance used in medicine as an antacid and laxative. Also, **magnesium oxide.** [ME, from ML (in alchemy), from Gk (*hē*) *Magnēsía* (*líthos*) (the) Magnesian (stone); i.e. stone from Magnesia in Thessaly] – **magnesian, magnesic,** *adj.*

**magnesite** /ˈmægnəsaɪt/, *n.* a mineral, magnesium carbonate, $MgCO_3$, usu. occurring in white masses.

**magnesium** /mægˈniziəm/, *n.* a light, ductile, silver-white metallic element which burns with a dazzling white light, used in lightweight alloys. *Symbol:* Mg; *at. wt:* 24.312; *at. no.:* 12; *sp. gr.:* 1.74 at 20°C. [NL, from *magnēsia* MAGNESIA]

**magnesium light** /– ˈlaɪt/, *n.* the strongly actinic white light produced when magnesium is burnt, used in photography, signalling, pyrotechnics, etc.

**magnesium oxide** /– ˈɒksaɪd/, *n.* →**magnesia.**

**magnesium sulphate** /– ˈsʌlfeɪt/, *n.* →**Epsom salts.**

**magnet** /ˈmægnət/, *n.* **1.** a body (as a piece of iron or steel) which possesses the property of attracting certain substances, esp. iron; any piece of metal with ferromagnetic properties. **2.** →**loadstone. 3.** a thing or person that attracts, as by some inherent power or charm. [late ME *magnete,* from L *magnes* loadstone, magnet, from Gk *Mágnēs* (*líthos*) (stone) of Magnesia (in Thessaly), loadstone. Cf. MAGNESIA]

**magnetic** /mægˈnɛtɪk/, *adj.* **1.** of or pertaining to a magnet or magnetism. **2.** having the properties of a magnet. **3.** capable of being magnetised or attracted by a magnet. **4.** pertaining to the earth's magnetism: *the magnetic equator.* **5.** exerting a strong attractive power or charm: *a magnetic personality.* Also, **magnetical.** – **magnetically,** *adv.*

**magnetic bearing** /– ˈbɛərɪŋ/, *n.* the bearing of an object in relation to the magnetic meridian.

**magnetic bottle** /– ˈbɒtl/, *n.* any configuration of magnetic fields used to contain a plasma in controlled thermo-nuclear reaction experiments.

**magnetic compass** /– ˈkʌmpəs/, *n.* a compass consisting of a magnetic needle which acts itself along the lines of the earth's magnetic field and thus indicates the direction of the earth's magnetic poles.

**magnetic core** /– ˈkɔ/, *n.* See **core** (def. 3c).

**magnetic declination** /– dɛkləˈneɪʃən/, *n.* →**declination** (def. 2). Also, **magnetic variation.**

**magnetic dipole** /– ˈdaɪpoul/, *n.* **1.** a current loop or magnet which tends to align itself with a magnetic field. **2.** a pair of equal and opposite magnetic poles.

**magnetic disc** /– ˈdɪsk/, *n.* a memory unit for computers consisting of a rapidly spinning magnetic disc on which information is recorded by magnetising the surface. See **magnetic drum.**

**magnetic drum** /– ˈdrʌm/, *n.* a memory unit for computers, consisting of a rapidly spinning cylinder on which information is recorded by magnetising the surface.

**magnetic element** /– ˈɛləmənt/, *n.* any one of the three quantities, magnetic declination, dip, or horizontal intensity, which define the earth's magnetic field at any point on the earth's surface.

**magnetic equator** /– əˈkweɪtə/, *n.* →**aclinic line.**

**magnetic field** /– ˈfild/, *n.* a condition of space in the vicinity of a magnet or electric current which manifests itself as a force on magnetic objects within that space.

magnetic field: iron filings aligned by magnetic fields of bar magnets

**magnetic field strength,** *n.* the strength of a magnetic field, in SI units measured in amperes per metre.

**magnetic flux** /mæg,nɛtɪk ˈflʌks/, *n.* **1.** the total magnetic induction through a given cross-section; the derived SI unit of magnetic flux is the weber. **2.** magnetomotive force divided by reluctance.

**magnetic induction** /– ɪnˈdʌkʃən/, *n.* **1.** the induction of magnetism in a body by an external magnetic field. **2.** the magnetic flux passing through unit area in a direction at right angles to the magnetic force; the derived SI unit of magnetic induction is the tesla.

**magnetic ink** /– ˈɪŋk/, *n.* a type of ink containing magnetic particles which can be read by a magnetic character reader.

**magnetic lens** /– ˈlɛnz/, *n.* a lens on a device, such as an electron microscope, with a set of magnets used to focus a beam.

**magnetic meridian** /– məˈrɪdiən/, *n.* an imaginary line on the earth's surface which coincides with the horizontal component of the earth's magnetic field.

**magnetic mine** /– ˈmaɪn/, *n.* a mine designed to be exploded when its mechanism is triggered by the presence of ferrous objects, as the metal hull of a ship.

**magnetic mirror** /– ˈmɪrə/, *n.* a particular form of magnetic bottle used to contain a plasma in controlled thermonuclear reaction experiments.

**magnetic moment** /– ˈmoʊmənt/, *n.* a quantity associated with a magnet, equal to the product of its pole strength and its length.

**magnetic monopole** /– ˈmɒnəpoʊl/, *n.* a hypothetical magnetic 'charge' analogous to electric charge.

**magnetic needle** /– ˈnidl/, *n.* a slender magnetised steel rod which, when adjusted to swing in a horizontal plane, as in a compass, indicates the direction of the earth's magnetic fields or the approximate north and south.

**magnetic north** /– ˈnɔθ/, *n.* the direction in which the needle of a compass points, differing in most places from true north.

**magnetic permeability** /– pɜmiəˈbɪləti/, *n.* a measure of the ratio of the magnetic induction in a body to the external magnetic field which induces it.

**magnetic pick-up** /– ˈpɪk-ʌp/, *n.* a gramophone pick-up in which stylus vibrations are conveyed to a coil moving in a magnetic field and there converted into electric impulses for amplification.

**magnetic pole** /– ˈpoʊl/, *n.* **1.** a pole of a magnet. **2.** either of the two points on the earth's surface where the dipping needle of a compass stands vertical, one in the Arctic, the other in the Antarctic.

magnetic north pole

**magnetic potential** /– pəˈtɛnʃəl/, *n.* a scalar quantity analogous to electric potential; the difference in magnetic potential between two points in a magnetic field being the work done in carrying unit magnetic pole from one point to the other.

**magnetic recorder** /– rəˈkɔdə/, *n.* a device for recording sound on magnetic tape; tape-recorder.

magnetic south pole

**magnetic sound** /– ˈsaʊnd/, *n.* sound which in filming is recorded on magnetic tape, either separately from the film or on the film itself.

**magnetic storm** /– ˈstɔm/, *n.* a sudden disturbance in the earth's magnetic field associated with sunspot activity.

**magnetic susceptibility** /– səsɛptəˈbɪləti/, *n.* the ratio of the intensity of magnetisation produced in a substance to the

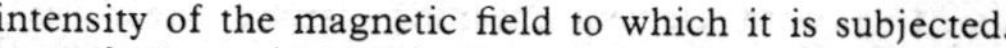

intensity of the magnetic field to which it is subjected.

**magnetic tape** /– ˈteɪp/, *n.* a plastic tape coated with a ferromagnetic powder, esp. iron oxide, used to record sound in a tape recorder, and video signals in a video recorder, to retain digital information in computing, and machine instructions in industrial and other control systems.

**magnetic tape unit,** *n.* a machine which holds a magnetic tape and transfers information between the tape and a computer.

**magnetic termite** /mæg,nɛtɪk ˈtɜmaɪt/, *n.* a termite, *Amitermes meridionalis,* named from the large nest built by a whole colony of the species, which is up to three metres in height, with narrow ends pointing approximately north and south, so that there is always some point of the nest which has an equable temperature.

**magnetic variation** /– vɛəriˈeɪʃən/, *n.* →**magnetic declination.** See **declination** (def. 2).

**magnetisation** /mægnətaɪˈzeɪʃən/, *n.* **1.** state or process of being magnetised. **2.** a measure of the magnetic moment per unit volume of a magnetised body.

**magnetise** /ˈmægnətaɪz/, *v.t.,* **-tised, -tising. 1.** to communicate magnetic properties to. **2.** to exert an attracting or compelling influence upon. **3.** *Obs.* →**mesmerise.** Also, **magnetize.** – **magnetiser,** *n.*

**magnetism** /ˈmægnətɪzəm/, *n.* **1.** the characteristic properties possessed by magnets; the molecular properties common to magnets. **2.** the agency producing magnetic phenomena. **3.** the science dealing with magnetic phenomena. **4.** magnetic or attractive power or charm.

**magnetite** /ˈmægnətaɪt/, *n.* a very common black iron oxide, $Fe_3O_4$, that is strongly attracted by a magnet; an important iron ore.

**magneto** /mægˈnitoʊ/, *n., pl.* **-tos.** a small electric generator, the poles of which are permanent magnets, as a hand-operated generator for telephone signalling, or the generator producing sparks in an internal-combustion engine. [short for MAGNETO-ELECTRIC (machine)]

**magneto-,** a combining form of **magnet** or **magnetic.**

**magneto-chemistry** /mæg,nitoʊ-ˈkɛməstri/, *n.* the study of magnetic and chemical phenomena in their relation to one another. – **magneto-chemical,** *adj.*

**magneto-electric** /mæg,nitoʊ-əˈlɛktrɪk/, *adj.* pertaining to the induction of electric currents by means of magnets. Also, **magneto-electrical.**

**magneto-electricity** /mæg,nitoʊ-əlɛkˈtrɪsəti/, *n.* electricity developed by the action of magnets.

**magneto-generator** /mæg,nitoʊ-ˈdʒɛnəreɪtə/, *n.* →**magneto.**

**magnetograph** /mægˈnɛtəgræf, -graf/, *n.* a magnetometer which makes a record of its measurements.

**magnetohydrodynamics** /mæg,nitoʊ,haɪdroʊdaɪˈnæmɪks/, *n.* (*construed as sing.*) **1.** the study of the flow of electrically conducting fluids through a magnetic field. **2.** a method of generating electricity by subjecting the free electrons in a high-temperature, high-velocity flame or plasma to a strong magnetic field. *Abbrev.:* M.H.D.

**magnetometer** /mægnəˈtɒmətə/, *n.* an instrument for measuring magnetic forces. – **magnetometry,** *n.*

**magnetomotive** /mæg,nitoʊˈmoʊtɪv/, *adj.* producing magnetic effects, or pertaining to such production.

**magnetomotive force** /– ˈfɔs/, *n.* the force which gives rise to magnetic effects or magnetic induction, calculated as the magnetic flux multiplied by reluctance.

**magneton** /ˈmægnətɒn, mægˈnitən/, *n.* a unit for measuring the magnetic moments of atomic or subatomic particles, measured in joules per tesla. *Symbols:* β, $m_B$ [MAGNET + (ELECTR)ON]

**magnetosphere** /mægˈnitoʊsfɪə/, *n.* the space surrounding the earth in which there is a magnetic field.

**magnetostatic** /mæg,nitoʊˈstætɪk/, *adj.* pertaining to steady magnetic fields.

**magnetostriction** /mæg,nitoʊˈstrɪkʃən/, *n.* the change in dimensions of a ferromagnetic substance on magnetisation.

**magnetron** /ˈmægnətrɒn/, *n.* a two-element radar valve in which the flow of electrons is under the influence of an external magnetic field; used to generate extremely short radio waves. [MAGNE(T) + (ELEC)TRON]

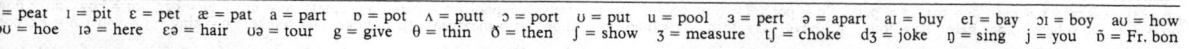

**magni-**, **1.** a word element meaning 'large', 'great', as in *magnify.* **2.** *Zool.* a word element denoting length. [L, combining form of *magnus* great]

**magnific** /mæg'nɪfɪk/, *adj. Archaic.* **1.** magnificent; imposing. **2.** grandiose; pompous. Also, **magnifical.** [L *magnificus*] – **magnifically,** *adv.*

**Magnificat** /mæg'nɪfɪkæt/, *n.* **1.** the hymn of the Virgin Mary in Luke, 1:46-55, beginning 'My soul doth magnify the Lord', used as a canticle at evensong or vespers. **2.** a musical setting of it. [ME, from L: doth magnify, the first word of the hymn in the Vulgate]

**magnification** /mægnəfə'keɪʃən/, *n.* **1.** the act of magnifying. **2.** the state of being magnified. **3.** the power to magnify. **4.** a magnified copy or reproduction. **5.** (of an optical instrument) the ratio of the linear dimensions of the final image to that of the object.

**magnificence** /mæg'nɪfəsəns/, *n.* **1.** the quality or state of being magnificent; splendour; grandeur; impressiveness; sublimity. **2.** impressiveness of surroundings. [ME, from OF, from L *magnificentia*]

**magnificent** /mæg'nɪfəsənt/, *adj.* **1.** making a splendid appearance or show: *a magnificent cathedral.* **2.** extraordinarily fine; superb: *a magnificent opportunity.* **3.** noble; sublime: *a magnificent poem.* **4.** great in deeds (now only as a title): *Lorenzo the Magnificent.* **5.** →**lavish.** [OF, from L *magnificent-* (recorded in compar., superl., and other forms), for *magnificus.* See MAGNIFIC] – **magnificently,** *adv.*

**magnifico** /mæg'nɪfɪkoʊ/, *n., pl.* **-coes. 1.** a Venetian grandee. **2.** any grandee or great personage. [It., from L *magnificus* MAGNIFIC]

**magnify** /'mægnəfaɪ/, *v.,* **-fied, -fying.** *–v.t.* **1.** to increase the apparent size of, as a lens does. **2.** to make greater in size; enlarge. **3.** to cause to seem greater or more important. **4.** *Archaic.* to extol; praise. *–v.i.* **5.** to increase or be able to increase the apparent size of an object, as a lens does. [ME *magnifie(n),* from L *magnificāre* make much of] – **magnifier,** *n.*

**magnifying glass** /'mægnəfaɪɪŋ glas/, *n.* a glass lens, usu. convex, or a combination of lenses used to produce a virtual image larger than the object being viewed.

**magniloquent** /mæg'nɪləkwənt/, *adj.* speaking or expressed in a lofty or grandiose style. [L *magniloquus* + -ENT] – **magniloquence,** *n.* – **magniloquently,** *adv.*

**magnitude** /'mægnətʃud/, *n.* **1.** size; extent: *to determine the magnitude of an angle.* **2.** great amount, importance, etc.: *affairs of magnitude.* **3.** greatness; great size: *the magnitude of the loss.* **4.** moral greatness: *magnitude of mind.* **5.** *Astron.* the brightness of a star expressed according to an arbitrary numerical system (the brightest degree being the first magnitude). Stars brighter than the sixth magnitude are visible to the unaided eye. [ME, from L *magnitūdo* greatness]

**magnolia** /mæg'noʊliə/, *n.* **1.** a large tree, *Magnolia grandiflora,* with large, spectacular, scented, creamy flowers. **2.** a small tree, *Magnolia × soulangiana,* much cultivated in gardens because of its pink to dark red flowers. **3.** any plant of the genus *Magnolia,* comprising shrubs and trees, usu. with fragrant flowers and an aromatic bark, much cultivated for ornament. **4.** the magnolia blossom. [NL; named from P. *Magnol,* 1638-1715, French botanist]

**magnoliaceous** /mæg,noʊli'eɪʃəs/, *adj.* belonging to the Magnoliaceae, or magnolia family of plants including the magnolias generally, the tulip trees, etc.

**magnum** /'mægnəm/, *n., pl.* **-nums.** a bottle for wine or spirits, holding about 2 quarts or 2.25 litres. [L, neut. of *magnus* great]

**magnum opus** /– 'oʊpəs/, *n.* **1.** a great work. **2.** one's chief work, esp. a literary or artistic work. [L]

**magpie** /'mægpaɪ/, *n.* **1.** any of several common black and white birds of the genus *Gymnorhina* with solid bodies, strong legs and large pointed bills, found throughout Australia and in New Guinea, as the **black-backed magpie,** *G. tibicen.* **2.** any of various currawongs (def. 1). **3.** any of various superficially similar but unrelated birds of the genus *Pica* and other genera of the family Corvidae as the **black-billed magpie,** *P. pica,* of Europe and North America. **4.** a chattering person. **5.** Also, **bowerbird.** one who collects useless objects. **6.** one who collects ideas from various sources and presents them as a whole original work; plagiarist. **7.** *Archery, Shooting.* **a.** the third ring or part from the centre of a target, between the inner and the outer. **b.** a shot which strikes this part. **c.** the score value of this part. **8.** *Colloq.* →**South Australian.** [from *Mag,* familiar var. of *Margaret,* woman's name + PIE[2]]

magpie (def. 1)

**magpie clothing** /'– kloʊðɪŋ/, *n.* (formerly) black and yellow convict's clothing. Also, **magpie dress.**

**magpie goose** /'– gus/, *n.* a large black and white anatine bird, *Anseranas semipalmata,* found in freshwater areas of northern Australia and adjacent islands.

**magpie lark** /'– lak/, *n.* a handsome and common Australian black and white bird, *Grallina cyanoleuca,* which builds its mud nest high in a tree; mudlark; peewee; peewit.

magpie lark

**M.Ag.Sc.,** Master of Agricultural Science.

**magsman** /'mægzmən/, *n. Colloq.* a person who tells stories; raconteur.

**maguey** /'mægweɪ/, *n.* **1.** any of several species of the family Agavaceae, esp. *Agave cantala* and species of the genus *Furcraea.* **2.** the fibre from these plants. [Sp., probably from Haitian]

**Magus** /'meɪgəs/, *n., pl.* **-gi** /-dʒaɪ/. **1.** (*also l.c.*) See **Magi** (def. 1). **2.** (*l.c.*) an ancient astrologer or magician. **3.** a Zoroastrian priest. [ME, from L, from Gk *Mágos,* from OPers. *magus*]

**mag wheel** /'mæg wil/, *n. Colloq.* a magnesium alloy wheel used for its lightness on some motor cars.

**Magyar** /'mægja/, *n.* **1.** a member of the ethnic group, of the Finno-Ugric stock, which forms the predominant element of the population of Hungary. **2.** the Hungarian language. *–adj.* **3.** of or pertaining to the Magyars or their language; Hungarian. [Hung.]

**maharaja** /mahə'radʒə/, *n.* the title of certain great ruling princes in India. Also, **maharajah.** [Skt: great raja]

**maharani** /mahə'rani/, *n.* **1.** the wife of a maharaja. **2.** a female sovereign in her own right. Also, **maharanee.** [Hind.: great queen]

**maharishi** /mahə'rɪʃi/, *n.* a Hindu teacher; a mystic. [Hindi, from *mahā* great + *rishi* inspired sage]

**mahatma** /mə'hatmə, -'hætmə/, *n.* **1.** an adept in Brahmanism. **2.** a wise and holy leader, esteemed for his saintliness. **3.** *Theosophy.* one of a class of reputed beings with preternatural powers. [Skt *mahātman* great-souled] – **mahatmaism,** *n.*

**Mahdi** /'madi/, *n., pl.* **-dis.** (in Muslim usage) the title of an expected spiritual and temporal ruler destined to establish a reign of righteousness throughout the world. [Ar. *mahdīy,* lit., the guided or directed one] – **Mahdism** /'madɪzəm/, *n.* – **Mahdist,** *n.*

**mah-jong** /'ma-dʒɒŋ/, *n.* **1.** a game of Chinese origin, usu. for four persons, with 136 (or sometimes 144) domino-like pieces or tiles (marked in suits) counters, and dice. *–v.i.* **2.** to win a game of mah-jong. Also, **mah-jongg.** [Chinese (Mandarin) *ma-ch'iao* sparrow (lit., hemp-bird), pictured on the first tiles of one of the suits]

**mahlstick** /'mɔlstɪk/, *n.* →**maulstick.**

**mahoe** /'mahoʊi/, *n.* a small New Zealand and Pacific Islands tree, *Melicytus ramiflorus;* whiteywood. [Maori]

**mahogany** /mə'hɒgəni/, *n., pl.* **-nies,** *adj.* *–n.* **1.** any of certain tropical American trees, esp. *Swietenia mahogani* and *S. macrophylla,* yielding a hard, reddish brown wood highly esteemed for making fine furniture, etc. **2.** the wood itself. **3.** any of various related or similar trees, as species of the genus *Dysoxylum,* and *Eucalyptus robusta,* swamp mahogany, or their timber. **4.** a reddish brown colour. *–adj.* **5.** pertaining to or made of mahogany. **6.** of the colour mahogany. [? from some non-Carib W Indian tongue]

**Mahometan** /mə'hɒmətən/, *adj., n.* →**Mohammedan.**

**mahonia** /mə'hoʊniə/, *n.* any of several evergreen shrubs of the genus *Mahonia,* as *M. aquifolium* with pinnate spiny leaves and clusters of yellow flowers.

**mahout** /mə'haʊt/, *n.* (in the East Indies) the keeper and driver of an elephant. [Hind. *mahāut*]

**Mahratta** /mə'ratə/, *n.* →**Maratha.**

**Mahratti** /mə'rati/, *n.* →**Marathi.**

**mahzor** /mak'zɔ/, *n.* a Hebrew prayer book containing the ritual for festivals. See **siddur.**

**mai** /maɪ/, *n. N.Z.* →**matai.** [Maori]

**maid** /meɪd/, *n.* **1.** a girl; young unmarried woman. **2.** a spinster (usu. in the expression *old maid*). **3.** a female servant. [apocopated var. of MAIDEN]

**maiden** /'meɪdn/, *n.* **1.** a maid; girl; young unmarried woman; virgin. **2.** a maiden speech. **3.** *Cricket.* a maiden over. **4.** →**maiden horse. 5.** →**maiden handicap.** *–adj.* **6.** of, pertaining to, or befitting a girl or unmarried woman. **7.** unmarried: *a maiden lady.* **8.** made, tried, appearing, etc., for the first time: *maiden voyage.* **9.** untried, as a knight, soldier, or weapon. [ME; OE *mægden,* from *mægd-* + *-en* -EN[5]]

**maidenhair** /'meɪdnhɛə/, *n.* any of the ferns constituting the genus *Adiantum,* of which the cultivated species have fine, glossy stalks and delicate, finely divided fronds.

**maidenhair tree** /'– tri/, *n.* →**ginkgo.**

**maiden handicap** /meɪdn 'hændikæp/, *n.* a race for horses which have never won a prize.

**maidenhead** /'meɪdnhɛd/, *n.* **1.** maidenhood; virginity. **2.** →**hymen.**

**maidenhood** /'meɪdnhʊd/, *n.* the state or time of being a maiden; virginity.

**maiden horse** /meɪdn 'hɔs/, *n.* a horse eligible to run in a maiden handicap. Also, **maiden-class horse.**

**maidenly** /'meɪdnli/, *adj.* **1.** pertaining to a maiden: *maidenly years.* **2.** characteristic of or befitting a maiden: *maidenly behaviour.* – **maidenliness,** *n.*

**maiden name** /'meɪdn neɪm/, *n.* a woman's surname before marriage.

**maiden over** /– 'oʊvə/, *n.* (in cricket) an over in which no runs are made.

**maiden pink** /– 'pɪŋk/, *n.* a small perennial caryophyllaceous herb with narrow leaves and pink or white flowers, *Dianthus deltoides,* widespread in grassland throughout temperate Europe and Asia.

**maiden speech** /– 'spitʃ/, *n.* a first speech, as the first speech of an M.P. in Parliament.

**maid of honour,** *n.* **1.** the chief unmarried attendant of a bride. **2.** an unmarried woman, usu. of noble birth, attendant on a queen or princess. **3.** a small tart with a curd or almond cream filling.

**maidservant** /'meɪdsɜvənt/, *n.* a female servant.

**maieutic** /meɪ'jutɪk/, *adj.* (of the Socratic mode of enquiry) bringing out ideas latent in the mind. [Gk *maieutikós* of midwifery]

**maigre** /'meɪgə/, *adj.* containing neither flesh nor its juices, as food permissible on days of religious abstinence. [F. See MEAGRE]

**maihem** /'meɪhɛm/, *n.* →**mayhem.**

**mail**[1] /meɪl/, *n.* **1.** letters, packages, etc., arriving or sent by post. **2.** the system of transmission of letters, etc., by post. **3.** a train or boat by which postal matter is carried. *–adj.* **4.** of or pertaining to mail: *a mailbag.* *–v.t.* **5.** to send by mail; place in a post office or postbox for transmission. [ME *male* bag, from OF, from Gmc; cf. OHG *malha* wallet]

**mail**[2] /meɪl/, *n.* **1.** flexible armour of interlinked rings, the ends riveted, butted, or soldered. **2.** defensive armour. *–v.t.* **3.** to clothe or arm with mail. [ME *maille,* from F, from L *macula* spot, mesh of a net]

**mailbag** /'meɪlbæg/, *n.* a bag in which mail is carried.

**mailbox** /'meɪlbɒks/, *n.* **1.** →**letterbox. 2.** →**post-box.**

**mailed** /meɪld/, *adj.* clad or armed with mail: *the mailed horseman.* [MAIL[2] + -ED[2]]

**mailed fist** /– 'fɪst/, *n.* armed force, esp. as a threat.

**mailing list** /'meɪlɪŋ lɪst/, *n.* a list consisting of the names and addresses of persons to whom information, etc., is sent by post.

**maillot** /meɪ'joʊ, 'meɪjoʊ/, *n.* **1.** tights. **2.** a tight-fitting one-piece swimming costume. [F: swaddling clothes; probably alteration of *maillol, maille* mesh, MAIL[2]]

**mailman** /'meɪlmən/, *n., pl.* **-men.** →**postman.**

**mail order** /'meɪl ɔdə/, *n.* **1.** an order for goods, etc., received and transmitted by post. **2.** the system of conducting a business by receiving orders and payment by mail for goods supplied to the buyers.

**mail-order** /'meɪl-ɔdə/, *v.t.* **1.** to send or receive (goods, etc.) by mail order. *–adj.* **2.** of or pertaining to a business, etc., dealing mainly in mail orders.

**maim** /meɪm/, *v.t.* **1.** to deprive of the use of some bodily member; mutilate; cripple. **2.** to impair; make essentially defective. *–n.* **3.** *Rare.* an injury or defect. [var. of MAYHEM] – **maimer,** *n.*

**mai mai** /'maɪ maɪ/, *n. N.Z.* a place of shelter or concealment made of interlaced branches, etc., esp. used by duck shooters. Also, **maimai, maemae, mimi.** [Aboriginal]

**main**[1] /meɪn/, *adj.* **1.** chief; principal; leading: *the main office.* **2.** sheer; utmost, as strength, force, etc.: *by main force.* **3.** of or pertaining to a broad expanse: *main sea.* **4.** *Gram.* See **main clause. 5.** *Obs.* strong or mighty. **6.** *Naut.* pertaining to the mainmast or mainsail. *–n.* **7.** a principal pipe or duct in a system used to distribute water, gas, etc. **8.** the principal wire or cable used to distribute electricity. **9.** strength; force; violent effort: *with might and main.* **10.** the chief or principal part or point. **11.** *Poetic.* the open ocean; high sea. **12.** →**mainland. 13. in the main,** for the most part. [ME *meyn,* OE *mægen* strength, power, c. Icel. *megin* strength, main part]

**main**[2] /meɪn/, *n.* a cockfighting match. [orig. uncert.]

**mainbrace** /'meɪnbreɪs/, *n.* **1.** a pennant and tackle secured to each end of the mainyard and led down to the main deck, used to haul the yard round to trim the mainsail to the wind. **2. splice the mainbrace,** *Colloq.* **a.** to order an issue of a tot of rum to a crew. **b.** to invite an assembly to have a drink. [def. 2 originated as a rare or unlikely order, the mainbrace being replaced rather than repaired by splicing]

**main clause** /'meɪn klɔz/, *n.* (in a complex sentence) the clause which may stand syntactically as a sentence by itself; independent clause. For example, in *I was out when he came in,* the main clause is *I was out.*

**main deck** /'– dɛk/, *n.* the upper deck in a vessel with two decks, and usu. the second deck down in a vessel with more than two decks.

**mainframe computer** /ˌmeɪnfreɪm kəm'pjutə/, *n.* a high-speed, general purpose computer with a large storage structured in 32 or 64 bit words.

**mainland** /'meɪnlænd, -lənd/, *n.* **1.** the principal land mass as distinguished from nearby islands and peninsulas. **2. the mainland,** *Tas.* continental Australia. – **mainlander,** *n.*

**main line** /meɪn 'laɪn/, *n.* a through railway route; a principal line of a railway as contrasted with a branch or secondary line.

**mainline** /'meɪnlaɪn/, *v.i.,* **-lined, -lining.** *Colloq.* to inject a narcotic drug directly into the vein.

**mainliner** /'meɪnlaɪnə/, *n. Colloq.* one who uses addictive drugs injected directly into the vein.

**mainly** /'meɪnli/, *adv.* **1.** chiefly; principally; for the most part. **2.** *Obs.* greatly.

**mainmast** /'meɪnmast/, *n.* **1.** the principal mast in a ship or other vessel. **2.** (in a schooner, brig, bark, etc.) the second mast from the bow. **3.** (in a yawl or ketch) the mast nearer the bow.

**main plane** /'meɪn pleɪn/, *n.* **1.** any of the main surfaces of an aeroplane, esp. a wing. **2.** the wings of a plane considered together.

**main-range** /'meɪn-reɪndʒ/, *adj.* (of skiing) cross country, esp. as undertaken in the main range of the Snowy Mountains.

**mainsail** /'meɪnsəl/, *n.* **1.** (in a square-rigged vessel) the sail bent to the mainyard. **2.** (in a fore-and-aft rigged vessel) the large sail set abaft the mainmast.

**mainsheet** /'meɪnʃit/, *n.* the sheet of a mainsail.

**mainspring** /ˈmeɪnsprɪŋ/, *n.* **1.** the principal spring in a mechanism, as in a watch. **2.** the chief motive power; the impelling cause.

**mainstay** /ˈmeɪnsteɪ/, *n.* **1.** *Naut.* the stay which secures the mainmast forward. **2.** a chief support.

**mainstream** /ˈmeɪnstrim/, *n.* **1.** the dominant trend; chief tendency: *she was in the mainstream of fashion.* *–adj.* **2.** of or pertaining to jazz which lies between traditional and modern in its stage of development.

**maintain** /meɪnˈteɪn, mən-/, *v.t.* **1.** to keep in existence or continuance; preserve; retain: *to maintain good relations with New Zealand.* **2.** to keep in due condition, operation, or force; keep unimpaired: *to maintain order, maintain public highways.* **3.** to keep in a specified state, position, etc. **4.** to affirm; assert (with a clause, or with an object and infinitive): *maintain that it is right, maintain it to be true.* **5.** to support in speech or argument, as a statement, etc. **6.** to keep or hold against attack: *to maintain one's ground.* **7.** to provide with the means of existence. [ME *mainten(en)*, from F *maintenir*, from L *manū tenēre* hold in the hand] – **maintainable**, *adj.* – **maintainer**, *n.*

**maintenance** /ˈmeɪntənəns/, *n.* **1.** the act of maintaining. **2.** the state of being maintained. **3.** means of provision for maintaining; means of subsistence. **4.** *Law.* the money paid either in a lump sum or by way of periodical payments for the support of the other spouse or infant children, usu. after divorce. **5.** *Law.* an officious intermeddling in a suit in which the meddler has no interest, by assisting either party with means to prosecute or defend it.

**maintop** /ˈmeɪntɒp/, *n.* a platform at the head of the lower mainmast.

**main-topgallant** /meɪn-təˈgæiənt, -tɒp-/, *n.* a sail on the main-topgallant mast.

**main-topgallant mast** /ˈ– məst/, *n.* the mast next above the main-topmast.

**main-topmast** /meɪn-ˈtɒpməst/, *n.* the mast next above the lower mainmast.

**main-topsail** /meɪn-ˈtɒpsəl/, *n.* the sail set on the main-topmast.

**mainyard** /ˈmeɪnjad, -jəd/, *n.* the lower yard on the mainmast.

**maire** /ˈmairi/, *n.* any New Zealand forest tree belonging to the olive genus, *Gymnelaea.* [Maori]

**maison** /ˈmeɪzɒn, meɪˈzõ/, *adj.* of the house, as *pâté maison,* the pâté of the house. [F]

**maisonette** /meɪzəˈnɛt/, *n.* **1.** a small house. **2.** *Brit.* a self-contained flat occupying two floors. Also, **maisonnette.**

**maître d** /meɪtrə ˈdi/, *n. Colloq.* →**maître d'hôtel.**

**maître d'hôtel** /meɪtrə doʊˈtɛl/, *n.* **1.** a steward or butler. **2.** a head waiter. **3.** (of foods) with a sauce of melted butter, minced parsley, and lemon juice or vinegar. [F: master of a house]

**maize** /meɪz/, *n.* **1.** a widely cultivated cereal plant, *Zea mays,* occurring in many varieties, bearing grain in large ears or spikes; Indian corn. **2.** its grain. **3.** a pale yellow colour. *–adj.* **4.** of the colour of maize. [Sp. *maíz,* from Antillean *maysi, mahiz,* from Arawak *marise*]

**Maj.**, Major.

**majestic** /məˈdʒɛstɪk/, *adj.* characterised by or possessing majesty; of lofty dignity or imposing aspect; stately; grand. Also, **majestical.** – **majestically**, *adv.*

**majesty** /ˈmædʒəsti/, *n., pl.* **-ties.** **1.** regal, lofty, or stately dignity; imposing character; grandeur. **2.** supreme greatness or authority; sovereignty. **3.** a royal personage, or royal personages collectively. **4.** (*usu. cap.*) a title used when speaking of or to a sovereign (prec. by *his, her, your,* etc.). [ME *maieste,* from F *majesté,* from L *mājestas* greatness, grandeur, majesty]

**Maj. Gen.**, Major General.

**majolica** /məˈdʒɒlɪkə, məˈjɒl-/, *n.* **1.** a kind of Italian pottery coated with enamel and decorated, often in rich colours. **2.** a more or less similar pottery made elsewhere. [It. *maiolica* Majorca, a Spanish island in the W Mediterranean]

**major** /ˈmeɪdʒə/, *n.* **1.** *Mil.* a commissioned officer ranking below a lieutenant colonel and above a captain. **2.** one of superior rank in a specified class. **3.** a person of full legal age. **4.** *Music.* a major interval, chord, scale, etc. **5.** a subject or field of study chosen by a student to represent his principal interest and upon which he concentrates a large share of his efforts. **6.** *Aus. Rules. Colloq.* a goal. *–adj.* **7.** greater, as in size, amount, extent, importance, rank, etc.: *the major part of the town, a major question.* **8.** of or pertaining to the majority. **9.** of full legal age. **10.** *Logic.* broader or more extensive: **a. major term** of a syllogism is the term that enters into the predicate of the conclusion. **b. major premise** is that premise of a syllogism which contains the major term. **11.** *Music.* **a.** (of an interval) being between the tonic and the second, third, sixth, and seventh degrees of a major scale: *the major third, sixth, etc.* **b.** (of a chord) having a major third between the root and the note next above it. **12.** *Brit.* elder; senior; in boys' schools designating the elder of two brothers, the eldest of three, or the second of four. **13.** denoting or pertaining to educational majors: *a major field of study.* *–v.i.* **14.** to pursue a major or principal subject or course of study (fol. by *in*). [ME, from L: greater, larger, superior, compar. of *magnus* great]

**major arcanum** /meɪdʒər aˈkeɪnəm/, *n.* →**trump**[1] (def. 1c).

**major axis** /ˈ– æksəs/, *n.* (in mathematics) the axis of an ellipse which passes through both foci. Cf. **minor axis.**

**major-domo** /meɪdʒə-ˈdoʊmoʊ/, *n., pl.* **-mos.** **1.** a man in charge of a great household, as that of a sovereign; a chief steward. **2.** a steward or butler. [Sp. *mayordomo,* or It. *maggiordomo,* from ML *mājor domūs* chief officer of the house]

**major general** /meɪdʒə ˈdʒɛnrəl/, *n.* **1.** an officer ranking below a lieutenant general and above a brigadier general. **2.** the rank. – **major-generalcy, major-generalship,** *n.*

**majority** /məˈdʒɒrəti/, *n., pl.* **-ties.** **1.** the greater part or number: *the majority of mankind.* **2.** a number of voters or votes, jurors, or others in agreement, constituting more than half the total number. **3.** the number by which votes cast for the leading candidate exceed those cast for the next candidate (opposed to *absolute majority*). **4.** the party or faction with the majority vote. **5.** the state or time of being of full legal age: *to attain one's majority.* **6.** the military rank or office of a major. [F *majorité,* from ML *mājōritas,* from L *mājor* MAJOR]

**majority carrier** /– ˈkæriə/, *n.* (in a semiconductor) the charge carrier which carries the greater proportion of the electric current.

**major key** /ˈmeɪdʒə ki/, *n.* a key based on a major scale.

**Major Mitchell** /meɪdʒə ˈmɪtʃəl/, *n.* a cockatoo, *Cacatua leadbeateri,* with white wings, pink underparts, neck and face, and white crown suffused with salmon pink and forward-curving scarlet crest, found throughout the arid and semi-arid regions of Australia; chockalott; Leadbeater's cockatoo; wee juggler; cocklerina.

**Major-Mitchell** /meɪdʒə-ˈmɪtʃəl/, *v.i.* (formerly) to travel across country in zig-zags.

**major orders** /meɪdʒər ˈɔdəz/, *n. pl.* See **order** (def. 15).

**major scale** /ˈmeɪdʒə skeɪl/, *n.* a musical scale whose third tone forms a major third with the root.

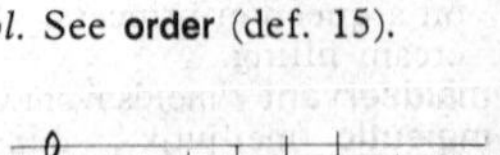

major scale (key of C)

**major suit** /– ˈsut/, *n. Bridge.* hearts or spades (because they have higher point values).

**major third** /– ˈθɜd/, *n. Music.* an interval of two whole tones.

**majuscule** /ˈmædʒəskjul/, *adj.* **1.** large, as letters (whether capital or uncial). **2.** written in such letters (opposed to *minuscule*). *–n.* **3.** a majuscule letter. [F, from L *mājusculus* somewhat greater or larger] – **majuscular** /məˈdʒʌskjələ/, *adj.*

**make** /meɪk/, *v.,* **made, making,** *n.* *–v.t.* **1.** to bring into existence by shaping material, combining parts, etc.: *to make a dress.* **2.** to produce by any action or causative agency: *to make trouble.* **3.** to cause to be or become; render: *to make an old man young.* **4.** to constitute; appoint: *to make someone a judge.* **5.** to put into proper condition for use: *to make a bed.* **6.** to bring into a certain form or condition: *to make bookcases out of orange boxes.* **7.** to cause, induce, or compel (to do something): *to make a horse go.* **8.** to give rise to; occasion. **9.** to produce, earn, or win for oneself: *to make a fortune.* **10.** to compose, as a poem. **11.** to draw up, as a legal document. **12.** to do; effect: *to make a bargain.* **13.** to fix; establish; enact: *to make laws.* **14.** to become by development; prove to be: *he will make a good lawyer.* **15.** to form in the mind, as a judgment, estimate, or plan. **16.** to judge or infer as to the truth, nature, meaning, etc.: *what do you make of it?* **17.** to estimate; reckon: *to make the distance ten metres.* **18.** (of material or parts) to compose; form: *two and two make four.* **19.** to bring to; bring up the total to: *to make a kilo.* **20.** to serve for or as: *to make good reading.* **21.** to be sufficient to constitute; be essential to. **22.** to assure the success or fortune of. **23.** to put forth; deliver: *to make a speech.* **24.** *U.S.* to accomplish by travelling, etc.: *to make one hundred kilometres an hour.* **25.** to arrive at or reach: *to make a port.* **26.** to arrive in time for: *to make the first show.* **27.** to achieve a position on or inclusion in (a list of honours, place of honour, or the like). **28.** *Colloq.* to seduce or have sexual intercourse with. **29.** *Colloq.* to secure a place on, as a team. **30.** *Cards.* **a.** to name (the trump). **b.** to achieve a trick with (a card). **c.** *Bridge.* to achieve (a bid). **d.** to mix up or shuffle (the cards). **31.** *Sport, Games.* to earn as a score. **32.** to close (an electric circuit). *–v.i.* **33.** to cause oneself, or something understood, to be as specified: *to make sure.* **34.** to show oneself in action or behaviour: *to make merry.* **35.** to direct or pursue the course; go: *to make for home.* **36.** to rise, as the tide, or as water in a ship, etc. *–v.* **37.** Some special verb phrases are:

**make a face,** to grimace.

**make as if** or **as though,** to act as if; pretend.

**make a splash,** to make a big impression socially, as by lavish entertainment, publicity stunts, etc.

**make at,** to attack or lunge towards: *he made at me with a knife.*

**make a wave,** *Surfing.* to catch a wave on the crest.

**make away with, 1.** to get rid of. **2.** to kill or destroy. **3.** to steal or abduct.

**make believe,** to pretend.

**make do,** to operate or carry on using minimal or improvised resources.

**make eyes,** to flirt (fol. by *at*).

**make for, 1.** to travel towards or attempt to reach. **2.** to help to promote or maintain: *to make for better international relations.*

**make good, 1.** to achieve (a goal). **2.** to become a success.

**make heavy weather, 1.** *Naut.* to roll and pitch in heavy seas. **2.** to have difficulty; progress laboriously (with) (oft. fol. by *of*): *to make heavy weather of a simple calculation.*

**make it, 1.** to achieve one's object. **2.** to have intercourse. (usu. fol. by *with*). **3.** to arrive successfully.

**make like, 1.** to imitate. **2.** to pretend.

**make love,** *Colloq.* to have sexual intercourse.

**make off,** to run away.

**make off with,** to steal.

**make one's alley good,** *Colloq.* to conciliate; placate (fol. by *with*).

**make out, 1.** to write out a bill, a cheque, etc. **2.** to prove; establish. **3.** to discern; decipher. **4.** to present as; impute to be: *he made me out a liar.* **5.** *Colloq.* to manage; do; perform. **6.** *Colloq.* to have sexual intercourse: *I made out last night.*

**make over, 1.** to make anew; alter: *to make over a dress.* **2.** to hand over into the possession or charge of another. **3.** to transfer the title of (property); convey.

**make public,** to reveal to the public.

**make time, 1.** to move quickly, esp. in an attempt to recover lost time. **2.** *Chiefly U.S.* to flirt: *make time with the hostess.*

**make tracks,** *Colloq.* to depart.

**make up, 1.** (of parts) to constitute; form. **2.** to put together; construct; compile. **3.** to concoct; invent. **4.** to compensate for; make good. **5.** to complete. **6.** to prepare; put in order. **7.** to bring to a definite conclusion, as one's mind. **8.** to settle amicably, as differences. **9.** Also, **make it up.** to become reconciled after a quarrel. **10.** *Print.* to arrange set type, etc., into columns or pages. **11.** to apply cosmetics to, as the face. **12.** to prepare for a part, as on the stage, by appropriate dress, cosmetics, etc. **13.** to adjust or balance, as accounts; to prepare, as statements. **14.** to assemble the component parts of a drill string. **15.** *Educ.* to repeat (a course or examination in which one has failed) or to take (an examination from which one has been absent). **16.** to give or work in lieu for; compensate for (time or work lost, etc.).

**make up to, 1.** *Colloq.* to try to be on friendly terms with; fawn on. **2.** to make advances or pay court to.

**make water,** to urinate.

**make waves,** to cause a disturbance; upset existing standards or notions.

*–n.* **38.** style or manner of being made; form; build. **39.** production with reference to the maker: *our own make.* **40.** disposition; character; nature. **41.** the act or process of making. **42. on the make,** *Colloq.* **a.** intent on gain or one's own advantage. **b.** looking for a sexual partner. **43.** quantity made; output. **44.** *Cards.* **a.** the act of naming the trump, or the suit named as trump. **b.** the act of shuffling the cards before dealing. **45.** *Elect.* the closing of an electric circuit (opposed to *break*). [ME *make(n)*, OE *macian*, c. LG and D *maken*, G *machen*]

**make and break,** *n.* a device for alternately making and breaking an electric circuit.

**make-believe** /ˈmeɪk-bəliv/, *n.* **1.** pretence; feigning; sham. **2.** a pretender; one who pretends. *–adj.* **3.** pretended; feigned; sham.

**make-do** /ˈmeɪk-du/, *adj.* of a temporary or substitute nature.

**makefast** /ˈmeɪkfast/, *n.* *U.S.* any structure to which a boat is tied up, as a bollard, buoy, etc.

**make-peace** /ˈmeɪk-pis/, *n.* *Rare.* a peacemaker.

**maker** /ˈmeɪkə/, *n.* **1.** one who makes. **2.** *Law.* the party executing a legal instrument, esp. a promissory note. **3.** *Bridge, etc.* **a.** the one who first designates the successful bid. **b.** the person whose turn it is to shuffle. **4.** *Archaic.* a poet.

**make-ready** /ˈmeɪk-rɛdi/, *n.* the final preparation of type blocks, offset plates, etc., before printing.

**makeshift** /ˈmeɪkʃɪft/, *n.* **1.** a temporary expedient; substitute. *–adj.* **2.** serving as a makeshift.

**make-up** /ˈmeɪk-ʌp/, *n.* **1.** cosmetics, as those used by a woman to enhance her features. **2.** the application of such cosmetics. **3.** the total effect achieved by such application. **4.** the way in which an actor or other person dresses himself, paints his face, etc., for a part. **5.** the manner of being made up or put together; composition. **6.** physical or mental constitution. **7.** *Print.* the arrangement of type, illustrations, etc., into columns or pages. **8.** a wharf labourer who supplements a gang as required.

**makeweight** /ˈmeɪkweɪt/, *n.* **1.** something put in a scale to complete a required weight. **2.** anything added to supply a lack.

**making** /ˈmeɪkɪŋ/, *n.* **1.** the act of one who or that which makes. **2.** the process by which something is made to be as it is. **3.** means or cause of success or advancement: *to be the making of someone.* **4.** (*oft. pl.*) material of which something may be made; potential. **5.** something made. **6.** the quantity made. **7. in the making,** being made; not yet finished. **8. the makings,** *Colloq.* the tobacco and paper used to hand roll a cigarette.

**mako** /ˈmeɪkoʊ/, *n.* **1.** Also, **blue pointer.** a very fast, vigorous shark, *Isurus glaucus,* of Indo-Pacific waters, having a blue back and a pointed snout and being highly esteemed as a game fish. **2.** the very similar sharp-nosed mackerel shark, *Isurus oxyrinchus,* of the Atlantic.

**makomako** /ˈmakəmakoʊ/, *n.* **1.** a small tree, *Aristotelia serrata* of the family Elaeocarpaceae, growing in forest clearings in New Zealand; wineberry. **2.** *N.Z.* →**bellbird.** [Maori]

**mal-,** a prefix having attributive relation to the second element, meaning 'bad', 'wrongful', 'ill', as in *maladjustment, malpractice.* [F, representing *mal,* adv. (from L *male* badly, ill), or *mal,* adj. (from L *malus* bad)]

**Mal.,** *Bible.* Malachi.

**Malabar rat** /mæləba ˈræt/, *n.* →**bandicoot.**

**Malacca cane** /məlækə ˈkeɪn/, *n.* a cane or walking stick made of the brown, often mottled or clouded stem of an East Indian rattan palm, *Calamus scipionum,* usu. highly polished. [named after *Malacca,* state in Malaysia, on the SW Malay Peninsula]

**malachite** /ˈmæləkaɪt/, *n.* a green mineral basic copper carbonate, $Cu_2CO_3(OH)_2$, an ore of copper, also used for making ornamental articles. [F, from Gk *maláchē* mallow + *-ite* -ITE[1]]

**malacology** /mæləˈkɒlədʒi/, *n.* the science dealing with the study of molluscs. [Gk *malakó(s)* soft (with reference to the soft body of the molluscs) + -LOGY] – **malacologist,** *n.*

**malacophilous** /mælə'kɒfələs/, *adj.* pollinated by snails or slugs.

**malacopterygian** /mælə,kɒptə'rɪdʒiən/, *adj.* of or pertaining to the Malacopterygii, a division of soft-finned teleost fishes. [Gk *malakó(s)* soft + *ptéryx* wing, fin + -IAN]

**malacostracan** /mælə'kɒstrəkən/, *adj.* **1.** Also, **malacostracous.** belonging to the Malacostraca, a subclass of crustaceans which have a comparatively complex organisation, including lobsters, shrimps, crabs, etc. –*n.* **2.** a malacostracan crustacean. [NL *Malacostraca* (from Gk *malakóstraka* (neut. pl.) soft-shelled) + -AN]

**maladdress** /mælə'drɛs/, *n.* gaucheness; awkwardness. [F *maldresse*]

**maladjusted** /mælə'dʒʌstəd/, *adj.* **1.** badly adjusted. **2.** *Psychol.* suffering from maladjustment.

**maladjustment** /mælə'dʒʌstmənt/, *n.* **1.** a faulty adjustment. **2.** *Psychol.* a failure to function successfully with regard to personal relationships and environment, often a symptom of mental disturbance.

**maladminister** /mæləd'mɪnəstə/, *v.t.* to manage (esp. public affairs) badly or inefficiently. – **maladministration** /mæləd,mɪnəs'treɪʃən/, *n.* – **maladministrator,** *n.*

**maladroit** /mælə'drɔɪt/, *adj.* lacking in adroitness; unskilful; awkward. [F. See MAL-, ADROIT] – **maladroitly,** *adv.* – **maladroitness,** *n.*

**malady** /'mælədi/, *n., pl.* **-dies. 1.** any bodily disorder or disease, esp. one that is chronic or deep-seated. **2.** any form of disorder: *social maladies.* [ME *maladie,* from OF, from *malade* sick, from LL *male habitus,* lit., ill-conditioned]

**malaga** /'mæləgə/, *n.* **1.** a sweet strong white wine with a pronounced muscat grape flavour, produced in the province of Málaga, Spain. **2.** any of the grapes grown in or exported from Málaga.

**Malagasy** /'mæləgæsi/, *n., pl.* **-gasy, -gasies,** *adj.* –*n.* **1.** a native of the Malagasy Republic. **2.** an Austronesian language, the language of the Malagasy Republic. –*adj.* **3.** of or pertaining to Malagasy.

**Malagasy Republic** /– rə'pʌblɪk/, *n.* former official name of **Madagascar.**

**malaguena** /mælə'geɪnjə/, *n.* a Spanish dance similar to the fandango, originating in Málaga. Also, **malagueña.**

**malaise** /mæ'leɪz/, *n.* a condition of indefinite bodily weakness or discomfort, often marking the onset of a disease. [F, from *mal* ill + *aise* EASE]

**malanders** /mə'lændəz/, *n.pl.* a dry, scabby or scurfy eruption or scratch behind the knee in horses. Also, **mallenders.** [late ME, from F *malandres,* from L *malandria* blisters on the neck]

**malapert** /'mæləpɜt/, *Archaic.* –*adj.* **1.** unbecomingly bold or saucy. –*n.* **2.** a malapert person. [ME, from OF, from *mal* badly + *appert,* for *espert,* from L *expertus* EXPERT] – **malapertly,** *adv.* – **malapertness,** *n.*

**malapropism** /'mæləprɒp,ɪzəm/, *n.* **1.** the act or habit of ridiculously misusing words. **2.** a word so misused. [from Mrs *Malaprop,* a character noted for her misapplication of words, in *The Rivals* (1775) by R.B. Sheridan, 1751-1816, Irish dramatist]

**malapropos** /mælæprə'poʊ/, *adj.* **1.** inappropriate. –*adv.* **2.** inappropriately. [F *mal à propos* not to the point. See MAL-, APROPOS]

**malar** /'meɪlə/, *adj.* **1.** of or pertaining to the cheekbone or cheek. –*n.* **2.** Also, **malar bone.** the cheekbone. [NL *mālāris,* from L *māla* cheekbone, cheek]

**malaria** /mə'lɛəriə/, *n.* **1.** any of a group of diseases, usu. intermittent or remittent, and characterised by attacks of chills, fever, and sweating; formerly supposed to be due to swamp exhalations, but now known to be caused by a species of parasitic protozoans which are transferred to the human blood by mosquitoes (genus *Anopheles*) and which occupy and destroy the red blood corpuscles. **2.** unwholesome or poisonous air. [It., contraction of *mala aria* bad air] – **malarial, malarian, malarious,** *adj.*

**malariologist** /məlɛəri'ɒlədʒəst/, *n.* one who is expert in the control of malaria, esp. in eradication procedures.

**malarky** /mə'laki/, *n.* nonsense; meaningless talk. Also, **malarkey.**

**malassimilation** /,mæləsɪmə'leɪʃən/, *n.* imperfect assimilation or nutrition.

**malate** /'mæleɪt, 'meɪl-/, *n.* a salt or ester of malic acid. [MAL(IC) + -ATE[2]]

**malathion** /mælə'θaɪən/, *n.* a powerful sulphur-containing organophosphorus insecticide, $C_{10}H_{19}O_6PS_2$, which has low toxicity for mammals. [Trademark]

**Malawi** /mə'lawi/, *n.* a republic in south-eastern central Africa.

**Malay** /mə'leɪ/, *adj.* **1.** of or pertaining to the Malays or their country or language. **2.** denoting or pertaining to the so-called 'brown' race, characterised by short stature, roundish skull, moderate prognathism, and straight black hair. –*n.* **3.** a member of the dominant people of the Malay Peninsula and adjacent islands. **4.** an Austronesian language, widespread in the East Indies as a language of commerce.

**Malayalam** /mæli'aləm/, *n.* a Dravidian language spoken in Kerala, a state in south-western India. Also, **Malayalaam.**

**Malayan** /mə'leɪən/, *adj.* **1.** Malay. –*n.* **2.** a Malay.

**Malayo-Polynesian** /mə,leɪoʊ-,pɒlə'niʒən/, *adj.* →**Austronesian.**

**Malaysia** /mə'leɪʒə/, *n.* a federation in South-East Asia. – **Malaysian,** *adj., n.*

**malcontent** /'mælkəntɛnt/, *adj.* **1.** discontented; dissatisfied. **2.** dissatisfied with the existing administration; inclined to rebellion. –*n.* **3.** a malcontent person. [OF. See MAL-, CONTENT[2]]

**mal de mer** /mæl də 'mɛə/, *n.* seasickness. [F]

**Maldives** /'mɔldɪvz/, *n.pl.* a country comprising a group of atolls in the Indian Ocean.

**male** /meɪl/, *adj.* **1.** belonging to the sex which begets young, or any division or group corresponding to it. **2.** pertaining to or characteristic of this sex; masculine. **3.** composed of males: *a male choir.* **4.** *Bot.* **a.** designating or pertaining to any reproductive structure which produces or contains elements that bring about the fertilisation of the female element. **b.** (of seed plants) staminate. **5.** *Mach.* designating some part, etc., which fits into a corresponding part. –*n.* **6.** a male human being; a man or boy. **7.** any animal of male sex. **8.** *Bot.* a staminate plant. [ME, from OF, from L *masculus*]

**maleate** /mə'liət, -'leɪ-/, *n.* a salt or ester of maleic acid.

**male chauvinist** /meɪl 'ʃoʊvənəst/, *n.* **1.** a man who discriminates against women by applying to them stereotyped ideas of female incompetence, inferiority, female roles, etc. **2.** a chauvinist for the male sex. **3. male chauvinist pig,** (*derog.*) an extreme male chauvinist. –*adj.* **4.** having the characteristics of a male chauvinist. – **male chauvinism,** *n.*

**malediction** /mælə'dɪkʃən/, *n.* **1.** a curse; the utterance of a curse. **2.** slander. [late ME, from L *maledictio* abuse] – **maledictory** /mælə'dɪktri, -təri/, *adj.*

**malefaction** /mælə'fækʃən/, *n.* an evil deed.

**malefactor** /'mæləfæktə/, *n.* **1.** an offender against the law; a criminal. **2.** one who does evil. [late ME, from L] – **malefactress** /'mæləfæktrəs/, *n. fem.*

**male fern** /'meɪl fɜn/, *n.* a variable, robust, rhizomatous fern with large dissected leaves, *Dryopteris filix-mas,* widespread in woods of temperate regions.

**malefic** /mə'lɛfɪk/, *adj.* productive of evil; malign. [L *maleficus* evil-doing]

**maleficence** /mə'lɛfəsəns/, *n.* **1.** the doing of evil or harm. **2.** maleficent or harmful character.

**maleficent** /mə'lɛfəsənt/, *adj.* doing evil or harm; harmful. [backformation from L *maleficientia* MALEFICENCE. Cf. BENEFICENT]

**maleic acid** /mə,liɪk 'æsəd/, *n.* crystalline dibasic acid, $C_2H_2(COOH)_2$, an isomer of fumaric acid.

**malerisch** /'malərɪʃ/, *adj.* →**painterly** (def. 2). [G: pictorial]

**malevolence** /mə'lɛvələns/, *n.* the state or feeling or being malevolent; ill will.

**malevolent** /mə'lɛvələnt/, *adj.* **1.** wishing evil to another or others; showing ill will: *his failure made him malevolent towards others.* **2.** *Astrol.* evil or malign in influence. [L *malevolens* wishing ill] – **malevolently,** *adv.*

**malfeasance** /mæl'fizəns/, *n.* the doing of an unlawful act, as a trespass. Cf. **misfeasance, nonfeasance.** [F *malfaisance* evil-doing, from *malfaisant,* from *mal* evil + *faisant,* ppr. of *faire* do, from L *facere*] – **malfeasant,** *adj., n.*

**malformation** /mælfɔ'meɪʃən, -fə-/, *n.* faulty or anomalous formation or structure, esp. in a living body.

**malformed** /mæl'fɔmd/, *adj.* faultily formed.

**malfunction** /mæl'fʌŋkʃən/, *v.i.* **1.** to fail to function properly. *–n.* **2.** failure to function properly. [MAL- + FUNCTION]

**Mali** /'mali/, *n.* a republic in western Africa.

**malibu board** /'mæləbu bɔd/, *n.* a lightweight surfboard, originally of balsa wood covered with fibreglass; a small manoeuvrable surfboard.

**malic** /'mælɪk/, *adj.* pertaining to or derived from apples. [F *malique,* from L *mālum* apple]

**malic acid** /– 'æsəd/, *n.* a crystalline, dibasic hydroxy acid, $C_2H_3OH(COOH)_2$, occurring in small amounts in almost all living cells as a component of the citric acid cycle, and in greater amounts in apples, grapes, and other fruits.

**malice** /'mæləs/, *n.* **1.** desire to inflict injury or suffering on another. **2.** *Law.* evil intent on the part of one who commits a wrongful act injurious to others, technically called *malitia praecogitata,* or *malice prepense* or *aforethought.* [ME, from OF, from L *malitia* badness, spite, malice]

**malicious** /mə'lɪʃəs/, *adj.* **1.** full of, characterised by, or showing malice; malevolent. **2.** *Law.* motivated by vicious, wanton, or mischievous purposes, as in malicious arrest, malicious injuries to persons or property, malicious prosecution, etc. – **maliciously,** *adv.* – **maliciousness,** *n.*

**malign** /mə'laɪn/, *v.t.* **1.** to speak ill of; slander. *–adj.* **2.** evil in effect; pernicious; baleful. **3.** having or showing an evil disposition; malevolent. [ME *maligne,* from OF, from L *malignus* ill-disposed] – **maligner,** *n.* – **malignly,** *adv.*

**malignant** /mə'lɪgnənt/, *adj.* **1.** disposed to cause suffering or distress; malicious. **2.** very dangerous; harmful in influence or effect. **3.** *Pathol.* deadly; tending to produce death, as a disease, tumour, etc. [LL *malignans,* ppr., injuring maliciously] – **malignance, malignancy,** *n.* – **malignantly,** *adv.*

**malignity** /mə'lɪgnəti/, *n., pl.* **-ties. 1.** the state or character of being malign; malevolence. **2.** (*pl.*) malignant feelings, actions, etc. [late ME, from L *malignitas*]

**malinger** /mə'lɪŋgə/, *v.i.* to feign sickness or injury, esp. in order to avoid duty, work, etc. [F *malingre* sickly, ailing, from *mal* bad(ly) + OF *heingre* haggard, of Gmc orig.] – **malingerer,** *n.*

**mall** /mɔl, mæl/, *n.* **1.** a shaded walk, usu. public. **2.** the mallet used in the game of pall-mall. **3.** the game. **4.** the place or alley where it was played. **5.** →**shopping complex.** [ME *malle,* from OF *ma(i)l,* from L *malleus* hammer]

**mallard** /'mælad/, *n., pl.* **-lards,** (*esp. collectively*) **-lard. 1.** a common, almost cosmopolitan, wild duck, *Anas platyrhynchos,* from which the domestic ducks are descended. **2.** a male of this species. [ME, from OF *malart,* probably from Gmc proper name *Madalhart,* given to the duck in a beast epic]

**malleable** /'mæliəbəl/, *adj.* **1.** capable of being extended or shaped by hammering or by pressure with rollers. **2.** adaptable or tractable. [ME *malliable,* from OF *malleable,* from L *malleāre* beat with a hammer. See -ABLE] – **malleability** /mæliə'bɪləti/, **malleableness,** *n.*

**malleable cast iron,** *n.* white cast-iron castings given a special heat treatment to make them tough.

**malleable iron** /mæliəbəl 'aɪən/, *n.* **1.** →**malleable cast iron. 2.** the purest form of commercial iron, easily welded or forged.

**mallee** /'mæli/, *n.* **1.** any of various Australian species of *Eucalyptus* having a number of almost unbranched stems arising from a large underground root stock as *E. dumosa.* **2. the mallee, a.** an area of scrub where the predominant species is a mallee. **b.** any remote, isolated or unsettled area. [Aboriginal]

**mallee fowl** /'– faʊl/, *n.* a greyish-brown, spotted, Australian bird, *Leipoa ocellata,* found in dry inland scrub areas; a mound builder; lowan. Also, **mallee bird, mallee hen.**

**mallee kangaroo** /– kæŋgə'ru/, *n.* →**western grey kangaroo.**

**mallee roots** /'– ruts/, *n.pl.* the roots and butts of certain eucalypts, used as fuel.

mallee fowl

**mallee snake** /'– sneɪk/, *n.* →**common brown snake.**

**mallemuck** /'mæləmʌk/, *n.* any of various oceanic birds, as the fulmar or albatross. Also, **mollymawk.** [D *mallemok,* from *mal* foolish + *mok* gull]

**mallenders** /'mæləndəz/, *n.pl.* →**malanders.**

**malleolar** /mə'liələ/, *adj.* pertaining to a malleolus. [MALLEOL(US) + -AR[1]]

**malleolus** /mə'liələs/, *n., pl.* **-li** /-li/. either of two bony protuberances, one on each side of the ankle, situated in man at the lower end of the fibula and tibia respectively. [L, diminutive of *malleus* hammer]

**mallet** /'mælət/, *n.* **1.** a hammer-like tool with a head commonly of wood but occasionally of rawhide, plastic, etc., used for driving any tool with a wooden handle, as a chisel. **2.** the wooden implement used to strike the balls in croquet. **3.** the stick used to drive the ball in polo. **4.** any of several species of the genus *Eucalyptus* in western Australia, esp. *E. occidentalis.* **5.** the wood of these trees. [ME *maylet,* from OF *maillet,* diminutive of *mail* MALL]

**malleus** /'mæliəs/, *n., pl.* **-lei** /-lii/. the outermost of three small bones in the middle ear of man and other mammals. [L: hammer]

**mallow** /'mæloʊ/, *n.* any of various plants of the family Malvaceae, as *Malva sylvestris,* **tall mallow,** and *Modiola carolineana,* **red-flowered mallow.** [ME *malue,* OE *mealwe,* from L *malva*]

**malm** /mam/, *n.* **1.** a kind of soft, friable limestone. **2.** a chalk-bearing soil of the south-eastern part of England. [ME *malme,* OE *mealm,* c. Icel. *mālmr* ore]

**malmsey** /'mamzi/, *n.* a strong, sweet wine of a strong flavour, originally made in Greece, but now in Madeira. [ME *malmesey,* from ML *malmasia,* from NGk, alteration of *Monemvasía* a seaport in S Greece]

**malnourished** /'mælnʌrɪʃt/, *adj.* **1.** poorly nourished. **2.** suffering from malnutrition.

**malnutrition** /mælnju'trɪʃən/, *n.* imperfect nutrition; lack of proper nutrition resulting from deficiencies in the diet or the process of assimilation.

**malocclusion** /mælə'kluʒən/, *n.* faulty occlusion, closing, or meeting, as of opposing teeth in the upper and lower jaws.

**malodorous** /mæl'oʊdərəs/, *adj.* having a bad smell. – **malodorously,** *adv.* – **malodorousness,** *n.*

**malodour** /mæl'oʊdə/, *n.* a bad smell; a stench. Also, *U.S.,* **malodor.**

**malolactic fermentation** /mæloʊˌlæktɪk fɜmɛn'teɪʃən/, *n.* the conversion in wine-making of malic acid to lactic acid resulting in a reduction in acidity.

**malonic acid** /məˌlɒnɪk 'æsəd, məˌloʊnɪk/, *n.* a dibasic acid, $CH_2(COOH)_2$, easily decomposed by heat. [F *malonique,* alteration of *malique* MALIC]

**malonic ester** /– 'ɛstə/, *n.* a colourless fluid, $CH_2(COOC_2H_5)_2$, used in organic syntheses; diethyl malonate.

**malonyl** /'mælənəl/, *n.* a divalent radical, $-OCCH_2CO-$, derived from malonic acid.

**malonyl urea** /– 'juriə/, *n.* →**barbituric acid.**

**Malpighian bodies** /mælˌpɪgiən 'bɒdiz/, *n. pl.* certain small, round bodies occurring in the cortical substance of the kidney, and the lymph nodules of the spleen. Also, **Malpighian corpuscles.** [from Marcello *Malpighi,* 1628-94, Italian physiologist]

**Malpighian layer** /– 'leɪə/, *n.* the layer of non-horny cells in the epidermis.

**Malpighian tubules** /– 'tjubjulz/, *n. pl.* the excretory organs of insects, tubular outgrowths of the alimentary canal near the junction of the ventriculus and intestine. Also, **Malpighian tubes, Malpighian vessels.**

**malposition** /mælpə'zɪʃən/, *n.* faulty or wrong position, esp. of a part or organ of the body or of a foetus in the uterus.

**malpractice** /mæl'præktəs/, *n.* **1.** improper professional action or treatment by a physician, as from reprehensible ignorance or neglect or with criminal intent. **2.** any improper conduct. – **malpractitioner** /mælpræk'tɪʃənə/, *n.*

**malt** /mɔlt, mɒlt/, *n.* **1.** germinated grain (usu. barley), used in brewing and distilling. **2.** liquor produced from malt by fermentation, as beer or ale. **3.** malt extract. *–v.t.* **4.** to convert (grain) into malt. **5.** to treat or mix with malt or malt product. **6.** to make (liquor) with malt. *–v.i.* **7.** to become malt. **8.** to produce malt from grain. [ME; OE *mealt,* c. G *Malz;* akin to MELT]

**Malta** /'mɔltə, 'mɒltə/, *n.* a republic consisting of the island of Malta and two adjacent islands, in the Mediterranean between Sicily and Africa.

**Malta fever** /– 'fivə/, *n.* undulant fever due to a bacterium, *Brucella melitensis.*

**maltase** /'mɔlteɪz/, *n.* an enzyme which converts maltose into glucose and causes similar cleavage of many other glucosides. [MALT + -ASE]

**malted milk** /mɔltəd 'mɪlk, mɒltəd/, *n.* **1.** a soluble powder made by dehydrating a mixture of milk and malted cereals. **2.** a beverage made from this powder dissolved, usu. in milk.

**Maltese** /mɔl'tiz, mɒl-/, *adj., n., pl.* **-tese.** *–adj.* **1.** of or pertaining to Malta, its people, or their language. *–n.* **2.** a native or inhabitant of Malta. **3.** the Arabic dialect spoken in Malta.

**Maltese cat** /– 'kæt/, *n.* a bluish grey variety of domestic cat.

**Maltese cockspur** /– 'kɒkspɜ/, *n.* an annual spiny-headed thistle-like plant, *Centaurea melitensis,* a widespread weed in temperate areas.

**Maltese cross** /– 'krɒs/, *n.* a cross having four equal arms that expand in width outwards.

**Maltese dog** /– 'dɒg/, *n.* one of a breed of toy dogs, with long silky coats, often white in colour.

**malt extract** /mɔlt 'ɛkstrækt, mɒlt/, *n.* a sweet gummy substance derived from an infusion of malt.

**maltha** /'mælθə/, *n.* **1.** any of various cements or mortars, bituminous or otherwise. **2.** →**ozocerite.** **3.** a viscous mineral liquid or semiliquid bitumen; a mineral tar. [late ME, from L, from Gk: mixture of wax and pitch]

**malthoid** /'mælθɔɪd/, *n.* a type of rubberised tar, laid over concrete, used for: **a.** the surfacing of cricket pitches, tennis courts, etc. **b.** the covering of floors, roofs, etc.

**Malthusian** /mæl'θjuziən/, *adj.* **1.** of or pertaining to T. R. Malthus, 1766-1834, an English political economist, who contended that population, tending to increase faster than the means of subsistence, should be checked by social and moral restraints. *–n.* **2.** a follower of Malthus. – **Malthusianism,** *n.*

**malt liquor** /'mɔlt lɪkə, 'mɒlt/, *n.* an alcoholic beverage, as beer, fermented from malt.

**malt loaf** /'– loʊf/, *n.* a loaf made from malt extract, syrup, etc., served sliced with butter.

**maltose** /'mɔltoʊz, -toʊs, 'mɒl-/, *n.* a white crystalline disaccharide, $C_{12}H_{22}O_{11}$, containing two glucose units, formed by the action of beta-amylase on starch. Also, **maltobiose, malt sugar.** [MALT + -OSE[2]]

**maltreat** /mæl'trit/, *v.t.* to treat badly; handle roughly or cruelly; abuse. [F *maltraiter.* See MAL-, TREAT, *v.*] – **maltreatment,** *n.*

**maltster** /'mɔltstə, 'mɒltstə/, *n.* a maker of or dealer in malt.

**malty** /'mɔlti, 'mɒlti/, *adj.* of, like, or containing malt.

**maluka** /mə'lukə/, *n.* **1.** the boss. **2.** (*cap.*) a form of address to one's superior. [Aboriginal]

**malvaceous** /mæl'veɪʃəs/, *adj.* belonging to the Malvaceae, or mallow family of plants, which includes the abutilon, althaea, hollyhock, okra, cotton plant, etc. [L *malvāceus* of mallows]

**Malvasia** /mælvə'siə/, *n.* a sweet grape from which malmsey wine is made. [It. See MALMSEY]

**malversation** /mælvə'seɪʃən/, *n.* improper or corrupt behaviour in office. [F, from *malverser,* from L *male versārī* behave wrongly]

**malvoisie** /'mælvɔɪzi, -və-/, *n.* **1.** →**malmsey.** **2.** (*cap.*) →**Malvasia.** [F; replacing ME *malvesie* MALMSEY, from OF]

**mama** /mə'ma/, *n.* mother; mamma.

**mamaku** /'mʌməku/, *n.* an edible New Zealand tree-fern, *Cyathea medullaris,* with black trunk from 6 to 15 metres in height supporting a crown of up to thirty curving fronds. [Maori]

**mamba** /'mæmbə/, *n.* any of the long, slender, arboreal African snakes of the genus *Dendroaspis,* whose bite causes almost certain death, and which are said to attack without provocation. [Zulu or Xhosa *imamba*]

**mambo** /'mæmboʊ/, *n., pl.* **-bos,** *v.* *–n.* **1.** a ballroom dance of Latin-American origin, somewhat resembling the rumba. *–v.i.* **2.** to dance the mambo. [W Ind. Creole]

**mamey** /mæ'mi/, *n.* →**mammee.**

**mamilla** /mæ'mɪlə/, *n., pl.* **-millae** /-'mɪli/. **1.** the nipple of the mamma or breast. **2.** any nipple-like process or protuberance. Also, *Chiefly U.S.,* **mammilla.** [L *mammilla,* diminutive of *mamma* MAMMA[2]]

**mamillary** /'mæmələri/, *adj.* of, pertaining to, or resembling a mamilla. Also, *Chiefly U.S.,* **mammillary.**

**mamillate** /'mæməleɪt, -lət/, *adj.* having a mamilla or mamillae. Also, **mamillated;** *Chiefly U.S.,* **mammillate.**

**mamma**[1] /'mʌmə, mə'ma/, *n.* (*esp. in children's speech*) mother. [reduplication of a syllable common in natural infantile utterance. Cf. F *maman,* L *mamma,* Gk *mámmē,* Russ. and Lith. *mama*]

**mamma**[2] /'mæmə/, *n., pl.* **mammae** /'mæmi/. the organ, characteristic of mammals, which in the female secretes milk; a breast or udder. [OE, from L: breast, pap]

**mammal** /'mæməl/, *n.* a member of the Mammalia, a class of vertebrates whose young feed upon milk from the mother's breast. Most species (except cetaceans) are more or less hairy, all have a diaphragm, and all (except the monotremes) are viviparous. [LL *mammālis* of the breast] – **mammal-like,** *adj.* – **mammalian,** *adj., n.*

**mammalogy** /mə'mælədʒi/, *n.* the science that deals with mammals. [MAMMA(L) + -LOGY]

**mammaplasty** /'mæməplæsti/, *n.* the alteration of the shape or size of a breast by means of plastic surgery. Also, **mammoplasty.**

**mammary** /'mæməri/, *adj.* of or pertaining to the mamma or breast; mamma-like.

**mammatus** /mə'matəs/, *adj.* of or pertaining to a cloud whose lower edges are in the form of pouches. [L: of the breast]

**mammee** /mæ'mi/, *n.* **1.** a tall, tropical American resin-yielding tree, *Mammea americana.* **2.** Also, **mammee apple.** its large, edible fruit. **3.** →**marmalade tree.** Also, **mamey.** [Sp. *mamey,* from Haitian]

**mammiferous** /mæ'mɪfərəs/, *adj.* having mammae; mammalian. [L *mamma* breast + -I- + -FEROUS]

**mammilla** /mæ'mɪlə/, *n., pl.* **-millae** /-'mɪli/. *Chiefly U.S.* →**mamilla.**

**mammillary** /'mæmələri/, *adj. Chiefly U.S.* →**mamillary.**

**mammillate** /'mæməleɪt/, *adj. Chiefly U.S.* →**mamillate.**

**mammogram** /'mæməgræm/, *n.* an X-ray taken of the breasts.

**mammography** /mæ'mɒgrəfi/, *n.* the screening of the breasts by X-ray, to detect any abnormality.

**mammon** /'mæmən/, *n.* **1.** *New Testament.* riches or material wealth. **2.** (*cap.*) a personification of riches as an evil spirit or deity. [LL *mammōna,* from Gk *mamōnâs,* from Aram. *māmōn(ā)* riches] – **mammonish,** *adj.*

**mammonism** /'mæmənɪzəm/, *n.* the greedy pursuit of riches. – **mammonist, mammonite,** *n.* – **mammonistic** /mæmə'nɪstɪk/, *adj.*

**mammoplasty** /'mæməplæsti/, *n.* →**mammaplasty.**

woolly mammoth

**mammoth** /'mæməθ/, *n.* **1.** a large, extinct species of elephant, *Mammuthus primigenius,* the **northern woolly mammoth,** which resembled the present Indian elephant but had a hairy coat and long, curved tusks. **2.** any of various related extinct species of elephant, as the **imperial mammoth,** *Mammuthus imperator,* the largest mammoth. *–adj.* **3.** huge; gigantic: *a mammoth enterprise.* [Russ. *mammot',* now *mamant'*]

**mammy** /'mæmi/, *n., pl.* **-mies.** **1.** (*in children's speech*) mother. **2.** *U.S.* a coloured female nurse or old family servant.

**man** /mæn/, *n., pl.* **men,** *v.,* **manned, manning.** *–n.* **1.** *Anthrop.* an individual (genus *Homo,* family Hominidae, class Mammalia) at the highest level of animal development, mainly characterised by his exceptional mentality. **2.** the human creature or being as representing the species or as distinguished from other beings, animals, or things; the human race; mankind. **3.** a human being; a person: *to elect a new man.* **4.** the male human being, as distinguished from woman. **5.** an adult male person. **6.** a husband: *man and wife.* **7.** one; anyone (prec. by *a*): *to give a man a chance.* **8.** employer; boss (prec. by *the*). **9.** a male follower, subordinate, or employee: *officers and men of the army.* **10.** one having manly qualities or virtues. **11.** one's representative in a specified place, country, etc. **12.** a male servant; a valet. **13.** a word of familiar address to a man. **14.** *Colloq.* a term of address to a man or woman. **15.** one of the pieces used in playing certain games, as chess or draughts. **16.** *Hist.* a liegeman; vassal. **17. man and boy,** from childhood. **18. the man on the land,** the farmer. **19. to a man,** all; to the last man. [ME and OE *mann, man* (pl *menn, men*), c. Icel. *madhr,* D *man,* G *Mann*] *–v.t.* **20.** to furnish with men, as for service or defence. **21.** to take one's place for service, as at a gun, post, etc. **22.** to make manly; brace. **23.** to accustom (a hawk) to the presence of men. [ME *manne(n),* OE *mannian*]

**mana** /ˈmanə/, *n.* **1.** *Anthrop.* impersonal, supernatural force which may be concentrated in objects or persons. **2.** authority; influence; power; prestige. [Maori or ? Polynesian]

**man about town,** *n.* a frequenter of theatres, clubs, etc.

**manacle** /ˈmænəkəl/, *n., v.,* **-cled, -cling.** *–n.* (*usu. pl.*) **1.** a shackle for the hand; handcuff. **2.** a restraint. *–v.t.* **3.** to handcuff; fetter. **4.** to hamper; restrain. [ME *manicle,* from OF: handcuff, from L *manicula,* diminutive of *manus* hand]

**manage** /ˈmænɪdʒ/, *v.,* **-aged, -aging.** *–v.t.* **1.** to bring about; succeed in accomplishing: *he managed to see the governor.* **2.** to take charge or care of: *to manage an estate.* **3.** to dominate or influence (a person) by tact, address, or artifice. **4.** to handle, direct, govern, or control in action or use. **5.** to wield (a weapon, tool, etc.). **6.** to succeed in accomplishing a task, purpose, etc. **7.** to contrive to get along. **8.** to handle or train (a horse) in the exercises of the manège. *–v.i.* **9.** to conduct affairs. [It. *maneggiare* handle, train (horses), from *mano* hand, from L *manus;* sense influenced by F *manège* act of managing and *ménage* household]

**manageable** /ˈmænɪdʒəbəl/, *adj.* that may be managed; contrivable; tractable. **– manageability** /ˌmænɪdʒəˈbɪləti/, **manageableness,** *n.* **– manageably,** *adv.*

**managed currency** /mænɪdʒd ˈkʌrənsi/, *n.* a form of money management where the purchasing power of a nation's currency is adjusted by the monetary authorities to influence business activity and prices (contrasted with the *gold standard*).

**management** /ˈmænɪdʒmənt/, *n.* **1.** the act or manner of managing; handling, direction, or control. **2.** skill in managing; executive ability. **3.** the person or persons managing an institution, business, etc.: *this shop is under new management.* **4.** executives collectively: *conflicts between labour and management.*

**manager** /ˈmænədʒə/, *n.* **1.** one who manages. **2.** one charged with the management or direction of an institution, a business or the like. **3.** one who manages resources and expenditures, as of a household. **4.** a person in charge of the business affairs of an entertainer or group of entertainers. **5.** a person in charge of the performance and training of a sporting individual or team. **– managership,** *n.*

**manageress** /mænədʒəˈrɛs, ˈmænədʒərəs/, *n.* a female manager.

**managerial** /mænəˈdʒɪəriəl/, *adj.* pertaining to management or a manager: *managerial functions.* **– managerially,** *adv.*

**manakin** /ˈmænəkən/, *n.* **1.** any of various songless passerine birds, family Pipridae, of the warmer parts of America, mostly small and brilliantly coloured. **2.** manikin. [var. of MANIKIN]

**mañana** /mænˈjana, mən-/, *n., adv.* tomorrow; the indefinite future. [Sp.]

**man-at-arms** /mæn-ət-ˈamz/, *n., pl.* **men-at-arms. 1.** a soldier. **2.** a heavily armed soldier on horseback.

**manatee** /mænəˈti/, *n.* any of various herbivorous, gregarious sirenians constituting the genus *Trichechus* found in the coastal waters of America, West India and Africa, having two flippers in front and a spoon-shaped tail. [Sp. *manatí,* from Carib *manatoui*] **– manatoid** /ˈmænətɔɪd/, *adj.*

**manatoka** /mænəˈtoʊkə/, *n.* →**boobialla.**

**manavelins** /məˈnævələnz/, *n.pl. Naut.* miscellaneous pieces of gear and material. Also, **manavilins.** [orig. unknown]

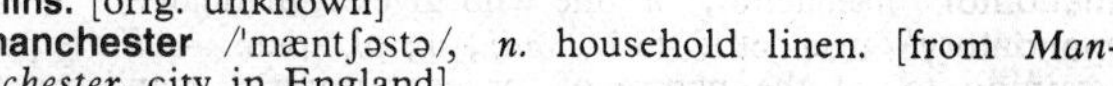

Florida manatee

**manchester** /ˈmæntʃəstə/, *n.* household linen. [from *Manchester,* city in England]

**Manchester terrier** /mæntʃəstə ˈtɛriə/, *n.* one of a breed of medium-sized terriers which originated in Manchester, England, having short, smooth, glossy black-and-tan coats.

**manchineel** /mæntʃəˈnil/, *n.* a tropical American tree or shrub, *Hippomane mancinella,* with a milky, highly caustic, poisonous sap. [F *mancenille,* from Sp. *manzanilla,* diminutive of *manzana* apple, from L (*māla*) *Matiāna* (apples) of Matius (author of a cooking manual)]

**manciple** /ˈmænsəpəl/, *n.* (in Britain) a steward or purveyor, esp. of a college or Inn of Court, or other institution. [ME, from OF: slave, servant, from L *manicipium* purchase, possession, a slave]

**-mancy,** a word element meaning 'divination', as in *necromancy.* [ME *-manci(e), -mancy(e),* from OF *mancie,* from LL *mantīa,* from Gk *manteía* divination]

**mandala** /mænˈdalə/, *n.* a mystic symbol of the universe, in the form of a circle enclosing a design; used chiefly by Hindus and Buddhists as an aid to meditation. [Skt: circle]

**mandamus** /mænˈdeɪməs/, *n.* **1.** *Law.* a writ from a superior court to an inferior court, or to an officer, a corporation, etc., commanding a specified thing to be done. **2.** (in early English law) any prerogative writ directing affirmative action. *–v.t.* **3.** *Colloq.* to intimidate or serve with such a writ. [L: we command]

mandala

**mandarin** /ˈmændərən, mændəˈrɪn/, *n.* **1.** (formerly) a member of any of the nine ranks of public officials in the Chinese Empire, each distinguished by a particular kind of button worn on the cap. **2.** an official or bureaucrat, esp. one who is in or makes himself in a high or inaccessible position. **3.** (*cap.*) standard Chinese. **4.** (*cap.*) the language of north China, esp. of Peking. **5.** a small, flattish citrus fruit of which the tangerine is one variety, native to south-western Asia, of a characteristic sweet and spicy flavour. **6.** the tree producing it, *Citrus reticulata,* and related species. [Chinese pidgin E, from Pg. *mandarim,* from *mandar* to command, b. with Malay and Hind. *mantrī,* from Skt *mantrin* counsellor, from *mantra* thought, counsel]

**mandarin collar** /– ˈkɒlə/, *n.* a type of high, single-piece, stand-up collar on a tunic or dress.

**mandarin duck** /– ˈdʌk/, *n.* a crested duck, *Aix galericulata,* with variegated plumage of purple, green, chestnut and white, native to China.

**mandarine** /mændəˈrin/, *n.* →**mandarin** (defs 5 and 6). Also, **mandarine orange.**

**mandata** /mænˈdatə/, *n.* a computer system for processing all personnel details and employment history of all Commonwealth public servants.

**mandatary** /ˈmændətəri/, *n., pl.* **-ries.** a person or nation holding a mandate. Also, **mandatory.** [LL *mandātārius,* from L *mandātum* MANDATE]

**mandate** /ˈmændeɪt/, *n., v.,* **-dated, -dating.** *–n.* **1.** a commission given to one nation (the mandatary) by an associated group of nations (such as the League of Nations) to administer the government and affairs of a people in a backward territory. **2.** a mandated territory. **3.** *Politics.* the instruction as to policy given or supposed to be given by electors to a legislative body or to one or more of its members. **4.** a command from a superior court or official to an inferior one. **5.** a command; order. **6.** an order issued by the pope, esp. one commanding the preferment of a certain person to a benefice. **7.** *Roman and Civil Law.* a contract by which one engages gratuitously to perform services for another. **8.** *Roman Law.* an order or decree by the emperor, esp. to governors of provinces. *–v.t.* **9.** to consign (a territory, etc.) to the charge of a particular nation under a mandate. [L *mandātum,* properly pp. neut. of *mandāre* commit, enjoin, command]

**mandator** /ˈmændeɪtə/, *n.* one who gives a mandate.

**mandatory** /ˈmændətri, -təri/, *adj., n., pl.* **-ries.** *–adj.* **1.** pertaining to, of the nature of, or containing a mandate. **2.** obligatory. **3.** *Law.* permitting no option. **4.** having received a mandate, as a nation. *–n.* **5.** →**mandatary.**

**mandible** /ˈmændəbəl/, *n.* **1.** the bone of the lower jaw. **2.** (in birds) **a.** the lower part of the beak; the lower jaw. **b.** (*pl.*) the upper and lower parts of the beak; the jaws. **3.** (in arthropods) one of the first pair of mouth-part appendages, typically a jawlike biting organ, but styliform or setiform in piercing and sucking species. [LL *mandibula, mandibulum* jaw]

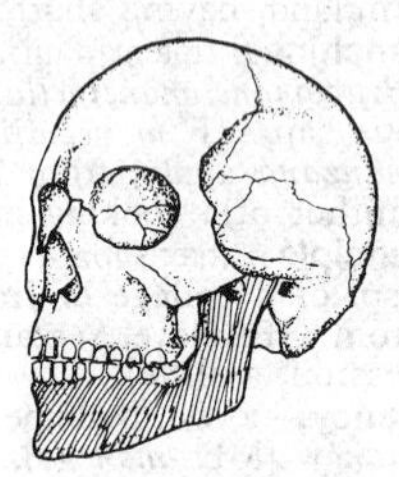

mandible (def. 1)

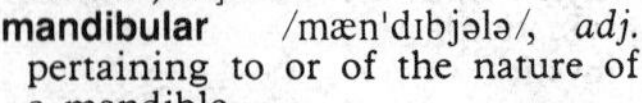

**mandibular** /mænˈdɪbjələ/, *adj.* pertaining to or of the nature of a mandible.

**mandibulate** /mænˈdɪbjələt, -leɪt/, *adj.* having mandibles.

**mandied** /ˈmændid/, *adj. Colloq.* under the influence of mandrax.

**Mandingo** /mænˈdɪŋgoʊ/, *n., pl.* **-gos, -goes,** *adj.* *–n.* **1.** a member of any of a number of Negro peoples forming an extensive linguistic group in western Africa. **2.** any language or dialect of these peoples. *–adj.* **3.** of the Mandingos or their languages.

**mandolin** /mændəˈlɪn/, *n.* a musical instrument with a pear-shaped wooden body (smaller than that of the lute) and a fretted neck, usu. having metal strings plucked with a plectrum. Also, **mandoline.** [F *mandoline,* from It. *mandolino,* diminutive of *mandola, mandora,* var. of *pandora.* See PANDORA, BANDORE] – **mandolinist,** *n.*

mandolin

**mandorla** /mænˈdɔlə/, *n.* a glory of light in an almond shape used in painting and sculpture, usu. shown surrounding the figure of Christ. [It.: lit., almond]

**mandragora** /mænˈdrægərə/, *n.* **1.** *Hist.* →**mandrake.** **2.** a mandrake root. [OE, from LL, in L *mandragoras,* from Gk]

**mandrake** /ˈmændreɪk/, *n.* a narcotic, short-stemmed European herb, *Mandragora officinarum,* with a fleshy, often forked root fancied to resemble a human form. [ME; popular etymological alteration of MANDRAGORA which was interpreted as MAN + *drake,* obs., dragon]

**mandrax** /ˈmændræks/, *n.* a sedative tablet, containing methaqualone and diphenhydramine hydrochloride. [Trademark]

**mandrel** /ˈmændrəl/, *n.* a spindle, axle, bar, or arbor, usu. tapered, pressed into a hole in a piece of work to support the work during the machining process, as between the centres of a lathe. Also, **mandril.** [F, dissimilated var. of *mandrin*]

**mandrill** /ˈmændrəl/, *n.* a large, ferocious-looking baboon, *Papio sphinx,* of western Africa, the male of which has the face marked with blue and scarlet and the muzzle ribbed. [MAN + DRILL[4]]

**manducate** /ˈmændʒukeɪt/, *v.t.,* **-cated, -cating.** *Rare.* to chew; masticate; eat. [L *mandūcātus,* pp.] – **manducation,** /mændʒuˈkeɪʃən/, *n.* – **manducatory,** *adj.*

**mandy** /ˈmændi/, *n., pl.* **mandies.** *Colloq.* →**mandrax.**

**mane** /meɪn/, *n.* **1.** the long hair growing on the back of or about the neck and neighbouring parts of some animals, as the horse, lion, etc. **2.** a long, bushy, often untended head of hair. [ME; OE *manu,* c. G *Mähne*] – **maned,** *adj.*

mandrill

**man-eater** /ˈmæn-itə/, *n.* **1.** a cannibal. **2.** an animal, esp. a tiger, lion, or shark, that eats or is said to eat men. **3.** the great white shark, *Carcharodon caracharias,* the shark reputedly most dangerous to man. **4.** a woman who habitually dominates lovers and then discards them.

**maned wolf** /meɪnd ˈwʊlf/, *n.* the largest wild South American dog, *Chrysocyon jubatus,* a red-coated, large-eared, long-legged fox, found in southern Brazil, Paraguay, and northern Argentina.

**manège** /mæˈneɪʒ/, *n.* **1.** the art of training and riding horses. **2.** the action or movements of a trained horse. **3.** a school for training horses and teaching horsemanship. Also, **manege.** [F. See MANAGE]

**manes** /ˈmaneɪz/, *n.pl.* **1.** (among the ancient Romans) the deified souls of the dead. **2.** the spirit or shade of a particular dead person. Also, **Manes.** [L]

**manet** /ˈmænət/, *v.i.* (he or she) remains (used as a stage direction to indicate that one character is to remain on stage, while others exit). [L]

**maneuver** /məˈnuvə/, *n., v.t., v.i.,* **-vered, -vering.** *U.S.* →**manoeuvre.**

**manful** /ˈmænfəl/, *adj.* having or showing manly spirit; resolute. – **manfully,** *adv.* – **manfulness,** *n.*

**mangabey** /ˈmæŋgəbi/, *n.* any primate of the genus *Cercocebus,* monkeys with white eyelids, which live in the forests of central Africa.

**manganate** /ˈmæŋgəneɪt/, *n.* a salt of manganic acid, as potassium manganate, $K_2MnO_4$.

**manganepidote** /mæŋgənˈɛpədoʊt/, *n.* →**piedmontite.**

**manganese** /mæŋgəˈniz/, *n.* a hard, brittle, greyish white metallic element used as an alloying agent with steel and other metals to give them toughness. *Symbol:* Mn; *at. wt:* 54.938; *at. no.:* 25; *sp. gr.:* 7.2 at 20°C. [F, from It., from ML *magnēsia* MAGNESIA]

**manganese bronze** /– ˈbrɒnz/, *n.* an alloy of 59 per cent copper, 1 per cent tin and up to 40 per cent manganese.

**manganese dioxide** /– daɪˈɒksaɪd/, *n.* a heavy black powder, $MnO_2$, occurring naturally as pyrolusite; used as a source of metallic manganese, as an oxidising agent, and as a catalyst. Also, **manganese peroxide.**

**manganese epidote** /– ˈɛpɪdoʊt/, *n.* →**piedmontite.**

**manganese steel** /– ˈstil/, *n.* a steel alloy containing 10 to 14 per cent of manganese, used for railway points and other devices involving heavy wear and strain.

**manganic** /mæŋˈgænɪk/, *adj.* of or containing manganese, esp. in the trivalent state.

**manganic acid** /– ˈæsəd/, *n.* an acid, $H_2MnO_4$, not known in the free state.

**manganin** /ˈmæŋgənən/, *n.* an alloy based on copper which contains manganese (up to 18 per cent) and nickel (up to 5 per cent), used extensively for electrical purposes as its resistance is only slightly affected by changes in temperature. [Trademark]

**manganite** /ˈmæŋgənaɪt/, *n.* **1.** a grey to black mineral, hydrous manganese oxide, MnO(OH), a minor ore of manganese. **2.** *Chem.* any of a series of salts containing tetravalent manganese, and derived from the acids $H_4MnO_4$ or $H_2MnO_3$. [MANGAN(ESE) + -ITE[1]]

**manganous** /ˈmæŋgənəs, mæŋˈgænəs/, *adj.* containing divalent manganese.

**mange** /meɪndʒ/, *n.* any of various skin diseases due to parasitic mites affecting animals and sometimes man, characterised by loss of hair and scabby eruptions. [late ME *manjewe,* from OF *manjue* itch, from *mangier* eat, from L *mandūcāre* chew]

**mangel-wurzel** /ˈmæŋgəl-wɜzəl/, *n.* a coarse variety of the common beet, *Beta vulgaris*, extensively cultivated as food for cattle, etc. Also, **mangel, mangold.** [G, var. of *Mangoldwurzel* beetroot]

**mangemange** /ˈmʌŋiˌmʌŋi/, *n.* a climbing New Zealand fern, *Lygodium articulatum.* [Maori]

**manger** /ˈmeɪndʒə/, *n.* a box or trough, as in a stable, from which horses or cattle eat. [ME, from OF *mangeoire*, from L *mandūcāre* chew]

**mangle**[1] /ˈmæŋgəl/, *v.t.*, **-gled, -gling.** **1.** to cut, slash, or crush so as to disfigure: *a corpse mangled in battle.* **2.** to mar; spoil: *to mangle a text by poor typesetting.* [ME *mangel(en)*, from AF *mangler*, ? frequentative of OF *mahaignier* MAIM] – **mangler,** *n.*

**mangle**[2] /ˈmæŋgəl/, *n., v.*, **-gled, -gling.** –*n.* **1.** a machine for smoothing, or pressing water, etc., out of cloth, household linen, etc., by means of rollers. **2. put through the mangle,** *Colloq.* exhausted, esp. emotionally. –*v.t.* **3.** to smooth with a mangle. [D *mangel;* ultimately akin to MANGONEL]

**mango** /ˈmæŋgoʊ/, *n., pl.* **-goes, -gos.** **1.** the oblong, slightly acid fruit of a tropical tree, *Mangifera indica*, which is eaten ripe, or preserved or pickled. **2.** the tree itself. [Pg. *manga*, from Malay *manggā*, from Tamil *mānkāy*]

**mangold** /ˈmæŋgoʊld/, *n.* →**mangel-wurzel.** Also, **mangold-wurzel.**

**mangonel** /ˈmæŋgənɛl/, *n.* a large ancient military engine, or powerful crossbow, for throwing arrows, darts, or stones. [ME, from OF, diminutive from LL *manganum*, from Gk *mánganon* engine of war]

**mangosteen** /ˈmæŋgoʊstin/, *n.* **1.** the juicy edible fruit of an East Indian resin-yielding tree, *Garcinia mangostana.* **2.** the tree itself. [Malay *mangustan*]

**mangrove** /ˈmæŋgroʊv, ˈmæn-/, *n.* a type of tree found in subtropical and tropical countries on salt or brackish, esp. estuarine, mudflats, and characterised by a strongly developed system of aeriferous spaces esp. in aerial roots and pneumatophores, as in species of the genera *Avicennia* and *Rhizophora.* [Sp. *mangle* (from Taino) + GROVE]

mangroves

**mangrove Jack** /– ˈdʒæk/, *n.* a reddish-brown, carnivorous, food and sport fish, *Lutjanus argentimaculatus*, of northern Australian rivers and mangrove-lined tidal creeks.

**mangy** /ˈmeɪndʒi/, *adj.*, **-gier, -giest.** **1.** having, caused by, or like the mange. **2.** contemptible; mean. **3.** squalid; shabby. – **mangily,** *adv.* – **manginess,** *n.*

**manhandle** /ˈmænhændl/, *v.t.*, **-dled, -dling.** **1.** to handle roughly. **2.** to move by force of men, without mechanical appliances.

**manhattan** /mænˈhætn/, *n.* a cocktail of whisky and sweet vermouth, often with a dash of bitters and a cherry. [named after *Manhattan*, the main island of New York City, U.S.]

**manhole** /ˈmænhoʊl/, *n.* a hole, usu. with a cover, through which a man may enter a sewer, drain, steam boiler, etc.

**manhood** /ˈmænhʊd/, *n.* **1.** the state of being a man or adult male person. **2.** manly qualities. **3.** men collectively. **4.** the state of being human. **5.** the human male genital organs.

**man-hour** /ˈmæn-aʊə/, *n.* an hour of work by one man, used as an industrial time unit.

**man-hunt** /ˈmæn-hʌnt/, *n.* a large scale search, usu. under the authority of the police, for a criminal or other wanted person.

**mania** /ˈmeɪniə/, *n.* **1.** great excitement or enthusiasm; craze. **2.** *Psychol.* a form of insanity characterised by great excitement, with or without delusions, and in its acute stage by great violence. [late ME, from L, from Gk: madness]

**-mania,** a combining form of **mania** (as in *megalomania*), extended to mean exaggerated desire or love for, as *balletomania.*

**maniac** /ˈmeɪniæk/, *n.* **1.** a raving lunatic; a madman. –*adj.* **2.** raving with madness; mad.

**maniacal** /məˈnaɪəkəl/, *adj.* of or pertaining to mania or a maniac. – **maniacally,** *adv.*

**manic** /ˈmænɪk/, *adj.* **1.** pertaining to mania. **2.** *Colloq.* pertaining to manic-depression. [Gk *manikós* insane]

**manic-depressive** /ˌmænɪk-dəˈprɛsɪv/, *adj.* **1.** having a mental disorder marked by cyclothymic manifestations of excitation and depression. –*n.* **2.** one who is suffering from this disorder. – **manic-depression,** *n.*

**Manichean** /mænəˈkiən/, *n.* **1.** an adherent of the religious system of the Persian teacher Mani or Manichaeus (A.D. 216?-276?), composed of Gnostic Christian, Buddhist, Zoroastrian, and various other elements, the principal feature being a dualistic theology which represented a conflict between light and darkness and included belief in the inherent evil of matter. –*adj.* **2.** of or pertaining to Mani or the Manicheans. Also, **Manichaean.** [LL *Manichaeus* (from LGk *Manichaíos;* from the name of the founder of the sect) + -AN] – **Manicheanism, Manicheism,** *n.*

**manicure** /ˈmænəkjuə/, *n., v.*, **-cured, -curing.** –*n.* **1.** professional care of the hands and fingernails. **2.** a manicurist. –*v.t.* **3.** to care for (the hands and fingernails). [F, from L *manus* hand + *cura* care]

**manicurist** /ˈmænəkjurəst/, *n.* a person who does manicuring.

**manifest** /ˈmænəfəst, -fɛst/, *adj.* **1.** readily perceived by the eye or the understanding; evident; obvious; apparent; plain: *a manifest error.* **2.** *Psychol.* apparent or disguising (used of conscious feelings and ideas which conceal and yet incorporate unconscious ideas and impulses): *the manifest content of a dream as opposed to the latent content which it conceals.* –*v.t.* **3.** to make manifest to the eye or the understanding; show plainly. **4.** to prove; put beyond doubt or question. **5.** to record in a ship's manifest. –*n.* **6.** a list of a ship's cargo signed by the master, for the information and use of the customs officers. **7.** a list of goods transported by land. **8.** a list of the cargo carried by an aeroplane. **9.** →**manifesto.** [ME, from L *manifestus* palpable, evident] – **manifestable,** *adj.* – **manifestly,** *adv.* – **manifestness,** *n.*

**manifestant** /mænəˈfɛstənt/, *n.* one who takes part in a public demonstration.

**manifestation** /mænəfɛsˈteɪʃən/, *n.* **1.** the act of manifesting. **2.** the state of being manifested. **3.** a means of manifesting; indication. **4.** a public demonstration, as for political effect. **5.** *Spiritualism.* a materialisation.

**manifestative** /mænəˈfɛstətɪv/, *adj.* showing clearly; manifesting.

**manifesto** /mænəˈfɛstoʊ/, *n., pl.* **-tos** or **-toes.** a public declaration, as of a sovereign or government, or of any person or body of persons taking important action, making known intentions, objects, motives, etc.; a proclamation. [It.: manifest, n.]

**manifold** /ˈmænəfoʊld/, *adj.* **1.** of many kinds, numerous and varied: *manifold duties.* **2.** having many different parts, elements, features, forms, etc. **3.** doing or operating several things at once. –*n.* **4.** something having many different parts or features. **5.** a copy or facsimile, as of writing, such as is made by manifolding. **6.** a pipe or chamber with a number of inlets or outlets. **7.** any very fine typing paper. –*v.t.* **8.** to make copies of, as with carbon paper. [ME *monifald*, OE *manigfeald.* See MANY, -FOLD] – **manifoldly,** *adv.* – **manifoldness,** *n.*

**manifolder** /ˈmænəfoʊldə/, *n.* a machine for making manifolds or copies, as of writing.

**maniform** /ˈmænəfɔm/, *adj.* having the shape of a hand.

**manikin** /ˈmænəkɪn, -ɪkən/, *n.* **1.** a little man; a dwarf; pygmy. **2.** mannequin. **3.** a model of the human body for teaching anatomy, demonstrating surgical operations, etc. Also, **manakin, mannikin.** [D *manneken*, diminutive of *man* man. Cf. MANNEQUIN]

**Manila** /məˈnɪlə/, *adj.* of or pertaining to envelopes, folders, etc., made from Manila or similar paper. Also, **manila.** [paper orig. made in *Manila*, the capital of the Philippines]

**Manila hemp** /mənɪlə ˈhɛmp/, *n.* a fibrous material obtained from the leaves of the abaca, *Musa textilis*, used for making ropes, fabrics, etc.

**Manila paper** /ˈ– peɪpə/, *n.* strong light brown paper, derived originally from Manila hemp, but now also from wood-pulp substitutes.

**Manila rope** /– ˈroʊp/, *n.* rope manufactured from Manila hemp.

**manilla** /məˈnɪlə/, *n.* **1.** →**Manila hemp.** **2.** →**Manila paper.**

**man in the street,** *n.* the average citizen.

**manioc** /ˈmænɪɒk/, *n.* →**cassava.** [representing Sp., Pg. *mandioca,* Tupi *manioca,* Guarani *mandio*]

**maniple** /ˈmænəpəl/, *n.* **1.** a subdivision of the Roman legion, consisting of either 120 or 60 men. **2.** *Eccles.* one of the Eucharistic vestments, consisting of an ornamental band or strip worn on the left arm near the wrist. [ME, from OF, from L *manipulus* handful, company]

**manipular** /məˈnɪpjələ/, *adj.* **1.** of or pertaining to the Roman maniple. **2.** of or pertaining to manipulation. *–n.* **3.** a soldier belonging to a maniple.

**manipulate** /məˈnɪpjəleɪt/, *v.t.,* **-lated, -lating. 1.** to handle, manage, or use, esp. with skill, in some process of treatment or performance. **2.** to manage or influence by artful skill, or deviousness: *to manipulate people; to manipulate prices.* **3.** to adapt or change (accounts, figures, etc.) to suit one's purpose or advantage. **4.** to stimulate (the genitalia). [backformation from MANIPULATION] **– manipulative, manipulatory,** *adj.* **– manipulator,** *n.*

**manipulation** /mənɪpjəˈleɪʃən/, *n.* **1.** skilful or artful management. **2.** the act of manipulating. **3.** the state or fact of being manipulated. **4.** *Med.* a treatment performed in physiotherapy, orthopaedics, and osteopathy to obtain forced passive movement of a joint beyond its active range of movement. [F, from L *manipulus* handful]

**mankind** /mænˈkaɪnd/ *for def. 1;* /ˈmænkaɪnd/ *for def. 2, n.* **1.** the human race; human beings collectively. **2.** men, as distinguished from women.

**manlike** /ˈmænlaɪk/, *adj.* **1.** resembling a man. **2.** belonging or proper to a man; manly: *manlike fortitude.*

**manly** /ˈmænli/, *adj.,* **-lier, -liest,** *adv. –adj.* **1.** possessing qualities proper to a man; strong; brave; honourable. **2.** pertaining to or befitting a man: *manly sports. –adv.* **3.** *Archaic.* in a manly manner. **– manlily,** *adv.* **– manliness,** *n.*

**man-made** /ˈmæn-meɪd/, *adj.* **1.** made or produced by man. **2.** produced artificially; not deriving from natural processes: *a man-made harbour.* **3.** *Textiles.* **a.** (of fibres) manufactured synthetically. **b.** (of fabrics) manufactured from man-made fibres.

**manna** /ˈmænə/, *n.* **1.** the food miraculously supplied to the children of Israel in the wilderness. **2.** divine or spiritual food. **3.** anything likened to the manna of the Israelites. **4.** an exudate of insects living on many Australian eucalypts, esp. *Eucalyptus viminalis,* once forming an important part of Aboriginal diet for limited periods. **5.** an exudate obtained by making an incision into the bark of the flowering ash, *Fraxinus ornus,* of southern Europe, and used as a mild laxative. **6. manna from heaven,** a welcome surprise. [OE, from LL, from Gk, from Heb. *mān*]

**manna gum** /ˈ– gʌm/, *n.* →**ribbon gum.**

**mannequin** /ˈmænəkən, -kwən/, *n.* **1.** a model of the human figure made of wood, wax, etc., used by tailors, dress designers, etc., for displaying or fitting clothes. **2.** →**model** (def. 5). [F, from D *manneken.* See MANIKIN]

**manner** /ˈmænə/, *n.* **1.** way of doing, being done, or happening; mode of action, occurrence, etc. **2.** characteristic or customary way of doing: *houses built in the Mexican manner.* **3.** (*pl.*) the prevailing customs, modes of living, etc., of a people, class, period, etc. **4.** a person's outward bearing; way of addressing and treating others. **5.** (*pl.*) ways of behaving, esp. with reference to polite standards: *bad manners.* **6.** (*pl.*) good or polite ways of behaving: *have you no manners?* **7.** outward bearing; way of behaving towards others: *the policeman had rather an awkward manner.* **8.** air of distinction: *he had quite a manner.* **9.** kind; sort: *all manner of things.* **10.** characteristic style in art, literature, or the like: *verses in the manner of Spenser.* **11.** mannered style; mannerism. **12.** *Obs.* nature; character; guise. **13. by all manner of means,** by all means; certainly. **14. in a manner,** after a fashion; so to speak; somewhat. **15. in a manner of speaking,** in a way; so to speak. **16. to the manner born, a.** accustomed or destined by birth (to a high position, etc.). **b.** naturally fitted for a position, duty, etc. [ME *manere,* from AF: orig., way of handling, from L *manuāria,* fem. of *manuārius* of or for the hand]

**mannered** /ˈmænəd/, *adj.* **1.** having (specified) manners: *ill-mannered.* **2.** having mannerisms; affected.

**mannerism** /ˈmænərɪzəm/, *n.* **1.** marked or excessive adherence to an unusual manner, esp. in literary work. **2.** a habitual peculiarity of manner. **3.** (*usu. cap.*) a style of late 16th century European art, mainly current in Italy. **– mannerist,** *n.* **– manneristic** /mænəˈrɪstɪk/, *adj.*

**mannerless** /ˈmænələs/, *adj.* without good manners.

**mannerly** /ˈmænəli/, *adj.* **1.** having or showing good manners; courteous; polite. *–adv. Archaic.* **2.** with good manners; courteously; politely. **– mannerliness,** *n.*

**mannikin** /ˈmænəkɪn, -ɪkən/, *n.* →**manikin.**

**manning scale** /ˈmænɪŋ skeɪl/, *n.* a schedule prescribing the number of men which an employer is required to employ on a particular machine or process in his establishment.

**mannish** /ˈmænɪʃ/, *adj.* **1.** resembling a man. **2.** imitating a man. **3.** (of a woman or her behaviour, clothes, etc.) characteristic of or natural to a man. **– mannishly,** *adv.* **– mannishness,** *n.*

**mannitol** /ˈmænətɒl/, *n.* a white sweetish crystalline, carbohydrate alcohol, $HOCH_2(CHOH)\ CH_2OH$, occurring in three optically different forms (the common one being found in the manna of the ash *Fraxinus ornus,* and in other plants), used in medicine as a diuretic and to assess renal function.

**mannose** /ˈmænoʊz, -oʊs/, *n.* a hexose, $C_6H_{12}O_6$, obtained from the hydrolysis of the ivory nut, and yielding mannitol on reduction. [MANN(A) + -OSE[2]]

**manoeuvre** /məˈnuvə/, *n., v.,* **-vred, -vring.** *–n.* **1.** a planned and regulated movement or evolution of troops, war vessels, etc. **2.** (*pl.*) a series of tactical exercises, usu. carried out in the field by large bodies of troops in imitation of war. **3.** an adroit move; skilful proceeding, measure, etc. *–v.t.* **4.** to change the position of (troops, etc.) by a manoeuvre. **5.** to bring, put, drive, or make by manoeuvres. **6.** to manipulate with skill or adroitness. *–v.i.* **7.** to perform a manoeuvre or manoeuvres. **8.** to scheme; intrigue. Also, *U.S.,* **maneuver.** [F: manipulation, from *manoeuvrer* work, from LL *manū operāre* work by hand] **– manoeuvrable,** *adj.* **– manoeuvrability** /məˌnuvrəˈbɪləti/, *n.* **– manoeuvrer,** *n.*

**man of God,** *n.* **1.** a saint, prophet, etc. **2.** *Colloq.* a clergyman.

**man of the people,** *n.* a public figure as a politician, who is seen to maintain a close rapport with his fellow men.

**man of the world,** *n.* a sophisticated man.

**man-of-war** /mæn-əv-ˈwɔ/, *n., pl.* **men-of-war. 1.** a warship. **2.** See **Portuguese man-of-war. Also, man-o'-war.**

**manometer** /məˈnɒmətə/, *n.* an instrument for determining the pressure of gases, vapours, or liquids. [F *manomètre,* from Gk *mānó(s)* thin, rare + F *-mètre* METER[1]] **– manometric** /mænəˈmɛtrɪk/, *adj.*

**manor** /ˈmænə/, *n.* **1.** a landed estate or territorial unit, originally of the nature of a feudal lordship, consisting of a lord's demesne and of lands within which he has the right to exercise certain privileges and exact certain fees, etc. **2.** the mansion of a lord with the land pertaining to it. **3.** the main house or mansion on an estate. [ME *manere,* from OF *manoir,* n. use of *manoir,* inf., dwell, from L *manēre* remain] **– manorial** /məˈnɔrɪəl/, *adj.*

**manor house** /ˈ– haʊs/, *n.* the house or mansion of the lord of a manor.

**man-o'-war** /mæn-ə-ˈwɔ/, *n.* →**man-of-war.**

**man-o'-war bird** /ˈ– bɜd/, *n.*→**frigatebird.**

**manpower** /ˈmænpaʊə/, *n.* **1.** the power supplied by the physical exertions of a man or men. **2.** a unit of power assumed to be equal to the rate at which a man can do mechanical work, commonly taken as $\frac{1}{10}$ horsepower. **3.** rate of work in terms of this unit. **4.** power in terms of men available or required: *the manpower of an army.*

**manqué** /ˈmɒŋkeɪ, mɒŋˈkeɪ/, *adj.* failed; unsuccessful; unfulfilled. [F]

**manriding transport** /ˈmænraɪdɪŋ ˌtrænspɔt/, *n.* transport devised for carrying miners underground, as distinct from the more common trains for hauling materials.

**manrope** /ˈmænroʊp/, *n.* a rope placed at the side of a ship's gangway, ladder, or the like, to serve as a rail.

**mansard roof** /ˈmænsad ruf, -səd/, *n.* a roof having two pitches, the upper slopes being flatter than the lower ones, usu. with rooms in the roof space having dormer windows. Also,

**mansard.** [named after F. *Mansart,* 1598-1666, French architect]

mansard roof

**manse** /mæns/, *n.* **1.** the house and land occupied by a minister or parson, usu. of nonconformist churches, as Uniting, Presbyterian, etc. **2.** (originally) the dwelling of a landholder, with the land attached. [late ME, from ML *mansa* dwelling, orig. pp. fem. of L *manēre* remain]

**manservant** /ˈmænsɜvənt/, *n., pl.* **menservants.** a male servant.

**-manship,** a suffix added to a noun, adverb, or (occasionally) to a verb, to signify proficiency in an activity, as *gamesmanship, one-upmanship, craftsmanship.*

**mansion** /ˈmænʃən/, *n.* **1.** an imposing or stately residence. **2.** (*pl.*) *Brit.* a block of flats. **3.** *Archaic.* a place of abode. **4.** *Astrol.* each of twenty-eight divisions of the ecliptic occupied by the moon on successive days. [ME, from OF, from L *mansio* a remaining, dwelling]

**man-sized** /ˈmæn-saɪzd/, *adj.* of a size or kind suitable for or appropriate to a man. Also, **man-size.**

**manslaughter** /ˈmænslɔtə/, *n.* **1.** the killing of a human being by another human being; homicide. **2.** *Law.* the killing of a human being unlawfully but without malice aforethought. See **malice** (def. 2). – **manslaughterer,** *n.*

**manslayer** /ˈmænsleɪə/, *n.* one who kills a human being; a homicide. – **manslaying,** *n., adj.*

**manta** /ˈmæntə/, *n.* **1.** (in Spain and Spanish America) a cloak or wrap. **2.** the type of blanket or cloth used on a horse or mule. **3.** *Mil.* Also, **mantelet, mantlet.** a movable shelter formerly used to protect besiegers. **4.** →**manta ray.** [Sp., from Pr.: blanket]

**manta ray** /ˈ– reɪ/, *n.* any of several rays of the genus *Manta,* widely distributed in warm seas, sometimes reaching a width of six metres, with ear-like flaps on either side of the head; devilfish. Also, **manta.**

**manteau** /ˈmæntoʊ/, *n. Archaic.* a mantle or cloak, esp. one worn by women. [F]

**mantelet** /ˈmæntlət, -tələt/, *n.* **1.** a short mantle. **2.** Also, **mantlet.** *Mil.* **a.** →**manta** (def. 3). **b.** any of various bullet-proof shelters or screens. [ME, from OF, diminutive of *mantle* MANTLE]

**mantelletta** /mæntəˈlɛtə/, *n.* a sleeveless vestment of silk or woollen stuff reaching to the knees, worn by Roman Catholic cardinals, bishops, abbots, etc. [It., diminutive of *mantello,* from L *mantellum* MANTLE]

**mantelpiece** /ˈmæntlpis/, *n.* the more or less ornamental structure above and about a fireplace, usu. having a shelf or projecting ledge. Also, **mantle.**

**mantelshelf** /ˈmæntlʃɛlf/, *n.* **1.** the projecting part of a mantelpiece. **2.** *Mountaineering.* a small ledge on the rock wall.

**manteltree** /ˈmæntltri/, *n.* a wooden beam or arch or a stone arch forming the lintel of a fireplace.

**mantic** /ˈmæntɪk/, *adj.* **1.** of or pertaining to divination. **2.** having the power of divination. [Gk *mantikós* prophetic] – **mantically,** *adv.*

**mantilla** /mænˈtɪlə/, *n.* **1.** a silk or lace head-scarf arranged over a high comb and falling over the back and shoulders, worn in Spain, Mexico, etc. **2.** a short mantle or light cape. [Sp., diminutive of *manta.* See MANTA]

**mantis** /ˈmæntəs/, *n., pl.* **-tises, -tes** /-tiz/. any of the carnivorous orthopterous insects constituting the family Mantidae, which have a long prothorax and which are remarkable for their manner of holding the forelegs doubled up as if in prayer. Also, **praying mantis.** [NL, from Gk: prophet, kind of insect]

praying mantis

**mantis crab** /ˈ– kræb/, *n.* any of the stomatopod crustaceans with appendages resembling those of the mantis. Also, **mantis shrimp.**

**mantissa** /mænˈtɪsə/, *n.* the decimal part of a logarithm. Cf. **characteristic** (def. 3). [L: an addition]

**mantle** /ˈmæntl/, *n., v.,* **-tled, -tling.** *–n.* **1.** Also, **mantua.** a loose, sleeveless cloak. **2.** something that covers, envelops, or conceals. **3.** a single or paired outgrowth of the body wall that lines the inner surface of the valves of the shell in molluscs and brachiopods. **4.** →**gas mantle. 5.** *Ornith.* the back, scapular, and inner wing feathers taken together, esp. when these are all of the same colour. **6.** the outer enveloping masonry of a blast furnace over the hearth. **7.** *Geol.* a layer of the earth between crust and core, consisting of solid rock. **8.** →**mantelpiece.** *–v.t.* **9.** to cover with or as with a mantle; envelop; conceal. *–v.i.* **10.** to spread like a mantle, as a blush over the face. **11.** to flush; blush. **12.** (of a hawk) to spread out first one wing and then the other over the corresponding outstretched leg. **13.** (of a liquid) to be or become covered with a coating; foam. [ME *mantel,* OE *mæntel,* from L *mantellum, mantēlum* cloak]

**mantle plume** /– ˈplum/, *n.* a fixed hot-spot occurring within the earth's mantle which generates heat upwards to the earth's surface, the presence of which may be indicated by volcanic activity.

**mantle rock** /– ˈrɒk/, *n.* the layer of disintegrated and decomposed rock fragments, including soil, just above the solid rock of the earth's crust; regolith.

**mantlet** /ˈmæntlət/, *n.* →**mantelet** (defs 2a and 2b).

**man-to-man** /ˈmæn-tə-mæn/, *adj.* (of a discussion, talk, etc., between two men) characterised by frankness or directness.

**Mantoux test** /mænˈtu tɛst, ˈmæntu/, *n.* a test to detect past and present tuberculosis infection, by injecting diluted tuberculin (intradermally). [named after Charles *Mantoux,* 1877-1947, French physician]

**mantra** /ˈmæntrə/, *n.* a word, phrase or verse intoned, often repetitively, as a sacred formula in Hinduism and Mahayana Buddhism. Also, **mantram.** [Skt *mantra,* lit. speech, hymn] – **mantric,** *adj.*

**mantrap** /ˈmæntræp/, *n.* **1.** a trap or snare for catching a man, esp. a trespasser. **2.** *Colloq.* a seductive woman.

**mantua** /ˈmæntʃuə/, *n.* **1.** a kind of loose gown formerly worn by women. **2.** a mantle. [from MANTEAU, by association with *Mantua,* town in N Italy]

**manual** /ˈmænjuəl/, *adj.* **1.** of or pertaining to the hand or hands. **2.** done or worked by the hand or hands. **3.** using or involving human energy, power, etc. **4.** of the nature of a manual or handbook. *–n.* **5.** a book, giving information or instructions. **6.** *Mil.* prescribed exercises in the handling of a rifle, etc. **7.** *Music.* the keyboard of an organ played with the hands. **8.** a car with a manual gear shift. [L *manuālis* of the hand (as n., ML *manuāle*); replacing ME *manuel,* from OF] – **manually,** *adv.*

**manual arts** /– ˈats/, *n.pl.* particular skills in the use of the hands, esp. metalwork, carpentry, etc., which are taught as school subjects to provide training for future employment in industry.

**manual training** /– ˈtreɪnɪŋ/, *n.* training in the various manual arts and crafts, esp. carpentry, metalwork, etc.

**manubrium** /məˈnjubriəm/, *n., pl.* **-bria** /-briə/, **-briums. 1.** *Anat., Zool.* a segment, bone, cell, etc., resembling a handle. **2.** *Anat.* **a.** the uppermost of the three portions of the sternum; the episternum. **b.** the long process of the malleus. [L: a handle]

**manucode** /ˈmænjəkoʊd/, *n.* an iridescent greenish bird, *Phonygammus keraudreni,* of Cape York and the island of New Guinea, with a powerful bass call; trumpet bird.

**manufactory** /mænjuˈfæktəri, -tri/, *n., pl.* **-ries.** *Archaic.* →**factory.**

**manufacture** /mænjəˈfæktʃə, ˈmænjəfæktʃə/, *n., v.,* **-tured, -turing.** *–n.* **1.** the making of goods or wares by manual labour or by machinery, esp. on a large scale. **2.** the making of anything. **3.** the thing or material manufactured. *–v.t.* **4.** to make or produce by hand or machinery, esp. on a large scale. **5.** to make anything. **6.** to work up (material) into form for use. **7.** to invent fictitiously; concoct; devise. **8.** to produce by mere mechanical industry without inspiration. [F, from L *manū,* abl. of *manus* hand + *factūra* a making] – **manufacturing,** *n.*

**manufacturer** /mænjəˈfæktʃərə/, *n.* **1.** one who owns or runs a manufacturing plant. **2.** one who manufacturers.

**manufg,** manufacturing.

**manuka** /məˈnukə, ˈmanəkə/, *n.* either of the New Zealand tea-trees, kahikatoa and kanuka, both valuable honey plants.

**manumission** /mænjəˈmɪʃən/, *n.* **1.** the act of manumitting. **2.** the state of being manumitted.

**manumit** /mænjəˈmɪt/, *v.t.*, **-mitted, -mitting.** to release from slavery or servitude. [L *manūmittere*] – **manumitter,** *n.*

**manure** /məˈnjuə/, *n., v.*, **-nured, -nuring.** *–n.* **1.** any natural or artificial substance for fertilising the soil. **2.** excrement, esp. of animals used as fertiliser. *–v.t.* **3.** to treat (land) with fertilising matter; apply manure to. [ME *maynour(en)*, v., from AF *maynoverer* work by hand, from OF *manuevre.* See MANOEUVRE, *n.*] – **manurer,** *n.* – **manurey,** *adj.*

**manus** /ˈmeɪnəs/, *n., pl.* **-nus. 1.** *Anat.* the distal segment of the forelimb of a vertebrate, including the carpus and the forefoot or hand. **2.** *Rom. Law.* power over persons, as that of the husband over the wife. [L: hand]

**manuscript** /ˈmænjəskrɪpt/, *n.* **1.** a book, document, letter, musical score, etc., written by hand. **2.** an author's copy of his work, written by hand or typewriter, which is used as the basis for typesetting. **3.** writing, as distinguished from print. *–adj.* **4.** written by hand or typed (not printed). [ML *manūscriptus,* lit., hand-written] – **manuscriptal,** *adj.*

**manward** /ˈmænwəd/, *adv.* **1.** Also, **manwards.** towards man. *–adj.* **2.** directed towards man.

**manway** /ˈmænweɪ/, *n.* →**catwalk.**

**Manx** /mæŋks/, *adj.* **1.** of or pertaining to the Isle of Man, its inhabitants, or their language. *–n.* **2.** (*construed as pl.*) the inhabitants of the Isle of Man. **3.** the Gaelic of the Isle of Man, virtually extinct. [metathetic and syncopated form of earlier *Maniske*]

**Manx cat** /– ˈkæt/, *n.* a tailless variety of the domestic cat.

**many** /ˈmɛni/, *adj.*, **more, most. 1.** constituting or forming a large number: *many people.* **2.** relatively numerous (after *as, so, too,* or *how*): *six may be too many.* **3.** being one of a large number (fol. by *a* or *an*): *many a day.* *–n.* **4.** a great or considerable number (oft. fol. by a noun with *of* expressed or understood): *a great many people.* **5.** (as a collective plural) many persons or things. **6. a good (great) many,** a large number. [ME *mani, manye,* etc., OE *manig,* c. G *manch*]

**manyfold** /ˈmɛnifoʊld/, *adv.* (multiplying or increasing) by many times: *in the years after the discovery of gold, Melbourne's population increased manyfold.* Also, **many-fold, many fold.** [MANY + -FOLD]

**manyplies** /ˈmɛniplaɪz/, *n.* the omasum (so called from the plies or folds of its membrane). [MANY + *plies,* pl. of PLY[2]]

**many-sided** /ˈmɛni-saɪdəd/, *adj.* **1.** having many sides. **2.** having many aspects, capabilities, etc.: *a many-sided man.* – **many-sidedness,** *n.*

**manzanilla** /mænzəˈnɪlə/, *n.* **1.** a pale, very dry Spanish sherry. **2.** a small kind of green olive, with a thin skin.

**Mao** /maʊ/, *adj.* of the simple, undecorative, practical style of clothing common in China since the 1949 revolution: *Mao suit, Mao cap.* [named after *Mao* Zedung. See MAOISM]

**Maoism** /ˈmaʊɪzəm/, *n.* the principles of Communism as expounded by Mao Zedung. [named after *Mao* Zedung, 1893-1976, Chinese statesman; chairman of the Chinese Communist Party 1943-76]

**Maoist** /ˈmaʊəst/, *n.* one who believes in the principles and practices of Maoism.

**Maori** /ˈmaʊri/, *n., pl.* **-ris, -ri,** *adj.* *–n.* **1.** a member of a brown-skinned Polynesian people of New Zealand. **2.** a Polynesian language, the language of the Maoris. *–adj.* **3.** of or pertaining to the Maoris or their language. **4.** *N.Z. Colloq.* rough; uncivilised. [Maori: lit., of the usual kind (as opposed to foreigners)]

**Maori basket** /– ˈbaskət/, *n. N.Z.* →**kit**[3].

**Maori beetle** /– ˈbitl/, *n.* a dark brown New Zealand cockroach, *Platyzosteria novae-zelandiae;* evil smelling when crushed. Also, **Maori bug.**

**Maori cabbage** /– ˈkæbɪdʒ/, *n. N.Z.* **1.** a wild form of cabbage, *Brassica oleracea.* **2.** →**puha.**

**Maori dog** /– ˈdɒg/, *n.* **1.** the extinct Polynesian dog of New Zealand. **2.** →**kuri**[1].

**Maoridom** /ˈmaʊridəm/, *n. N.Z.* the Maori race or people.

**Maori-head** /ˈmaʊri-hɛd/, *n. N.Z.* →**niggerhead** (def. 4).

**Maori hen** /maʊri ˈhɛn/, *n. N.Z.* →**weka.**

**Maoriland** /ˈmaʊrilænd/, *n.* →**New Zealand.** – **Maorilander,** *n.*

**Maori oven** /maʊri ˈʌvən/, *n. N.Z.* →**hangi.**

**Maori P.T.** /– pi ˈti/, *n. N.Z. Colloq.* a rest; spell. [MAORI + P.T.]

**Maori rat** /– ˈræt/, *n.* the rat, *Mus maorium,* introduced by the Maoris to New Zealand; kiore.

**Maoritanga** /ˈmaʊritʌŋə/, *n.* the qualities inherent in being a Maori, relating to heritage, culture, etc. [Maori]

**map** /mæp/, *n., v.*, **mapped, mapping.** *–n.* **1.** a representation, on a flat surface, of a part or the whole of the earth's surface, the heavens, or a heavenly body. **2.** a maplike representation of anything. **3. off the map,** out of existence, into oblivion: *whole cities were wiped off the map.* **4. put on the map,** to make widely known; make famous. *–v.t.* **5.** to represent or delineate in or as in a map. **6.** to sketch or plan (oft. fol. by *out*): *to map out a new career.* [ML *mappa* (*mundī*) map (of the world), from L *mappa* napkin]

**maple** /ˈmeɪpəl/, *n.* **1.** any tree of the genus *Acer,* of the north temperate zone, species of which are valued for shade and ornament, for their wood, or for their sap, from which a syrup (**maple syrup**) and a sugar (**maple sugar**) are obtained. **2.** the wood of any such tree. [ME *mapel,* OE *mapel-* in *mapeltrēow* maple tree]

**mapou** /ˈmapoʊ/, *n.* a small New Zealand tree, *Myrsine australis,* with aromatic leaves. Also, **matipo.** [Maori]

**map projection** /ˈmæp prədʒɛkʃən/, *n.* →**projection** (def. 5).

**map-reading** /ˈmæp-ridɪŋ/, *n.* **1.** the technique of reading a map. **2.** the act of reading a map.

**maquette** /maˈkɛt/, *n.* a model of a contemplated structure, as a wax or clay model of a piece of sculpture. [F: model]

**maquis** /maˈki/, *n., pl.* **maquis.** (*oft. cap.*) a member of one of the French underground groups resisting the Germans in World War II. [F, special use of *maquis, makis* wild, bushy land (Corsican d.)]

**mar** /ma/, *v.t.*, **marred, marring. 1.** to damage; impair; ruin. **2.** to disfigure; deface. [ME *marre,* OE *merran* hinder, waste, c. OHG *merren,* OS *merrian* hinder]

**mar.,** **1.** marine. **2.** maritime. **3.** married.

**Mar.,** March.

**marabou** /ˈmærəbu/, *n.* **1.** any of three large storks, *Leptoptilus crumeniferus* of Africa, *L. dubius,* the adjutant bird, and *L. javanicus* of the East Indies, having under the wings and tail soft, downy feathers that are used in millinery and for making a furlike trimming or material. **2.** one of the feathers. **3.** the trimming or material made of them. Also, **marabout.** [F *marabout,* orig. a Muslim hermit]

**maraca** /məˈrækə/, *n.* a gourd filled with pebbles, seeds, etc., and used as a percussion instrument in Latin-American bands.

**marae** /məˈraɪ/, *n.* enclosed space in front of a Maori meeting house; a Maori place of meeting. [Maori]

**marasca** /məˈræskə/, *n.* a wild cherry, *Prunus cerasus* var. *marasca,* with small, acid, bitter fruit, from which maraschino is made.

**maraschino** /mærəˈskinoʊ, -ˈʃinoʊ/, *n.* a cordial or liqueur distilled from marascas. [It., from *(a)marasca* kind of cherry, from *amaro* bitter, from L *amārus*]

**maraschino cherry** /– ˈtʃɛri/, *n.* a cherry cooked in coloured syrup and flavoured with imitation maraschino.

**marasmus** /məˈræzməs/, *n.* gradual loss of flesh and strength, as from malnutrition, old age, etc., rather than from actual disease. [NL, from Gk *marasmós* a wasting] – **marasmic,** *adj.*

**Maratha** /məˈratə/, *n.* a member of a Hindu people inhabiting central and western India. Also, **Mahratta.** [Hind. *marhatá*]

**Marathi** /məˈrati/, *n.* the language of the Marathas; an Indic language of western India. Also, **Mahratti.**

**marathon** /ˈmærəθɒn, -θən/, *n.* **1.** any long-distance race. **2.** a foot race of 26 miles or 42 195 metres. **3.** any long contest with endurance as the primary factor: *a dance marathon.* [named after the plain of *Marathon* in Greece, where the Athenians defeated the Persians in 490 B.C., and from which a runner took the news to Athens, about 40 kilometres away]

**maraud** /məˈrɔd/, *v.i.* **1.** to rove in quest of plunder; make a raid for booty. *–v.t.* **2.** to raid for plunder. *–n.* **3.** the act of marauding. [F *marauder,* from *maraud* rogue, vagabond] – **marauder,** *n.* – **marauding,** *adj.*

**marble** /ˈmabəl/, *n., adj., v.*, **-bled, -bling.** *–n.* **1.** limestone in a more or less crystalline state and capable of taking a polish, occurring in a wide range of colours and variegations, and much used in sculpture and architecture. **2.** a variety of this stone. **3.** a piece of this stone. **4.** a work of art carved in marble. **5.** a marbled appearance or pattern; marbling. **6.** something resembling marble in hardness, coldness, smoothness, etc. **7.** *Games.* **a.** a little ball of stone, baked clay, glass, etc., used in a children's game. **b.** (*pl. construed as sing.*) the game itself. **8. make one's marble good,** *Colloq.* ingratiate oneself (fol. by *with*). **9. pass in one's marble,** *Colloq.* to die. **10. lose one's marbles,** *Colloq.* to act irrationally; go mad. *–adj.* **11.** consisting of marble. **12.** like marble, as being hard, cold, unfeeling, etc. **13.** of variegated or mottled colour. *–v.t.* **14.** to colour or stain like a variegated marble. [dissimilated var. of ME *marbre,* from OF, from L *marmor*]

**marble cake** /'– keɪk/, *n.* a cake given a marble-like appearance by the use of combinations of dark and light mixture.

**marble fish** /'– fɪʃ/, *n.* →**congolli.**

**marble orchard** /– 'ɔtʃəd/, *n. Colloq.* a cemetery.

**marble wood** /'– wʊd/, *n.* a tree of the genus *Albizia* with mottled timber.

**marbling** /'mablɪŋ/, *n.* **1.** the act, process, or art of colouring or staining in imitation of variegated marble. **2.** an appearance like that of variegated marble. **3.** *Bookbinding.* marble-like decoration on the paper edges, lining, or binding boards of a book. **4.** *Meat Industry.* the distribution of fat in the muscular tissue of a cut of meat, giving a spotted or streaked appearance.

**marbly** /'mabli/, *adj.* rigid, cold, etc., like marble.

**marc** /mak/, *n.* **1.** the grapes contained in the winepress, and the residue (skins and pips) remaining after the juice is expressed. **2.** the brandy distilled from grape pomace. [F, from *marcher* treat, press]

**marcasite** /'makəsaɪt/, *n.* **1.** a common mineral (**white iron pyrites**), iron disulphide ($FeS_2$), of the same composition as pyrite, but differing in crystal system. **2.** (formerly) any of the crystallised forms of iron pyrites, much used in the 18th century for ornaments. **3.** a specimen or ornament of this substance. [ML *marcasīta,* from Ar. *marqashītā,* from Aram.]

**marcato** /ma'katoʊ/, *adv.* (a musical direction) in a marked manner. [It.] – **marcate,** *adj.*

**marcel** /ma'sɛl/, *v.,* **-celled, -celling,** *n. –v.t.* **1.** to wave (the hair) by means of special irons, producing the effect of regular, continuous waves (**marcel waves**). *–n.* **2.** a marcelling. **3.** a marcelled condition. [from *Marcel* Grateau, 1852-1936, French hairdresser, the originator]

**marcescent** /ma'sɛsənt/, *adj.* withering but not falling off, as a part of a plant. [L *marcescens,* ppr., withering] – **marcescence,** *n.*

**march**[1] /matʃ/, *v.i.* **1.** to walk with regular and measured tread, as soldiers; advance in step in an organised body. **2.** to walk in a stately or deliberate manner. **3.** to proceed; advance. *–v.t.* **4.** to cause to march. *–n.* **5.** the act or course of marching. **6.** the distance traversed in a single course of marching. **7.** advance; forward movement: *the march of progress.* **8.** a piece of music with a rhythm suited to accompany marching. **9. steal a march,** to gain an advantage secretly or slyly (usu. fol. by *on* or *upon*). [F *marcher* walk, march, go, earlier trample, from L *marcus* hammer]

**march**[2] /matʃ/, *n.* **1.** a tract of land along a border of a country; frontier. *–v.i.* **2.** to touch at the border; border (fol. by *upon, with,* etc.). [ME *marche,* from OF, from Gmc; cf. OHG *marka*]

**March** /matʃ/, *n.* the third month of the year, containing 31 days. [ME, from AF *marche,* c. OF *marz,* from L *Martius,* lit., month of Mars]

**marcher**[1] /'matʃə/, *n.* one who marches (on foot). [MARCH[1] + -ER[1]]

**marcher**[2] /'matʃə/, *n.* an inhabitant of, or an officer or lord having jurisdiction over, marches or border territory. [MARCH[2] + -ER[1]]

**marchesa** /ma'keɪzə/, *n., pl.* **-se** /-zeɪ/. (in Italy) a marchioness. [It., fem. of *marchese*]

**marchese** /ma'keɪzə/, *n., pl.* **-si** /-zi/. (in Italy) a marquess. [It.]

**march fly** /'matʃ flaɪ/, *n.* any of certain members of the large family Tabanidae, which suck the blood of mammals and inflict a painful bite; horsefly.

**march fracture** /'matʃ fræktʃə/, *n.* fracture of the 2nd, 3rd, or 4th metatarsal bones, occurring after unaccustomed walking or marching.

**marching girl** /'matʃɪŋ gɜl/, *n.* a girl who marches in formation with other girls, as a form of exercise or public entertainment.

**marching orders** /– ɔdəz/, *n.pl.* **1.** *Mil.* directions to soldiers to proceed in order to take position for battle, etc.: *the brigade received its marching orders shortly after the general's visit.* **2.** *Colloq.* orders to leave; dismissal (from a job, etc.).

**marchioness** /maʃə'nɛs/, *n.* **1.** the wife or widow of a marquess. **2.** a lady holding in her own right the rank equal to that of a marquess. [ML *marchiōnissa,* fem. of *marchio* MARQUESS]

**marchpane** /'matʃpeɪn/, *n. Obs.* marzipan. [F, d. var. of *massepain, marcepain,* from It. *marzapane,* orig. box of sweets, from Ar. *martabân* glazed vessel]

**march-past** /matʃ-'past/, *n.* a ceremonial parade or procession, esp. of troops past a saluting base.

**Mardi gras** /'madi gra/, *n.* Shrove Tuesday; the last day before Lent which is celebrated with special carnival festivities. [F: meat-eating Tuesday]

**mardo** /'madoʊ/, *n.* the yellow-footed marsupial mouse, *Antechinus flavipes.*

**mare**[1] /mɛə/, *n.* a female horse, fully grown and past its fourth birthday. [ME *mare, mere,* OE *mere, myre* (c. Icel. *merr*), fem. of *mearh* horse (c. OHG, *marah.* Icel. *marr*). Cf. MARSHAL]

**mare**[2] /mɛə/, *n. Obs.* **1.** the evil spirit supposed to cause bad dreams. **2.** →**nightmare.** [ME and OE, c. Icel. *mara*]

**mare**[3] /'mareɪ/, *n., pl.* **maria** /'mariə/. **1.** any of several large, dark plains on the moon. **2.** any of several dark areas on the planet Mars. [L: sea]

**maremma** /mə'rɛmə/, *n., pl.* **-remme** /-'rɛmi/. **1.** a marshy, unhealthy region near the seashore, as in Italy. **2.** the miasma associated with such a region. [It., from L *maritima,* fem. of *maritimus* maritime]

**marengo** /mə'rɛŋgoʊ/, *adj.* (of a chicken, or veal dish) browned in oil, and sauteed in a sauce of tomatoes, mushrooms, garlic or onions, and white wine. [probably from a chicken dish created for Napoleon after his victory at *Marengo* (1800), village in Italy]

**mare's-nest** /'mɛəz-nɛst/, *n.* something imagined to be an extraordinary discovery but proving to be a delusion or a hoax.

**mare's-tail** /'mɛəz-teɪl/, *n.* **1.** an erect aquatic Old World plant, *Hippuris vulgaris,* with crowded whorls of narrow, hairlike leaves. **2.** a cirrus cloud resembling a horse's tail.

**marg** /madʒ/, *n. Colloq.* →**margarine.**

**margaric acid** /ma,gærɪk 'æsəd/, *n.* a white fatty acid, $CH_3(CH_2)_{15}COOH$, resembling stearic acid and obtained from lichens or synthetically. [Gk *márgaron* pearl + -IC]

**margarine** /madʒə'rin, mag-, 'madʒərən/, *n.* **1.** a butter-like product made from refined vegetable or animal oils or various mixtures of both, and emulsifiers, colouring matter, etc. **2.** Also, **table margarine.** the more palatable kind of margarine intended for use on bread, biscuits, etc. **3.** Also, **cooking margarine.** a cheaper margarine intended for use in cooking. Also, **marg.** [F, from Gk *margáron* white of pearl + *-ine* -INE[2]]

**margarite** /'magəraɪt/, *n.* **1.** an aggregate of small crystals, found in a bead-like row in some glassy igneous rocks. **2.** a mineral, hydrated aluminium calcium silicate, occurring in grey or yellow monoclinic crystals.

**margay** /'mageɪ/, *n.* a small tiger cat, *Felis wiedi,* of tropical America. [F *margai,* from Pg. *maracajá,* from Tupi *mbaracajá*]

**marge** /madʒ/, *n. Colloq.* margarine.

**margin** /'madʒən/, *n.* **1.** a border or edge. **2.** the space bordering the printed or written matter on a page. **3.** a limit, or a condition, etc., beyond which something ceases to exist or be possible: *the margin of consciousness.* **4.** an amount allowed or available beyond what is actually necessary: *a margin of error.* **5.** *Finance.* **a.** a security, as a percentage in money, deposited with a broker as a provision against loss on transactions on behalf of his principal. **b.** the amount representing the customer's investment or equity in such an account. **6.** *Comm.* the difference between the cost and the selling price. **7.** *Econ.* the point at which the return from economic activity barely covers the cost of production, and below which production is unprofitable. **8.** *Banking.* the excess value of the relative security over the loan for which it is collateral. **9.** that part of a wage, additional to the basic wage, which is offered to account for the employee's particular skills; secondary wage. **10.** an allowance made in estimation or performance as a safety precaution: *margin of safety.* *–v.t.* **11.** to provide with a margin or border. **12.** to furnish with marginal notes, as a document. **13.** to enter in the margin, as of a book. **14.** *Finance.* to deposit a margin upon. [ME *margyn,* from L *margo* border, edge]

**marginal** /ˈmadʒənəl/, *adj.* **1.** pertaining to a margin. **2.** situated on the border or edge. **3.** written or printed in the margin of a page: *a marginal note.* **4.** minimal for requirements; barely sufficient. **5.** *Econ.* **a.** supplying goods at a rate merely covering the cost of production. **b.** of or pertaining to goods produced and marketed at margin: *marginal profits.* **6.** denoting or pertaining to an electoral division in which a poll is likely to result in victory by a narrow margin. **7.** (of land) difficult and unprofitable to cultivate. **8.** of or pertaining to the rate at which the margin (def. 9) is paid. [NL *marginālis,* from L *margo* MARGIN] – **marginally,** *adv.*

**marginalia** /madʒəˈneɪliə/, *n.pl.* marginal notes. [NL]

**marginalism** /ˈmadʒənəlɪzəm/, *n.* a type of economic analysis which places stress on marginal factors in the economy.

**marginal man** /madʒənəl ˈmæn/, *n.* a person who lives on the margins of two cultural groups, but identifies with neither.

**marginate** /ˈmadʒəneɪt/, *adj., v.,* **-nated, -nating.** *–adj.* Also, **marginated. 1.** having a margin. **2.** *Entomol.* having the margin of a distinct colour: *marginate with purple.* *–v.t.* **3.** to furnish with a margin; border. [L *margināt us,* pp.] – **margination** /madʒəˈneɪʃən/, *n.*

**margravate** /ˈmagrəvət/, *n.* the province of a margrave. Also, **margraviate** /maˈgreɪviət/.

**margrave** /ˈmagreɪv/, *n.* **1.** the hereditary title of the rulers of certain states. **2.** *Hist.* a hereditary German title, equivalent to *marquess.* **3.** (originally) a German military governor of a mark, or border province. [MD *markgrave* mark or border count]

**margravine** /ˈmagrəvin/, *n.* the wife of a margrave.

**marguerite** /magəˈrit/, *n.* **1.** any of several flowers of the daisy family, esp. *Chrysanthemum frutescens,* cultivated for its numerous white-rayed, yellow-centred flowers. **2. chase marguerites,** *Colloq.* to clean fly-struck sheep. [F: daisy, pearl, from L *margarīta* pearl]

**mariage de convenance** /mari,aʒ də kõvəˈnõs/, *n.* →**marriage of convenience.**

**Marian** /ˈmɛəriən/, *adj.* **1.** of or pertaining to the Virgin Mary. **2.** of or pertaining to some other Mary, as Mary, queen of England, or Mary, queen of Scots. *–n.* **3.** one who has a particular devotion to the Virgin Mary.

**mariculture** /ˈmærikʌltʃə/, *n.* the cultivation of the sea's resources, esp. fish, for food.

**marigold** /ˈmærigould/, *n.* **1.** any of the various chiefly golden-flowered plants esp. of the genus *Tagetes,* as *T. erecta,* with strong-scented foliage. **2.** any of various other plants, esp. of the genus *Calendula,* as C. *officinalis,* a common garden plant of some use in dyeing and medicine. [ME, from MARY (the Virgin) + GOLD]

**marigraph** /ˈmærəgræf/, *n.* a device for registering the rise and fall of the tide.

marijuana

**marijuana** /mærəˈwanə/, *n.* **1.** the Indian hemp, *Cannabis sativa.* **2.** its dried leaves and flowers, used in cigarettes and food as a narcotic and intoxicant. Also, **marihuana.** [Amer. Sp.; ? native word, b. with *Maria Juana* Mary Jane]

**marimba** /məˈrɪmbə/, *n.* a musical instrument, originating in Africa but popularised and modified in Central America, formed of strips of wood of various sizes (often having resonators beneath to reinforce the sound), struck by hammers or sticks. [E African lang. (cf. Chopi *mbila*)]

**marina** /məˈrinə/, *n.* a boat basin offering dockage and other service for small craft. [It. and Sp.: of the sea]

**marinade** /mærəˈneɪd/, *n.;* /ˈmærəneɪd/, *v.,* **-naded, -nading.** *–n.* **1.** a liquid, esp. wine or vinegar with oil and seasonings, in which meat, fish, vegetables, etc., may be steeped before cooking. **2.** a liquid, as brandy, in which fruits, etc., may be steeped before serving. **3.** the food so treated. *–v.t.* **4.** →**marinate.** [F, from *mariner* pickle in brine, from *marin* MARINE]

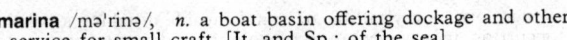

**marinara** /mærəˈnarə/, *adj.* having a sauce based on seafood, as prawns, mussels, etc. [It. *(alla) marinara* in the manner of sailors, from *marinaio* sailor, from L *mare* sea]

marimba

**marinate** /ˈmærəneɪt/, *v.t.,* **-nated, -nating. 1.** to let stand in a liquid before cooking or serving in order to impart flavour; marinade. **2.** to apply French dressing to (a salad). [F *mariner* (see MARINADE) + -ATE[1]] – **marination** /mærəˈneɪʃən/, *n.*

**marine** /məˈrin/, *adj.* **1.** of or pertaining to the sea; existing in or produced by the sea. **2.** pertaining to navigation or shipping; nautical; naval; maritime. **3.** serving on shipboard, as soldiers. **4.** of or belonging to the marines. **5.** adapted for use at sea: *a marine barometer.* *–n.* **6.** seagoing vessels collectively, esp. with reference to nationality or class; shipping in general. **7.** one of a class of naval troops serving both on shipboard and on land. **8.** a picture with a marine subject. **9.** naval affairs, or the department of a government (as in France) having to do with such affairs. **10. dead marine,** *Colloq.* an empty and discarded beer, wine or spirits bottle. **11. tell it** (or **that**) **to the marines!** (an expression of disbelief, esp. at an unlikely story). [ME *maryne,* from F *marin* (fem. *marine*), from L *marīnus* of the sea]

**marine biologist** /– baɪˈɒlədʒəst/, *n.* one who studies marine biology.

**marine biology** /– baɪˈɒlədʒi/, *n.* the study of plant and animal life in the sea.

**marine insurance** /– ɪnˈʃɔrəns/, *n.* insurance covering loss or damage to maritime property occasioned by any of the numerous perils on and of the sea.

**marineland** /məˈrinlænd/, *n.* a zoo for the purpose of exhibiting and preserving marine animals.

**mariner** /ˈmærənə/, *n.* one who directs or assists in the navigation of a ship; seaman; sailor. [ME, from AF, from F *marin* MARINE]

**marine stinger** /mərin ˈstɪŋə/, *n. Colloq.* →**sea wasp.**

**mariniere** /mærɪˈnjɛə/, *adj. Cookery.* **1.** (of mussels and other shellfish), cooked in a little water with seasonings. **2.** (of a fish dish), cooked in wine with mussels. [F *marinière*]

**Mariolatry** /mɛəriˈɒlətri/, *n.* *(derog.)* excessive veneration of the Virgin Mary. [MARY + -OLATRY] – **Mariolater,** *n.* – **Mariolatrous,** *adj.*

**Mariology** /mɛəriˈɒlədʒi/, *n.* the body of belief, doctrine, and opinion concerning the Virgin Mary.

**marionette** /mæriəˈnɛt/, *n.* a puppet moved by strings attached to its jointed limbs. [F, from *Marion,* diminutive of *Marie* Mary]

marionette

**marish** /ˈmærɪʃ/, *Archaic or Poetic.* *–n.* **1.** →**marsh.** *–adj.* **2.** →**marshy.** [ME *mareis,* from OF. See MORASS]

**Marist** /ˈmarəst, ˈmærəst/, *n.* a member of the 'Society of Mary', founded in 1816 for missionary and educational work in the name of the Virgin Mary.

**marital** /ˈmærətəl/, *adj.* **1.** of or pertaining to marriage. **2.** of or pertaining to a husband. [L *marītālis* pertaining to married people] – **maritally,** *adv.*

**maritime** /ˈmærətaɪm/, *adj.* **1.** connected with the sea in relation to navigation, shipping, etc.: *maritime law.* **2.** of or pertaining to the sea. **3.** bordering on the sea. **4.** living near the sea. **5.** characteristic of a seaman; nautical. [L *maritimus* of the sea]

i = peat ɪ = pit ɛ = pet æ = pat a = part ɒ = pot ʌ = putt ɔ = port ʊ = put u = pool ɜ = pert ə = apart aɪ = buy eɪ = bay ɔɪ = boy aʊ = how
oʊ = hoe ɪə = here ɛə = hair ʊə = tour g = give θ = thin ð = then ʃ = show ʒ = measure tʃ = choke dʒ = joke ŋ = sing j = you õ = Fr. bon

**maritime climate** /– 'klaımət/, *n.* a type of climate characterised by little temperature change, high cloud cover, and precipitation, and associated with coastal areas.

**maritime pine** /– 'paın/, *n.* a tall conifer with large cones, *Pinus pinaster,* native to western and south-western Europe on sandy soils near the sea, naturalised in south-western England.

**marjoram** /'madʒərəm/, *n.* any plant of the mint family belonging to the genera *Origanum* or *Majorana,* esp. the species *M. hortensis* (**sweet marjoram**) used in cookery, or *O. vulgare,* a wild species native to Europe and naturalised elsewhere. [ME *majorane,* from OF, from L *amāracus*]

**mark**[1] /mak/, *n.* **1.** a visible trace or impression upon anything, as a line, cut, dent, stain, bruise, etc.: *a birthmark.* **2.** a badge, brand, or other visible sign assumed or imposed. **3.** a symbol used in writing or printing: *a punctuation mark.* **4.** a sign, usu. a cross, made by an illiterate person by way of signature. **5.** an affixed or impressed device, symbol, inscription, etc., serving to give information, identify, indicate origin or ownership, attest to character or comparative merit, or the like. **6.** a sign, token, or indication. **7.** a symbol used in rating conduct, proficiency, attainment, etc., as of pupils in a school. **8.** something serving as an indication of position, as a bookmark. **9.** a recognised or required standard: *to be below the mark.* **10.** repute; note; importance, or distinction: *a man of mark.* **11.** a distinctive trait. **12.** (*usu. cap.*) a designation for a model of a weapon, an item of military equipment, a motor vehicle, or the like, generally used together with a numeral: *the Mark-4 weapon-carrier.* **13.** an object aimed at, as a target. **14.** an object or end desired or striven for, as a goal. **15.** an object of derision, scorn, hostile schemes, swindling, etc.: *an easy mark.* **16.** *Athletics.* the starting point allotted to a contestant. **17.** *Boxing.* the middle of the stomach. **18.** *Bowls.* See **jack**[1] (def. 7). **19.** (on a nautical lead line) one of the measured indications of depth, consisting of a white, blue, or red rag, a bit of leather, or a knot of small line. **20.** a tract of land held in common by a medieval community of freemen. **21.** *Rugby Football.* **a.** →**fair catch. b.** the mark on the turf made by the heel as the player calls 'mark' while taking a fair catch as a claim for a free kick. **c.** the place from or behind which a free kick or penalty kick is taken. **22.** *Aus. Rules.* **a.** the action of catching the ball on the full, after it has travelled not less than nine metres directly from the kick of another player without it having been touched while in transit from kick to catch. **b.** the place on the field where the mark was made, or where an infringement resulting in a free kick took place, and from or behind which the player must then kick. **c.** the field umpire's decision that the catch has been fairly taken. **23.** Some special noun phrases are:

**be quick off the mark, 1.** (of a competitor in a race) to start promptly. **2.** to be prompt in recognising and acting upon the possibilities of a situation.

**be slow off the mark, 1.** (of a competitor in a race) to start slowly. **2.** to be sluggish or slow to start something.

**give (someone) a good (bad) mark,** to approve (disapprove) of (someone).

**give full (top) marks,** to approve warmly (fol. by *to*).

**leave one's mark,** to effect lasting changes.

**make one's mark,** to become famous or successful.

**on your mark** or **marks!** (addressed to competitors at the beginning of a race) take your places!

**overshoot the mark,** to err by overestimating the requirements of a situation.

**overstep the mark, 1.** (of a competitor in a race) to break the rules by placing a foot over or beyond the mark before the start of the race. **2.** to go beyond the bounds of convention or accepted standards.

**up to the mark,** of the required standard.

**wide of the mark,** inaccurate; irrelevant.

*–v.t.* **24.** to be a distinguishing feature of: *a day marked by rain.* **25.** to put a mark or marks on. **26.** to attach or affix to (something) figures or signs indicating price, quality, brandname, etc. **27.** to castrate (a lamb, calf, etc.). **28.** to trace or form by or as by marks (oft. fol. by *out*). **29.** to indicate or designate by or as by marks. **30.** to single out; destine (oft. fol. by *out*). **31.** to record, as a score. **32.** to make manifest. **33.** to give heed or attention to. **34.** to notice or observe. **35.** *Sport.* to observe and keep close to (an opponent) with the intention of obtaining advantage. **36.** *Football.* to catch the ball so as to be awarded a mark (def. 21). *–v.i.* **37.** to take notice; give attention; consider. *–v.* **38.** Some special verb phrases are:

**mark down,** to reduce the price of.

**mark off,** to separate, as by a line or boundary.

**mark time, 1.** to suspend advance or progress temporarily as while awaiting development. **2.** *Mil.* to move the feet alternately as in marching, but without advancing.

**mark up, 1.** to mark with notations or symbols. **2.** to increase the price of. [ME; OE *mearc* boundary, landmark, c. G *Mark;* akin to L *margo* border]

**mark**[2] /mak/, *n.* **1.** a former silver coin of Germany, until 1924 the monetary unit. **2.** →**deutschmark. 3. Mark der Deutschen Notenbank,** the monetary unit of East Germany. **4.** →**markka.** [ME; OE *m(e)arc,* c. G *Mark*]

**mark**[3] /mak/, *v.i.* (in opera singing) to go through a rehearsal performance without taxing one's vocal powers. [G *markien* to simulate]

**markdown** /'makdaʊn/, *n.* **1.** a reduction in price. **2.** the amount by which a price is reduced.

**marked** /makt/, *adj.* **1.** strikingly noticeable; conspicuous: *with marked success.* **2.** *Linguistics.* (of a phonetic or syntactic unit) abnormal; more complex or more unexpected than an opposed unit. **3.** watched as an object for suspicion or vengeance: *a marked man.* **4.** having a mark or marks. – **markedly** /'makədli/, *adv.* – **markedness,** *n.*

**marker** /'makə/, *n.* **1.** one who or that which marks. **2.** something used as a mark or indication, as a bookmark, etc. **3.** one who records a score, as in a game, etc. **4.** a counter used in card-playing. **5.** *Colloq.* an I.O.U.

**market** /'makət/, *n.* **1.** a meeting of people for selling and buying. **2.** the assemblage of people at such a meeting. **3.** an open space or a covered building where such meetings are held, esp. for the sale of food, etc. **4.** a store for the sale of food. **5.** trade or traffic, esp. as regards a particular commodity. **6.** a body of persons carrying on extensive transactions in a specified commodity: *the cotton market.* **7.** the field of trade or business: *the best shoes on the market.* **8.** demand for a commodity: *an unprecedented market for leather.* **9.** a region where anything is or may be sold: *the foreign market.* **10.** current price or value: *a rising market.* **11. at the market,** at the best obtainable price in the open market. **12. in the market,** of a racehorse, etc., considered to have a chance of winning, consequently causing the betting odds to be short. **13. in the market for,** ready to buy; seeking to buy. **14. on the market,** for sale; available. **15. play the market,** to speculate on the stock exchange. **16. go to market,** *Colloq.* to become angry, excited, unmanageable. *–v.i.* **17.** to deal (buy or sell) in a market. *–v.t.* **18.** to carry or send to market for disposal. **19.** to dispose of in a market; sell. [ME and late OE, from VL *marcātus,* L *mercātus* trading, traffic, market]

**marketable** /'makətəbəl/, *adj.* **1.** readily saleable. **2.** of or pertaining to selling or buying. – **marketability** /makətə'bıləti/ **marketableness,** *n.*

**marketable parcel** /'– pasəl/, *n.* the minimum number of shares necessary for a normal market transaction.

**market economy** /makət ə'kɒnəmi/, *n.* an economic structure in which the allocation of resources is achieved by the interdependent decisions of persons supplying and demanding those resources rather than by the decisions of a centralised planning agency such as a bureaucracy.

**marketeer** /makə'tıə/, *n.* one active in or advocating a market as specified: *black marketeer, Common Marketeer.*

**market garden** /makət 'gadn/, *n.* a garden or smallholding where vegetables and fruit are grown for sale. – **market gardener,** *n.* – **market gardening,** *n.*

**marketing** /'makətıŋ/, *n.* **1.** the total process whereby goods are put on to the market. **2.** the act of buying or selling in a market.

**market order** /makət 'ɔdə/, *n.* an order to purchase or sell at the current market price.

**market overt** /– 'oʊvɜt/, *n.* the tenet that all sales are binding, not only on parties to sale but on all other persons; thus a purchaser acting in good faith acquires a valid title to goods even if they are stolen unless the true owner has prosecuted the thief to conviction.

**marketplace** /'makətpleɪs/, *n.* **1.** a place, esp. an open space in a town, where a market is held. **2.** the world of business, esp. regarded as a place where monetary value is established.

**market price** /'makət praɪs/, *n.* the price at which a commodity, security, or service is selling in the open market. Also, **market value.**

**market research** /– rə'sɜtʃ, 'ri-/, *n.* the gathering of information by a firm about the preferences, purchasing powers, etc., of consumers, esp. as a preliminary to putting a product on the market.

**market town** /'– taʊn/, *n.* a town where a market is held.

**markhor** /'makɔ/, *n.* the largest of the wild goats, *Capra falconeri,* living in and around the Himalayas. [Pers.: lit., snake-eater]

**marking** /'makɪŋ/, *n.* **1.** a mark, or a number or pattern of marks. **2.** the act of one who or that which marks: *the marking of papers.* **3.** (*usu. pl.*) *Agric.* **a.** identification marks as brands, etc., placed on animals. **b.** the characteristic natural mark patterns on animals, as on Hereford cattle.

**marking-ink** /'makɪŋ-ɪŋk/, *n.* an indelible ink used for marking names on linen, etc.

**marking tape** /'makɪŋ teɪp/, *n.* a piece of material sewn or ironed onto clothes, etc., used for recording a person's name.

**markka** /'makə/, *n.pl.* the monetary unit of Finland. *Abbrev.:* mk. [Finn., from Swed. *mark*]

**marksman** /'maksmən/, *n., pl.* **-men. 1.** one skilled in shooting at a mark; one who shoots well. **2.** *Law.* person unable to write who signs with a mark, usu. X. **–marksmanship,** *n.* **–markswoman,** *n. fem.*

**mark-up** /'mak-ʌp/, *n.* the amount or percentage added to the cost of the article in fixing the selling price: *a 50 per cent mark-up on cameras.*

**marl**[1] /mal/, *n.* **1.** a soil or earthy deposit consisting of clay and calcium carbonate, used esp. as a fertiliser. **2.** compact, impure limestones. **3.** *Poetic.* earth. *–v.t.* **4.** to fertilise with marl. [ME, from OF, from LL *margila,* diminutive of L *marga*] **–marlaceous** /ma'leɪʃəs/, **marly,** *adj.*

**marl**[2] /mal/, *v.t. Naut.* to wind (a rope, etc.) with marline, usu. every turn being secured by a hitch. [D *marlen,* apparently frequentative of *marren* tie. Cf. MARLINESPIKE]

**marl**[3] /mal/, *n.* →**barred bandicoot.**

**marlin** /'malən/, *n.* any of various species of large, powerful, game-fishes having the upper jaw elongated into a rounded spear, as the **striped marlin,** *Makaira audax,* which is found seasonally in coastal waters of eastern Australia. [short for MARLINESPIKE]

marlin

**marline** /'malən/, *n.* small cord of two loosely twisted strands, used for seizing. [half adoption, half translation of D *marlijn,* from *marr(en)* tie + *lijn* LINE[1]]

**marlinespike** /'malənspaɪk/, *n.* a pointed metal implement used in marling, separating the strands of rope in splicing, etc. [orig. **marling spike.** See MARL[2], SPIKE[1]]

**marlock** /'malɒk/, *n.* a medium-height tree, *Eucalyptus redunca,* with thick, narrow or elliptical leaves, horn-shaped buds, and mottled bark, found in south-western Australia.

A, marlinespike; B, marlinespike separating strands of rope

**marmalade** /'maməleɪd/, *n.* a jelly-like preserve with fruit (usu. citrus) suspended in small pieces. [late ME, from F *marmelade,* from Pg. *marmelada,* from *marmelo* quince, from L *melimēlum,* from Gk *melímēlon,* lit., honey apple]

**marmalade tree** /'– tri/, *n.* a sapotaceous tree, *Calocarpum sapota,* of tropical America, with a durable wood resembling mahogany and a fruit used in preserving.

**marmite** /'mamaɪt/, *n.* **1.** a type of covered cooking pot. **2.** broth cooked in such a pot. [F *marmite* pot]

**marmoreal** /ma'mɔriəl/, *adj.* of or like marble. Also, **marmorean.** [L *marmoreus* of marble + -AL[1]]

**marmoset** /'maməsɛt/, *n.* any of various small, squirrel-like South and Central American monkeys, genera *Callithrix* and *Leontocebus,* and allied genera, with soft fur and a long, slightly furry, non-prehensile tail. [ME *marmusette,* from OF *marmouset* grotesque little figure, from OF *merme* under age, from L *minimus* least, b. with Gk *mormōtós* frightful]

marmoset

**marmot** /'mamət/, *n.* **1.** any of the bushy-tailed, thickset rodents constituting the genus *Marmota,* as the common woodchuck. **2.** any of certain related animals, as the prairie dogs. [F *marmotte,* backformation from *marmottaine,* L *mūsmontānus,* from *mūs* mouse + *montānus* of the mountains]

marmot (def. 1)

**marocain** /'mærəkeɪn/, *n.* a ribbed crepe fabric made of silk, wool, or rayon, or a combination of these materials. [F: Moroccan]

**maroon**[1] /mə'roʊn, mə'run/, *n.* **1.** dark brownish red. **2.** a firework exploding with a loud report, esp. one used as a warning or distress signal. *–adj.* **3.** of a dark brownish red colour. [F *marron,* from It. *marrone* chestnut]

**maroon**[2] /mə'run/, *v.t.* **1.** to put ashore and leave on a desolate island or coast by way of punishment, as was done by buccaneers, etc. **2.** to isolate as if on a desolate island. *–n.* **3.** one of a group of Negroes, originally fugitive slaves, living in the wilder parts of the West Indies and the Guianas. **4.** one who is marooned. [F *marron.* Cf. Sp. *cimarrón* wild, from *cimarra* bushes]

**marplot** /'maplɒt/, *n.* one who mars or defeats a plot, design, or project by officious interference.

**marquee** /ma'ki/, *n.* **1.** a large tent or tentlike shelter, sometimes with open sides, esp. one for temporary use providing refreshment, entertainment, etc. **2.** *U.S.* →**marquise** (def. 4). [assumed sing. of MARQUISE taken as pl.]

**marquess** /'makwəs/, *n.* a nobleman ranking next below a duke and above an earl or count. Also, **marquis.** [var. of MARQUIS]

**marquetry** /'makətri/, *n.* inlaid work of variously coloured woods or other materials, esp. in furniture. Also, **marqueterie** /'makətri/. [F *marqueterie,* from *marqueter* mark, chequer, inlay, from *marque* MARK[1]]

**marquis** /'makwəs, ma'ki/, *n.* →**marquess.** [F replacing ME *markis,* from OF *marchis,* from *marche* MARCH[2]]

**marquisate** /'makwəzət/, *n.* **1.** the rank of a marquess. **2.** the territory ruled by a marquess or a margrave.

**marquise** /ma'kiz/, *n.* **1.** the wife or widow of a marquess. **2.** a lady holding the rank equal to that of a marquess. **3.** a common diamond shape, pointed oval, usu. with normal brilliant facets. **4.** a rooflike shelter or canopy, as of glass, projecting above the outer door of a building and over a pavement or terrace. **5.** →**marquee.** [F, fem. of MARQUIS]

**marquisette** /makwə'zɛt, -kə-/, *n.* a lightweight open fabric of leno weave in cotton, rayon, silk, or nylon. [F, diminutive of MARQUISE]

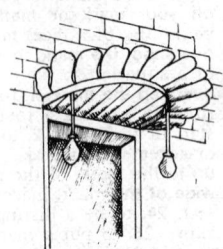

marquise (def. 4)

**marram grass** /'mærəm gras/, *n.* a stout perennial grass with creeping stems and stiff leaves, *Ammophila arenaria,* abundant in coastal sand-dunes.

**marri** /ˈmæri/, *n.* a tree, *Eucalyptus calophylla,* endemic to western Australia which, together with its hybrids with *E. ficifolia,* flame gum, is widely cultivated for its coloured flowers.

**marriage** /ˈmærɪdʒ/, *n.* **1.** the legal union of a man with a woman for life; state or condition of being married; the legal relation of spouses to each other; wedlock. **2.** the legal or religious ceremony that sanctions or formalises the decision of a man and woman to live as husband and wife. **3.** any intimate union. **4.** *Econ.* the offsetting of a buying order and a selling order in a broker's office, both orders having been received by the broker's clients. [ME *mariage,* from OF, from *marier* MARRY[1]]

**marriageable** /ˈmærədʒəbəl/, *adj.* fit, esp. old enough, for marriage. – **marriageability** /mærədʒəˈbɪləti/, **marriageableness,** *n.*

**marriage celebrant** /ˈmærɪdʒ sɛləbrənt/, *n.* one who performs a marriage, esp. in a civil service.

**marriage certificate** /ˈ– sətɪfəkət/, *n.* a certificate issued compulsorily by a registrar upon the legal marriage of two people.

**marriage guidance** /ˈ– gaɪdns/, *n.* advice on problems connected with marriage. Also, **marriage counselling.**

**marriage guidance counsellor,** *n.* a person trained to advise on problems connected with marriage.

**marriage of convenience,** *n.* a marriage of expediency, usu. for money or position. Also, **mariage de convenance.**

**marriage portion** /ˈmærɪdʒ pɔʃən/, *n.* →**dowry.**

**marriage settlement** /ˈ– sɛtlmənt/, *n.* an arrangement for the conveyance of property for the benefit of the parties to, and the prospective children of, a marriage.

**married** /ˈmærid/, *adj.* **1.** united in wedlock; wedded. **2.** pertaining to marriage or married persons.

**marron**[1] /ˈmærən/, *n.* a chestnut; esp. as used in cookery, or candied or preserved in syrup. [F. See MAROON[1]]

**marron**[2] /ˈmærən/, *n.* a large freshwater crayfish of western Australia, *Cherax tenuimanus.* [Aboriginal]

**marrons glacés** /mærɔ̃ ˈglaseɪ/, *n.pl.* chestnuts glazed or coated with sugar.

**marrow** /ˈmæroʊ/, *n.* **1.** a soft, fatty vascular tissue in the interior cavities of bones. **2.** the inmost or essential part. **3.** strength or vitality. **4.** rich and nutritious food. **5.** the elongated fruit of a cultivated variety of *Cucurbita pepo,* widely used as a cooked vegetable; vegetable marrow. [ME *marowe, marw(e),* OE *mearg,* c. G *Mark*]

**marrowbone** /ˈmæroʊboʊn/, *n.* **1.** a bone containing edible marrow. **2.** (*pl.*) (*joc.*) the knees. **3.** (*pl.*) →**crossbones.**

**marrow squash** /mæroʊ ˈskwɒʃ/, *n.* *U.S.* any of several squashes with a smooth surface, oblong shape, and hard rind.

**marry**[1] /ˈmæri/, *v.,* **-ried, -rying.** *–v.t.* **1.** to take in marriage. **2.** to unite in wedlock. **3.** to give in marriage. **4.** to unite intimately. **5.** *Naut.* **a.** to join together, as two ropes, end to end without increasing the diameter. **b.** to force the two parts of (a hatch) into place. *–v.i.* **6.** to take a husband or wife; wed. [ME *marie(n),* from F *marier,* from L *marītāre* wed] – **marrier,** *n.*

**marry**[2] /ˈmæri/, *interj. Archaic.* (an exclamation of surprise, etc.). [euphemistic var. of MARY (the Virgin)]

**Mars** /maz/, *n.* the planet next outside the earth, fourth in order from the sun. [from *Mars,* the ancient Roman god of war]

**marsala** /məˈsalə, ma-/, *n.* a sweet, dark, fortified wine. [from *Marsala,* town in Italy]

**Marseillaise** /masəˈleɪz/, *n.* the French national anthem, written in 1792 by Rouget de Lisle.

**marsh** /maʃ/, *n.* a tract of low, wet land; a swamp. [ME *mershe,* OE *mersc,* syncopated var. of *merisc* (c. G *Marsch*), from *mere* pool + *-isc* -ISH[1]. See MERE[2]]

**marshal** /ˈmaʃəl/, *n., v.,* **-shalled, -shalling** or (*U.S.*) **-shaled, -shaling.** *–n.* **1.** a military officer of the highest rank. In many countries the title is modified by some other term, as in Australia *field marshal,* and in France *marshal of France.* **2.** *U.S.* an administrative officer of a judicial district who performs duties similar to those of a sheriff. **3.** an officer who attends a judge on the assizes. **4.** the title of various officials having certain police duties. **5.** a high officer of a royal household or court. **6.** a person charged with the arrangement or regulation of ceremonies, etc. *–v.t.* **7.** to arrange in due or proper order; set out in an orderly manner. **8.** to array for battle, etc. **9.** to usher or lead. **10.** *Her.* to combine (two or more coats of arms) on a single escutcheon. [ME *mareschal,* from OF, from VL *mariscalcus* groom, from Gmc; cf. OE *mearh* horse, *scealc* servant] – **marshalcy, marshalship,** *n.* – **marshaller,** *n.*

**marshalling yard** /ˈmaʃəlɪŋ jad/, *n.* a system of parallel tracks, crossings, points, etc., where cars are shunted and made up into trains, and where carriages, locomotives, and other rolling stock are kept when awaiting repairs or when not in use.

**Marshall's fig-parrot** /maʃəlz ˈfɪg-pærət/, *n.* a small fig-parrot, *Psittaculirostris diophthalma marshalli,* green with a red crown and a blue spot above and in front of the eye, found only on the Cape York peninsula; lorilet.

**marsh fern** /ˈmaʃ fɜn/, *n.* a fern with a slender creeping rhizome and erect pinnate leaves, *Thelypteris palustris,* widespread in wet places throughout temperate regions.

**marsh gas** /ˈ– gæs/, *n.* a gaseous decomposition product of organic matter, consisting largely of methane.

**marsh harrier** /ˈ– hæriə/, *n.* an Old World harrier, *Circus aeruginosus,* having a cream-coloured head.

**marsh hen** /ˈ– hɛn/, *n.* any of various rails or rail-like birds.

**marsh horsetail** /– ˈhɔsteɪl/, *n.* →**horsetail.**

**marshland** /ˈmaʃlænd/, *n.* a district or region characterised by marshes, swamps, etc.

**marsh light** /ˈmaʃ laɪt/, *n.* →**ignis fatuus.**

**marsh mallow** /maʃ ˈmæloʊ/, *n.* an Old World mallow, *Althaea officinalis,* with pink flowers, found in marshy places.

**marshmallow** /ˈmaʃmæloʊ, -mɛl-/, *n.* confection with an elastic, spongy texture, sometimes tinted pink or other colours, usu. containing gelatine, sugar, and flavouring. [ME *marshmalue,* OE *merscmealwe.* See MARSH, MALLOW]

**marsh marigold** /maʃ ˈmærigoʊld/, *n.* a species of kingcup, *Caltha palustris.*

**marsh saltbush** /– ˈsɒltbʊʃ/, *n.* a narrow plant, *Atriplex paludosa,* family Chenopodiaceae, of coastal and inland salty marshes of south-eastern Australia and Tasmania.

**marshy** /ˈmaʃi/, *adj.,* **-shier, -shiest.** **1.** like a marsh; soft and wet. **2.** pertaining to a marsh. **3.** consisting of or constituting marsh. – **marshiness,** *n.*

**marsupial** /maˈsupiəl, -ˈsjup-/, *adj.* **1.** pertaining to, resembling, or having a marsupium. **2.** of or pertaining to the marsupials. *–n.* **3.** any of the Marsupialia, the order which includes all of the viviparous, but non-placental mammals such as kangaroos, wombats, possums and related animals, found chiefly in the Australian region and in South and Central America. The female of most species has a marsupium. [NL *marsūpiālis,* from L *marsūpium.* See MARSUPIUM]

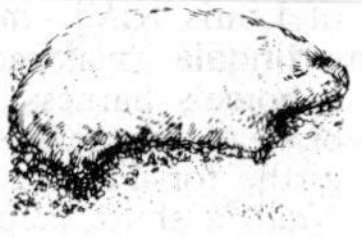

marsupial mole

**marsupial cat** /– ˈkæt/, *n.* →**native cat.**

**marsupial fence** /maˈsjupiəl fɛns/, *n.* →**kangaroo fence.**

**marsupial mole** /– ˈmoʊl/, *n.* a small, Australian, burrowing marsupial of arid regions, *Notoryctes typhlops,* whose habits, shape and size closely parallel those of placental moles.

**marsupial mouse** /– ˈmaʊs/, *n.* any of various small, Australian, carnivorous marsupials superficially resembling mice or small rats.

marsupial mouse

**marsupium** /maˈsupiəm, -sjup-/, *n., pl.* **-pia** /-piə/. **1.** the pouch or fold of skin on the abdomen of a female marsupial which contains the mammary glands and serves as a receptacle for the developing young. **2.** a structure in certain other animals for enclosing eggs or young. [L: pouch, from Gk *marsýpion, marsípion,* diminutive of *mársipos* bag, pouch]

**mart** /mat/, *n.* **1.** market; trading centre. **2.** a shop. **3.** *Archaic.* →**fair**[2]. [D, spoken var. of *markt* MARKET]

**martagon lily** /matəgən 'lɪli/, *n.* a commonly cultivated perennial plant, *Lilium martagon,* with large, dull purple flowers.

**martellato** /matə'latoʊ/, *adv.* **1.** (a musical direction) in a heavily accented manner. *–adj.* **2.** heavily accented.

**Martello tower** /ma,tɛloʊ 'taʊə/, *n.* a circular, tower-like fort with guns on the top. Also, **martello.** [alteration of *Mortella Tower,* a fort on Corsica]

**marten** /'matn/, *n., pl.* **-tens,** (*esp. collectively*) **-ten. 1.** any of various slender, fur-bearing carnivores of the genus *Martes,* as the American **pine marten,** *M. americana,* of the northern U.S. and Canada. **2.** the fur of such an animal, generally a dark brown. [ME *martren,* from OF *martrine,* properly the fur, n. use of *martrin,* adj., from *martre* marten; from Gmc (cf. G *Marder*)]

marten

**martensite** /'matnzaɪt/, *n.* the hard constituent produced when steel is cooled from the hardening temperature at a greater speed than its critical cooling rate.

**martial** /'maʃəl/, *adj.* **1.** inclined or disposed to war; warlike; brave. **2.** pertaining to or connected with the army and navy. **3.** pertaining to or appropriate for war: *martial music.* **4.** characteristic of or befitting a warrior: *a martial stride.* [ME, from L *martiālis* of Mars] **– martially,** *adv.* **– martialness,** *n.*

**martial law** /– 'lɔ/, *n.* the law imposed upon an area by military forces when civil authority has broken down.

**Martian** /'maʃən/, *adj.* **1.** pertaining to the planet Mars. *–n.* **2.** a supposed inhabitant of the planet Mars. [L *Martius* of Mars + -AN]

**martie** /'mati/, *n. Colloq.* a tomato. Also, **marty.**

**martin** /'matn/, *n.* any of various small, insectivorous birds, resembling and related to the swallows, which breed in colonies, as the tree martin, *Petrochelidon nigricans,* and the fairy martin, *Petrochelidon ariel,* widely distributed in Australia, or the common European house martin, *Chelidon urbica.* [late ME, from *Martin* man's name]

**martinet** /matə'nɛt/, *n.* a rigid disciplinarian, esp. a military one. [from General *Martinet,* French drillmaster of the reign of Louis XIV] **– martinetish,** *adj.* **– martinetism,** *n.*

**martingale** /'matəngeɪl/, *n.* **1.** a strap of a horse's harness passing from the bit or headgear, between the forelegs, to the girth, for holding the head down. **2.** *Naut.* a short, perpendicular spar under the bowsprit end, used for staying the jib boom. **3.** a gambling system in which the stakes are doubled after each loss. **4.** *Fencing.* a leather strap attached to the handle of a foil or épée and looped around the hand as a safety precaution in the event of a disarm. [F, of unknown orig.]

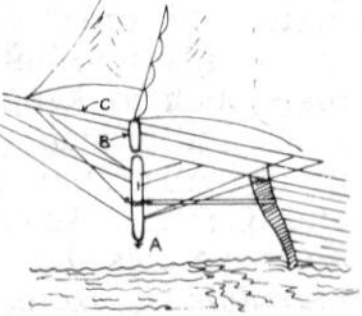

martingale (def. 2): A, martingale; B, bowsprit; C, jib boom

**martini** /ma'tini/, *n.* →**dry martini.** [from *Martini* and Rossi, Italian winemakers]

**martlet** /'matlət/, *n.* **1.** →**house martin. 2.** *Her.* a representation of a swallow without legs, used esp. as the fourth son's mark of status. [F *martelet,* var. of *martinet,* diminutive of *martin* MARTIN]

martlet (def. 2)

**martyr** /'matə/, *n.* **1.** one who willingly suffers death rather than renounce his religion. **2.** one who is put to death or endures great suffering on behalf of any belief, principle, or cause. **3.** one undergoing severe or constant suffering. **4.** one who suffers from a martyr complex. *–v.t.* **5.** to put to death as a martyr. **6.** to make a martyr of. **7.** to torment or torture. [ME *marter,* OE *martyr,* from L, from Gk *mártys,* orig., witness]

**martyr complex** /'– kɒmplɛks/, *n.* a desire to put oneself to considerable trouble for the sake of another person, organisation, project, etc., so that one will feel exceedingly self-righteous and compel the sympathy of others.

**martyrdom** /'matədəm/, *n.* **1.** the condition, sufferings, or death of a martyr. **2.** extreme suffering.

**martyrise** /'matəraɪz/, *v.t.,* **-rised, -rising. 1.** to make a martyr of. **2.** to torment. Also, **martyrize. – martyrisation** /matəraɪ'zeɪʃən/, *n.*

**martyrology** /matə'rɒlədʒi/, *n., pl.* **-gies. 1.** the branch of knowledge dealing with the lives of martyrs. **2.** an account or history of martyrs. **3.** such histories collectively. **4.** a list of martyrs. **– martyrological** /matərə'lɒdʒɪkəl/, *adj.* **– martyrologist,** *n.*

**martyry** /'matəri/, *n., pl.* **-ries.** a shrine, chapel, or the like, erected in honour of a martyr. [LL *martyrium,* from LGk *martýrion*]

**marula** /mə'rulə/, *n.* a large shrub of southern Africa, *Sclerocarya caffra,* having spiky flowers and walnut-sized drupes. [? from Tswana, a Bantu language]

**marvel** /'mavəl/, *n., v.,* **-velled, -velling** or (*U.S.*) **-veled, -veling.** *–n.* **1.** a wonderful thing; a wonder or prodigy; something that arouses wonder or admiration. **2.** *Archaic.* the feeling of wonder. *–v.t.* **3.** to wonder at (usu. fol. by a clause as object). **4.** to wonder or be curious about (usu. fol. by a clause as object). *–v.i.* **5.** to be affected with wonder, as at something surprising or extraordinary. [ME *merveille,* from F, from L *mīrābilia* wonderful things, properly neut. pl. of *mīrābilis* wonderful]

**marvellous** /'mavələs/, *adj.* **1.** such as to excite wonder; surprising, extraordinary. **2.** excellent; superb. **3.** improbable or incredible (often used absolutely in the phrase *the marvellous*). **– marvellously,** *adv.* **– marvellousness,** *n.*

**marvel-of-Peru** /mavəl-əv-pə'ru/, *n.* →**four-o'clock** (def. 1).

**Marxian** /'maksiən/, *adj.* of or pertaining to Karl Marx or his theories. **– Marxianism,** *n.*

**Marxism** /'maksɪzəm/, *n.* the system of thought developed by Karl Marx, together with Friedrich Engels, esp. the doctrine that the state throughout history has been a device for the exploitation of the masses by a dominant class, that class struggle has been the main agency of historical change, and that the capitalist state contained from the first the 'seeds of its own decay' and will inevitably, after a transitional period known as 'the dictatorship of the proletariat', be superseded by a socialist order and a classless society. [named after Karl *Marx,* 1818-83, German philosopher, economist and political theorist]

**Marxism-Leninism** /,maksɪzəm-'lɛnənɪzəm/, *n.* a form of Marxism, as modified by Lenin, which holds that imperialism is an advanced kind of capitalism.

**Marxist** /'maksəst/, *n.* **1.** an adherent of Karl Marx or his theories. *–adj.* **2.** of Karl Marx or his theories.

**mary** /'mɛəri/, *n. Colloq.* a woman, esp. a black woman.

**Mary** /'mɛəri/, *n.* the mother of Jesus, often called the **Virgin Mary** or **Saint Mary.** [ME *Marie,* OE *Maria,* from L, from Gk, from Heb. *Miryām*]

**Mary Jane** /– 'dʒeɪn/, *n. Colloq.* →**marijuana.** Also, **Mary Jay** /mɛəri 'dʒeɪ/.

**marzipan** /'mazəpæn/, *n.* a confection made of almonds reduced to a paste with sugar, etc., and moulded into various forms, usu. diminutive fruits and vegetables. Also, **marchpane.** [G. See MARCHPANE]

**-mas,** a final element in certain names of holidays and Christian feasts, as *Michaelmas.* [combining form of MASS[2]]

**masc.,** masculine.

**mascara** /mæs'karə/, *n.* a substance used as a cosmetic to colour the eyelashes. [Sp.: a mask]

**mascle** /'mæskəl/, *n.* a lozenge represented as having a lozenge-shaped hole at the centre. [ME, probably for OF *macle,* from L *macula* spot, mesh of a net. Cf. MAIL[2]]

**mascon** /'mæskɒn/, *n.* any of several local concentrations of mass below the surface of the moon. [MAS(S)[1] + CON(CENTRATION)]

**mascot** /'mæskɒt/, *n.* a person, animal, or thing supposed to bring good luck. [F *mascotte,* diminutive of Pr. *masco* witch; of Gmc orig.]

**masculine** /'mæskjələn/, *adj.* **1.** having manlike qualities;

strong; manly: *a masculine voice.* **2.** pertaining to or characteristic of a man or men: *masculine attire.* **3.** *Gram.* denoting or pertaining to one of the three genders of Latin, German, Greek, etc., or one of the two of French, Spanish, etc., so termed because most or all nouns denoting males belong to it, as well as other nouns, as French *crayon* 'pencil' or Spanish *dedo* 'finger'. **4.** (of a woman) mannish. *–n.* **5.** *Gram.* the masculine gender. **6.** a noun or another element marking that gender. [ME *masculin,* from L *masculīnus* male] **– masculinely,** *adv.* **– masculinity** /mæskjə'lɪnəti/, **masculineness,** *n.*

**masculine rhyme** /– 'raɪm/, *n.* a rhyme of but a single stressed syllable; single rhyme, as in *disdain, complain.*

**maser** /'meɪsə/, *n.* a device for obtaining low noise amplification of microwave oscillations of precisely determined frequencies. [short for *m(icrowave) a(mplification by) s(timulated) e(mission of) r(adiation)*]

**mash** /mæʃ/, *n.* **1.** a soft, pulpy mass. **2.** pulpy condition. **3.** a mess of boiled grain, bran, meal, etc., fed warm to horses and cattle. **4.** crushed malt or meal of grain mixed with hot water to form wort. **5.** mashed potatoes. **6.** *Obs. Colloq.* **a.** sweetheart; object of admiration. **b.** masher. **7. do a mash,** *Obs. Colloq.* to flirt (fol. by *with*). *–v.t.* **8.** to crush. **9.** to reduce to a soft, pulpy mass, as by heating or pressure. **10.** to mix (crushed malt, etc.) with hot water to form wort. **11.** *Obs. Colloq.* to flirt with; seek to attract or fascinate (one of the opposite sex). *–v.i.* **12.** *Obs. Colloq.* to flirt. [ME *masche,* OE *māsc-* (in compounds), c. G *Maische*]

**masher** /'mæʃə/, *n.* **1.** one who or that which mashes. **2.** *Obs. Colloq.* a lady-killer, esp. one who dresses showily; a flirtatious dandy.

**mashie** /'mæʃi/, *n.* a golf club (No. 5 iron) having a short head with a sloping face for making lofting shots. Also, **mashy.** [alteration of F *massue* club]

**mask** /mask/, *n.* **1.** a covering for the face, esp. one worn for disguise; a false face. **2.** a piece of cloth, silk, or plastic material, covering the face of an actor, to symbolise the character he represents, used in Greek and Roman drama and in some modern plays. **3.** anything that disguises or conceals; a disguise; a pretence. **4.** a person wearing a mask. **5.** a masquerade or revel. **6.** →**masque** (defs 1 and 2). **7.** a likeness of a face, as one moulded in plaster after death. **8.** the face or head, as of a fox. **9.** a representation of a face or head, generally grotesque, used as an ornament. **10.** a covering of wire, gauze, tinted glass, cloth, etc., to protect the face, as from splinters, dust, sparks, glare, fumes, polluted air, etc. **11.** →**gasmask. 12.** any of various devices, usu. consisting of rubber, glass, and plastic material, used by skindivers to protect the face. **13.** *Fort.* a screen, as of earth or brush, for concealing or protecting a battery or any military operation. **14.** *Photog.* any device used to limit the amount of light reaching a sensitised surface. *–v.t.* **15.** to disguise or conceal. **16.** to cover with a mask. **17.** *Fort.* to conceal (a battery or any military operation) from the enemy. **18.** to hinder (an army, etc.) from conducting an operation. **19.** *Photog.* to restrict the amount of light reaching (a sensitised surface). *–v.i.* **20.** to put on a mask; disguise oneself. [F *masque,* from It. *maschera,* from LL *masca*]

**masked ball** /maskt 'bɔl/, *n.* a ball at which masks are worn.

**masker** /'maskə/, *n.* one who masks; one who takes part in a masque. Also, **masquer.**

**masking tape** /'maskɪŋ teɪp/, *n.* an adhesive tape used for defining edges and protecting surfaces not to be painted.

**masochism** /'mæsəkɪzəm/, *n.* **1.** the condition in which sexual gratification depends on suffering. **2.** a condition in which one compulsively seeks, and sometimes derives pleasure from, suffering, as humiliation, pain, etc. [named after Leopold von Sacher *Masoch,* 1836-95, Austrian novelist, who described it] **– masochist,** *n.* **– masochistic** /mæsə'kɪstɪk/, *adj.*

**mason** /'meɪsən/, *n.* **1.** one who builds or works with stone. **2.** one who dresses stone. **3.** *U.S.* a bricklayer. **4.** *U.S.* one who dresses bricks. **5.** *(oft. cap.)* →**Freemason.** *-v.t.* **6.** to construct of or strengthen with masonry. [ME, from OF *maçon,* from LL *maccāre* beat; of Gmc orig.]

**mason bee** /'– bi/, *n.* any of certain bees of the family Megachilidae, which construct their nests of clay.

**masonic** /mə'sɒnɪk/, *adj.* *(oft. cap.)* pertaining to or characteristic of Freemasons or Freemasonry.

**masonite** /'meɪsənaɪt/, *n.* a kind of wood-fibre material, pressed in sheets and used for partitions, insulation, etc. [Trademark]

**masonry** /'meɪsənri/, *n., pl.* **-ries. 1.** the art or occupation of a mason. **2.** work constructed by a mason. **3.** *(oft. cap.)* →**freemasonry.**

**mason wasp** /'meɪsən wɒsp/, *n.* any of a number of species of wasps of the genus *Odynerus,* which build mud cells in which to store food for their larvae; mud dauber.

**masque** /mask/, *n.* **1.** a form of aristocratic entertainment in 16th and 17th century England, originally consisting of pantomime and dancing but later with dialogue and song, in elaborate productions given by amateur and professional actors. **2.** a dramatic composition for such entertainment. **3.** a masquerade; a revel. Also, **mask.** [See MASK]

**masquer** /'maskə/, *n.* →**masker.**

**masquerade** /mæskə'reɪd, mas-/, *n., v.,* **-raded, -rading.** *–n.* **1.** an assembly of persons wearing masks and other disguises, and often elaborate or fantastic costumes, for dancing, etc. **2.** disguise such as is worn at such an assembly. **3.** disguise, or false outward show. **4.** a going about under false pretences. *–v.t.* **5.** to go about under false pretences or a false character. **6.** to disguise oneself. **7.** to take part in a masquerade. [F *mascarade,* from It. *mascherata,* from *maschera* MASK] **– masquerader,** *n.*

**mass**[1] /mæs/, *n.* **1.** a body of coherent matter, usu. of indefinite shape and often of considerable size: *a mass of dough.* **2.** an aggregation of incoherent particles, parts, or objects regarded as forming one body: *a mass of sand.* **3.** a considerable assemblage, number, or quantity: *a mass of errors, a mass of troops.* **4.** an expanse, as of colour, light, or shade in a painting. **5.** the main body, bulk, or greater part of anything: *the great mass of Australian products.* **6.** bulk, size, or massiveness. **7.** *Physics.* that property of a body, commonly but inadequately defined as the measure of the quantity of matter in it, to which its inertia is ascribed, and expressed as the quotient of the weight of the body and the acceleration due to gravity. **8.** *Pharm.* a preparation of thick, pasty consistency, from which pills are made. **9. in the mass,** in the main; as a whole. **10. the masses,** the great body of the common people; the working classes or lower social orders. *–v.i.* **11.** to come together in or form a mass or masses: *the clouds are massing in the west.* *–v.t.* **12.** to gather into or dispose in a mass or masses; assemble: *the houses are massed in blocks, to mass troops.* [ME *masse,* from L *massa* mass, lump]

**mass**[2] /mæs/, *n.* **1.** the celebration of the Eucharist. See **high mass, low mass. 2.** a musical setting of certain parts of this service (now chiefly as celebrated in the Roman Catholic Church), as the Kyrie eleison, Gloria, Credo, Sanctus, Benedictus and Agnus Dei. Also, **Mass.** [ME *masse,* OE *mæsse,* from VL *messa,* L *missa;* orig. application of L term uncert.]

**massacre** /'mæsəkə/, *n., v.,* **-cred, -cring.** *–n.* **1.** the unnecessary, indiscriminate killing of a number of human beings, as in barbarous warfare or persecution, or for revenge or plunder. **2.** a general slaughter of human beings. *–v.t.* **3.** to kill indiscriminately or in a massacre. [F, from OF *macecler* to butcher, from *mache-col* butcher, from *macher* smash (from *maccāre* to strike; of Gmc orig.) + *col* neck (from L *collum*); ? also influenced by *masselier* butcher, from L *macellārius*] **– massacrer,** *n.*

**massage** /'mæsaʒ, 'mæsadʒ/, *n., v.,* **-saged, -saging.** *–n.* **1.** the act or art of treating the body by rubbing, kneading, or the like, to stimulate circulation, increase suppleness, etc. *–v.t.* **2.** to treat by massage. [F, from *masser* knead, from *masse* mass] **– massager, massagist,** *n.* **– massageuse** /mæsa'ʒɜz/, *n. fem.*

**massage parlour** /'– palə/, *n.* **1.** an establishment providing massage for its clients. **2.** such an establishment which in addition illegally provides for the sexual gratification of its clients.

**massasauga** /mæsə'sɔgə/, *n.* a venomous rattlesnake, *Sistrurus catenatus,* of North America.

**masscult** /'mæskʌlt/, *Chiefly U.S.* *–n.* **1.** mass culture, as most television programs, cinema entertainment, major newspapers, etc. *–adj.* **2.** of or pertaining to productions of such a kind.

**mass defect** /ˈmæs ˌdifɛkt/, *n.* the difference between the mass of a nucleus and the total mass of its constituent particles, due to the equality of mass and energy.

**massé** /ˈmæsi/, *n.* a stroke made in billiards by hitting the cue ball with the cue held almost or quite perpendicular to the table. Also, **massé shot.** [F, pp. of *masser* strike by a massé, from *masse* kind of cue, MACE[1]]

**mass-energy equivalence** /mæs-ˌɛnədʒi iˈkwɪvələns/, *n.* the theory that mass and energy are connected and equivalent. Equivalent to a given mass is an energy equal to the mass times the square of the velocity of light.

**masseter** /mæˈsitə/, *n.* an important masticatory muscle which serves to close the jaws by raising the mandible. [NL, from Gk *masētḗr* a chewer] – **masseteric** /mæsəˈtɛrɪk/, *adj.*

**masseur** /mæˈsɜ/, *n.* a man who practises massage. [F, from *masser* to massage] – **masseuse** /mæˈsɜz/, *n. fem.*

**massicot** /ˈmæsəkɒt/, *n.* monoxide of lead, PbO, in the form of a yellow powder, used as a pigment and drier. [F, from Sp. *mazacote* soda, from Ar. *shabb qubṭī* Egyptian alum]

**massif** /ˈmæsif/, *n.* **1.** a compact portion of a mountain range, containing one or more summits. **2.** an extensive block of mountain country rising to one or two dominant heights, with longitudinal and transverse valleys, raised or depressed as a unit and bounded by series of faults; an extensive horst. [F, n. use of *massif* MASSIVE]

**massive** /ˈmæsɪv/, *adj.* **1.** consisting of or forming a large mass; bulky and heavy. **2.** large, as the head or forehead. **3.** solid or substantial; great or imposing. **4.** *Mineral.* without outward crystal form, although perhaps crystalline in internal structure. **5.** *Geol.* →**homogeneous. 6.** *Med.* affecting a large continuous mass of bodily tissue, as a disease. **7.** *Colloq.* tremendous; extraordinary; unusual. [ME *massiffe*, from F *massif*, from *masse* MASS[1]] – **massively,** *adv.* – **massiveness,** *n.*

**mass media** /mæs ˈmidiə/, *n.* the means of communication, as radio, television, newspapers, magazines, etc., that reach large numbers of people. Also, **the media.**

**mass meeting** /– ˈmitɪŋ/, *n.* a large or general assembly to discuss or hear discussed some matter of common interest.

**mass noun** /ˈ– naʊn/, *n.* a noun referring to an object which is being thought of as existing in bulk and not as one of a series which can be counted, as *wheat, butter.* Cf. **count noun.**

**mass number** /ˈ– nʌmbə/, *n.* the number of nucleons in the nucleus of an atom.

**mass observation** /– ɒbzəˈveɪʃən/, *n.* research or poll on public opinion and behaviour. *Abbrev.:* M.O.

**massotherapy** /mæsoʊˈθɛrəpi/, *n.* treatment by massage. [F *mass(er)*, v., massage + -o- + THERAPY]

**mass-produce** /mæs-prəˈdjus/, *v.t.*, **-duced, -ducing.** to manufacture in large quantities by standardised mechanical processes.

**mass production** /mæs prəˈdʌkʃən/, *n.* the production or manufacture of goods in large quantities by standardised mechanical processes.

**mass ratio** /ˈ– reɪʃioʊ/, *n.* the ratio of the total mass of a rocket to the mass when all the propellant has been consumed.

**mass spectrograph** /– ˈspɛktrəgræf/, *n.* a mass spectrometer with a means of recording photographically the mass spectrum found.

**mass spectrometer** /– spɛkˈtrɒmətə/, *n.* a device for separating atoms or molecules of different masses by utilising the fact that the ions of such entities are deflected in a magnetic field by an amount which depends on the mass. Also, **mass spectroscope.**

**mass spectrum** /– ˈspɛktrəm/, *n.* a spectrum obtained with a mass spectrograph or mass spectrometer, which displays the isotopes present in a sample in order of increasing charge to mass ratio.

**massy** /ˈmæsi/, *adj.*, **-sier, -siest.** →**massive.** – **massiness,** *n.*

**mast**[1] /mast/, *n.* **1.** a tall spar rising more or less vertically from the keel or deck of a vessel, which supports the yards, sails, etc. **2.** any upright pole, as a support for an aerial, etc. **3.** the upright member in a derrick from which the jib is supported. **4. before the mast,** *Naut.* an unlicensed seaman (named from the quarters of seamen forward of the foremast in the forecastle). *–v.t.* **5.** to provide with a mast or masts. [ME; OE *mæst*, c. G *Mast;* akin to L *mālus*] – **mastlike,** *adj.*

**mast**[2] /mast/, *n.* the fruit (acorns, chestnuts, beechnuts, etc.) of certain forest trees, esp. as food for swine. [ME; OE *mæst*, c. G *Mast;* akin to MEAT]

**mast-,** variant of **masto-,** before vowels, as in *mastectomy.*

**mastaba** /ˈmæstəbə/, *n.* an ancient Egyptian tomb, rectangular in plan, with sloping sides and a flat roof. Also, **mastabah.** [Ar. (Egypt. d.): bench]

**mast cell** /ˈmast sɛl/, *n.* a cell found in the connective tissues of vertebrates, and thought to produce histamines. [part-translation of G *Mastzelle*, from *Mast* MAST[2] + *Zelle* cell]

**mastectomy** /mæsˈtɛktəmi/, *n., pl.* **-mies.** the operation of removing the breast or mamma. [MAST- + -ECTOMY]

**master** /ˈmastə/, *n.* **1.** one who has the power of controlling, using, or disposing of something: *a master of several languages.* **2.** an employer of workmen or servants. **3.** Also, **master mariner.** the commander of a merchant vessel. **4.** the male head of a household. **5.** an owner of a slave, horse, dog, etc. **6.** a presiding officer. **7.** a male teacher, tutor, or schoolmaster. **8.** a person whose teachings one accepts or follows. **9.** (*cap.*) Christ (prec. by *the, our,* etc.). **10.** a victor. **11.** a workman qualified to teach apprentices and to carry on his trade independently. **12.** a person eminently skilled in something, as an occupation, art, or science. **13.** a title given to a bridge or chess player who has won or been placed high in a certain number of officially recognised tournaments. **14.** one holding this title. **15.** *Law.* an officer of the Supreme Court of Judicature whose main function is to decide preliminary issues in High Court cases. **16.** *Educ.* one who has been awarded a master's degree. **17.** a boy or young man (used chiefly as a term of address). **18.** the title given to the head of a college at certain universities. **19.** the head teacher in a particular subject department in a secondary school: *the history master.* **20.** an original matrix, esp. the first pressing of a gramophone record. **21. a.** the original tape of a recording. **b.** the final mix of a multitrack recording. **22. be master in one's own house,** to manage one's own affairs without interference. **23. be one's own master,** to be completely free and independent. **24. master and servant,** *Law.* the relationship which exists when the master or employer has the right to direct the servant or employee what to do, and to control how he does it; a master is liable for a tort committed by his servant in the course of his employment. *–adj.* **25.** being master, or exercising mastery. **26.** chief or principal: *the master bedroom.* **27.** directing or controlling. **28.** dominating or predominant. **29.** being a master carrying on his trade independently, rather than a workman employed by another. **30.** being a master of some occupation, art, etc.; eminently skilled. **31.** characteristic of a master; showing mastery. *–v.t.* **32.** to conquer or subdue; reduce to subjection. **33.** to rule or direct as master. **34.** to make oneself master of; to become an adept in. [ME *maister*, OE *magister*, from L] – **masterdom,** *n.* – **masterless,** *adj.*

**master-at-arms** /mastər-ət-ˈamz/, *n. Naut.* **1.** a petty officer in the navy responsible for the maintenance of disciplinary regulations on board ship. **2.** an officer on a merchant ship performing the same function.

**master builder** /mastə ˈbɪldə/, *n.* a person who is qualified to contract for and supervise building construction.

**master-craftsman** /mastə-ˈkraftsmən/, *n.* a craftsman who is highly skilled in his trade.

**masterful** /ˈmastəfəl/, *adj.* **1.** having or showing the qualities of a master; authoritative; domineering. **2.** showing mastery or skill; masterly. – **masterfully,** *adv.* – **masterfulness,** *n.*

**master hand** /mastə ˈhænd/, *n.* **1.** an expert. **2.** great expertness.

**master key** /ˈ– ki/, *n.* a key that will open a number of locks whose proper keys are not interchangeable. Also, **pass key.**

**masterly** /ˈmastəli/, *adj.* **1.** like or befitting a master, as in skill or art. *–adv.* **2.** in a masterly manner. – **masterliness,** *n.*

**master mariner** /mastə ˈmærənə/, *n.* →**master** (def. 3).

**master mason** /– ˈmeɪsən/, *n.* **1.** a Freemason who has reached the third degree. **2.** an expert mason.

**master mechanic** /– mə'kænɪk/, *n.* a mechanic in charge of other mechanics.

**mastermind** /'mastəmaɪnd/, *v.t.* **1.** to plan and direct activities skilfully: *the revolt was masterminded by two colonels.* *–n.* **2.** one who originates or is mainly responsible for the carrying out of a particular project, scheme, etc.

**Master of Arts,** *n.* **1.** a second university degree, usu. in a branch of the humanities or social sciences, normally awarded to one who has completed at least one year's post-graduate study. **2.** one holding this degree. *Abbrev.:* M.A.

**master of ceremonies,** *n.* a person who directs the entertainment at a party, dinner, etc.

**Master of Science,** *n.* **1.** an academic degree similar to the Master of Arts, but taken in the field of natural sciences or mathematics. **2.** one holding this degree. *Abbrev.:* M.Sc.

**masterpiece** /'mastəpis/, *n.* **1.** one's most excellent production, as in an art: *the masterpiece of a painter.* **2.** any production of masterly skill. **3.** a consummate example of skill or excellence of any kind.

**master race** /'mastə reɪs/, *n.* a race or nation, as the Aryan Germans during the Nazi period, who consider themselves superior to other races or nations and therefore fitted to rule or enslave them.

**master's certificate** /'mastəz sətɪfəkət/, *n.* a certificate of competency entitling the holder to be the master of a merchant vessel.

**mastership** /'mastəʃɪp/, *n.* **1.** the office, function, or authority of a master. **2.** control. **3.** mastery, as of a subject. **4.** masterly skill or knowledge.

**masterstroke** /'mastəstroʊk/, *n.* a masterly action or achievement.

**masterwork** /'mastəwɜk/, *n.* →**masterpiece.**

**master workman** /mastə 'wɜkmən/, *n.* one who is master of his craft.

**mastery** /'mastəri/, *n., pl.* **-ries.** **1.** the state of being master; power of command or control. **2.** command or grasp, as of a subject. **3.** victory. **4.** the action of mastering, as a subject, etc. **5.** expert skill or knowledge. [MASTER + -Y[3]; replacing ME *maistrie,* from OF, from *maistre* MASTER]

**masthead** /'masthɛd/, *n.* **1.** the top or head of the mast of a ship or vessel; usu. the top of the highest mast in one vertical line. **2.** a statement printed at the top of the front page in all issues of a newspaper, magazine, etc., giving the name, owner, staff, etc. *–v.t. Naut.* **3.** to hoist to the top or head of a mast. **4.** to send to the masthead as a punishment.

**mastic** /'mæstɪk/, *n.* **1.** an aromatic, astringent resin obtained from a small evergreen tree, *Pistacia lentiscus,* native to the Mediterranean region, used in making varnish. **2.** a similar resin yielded by other trees of the same genus, or a resin likened to it. **3.** a tree yielding a mastic, esp. *Pistacia lentiscus.* **4.** *Bldg Trades.* **a.** any of various preparations used for sealing joints, window frames, etc. **b.** a pasty form of cement used for filling holes in masonry or plastered walls. [ME *mastyk,* from OF *mastic,* from L *mastichum,* from Gk *mastíchē*]

**masticate** /'mæstəkeɪt/, *v.t., v.i.,* **-cated, -cating.** **1.** to chew. **2.** to reduce to a pulp by crushing or kneading, as rubber. [LL *masticātus,* pp., chewed] – **mastication** /mæstə'keɪʃən/, *n.* – **masticator,** *n.*

**masticatory** /'mæstəkeɪtəri/, *adj., n., pl.* **-tories.** *–adj.* **1.** of, pertaining to, or used in or for mastication. *–n.* **2.** a medicinal substance to be chewed, as to promote the secretion of saliva.

**mastiff** /'mæstɪf/, *n.* one of a breed of large, powerful, short-haired dogs having an apricot, fawn, or brindled coat. [ME, from OF, b. *mastin* mastiff and *mestif* mongrel]

mastiff

**mastitis** /mæs'taɪtəs/, *n.* **1.** *Pathol.* inflammation of the breast. **2.** *Vet. Sci.* →**garget.** [NL; see MAST(O)-, -ITIS]

**masto-,** a word element meaning the breast, mastoid. Also, **mast-.** [Gk, combining form of *mastó* breast]

**mastodon** /'mæstədɒn/, *n.* any of various species of large, extinct mammals (genus *Mammut,* etc.) of the elephant kind, characterised by nipple-like elevations on the molar teeth. [NL, from Gk, from *mast-* MAST- + *odoús* tooth]

mastodon

**mastoid** /'mæstɔɪd/, *adj.* **1.** resembling a breast or nipple. **2.** denoting the nipple-like process of the temporal bone behind the ear. **3.** of or pertaining to the mastoid process. *–n.* **4.** the mastoid process. [Gk *mastoeidēs* like the breast]

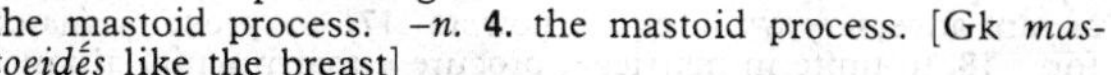

**mastoidectomy** /mæstɔɪ'dɛktəmi/, *n., pl.* **-mies.** any operation for the relief of inflammation of or within the mastoid process, esp. by the removal of part of a mastoid bone.

**mastoiditis** /mæstɔɪ'daɪtəs/, *n.* inflammation of the mastoid process of the temporal bone of the skull. [MASTOID + -ITIS]

**masturbate** /'mæstəbeɪt/, *v.,* **-bated, -bating.** *–v.i.* **1.** to engage in masturbation. *–v.t.* **2.** to practise masturbation upon. – **masturbator,** *n.*

**masturbation** /mæstə'beɪʃən/, *n.* the stimulation by friction of the genitals resulting in orgasm; sexual self-gratification; onanism (def. 2). [L *masturbātio*]

**masurium** /mə'suriəm/, *n.* former name of **technetium.** [from *Masur(ia),* region in NE Poland + -IUM]

**mat**[1] /mæt/, *n., v.,* **matted, matting.** *–n.* **1.** a piece of fabric made of plaited or woven rushes, straw, hemp, or other fibre, used to cover a floor, to wipe the shoes on, etc. **2.** a small piece of material, often ornamental, set under a dish of food, a lamp, vase, etc. **3.** a thick covering, as of padded canvas, laid on a floor on which wrestlers contend. **4.** *N.Z.* a Maori cloak. **5.** a thickly growing or thick and tangled mass, as of hair or weeds. **6.** *Print.* **a.** the intaglio (usu. of papier-mâché or plastic), impressed from type or cut, from which a stereotype plate is cast or from which plastic and rubber plates are made for letterpress printing. **b.** the brass die used in a linotype, each carrying a letter in intaglio. **7. put on the mat,** to reprimand. *–v.t.* **8.** to cover with or as with mats or matting. **9.** to form into a mat, as by interweaving. **10.** to reprimand. *–v.i.* **11.** to become entangled; from tangled masses. [ME *matte,* OE *meatt(e),* from LL *matta*]

**mat**[2] /mæt/, *n., v.,* **matted, matting.** *–n.* **1.** a piece of cardboard or other material placed round a photograph, painting, etc., to serve as a frame or border. *–v.t.* **2.** to provide (a picture) with a mat. [F. See MAT[1], MAT[3], *adj.*]

**mat**[3] /mæt/, *adj., n., v.* →**matt.** Also, *U.S.,* **matte.**

**matador** /'mætədɔ/, *n.* **1.** the bullfighter who has the principal role and who kills the bull in a bullfight. **2.** one of the principal cards in skat and certain other games. [Sp., from L *mactātor* slayer]

**matagouri** /mætə'guri/, *n.* a thorny bush or small tree of New Zealand, *Discaria toumatou,* forming thickets on waste-lands; Irishman; wild Irishman. Also, **tumatakuru, matagory, matagowry.** [Maori]

**Mata Hari** /mætə 'hari/, *n.* an attractive, mysterious woman, esp. one who might possibly disadvantage or betray male associates. [from *Mata Hari* (Gertrud Margareta Zelle), 1876-1917, Dutch dancer in France; executed as a spy by the French]

**matai** /'mætaɪ/, *n.* a coniferous, evergreen tree of New Zealand, *Podocarpus spicatus,* with a bluish bark and small, narrow leaves, reaching a height of 20-25 metres. [Maori]

**matamata** /mætəmə'ta/, *n.* a common freshwater turtle, *Chelus fimbriata,* of the rivers of Brazil and the Guianas, growing to about 60 cm in length.

**Mataro** /mə'taroʊ/, *n.* a red variety of grape used in the production of both dry and sweet wines.

**match**[1] /mætʃ/, *n.* **1.** a short, slender piece of wood or other material tipped with a chemical substance which produces fire when rubbed on a rough or chemically prepared surface. **2.** a wick, cord, or the like, prepared to burn at an even rate, used to fire cannon, etc. [ME *matche,* from OF *meiche;*

orig. uncert.]

**match**$^{2}$ /mætʃ/, *n.* **1.** a person or thing that equals or resembles another in some respect. **2.** a person or thing that is an exact counterpart of another. **3.** one able to cope with another as an equal: *to meet one's match.* **4.** a corresponding or suitably associated pair. **5.** a contest or game. **6.** an engagement for a contest or game. **7.** a person considered with regard to suitability as a partner in marriage. **8.** a matrimonial compact or alliance. *–v.t.* **9.** to equal, or be equal to. **10.** to be the match or counterpart of: *the colour of the skirt does not match that of the coat.* **11.** to adapt; make to correspond. **12.** to fit together, as two things. **13.** to procure or produce an equal to. **14.** to place in opposition or conflict. **15.** to provide with an adversary or competitor of equal power: *the teams were well matched.* **16.** to encounter as an adversary with equal power. **17.** to prove a match for. **18.** to unite in marriage; procure a matrimonial alliance for. *–v.i.* **19.** to be equal or suitable. **20.** to correspond; be of corresponding size, shape, colour, pattern, etc. **21.** to ally oneself in marriage. [ME *macche,* OE *gemæcca* mate, fellow] – **matchable,** *adj.* – **matcher,** *n.*

**matchboard** /ˈmætʃbɔd/, *n.* a board which has a tongue cut along one edge, and a groove in the opposite edge, used in making floors, etc., the tongue of one such board fitting into the groove of the next.

**matchbox** /ˈmætʃbɒks/, *n.* **1.** a small box, usu. of wood, for holding matches, usu. with a striking surface on one side. **2.** *Colloq.* an improvised pipe made from a matchbox by inserting a cigarette in a hole at the top.

**matchbox bean** /ˈ– bin/, *n.* a tropical climbing vine, *Entada phaesoloides,* with beans a metre or more long and 10 cm broad, found in Queensland; Queensland bean.

**matchbox toy** /ˈ– tɔɪ/, *n.* **1.** a miniature model of a motor vehicle. **2.** a toy small enough to fit into a matchbox. [Trademark]

**matchless** /ˈmætʃləs/, *adj.* having no equal; peerless: *matchless courage.* – **matchlessly,** *adv.* – **matchlessness,** *n.*

**matchlock** /ˈmætʃlɒk/, *n.* **1.** an old form of gunlock in which the priming was ignited by a slow match. **2.** a hand gun, usu. a musket, with such a lock.

**matchmaker**$^{1}$ /ˈmætʃmeɪkə/, *n.* **1.** one who makes, or seeks to bring about, matrimonial matches. **2.** one who makes or arranges matches for athletic contests, etc. [MATCH$^{2}$ + MAKER] – **matchmaking,** *n., adj.*

**matchmaker**$^{2}$ /ˈmætʃmeɪkə/, *n.* one who makes matches for burning. [MATCH$^{1}$ + MAKER] – **matchmaking,** *n., adj.*

**matchmark** /ˈmætʃmak/, *n.* **1.** a mark on each of two adjacent parts of an engine, etc., which help in positioning the parts being assembled. *–v.t.* **2.** to stamp or draw matchmarks on.

**match-of-the-day** /mætʃ-əv-ðə-ˈdeɪ/, *n.* **1.** the most important match (usu. of football) played on a particular day. **2.** the match being covered by a radio or television station on a particular day.

**match play** /ˈmætʃ pleɪ/, *n.* (in golf) play in which the score is reckoned by counting the holes won by each side.

**match point** /ˈ– pɔɪnt/, *n.* the final point needed to win a contest.

**match race** /ˈ– reɪs/, *n.* a race in which there are only two contestants.

**matchstick** /ˈmætʃstɪk/, *n.* a short, slender fairly rigid length of wood or other similar material, used in making matches.

**matchwood** /ˈmætʃwʊd/, *n.* **1.** wood suitable for matches. **2.** splinters.

**mate**$^{1}$ /meɪt/, *n., v.,* **mated, mating.** *–n.* **1.** one joined with another in any pair. **2.** a counterpart. **3.** husband or wife. **4.** one of a pair of mated animals. **5. a.** a habitual associate; comrade; friend; intimate: *they've been good mates from way back.* **b.** (a form of address amongst men): *how are you going, mate?* **6.** an officer of a merchant vessel who ranks below the captain or master (called **first mate, second mate,** etc., when there are more than one on a ship. **7.** an assistant to a tradesman. **8.** *Archaic.* a suitable associate. **9. be mates with,** to be good friends with. *–v.t.* **10.** to join as a mate or as mates. **11.** to match or marry. **12.** to pair, as animals. **13.** to join suitably, as two things. **14.** to treat as comparable, as one thing with another. *–v.i.* **15.** to associate as a mate or as mates. **16.** to marry. **17.** to pair. **18.** to consort; keep company. **19.** (of animals) to copulate. [ME, from MLG, var. of *gemate;* akin to OE *gemetta* sharer of food, guest. See MEAT]

**mate**$^{2}$ /meɪt/, *n., v.t.,* **mated, mating.** →**checkmate.** [ME *mate(n)* from OF *mater,* from *mat* checkmated, overcome, from Ar. See MAT$^{3}$, CHECKMATE]

**maté** /ˈmateɪ, ˈmæteɪ/, *n.* **1.** a tealike South American beverage made from the leaves of a species of holly, *Ilex paraguayensis,* native to Paraguay and Brazil. **2.** the plant itself. Also, **mate.** [Sp.: properly, a vessel, from Quechua *mat* calabash]

**matelassé** /mætˈlæseɪ/, *n.* a heavy type of cloth, with figuring in geometrical forms in a variety of weaves. [F, pp. of *matelasser* to quilt]

**matelot** /ˈmætəloʊ, ˈmætloʊ/, *n. Colloq.* a sailor. [F]

**matelote** /ˈmætəlɒt/, *n.* **1.** a savoury fish stew cooked with wine. **2.** a wine sauce for fish. [F *(sauce) matelote* sailor (sauce)]

**mater** /ˈmeɪtə/, *n.* mother. [L]

**mater dolorosa** /– dɒləˈroʊsə/, *n.* **1.** the sorrowful mother. **2.** *(cap.)* the mother of Christ sorrowing for her son, esp. as represented in art. [L]

**materfamilias** /meɪtəfəˈmɪliæs/, *n.* the mother of a family. [L]

**material** /məˈtɪəriəl/, *n.* **1.** the substance or substances of which a thing is made or composed. **2.** any constituent element of a thing. **3.** anything serving as crude or raw matter for working upon or developing. **4.** a person demonstrating potential in a particular skill or occupation: *he's good foreman material.* **5.** information, ideas, or the like on which a report, thesis, etc., is based. **6.** a textile fabric. **7.** *(pl.)* articles of any kind requisite for making or doing something: *writing materials.* *–adj.* **8.** formed or consisting of matter; physical; corporeal: *the material world.* **9.** relating to, concerned with, or involving matter: *material force.* **10.** concerned or occupied unduly with corporeal things or interests. **11.** pertaining to the physical rather than the spiritual or intellectual aspect of things: *material civilisation.* **12.** of substantial import or much consequence. **13.** pertinent or essential (fol. by *to*). **14.** *Law.* (of evidence, etc.) likely to influence the determination of a cause. **15.** *Philos.* of or pertaining to matter as distinguished from form. [ME, from LL *māteriālis,* from *māteria* matter] – **materialness,** *n.*

**materialisation** /mətɪəriəlaɪˈzeɪʃən/, *n.* **1.** the process of taking on material form. **2.** an appearance (as of a spirit) in bodily form; apparition. **3.** something materialised.

**materialise** /məˈtɪəriəlaɪz/, *v.,* **-lised, -lising.** *–v.t.* **1.** to give material form to. **2.** to invest with material attributes. **3.** to make physically perceptible. **4.** to render materialistic. *–v.i.* **5.** to assume material or bodily form. **6.** to come into perceptible existence; appear. Also, **materialize.** – **materialiser,** *n.*

**materialism** /məˈtɪəriəlɪzəm/, *n.* **1.** the philosophical theory which regards matter and its motions as constituting the universe, and all phenomena, including those of mind, as due to material agencies. **2.** *Ethics.* the doctrine that the self-interest of the individual is or ought to be the first law of life; egoistic, as opposed to universalistic, hedonism. **3.** devotion to material rather than spiritual objects, needs, and considerations.

**materialist** /məˈtɪəriələst/, *n.* **1.** an adherent of philosophical materialism. **2.** one absorbed in material interests; one who takes a material view of life. – **materialistic** /mətɪəriəˈlɪstɪk/, *adj.* – **materialistically** /mətɪəriəˈlɪstɪkli/, *adv.*

**materiality** /mətɪəriˈæləti/, *n., pl.* **-ties. 1.** material nature or quality. **2.** something material.

**materially** /məˈtɪəriəli/, *adv.* **1.** to an important degree; considerably. **2.** with reference to matter or material things; physically. **3.** *Philos.* with regard to matter or substance as distinguished from form.

**materia medica** /məˌtɪəriə ˈmɛdɪkə/, *n.* **1.** the remedial substances employed in medicine. **2.** the branch of medicine treating of these. [ML: medical material]

**matériel** /məˈtɪəriəl/, *n.* **1.** the aggregate of things used or needed in any business, undertaking, or operation (distinguished from *personnel*). **2.** *Mil.* arms, ammunition, and equipment in general. [F. See MATERIAL]

**maternal** /məˈtɜnəl/, *adj.* **1.** of or pertaining to, befitting, having the qualities of, or being a mother. **2.** derived from a mother. **3.** related through a mother: *his maternal aunt.* [late ME, from L *māternus* of a mother + -AL[1]] – **maternally,** *adv.*

**maternity** /mə'tɜnəti/, *n.* **1.** the state of being a mother; motherhood. **2.** motherliness. *–adj.* **3.** belonging to or characteristic of motherhood or of the period of pregnancy.

**maternity clothes** /'– kloʊðz/, *n.pl.* loose-fitting clothes designed for pregnant women.

**maternity dress** /'– drɛs/, *n.* a full dress, often adjustable in girth, designed to be worn by pregnant women.

**maternity hospital** /'– hɒspɪtl/, *n.* a hospital for the care of women before and during confinement in childbirth.

**maternity leave** /'– liv/, *n.* time off from one's job, usu. with pay, in order to have a baby.

**mateship** /'meɪtʃɪp/, *n.* **1.** the quality or state of being a mate. **2.** a code of conduct among men stressing equality and fellowship.

**matey** /'meɪti/, *Colloq. –adj.* **1.** comradely; friendly. *–n.* **2.** (a form of address) comrade; chum.

**mateyness** /'meɪtinəs/, *n. Colloq.* hearty, good-natured friendship.

**mat-grass** /'mæt-gras/, *n.* **1.** a grass, *Hemarthria uncinata,* of dense prostrate growth. **2.** any other mat-forming grass as *Axonopus affinis* and *Nardus stricta.*

**math.,** **1.** mathematical. **2.** *U.S.* mathematics.

**mathematical** /mæθə'mætɪkəl/, *adj.* **1.** of, pertaining to, or of the nature of mathematics. **2.** employed in the operations of mathematics. **3.** having the exactness or precision of mathematics. Also **mathematic.** [*mathematic* MATHEMATICS + -AL[1]] – **mathematically,** *adv.*

**mathematical expectation** /– ɛkspɛk'teɪʃən/, *n. Statistics.* the average of a set of possible values of a variable, the values weighted by the probabilities associated with these values.

**mathematical logic** /– 'lɒdʒɪk/, *n.* a modern development of formal logic employing a special notation or symbolism capable of manipulation in accordance with precise rules; symbolic logic.

**mathematician** /mæθəmə'tɪʃən/, *n.* a student of or an expert in mathematics.

**mathematics** /mæθə'mætɪks/, *n.* the science that treats of the measurement, properties, and relations of quantities, including arithmetic, geometry, algebra, etc. [pl. of *mathematic,* from L *mathēmaticus,* from Gk *mathēmatikós* pertaining to science. See -ICS]

**maths** /mæθs/, *n.* →**mathematics.**

**matilda** /mə'tɪldə/, *n. Colloq.* a swag. [see WALTZ[2]]

**matin** /'mætn/, *n.* **1.** (*pl.*) *Eccles.* **a.** the first of the seven canonical hours, or the service for it, properly beginning at midnight, sometimes at daybreak. **b.** the order for public morning prayer in the Anglican Church. **2.** *Poetic.* a morning song, esp. of a bird. *–adj.* **3.** Also, **matinal.** pertaining to the morning or to matins. Also, **mattin.** [ME *matyn* (pl. *matines*), from OF *matin* morning, from L *mātūtīnus* of or in the morning]

**matinee** /'mætəneɪ/, *n.* an entertainment, as a dramatic or musical performance, film, etc., held in the daytime, usu. in the afternoon. Also, **matinée.** [F, from *matin* morning. See MATIN]

**matinee coat** /'– koʊt/, *n.* a jacket of wool or warm material, esp. to be worn in bed. Also, **matinee jacket.**

**matinee idol** /'– aɪdəl/, *n.* the handsome and romantic hero of a movie such as might once have appealed to the largely female cinema audiences of matinee sessions.

**matipo** /'matipoʊ/, *n.* either of two trees of New Zealand: **a.** Also, **black matipo.** an evergreen tree, *Pittosporum tenuifolium.* **b.** Also, **red matipo.** →**mapou.**

**matrass** /'mætrəs/, *n.* (formerly) a rounded, long-necked glass vessel, used for distilling, etc. Also, **mattrass.**

**matri-,** a word element meaning 'mother'. [L, combining form of *māter*]

**matriarch** /'meɪtriak, 'mæt-/, *n.* **1.** a woman holding a position of leadership in a family or tribe. **2.** a woman who dominates any group or field of activity. [MATRI- + -ARCH; modelled on PATRIARCH] – **matriarchal, matriarchic,** *adj.*

**matriarchate** /'meɪtriakət, 'mæt-, -keɪt/, *n.* **1.** a matriarchal system or community. **2.** *Sociol.* a social order believed to have preceded patriarchal tribal society in the early period of human communal life, embodying rule by the mothers, or by all adult women.

**matriarchy** /'meɪtriaki, 'mæt-/, *n., pl.* **-chies.** the matriarchal system; a form of social organisation, as in certain primitive tribes, in which the mother is head of the family, and in which descent is reckoned in the female line, the children belonging to the mother's clan.

**matric.,** **1.** matriculated. **2.** matriculation.

**matrices** /'meɪtrəsiz/, *n.* plural form of **matrix.**

**matricide** /'meɪtrəsaɪd, 'mæt-/, *n.* **1.** one who kills his mother. **2.** the act of killing one's mother. [L *mātrīcīdium* (def. 2), *mātrīcīda* (def. 1). See MATRI-, -CIDE] – **matricidal** /meɪtrə'saɪdl, mæt-/, *adj.*

**matriclinous** /mə'trɪklənəs/, *adj.* derived or inherited from the mother and her line. Cf. **patriclinous.** [MATRI- + *-clinous,* from Gk *-clinēs* leaning, bending]

**matriculant** /mə'trɪkjələnt/, *n.* one who matriculates; a candidate for matriculation.

**matriculate** /mə'trɪkjəleɪt/, *v.,* **-lated, -lating;** /mə'trɪkjələt/, *n.* *–v.i.* **1.** to be admitted to membership, esp. of a university or similar institution as a college of advanced education. **2.** to pass matriculation (def. 2). *–v.t.* **3.** to enrol or admit. *–n.* **4.** one who has matriculated. [LL *mātrīcula,* diminutive of *mātrix* public register, roll + -ATE[1]] – **matriculator,** *n.*

**matriculation** /mətrɪkjə'leɪʃən/, *n.* **1.** the process of being formally enrolled in or admitted to certain universities, or similar tertiary education institutions. **2.** a secondary-school examination in which a required level must be reached before qualification for admission to a tertiary education institution.

**matrilineal** /mætrə'lɪniəl/, *adj.* of, pertaining to, or founded on the recognition of kinship and descent through the female line. Also, **matrilinear.** – **matriline,** *n.*

**matrimonial** /mætrə'moʊniəl/, *adj.* of or pertaining to matrimony; nuptial. – **matrimonially,** *adv.*

**matrimonial cause** /– 'kɔz/, *n.* any legal action for divorce, nullity, judicial separation, jactitation of marriages, or restitution of conjugal rights.

**matrimony** /'mætrəməni/, *n., pl.* **-nies.** the rite, ceremony, or sacrament of marriage. [ME *matrimonye,* from L *mātrimōnium* marriage]

**matrimony vine** /'– vaɪn/, *n.* any of the plants constituting the genus *Lycium,* species of which are cultivated for their foliage, flowers, and berries; boxthorn.

**matrix** /'meɪtrɪks/, *n., pl.* **matrices** /'meɪtrəsiz/, **matrixes. 1.** that which gives origin or form to a thing, or which serves to enclose it. **2.** *Anat.* a formative part, as the corium beneath a fingernail. **3.** *Biol.* the intercellular substance of a tissue. **4.** the rock in which a crystallised mineral is embedded. **5.** *Mining.* →**gangue. 6.** *Print.* **a.** a mould for casting typefaces. **b.** →**mat**[1] (def. 6). **7.** a positive or negative copy of an original disc recording, used in reproducing other copies. **8.** in a punching machine, a perforated block upon which the object to be punched is rested. **9.** *Maths, Computers.* a rectangular array of numbers. **10.** *Computers.* a rectangular array of logical elements acting as a selection system. **11.** *Geol.* the smaller grainsize material in a sedimentary rock containing material of two distinct grainsizes. **12.** *Mining.* partially porous grey or brown low-grade rocky material with thin streaks of opal through it. Also, **mother-o'-opal.** [L: breeding animal, LL womb, source]

**matron** /'meɪtrən/, *n.* **1.** a married woman, esp. one of ripe years and staid character or established position. **2.** a woman in charge of the domestic arrangements in an institution, as a school, hospital, prison, etc. **3.** a woman in charge of nursing, etc., in a hospital. **4.** a brood mare. [ME *matrone,* from OF, from L *mātrōna* married woman] – **matronal,** *adj.*

**matronage** /'meɪtrənɪdʒ/, *n.* **1.** the state of being a matron. **2.** guardianship by a matron. **3.** matrons collectively.

**matronly** /'meɪtrənli/, *adj.* **1.** like a matron, or having the characteristics of a matron. **2.** characteristic of or suitable for a matron. – **matronliness,** *n.*

**matron of honour,** *n.* a married woman acting as the principal attendant of the bride at a wedding.

**mat-rush** /'mæt-rʌʃ/, *n.* a tussocky plant, *Lomandra longifolia,* usu. found along creek banks, and having small, creamy flowers with sharp spines and long, tough, narrow leaves, used by Aborigines for making dilly-bags, widely distributed throughout eastern Australia.

**matt** /mæt/, *adj.* **1.** lustreless and dull in surface. *–n.* **2.** a dull or dead surface, without lustre, produced on metals, etc.; a roughened or frosted surface. **3.** a tool, as a punch, for producing such a surface. *–v.t.* **4.** to finish with a matt surface. Also, **mat;** *U.S.,* **matte.** [F, from *mater* make dull or weak, from *mat* dead. See CHECKMATE]

**Matt.,** *Bible.* Matthew.

**matte**[1] /mæt/, *n.* an unfinished metallic product of the smelting of certain sulphide ores, esp. those of copper. [F. See MATT]

**matte**[2] /mæt/, *adj., n., v. U.S.* →**matt.**

**matted**[1] /ˈmætəd/, *adj.* **1.** covered with a dense growth or a tangled mass. **2.** covered with mats or matting. **3.** formed into a mat; entangled in a thick mass. **4.** formed of mats, or of woven material. [MAT[1] + -ED[2]]

**matted**[2] /ˈmætəd/, *adj.* having a dull finish. [MATT + -ED[2]]

**matter** /ˈmætə/, *n.* **1.** the substance or substances of which physical objects consist or are composed. **2.** physical or corporeal substance in general (whether solid, liquid, or gaseous), esp. as distinguished from incorporeal substance (as spirit or mind), or from qualities, actions, etc. **3.** whatever occupies space. **4.** a particular kind of substance: *colouring matter.* **5.** some substance excreted by a living body, esp. pus. **6.** the material or substance of a discourse, book, etc., often as distinguished from the form. **7.** things written or printed: *printed matter.* **8.** a thing, affair, or business: *a matter of life and death.* **9.** an amount or extent reckoned approximately: *a matter of ten kilometres.* **10.** something of consequence: *it is no matter.* **11.** importance or significance: *what matter?* **12.** the trouble or difficulty (prec. by *the*): *there is nothing the matter.* **13.** ground, reason, or cause. **14.** *Law.* statement or allegation. **15.** *Print.* **a.** material for work; copy. **b.** type set up. **16. as a matter of fact,** actually; in reality. **17. for that matter,** as far as that is concerned. **18. matter of course,** the logical and inevitable outcome of a sequence of events. *–v.i.* **19.** to be of importance; signify: *it matters little.* **20.** →**suppurate.** [ME *matere,* from OF, from L *māteria* stuff, material]

**matter-of-course** /mætər-əv-ˈkɔs/, *adj.* occurring or proceeding as if in the natural course of things.

**matter-of-fact** /mætər-əv-ˈfækt/, *adj.* adhering to actual facts; not imaginative; prosaic; commonplace.

**mattin** /ˈmætn/, *n., adj.* →**matin.**

**matting**[1] /ˈmætɪŋ/, *n.* **1.** a coarse fabric of rushes, grass, straw, hemp, or the like, used for covering floors, wrapping, etc. **2.** material for mats. [MAT[1] + -ING[1]]

**matting**[2] /ˈmætɪŋ/, *n.* a dull, slightly roughened surface, free from polish, produced by the use of the mat. [MATT + -ING[1]]

**matting wicket** /– ˈwɪkət/, *n.* (in cricket) a wicket made of a coir mat laid over a concrete or dirt foundation.

**mattock** /ˈmætək/, *n.* an instrument for loosening the soil in digging, shaped like a pickaxe, but having one end broad instead of pointed. [ME *mattok,* OE *mattuc*]

**mattoid** /ˈmætɔɪd/, *n.* a person of abnormal mentality bordering on insanity. [It. *mattoide,* from *matto* mad, from L *mattus* intoxicated]

**mattrass** /ˈmætrəs/, *n.* →**matrass.**

**mattress** /ˈmætrəs/, *n.* **1.** a case filled with soft material, as straw, cotton, etc., often reinforced with springs, and usu. quilted or fastened together at intervals, used as or on a bed. **2.** a mat woven of brush, poles, or similar material used to prevent erosion of the surface of dykes, jetties, embankments, dams, etc. [ME *materas,* from OF, from It. *materasso,* from Ar. *(al) maṭraḥ* (the) mat, cushion]

**matuku** /məˈtuku/, *n.* a brown bittern, of New Zealand, *Botaurus poiciloptilus.* [Maori]

**maturate** /ˈmætʃəreɪt, -tʃu-/, *v.i.,* **-rated, -rating. 1.** →**suppurate. 2.** →**mature.** [L *mātūrātus,* pp., ripened] – **maturative** /məˈtjurətɪv/, *adj.*

**maturation** /mætʃəˈreɪʃən, -tʃu-/, *n.* **1.** the act or process of maturating. **2.** *Biol.* the second phase of gametogenesis resulting in the production of mature eggs and sperms from oogonia and spermatogonia.

**mature** /məˈtjuə/, *adj., v.,* **-tured, -turing.** *–adj.* **1.** complete in natural growth or development, as plant and animal forms, cheese, wine, etc. **2.** ripe, as fruit. **3.** fully developed in body or mind, as a person. **4.** pertaining to or characteristic of full development: *a mature appearance.* **5.** completed, perfected, or elaborated in full by the mind: *mature plans.* **6.** *Comm.* having reached the limit of its time; having become payable or due, as a note. **7.** *Med.* in a state of perfect suppuration, esp. of a boil which has come to a head. **8.** *Phys. Geog.* (of topographical features) exhibiting the stage of maximum stream development, as in the process of erosion of a land surface. *–v.t.* **9.** to make mature; esp., to ripen. **10.** to bring to full development. **11.** to complete or perfect. *–v.i.* **12.** to become mature, esp. to ripen. **13.** to come to full development. **14.** *Comm.* to become due, as a note, insurance policy, etc. [late ME, from L *mātūrus* ripe, timely, early] – **maturely,** *adv.* – **matureness,** *n.*

**mature age student,** *n.* an adult who has taken up a course of study at a later age than normal.

**maturity** /məˈtjurəti/, *n.* **1.** the state of being mature; ripeness. **2.** full development; perfected condition. **3.** *Physiol.* period following attainment of full development of bodily structure and reproductive faculty. **4.** *Comm.* **a.** the state of being due. **b.** the time when a note or bill of exchange becomes due.

**matutinal** /mætʃəˈtaɪnəl/, *adj.* pertaining to or occurring in the morning; early in the day. [L *mātūtīnālis* of the morning] – **matutinally,** *adv.*

**matzo** /ˈmætsoʊ/, *n., pl.* **matzoth** /ˈmætsoʊθ/, **matzos** /ˈmætsoʊz/. a biscuit of unleavened bread, eaten by Jews during the Feast of Passover. [Heb. *matstsāh* cake of unleavened bread]

**matzoon** /ˈmætsun/, *n.* a food, resembling yoghurt, made of fermented milk. Also, **madzoon.** [Armenian *madzun*]

**maudlin** /ˈmɔdlən/, *adj.* **1.** tearfully or weakly emotional or sentimental. **2.** tearfully or emotionally silly from drink. [from *Maudlin,* familiar var. of *Magdalen* (Mary Magdalene), often represented in art as weeping] – **maudlinly,** *adv.* – **maudlinness,** *n.*

**maul** /mɔl/, *n.* **1.** a heavy hammer as for driving piles. **2.** *Obs.* a heavy club or mace. **3.** *Rugby Football,* a loose scrum around the ball carrier. *–v.t.* **4.** to handle roughly; to injure by rough treatment. **5.** *U.S.* to split with a maul and a wedge, as a rail. [var. of MALL] – **mauler,** *n.*

**maulstick** /ˈmɔlstɪk/, *n.* a painter's stick, used as a support for the hand which holds the brush. Also, **mahlstick.** [D *maalstok*]

**maunder** /ˈmɔndə/, *v.i.* **1.** to talk in a rambling, foolish, or imbecile way. **2.** to move, go, or act in an aimless, confused manner. [? OF *mendier* beg, from L *mendīcāre*] – **maunderer,** *n.*

**maundy** /ˈmɔndi/, *n.* **1.** the ceremony of washing the feet of the poor, esp. commemorating Jesus's washing of His disciples' feet on Maundy Thursday. **2.** Also, **maundy money.** *Brit.* money distributed as alms in conjunction with the ceremony of maundy or on Maundy Thursday. [ME *maunde,* from OF *mande,* from L *mandātum* a command, mandate]

**Mauritania** /mɔrəˈteɪniə/, *n.* a republic in north-western Africa. – **Mauritanian,** *adj., n.*

**Mauritius** /məˈrɪʃəs/, *n.* a country comprising the island of Mauritius and its dependencies. – **Mauritian,** *adj., n.*

**Mauser** /ˈmaʊzə/, *n.* **1.** a high velocity repeating rifle made in Germany and used in the two World Wars. **2.** an automatic pistol. [Trademark; named after P.P. von *Mauser,* 1838-1914, German firearms inventor]

**mausoleum** /mɔsəˈliəm, mɔz-/, *n., pl.* **-leums, -lea** /-ˈliə/. **1.** a stately and magnificent tomb. **2.** *Colloq.* a large, old, gloomy building. [L, from Gk *mausōleîon* the tomb of Mausolus (king of Caria)] – **mausolean,** *adj.*

**mauve** /moʊv/, *n.* **1.** pale bluish purple. **2.** a purple dye obtained from aniline, the first of the coal-tar dyes (discovered in 1856). *–adj.* **3.** of the colour of mauve: *a mauve dress.* [F: orig., mallow, from L *malva* MALLOW]

**maverick** /ˈmævərɪk/, *n.* **1.** *U.S.* (in cattle-raising regions) **a.** an animal found without an owner's brand. **b.** a calf separated from its dam. **2.** a dissenter; loner. [probably named after Samuel *Maverick,* 1803-70, a Texas (U.S.) cattle-raiser who neglected to brand his cattle]

**mavis** /ˈmeɪvəs/, *n.* the European throstle or song thrush, *Turdus philomelus.* [ME *mavys,* from OF *mauvis;* of Celtic orig.]

**mavourneen** /məˈvɔnin/, *n.* my darling. Also, **mavournin.** [Irish *mo mhuirnīn*]

**maw** /mɔ/, *n.* **1.** the mouth, throat, or gullet as concerned in devouring (now chiefly of animals or in figurative use). **2.** the crop or craw of a fowl. **3.** the stomach. [ME *mawe,* OE *maga,* c. G *Magen*]

**mawkish** /ˈmɔkɪʃ/, *adj.* **1.** sickly or slightly nauseating. **2.** characterised by sickly sentimentality. [*mawk* maggot (from Scand.; cf. Icel. *madhkr*) + -ISH[1]] – **mawkishly,** *adv.* – **mawkishness,** *n.*

**max.,** maximum.

**maxi** /ˈmæksi/, *adj.* **1.** of or pertaining to a dress, skirt, or coat for day wear, which is full-length. *–n.* **2.** such a dress, skirt, or coat.

**maxilla** /mækˈsɪlə/, *n., pl.* **maxillae** /mækˈsɪli/. **1.** a jaw or jawbone, esp. the upper. **2.** one of the paired appendages immediately behind the mandibles of arthropods. [L: jaw]

**maxillary** /mækˈsɪləri/, *adj., n., pl.* **-laries.** *–adj.* **1.** of or pertaining to a jaw, jawbone, or maxilla. *–n.* **2.** a maxilla or maxillary bone.

**maxim** /ˈmæksəm/, *n.* **1.** an expression, esp. an aphoristic or sententious one, of a general truth, esp. as to conduct. **2.** a principle of conduct. [ME *maxime,* from OF, from L *maxima* (*prōpositio*), lit., greatest (proposition)]

**maxima** /ˈmæksəmə/, *n.* a plural form of **maximum.**

**maximal** /ˈmæksəməl/, *adj.* of or being a maximum; greatest possible; highest. – **maximally,** *adv.*

**maximalise** /ˈmæksəməlaɪz/, *v.t.,* **-lised, -lising.** to make maximal.

**maximise** /ˈmæksəmaɪz/, *v.t.,* **-mised, -mising.** to increase to the greatest possible amount or degree. Also, **maximize.** [L *maximus* greatest + -ISE[1]] – **maximisation** /mæksəmaɪˈzeɪʃən/, *n.* – **maximiser,** *n.*

**maximite** /ˈmæksəmaɪt/, *n.* a powerful explosive consisting largely of picric acid. [named after Hudson *Maxim,* 1853-1927, U.S. inventor. See -ITE[1]]

**maximum** /ˈmæksəməm/, *n., pl.* **-ma** /-mə/, **-mums,** *adj.* *–n.* **1.** the greatest quantity or amount possible, assignable, allowable, etc.; the highest amount, value or degree attained or recorded (opposed to *minimum*). **2.** *Maths.* a value of a function at a certain point which is not exceeded in the immediate vicinity of that point. *–adj.* **3.** that is a maximum; greatest possible; highest. **4.** pertaining to a maximum or maximums. [L, neut. of *maximus* greatest]

**maximum and minimum thermometer,** *n.* a type of differential thermometer, used for measuring the highest and lowest temperatures over a period of time, usu. 24 hours.

**maximum-security** /mæksəməm-səˈkjurəti/, *adj.* **1.** of or pertaining to institutions in which the maximum restrictions are placed on prisoners, as in a secured gaol. **2.** of or pertaining to procedures for protecting a public figure, in which the greatest precautions are deemed necessary. Cf. **minimum-security.**

**maximus** /ˈmæksəməs/, *adj.* **1.** that is greatest. **2.** *Brit.* (in boys' schools) designating the eldest of four brothers.

**maxiskirt** /ˈmæksiskɜt/, *n.* a long skirt (contrasted with *miniskirt*).

**maxwell** /ˈmækswəl/, *n.* a non-SI unit of magnetic flux, equal to $10 \times 10^{-9}$ weber. *Symbol:* Mx [named after James Clerk *Maxwell,* 1831-79, Scottish physicist]

**Maxwell-Boltzmann distribution** /ˌmækswəl-ˌbɒltzmən dɪstrəˈbjuʃən/, *n.* a statistical equation for expressing the velocities of particles or their positions in a gas. [named after J. C. *Maxwell,* see MAXWELL, and L. *Boltzmann,* 1844-1906, Austrian physicist]

**Maxwell's equations** /mækswəlz əˈkweɪʒənz/, *n.pl.* the basic equations of electromagnetism, relating charges, currents, electric fields, and magnetic fields, and predicting the behaviour of electromagnetic waves. [See MAXWELL]

**may**[1] /meɪ/, *v., pres.* 1 **may,** 2 (*Archaic*) **mayest** *or* **mayst,** 3 **may,** *pl.* **may;** *p.t.* **might.** used as an auxiliary to express: **a.** possibility, opportunity, or permission: *you may enter.* **b.** wish or prayer: *may you live long.* **c.** contingency, esp. in clauses expressing condition, concession, purpose, result, etc. **d.** *Archaic.* ability or power (more commonly *can*). [OE *mæg,* 1st and 3rd pers. sing. pres. ind. of *magan,* c. G *mögen*]

**may**[2] /meɪ/, *n.* **1.** (*cap.*) the fifth month of the year, containing 31 days. **2.** →**hawthorn.** **3.** any of several, usu. white-flowered, species of the genus *Spiraea.* *–v.i.* **4.** to gather flowers in the northern spring. [ME; OE Maius, from L]

**maya** /ˈmaɪə/, *n.* (in the Veda) a powerful force that creates the cosmic illusion that the phenomenal world is real. [Skt *māyā*]

**Maya** /ˈmaɪə, ˈmeɪə/, *n.* **1.** a member of an aboriginal people of Yucatán which had attained a relatively high civilisation in pre-European America. **2.** the historical and modern language of the Mayas, of Mayan stock. – **Mayan,** *adj.*

**May apple** /ˈmeɪ æpəl/, *n.* **1.** an American perennial herb, *Podophyllum peltatum,* of the family Podophyllaceae, bearing an edible, yellowish, egg-shaped fruit. **2.** the fruit.

**maybe** /ˈmeɪbi, meɪˈbi/, *adv.* perhaps. [short for *it may be*]

**May blobs** /ˈmeɪ blɒbz/, *n.pl.* →**kingcup.**

**May Day** /ˈmeɪ deɪ/, *n.* the first day of May, long celebrated with various festivities, as the crowning of the May queen, dancing round the maypole, etc., and, in recent years, often marked by labour rallies.

**Mayday** /ˈmeɪdeɪ/, *n.* (according to international radio regulations) the radio telephonic distress signal used by ships or aircraft. [F: alteration of *m'aidez* help me]

**mayfly** /ˈmeɪflaɪ/, *n.* **1.** any of the Ephemerida, an order of delicate-winged insects having the forewings much larger than the hind wings, the larvae being aquatic, and the winged adults very short-lived; ephemerid. **2.** an artificial fly made in imitation of this fly.

**maygo** /ˈmeɪgoʊ/, *n.* the document issued by an authority, as Customs, which allows delivery of goods from government control, bond, etc. [short for *it may go*]

**mayhap** /ˈmeɪhæp, meɪˈhæp/, *adv. Archaic.* perhaps. [short for *it may hap*]

**mayhem** /ˈmeɪhɛm/, *n.* **1.** *Law.* the crime of violently inflicting a bodily injury rendering a man less able to defend himself or to annoy his adversary (now often extended by statute to include any wilful mutilation of another's body). **2.** any tumult, fracas, or fight. Also, **maihem.** **3. be mayhem,** *Colloq.* to be in a state of disorder of confusion. **4. in (a state of) mayhem,** *Colloq.* in disorder or confusion. [ME *maheym,* from AF, var. of OF *mahaigne* injury. See MAIM]

**May lily** /ˈmeɪ lɪli/, *n.* a small, rhizomatous, liliaceous herb with dense heads of white flowers, *Maianthemum bifolium,* occurring in woods of Europe and northern Asia.

**mayonnaise** /meɪəˈneɪz/, *n.* a thick dressing of egg yolks, vinegar or lemon juice, seasonings, and oil, used for salads or vegetables. [F: earlier *magnonaise, mahonnaise,* from *Mahon,* a port of the Balearic Islands]

**mayor** /mɛə/, *n.* the principal officer of a municipality; the chief magistrate of a city or borough. [ME *maire,* from F, from L *mājor* greater. Cf. MAJOR] – **mayorship,** *n.*

**mayoralty** /ˈmɛərəlti/, *n., pl.* **-ties.** **1.** the office of a mayor. **2.** the period of office of a mayor.

**mayoress** /ˈmɛərɛs, -rəs, mɛəˈrɛs/, *n.* **1.** the wife of a mayor or the deputy of a lady mayor. **2.** a woman mayor.

**maypole** /ˈmeɪpoʊl/, *n.* a high pole, decorated with flowers or ribbons, for the merrymakers to dance round at May Day (or May) festivities.

**May queen** /ˈmeɪ kwin/, *n.* a girl or young woman crowned with flowers and honoured as queen in the celebrations of May Day.

**mayst** /meɪst/, *v. Archaic.* 2nd person singular present indicative of **may.** Also, **mayest.**

**Maytime** /ˈmeɪtaɪm/, *n.* the month of May. Also, **Maytide** /ˈmeɪtaɪd/.

**maytree** /ˈmeɪtri/, *n.* →**hawthorn.**

**mayweed** /ˈmeɪwid/, *n.* a herb, *Anthemis cotula,* native to Europe and Asia, and naturalised elsewhere, having ill-scented foliage, and flower heads with a yellow disc and white rays. [from obs. *mayth* mayweed (OE *mægtha*) + WEED[1], with loss of *-th*]

**mazard** /ˈmæzəd/, *n.* a wild sweet cherry, *Prunus avium,* used as a rootstock for cultivated varieties of cherries. Also, **mazzard.** [earlier *mazer,* from OF *masere,* from Gmc (cf. MHG *maser* maple)]

**maze** /meɪz/, *n., v.,* **mazed, mazing.** *–n.* **1.** a confusing network of intercommunicating paths or passages; a labyrinth. **2.** a state of bewilderment or confusion. **3.** a winding movement, as in dancing. *–v.t.* **4.** *Archaic.* to stupefy or daze. [ME *mase(n)*; aphetic var. of AMAZE] – **mazement,** *n.* – **mazelike,** *adj.*

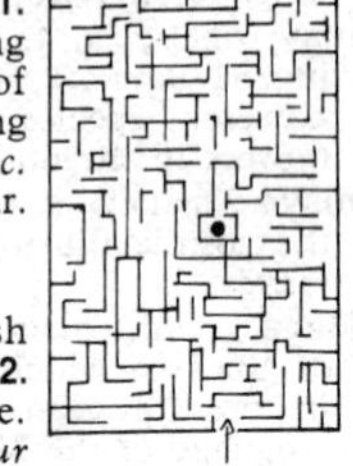
maze (def. 1)

**mazuma** /məˈzumə/, *n. Colloq.* money.

**mazurka** /məˈzɜkə/, *n.* **1.** a lively Polish dance in moderate quick triple rhythm. **2.** music for, or in the rhythm of, this dance. Also, **mazourka.** [Pol.: equivalent to *Mazur* of Mazovia (district in Poland) + *-ka* fem. adj. suffix]

**mazy** /ˈmeɪzi/, *adj.,* **-zier, -ziest.** mazelike; full of intricate windings. – **mazily,** *adv.* – **maziness,** *n.*

**mb,** millibar.

**M.B.,** Bachelor of Medicine. [L *Medicinae Baccalaureus*]

**M.B.A.** /ɛm bi ˈeɪ/, **1.** Master Builders Association. **2.** Master of Business Administration.

**M.B.E.** /ɛm bi ˈi/, Member of the Order of the British Empire.

**m.c.,** medical certificate.

**Mc-,** variant of **Mac-.**

**M.C.** /ɛm ˈsi/, **1.** Master of Ceremonies. **2.** Military Cross. **3.** Marriage Certificate.

**McCarthyism** /məˈkaθiˌɪzəm/, *n.* **1.** public accusation of disloyalty, esp. of pro-Communist activity, in many instances unsupported by proof or based on slight, doubtful, or irrelevant evidence. **2.** unfairness in investigative technique. **3.** persistent search for and exposure of disloyalty, esp. in government offices. [named after Joseph R. *McCarthy,* 1909-57, U.S. politician]

**McCoy** /məˈkɔɪ/, *n. in the phrase* **the real McCoy,** the genuine article.

**M.C.G.** /ɛm si ˈdʒi/, *n.* Melbourne Cricket Ground.

**M. Ch.,** Master of Surgery. [L *Master Chirugiae*]

**MCP** /ɛm si ˈpi/, *n.* male chauvinist pig.

**McPherson strut suspension,** *n.* →**strut suspension.**

**M.C.P.S.,** megacycles per second.

**m.d.,** *Music.* right hand. [It. *mano destra;* in French music, F *main droite*]

**Md,** *Chem.* mendelevium.

**M.D.** /ɛm ˈdi/, **1.** Doctor of Medicine. [L *Medicīnae Doctor*] **2.** Managing Director.

**m.d.o.** /ɛm di ˈoʊ/, *n. N.Z. Colloq.* →**sickie.** [*M(aori) d(ay) o(ff)*]

**M.D.S.** /ɛm di ˈɛs/, Master of Dental Surgery.

**me**[1] /mi/, *pers. pron.* objective case of the pronoun *I.* [ME *mē,* OE *me,* dat. sing. (c. D *mij,* G *mir*); akin to L *mē* (acc.), etc.]

**me**[2] /mi/, *n.* the syllable used for the third note of the scale in solfa. Also, **mi.** See **solfa.**

**Me,** *Chem.* methyl.

**ME,** Middle English. Also, **M.E.**

**M.E., 1.** Marine Engineer. **2.** Mechanical Engineer. **3.** Middle English. **4.** Mining Engineer. **5.** Most Excellent.

**meaconing** /ˈmikənɪŋ/, *n.* a system of receiving radio beacon signals and rebroadcasting them on the same frequency to confuse navigation.

**mead**[1] /mid/, *n. Poetic.* →**meadow.** [ME *mede,* OE *mǣd.* See MEADOW]

**mead**[2] /mid/, *n.* **1.** an alcoholic liquor made by fermenting honey and water. **2.** *U.S.* any of various non-alcoholic beverages. [ME *mede,* OE *medu,* c. G *Met*]

**meadow** /ˈmɛdoʊ/, *n.* **1.** *Chiefly Brit.* a piece of grassland, whether used for raising of hay or for pasture. **2.** *U.S.* a low, level tract of uncultivated ground, as along a river, producing coarse grass. [ME *medwe,* OE *mǣdw-,* in inflectional forms of *mǣd* (cf. MEAD[1]); akin to G *Matte*]

**meadow cake** /ˈ– keɪk/, *n. Colloq.* →**cow pat.**

**meadow grass** /ˈ– gras/, *n.* any of a number of species of the genus *Poa,* as annual meadow grass, *P. annua.*

**meadow lark** /ˈ– lak/, *n.* a common American songbird of the genus *Sturnella* (family Icteridae), esp. the **eastern meadow lark,** *S. magna,* and **western meadow lark,** *S. neglecta,* both of which are robust, yellow-breasted birds about the size of the thrush.

**meadow rue** /ˈ– ru/, *n.* any perennial herb of the genus *Thalictrum,* as *T. flavum,* the common meadow rue of Europe and temperate Asia.

**meadow saffron** /– ˈsæfrən/, *n.* the autumn crocus, *Colchicum autumnale.*

**meadowsweet** /ˈmɛdoʊswit/, *n.* a perennial herb, *Filipendula ulmaria,* with dense heads of small, cream-coloured flowers, widespread on wet ground in Europe and temperate Asia.

**meadowy** /ˈmɛdoʊi/, *adj.* pertaining to, resembling, or consisting of meadow.

**meagre** /ˈmigə/, *adj.* **1.** deficient in quantity or quality, or without fullness or richness. **2.** having little flesh, lean, or thin. **3.** →**maigre.** *–n.* **4.** a long, thin fish of the genus *Sciaena,* sometimes found in British waters; up to 1.5 metres long. Also, *U.S.,* **meager.** [ME *megre,* from OF *maigre,* from L *macer* lean] – **meagrely,** *adv.* – **meagreness,** *n.*

**meal**[1] /mil/, *n.* **1.** one of the regular repasts of the day, as breakfast, lunch, or dinner. **2.** the food eaten or served for a repast. [ME; OE *mǣl* measure, fixed time, occasion, meal, c. G *Mal* time, *Mahl* meal]

**meal**[2] /mil/, *n.* **1.** the edible part of any grain (now usu. excluding wheat) or pulse ground to a (coarse) powder and unbolted. **2.** *U.S.* coarse, unbolted grain. **3.** any ground or powdery substance, as of nuts or seeds, resembling this. [ME *mele,* OE *melu,* c. G *Mehl*]

**meal allowance** /ˈ– əlaʊəns/, *n.* an allowance paid to employees required to work overtime in excess of a specified number of hours or during a particular period of the day.

**mealie** /ˈmili/, *n.* (*usu. pl.*) *S. African.* maize. Also, **mealy.** [Afrikaans *milje*]

**meals on wheels,** *n.* a voluntary service delivering meals to the sick and the aged at home.

**meal ticket** /ˈmil tɪkət/, *n.* **1.** a ticket entitling the holder to a meal. **2.** *Colloq.* any means or source of financial support, as a pimp's prostitute, a spouse, a university degree, etc.

**mealtime** /ˈmiltaɪm/, *n.* **1.** the usual time for a meal. **2.** any time at which one eats.

**mealworm** /ˈmilwɜm/, *n.* the larva of the beetle *Tenebrio molitor,* which infests granaries, and is cultivated in great numbers as food for birds and animals.

**mealy** /ˈmili/, *adj.,* **-lier, -liest. 1.** having the qualities of meal; powdery; soft, dry, and crumbly: *mealy potatoes.* **2.** of the nature of, or containing, meal; farinaceous. **3.** covered with or as with meal or powder. **4.** flecked as if with meal, or spotty. **5.** pale, as the complexion. – **mealiness,** *n.*

**mealy bug** /ˈ– bʌg/, *n.* any hemipterous, plant-sucking insect of the family Coccidae, so called because of the powdery wax which covers the body.

**mealy-mouthed** /ˈmili-maʊðd/, *adj.* **1.** avoiding the use of plain terms, as from timidity, excessive delicacy, or hypocrisy. **2.** using soft words.

**mealy saltbush** /mili ˈsɒltbʊʃ/, *n.* →**old-man saltbush.**

**mean**[1] /min/, *v.,* **meant, meaning.** *–v.t.* **1.** to have in the mind as in intention or purpose (often with an infinitive as object): *I mean to talk to him.* **2.** to intend for a particular purpose, destination, etc.: *they were meant for each other.* **3.** to intend to express or indicate: *by 'liberal' I mean...* **4.** (of words, things, etc.) to have as the signification; signify. *–v.i.* **5.** to be minded or disposed; have intentions: *he means well.* [ME *mene(n),* OE *mǣnan,* c. G *meinen*]

**mean**[2] /min/, *adj.* **1.** inferior in grade, quality or character: *he is no mean performer.* **2.** low in station, rank, or dignity. **3.** of little importance or consequence. **4.** unimposing or shabby: *a mean abode.* **5.** without moral dignity; small-minded or ignoble: *mean motives.* **6.** penurious, stingy, or miserly: *a man who is mean about money.* **7.** pettily offensive or unaccommodating; nasty. **8.** *Colloq.* small, humiliated, or ashamed: *to feel mean over some ungenerous action.* **9.** *Colloq.* troublesome or vicious, as a horse. **10.** (of one involved in a competitive activity, as sport, business, warfare, etc.) sufficiently accomplished and determined to make success very difficult for an opponent: *he's a mean bowler.* **11.** *Colloq.* powerful, effective, having a vicious energy: *a big mean* *motor.* [ME *mene,* aphetic. var. of *imene,* OE *gemǣne,* c. G *gemein* common]

**mean**[3] /min/, *n.* **1.** (*usu. pl. but oft. construed as sing.*) an agency, instrumentality, method, etc., used to attain an end: *a means of communication.* **2.** (*pl.*) disposable resources, esp. pecuniary resources: *to live beyond one's means.* **3.** (*pl.*) considerable pecuniary resources: *a man of means.* **4.** something intermediate; that which is midway between two extremes. **5.** *Maths.* **a.** a quantity having a value intermediate between the values of other quantities; an average, esp. the arithmetic mean. **b.** either the second or third term in a proportion of four terms. **6.** *Logic, Obs.* the middle term in a syllogism. **7. by all means, a.** at any cost; without fail. **b.** (in emphasis) certainly: *go, by all means.* **8. by any means,** in any way; at all. **9. by means of,** employing the method of; by the use of. **10. by no means,** in no way; not at all; certainly not: *a practice by no means to be recommended.* *–adj.* **11.** occupying a middle position or an intermediate place. **12.** intermediate in kind, quality, degree, time, etc. [ME *mene,* from OF *meien,* from LL *mediānus* in the middle]

**meander** /mi'ændə/, *v.i.* **1.** to proceed by a winding course. **2.** to wander aimlessly. *–n.* **3.** (*usu. pl.*) a turning or winding; a winding; a winding path or course. **4.** a circuitous movement or journey. **5.** an intricate variety of fret or fretwork. [L, from Gk *maíandros* a winding, orig. the name of a winding river (now Mendere) in W Asia Minor] – **meanderingly,** *adv.*

**mean deviation** /min divi'eɪʃən/, *n.* the average of the absolute values of a set of deviations from an accepted norm in a statistical distribution.

**mean distance** /min 'dɪstns/, *n.* the arithmetic mean of the greatest and least distances of a planet from the sun, called the semi-major axis, and used in stating the size of an orbit.

**mean free path,** *n.* **1.** the average distance travelled by a particle, atom, or molecule between collisions. **2.** the average distance travelled by a soundwave between successive reflections.

**meanie** /'mini/, *n. Colloq.* a mean person.

**meaning** /'minɪŋ/, *n.* **1.** that which is intended to be, or actually is, expressed or indicated; signification; import. *–adj.* **2.** intending: *he is very well-meaning.* **3.** expressive or significant: *a meaning look.* – **meaningly,** *adv.*

**meaningful** /'minɪŋfəl/, *adj.* full of meaning; significant.

**meaningless** /'minɪŋləs/, *adj.* without meaning or significance. – **meaninglessly,** *adv.* – **meaninglessness,** *n.*

**meanly** /'minli/, *adv.* in a mean manner; poorly; basely; stingily. [MEAN[2] + -LY]

**meanness** /'minnəs/, *n.* **1.** the state or quality of being mean. **2.** a mean act.

**mean noon** /min 'nun/, *n.* the moment when the mean sun's centre crosses the meridian.

**mean sea-level** /– 'si-lɛvəl/, *n.* the average level of the sea as calculated from a long series of observations of tidal oscillations taken at equal time intervals.

**mean solar day,** *n.* See **day** (def. 3b).

**mean solar time,** *n.* →**mean time.**

**means test** /'minz tɛst/, *n.* **1.** an evaluation of the income and resources of a person, or of those upon whom he or she is dependent, in order to determine eligibility for part or all of a pension, grant, allowance, etc. *–v.t.* **2.** to make such an evaluation of (a person's income, etc.). Also, **means-test.** – **means-testable,** *adj.*

**mean sun** /min 'sʌn/, *n.* an imaginary sun moving uniformly in the celestial equator and taking the same time to make its annual circuit as the true sun does in the ecliptic.

**meant** /mɛnt/, *v.* past tense and past participle of **mean**[1].

**mean time** /'min taɪm/, *n.* the time at a given place on earth based on a day of 24 hours; the interval between successive local noons on which local time is based varies and so an average day of 24 hours is used, giving mean time. Also, **mean solar time.**

**meantime** /'mintaɪm/, *n.* **1.** the intervening time: *in the meantime.* *–adv.* **2.** meanwhile.

**meanwhile** /'minwaɪl, min'waɪl/, *adv.* in the intervening time; during the interval; at the same time.

**meas.,** measure.

**measled** /'mizəld/, *adj.* (of animals) affected with measles (def. 3).

**measles** /'mizəlz/, *n.* **1.** an acute infectious disease occurring mostly in children, characterised by catarrhal and febrile symptoms and an eruption of small red spots; rubeola. **2.** any of certain other eruptive diseases, as rubella (**German measles**). **3.** a disease in swine and other animals caused by the larvae of certain tapeworms of the genus *Taenia.* **4.** (*pl.*) the larvae which cause measles. [partly ME *maseles,* c. D *mazelen,* akin to G *Masern* measles, pl. of *Maser* spot; partly ME *mesels,* akin to OHG *māsa* spot]

**measly** /'mizli/, *adj.,* **-lier, -liest.** **1.** infected with measles, as an animal or its flesh. **2.** pertaining to or resembling measles. **3.** (of beef or pork) infected with cysts or tapeworms of the genus *Taenia.* **4.** *Colloq.* wretchedly poor or unsatisfactory; very small.

**measurable** /'mɛʒrəbəl, -ərəbəl/, *adj.* that may be measured. – **measurability** /mɛʒərə'bɪləti/, **measurableness,** *n.* – **measurably,** *adv.*

**measure** /'mɛʒə/, *n., v.,* **-ured, -uring.** *–n.* **1.** the act or process of ascertaining the extent, dimensions, quantity, etc., of something, esp. by comparison with a standard. **2.** size, dimensions, quantity, etc., as thus ascertained. **3.** an instrument, as a graduated rod or a vessel of standard capacity, for measuring. **4.** a unit or standard of measurement. **5.** a definite or known quantity measured out. **6.** a system of measurement. **7.** *Print.* the width of a page or column, usu. measured in ems or picas. **8.** any standard of comparison, estimation, or judgment. **9.** a quantity, degree, or proportion. **10.** a limit, or an extent or degree not to be exceeded: *to know no measure.* **11.** reasonable bounds or limits: *beyond measure.* **12.** a legislative bill or enactment. **13.** an action or procedure intended as a means to an end: *to take measures to avert suspicion.* **14.** a short rhythmical movement or arrangement, as in poetry or music. **15.** a particular kind of such arrangement. **16.** a metrical unit. **17.** *Poetic.* an air or melody. **18.** *U.S. Music.* →**bar**[1] (def. 10). **19.** (*pl.*) *Geol.* beds; strata. **20.** *Archaic.* a slow, stately dance or dance movement. **21. for good measure,** as an extra and probably unnecessary act, precaution, etc.: *he padlocked the door for good measure.* **22. get someone's measure,** *Colloq.* to gain ascendancy over someone. **23. get the measure of someone,** to achieve equality with someone, esp. a competitor. *–v.t.* **24.** to ascertain the extent, dimensions, quantity, capacity, etc., of, esp. by comparison with a standard. **25.** to mark or lay off or out, or deal out, with reference to measure (oft. fol. by *off* or *out*). **26.** to estimate the relative amount, value, etc., of, by comparison with some standard. **27.** to judge of or appraise by comparison with something else. **28.** to serve as the measure of. **29.** to adjust or proportion. **30.** to bring into comparison or competition. **31.** to travel over or traverse. **32. measure one's length,** to fall flat on one's face. **33. measure up to,** to be adequate for. *–v.i.* **34.** to take measurements. **35.** to admit of measurement. **36.** to be of a specified measure. [ME *mesure(n),* from OF *mesurer,* from L *mensūrāre*] – **measurer,** *n.*

**measured** /'mɛʒəd/, *adj.* **1.** ascertained or apportioned by measure. **2.** accurately regulated or proportioned. **3.** regular or uniform, as in movement; rhythmical. **4.** deliberate and restrained: *measured speech.* **5.** in the form of metre or verse; metrical. – **measuredly,** *adv.*

**measureless** /'mɛʒələs/, *adj.* without bounds; unlimited; immeasurable: *caverns measureless to man.* – **measurelessly,** *adv.* – **measurelessness,** *n.*

**measurement** /'mɛʒəmənt/, *n.* **1.** the act of measuring. **2.** an ascertained dimension. **3.** extent, size, etc., ascertained by measuring. **4.** a system of measuring or of measures. **5.** *Survey.* the estimation by a quantity surveyor, civil engineer, or the like, of the work to be done and billed, and later the measuring on the site of the work done and to be paid for.

**measuring cup** /'mɛʒərɪŋ kʌp/, *n.* a graduated cup or jug for measuring quantities of cooking ingredients, etc.

**measuring worm** /'mɛʒərɪŋ wɜm/, *n.* the larva of any geometrid moth, which progresses by bringing the rear end of the body forward and then advancing the front end; a looper; an inchworm.

**meat** /mit/, *n.* **1.** the flesh of animals as used for food. **2.**

food in general: *meat and drink.* **3.** the edible part of anything, as a fruit, nut, etc. **4.** *Archaic.* the principal meal: *to say grace before meat.* **5.** the main substance of something, as an argument. **6.** *Colloq.* male or female genitalia. **7.** **strong meat,** books, films, etc., which would shock anyone with a nervous or squeamish disposition, as those depicting violence. [ME and OE *mete,* c. OHG *maz*] – **meatless,** *adj.*

**meat ant** /'– ænt/, *n.* any of various ants of the genus *Leptomyrmex,* characteristically swarming to meat or carrion. Also, **beef ant, mound ant.**

**meataxe** /'mitæks/, *n.* **1.** →**cleaver.** **2.** **mad as a meat-axe,** *Colloq.* **a.** angry. **b.** eccentric; behaving erratically.

**meatball** /'mitbɔl/, *n.* a small rissole.

**meat-head** /'mit-hɛd/, *n. Chiefly U.S.* a stupid person.

**meat loaf** /'mit loʊf/, *n.* a mixture of minced meat and seasonings with breadcrumbs, rice, etc., shaped like a loaf, and baked.

**meat pie** /– 'paɪ/, *n.* a pie made from stewed meat enclosed in a square or round pastry case.

**meat-pie western** /mit-paɪ 'wɛstən/, *n.* a film made in Australia in the genre of a U.S western.

**meat tag** /'mit tæg/, *n. Colloq.* →**identity disc.** Also, **meat ticket.**

**meatus** /mi'eɪtəs/, *n., pl.* **-tuses, -tus.** an opening or foramen, esp. in a bone or bony structure, as the opening of the ear, nose, etc. [L: passage]

**meatworker** /'mitwɜkə/, *n.* a man employed at an abattoirs or a meatworks.

**meatworks** /'mitwɜks/, *n.* a place where meat is packed, tinned, or otherwise processed, often part of an abattoirs.

**meaty** /'miti/, *adj.,* **-tier, -tiest.** **1.** of or like meat. **2.** abounding in meat. **3.** full of substance; pithy. – **meatiness,** *n.*

**M.Ec.** /ɛm i 'si/, Master of Economics.

**Mecca** /'mɛkə/, *n.* **1.** a place regarded as a centre of interest or activity or visited by many people. **2.** (*also l.c.*) any goal to which people aspire. [from *Mecca,* city in Saudi Arabia, to which Moslem pilgrims journey]

**meccano set** /mə'kanoʊ sɛt/, *n.* perforated metal strips and a kit of components which can be bolted together as a framework for constructing models. [Trademark]

**mech.,** **1.** mechanical. **2.** mechanics. **3.** mechanism.

**mechanic** /mə'kænɪk/, *n.* **1.** a skilled worker with tools or machines. **2.** one who repairs machinery. [ME, from L *mēchanicus,* from Gk *mēchanikós* of machines]

**mechanical** /mə'kænɪkəl/, *adj.* **1.** having to do with machinery. **2.** of the nature of a device or contrivance for controlling or utilising material forces, or of a mechanism or machine. **3.** acting or operated by means of such a contrivance, or of a mechanism or machine. **4.** produced by such means. **5.** acting or performed without spontaneity, spirit, individuality, etc. **6.** belonging or pertaining to the subject matter of mechanics. **7.** pertaining to, or controlled or effected by, physical forces. **8.** **a.** explanatory of phenomena, as due to mechanism (defs 8 and 9). **b.** of or pertaining to those who advocate such explanations, or to their theories. **9.** subordinating the spiritual to the material; materialistic. **10.** involving the material objects or physical conditions: *hindered by mechanical difficulties.* **11.** pertaining to or concerned with the use of tools and the like, or the contrivance and construction of machines or mechanisms. **12.** pertaining to or concerned with manual labour or skill. **13.** exhibiting skill in the use of tools and the like, in the contrivance of machines, etc.: *a mechanical genius.* – **mechanically,** *adv.* – **mechanicalness,** *n.*

**mechanical advantage** /– əd'væntɪdʒ/, *n.* the ratio of the force performing the work done by a mechanism to the input force.

**mechanical drawing** /– 'drɔ-ɪŋ/, *n.* drawing, as of machinery, done with the aid of rulers, scales, compasses, etc.

**mechanical engineer** /– ɛndʒə'nɪə/, *n.* one versed in the design and construction of engines and machines.

**mechanical engineering** /– ɛndʒə'nɪərɪŋ/, *n.* action, work, or profession of a mechanical engineer.

**mechanical equivalent of heat,** *n. Obs.* the relation of 'heat' units to mechanical units of work or energy, thus if 1 calorie = 4.186 joules, 4.186 was called the mechanical equivalent of heat. In SI all forms of energy are measured in the same units (joules).

**mechanician** /mɛkə'nɪʃən/, *n.* one skilled in constructing, working, or repairing machines.

**mechanics** /mə'kænɪks/, *n.* **1.** the branch of knowledge concerned (both theoretically and practically) with machinery or mechanical appliances. **2.** the science dealing with the action of forces on bodies and with motion, and comprising kinematics, statics and dynamics. **3.** (*construed as pl.*) the mechanical or technical part or aspect. **4.** (*construed as pl.*) methods of operation, procedures, and the like.

**mechanics' hall** /– 'hɔl/, *n.* →**school of arts.** Also, **mechanics' institute.**

**mechanise** /'mɛkənaɪz/, *v.t.,* **-nised, -nising.** **1.** to make mechanical. **2.** to operate or perform by or as if by machinery. **3.** to introduce machinery into (an industry, etc.). **4.** *Mil.* to equip with tanks and other armoured motor vehicles. Also, **mechanize.** – **mechanisation** /mɛkənaɪ'zeɪʃən/, *n.*

**mechanism** /'mɛkənɪzəm/, *n.* **1.** a piece of machinery. **2.** the machinery, or the agencies or means, by which a particular effect is produced or a purpose is accomplished. **3.** machinery or mechanical appliances in general. **4.** the structure, or arrangement of parts, of a machine or similar device, or of anything analogous. **5.** such parts collectively. **6.** the way in which a thing works or operates. **7.** mechanical execution, as in painting or music; technique. **8.** the theory that everything in the universe is produced by matter in motion. Cf. **vitalism** (def. 1). **9.** *Philos., Biol.* a natural process interpreted as machine-like or as explicable in terms of Newtonian physics. **10.** *Psychoanal.* (used as an analogy drawn from mechanics) the operation and interaction of psychological forces: *the mechanism of sexual desire.* [NL *mēchanismus,* from Gk *mēchanē* machine + *-ismos* -ISM]

**mechanist** /'mɛkənəst/, *n.* **1.** one who believes in philosophical or biological mechanism (defs 8 and 9). **2.** *Rare.* →**mechanician.**

**mechanistic** /mɛkə'nɪstɪk/, *adj.* pertaining to mechanists or mechanism, or to mechanics (def. 1), or to mechanical theories in philosophy, etc.

**mechanotherapy** /mɛkənoʊ'θɛrəpi/, *n.* curative treatment by mechanical means. [Gk *mēchanē* machine + -O- + THERAPY]

**Mechlin lace** /mɛklən 'leɪs/, *n.* **1.** (originally) handmade bobbin lace with raised cord, made in Flanders. **2.** (now) a similar lace copied by machine. Also, **malines.** [from *Mechlin* (Fr. *Malines*), city in Belgium]

**meconic acid** /məkɒnɪk 'æsəd/, *n.* a white crystalline solid, $C_7H_4O_7$, present in opium and used as a test for opium poisoning as it gives a dark red stain with ferric chloride. [*meconic* from Gk *mēkōn* poppy + -IC]

**meconium** /mə'koʊniəm/, *n.* **1.** the blackish green contents of the bowel of a foetus, discharged soon after birth as the baby's first bowel movement. **2.** opium, or opium poppy juice. **3.** a green discharge from certain larvae. [L: poppy juice (which is dark green in colour)]

**med.,** **1.** medical. **2.** medicine. **3.** medieval. **4.** medium.

**M.Ed.** /ɛm i 'di/, Master of Education.

**medal** /'mɛdl/, *n., v.,* **-alled, -alling** or (*U.S.*) **-aled, -aling.** –*n.* **1.** a flat piece of metal, usu. in the shape of a disc, star, cross, or the like, bearing an inscription, device, etc., issued to commemorate a person, action, or event, or given to serve as a reward for bravery, merit, or the like. –*v.t.* **2.** to decorate or honour with a medal. [F *médaille,* from It. *medaglia,* from L *metallum* metal]

**medallic** /mə'dælɪk/, *adj.* of or pertaining to medals.

**medallion** /mə'dæljən/, *n.* **1.** a large medal. **2.** *Archit.* **a.** a tablet, usu. rounded, often bearing objects represented in relief. **b.** a member in a decorative design resembling a panel. [F *médaillon,* from It. *medaglione,* augmentative of *medaglia* MEDAL]

**medallion steak** /'– steɪk/, *n.* a standard cut of meat taken from a trimmed skinless loin of a superporker.

**medallist** /'mɛdələst/, *n.* **1.** one to whom a medal has been awarded. **2.** a designer, engraver, or maker of medals. Also, *Chiefly U.S.,* **medalist.**

**medal play** /'mɛdl pleɪ/, *n.* (in golf) play in which the score is reckoned by counting the strokes taken to complete the round. Also, **stroke play.**

**meddle** /ˈmɛdl/, *v.i.*, **-dled, -dling.** to concern or busy oneself with or in something without warrant or necessity; interfere. [ME *medle(n)*, from OF *medler*, from L *miscēre* mix] – **meddler,** *n.*

**meddlesome** /ˈmɛdlsəm/, *adj.* given to meddling. – **meddlesomely,** *adv.* – **meddlesomeness,** *n.*

**Mede** /mid/, *n.* a native or inhabitant of Media, an ancient kingdom, south of the Caspian Sea, which built an empire in south-western Asia in the 7th and 6th centuries B.C.

**media**[1] /ˈmidiə/, *n.* **1.** a plural of medium. **2.** →**mass media.**

**media**[2] /ˈmidiə/, *n., pl.* **-diae** /-dii/. **1.** (in various scientific uses) something medial. **2.** *Anat.* the middle layer of an artery or lymphatic vessel. [L: middle (fem. adj.)]

**mediacy** /ˈmidiəsi/, *n.* the state of being mediate.

**mediaeval** /mɛdiˈivəl/, *adj.* →**medieval.** – **mediaevalism,** *n.* – **mediaevalist,** *n.*

**medial** /ˈmidiəl/, *adj.* **1.** situated in or pertaining to the middle; median; intermediate. **2.** pertaining to a mean or average; average. **3.** ordinary. **4.** within a word or syllable; neither initial nor final. –*n.* **5.** a medial linguistic element. [LL *mediālis*, from L *medius* middle] – **medially,** *adv.*

**median** /ˈmidiən/, *adj.* **1.** denoting or pertaining to a plane dividing something into two equal parts, esp. one dividing an animal into right and left halves. **2.** situated in or pertaining to the middle; medial. –*n.* **3.** the middle number in a given sequence of numbers: *4 is the median of 1, 3, 4, 8, 9.* **4.** a line through a vertex of a triangle bisecting the opposite side. [L *mediānus* in the middle] – **medianly,** *adv.*

**median lethal dose,** *n.* the dose of ionising radiation which would kill 50 per cent of a large batch of organisms within a specified period. *Abbrev.:* LD-50.

**median strip** /ˈmidiən strɪp/, *n.* a dividing area, often raised or landscaped between opposing traffic lanes on a highway.

**mediant** /ˈmidiənt/, *n.* the third degree of a scale.

**mediastinum** /midiəˈstaɪnəm/, *n., pl.* **-stina** /-ˈstaɪnə/. **1.** a median septum or partition between two parts of an organ, or paired cavities of the body. **2.** the partition separating the right and left thoracic cavities, formed of the two inner pleural walls, and, in man, containing all the viscera of the thorax except the lungs. [ML, properly neut. of ML *mediastīnus* in the middle, from L *medius* middle] – **mediastinal,** *adj.*

**mediate** /ˈmidieɪt/, *v.*, **-ated, -ating;** /ˈmidiət/, *adj.* –*v.t.* **1.** to bring about (an agreement, peace, etc.) between parties by acting as mediator. **2.** to settle (disputes, etc.) by mediation; reconcile. **3.** to effect (a result), convey (a gift), etc., as or by an intermediary or medium. –*v.i.* **4.** to act between parties to effect an agreement, compromise, or reconciliation. **5.** to occupy an intermediate place or position. –*adj.* **6.** acting through, dependent on, or involving an intermediate agency; not direct or immediate. [ME, from LL *mediātus*, pp., divided, situated in the middle] – **mediately,** *adv.*

**mediation** /midiˈeɪʃən/, *n.* action in mediating between parties, as to effect an agreement or reconciliation.

**mediatise** /ˈmidiətaɪz/, *v.t.*, **-tised, -tising.** to annex (a principality) to another state (while allowing certain rights to its former sovereign). Also, **mediatize.** [F *médiatiser*, or from G *mediatisieren*, from LL *mediātus*, pp., divided] – **mediatisation** /ˌmidiətaɪˈzeɪʃən/, *n.*

**mediative** /ˈmidiətɪv/, *adj.* mediating; mediatory.

**mediator** /ˈmidiˌeɪtə/, *n.* **1.** one who mediates. **2.** one who mediates between parties at variance.

**mediatory** /ˈmidiətri, -ətəri /, *adj.* **1.** pertaining to mediation. **2.** having the function of mediating. Also, **mediatorial** /midiəˈtɔriəl/.

**medic**[1] /ˈmɛdɪk/, *n. Chiefly U.S. Colloq.* a doctor, medical student, or medical orderly.

**medic**[2] /ˈmɛdɪk/, *n.* any papilionaceous herb of the genus *Medicago*, widespread in temperate grasslands, as burr medic. Also, **medick.** [L *mēdica*, from Gk *(póa) Mēdikḗ* Median (grass), i.e., from the ancient country of Media (now NW Iran)]

**medicable** /ˈmɛdɪkəbəl/, *adj.* susceptible of medical treatment; curable. [L *medicābilis*]

**medical** /ˈmɛdɪkəl/, *adj.* **1.** of or pertaining to the science or practice of medicine. **2.** curative; medicinal; therapeutic: *medical properties.* –*n.* **3.** a medical examination. [LL *medicālis*, from L *medicus* of healing] – **medically,** *adv.*

**medical certificate** /– səˈtɪfəkət/, *n.* a certificate made out by a doctor testifying to the state of a person's health.

**medical jurisprudence** /– dʒurəsˈprudəns/, *n.* the science of the application of medical knowledge to the law; forensic medicine.

**medical orderly** /– ˈɔdəli/, *n.* See **orderly** (def. 8).

**medicament** /məˈdɪkəmənt/, *n.* a curative or healing substance. [L *medicāmentum*] – **medicamental** /mədɪkəˈmɛntəl/, **medicamentary** /mədɪkəˈmɛntəri/, *adj.*

**medicate** /ˈmɛdəkeɪt/, *v.t.*, **-cated, -cating. 1.** to treat with medicine or medicaments. **2.** to impregnate with a medicine. [L *medicātus*, pp., cured]

**medication** /mɛdəˈkeɪʃən/, *n.* **1.** the use or application of medicine. **2.** a medicament; a medicinal agent.

**medicative** /ˈmɛdəkətɪv, -keɪ-/, *adj.* →**medicinal.**

**medicheck** /ˈmɛditʃɛk/, *n.* a multiphasic screening.

**medicinal** /məˈdɪsənəl/, *adj.* pertaining to, or having the properties of, a medicine; curative; remedial: *medicinal properties, medicinal substances.* [ME, from L *medicīnālis* of medicine] – **medicinally,** *adv.*

**medicine** /ˈmɛdəsən, ˈmɛdsən/, *n., v.*, **-cined, -cining.** –*n.* **1.** any substance or substances used in treating disease; a medicament; a remedy. **2.** the art or science of restoring or preserving health or due physical condition, as by means of drugs, surgical operations or appliances, manipulations, etc. (often divided into medicine proper, surgery, and obstetrics). **3.** the art or science of treating disease with drugs or curative substances (distinguished from *surgery* and *obstetrics*). **4.** the medical profession. **5.** any object or practice regarded by primitive peoples as of magical efficacy. **6.** any unpleasant treatment or experience, esp. one that is difficult to accept. **7. a taste** (or **dose**) **of one's own medicine,** any unpleasant treatment meted out to one who usu. punishes, bullies, etc. –*v.t.* **8.** to administer medicine to. [ME, from L *medicīna*]

**medicine ball** /ˈ– bɔl/, *n.* a large, solid, leather-covered ball, thrown from one person to another for exercise.

**medicine box** /ˈ– bɒks/, *n.* →**medicine chest.**

**medicine chest** /ˈ– tʃɛst/, *n.* a box, carry-bag, small cupboard, etc., used to store household medicines, bandages, etc. Also, **medicine box.**

**medicine man** /ˈ– mæn/, *n.* (esp. among American Indians) a man supposed to possess mysterious or supernatural powers.

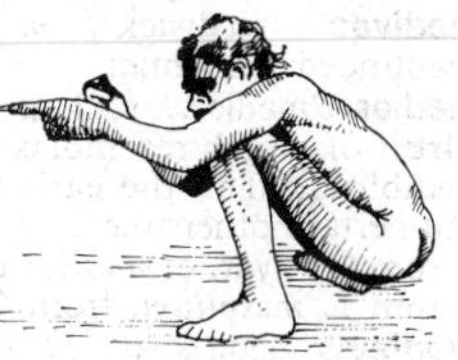

Aboriginal medicine man pointing the bone

**medick** /ˈmɛdɪk/, *n.* →**medic**[2].

**medico** /ˈmɛdɪkoʊ/, *n., pl.* **-cos.** *Colloq.* a doctor. [It. and Sp., from L *medicus* a physician]

**medieval** /mɛdiˈivəl/, *adj.* of or pertaining to, characteristic of, or in the style of the Middle Ages: *medieval architecture.* See **Middle Ages.** Also, **mediaeval.** [NL *medi(um) aev(um)* middle age + -AL[1]] – **medievally,** *adv.*

**Medieval Greek** /mɛdiˌivəl ˈgrik/, *n.* the Greek language of the Middle Ages, usu. dated A.D. 700-1500. Also, **Middle Greek.**

**medievalism** /mɛdiˈivəlɪzəm/, *n.* **1.** the spirit, practices, or methods of the Middle Ages. **2.** devotion to or adoption of medieval ideals or practices. **3.** a medieval belief, practice, or the like. Also, **mediaevalism.**

**medievalist** /mɛdiˈivələst/, *n.* **1.** an expert in medieval history and affairs. **2.** one in sympathy with the spirit and methods of the Middle Ages. Also, **mediaevalist.**

**Medieval Latin** /mɛdiˌivəl ˈlætən/, *n.* the Latin language of the literature of the Middle Ages (usu. dated A.D. 700 to 1500), including many Latinised words from other languages.

**mediocre** /midiˈoʊkə, ˈmidioʊkə/, *adj.* of middling quality; of only moderate excellence; neither good nor bad; indifferent; ordinary: *a person of mediocre abilities.* [F, from L *mediocris* in a middle state]

**mediocrity** /midiˈɒkrəti, mɛdi-/, n., pl. **-ties. 1.** the state or quality of being mediocre. **2.** mediocre ability or accomplishment. **3.** a person of only moderate ability.

**meditate** /ˈmɛdəteɪt/, *v.*, **-tated, -tating.** *–v.t.* **1.** to consider in the mind as something to be done or effected; to intend or purpose. *–v.i.* **2.** to engage in thought or contemplation; reflect. [L *meditātus,* pp.] – **meditator,** *n.*

**meditation** /mɛdəˈteɪʃən/, *n.* **1.** the act of meditating. **2.** continued thought; reflection; contemplation.

**meditative** /ˈmɛdəteɪtɪv, ˈmɛdətətɪv/, *adj.* given to, characterised by, or indicative of meditation. – **meditatively,** *adv.* – **meditativeness,** *n.*

**Mediterranean climate** /ˌmɛdətəreɪniən ˈklaɪmət/, *n.* the type of climate experienced by the lands bordering the Mediterranean Sea and also by other regions in both hemispheres, characterised by sunny, hot summers, and warm winters with rainfall in the winter half of the year.

**Mediterranean fever,** /– ˈfivə/, *n.* →**undulant fever.**

**medium** /ˈmidiəm/, *n., pl.* **-dia** /-diə/, **-diums,** *adj.* *–n.* **1.** a middle state or condition; a mean. **2.** something intermediate in nature or degree. **3.** *Print.* a size of printing paper, 18 × 23 inches, most commonly in use before metrication. **4.** an intervening substance, as air, etc., through which a force acts or an effect is produced. **5.** the element in which an organism has its natural habitat. **6.** one's environment; surrounding things, conditions, or influences. **7.** an agency means, or instrument: *newspapers as an advertising medium.* **8.** *Biol.* the substance by which specimens are displayed or preserved. **9.** *Bacteriol.* a nutritive substance containing protein, carbohydrates, salts, water, etc., either liquid or solidified through the addition of gelatine or agar-agar, in or upon which micro-organisms are grown for study. **10.** *Painting.* **a.** a liquid with which pigments are mixed for application. **b.** the material or technique which an artist uses. **11.** a person serving or conceived as serving, as an instrument for the manifestation of another personality or of some alleged supernatural agency: *a spiritualist medium.* *–adj.* **12.** intermediate in degree, quality, etc.: *a man of medium size.* [L: (neut. adj.) middle, intermediate]

**medium frequency** /– ˈfrikwənsi/, *n.* a radio frequency of between 30 and 300 kilohertz. *Abbrev.:* m.f.

**mediumistic** /midiəmˈɪstɪk/, *adj.* of or pertaining to a spiritualist medium.

**medium shot** /ˈmidiəm ʃɒt/, *n.* (in film or television) half-way between a close-up and a long shot.

**medium wave** /ˈmidiəm weɪv/, *n.* an electromagnetic wave with a wavelength of 200-1000 metres. – **medium-wave,** *adj.*

**medivac** /ˈmɛdivæk/, *n. Colloq.* evacuation by aircraft of wounded personnel.

**medlar** /ˈmɛdlə/, *n.* **1.** a small tree, *Mespilus germanica,* the fruit of which resembles an open-topped crab-apple and is not edible until in the early stages of decay. **2.** its fruit. **3.** any of certain other trees. **4.** the fruit of such a tree. [ME *medler,* from OF, var. of *meslier* the medlar tree, from *mesle,* the fruit, from L *mespilum,* from Gk *méspilon*]

**medley** /ˈmɛdli/, *n., pl.* **-leys,** *adj.* *–n.* **1.** a mixture, esp. of heterogeneous elements; a jumble. **2.** a piece of music combining airs or passages from various sources. **3.** *Swimming.* a race in which a competitor swims butterfly stroke, backstroke and freestyle in that order. *–adj.* **4.** mixed; mingled; motley. [ME *medlee,* from OF, var. of *meslee* a mixing, orig. pp. fem. of *mesler* mix]

**medley relay** /– ˈrileɪ/, *n.* **1.** *Athletics.* a relay race in which each member of a team runs a different distance. **2.** *Swimming.* a relay race in which each member of a team uses a different stroke.

**medulla** /məˈdʌlə/, *n., pl.* **-dullae** /-ˈdʌli/. **1.** *Anat.* **a.** the marrow of bones. **b.** the soft marrow-like centre of an organ, such as the kidney, suprarenal, etc. **c.** the medulla oblongata. **2.** *Bot.* the pith of plants. [L: marrow, pith]

**medulla oblongata** /– ɒblɒŋˈgatə/, *n.* the lowest or hindmost part of the brain, continuous with the spinal cord. [NL: prolonged medulla]

**medullary** /məˈdʌləri/, *adj.* pertaining to, consisting of, or resembling the medulla of an organ or the medulla oblongata.

**medullary ray** /ˈ– reɪ/, *n.* (in the stems of exogenous plants) one of the vertical bands of plates of parenchymatous tissue which radiate between the pith and the bark.

**medullary sheath** /ˈ– ʃiθ/, *n.* **1.** a narrow zone made up of the innermost layer of woody tissue immediately surrounding the pith in plants. **2.** →**myelin.**

**medullated** /ˈmɛdəleɪtəd, məˈdʌleɪtəd/, *adj.* covered by a medullary substance; possessing myelin sheaths.

**medusa** /məˈdjusə/, *n., pl.* **-sas, -sae** /-si/. →**jellyfish.** – **medusoid,** *adj.*

**medusan** /məˈdjusən/, *adj.* **1.** pertaining to a medusa or jellyfish. *–n.* **2.** a medusa or jellyfish.

**meed** /mid/, *n. Archaic.* a reward or recompense for service or desert (good or bad). [ME *mede,* OE *mēd,* c. G *Miete* hire]

**meek** /mik/, *adj.* **1.** humbly patient or submissive, as under provocation from others. **2.** unduly patient or submissive; spiritless; tame. [ME *meke, meoc,* from Scand.; cf. Icel. *mjūkr* soft, mild, meek] – **meekly,** *adv.* – **meekness,** *n.*

**meerkat** /ˈmɪəkæt/, *n.* any of several small, burrowing, southern African carnivores, esp. *Suricata suricatta,* with dark bands across the back, related to the mongoose. Also, **suricate.** [Afrikaans: lit., sea cat]

meerkat

**meerschaum** /ˈmɪəʃəm/, *n.* **1.** *Geol.* a clay mineral, hydrous magnesium silicate $H_4Mg_2Si_3O_{10}$ occurring in white, compact, spongy or fibrous masses, used for ornamental carvings for pipe bowls etc.; sepiolite. **2.** a tobacco pipe the bowl of which is made of this substance. [G: sea foam]

**meet**[1] /mit/, *v.,* **met, meeting,** *n.* *–v.t.* **1.** to come into contact, junction, or connection with. **2.** to come before or to (the eye, gaze, ear, etc.). **3.** to come upon or encounter; come face to face with or into the presence of. **4.** to go to the place of arrival of, as to welcome, speak with, accompany, etc.: *to meet one's guests at the door.* **5.** to come into the company of (a person, etc.) in intercourse, dealings, conference, etc. **6.** to come into personal acquaintance with, as by formal presentation: *to meet the governor.* **7.** to face, eye, etc., directly or without avoidance. **8.** to encounter in opposition or conflict. **9.** to oppose: *to meet charges with countercharges.* **10.** to cope or deal effectively with (an objection, difficulty, etc.). **11.** to satisfy (needs, obligations, demands, etc.): *to meet a cheque.* **12.** to come into conformity with (wishes, expectations, views, etc.). **13.** to encounter in experience: *to meet hostility.* **14. meet (someone) halfway,** to reach an agreed compromise. *–v.i.* **15.** to come together, face to face, or into company: *we met in the street.* **16.** to assemble, as for action or conference as a committee, a legislature, a society, etc. **17.** to become personally acquainted. **18.** to come into contact or form a junction, as lines, planes, areas, etc. **19.** to be conjoined or united. **20.** to concur or agree. **21.** to come together in opposition or conflict, as adversaries, hostile forces, etc. **22. meet with, a.** to encounter; come across. **b.** to experience; undergo; receive (praise, blame, etc.). *–n.* **23.** a meeting, as of huntsmen for a hunt, or cyclists for a ride, etc. **24.** those assembled at such a meeting. **25.** the place of meeting. [ME *mete(n),* OE *mētan, gemētan,* from *mōt, gemōt* meeting. See MOOT]

**meet**[2] /mit/, *adj. Archaic.* suitable; fitting; proper. [ME *mete,* representing OE form, replacing OE *gemǣte* suitable, c. G *gemäss* conformable]

**meeting** /ˈmitɪŋ/, *n.* **1.** a coming together. **2.** an assembling, as of persons for some purpose. **3.** an assembly or gathering held. **4.** →**race meeting.** **5.** the persons present. **6.** a hostile encounter; a duel. **7.** an assembly for religious worship, esp. of Quakers. **8.** a coming into or being in contact, as of things; junction or union.

**meeting house** /ˈ– haʊs/, *n.* **1.** a house or building for religious worship. **2.** a house of worship of Quakers. **3.** *N.Z.* the central community building on a Maori marae.

**meeting point** /ˈmitɪŋ pɔɪnt/, *n.* **1.** a place where things meet: *the meeting point of the rivers.* **2.** something which a group of people have in common: *their religion is their only meeting point.*

**meetly** /ˈmitli/, *adv.* suitably; fittingly; properly.

**mega-** /ˈmɛgə-/, **1.** a prefix denoting $10^6$ of a given unit, as in *megawatt.* *Symbol:* M **2.** a prefix meaning 'great', 'huge', as in *megalith.* Also, before vowels, **meg-**. **3.** *Colloq.* to a very great degree: *a megatrendy.* [Gk, combining form of *mégas*]

**megacephalic** /mɛgəsə'fælɪk/, *adj.* **1.** having a skull with a large cranial capacity or one exceeding the mean. Cf. **microcephalic. 2.** large-headed. Also, **megacephalous** /mɛgə'sɛfələs/. [MEGA- + Gk *kephalḗ* head + -IC]

**megadeath** /'mɛgədɛθ/, *n.* the death of a million persons, esp. as the result of an act of nuclear warfare.

**megagamete** /mɛgə'gæmit/, *n.* →**macrogamete.**

**megalith** /'mɛgəlɪθ/, *n.* a stone of great size, esp. in ancient constructive work or in primitive monumental remains (as menhirs, dolmens, cromlechs, etc.). – **megalithic** /mɛgə'lɪθɪk/, *adj.*

**megalo-,** a word element denoting bigness or exaggeration. [Gk, combining form of *mégas* great]

**megalocephalic** /mɛgəlousə'fælɪk/, *adj.* →**megacephalic.** Also, **megalocephalous** /mɛgəlou'sɛfələs/. – **megalocephaly,** *n.*

**megalomania** /mɛgəlou'meɪniə/, *n.* **1.** a form of mental alienation marked by delusions of greatness, wealth, etc. **2.** a mania for big or great things. [NL. See MEGALO-, -MANIA]

**megalomaniac** /mɛgəlou'meɪniæk/, *n.* one who is afflicted with megalomania. – **megalomaniacal** /mɛgəloumə'naɪəkəl/, *adj.*

**megalopolis** /mɛgə'lɒpələs/, *n.* a large urban region, often consisting of adjoining towns and suburbs which have merged. – **megalopolitan** /mɛgələ'pɒlətən/, *adj.*

**megalosaur** /'mɛgələsɔ/, *n.* any of the gigantic carnivorous dinosaurs that constitute the extinct genus *Megalosaurus.* [NL *megalosaurus*] – **megalosaurian** /mɛgələ'sɔriən/, *adj., n.*

**megamachine** /'mɛgəməʃin/, *n.* a social system dominated by technology which functions with little or no regard for essentially human needs.

**megaphone** /'mɛgəfoun/, *n.* a device for magnifying sound, or for directing it in increased volume, as a large funnel-shaped instrument used in addressing a large audience out of doors or in calling to a distance. – **megaphonic** /mɛgə'fɒnɪk/, *adj.*

**megapod** /'mɛgəpɒd/, *adj.* having large feet.

**megapode** /'mɛgəpoud/, *n.* any of the Megapodiidae, a family of large-footed gallinaceous birds, of the East Indies, Australasia and Polynesia, which constructs a mound of earth or vegetation either for use in display, as the superb lyrebird, or as an incubator for its eggs, as the brush turkey, the lowan and the jungle fowl; mound bird; mound builder.

**megaron** /'mɛgərɒn/, *n.* the main hall of an ancient Mycenean house, consisting basically of a rectangular room with the side walls projecting beyond the forward end to form a porch which may be pillared.

**megasporangium** /mɛgəspə'rændʒiəm/, *n., pl.* **-gia** /-dʒiə/. a sporangium containing megaspores.

**megaspore** /'mɛgəspɔ/, *n.* **1.** the larger of the two kinds of spores produced by some pteridophytes. **2.** the embryo sac of a flowering plant.

**megasporophyll** /mɛgə'spɔrəfɪl/, *n.* a sporophyll producing megasporangia only.

**megastructure** /'mɛgəstrʌktʃə/, *n.* a huge construction or complex, esp. one consisting of many buildings.

**megathere** /'mɛgəθɪə/, *n.* any of the huge slothlike animals that constitute the extinct genus *Megatherium.* [NL *megathērium,* from Gk *mega-* MEGA- + *thēríon* beast]

**megaton** /'mɛgətʌn/, *n* **1.** one million tons. **2.** an explosive force equal to that of one million tons of TNT.

**megaton weapon** /'– wɛpən/, *n.* a nuclear weapon, the yield of which is measured in terms of millions of tons of trinitrotoluene explosive equivalents.

**megrim** /'migrəm/, *n.* **1.** (*pl.*) morbid low spirits. **2.** (*pl.*) →**blind staggers. 3.** *Archaic.* a whim or caprice. **4.** *Obs.* →**migraine.** [ME *migraine,* from F, from LL *hemicrānia* HEMICRANIA]

**meiosis** /maɪ'ousəs/, *n.* the maturation process of gametes, consisting of chromosome conjugation and two cell divisions, in the course of which the diploid chromosome number becomes reduced to the haploid. [Gk: a lessening] – **meiotic,** *adj.*

**mel** /mɛl/, *n.* honey of a very pure kind used for pharmaceutical products. [L]

**melaleuca** /mɛlə'lukə/, *n.* any tree or shrub of the predominantly Australian genus *Melaleuca,* family Myrtaceae, many of which are found on river banks or in swamps; paperbark; tea tree. [NL, from Gk *méla(s)* black + *leukós* white, with reference to the black trunk and white branches]

**melamine** /'mɛləmin/, *n.* a white crystalline solid, $C_3H_6N_6$, used in synthetic resins, esp. with formaldehyde, for making cups, plates, basins, etc.

**melan-,** variant of **melano-**, as in *melancholy.*

**melancholia** /mɛlən'kouliə/, *n.* mental disease characterised by great depression of spirits and gloomy forebodings. [LL. See MELANCHOLY]

**melancholiac** /mɛlən'kouliæk/, *adj.* **1.** affected with melancholia. *–n.* **2.** one affected with melancholia.

**melancholic** /mɛlən'kɒlɪk/, *adj.* **1.** disposed to or affected with melancholy; gloomy; melancholy. **2.** pertaining to melancholia. – **melancholically,** *adv.*

**melancholy** /'mɛlənkɒli/, *n., pl.* **-cholies,** *adj. –n.* **1.** a gloomy state of mind, esp. when habitual or prolonged; depression. **2.** sober thoughtfulness; pensiveness. **3.** *Archaic.* **a.** condition of having too much black bile. **b.** the bile itself. *–adj.* **4.** affected with, characterised by, or showing melancholy: *a melancholy mood.* **5.** attended with or inducing melancholy or sadness: *a melancholy occasion.* **6.** soberly thoughtful; pensive. [ME *melancholie,* from LL *melancholia,* from Gk: black bile]

**Melanesia** /mɛlə'niʒə/, *n.* one of the three principal divisions of Oceania, comprising the island groups in the South Pacific, north-east of Australia. [Gk *méla(s)* black + Gk *nêsos* island + -IA; ? so named from black appearance of the islands seen from the sea]

**Melanesian** /mɛlə'niʒən/, *adj.* **1.** of or pertaining to Melanesia, its inhabitants, or their languages. *–n.* **2.** a member of any of the dark-skinned, frizzy-haired peoples inhabiting Melanesia. **3.** any of the Austronesian languages of Melanesia.

**Melanesian pidgin** /– 'pɪdʒən/, *n.* →**Neo-Melanesian.**

**melange** /meɪ'lɒnʒ/, *n.* a mixture; medley. Also, **mélange.** [F, from *mêler* mix. See MEDDLE]

**melange printing** /– 'prɪntɪŋ/, *n.* a process of printing stripes of colour onto slivers of unspun wool, which causes perfect blending of the colour during spinning.

**melanin** /'mɛlənən/, *n.* the dark pigment in the body of man and certain animals, $C_{17}H_{98}O_{33}N_{14}S$, as that occurring in the hair, epidermis, etc., of coloured races, or one produced in certain diseases. [MELAN- + -IN[2]]

**melanism** /'mɛlənɪzəm/, *n.* the condition of having a high amount of dark or black pigment granules in the skin, hair, and eyes of a human being or the skin and surface structures of any other animal. – **melanistic** /mɛlə'nɪstɪk/, *adj.*

**melanite** /'mɛlənaɪt/, *n.* a deep-black variety of garnet. [MELAN- + -ITE[1]]

**melano** /mə'lanou/, *n.* an animal characterised by an abnormal development of black pigment in the epidermis, hair, feathers, etc. (opposed to *albino*).

**melano-,** a word element meaning 'black'. [Gk, combining form of *mélas* black]

**melanoid** /'mɛlənɔɪd/, *adj.* **1.** of or characterised by melanosis. **2.** resembling the colour of melanin.

**melanoma** /mɛlə'noumə/, *n.* a malignant tumour derived from pigment-containing cells esp. in skin. [NL. See MELAN-, -OMA]

**melanosis** /mɛlə'nousəs/, *n.* **1.** morbid deposition or development of black or dark pigment in the tissues, sometimes leading to the production of malignant pigmented tumours. **2.** a discolouration caused by this. [NL, from Gk: a blackening] – **melanotic,** *adj.*

**Melb.,** Melbourne.

**Melba sauce** /mɛlbə 'sɔs/, *n.* a sauce, made from sweetened pureed raspberries. [named after Dame Nellie *Melba* (Mrs. Nellie Mitchell Armstrong), 1861-1931, Australian soprano]

**Melba toast** /– 'toust/, *n.* very thinly sliced bread, baked in the oven until crisp; fairy bread. [named after Dame Nellie *Melba.* See MELBA SAUCE]

**Melbourne Cup** /mɛlbən 'kʌp/, *n. N.Z. Colloq.* →**chamber-pot.** [from *Melbourne Cup,* a major Australian horserace, first run 1861]

**Melburnian** /mɛl'bɜniən/, *n.* **1.** one who was born in Melbourne, the capital city of Victoria, or who has come to regard it as his hometown. *–adj.* **2.** of or pertaining to the city of Melbourne. Also, **Melbournian.**

**meld**[1] /mɛld/, *Cards. –v.t.* **1.** to announce and display (a counting combination of cards in the hand) for a score. *–v.i.* **2.** to present a meld. *–n.* **3.** the act of melding. **4.** any combination of cards to be melded. [G *melden* announce]

**meld**[2] /mɛld/, *v.t.* **1.** to cause to merge or blend. *–v.i.* **2.** to blend or combine. [b. MELT + WELD[1]]

**melee** /mɛ'leɪ, -'li/, *n.* **1.** a confused general hand-to-hand fight. **2.** any noisy or confused situation. [F. See MEDLEY]

**meliaceous** /mili'eɪʃəs/, *adj.* belonging to the Meliaceae, a family of trees and shrubs including the mahogany, red cedar, etc. [NL *Melia* the typical genus (from Gk: ash tree) + -ACEOUS]

**melic** /'mɛlɪk/, *adj.* **1.** intended to be sung. **2.** denoting or pertaining to the more elaborate form of Greek lyric poetry, as distinguished from iambic and elegiac poetry. [Gk *melikós,* from *mélos* song]

**melilot** /'mɛləlɒt/, *n.* any of the tall papilonaceous herbs of the genus *Melilotus,* as Bokhara clover and Hexham scent. [ME *mellilot,* from OF, from L *melilōtos,* from Gk: a kind of clover]

**melinite** /'mɛlənaɪt/, *n.* a high explosive containing picric acid. [Gk *mélinos* quince-yellow + -ITE[1]]

**meliorate** /'miliəreɪt/, *v.,* **-rated, -rating.** *–v.t.* **1.** to make better; ameliorate. *–v.i.* **2.** to become better; improve. [LL *meliōrātus,* pp.] – **melioration** /miliə'reɪʃən/, *n.* – **meliorative,** *adj.* – **meliorator,** *n.*

**meliorative** /'miliərətɪv/, *adj.* (of lexical items) giving or acquiring a more favourable meaning or connotation.

**meliorism** /'miliərɪzəm/, *n.* the doctrine that the world tends to become better, or may be made better by human effort. [L *melior* better + -ISM] – **meliorist,** *n., adj.* – **melioristic** /miliə'rɪstɪk/, *adj.*

**meliority** /mili'ɒrəti/, *n.* →**superiority.**

**melisma** /mə'lɪzmə/, *n.* a group of musical notes sung to one syllable.

**melliferous** /mə'lɪfərəs/, *adj.* yielding or producing honey. [L *mellifer* honey-bearing + -OUS]

**mellifluent** /mə'lɪfluənt/, *adj.* →**mellifluous.** [LL *mellifluens* flowing with honey] – **mellifluence,** *n.* – **mellifluently,** *adv.*

**mellifluous** /mə'lɪfluəs/, *adj.* **1.** sweetly or smoothly flowing: *mellifluous tones.* **2.** flowing with honey; sweetened with or as with honey. [ME, from LL *mellifluus* flowing with honey] – **mellifluously,** *adv.* – **mellifluousness,** *n.*

**mellophone** /'mɛləfoun/, *n.* a simplified French horn used in dance bands.

**mellow** /'mɛlou/, *adj.* **1.** soft and full-flavoured from ripeness, as fruit. **2.** well-matured, as wines. **3.** softened, toned down or improved as if by ripening. **4.** soft and rich, as sound, tones, colour, light, etc. **5.** genial; jovial. **6.** friable or loamy, as soil. *–v.t., v.i.* **7.** to make or become mellow; soften by or as by ripening. [ME *mel(o)we,* OE *meru* tender, soft, with change of *r* to *l,* presumably by dissimilation in sequence *melowe fruit*] – **mellowly,** *adv.* – **mellowness,** *n.*

**melodeon** /mə'loudiən/, *n.* **1.** a small reed organ. **2.** a kind of accordion. [pseudo-Gk var. of *melodium* (from MELODY). Cf. ACCORDION]

**melodic** /mə'lɒdɪk/, *adj.* **1.** melodious. **2.** pertaining to melody as distinguished from harmony and rhythm. – **melodically,** *adv.*

**melodics** /mə'lɒdɪks/, *n.* that branch of musical science concerned with the pitch and succession of tones.

**melodious** /mə'loudiəs/, *adj.* **1.** of the nature of or characterised by melody; tuneful. **2.** producing melody or sweet sound. – **melodiously,** *adv.* – **melodiousness,** *n.*

**melodise** /'mɛlədaɪz/, *v.,* **-dised, -dising.** *–v.t.* **1.** to make melodious. *–v.i.* **2.** to make melody. **3.** to blend melodiously. Also, **melodize.** – **melodiser,** *n.*

**melodist** /'mɛlədəst/, *n.* a composer or a singer of melodies.

**melodrama** /'mɛlədramə/, *n.* **1.** a play which does not observe the dramatic laws of cause and effect and which intensifies sentiment and exaggerates passion. **2.** (in the 17th, 18th, and early 19th centuries) a romantic dramatic composition with music interspersed. [F *mélodrame,* from It. *melodramma* musical drama, from Gk, from *mélo(s)* song, music + *dráma* DRAMA] – **melodramatise** /mɛlə'dræmətaɪz/, *v.t.* – **melodramatist** /mɛlə'dræmətəst/, *n.*

**melodramatic** /mɛlədrə'mætɪk/, *adj.* **1.** of, like, or befitting melodrama; sentimental and exaggerated. *–n.* **2.** (*pl.*) melodramatic behaviour. – **melodramatically,** *adv.*

**melody** /'mɛlədi/, *n., pl.* **-dies.** **1.** musical sounds in agreeable succession or arrangement. **2.** *Music.* **a.** the succession of single notes in musical compositions, as distinguished from harmony and rhythm. **b.** the principal part in a harmonic composition; the air. **c.** a succession of tones arranged in some intuitive or logical order so as to make up a particular musical phrase or idea. [ME *melodie,* from OF, from LL *melōdia,* from Gk *melōidía* singing, choral song]

**meloid** /'mɛlɔɪd/, *n.* **1.** →**blister beetle.** *–adj.* **2.** of or pertaining to a blister beetle. [NL *Meloïdae* the typical genus, from *meloē* beetle]

**melon** /'mɛlən/, *n.* **1.** the fruit of any of various members of the family Cucurbitaceae as the paddy melon, *Cucumis myriocarpus.* **2.** *Colloq.* a head. **3.** *Colloq.* a stupid person; fool. **4. cut a melon,** *U.S. Colloq.* to declare a large extra dividend to shareholders. [ME, from OF, from LL *mēlo,* from Gk *mēlopé pōn* apple-like gourd]

**melonhead** /'mɛlənhɛd/, *n. Colloq.* a fool; idiot.

**melon hole** /'mɛlən houl/, *n.* →**namma hole.**

**melt** /mɛlt/, *v.,* **melted, melted** or **molten, melting,** *n.* *–v.i.* **1.** to become liquefied by heat, as ice, snow, butter, metal, etc. **2.** (not in scientific use) to become liquid; dissolve. **3.** to pass, dwindle or fade gradually. **4.** to pass, change, or blend gradually (oft. fol. by *into*). **5.** to become softened in feeling by pity, sympathy, love, or the like. **6.** *Archaic.* to fail; to faint, as the heart or soul, from fear, grief, etc. *–v.t.* **7.** to reduce to a liquid state by heat; fuse. **8.** to cause to pass or fade (*away*). **9.** to cause to pass or blend gradually. **10.** to soften in feeling, as a person, the heart, etc. *–n.* **11.** the act or process of melting. **12.** the state of being melted. **13.** that which is melted. **14.** a quantity melted at one time. **15.** Also, **milt.** the spleen of an animal, esp. a pig, ox, etc. [ME *melte(n),* OE *meltan,* v.i., *m(i)eltan,* v.t.; akin to Icel. *melta* digest, Gk *méldein* melt] – **melter,** *n.*

**meltage** /'mɛltɪdʒ/, *n.* the amount melted or the result of melting.

**meltdown** /'mɛltdaun/, *n.* the melting of the insulation of a nuclear reactor, resulting in exposure of the fuel.

**melting point** /'mɛltɪŋ pɔɪnt/, *n.* the equilibrium temperature of the solid and liquid phases of a substance in the presence of a specified gas at a specified pressure (usu. air at a pressure of 101.325 kilopascals).

**melting pot** /'– pɒt/, *n.* **1.** a pot in which metals or other substances are melted or fused. **2.** any situation in which a mixture of diverse elements or ideas occurs, as a multi-racial community.

**melton** /'mɛltn/, *n.* a smooth heavy woollen cloth, used for coats, hunting jackets, etc. [from *Melton* Mowbray, town in Leicestershire, England]

**melt-water** /'mɛlt-wɔtə/, *n.* water deriving from melted snow or ice.

**mem.,** **1.** member. **2.** memorandum.

**member** /'mɛmbə/, *n.* **1.** each of the persons composing a society, party, community, or other body. **2.** each of the persons included in the membership of a legislative body, as parliament. **3.** a part or organ of an animal body; a limb, as a leg, arm, or wing. **4.** a constituent part of any structural or composite whole, as a subordinate architectural feature of a building or the like. **5.** either side of an algebraic equation. [ME *membre,* from OF, from L *membrum* limb, part]

**membership** /'mɛmbəʃɪp/, *n.* **1.** the state of being a member, as of a society. **2.** the status of a member. **3.** the total number of members belonging to a body.

**membrane** /'mɛmbreɪn/, *n.* **1.** a thin, pliable sheet or layer of animal or vegetable tissue, serving to line an organ, connect parts, etc. **2.** *Chem.* a thin sheet of material, natural or synthetic, which allows substances in solution to pass through it. **3.** a piece of parchment. **4.** any thin connecting layer. [L *membrāna* the skin that covers the several members of the body, parchment]

**membrane bone** /'– boʊn/, *n.* a bone which originates in membranous tissue (distinguished from *cartilage bone*).

**membranous** /'mɛmbrənəs, mɛm'breɪnəs/, *adj.* **1.** consisting of, of the nature of, or resembling membrane. **2.** characterised by the formation of a membrane. Also, **membranaceous** /mɛmbrə'neɪʃəs/.

**memento** /mə'mɛntoʊ/, *n., pl.* **-tos, -toes. 1.** something that serves as a reminder of what is past or gone. **2.** anything serving as a reminder or warning. [L, impv. of *meminisse* remember]

**memento mori** /– 'mɔri/, *n.* an object, as a skull or the like, serving as a reminder of death. [L: remember that you must die (lit., to die)]

**memo** /'mɛmoʊ, 'mi-/, *n., pl.* **memos.** →**memorandum.**

**memoir** /'mɛmwa/, *n.* **1.** (*pl.*) records of facts or events in connection with a particular subject, historical period, etc., as known to the writer or gathered from special sources. **2.** (*pl.*) records of one's own life and experiences. **3.** →**biography. 4.** (*pl.*) a collection of reports made to a scientific or other learned society. [F *mémoire,* masc., memorandum, memorial, *mémoire,* fem., MEMORY]

**memorabilia** /mɛmərə'bɪliə/, *n.pl., sing.* **-rabile** /-'ræbəli/. matters or events worthy to be remembered. [L, neut. pl. of *memorābilis* memorable]

**memorable** /'mɛmrəbəl, -ərəbəl/, *adj.* **1.** worthy to be remembered; notable: *a memorable speech.* **2.** easy to be remembered. [L *memorābilis*] – **memorability** /mɛmərə'bɪləti/, **memorableness,** *n.* – **memorably,** *adv.*

**memorandum** /mɛmə'rændəm/, *n., pl.* **-dums, -da** /-də/. **1.** a note made of something to be remembered, as in future action. **2.** a record or written statement of something. **3.** a note, as one sent from one member of a firm to another, regarding policy or the like. **4.** *Law.* a writing, usu. informal, containing the terms of a transaction. **5.** *Diplomacy.* a summary of the state of a question, the reasons for a decision agreed on, etc. **6.** a document which includes the main terms of a shipment of unsold goods and authorises their return within a specified time. [L, neut. of *memorandus* (ger.) that is to be remembered]

**memorandum of association,** *n.* a formal document constituting the charter of incorporation of a company.

**memorial** /mə'mɔriəl/, *n.* **1.** something designed to preserve the memory of a person, event, etc., as a monument, a periodic observance, etc. **2.** a written statement of facts presented to a sovereign, a legislative body, etc., as the basis of, or expressed in the form of, a petition or remonstrance. *–adj.* **3.** preserving the memory of a person or thing; commemorative: *memorial services.* **4.** of or pertaining to the memory. [ME, from L *memoriālis* of memory] – **memorially,** *adv.*

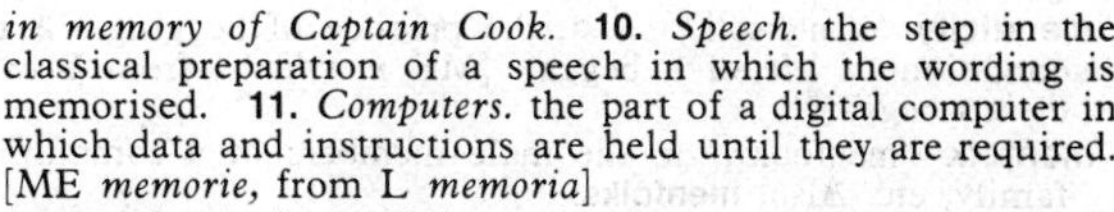

war memorial, Canberra

**memorialise** /mə'mɔriəlaɪz/, *v.t.,* **-lised, -lising. 1.** →**commemorate. 2.** to present a memorial to. Also, **memorialize.** – **memorialisation** /mə,mɔriəlaɪ'zeɪʃən/, *n.* – **memorialiser,** *n.*

**memorise** /'mɛməraɪz/, *v.t.,* **-rised, -rising.** to commit to memory, or learn by heart: *he finally memorised the poem.* Also, **memorize.** – **memorisable,** *adj.* – **memorisation** /mɛməraɪ'zeɪʃən/, *n.* – **memoriser,** *n.*

**memory** /'mɛməri/, *n., pl.* **-ries. 1.** the mental capacity or faculty of retaining and reviving impressions, or of recalling or recognising previous experiences. **2.** this faculty as possessed by a particular individual: *to have a good memory.* **3.** the act or fact of retaining mental impressions; remembrance; recollection: *to draw from memory.* **4.** the length of time over which recollection extends: *a time within the memory of living men.* **5.** a mental impression retained; a recollection: *one's earliest memories.* **6.** the reputation of a person or thing, esp. after death. **7.** the state or fact of being remembered. **8.** a person or thing remembered. **9.** commemorative remembrance; commemoration: *a monument in memory of Captain Cook.* **10.** *Speech.* the step in the classical preparation of a speech in which the wording is memorised. **11.** *Computers.* the part of a digital computer in which data and instructions are held until they are required. [ME *memorie,* from L *memoria*]

**memory bank** /'– bæŋk/, *n.* the primary storage inside the main part of a computer to which fast random access is available.

**memory cycle** /'– saɪkəl/, *n.* the process of replacing one unit of data in the memory bank of a computer by another.

**memory snatch** /'– snætʃ/, *n.* the accessing of a computer memory in the interval between two computer instructions.

**memory span** /'– spæn/, *n.* the period of time during which particular material can be remembered esp. after having been learned under experimental conditions.

**mem-sahib** /'mɛm-sa-ɪb, -sahɪb/, *n.* (in India, formerly) a native term of address to a European lady. [Hind. *mem* (from E *ma'am*) + *sāhib* master]

**men** /mɛn/, *n.* plural of **man.**

**menace** /'mɛnəs/, *n., v.,* **-aced, -acing.** *–n.* **1.** something that threatens to cause evil, harm, injury, etc.; a threat. **2.** *Colloq.* →**nuisance.** *–v.t.* **3.** to utter or direct a threat against; threaten. **4.** to serve as a probable cause of evil, etc., to. [ME, from OF, from L *minācia* a threat] – **menacer,** *n.* – **menacingly,** *adv.*

**menad** /'minæd/, *n.* →**maenad.**

**menadione** /mɛnə'daɪoʊn/, *n.* a yellow crystalline compound, related to vitamin K.

**ménage** /meɪ'naʒ/, *n.* **1.** a household; a domestic establishment. **2.** housekeeping. Also, **menage.** [F, from L *mansio* MANSION]

**ménage à trois** /meɪ,naʒ a 'trwa/, *n.* a household of three people, at least one of whom is having a sexual relationship with the other two. [F]

**menagerie** /mə'nædʒəri/, *n.* **1.** a collection of wild or strange animals, esp. for exhibition. **2.** a place where they are kept or exhibited. [F: management of a household, menagerie, from *ménage* MÉNAGE]

**menaquinone** /mɛnəkwɪ'noʊn/, *n.* the common inactive form of vitamin K found in mammalian liver.

**menarche** /'mɛnak/, *n.* the onset of menstruation in a young woman. Cf. **menopause.** [NL, from Gk *mḗn* month + *archḗ* beginning]

**mend** /mɛnd/, *v.t.* **1.** to make whole or sound by repairing, as something broken, worn, or otherwise damaged; repair: *to mend clothes, to mend a road.* **2.** to remove or correct defects or errors in. **3.** to remove or correct (a defect, etc.). **4.** to set right; make better; improve: *to mend matters.* *–v.i.* **5.** to progress towards recovery, as a sick person. **6.** (of conditions) to improve. *–n.* **7.** the act of mending; repair or improvement. **8.** a mended place. **9.** **on the mend, a.** recovering from sickness. **b.** improving in state of affairs. [aphetic var. of AMEND] – **mendable,** *adj.* – **mender,** *n.*

**mendacious** /mɛn'deɪʃəs/, *adj.* **1.** false or untrue: *a mendacious report.* **2.** lying or untruthful. [MENDACI(TY) + -OUS] – **mendaciously,** *adv.* – **mendaciousness,** *n.*

**mendacity** /mɛn'dæsəti/, *n., pl.* **-ties. 1.** the quality of being mendacious. **2.** a falsehood; a lie. [LL *mendācitas*]

**mendelevium** /mɛndə'liviəm/, *n.* a synthetic, radioactive element. *Symbol:* Md; *at. no.:* 101; *half life*: 1.5 hrs. [named after Dmitri *Mendelyeev,* 1834-1907, Russian chemist, + -IUM]

**Mendelism** /'mɛndəlɪzəm/, *n.* the theories of heredity advanced in Mendel's laws. Also, **Mendelianism** /mɛn'diliənɪzəm/.

**Mendel's laws** /'mɛndəlz lɔz/, *n.pl.* the basic principles of heredity, showing that alternative hereditary factors of hybrids exhibit a clean-cut separation or segregation from one another, and that different pairs of hereditary traits are independently assorted from each other. [from Gregor *Mendel,* 1822-88, Austrian biologist] – **Mendelian,** *adj.*

**mendicant** /'mɛndəkənt/, *adj.* **1.** begging, practising begging, or living on alms. **2.** pertaining to or characteristic of a beggar. *–n.* **3.** one who lives by begging; a beggar. **4.** a mendicant friar. [L *mendīcans,* ppr., begging] – **mendicancy,** *n.*

**mendicity** /mɛn'dɪsəti/, *n.* **1.** the practice of begging. **2.** the condition of life of a beggar. [ME *mendicite,* from L *mendīcitas* beggary]

**menfolk** /'mɛnfoʊk/, *n.* the male members of a community, family, etc. Also, **menfolks.**

**menhaden** /mɛn'heɪdn/, *n., pl.* **-den.** any marine clupeoid fish of the genus *Brevoortia,* esp. *B. tyrannus,* having the appearance of a shad but with a more compressed body, common along the eastern coast of the U.S., and used for making oil and fertiliser. [Narragansett (N. Amer. Ind. language): they manure]

**menhir** /'mɛnhɪə/, *n.* an upright monumental stone, standing either alone or with others, as in a cromlech, found in various parts of Europe, also in Africa and Asia. [Breton *men hir* long stone]

**menial** /'miniəl/, *adj.* **1.** pertaining or proper to domestic servants. **2.** →**servile.** –*n.* **3.** a domestic servant. **4.** a servile person. [ME, from AF, from *meiniee,* from L *mansio* household, MANSION] – **menially,** *adv.*

**Ménière's syndrome** /'mɛniɛəz ˌsɪndroʊm/, *n.* a disease of the internal ear characterised by deafness, vertigo and tinnitus with occasional nausea. [named after Prosper *Ménière,* 1799-1862, French physician]

**Menindie clover** /mənɪndi 'kloʊvə/, *n.* a herbaceous plant, *Trigonella suavissima,* with trifoliate leaves and pale yellow flowers, native to Australia where it is found in inland areas subject to flooding. [from *Menindee* (formerly *Menindie*), a town on the Darling River, N.S.W.]

**meninges** /mə'nɪndʒiz/, *n.pl., sing.* **meninx** /'minɪŋks/. the three membranes (dura mater, arachnoid, and pia mater) investing the brain and spinal cord. [NL, pl. of *mēninx,* from Gk *mêninx* membrane, esp. of the brain] – **meningeal,** *adj.*

**meningitis** /mɛnən'dʒaɪtəs/, *n.* inflammation of the meninges, esp. of the pia mater and arachnoid. [NL, from Gk *mêninx* membrane + *-ītis* -ITIS] – **meningitic** /mɛnən'dʒɪtɪk/, *adj.*

**meniscus** /mə'nɪskəs/, *n., pl.* **-nisci** /-'nɪsaɪ/. **1.** a crescent or crescent-shaped body. **2.** a lens with a crescent-shaped section. **3.** the convex or concave upper surface of a column of liquid, the curvature of which is caused by capillarity. **4.** a disc of cartilage between the articulating ends of the bones in a joint. [NL, from Gk *mēnískos* crescent, diminutive of *mḗnē* moon] – **meniscoid,** *adj.*

menisci (def. 3): A, concave water meniscus; B, convex mercury meniscus

**meno** /'mɛnoʊ/, *adv.* (a musical direction) less. [It., from L *minus*]

**meno-,** a word element meaning 'month'. [Gk, combining form of *mḗn*]

**menology** /mə'nɒlədʒi/, *n., pl.* **-gies. 1.** a calendar of the months. **2.** a record or account, as of saints, arranged in the order of a calendar. [NL *mēnologium,* from LGk *mēnológion,* from *mēno-* MENO- + *lógion* saying]

**menopause** /'mɛnəpɔz/, *n.* the period of irregular menstrual cycles prior to the final cessation of the menses, occurring usu. between the ages of 45 and 50. [MENO- + PAUSE] – **menopausic** /ˌmɛnə'pɔzɪk/, *adj.*

**menorah** /mə'nɔrə/, *n.* (in Judaism) a candelabrum, originally holding seven candles, used in Jewish religious services. [Heb.]

menorah

**menorrhagia** /mɛnə'reɪdʒiə/, *n.* excessive menstrual discharge. [NL. See MENO-, -RRHAGIA]

**mensal**[1] /'mɛnsəl/, *adj.* →**monthly.** [L *mēnsis* month + -AL[1]]

**mensal**[2] /'mɛnsəl/, *adj.* of, pertaining to, or used at the table. [ME, from LL *mensālis* of a table]

**menses** /'mɛnsiz/, *n.pl.* the (approximately) monthly discharge of blood and mucosal tissue from the uterus. [L, pl. of *mensis* month]

**Menshevik** /'mɛnʃəvɪk/, *n., pl.* **-viki** /-vɪ'ki/, **-viks.** (formerly) a member of a less radical socialistic party or group of the

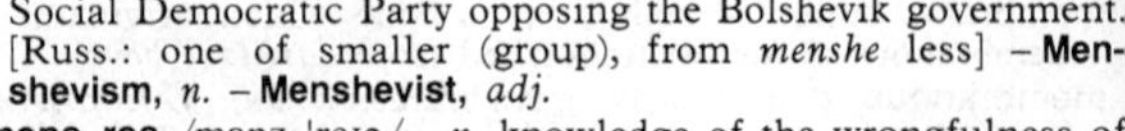
Social Democratic Party opposing the Bolshevik government. [Russ.: one of smaller (group), from *menshe* less] – **Menshevism,** *n.* – **Menshevist,** *adj.*

**mens rea** /mɛnz 'reɪə/, *n.* knowledge of the wrongfulness of an act at the time of its commission. [NL *non actus reus nisi mens sit rea* the accused is not guilty unless his mind is guilty]

**menstrual** /'mɛnstruəl/, *adj. Physiol.* of or pertaining to the menses. [L *menstruālis* monthly]

**menstruate** /'mɛnstrueɪt/, *v.i.,* **-ated, -ating.** to discharge the menses.

**menstruation** /mɛnstru'eɪʃən/, *n.* **1.** the act of discharging the menses. **2.** the period of menstruating.

**menstruous** /'mɛnstruəs/, *adj.* pertaining to menstruation. [L *menstruus* monthly]

**menstruum** /'mɛnstruəm/, *n., pl.* **-struums, -strua** /-struə/. a solvent. [ML, properly neut. of L *menstruus* monthly]

**mensurable** /'mɛnʃərəbəl/, *adj.* →**measurable.** [LL *mensūrābilis*] – **mensurability** /mɛnʃərə'bɪləti/, *n.*

**mensural** /'mɛnʃərəl/, *adj.* pertaining to measure.

**mensuration** /mɛnʃə'reɪʃən/, *n.* **1.** that branch of mathematics which deals with the determination of length, area, and volume. **2.** the act, art, or process of measuring. [LL *mensūrātio*]

**mensurative** /'mɛnʃərətɪv/, *adj.* adapted for or concerned with measuring.

**menswear** /'mɛnzwɛə/, *n.* clothing for men.

**-ment,** a suffix of nouns, often concrete, denoting an action or state resulting (*abridgment, refreshment*), a product (*fragment*), or means (*ornament*). [F, from L *-mentum,* suffix forming nouns, usu. from verbs]

**mental**[1] /'mɛntl/, *adj.* **1.** of or pertaining to the mind. **2.** performed by or existing in the mind: *mental arithmetic.* **3.** pertaining to the intellect; intellectual. **4.** denoting a disorder of the mind. **5.** designated for or pertaining to the care of those with disordered minds: *mental hospital, mental nurse.* **6.** *Colloq.* foolish or mad. –*n.* **7. chuck a mental,** *Colloq.* to manifest mental disturbance, esp. with conscious purpose. [ME, from LL *mentālis*]

**mental**[2] /'mɛntl/, *adj.* of or pertaining to the chin. [L *mentum* chin + -AL[1]]

**mental age** /'– eɪdʒ/, *n.* the degree of mental development or intelligence of an individual in comparison with the average intelligence of normal children at different ages. It is determined by a graded series of tests, in the form of tasks or questions, designed to measure native ability rather than the result of education: *a child of 10 years old with a mental age of 12.*

**mental block** /– 'blɒk/, *n.* an obstruction to the thought processes, usu. caused by psychological factors: *I had a mental block about his name.*

**mental cruelty** /– 'kruəlti/, *n.* conduct which inflicts suffering on another's mind, formerly grounds for legal separation or divorce.

**mental defective** /– də'fɛktɪv/, *n.* one who is mentally deficient.

**mental deficiency** /– də'fɪʃənsi/, *n.* the condition of one who is mentally deficient. It embraces all types of idiocy, imbecility, and moronity.

**mental healing** /– 'hilɪŋ/, *n.* the healing of any ailment or disorder by mental concentration and suggestion.

**mental health** /– 'hɛlθ/, *n.* the general condition of the mind with reference to sanity and vigour.

**mental hospital** /'– hɒspɪtl/, *n.* →**psychiatric hospital.** Also, **mental asylum, mental home.**

**mentalism** /'mɛntəlɪzəm/, *n.* a philosophical doctrine which teaches that the mind is the fundamental reality and that objects and all the things of experience exist only in the mind of the observer.

**mentality** /mɛn'tæləti/, *n., pl.* **-ties. 1.** mental capacity or endowment; intellectuality; mind: *she was of average mentality.* **2.** outlook; frame of mind: *of a vulgar mentality.*

**mentally** /'mɛntəli/, *adv.* **1.** in or with the mind or intellect; intellectually. **2.** with regard to the mind.

**mentally deficient** /– də'fɪʃənt/, *adj.* characterised by subnormal intelligence which is a handicap to the individual in his school or adult life; feeble-minded.

**mentally handicapped** /– 'hændikæpt/, *adj.* →**mentally deficient.**

**menthene** /'mɛnθin/, *n.* a colourless liquid, $C_{10}H_{18}$, synthetically obtainable from menthol. [G *Menthen,* from L *mentha* MINT[1] + *-en* -ENE]

**menthol** /'mɛnθɒl/, *n.* a colourless, crystalline alcohol, $C_{10}H_{20}O$, present in peppermint oil, used in perfume, cigarettes, and confectionery, and for colds and nasal disorders because of its cooling effect on mucous membranes. [G, from L *mentha* MINT[1] + *-ol* -OL[1]]

**mentholated** /'mɛnθəleɪtəd/, *adj.* **1.** covered or treated with menthol. **2.** saturated with or containing menthol.

**mention** /'mɛnʃən/, *v.t.* **1.** to refer briefly to; refer to by name incidentally; name, specify, or speak of. **2.** to cite as for some meritorious act. **3. not to mention,** to say nothing of; in addition to. *–n.* **4.** a speaking of or mentioning; a reference, direct or incidental. **5.** recognition, as for a meritorious act or achievement. [L *mentio* a calling to mind, mention; replacing ME *mencioun,* from OF] **– mentionable,** *adj.* **– mentioner,** *n.*

**mentor** /'mɛntɔ/, *n.* **1.** a wise and trusted counsellor. **2.** a trainer in dogracing, horseracing, etc. [from *Mentor,* friend of Odysseus and guardian of his household when he went to Troy]

**menu** /'mɛnju, 'minju/, *n.* **1.** a list of the dishes served at a meal; a bill of fare. **2.** the dishes served. **3.** *Computers.* a range of optional procedures presented to an operator by a computer. [F: detailed list, orig. adj., small, from L *minūtus* MINUTE[2]]

**menu-driven device** /ˌmɛnju-drɪvən də'vaɪs/, *n.* a computerised device which has a form of operator communication designed to make the operator's task easier by providing him with a list of optional procedures.

**menu-oriented** /mɛnju-'ɒriɛntəd/, *adj.* of or pertaining to a computerised machine which is programmed to prompt the operator by presenting him with a number of optional procedures.

**meow** /mi'aʊ/, *v.i.* →**miaow.**

**mepacrine** /'mɛpəkrin/, *n.* a substance used in the treatment of malaria and of infestations with worms, such as tapeworms.

**mephistophelian** /ˌmɛfɪstə'filiən/, *adj.* crafty, cunning. [from *Mephistopheles,* one of the seven chief devils]

**mephitic** /mə'fɪtɪk/, *adj.* **1.** offensive to the smell. **2.** noxious; pestilential; poisonous. **– mephitically,** *adv.*

**mephitis** /mə'faɪtəs/, *n.* **1.** a noxious or pestilential exhalation, esp. from the earth. **2.** a noisome or poisonous stench. [L]

**meprobamate** /mə'proʊbəmeɪt, mɛproʊ'bæmeɪt/, *n.* a tranquilliser used in the treatment of anxiety states. [ME(THYL) + PRO(PYL) + (*car*)*bamate* (see CARBAMIC ACID)]

**mer.,** meridian.

**mercantile** /'mɜkəntaɪl/, *adj.* **1.** of or pertaining to merchants or to trade; commercial. **2.** engaged in trade or commerce. **3.** *Econ.* of or pertaining to the mercantile system. [F, from It., *mercante,* from L *mercans,* ppr., trading]

**mercantile agency** /'– eɪdʒənsi/, *n.* a concern which obtains information concerning the financial standing, business reputation, and credit ratings of individuals, firms and companies for the benefit of its subscribers.

**mercantile marine** /– mə'rin/, *n.* →**merchant navy.**

**mercantile paper** /'– peɪpə/, *n.* negotiable commercial paper, as promissory notes given by merchants for goods purchased, drafts drawn against purchasers, etc.

**mercantile system** /'– sɪstəm/, *n.* a system of political and economic policy, evolving with the modern national state, which sought to secure the political supremacy of a state in its rivalry with other states. According to this system, money was regarded as a store of wealth, and the great object of a state was the importation of the precious metals, by exporting the utmost possible quantity of its products and importing as little as possible, thus establishing a favourable balance of trade.

**mercantilism** /mə'kæntəlɪzəm, 'mɜkəntaɪlɪzəm/, *n.* **1.** the mercantile spirit. **2.** the mercantile system. **– mercantilist,** *n.*

**mercaptan** /mɜ'kæptən/, *n.* any of a class of sulphur-containing compounds, with the type formula RSH, the low-boiling members of which have an extremely offensive smell, esp. **ethyl mercaptan,** $C_2H_5SH$, a colourless liquid, with an offensive, garlic-like smell. [G: arbitrary abbrev. of L expression (*corpus*) *mer*(*curium*) *captan*(*s*) body-catching mercury]

**mercaptide** /mə'kæptaɪd, mɜ-/, *n.* the salt of a mercaptan.

**Mercator's projection** /mɜˌkeɪtəz prə'dʒɛkʃən/, *n.* a map projection with rectangular grid which is conformable and on which any rhumb line is represented as a straight line. It is particularly useful for navigation, though the scale varies notably with latitude and areal size, and the shapes of large areas are greatly distorted. Also, **Mercator projection.** [named after Gerhardus *Mercator,* 1512-94, Flemish cartographer and geographer]

Mercator's projection

**mercenary** /'mɜsənri, -sənəri/, *adj., n., pl.* **-naries.** *–adj.* **1.** working or acting merely for gain. **2.** hired (now only of soldiers serving in a foreign army). *–n.* **3.** a professional soldier serving in a foreign army. **4.** any hireling. [L *mercēnārius* hired for pay] **– mercenarily,** *adv.* **– mercenariness,** *n.*

**mercer** /'mɜsə/, *n.* a dealer in textile fabrics, esp. silks, etc. [ME, from OF *mercier,* from OF *merz* goods, wares, from L *merx*]

**mercerise** /'mɜsəraɪz/, *v.t.,* **-rised, -rising.** to treat (cotton yarns or fabric) with caustic alkali under tension, increasing strength, lustre and affinity for dye. Also, **mercerize.** [from J. *Mercer,* English calico printer, the patentee (1850) of the process. See -ISE[1]] **– mercerisation** /mɜsəraɪ'zeɪʃən/, *n.*

**mercery** /'mɜsəri/, *n., pl.* **-ries. 1.** a mercer's shop. **2.** mercers' wares. [ME *mercerie,* from OF, from *mercier* MERCER]

**merchandise** /'mɜtʃəndaɪs/, *n.;* /'mɜtʃəndaɪz/, *v.* **-dised, -dising.** *–n.* **1.** goods; commodities; esp. manufactured goods. **2.** the stock of a store. *–v.i.* **3.** to trade. *–v.t.* **4.** to trade in; buy and sell. [ME *marchandise,* from OF *marchand* MERCHANT] **– merchandiser,** *n.*

**merchandising** /'mɜtʃəndaɪzɪŋ/, *n.* the promotion and planning of the sales of a product, by using all available techniques of display, advertising and marketing.

**merchant** /'mɜtʃənt/, *n.* **1.** one who buys and sells commodities for profit; a wholesaler. **2.** *U.S.* a shopkeeper. *–adj.* **3.** pertaining to trade or commerce: *a merchant ship.* **4.** pertaining to the merchant navy. **5.** (*usu. prec. by a defining term*) *Colloq.* a person noted or notorious for the specified aspect of his behaviour: *panic merchant, standover merchant.* [ME, from OF *marcheant,* from L *mercārī* trade]

**merchantable** /'mɜtʃəntəbəl/, *adj.* marketable: *merchantable war-surplus goods.*

**merchant bank** /mɜtʃənt 'bæŋk/, *n.* a private banking firm engaged chiefly in accepting and endorsing bills of exchange, underwriting new issues of securities and advising on corporate strategy. **– merchant banker,** *n.* **– merchant banking,** *n.*

**merchant flag** /– 'flæg/, *n.* →**red ensign.**

**merchantman** /'mɜtʃəntmən/, *n., pl.* **-men.** a trading vessel.

**merchant navy** /mɜtʃənt 'neɪvi/, *n.* **1.** the vessels of a nation engaged in commerce. **2.** the officers and crews of merchant vessels. Also, **mercantile marine, merchant marine.**

**merchant prince** /– 'prɪns/, *n.* a merchant of great wealth, power, or position.

**merci** /mɜ'si, mɛə'si/, *interj.* thank (you). [F]

**merci beaucoup** /– boʊ'ku/, *interj.* thank (you) very much. [F]

**merciful** /'mɜsəfəl/, *adj.* exercising, or characterised by, mercy; compassionate. **– mercifully,** *adv.* **– mercifulness,** *n.*

**merciless** /'mɜsələs/, *adj.* without any mercy; pitiless. **– mercilessly,** *adv.* **– mercilessness,** *n.*

**mercurate** /'mɜkjəreɪt/, *v.t.,* **-rated, -rating. 1.** to add mercury to (a compound). **2.** *Obsolesc.* to expose to the action of mercury.

**mercurial** /mɜ'kjuriəl/, *adj.* **1.** pertaining to, consisting of or containing, or caused by the metal mercury. **2.** sprightly; volatile. **3.** flighty; fickle; changeable. *–n.* **4.** a preparation of mercury used as a drug. [L *mercuriālis* of Mercury. See MERCURY] – **mercurially,** *adv.* – **mercurialness,** *n.*

**mercurialise** /mɜ'kjuriəlaɪz/, *v.t.,* **-lised, -lising. 1.** to make mercurial. **2.** to treat or impregnate with mercury or one of its compounds. Also, **mercurialize.** – **mercurialisation** /mɜˌkjuriəlaɪ'zeɪʃən/, *n.*

**mercurialism** /mɜ'kjuriəlɪzəm/, *n.* a morbid condition caused by mercury.

**mercuric** /mɜ'kjurɪk/, *adj.* of or containing mercury, esp. in the divalent state.

**mercuric chloride** /– 'klɔraɪd/, *n.* a strongly acrid, highly poisonous, white crystalline soluble salt, $HgCl_2$, prepared by sublimation of chlorine with mercury, much used as an antiseptic; corrosive sublimate. Also, **bichloride of mercury, mercury chloride.**

**mercuric cyanate** /– 'saɪəneɪt/, *n. Chem.* →**mercury fulminate.**

**mercuric oxide** /– 'ɒksaɪd/, *n.* a soluble, poisonous solid, HgO, occurring as a red or yellow powder; used as a pigment and an antiseptic.

**mercurous** /'mɜkjərəs/, *adj.* containing monovalent mercury.

**mercury** /'mɜkjəri/, *n., pl.* **-ries. 1.** *Chem.* a heavy, silver-white metallic element, remarkable for its fluidity at ordinary temperatures; quicksilver. *Symbol:* Hg (for **hydrargyrum**); *at. wt:* 200.59; *at. no.:* 80; *sp. gr.:* 13.546 at 20°C; *freezing point:* –38.9°C; *boiling point:* 357°C. **2.** a preparation of mercury (metal) used in medicine. **3.** (*cap.*) *Astron.* the planet nearest the sun. **4.** a messenger, or carrier of news (sometimes used as the name of a newspaper or periodical). **5.** any herb of the euphorbiaceous genus *Mercurialis,* as *M. perennis* **(dog's mercury),** a poisonous weed. [from *Mercury,* a Roman deity, messenger of the gods; ME, from L *Mercurius*]

**mercury cell** /'– sɛl/, *n.* a primary cell consisting of a zinc anode and a cathode of mercuric oxide mixed with graphite; the electrolyte is potassium hydroxide saturated with zinc oxide. The cell produces about 1.3 volts.

**mercury chloride** /– 'klɔraɪd/, *n.* →**mercuric chloride.**

**mercury fulminate** /– 'fʊlməneɪt/, *n.* the mercury salt of fulminic acid, $Hg(ONC)_2$, which explodes as a result of very slight friction or shock when dry, used as a detonator; mercuric cyanate.

**mercury-vapour lamp** /mɜkjəri-'veɪpə læmp/, *n.* a lamp producing a light with a high ultraviolet content by means of an electric arc in mercury vapour.

**mercy** /'mɜsi/, *n., pl.* **-cies. 1.** compassionate or kindly forbearance shown towards an offender, an enemy, or other person in one's power; compassion, pity, or benevolence. **2.** disposition to be merciful: *an adversary wholly without mercy.* **3.** discretionary power as to clemency or severity, pardon or punishment, or the like: *be at the mercy of a conqueror.* **4.** an act of forbearance, compassion, or favour, esp. of God towards his creatures. **5. at the mercy of,** defenceless; unprotected. [ME, from OF *merci,* fem., favour, mercy; masc., thanks, from L *merces* pay, ML mercy]

**mercy flight** /'– flaɪt/, *n.* a flight made to meet an emergency, as to transport a person in urgent need of medical attention, or to rescue a person from a dangerous situation.

**mercy killing** /'– kɪlɪŋ/, *n.* →**euthanasia.**

**mercy seat** /'– sit/, *n.* **1.** the gold covering on the ark of the covenant, regarded as the resting place of God (see Ex. 25:17-22). **2.** the Throne of God.

**mere**[1] /mɪə/, *adj., superl.* **merest. 1.** being nothing more nor better than what is specified; pure and simple. **2.** *Chiefly Law.* belonging or pertaining to a single individual or group, or sole. [ME, from L *merus* pure, unmixed, mere]

**mere**[2] /mɪə/, *n.* a lake; a pond. [ME and OE, c. G *Meer;* akin to L *mare* sea]

**mere**[3] /'mɛrə, 'mɛri/, *n. N.Z.* a Maori club for hand-to-hand fighting. [Maori]

**-mere,** a word element meaning 'part', as in *blastomere.* [combining form representing Gk *méros*]

**merely** /'mɪəli/, *adv.* only as specified, and nothing more; simply: *merely as a matter of form.*

**meretricious** /mɛrə'trɪʃəs/, *adj.* **1.** alluring by a show of false attractions; showily attractive; tawdry. **2.** insincere. **3.** *Archaic.* of, pertaining to, or characteristic of a prostitute. [L *meretrīcius* of prostitutes] – **meretriciously,** *adv.* – **meretriciousness,** *n.*

**merganser** /mɜ'gænsə/, *n., pl.* **-sers,** (*esp. collectively*) **-ser.** any of several saw-billed, fish-eating, diving ducks of the subfamily Merginae, as the **red-breasted merganser,** *Mergus serrator,* a partial migrant of northern Europe. [NL, from L *mergus* diver (bird) + *anser* goose]

**merge** /mɜdʒ/, *v.,* **merged, merging.** *–v.t.* **1.** to unite or combine. **2.** to cause to be swallowed up or absorbed; to sink the identity of by combination (oft. fol. by *in* or *into*). *–v.i.* **3.** to become swallowed up or absorbed; lose identity by absorption (oft. fol. by *in* or *into*). [L *mergere* dip, plunge, sink] – **mergence** /'mɜdʒəns/, *n.*

**merger** /'mɜdʒə/, *n.* **1.** a statutory combination of two or more companies by the transfer of the properties to one surviving company. **2.** any combination of two or more business enterprises into a single enterprise. **3.** the act of merging. [MERG(E) + -ER[3]]

**mericarp** /'mɛrikap/, *n.* a single-seeded portion of a schizocarpous fruit, as in umbelliferous plants.

**meridian** /mə'rɪdiən/, *n.* **1.** *Geog.* a line of longitude or half of one of the Great Circles which pass through the poles and cut the equator at right angles. **2.** →**magnetic meridian. 3.** *Astron.* the great circle of the celestial sphere which passes through its poles and the observer's zenith. **4.** a point or period of highest development, greatest prosperity, or the like. *–adj.* **5.** of or pertaining to a meridian. **6.** of or pertaining to midday or noon: *the meridian hour.* **7.** pertaining to a period of greatest elevation, prosperity, splendour, etc.; culminating. [L *merīdiānus* of midday, of the south; replacing ME *meridian,* from OF]

meridians (def. 1): earth encircled by meridians

**meridional** /mə'rɪdiənəl/, *adj.* **1.** of, pertaining to, or resembling a meridian. **2.** characteristic of the south or people inhabiting the south, esp. of France. **3.** southern; southerly. *–n.* **4.** an inhabitant of the south, esp. of France. [ME, from LL *merīdiōnālis* of midday] – **meridionally,** *adv.*

**meridional part** /– 'pat/, *n.* a unit of measurement equal to one minute of longitude at the equator.

**meringue** /mə'ræŋ/, *n.* **1.** a mixture of sugar and beaten eggwhites formed into small cakes and baked, or spread over pastry, etc. **2.** a dish, cake, or shell made with it. [F, ? from G *Meringe,* lit., cake of Mehringen]

**merino** /mə'rinoʊ/, *n., pl.* **-nos,** *adj.* *–n.* **1.** (*cap.*) one of a variety of sheep, originating in Spain, valued for its fine wool. **2.** wool from such sheep. **3.** a knitted fabric made of wool or wool and cotton. **4.** a variety of potato. **5. pure merino,** (formerly) a free settler (opposed to *legitimate*). **6.** made of merino wool, yarn, or cloth. [Sp., from L (*ariēs*) *mājōrīnus* (male sheep) of the larger sort, from *mājor* MAJOR]

merino

**meristem** /'mɛristɛm/, *n.* embryonic tissue; undifferentiated, growing, actively dividing cells. [Gk *meristós* divided + *-ēm(a),* n. suffix] – **meristematic** /mɛrəstə'mætɪk/, *adj.*

**meristic** /mə'rɪstɪk/, *adj.* **1.** of or pertaining to the number of parts of a body: *meristic change.* **2.** divided into segments or parts, as worms.

**merit** /'mɛrət/, *n.* **1.** claim to commendation; excellence; worth. **2.** something that entitles to reward or commendation; a commendable quality, act, etc.: *the merits of a book* *or a play.* **3.** (*pl.*) the substantial right and wrong of a matter unobscured by technicalities: *the merits of a case.* **4.** the state or fact of deserving well; good desert. **5.** that which is deserved, whether good or bad. **6.** (*sometimes pl.*) the state or fact of deserving, or desert: *to treat a person according to his merits.* –*v.t.* **7.** to be worthy of; deserve. –*v.i.* **8.** *Chiefly Theol.* to acquire merit. [ME *merite,* from F, from L *meritum,* properly pp. neut., deserved, earned]

**merited** /ˈmɛrətəd/, *adj.* deserved. – **meritedly,** *adv.*

**merit money** /ˈmɛrət mʌni/, *n.* a sum of money paid to an employee in recognition of his possessing experience, extra skill, adaptability or aptitude.

**meritocracy** /mɛrəˈtɒkrəsi/, *n.* **1.** persons collectively who have reached positions of authority by reason of real or supposed merit (contrasted with *aristocracy,* etc.). **2.** government or administration by such persons. [MERIT + -O- + -CRACY, modelled on ARISTOCRACY]

**meritorious** /mɛrəˈtɔriəs/, *adj.* deserving of reward or commendation; possessing merit. [ME, from ML *meritōrius* meritorious, L serving to earn money] – **meritoriously,** *adv.* – **meritoriousness,** *n.*

**merle**[1] /mɜl/, *n.* *Chiefly Scot. and Poetic.* the common European blackbird, *Turdus merula.* Also, **merl.** [F, from L *merula, merulus*]

**merle**[2] /mɜl/, *adj.* **1.** coloured bluish grey with black mottling, esp. of the coat of an animal, as a dog. –*n.* **2.** this colour.

**merlin** /ˈmɜlən/, *n.* any of various bold small hawks of the genus *Falco,* esp. the **European merlin,** *F. columbarius aesalon,* and the closely related North American pigeon-hawk, *F. c. columbarius.* [ME *merlion,* from AF *merilun,* from OF *esmeril,* from Gmc; cf. OHG *smirl*]

**merlon** /ˈmɜlən/, *n.* (in a battlement) the solid part between two crenels. [F, from It. *merlone,* from L *mergae* fork]

**mermaid** /ˈmɜmeɪd/, *n.* **1.** an imaginary female marine creature typically having the head and trunk of a woman and the tail of a fish. **2.** *Colloq.* an inspector at a weighbridge who is in charge of the scales. [ME *mermayde.* See MERE[2], MAID]

**mermaid's-purse** /mɜmeɪdz-ˈpɜs/, *n.* →**sea-purse.**

**merman** /ˈmɜmæn/, *n., pl.* **-men.** an imaginary man of the sea, corresponding to a mermaid.

**meroblastic** /mɛrəˈblæstɪk/, *adj.* (of large eggs) undergoing partial cleavage (opposed to *holoblastic*). [Gk *méro(s)* part + BLAST + -IC]

**merogony** /məˈrɒgəni/, *n.* the development of egg fragments. [Gk *méro(s)* part + -GONY]

**merozoite** /mɛrəˈzoʊaɪt/, *n.* one of the products of reproduction in the asexual phase of parasitic protozoans of the class Sporozoa, as malaria parasites. [Gk *méro(s)* part + stem of Gk *zōḗ* life + -ITE[1]]

**merriment** /ˈmɛrimənt/, *n.* **1.** merry gaiety; mirth; hilarity; laughter. **2.** *Obs.* merrymaking.

**merrin** /ˈmɛrən/, *n.* a nail-tailed wallaby, *Onychogalea fraenata,* of New South Wales and Queensland, with distinctive bridle-like markings.

**merry** /ˈmɛri/, *adj.,* **-rier, -riest.** **1.** full of cheer or gaiety; festive; joyous in disposition or spirit. **2.** laughingly gay; mirthful; hilarious. **3.** *Archaic.* pleasant or delightful: *merry England.* **4.** *Colloq.* slightly intoxicated. **5. make merry,** to be gay or festive. [ME *meri(e), myrie, murie,* OE *myr(i)ge* pleasant, delightful] – **merrily,** *adv.* – **merriness,** *n.*

**merry-andrew** /mɛri-ˈændru/, *n.* a clown; buffoon.

**merry-go-round** /ˈmɛri-goʊ-ˌraʊnd/, *n.* **1.** a revolving machine, as a circular platform fitted with wooden horses, etc., on which persons, esp. children, ride for amusement. **2.** any whirl or rapid round of events, social activities, etc.

**merrymaker** /ˈmɛrimeɪkə/, *n.* one who is making merry.

**merrymaking** /ˈmɛrimeɪkɪŋ/, *adj.* **1.** the act of making merry. **2.** a merry festivity; a revel. –*adj.* **3.** producing mirth; gay; festive.

**merrythought** /ˈmɛriθɔt/, *n.* the wishbone of a bird. [from the custom of two persons pulling the bone until it breaks; the person holding the longer (sometimes shorter) piece will supposedly marry first or will be granted a wish made at the time]

**Mersey Valley cheese** /ˌmɜzi væli ˈtʃiz/, *n.* a cheese combining qualities of several different styles of Continental cheeses, manufactured in Burnie, Tasmania. [named after the *Mersey Valley,* Tas.]

**mes-,** variant of **meso-,** sometimes used before vowels, as in *mesencephalon.*

**mesa** /ˈmeɪsə/, *n.* a land form having a relatively flat top and bounded wholly or in part with steep rock walls, common in arid and semi-arid parts of the south-western U.S. but also occurring in areas of inland Australia. [Sp., from L *mensa* table]

**mésalliance** /meˈzæliəns/, *n.* a marriage with a social inferior; a misalliance. [F, from *més-* MIS-[1] + *alliance* ALLIANCE]

**mesarch** /ˈmɛsak/, *adj.* referring to a strand or cylinder of primary xylem in a stem or root with the xylem other than at the edge.

**mesc** /mɛsk/, *n.* *Colloq.* →**mescaline.**

**mescal** /mɛsˈkæl/, *n.* **1.** either of two species of cactus, *Lophophora williamsii* or *L. lewinii,* of the southern U.S. and northern Mexico, whose button-like tops (**mescal buttons**) are dried and used as a stimulant, esp. by the American Indians. **2.** an intoxicating spirit distilled from the fermented juice of certain species of agave. **3.** any agave yielding this spirit. [Sp. *mezcal,* from Nahuatl *mexcalli,* from *metl* maguey]

**mescaline** /ˈmɛskələn, -lən/, *n.* a white water-soluble crystalline powder, $C_{11}H_{17}NO_3$, obtained from mescal buttons, used to produce hallucinations. Also, **mescalin.**

**mesdames** /ˈmeɪdam/, *n.* plural of **madame.** [F]

**mesdemoiselles** /mɛdəmwaˈzɛl/, *n.* plural of **mademoiselle.** [F]

**mesembryanthemum** /ˌmɛzəmbriˈænθəməm/, *n.* any of various small succulent plants of a number of genera of the family Ficoidaceae (Aizoaceae), esp. species of the genera *Lampranthus* and *Carpobrotus,* often cultivated for their showy flowers. Also, **mesembrianthemum.** [NL, from Gk *mesēbria* noon + *ánthemon* flower]

**mesencephalon** /mɛsɛnˈsɛfəlɒn/, *n., pl.* **-la** /-lə/. the middle segment of the brain; the midbrain. [NL. See MES-, ENCEPHALON] – **mesencephalic** /ˌmɛsɛnsəˈfælɪk/, *adj.*

**mesenchyme** /ˈmɛsɛŋkaɪm/, *n.* the nonepithelial mesoderm. Also, **mesenchyma** /mɛsˈɛŋkəmə/. [NL, from Gk *mes-* MES- + *énchyma* infusion] – **mesenchymal, mesenchymatous** /mɛsɛŋˈkɪmətəs/, *adj.*

**mesentery** /ˈmɛsəntəri, ˈmɛz-/, *n., pl.* **-ries.** a fold or doubling of the peritoneum, investing and attaching to the posterior wall of the abdomen. [NL *mesenterium,* from Gk *mesentérion* the middle intestine] – **mesenteric** /mɛsənˈtɛrɪk, mɛz-/, *adj.*

**mesh** /mɛʃ/, *n.* **1.** one of the open spaces of network of a net. **2.** (*pl.*) the threads that bound such spaces. **3.** (*pl.*) means of catching or holding fast: *caught in the meshes of the law.* **4.** a network or net. **5.** a knitted, woven, or knotted fabric, with open spaces between the threads. **6.** light woven or welded interlocking links or wires, as used for reinforcement, for sieves, etc. **7.** *Mach.* **a.** the engagement of gear teeth. **b. in mesh,** with gears engaged. –*v.t.* **8.** to catch or entangle in or as in the meshes of a net; enmesh. **9.** to form with meshes, as a net. **10.** to cause to coordinate or interlock. **11.** *Mach.* to engage, as gear teeth. –*v.i.* **12.** to become enmeshed. **13.** to interlock or coordinate. **14.** *Mach.* to become or be engaged, as the teeth of one wheel with those of another. [cf. OE *māx* and *mǣscre* net]

**meshwork** /ˈmɛʃwɜk/, *n.* meshed work; network.

**meshy** /ˈmɛʃi/, *adj.* formed with meshes; meshed.

**mesial** /ˈmiziəl/, *adj.* medial. [MES- + -IAL] – **mesially,** *adv.*

**mesic** /ˈmizɪk/, *adj.* pertaining to an environment containing, or characterised by, a moderate amount of moisture. Cf. **hydric** (def. 2), **xeric.**

**mesitylene** /məˈsɪtəlin, ˈmɛsətəlin/, *n.* a colourless, liquid, aromatic hydrocarbon, $C_6H_3(CH_3)_3$, found in coal tar but prepared from acetone. [*mesityl* (from Gk *mesítēs* go-between + -YL) + -ENE]

**mesmeric** /mɛzˈmɛrɪk/, *adj.* **1.** hypnotic. **2.** fascinating; spellbinding. – **mesmerically,** *adv.*

**mesmerise** /ˈmɛzməraɪz/, *v.t.,* **-rised, -rising.** **1.** to hypnotise. **2.** to fascinate; dominate; spellbind. Also, **mesmerize.**

– **mesmerisation** /mɛzmərai'zeɪʃən/, *n.* – **mesmeriser,** *n.*

**mesmerism** /'mɛzmərɪzəm/, *n.* **1.** hypnotism. **2.** compelling fascination. [named after F. A. *Mesmer,* 1733-1815, German physician and hypnotist. See -ISM] – **mesmerist,** *n.*

**mesnalty** /'minəlti/, *n. Law.* the estate of a mesne lord. [AF *mesnalte,* from OF *mesne* MESNE]

**mesne** /min/, *adj. Law.* intermediate or intervening. [F, altered spelling of AF *meen* MEAN[3]]

**mesne lord** /'– lɔd/, *n.* a feudal lord who holds estate from a superior lord, and to whom his own tenants and vassals are inferior.

**mesne process** /'– proʊsɛs/, *n. Law.* an intervening process in the progress of a suit or action between its beginning and end.

**meso-,** a word element meaning 'middle', used in combination, chiefly in scientific terms. Also, **mes-.** [Gk, combining form of *mésos* middle]

**mesoblast** /'mɛsoʊblast, 'miz-/, *n.* the prospective mesoderm. – **mesoblastic** /mɛsə'blæstɪk, miz-/, *adj.*

**mesocarp** /'mɛsoʊkap, 'miz-/, *n.* the middle layer of pericarp, as the fleshy part of certain fruits.

**mesocephalic** /mɛsoʊsə'fælɪk, miz-/, *adj.* having a head with a cephalic index between that of dolichocephaly and brachycephaly.

**mesocranic** /mɛsoʊ'kreɪnɪk, 'miz-/, *adj.* having a skull with a cranial index between that of dolichocranic and brachycranic skulls.

**mesoderm** /'mɛsoʊdɜm, 'miz-/, *n.* the middle germ layer of a metazoan embryo. – **mesodermal** /mɛsoʊ'dɜməl, miz-/, **mesodermic,** *adj.*

**mesogastrium** /mɛsoʊ'gæstriəm, miz-/, *n.* the mesentery of the embryonic stomach. [NL, from *meso-* MESO- + Gk *gastḗr* belly + *-ium* -IUM] – **mesogastric,** *adj.*

**mesoglea** /mɛsoʊ'gliə, miz-/, *n.* a jelly-like non-living material between the ectoderm and endoderm of coelenterates. Also, **mesogloea.** [NL, from *meso-* MESO- + Gk *gloía* glue]

**mesognathous** /mə'sɒgnəθəs, mə'zɒg-/, *adj.* **1.** having medium, slightly protruding jaws. **2.** having a moderate or intermediate gnathic index of from 98 to 103. – **mesognathism, mesognathy,** *n.*

**Mesolithic** /mɛsoʊ'lɪθɪk, miz-/, *adj.* (*sometimes l.c.*) of, pertaining to, or characteristic of an intermediate period between the Palaeolithic and Neolithic periods of the Stone Age.

**mesomerism** /mə'soʊmərɪzəm, -'zoʊ-/, *n. Chem.* →**resonance** (def. 6).

**mesomorph** /'mɛsoʊmɔf, 'miz-/, *n.* a person of mesomorphic type.

**mesomorphic** /mɛsoʊ'mɔfɪk, miz-/, *adj.* having a muscular or sturdily built body characterised by the relative prominence of structures developed from the embryonic mesoderm (distinguished from *ectomorphic, endomorphic*).

**mesomorphous** /mɛsoʊ'mɔfəs, miz-/, *adj.* denoting or pertaining to a substance which exists in a state midway between that of a crystalline solid and an amorphous solid.

**meson** /'mizɒn/, *n.* any of a group of elementary particles, all of which have rest masses between that of the electron and the proton. Also, **mesotron.**

**mesonephros** /mɛsoʊ'nɛfrəs, miz-/, *n.* the middle kidney, developing between the pronephros and the metanephros, in proximity with the sex glands. In males of the higher vertebrates, it becomes a part of the epididymis. [NL, from Gk *meso-* MESO- + *nephrós* kidney] – **mesonephric,** *adj.*

**mesophile** /'mizəfaɪl/, *n.* an organism which flourishes at medium temperatures. Cf. **psychrophile, thermophile.** [MESO- + -PHILE] – **mesophilic** /mizə'fɪlɪk/, *adj.*

**mesophyll** /'mɛsoʊfɪl, 'miz-/, *n.* the parenchyma which forms the interior parts of a leaf, usu. containing chlorophyll.

**mesophyte** /'mɛsoʊfaɪt, 'miz-/, *n.* a plant growing under conditions of well-balanced moisture supply. Cf. **hydrophyte** and **xerophyte.** – **mesophytic** /mɛsoʊ'fɪtɪk, miz-/, *adj.*

**mesorrhine** /'mɛsəraɪn, -rən, 'mɛz-/, *adj.* having a moderately broad and high-bridged nose. [MESO- + Gk *rhís* nose]

**mesosphere** /'mɛsoʊsfɪə, 'miz-/, *n.* **1.** the stratum of atmosphere between the ionosphere and the exosphere (400 to 950 km). **2.** the stratum of atmosphere between the top of the stratosphere and an unnamed layer where the minimum of temperature occurs (30 to 80 km); chemosphere. [MESO- + SPHERE] – **mesospheric** /mɛsoʊ'sfɛrɪk, miz-/, *adj.*

**mesothelium** /mɛsoʊ'θiliəm, miz-/, *n., pl.* **-lia** /-liə/. epithelium of mesodermal origin, which lines the body cavities. [MESO- + *-thelium* as in EPITHELIUM] – **mesothelial,** *adj.*

**mesothorax** /mɛsoʊ'θɔræks, miz-/, *n., pl.* **-raxes, -races** /-rəsiz/. the middle one of three divisions of an insect's thorax, bearing the second pair of legs and first pair of wings. – **mesothoracic** /mɛsoʊθɔ'ræsɪk, miz-/, *adj.*

**mesothorium** /mɛsoʊ'θɔriəm, miz-/, *n.* **1. mesothorium** I, →**radium-228. 2. mesothorium** II, →**actinium-228.**

**mesotron** /'mɛsətrɒn, 'miz-/, *n. Physics. Obs.* →**meson.**

**Mesozoic** /mɛsə'zoʊɪk, miz-/, *Geol.* –*adj.* **1.** pertaining to the geological era of rocks intermediate between Palaeozoic and Cainozoic; the era of reptiles. –*n.* **2.** the era or rocks comprising the Triassic, Jurassic, and Cretaceous periods or systems. [MESO- + stem of Gk *zōḗ* + -IC]

**mesquite** /mɛs'kit, 'mɛskit/, *n.* any of several south-western U.S. and Mexican trees and shrubs of the genus *Prosopis,* family Mimosaceae, of tropical and subtropical regions, having beanlike pods rich in sugar and useful as fodder, but tending to form dense, impenetrable thickets, esp. the honey locust.

**mess** /mɛs/, *n.* **1.** a dirty or untidy condition: *the room was in a mess.* **2.** a state of embarrassing confusion: *his affairs are in a mess.* **3.** an unpleasant or difficult situation: *to get into a mess.* **4.** a dirty or untidy mass, litter, or jumble: *a mess of papers.* **5.** excrement, esp. of an animal. **6.** a place where service personnel, etc., eat together. **7.** a place used by officers and senior NCOs for eating, recreation, and entertaining. **8.** *Navy.* the living quarters of the crew. **9.** a group regularly taking meals together. **10.** the meal so taken. **11.** a sloppy or unappetising preparation of food. **12.** a dish or quantity of soft or liquid food. **13.** *Colloq.* a person whose life is confused or without coherent purpose, often due to psychological difficulties. –*v.t.* **14.** to make dirty or untidy (oft. fol. by *up*): *mess up a room.* **15.** to make a mess of, or muddle (affairs, etc.). **16. mess someone around** or **about,** *Colloq.* to cause inconvenience to (a person). –*v.i.* **17.** to eat in company, esp. as a member of a mess. **18.** to make a dirty or untidy mess. **19. mess around** or **about,** *Colloq.* **a.** to busy oneself in a untidy or confused way. **b.** to waste time. **c.** to play the fool. **d.** to associate, esp. for immoral or illegal purposes (fol. by *with*). **20. mess in,** *Colloq.* to meddle officiously. **21. mess with,** *Colloq.* to associate with; have dealings with: *don't mess with him, he's trouble.* [ME *mes,* OF: lit., put (on the table), from L *missum,* pp. neut., sent, put]

**message** /'mɛsɪdʒ/, *n.* **1.** a communication, as of information, advice, direction, or the like, transmitted through a messenger or other agency. **2.** an inspired communication of a prophet. **3.** the moral or meaning intended to be conveyed by a book, film, play, or the like. **4.** an errand or mission, as shopping. **5. do the messages,** to do errands. **6. get the message,** *Colloq.* to understand. [ME, from OF, *mes* envoy, from L *missus,* pp., sent]

**message stick** /'– stɪk/, *n.* a carved stick or block of wood used among some primitive peoples when conveying messages.

message stick

**messaline** /mɛsə'lin, 'mɛsəlin/, *n.* a thin, soft, silk fabric with a twilled or a satin weave. [F]

**mess allowance** /'mɛs əlaʊəns/, *n.* monies allowed to augment rations in a mess.

**mess deck** /'– dɛk/, *n.* the deck where the crew of a ship eat.

**Messeigneur** /meɪsɛn'jɜ/, *n.* plural form of **monseigneur.**

**messenger** /'mɛsəndʒə/, *n.* **1.** one who bears a message or goes on an errand, esp. as a matter of duty or business. **2.** one employed to convey official dispatches or to go on other official or special errands: *a bank messenger.* **3.** *Archaic.* a herald or harbinger. **4.** anything regarded as sent on an errand. **5.** *Naut.* **a.** any light line used to haul a heavier line. **b.** a weight or other device which travels along a line to activate a remote device. [ME *messanger, messager,* from

OF *messager,* from *message* MESSAGE]

**messenger RNA** /– ar ɛn 'eɪ/, *n.* the RNA containing the information to form specific proteins by the process of protein synthesis.

**Messiah** /mə'saɪə/, *n.* **1.** the title applied to an expected deliverer of the Jewish people, and hence to Jesus (see John 4:25, 26). **2.** any expected deliverer. [var. of L *Messīas* (Vulgate), from Gk Hellenised form of Heb. *māshīah* anointed] – **Messiahship,** *n.* – **Messianic** /mɛsi'ænɪk/, *adj.*

**messieurs** /mɛs'jɜz/, *n.* plural of **monsieur.**

**mess jacket** /'mɛs dʒækət/, *n.* a short jacket cut to a point at the back and reaching only to the waist, worn at dinner in the officers' mess on special occasions.

**mess kit** /'– kɪt/, *n.* formal dress, including a mess jacket, worn by officers on special occasions.

**messmate**[1] /'mɛsmeɪt/, *n.* a fellow member of a mess.

**messmate**[2] /'mɛsmeɪt/, *n.* any of a number of Australian trees of the genus *Eucalyptus,* esp. *E. obliqua* of the tablelands of New South Wales.

**Messrs,** messieurs (used as if a plural of *Mr*).

**mess tin** /'mɛs tɪn/, *n.* a portable metal dish, used as a plate, cup, and cooking utensil by a soldier in the field.

**messuage** /'mɛswɪdʒ/, *n. Law.* a dwelling house with its adjacent buildings and the lands appropriated to the use of the household. [ME *mesuage,* from AF *me(s)suage,* probably from *mesnage.* See MÉNAGE]

**mess-up** /'mɛs-ʌp/, *n.* a confusion arising from a mistake, misadventure, etc.

**messy** /'mɛsi/, *adj.,* **-sier, -siest. 1.** of the nature of a mess: *a messy concoction.* **2.** being in a mess: *a messy table.* **3.** attended with or making a mess; dirty; untidy: *messy work.* – **messiness,** *n.*

**mestee** /mɛs'ti/, *n.* →**mustee.**

**mestizo** /mɛs'tizoʊ/, *n., pl.* **-zos, -zoes. 1.** a person of mixed blood. **2.** (in Spanish America) one who has Spanish and American Indian blood. **3.** one of European and East Indian, Negro, or Malay blood. **4.** a Philippine Island native with Chinese blood. [Sp., from LL *mixtīcius* of mixed race] – **mestiza** /mɛs'tizə/, *n. fem.*

**met** /mɛt/, *v.* past tense and present participle of **meet.**

**met.,** **1.** metaphor. **2.** metaphysics. **3.** metropolitan.

**meta-,** **1.** a prefix meaning 'among', 'together with', 'after', 'behind', and often denoting change, found chiefly in scientific words. **2.** *Chem.* **a.** a prefix meaning 'containing least water', used of acids and salts, as in *meta-antimonic,* $HSbO_3$, *meta-antimonous,* $HSbO_2$. **b.** a prefix indicating that an organic compound contains a benzene ring substituted in the 1, 3 positions. [Gk, representing *metá,* prep., with, after]

**metabolise** /mə'tæbəlaɪz/, *v.t.,* **-lised, -lising.** to subject to metabolism; change by metabolism. Also, **metabolize.**

**metabolism** /mə'tæbəlɪzəm/, *n.* the sum of the processes or chemical changes in an organism or a single cell by which food is built up (*anabolism*) into living protoplasm and by which protoplasm is broken down (*catabolism*) into simpler compounds with the exchange of energy. [META- + stem of Gk *bolḗ* change + -ISM] – **metabolic** /mɛtə'bɒlɪk/, *adj.*

**metabolite** /mə'tæbəlaɪt/, *n.* a substance acted upon or produced in metabolism.

**metacarpal** /mɛtə'kapəl/, *adj.* **1.** of or pertaining to the metacarpus. *–n.* **2.** a metacarpal bone.

**metacarpus** /mɛtə'kapəs/, *n., pl.* **-pi** /-paɪ/. the part of a hand or forelimb (esp. of its bony structure) included between the wrist or carpus and the fingers or phalanges. [NL (see META-, CARPUS); replacing *metacarpium,* from Gk *metakárpion*]

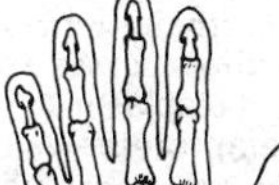

metacarpus

**metacentre** /'mɛtəsɛntə/, *n.* the point where the vertical line through the centre of buoyancy of a floating body (as a ship) in equilibrium meets the vertical line through the new centre of buoyancy when the body is in a slightly inclined position (less than one degree). The equilibrium of the body is stable when this point is above its centre of gravity, and unstable when it is below. Also, U.S., **metacenter.** [F *métacentre,* from Gk *meta-* META- + *kéntron* CENTRE] – **metacentric** /mɛtə'sɛntrɪk/, *adj.*

**metacentric height** /,mɛtəsɛntrɪk 'haɪt/, *n.* the distance between a vessel's centre of gravity and its metacentre; a measure of a vessel's stability. If the metacentre is above the centre of gravity, stability is positive and the vessel is stable.

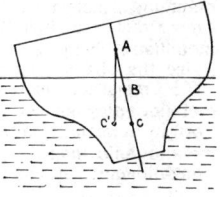

metacentre of a boat: A, metacentre; B, centre of gravity; C, centre of buoyancy; C[1], centre of buoyancy when boat is inclined

**metachromatism** /mɛtə'kroʊmətɪzəm/, *n.* change of colour, esp. that due to variation in the temperature of a body. [META- + stem of Gk *chrôma* colour + -ISM] – **metachromatic** /mɛtəkroʊ'mætɪk/, *adj.*

**metagalaxy** /mɛtə'gæləksi/, *n., pl.* **-axies.** the complete system of external galaxies, or extragalactic nebulae.

**metage** /'mitɪdʒ/, *n.* **1.** the official measurement of contents or weight. **2.** the charge for it. [METE[1] + -AGE]

**metagenesis** /mɛtə'dʒɛnəsəs/, *n.* reproduction characterised by the alternation of a sexual generation and a generation which reproduces asexually by budding. – **metagenetic** /mɛtədʒə'nɛtɪk/, *adj.*

**metagnathous** /mə'tægnəθəs/, *adj. Ornith.* having the tips of the mandibles crossed, as the crossbills. – **metagnathism,** *n.*

**metagnomy** /mə'tægnəmi/, *n.* →**divination.**

**metal** /'mɛtl/, *n., v.,* **-alled, -alling** or (*U.S.*) **-aled, -aling.** *–n.* **1.** any of a class of elementary substances, as gold, silver, copper, etc., all of which are crystalline when solid and many of which are characterised by opacity, ductility, conductivity, and a peculiar lustre when freshly fractured. **2.** an alloy or mixture composed wholly or partly of such substances. **3.** *Chem.* **a.** a metal (def. 1) in its pure state, as distinguished from alloys. **b.** an element yielding positively charged ions in aqueous solutions of its salts. **4.** formative material; mettle. **5.** *Print., etc.* **a.** type metal. **b.** the state of being set up in type. **6.** Also, **road metal.** broken stone used for ballast on railway tracks or for surfacing roads; blue metal. **7.** (*pl.*) rails. **8.** molten glass in the pot or melting tank. **9.** *Her.* either of the tinctures gold (*or*) and silver (*argent*). *–v.t.* **10.** to furnish or cover with metal. [ME, from OF, from L *metallum* mine, mineral, metal, from Gk *métallon* mine]

**metal.,** **1.** metallurgical. **2.** metallurgy.

**metalanguage** /'mɛtəlæŋgwɪdʒ/, *n.* **1.** a language or code used to discuss a given object language or some aspect of it, as the syntax. **2.** a language which encodes ideas other than one of the naturally occurring languages.

**metaldehyde** /mə'tældəhaɪd/, *n.* a white, crystalline, poisonous, solid polymer of acetaldehyde; used as a fuel in small heaters, and as a snail killer.

**metal fabricator** /mɛtl 'fæbrəkeɪtə/, *n.* a tradesman who combines the skills of a boilermaker and a welder in the construction of items made from metal cylinders, as tubular furniture, buildings, etc.

**metalflake duco** /mɛtəlfleɪk 'djukoʊ/, *n.* a type of duco in which is embedded small flakes of metal which reflect the light.

**metal hare** /mɛtl 'hɛə/, *n.* →**lure** (def. 4).

**metalinguistics** /mɛtəlɪŋ'gwɪstɪks/, *n.* **1.** the study of metalanguages. **2.** the study of the relation of language to other culture-mediated behaviour.

**metall.,** metallurgy.

**metallic** /mə'tælɪk/, *adj.* **1.** of, pertaining to, or consisting of metal. **2.** of the nature of metal: *metallic lustre, metallic sounds.* **3.** *Chem.* **a.** (of a metal element) being in the free or uncombined state: *metallic iron.* **b.** containing or yielding metal. – **metallically,** *adv.*

**metallic soap** /– 'soʊp/, *n.* any of several salts of a monocarboxylic acid and certain metals, which, though insoluble in water, dissolve in benzene, and are used as a basis for ointments, fire- and water-proofing agents, driers, lubricants and fungicides.

**metallic starling** /'– stalɪŋ/, *n.* a bird native to north Queensland, *Aplonis metallica,* glossy black with a green and purple lustre, and with bright red eyes. Also, **shining starling.**

**metalliferous** /mɛtəˈlɪfərəs/, *adj.* containing or yielding metal. [L *metallifer* yielding metals + -OUS]

**metalline** /ˈmɛtəlaɪn/, *adj.* **1.** metallic. **2.** containing one or more metals or metallic salts.

**metallise** /ˈmɛtəlaɪz/, *v.t.*, **-lised, -lising.** to make metallic; give the characteristics of metal to. Also, **metallize;** *Chiefly U.S.,* **metalize.** – **metallisation** /mɛtəlaɪˈzeɪʃən/, *n.*

**metallogenic** /mɛtəloʊˈdʒɛnɪk, mətælə-/, *adj.* pertaining to the origin of metallic minerals.

**metallogenic map** /– ˈmæp/, *n.* a map showing the limits of metallogenic provinces and the particular minerals which occur.

**metallogenic province** /– ˈprɒvəns/, *n.* a localised area in which mineralisation has been active at one or more periods of geological time.

**metallography** /mɛtəˈlɒgrəfi/, *n.* **1.** the microscopic study of the structure of metals and alloys. **2.** an art or process allied to lithography, in which metallic plates are substituted for stones. – **metallographic** /mətæləˈgræfɪk/, *adj.*

**metalloid** /ˈmɛtəlɔɪd/, *n.* **1.** a non-metal. **2.** an element which is both metallic and non-metallic, as arsenic, silicon, or bismuth. *–adj.* **3.** of or pertaining to a metalloid. **4.** resembling both a metal and non-metal.

**metallurgy** /ˈmɛtələdʒi, məˈtælədʒi/, *n.* **1.** the art or science of separating metals from their ores. **2.** the art or science of making and compounding alloys. **3.** the art or science of working or heat-treating metals so as to give them certain desired shapes or properties. [NL *metallurgia,* from Gk *metallourgós* mineworker + *-ia* (suffix)] – **metallurgic** /mɛtəˈlɜdʒɪk/, **metallurgical** /mɛtəˈlɜdʒɪkəl/, *adj.* – **metallurgically** /mɛtəˈlɜdʒɪkli/, *adv.* – **metallurgist** /məˈtælədʒəst, ˈmɛtələdʒəst/, *n.*

**metal oxide semiconductor,** *n.* →**MOS.**

**metal road** /mɛtl ˈroʊd/, *n.* a road surfaced with blue metal.

**metal spinning** /ˈ– spɪnɪŋ/, *n.* a process in which molten metal is spread by centrifugal force onto the surface of a die to make items with a basic cylindrical shape, as a saucepan.

**metal spraying** /– ˈspreɪɪŋ/, *n.* a process in which one metal is sprayed, in a molten state, onto another.

**metalwork** /ˈmɛtlwɜkɪŋ/, *n.* **1.** the art or craft of working with metal. **2.** objects produced by metalwork. – **metalworking,** *n.* – **metalworker,** *n.*

**metamere** /ˈmɛtəmɪə/, *n.* →**somite.** – **metameral** /məˈtæmərəl/, **metameric** /mɛtəˈmɛrɪk/, *adj.*

**metamerism** /məˈtæmərɪzəm/, *n.* **1.** *Zool.* division into metameres, the developmental process of somite formation. **2.** *Zool.* the condition of consisting of metameres. **3.** *Chem.* a type of isomerism caused by the attachment of different radicals to the same central atom or group, as $(C_2H_5)_2O$ and $CH_3OC_3H_7$.

**metamorphic** /mɛtəˈmɔfɪk/, *adj.* **1.** pertaining to or characterised by change of form, or metamorphosis. **2.** *Geol.* pertaining to or exhibiting structural change, or metamorphism.

**metamorphic rock** /– ˈrɒk/, *n.* See **rock**[1] (def. 2a).

**metamorphism** /mɛtəˈmɔfɪzəm/, *n.* **1.** →**metamorphosis. 2.** *Geol.* a change in the structure or constitution of a rock, due to natural agencies, as pressure and heat, esp. when the rock becomes harder and more completely crystalline.

**metamorphose** /mɛtəˈmɔfoʊz/, *v.t.*, **-phosed, -phosing. 1.** to transform. **2.** to subject to metamorphosis or metamorphism.

**metamorphosis** /mɛtəˈmɔfəsəs/, *n., pl.* **-ses** /-siz/. **1.** change of form, structure, or substance, as transformation by magic or witchcraft. **2.** any complete change in appearance, character, circumstances, etc. **3.** a form resulting from any such change. **4.** a change of form during the postembryonic or embryonic growth of an animal by which it is adapted temporarily to a special environment or way of living usu. different from that of the preceding stage: *the metamorphosis of tadpoles into frogs.* **5.** *Pathol.* **a.** a type of alteration or degeneration in which tissues are changed: *fatty metamorphosis of the liver.* **b.** the resultant form. **6.** *Bot.* the structural or functional modification of a plant organ or structure during its development. [L, from Gk: transformation]

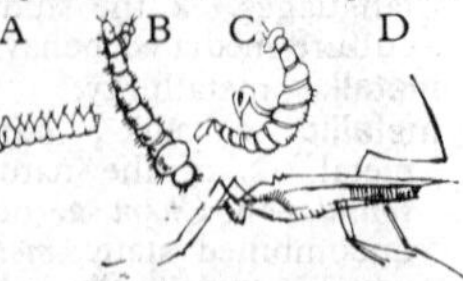

metamorphosis (def. 4) mosquito A, eggs; B, larva; C, pupa; D, adult

**metamorphous** /mɛtəˈmɔfəs/, *adj.* →**metamorphic.**

**metanephros** /mɛtəˈnɛfrɒs/, *n.* the pelvic kidney, developing from the lowest portion of the renal blastema cords. [NL, from Gk *meta-* META- + *nephrós* kidney]

**metaph.,** **1.** metaphysical. **2.** metaphysics.

**metaphase** /ˈmɛtəfeɪz/, *n.* the middle stage in mitotic cell division, in which the chromosomes in the equatorial plane of the cell split.

**metaphor** /ˈmɛtəfə, -fɔ/, *n.* **1.** a figure of speech in which a term or phrase is applied to something to which it is not literally applicable, in order to suggest a resemblance, as *A mighty fortress is our God.* **2. mixed metaphor,** a figurative expression in which two or more metaphors are employed, producing an incongruous assemblage of ideas, as *The king put the ship of state on its feet.* [L *metaphora,* from Gk: a transfer] – **metaphorical** /mɛtəˈfɒrɪkəl/, **metaphoric** /mɛtəˈfɒrɪk/, *adj.* – **metaphorically** /mɛtəˈfɒrɪkli/, *adv.*

**metaphosphoric acid** /mɛtəfɒsˌfɒrɪk ˈæsəd/, *n.* an acid, $HPO_3$, derived from phosphorous pentoxide, and containing the least water of the phosphoric acids. See **phosphoric acid.**

**metaphrase** /ˈmɛtəfreɪz/, *n., v.,* **-phrased, -phrasing.** *–n.* **1.** a translation. *–v.t.* **2.** to translate, esp. literally. **3.** to change the phrasing or literary form of. [NL *metaphrasis,* from Gk: a translation]

**metaphys.,** metaphysics.

**metaphysical** /mɛtəˈfɪzɪkəl/, *adj.* **1.** pertaining to or of the nature of metaphysics. **2.** *Philos.* **a.** concerned with abstract thought or subjects, as existence, causality, truth, etc. **b.** concerned with first principles and ultimate grounds, as being, time, substance. **3.** highly abstract or abstruse. **4.** designating or pertaining esp. to that school of early 17th century English poets of whom John Donne was the chief, whose characteristic style is highly intellectual, philosophical, and crowded with ingenious conceits and turns of wit. **5.** *Archaic.* imaginary. – **metaphysically,** *adv.*

**metaphysical painting** /– ˈpeɪntɪŋ/, *n.* an art movement current in Italy, from 1917 to 1919 which sought to represent pictorially the inner and spiritual aspects of things, and which was an important influence on the surrealist movement. [It. *pittura metafisica*]

**metaphysician** /mɛtəfəˈzɪʃən/, *n.* one versed in metaphysics. Also, **metaphysicist** /mɛtəˈfɪzəsəst/.

**metaphysics** /mɛtəˈfɪzɪks/, *n.* **1.** that branch of philosophy which treats of first principles, including the sciences of being (*ontology*) and of the origin and structure of the universe (*cosmology*). It is always intimately connected with a theory of knowledge (*epistemology*). **2.** philosophy, esp. in its more abstruse branches. [ML representing *metaphysica,* from MGk (*tà*) *metaphysiká* (neut. pl.), representing *tà metà tà physiká* the (works) after the physics; with reference to the arrangement of Aristotle's writings]

**metaplasia** /mɛtəˈpleɪziə/, *n.* tissue transformation, as from one form of tissue to another.

**metaplasm** /ˈmɛtəplæzəm/, *n.* **1.** *Biol.* the lifeless matter or inclusions (as starch, pigment, etc.) in the protoplasm of a cell. **2.** a change in the structure of a word by adding, removing, or transposing the sounds of which it is composed or their representation in spelling. **3.** the formation of oblique cases from a stem other than that of the nominative. – **metaplasmic** /mɛtəˈplæzmɪk/, *adj.*

**metaprotein** /mɛtəˈproʊtin/, *n.* a hydrolytic derivative of protein, insoluble in water, but soluble in dilute acids or alkalis.

**metapsychology** /ˌmɛtəsaɪˈkɒlədʒi/, *n.* the branch of psychology which deals with philosophical questions which cannot be answered by experimental means, as the relationship between mind and body.

**metasediment** /mɛtəˈsɛdəmənt/, *n.* slightly metamorphosed sedimentary rock.

**metasomatism** /mɛtəˈsoʊmətɪzəm/, *n. Geol.* **1.** the processes whereby minerals or rocks are replaced by others of different chemical composition as a result of the introduction of material, usu. in very hot aqueous solutions, from sources external to the formation undergoing change. **2.** →**replace-**

ment (def. 4). [META- + Gk *sôma* body + -ISM]

**metastable** /mɛtəˈsteɪbəl/, *adj.* **1.** *Chem.* (of a body or system) existing in an apparently stable state although the addition of a small quantity of energy would convert it to a more stable state, as supercooled water will remain liquid below 0°C until a crystal of ice is introduced. **2.** *Physics.* (of an atom or nucleus) being in an excited state for a relatively long period. – **metastability** /mɛtəstəˈbɪləti/, *n.*

**metastasis** /məˈtæstəsəs/, *n., pl.* **-ses** /-siz/. **1.** *Physiol., Pathol.* transference of a fluid, disease, or the like, from one part of the body to another. **2.** *Chiefly Pathol.* the translocation of cancerous cells to other parts of the body via the circulation, lymphatics, or membranous surfaces. **3.** a transformation. **4.** *Rhet.* a rapid transition, as from one subject to another. [LL, from Gk: removal] – **metastatic** /mɛtəˈstætɪk/, *adj.*

**metastasise** /məˈtæstəsaɪz/, *v.i.,* **-sised, -sising.** (esp. of cells of malignant tumours, or micro-organisms) to spread to other regions by dissemination through the circulation or other channels. Also, **metastasize.**

**metatarsal** /mɛtəˈtasəl/, *adj.* **1.** of or pertaining to the metatarsus. *–n.* **2.** a metatarsal bone.

**metatarsus** /mɛtəˈtasəs/, *n., pl.* **-si** /-si/. **1.** the part of a foot or hind limb (esp. of its bony structure) included between the tarsus and the toes or phalanges. **2.** (in birds) a bone composed of both tarsal and metatarsal elements, extending from the tibia to the phalanges. [NL. See META-, TARSUS]

**metatherian** /mɛtəˈθɪəriən/, *n.* a subdivision of the mammals which includes those in which the young are neither hatched from eggs nor nourished by means of a placenta, but are born at a very immature stage and usu. carried in a pouch; marsupial.

**metathesis** /məˈtæθəsəs/, *n., pl.* **-ses** /-siz/. **1.** the transposition of letters, syllables, or sounds in a word. **2.** *Chem.* a double decomposition, as when two compounds interreact to form two other compounds. [LL, from Gk: transposition] – **metathetic** /mɛtəˈθɛtɪk/, **metathetical** /mɛtəˈθɛtɪkəl/, *adj.*

**metathorax** /mɛtəˈθɔræks/, *n., pl.* **-thoraxes, -thoraces** /-ˈθɔrəsiz/. the posterior division of an insect's thorax, bearing the third pair of legs and the second pair of wings. – **metathoracic** /mɛtəθəˈræsɪk/, *adj.*

**metavolcanic** /mɛtəvɒlˈkænɪk/, *n.* **1.** slightly metamorphosed volcanic rock. *–adj.* **2.** pertaining to slightly metamorphosed volcanic rocks.

**metaxylem** /mɛtəˈzaɪləm/, *n.* that part of the primary xylem of a vascular strand which is formed after elongation has ceased.

**metazoan** /mɛtəˈzoʊən/, *adj.* **1.** belonging or pertaining to the phylum Metazoa, comprising all the animals above the protozoans, i.e., those organisms which, although originating from a single cell, are composed of many cells. *–n.* **2.** any member of this phylum. [NL, pl. of *metazōōn*, from Gk *meta-* META- + *zôion* animal] – **metazoic,** *adj.*

**mete**[1] /mit/, *v.t.,* **meted, meting.** **1.** to distribute or apportion by measure; allot (usu. fol. by *out*). **2.** *Archaic.* to measure. [ME; OE *metan*, c. G *messen*]

**mete**[2] /mit/, *n.* **1.** a limiting mark. **2.** a limit. [ME, from OF, from L *mēta* goal-mark, turning post]

**metempiric** /mɛtəmˈpɪrɪk/, *n.* a supporter of the metempirical philosophy. [MET(A)- + EMPIRIC]

**metempirical** /mɛtəmˈpɪrɪkəl/, *adj.* **1.** beyond or outside the field of experience. **2.** of or pertaining to metempirics.

**metempirics** /mɛtəmˈpɪrɪks/, *n.* the philosophy of things the existence of which is, even in principle, beyond the field of experience. – **metempiricist,** *n.*

**metempsychosis** /mɛtəmsaɪˈkoʊsəs/, *n., pl.* **-ses** /-siz/. **1.** the passage of the soul from one body to another. **2.** the rebirth of the soul at death in another body either of human or animal form. [L, from Gk]

**metencephalon** /mɛtɛnˈsɛfəlɒn/, *n., pl.* **-la** /-lə/. the segment of the brain including the cerebellum and pons and the upper portion of the medulla oblongata; the hindbrain. [NL. See MET(A)-, ENCEPHALON] – **metencephalic** /ˌmɛtɛnsəˈfælɪk/, *adj.*

**meteor** /ˈmitiə, -ɔ/, *n.* **1.** a transient fiery streak in the sky produced by a meteoroid passing through the earth's atmosphere; a bolide or shooting star. **2.** any meteoroid or meteorite. **3.** a brief, dazzling success, as of a person or object. **4.** *Obs.* any atmospheric phenomenon, as hail, a typhoon, etc. [late ME, from NL *meteōrum*, from Gk *metéōron* (pl. *metéōra* phenomena in the heavens), neut. adj., raised, high in air]

**meteor.,** **1.** meteorological. **2.** meteorology.

**meteoric** /mitiˈɒrɪk/, *adj.* **1.** pertaining to or like a meteor. **2.** consisting of meteors: *a meteoric shower.* **3.** flashing like a meteor; transiently brilliant: *a meteoric career.* **4.** swift or rapid. **5.** of the atmosphere; meteorological. – **meteorically,** *adv.*

**meteorite** /ˈmitiəraɪt/, *n.* **1.** a mass of stone or metal that has reached the earth from outer space; a fallen meteoroid. **2.** a meteor or a meteoroid. – **meteoritic** /mitiəˈrɪtɪk/, *adj.*

**meteorogram** /ˈmitiərəgræm/, *n.* the record produced by a meteorograph.

**meteorograph** /ˈmitiərəgræf, -graf/, *n.* an instrument for automatically recording various meteorological conditions simultaneously, as pressure, temperature, etc.

**meteoroid** /ˈmitiərɔɪd/, *n.* any of the small bodies, often remnants of comets, travelling through space, which, when encountering the earth's atmosphere, are heated to luminosity, thus becoming meteors.

**meteorol.,** **1.** meteorological. **2.** meteorology.

**meteorological** /mitiərəˈlɒdʒɪkəl/, *adj.* pertaining to meteorology, or to phenomena of the atmosphere or weather. Also, **meteorologic.** – **meteorologically,** *adv.*

**meteorology** /mitiəˈrɒlədʒi/, *n.* the science dealing with the atmosphere and its phenomena, esp. as relating to weather. [Gk *meteōrologia.* See METEOR, -LOGY] – **meteorologist,** *n.*

**meteoromancy** /ˈmitiərəˌmænsi/, *n.* study of omens dependent on meteors and similar phenomena.

**meter**[1] /ˈmitə/, *n.* **1.** an instrument that measures, esp. one that automatically measures and records the quantity of gas, water, electricity, or the like, passing through it or actuating it. *–v.t.* **2.** to measure by means of a meter. [ME; from METE[1] + -ER[1]]

**meter**[2] /ˈmitə/, *n. U.S.* →**metre**[1].

**meter**[3] /ˈmitə/, *n. U.S.* →**metre**[2].

**-meter**[1], a word element used in names of instruments for measuring quantity, extent, degree, etc., as in *altimeter, barometer.* [NL *-metrum*, from Gk (see METRE[1]). Cf. METER[1]]

**-meter**[2], (in words taken from Greek or Latin) a word element denoting a certain poetic measure or rhythmic pattern, depending on the number of feet constituting the verse, as in *pentameter, trimeter.* [See METRE[2]]

**-meter**[3], *U.S.* →**-metre.**

**meter maid** /ˈ– meɪd/, *n.* **1.** *Brit. Colloq.* a female traffic warden. **2.** an attractive young woman employed at a holiday resort to put coins in the parking meters of visiting motorists.

**meth** /mɛθ/, *n. Colloq.* →**methedrine.**

**meth.,** methylated.

**methacrylate** /məˈθækrəleɪt/, *n.* an ester or salt derived from methacrylic acid.

**methacrylic acid** /ˌmɛθəkrɪlɪk ˈæsəd/, *n.* a colourless liquid acid, $CH_2C(CH_3)COOH$, produced synthetically, the esters of which are used in making plastics.

**methadone** /ˈmɛθədoʊn/, *n.* a powerful analgesic drug used for the treatment of drug withdrawal symptons.

**methaemoglobin** /mətˌhiməˈgloʊbən/, *n.* a brownish compound formed when haemoglobin is oxidised by oxygen. Also, *U.S.,* **methemoglobin.** [MET(A)- + HAEMOGLOBIN]

**methaglyn** /ˈmɛθəglɪn/, *n.* a drink made from fermented honey; a kind of mead. Also, **metheglin.**

**methanal** /ˈmɛθənæl/, *n. Chem.* →**formaldehyde.**

**methane** /ˈmiθeɪn/, *n.* a colourless, odourless, inflammable gas, $CH_4$, the main constituent of marsh gas and the firedamp of coal mines, and obtained commercially from natural gas; the first member of the methane or paraffin series of hydrocarbons. [METH(YL) + -ANE]

**methane series** /– ˈsɪəriz/, *n.* a homologous series of saturated aliphatic hydrocarbons, having the general formula $C_nH_{2n+2}$, as *methane* ($CH_4$), *ethane* $C_2H_6$), etc.; paraffin series; alkanes.

**methanoic acid** /ˌmɛθənoʊɪk ˈæsəd/, *n. Chem.* →**formic acid.**

**methanol** /ˈmɛθənɒl/, *n.* methyl alcohol, or wood alcohol. [METHAN(E) + -OL[1]]

**methanoyl** /mɛθəˈnoʊaɪl/, *n. Chem.* →**formyl.**

**methaqualome** /məˈθækwəloʊm/, *n.* a sedative drug, component of mandrax.

**methedrine** /ˈmɛθədrin, -aɪn/, *n.* a potent stimulant of the central nervous system; methyl amphetamine. [Trademark]

**methenamine** /məˈθinəmin, -maɪn/, *n. U.S.* →**hexamethylene tetramine.**

**methinks** /miˈθɪŋks/, *v. impers.; pt.* **methought.** *Archaic and Poetic.* it seems to me. [ME *me thinketh,* OE *me thyncth* it seems to me]

**methionine** /məˈθaɪənin/, *n.* an essential amino acid, $CH_3SCH_2CH_2CH(NH_3^+)COO^-$, found in proteins, particularly casein, wool, gelatine.

**metho** /ˈmɛθoʊ/, *n. Colloq.* **1.** methylated spirits. **2.** one addicted to drinking methylated spirits. [METH(YLATED SPIRIT) + -O]

**Metho** /ˈmɛθoʊ/, *n. Colloq.* a Methodist.

**method** /ˈmɛθəd/, *n.* **1.** a mode of procedure, esp. an orderly or systematic mode: *a method of instruction.* **2.** a way of doing something, esp. in accordance with a definite plan. **3.** order or system in doing anything: *to work with method.* **4.** orderly or systematic arrangement. **5. method in one's madness,** reason or sense underlying one's apparent stupidity. **6.** (*usu. cap.*) Also, **Stanislavsky Method, Stanislavsky System.** a way of acting in which the actor first explores the inner motivation of the character to be portrayed and builds his character study outwards: the actor's external reactions are therefore spontaneously created rather than intellectually imposed. *–adj.* **7.** (*usu. cap.*) of, pertaining to, or employing the Method. [L *methodus* mode of procedure, method, from Gk *méthodos* a following after, method]

**methodical** /məˈθɒdɪkəl/, *adj.* performed, disposed, or acting in a systematic way; systematic; orderly: *a methodical man.* Also, **methodic.** – **methodically,** *adv.* – **methodicalness,** *n.*

**methodise** /ˈmɛθədaɪz/, *v.t.,* **-dised, -dising. 1.** to reduce to method. **2.** to arrange with method. Also, **methodize.** – **methodiser,** *n.*

**Methodism** /ˈmɛθədɪzəm/, *n.* the doctrines, polity, and worship of the Methodist Church.

**Methodist** /ˈmɛθədəst/, *n.* **1.** a member of one of the Christian denominations which grew out of the revival of religion led by John Wesley. *–adj.* **2.** of or pertaining to the Methodists or Methodism. – **Methodistic** /mɛθəˈdɪstɪk/, *adj.*

**methodology** /mɛθəˈdɒlədʒi/, *n., pl.* **-gies.** the science of method, esp.: **a.** a branch of logic dealing with the logical principles underlying the organisation of the various special sciences, and the conduct of scientific enquiry. **b.** *Educ.* a branch of pedagogics concerned with analysis and evaluation of subject matter and methods of teaching.

**methought** /miˈθɔt/, *v.* past tense of **methinks.**

**meths** /mɛθs/, *n. Brit. Colloq.* →**methylated spirits.**

**methuselah** /məˈθuzələ/, *n.* **1.** a very aged person. **2.** a large wine bottle, having a capacity of 6 to 8 normal bottles. [Heb. *M'thūshelah* a biblical patriarch who according to tradition lived 969 years. Gen. 5:27]

**methyl** /ˈmɛθəl/, *n.* a univalent hydrocarbon radical, $CH_3$, derived from methane. [F *méthyle,* backformation from *méthylène* METHYLENE]

**methyl acetate** /– ˈæsəteɪt/, *n.* a colourless, combustible, volatile liquid, $CH_3COOCH_3$, having a fragrant odour, used as a solvent; the methyl ester of acetic acid.

**methylal** /ˈmɛθəlæl/, *n.* a liquid compound with a pleasant odour, $CH_2(OCH_3)_2$, used in medicine as a hypnotic; dimethoxymethane. [METHYL + AL(COHOL)]

**methyl alcohol** /mɛθəl ˈælkəhɒl/, *n.* a colourless, inflammable, poisonous liquid, $CH_3OH$, of the alcohol class, formerly obtained by the distillation of wood, but now produced synthetically from carbon monoxide and hydrogen, used as a fuel, solvent, etc.; wood alcohol.

**methylamine** /məˈθaɪləmin/, *n.* any of three derivatives of ammonia in which one or all of the hydrogen atoms are replaced by methyl radicals; esp., a gas, $CH_3NH_2$, with an ammonia-like smell, the simplest alkyl derivative of ammonia and, like the latter, forming a series of salts.

**methyl amphetamine** /mɛθəl æmˈfɛtəmin/, *n.* →**methedrine.**

**methylate** /ˈmɛθəleɪt/, *n., v.,* **-lated, -lating.** *–n.* **1.** a methyl alcohol derivative in which the hydrogen of the hydroxyl group has been replaced by a metal. *–v.t.* **2.** to combine with methyl. **3.** to mix with methyl alcohol as in the denaturation of ethyl alcohol: *methylated spirits.* [METHYL + -ATE[2]]

**methylated spirits** /mɛθəleɪtəd ˈspɪrəts/, *n.* ethyl alcohol denatured with 5-10 per cent of methyl alcohol to prevent its use as a beverage; sometimes also contains pyridine and methyl violet dye although the industrial spirit is normally free of these additives.

**methylation** /mɛθəˈleɪʃən/, *n.* the process of replacing a hydrogen atom with a methyl radical.

**methyl benzoic acid,** *n. Chem.* →**toluic acid.**

**methylcellulose** /mɛθəlˈsɛljəloʊz, -oʊs/, *n.* a semisynthetic derivative of wood pulp or chemical cotton used as a laxative.

**methyl chloride** /mɛθəl ˈklɔraɪd/, *n.* →**chloromethane.**

**methylene** /ˈmɛθəlin/, *n.* a bivalent hydrocarbon radical, $CH_2$, derived from methane. [F, from Gk *méthy* wine + *-yl* -YL + *-ène* -ENE]

**methylene blue** /– ˈblu/, *n.* a thiazine dye, $C_{16}H_{18}ClN_3S \cdot 3H_2O$, also used as an antidote for cyanide poisoning.

**methylene chloride** /– ˈklɔraɪd/, *n.* →**dichloromethane.**

**methyl methacrylate** /mɛθəl məˈθækrəleɪt/, *n.* a colourless volatile liquid, $CH_2C(CH_3)COOCH_3$, which polymerises to form a clear, transparent thermoplastic. Cf. **plexiglas, perspex.**

**methylnaphthalene** /mɛθəlˈnæfθəlin/, *n.* a compound, $C_{11}H_{10}$, the alpha form of which, a colourless liquid, is used in determining cetane numbers. Cf. **cetane number.**

**methylpropane** /mɛθəlˈproʊpeɪn/, *n. Chem.* →**isobutane.**

**methylpropene** /mɛθəlˈproʊpin/, *n. Chem.* →**isobutylene.**

**meticulous** /məˈtɪkjələs/, *adj.* solicitous about minute details; minutely or finically careful: *he was meticulous about his personal appearance.* [L *meticulōsus* fearful] – **meticulousness,** *n.* – **meticulously,** *adv.*

**metier** /ˈmɛtieɪ/, *n.* trade; profession; line of work or activity. Also, **métier.** [F, from L *ministerium* MINISTRY]

**métis** /meɪˈtis/, *n.* **1.** any person of mixed ancestry. **2.** *U.S.* a person of one-eighth Negro ancestry; an octoroon. **3.** *Canadian.* a half-breed of white, esp. French, and North American Indian parentage. Also, **métif** /meɪˈtif/. [F, from LL *mixtīcius* of mixed blood] – **métisse,** *n. fem.*

**metol** /ˈmitɒl/, *n.* a soluble white powder used as a developer, $C_{14}H_{18}N_2O_2 \cdot H_2SO_4$.

**Metonic cycle** /mətɒnɪk ˈsaɪkəl/, *n.* a cycle of nineteen years, after which the new moon recurs on the same day of the year as at the beginning of the cycle. [named after the discoverer, *Meton,* 5th-cent. B.C. Athenian astronomer. See -IC]

**metonym** /ˈmɛtənɪm/, *n.* a word used in metonymy.

**metonymical** /mɛtəˈnɪmɪkəl/, *adj.* having the nature of metonymy. Also, **metonymic.** – **metonymically,** *adv.*

**metonymy** /məˈtɒnəmi/, *n.* (in rhetoric) the use of the name of one thing for that of another to which it has some logical relation, as 'sceptre' for 'sovereignty' or 'the bottle' for 'strong drink'. [LL *metōnymia,* from Gk: a change of name]

**metope** /ˈmɛtoʊp, ˈmɛtəpi/, *n.* **1.** *Archit.* one of the square spaces, either decorated or plain, between triglyphs in the Doric frieze. **2.** *Anat.* the face, forehead, or frontal surface in general. [Gk] – **metopic** /məˈtɒpɪk/, *adj.*

B A B

metope: A, metope; B, triglyph

**metoposcopy** /mɛtəˈpɒskəpi/, *n.* the reading of a person's character from the lines of the forehead.

**metre**[1] /ˈmitə/, *n.* the base SI unit of measurement of length equal to 1 650 763.73 wavelengths in vacuum of the (orange-red) radiation corresponding to the transition between the levels $2p_{10}$ and $5d_5$ of the krypton-86 atom; originally intended to be one ten millionth of the distance from the north pole to the equator measured on a meridian and in 1889 defined as the distance between lines on a standard bar, kept at the International Bureau of Weights and Measures in Sèvres, France. *Symbol:* m Also, *U.S.,* **meter.** [F *mètre,* from Gk *métron* measure]

**metre**[2] /ˈmitə/, *n.* a poetic measure; arrangement of words in regularly measured or patterned or rhythmic lines or verses.

Also, *U.S.,* **meter**. [ME, from F *mètre,* from L *metrum;* replacing OE *meter,* from L *metrum* poetic metre, verse, from Gk *métron* measure]

**-metre,** a word element meaning metres; of or pertaining to a metre, as in *kilometre.* [See METRE[1]]

**metre-kilogram-second system** /ˌmitə-kɪləgræm-ˈsɛkənd sɪstəm/, *n.* a system of units used in science, based on the metre, kilogram, and second as the fundamental units of length, mass, and time. *Abbrev.:* MKS (system). See **SI unit.**

**metric**[1] /ˈmɛtrɪk/, *adj.* pertaining to the metre or to the system of measures and weights originally based upon it. [F *métrique,* from *mètre* METRE[1]]

**metric**[2] /ˈmɛtrɪk/, *adj.* →**metrical.** [L *metricus,* from Gk *metrikós* pertaining to metre or measure]

**metrical** /ˈmɛtrɪkəl/, *adj.* **1.** pertaining to metre or poetic measure. **2.** composed in metre or verse. **3.** pertaining to measurement. Also, **metric.** – **metrically,** *adv.*

**metrical psalm** /– ˈsam/, *n.* a verse translation of a psalm, sung as a hymn.

**metricate** /ˈmɛtrəkeɪt/, *v.t.* to convert to metric units.

**metrication** /mɛtrəˈkeɪʃən/, *n.* the process of conversion from British or imperial units to the metric system.

**metric carat** /mɛtrɪk ˈkærət/, *n.* a unit of mass for commercial transactions in precious stones and fine pearls, equal to $2 \times 10^{-4}$ kg.

**metrician** /mɛˈtrɪʃən/, *n.* →**metrist.**

**metrics** /ˈmɛtrɪks/, *n.* **1.** the science of metre. **2.** the art of metrical composition.

**metric system** /ˈmɛtrɪk sɪstəm/, *n.* a decimal system of measurement, first adopted in France in 1795, and adopted internationally by the Metric Convention in 1875. The modern metric system, known as the International System of Units (SI), was adopted in 1960 and introduced in Australia in 1970. It comprises seven *base units,* the metre (m), kilogram (kg), second (s), ampere (A), kelvin (k), mole (mol), and candela (cd), two *supplementary units,* the radian (rad) and the steradian (sr), and *derived units,* formed by combining base and supplementary units according to the algebraic relations linking the corresponding physical quantities. Thus the SI unit of density, mass per unit volume, is the *kilogram per cubic metre* (kg/m$^3$). Special names have been given to some derived units; thus the unit of power, defined as a joule per second, is called a *watt* (W). Decimal multiples and submultiples of SI units may be formed by means of the following prefixes:

| *Prefix* | *Symbol* | *Factor* | *Prefix* | *Symbol* | *Factor* |
|---|---|---|---|---|---|
| deka | da | 10 | deci | d | $10^{-1}$ |
| hecto | h | $10^2$ | centi | c | $10^{-2}$ |
| kilo | k | $10^3$ | milli | m | $10^{-3}$ |
| mega | M | $10^6$ | micro | μ | $10^{-6}$ |
| giga | G | $10^9$ | nano | n | $10^{-9}$ |
| tera | T | $10^{12}$ | pico | p | $10^{-12}$ |
| peta | P | $10^{15}$ | femto | f | $10^{-15}$ |
| exa | E | $10^{18}$ | atto | a | $10^{-18}$ |

Thus 1 000 000 watts ($10^6$W) may be expressed as 1 megawatt (1 MW). Each SI unit name and each prefix has an internationally uniform symbol associated with it.

**metric ton** /mɛtrɪk ˈtʌn/, *n.* →**tonne.**

**metrify** /ˈmɛtrəfaɪ/, *v.t.,* **-fied, -fying.** to put into metre; compose in verse. [F *métrifier,* from ML *metrificāre* put in metre, from *metri-* (combining form of *metrum* metre) + *-ficāre* -FY] – **metrifier,** *n.*

**metrist** /ˈmɛtrəst/, *n.* one versed in the use of poetic metres. [ML *metrista,* from L *metrum* METRE[2]]

**metritis** /məˈtraɪtəs/, *n.* inflammation of the uterus. [NL, from Gk *mētra* uterus + *-ītis-* -ITIS]

**metro** /ˈmɛtroʊ/, *n.* an underground railway system in certain cities, esp. Paris. [F *métro*]

**metrology** /məˈtrɒlədʒi/, *n., pl.* **-gies.** the science of measures and weights [Gk *métro(n)* measure + -LOGY] – **metrological** /mɛtrəˈlɒdʒɪkəl/, *adj.* – **metrologist,** *n.*

**metronome** /ˈmɛtrənoʊm/, *n.* a mechanical contrivance for marking time, as for music. [Gk *métro(n)* measure + stem of *nómos* law] – **metronomic** /mɛtrəˈnɒmɪk/, *adj.*

**metronymic** /mɛtrəˈnɪmɪk/, *adj.* **1.** derived from the name of a mother or other female ancestor. *–n.* **2.** a metronymic name. [Gk *mētrōnymikós* named after one's mother]

**metrop.,** **1.** metropolis. **2.** metropolitan.

**metropolis** /məˈtrɒpələs/, *n., pl.* **-lises** /-ləsiz/. **1.** the chief city (not necessarily the capital) of a country, state, or region. **2.** a central or principal point, as of some activity. **3.** the mother city or parent state of an ancient Greek (or other) colony. **4.** the chief see of an ecclesiastical province. [LL, from Gk: a mother state or city]

**metropolitan** /mɛtrəˈpɒlətən/, *adj.* **1.** of, pertaining to, or characteristic of a metropolis or chief city, or of its inhabitants. **2.** pertaining to or constituting a mother country. **3.** pertaining to an ecclesiastical metropolis. *–n.* **4.** an inhabitant of a metropolis or chief city. **5.** one having metropolitan manners, etc. **6.** the next highest rank to patriarch in the Russian Orthodox Church.

**metrorrhagia** /mitrɔˈreɪdʒiə, mɛtrɔ-/, *n.* nonmenstrual discharge of blood from the uterus; uterine haemorrhage. [NL, from Gk *mētra* uterus + *-rrhagía* -RRHAGIA]

**-metry,** a word element denoting the process of measuring, abstract for *-meter,* as in *anthropometry, chronometry.* [Gk *-metria,* from *-metros* measuring]

**mettle** /ˈmɛtl/, *n.* **1.** the characteristic disposition or temper: *to try a man's mettle.* **2.** spirit; courage. **3. on one's mettle,** incited to do one's best. [var. of METAL]

**mettlesome** /ˈmɛtlsəm/, *adj.* spirited; courageous. Also, **mettled** /ˈmɛtld/.

**meunière** /mɜniˈɛə/, *adj.* (usu. of fish), floured, fried in butter and served in a sauce of hot butter and lemon juice. Also, **à la meunière.** [F: miller's wife]

**MeV,** *Physics.* million electron-volts. Also, **Mev.**

**mew**[1] /mju/, *n.* **1.** the sound a cat makes. *–v.i.* **2.** to make this sound. [imitative]

**mew**[2] /mju/, *n.* a seagull, esp. the common gull, *Larus canus,* of Europe. [OE, c. G *Möwe*]

**mew**[3] /mju/, *n.* **1.** a cage for hawks, esp. while moulting. **2.** a place of retirement or concealment. **3.** →**mews.** *–v.t.* **4.** to shut up in or as in a mew; to confine; conceal (oft. fol. by *up*). [ME *mue,* from OF, from *meur* MEW[4]]

**mew**[4] /mju/, *v.i.* to shed feathers; to moult. [ME *mewe(n),* from OF *muer* moult, change, from L *mūtāre*]

**mewl** /mjul/, *v.i.* to cry, as a young child. [imitative]

**mews** /mjuz/, *n.pl. usu. construed as sing.* **1.** a set of stables or garages, usu. with living accommodation attached, around a yard, court, or alley. **2.** a street, yard, or court lined by buildings originally used as stables and servants' quarters. [orig. pl. of MEW[3]]

**Mex.,** **1.** Mexico. **2.** Mexican.

**Mexican** /ˈmɛksɪkən/, *adj.* **1.** of or pertaining to Mexico. **2.** of a style of cooking common in Mexico, which frequently uses tomatoes, chillies, garlic, onions, etc. *–n.* **3.** a native or inhabitant of Mexico. **4.** *N.S.W. Colloq.* a Victorian (one south of the border).

**Mexican hairless** /– ˈhɛələs/, *n.* a medium-sized dog which has hair only on the skull and the end of the tail.

**Mexican poppy** /– ˈpɒpi/, *n.* a tall, prickly weed, *Argemone mexicana,* from Mexico, with bluish-coloured leaves and stems, and pale yellow flowers.

**Mexican stand-off** /– ˈstænd-ɒf/, *n. Colloq.* a situation in which two opponents threaten each other loudly but neither makes any attempt to resolve the conflict.

**Mexican tea** /– ˈti/, *n.* an erect herbaceous weed, *Chenopodium ambrosioides,* widespread in temperate regions.

**Mexico** /ˈmɛksɪkoʊ/, *n.* a republic in southern North America.

**mezereon** /mɛˈzɪəriən/, *n.* an Old World shrub, *Daphne mezereum,* cultivated for its fragrant purplish pink flowers, which appear in early spring. [ML, from Ar. *māzaryūn* the camellia]

**mezzanine** /ˈmɛzənin, mɛzəˈnin/, *n.* a low storey between two other storeys of greater height, esp. when the low storey and the one beneath it form part of one composition; entresol. [F, from It. *mezzanino,* diminutive of *mezzano* middle, from L *mediānus* MEDIAN]

**mezzo** /ˈmɛtsoʊ/, *adj.* **1.** middle; medium; half. *–n.* **2.** *Colloq.* a mezzosprano. [It., from L *medius* middle]

**mezzo-rilievo** /mɛtsoʊ-rəˈlivoʊ, -rəlˈjeɪvoʊ/, *n.* →**demirelief.** Also, **mezzo-relievo.** [It.]

**mezzosoprano** /mɛtsousəˈpranou/, *n., pl.* **-nos, -ni** /-ni/. **1.** a voice or voice part intermediate in compass between soprano and contralto. **2.** a person having such a voice. [It.]

**mezzotint** /ˈmɛtsoutɪnt/, *n.* **1.** a method of engraving on copper or steel by burnishing or scraping away a uniformly roughened surface. **2.** a print produced by this method. *–v.t.* **3.** to engrave in mezzotint. [It. *mezzotinto* half-tint]

**mf.,** /ɛm ˈɛf/, *Music.* moderately loud. [It. *mezzoforte*]

**m.f.,** medium-frequency.

**MF,** Middle French. Also, **M.F.**

**mfd,** manufactured.

**mfg,** manufacturing.

**M.F.N.,** Most Favoured Nation.

**mg,** milligram; milligrams.

**m.g.,** *Music.* left hand. [F *main gauche*]

**Mg,** magnesium.

**MGk,** Medieval Greek.

**mgr,** manager.

**Mgr,** Monsignor.

**MHA** /ɛm eɪtʃ ˈeɪ/, Member of the House of Assembly.

**MHG,** Middle High German.

**mho** /mou/, *n. Obs.* →**siemens.** [coined by Lord Kelvin, 1824-1907, British physicist; reversed spelling of OHM]

**MHR,** /ɛm eɪtʃ ˈa/, Member of the House of Representatives.

**mi** /mi/, *n.* **1.** the syllable used for the third note of the scale in solfège. See **solfège. 2.** →**me**[2].

**MIA** /ɛm aɪ ˈeɪ/, Murrumidgee Irrigation Area.

**mia-mia** /ˈmaɪə-maɪə, ˈmiə-miə/, *n.* a temporary bush shelter used by Aborigines; gunyah; humpy; wurley. [Aboriginal]

**miaow** /miˈaʊ, mjaʊ/, *n.* **1.** the sound a cat makes. *–v.i.* **2.** to make such a sound. Also, **meow, miaou, miaul** /miˈaʊl/. [imitative]

**miasma** /miˈæzmə/, *n., pl.* **-mata** /-mətə/, **-mas.** noxious exhalations from putrescent organic matter; poisonous effluvia or germs infecting the atmosphere. [NL, from Gk: pollution] **– miasmal, miasmatic** /miəzˈmætɪk/, **miasmatical** /miəzˈmætɪkəl/, **miasmic,** *adj.*

**Mic.,** *Bible.* Micah.

**mica** /ˈmaɪkə/, *n.* any member of a group of minerals, hydrous disilicates of aluminium with other bases, chiefly potassium, magnesium, iron, and lithium, that separate readily (by cleavage) into thin, tough, often transparent, and usu. elastic laminae. [NL, special use of L *mīca* crumb, grain, little bit]

**micaceous** /maɪˈkeɪʃəs/, *adj.* **1.** consisting of, containing, or resembling mica. **2.** of or pertaining to mica.

**mice** /maɪs/, *n.* plural of **mouse.**

**micelle** /məˈsɛl/, *n.* a colloidal particle formed by the reversible aggregation of dissolved molecules. Electrically charged micelles form colloidal electrolytes, as soaps and detergents. [NL *mīcella,* diminutive of L *mīca* crumb]

**michael** /ˈmaɪkəl/, *n. Colloq.* female pudendum. Also, **mick.**

**Michaelmas** /ˈmɪkəlməs/, *n.* a festival celebrated on 29 September in honour of the archangel Michael. Also, **Michaelmas Day.** [OE (*Sanct*) *Michaeles masse* St Michael's mass]

**Michaelmas daisy** /– ˈdeɪzi/, *n.* any of a number of plants of the genus *Aster,* with many cultivated varieties and hybrids.

**Michaelmas term** /ˈ– tɜm/, *n.* the last term of the academic year at some Australian schools and universities.

**mick**[1] /mɪk/, *n. Colloq.* **1.** the obverse side of a coin; head. **2.** the reverse side of a coin; tail. *–v.t.* **3.** to throw (the coins) in two-up so that both tails are facing up. [orig. unknown]

**mick**[2] /mɪk/, *n. Colloq.* female pudendum.

**Mick** /mɪk/, *n. Colloq.* **1.** a Roman Catholic (esp. of Irish extraction). **2.** an Irishman.

**mickery**[1] /ˈmɪkəri/, *n.* a soakage in the sandy bed of an inland river. [orig. unknown]

**mickery**[2] /ˈmɪkəri/, *n.* (*oft. cap.*) *Colloq.* behaviour allegedly typical of Roman Catholics; Roman Catholic influence: *there's a lot of mickery in that Party.* [MICK + -ERY]

**mickery country** /ˈ– kʌntri/, *n.* country that holds water after rain.

**mickey**[1] /ˈmɪki/, *n.* →**micky**[1].

**mickey**[2] /ˈmɪki/, *n.* →**micky**[2].

**mickey**[3] /ˈmɪki/, *n.* →**mickey finn.**

**mickey**[4] /ˈmɪki/, *n.* →**micky**[3].

**Mickey** /ˈmɪki/, *n. Colloq.* a policeman.

**Mickey Doolan** /- ˈdulən/, *n. N.Z. Colloq.* a Roman Catholic (esp. of Irish extraction).

**mickey finn** /– ˈfɪn/, *n. Colloq.* a drink, usu. alcoholic, which has been surreptiously laced so as to cause to fall asleep, to discomfort or in some way to incapacitate the person who drinks it. Also, **Mickey Finn, mickey.** [orig. unknown]

**mickey mouse**[1] /– ˈmaʊs/, *Colloq. –adj.* **1.** insubstantial, lacking serious worth but amusing, as of certain light music, courses of instruction, etc. **2.** (of cross-bred dairy and beef cattle) part Friesian with white faces and mainly black bodies. *–n.* **3.** a beast of this breed. [from *Mickey Mouse,* a cartoon character created by Walt Disney, 1901-66, U.S. animator and film producer]

**mickey mouse**[2] /– ˈmaʊs/, *adj. Colloq.* splendid, excellent. [rhyming slang, *Mickey Mouse* GROUSE[3]. See MICKEY MOUSE[1]]

**Mickhead** /ˈmɪkhɛd/, *n. Colloq.* a Roman Catholic.

**mickle** /ˈmɪkəl/, *adj. Scot.* great; large; much. Also, **muckle.** [ME *mikel,* OE *micul,* var. of *micel* MUCH]

**micky**[1] /ˈmɪki/, *n. Colloq.* a young, wild bull. Also, **mickey.** [? from MICK an Irishman (by association with a wild bull)]

**micky**[2] /ˈmɪki/, *n.* →**noisy miner.** Also, **mickey.**

**micky**[3] /ˈmɪki/, *n. in the phrase* **take the micky out of,** *Colloq.* to make seem foolish; tease.

**micky quick** /– ˈkwɪk/, *v.i. Colloq.* to depart in a hurry.

**micra** /ˈmaɪkrə/, *n.* a plural of **micron.**

**MICR encoding** /maɪkər ənˈkoudɪŋ/, *n.* a machine-reading system by which ferrous-impregnated ink characters encoded on documents, as cheques, are read by a magnetically-sensitive device. [*M*(*agnetic*) *I*(*nk*) *C*(*haracter*) *R*(*ecognition*)]

**micrify** /ˈmaɪkrəfaɪ/, *v.t.,* **-fied, -fying.** to make small or insignificant. [MICR(O)- + -IFY; modelled on MAGNIFY]

**micro-** /ˈmaɪkrou-/, **1.** a prefix meaning **a.** 'very small', as in *micro-organism, microcosm.* **b.** 'enlarging' or 'amplifying', as in *microphone, microscope, microbarograph.* Also, before vowels, **micr-. 2.** a prefix denoting $10^{-6}$ of a given unit, as in *microvolt. Symbol:* μ [GK *mīkro-,* combining form of *mikrós* small]

**microanalysis** /ˌmaɪkrouəˈnæləsəs/, *n., pl.* **-ses** /-siz/. the chemical analysis of extremely small quantities. **– microanalytical** /ˌmaɪkrouænəˈlɪtɪkəl/, *adj.*

**microbalance** /ˈmaɪkrouˌbæləns/, *n.* a balance for weighing very small quantities of material, esp. of the order of a thousandth to a millionth of a gram.

**microbarograph** /maɪkrouˈbærəgræf, -graf/, *n.* a barograph for recording minute fluctuations of atmospheric pressure.

**microbe** /ˈmaɪkroub/, *n.* **1.** a micro-organism, usu. one of vegetable nature; a germ. **2.** a bacterium, esp. one causing disease. [F, from Gk *mīkro-* MICRO- + *bíos* life] **– microbial** /maɪˈkroubiəl/, **microbic** /maɪˈkroubɪk/, *adj.*

**microbiology** /ˌmaɪkroubaɪˈɒlədʒi/, *n.* the science concerned with the occurrence, activities, and utilisation of the extremely small, microscopic and submicroscopic organisms. **– microbiological** /ˌmaɪkroubaɪəˈlɒdʒɪkəl/, *adj.* **– microbiologist,** *n.*

**microcentrifuge** /maɪkrouˈsɛntrəfjudʒ, -fjuʒ/, *n.* a centrifuge capable of separating the constituents of very small volumes of fluid.

**microcephalic** /maɪkrousəˈfælɪk/, *adj.* **1.** *Anat.* having a skull with a small cranial capacity. **2.** *Pathol.* having an abnormally small skull. Also, **microcephalous**/maɪkrouˈsɛfələs/. **– microcephaly** /maɪkrouˈsɛfəli/, *n.*

**microchemistry** /maɪkrouˈkɛməstri/, *n.* chemistry as concerned with minute or microscopic objects or quantities. **– microchemical,** *adj.*

**microcircuit** /ˈmaɪkrouˌsɜkət/, *n.* a tiny electronic circuit, esp. one which includes a chip (def. 6). **– microcircuitry** /maɪkrouˈsɜkətri/, *n.*

**microclimate** /ˈmaɪkrouˌklaɪmət/, *n.* the climate of a very small or confined area. **– microclimatic** /ˌmaɪkroukla ɪˈmætɪk/, *adj.* **– microclimatically** /ˌmaɪkrouklaɪˈmætɪkli/, *adv.*

**microclimatology** /maɪkrouˌklaɪməˈtɒlədʒi/, *n.* a branch of climatology dealing with studies of small-scale climatic conditions, as local climatic changes induced by planting trees as a windbreak.

**microcline** /ˈmaɪkrouˌklaɪn/, *n.* a mineral of the felspar group, potassium aluminium silicate, $KAlSi_3O_8$, identical in composition with orthoclase but differing in crystal system, used in making porcelain. [G *Mikroklin,* from Gk *mīkro-* MICRO- + *klínein* incline]

**micrococcus** /maɪkroʊˈkɒkəs/, *n., pl.* **-cocci** /-ˈkɒksaɪ/. any member of the genus *Micrococcus,* comprising globular or oval bacterial organisms, of which certain species cause disease, and others produce fermentation, colouration, etc. [NL. See MICRO-, COCCUS]

**microcomputer** /ˈmaɪkroʊkəmˌpjutə/, *n.* a computer which has its central processor functions contained on a single printed circuit board constituting a stand-alone module; usu. small in size and cost.

**microcopy** /ˈmaɪkroʊˌkɒpi/, *n., pl.* **-ies.** a greatly reduced photographic copy of a book, page, etc., usu. read by enlargement on a ground-glass screen.

**microcosm** /ˈmaɪkrəkɒzəm/, *n.* **1.** a little world (opposed to *macrocosm*). **2.** anything regarded as a world in miniature. **3.** man viewed as an epitome of the universe. [F *microcosme,* from LL *mīcrocosmus,* from LGk *mīkrós kósmos* little world] – **microcosmic** /maɪkrəˈkɒzmɪk/, **microcosmical** /maɪkrəˈkɒzmɪkəl/, *adj.*

**microcosmic salt** /maɪkrəˌkɒzmɪk ˈsɒlt/, *n.* a phosphate of sodium and ammonium, $NaNH_4HPO_4 \cdot 4H_2O$, originally obtained from human urine, much used as a blowpipe flux in testing metallic oxides.

**microcrystalline** /maɪkroʊˈkrɪstəlaɪn/, *adj.* minutely crystalline; composed of microscopic crystals.

**microcyte** /ˈmaɪkroʊsaɪt/, *n.* **1.** a minute cell or corpuscle. **2.** *Pathol.* an abnormally small-sized red blood cell, usu. deficient in haemoglobin. – **microcytic** /maɪkroʊˈsɪtɪk/, *adj.*

**microdetector** /ˌmaɪkroʊdəˈtɛktə/, *n.* **1.** an instrument measuring small quantities or changes. **2.** *Elect.* a sensitive galvanometer.

**microdont** /ˈmaɪkroʊdɒnt/, *adj.* **1.** having small or short teeth. –*n.* **2.** a small or short tooth. – **microdontous** /maɪkroʊˈdɒntəs/, *adj.*

**microdot** /ˈmaɪkroʊˌdɒt/, *n.* **1.** a microphotograph reduced to the size of a printed or typed dot. **2.** *Colloq.* LSD in tablet form.

**micro-economic** /ˌmaɪkroʊ-ɛkəˈnɒmɪk/, *adj.* of or pertaining to one small section of the economy.

**micro-economics** /ˌmaɪkroʊ-ɛkəˈnɒmɪks/, *n.* a study of the economic system in terms of its different sectors (opposed to *macro-economics*). [MICRO- + ECONOMICS]

**microelectronics** /maɪkroʊˌɛlɛkˈtrɒnɪks/, *n.* the branch of electronics concerned with the development and application of very small circuits, as those formed on a surface by etching. – **microelectronic,** *adj.*

**microfauna** /ˈmaɪkroʊfɔnə/, *n.* **1.** fauna comprising extremely small animals, as protozoa. **2.** fauna found in a microhabitat.

**microfiche** /ˈmaɪkroʊfiʃ/, *n.* a microfilmed transparency about the size and shape of a filing card which may have on it many pages of print. [F *micro-* MICRO- + *fiche* slip of paper, index card]

**microfilm** /ˈmaɪkroʊfɪlm/, *n.* **1.** a narrow film, esp. of motion-picture stock, on which microcopies are made. **2.** →**microphotograph.** –*v.t.* **3.** to record on microfilm.

**microform** /ˈmaɪkroʊfɔm/, *n.* any arrangement of images reduced in size, as on microfilm.

**microgamete** /maɪkroʊˈgæmit/, *n.* (in heterogamous reproduction) the smaller of the two gametes, usu. the male cell.

**micrograph** /ˈmaɪkroʊgræf, -graf/, *n.* **1.** an instrument for executing extremely minute writing or engraving. **2.** a photograph or a drawing of an object as seen through a microscope.

**micrography** /maɪˈkrɒgrəfi/, *n.* **1.** the description or delineation of microscopic objects. **2.** examination or study with the microscope. **3.** the art or practice of writing in very small characters. – **micrographic** /maɪkrəˈgræfɪk/, *adj.*

**microgroove** /ˈmaɪkrəgruv/, *n.* **1.** (in a long-playing gramophone record) a narrow groove which accepts a stylus of the order of thousandths of a centimetre in diameter. **2.** a record with such grooves.

**microhabitat** /maɪkroʊˈhæbətæt/, *n.* a very small, usu. confined and isolated habitat, as a tree stump.

**microhardness** /maɪkroʊˈhadnəs/, *n.* the hardness of a substance, as a metal, measured by its resistance to indentation by an indentor which is able to penetrate microscopic areas.

**microinch** /ˈmaɪkroʊɪntʃ/, *n.* a unit of length in the imperial system, equal to a millionth of an inch or $25.4 \times 10^{-9}$ m. *Symbol:* μin

**micrology** /maɪˈkrɒlədʒi/, *n.* excessive attention to petty details or distinctions. [Gk *mīkrología.* See MICRO-, -LOGY]

**micro-meteorology** /maɪkroʊ-ˌmitiəˈrɒlədʒi/, *n.* that portion of the science of meteorology that deals on the smallest scale with the observation and explanation of physical and dynamic occurrences within the atmosphere.

**micrometer** /maɪˈkrɒmətə/, *n.* **1.** any of various devices for measuring minute distances, angles, etc., as in connection with a telescope or microscope. **2.** a U-shaped gauge for measuring thicknesses or short lengths in which the gap between the measuring faces is adjusted by a finely threaded screw, the end of which forms one face; a micrometer gauge. [F *micromètre,* from *micro-* MICRO- + *-mètre* -METER[1]]

**micrometer screw** /ˈ– skru/, *n.* a screw with a very fine thread and a graduated head, used in micrometers, etc.

**micrometry** /maɪˈkrɒmətri/, *n.* the method or art of measuring with a micrometer.

**microminiaturisation** /maɪkroʊˌmɪnətʃəraɪˈzeɪʃən/, *n.* the development and application of very small electronic circuits, as those formed on a surface by etching. Also, **microminiaturization.**

**micron** /ˈmaɪkrɒn/, *n., pl.* **-cra** /-krə/, **-cras. 1.** *Obs.* the millionth part of a metre; micrometre. *Symbol:* μ **2.** *Phys. Chem.* a colloidal particle whose diameter is between 0.2 and 10 micrometres. Also, **mikron.** [NL, from Gk *mīkrón* (neut. adj.) small]

**Micronesia** /maɪkrəˈniʒə/, *n.* groups of small Pacific islands, north of the equator, east of the Philippine Islands. The main groups included are the Marianas, the Caroline, and the Marshall islands. [MICRO- + Gk *nêsos* island + -IA]

**Micronesian** /maɪkrəˈniʒən/, *adj.* **1.** of Micronesia, its inhabitants, or their languages. –*n.* **2.** a native of Micronesia. **3.** any of the Austronesian languages or dialects spoken in the Micronesian islands.

**micronutrient** /maɪkroʊˈnjutrɪənt/, *n.* a vitamin, mineral or other substance essential for good health, but required in tiny amounts only. Cf. **macronutrient.**

**micro-organism** /maɪkroʊ-ˈɔgənɪzəm/, *n.* a microscopic (animal or vegetable) organism.

**micro-oven** /ˈmaɪkroʊ-ʌvən/, *n.* →**microwave oven.**

**microparasite** /maɪkroʊˈpærəsaɪt/, *n.* a parasitic microorganism. – **microparasitic** /maɪkroʊˌpærəˈsɪtɪk/, *adj.*

**microphone** /ˈmaɪkrəfoʊn/, *n.* an instrument which is capable of transforming the air-pressure waves of sound into changes in electric currents or voltages. Qualifying adjectives, as *condenser, crystal, velocity,* etc., describe the method of developing the electric quantity. – **microphonic** /maɪkrəˈfɒnɪk/, *adj.*

**microphotograph** /maɪkroʊˈfoʊtəgræf/, *n.* **1.** a small photograph requiring optical enlargement to render it visible in detail. **2.** a film reproduction of a large or bulky publication, as a file of newspapers, used to conserve space or to copy material which is difficult to obtain. **3.** →**photomicrograph.** – **microphotographic** /maɪkroʊˌfoʊtəˈgræfɪk/, *adj.* – **microphotography** /ˌmaɪkroʊfəˈtɒgrəfi/, *n.*

**microphysics** /ˈmaɪkroʊˌfɪzɪks, ˌmaɪkroʊˈfɪzɪks/, *n.* that area of physics concerned with studying phenomena on a microscopic or smaller scale, esp. with molecules, atoms, and sub-atomic particles.

**microphyte** /ˈmaɪkroʊfaɪt/, *n.* **1.** a microscopic plant, esp. a parasite. **2.** a plant dwarfed by malnourishment.

**microprocessor** /maɪkroʊˈproʊsɛsə/, *n.* a small stand-alone computer, often dedicated to specific functions, as directing a quality-control inspection in a factory or regulating a domestic procedure such as the keeping of a record of engagements, etc.

**micropublishing** /ˈmaɪkroʊˌpʌbləʃɪŋ/, *n.* the publishing of material in microfiche form.

**micropyle** /ˈmaɪkroʊpaɪl/, *n.* **1.** *Zool.* any minute opening in the coverings of an ovum, through which spermatozoa may gain access to the interior. **2.** *Bot.* the minute orifice or opening in the integuments of an ovule. [F, from Gk *mīkro-* MICRO- + *pýlē* gate, orifice] – **micropylar** /maɪkroʊ'paɪlə/, *adj.*

**micropyrometer** /ˌmaɪkroʊpaɪ'rɒmətə/, *n.* an optical pyrometer for use with small glowing bodies.

**micros.**, microscopy.

**microscope** /'maɪkrəskoʊp/, *n.* an optical instrument having a magnifying lens or a combination of lenses for inspecting objects too small to be seen, or to be seen distinctly and in detail, by the naked eye. [NL *mīcroscopium,* from *mīcro-* MICRO- + Gk *skopeîn* view + *-ium* -IUM]

**microscopic** /maɪkrə'skɒpɪk/, *adj.* **1.** so small as to be invisible or indistinct without the use of the microscope. **2.** very small; tiny. **3.** of or pertaining to the microscope or its use. **4.** performing the work of a microscope. **5.** suggestive of the use of the microscope: *microscopic exactness.* Also, **microscopical.** – **microscopically,** *adv.*

**microscopy** /maɪ'krɒskəpi/, *n.* **1.** the use of the microscope. **2.** microscopic investigation. – **microscopist,** *n.*

**microseism** /'maɪkroʊsaɪzəm/, *n.* a vibration of the ground recorded by seismographs but not believed to be due to an earthquake. [MICRO- + Gk *seismós* earthquake] – **microseismic** /maɪkroʊ'saɪzmɪk/, **microseismical** /maɪkroʊ'saɪzmɪkəl/, *adj.*

**microsome** /'maɪkrəsoʊm/, *n.* one of the minute granules, smaller than mitochondria and lysosomes, present in living cells, and containing ribonucleic acid and enzymes involved in protein synthesis. [NL *mīcrosōma.* See MICRO-, -SOME[3]] – **microsomal** /maɪkroʊ'soʊməl/, *adj.*

**microsporangium** /ˌmaɪkroʊspɔ'rændʒiəm/, *n., pl.* **-gia** /-dʒiə/. a sporangium containing microspores. [NL. See MICRO-, SPORANGIUM]

**microspore** /'maɪkroʊspɔ/, *n.* **1.** the smaller of two kinds of spores produced by some heterosporous pteridophytes. **2.** a pollen grain.

**microsporophyll** /maɪkroʊ'spɔrəfɪl/, *n.* a sporophyll bearing microsporangia.

**microstomatous** /maɪkroʊ'stɒmətəs/, *adj.* having or pertaining to a very small mouth. Also, **microstomous** /maɪ'krɒstəməs/. [MICRO- + Gk *stóma* mouth + -OUS]

**microstructure** /'maɪkroʊstrʌktʃə/, *n.* the structure of metals and alloys as revealed, after polishing and etching, by examination under a microscope.

**microsurgery** /'maɪkroʊˌsɜdʒəri/, *n.* surgery performed on very small parts of the body, as the nerve fibres, etc., of a severed hand being restored to its wrist, often requiring special instruments to enable the surgeon to see and manipulate those parts.

**microtome** /'maɪkroʊtoʊm/, *n.* an instrument for cutting very thin sections, as of organic tissue, for microscopic examination.

**microtomy** /maɪ'krɒtəmi/, *n.* the cutting of very thin sections, as with the microtome. – **microtomic** /maɪkrə'tɒmɪk/, **microtomical** /maɪkrə'tɒmɪkəl/, *adj.* – **microtomist,** *n.*

**microtone** /'maɪkrətoʊn/, *n. Music.* an interval less than a semitone.

**microtrauma** /'maɪkroʊtrɔmə/, *n.* bodily injury from repeated minor traumata, which individually are not recognisably injurious.

**microwave** /'maɪkrəweɪv/, *n.* an electromagnetic wave of extremely high frequency, approximately comprising the wavelength range from 50 cm to 1 mm.

**microwave oven** /– 'ʌvən/, *n.* an oven which cooks with unusual rapidity, by passing microwaves through food and generating heat inside it.

**microwave spectroscopy** /– spɛk'trɒskəpi/, *n.* the measurement of the absorption or emission of microwave radiation by atomic or molecular systems, which provides information regarding their structure.

**micturate** /'mɪktʃəreɪt/, *v.i.,* **-rated, -rating.** to pass urine; urinate. [L *micturīre* desire to urinate + -ATE[1]]

**micturition** /mɪktʃə'rɪʃən/, *n.* the act of passing urine. [L *micturītus,* pp. of *micturīre* desire to urinate + -ION]

**mid**[1] /mɪd/, *adj.* **1.** central; at or near the middle point: *in the mid nineties of the last century.* **2.** *Phonet.* having a tongue position intermediate between high and low: *beet, bet,* and *bat* have high, mid, and low vowels respectively. [ME; OE *midd,* c. OHG *mitti,* Icel. *midhr,* Goth. *midjis* middle; akin to L *medius,* Gk *mésos,* Skt *madhya* middle]

**mid**[2] /mɪd/, *prep.* →**amid.** Also, **'mid.**

**mid-,** a combining form of 'middle'.

**mid.,** middle.

**midafternoon** /mɪdaftə'nun/, *n.* **1.** a point or time about midway through the afternoon, as between 3 p.m. and 4 p.m. *–adj.* **2.** of, pertaining to, or taken at or during midafternoon.

**midair** /mɪd'ɛə/, *n.* **1.** any elevated position above the ground. *–adv.* **2.** in a state of suspension.

**Midas touch** /'maɪdəs tʌtʃ/, *n.* a great ability to make money. [from *Midas,* a legendary Phrygian king, who was given by Dionysus the power of turning into gold whatever he touched]

**mid-Atlantic** /mɪd-ət'læntɪk/, *adj.* of a form of spoken English, usu. readily accepted as agreeable, in which both British and American influences are apparent.

**midbrain** /'mɪdbreɪn/, *n.* →**mesencephalon.**

**midcult** /'mɪdkʌlt/, *Chiefly U.S.* (*derog.*) *–n.* **1.** a form of culture or a cultural manifestation, which, aiming only at inoffensive and undemanding popularity, avoids any dangerous vulgarity and simplifies any complexity. *–adj.* **2.** of or pertaining to such culture. [coined by Dwight Macdonald, b. 1906, U.S. critic, from MID(DLEBROW) + CULT(URE)]

**midday** /'mɪddeɪ/, *n.* **1.** the middle of the day; noon. *–adj.* **2.** of or pertaining to the middle part of the day. [ME; OE *middæg*]

**midden** /'mɪdn/, *n.* **1.** a dunghill or refuse heap. **2.** a mound consisting of shells of edible molluscs and other refuse, marking the site of prehistoric human habitation. [ME *myd(d)yng,* from Scand.; cf. Dan. *mödding*]

**middle** /'mɪdl/, *adj.* **1.** equally distant from extremes or limits: *the middle point of a line.* **2.** intervening or intermediate: *the middle distance.* **3.** medium: *a man of middle size.* **4.** (*cap.*) (in the history of a language) intermediate between periods classified as Old and New or Modern: *Middle English.* **5.** *Gram.* (in some languages) denoting a voice of verb inflection, in which the subject is represented as acting on or for itself, in contrast to the active voice in which the subject acts, and the passive, in which the subject is acted upon, as in Greek *gráphomai* 'I write for myself', *gráphō* 'I write'. **6.** (*oft. cap.*) *Geol.* denoting the division intermediate between the Upper and Lower divisions of a period, system, or the like. **7.** *Rare.* at or near its middle. *–n.* **8.** the point, part, etc., equidistant from extremes or limits. **9.** the waist, or middle part of the human body. **10.** something intermediate; a mean. *–v.t.* **11.** to place in the middle. **12.** *Tennis, Cricket, etc.* to hit (the ball) squarely in the centre of the racquet, bat, etc. **13.** *Chiefly Naut.* to fold in half. [ME and OE *middel,* c. G *Mittel*]

**middle age** /– 'eɪdʒ/, *n.* the period between youth and old age.

**middle-aged** /'mɪdl-eɪdʒd/, *adj.* **1.** intermediate in age between youth and old age; commonly, from about 45 to about 60 years old. **2.** characteristic of or suitable for middle-aged people.

**middle-aged spread** /– 'sprɛd/, *n.* the visible effects of weight gained in middle age, esp. around the stomach and hips.

**Middle Ages** /mɪdl 'eɪdʒəz/, *n.pl.* the time in European history between classical antiquity and the Italian Renaissance (from the late 5th century to about A.D. 1350); sometimes restricted to the later part of this period (after 1100); sometimes extended to 1450 or 1500.

**middlebrow** /'mɪdlbraʊ/, *Colloq. –n.* **1.** a person of mediocre or limited intellectual calibre or culture. **2.** a person of middle-class or bourgeois taste. *–adj.* **3.** mediocre; bourgeois.

**middle C** /mɪdl 'si/, *n. Music.* the note indicated by the first ledger line above the bass stave and the first below the treble stave.

**middle class** /'mɪdl klas/, *n.* a social class intermediate between the upper and lower classes as **a.** a fluid socio-economic grouping comprising esp. business and professional people and public servants of middle income, who do not have an upper-class or establishment background. **b.** *Brit.* a class which in the social hierarchy is between the aristocracy and the working class. **c.** a class identified with merchants, the emergence of which marked the change from medieval to modern economy.

**middle-class** /'mɪdl-klas/, *adj.* belonging or pertaining to or characteristic of the middle class; bourgeois.

**middle distance** /mɪdl 'dɪstns/, *n.* **1.** (in painting, etc.) the space between the foreground and the background or distance. **2.** a division of competitive running, usu. ranging from 800 to 1500 metres.

**middle ear** /– 'ɪə/, *n.* the section of the ear recessed into the temporal bone, lying between the inner ear and the eardrum and containing the three ossicles which join them; tympanum.

**middle eight** /– 'eɪt/, *n.* a group of eight bars in popular music, with a freely chosen chord progression, and usu. played between two twelve-bar patterns.

**Middle English** /mɪdl 'ɪŋglɪʃ/, *n.* the English language of the period approximately 1100-1450.

**Middle French** /– 'frɛntʃ/, *n.* the French language of the period approximately 1400-1600.

**middle game** /'mɪdl geɪm/, *n.* (in chess) that section between the opening and the endgame, characterised by the play of pieces in deployment, while the board is still relatively full.

**Middle Greek** /mɪdl 'grik/, *n.* →**Medieval Greek.**

**Middle High German,** *n.* the High German language from approximately 1100-1450.

**middle-income** /mɪdl-'ɪŋkʌm/, *adj.* earning an average income.

**Middle Irish** /mɪdl 'aɪrɪʃ/, *n.* the Irish language from approximately 900-1200.

**Middle Low German,** *n.* Low German of the period approximately 1100-1500.

**middleman** /'mɪdlmæn/, *n., pl.* **-men. 1.** a trader who makes a profit by buying from producers and selling to retailers or consumers. Also, **middle man. 2.** one who acts as an intermediary between others.

**middlemost** /'mɪdlmoʊst/, *adj.* →**midmost.**

**middle name** /'mɪdl neɪm/, *n.* the name between the Christian or first name and the surname.

**middle-of-the-road** /mɪdl-əv-ðə-'roʊd/, *adj.* **1.** between extremes; moderate. **2.** middlebrow; non-committal. **3.** Also, **M.O.R.** of or pertaining to light or sentimental music, written to appeal to a wide audience. – **middle-of-the-roader,** *n.*

**middle term** /mɪdl 'tɜm/, *n.* (in logic) that term of a syllogism which appears twice in the premises, but is eliminated from the conclusion.

**middle watch** /– 'wɒtʃ/, *n. Naut.* the watch from midnight to 4 a.m.

**middleweight** /'mɪdlweɪt/, *n.* **1.** a boxer weighing between 71 and 75 kg (in the amateur ranks) or between 69.853 and 72.574 kg (in the professional ranks). **2.** a professional wrestler weighing between 76.204 and 78.925 kg.

**middling** /'mɪdlɪŋ/, *adj.* **1.** medium in size, quality, grade, rank, etc.; moderately large, good, etc. **2.** *Colloq.* in fairly good health. **3.** *Colloq.* mediocre; second-rate. **4. fair to middling,** *Colloq.* in average health or spirits; so-so. *–adv.* **5.** *Colloq.* moderately; fairly. *–n.* **6.** (*pl.*) any of various products or commodities of intermediate quality, grade, etc., as the coarser particles of ground wheat mingled with bran. – **middlingly,** *adv.*

**middy** /'mɪdi/, *n., pl.* **-dies. 1.** a medium size glass, primarily used for serving beer; pot. **2.** *Colloq.* →**midshipman.**

**midge** /mɪdʒ/, *n.* **1.** any of various small dipterous insects esp. the non-biting Chironomidae, or the biting midges of the family Ceratopogonidae. See **gnat. 2.** *Colloq.* a small or diminutive person. [ME *mydge,* OE *mycg,* c. G *Mücke*]

**midge orchid** /'– ɔkəd/, *n.* any of a group of small flowered species of the terrestrial orchid genus *Prasophyllum,* of Australia and New Zealand.

**midget** /'mɪdʒət/, *n.* **1.** a very small person. **2.** something very small of its kind. [MIDGE + -ET]

**midgut** /'mɪdgʌt/, *n.* the middle part of the alimentary canal.

**midi** /'mɪdi/, *adj.* **1.** of or pertaining to a dress, skirt, or coat, with a hemline just below the knee. *–n.* **2.** such a dress, skirt, or coat.

**mid-iron** /'mɪd-aɪən/, *n.* (in golf) an iron (No. 2 iron) whose face has a medium loft, used for far approaches.

**midland** /'mɪdlənd/, *n.* **1.** the middle or interior part of a country. *–adj.* **2.** in or of the midland; inland.

**mid-leg** /mɪd-'lɛg/, *n.* **1.** the middle part of the leg. **2.** one of the second pair of legs of an insect. *–adv.* **3.** at the middle of the leg.

**mid loin** /mɪd 'lɔɪn/, *n.* a standard cut of lamb or pork which is the portion from the last rib to the top of the hip bone.

**midmorning** /mɪd'mɔnɪŋ/, *n.;* /'mɪdmɔnɪŋ/, *adj. –n.* **1.** the period between breakfast and lunch. **2.** a point about halfway through this period, as about 11 a.m. *–adj.* **3.** of, pertaining to or taken at or during midmorning.

**midmost** /'mɪdmoʊst/, *adj.* **1.** being in the very middle; middlemost; middle. **2.** at or near its middle point. *–adv.* **3.** in the midmost part; in the midst.

**midnight** /'mɪdnaɪt/, *n.* **1.** the middle of the night; 12 o'clock at night. *–adj.* **2.** of or pertaining to midnight. **3.** resembling midnight, as in darkness. **4. burn the midnight oil,** to study or work far into the night. – **midnightly,** *adj., adv.*

**midnight feast** /– 'fist/, *n.* a feast at midnight, esp. a secret feast in a school dormitory or children's bedroom.

**midnight sun** /– 'sʌn/, *n.* the sun visible at midnight in midsummer in arctic and antarctic regions.

**midnoon** /mɪd'nun/, *n.* midday; noon.

**mid-off** /mɪd-'ɒf/, *n.* **1.** (in cricket) a fielding position on the off side, near the bowler. **2.** a fielder in this position.

**mid-on** /mɪd-'ɒn/, *n.* **1.** (in cricket) a fielding position on the on side near the bowler. **2.** a fielder in this position.

**midpoint** /'mɪdpɔɪnt/, *n.* **1.** a point midway between the start and the end of a line. **2.** *Geom.* a point at the centre of any geometric figure. **3.** a point in time halfway between the start and the end as of an event, situation, etc.

**mid-range** /'mɪd-reɪndʒ/, *adj.* of or pertaining to a loudspeaker designed to reproduce sounds in the middle of the audible frequency range.

**midrash** /'mɪdræʃ/, *n., pl.* **midrashim** /mɪd'raʃɪm/, **midrashoth** /mɪd'raʃoʊθ/. *Hebrew Literature.* **1.** the traditional Jewish interpretation of Scripture, whether of its legal or its nonlegal portions. **2.** (*cap.*) a series of books, of various titles, containing the traditional Jewish interpretation of Scripture, arranged in the form of commentaries or homilies upon certain books of the Bible or upon selected passages from various books of the Bible. [Heb.: commentary]

**midrib** /'mɪdrɪb/, *n.* the central or middle vein of a leaf.

**midriff** /'mɪdrɪf/, *n.* **1.** the diaphragm (in the human body). **2.** the middle part of the body, between the chest and the waist. *–adj.* **3.** of a dress, blouse etc., which exposes this part of the body. [ME *mydryf,* OE *midhrif,* from *midd* mid + *hrif* belly]

**midship** /'mɪdʃɪp/, *adj.* in or belonging to the middle part of a ship.

**midshipman** /'mɪdʃɪpmən/, *n., pl.* **-men. 1.** a probationary rank held by naval cadets before qualifying as officers. **2.** (formerly) one of a class of boys or young men who had various minor duties and who formed the group from which officers were chosen.

**midships** /'mɪdʃɪps/, *adv.* →**amidships.**

**midst**[1] /mɪdst/, *n.* **1.** the position of anything surrounded by other things or parts, or occurring in the middle of a period of time, course of action, etc. **2.** the middle point, part, or stage. **3. in our (your, their) midst,** in the midst of us (you, them). [alteration of ME *middes* middle, by association with -EST, superl. suffix]

**midst**[2] /mɪdst/, *prep. Poetic.* →**amid.**

**midstream** /mɪd'strim/, *n., adv.;* /'mɪdstrim/, *adj. –n.* **1.** the middle of the stream. **2. in midstream,** *Colloq.* in the middle; at a critical point. *–adv.* **3.** in the middle of the stream: *we canoed midstream. –adj.* **4.** of or pertaining to the middle of the stream.

**midsummer** /mɪd'sʌmə/, *n.;* /'mɪdsʌmə/, *adj. –n.* **1.** the middle of summer. *–adj.* **2.** of, pertaining to, or occurring in the middle of summer: *a midsummer barbecue.*

**midsummer disease** /– də'ziz/, *n. Colloq.* →**amoebic meningitis.**

**midsummer madness** /– 'mædnəs/, *n. Colloq.* a temporary lapse into folly or foolishness, esp. during the summer.

**mid-Victorian** /'mɪd-vɪktɔriən, mɪd-vɪk'tɔriən/, *adj.*; /mɪd-vɪk'tɔriən/, *n.* –*adj.* **1.** of, pertaining to, or characteristic of the middle portion of the reign of Queen Victoria (reigned 1837-1901) in England: *mid-Victorian writers or ideas.* –*n.* **2.** a person, as a writer, belonging to the mid-Victorian time. **3.** a person of mid-Victorian ideas, tastes, etc.

**midway** /mɪd'weɪ/, *adv.*; /'mɪdweɪ/, *adj.*, *n.* –*adv.* **1.** to the middle of the way or distance; halfway. –*adj.* **2.** in the middle. –*n.* **3.** *Obs.* a place or part situated midway. **4.** *U.S.* a place for sideshows and other amusements at any fair or the like. [ME *mydwaye,* OE *midweg*]

**midweek** /mɪd'wik/, *n.*; /'mɪdwik/, *adj.* –*n.* **1.** the middle of the week. –*adj.* **2.** occurring in the middle of the week.

**midweekly** /'mɪdwikli/, *adj.*; /mɪd'wikli/, *adv.* –*adj.* **1.** midweek. –*adv.* **2.** in the middle of the week.

**mid wicket** /mɪd 'wɪkət/, *n.* **1.** (in cricket) an on-side fielding position between square leg and mid-on. **2.** a fielder in this position.

**midwife** /'mɪdwaɪf/, *n.*, *pl.* **-wives** /-waɪvz/. a woman who assists women in childbirth. [ME, from *mid* with, adv. (OE *mid,* c. G *mit*) + WIFE]

**midwifery** /'mɪdwɪfəri/, *n.* the art or practice of assisting women in childbirth.

**midwinter** /mɪd'wɪntə/, *n.*; /'mɪdwɪntə/, *adj.* –*n.* **1.** the middle of winter. –*adj.* **2.** occurring in the middle of winter.

**midyear** /mɪd'jɪə/, *n.*; /'mɪdjɪə/, *adj.* –*n.* **1.** the middle of the year. –*adj.* **2.** pertaining to or occurring in midyear.

**mien** /min/, *n.* air, bearing, or aspect, as showing character, feeling, etc.: *a man of noble mien.* [*demean,* v., influenced by F *mine* aspect, from Breton *min* beak]

**miersite** /'maɪəsaɪt/, *n.* an iodide of silver and copper, first found as yellow isometric crystals, at Broken Hill in New South Wales. [named after Sir Henry Alexander *Miers,* 1858-1942, English mineralogist]

**miff** /mɪf/, *n. Colloq.* **1.** petulant displeasure; a petty quarrel. –*v.t. Colloq.* **2.** to give offence to; offend. –*v.i.* **3.** (of plants) to die or wither.

**miffed** /mɪft/, *adj. Colloq.* annoyed; displeased.

**miffy** /'mɪfi/, *adj.* **1.** (of certain plants) difficult to cultivate except under ideal conditions. **2.** *Colloq.* extremely sensitive; easily offended.

**might**[1] /maɪt/, *v.* past tense of **may.** [ME; OE *mihte*]

**might**[2] /maɪt/, *n.* **1.** power to do or accomplish; ability. **2.** effective power or force of any kind. **3.** superior power: *the doctrine that might makes right.* **4. with might and main,** with utmost strength, vigour, force, or effort. [ME *myghte,* OE *miht, meaht,* c. G *Macht*]

**mightily** /'maɪtəli/, *adv.* **1.** in a mighty manner; powerfully; vigorously. **2.** to a great extent or degree; very much.

**mighty** /'maɪti/, *adj.*, **-tier, -tiest.** **1.** having, characterised by, or showing might or power: *mighty rulers.* **2.** of great size; huge: *a mighty oak.* **3.** *Colloq.* great in amount, extent, degree, or importance. –*adv.* **4.** *U.S. Colloq.* very: *to be mighty pleased.* – **mightiness,** *n.*

**mignon** /'mɪnjɒn, mɪn'jɒn/, *adj.* small and pretty; delicately pretty. [from F, from stem *mign-,* akin to MINION. Cf. Celt. *mīno* tender, soft]

**mignonette** /mɪnjə'nɛt/, *n.* **1.** a plant, *Reseda odorata,* common in gardens, having racemes of small, fragrant, greenish white flowers with prominent reddish yellow or brownish anthers. **2.** light green as of reseda plants. **3.** a perfume derived from the flowers of the mignonette. [F *mignonnette,* diminutive of *mignon* small, pretty]

**mignonette orchid** /– 'ɔkəd/, *n.* a terrestrial orchid, *Microtis alba,* endemic in the south-west part of Western Australia.

**mignonette vine** /'– vaɪn/, *n.* →**Madeira vine.**

**migraine** /'maɪgreɪn, 'migreɪn/, *n.* a paroxysmal headache often confined to one side of the head and usu. associated with nausea; hemicrania. [F. See MEGRIM]

**migrant** /'maɪgrənt/, *n.* **1.** one who migrates. **2.** an immigrant. **3.** an animal or bird which migrates. **4.** a plant whose distribution has changed or extended. –*adj.* **5.** of or pertaining to migration or migrants. [L *migrans,* ppr.]

**migrate** /maɪ'greɪt/, *v.i.*, **-grated, -grating.** **1.** to pass periodically from one region to another, as certain birds, fishes, and animals. [L *migrātus,* pp.] – **migrator,** *n.*

**migration** /maɪ'greɪʃən/, *n.* **1.** the action of migrating: *the right of migration.* **2.** a migratory movement: *preparations for the migration.* **3.** a number or body of persons or animals migrating together. **4.** *Chem.* a movement or change of place of atoms within a molecule. [L *migrātio*] – **migrational,** *adj.*

**migration of ions,** *n.* the movement of ions towards an electrode, during electrolysis.

**migratory** /maɪ'greɪtəri, 'maɪgrətri/, *adj.* **1.** migrating: *migratory species.* **2.** pertaining to a migration: *migratory movements of birds.* **3.** roving or nomad.

**mihrab** /'miræb, -rəb/, *n.* a niche in a mosque, indicating the direction of Mecca.

**mikado** /mə'kadoʊ/, *n.*, *pl.* **-dos.** (*oft. cap.*) (formerly) a title of the emperor of Japan. [Jap.: lit., exalted gate]

**mike**[1] /maɪk/, *Colloq.* –*n.* **1.** →**microphone.** –*v.t.* **2.** to place a microphone in or near for the purpose of recording or amplifying.

**mike**[2] /maɪk/, *n. Colloq.* a microgram, esp. of LSD.

**mikron** /'maɪkrɒn/, *n.*, *pl.* **-kra, -kras.** →**micron.**

**mil** /mɪl/, *n.* **1.** a millilitre (0.001 of a litre), or cubic centimetre. **2.** a unit of length equal to 0.001 of an inch, used in measuring the diameter of wires. **3.** *Mil.* unit of angle used in artillary equal to the angle subtended by an arc of 1/6400 of a circumference. [short for L *millēsimus* thousandth]

**mil.,** military.

**milady** /mə'leɪdi/, *n.*, *pl.* **-dies.** a Continental rendering of English *my lady,* used in speaking to or of an English noblewoman. Also, **miladi.**

**milage** /'maɪlɪdʒ/, *n.* →**mileage.**

**milanese** /mɪlə'niz/, *n.* a fine, light-weight, warp-knitted fabric usu. of silk, rayon or nylon used extensively in the manufacture of women's underwear, etc. [from *Milan,* a city in Italy]

**milch** /mɪltʃ/, *adj.* (of a cow, goat, or other animal) producing milk; kept for milk-production. [ME *milche;* akin to MILK]

**mild** /maɪld/, *adj.* **1.** amiably gentle or temperate in feeling or behaviour towards others. **2.** characterised by or showing such gentleness, as manners, speech, etc. **3.** not cold, severe, or extreme, as air, weather, etc. **4.** gentle or moderate in force or effect: *mild penalties.* **5.** softly shining, as light, etc. **6.** not sharp, pungent, or strong: *mild flavour.* **7.** not acute, as disease, etc. **8.** moderate in intensity, degree, or character: *mild regret.* **9.** easily worked, as soil, stone, wood, etc. **10.** *Obs.* kind or gracious. –*n.* **11.** a dark, full-flavoured beer brewed from malt which has been heated on the kiln to a higher temperature than malt for pale ale, which gives it a characteristic burnt flavour. [ME and OE, c. G *mild*] – **mildly,** *adv.* – **mildness,** *n.*

**mild ale** /– 'eɪl/, *n. Chiefly Brit.* →**mild** (def. 11).

**milden** /'maɪldən/, *v.i.* **1.** to become mild or milder. –*v.t.* **2.** to cause to become mild.

**mildew** /'mɪldju/, *n.* **1.** a plant disease usu. characterised by a whitish coating or a discolouration on the surface, caused by any of various parasitic fungi. **2.** any of these fungi. **3.** similar coating or discolouration, due to fungi, on cotton and linen fabrics, paper, leather, etc., when exposed to moisture. –*v.t.* **4.** to affect with mildew. –*v.i.* **5.** to become affected with mildew. [ME; OE *mildēaw, meledēaw,* lit., honeydew] – **mildewy,** *adj.*

**mild steel** /maɪld 'stil/, *n.* a tough ductile form of steel containing between 0.12 and 0.25 per cent of carbon.

**mile** /maɪl/, *n.* **1.** a unit of measurement of length in the imperial system, equal to 5280 feet (1609.34 m). **2. nautical, international nautical** or **sea mile,** a unit of measurement of length used in marine or aeronautical navigation, equal to 1852 m. The Admiralty nautical mile, used until recently, is 6080 feet (approx 1853.2 m). **3.** any of various other lengths ascribed to the mile in different periods and in different countries. **4.** (*oft. pl.*) a large distance or quantity. [ME *myle,* OE *mīl,* from L *mīlia* (*passuum*) a thousand (paces)]

**mileage** /'maɪlɪdʒ/, *n.* **1.** the total length or distance expressed in miles. **2.** the aggregate number of miles travelled in a given time. **3.** an allowance for travelling expenses, at a specified rate per mile. **4.** the number of miles travelled by a motor vehicle on a specified quantity of fuel. **5. get mileage out of,** *Colloq.* to gain advantage from. Also, **milage.**

**mileometer** /maɪl'ɒmətə/, *n.* a device used for measuring the distance travelled esp. in miles as by a motor vehicle. Cf. **odometer.**

**mile post** /'maɪl poust/, *n.* **1.** a post functioning as a milestone. **2.** *Racing.* a post marking a point one mile from the finish.

**miler** /'maɪlə/, *n.* a participant in a race over one mile, or an athlete or racehorse, specialising in such races.

**milestone** /'maɪlstoun/, *n.* **1.** a stone set up to mark the distance to or from a town, as along a highway or other line of travel. **2.** a birthday or some event regarded as marking a significant point in one's life or career.

**milfoil** /'mɪlfɔɪl/, *n.* **1.** a herbaceous plant, *Achillea millefolium,* with finely divided leaves and small white to red flowers, sometimes used in medicine as a tonic and astringent; yarrow. **2.** any of a number of species of *Myriophyllum,* esp. water milfoil, *M. brasiliense.* [ME, from OF, from L *mīlifolium, millefolium,* lit., thousand leaves]

**miliaria** /mɪli'ɛəriə/, *n.* an inflammatory disease of the skin, located about the sweat glands, marked by the formation of vesicles or papules resembling millet seeds; miliary fever. [NL, properly fem. of L *miliārius* MILIARY]

**miliary** /'mɪljəri/, *adj.* **1.** resembling a millet seed or seeds. **2.** *Pathol.* accompanied by spots (papules) or vesicles resembling millet seeds: *miliary fever.* [L *miliārius* of millet]

**miliary tuberculosis** /– təbɜkju'lousəs/, *n.* tuberculosis in which the bacilli are spread by the blood from one point of infection, producing small tubercles in other parts of the body.

**milieu** /mi'ljɜ/, *n.* medium or environment. [F, from *mi* (from L *medius*) middle + *lieu* (from L *locus*) place]

**milit.,** military.

**militant** /'mɪlətənt/, *adj.* **1.** combative; aggressive: *a militant reformer.* **2.** engaged in warfare; warring. *–n.* **3.** one engaged in warfare or strife. **4.** a militant person. [ME, from L *mīlitans,* ppr., serving as a soldier] **– militancy,** *n.* **– militantly,** *adv.*

**militarise** /'mɪlətəraɪz/, *v.t.,* **-rised, -rising. 1.** to make military. **2.** to imbue with militarism. Also, **militarize. – militarisation** /mɪlətəraɪ'zeɪʃən/, *n.*

**militarism** /'mɪlətərɪzəm/, *n.* **1.** military spirit or policy. **2.** the principle of keeping a large military establishment. **3.** the tendency to regard military efficiency as the supreme ideal of the state, and to subordinate all other interests to those of the military.

**militarist** /'mɪlətərəst/, *n.* **1.** one imbued with militarism. **2.** one skilled in the art of war. **– militaristic** /mɪlətə'rɪstɪk/, *adj.* **– militaristically** /mɪlətə'rɪstɪkli/, *adv.*

**military** /'mɪlətri, -təri/, *adj.* **1.** of or pertaining to the army, armed forces, affairs of war, or a state of war. **2.** of or pertaining to soldiers. **3.** befitting a soldier. **4.** following the life of a soldier. **5.** having the characteristics of a soldier; soldierly. *–n.* **6.** soldiers generally; the armed forces. [L *mīlitāris*] **– militarily,** *adv.*

**military fern** /'– fɜn/, *n.* →**artillery-plant.**

**military law** /– 'lɔ/, *n.* rules and regulations applicable to persons in the armed forces.

**military police** /– pə'lis/, *n.* soldiers who perform police duties within the army. *Abbrev.:* M.P.

**militate** /'mɪləteɪt/, *v.i.,* **-tated, -tating.** to operate (*against* or *in favour of*); have effect or influence: *every fact militated against his argument.* [L *mīlitātus,* pp. of *mīlitāre* be a soldier] **– militation** /mɪlə'teɪʃən/, *n.*

**militia** /mə'lɪʃə/, *n.* **1.** a body of men enrolled for military service, called out periodically for drill and exercise but for actual service only in emergencies. **2.** a body of citizen soldiers as distinguished from professional soldiers. **3.** *U.S.* all able-bodied males who are or are eligible to become citizens, and are more than 18 and not more than 45 years of age. [L: military service, soldiery]

**militiaman** /mə'lɪʃəmən/, *n., pl.* **-men.** one serving in the militia.

**milium** /'mɪliəm/, *n., pl.* **milia** /'mɪliə/. a small white or yellowish nodule resembling a millet seed, produced in the skin by the retention of a sebaceous secretion. [L: millet]

**miljee** /'mɪldʒi/, *n.* a small tree, *Acacia oswaldii,* widely distributed in inland Australia.

**milk** /mɪlk/, *n.* **1.** an opaque white or bluish white liquid secreted by the mammary glands of female mammals, serving for the nourishment of their young, and, in the case of the cow and some other animals, used for food or as a source of dairy products. **2.** any liquid resembling this, as the liquid within a coconut, the juice or sap (latex) of certain plants, or various pharmaceutical preparations. **3. cry over spilt milk,** to lament something which cannot be changed. *–v.t.* **4.** to press or draw milk by hand or machine from the udder of (a cow or other animal). **5.** to draw venom from (a spider, snake, etc.). **6.** to extract (the sap) from certain plants. **7.** to extract (something) as if by milking; draw: *to milk applause from an audience.* **8.** to extract something from, as if by milking; to siphon: *to milk a car.* **9.** to drain strength, information, wealth, etc., from; exploit. **10. milk the till,** *Colloq.* to steal money from a cash register. *–v.i.* **11.** to yield milk, as a cow. **12.** to milk a cow or other animal. [ME; OE *milc, meolc,* c. G *Milch*]

**milk and honey,** *n.* **1.** abundance; plenty. **2.** luxury.

**milk-and-water** /mɪlk-n-'wɔtə/, *adj.* weak or insipid; wishy-washy.

**milk bar** /'mɪlk ba/, *n.* **1.** a shop, often with an open front, where milk drinks, ice-cream, sandwiches, etc., are sold. **2. milk bar cowboy,** *Colloq.* a bikie who frequents a milk bar meeting place.

**milk board** /'– bɔd/, *n.* a government authority which supervises the orderly marketing of milk.

**milk bread** /'– brɛd/, *n.* →**milk loaf.**

**milk-bush** /'mɪlk-bʊʃ/, *n.* any of various succulent shrubs or herbs which have a milky latex, esp. a euphorbia.

**milk can** /'mɪlk kæn/, *n.* a large container for holding milk for transportation.

**milk-carton** /'mɪlk-katən/, *n.* a waxed cardboard box in which milk is packaged and sold.

**milk chocolate** /mɪlk 'tʃɒklət/, *n.* eating chocolate that has been made with milk.

**milk coffee** /– 'kɒfi/, *n.* coffee made with hot milk rather than water.

**milker** /'mɪlkə/, *n.* **1.** one who milks. **2.** milking machine. **3.** a cow or other animal that gives milk.

**milk fever** /'– fivə/, *n.* →**hypocalcaemia.**

**milkfish** /'mɪlkfɪʃ/, *n., pl.* **-fishes,** (*esp. collectively*) **-fish.** a large, silvery, food fish, *Chanos chanos,* widely distributed in warmer waters of the Indian and Pacific Oceans and extensively cultivated in south-east Asia.

**milk float** /'mɪlk flout/, *n.* →**float** (def. 25).

**milk-ice** /mɪlk-'aɪs/, *n.* a milk-flavoured iceblock on a stick.

**milkie** /'mɪlki/, *n. N.Z. Colloq.* →**milkman.**

**milking machine** /'mɪlkɪŋ məʃin/, *n.* an apparatus for milking cows.

**milking stool** /'– stul/, *n.* a low, three-legged stool with a seat in the shape of a half-circle or three-quarter circle.

**milk leg** /'mɪlk lɛg/, *n. Obs.* a painful swelling of the leg, due to thrombosis of the large veins, occurring most frequently in connection with parturition. Also, **white leg.**

**milk loaf** /'– louf/, *n.* a loaf of white bread made with a specified minimum percentage by weight of whole milk solids.

**milkmaid** /'mɪlkmeɪd/, *n.* **1.** a woman who milks cows or is employed in a dairy. **2.** (*pl.*) *Bot.* either of two species of the genus *Burchardia,* family Liliaceae, native to Australia.

**milkman** /'mɪlkmən/, *n., pl.* **-men.** a man who sells or delivers milk.

**milko** /'mɪlkou/, *n. Colloq.* →**milkman.**

**milk of magnesia,** *n.* a liquid suspension of magnesium hydroxide, $Mg(OH)_2$, used medicinally as an antacid or laxative.

**milk run** /'mɪlk rʌn/, *n.* **1.** the route over which a milkman delivers milk to houses, etc. **2.** *Airforce Colloq.* a routine or uneventful flight in an aeroplane, esp. if regular. **3.** a routine trip taken in turn by each one in a group of mothers to take their children to and from school.

**milkshake** /'mɪlkʃeɪk/, *n.* a frothy drink made of milk, flavouring, and sometimes ice-cream, shaken together. Also, **milk shake.**

**milksop** /ˈmɪlksɒp/, *n.* **1.** a dish of bread, etc., soaked in milk, as given to children and invalids. **2.** an effeminate man or youth. – **milksopism,** *n.*

**milk sugar** /ˈmɪlk ʃʊgə/, *n.* →**lactose.**

**milk thistle** /ˈ– θɪsəl/, *n.* **1.** an annual or biennial herb with spiny leaves and reddish purple capitula, *Silybum marianum,* widespread in temperate grasslands and waste places. **2.** any of several species of the genus *Sonchus,* with yellow flower heads and containing a milky juice, as *S. oleraceus,* a widespread weed of cultivated land in temperate regions.

**milk tooth** /ˈ– tuθ/, *n.* one of the temporary teeth of a mammal which are replaced by the permanent teeth.

**milk tree** /ˈ– tri/, *n.* a tree, *Paratrophis microphylla,* with a milky sap, found in lowland forests in New Zealand.

**milk vetch** /ˈ– vɛtʃ/, *n.* any small herb of the northern hemisphere genus *Astragalus,* esp. *A. hamosus,* naturalised in Australian pastures.

**milkweed** /ˈmɪlkwid/, *n.* any of various plants with milky juice, as the widely distributed herbs or shrubs of the genus *Asclepias.*

**milk-white** /ˈmɪlk-waɪt/, *adj.* of a white or slightly blue-white colour, such as that of milk.

**milk-wood** /ˈmɪlk-wʊd/, *n.* **1.** any of various trees which have a milky latex, as milky pine. **2.** →**paperbark.**

**milkwort** /ˈmɪlkwɜt/, *n.* any of the herbs and shrubs constituting the genus *Polygala,* having (mostly) spikes or spikelike racemes of variously coloured flowers, formerly reputed to increase the secretion of milk.

**milky** /ˈmɪlki/, *adj.,* **-kier, -kiest.** **1.** resembling milk in colour or consistency. **2.** of a chalky white. **3.** giving a good supply of milk. **4.** filled with or yielding any substance resembling milk: *dandelions are milky weeds.* **5.** meek, tame, or spiritless. – **milkiness,** *n.*

**milky pine** /– ˈpaɪn/, *n.* a tall rainforest tree with soft whitish timber, *Alstonia scholaris,* which grows in north Queensland rainforests, in the Malay archipelago and in the Pacific Islands.

**Milky Way** /mɪlki ˈweɪ/, *n.* the faintly luminous band stretching across the heavens, composed of innumerable stars too faint for unassisted vision; the Galaxy. [translation of L *via lactea*]

**mill** /mɪl/, *n.* **1.** a building or establishment fitted with machinery, in which any of various mechanical operations or forms of manufacture is carried on, esp. the spinning or weaving of cotton or wool. **2.** a mechanical appliance or a building or establishment equipped with appliances for grinding corn into flour. **3.** a machine for grinding, crushing, pulverising, or extracting liquid from, any solid substance: *a coffee mill, a cider mill.* **4.** a steel roller for receiving and transferring an impressed design, as to a calico-printing cylinder or a banknote-printing plate. **5.** a machine which does its work by rotary motion, as one used by a lapidary for cutting and polishing precious stones. **6.** any of various other apparatuses for working materials into due form or performing other mechanical operations. **7.** any institution or machine that churns out mass produced goods: *college is a diploma mill.* **8. go through the mill,** to undergo a gruelling or difficult experience. **9. run of the mill,** conventional; commonplace. *–v.t.* **10.** to grind, work, treat, or shape in or with a mill. **11.** to finish the edge of (a coin, etc.) with a series of fine notches or transverse grooves. **12.** to beat or stir, as to a froth: *to mill chocolate.* *–v.i.* **13.** to move confusedly in a circle, as a herd of cattle (oft. fol. by *about*). [ME *mille, myln,* OE *mylen,* from LL *molīnum,* from L *mola* millstone, mill]

**mill.,** **1.** million. **2.** millions.

**millboard** /ˈmɪlbɔd/, *n.* a strong, thick pasteboard used to make book covers.

**milldam** /ˈmɪldæm/, *n.* a dam built in a stream to furnish a head of water for turning a millwheel.

**milled** /mɪld/, *adj.* **1.** having undergone the operations of a mill. **2.** (of the edge of a coin) serrated.

**millefiori** /mɪlifiˈɔri/, *n.* ornamental glass made by fusing coloured glass rods in a kiln. [It., lit., a thousand flowers]

**millenarian** /mɪləˈnɛəriən/, *adj.* **1.** of or pertaining to a thousand, esp. the thousand years of the prophesied millennium. *–n.* **2.** a believer in the millennium.

**millenary** /məˈlɛnəri/, *adj., n., pl.* **-ries.** *–adj.* **1.** consisting of or pertaining to a thousand, esp. a thousand years. **2.** pertaining to the millennium. *–n.* **3.** an aggregate of a thousand. **4.** millennium. **5.** millenarian. [LL *millēnārius,* of a thousand, from L *millēnī,* a thousand each, from *mīlle,* thousand]

**millennial** /məˈlɛniəl/, *adj.* **1.** of or pertaining to a millennium or the millennium. **2.** worthy or suggestive of the millennium. – **millennially,** *adv.*

**millennium** /məˈlɛniəm/, *n., pl.* **-niums, -nia** /-niə/. **1.** a period of a thousand years. **2.** a thousandth anniversary. **3.** the period of 'a thousand years' (a phrase variously interpreted) during which Christ is to reign on earth, according to the prophetic statement in Rev. 20:1-7. **4.** a period of general righteousness and happiness, esp. in the indefinite future. [NL, from L *mīlle* thousand + *-ennium* as in BIENNIUM]

**millepede** /ˈmɪləpid/, *n.* →**millipede.**

**millepore** /ˈmɪləpɔ/, *n.* a coralline hydrozoan of the genus *Millipora,* having a smooth calcareous surface with many perforations. [NL *millepora,* from L *mille* thousand + *porus* PORE[2]]

**miller** /ˈmɪlə/, *n.* **1.** one who keeps or operates a mill, esp. a corn mill. **2.** a milling machine. **3.** →**floury baker.** [ME; replacing OE *myle(n)weard* (see MILL[1], WARD)]

**millerite** /ˈmɪləraɪt/, *n.* a mineral, nickel sulphide (NiS), occurring in bronze-coloured slender crystals, a minor ore of nickel. [named after W. H. *Miller,* 1801-80, English crystallographer. See -ITE[1]]

**miller's thumb** /mɪləz ˈθʌm/, *n.* any small freshwater European fish of the family Cottidae; bullhead.

**millesimal** /məˈlɛsəməl/, *adj.* **1.** thousandth. **2.** consisting of thousandth parts. *–n.* **3.** a thousandth part. [L *millēsimus* thousandth + -AL[1]]

**millet** /ˈmɪlət/, *n.* **1.** a cereal grass, *Setaria italica,* extensively cultivated in Asia and in southern Europe for its small seed or grain (used as a food for man and fowls), but in the U.S. grown chiefly for fodder. **2.** any of various related or similar grasses, esp. those cultivated as grain plants or forage plants, as durra, and pearl millet. **3.** the grain of any of these grasses. [ME, from F, diminutive of *mil,* from L *milium*]

**milli-** /ˈmɪli-/, a prefix denoting $10^{-3}$ of a given unit, as in *milligram. Symbol:* m [L, combining form of *mille* a thousand]

**milliard** /ˈmɪliad, ˈmɪljad/, *n.* a thousand millions. [F, from L *mille* thousand]

**milliary** /ˈmɪljəri/, *adj.* **1.** pertaining to the ancient Roman mile of a thousand paces. **2.** marking a mile. [L *milliārius* containing a thousand]

**millibar** /ˈmɪliba/, *n.* a widely used unit of atmospheric pressure, equal to 0.001 bar or 100 pascals.

**millimetre of mercury,** *n.* a non-SI unit of measurement of pressure, approx. equal to 133.3 pascals. *Symbol:* mmHg

**milliner** /ˈmɪlənə/, *n.* one who makes or sells hats for women. [var. of obs. *Milaner* an inhabitant of Milan, a dealer in articles from Milan]

**millinery** /ˈmɪlənri, -nəri/, *n.* **1.** articles made or sold by milliners. **2.** the business or trade of a milliner.

**milling** /ˈmɪlɪŋ/, *n.* **1.** the act of subjecting something to the operation of a mill. **2.** the process of producing plane and formed surfaces. **3.** the process of finishing the edge of a coin, etc., with fine notches or transverse grooves. **4.** *Colloq.* →**thrashing** (def. 1).

**milling machine** /ˈ– məʃin/, *n.* a machine tool used to produce plane and formed surfaces.

**million** /ˈmɪljən/, *n.* **1.** a cardinal number, one thousand times one thousand, or $10^6$. **2.** the amount of a thousand thousand units of money, as pounds, dollars, or francs. **3.** a very great number. **4.** the multitude, or the mass of the common people (prec. by *the*). **5. gone a million,** ruined; lost; done for. **6. one in a million,** someone or something of great rarity or worth. *–adj.* **7.** amounting to one million in numbers. [ME *millioun,* from OF *million,* from It. *mil(l)ione,* augmentative of *mille* thousand, from L *mille*]

**millionaire** /mɪljəˈnɛə/, *n.* **1.** a person worth a million or millions, as of pounds, dollars, or francs. **2.** a very rich person. [F *millionnaire,* from *million* MILLION] – **millionairess,** *n. fem.*

**millionth** /ˈmɪljənθ/, *adj.* **1.** coming last in a series of a million. **2.** being one of a million equal parts. *–n.* **3.** the millionth member of a series; a millionth part, esp. of one (1/1 000 000).

**millipede** /ˈmɪləpid/, *n.* any one of the many arthropods belonging to the class Diplopoda. These are slow-moving, mostly herbivorous, myriapods having a cylindrical body of numerous segments, most of which bear two pairs of legs. Also, **millepede.** [L *millepeda* wood louse, from *mille* thousand + *pēs* foot]

**millisecond** /ˈmɪlisɛkənd/, *n.* one thousandth of a second.

**millpond** /ˈmɪlpɒnd/, *n.* **1.** a pond for supplying water to drive a millwheel. **2.** an area of very calm water.

**millrace** /ˈmɪlreɪs/, *n.* **1.** the channel in which the current of water driving a millwheel flows to the mill. **2.** the current itself.

**mill-run** /ˈmɪl-rʌn/, *adj.* **1.** not specially prepared; unsorted as to quality; taken from production. **2.** →**run-of-the-mill.**

**millrun** /ˈmɪlrʌn/, *n.* **1.** →**millrace.** **2.** a test of the mineral content or quality of a rock or ore consisting of the actual milling of a sample. **3.** the mineral so obtained.

**Mills bomb** /ˈmɪlz bɒm/, *n.* a type of high-explosive grenade weighing about 700 grams. Also, **Mills grenade.** [named after the inventor, Sir William *Mills,* 1856-1932]

**millstone** /ˈmɪlstoʊn/, *n.* **1.** either of a pair of circular stones between which grain or other substance is ground, as in a mill. **2.** something that grinds or crushes. **3.** a heavy burden, esp. in the phrase *a millstone around one's neck* (in allusion to Matt. 18:6).

**millstream** /ˈmɪlstrim/, *n.* the stream in a millrace.

**millwheel** /ˈmɪlwil/, *n.* a wheel, esp. a waterwheel, to drive a mill.

**millwork** /ˈmɪlwɜk/, *n.* **1.** ready-made carpentry work from a mill. **2.** work done in a mill.

**millwright** /ˈmɪlraɪt/, *n.* one who designs, builds, or sets up mills or mill machinery.

**milo** /ˈmaɪloʊ/, *n., pl.* **-los.** any of various forms of *Sorghum* grown for their grain. [from a Bantu language of Lesotho]

**milord** /məˈlɔd/, *n.* (a Continental rendering of English *my lord,* used as a term of address.).

**milquetoast** /ˈmɪlktoʊst/, *n. U.S.* a very timid person. [named after Caspar *Milquetoast,* a comic-strip character]

**milt** /mɪlt/, *n.* **1.** the secretion of the male generative organs of fishes. **2.** the organs themselves. **3.** →**melt** (def. 15). *–v.t.* **4.** to extract the eggs or sperm from (a fish) for artificial spawning. [ME and OE *milte,* c. G *Milz,* etc.; akin to MELT]

**milter** /ˈmɪltə/, *n.* a male fish in breeding time.

**Miltonic** /mɪlˈtɒnɪk/, *adj.* of or pertaining to the English poet Milton, 1608-74, or resembling his majestic style. Also, **Miltonian** /mɪlˈtoʊniən/.

**mime** /maɪm/, *n., v.,* **mimed, miming.** *–n.* **1.** the art or technique of expressing emotion, character, action, etc., by mute gestures and bodily movements. **2.** a play or entertainment in which the performers express themselves by such gestures and movements. **3.** a comedian or clown, esp. one who entertains by mute gesture, facial expression, bodily movement, etc. **4.** a player in an ancient Greek or Roman kind of farce which depended for effect largely upon ludicrous actions and gestures. **5.** such a farce. **6.** the dialogue for such a player. *–v.t.* **7.** →**mimic.** *–v.i.* **8.** to play a part by mimicry, esp. without words. [L *mīmus,* from Gk *mîmos*] – **mimer,** *n.*

**mimeograph** /ˈmɪmiəgræf, -graf/, *n.* **1.** a stencil device for duplicating letters, drawings, etc. *–v.t.* **2.** to make copies of, using a mimeograph. [*mimeo-* (representing Gk *mīméomai* I imitate; cf. MIME) + -GRAPH]

**mimesis** /məˈmisəs/, *n.* **1.** *Rhet.* imitation or reproduction of the supposed words of another, as in order to represent his character. **2.** (in the arts) the imaginative representation of the actions, motives, or natures of men or of their environments. **3.** *Biol.* →**imitation** (def. 3). **4.** *Zool.* →**mimicry** (def. 2). **5.** *Pathol.* the imitation of one disease by another; hysterical simulation. [NL, from Gk: imitation]

**mimetic** /məˈmɛtɪk/, *adj.* **1.** characterised by, exhibiting, or of the nature of mimicry or mimesis: *mimetic gestures.* **2.** mimic or make-believe. [Gk *mīmētikós*] – **mimetically,** *adv.*

**mimetic diagram** /– ˈdaɪəgræm/, *n.* an animated diagram indicating by coloured lights, recorders, and other devices, the state of a large industrial process or other complicated operation.

**mimetite** /ˈmɪmətaɪt, ˈmaɪmə-/, *n.* a mineral, lead chloroarsenate, $Pb_5As_3O_{12}Cl$, occurring in yellow to brown prismatic crystals or globular masses; a minor ore of lead. [G *Mimetit,* from Gk *mīmētḗs* imitator + *-it* -ITE[1]]

**mimic** /ˈmɪmɪk/, *v.,* **-icked, -icking,** *n., adj.* *–v.t.* **1.** to imitate or copy in action, speech, etc., often playfully or derisively. **2.** to imitate unintelligently or servilely; ape. **3.** (of things) to be an imitation of; simulate. *–n.* **4.** one apt at imitating or mimicking the characteristic voice or gesture of others. **5.** one who or that which imitates or mimics; an imitator or imitation. **6.** *Obs.* →**mime** (def. 3). *–adj.* **7.** being merely an imitation or reproduction of the true thing, often on a smaller scale: *a mimic battle.* **8.** apt at or given to imitating; imitative. [L *mīmicus,* from Gk *mīmikós* belonging to mimes]

**mimicry** /ˈmɪməkri/, *n., pl.* **-ries.** **1.** the act, practice, or art of mimicking. **2.** *Zool.* the close external resemblance, as if from imitation or simulation, of an animal to some different animal or to surrounding objects, esp. as serving for protection or concealment. **3.** an instance, performance, or result of mimicking.

**mimosa** /məˈmoʊsə/, *n.* **1.** any plant of the genus *Mimosa,* native to tropical or warm regions, and comprising trees, shrubs, and plants having usu. bipinnate and often sensitive leaves, and small flowers in globular heads or cylindrical spikes, esp. the sensitive plant, *M. pudica.* **2.** the species *Acacia farnesiana,* widespread in the Old World and used in perfumery. **3.** *Obs.* →**wattle.** [NL, from L *mīmūs* MIME; apparently so named from seeming mimicry of animal life in closing its leaves when touched]

**mimosaceous** /mɪməˈseɪʃəs, maɪmə-/, *adj.* belonging to the Mimosaceae, or mimosa family which includes the genus *Acacia,* wattle.

**min.,** **1.** minim. **2.** minute; minutes. **3.** *Music.* minor key.

**Min.,** **1.** Minister. **2.** Ministry.

**mina** /ˈmaɪnə/, *n.* →**myna.**

**minacious** /məˈneɪʃəs/, *adj.* menacing; threatening. [L *minăciae* threats + -OUS] – **minaciously,** *adv.* – **minaciousness, minacity** /məˈnæsəti/, *n.*

**minaret** /mɪnəˈrɛt, ˈmɪnərɛt/, *n.* a lofty, often slender, tower or turret attached to a Muslim mosque, surrounded by or furnished with one or more balconies, from which the muezzin calls the people to prayer. [Sp. *minarete,* from Ar. *manāra(t),* orig., lighthouse]

minaret

**minatory** /ˈmɪnətəri, -tri/, *adj.* menacing; threatening. Also, **minatorial** /mɪnəˈtɔriəl/. [LL *minātōrius,* from L *minārī* threaten] – **minatorily,** *adv.*

**minbar** /ˈmɪnba/, *n.* the high pulpit in a mosque.

**mince** /mɪns/, *v.,* **minced, mincing,** *n.* *–v.t.* **1.** to cut or chop into very small pieces. **2.** to subdivide minutely, as land, a subject, etc. **3.** to soften or moderate (one's words, etc.) to a milder form. **4.** to speak of (matters) in polite or euphemistic terms. **5.** to perform or utter with affected elegance. *–v.i.* **6.** to walk or move with short, affectedly dainty steps. **7.** to act, behave, or speak with affected elegance. *–n.* **8.** minced meat. [ME *mynce(n),* OF *mincier* make small, from L *minūtus* small]

**mincemeat** /ˈmɪnsmit/, *n.* **1.** a mixture composed of minced apples, suet (and sometimes meat), candied peel, etc., with raisins, currants, etc., for filling a pie (mince pie). **2.** minced meat. **3.** anything cut up very small. **4. make mincemeat of,** *Colloq.* **a.** assault and do harm to. **b.** to make a successful verbal attack on; berate.

**mince pie** /mɪns ˈpaɪ/, *n.* a covered tart filled with mincemeat (def. 1).

**mincer** /ˈmɪnsə/, *n.* one who or that which minces, esp. a machine for mincing meat.

**mincing** /ˈmɪnsɪŋ/, *adj.* **1.** affectedly nice or elegant, as gait, behaviour, air, speech, etc. **2.** walking, acting, or speaking in an affectedly nice or elegant manner. – **mincingly,** *adv.*

**mind** /maɪnd/, *n.* **1.** that which thinks, feels, and wills, exercises perception, judgment, reflection, etc., as in a human or other conscious being: *the processes of the mind.* **2.** *Psychol.* the psyche; the totality of conscious and unconscious activities of the organism. **3.** the intellect or understanding, as distinguished from the faculties of feeling and willing; the intelligence. **4.** a particular instance of the intellect or intelligence, as in a person. **5.** a person considered with reference to intellectual power: *the greatest minds of the time.* **6.** intellectual power or ability. **7.** reason, sanity, or sound mental condition: *to lose one's mind.* **8.** way of thinking and feeling, disposition, or temper: *many men, many minds.* **9.** opinion or sentiments: *to read someone's mind.* **10.** inclination or desire. **11.** purpose, intention, or will. **12.** psychic or spiritual being, as opposed to matter. **13.** a conscious or intelligent agency or being: *the doctrine of a mind pervading the universe.* **14.** remembrance or recollection: *to keep in mind.* **15.** *Rom. Cath. Ch.* commemoration (def. 2). **16.** Some special noun phrases are:

**a piece of one's mind, 1.** an uncomplimentary opinion. **2.** a reprimand or browbeating.

**have a good** (or **great**) **mind to,** to firmly intend to.

**have half a mind to,** to be almost decided to.

**make up one's mind,** to come to a decision.

**out of one's mind,** demented; delirious.

**presence of mind,** alacrity in controlled reaction when faced with danger or difficulty.

**put in mind,** to cause to remember; remind.

**to one's mind,** in one's opinion or judgment.

*–v.t.* **17.** to pay attention to, heed, or obey (a person, advice, instructions, etc.). **18.** to apply oneself or attend to: *to mind one's own business.* **19.** to look after; take care of; tend: *to mind the baby.* **20.** to be careful, cautious, or wary concerning: *mind what you say.* **21.** to care about or feel concern at. **22.** (*in negative and interrogative expressions*) to feel disturbed or inconvenienced by; object to: *you don't mind if I sit here?* **23.** to regard as concerning oneself or as mattering: *never mind what he does.* **24.** to perceive or notice. **25.** *Archaic.* to remember. **26.** *Archaic.* to remind. *–v.i.* **27.** (*chiefly in the imperative*) to take notice, observe, or understand: *mind you, I think he's wrong.* **28.** to obey. **29.** to be careful or wary. **30.** (*often in negative and interrogative expressions*) to care, feel concern, or object: *mind if I go?* **31.** to regard a thing as concerning oneself or as mattering: *never mind about them.* [ME *mind(e),* OE *gemynd* memory, thought, c. Goth. *gamunds* memory; akin to L *mens* mind]

**mind-blowing** /ˈmaɪnd-bloʊɪŋ/, *adj. Colloq.* exceptionally exciting, stimulating, euphoric: *a mind-blowing experience.* Also, **mind-bending.**

**mind-boggling** /ˈmaɪnd-bɒglɪŋ/, *adj.* overwhelming; stupendous.

**minded** /ˈmaɪndəd/, *adj.* **1.** having a certain kind of mind (usu. used in combination): *strong-minded.* **2.** inclined or disposed.

**minder** /ˈmaɪndə/, *n.* one whose occupation is to mind or tend something (usu. used in combination): *machine-minder, baby-minder.*

**mind-expanding** /ˈmaɪnd-əksˌpændɪŋ/, *adj.* increasing one's mental powers or awareness, as of a psychedelic drug.

**mindful** /ˈmaɪndfəl/, *adj.* attentive; careful (usu. fol. by *of*). – **mindfully,** *adv.* – **mindfulness,** *n.*

**mindless** /ˈmaɪndləs/, *adj.* **1.** without intelligence; senseless. **2.** unmindful, careless, or heedless. – **mindlessly,** *adv.* – **mindlessness,** *n.*

**mind-reading** /ˈmaɪnd-ridɪŋ/, *n.* reading or discerning of the thoughts in the minds of others, esp. by some apparently supernormal power. – **mind-reader,** *n.*

**mind's eye** /maɪndz ˈaɪ/, *n.* →**imagination.**

**mind-your-own-business** /maɪnd-jər-oʊn-ˈbɪznəs/, *n.* a small, much-cultivated urticaceous herb, *Helxine soleirolii,* native to Mediterranean islands; mother-of-thousands.

**mine**[1] /maɪn/, *pron.* **1.** possessive form of *I,* used predicatively or without a noun following. **2.** the person(s) or thing(s) belonging to me: *that book is mine, a friend of mine.* *–adj.* **3.** *Archaic.* my (used before a vowel or *h,* or after a noun): *mine eyes, lady mine.* [ME; OE *mīn,* poss. adj. and pron. of first person]

**mine**[2] /maɪn/, *n., v.,* **mined, mining.** *–n.* **1.** an excavation made in the earth for the purpose of getting out ores, precious stones, coal, etc. **2.** a place where such minerals may be obtained, either by excavation or by washing the soil. **3.** a deposit of such minerals, either under the ground or at its surface. **4.** an abounding source or store of anything: *this book is a mine of information.* **5.** a subterranean passage made to extend under an enemy's works or position, as for the purpose of securing access or of depositing explosives for blowing up the position. **6.** a device containing a large charge of explosive in a watertight casing floating on or moored beneath the surface of the water for the purpose of blowing up an enemy vessel which touches it or passes in close proximity to it. **7.** a similar device used on land; a landmine. *–v.i.* **8.** to dig in the earth for the purpose of extracting ores, coal, etc.; make a mine. **9.** to extract ores, etc., from mines. **10.** to make subterranean passages. **11.** to dig or lay mines, as in military operations. *–v.t.* **12.** to dig in (earth, etc.) in order to obtain ores, coal, etc. **13.** to extract (ores, coal, etc.) from a mine. **14.** to make subterranean passages in or under; burrow. **15.** to make (passages, etc.) by digging or burrowing. **16.** to dig away or remove the foundations of. **17.** to attack, ruin, or destroy by secret or slow methods. **18.** to dig or lay military mines under. [ME, from OF, of Celtic orig.]

**minefield** /ˈmaɪnfild/, *n.* an area on land or water throughout which mines have been laid.

**mine-layer** /ˈmaɪn-leɪə/, *n.* a naval vessel with special equipment for laying mines in water.

**miner**[1] /ˈmaɪnə/, *n.* **1.** one who works in a mine, esp. a coalmine. **2.** *Stock Exchange.* a mining company, or the shares in that company. **3.** *Obs.* one who digs or lays military mines.

**miner**[2] /ˈmaɪnə/, *n.* any bird of the genus *Manorina,* of the honeyeater family Meliphagidae, with a yellow beak and yellow or yellow-brown legs, which lives in colonies, as the noisy miner or bellbird.

**mineral** /ˈmɪnərəl, ˈmɪnrəl/, *n.* **1.** a substance obtained by mining; ore. **2.** any of a class of substances occurring in nature, usu. comprising inorganic substances (as quartz, felspar, etc.) of definite chemical composition and definite crystal structure, but sometimes taken to include aggregations of these substances (more correctly called rocks) and also certain natural products of organic origin, as asphalt, coal, etc. **3.** a substance neither animal nor vegetable. **4.** (*usu. pl.*) mineral water. *–adj.* **5.** of the nature of a mineral; pertaining to minerals. **6.** impregnated with a mineral or minerals. **7.** neither animal nor vegetable; inorganic: *the mineral kingdom.* [late ME, from ML *minerālis,* from *minera* mine, from OF *miniere,* from *mine* MINE[2]]

**mineral.,** **1.** mineralogical. **2.** mineralogy.

**mineral block** /ˈmɪnərəl blɒk/, *n.* **1.** *Agric.* a block of salt with added minerals placed in the paddock for animals to lick. **2.** *Vet. Sci.* a calculus or stone formed in the bodies of animals which may block the function of a vital organ.

**mineral caoutchouc** /– ˈkaʊtʃʊk/, *n.* soft elastic brown solid bitumen, much like India-rubber in its physical properties; elaterite; elastic bitumen.

**mineralisation** /mɪnərəlaɪˈzeɪʃən, mɪnrəl-/, *n.* the presence of ore minerals in an area.

**mineralise** /ˈmɪnərəlaɪz, ˈmɪnrə-/, *v.,* **-lised, -lising.** *–v.t.* **1.** to convert into a mineral substance. **2.** to transform (a metal) into an ore. **3.** to impregnate or supply with mineral substances. *–v.i.* **4.** to collect and study mineral specimens, esp. of a particular region. Also, **mineralize.** – **mineraliser,** *n.*

**mineral jelly** /mɪnərəl ˈdʒɛli/, *n.* a gelatinous product made from petroleum, used to stabilise some explosives.

**mineralogist** /mɪnəˈrælədʒəst, -ˈrɒl-/, *n.* a specialist in mineralogy.

**mineralogy** /mɪnəˈrælədʒi, -ˈrɒl-/, *n.* the science of minerals. – **mineralogical** /mɪnərəˈlɒdʒɪkəl/, *adj.* – **mineralogically,** *adv.*

**mineral oil** /mɪnərəl ˈɔɪl/, *n.* any of a class of oils of mineral origin, as petroleum, consisting of mixtures of hydrocarbons, and used as illuminants, fuels, etc., and in medicine.

**mineral pitch** /– 'pɪtʃ/, *n.* →**asphalt** (bituminous substance).

**mineral sand** /'– sænd/, *n.* sand containing valuable minerals such as rutile, zircon, tin, gold, etc.

**mineral spring** /– 'sprɪŋ/, *n.* a spring of water which has in it a high proportion of naturally occurring mineral salts.

**mineral tar** /– 'ta/, *n.* bitumen of the consistency of tar; maltha.

**mineral water** /'– wɔtə/, *n.* **1.** water containing dissolved mineral salts or gases. **2.** carbonated water.

**mineral wax** /– 'wæks/, *n.* →**ozokerite.**

**mineral wool** /'– wʊl/, *n.* an insulating material consisting of woolly fibres made from melted slag.

**miner's right** /maɪnəz 'raɪt/, *n.* an official licence to dig for gold.

**minestrone** /mɪnə'stroʊni/, *n.* a soup containing vegetables, herbs, pasta, etc., in chicken or meat stock. [It., augmentative of *minestra* soup, from *minestrare,* from L *ministrāre* MINISTER, *v.*]

**minesweeper** /'maɪnswipə/, *n.* a vessel or ship used for dragging a body of water in order to remove enemy mines.

**minette** /mɪ'nɛt/, *n.* **1.** a lamprophyre comprised of biotite and orthoclase occurring in dykes associated with major intrusions. **2.** a phosphatic iron ore occurring in the Middle Jurassic of Lorraine and Luxembourg.

**mineworker** /'maɪnwɜkə/, *n.* →**miner.** (def. 1).

**Ming** /mɪŋ/, *adj.* denoting the objects, esp. a type of porcelain produced under the Ming dynasty which ruled China from 1368 to 1644.

**mingle** /'mɪŋgəl/, *v.,* **-gled, -gling.** *–v.i.* **1.** to become mixed, blended, or united. **2.** to associate or mix in company. **3.** to take part with others; participate. *–v.t.* **4.** to mix or combine; put together in a mixture; blend. **5.** to unite, join, or conjoin: *joy mingled with pain.* **6.** to associate in company. **7.** to form by mixing; compound; concoct. [ME *myngle, mengle,* frequentative of *menge(n)*; OE *mengan*] **– mingler,** *n.*

**mingy** /'mɪndʒi/, *adj. Colloq.* mean and stingy. [b. M(EAN[2]) + (ST)INGY[1]]

**mini** /'mɪni/, *Colloq. –n.* **1.** something small in size or dimension, as a skirt or motor vehicle. *–adj.* **2.** small; miniature.

**mini-,** a word element meaning 'small' or 'miniature', as in *miniskirt.* [abbrev. of MINIATURE]

**miniature** /'mɪnətʃə/, *n.* **1.** a representation or image of anything on a very small scale. **2.** greatly reduced or abridged form. **3.** a very small painting, esp. a portrait, on ivory, vellum, or the like. **4.** the art of executing such painting. **5.** an illumination, as in manuscripts. *–adj.* **6.** on a very small scale; reduced. [It. *miniatura,* from L *miniāre* rubricate]

**miniature camera** /– 'kæmrə/, *n.* a small camera using film of 35 mm width or less.

**miniaturise** /'mɪnətʃəraɪz/, *v.t.,* **-rised, -rising.** to reduce in size; to produce an exact working copy in reduced scale. Also, **miniaturize.** [MINIATUR(E) + -ISE[1]] **– miniaturisation** /mɪnətʃəraɪ'zeɪʃən/, *n.*

**mini-budget** /'mɪni-bʌdʒət/, *n.* a budget which seeks to implement government fiscal policies decided upon after the normal budget session.

**minibus** /'mɪnibʌs/, *n.* a motor vehicle for carrying between five and ten passengers.

**minify** /'mɪnəfaɪ/, *v.t.,* **-fied, -fying.** **1.** to make less. **2.** →**minimise.** [L *min(us)* less + -(I)FY]

**minigolf** /'mɪnigɒlf/, *n.* a form of golf played on a very small course with fancifully-contrived obstacles and hazards. [shortened form of *mini(ature) golf*]

**minikin** /'mɪnəkən/, *n.* **1.** a person or object that is delicate or diminutive. *–adj.* **2.** delicate; dainty; mincing. [MD *minnekijn,* diminutive of *minne* love. See -KIN]

**minim** /'mɪnəm/, *n.* **1.** the smallest unit of liquid measure in the imperial system, equal to 59.193 880 × $10^{-6}$ litres. **2.** *Music.* a note, formerly the shortest in use, but now equivalent in time value to one half of a semibreve. **3.** the least quantity or jot of anything. **4.** something very small or insignificant. **5.** a single downward stroke of the pen in handwriting. *–adj.* **6.** smallest; very small. [ME, from L *minimus* least, smallest, superl. of *minor* MINOR]

**minimal** /'mɪnəməl/, *adj.* **1.** pertaining to or being a minimum. **2.** least possible. **3.** smallest; very small. [L *minimus* least + -AL[1]]

**minimal art** /– 'at/, *n.* a style of abstract painting which rejects emotionalism in art and concentrates in a restrained, uninvolved manner on the visual effects of colour and shape.

**minimise** /'mɪnəmaɪz/, *v.t.,* **-mised, -mising.** **1.** to reduce to the smallest possible amount or degree. **2.** to represent at the lowest possible estimate; to belittle. Also, **minimize. – minimisation** /mɪnəmaɪ'zeɪʃən/, *n.* **– minimiser,** *n.*

**minimum** /'mɪnəməm/, *n., pl.* **-mums, -ma** /-mə/, *adj. –n.* **1.** the least quantity or amount possible, assignable, allowable, etc. **2.** the lowest amount, value, or degree attained or recorded (opposed to *maximum*). **3.** *Maths.* a value of a function at a certain point which is less than or equal to the value attained at nearby points. *–adj.* **4.** that is a minimum. **5.** least possible. **6.** lowest: *a minimum rate.* **7.** pertaining to a minimum or minimums. [L, neut. of *minimus.* See MINIM]

**minimum-security** /mɪnəməm-sə'kjurəti/, *adj.* **1.** of or pertaining to institutions in which minimum restrictions are placed on prisoners, as certain gaols, prison farms, etc. **2.** of or pertaining to procedures for protecting a public figure in which little more than routine measures are deemed necessary. Cf. **maximum-security.**

**minimum wage** /mɪnəməm 'weɪdʒ/, *n.* the lowest wage legally payable to any adult employee covered by a particular award or agreement.

**minimus** /'mɪnəməs/, *n.* **1.** a being that is the smallest or least significant. **2.** *Anat.* the little finger or little toe. *–adj.* **3.** *Brit.* youngest; in boys' schools, designating the youngest of three brothers.

**mining** /'maɪnɪŋ/, *n.* **1.** the action, process, or industry of extracting ores, etc., from mines. **2.** the action of laying explosive mines.

**minion** /'mɪnjən/, *n.* **1.** a servile or base favourite of a prince or any patron. **2.** any favourite. **3.** →**catamite.** *–adj.* **4.** dainty; elegant; trim; pretty. [F *mignon* MIGNON]

**minipill** /'mɪnipɪl/, *n.* a contraceptive pill of low dosage, containing only progesterone.

**miniskirt** /'mɪniskɜt/, *n.* a very short skirt.

**minister** /'mɪnəstə/, *n.* **1.** one authorised to conduct religious worship; a clergyman; a pastor. **2.** one authorised to administer sacraments, as at mass. **3.** one appointed by (or under the authority of) the sovereign or executive head of a government to some high office of state, esp. to that of head of an administrative department: *the Minister of Education.* **4.** a diplomatic representative accredited by one government to another ranking below an ambassador, esp. an envoy. **5.** one acting as the agent or instrument of another. *–v.t.* **6.** to administer or apply. **7.** *Archaic.* to furnish; supply. *–v.i.* **8.** to give service, care, or aid; attend, as to wants, necessities, etc. **9.** to contribute, as to comfort, happiness, etc. [L: servant; replacing ME *menistre,* from OF]

**ministerial** /mɪnəs'tɪəriəl/, *adj.* **1.** pertaining to the ministry of religion, or to a minister or clergyman. **2.** pertaining to a ministry or minister of state. **3.** pertaining to or invested with delegated executive authority. **4.** of ministry or service. **5.** instrumental. **– ministerially,** *adv.*

**minister plenipotentiary** /mɪnəstə ˌplɛnɪpoʊ'tɛnʃəri/, *n., pl.* **ministers plenipotentiary.** →**plenipotentiary.**

**minister resident** /– 'rɛzədənt/, *n., pl.* **ministers resident.** a diplomatic representative in a minor country, ranking below an ambassador.

**minister without portfolio,** *n., pl.* **ministers without portfolio.** *Brit.* a member of a ministry with no specific departmental responsibilities.

**ministrant** /'mɪnəstrənt/, *adj.* **1.** ministering. *–n.* **2.** one who ministers. [L *ministrans,* ppr.]

**ministration** /mɪnəs'treɪʃən/, *n.* **1.** the act of ministering care, aid, religious service, etc. **2.** an instance of it. **– ministrative** /'mɪnəstrətɪv/, *adj.*

**ministry** /'mɪnəstri/, *n., pl.* **-tries.** **1.** the service, functions, or profession of a minister of religion. **2.** the body or class of ministers of religion; the clergy. **3.** the service, function, or office of a minister of state. **4.** the policy-forming executive officials in a country taken collectively. **5.** any of the administrative departments of state in certain countries. **6.** the building which houses such a department. **7.** the term of office of a minister. **8.** the act of ministering; ministration; service. [ME *ministerie,* from L *ministerium* office, service]

**minitrack** /ˈmɪnitræk/, *n.* the procedure of tracking the orbit of an artificial satellite and of recording its signals by telemetry.

**minium** /ˈmɪniəm/, *n.* red lead, $Pb_3O_4$. [L: native cinnabar, red lead]

**mini-van** /ˈmɪni-væn/, *n.* a very small, fully enclosed truck for transporting goods, etc.

**miniver** /ˈmɪnəvə/, *n.* (in medieval times) a fur of white or spotted white and grey used for linings or trimmings. [ME *meniver,* OF *menu vair* small vair. See MENU, VAIR]

**mink** /mɪŋk/, *n., pl.* **minks,** (*esp. collectively*) **mink. 1.** a semi-aquatic weasel-like animal of the genus *Mustela,* esp. the North American *M. vison.* **2.** the valuable fur of this animal, brownish with lustrous outside hairs and thick, soft undercoat. [apparently from Sw. *mänk*]

mink

**Minkowski world** /mɪnˌkɒfski ˈwɜld/, *n.* a four-dimensional space in which the fourth coordinate is time and in which a single element is presented as a point. Also, **Minkowski universe.** [from Herman *Minkowski,* 1864-1909, German mathematician]

**min min** /ˈmɪn mɪn/, *n.* a will-o'-the-wisp, allegedly seen in outback areas. [Aboriginal]

**minnesinger** /ˈmɪnəsɪŋə/, *n.* one of a class of German lyric poets and singers of the 12th, 13th, and 14th centuries. [G: love singer]

**minnow** /ˈmɪnoʊ/, *n., pl.* **-nows,** (*esp. collectively*) **-now. 1.** a small European cyprinoid fish, *Phoxinus phoxinus.* **2.** any of various other small silvery fishes. **3.** *U.S.* any fish of the family Cyprinidae, mostly small but including some large species, as the carp. **4.** an unimportant, insignificant person or thing. [ME *men(a)we,* late OE *myne* (for *mynu*), c. OHG *munewa* kind of fish]

**Minoan** /məˈnoʊən/, *adj.* **1.** of or pertaining to the ancient advanced civilisation of Crete, dating (approximately) from 3000 to 1100 B.C. *–n.* **2.** an inhabitant of ancient Crete. [*Mino(s),* in Greek mythology the king of Crete, + -AN]

**minor** /ˈmaɪnə/, *adj.* **1.** lesser, as in size, extent, or importance, or being the lesser of two: *a minor share, minor faults.* **2.** under legal age. **3.** *Brit.* younger; junior; in boys' schools, denoting the younger of two brothers, the second of three, or the third of four. **4.** of or pertaining to the minority. **5.** *Logic.* less broad or extensive: **a. minor term,** (in a syllogism) the term that is the subject of the conclusion. **b. minor premise,** the premise that contains the minor term. **6.** *Music.* **a.** (of an interval) smaller by a semitone than the corresponding major interval. **b.** (of a chord) having a minor third between the root and the note next above it. **7.** *U.S.* denoting or pertaining to educational minors: *a minor subject.* *–n.* **8.** a person under legal age. **9.** one of inferior rank or importance in a specified class. **10.** *Music.* a minor interval, chord, scale, etc. **11.** *U.S.* **a.** a subject or a course of study pursued by a student, esp. a candidate for a degree, subordinately or supplementarily to a major or principal subject or course. **b.** a subject for which less credit than a major is granted in colleges or occasionally in high school. *–v.i.* **12.** *U.S.* to pursue a minor or subordinate subject or course of study (fol. by *in*). [L: less, smaller, inferior, younger, a compar. form; replacing ME *menour,* from OF]

**minor axis** /maɪnər ˈæksəs/, *n.* the axis of an ellipse perpendicular to the major axis. Cf. **major axis.**

**minority** /maɪˈnɒrəti, mə-/, *n., pl.* **-ties,** *adj.* *–n.* **1.** the smaller part or number; a number forming less than half the whole. **2.** a smaller party or group opposed to a majority, as in voting or other action. **3.** a group having in common ethnic, religious, or other ties different from those of the majority of the inhabitants of a country. **4.** the state or period of being a minor or under legal age. *–adj.* **5.** of or pertaining to a minority.

**minor key** /maɪnə ˈki/, *n.* a musical key based on a minor scale.

**minor order** /maɪnər ˈɔdə/, *n.* See **order** (def. 15).

**minor planet** /maɪnə ˈplænət/, *n.* →**asteroid.**

**minor scale** /– ˈskeɪl/, *n.* a musical scale whose third tone forms a minor third with the root.

**minor suit** /– ˈsut/, *n.* (in bridge) diamonds or clubs.

**minor third** /– ˈθɜd/, *n.* a musical interval of three semitones.

**mins,** minutes.

**minster** /ˈmɪnstə/, *n.* **1.** a church actually or originally connected with a monastic establishment. **2.** any large or important church, as a cathedral. [ME and OE *mynster,* c. G *Münster,* of doubtful orig. Cf. LL *monastērium* MONASTERY]

**minstrel** /ˈmɪnstrəl/, *n.* **1.** one of a class of medieval musicians who sang or recited to the accompaniment of instruments. **2.** *Poetic.* any musician, singer, or poet. **3.** one of a troupe of comedians, usu. white men made up as Negroes, presenting songs, jokes, etc. [ME *menestral, minstral,* from OF *menestrel,* orig., servant, from LL *ministeriālis* ministerial]

**minstrelsy** /ˈmɪnstrəlsi/, *n., pl.* **-sies. 1.** the art or practice of a minstrel. **2.** minstrels' songs, ballads, etc.: *a collection of Scottish minstrelsy.*

**mint**[1] /mɪnt/, *n.* **1.** any plant of the genus *Mentha,* comprising aromatic herbs with opposite leaves and small verticillate flowers, as spearmint, peppermint and horsemint. **2.** a soft or hard confection flavoured with peppermint or other similar flavouring. *–adj.* **3.** flavoured with or containing mint: *mint sauce.* [ME and OE *minte* (c. OHG *minza*), from L *ment(h)a,* from Gk *mínthē*]

**mint**[2] /mɪnt/, *n.* **1.** a place where money is coined by public authority. **2.** a vast amount, esp. of money. *–adj.* **3.** *Philately.* (of a stamp) as issued by the Post Office: *in mint condition.* *–v.t.* **4.** to coin (money). **5.** *Colloq.* to make or gain money rapidly. **6.** to make or fabricate as if by coining: *mint words.* [ME *mynt,* OE *mynet* coin (c. G *Münze*), from L *monēta* mint, MONEY] – **minter,** *n.*

**mintage** /ˈmɪntɪdʒ/, *n.* **1.** the act or process of minting. **2.** the product or result of minting; coinage. **3.** the charge for or cost of minting or coining. **4.** the output of a mint. **5.** a stamp or character impressed.

**mint-bush** /ˈmɪnt-bʊʃ/, *n.* any of several strongly scented, evergreen shrubs of the genus *Prostanthera,* native to Australia.

**mint julep** /mɪnt ˈdʒuləp/, *n.* *U.S.* a long drink made of bourbon whiskey, sugar, crushed ice, and sprigs of fresh mint.

**mintweed** /ˈmɪntwid/, *n.* a North American species of *Salvia, S. reflexa,* an annual plant with greyish-coloured leaves and blue flowers, which is poisonous to stock.

**minuend** /ˈmɪnjuɛnd/, *n.* (in mathematics) the number from which another (the subtrahend) is to be subtracted. [L *minuendus,* ger. of *minuere* make smaller]

**minuet** /mɪnjuˈɛt/, *n.* **1.** a slow stately dance of French origin. **2.** a piece of music for such a dance or in its rhythm. [F *menuet,* orig. adj., very small (with reference to the small steps taken in the dance), diminutive of *menu* small. See MENU]

**minus** /ˈmaɪnəs/, *prep.* **1.** less by the subtraction of; decreased by: *ten minus six.* **2.** lacking or without: *a book minus its titlepage.* *–adj.* **3.** involving or denoting subtraction: *the minus sign.* **4.** algebraically negative: *a minus quantity.* **5.** *Colloq.* lacking: *the profits were minus.* **6.** *Bot.* (in heterothallic fungi) designating, in the absence of morphological differentiation, one of the two strains or mycella which must unite in the sexual process. *–n.* **7.** →**minus sign. 8.** a minus quantity. **9.** a deficiency or loss. [L, adj., neut. of *minor* MINOR]

**minuscule** /ˈmɪnəskjul/, *adj.* **1.** small, as letters not capital or uncial. **2.** written in such letters (opposed to *majuscule*). **3.** very small; tiny. *–n.* **4.** a minuscule letter. **5.** a small cursive script developed in the 7th century from the uncial, which it afterwards superseded. [L *minusculus* rather small, diminutive of *minor* MINOR] – **minuscular** /məˈnʌskjulə/, adj.

**minus sign** /ˈmaɪnəs saɪn/, *n.* the symbol (−) denoting subtraction or a minus quantity.

**minute**[1] /ˈmɪnət/, *n., v.,* **-uted, -uting,** *adj.* *–n.* **1.** the sixtieth part of an hour; sixty seconds. **2.** an indefinitely short space of time: *wait a minute.* **3.** a point of time, an instant, or moment: *come here this minute!* **4.** a rough draft, as of a document. **5.** a written summary, note, or memorandum. **6.** (*pl.*) the official record of the proceedings at a meeting of a society, board, committee, council, or other body. **7.** *Geom., etc.* the sixtieth part of a degree, or sixty seconds, equivalent to 290.888 21 × $10^{-6}$ radians (often represented by the sign ′), as 12°10′ (twelve degrees and ten minutes). **8. up to the minute,** very modern; latest; most up to date. *–v.t.* **9.** to time exactly, as movements, speed, etc. **10.** to make a draft of (a document, etc.). **11.** to record (something) in a memorandum; note down. **12.** to enter in the minutes of a society or other body. *–adj.* **13.** prepared in a very short time: *minute steak.* [ME, from OF, from ML *minūta* small part or division, properly fem. of L *minūtus* MINUTE[2]]

**minute**[2] /maɪˈnjut/, *adj.*, **-nuter, -nutest. 1.** extremely small, as in size, amount, extent, or degree: *minute differences.* **2.** of very small scope or individual importance: *minute particulars of a case.* **3.** attentive to or concerned with even very small details or particulars: *a minute observer or report.* [ME, from L *minūtus,* pp., made smaller] – **minuteness,** *n.*

**minute gun** /ˈmɪnət gʌn/, *n.* (formerly) a gun fired at intervals of a minute, as in token of mourning or of distress.

**minute hand** /ˈ– hænd/, *n.* the hand that indicates the minutes on a clock or watch.

**minutely**[1] /ˈmɪnətli/, *adj.* **1.** occurring every minute. *–adv.* **2.** every minute; minute by minute. [MINUTE[1] + -LY]

**minutely**[2] /maɪˈnjutli/, *adv.* in a minute manner, form, or degree; in minute detail. [MINUTE[2] + -LY]

**minute man** /ˈmɪnət mæn/, *n.* **1.** *Cycling.* the competitor who finishes immediately before another in a time trial. **2.** *Colloq.* (*oft. derog.*) a man who, in intercourse, ejaculates after a very short time. **3.** *U.S.* **a.** one who was prepared to take up arms at a minute's notice during the American War of Independence. **b.** one who now shares a similar spirit and is willing to take instant action.

minute man (def. 3a) from drawing of minute man statue, Concord, Massachusetts

**minutia** /maɪˈnjuʃə, -tiə/, *n., pl.* **-tiae** /-ʃii, -tii/. (*usu. pl.*) a small or trivial detail; a trifling circumstance or matter. [L: smallness]

**minx** /mɪŋks/, *n.* a pert, impudent, or flirtatious girl. [? alternative of *minikins* MINIKIN + hypocoristic *-s*]

**Miocene** /ˈmaɪəsin/, *adj.* **1.** pertaining to a series of the Tertiary period or system. *–n.* **2.** a division of the Tertiary following Oligocene and preceding Pliocene. [*mio-* (representing Gk *meíōn* less) + -CENE]

**miosis** /maɪˈoʊsəs/, *n.* excessive contraction of the pupil of the eye, as the result of disease, drugs, or the like. Also, **myosis.** [NL, from Gk *mýein* close (the eyes) + *-ōsis* -OSIS]

**miotic** /maɪˈɒtɪk/, *adj.* **1.** pertaining to, producing, or suffering from miosis. *–n.* **2.** a miotic drug. Also, **myotic.**

**M.I.P.,** magnetic induced polarisation.

**mirabile dictu** /mɪˌrabəleɪ ˈdɪktu/, strange to say; marvellous to relate. [L]

**mirabilia** /mɪrəˈbɪliə/, *n.pl.* marvels; miracles. [L]

**miracidium** /maɪrəˈsɪdiəm/, *n., pl.* **-cidia** /-ˈsɪdiə/. the larva that hatches from the egg of a trematode worm or fluke. – **miracidial,** *adj.*

**miracle** /ˈmɪrəkəl/, *n.* **1.** an effect in the physical world which surpasses all known human or natural powers and is therefore ascribed to supernatural agency. **2.** a wonderful thing; a marvel. **3.** a wonderful or surpassing example of some quality. **4.** →**miracle play.** [ME, from OF, from L *mīrāculum*]

**miracle play** /ˈ– pleɪ/, *n.* a medieval dramatic form dealing with religious subjects such as biblical stories or saints' lives, usu. presented in a series or cycle by the craft guilds.

**miraculous** /məˈrækjələs/, *adj.* **1.** of the nature of a miracle; marvellous. **2.** performed by or involving a supernatural power: *a miraculous cure.* **3.** having power to work miracles or wonders: *miraculous drugs.* [ML *mīrāculōsus,* from L *mīrāculum* miracle] – **miraculously,** *adv.* – **miraculousness,** *n.*

**miraculous fruit** /ˈ– frut/, *n.* **1.** either of two tropical African fruits that have a lingering sweetish aftertaste. **2.** a plant yielding miraculous fruit.

**mirage** /məˈraʒ/, *n.* **1.** an optical illusion, due to atmospheric conditions, by which reflected images of distant objects are seen, often inverted. **2.** something illusory or unreal. [F, from (*se*) *mirer* look at (oneself) in a mirror, see reflected, from VL *mīrāre.* See MIRROR, ADMIRE]

**mire** /ˈmaɪə/, *n., v.,* **mired, miring.** *–n.* **1.** a piece of wet, swampy ground. **2.** ground of this kind; wet, slimy soil of some depth, or deep mud. *–v.t.* **3.** to plunge and fix in mire; cause to stick fast in mire. **4.** to involve in difficulties. **5.** to soil with mire or filth; bespatter with mire. *–v.i.* **6.** to sink in mire; stick in mud. [ME *myre,* from Scand.; cf. Icel. *mȳrr*]

**mirepoix** /mɪəˈpwa/, *n.* a mixture of carrots, celery, onion, etc., cut into large pieces, fried, and used as a bed on which to braise meat. [after the Duke of *Mirepoix,* 18th-century French diplomat]

**mirk** /mɜk/, *n., adj.* →**murk.**

**mirky** /ˈmɜki/, *adj.,* **-kier, -kiest.** →**murky.**

**mirliton** /ˈmɜlətən/, *n.* →**kazoo.** [F, ? imit.]

**miro** /ˈmɪəroʊ/, *n.* a coniferous timber tree, *Podocarpus ferrugineus,* native to New Zealand. [Maori]

**mirrnyong**[1] /ˈmɜnjɒŋ/, *n.* a mound of shells, ashes, etc., accumulated in a place used for cooking by the Aborigines; a kitchen-midden. [Aboriginal]

**mirrnyong**[2] /ˈmɜnjɒŋ/, *n.* →**murrnong.**

**mirror** /ˈmɪrə/, *n.* **1.** a reflecting surface, originally polished metal, now usu. glass with a metallic or amalgam backing; a looking glass. **2.** such a surface set into an ornamental frame, esp. one with a handle, used chiefly by women. **3.** any reflecting surface, as that of calm water. **4.** *Optics.* a surface (plane, concave, or convex) for reflecting rays of light; a speculum. **5.** something that gives a faithful reflection or true picture of something else. **6.** a pattern for imitation; exemplar. **7.** *Archaic.* a glass, crystal, or the like used by magicians, etc. **8. done with mirrors,** *Colloq.* done by sleight of hand or subterfuge. *–v.t.* **9.** to reflect in or as in a mirror, or as a mirror does. [ME *mirour,* from OF, from ML *mīrāre* wonder at, admire, replacing L *mīrārī*]

**mirror carp** /ˈ– kap/, *n.* a carp, characterised by its large, shiny scales.

**mirror exercise** /ˈ– ɛksəsaɪz/, *n.* an exercise in acting, miming or dancing which involves two people mirroring exactly each other's actions.

**mirror image** /– ˈɪmɪdʒ/, *n.* **1.** the image of an object as viewed in a mirror. **2.** an object reversed in such a way that it bears the same relationship to another object as a right hand bears to a left hand.

**mirror writing** /ˈ– raɪtɪŋ/, *n.* backward writing which forms a mirror image of normal writing.

**mirth** /mɜθ/, *n.* **1.** rejoicing; joyous gaiety; festive jollity. **2.** humorous amusement, as at something ludicrous, or laughter excited by it. [ME; OE *myr(g)th, myrigth,* from *myrige* MERRY. See -TH[1]]

**mirthful** /ˈmɜθfəl/, *adj.* **1.** full of mirth; joyous; jolly; laughingly gay or amused. **2.** affording mirth; amusing. – **mirthfully,** *adv.* – **mirthfulness,** *n.*

**mirthless** /ˈmɜθləs/, *adj.* without mirth; joyless; gloomy. – **mirthlessly,** *adv.* – **mirthlessness,** *n.*

**miry** /ˈmaɪri/, *adj.,* **-rier, -riest. 1.** of the nature of mire; swampy: *miry ground.* **2.** abounding in mire; muddy. **3.** covered or bespattered with mire. **4.** dirty; filthy. – **miriness,** *n.*

**mirza** /ˈmɜzə/, *n.* (in Persia) **1.** a royal prince (as a title, placed after the name). **2.** a title of honour for men (prefixed to the name). [Pers. apocopated var. of *mīrzād,* from *mīr* prince (from Ar. *amīr* EMIR) + *zād* born]

**mis-**[1], a prefix applied to various parts of speech, meaning 'ill', 'mistaken', 'wrong', or simply negating, as in *mistrial, misprint, mistrust.* [ME and OE *mis(s)-,* c. G *miss-* (see MISS[1], *v.*); often replacing ME *mes-,* from OF, from L *minus* (see MINUS)]

**mis-**[2], variant of **miso-**, before some vowels, as in **misanthrope.**

**misaddress** /mɪsəˈdrɛs/, *v.t.* to address wrongly or mistakenly.

**misadventure** /mɪsədˈvɛntʃə/, *n.* **1.** a piece of ill fortune; a mishap. **2.** ill fortune. **3.** *Law.* an accident, as where a man doing a lawful act, without any intention of hurt, kills another.

**misadvise** /mɪsəd'vaɪz/, *v.t.*, **-vised, -vising.** to advise wrongly.

**misalliance** /mɪsə'laɪəns/, *n.* an improper alliance or association, esp. in marriage; a mésalliance. [half adoption, half translation of F *mésalliance*]

**misally** /mɪsə'laɪ/, *v.t.*, **-lied, -lying.** to ally improperly or unsuitably.

**misandry** /mɪs'ændri/, *n.* the hatred of males. [Gk *mīsandría*]

**misanthrope** /'mɪzənθroʊp/, *n.* a hater of mankind. Also, **misanthropist** /mɪ'zænθrəpəst/. [Gk *misánthrōpos* hating mankind]

**misanthropic** /mɪzən'θrɒpɪk/, *adj.* **1.** of, pertaining to, or characteristic of a misanthrope. **2.** having the character of, or resembling, a misanthrope. Also, **misanthropical.** – **misanthropically,** *adv.*

**misanthropy** /mə'zænθrəpi/, *n.* hatred, dislike, or distrust of mankind.

**misapplied** /mɪsə'plaɪd/, *adj.* mistakenly applied; used wrongly.

**misapply** /mɪsə'plaɪ/, *v.t.*, **-plied, -plying.** to make a wrong application or use of. – **misapplication** /mɪsæplə'keɪʃən/, *n.*

**misapprehend** /mɪsæprə'hɛnd/, *v.t.* →**misunderstand.** – **misapprehensive,** *adj.* – **misapprehensively,** *adv.* – **misapprehensiveness,** *n.*

**misapprehension** /mɪsæprə'hɛnʃən/, *n.* misunderstanding.

**misappropriate** /mɪsə'proʊprieɪt/, *v.t.*, **-ated, -ating.** **1.** to put to a wrong use. **2.** to apply wrongfully or dishonestly to one's own use, as funds entrusted to one. – **misappropriation** /mɪsəˌproʊpri'eɪʃən/, *n.*

**misarrange** /mɪsə'reɪndʒ/, *v.t.*, **-ranged, -ranging.** to arrange wrongly. – **misarrangement,** *n.*

**misbecome** /mɪsbə'kʌm/, *v.t.*, **-came, -come, -coming.** to be unsuitable, unbecoming, or unfit for.

**misbegotten** /mɪsbə'gɒtn/, *adj.* unlawfully or irregularly begotten; illegitimate. Also, **misbegot.**

**misbehave** /mɪsbə'heɪv/, *v.i.*, **-haved, -having.** to behave badly. – **misbehaviour,** *n.*

**misbelief** /mɪsbə'lif/, *n.* **1.** erroneous belief; false opinion. **2.** erroneous or unorthodox religious belief.

**misbelieve** /mɪsbə'liv/, *v.*, **-lieved, -lieving.** *Obs.* –*v.i.* **1.** to believe wrongly; hold an erroneous belief. –*v.t.* **2.** to disbelieve; doubt. – **misbeliever,** *n.*

**misbestow** /mɪsbə'stoʊ/, *v.t.* to bestow improperly.

**misc.,** **1.** miscellaneous. **2.** miscellany.

**miscalculate** /mɪs'kælkjəleɪt/, *v.t., v.i.*, **-lated, -lating.** to calculate wrongly. – **miscalculation** /mɪskælkjə'leɪʃən/, *n.*

**miscall** /mɪs'kɔl/, *v.t.* **1.** to call by a wrong name. **2.** *Bridge, etc.* to call incorrectly.

**miscarriage** /mɪs'kærɪdʒ, 'mɪskærɪdʒ/, *n.* **1.** failure to attain the right or desired result: *a miscarriage of justice.* **2.** a transmission of goods not in accordance with the contract of shipment. **3.** failure of a letter, etc., to reach its destination. **4.** premature expulsion of a foetus from the uterus, esp. before it is viable.

**miscarry** /mɪs'kæri/, *v.i.*, **-ried, -rying.** **1.** to fail to attain the right end; be unsuccessful. **2.** to go astray or be lost in transit, as a letter. **3.** to have a miscarriage.

**miscast** /mɪs'kast/, *v.t.*, **-cast, -casting.** **1.** *Theat.* to allot an unsuitable part in a play to (an actor), or to select an unsuitable actor or unsuitable actors for (a part or play). **2.** *Metall.* to cast (metal) badly or into a faulty shape.

**miscegenation** /mɪ'sɛdʒəneɪʃən, mɪsɛdʒə'neɪʃən/, *n.* **1.** mixture of races by sexual union. **2.** interbreeding between different races. [L *miscē(re)* mix + L *gen(us)* race + -ATION] – **miscegenetic** /mɪsɛdʒə'nɛtɪk/, *adj.*

**miscellanea** /mɪsə'leɪniə/, *n.pl.* a miscellaneous collection, esp. of literary compositions. [L, neut. pl. of *miscellāneus* MISCELLANEOUS]

**miscellaneous** /mɪsə'leɪniəs/, *adj.* **1.** consisting of members or elements of different kinds: *miscellaneous volumes.* **2.** of mixed character. **3.** having various qualities or aspects; dealing with various subjects. [L *miscellāneus,* from *miscellus* mixed] – **miscellaneously,** *adv.* – **miscellaneousness,** *n.*

**miscellany** /mə'sɛləni/, *n.*, *pl.* **-nies.** **1.** a miscellaneous collection of literary compositions or pieces by several authors, dealing with various topics, assembled in a volume or book. **2.** (*oft. pl.*) a miscellaneous collection of articles or entries, as in a book. [Anglicised var. of MISCELLANEA]

**mischance** /mɪs'tʃæns, -'tʃans/, *n.* ill luck; a mishap or misfortune. [ME *meschance,* from OF *mescheance.* See MIS-[1], CHANCE]

**mischief** /'mɪstʃəf/, *n.* **1.** conduct such as to tease or cause playfully petty annoyance. **2.** a tendency or disposition to tease or vex. **3.** teasing, vexatious, or annoying action. **4.** harm or trouble, esp. as due to an agent or cause. **5.** an injury caused by a person or other agent, or an evil due to some cause. **6.** a cause or source of harm, evil, or annoyance. **7.** *Obs.* the devil. [ME *meschief,* from OF, from *meschever* succeed ill, from *mes-* MIS-[1] + *chever* come to an end, from *chef* head, end (see CHIEF)]

**mischief-maker** /'mɪstʃəf-meɪkə/, *n.* one who makes mischief; one who stirs up discord, as by tale-bearing. – **mischief-making,** *adj., n.*

**mischievous** /'mɪstʃəvəs/, *adj.* **1.** fond of mischief, as children. **2.** roguishly or archly teasing, as speeches, glances, etc. **3.** maliciously or playfully annoying, as persons, actions, etc. **4.** harmful or injurious. – **mischievously,** *adv.* – **mischievousness,** *n.*

**mischmetal** /'mɪʃmɛtl/, *n.* an alloy of cerium with small amounts of other rare-earth metals; used as a flint in automatic lighters. [G *Mischmetall,* equivalent to *misch(en)* MIX + *Metall* METAL]

**miscible** /'mɪsəbəl/, *adj.* capable of being mixed. [L *miscēre* mix + -IBLE] – **miscibility** /mɪsə'bɪləti/, *n.*

**miscolour** /mɪs'kʌlə/, *v.t.* **1.** to give a wrong colour to. **2.** to misrepresent.

**misconceive** /mɪskən'siv/, *v.t., v.i.*, **-ceived, -ceiving.** to conceive wrongly; misunderstand. – **misconceiver,** *n.*

**misconception** /mɪskən'sɛpʃən/, *n.* erroneous conception; a mistaken notion.

**misconduct** /mɪs'kɒndʌkt/, *n.*; /mɪskən'dʌkt/, *v.* –*n.* **1.** improper conduct; wrong behaviour. **2.** unlawful conduct by an official in regard to his office, or by a person in the administration of justice, such as a lawyer, witness, or juror. –*v.t.* **3.** →**mismanage.** **4. misconduct oneself,** to misbehave.

**misconstruction** /mɪskən'strʌkʃən/, *n.* **1.** wrong construction; misinterpretation. **2.** the act of misconstruing.

**misconstrue** /mɪskən'stru/, *v.t.*, **-strued, -struing.** to construe wrongly; take in a wrong sense; misinterpret; misunderstand.

**miscounsel** /mɪs'kaʊnsəl/, *v.t.*, **-selled, -selling** or (*U.S.*) **-seled, -seling.** to advise wrongly.

**miscount** /mɪs'kaʊnt/, *v.*; /'mɪskaʊnt/, *n.* –*v.t., v.i.* **1.** to count erroneously; miscalculate. –*n.* **2.** an erroneous counting or a miscalculation.

**miscreance** /'mɪskriəns/, *n. Archaic.* wrong belief; misbelief; false religious faith.

**miscreancy** /'mɪskriənsi/, *n. Archaic.* **1.** →**miscreance.** **2.** the state or condition of a miscreant; turpitude.

**miscreant** /'mɪskriənt/, *adj.* **1.** depraved, villainous, or base. **2.** *Archaic.* misbelieving; holding a false religious belief. –*n.* **3.** a vile wretch; villain. **4.** *Archaic.* a misbelieving person, as a heretic or an infidel. [ME *miscreaunt,* from OF *mescreant,* from *mes-* MIS-[1] + *creant,* ppr. of *creire* believe, from L *crēdere*]

**miscreate** /mɪskri'eɪt/, *v.*, **-ated, -ating,** *adj.* –*v.t., v.i.* **1.** *Rare.* to create amiss. –*adj.* **2.** *Archaic.* miscreated. – **miscreation,** *n.*

**miscreated** /mɪskri'eɪtəd/, *adj.* wrongly created; misshapen; monstrous.

**miscue** /mɪs'kju/, *n., v.*, **-cued, -cuing.** –*n.* **1.** *Billiards, etc.* a slip of the cue, causing it to strike the ball improperly or not at all. **2.** *Colloq.* a mistake or blunder, usu. caused by faulty judgment or timing. –*v.i.* **3.** to make a miscue. **4.** *Theat.* to fail to answer one's cue or to answer another's cue.

**misdate** /mɪs'deɪt/, *v.*, **-dated, -dating;** /'mɪsdeɪt/, *n.* –*v.t.* **1.** to date wrongly; assign or affix a wrong date to. –*n.* **2.** a wrong date.

**misdeal** /mɪs'dil/, *v.*, **-dealt, -dealing;** /'mɪsdil/, *n.* –*v.t.* **1.** to deal wrongly, esp. at cards. –*v.i.* **2.** to deal cards improperly or in the wrong order. –*n.* **3.** a wrong deal. – **misdealer,** *n.*

**misdeed** /mɪs'did/, *n.* a bad deed; a wicked action.

**misdeliver** /mɪsdə'lɪvə/, *v.t.* to deliver wrongly, as to a wrong address.

**misdemeanour** /mɪsdə'minə/, *n.* **1.** misbehaviour; a misdeed. **2.** *Law.* any criminal offence, esp. (before 1967) one not classified as a felony or treason. Also, *esp. U.S.,* **misdemeanor.**

**misderive** /mɪsdə'raɪv/, *v.t., v.i.,* **-rived, -riving.** to derive wrongly; assign a wrong derivation to.

**misdescribe** /mɪsdə'skraɪb/, *v.t., v.i.,* **-scribed, -scribing.** to describe incorrectly or falsely. – **misdescription** /mɪsdə'skrɪpʃən/, *n.*

**misdirect** /mɪsdə'rɛkt/, *v.t.* to direct or charge wrongly.

**misdirection** /mɪsdə'rɛkʃən/, *n.* **1.** a wrong indication, guidance, or instruction. **2.** *Law.* an erroneous charge to the jury by a judge.

**misdo** /mɪs'du/, *v.t.,* **-did, -done, -doing.** to do wrongly. [ME *misdo(n),* OE *misdōn.* See MIS-[1], DO[1]] – **misdoer,** *n.*

**misdoubt** /mɪs'daʊt/, *Archaic.* –*v.t.* **1.** to doubt or suspect. –*v.i.* **2.** to be wary or fearful. –*n.* **3.** doubt or suspicion.

**mise** /miz, maɪz/, *n.* a settlement or agreement. [late ME, from AF, from *mettre* put, set, from L *mittere* send]

**mise en scène** /miz õ 'seɪn, 'sin/, *n.* **1.** the act or art of placing a play, scene, etc., on the stage, esp. with regard to the equipment necessary. **2.** stage setting, as of a play. **3.** the surroundings amid which anything is seen. [F]

**misemploy** /mɪsəm'plɔɪ/, *v.t.* to employ wrongly or improperly; misuse. – **misemployment,** *n.*

**miser**[1] /'maɪzə/, *n.* **1.** one who lives in wretched circumstances in order to save and hoard money. **2.** a niggardly, avaricious person. **3.** *Obs.* a wretched or unhappy person. [L: wretched, unhappy, sick, bad]

**miser**[2] /'maɪzə/, *n.* a large hand auger. [orig. uncert.]

**miserable** /'mɪzrebəl, -zərəbəl/, *adj.* **1.** wretchedly unhappy, uneasy, or uncomfortable. **2.** wretchedly poor; needy. **3.** of wretched character or quality; contemptible; wretchedly bad. **4.** attended with or causing misery: *a miserable existence.* **5.** manifesting misery. **6.** worthy of pity; deplorable: *a miserable failure.* **7. miserable as a bandicoot,** *Colloq.* very miserable. [L *miserābilis* pitiable] – **miserableness,** *n.* – **miserably,** *adv.*

**misère** /mə'zɛə/, *n. Cards.* **1.** a hand which contains no winning card. **2.** a bid made by a player who has such a hand, declaring that he will take no tricks. [F: lit., misery]

**Miserere** /mɪzə'rɛəreɪ, -'rɪə-, -'reɪri/, *n.* **1.** the 51st psalm (50th in the Vulgate and Douay versions), one of the penitential psalms. **2.** a musical setting for it. **3.** (*l.c.*) a prayer or expression asking for mercy. **4.** (*l.c.*) →**misericord** (def. 3). [L: have pity; the first word of the psalm in the Vulgate]

**misericord** /mɪ'zɛrəkɔd/, *n.* **1.** a relaxation of a monastic rule. **2.** a room in a monastery where such relaxations are permitted. **3.** a small projection on the underside of a hinged seat of a church stall, which when the seat was thrown back, gave support to a person standing in the stall. **4.** a medieval dagger, used for the mercy stroke to a wounded foe. Also, **misericorde.** [ME *misericorde,* from OF, from L *misericordia* mercy]

misericord (def. 4)

**misericordia** /mɪzərə'kɔdiə/, *n.* compassion; mercy. [L]

**miseries** /'mɪzəriz/, *n.* **1.** plural form of **misery. 2. in the miseries,** *Colloq.* unhappy; unwell; depressed.

**miserly** /'maɪzəli/, *adj.* of, like, or befitting a miser; penurious; niggardly. – **miserliness,** *n.*

**misery** /'mɪzəri/, *n., pl.* **-ries. 1.** great distress of mind; extreme unhappiness. **2.** a cause or source of wretchedness. **3.** distress caused by privation or poverty. **4.** wretchedness of condition or circumstances. **5. misery me,** (an exclamation expressing unhappiness or self-pity). **6. put out of misery, a.** to remedy a distressful circumstance: *she put the candidate out of his misery by telling him he would certainly pass.* **b.** to kill or render unconscious a person or animal so as to end bodily suffering.

**miseryguts** /'mɪzərigʌts/, *n. Colloq.* a person who is always whinging or complaining.

**misesteem** /mɪsəs'tim/, *v.t.* to esteem wrongly; fail to esteem or respect properly.

**misestimate** /mɪs'ɛstəmeɪt/, *v.,* **-mated, -mating;** /mɪs'ɛstəmət/, *n.* –*v.t.* **1.** to estimate wrongly or incorrectly. –*n.* **2.** wrong estimate.

**misfeasance** /mɪs'fizəns/, *n. Law.* **1.** wrong, actual or alleged, arising from or consisting of affirmative action (contrasted with *nonfeasance*). **2.** the wrongful performance of a normally lawful act; the wrongful and injurious exercise of lawful authority. Cf. **malfeasance, nonfeasance.** [AF *mesfesance,* from *mesfaire* misdo. See MIS-[1], MALFEASANCE]

**misfeasor** /mɪs'fizə/, *n. Law.* one guilty of misfeasance.

**misfield** /mɪs'fild/, *v.;* /'mɪsfild/, *n. Cricket.* –*v.t.* **1.** to fail to stop (the ball) cleanly when fielding. –*v.i.* **2.** to make a mistake in fielding, esp. in stopping the ball. –*n.* **3.** a fielding error, esp. a failure to stop the ball cleanly.

**misfile** /mɪs'faɪl/, *v.t.,* **-filed, -filing.** to file (papers, etc.) incorrectly or in the wrong place.

**misfire** /mɪs'faɪə/, *v.,* **-fired, -firing;** /'mɪsfaɪə/, *n.* –*v.i.* **1.** (of a gun or projectile, etc.) to fail to fire or explode. **2.** (of an internal combustion engine) to fail to fire; to fire at the wrong time. **3.** to fail to have a desired effect; be unsuccessful. –*n.* **4.** (of a gun or projectile, etc.) a failure to explode or fire, or to explode or fire properly.

**misfit** /mɪs'fɪt/, *v.,* **-fitted, -fitting;** /'mɪsfɪt/, *n.* –*v.t., v.i.* **1.** to fit badly. –*n.* **2.** a bad fit, as an ill-fitting garment, etc. **3. a.** a badly adjusted person. **b.** one who feels ill at ease or out of place in a given environment, as a family, a school, a job, or society as a whole.

**misfortune** /mɪs'fɔtʃən/, *n.* **1.** ill or adverse fortune; ill luck. **2.** an instance of this; a mischance or mishap.

**misgive** /mɪs'gɪv/, *v.,* **-gave, -given, -giving.** –*v.t.* **1.** (of one's mind, heart, etc.) to give doubt or apprehension to. –*v.i.* **2.** to be apprehensive.

**misgiving** /mɪs'gɪvɪŋ/, *n.* a feeling of doubt, distrust, or apprehension.

**misgovern** /mɪs'gʌvən/, *v.t.* to govern or manage badly. – **misgovernment,** *n.* – **misgovernor,** *n.*

**misguide** /mɪs'gaɪd/, *v.t.,* **-guided, -guiding.** to guide wrongly; mislead. – **misguidance,** *n.* – **misguider,** *n.*

**misguided** /mɪs'gaɪdəd/, *adj.* misled; deluded. – **misguidedly,** *adv.*

**mishandle** /mɪs'hændl/, *v.t.,* **-dled, -dling. 1.** to handle badly; maltreat. **2.** to mismanage.

**mishap** /'mɪshæp/, *n.* an unfortunate accident.

**mishear** /mɪs'hɪə/, *v.t.,* **-heard, -hearing.** to hear incorrectly or imperfectly.

**mishit** /mɪs'hɪt/, *v.;* /'mɪshɪt/, *n. Cricket, Golf, Tennis, etc.* –*v.t.* **1.** to hit (the ball) faultily, as when batting. –*v.i.* **2.** to make a faulty stroke. –*n.* **3.** a faulty stroke.

**mishmash** /'mɪʃmæʃ/, *n.* a hotchpotch; jumble.

**misinform** /mɪsɪn'fɔm/, *v.t.* to give false or misleading information to. – **misinformant, misinformer,** *n.* – **misinformation** /mɪsɪnfə'meɪʃən/, *n.*

**misinterpret** /mɪsɪn'tɜprət/, *v.t.* to interpret, explain, or understand incorrectly. – **misinterpretation** /mɪsɪn,tɜprə'teɪʃən/, *n.*

**misjoinder** /mɪs'dʒɔɪndə/, *n.* a joining in one law suit or action of causes or of parties not permitted to be so joined.

**misjudge** /mɪs'dʒʌdʒ/, *v.,* **-judged, -judging.** –*v.t.* **1.** to make an error in the judgment of. –*v.i.* **2.** to make an error in judging. – **misjudgment,** *n.*

**mislay** /mɪs'leɪ/, *v.t.,* **-laid, -laying. 1.** to put in a place afterwards forgotten. **2.** to lay or place wrongly; misplace. – **mislayer,** *n.*

**mislead** /mɪs'lid/, *v.t.,* **-led, -leading. 1.** to lead or guide wrongly; lead astray. **2.** to lead into error of conduct, thought, or judgment. – **misleader,** *n.* – **misleading,** *adj.* – **misleadingly,** *adv.*

**mismanage** /mɪs'mænɪdʒ/, *v.t.,* **-aged, -aging.** to manage incompetently or dishonestly. – **mismanagement,** *n.*

**mismarriage** /mɪs'mærɪdʒ/, *n.* an unsuitable or unhappy marriage.

**mismatch** /mɪs'mætʃ/, *v.;* /'mɪsmætʃ, mɪs'mætʃ/, *n.* –*v.t.* **1.** to match badly or unsuitably. –*n.* **2.** a bad or unsatisfactory match.

**mismate** /mɪs'meɪt/, *v.t., v.i.*, **-mated, -mating.** to mate amiss or unsuitably.

**mismeasure** /mɪs'mɛʒə/, *v.t.*, **-sured, -suring.** to measure wrongly. – **mismeasurement,** *n.*

**mismother** /mɪs'mʌðə/, *v.t.* (usu. of sheep) to neglect (offspring) causing death by starvation, as when the wrong lamb is placed with a ewe or when for some other reason either the ewe or the lamb lacks interest in suckling. – **mismothering,** *n.*

**mismove** /mɪs'muv/, *n.* a wrong move, as in a game or any course of procedure.

**misname** /mɪs'neɪm/, *v.t.*, **-named, -naming.** to call by a wrong name.

**misnomer** /mɪs'noʊmə/, *n.* **1.** a misapplied name or designation. **2.** an error in naming a person or thing. [ME *misnoumer,* from OF *mesnommer,* n. use of inf., from *mes-* MIS-[1] + *nommer* name, from L *nōmināre.* See NOMINATE]

**miso** /'misoʊ/, *n.* a paste of rice, soya beans, and salt fermented in brine, used as flavouring for soups and savoury dishes. [Jap.]

**miso-,** a word element referring to hate. [Gk, combining form of *miseîn* to hate, *mîsos* hatred]

**misogamy** /mə'sɒgəmi/, *n.* hatred of marriage. – **misogamist,** *n.*

**misogyny** /mə'sɒdʒəni/, *n.* hatred of women. [Gk *mīsogynia*] – **misogynist,** *n.* – **misogynous,** *adj.*

**misology** /mə'sɒlədʒi, maɪ-/, *n.* hatred of reason or reasoning. [Gk *mīsología* hatred of argument] – **misologist,** *n.*

**misoneism** /mɪsoʊ'niɪzəm, maɪsoʊ-/, *n.* hatred or dislike of what is new. [It. *misoneismo,* from *miso-* MISO- + Gk *néos* new + *-ismo* -ISM] – **misoneist,** *n.*

**mispickel** /'mɪspɪkəl/, *n.* →**arsenopyrite.** [G]

**misplace** /mɪs'pleɪs, 'mɪspleɪs/, *v.t.*, **-placed, -placing. 1.** to put in a wrong place. **2.** to place or bestow improperly, unsuitably, or unwisely. – **misplacement,** *n.*

**misplay** /mɪs'pleɪ/, *v.;* /'mɪspleɪ/, *n.* *Games.* –*v.t.* **1.** to play wrongly, badly, or against the rules. –*n.* **2.** a wrong play, move or stroke.

**misplead** /mɪs'plid/, *v.t., v.i.* to plead incorrectly.

**mispleading** /mɪs'plidɪŋ/, *n.* *Law.* a mistake in pleading, as a misjoinder of parties, a misstatement of a cause of action, etc.

**misprint** /'mɪsprɪnt/, *n.;* /mɪs'prɪnt/, *v.* –*n.* **1.** a mistake in printing. –*v.t.* **2.** to print incorrectly.

**misprise** /mɪs'praɪz/, *v.t.*, **-prised, -prising.** to despise; undervalue; slight; scorn. Also, **misprize.** [OF *mesprisier,* from *mes-* MIS-[1] + *prisier* PRIZE[2]]

**misprision**[1] /mɪs'prɪʒən/, *n.* **1.** a wrongful action or commission, esp. by a public official. **2.** the act of concealing one's knowledge of a treason or felony. [ME, from OF, from *mesprendre* mistake, do wrong, from *mes-* MIS-[1] + *prendre* take, from L *prehendere*]

**misprision**[2] /mɪs'prɪʒən/, *n.* scorn; contempt; low estimation. [*misprise* (see MISPRISE) + -ION]

**mispronounce** /mɪsprə'naʊns/, *v.t., v.i.*, **-nounced, -nouncing.** to pronounce incorrectly. – **mispronunciation,** /ˌmɪsprənʌnsi'eɪʃən/, *n.*

**mispunctuate** /mɪs'pʌŋktʃueɪt/, *v.t., v.i.*, **-ated, -ating.** to punctuate wrongly. – **mispunctuation** /mɪsˌpʌŋktʃu'eɪʃən/, *n.*

**misquotation** /mɪskwoʊ'teɪʃən/, *n.* an inaccurate quotation.

**misquote** /mɪs'kwoʊt/, *v.;* /mɪs'kwoʊt, 'mɪskwoʊt/, *n.* –*v.t., v.i.* **1.** to quote incorrectly. –*n.* **2.** *Colloq.* →**misquotation.**

**misread** /mɪs'rid/, *v.t., v.i.*, **-read** /–'rɛd/, **reading.** to read wrongly; misinterpret.

**misreckon** /mɪs'rɛkən/, *v.t.* **1.** to reckon incorrectly; miscalculate. –*v.i.* **2.** to make a faulty reckoning.

**misrelate** /mɪsrə'leɪt/, *v.t.*, **-lated, -lating.** to relate incorrectly. – **misrelation** /mɪsrə'leɪʃən/, *n.*

**misrelated participle** /ˌmɪsrəleɪtəd 'patəsɪpəl/, *n.* a participle related grammatically to a word which it was not intended to modify, as *coming* in: *coming round the corner, the church sprang into view.* Also, **hanging participle.**

**misremember** /mɪsrə'mɛmbə/, *v.t.* **1.** to remember incorrectly. **2.** to fail to remember.

**misreport** /mɪsrə'pɔt/, *v.t.* **1.** to report incorrectly or falsely. –*n.* **2.** an incorrect or false report. – **misreporter,** *n.*

**misrepresent** /mɪsrɛprə'zɛnt/, *v.t.* to represent (a person, facts, etc.) incorrectly, improperly, or falsely. – **misrepresentation** /mɪsˌrɛprəzɛn'teɪʃən/, *n.* – **misrepresenter,** *n.* – **misrepresentative,** *adj.*

**misrule** /mɪs'rul/, *n., v.*, **-ruled, -ruling.** –*n.* **1.** bad or unwise rule; misgovernment. **2.** disorder or lawless tumult. –*v.t., v.i.* **3.** to misgovern. – **misruler,** *n.*

**misrun** /'mɪsrʌn/, *n.* a metal casting marred by premature solidification before the mould is filled.

**miss**[1] /mɪs/, *v.t.* **1.** to fail to hit, light upon, meet, catch, receive, obtain, attain, accomplish, see, hear, etc.: *to miss a train.* **2.** to fail to perform, attend to, be present at, etc.: *to miss an appointment.* **3.** to perceive the absence or loss of, often with regret. **4.** to escape or avoid: *he just missed being caught.* **5.** to fail to perceive or understand: *to miss the point of a remark.* **6. miss fire,** *Obs.* to fail to go off, as a firearm; misfire. **7. miss the boat** or **bus,** *Colloq.* to be too late; fail to grasp an opportunity. **8. not (never) miss a trick,** *Colloq.* (*oft. derog.*) never to fail to exploit an opportunity, press an advantage, etc. –*v.i.* **9.** to fail to hit, light upon, receive, or attain something. **10.** to fail of effect or success; be unsuccessful. **11. miss out,** to fail to be present, as at a function, or to fail to receive, esp. something desired (oft. fol. by *on*). **12.** *Colloq.* (of an internal combustion engine) to fail to fire in one or more cylinders. **13.** *Colloq.* to fail to menstruate at the usual time. –*n.* **14.** a failure to hit, meet, obtain, or accomplish something. **15.** *Colloq.* an omission or neglect, usu. deliberate: *give it a miss.* [ME *misse,* OE *missan,* c. D and G *missen*]

**miss**[2] /mɪs/, *n., pl.* **misses. 1.** (*cap.*) the conventional title of respect for an unmarried woman, prefixed to the name. **2.** (without the name) a term of address to a woman, married or unmarried, esp. one in a position of authority, as a teacher. **3.** a young unmarried woman; a girl. **4.** the title of respect often retained (with maiden names or assumed names) by married women in public life, as actresses, writers, etc.

**missal** /'mɪsəl/, *n.* *Rom. Cath. Ch.* the book containing the prayers and rites for celebrating mass for a complete year, used by the priest at the altar. [ME, from ML *missāle,* neut. of *missālis,* from LL *missa* MASS[2]]

**missel thrush** /'mɪsəl θrʌʃ/, *n.* a large European thrush, *Turdus viscivorus,* which feeds on the berries of the mistletoe. Also, **missel, mistle thrush.** [See MISTLE(TOE), THRUSH[1]]

**misshape** /mɪs'ʃeɪp/, *v.t.*, **-shaped, -shaped** or **-shapen, -shaping.** to shape badly; deform.

**misshapen** /mɪs'ʃeɪpən/, *adj.* badly shaped; deformed. – **misshapenly,** *adv.* – **misshapenness,** *n.*

**missile** /'mɪsaɪl/, *n.* **1.** an object or weapon that can be thrown, hurled, or shot, as a stone, a bullet, a lance, or an arrow. **2.** a guided missile. –*adj.* **3.** capable of being thrown, hurled, or shot, as from the hand, a gun, etc. **4.** that discharges missiles. [L: something which can be thrown]

**missing** /'mɪsɪŋ/, *adj.* lacking; absent; not found.

**missing link** /– 'lɪŋk/, *n.* **1.** a hypothetical form of animal formerly assumed to have constituted a connecting link between the anthropoid apes and man. **2.** something lacking for the completion of a series or sequence of any kind.

**mission** /'mɪʃən/, *n.* **1.** a body of persons sent to a foreign country to conduct negotiations, establish relations, or the like. **2.** the business with which an agent, envoy, etc., is charged. **3.** a permanent diplomatic establishment abroad: *chief of mission.* **4.** *Mil.* an operation on land, sea, or in the air, carried out by an armed force against an enemy. **5.** a body of persons sent into a foreign land for religious work among a heathen people, or into any region for the religious conversion or betterment of the inhabitants. **6.** an establishment of missionaries in a foreign land; a missionary post or station. **7.** the district assigned to a missionary priest. **8.** missionary duty or work. **9.** (*pl.*) organised missionary work or activities in any country, region, or field: *foreign missions.* **10.** a district for which no ecclesiastical establishment has been set up, having temporary buildings and offices. **11.** a series of special religious services for increasing piety and converting unbelievers. **12.** a self-imposed or assigned duty. **13.** a sending or being sent for some duty or purpose. **14.** those sent. [L *missio* a sending]

**missionary** /'mɪʃənri/, *n., pl.* **-ries,** *adj.* –*n.* **1.** a person sent to work for the propagation of his religious faith in a heathen land or a newly settled district. **2.** one sent on a mission. *–adj.* **3.** pertaining to or connected with religious missions. **4.** engaged in such a mission, or devoted to work connected with missions. **5.** *N.Z.* →**sweetbriar.** [MISSION + -ARY[1]]

**missionary position** /'– pəzɪʃən/, *n. Colloq.* a position of sexual intercourse in which the male is on top of and face to face with the female.

**missioner** /'mɪʃənə/, *n.* the conductor of a crusade or mission designed to stimulate and renew faith in an already Christian context.

**missish** /'mɪsɪʃ/, *adj.* prim; affected; prudish.

**missive** /'mɪsɪv/, *n.* **1.** a written message; a letter. *–adj.* **2.** sent, esp. from an official source. [late ME, from ML *missīvus,* from L *missus,* pp., sent]

**misspeak** /mɪs'spik/, *v.t., v.i.,* **-spoke, -spoken, -speaking.** to speak, utter, or pronounce incorrectly.

**misspell** /mɪs'spɛl/, *v.t., v.i.,* **-spelt** or **-spelled, -spelling.** to spell incorrectly. – **misspelling,** *n.*

**misspend** /mɪs'spɛnd/, *v.t.,* **-spent, -spending.** to spend improperly; squander; waste. – **misspender,** *n.*

**misstate** /mɪs'steɪt/, *v.t.,* **-stated, -stating.** to state wrongly or misleadingly; make a wrong statement about. – **misstatement,** *n.*

**misstep** /mɪs'stɛp/, *n.* **1.** a wrong step. **2.** an error or slip in conduct.

**missus** /'mɪsəs, -səz/, *n. Colloq.* **1.** a man's wife; the woman with whom a man cohabits. **2.** the mistress of a household. **3.** *Colloq.* (in address, without the name) madam. Also, **missis.** [spoken form of MRS]

**missy** /'mɪsi/, *n.* **1.** an appellation for a young girl. **2.** a forward young girl; a disagreeably pert girl or woman. [MISS[2] + -Y[2]]

**mist** /mɪst/, *n.* **1.** a cloudlike aggregation of minute globules of water suspended in the atmosphere at or near the earth's surface. **2.** *Meteorol.* (by international agreement) a very thin fog in which the horizontal visibility is greater than 1 km. **3.** a cloud of particles resembling a mist. **4.** something which dims, obscures, or blurs. **5.** a hazy appearance before the eyes, as due to tears or to bodily disorders. **6.** a suspension of a liquid in a gas. *–v.i.* **7.** to be or become misty. *–v.t.* **8.** to make misty. [ME and OE, c. D, LG, and Sw. *mist*]

**mistake** /mə'steɪk/, *n., v.,* **-took, -taken, -taking.** *–n.* **1.** an error in action, opinion or judgment. **2.** a misconception or misapprehension. **3.** *Colloq.* an unplanned or unwanted pregnancy. *–v.t.* **4.** to take or regard as something or somebody else. **5.** to conceive of or understand wrongly; misapprehend; misunderstand; misjudge. *–v.i.* **6.** to be in error. [ME *mistake(n),* v., from Scand.; cf. Icel. *mistaka* take by mistake. See MIS-[1], TAKE]

**mistakeable** /mə'steɪkəbəl/, *adj.* that may be mistaken or misunderstood. Also, **mistakable.** – **mistakeably,** *adv.*

**mistaken** /mə'steɪkən/, *adj.* **1.** wrongly conceived, entertained, or done: *a mistaken notion.* **2.** erroneous; wrong. **3.** having made a mistake; being in error. – **mistakenly,** *adv.*

**misteach** /mɪs'titʃ/, *v.t.,* **-taught, -teaching.** to teach wrongly or badly.

**mistelle** /mɪs'tɛl/, *n.* a fortified liquor made by adding alcohol to grape juice before it ferments; used as a sweetening agent for wine. [F]

**mister** /'mɪstə/, *n.* **1.** (*cap.*) the conventional title of respect for a man, prefixed to the name and to certain official designations (usu. written *Mr*). **2.** *Colloq.* (in address, without the name) sir. **3.** the official title used in addressing: **a.** *Mil.* a junior officer. **b.** *Navy.* a warrant officer or midshipman. **c.** *Naut.* any officer other than the captain. **4.** (a title used in addressing a surgeon as opposed to *doctor*). *–v.t.* **5.** *Colloq.* to address or speak of as 'mister' or 'Mr'. [var. of MASTER]

**mist flower** /'mɪst flaʊə/, *n.* a troublesome weed, *Eupatorium riparium,* native to America but naturalised in eastern Australia; small crofton weed.

**mistime** /mɪs'taɪm/, *v.t.,* **-timed, -timing.** to time wrongly; perform, say, etc., at a wrong time.

**mistle thrush** /'mɪsəl θrʌʃ/, *n.* →**missel thrush.**

**mistletoe** /'mɪsəltoʊ/, *n.* any of various plants of the family Loranthaceae which grow parasitically on other plants, esp. *Viscum album* of Europe, much used in Christmas decorations. [ME *mistelto,* OE *misteltān* (c. Icel. *mistilteinn*), from *mistel* mistletoe + *tān* twig]

**mistletoe bird** /'– bɜd/, *n.* a small bird, *Dicaeum hirundinaceum,* which builds a nest of plant down and spiderweb in treetops, and is common in most parts of mainland Australia.

**mistook** /mɪs'tʊk/, *v.* past tense of **mistake.**

**mistral** /'mɪstrəl/, *n.* a cold, dry, northerly wind common in southern France and neighbouring regions. [F: lit., master wind, from Pr.: important, from L *magistrālis* MAGISTRAL]

**mistranslate** /mɪstrænz'leɪt, -tranz-/, *v.t., v.i.,* **-lated, -lating.** to translate incorrectly. – **mistranslation,** *n.*

**mistreat** /mɪs'trit/, *v.t.* to treat badly or wrongly. – **mistreatment,** *n.*

**mistress** /'mɪstrəs/, *n.* **1.** a woman who has authority or control; the female head of a household or some other establishment. **2.** a woman employing, or in authority over, servants or attendants. **3.** a female owner, as of a slave, horse, dog, etc. **4.** a woman who has the power of controlling or disposing of something at pleasure. **5.** something regarded as feminine which has control or supremacy: *England was the mistress of the seas.* **6.** a female head teacher in a particular subject department in a secondary school. **7.** a woman who has a continuing sexual relationship with one man outside marriage. **8.** *Archaic or Poetic.* sweetheart. **9.** *Archaic.* a term of address for a woman. Cf. **Mrs** and **miss.** [ME *maistresse,* from OF, fem. of *maistre* MASTER]

**mistrial** /mɪs'traɪəl/, *n. Law.* **1.** a trial terminated without conclusion on the merits because of some error. **2.** *U.S.* an inconclusive trial, as where the jury cannot agree.

**mistrust** /mɪs'trʌst/, *n.* **1.** lack of trust or confidence; distrust. *–v.t.* **2.** to regard with mistrust; distrust. *–v.i.* **3.** to be distrustful. – **mistruster,** *n.* – **mistrustingly,** *adv.*

**mistrustful** /mɪs'trʌstfəl/, *adj.* full of mistrust; suspicious. – **mistrustfully,** *adv.* – **mistrustfulness,** *n.*

**misty** /'mɪsti/, *adj.,* **-tier, -tiest.** **1.** abounding in or clouded by mist. **2.** of the nature of or consisting of mist. **3.** appearing as if seen through mist; indistinct in form or outline. **4.** obscure; vague. [ME; OE *mistig*] – **mistily,** *adv.* – **mistiness,** *n.*

**misunderstand** /ˌmɪsʌndə'stænd, mɪsˌʌn-/, *v.,* **-stood, -standing.** *–v.t.* **1.** to misinterpret the words or actions of (a person). *–v.i.* **2.** to understand wrongly.

**misunderstanding** /ˌmɪsʌndə'stændɪŋ, mɪsˌʌn-/, *n.* **1.** disagreement or dissension. **2.** failure to understand; mistake as to meaning.

**misunderstood** /ˌmɪsʌndə'stʊd, mɪsˌʌn-/, *adj.* **1.** improperly interpreted. **2.** unappreciated.

**misusage** /mɪs'juzɪdʒ, -sɪdʒ/, *n.* **1.** wrong or improper usage, as of words; abusage. **2.** ill-use; bad treatment.

**misuse** /mɪs'jus/, *n.;* /mɪs'juz/, *v.,* **-used, -using.** *–n.* **1.** wrong or improper use; misapplication. **2.** *Obs.* ill-use. *–v.t.* **3.** to use wrongly or improperly; misapply. **4.** to ill-use; maltreat.

**misuser** /mɪs'juzə/, *n.* **1.** *Law.* abuse of a liberty or benefit or thing. **2.** one who misuses.

**misvalue** /mɪs'vælju/, *v.t.,* **-ued, -uing.** to value wrongly.

**misword** /mɪs'wɜd/, *v.t.* to word wrongly.

**miswrite** /mɪs'raɪt/, *v.t.,* **-wrote, -written, -writing.** to write incorrectly.

**Mitchell grass** /'mɪtʃəl gras/, *n.* a drought-resistant native pasture grass, of the genus *Astrebla,* mainly distinguished by its hard seed-coverings; plentiful on the western plains of Queensland and New South Wales, and once a staple of Aboriginal diet.

Mitchell grass

**mite**[1] /maɪt/, *n.* any of various small arachnids (order Acari) with a saclike body, many being parasitic on plants and animals, others living in cheese, flour, unrefined sugar, etc. [ME *myte,* OE *mīte,* c. MD *mīte* (D *mijt*)]

**mite**[2] /maɪt/, *n.* **1.** a small contribution, but all that one can afford (in allusion to Mark 12:41-44): *to contribute one's mite.* **2.** a very small sum of money. **3.** a coin of very small value. **4.** a very small object. **5.** a very small creature. **6.** a very small child. *–adv.* **7.** to a limited extent; somewhat (prec. by *a*): *a mite stupid.* [ME, from MD ultimately identical with MITE[1]]

**miter** /ˈmaɪtə/, *n., v.t. U.S.* →**mitre.**

**Mithraism** /ˈmɪθreɪˌɪzəm/, *n.* an ancient Persian religion worshipping Mithras the god of light and truth and later of the sun, seen as a source of some Christian moral teaching. Also, **Mithraicism** /mɪθˈreɪəsɪzəm/. – **Mithraic** /mɪθˈreɪɪk/, **Mithraistic** /mɪθreɪˈɪstɪk/, *adj.* – **Mithraist,** *n.*

**mithridate** /ˈmɪθrədeɪt/, *n. Obs.* a compound believed to be a universal antidote against every poison and disease. [ML *mithridatum,* var. of *mithridatium* (neut. sing.) of or pertaining to *Mithridates.* See MITHRIDATISM]

**mithridatise** /mɪθrəˈdeɪtaɪz/, *v.t.,* **-tised, -tising.** to induce a state of mithridatism in. Also, **mithridatize.**

**mithridatism** /ˈmɪθrədeɪtɪzəm/, *n.* the production of immunity against the action of a poison by taking the poison in gradually increased doses. [named after *Mithradates VI,* c. 132-63 B.C., king of Pontus, said to have so immunised himself] – **mithridatic** /mɪθrəˈdætɪk, -ˈdeɪtɪk/, *adj.*

**miticide** /ˈmaɪtəsaɪd/, *n.* →**acaricide.** [MIT(E)[1] + -I- + -CIDE]

**mitigate** /ˈmɪtəgeɪt/, *v.,* **-gated, -gating.** *–v.t.* **1.** to lessen in force or intensity (wrath, grief, harshness, pain, etc.). **2.** to moderate the severity of (anything distressing). **3.** *Rare.* to make milder or more gentle; mollify. *–v.i.* **4.** to become milder; moderate in severity. [ME, from ML *mītigātus,* pp.] – **mitigative, mitigatory** /ˈmɪtəgeɪtəri/, *adj.* – **mitigator,** *n.*

**mitigation** /mɪtəˈgeɪʃən/, *n.* **1.** the act or fact of mitigating. **2.** *Law.* a reduction or attempt to secure a reduction in damages or punishment, as in a speech made to a judge after a verdict or plea of guilty.

**mitis** /ˈmaɪtəs, ˈmi-/, *n.* **1.** Also, **mitis metal.** a malleable iron produced by fusing wrought iron with a small amount of aluminium rendering the product fluid enough to cast. *–adj.* **2.** designating or pertaining to mitis. [L: mild]

**mitochondrion** /maɪtoʊˈkɒndriən/, *n., pl.* **-ia** /-iə/. one of the minute granules, larger than lysosomes or microsomes, present in living cells, regarded as responsible for respiration and energy production. [Gk *mítos* a thread + *chóndrion* granule, diminutive of *chóndros* grain] – **mitochondrial,** *adj.*

**mitosis** /məˈtoʊsəs, maɪ-/, *n.* the usual (indirect) method of cell division, characterised typically by the resolving of the chromatin of the nucleus into a thread-like form, which separates into segments or chromosomes, each of which separates longitudinally into two parts, one part of each chromosome being retained in each of two new cells resulting from the original cell. [NL, from Gk *mítos* a thread + *-osis* -OSIS] – **mitotic,** *adj.* – **mitotically,** *adv.*

**mitral** /ˈmaɪtrəl/, *adj.* of or resembling a mitre.

**mitral valve** /ˈ– vælv/, *n.* the valve between the left auricle and ventricle of the heart which prevents the blood from flowing back into the auricle.

**mitre** /ˈmaɪtə/, *n., v.,* **-tred, -tring.** *–n.* **1.** the ceremonial headdress of a bishop symbolising his apostolic authority. In the Roman Catholic Church it is by courtesy extended as a mark of distinction to the heads of certain religious houses for men. In the Western Church it can lie flat when not in use and takes the form of a tall divided cap with two ribbons hanging at the back, often richly jewelled and embroidered. In the Eastern Church it takes various forms, but is invariably a solid structure of metal of rounded shape. **2.** the office or rank of bishop; bishopric. **3.** the ceremonial cap of the ancient Jewish high priest. **4.** a kind of headdress formerly worn by Asiatics. **5.** the abutting surface or bevel on either of the pieces joined in a mitre-joint. *–v.t.* **6.** to bestow a mitre upon, or raise to a rank entitled to it. **7.** to join with a mitre-joint. **8.** to make a mitre-joint in; cut to a mitre. Also, *U.S.,* **miter.** [ME *mitre,* from L *mitra,* from Gk: belt, headband, headdress]

mitre (def. 1)

**mitre box** /ˈ– bɒks/, *n.* a box or apparatus for use in cutting mitres (def. 5).

**mitred** /ˈmaɪtəd/, *adj.* **1.** shaped like a bishop's mitre or having a mitre-shaped apex. **2.** wearing, or entitled or privileged to wear, a mitre. Also, *U.S.,* **mitered.**

**mitre-joint** /ˈmaɪtə-dʒɔɪnt/, *n.* a joint formed when two pieces of identical cross-section are joined at the ends, and where the joined ends are bevelled at equal angles.

mitre-joint

**mitre wheel** /ˈmaɪtə wil/, *n.* one of a pair of cogwheels each having bevelled faces.

**mitriform** /ˈmaɪtrəfɔm/, *adj.* shaped like a mitre.

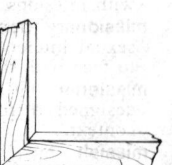

**mitt** /mɪt/, *n.* **1.** a kind of glove extending only to, or slightly over, the fingers, esp. as worn by women. **2.** *Baseball.* a kind of glove having the side next to the palm of the hand protected by a large, thick mitten-like pad. **3.** a mitten. **4.** *Colloq.* a hand. [apocopated var. of MITTEN]

**mitten** /ˈmɪtn/, *n.* **1.** a kind of hand-covering enclosing the four fingers together and the thumb separately. **2.** a mitt (def. 1). **3.** (*pl.*) *Colloq.* boxing gloves. [ME *myteyne,* from OF *mitaine,* from Gallo-Rom. *medietāna* half (glove), from L *medius* middle] – **mitten-like,** *adj.*

**mittimus** /ˈmɪtəməs/, *n. Law.* **1.** a warrant of commitment to prison. **2.** a writ for removing a suit or a record from one court to another. [L: we send, first word of such a writ in Latin]

**mitzvah** /ˈmɪtsva/, *n., pl.* **-voth** /-voʊθ/. *Judaism.* **1.** an order or commandment from the Bible or the rabbis. **2.** a religious act; a meritorious deed. Also, **mitsvah.** [Heb. *miswāh* commandment]

**mix** /mɪks/, *v.,* **mixed** or **mixt, mixing,** *n.* *–v.t.* **1.** to put together (substances or things, or one substance or thing with another) in one mass or assemblage with more or less thorough diffusion of the constituent elements among one another. **2.** to put together indiscriminately or confusedly (oft. fol. by *up*). **3.** to combine, unite, or join: *to mix business and pleasure.* **4.** to put in as an added element or ingredient: *to mix a little baking powder into the flour.* **5.** to form by combining ingredients: *to mix a cake, to mix mortar.* **6.** to crossbreed. **7.** to confuse completely (fol. by *up*). **8. mix one's drinks,** to drink a range of alcoholic liquors indiscriminately, usu. resulting in a hangover. **9.** to put together (the separate tracks of a recording). **10. mix up in,** to involve in. *–v.i.* **11.** to become mixed: *oil and water will not mix.* **12.** to associate, as in company. **13.** to be crossbred, or of mixed breeding. **14.** *Colloq.* to fight vigorously, as with the fists (sometimes fol. by *it*). **15. mix with,** to associate socially with. *–n.* **16.** a mixing, or a mixed condition; a mixture. **17.** *Colloq.* a muddle or mess. **18.** a commercially prepared blend of ingredients to which it is only necessary to add liquid and stir, before baking, cooking, serving, etc. **19.** a recording made by combining tracks separately recorded in a mixer. [backformation from *mixt* mixed, from F *mixte,* from L *mixtus,* pp.]

**mixed** /mɪkst/, *adj.* **1.** put together or formed by mixing. **2.** composed of different constituents or elements. **3.** composed of male and female together: *a mixed school, mixed doubles.* **4.** of different kinds combined: *mixed sweets.* **5.** comprising persons of different sexes, or of different classes, status, character, opinions, race, etc.: *mixed company.* **6.** *Law.* involving more than one issue or aspect: *a mixed question of law and fact.* **7.** *Colloq.* mentally confused (fol. by *up*). **8.** *Phonet.* (of a vowel) central.

**mixed bag** /– ˈbæg/, *n.* (*oft. pejor.*) an assortment of people or objects of different kinds and varying quality.

**mixed blessing** /– ˈblɛsɪŋ/, *n.* an event, thing, situation, etc., which has disadvantages, esp. unexpected disadvantages, which offset the advantages.

**mixed business** /– ˈbɪznəs/, *n.* a small grocery shop which also sells a selection of other types of merchandise.

**mixed crystal** /– ˈkrɪstəl/, *n.* a crystal in which some of the atoms of one constituent element are replaced by those of another element.

**mixed farming** /– ˈfamɪŋ/, *n.* combined agriculture and

i = peat ɪ = pit ɛ = pet æ = pat a = part ɒ = pot ʌ = putt ɔ = port ʊ = put u = pool ɜ = pert ə = apart aɪ = buy eɪ = bay ɔɪ = boy aʊ = how oʊ = hoe ɪə = here ɛə = hair ʊə = tour g = give θ = thin ð = then ʃ = show ʒ = measure tʃ = choke dʒ = joke ŋ = sing j = you õ = Fr. bon

pastoral farming.

**mixed functions** /– ˈfʌŋkʃənz/, *n.pl.* duties undertaken by an employee at a level above or below those of his normal work classification and for the performance of which he may be paid an allowance.

**mixed grill** /– ˈgrɪl/, *n.* a dish of several kinds of meat, etc., grilled and served together, usu. with grilled vegetables.

**mixed industry** /– ˈɪndəstri/, *n.* an industry in which employees are engaged under a number of separate awards and/or agreements, the particular provisions of which may not be uniform in regard to conditions of employment.

**mixed marriage** /– ˈmærɪdʒ/, *n.* a marriage between persons of different religions or races.

**mixed metaphor** /– ˈmɛtəfɔ/, *n.* See **metaphor** (def. 2).

**mixed number** /– ˈnʌmbə/, *n.* a number consisting of a whole number and a fraction, as $4\frac{1}{2}$.

**mixed train** /– ˈtreɪn/, *n.* a railway train made up partly of passenger carriages and partly of goods wagons.

**mixed-up** /ˈmɪkst-ʌp/, *adj.* emotionally confused: *she's just a crazy, mixed-up kid.*

**mixer** /ˈmɪksə/, *n.* **1.** one who or that which mixes. **2.** *Colloq.* a person with reference to his sociability: *a good mixer.* **3.** a kitchen utensil or electrical appliance used for beating. **4.** an electrical system, as in a broadcasting studio providing for the mixing, etc., of sounds from various sources, as from studio microphones, discs, tapes, etc. **5.** *Radio, T.V.* a technician who controls the sound mixer in a studio.

**mixing valve** /ˈmɪksɪŋ vælv/, *n.* a valve controlling a single outlet receiving water from both hot-water and cold-water pipes. Also, **mixing tap, mixing faucet.**

**Mixolydian mode** /mɪksoʊˈlɪdiən moʊd/, *n.* a scale represented by the white keys of a keyboard instrument, beginning on G. [Gk *mixolýdios* mixed LYDIAN + -AN]

**mixture** /ˈmɪkstʃə/, *n.* **1.** a product of mixing. **2.** any combination of differing elements, kinds, qualities, etc.: *a curious mixture of eagerness and terror.* **3.** *Chem., Physics.* an aggregate of two or more substances which are not chemically united, and which exist in no fixed proportion to each other. **4.** a fabric woven of yarns combining various colours: *a heather mixture.* **5.** the act of mixing. **6.** the state of being mixed. **7.** an added element or ingredient; an admixture. **8.** *Music.* a type of organ stop, with several ranks of pipes, giving harmonics. [L *mixtūra*]

**mix-up** /ˈmɪks-ʌp/, *n.* **1.** a confused state of things; a muddle; a tangle. **2.** *Colloq.* a fight.

**mizzen** /ˈmɪzən/, *Naut.* –*n.* **1.** the lower sail set on the mizzenmast. **2.** →**mizzenmast.** –*adj.* **3.** of, relating to, or set on the mizzenmast. Also, **mizen.** [ME *meseyn,* from F *misaine,* from It. *mezzana,* properly fem. of *mezzano* middle, from L *mediānus.* See MEDIAN]

**mizzenmast** /ˈmɪzənmast, -məst/, *n.* **1.** the aftermost mast of a three-masted vessel, or the third on a vessel with more than three masts. **2.** the after and shorter of the two masts of a yawl or ketch. Also, **mizenmast.**

**Mk**[1], mark[2].

**Mk**[2], *Bible.* Mark

**MKS** /ɛm keɪ ˈɛs/, *n.* →**metre-kilogram-second (system).**

**ml,** millilitre; millilitres.

**ML,** Medieval Latin. Also, **M.L.**

**MLA** /ɛm ɛl ˈeɪ/, Member of the Legislative Assembly.

**MLC** /ɛm ɛl ˈsi/, Member of the Legislative Council.

**M.Litt.** /ɛm ˈlɪt/, Master of Letters. [L *Magister Litterae*]

**Mlle,** *pl.* **Mlles.** Mademoiselle.

**mm,** millimetre; millimetres.

**MM.,** Messieurs.

**M.M.,** Military Medal.

**Mme,** *pl.* **Mmes.** madame.

**mmHg,** millimetre of mercury.

**Mn,** *Chem.* manganese.

**M.N.,** Merchant Navy.

**MnE,** Modern English.

**mnemonic** /nəˈmɒnɪk/, *adj.* **1.** assisting, or intended to assist, the memory. **2.** pertaining to mnemonics or to memory. –*n.* **3.** a verse or the like intended to assist the memory. [Gk *mnēmonikós* of memory]

**mnemonics** /nəˈmɒnɪks/, *n.* the art of improving or developing the memory. Also, **mnemotechnics** /nimoʊˈtɛknɪks/.

**Mngr,** Monsignor.

**mo**[1] /moʊ/, *n. Colloq.* **1.** a moment. **2. half a mo,** just a moment.

**mo**[2] /moʊ/, *n. Colloq.* **1.** a moustache. **2. curl the (a) mo!** (an exclamation of admiration, delight, etc.)

**-mo,** the final element of a series of compounds referring to book sizes by numbering the times the sheets are folded, as in *12mo* or *duodecimo.*

**mo.,** month.

**Mo,** *Chem.* molybdenum.

**M.O.,** **1.** mail order. **2.** Medical Officer. **3.** Also, **m.o.** money order.

**moa** /ˈmoʊə/, *n.* any of various extinct, flightless birds of New Zealand, constituting the family Dinornithidae, allied to the apteryx but resembling an ostrich. [Maori]

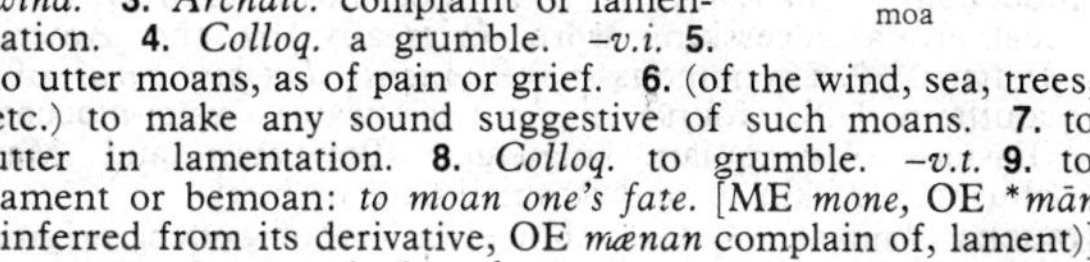

moa

**moa hunter** /ˈ– hʌntə/, *n.* a member of the Polynesian culture in New Zealand earlier than the classical Maori culture, associated with moa-bone discoveries.

**moan** /moʊn/, *n.* **1.** a prolonged, low, inarticulate sound uttered from or as if from physical or mental suffering. **2.** any similar sound: *the moan of the wind.* **3.** *Archaic.* complaint or lamentation. **4.** *Colloq.* a grumble. –*v.i.* **5.** to utter moans, as of pain or grief. **6.** (of the wind, sea, trees, etc.) to make any sound suggestive of such moans. **7.** to utter in lamentation. **8.** *Colloq.* to grumble. –*v.t.* **9.** to lament or bemoan: *to moan one's fate.* [ME *mone,* OE **mān* (inferred from its derivative, OE *mænan* complain of, lament)] –**moaner,** *n.* –**moaningly,** *adv.*

**moat** /moʊt/, *n.* **1.** a deep, wide trench surrounding a fortified place, as a town or a castle, usu. filled with water. –*v.t.* **2.** to surround with, or as with, a moat. [ME *mote* moat, (earlier) mound, from OF: mound, eminence; probably from Celtic or Gmc]

**mob** /mɒb/, *n., adj., v.,* **mobbed, mobbing.** –*n.* **1. a.** a large number, esp. of people: *there was a mob of people in the streets to see the procession.* **b.** a group of people, as friends, not necessarily large: *we'll invite the mob over for Saturday night.* **2.** a collection of animals: *a mob of sheep.* **3.** a disorderly, riotous or destructive group of people: *the mob packed the presidential palace.* **4.** (*oft. derog.*) any assemblage or aggregation of persons, animals, or things; a crowd. **5.** the common mass of people; the populace or multitude. **6. a big mob, a.** a large number. **b.** a great amount. –*adj.* **7.** of, pertaining to, characteristic of, or suitable for a mob: *mob violence, mob oratory.* –*v.t.* **8.** to crowd around tumultuously: *the pop star was mobbed by his fans at the airport.* **9.** to surround and attack with riotous violence: *the peasants mobbed the coach, destroying it.* [short for L *mōbile vulgus* the movable (i.e., excitable) common people] –**mobber,** *n.* –**mobbish,** *adj.*

**mob-cap** /ˈmɒb-kæp/, *n. Obs.* a large, full cap fitting down over the ears, formerly much worn indoors by women.

**mobile** /ˈmoʊbaɪl/, *adj.* **1.** movable; moving readily. **2.** *Mil.* permanently equipped with vehicles for transport. **3.** flowing freely, as a liquid. **4.** changing easily in expression, as features. **5.** quickly responding to impulses, emotions, etc., as the mind; versatile. **6.** characterised by social mobility. **7.** of or pertaining to a mobile. –*n.* **8.** a construction or sculpture of delicately balanced movable parts (of metal, wood, etc.) which describe rhythmic patterns through their motion. [L: movable (neut.)]

**mobile barrier** /– ˈbæriə/, *n.* a barrier on a trotting or pacing track, consisting of retractable arms mounted on the back of a motor vehicle, used for starts in which the contestants are all moving at an even rate.

**mobile library** /– ˈlaɪbri/, *n.* a van, fitted out inside as a library, which takes its facilities to people who for reasons of distance or disability would not otherwise have access to a library.

**mobilise** /ˈmoʊbəlaɪz/, *v.,* **-lised, -lising.** –*v.t.* **1.** to put (armed forces) into readiness for active service. **2.** to organise or adapt (industries, etc.) for service to the government in time of war. **3.** to marshal, as for a task: *to mobilise one's energies.* **4.** to put into motion, circulation, or use: *mobilise the wealth of a country.* *–v.i.* **5.** to be assembled, organised, etc., for war. Also, **mobilize.** [F *mobiliser,* from *mobile* MOBILE] **– mobilisation** /moʊbəlaɪˈzeɪʃən/, *n.*

**mobility** /moʊˈbɪləti, mə-/, *n.* **1.** the quality of being mobile. **2.** *Sociol.* the movement of people in a population, as from place to place, or job to job, or social class to social class. **3.** the ability to apply for a job in any department of the public service.

**möbius strip** /ˈmɜbiəs strɪp/, *n.* a continuous one-sided surface, as formed by half-twisting a strip, as of paper or cloth, and joining the ends. [named after August Ferdinand *Möbius,* 1790-1868, German mathematician]

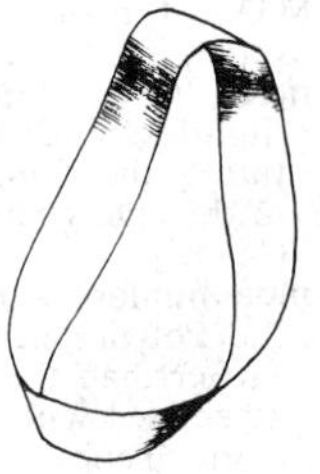
möbius strip

**mobocracy** /mɒˈbɒkrəsi/, *n., pl.* **-cies. 1.** rule by the mob; political control by a mob. **2.** the mob as a ruling class. [MOB, *n.* + -(O)CRACY; modelled on DEMOCRACY, etc.] **– mobocratic** /mɒboʊˈkrætɪk/, **mobocratical** /mɒboʊˈkrætɪkəl/, *adj.*

**mobster** /ˈmɒbstə/, *n. U.S.* a member of a gang of criminals. [MOB + -STER]

**moccasin** /ˈmɒkəsən/, *n.* **1.** a shoe made entirely of soft leather, as deerskin, worn originally by the American Indians. **2.** a venomous snake, *Ancistrodon piscivorus,* of the southern U.S., found in or near water (**water-moccasin**). [Eastern Algonquian languages (Powhatan and Massachusetts); ? akin to *makak* small case or box]

**mocha** /ˈmɒkə/, *n.* **1.** a choice variety of coffee, originally coming from Mocha, a seaport in south-west Yemen, a republic in Arabia. **2.** a flavouring obtained from coffee infusion or combined chocolate and coffee infusion. **3.** a glove leather, finer and thinner than doeskin, the best grades of which are made from Arabian goatskins. **4.** a cake or pudding flavoured with a combined coffee and chocolate mixture. **5.** a dark chocolate colour. Also, **mokha.**

**mock** /mɒk/, *v.t.* **1.** to assail or treat with ridicule or derision. **2.** to ridicule by mimicry of action or speech; mimic derisively. **3.** to mimic, imitate, or counterfeit. **4.** to defy; set at naught. **5.** to deceive, delude, or disappoint. **6. mock up,** to build or construct, esp. quickly, as a mock-up. *–v.i.* **7.** to use ridicule or derision; scoff; jeer (oft. fol. by *at*). *–n.* **8.** a mocking or derisive action or speech; mockery or derision. **9.** something mocked or derided; an object of derision. **10.** imitation. *–adj.* **11.** being an imitation or having merely the semblance of something: *a mock battle.* [ME *mokken,* from OF *mocquer;* orig. uncert.] **– mocker,** *n.* **– mockingly,** *adv.*

**mock cream** /– ˈkrim/, *n.* a cake filling with a creamy consistency, made by creaming butter and icing sugar with flavouring.

**mocker**[1] /ˈmɒkə/, *n. in the phrase* **put the mocker(s) on,** to bring bad luck to ; jinx. Also, **put the mock(s) on.**

**mocker**[2] /ˈmɒkə/, *Colloq. –n.* **1.** clothing. *–v.i.* **2. mocker up,** to dress up: *he's all mockered up.*

**mocker**[3] /ˈmɒkə/, *n. N.Z. Colloq.* →**bellbird** (def. 2). [Maori *makomako*]

**mockery** /ˈmɒkəri/, *n., pl.* **-ries. 1.** ridicule or derision. **2.** a derisive action or speech. **3.** a subject or occasion of derision. **4.** an imitation, esp. of a ridiculous or unsatisfactory kind. **5.** a mere travesty, or mocking pretence. **6.** something absurdly or offensively inadequate or unfitting.

**mock-heroic** /mɒk-həˈroʊɪk/, *adj.* **1.** exaggerating of low or insignificant material in a literary work to heroic proportions or in a heroic style in order to ridicule it. *–n.* **2.** the literary device or style which employs this technique. **– mock-heroically,** *adv.*

**mockingbird** /ˈmɒkɪŋbɜd/, *n.* **1.** in Australia, the small, elusive, rufous scrub-bird, *Atrichornis rufescens,* noted for its ability as a mimic. **2.** elsewhere, any of several grey, black, and white songbirds of the genus *Mimus,* remarkable for their imitative powers, esp. the celebrated mocker, *M. polyglottos,* of the southern U.S. and Mexico. **3.** any of various allied or similar birds, as the **blue mockingbird,** *Melanotis caerulescens,* of Mexico.

mockingbird

**mock moon** /mɒk ˈmun/, *n.* →**paraselene.**

**mock-olive** /mɒk-ˈɒləv/, *n.* any species of the genus *Notelaea,* of the olive family, of eastern Australia.

**mock orange** /mɒk ˈɒrɪndʒ/, *n.* any of several species of *Philadelphus,* esp. *P. coronaria,* shrubs grown in gardens for their sweet-scented white flowers; syringa (def.1).

**mock sun** /– ˈsʌn/, *n.* →**parhelion.**

**mock turtle soup,** *n.* a brown soup prepared from a calf's head, supposed to resemble real turtle soup.

**mock-up** /ˈmɒk-ʌp/, *n.* **1.** a model, built to scale, of a machine, apparatus, or weapon, used in studying the construction and in testing a new development, or in teaching men how to operate the actual machine, apparatus, or weapon. **2.** a model of a finished book or magazine with the essential detail only sketched in.

**mod** /mɒd/, *Colloq. –adj.* **1.** modern. **2.** of or pertaining to a style of dress, furnishing, behaviour, etc., which is fashionable to the point of being unconventional. *–n.* **3.** a young person of the early 1960s, esp. in Britain, who was neatly dressed, had ungreased hair, and who usu. rode a motor scooter in preference to a motor bike. Cf. **rocker.**

**mod.,** **1.** moderate. **2.** *Music.* moderato.

**modal** /ˈmoʊdl/, *adj.* **1.** of or pertaining to mode, manner, or form. **2.** *Music.* pertaining to mode. **3.** *Gram.* denoting or pertaining to mood. **4.** *Philos.* pertaining to mode as distinguished from substance, matter, or basic attribute. **5.** *Logic.* exhibiting or expressing some phase of modality. [ML *modālis,* from L *modus* MODE[1]] **– modally,** *adv.*

**modality** /moʊˈdæləti/, *n., pl.* **-ties. 1.** modal quality or state. **2.** a modal attribute or circumstance. **3.** *Logic.* **a.** that fourfold classification of propositions according to whether the truth of what they assert is either *contingent, possible, impossible* or *necessary.* **b.** (in Kantian logic) that threefold classification of judgments according to whether they are either *problematic, assertoric,* or *apodictic.* **4.** *Med.* the application of a therapeutic agent, usu. a physical therapeutic agent.

**mod cons** /mɒd ˈkɒnz/, *n. pl. Colloq.* modern conveniences.

**mode**[1] /moʊd/, *n.* **1.** manner of acting or doing; a method; a way. **2.** the natural disposition or the manner of existence or action of anything; a form: *heat is a mode of motion.* **3.** *Philos.* appearance, form, or disposition taken by a single reality or by an essential property or attribute of it. **4.** *Logic.* any one of the various forms (four in Scholastic logic, three in Kant) of modal propositions. **5.** *Music.* **a.** any of various arrangements of the diatonic tones of an octave, differing from one another in the order of the major seconds and minor seconds. **b.** an ordered selection of tones from all the tones available in the octave of a particular tonal system; thus the major scale and the whole-tone scale are two of the modes of the chromatic system. **6.** *Gram.* mood. **7.** *Statistics.* (in a statistical population) the category, value, or interval of the variable having the greatest frequency. **8.** *Geol.* the actual mineral composition of a rock, expressed in percentages by weight. **9.** *Engineering.* a resonant oscillation in a system. [ME, from L *modus* measure, due measure, manner]

**mode**[2] /moʊd/, *n.* **1.** customary or conventional usage in manners, dress, etc., esp. as observed by persons of fashion. **2.** a prevailing style or fashion. [F, from L *modus* MODE[1]]

**model** /ˈmɒdl/, *n., adj., v.,* **-elled, -elling** or (*U.S.*) **-eled, -eling.** *–n.* **1.** a standard or example for imitation or comparison; a pattern. **2.** a representation, generally in miniature, to show the construction or serve as a copy of something. **3.** an image in clay, wax, or the like to be reproduced in more durable material. **4.** a person, esp. a young woman, who poses for a painter, photographer, sculptor, etc. **5.** one employed to put on articles of apparel to display them to customers; a mannequin. **6.** (euphemistically) a prostitute. **7.** mode of structure or formation. **8.** a typical or specific form or style. *–adj.* **9.** serving as a model. **10.** worthy to serve as a model; exemplary. *–v.t.* **11.** to form or plan according to a model. **12.** to give shape or form to; fashion. **13.** to make a model or representation of. **14.** to fashion in clay, wax, or the like. **15.** to display, esp. by wearing: *to model evening dresses.* *–v.i.* **16.** to make models. **17.** to produce designs in some plastic material. **18.** to assume a typical or natural appearance, as the parts of a drawing in progress. **19.** to serve or be employed as a model. [F *modèle,* from It. *modello,* diminutive of *modo,* from L *modus* MODE[1]] – **modeller,** *n.*

**modelling** /'mɒdəlɪŋ, 'mɒdlɪŋ/, *n.* **1.** the act or art of one who models. **2.** the process of producing sculptured form with plastic material, usu. clay, as for reproduction in a more durable material. **3.** *Graphic Arts.* the process of rendering the illusion of the third dimension. **4.** the undulations of form in sculpture.

**modem** /'moʊdəm/, *n.* a device which enables one to connect a peripheral device to a computer.

**moderate** /'mɒdrət, -ərət/, *adj., n.;* /'mɒdəreɪt/, *v.,* **-rated, -rating.** *–adj.* **1.** kept or keeping within due bounds; not extreme, excessive, or intense: *a moderate request.* **2.** of medium quantity, extent, etc.: *a moderate income.* **3.** mediocre; fair: *moderate ability.* **4.** of or pertaining to moderates, as in politics or religion. *–n.* **5.** one who is moderate in opinion or action, or opposed to extreme views and courses, esp. in politics or religion. **6.** (*usu. cap.*) a member of a political party advocating moderate reform. *–v.t.* **7.** to reduce the excessiveness of; make less violent, severe, intense, or rigorous. **8.** to preside over or at, as a public meeting. *–v.i.* **9.** to become less violent, severe, intense, or rigorous. **10.** to act as moderator; preside. [ME, from L *moderātus,* pp.] – **moderately,** *adv.* – **moderateness,** *n.*

**moderate breeze** /'– briz/, *n.* a wind of Beaufort scale force 4, i.e. one with average wind speed of 11 to 16 knots, or 20 to 28 km/h.

**moderation** /mɒdə'reɪʃən/, *n.* **1.** the quality of being moderate; restraint; avoidance of extremes; temperance. **2.** the act of moderating. **3.** *Physics.* the slowing down of neutrons on passing through matter, owing to repeated collisions with nuclei. **4. in moderation,** without excess; moderately.

**moderato** /mɒdə'ratoʊ/, *adv.* **1.** (a musical direction) moderately; in moderate time. *–adj.* **2.** moderate.

**moderator** /'mɒdəreɪtə/, *n.* **1.** one who or that which moderates. **2.** a presiding officer, as over a public forum, a legislative body, or an ecclesiastical body in the Presbyterian Church. **3.** *Physics.* a substance, as graphite or heavy water, used to slow down neutrons from the high energies at which they are released in fission to speeds suitable for further fission. **4.** →**chairman.** – **moderatorship,** *n.*

**modern** /'mɒdn/, *adj.* **1.** of or pertaining to present and recent time; not ancient or remote. **2.** characteristic of present and recent time; not antiquated or obsolete. **3.** of or pertaining to various styles of jazz, evolved in the 1940s and much developed since then, characterised by complex harmonies and rhythms, free improvisation, and usu. played by small groups. Cf. **bebop.** **4.** (of a living language) in its most recent period; in the latest stage of its development; new. *–n.* **5.** a person of modern times. **6.** one whose views and tastes are modern. **7.** *Print.* a type style differentiated from *old style* by heavy vertical strokes and straight serifs. [LL *modernus,* from L *modō* just now (orig. abl. of *modus* MODE[1])] – **modernly,** *adv.* – **modernness,** *n.*

**modern dance** /– 'dæns/, *n.* a form of dance originating in ballet and incorporating many of its movements, but disregarding some of its conventions.

**Modern English** /mɒdn 'ɪŋglɪʃ/, *n.* the English language since *c.* 1475.

**modern figure** /mɒdn 'fɪgə/, *n. Print.* →**lining figure.**

**Modern French** /mɒdn 'frɛntʃ/, *n.* the French language since *c.* 1600.

**Modern Greek** /– 'grik/, *n.* the Greek language since *c.* 1500.

**Modern Hebrew** /– 'hibru/, *n.* the language of modern Israel, a revived form of ancient Hebrew.

**modern history** /mɒdn 'hɪstri/, *n.* **1.** history since the Renaissance. **2.** history since the French Revolution (1789).

**modernise** /'mɒdənaɪz/, *v.,* **-nised, -nising.** *–v.t.* **1.** to make modern; give a modern character or appearance to. *–v.i.* **2.** to become modern; adopt modern ways, views, etc. Also, **modernize.** – **modernisation** /mɒdənaɪ'zeɪʃən/, *n.* – **moderniser,** *n.*

**modernism** /'mɒdənɪzəm/, *n.* **1.** modern character; modern tendencies; sympathy with what is modern. **2.** a modern usage or characteristic. **3.** *Theol.* **a.** (*cap.*) a Roman Catholic movement which interpreted the teachings of the church in the light of the philosophy and science of the late 19th and early 20th centuries; condemned by Pope Pius X in 1907. **b.** the liberal theological tendency in Protestantism (opposed to *fundamentalism*).

**modernist** /'mɒdənəst/, *n.* **1.** one who follows or favours modern ways, tendencies, etc. **2.** one who advocates the study of modern subjects in preference to ancient classics. **3.** an adherent of modernism in theological questions. *–adj.* **4.** of modernists or modernism.

**modernistic** /'mɒdənɪstɪk/, *adj.* **1.** modern. **2.** of or pertaining to modernism or modernists: *a modernistic painting.*

**modernity** /mə'dɜnəti/, *n., pl.* **-ties.** **1.** the quality of being modern. **2.** something modern.

**modest** /'mɒdəst/, *adj.* **1.** having or showing a moderate or humble estimate of one's merits, importance, etc.; free from vanity, egotism, boastfulness, or great pretensions. **2.** free from ostentation or showy extravagance: *a modest house.* **3.** moderate. **4.** having or showing regard for the decencies of behaviour, speech, dress, etc.; decent. [L *modestus* keeping due measure] – **modestly,** *adv.*

**modesty** /'mɒdəsti/, *n., pl.* **-ties.** **1.** the quality of being modest; freedom from vanity, boastfulness, etc. **2.** regard for decency of behaviour, speech, dress, etc. **3.** simplicity; moderation.

**modicum** /'mɒdəkəm/, *n.* a moderate or small quantity. [late ME, from L, neut. of *modicus* moderate]

**modification** /mɒdəfə'keɪʃən/, *n.* **1.** the act of modifying. **2.** the state of being modified; partial alteration. **3.** a modified form; a variety. **4.** *Biol.* a change in a living organism acquired from its own activity or environment and not transmitted to its descendants. **5.** limitation or qualification. **6.** *Gram.* **a.** the use of a modifier in a construction, or of modifiers in a class of constructions or in a language. **b.** the meaning of a modifier, esp. as it affects the meaning of the word or other form modified: *limitation is one kind of modification.* **c.** a change in the phonemic shape of a morpheme, word, or other form when it functions as an element in a construction, as the change of *not* to *-n't* in the phrase *doesn't.* **d.** the feature of a construction resulting from such a change, as in the phrases *doesn't* and *does not* which differ in modification. **e.** an adjustment in the form of a word as it passes from one language to another.

**modificatory** /'mɒdəfəkeɪtəri/, *adj.* modifying. Also, **modificative.**

**Modified Australian** /ˌmɒdəfaɪd ɒ'streɪljən/, *n.* that pronunciation of Australian English which seeks to imitate British upper class speech, usu. considered affected and unacceptable.

**modifier** /'mɒdəfaɪə/, *n.* **1.** one who or that which modifies. **2.** *Gram.* a word, phrase, or sentence element which limits or qualifies the sense of another word, phrase, or element in the same construction: *adjectives are modifiers.*

**modify** /'mɒdəfaɪ/, *v.,* **-fied, -fying.** *–v.t.* **1.** to change somewhat the form or qualities of; alter somewhat. **2.** *Gram.* (of a word or larger linguistic form) to stand in a subordinate relation to (another form called the *head*) usu. with descriptive, limiting, or particularising meaning, as in *a good man,* where good modifies the head *man.* **3.** to be the modifier or attribute of. **4.** to change (a vowel) by umlaut. **5.** to reduce in degree; moderate; qualify. *–v.i.* **6.** to change; to become changed. [ME *modifie(n),* from L *modificāre, modificārī* set limits to] – **modifiable,** *adj.*

**modillion** /mə'dɪljən/, *n.* one of a series of ornamental blocks or brackets placed under the corona of a cornice in the Corinthian and other orders. [It. *modiglione,* from L *mūtulus*]

**modiolus** /mə'diələs, moʊ-/, *n., pl.* **-li** /-laɪ/. the central conical axis round which the cochlea of the ear winds. [NL, diminutive of L *modius* measure for grain]

modillion

**modish** /ˈmoʊdɪʃ/, *adj.* in accordance with the prevailing mode; fashionable; stylish. – **modishly,** *adv.* – **modishness,** *n.*

**modiste** /moʊˈdist/, *n.* a maker of or dealer in articles of fashionable attire, esp. women's dresses, millinery, etc. [F, from *mode* MODE[2]]

**mod squad** /ˈmɒd skwɒd/, *n. Prison Colloq.* plain-clothes warders who handle sudden transfers of prisoners to other gaols.

**modular** /ˈmɒdʒələ/, *adj.* **1.** of or pertaining to a module or modulus. **2.** composed of standardised units or sections for easy construction or flexible arrangement: *a modular home, modular furniture.*

**modulate** /ˈmɒdʒəleɪt/, *v.*, **-lated, -lating.** *–v.t.* **1.** to regulate by or adjust to a certain measure or proportion; soften; tone down. **2.** to alter or adapt (the voice) fittingly in utterance. **3.** *Music.* **a.** to attune to a certain pitch or key. **b.** to vary the volume of (tone). **4.** *Radio.* to cause the amplitude, frequency, phase, or intensity of (the carrier wave) to vary in accordance with the soundwaves or other signals, the frequency of the signal wave usu. being very much lower than that of the carrier; frequently applied to the application of soundwave signals to a microphone to change the characteristic of a transmitted radio wave. *–v.i.* **5.** *Radio.* to modulate a carrier wave. **6.** *Music.* to pass from one key to another. [L *modulātus,* pp., having measured] – **modulative,** *adj.*

**modulation** /mɒdʒəˈleɪʃən/, *n.* **1.** the act of modulating. **2.** the state of being modulated. **3.** *Music.* transition from one key to another. **4.** *Gram.* **a.** the use of a particular distribution of stress or pitch in a construction, as the use of rising pitch on the last word of *John is here?* **b.** the feature of a construction resulting from such a use, as in the question *John is here?* which differs from the statement *John is here* only in modulation.

**modulator** /ˈmɒdʒəleɪtə/, *n.* **1.** one who or that which modulates. **2.** *Radio.* a device for modulating a carrier wave. Cf. **modulate** (def. 4).

**module** /ˈmɒdʒul/, *n.* **1.** a standard or unit for measuring. **2.** a selected unit of measure, ranging in size from a few inches to several feet, used as a basis for planning and standardisation of building materials. **3.** a structural component, as a plexiglass cube, used as a basic unit for do-it-yourself furniture. **4.** a self-contained unit within a course of study. **5.** *Archit.* the size of some part, as the semidiameter of a column at the base of the shaft, taken as a unit of measure. **6.** *Electronics.* a small, standard unit which can be used in the construction of a piece of equipment. **7.** *Astronautics.* a detachable section of a space vehicle: *command module.* [L *modulus,* diminutive of *modus* measure, MODE[1]]

**modulus** /ˈmɒdʒələs/, *n., pl.* **-li** /-laɪ/. **1.** *Maths.* **a.** (of a number, esp. a complex number) magnitude or absolute value. **b.** See **congruent** (def. 3). **2.** *Physics.* →**coefficient** (def. 3). [L: a small measure. See MODULE]

**modulus of elasticity,** *n.* the ratio of the stress to the strain in a particular material.

**modulus of rigidity,** *n.* the modulus of elasticity applied to a body under a shearing strain; shear modulus.

**modus operandi** /ˌmoʊdəs ɒpəˈrændi/, *n.* mode of operating or working. [L]

**modus vivendi** /moʊdəs vəˈvɛndi/, *n.* **1.** mode of living. **2.** a temporary arrangement between persons or parties pending a settlement of matters in debate. [L]

**mofette** /moʊˈfɛt/, *n.* **1.** a noxious emanation, consisting chiefly of carbon dioxide, escaping from the earth in regions of nearly extinct volcanic activity. **2.** one of the openings or fissures from which this emanation issues. Also, **moffette.** [F, from It. (Naples d.) *mofetta*]

**moggy** /ˈmɒgi/, *n. Brit. Colloq.* a cat. Also, **mog, moggie.**

**mogo** /ˈmoʊgoʊ/, *n.* an Aboriginal stone hatchet. [Aboriginal]

**mogul** /ˈmoʊgəl/, *n.* **1.** an important person. **2.** a steam locomotive with a particular wheel arrangement consisting of a two wheel truck at the front, and three pairs of driving wheels. **3.** (*cap.*) a Mongol or Mongolian. *–adj.* **4.** (*cap.*) of or pertaining to the Moguls or their empire. [from one of the Mongol conquerors of India who ruled from 1526 to 1857; from Ar. and Pers. *Mughul* Mongol]

**mohair** /ˈmoʊhɛə/, *n.* **1.** the coat or fleece of an Angora goat. **2.** a fabric made of yarn from this fleece, in a plain weave for draperies and in a pile weave for upholstery. **3.** a garment made of this fabric. [obs. *mo(cayare)* mohair (from Ar. *mukhayyar*) + HAIR]

**Mohammedan** /məˈhæmədən/, *adj.* **1.** of or pertaining to Mohammed, A.D. 570?-632, Arab prophet, or his religious system; Islamic; Muslim. *–n.* **2.** a follower of Mohammed; a Muslim. Also, **Mahometan, Muhammadan, Muhammedan.**

**Mohammedanise** /məˈhæmədənaɪz/, *v.t.*, **-nised, -nising.** →**Islamise.** Also, **Mohammedanize.**

**Mohammedanism** /məˈhæmədənɪzəm/, *n.* the Mohammedan religion; Islam.

**Mohole** /ˈmoʊhoʊl/, *n.* any hole drilled through the earth's crust with the intention of penetrating the Mohorovicic discontinuity. [MO(HOROVICIC DISCONTINUITY) + HOLE]

**Mohorovicic discontinuity** /moʊhəˌroʊvətʃɪtʃ dɪskɒntənˈjuəti/, *n.* the dividing line between the earth's crust and mantle where an abrupt change occurs in the velocity of earthquake waves. Also, **moho.** [named after A. *Mohorovičić,* 1857-1936, Yugoslavian geologist]

**Mohs scale** /ˈmoʊz skeɪl/, *n.* a scale for measuring the hardness of a mineral by determining its resistance to scratching by other minerals of known hardness. [after F. *Mohs,* 1773-1839, German mineralogist]

**moiety** /ˈmɔɪəti/, *n., pl.* **-ties.** **1.** a half. **2.** an indefinite portion. **3.** *Anthrop.* one of two units into which a tribe is divided on the basis of unilateral descent. [ME *moit(i)e,* from OF, from LL *medietas* half, L the middle]

**moil** /mɔɪl/, *v.i.* **1.** to work hard; toil; drudge. *–n.* **2.** toil or drudgery. **3.** confusion, turmoil, or trouble. [ME *moile(n),* from OF *moillier* wet, moisten, from L *mollis* soft] – **moiler,** *n.*

**moire** /mwa/, *n.* a watered fabric, as of silk or wool. [F, from E MOHAIR]

**moiré** /ˈmwareɪ/, *adj.* **1.** watered as silk; having a wavelike pattern. *–n.* **2.** a design pressed on silk, rayon, etc., by engraved rollers. **3.** →**moire.**

**moist** /mɔɪst/, *adj.* **1.** moderately or slightly wet; damp; humid. **2.** (of the eyes) tearful. **3.** accompanied by or connected with liquid or moisture. [ME *moiste,* from OF: moist, mouldy. Cf. L *mūcidus* mouldy, musty] – **moistly,** *adv.* – **moistness,** *n.*

**moisten** /ˈmɔɪsən/, *v.t.* **1.** to make moist. *–v.i.* **2.** to become moist. – **moistener,** *n.*

**moisture** /ˈmɔɪstʃə/, *n.* water or other liquid rendering anything moist.

**moisturise** /ˈmɔɪstʃəraɪz/, *v.*, **-rised, -rising.** *–v.t.* **1.** to impart or restore moisture to: *to moisturise one's skin with cream.* *–v.i.* **2.** to make something moist: *an airconditioner that moisturises effectively.* Also, **moisturize.** – **moisturiser,** *n.*

**moity** /ˈmɔɪti/, *n.* wool which contains vegetable matter other than seed or burr, such as fern, bark, straw, etc.

**moke** /moʊk/, *n. Colloq.* **1.** a donkey. **2.** an inferior horse. **3.** *U.S.* (*derog.*) a Negro.

**mokha** /ˈmɒkə/, *n.* →**mocha.**

**moki** /ˈmoʊki/, *n. N.Z.* any of several common food fishes as the **blue moki,** *Latridopsis ciliaris,* and the **red moki,** *Cheilodactylus spectabilis.* [Maori]

**moko** /ˈmoʊkoʊ/, *n. N.Z.* Maori facial or body tattoo. [Maori]

**mol,** mole[4].

**molal** /ˈmoʊləl/, *adj.* **1.** pertaining to gram-molecular weight, or containing a mole. **2.** pertaining to a solution containing one mole of solute per 1000 grams of solvent.

**molality** /məˈlæləti/, *n.* the number of moles of solute per 1000 grams of solvent.

**molar**[1] /ˈmoʊlə/, *n.* **1.** a tooth adapted for grinding with a broad biting surface as in human dentition, which has twelve molar teeth, three in each quadrant. *–adj.* **2.** adapted for grinding, as teeth, esp. those in man, with a broad biting surface, situated behind the bicuspids. **3.** pertaining to such teeth. [L *molāris* grinder]

**molar**[2] /'moulə/, *adj.* **1.** *Physics.* pertaining to a body of matter as a whole, and contrasted with molecular and atomic. **2.** *Chem.* pertaining to a solution containing one mole of solute per litre of solution. [L *mōles* mass + -AR[1]]

**molarity** /mə'lærəti/, *n.* the number of moles of solute per litre of solution.

**molasses** /mə'læsəz/, *n.* **1.** the uncrystallised syrup drained from raw sugar. **2.** *U.S.* →**treacle** (def. 1). [Pg. *melaco,* from LL *mellāceum* must, from *mel* honey]

**mold** /mould/, *n., v.t., v.i. U.S.* →**mould.**

**moldavite** /'mɒldəvaɪt/, *n.* a natural green glass, found in Bohemia, an area in Czechoslovakia, and thought to be of possible meteoritic origin. Cf. **tektite.**

**moldboard** /'mouldbɔd/, *n. U.S.* →**mouldboard.**

**molder** /'mouldə/, *v.i., v.t., n. U.S.* →**moulder.**

**molding** /'mouldɪŋ/, *n. U.S.* →**moulding.**

**molding board** /'– bɔd/, *n. U.S.* →**moulding board.**

**moldy** /'mouldi/, *adj. U.S.* →**mouldy.**

**mole**[1] /moul/, *n.* **1.** a small congenital spot or blemish on the human skin, usu. of a dark colour and slightly elevated, and often hairy. **2.** a pigmented naevus. [ME; OE *māl,* c. OHG *meil* wrinkle, blemish]

**mole**[2] /moul/, *n.* **1.** any of various small insectivorous mammals, of Europe, Asia, and North America, esp. of the family Talpidae, living chiefly underground, and having velvety fur, very small eyes, and strong, fossorial forefeet. **2.** a person who establishes himself in the bureaucracy of the enemy so that he can act as a spy when required. [ME *molle,* c. MD and MLG *mol*]

mole[2]

**mole**[3] /moul/, *n.* **1.** a massive structure, esp. of stone, set up in the water, as for a breakwater or a pier. **2.** an anchorage or harbour protected by such a structure. [L *mōles* mass, dam]

**mole**[4] /moul/, *n.* the SI base unit of measurement of amount of substance equal to the amount of substance of a system which contains as many elementary entities as there are atoms in 0.012 kg of carbon-12. *Symbol:* mol [G, from *Molekül* MOLECULE]

**mole**[5] /moul/, *n.* a fleshy mass in the uterus formed by a haemorrhagic dead ovum. [L *mola* false conception, millstone]

**mole cricket** /'– krɪkət/, *n.* a burrowing insect of the genus *Gryllotalpa,* brown in colour, related to the true cricket, but with front claws adapted for digging in order to eat the roots of grasses and other plants.

**molecular** /mə'lɛkjələ/, *adj.* pertaining to, caused by or consisting of molecules. [NL *mōlēcula* MOLECULE + -AR[1]] – **molecularly,** *adv.*

**molecular beam** /– 'bim/, *n.* a stream of molecules in a vacuum moving in directions almost parallel, produced experimentally by passing the molecules through a series of narrow openings. Also, **molecular ray.**

**molecular biology** /– baɪ'ɒlədʒi/, *n.* the study of the structure and activity of biological macromolecules at a molecular level.

**molecular distillation** /– dɪstə'leɪʃən/, *n.* vacuum distillation in which the mean free path of the distillate molecules is of the same order as the distance between the heating and condensing surfaces; used for isotope separation.

**molecular film** /– 'fɪlm/, *n.* a film or layer one molecule thick.

**molecular formula** /– 'fɔmjələ/, *n.* the formula of a chemical compound showing the number and kind of atoms present in the molecule, but not their arrangement.

**molecular volume** /– 'vɒljum/, *n.* the volume occupied by one mole of a substance.

**molecular weight** /– 'weɪt/, *n.* the average weight of a molecule of an element or compound measured in units based on one twelfth of the weight of an atom of carbon-12; the sum of the atomic weights of all the atoms in a molecule.

**molecule** /'mɒləkjul/, *n.* **1.** *Chem., Physics.* the smallest physical unit of an element or compound, consisting of one or more like atoms in the first case, and two or more different atoms in the second case. **2.** a quantity of a substance, the weight of which, measured in any chosen unit, is numerically equal to the molecular weight; gram molecule. **3.** any very small particle. [NL *mōlēcula,* diminutive of L *mōles* mass. Cf. MOLE[3], MOLE[4]]

**molehill** /'moulhɪl/, *n.* **1.** a small mound or ridge of earth raised up by moles burrowing under the ground. **2. make a mountain out of a molehill,** to make something insignificant into a major obstacle or difficulty.

**moleskin** /'moulskɪn/, *n.* **1.** the fur of the mole, soft, deep grey in colour, and very fragile. **2.** a stout, napped, twilled cotton fabric used for sportsmen's and labourers' clothing. **3.** (*pl.*) garments, esp. trousers, of this fabric.

**molest** /mə'lɛst/, *v.t.* to interfere with annoyingly, injuriously, or with hostile intent. [ME *moleste(n),* from L *molestāre*] – **molestation** /mɒləs'teɪʃən/, *n.* – **molester,** *n.*

**moll**[1] /mɒl/, *n. Colloq.* **1.** the girlfriend or mistress of a gangster, thief, etc. **2.** →**tart**[2] (defs 3 and 4). **3.** →**prostitute. 4.** the girlfriend of a surfie, bikie, etc. [short for *Molly,* var. of MARY]

**moll**[2] /mɒl/, *adj. Music.* →**minor.** [G]

**mollescent** /mə'lɛsənt/, *adj.* producing less hardness or firmness; softening. [L *mollescens,* ppr.] – **mollescence,** *n.*

**mollify** /'mɒləfaɪ/, *v.t.,* **-fied, -fying. 1.** to soften in feeling or temper, as a person, the heart or mind, etc. **2.** to mitigate or appease, as rage. [ME *mollifie(n),* from L *mollificāre* soften] – **mollification** /mɒləfə'keɪʃən/, *n.* – **mollifier,** *n.* – **mollifyingly,** *adv.* – **mollifiable,** *adj.*

**mollusc** /'mɒləsk/, *n.* any invertebrate of the phylum Mollusca, characterised by a calcareous shell (sometimes lacking) of one, two, or more pieces that wholly or partly encloses the soft unsegmented body and including the chitons, snails, bivalves, squids, octopuses, etc. Also, *U.S.,* **mollusk.** [NL *mollusca,* pl., in L neut. pl. of *molluscus* soft (applied to a thin-shelled nut)] – **molluscan** /mə'lʌskən/, *adj., n.* – **mollusc-like,** *adj.*

**molluscoid** /mə'lʌskɔɪd/, *adj.* denoting or pertaining to an animal group comprising the bryozoans and brachiopods. Also, **molluscoidal** /mɒləs'kɔɪdl/.

**molluscum** /mə'lʌskəm/, *n., pl.* **-ca** /-kə/. any of various soft, rounded, cutaneous tumours.

**molly** /'mɒli/, *n., pl.* **mollies.** a livebearing fish of the genus *Mollienisia,* often kept in aquariums. [shortened form of NL *Mollienisia,* named after Comte de *Mollien,* 1758-1850]

**mollycoddle** /'mɒlikɒdl/, *v.t.,* **-dled, -dling.** to coddle; pamper. [*Molly* (var. of MARY) + CODDLE] – **mollycoddler,** *n.*

**mollydooker** /mɒli'dukə/, *n. Colloq.* a left-handed person. Also, **mollydook.**

**mollygrubber** /'mɒligrʌbə/, *n.* →**mullygrubber.**

**mollymawk** /'mɒlimɔk/, *n.* →**mallemuck.**

**molo** /'mɒlou/, *adj. Colloq.* drunk.

**moloch** /'moulɒk/, *n.* **1.** (*cap.*) Also, **Molech.** anything conceived as requiring terrible sacrifice: *the Moloch of War.* **2.** a spiny Australian lizard, *Moloch horridus.* **3.** →**mountain devil.** [from a Semitic deity whose worship was marked by the sacrificial burning of children offered by their own parents; from L (Vulgate), from Gk (Septuagint), from Heb. *Mōlek,* orig. *melek* king]

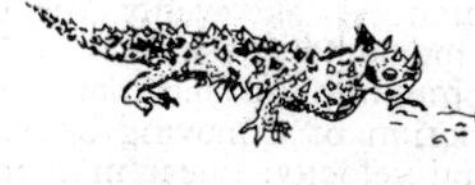
moloch (def. 2)

**Molotov cocktail** /mɒlətɒv 'kɒkteɪl/, *n.* an incendiary bomb consisting of a bottle filled with an inflammable liquid, usu. petrol, and a saturated wick which is ignited before the bottle is thrown. [named after Viacheslav Mikhailovich *Molotov,* b. 1890, Soviet statesman]

**molt** /moult/, *v., n. U.S.* →**moult.**

**molten** /'moultn/, *v.* **1.** a past participle of **melt.** –*adj.* **2.** liquefied by heat; in a state of fusion. **3.** produced by melting and casting: *a molten image.*

**molto** /'mɒltou/, *adv.* (a musical direction) much; very: *molto allegro.* [It., from L *multum*]

**Molucca balm** /məlʌkə 'bam/, *n.* an erect annual plant, *Molucella laevis,* with tall flower spikes which, owing to their green funnel-shaped calyces, are much used by florists;

bells-of-Ireland.

**mol. wt,** molecular weight.

**molybdate** /mə'lɪbdeɪt/, *n.* a salt of any molybdic acid.

**molybdenite** /mə'lɪbdənaɪt/, *n.* a soft, graphite-like mineral, molybdenum sulphide, $MoS_2$, occurring in foliated masses or scales; principal ore of molybdenum. [obs. *molybdena* MOLYBDENUM + -ITE[1]]

**molybdenous** /mə'lɪbdənəs/, *adj.* containing divalent molybdenum.

**molybdenum** /mə'lɪbdənəm/, *n.* a silver-white high-melting metalloid, alloyed with iron in making hard, high-speed cutting tools. *Symbol:* Mo; *at. wt:* 95.94; *at. no.:* 42; *sp. gr.:* 10.2. [NL, from L *molybdaena,* from Gk *molýbdaina* galena]

**molybdenum trioxide** /– traɪ'ɒksaɪd/, *n.* a white crystalline powder, $MoO_3$, which is the anhydride of molybdic acid; used in the manufacture of molybdenum compounds. Also, **molybdic anhydride, molybdic oxide.**

**molybdic** /mə'lɪbdɪk/, *adj.* of or containing molybdenum, esp. in the trivalent or hexavalent states.

**molybdic acid** /– 'æsəd/, *n.* a yellowish crystalline solid, $MoO_3$ $2H_2O$.

**molybdite** /mə'lɪbdaɪt/, *n.* a hydrous ferric molybdate, occurring in molybdenite. Also, **molybdic ochre.**

**mom** /mɒm/, *n. U.S. Colloq.* →**mother**[1].

**moment** /'moʊmənt/, *n.* **1.** an indefinitely short space of time; an instant: *wait a moment.* **2.** the present or other particular instant: *I cannot recall his name at the moment.* **3.** a definite stage, as in a course of events. **4.** importance or consequence: *of great moment.* **5.** *Statistics.* the average of a given power of the values of a set of variates. **6.** (of a physical quantity about an axis) the product of the quantity and its perpendicular distance from an axis: *moment of inertia, electric dipole moment, etc.* [ME, from L *mōmentum* movement, moment of time, etc.]

**momentarily** /'moʊməntrəli/; *Chiefly U.S.,* /moʊmən'terəli/, *adv.* **1.** for a moment: *to hesitate momentarily.* **2.** every moment; from moment to moment: *danger momentarily increasing.* **3.** at any moment: *momentarily liable to occur.*

**momentary** /'moʊməntri/, *adj.* **1.** lasting but a moment; very brief: *a momentary glimpse.* **2.** occurring at any moment: *to live in fear of momentary exposure.* **3.** constant; occurring at every moment. – **momentariness,** *n.*

**momently** /'moʊməntli/, *adv.* **1.** every moment; from moment to moment. **2.** for a moment; momentarily.

**moment of inertia,** *n.* the sum of the products of the mass of each element of a body and the square of its distance from an axis about which the body rotates.

**moment of truth,** *n.* **1.** the climax of a bullfight when the matador is about to kill the animal. **2.** any moment when a person's character, courage, skill, etc., are put to a severe test.

**momentous** /moʊ'mentəs, mə-/, *adj.* of great importance or consequence; fraught with serious or far-reaching consequences, as events, decisions, etc. – **momentously,** *adv.* – **momentousness,** *n.*

**momentum** /mə'mentəm/, *n., pl.* **ta** /-tə/. **1.** the quantity of motion of a moving body, equal to the product of its mass and velocity; linear momentum. **2.** impetus, as of a moving body. [L. See MOMENT]

**mon-,** variant of **mono-,** before vowels.

**Mon** /moʊn/, *n.* one of the Mon-Khmer languages.

**Mon.,** Monday.

**monachal** /'mɒnəkəl/, *adj.* →**monastic.** [ML *monachālis,* from LL *monachus* MONK]

**monachism** /'mɒnəkɪzəm/, *n.* →**monasticism.**

**Monaco** /mə'nakoʊ/, *n.* a principality on the Mediterranean coast, bordering south-eastern France.

**monad** /'moʊnæd/, *n.* **1.** *Biol.* **a.** any simple single-celled organism, **b.** a certain type of small, flagellate, colourless, naked amoeboid with one to three flagella. **2.** *Chem.* an element, atom or radical having a valency of one. **3.** *Philos.* an entity, conceived after the fashion of the self, and regarded as the ultimate unit of being or as a microcosm. **4.** a single unit or entity. **5.** →**atman.** [LL *monas,* from Gk: unit] – **monadic** /mə'nædɪk/, **monadical,** *adj.* – **monadically,** *adv.*

**monadelphous** /mɒnə'delfəs/, *adj.* **1.** (of stamens) united into one bundle or set by their filaments. **2.** (of a plant or flower) having the stamens so united. [MON- + Gk *adelphós* brother + -OUS]

**monadism** /'mɒnədɪzəm, 'moʊnə-/, *n. Philos.* **1.** the doctrine of monads as ultimate units of being. **2.** the philosophy of Gottfried Wilhelm von Leibnitz, 1646-1716, German philosopher, writer, and mathematician. Also, **monadology** /mɒnə'dɒlədʒi, moʊnə-/. – **monadistic** /mɒnə'dɪstɪk, moʊnə-/, *adj.*

**monadnock** /mə'nædnɒk/, *n.* a residual hill or mountain standing well above the surface of the surrounding eroded country. [named after Mount *Monadnock,* New Hampshire, U.S.A.; from N. Amer. Ind: (object) standing out, isolated]

**Mona Lisa smile,** *n.* an enigmatic smile, similar to that of the woman in the famous portrait by Leonardo da Vinci, 1452-1519, painter and sculptor.

**monandrous** /mə'nændrəs/, *adj.* **1.** having only one husband at a time. **2.** of or characterised by monandry: *the monandrous system.* **3.** *Bot.* **a.** (of a flower) having only one stamen. **b.** (of a plant) having such flowers. [Gk *mónandros* having one husband]

**monandry** /mə'nændri/, *n.* the practice or the condition of having only one husband at a time.

**monarch** /'mɒnək, -ak/, *n.* **1.** a hereditary sovereign with more or less limited powers, as a king, queen, emperor, etc. **2.** a sole and absolute ruler of a state. **3.** one who or that which holds a dominating or pre-eminent position. **4.** a large migratory reddish brown butterfly, *Danaus plexippus,* having black and white markings, whose larva feeds on milkweed; wanderer. [late ME, from LL *monarcha,* from Gk *monárchēs* ruling alone]

**monarchal** /mə'nakəl/, *adj.* **1.** pertaining to, characteristic of, or befitting a monarch. **2.** having the status of a monarch. Also, **monarchial** /mə'nakiəl/. – **monarchally,** *adv.*

**Monarchian** /mə'nakiən/, *Theol.* –*n.* **1.** one who holds that God must be understood as being a single deity, and rejecting the doctrine of the Trinity. Cf. **Unitarian. 2.** an adherent of a 2nd-3rd century heresy teaching this. –*adj.* **3.** denoting or pertaining to this doctrine or heresy. – **Monarchianism,** *n.*

**monarchical** /mə'nakɪkəl/, *adj.* **1.** of a monarch or monarchy. **2.** characterised by or favouring monarchy. Also, **monarchic.** – **monarchically,** *adv.*

**monarchism** /'mɒnəkɪzəm/, *n.* **1.** the principles of monarchy. **2.** advocacy of monarchical principles. – **monarchist,** *n., adj.* – **monarchistic** /mɒnə'kɪstɪk/, *adj.*

**monarchy** /'mɒnəki/, *n., pl.* **-chies. 1.** a government or state in which the supreme power is actually or nominally lodged in a monarch (known as an **absolute** or **despotic monarchy** when the monarch's authority is not limited by laws or a constitution, and as a **limited** or **constitutional monarchy** when the monarch's authority is so limited). **2.** supreme power or sovereignty wielded by a single person. [ME *monarchie,* from LL *monarchia,* from Gk]

**monas** /'mɒnæs, 'moʊ-/, *n., pl.* **monades** /'mɒnədiz/. →**monad.** [LL]

**monastery** /'mɒnəstri, -təri/, *n., pl.* **-teries. 1.** a house or place of residence occupied by a community of persons, esp. monks, living in seclusion from the world under religious vows. **2.** the community of persons living in such a place. [ME, from LL *monastērium,* from LGk *monastḗrion* solitary dwelling] – **monasterial** /mɒnəs'tɪəriəl/, *adj.*

**monastic** /mə'næstɪk/, *adj.* Also, **monastical. 1.** of or pertaining to monasteries: *monastic architecture.* **2.** of, pertaining to, or characteristic of monks, or other persons living in seclusion from the world under religious vows: *monastic vows of poverty, chastity, and obedience.* –*n.* **3.** a member of a monastic community or order; a monk. [ML *monasticus,* from LGk *monastikós* living in solitude] – **monastically,** *adv.*

**monasticism** /mə'næstəsɪzəm/, *n.* the monastic system, condition, or mode of life.

**monatomic** /mɒnə'tɒmɪk/, *adj.* **1.** having one atom in the molecule. **2.** containing one replaceable atom or group. **3.** having a valency of one.

**monaural** /mɒn'ɔrəl/, *adj.* of or pertaining to one ear.

**monaxial** /mɒn'æksiəl/, *adj. Bot.* **1.** →**uniaxial. 2.** having flowers that grow on the primary axis.

**monazite** /'mɒnəzaɪt/, *n.* a reddish brown or yellow brown mineral, a phosphate of cerium and lanthanum (Ce, La)$PO_4$, commonly containing thorium; the principal ore of the rare earths and thorium. [G *Monazit,* from Gk *monázein* be alone + *-it* -ITE[1]]

**Monday** /ˈmʌndeɪ, -di/, *n.* the second day of the week, following Sunday. [ME *Mone(n)day,* OE *mōn(an)dæg* moon's day, used to render LL *Lūnae dies*]

**Mondayise** /ˈmʌndeɪaɪz/, *v.t.,* **-ised, -ising.** *N.Z. Colloq.* to shift (a public holiday) falling during a weekend to the following Monday.

**Mondayitis** /mʌndeɪˈaɪtəs/, *n. Colloq.* lassitude and general reluctance to work as is often experienced on Mondays.

**Mond process** /ˈmɒnd ˌproʊsɛs/, *n.* a method of extracting pure nickel from the impure metal by reacting carbon monoxide with the metal to form the carbonyl which is decomposed by heating into pure nickel and carbon monoxide. [named after Ludwig *Mond,* 1839-1909, British chemist, born in Germany]

**Mondurup bell** /ˈmɒndərʌp bɛl/, *n.* a shrub of the family Myrtaceae, *Darwinia meeboldii,* with drooping flower-heads and red-tipped bracts.

**monecious** /məˈniʃəs/, *adj.* →**monoecious.**

**Monegasque** /mɒnəˈgæsk/, *adj.* **1.** of or pertaining to Monaco or its inhabitants. *–n.* **2.** a native or inhabitant of Monaco.

**Monel metal** /mɒˈnɛl mɛtəl/, *n.* **1.** a non-rusting, silvery-white alloy containing about 67 per cent nickel, 28 per cent copper, and 5 per cent other metals, produced from the nickeliferous ores of the Sudbury district in Canada, and used for a great number of purposes. **2.** a trademark for this metal. Also, **Monell metal.** [named after Ambrose *Monell,* d. 1921, of New York]

**monetary** /ˈmʌnətri, -təri/, *adj.* **1.** of or pertaining to the coinage or currency of a country. **2.** of or pertaining to money, or pecuniary matters: *monetary consideration.* [L *monētārius* pertaining to the mint] – **monetarily,** *adv.*

**monetary unit** /ˈ– junət/, *n.* the standard unit of value of the currency of a country.

**monetise** /ˈmʌnətaɪz/, *v.t.,* **-tised, -tising.** **1.** to legalise as money. **2.** to coin into money: *to monetise gold.* **3.** to give the character of money to. Also, **monetize.** – **monetisation** /mʌnətaɪˈzeɪʃən/, *n.*

**money** /ˈmʌni/, *n., pl.* **-eys, -ies.** **1.** gold, silver, or other metal in pieces of convenient form stamped by public authority and issued as a medium of exchange and measure of value. **2.** current coin. **3.** coin or certificate (as banknotes, etc.) generally accepted in payment of debts and current transactions. **4.** any article or substance similarly used. **5.** a particular form or denomination of currency. **6.** a money of account. **7.** property considered with reference to its pecuniary value. **8.** an amount or sum of money. **9.** wealth reckoned in terms of money. **10.** (*pl.*) *Archaic or Law.* pecuniary sums. **11.** pecuniary profit. **12. for one's money,** as far as one's own choice or preference is concerned; in one's own opinion. **13. in the money,** *Colloq* rich. **14. make money,** to become rich. **15. money's worth,** full value; greatest possible advantage. **16. put money into,** to invest in. [ME *moneye,* from OF *moneie,* from L *monēta* mint, money, from *Jūno Monēto* Juno the Adviser, in whose temple at Rome money was coined]

**moneybag** /ˈmʌnibæg/, *n.* **1.** a bag for money. **2.** (*pl. construed as sing.*) a wealthy person.

**money bill** /ˈmʌni bɪl/, *n.* a bill imposing taxation or appropriating public moneys for expenditure.

**moneybox** /ˈmʌnibɒks/, *n.* a closed or locked box into which coins are dropped through a slit, used for savings, collecting contributions to charities, etc.

**moneychanger** /ˈmʌnitʃeɪndʒə/, *n.* one whose business it is to change money at a fixed or official rate.

**moneyed** /ˈmʌnid/, *adj.* **1.** having money; wealthy. **2.** consisting of or representing money: *moneyed interests.*

**money-grubber** /ˈmʌni-grʌbə/, *n. Colloq.* an avaricous person; one devoted entirely to the making of money. – **money-grubbing,** *adj.*

**moneylender** /ˈmʌnilɛndə/, *n.* one whose business it is to lend money at interest.

**moneymaker** /ˈmʌnimeɪkə/, *n.* **1.** one engaged in or successful at gaining money. **2.** something that yields pecuniary profit. – **moneymaking,** *n., adj.*

**money market** /ˈmʌni makət/, *n.* a market in which large amounts of money (usu. more than $50 000) are borrowed and lent for short periods of time (usu. less than a month).

**money-minded** /ˈmʌni-maɪndəd/, *adj.* **1.** having a strong sense of the financial worth or pecuniary advantage to be gained from any action. **2.** taking a great interest in the exact cost of things; judging worth by financial value only.

**money order** /ˈmʌni ɔdə/, *n.* an order for the payment of money, as one issued by one post office and payable at another, usu. for a sum larger than ten dollars, and requiring proof of ownership before being cashed. Cf. **postal order.**

**money spider** /ˈ– spaɪdə/, *n.* any spiderling, popularly considered a harbinger of riches.

**money-spinner** /ˈmʌni-spɪnə/, *n. Colloq.* a business enterprise or property which is very profitable.

**money wages** /ˈmʌni weɪdʒəz/, *n. pl.* the actual amount of money paid out as wages for work done (opposed to *real wages*).

**mong** /mʌŋ/, *n. Colloq.* a mongrel dog.

**mongan** /ˈmɒŋgən/, *n.* a dark brown, ring-tail possum, *Pseudocheirus herbertensis,* of the Herbert river district of Queensland. [Aboriginal]

**monger** /ˈmʌŋgə/, *n.* (*usu. in compounds*) **1.** a dealer in some commodity: *a fishmonger.* **2.** one who busies himself with something in a sordid or petty way: *a scandalmonger.* [ME *mongere,* OE *mangere* (c. Icel. *mangari*), from L *mang(o)* trader + *-ere* -ER[1]] – **mongering,** *n., adj.*

**Mongol** /ˈmɒŋgəl/, *n.* **1.** one of an Asian people now living chiefly in Mongolia. **2.** one having Mongoloid characteristics. **3.** any Mongolian language. **4.** (*oft. l.c.*) *Pathol.* one afflicted with Down's syndrome. *–adj.* **5.** Mongolian. **6.** (*oft. l.c.*) *Pathol.* of or pertaining to Down's syndrome.

**Mongolia** /mɒŋˈgoʊliə/, *n.* **1.** a vast region of east-central Asia, consisting of the Mongolian People's Republic (Outer Mongolia) and the Inner Mongolian Autonomous Region of China.

**Mongolian** /mɒŋˈgoʊliən/, *adj.* **1.** pertaining to Mongolia. **2.** of or pertaining to the Mongol people of inner Asia. **3.** *Anthrop.* Mongoloid. **4.** (*oft. l.c.*) *Pathol.* affected with Down's syndrome. **5.** of or pertaining to Mongolian (def. 9). *–n.* **6.** a member of the Mongoloid peoples of Asia. **7.** a native or inhabitant of Inner Mongolia. **8.** a native or inhabitant of the Mongolian People's Republic. **9.** a subfamily of languages, including the languages of the Mongols, a member of the Altaic linguistic family. **10.** any of the languages of this family.

**Mongolian People's Republic,** *n.* a republic in the northern part of Mongolia. Formerly, **Outer Mongolia.**

**Mongolic** /mɒŋˈgɒlɪk/, *adj.* **1.** Mongolian. *–n.* **2.** →**Mongolian** (def. 9).

**Mongolism** /ˈmɒŋgəlɪzəm/, *n.* (*oft. l.c.*) →**Down's syndrome.**

**Mongoloid** /ˈmɒŋgəlɔɪd/, *adj.* **1.** resembling the Mongols. **2.** *Anthrop.* of, pertaining to, or characteristic of a racial division of mankind, characterised chiefly by yellowish complexion, prominent cheekbones, epicanthic folds about the eyes, short nose, straight black hair, and scanty facial hair, and including the Mongols, Manchus, Chinese, Koreans, Japanese, Annamese, Thais, Burmese and Tibetans. **3.** (*oft. l.c.*) *Pathol.* of, pertaining to, or characteristic of Down's syndrome. *–n.* **4.** a person of a Mongoloid race. **5.** (*oft. l.c.*) *Pathol.* one afflicted with Down's syndrome.

**mongoose** /ˈmɒŋgus/, *n., pl.* **-gooses.** a slender ferret-like carnivore, typified by *Herpestes edwardsii,* of India, of the same genus as the common ichneumon, used for destroying rats, etc., and noted for its ability to kill certain venomous snakes. [Marathi (a language of West India) *mangūs*]

mongoose

**mongrel** /ˈmʌŋgrəl/, *n.* **1.** any animal or plant resulting from the crossing of different breeds or varieties. **2.** any cross between different things. **3.** a dog of mixed or uncertain breed. *–adj.* **4.** of or like a mongrel: *of mixed breed, race, origin, nature, etc.* **5.** inferior. [obs. *mong* mixture (OE *gemang*) + -REL] – **mongrelism, mongrelness,** *n.* – **mongrelly,** *adv.*

**mongrelise** /ˈmʌŋgrəlaɪz/, *v.t.,* **-lised, -lising.** to subject (a breed, race, etc.) to crossbreeding, esp. with a breed or race considered inferior; to make mongrel in race, composition, character, etc. Also, **mongrelize.** – **mongrelisation** /mʌŋgrəlaɪˈzeɪʃən/, *n.* – **mongreliser,** *n.*

**mongst** /mʌŋst/, *prep. Poetic.* →**amongst.**

**moniker** /ˈmɒnəkə/, *n. Colloq.* a person's name; a nickname. Also, **monicker, monniker.** [b. MONOGRAM and MARKER]

**monilia** /məˈnɪliə/, *n.* **1.** a yeast-like fungus, *Candida albicans,* which occasionally causes a condition of infection, mainly in the mouth and vagina. **2.** Also, **moniliasis.** the condition caused by the monilia organism; candidiasis; thrush.

**moniliform** /məˈnɪləfɔm/, *adj.* **1.** *Bot., Zool.* consisting of or characterised by a series of beadlike swellings alternating with contractions, as certain roots, stems, etc. **2.** resembling a string of beads. [L *monīle* necklace + -(I)FORM]

moniliform fruits

**monism** /ˈmɒnɪzəm/, *n.* **1.** the doctrine of one ultimate substance or principle, as mind (*idealism*) or matter (*materialism*), or something that is neither mind nor matter but the ground of both. **2.** the theory that reality is one (opposed to *pluralism*). [NL *monismus,* from Gk *mónos* single] – **monist,** *n.* – **monistic** /məˈnɪstɪk/, *adj.* – **monistically** /məˈnɪstɪkli/, *adv.*

**monition** /məˈnɪʃən/, *n.* **1.** admonition; warning; caution. **2.** an official or legal notice. **3.** *Obs. Law.* a court order summoning a party, either to commence suit by appearance and answer or to answer contempt charges. **4.** an old process analagous to a writ of summons, by which a cause for the condemnation of a ship was commenced. **5.** a formal notice from a bishop requiring the amendment of an ecclesiastical offence. [ME, from L *monitio* a reminding]

**monitor** /ˈmɒnətə/, *n.* **1.** one who admonishes, esp. with reference to conduct. **2.** something that serves to remind or give warning. **3.** a device used to check, observe, or record the operation of a machine or system. **4.** (formerly) an ironclad warship with a low freeboard and one or more revolving turrets, each containing one or more large-calibre guns. **5.** (in hydraulic mining) a nozzle for projecting water at and breaking up sand or gravel; giant. **6.** *U.S.* a raised construction on a roof having windows for lighting or ventilating a building, as a factory or warehouse. **7.** any of the large lizards constituting the genus *Varanus* and family Varanidae of Africa, the East Indies, and Australia, supposed to give warning of the presence of crocodiles. **8.** *Television.* a screen or set of screens used, as in a studio, to check the transmission. *–v.t.* **9.** *Radio, T.V.* **a.** to listen to or watch (transmitted signals) using a receiving set in order to check the quality of the transmission. **b.** to listen to (broadcasts) for operating compliance, censorship, propaganda analysis, and similar purposes. **10.** to check, observe, or record, the operation of (a machine, etc.), without interfering with the operation. **11.** to supervise; observe critically. [L] – **monitorship,** *n.*

**monitorial** /mɒnəˈtɔriəl/, *adj.* **1.** of or pertaining to a monitor. **2.** monitory.

**monitory** /ˈmɒnətəri, -tri/, *adj., n., pl.* **-ries.** *–adj.* **1.** serving to admonish or warn; admonitory. **2.** giving monition. *–n.* **3.** Also, **monitory letter.** a letter, as one from a bishop, containing a monition. [late ME, from L *monitōrius,* adj.]

**monitress** /ˈmɒnətrəs/, *n.* a female monitor.

**monk** /mʌŋk/, *n.* a man who has withdrawn from the world from religious motives, either as an eremite or, esp., as a member of an order of coenobites living under vows of poverty, chastity, and obedience, according to a rule. [ME; OE *munuc,* from LL *monachus,* from LGk *monachós,* adj., solitary (as n., monk)]

**monkery** /ˈmʌŋkəri/, *n., pl.* **-ries. 1.** the way of life, behaviour, etc., of monks. **2.** (*derog.*) the practices, beliefs, etc., of monks.

**monkey**[1] /ˈmʌŋki/, *n., pl.* **-keys,** *v.,* **-keyed, -keying.** *–n.* **1.** any member of the mammalian order Primates, including the guenons, macaques, langurs, capuchins, etc., but excluding man, the anthropoid apes, and usu., the lemurs. **2.** a person likened to such an animal, as a mischievous child, a mimic, etc. **3.** the fur of certain species of long-haired monkeys. **4.** *Colloq.* a sheep. **5.** any of various mechanical devices, as the ram of a pile-driving apparatus, or of a wool press. **6.** *U.S. Colloq.* an addiction to narcotic drugs, seen as a burden or affliction: *have a monkey on one's back.* **7.** *Colloq.* **a.** (formerly) the sum of £500. **b.** the sum of $500. **8.** *N.Z. Colloq.* →**mortgage. 9. get one's monkey up,** *Colloq.* to become angry or enraged. **10. make a monkey of,** to make a fool of. **11. monkey business,** trickery; underhand dealing. **12. monkey tricks,** mischief. *–v.i.* **13.** *Colloq.* to play or trifle idly; fool (oft. fol. by *about with* or *with*). *–v.t.* **14.** to imitate as a monkey does; ape; mimic. **15.** to mock. [apparently from LG. Cf. MLG *Moneke* (name of son of Martin the Ape in story of Reynard), from *mone-* (akin to Sp. and Pg. *mono* ape) + *-ke* (diminutive suffix)]

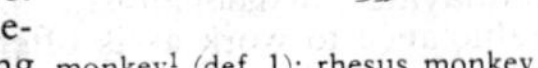

monkey[1] (def. 1): rhesus monkey

**monkey**[2] /ˈmʌŋki/, *n.* a looped strap which an inexperienced buckjumper grips with his right hand. [short for MONKEY ROPE]

**monkey bars** /ˈ– baz/, *n.pl. Colloq.* →**jungle gym.**

**monkey-block** /ˈmʌŋki-blɒk/, *n. Naut.* a small block that swivels.

**monkey-bread** /ˈmʌŋki-brɛd/, *n.* **1.** the gourdlike fruit of the baobab, eaten by monkeys. **2.** the tree itself.

**monkey-faced owl** /mʌŋki-feɪst ˈaʊl/, *n.* →**barn owl.**

**monkey-flower** /ˈmʌŋki-flaʊə/, *n.* any plant of the genus *Mimulus,* as the monkey musk, *M. moschatus.*

**monkey-gaff** /ˈmʌŋki-gæf/, *n.* a small gaff for supporting a flag on a ship.

**monkey island** /ˈmʌŋki aɪlənd/, *n.* the top of the pilot house on a ship.

**monkey-jacket** /ˈmʌŋki-dʒækət/, *n.* **1.** →**mess jacket. 2.** a short, close-fitting jacket, formerly worn by sailors. [from its resemblance to the jackets worn by performing monkeys]

**monkey nut** /ˈmʌŋki nʌt/, *n.* a small, edible black nut.

**monkeypot** /ˈmʌŋkipɒt/, *n.* the woody, operculate seed vessel of any of certain large South American trees of the genus *Lecythis.*

**monkey-puzzle tree** /ˈmʌŋki-pʌzəl tri/, *n.* a South American coniferous tree, *Araucaria araucana,* with candelabra-like branches, stiff sharp leaves, and edible nuts. Also, **monkey-puzzle.**

**monkey rope** /ˈmʌŋki roʊp/, *n.* **1.** a rope tied around a sailor's waist to secure him as he goes down the ship's side. **2.** a robust, woody, apocynaceous climber, *Parsonsia straminea,* found in rainforests of eastern Australia, and having cream, brown or mauve fragrant flowers.

**monkeyshine** /ˈmʌŋkiʃaɪn/, *n. U.S. Colloq.* a mischievous or clownish trick or prank.

**monkey suit** /ˈmʌŋki sut/, *n. Colloq.* →**dinner suit.**

**monkey-wrench** /ˈmʌŋki-rɛntʃ/, *n.* a spanner or wrench with an adjustable jaw, for turning nuts of different sizes, etc.

**monkfish** /ˈmʌŋkfɪʃ/, *n.* a thin, flat fish, *Rhina squatina,* related to the sharks and rays, found in the waters around the British Isles. [so named from the cowled appearance of the head]

**Mon-Khmer** /moʊn-ˈkmɛə/, *adj.* **1.** of or pertaining to a group of related languages of south-east Asia, including Mon and Khmer. *–n.* **2.** these languages collectively.

**monkhood** /ˈmʌŋkhʊd/, *n.* **1.** the condition or profession of a monk. **2.** monks collectively.

**monkish** /ˈmʌŋkɪʃ/, *adj.* (*oft. derog.*) of or pertaining to, characteristic of, or resembling a monk. – **monkishly,** *adv.* – **monkishness,** *n.*

**monk's cloth** /ˈmʌŋks klɒθ/, *n.* a heavy cotton fabric in a basket weave, used for curtains, bedspreads, etc.

**monkshood** /ˈmʌŋkshʊd/, *n.* a plant of the genus *Aconitum*, esp. *A. napellus* (so called from the hooded flowers). See **aconite.**

**mono** /ˈmɒnoʊ/, *n., pl.* **monos,** *adj.* *–n.* **1.** a recording not adapted for stereophonic reproduction. *–adj.* **2.** →**monophonic.**

**mono-,** a word element: **1.** meaning 'alone', 'single', 'one'. **2.** denoting a monomolecular thickness, as in *monofilm, monolayer,* etc. **3.** adapted in chemistry to apply to compounds containing one atom of a particular element. Also, **mon-.** [Gk, combining form of *mónos* alone]

**monoamine oxidase** /ˌmɒnoʊəmin ˈɒksədeɪz, -eɪs/, *n.* a nonspecific enzyme which removes by oxidation metabolically active amines, esp. adrenalin and serotonin, from the circulation.

**monobasic** /mɒnoʊˈbeɪsɪk/, *adj.* **1.** *Chem.* (of an acid) containing one replaceable hydrogen atom. **2.** *Biol.* →**monotypic.**

**monocable** /ˈmɒnoʊkeɪbəl/, *n.* an aerial ropeway with a single moving cable.

**monocarp** /ˈmɒnoʊkap/, *n.* a plant that dies after having once borne fruit.

**monocarpellary** /mɒnoʊˈkapələri/, *adj.* consisting of a single carpel.

**monocarpic** /mɒnoʊˈkapɪk/, *adj.* (of a plant) producing fruit once only and then dying.

**monocarpous** /mɒnoʊˈkapəs/, *adj.* **1.** having a gynoecium which forms only a single ovary. **2.** monocarpic.

**monochasium** /mɒnoʊˈkeɪziəm/, *n., pl.* **-sia** /-ziə/. a form of cymose inflorescence in which the main axis produces only a single branch. [NL *mono-* MONO- + Gk *chásis* separation + *-ium* -IUM] – **monochasial,** *adj.*

**monochord** /ˈmɒnoʊkɔd/, *n.* an acoustical instrument consisting of an oblong wooden sounding box, usu. with a single string, used for the mathematical determination of musical intervals. [ME *monocorde,* from OF, from L *monochordon,* from Gk: having a single string]

**monochroic** /mɒnəˈkroʊɪk/, *adj.* of one colour. [Gk *monóchroos* of one colour + -IC]

**monochromasia** /mɒnəkroʊˈmeɪziə/, *n.* a defect of vision in which all colours are perceived as a single colour. Also, **monochromasy** /mɒnəˈkroʊməsi/, **monochromatism** /mɒnəˈkroʊmətɪzəm/.

**monochromat** /mɒnəˈkroʊmæt/, *n.* one afflicted with monochromasia. Also, **monochromate.**

**monochromatic** /mɒnəkroʊˈmætɪk/, *adj.* **1.** of, producing, or pertaining to one colour or one wavelength. **2.** *Opthalm.* of or pertaining to monochromasia. – **monochromatically,** *adv.*

**monochromator** /mɒnəˈkroʊmətə/, *n.* a device for looking at one narrow region of the (visible) spectrum.

**monochrome** /ˈmɒnəkroʊm/, *n.* **1.** a painting or drawing in different shades of a single colour. **2.** the art or method of making these. **3.** the state or condition of being painted, decorated, etc., in shades of a single colour. **4.** a black and white photograph. *–adj.* **5.** monochromatic. [Gk *monóchrōmos* of one colour] – **monochromic** /mɒnəˈkroʊmɪk/, **monochromical** /mɒnəˈkroʊmɪkəl/, *adj.* – **monochromist,** *n.*

**monocle** /ˈmɒnəkəl/, *n.* an eyeglass for one eye. [F, from LL *monoculus* one-eyed] – **monocled,** *adj.*

**monoclinal** /mɒnoʊˈklaɪnəl/, *adj.* **1.** dipping in one direction, as strata of rocks. **2.** pertaining to strata which dip in the same direction. *–n.* **3.** monocline. – **monoclinally,** *adv.*

**monocline** /ˈmɒnoʊklaɪn/, *n.* a monoclinal structure or fold. [MONO- + Gk *klī́nein* incline]

**monoclinic** /mɒnoʊˈklɪnɪk/, *adj.* denoting or pertaining to crystallisation in which the crystals have three unequal axes, with one oblique intersection.

**monoclinous** /mɒnoʊˈklaɪnəs, ˈmɒnəklaɪnəs/, *adj.* (of a plant species, etc.) having both the stamens and pistils in the same flower.

**monocoque** /ˈmɒnoʊkɒk/, *adj.* a form of aeroplane fuselage or motor vehicle body construction in which all or most of the stresses are carried by the skin. [F *mono-* MONO- + *coque* shell (from L *coccum*)]

**monocotyledon** /ˌmɒnoʊkɒtəˈlidən/, *n.* **1.** a plant with only one cotyledon. **2.** a member of the group Monocotyledonae, one of the two subclasses of angiospermous plants, characterised in the main by producing seeds with a single cotyledon or seed leaf, and by an endogenous mode of growth. – **monocotyledonous,** *adj.*

**monocracy** /mɒˈnɒkrəsi/, *n., pl.* **-cies.** government by a single person; autocracy. – **monocratic** /mɒnəˈkrætɪk/, *adj.*

**monocrat** /ˈmɒnəkræt/, *n.* one favouring monocracy.

**monocular** /mɒˈnɒkjələ/, *adj.* **1.** having only one eye. **2.** pertaining to or intended for one eye: *a monocular microscope.* [LL *monoculus* one-eyed + -AR[1]]

**monoculture** /ˈmɒnoʊkʌltʃə/, *n.* the use of land for growing only one kind of crop.

**monocyclic** /mɒnoʊˈsaɪklɪk/, *adj.* **1.** having one cycle. **2.** *Bot.* arranged in a single whorl, as the parts of certain flowers.

**monocyte** /ˈmɒnoʊsaɪt/, *n.* the largest unicellular leucocyte in the blood, having a bean-shaped nucleus.

**monocytosis** /ˌmɒnoʊsaɪˈtoʊsəs/, *n.* an increase in the circulating monocytes in the blood, found in various bacterial infections, etc.

**monodactylous** /mɒnoʊˈdæktələs/, *adj.* (of animals, birds, etc) having only one digit or claw. Also, **monodactyl.** [Gk *monodáktylos*]

**monodic** /mɒˈnɒdɪk/, *adj.* pertaining to monody or homophony. Also, **monodical.** [Gk *monōidikós*] – **monodically,** *adv.*

**monodrama** /ˈmɒnoʊdramə/, *n.* a dramatic piece for a single performer. – **monodramatic** /ˌmɒnoʊdrəˈmætɪk/, *adj.*

**monody** /ˈmɒnədi/, *n., pl.* **-dies. 1.** a Greek ode sung by a single voice, as in a tragedy; a lament. **2.** a poem in which one person laments another's death. **3.** *Music.* **a.** a style of composition in which one part or melody predominates; homophony, as distinguished from polyphony. **b.** a piece in this style. [LL *monōdia,* from Gk *monōidía* a solo, lament] – **monodist,** *n.*

**monoecious** /mɒˈniʃəs/, *adj.* **1.** *Biol.* having both male and female organs in the same individual; hermaphroditic. **2.** *Bot.* (of a plant species, etc.) having the stamens and the pistils in separate flowers on the same plant. Also, **monecious.** [MON- + Gk *oikíon* house + -OUS]

A
B
branch of a monoecious tree: A, female catkins; B, male catkins

**monofil** /ˈmɒnəfɪl/, *n.* a single strand of synthetic fibre. Also, **monofilament** /mɒnəˈfɪləmənt/.

**monogamist** /məˈnɒgəməst/, *n.* one who practises or advocates monogamy. – **monogamistic** /mənɒgəˈmɪstɪk/, *adj.*

**monogamous** /məˈnɒgəməs/, *adj.* **1.** practising or advocating monogamy. **2.** pertaining to monogamy. [LL *monogamus,* from Gk *monógamos*]

**monogamy** /məˈnɒgəmi/, *n.* **1.** marriage of one woman with one man. **2.** *Zool.* the habit of having only one mate. **3.** the practice of marrying only once during life.

**monogenesis** /mɒnoʊˈdʒɛnəsəs/, *n.* **1.** the theoretical descent of all living things from a single ancestral organism. **2.** the theoretical descent of the whole human race from a single pair. **3.** *Biol.* development of an ovum into an organism similar to its parent, without metamorphosis. Also, **monogeny** /məˈnɒdʒəni/.

**monogenetic** /ˌmɒnoʊdʒəˈnɛtɪk/, *adj.* **1.** of or pertaining to monogenesis. **2.** having only one generation in the life cycle; without intermediate non-sexual generations, as applied to trematode worms of the subclass Monogenea. **3.** *Geol.* resulting from one genetic process.

**monogram** /ˈmɒnəgræm/, *n.* a character consisting of two or more letters combined or interlaced, commonly one's initials, often printed on stationery, embroidered on clothing, handkerchiefs, etc. [LL *monogramma,* from LGk *monógrammon* single-lettered character. See MONO-, -GRAM[1]] – **monogrammatic** /mɒnəgrəˈmætɪk/, *adj.*

**monograph** /ˈmɒnəgræf, -graf/, *n.* **1.** a treatise on a particular subject. **2.** an account of a single thing or class of things, as of a species of animals or plants. – **monographic** /mɒnəˈgræfɪk/, *adj.* – **monographically** /mɒnəˈgræfəkli/, *adv.*

**monographer** /mɒˈnɒgrəfə/, *n.* the writer of a monograph.

**monogyny** /mɒˈnɒdʒəni/, *n.* the practice or the condition of having only one wife at a time. [MONO- + Gk *-gynía*, from *gynḗ* woman]

**monohull** /ˈmɒnoʊhʌl/, *n.* a boat with one hull. [MONO- + HULL[2]]

**monohybrid** /mɒnoʊˈhaɪbrəd/, *n.* a hybrid of two parents which differ in respect of only one set of genes.

**monohydric** /mɒnoʊˈhaɪdrɪk/, *adj.* (of a chemical compound, usu. an alcohol) having a single hydroxyl radical.

**monokini** /ˈmɒnoʊkini/, *n.* the bottom half of a bikini worn without a top. [MONO- + (BI)KINI]

**monolatry** /mɒˈnɒlətri/, *n.* the worship of one god only, when other gods are recognised as existing. [MONO- + Gk *latreía* worship] – **monolater** /mɒˈnɒlətə/, **monolatrist,** *n.* – **monolatrous,** *adj.*

**monolingual** /mɒnoʊˈlɪŋgwəl/, *adj.* **1.** able to speak only one language. **2.** written in one language only: *a monolingual dictionary.* –*n.* **3.** a monolingual person.

**monolith** /ˈmɒnəlɪθ/, *n.* **1.** a single block or piece of stone of considerable size, whether in the natural state, as of Ayers Rock, Northern Territory, or fabricated, as in architecture or sculpture. **2.** an obelisk, column, statue, etc., formed of a single block of stone. **3.** *Engineering.* a concrete, stone, or brick foundation sunk as an open caisson and excavated by a grabbing crane. **4.** something resembling a large block of stone, esp. in having a massive, uniform, or unyielding quality or character. [LL *monolithus,* from Gk *monólithos* made of one stone]

monolith (def. 1)

**monolithic** /mɒnəˈlɪθɪk/, *adj.* **1.** of or pertaining to a monolith. **2.** made of only one stone or a single block. **3.** characterised by massiveness and uniformity; undifferentiated. **4.** *Elect.* (of an integrated circuit) built on a single crystal.

**monologue** /ˈmɒnəlɒg/, *n.* **1.** a prolonged talk or discourse by a single speaker. **2.** any composition, as a poem, in which a single person speaks alone. **3.** a part of a drama in which a single actor speaks alone. **4.** a form of dramatic entertainment by a single speaker. [F, from Gk *monólogos* speaking alone] – **monologic** /mɒnəˈlɒdʒɪk/, **monological** /mɒnəˈlɒdʒɪkəl/, *adj.* – **monologist** /ˈmɒnəlɒgəst, məˈnɒləgəst/, *n.*

**monology** /məˈnɒlədʒi/, *n., pl.* **-gies. 1.** the act or habit of soliloquising. **2.** *Obs.* a monologue. [Gk *monología*]

**monomania** /mɒnoʊˈmeɪniə/, *n.* **1.** insanity in which the patient is irrational on one subject only. **2.** an exaggerated zeal for, or interest in, some one thing; a craze. – **monomaniac** /mɒnoʊˈmeɪniæk/, *n.* – **monomaniacal** /mɒnoʊməˈnaɪəkəl/, *adj.*

**monomer** /ˈmɒnəmə/, *n.* a molecule of low molecular weight capable of reacting with identical or indifferent monomers to form a polymer. – **monomeric** /mɒnəˈmɛrɪk/, *adj.*

**monomerous** /mɒˈnɒmərəs/, *adj.* (of flowers) having one member in each whorl. [Gk *monomerḗs* consisting of one part + -OUS]

**monometallic** /mɒnoʊməˈtælɪk/, *adj.* **1.** of or using one metal. **2.** pertaining to monometallism.

**monometallism** /mɒnoʊˈmɛtəlɪzəm/, *n.* **1.** the use of one metal only (as gold or silver) as the monetary standard. **2.** the doctrine or actions supporting such a standard. – **monometalist,** *n.*

**monometer** /mɒˈnɒmətə/, *n.* a line of verse, poetry, etc. having one measure or foot.

**monomial** /mɒˈnoʊmiəl/, *adj.* **1.** *Alg.* consisting of one term only. **2.** *Biol.* denoting or pertaining to a name which consists of a single word or term. –*n.* **3.** *Alg.* a monomial expression or quantity. [irregularly from MO(NO)- + *-nomial,* after BINOMIAL]

**monomolecular** /mɒnoʊməˈlɛkjələ/, *adj.* indicating a thickness of one molecule.

**monomorphic** /mɒnoʊˈmɔfɪk/, *adj.* **1.** *Biol.* having only one form. **2.** of the same or of an essentially similar type of structure. Also, **monomorphous.**

**mononuclear** /mɒnoʊˈnjukliə/, *adj.* **1.** having only one nucleus. –*n.* **2.** a cell having only one nucleus, esp. a monocyte. Also, **mononucleate** /mɒnoʊˈnjukliət/.

**mononucleosis** /mɒnoʊˌnjukliˈoʊsəs/, *n.* →**glandular fever.**

**monopetalous** /mɒnoʊˈpɛtələs/, *adj.* **1.** →**gamopetalous. 2.** having only one petal, as a corolla.

**monophagia** /mɒnoʊˈfeɪdʒiə/, *n.* the eating of or the desire for only one kind of food. Also, **monophagy.**

**monophagous** /məˈnɒfəgəs/, *adj.* (esp. of insects) eating only one kind of food. – **monophagy,** *n.*

**monophobia** /mɒnəˈfoʊbiə/, *n.* morbid dread of being alone.

**monophonic** /mɒnəˈfɒnɪk/, *adj.* **1.** of or pertaining to monophony. **2.** of or denoting a system of sound reproduction through only one loudspeaker (opposed to *stereophonic*).

**monophony** /məˈnɒfəni/, *n.* a musical style consisting of a single line of melody without accompaniment.

**monophthong** /ˈmɒnəfθɒŋ/, *n.* a single, simple vowel sound. [Gk *monóphthongos* with one sound] – **monophthongal** /mɒnəfˈθɒŋəl, -ˈθɒŋgəl/, *adj.*

**monophthongise** /ˈmɒnəfθɒŋˌaɪz/, *v.,* **-gised, -gising.** –*v.t.* **1.** to change into or pronounce as a monophthong. –*v.i.* **2.** to become a monophthong. Also, **monophthongize.** – **monophthongisation** /ˌmɒnəfθɒŋaɪˈzeɪʃən/, *n.*

**monophyletic** /ˌmɒnoʊfaɪˈlɛtɪk/, *adj.* **1.** of or pertaining to a single tribe or stock. **2.** developed from a single ancestral type, as a group of animals. [MONO- + Gk *phyletikós* belonging to a tribesman]

**monophyllous** /mɒnoʊˈfɪləs/, *adj.* **1.** consisting of one leaf, as a calyx. **2.** having only one leaf. [Gk *monóphyllos*]

**Monophysite** /mɒˈnɒfəsaɪt/, *n.* one holding that there is in Christ one composite nature, partly divine and partly human. [LGk *monophysī́tēs,* from *mono-* MONO- + *phýs(is)* nature + *-ī́tēs* -ITE[1]] – **Monophysitic** /mɒnɒfəˈsɪtɪk/, *adj.* – **Monophysitism,** *n.*

**monoplane** /ˈmɒnəpleɪn/, *n.* an aeroplane with a single sustaining wing.

**monoplegia** /mɒnoʊˈplidʒiə/, *n.* paralysis of only one extremity, muscle, or group of muscles. [NL. See MONO-, -PLEGIA] – **monoplegic** /mɒnoʊˈplidʒɪk/, *adj.*

**monoploid** /ˈmɒnoʊplɔɪd/, *adj.* **1.** having or being a chromosome number which is the haploid number. –*n.* **2.** a cell or organism which is monoploid.

**monopode** /ˈmɒnəpoʊd/, *adj.* **1.** having only one foot. –*n.* **2.** a creature having only one foot. **3.** one of a legendary race of men having only one leg. **4.** *Bot.* →**monopodium.** [Gk *monópous* one-footed]

**monopodium** /mɒnəˈpoʊdiəm/, *n., pl.* **-dia** /diə/. a single main axis which continues to extend at the apex in the original line of growth, giving off lateral branches beneath in acropetal succession. [NL, from Gk *mono-* MONO- + *pódion* foot] – **monopodial,** *adj.*

**monopolise** /məˈnɒpəlaɪz/, *v.t.,* **-lised, -lising. 1.** to acquire, have, or exercise a monopoly of (a market, commodity, etc.). **2.** to obtain exclusive possession of; keep entirely to oneself: *she tried to monopolise his time.* Also, **monopolize.** – **monopolisation** /mənɒpəlaɪˈzeɪʃən/, *n.* – **monopoliser,** *n.*

**monopolism** /məˈnɒpəlɪzəm/, *n.* the existence or prevalence of monopolies.

**monopolist** /məˈnɒpələst/, *n.* **1.** one who has a monopoly. **2.** an advocate of monopoly. – **monopolistic** /mənɒpəˈlɪstɪk/, *adj.* – **monopolistically** /mənɒpəˈlɪstɪkli/, *adv.*

**monopoly** /məˈnɒpəli/, *n., pl.* **-lies. 1.** exclusive control of a commodity or service in a particular market, or a control that makes possible the manipulation of prices. **2.** an exclusive privilege to carry on a traffic or service, granted by a sovereign, state, etc. **3.** the exclusive possession or control of something. **4.** something which is the subject of such control; a commodity, service, etc., which is exclusively controlled. **5.** a company or the like having such control. **6.** (*usu. cap.*) a game played with counters, cards, etc., with the object of one player gaining monopoly controls over the others. [L *monopōlium,* from Gk *monopṓlion* a right of exclusive sale]

**monopropellant** /ˌmɒnoʊprəˈpɛlənt/, *n.* a rocket propellant consisting of a single substance, either liquid or solid, which contains both the fuel and oxidant.

**monopsony** /mɒnˈɒpsəni/, *n., pl.* **-nies.** a market situation where there is a single buyer of a product or service from a large number of sellers. [MON- + Gk *opsōnía* purchase of victuals, catering] – **monopsonist,** *n.* – **monopsonistic** /mənɒpsəˈnɪstɪk/, *adj.*

**monorail** /ˈmɒnoʊreɪl/, *n.* a railway with coaches running on a single (usu. overhead) rail.

**monosaccharide** /mɒnoʊˈsækəraɪd, -rəd/, *n.* a simple sugar, such as glucose, fructose, arabinose, and ribose, occurring in nature or obtained by the hydrolysis of glucosides or polysaccharides.

**monosaccharose** /mɒnoʊˈsækəroʊz, -oʊs/, *n.* →**monosaccharide.**

**monosepalous** /mɒnoʊˈsɛpələs/, *adj.* **1.** →**gamosepalous.** **2.** having only one sepal, as a calyx.

**monosilane** /mɒnoʊˈsaɪleɪn/, *n.* a gas, $SiH_4$, formed by the action of hydrochloric acid on magnesium silicide; silicomethane; silicane.

**monosodium glutamate** /mɒnəˌsoʊdiəm ˈglutəmeɪt/, *n.* a sodium salt of glutamic acid used in cooking to enhance the natural flavour of a dish; ve-tsin; ajinomoto; taste powder; Chinese salt.

**monospermous** /mɒnoʊˈspɜməs/, *adj.* (of plants, etc.) one-seeded. Also, **monospermal.**

**monostable** /ˈmɒnoʊsteɪbəl/, *adj.* denoting a circuit which may have several states, but always reverts to the same state in the absence of external forces.

**monostich** /ˈmɒnəstɪk/, *n.* **1.** a poem or epigram consisting of a single metrical line. **2.** a single line of poetry. [LL *monostichum,* from Gk *monóstichon,* adj. neut., consisting of one line]

**monostome** /ˈmɒnəstoʊm/, *adj.* having a single mouth, pore, or stoma. Also, **monostomous** /mɒnˈɒstəməs/. [Gk *monóstomos* with one mouth]

**monostrophe** /məˈnɒstrəfi, mɒnəsˈtroʊfi/, *n.* a poem in which all the strophes or stanzas are of the same metrical form. [Gk *monóstrophos.* See MONO-, STROPHE] – **monostrophic** /mɒnəsˈtrɒfɪk/, *adj.*

**monostylous** /mɒnoʊˈstaɪləs/, *adj.* (of plants, etc.) having only one style.

**monosyllabic** /mɒnəsəˈlæbɪk/, *adj.* **1.** having only one syllable, as the word *no.* **2.** having a vocabulary composed exclusively of monosyllables; uncommunicative. **3.** using or uttering monosyllables. – **monosyllabically,** *adv.*

**monosyllabism** /mɒnəˈsɪləbɪzəm/, *n.* **1.** monosyllabic character. **2.** use of monosyllables.

**monosyllable** /ˈmɒnəsɪləbəl/, *n.* a word of one syllable, as *yes* and *no.* [MONO- + SYLLABLE. Cf. L *monosyllabon,* from Gk]

**monotheism** /ˈmɒnoʊθiˌɪzəm, mɒnoʊˈθiɪzəm/, *n.* the doctrine or belief that there is only one God. [MONO- + Gk *theós* god + -ISM] – **monotheist,** *n., adj.* – **monotheistic** /ˌmɒnoʊθiˈɪstɪk/, *adj.* – **monotheistically** /ˌmɒnoʊθiˈɪstɪkli/, *adv.*

**Monothelite** /mɒnəˈθɛlaɪt/, *n.* **1.** one who believes that the incarnate Christ had only a single will or faculty of choice. **2.** an adherent of a 7th-century sect holding this opinion. –*adj.* **3.** denoting or pertaining to this opinion. Also, **Monothelete** /mɒnəˈθɛlit/. – **Monothelitism, Monothelism,** *n.*

**monothematic** /ˌmɒnoʊθəˈmætɪk/, *adj.* (of music) having only a single theme.

**monotone** /ˈmɒnətoʊn/, *n.* **1.** a vocal utterance, or series of speech sounds in a single unvaried tone. **2.** a single tone without harmony or variation in pitch. **3.** recitation or singing of words in such a tone. **4.** a person who sings in such manner. **5.** sameness of style, as in composition or writing. –*adj.* **6.** monotonous. **7.** *Maths.* →**monotonic.** [NL *monotonus,* from LGk *monótonos* of one tone]

**monotonic** /mɒnəˈtɒnɪk/, *adj. Maths.* (of a function) steadily increasing or steadily decreasing. Also, **monotone.**

**monotonous** /məˈnɒtənəs/, *adj.* **1.** unvarying in any respect, lacking in variety, or tiresomely uniform. **2.** characterising a sound continuing on one note. **3.** having very little inflection; limited to a narrow pitch range. [MONOTONE + -OUS] – **monotonously,** *adv.* – **monotonousness,** *n.*

**monotony** /məˈnɒtəni/, *n.* **1.** lack of variety, or wearisome uniformity, as in occupation, scenery, etc. **2.** the continuance of an unvarying sound; monotone. **3.** sameness of tone or pitch, as in utterance. [LGk *monotonía*]

**monotrematous** /mɒnəˈtrimətəs/, *adj.* of or pertaining to a monotreme.

**monotreme** /ˈmɒnətrim/, *n.* any of the Monotremata, the lowest order of mammals, restricted to the Australian region and comprising only the platypus and the echidnas, oviparous mammals in which the genital, urinary, and digestive organs have a common opening. [MONO- + Gk *trêma* hole]

monotreme: platypus

**monotricha** /mɒˈnɒtrɪkə/, *n.pl.* bacteria having the organs of locomotion at one pole. [MONO- + Gk *thríx* hair + *-a* (representation of L and Gk neut. pl. suffix *-a*)] – **monotrichic** /mɒnoʊˈtrɪkɪk/, **monotrichous,** *adj.*

**monotropic** /mɒnoʊˈtrɒpɪk/, *adj.* existing chemically in only one stable physical form.

**monotype** /ˈmɒnətaɪp/, *n.* **1.** *Print.* **a.** type composed and cast on separate keyboard and casting machines which produce each character on an individual body. **b.** a machine on which such type is set or cast. **2.** a print from a metal plate on which a picture is painted, as in oil colour or printing ink. **3.** the method of producing such a print. **4.** *Biol.* the only or sole type of its group, as a single species constituting a genus. – **monotyper,** *n.*

**monotypic** /mɒnoʊˈtɪpɪk/, *adj.* **1.** having only one type. **2.** of the nature of a monotype. **3.** *Biol.* (of genera) established on the basis of a single species or genus.

**mono-unsaturated fat** /mɒnoʊ-ʌnˌsætʃəreɪtəd ˈfæt/, *n.* a fat or oil based on fatty acids having only one double bond per molecule, as oleic acid in olive oil.

**monovalent** /mɒnoʊˈveɪlənt/, *adj.* **1.** *Chem.* having a valency of one; univalent. **2.** *Bacteriol.* (of a serum, tissue, etc.) capable of resisting a specific disease organism because of the presence of the proper antibodies or antigens. [MONO- + -VALENT] – **monovalence, monovalency,** *n.*

**monoxide** /məˈnɒksaɪd/, *n.* an oxide containing one oxygen atom to the molecule.

**monozygotic** /ˌmɒnoʊzaɪˈgɒtɪk/, *adj.* (of twins, etc.) produced from a single zygote; identical (opposed to *dizygotic*).

**mons** /mɒnz/, *n.* a rounded eminence of fatty tissue, covered with hair, over the pubic symphysis of the adult human, called the **mons veneris** in the female, the **mons pubis** in the male.

**monseigneur** /mõseɪˈnjɜ/, *n., pl.* **messeigneurs** /meɪsɛnˈjɜ/. **1.** a French title of honour given to princes, bishops, and other persons of eminence. **2.** a person bearing this title. [F: my lord]

**monsieur** /məˈsjɜ/, *n., pl.* **messieurs** /meɪˈsjɜ/. the conventional French title of respect and term of address for a man, corresponding to *Mr* and to *Sir.* [F: my lord (orig. applied to men of high station). See SIRE]

**Monsignor** /mɒnˈsinjə/, *n., pl.* **Monsignors, Monsignori** /mɒnsinˈjɔri/. *Rom. Cath. Ch.* **1.** a title conferred upon certain dignitaries. **2.** a person bearing this title. Also, **monsignor.** *Abbrev.:* Mgr [It., from F *mon* my + It. *signor(e)* lord]

**monsoon** /mɒnˈsun/, *n.* **1.** the seasonal wind of the Indian Ocean and Indonesia, blowing in the northern hemisphere from the south-west in summer and from the north-east in winter, and in the southern hemisphere from the south-east in winter and from the north-west in summer. **2.** the rainy season of the summer monsoon, from April to October in the northern hemisphere, esp. India, and from December to February in the southern hemisphere, esp. northern Australia. **3.** a wind system that reverses with the seasons. [D (early colonial period) *monssoen,* from Portuguese *monçao,* from Ar. *mausim* season, seasonal wind, monsoon] – **monsoonal,** *adj.*

**monster** /ˈmɒnstə/, *n.* **1.** a legendary animal compounded of brute and human shape or of the shapes of various brutes, as a centaur, a griffin, or a sphinx. **2.** an animal or a plant of abnormal form or structure, as from marked malformation, the absence of certain parts or organs, etc. **3.** something unnatural or monstrous. **4.** a person who excites horror, as by wickedness, cruelty, etc. **5.** any animal or thing of huge size. *–adj.* **6.** huge; enormous; monstrous. *–v.t.* **7.** to rebuke or attack (someone), esp. in politics. [ME *monstre,* from OF, from L *monstrum* omen, prodigy, monster]

**monstera deliciosa** /mɒnˌstɪərə dəlɪsi'ousə/, *n.* **1.** a plant of the genus *Monstera,* native to tropical America but widely grown elsewhere, having large, deeply incised and perforated leaves and an edible fruit. **2.** the elongate, conical fruit of this plant, which has a thick rind and pulpy, sweet-smelling flesh; fruit salad plant; ceriman.

**monstrance** /'mɒnstrəns/, *n.* (in the Roman Catholic Church) a receptacle in which the consecrated host is exposed for adoration. [ME, from ML *monstrantia,* from L *monstrāre* show]

**monstrosity** /mɒn'strɒsəti/, *n., pl.* **-ties.** **1.** the state or character of being monstrous. **2.** something monstrous. **3.** a monster. [LL *monstrōsitas*]

**monstrous** /'mɒnstrəs/, *adj.* **1.** huge; extremely great: *a monstrous sum.* **2.** frightful or hideous; extremely ugly. **3.** revolting; outrageous; shocking: *a monstrous proposal.* **4.** deviating greatly from the natural or normal form or type. **5.** having the nature or appearance of a legendary monster. [late ME, from LL *monstrōsus* strange] – **monstrously,** *adv.* – **monstrousness,** *n.*

**montage** /mɒn'taʒ/, *n.* **1.** the art or method of arranging in one composition pictorial elements borrowed from several sources so that the elements are both distinct and blended into a whole, through techniques such as superimposition. **2.** a picture made in this way. **3.** *Films, T.V.* **a.** a technique of film editing in which several shots are juxtaposed or partially superimposed to form a single image. **b.** a method of film-making in which a single idea is expressed by the combining of different elements. **c.** a section of film using either process. [F: mounting, putting together]

**montane** /'mɒnteɪn/, *adj.* **1.** pertaining to mountain conditions. *–n.* **2.** the lower vegetation belt on mountains. [L *montānus* of a mountain]

**montan wax** /'mɒntæn wæks/, *n.* a dark brown bituminous wax extracted from lignite and peat; used in various polishes. Also, **lignite wax.** [*montan* (from L *montānus* of a mountain) + WAX[1]]

**mont-de-piété** /mɒnt-də-pi'eɪteɪ/, *n., pl.* **monts-de-piété** /mɒnt-də-pi'eɪteɪ/. a public pawnbroking establishment for lending money on reasonable terms, esp. to the poor. [F, from It. *monte di pietà,* lit., mountain (fund) of pity]

**monte** /'mɒnti/, *n.* **1.** a gambling game at cards. **2.** *Colloq.* a certainty: *a monte to win.* **3. for a monte,** for certain. Also, **monty.** [Sp.: mountain, heap (of cards), from L *mons* MOUNT[2]]

**Monte Carlo method,** *n.* a method of computer simulation in which probabilistic methods are employed to estimate a solution to problems too complex or ill-defined to program directly. [named after *Monte Carlo,* the gambling resort]

**monteith** /mɒn'tiθ/, *n.* a large bowl commonly of silver, often with a rim for suspending drinking glasses in the cool water within the bowl; also used as a punchbowl. [orig. proper name]

**monterey** /'mɒntəreɪ/, *n.* a cheese similar to cheddar, but paler and softer, with a milder flavour; jack. [named after *Monterey,* California, U.S.A.]

**Monterey pine** /mɒntəreɪ 'paɪn/, *n.* →**radiata pine.**

**Montessori method** /mɒntə'sɔri meθəd/, *n.* a system for training and instructing young children, of which the fundamental aim is self-education by the children themselves, accompanied by special emphasis on the training of the senses. Also, **Montessori system.** [named after Maria *Montessori,* 1870-1952, Italian educational reformer]

**montgolfier** /mɒnt'gɒlfiə/, *n.* a balloon raised by heated air provided by a fire in the lower section. [named after Jacques Étienne *Montgolfier,* 1745-99, and his brother, Joseph Michel, 1740-1810, inventors of the first balloon to make a successful flight]

**month** /mʌnθ/, *n.* **1.** approximately one twelfth of a tropical or solar year (**solar month**). **2.** any of the twelve parts (January, February, etc.) into which the calendar year is divided **(calendar month).** **3.** the time from any day of one calendar month to the corresponding day of the next. **4.** a period of four weeks or of thirty days. **5.** the period **(lunar month)** of a complete revolution of the moon with regard to some point, usu. the interval **(synodic month)** from one new moon to the next, equivalent to 29 days, 12 hours, 44 minutes, and 2.7 seconds. [ME *mon(e)th,* OE *mōnath,* c. G *Mond* MOON]

**monthly** /'mʌnθli/, *adj., n., pl.* **-lies,** *adv.* *–adj.* **1.** pertaining to a month, or to each month. **2.** done, happening, appearing, etc., once a month, or every month. **3.** continuing or lasting for a month. *–n.* **4.** a periodical published once a month. **5.** *Colloq.* a menstrual period. *–adv.* **6.** once a month; by the month.

**monticule** /'mɒntəkjul/, *n.* **1.** a small mountain, hill, or mound. **2.** a subordinate volcano cone. [F, from LL *monticulus,* diminutive of L *mons* MOUNT[2]]

**monument** /'mɒnjəmənt/, *n.* **1.** something erected in memory of a person, event, etc., as a pillar, statue, or the like. **2.** any building, megalith, etc., surviving from a past age, and regarded as of historical or archaeological importance. **3.** any work, writing, or the like by a person, regarded as a memorial of him after his death. **4.** any enduring evidence or notable example of something. **5.** a building, esp. one that is not necessary or functional, erected at public expense at the initiative of a public leader to gain personal kudos. **6.** *U.S.* an object, as a stone shaft, set in the ground to mark the boundaries of real property. **7.** a written document or record; legal instrument. **8.** *Obs.* a tomb; place of burial. **9.** *Obs.* a statue. [ME, from L *monumentum*]

monument (def. 1): war memorial, Hyde Park, Sydney

**monumental** /mɒnjə'mɛntl/, *adj.* **1.** resembling a monument; massive or imposing. **2.** (of a work of art) **a.** of great physical size. **b.** elevated in idea. **c.** noble in conception and execution. **d.** of lasting significance. **3.** historically prominent: *a monumental event.* **4.** *Colloq.* conspicuously great or gross. **5.** of a monument or monuments. **6.** serving as a monument. – **monumentally,** *adv.*

**monumentalise** /mɒnjə'mɛntəlaɪz/, *v.t.,* **-lised, -lising.** to establish an enduring memorial or record of. Also, **monumentalize.**

**-mony,** a noun suffix indicating result or condition, as in *parsimony;* but sometimes having the same function as **-ment.** [L *-mōnia, -mōnium*]

**monzonite** /'mɒnzənaɪt/, *n.* any of a group of granular igneous rocks intermediate in composition between syenite and diorite. [G *Monzonit,* from *Monzoni* (name of mountain in Tyrol) + *-it* -ITE[1]] – **monzonitic** /mɒnzə'nɪtɪk/, *adj.*

**moo** /mu/, *n.* **1.** the sound a cow makes. **2.** *Brit. Colloq.* a stupid person, esp. a woman. *–v.i.* **3.** to make such a sound; low. [imitative]

**mooch** /mutʃ/, *Colloq.* *–v.i.* **1.** to skulk or sneak. **2.** to hang or loiter about. **3.** to slouch or saunter along. **4. mooch off,** to depart. *–v.t.* **5.** to steal. **6.** to get without paying or at another's expense; cadge. Also, **mouch.** [ME, ? from OF *muchier*] – **moocher,** *n.*

**moo-cow** /'mu-kaʊ/, *n.* *(in children's speech)* a cow.

**mood**[1] /mud/, *n.* **1.** frame of mind, or state of feeling, as at a particular time. **2.** *(pl.)* fits of uncertainty, gloominess, or sullenness. [ME; OE *mōd* mind, spirit, mood, c. G *Mut* spirit, courage]

**mood**[2] /mud/, *n.* **1.** *Gram.* **a.** (in many languages) a set of categories of verb inflection, whose selection depends either on the syntactic relation of the verb to other verbs in the sentence, or on a difference in the speaker's attitude towards the action expressed by the verb (e.g., certainty *v.* uncertainty, question *v.* statement, wish *v.* command, emphasis *v.* hesitancy). **b.** (in some languages, including English) a similar set of categories marked by the use of special auxiliary words (Eng. *can, could, may, might,* etc.) instead of by, or in addition to, inflection. **c.** any category of such a set: *the Greek indicative, imperative, optative, and subjunctive moods.* **2.** *Logic.* any of the various forms of valid categorical syllogisms, depending on the quantity and quality of their constituent propositions. [special use of MOOD[1], influenced by MODE[1]]

**moody** /ˈmudi/, *adj.*, **-dier, -diest.** **1.** given to gloomy or sullen moods; ill-humoured. **2.** proceeding from or showing such a mood: *a moody silence.* **3.** exhibiting sharply varied moods; temperamental. – **moodily,** *adv.* – **moodiness,** *n.*

**moog** /moʊg, mug/, *n.* →**synthesiser** (def. 2). [Trademark]

**moolah** /ˈmulə/, *n. Colloq.* money. Also, **moola.**

**moon** /mun/, *n.* **1.** the body which revolves around the earth monthly at a mean distance of 384 403 km, accompanying the earth in its annual revolution about the sun. It is 3 466 km in diameter, and its mass is 0.0123 that of the earth. **2.** this heavenly body during a particular lunar month, or during a certain period of time, or at a certain point of time, regarded as a distinct object or entity. **a. new moon,** the moon when in conjunction with the sun and hence invisible, or the phase so represented, or the moon soon afterwards when visible as a slender crescent. **b. half-moon,** the moon when half its disc is illuminated, occurring when at either quadrature, or quarter. **c. full moon,** the moon when the whole of its disc is illuminated, occurring when in opposition to the sun, or the phase so represented. **d. old moon,** the waning moon. **e. waxing moon,** the moon at any time before it is full, so called because its illuminated area is increasing. **f. waning moon,** the moon at any time after it has been full, so called because its illuminated area is decreasing. **3.** a lunar month, or, in general, a month. **4.** any planetary satellite. **5.** something shaped like an orb or a crescent. **6. once in a blue moon,** seldom; very rarely. *–v.i.* **7.** *Colloq.* to wander about or gaze idly, dreamily, or listlessly (oft. fol. by *about*). *–v.t.* **8.** to spend (time) idly. [ME *mone,* OE *mōna,* c. OHG *māno;* akin to Gk *mḗnē* moon, *mḗn* month, L *mensis* month]

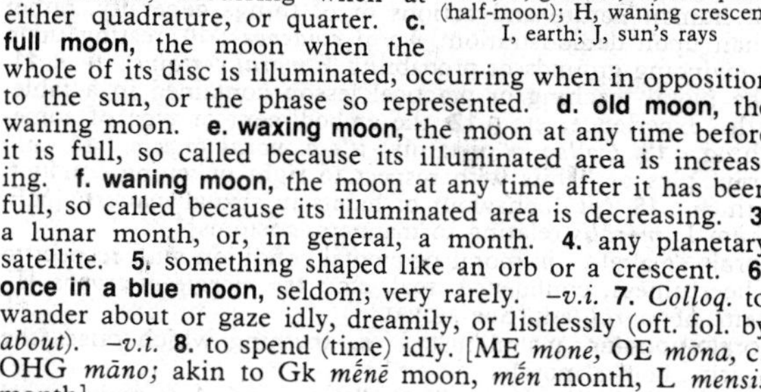

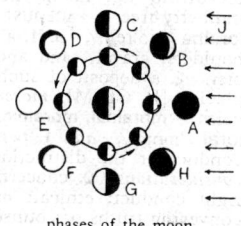

phases of the moon
the figures on the inner circle show the moon in its orbit round the earth, those on the outer circle represent the moon's corresponding phases as seen from the earth: A, new moon (invisible); B, waxing crescent; C, first quarter; D, gibbous; E, full moon; F, gibbous; G, last quarter (half-moon); H, waning crescent; I, earth; J, sun's rays

**moonah** /ˈmunə/, *n.* a shrub or small tree, *Melaleuca lanceolata,* widespread in the southern half of Australia.

**moonbeam** /ˈmunbim/, *n.* a ray of moonlight.

**moonbird** /ˈmunbɜd/, *n.* →**white-fronted chat.**

**moon-blind** /ˈmun-blaɪnd/, *adj.* (of horses) afflicted with moon blindness. Also, **moon-eyed** /ˈmun-aɪd/.

**moon blindness** /ˈmun blaɪndnəs/, *n.* a specific, probably non-infectious disease of horses, of unknown cause, in which the eyes suffer from recurring attacks of inflammation, and which eventually results in opacity and blindness.

**mooncalf** /ˈmunkaf/, *n.* a congenital imbecile. [lit., a child influenced by the moon]

**moon daisy** /ˈmun deɪzi/, *n.* a perennial composite herb, *Chrysanthemum leucanthemum,* with single capitula having yellow disc florets and white ray florets; a grassland species of the Old World introduced elsewhere.

**mooned** /mund/, *adj.* **1.** ornamented with moons or crescents. **2.** shaped like a moon or crescent.

**mooneye** /ˈmunaɪ/, *n.* **1.** a freshwater fish, *Hiodon tergisus,* of central North America with large eyes. **2.** *Vet. Sci.* an eye of a horse affected with moon blindness.

**moon-face** /ˈmun-feɪs/, *n.* one with a very round face: *he's a moon-face.* – **moon-faced,** *adj.*

**moonfish** /ˈmunfɪʃ/, *n., pl.* **-fishes,** (*esp. collectively*) **-fish.** **1.** in Australia, **a.** →**opah. b.** a silvery, tropical fish, *Drepanichthys punctatus,* of coastal waters. **2.** elsewhere, **a.** any of certain fishes having a deep, sharply compressed, silvery body, as of the carangoid genera *Selene* and *Vomer,* as *S. vomer* and *V. setipinnis* of the warmer coastal waters of North and South America. **b.** a minnow, *Platypoecilus maculatus.*

**moonflower** /ˈmunflaʊə/, *n.* a night-blooming convolvulaceous plant, *Calonyction aculeatum,* with fragrant white flowers.

**moonlight** /ˈmunlaɪt/, *n.* **1.** the light of the moon. *–adj.* **2.** pertaining to moonlight. **3.** illuminated by moonlight. **4.** occurring by moonlight, or by night. **5.** of or pertaining to a person who is moonlighting. *–v.i.* **6.** to work at a second job, often at night, in addition to one's regular employment.

**moonlighter** /ˈmunlaɪtə/, *n. Colloq.* one who does a job in addition to regular employment. [orig. a person who under cover of night engaged in illegal activities]

**moonlight flit** /munlaɪt ˈflɪt/, *n. Colloq.* **1.** a departure by night with one's possessions in order to avoid payment of rent. **2.** any sudden departure, esp. to avoid a disagreeable circumstance. – **moonlight flitting,** *n.*

**moonlighting** /ˈmunlaɪtɪŋ/, *n.* **1.** the carrying on of activities, esp. illegal ones, by moonlight. **2.** *Colloq.* working at a job in addition to one's regular, full-time employment.

**moonlit** /ˈmunlɪt/, *adj.* illuminated by moonlight.

**moonquake** /ˈmunkweɪk/, *n.* a tremor on the moon's surface, similar to that experienced on earth in an earthquake.

**moonraker** /ˈmunreɪkə/, *n.* →**moonsail.**

**moonrat** /ˈmunræt/, *n.* a hairy hedgehog, *Echinosorex gymnuras,* the largest living insectivores, found in south-eastern Asia.

**moonrise** /ˈmunraɪz/, *n.* **1.** the rising of the moon above the horizon. **2.** the time at which the moon rises above the horizon.

**moonsail** /ˈmunsəl, -seɪl/, *n.* a small sail carried above the skysail. Also, **moonraker.**

**moonscape** /ˈmunskeɪp/, *n.* a view of the moon, as by photograph, painting, etc. Cf. **landscape.**

**moonseed** /ˈmunsid/, *n.* any of the climbing herbs constituting the genus *Menispermum* (family Menispermaceae) with greenish white flowers, so called from the crescent-shaped seeds.

**moonset** /ˈmunsɛt/, *n.* **1.** the setting of the moon below the horizon. **2.** the time at which the moon disappears below the horizon.

**moonshine** /ˈmunʃaɪn/, *n.* **1.** the light of the moon. **2.** empty or foolish talk, ideas, etc.; nonsense. **3.** *Colloq.* smuggled or illicitly distilled liquor.

**moonshiner** /ˈmunʃaɪnə/, *n. Colloq.* **1.** an illicit distiller. **2.** one who pursues an illegal trade at night.

**moonshiny** /ˈmunʃaɪni/, *adj.* **1.** like moonlight. **2.** moonlit. **3.** without sense; fictitious; visionary.

**moonshot** /ˈmunʃɒt/, *n.* **1.** the launching of a missile to the moon. **2.** the missile itself.

**moonstone** /ˈmunstoʊn/, *n.* a white translucent variety of felspar with a bluish pearly lustre, used as a gem.

**moonstruck** /ˈmunstrʌk/, *adj.* injuriously affected in mind (or otherwise), supposedly by the influence of the moon; dazed; crazed. Also, **moonstricken** /ˈmunstrɪkən/.

**moonwort** /ˈmunwɜt/, *n.* **1.** any fern of the genus *Botrychium,* esp. *B. lunaria,* whose fronds have crescent-shaped pinnae. **2.** →**honesty** (def. 4).

**moony** /ˈmuni/, *adj.,* **-nier, -niest.** **1.** pertaining to or characteristic of the moon. **2.** resembling the moon in shape. **3.** moonlit. **4.** resembling moonlight. **5.** *Colloq.* dreamy, listless, or silly.

**moor**[1] /mɔ/, *n.* **1.** a tract of open, peaty, waste land, often overgrown with heath, common in high latitudes and altitudes where drainage is poor; a heath. **2.** a tract of land preserved for shooting game. [ME *more,* OE *mōr,* c. G *Moor* marsh]

**moor**[2] /mɔ/, *v.t.* **1.** to secure (a ship, etc.) in a particular place, as by cables and anchors (esp. two or more) or by lines. **2.** to secure, or fix firmly. *–v.i.* **3.** to moor a ship, etc. **4.** to take up a position or be made secure by anchors or the like, as a ship. [late ME *more,* OE *mār-* (in *mārels* mooring rope), c. MD *mâren* moor, tie up]

**Moor** /mɔ/, *n.* **1.** a Muslim of the mixed Berber and Arab people inhabiting north-west Africa. **2.** one belonging to that group of this people which in the 8th century invaded and conquered Spain. **3.** *Archaic.* →**blackamoor.** [ME *More,* from OF, var. of *Maure,* from L *Maurus,* from Gk *Maûros*]

**moorage** /ˈmɔrɪdʒ/, *n.* **1.** the act of mooring. **2.** the state of being moored. **3.** a place for mooring. **4.** a charge or payment for the use of moorings.

**moorhen** /ˈmɔhɛn/, *n.* **1.** →**dusky moorhen. 2.** a common

European gallinule, *Gallinula chloropus.*

**mooring** /ˈmɔrɪŋ/, *n.* **1.** the act of one who or that which moors. **2.** (*usu. pl.*) something by which a ship or the like is moored, as a cable, line, etc. **3.** (*pl.*) the place where a vessel is or may be moored.

**mooring buoy** /ˈ– bɔɪ/, *n.* a buoy to which vessels can be moored.

**mooring mast** /ˈ– mast/, *n.* the mast or tower to which a dirigible is moored. Also, **mooring tower.**

**Moorish** /ˈmɔrɪʃ/, *adj.* **1.** of or pertaining to the Moors. **2.** in the style of the Moors, as architecture, decoration, etc.

**moorish idol** /mɔrɪʃ ˈaɪdl/, *n.* a small, handsome, boldly marked fish, *Zanclus canescens,* found in Australian waters and elsewhere.

**moorland** /ˈmɔlænd/, *n.* land consisting of a moor.

**moort** /mɔt/, *n.* a large shrub or small tree, *Eucalyptus platypus,* found in southern coastal areas of western Australia, which has dense foliage, providing shelter near the ground.

**moose** /mus/, *n., pl.* **moose. 1.** a large animal, *Alces americanus,* of the deer family, inhabiting Canada and the northern U.S., the male of which has enormous palmate antlers, long legs, and a large head. **2.** a similar species, *A. gigas,* found in Alaska. **3.** the European elk, *A. machlis.* [N Amer. Ind.; cognate forms in Algonquian, Narragansett, Delaware, etc., meaning 'he strips or eats off']

**moosh** /mʊʃ/, *n. Colloq.* **1.** the mouth; the face. **2.** prison food, esp. porridge. Also, **mush.**

**moot** /mut/, *adj.* **1.** subject to argument or discussion; debatable; doubtful: *a moot point.* –*v.t.* **2.** to bring forward (any point, subject, project, etc.) for discussion. **3.** *Obs.* to argue (a case, etc.), esp. in a mock court. –*n.* **4.** an early English assembly of the people, exercising political, administrative, and judicial powers. **5.** an argument or discussion, esp. of a hypothetical legal case. [ME *mote,* OE *mōt, gemōt* meeting, assembly, c. Icel. *mōt,* D *gemoet*] – **mooter,** *n.*

**moot court** /ˈ– kɔt/, *n.* a mock court for the conduct of hypothetical legal cases, as for practice for students of law.

**moot hall** /ˈ– hɔl/, *n.* (in an English village) a historic building where a moot (def. 4) was once held.

**mop** /mɒp/, *n., v.,* **mopped, mopping.** –*n.* **1.** a bundle of coarse yarn, a piece of cloth, or the like, fastened at the end of a stick or handle, used for washing floors, dishes, etc. **2.** a thick mass, as of hair. –*v.t.* **3.** to rub, wipe, clean, or remove with a mop. **4.** to wipe: *to mop the face with a handkerchief.* **5. mop up, a.** to clean up. **b.** *Mil.* to clear (ground, trenches, towns, etc.) of scattered or remaining enemy combatants, after attacking forces have gone beyond the place. [earlier *map,* ME *mappe.* Cf. L *mappa* napkin, cloth. ? in ML mop]

**mope** /moʊp/, *v.,* **moped, moping,** *n.* –*v.i.* **1.** to be sunk in listless apathy or dull dejection. –*v.t.* **2.** to make listless and dispirited. –*n.* **3.** a person who mopes or is given to moping. **4.** (*pl.*) low spirits. [var. of obs. *mop* make a wry face. Cf. D *moppen* pout] – **moper,** *n.* – **mopey,** *adj.* – **mopingly,** *adv.*

**moped** /ˈmoʊpɛd/, *n.* a light, low-powered motorcycle equipped with pedals for starting and assisting the motor.

**mopish** /ˈmoʊpɪʃ/, *adj.* given to moping; listless and dejected. – **mopishly,** *adv.* – **mopishness,** *n.*

**mopoke** /ˈmoʊpoʊk/, *n.* **1.** an owl of the genus *Ninox,* esp. the boobook, found in Australia and New Zealand and having a call which resembles the word 'mopoke'. In Australia the tawny frogmouth is often wrongly identified as the mopoke. **2.** *Colloq.* a slow, stupid or miserable-looking person. Also, **morepork** /ˈmɔpɔk/. [imitative]

mopoke (def. 1)

**moppet** /ˈmɒpət/, *n.* **1.** a child or a young girl. **2.** *Colloq.* a doll. [(obs.) *mop* baby, rag doll + -ET]

**moquette** /mɒˈkɛt, moʊ-/, *n.* a kind of fabric with a thick velvety pile used for carpets and upholstery. [F; orig. uncert.]

**M.O.R.** /ɛm oʊ ˈa/, *adj.* →**middle-of-the-road** (def. 3). Also, **MOR.**

**mora** /ˈmɔrə/, *n., pl.* **morae** /ˈmɔri/, **moras.** in quantitive verse, the unit of time equivalent to the ordinary or normal short sound or syllable. [L: delay]

**moraceous** /mɔˈreɪʃəs/, *adj.* belonging to the Moraceae, or mulberry family of plants, which includes the mulberry, breadfruit, fig, hemp, hop, Osage orange, etc. [L *mōrus* mulberry tree + -ACEOUS]

**moraine** /mɔˈreɪn/, *n.* **1.** a ridge, mound, or irregular mass of boulders, gravel, sand and clay, transported in or on a glacier. **2.** a deposit of such material left on the ground by a glacier. [F. Cf. ML *morena* embankment of stakes, It. *mora* cairn] – **morainal, morainic,** *adj.*

**moral** /ˈmɒrəl/, *adj.* **1.** pertaining to or concerned with right conduct or the distinction between right or wrong: *moral considerations.* **2.** concerned with the principles or rules of right conduct; ethical: *moral philosophy.* **3.** expressing or conveying truths or counsel as to right conduct, as a speaker, a literary work, etc.; moralising. **4.** founded on the fundamental principles of right conduct rather than on enactment or custom: *moral rights.* **5.** capable of conforming to the rules of right conduct. **6.** conforming to the rules of right conduct (opposed to *immoral*): *a moral man.* **7.** sexually virtuous; chaste. **8.** of, pertaining to, or producing an effect upon the mind, feelings, or on results generally: *a moral victory; moral support.* **9.** depending upon what is observed of human nature and actions or of things generally, rather than upon demonstration: *moral evidence.* **10.** resting upon convincing grounds of probability: *a moral certainty.* –*n.* **11.** the moral teaching or practical lesson contained in a fable, tale, experience, etc. **12.** the embodiment or type of something. **13.** *Colloq.* a certainty: *it's a moral to win.* **14.** (*pl.*) principles or habits with respect to right or wrong conduct; ethics. **15.** (*pl.*) behaviour or habits in sexual matters. [ME, from L *mōrālis* relating to manners, customs]

**morale** /məˈral/, *n.* moral or mental condition with respect to cheerfulness, confidence, zeal, etc.: *the morale of troops.* [F, fem. of *moral,* adj. See MORAL]

**morale-booster** /məˈral-bustə/, *n.* anything which raises the spirits, boosts morale.

**moralise** /ˈmɒrəlaɪz/, *v.,* **-lised, -lising.** –*v.i.* **1.** to make moral reflections. –*v.t.* **2.** to explain in a moral sense, or draw a moral from. **3.** to improve the morals of. Also, **moralize.** – **moralisation** /mɒrəlaɪˈzeɪʃən/, *n.* – **moraliser,** *n.* – **moralisingly,** *adv.*

**moralism** /ˈmɒrəlɪzəm/, *n.* **1.** the habit of moralising. **2.** a moral maxim. **3.** the practice of morality, as distinct from religion.

**moralist** /ˈmɒrələst/, *n.* **1.** one who teaches or inculcates morality. **2.** one who practises morality. – **moralistic** /mɒrəˈlɪstɪk/, *adj.*

**morality** /məˈrælətі/, *n., pl.* **-ties. 1.** conformity to the rules of right conduct; moral or virtuous conduct. **2.** sexual virtue; chastity. **3.** moral quality or character. **4.** a doctrine or system of morals; ethics; duties. **5.** moral instruction; a moral lesson or precept; a moralising discourse or utterance. **6.** →**morality play.**

**morality play** /ˈ– pleɪ/, *n.* a form of allegorical drama in vogue from the 14th to the 16th centuries, employing personifications of virtues and vices.

**morally** /ˈmɒrəli/, *adv.* **1.** in a moral manner. **2.** from a moral point of view. **3.** virtuously. **4.** virtually; practically.

**moral philosophy** /mɒrəl fəˈlɒsəfi/, *n.* →**ethics.**

**moral sense** /– ˈsɛns/, *n.* the ability to distinguish between right and wrong.

**moral support** /– səˈpɔt/, *n.* a person who or that which provides reassurance and encouragement.

**moral theology** /– θiˈɒlədʒi/, *n.* that branch of theology dealing with principles of moral conduct treated with reference to a divine origin.

**morass** /məˈræs/, *n.* **1.** a tract of low, soft, wet ground. **2.** a marsh or bog. **3.** marshy ground. [D *moeras,* in MD *maras,* from OF *marais,* of Gmc orig. See MARSH]

**moratorium** /mɒrəˈtɔriəm/, *n., pl.* **-toria** /-ˈtɔriə/, **-toriums. 1.** a legal authorisation to delay payment of money due, as in an emergency. **2.** the period during which such authorisation is in effect. **3.** a respite; a temporary cessation of activity, for the purpose of deferring a decision on a particular course of action in politics. [NL, properly neut. of LL *morātōrius* MORATORY]

**moratory** /ˈmɒrətəri, -tri/, *adj.* authorising delay of payment: *a moratory law.* [LL *morātōrius* delaying, from L *morārī* delay]

**moray** /ˈmɔreɪ/, *n., pl.* **-rays.** *n.* any of numerous eels of the family Muraenidae, often found lurking amongst rocks and weeds, as the **long-tailed eel,** *Evenchelys macrurus* of northern Australia, or *Muraena helena,* common in the Mediterranean and valued as a food fish.

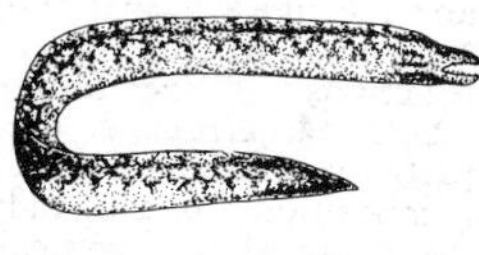
moray eel

**morbid** /ˈmɔbəd/, *adj.* **1.** suggesting an unhealthy mental state; unwholesomely gloomy, sensitive, extreme, etc. **2.** affected by, proceeding from, or characteristic of disease. **3.** pertaining to diseased parts: *morbid anatomy.* [L *morbidus* sickly] – **morbidly,** *adv.* – **morbidness,** *n.*

**morbidity** /mɔˈbɪdəti/, *n.* **1.** morbid state or quality. **2.** the proportion of sickness in a locality.

**morbific** /mɔˈbɪfɪk/, *adj.* causing disease. Also, **morbifical.** [NL *morbificus,* from L *morbus* disease] – **morbifically,** *adv.*

**morbilli** /mɔˈbɪlaɪ/, *n.pl.* →**measles.** [ML, pl. of *morbillus,* diminutive of L *morbus* disease]

**morceau** /mɔˈsoʊ/, *n., pl.* **-ceaux** /-ˈsoʊ/. **1.** morsel. **2.** an excerpt or passage of poetry or music.

**mordacious** /mɔˈdeɪʃəs/, *adj.* biting; given to biting. [L *mordācitas* power of biting + -OUS] – **mordaciously,** *adv.* – **mordacity** /mɔˈdæsəti/, *n.*

**mordancy** /ˈmɔdnsi/, *n.* mordant quality.

**mordant** /ˈmɔdnt/, *adj.* **1.** caustic or sarcastic, as wit, a speaker, etc. **2.** having the property of fixing colours, as in dyeing. *–n.* **3.** a substance used in dyeing to fix the colouring matter, esp. a metallic compound, as an oxide or hydroxide, which combines with the organic dye and forms an insoluble coloured compound or lake in the fibre. **4.** an acid or other corrosive substance used in etching to eat out the lines, etc. *–v.t.* **5.** to impregnate or treat with a mordant. [ME, from OF, ppr. of *mordre,* from L *mordēre* bite] – **mordantly,** *adv.*

**mordent** /ˈmɔdnt/, *n.* **1.** a melodic embellishment consisting of a rapid alternation of a principal note with a supplementary note a semitone below it, called *single* or *short* when the supplementary note occurs only once, and *double* or *long* when this occurs twice or oftener. **2.** See **inverted mordent.** [G, from It. *mordente,* properly ppr. of *mordere,* from L *mordēre* bite]

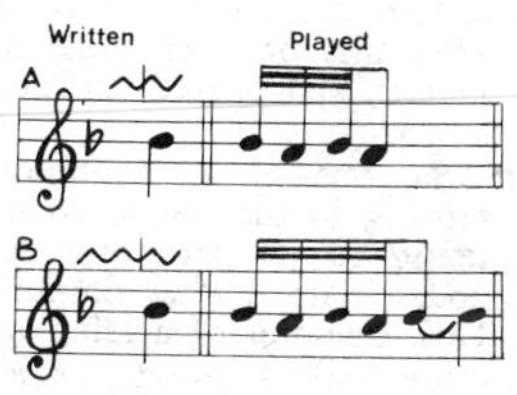

mordents: A, single; B, double

**more** /mɔ/, *adj., superl.* **most,** *n., adv.* *–adj.* **1.** in greater quantity, amount, measure, degree, or number (as the comparative of *much* and *many,* with the superlative *most*): *more money.* **2.** additional or further: *do not lose any more time.* *–n.* **3.** an additional quantity, amount, or number. **4.** a greater quantity, amount, or degree. **5.** something of greater importance. **6.** (*construed as pl.*) a greater number of a class specified, or the greater number of persons. *–adv.* **7.** in or to a greater extent or degree: *more rapid.* **8.** in addition; further; longer; again. **9. more or less,** to a certain extent; approximately. [ME; OE *māra,* c. OS and OHG *mēro.* See MOST]

**moreen** /mɒˈrin/, *n.* a heavy fabric of wool, or wool and cotton, commonly watered, used for curtains, petticoats, etc. [? akin to MOIRE]

**more-ish** /ˈmɔr-ɪʃ/, *adj.* of or pertaining to something of which one would like more; tempting; delicious: *that cake is very more-ish.*

**morel** /mɒˈrɛl/, *n.* an edible mushroom of the genus *Morchella,* an ascomycetous group in which the fruit body has the aspect of a stalked sponge. [ME *morele,* from OF, from L *mōrum* a mulberry]

**morello** /məˈrɛloʊ/, *n., pl.* **-los.** a sour cherry, *Prunus cerasus,* var. *austera,* with a dark-coloured skin and juice. Also, *U.S.,* **amarelle.** [It.: dark-coloured (from L *maurus* moor), ? b. with It. *amarello,* diminutive of *amaro* bitter (from L *amārus*)]

**moreover** /mɔrˈoʊvə/, *adv.* beyond what has been said; further; besides.

**morepork** /ˈmɔpɔk/, *n.* →**mopoke.**

**mores** /ˈmɔreɪz/, *n.pl.* customs or conventions accepted without question and embodying the fundamental moral views of a group. [L: customs]

**Moresque** /məˈrɛsk/, *adj.* →**Moorish.** [F, from It. *moresco,* from *Moro* MOOR]

**Moreton Bay bug,** *n.* →**Balmain bug.**

**Moreton Bay chestnut,** *n.* →**black bean.**

**Moreton Bay fig,** *n.* a massive umbrageous tree, *Ficus macrophylla,* native to the east coast of Australia which bears small, purplish, non-edible fruit.

Moreton Bay fig

**morganatic** /mɔgəˈnætɪk/, *adj.* designating or pertaining to a form of marriage in which a man of high rank takes to wife a woman of lower station with the stipulation that neither she nor the issue (if any) shall have any claim to his rank or property. Also, *Rare,* **morganic** /mɔˈgænɪk/. [NL *morganāticus,* from ML (*mātrimōnium ad*) *morganāticam* (marriage with) morning gift (in lieu of a share in the husband's possessions), from OHG *morgan* morning. The morning gift was a gift from a husband to his wife the morning after their marriage] – **morganatically,** *adv.*

**morgue** /mɔg/, *n.* **1.** a place in which the bodies of persons found dead are exposed for identification. **2.** *Journalism. Colloq.* **a.** the reference library of clippings, mats, books, etc., kept by a newspaper, etc. **b.** the room for it. [F; orig. name of building in Paris so used]

**moribund** /ˈmɒrəbʌnd/, *adj.* **1.** in a dying state. **2.** on the verge of extinction or termination. [L *moribundus*] – **moribundity** /mɒrəˈbʌndəti/, *n.* – **moribundly,** *adv.*

**morion**[1] /ˈmɒriən/, *n.* an open helmet with a tall comb and a curved brim merging into a peak at front and back. [F, from Sp. *morrión,* from *morra* crown of the head]

morion[1]

**morion**[2] /ˈmɒriən/, *n.* a variety of smoky quartz of a dark brown or nearly black colour. [L misreading (in early editions of Pliny's Nat. Hist.) of *mormorion*]

**Moriori** /mɒriˈɔri/, *n.* **1.** a Polynesian culture in New Zealand and the Chatham Islands, earlier than Maori culture; the culture of the moa hunters. **2.** the language of the Moriori.

**Mormon** /ˈmɔmən/, *n.* **1.** a member of a religious body founded in the U.S. in 1830 by Joseph Smith and calling itself 'The Church of Jesus Christ of Latter-day Saints'. **2. The Book of Mormon,** a sacred book of the Mormon Church, supposed to be an abridgment by a prophet (**Mormon**) of a record of certain ancient peoples in America, written on golden plates, and discovered and translated (1827-30) by Joseph Smith. *–adj.* **3.** of or pertaining to the Mormons or their religious system: *the Mormon view of Creation.* – **Mormonism,** *n.*

**morn** /mɔn/, *n. Poetic.* morning. [ME *morn(e),* OE *morne* (dat. of *morgen* morning), c. D *morgen* and G *Morgen*]

**mornay** /ˈmɔneɪ/, *adj.* **1.** covered with a thick white sauce which has grated cheese added to it. *–n.* **2.** a dish made with such a sauce. [orig. uncert.]

**morning** /ˈmɔnɪŋ/, *n.* **1.** the beginning of day; the dawn. **2.** the first part or period of the day, extending from dawn, or from midnight, to noon. **3.** the first or early period of anything. *–adj.* **4.** of or pertaining to morning: *the morning hours.* **5.** occurring, appearing, coming, used, etc., in the morning: *the morning sun.* [ME. See MORN, -ING[1], modelled on EVENING]

**morning after** /– 'aftə/, *n. Colloq.* the morning after a drinking bout.

**morning-after** /mɔnɪŋ-'aftə/, *adj. Colloq.* pertaining to a hangover: *that morning-after feeling.*

**morning-after pill** /'– pɪl/, *n.* a birth-control pill based on a prostaglandin.

**morning coat** /'mɔnɪŋ koʊt/, *n.* a black coat with tails, forming part of morning dress.

**morning dress** /'– drɛs/, *n.* formal dress used in daytime, as at weddings, etc., consisting for men typically of morning coat, light grey striped trousers, a light-coloured top-hat, etc.

**morning glory** /mɔnɪŋ 'glɔri/, *n., pl.* **-ries.** **1.** any of various climbing plants of the family Convolvulaceae, esp. of the genera *Ipomoea* and *Convolvulus,* as *I. purpurea,* a twining plant with cordate leaves and funnel-shaped flowers of various colours. **2.** *Horseracing Colloq.* a horse which performs well in morning track work, but not in races. **3.** *Colloq.* sexual intercourse had upon awakening.

morning glory

**morning piece** /'mɔnɪŋ pis/, *n. W.A.* →**playlunch.**

**morning room** /'– rum/, *n.* a room in a house, usu. adjoining the kitchen, used esp. for eating breakfast. Also, **breakfast room.**

**morning sickness** /'– sɪknəs/, *n.* nausea occurring often in the early part of the day, as a characteristic symptom in the first months of pregnancy.

**morning star** /'– sta/, *n.* a bright planet, seen in the east before sunrise.

**morning sticks** /'– stɪks/, *n.pl.* →**kindling** (def. 1). Also, **mornings wood.**

**morning tea** /– 'ti/, *n.* a very light meal, as of a biscuit and a cup of tea or coffee, etc., taken in the mid-morning.

**morocco** /mə'rɒkoʊ/, *n.* **1.** a fine leather made from goatskins tanned with sumac, originally in Morocco. **2.** any leather made in imitation of this. Also, **morocco leather.**

**Morocco** /mə'rɒkoʊ/, *n.* a kingdom in north-western Africa. – **Moroccan,** *adj., n.*

**moron** /'mɔrɒn/, *n.* **1.** a person of arrested intelligence whose mentality is judged incapable of developing beyond that of a normal child of 8 to 12 years of age. **2.** *Colloq.* a stupid person. [Gk, neut. of *mōrós* dull, foolish] – **moronic** /mə'rɒnɪk/, *adj.* – **moronism, moronity** /mə'rɒnəti/, *n.*

**morose** /mə'roʊs/, *adj.* gloomily or sullenly ill-humoured as a person, mood, etc. [L *mōrōsus* fretful, morose, particular] – **morosely,** *adv.* – **moroseness,** *n.*

**morph**[1] /mɔf/, *n.* (in linguistics) a group of phonemes linked together to make a linguistic sign or a part thereof, as /æp/ taken from the sign /æpəl/, for *apple.*

**morph**[2] /mɔf/, *n. Colloq.* →**morphine.**

**morph-,** variant of **morpho-** before vowels.

**-morph,** a word element meaning 'form', as in *isomorph.* [Gk *morphḗ* form]

**morph.,** morphology.

**morpheme** /'mɔfim/, *n.* (in linguistics) any of the minimum meaningful elements in a language, not further divisible into smaller meaningful elements, usu. recurring in various contexts with relatively constant meaning: either a word, as *girl, world,* or part of a word, as *-ish* or *-ly* in *girlish* and *worldly.* [MORPH(O)- + *-eme,* as in *phoneme*] – **morphemic** /mɔ'fimɪk/, *adj.*

**-morphic,** a word element used as adjective termination corresponding to **-morph,** as in *anthropomorphic.* [Gk *morphḗ* form + -IC]

**morphine** /'mɔfin/, *n.* a bitter crystalline alkaloid, $C_{17}H_{19}NO_3 \cdot H_2O$, the most important narcotic principle of opium, used in medicine (usu. in the form of a sulphate or other salt) to dull pain, induce sleep, etc. Also, **morphia** /'mɔfiə/. [F, from G *Morphin,* from *Morph(eus)* the Greek god of sleep + *-in* -INE[2]]

**morphinism** /'mɔfənɪzəm/, *n.* **1.** a morbid condition induced by the habitual use of morphine. **2.** the habit inducing it.

**morpho-,** initial word element corresponding to **-morph.**

**morphogenesis** /mɔfoʊ'dʒɛnəsəs/, *n.* the structural development of an organism or part. Also, **morphosis.** – **morphogenetic** /,mɔfoʊdʒə'nɛtɪk/, **morphogenic** *adj.*

**morphology** /mɔ'fɒlədʒi/, *n.* **1.** the study of form, structure, and the like. **2.** that branch of biology which deals with the form and structure of animals and plants, without regard to functions. **3.** the form of an organism considered as a whole. **4.** *Gram.* **a.** the patterns of word formation in a particular language, including inflection, derivation, and composition. **b.** the study and description thereof. **5.** *Geog.* the study of the physical form of lands, regions, or towns. – **morphologic** /mɔfə'lɒdʒɪk/, **morphological** /mɔfə'lɒdʒɪkəl/, *adj.* – **morphologically** /mɔfə'lɒdʒɪkli/, *adv.* – **morphologist,** *n.*

**morphophonemics** /,mɔfoʊfə'nimɪks/, *n.* **1.** the study of the phonological variation of morphemes as they appear in different contexts. The negative prefix *in-* shows such variation in *inelegant, impossible, illegible.* **2.** the structure displayed by such patterned variation. – **morphophonemic,** *adj.*

**morphosis** /mɔ'foʊsəs/, *n.* structural changes in an organism or its parts that may occur in the course of its development. [NL, from Gk *morphḗ* form + -OSIS]

**morphotectonics** /,mɔfoʊtɛk'tɒnɪks/, *n.* the study of the form and make-up of large geological structures such as continents, mountain ranges, etc.

**-morphous,** a word element used as adjective termination corresponding to **-morph,** as in *amorphous.* [Gk *-morphos,* from *morphḗ* form]

**morrell** /mə'rɛl/, *n.* a tall tree, *Eucalyptus longicornis,* with pointed buds, found in south-western Australia.

**morrie** /'mɒri/, *n.* **1.** a watered fabric, as of silk or wool. **2.** *Print.* a pattern formed when two screens are at conflicting angles.

**morris dance** /'mɒrəs dæns/, *n.* a folk dance, performed by persons in costume, often representing personages of the Robin Hood legend, formerly common in England, esp. in May Day festivities. Also, **morris.** [late ME *moreys daunce* Moorish dance]

**morrison** /'mɒrəsən/, *n.* a brightly coloured flower of the genus *Verticordia,* as *V. nitens* of western Australia.

**morrow** /'mɒroʊ/, *n. Archaic.* **1.** morning. **2.** the day next after this or after some other particular day or night. [ME *morwe,* apocopated var. of *morwen,* OE *morgen* morning. See MORN]

**morse** /mɔs/, *n.* **1.** →**morse code.** *–adj.* **2.** denoting or pertaining to the morse code or the system of communications using it. **3.** pertaining to any code resembling the morse code. [named after Samuel Finley Breeze *Morse,* 1791-1872, U.S. inventor of a telegraph system]

**morse code** /– 'koʊd/, *n.* a system of dots, dashes, and spaces, or the corresponding sounds or the like, used in telegraphy and signalling to represent the letters of the alphabet, numerals, etc. Also, **morse alphabet.**

**morsel** /'mɔsəl/, *n.* **1.** a bite, mouthful, or small portion of food or the like. **2.** a small piece, quantity, or amount of anything; a scrap; a bit. *–v.t.* **3.** to distribute in or divide into tiny portions. [ME, from OF, diminutive of *mors* a bite, from L *morsum,* pp. neut. of *mordēre* bite]

**mort** /mɔt/, *n.* **1.** the note blown on the hunting horn to signify the death of the animal hunted. **2.** *Obs.* death. [ME, from OF, from L *mors*]

**mort.,** **1.** mortgage. **2.** mortuary.

**mortadella** /mɔtə'dɛlə/, *n.* a large cooked and smoked sausage made of chopped beef and pork seasoned with garlic and pepper. [It., from L *murtātum* sausage seasoned with myrtleberries]

**mortal** /'mɔtl/, *adj.* **1.** liable or subject to death: *all mortal creatures.* **2.** of or pertaining to man as subject to death; human: *this mortal life.* **3.** belonging to this world. **4.** pertaining to death: *mortal throes.* **5.** involving spiritual death (opposed to *venial*): *a mortal sin.* **6.** causing death; fatal: *a mortal wound.* **7.** to the death: *mortal combat.* **8.** deadly or implacable: *a mortal enemy.* **9.** dire, grievous, or bitter: *in mortal fear.* **10.** *Colloq.* extreme; very great: *in a mortal* *hurry.* **11.** *Colloq.* possible or conceivable: *of no mortal use.* *–n.* **12.** a human being; a being subject to death. [ME, from L *mortālis* subject to death] – **mortally,** *adv.*

**mortality** /mɔ'tæləti/, *n., pl.* **-ties. 1.** the condition of being mortal or subject to death; mortal character, nature, or existence. **2.** mortal beings collectively; humanity. **3.** relative frequency of death, or death rate, as in a district or community. **4.** death or destruction on a large scale, as from war, plague, famine, etc. **5.** *Obs.* death.

**mortality rate** /'– reɪt/, *n.* the rate at which members of a given population die, usu. expressed as a ratio of deaths to total population. Also, **death rate.**

**mortality table** /'– teɪbəl/, *n.* an actuarial table compiled by an insurance company from statistics on the life spans of an arbitrarily selected population group or of former policy-holders.

**mortar**[1] /'mɔtə/, *n.* **1.** a vessel of hard material, having a bowl-shaped cavity, in which drugs, etc., are reduced to powder with a pestle. **2.** any of various mechanical appliances in which substances are pounded or ground. **3.** a cannon very short in proportion to its bore, for throwing shells at high angles. **4.** some similar contrivance, as for throwing pyrotechnic bombs or a lifeline. [ME and OE *mortere,* from L *mortārium* vessel in which substances are pounded, or one in which MORTAR[2] is made; in defs 3 and 4, trans. of F *mortier*]

mortar[1] and pestle: A, pestle; B, mortar

**mortar**[2] /'mɔtə/, *n.* **1.** a material which binds bricks, stones, etc., into a compact mass. **2.** a mixture, as of quicklime, cement, etc., sand, and water, which hardens in the air and is used for binding bricks, etc., together. *–v.t.* **3.** to plaster or fix with mortar. [ME *morter,* from F *mortier,* from L *mortārium.* See MORTAR[1]]

**mortarboard** /'mɔtəbɔd/, *n.* **1.** a board, commonly square, used by masons to hold mortar. **2.** a kind of cap with a close-fitting crown surmounted by a stiff, flat, cloth-covered, square piece, worn by university students, graduates, teachers, etc.

mortarboard

**mortgage** /'mɔgɪdʒ/, *n.* **1.** *Law.* a security by way of conveyance or assignment of property securing the payment of a debt or the performance of an obligation where the property is redeemable upon payment or performance. **2.** **legal mortgage,** a mortgage where the legal estate in property is conveyed or assigned. **3.** **equitable mortgage, a.** a charge on property enforceable as a right in equity where the legal estate in the mortgaged property remains in the mortgagor. **b.** a mortgage of equitable property. **4.** the deed by which such a transaction is effected. **5.** the rights conferred by it, or the state of the property conveyed. *–v.t.* **6.** to convey or place (property, esp. houses or land) under a mortgage. **7.** →**pledge.** [ME *mor-gage,* from OF, from *mort* dead + *gage* pledge, GAGE[1], *n.*]

**mortgage debenture** /– də'bɛntʃə/, *n.* →**debenture** (def. 2).

**mortgagee** /mɔgə'dʒi/, *n.* one to whom property is mortgaged.

**mortgagee clause** /'– klɔz/, *n.* a clause attached to a fire-insurance policy, designed to protect the mortgagee against loss or damage.

**mortgagor** /'mɔgədʒə, mɔgə'dʒɔ/, *n.* one who mortgages property. Also, **mortgager.**

**mortice** /'mɔtəs/, *n., v.,* **-ticed, -ticing.** *–n.* **1.** a rectangular cavity of considerable depth in one piece of wood, etc., for receiving a corresponding projection (tenon) on another piece, so as to form a joint (**mortice and tenon joint**). **2.** *Print.* the portion cut away from a letterpress printing plate for the insertion of type or another plate. *–v.t.* **3.** to fasten by, or as by, a mortice. **4.** to cut or otherwise form a mortice in, to fit a prescribed tenon. **5.** to fasten or join securely. **6.** *Print.* to cut away part of a letterpress printing plate in order to insert type or another plate in its place. Also, **mortise.** [ME *mortas,* from OF *mortaise,* ? from Ar. *murtazz* made fast]

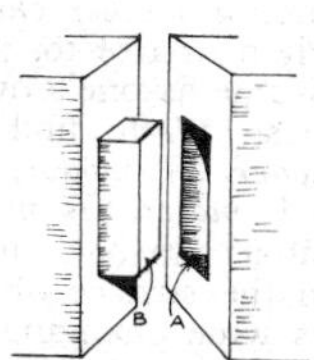

A, mortice; B, tenon

**mortician** /mɔ'tɪʃən/, *n.* →**undertaker.** [MORT(UARY) + -ICIAN, modelled on PHYSICIAN]

**mortification** /mɔtəfə'keɪʃən/, *n.* **1.** humiliation in feeling, as by some wound to pride. **2.** a cause or source of such humiliation. **3.** the practice of asceticism by penitential discipline to overcome desire for sin and to strengthen the will. **4.** *Pathol.* the death of one part of the body while the rest is alive; gangrene.

**mortify** /'mɔtəfaɪ/, *v.,* **-fied, -fying.** *–v.t.* **1.** to humiliate in feeling, as by a severe wound to the pride or self-complacency. **2.** to bring (the body, passions, etc.) into subjection by abstinence, ascetic discipline, or rigorous austerities. **3.** *Pathol.* to affect with gangrene or necrosis. *–v.i.* **4.** to practise mortification or disciplinary austerities. **5.** *Pathol.* to undergo mortification, or become gangrened or necrosed. [ME *mortifie(n),* from OF *mortifier,* from LL *mortificāre* kill, destroy] – **mortifier,** *n.* – **mortifyingly,** *adv.*

**mortise** /'mɔtəs/, *n., v.t.,* **-tised, -tising.** →**mortice.**

**mortmain** /'mɔtmeɪn/, *n.* **1.** the condition of lands or tenements held without right of alienation, as by an ecclesiastical corporation; inalienable ownership. **2.** the holding of land by a corporation or charitable trust beyond the period of time or in violation of the conditions authorised by law; dead hand. [ME *mort(e)mayn(e),* from OF *mortemain,* trans. of ML *mortua manus* dead hand]

**mortuary** /'mɔtʃəri/, *n., pl.* **-ries,** *adj.* *–n.* **1.** a place for the temporary reception of the dead. **2.** a customary gift formerly claimed by and due to the incumbent of an English parish from the estate of a deceased parishioner. *–adj.* **3.** of or pertaining to the burial of the dead. **4.** pertaining to or connected with death. [ME, from ML *mortuārium,* properly neut. of L *mortuārius* belonging to the dead]

**morula** /'mɒrulə/, *n., pl.* **-lae** /-li/. the mass of cells resulting from the cleavage of the ovum before the formation of a blastula. [NL, diminutive of L *mōrum* mulberry] – **morular,** *adj.*

**morwong** /'mɔwɒŋ/, *n.* any of a number of species of marine food fishes of the family Cheilodactylidae, esp. *Nemadactylus douglasii,* of southern Australian and New Zealand waters; black perch.

**MOS** /mɒs/, *n.* a FET which is characterised by extremely high input resistance. Also, **metal oxide semiconductor.**

**mosaic** /moʊ'zeɪɪk, mə'zeɪɪk/, *n.* **1.** a picture or decoration made of small pieces of stone, glass, etc., of different colours, inlaid to form a design. **2.** the process of producing it. **3.** something resembling a mosaic in composition. **4.** *Aerial Survey.* an assembly of aerial photographs taken vertically and matched in such a way as to show a continuous photographic representation of an area (**mosaic map**). **5.** *Plant Pathol.* a symptom of various virus diseases, a patchy variation of colour. **6.** *Genetics.* an organism, usu. animal, composed of a mixture of genetically distinct tissues; chimera. *–adj.* **7.** pertaining to or resembling a mosaic or mosaic work. **8.** composed of diverse elements combined. [ME, from ML *mosaicus,* var. of *mūsaicus,* lit., of the Muses, artistic] – **mosaicist** /moʊ'zeɪəsəst/, *n.*

**Mosaic** /moʊ'zeɪɪk/, *adj.* of or pertaining to the writings and institutions attributed to Moses, the leader of the Israelites in their flight from Egypt. Also, **Mosaical.** [NL *Mosaicus*]

**mosaic fleece** /moʊzeɪɪk 'flis/, *n.* a fleece made up of at least two distinct types of wool, one of which occurs in patches over the fleece and may be finer or coarser, longer or shorter than the rest of the fleece.

**mosaic gold** /'– goʊld/, *n.* **1.** →**stannic sulphide. 2.** →**ormolu** (def. 1).

**mosaicism** /mə'zeɪəsɪzəm/, *n.* the condition of a mosaic (def. 6).

**Mosaic Law** /moʊ,zeɪɪk 'lɔ/, *n.* **1.** the ancient law of the Hebrews, attributed to Moses. **2.** the part of the Scripture containing this law; the Pentateuch.

**mosaic-tailed rat** /moʊ,zeɪɪk-teɪld 'ræt/, *n.* any of a number of Australian rodents of the genera *Melomys* and *Uromys* in which the scale pattern of the tail is a series of plates rather than the more usual ring formation.

**moschate** /ˈmɒskeɪt/, *adj.* having a musky smell. [NL *moschātus,* from ML *moschus* musk]

**Moscow** /ˈmɒskoʊ/, *Colloq.* –*n.* **1.** a pawnshop. **2. gone to** or **in Moscow,** in pawn. –*v.t.* **3.** to pawn.

**moselle** /moʊˈzɛl/, *n.* **1.** a light white wine made along the Moselle river in West Germany. **2.** a similar wine made elsewhere. [G *Mosel,* a river in W West Germany]

**Moses basket** /ˈmoʊzəs baskət/, *n.* →**car-basket.**

**mosey** /ˈmoʊzi/, *v.i. U.S. Colloq.* to stroll; saunter (fol. by *along, up, down, off,* etc.).

**Moslem** /ˈmɒzləm, ˈmʊz-/, *adj., n., pl.* **-lems, -lem.** →**Muslim.** – **Moslemic** /mɒzˈlɛmɪk, mʊz-/, *adj.*

**Moslemism** /ˈmɒzləmɪzəm, ˈmʊz-/, *n.* the Muslim religion; Islam.

**mosque** /mɒsk/, *n.* a Muslim temple or place of worship. [F *mosquée,* from It. *moschea,* from Ar. *masjid,* from *sajada* prostrate oneself, worship]

**mosquito** /məsˈkitoʊ/, *n., pl.* **-toes, -tos.** any of various dipterous insects of the family Culicidae (genera *Culex, Anopheles,* etc.), the females of which have a long proboscis, by means of which they puncture the skin of animals (including man) and draw blood, some species transmitting certain diseases, as malaria and yellow fever. [Sp., diminutive of *mosca,* from L *musca* a fly]

mosque

**mosquito hawk** /ˈ– hɔk/, *n.* →**nighthawk** (def. 2).

**mosquito net** /ˈ– nɛt/, *n.* a screen, curtain, or canopy of net, gauze, or the like **(mosquito netting),** for keeping out mosquitoes.

**mosquito orchid** /ˈ– ɔkəd/, *n.* a small terrestrial orchid, *Acianthus exsertus,* whose flowers resemble a mosquito.

**moss** /mɒs/, *n.* **1.** any of the cryptogamic plants which belong to the class Musci, of the bryophytes, comprising small leafy-stemmed plants growing in tufts, sods, or mats on moist ground, tree trunks, rocks, etc. **2.** a growth of such plants. **3.** any of various similar plants, as certain lichens (see **Iceland moss**), the lycopods (see **club moss**), etc. –*v.t.* **4.** to cover with a growth of moss. [ME *mos(se),* OE *mos* bog, c. D *mos* moss, G *Moos* bog, moss] – **mosslike,** *adj.*

**moss agate** /ˈ– ægət/, *n.* a kind of agate or chalcedony containing brown or black mosslike dendritic markings from various impurities.

**mossback** /ˈmɒsbæk/, *n. U.S. Colloq.* **1.** a person attached to antiquated notions. **2.** an extreme conservative.

**Mössbauer effect** /ˈmɒsbaʊər əfɛkt/, *n.* a discovery made in 1957, that in certain cases appreciable fractions of the gamma-ray spectrum emitted by some excited nuclei may be undisturbed by nuclear recoil or lattice vibrations. [named after R. L. *Mössbauer,* b. 1922, German physicist]

**moss-grown** /ˈmɒs-groʊn/, *adj.* **1.** overgrown with moss. **2.** old-fashioned.

**mossie**[1] /ˈmɒsi/, *n.* a bird of southern Africa, *Passer melanurus,* of the family Ploceidae, common in the vicinity of human dwellings; Cape Sparrow.

**mossie**[2] /ˈmɒzi/, *n.* →**mozzie.**

**mosso** /ˈmɒsoʊ/, *adv.* (a musical direction) in a fast manner. [It., pp. of *muovere* move]

**moss rose** /ˈmɒs roʊz/, *n.* a cultivated variety of rose with a mosslike growth on the calyx and stem.

**mosstrooper** /ˈmɒstrupə/, *n.* **1.** one of the class of marauders who infested the mosses or bogs of the border between England and Scotland in the 17th century. **2.** any marauder. – **mosstrooping,** *n., adj.*

**mossy** /ˈmɒsi/, *adj.,* **-sier, -siest.** **1.** overgrown with, or abounding in, moss. **2.** covered with a mosslike growth. **3.** appearing as if covered with moss. **4.** resembling moss. – **mossiness,** *n.*

**most** /moʊst/, *adj., superl.* of **more,** *n., adv.* –*adj.* **1.** in the greatest quantity, amount, measure, degree, or number (used as the superlative of *much* and *many,* with the comparative *more*): *the most votes.* **2.** in the majority of instances: *most exercise is beneficial.* **3.** greatest, as in size or extent: *the most part.* –*n.* **4.** the greatest quantity, amount, or degree; the utmost. **5.** the greatest number or the majority of a class specified. **6.** the greatest number. **7.** the majority of persons (*construed as pl.*). –*adv.* **8.** in or to the greatest extent or degree (in this sense much used before adjectives and adverbs, and regularly before those of more than two syllables, to form superlative phrases having the same force and effect as the superlative degree formed by the termination *-est*): *most rapid, most wisely.* **9.** *U.S.* almost or nearly. [ME *most(e),* OE *māst* (replacing ME *mest(e),* OE *mǣst*), c. G *meist,* etc.]

**-most,** a suffixal use of *most* found in a series of superlatives, as in *utmost, foremost.* [ME *-most,* replacing ME and OE *-mest,* a double superl. suffix, from *-ma* + *-est,* both forming superlatives]

**most common fee,** *n.* the charge judged to be most usual for any particular medical service and used as the basis for the reimbursement of medical costs under the Government health scheme. Also, **common fee.**

**most favoured nation,** *n.* a country with which trade is carried on under conditions which are no less favourable than those pertaining to trade with any other country. *Abbrev.:* M.F.N.

**mostly** /ˈmoʊstli/, *adv.* **1.** for the most part; in the main: *the work is mostly done.* **2.** chiefly.

**mot** /moʊ/, *n.* a pithy or witty remark. [F: word, saying, note of a horn, etc., from L *muttum* a mutter, grunt]

**mote** /moʊt/, *n.* a particle or speck, esp. of dust. [ME; OE *mot* speck, c. D *mot* grit, sawdust]

**motel** /moʊˈtɛl/, *n.* **1.** a roadside hotel which provides accommodation for travellers in self-contained, serviced units, with parking for their vehicles. **2.** *N.Z.* such a unit. [M(OTOR) + (H)OTEL]

**motelier** /moʊˈtɛliə/, *n.* the proprietor of a motel.

**motet** /moʊˈtɛt/, *n.* a vocal composition in polyphonic style, on a biblical or similar prose text, intended for use in a church service. [ME, from OF, diminutive of *mot* word]

**moth** /mɒθ/, *n., pl.* **moths.** **1.** any of a very large group of lepidopterous insects, generally distinguished from the butterflies by not having their antennae clubbed and by their (mainly) nocturnal or crepuscular habits. **2.** a clothes moth. [ME *motthe,* OE *moththe,* c. G *Motte*]

**mothball** /ˈmɒθbɔl/, *n.* **1.** a small ball of naphthalene or (sometimes) camphor which repels moths for the protection of clothing. **2. in mothballs, a.** no longer in use; in reserve. **b.** out of commission, as a ship. –*v.t.* **3.** to put out of use; place in reserve.

**moth-eaten** /ˈmɒθ-itn/, *adj.* **1.** eaten or damaged by or as by moths. **2.** decayed. **3.** out of fashion.

**mother**[1] /ˈmʌðə/, *n.* **1.** a female parent. **2.** (*oft. cap.*) one's own mother. **3.** *Colloq.* a mother-in-law, step-mother, or adoptive mother. **4.** a term of familiar address for an old or elderly woman. **5.** the head or superior of a female religious community. **6.** a woman looked upon as a mother, or exercising control or authority like that of a mother. **7.** the qualities characteristic of a mother, or maternal affection. **8.** something that gives rise to, or exercises protecting care over, something else. **9.** *Colloq.* →**mother-fucker.** –*adj.* **10.** that is a mother: *a mother bird.* **11.** pertaining to or characteristic of a mother: *mother love.* **12.** derived from one's mother; native: *mother tongue.* **13.** bearing a relation like that of a mother, as in giving origin or rise, or in exercising protective care: *a mother church.* –*v.t.* **14.** to be the mother of; give origin or rise to. **15.** to acknowledge oneself the author of; assume as one's own. **16.** to care for or protect as a mother does. **17.** to find a substitute mother for (a lamb.). [ME *moder,* OE *mōdor,* c. D *moeder,* G *Mutter,* Icel. *mōdhir;* akin. to L *māter,* Gk *mḗtēr,* Skt *mātar-*] – **motherless,** *adj.*

**mother**[2] /ˈmʌðə/, *n.* a stringy, mucilaginous substance formed on the surface of a liquid undergoing acetous fermentation (as wine changing to vinegar), and consisting of the various bacteria, esp. *Mycoderma aceti,* which cause such fermentation. Also, **mother of vinegar.** [special use of MOTHER[1]]

**Mother Carey's chicken** /ˌmʌðə kɛəriz ˈtʃɪkən/, *n.* any of various storm-petrels.

**mothercraft** /ˈmʌðəkraft/, *n.* the knowledge and skill associated with the rearing of children.

**mother-fucker** /'mʌðə-fʌkə/, *n. U.S. Colloq.* a person or thing which arouses exasperation, irritation, contempt, etc. Also, **mother.** – **mother-fucking,** *adj.*

**mother hair** /'mʌðə-hɛə/, *n.* long coarse harsh chalky kemp which sometimes occurs on new born lambs. It is shed and may or may not be replaced by normal wool fibres in the same follicle.

**motherhood** /'mʌðəhʊd/, *n.* **1.** the state of being a mother; maternity. **2.** mothers collectively. **3.** the qualities or spirit of a mother.

**Mother Hubbard** /mʌðə 'hʌbəd/, *n.* a kind of full, loose gown worn by women. [from the nursery rhyme character, *Mother Hubbard*]

**mothering** /'mʌðərɪŋ/, *n.* **1.** the process of acting as a mother to a child. **2.** sympathetic treatment, as if to a child. **3.** *Brit.* the custom of visiting one's parents on Mid-Lent Sunday (Mothering Sunday) and giving a small gift.

**Mothering Sunday** /mʌðərɪŋ 'sʌndeɪ/, *n.* a Sunday in mid-Lent on which in British tradition one visits one's parents and presents them with a gift.

**mother-in-law** /'mʌðər-ən-lɔ/, *n., pl.* **mothers-in-law.** the mother of one's husband or wife.

**motherland** /'mʌðəlænd/, *n.* **1.** one's native country. **2.** the land of one's ancestors.

**motherless** /'mʌðələs/, *adj.* **1.** without a mother. *–adv.* **2.** (an intensive): *stone motherless broke.*

**mother lode** /'mʌðə loʊd/, *n.* a rich or principal lode.

**motherly** /'mʌðəli/, *adj.* **1.** pertaining to, characteristic of, or befitting a mother: *motherly affection.* **2.** having the character, etc., of a mother. *–adv.* **3.** in the manner of a mother. – **motherliness,** *n.*

**Mother of God,** *n.* a designation of the Virgin Mary.

**mother-of-opal** /mʌðər-əv-'oʊpəl/, *n.* →**matrix** (def. 12.)

**mother-of-pearl** /mʌðər-əv-'pɜl/, *n.* a hard, iridescent substance which forms the inner layer of certain shells, as that of the pearl oyster; nacre.

**mother-of-thousands** /mʌðər-əv-'θaʊzənz/, *n.* →**mind-your-own-business.**

**mother of vinegar,** *n.* →**mother**[2].

**mother's boy** /'mʌðəz bɔɪ/, *n.* a boy or man who is excessively attached to his mother and often somewhat effeminate.

**Mother's Day** /'mʌðəz deɪ/, *n.* a day for acts of grateful affection or remembrance by each person towards his mother, observed annually on the second Sunday in May.

**mother's help** /mʌðəz 'hɛlp/, *n.* a girl or woman either living with a family or coming daily, who is paid to help with light housework and look after children.

**mother's ruin** /– 'ruən/, *n. Colloq. (joc.)* gin; aunty's downfall.

**mother superior** /mʌðə sə'pɪəriə/, *n.* the head of a female religious community.

**mother-to-be** /mʌðə-tə-'bi/, *n.* a pregnant woman.

**mother tongue** /'mʌðə tʌŋ/, *n.* **1.** the language first learned by a person; native language. **2.** a parent language.

**mother wit** /– 'wɪt/, *n.* →**commonsense.**

**mothy** /'mɒθi/, *adj.,* **-ier, -iest.** **1.** containing moths. **2.** moth-eaten.

**motif** /moʊ'tif, 'moʊtəf/, *n.* **1.** a recurring subject or theme for development or treatment, as in art, literature, or music. **2.** a distinctive figure in a design, as of wallpaper. **3.** a dominant idea or feature. [F. See MOTIVE]

**motile** /'moʊtaɪl/, *adj.* **1.** *Biol.* moving, or capable of moving, spontaneously: *motile cells or spores.* *–n.* **2.** *Psychol.* one in whose mind motor images are predominant or esp. distinct. [L *mōtus,* pp., moved + -ILE] – **motility** /moʊ'tɪləti/, *n.*

**motion** /'moʊʃən/, *n.* **1.** the process of moving, or changing place or position. **2.** a movement. **3.** power of movement, as of a living body. **4.** the action or manner of moving the body in walking, etc.; gait. **5.** a bodily movement or change of posture; a gesture. **6.** a proposal formally made to a deliberative assembly: *to make a motion to adjourn.* **7.** *Law.* an application made to a court or judge for an order, ruling, or the like. **8.** a suggestion or proposal. **9.** an inward prompting or impulse; inclination: *of one's own motion.* **10.** *Music.* melodic progression, as the change of a voice part from one pitch to another. **11.** *Mach.* **a.** a piece of mechanism with a particular action or function. **b.** the action of such mechanism. **12.** →**faeces** (def. 1). **13.** **in motion,** in active operation; moving. *–v.t.* **14.** to direct by a significant motion or gesture, as with the hand: *to motion a person to a seat.* *–v.i.* **15.** to make a significant motion; gesture, as with the hand for the purpose of directing: *to motion to a person.* [ME, from L *mōtio* a moving]

**motionless** /'moʊʃənləs/, *adj.* without, or incapable of, motion. – **motionlessly,** *adv.* – **motionlessness,** *n.*

**motion picture** /moʊʃən 'pɪktʃə/, *n.* →**film** (def. 4).

**motivate** /'moʊtəveɪt/, *v.t.,* **-vated, -vating.** to provide with a motive or motives.

**motivated** /'moʊtəveɪtəd/, *adj.* ambitious; determined; energetic: *the prime minister is a highly motivated person.*

**motivation** /moʊtə'veɪʃən/, *n.* a motivating; a providing of a motive; inducement. – **motivational,** *adj.*

**motivational research** /moʊtə,veɪʃənəl rə'sɜtʃ/, *n.* the application of the knowledge and techniques of the social sciences (esp. psychology and sociology) to understanding consumer attitudes and behaviour; used as a guide in advertising and marketing. Also, **motivation research.**

**motive** /'moʊtɪv/, *n., adj., v.,* **-tived, -tiving.** *–n.* **1.** something that prompts a person to act in a certain way or that determines volition; an incentive. **2.** the goal or object of one's actions: *his motive was revenge.* **3.** (in art, literature, and music) a motif. *–adj.* **4.** causing, or tending to cause, motion. **5.** pertaining to motion. **6.** prompting to action. **7.** constituting a motive or motives. *–v.t.* **8.** to provide with a motive. **9.** to motivate. **10.** to relate to a motif or a principal theme or idea in a work of art. [ML *mōtīvum* a moving cause, properly neut. of *mōtīvus* serving to move, from L *mōtus,* pp., moved; replacing ME *motif,* from OF]

**motive power** /– paʊə/, *n.* **1.** any power used to impart motion. **2.** a source of mechanical energy. **3.** *Railways.* locomotives, etc., which supply tractive power.

**motivity** /moʊ'tɪvəti/, *n.* the power of initiating or producing motion.

**mot juste** /moʊ 'dʒust, ʒust/, *n.* the exact or appropriate word.

**motley** /'mɒtli/, *adj., n., pl.* **-leys.** *–adj.* **1.** exhibiting great diversity of elements; heterogeneous: *a motley crowd.* **2.** being of different colours combined; particoloured. **3.** wearing a particoloured garment: *a motley fool.* *–n.* **4.** a combination of different colours. **5.** a particoloured effect of colour. **6.** the motley or particoloured garment of the medieval professional fool or jester: *to wear the motley.* **7.** a heterogeneous assemblage. **8.** a medley. [ME, unexplained derivative of MOTE]

**motmot** /'mɒtmɒt/, *n.* any of the tropical and subtropical American birds constituting the family Momotidae, related to the kingfishers, and having a serrate bill and chiefly greenish and bluish plumage. [Amer. Sp.; imitative]

**motocross** /'moʊtəkrɒs/, *n.* a short distance motorcycle race of at least two laps on a circuit presenting a variety of surfaces and terrain. Cf. **scramble** (def. 10). [F *moto* motorcycle + CROSS(-COUNTRY)]

**motor** /'moʊtə/, *n.* **1.** a comparatively small and powerful engine, esp. an internal-combustion engine in a motor car, motor boat, or the like. **2.** any self-powered vehicle. **3.** one who or that which imparts motion, esp. a contrivance (as a steam engine), which receives and modifies energy from some natural source in order to utilise it in driving machinery, etc. **4.** *Elect.* a machine which converts electrical energy into mechanical energy: *an electric motor.* *–adj.* **5.** causing or imparting motion. **6.** pertaining to or operated by a motor. **7.** used in or for, or pertaining to, motor vehicles. **8.** *Physiol.* conveying an impulse that results or tends to result in motion, as a nerve. **9.** *Physiol., Psychol.* denoting the effect or phase of any mental process, as the innervation of muscles and glands. **10.** *Psychol.* pertaining to or involving action: *motor images.* *–v.i.* **11.** to ride or travel in a motor car. *–v.t.* **12.** to convey (someone) by a motor car. [L: one who moves]

**motorbike** /'moʊtəbaɪk/, *n. Colloq.* →**motorcycle.**

**motor boat** /'moʊtə boʊt/, *n.* a boat propelled by its own mechanical power. – **motor-boating,** *n.*

**motorbus** /'moʊtəbʌs/, *n.* **1.** a bus. **2.** *U.S.* a motor coach.

**motorcade** /'moʊtəkeɪd/, *n.* a procession or parade of motor cars. Also, *U.S.,* **autocade.** [MOTOR and (CAVAL)CADE]

**motor camp** /ˈmoʊtə kæmp/, *n. N.Z.* →**camping ground.**

**motor car** /ˈ– ka/, *n.* a vehicle, esp. one for passengers, carrying its own power-generating and propelling mechanism, usu. an internal-combustion engine, for travel on ordinary roads.

**motor coach** /ˈ– koʊtʃ/, *n.* →**coach** (def. 3).

**motorcycle** /ˈmoʊtəsaɪkəl/, *n.* a motor vehicle resembling a bicycle, for one or two riders, sometimes with a sidecar attached. – **motorcyclist,** *n.*

**motor drive** /ˈmoʊtə draɪv/, *n.* the mechanical system, including an electric motor, used to operate a machine or machines.

**motored** /ˈmoʊtəd/, *adj.* having a motor or motors, esp. of specified number or type: *a two-motored tape-recorder.*

**motor generator** /moʊtə ˈdʒɛnəreɪtə/, *n.* an electric motor coupled to a generator for altering the voltage, frequency, or number of phases of an electric supply.

**motorise** /ˈmoʊtəraɪz/, *v.t.,* **-rised, -rising.** **1.** to furnish with a motor or motors, as vehicles. **2.** to supply with motor-driven vehicles in the place of horses and horse-drawn vehicles. Also, **motorize.** – **motorisation** /moʊtəraɪˈzeɪʃən/, *n.*

**motorist** /ˈmoʊtərəst/, *n.* **1.** one who drives a motor car. **2.** the user of a privately owned motor car.

**motorkhana** /moʊtəˈkanə/, *n.* →**gymkhana** (def. 3).

**motorman** /ˈmoʊtəmən/, *n., pl.* **-men.** **1.** *Brit.* one who drives an electric train or tram. **2.** one who operates a motor.

**motor scooter** /ˈmoʊtə skutə/, *n.* a low-built motorcycle having small wheels, footboards, and an enclosed engine. Also, **scooter.**

**motor starter** /ˈ– statə/, *n.* a device for starting and accelerating an electric motor up to its normal running speed.

**motor vehicle** /ˈ– viɪkəl/, *n.* a road vehicle driven by a motor, usu. an internal-combustion engine, as a motor car, motorcycle, or the like.

**motor vessel** /ˈ– vɛsəl/, *n.* a ship driven by internal-combustion engines, usu. diesel. Also, *U.S.,* **motor ship.**

**motorway** /ˈmoʊtəweɪ/, *n.* an expressway; freeway.

**motown** /ˈmoʊtaʊn/, *n.* **1.** a form of commercial soul and blues music. *–adj.* **2.** of or pertaining to such music. [from *Motown* (short for *motor town*), a recording company in Detroit, centre of the U.S. car industry]

**motser** /ˈmɒtsə/, *n. Colloq.* a large amount of money, esp. a gambling win. Also, **motza, motzer.**

**mottle** /ˈmɒtl/, *v.,* **-tled, -tling,** *n.* *–v.t.* **1.** to diversify with spots or blotches of a different colour or shade. *–n.* **2.** a diversifying spot or blotch of colour. **3.** mottled colouring or pattern. [backformation from MOTLEY]

**mottled** /ˈmɒtld/, *adj.* spotted or blotched in colouring.

**mottled sandstone** /–ˈsændstoʊn/, *n.* →**speckled hen.**

**motto** /ˈmɒtoʊ/, *n., pl.* **-toes, -tos.** **1.** a maxim adopted as expressing one's guiding principle. **2.** a sentence, phrase, or word attached to or inscribed on anything as appropriate to it. [It.]

**motza** /ˈmɒtsə/, *n.* →**motser.** Also, **motzer.**

**mouch** /mutʃ/, *v.i., v.t. Colloq.* →**mooch.**

**moue** /mu/, *n.* a pouting grimace. [see MOW[3]]

**mouflon** /ˈmuflɒn/, *n.* a wild sheep, *Ovis musimon,* inhabiting the mountainous regions of south-western Europe, esp. Sardinia, Corsica, etc., the male of which has large curving horns. Also, **moufflon.** [F, from Corsican, from LL *mufro*]

**mouillé** /ˈmwieɪ, ˈmuieɪ/, *adj.* **1.** palatal or palatalised, esp. referring to sounds spelt *ll* and *ñ* in Spanish, *gl* and *gn* in Italian, etc. **2.** (of French sounds) spelt *l* or *ll* and pronounced as a *y* sound. [F, pp. of *mouiller* wet, moisten, from L *mollis* soft]

**moujik** /ˈmuʒɪk/, *n.* →**muzhik.**

**moulage** /muˈlaʒ/, *n.* **1.** the making of a mould in plaster of Paris, etc., of objects, footprints, tyre tracks, etc., esp. for identification. **2.** the mould itself. [F]

**mould**[1] /moʊld/, *n.* **1.** a hollow form or matrix for giving a particular shape to something in a molten or plastic state. **2.** that on or about which something is formed or made. **3.** something formed in or on a mould: *a mould of jelly.* **4.** the shape imparted to a thing by a mould. **5.** shape or form. **6.** distinctive nature, or native character. **7.** *Archit.* **a.** a moulding. **b.** a group of mouldings. *–v.t.* **8.** to work into a required shape or form; shape. **9.** to shape or form in or on a mould. **10.** *Foundry.* to form a mould of or from, in order to make a casting. **11.** to produce by or as if by shaping material; form. **12.** to fashion; model the character of. **13.** to ornament with mouldings. Also, *U.S.,* **mold.** [ME, from OF *modle,* from L *modulus* MODULE] – **mouldable,** *adj.*

**mould**[2] /moʊld/, *n.* **1.** a growth of minute fungi forming on vegetable or animal matter, commonly as a downy or furry coating, and associated with decay. **2.** any of the fungi that produce such a growth. *–v.i.* **3.** to become mouldy. Also, *U.S.,* **mold.** [ME *mowlde,* apparently var. of *mowled, mouled,* pp. of *moulen,* earlier ME *muwlen,* c. d. Dan. *mugle* grow mouldy]

**mould**[3] /moʊld/, *n.* **1.** loose, friable earth, esp. such as is rich in organic matter and favourable to the growth of plants. **2.** *Poetic.* the ground or earth. Also, *U.S.,* **mold.** [ME and OE *molde,* c. OHG *molta* mould, dust]

**mouldboard** /ˈmoʊldbɔd/, *n.* the curved board or metal plate in a plough, which turns over the earth from the furrow. Also, *U.S.,* **moldboard.**

**moulder**[1] /ˈmoʊldə/, *v.i.* **1.** to turn to dust by natural decay; crumble; waste away. *–v.t.* **2.** to cause to moulder. Also, *U.S.,* **molder.** [frequentative of obs. *mold,* v., moulder, crumble away (v. use of MOULD[3]). See -ER[6]]

**moulder**[2] /ˈmoʊldə/, *n.* one who moulds; a maker of moulds. Also, *U.S.,* **molder.** [MOULD[1], *v.* + -ER[1]]

**moulding** /ˈmoʊldɪŋ/, *n.* **1.** the act or process of one who or that which moulds. **2.** something moulded. **3.** *Archit., etc.* **a.** a decorative variety of contour or outline given to cornices, jambs, strips of woodwork, etc. **b.** a shaped member introduced into a structure to afford such variety or decoration. **4.** shaped material in the form of a strip, used for supporting pictures, covering electric wires, etc. Also, *U.S.,* **molding.**

**moulding board** /ˈ– bɔd/, *n.* the board upon which bread is kneaded. Also, *U.S.,* **molding board.**

**mouldy** /ˈmoʊldi/, *adj.,* **-dier, -diest.** **1.** overgrown or covered with mould. **2.** musty, as from decay or age. Also, *U.S.,* **moldy.** [MOULD[2] + -Y[1]] – **mouldiness,** *n.*

**moulin** /ˈmulən/, *n.* a nearly vertical shaft or cavity worn in a glacier by surface water falling through a crack in the ice. [F, from LL *molīnum* mill. See MILL]

**moult** /moʊlt/, *v.i.* **1.** (of birds, insects, reptiles, etc.) to cast or shed the feathers, skin, or the like, to be succeeded by a new growth. *–v.t.* **2.** to cast or shed (feathers, etc.) in the process of renewal. *–n.* **3.** the act or process of moulting. Also, *U.S.,* **molt.** [ME *mout,* OE *-mūtian* change (in *bemūtian* exchange for), from L *mūtāre* change. Cf. MEW[4]] – **moulter,** *n.*

**mound** /maʊnd/, *n.* **1.** an elevation formed of earth or sand, debris, etc., overlying ruins, a grave, etc. **2.** a tumulus or other raised work of earth dating from a prehistoric or long-past period. **3.** a natural elevation of earth; a hillock or knoll. **4.** an artificial elevation of earth, as for a defence work, a dam or barrier, or any other purpose; an embankment. **5.** a heap or raised mass: *a mound of hay.* **6.** an artificial platform of earth, twigs, etc. constructed by a mound bird. **7.** *Baseball.* the slightly elevated ground from which the pitcher delivers the ball and which slopes gradually to the baselines. *–v.t.* **8.** to furnish with a mound of earth, as for a defence. **9.** to form into a mound; heap up. [OE *mund* hand, protection]

**mound ant** /ˈ– ænt/, *n.* →**meat ant.**

**mound bird** /ˈ– bɜd/, *n.* →**megapode.** Also, **mound-builder** /ˈmaʊnd-bɪldə/.

**mount**[1] /maʊnt/, *v.t.* **1.** to go up or ascend: *to mount the stairs.* **2.** to get up on (a platform, a horse, etc.) **3.** to set or place at an elevation: *to be mounted on stilts.* **4.** to furnish with a horse or other mount for riding. **5.** to set on horseback. **6.** to raise or put into position for use, as a gun. **7.** to have or carry (guns) in position for use, as a fortress or a vessel does. **8.** to go or put on (guard), as a sentry or watch. **9.** (of a male animal) to climb up on (a female) for copulation. **10.** to fix on or in a support, backing, setting, etc: *to mount a photograph.* **11.** to provide (a play, etc.) with scenery, costumes, and other appurtenances for production. **12.** to prepare (an animal body or skeleton) as a specimen. **13.** *Microscopy.* **a.** to prepare (a slide) for microscopic investigation. **b.** to prepare (a sample, etc.) for examination by a microscope, as by placing it on a slide. *–v.i.* **14.** to rise or go to a higher position, level, degree, etc.; ascend. **15.** to rise in amount (oft. fol. by *up*): *the costs are steadily mounting.* **16.** to get up on the back of a horse, etc., for riding. **17.** to get up on something, as a platform. *–n.* **18.** the act or manner of mounting. **19.** a horse or other animal (or sometimes a bicycle) used, provided, or available for riding. **20.** an act or occasion of riding a horse, esp. in a race. **21.** a support, backing, setting, or the like, on or in which something is, or is to be, mounted or fixed: *a stamp mount.* **22.** *Microscopy.* the prepared slide. **23.** (in palmistry) one of nine sections of the palm. [ME *monte(n)*, from OF *monter,* from L *mons* mountain]

**mount**[2] /maʊnt/, *n.* a mountain or hill (now chiefly poetic, except in proper names, as *Mount Wellington*). [ME *mont, munt,* OE *munt,* from L *mons*]

**mountain** /ˈmaʊntən/, *n.* **1.** a natural elevation of the earth's surface rising more or less abruptly to a summit, and attaining an altitude greater than that of a hill. **2.** something resembling this, as in size: *a mountain of ice.* **3.** a huge amount. **4. make a mountain out of a molehill,** to complain to a degree out of proportion to the magnitude of the inconvenience, imposition or offence. *–adj.* **5.** of mountains: *mountain air.* **6.** living, growing, or found on mountains: *mountain people, mountain plants.* **7.** resembling or suggesting a mountain, as in size. [ME, from OF *montaigne,* from *mont* mountain, from L *mons*]

**mountain ash** /– ˈæʃ/, *n.* **1.** any of several eucalypts, as *Eucalyptus regnans* of Australia. **2.** any of various small trees of the genus *Sorbus,* as the European rowan, *S. aucuparia,* and the American *S. americana,* both having pinnate leaves and bearing small white corymbose flowers succeeded by bright red to orange berries.

**mountain beauty** /– ˈbjuti/, *n.* a tall shrub, *Hovea rosmarinifolia,* with purple pea-shaped flowers, found in south-eastern Australia.

**mountain blue butterfly,** *n.* a large, metallic-blue swallowtail butterfly, occurring in rainforest areas of northern Queensland and certain other tropical areas beyond Australia; Ulysses butterfly.

**mountain cat** /ˈmaʊntən kæt/, *n.* **1.** →**puma.** **2.** →**bobcat.**

**mountain cedar wattle,** *n.* →**cedar wattle.**

**mountain chain** /ˈmaʊntən tʃeɪn/, *n.* **1.** a connected series of mountains. **2.** two or more mountain ranges of close geographical relation.

**mountain daisy** /– ˈdeɪzi/, *n.* a montane and sub-alpine daisy of the genus *Celmisia,* as *C. coriacea* of New Zealand.

**mountain devil** /ˈ– dɛvəl/, *n.* **1.** Also, **moloch.** a spiny, grotesque-looking lizard, *Moloch horridus,* occurring in lowland as well as mountain regions of southern, central and western Australia. **2.** a woody shrub, *Lambertia formosa,* of sandstone areas of New South Wales. **3.** a small doll-like figure with a body usu. of wool wound around pipe cleaners and a head formed from the woody fruit of *Lambertia formosa* which fancifully resembles the head of the Devil.

mountain devil (def. 2)

**mountain dew** /– ˈdju/, *n. Colloq.* **1.** →**Scotch whisky.** **2.** any whisky, esp. when illicitly distilled.

**mountaineer** /maʊntəˈnɪə/, *n.* **1.** a climber of mountains. **2.** an inhabitant of a mountainous district. *–v.i.* **3.** to climb mountains. – **mountaineering,** *n.*

**mountain goat** /ˈmaʊntən goʊt/, *n.* →**Rocky Mountain goat.**

**mountain ibex** /– ˈaɪbɛks/, *n.* →**tahr.**

**mountain laurel** /– ˈlɒrəl/, *n.* →**laurel** (def. 3).

**mountain lion** /ˈ– laɪən/, *n.* →**puma.**

**mountainous** /ˈmaʊntənəs/, *adj.* **1.** abounding in mountains. **2.** of the nature of a mountain. **3.** resembling a mountain or mountains; large and high; huge: *mountainous waves.* – **mountainously,** *adv.*

**mountain oysters** /maʊntən ˈɔɪstəz/, *n.pl. N.Z. Colloq.* the testicles of a lamb.

**mountain pine** /– ˈpaɪn/, *n.* a small non-deciduous tree of New Zealand, *Dacrydium bidwillii.*

**mountain possum** /ˈ– pɒsəm/, *n.* →**bobuck.**

**mountain range** /ˈ– reɪndʒ/, *n.* **1.** a series of more or less connected mountains ranged in a line. **2.** a series of mountains, or of more or less parallel lines of mountains, closely related in origin, etc. **3.** an area in which the greater part of the land surface is in considerable degree or slope, upland summits are small or narrow, and there are great differences in elevations within the area (commonly over 1200 metres).

**mountain sheep** /ˈ– ʃip/, *n.* **1.** the bighorn, *Ovis canadensis,* found in the Rocky Mountains, U.S., and in northern Asia. **2.** any of various wild sheep inhabiting mountains.

**mountain sickness** /ˈ– sɪknəs/, *n.* a morbid condition characterised by difficult breathing, headache, nausea, etc., due to the rarefaction of the air at high altitudes.

**Mount Cook lily,** *n.* a large white buttercup, *Ranunculus lyallii,* native to South Island alpine districts of New Zealand.

**mountebank** /ˈmaʊntəbæŋk/, *n.* **1.** one who sells quack medicines from a platform in public places, appealing to his audience by tricks, storytelling, etc. **2.** any charlatan or quack. *–v.i.* **3.** to play the mountebank. [It. *montambanco,* contraction of *monta in banco* mount-on-(a)-bench] – **mountebankery** /maʊntəˈbæŋkəri/, *n.*

**mounted** /ˈmaʊntəd/, *adj.* **1.** seated or riding on a horse or the like. **2.** serving on horseback, or on some special mount, as soldiers, police, etc. **3.** *Mil.* permanently equipped with trucks, tanks, or other vehicles, or horses as means of transport. **4.** fixed on or in a support, backing, setting, or the like: *mounted gems.* **5.** put into position for use, as guns.

**mounted drill** /– ˈdrɪl/, *n.* military drill performed when mounted on horses or in vehicles.

**mounter** /ˈmaʊntə/, *n.* one who or that which mounts.

**mounting** /ˈmaʊntɪŋ/, *n.* **1.** the act of one who or that which mounts. **2.** something that serves as a mount, support, setting, or the like.

**mourn** /mɔn/, *v.i.* **1.** to feel or express sorrow or grief. **2.** to grieve or lament for the dead. **3.** to display the conventional tokens of sorrow after a person's death. *–v.t.* **4.** to feel or express sorrow or grief over (misfortune, loss, or anything regretted); deplore. **5.** to grieve or lament over (the dead). **6.** to utter in a sorrowful manner. [ME *mo(u)rne,* OE *murnan,* c. OHG *mornên*]

**mourner** /ˈmɔnə/, *n.* **1.** one who mourns. **2.** one who attends a funeral as a mourning friend or relative of the deceased. **3.** *U.S.* (at religious revival meetings) one who professes penitence for sin, with desire for salvation.

**mourners' bench** /ˈmɔnəz bɛntʃ/, *n. U.S.* (at religious revival meetings) a bench or seat at the front of the church or room, set apart for mourners or penitent sinners seeking salvation.

**mournful** /ˈmɔnfəl/, *adj.* **1.** full of, expressing, or showing sorrow or grief, as persons, the tone, etc.; sorrowful; sad. **2.** expressing, or used in, mourning for the dead. **3.** causing, or attended with, sorrow or mourning: *a mournful occasion.* **4.** gloomy, sombre or dreary, as in appearance or character: *mournful shadows.* – **mournfully,** *adv.* – **mournfulness,** *n.*

**mourning** /ˈmɔnɪŋ/, *n.* **1.** the act of one who mourns; sorrowing or lamentation. **2.** the conventional manifestation of sorrow for a person's death, esp. by the wearing of black, the hanging of flags at half-mast, etc. **3.** the outward tokens of such sorrow, as black garments, etc. **4. in mourning,** recently bereaved, esp. if showing the traditional outward tokens of grief. *–adj.* **5.** of, pertaining to, or used in mourning. – **mourningly,** *adv.*

**mourning band** /ˈ– bænd/, *n.* a black arm-band worn to show that one is in mourning.

**mourning cloak** /ˈ– kloʊk/, *n.* a European and American butterfly, *Nymphalis antiopa,* having dark wings with a yellow border.

**mouse** /maʊs/, *n., pl.* **mice** /maɪs/; /maʊz/, *v.,* **moused, mousing.** *–n.* **1.** any of various small rodents of the family Muridae, esp. of the genus *Mus,* as *M. musculus,* which infests houses. **2.** any similar animal of some other family, as the Cricetidae. **3.** *Colloq.* →**black eye.** **4.** *Colloq.* a person who is very quiet and shy, esp. a girl or woman. *–v.i.* **5.** to hunt for or catch mice. **6.** to prowl (about, etc.), as if seeking something. **7.** to seek or search stealthily or watchfully, as if for prey. *–v.t.* **8.** *Chiefly U.S.* to hunt out, as a cat hunts out mice. **9.** *Naut.* to secure with a mousing. [ME *mous,* OE *mūs* (pl. *mȳs*), c. G *Maus,* L *mūs*]

mouse

**mousebird** /ˈmaʊsbɜd/, *n.* a coly; any bird of the African family Coliidae.

**mouse cheese** /ˈmaʊs tʃiz/, *n. Colloq.* any type of cheddar cheese.

**mousedeer** /ˈmaʊsdɪə/, *n.* →**chevrotain.**

**mouse-dun** /ˈmaʊs-dʌn/, *n.* dark brownish grey.

**mouse-ear** /ˈmaʊs-ɪə/, *n.* any of various plants with small hairy leaves, as mouse-ear chickweed, *Cerastium glomeratum.*

**mouser** /ˈmaʊsə/, *n.* **1.** an animal that catches mice (commonly used with a qualifying term or with reference to the animal's ability to catch mice). **2.** one who mouses, or seeks or prowls as if for prey.

**mouse spider** /ˈmaʊs spaɪdə/, *n.* a robust, Australian, ground-tunnelling spider, *Missulena occatoria.* The female is blackish-brown but the male has a scarlet head.

**mousetail** /ˈmaʊsteɪl/, *n.* any plant of the genus *Myosurus,* esp. *M. minimus,* the flowers of which have a tail-like torus.

**mouse-trap** /ˈmaʊs-træp/, *n.* **1.** a trap used for catching mice in houses. **2.** Also, **mouse-trap cheese.** *Colloq.* an inexpensive, often tasteless, type of cheese.

**mousey** /ˈmaʊsi/, *adj.* →**mousy.**

**mousing** /ˈmaʊzɪŋ/, *n. Naut.* several turns of small rope or the like, uniting the shank and point of a hook, to prevent the unhooking of the lead.

**moussaka** /muˈsakə/, *n.* a Balkan and Middle Eastern dish based on minced lamb, tomatoes and aubergines, layered, topped with a thick white sauce and baked. [Ar. *musakk'a,* from Turk.]

**mousse** /mus/, *n.* any of various preparations of whipped cream, beaten eggs, gelatine, etc., flavoured (sweet or savoury) and usu. chilled. [F *mousse* froth]

**mousseline** /musəˈlin/, *n.* →**muslin.**

**mousseline de laine** /– də ˈleɪn/, *n.* →**delaine.** [F: lit., woollen muslin]

**mousseline de soie** /– də ˈswa/, *n.* a thin, stiff silk or rayon fabric. [F. lit., silken muslin]

**mousseline sauce** /– ˈsɔs/, *n.* a hollandaise sauce to which whipped cream has been added just before serving.

**moustache** /məˈstaʃ/, *n.* **1.** the hair growing on the upper lip, or on either half of the upper lip, of men. **2.** such hair when allowed to grow without shaving, and usu. trimmed to a particular shape. **3.** hair or bristles growing near the mouth of an animal. **4.** a stripe of colour, or elongated feathers, suggestive of a moustache on either side of the head of a bird. Also, *U.S.,* **mustache.** [F, from It. *mostaccio,* from Gk *mýstax* upper lip, moustache]

**Mousterian** /musˈtɪəriən/, *adj.* **1.** of or pertaining to the flint industry associated with Neanderthal man. **2.** the general culture of this period of the Palaeolithic. **3.** pertaining to human relics of this part of the Palaeolithic, c. 70 000 B.C. to 32 000 B.C. [from Le *Moustier,* a cave in SW France, containing flint implements of this period, + -IAN]

**mousy** /ˈmaʊsi/, *adj.,* **-sier, -siest. 1.** resembling or suggesting a mouse, as in colour, smell, etc. **2.** drab and colourless. **3.** quiet as a mouse. **4.** infested with mice. Also, **mousey.**

**mouth** /maʊθ/, *n., pl.* **mouths** /maʊðz/; /maʊð/, *v.* *–n.* **1.** the opening through which an animal takes in food, or the cavity containing or the parts including the masticating apparatus. **2.** the masticating and tasting apparatus. **3.** a person or other animal as requiring food. **4.** the oral opening or cavity considered as the source of vocal utterance. **5.** utterance or expression: *to give mouth to one's thoughts.* **6.** a grimace made with the lips. **7.** an opening leading out of or into any cavity or hollow place or thing: *the mouth of a cave.* **8.** a part of a river or the like where its waters are discharged into some other body of water: *the mouth of the Nile.* **9.** the opening between the jaws of a vice or the like. **10.** the lateral hole of an organ pipe. **11.** the lateral blowhole of a flute. **12. by word of mouth,** orally, as opposed to *in writing.* **13. down in the mouth,** depressed; unhappy. **14. shut one's mouth,** *Colloq.* to be quiet. *–v.t.* **15.** to utter in a sonorous, oratorical, or pompous manner, or with unnecessarily noticeable use of the mouth or lips. **16.** to put or take into the mouth, as food. **17.** to press, rub, or mumble with the mouth or lips. **18.** to accustom (a horse) to the use of the bit and bridle. *–v.i.* **19.** to speak or declaim sonorously and oratorically, or with mouthing of the words. **20.** to grimace with the lips. [ME; OE *mūth,* c. G *Mund*]

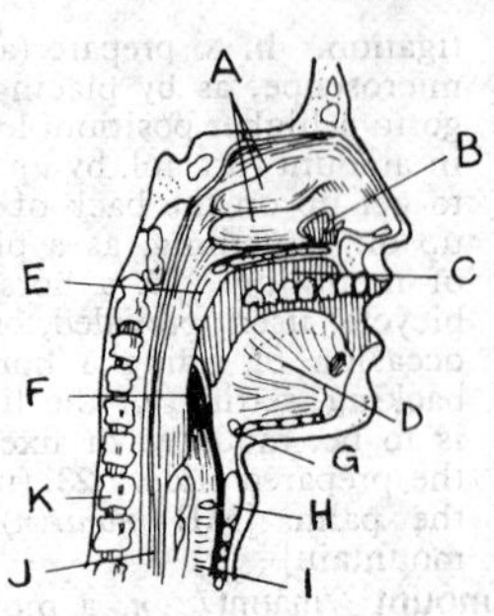


mouth and nose (section): A, turbinate bones; B, lachrymal duct; C, hard palate; D, tongue; E, uvula; F, epiglottis; G, hyoid bone; H, larynx; I, trachea; J, oesophagus; K, cervical vertibrae

**mouth-breeder** /ˈmaʊθ-bridə/, *n.* **1.** any aquarium fish, of the genera *Tilapia* and *Haplochromis,* which care for their young by holding them in the mouth. **2.** any of various other fishes, particularly those inhabiting warm fresh water where oxygen supply tends to be precarious, which incubate their eggs in the mouth or gill chambers.

**mouthful** /ˈmaʊθfʊl/, *n., pl.* **-fuls. 1.** as much as a mouth can hold. **2.** as much as is taken into the mouth at one time. **3.** a small quantity.

**mouthguard** /ˈmaʊθgad/, *n.* a protective device for the mouth, worn esp. by people playing sports, as football, basketball, etc.

**mouthman** /ˈmaʊθmæn/, *n. Prison Colloq.* a con man.

**mouth organ** /ˈmaʊθ ɔgən/, *n.* →**harmonica** (def. 1).

**mouthpart** /ˈmaʊθpat/, *n.* a structure in the region of the mouth of arthropods.

**mouthpiece** /ˈmaʊθpis/, *n.* **1.** a piece placed at or forming the mouth, as of a receptacle, tube, or the like. **2.** a piece or part, as of an instrument, to which the mouth is applied or which is held in the mouth: *the mouthpiece of a trumpet.* **3.** the part of a bit or bridle, as for a horse, that passes through the animal's mouth. **4.** *Boxing.* an appliance placed in the mouth to protect teeth and gums; a gumshield. **5.** *Colloq.* a legal representative or adviser; an official spokesperson, usu. for clients operating outside the law. **6.** a person, a newspaper, or the like that voices or communicates the sentiments, decisions, etc., of another or others; a spokesperson.

**mouth-to-mouth** /maʊθ-tə-ˈmaʊθ/, *adj.* denoting a method of artificial respiration in which air is breathed rhythmically into the mouth of the patient.

**mouthwash** /ˈmaʊθwɒʃ/, *n.* a medicated solution used for gargling and cleansing the mouth.

**mouth-watering** /ˈmaʊθ-wɔtərɪŋ/, *adj.* (of food, etc.) appetising: *a mouth-watering smell of cooking.*

**mouthy** /ˈmaʊði/, *adj.,* **-thier, -thiest.** loud-mouthed; ranting; bombastic. **– mouthily,** *adv.* **– mouthiness,** *n.*

**moutonnée** /ˈmutəneɪ/, *adj.* designating scattered knobs of rock rounded and smoothed by glacial action. Also, **moutonnéed.** [F lit., rounded like a sheep's back, pp. fem. of *moutonner,* from *mouton* sheep. See MUTTON]

**movable** /ˈmuvəbəl/, *adj.* **1.** capable of being moved; not fixed in one place, position, or posture. **2.** changing from one date to another in different years: *movable feast.* **3.** *Law.* →**moveable. 4.** *Print.* (of type or matrices) separate and capable of being rearranged. *–n.* **5.** an article of furniture which is not fixed in place. **6.** (*usu. pl.*) *Law.* →**moveable. – movableness, movability** /muvəˈbɪləti/, *n.* **– movably,** *adv.*

**move** /muv/, *v.,* **moved, moving,** *n.* *–v.i.* **1.** to change place or position; pass from one place or situation to another. **2.** to change one's abode; go from one place of residence to another. **3.** to advance, progress, or make progress. **4.** to have a regular motion, as an implement or a machine; turn; revolve. **5.** *Comm.* to be disposed of by sale, as goods in stock. **6.** *Colloq.* to start off, or depart: *it's time to be moving.* **7.** (of the bowels) to operate. **8.** to be active in a particular sphere: *to move in society.* **9.** to take action, or act, as in an affair. **10.** to make a formal request, application, or proposal: *to move for a new trial.* **11. move in,** to take up residence in a new home. **12. move out,** to leave a home. **13. move with the times,** to alter one's own attitudes or ideas in conjunction with changes in society. *–v.t.* **14.** to change the place or position of; take from one place, posture, or situation to another. **15.** to set or keep in motion; stir or shake. **16.** to prompt, actuate, or impel to some action: *what moved you to do this?* **17.** to cause (the bowels) to act or operate. **18.** to arouse or excite the feelings or passions of; affect with emotion; excite (*to*). **19.** to affect with tender or compassionate emotion; touch. **20.** to propose formally, as to a court or judge, or for consideration by a deliberative assembly. **21.** to submit a formal request or proposal to (a ruler, a court, etc.). **22. move heaven and earth,** to do one's utmost. *–n.* **23.** the act of moving; a movement. **24.** a change of abode or residence. **25.** an action towards an end; a step. **26.** *Games, etc.* the right or turn to move. **27. get a move on,** *Colloq.* hurry up. **28. on the move,** moving. [ME *move(n),* from AF *mover,* from L *movēre*] **– mover,** *n.*

**moveable** /ˈmuvəbəl/, *adj.* **1.** →**movable. 2.** *Law.* (of property) **a.** not permanent in place; capable of being moved without injury or damage. **b.** personal, as distinguished from real. *–n.* **3.** →**movable. 4.** (*usu. pl.*) *Law.* an article of personal property not attached to land. **– moveableness, moveability** /muvəˈbɪləti/, *n.* **– moveably,** *adv.*

**movement** /ˈmuvmənt/, *n.* **1.** the act or process or result of moving. **2.** a particular manner of moving. **3.** (*Chiefly pl.*) an action or activity, as of a person or a body of persons. **4.** *Mil., Navy.* a change of position or location of troops or ships. **5.** rapid progress of events, or abundance of events or incidents. **6.** the progress of events, as in a narrative or drama. **7.** the suggestion of action, as in a painting or the like. **8.** a series of actions or activities directed or tending towards a particular end: *the anti-slavery movement.* **9.** the course, tendency, or trend, of affairs in a particular field. **10.** the price change in the market of some commodity or security. **11.** an evacuation of the bowels. **12.** the material evacuated. **13.** the works, or a distinct portion of the works, of a mechanism, as a watch. **14.** *Music.* **a.** a principal division or section of a sonata, symphony, or the like. **b.** motion; rhythm; time; tempo. **15.** *Pros.* rhythmical structure or character.

**movie** /ˈmuvi/, *n.* **1.** →**film** (def. 4b). **2. the movies,** →**film** (def. 4c).

**moving** /ˈmuvɪŋ/, *adj.* **1.** that moves. **2.** causing or producing motion. **3.** actuating, instigating, or impelling: *the moving cause of a dispute.* **4.** that excites the feelings or affects with emotion, esp. touching or pathetic. **– movingly,** *adv.* **– movingness,** *n.*

**moving pathway** /– ˈpaθweɪ/, *n.* a type of conveyor belt on which people stand and are borne from one point to another, as at an airport, parking station, etc. Also, **moving footpath.**

**moving picture** /– ˈpɪktʃə/, *n. Chiefly U.S.* →**film** (def. 4).

**moving staircase** /– ˈstɛəkeɪs/, *n.* →**escalator.**

**mow**[1] /moʊ/, *v.,* **mowed, mown** or **mowed, mowing.** *–v.t.* **1.** to cut down (grass, grain, etc.) with a scythe or a machine. **2.** to cut grass, grain, etc., from. **3.** to cut down, destroy, or kill indiscriminately or in great numbers, as men in battle (fol. by *down*). *–v.i.* **4.** to cut down grass, grain, etc. [ME *mowe(n),* OE *māwan,* c. G *mähen*] **– mower,** *n.*

**mow**[2] /moʊ/, *n. U.S.* **1.** the place in a barn where hay, sheaves of grain, etc., are stored. **2.** a heap or pile of hay or of sheaves of grain in a barn. [ME *mowe,* OE *mūga, mūha,* c. Icel. *mūgi* swath]

**mow**[3] /moʊ/, *Archaic.* *–n.* **1.** a wry or derisive grimace. *–v.i.* **2.** to make mows, mouths, or grimaces. [ME *mowe,* from OF *moe* a pouting grimace]

**mowe** /moʊ/, *n., v.i.,* **mowed, mowing.** *Archaic.* →**mow**[3].

**mowing** /ˈmoʊɪŋ/, *n.* **1.** the act of levelling or cutting down grass with a mowing machine or scythe. **2.** as much grass as is cut in any specified period.

**mowing machine** /ˈ– məʃin/, *n.* a machine for mowing or cutting down standing grass, etc.

**mown** /moʊn/, *v.* past participle of **mow**[1].

**moxa** /ˈmɒksə/, *n.* **1.** a wormwood, *Artemisia moxa,* of eastern Asia. **2.** a preparation made from the leaves of this plant, used esp. in Japanese popular medicine as a cautery by being ignited on the skin. [NL, from Jap. *mogusa*]

**moxie** /ˈmɒksi/, *n. U.S. Colloq.* courage; audacity; liveliness. [from *Moxie,* the name of a U.S. soft drink]

**Mozambique** /moʊzæmˈbik/, *n.* a republic in south-eastern Africa.

**mozz** /mɒz/, *Colloq. –n.* **1.** a hex. **2. put the mozz on** (someone), to hex (someone). *–v.t.* **3.** to hex. **4.** to inconvenience; hinder. [short for MOZZLE]

**mozzarella** /mɒtsəˈrɛlə/, *n.* a soft, white, ripened cheese, with a plastic curd, giving it a smooth, close texture. It is formed into pear shapes and covered with a heat-shrinkable plastic coating. [It. *mozza* a slice]

**mozzetta** /moʊˈzɛtə/, *n.* a short cape which covers the shoulders and can be buttoned over the breast, and to which a hood is attached, worn by the pope and by cardinals, bishops, abbots, and other dignitaries. Also, **mozetta.** [It., shortened form of *almozetta,* from L *almutia* AMICE[1]]

**mozzie** /ˈmɒzi/, *n. Colloq.* →**mosquito.** [shortened form of MOSQUITO + -IE]

**mozzle** /ˈmɒzəl/, *n.* luck, esp. bad luck. [Heb. *mazzal* luck]

**mp,** *Music.* moderately soft. [It. *mezzopiano*]

**MP** /ɛm ˈpi/, *n.* **1.** Member of Parliament. **2.** Military Police.

**m.p.g.,** miles per gallon.

**m.p.h.,** miles per hour.

**m.p.s.,** miles per second.

**Mr** /ˈmɪstə/, *n., pl.* **Messrs** /ˈmɛsəz/. mister; a title prefixed to a man's name or position: *Mr Lawson, Mr Prime Minister.* [abbrev. of MISTER]

**Mrs** /ˈmɪsəz/, *n.* mistress; a title prefixed to the name of a married woman: *Mrs Jones.* [var. of MISTRESS. Cf. MISSUS]

**m.s.,** (a musical direction) left hand. [It. *mano sinistra*]

**Ms** /məz/, a title prefixed to the name of a woman, used to avoid reference to marital status: *Ms Smith.* [var. of MISTRESS]

**MS.,** *pl.* **MSS.** manuscript. Also, **ms.**

**M.S.** /ɛm ˈɛs/, Multiple Sclerosis. Also, **MS.**

**MSc** /ɛm ɛs ˈsi/, Master of Science.

**m'sieur** /məˈsjɜ/, *n.* contraction of *monsieur.*

**Ms-Th,** *Chem.* mesothorium.

**Mt,** *pl.* **Mts. 1.** mount: *Mt Kosciusko.* **2.** mountain. Also, **mt.**

**Mt.,** *Bible.* Matthew.

**mtg,** **1.** meeting. **2.** mortage.

**mu** /mju/, *n.* the twelfth letter of the Greek alphabet (M, μ).

**much** /mʌtʃ/, *adj.,* **more, most,** *n., adv.* *–adj.* **1.** in great quantity, amount, measure, or degree: *much work.* *–n.* **2.** a great quantity or amount; a great deal: *much of this is true.* **3.** a great, important, or notable thing or matter: *the house is not much to look at.* **4. to make much of, a.** to treat, represent, or consider as of great importance. **b.** to treat (a person) with great, flattering, or fond consideration. **5. as much,** the same; precisely that. **6. much of a muchness,** (of two or more objects, concepts, etc.) very similar; having little to choose between them. *–adv.* **7.** to a great extent or degree; greatly; far: *much pleased.* **8.** nearly, approximately, or about: *this is much the same as the others.* **9. not to go much for,** to be unenthusiastic about. [ME *muche, moche,* apocopated var. of *muchel, mochel,* OE *mycel;* replacing ME *miche(l),* OE *micel* great, much, c. Icel. *mikill,* Goth. *mikils,* Gk *megalo-* great]

**muchness** /ˈmʌtʃnəs/, *n.* greatness, as in quantity, measure, or degree.

**mucic acid** /mjusɪk ˈæsəd/, *n.* a dibasic crystalline acid, $HOOC(CHOH)_4COOH$, obtained by oxidising certain gums, milk sugar, or galactose.

**mucid** /ˈmjusəd/, *adj.* mouldy; musty. [L *mūcidus*] **– mucidness,** *n.*

**mucilage** /ˈmjusəlɪdʒ/, *n.* **1.** any of various preparations of gum, glue, or the like, for causing adhesion. **2.** any of various gummy secretions or gelatinous substances present in plants. [ME, from F, from LL *mucilāgo* a musty juice]

**mucilaginous** /mjusəˈlædʒənəs/, *adj.* **1.** of the nature of or resembling mucilage; moist, soft, and viscid. **2.** *Chiefly U.S.* of, pertaining to, or secreting mucilage.

**mucin** /ˈmjusən/, *n.* any of a group of nitrogenous substances found in mucous secretions, etc., and of varying composition according to their source. [L *mūcus* MUCUS + -IN[2]] **– mucinous,** *adj.*

**muck** /mʌk/, *n.* **1.** farmyard dung, decaying vegetable matter, etc., in a moist state; manure. **2.** a highly organic soil, less than fifty per cent combustible, often used as manure. **3.** filth; dirt. **4.** *Colloq.* something of no value; trash. **5.** *Civ. Engineering, Mining, etc.* earth, rock or other useless matter to be removed in order to get out the mineral or other substances sought. **6. make a muck of,** *Colloq.* to spoil; impair; disrupt. *–v.t.* **7.** to manure. **8.** to make dirty; soil. **9.** to remove muck from (oft. fol. by *out*). **10.** *Colloq.* to spoil; make a mess of. **11. muck in,** *Colloq.* **a.** to share, esp. living accommodation. **b.** to join in. **12. muck up,** *Colloq.* to spoil. *–v.i.* **13. muck about, or around,** *Colloq.* to idle; potter; fool about. **14. muck up,** *Colloq.* to misbehave. [ME *muk,* from Scand.; cf. Icel. *myki* cow dung]

**mucker** /ˈmʌkə/, *n.* **1.** a person who is messy and untidy. **2.** →**muckshifter.** **3.** *Brit. Colloq.* a vulgar ill-bred person. **4.** *Brit. Colloq.* a friend.

**muckle** /ˈmʌkəl/, *adj.* →**mickle.**

**muck rake** /ˈmʌk reɪk/, *n.* a rake for use on muck or filth.

**muckrake** /ˈmʌkreɪk/, *v.i.*, **-raked, -raking.** *Colloq.* to expose, esp. in print, political or other corruption, real or alleged. [MUCK + RAKE¹] – **muckraker,** *n.* – **muckraking,** *n.*

**muck-raker** /ˈmʌk-reɪkə/, *n.* one who attempts to discover and disseminate information unfavourable to an associate, enemy, etc.

**muckshifter** /ˈmʌkʃɪftə/, *n.* **1.** *Civ. Eng., Mining, etc.* one who removes muck (def. 5). **2.** *Bldg Trades. Colloq.* an excavation worker.

**muck soil** /ˈmʌk sɔɪl/, *n.* peaty soil requiring to be drained for agriculture.

**muck-up** /ˈmʌk-ʌp/, *n. Colloq.* **1.** fiasco; muddle. **2.** (*in children's speech*) one who misbehaves, esp. in school.

**muck-up day** /ˈ– deɪ/, *n.* the last day of attendance at high school, traditionally a day of student pranks.

**mucky** /ˈmʌki/, *adj.*, **-ier, -iest.** **1.** of or like muck. **2.** filthy; dirty.

**mucoid** /ˈmjukɔɪd/, *n.* any of a group of substances resembling the mucins, occurring in connective tissue, etc. [MUC(IN) + -OID]

**muconic acid** /mjuˌkɒnɪk ˈæsəd/, *n.* a white crystalline solid, HOOCCH:CHCH:CHCOOH, formed from certain aromatic amino acids.

**mucoprotein** /mjukoʊˈproʊtin/, *n.* a compound containing protein and a carbohydrate group.

**mucosa** /mjuˈkoʊsə/, *n., pl.* **-sae** /-si/. a mucous membrane. [NL, fem. of L *mūcosus* MUCOUS] – **mucosal,** *adj.*

**mucous** /ˈmjukəs/, *adj.* **1.** pertaining to, consisting of, or resembling mucus. **2.** containing or secreting mucus: *the mucous membrane.* [L *mūcōsus* slimy] – **mucosity** /mjuˈkɒsəti/, *n.*

**mucous membrane** /– ˈmɛmbreɪn/, *n.* a lubricating membrane lining an internal surface or an organ, such as the alimentary, respiratory, and genito-urinary canals.

**mucro** /ˈmjukroʊ/, *n., pl.* **mucrones** /mjuˈkroʊniz/. a short point projecting abruptly, as at the end of a leaf. [L: point]

**mucronate** /ˈmjukrənət, -neɪt/, *adj.* having an abruptly projecting point, as a feather, leaf, etc. Also, **mucronated.** [L *mūcrōnātus* pointed]

**mucus** /ˈmjukəs/, *n.* a viscid secretion of the mucous membranes. [L]

**mud** /mʌd/, *n.* **1.** wet, soft earth or earthy matter, as on the ground after rain, at the bottom of a pond, or among the discharges from a volcano; mire. **2.** *Colloq.* →**mortar**². **3. one's name is mud,** *Colloq.* one is in disgrace. **4. throw (sling) mud at,** *Colloq.* speak ill of; abuse; vilify. [ME *mudde, mode,* c. MLG *mudde*]

**mud bath** /ˈ– baθ/, *n.* a bath in mud containing certain salts, for medicinal purposes.

**mud crab** /ˈ– kræb/, *n.* a large edible crab, *Scylla serrata,* of the mangrove regions of New South Wales and Queensland. Also, **muddie.**

**mud dauber** /ˈ– dɔbə/, *n.* any of certain wasps of the families Eumenidae and Sphecidae, which construct mud cells for their larvae and provision them with insects.

**muddle** /ˈmʌdl/, *v.*, **-dled, -dling,** *n., adj.* *–v.t.* **1.** to mix up or jumble together in a confused or bungling way. **2.** to render confused mentally, or unable to think clearly. **3.** to render confused or stupid with drink, or as drink does. **4.** to make muddy or turbid, as water. **5.** *U.S.* to mix or stir. *–v.i.* **6. muddle through,** to come to a satisfactory conclusion without planned direction. *–n.* **7.** a muddled condition; a confused mental state. **8.** a confused, disordered, or embarrassing state of affairs, or a mess. *–adj.* **9. muddling pace,** (of a horse) a very slow pace. [MUD + *-le,* frequentative and diminutive suffix]

**muddle-head** /ˈmʌdl-hɛd/, *n.* a confused or muddled person.

**muddle-headed** /ˈmʌdl-hɛdəd/, *adj.* vague; illogical; confused. – **muddle-headedness,** *n.*

**muddler** /ˈmʌdlə/, *n.* **1.** one who muddles or muddles through. **2.** *U.S.* a stick for stirring drinks.

**muddy** /ˈmʌdi/, *adj.*, **-dier, -diest,** *v.*, **-died, -dying.** *–adj.* **1.** abounding in or covered with mud. **2.** not clear or pure, as colour. **3.** dull, as the complexion. **4.** not clear mentally. **5.** obscure or vague, as thought, expression, literary style, etc. *–v.t.* **6.** to make muddy; soil with mud. **7.** to make turbid. **8.** to render confused or obscure. *–v.i.* **9.** to become muddy or turbid. – **muddily,** *adv.* – **muddiness,** *n.*

**mud eye** /ˈmʌd aɪ/, *n. Colloq.* the aquatic nymph of a dragon fly.

**mudflap** /ˈmʌdflæp/, *n.* a flexible appendage to the rear mudguard of a vehicle, hanging down to prevent mud, etc., from being thrown out backwards.

**mudflat** /ˈmʌdflæt/, *n.* an area of muddy ground covered by water at high tide.

**mudflow** /ˈmʌdfloʊ/, *n.* **1. a.** mixture of water and volcanic matter, flowing from a volcano. **b.** a body of rock formed from this. **2.** a flow of mud from a mud volcano. **3.** a fluid mass of soil, which becomes unstable as a result of heavy rain or melting snow.

**mudgerabah** /ˈmʌdʒərəba/, *n.* →**blackwood.**

**mudguard** /ˈmʌdgad/, *n.* a guard or shield shaped to fit over the wheels of a motor vehicle or a bicycle to prevent splashing of water, mud etc.

**mudhook** /ˈmʌdhʊk/, *n. Colloq.* →**anchor** (def. 1).

**mudlark** /ˈmʌdlak/, *n.* **1.** →**magpie lark.** **2.** Also, **mudrunner.** *Horseracing.* a horse that performs very well on wet tracks. **3.** *Brit. Colloq.* →**guttersnipe.**

**mud map** /ˈmʌd mæp/, *n.* a map drawn in soft earth.

**mud-mat** /ˈmʌd-mæt/, *n.* any of the very small plants belonging to the genus *Glossostigma,* family Scrophulariaceae.

**mud pack** /ˈmʌd pæk/, *n.* a cosmetic preparation for the complexion.

**mudpie** /mʌdˈpaɪ/, *n.* **1.** (in children's games) a pat of mud moulded to the shape of a pie. **2. make mudpies,** to smear or besmirch, esp. with mud-like substances.

**mud puppy** /ˈ– pʌpi/, *n.* **1.** any of the large North American aquatic salamanders of the genus *Necturus,* which have bushy red gills and well-developed limbs. **2.** any of various American salamanders of the genus *Ambystoma.*

**mudsill** /ˈmʌdsɪl/, *n.* →**groundsel**².

**mudskipper** /ˈmʌdskɪpə/, *n.* any of several tropical Australian fishes mainly of the family Periopthalmidae with bulging eyes and stiffened pectoral fins which enable them to skip over mudflats and climb over rocks and mangrove roots. Also, **mudhopper.**

mudskipper

**mud-slinger** /ˈmʌd-slɪŋə/, *n.* a person who sets out to discredit an opponent, esp. one in public office, by hurling abusive accusations at him.

**mudstone** /ˈmʌdstoʊn/, *n.* a clayey rock of nearly uniform texture throughout, with little or no lamination.

**mud turtle** /ˈmʌd tɜtl/, *n.* any of various freshwater turtles of North America, as *Kinosternon subrubrum,* or *Chrysemys picta.*

**mud volcano** /– vɒlˈkeɪnoʊ/, *n.* **1.** a cone of mud built up by ejection of hot water and mud from a volcanic vent. **2.** a soft slurry of mud caused by an escape of gases through a layer of clay; often associated with oil deposits.

**mudwort** /ˈmʌdwɜt/, *n.* any species of the genus *Limosella,* family Scrophulariaceae, as *Limosella australis,* a small plant found on wet mud on pool margins in temperate regions.

**muesli** /ˈmjuzli/, *n.* a breakfast cereal of various mixed products such as oats, wheatgerm, chopped fruit and nuts, etc. [Swiss G.]

**muezzin** /muˈɛzən/, *n.* (in Muslim communities) the crier who, from a minaret or other part of a mosque, at stated hours five times daily, intones aloud the call summoning the faithful to prayer. [Ar. *muazzin,* d. var. of *muadhdhin*]

**muff** /mʌf/, *n.* **1.** a kind of thick tubular case covered with fur or other material, in which the hands are placed for warmth. **2.** a tuft of feathers on the sides of the head of certain fowls. **3.** *Colloq.* the female pudendum. **4.** *Colloq.* any failure. *–v.t.* **5.** *Colloq.* to perform clumsily, or bungle. **6.** *Sports.* to fail to play (a stroke) successfully, to catch (a ball) properly, etc. *–v.i.* **7.** *Colloq.* to bungle. [D *mof,* from F *moufle;* akin to MUFFLE, *n.*]

**muff-diver** /ˈmʌf-daɪvə/, *n. Colloq.* a person who practises cunnilingus.

**muffin** /ˈmʌfən/, *n.* **1.** a thick, flat yeast cake, made from a soft, risen dough, baked without browning, served cut open, grilled, with butter. **2.** *U.S.* a small cake-like bread, baked in special muffin-cake pans, usu. served hot.

**muffle** /ˈmʌfəl/, *v.,* **-fled, -fling,** *n. –v.t.* **1.** to wrap or envelop in a cloak, shawl, scarf, or the like disposed about the person, esp. about the face and neck (oft. fol. by *up*). **2.** to wrap with something to deaden or prevent sound: *to muffle drums.* **3.** to deaden (sound) by wrappings or other means. *–v.i.* **4.** to muffle oneself (*up*) as in garments or other wrappings. *–n.* **5.** something that muffles. **6.** muffled sound. **7.** an oven or arched chamber in a furnace or kiln, used for heating substances without direct contact with the fire: *muffle furnace.* **8.** the thick, bare part of the upper lip and nose of ruminants and rodents. [ME *mufle(n),* apparently from OF. Cf. OF *emmouflé* wrapped up]

**muffle-faced** /ˈmʌfəl-feɪst/, *adj.* (of sheep) excessively wrinkled on the wool-covered muzzle which collects grass seeds, etc., necessitating frequent wigging.

**muffler** /ˈmʌflə/, *n.* **1.** a heavy neck scarf used for warmth. **2.** any device that reduces noise, esp. that on the exhaust of an internal combustion engine.

**mufti** /ˈmʌfti/, *n., pl.* **-tis. 1.** civilian dress as opposed to military or other uniform, or as worn by one who usu. wears a uniform. **2.** a Muslim legal adviser consulted in applying the religious law. [Ar.: lit., one who delivers a judgment; orig. Ar. meaning def. 2. Def. 1 from the fact that a mufti is a civil official]

**mug** /mʌg/, *n., v.,* **mugged, mugging.** *–n.* **1.** a drinking cup, usu. cylindrical and commonly with a handle. **2.** the quantity it holds. **3.** *Colloq.* the face. **4.** *Brit. Colloq.* the mouth. **5.** *Brit. Colloq.* a grimace. **6.** *Colloq.* a fool; one who is easily duped. **7. a mug's game,** *Colloq.* an activity in which one is bound to lose. *–v.t.* **8.** *Colloq.* to study hard (fol. by *up*). **9.** *Colloq.* to assault by hitting in the face. **10.** *Colloq.* to assault and rob. **11.** *U.S. Colloq.* to take a photograph of a (person), esp. in compliance with an official or legal requirement. *–v.i.* **12.** *Brit. Colloq.* to grimace. *–adj.* **13.** *Colloq.* stupid: *a mug lair, a mug copper, a mug alec.* [ME *mogge,* from Scand.; cf. Swed. *mugg,* D *mugge*]

**mug alec** /ˈ– ælək/, *n. Colloq.* a foolish man, often loudmouthed.

**mugga** /ˈmʌgə/, *n.* a striking tree with dark, fissured bark, the pink-flowering ironbark, *Eucalyptus sideroxylon,* native to eastern Australia.

**mugger**[1] /ˈmʌgə/, *n.* one who mugs.

**mugger**[2] /ˈmʌgə/, *n.* a broad-snouted crocodile, *Crocodilus palustris,* of India, etc., growing to about 3.5 metres in length. Also, **muggar, muggur.** [Hind *magar*]

**muggins** /ˈmʌgənz/, *n.* **1.** a convention in the card game of cribbage in which a player scores points overlooked by an opponent. **2.** a game of dominoes in which any player, if he can make the sum of the two ends of the line equal five or a multiple of five, adds the number so made to his score. **3.** *Colloq.* a fool, often used comically by a speaker to refer to himself: *and who has to finish the job? muggins!* [? orig. surname *Muggins*]

**muggy** /ˈmʌgi/, *adj.,* **-gier, -giest.** (of the atmosphere, weather, etc.) damp and close; humid and oppressive. [d. *mug* mist (from Scand.; cf. Icel. *mugga*) + -Y[1]] – **mugginess,** *n.*

**mug lair** /mʌg ˈlɛə/, *n.* one who is vulgarly flamboyant in dress and behaviour. Cf. **lair**[2].

**mug's game** /ˈmʌgz geɪm/, *n. Colloq.* any activity which is unrewarding, not worth doing: *door-to-door selling is a mug's game.*

**mug shot** /ˈmʌg ʃɒt/, *n.* a photograph, usu. of the head only, taken for police records.

**mugwort** /ˈmʌgwɜt/, *n.* a perennial herb, *Artemisia vulgaris,* with aromatic leaves, widespread in waste places. [ME, OE *mucgwyrt.* See MIDGE, WORT[2]]

**mugwump** /ˈmʌgwʌmp/, *n. U.S.* one who acts as an independent or affects superiority, esp. in politics. [from a name given to those Republicans who refused to support the party nominee in the U.S. presidential campaign of 1884; Algonquian (Massachusetts) *Mukquomp* leader, chief, great man, from *moqki* great + *-omp* man] – **mugwumpery,** *n.*

**Muhammadan** /məˈhæmədən/, *adj., n.* →**Mohammedan.** Also, **Muhammedan.**

**mujik** /ˈmuʒɪk/, *n.* →**muzhik.**

**mulatto** /mjuˈlætoʊ, mə-/, *n., pl.* **-tos** or **-toes,** *adj. –n.* **1.** the offspring of parents of whom one is white and the other a Negro. *–adj.* **2.** having a light brown colour (similar to the skin of a mulatto). [Sp. and Pg. *mulato,* from *mulo,* from L *mūlus* MULE[1]; so called from the hybrid origin]

**mulberry** /ˈmʌlbəri, -bri/, *n., pl.* **-ries. 1.** the edible, berry-like collective fruit of any tree of the genus *Morus.* **2.** a tree of this genus, as *M. rubra* (**red** or **American mulberry**), with dark purple fruit, *M. nigra* (**black mulberry**), with dark-coloured fruit, and *M. alba* (**white mulberry**), with fruit nearly white and with leaves esp. valued as food for silkworms. **3.** a dull, dark, reddish purple colour. [ME *mulberie,* dissimilated var. of *murberie,* OE *mōrberie,* L *mōrum* mulberry + *berie* BERRY]

**mulberry bird** /ˈ– bɜd/, *n.* →**southern figbird.**

**mulch** /mʌltʃ/, *n.* **1.** straw, leaves, loose earth, etc., spread on the ground or produced by tillage to protect the roots of newly planted trees, crops, etc. *–v.t.* **2.** to cover with mulch. [n. use of (obs.) *mulch,* adj., ME *molsh* soft, OE *myl(i)sc* mellow; akin to d. G *molsch* soft, overripe]

**mulct** /mʌlkt/, *n.* **1.** a fine; a penalty. *–v.t.* **2.** to punish (a person, or formerly, an offence) by fine or forfeiture. **3.** to deprive of something as a penalty. **4.** to deprive of something by trickery. [L *mulcta* fine]

**mule**[1] /mjul/, *n.* **1.** the offspring of a male donkey and a mare, used esp. as a beast of burden because of its patience, surefootedness, and hardiness. **2.** any hybrid between the donkey and the horse. **3.** *Colloq.* a stupid or stubborn person. **4.** an infertile hybrid of any genetic cross. **5.** a machine which spins cotton, etc., into yarn and winds it on spindles. [ME *mule,* from OF, from L *mūla;* replacing OE *mūl,* from L *mūlus*]

mule[1]

**mule**[2] /mjul/, *n.* a kind of slipper which leaves the heel exposed. [ME, from F]

**mule deer** /ˈ– dɪə/, *n.* a deer, *Odocoileus hemionus,* with large ears, common in western North America.

**mulesing** /ˈmjulzɪŋ/, *n.* the surgical removal of folds of skin in the breech of ewes as a measure against flystrike. [from J. H. W. *Mules,* who invented the technique]

**mule-skinner** /ˈmjul-skɪnə/, *n. U.S. Colloq.* →**muleteer.**

**muleteer** /mjuləˈtɪə/, *n.* **1.** a driver of mules. **2.** *Colloq.* a half-caste. [F *muletier,* from *mulet,* diminutive of OF *mul* MULE[1]]

**muley** /ˈmjuli/, *adj., n., pl.* **-leys.** *–adj.* **1.** (of cattle) hornless; polled. *–n.* **2.** any cow. Also, **mulley.** [var. of d. *moiley,* from Irish *maol,* or from Welsh *moel,* lit., bald]

**muley saw** /ˈ– sɔ/, *n. U.S. Colloq.* a saw having a long, stiff blade which is not stretched in a gate but whose motion is directed by clamps at each end mounted on guide rails.

**mulga** /ˈmʌlgə/, *n.* **1.** any of several species of *Acacia,* esp. *A. aneura,* found in drier parts of Australia. **2.** the wood of the tree. **3.** the bush; back country. **4.** an Aborigine's shield. **5. up (in) the mulga,** in the bush. *–adj.* **6.** of or pertaining to trees, grass, etc. which grows typically in the mulga. [Aboriginal]

mulga

**mulga grass** /ˈ– gras/, *n.* any of a number of species of small, native, drought-resistant grasses, of the species *Neurachne,* found typically in mulga country.

**mulgara** /mʌlˈgarə/, *n.* →**crest-tailed marsupial mouse.** [Aboriginal]

**mulga snake** /ˈmʌlgə sneɪk/, *n.* a large, brown, aggressive and dangerous snake, *Pseudechis australis,* distributed in Australia generally and often confused with the common brown snake; king brown snake.

**mulga wire** /ˈ– waɪə/, *n. Colloq.* →**bush telegram.**

**muliebrity** /mjuliˈɛbrəti/, *n.* **1.** womanly nature or qualities. **2.** womanhood. [LL *muliebritas,* from L *muliebris* womanly]

**mulish** /ˈmjulɪʃ/, *adj.* like a mule; characteristic of a mule; stubborn, obstinate, or intractable. – **mulishly,** *adv.* – **mulishness,** *n.*

**mull**[1] /mʌl/, *v.t.* **1.** to study or ruminate (*over*), esp. in an ineffective way; ponder upon. **2.** to make a mess or failure of. [? orig. Brit. d.: muddle, crumble, from MD *mail, mol.* See MULLER]

**mull**[2] /mʌl/, *v.t.* to heat, sweeten, and spice for drinking, as ale, wine, etc.: *mulled cider.* [orig. uncert.]

**mull**[3] /mʌl/, *n.* **1.** a soft, thin kind of muslin. **2.** *Bookbinding.* a loosely woven material used to reinforce the spine of a bound book. [earlier *mulmul,* from Hind. *malmal*]

**mull**[4] /mʌl/, *n. Scot.* a promontory or headland. [Scand.; cf. Icel. *mūli.* Cf. also Gaelic *maol*]

**mullah** /ˈmʌlə, ˈmʊlə/, *n.* (in Muslim countries) a title of respect for one who is learned in, teaches, or expounds the sacred law. Also, **mulla.** [Turk., Pers., and Hind. *mullā,* from Ar. *mawlā* patron, lord]

**mullein** /ˈmʌlən/, *n.* any of a number of plants of the genus *Verbascum,* as the twiggy mullein, *V. virgatum.* Also, **mullen.** [ME *moleyn,* from AF *moleine,* from Celtic. Cf. Breton *melen* yellowish]

**mullenise** /ˈmʌlənaɪz/, *v.t.,* **-ised, -ising.** to clear (scrub-covered land) by pushing down the undergrowth with a roller. [after *Mullens,* an Irish settler near Adelaide, S.A.]

**mullentypery** /mʌlənˈtɪpəri/, *n.* →**long-necked tortoise.** [Aboriginal]

**muller** /ˈmʌlə/, *n.* **1.** an implement of stone or other substance with a flat base for grinding paints, powders, etc., on a slab of stone or the like. **2.** any of various mechanical devices for grinding. [? orig. meaning powderer (from ME *mul* powder, OE *myl* dust, c. G *Müll.* See MULL[1])]

**Müller Thurgau** /mjulə ˈθзgaʊ/, *n.* a hybrid grape variety used in wine-making.

**mullet** /ˈmʌlət/, *n., pl.* **-lets,** (*esp. collectively*) **-let. 1.** any fish of the family Mugilidae, which includes various marine and freshwater species with a nearly cylindrical body and generally greyish-silver colouration as the sea mullet, *Mugil cephalus* widely distributed in Australian waters. **2.** →**goatfish. 3.** any of various other fishes. [ME *mulet,* from OF, from L *mullus* red mullet]

**mulley** /ˈmjuli/, *adj., n.* →**muley.**

**mulligan stew** /mʌlɪgən ˈstju/, *n.* →**hashmagandy.** [from *mulligan,* U.S., a kind of stew, apparently from a proper name]

**mulligatawny** /mʌləgəˈtɔni/, *n.* a soup of East Indian origin, flavoured with curry. [Tamil *milagutannīr* pepper water]

**mullion** /ˈmʌliən, ˈmʌljən/, *n.* **1.** a vertical member, as of stone or wood, between the lights of a window, the panels in wainscoting, or the like. *–v.t.* **2.** to furnish with, or to form into divisions by the use of, mullions. [metathetic var. of *monial,* from OF; orig. uncert.]

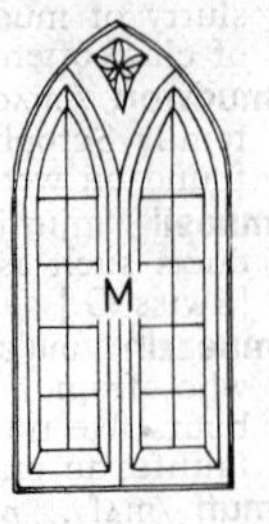


M, mullion

**mullock** /ˈmʌlək/, *n.* **1.** mining refuse; muck. **2.** anything valueless. **3. poke mullock at,** to ridicule; make fun of. *–v.i.* **4.** *Colloq.* to work in a slipshod way. [Brit. d. *mull* rubbish (see MULLER) + -OCK]

**mullocker** /ˈmʌləkə/, *n.* a clumsy or slipshod person.

**mullocky reef** /ˈmʌləki rif/, *n.* a reef which yields gold, but which also contains a large proportion of useless gangue.

**mulloway** /ˈmʌləweɪ/, *n.* a large Australian marine fish, *Sciaena antarctica,* important as a game and food fish; jewfish. [orig. uncert.]

**Mullumbimby couch** /mʌləmbɪmbi ˈkutʃ/, *n.* a sedge, *Kyllinga brevifolia,* having globular seed heads and mainly found as a lawn weed. [from *Mullumbimby,* town in N.S.W.]

**mullygrubber** /ˈmʌligrʌbə/, *n. Cricket, etc.* a ball delivered in such a manner that on contact with the ground it does not bounce. Also, **grubber.**

**multi-,** a word element meaning 'many'. [L, combining form of *multus* much, many]

**multicellular** /mʌltiˈsɛljələ/, *adj.* composed of several or many cells.

**multicoil** /ˈmʌltikɔɪl/, *adj.* having more than one coil, as an electrical device.

**multicoloured** /ˈmʌltikʌləd/, *adj.* of many colours.

**multicultural** /mʌltiˈkʌltʃərəl/, *adj.* of or pertaining to a society which embraces a number of minority cultures.

**multiculturalism** /mʌltiˈkʌltʃərəlɪzəm/, *n.* the theory that it is beneficial to a society to maintain more than one culture within its structure.

**multicylinder** /mʌltiˈsɪləndə/, *adj.* having more than one cylinder, as an internal-combustion or steam engine. Also, **multicylindered.**

**multidentate** /mʌltiˈdɛnteɪt/, *adj.* having many teeth or toothlike processes.

**multifaceted** /mʌltiˈfæsətəd/, *adj.* **1.** (of a gem) having many facets. **2.** having many aspects or phases.

**multifarious** /mʌltəˈfɛəriəs/, *adj.* **1.** having many different parts, elements, forms, etc. **2.** of many kinds, or numerous and varied; manifold (modifying a plural noun): *multifarious activities.* [L *multifārius* manifold] – **multifariously,** *adv.* – **multifariousness,** *n.*

**multifid** /ˈmʌltifɪd/, *adj.* cleft into many parts, divisions, or lobes. Also, **multifidous** /mʌlˈtɪfədəs/. [L *multifidus*]

**multiflorous** /mʌltiˈflɔrəs/, *adj.* bearing many flowers, as a peduncle.

**multifoil** /ˈmʌltifɔɪl/, *n.* See **foil**[2] (def. 5).

**multifoliate** /mʌltiˈfoʊliət, -eɪt/, *adj.* having many leaves or leaflets.

**multiform** /ˈmʌltifɔm/, *adj.* having many forms; of many different forms or kinds. [L *multiformis*] – **multiformity** /mʌltiˈfɔməti/, *n.*

**multigrade** /ˈmʌltigreɪd/, *adj.* denoting a motor oil with a stable viscosity level over a wide range of temperatures.

**multigrips** /ˈmʌltigrɪps/, *n. pl.* adjustable pliers which can be used for a variety of purposes, as for loosening pipes, nuts, bolts, etc.

**multilaminate** /mʌltiˈlæmənət, -neɪt/, *adj.* having many laminae or layers.

**multilateral** /mʌltiˈlætərəl, -ˈlætrəl/, *adj.* **1.** having many sides; many-sided. **2.** *Govt.* denoting an agreement or other instrument in which three or more nations participate; multipartite. – **multilaterally,** *adv.*

**multilingual** /mʌltiˈlɪŋgwəl/, *adj.* **1.** able to speak one's native language and at least two others with approximately equal facility. **2.** expressed or contained in three or more different languages. *–n.* **3.** a multilingual person. – **multilingualism,** *n.*

**multilobular** /mʌltiˈlɒbjələ/, *adj.* having many lobules.

**multimeter** /ˈmʌltimitə/, *n.* a meter for measuring voltages, currents and resistances.

**multimillionaire** /ˌmʌltimɪljəˈnɛə/, *n.* one with a fortune of several million dollars.

**multimotored** /mʌlti'moʊtəd/, *adj.* with a number of motors or engines.

**multinational** /mʌlti'næʃənəl/, *adj.* of, pertaining to, or spreading across many nations: *multinational corporation or company.*

**multinominal** /mʌlti'nɒmənəl/, *adj.* having many names.

**multinuclear** /mʌlti'njukliə/, *adj.* having many or several nuclei, as a cell. Also, **multinucleate.**

**multipaned window** /ˌmʌltipeɪnd 'wɪndoʊ/, *n.* a window made of numerous small panes of glass.

**multipara** /mʌl'tɪpərə/, *n., pl.* **-rae** /-ri/. a woman who has borne two or more children, or who is parturient the second time. [NL, fem. of *multiparus* MULTIPAROUS]

**multiparous** /mʌl'tɪpərəs/, *adj.* **1.** producing many, or more than one, at a birth. **2.** *Bot.* (of a cyme) having many lateral axes. [NL *multiparus.* See MULTI-, -PAROUS]

**multipartite** /mʌlti'pataɪt/, *adj.* **1.** divided into many parts; having many divisions. **2.** *Govt.* →**multilateral** (def. 2). [L *multipartītus* much-divided]

**multiped** /'mʌltipɛd/, *adj.* **1.** having many feet. *–n.* **2.** a creature that has many feet. Also, **multipede** /'mʌltipid/. [L *multipēs,* adj. and n., many-footed]

**multiphase** /'mʌltifeɪz/, *adj.* having many phases.

**multiphasic screening** /ˌmʌltifeɪzɪk 'skrinɪŋ/, *n.* a medical check involving tests of a number of different bodily functions.

**multiple** /'mʌltəpəl/, *adj.* **1.** consisting of, having, or involving many individuals, parts, elements, relations, etc.; manifold. **2.** *Elect.* denoting two or more circuits connected in parallel. **3.** *Bot.* (of a fruit) collective. *–n.* **4.** *Maths.* a number which contains another number some number of times without a remainder: *12 is a multiple of 3.* **5.** *Elect.* **a.** a group of terminals arranged to make a circuit or group of circuits accessible at a number of points at any one of which connection can be made. **b. in multiple,** in parallel. See **parallel** (def. 13). **6.** a work of art produced by any of the printing processes, in any quantity and replaceable at any time whose value lies in the fact that it reaches a vast audience. [F, from LL *multiplus* manifold]

**multiple alleles** /– ə'lilz/, *n.pl.* a series of three or more alternative or allelic forms of a gene, only two of which can exist in any normal, diploid individual.

**multiple-choice** /'mʌltəpəl-tʃɔɪs/, *adj.* **1.** offering a number of choices. **2.** composed of multiple-choice questions: *a multiple-choice exam.*

**multiple-choice question** /– 'kwɛstʃən/, *n.* a question with several answers given, from which the correct one must be selected.

**multiple cropping** /mʌltəpəl 'krɒpɪŋ/, *n.* the use of the same field for two or more separate crops, whether of the same or of different kinds, successively during a single year.

**multiple factors** /– 'fæktəz/, *n.pl.* a series of two or more pairs of genes responsible for the development of complex, quantitative characters such as size, yield, etc.

**multiple-hire** /mʌltəpəl-'haɪə/, *v.i.,* **-hired, hiring.** (of taxis) to pick up additional paying passengers after accepting the first.

**multiple neuritis** /mʌltəpəl nju'raɪtəs/, *n.* inflammation of several nerves at the same time.

**multiple personality** /– pɜsən'æləti/, *n.* a form of schizophrenia in which the victim develops several distinct personalities which emerge in different situations.

**multiple sclerosis** /– sklə'roʊsəs/, *n.* a disease of the nervous system, usu. progressive, characterised by remissions and exacerbations, and caused by plaques of demyelisation of the white matter of the nervous system. Also, **disseminated sclerosis.** *Abbrev.:* M.S.

**multiple star** /– 'sta/, *n.* three or more stars lying close together in the celestial sphere and usu. united in a single gravitational system.

**multiple unit** /– 'junət/, *n.* two or three diesel locomotives coupled together for pulling a train.

**multiplex** /'mʌltiplɛks/, *adj.* **1.** manifold; multiple: *multiplex telegraphy.* *–v.t.* **2.** *Elect.* to arrange a circuit for use by multiplex telegraphy. [L: manifold]

**multiplexer** /'mʌltiplɛksə/, *n.* a device for distributing each of a number of consecutive signals in one channel to one of a set of different channels, or for performing the reverse operation.

**multiplex telegraphy** /mʌltiplɛks tə'lɛgrəfi/, *n.* a system for sending many messages in each direction, simultaneously, over the same wire or communications channel.

**multipliable** /'mʌltəplaɪəbəl/, *adj.* that may be multiplied. Also, **multiplicable.**

**multiplicand** /mʌltəplə'kænd/, *n.* the number to be multiplied by another. [L *multiplicandus,* gerundive of *multiplicāre* MULTIPLY]

**multiplicate** /'mʌltəpləkeɪt/, *adj.* multiple; manifold. [ME L *multiplicātus,* pp., multiplied]

**multiplication** /ˌmʌltəplə'keɪʃən/, *n.* **1.** the act or process of multiplying. **2.** the state of being multiplied. **3.** *Arith.* the process of finding the number (the product) resulting from the addition of a given number (the multiplicand) taken as many times as there are units in another given number (the multiplier). *Symbol:* × **4.** *Maths.* any generalisation of this operation applicable to numbers other than integers, such as fractions, irrationals, vectors, etc. **5.** *Physics.* the process by which additional neutrons are produced by a chain reaction in a nuclear reactor. – **multiplicational,** *adj.*

**multiplication constant** /'– kɒnstənt/, *n.* (of a nuclear reactor) the ratio of the average number of neutrons produced by fission per unit time, to the total number of neutrons absorbed or leaking out in the same time.

**multiplication table** /'– teɪbəl/, *n.* a table in which the product of any two numbers of a set are given; usu. of the integers 1 to 12.

**multiplicative** /'mʌltəpləkeɪtɪv, mʌltə'plɪkətɪv/, *adj.* **1.** tending to multiply or increase. **2.** having the power of multiplying. – **multiplicatively,** *adv.*

**multiplicity** /mʌltə'plɪsəti/, *n., pl.* **-ties. 1.** a multitude or great number. **2.** the state of being multiplex or manifold; manifold variety. [LL *multiplicitas*]

**multiplier** /'mʌltəplaɪə/, *n.* **1.** one who or that which multiplies. **2.** *Maths.* the number by which another is to be multiplied. **3.** *Physics.* a device for intensifying some phenomenon. **4.** an indicator of the relative sizes of a given initial increase in investment and the total ultimate increase in income.

**multiply** /'mʌltəplaɪ/, *v.,* **-plied, -plying.** *–v.t.* **1.** to make many or manifold; increase the number, quantity, etc., of. **2.** *Maths.* to take by addition a given number of times; find the product of by multiplication. **3.** to produce (animals or plants) by propagation. **4.** to increase by procreation. *–v.i.* **5.** to grow in number, quantity, etc.; increase. **6.** *Maths.* to perform the process of multiplication. **7.** to increase in number by procreation or natural generation. [ME *multiplie(n),* from OF *multiplier,* from L *multiplicāre*]

**multipolar** /mʌlti'poʊlə/, *adj.* having many poles.

**multipurpose** /mʌlti'pɜpəs/, *adj.* having various different uses.

**multi-racial** /mʌlti-'reɪʃəl/, *adj.* of or pertaining to more than one race or extraction. [MULTI- + RACIAL]

**multiseriate** /mʌlti'sɛriət/, *adj.* having, or consisting of, more than one row or layer of cells. – **multiseriately,** *adv.*

**multistage** /'mʌltisteɪdʒ/, *adj.* (of a rocket, guided missile, etc.) having more than one stage.

**multistorey** /mʌlti'stɔri/, *adj.* (of a building) having a considerable number of storeys. Also, *Chiefly U.S.,* **multistory.**

**multi-tracking** /'mʌlti-trækɪŋ/, *n.* a recording technique whereby the various instruments and voices of a combination can be recorded separately, and later joined.

**multitude** /'mʌltətjud/, *n.* **1.** a great number; host: *a multitude of friends.* **2.** a great number of persons gathered together; a crowd or throng. **3. the multitude,** the common people. **4.** the state or character of being many. [ME, from L *multitūdo*]

**multitudinous** /mʌltə'tjudənəs/, *adj.* **1.** forming a multitude or great number, or existing, occurring, or present in great numbers; very numerous. **2.** comprising many items, parts, or elements. **3.** *Poetic.* crowded or thronged. – **multitudinously,** *adv.* – **multitudinousness,** *n.*

**multivalent** /mʌlti'veɪlənt/, *adj.* having a valency of three or higher. Cf. **polyvalent.** – **multivalence,** *n.*

**multivibrator** /mʌlti'vaɪbreɪtə/, *n.* an electronic device con-

M-N ↔

i = peat ɪ = pit ɛ = pet æ = pat a = part ɒ = pot ʌ = putt ɔ = port ʊ = put u = pool ɜ = pert ə = apart aɪ = buy eɪ = bay ɔɪ = boy aʊ = how oʊ = hoe ɪə = here ɛə = hair ʊə = tour g = give θ = thin ð = then ʃ = show ʒ = measure tʃ = choke dʒ = joke ŋ = sing j = you õ = Fr. bon

sisting of two oscillators feeding into each other, used for generating audible tones, electronic switching, etc.

**mum**[1] /mʌm/, *adj.* **1.** silent; not saying a word: *to keep mum.* –*interj.* **2.** Say nothing! Be silent! –*n.* **3.** silence: *mum's the word.* [ME; imitative. Cf. G *mumm*]

**mum**[2] /mʌm/, *v.i.*, **mummed, mumming.** **1.** to say 'mum'; call for silence. **2.** to act as a mummer. Also, **mumm.** [v. use of MUM[1]. Cf. OF *momer* mask oneself]

**mum**[3] /mʌm/, *n. Colloq.* mother.

**mumble** /ˈmʌmbəl/, *v.*, **-bled, -bling,** *n.* –*v.i.* **1.** to speak indistinctly or unintelligibly, as with partly closed lips; mutter low, indistinct words. **2.** to chew ineffectively, as from loss of teeth: *to mumble on a crust.* –*v.t.* **3.** to utter indistinctly, as with partly closed lips. **4.** to chew, or try to eat, with difficulty, as from loss of teeth. –*n.* **5.** a low, indistinct utterance or sound. [ME *momele,* frequentative of (obs.) *mum,* v., make inarticulate sounds. Cf. G *mummeln*] – **mumbler,** *n.* – **mumblingly,** *adv.*

**mumbo jumbo** /ˌmʌmboʊ ˈdʒʌmboʊ/, *n.* **1.** meaningless incantation or ritual. **2.** an object of superstitious awe or reverence. **3.** unintelligible speech or writing, often intended to be impressive; gibberish. **4.** *Colloq.* superstition; witchcraft. [from the name of a deity formerly worshipped by certain W African tribes]

**mu-meson** /ˈmju-mizɒn/, *n.* →**muon.**

**mu-metal** /ˈmju-mɛtl/, *n.* an alloy of high magnetic permeability containing up to 78 per cent nickel in addition to iron, copper, and manganese.

**mummer** /ˈmʌmə/, *n.* **1.** one who wears a mask or fantastic disguise, esp. as formerly at Christmas and other festive seasons. **2.** (*joc.*) an actor. [late ME, from OF *momeur,* from *momer* MUM[2]]

**mummery** /ˈmʌməri/, *n., pl.* **-meries.** **1.** performance of mummers. **2.** any mere theatrical performance or ceremony or empty spectacular pretence, or what is regarded as such. [F *momerie*]

**mummify** /ˈmʌməfaɪ/, *v.*, **-fied, -fying.** –*v.t.* **1.** to make (a dead body) into a mummy, as by embalming and drying. **2.** to make like a mummy. –*v.i.* **3.** to dry or shrivel up. – **mummification** /mʌməfəˈkeɪʃən/, *n.*

**mummy**[1] /ˈmʌmi/, *n., pl.* **-mies,** *v.*, **-mied, -mying.** –*n.* **1.** the dead body of a human being or animal preserved by the ancient Egyptian (or some similar) method of embalming. **2.** a dead body dried and preserved by the agencies of nature. **3.** a withered or shrunken living being. –*v.t.* **4.** to make into or like a mummy; mummify. [ME *mumie,* from ML *mumia,* from Ar. *mūmiya,* from Pers. *mūmiyā* asphalt]

**mummy**[2] /ˈmʌmi/, *n. Colloq.* mother.

**mumps** /mʌmps/, *n.pl., construed as sing.* a specific infectious viral disease characterised by inflammatory swelling of the parotid and (usu.) other salivary glands, and sometimes by inflammation of the testicles, ovaries, etc. [orig. meaning 'grimace'; imitative]

**munch** /mʌntʃ/, *v.t.* **1.** to chew with steady or vigorous working of the jaws, and often audibly. –*v.i.* **2.** to chew steadily or vigorously, and often audibly. [ME *monche,* nasalised var. of obs. *mouch* eat, chew; orig. unknown] – **muncher,** *n.*

**munchies** /ˈmʌntʃiz/, *n. pl. Colloq.* **1.** anything to eat, esp. snacks between meals. **2. have the munchies,** to experience a craving for food, esp. one resulting from smoking marijuana.

**mundane** /ˈmʌndeɪn, mʌnˈdeɪn/, *adj.* **1.** of or pertaining to the world, universe, or earth esp. as contrasted with heaven; worldly; earthly: *mundane affairs.* **2.** ordinary; pedestrian; boring. [L *mundānus* of the world; replacing ME *mondeyne,* from OF] – **mundanely,** *adv.*

**mundarda** /mʌnˈdadə/, *n.* a small possum, *Cercartetus concinnus,* of southern Australia. [Aboriginal]

**mundic** /ˈmʌndɪk/, *n.* →**iron pyrites.** Also, **mundick.** [Corn. d.]

**munga** /ˈmʌŋgə/, *n. Orig. Mil. Colloq.* food. [? F *manger* to eat]

**mung bean** /ˈmʌŋ bin/, *n.* a bushy annual herb, *Phaseolus aureus,* family Papilionaceae, probably originally from India, cultivated there as a food crop, and elsewhere in eastern Asia as the chief source of beansprouts; green gram.

**mungo** /ˈmʌŋgoʊ/, *n.* **1.** →**shoddy** (def. 1). **2.** wool fibres recovered from clippings of felting or worsted, and used in re-manufacturing. [? obs. *mung, mong* mixture, from OE *gemang*]

**municipal** /mjuˈnɪsəpəl, mjunəˈsɪpəl/, *adj.* **1.** of or pertaining to a municipality, its government, facilities, etc: *municipal library; municipal elections.* **2.** *Brit.* pertaining to the internal affairs of a state or nation rather than to international affairs. [L *mūnicipālis,* from *mūniceps* citizen of a privileged (sometimes self-governing) town standing in a certain relation to Rome] – **municipally,** *adv.*

**municipal district** /– ˈdɪstrɪkt/, *n. Tas.* an area of land delineated for the purposes of local government; three such areas, Hobart, Launceston and Glenorchy, are also cities.

**municipalise** /mjuˈnɪsəpəlaɪz/, *v.t.*, **-lised, -lising.** **1.** to make a municipality of. **2.** to bring under municipal ownership, direction, or control. Also, **municipalize.** – **municipalisation** /mjuˌnɪsəpəlaɪˈzeɪʃən/, *n.*

**municipality** /mjunəsəˈpæləti/, *n., pl.* **-ties.** **1.** an area of land delineated for the purposes of local government and which, when first defined in New South Wales in 1858, was to be no larger than ten square miles with a minimum population of 500; (in Victoria) borough. **2.** a community under municipal jurisdiction. **3.** the governing body of such a district or community.

**munificent** /mjuˈnɪfəsənt/, *adj.* **1.** extremely liberal in giving or bestowing; very generous. **2.** (of a gift, or the like) characterised by great generosity. [backformation from L *mūnificentia* munificence] – **munificence,** *n.* – **munificently,** *adv.*

**muniment** /ˈmjunəmənt/, *n.* **1.** (*pl.*) *Law.* a document, as a titledeed or a charter, by which rights or privileges are defended or maintained. **2.** a defence or protection. [ME, from ML *mūnīmentum* document, title deed, L fortification]

**munition** /mjuˈnɪʃən/, *n.* **1.** (*usu. pl.*) materials used in war, esp. weapons and ammunition. **2.** material or equipment for carrying on any undertaking. –*v.t.* **3.** to provide with munitions. [L *mūnītio* fortification]

**munning** /ˈmʌnɪŋ/, *n.* a small hare-wallaby, *Lagostrophus fasciatus,* of the south-western regions of Australia, having thick grey fur with conspicuous bands of black and white across the back. [orig. uncert.]

**munnion** /ˈmʌnjən/, *n.* →**mullion.**

**muntjac** /ˈmʌntdʒæk/, *n.* **1.** any of various small deer constituting the genus *Muntiacus,* of southern and eastern Asia and the adjacent islands, esp. *M. muntjac,* of Java, India, etc., having well-developed horns on bony pedicels. **2.** any of the small deer of the related genus *Elaphodus,* of China and Tibet, having minute horns. Also, **muntjak.** [Sunda (a language of Indonesia) *minchek*]

**muntries** /ˈmʌntriz/, *n.* a prostrate shrub, *Kunzea pomifera,* family Myrtaceae, found in dry sandy areas of western Victoria and in South Australia.

**Muntz metal** /ˈmʌnts mɛtl/, *n.* an alloy containing approximately 60 per cent copper and 40 per cent zinc, harder and stronger than brass. [named after G. F. *Muntz,* 19th C English metallurgist]

**muon** /ˈmjuɒn/, *n.* an elementary particle with a mass 207 times that of an electron, which may have a positive or negative charge; mu-meson.

**mural** /ˈmjurəl/, *adj.* **1.** of or pertaining to a wall; resembling a wall. **2.** executed on or affixed to a wall (of a decoration, or the like). –*n.* **3.** a mural painting. [F, from L *mūrālis*]

**murder** /ˈmɜdə/, *n.* **1.** *Law.* the unlawful killing of another human being with malice aforethought. **2. scream (yell) (cry) blue murder,** *Colloq.* to make a commotion; complain vociferously. **3.** *Colloq.* an uncommonly laborious or difficult task: *gardening in the heat is murder.* –*v.t.* **4.** *Law.* to kill by an act constituting murder. **5.** to kill or slaughter inhumanly or barbarously. **6.** to spoil or mar by bad execution, representation, pronunciation, etc. –*v.i.* **7.** to commit murder. [var. of obs. *murther,* from ME *morther,* OE *morthor,* c. Goth. *maurthr*] – **murderer,** *n.* – **murderess,** *n. fem.*

**murderous** /ˈmɜdərəs/, *adj.* **1.** of the nature of or involving murder: *a murderous deed.* **2.** guilty of, bent on, or capable of murder: *murderous thoughts.* **3.** intentionally deadly. – **murderously,** *adv.* – **murderousness,** *n.*

**murex** /ˈmjurɛks/, *n., pl.* **murices** /ˈmjurəsiz/, **murexes.** **1.** any of the marine gastropods, common in tropical seas, constituting the genus *Murex* or the family Muricidae, certain species of which yielded the celebrated purple dye of the ancients. **2.** a shell used as a trumpet, as in representations of Tritons in art. **3.** purplish red. [L: the purple fish]

murex

**muriate** /ˈmjuriət, -eɪt/, *n.* (in industry) any chloride, esp. potassium chloride, KCl, used as a fertiliser. [L *muria* brine + -ATE[2]]

**muriated** /ˈmjurieɪtəd/, *adj. Obs.* charged with or containing a chloride or chlorides, as mineral waters.

**muriatic acid** /mjuriˌætɪk ˈæsəd/, *n.* the commercial name for hydrochloric acid.

**muricate** /ˈmjurəkeɪt/, *adj.* **1.** shaped like the murex. **2.** covered with short, hard-pointed protuberances.

**murine** /ˈmjuraɪn, -rən/, *adj.* **1.** belonging or pertaining to the Muridae, the family of rodents that includes the mice and rats, or to the Murinae, the subfamily that includes the domestic species. *–n.* **2.** a murine rodent. [L *mūrīnus* of a mouse]

**murk** /mɜk/, *n.* **1.** darkness. *–adj.* **2.** *Archaic.* dark, or with little light, as night, etc.; murky. Also, **mirk.** [ME *mirke,* OE *myrce,* c. Icel. *myrkr* gloomy]

**murky** /ˈmɜki/, *adj.,* **-kier, -kiest. 1.** intensely dark, gloomy, and cheerless. **2.** obscure or thick with mist, haze, or the like, as the air, etc. Also, **mirky.** – **murkily,** *adv.* – **murkiness,** *n.*

**murmur** /ˈmɜmə/, *n.* **1.** any low, continuous sound, as of a brook, the wind, trees, etc., or of low indistinct voices. **2.** a mumbled or private expression of discontent. **3.** *Med.* an abnormal sound heard on listening over the heart, usu. through a stethoscope, and produced by vibrations of the valves and walls of the heart and great vessels. *–v.i.* **4.** to make a low or indistinct continuous sound. **5.** to speak in a low tone or indistinctly. **6.** to complain in a low tone, or in private. *–v.t.* **7.** to sound by murmurs. **8.** to utter in a low tone. [ME, from L *murmurāre*] – **murmurer,** *n.* – **murmuring,** *adj., n.* – **murmuringly,** *adv.*

**murmuration** /mɜməˈreɪʃən/, *n.* **1.** the act or instance of murmuring. **2.** a flock of starlings.

**murmurous** /ˈmɜmərəs/, *adj.* **1.** abounding in or characterised by murmurs. **2.** murmuring: *murmurous waters.* – **murmurously,** *adv.*

**murning** /ˈmɜnɪŋ/, *n.* →**murrnong.**

**murphy** /ˈmɜfi/, *n., pl.* **-phies.** *Colloq.* →**potato.** [special use of *Murphy,* Irish surname]

**Murphy's Law** /ˈmɜfiz lɔ/, *n.* a principle supposed to operate in all circumstances to produce the least desirable result, usu. stated as "if anything can go wrong, it will". [? named after *Murphy,* a character in a series of educational cartoons published by the U.S. Navy, who always made mistakes]

**murrain** /ˈmʌreɪn/, *n.* **1.** any of various diseases of cattle, as anthrax, foot-and-mouth disease, etc. **2.** *Archaic.* a plague or pestilence (esp. in curses). [ME *moryne,* from F *morine* plague, from L *morī* die]

**Murray cod**[1] /mʌri ˈkɒd/, *n.* a large Australian freshwater fish, *Maccullochella macquariensis,* principally of the Murray-Darling river system, related to the marine gropers of genus *Polyprion.*

**Murray cod**[2] /mʌri ˈkɒd/, *n. in the phrase* **give someone the Murray cod,** *Colloq.* to indicate to someone to proceed. [rhyming slang *give the nod.* See NOD]

**Murray Grey** /– ˈgreɪ/, *n.* one of a breed of beef cattle developed in Victoria and recognised for registration in 1962. It is the result of mating a very light roan Shorthorn cow with an Aberdeen Angus bull, the progeny of this cross being grey in colour.

**Murray lily** /– ˈlɪli/, *n.* →**Darling lily.**

**Murray perch** /– ˈpɜtʃ/, *n.* →**golden perch.**

**Murray tortoise** /– ˈtɔtəs/, *n.* an Australian side-necked water tortoise, *Emydura macquarri,* of the southern regions of the Murray-Darling river system; ware.

**Murray Valley encephalitis,** *n.* a strain of encephalitis carried by mosquitoes in the Murray Valley.

**murre** /mɜ/, *n.* **1.** either of two species of diving birds of the genus *Uria,* of northern seas. **2.** *Colloq.* the razor-billed auk.

**murrelet** /ˈmɜlət/, *n.* any of several small, chunky diving birds found chiefly on coasts of the north Pacific, as the **marbled murrelet,** *Brachyramphus marmoratus.*

**murrey** /ˈmʌri/, *n.* a dark purplish red colour. [ME *morrey,* from OF *more,* from L *mōrum* mulberry]

**murrhine** /ˈmʌraɪn, -rən/, *adj.* **1.** pertaining to a stone or stonelike substance of Roman times used for wine cups and other vessels. *–n.* **2.** the substance. Also, **murrine.** [L *mur-r(h)inus*]

**murrhine glass** /ˈ– glas/, *n.* **1.** any kind of glassware supposed to resemble the Roman cups of murrhine. **2.** a ware composed of glass in which metals, precious stones, or the like are embedded.

**murri** /ˈmʊri/, *n.* an Aboriginal. [Aboriginal]

**murrnong** /ˈmɜnɒŋ/, *n.* →**blackfellow's yam.** Also, **mirrnyong, murning.** [Aboriginal]

**Murrumbidgee jam** /ˌmʌrəmbɪdʒi ˈdʒæm/, *n. Colloq.* brown sugar added to a little cold tea to form a thick syrup to be spread on damper.

**Murrumbidgee oyster** /– ˈɔɪstə/, *n. Colloq.* →**prairie oyster.**

**Murrumbidgee whaler** /– ˈweɪlə/, *n.* a swagman frequenting the Australian inland rivers, who sustains himself by begging and fishing. [from *Murrumbidgee,* a river in N.S.W., + WHALER (def. 2)] – **Murrumbidgee whaling,** *n.*

**Mus.,** **1.** museum. **2.** music. **3.** musical. **4.** musician.

**musaceous** /mjuˈzeɪʃəs/, *adj.* belonging to the Musaceae, or banana family of plants. [NL *Mūsāceae* (from *Musa,* the typical genus, from Ar. *mawza* banana, probably of E Ind. orig.) + -OUS]

**muscadel** /mʌskəˈdɛl/, *n.* →**muscatel.** Also, **muscadelle.**

**muscadet** /ˈmʌskədeɪ/, *n.* a white wine of the muscatel type from the lower reaches of the Loire.

**muscae volitantes** /mʌski vɒləˈtæntiz/, *n.pl.* specks that seem to dance in the air before the eyes, due to defects in the vitreous humour of the eye or other causes. [NL: flies flying about]

**muscat** /ˈmʌskət/, *n.* **1.** (*cap.*) a grape variety with pronounced pleasant sweet aroma and flavour, much used for making wine. **2.** the vine bearing this grape. **3.** a sweet wine made from this grape. [F, from Pr., from LL *muscus* MUSK]

**Muscat and Oman,** *n.* →**Oman.**

**muscatel** /mʌskəˈtɛl/, *n.* **1.** the muscat grape, esp. in the dried form as a raisin. **2.** →**muscat** (def. 3). [ME, from OF, from Pr. *muscat* MUSCAT]

**muscid** /ˈmʌsəd/, *adj.* **1.** belonging or pertaining to the Muscidae, the family of dipterous insects that includes the common housefly. *–n.* **2.** any muscid fly. [NL *Muscidae,* pl., from L *musca* a fly]

**muscle** /ˈmʌsəl/, *n., v.,* **-cled, -cling.** *–n.* **1.** a discrete bundle or sheet of contractile fibres having the function of producing movement in the animal body. **2.** the tissue of such an organ. **3.** muscular strength; brawn. **4. put the muscle in,** *Colloq.* to throw one's weight around. **5.** political or financial strength, esp. when exercised in a ruthless fashion. *–v.i.* **6.** *Colloq.* to make or shove one's way by sheer brawn or force. **7. muscle in (on),** to force one's way in(to), esp. by violent means, trickery, or in the face of hostility, in order to obtain a share of something. [F, from L *musculus* muscle, lit., little mouse (from the appearance of certain muscles)] – **muscly,** *adj.*

**muscle-bound** /ˈmʌsəl-baʊnd/, *adj.* having muscles enlarged and inelastic, as from excessive exercise.

**muscle fibre** /ˈmʌsəl faɪbə/, *n.* any of the long contractible cells which comprise striated muscles.

**muscle man** /ˈ– mæn/, *n. Colloq.* **1.** a very strong man; a man of unusually impressive and powerful physique. **2.** a man who regularly uses violence, or the threat of violence, to further the interests of his employer or himself.

**muscle spindles** /ˈ– spɪndlz/, *n.* the sensory end organs in skeletal muscle.

**muscone** /ˈmʌskoun/, *n.* a large cyclic ketone, $C_{16}H_{30}O$, obtained from musk and used in the perfume industry.

**muscovado** /mʌskəˈvadou/, *n.* raw or unrefined sugar, obtained from the juice of the sugar cane by evaporation and draining off the molasses. [Pg. *(açucar) mascavado* (sugar) of inferior quality, pp. of *mascavar* diminish]

**muscovite** /ˈmʌskəvaɪt/, *n.* common light-coloured mica, essentially $KAl_3Si_3O_{10}(OH)_2$, used as an electrical insulator.

**Muscovy duck** /mʌskəvi ˈdʌk/, *n.* a large, crested, neotropical duck, *Cairina moschata,* which has been widely domesticated. When wild it is glossy black with a large white patch on each wing. [erroneous var. of MUSK DUCK]

**muscular** /ˈmʌskjələ/, *adj.* **1.** of or pertaining to muscle or the muscles. **2.** dependent on or affected by the muscles. **3.** having well-developed muscles; brawny. – **muscularity** /mʌskjəˈlærəti/, *n.* – **muscularly,** *adv.*

**muscular dystrophy** /– ˈdɪstrəfi/, *n.* a disease of unknown origin which produces a progressive muscular deterioration and wasting, robbing the muscles of all vitality until the patient is completely helpless.

**musculature** /ˈmʌskjələtʃə/, *n.* the muscular system of the body or of its parts. [F, from L *musculus* MUSCLE]

**muse**[1] /mjuz/, *v.,* **mused, musing.** *–v.i.* **1.** to reflect or meditate in silence, as on some subject, often as in a reverie. **2.** to gaze meditatively or wonderingly. *–v.t.* **3.** to meditate on. [ME *muse(n),* from OF *muser* ponder, loiter, trifle (cf. AMUSE), from *muse* muzzle] – **muser,** *n.*

**muse**[2] /mjuz/, *n.* **1.** the goddess thought to inspire a poet. **2.** a poet's characteristic genius or powers. Also, **Muse.** [from the *Muses,* the nine sister goddesses of classical mythology; ME, from OF, from L *Mūsa,* from Gk *Moûsa*]

**museful** /ˈmjuzfəl/, *adj.* deeply thoughtful.

**muselage** /ˈmjuzəlɪdʒ/, *n.* the wire hood holding the cork in a champagne bottle. [F, from *museler* to muzzle]

**musette** /mjuˈzɛt/, *n.* **1.** an ancient French double-reed instrument, resembling a bagpipe, sometimes with a drone and windbag. **2.** a simple tune suitable for a musette. [ME, from MF, diminutive of *muse* bagpipe]

**musette bag** /ˈ– bæg/, *n. U.S.* a haversack, esp. one used by officers.

**museum** /mjuˈziəm/, *n.* a building or place for the keeping, exhibition, and study of objects of scientific, artistic, and historical interest. [L, from Gk *mouseîon* seat of the Muses, place of study, library]

**museum piece** /ˈ– pis/, *n.* **1.** an object suitable for keeping and exhibiting in a museum. **2.** *Colloq.* anything old-fashioned or which has outlived its usefulness.

**mush**[1] /mʌʃ/, *n.* **1.** meal, esp. corn meal, boiled in water or milk until it forms a thick, soft mass. **2.** any thick, soft mass. **3.** anything unpleasantly lacking in firmness, force, dignity, etc. **4.** *Colloq.* weak or maudlin sentiment or sentimental language. [b. (obs.) *moose* thick vegetable porridge (from D *moes*) and MASH, *n.*]

**mush**[2] /mʌʃ/, *v.t.* **1.** to go or travel on foot, esp. over the snow with a dog team. *–interj.* **2.** (an order to start or speed up a dog team.) *–n.* **3.** a journey on foot, esp. over the snow with a dog team. [? from F *marche* or *marchons,* impv. of *marcher* advance] – **musher,** *n.*

**mush**[3] /mʊʃ/, *n. Colloq.* →**moosh.**

**mushie** /ˈmʌʃi/, *n. Colloq.* →**mushroom.** Also, **mushy.**

**mushroom** /ˈmʌʃrum/, *n.* **1.** any of various fleshy fungi including the toadstools, puffballs, coral fungi, morels, etc. **2.** any of certain edible species belonging to the family Agaricaceae, usu. of umbrella shape. Cf. **toadstool. 3.** the **common field mushroom,** *Agaricus campestris,* or related forms grown for the market. **4.** anything of similar shape or correspondingly rapid growth. **5.** *Colloq.* a person who is deliberately kept ignorant and misinformed. [from the practice of growing mushrooms in the dark and feeding them with manure] *–adj.* **6.** of, pertaining to, or made of mushrooms. **7.** resembling or suggesting a mushroom in shape. **8.** of rapid growth and, often, brief duration: *mushroom fame.* *–v.i.* **9.** to gather mushrooms. **10.** to have or assume the shape of a mushroom. **11.** to spread or grow quickly, as mushrooms. [late ME, from F *mousseron,* from LL *mussirio*]

**mushy** /ˈmʌʃi/, *adj.,* **-ier, -iest. 1.** mushlike; pulpy. **2.** *Colloq.* weakly sentimental: *a mushy valentine.* **3.** (of wool) lacking character, open, badly weathered, and very noily. – **mushily,** *adv.* – **mushiness,** *n.*

**music** /ˈmjuzɪk/, *n.* **1.** an art of organising sound in significant forms to express ideas and emotions through the elements of rhythm, melody, harmony, and colour. **2.** the tones or sounds employed, occurring in single line (melody) or multiple lines (harmony). **3.** musical work or compositions for singing or playing. **4.** the written or printed score of a musical composition. **5.** such scores collectively. **6.** any sweet, pleasing, or harmonious sounds or sound: *the music of the waves.* **7.** appreciation of or responsiveness to musical sounds or harmonies. **8. face the music,** to face the consequences, usu. unpleasant, of one's actions; accept responsibility for what one has done. [ME *musik,* from L *mūsica,* from Gk *mousikḗ (téchnē)* orig., any art over which the Muses presided]

**musical** /ˈmjuzɪkəl/, *adj.* **1.** of, pertaining to, or producing music: *a musical instrument.* **2.** of the nature of or resembling music; melodious; harmonious. **3.** fond of or skilled in music. **4.** set to or accompanied by music: *a musical melodrama.* *–n.* **5.** a play or film, often of a light romantic variety, in which songs, choruses, dances, etc., in a popular musical idiom, form a substantial and essential part. – **musically,** *adv.* – **musicality** /mjuzəˈkæləti/, **musicalness,** *n.*

**musical box** /ˈ– bɒks/, *n.* a box or case containing an apparatus for producing music mechanically, as by means of a comblike steel plate with tuned teeth sounded by small pegs or pins in the surface of a revolving cylinder or disc. Also, **music box.**

**musical chairs** /– ˈtʃɛəz/, *n.pl. (construed as sing.)* a children's game in which the players walk to music around a number of chairs (one less than the number of players), with the object of finding a seat when the music stops. The player failing to do so is eliminated, and one chair removed before the next round.

**musical comedy** /– ˈkɒmədi/, *n.* a musical of light character, often of a whimsical or satirical nature with music of obvious tunefulness.

**musical flags** /– ˈflægz/, *n.pl. (construed as sing.)* a game used as a training exercise for lifesavers, in which six or so players race a set distance towards two flags, the object of each player being to gain possession of a flag. Cf. **musical chairs.**

**musical milk** /– ˈmɪlk/, *n. Colloq.* methylated spirits.

**music appreciation** /ˌmjuzɪk əpriʃiˈeɪʃən/, *n.* training intended to develop an understanding of music through listening skills.

**music drama** /ˈ– dramə/, *n.* that form of opera, as conceived by Richard Wagner, in which the music is used to develop the drama in a symphonic manner, without the use of formal divisions, repeats, etc., and in which themes, characters, etc., are introduced by means of a leitmotiv.

**music hall** /ˈ– hɔl/, *n.* a theatre or hall for variety entertainment.

**musician** /mjuˈzɪʃən/, *n.* **1.** one who makes music a profession, esp. as a performer on an instrument. **2.** one skilled in playing a musical instrument. – **musicianly,** *adj.*

**musicianship** /mjuˈzɪʃənʃɪp/, *n.* skill and sensitivity in performing or perception in appreciating music.

**music of the spheres,** *n.* a harmony supposed by the Pythagoreans to be made by the vibrations of crystal spheres upon which, they believed, the planets and stars revolved.

**musicology** /mjuzəˈkɒlədʒi/, *n.* the scholarly or scientific study of music, as in historical research, musical theory, ethnic music, the physical nature of sound, etc. – **musicological** /mjuzəkəˈlɒdʒɪkəl/, *adj.* – **musicologist,** *n.*

**music roll** /ˈmjuzɪk roul/, *n.* a roll of perforated paper for use in a pianola.

**music stand** /ˈ– stænd/, *n.* an adjustable stand for holding a music score in position for reading during a performance.

**music sticks** /ˈ– stɪks/, *n.pl.* claves, esp. as used by Aboriginal tribesmen. Also, **songsticks.**

**music stool** /ˈ– stul/, *n.* a stool, usu. adjustable, used when playing a piano.

**music synthesiser** /– ˈsɪnθəsaɪzə/, *n.* →**synthesiser** (def.2).

**music system** /ˈ– sɪstəm/, *n.* →**audio system.**

**music theatre** /ˈ– θɪətə/, *n.* **1.** the presentation of compositions in a theatrical way with the aid of light, properties and gesture, etc. **2.** contemporary or radical works for opera companies.

**musing** /ˈmjuzɪŋ/, *adj.* **1.** absorbed in thought; meditative. –*n.* **2.** contemplation. – **musingly,** *adv.*

**musique concrete** /mjuˌzik kɒnˈkreɪt/, *n.* →**concrete music.**

**musk** /mʌsk/, *n.* **1.** a substance secreted in a glandular sac under the skin of the abdomen of the male musk deer, having a strong smell, and used in perfumery. **2.** a synthetic imitation of the substance. **3.** a similar secretion of other animals, as the civet, muskrat, otter, etc. **4.** the smell, or some similar smell. **5.** *Bot.* any of several plants, as the monkey-flower, having a musky fragrance. [ME *muske,* var. of *musco,* from LL, abl. of *muscus,* from LGk *móschos,* from Pers. *mushk*]

**musk deer** /ˈ– dɪə/, *n.* a small, hornless animal of the deer kind, *Moschus moschiferus,* of central Asia, the male of which secretes musk and has large canine teeth.

**musk duck** /ˈ– dʌk/, *n.* **1.** a southern Australian anatine bird, *Biziura lobata,* the drake of which emits a distinct odour of musk. **2.** →**Muscovy duck.**

**musket** /ˈmʌskət/, *n.* **1.** a hand-gun for infantry soldiers, introduced in the 16th century, the predecessor of the modern rifle. **2.** the male sparrowhawk, *Accipiter nisus.* [F *mousquet,* from It. *moschetto* (orig. sense: def. 2), from *mosca* a fly, from L *musca*]

**musketeer** /mʌskəˈtɪə/, *n.* a soldier armed with a musket. [MUSKET + -EER, modelled on F *mousquetaire*]

**musketry** /ˈmʌskətri/, *n.* **1.** *Mil.* instruction in the art of using small arms. **2.** *Obs.* muskets collectively. **3.** *Obs.* troops armed with muskets.

**musk lorikeet** /mʌsk ˈlɒrəkit/, *n.* the small nomadic Australian parrot, *Glossopsitta concinna,* occurring in large flocks and having a characteristic musky odour.

**muskmelon** /ˈmʌskmɛlən/, *n.* **1.** a kind of melon, of many varieties, a round or oblong fruit with a juicy, often aromatically sweet, edible flesh (yellow, white, or green). **2.** the plant, *Cucumis melo,* bearing it.

**musk ox** /ˈmʌsk ɒks/, *n.* a bovine ruminant, *Ovibos moschatus,* between the ox and the sheep in size and anatomy, and having a musky smell, native to arctic America.

musk ox

**muskrat** /ˈmʌskræt/, *n., pl.* **-rats,** (*esp. collectively*) **-rat. 1.** a large aquatic North American rodent, *Ondatra zibethica,* with a musky smell. **2.** its thick, light brown fur.

**musk rat-kangaroo** /ˌmʌsk ræt-kæŋgəˈru/, *n.* a small rat-kangaroo, *Hypsiprymnodon moschatus,* of the north-eastern coastal regions of Queensland.

**musk rose** /ˈ– roʊz/, *n.* a species of rose, *Rosa moschata,* having fragrant white flowers.

**musky** /ˈmʌski/, *adj.,* **-kier, -kiest.** of or like musk, as smells; having a smell like that of musk. [MUSK + -Y[1]]

**Muslim** /ˈmʊzləm, ˈmʌz-/, *adj., n., pl.* **-lims, -lim.** –*adj.* **1.** of or pertaining to the religion, law, or civilisation of Islam. –*n.* **2.** an adherent of Islam. Also, **Moslem.** [Ar.: one who accepts *Islam,* lit., submission]

muskrat

**Muslimism** /ˈmʊzləmɪzəm, ˈmʌz-/, *n.* the Mohammedan religion; Islam. Also, **Moslemism.**

**muslin** /ˈmʌzlən/, *n.* a cotton fabric made in various degrees of fineness, and often printed, woven or embroidered in patterns; esp., a cotton fabric of plain weave, used for curtains and for a variety of other purposes. [F *mousseline,* from It. *mussolina* muslin, from *Mussolo* Mosul, city in Iraq]

**muso** /ˈmjuzoʊ/, *n. Colloq.* →**musician.**

**musquash** /mʌsˈkwɒʃ/, *n.* →**muskrat.** [Algonquian: it is red]

**muss** /mʌs/, *Chiefly U.S. Colloq.* –*n.* **1.** a state of disorder or confusion. –*v.t.* **2.** to put into disorder; make untidy or messy; rumple (oft. fol. by *up*). [alteration of MESS]

**mussel** /ˈmʌsəl/, *n.* any bivalve mollusc, esp. an edible marine bivalve of the family Mytilidae and a freshwater bivalve of the family Unionidae. [MLG; replacing ME and OE *muscle,* from LL *muscula,* var. of L *musculus* MUSCLE, mussel]

**Mussulman** /ˈmʌsəlmən/, *n. Archaic.* →**Muslim.** [Pers. *musulmān,* from *muslim* MUSLIM, from Ar. (with the Pers. pl. ending *-ān*)]

**mussy** /ˈmʌsi/, *adj.,* **-sier, -siest.** *Chiefly U.S. Colloq.* untidy, messy or rumpled.

**must**[1] /mʌst, mʌs/; *weak forms* /məst, məs/ *aux. v.* **1.** to be bound by some imperative requirement to: *I must keep my word.* **2.** to be obliged or compelled to, as by some constraining force or necessity: *man must eat to live.* **3.** may reasonably be supposed to: *she must be nearly fifty.* **4.** to be inevitably certain to: *man must die.* **5.** to have to; ought to; should: *I must go soon.* **6.** *Archaic.* (sometimes used with ellipsis of *go, get,* or some similar verb readily understood from the context): *we must away.* –*n. Colloq.* **7.** anything necessary or vital: *this law is a must.* [ME *most(e),* OE *mōste,* pret. (pres. *mōt*); akin to D *moeten,* G *müssen* be obliged]

**must**[2] /mʌst/, *n.* new wine; the unfermented juice as pressed from the grape or other fruit. [ME and OE, from L *mustum,* short for *vinum mustum* fresh wine]

**must**[3] /mʌst/, *n.* mould; mustiness. [backformation from MUSTY]

**must**[4] /mʌst/, *n.* →**musth.**

**mustache** /məsˈtaʃ, ˈmʌstæʃ/, *n. U.S.* →**moustache.**

**mustachio** /məˈstaʃioʊ/, *n., pl.* **-os.** →**moustache.** [Sp. *mostaccho* and It. *mustaccio* MOUSTACHE]

**mustang** /ˈmʌstæŋ/, *n.* the small, wild or half-wild horse of the American plains, descended from Spanish stock. [Sp. *mestengo* wild]

**mustard** /ˈmʌstəd/, *n.* **1.** a pungent powder or paste prepared from the seed of the mustard plant, much used as a food seasoning or condiment, and medicinally in plasters, poultices, etc. **2.** any of various species of *Brassica* and allied genera, as *B. juncea,* **Indian mustard,** and *Sisymbrium officinale,* **hedge mustard. 3. keen as mustard,** extremely keen or eager. –*adj.* **4.** brownish-yellow in colour. [ME, from OF *moustarde,* orig. powdered mustard seed and must, from *moust,* from L *mustum* MUST[2]]

**mustard bush** /ˈ– bʊʃ/, *n.* a plant of tropical inland Australia, *Apophyllum anomalum,* family Capparidaceae, bearing small, fragrant flowers, and leaves which make good stock feed, and whose young shoots have a flavour like mustard. Also, **mustard tree.**

**mustard gas** /ˈ– gæs/, *n.* a chemical-warfare agent, $(ClCH_2CH_2)_2S$, stored in liquid form, producing burns, blindness, and death, introduced by the Germans in World War I; yperite.

**mustard oil** /ˈ– ɔɪl/, *n.* oil expressed from the seed of mustard, esp. a carbylamine (a drying oil) used in making soap.

**mustard plaster** /ˈ– plastə/, *n.* a powdered, black, mustard and rubber solution mixture placed on a cloth and used as a counter-irritant.

**mustee** /mʌsˈti, ˈmʌsti/, *n.* **1.** the offspring of a white person and a quadroon. **2.** a half-breed. Also, **mestee.** [Sp. *mestizo*]

**musteline** /ˈmʌstəlaɪn, -lin/, *adj.* **1.** belonging or pertaining to the family Mustelidae, including the martens, skunks, minks, weasels, badgers, otters, etc. **2.** weasel-like. **3.** tawny or brown, like a weasel in summer. [L *mustēlinus* belonging to a weasel]

**muster** /ˈmʌstə/, *v.t.* **1.** to assemble (troops, a ship's crew, etc.), as for battle, display, inspection, orders, discharge, etc. **2.** to round up livestock for shearing, branding, etc. **3.** to gather or summon (oft. fol. by *up*): *he mustered up all his courage.* **4.** *Naut.* to call the roll of. –*v.i.* **5.** to assemble for inspection, service, etc., as troops or forces. **6.** to come together, collect, or gather. **7. muster in or out,** *U.S.* to enlist into or discharge from military service. –*n.* **8.** an assembling of troops or men for inspection or other purposes. **9.** an assemblage or collection. **10.** the act of mustering. **11.**

Also, **muster roll.** (formerly) a list of the men enrolled in a military or naval unit. **12. pass muster,** to measure up to specified standards. [ME *mostre(n)*, from OF *mostrer,* from L *monstrāre* show] – **musterer,** *n.* – **mustering,** *n.*

**musth** /mʌst/, *n.* a condition periodically typical in all mature male elephants and some females, characterised by discharge from a facial gland accompanied by frenzied emotional disturbance. Also, **must.** [Urdu, from Pers. *mast*]

**musty** /'mʌsti/, *adj.*, **-tier, -tiest. 1.** having a smell or flavour suggestive of mould, as old buildings, long-closed rooms, food, etc. **2.** made stale by time, or antiquated: *musty laws.* **3.** dull; apathetic. [var. of *moisty* (from MOIST + -Y[1]), with loss of *i* before *s*] – **mustily,** *adv.* – **mustiness,** *n.*

**mutable** /'mjutəbəl/, *adj.* **1.** liable or subject to change or alteration. **2.** given to changing, or ever changing; fickle or inconstant: *the mutable ways of fortune.* [ME, from L *mūtābilis*] – **mutability** /mjutə'bɪləti/, **mutableness,** *n.* – **mutably,** *adv.*

**mutant** /'mjutnt/, *adj.* **1.** undergoing mutation; resulting from mutation. *–n.* **2.** a new type of organism produced as the result of mutation. [L *mūtans*, ppr., changing]

**mutarotation** /mjutəroʊ'teɪʃən/, *n. Chem.* a change in the optical rotation of fresh solutions of reducing sugars over a period of time. [MUTA(TION) + ROTATION]

**mutate** /mju'teɪt/, *v.*, **-tated, -tating.** *–v.t.* **1.** to change; alter. **2.** *Phonet.* to change by umlaut. *–v.i.* **3.** to change; undergo mutation. – **mutative** /'mjutətɪv, mju'teɪtɪv/, *adj.*

**mutation** /mju'teɪʃən/, *n.* **1.** the act or process of changing. **2.** a change or alteration, as in form, qualities, or nature. **3.** *Biol.* **a.** a sudden departure from the parent type, as when an individual differs from its parents in one or more heritable characteristics, caused by a change in a gene or a chromosome. **b.** an individual, species, or the like, resulting from such a departure. **4.** *Phonet.* →**umlaut.** [ME, from L *mūtātio*] – **mutational,** *adj.*

**mutatis mutandis** /mjuˌteɪtəs mju'tændəs/, *adv.* with things changed that must be changed. [L]

**mute**[1] /mjut/, *adj.*, *n.*, *v.*, **muted, muting.** *–adj.* **1.** silent; refraining from speech or utterance. **2.** not emitting or having sound of any kind. **3.** incapable of speech; dumb. **4.** *Gram.* (of letters) silent; not pronounced. **5.** *Fox Hunting.* (of a hound) not giving tongue while hunting. **6. stand mute,** *Law.* (of a prisoner) to make no response when arraigned, now resulting in the entry of a plea of not guilty. *–n.* **7.** one unable to utter words. **8.** an actor whose part is confined to dumb show. **9.** *Law.* a person who makes no response when arraigned. **10.** a hired attendant at a funeral; a professional mourner. **11.** a mechanical device of various shapes and materials for muffling the tone of a musical instrument. **12.** *Phonet.* a stop (def. 34). *–v.t.* **13.** to deaden or muffle the sound of (a musical instrument, etc.). **14.** to reduce, as in volume; soften. [L *mūtus* silent, dumb; replacing ME *muet,* from OF] – **mutely,** *adv.* – **muteness,** *n.*

**mute**[2] /mjut/, *n. Banking Colloq.* a mutilated banknote.

**mute negative** /– 'nɛgətɪv/, *n.* the negative of a film without its soundtrack.

**mute print** /– 'prɪnt/, *n.* positive film print of the picture part of a sound film without the soundtrack.

**mutilate** /'mjutəleɪt/, *v.t.*, **-lated, -lating. 1.** to deprive (a person or animal, the body, etc.) of a limb or other important part or parts. **2.** →**castrate. 3.** to injure, disfigure, or make imperfect by removing or irreparably damaging parts. [L *mutilātus,* pp., cut off, maimed] – **mutilation** /mjutə'leɪʃən/, *n.* – **mutilative,** *adj.* – **mutilator,** *n.*

**mutineer** /mjutə'nɪə/, *n.* one who mutinies. [F (obs.) *mutinier,* from *mutin* rebellious, from OF *muete* rebellion, orig. pp., from L *movēre* move]

**mutinous** /'mjutənəs/, *adj.* **1.** disposed to, engaged in, or involving revolt against constituted authority. **2.** characterised by mutiny; rebellious. – **mutinously,** *adv.* – **mutinousness,** *n.*

**mutiny** /'mjutəni/, *n.*, *pl.* **-nies,** *v.*, **-nied, -nying.** *–n.* **1.** revolt, or a revolt or rebellion, against constituted authority, esp. by soldiers or seamen against their officers. *–v.i.* **2.** to commit the offence of mutiny; revolt against constituted authority. [(obs.) *mutin,* adj., mutinous (from F) + -Y[3]]

**mutism** /'mjutɪzəm/, *n.* a conscious or unconscious refusal to respond verbally to interrogation, present in some mental disorders. [F *mutisme,* from L *mūtus* mute, adj.]

**mutt** /mʌt/, *n. Colloq.* **1.** a dog, esp. a mongrel. **2.** a simpleton; a stupid person. [orig. uncert; ? shortened from *muttonhead*]

**mutter** /'mʌtə/, *v.i.* **1.** to utter words indistinctly or in a low tone, often in talking to oneself or in making obscure complaints, threats, etc.; murmur; grumble. **2.** to make a low, rumbling sound. *–v.t.* **3.** to utter indistinctly or in a low tone. *–n.* **4.** the act or utterance of one who mutters. [ME *moter(e)*, ? frequentative of (obs.) *moot,* v., speak, murmur, OE *mōtian* speak in public. Cf. d. G *muttern*] – **mutterer,** *n.* – **mutteringly,** *adv.*

**muttlegar** /'mʌtlga/, *n.* a species of *Eucalyptus, E. macrocarpa,* of western Australia, with fruits up to 10 cm long.

**mutton** /'mʌtn/, *n.* **1.** the flesh of sheep, used as food. **2.** the flesh of the well-grown or more mature sheep, as distinguished from lamb, and hogget. **3.** *Colloq.* the penis. [ME *moton,* from OF; of Celtic orig.] – **muttony,** *adj.*

**mutton-bird** /'mʌtn-bɜd/, *n.* **1.** any of various species of petrel, including the short-tailed shearwater, *Puffinus tenuirostris,* which inhabits the Pacific Ocean, and in summer nests in Tasmania, South Australia, Victoria, and the islands of Bass Strait. **2.** *Colloq.* Also, **mutton-bird eater.** an inhabitant of northern Tasmania. Also, **muttonbird.**

mutton-bird (def. 1)

**mutton-birder** /'mʌtn-bɜdə/, *n.* one who hunts mutton-birds.

**mutton-birding** /'mʌtn-bɜdɪŋ/, *n.* the hunting of mutton birds.

**mutton chain** /'mʌtn tʃeɪn/, *n.* a chain (def. 11a) in a meatworks carrying sheep carcasses.

**mutton-chops** /'mʌtn-tʃɒps, mʌtn-'tʃɒps/, *n.pl.* side-whiskers narrow at the top, and broad and trimmed short at the bottom, the chin being shaved both in front and beneath. Also, **mutton-chop whiskers.** [from similarity in shape to mutton chops]

**mutton-fish** /'mʌtn-fɪʃ/, *n.* →**abalone.**

**mutton-fist** /'mʌtn-fɪst/, *n.* a large, coarse hand.

**mutton-head** /'mʌtn-hɛd/, *n. Colloq.* a stupid or dull person.

**mutton-wood** /'mʌtn-wʊd/, *n.* any of several small trees of the genus *Rapanea,* family Myrsinaceae, found in Victoria and New South Wales.

**mutual** /'mjutʃuəl/, *adj.* **1.** possessed, experienced, performed, etc., by each of two or more with respect to the other or others; reciprocal: *mutual aid.* **2.** having the same relation each towards the other or others: *mutual foes.* **3.** of or pertaining to each of two or more, or common: *mutual acquaintance.* **4.** pertaining to mutual insurance: *a mutual company.* [late ME, from L *mūtuus* reciprocal + -AL[1]] – **mutually,** *adv.*

**mutual fund** /– 'fʌnd/, *n.* an investment trust which pools the money of a large number of investors and invests on their behalf.

**mutual inductance** /– ɪn'dʌktəns/, *n.* the ratio of the electromotive force in one circuit to the rate of change of current in another circuit which is magnetically linked to the first circuit; coefficient of mutual induction.

**mutual induction** /– ɪn'dʌkʃən/, *n.* the induction of an electromotive force in one circuit as a result of a changing current in a separate circuit with which it is magnetically linked.

**mutual insurance** /– ɪn'ʃɔrəns/, *n.* insurance in which those insured become members of a company who reciprocally engage, by payment of certain amounts into a common fund, to indemnify one another against loss.

**mutualise** /'mjutʃuəlaɪz/, *v.*, **-lised, -lising.** *Chiefly U.S.* *–v.t.* **1.** to make mutual. *–v.i.* **2.** to become mutual. Also, **mutualize.** – **mutualisation** /ˌmjutʃuəlaɪ'zeɪʃən/, *n.*

**mutualism** /'mjutʃuəlɪzəm/, *n.* **1.** the attainment of individual and collective well-being through mutual dependence. **2.** *Biol.* →**symbiosis.**

**mutuality** /mjutʃu'æləti/, *n.* condition or quality of being mutual; reciprocity; mutual dependence.

**mutual savings bank,** *n.* a non-capitalised savings bank distributing its profits to depositors.

**mutule** /ˈmjutjul/, *n.* a projecting flat block under the corona of the Doric cornice, corresponding to the modillion of other orders. [F, from L *mūtulus* modillion]

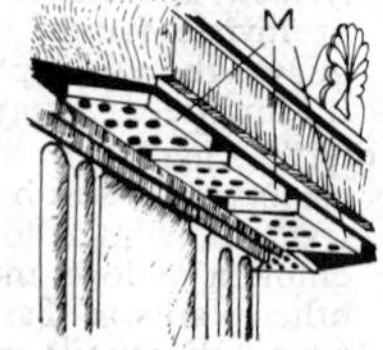

M, mutule

**muu-muu** /ˈmu-mu/, *n.* a long, loose dress, usu. brightly coloured. [Hawaiian *mu'u mu'u*]

**muzak** /ˈmjuzæk/, *n.* recorded background music played, usu. continuously, in places of work, hotels, restaurants, etc., designed to increase efficiency or create a feeling of well-being. [Trademark]

**muzhik** /ˈmuʒɪk/, *n.* a Russian peasant. Also, **moujik, mujik, muzjik.** [Russ.]

**muzzle** /ˈmʌzəl/, *n., v.,* **-zled, -zling.** *–n.* **1.** the mouth, or end for discharge, of the barrel of a gun, pistol, etc. **2.** the projecting part of the head of an animal, including jaws, mouth, and nose. **3.** a device, usu. an arrangement of straps or wires, placed over an animal's mouth to prevent the animal from biting, eating, etc. *–v.t.* **4.** to put a muzzle on (an animal or its mouth) so as to prevent biting, eating, etc. **5.** to restrain (by physical, legal, or procedural means) from speech or the expression of opinion; gag: *they tried to muzzle him but he insisted on finishing his speech.* [ME *mosel,* from OF *musel,* diminutive of *muse* muzzle; orig. uncert.] – **muzzler,** *n.*

**muzzle brake** /ˈ– breɪk/, *n.* a device attached to the muzzle of a weapon which utilises escaping gas to reduce recoil.

**muzzle-loader** /ˈmʌzəl-loʊdə/, *n.* a firearm which is loaded through the muzzle. – **muzzle-loading,** *adj.*

**muzzle velocity** /ˈmʌzəl vəlɒsəti/, *n.* the speed of a projectile as it leaves a gun muzzle.

**muzzy** /ˈmʌzi/, *adj.,* **-zier, -ziest.** *Colloq.* confused; dazed; tipsy. – **muzzily,** *adv.* – **muzziness,** *n.*

**Mv,** **1.** *Elect.* megavolt. **2.** *Chem.* mendelevium.

**M.V.,** **1.** Merchant Vessel. **2.** Motor Vessel.

**M.V.O.,** Member (fourth or fifth class) of the Royal Victorian Order.

**M.V.Sc.,** Master of Veterinary Science.

**Mw,** *Elect.* megawatt.

**Mx,** maxwell.

**my** /maɪ/; *weak forms* /mi, mə/, *pron.* **1.** the possessive form corresponding to *I* and *me,* used before a noun: *my house.* *–interj.* **2.** *Colloq.* (an exclamation of surprise): *Oh my!* [ME *mī,* apocopated var. of *mīn,* OE *mīn.* See MINE[1]]

**my-,** a word element meaning 'muscle'. Also, **myo-.** [Gk, combining form of *mŷs*]

**myalgia** /maɪˈældʒə/, *n.* pain in the muscles; muscular rheumatism.

**myall**[1] /ˈmaɪɔl/, *n.* **1.** any of several wattle trees as the weeping myall, the yarran, the bastard myall. **2.** the hard fine-grained wood of such a tree used for carving. [Aboriginal]

**myall**[2] /ˈmaɪɔl/, *n.* **1.** an Aboriginal living in a traditional tribal way, outside European civilisation. **2.** anything wild or uncivilised. *–adj.* **3.** wild or uncivilised. [Aboriginal]

**myall snake** /ˈ– sneɪk/, *n.* a small, elapid snake, *Denisonia suta,* of southern and inland Australia; not considered dangerous; salt-bush snake.

**myasthenia** /maɪəsˈθiniə/, *n.* muscle weakness.

**myc-,** a word element meaning 'fungus'. Also, **myco-.** [combining form representing Gk *mýkēs*]

**mycelium** /maɪˈsiliəm/, *n., pl.* **-lia** /-liə/. the vegetative part or thallus of the fungi, when composed of one or more filamentous elements, or hyphae. [NL, from Gk *mýkēs*] – **myceloid** /ˈmaɪsələɪd/, *adj.*

**Mycenaean** /maɪsəˈniən/, *adj.* **1.** of or pertaining to the ancient southern Greek city of Mycenae. **2.** denoting or pertaining to the Aegean civilisation which flourished at Mycenae (*c.* 1600 B.C. to *c.* 1100 B.C.).

**-mycetes,** a word element meaning 'fungus', as in *myxomycetes.* [combining form representing pl. of Gk *mýkēs* fungus]

**mycetoma** /maɪsəˈtoʊmə/, *n.* localised mycosis of subcutaneous and deeper tissues.

**mycetozoan** /maɪˌsitəˈzoʊən/, *adj.* **1.** of or pertaining to the Mycetozoa. *–n.* **2.** any of the Mycetozoa (Myxomycetes, slime moulds), a group of very primitive organisms lying near the borderline between the plant and animal worlds. [*myceto-,* var. of MYC- + -ZOAN]

**myco-,** variant of **myc-,** before consonants, as in *mycology.*

**mycobacterium** /ˌmaɪkoʊbækˈtɪəriəm/, *n., pl.* **-teria** /-ˈtɪəriə/. any of a group of bacteria, difficult to stain but which, once stained, hold stain tenaciously and are acid- and alcohol-fast. Mycobacteria produce human and bovine or mammalian tuberculosis, avian tuberculosis, tuberculosis of cold-blooded animals, and leprosy. [NL. See MYCO-, BACTERIUM]

**mycol.,** **1.** mycological. **2.** mycology.

**mycology** /maɪˈkɒlədʒi/, *n.* **1.** the branch of botany that treats of fungi. **2.** the fungi found in an area. – **mycologist,** *n.*

**mycorrhiza** /maɪkəˈraɪzə/, *n.* a non-pathogenic association of a fungus with a vascular plant or bryophyte.

**mycosis** /maɪˈkoʊsəs/, *n.* **1.** *Pathol.* the presence of parasitic fungi in or on any part of the body. **2.** a disease caused by them. [NL. See MYC-, -OSIS] – **mycotic** /maɪˈkɒtɪk/, *adj.*

**mycostatin** /maɪkoʊˈstætn/, *n.* an antifungal substance produced commercially from the growth of *Streptomyces noursei* and used to treat monilia infections. [Trademark]

**mycotic dermatitis** /maɪˌkɒtɪk dɜməˈtaɪtəs/, *n.* →**lumpy wool.**

**mydriasis** /mɪˈdraɪəsəs, maɪ-/, *n.* excessive dilatation of the pupil of the eye, as the result of disease, drugs, or the like. [L, from Gk]

**mydriatic** /mɪdriˈætɪk/, *adj.* **1.** pertaining to or producing mydriasis. *–n.* **2.** a mydriatic drug.

**myel-,** a word element meaning 'marrow' or 'of the spinal cord'. Also (before consonants), **myelo-.** [Gk, combining form of *myelós* marrow]

**myelencephalon** /maɪəlɛnˈsɛfəlɒn/, *n.* the posterior segment of the brain, practically co-extensive with the medulla oblongata; the afterbrain.

**myelin** /ˈmaɪələn/, *n.* a soft, white, fatty substance encasing the axis cylinder of certain nerve fibres. Also, **myeline** /ˈmaɪəlin/. [G. See MYEL-, -IN[2]]

**myelitis** /maɪəˈlaɪtəs/, *n.* **1.** inflammation of the substance of the spinal cord. **2.** inflammation of the bone marrow.

**myelocele** /ˈmaɪələsil/, *n.* **1.** a protrusion of the spinal cord through a defect in the spinal column, forming a round swelling usu. at the base of the spine. **2.** a condition in which an area of the spinal cord lies exposed. **3.** the area thus exposed. [MYELO- + *-cele* (from Gk *kēlē* rupture)]

**myelocoele** /ˈmaɪələsil/, *n.* the central cavity of the spinal cord. Also, **myelocele.** [MYELO- + *-coele* (from Gk *koilía* cavity of the body)]

**myeloid** /ˈmaɪələɪd/, *adj.* **1.** pertaining to the spinal cord. **2.** marrow-like. **3.** pertaining to marrow.

**mylonite** /ˈmaɪlənaɪt, ˈmɪlə-/, *n.* a rock that has been crushed and rolled out to such an extent that the original structure has been destroyed. [Gk *mylṓn* mill + -ITE[1]]

**myna** /ˈmaɪnə/, *n.* **1.** Also, **Indian myna.** the semi-domesticated bird, *Acridotheres tristis,* a noisy, chocolate-brown scavenger with a black head, and yellow beak and legs, introduced from Asia and now common around large cities and cane-growing areas in eastern Australia. **2.** any of various Asian birds of the starling family (Sturnidae), esp. those of the genera *Acridotheres* and *Eulabes,* some of which are well-known cagebirds and can learn to talk. Also, **mina, mynah.** [Hind. *mainā* a starling]

**Mynheer** /məˈnɪə/, *n.* **1.** the Dutch term of address and title of respect corresponding to *sir* and *Mr.* **2.** (*l.c.*) *Colloq.* a Dutchman. [D *mijnheer,* from *mijn* my + *heer* lord, gentleman]

**myo-,** variant of **my-,** before consonants.

**myocardiogram** /maɪoʊˈkadiəgræm/, *n.* a tracing representing cardiac muscular activity, made by a myocardiograph.

**myocardiograph** /maɪoʊˈkadiəgræf/, *n.* an apparatus which records the movements of the heart muscle.

**myocarditis** /ˌmaɪoʊkaˈdaɪtəs/, *n.* inflammation of the myocardium. [MYOCARD(IUM) + -ITIS]

**myocardium** /maɪoʊˈkadiəm/, *n.* the muscular substance of the heart. [NL. See MYO-, CARDIO-] – **myocardial,** *adj.*

**myoclonus** /maɪəˈklounəs/, *n.* clonic spasm of a muscle or group of muscles. – **myoclonic** /maɪəˈklɒnɪk/, *adj.*

**myogenic** /maɪouˈdʒɛnɪk/, *adj.* of or pertaining to muscle: *myogenic pain.*

**myoglobin** /maɪouˈgloubən/, *n.* a muscle protein that, like haemoglobin, can combine reversibly with oxygen.

**myogram** /ˈmaɪəgræm/, *n.* a tracing representing muscular activity, made by a myograph.

**myograph** /ˈmaɪəgræf/, *n.* an instrument for taking tracings of muscular contractions and relaxations.

**myography** /maɪˈɒgrəfi/, *n.* **1.** the science of describing muscles; the descriptive aspect of myology. **2.** the process of using a myograph. – **myographic** /maɪəˈgræfɪk/, *adj.*

**myology** /maɪˈɒlədʒi/, *n.* the science of muscles; the branch of anatomy that treats of muscles.

**myoma** /maɪˈoumə/, *n., pl.* **-mata** /-mətə/, **-mas** /-məz/. a tumour composed of muscular tissue. [NL. See MY-, -OMA] – **myomatous** /maɪˈɒmətəs, -ˈoumə-/, *adj.*

**myomancy** /ˈmaɪəmænsi/, *n.* the study of rats and mice, esp. the cries they give and the destruction they cause, as prophetic tokens.

**myopia** /maɪˈoupiə/, *n.* a condition of the eye in which parallel rays are focused in front of the retina, so that only near objects are seen clearly; near-sightedness (opposed to *hypermetropia*). [NL, from Gk *mýōps* short-sighted + *ia* -IA] – **myopic** /maɪˈɒpɪk/, *adj.*

**myoscope** /ˈmaɪəskoup/, *n.* an apparatus or instrument for observing muscular contraction.

**myosin** /ˈmaɪəsən/, *n.* a globulin occurring in muscle plasma. [MY- + -OS(E)[2] + -IN[2]]

**myosis** /maɪˈousəs/, *n.* →**miosis.**

**myosotis** /maɪəˈsoutəs/, *n.* any plant of the boraginaceous genus *Myosotis,* as the common forget-me-not. Also, **myosote** /ˈmaɪəsout/. [L, from Gk: the plant mouse-ear]

**myotic** /maɪˈɒtɪk/, *adj.* →**miotic.**

**myriad** /ˈmɪriəd/, *n.* **1.** an indefinitely great number. **2.** a very great number of persons or things. **3.** ten thousand. *–adj.* **4.** of an indefinitely great number; innumerable. **5.** having innumerable phases, aspects, etc.: *the myriad mind of Shakespeare.* **6.** ten thousand. [Gk *mȳriás* a number of ten thousand]

**myriapod** /ˈmɪriəpɒd/, *n.* **1.** any arthropod of the group Myriapoda, having an elongated, segmented, body with numerous three-jointed legs; formerly treated as a class embracing chiefly the centipedes and millipedes. *–adj.* Also, **myriapodous** /mɪriˈæpədəs/. **2.** belonging or pertaining to the Myriapoda. **3.** having very numerous legs. [NL *Myriapoda,* pl., from Gk *mȳriá(s)* MYRIAD + *poús* foot + *-a,* neut. pl. ending]

**myrmeco-,** a word element meaning 'ant'. [Gk, combining form of *mýrmēx*]

**myrmecology** /mɜməˈkɒlədʒi/, *n.* the branch of entomology that treats of ants. – **myrmecological** /mɜməkəˈlɒdʒɪkəl/, *adj.* – **myrmecologist,** *n.*

**myrmecophagous** /mɜməˈkɒfəgəs/, *adj.* adapted for feeding on ants or termites, as the jaws, teeth, etc., of various anteaters.

**myrmecophile** /ˈmɜməkəfaɪl/, *n.* any species of foreign insect that lives more or less permanently in an ant colony.

**myrmecophilous** /mɜməˈkɒfələs/, *adj.* **1.** of myrmecophiles. **2.** of plants frequented by ants.

**myrmecophyte** /ˈmɜməkəfaɪt/, *n.* a plant with an adaptation for attracting ants.

**myrmidon** /ˈmɜmədɒn/, *n.* one who executes without scruple his master's commands. [in Greek mythology, a Thessalonian subject of Achilles]

**myrnonger** /ˈmɜnɒŋgə/, *n.* an Aboriginal. [var. MURRNONG + -ER[1]]

**myrobalan** /maɪˈrɒbələn, mə-/, *n.* the dried plumlike fruit of certain tropical trees of the genus *Terminalia,* used in dyeing and making ink. [L *myrobalanum,* from Gk *myrobálanos* kind of fruit or nut]

**myrrh** /mɜ/, *n.* an aromatic resinous exudation from certain plants of the genus *Commiphora,* esp. *C. myrrha,* a spiny shrub, used for incense, perfume, etc. [ME *mirre,* OE *myrre,* from L *myrrha, murra,* from Gk *mýrra,* from Akkadian *murrû;* cf. Heb. *mor,* akin to *mar* bitter]

**myrrnong** /ˈmɜnɒŋ/, *n.* →**blackfellow's yam.** Also, **murrnong.** [Aboriginal]

**myrtaceous** /mɜˈteɪʃəs/, *adj.* **1.** belonging to the Myrtaceae, or myrtle family of plants, which includes the myrtle, the guava, the eucalypts, etc. **2.** of, pertaining to, or resembling the myrtle. [LL *myrtāceus* of myrtle]

**myrtle** /ˈmɜtl/, *n.* **1.** any plant of the genus *Myrtus,* esp. *M. communis,* a shrub of southern Europe with evergreen leaves, fragrant white flowers, and aromatic berries, used as an emblem of love and held sacred to Venus. **2.** any of certain other plants as Tasmanian myrtle, *Diospyros pentandra.* [ME, from OF *mirtile* myrtle berry, diminutive of L *myrtus,* from Gk *mýrtos* myrtle]

**myself** /maɪˈsɛlf, məˈsɛlf/, *pron.* **1.** a reflexive form of *me: I cut myself.* **2.** an emphatic form of *me* or *I,* used: **a.** as object: *I used it for myself.* **b.** in apposition to a subject or object: *I myself did it.* **3.** one's proper or normal self; one's normal state of mind (used after, *be, become,* or *come to*): *I am myself again.*

**Mysore thorn** /ˌmaɪsɔ ˈθɔn/, *n.* a climbing plant, *Caesalpinia sepiaria,* a troublesome weed in tropical areas, with strong recurved prickles.

**mystagogue** /ˈmɪstəgɒg/, *n.* one who instructs persons before initiation into religious mysteries or before participation in the sacraments. [L *mystagōgus,* from Gk *mystagōgós*] – **mystagogy** /ˈmɪstəgɒdʒi/, *n.* – **mystagogic** /mɪstəˈgɒdʒɪk/, *adj.*

**mysterious** /məsˈtɪəriəs/, *adj.* **1.** full of, characterised by, or involving mystery: *a mysterious stranger.* **2.** of obscure nature, meaning, origin, etc.; puzzling; inexplicable. **3.** implying or suggesting a mystery: *a mysterious smile.* [L *mystērium* MYSTERY[1] + -OUS] – **mysteriously,** *adv.* – **mysteriousness,** *n.*

**mystery**[1] /ˈmɪstri, -təri/, *n., pl.* **-ries. 1.** anything that is kept secret or remains unexplained or unknown: *the mysteries of nature.* **2.** any affair, thing, or person that presents features or points so obscure as to arouse curiosity or speculation: *a mystery story.* **3.** obscurity, as of something unexplained or puzzling: *proceedings wrapped in mystery.* **4.** obscure, puzzling, or mysterious quality or character. **5.** any truth unknowable except by divine revelation. **6.** (in the Christian religion) **a.** a sacramental rite. **b.** (*pl.*) the consecrated elements. **c.** →**Eucharist. 7.** an incident or scene in connection with the life of Christ, regarded as of special significance: *the mysteries of the Passion.* **8.** (*pl.*) ancient religions which admitted candidates by secret rites the meaning of which only the initiated might know. **9.** (*pl.*) rites or secrets known only to those specially initiated: *the mysteries of freemasonry.* **10.** a mystery play. [ME *mysterie,* from L *mystērium,* from Gk *mystḗrion*]

**mystery**[2] /ˈmɪstri, -təri/, *n., pl.* **-ries. 1.** *Archaic.* a craft or trade. **2.** *Archaic. or Hist.* a guild, as of craftsmen, merchants, or the like. [ME *misterye,* from ML *misterium,* L *ministerium* MINISTRY]

**mystery play** /ˈ– pleɪ/, *n.* a medieval religious drama originating in the liturgy and usu. dealing with the life, death, and resurrection of Christ.

**mystery tour** /ˈ– tʊə/, *n.* a tour or excursion undertaken in ignorance of its destination.

**mystic** /ˈmɪstɪk/, *adj.* **1.** spiritually significant or symbolic, as the dove used in religious art to symbolise the Holy Ghost. **2.** of the nature of or pertaining to mysteries known only to the initated: *mystic rites.* **3.** of occult character, power, or significance: *a mystic formula.* **4.** of obscure or mysterious character or significance. **5.** of or pertaining to mystics or mysticism. *–n.* **6.** one initiated into mysteries. **7.** one who claims to attain, or believes in the possibility of attaining, insight into mysteries transcending ordinary human knowledge, as by immediate intuition in a state of spiritual ecstasy. [ME *mystik,* from L *mysticus,* from Gk *mystikós* mystic, secret]

**mystical** /ˈmɪstɪkəl/, *adj.* **1.** mystic; occult. **2.** of or pertaining to mystics or mysticism: *mystical doctrines.* **3.** spiritually symbolic. **4.** *Rare.* mysterious; obscure in meaning. – **mystically,** *adv.* **mysticalness,** *n.*

**mysticise** /ˈmɪstəsaɪz/, *v.t.,* **-cised, -cising.** to make mystical; give a mystical significance to. Also, **mysticize.**

**mysticism** /ˈmɪstəsɪzəm/, *n.* **1.** the beliefs, ideas, or mode of thought of mystics. **2.** the doctrine of an immediate spiritual intuition of truths believed to transcend ordinary understanding, or of a direct, intimate union of the soul with the Divinity through contemplation and love. **3.** obscure thought or speculation.

**mystify** /ˈmɪstəfaɪ/, *v.t.*, **-fied, -fying.** **1.** to impose upon (a person) by playing upon his credulity; bewilder purposely. **2.** to involve (a subject, etc.) in mystery or obscurity. [F *mystifier,* from *mysti(que)* mystic + *-fier* -FY] – **mystification** /mɪstəfəˈkeɪʃən/, *n.*

**mystique** /mɪsˈtik/, *n.* **1.** an air of mystery or mystical power surrounding a particular person, object, pursuit, belief, etc. **2.** an incommunicable or esoteric quality; a secret known only to the devotees of a cult, etc. [F]

**myth** /mɪθ/, *n.* **1.** a traditional story, usu. concerning some superhuman being or some alleged person or event, and which attempts to explain natural phenomena; esp. a traditional story about deities or demigods and the creation of the world and its inhabitants. **2.** stories or matter of this kind: *in the realm of myth.* **3.** any invented story. **4.** an imaginary or fictitious thing or person. **5.** *Sociol.* a collective belief that is built up in response to the wishes of the group rather than an analysis of the basis of the wishes. [NL *mȳthus,* mod. var. of LL *mȳthos,* from Gk: word, speech, tale, legend, myth]

**myth.,** **1.** mythological. **2.** mythology.

**mythical** /ˈmɪθɪkəl/, *adj.* **1.** pertaining to, of the nature of, or involving a myth or myths. **2.** dealt with in myth, as a period in history. **3.** dealing with myths, as a writer. **4.** existing only in myth, as a person. **5.** having no foundation in fact; imaginary; fictitious: *his claim to be of royal blood is completely mythical.* Also, **mythic.** – **mythically,** *adv.*

**mythicise** /ˈmɪθəsaɪz/, *v.t.*, **-cised, -cising.** to turn into, or treat or explain as, a myth. Also, **mythicize.**

**mytho-,** a word element meaning 'myth.' [Gk, combining form of *mȳthos*]

**mythol.,** **1.** mythological. **2.** mythology.

**mythological** /mɪθəˈlɒdʒɪkəl/, *adj.* of or pertaining to mythology. Also, **mythologic.** – **mythologically,** *adv.*

**mythologise** /məˈθɒlədʒaɪz/, *v.*, **-gised, -gising.** *–v.i.* **1.** to classify, explain, or write about myths. **2.** to construct or relate myths. *–v.t.* **3.** to make into or explain as a myth; make mythical. Also, **mythologize.** – **mythologiser,** *n.*

**mythologist** /məˈθɒlədʒəst/, *n.* **1.** an expert in mythology. **2.** a writer of myths.

**mythology** /məˈθɒlədʒi/, *n., pl.* **-gies.** **1.** a body of myths, as that of a particular people, or that relating to a particular person: *Greek mythology.* **2.** myths collectively. **3.** the science of myths. [ME, from LL *mȳthologia,* from Gk: legend]

**mythomania** /mɪθəˈmeɪniə/, *n.* lying or exaggerating to an abnormal degree. – **mythomaniac** /mɪθəˈmeɪniæk/, *n., adj.*

**mythopoeic** /mɪθəˈpiɪk/, *adj.* myth-making; pertaining to the making of myths. [Gk *mȳthopoiós* making myths + -IC] – **mythopoeism,** *n.* – **mythopoeist,** *n.*

**myx-,** a word element meaning 'slimy'. Also, **myxo-.** [Gk, combining form of *mýxa* slime, mucus]

**myxo** /ˈmɪksoʊ/, *n. Colloq.* →**myxomatosis.**

**myxoedema** /mɪksəˈdimə/, *n.* a disease characterised by thickening of the skin, blunting of the senses and intellect, laboured speech, etc., associated with diminished functional activity of the thyroid gland. Also, *U.S.,* **myxedema.** [NL. See MYX-, OEDEMA] – **myxoedematous** /mɪksəˈdɛmətəs, -ˈdimə-/, *adj.* – **myxoedemic** /mɪksəˈdɛmɪk/, *adj.*

**myxomatosis** /mɪksəməˈtoʊsəs/, *n.* a highly infectious viral disease of rabbits, artificially introduced into Britain and Australia to reduce the rabbit population. [MYX- + -OMAT(A) + -OSIS]

**myxomycete** /ˌmɪksoʊmaɪˈsit/, *n.* any one of the slime moulds (Myxomycetes, Mycetozoa), primitive organisms whose characteristics place them at the borderline between the plant and animal kingdoms.

**myxomycetous** /ˌmɪksoʊmaɪˈsitəs/, *adj.* belonging or pertaining to the Myxomycetes, or slime moulds (sometimes regarded as a distinct phylum, Myxophyta, and sometimes as a class of Thallophyta), having characteristics of both animals and plants. [NL *Myxomycētes,* pl. (see MYXO-, -MYCETES) + -OUS]

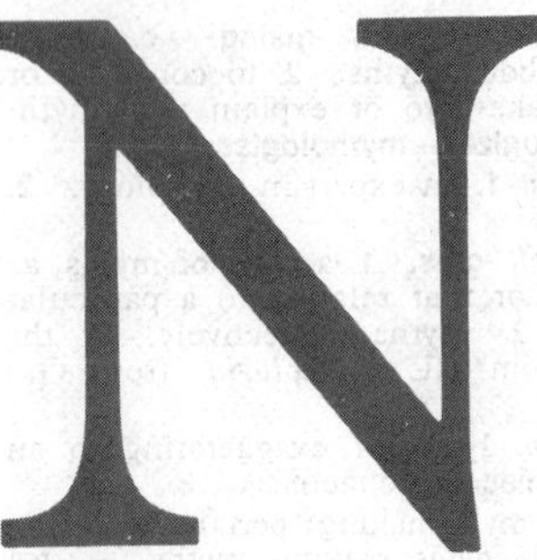

Nn Roman TROOPER Nn Sans Serif GROTESQUE Nn Script MUSKETEER Nn Decorative FREDDY

*Although there are numerous typefaces in the world they can be divided into four main classifications. These are:*

*ROMAN or SERIF. This typeface came into being from the technique of the Roman masons who, working in stone, finished off each letter with a serif or small stroke projecting from the top or bottom. This was done to correct any feeling of unevenness or imbalance they may have created in cutting the characters in stone.*

*SANS SERIF (without serif). This typeface is geometric in design and has straight-edged characters and lines of a regular thickness.*

*SCRIPT. Based on the movement of the hand, this typeface is often italicised or slanted, as if drawn by a brush or quill pen.*

*DECORATIVE. Any typeface that exaggerates the characteristics of any of the other three classifications to a degree that places it outside of them.*

*The dictionary entries in this book use a SANS SERIF typeface called Helvetica (set in a bold face for the head words) and a SERIF typeface Plantin (used throughout the body of the entries).*

**N, n** /ɛn/, *n., pl.* **N's** or **Ns, n's** or **ns. 1.** a consonant, the 14th letter of the English alphabet. **2.** *Maths.* an indefinite constant whole number, esp. the degree of a quantic or an equation, or the order of a curve. **3.** *Print.* →**en. 4.** *Chess.* →**knight.**

**n-,** *Chem.* normal (indicating an unbranched carbon chain in an aliphatic molecule): *an n-butyl ester.* Cf. **iso-** (def. 2).

**n., 1.** born. [L *nātus*] **2.** neuter. **3.** noon. **4.** *Chem.* normal (strength solution). **5.** noun. **6.** nominative. **7.** nominal.

**N, 1.** *Chem.* nitrogen. **2.** north. **3.** northern. **4.** newton.

**N., 1.** navy. **2.** *Chem.* normal (strength solution). **3.** Norse. **4.** north. **5.** northern.

**n/a, 1.** no account. **2.** no answer. **3.** not applicable. **4.** not available.

**n.a., 1.** not applicable. **2.** not available.

**Na,** *Chem.* sodium. [L *natrium*]

**N.A.,** *Physics.* numerical aperture.

**nab** /næb/, *v.t.,* **nabbed, nabbing.** *Colloq.* **1.** to catch or seize, esp. suddenly. **2.** to capture or arrest. [earlier *nap.* Cf. OE *hnæppan* strike]

**Nabis** /na'bi/, *n.pl.* a group of late 19th-century French painters, led by Pierre Bonnard, 1867-1947. [Heb. *nābhi* prophet]

**nabob** /'neɪbɒb/, *n.* **1.** an Englishman who has grown rich in India. **2.** any very wealthy and powerful person. **3.** →**nawab.** [Hind. *nawwab.* See NAWAB] – **nabobery** /'neɪbɒbəri, neɪ'bɒbəri/, **nabobism,** *n.* – **nabobish,** *adj.*

**nacelle** /næ'sɛl/, *n.* **1.** the enclosed part of an aeroplane, dirigible, etc., in which the engine is housed or passengers, etc., are carried. **2.** the car of a balloon. [F, from LL *nāvicella,* diminutive of L *nāvis* ship]

**nacre** /'neɪkə/, *n.* →**mother-of-pearl.** [F, from ML *nacrum,* var. of *nacara,* ? from Pers. (Kurdish) *nakāra* pearl oyster]

**nacreous** /'neɪkriəs/, *adj.* **1.** of or pertaining to nacre. **2.** (of minerals) having a lustre resembling that of pearl.

**nadir** /'neɪdɪə/, *n.* **1.** the point of the celestial sphere vertically beneath any place or observer and diametrically opposite to the zenith. **2.** the lowest point, as of adversity. [ME, from Ar. *nazīr* corresponding, opposite (i.e., to the zenith)]

**nae** /neɪ/, *adj., adv. Scot.* **1.** no. **2.** not. [var. of NO[1]]

**naevus** /'nivəs/, *n., pl.* **-vi** /-vaɪ/. any congenital anomaly, including various types of birthmarks and all types of moles. Also, *U.S.,* **nevus.** [L] – **naevoid** /'nivɔɪd/, *adj.*

**nag**[1] /næg/, *v.,* **nagged, nagging.** –*v.t.* **1.** to torment by persistent fault-finding, complaints, or importunities. –*v.i.* **2.** to keep up an irritating or wearisome fault-finding, complaining, or the like (oft. fol. by *at*). **3.** to cause continual pain, discomfort, or depression, as a headache, feeling of guilt, etc. [cf. MLG *naggen* irritate, provoke, Icel. *nagga* grumble, *nagg* grumbling] – **nagger,** *n.* – **naggingly,** *adv.*

**nag**[2] /næg/, *n.* **1.** a small horse, or pony, esp. for riding. **2.** *Colloq.* a horse. **3.** an old or inferior horse. [ME *nagge,* c. D *negge;* akin to NEIGH]

**Nah.,** *Bible.* Nahum.

**Nahuatl** /na'watl/, *n.* **1.** a group of peoples of southern Mexico and central America, including the Aztecs. **2.** a member of such peoples. **3.** any of a subgroup of Uto-Aztecan languages of these peoples. –*adj.* **4.** of or pertaining to the Nahuatl language or peoples.

**naiad** /'naɪæd/, *n., pl.* **-ads, -ades** /-ə'diz/. **1.** (*also cap.*) *Class. Myth.* one of a class of water-nymphs fabled to dwell in and preside over streams and springs. **2.** *Bot.* a submerged water plant of the genus *Najas,* or the family Najadaceae. **3.** *Biol.* the aquatic larva or nymph of such insects as dragonflies, mayflies, etc. [L *Nāias,* from Gk]

**naïf** /na'if/, *adj.* →**naive.** [F (masc.). See NAIVE]

**nail** /neɪl/, *n.* **1.** a slender piece of metal, usu. with one end pointed and the other enlarged, for driving into or through wood, etc., as to hold separate pieces together. **2.** a thin, horny plate, consisting of modified epidermis, growing on the upper side of the end of a finger or toe. **3.** a measure of length for cloth, equal to 2¼ inches or 57.15 millimetres. **4. hard as nails,** (of a person) stern; tough. **5. hit the nail on the head,** to say or do exactly the right thing. **6. on the nail,** *Colloq.* on the spot, or at once. –*v.t.* **7.** to fasten with a nail or nails: *to nail the cover on a box.* **8.** to stud with or as with nails driven in. **9.** to shut within something by driving nails in (fol. by *up*): *to nail goods up in a box.* **10.** to make fast or keep firmly in one place or position: *fear nailed him to the spot.* **11.** *Colloq.* to secure by prompt action; catch or seize. **12.** *Colloq.* to catch (a person) in some difficulty, a lie, etc. **13.** *Colloq.* to detect and expose (a lie, etc.). [ME; OE *nægl,* c. D *nagel* and G *Nagel*] – **nailer,** *n.*

**nail-biting** /'neɪl-baɪtɪŋ/, *n.* **1.** a habitual biting of the fingernails. –*adj.* **2.** suspenseful; exciting.

**nailbrush** /'neɪlbrʌʃ/, *n.* a small brush with hard bristles, used for scrubbing fingernails.

**nailfile** /'neɪlfaɪl/, *n.* a small file for trimming or shaping fingernails.

**nail harmonica** /ˈneɪl haˈmɒnɪkə/, *n.* →**nail violin.**

**nail polish** /ˈ– pɒlɪʃ/, *n.* a varnish, either colourless or of varying shades, used by women to paint their nails. Also, **nail varnish.**

**nailrod** /ˈneɪlrɒd/, *n.* **1.** an iron strip from which nails are cut. **2.** coarse dark tobacco in the form of a long, thin plug.

**nail scissors** /ˈneɪl sɪzəz/, *n.* a small pair of scissors, often with a curved blade, used for trimming fingernails, etc.

**nail set** /ˈ– sɛt/, *n.* a short tapering rod of steel used to drive a nail below, or flush with, the surface. Also, **nail punch, nail sett.**

**nail-tail** /ˈneɪl-teɪl/, *n.* a condition seen in many animals in which the tip of the tail is either equipped with a nail-like hardening of the skin or exposes the terminal vertebrae.

**nail-tailed wallaby** /ˌneɪl-teɪld ˈwɒləbi/, *n.* any of three species of wallabies, the karrabul, wurrung and the merrin, characterised by a horny nail-like tip at the end of a long, slender tail.

**nail varnish** /ˈneɪl vanɪʃ/, *n.* →**nail polish.**

**nail violin** /– vaɪəˈlɪn/, *n.* a musical instrument on which a set of nails around the perimeter of a soundboard is made to vibrate by the use of a violin bow. Also, **nail harmonica.**

**nainsook** /ˈneɪnsʊk, ˈnæn-/, *n.* a fine, soft-finished cotton fabric, usu. white, used for lingerie and infants' wear. [Hind. *nainsukh,* lit., eye pleasure]

**naive** /naɪˈiv, na-/, *adj.* having or showing natural simplicity of nature; unsophisticated; ingenuous. Also, **naïf, naïve.** [F, fem. of *naïf,* from L *nātīvus* native, natural] – **naively,** *adv.*

**naivety** /naɪˈivəti/, *n.* **1.** the quality of being naive; artless simplicity. **2.** a naive action, remark, etc. Also, **naiveté, naïveté** /naˈivteɪ/. [F *naïveté,* from *naive*]

**naked** /ˈneɪkəd/, *adj.* **1.** without clothing or covering; nude. **2.** without adequate clothing. **3.** bare of any covering, overlying matter, vegetation, foliage, or the like: *naked fields.* **4.** bare, stripped, or destitute (*of* something specified): *trees naked of leaves.* **5.** without a sheath or customary covering: *a naked sword.* **6.** without carpets, hangings, or furnishings, as rooms, walls, etc. **7.** (of the eye, sight, etc.) unassisted by a microscope, telescope, or other instrument. **8.** defenceless or unprotected; unguarded; exposed, as to attack or harm. **9.** simple; unadorned: *the naked truth.* **10.** not accompanied or supplemented by anything else: *a naked outline of facts.* **11.** exposed to view or plainly revealed: *a naked vein.* **12.** plain-spoken; blunt. **13.** *Bot.* **a.** (of seeds) not enclosed in an ovary. **b.** (of flowers) without a calyx or perianth. **c.** (of stalks, etc.) without leaves. **d.** (of stalks, leaves, etc.) without hairs or pubescence. **14.** *Zool.* having no covering of hair, feathers, shell, etc. **15.** *Law. Obs.* unsupported, as by authority or consideration: *a naked assertion.* [ME *naked(e),* OE *nacod,* c. G *nackt*] – **nakedly,** *adv.* – **nakedness,** *n.*

**naked-nose wombat** /ˌneɪkəd-noʊz ˈwɒmbæt/, *n.* a wombat of the genus *Vombatus,* having no hair on the muzzle and a coarse coat.

**namable** /ˈneɪməbəl/, *adj.* →**nameable.**

**namby-pamby** /ˈnæmbi-ˌpæmbi/, *adj., n., pl.* **-bies.** *–adj.* **1.** weakly simple or sentimental; insipid. *–n.* **2.** namby-pamby verse or prose. **3.** a namby-pamby person. **4.** namby-pamby sentiment. [orig. a nickname, *Namby Pamby,* for Ambrose Philips, d. 1749, English poet; first used by Henry Carey in 1726 as title of poem ridiculing Philips' verses]

**name** /neɪm/, *n., v.,* **named, naming.** *–n.* **1.** a word or a combination of words by which a person, place, or thing, a body or class, or any object of thought, is designated or known. **2.** mere designation as distinguished from fact: *king in name only.* **3.** an appellation, title, or epithet, applied descriptively, in honour, abuse, etc.: *to call him bad names.* **4.** a reputation of a particular kind given by common report: *a bad name.* **5.** a distinguished, famous, or great reputation; fame: *to seek a name for oneself.* **6.** a widely known or famous person. **7.** a personal or family name as exercising influence or bringing distinction. **8.** a body of persons grouped under one name, as a family or race. **9.** the verbal or other symbolic representation of a thing, event, property, relation, or concept. A **proper name** represents some particular thing or event. A **common name** (e.g. 'man') is the name of anything which satisfies certain indicated conditions. **10. in the name of, a.** with appeal to: *in the name of mercy, stop screaming!* **b.** by the authority of: *open in the name of the law!* **c.** on behalf of: *to vote in the name of others.* **d.** under the name of: *money deposited in the name of a son.* **e.** under the designation of; in the character of: *murder in the name of mercy.* **11. to one's name,** belonging to one: *not a cent to my name.* *–v.t.* **12.** to give a name to: *name a baby.* **13.** to call by a specified name: *to name a child Regina.* **14.** to specify or mention by name: *three persons were named in the report.* **15.** to designate for some duty or office; nominate or appoint: *I have named you for the position.* **16.** to specify: *to name a price.* **17.** to tell the name of: *name the capital of France.* **18.** to speak of. **19.** (in sittings of Parliament) to cite (a member) for contempt. **20. the name of the game,** *Colloq.* the central issue or the essential part of an operation, business, etc. [ME; OE *nama,* c. G *Name;* akin to L *nōmen,* Gk *ónoma*] – **namer,** *n.*

**nameable** /ˈneɪməbəl/, *adj.* that may be named. Also, **namable.**

**name-calling** /ˈneɪm-kɔlɪŋ/, *n.* abusive remarks directed at an opponent himself rather than at the argument which he put forward: *the interview degenerated into mere name-calling.*

**name-day** /ˈneɪm-deɪ/, *n.* **1.** Also, **ticket day.** the day on which buying stockbrokers pass to selling brokers the names of the purchasers of the stocks since the last settlement. **2.** the celebration of the mass-day of the Saint whose name one bears.

**name-dropper** /ˈneɪm-drɒpə/, *n.* one who introduces casually into a conversation names of prominent people as though they are personal friends, in order to impress. – **namedropping,** *n.*

**nameless** /ˈneɪmləs/, *adj.* **1.** unknown to fame; obscure. **2.** having no name. **3.** left unnamed: *a certain person who shall be nameless.* **4.** anonymous: *a nameless writer.* **5.** having no legitimate paternal name, as a child born out of wedlock. **6.** that cannot be specified or described: *a nameless charm.* **7.** too shocking or vile to be specified. – **namelessly,** *adv.* – **namelessness,** *n.*

**namely** /ˈneɪmli/, *adv.* that is to say; to wit: *two cities, namely, Sydney and Melbourne.*

**nameplate** /ˈneɪmpleɪt/, *n.* a plate outside a house bearing the name and usu. the profession of the occupant, as used by doctors, dentists, etc.

**namesake** /ˈneɪmseɪk/, *n.* **1.** one having the same name as another. **2.** one named after another. [alteration of *name's sake*]

**name tag** /ˈneɪm tæg/, *n.* **1.** a small disc or strip attached to the collar of a dog, cat, or other pet, stating owner, address, etc. **2.** a tape on an article of clothing bearing the owner's name (used esp. for children at school).

**namma hole** /ˈnæmə hoʊl/, *n.* a depression in the ground forming a natural reservoir; melon hole. Also, **gnamma hole.** [Aboriginal]

A, namma hole; B, cross-section.

**nana**[1] /ˈnanə/, *n.* **1.** the name of a men's hairstyle briefly popular in the 1920s in which the hair was worn long at the sides and very short at the back. **2. do one's nana,** to lose one's temper. [shortened form of BANANA]

**nana**[2] /ˈnænə/, *n.* →**nanna.**

**nancy boy** /ˈnænsi bɔɪ/, *n. Chiefly Brit. Colloq.* **1.** an effeminate man. **2.** homosexual.

**nandina** /nænˈdinə/, *n.* a shrub, *Nandina domestica,* family Berberidaceae, native to China, much planted for its graceful bipinnate foliage which is produced on bamboo-like stems.

**nanism** /ˈneɪnɪzəm/, *n.* a condition of abnormal smallness in size or stature.

**nankeen** /næŋˈkin/, *n.* **1.** a firm, durable, yellow or buff fabric, made originally from a natural-coloured Chinese cotton but now from other cotton and dyed. **2.** (*pl.*) garments made of this material. **3.** a yellow or buff colour. **4.** a type of porcelain, blue on a white background. Also, **nankin.** [named after *Nankin* Nanjing, a port on the Chang Jing (Yangtze) river in E China]

**nankeen kestrel** /– ˈkɛstrəl/, *n.* a small falcon, *Falco cenchroides,* reddish brown above and white below, found in

Australia, Tasmania and New Guinea; the most common of the smaller Australian raptorial birds; windhover; sparrowhawk.

nankeen kestrel

**nankeen night heron,** *n.* a small chestnut-brown, nocturnal heron, *Nycticorax caledonicus,* of Australia and Tasmania. Also, **nankeen crane.**

**nankin** /næŋ'kɪn/, *n.* →**nankeen.**

**nanna** /'nænə/, *n. Colloq.* a grandmother. Also, **nana.**

**nanny** /'næni/, *n., pl.* **-ies. 1.** a nurse for children. **2.** a grandmother. **3.** →**nanny-goat.** [alteration of female Christian name *Ann.* See -Y[2]]

**nannygai** /'nænigaɪ/, *n.* a handsome fish of fine flavour, *Centroberyx affinis,* found around the southern half of the Australian coast; redfish. [Aboriginal]

**nanny-goat** /'næni-goʊt/, *n.* a female goat.

**nano-** /'nænoʊ-/, **1.** a prefix denoting $10^{-9}$ of a given unit, as in *nanometre. Symbol:* n **2.** a prefix indicating very small size, as *nanoplankton.* [combining form of L *nānus* dwarf; from Gk *nânos*]

**nanoplankton** /'nænoʊˌplæŋktən/, *n.* plankton of such a size that they can be seen only with the aid of a microscope.

**nanosecond** /'nænoʊˌsɛkənd/, *n.* one thousand-millionth part of a second.

**nanto** /'næntoʊ/, *n.* a horse. [Aboriginal: the nose distended after hard riding]

**naos** /'neɪɒs/, *n.* **1.** a temple. **2.** *Archit.* the central chamber, or cella, of an ancient temple. [Gk: temple]

**nap**[1] /næp/, *v.,* **napped, napping,** *n.* *–v.i.* **1.** to have a short sleep; doze. **2.** to be off one's guard: *I caught him napping.* *–n.* **3.** a short sleep; a doze. [ME *nappe(n),* OE *hnappian,* c. MHG *napfen*]

**nap**[2] /næp/, *n., v.,* **napped, napping.** *–n.* **1.** the short fuzzy ends of fibres on the surface of cloth drawn up in napping. **2.** *Colloq.* blankets. **3.** any downy coating, as on plants. **4.** *Golf, etc.* the surface of a green as determined by the way the grass grows, is mown, etc., and which affects the movement of a ball being putted across it. *–v.t.* **5.** to raise a nap on. [ME *noppe,* OE *-hnoppa* (in *wullcnoppa,* mistake for *wullhnoppa* tuft of wool), c. MD and MLG *noppe;* akin to OE *hnoppian* pluck] – **napless,** *adj.*

**nap**[3] /næp/, *n.* **1.** *Cards.* **a.** a game in which the players bid for the tricks they propose to win. **b.** a bid in this game to take all five tricks of a hand. **2. go nap,** to undertake to win all five tricks. **3. not to go nap on,** *Colloq.* to be unenthusiastic about. [shortened form of *Napoleon.* See NAPOLEON]

**nap**[4] /næp/, *n., v.,* **napped, napping.** *Horseracing.* *–n.* **1.** a good tip. *–v.t.* **2.** to name (a certain horse) as the winner of a race. [special use of NAP[3]]

**nap**[5] /næp/, *n. N.Z. Colloq.* →**nappy**[4].

**napalm** /'neɪpam, 'næpam/, *n.* **1.** an aluminium soap, in the form of a granular powder, which is a mixture of oleic, naphthenic and coconut fatty acids; mixed with petrol it forms a sticky gel, stable from −40°C to 100°C, used in flame throwers and fire bombs. **2.** the gel made by the addition of napalm to petrol. [NA(PHTHA) + PALM(ITATE)]

**nape** /neɪp/, *n.* the back (of the neck). [ME]

**napery** /'neɪpəri/, *n.* **1.** table linen; tablecloths, napkins, etc. **2.** linen for household use. [ME *naperie,* from OF, from *nape* tablecloth. See NAPKIN]

**naphtha** /'næfθə/, *n.* **1.** a colourless, volatile liquid, a petroleum distillate (esp. a product intermediate between gasoline and benzine), used as a solvent, fuel, etc. **2.** any of various similar liquids distilled from other products. **3.** *Obs.* petroleum. [L, from Gk]

**naphthalene** /'næfθəlin/, *n.* a white crystalline hydrocarbon, $C_{10}H_8$, usu. prepared from coal tar, used in making dyes, as a moth repellent, etc. Also, **naphthaline, naphthalin** /'næfθələn/. [NAPHTH(A) + AL(COHOL) + -ENE]

**naphthene** /'næfθin/, *n. Obsolesc.* any of a group of hydrocarbon ring compounds of the general formula, $C_nH_{2n}$, derivatives of cyclopentane and cyclohexane, found in certain petroleums. – **naphthenic** /næf'θinɪk/, *adj.*

**naphthol** /'næfθɒl/, *n.* **1.** either of two isomeric derivatives of naphthalene, having the formula $C_{10}H_7OH$, and occurring in coal tar, used as antiseptics and in dye manufacture. See **beta-naphthol. 2.** any of certain hydroxyl derivatives of naphthalene. Also, **naphtol** /'næftɒl/. [NAPHTH(A) + -OL[2]]

**naphthyl group** /'næfθəl grup/, *n.* the univalent group $C_{10}H_7-$. Also, **naphthyl radical.**

**Napierian logarithm** /nəˌpɪəriən 'lɒgərɪðəm/, *n.* →**natural logarithm.** [named after John *Napier,* 1550-1617, Scottish mathematician and inventor of logarithms]

**napiform** /'neɪpəfɔm/, *adj.* turnip-shaped, as a root. [L *nāpus* turnip + -I- + -FORM]

**napkin** /'næpkən/, *n.* **1.** →**serviette. 2.** a square or oblong piece of linen, cotton cloth or paper as for **a.** a towel. **b.** a baby's nappy. [late ME *napekyn,* diminutive of *nape* tablecloth, from F *nappe,* from L *mappa* cloth. Cf. MAP]

**napkin ring** /'– rɪŋ/, *n.* →**serviette ring.**

**Naples yellow** /neɪpəlz 'jɛloʊ/, *n.* **1.** a yellow pigment made from lead antimoniate. **2.** the colour of this. [from *Naples,* a city in S Italy where it was first manufactured]

**napoleon** /nə'poʊliən/, *n.* **1.** *Cards.* →**nap**[3] (def. 1). **2.** a rectangular piece of pastry, iced on top, with crisp, flaky layers filled with custard, cream or jam. [named after *Napoleon* Bonaparte, 1769-1821, emperor of France]

**Napoleonic** /nəpoʊli'ɒnɪk/, *adj.* pertaining to, resembling, or suggestive of Napoleon I, or, less often, Napoleon III, or their dynasty.

**napolitaine** /næpɒlɪ'teɪn/, *adj.* with a sauce, of Italian origin, made from tomatoes, garlic, parsley, oil, and marsala. Also, **à la Napolitaine.** [F *à la Napolitaine* in the manner of Naples (city in S Italy)]

**napoo** /næ'pu/, *adj. Colloq.* **1.** finished; used up. **2.** doomed; done for. [alteration of F *il n'y a plus* there is no more]

**nappa** /'næpə/, *n.* soft, rough-surfaced leather, coarser than suede.

**nappe** /næp/, *n.* a large overturned anticlinal fold of rock strata, often thrust away from its roots by earth movements.

**napper**[1] /'næpə/, *n.* **1.** one who raises a nap on cloth. **2.** a machine for putting a nap on cloth. [NAP[2] + -ER[1]]

**napper**[2] /'næpə/, *n.* one who naps or dozes. [NAP[1] + -ER[1]]

**nappy**[1] /'næpi/, *adj. Brit.* heady or strong, as ale. [probably special use of NAPPY[3]]

**nappy**[2] /'næpi/, *n., pl.* **-pies.** *U.S.* a small dish, usu. round and often of glass, with a flat bottom and sloping sides, for food, etc. Also, **nappie.** [orig. obscure]

**nappy**[3] /'næpi/, *adj.,* **-pier, -piest.** covered with nap; downy. [NAP[2] + -Y[1]]

**nappy**[4] /'næpi/, *n., pl.* **-pies.** a piece of muslin, cotton, or some disposable material, fastened round a baby to absorb and contain its excrement. [alteration of NAPKIN]

**nappy**[5] /'næpi/, *adj.* (of horses) nervy; recalcitrant. [from obs. *nab* (or *nap*) *the rust* become restless (of a horse)]

**nappy liner** /'– laɪnə/, *n.* a piece of disposable material used to line a baby's nappy.

**nappy rash** /'– ræʃ/, *n.* dermatitis of thighs and buttocks due to ammonia produced in decomposing urine in an infant's nappy.

**naprapathy** /nə'præpəθi/, *n.* a system of treatment based on the belief that all diseases are caused by connective tissue and ligament disorders and can be cured by massage. [Czech *napra(va)* correction (cf. Russ. *napravit'* direct, guide) + -PATHY] – **naprapath** /'næprəpæθ/, *n.*

**narangy** /nə'ræŋi/, *n.* a person on a station whose status is between that of the boss and that of the stationhands. [Aboriginal]

**narc** /nak/, *n. Colloq.* a member of the narcotics squad in the police force. [shortened form of *narc(otics);* ? pun on NARK]

**narceine** /'nasin/, *n.* a bitter, white, crystalline narcotic alkaloid, $C_{23}H_{27}NO_8 \cdot 3H_2O$, contained in opium, having a muscle-relaxing action. [L *narcē* (from Gk *nárkē* numbness, torpor) + -INE[2]]

**narcissism** /'nasəsɪzəm/, *n.* **1.** extreme admiration for oneself or one's own attributes; egoism; self-love. **2.** *Psychol.* sexual excitement through admiration of oneself. **3.** *Psychol.* erotic gratification derived from admiration of one's own physical or mental attributes, a normal condition at the infantile level of personality development. Also, **narcism** /ˈnasɪzəm/. [G *Narzissismus,* from *Narcissus,* in Greek mythology a beautiful youth who fell in love with his own reflection, pined away, and was metamorphosed into the flower that bears his name] – **narcissist,** *n.* – **narcissistic** /nasəˈsɪstɪk/, *adj.*

**narcissus** /naˈsɪsəs/, *n., pl.* **-cissuses, -cissi** /-ˈsɪsaɪ/. any plant of the genus *Narcissus,* which comprises bulbous plants bearing showy flowers with a cup-shaped corona, as the narcissus, *N. poeticus,* and the wild daffodil, *N. pseudonarcissus.* [L, from Gk *nárkissos* the plant (so named from its narcotic properties)]

**narco-,** a word element meaning 'stupor' or 'narcosis'. [Gk *nárko-,* combining form of *nárkē* numbness]

**narcolepsy** /ˈnakəlɛpsi/, *n.* a condition characterised by an uncontrollable desire for, and short attacks of, sleep on all occasions. [b. NARCO(SIS) and (EPI)LEPSY] – **narcoleptic** /nakəˈlɛptɪk/, *adj.*

**narcosis** /naˈkoʊsəs/, *n.* **1.** a state of sleep or drowsiness. **2.** a temporary state of stupor or unconsciousness, esp. produced by a drug. [NL, from Gk *nárkōsis* a benumbing]

**narcosynthesis** /nakoʊˈsɪnθəsəs/, *n.* a treatment for psychiatric disturbances which uses narcotics.

**narcotic** /naˈkɒtɪk/, *adj.* **1.** having the power to produce narcosis, as a drug. **2.** pertaining to or of the nature of narcosis. **3.** pertaining to narcotics or their use. **4.** for the use or treatment of narcotic addicts. *–n.* **5.** any of a class of substances that blunt the senses, relieving pain, etc., and inducing sleep, and in large quantities producing complete insensibility, often used habitually to satisfy morbid appetite. **6.** an individual inclined towards the habitual use of such substances. [Gk *narkōtikós* making stiff or numb]

**narcotise** /ˈnakətaɪz/, *v.t.,* **-tised, -tising.** to subject to a narcotic; stupefy. Also, **narcotize.** – **narcotisation** /nakətaɪˈzeɪʃən/, *n.*

**narcotism** /ˈnakətɪzəm/, *n.* **1.** the habit of taking narcotics. **2.** the action or influence of narcotics. **3.** →**narcosis. 4.** an abnormal inclination to sleep.

**nard** /nad/, *n.* **1.** an aromatic Himalayan plant, supposedly *Nardostachys jatamansi* (spikenard), the source of an ointment used by the ancients. **2.** the ointment. [ME, from L *nardus,* from Gk *nárdos*]

**nardoo** /naˈdu/, *n.* **1.** any of the Australian species of the mud-loving or aquatic genus of ferns, *Marsilea.* **2.** the sporocarps of such a plant ground into a flour and eaten by Australian Aborigines. [Aboriginal]

**nares** /ˈnɛəriz/, *n.pl., sing.* **naris** /ˈnɛərəs/. the nostrils or the nasal passages. [L, pl. of *nāris*]

**narghile** /ˈnagəli/, *n.* →**hookah.** [F *narguilé,* from Pers. *nārgīleh* a pipe]

**narial** /ˈnɛəriəl/, *adj.* of or pertaining to the nares or nostrils. Also, **narine** /ˈnɛərən, -raɪn/.

**nark** /nak/, *n.* **1.** *Colloq.* an informer; a spy, esp. for the police. **2.** a scolding, complaining person; one who is always interfering and spoiling the pleasure of others. *–v.t.* **3.** to nag; irritate; annoy. *–v.i.* **4.** to act as an informer. [Gipsy *nāk* nose] – **narky,** *adj.*

**narked** /nakt/, *adj. Colloq.* upset; irritated; angry.

**narrate** /nəˈreɪt/, *v.,* **-rated, -rating.** *–v.t.* **1.** to give an account of or tell the story of (events, experiences, etc.). *–v.i.* **2.** to relate or recount events, etc., in speech or writing. [L *narrātus,* pp.] – **narratable,** *adj.* – **narrator,** *n.*

**narration** /nəˈreɪʃən/, *n.* **1.** an account or story. **2.** the act or process of narrating. **3.** words or matter narrating something. **4.** *Rhet.* (in a classical speech) the third part, the exposition of the question.

**narrative** /ˈnærətɪv/, *n.* **1.** a story of events, experiences, or the like, whether true or fictitious. **2.** narrative matter, as in literary work. **3.** the act or process of narrating. *–adj.* **4.** that narrates: *a narrative poem.* **5.** of or pertaining to narration: *narrative skill.* – **narratively,** *adv.*

**narrawa burr** /nærəwa ˈbɜ/, *n.* a hoary spiny plant, *Solanum cinereum,* with blue flowers and globular yellow berries.

**narrow** /ˈnæroʊ/, *adj.* **1.** of little breadth or width; not broad or wide: *a narrow room.* **2.** limited in extent or space, or affording little room: *narrow quarters.* **3.** limited in range or scope. **4.** lacking breadth of view or sympathy, as persons, the mind, ideas, etc. **5.** limited in amount, small, or meagre: *narrow resources.* **6.** straitened, as circumstances. **7.** barely sufficient or adequate; being barely that: *a narrow escape.* **8.** careful; minute, as a scrutiny, search or inquiry. **9.** *Phonet.* pronounced with relatively tense muscles. **10.** *Phonet.* (of a transcription) **a.** representing sounds in a detailed manner and showing non-phonemic differences between sounds, using symbols and diacritics. **b.** representing each phoneme by a separate symbol. Cf. **broad**[1] (def. 14). *–v.i.* **11.** to become narrower. *–v.t.* **12.** to make narrower. **13.** to limit or restrict. **14.** to make narrow-minded. *–n.* **15.** a narrow part, place or thing. **16.** (*pl.*) a narrow part of a strait, river, ocean current, etc. [ME; OE *nearu,* c. OS *naru* narrow, D *naar* unpleasant] – **narrowly,** *adv.* – **narrowness,** *n.*

**narrow gauge** /– ˈgeɪdʒ/, *n.* See **gauge** (def. 13).

**narrow-gauge** /ˈnæroʊ-geɪdʒ/, *adj.* (of a railway line) having a lesser gauge than standard gauge.

**narrow-minded** /ˈnæroʊ-maɪndəd/, *adj.* having or showing a prejudiced mind, as persons, opinions, etc. – **narrow-mindedly,** *adv.* – **narrow-mindedness,** *n.*

**narthex** /ˈnaθɛks/, *n.* a vestibule along the facade of an early Christian or Byzantine church. [LGk; in Gk: giant fennel]

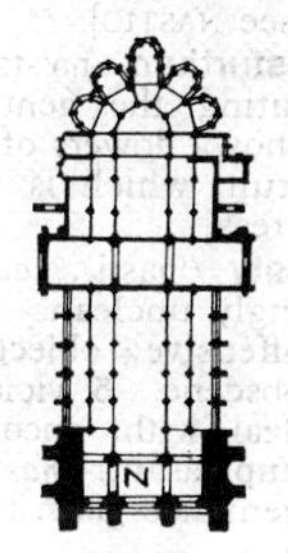

N, narthex

**narwhal** /ˈnawəl/, *n.* an arctic cetacean, *Monodon monoceros,* the male of which has a long, spirally twisted tusk extending forwards from the upper jaw. Also, **narwal, narwhale.** [Swed. or Dan. *narhval* (from *nar* + *hval* whale). Cf. Icel. *nāhvalr,* lit., corpse whale (from corpselike colour of belly)]

**nary** /ˈnɛəri/, *adv. U.S., Brit.* never: *nary a fish did I catch.* [U.S. regional; also Brit. d.; contraction of *ne'er a*]

**nasal**[1] /ˈneɪzəl/, *adj.* **1.** of or pertaining to the nose. **2.** *Phonet.* with the voice issuing through the nose, either partly (as in French nasal vowels) or entirely (as in *m, n,* or the *ng* of *song*). *–n.* **3.** *Phonet.* a nasal speech sound. [NL *nāsālis,* from L *nāsus* nose. See NOSE] – **nasality** /neɪˈzæləti/, *n.* – **nasally,** *adv.*

**nasal**[2] /ˈneɪzəl/, *n.* a part of a helmet, protecting the nose and adjacent parts of the face. [late ME, from OF, from L *nāsus* nose]

**nasal feed** /– ˈfid/, *n.* the administration of nutrient liquids by means of a tube passed through the nose into the stomach.

narwhal

**nasal index** /– ˈɪndɛks/, *n.* **1.** (of the skull) the ratio of the distance from the nasion to the lower margin of the nasal aperture to that of the maximum breadth of the nasal aperture. **2.** (of the head) the ratio of the maximum breadth of the external nose to its height from the nasal root to where the septum is confluent with the upper lip.

**nasalise** /ˈneɪzəlaɪz/, *v.,* **-lised, -lising.** *Phonet. etc. –v.t.* **1.** to pronounce as a nasal sound by allowing some of the voice to issue through the nose. *–v.i.* **2.** to nasalise normally oral sounds. Also, **nasalize.** – **nasalisation** /neɪzəlaɪˈzeɪʃən/, *n.*

**nascent** /ˈnæsənt/, *adj.* **1.** beginning to exist or develop: *the nascent republic.* **2.** *Chem.* (of an element) being in the nascent state. [L *nascens,* ppr., being born] – **nascence, nascency,** *n.*

**nascent state** /– ˈsteɪt/, *n.* the condition of an element at the instant it is set free from a combination in which it has previously existed. Also, **nascent condition.**

**naseberry** /ˈneɪzbɛri/, *n., pl.* **-ries. 1.** the fruit of the sapodilla, *Achras zapota.* **2.** →**sapodilla.** [Sp. *néspera* medlar, from L *mespila.* See MEDLAR]

**nasho** /ˈnæʃoʊ/, *n. Colloq.* **1.** →**national service. 2.** one who has been called up for national service. [abbrev. of NATIONAL SERVICE]

**nasi goreng** /nazi ˈgɒrɛŋ, ˈgɔrɛŋ/, *n.* a dish of Indonesian origin consisting of cooked rice, fried in seasoned oil, garnished with hot chillies, beef shreds or slices, fried onions and sliced omelette. [Bahasa Indonesia]

**nasion** /ˈneɪziən/, *n. Anat.* the intersection of the internasal suture with the nasofrontal suture, in the midsagittal plane. [NL, from L *nāsus* nose] – **nasial,** *adj.*

**nasofrontal** /neɪzoʊˈfrʌntl/, *adj.* of or pertaining to the nose and frontal bone.

**nasopharyngeal port** /neɪzoʊfəˌrɪndʒiəl ˈpɔt/, *n.* the passageway joining the nasal cavity and the nasopharynx.

**nasopharynx** /neɪzoʊˈfærɪŋks/, *n., pl.* **-pharynges** /-fəˈrɪndʒiz/, **-pharynxes.** the part of the pharynx behind and above the soft palate or velum, directly continuous with the nasal passages (distinguished from *oropharynx*). – **nasopharyngeal** /neɪzoʊfəˈrɪndʒiəl/, *adj.*

**nassella tussock** /nəˌsɛlə ˈtʌsək/, *n.* →**serrated tussock.**

**nastic** /ˈnæstɪk/, *adj.* (in botany) of or showing sufficiently greater cellular force or growth on one side of an axis to change the form or position of the axis. [Gk *nastós* squeezed together + -IC]

**-nastic,** a suffix forming adjectives of words ending in **-nasty.** [see NASTIC]

**nasturtium** /nəˈstɜʃəm/, *n.* any of the garden plants constituting the genus *Tropaeolum,* much cultivated for their showy flowers of yellow, red, and other colours, and for their fruit, which is picked and used like capers. [L: a kind of cress]

**nasty** /ˈnasti/, *adj.,* **-tier, -tiest. 1.** physically filthy; disgustingly unclean. **2.** offensive to taste or smell; nauseous. **3.** offensive; objectionable: *a nasty habit.* **4.** morally filthy; obscene. **5.** vicious, spiteful, or ugly: *a nasty dog.* **6.** bad to deal with, encounter, undergo, etc.: *a nasty cut.* **7.** very unpleasant: *nasty weather.* *–n.* **8.** (*pl.*) *Brit. Colloq.* the genital organs. [ME, orig. uncert.] – **nastily,** *adv.* – **nastiness,** *n.*

**-nasty,** a suffix indicating irregularity of cellular growth because of some pressure. [Gk *nastós* squeezed together + -Y[3]]

**nat., 1.** national. **2.** native. **3.** natural.

**natal**[1] /ˈneɪtl/, *adj.* **1.** of or pertaining to one's birth: *one's natal day.* **2.** presiding over or affecting one at birth: *natal influences.* [ME, from L *nātālis*]

**natal**[2] /ˈneɪtl/, *adj.* of or pertaining to the buttocks. [L *natis* buttock + -AL[1]]

**natal cleft** /– ˈklɛft/, *n.* a cleft between the buttocks.

**natality** /nəˈtæləti/, *n.* →**birthrate.**

**Natal red-grass** /nəˌtal ˈrɛd-gras/, *n.* a tufted perennial grass, *Rhynchelytrum repens,* native to southern Africa but common along roadsides in temperate Australia.

**natant** /ˈneɪtənt/, *adj.* **1.** swimming; floating. **2.** *Bot.* floating on water, as the leaf of an aquatic plant. [L *natans,* ppr.]

**natation** /neɪˈteɪʃən, nə-/, *n.* the act or art of swimming. [L *natātio*] – **natational,** *adj.*

**natatorial** /neɪtəˈtɔriəl/, *adj.* pertaining to, adapted for, or characterised by swimming: *natatorial birds.* Also, **natatory** /ˈneɪtətəri, -tri/. [LL *natātōrius* + -AL[1]]

**natatorium** /neɪtəˈtɔriəm/, *n., pl.* **-toriums, -toria** /-ˈtɔriə/. *U.S.* →**swimming pool.** [LL]

**nates** /ˈneɪtiz/, *n.pl.* the buttocks. [L, pl. of *natis*]

**nation** /ˈneɪʃən/, *n.* **1.** an aggregation of persons of the same ethnic family, speaking the same language or cognate languages. **2.** a body of people associated with a particular territory who are sufficiently conscious of their unity to seek or to possess a government peculiarly their own. [ME, from L *nātio* race, people, nation; orig., birth] – **nationhood,** *n.* – **nationless,** *adj.*

**national** /ˈnæʃnəl, ˈnæʃənəl/, *adj.* **1.** of, pertaining to, or maintained by a nation as an organised whole or independent political unit: *national affairs.* **2.** peculiar or common to the whole people of a country: *national customs.* **3.** devoted to one's own nation, its interests, etc.; patriotic. *–n.* **4.** a citizen or subject of a particular nation, entitled to its protection. – **nationally,** *adv.*

**national anthem** /– ˈænθəm/, *n.* a patriotic hymn played or sung at public gatherings, official ceremonies, etc.

**National Assembly** /næʃnəl əˈsɛmbli/, *n.* any of various national legislative bodies, esp. in French-speaking countries.

**national code** /næʃnəl ˈkoʊd/, *n.* →**Australian Rules.**

**national debt** /– ˈdɛt/, *n.* the financial indebtedness of a country in respect of money borrowed from individuals for national purposes, as opposed to the personal liabilities of its inhabitants.

**national flag** /– ˈflæg/, *n.* →**Australian national flag.**

**national income** /– ˈɪŋkʌm/, *n.* the total net value of commodities produced and services rendered by all the people of a nation during a specified period.

**national insurance** /– ɪnˈʃɔrəns/, *n.* a scheme of state insurance by which, for weekly contributions paid by both employee and his employer, the employee is insured against sickness, unemployment, retirement, etc.

**nationalise** /ˈnæʃnəlaɪz/, *v.t.,* **-lised, -lising. 1.** to bring under the control or ownership of a government as industries, land, etc. **2.** to make nationwide. **3.** →**naturalise** (def. 1). **4.** to make into a nation. Also, **nationalize.** – **nationalisation** /næʃnəlaɪˈzeɪʃən/, *n.* – **nationaliser,** *n.*

**nationalism** /ˈnæʃnəlɪzəm/, *n.* **1.** national spirit or aspirations. **2.** devotion to the interests of one's own nation. **3.** desire for national advancement or independence. **4.** the policy of asserting the interests of a nation, viewed as separate from the interests of other nations or the common interests of all nations.

**nationalist** /ˈnæʃnələst/, *n.* **1.** one inspired with nationalism. **2.** an advocate of national independence. *–adj.* **3.** Also, **nationalistic** /næʃnəˈlɪstɪk/. of or pertaining to nationalism or nationalists. – **nationalistically** /næʃnəˈlɪstɪkli/, *adv.*

**Nationalist China** /næʃnələst ˈtʃaɪnə/, *n.* a country consisting mainly of the island of Taiwan, off the south-eastern coast of the mainland of China. Official name: **Nationalist Republic of China.**

**nationality** /næʃəˈnæləti, næʃˈnæl-/, *n., pl.* **-ties. 1.** the quality of membership in a particular nation (original or acquired): *the nationality of an immigrant.* **2.** relationship of property, etc., to a particular nation, or to one or more of its members: *the nationality of a ship.* **3.** →**nationalism. 4.** existence as a distinct nation; national independence. **5.** nation or people: *the various nationalities of America.* **6.** national quality or character.

**national park** /næʃnəl ˈpak/, *n.* a flora and fauna reserve open to the general public.

**national service** /– ˈsɜvəs/, *n.* (in many countries) compulsory service in the armed forces for a period of varying duration.

**nation-state** /ˈneɪʃən-steɪt/, *n.* an independent state where the population is all of one nationality.

**nationwide** /ˈneɪʃənwaɪd/, *adj.* extending throughout the nation: *a nationwide campaign against cancer.*

**native** /ˈneɪtɪv/, *adj.* **1.** being the place or environment in which one was born or a thing came into being: *one's native land.* **2.** belonging to a person or thing by birth or nature; inborn; inherent; natural (oft. fol. by *to*). **3.** belonging by birth to a people regarded as natives, esp. outside the general body of white peoples: *native policemen in India.* **4.** of indigenous origin, growth, or production (oft. fol. by *to*): *native pottery.* **5.** of, pertaining to, or characteristic of natives: *native customs in Java.* **6.** under the rule of natives: *the native states of India.* **7.** occupied by natives: *the native quarter of Algiers.* **8.** belonging or pertaining to one by reason of one's birthplace or nationality: *one's native language.* **9.** born in a particular place or country: *native Frenchmen.* **10.** remaining in a natural state; unadorned; untouched by art: *native beauty.* **11.** forming the source or origin of a person or thing. **12.** originating naturally in a particular country or region, as animals or plants. **13.** found in nature rather than produced artificially, as a mineral substance. **14.** occurring in nature pure or uncombined, as metals, etc.: *native copper.* **15.** belonging to one as a possession by virtue of his birth: *native rights.* **16.** *Archaic.* closely related, as by birth. *–n.* **17.** one of the original inhabitants of a place or country, esp. as distinguished from strangers, foreigners, colonisers, etc.: *the natives of Chile.* **18.** one born in a particular place or country: *a native of Muswellbrook.* **19.** an animal or plant indigenous to a particular region. **20.** *Astrol.* one born under a particular planet. [L *nātīvus* native, innate, natural; replacing ME *natif,* from OF] – **natively,** *adv.* – **nativeness,** *n.*

**native apricot** /– 'eɪprikɒt/, *n.* →**native willow.**

**native bear** /– 'bɛə/, *n.* →**koala.**

**native-born** /'neɪtɪv-bɔn/, *adj.* born in a place or country indicated.

**native cat** /neɪtɪv 'kæt/, *n.* any of several cat-sized, predatory marsupials of the genus *Dasyurus,* having slender, white-spotted bodies and very pointed snouts; marsupial cat.

**native cherry** /– 'tʃɛri/, *n.* any of a number of unrelated Australian trees bearing fruit thought to resemble a cherry, as *Exocarpos cupressiformis.*

**native companion** /– kəm'pænjən/, *n.* →**brolga.**

**native dandelion** /– 'dændilaɪən/, *n.* →**blackfellow's yam.**

**native elder** /– 'ɛldə/, *n.* a shrub, *Sambucus gaudichaudiana,* family Caprifoliaceae, of temperate eastern Australia, having clusters of white flowers and small yellowish-white fruit. Also, **white elder.**

**native fuchsia** /– 'fjuʃə/, *n.* any of a number of Australian plants whose flowers have tubular corollas, esp. *Eremophila maculata* of inland areas, *Correa reflexa* of south-eastern coastal areas and *Epacris longiflora* of the Sydney district.

**native millet** /– 'mɪlət/, *n.* a native perennial grass, *Panicum decompositum,* found in many low-rainfall zones of Australia and reaching one metre in height; the seeds were once a staple of Aboriginal diet.

**native mouse** /– 'maʊs/, *n.* any of a number of small rodents of the genus *Pseudomys,* indigenous to Australia.

**native mulberry** /– 'mʌlbəri/, *n.* a small, soft-wooded coastal tree, *Pipturus argenteus,* with sweet fleshy white fruit; pigeonberry.

**native oak** /– 'oʊk/, *n.* →**casuarina.**

**native pheasant** /– 'fɛzənt/, *n.* →**superb lyrebird.**

**native poplar** /– 'pɒplə/, *n.* →**bell-fruit tree.**

**native rat** /– 'ræt/, *n.* any of various rodents indigenous to Australia.

**native rose** /– 'roʊz/, *n.* a shrub, *Boronia serrulata,* with rose-pink scented flowers found in sandstone areas near Sydney; Sydney rose; Port Jackson rose.

**native rosella** /– roʊ'zɛlə/, *n.* a tall shrub of moist eucalypt forests, *Hibiscus heterophyllus,* having lobed leaves and large white flowers, the young shoots and buds of which are eaten cooked or uncooked; native sorrel.

**native sorrel** /– 'sɒrəl/, *n.* →**native rosella.**

**native speaker** /– 'spikə/, *n.* one who speaks (a language) as his native tongue: *a native speaker of French.*

**native trout** /– 'traʊt/, *n.* →**galaxias.**

**native willow** /– 'wɪloʊ/, *n.* a slender, drooping tree, *Pittosporum phylliraeoides,* family Pittosporaceae, of mainland Australia, having bright orange capsules which split to expose sticky red seeds; berrigan; native apricot.

**nativism** /'neɪtəvɪzəm/, *n.* **1.** *U.S.* the policy of protecting the interests of native inhabitants against those of immigrants. **2.** *Philos.* the doctrine of innate ideas. – **nativist,** *n.* – **nativistic** /neɪtə'vɪstɪk/, *adj.*

**nativity** /nə'tɪvəti/, *n., pl.* **-ties,** *adj.* –*n.* **1.** birth. **2.** birth with reference to place or attendant circumstances: *of Irish nativity.* **3.** (*cap.*) the birth of Christ. **4.** (*cap.*) the church festival commemorating the birth of Christ; Christmas. **5.** (*cap.*) a representation of the birth of Christ, as in art. **6.** *Astrol.* a horoscope. –*adj.* **7.** (*cap.*) of or pertaining to the Nativity: *Nativity play, Nativity painting.* [ME *nativite,* from LL *nātīvitas*]

**Natl,** National.

**natrolite** /'nætrəlaɪt, 'neɪtrə-/, *n.* a zeolite mineral, a hydrous silicate of sodium and aluminium, $Na_2Al_2Si_3O_{10}\cdot 2H_2O$, occurring usu. in white or colourless, often acicular, crystals. [NATRO(N) + -LITE]

**natron** /'neɪtrən/, *n.* a mineral, hydrated sodium carbonate, $Na_2CO_3\cdot 10H_2O$. [F, from Sp., from Ar. *natrūn,* from Gk *nítron* natron. See NITRE]

**natter** /'nætə/, *v.i. Colloq.* **1.** to chatter; gossip. –*n.* **2.** a chat.

**natterjack** /'nætədʒæk/, *n.* a common European toad, *Bufo calamita.*

**natty** /'næti/, *adj.,* **-tier, -tiest.** neatly smart in dress or appearance; spruce; trim: *a natty white uniform.* [? akin to NEAT[1]] – **nattily,** *adv.* – **nattiness,** *n.*

**natural** /'nætʃərəl, 'nætʃrəl/, *adj.* **1.** existing in or formed by nature; not artificial: *a natural bridge.* **2.** based on the state of things in nature; constituted by nature: *the natural day.* **3.** of or pertaining to nature or the created universe: *a natural science.* **4.** occupied with the study of natural science. **5.** in a state of nature; uncultivated, as land. **6.** growing spontaneously, as vegetation. **7.** having a real or physical existence, as opposed to one that is spiritual, intellectual, fictitious, etc. **8.** of, pertaining to, or proper to the nature or essential constitution: *natural ability.* **9.** proper to the circumstances of the case. **10.** free from affectation or constraint: *a natural manner.* **11.** essentially pertaining; coming easily or spontaneously: *a manner natural to an aristocrat.* **12.** consonant with the nature or character of. **13.** in accordance with the nature of things: *it was natural that he should hit back.* **14.** based upon the innate moral feeling of mankind: *natural justice.* **15.** having or showing the nature, disposition, feelings, etc., befitting a person. **16.** in conformity with the ordinary course of nature; not unusual or exceptional. **17.** happening in the ordinary course of things, without the intervention of accident, violence, etc.: *a natural death.* **18.** by birth merely, and not legally recognised; illegitimate. **19.** based on what is learned from nature, rather than on revelation: *natural religion.* **20.** true to nature, or closely imitating nature. **21.** unenlightened or unregenerate: *the natural man.* **22.** being such by nature; born such: *a natural fool.* **23.** *Music.* **a.** neither sharp nor flat; without sharps or flats. **b.** changed in pitch by the sign ♮. **24.** *Maths.* of or pertaining to a sine, tangent, etc., which is expressed as the actual value, not the logarithim. –*n.* **25.** *Music.* (of horns and trumpets) having no mechanism and thus able to produce only the notes of the harmonic series. **26.** *Colloq.* a thing or a person that is by nature satisfactory or successful. **27.** *Music.* **a.** a white key on the pianoforte, etc. **b.** the sign ♮, placed before a note cancelling the effect of a previous sharp or flat. **c.** a note affected by a ♮, or a note thus represented. [ME, from L *nātūrālis* by birth, in accordance with nature] – **naturally,** *adv.* – **naturalness,** *n.*

**natural abundance** /– ə'bʌndəns/, *n.* the abundance of each isotope in an element as it is found in nature.

**natural childbirth** /–' tʃaɪldbɜθ/, *n.* childbirth without the use of anaesthetics or surgical intervention, usu. involving prenatal education of the mother, as with breathing exercises, psychological conditioning, etc.

**natural foot** /'– fʊt/, *n.* a surfer who rides with the left foot in front of the right.

**natural frequency** /– 'frikwənsi/, *n.* the frequency of free oscillation of a system.

**natural gas** /– 'gæs/, *n.* combustible gas formed naturally in the earth, as in regions yielding petroleum, and consisting typically of methane with certain amounts of hydrogen and other gases, used as a fuel, etc.

**natural history** /– 'hɪstri/, *n.* **1.** the science or study dealing with all objects in nature. **2.** the aggregate of knowledge connected with such objects.

**naturalise** /'nætʃrəlaɪz/, *v.,* **-lised, -lising.** –*v.t.* **1.** to invest (an alien) with the rights and privileges of a subject or citizen; confer the rights and privileges of citizenship upon. **2.** to introduce (animals or plants) into a region and cause to flourish as if native. **3.** to introduce or adopt (foreign practices, words, etc.) into a country or into general use: *to naturalise a French phrase.* **4.** to bring into conformity with nature. **5.** to regard or explain as natural rather than supernatural: *to naturalise miracles.* **6.** to adapt or accustom to a place or to new surroundings. –*v.i.* **7.** to become naturalised, or as if native. Also, **naturalize.** – **naturalisation** /nætʃrəlaɪ'zeɪʃən/, *n.*

**naturalism** /'nætʃrəlɪzəm/, *n.* **1.** (in literature) **a.** a theory of writing developed originally in France in the late 19th century and used esp. of the novel. It purports to apply scientific methods to the objective description in detail of human actions and character, presenting a determinist view of life. **b.** any writing which represents life, actions, environment, etc., in naturalistic detail. **2. a.** (in the arts) a method of presenting nature in an accurate and lifelike form. **b.** a style of painting characterised by a close fidelity to nature. **3.** action arising from or based on natural instincts and desires alone. **4.** *Philos.* **a.** the view of the world which takes account only of natural elements and forces, excluding the supernatural or spiritual. **b.** the belief that all phenomena are covered by laws of science and that all teleological explanations are therefore without value. **c.** positivism or materialism. **5.** *Theol.* **a.** the doctrine that mankind apprehends eternal truths only by observation and deduction and never from direct revelation. **b.** the doctrine that man may be saved by his perception of, and actions directed by, verities so revealed to him. **6.** adherence or attachment to what is natural.

**naturalist** /ˈnætʃrələst/, *n.* **1.** one who is versed in or devoted to natural history, esp. a zoologist or botanist. **2.** an adherent of naturalism.

**naturalistic** /nætʃrəˈlɪstɪk/, *adj.* **1.** imitating nature or usual natural surroundings. **2.** pertaining to naturalists or natural history. **3.** pertaining to naturalism, esp. in art and literature.

**natural law** /nætʃərəl ˈlɔ/, *n.* the expression of right reason or of religion, inhering in nature and man, and having ethically a binding force as a rule of civil conduct.

**natural logarithm** /– ˈlɒgərɪðəm/, *n.* a logarithm using the number 2.71828128... as a base; Napierian logarithm. *Symbol*: *e*

**natural number** /– ˈnʌmbə/, *n.* any of the numbers 1, 2, 3, etc.

**natural philosophy** /– fəˈlɒsəfi/, *n.* the branch of physical science which treats of those properties and phenomena of bodies which are unaccompanied by an essential change in the bodies themselves, including the sciences classed under physics.

**natural region** /– ˈridʒən/, *n.* an area of the earth's surface with general similarity of landscape and characterised by a degree of uniformity of physical characteristics such as structure, relief, climate, and vegetation.

**natural resources** /– rəˈzɔsəz/, *n. pl.* the wealth of a country consisting of land, forests, mines, water and energy resources.

**natural science** /– ˈsaɪəns/, *n.* science or knowledge dealing with objects in nature, as distinguished from mental or moral science, abstract mathematics, etc.

**natural selection** /– səˈlɛkʃən/, *n.* the elimination of the unfit and the survival of the fit in the struggle for existence, resulting in the adaptation of a species to a specific environment.

**natural sine (tangent, etc.),** *n.* the actual value, not the logarithm, of a sine (tangent, etc.).

**natural vegetation** /nætʃərəl vɛdʒəˈteɪʃən/, *n.* the indigenous flora of an area unaltered by man's activities.

**nature** /ˈneɪtʃə/, *n.* **1.** the particular combination of qualities belonging to a person or thing by birth or constitution; native or inherent character: *the nature of atomic energy.* **2.** the instincts or inherent tendencies directing conduct: *a man of good nature.* **3.** character, kind, or sort: *a book of the same nature.* **4.** a person of a particular character or disposition. **5.** the material world, esp. as surrounding man and existing independently of his activities. **6.** the universe, with all its phenomena. **7.** the sum total of the forces at work throughout the universe. **8.** reality, as distinguished from any effect of art: *true to nature.* **9.** the physical being. **10.** the vital powers: *food sufficient to sustain nature.* **11.** a primitive, wild condition; an uncultivated state. **12.** *Theol.* the moral state as unaffected by grace. **13. by nature,** as a result of inherent qualities. **14. of** or **in the nature of,** having the qualities of. [ME *natur,* from L *nātūra* birth, natural character, nature]

**nature lover** /ˈ– lʌvə/, *n.* one who enjoys exploring the natural environment, esp. when unspoiled by contact with human civilisation.

**nature reserve** /ˈ– rəzɜv/, *n.* **1.** a region set aside for the preservation of flora and fauna. **2.** a region set aside for the observation of flora and fauna, open only at restricted times to the general public.

**nature strip** /ˈ– strɪp/, *n.* **1.** →**verge**[1] (def. 4a). **2.** a narrow strip of land between two carriageways, where grass, shrubs, etc., are planted.

**nature study** /ˈ– stʌdi/, *n.* the study of physical nature, esp. in primary schools.

**nature trail** /ˈ– treɪl/, *n.* a rough path designed to allow people to walk through bush or other natural environments.

**naturism** /ˈneɪtʃərɪzəm/, *n.* →**nudism.** – **naturist,** *n., adj.*

**naught** /nɔt/, *n.* **1.** *Archaic or Poetic.* nothing. **2.** destruction, ruin, or complete failure: *to bring or come to naught.* **3.** *Chiefly U.S.* →**nought** (def. 1). **4. set at naught,** to regard or treat as of no importance. *–adj. Obs. or Archaic.* **5.** worthless; useless. **6.** lost; ruined. **7.** morally bad; wicked. *–adv.* **8.** *Obs. or Archaic.* in no respect or degree. Also, **nought.** [ME; OE *nauht, nāwiht,* from *nā* NO[1] + *wiht* thing. See NOUGHT, WIGHT, WHIT]

**naughty** /ˈnɔti/, *adj.,* **-tier, -tiest,** *n. –adj.* **1.** disobedient; mischievous (esp. in speaking to or about children): *a naughty child.* **2.** improper; obscene: *a naughty word.* **3.** *Obs.* wicked; evil. *–n.* **4.** *Colloq.* sexual intercourse: *a nightly naughty.* [ME, from NAUGHT (def. 7) + -Y[1]] – **naughtily,** *adv.* – **naughtiness,** *n.*

**naughty forty-eight** /ˌnɔti fɔti-ˈeɪt/, *n. Colloq.* →**dirty weekend.**

**naumachia** /nɔˈmeɪkiə/, *n., pl.* **-chiae** /-kiˌi/, **-chias.** **1.** a mock sea-fight, given as a spectacle among the ancient Romans. **2.** a place for presenting such spectacles. [L, from Gk] Also, **naumachy** /ˈnɔməki/.

**nauplius** /ˈnɔpliəs/, *n., pl.* **-plii** /-pliˌi/. (in many crustaceans) a larval form with three pairs of appendages and a single median eye, occurring (usu.) as the first stage of development after leaving the egg. [L: kind of shellfish]

**Nauru** /naˈru/, *n.* an island republic in the Pacific near the equator.

**nausea** /ˈnɔziə, ˈnɔsiə/, *n.* **1.** sickness at the stomach; a sensation of impending vomiting. **2.** extreme disgust. **3.** *Obs.* seasickness. [L, var. of *nausia,* from Gk]

**nauseate** /ˈnɔzieɪt, ˈnɔsi-/, *v.,* **ated, -ating.** *–v.t.* **1.** to affect with nausea; sicken. **2.** to feel extreme disgust at; loathe. *–v.i.* **3.** to become affected with nausea. [L *nauseātus,* pp., having been seasick] – **nauseation** /nɔziˈeɪʃən, nɔsi-/, *n.*

**nauseous** /ˈnɔziəs, ˈnɔsi-, ˈnɔʃəs/, *adj.* **1.** causing nausea, or sickening. **2.** disgusting; loathsome. [L *nauseōsus*] – **nauseously,** *adv.* – **nauseousness,** *n.*

**naut.,** nautical.

**nautch** /nɔtʃ/, *n.* an Indian exhibition of dancing by professional dancing girls (**nautch girls**). [Hind. *nāch,* from Prakrit *nachcha* dancing]

**nautical** /ˈnɔtɪkəl/, *adj.* of or pertaining to seamen, ships, or navigation: *nautical terms.* [L *nauticus* (from Gk *nautikós* pertaining to ships or sailors) + -AL[1]] – **nautically,** *adv.*

**nautical mile** /– ˈmaɪl/, *n.* a unit of measurement of length, used in marine and aeronautical navigation, equal to 1852 m, originally defined as one minute of latitude. Formerly, **international nautical mile.**

**nautilus** /ˈnɔtələs/, *n., pl.* **-luses, -li** /-laɪ/. **1.** any of the tetrabranchiate cephalopods that constitute the genus *Nautilus,* having a spiral, chambered shell with pearly septa; pearly nautilus. **2.** →**paper nautilus.** [L, from Gk *nautílos,* lit., sailor]

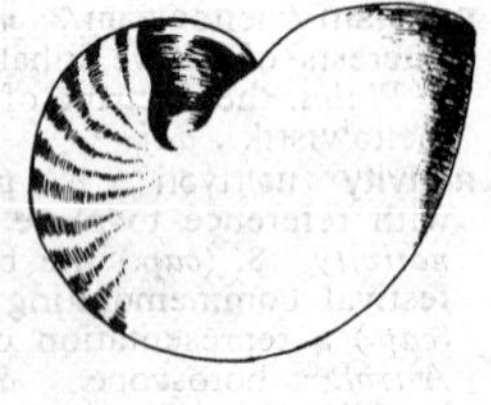
nautilus

**nav.,** **1.** naval. **2.** navigation. **3.** navy.

**navaid** /ˈnæveɪd/, *n.* a navigational device in a ship, aeroplane, etc. [NAV(IGATION) + AID]

**naval** /ˈneɪvəl/, *adj.* **1.** of or pertaining to ships, now only ships of war: *a naval battle.* **2.** belonging to, pertaining to, or connected with, a navy: *naval affairs.* **3.** possessing a navy: *the great naval powers.* [L *nāvālis* pertaining to a ship]

**naval college** /ˈ– kɒlɪdʒ/, *n.* a collegiate institution for training naval officers. Also, *U.S.,* **naval academy.**

**navarin** /ˈnævərɪn/, *n.* a French mutton stew with small onions, potatoes, and sometimes spring vegetables. [F]

**nave**[1] /neɪv/, *n.* the main body, or middle part, lengthwise, of a church, flanked by the aisles and extending typically from the entrance to the apse or chancel. [ML *nāvis* nave of a church, in L: ship]

**nave**[2] /neɪv/, *n.* **1.** the central part of a wheel; the hub. **2.** *Obs.* →**navel.** [ME; OE *nafu,* c. G *Nabe*]

**navel** /ˈneɪvəl/, *n.* **1.** a pit or depression in the middle of the surface of the belly; the umbilicus. **2.** the central point or middle of any thing or place. [ME; OE *nafela,* c. G *Nabel*] – **navel-like,** *adj.*

nave[1]

**navel orange** /–ˈɒrɪndʒ/, *n.* a kind of orange having at the apex a navel-like formation containing a small secondary fruit.

**navel pipe** /ˈ– paɪp/, *n.* →**spurling pipe.** Also, **naval pipe.**

**navelwort** /ˈneɪvəlwɜt/, *n.* a perennial, fleshy, saxifragaceous herb with peltate leaves and spikes of small yellow-green flowers, *Umbilicus rupestris,* occurring on rocks and walls in western Europe and Mediterranean regions.

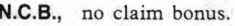

**navicert** /ˈnævəsɜt/, *n.* a certificate granted by a belligerent in wartime, specifying the character of a neutral ship's cargo, etc. [L *nāvi(s)* ship + CERT(IFICATE)]

**navicular** /nəˈvɪkjələ/, *adj.* **1.** (of certain bones, etc.) boat-shaped. *–n.* Also, **naviculare** /nəvɪkjəˈlari/. **2.** the bone at the radial end of the proximal row of the bones of the carpus. **3.** the bone in front of the talus, or anklebone, on the inner side of the foot. [LL *nāviculāris* relating to ships]

**navig.,** **1.** navigation. **2.** navigator.

**navigable** /ˈnævɪgəbəl/, *adj.* that may be navigated, as waters, or vessels or aircraft. – **navigability** /nævɪgəˈbɪləti/, **navigableness,** *n.* – **navigably,** *adv.*

**navigate** /ˈnævəgeɪt/, *v.,* **-gated, -gating.** *–v.t.* **1.** to traverse (the sea, a river, etc.) in a vessel, or (the air) in an aircraft. **2.** to direct or manage (a ship, aircraft, etc.) on its course. **3.** to pass over (the sea, etc.), as a ship does. *–v.i.* **4.** to direct or manage a ship, aircraft, etc., on its course. **5.** to travel by using a ship or boat, as over the water; sail. **6.** to pass over the water, as a ship does. [L *nāvigātus,* pp.]

**navigation** /nævəˈgeɪʃən/, *n.* **1.** the act or process of navigating. **2.** the art or science of directing the course of a ship or aircraft. **3.** an artificial waterway; a canal. – **navigational,** *adj.*

**navigator** /ˈnævəgeɪtə/, *n.* **1.** one who navigates. **2.** one who practises, or is skilled in, navigation of ships, aircraft, etc. **3.** one who conducts explorations by sea. **4.** *Brit.* a labourer employed building canals. [L]

**navvy** /ˈnævi/, *n., pl.* **-vies.** a labourer employed in making roads, railways, canals, etc. [short for NAVIGATOR (def. 4)]

**navy** /ˈneɪvi/, *n., pl.* **-vies. 1.** the whole body of warships and auxiliaries belonging to a country or ruler. **2.** such a body of warships together with their officers and men, equipment, yards, etc. **3.** Also, **navy blue.** a dark blue, as of a naval uniform. **4.** *Archaic.* a fleet of ships. [ME *navie,* from OF, from L *nāvis* ship]

**navy yard** /ˈ– jad/, *n. U.S.* →**dockyard.**

**nawab** /nəˈwɒb, nəˈwab/, *n.* **1.** a viceroy or deputy governor under the former Mogul empire in India. **2.** an honorary title conferred upon Muslims of distinction in India. Cf. **rajah. 3.** →**nabob.** [Hind. *nawwāb,* from Ar., pl. of *nā'ib* deputy, viceroy]

**nay** /neɪ/, *adv.* **1.** no (used in dissent, denial, or refusal). **2.** also; and not only so; but: *many good, nay, noble qualities.* *–n.* **3.** a denial or refusal. **4.** a negative vote or voter. [ME *nai, nei,* from Scand.; cf. Icel. *nei* no, from *ne* not + *ei* ever]

**naze** /neɪz/, *n.* →**headland** (def. 1).

**Nazi** /ˈnatsi/, *n., pl.* **-zis. 1.** a member of the National Socialist German Workers' Party, founded in 1919 in Germany and brought to power in 1933 under Adolf Hitler. **2.** (*oft. l.c.*) one who believes in or sympathises with policies characteristic of this party. *–adj.* **3.** of or pertaining to Nazis. [G, short for *Nazi(onalsozialist)* National Socialist]

**Nazism** /ˈnatsɪzəm/, *n.* the beliefs and practices of Nazis, esp. the policy of state control over the economy, racist nationalism and national expansion. Also, **Naziism.**

**n.b.,** (in cricket) no ball.

**Nb,** *Chem.* niobium.

**N.B.** /ɛn ˈbi/, nota bene. Also, **NB.**

**nbg** /ɛn bi ˈdʒi/, *adj. Colloq.* no bloody good.

**N.C.B.,** no claim bonus.

**N.C.O.** /ɛn si ˈoʊ/, *n.* a non-commissioned officer. Also, **NCO.**

**N.C.P.,** National Country Party.

**n.c.v.,** no commercial value.

**n.d. 1.** no date. **2.** not dated.

**Nd,** *Chem.* neodymium.

**Ne,** *Chem.* neon.

**NE, 1.** north-east. **2.** north-eastern. Also, **n.e.**

**nealie** /ˈnili/, *n.* **1.** a small, umbrella-like tree, *Acacia loderi,* of calcareous inland plains of south-eastern Australia. **2.** a small tree, *Acacia oswaldii,* of inland Australia. Also, **nelia.** [orig. uncert.]

**Neanderthal** /niˈændəθəl, -tal/, *adj.* **1.** of or pertaining to the Neanderthal man. **2.** primitive; archaic.

Neanderthal man: probable appearance reconstructed from a study of skeletal remains

**Neanderthal man** /– ˈmæn/, *n.* the species of primeval man widespread in Europe in the Palaeolithic period. [so called because earliest evidence was discovered at *Neanderthal,* a valley near Düsseldorf, Germany]

**Neanderthaloid** /niˌændəˈθælɔɪd, -ˈtalɔɪd/, *adj.* **1.** characteristic of the Neanderthal man. *–n.* **2.** a species of primeval man, having the characteristics of the Neanderthal man.

**neap** /nip/, *adj.* **1.** designating those tides, midway between spring tides, which attain the least height. *–n.* **2.** a neap tide. [ME *neep,* OE *nēp,* in *nēpflōd* neap flood]

**Neapolitan** /niəˈpɒlətən/, *adj.* **1.** of or pertaining to Naples, a city in southern Italy. **2.** (*l.c.*) (of ice cream) variously flavoured and coloured, frequently arranged in layers of strawberry, vanilla and chocolate. [ME, from L *Neāpolītānus*]

**neap tide** /ˈnip taɪd/, *n.* a tide which is neap.

**near** /nɪə/, *adv.* **1.** close: *near by.* **2.** nigh; at, within, or to a short distance: *to stand near.* **3.** close at hand in time: *New Year's Day is near.* **4.** close in relation; closely with respect to connection, similarity, etc. **5.** *Chiefly Colloq.* all but; almost: *a period of near thirty years.* **6.** *Naut.* close to the wind. **7. near at hand,** close by. *–adj.* **8.** being close by; not distant: *the near meadows.* **9.** less distant: *the near side.* **10.** short or direct: *the near road.* **11.** close in time: *the near future.* **12.** closely related or connected: *our nearest relation.* **13.** close to an original: *a near translation.* **14.** closely affecting one's interests or feelings: *a matter of near consequence to one.* **15.** intimate or familiar: *a near friend.* **16.** narrow: *a near escape.* **17.** parsimonious or niggardly: *a near man.* **18.** (in riding or driving) on the left (opposed to *off*): *the near wheel; the near hind leg.* *–prep.* (*strictly, the adverb with 'to' understood*). **19.** at, within, or to a short distance, or no great distance, from: *regions near the equator.* **20.** close upon in time: *near the beginning of the year.* **21.** close upon (a condition, etc.): *a task near completion.* **22.** close to in similarity, resemblance, etc.: *near beer.* **23.** close to (doing something): *this act came near spoiling his chances.* *–v.t.* **24.** to come or draw near (to); approach. [ME *nere,* OE *nēar,* compar. of *nēah* NIGH] – **nearness,** *n.*

**nearby** /ˈnɪəbaɪ/, *adj.;* /nɪəˈbaɪ/, *adv.* *–adj.* **1.** close at hand; not far off; adjacent; neighbouring: *a nearby village.* *–adv.* **2.** close at hand; not far off.

**Nearctic** /niˈaktɪk/, *adj.* (in biogeography) belonging to the northern division of the New World (temperate and arctic North America, with Greenland).

**Near East** /nɪər ˈist/, *n.* an indefinite geographical or regional term, usu. referring to the Balkan States, Egypt, and the countries of south-western Asia.

**near gale** /nɪə ˈgeɪl/, *n.* a wind of Beaufort scale force 7, i.e. one with average wind speed of 28-33 knots or 50 to 61 km/h.

**near infra-red** /ˌnɪər ɪnfrəˈrɛd/, *n.* **1.** the part of the electromagnetic spectrum with wavelengths just above those of visible red, about 800 millimicrons, to about 2.5 microns. *–adj.* **2.** of or pertaining to this part of the electromagnetic spectrum.

**nearly** /ˈnɪəli/, *adv.* **1.** all but; almost: *nearly dead with cold.* **2.** with close approximation. **3.** with close agreement or resemblance: *a case nearly approaching this one.* **4.** with close kinship, interest, or connection; intimately. **5.** with parsimony.

**near miss** /nɪə ˈmɪs/, *n.* **1.** a narrow escape, as from a crash. **2.** a bomb, shell, etc., which does not score a direct hit on a target, but lands close enough to damage it. **3.** *Colloq.* anything which just fails to achieve an object or aim.

**nearside** /ˈnɪəsaɪd/, *adj.* **1.** of or pertaining to the left-hand side of a motor vehicle in a country where traffic drives on the left. **2.** of or pertaining to the side of a road nearer to the footpath. *–n.* **3.** the left-hand side of a road, vehicle, or the like.

**near-sighted** /ˈnɪə-saɪtəd/, *adj.* seeing distinctly at a short distance only; myopic. – **nearsightedly,** *adv.* – **nearsightedness,** *n.*

**near thing** /nɪə ˈθɪŋ/, *n.* →**close call.**

**neat**[1] /nit/, *adj.* **1.** in a pleasingly orderly condition: *a neat room.* **2.** habitually orderly in appearance, etc. **3.** of a simple, pleasing appearance: *a neat cottage.* **4.** cleverly effective in character or execution: *a neat scheme.* **5.** clever, dexterous, or apt: *a neat characterisation.* **6.** unadulterated or undiluted, as liquors. **7.** net: *neat profits.* **8.** *Colloq.* fine, pleasing, excellent. [F *net* clean, from L *nitidus* bright, fine, neat] – **neatly,** *adv.* – **neatness,** *n.*

**neat**[2] /nit/, *n., pl.* **neat.** *Obs.* cattle of the genus *Bos.* [ME *neet,* OE *nēat,* c. Icel. *naut*]

**neaten** /ˈnitən/, *v.t.* to make (something) neat.

**neath** /niθ/, *prep. Poetic or Scot.* beneath. Also, **'neath.**

**neat's-foot oil** /nits-fʊt ˈɔɪl/, *n.* a pale yellow fixed oil made by boiling the feet and shinbones of cattle, used chiefly as a dressing for leather. [see NEAT[2]]

**neb** /nɛb/, *n.* **1.** a bill or beak, as of a bird. **2.** the nose, esp. of an animal. **3.** the tip or pointed end of anything. **4.** the nib of a pen. [ME *nebbe,* OE *nebb,* c. MD and MLG *nebbe*]

**N.E.B.,** New English Bible.

**nebbie** /ˈnɛbi/, *n. Colloq.* →**nembutal.**

**nebuchadnezzar** /nɛbjəkədˈnɛzə/, *n.* a large wine bottle having a capacity of 20 ordinary bottles and used mainly for display purposes. [from *Nebuchadnezzar,* king of Babylonia, 604?-561? B.C.]

**nebula** /ˈnɛbjələ/, *n., pl.* **-lae** /-li/, **-las. 1.** *Astron.* **a.** a cloudlike luminous patch in the sky, consisting of a galaxy of stars, or of the materials from which a galaxy is formed; an extra-galactic nebula. **b.** a small regular disc resembling a planet, consisting of a gaseous envelope enclosing a central star; a planetary nebula. **c.** an irregular, luminous, or dark patch in the sky consisting only of gases and dust; a diffuse nebula, an irregular nebula. **2.** *Pathol.* **a.** a faint opacity in the cornea. **b.** cloudiness in the urine. [L: mist, vapour, cloud] – **nebular,** *adj.*

**nebular hypothesis** /ˈ– haɪˌpɒθəsəs/, *n.* the theory that the solar system has been evolved from a mass of nebulous matter (a theory prominent in the 19th century following its precise formulation by Marquis de Pierre Simon Laplace, 1749-1827, French astronomer and mathematician.)

**nebulise** /ˈnɛbjəlaɪz/, *v.t.,* **-lised, -lising.** to reduce to fine spray; atomise. Also, **nebulize.** – **nebuliser,** *n.*

**nebulose** /ˈnɛbjəloʊs/, *adj.* **1.** nebulous; cloudlike. **2.** hazy or indistinct. **3.** having cloudlike markings.

**nebulosity** /nɛbjəˈlɒsəti/, *n., pl.* **-ties. 1.** nebulous or nebular matter. **2.** nebulous state.

**nebulous** /ˈnɛbjələs/, *adj.* **1.** hazy, vague, indistinct, or confused: *a nebulous recollection.* **2.** cloudy or cloudlike. **3.** of or characteristic of a nebula. [ME, from L *nebulōsus*] – **nebulously,** *adv.* – **nebulousness,** *n.*

**necessarian** /nɛsəˈsɛəriən/, *n., adj.* →**necessitarian.** – **necessarianism,** *n.*

**necessarily** /nɛsəˈsɛrəli/, *adv.* **1.** by or of necessity: *you need not necessarily go to the party.* **2.** as a necessary result.

**necessary** /ˈnɛsəsɛri, ˈnɛsəsri/, *adj., n., pl.* **-saries.** *–adj.* **1.** that cannot be dispensed with: *a necessary law.* **2.** happening or existing by necessity. **3.** acting or proceeding from compulsion or necessity; not free; involuntary: *a necessary agent.* **4.** *Logic.* **a.** (of propositions) denoting that the denial of that proposition involves a self-contradiction (opposed to *contingent*). **b.** (of inferences or arguments) denoting that it is impossible for the premises of an inference or argument to be true and its conclusion false. **5.** *Archaic.* rendering indispensable or useful services. *–n.* **6.** something necessary, indispensable, or requisite. **7.** (*pl.*) *Law.* food, clothing, etc., required by a dependant or incompetent and varying with his social or economic position or that of the person upon whom he is dependent. [ME, from L *necessārius* unavoidable, indispensable]

**necessitarian** /nəsɛsəˈtɛəriən/, *n.* **1.** one who maintains that the action of the will is a necessary effect of antecedent causes (opposed to *libertarian*). *–adj.* **2.** pertaining to necessitarians or necessitarianism.

**necessitarianism** /nəsɛsəˈtɛəriənɪzəm/, *n.* the doctrine of the determination of the will by antecedent causes, as opposed to that of the freedom of the will.

**necessitate** /nəˈsɛsəteɪt/, *v.t.,* **-tated, -tating. 1.** to make necessary: *the breakdown of the motor necessitated a halt.* **2.** to compel, oblige, or force: *the rise in prices necessitated greater thrift.* – **necessitation** /nəsɛsəˈteɪʃən/, *n.* – **necessitative,** *adj.*

**necessitous** /nəˈsɛsətəs/, *adj.* being in or involving necessity; needy; indigent. – **necessitously,** *adv.* – **necessitousness,** *n.*

**necessity** /nəˈsɛsəti/, *n., pl.* **-ties. 1.** something necessary or indispensable: *the necessities of life.* **2.** the fact of being necessary or indispensable; indispensableness. **3.** an imperative requirement or need for something: *necessity for a decision.* **4.** the state or fact of being necessary or inevitable. **5.** an unavoidable compulsion to do something. **6.** a state of being in difficulty or need; poverty. **7. agent of necessity,** *Law.* a person who, in urgent necessity but without authority, makes a contract for another that will bind that other. **8.** *Philos.* **a.** constraint viewed as a principle of universal causation, determining even the action of the will. **b.** the relation of the inevitable to the nature of its conditions; inevitable connection. [ME *necessite,* from L *necessitas* exigency]

**neck** /nɛk/, *n.* **1.** that part of an animal's body which is between the head and the trunk and connects these parts. **2. a.** a standard cut of meat, esp. lamb, from this area, used mainly for chops, stews, etc. **b. best neck,** the section between the upper cervical vertebrae. **3.** the part of a garment covering the neck or extending about it. **4.** the length of the neck of a horse or other animal as a measure in racing. **5.** the slender part of a bottle, retort, or any similar object. **6.** that part of a golf club head by which this joins the shaft. **7.** any narrow, connecting, or projecting part suggesting the neck of an animal. **8.** the longer slender part of a violin or the like, extending from the body to the head. **9.** *Anat.* a constricted part of a bone, organ, or the like. **10.** *Dentistry.* the junction between enamel of crown and cementum of the root of a tooth. **11.** *Print.* →**beard** (def. 5). **12.** (*usu. pl.*). skirtings of wool which are removed from the neck of a fleece in the process of wool rolling. **13.** *Archit.* the lowest part of the capital of a column, above the astragal at the head of the shaft. **14.** a narrow strip of land, as an isthmus or a cape. **15.** →**strait** (def. 1). **16. get it in the neck,** to be reprimanded or punished severely. **17. go under someone's neck,** to act without regard for someone's authority or responsibility. **18. neck and crop,** entirely; completely. **19. neck and neck,** just even. **20. neck of the woods,** a specific area, particular place: *we don't often see you in this neck of the woods.* **21. neck or nothing,** at every risk; desperately. **22. pull one's neck in,** to withdraw; to mind one's own business. **23. stick one's neck out,** to act, express an opinion, etc., so as to expose oneself to criticism, hostility, danger, etc. **24. win by a neck,** *Horseracing, etc.* to be first by a head and neck; finish closely. *–v.i.* **25.** *Colloq.* to play amorously. *–v.t.* **26.** to strangle or behead. [ME *nekke,* OE *hnecca,* c. D *nek;* akin to G *Nacken* nape of the neck]

**neckband** /ˈnɛkbænd/, *n.* **1.** a band of cloth at the neck of a garment. **2.** a band worn round the neck.

**neckcloth** /ˈnɛkklɒθ/, *n. Archaic.* →**cravat.**

**neckerchief** /ˈnɛkətʃif/, *n.* a cloth worn round the neck by women or men. [NECK + KERCHIEF]

**neckful** /ˈnɛkfʊl/, *n. Colloq.* an extreme amount: *I've had a* *neckful of my mother-in-law.*

**necking** /ˈnɛkɪŋ/, *n.* **1.** *Archit.* **a.** a moulding or group of mouldings between the projecting part of a capital of a column and the shaft. **b.** →**gorgerin.** **2.** *Colloq.* the act of playing amorously.

**necklace** /ˈnɛkləs/, *n.* an ornament of precious stones, beads, or the like, worn esp. by women round the neck. Also, **necklet** /ˈnɛklət/. [NECK + LACE string]

**necklace fern** /ˈ– fɜn/, *n.* a terrestrial fern, *Asplenium flabellifolium,* found on rocks in forest in Australia and New Zealand.

**neckline** /ˈnɛklaɪn/, *n.* the shape of the edge of a garment at or near the neck.

**neckpiece** /ˈnɛkpis/, *n.* a piece of material, fur, etc., covering, bordering, or worn round the neck.

**neck roll** /ˈnɛk roʊl/, *n.* →**forward roll.**

**necktie** /ˈnɛktaɪ/, *n.* **1.** a band of woven or knitted material placed round the neck and tied in front. **2.** *Chiefly U.S.* →**tie** (def. 21). **3.** *U.S. Colloq.* a hangman's rope.

**neck-to-knees** /nɛk-tə-ˈniz/, *n.* an old-fashioned swimming costume, covering the body from the neck to the knees.

**neckwear** /ˈnɛkwɛə/, *n.* articles of dress worn round or at the neck.

**necr-,** a word element meaning 'dead', 'corpse', 'death'. Also, before consonants, **necro-**. [Gk *nekr-, nekro-,* combining forms of *nekrós* person, corpse]

**necrobacillus** /nɛkroʊbəˈsɪləs/, *n.* any disease of cattle, horses, sheep, and pigs marked by necrotic areas in which a bacillus, *Actinomyces necrophorus,* is found.

**necrolatry** /nɛˈkrɒlətri/, *n.* worship of the dead.

**necrology** /nɛˈkrɒlədʒi/, *n., pl.* **-gies.** **1.** an obituary notice. **2.** a list of persons who have died within a certain time. [ML *necrologium,* from Gk (see NECRO-, -LOGY)] – **necrological** /nɛkrəˈlɒdʒɪkəl/, *adj.* – **necrologically** /nɛkrəˈlɒdʒɪkli/, *adv.* – **necrologist,** *n.*

**necromancy** /ˈnɛkrəˌmænsi/, *n.* **1.** magic in general; enchantment; conjuration. **2.** the pretended art of divination through communication with the dead; the black art. [L *necromantīa,* from Gk *necromanteía;* replacing ME *nigromancie,* from ML *nigromantīa,* alteration of L *necromantīa* by association with L *niger* black. Cf. BLACK ART] – **necromancer,** *n.* – **necromantic** /nɛkrəˈmæntɪk/, *adj.*

**necromania** /nɛkrəˈmeɪniə/, *n.* →**necrophilia.**

**necrophilia** /nɛkrəˈfɪliə/, *n.* morbid attraction to corpses. Also, **necrophilism** /nəˈkrɒfəlɪzəm/. – **necrophiliac,** *n.* – **necrophilic,** *adj.*

**necrophobia** /nɛkrəˈfoʊbiə/, *n.* **1.** morbid fear of death. **2.** a morbid aversion to, or fear of, dead bodies.

**necropolis** /nəˈkrɒpələs/, *n., pl.* **-lises.** **1.** a cemetery, often of large size. **2.** an old or prehistoric burial ground, as of an ancient people. [NL, from Gk *nekrópolis,* lit., city of the dead]

**necropsy** /ˈnɛkrɒpsi/, *n., pl.* **-sies.** the examination of a body after death; an autopsy. Also, **necroscopy** /nəˈkrɒskəpi/. [NECR- + Gk *ópsis* sight + -Y[3]]

**necrose** /nəˈkroʊs, ˈnɛkroʊs/, *v.t., v.i.,* **-crosed, -crosing.** to affect or be affected with necrosis.

**necrosis** /nəˈkroʊsəs/, *n.* **1.** *Pathol.* death of a circumscribed piece of tissue or of an organ. **2.** *Bot.* a diseased condition in plants resulting from the death of the tissue. [NL, from Gk *nékrōsis* a killing] – **necrotic** /nəˈkrɒtɪk/, *adj.*

**necrotic enteritis** /nəˌkrɒtɪk ɛntəˈraɪtəs/, *n.* a disease of pigs characterised by extensive ulceration of the intestine.

**necrotomy** /nəˈkrɒtəmi/, *n., pl.* **-mies.** **1.** the excision of necrosed bone. **2.** dissection of dead bodies.

**nectar** /ˈnɛktə/, *n.* **1.** *Bot.* the saccharine secretion of a plant which attracts the insects or birds that pollinate the flower, collected by bees in whose body it is elaborated into honey. **2.** the drink, or less properly, the food, of the gods of classical mythology. **3.** any delicious drink. [L, from Gk *néktar*]

**nectareous** /nɛkˈtɛəriəs/, *adj.* **1.** of the nature of or resembling nectar. **2.** delicious; sweet. Also, **nectarean, nectarous** /ˈnɛktərəs/. [L *nectareus,* from Gk *nektáreos*]

**nectarine** /ˈnɛktərən, nɛktəˈrin/, *n.* a form of the common peach, having a skin destitute of down. [n. use of *nectarine,* adj., from NECTAR + -INE[1]]

**nectary** /ˈnɛktəri/, *n., pl.* **-ries.** **1.** *Bot.* an organ or part, usu. of a flower, that secretes nectar. **2.** *Entomol.* one of a pair of small abdominal tubes from which aphids secrete honeydew. – **nectarial** /nɛkˈtɛəriəl/, *adj.*

**neddy** /ˈnɛdi/, *n., pl.* **-dies.** *Colloq.* a horse.

**nee** /neɪ/, *adj.* born (placed after the name of a married woman to introduce her maiden name): *Mrs Smith nee Brown.* Also, **née** /neɪ/. [F, fem. of *né,* pp. of *naître* to be born, from L *nascī*]

**need** /nid/, *n.* **1.** a case or instance in which some necessity or want exists; a requirement: *to meet the needs of the occasion.* **2.** urgent want, as of something requisite: *he has no need of your kindness.* **3.** necessity arising from the circumstances of a case: *there is no need to worry.* **4.** a situation or time of difficulty; exigency: *a friend in need.* **5.** a condition marked by the lack of something requisite: *the need for leadership.* **6.** destitution; extreme poverty. *–v.t.* **7.** to have need of; require: *to need money.* **8. need like a hole in the head,** *Colloq.* to be severely inconvenienced or distressed by. *–v.i.* **9.** to be necessary: *there needs no apology.* **10.** to be under a necessity (fol. by infinitive, in certain cases without *to;* in the 3rd pers. sing. the form is *need,* not *needs*): *he need not go.* **11.** to be in need or want. [ME *nede,* d. OE *nēd;* replacing ME *nud(e),* OE *nȳd, nīed;* akin to G *Not*] – **needer,** *n.*

**needful** /ˈnidfəl/, *adj.* **1.** necessary: *needful supplies.* **2.** *Rare.* needy. – **needfully,** *adv.* – **needfulness,** *n.*

**neediness** /ˈnidinəs/, *n.* needy state; indigence.

**needle** /ˈnidl/, *n., v.,* **-dled, -dling.** *–n.* **1.** a small, slender, pointed instrument, now usu. of polished steel, with an eye or hole for thread, used in sewing. **2.** a slender, rodlike implement for use in knitting, or one hooked at the end for use in crocheting, etc. **3.** *Med.* **a.** a slender, pointed, steel instrument used in sewing or piercing tissues. **b.** hypodermic needle. **4.** any of various objects resembling or suggesting a needle. **5.** a small, slender, pointed instrument, usu. of polished steel or some other material, used to transmit vibratory motions as from a gramophone record. **6.** →**magnetic needle.** **7.** a pointed instrument used in engraving, etc. **8.** *Bot.* a needle-shaped leaf, as of a conifer: *a pine needle.* **9.** *Zool.* a slender sharp spicule. **10.** *Chem., Mineral.* a needle-like crystal. **11.** a sharp-pointed mass or pinnacle of rock. **12.** an obelisk, or tapering, four-sided shaft of stone. **13.** Also, **needle beam.** *Bldg Trades.* a beam of steel or wood passed through the wall of a house and supported at each end on shores. **14.** *Colloq.* **a.** tension. **b.** aggression; unpleasantness. *–adj. Colloq.* **15.** involving unpleasantness or aggression: *a needle game.* *–v.t.* **16.** to sew or pierce with or as with a needle. **17.** to prod or goad. **18.** to tease or heckle. *–v.i.* **19.** to form needles in crystallisation. **20.** to work with a needle. [ME *nēdle,* d. OE *nēdl;* replacing OE *nǣdl,* c. G *Nadel*] – **needle-like,** *adj.*

**needle burr** /ˈ– bɜ/, *n.* an annual plant, *Amaranthus spinosus,* with prominent spinescent bracts and bracteoles.

**needlefish** /ˈnidlfɪʃ/, *n., pl.* **-fishes,** (*esp. collectively*) **-fish.** **1.** any fish of the family Belonidae, with a long sharp beak and needle-like teeth, found in all warm seas and in some coastal fresh waters. **2.** →**pipefish.**

**needleful** /ˈnidlfʊl/, *n., pl.* **-fuls.** a suitable length of thread for using at one time with a needle.

**needle point** /ˈnidl pɔɪnt/, *n.* embroidery on canvas worked to cover the area completely with even stitches to resemble tapestry.

**needle-point** /ˈnidl-pɔɪnt/, *adj.* denoting a kind of lace (**needle-point lace**) in which a needle works out the design upon parchment or paper.

**needless** /ˈnidləs/, *adj.* not needed or wanted; unnecessary: *a needless waste of food.* – **needlessly,** *adv.* – **needlessness,** *n.*

**needle valve** /ˈnidl vælv/, *n.* a valve with a needle-like part, a fine adjustment, or a small opening, esp. a valve in which the opening is controlled by a needle-like or conical point which fits into a conical seat.

**needlewoman** /ˈnidlwʊmən/, *n., pl.* **-women.** a woman who does needlework.

**needlewood** /ˈnidlwʊd/, *n.* any species of *Hakea* with cylindrical, pungent, pointed leaves, esp. *H. leucoptera,* a small tree of inland dry sandy ridges. Also, **needlebush.**

**needlework** /ˈnidlwɜk/, *n.* the process or the product of working with a needle as in sewing or embroidery.

**needn't** /ˈnidnt/, *v.* contraction of *need not.*

**needs** /nidz/, *adv.* of necessity; necessarily (usu. with *must*). [ME *needes,* OE *nēdes,* orig. gen. of *nēd* NEED]

**needy** /ˈnidi/, *adj.,* **-dier, -diest.** in, or characterised by, need or want; very poor: *a needy family.*

**neenish tart** /ninɪʃ ˈtat/, *n.* a small tart, sometimes made with almond flavoured pastry, with a mock cream filling, and a two colour topping.

**neep** /nip/, *n. Scot.* a turnip. [ME *nepe,* d. OE *nēp;* r. OE *nǣp,* from L *nāpus*]

**ne'er** /nɛə/, *adv. Chiefly Poetic.* contraction of *never.*

**ne'er-do-well** /ˈnɛə-du-wɛl/, *n.* **1.** a worthless person. *–adj.* **2.** worthless; good-for-nothing.

**nefarious** /nəˈfɛəriəs/, *adj.* extremely wicked; iniquitous: *nefarious practices.* [L *nefārius* impious] – **nefariously,** *adv.* – **nefariousness,** *n.*

**neg.,** **1.** negative. **2.** negatively.

**negate** /nəˈgeɪt/, *v.t.,* **-gated, -gating.** to deny; nullify. [L *negātus,* pp.]

**negation** /nəˈgeɪʃən/, *n.* **1.** the act of denying. **2.** a denial. **3.** a negative thing; a nonentity. **4.** the absence or opposite of what is actual, positive, or affirmative; denial as opposed to assertion. **5.** a statement, idea, etc., consisting in the absence of something positive.

**negative** /ˈnɛgətɪv/, *adj., n., v.,* **-tived, -tiving.** *–adj.* **1.** expressing or containing negation or denial: *a negative statement.* **2.** expressing refusal to do something. **3.** refusing consent, as to a proposal. **4.** prohibitory, as an order or command. **5.** characterised by the absence of distinguishing or marked qualities or features; lacking positive attributes: *a negative character.* **6.** *Maths, Physics.* **a.** involving or denoting subtraction; minus. **b.** measured or proceeding in the opposite direction to that which is considered as positive. **7.** *Bacteriol.* failing to show a positive result in a test for a specific disease caused by either bacteria or viruses. **8.** *Photog.* denoting an image in which the gradations of light and shade are represented in reverse. **9.** *Physiol.* responding in a direction away from the stimulus. **10.** *Elect.* denoting or pertaining to the kind of electricity developed on resin, amber, etc., when rubbed with flannel, or that present at the pole from which electrons leave an electric generator or battery, having an excess of electrons. **11.** denoting or pertaining to the south-seeking pole of a magnet. **12.** *Chem.* (of an element or radical) tending to gain electrons and become negatively charged. **13.** *Logic.* denoting a proposition or judgment that denies a relation between its terms, or denies that the predicate applies to the subject. *–n.* **14.** a negative statement, answer, word, gesture, etc. **15.** a refusal of assent. **16.** that side of a question which denies what the opposite side affirms. **17.** the negative form of statement (opposed to *affirmative*). **18.** *Maths.* a negative quantity or symbol. **19.** *Photog.* a negative image, as on a film or plate, used chiefly for printing positive pictures. **20.** *Archaic.* a negative quality or characteristic. **21.** *Obs.* →**veto.** **22.** *Elect.* the negative plate or element in a voltaic cell. *–v.t.* **23.** to deny; contradict. **24.** to disprove. **25.** to refuse assent or consent to; pronounce against; veto. **26.** to neutralise or counteract. [ME, from L *negātīvus* that denies] – **negatively,** *adv.* – **negativeness,** – **negativity,** *n.*

**negative catalyst** /– ˈkætələst/, *n.* →**inhibitor** (def. 1).

**negative feedback** /– ˈfidbæk/, *n.* See **feedback** (def. 3).

**negative geotropism** /– dʒiˈɒtrəpɪzəm/, *n.* geotropism orientated against gravity as a plant which grows upwards regardless of its spatial orientation. See **positive geotropism.**

**negative ion** /–ˈaɪən/, *n.* →**anion.**

**negative resistance** /– rəˈzɪstəns/, *n.* the property of certain devices in which an increase in the voltage applied causes a decrease in the current passing through them.

**negativism** /ˈnɛgətəvɪzəm/, *n.* **1.** negativistic behaviour. **2.** any system of philosophy in which denial is the prominent feature of its conclusions, as agnosticism, scepticism, etc. – **negativist,** *n.*

**negativistic** /nɛgətəˈvɪstɪk/, *adj.* marked by resistance to a stimulus; reacting in the opposite way to any suggestion.

**negatory** /nəˈgeɪtəri/, *adj.* denying; negative.

**negatron** /ˈnɛgətrɒn/, *n. Obs.* →**electron.**

**neglect** /nəˈglɛkt/, *v.t.* **1.** to pay no attention to; disregard: *a neglected genius.* **2.** to be remiss in care for or treatment of: *to neglect one's family.* **3.** to omit (doing something), through indifference or carelessness. **4.** to fail to carry out or perform (orders, duties, etc.). **5.** to fail to take or use: *to neglect no precaution.* *–n.* **6.** the act or fact of neglecting; disregard. **7.** the fact or state of being neglected; negligence. [L *neglectus,* pp., unheeded] – **neglecter,** *n.*

**neglectful** /nəˈglɛktfəl/, *adj.* characterised by neglect; disregardful; careless; negligent (oft. fol. by *of*). – **neglectfully,** *adv.* – **neglectfulness,** *n.*

**negligee** /ˈnɛgləʒeɪ/, *n.* **1.** a woman's dressing-gown, esp. a very flimsy one, of nylon, or the like. **2.** easy, informal attire. Also, **négligé.** [F *négligé,* orig. pp. of *négliger* neglect, from L *negligere*]

**negligence** /ˈnɛglədʒəns/, *n.* **1.** the state or fact of being negligent; neglect. **2.** an instance of being negligent; a defect due to carelessness. **3.** *Law.* the failure to exercise that degree of care which, in the circumstances, the law requires for the protection of those interests of other persons which may be injuriously affected by the want of such care.

**negligent** /ˈnɛglədʒənt/, *adj.* guilty of or characterised by neglect, as of duty: *negligent officials.* [ME, from L *negligens,* ppr., neglecting] – **negligently,** *adv.*

**negligible** /ˈnɛglədʒəbəl/, *adj.* that may be neglected or disregarded; very little. – **negligibility** /nɛglədʒəˈbɪləti/, **negligibleness,** *n.* – **negligibly,** *adv.*

**negotiable** /nəˈgoʊʃəbəl/, *adj.* **1.** capable of being negotiated. **2.** (of bills, etc.) transferable by delivery, with or without endorsement, according to the circumstances, the title passing to the transferee. – **negotiability** /nəgoʊʃəˈbɪləti/, *n.*

**negotiant** /nəˈgoʊʃiənt/, *n.* one who negotiates.

**negotiate** /nəˈgoʊʃieɪt/, *v.,* **-ated, -ating.** *–v.i.* **1.** to treat with another or others, as in the preparation of a treaty, or in preliminaries to a business deal. *–v.t.* **2.** to arrange for or bring about by discussion and settlement of terms: *to negotiate a loan.* **3.** to conduct (an affair, etc.). **4.** to clear or pass (an obstacle, etc.). **5.** to transfer (a bill of exchange, etc.) by assignment, endorsement, or delivery. **6.** to dispose of by sale or transfer: *to negotiate securities.* [L *negōtiātus,* pp.] – **negotiator,** *n.*

**negotiation** /nəgoʊʃiˈeɪʃən, -goʊsi-/, *n.* mutual discussion and arrangement of the terms of a transaction or agreement: *the negotiation of a treaty.*

**negritude** /ˈnigrətjud, ˈnɛg-/, *n.* **1.** the fact of being Negro. **2.** the character or spirit of the Negro, in politics, literature, art, etc. Also, **nigritude.** [F *négritude,* from L *nigritūdo* blackness]

**Negro** /ˈnigroʊ/, *n., pl.* **-groes,** *adj.* *–n.* **1.** a member of the Negro race. **2.** a person having some Negro ancestry. *–adj.* **3.** of, denoting, or pertaining to the so-called black race of Africa and its descendants elsewhere, characterised by a brown-black complexion, broad and flat nose, projecting jaws, everted lips, and crisp or woolly hair. Also, **negro.** [Sp. and Pg.: a black person, Negro, from L *niger* black] – **Negress** /ˈnigrəs/, *n. fem.*

**negroid** /ˈnigrɔɪd/, *adj.* **1.** resembling, or akin to, the Negro race and presumably allied to it in origin. *–n.* **2.** a person of a negroid race.

**Negrophil** /ˈnigroʊfɪl/, *adj.* **1.** friendly to or liking Negroes. *–n.* **2.** one who is friendly to and likes Negroes. Also, **Negrophile** /ˈnigroʊfaɪl/. – **Negrophilism** /niˈgrɒfəlɪzəm/, *n.*

**Negrophobe** /ˈnigroʊfoʊb/, *n.* one who fears, or has strong antipathy to, Negroes.

**Negrophobia** /nigroʊˈfoʊbiə/, *n.* fear of, or strong antipathy to, Negroes.

**negus**[1] /ˈnigəs/, *n.* **1.** a royal title in Ethiopia, also Abyssinia, a kingdom in East Africa. **2.** (*cap.*) the emperor of Ethiopia. [Amharic, a Semitic language: king]

**negus**[2] /ˈnigəs/, *n.* a beverage made of wine and hot water, with sugar, nutmeg, and lemon. [named after Colonel Francis *Negus,* d. 1732, its reputed inventor]

**Neh.,** *Bible.* Nehemiah.

**neigh** /neɪ/, *n.* **1.** the sound a horse makes; a whinny. *–v.i.* **2.** to make such a sound; to whinny. [ME *neyghe,* OE *hnǣgan,* c. MHG *nēgen.* See NAG², *n.*]

**neighbour** /ˈneɪbə/, *n.* **1.** one who lives near another. **2.** a person or thing that is near another. **3.** a fellow being subject to the obligations of humanity. *–adj.* **4.** *U.S.* living or situated near to another. *–v.t.* **5.** to place or bring near. **6.** to live or be situated near to; adjoin; border on. *–v.i.* **7.** to associate on the terms of neighbours; be neighbourly or friendly (fol. by *with*). **8.** to live or be situated nearby. Also, *U.S.,* **neighbor.** [ME *neighebour,* OE *nēahgebūr,* from *nēah* nigh + *gebūr* dweller, countryman, c. G *Nachbar*]

**neighbourhood** /ˈneɪbəhʊd/, *n.* **1.** the region near or about some place or thing; the vicinity. **2.** a district or locality, often with reference to its character or inhabitants: *a fashionable neighbourhood.* **3.** a number of persons living near one another or in a particular locality: *the whole neighbourhood was there.* **4.** *Town Planning.* the number of dwellings which will require and support communal facilities such as shops, a school, etc. **5.** *Archaic.* neighbourly feeling or conduct. **6.** nearness; proximity. **7. in the neighbourhood of,** nearly; about.

**neighbouring** /ˈneɪbərɪŋ/, *adj.* living or situated near.

**neighbourly** /ˈneɪbəli/, *adj.* befitting or acting as befits a neighbour; friendly. – **neighbourliness,** *n.*

**neinei** /ˈneɪneɪ/, *n. N.Z.* a shrub with long, tapering leaves, *Dracophyllum latifolium.* [Maori]

**neither** /ˈnaɪðə, ˈniðə/, *adj.* **1.** not either; not the one or the other: *neither statement is true.* *–pron.* **2.** not either; not the one or the other: *neither of the statements is true.* *–conj.* **3.** not either (a disjunctive connective preceding a series of two or more alternative words, etc., connected by the correlative *nor*): *neither you nor I nor anybody else knows the answer.* **4.** nor yet: *Ye shall not eat of it, neither shall ye touch it.* [ME *neither* (from *ne* not + EITHER); replacing ME *nauther,* OE *nāwther,* contracted var. of *nāhwæther,* from *nā* not + *hwæther* either, WHETHER]

**nekton** /ˈnɛktɒn/, *n.* the aggregate of actively swimming organisms at the surface of the sea. [G, from Gk (neut.): swimming] – **nektonic** /nɛkˈtɒnɪk/, *adj.*

**nelia** /ˈniliə/, *n.* →**nealie.**

**Nellie Bly** /nɛli ˈblaɪ/, *n. Colloq.* a pie¹. [rhyming slang]

**nelly** /ˈnɛli/, *n. Colloq.* **1.** cheap wine, esp. red wine. **2.** *in the phrase* **not on your nelly!,** absolutely not! [from *Nelly,* a girl's name]

**nelson** /ˈnɛlsən/, *n.* See **full nelson** and **half-nelson.**

**nelumbo** /nəˈlʌmboʊ/, *n., pl.* **-bos.** →**lotus** (def. 3). [NL, from Singhalese *nelumbu*]

**nemat-,** a word element referring to threadlike things, esp. to *nematodes.* Also, before consonants, **nemato-.** [Gk, combining form of *nêma* thread]

**nemathelminth** /nɛməˈθɛlmɪnθ/, *n.* any of the Nemathelminthes, a phylum of worms (now usu. broken up into several phyla), including the nematodes, etc., characterised by an elongated, unsegmented cylindrical body. [Gk *nêma* thread + *hélmins* worm]

**nematic** /nəˈmætɪk/, *adj.* of or pertaining to one of the forms of liquid crystals.

**nematocyst** /ˈnɛmətəsɪst/, *n.* an organ of offence and defence peculiar to coelenterates, consisting of a minute capsule containing a thread capable of being ejected and of causing a sting.

**nematode** /ˈnɛmətoʊd/, *n.* any of the Nematoda, the roundworms, a group variously considered a phylum or class. They are elongated smooth worms of cylindroid shape, parasitic or free-living, as ascarids, trichinae, vinegar eels, etc.

**nembutal** /ˈnɛmbjətæl/, *n.* (*also cap.*) a form of sleeping pill; pentobarbitone. Also, **nebbie.** [Trademark]

**nem. con.** /nɛm ˈkɒn/, *adv.* no-one contradicting; unanimously. [L *nēmine contrādīcente*]

**nem. diss.** /nɛm ˈdɪs/, *adv.* no-one dissenting; unanimously. [L *nēmine dissentiente*]

**nemertean** /nəˈmɜtiən/, *adj.* **1.** of or pertaining to the Nemertinea, a group of unsegmented, chiefly marine worms, considered either a class of Platyhelminthes or an independent phylum, having soft flattened, often brightly coloured bodies, and characterised by the long proboscis that can be extruded from the anterior end. *–n.* **2.** a nemertean worm; ribbon worm. Also, **nemertine, nemertinean** /nɛməˈtɪniən/. [NL *Nemertea,* pl. (from Gk *Nēmertēs* name of a nereid) + -AN]

**nemesia** /nəˈmisiə, -ˈmiʃə/, *n.* any plant of the genus *Nemesia,* cultivated for its flowers in a variety of colours. [NL, from Gk]

**nemesis** /ˈnɛməsəs/, *n., pl.* **-ses** /-siz/. an agent of retribution or punishment. [named after *Nemesis,* who, in classical mythology, was the goddess of retribution or vengeance; L, from Gk]

**neo-,** a word element meaning 'new', 'recent', used in combination, as in *Neo-Darwinism* (a new or modified form of Darwinism), *Neo-Gothic* (Gothic after a new or modern style), *Neo-Hebraic* (pertaining to Hebrew of the modern period). [Gk, combining form of *néos*]

**neoarsphenamine** /nioʊasˈfɛnəmin/, *n.* an orange medicinal powder, $H_2NC_6H_3(OH)As_2C_6H_3(OH)NHCH_2OSONa$, used chiefly in the treatment of syphilis and yaws, and prepared from, but less toxic than, salvarsan; neosalvarsan.

**Neocene** /ˈniəsin/, *adj.* **1.** of or pertaining to the later of two epochs into which the Tertiary period was formerly divided, comprising the Miocene and Pliocene. Also, **Neogene.** *–n.* **2.** (formerly) a division of the Tertiary period.

**neoclassical** /nioʊˈklæsɪkəl/, *adj.* belonging or pertaining to a revival of classical style, as in art. Also, **neoclassic.**

**neoclassicism** /nioʊˈklæsəsɪzəm/, *n.* a late 18th- and early 19th-century revivalist art and architectural style, deriving directly from classical models.

**neo-colonialism** /ˌnioʊ-kəˈloʊniəlɪzəm/, *n.* the control, esp. political, by a powerful nation of a smaller one which is technically independent.

**neocortex** /nioʊˈkɔtɛks/, *n.* the part of the cerebral cortex which is phylogenetically the most recent in development, including all of the cortex except the olfactory portions, hippocampal and piriform areas.

**Neo-Darwinism** /nioʊ-ˈdawənɪzəm/, *n.* the theory of evolution as expounded by later students of Darwin, esp. Weismann, who hold that natural selection accounts for evolution and deny the inheritance of acquired characteristics.

**neodymium** /nioʊˈdɪmiəm/, *n.* a rare-earth, metallic, trivalent element occurring with cerium and other rare-earth metals, and having rose- to violet-coloured salts. *Symbol:* Nd; *at. wt:* 144.24; *at. no.:* 60; *sp. gr.:* 6.9 at 20°C. [NL; see NEO-, (DI)DYMIUM]

**Neo-Fascism** /nioʊ-ˈfæʃɪzəm/, *n.* a political movement incorporating the principles of Fascism, founded after World War II. – **Neo-Fascist,** *n.*

**Neogaea** /nioʊˈdʒiə/, *n.* →**Neotropical realm.**

**Neogene** /ˈniədʒin/, *n.* the later of the two periods into which the Cainozoic era is divided in an international classification, comprising the Miocene, Pliocene, Pleistocene and Recent epochs.

**neo-impressionism** /ˌnioʊ-ɪmˈprɛʃənɪzəm/, *n.* a movement in art in the 1880s and 1890s, characterised by the use of pointillism in the application of colour and by strict and formal composition.

**Neo-Lamarckism** /ˌnioʊ-ləˈmakɪzəm/, *n.* the theory of Lamarckism as expounded by later biologists who hold especially that some acquired characters of organisms may be transmitted to descendants, but that natural selection also is a factor in evolution. – **Neo-Lamarckian,** *adj., n.*

**Neo-Latin** /nioʊ-ˈlætn/, *n.* →**New Latin.**

**neolith** /ˈniəlɪθ/, *n.* a neolithic stone implement.

**Neolithic** /niəˈlɪθɪk/, *n.* **1.** Also, **Neolithic Period.** the later Stone Age or New Stone Age, characterised by well-finished polished implements of flint and other stone; it includes the Holocene (or Recent) Epoch of the post-glacial period, until the beginning of the Bronze Age, and is sometimes regarded as including the Mesolithic. *–adj.* **2.** (*sometimes l.c.*) of or pertaining to the Neolithic.

**neologise** /niˈɒlədʒaɪz/, *v.i.,* **-gised, -gising.** to create neologisms. Also, **neologize.**

**neologism** /niˈɒlədʒɪzəm/, *n.* **1.** a new word or phrase. **2.** the introduction or use of new words, or new senses of words. **3.** a new doctrine. [F *néologisme,* from *néologie.* See NEO-, -LOGY]

–**neologist,** *n.* –**neologistic** /niˌɒlə'dʒɪstɪk/, **neologistical** /niˌɒlə'dʒɪstɪkəl/, *adj.*

**neology** /ni'ɒlədʒi/, *n.*, *pl.* **-gies.** →**neologism.** –**neological** /niə'lɒdʒɪkəl/, *adj.*

**Neo-Melanesian** /ˌnioʊ-mɛlə'niʒən/, *n.* **1.** a pidgin language based on English, spoken in Melanesia and New Guinea. –*adj.* **2.** denoting or pertaining to this language.

**neomycin** /nioʊ'maɪsən/, *n.* a mixture of closely related antibiotics, similar to streptomycin but more effective in combating certain infections, particularly those of the urinary tract.

**neon** /'niɒn/, *n.* a chemically inert gaseous element occurring in small amounts in the earth's atmosphere, and chiefly used in orange-red tubular electrical discharge lamps. *Symbol:* Ne; *at. wt:* 20.183; *at. no.:* 10; *weight of one litre of the gas at* 0°C *and at* 760 *mm pressure:* 0.9002 gr. [NL, from Gk (neut.): new]

**neonatal** /nioʊ'neɪtl/, *adj.* of or pertaining to a newborn child.

**neonate** /'nioʊneɪt/, *n.* a newborn child.

**neon lamp** /niɒn 'læmp/, *n.* an electric discharge lamp consisting of a glass tube containing neon gas which gives a red glow when a voltage is applied across the electrodes; widely used in advertising signs. Also, **neon light.**

**neophyte** /'nioʊfaɪt/, *n.* **1.** converted heathen, heretic, etc. **2.** a newly ordained Roman Catholic priest. **3.** a novice belonging to a religious order. **4.** a beginner. [LL *neophytus,* from Gk *neóphytos,* newly planted] –**neophytic** /nioʊfɪtɪk/, *adj.*

**neoplasm** /'nioʊplæzəm/, *n.* a new growth of different or abnormal tissue; a tumour. –**neoplastic** /nioʊ'plæstɪk/, *adj.*

**neoplasty** /'nioʊplæsti/, *n.* the repairing or restoration of a part by plastic surgery.

**neoplatonism** /nioʊ'pleɪtənɪzəm/, *n.* a philosophical system founded chiefly on platonic doctrine and oriental mysticism, later influenced by Christianity, which originated in the 3rd-century A.D. Also, **Neo-Platonism.** –**neoplatonic** /ˌnioʊplə'tɒnɪk/, *adj.* –**neoplatonist,** *n.*

**neoprene** /'nioʊprin/, *n.* an oil-resistant synthetic rubber $(C_4H_7Cl)_n$ made by polymerising chloroprene.

**neosalvarsan** /nioʊ'sælvəsən/, *n.* (*also cap.*) →**neoarsphenamine.** [Trademark]

**Neo-Scholasticism** /nioʊ-skə'læstəsɪzəm/, *n.* a contemporary application of scholasticism to modern problems and life. –**Neo-Scholastic,** *adj.*

**neo-synephrine** /nioʊ-'sɪnəfrin/, *n.* →**phenylephrine.** Also, **Neo-Synephrine.** [Trademark]

**neoteny** /ni'ɒtəni/, *n.* the capacity or phenomenon of becoming sexually mature in the larval state. [NL *neotēnia,* from Gk *neo-* NEO- + *teínein* extend + *-ia* -IA] –**neotenous,** *adj.*

**neoteric** /nioʊ'tɛrɪk/, *adj.* **1.** modern. –*n.* **2.** a modern writer, thinker, etc. [LL *neōtericus,* from Gk *neōterikós* youthful] –**neoterically,** *adv.*

**neotropical** /nioʊ'trɒpɪkəl/, *adj.* belonging to that part of the New World extending from the tropic of Cancer southwards.

**Neotropical realm** /nioʊˌtrɒpɪkəl 'rɛlm/, *n.* the biogeographical realm extending from Mexico through the whole of South America and including islands such as the West Indies, Galapagos, Tierra del Fuego and the Falkland islands. Also, **Neogaea.**

**neoytterbium** /ˌnioʊɪ'tɜbiəm/, *n.* →**ytterbium.**

**Neozoic** /nioʊ'zoʊɪk/, *adj.* of or pertaining to the geological era lasting from the end of the Mesozoic to the present time.

**nep** /nɛp/, *n.* (*usu. pl.*) a small knot of tangled fibre removed in the process of combing wool.

**Nepal** /nə'pɔl/, *n.* a constitutional monarchy in the Himalayas between northern India and Tibet.

**Nepalese** /nɛpə'liz/, *n.* **1.** a native of or resident in Nepal. **2.** the language spoken in Nepal. –*adj.* **3.** of or pertaining to the country, inhabitants, or language of Nepal.

**nepenthe** /nə'pɛnθi/, *n.* **1.** a drug or draught (or the plant yielding it) mentioned by ancient writers as capable of bringing forgetfulness of sorrow or trouble. **2.** anything inducing easeful forgetfulness. Also, **nepenthes** /nə'pɛnθiz/. [L *nēpenthes,* from Gk (neut.): banishing sorrow] –**nepenthean,** *adj.*

**neper** /'neɪpə, 'nipə/, *n.* a unit used to compare two scalar quantities, esp. currents or voltages, defined as the natural logarithm of the ratio of the two quantities; equivalent to 8.686 decibels. Also, **napier.** [var. of *napier,* named after John *Napier,* 1550-1617, Scottish mathematician and inventor of logarithms]

**nephanalysis** /nɛfə'næləsəs/, *n.* **1.** the analysis and interpretation of cloud formations. **2.** a map showing cloud patterns and distribution, esp. such a map drawn from photographs taken by artificial satellites. [Gk *néphos* cloud + ANALYSIS]

**nepheline** /'nɛfəlin, -lən/, *n.* a mineral, essentially sodium aluminium silicate, $NaAlSiO_4$, occurring in alkali-rich volcanic rocks. Also, **nephelite** /'nɛfəlaɪt/. [F, from Gk *nephélē* cloud + *-ine* -INE[2]]

**nephelinite** /'nɛfələnaɪt/, *n.* a fine-grained, dark rock of volcanic origin, essentially a basalt containing nepheline but no felspar and little or no olivine.

**nephelometer** /nɛfə'lɒmətə/, *n.* **1.** *Bacteriol.* an apparatus containing a series of barium chloride standards used to determine the number of bacteria in a suspension. **2.** *Chem., etc.* a device for studying the nature of suspensions by the use of diffuse reflected light. [Gk *nephélē* cloud + -O- + -METER[1]]

**nephew** /'nɛfju, 'nɛvju/, *n.* **1.** a son of one's brother or sister. **2.** a son of one's husband's or wife's brother or sister. **3.** (*euph.*) an illegitimate son of a celibate ecclesiastic. [ME *nevew,* from OF *neveu,* from L *nepos* grandson, nephew]

**nepho-,** a word element meaning 'cloud'. [Gk, combining form of *néphos* cloud]

**nephogram** /'nɛfəgræm/, *n.* a photograph of a cloud or clouds.

**nephograph** /'nɛfəgræf, -graf/, *n.* an instrument for photographing clouds.

**nephology** /nə'fɒlədʒi/, *n.* the branch of meteorology that treats of clouds. –**nephological** /nɛfə'lɒdʒɪkəl/, *adj.*

**nephoscope** /'nɛfəskoʊp/, *n.* an instrument for determining the altitude of clouds and the velocity and direction of their motion.

**nephr-,** variant of **nephro-,** before vowels.

**nephralgia** /nə'frældʒə/, *n.* pain in the kidney or kidneys.

**nephrectomy** /nə'frɛktəmi/, *n.*, *pl.* **-mies.** excision or removal of a kidney.

**nephric** /'nɛfrɪk/, *adj.* →**renal.**

**nephridium** /nə'frɪdiəm/, *n.*, *pl.* **-phridia** /-'frɪdiə/. the excretory organ of invertebrates consisting of a tubule with an open or closed motile apparatus at its inner end. [NL, from *nephr-* NEPHR- + *-idium* (diminutive suffix)] –**nephridial,** *adj.*

**nephrism** /'nɛfrɪzəm/, *n.* the unhealthy state produced by a chronic kidney disease.

**nephrite** /'nɛfraɪt/, *n.* a mineral, a compact or fibrous variety of actinolite, varying from whitish to dark green in colour. See **jade**[1] (def. 1). [G *Nephrit,* from *nephr-* NEPHR- + *-it* -ITE[1]]

**nephritic** /nə'frɪtɪk/, *adj.* of, pertaining to, or affected with nephritis. [LL *nephriticus,* from Gk *nephritikós* affected with nephritis]

**nephritis** /nə'fraɪtəs/, *n.* inflammation of the kidneys. [LL, from Gk]

**nephro-,** a word element referring to the kidneys. Also, **nephr-.** [Gk, combining form of *nephrós* kidney]

**nephrolith** /'nɛfrəlɪθ/, *n.* →**kidney stone.**

**nephrosis** /nə'froʊsəs/, *n.* kidney disease, esp. marked by non-inflammatory degeneration of the tubular system. [NEPHR- + -OSIS] –**nephrotic** /nə'frɒtɪk/, *adj.*

**nephrotomy** /nə'frɒtəmi/, *n.*, *pl.* **-mies.** incision into the kidney, as for the removal of a calculus.

**ne plus ultra** /neɪ plʊs 'ʊltrə, ni plʌs 'ʌltrə/, *n.* the acme; the extreme or utmost point; culmination. [L: no more beyond]

**nepotism** /'nɛpətɪzəm/, *n.* patronage bestowed in consideration of family relationship and not of merit. [F *népotisme,* from It. *nepotismo,* from L *nepos* descendant. See -ISM] –**nepotic** /nə'pɒtɪk/, *adj.* –**nepotist,** *n.*

**Neptune** /'nɛptʃun/, *n.* **1.** the sea or ocean. **2.** *Astron.* the eighth planet in order from the sun. [from *Neptune,* in Roman mythology, the god of the sea]

**Neptune's necklace** /ˌnɛptʃunz 'nɛkləs/, *n.* a marine alga, *Hormosira banksii,* found on rock platforms in south-eastern Australia.

**Neptunian** /nɛp'tjuniən/, *adj.* **1.** of or pertaining to the sea. **2.** (*oft. l.c.*) *Geol.* formed by the action of water.

**neptunium** /nɛp'tjuniəm/, *n.* a radioactive transuranic element, not found in nature, produced artificially by the neutron bombardment of U-238. It decays rapidly to plutonium and then to U-235. *Symbol:* Np; *at. no.:* 93; *at. wt:* 237.

**nerd** /nɜd/, *n. Colloq.* (*derog.*) an idiot; fool. Also, **nurd.**

**nereid** /ˈnɪəriəd/, *n.* a marine free-living annelid worm of the genus *Nereis.* [named after the *Nereids,* who in Greek mythology were the daughters of the sea god Nereus; L *Nērēis,* from Gk]

nereid

**nerine** /nəˈrin/, *n.* any plant of the southern African genus *Nerine,* many species of which are grown for their umbels of coloured flowers produced in autumn.

**neritic** /nəˈrɪtɪk/, *adj.* of or pertaining to the shallow waters near land.

**nerol** /ˈnɪərɒl/, *n.* a colourless alcohol, $C_{10}H_{17}OH$, contained in neroli oil.

**neroli oil** /ˈnɪərəli ˌɔɪl/, *n.* an essential oil consisting of citral, limonene, linalool, etc., derived from orange blossoms of the tree *Citrus aurantium,* and used in the perfume industry. [F, from It.; named after Anne Marie de la Tremoïlle of *Neroli,* Italian princess said to have discovered it]

**nervate** /ˈnɜveɪt/, *adj.* (of leaves) having nerves or veins; nerved.

**nervation** /nɜˈveɪʃən/, *n.* →**venation.**

**nerve** /nɜv/, *n., v.,* **nerved, nerving.** *–n.* **1.** one or more bundles of fibres, forming part of a system which conveys impulses of sensation, motion, etc., between the brain or spinal cord and other parts of the body. **2.** *Dentistry.* **a.** the nerve tissue in the pulp of a tooth. **b.** (popularly but incorrectly) pulp tissue of a tooth. **3.** strength, vigour, or energy. **4.** firmness or courage in trying circumstances: *a position requiring nerve.* **5.** (*pl.*) nervousness: *a fit of nerves.* **6.** *Obs.* a sinew or tendon. **7.** *Colloq.* impertinent assurance. **8.** *Bot.* a vein, as in a leaf. **9.** a line or one of a system of lines traversing something. **10. get on one's nerves,** to irritate. *–v.t.* **11.** to give strength, vigour, or courage to. [ME, from L *nervus,* akin to Gk *neûron* sinew, tendon, nerve]

**nerve agent** /ˈ– eɪdʒənt/, *n.* a lethal chemical agent which, when absorbed into the body, disrupts the nervous and respiratory functions.

**nerve cell** /ˈ– sɛl/, *n.* **1.** any of the cells constituting the cellular element of nervous tissue. **2.** one of the essential cells of a nerve centre. Also, **neurone.**

**nerve centre** /ˈ– sɛntə/, *n.* **1.** *Anat., Physiol.* a group of nerve cells closely connected with one another and acting together in the performance of some function. **2.** (of a large company, movement, or organisation) the centre from which plans, policies, and movements are directed.

nerve cell: A, cell; B, nucleus; C, dendrites; D, axon

**nerve fibre** /ˈ– faɪbə/, *n.* a process, axon, or dendrite of a nerve cell.

**nerve gas** /ˈ– gæs/, *n.* a type of gas, used during warfare, which has a paralysing, often fatal, effect on the central nervous system.

**nerve impulse** /ˈ– ɪmpʌls/, *n.* a wave of electrical and chemical activity progressing along nerve fibres and acting as a stimulus to muscle, gland, or other nerve cells.

**nerveless** /ˈnɜvləs/, *adj.* **1.** *Anat., Bot., etc.* without nerves. **2.** lacking strength or vigour; feeble; weak. **3.** lacking firmness or courage; spiritless; pusillanimous. – **nervelessly,** *adv.* – **nervelessness,** *n.*

**nerve-racking** /ˈnɜv-rækɪŋ/, *adj.* extremely trying.

**nervine** /ˈnɜvin, -vaɪn/, *adj.* **1.** of or pertaining to the nerves. **2.** acting on, or relieving disorders of the nerves; soothing the nerves. *–n.* **3.** a nervine medicine.

**nerving** /ˈnɜvɪŋ/, *n. Vet. Sci.* the excision of part of a nerve trunk.

**nervous** /ˈnɜvəs/, *adj.* **1.** of or pertaining to the nerves. **2.** having or containing nerves of sensation, etc. **3.** affecting the nerves, as diseases. **4.** suffering from, characterised by, or proceeding from disordered nerves. **5.** highly excitable; unnaturally or acutely uneasy or apprehensive. **6.** characterised by or attended with acute uneasiness or apprehension. [ME, from L *nervōsus* sinewy] – **nervously,** *adv.* – **nervousness,** *n.*

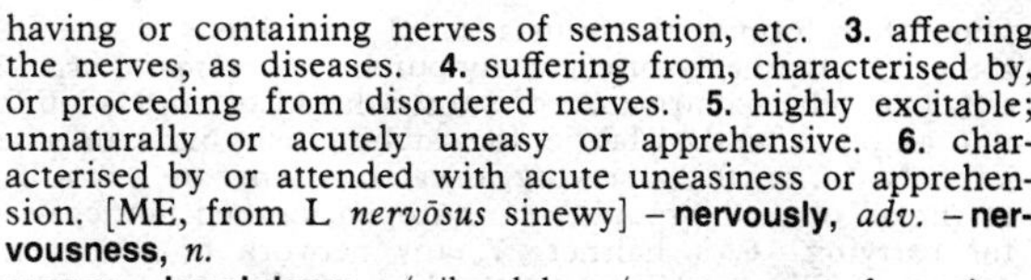

**nervous breakdown** /– ˈbreɪkdaʊn/, *n.* any of various psychiatric illnesses, esp. those attended by nervous debility and exhaustion and undefined physical complaints.

**nervous system** /ˈ– sɪstəm/, *n.* **1.** the system of nerves and nerve centres in an animal. **2.** a particular part of this system: **a.** the **central** or **cerebrospinal nervous system,** the brain and spinal cord. **b.** the **peripheral nervous system,** the system of nerves and ganglia derived from the central system, comprising the cranial nerves, the spinal nerves, the various sense organs, etc. **c.** the **autonomic nervous system,** the system of nerves and ganglia which supply the walls of the vascular system and the various viscera and glands.

**nervure** /ˈnɜvjuə/, *n.* a vein, as of an insect's wing. [F, from L *nervus* NERVE]

**nervy** /ˈnɜvi/, *adj.,* **-vier, -viest. 1.** nervous. **2.** excitable; irritable. **3.** requiring nerve. **4.** having or showing courage; audacious; bold. **5.** strong or vigorous.

**nescience** /ˈnɛsiəns/, *n.* **1.** lack of knowledge; ignorance. **2.** →**agnosticism.** [LL *nescientia,* from L *nesciens,* ppr., being ignorant] – **nescient,** *adj., n.*

**-ness,** a suffix used to form, from adjectives and participles, nouns denoting quality or state (also often, by extension, something exemplifying a quality or state), as in *darkness, goodness, kindness, obligingness, preparedness.* [ME *-nes(se),* OE *-nes(s),* c. G *-niss*]

**nesselrode** /ˈnɛsəlroʊd/, *n.* a rich and elaborate frozen dessert made from chestnuts, egg yolks, cream, and sometimes candied fruits. [named after Count Karl R. *Nesselrode,* 1780-1862, Russian diplomat]

**Nessler's solution** /ˈnɛsləz səluʃən/, *n.* a solution of potassium mercuric iodide in potassium hydroxide; used as a test for ammonia, in the presence of which it forms a brown precipitate. [named after Julius *Nessler,* 1827-1905, German chemist]

**nest** /nɛst/, *n.* **1.** a structure formed or a place used by a bird for incubation and the rearing of its young. **2.** a place used by insects, fishes, turtles, rabbits, or the like, for depositing their eggs or young. **3.** a number of birds or animals inhabiting one such place. **4.** a snug retreat, or resting place. **5.** an assemblage of things lying or set close together, as a series of tables, trays, etc., that fit within each other. **6.** a place where something bad is fostered or flourishes: *a robbers' nest.* **7.** the occupants or frequenters of such a place. *–v.t.* **8.** to settle or place in or as in a nest. **9.** to fit or place one within another. *–v.i.* **10.** to build or have a nest: *the swallows nested under the eaves.* **11.** to settle in or as in a nest. **12.** to search for nests: *to go nesting.* **13.** to fit together or one within another. [ME and OE, c. G *Nest;* akin to L *nīdus*]

**nest egg** /ˈ– ɛg/, *n.* **1.** an egg (usu. artificial) left in a nest to induce a hen to continue laying eggs there. **2.** money saved as the basis of a fund or for emergencies.

**nester** /ˈnɛstə/, *n. N.Z.* a baby rabbit still in the breeding nest.

**nestle** /ˈnɛsəl/, *v.,* **-tled, -tling.** *–v.i.* **1.** to lie close and snug, like a bird in a nest; snuggle or cuddle. **2.** to lie in a sheltered or pleasant situation. **3.** *Obs.* to make or have a nest. *–v.t.* **4.** to provide with or settle in a nest, as birds. **5.** to settle or ensconce snugly. **6.** to put or press confidingly or affectionately. [ME *nestle(n),* OE *nestlian* (c. D *nestelen*), from *nest* NEST] – **nestler,** *n.*

**nestling** /ˈnɛslɪŋ/, *n.* **1.** a young bird in the nest. **2.** a young child.

**Nestorian** /nɛsˈtɔriən/, *n.* one of a sect of Christians, followers of Nestorius, died A.D. *c.* 451, patriarch of Constantinople A.D. 428-431, who denied the hypostatic union and were represented as maintaining the existence of two distinct persons in Christ. – **Nestorianism,** *n.*

**net**[1] /nɛt/, *n., v.,* **netted, netting,** *adj.* *–n.* **1.** a lacelike fabric with a uniform mesh of cotton, silk, rayon, nylon, or other

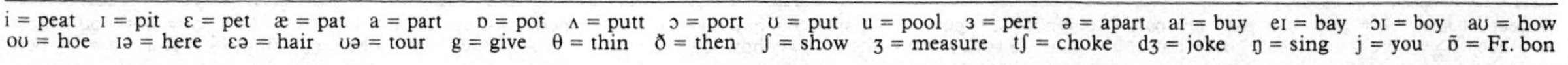

fibre, often forming the foundation of many kinds of lace. **2.** a piece of meshed fabric for any purpose: *a mosquito net.* **3.** a bag or other contrivance of strong thread or cord wrought into an open, meshed fabric, for catching fish, birds, or other animals. **4.** anything serving to catch or ensnare. **5.** a bag of thread or cord wrought into an open meshed fabric, used for carrying. **6.** a hairnet. **7.** any network or reticulated system of filaments, lines, or the like. **8.** *Tennis, etc.* a ball that hits the net. **9.** *Cricket.* a pitch surrounded by netting, used for practice in batting and bowling. **10.** *Soccer, Hockey, etc.* the goal. *–v.t.* **11.** to cover, screen, or enclose with a net or netting. **12.** to take with a net: *to net fish.* **13.** to set or use nets in (a river, etc.), as for fish. **14.** to catch or ensnare. **15.** *Tennis, etc.* to hit (the ball) into the net. **16.** *Soccer, Hockey, etc.* to kick or hit into the goal; score. *–adj.* **17.** made in the form of or resembling a net. [ME *net(te)*, OE *net(t)*, c. G *Netz*] – **netlike,** *adj.*

**net**[2] /nɛt/, *adj., n., v.,* **netted, netting.** *–adj.* **1.** exclusive of deductions, as for charges, expenses, loss, discount, etc.: *net earnings.* **2.** sold at net prices. **3.** ultimate; conclusive: *the net result.* *–n.* **4.** net income, profits, or the like. *–v.t.* **5.** to gain or produce as clear profit. Also, **nett.** [F: clean, clear. See NEAT[1]]

**netball** /ˈnɛtbɔl/, *n.* a game similar to basketball played, usu. by women, by two teams of seven players.

**net fungus** /ˈnɛt fʌŋgəs/, *n.* a New Zealand fungus, *Clathrus cibarius,* resembling a hollow lattice ball; fairies' closet.

**nether** /ˈnɛðə/, *adj.* **1.** lying, or conceived as lying, beneath the earth's surface; infernal: *the nether world.* **2.** lower or under: *his nether lip.* [ME; OE *neothera,* earlier *ni(o)ther(r)a* (c. G *nieder*), from *nither,* adv., downwards, down (a compar. form)]

**Netherlands** /ˈnɛðələndz/, **The,** *n.pl.* a kingdom in western Europe, bordering on the North Sea, West Germany, and Belgium. – **Netherlander,** *n.*

**nethermost** /ˈnɛðəmoʊst/, *adj.* lowest.

**nether world** /ˈnɛðə wɜld/, *n.* **1.** hell. **2.** the afterworld.

**netsuke** /ˈnɛtsʊki/, *n.* a small object of ivory, wood, etc., usu. carved or decorated, used in Japanese dress as a toggle to prevent a pouch or other article, to which it is attached by a cord, from slipping through the girdle.

netsuke and cord supporting lacquer case

**nett** /nɛt/, *adj., n., v.t.* →**net**[2].

**netting** /ˈnɛtɪŋ/, *n.* any of various kinds of net fabric: *fish netting, mosquito netting.*

**nettle** /nɛtl/, *n., v.,* **-tled, -tling.** *–n.* **1.** any plant of the genus *Urtica,* comprising widely distributed herbs armed with stinging hairs. **2.** any of various allied or similar plants, as Gympie nettle. **3. grasp the nettle,** *Colloq.* to approach an unpleasant task with courage and resolution. *–v.t.* **4.** to irritate, irk, provoke, or vex. **5.** to sting as a nettle does. [ME; OE *netele,* c. G *Nessel*]

**nettlecloth** /ˈnɛtlklɒθ/, *n.* a type of heavy cotton fabric finished in lacquer or enamel to imitate leather; used for waist belts, etc.

**nettle rash** /ˈnɛtl ræʃ/, *n.* urticaria caused by contact with various plants causing local irritation.

**nettle tree** /ˈ– tri/, *n.* any of several stinging trees of the family Urticaceae, native to Australia.

**net tonnage** /ˈnɛt tʌnɪdʒ/, *n.* →**register tonnage.**

**network** /ˈnɛtwɜk/, *n.* **1.** any netlike combination of filaments, lines, passages, or the like. **2.** a netting or net. **3.** a group of affiliated radio or television stations, sometimes commonly owned, and from which at times the same program may be broadcast. **4.** *Elect.* a system of interconnected electrical elements, units, or circuits. **5.** *Computers.* a system of connecting computer systems or peripheral devices, each one remote from the others.

**networking** /ˈnɛtwɜkɪŋ/, *n.* the creation of networks (def. 3) by purchase or agreement.

**neufchâtel** /nɜfʃəˈtɛl/, *n.* a soft, white cheese similar to cream cheese, made from whole or partly skimmed milk. [from *Neufchâtel,* town in N France where first produced]

**neume** /njum/, *n.* any of various symbols used in medieval musical notation, and still used for noting Gregorian chant, etc. [ME, from ML *neuma,* from Gk *pneûma* breath] – **neumic,** *adj.*

**neur-,** variant of **neuro-,** before vowels.

**neural** /ˈnjurəl/, *adj.* of or pertaining to a nerve or the nervous system. – **neurally,** *adv.*

**neuralgia** /njuˈrældʒə/, *n.* sharp and paroxysmal pain along the course of a nerve. [NL. See NEUR-, -ALGIA] – **neuralgic,** *adj.*

**neurasthenia** /njurəsˈθiniə/, *n.* nervous debility or exhaustion, as from overwork or prolonged mental strain, characterised by vague complaints of a physical nature in the absence of objectively present causes or lesions.

**neurasthenic** /njurəsˈθɛnɪk/, *adj.* **1.** pertaining to or suffering from neurasthenia. *–n.* **2.** a person suffering from neurasthenia.

**neuration** /njuˈreɪʃən/, *n.* →**venation.**

**neurectomy** /njuˈrɛktəmi/, *n., pl.* **-mies.** the removal of a nerve or part thereof.

**neurilemma** /njurəˈlɛmə/, *n.* the delicate membranous sheath of a nerve fibre. Also, **neurolemma.** [var. (by association with LEMMA[2] husk, outer layer) of *neurilema,* from NEUR- + Gk *eílēma* covering]

**neuritis** /njuˈraɪtəs/, *n.* **1.** inflammation of a nerve. **2.** continuous pain in a nerve associated with its paralysis and sensory disturbances. [NL. See NEUR-, -ITIS] – **neuritic** /njuˈrɪtɪk/, *adj.*

**neuro-,** a word element meaning 'tendon', 'nerve'. Also, **neur-.** [Gk, combining form of *neûron*]

**neuroanatomy** /ˌnjuroʊəˈnætəmi/, *n., pl.* **-mies.** the anatomy of the nervous system. – **neuroanatomical** /ˌnjuroʊænəˈtɒmɪkəl/, *adj.* – **neuroanatomically** /ˌnjuroʊænəˈtɒmɪkli/, *adv.* – **neuroanatomist,** *n.*

**neuroblast** /ˈnjurəblæst/, *n.* one of the cells in the embryonic brain and spinal cord of vertebrates, which eventually give rise to nerve cells.

**neurocoele** /ˈnjurəsil/, *n.* the cavity (ventricles and central canal) of the embryonic brain and spinal cord.

**neurofibril** /njurəˈfaɪbrəl/, *n.* one of many threadlike processes found in the cytoplasm of nerve cells. – **neurofibrilar,** *adj.*

**neurofibroma** /njurəfaɪˈbroʊmə/, *n.* a tumour consisting of nerve and fibrous tissue.

**neurogenic** /njurəˈdʒɛnɪk/, *adj.* pertaining to the formation of nervous tissue.

**neuroglia** /njuˈrɒgliə/, *n.* the delicate connective tissue which supports and binds the essential elements of nervous tissue in the central nervous system. [NL, from Gk *neuro-* NEURO- + *glía* glue]

**neurohypophysis** /ˌnjuroʊhaɪˈpɒfəsəs/, *n.* the posterior lobe of the pituitary gland which releases hormones that regulate the function of specific organs, as the contracting of the uterus. [NEURO- + HYPOPHYSIS]

**neurolemma** /njurəˈlɛmə/, *n.* →**neurilemma.**

**neurology** /njuˈrɒlədʒi/, *n.* the science of the nerves or the nervous system, esp. the diseases thereof. – **neurological** /njurəˈlɒdʒɪkəl/, *adj.* – **neurologist,** *n.*

**neuroma** /njuˈroʊmə/, *n., pl.* **-mata** /-mətə/, **-mas.** a tumour formed of nervous tissue. [NL. See NEUR-, -OMA]

**neuromuscular** /njuroʊˈmʌskjələ/, *adj.* concerning both nerves and muscles.

**neurone** /ˈnjuroʊn/, *n.* →**nerve cell.** Also, **neuron** /ˈnjurɒn/. [Gk *neûron* nerve] – **neuronic** /njuˈrɒnɪk/, *adj.*

**neuropath** /ˈnjurəpæθ/, *n.* a person subject to or affected with a functional nervous disease; a neurotic person.

**neuropathic** /njurəˈpæθɪk/, *adj.* →**neurotic.**

**neuropathology** /ˌnjuroʊpəˈθɒlədʒi/, *n.* the pathology of the nervous system. – **neuropathologist,** *n.*

**neuropathy** /njuˈrɒpəθi/, *n.* disease of the nervous system. [NEURO- + -PATHY]

**neurophysiology** /ˌnjuroʊfɪziˈɒlədʒi/, *n.* the study of the physiology of the nervous system.

**neuropsychiatry** /ˌnjuroʊsəˈkaɪətri/, *n.* the branch of medicine dealing with diseases involving the mind and nervous system. – **neuropsychiatric** /ˌnjuroʊsaɪkiˈætrɪk/, *adj.*

**neuropsychosis** /ˌnjuroʊsaɪˈkoʊsəs/, *n., pl.* **-ses** /-siz/. mental derangement in association with nervous disease.

**neuropterous** /njuˈrɒptərəs/, *adj.* belonging to an order of insects, the Neuroptera, that includes the antlions and lacewings, characterised by two pairs of membranous wings with netlike venation. [NEURO- + Gk *pterón* wing + -OUS]

**neurosis** /nju'rousəs/, *n., pl.* **-ses** /-siz/. psychoneurosis; an emotional disorder in which feelings of anxiety, obsessional thoughts, compulsive acts, and physical complaints without objective evidence of disease, in various patterns, dominate the personality.

**neurosurgery** /njurou'sɜdʒəri/, *n.* the branch of medicine pertaining to the surgery of the nervous system. – **neurosurgical,** *adj.*

**neurotic** /nju'rɒtɪk/, *adj.* **1.** having a neurosis. **2.** pertaining to the nerves or to nervous disease. *–n.* **3.** a person affected with neurosis. – **neurotically,** *adv.*

**neurotomy** /nju'rɒtəmi/, *n., pl.* **-mies.** surgical cutting of a nerve, as to relieve neuralgia.

**neurovascular** /njurou'væskjələ/, *adj.* of or pertaining to both nerves and blood vessels.

**neut.,** neuter.

**neuter** /'njutə/, *adj.* **1.** *Gram.* **a.** denoting or pertaining to one of the three genders of Latin, German, Greek, etc., or one of the two of Dutch, Swedish, etc., so termed because few if any nouns denoting males or females belong to it, or (as in German) purely for traditional reasons. For example: Latin *nōmen* 'name', *cor* 'heart', *bellum* 'war' are all neuter gender. **b.** (of verbs) intransitive. **2.** sexless, apparently sexless, or of indeterminate sex, as a hermaphrodite or castrated person. **3.** *Zool.* having imperfectly developed sexual organs, as the workers among bees and ants. **4.** *Bot.* having neither stamens nor pistils; asexual. **5.** *Archaic.* neutral. *–n.* **6.** *Gram.* **a.** the neuter gender. **b.** a noun of that gender. **c.** another element marking that gender. **d.** an intransitive verb. **7.** an animal made sterile by castration. **8.** a neuter insect. **9.** a person of no or of indeterminate sex. **10.** *Bot.* a plant with neither stamens nor pistils. **11.** *Archaic.* a neutral. *–v.t.* **12.** to castrate. [L: neither; replacing ME *neutre,* from OF]

**neutral** /'njutrəl/, *adj.* **1.** (of a person or state) refraining from taking part in a controversy or war between others. **2.** of no particular kind, colour, characteristics, etc.; indefinite. **3.** grey; without hue; of zero chroma; achromatic. **4.** having no definite colour, so as to match well with other colours. **5.** *Phonet.* pertaining to the vowel schwa (ə); pronounced with the tongue in a central position. **6.** *Phonet.* pertaining to the lip shape in articulation in which the lips are neither spread nor rounded, as in the vowels of *cat* and *cart.* **7.** *Biol.* neuter. **8.** *Chem.* exhibiting neither acid nor alkaline qualities: *neutral salts.* **9.** *Elect.* neither positive nor negative; not electrified; not magnetised. *–n.* **10.** a person or a state that remains neutral, as in a war. **11.** a citizen of a neutral nation. **12.** *Mach.* the position or state of disengaged gears or other interconnecting parts: *in neutral.* [late ME, from L *neutrālis* neuter] – **neutrally,** *adv.*

**neutral corner** /– 'kɔnə/, *n.* **1.** *Boxing.* one of the two corners of the ring not occupied by contestants between rounds and to which a boxer must retire when his opponent is knocked down. **2.** at a social gathering, a position where one is less likely to have to talk with fellow guests.

**neutralise** /'njutrəlaɪz/, *v.t.,* **-lised, -lising.** **1.** to make neutral. **2.** to render ineffective; counteract. **3.** *Mil.* to put out of action or make incapable of action. **4.** to declare neutral; invest with neutrality. **5.** *Chem.* to render inert the peculiar properties of. **6.** *Elect.* to render electrically neutral. Also, **neutralize.** – **neutralisation** /njutrəlaɪ'zeɪʃən/, *n.* – **neutraliser,** *n.*

**neutralism** /'njutrəlɪzəm/, *n.* the policy of remaining strictly neutral in foreign affairs. – **neutralist,** *n.*

**neutrality** /nju'træləti/, *n.* **1.** the state of being neutral. **2.** the attitude or status of a nation which does not participate in a war between other nations: *the continuous neutrality of Switzerland.* **3.** neutral status, as of a seaport during a war.

**neutretto** /nju'trɛtou/, *n. Obs.* a neutral meson.

**neutrino** /nju'trinou/, *n., pl.* **-nos.** an elementary particle with zero electric charge and zero rest mass.

**neutron** /'njutrɒn/, *n.* an elementary particle which is a constituent of all atomic nuclei except normal hydrogen. It has zero electric charge and approximately the same mass as the proton. [NEUTR(AL) neither positive nor negative + *-on* (after ELECTRON, PROTON)]

**neutron bomb** /– 'bɒm/, *n.* a nuclear weapon which releases a shower of neutrons but relatively little blast, thus killing people but causing relatively little damage to property. Also, **clean bomb.**

**neutron excess** /– 'ɛksɛs/, *n.* →**isotopic number.**

**neutron star** /– 'sta/, *n.* a hypothetical star with an estimated density 10 times greater than a white dwarf; postulated as the result of a gravitational collapse in which pressure is so great that electrons and protons coalesce into neutron.

**neutron temperature** /– 'tɛmprətʃə/, *n.* the energy of neutrons, in thermal equilibrium with their surroundings, expressed as a temperature on the assumption that they behave as a monotomic gas.

**neutropenia** /njutrə'piniə/, *n.* an abnormally low number of neutrophils in the blood.

**neutrophil** /'njutrəfɪl/, *adj.* **1.** (of a cell or cell part) having an affinity for neutral dyes. *–n.* **2.** *Anat.* a phagocytic leucocyte having a nucleus and neutrophil granules in the cytoplasm.

**névé** /'nɛveɪ/, *n.* **1.** granular snow accumulated on high mountains and subsequently compacted into glacial ice. **2.** a field of such snow. Also, **firn.** [F, var. of d. F *nevé,* from O South-eastern F *neif,* from L *nix* snow]

**never** /'nɛvə/, *adv.* **1.** not ever; at no time. **2.** not at all; absolutely not; not even. **3.** to no extent or degree. [ME; OE *nǣfre,* from *ne* not + *ǣfre* EVER]

**neverfail grass** /'nɛvəfeɪl gras/, *n.* **1.** any of various species of grasses which remain green even during prolonged drought periods. **2.** a drought resistant native perennial, *Eragrostis setifolia,* with slender, wiry stems and leaves which are bristly on the upper surface.

**nevermore** /nɛvə'mɔ/, *adv.* never again.

**never-never** /'nɛvə-nɛvə/, *Colloq. –n.* **1.** (*sometimes cap.*) sparsely inhabited desert country; a remote and isolated region. **2.** *Orig. Brit.* the hire-purchase system: *on the never-never.* *–adj.* **3.** imaginary: *never-never land.*

**nevertheless** /nɛvəðə'lɛs/, *adv.* nonetheless; notwithstanding; however.

**nevus** /'nivəs/, *n., pl.* **-vi** /-vaɪ/. *U.S.* →**naevus.** – **nevoid** /'nivɔɪd/, *adj.*

**new** /nju/, *adj.* **1.** of recent origin or production, or having only lately come or been brought into being: *a new book.* **2.** of a kind now existing or appearing for the first time; novel. **3.** having only lately or only now come into knowledge: *a new chemical element.* **4.** unfamiliar or strange (fol. by *to*): *ideas new to us.* **5.** recently arrived: *New Australians.* **6.** having only lately come to a position, status, etc.: *a new minister.* **7.** unaccustomed (fol. by *to*): *men new to such work.* **8.** coming or occurring afresh; further; additional: *new gains.* **9.** fresh or unused: *a new sheet.* **10.** different and better, physically or morally: *the operation made a new man of him.* **11.** other than the former or the old: *a new era.* **12.** being the later or latest of two or more things of the same kind: *the New Testament.* **13.** (of a language) in its latest known period, esp. as a living language at the present time: *New Latin.* *–adv.* **14.** recently or lately. **15.** freshly; anew or afresh. *–n.* **16.** something new. [ME and OE *newe,* c. G *neu,* L *novus,* Gk *néos*] – **newness,** *n.*

**New Australian** /nju ɒ'streɪljən/, *n. Colloq.* an immigrant, esp. one whose native tongue is not English; migrant.

**new beer** /'nju bɪə/, *n.* beer brewed by the bottom fermentation method, usu. light in colour.

**newborn** /'njubɔn/, *adj.* **1.** recently or only just born. **2.** born anew; reborn.

**Newcastle disease** /'njukasəl dəziz, 'njukæs-/, *n.* a specific, virus-induced disease of chickens, etc., marked by loss of egg production in old birds and by paralysis in chickens.

**new chum** /'nju tʃʌm/, *n.* **1.** a novice; one inexperienced in some field: *a new chum on the job.* **2.** (formerly) **a.** a newly transported convict. **b.** a newly arrived British immigrant.

**newcomer** /'njukʌmə/, *n.* one who has newly come; a new arrival.

**newel** /'njuəl/, *n.* **1.** a central pillar or upright from which the steps of a winding stair radiate. **2.** a post at the head or foot of a stair, supporting the handrail. [ME *nowell,* from OF *noiel* kernel, newel (from LL *nucāle,* neut. of *nucālis* of or like a nut), b. with *noel* bud, trickle-ornament, from LL *nōdellus,* diminutive of L *nōdus* knot]

**newfangled** /ˈnjufæŋgəld/, *adj.* **1.** (*pejor.*) new-fashioned; of a new kind: *newfangled ideas.* **2.** fond of novelty. [ME *newefangel,* from *newe* NEW + *fangel,* from OE *fōn* take]

**new-fashioned** /ˈnju-fæʃənd/, *adj.* lately come into fashion; of a new fashion.

**newfoundland** /njuˈfaʊndlənd, ˈnjufəndlənd/, *n.* one of a breed of large, shaggy dogs, noted for their sagacity, docility, swimming powers, etc. [orig. from *Newfoundland,* large island in E canada]

newfoundland

**new ground** /nju ˈgraʊnd/, *n.* **1.** *Mining.* that portion of a goldfield not previously worked. **2. break new ground,** to pioneer a new development. **3. cover new ground,** to handle new subject matter.

**New Guinea** /nju ˈgɪni/, *n.* a large island north of Australia comprising the independent state of Papua New Guinea and the Indonesian province of Irian Jaya.

**New Hebrides** /– ˈhɛbrədiz/, *n.* former name of Vanuatu.

**New Holland** /– ˈhɒlənd/, *n.* (formerly) the name given to Australia by the Dutch explorers.

**New Holland sloth,** *n. Obs.* →**koala.**

**newie** /ˈnjui/, *n. Colloq.* something or someone new.

**newish** /ˈnjuɪʃ/, *adj.* rather new.

**New Jerusalem** /nju dʒəˈrusələm/, *n.* the heavenly city; the abode of God and His saints.

**new-laid** /ˈnju-leɪd/, *adj.* **1.** fresh; having just been laid: *new-laid eggs.* **2.** *Colloq.* inexperienced; immature in judgment; green.

**New Latin** /nju ˈlætn/, *n.* the Latin which became current (notably in scientific literature) after the Renaissance (approx. 1500). Also, **Neo-Latin.**

**New Learning** /– ˈlɜnɪŋ/, *n.* the studies, chiefly in classical literature, of the Renaissance, esp. in the 16th century in England.

**new look** /nju ˈlʊk/, *n.* a complete and radical change in appearance or form.

**newly** /ˈnjuli/, *adv.* **1.** recently; lately: *a newly wedded couple.* **2.** anew or afresh: *a newly repeated slander.* **3.** in a new manner or form. [ME; OE *nīwlice*]

**newlywed** /ˈnjuliwɛd/, *n.* a recently married person.

**new moon** /nju ˈmun/, *n.* →**moon** (def. 2a).

**New Orleans** /nju ˈɔlianz, ɔˈlinz/, *n.* traditional jazz. [after a seaport on the Mississippi in SE Louisiana, U.S., where it originated]

**new penny** /nju ˈpɛni/, *n.* →**penny** (def. 4).

**new-rich** /nju-ˈrɪtʃ/, *adj.* **1.** characteristic of the nouveau riche. *–n.* **2.** →**nouveau riche.**

**news** /njuz/, *n.pl.* (*construed as sing.*) **1.** a report of any recent event, situation, etc. **2.** the report of events published in a newspaper, journal, radio, television, or any other medium. **3.** information, events, etc., considered as suitable for reporting: *it's very interesting, but it's not news.* **4.** information not previously known: *that's news to me.* **5.** newsprint or newspaper. **6. bad news,** *Colloq.* someone or something from whom or which nothing good is to be expected. [ME *news,* pl. of ME, OE *newe* that which is new, n. use of *newe,* adj.]

**news agency** /ˈ– eɪdʒənsi/, *n.* an organisation which collects news and supplies it to newspapers, television and radio stations, etc.

**newsagency** /ˈnjuzeɪdʒənsi/, *n.* **1.** the franchise to sell newspapers. **2.** a shop which sells principally newspapers, magazines, stationery and books.

**newsagent** /ˈnjuzeɪdʒənt/, *n.* the proprietor of a newsagency.

**newsboy** /ˈnjuzbɔɪ/, *n.* →**newspaper-boy.**

**newscast** /ˈnjuzkast/, *n., v.,* **-cast, -casting.** *–n.* **1.** a radio or television broadcast of news reports. *–v.i.* **2.** to broadcast a news bulletin. – **newscaster,** *n.*

**newsdealer** /ˈnjuzdilə/, *n. U.S.* →**newsagent.**

**newshawk** /ˈnjuzhɔk/, *n. Colloq.* a newspaper reporter, esp. one with a keen eye for news. Also, **newshound** /ˈnjuzhaʊnd/.

**newsletter** /ˈnjuzlɛtə/, *n.* **1.** an informal bulletin, as one circulating among people with a common interest. **2.** a confidential report and analysis of the news.

**newsman** /ˈnjuzmæn/, *n.* **1.** one who sells or distributes newspapers, periodicals, etc. **2.** a newspaperman; a reporter on a newspaper.

**newsmonger** /ˈnjuzmʌŋgə/, *n.* a spreader of news by oral or written means, esp. a gossip.

**New South Wales,** *n.* a state in eastern Australia. *Abbrev.:* N.S.W., NSW

**New South Welshman,** *n.* one who was born in New South Wales, one of the six States of Australia, or who has come to regard it as his home State.

New South Wales: coat of arms

**newspaper** /ˈnjuzpeɪpə/, *n.* **1.** a printed publication issued at regular intervals, usu. daily or weekly, and commonly containing news, comment, features, and advertisements. **2.** the organisation publishing a newspaper. **3.** a single copy or issue of a newspaper.

**newspaper-boy** /ˈnjuzpeɪpə-bɔɪ/, *n.* a boy who sells or delivers newspapers.

**newspaperman** /ˈnjuzpeɪpəmæn/, *n.* **1.** a reporter or other employee of a newspaper. **2.** a seller of newspapers.

**newsposter** /ˈnjuzpoʊstə/, *n.* →**poster**[1] (def. 2).

**newsprint** /ˈnjuzprɪnt/, *n.* paper used or made to print newspapers on.

**newsreader** /ˈnjuzridə/, *n.* one who reads the news bulletin on radio or television.

**newsreel** /ˈnjuzril/, *n.* a short film presenting current news events.

**newsroom** /ˈnjuzrum/, *n.* **1.** a room in a newspaper office, a television studio, or the like, dealing exclusively with the collection, analysis, and presentation of news. **2.** a room in a library where newspapers, etc., are available for reading.

**news-sheet** /ˈnjuz-ʃit/, *n.* a short newspaper, usu. one printed on a single sheet.

**newsstand** /ˈnjuzstænd/, *n.* **1.** →**paperstand. 2.** →**bookstall** (def. 1).

**new-Stater** /nju-ˈsteɪtə/, *n.* one who supports the creation of new States within Australia. – **new-Statism,** *n.*

**New Stone Age,** *n.* the neolithic era.

**newsvendor** /ˈnjuzvɛndə/, *n.* a seller of newspapers, etc.

**newsworthy** /ˈnjuzwɜði/, *adj.* of sufficient interest to appear in a newspaper. – **newsworthiness,** *n.*

**newsy** /ˈnjuzi/, *adj.,* **-sier, -siest.** *Colloq.* full of news. – **newsiness,** *n.*

**newt** /njut/, *n.* any of various small, semi-aquatic salamanders of the genus *Triturus* and related genera, of Europe, North America, and northern Asia. [ME *newte,* for *ewte* (*an ewte* being taken as *a newte*), var. of *evet,* OE *efete*]

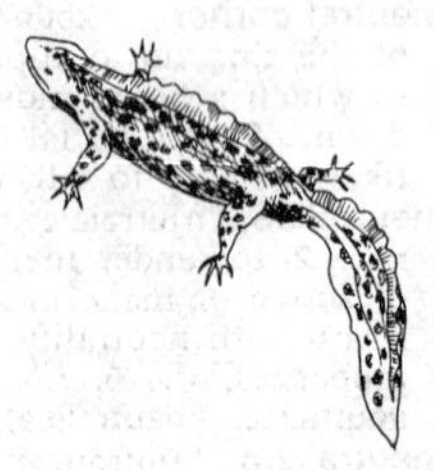
newt

**New Testament** /nju ˈtɛstəmənt/, *n.* those books in the Bible which were produced by the early Christian Church, and were added to the Jewish scriptures (Old Testament).

**newton** /ˈnjutn/, *n.* the derived SI unit of force; the force required to give an acceleration of one metre per second to a mass of one kilogram. *Symbol:* N [named after Sir Isaac *Newton,* 1642-1727, English scientist, mathematician and philosopher, formulator of the law of gravity]

**Newtonian telescope** /nju,toʊniən ˈtɛləskoʊp/, *n.* a telescope employing a reflecting parabolic objective mirror. [named after Sir Isaac *Newton.* See NEWTON]

**Newton's law of gravitation,** *n.* a law stating that the attractive force of gravitation between any two bodies is proportional to the product of their masses and inversely proportional to the square of the distance between them, the constant of proportionality being known as the **gravitational constant.** [see NEWTON]

**Newton's laws** /ˈnjutnz lɔz/, *n. pl.* three laws of motion which form the basis of classical dynamics: **1.** all bodies continue in a state of rest or uniform motion unless they are acted upon by external forces to change that state. **2.** the rate of change of momentum of a body is proportional to the force applied to it. **3.** to every action there is an equal and opposite reaction. [see NEWTON]

**Newton's rings** /ˈ– rɪŋz/, *n. pl.* coloured concentric rings which are produced round the point of contact of a convex lens and a plane reflecting surface. [see NEWTON]

**new wave** /nju ˈweɪv/, *n.* **1.** a movement or trend to break with traditional concepts in art, literature, politics, etc. **2.** →**nouvelle vague. 3.** a form of rock music of the 1970s in the style of punk rock, but characterised by greater imaginativeness and performance skills.

**New World, The,** *n.* the Western Hemisphere; the American continents.

**new year** /nju ˈjɪə/, *n.* **1.** the year approaching or newly begun. **2.** (*caps*) the first day or days of a year. **3.** (*caps*) New Year's Day.

**New Year's Day,** *n.* the first day of the year; 1 January.

**New Year's Eve,** *n.* the night of 31 December, usu. observed with merrymaking.

**New Zealand** /nju ˈzilənd/, *n.* a country in the South Pacific; an independent member of the Commonwealth.

**New Zealand beech,** *n.* any New Zealand forest tree of the genus *Nothofagus;* beech.

**New Zealander** /nju ˈziləndə/, *n.* a person native to or resident in New Zealand.

**New Zealand flax,** *n.* a New Zealand plant, *Phormium tenax,* with a rosette of long stiff leaves from which is obtained a fibre used in making rope and twine. Also, **New Zealand hemp.**

**New Zealand lilac,** *n.* an attractive New Zealand shrub, *Hebe hulkeana,* with lilac-like flowers.

**New Zealand realm,** *n.* a biogeographical realm centred on the New Zealand islands but including Norfolk, Lord Howe and Kermadec islands to the north, the Chatham Islands to the east and Macquarie Island to the south, and characterised by the lack of endemic mammals and a high proportion of flightless birds.

**New Zealand spinach,** *n.* a prostrate succulent plant, *Tetragonia tetragonioides,* common on sea shores in Australia and New Zealand.

**next** /nɛkst/, *adj.* (*superl. of* **nigh**), *adv.* *–adj.* **1.** immediately following in time, order, importance, etc.: *the next day.* **2.** nearest in place or position: *the next room.* **3.** nearest in relationship or kinship. **4.** *Archaic.* immediately preceding: *the Sunday next before Easter.* *–adv.* **5.** in the nearest place, time, importance, etc. **6.** on the first subsequent occasion: *when next we meet.* [ME *nexte,* OE *nēxt,* var. of *nēhst,* superl. of *nēah* NIGH]

**next-door** /ˈnɛkst-dɔ, nɛkst-ˈdɔ/, *adj.;* /nɛkst-ˈdɔ/, *adv.* *–adj.* **1.** dwelling in or occupying the next house, flat, shop, etc. **2. the boy (girl) next-door, a.** a boy (girl), often associated with one's family circle, whose virtues or attractions tend to be overlooked. **b.** an unsophisticated, wholesome boy (girl). *–adv.* **3.** at, in, or to the next house, etc.

**next friend** /nɛkst ˈfrɛnd/, *n.* a person bringing action in a court of law on behalf of a minor or person of unsound mind.

**next of kin,** *n.* **1.** a person's nearest relative or relatives. **2.** *Law.* the nearest relative(s), to whom the personal property passes upon the death of an intestate.

**nexus** /ˈnɛksəs/, *n., pl.* **nexus. 1.** a tie or link; a means of connection. **2.** a connected series. **3.** *Parl. Proc.* a constitutional condition which requires (as nearly as practicable) the ratio of two House of Representative members to one Senate member, in order to safeguard the numerical strength and constitutional power of the Senate. [L]

**NF,** Norman French.

**N.G.,** New Guinea.

**ngaio** /ˈnaɪoʊ/, *n.* a small coastal tree or shrub of New Zealand, *Myoporum laetum,* with narrow leaves and small white flowers marked with purple spots. [Maori]

**NGk,** New Greek. Also, **N.Gk.**

**Ni,** *Chem.* nickel.

**N.I.,** Norfolk Island.

**niacin** /ˈnaɪəsən/, *n.* →**nicotinic acid.** [Trademark; NI(COTINIC) AC(ID) + -IN[2]]

**nib** /nɪb/, *n., v.,* **nibbed, nibbing.** *–n.* **1.** the point of a pen, esp. a small, tapering metallic device having a split tip for drawing up ink and for writing. **2.** either of the divisions of a nib. **3.** a bill or beak, as of a bird; a neb. **4.** a point of anything. **5.** any pointed extremity. **6.** (*pl.*) crushed cocoa beans. *–v.i.* **7.** to furnish with a nib or point. **8.** *Obs.* to mend or trim the nib of (a quill pen). [OE *nybba* point (in a place name), c. Icel. *nibba* sharp point]

**nibble** /ˈnɪbəl/, *v.,* **-bled, -bling,** *n.* *–v.i.* **1.** to bite off small bits. **2.** to eat or feed by biting off small pieces. **3.** to bite slightly or gently (fol. by *at*). **4.** to evince interest (*at*) without actually accepting. *–v.t.* **5.** to bite off small bits of (a thing). **6.** to eat by biting off small pieces. **7.** to bite (*off,* etc.) in small pieces. *–n.* **8.** a small morsel or bit: *each nibble was eaten with the air of an epicure.* **9.** the act or an instance of nibbling. [late ME; cf. LG *nibbelen*] – **nibbler,** *n.*

**niblick** /ˈnɪblɪk/, *n.* a golf club (No. 8 iron) with a short, rounded, flat head whose face slopes greatly from the vertical.

**nibs** /nɪbz/, *n.pl.* (*construed as sing.*) *in the phrase* **his nibs,** *Colloq.* an arrogant or self-important man.

**Nicaragua** /nɪkəˈrægjuə/, *n.* a republic in Central America. – **Nicaraguan,** *adj., n.*

**niccolite** /ˈnɪkəlaɪt/, *n.* a pale copper-red mineral of a metallic lustre, nickel arsenide (Ni As), usu. occurring massive. [NL *niccolum* nickel + -ITE[1]]

**nice** /naɪs/, *adj.,* **nicer, nicest. 1.** pleasing; agreeable; delightful: *a nice visit.* **2.** amiably pleasant; kind: *they are always nice to strangers.* **3.** characterised by or requiring great accuracy, precision, skill, or delicacy: *nice workmanship.* **4.** requiring or showing tact or care; delicate. **5.** showing minute differences; minutely accurate, as instruments. **6.** minute, fine, or subtle, as a distinction. **7.** having or showing delicate and accurate perception: *a nice sense of colour.* **8.** refined as to manners, language, etc. **9.** suitable or proper: *not a nice song.* **10.** carefully neat as to dress, habits, etc. **11.** dainty or delicious, as food. **12.** dainty as to taste. **13.** *Obs.* coy, shy, or reluctant. **14.** *Obs.* →**wanton. 15.** *Obs.* foolish. [ME, from OF: simple, from L *nescius* not knowing] – **nicely,** *adv.* – **niceness,** *n.*

**nicety** /ˈnaɪsəti/, *n., pl.* **-ties. 1.** a delicate or fine point: *niceties of protocol.* **2.** a fine distinction; subtlety. **3.** (*oft. pl.*) something nice; a refinement or elegance, as of manners or living. **4.** the quality of being nice. **5.** delicacy of character, as of something requiring care or tact: *a matter of considerable nicety.* **6. to a nicety,** in great detail; with precision. [ME *nycete,* from OF *nicete,* from *nice* NICE]

**niche** /nɪtʃ/, *n., v.,* **niched, niching.** *–n.* **1.** an ornamental recess in a wall, etc., usu. round in section and arched, as for a statue or other decorative object. **2.** a place or position suitable or appropriate for a person or thing. **3.** *Ecol.* the position or function of an organism in a community of plants and animals. *–v.t.* **4.** to place in a niche. [F, from *nicher* to make a nest, from Gallo-Rom. *nīdicāre,* from L *nīdus* nest]

niche (def. 1)

**nichrome** /ˈnaɪkroʊm/, *n.* a nickel-based alloy, containing chromium and iron, having high electrical resistance and stability at high temperatures.

**nick**[1] /nɪk/, *n.* **1.** a notch, groove, or the like, cut into or existing in a thing. **2.** a hollow place produced in an edge or surface, as of a dish, by breaking. **3.** a small groove on one side of the shank of a printing type, serving as a guide in setting or to distinguish different types. **4.** *Horseracing.* a breeding connection: *that horse has a double nick to a famous sire.* **5. in good nick,** in good physical condition. **6.** *Colloq.* prison. **7. in the nick of time,** at the vital or last possible moment. **8.** *Colloq.* the act of stopping work and leaving the job, esp. one finished ahead of schedule: *the nick's* *on, the 4 o'clock nick.* **9.** *Squash.* the corner between the floor boards and the wall of a squash court. **10.** *Cricket.* →**snick.** *–v.t.* **11.** to make a nick or nicks in; notch. **12.** to record by means of a notch or notches. **13.** to cut through or into. **14.** to incise certain tendons at the root of (a horse's) tail when setting it, to cause him to carry it higher. **15.** *Horseracing.* to breed through certain successful racing bloodlines. **16.** to hit, guess, catch, etc., exactly. **17.** *Colloq.* to capture or arrest. **18.** to trick, cheat, or defraud. **19.** *Colloq.* to steal. **20.** *Cricket.* →**snick.** *–v.i.* **21. nick off,** *Colloq.* to leave, disappear. **22. nick out,** *Colloq.* to go out for a short period. [late ME; cf. OE *gehnycned* wrinkled]

**nick**[2] /nɪk/, *n. Colloq. in the phrase* **in the nick,** in the nude; naked. [orig. uncert.; ? *nix* nothing]

**nicked** /nɪkt/, *v.* **1.** past tense and past participle of **nick**[1]. *–adj.* **2. get nicked,** *Colloq.* **a.** to go away. **b.** to be caught.

**nickel** /ˈnɪkəl/, *n., v.,* **-elled, -elling** or (*U.S.*) **-eled, -eling.** *–n.* **1.** *Chem.* a hard, silvery white, ductile and malleable metallic element, allied to iron and cobalt, not readily oxidised, and much used in the arts, in making alloys, etc. *Symbol:* Ni; *at. wt:* 58.71; *at. no.:* 28; *sp. gr.:* 8.9 at 20°C. **2.** *U.S.* a coin composed of or containing nickel, now a five-cent piece. *–v.t.* **3.** to cover or coat with nickel. [Swed., short for *kopparnickel* niccolite, from G, half-translation, half-adoption of *Kupfernickel,* said to mean copper demon, since it looks like copper but yields none]

**nickel bloom** /ˈ– blum/, *n.* **1.** a monoclinic mineral $Ni_3(AsO_4)_2 \cdot 8H_2O$, usu. found as green encrustations as an alteration product of nickel arsenides; annabergite. **2.** a hydrated and oxidised green patina on outcropping rocks indicating the existence of primary nickel minerals; nickel indicator.

**nickel carbonyl** /– ˈkabənəl/, *n.* a volatile liquid, $Ni(CO)_4$, used in nickel plating and formed in the Mond process for purifying nickel.

**nickelic** /nɪˈkɛlɪk/, *adj.* of or containing nickel, esp. in the trivalent state.

**nickeliferous** /nɪkəˈlɪfərəs/, *adj.* containing or yielding nickel.

**nickelodeon** /nɪkəˈloʊdiən/, *n.* **1.** *U.S.* (formerly) a place of amusement with a film or variety show, etc., to which the price of admission was five cents. **2.** an early jukebox. [NICKEL (def. 2) + *odeon,* var. of ODEUM]

**nickelous** /ˈnɪkələs/, *adj.* containing bivalent nickel.

**nickel plate** /nɪkəl ˈpleɪt/, *n.* a thin coating of nickel deposited on the surface of a piece of metal by electroplating or otherwise.

**nickel-plate** /nɪkəl-ˈpleɪt/, *v.t.,* **-plated, -plating.** to coat with nickel by electroplating or otherwise.

**nickel silver** /ˈnɪkəl sɪlvə/, *n.* a silver-white alloy containing copper (52-80%), zinc (10-35%) and nickel (5-35%), used for making utensils, drawing instruments, etc.; German silver.

**nick-nack** /ˈnɪk-næk/, *n.* →**knick-knack.**

**nickname** /ˈnɪkneɪm/, *n., v.,* **-named, -naming.** *–n.* **1.** a name added to or substituted for the proper name of a person, place, etc., as in ridicule or familiarity. **2.** a familiar form of a proper name, as *Jim* for *James.* *–v.t.* **3.** to give a nickname to, or call by a specified nickname. **4.** to call by an incorrect or improper name. [ME *nekename,* for *ekename* (*an ekename* being taken as *a nekename*). See EKE[2], NAME]

**nicky** /ˈnɪki/, *v.t.,* **nickied, nickying.** *Colloq.* to improve, esp. superficially, the appearance of (a car, house, etc.) (fol. by *up*). [from NICK[1]]

**niçoise** /nɪˈswaz/, *adj.* (of a salad) prepared with lettuce, olives, anchovies, tuna, tomatoes, orange, hard-boiled eggs, potatoes, etc., and French dressing. [F *Niçoise* of Nice, city in S France]

**nicotinamide** /nɪkəˈtɪnəmaɪd/, *n.* a colourless crystalline solid, $C_6H_4NCONH_2$, the amide of nicotinic acid and a component of the vitamin B complex.

**nicotinamide adenine dinucleotide,** *n.* an important cofactor produced from niacin involved in reactions catalysed by many dehydrogenases.

**nicotine** /nɪkəˈtin, ˈnɪkətin/, *n.* a poisonous alkaloid, $C_{10}H_{14}N_2$, the active principle of tobacco, obtained as a colourless or nearly colourless, oily, acrid liquid. Also, **nicotin** /ˈnɪkətən/. [F, from Jacques *Nicot,* 1530-1600, who introduced tobacco into France in 1560]

**nicotinic acid** /nɪkətɪnɪk ˈæsəd, -tin-/, *n.* an acid derived from the oxidation of nicotine, $(C_5H_4N)COOH$, found in fresh meat, yeast, etc., and which is the component of the vitamin B complex which counteracts pellagra; niacin.

**nicotinism** /ˈnɪkətinɪzəm/, *n.* a pathological condition caused by excessive use of tobacco.

**nictitate** /ˈnɪktəteɪt/, *v.i.,* **-tated, -tating.** →**wink**[1]. Also, **nictate** /ˈnɪkteɪt/. [ML *nictitātus,* pp. of *nictitāre,* frequentative of L *nictāre* wink] – **nictitation** /nɪktəˈteɪʃən/, **nictation** /nɪkˈteɪʃən/, *n.*

**nictitating membrane** /ˌnɪktəteɪtɪŋ ˈmɛmbreɪn/, *n.* a thin membrane, or inner of third eyelid, present in many animals, capable of being drawn across the eyeball, as for protection.

**niddering** /ˈnɪdərɪŋ/, *Archaic.* *–n.* **1.** a cowardly or base person. *–adj.* **2.** cowardly; base. Also, **nidering.** [erroneous var. of *nithing,* from Scand.; cf. Icel. *nīdhingr*]

**nide** /naɪd/, *n.* a nest or brood, esp. of pheasants. [L *nīdus* nest]

**nidicolous** /nɪˈdɪkələs/, *adj.* denoting birds which are helpless when hatched and remain in the nest for some time.

**nidificate** /ˈnɪdəfəkeɪt/, *v.i.,* **-cated, -cating.** to build a nest. Also, **nidify.** [L *nīdificātus,* pp.] – **nidification** /nɪdəfəˈkeɪʃən/, *n.*

**nidifugous** /nɪˈdɪfjəgəs/, *adj.* denoting birds which are active soon after hatching and leave the nest almost at once.

**nidify** /ˈnɪdəfaɪ/, *v.i.,* **-fied, -fying.** →**nidificate.**

**nidus** /ˈnaɪdəs/, *n., pl.* **-di** /-daɪ/. **1.** a nest, esp. one in which insects, etc., deposit their eggs. **2.** a place or point in a living organism where a germ, whether proper or foreign to the organism, normal or morbid, may find means of development. [L. See NEST]

**niece** /nis/, *n.* **1.** a daughter of one's brother or sister. **2.** a daughter of one's husband's or wife's brother or sister. **3.** (*euph.*) an illegitimate daughter of a celibate ecclesiastic. [ME *nece, nice,* from OF *niece,* from VL *neptia,* replacing L *neptis* granddaughter, niece]

**niello** /niˈɛloʊ/, *n., pl.* **nielli** /niˈɛli/, **niellos,** *v.,* **-loed, -loing.** *–n.* **1.** a black metallic composition, consisting of silver, copper, lead, and sulphur, with which an incised design is filled in to produce an ornamental effect. **2.** ornamental work produced by this process. **3.** a specimen of such work. *–v.t.* **4.** to decorate by means of niello; treat with niello or by the niello process. [It., from L *nigellus* blackish]

**Nietzscheism** /ˈnitʃiˌɪzəm/, *n.* the philosophy of Friedrich Wilhelm Nietzsche, 1844-1900, emphasising self-aggrandisement, or the will to power, as the chief motivating force of both the individual and society. Also, **Nietzscheanism.** – **Nietzschean,** *n., adj.*

**Ni-Fe accumulator** /naɪ-ˌfi əˈkjumjəleɪtə/, *n.* →**Edison accumulator.** [Trademark; from the chemical symbols NI + FE]

**niff** /nɪf/, *n. Colloq.* an unpleasant smell.

**nifty** /ˈnɪfti/, *adj.,* **-tier, -tiest,** *n., pl.* **-ties.** *Colloq.* *–adj.* **1.** smart; stylish; fine: *a nifty little car.* *–n.* **2.** *Chiefly U.S.* something nifty, as a smart or clever remark. [orig. theatrical slang]

**nig** /nɪg/, *n. Colloq.* (*derog.*) a negro. [short for NIGGER]

**Niger** /ˈnaɪdʒə/, *n.* a republic in north-western Africa.

**Nigeria** /naɪˈdʒɪəriə/, *n.* a republic in western Africa. – **Nigerian,** *adj., n.*

**niggard** /ˈnɪgəd/, *n.* **1.** an excessively parsimonious or stingy person. *–adj.* **2.** niggardly. [ME, from (obs.) *nig* niggard (from Scand.; cf. d. Swed. *nygg*) + -ARD]

**niggardly** /ˈnɪgədli/, *adj.* **1.** parsimonious; stingy. **2.** meanly small or scanty: *a niggardly allowance.* *–adv.* **3.** in the manner of a niggard. – **niggardliness,** *n.*

**nigger** /ˈnɪgə/, *n.* **1.** (*derog.*) a Negro. **2.** (*derog.*) a member of any dark-skinned race. **3.** →**blackfish** (def. 1). **4. nigger in the woodpile,** a hidden snag. *–adj.* **5.** (*derog.*) denoting or pertaining to a Negro or dark-skinned person. [var. of *neger,* from F *nègre,* from Sp. *negro* NEGRO]

**niggerhead** /ˈnɪgəhɛd/, *n.* **1.** a hard black stone, spherical and often concretionary, common in coal measures. **2.** a block of black coral standing above water. **3.** any of a number of species of hardy, dry-weather resistant, nine-awned, native grasses of the genus *Enneapogon,* with tufted seedheads often blackish in colour. **4.** Also, **Maori-head.** *N.Z.* a blackened, matted clump of a swamp tussock grass, esp. a grass of the genus *Carex*. **5.** the spiny head of a saltwort. **6.** (formerly) a stick of coarse dark tobacco.

**nigger-head beech** /ˈnɪgə-hɛd ˈbitʃ/, *n.* the northernmost Australian species of *Nothofagus*, *N. moorei*, which forms forests on high eastern mountain slopes in northern New South Wales and southern Queensland.

**niggle** /ˈnɪgəl/, *v.*, **-gled, -gling.** *–v.i.* **1.** to trifle; work ineffectively. **2.** to make constant petty criticisms. *–v.t.* **3.** to irritate; annoy. [apparently from Scand.; cf. Norw. *nigla*] – **niggler,** *n.*

**niggling** /ˈnɪglɪŋ/, *adj.* **1.** worrying; persistent; nagging: *a niggling thought.* **2.** petty; overly concerned with trifling details. Also, **niggly.**

**nigh** /naɪ/, *adv., adj.* **nigher, nighest** or **next,** *prep.* *–adv.* **1.** near in space, time, or relation. **2.** *Archaic.* nearly or almost. *–adj.* **3.** being near; not distant; near in relationship. **4.** short or direct. **5.** *Archaic.* (with reference to animals or vehicles) left or near. **6.** *Archaic.* parsimonious. *–prep.* **7.** near. [ME *nigh(e), neye,* OE *nēah, nēh,* c. G *nahe*]

**night** /naɪt/, *n.* **1.** the interval of darkness between sunset and sunrise. **2.** nightfall. **3.** the darkness of night; the dark. **4.** a state or time of obscurity, ignorance, misfortune, etc. [ME; OE *niht, neaht,* c. G *Nacht*]

**night-and-day** /naɪt-ən-ˈdeɪ/, *n.* a couch with a mechanism which allows the back to be made level with the seat to form a bed.

**night-bird** /ˈnaɪt-bɜd/, *n.* **1.** any bird of nocturnal habits. **2.** *Colloq.* one who is habitually up or prowling at night; a nighthawk.

**night blindness** /ˈnaɪt blaɪndnəs/, *n.* →**nyctalopia.**

**nightcap** /ˈnaɪtkæp/, *n.* **1.** (formerly) a cap for the head, worn in bed. **2.** *Colloq.* an alcoholic or other drink, esp. a hot one, taken before going to bed.

**night cart** /ˈnaɪt kat/, *n. Colloq.* →**sanitary cart.**

**night chemist** /ˈ– kɛməst/, *n.* a chemist's shop or pharmacy which is open at night.

**nightclothes** /ˈnaɪtkloʊðz/, *n. pl.* garments designed to be worn in bed.

**nightclub** /ˈnaɪtklʌb/, *n.* a place of entertainment, open until late, offering food, drink, cabaret, dancing, etc.

**nightdress** /ˈnaɪtdrɛs/, *n.* **1.** dress or clothing for wearing in bed. **2.** a loose, full-length garment, worn in bed by women and children.

**nightfall** /ˈnaɪtfɔl/, *n.* the coming of night.

**nightgown** /ˈnaɪtgaʊn/, *n.* a nightdress or nightshirt.

**nighthawk** /ˈnaɪthɔk/, *n.* **1.** a nightjar, *Eurostopodus mystacalis,* of coastal eastern Australia. **2.** elsewhere, any of various goatsuckers, esp. the **common nighthawk,** mosquito hawk, or bullbat, *Chordeiles minor.* **3.** *Colloq.* one who is habitually up or prowling about at night.

**night heron** /ˈnaɪt hɛrən/, *n.* any of certain thick-billed herons of crepuscular or nocturnal habits, of the genus *Nycticorax* and allied genera, as the **nankeen night heron,** *Nycticorax caledonicus.*

**night-horse** /ˈnaɪt-hɔs/, *n.* a quiet, old horse kept near the homestead overnight, often hobbled, so that he can be used to catch the other horses in the morning.

**nightie** /ˈnaɪti/, *n.* →**nightdress.** Also, **nighty.**

**nightingale** /ˈnaɪtɪŋgeɪl/, *n.* a small migratory bird of the thrush family, esp. the common nightingale, *Luscinia megarhyncha,* of Europe, noted for the melodious song of the male given chiefly at night during the breeding season. [ME *nightyngale,* nasalised var. of *nightegale,* OE *nihtegale,* c. G *Nachtigall,* lit., night singer (cf. OE *galan* sing)]

**nightjar** /ˈnaɪtdʒa/, *n.* **1.** any of various nocturnal insect-eating birds of the widely distributed family Caprimulgidae, as the spotted nightjar, *Eurostopodus guttatus,* found throughout Australia. **2.** →**owlet-nightjar.** **3.** the common European nightjar, *Caprimulgus europaeus.*

**night latch** /ˈnaɪt lætʃ/, *n.* a spring latch for a door or the like, which when adjusted for use, as at night, prevents the door from being opened from outside except by a key.

**night-life** /ˈnaɪt-laɪf/, *n.* the entertainments and activity of a place at night, as in nightclubs, etc.

**night-light** /ˈnaɪt-laɪt/, *n.* a dim light left burning throughout the night.

**nightline** /ˈnaɪtlaɪn/, *n.* a fishing line left in a river, etc., overnight.

**nightlong** /ˈnaɪtlɒŋ/, *adj.* **1.** lasting all night. *–adv.* **2.** throughout the whole night.

**nightly** /ˈnaɪtli/, *adj.* **1.** coming, occurring, appearing, or active at night: *nightly revels.* **2.** coming or occurring each night. **3.** of, pertaining to, or characteristic of night. *–adv.* **4.** at or by night. **5.** on every night: *for one week only, performances will be given nightly.*

**nightmare** /ˈnaɪtmɛə/, *n.* **1.** a condition during sleep, or a dream, marked by a feeling of suffocation or distress, with acute fear, anxiety, or other painful emotion. **2.** a condition, thought, or experience suggestive of a nightmare in sleep. **3.** a monster or evil spirit formerly supposed to oppress persons during sleep. [ME. See NIGHT, MARE[2]] – **nightmarish,** *adj.*

**night-night** /naɪt-ˈnaɪt/, *interj.* (*in children's speech*) good night. Also, **nightie-night.**

**night out** /naɪt ˈaʊt/, *n.* an evening visit to a restaurant, theatre, etc., seen as a pleasurable release from the habit of staying at home.

**night owl** /ˈ– aʊl/, *n. Colloq.* a person who often stays up late.

**night parrot** /ˈ– pærət/, *n.* either of two small Australian parrots that feed and drink after dusk: **1.** a rare green and yellow parrot, *Geopsittacus occidentalis.* **2.** →**Bourke parrot.**

**night-porter** /ˈnaɪt-pɔtə/, *n.* a porter or doorkeeper on duty at night.

**night raven** /ˈnaɪt reɪvən/, *n.* **1.** *Poetic.* a bird that cries in the night; an ill omen. **2.** →**night heron.**

**nightrider** /ˈnaɪtraɪdə/, *n. U.S.* one of a band of mounted men committing deeds of violence at night, as for purposes of intimidation or vengeance. – **nightriding,** *n.*

**nightrobe** /ˈnaɪtroʊb/, *n.* **1.** →**dressing-gown.** **2.** →**nightdress.**

**nights** /naɪts/, *adv. Colloq.* at night.

**night school** /ˈnaɪt skul/, *n.* a school held in the evening, esp. for those who cannot attend a day school; evening class.

**nightshade** /ˈnaɪtʃeɪd/, *n.* **1.** any of various plants of the genus *Solanum,* as black nightshade. **2.** any of various other plants, as deadly nightshade. [ME; OE *nihtscada.* See NIGHT, SHADE]

**night shift** /ˈnaɪt ʃɪft/, *n.* **1.** a work period during the night, esp. the shift between late evening and early morning. **2.** the group of workers working this shift.

**nightshirt** /ˈnaɪtʃɜt/, *n.* a knee-length shirt or loose garment worn in bed by men or boys.

**nightsoil** /ˈnaɪtsɔɪl/, *n.* the contents of privies, cesspools, etc., used as manure.

**nightspot** /ˈnaɪtspɒt/, *n.* →**nightclub.**

**nightstick** /ˈnaɪtstɪk/, *n. U.S.* a heavy stick or long club carried by a policeman at night, and sometimes in the daytime.

**night tiger** /ˈnaɪt taɪgə/, *n.* →**broad-headed snake.**

**night-time** /ˈnaɪt-taɪm/, *n.* the time between evening and morning. Also, *Poetic,* **night-tide.**

**nightwalker** /ˈnaɪtwɔkə/, *n.* one who walks or prowls about in the night, as a thief, a prostitute, etc. – **nightwalking,** *n.*

**night watch** /ˈnaɪt wɒtʃ/, *n.* **1.** a watch or guard kept during the night. **2.** the person or persons keeping such a watch. **3.** (*usu. pl.*) a period or division of the night.

**nightwatchman** /naɪtˈwɒtʃmən/, *n., pl.* **-men** /-mən/. **1.** a man employed to guard property, etc., at night. **2.** *Cricket Colloq.* a low order batsman, who is sent in to bat late in the afternoon when the batting-side captain wishes to preserve his better batsmen for the next day's play.

**nightwear** /ˈnaɪtwɛə/, *n.* clothes for wearing in bed.

**nighty** /ˈnaɪti/, *n., pl.* **nighties.** →**nightie.**

**nig-nog** /ˈnɪg-nɒg/, *n. Colloq.* (*derog.*) **1.** a simpleton. **2.** *Brit.* a black person.

**nigrescent** /naɪˈgrɛsənt/, *adj.* blackish. [L *nigrescens,* ppr., becoming black] – **nigrescence,** *n.*

**nigrify** /ˈnɪgrəfaɪ/, *v.t.,* **-fied, -fying.** to make black.

**nigritude** /ˈnɪgrətjud/, *n.* **1.** blackness. **2.** something black. **3.** →**negritude.** [L *nigritūdo*]

**nigrosine** /ˈnɪgrəsin/, *n.* any of a class of black dyestuffs based on the oxidation products of aniline, used as pigments in ink, shoe polish, etc. and as a shark repellent.

**nihil** /ˈnaɪhɪl, ˈni-/, *n.* nothing; a thing of no value. [L]

**nihilism** /ˈnaɪəlɪzəm, ˈni-/, *n.* **1.** total disbelief in religion or moral principles and obligations, or in established laws and institutions. **2.** *Philos.* **a.** a belief that there is no objective basis of truth. **b.** an extreme form of scepticism, denying all real existence. **c.** nothingness or non-existence. **3.** (*sometimes cap.*) the principles of a Russian revolutionary group, active in the latter half of the 19th century, holding that existing social and political institutions must be destroyed in order to clear the way for a new state of society, and in its extreme measures employing terrorism, assassination, etc. **4.** terrorism or revolutionary activity. [L *nihil* nothing + -ISM] – **nihilist,** *n.* – **nihilistic** /naɪəˈlɪstɪk, ni-/, *adj.*

**nihility** /naɪˈhɪləti, ni-/, *n.* nothingness.

**nihil obstat** /naɪhɪl ˈɒbstæt/, (a phrase used by an official Roman Catholic censor to grant permission for publication of a book containing nothing contrary to faith or morals). [L: nothing hinders]

**nikau** /ˈnikaʊ/, *n.* the only palm native to New Zealand, *Rhopalostylus sapida.* [Maori]

**nikethamide** /nəˈkɛθəmaɪd/, *n.* a drug used as a respiratory stimulant.

**nil** /nɪl/, *n.* nothing. [L, contraction of *nihil*]

**Nile blue** /naɪl ˈblu/, *n.* a pale greenish-blue colour.

**Nile green** /– ˈgrin/, *n.* a pale bluish-green colour.

**nilgai** /ˈnɪlgaɪ/, *n., pl.* **-gais,** (*esp. collectively*) **-gai.** a large antelope of eastern India, *Boselaphus tragocamelus,* the male coloured bluish grey, the hornless female tawny. Also, **nylghai.** [Hind.: lit., blue cow]

nilgai

**nill** /nɪl/, *Archaic.* *–v.t.* **1.** not to will; not to want. *–v.i.* **2.** to be unwilling. [ME *nille(n),* OE *nyllan,* from *ne* not + *willan* will]

**nim**[1] /nɪm/, *v.t.,* **nam** or **nimmed; nomen, nome,** or **nimmed; nimming.** *Archaic.* **1.** to take. **2.** to steal. [ME; OE *niman,* c. G *nehmen,* Goth. *niman*]

**nim**[2] /nɪm/, *n.* a game in which two players take counters, matches, etc., in turns from piles or patterns, the object being either to draw the last match, etc., or to avoid drawing it. [special use of NIM[1]]

**nimble** /ˈnɪmbəl/, *adj.,* **-bler, -blest. 1.** quick and light in movement; moving with ease; agile; active; rapid: *nimble feet.* **2.** quick in apprehending, devising, etc.: *nimble wits.* **3.** cleverly contrived. [ME *nymel,* representing OE var. (unrecorded) of *numol* quick at taking, from *niman* take] – **nimbleness,** *n.* – **nimbly,** *adv.*

**nimbostratus** /nɪmboʊˈstreɪtəs/, *n.* a low, formless cloud layer, of a nearly uniform dark grey; a layer type of rain cloud. [*nimbo-* (combining form of NIMBUS) + STRATUS]

**nimbus** /ˈnɪmbəs/, *n., pl.* **-bi** /-baɪ/, **-buses. 1.** a bright cloud anciently conceived of as surrounding a deity of the classical mythology when appearing on earth. **2.** a cloud or atmosphere of some kind surrounding a person or thing. **3.** *Art.* a disc or otherwise shaped figure representing a radiance about the head of a divine or sacred personage, a medieval sovereign, etc.; a halo. **4.** *Obs.* the type of cloud or mass of clouds, dense, with ragged edges, which yields rain or snow; a rain cloud. [L: rainstorm, thunder-cloud]

**nimiety** /nɪˈmaɪəti/, *n.* excess. [LL *nimietas*]

**niminy-piminy** /nɪməni-ˈpɪməni/, *adj.* mincing; affectedly nice or refined. [imitative of a mincing utterance]

**Nimrod** /ˈnɪmrɒd/, *n.* (*also l.c.*) one expert in or devoted to hunting. [orig. with ref. to *Nimrod,* a 'mighty hunter', the great-grandson of Noah (Gen. 10: 8, 9)]

**nincompoop** /ˈnɪŋkəmpup/, *n.* a fool or simpleton.

**nine** /naɪn/, *n.* **1.** a cardinal number, eight plus one. **2.** a symbol for this number, as 9 or IX. **3.** a set of nine persons or things. **4.** a team of baseball players. **5.** a playing card with nine pips. **6.** a small keg of beer (a firkin), formerly approx. 9 gallons, now 40.5 litres. **7. dressed (up) to the nines,** *Colloq.* smartly dressed or overdressed. *–adj.* **8.** amounting to nine in number. [ME; OE *nigen,* var. of *nigon,* c. G *neun*]

**nine day wonder,** *n.* an event, etc., that arouses great but short-lived popular interest. Also, **nine days' wonder.**

**ninefold** /ˈnaɪnfoʊld/, *adj.* **1.** nine times as much. **2.** having nine parts. *–adv.* **3.** nine times as much.

**ninepins** /ˈnaɪnpɪnz/, *n.pl.* **1.** (*construed as sing.*) a game played with nine wooden pins at which a ball is bowled to knock them down; skittles. **2.** the pins used in this game; the skittles.

**nineteen** /naɪnˈtin, ˈnaɪntin/, *n.* **1.** a cardinal number, ten plus nine. **2.** a symbol for this number, as 19 or XIX. **3. talk nineteen to the dozen,** to talk very quickly or excitedly. *–adj.* **4.** amounting to nineteen in number. [ME *nintene,* representing d. OE var. (unrecorded) of OE *nigontȳne*] – **nineteenth,** *adj., n.*

**nineteenth hole** /naɪntinθ ˈhoʊl/, *n. Colloq.* the bar in a golf clubhouse.

**nineteenth man** /– ˈmæn/, *n.* (in Australian Rules) the first of the two reserves who may be used to replace any player already on the field.

**ninety** /ˈnaɪnti/, *n., pl.* **-ties,** *adj.* *–n.* **1.** a cardinal number, ten times nine. **2.** a symbol for this number, as 90 or XC. **3.** (*pl.*) the numbers from 90 to 99 of a series, esp. with reference to the years of a person's age, or the years of a century, esp. the nineteenth. *–adj.* **4.** amounting to ninety in number. [ME *nineti,* OE *nigontig*] – **ninetieth** *adj., n.*

**ning-nong** /ˈnɪŋ-nɒŋ/, *n. Colloq.* a simpleton.

**ninhydrin** /nɪnˈhaɪdrən/, *n.* an organic compound, $C_9H_6O_4$, widely used to detect small amounts of amino acids by the colour produced.

**ninny** /ˈnɪni/, *n., pl.* **-nies.** a fool; a simpleton.

**ninon** /ˈninɒn, ˈnɪnɒn/, *n.* a fine semitransparent silk fabric, used mostly for expensive lingerie.

**ninth** /naɪnθ/, *adj.* **1.** next after the eighth. **2.** being one of nine equal parts. *–n.* **3.** a ninth part, esp. of one ($\frac{1}{9}$). **4.** the ninth member of a series. **5.** *Music.* **a.** a note distant from another note by an interval of an octave and a second. **b.** the interval between such notes. **c.** harmonic combination of such notes. – **ninthly,** *adv.*

**ninth chord** /– ˈkɔd/, *n.* a musical chord formed by the superposition of four thirds.

**niobate** /ˈnaɪəbeɪt/, *n.* a salt of any niobic acid. [NIOB(IUM) + -ATE[2]]

**niobic** /naɪˈoʊbɪk, -ˈɒbɪk/, *adj.* **1.** containing pentavalent niobium, as *niobic acid,* $Nb_2O_5 \cdot nH_2O$. **2.** of or pertaining to niobium.

**niobium** /naɪˈoʊbiəm/, *n.* a steel-grey metallic element resembling tantalum in its chemical properties. *Symbol:* Nb; *at. no.:* 41; *at. wt:* 92.906; *sp. gr.:* 8.57 at 20°C. Formerly, **columbium.** [NL; named after *Niobe,* in Greek mythology daughter of Tantalus, because found with tantalum. See -IUM]

**niobous** /naɪˈoʊbəs/, *adj.* **1.** containing trivalent niobium, as *niobous chloride,* $NbCl_3$. **2.** of or pertaining to niobium.

**nip**[1] /nɪp/, *v.,* **nipped, nipping,** *n.* *–v.t.* **1.** to compress sharply between two surfaces or points; pinch or bite. **2.** to take off by pinching, biting, or snipping (usu. fol. by *off*). **3.** to check in growth or development: *to nip a plot in the bud.* **4.** to affect sharply and painfully or injuriously, as cold does. **5.** *Naut.* to secure (a rope) by holding it with a smaller rope. **6.** *Colloq.* to snatch or take suddenly or quickly (fol. by *away, up,* etc.). **7.** *Colloq.* to steal. *–v.i.* **8.** *Colloq.* to move or go suddenly or quickly, or slip (fol. by *away, off, up,* etc.). *–n.* **9.** the act of nipping; a pinch. **10.** a sharp or biting remark. **11.** a biting quality, as in cold or frosty air. **12.** sharp cold; a sharp touch of frost. **13.** biting taste or tang, as in cheese. **14.** a small bit or quantity of anything. **15.** *Naut.* pressure exerted by pack-ice on the sides of a vessel. **16.** *Naut.* the grip of a rope at the point where it is twisted round something. **17. nip and tuck,** *U.S.* (in a race or other contest) with one competitor equalling the speed or efforts of another; neck and neck. **18. put the nips in,** *Colloq.* to extract money, etc, by putting pressure on someone. [ME *nyp(pen)*; akin to obs. *nipe,* c. D *nijpen*]

**nip**[2] /nɪp/, *n., v.,* **nipped, nipping.** *–n.* **1.** a small drink; a sip. **2.** a small measure of spirits. *–v.t.* **3.** to drink (spirits, etc.) in small sips. *–v.i.* **4.** to take a nip or nips, esp.

repeatedly. [short for *nipperkin,* ? from D or LG]

**Nip** /nɪp/, *n. Colloq.* (*derog.*) a Japanese, esp. a Japanese soldier. [short for NIPPONESE]

**nipa** /ˈnipə, ˈnaɪpə/, *n.* a palm, *Nypa fruticans,* of the East Indies, the Philippines, etc., whose foliage is much used for thatching, etc. [Malay *nīpah*]

**nipper** /ˈnɪpə/, *n.* **1.** one who or that which nips. **2.** (*usu. pl.*) a device for nipping, as pincers or forceps. **3.** one of the large claws of a crustacean. **4.** (*pl.*) *Colloq.* handcuffs. **5.** *Colloq.* a small boy or younger brother. **6.** (*pl.*) *Colloq.* children. **7.** *Bldg Trades Colloq.* one employed on a construction site to do small odd jobs, as make tea, buy lunch, etc. **8.** a junior lifesaver.

**nipping** /ˈnɪpɪŋ/, *adj.* **1.** that nips. **2.** sharp or biting, as cold, etc. **3.** sarcastic. – **nippingly,** *adv.*

**nipple** /ˈnɪpəl/, *n.* **1.** a protuberance of the mamma or breast where, in the female, the milk ducts discharge; a teat. **2.** something resembling it, as the mouthpiece of a nursing bottle. **3.** a short piece of pipe with threads on each end, used for joining valves, etc. **4.** *Mach.* a small drilled bush containing a one-way valve through which a lubricant can be supplied to a bearing, esp. by a grease gun. [orig. uncert.]

**nipplewort** /ˈnɪpəlwɜt/, *n.* a slender, erect annual with yellow capitula, *Lapsana communis,* widespread in hedges and waste places of the temperature zone.

**Nippon** /ˈnɪpɒn/, *n.* Japanese name of Japan. [short for *Nippon-koku,* lit., land of the origin of the sun]

**Nipponese** /nɪpənˈiz/, *n., pl.* **-ese,** *adj.* →**Japanese.** [NIPPON + -ESE]

**nippy** /ˈnɪpi/, *adj.,* **-pier, -piest. 1.** apt to nip; sharp; biting. **2.** biting, as the cold. **3.** *Colloq.* nimble; active.

**nirvana** /nɜˈvanə, nɪə-/, *n.* **1.** (*oft. cap.*) (in Buddhism) **a.** the extinguishing of the restlessness and heat of one's emotions. **b.** the passionless peace of imperturbability, attained through the annihilation of disturbing desires. **2.** freedom from pain, worry, and the external world. [Skt: a blowing out (as of a light)]

**nisi** /ˈnaɪsaɪ/, *conj.* **1.** unless. *–adj.* **2.** *Law.* (of a court order, decree, etc.) conditional; not coming into effect unless a person or persons fail to show cause against it within a certain time. [L]

**nisi prius** /– ˈpraɪəs/, *n.* **1.** a trial before a single judge with a jury, hearings at nisi prius being part of the jurisdiction of the Supreme Court. *–adj.* **2.** denoting such a trial. **3.** *U.S.* designating a court of first instance. [L: unless previously]

**Nissen hut** /ˈnɪsən hʌt/, *n.* a prefabricated shelter with the shape of a long, slightly flattened cylinder, usu. built of steel sheet, esp. for use by soldiers. [named after Colonel P. N. *Nissen,* 1871-1930, British mining engineer, the inventor]

**nisus** /ˈnaɪsəs/, *n., pl.* **-sus.** effort; impulse. [L: effort]

**nit**[1] /nɪt/, *n.* **1.** the egg of a parasitic insect attached to a hair, or fibre of clothing; particularly the egg of a louse. **2.** the insect while young. **3.** *Colloq.* a foolish or stupid person. [ME *nite,* OE *hnitu,* c. G *Niss*]

**nit**[2] /nɪt/, *n.* →**candela per square metre.** [L *nitor* brightness]

**nit**[3] /nɪt/, *n. Colloq.* watch; guard: *to keep nit.* [orig. uncert.]

**nite** /naɪt/, *n. Colloq.* night.

**nitgrass** /ˈnɪtgras/, *n.* a small annual tufted grass, *Gastridium ventricosum,* occurring mostly in dry places near the sea in south-western Europe and the Mediterranean region.

**nit-keeper** /ˈnɪt-kipə/, *n. Colloq.* a person who keeps watch; a lookout.

**niton** /ˈnaɪtɒn/, *n.* an early name for the element radon. *Symbol:* Nt [NL, from L *nitēre* shine]

**nitpick** /ˈnɪtpɪk/, *v.i.* to be unduly critical, concerned with insignificant details. [NIT[1] + PICK[1]] – **nitpicker,** *n.* – **nitpicking,** *n., adj.*

**nitr-,** variant of **nitro-,** before vowels.

**nitramine** /ˈnaɪtrəmin, -mən/, *n.* any of a class of amines containing a nitro group, and having the general formula $R \cdot NH \cdot NO_2$.

**nitrate** /ˈnaɪˌtreɪt/, *n., v.,* **-trated, -trating.** *–n.* **1.** *Chem.* a salt or ester of nitric acid, or any compound containing the $-NO_3$ radical. **2.** fertiliser consisting of potassium nitrate or sodium nitrate. *–v.t.* **3.** to treat with nitric acid or a nitrate. **4.** to convert into a nitrate. [NITRE + -ATE[2]]

**nitration** /naɪˈtreɪʃən/, *n.* →**nitrification.**

**nitre** /ˈnaɪtə/, *n.* **1.** nitrate of potassium, $KNO_3$, a white salt used in making gunpowder, etc.; saltpetre. **2.** nitrate of sodium, $NaNO_3$; Chile saltpetre. Also, *U.S.* **niter.** [ME, from L *nitrum,* from Gk *nítron* natron, native sodium carbonate]

**nitric** /ˈnaɪtrɪk/, *adj.* **1.** *Chem.* containing nitrogen, usu. in the pentavalent state. **2.** of or pertaining to nitre. [F *nitrique.* See NITRE, -IC]

**nitric acid** /– ˈæsəd/, *n.* a corrosive liquid, $HNO_3$, with powerful oxidising properties.

**nitric bacteria** /– bækˈtɪəriə/, *n.pl.* →**nitrobacteria.**

**nitric ether** /– ˈiθə/, *n.* →**ethyl nitrate.**

**nitric oxide** /– ˈɒksaɪd/, *n.* a colourless gaseous compound of nitrogen and oxygen, NO, formed when copper is treated with dilute nitric acid.

**nitride** /ˈnaɪˌtraɪd/, *n.* a compound, usu. containing two elements only, of which the more electronegative one is nitrogen. Also, **nitrid** /ˈnaɪtrəd/. [NITRE + -IDE]

**nitriding** /ˈnaɪˌtraɪdɪŋ/, *n.* the introduction of nitrogen into the surface of certain types of steel by heating in contact with partially dissociated ammonia, a form of case-hardening.

**nitrification** /naɪtrəfəˈkeɪʃən/, *n.* **1.** the act of nitrifying. **2.** the introduction of an $NO_2$ radical into an organic compound, usu. by means of mixed nitric and sulphuric acids. Also, **nitration.**

**nitrify** /ˈnaɪtrəfaɪ/, *v.t.,* **-fied, -fying. 1.** to oxidise (ammonia compounds, etc.) to nitrites or nitrates, esp. by bacterial action. **2.** to impregnate (soil, etc.) with nitrates. **3.** to treat or combine with nitrogen or its compounds. **4.** *Obsolesc.* to convert into nitre. [F *nitrifier.* See NITRE, -FY]

**nitrile** /ˈnaɪtrəl, -traɪl/, *n.* any of a class of organic compounds with the general formula RCN. Also, **nitril** /ˈnaɪtrəl/. [NIT-R(OGEN) + -ILE]

**nitrile rubber** /– ˈrʌbə/, *n.* any of a class of synthetic rubbers which are copolymers of butadiene and acrylonitrile, used esp. where oil resistance is required.

**nitrite** /ˈnaɪˌtraɪt/, *n.* a salt of nitrous acid.

**nitro** /ˈnaɪtroʊ/, *n. Colloq.* →**nitroglycerine.**

**nitro-, 1.** a word element indicating the group $NO_2$. **2.** a misnomer for the nitrate group ($NO_3$), as in *nitrocellulose.* Also, **nitr-.** [Gk, combining form of *nítron* native sodium carbonate]

**nitrobacteria** /ˌnaɪtroʊbækˈtɪəriə/, *n.pl.* certain bacteria of the soil, concerned in nitrifying processes. Also, **nitric bacteria.**

**nitrobenzene** /naɪtroʊˈbɛnzin/, *n.* a light yellowish liquid, $C_6H_5NO_2$, a derivative of benzene, used in the manufacture of aniline.

**nitrocellulose** /naɪtroʊˈsɛljəloʊz, -oʊs/, *n.* →**cellulose nitrate.**

**nitrochalk** /naɪtroʊˈtʃɔk/, *n.* a mixture of calcium carbonate and ammonium nitrate, used as a fertiliser.

**nitrochloroform** /naɪtroʊˈklɒrəfɔm/, *n.* →**chloropicrin.**

**nitrogen** /ˈnaɪtrədʒən/, *n.* a colourless, odourless, gaseous element which forms about four-fifths of the volume of the atmosphere and is present (combined) in animal and vegetable tissues, chiefly in proteins. It is used in compounds, as fertiliser, in explosives, and in dyes. *Symbol:* N; *at. wt:* 14.0067; *at. no:* 7. [F *nitrogène.* See NITRO-, -GEN]

**nitrogen cycle** /ˈ– saɪkəl/, *n.* the continuous circulation of nitrogen and nitrogen compounds in nature between the atmosphere, the soil, and the various organisms to which nitrogen is essential.

**nitrogen dioxide** /– daɪˈɒksaɪd/, *n.* a dark brown toxic gas, $NO_2$, used as a nitrating and oxidising agent.

**nitrogen fixation** /– fɪkˈseɪʃən/, *n.* **1.** any process of combining free nitrogen from the air with other elements, either by chemical means or by bacterial action, used esp. in the preparation of fertilisers, industrial products, etc. **2.** this process as performed by bacteria (**nitrogen fixers**) found in the nodules of leguminous plants, which make the resulting nitrogenous compounds available to their host plants. – **nitrogen-fixing,** *adj.*

**nitrogenise** /naɪˈtrɒdʒənaɪz/, *v.t.,* **-nised, -nising.** to combine with nitrogen or add nitrogenous material to. Also, **nitrogenize.**

**nitrogenous** /naɪˈtrɒdʒənəs/, *adj.* containing nitrogen.

**nitrogen peroxide** /naɪtrədʒən pəˈrɒksaɪd/, *n.* a misnomer for nitrogen dioxide.

**nitroglycerine** /naɪtroʊˈglɪsərin/, *n.* a colourless, highly explosive oil, $C_3H_5(ONO_2)_3$, a principal constituent of dynamites and certain propellent and rocket powders; a nitration product of glycerine. Also, **nitroglycerin** /naɪtroʊˈglɪsərən/.

**nitro group** /ˈnaɪtroʊ grup/, *n.* the univalent $-NO^2$ radical.

**nitrolic** /naɪˈtrɒlɪk/, *adj.* of or denoting a series of acids of the type $RC(:NOH)NO_2$, whose salts form deep red solutions. [NITR- + -OL[1] + -IC]

**nitrometer** /naɪˈtrɒmətə/, *n.* an apparatus for determining the amount of nitrogen or nitrogen compounds in a substance or mixture. [NITRO- + -METER[1]]

**nitroparaffin** /naɪtroʊˈpærəfən/, *n.* any of a class of compounds derived from the methane series replacing a hydrogen atom by the nitro group.

**nitrosamine** /ˌnaɪtroʊsəˈmin, naɪtroʊsˈæmən/, *n.* any of a series of oily compounds with the type formula $R_2NNO$. Also, **nitrosamin** /naɪtroʊsˈæmən/.

**nitroso** /naɪˈtroʊsoʊ/, *adj.* containing the group NO−; nitrosyl.

**nitrosyl** /naɪˈtroʊsəl, ˈnaɪtrəsəl/, *adj.* →**nitroso.**

**nitrous** /ˈnaɪtrəs/, *adj.* **1.** of or pertaining to compounds obtained from nitre, usu. containing less oxygen than the corresponding nitric compounds. **2.** containing nitrogen, usu. trivalent. [L *nitrōsus* full of natron. See NITRE]

**nitrous acid** /– ˈæsəd/, *n.* an acid, $HNO_2$, known only in solution.

**nitrous bacteria** /– bækˈtɪəriə/, *n.pl.* nitrobacteria which convert ammonia derivatives into nitrites by oxidation.

**nitrous ether** /– ˈiθə/, *n.* →**ethyl nitrite.**

**nitrous oxide** /– ˈɒksaɪd/, *n.* laughing gas, $N_2O$, used as an anaesthetic.

**nitty** /ˈnɪti/, *adj.*, **-tier, -tiest. 1.** full of nits. **2.** *Colloq.* foolish.

**nitty-gritty** /ˈnɪti-ˌgrɪti/, *n. Colloq.* **1.** the hard core of a matter: *let's get down to the nitty-gritty.* **2.** *Music.* similar to blue grass and delta blues music. [orig. uncert.]

**nitwit** /ˈnɪtwɪt/, *n.* a slow-witted or foolish person.

**Niu Gini** /nju ˈgɪni/, *n.* →**New Guinea.**

**nivation** /nɪˈveɪʃən/, *n.* the disintegration of rocks around a patch of snow, brought about by alternate freezing and thawing.

**niveous** /ˈnɪviəs/, *adj.* snowy; resembling snow. [L *niveus*]

**nix**[1] /nɪks/, *Colloq.* *–n.* **1.** nothing. *–adv.* **2.** no. *–interj.* **3.** *U.S.* (used as a signal warning of someone's approach): *nix, the cops!* [G, var. of *nichts* nothing]

**nix**[2] /nɪks/, *n., pl.* **nixes.** a water-sprite, usu. small, and either in human form, or half human, half fish. [G, var. of *nichs,* OHG *nichus,* c. OE *nicor* fabulous sea-monster] – **nixie** /ˈnɪksi/, *n. fem.*

**n.l., 1.** *Print.* new line. **2.** it is not permitted. [L *nōn licet*] **3.** it is not clear or evident. [L *nōn liquet*]

**NL, 1.** (of companies) no liability. **2.** New Latin or Neo-Latin. Also, **N.L.**

**N Lat.,** north latitude.

**n mile,** nautical mile.

**NMR,** *Physics.* nuclear magnetic resonance.

**NNE,** north-north-east. Also, **N.N.E.**

**n-nonoic acid** /ɛn-nəˌnoʊɪk ˈæsəd/, *n.* →**nonanoic acid.**

**n-nonylic acid** /ɛn-nəˌnɪlɪk ˈæsəd/, *n.* →**pelargonic acid.**

**NNW,** north-north-west. Also, **N.N.W.**

**no**[1] /noʊ/, *adv., n., pl.* **noes.** *–adv.* **1.** a word used: **a.** to express dissent, denial, or refusal, as in response (opposed to *yes*). **b.** to emphasise a previous negative or qualify a previous statement. **2.** not in any degree; not at all (used with a comparative): *he is no better.* **3.** not: *whether or no.* *–n.* **4.** an utterance of the word 'no'. **5.** a denial or refusal. **6.** a negative vote or voter. [ME; OE *nā* (c. Icel. *nei*), from *ne* not + *ā* ever. See AYE[1]]

**no**[2] /noʊ/, *adj.* **1.** not any: *no money.* **2.** not at all; very far from being; not at all a: *he is no genius.* [var. of NONE]

**No,** *Chem.* nobelium.

**No** /noʊ/, *n., pl.* **No.** a type of highly stylised Japanese classical drama, first developed in the 15th century, employing music, dancing, a chorus, symbolic scenery, and elaborate costumes and masks. Also, **Noh, Nō.** [Jap.: lit., ability]

**No., 1.** north. **2.** northern. **3.** number.

**N.O.** /ɛn ˈoʊ/, Naval Officer.

**Noahs** /ˈnoʊəz/, *n., pl.* **Noahs.** *Colloq.* a shark. [rhyming slang, *Noah's ark* shark]

**nob**[1] /nɒb/, *n.* **1.** *Colloq.* the head. **2.** *Cribbage.* the knave of the same suit as the card turned up, counting one to the holder. **3.** a double-headed coin. [? var. of KNOB]

**nob**[2] /nɒb/, *n. Colloq.* a member of a social elite. [orig. uncert.]

**no-ball** /noʊ-ˈbɔl/, *n.* **1.** (in cricket) a ball bowled in a way disallowed by the rules and automatically giving the batsman a score of one run. *–interj.* **2.** (a call by the umpire as the bowler bowls indicating that he has infringed the rules.) *–v.t.* **3.** to deliver a no-ball to (a batsman).

**nobble** /ˈnɒbəl/, *v.t.*, **-bled, -bling.** *Colloq.* **1.** to disable (a horse), as by drugging it. **2.** to win (a person, etc.) over by underhand means. **3.** to swindle. **4.** to catch or seize. **5.** to give someone a task, etc. which they may be unwilling to perform (fol. by *with*): *the headmaster nobbled him with the task of reorganisation.* [backformation from *nobbler,* var. of HOBBLER (*an 'obbler* being taken as *a nobbler*)]

**nobbler** /ˈnɒblə/, *n.* **1.** one who or that which nobbles. **2.** any small glass of spirits.

**nobby**[1] /ˈnɒbi/, *adj.*, **-bier, -biest.** *Colloq.* **1.** smart; elegant. **2.** first-rate. [NOB[2] + -Y[1]]

**nobby**[2] /ˈnɒbi/, *n. Colloq.* an opal. Also, **knobby.**

**nobelium** /noʊˈbiliəm/, *n.* a synthetic, radioactive element. *Symbol:* No; *at. no.:* 102. [*Nobel* Institute, where first identified + -IUM]

**nobiliary** /noʊˈbɪljəri/, *adj.* of or pertaining to the nobility. [F *nobiliaire,* from L *nōbilis* noble]

**nobility** /noʊˈbɪləti/, *n., pl.* **-ties. 1.** the noble class, or the body of nobles, in a country. **2.** the state or quality of being noble. **3.** noble birth or rank. **4.** exalted moral excellence. **5.** grandeur. [ME *nobilite,* from OF, from L *nōbilitas*]

**noble** /ˈnoʊbəl/, *adj.*, **nobler, noblest,** *n.* *–adj.* **1.** distinguished by birth, rank, or title. **2.** of or pertaining to persons so distinguished: *noble birth.* **3.** belonging to or constituting a class (the nobility) possessing a hereditary social or political pre-eminence in a country or state. **4.** of an exalted moral character or excellence: *a noble thought.* **5.** admirable in dignity of conception, or in the manner of expression, execution, or composition: *a noble poem.* **6.** imposing in appearance; stately; magnificent: *a noble monument.* **7.** of an admirably high quality; notably superior. **8.** *Chem.* inert; chemically inactive. **9.** (of some metals, as gold and platinum) not altered on exposure to the air, not rusting easily, and much scarcer and more valuable than the so-called useful metals. **10.** *Falconry.* denoting the long-winged falcons which stoop to the quarry at a single swoop (opposed to *ignoble*). *–n.* **11.** a person of noble birth or rank; a nobleman. [ME, from OF, from L *nōbilis* well-known, highborn] – **nobleness,** *n.*

**noble art** /– ˈat/, *n.* →**boxing**[2].

**noble gas** /ˈ– gæs/, *n.* →**rare gas.**

**nobleman** /ˈnoʊbəlmən/, *n., pl.* **-men.** a man of noble birth or rank; a noble. – **noblewoman,** *n. fem.*

**noble rot** /noʊbəl ˈrɒt/, *n.* →**botrytis cinerea.**

**noblesse** /noʊˈblɛs/, *n.* **1.** noble birth or condition. **2.** the nobility. [ME, from OF, from L *nōbilis* noble]

**noblesse oblige** /– oʊˈbliʒ/, (the nobility has an obligation to display generous and honourable conduct). [F: lit., nobility obliges]

**nobly** /ˈnoʊbli/, *adv.* **1.** in a noble manner. **2.** courageously. **3.** splendidly; superbly. **4.** of noble ancestry.

**nobody** /ˈnoʊbɒdi, -bədi/, *pron., n., pl.* **-bodies.** *–pron.* **1.** no person. *–n.* **2.** a person of no importance, esp. socially. **3. like nobody's business,** energetically; intensively: *to work like nobody's business.*

**nocent** /ˈnoʊsənt/, *adj.* **1.** hurtful; harmful; injurious. **2.** guilty. [L *nocens,* ppr., harming]

**nock** /nɒk/, *n.* **1.** a metal or plastic piece at the end of an arrow, with a notch for the bowstring. **2.** the notch or groove itself. **3.** a notch or groove at each end of a bow, to hold the bowstring in place. **4.** *Naut.* the forward upper corner of a fore-and-aft boom sail; throat. *–v.t.* **5.** to furnish with a nock. **6.** to adjust (the arrow) to the bowstring, in readiness to shoot. [ME *nocke;* ? from D *nok,* or LG *nokk* tip or projection]

**no-claim bonus** /noʊ-ˈkleɪm boʊnəs/, *n.* a reduction in premium payments for insurance offered to policy holders who have made no claim on the insurance company for some time.

**no-confidence** /noʊ-ˈkɒnfədəns/, *adj.* of or pertaining to a motion or vote which expresses lack of confidence in the governing party of a parliament or a similar body of a representative nature.

**noctambulism** /nɒkˈtæmbjəlɪzəm/, *n.* →**somnambulism.** Also, **noctambulation** /nɒkˌtæmbjəˈleɪʃən/. [L *nox* night + *ambulāre* walk about + -ISM] – **noctambulist,** *n.*

**nocti-,** a word element meaning 'night'. Also (before a vowel), **noct-.** [L, combining form of *nox*]

**noctiluca** /nɒktəˈlukə/, *n., pl.* **-cae** /-si/. a pelagic flagellate protozoan, genus *Noctiluca,* notable for its phosphorescence. [L: something that shines by night]

**noctilucent** /nɒktəˈlusənt/, *adj.* **1.** shining at night; phosphorescent. **2.** *Meteorol.* (of clouds) very high and cirrus-like, visible during the short night of summer and believed to be of meteor dust shining with reflected sunlight. – **noctilucence,** *n.*

**noctivagant** /nɒkˈtɪvəgənt/, *adj.* wandering at night. [L *nocti-* NOCTI- + *vagans,* ppr., wandering]

**noctuid** /ˈnɒktʃuɪd/, *n.* **1.** any of the Noctuidae, a large family of dull-coloured moths, the larvae of which include the highly destructive army worms and cutworms. –*adj.* **2.** belonging or pertaining to the Noctuidae. [NL *Noctuidae,* pl., from L *noctua* night owl]

**noctule** /ˈnɒktʃul/, *n.* a large reddish insectivorous bat, *Nyctalus noctula,* common to Europe and Asia. [F, from It. *nottola* bat, from *notte* night, from L *nox*]

**nocturnal** /nɒkˈtɜnəl/, *adj.* **1.** of or pertaining to the night. **2.** done, occurring, or coming by night. **3.** active by night, as many animals. **4.** opening by night and closing by day, as certain flowers. [late ME, from LL *nocturnālis,* from L *nocturnus* of or in the night] – **nocturnally** /nɒkˈtɜnəli/, *adv.*

**nocturne** /ˈnɒktɜn/, *n.* **1.** *Music.* a piece appropriate to the night or evening. **2.** *Music.* an instrumental composition of a dreamy or pensive character. **3.** *Painting.* a night scene. [F, from LL *nocturna* (fem.) of the night]

**nocuous** /ˈnɒkjuəs/, *adj.* injurious; noxious. [L *nocuus*] – **nocuously,** *adv.* – **nocuousness,** *n.*

**nod** /nɒd/, *v.,* **nodded, nodding,** *n.* –*v.i.* **1.** to make a slight, quick inclination of the head, as in assent, greeting, command, etc. **2.** to let the head fall forwards with a sudden, involuntary movement when sleepy. **3.** to grow careless, inattentive, or dull. **4.** (of trees, flowers, plumes, etc.) to droop, bend, or incline with a swaying motion. **5. nod off,** *Colloq.* to go to sleep. –*v.t.* **6.** to incline (the head) in a short, quick movement, as of assent, greeting, etc. **7.** to express or signify by such a movement of the head: *to nod assent.* **8.** to summon, bring, or send by a nod of the head. **9.** to incline or cause to lean or sway. **10.** *Soccer.* to head (the ball) with a quick, downward movement. **11. nod one's head,** *Prison Colloq.* to plead guilty. –*n.* **12.** a short, quick inclination of the head, as in assent, greeting, command, or drowsiness. **13.** a bending or swaying movement of anything. **14.** a nap. **15. get the nod,** *Colloq.* **a.** to gain approval or permission. **b.** to get unofficial assurance of a job, position, etc. **16. give the nod,** *Colloq.* **a.** to permit. **b.** to make a signal to. **17. on the nod.** *Colloq.* on credit. **18. go to the land of nod,** to fall asleep. [ME; orig. obscure] – **nodder,** *n.*

**nodal** /ˈnoʊdl/, *adj.* of or of the nature of a node. – **nodality** /noʊˈdæləti/, *n.*

**nodal point** /ˈ– pɔɪnt/, *n.* either of two points on the axis of a lens system, such that if the incident ray passes through one, travelling in a given direction, the emergent ray passes through the other, in a parallel direction.

**nodding** /ˈnɒdɪŋ/, *v.* **1.** present participle of **nod.** –*adj.* **2.** slight; such as to give rise to no more than a brief salutation: *a nodding acquaintance.*

**noddle**[1] /ˈnɒdl/, *n. Colloq.* the head. [ME *nodel, nodul;* orig. uncert.]

**noddle**[2] /ˈnɒdl/, *v.t., v.i.,* **-dled, -dling.** to nod lightly or frequently. [frequentative of NOD]

**noddy**[1] /ˈnɒdi/, *n., pl.* **-dies.** **1.** any of several dusky, white-capped terns of the genus *Anous,* frequenting warm coastal and offshore areas, usu. so fearless of man as to seem stupid. **2.** a fool or simpleton. [? n. use of *noddy,* adj., silly; orig. uncert.]

**noddy**[2] /ˈnɒdi/, *n. N.Z. Railways.* a four-wheeled barrow or small wagon for passenger luggage. [orig. uncert.]

**node** /noʊd/, *n.* **1.** a knot, protuberance, or knob. **2.** a complication; difficulty. **3.** a centring point of component parts. **4.** *Bot.* **a.** a joint in a stem. **b.** a part of a stem which normally bears a leaf. **5.** *Geom.* a point on a curve or surface, at which there can be more than one tangent line or plane. **6.** *Physics.* a point, line, or region in a vibrating medium at which there is comparatively no variation of the disturbance which is being transmitted through the medium. **7.** *Astron.* either of the two points at which the orbit of a heavenly body cuts the plane of the ecliptic, equator, or other properly defined plane (that passed as the body goes to the north being called the **ascending node,** and that passed as it goes to the south being called the **descending node**). **8.** *Pathol.* a circumscribed swelling. **9.** *Gram.* the labelled intersection of two or more branches in a tree diagram. **10.** *Computers.* an end point of a branch or junction of two or more branches in a network (def. 5). [L *nōdus* knot]

N, nodes (def. 4)

**nodical** /ˈnoʊdɪkəl, ˈnɒd-/, *adj. Astron.* of or pertaining to the nodes: *the nodical month.*

**nodose** /ˈnoʊdoʊs, noʊˈdoʊs/, *adj.* having nodes. [L *nōdōsus*] – **nodosity** /noʊˈdɒsəti/, *n.*

**no doubt** /noʊ ˈdaʊt/, *adv.* certainly or almost certainly.

**nodous** /ˈnoʊdəs/, *adj.* full of knots. [L *nōdōsus*]

**nodular** /ˈnɒdʒələ/, *adj.* having, relating to, or shaped like nodules.

**nodule** /ˈnɒdʒul/, *n.* **1.** a small node, knot, or knob. **2.** a small rounded mass or lump. **3.** *Bot.* →**tubercle.** [L *nōdulus,* diminutive of *nōdus* node]

**nodulous** /ˈnɒdʒələs/, *adj.* having nodules. Also, **nodulose** /ˈnɒdʒəloʊs/.

**nodus** /ˈnoʊdəs/, *n., pl.* **-di** /-daɪ, -di/. a difficult or intricate point, situation, plot, etc. [L: a knot]

**Noel** /noʊˈɛl/, *n.* **1.** Christmas. **2.** (*l.c.*) a Christmas song or carol. [F *noël* Christmas carol, *Noël* Christmas, from L *nātālis* birthday (orig. adj.)]

**noesis** /noʊˈisəs/, *n.* **1.** *Philos.* a thing grasped by the intellect alone. **2.** *Psychol.* cognition; the functioning of the intellect. [Gk: a perception]

**noetic** /noʊˈɛtɪk/, *adj.* **1.** of or pertaining to the mind. **2.** originating in and apprehended by the reason.

**no-fault** /ˈnoʊ-fɔlt/, *adj.* of or pertaining to legislation, insurance, etc., which does not depend on the assignation of guilt or blame to any of the parties involved.

**no-fines** /ˈnoʊ-faɪnz/, *n.* concrete made without fine aggregate such as sand.

**nog**[1] /nɒg/, *n.* **1.** any beverage made with beaten eggs, usu. with alcoholic liquor; eggnog. **2.** *Obs.* a kind of strong ale. Also, **nogg.** [orig. uncert.]

**nog**[2] /nɒg/, *n., v.,* **nogged, nogging.** –*n.* **1.** a brick-shaped piece of wood built into a wall, esp. as a hold for nails. **2.** any wooden peg, pin, or block. –*v.t.* **3.** to fill in (a wall, etc.) with brickwork. –*v.i.* **4.** to construct nogging. [orig. uncert.; ? var. of obs. *knag,* ME *knagge* spur, peg]

**nog**[3] /nɒg/, *n. Colloq.* (*derog.*) a coloured person, esp. a Vietnamese. Also, **noggy.** [contraction of NIG-NOG]

**noggin** /ˈnɒgən/, *n.* **1.** a small cup or mug. **2.** a small measure of spirits. **3.** *Colloq.* the head. **4.** →**nogging.**

**nogging** /ˈnɒgɪŋ/, *n.* **1.** the brick filling to a wooden-framed partition. **2.** the horizontal short timbers in stud positions, used to stiffen the vertical members of a framed partition. Also, **noggin.**

**no-good** /ˈnoʊ-gʊd/, *adj. Colloq.* worthless.

**Noh** /noʊ/, *n.* →**No.**

**no-hoper** /noʊ-ˈhoʊpə/, *n. Colloq.* **1.** one who displays marked incompetence: *he is a real no-hoper at tennis.* **2.** a social misfit. **3.** a social outcast, vagrant. **4.** an unpromising animal, as a second-rate racehorse, greyhound, etc.

**nohow** /ˈnoʊhaʊ/, *adv.* (*in non-standard use*) in no manner; not at all.

**noil** /nɔɪl/, *n.* **1.** a short fibre of wool or silk separated from the long fibres in combing. **2.** *Wool.* a short, tangled and broken fibre which may contain vegetable matter, removed from wool during combing. [? F *noel,* from ML *nōdellus,* diminutive of L *nōdus* knot, NODE] – **noily,** *adj.*

**noise** /nɔɪz/, *n., v.,* **noised, noising.** *–n.* **1.** sound, esp. of a loud, harsh, or confused kind: *deafening noises.* **2.** a sound of any kind. **3.** loud shouting, outcry, or clamour. **4.** *Physics.* the combination of a non-harmonious group of frequencies of very short duration. **5.** *Electronics.* interference which degrades the useful information in a signal. **6.** *Archaic.* rumour. **7. big noise,** *Colloq.* an important person. *–v.t.* **8.** to spread the report or rumour of. **9.** to spread (a report, rumour, etc.). *–v.i.* **10.** to talk much or publicly (fol. by *off*). **11.** to make a noise, outcry, or clamour. [ME, from OF, from L *nausea* seasickness]

**noise gate** /ˈ– geɪt/, *n.* an electronic device which reduces the gain of an amplifier when an incoming signal, as from an electronic musical instrument, drops below a preset level and increases it when the signal rises above it again, thereby reducing the nuisance of noise inherent in the system.

**noiseless** /ˈnɔɪzləs/, *adj.* making, or attended with, no noise; silent; quiet: *a noiseless step.* – **noiselessly,** *adv.* – **noiselessness,** *n.*

**noisemaker** /ˈnɔɪzmeɪkə/, *n.* a person or thing that makes noise, as a hooter, whistle, etc., used in merrymaking. – **noisemaking,** *n., adj.*

**noisette** /nwaˈzɛt/, *n.* a boned cutlet of lamb, veal, pork, etc. [F]

**noisome** /ˈnɔɪsəm/, *adj.* **1.** offensive or disgusting, often as to smell. **2.** harmful, injurious, or noxious. [ME, from obs. or d. *noy* (aphetic var. of ANNOY) + -SOME[1]] – **noisomely,** *adv.* – **noisomeness,** *n.*

**noisy** /ˈnɔɪzi/, *adj.,* **noisier, noisiest.** **1.** making much noise: *a noisy crowd.* **2.** abounding in noise: *a noisy street.* – **noisily,** *adv.* – **noisiness,** *n.*

**noisy friar-bird** /– ˈfraɪə-bɜd/, *n.* one of the friar-birds, *Philemon corniculatus,* with a bare black head, grey-brown body and silvery-white breast, found along the eastern coastal regions from Cape York to Victoria; four-o'clock; leatherhead.

**noisy miner** /– ˈmaɪnə/, *n.* a miner of eastern Australia, *Manorina melanocephela,* marked by its brown wings with grey-white plumage and noted for its raucous cries; soldier bird; micky.

**noisy pitta** /– ˈpɪtə/, *n.* a brightly-coloured pitta, *Pitta versicolor,* found in the rainforests of north-eastern Australia, which makes loud, melodious whistling calls; dragoon bird.

**no-liability company** /ˌnoʊ-laɪəˈbɪləti ˌkʌmpəni/, *n.* an exploration company in which the acceptance or purchase of a partly paid share does not legally bind the holder to pay up the uncalled part of the capital.

**noli-me-tangere** /ˌnoʊli-meɪ-ˈtæŋgəri/, *n.* **1.** one who or that which must not be touched or interfered with. **2.** a picture representing Jesus appearing to Mary Magdalene after his resurrection. [L: touch me not]

**nolle prosequi** /nɒli ˈprɒsəkwi/, *n.* an entry made upon the records of a court when the plaintiff or prosecutor will proceed no further in a suit or action. [L: to be unwilling to pursue (prosecute)]

**nol. pros.,** nolle prosequi.

**nom.,** nominative.

**noma** /ˈnoʊmə/, *n.* a gangrenous ulceration of the mouth and cheeks (and sometimes other parts), occurring mainly in debilitated children. [NL, from Gk *nomḗ* a corroding sore]

**nomad** /ˈnoʊmæd/, *n.* **1.** one of a race or tribe without fixed abode, but moving about from place to place according to the state of the pasturage or food supply. **2.** any wanderer. *–adj.* **3.** nomadic. [L *nomas,* from Gk: roaming (like cattle)] – **nomadism,** *n.*

**nomadic** /noʊˈmædɪk/, *adj.* of, pertaining to, or characteristic of nomads. – **nomadically,** *adv.*

**no-man's-land** /ˈnoʊ-mænz-lænd/, *n.* **1.** a region not possessed by any power, as the area between opposing armies. **2.** something chaotic or out of order, as a desk, room, etc. **3.** a place not frequented by man; wilderness; place to be avoided as dangerous. **4.** a state of insecurity resulting from the lack or disruption of a cultural heritage, as of a displaced tribe. **5.** a state of mind resulting from the loss of spiritual or cultural landmarks. **6.** a barren or infertile period in one's life, characterised by insecurity or loss of identity.

**nomarch** /ˈnɒmak/, *n.* the governor of a nome or a nomarchy. [Gk *nomárchēs*]

**nomarchy** /ˈnɒmaki, -əki/, *n., pl.* **-chies.** one of the provinces into which modern Greece is divided. Also, **nome.**

**nombril** /ˈnɒmbrəl/, *n.* the point in an escutcheon between the middle of the base and the fess point. [F: navel]

**nom de guerre** /nɒm də ˈgɛə/, *n.* an assumed name; pseudonym. [F: war name]

**nom de plume** /ˈnɒm də plum/, *n.* →**pen-name.** [coined in E from F words; lit., pen name]

**nome** /noʊm/, *n.* **1.** one of the provinces of ancient Egypt. **2.** →**nomarchy.** [Gk *nomós* territorial division]

**nomenclator** /ˈnoʊmənkleɪtə/, *n.* **1.** one who calls or announces things or persons by their names. **2.** one who assigns names, as in scientific classification. [L]

**nomenclature** /nəˈmɛnklətʃə, ˈnoʊmənkleɪtʃə/, *n.* **1.** a set or system of names or terms, as those used in a particular science or art by an individual or community, etc. **2.** the names or terms forming a set or system. [L *nōmenclātūra*] – **nomenclative, nomenclatorial** /nəmɛnkləˈtɔriəl/, **nomenclatural,** *adj.*

**nominal** /ˈnɒmənəl/, *adj.* **1.** being such in name only; so-called: *nominal peace.* **2.** (of a price, consideration, etc.) named as a mere matter of form, being trifling in comparison with the actual value. **3.** of, pertaining to, or consisting in a name or names. **4.** *Gram.* **a.** of, pertaining to, or producing a noun or nouns. **b.** used as or like a noun. **5.** assigned to a person by name: *nominal shares of stock.* **6.** containing, bearing, or giving a name or names. **7.** *U.S.* satisfactory; within acceptable limits, as of the launch of a spacecraft. [ME, from L *nominālis* pertaining to names]

**nominalise** /ˈnɒmənəlaɪz/, *v.t.,* **-lised, -lising.** to give a word or phrase the form or force of a noun. Also, **nominalize.** – **nominalisation** /nɒmənəlaɪˈzeɪʃən/, *n.*

**nominalism** /ˈnɒmənəlɪzəm/, *n.* the philosophical doctrine that universals are reducible to names without any objective existence corresponding to them. In the strict sense of the doctrine there are no universals either in the mind or in the external world but words operate as symbols. Cf. **conceptualism.** – **nominalist,** *n., adj.* – **nominalistic** /nɒmənəˈlɪstɪk/, *adj.* – **nominalistically** /nɒmənəˈlɪstɪkli/, *adv.*

**nominally** /ˈnɒmənəli/, *adv.* in a nominal manner; by or as regards name; in name; only in name; ostensibly.

**nominal value** /nɒmənəl ˈvælju/, *n.* book or par value; face value.

**nominal wages** /– ˈweɪdʒəz/, *n.pl.* wages measured in terms of money and not by their ability to command goods and services. Cf. **real wages.**

**nominal weapon** /– ˈwɛpən/, *n.* a nuclear weapon producing a yield of approximately twenty kilotons.

**nominate** /ˈnɒməneɪt/, *v.,* **-nated, -nating;** /ˈnɒmənət/, *adj.* *–v.t.* **1.** to propose as a proper person for appointment or election to an office. **2.** to appoint for a duty or office. **3.** to enter (a horse, etc.) in a race. **4.** *Archaic.* to entitle; name. **5.** *Obs.* to specify. *–adj.* **6.** having a particular name. [L *nōminātus,* pp., named] – **nominator,** *n.*

**nomination** /nɒməˈneɪʃən/, *n.* **1.** the act of nominating, esp. to office: *the nomination of candidates for the governorship.* **2.** the state of being nominated.

**nominative** /ˈnɒmənətɪv, ˈnɒmnə-/, *adj.* **1.** *Gram.* **a.** denoting a case which by its form, position, or function indicates that it serves as the subject of a finite verb, as in 'we enjoyed the meal and the men washed up', where *we* and *men* are in the nominative case. **b.** similar to such a case form in function or meaning. **2.** nominated; appointed by nomination. *–n.* **3.** *Gram.* the nominative case, a word in that case, or a form or construction of similar function or meaning. [L *nōmināt-*

*īvus* serving to name; replacing ME *nominatif,* from OF]

**nominative absolute** /– 'æbsəlut/, *n.* a group of words including a substantive together with a participial modifier, not grammatically related to any other element in the sentence. In the following sentence, 'the sun having set' is a nominative absolute construction: *the sun having set, we ate dinner.*

**nominative of address,** *n.* a noun naming the person to whom one is speaking. See **vocative.**

**nominee** /nɒmə'ni/, *n.* **1.** one nominated as to fill an office or stand for election. **2.** a person appointed by another to act as his agent. [NOMIN(ATE) + -EE]

**nomism** /'noʊmɪzəm/, *n.* conduct in a religion based on a law or laws. [Gk *nómos* law + -ISM] – **nomistic** /noʊ'mɪstɪk/, *adj.*

**nomogram** /'nɒməgræm, 'noʊm-/, *n.* a graph containing, usu., three parallel scales graduated for different variables so that when a straight line connects values of any two, the related value may be read directly from the third at the point intersected by the line. Also, **nomograph** /-græf, -graf/. [Gk *nomó(s)* law + -GRAM[1]]

**nomography** /nɒ'mɒgrəfi/, *n.* **1.** the art of drawing up laws. **2.** the art of making and using a nomogram for solving a succession of nearly identical problems. [Gk *nomographía* a writing of laws] – **nomographer,** *n.* – **nomographic** /nɒmə'græfɪk/, **nomographical** /nɒmə'græfɪkəl/, *adj.* – **nomographically** /nɒmə'græfɪkli/, *adv.*

**nomology** /nɒ'mɒlədʒi/, *n.* **1.** the science of law or laws. **2.** the science of the laws of the mind. [*nomo-* (from Gk, combining form of *nómos* law) + -LOGY] – **nomological** /nɒmə'lɒdʒɪkəl/, *adj.* – **nomologist,** *n.*

**nomothetic** /nɒmə'θɛtɪk/, *adj.* **1.** lawgiving; legislative. **2.** pertaining to or based on laws, esp. religious laws; nomistic. **3.** *Psychol.* of or pertaining to the search for general laws (opposed to *idiographic*). Also, **nomothetical.** [Gk *nomothetikós*]

**-nomy,** a final word element meaning 'distribution', 'arrangement', 'management', or having reference to laws or government, as in *astronomy, economy, taxonomy.* [Gk *-nomía,* from *nómos* custom, law. See -IA]

**non-,** a prefix indicating: **1.** exclusion from a specified class or group: *non-Jew, non-passerine.* **2.** objective negation or opposition: *non-porous, non-recurrent.* **3.** spuriousness or failure to fulfil a claim: *non-event, non-hero.* **4.** the absence of activity or achievement in the area named: *non-arrival, non-publication.* [representing L *nōn* not; not a L prefix]

**non-access** /nɒn-'æksɛs/, *n.* the absence of opportunity for sexual intercourse, as when a husband, because of absence, could not have fathered his wife's child.

**nonachiever** /nɒnə'tʃivə/, *n.* a person who does not succeed in the various established tests designed to measure performance; a failure.

**nonage** /'noʊnɪdʒ/, *n.* **1.** the period of legal minority. **2.** any period of immaturity. [ME *nounage,* from AF, from *noun-* NON- + *age* AGE]

**nonagenarian** /nɒnədʒə'nɛəriən, noʊ-/, *adj.* **1.** of the age of 90 years, or between 90 and 100 years old. *–n.* **2.** a nonagenarian person. [L *nōnāgēnārius* containing ninety + -AN]

**nonaggression** /nɒnə'grɛʃən/, *n.* **1.** deliberate avoidance of aggression, esp. where hostility exists. *–adj.* **2.** of or pertaining to nonaggression: *a nonaggression policy.*

**nonagon** /'nɒnəgɒn, -gən/, *n.* a polygon having nine angles and nine sides; enneagon. [L *nōnus* ninth + *-agon* (after OCTAGON)] – **nonagonal** /nɒn'ægənəl/, *adj.*

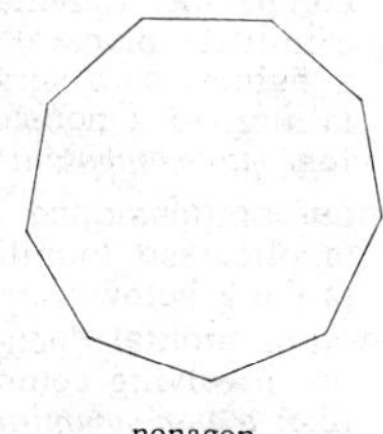
nonagon

**non-alignment** /nɒn-ə'laɪnmənt/, *n.* the political attitude of a state which does not associate, ally, or identify itself with the political ideology or objective espoused by other states, groups of states, or international causes, or with the foreign policies stemming therefrom. – **non-aligned,** *adj.*

**nonanoic acid** /nɒnənoʊɪk 'æsəd/, *n.* →**pelargonic acid.** Also, **n-nonoic acid.** [L *nōnus* ninth. See -ANE, -IC]

**non-appearance** /nɒn-ə'pɪərəns/, *n.* failure or neglect to appear, as in a court.

**non-art** /nɒn-'at/, *n.* **1.** the absence of art; something which lacks art. **2.** a kind of art in which the creator tries to avoid artifice and conventional artistic devices.

**nonce** /nɒns/, *n.* **1.** the one or particular occasion or purpose. **2. for the nonce,** for this one occasion only; for the time being. [ME *nones,* in phrase *for the nones,* orig., *for then one(s),* lit., for the once]

**nonce word** /'– wɜd/, *n.* a word coined and used only for the particular occasion.

**nonch** /nɒntʃ/, *n. Prison Colloq.* **1.** a method of shop-lifting in which the goods stolen are concealed in a coat or jacket not worn but nonchalantly draped over one shoulder, ostensibly because of the heat. *–v.t.* **2.** steal in such a manner.

**nonchalance** /'nɒnʃələns/, *n.* the quality of being nonchalant; cool unconcern or indifference; casualness. [F, from *nonchalant* NONCHALANT]

**nonchalant** /'nɒnʃələnt/, *adj.* coolly unconcerned, indifferent, or unexcited; casual. [F, from *non-* NON- + *chalant* (ppr. of *chaloir* have concern for, from L *calēre* be hot)] – **nonchalantly,** *adv.*

---

**non-abrasive,** *adj.*
**non-abrasively,** *adv.*
**non-abrasiveness,** *n.*
**non-absorbent,** *adj., n.*
**non-academic,** *adj., n.*
**non-acceptance,** *n.*
**non-achievement,** *n.*
**non-activity,** *n.*
**non-addictive,** *adj.*
**non-adherence,** *n.*
**non-adherent,** *n., adj.*
**non-adjacent,** *adj.*
**non-adjacently,** *adv.*
**non-admission,** *n.*
**non-aggression,** *n., adj.*
**non-aggressive,** *adj.*
**non-agricultural,** *adj.*
**non-alcoholic,** *adj.*
**non-allegiance,** *n.*
**non-allergic,** *adj.*
**non-alliance,** *n.*
**non-allelic,** *adj.*
**non-amortising,** *adj.*
**non-aquatic,** *adj.*
**non-arrival,** *n.*
**non-Aryan,** *n., adj.*
**non-assessable,** *adj.*
**non-assimilation,** *n.*
**non-attendance,** *n.*
**non-automatic,** *adj., n.*
**non-availability,** *n.*
**non-being,** *n.*
**non-believer,** *n.*
**non-believing,** *adj.*
**non-believingly,** *adv.*
**non-belligerent,** *n., adj.*
**non-belligerency,** *n.*
**non-breakable,** *adj.*
**non-cancellable,** *adj.*
**non-candidate,** *n.*
**non-canonical,** *adj.*
**non-Catholic,** *n., adj.*
**non-cellular,** *adj.*
**non-central,** *adj.*
**non-centrally,** *adv.*
**non-Christian,** *adj., n.*
**non-civilised,** *adj.*
**non-clearance,** *n.*
**non-clerical,** *adj.*
**non-coalition,** *n.*
**non-cognition,** *n.*
**non-collapsible,** *adj.*
**non-collection,** *n.*
**non-colloidal,** *adj.*
**non-collusive,** *adj.*
**non-colonial,** *adj.*
**non-combat,** *n.*
**non-combining,** *adj.*
**non-combustible,** *adj., n.*
**non-combustion,** *n.*
**non-combustive,** *adj.*
**non-commercial,** *adj., n.*
**non-commercially,** *adv.*
**non-commitment,** *n.*
**non-communicable,** *adj.*
**non-communication,** *n.*
**non-communicative,** *adj.*
**non-communicatively,** *adv.*
**non-communist,** *n., adj.*
**non-competitive,** *adj.*
**non-completion,** *n.*
**non-complicity,** *n.*
**non-comprehension,** *n.*
**non-compulsion,** *n.*
**non-compulsory,** *adj.*

**non-chaser** /nɒn-'tʃeɪsə/, *n.* a dog in a race which displays little interest in chasing the lure.

**non-claim** /nɒn-'kleɪm/, *n.* the failure to make a claim within a time limited by law.

**non-collegiate** /nɒn-kə'lidʒiət/, *adj.* **1.** belonging to the body of students in a university not attached to any particular college or hall. **2.** below the level usu. associated with college or university study. **3.** (of a university) not composed of colleges.

**non-com** /'nɒn-kɒm/, *n. Colloq.* a non-commissioned officer.

**non-combatant** /nɒn-'kɒmbətənt/, *n.* **1.** one who is not a combatant; a civilian in time of war. **2.** one connected with a military or naval force in some capacity other than that of a fighter, as a surgeon, a chaplain, etc. *–adj.* **3.** of or pertaining to a non-combatant: *pacifists were ordered to undertake non-combatant duties in the armed forces.*

**non-commissioned** /'nɒn-kəmɪʃənd/, *adj.* not commissioned (applied esp. to military personnel, as sergeants and corporals, ranking below warrant officer).

**non-committal** /'nɒn-kəmɪtl/, *adj.* not committing oneself, or not involving committal, to a particular view, course, or the like: *a non-committal answer.*

**non-communicant** /nɒn-kə'mjunəkənt/, *n.* **1.** one who is not a communicant. **2.** one who does not communicate.

**non-compliance** /nɒn-kəm'plaɪəns/, *n.* failure or refusal to comply. – **non-compliant,** *adj., n.* – **non-complier,** *n.*

**non compos** /nɒn 'kɒmpəs/, *adj. Colloq.* **1.** in a vague or dazed state of mind. **2.** unconscious, as from alcoholic drink. **3.** not of sound mind; mentally incapable. [short for L *non compos mentis*]

**non-conductor** /nɒn-kən'dʌktə/, *n.* a substance which does not readily conduct or transmit heat, sound, electricity, etc.; an insulator. – **non-conducting,** *adj.*

**nonconformance** /nɒnkən'fɔməns/, *n.* lack of conformity.

**nonconformist** /nɒnkən'fɔməst/, *n.;* /'nɒnkənfɔməst/, *adj.* *–n.* **1.** one who refuses to conform, esp. to an established Church. **2.** one belonging to an originally British protestant church which at no time acknowledged the established church in England, as a Methodist, Presbyterian, etc. **3.** one who does not conform to accepted social standards of behaviour, etc. *–adj.* **4.** of or pertaining to a nonconformist, or to nonconformists as a group: *nonconformist beliefs.* – **nonconforming,** *adj.*

**nonconformity** /nɒnkən'fɔməti/, *n.* **1.** lack of conformity or agreement. **2.** failure or refusal to conform, as to an established Church.

**non-cooperation** /ˌnɒn-koʊɒpə'reɪʃən/, *n.* **1.** failure or refusal to cooperate. **2.** a method or practice, established in India by Mahatma Gandhi, of showing opposition to acts or policies of the government by refusing to participate in civic and political life or to obey governmental regulations. – **non-cooperative** /nɒn-koʊ'ɒpərətɪv/, *adj.* – **non-cooperator** /nɒn-koʊ'ɒpəreɪtə/, *n.*

**nonda** /'nɒndə/, *n.* a tree, *Parinari nonda,* with a yellow edible fruit which is astringent to taste, found in Queensland and the Northern Territory.

**nondescript** /'nɒndəskrɪpt/, *adj.* **1.** of no recognised, definite, or particular type or kind: *a nondescript garment.* *–n.* **2.** a person or a thing of no particular type or kind. [NON- + L *dēscriptus,* pp., described]

**non-disjunction** /nɒn-dɪs'dʒʌŋkʃən/, *n.* the failure of chromosomes to follow normal separation into daughter cells at division.

**none** /nʌn/, *pron.* **1.** no one; not one: *there is none to help.* **2.** not any, as of something indicated: *that is none of your business.* **3.** no part; nothing. **4.** (*construed as pl.*) no, or not any, persons or things: *none come to the feasts.* *–adv.* **5.** to no extent; in no way; not at all: *the supply is none too great.* *–adj.* **6.** *Archaic.* not any; no (in later use only before a vowel or *h*): *Thou shalt have none other gods before me.* [ME *non,* OE *nān,* from *ne* not + *ān* one]

**non-effective** /'nɒn-əfɛktɪv/, *adj.* **1.** not effective. **2.** not fit for duty or active service, as a soldier or sailor. *–n.* **3.** a non-effective person.

**non-ego** /nɒn-'igoʊ/, *n.* all that is not the ego or conscious self; object as opposed to subject.

**nonentity** /nɒn'ɛntəti/, *n., pl.* **-ties.** **1.** a person or thing of no importance. **2.** something which does not exist, or exists only in imagination. **3.** non-existence. [NON- + ENTITY]

**nones**[1] /noʊnz/, *n.* the fifth of the seven canonical hours, or the service for it, originally fixed for the ninth hour of the day (or 3 p.m.). [OE *nōn,* from L *nōna* (*hōra*). See NOON]

**nones**[2] /noʊnz/, *n.pl., sing.* **none.** (in the ancient Roman calendar) the ninth day before the ides, both days included, thus being the 7th of March, May, July, and October, and the 5th of the other months. [ME, from L *nōnae,* orig. fem. pl. of *nōnus* ninth]

**non-essential** /nɒn-ə'sɛnʃəl/, *adj.* **1.** not essential; not necessary: *non-essential use of petrol.* *–n.* **2.** a non-essential thing or person.

**non est factum** /nɒn ɛst 'fæktəm/, *n. Law.* **1.** denial of a party that the deed in question was executed by him. **2.** a defence used when a defendant says he signed a document fundamentally different in nature from what he believed it to be. [L: it is not (his) deed]

---

**non-concealment,** *n.*
**non-concurrence,** *n.*
**non-conducive,** *adj.*
**non-confidence,** *n.*
**non-congruence,** *n.*
**non-consecutive,** *adj.*
**non-consecutively,** *adv.*
**non-consecutiveness,** *n.*
**non-consent,** *n.*
**non-consequence,** *n.*
**non-conservative,** *adj., n.*
**non-consideration,** *n.*
**non-constitutional,** *adj.*
**non-consummation,** *n.*
**non-contagious,** *adj.*
**non-contagiously,** *adv.*
**non-contagiousness,** *n.*
**non-contemporary,** *adj., n.*
**non-contentious,** *adj.*
**non-contentiously,** *adv.*
**non-continuance,** *n.*
**non-continuous,** *adj.*
**non-continuously,** *adv.*
**non-contraband,** *n., adj.*
**non-contradictory,** *adj., n.*
**non-contributory,** *adj., n.*
**non-controversial,** *adj.*
**non-corrosive,** *adj.*
**non-creative,** *adj.*
**non-creatively,** *adv.*
**non-creativeness,** *n.*
**ncn-critical,** *adj.*
**non-critically,** *adv.*
**non-crystalline,** *adj.*
**non-cumulative,** *adj.*
**non-curdling,** *adj.*
**non-dancer,** *n.*
**non-deceptive,** *adj.*
**non-deceptively,** *adv.*
**non-deceptiveness,** *n.*
**non-deciduous,** *adj.*
**non-deciduously,** *adv.*
**non-deciduousness,** *n.*
**non-decisive,** *adj.*
**non-decisively,** *adv.*
**non-decisiveness,** *n.*
**non-decreasing,** *adj.*
**non-deist,** *n.*
**non-delivery,** *n.*
**non-democratic,** *adj., n.*
**non-denominational,** *adj.*
**non-detachable,** *adj.*
**non-determinist,** *n., adj.*
**non-deterrent,** *adj.*
**non-destructive,** *adj.*
**non-destructively,** *adv.*
**non-destructiveness,** *n.*
**non-deviant,** *n., adj.*
**non-diplomatic,** *adj.*
**non-diplomatically,** *adv.*
**non-directional,** *adj.*
**non-directive,** *adj.*
**non-dirigible,** *adj., n.*
**non-disciplinary,** *adj.*
**non-disclosure,** *n.*
**non-discrimination,** *n.*
**non-discriminatory,** *adj.*
**non-disposable,** *adj.*
**non-disposal,** *n.*
**non-distinctive,** *adj.*
**non-distribution,** *n.*
**non-distributive,** *adj.*
**non-distributively,** *adv.*
**non-divergence,** *n.*
**non-divergent,** *adj.*

**nonesuch** /ˈnʌnsʌtʃ/, *n.* **1.** a person or thing without equal; a paragon. **2.** black medic. See **medic**[2]. Also, **nonsuch.**

**nonet** /noʊˈnɛt, nɒˈnɛt/, *n.* **1.** a composition for nine voices or instruments. **2.** a group of nine performers. Also, **nonette.**

**nonetheless** /nʌnðəˈlɛs/, *adv.* however; nevertheless. Also, **none the less.**

**non-event** /nɒn-əˈvɛnt/, *n.* an occurrence of little significance or importance, esp. one which was expected to have great importance.

**non-existence** /nɒn-əgˈzɪstəns/, *n.* **1.** absence of existence. **2.** a thing that has no existence. – **nonexistent,** *adj.*

**nonfeasance** /nɒnˈfizəns/, *n. Law.* the omission of some act which ought to have been performed. Cf. **malfeasance, misfeasance.**

**nonferrous** /nɒnˈfɛrəs/, *adj.* **1.** of or pertaining to any metal except iron. **2.** containing no iron: *nonferrous compound.*

**non-fiction** /nɒn-ˈfɪkʃən/, *n.* **1.** a class of writing comprising works dealing with facts and events, rather than imaginative narration: *we publish only non-fiction.* –*adj.* **2.** Also, **non-fictional.** denoting or pertaining to writing of this class.

**non-figurative** /nɒn-ˈfɪgjərətɪv/, *adj.* (of art) not figurative; abstract.

**nonflammable** /nɒnˈflæməbəl/, *adj.* not easily set alight; slow-burning; not flammable.

**non-forfeiture** /nɒn-ˈfɔfətʃə/, *n.* a clause written into an insurance policy whereby the policy is not voided by non-payment of a premium.

**nong** /nɒŋ/, *n. Colloq.* a fool; an idiot. [orig. uncert.]

**non-government school** /ˌnɒn-gʌvənmənt ˈskul/, *n.* any school which is owned and controlled by a private body, as a church. Also, **non-state school.**

**non-harmonic** /ˈnɒn-hamɒnɪk/, *adj.* denoting or pertaining to a note sounding with a chord of which it is not a chord note.

**non-hero** /nɒn-ˈhɪəroʊ/, *n.* →**antihero.**

**nonillion** /noʊˈnɪljən/, *n.* **1.** a cardinal number represented by one followed by 54 zeroes (in the U.S. and France, by one followed by 30 zeroes). –*adj.* **2.** amounting to one nonillion in number. [F, from *non-* (from L *nōnus* ninth) + *(m)illion* MILLION] – **nonillionth,** *n., adj.*

**non-inductive** /nɒn-ɪnˈdʌktɪv/, *adj. Elect.* not inductive: *a non-inductive resistance.*

**non-intervention** /ˌnɒn-ɪntəˈvɛnʃən/, *n.* **1.** abstention by a state from interference in the affairs of other states or in those of its own political subdivisions. **2.** failure or refusal to intervene. – **non-interventionist,** *n.*

**non-iron** /nɒn-ˈaɪən/, *adj.* (of clothing) not requiring ironing; drip-dry.

**non-joinder** /nɒn-ˈdʒɔɪndə/, *n. Law.* omission to join, as of one who should have been a party to an action.

**nonjuror** /nɒnˈdʒʊərə/, *n.* one who refuses to take a required oath, as of allegiance.

**non-legal** /nɒn-ˈligəl/, *adj.* not (definitely) legal; having no legal aspect (distinguished from *illegal*): *a completely non-legal controversy.*

**non-linear** /ˈnɒn-lɪniə/, *adj.* (of a mathematical equation) not of the first degree. See **linear.**

**non-linearity** /ˌnɒn-lɪniˈærəti/, *n.* the deviation of a mathematical equation from the linear.

**non-metal** /nɒn-ˈmɛtl/, *n.* **1.** an element not having the character of a metal, as carbon, nitrogen, etc. **2.** an element incapable of forming simple positive ions in solution.

**non-metallic** /nɒn-məˈtælɪk/, *adj.* **1.** of or relating to non-metal. **2.** not of a metallic quality: *a non-metallic appearance.*

**non-moral** /nɒn-ˈmɒrəl/, *adj.* having no relation to morality; neither moral nor immoral: *a completely non-moral problem of society.*

**non-nitrogenous** /nɒn-naɪˈtrɒdʒənəs/, *adj.* containing no nitrogen.

**non-nuclear** /ˈnɒn-njukliə/, *adj.* **1.** (of military weapons and equipment) not activated or powered by nuclear fission. **2.** not possessing nuclear technology, weapons, or equipment: *non-nuclear nations.*

**no-no** /ˈnoʊ-noʊ/, *n., pl.* **no-noes.** *Colloq.* **1.** something not to be done on any account: *in this house smoking is a no-no.* **2.** an impossible undertaking. **3.** a complete failure.

**non-objective** /nɒn-əbˈdʒɛktɪv/, *adj.* (of a work of art) not representing or containing objects known in physical nature; abstract or non-representational.

**non obstante** /nɒn ɒbˈstænti/, *prep.* notwithstanding. [L]

**no-nonsense** /ˈnoʊ-nɒnsəns/, *adj. Colloq.* **1.** practical. **2.** strict. **3.** unpretentious.

**nonpareil** /ˈnɒnpərɛl, -reɪl/, *adj.* **1.** having no equal; peerless. –*n.* **2.** a person or thing having no equal; something unique. **3.** *Print.* **a.** a size of type (6 point). **b.** a slug occupying 6 points of space between lines. **4.** *(pl.)* →**hundreds and thousands.** [late ME, from F, from *non-* NON- + *pareil* equal (from L *pār*)]

**non-parole** /nɒn-pəˈroʊl/, *adj.* of or pertaining to that portion of a prison sentence in which the prisoner is not eligible for parole.

**non-parous** /nɒn-ˈparəs/, *adj.* having borne no children.

**non-participating** /nɒn-paˈtɪsəpeɪtɪŋ/, *adj.* **1.** not participating. **2.** *Insurance.* having no right to dividends or to a distribution of surplus.

**non-partisan** /nɒn-ˈpatəzən/, *adj.* **1.** not partisan; disin-

---

**non-divergently,** *adv.*
**non-divisible,** *adj.*
**non-dogmatic,** *adj.*
**non-dramatic,** *adj.*
**non-drinkable,** *adj.*
**non-drinker,** *n.*
**non-driver,** *n.*
**non-durable,** *adj.*
**non-dutiable,** *adj.*
**non-dwelling,** *adj.*
**non-edible,** *adj., n.*
**non-educable,** *adj.*
**non-educational,** *adj.*
**non-efficient,** *adj.*
**non-efficiently,** *adv.*
**non-elastic,** *adj.*
**non-election,** *n.*
**non-elective,** *adj.*
**non-emotional,** *adj.*
**non-emotionally,** *adv.*
**non-enforcement,** *n.*
**non-equivalent,** *n., adj.*
**non-equivalently,** *adv.*
**non-establishment,** *n.*
**non-ethical,** *adj.*
**non-ethically,** *adv.*
**non-Euclidean,** *adj.*
**non-European,** *adj.*
**non-exchangeable,** *adj.*
**non-exclusive,** *adj.*
**non-exemption,** *n.*
**non-existing,** *adj.*
**non-explosive,** *adj., n.*
**non-explosively,** *adv.*
**non-explosiveness,** *n.*
**non-exportable,** *adj.*
**non-exportation,** *n.*
**non-extraditable,** *adj.*
**non-factual,** *adj.*
**non-factually,** *adv.*
**non-farm,** *adj.*
**non-fat,** *adj.*
**non-fatal,** *adj.*
**non-fatally,** *adv.*
**non-federal,** *adj.*
**non-federated,** *adj.*
**non-ferrous,** *adj.*
**non-festive,** *adj.*
**non-festively,** *adv.*
**non-feudal,** *adj.*
**non-finite,** *adj.*
**non-fiscal,** *adj.*
**non-fiscally,** *adv.*
**non-fissile,** *adj.*
**non-fissionable,** *adj.*
**non-flammable,** *adj.*
**non-formal,** *adj.*
**non-fossiliferous,** *adj.*
**non-fouling,** *adj.*
**non-freezing,** *adj.*
**non-fulfilment,** *n.*
**non-functional,** *adj.*
**non-functionally,** *adv.*
**non-gaseous,** *adj.*
**non-geometric,** *adj.*
**non-government,** *adj.*
**non-grammatical,** *adj.*
**non-green,** *adj.*
**non-habitable,** *adj.*
**non-habitably,** *adv.*
**non-happening,** *n.*
**non-hereditary,** *adj.*
**non-heretical,** *adj.*
**non-heretically,** *adv.*
**non-heritable,** *adj.*

---

terested. 2. not supporting any of the established or regular parties. Also, **nonpartizan.**

**non-person** /nɒn-'pɜsən/, *n.* an insignificant or unimpressive person.

**nonplus** /nɒn'plʌs/, *v.*, **-plussed, -plussing** or (*U.S.*) **-plused, -plusing,** *n.* *–v.t.* **1.** to bring to a nonplus; puzzle completely. *–n.* **2.** a state of utter perplexity. [L *nōn plūs* not more, no further]

**non-polluting** /'nɒn-pəlutɪŋ/, *adj.* of or pertaining to products, machines, etc., which do not pollute the environment.

**non-pro** /nɒn-'proʊ/, *n., adj. Colloq.* non-professional.

**non-productive** /'nɒn-prədʌktɪv/, *adj.* **1.** not producing goods directly, as employees in charge of personnel, inspectors, etc. **2.** unproductive. **– non-productively,** *adv.* **– non-productiveness, non-productivity** /ˌnɒn-prɒdʌk'tɪvəti/, *n.*

**non-profit-making** /nɒn-'prɒfət-meɪkɪŋ/, *adj.* not yielding a return; established or entered into for some motive other than the hope of making a profit. Also, **non-profit.**

**non-proliferation** /ˌnɒn-prəlɪfə'reɪʃən/, *n.* **1.** the attempt to prevent countries which do not possess nuclear weapons from acquiring them. *–adj.* **2.** of or pertaining to non-proliferation: *the non-proliferation treaty.*

**non pros.,** non prosequitur.

**non prosequitur** /nɒn proʊ'sɛkwətɜ/, *n.* a judgment entered against the plaintiff in a suit when he does not appear to prosecute it. [L: he does not pursue (prosecute)]

**non-renounceable issue** /nɒn-rəˌnaʊnsəbəl 'ɪʃu/, *n.* →**entitlement issue.**

**non-representational** /ˌnɒn-rɛprəzɛn'teɪʃənəl/, *adj.* not resembling any object in physical nature: *a non-representational painting.*

**non-resident** /nɒn-'rɛzədənt/, *adj.* **1.** not resident in a particular place. **2.** not residing where one is required to perform official duties: *a non-resident hospital nurse.* *–n.* **3.** one who is non-resident. **– non-residence, non-residency,** *n.*

**non-resistant** /nɒn-rə'zɪstənt/, *adj.* **1.** not resistant; passively obedient. *–n.* **2.** one who does not resist authority or force. **3.** one who maintains that violence should not be resisted by force. **– non-resistance,** *n.*

**non-restraint** /nɒn-rə'streɪnt/, *n.* **1.** *Psychiatry.* the treatment of the mentally ill without mechanical means of restraint. **2.** absence of restraint.

**non-restrictive** /'nɒn-rəstrɪktɪv/, *adj.* **1.** not restrictive or limiting: *non-restrictive practices.* **2.** *Gram.* (of a word or clause) purely descriptive rather than limiting in its application to the sentence element it modifies. 'Mr Owen, *who was here yesterday,* is a farmer' illustrates a non-restrictive clause. 'The man who was here yesterday is a farmer' shows the same clause employed to restrict the meaning of *the man.*

**non-rigid** /'nɒn-rɪdʒəd/, *adj.* **1.** not rigid. **2.** designating a type of airship having a flexible gas container without a supporting structure and held in shape only by the pressure of the gas within.

**non-sectarian** /nɒn-sɛk'tɛəriən/, *adj.* not affiliated to any specific religious denomination.

**nonsense** /'nɒnsəns/, *n.* **1.** that which makes no sense or is lacking in sense. **2.** words without sense or conveying absurd ideas. **3.** senseless or absurd action; foolish conduct, notions, etc.: *to stand no nonsense from a person.* **4.** absurdity: *the nonsense of an idea.* **5.** stuff, trash, or anything useless. **– nonsensical** /nɒn'sɛnsɪkəl/, *adj.* **– nonsensically** /nɒn'sɛnsɪkli/, *adv.* **– nonsensicalness** /nɒn'sɛnsɪkəlnəs/, **nonsensicality** /ˌnɒnsɛnsə'kæləti/, *n.*

**nonsense verse** /'– vɜs/, *n.* verse conveying deliberately absurd ideas or using specially coined words, usu. humorous, as the verse of the English humorist, Edward Lear, 1812-88.

**non seq.,** non sequitur.

**non sequitur** /nɒn 'sɛkwɪtə/, *n.* an inference or a conclusion which does not follow from the premises. [L: it does not follow]

**non-skid** /'nɒn-skɪd/, *adj.* having the wheel rim or tyre with a ridged or otherwise skid-resistant surface.

**non-slip** /'nɒn-slɪp/, *adj.* designed or constructed in such a way as to minimise danger of slipping.

**non-smoker** /nɒn-'smoʊkə/, *n.* **1.** a person who does not smoke. **2.** a compartment of a railway carriage in which smoking is forbidden.

**non-smoking** /nɒn-'smoʊkɪŋ/, *adj.* **1.** of a person who does not smoke. **2.** of a place, as a railway carriage, tram, theatre, etc., where smoking is not allowed. *–n.* **3.** the practice of not smoking.

**non-specific urethritus** /ˌnɒn-spəsɪfɪk jurə'θraɪtəs/, *n.* a urethritus resulting from an unidentifiable cause. *Abbrev.:* N.S.U.

**non-starter** /nɒn-'statə/, *n.* **1.** a person, animal, vehicle, etc., which does not start in a race. **2.** *Colloq.* something which has no chance of success, as an idea that is discounted as inherently impracticable.

**non-state school** /ˌnɒn-steɪt 'skul/, *n.* →**non-government school.**

**non-stick** /'nɒn-stɪk/, *adj.* (of frying pans, etc.) coated on the inside with a substance (as polytetrafluoroethylene) to prevent food sticking during cooking.

**non-stop** /nɒn-'stɒp/, *adv.*; /'nɒn-stɒp/, *adj.* *–adv.* **1.** without stopping; continuously: *it rained non-stop yesterday.* *–adj.* **2.** without a single stop: *a non-stop flight from Sydney to Perth.*

---

**non-heritably,** *adv.*
**non-historic,** *adj.*
**non-historical,** *adj.*
**non-human,** *adj., n.*
**non-humorous,** *adj.*
**non-humorously,** *adv.*
**non-ideal,** *adj.*
**non-identical,** *adj.*
**non-identity,** *n.*
**non-ideological,** *adj.*
**non-idiomatic,** *adj.*
**non-immunity,** *n.*
**non-importation,** *n.*
**non-impeachable,** *adj.*
**non-imperialist,** *adj., n.*
**non-implementation,** *n.*
**non-impregnated,** *adj.*
**non-incident,** *n., adj.*
**non-inclusive,** *adj.*
**non-inclusively,** *adv.*
**non-indictable,** *adj.*
**non-indictment,** *n.*
**non-indigenous,** *adj.*
**non-industrial,** *adj., n.*
**non-industrially,** *adv.*
**non-infection,** *n.*
**non-infectious,** *adj.*
**non-inflammable,** *adj.*
**non-inflammably,** *adv.*
**non-inflected,** *adj.*
**non-informative,** *adj.*
**non-informatively,** *adv.*
**non-inheritable,** *adj.*
**non-intellectual,** *adj., n.*
**non-intercourse,** *n.*
**non-interference,** *n.*
**non-intersecting,** *adj.*
**non-intoxicant,** *adj., n.*
**non-intoxicating,** *adj.*
**non-intoxicatingly,** *adv.*
**non-involvement,** *n.*
**non-ionic,** *adj.*
**non-irrigable,** *adj.*
**non-irritant,** *adj.*
**non-irritating,** *adj.*
**non-issuable,** *adj.*
**non-issuably,** *adv.*
**non-labour,** *adj.*
**non-liberation,** *n.*
**non-life,** *n.*
**non-literary,** *adj.*
**non-literate,** *adj.*
**non-living,** *adj.*
**non-luminous,** *adj.*
**non-luminously,** *adv.*
**non-magnetic,** *adj.*
**non-malignant,** *adj.*
**non-malignantly,** *adv.*
**non-malleable,** *adj.*
**non-mandatory,** *adj.*
**non-manufacturing,** *adj.*
**non-marrying,** *adj.*
**non-martial,** *adj.*
**non-martially,** *adv.*
**non-material,** *adj.*
**non-mathematician,** *n.*
**non-measurable,** *adj.*
**non-measurably,** *adv.*
**non-mechanical,** *adj.*
**non-mechanically,** *adv.*
**non-medical,** *adj.*
**non-medically,** *adv.*
**non-medicinal,** *adj.*
**non-medicinally,** *adv.*
**non-melodic,** *adj.*

**non-striated** /nɒn-straɪ'eɪtəd/, *adj.* not striated; unstriped, as muscular tissue.

**non-striker** /nɒn-'straɪkə/, *n.* **1.** one who does not strike. **2.** *Cricket.* the batsman who is at the bowler's wicket. – **non-striking,** *n.*

**nonsuch** /'nʌnsʌtʃ/, *n.* →**nonesuch.**

**nonsuit** /nɒn'sut/, *n.* **1.** a judgment given against a plaintiff who neglects to prosecute, or who fails to show a legal cause of action or to bring sufficient evidence. *–v.t.* **2.** to subject to a nonsuit.

**non-swimmer** /nɒn-'swɪmə/, *n.* a person who is unable to swim.

**non troppo** /nɒn 'trɒpoʊ/, *adv.* (a musical direction) not too much: *non troppo lento* (not too slow). [It.]

**non-U** /nɒn-'ju/, *adj. Colloq.* not appropriate to or characteristic of the upper class. [NON- + *U(pper class)*]

**non-union** /'nɒn-junjən/, *adj.* **1.** not belonging to or not in accordance with the rules of, a trade union. *–n.* **2.** *Pathol.* failure of a broken bone to heal.

**non-unionism** /nɒn-'junjənɪzəm/, *n.* disregard of or opposition to trade unions. – **non-unionist,** *n.*

**non-union shop** /ˌnɒn-junjən 'ʃɒp/, *n.* a factory, office, or other workplace, in which there are no union members.

**non-user** /nɒn-'juzə/, *n.* **1.** one who does not use. **2.** *Law.* ceasing to exercise a right.

**nonverbal communication** /nɒnˌvɜbəl kəmjunə'keɪʃən/, *n.* communication without words, as by gesture, stance, inflectional patterns, etc.

**non-violence** /nɒn-'vaɪələns/, *n.* **1.** the principle of avoiding the use of violence in all circumstances. **2.** the practice of this principle.

**non-violent** /'nɒn-vaɪələnt/, *adj.* **1.** upholding or applying the principles of non-violence. **2.** peaceable; equable. – **non-violently,** *adv.*

**non-word** /nɒn-'wɜd/, *n.* a word which is not recorded; a word to which a person or authority refuses to grant status, recognition or acceptance.

**noodle**[1] /'nudl/, *n.* a type of pasta, cut into long, narrow, flat strips and served in soups or, with a sauce, as a main dish. [G *Nudel*]

**noodle**[2] /'nudl/, *n.* **1.** *Colloq.* the head. **2.** a simpleton. **3.** **use one's noodle,** *Colloq.* to think for oneself. [? var. of NODDLE[1] (with *oo* from FOOL[1])]

**noodle**[3] /'nudl/, *v.t.,* **noodled, noodling. 1.** to search carefully for opal through a bucket of dirt sent up to the surface. **2.** to sift dumps or mullock heaps searching for opal missed by the miner. – **noodler,** *n.*

**Noogoora burr** /nəgurə 'bɜ/, *n.* a tall herbaceous plant with large spiny burrs, *Xanthium chinense,* which is poisonous to young livestock. [from *Noogoora,* sheep station in Qld]

Noogoora burr

**nook** /nʊk/, *n.* **1.** a corner, as in a room. **2.** any secluded or obscure corner. **3.** any small recess. **4.** a remote spot. [ME *noke.* Cf. d. Norw. *nok* hook]

**nooky**[1] /'nʊki/, *adj.* **1.** having many nooks. **2.** shaped like a nook. Also, **nookie.**

**nooky**[2] /'nʊki/, *n. Colloq.* sexual intercourse. Also, **nookie.** [orig. uncert.]

**noolbenger** /'nulbɛŋgə/, *n.* →**honey possum.**

**noon** /nun/, *n.* **1.** midday. **2.** twelve o'clock in the daytime. **3.** the highest, brightest, or finest point or part. [ME *none,* OE *nōn,* from L *nōna* ninth hour. See NONES[1]]

**noonday** /'nundeɪ/, *adj.* **1.** of or at noon. *–n.* **2.** midday; noon.

**no-one** /'noʊ-wʌn/, *pron.* **1.** nobody. *–n.* **2.** no person. Also, **no one.**

**noongar** /'nuŋgə/, *n. W.A. Colloq.* an Aborigine. [Aboriginal]

**noontide** /'nuntaɪd/, *n.* **1.** the time of noon: midday. **2.** the highest or best point or part. [ME *nonetyde,* OE *nōntīd*]

**noontime** /'nuntaɪm/, *n.* the time of noon.

**noose** /nus/, *n., v.,* **noosed, noosing.** *–n.* **1.** a loop with a running knot, as in a snare, lasso, hangman's halter, etc., which tightens as the rope is pulled. **2.** a tie or bond; a snare. *–v.t.* **3.** to secure by or as by a noose. **4.** to make a noose with or in (a rope, etc.). [probably from OF *nos,* from *noer* to knit, from L *nōdāre,* from *nōdus* knot]

noose

**nopal** /'noʊpəl/, *n.* **1.** any cactus or fruit of the genera *Opuntia* and *Nopalea.* **2.** →**prickly pear.** [Sp., from Nahuatl *nopalli* cactus]

**no-par** /'noʊ-pa/, *adj.* without par, or face, value.

**nope** /noʊp/, *adv. Colloq.* an emphatic form of **no**[1].

**nor** /nɔ/, *conj.* a negative conjunction used: **a.** as the correlative to a preceding *neither: he could neither read nor write.* **b.** to continue the force of a negative, such as *not, no, never,* etc., occurring in a preceding clause: *he left and I never saw him again, nor did I regret it.* **c.** after an affirmative clause, or as a continuative, in the sense of *and...not: they are happy; nor need we mourn.* **d.** *Archaic or Poetic.* with omission of a preceding *neither,* its negative force being understood: *he nor I was there.* **e.** *Chiefly Poetic.* instead of *neither,* as correlative to

**non-melodically,** *adv.*
**non-melodious,** *adj.*
**non-melodiously,** *adv.*
**non-melting,** *adj.*
**non-member,** *n.*
**non-membership,** *n.*
**non-mental,** *adj.*
**non-metaphorical,** *adj.*
**non-metaphysical,** *adj.*
**non-metrical,** *adj.*
**non-metrically,** *adv.*
**non-metropolitan,** *adj.*
**non-migratory,** *adj.*
**non-militant,** *adj.*
**non-militantly,** *adv.*
**non-military,** *adj.*
**non-miscible,** *adj.*
**non-miscibility,** *n.*
**non-molecular,** *adj.*
**non-monetary,** *adj.*
**non-mortal,** *adj.*
**non-mortally,** *adv.*
**non-motile,** *adj.*
**non-muscular,** *adj.*
**non-muscularly,** *adv.*
**non-musical,** *adj.*
**non-musically,** *adv.*
**non-natural,** *adj.*
**non-naturally,** *adv.*
**non-naturalistic,** *adj.*
**non-navigable,** *adj.*
**non-navigably,** *adv.*
**non-necessary,** *adj.*
**non-necessity,** *n.*
**non-negotiable,** *adj.*
**non-neutral,** *adj.*
**non-nutritious,** *adj.*
**non-obedience,** *n.*
**non-obligatory,** *adj.*
**non-observance,** *n.*
**non-occurrence,** *n.*
**non-odorous,** *adj.*
**non-odorously,** *adv.*
**non-offender,** *n.*
**non-offensive,** *adj.*
**non-offensively,** *adv.*
**non-official,** *adj.*
**non-officially,** *adv.*
**non-operational,** *adj.*
**non-organic,** *adj.*
**non-orthodox,** *adj.*
**non-orthodoxly,** *adv.*
**non-parishioner,** *n.*
**non-parliamentary,** *adj.*
**non-parochial,** *adj.*
**non-parochially,** *adv.*
**non-participant,** *n.*
**non-participation,** *n.*
**non-participatory,** *adj.*
**non-party,** *adj.*
**non-passerine,** *adj.*
**non-paying,** *adj.*
**non-payment,** *n.*
**non-performance,** *n.*
**non-perishable,** *adj.*
**non-permanent,** *adj.*
**non-permanently,** *adv.*
**non-permeable,** *adj.*
**non-perpendicular,** *adj., n.*
**non-perpendicularly,** *adv.*
**non-persistance,** *n.*
**non-phallic,** *adj.*
**non-philosophical,** *adj.*
**non-philosophically,** *adv.*
**non-phonetic,** *adj.*

a following *nor: nor he nor I was there.* [ME *nor,* contraction of *nother,* OE *nōther,* from *ne* not + *ōther* (contraction of *ōhwæther* either)]

**nor'** /nɔ/, *n., adj., adv. Chiefly Naut.* north.

**nor-,** a word element meaning 'normal'. [short for NORMAL]

**Nor., 1.** Norman. **2.** North. **3.** Norway. **4.** Norwegian.

**noradrenaline** /nɔrə'drɛnələn/, *n.* a hormone, $(HO)_2C_6H_3CH(OH)CH_2NH_2$, produced by the adrenal medulla, which causes dilatation of blood vessels in skeletal muscle and effects carbohydrate and lipid metabolism. Also, **norepinephrine.**

**Nordhausen acid** /ˌnɔdhaʊzən 'æsəd/, *n.* →**fuming sulphuric acid.**

**Nordic** /'nɔdɪk/, *adj.* **1.** *Ethnol.* designating, or belonging or pertaining to, a race of men or a Caucasian racial subtype characterised by tall stature, blond hair, blue eyes, and elongated head, exemplified most markedly by Scandinavians and Britons and their descendants. **2.** (*also l.c.*) of or pertaining to a type of skiing which involves travelling across country. *–n.* **3.** a member of the Nordic race. [F *nordique,* from *nord* north, from Gmc, and akin to NORTH. See -IC]

**nor'-easter** /nɔr-'istə/, *n.* **1.** →**north-easter. 2. black nor'-easter.** an unpleasant, persistent north-easterly wind blowing from the sea, which deposits a dirty salty moistness on everything near the waterfront.

**Norfolk Island** /nɔfək 'aɪlənd/, *n.* an island in the South Pacific Ocean, east of Australia, a territory of Australia.

**Norfolk Island hibiscus,** *n.* an evergreen tree with a greyish foliage, *Lagunaria patersonia,* commonly planted in conditions which expose it to sea air, the fruit capsule of which splits to produce fine hairs which may cause irritation; cow-itch tree. Also, **Norfolk Island hibiscus tree.**

**Norfolk Island pine,** *n.* a tall coniferous tree, *Araucaria heterophylla,* native to Norfolk Island, but often cultivated elsewhere on deep sands in coastal areas.

Norfolk Island pine

**Norfolk jacket** /'nɔfək dʒækət/, *n.* a loosely belted single-breasted jacket, with box pleat at front and back.

**noria** /'nɔriə/, *n.* a device consisting of a series of buckets on a wheel, used in Spain and the Orient for raising water. [Sp., from Ar. *nā'ūra*]

**norks** /nɔks/, *n.pl. Colloq.* breasts. [orig. uncert.]

**norm** /nɔm/, *n.* **1.** a standard, model, or pattern. **2.** a mean or average. **3.** *Educ.* **a.** a designated standard of average performance of people of a given age, background, etc. **b.** a standard of average performance by a person. [L *norma* carpenter's square, rule, pattern]

**norm.,** normalised.

**normal** /'nɔməl/, *adj.* **1.** conforming to the standard or the common type; regular, usual, natural, or not abnormal: *the normal procedure.* **2.** serving to fix a standard. **3.** *Psychol.* **a.** approximately average in respect to any psychological trait, such as intelligence, personality, emotional adjustment, etc. **b.** without any mental aberrations; sane. **4.** *Maths.* **a.** being at right angles, as a line; perpendicular. **b.** of the nature of or pertaining to a mathematical normal. **5.** *Chem.* **a.** (of a solution) containing one equivalent weight of the constituent in question in one litre of solution. **b.** pertaining to an aliphatic hydrocarbon having a straight unbranched carbon chain, each carbon atom of which is joined to no more than two other carbon atoms. **c.** pertaining to a normal element. **6.** *Biol., Med., etc.* **a.** free from any infection or experimental therapy. **b.** of natural occurrence. *–n.* **7.** the standard or type. **8.** the normal form or state; the average or mean. **9.** *Maths.* a perpendicular line or plane, esp. one perpendicular to a tangent line of a curve, or a tangent plane of a surface, at the point of contact. [L *normālis* made according to a carpenter's square or rule]

**normal curve** /– 'kɜv/, *n.* a bell-shaped curve giving the distribution of probability associated with the different values of a variable.

**normalcy** /'nɔməlsi/, *n.* the character or state of being normal; normality: *back to normalcy.*

**normal distribution** /– dɪstrə'bjuʃən/, *n.* a form of statistical distribution in which the highest frequency is at the mean score, or in which the mean, median and mode are equal. Also, **Gaussian distribution.**

**normalise** /'nɔməlaɪz/, *v.t.,* **-lised, -lising. 1.** to make normal. **2.** *Metall.* to heat-treat a steel, in order to relieve its internal stresses, by heating to above the critical temperature and allowing it to cool in air. **3. normalise relations,** to re-establish normal diplomatic relations with a country. Also, **normalize. – normalisation** /nɔməlaɪ'zeɪʃən/, *n.* **– normaliser,** *n.*

**normality** /nɔ'mæləti/, *n.* **1.** the character or state of being normal. **2.** *Psychol.* **a.** the quality of being approximately average with respect to any psychological trait. **b.** sanity; freedom from mental aberration. **3.** *Chem.* the concentration of a solution expressed in gram equivalents of active reagent per litre of solution. **4.** *Biol., Med., etc.* freedom from infection.

**normally** /'nɔməli/, *adv.* as a rule; regularly; according to rule, general custom, etc.

---

**non-physical,** *adj.*
**non-pinaceous,** *adj.*
**non-poetic,** *adj.*
**non-poisonous,** *adj.*
**non-poisonously,** *adv.*
**non-polar,** *adj.*
**non-political,** *adj.*
**non-politically,** *adv.*
**non-porous,** *adj.*
**non-possession,** *n.*
**non-predatory,** *adj.*
**non-predictable,** *adj.*
**non-prehensile,** *adj.*
**non-prepositional,** *adj.*
**non-prescriptive,** *adj.*
**non-priority,** *n.*
**non-problem,** *n.*
**non-producing,** *adj.*
**non-production,** *n.*
**non-professional,** *adj., n.*
**non-professorial,** *adj.*
**non-proficiency,** *n.*
**non-proficient,** *adj.*
**non-profiteering,** *adj.*
**non-progressive,** *adj.*
**non-progressively,** *adv.*
**non-proportionate,** *adj.*
**non-protective,** *adj.*
**non-protectively,** *adv.*
**non-punishable,** *adj.*
**non-racial,** *adj.*
**non-racially,** *adv.*
**non-radioactive,** *adj.*
**non-rational,** *adj.*
**non-rationality,** *n.*
**non-reader,** *n.*
**non-realistic,** *adj.*
**non-reality,** *n.*
**non-reciprocal,** *adj.*
**non-reciprocally,** *adv.*
**non-recognition,** *n.*
**non-recurrence,** *n.*
**non-recurrent,** *adj.*
**non-recurrently,** *adv.*
**non-recurring,** *adj.*
**non-reduction,** *n.*
**non-refillable,** *adj.*
**non-reflecting,** *adj.*
**non-reflexive,** *adj.*
**non-refuelling,** *adj.*
**non-regimented,** *adj.*
**non-reigning,** *adj.*
**non-religious,** *adj.*
**non-religiously,** *adv.*
**non-remunerated,** *adj.*
**non-remunerative,** *adj.*
**non-remuneratively,** *adv.*
**non-renewable,** *adj.*
**non-representative,** *adj.*
**non-reproducible,** *adj.*
**non-residential,** *adj.*
**non-restricted,** *adj.*
**non-restrictedly,** *adv.*
**non-returnable,** *adj.*
**non-reversible,** *adj.*
**non-reversibly,** *adv.*
**non-revolutionary,** *adj.*
**non-rhyming,** *adj.*
**non-rhythmic,** *adj.*
**non-rural,** *adj.*
**non-rurally,** *adv.*
**non-rust,** *adj.*
**non-salaried,** *adj.*
**non-saleable,** *adj.*
**non-scheduled,** *adj.*

**normal solution** /nɔməl sə'luʃən/, *n.* a solution of a chemical substance in water which contains the equivalent weight of that substance in one litre of solution.

**Norman** /'nɔmən/, *adj.* **1.** of or pertaining to the Normans, a mixed Scandinavian and French people. **2.** *Archit.* denoting or pertaining to a variety of the Romanesque style of architecture introduced from Normandy into Britain before and during the Norman Conquest. [ME, backformation from OF *Normans,* pl. of *Normant* Northman]

**Norman French** /– 'frɛntʃ/, *n.* **1.** the French of the Normans or of Normandy. **2.** the legal jargon of England, now extinct except in phrases, originally a dialect of Old French.

**normative** /'nɔmətɪv/, *adj.* **1.** concerning a norm, esp. an assumed norm regarded as the standard of correctness in speech and writing. **2.** tending or attempting to establish such a norm esp. by the prescription of rules: *normative grammar.* **3.** reflecting the assumption of such a norm, or favouring its establishment. – **normatively,** *adv.*

**norm-formation** /'nɔm-fɔˌmeɪʃən/, *n.* (in sociology) the development of common behaviour and beliefs by general agreement within a reference group.

**normocyte** /'nɔməsaɪt/, *n.* a red blood cell of normal size.

**normotensive** /nɔmoʊ'tɛnsɪv/, *adj.* having a normal blood pressure.

**Norse** /nɔs/, *adj.* **1.** belonging or pertaining to Norway, esp. ancient Norway with its colonies (as in Iceland), or to ancient Scandinavia generally. *–n.* **2.** (*construed as pl.*) the Norwegians. **3.** (*construed as pl.*) the ancient Norwegians. **4.** (*construed as pl.* ) the Northmen or ancient Scandinavians generally. **5.** the Norwegian language, esp. in its older forms. See **Old Norse.** [probably from D *noorsch,* var. of *noordsch,* from *noord* north. Cf. Norw., Swed., Dan. *Norsk* Norwegian, Norse]

**north** /nɔθ/, *n.* **1.** a cardinal point of the compass lying in the plane of the meridian and to the right of a person facing the setting sun or west. **2.** the direction in which this point lies. **3.** →**magnetic north. 4.** (*l.c. or cap.*) a quarter or territory situated in this direction. **5.** *Chiefly Poetic.* the north wind. *–adj.* **6.** lying towards or situated in the north. **7.** directed or proceeding towards the north. **8.** coming from the north, as a wind. **9.** (*cap.*) designating the northern part of a region, nation, country, etc.: *North Atlantic.* *–adv.* **10.** towards or in the north. **11.** from the north. Also, *esp. Naut.,* **nor'**. [ME and OE, c. G *Nord*]

**North America** /nɔθ ə'mɛrɪkə/, *n.* the northernmost continent of the Western Hemisphere, extending from Central America to the Arctic Ocean. – **North American,** *adj.,n.*

**north and south,** *n. Colloq.* a mouth. [rhyming slang]

**northbound** /'nɔθbaʊnd/, *adj.* travelling towards the north.

**north by east,** *n. Navig., Survey.* 11° 15′ (one point) east of north. *Abbrev.:* N by E. Also, *esp. Naut.,* **nor' by east.**

**north by west,** *n. Navig., Survey.* 11° 15′ (one point) west of north; 348° 45′ from due north. *Abbrev.:* N by W. Also, *esp. Naut.,* **nor' by west.**

**north-east** /nɔθ-'ist/, *n., adv.*; /'nɔθ-ist/, *adj.* *–n.* **1.** the point or direction midway between north and east. **2.** a region in this direction. *–adv.* **3.** towards or in the north-east. **4.** from the north-east. *–adj.* **5.** lying towards or situated in the north-east. **6.** directed or proceeding towards the north-east. **7.** coming from the north-east, as a wind. Also, *esp. Naut.,* **nor'-east.** – **north-easterner,** *n.*

**north-east by east,** *n. Navig., Survey.* 11° 15′ (one point) east of north-east; 56° 15′ from due north. *Abbrev.:* NE by E. Also, *esp. Naut.,* **nor'-east by east.**

**north-east by north,** *n. Navig., Survey.* 11° 15′ (one point) north of north-east; 33° 45′ from due north. *Abbrev.:* NE by N. Also, *esp. Naut.,* **nor'-east by nor'.**

**north-easter** /nɔθ-'istə/, *n.* a wind or gale from the north-east. Also, *esp. Naut.,* **nor'-easter.**

**north-easterly** /nɔθ-'istəli/, *adj.* **1.** of or situated in the north-east. **2.** towards or from the north-east. *–adv.* **3.** towards or from the north-east. Also, *esp. Naut.,* **nor'-easterly.** *–n.* **4.** a wind or gale from the north-east.

**north-eastern** /nɔθ-'istən/, *adj.* situated in, proceeding towards, or coming from the north-east. Also, *esp. Naut.,* **nor'-eastern.**

**north-eastward** /nɔθ-'istwəd/, *adv., adj.* **1.** Also, **north-eastwardly,** *esp. Naut.,* **nor'-eastwardly.** towards the north-east. *–n.* **2.** the north-east. Also, *esp. Naut.,* **nor'-eastward.**

**north-eastwards** /nɔθ-'istwədz/, *adv.* north-eastward. Also, *esp. Naut.,* **nor'-eastwards.**

**northerly** /'nɔðəli/, *adj.* **1.** moving, directed, or situated towards the north. **2.** coming from the north, as a wind. *–adv.* **3.** towards the north. **4.** from the north. – **northerliness,** *n.*

**northern** /'nɔðən/, *adj.* **1.** lying towards or situated in the north. **2.** directed or proceeding northwards. **3.** coming from the north, as a wind. **4.** (*cap.*) of or pertaining to the North. **5.** *Astron.* north of the celestial equator or of the zodiac: *a northern constellation.* [ME and OE *northerne.* See -ERN]

**northerner** /'nɔðənə/, *n.* a native or inhabitant of a northern country or region.

**Northern Hemisphere** /nɔðən 'hɛməsfɪə/, *n.* the half of the earth between the North Pole and the equator.

**Northern Ireland** /– 'aɪələnd/, *n.* a political division of the

---

**non-scientific,** *adj.*
**non-scientist,** *n.*
**non-scriptural,** *adj.*
**non-seasonal,** *adj.*
**non-sectional,** *adj.*
**non-sectionally,** *adv.*
**non-selective,** *adj.*
**non-self-governing,** *adj.*
**non-sensitive,** *adj.*
**non-sensitively,** *adv.*
**non-sensory,** *adj.*
**non-sensuous,** *adj.*
**non-sensuously,** *adv.*
**non-sexual,** *adj.*
**non-sexually,** *adv.*
**non-Shakespearian,** *adj.*
**non-sharing,** *adj.*
**non-shatter,** *adj.*
**non-shrink,** *adj.*
**non-shrinkable,** *adj.*
**non-significant,** *adj.*
**non-significantly,** *adv.*
**non-social,** *adj.*
**non-socialist,** *adj., n.*
**non-socially,** *adv.*
**non-solvent,** *adj.*
**non-solvency,** *n.*
**non-sparkling,** *adj.*
**non-spatial,** *adj.*
**non-specialist,** *n., adj.*
**non-specialised,** *adj.*
**non-specific,** *adj.*
**non-spherical,** *adj.*
**non-spiritual,** *adj.*
**non-spiritually,** *adv.*
**non-spore-forming,** *adj.*
**non-stainable,** *adj.*
**non-staining,** *adj.*
**non-standard,** *adj.*
**non-standardised,** *adj.*
**non-State,** *adj.*
**non-statistical,** *adj.*
**non-statutory,** *adj.*
**non-stimulating,** *adj.*
**non-strategic,** *adj.*
**non-stretch,** *adj.*
**non-structural,** *adj.*
**non-submissive,** *adj.*
**non-submissively,** *adv.*
**non-subscriber,** *n.*
**non-substantial,** *adj.*
**non-substantially,** *adv.*
**non-successive,** *adj.*
**non-successively,** *adv.*
**non-supporter,** *n.*
**non-survival,** *n.*
**non-sustainable,** *adj.*
**non-sustaining,** *adj.*
**non-swimmer,** *n.*
**non-swimming,** *adj.*
**non-symbolic,** *adj.*
**non-symmetrical,** *adj.*
**non-synthetic,** *adj.*
**non-systematic,** *adj.*
**non-taxable,** *adj.*
**non-taxably,** *adv.*
**non-teachable,** *adj.*
**non-technical,** *adj.*
**non-technically,** *adv.*
**non-terrestrial,** *adj.*
**non-territorial,** *adj.*
**non-territorially,** *adv.*
**non-textual,** *adj.*
**non-textually,** *adj.*
**non-theological,** *adj.*

United Kingdom in north-eastern Ireland.
**northern lights** /nɔðən 'laɪts/, *n.pl.* →**aurora borealis.**
**northernmost** /'nɔðənmoʊst/, *adj.* farthest north.
**northern native cat,** *n.* the smallest of the Australian native cats, *Dasyurus hallucatus,* of northern Australia, having a yellow-brown white-spotted body; satanellus.
**Northern Rhodesia** /nɔðən roʊ'diʒə/, *n.* former name of Zambia.
**Northern Territory** /– 'tɛrətri/, *n.* a territory in central north Australia. *Abbrev.:* N.T.
**North Germanic** /nɔθ dʒə'mænɪk/, *n.* the Scandinavian subgroup of Germanic languages.
**northing** /'nɔðɪŋ/, *n.* **1.** the difference in latitude to the north between two positions on a map as a result of progress to the north. **2.** progress in a northerly direction. **3.** the north coordinate which together with the easting identifies a position on a map.
**North Korea** /nɔθ kə'riə/, *n.* a republic in eastern Asia, formed in 1948 after the division of Korea at 38°N. Official name: **Democratic People's Republic of Korea.**
**northland** /'nɔθlænd/, *n.* **1.** the land or region in the north. **2.** the northern part of a country. [ME and OE, c. G, Dan., Swed. *nordland*] – **northlander,** *n.*
**northlight roof** /ˌnɔθlaɪt 'ruf/, *n.* (in the northern hemisphere) a sawtooth roof in which the spandrels are glazed and face north, giving light without glare.
**north-north-east** /ˌnɔθ-nɔθ-'ist/, *Navig., Survey.* –*n.* **1.** the point of the compass midway between north and north-east; 22°30′ from north. –*adj.* **2.** lying or situated in this direction. –*adv.* **3.** to, in, or from this direction. *Abbrev.:* NNE. Also, *esp. Naut.,* **nor'-nor'-east** /nɔ-nɔr-'ist/.
**north-north-west** /ˌnɔθ-nɔθ-'wɛst/, *Navig., Survey.* –*n.* **1.** the point of the compass midway between north and north-west; 337°30′ from north. –*adj.* **2.** lying or situated in this direction. –*adv.* **3.** to, in, or from this direction. *Abbrev.:* NNW. Also, *esp. Naut.,* **nor'-nor'-west** /nɔ-nɔ-'wɛst/.
**North Pole** /nɔθ 'poʊl/, *n.* **1.** that end of the earth's axis of rotation marking the northernmost point on the earth. **2.** *Astron.* the zenith of the earth's north pole.
**northward** /'nɔθwəd/, *adj.* **1.** moving, bearing, facing, or situated towards the north. –*n.* **2.** the northward part, direction, or point. –*adv.* **3.** northwards. – **northwardly,** *adj., adv.*
**northwards** /'nɔθwədz/, *adv.* towards the north. Also, **northward.**
**north-west** /nɔθ-'wɛst/, *n.;* /'nɔθ-wɛst/, *adj.;* /nɔθ-'wɛst/, *adv.* –*n.* **1.** the point or direction midway between north and west. **2.** a region in this direction. –*adj.* **3.** lying towards or situated in the north-west. **4.** directed or proceeding towards the north-west. **5.** coming from the north-west, as a wind. –*adv.* **6.** in the direction of a point midway between north and west. **7.** from this direction. Also, *esp. Naut.,* **nor'-west.**
**north-west by north,** *n. Navig., Survey.* 11°15′ (one point) north of north-west; 326°15′ from due north. *Abbrev.:* NW by N. Also, *esp. Naut.,* **nor'-west by nor'.**
**north-west by west,** *n. Navig., Survey.* 11°15′ (one point) west of north-west; 303°45′ from due north. *Abbrev.:* NW by W. Also, *esp. Naut.,* **nor'-west by west.**
**north-wester** /nɔθ-'wɛstə/, *n.* a wind or gale from the north-west. Also, *esp. Naut.,* **nor'-wester.**
**north-westerly** /nɔθ-'wɛstəli/, *adj., adv.* **1.** towards or from the north-west. –*n.* **2.** a wind or gale from the north-west. Also, *esp. Naut.,* **nor'-westerly.**
**north-western** /nɔθ-'wɛstən/, *adj.* situated in, proceeding towards, or coming from the north-west. Also, *esp. Naut.,* **nor'-western.**
**north-westward** /nɔθ-'wɛstwəd/, *adv., adj.* **1.** Also, **north-westwardly,** *esp. Naut.,* **nor'-westwardly.** towards the north-west. –*n.* **2.** the north-west. Also, *esp. Naut.,* **nor'westward.**
**north-westwards** /nɔθ-'wɛstwədz/, *adv.* north-westward. Also, *esp. Naut.,* **nor'-westwards.**
**Norw.,** **1.** Norway. **2.** Norwegian.
**Norway** /'nɔweɪ/, *n.* a kingdom in northern Europe, in the western part of the Scandinavian peninsula.
**Norway spruce** /– 'sprus/, *n.* a coniferous tree, *Picea abies,* native of northern and central Europe, much planted for forestry elsewhere.
**Norwegian** /nɔ'widʒən/, *adj.* **1.** of or pertaining to Norway, its inhabitants, or their language. –*n.* **2.** a native or inhabitant of Norway. **3.** the speech of Norway in any of its forms, whether Dano-Norwegian, or the local dialects, or the standard language based on these, all being closely related to one another and to the other Scandinavian languages.
**Norwegian elkhound** /– 'ɛlkhaʊnd/, *n.* See **elkhound.**
**Norwich terrier** /ˌnɒrɪtʃ 'tɛriə/, *n.* a small, short-legged terrier, having a wiry red or black-and-tan coat.
**nos-,** variant of **noso-,** before vowels.
**Nos,** numbers. Also, **nos.**
**nose** /noʊz/, *n., v.,* **nosed, nosing.** –*n.* **1.** the part of the face or head which contains the nostrils, affording passage for air in respiration, etc. **2.** this part as the organ of smell: *the aroma of coffee greeted his nose.* **3.** the sense of smell: *a dog with a good nose.* **4.** a faculty of perceiving or detecting: *a nose for news.* **5.** the quality of prying or interfering: *keep your nose out of it.* **6.** something regarded as resembling the nose of a person or animal, as a spout or nozzle. **7.** the prow of a ship. **8.** the forward end of an aircraft. **9.** a projecting part of anything. **10.** (of wines) →**bouquet** (def. 2). **11.** the length of the nose of a horse or other animal as a measure in racing. Cf. **neck. 12.** Some special noun phrases are:
**by a nose,** *Colloq.* by a very narrow margin.
**cut off one's nose to spite one's face,** to damage one's own interests by a spiteful or vengeful action.
**follow one's nose,** to find one's own way, as by instinct.
**keep one's nose to the grindstone,** to force one to work without respite.
**lead by the nose,** to exercise complete control over.
**look down one's nose at,** to despise; disdain.
**on the nose,** *Colloq.* **1.** smelly, objectionable, decayed, stinking (esp. of rotten organic matter, as food). **2.** unpleasant, distasteful.
**pay through the nose,** to pay an excessive amount.
**put someone's nose out of joint,** to thwart or upset a person.
**turn one's nose up,** to be contemptuous or ungrateful.

---

**non-tidal,** *adj.*
**non-totalitarian,** *adj.*
**non-toxic,** *adj.*
**non-trading,** *adj.*
**non-traditional,** *adj.*
**non-transferable,** *adj.*
**non-transient,** *adj.*
**non-transiently,** *adv.*
**non-tributary,** *adj.*
**non-tropical,** *adj.*
**non-truth,** *n.*
**non-typical,** *adj.*
**non-typically,** *adv.*
**non-uniform,** *adj.*
**non-united,** *adj.*
**non-universal,** *adj.*
**non-universally,** *adv.*
**non-urban,** *adj.*
**non-utilitarian,** *adj.*
**non-utility,** *n.*
**non-utterance,** *n.*
**non-validity,** *n.*
**non-venomous,** *adj.*
**non-venomously,** *adv.*
**non-verbal,** *adj.*
**non-verbally,** *adv.*
**non-vertical,** *adj., n.*
**non-vertically,** *adv.*
**non-viable,** *adj.*
**non-violation,** *n.*
**non-visual,** *adj.*
**non-vocal,** *adj.*
**non-vocally,** *adv.*
**non-vocalic,** *adj.*
**non-vocational,** *adj.*
**non-vocationally,** *adv.*
**non-volatile,** *adj.*
**non-voluntary,** *adj.*
**non-voter,** *n.*
**non-voting,** *adj.*
**non-western,** *adj.*
**non-white,** *adj., n.*
**non-worker,** *n.*
**non-woven,** *adj.*
**non-writer,** *n.*
**non-yielding,** *adj.*

**under one's nose,** in an obvious place. *–v.t.* **13.** to perceive by or as by the nose or the sense of smell. **14.** to bring the nose close to, as in smelling or examining; sniff. **15.** to move or push forward. **16.** to touch or rub with the nose; nuzzle. *–v.i.* **17.** to smell or sniff. **18.** to seek as if by smelling or scent (fol. by *after, for,* etc.); pry (fol. by *about, into,* etc.). **19.** to move or push forwards. **20.** to meddle or pry. [ME; OE *nosu*, c. MD and MLG *nose*. Cf. L *nāsus*]

**nosebag** /ˈnoʊzbæg/, *n.* a bag for feeding horses, placed before the mouth with straps around the head.

**noseband** /ˈnoʊzbænd/, *n.* that part of a bridle or halter which passes over an animal's nose. Also, **nosepiece.**

**nosebleed** /ˈnoʊzblid/, *n.* a bleeding from the nose.

**nose-cone** /ˈnoʊz-koʊn/, *n.* the separable cone-shaped leading end of a rocket, containing equipment or a warhead, built to withstand high temperatures.

**nosedive** /ˈnoʊzdaɪv/, *n., v.,* **-dived, -diving.** *–n.* **1.** a plunge of an aeroplane with the fore part of the craft vertically downwards. **2.** any sudden drop. *–v.i.* **3.** to execute a nosedive.

**nosegay** /ˈnoʊzgeɪ/, *n.* a bunch of flowers, or herbs; a bouquet; a posy. [ME; lit., a *gay* (obs., something pretty) for the NOSE (i.e., to smell)]

**nosepiece** /ˈnoʊzpis/, *n.* **1.** a protective cover for the nose. **2.** the part of a microscope where the object slide is attached. **3.** →**noseband.**

**nose rag** /ˈnoʊz ræg/, *n. Colloq.* →**handkerchief.**

**nose riding** /ˈ– raɪdɪŋ/, *n.* a surfing manoeuvre in which the surfer stands on the very front of the surfboard.

**nosey** /ˈnoʊzi/, *adj.,* **-sier, -siest.** →**nosy.**

**nosey parker** /– ˈpakə/, *n.* →**nosy parker.**

**nosh** /nɒʃ/, *Colloq.* *–v.i.* **1.** to eat; have a snack or a meal. *–n.* **2.** anything eaten, esp. a snack. **3.** a titbit eaten between meals. [Yiddish; cf. G *naschen* nibble]

**nosh-up** /ˈnɒʃ-ʌp/, *n. Colloq.* a meal.

**no-side** /noʊ-ˈsaɪd/, *n.* (in rugby football) the end of the period of play.

**nosing** /ˈnoʊzɪŋ/, *n.* a projecting edge, as the part of the tread of a step extending beyond the riser, or a projecting part of a buttress.

**noso-,** a word element meaning 'disease'. Also, **nos-.** [Gk, combining form of *nósos*]

**nosogeography** /ˌnɒsoʊdʒiˈɒgrəfi/, *n.* the study of the causes and occurrence of diseases in relation to geographical factors. – **nosogeographic** /ˌnɒsoʊdʒiəˈgræfɪk/, **nosogeographical** /ˌnɒsoʊdʒiəˈgræfɪkəl/, *adj.* – **nosogeographically,** *adv.*

**nosography** /nɒˈsɒgrəfi/, *n.* the systematic description of diseases. – **nosographer,** *n.* – **nosographic** /nɒsəˈgræfɪk/, **nosographical,** /nɒsəˈgræfɪkəl/, *adj.* – **nosographically** /nɒsəˈgræfɪkli/, *adv.*

**nosology** /nɒˈsɒlədʒi/, *n.* **1.** the systematic classification of diseases. **2.** the knowledge of a disease. – **nosological** /nɒsəˈlɒdʒɪkəl/, *adj.* – **nosologically** /nɒsəˈlɒdʒɪkli/, *adv.* – **nosologist,** *n.*

**nosophobia** /nɒsoʊˈfoʊbiə/, *n.* morbid fear of disease.

**nostalgia** /nɒsˈtældʒə/, *n.* a longing and desire for home, family and friends, or the past. [NL, from Gk *nóstos* a return to home + *-algia* -ALGIA] – **nostalgic,** *adj.* – **nostalgically,** *adv.*

**nostology** /nɒsˈtɒlədʒi/, *n.* →**geriatrics.** [Gk *nósto(s)* a return to home (with ref. to 'second childhood') + -LOGY] – **nostologic** /nɒstəˈlɒdʒɪk/, *adj.*

**nostril** /ˈnɒstrəl/, *n.* one of the external openings of the nose. [ME *nostrill*, OE *nosterl*, var. of *nosthyrl*, from *nosu* nose + *-thyrel* hole]

**nostrum** /ˈnɒstrəm/, *n.* **1.** a patent medicine. **2.** a quack medicine. **3.** a medicine made by the person who recommends it. **4.** a pet scheme or device for effecting something. [L, neut. of *noster* our, ours (cf. def. 3)]

**nosy** /ˈnoʊzi/, *adj.,* **-sier, -siest.** *Colloq.* prying; inquisitive. Also, **nosey.** – **nosily,** *adv.* – **nosiness,** *n.*

**nosy parker** /– ˈpakə/, *n.* a person who continually pries; a meddler; a stickybeak. Also, **nosey parker.**

**not** /nɒt/, *adv.* (a word expressing negation, denial, refusal, or prohibition): *not far; you must not do that.* [ME, reduced form of *noht, nouht.* See NOUGHT]

**nota bene** /noʊtə ˈbɛni, ˈbeɪneɪ/, note well. [L]

**notabilia** /noʊtəˈbɪliə/, *n. pl.* **1.** noteworthy things. **2.** noteworthy sayings. [L]

**notability** /noʊtəˈbɪləti/, *n., pl.* **-ties.** **1.** the quality of being notable. **2.** a notable person.

**notable** /ˈnoʊtəbəl/, *adj.* **1.** worthy of note or notice; noteworthy: *a notable success.* **2.** prominent, important, or distinguished, as persons. **3.** *Archaic.* capable, thrifty, and industrious, as a housewife. *–n.* **4.** a notable person; a prominent or important person. **5.** *Obs.* a notable thing. [ME, from L *notābilis*] – **notableness,** *n.* – **notably,** *adv.*

**notarial** /noʊˈtɛəriəl/, *adj.* of or pertaining to, or drawn up or executed by, a notary. – **notarially,** *adv.*

**notarise** /ˈnoʊtəraɪz/, *v.t.,* **-rised, -rising.** to authenticate (a contract, etc.). Also, **notarize.**

**notary** /ˈnoʊtəri/, *n., pl.* **-ries.** →**notary public.** [ME, from L *notārius* shorthand writer, clerk, secretary]

**notary public** /– ˈpʌblɪk/, *n., pl.* **notaries public.** an official, usu. a solicitor, authorised to certify contracts, acknowledge deeds, take affidavits, protest bills of exchange, take depositions, etc.

**notate** /noʊˈteɪt/, *v.t.,* **-tated, -tating.** to record (a piece of music) by a notation. [backformation from NOTATION]

**notation** /noʊˈteɪʃən/, *n.* **1.** a system of graphic symbols for a specialised use, other than ordinary writing: *musical notation.* **2.** the process of noting or setting down by means of a special system of signs or symbols. **3.** the act of noting, marking, or setting down in writing. **4.** a note, jotting, or record. [L *notātio* a marking] – **notational,** *adj.*

**notch** /nɒtʃ/, *n.* **1.** a more or less angular cut, indentation, or hollow in a narrow object or surface or an edge. **2.** a cut or nick made in a stick or other object for record, as in keeping a score. **3.** *U.S.* a deep, narrow opening or pass between mountains. **4.** *Colloq.* a step or degree. *–v.t.* **5.** to cut or make a notch or notches in. **6.** to make notches in by way of record. **7.** to record by a notch or notches. **8.** to score, as in a game (fol. by *up*): *he notched up three more deals before Saturday.* [AF *anocher*, var. of OF *enochier*, from *oche* notch]

**notch graft** /ˈ– graft/, *n.* a type of plant graft in which the scion is inserted into a slit in a thicker stock.

**note** /noʊt/, *n., v.,* **noted, noting.** *–n.* **1.** a brief record of something set down to assist the memory, or for reference or development. **2.** (*pl.*) a record of a speech, statement, testimony, etc., or of one's impressions of something. **3.** an explanatory or critical comment, or a reference to authority quoted, appended to a passage in a book or the like. **4.** a brief written or printed statement giving particulars or information. **5.** *Bibliog.* additional information about a book, such as its special series or some other significant identification, entered on the library catalogue card. **6.** a short informal letter. **7.** a formal diplomatic or official communication in writing. **8.** a paper acknowledging a debt and promising payment; promissory note; note of hand. **9.** a certificate, as of a government or a bank, passing current as money; a banknote. **10.** eminence or distinction: *a man of note.* **11.** importance or consequence: *no other thing of note this year.* **12.** notice, observation, or heed. **13.** a characteristic or distinguishing feature. **14.** a mark, token, or indication of something, or from which something may be inferred. **15.** a sound or tone. **16.** *Music.* a sign or character used to represent a sound, its position and form indicating the pitch and duration. **17.** *Music.* a key, as of a piano. **18.** *Archaic.* a melody, tune, or song. **19.** a sound of musical quality uttered by a bird. **20.** any call, cry, or sound of a bird, fowl, etc. **21.** a tone sounded on a trumpet or other musical instrument as a signal. **22.** a signal, announcement, or intimation: *a note of warning.* **23.** *Colloq.* a new or unexpected element in a situation. **24.** way of speaking or thinking: *to change one's note.* **25.** a mark or sign, as of punctuation, used in writing or printing. *–v.t.* **26.** to mark

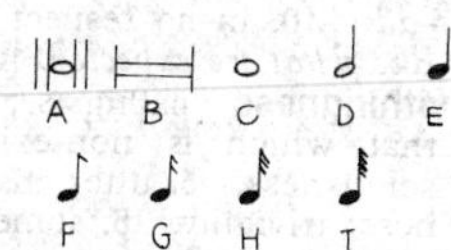


notes (def. 16): A, B, breve; C, semibreve; D, minim; E, crotchet; F, quaver; G, semiquaver; H, demisemiquaver; I, hemidemisemiquaver

down, as in writing; make a memorandum of. **27.** to make particular mention of in a writing. **28.** to annotate. **29.** to observe carefully; give attention or heed to. **30.** to take notice of; perceive. **31.** to set down in or furnish with musical notes. **32.** to indicate or designate; signify or denote. [ME, from L *nota* a mark] – **noter,** *n.*

**notebook** /ˈnoʊtbʊk/, *n.* **1.** a book of or for notes. **2.** a book in which promissory notes are registered.

**notecase** /ˈnoʊtkeɪs/, *n.* a wallet usu. of leather, for carrying paper money, personal cards, etc.

**noted** /ˈnoʊtəd/, *adj.* **1.** celebrated; famous. **2.** specially observed or noticed. – **notedly,** *adv.* – **notedness,** *n.*

**noteless** /ˈnoʊtləs/, *adj.* **1.** of no note; undistinguished; unnoticed. **2.** unmusical or voiceless.

**notelet** /ˈnoʊtlət/, *n.* a small folded card with a printed design on the front, used for informal notes or letters.

**note of hand,** *n.* →**promissory note.**

**notepad** /ˈnoʊtpæd/, *n.* a pad of paper for making notes.

**notepaper** /ˈnoʊtpeɪpə/, *n.* paper used for correspondence.

**note-row** /ˈnoʊt-roʊ/, *n.* (in music) →**tone row.**

**noteworthy** /ˈnoʊtwɜði/, *adj.* worthy of note or notice; notable. – **noteworthily,** *adv.* – **noteworthiness,** *n.*

**not guilty** /nɒt ˈgɪlti/, *n.* the appropriate plea to an indictment where the prisoner wishes to deny or justify everything and let the prosecution prove what they can.

**nothing** /ˈnʌθɪŋ/, *n.* **1.** no thing; not anything; naught: *say nothing.* **2.** no part, share, or trace (fol. by *of*): *the place shows nothing of its former magnificence.* **3.** that which is non-existent. **4.** something of no importance or significance. **5.** a trivial action, matter, circumstance, thing, or remark. **6.** a person of no importance. **7.** that which is without quantity or magnitude. **8.** a cipher or nought. **9.** Some special noun phrases are:
**for nothing,** free of charge.
**in nothing flat,** *Colloq.* in no time at all; very quickly.
**make nothing of, a.** to be unable to understand. **b.** to cope easily with; treat lightly.
**next to nothing,** very little.
**nothing doing,** *Colloq.* definitely no or not.
**nothing for it,** no other course of action is open.
**nothing to write home about,** not worthy of special mention; ordinary.
*–adv.* **10.** in no respect or degree; not at all: *it was nothing like what we expected.* [orig. two words. See NO[1], THING]

**nothingness** /ˈnʌθɪŋnəs/, *n.* **1.** the state of being nothing. **2.** that which is non-existent. **3.** non-existence. **4.** unconsciousness. **5.** utter insignificance, emptiness, or worthlessness; triviality. **6.** something insignificant.

**notice** /ˈnoʊtəs/, *n., v.,* **-ticed, -ticing.** *–n.* **1.** information or intelligence: *to give notice of a thing.* **2.** an intimation or warning. **3.** a note, placard, or the like conveying information or warning. **4.** a notification of the termination, at a specified time, of an agreement, as for renting or employment, given by one of the parties to the agreement. **5.** observation, perception, attention, or heed: *worthy of notice.* **6.** interested or favourable attention. **7.** a single observation or perception. **8.** a brief written mention or account, as of a newly published book; a review. *–v.t.* **9.** to pay attention to or take notice of. **10.** to perceive: *did you notice her hat?* **11.** to treat with attention, politeness, or favour. **12.** to acknowledge acquaintance with. **13.** to mention or refer to; point out, as to a person. **14.** *Chiefly U.S.* to give notice to; serve with a notice. [late ME, from OF, from L *nōtitia* a being known, fame, knowledge] – **noticer,** *n.*

**noticeable** /ˈnoʊtəsəbəl/, *adj.* that may be noticed; such as to attract notice. – **noticeably,** *adv.*

**noticeboard** /ˈnoʊtəsbɔd/, *n.* a board, located centrally in a school, office, etc., designed for the display of notices and other information of general interest.

**notice paper** /ˈnoʊtəs peɪpə/, *n.* a daily document giving notice of business before a house of parliament, including the order in which this business is to be handled.

**notification** /noʊtəfəˈkeɪʃən/, *n.* **1.** the act of notifying, making known, or giving notice. **2.** a formal notifying, or informing. **3.** a notice.

**notify** /ˈnoʊtəfaɪ/, *v.t.,* **-fied, -fying.** **1.** to give notice to, or inform, of something. **2.** to make known; give information of: *the sale was notified in the newspapers.* [ME *notifie(n),* from OF *notifier,* from L *nōtificāre* make known] – **notifiable,** *adj.* – **notifier,** *n.*

**notion** /ˈnoʊʃən/, *n.* **1.** a more or less general, vague or imperfect conception or idea of something: *notions of beauty.* **2.** an opinion, view, or belief. **3.** conception or idea. **4.** a fanciful or foolish idea; whim. **5.** (*pl.*) small wares, esp. pins, needles, thread, tapes, etc.; haberdashery. [L *nōtio* a becoming acquainted, conception, notion]

**notional** /ˈnoʊʃənəl/, *adj.* **1.** pertaining to or expressing a notion or idea. **2.** of the nature of a notion. **3.** abstract or speculative, as reflective thought. **4.** ideal or imaginary; not real. **5.** *Chiefly U.S.* given to or full of notions, as a person; fanciful. **6.** *Gram.* **a.** relating to the meaning expressed by a linguistic form. **b.** having full lexical meaning, in contrast to relational. **7.** *Semantics.* →**presentive.** – **notionally,** *adv.*

**not negotiable** /nɒt nəˈgoʊʃəbəl/, *adj.* of or pertaining to a cheque which is crossed, indicating that the person to whom it is given has no better title to it than the person had from whom he received it; popularly and inaccurately held to mean that the cheque can be paid only into the account, the name of which appears on the cheque.

**notochord** /ˈnoʊtəkɔd/, *n.* a rodlike stiffening structure found in the bodies of the protochordates, as along the back of the lancelet, and also found in the embryos of the vertebrates, and presumed to represent an ancestral stage of the spinal column. [*noto-* (from Gk, combining form of *nôton* back) + CHORD[1]] – **notochordal** /noʊtəˈkɔdl/, *adj.*

**Notogaea** /noʊtəˈdʒiə/, *n.* a biogeographical area of the earth's land area including Australia, New Zealand, part of the East Indies, and the islands of the Pacific. Formerly, Central and South America were also included. [NL, from Gk *nóto(s)* the south + *gaîa* land, earth] – **Notogaean,** *n., adj.*

**notoriety** /noʊtəˈraɪəti/, *n., pl.* **-ties.** **1.** the state or character of being notorious or widely known: *a craze for notoriety.* **2.** a widely known or well-known person.

**notorious** /nəˈtɔriəs/, *adj.* **1.** widely but unfavourably known: *a notorious gambler.* **2.** publicly or generally known: *notorious crimes.* [ML *nōtōrius,* from L *nōtus,* pp., known] – **notoriously,** *adv.* – **notoriousness,** *n.*

**notornis** /noʊˈtɔnəs/, *n.* any of the rare flightless birds constituting the genus *Notornis,* chiefly of New Zealand. [NL, from Gk *nôtos* the south + *órnis* bird]

notornis

**notoungulate** /noʊˈtʌŋgjulət/, *adj.* →**notungulate.**

**not out** /nɒt ˈaʊt/, *adj. Cricket.* **1.** (of a team) still batting. **2.** (of a batsman) not having been put out by the end of an innings; undefeated. **3.** (of a score) made without the wicket having been taken.

**no-trump** /ˈnoʊ-trʌmp/, *Bridge, etc.* *–adj.* **1.** denoting a bid or play without any trump suit. *–n.* **2.** Also, **no-trumps.** the play, or the bid to play, without any trump suit.

**no-trumper** /ˈnoʊ-trʌmpə/, *n.* (in bridge) a game or hand played in no-trumps.

**notum** /ˈnoʊtəm/, *n., pl.* **-ta** /-tə/. a scleritic segmental plate on the thorax or back of an insect. [NL, from Gk *nôton* the back] – **notal,** *adj.*

**notungulate** /noʊˈtʌŋgjulət/, *adj.* of an order, Notungulata, of extinct herbivorous mammals. Also, **notoungulate.**

**not up** /nɒt ˈʌp/, *adj.* (of a squash ball) failing to hit the front wall above the board.

**notwithstanding** /ˌnɒtwɪθˈstændɪŋ/, *prep.* **1.** without being withstood or prevented by; in spite of. *–adv.* **2.** nevertheless; yet (used after the statement it modifies). *–conj.* **3.** in spite of the fact that; although. [ME]

**nougat** /ˈnuga/, *n.* a hard, pastelike sweet, usu. white or pink, containing almonds or other nuts. [F, from Pr., from *noga,* from LL *nuca* nut, replacing L *nux*]

**nought** /nɔt/, *n.* **1.** a cipher (0); zero. *–adj., adv. Obs. or Archaic.* **2.** →**naught.** [ME *noht, nouht,* OE *nōht,* syncopated var. of *nōwiht*]

**noughts-and-crosses** /nɒts-ən-ˈkrɒsəz/, *n.pl.* (*construed as sing.*) a commonly played children's game in which two players set down alternately, in the nine compartments of a figure made of crossed lines, the one a cross, and the other a nought, the object of the game being to be the first to get 3 crosses or 3 noughts in a row. Also, *U.S.*, **tick-tack-toe.**

**noumenon** /ˈnumənɒn, ˈnaʊ-/, *n., pl.* **-na** /-nə/. **1.** (in Kantian philosophy) that which can be the object only of a purely intellectual (non-sensuous) intution; essentially, a postulate. **2.** the transexperiential object to which a phenomenon is referred as to the basis or cause of its sense content. **3.** a thing in itself, as distinguished from a phenomenon or thing as it appears to us. [Gk *nooúmenon,* neut. ppr. pass., (anything) perceived] – **noumenal,** *adj.* – **noumenally,** *adv.* – **noumenalism,** *n.* – **noumenalist,** *n.*

**noun** /naʊn/, *n.* **1.** (in most languages) one of the major form classes, or 'parts of speech', comprising words denoting person, places, things, and such other words as show similar grammatical behaviour, as English *friend, city, desk, whiteness, virtue.* **2.** any such word. *–adj.* **3.** Also, **nounal.** pertaining to or resembling a noun. [ME *nowne,* from AF *noun,* from L *nōmen* name]

**nourish** /ˈnʌrɪʃ/, *v.t.* **1.** to sustain with food or nutriment; supply with what is necessary for maintaining life. **2.** to foster or promote. [ME *norische(n),* from OF *noriss-,* stem of *norir,* from L *nūtrīre* suckle, feed, maintain] – **nourishable,** *adj.* – **nourisher,** *n.* – **nourishingly,** *adv.*

**nourishment** /ˈnʌrɪʃmənt/, *n.* **1.** that which nourishes; food, nutriment, or sustenance. **2.** the act of nourishing. **3.** the state of being nourished.

**nous** /naʊs/, *n.* **1.** *Colloq.* common sense. **2.** in Neoplatonism, the absolute reason and absolute subject into which the absolute first differentiates itself. [Gk: mind, intellect]

**nouveau riche** /nuvoʊ ˈriʃ/, *n., pl.* **nouveaux riches** /nuvoʊ ˈriʃ/. one who has newly become rich, esp. a boorish person. [F]

**nouvelle vague** /nuvɛl ˈvag/, *n., pl.* **nouvelles vagues** /nuvɛl ˈvag/. a new style or trend in an art form, esp. the style of film-making current in France after about 1960. [F: lit., new wave]

**Nov.,** November.

**nova** /ˈnoʊvə/, *n., pl.* **-vas, -vae** /-vi/. a star which suddenly emits an outburst of light, sometimes seen by the naked eye as a new star. [NL (fem.): new]

**novaculite** /noʊˈvækjəlaɪt/, *n.* a very hard, compact, siliceous rock, probably sedimentary, used for hones, etc. [L *novācula* sharp knife, razor + -ITE[1]]

**novation** /noʊˈveɪʃən/, *n.* **1.** *Law.* the substitution of a new obligation for an old one, usu. by the substitution of a new debtor or of a new creditor. **2.** *Rare.* the introduction of something new; an innovation.

**novecento** /nɒvəˈtʃɛntoʊ/, *n.* the 20th century, used commonly with reference to Italian art and literature of that period. [It.: nine hundred, short for *mille novecento,* one thousand nine hundred]

**novel**[1] /ˈnɒvəl/, *n.* **1.** a fictitious prose narrative of considerable length, usu. having a plot that is developed by the actions, thoughts, speech, etc., of the characters. **2.** (formerly) a short story or a novella. [It. *novella,* from L (apparently short for *novella narrātio* new kind of story)]

**novel**[2] /ˈnɒvəl/, *adj.* of a new kind, or different from anything seen or known before: *a novel idea.* [ME, from L *novellus* new] – **novelly,** *adv.*

**novel**[3] /ˈnɒvəl/, *n.* **1.** *Roman Law.* **a.** a constitution with imperial authority, subsequent to publication of a code. **b.** (*pl., cap.*) the constitutions of Justinian and later emperors before A.D. 582, issued after promulgation of the Justinian Code. **2.** *Civil Law.* an amendment to a statute. [LL, short for *novella* (*constitūtio*) new (regulation)]

**novelette** /nɒvəˈlɛt/, *n.* **1.** a short novel, esp. one that is trite and sentimental. **2.** a piece of music like this.

**novelettish** /nɒvəˈlɛtɪʃ/, *adj.* trite and sentimental, as in a novelette.

**novelise** /ˈnɒvəlaɪz/, *v.t.,* **-lised, -lising.** to put into the form of a novel. Also, **novelize.** – **novelisation** /nɒvəlaɪˈzeɪʃən/, *n.*

**novelist** /ˈnɒvələst/, *n.* a writer of novels.

**novelistic** /nɒvəˈlɪstɪk/, *adj.* of, pertaining to, or characteristic of novels. – **novelistically,** *adv.*

**novella** /nɒˈvɛlə/, *n., pl.* **-le** /-li/. **1.** a tale or short story of the type of those contained in the *Decameron* of Boccaccio, etc. **2.** a short novel, more complex than a short story. [It. See NOVEL[1]]

**novelty** /ˈnɒvəlti/, *n., pl.* **-ties. 1.** novel character, newness, or strangeness. **2.** a novel thing, experience, or proceeding. **3.** a new or novel article of trade; a variety of goods differing from the staple kinds. **4.** a decorative and usu. worthless trinket. *–adj.* **5.** of or pertaining to a novel game, article, etc: *a novelty toy.* [ME *novelte,* from OF *novelte,* from LL *novellitas* newness]

**November** /noʊˈvɛmbə, nə-/, *n.* the eleventh month of the year, containing 30 days. [ME and OE, from L: the ninth month of the early Roman year]

**novena** /noʊˈvinə/, *n., pl.* **-nae** /-ni/. (in the Roman Catholic Church) a devotion consisting of prayers or services on nine consecutive days. [ML, properly fem. of L *novēnus* nine each]

**novercal** /noʊˈvɜkəl/, *adj.* of, like, or befitting a stepmother. [L *novercālis,* from *noverca* stepmother]

**novice** /ˈnɒvəs/, *n.* **1.** one who is new to the circumstances, work, etc., in which he is placed; a tyro: *a novice in politics.* **2.** one who has been received into a religious order or congregation for a period of probation before taking vows. **3.** a person newly become a church member. **4.** a recent convert to Christianity. **5.** *Sport.* a sportsman who has not qualified for junior or senior status, as an oarsman who has never been a member of a winning crew at an open regatta. **6.** →**novice handicap. 7.** →**novice horse.** [ME *novise,* from OF *novice,* from L *novīcius* new]

**novice handicap** /– ˈhændikæp/, *n.* a restricted race for horses which are specified as being in the novice class in accordance with the rules operating in each State in Australia.

**novice horse** /– ˈhɔs/, *n.* a horse eligible to run in a novice handicap. Also, **novice-class horse.**

**novitiate** /noʊˈvɪʃiət, -ieɪt/, *n.* **1.** the state or period of being a novice of a religious order or congregation. **2.** the quarters occupied by religious novices during probation. **3.** the state or period of being a beginner in anything. **4.** a novice. Also, **noviciate.** [ML *nōvītiātus,* from L *novītius* new. See -ATE[3]]

**novobiocin** /noʊvoʊˈbaɪəsən/, *n.* an antibiotic similar to streptomycin.

**novocaine** /ˈnoʊvəkeɪn/, *n.* a non-irritant local anaesthetic, $C_{13}H_{20}N_2O_2HCl$, a synthetic and much less toxic substitute for cocaine; procaine. Also, **novocain.** [Trademark; *novo-* (combining form representing L *novus* new) + (CO)CAINE]

**Novocastrian** /noʊvəˈkæstriən/, *n.* **1.** one who was born in Newcastle, a city in New South Wales, or who has come to regard it as his home town. *–adj.* **2.** of or pertaining to the city of Newcastle.

**novus actus interveniens** /ˌnoʊvəs æktəs ɪntəˈveniənz/, *n. Law.* a new act by a third person which intervenes between a first person's act and the damage it causes a second person, and which renders the first person no longer liable for damage. [L]

**now** /naʊ/, *adv.* **1.** at the present time or moment: *he is here now.* **2.** (more emphatically) immediately or at once: *now or never.* **3.** at this time or juncture in some period under consideration or in some course of proceedings described: *the case now passes to the jury.* **4.** at the time or moment only just past: *I saw him just now in the street.* **5.** in these present times; nowadays. **6.** in the present or existing circumstances; as matters stand. **7.** (often used as a preliminary word before some statement, question, or the like): *now, what does he mean?* **8.** (to strengthen a command, entreaty, or the like): *come, now, stop that!* **9. now and again** or **now and then,** occasionally. **10. now that,** inasmuch as. *–conj.* **11.** now that; since, or seeing that. *–n.* **12.** the present time or moment: *the here and now. –interj.* **13. now, now!** (an expression used to reprove or placate someone.) [ME; OE *nū,* c. Icel. and Goth. *nū*]

**nowadays** /ˈnaʊədeɪz/, *adv.* **1.** at the present day; in these times. *–n.* **2.** the present. [ME; from NOW + *adays* by day (from *a* in + *days* by day, adv. gen.)]

**noway** /ˈnoʊweɪ/, *adv.* in no way, respect, or degree; not at all. Also, *U.S.,* **noways.**

**nowhere** /ˈnoʊwɛə/, *adv.* **1.** in, at, or to no place; not anywhere. *–n.* **2.** a state of apparent non-existence; a place unknown: *he disappeared into nowhere.* **3.** a state of anonymity. **4. get nowhere,** to achieve nothing. [ME; OE *nāhwær* (also *nōhwær*)]

**no-win** /noʊ-ˈwɪn/, *adj.* of or pertaining to a situation, argument, etc., which cannot be resolved in a way that will be advantageous to any of the participants.

**nowise** /ˈnoʊwaɪz/, *adv.* in no wise; noway; not at all.

**nowt** /naʊt/, *n. Colloq.* naught; nothing.

**noxious** /ˈnɒkʃəs/, *adj.* **1.** harmful or injurious to health or physical well-being: *noxious vapours.* **2.** morally harmful; pernicious. **3.** (of an animal, insect, plant, etc.) declared harmful by statute law for compulsory eradication. [L *noxius* hurtful] – **noxiously,** *adv.* – **noxiousness,** *n.*

**noyau** /ˈnwaɪoʊ/, *n.* a sweet liqueur, either white or pink in colour, originating in France.

**nozzle** /ˈnɒzəl/, *n.* **1.** a projecting spout, terminal discharging pipe, or the like, as of a hose or rocket. **2.** the socket of a candlestick. **3.** the spout of a teapot. **4.** *Colloq.* the nose. [NOSE + *-le,* diminutive suffix]

**np.,** **1.** new penny. **2.** new pence.

**Np,** *Chem.* neptunium.

**nr,** near.

**NRC** /ɛn a ˈsi/, (of a film) not recommended for children.

**n.s.,** **1.** near side. **2.** non-stop. **3.** not specified.

**N.S.** **1.** National Service. **2.** New Series.

**N.S.U.** /ɛn ɛs ˈju/, non-specific urethritis.

**N.S.W.,** New South Wales. Also, **NSW.**

**-n't,** a combining form of *not,* as in *didn't, won't, can't.*

**Nt,** *Chem.* niton.

**N.T.,** **1.** New Testament. **2.** Northern Territory. Also, **NT.**

**nth** /ɛnθ/, *adj.* **1.** denoting the last in a series of infinitely decreasing or increasing values, amounts, etc. **2. the nth degree** or **power, a.** a high (sometimes, any) degree or power. **b.** the utmost extent.

**N.T.P.** /ɛn ti ˈpi/, *n.* normal temperature and pressure; a temperature of 0° C and a pressure of 101 325 pascals. Also, **S.T.P.**

**nt wt,** net weight.

**n-type** /ˈɛn-taɪp/, *adj.* (in electronics) pertaining to semiconductor material with donor impurities.

**nu** /nju/, *n.* the thirteenth letter (N, ν = English N, n) of the Greek alphabet.

**nuance** /ˈnjuɒns, njuˈans/, *n.* a shade of colour, expression, meaning, feeling, etc. [F, b. OF *muance* variation (from *muer* to change, from L *mūtāre*), and *nue* cloud]

**nub** /nʌb/, *n.* **1.** a knob or protuberance. **2.** a lump or small piece. **3.** *Colloq.* the point or gist of anything. [var. of KNOB]

**nubbin** /ˈnʌbən/, *n. U.S.* **1.** a small lump or piece. **2.** a small or imperfect ear of maize. **3.** an undeveloped fruit. [diminutive of NUB]

**nubble** /ˈnʌbəl/, *n.* **1.** a small lump or piece. **2.** a small knob or protuberance. [NUB + *-le,* diminutive suffix]

**nubbly** /ˈnʌbli/, *adj.* **1.** full of small protuberances. **2.** in the form of small lumps.

**nubia** /ˈnjubiə/, *n.* a woman's light knitted or crocheted woollen scarf for the head and shoulders. [L *nūbes* cloud + -IA]

**Nubian** /ˈnjubiən/, *n.* Also, **Nuba. 1.** one of a Negroid people, of mixed descent, inhabiting Nubia, a region in what is now southern Egypt and northern Sudan. **2.** a language of the Nile valley below Khartoum. **3.** a Nubian or Negro slave. **4.** a Nubian horse. *–adj.* **5.** of or pertaining to Nubia.

**nubian goat** /njubiən ˈgoʊt/, *n.* one of a breed of long-legged, Roman-nosed, brown or black goats of northern Africa.

**nubile** /ˈnjubaɪl/, *adj.* (of a girl or young woman) marriageable, esp. as to age or physical development. [L *nūbilis*] – **nubility** /njuˈbɪləti/, *n.*

**nubilous** /ˈnjubələs/, *adj.* **1.** cloudy or foggy. **2.** obscure; indefinite. [L *nūbilus* cloudy]

**nucellus** /njuˈsɛləs/, *n., pl.* **-celli** /-ˈsɛlaɪ/. the central cellular mass of the body of the ovule, containing the embryo sac. [NL, diminutive of L *nux* nut] – **nucellar,** *adj.*

**nucha** /ˈnjukə/, *n., pl.* **-chae** /-ki/. the nape of the neck. [ME, from ML, from Ar. *nukhā* spinal marrow] – **nuchal,** *adj.*

**nuclear** /ˈnjukliə/, *adj.* **1.** of, pertaining to, or forming a nucleus. **2.** pertaining to, involving, or powered by atomic energy: *nuclear war, nuclear submarine.* **3.** armed with nuclear weapons: *a nuclear power.*

**nuclear bomb** /– ˈbɒm/, *n.* →**atomic bomb.**

**nuclear cloud** /– ˈklaʊd/, *n.* the volume of hot gases, smoke, dust, and other particulate matter from a nuclear bomb and from its environment, which is carried aloft in conjunction with the rise of the fireball produced by the detonation of the nuclear weapon.

**nuclear column** /– ˈkɒləm/, *n.* **1.** a hollow cylinder of water and spray thrown up from an underwater burst of a nuclear weapon, through which the hot high-pressure gases formed in the explosion are vented to the atmosphere. **2.** a similar column of dirt formed in an underground nuclear explosion.

**nuclear energy** /njukliər ˈɛnədʒi/, *n.* →**atomic energy.**

**nuclear enrichment** /– ənˈrɪtʃmənt/, *n.* the process of enriching uranium with its uranium 235 isotope.

**nuclear family** /njukliə ˈfæmli/, *n.* **1.** the family as a unit of social organisation, comprising only parents and children, where the children are the responsibility of the parents alone. **2.** the stereotype of this unit, typically seen as husband, wife, and two children.

**nuclear fission** /– ˈfɪʃən/, *n.* the breakdown of an atomic nucleus of an element of relatively high atomic number into two or more nuclei of lower atomic number, with conversion of part of its mass into energy.

**nuclear fuel** /– ˈfjuəl/, *n.* a substance which undergoes nuclear fission in a nuclear reactor.

**nuclear fusion** /– ˈfjuʒən/, *n.* the coming together of two atomic nuclei to form a single nucleus with a consequent release of energy.

**nuclear gap** /– ˈgæp/, *n.* the area forward of friendly troops which cannot, for safety reasons, be neutralised by nuclear fire.

**nuclear isomer** /– ˈaɪsəmə/, *n.* an atomic nucleus which has the same mass and charge as another nucleus, but a different rate of radioactive decay.

**nuclear magnetic resonance,** *n.* a change in energy state of a nucleus in a magnetic field which occurs when the nucleus absorbs energy at a particular radiofrequency, and which provides information about the configuration of complex molecules. Also, **NMR.**

**nuclear physics** /njukliə ˈfɪzɪks/, *n.* the branch of physics dealing with the structure and nature of the atomic nucleus and the behaviour of subatomic particles. – **nuclear physicist,** *n.*

**nuclear power** /– ˈpaʊə/, *n.* →**atomic power.**

**nuclear reaction** /– riˈækʃən/, *n.* any reaction which involves a change in the structure or energy state of the nuclei of the interacting atoms.

**nuclear reactor** /– riˈæktə/, *n.* any device in which a selfsustaining chain reaction is maintained and controlled for the production of nuclear energy, fissile material, or radioactive isotopes.

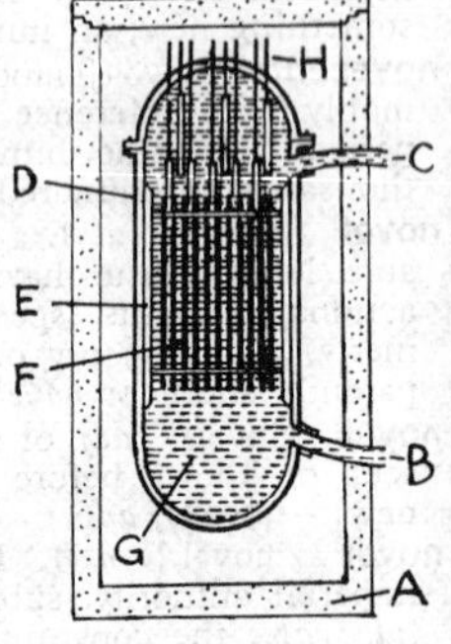

nuclear reactor: A, biological shield; B, coolant in; C, coolant out; D, reactor vessel; E, thermal shield; F, core of solid fuel elements; G, water as coolant and neutron moderator; H, control rods

**nuclear warfare** /– ˈwɔfɛə/, *n.* warfare in which nuclear weapons are used.

**nuclear warhead** /– ˈwɔhɛd/, *n.* a warhead which consists of, or contains, a nuclear weapon.

**nuclear weapon** /– ˈwɛpən/, *n.* any weapon in which the explosive power is derived from nuclear fission, nuclear fusion, or a combination of both.

**nuclear yields** /– ˈjildz/, *n.pl.* the energy released in the detonation of a nuclear weapon, measured in terms of the kilotons or megatons of trinitrotoluene (TNT) required to produce the same energy released.

**nuclease** /ˈnjuklieɪz/, *n.* any enzyme which catalyses the hydrolysis of nucleic acids to nucleotides, as ribonuclease.

**nucleate** /ˈnjukliət, -eɪt/, *adj.;* /ˈnjuklieɪt/, *v.,* **-ated, -ating.** *–adj.* **1.** having a nucleus. *–v.t.* **2.** to form (something) into a nucleus. *–v.i.* **3.** to form a nucleus. [L *nūcleātus* having a kernel or stone]

**nuclei** /ˈnjukliaɪ/, *n.* plural of **nucleus.**

**nucleic acid** /njuˌkliɪk ˈæsəd/, *n.* any polynucleotide of high molecular weight, occurring in all living cells and viruses. There are two main types, ribonucleic acid and deoxyribonucleic acid.

**nucleide** /ˈnjukliaɪd/, *n.* →**nuclide.**

**nuclein** /ˈnjukliən/, *n.* any of several proteins found in all living cell nuclei.

**nucleolar** /njuˈkliələ/, *adj.* relating or pertaining to the nucleolus.

**nucleolated** /ˈnjukliəleɪtəd/, *adj.* containing a nucleolus or nucleoli. Also, **nucleolate.**

**nucleolus** /njuˈkliələs/, *n., pl.* **-li** /-laɪ/. a conspicuous, often rounded body within the nucleus of a cell. Also, **nucleole** /ˈnjukliˌoul/. [L: little nut, diminutive of *nūcleus.* See NUCLEUS]

**nucleon** /ˈnjukliɒn/, *n.* one of the elementary particles (protons and neutrons) of atomic nuclei.

**nucleonics** /njukliˈɒnɪks/, *n.* the techniques of applying nuclear science to industry and to biology, physics, chemistry, and other sciences.

**nucleoplasm** /ˈnjukliəˌplæzəm/, *n.* →**karyoplasm.** [*nucleo-* (combining form of NUCLEUS) + -PLASM] – **nucleoplasmic** /njukliəˈplæzmɪk/, *adj.*

**nucleoprotein** /ˌnjuklioʊˈproutin/, *n.* any of a group of compounds of high molecular weight containing both nucleic acid and protein.

**nucleor** /ˈnjukliɔ/, *n.* the core of an atomic nucleus.

**nucleoside** /ˈnjukliəsaɪd/, *n.* any of several compounds of either a purine or a pyrimidine base with either ribose or deoxyribose, and present in combined form in nucleic acids.

**nucleotide** /ˈnjukliətaɪd/, *n.* the phosphate of any nucleoside, present in combined form in nucleic acids.

**nucleus** /ˈnjukliəs/, *n., pl.* **-clei** /-kliaɪ/ **-cleuses. 1.** a central part or thing about which other parts or things are grouped. **2.** anything constituting a central part, foundation, or beginning. **3.** *Biol.* a differentiated mass (usu. rounded) of protoplasm, encased in a delicate membrane, present in the interior of nearly all living cells and forming an essential element in their growth metabolism and reproduction. **4.** *Anat.* a mass of grey matter in the brain and spinal cord in which incoming nerve fibres form connections with outgoing fibres. **5.** *Chem.* a fundamental arrangement of atoms, as the benzene ring, which may occur in many compounds by substitution of atoms without a change in structure. **6.** *Physics.* the central core of an atom, composed of protons and neutrons. It has a net positive charge equal to the number of protons. **7.** *Astron.* the more condensed portion of the head of a comet. **8.** *Meteorol.* a particle upon which condensation of water vapour occurs to form water drops. **9.** *Phonet.* the central, vocalic constituent of a syllable, often a vowel, as the *o* sound in *dog.* [L: nut, kernel, fruit stone]

**nuclide** /ˈnjuklaɪd/, *n.* **1.** an atomic species which is characterised by its mass number, atomic number, and energy state. **2.** any individual atom of such a species. Also, **nucleide.**

**nuddy** /ˈnʌdi/, *n. in the phrase* **in the nuddy,** *Colloq.* in the nude.

**nude** /njud/, *adj.* **1.** naked or unclothed, as a person, the body, etc. **2.** without the usual coverings, furnishings, etc.; bare. **3.** *Law.* unsupported; made without a consideration: *a nude pact.* *–n.* **4. the nude, a.** the condition of being undraped. **b.** the undraped human figure. **5.** a nude figure as represented in art. [L *nūdus* bare] – **nudely,** *adv.* – **nudeness,** *n.*

**nudge** /nʌdʒ/, *v.,* **nudged, nudging,** *n.* *–v.t.* **1.** to push slightly or jog, esp. with the elbow, as in calling attention or giving a hint or with sly meaning. **2. nudge the bottle,** to drink alcoholic liquor to excess. *–n.* **3.** a slight push or jog. **4. give it a nudge,** to make an attempt; have a try at something. [orig. obscure]

**nudi-,** a word element meaning 'bare'. [L, combining form of *nūdus*]

**nudibranch** /ˈnjudəbræŋk/, *n.* a shell-less type of marine snail with external respiratory appendages, noted for its beautiful colouring and graceful form. [F *nudibranche,* from *nudi-* NUDI- + *branche* gills, from L *branchia* BRANCHIA]

**nudicaul** /ˈnjudəkɔl/, *adj.* having leafless stems. Also, **nudicaulous.** [NUDI- + L *caulus* stem]

**nudism** /ˈnjudɪzəm/, *n.* the practice of going nude as a means of healthful living; naturism.

**nudist** /ˈnjudəst/, *n.* **1.** one who advocates or practices nudism. *–adj.* **2.** of or pertaining to the principles or practice of nudism.

**nudity** /ˈnjudəti/, *n., pl.* **-ties. 1.** the state or fact of being nude; nakedness. **2.** something nude or naked. **3.** a nude figure, esp. as represented in art.

**nudum pactum** /ˌnudʊm ˈpæktʊm/, *n.* (in law) a simple contract or promise with no consideration involved. [L: bare agreement]

**nugatory** /ˈnjugətəri, -tri/, *adj.* **1.** trifling; of no real value; worthless. **2.** of no force or effect; futile; vain. [L *nūgātōrius* worthless]

**nugget** /ˈnʌgət/, *n.* **1.** a lump of something. **2.** a lump of native gold. **3.** *N.Z.* a lump of kauri gum. **4.** *Colloq.* a short muscular young man or animal. [apparently from Brit. d. *nug* lump, block]

**nuggetty** /ˈnʌgəti/, *adj.* **1.** of or resembling a nugget. **2.** *Colloq.* short; thickset.

**nuisance** /ˈnjusəns/, *n.* **1.** a highly obnoxious or annoying thing or person. **2.** something offensive or annoying to individuals or to the community, to the prejudice of their legal rights. [ME *nusance,* from OF *nuisance,* from *nuire* harm, from L *nocēre*]

**nuke** /njuk/, *n. Chiefly U.S. Colloq.* a nuclear device.

**null** /nʌl/, *adj.* **1.** of no effect, consequence, or significance. **2.** being none, lacking, or non-existent. **3. null and void,** having no legal force or effect. **4.** zero. [L *nullus* no, none]

**nullah** /ˈnʌlə/, *n.* **1.** a ravine. **2.** a watercourse. [Hind. *nālā*]

**nulla-nulla** /ˈnʌlə-nʌlə/, *n.* an Aboriginal club or heavy weapon. Also, **nulla.** [Aboriginal]

**nulli-,** a word element meaning 'none'. [L, combining form of *nullus*]

**nullification** /nʌləfəˈkeɪʃən/, *n.* **1.** the act of nullifying. **2.** the state of being nullified. **3.** *U.S.* failure of a state to aid in enforcement of federal laws within its limits. – **nullificationist,** *n.*

**nullifidian** /nʌləˈfɪdiən/, *n.* one who has no faith or religion; sceptic. [NULLI- + L *fides* faith + -IAN]

**nullify** /ˈnʌləfaɪ/, *v.t.,* **-fied, -fying. 1.** to make ineffective, futile, or of no consequence. **2.** to render or declare legally void or inoperative: *to nullify a contract.* [LL *nullificāre* make null, dispose] – **nullifier,** *n.*

**nullipara** /nʌˈlɪpərə/, *n., pl.* **-rae** /-ri/. a woman who has never borne a child. [NL, from *nulli-* NULLI- + *-para,* fem. of *-parus* -PAROUS] – **nulliparous,** *adj.*

**nullipore** /ˈnʌlɪpɔ/, *n.* any of the coralline algae with a crustlike plant body. [NULLI- + PORE[2]]

**nullity** /ˈnʌləti/, *n., pl.* **-ties. 1.** the state of being null; nothingness; invalidity. **2.** something null. **3.** something of no legal force or validity. [ML *nullitas*]

**nullity of marriage,** *n.* a petition to have a marriage judicially declared null and void.

**null set** /nʌl ˈsɛt/, *n.* a mathematical set having no elements; empty set.

**num.,** **1.** numeral. **2.** numerals.

**Num.,** *Bible.* Numbers.

**numb** /nʌm/, *adj.* **1.** deprived of or deficient in the power of sensation and movement: *fingers numb with cold.* **2.** of the nature of numbness: *a numb sensation.* *–v.t.* **3.** to make numb. [ME *nome,* lit., taken, seized, apocopated var. of ME *nomen, numen,* OE *numen,* pp. of *niman* take] – **numbly,** *adv.* – **numbness,** *n.*

**numbat** /ˈnʌmbæt/, *n.* a small, slender reddish-brown, insectivorous marsupial, *Myrmecobius fasciatus,* with a long, bushy tail, a pointed snout and conspicuous white stripes across the back, found in certain areas of south-western

Australia; banded anteater. [Aboriginal]

numbat

**number** /ˈnʌmbə/, *n.* **1.** the sum, total, count, or aggregate of a collection of units or any generalisation of this concept. **2.** →**integer.** **3.** →**numeral.** **4.** →**arithmetic.** **5.** the particular numeral assigned to anything in order to fix its place in a series: *a house number.* **6.** a word or symbol, or a combination of words or symbols, used in counting or to denote a total. **7.** one of a series of things distinguished by numerals. **8.** a single part of a book published in parts. **9.** a single issue of a periodical. **10.** any of a collection of poems or songs. **11.** a single part of a program made up of a number of parts. **12.** the full count of a collection or company. **13.** a collection or company. **14.** a quantity (large or small) of individuals. **15.** a certain collection, company, or quantity not precisely reckoned, but usu. considerable or large. **16.** (*pl.*) considerable collections or quantities. **17.** (*pl.*) numerical strength or superiority, as in a political party, organisation, etc. **18.** quantity as composed of units. **19.** *Gram.* (in many languages) a category of the inflection of nouns, verbs, and related word classes, usu. expressing the number of persons or objects referred to, comprising as subcategories the *singular* and *plural* and in some languages one or two intermediate subcategories (the *dual*, referring to two, and the *trial*, referring to three). **20.** (*pl.*) metrical feet, or verse. **21.** (*pl.*) musical periods, measures, or groups of notes. **22.** a distinct part of an extended musical work, or one in a sequence of compositions. **23.** *Obs.* conformity in music or verse to regular beat or measure; rhythm. **24.** an article of merchandise. **25.** *Colloq.* a marijuana joint. **26. do a number,** to perform a specified piece, or routine. **27. have someone's number,** to have the measure of someone. **28. one's number is up,** *Colloq.* **a.** one is in serious trouble. **b.** one is due to die. **29. without number,** of which the number is unknown or too great to be counted: *stars without number.* *–v.t.* **30.** to ascertain the number of. **31.** to mark with or distinguish by a number or numbers. **32.** to count over one by one. **33.** to mention one by one; enumerate. **34.** to fix the number of, limit in number, or make few in number. **35.** to reckon or include in a number. **36.** to mark with or distinguish by a number or numbers. **37.** to live or have lived (so many years). **38.** to have or comprise in number. **39.** to amount to in number: *a crew numbering fifty men.* **40.** *Obs.* to appoint or allot. *–v.i.* **41.** *Poetic.* to make enumeration; count. **42.** to be numbered or included. [ME *nombre,* from OF, from L *numerus*] **– numberer,** *n.*

**number crunching** /ˈ– krʌntʃɪŋ/, *Colloq. n.* long, laborious, recursive mathematical computation, esp. as done by computers.

**number eight forward,** *n. N.Z. Rugby Football.* →**lock**[1] (def. 8a). Also, **number eight.**

**numberless** /ˈnʌmbələs/, *adj.* **1.** innumerable; countless; myriad. **2.** without a number or numbers.

**number one** /nʌmbə ˈwʌn/, *n.* **1.** oneself. **2.** the person with highest authority; boss. **3.** *Navy Colloq.* the first officer. **4.** (*pl.*) *Navy Colloq.* dress uniform. **5.** *Colloq.* urination. *–adj.* **6.** chief; foremost: *television is the number one medium for advertising.*

**numberplate** /ˈnʌmbəpleɪt/, *n.* an identifying plate, carried by motor vehicles, bearing a registration number. Also, **registration plate.**

**number theory** /ˈnʌmbə θɪəri/, *n.* the study of numbers (integers) and of the relations which hold between them.

**number two** /– ˈtu/, *n.* **1.** the person second in rank or importance. **2.** *Colloq.* defecation.

**numbfish** /ˈnʌmfɪʃ/, *n., pl.* **-fishes,** (*esp. collectively*) **-fish.** an electric ray (fish), so called from its power of numbing its prey by means of electric shocks.

**numbles** /ˈnʌmbəlz/, *n.pl. Archaic.* certain of the inward parts of an animal, esp. of a deer, used as food. Also, **nombles, umbles.** [ME *noumbles,* from OF *nombles,* from L *lumbulus,* diminutive of *lumbus* loin]

**numbskull** /ˈnʌmskʌl/, *n. Colloq.* a dull-witted person; a dunce; a dolt. Also, **numskull.** [NUMB + SKULL]

**numen** /ˈnjumən/, *n., pl.* **-mina** /-mənə/. a deity; a divine power or spirit. [L]

**numerable** /ˈnjumərəbəl/, *adj.* that may be numbered or counted. [L *numerābilis*] **– numerably,** *adv.*

**numeracy** /ˈnjumərəsi/, *n.* basic competence in mathematics.

**numeral** /ˈnjumərəl/, *n.* **1.** a word or words expressing a number: *cardinal numerals.* **2.** a letter or figure, or a group of letters or figures, denoting a number: *the Roman numerals.* *–adj.* **3.** of or pertaining to number; consisting of numbers. **4.** expressing or denoting number. [LL *numerālis,* from L *numerus* number]

**numerary** /ˈnjumərəri, ˈnjumrəri/, *adj.* of or pertaining to a number or numbers.

**numerate** /ˈnjuməreɪt/, *v.,* **-rated, -rating;** /ˈnjumərət/, *adj.* *–v.t.* **1.** to number; count; enumerate. **2.** to read (an expression in numbers). *–adj.* **3.** having some knowledge of or versed in mathematics. [L *numerātus,* pp.] **– numeracy** /ˈnjumərəsi/, *n.*

**numeration** /njuməˈreɪʃən/, *n.* **1.** the act, process, or result of numbering or counting. **2.** the process or a method of reckoning or calculating. **3.** the act, art, or method of reading numbers in numerals or figures.

**numerator** /ˈnjuməreɪtə/, *n.* **1.** *Maths.* that term (usu. written above the line) of a fraction which shows how many parts of a unit are taken. **2.** one who or that which numbers. [LL: a counter]

**numerical** /njuˈmerɪkəl/, *adj.* **1.** of or pertaining to number; of the nature of number. **2.** denoting number or a number: *numerical symbols.* **3.** bearing, or designated by, a number. **4.** expressed by a number or figure, or by figures, and not by a letter or letters. **5.** *Maths.* denoting value or magnitude irrespective of sign: *the numerical value of −10 is greater than that of −5.* Also, **numeric. – numerically,** *adv.*

**numerical analysis** /– əˈnæləsəs/, *n.* the use of numerical methods for the analysis of problems and the ascertaining of margins of error, usu. with the aid of a computer.

**numerical aperture** /– ˈæpətʃə/, *n.* a measure of the resolving power of a microscope, equal to the product of the refractive index of the medium in which the object is placed and the size of the angle between the axis and the most oblique ray entering the instrument; the resolving power is proportional to the numerical aperture. *Abbrev.:* N.A.

**numerology** /njuməˈrɒlədʒi/, *n.* the study of numbers (as one's birth year, etc.), supposedly to determine their influence on one's life and future. [L *numerus* number + -O- + -LOGY] **– numerological** /njumərəˈlɒdʒɪkəl/, *adj.*

**numero uno** /numəroʊ ˈunoʊ, nju-/, *n. Colloq.* **1.** oneself. **2.** the leader or most important person in any situation. [It.: number one]

**numerous** /ˈnjumərəs/, *adj.* **1.** very many; forming a great number. **2.** consisting of or comprising a great number of units or individuals. [L *numerōsus*] **– numerously,** *adv.* **– numerousness,** *n.*

**Numidian crane** /nju͵mɪdiən ˈkreɪn/, *n.* →**demoiselle** (def. 2).

**numinous** /ˈnjumənəs/, *adj.* **1.** of or pertaining to a numen. **2.** arousing elevated or religious feelings.

**numis.,** numismatics.

**numismatic** /njuməzˈmætɪk/, *adj.* **1.** of or pertaining to, or consisting of, coins and medals. **2.** pertaining to numismatics. Also, **numismatical.** [F *numismatique,* from L *nomisma* coin, from Gk]

**numismatics** /njuməzˈmætɪks/, *n.* the science of coins and medals. **– numismatist** /njuˈmɪzmətəst/, *n.*

**numismatology** /njuməzməˈtɒlədʒi/, *n.* →**numismatics.** **– numismatologist,** *n.*

**nummary** /ˈnʌməri/, *adj.* **1.** of or pertaining to coins or money. **2.** occupied with coins or money.

**nummular** /ˈnʌmjələ/, *adj.* **1.** pertaining to coins or money; nummary. **2.** coin-shaped. [L *nummulus* (diminutive of *nummus* coin) + -AR[1]]

**nummulite** /ˈnʌmjəlaɪt/, *n.* any of the foraminifers (mostly fossil) that constitute the family Nummulitidae, having a somewhat coinlike shell. [NL *nummulītes,* from L *nummulus,* diminutive of *nummus* coin] **– nummulitic** /nʌmjəˈlɪtɪk/, *adj.*

**nummy** /ˈnʌmi/, *adj. Colloq.* (of food) tasty; delectable.

**num-num**[1] /ˈnʌm-nʌm/, *n.* a spiny shrub, *Carissa arduina,* of southern Africa, bearing scarlet edible berries. [Zulu *inamunamu* something sticky, specifically a herb with edible roots]

**num-num**[2] /nʌm-ˈnʌm/, *interj.;* /ˈnʌm-nʌm/, *n. Colloq.* (*esp. in children's speech*) *–interj.* **1.** Also, **nummy-nummy.** (an exclamation of delight at a particularly pleasing food.) *–n.* **2.** a particularly delectable food. **3.** (*pl.*) food. Also, **nyum-nyum.**

**numskull** /ˈnʌmskʌl/, *n.* →**numbskull.**

**nun** /nʌn/, *n.* **1.** a woman devoted to a religious life under vows. **2.** a woman living in a convent under solemn vows of poverty, chastity, and obedience. **3.** →**white-fronted chat.** [ME and OE *nunne,* from LL *nonna,* fem. of *nonnus* monk]

**nunatak** /ˈnʌnətæk/, *n.* an isolated rocky peak completely encircled by a glacier or icesheet. [Eskimo]

**Nunc Dimittis** /nʊŋk dəˈmɪtəs/, *n.* **1.** the canticle of Simeon (Luke 2:29-32), beginning 'Lord, now lettest thou thy servant depart in peace'. **2.** a musical setting of this. **3.** (*l.c.*) permission to depart; dismissal; departure. [L; the first words as given in the Vulgate]

**nunciature** /ˈnʌnsiətʃə/, *n.* the office or the term of service of a papal nuncio. [It. *nunziatura,* from *nunzio* NUNCIO]

**nuncio** /ˈnʌnsioʊ/, *n., pl.* **-cios.** a permanent diplomatic representative of the pope at a foreign court or capital. [It., from L *nuntius* messenger]

**nuncupative** /ˈnʌŋkju,peɪtɪv, nʌŋˈkjupətɪv/, *adj.* (of wills, etc.) oral, rather than written. [LL *nuncupātīvus* nominal]

**nunnery** /ˈnʌnəri/, *n., pl.* **-neries.** a religious house for nuns; a convent.

**nun's veiling** /ˈnʌnz veɪlɪŋ/, *n.* a thin, plain-woven, worsted fabric, originally for nun's veils but now for dresses, nightdresses and baby clothes.

**nunty** /ˈnʌnti/, *adj. Colloq.* dowdy; out of fashion.

**nuptial** /ˈnʌpʃəl/, *adj.* **1.** of or pertaining to marriage or the marriage ceremony: *the nuptial day.* *–n.* **2.** (*usu. pl.*) marriage; wedding. [L *nuptiālis* pertaining to marriage]

**nurse** /nɜs/, *n., v.,* **nursed, nursing.** *–n.* **1.** a person (woman or man) who has the care of the sick or infirm. **2.** a woman who has the general care of a child or children. **3.** a woman employed to suckle an infant; wet nurse. **4.** any fostering agency or influence. **5.** a worker that attends the young in a colony of social insects. **6.** *Billiards.* the act of nursing the balls. *–v.t.* **7.** to tend in sickness or infirmity. **8.** to seek to cure (a cold, etc.) by taking care of oneself. **9.** to look after carefully so as to promote growth, development, etc.; foster; cherish (a feeling, etc.). **10.** to treat or handle with adroit care in order to further one's own interests. **11.** to bring up, train, or nurture. **12.** to clasp or handle, as fondly or tenderly. **13.** to hold in the lap while travelling: *you can nurse this box; there's no room on the floor.* **14.** to suckle (an infant). **15.** to feed and tend in infancy. **16.** *Billiards.* to gather and keep (the balls) together for a series of canons. *–v.i.* **17.** to act as nurse; tend the sick or infirm. **18.** to suckle a child. **19.** (of a child) to take the breast. [ME *norse, nourice,* from OF, from LL *nūtrīcia* nurse, properly fem. of *nūtrīcius* that nourishes] – **nurser,** *n.*

**nurseling** /ˈnɜslɪŋ/, *n.* →**nursling.**

**nursemaid** /ˈnɜsmeɪd/, *n.* a maidservant employed to take care of children. Also, **nurserymaid.**

**nursery** /ˈnɜsri/, *n., pl.* **-eries.** **1.** a room or place set apart for young children. **2.** →**nursery school.** **3.** any place in which something is bred, nourished, or fostered. **4.** any situation, condition, circumstance, practice, etc., serving to foster something. **5.** a place where young trees or other plants are raised for transplanting or for sale.

**nursery handicap** /– ˈhændikæp/, *n.* a handicap race for two year old horses.

**nurseryman** /ˈnɜsrimən/, *n., pl.* **-men.** one who owns or conducts a nursery for plants.

**nursery rhyme** /ˈnɜsri raɪm/, *n.* a short, simple poem or song for children.

**nursery school** /ˈ– skul/, *n.* a school for children from three years (sometimes two years) of age to five years.

**nursery slope** /ˈ– sloʊp/, *n.* a gently inclining slope suitable for beginners at skiing.

**nurse shark** /ˈnɜs ʃak/, *n.* any shark of the widely distributed family Ovectolobidae, having a groove on each side of the head.

**nursing aid** /ˈnɜsɪŋ eɪd/, *n.* an untrained person who helps the nurses perform routine work, as serving meals, cleaning, etc.

**nursing home** /ˈ– hoʊm/, *n.* a nursing residence equipped for the care of patients who have chronic or terminal diseases, or who are handicapped in some way.

**nursing mother** /– ˈmʌðə/, *n.* **1.** a mother with a young child whom she is breast feeding. **2.** →**wet nurse.**

**nursling** /ˈnɜslɪŋ/, *n.* **1.** an infant or child under a nurse's care. **2.** any person or thing under fostering care, influences, or conditions. Also, **nurseling.**

**nurture** /ˈnɜtʃə/, *v.,* **-tured, -turing,** *n.* *–v.t.* **1.** to feed, nourish, or support during the stages of growth, as children or young; rear. **2.** to bring up; train; educate. *–n.* **3.** upbringing or training. **4.** education; breeding. **5.** nourishment or food. [ME, from OF, var. of *nourriture,* from *nourrir* to nourish, from L *nūtrīre*] – **nurturer,** *n.*

**nut** /nʌt/, *n., v.,* **nutted, nutting.** *–n.* **1.** a dry fruit consisting of an edible kernel or meat enclosed in a woody or leathery shell. **2.** the kernel itself. **3.** *Bot.* a hard, indehiscent, one-seeded fruit, as the chestnut or the acorn. **4.** any of various devices or parts supposed in some way to resemble a nut. **5.** a small lump of coal. **6.** *N.Z.* a small lump of kauri resin. **7.** a small, hard biscuit. **8.** *Colloq.* the head. **9.** *Colloq.* an enthusiast. **10.** *Colloq.* a foolish or eccentric person. **11.** *Colloq.* an insane person. **12.** a perforated block (usu. of metal) with an internal thread or female screw, used to screw on the end of a bolt, etc. **13.** (in musical instruments of the violin type) **a.** the ledge, as of ebony, at the upper end of the fingerboard, over which the strings pass. **b.** the movable piece at the lower end of the bow, by means of which the hairs may be slackened or tightened. **14.** *Colloq.* a testicle. **15.** *Print.* →**en.** **16. do one's nut,** *Colloq.* to be very angry, anxious, or upset. **17. hard nut to crack, a.** a difficult question, undertaking, or problem. **b.** a person who is difficult to convince, understand, or know. **18. off one's nut,** *Colloq.* **a.** mad; insane. **b.** crazy; foolish. **19. work one's nut,** to scheme. *–v.i.* **20.** to look for or gather nuts. *–v.t.* **21. nut out,** to think out; solve (a problem, a plan of action, etc.). *–adj.* **22.** made of or denoting the wood of any nut-bearing tree, as walnut, hickory, etc. [ME *nute,* OE *hnutu,* c. G *Nuss*] – **nutlike,** *adj.*

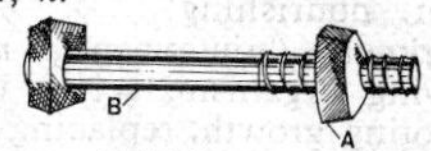

nut (def. 12): A, nut; B, bolt

**nutant** /ˈnjutnt/, *adj.* drooping; nodding. [L *nūtans,* ppr.]

**nutation** /njuˈteɪʃən/, *n.* **1.** a nodding of the head. **2.** *Bot.* spontaneous movements of plant parts during growth. **3.** *Astron.* the periodic oscillation in the precessional motion of the earth's axis or of the equinoxes. [L *nūtātio* a nodding] – **nutational,** *adj.*

**nutbrown** /ˈnʌtbraʊn/, *adj.* brown in colour, as many nuts when ripe.

**nut case** /ˈnʌt keɪs/, *n. Colloq.* a foolish or eccentric person.

**nutcracker** /ˈnʌtkrækə/, *n.* **1.** (*oft. pl.*) an instrument for cracking nuts. **2.** any of several corvine birds of the genus *Nucifraga* which feed on nuts, as the common nutcracker, *N. caryocatactes,* of Europe.

nutcracker and walnut

**nut factory** /ˈnʌt fæktri/, *n. Colloq.* →**mental hospital.**

**nut-gall** /ˈnʌt-gɔl/, *n.* **1.** a nutlike gall or excrescence, esp. one formed on an oak. **2.** →**Aleppo gall.**

**nutgrass** /ˈnʌtgras/, *n.* any of various sedges of the genus *Cyperus* bearing small nut-like tubers, esp. *C. rotundus,* a troublesome weed. Also, **nut grass.**

**nuthatch** /ˈnʌthætʃ/, *n.* any of numerous small short-tailed sharp-beaked birds constituting the family Sittidae, which creep on trees and feed on small nuts and insects. [ME *notehache, nuthage, nuthake,* lit., nut-hacker]

**nuthouse** /ˈnʌthaʊs/, *n. Colloq.* →**mental hospital.**

**nutlet** /ˈnʌtlət/, *n.* **1.** a small nut; a small nutlike fruit or seed. **2.** the stone of a drupe.

**nut loaf** /'nʌt loʊf/, *n.* →**date loaf.**

**nut man** /'– mæn/, *n. Colloq.* a homosexual.

**nutmeg** /'nʌtmɛg/, *n.* **1.** the hard, aromatic seed of the fruit of an East Indian tree, *Myristica fragrans,* used as a spice. **2.** the tree itself. **3.** the similar product of certain other trees of the same genus or other genera. [ME *notemuge,* from *note* nut + OF *mug(u)e* musk, from LL *muscus*]

**nut oil** /'nʌt ɔɪl/, *n.* edible oil made from nuts.

**nut pine** /'– paɪn/, *n.* any of various trees of the south-western U.S. and Rocky Mountains, as *Pinus monophylla, P. edulis,* etc., bearing edible nuts.

**nutria** /'njutriə/, *n.* **1.** →**coypu.** **2.** the fur of this animal, resembling beaver. [Sp.: otter, from L *lūtra* otter]

**nutrient** /'njutriənt/, *adj.* **1.** containing or conveying nutriment, as solutions or vessels of the body. **2.** nourishing; affording nutriment. *–n.* **3.** a nutrient substance. [L *nūtriens,* ppr., nourishing]

**nutriment** /'njutrəmənt/, *n.* **1.** any matter that, taken into a living organism, serves to sustain it in its existence, promoting growth, replacing loss, and providing energy. **2.** that which nourishes; nourishment, food, or aliment. [L *nūtrīmentum*]

**nutrition** /nju'trɪʃən/, *n.* **1.** the act or process of nourishing or of being nourished. **2.** food; nutriment. **3.** the process by which the food material taken into an organism is converted into living tissue, etc. – **nutritional,** *adj.* – **nutritionally,** *adv.*

**nutritionist** /nju'trɪʃənəst/, *n.* one who studies problems of food and nutrition.

**nutritious** /nju'trɪʃəs/, *adj.* nourishing, esp. in a high degree. [L *nūtrīcius, nūtrītius*] – **nutritiously,** *adv.* – **nutritiousness,** *n.*

**nutritive** /'njutrətɪv/, *adj.* **1.** serving to nourish; affording nutriment. **2.** of or concerned in nutrition. – **nutritively,** *adv.* – **nutritiveness,** *n.*

**nuts** /nʌts/, *Colloq. –interj.* **1.** (an expression of defiance, disgust, etc.) *–adj.* **2.** crazy; insane. **3.** overwhelmingly attracted (fol. by *on* or *over*): *I'm nuts over her.*

**nuts and bolts,** *n.pl.* the most basic components; the essentials of a situation.

**nuts-and-bolts man** /nʌts-ən-'boʊlts mæn/, *n. Colloq.* **1.** a man whose interests and aptitudes are essentially practical. **2.** a person who puts emphasis on analysing the essential factors of a situation, policy, plan, etc.

**nutshell** /'nʌtʃɛl/, *n.* **1.** the shell of a nut. **2. in a nutshell,** in very brief form; in a few words: *just tell me the story in a nutshell.*

**nut steak** /nʌt 'steɪk/, *n.* food made from nuts but contrived to resemble a steak in both shape and flavour. Also, **nut cutlet.**

**nutter** /'nʌtə/, *n.* **1.** one who gathers nuts. **2.** *Colloq.* crazy or foolish person.

**nutting** /'nʌtɪŋ/, *n.* the act of seeking or gathering nuts.

**nutty** /'nʌti/, *adj.,* **-tier, -tiest.** **1.** abounding in or producing nuts. **2.** nutlike, esp. in taste. **3.** *Colloq.* silly or stupid; crazy. **4.** *Colloq.* overwhelmingly attracted (fol. by *over*). **5. nutty as a fruitcake,** *Colloq.* completely mad. – **nuttiness,** *n.*

**nutwood** /'nʌtwʊd/, *n. Chiefly U.S.* **1.** any one of various species of nut-bearing trees, as walnut, hickory, etc. **2.** a tree or the wood of a tree of such a species. Also, **nut wood.**

**nuvistor** /'njuvɪstə/, *n.* a metal and ceramic vacuum tube which is mechanically very rigid.

**nux-vomica** /nʊks-'vɒmɪkə/, *n.* **1.** the strychnine-containing seed (used in medicine) of the orangelike fruit borne by an East Indian tree, *Strychnos nux-vomica.* **2.** the tree itself. [NL: vomiting nut, from L *nux* nut + NL *vomica,* from L *vomere* vomit]

**nuzzle** /'nʌzəl/, *v.,* **-zled, -zling.** *–v.i.* **1.** to burrow or root with the nose, as an animal does. **2.** to thrust the nose (fol. by *against, in, up,* etc.): *the pup nuzzled up close to the sick child.* **3.** to snuggle or cuddle up with someone or something. *–v.t.* **4.** to root up with the nose. **5.** to touch or rub with the nose. **6.** to thrust the nose against or into. **7.** to thrust (the nose or head), as into something. [ME *nosele;* frequentative of NOSE; to some extent confused with NESTLE]

**NW,** **1.** north-west. **2.** north-western. Also, **N.W., n.w.**

**nyala** /ən'jalə/, *n.* →**inyala.**

**nyckelharpa** /'nɪkəlhapə/, *n.* a former Swedish stringed musical instrument, similar to the hurdy-gurdy but sounded with a bow instead of a wheel.

**nyct-,** a word element meaning 'night'. [Gk *nykt-,* combining form of *nýx*]

**nyctalopia** /nɪktə'loʊpiə/, *n.* a condition of the eyes in which sight is normal in the day or in a strong light, but is abnormally poor or wholly gone at night or in a dim light; night blindness. [LL, from Gk *nyktálōps* blind by night + *-ia* -IA] – **nyctalopic** /nɪktə'lɒpɪk/, *adj.*

**nyctitropic** /nɪktə'trɒpɪk/, *adj.* tending to assume at or just before nightfall positions unlike those maintained during the day, as the leaves of certain plants. [*nycti-* (var. of NYCT-) + -TROPIC] – **nyctitropism** /nɪk'tɪtrəpɪzəm/, *n.*

**nyctophobia** /nɪktə'foʊbiə/, *n.* a morbid or abnormal fear of night or darkness.

**nylon** /'naɪlɒn/, *n.* **1.** a synthetic polyamide capable of extrusion when molten into fibres, sheets, etc., of extreme toughness, strength, and elasticity, used for yarn (as for hosiery), for bristles (as for brushes), etc. It is a thermoplastic product, made by interaction of a dicarboxylic acid with a diamine. **2.** (*pl.*) stockings made of nylon. [Trademark]

**nymph** /nɪmf/, *n.* **1.** one of a numerous class of inferior divinities of mythology, conceived as beautiful maidens inhabiting the sea, rivers, woods, trees, mountains, meadows, etc., and frequently mentioned as attending a superior deity. **2.** a beautiful or graceful young woman. **3.** *Chiefly Poetic.* a maiden. **4.** *Entomol.* **a.** Also, **nympha.** the young of an insect without metamorphosis. **b.** →**pupa.** [ME *nimphe,* from OF, from L *nympha,* from Gk *nýmphē* nymph, pupa] – **nymphal, nymphean,** *adj.*

**nympha** /'nɪmfə/, *n., pl.* **-phae** /-fi/. **1.** (*pl.*) *Anat.* the labia minora (see **labium** def. 2b). **2.** →**nymph** (def. 4a). [L. See NYMPH]

**nymphalid** /'nɪmfəlɪd/, *n.* any of the numerous butterflies of the family Nymphalidae, characterised by small useless forelegs, and including the fritillaries, etc. [NL, from *Nymphālis* genus name, from L *nympha* NYMPH + *-idae* -IDAE]

**nymphette** /nɪm'fɛt/, *n.* **1.** a young nymph. **2.** a very young girl with strong sexual attraction. Also, **nymphet** /'nɪmfət/.

**nympho** /'nɪmfoʊ/, *n., pl.* **-phos.** *Colloq.* a nymphomaniac.

**nympholepsy** /'nɪmfəlɛpsi/, *n., pl.* **-sies.** **1.** an ecstasy supposed to be inspired by nymphs. **2.** a frenzy of emotion, as for something unattainable. [b. NYMPHOLEPT and EPILEPSY] – **nympholeptic** /nɪmfə'lɛptɪk/, *adj.*

**nympholept** /'nɪmfəlɛpt/, *n.* one seized with nympholepsy. [Gk *nympholēptos* caught by nymphs]

**nymphomania** /nɪmfə'meɪniə/, *n.* uncontrollable sexual desire in women. [NL, from Gk *nýmphē* NYMPH + -MANIA] – **nymphomaniac,** *adj., n.*

**Nynorsk** /'ninɔsk/, *n.* an official language of Norway, based on the dialects of western Norway and Old Norse. Also, **Landsmål.** Cf. **Bokmål.**

**nystagmus** /nɪs'tægməs/, *n.* an involuntary oscillation of the eyeball, usu. lateral but sometimes rotatory or vertical, occurring esp. among miners and human albinos and in certain diseases. [NL, from Gk *nystagmós* nodding] – **nystagmic,** *adj.*

**nyum-nyum** /'njʌm-njʌm/, *interj., n.* →**num-num**[2].

**N.Z.** /ɛn 'zɛd/, *n.* New Zealand.

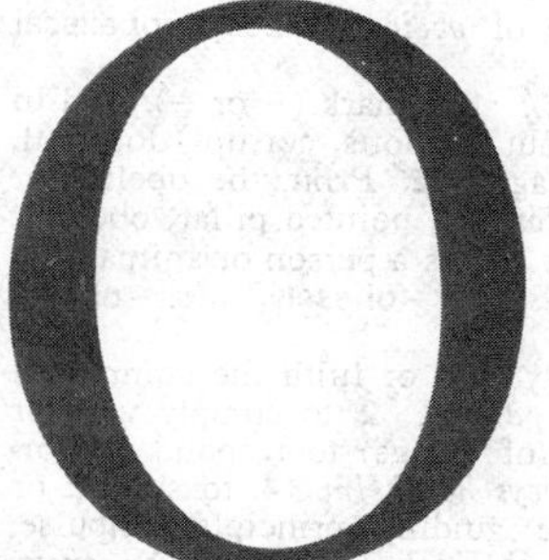

Oo Roman BASKERVILLE

Oo Sans Serif TRADE GOTHIC

Oo Script OBLIQUE

Oo Decorative PEKIN

*Although there are numerous typefaces in the world they can be divided into four main classifications. These are:*

*ROMAN or SERIF. This typeface came into being from the technique of the Roman masons who, working in stone, finished off each letter with a serif or small stroke projecting from the top or bottom. This was done to correct any feeling of unevenness or imbalance they may have created in cutting the characters in stone.*

*SANS SERIF (without serif). This typeface is geometric in design and has straight-edged characters and lines of a regular thickness.*

*SCRIPT. Based on the movement of the hand, this typeface is often italicised or slanted, as if drawn by a brush or quill pen.*

*DECORATIVE. Any typeface that exaggerates the characteristics of any of the other three classifications to a degree that places it outside of them.*

*The dictionary entries in this book use a SANS SERIF typeface called Helvetica (set in a bold face for the head words) and a SERIF typeface Plantin (used throughout the body of the entries).*

**O, o** /oʊ/, *n., pl.* **O's** or **Os; o's, os,** or **oes. 1.** a vowel, the 15th letter of the English alphabet. **2.** something resembling the letter O in shape. **3.** the Arabic cipher; zero; nought (o). **4.** a mere nothing. **5. the big O,** *Colloq.* female orgasm.

**o'** /ə/, *prep.* **1.** an abbreviated form of *of,* now chiefly dialectal or colloquial, except in *o'clock, will-o'-the-wisp,* etc. **2.** an abbreviated form of *on.*

**o-**[1], *Chem.* an abridgment of **ortho-.**

**o-**[2], variant of **ob-,** before *m,* as in *omission.*

**-o-,** an ending for the first element of many compounds, originally found in the combining forms of many Greek words, but often used in English as a connective irrespective of etymology, as in *Franco-Italian, speedometer,* etc.

**-o,** a suffix used: **1.** in colloquial abbreviations, as *arvo,* afternoon; *combo,* combination; *commo,* communist; *compo,* compensation; *demo,* demonstration; *kero,* kerosene; *metho,* methylated spirits; *nasho,* National Service (man). **2.** to refer to a person **a.** in a particular occupation, as *bottle-o,* bottle collector; *garbo,* garbageman; *journo,* journalist; *milko,* milkman; *scripto,* scriptwriter. **b.** of particular habits, as *weirdo,* one whose behaviour borders on perversion or eccentricity; *wino,* a wine addict. **3.** in colloquial responses showing compliance or agreement, as *goodo, righto.*

**O, 1.** *Elect.* ohm. **2.** *Chem.* oxygen.

**O** /oʊ/, *interj.* **1.** (a word used before a name in address, esp., as in solemn or poetic language, to lend earnestness to an appeal): *Praise the Lord, O Jerusalem.* **2.** (an expression of surprise, pain, longing, gladness, etc.).

**O'** /oʊ/, a prefix meaning 'descendant', in Irish family names: *O'Brien, O'Connor.* [representing Irish ō descendant]

**O., 1.** Ocean. **2.** Office. **3.** Officer. **4.** Order. **5.** Old.

**O.A.,** Order of Australia.

**oaf** /oʊf/, *n.* **1.** a simpleton or blockhead. **2.** a lout. **3.** a deformed or mentally deficient child; an idiot. **4.** →**changeling.** [var. of *auf,* ME *alfe,* OE *ælf* elf, c. G *Alp* nightmare] – **oafish,** *adj.* – **oafishly,** *adv.* – **oafishness,** *n.*

**oak** /oʊk/, *n.* **1.** any tree or shrub of the large fagaceous genus *Quercus,* including many forest trees with hard, durable wood, bearing the acorn as fruit. **2.** the wood of an oak tree. **3.** the leaves of the oak tree, esp. as worn in a chaplet. **4.** anything made of oak, as furniture, a door, etc. [ME *ook,* OE *āc,* c. D *eik,* G *Eiche*]

**oak-apple** /ˈoʊk-æpəl/, *n.* any of various roundish galls produced on oaks. Also, **oak-gall** /ˈoʊk-gɔl/.

**oaken** /ˈoʊkən/, *adj.* **1.** made of oak: *the old oaken bucket.* **2.** of or pertaining to the oak.

**oakum** /ˈoʊkəm/, *n.* loose fibre obtained by untwisting and picking apart old ropes, used for caulking the seams of ships, etc. [ME *okom(e),* OE *ācum(a),* var. of *ācumba,* lit., offcombings. See COMB[1]]

**O.A.M.,** Medal of the Order of Australia.

**Oamaru stone** /ˈoʊmərʊ stoʊn/, *n.* a white, granular limestone used in building, which is quarried in the Oamaru district of the east coast of the South Island of New Zealand.

**oar** /ɔ/, *n.* **1.** an instrument for propelling a boat, sometimes used also for steering, consisting of a long shaft of wood with a blade at one end. **2.** something resembling this or used for a similar purpose. **3.** →**oarsman. 4. put one's oar in,** to interfere; meddle. **5. rest on one's oars,** to relax; take things easily. *–v.t.* **6.** to propel with or as with oars; row. **7.** to traverse (the sea, etc.), or make (one's way), by or as if by rowing. *–v.i.* **8.** to move or advance as if by rowing. [ME *ore,* OE *ār,* c. Icel. *ār*] – **oarless,** *adj.* – **oarlike,** *adj.*

**oared** /ɔd/, *adj.* furnished with oars.

**oarfish** /ˈɔfɪʃ/, *n., pl.* **-fishes,** (*esp. collectively*) **fish.** a marine fish, *Regalecus glesne,* of temperate seas, having a long, compressed, tapelike body up to 9 metres in length, a dorsal fin running the whole length of the body, and red-tipped rays above the head.

oarfish

**oarlock** /ˈɔlɒk/, *n.* →**rowlock.** [ME *orlok,* OE *ārloc.* See OAR, LOCK[1]]

**oarsman** /ˈɔzmən/, *n., pl.* **-men.** one who rows a boat; a rower.

**oarsmanship** /ˈɔzmənʃɪp/, *n.* the art of rowing; skill in rowing.

**OAS** /oʊ eɪ ˈɛs/, on active service.

**oasis** /oʊˈeɪsəs/, *n., pl.* **oases** /-siz/. a fertile place in a desert region where ground water brought to the surface or surface water from other areas provides for humid vegetation. [L, from Gk, ? from Egyptian *wāh*]

**oast** /oʊst/, *n.* a kiln for drying hops or malt. [ME *ost,* OE *āst,* c. D *eest*]

**oast-house** /ˈoʊst-haʊs/, *n.* a building containing an oast.

**oat** /oʊt/, *n.* **1.** (*usu. pl.*) a cereal grass, *Avena sativa,* cultivated for its edible seed, which is used in making oatmeal and as a food for horses, etc. **2.** (*pl.*) the seeds. **3.** any species of the same genus, as *A. fatua,* the common **wild oat.** **4. feel one's oats, a.** to feel gay or lively. **b.** to be aware of and use one's importance and power. **5. sow (one's) wild oats,** to indulge in the excesses or follies of youth, esp. in sexual promiscuity. [ME *ote,* OE *āte*]

**oatcake** /ˈoutkeɪk/, *n.* a cake, usu. thin and brittle, made of oatmeal.

**oaten** /ˈoutn/, *adj.* **1.** made of oats or of oatmeal. **2.** of or pertaining to the oat. **3.** made of an oat straw.

**oatgrass** /ˈoutgras/, *n.* **1.** any of certain native Australian oat-like grasses, as *Themeda avenacea.* **2.** any wild species of oat.

**oath** /ouθ/, *n., pl.* **oaths** /ouðs/. **1.** a solemn appeal to God, or to some revered person or thing, in attestation of the truth of a statement or the binding character of a promise: *to testify upon oath.* **2.** a statement or promise strengthened by such an appeal. **3.** a formally affirmed statement or promise accepted as an equivalent. **4.** the form of words in which such a statement or promise is made: *the Hippocratic oath.* **5.** an irreverent or blasphemous use of the name of God or anything sacred. **6.** any profane expression; a curse. **7. blood oath, my (colonial) oath,** (an asseveration of agreement). **8. on oath, under oath,** *Law.* having sworn on the Bible to tell the truth. [ME *ooth,* OE *āth,* c. G *Eid*]

**oatmeal** /ˈoutmil/, *n.* **1.** meal made from oats and used in porridge, oatcakes, etc. **2.** oatmeal porridge.

**ob-,** a prefix meaning 'towards', 'to', 'on', 'over', 'against', originally occurring in loan words from Latin, but now used also, with the sense of 'reversely' or 'inversely', to form Neo-Latin and English scientific terms. Also, **o-, oc-, of-, op-.** [L, representing *ob,* prep., towards, to, about, before, on, over, against]

**ob.,** **1.** obiit. **2.** incidentally. [L *obiter*] **3.** oboe.

**OB** /ou ˈbi/, Outside Broadcast.

**Obad.,** *Bible.* Obadiah.

**obb.,** obbligato.

**obbligato** /ɒbləˈgatou/, *adj., n., pl.* **-tos, -ti** /-ti/. *Music.* *–adj.* **1.** obligatory or indispensable; so important that it cannot be omitted (opposed to *ad libitum*). *–n.* **2.** an obbligato part or accompaniment. Also, **obligato.** [It.: obliged]

**obcordate** /ɒbˈkɔdeɪt/, *adj.* heart-shaped, with the attachment at the pointed end, as a leaf.

**obdurate** /ˈɒbdʒərət/, *adj.* **1.** hardened against persuasions or tender feelings; hard-hearted. **2.** hardened against moral influence; persistently impenitent: *an obdurate sinner.* [ME, from L *obdūrātus,* pp., hardened] **– obduracy** /ˈɒbdʒərəsi/, **obdurateness,** *n.* **– obdurately,** *adj.*

**O.B.E.** /ou bi ˈi/, **1.** Officer (of the Order) of the British Empire. **2.** Order of the British Empire.

**obeah** /ˈoubiə/, *n.* →**obi**[2].

**obedience** /əˈbidiəns/, *n.* **1.** the state or fact of being obedient. **2.** the act or practice of obeying; dutiful or submissive compliance (fol. by *to*). **3.** a sphere of authority, or a body of persons, etc., subject to some particular authority, esp. ecclesiastical. **4.** authority or rule, esp. ecclesiastical, as over those who should obey.

**obedient** /əˈbidiənt/, *adj.* obeying, or willing to obey; submissive to authority or constraint. [ME, from L *oboediens,* ppr.] **– obediently,** *adv.*

**obeisance** /ouˈbeɪsəns/, *n.* **1.** a movement of the body expressing deep respect or deferential courtesy, as before a superior; a bow or curtsy. **2.** deference or homage. [ME *obeisaunce,* from OF *obeissance* obedience, from *obeir* OBEY] **– obeisant,** *adj.*

**obelise** /ˈɒbəlaɪz/, *v.t.,* **-lised, -lising.** to mark (a word or passage) with an obelus. Also, **obelize.**

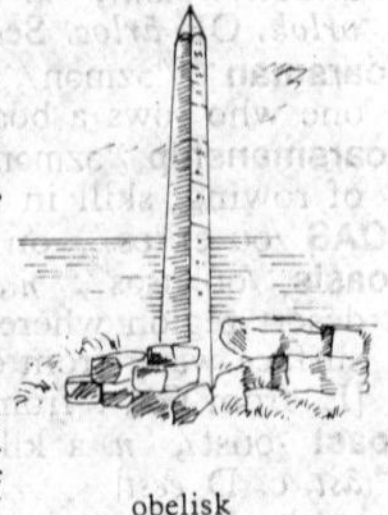
obelisk

**obelisk** /ˈɒbələsk/, *n.* **1.** a tapering, four-sided shaft of stone, usu. monolithic and having a pyramidal apex, of which notable examples are seen among the monuments of ancient Egypt. **2.** something resembling such a shaft. **3.** →**obelus.** **4.** *Print.* the dagger (†), used esp. as a reference mark. [L *obeliscus,* from Gk *obelískos,* diminutive of *obelós* OBELUS] **– obeliscal** /ɒbəˈlɪskəl/, *adj.*

**obelus** /ˈɒbələs/, *n., pl.* **-li** /-laɪ/. **1.** a mark (– or ÷) used in ancient manuscripts to point out spurious, corrupt, doubtful, or superfluous words or passages. **2.** *Print.* the obelisk or dagger (†). [LL, from Gk *obelós* spit, pointed pillar, obelus]

**obese** /ouˈbis/, *adj.* excessively fat, as a person or animal, the body, etc.; corpulent. [L *obēsus,* pp.] **– obesely,** *adv.* **– obeseness, obesity** /ouˈbisəti/, *n.*

**obey** /ouˈbeɪ/, *v.t.* **1.** to comply with or fulfil the commands or instructions of: *obey your parents.* **2.** to comply with or fulfil (a command, etc.). **3.** (of things) to respond conformably in action to: *a ship obeys her helm.* **4.** to submit or conform in action to (some guiding principle, impulse, etc.). *–v.i.* **5.** to be obedient. [ME *obei(en),* from OF *obeir,* from L *oboedīre*] **– obeyer,** *n.*

**obfuscate** /ˈɒbfəskeɪt/, *v.t.,* **-cated, -cating.** **1.** to confuse or stupefy. **2.** to darken or obscure. [LL *obfuscātus,* pp.] **– obfuscation** /ɒbfəsˈkeɪʃən/, *n.*

**obi**[1] /ˈoubi/, *n., pl.* **obis.** a long, broad sash worn by Japanese women and children. [Jap.]

**obi**[2] /ˈoubi/, *n., pl.* **obis.** **1.** a kind of sorcery practised by the Negroes of Africa, the West Indies, etc. **2.** a fetish or charm used in it. Also, **obeah.** [from a W African language (probably Efik; cf. Efik *abia* practitioner, *ubio* evil charm)]

**obiit** /ˈɒbiɪt, ˈoubi-/, he or she died. [L]

**obit** /ˈoubɪt, ˈɒbɪt/, *n.* **1.** the date of a person's death. **2.** an obituary notice. [ME, from L *obitus* death]

**obiter dictum** /ˌoubɪtə ˈdɪktəm, ˌɒbɪtə/, *n., pl.* **obiter dicta** /ˈdɪktə/. **1.** an incidental opinion; a passing remark. **2.** *Law.* an opinion by a judge in deciding a case, upon a matter not essential to the decision, and therefore not binding. [L: (something) said by the way]

**obituarise** /əˈbɪtʃəraɪz/, *v.t.,* **-ised, -ising.** to write an obituary on.

**obituary** /əˈbɪtʃəri/, *n., pl.* **-aries,** *adj.* *–n.* **1.** a notice of the death of a person, often with a brief biographical sketch, as in a newspaper. *–adj.* **2.** pertaining to or recording a death: *an obituary notice.* [NL *obituārius,* from L *obitus* death]

**obj.,** **1.** object. **2.** objection. **3.** objective.

**object** /ˈɒbdʒɛkt/, *n.;* /əbˈdʒɛkt/, *v.* *–n.* **1.** something that may be perceived by the senses, esp. by sight or touch; a visible or tangible thing. **2.** a thing or person to which attention or action is directed: *an object of study.* **3.** anything that may be presented to the mind: *objects of thought.* **4.** a thing with reference to the impression it makes on the mind: *an object of curiosity.* **5.** the end towards which effort is directed: *the object of our visit.* **6.** a person treated in terms of meeting a specific need in others: *a love object, sex object.* **7.** a person or thing which arouses feelings of pity, disgust, etc. **8.** *Gram.* (in English and many other languages) the noun or its substitute which represents the goal of an action (in English either *direct* or *indirect*) or the ending point of a relation (in English expressed by a preposition). **9.** *Metaphys.* that towards which a cognitive act is directed; the non-ego. **10. no object,** *Colloq.* not an obstacle or hindrance: *money is no object.* *–v.i.* **11.** to offer a reason or argument in opposition. **12.** to express or feel disapproval; be averse. *–v.t.* **13.** to bring as a charge; attribute as a fault. [ME, from ML *objectum,* properly neut. of L *objectus,* pp., thrown before, presented, exposed, opposed, reproached with] **– objector,** *n.*

**object.,** **1.** objection. **2.** objective.

**object ball** /ˈɒbdʒɛkt bɔl/, *n. Billiards, etc.* the ball which the striker aims to hit with the cue ball; any ball except the striker's.

**object glass** /ˈ– glas/, *n.* →**objective** (def. 3).

**objectify** /əbˈdʒɛktəfaɪ/, *v.t.,* **-fied, -fying.** to present as an object, esp. of sense; make objective; externalise. [ML *objectum* an object + -IFY] **– objectification** /əbdʒɛktəfəˈkeɪʃən/, *n.*

**objection** /əbˈdʒɛkʃən/, *n.* **1.** something adduced or said in disagreement or disapproval; an adverse reason. **2.** the act of objecting. **3.** a ground or cause of objecting. **4.** a feeling of disapproval or dislike.

**objectionable** /əbˈdʒɛkʃənəbəl/, *adj.* that may be objected to; unpleasant; offensive: *objectionable remarks; an objectionable smell.* **– objectionably,** *adv.*

**objective** /əb'dʒɛktɪv/, *n.* **1.** an end towards which efforts are directed; something aimed at. **2.** *Gram.* **a.** the objective case. **b.** a word in that case. **3.** (in a telescope, microscope, etc.) the lens or combination of lenses which first receives the rays from the object and forms the image viewed through the eyepiece or photographed. *–adj.* **4.** being the object of perception or thought; belonging to the object of thought rather than to the thinking subject (opposed to *subjective*). **5.** free from personal feelings or prejudice; unbiased. **6.** being the object of one's endeavours or actions. **7.** intent upon or dealing with things external to the mind rather than thoughts or feelings, as a person, a book, etc. **8.** of or pertaining to that which can be known, or to that which is an object or a part of an object. **9.** *Art.* **a.** of or pertaining to an object or objects (opposed to *non-objective* and *non-representational*). **b.** being, or pertaining to, the object whose perspective delineation is required: *an objective plane.* **10.** *Med.* (of a symptom) discernible to others as well as the patient. **11.** *Gram.* **a.** pertaining to the use of a form as object of a verb or preposition. **b.** (in English and some other languages) denoting a case specialised for that use: in *the boy hit him, him* is in the objective case. **c.** similar to such a case in meaning. [ML *objectīvus,* adj.] – **objectively,** *adv.* – **objectiveness,** *n.*

**objective complement** /– 'kɒmpləmənt/, *n.* a word or a group of words qualifying or modifying a direct object, as *the manager* in *they made him the manager.*

**objectivise** /əb'dʒɛktəvaɪz/, *v.t.,* **-vised, -vising.** to render objective; objectify. Also, **objectivize.**

**objectivism** /əb'dʒɛktəvɪzəm/, *n.* **1.** a tendency to lay stress on the objective or external elements of cognition. **2.** the tendency to deal with things external to the mind rather than thoughts or feelings, as in a writer. **3.** a doctrine characterised by this tendency. – **objectivist,** *n., adj.* – **objectivistic** /əbdʒɛktə'vɪstɪk/, *adj.*

**objectivity** /,ɒbdʒɛk'tɪvəti/, *n.* **1.** the state or quality of being objective. **2.** intentness on objects external to the mind. **3.** external reality.

**object language** /'ɒbdʒɛkt læŋgwɪdʒ/, *n.* **1.** a language which is the object of discussion, as opposed to a metalanguage in which the discussion might take place. **2.** a language which relates to objects or entities separate from itself.

**objectless** /'ɒbdʒɛktləs/, *adj.* **1.** having no object. **2.** not directed towards any object; purposeless.

**object lesson** /'ɒbdʒɛkt lɛsən/, *n.* **1.** a practical illustration of a principle, esp. one serving as a warning. **2.** a lesson in which instruction is conveyed by means of a material object.

**objet d'art** /ɒbʒɛ 'da/, *n., pl.* **objets d'art** /ɒbʒɛ 'da, ɒbjeɪ/. an article of artistic worth. [F]

**objurgate** /'ɒbdʒəgeɪt/, *v.t.,* **-gated, -gating.** to reproach vehemently; upbraid violently; berate. [L *objurgātus,* pp.] – **objurgation** /ɒbdʒə'geɪʃən/, *n.* – **objurgatory** /ɒb'dʒɜgətəri, ɒbdʒə'geɪtəri/, *adj.*

**obl.,** **1.** oblique. **2.** oblong.

**oblanceolate** /ɒb'lænsiəleɪt/, *adj.* inversely lanceolate, as a leaf.

**oblast** /'ɒblast/, *n.* an administrative subdivision of a republic in the Soviet Union. [Russ.]

**oblate**[1] /'ɒbleɪt/, *adj.* flattened at the poles, as a spheroid generated by the revolution of an ellipse about its shorter axis (opposed to *prolate*). [NL *oblātus,* from *ob-* OB- + *-lātus,* modelled on *prolātus* PROLATE] – **oblately,** *adv.*

**oblate**[2] /'ɒbleɪt/, *n.* **1.** a person offered to the service of a monastery, but not under monastic vows. **2.** a member of any of various Roman Catholic societies devoted to special religious work. [ML *oblātus,* properly pp. of *offerre* OFFER]

**oblation** /oʊ'bleɪʃən, ɒ-/, *n.* **1.** the offering to God of the elements of bread and wine in the Eucharist. **2.** the whole office of the Eucharist. **3.** the act of making an offering, now esp. to God or a deity. **4.** any offering for religious or charitable uses. [ME *oblacion,* from LL *oblātio*] – **oblatory** /'ɒblətəri, ɒb'leɪtəri/, *adj.*

**obligate** /'ɒbləgeɪt/, *v.,* **-gated, -gating;** /'ɒbləgət, -geɪt/, *adj.* *–v.t.* **1.** to oblige or bind morally or legally: *to obligate oneself to fulfil certain conditions.* **2.** *U.S.* to pledge, commit (funds, etc.). *–adj.* **3.** *U.S.* morally or legally bound or constrained. **4.** *U.S.* necessary; essential. **5.** *Biol.* restricted to a particular condition of life, as certain parasites which must live in close association with their usual hosts in order to survive (opposed to *facultative*). [ME, from L *obligātus,* pp.] – **obligator,** *n.*

**obligation** /ɒblə'geɪʃən/, *n.* **1.** a binding requirement as to action; duty: *to fulfil every obligation.* **2.** the binding power or force of a promise, law, duty, agreement, etc. **3.** a binding promise or the like. **4.** the act of binding oneself by a promise, contract, etc. **5.** *Law.* **a.** an agreement enforceable by law, originally applied to promises under seal. **b.** a document containing such an agreement. **c.** a bond containing a penalty, with a condition annexed for payment of money, performance of covenants, etc. **d.** any bond, note, bill, certificate, or the like, as of a government or a company, serving as security for payment of indebtedness. **6.** a benefit, favour, or service, for which gratitude is due. **7.** a debt of gratitude. **8.** the state or fact of being indebted for a benefit, favour, or service.

**obligato** /ɒblə'gatoʊ/, *adj., n., pl.* **-tos, -ti** /-ti/. →**obbligato.**

**obligatory** /ɒ'blɪgətəri, -tri/, *adj.* **1.** imposing obligation, morally or legally; binding: *an obligatory promise.* **2.** required as a matter of obligation: *a reply is expected but not obligatory.* **3.** incumbent or compulsory (fol. by *on* or *upon*): *duties obligatory on all.* **4.** creating or recording an obligation, as a writing. [ME, from LL *obligātōrius*] – **obligatorily,** *adv.*

**oblige** /ə'blaɪdʒ/, *v.,* **obliged, obliging.** *–v.t.* **1.** to require or constrain, as by law, command, conscience, or necessity. **2.** to bind (a person, etc.) morally or legally, as by a promise, contract, or the like. **3.** to make (an action, course, etc.) incumbent or obligatory. **4.** to place under a debt of gratitude for some benefit, favour, or service. **5.** to favour or accommodate (fol. by *with*): *he obliged us with a song.* *–v.i.* **6.** to do something as a favour: *he'll do anything to oblige.* [ME *oblige(n),* from OF *obligier,* from L *obligāre* bind or tie around] – **obliger,** *n.*

**obligee** /ɒblə'dʒi/, *n.* **1.** *Law.* **a.** one to whom another is bound. **b.** the person to whom a bond is given. **2.** one who is under obligation for a benefit or favour.

**obliging** /ə'blaɪdʒɪŋ/, *adj.* **1.** disposed to do favours or services, as a person: *the clerk was most obliging.* **2.** that obliges. – **obligingly,** *adv.* – **obligingness,** *n.*

**obligor** /ɒblə'gɔ/, *n.* **1.** one who is bound to another. **2.** the person who gives a bond.

**oblique** /ə'blik/, *adj., v.,* **obliqued, obliquing,** *n.* *–adj.* **1.** neither perpendicular nor parallel to a given line or surface; slanting; sloping. **2.** (of a solid) not having the axis perpendicular to the plane of the base. **3.** designating a method of projection in which neither side of the principal object is parallel to the plane of delineation. **4.** diverging from a given straight line or course. **5.** not straight or direct, as a course, etc. **6.** indirectly stated or expressed: *certain oblique hints.* **7.** indirectly aimed at or reached, as ends, results, etc. **8.** *Rhet.* indirect (applied to discourse in which the original words of a speaker or writer are assimilated to the language of the reporter). **9.** *Gram.* denoting or pertaining to any case of noun inflection except nominative and vocative, or except these two and accusative: *Latin genitive, dative, and ablative cases are said to be oblique.* **10.** not honest, deceptive, evasive: *oblique answers.* **11.** *Anat.* pertaining to muscles running obliquely in the body as opposed to those running transversely or longitudinally. **12.** *Bot.* having unequal sides, as a leaf. *–v.i.* **13.** to have or take an oblique direction; slant: *the wall obliques from the gate at a sharp angle.* **14.** *Mil.* to advance obliquely. *–n.* **15.** *Gram.* the oblique case. **16.** something which is oblique. [ME *oblike,* from L *oblīquus*] – **obliquely,** *adv.* – **obliqueness,** *n.*

**oblique angle** /– 'æŋgəl/, *n.* an angle that is not a right angle.

**oblique motion** /– 'moʊʃən/, *n.* (in music) the relative motion of two melodic parts in which one remains in place while the other moves.

**oblique sailing** /– 'seɪlɪŋ/, *n.* navigation along a course other than directly north, south, east, or west.

**obliquity** /ə'blɪkwəti/, *n., pl.* **-ties.** **1.** the state of being oblique. **2.** divergence from moral rectitude. **3.** a moral delinquency. **4.** mental perversity. **5.** an instance of mental perversity. **6.** inclination, or degree of inclination. **7.** Also,

**obliquity of the ecliptic.** *Astron.* the angle between the plane of the earth's orbit and that of the earth's equator, equal to about 23°27′. – **obliquitous,** *adj.*

**obliterate** /əˈblɪtəreɪt/, *v.t.*, **-rated, -rating. 1.** to remove all traces of; do away with; destroy. **2.** to blot out or render undecipherable (writing, marks, etc.); cancel; efface. [L *oblit(t)erātus,* pp., erased] – **obliteration** /əblɪtəˈreɪʃən/, *n.* – **obliterative** /əˈblɪtərətɪv/, *adj.*

**oblivion** /əˈblɪviən/, *n.* **1.** the state of being forgotten, as by the world. **2.** the forgetting, or forgetfulness, of something: *five minutes of oblivion.* **3.** disregard or overlooking: *oblivion of political offences.* [ME, from L *oblīvio*]

**oblivious** /əˈblɪviəs/, *adj.* **1.** forgetful; without remembrance: *oblivious of my former failure.* **2.** unmindful; unconscious (fol. by *of* or *to*): *she was oblivious of his adoration.* **3.** inducing forgetfulness. [ME, from L *oblīviōsus*] – **obliviously,** *adv.* – **obliviousness,** *n.*

**obliviscence** /ɒbləˈvɪsəns/, *n.* the fact or state of having forgotten; forgetfulness.

**oblong** /ˈɒblɒŋ/, *adj.* **1.** elongated, usu. from the square or circular form. **2.** in the form of a rectangle of greater length than breadth. –*n.* **3.** an oblong figure. [ME, from L *oblongus* rather long, oblong]

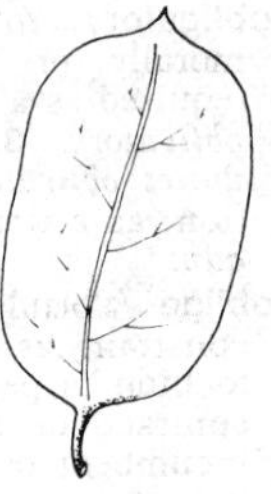

oblong leaf

**obloquy** /ˈɒbləkwi/, *n., pl.* **-quies. 1.** the discredit or disgrace resulting from public blame or revilement. **2.** censure, blame, or abusive language aimed at a person, etc., esp. by numbers of persons or by the public generally. [late ME *obloqui,* from LL *obloquium* contradiction]

**obnoxious** /əbˈnɒkʃəs, ɒb-/, *adj.* **1.** objectionable; offensive; odious: *obnoxious remarks.* **2.** exposed or liable (to harm, evil, or anything objectionable). **3.** *Obs.* liable to punishment or censure; reprehensible. [L *obnoxius* exposed to harm] – **obnoxiously,** *adv.* – **obnoxiousness,** *n.*

**oboe** /ˈoʊboʊ/, *n.* **1.** a woodwind instrument in the form of a slender conical tube, in which the tone is produced by a double reed. **2.** a reed stop in an organ which sounds like an oboe. [It., from F *hautbois* HAUTBOY]

oboe

**oboist** /ˈoʊboʊəst/, *n.* a player on the oboe.

**obovate** /ɒbˈoʊveɪt/, *adj.* inversely ovate; ovate with the narrow end at the base.

**obovoid** /ɒbˈoʊvɔɪd/, *adj.* inversely ovoid, ovoid with the narrow end at the base, as certain fruits.

**obs.,** **1.** observation. **2.** observatory. **3.** obsolete.

**obscene** /əbˈsin, ɒb-/, *adj.* **1.** offensive to modesty or decency; indecent; inciting to lust or sexual depravity; lewd: *obscene pictures.* **2.** abominable; disgusting; repulsive. [L *obscēnus, obscaenus* of evil omen, offensive, disgusting] – **obscenely,** *adv.* – **obsceneness,** *n.*

**obscenity** /əbˈsɛnəti, ɒb-/, *n., pl.* **-ties. 1.** obscene quality or character; indecency. **2.** something obscene, as language, a remark, an expression, etc. **3.** *Colloq.* an action or state of affairs that is degrading and offensive to one's moral or aesthetic sense: *war is an obscenity.*

**obscurant** /əbˈskjurənt, -ˈskʊə-/, *n.* **1.** one who strives to prevent inquiry and enlightenment. **2.** one who obscures. –*adj.* **3.** pertaining to or characteristic of obscurants. [L *obscūrans,* ppr.]

**obscurantism** /ɒbskjəˈræntɪzəm/, *n.* **1.** opposition to inquiry and enlightenment. **2.** the principle or practice of obscurants. – **obscurantist,** *n., adj.*

**obscuration** /ɒbskjuˈreɪʃən/, *n.* **1.** the act of obscuring. **2.** the state of being obscured.

obovate leaf

**obscure** /əbˈskjuə, -ˈskjʊə/, *adj.*, **-scurer, -scurest,** *v.*, **-scured, -scuring,** *n.* –*adj.* **1.** (of meaning) not clear or plain; uncertain. **2.** (of language, style, a speaker, etc.) not expressing the meaning clearly or plainly. **3.** inconspicuous or unnoticeable: *the obscure beginnings of a great movement.* **4.** of no prominence, note, or distinction. **5.** not readily seen; remote; retired, as a place. **6.** indistinct to the sight, or to some other sense. **7.** dark, as from lack of light or illumination; murky; dim. **8.** enveloped in, concealed by, or frequenting darkness. **9.** dark, dull, or not bright or lustrous, as colour or appearance. **10.** not clear to the mind; imperfectly understood; ambiguous; uncertain. –*v.t.* **11.** to make obscure, dark, dim, indistinct, etc. –*n.* **12.** darkness or obscurity. [ME, from L *obscūrus* dark, dim, unknown, ignoble] – **obscurely,** *adv.* – **obscureness,** *n.*

**obscurity** /əbˈskjurəti/, *n., pl.* **-ties. 1.** the state or quality of being obscure. **2.** uncertainty of meaning or expression. **3.** the condition of being unknown. **4.** an unknown or unimportant person or thing. **5.** darkness; dimness; indistinctness.

**obsecrate** /ˈɒbsəkreɪt/, *v.t.*, **-crated, -crating.** to entreat (a person, etc.) solemnly; beseech; supplicate. [L *obsecrātus,* pp.] – **obsecration** /ɒbsəˈkreɪʃən/, *n.*

**obsequious** /əbˈsikwiəs, ɒb-/, *adj.* **1.** servilely compliant or deferential: *obsequious servants.* **2.** characterised by or showing servile complaisance or deference: *an obsequious bow.* **3.** *Rare.* compliant; obedient; dutiful. [ME, from L *obsequiōsus*] – **obsequiously,** *adv.* – **obsequiousness,** *n.*

**obsequy** /ˈɒbsəkwi/, *n., pl.* **-quies.** (*usu. pl.*) a funeral rite or ceremony. [ME *obsequies,* from ML *obsequiae,* pl., (L *exsequiae*) funeral rites]

**observable** /əbˈzɜvəbəl/, *adj.* **1.** that may be or is to be noticed; noticeable; noteworthy. **2.** that may be or is to be followed or kept. – **observably,** *adv.*

**observance** /əbˈzɜvəns/, *n.* **1.** the action of conforming to, obeying or following: *observance of laws.* **2.** a keeping or celebration by appropriate procedure, ceremonies, etc. **3.** a procedure, ceremony, or rite, as for a particular occasion: *patriotic observances.* **4.** a rule or custom to be observed. **5.** *Rom. Cath. Ch.* **a.** a rule or discipline for a religious house or order. **b.** such a house or order. **6.** observation. **7.** respectful attention or service. **8.** *Archaic.* respectful or courteous attention; deference.

**observant** /əbˈzɜvənt/, *adj.* **1.** observing or regarding attentively; watchful. **2.** quick to notice or perceive; alert. **3.** careful in the observing of a law, custom, or the like. –*n.* **4.** an observer of law or rule. [ME, from L *observans,* ppr.] – **observantly,** *adv.*

**observation** /ɒbzəˈveɪʃən/, *n.* **1.** the act of noticing or perceiving. **2.** the act of regarding attentively or watching. **3.** the faculty or habit of observing or noticing. **4.** notice: *to escape a person's observation.* **5.** the act of viewing or noting something, for some scientific or other special purpose. **6.** the information or record secured thereby. **7.** that which is learned by observing. **8.** the fact or condition of being observed. **9.** an utterance by way of remark or comment. **10.** *Naut.* **a.** the measurement of the altitude of a celestial body to deduce a line of position for a vessel at sea. **b.** the result obtained. **11.** *Obs. or Rare.* observance, as of law, etc.

**observational** /ɒbzəˈveɪʃənəl/, *adj.* of, pertaining to, or founded on observation, esp. as contrasted with experiment.

**observation car** /ɒbzəˈveɪʃən ka/, *n.* a railway carriage usu. attached to the rear of a passenger train, designed to afford passengers an unobstructed view of passing scenery.

**observation post** /ˈ– poʊst/, *n.* a lookout position from which military targets may be observed and effective fire directed.

**observatory** /əbˈzɜvətri/, *n., pl.* **-tories. 1.** a place or building designed for making observations of astronomical, meteorological, or other natural phenomena, usu. equipped with a powerful telescope. **2.** an institution which controls or carries on the work of an observatory. **3.** a place or structure affording an extensive view.

**observe** /əbˈzɜv/, *v.*, **-served, -serving.** –*v.t.* **1.** to see, perceive, or notice. **2.** to regard with attention, so as to see or learn something. **3.** to make or take an observation of; to watch, view, or note for some scientific, official, or other special purpose: *to observe an eclipse.* **4.** to remark; comment. **5.** to keep or maintain in one's action, conduct, etc.: *you must observe the formalities.* **6.** to obey; comply with; conform to: *to observe a law.* **7.** to show regard for by some appropriate procedure, ceremonies, etc.: *to observe a holiday.* **8.** to perform duly, or solemnise (ceremonies, rites, etc.). –*v.i.* **9.** to notice. **10.** to act as an observer. **11.** to remark or comment (usu. fol. by *on* or *upon*). [ME *observe(n),* from L *observāre* watch, comply with, observe] – **observingly,** *adv.*

**observer** /əb'zɜvə/, *n.* **1.** one who or that which observes. **2.** one who accompanies the pilot of an aeroplane in order to observe. **3.** one who attends a meeting, etc. but does not take any official part in its activities.

**obsess** /əb'sɛs, ɒb-/, *v.t.* to beset, trouble, or dominate the thoughts, feelings, etc.; haunt: *obsessed by a fear of cancer.* [L *obsessus,* pp., besieged, beset] – **obsessive,** *adj.*

**obsession** /əb'sɛʃən/, *n.* **1.** the besetting or dominating action or influence of a persistent feeling, idea, or the like, which a person cannot escape. **2.** the feeling or idea itself. **3.** the state of being obsessed. **4.** the act of obsessing. – **obsessional,** *adj.*

**obsessive** /əb'sɛsɪv/, *adj.* **1.** of, pertaining to, or resembling an obsession. **2.** causing an obsession. **3.** excessive; extreme.

**obsidian** /ɒb'sɪdiən/, *n.* a volcanic glass, usu. of a dark colour and with a conchoidal fracture. [L *obsidiānus,* properly *obsiānus,* pertaining to *Obsius,* reputed discoverer of a similar mineral]

**obsolesc.,** obsolescent.

**obsolescent** /ɒbsə'lɛsənt/, *adj.* **1.** becoming obsolete; passing out of use, as a word. **2.** tending to become out of date, as machinery, weapons, etc. **3.** *Biol.* gradually disappearing, or imperfectly developed, as organs, marks, etc. [L *obsolescens,* ppr.] – **obsolescence,** *n.* – **obsolescently,** *adv.*

**obsolete** /'ɒbsəlit/, *adj.* **1.** fallen into disuse, or no longer in use: *an obsolete word.* **2.** of a discarded type; out of date: *an obsolete battleship.* **3.** effaced by wearing down or away. **4.** *Biol.* imperfectly developed or rudimentary in comparison with the corresponding character in other individuals, as of the opposite sex or of a related species. [L *obsolētus,* pp.] – **obsoletely,** *adv.* – **obsoleteness,** *n.*

**obstacle** /'ɒbstəkəl/, *n.* something that stands in the way or obstructs progress. [ME, from OF, from L *obstāculum*]

**obstacle race** /'– reɪs/, *n.* a race in which runners have to contend with both natural and artificial obstacles.

**obstet.,** **1.** obstetric. **2.** obstetrics.

**obstetric** /ɒb'stɛtrɪk, əb-/, *adj.* **1.** of or pertaining to the care and treatment of women in childbirth and during the period before and after delivery. **2.** of or pertaining to obstetrics. Also, **obstetrical.** [NL *obstētrīcus,* var. of L *obstētrīcius* pertaining to a midwife] – **obstetrically,** *adv.*

**obstetrician** /ɒbstə'trɪʃən/, *n.* one trained in obstetrics.

**obstetrics** /ɒb'stɛtrɪks, əb-/, *n.* the branch of medical art or science concerned with caring for and treating women in, before, and after childbirth; midwifery.

**obstinacy** /'ɒbstənəsi/, *n., pl.* **-cies. 1.** the quality or state of being obstinate. **2.** obstinate adherence to purpose, opinion, etc. **3.** stubborn persistence: *the soldiers fought with incredible obstinacy.* **4.** unyielding nature, as of a disease. **5.** an obstinate action; an instance of being obstinate. [ME, from ML *obstinātia*]

**obstinate** /'ɒbstənət/, *adj.* **1.** firmly and often perversely adhering to one's purpose, opinion, etc.; not yielding to argument, persuasion, or entreaty. **2.** inflexibly persisted in or carried out: *obstinate resistance.* **3.** not easily controlled: *the obstinate growth of weeds.* **4.** not yielding readily to treatment, as a disease. [ME *obstinat,* from L *obstinātus,* pp., determined] – **obstinately,** *adv.* – **obstinateness,** *n.*

**obstipant** /'ɒbstəpənt/, *n.* a substance that produces obstipation.

**obstipation** /ɒbstə'peɪʃən/, *n.* obstinate constipation. [L *obstipātio*]

**obstreperous** /əb'strɛpərəs, ɒb-/, *adj.* **1.** resisting control in a noisy manner; unruly. **2.** noisy or clamorous; boisterous. [L *obstreperus* clamorous] – **obstreperously,** *adv.* – **obstreperousness,** *n.*

**obstruct** /əb'strʌkt/, *v.t.* **1.** to block or close up, or make difficult of passage, with obstacles, as a way, road, channel, or the like. **2.** to interrupt, make difficult, or oppose the passage, progress, course, etc., of. **3.** to come in the way of or shut out (a view, etc.). [L *obstructus,* pp.] – **obstructer, obstructor,** *n.* – **obstructive,** *adj.* – **obstructively,** *adv.* – **obstructiveness,** *n.*

**obstruction** /əb'strʌkʃən/, *n.* **1.** something that obstructs; an obstacle or hindrance: *obstructions to navigation.* **2.** the act of obstructing. **3.** the retarding of business before a legislative group by parliamentary devices, or an attempt at such a retarding. **4.** the state of being obstructed. **5.** *Football, Hockey, etc.* a foul or infringement whereby a player interposes his body between an opponent and the ball so as to form an obstacle.

**obstructionist** /əb'strʌkʃənəst/, *n.* a person who obstructs something, esp. legislative business. – **obstructionism,** *n.*

**obstruent** /'ɒbstruənt/, *adj.* **1.** *Med.* (of a substance) producing an obstruction. **2.** *Phonet.* (of consonants) characterised by partial or complete constriction of the air stream as fricatives *f, z,* or stops *p, d,* etc. *–n.* **3.** *Med.* a medicine that closes the natural passages of the body. **4.** *Phonet.* an obstruent consonant. [L *obstruens,* ppr., blocking up]

**obtain** /əb'teɪn/, *v.t.* **1.** to come into possession of; get or acquire; procure, as by effort or request: *he obtained a knowledge of Greek.* **2.** *Obs. or Archaic.* to attain or reach. *–v.i.* **3.** to be prevalent, customary, or in vogue; hold good or be valid: *the morals that obtained in Rome.* **4.** *Obs. or Archaic.* to succeed. [ME *obteine(n),* from OF *obtenir,* from L *obtinēre* take hold of, get, prevail, continue] – **obtainable,** *adj.* – **obtainer,** *n.* – **obtainment,** *n.*

**obtect** /əb'tɛkt/, *adj.* denoting any insect pupa in which the antennae, legs, and wings are glued to the surface of the body by a hardened secretion. Also, **obtected.** [L *obtectus,* pp., covered over]

**obtest** /ɒb'tɛst/, *v.t.* **1.** to invoke as witness. **2.** to supplicate earnestly; beseech. *–v.i.* **3.** to protest. [L *obtestārī* call as a witness] – **obtestation** /ɒbtɛs'teɪʃən/, *n.*

**obtrude** /əb'trud/, *v.,* **-truded, -truding.** *–v.t.* **1.** to thrust forward or upon a person, esp. without warrant or invitation: *to obtrude one's opinions upon others.* **2.** to thrust forth; push out. *–v.i.* **3.** to thrust oneself or itself forward, esp. unduly; intrude. [L *obtrūdere* thrust upon or into] – **obtruder,** *n.*

**obtrusion** /əb'truʒən/, *n.* **1.** the act of obtruding. **2.** something obtruded.

**obtrusive** /əb'trusɪv, -zɪv/, *adj.* **1.** having or showing a disposition to obtrude. **2.** (of a thing) obtruding itself. **3.** projecting. **4.** showy; undesirably obvious. – **obtrusively,** *adv.* – **obtrusiveness,** *n.*

**obtund** /ɒb'tʌnd/, *v.t.* to blunt; dull; deaden. [ME, from L *obtundere* beat, strike at] – **obtundent,** *adj.*

**obturate** /'ɒbtʃəreɪt/, *v.t.,* **-rated, -rating. 1.** to stop up; close. **2.** *Ordn.* to seal (a gunbreach) to prevent gas from escaping when the gun is fired. [L *obtūrātus,* pp.] – **obturation** /ɒbtʃə'reɪʃən/, *n.*

**obturator** /'ɒbtʃəreɪtə/, *n.* **1.** that which stops or closes. **2.** a prosthesis used by those with cleft palates in an attempt to provide more normal naso-pharyngeal function. [OBTURATE + -OR[2]]

**obtuse** /əb'tjus, ɒb-/, *adj.* **1.** blunt in form; not sharp or acute. **2.** (of a leaf, petal, etc.) rounded at the extremity. **3.** not sensitive or observant; stupid; dull in perception, feeling, or intellect. **4.** indistinctly felt or perceived, as pain, sound, etc. [L *obtūsus,* pp., dulled] – **obtusely,** *adv.* – **obtuseness,** *n.*

**obtuse angle** /– 'æŋgəl/, *n.* an angle exceeding 90° but less than 180°.


ADE, obtuse angle; BDE, right angle; CDE, straight line

**obv.,** obverse.

**obverse** /'ɒbvɜs/, *n.* **1.** that side of a coin, medal, etc., which bears the head or principal design (opposed to *reverse*). **2.** the front or principal face of anything. **3.** a counterpart. **4.** *Logic.* a proposition obtained from another by obversion. *–adj.* **5.** turned towards or facing one. **6.** corresponding to something else as a counterpart. **7.** having the base narrower than the top, as a leaf. [L *obversus,* pp., turned towards or against] – **obversely** /ɒb'vɜsli/, *adv.*

**obversion** /ɒb'vɜʒən/, *n.* **1.** the act or result of obverting. **2.** *Logic.* a form of inference in which a negative proposition is inferred from an affirmative or an affirmative from a negative.

**obvert** /ɒb'vɜt/, *v.t.* **1.** to turn (something) towards an object. **2.** *Logic.* to change (a proposition) by obversion. [L *obvertere* turn towards or against]

**obviate** /ˈɒbvieɪt/, *v.t.*, **-ated, -ating.** to meet and dispose of or prevent (difficulties, objections, etc.) by effective measures: *to obviate the necessity of beginning again.* [LL *obviātus*, pp., met., opposed, prevented] – **obviation** /ɒbviˈeɪʃən/, *n.*

**obvious** /ˈɒbviəs/, *adj.* **1.** clearly perceptible or evident; easily recognised or understood; open to view or knowledge: *an obvious advantage.* **2.** *Obs.* being or standing in the way. [L *obvius* in the way, meeting] – **obviously,** *adv.* – **obviousness,** *n.*

**obvolute** /ˈɒbvəlut/, *adj.* **1.** rolled or turned in. **2.** *Bot.* denoting or pertaining to a kind of vernation in which two leaves are folded together in the bud so that one half of each is exterior and the other interior. [L *obvolūtus*, pp., wrapped up] – **obvolution** /ɒbvəˈluʃən/, *n.* – **obvolutive,** *adj.*

**oc-,** variant of **ob-** (by assimilation) before *c*, as in *Occident.*

**o.c.,** in the work cited. [L *opere citātō*]

**Oc.,** ocean. Also, **oc.**

**O.C.** /oʊ ˈsi/, Officer Commanding.

**ocarina** /ɒkəˈrinə/, *n.* a simple musical wind instrument shaped somewhat like an elongated egg, with finger holes. [probably diminutive of It. *oca* goose, with reference to the shape]

**Occam's razor** /ɒkəmz ˈreɪzə/, *n.* the principle that entities must not be unnecessarily multiplied, which as the principle of economy of hypothesis, is applicable to scientific research. [from William of *Occam,* d. 1349 ?, English scholastic philospher]

**occas.,** **1.** occasion.

**occasion** /əˈkeɪʒən/, *n.* **1.** a particular time, esp. as marked by certain circumstances or occurrences: *on several occasions.* **2.** a special or important time, event, ceremony, function, etc. **3.** a convenient or favourable juncture or time; opportunity. **4.** the ground, reason, immediate or incidental cause of some action or result. **5.** (*usu. pl.*) *Obs.* need or necessity. **6.** (*pl.*) *Obs.* necessary business matters: *to go about one's lawful occasions.* **7. on occasion,** now and then; occasionally. **8. rise to the occasion,** to show oneself equal to a task. *–v.t.* **9.** to give occasion or cause for; bring about. [ME, from L *occāsio* opportunity, fit time]

**occasional** /əˈkeɪʒənəl/, *adj.* **1.** occurring or appearing on one occasion or another or now and then: *an occasional visitor.* **2.** intended for use whenever needed: *an occasional table.* **3.** pertaining to, arising out of, or intended for a special occasion, ceremony, etc.: *occasional verses; occasional decrees.* **4.** acting or serving for the occasion or on particular occasions. **5.** serving as the occasion or incidental cause.

**occasionalism** /əˈkeɪʒənəlɪzəm/, *n.* the doctrine that the apparent interaction of mind and matter is to be explained by the supposition that God takes an act of the will as the occasion of producing a corresponding movement of the body, and a state of the body as the occasion of producing a corresponding mental state. – **occasionalist,** *n.*

**occasionally** /əˈkeɪʒənəli/, *adv.* at times; now and then.

**Occident** /ˈɒksədənt/, *n.* **1.** countries in Europe and America (contrasted with the *Orient*). **2.** the Western Hemisphere. **3.** (*l.c.*) the west; the western regions. [ME, from L *occidens* the west, sunset; properly ppr., going down]

**occidental** /ɒksəˈdɛntl/, *adj.* **1.** (*usu. cap.*) of, pertaining to, or characteristic of the Occident. **2.** western. *–n.* **3.** (*usu. cap.*) a native or inhabitant of the Occident. [ME, from L *occidentālis* western] – **occidentally,** *adv.*

**Occidentalise** /ɒksəˈdɛntəlaɪz/, *v.t.*, **-lised, -lising.** to make Occidental. Also, **Occidentalize.** – **Occidentalisation** /ˌɒksədɛntəlaɪˈzeɪʃən/, *n.*

**Occidentalism** /ɒksəˈdɛntəlɪzəm/, *n.* Occidental character or characteristics. – **Occidentalist,** *n., adj.*

**occipital** /ɒkˈsɪpətl/, *adj.* of or pertaining to the back of the head. [ML *occipitālis,* from *occiput* OCCIPUT]

**occipital bone** /ˈ– boʊn/, *n.* a compound bone which forms the lower posterior part of the skull.

**occipito-,** a word element meaning 'occiput', as in *occipitofrontal* (pertaining to both occiput and forehead), *occipitohyoid* (pertaining to both the occipital and the hyoid bone), *occipitoparietal, occipitosphenoid.* [combining form representing L *occiput*]

**occiput** /ˈɒksɪpʊt/, *n., pl.* **occipita** /ɒkˈsɪpətə/. the back part of the head or skull. [ME, from L]

**occlude** /əˈklud/, *v.,* **-cluded, -cluding.** *–v.t.* **1.** to close, shut, or stop up (a passage, etc.). **2.** to shut in, out, or off. **3.** *Chem.* (of certain metals and other solids) to absorb and retain gases or liquids, in minute pores. *–v.i.* **4.** *Dentistry.* to shut or close against each other, as the opposing teeth of the upper and lower jaws. [L *occlūdere* shut up, close up] – **occludent,** *adj.*

**occluded front** /əkludəd ˈfrʌnt/, *n. Meteorol.* the residual front after the cold front of a depression has overtaken the warm front and the warm sector has been lifted. Also, **occlusion.**

**occlusion** /əˈkluʒən/, *n.* **1.** the action of occluding or fact of being occluded. **2.** *Dentistry.* the contact between the teeth of the upper and lower jaws when the jaws are closed. **3.** *Phonet.* the complete closure of the breath passage in the articulation of a sound. **4.** *Meteorol.* **a.** the forming of an occluded front. **b.** an occluded front.

**occlusive** /əˈklusɪv/, *adj.* **1.** occluding or tending to occlude. **2.** *Phonet.* of or pertaining to a consonant made by the complete closure of the breath passage. *–n.* **3.** a consonant made by a complete closure of the breath passage; a plosive or a stop consonant.

**occult** /ˈɒkʌlt, əˈkʌlt/, *adj.* **1.** beyond the bounds of ordinary knowledge; mysterious. **2.** not disclosed; secret; communicated only to the initiated. **3.** (in early science) **a.** not apparent on mere inspection but discoverable by experimentation. **b.** of a nature not understood, as physical qualities. **c.** dealing with such qualities; experimental: *occult science.* **4.** of the nature of, or pertaining to, certain reputed sciences, as magic, astrology, etc., involving the alleged knowledge or employment of secret or mysterious agencies. **5.** *Obs. or Rare.* hidden from view. *–n.* **6.** occult studies or sciences. **7.** the supernatural. **8.** anything occult. *–v.t.* **9.** to hide; shut off (an object) from view. **10.** *Astron.* to hide (a body) by occultation. *–v.i.* **11.** to become hidden or shut off from view. **12.** (of a light) to shut off periodically, as in lighthouses, etc. [L *occultus*, pp., covered over, concealed] – **occulter,** *n.*

**occultation** /ɒkʌlˈteɪʃən/, *n.* **1.** *Astron.* the passage of one celestial body in front of a second, thus hiding the second from view (applied esp. to the moon's coming between an observer and a star or planet). **2.** disappearance from view or notice. **3.** the act of occulting. **4.** the resulting state.

**occultism** /ˈɒkʌltɪzəm/, *n.* the doctrine or study of the occult. – **occultist,** *n., adj.*

**occupancy** /ˈɒkjəpənsi/, *n.* **1.** the fact or condition of being an occupant. **2.** the act of taking possession. **3.** actual possession. **4.** the term during which one is an occupant. **5.** exercise of dominion over a thing which has no owner so as to become legal owner.

**occupant** /ˈɒkjəpənt/, *n.* **1.** one who occupies. **2.** a tenant of a house, estate, office, etc. **3.** *Law.* an owner through occupancy. [L *occupans,* ppr.]

**occupation** /ɒkjəˈpeɪʃən/, *n.* **1.** one's habitual employment; business, trade, or calling. **2.** that in which one is engaged. **3.** possession, as of a place. **4.** the act of occupying. **5.** the state of being occupied. **6.** tenure, as of an office. **7.** seizure, esp. of the territory of a foreign country, as by invasion. **8.** the period during which a country is under the control of foreign military forces. [ME *occupacion,* from L *occupātio* seizing, employment]

**occupational** /ɒkjəˈpeɪʃənəl/, *adj.* **1.** of or pertaining to occupation. **2.** of, pertaining to, arising from, or connected with an occupation, trade, or calling: *an occupational disease, occupational guidance, occupational hazard.*

**occupational psychology** /– saɪˈkɒlədʒi/, *n.* the branch of psychology which deals with people at work, esp. in relationship to environmental influences, stress, worker-management relationships, etc.

**occupational therapy** /– ˈθɛrəpi/, *n.* a method of therapy consisting of some kind of light work, such as basketry, carpentry, etc., which provides mental diversion or relaxation for the patient, and frequently serves to exercise an affected part or to give vocational training.

**occupier** /ˈɒkjəpaɪə/, *n.* a person having the legal right to reside, or who is residing, in a house, land. etc.

**occupy** /ˈɒkjəpaɪ/, *v.*, **-pied, -pying.** *–v.t.* **1.** to take up (space, time, etc.). **2.** to engage or employ (the mind, attention, etc., or the person). **3.** to take possession of (a place), as by invasion. **4.** to hold (a position, office, etc.). **5.** to be resident or established in (a place) as its tenant; to tenant. *–v.i.* **6.** *Rare or Obs.* to take or hold possession. [ME *occupie(n)*, from OF *occuper*, from L *occupāre* take possession of, take up, employ]

**occur** /əˈkɜ/, *v.i.*, **-curred, -curring.** **1.** to come to pass, take place, or happen. **2.** to be met with or found; present itself; appear. **3.** to suggest itself in thought (usu. fol. by *to*): *an idea occurred to me.* [earlier *occurr*, from L *occurrere* run against, go up to, meet, befall]

**occurrence** /əˈkʌrəns/, *n.* **1.** the action or fact of occurring. **2.** something that occurs; an event or incident: *a daily occurrence.* – **occurrent,** *adj.*

**ocean** /ˈoʊʃən/, *n.* **1.** the vast body of salt water which covers almost three fourths of the earth's surface. **2.** any of the geographical divisions of this body (commonly given as five: the Atlantic, Pacific, Indian, Arctic, and Antarctic oceans). **3.** a vast expanse or quantity: *an ocean of grass.* [L *ōceanus*, from Gk *ōkeanós* the ocean, orig. the great stream supposed to encompass the earth; replacing ME *occean*, from OF] – **ocean-like,** *adj.*

**oceanarium** /oʊʃənˈɛəriəm/, *n.* an enclosed part of the sea or a large salt-water pool, in which dolphins, porpoises, and other sea fauna are kept.

**oceanaut** /ˈoʊʃənɔt/, *n.* an aqualung diver who lives in an underwater shelter for long periods, esp. to study or exploit the resources of the sea.

**ocean beach** /ˈoʊʃən bitʃ/, *n.* →**surf beach.**

**ocean-going** /ˈoʊʃən-goʊɪŋ/, *adj.* denoting any vessel designed for sailing on the open sea.

**Oceania** /oʊʃiˈeɪniə, oʊsi-/, *n.* the islands of the Pacific grouped collectively, sometimes including Australia.

**oceanic** /oʊʃiˈænɪk, oʊsi-/, *adj.* **1.** of or belonging to the ocean; pelagic. **2.** ocean-like; vast.

**oceanics** /oʊʃiˈænɪks, oʊsi-/, *n.* the scientific study of oceans.

**oceanid** /oʊˈʃiənəd/, *n.* an ocean nymph. [Gk *Okeanís* from *Okeanós*, Oceanus, the god of the ocean]

**oceanog.,** oceanography.

**oceanography** /oʊʃənˈɒgrəfi/, *n.* the branch of physical geography dealing with the ocean. – **oceanographer,** *n.* – **oceanographic** /oʊʃənəˈgræfɪk/, **oceanographical** /oʊʃənəˈgræfɪkəl/, *adj.* – **oceanographically** /oʊʃənəˈgræfɪkli/, *adv.*

**ocellar** /oʊˈsɛlə/, *adj.* pertaining to an ocellus.

**ocellated** /ˈɒsəleɪtəd, oʊˈsɛleɪtəd/, *adj.* **1.** (of a spot or marking) eyelike. **2.** having ocelli, or eyelike spots. Also, **ocellate** /ˈɒsəleɪt, oʊˈsɛlət, -eɪt/. [L *ocellātus* having little eyes + -ED[2]]

**ocellation** /ɒsəˈleɪʃən/, *n.* an eyelike spot or marking.

**ocellus** /oʊˈsɛləs/, *n.*, *pl.* **ocelli** /oʊˈsɛlaɪ/. **1.** a type of eye common to invertebrates, consisting of retinal cells, pigments, and nerve fibres. **2.** an eyelike spot, as on a peacock feather. [L, diminutive of *oculus* eye]

**ocelot** /ˈɒsəlɒt/, *n.* a spotted, leopard-like cat, *Felis paradalis*, ranging from the central southern U.S. to central South America. [F, from Nahuatl *ocelotl* field tiger]

**ochlocracy** /ɒkˈlɒkrəsi/, *n.*, *pl.* **-cies.** government by the mob; mobocracy; mob rule. [Gk *ochlokratía* mob rule] – **ochlocrat** /ˈɒkləkræt/, *n.* – **ochlocratic** /ɒkləˈkraetɪk/, **ochlocratical** /ɒkləˈkrætɪkəl/, *adj.*

**ochlophobia** /ɒkləˈfoʊbiə/, *n.* fear of crowds. [Gk *óchlos* crowd, mob + -PHOBIA]

**ochna** /ˈɒknə/, *n.* any tree or shrub of the large tropical genus *Ochna*, as *O. atropurpurea*, a shrub with toothed leaves, yellow flowers, red sepals, and black drupes surrounding a bright-red receptacle.

**ochre** /ˈoʊkə/, *n.*, *adj.*, *v.*, **ochred, ochring.** *–n.* **1.** any of a class of natural earths, mixtures of hydrated oxide of iron with various earthy materials, ranging in colour from pale yellow to orange and red, and used as pigments. **2.** the colour of this, ranging from pale yellow to an orange or reddish yellow. *–adj.* **3.** of the colour of ochre. *–v.t.* **4.** to colour or mark with ochre. Also, *U.S.*, **ocher.** [ME *oker*, from OF *ocre*, from L *ōchra*, from Gk: yellow ochre] – **ochreous** /ˈoʊkriəs, ˈoʊkərəs/, **ochrous** /ˈoʊkrəs/, **ochry** /ˈoʊkəri, ˈoʊkri/, *adj.*

**ochroid** /ˈoʊkrɔɪd/, *adj.* yellow as ochre. [Gk *ōchroeidḗs* pallid]

**-ock,** a noun suffix used to make descriptive names, as in *ruddock* (lit., the red one); diminutives, as in *hillock;* etc. [ME *-ok*, OE *-oc, -uc*]

**ocker** /ˈɒkə/, *n. Colloq.* **1.** the archetypal uncultivated Australian working man. **2.** a boorish, uncouth, chauvinistic Australian. **3.** an Australian male displaying qualities considered to be typically Australian, as good humour, helpfulness, and resourcefulness. *–adj.* **4.** of or pertaining to an ocker. **5.** distinctively Australian: *an ocker sense of humour.* Also, **okker.** [var. of *Oscar*, esp. the character in the television program by Ron Frazer] – **ockerish,** *adj.*

**ockerdom** /ˈɒkədəm/, *n. Colloq.* (*derog.*) the society of ockers (def. 2).

**ockerina** /ɒkəˈrinə/, *n. Colloq.* (*joc.*) an ocker's female counterpart.

**ockie strap** /ˈɒki stræp/, *n. Colloq.* →**octopus strap.**

**o'clock** /əˈklɒk/, *adv.* of or by the clock (used in specifying or enquiring the hour of the day): *it is now one o'clock.*

**OCR** /ˈoʊkə/, *n.* a system of machine reading by a light-sensitive electrical cell of standard character sets encoded on documents such as gas bills, etc. [*O(ptical) C(haracter) R(ecognition)*]

**ocrea** /ˈɒkriə/, *n.*, *pl.* **ocreae** /ˈɒkrii/. a sheathing part, as a pair of stipules united about a stem. Also, **ochrea.** [L: greave, legging]

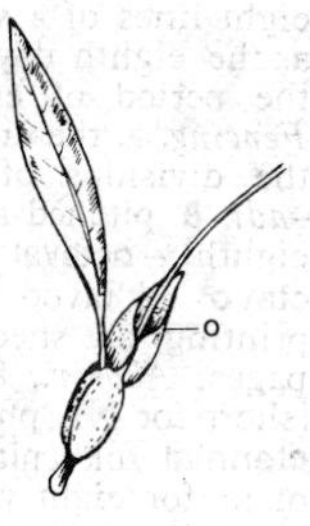

O, ocrea

**ocreate** /ˈɒkriət, -eɪt/, *adj.* having an ocrea or ocreae; sheathed.

**oct-,** variant of **octa-** or **octo-** before a vowel.

**oct.,** octavo.

**Oct.,** October.

**octa-,** a word element meaning 'eight'. Also, **oct-, octo-.** [Gk, combining form of *oktṓ*]

**octad** /ˈɒktæd/, *n.* **1.** a group or series of eight. **2.** *Chem.* an element, atom, or radical having a valency of eight. [LL *octas*, from Gk *oktás*] – **octadic** /ɒkˈtædɪk/, *adj.*

**octagon** /ˈɒktəgɒn, -gən/, *n.* a polygon having eight angles and eight sides. [Gk *oktágōnos* octangular. See OCTA-, -GON]

octagon

**octagonal** /ɒkˈtægənəl/, *adj.* having eight angles and eight sides. – **octagonally,** *adv.*

**octahedral** /ɒktəˈhidrəl/, *adj.* having the form of an octahedron.

**octahedrite** /ɒktəˈhidraɪt/, *n.* →**anatase.**

**octahedron** /ɒktəˈhidrən/, *n.*, *pl.* **-drons, -dra** /-drə/. a solid figure having eight faces. [Gk *oktáedron.* See OCTA-, -HEDRON]

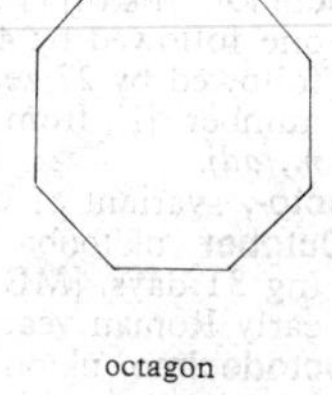
regular octahedrons

**octal** /ˈɒktl/, *adj.* of or pertaining to a number system based on the number 'eight'.

**octamerous** /ɒkˈtæmərəs/, *adj.* consisting of or divided into eight parts. [Gk *oktamerḗs* of eight parts + -OUS]

**octameter** /ɒkˈtæmətə/, *adj.* **1.** having eight measures or feet to a line of verse. *–n.* **2.** an octameter verse. [LL, from Gk *oktámetros* of eight measures]

**octan** /ˈɒktən/, *adj.* recurring every eighth day.

**octane** /ˈɒkteɪn/, *n.* any of eighteen isomeric saturated hydrocarbons, $C_8H_{18}$, some of which are obtained in the distillation and cracking of petroleum. [OCT- + -ANE]

**octane number** /ˈ– nʌmbə/, *n.* (of a grade of petrol) a designation of antiknock quality, numerically equal to the percentage of iso-octane by volume in a mixture of iso-octane and normal heptane that matches the given grade of petrol in antiknock characteristics. Also, **octane rating.**

**octangular** /ɒk'tæŋgjələ/, *adj.* having eight angles. [L *octangulus* eight-angled + -AR[1]]

**octant** /'ɒktənt/, *n.* **1.** the eighth part of a circle. **2.** *Maths.* each of the eighths into which three mutually perpendicular planes with a common point divide space. **3.** an instrument similar to a sextant, having a graduated arc of 45°, used for measuring angles, esp. in navigation. **4.** the position of one heavenly body when 45° distant from another. [L *octans*] – **octantal** /ɒk'tæntl/, *adj.*

**octarchy** /'ɒktaki/, *n., pl.* **-chies. 1.** a government by eight persons. **2.** a group of eight states or kingdoms.

**octastyle** /'ɒktəstaɪl/, *adj.* denoting a portico having eight frontal columns.

**octave** /'ɒktɪv/; *for def. 6,* /'ɒktəɪv/. *n.* **1.** *Music.* **a.** a note on the eighth degree from a given note (counted as the first). **b.** the interval between such notes. **c.** the harmonic combination of such notes. **d.** a series of notes, or of keys of an instrument, extending through this interval. **2.** (in organ building) a stop whose pipes give notes an octave above the normal pitch of the keys used. **3.** a series or group of eight. **4.** *Pros.* a group or a stanza of eight lines, as the first eight lines of a sonnet. **5.** the eighth of a series. **6.** *Eccles.* **a.** the eighth day from a feast day (counted as the first). **b.** the period of eight days beginning with a feast day. **7.** *Fencing.* **a.** the eighth of eight defensive positions. **b.** one of the divisions of the target area on an opponent's body. *–adj.* **8.** pitched an octave higher. [ME, from L *octāva* (fem.) eighth] – **octaval** /ɒk'teɪvəl, 'ɒktəvəl/, *adj.*

**octavo** /ɒk'tavoʊ, -'teɪv-/, *n.* **1.** a book size determined by printing on sheets folded to form eight leaves or sixteen pages. *Abbrev.:* 8vo *or* 8° *–adj.* **2.** in octavo. Also, **eightvo.** [short for NL phrase *in octāvō* in an eighth (of a sheet)]

**octennial** /ɒk'tɛniəl/, *adj.* **1.** occurring every eight years. **2.** of or for eight years. [LL *octennium* a period of eight years + -AL[1]] – **octennially,** *adv.*

**octet** /ɒk'tɛt/, *n.* **1.** a company of eight singers or players. **2.** a musical composition for eight voices or instruments. **3.** *Pros.* a group of eight lines of verse, esp. the first eight lines (octave) of a sonnet. **4.** *Chem.* a stable group of eight electrons which form a shell surrounding an atomic nucleus. **5.** any group of eight. Also, **octette.** [OCT(O)- + *-et* as in *duet*]

**octillion** /ɒk'tɪljən/, *n.* **1.** a cardinal number represented by one followed by 48 zeros or (in the U.S. and France) by one followed by 27 zeros. *–adj.* **2.** amounting to one octillion in number. [F, from *oct-* OCT- + *(m)illion* MILLION] – **octillionth,** *n., adj.*

**octo-,** variant of **octa-.**

**October** /ɒk'toʊbə/, *n.* the tenth month of the year, containing 31 days. [ME and OE, from L: the eighth month of the early Roman year]

**octodecimo** /ɒktoʊ'dɛsəmoʊ/, *n., pl.* **-mos,** *adj.* *–n.* **1.** a book size determined by printing on sheets folded to form eighteen leaves or thirty-six pages; eighteenmo. *Abbrev.:* 18mo *or* 18° *–adj.* **2.** in octodecimo. [short for NL phrase *in octōdecimō* in an eighteenth (of a sheet)]

**octogenarian** /,ɒktoʊdʒə'nɛəriən/, *adj.* Also, **octogenary** /ɒk'tɒdʒənəri/. **1.** of the age of 80 years. **2.** between 80 and 90 years old. *–n.* **3.** an octogenarian person. [L *octōgēnārius* containing eighty + -AN]

**octonary** /'ɒktənəri/, *adj., n., pl.* **-naries.** *–adj.* **1.** pertaining to the number eight. **2.** consisting of eight. **3.** proceeding by eights. *–n.* **4.** a group of eight; an ogdoad. **5.** *Pros.* eight lines, as a stanza. [L *octōnārius* containing eight]

**octopod** /'ɒktəpɒd/, *n.* any of the Octopoda, an order or suborder of eight-armed dibranchiate cephalopods that includes the octopuses and paper nautiluses.

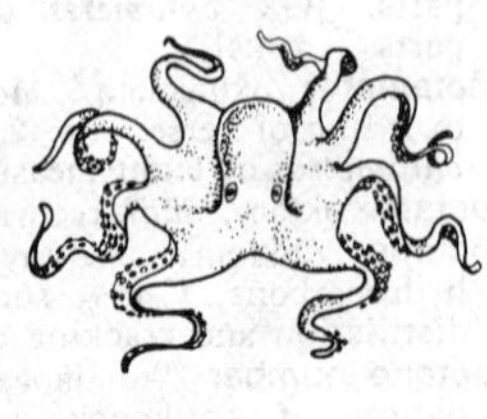
octopus

**octopus** /'ɒktəpəs, -pʊs/, *n., pl.* **-puses, -pi** /-paɪ/. **1.** any animal of the genus *Octopus,* comprising octopods with a soft, oval body and eight suckerbearing arms, and living mostly on the sea bottom. **2.** →**spider** (def. 4). **3.** any octopod. **4.** anything likened to an octopus. [NL, from Gk *oktṓpous* eight-footed]

**octopus clamp** /'– klæmp/, *n.* a complex leg-hold formerly used in professional wrestling.

**octopus strap** /'– stræp/, *n.* a stretchable rope with hooks on either end used for securing luggage to roof-racks, etc.

**octoroon** /ɒktə'run/, *n.* a person having one-eighth Negro ancestry; offspring of a quadroon and a white. [OCTO- + *-roon,* modelled on QUADROON]

**octosyllable** /'ɒktoʊ,sɪləbəl/, *n.* a word or a line of verse of eight syllables. – **octosyllabic** /,ɒktoʊsə'læbɪk/, *adj.*

**octuple** /'ɒktəpəl, ɒk'tjupəl/, *adj., v.,* **-pled, -pling.** *–adj.* **1.** eightfold; eight times as great. **2.** having eight effective units or elements. *–v.t.* **3.** to make eight times as great. [L *octuplus* eightfold]

**octuplet** /ɒk'tʌplət, -'tju-/, *n.* **1.** any group or combination of eight related items. **2.** *Music.* a group of eight notes to be played or sung in the time of six.

**ocular** /'ɒkjələ/, *adj.* **1.** of or pertaining to the eye: *ocular movements.* **2.** of the nature of an eye: *an ocular organ.* **3.** performed or perceived by the eye or eyesight. *–n.* **4.** the eyepiece of an optical instrument. [LL *oculāris* of the eyes] – **ocularly,** *adv.*

**oculist** /'ɒkjələst/, *n.* a doctor of medicine skilled in the examination and treatment of the eye; an ophthalmologist. [F *oculiste,* from L *oculus* eye + *-iste* -IST]

**oculomotor** /ɒkjəloʊ'moʊtə/, *adj.* moving the eyeball. [*oculo-* (combining form representing L *oculus* eye) + MOTOR]

**oculomotor nerve** /– 'nɜv/, *n.* either of the two cranial nerves which supply most of the muscles of the eyeball.

**oculus** /'ɒkjələs/, *n.* a decorative motif consisting of paired circles or spirals.

**o.d.,** overdose.

**Od** /ɒd/, *interj. Archaic.* reduced form of **God,** used interjectionally and in minced oaths. Also, **'Od, Odd.**

**OD** /oʊ 'di/, *n., v.,* **OD'd, OD-ing.** *Colloq.* *–n.* **1.** an overdose, esp. of an injected addictive drug, as heroin. **2.** *(joc.)* a surfeit. *–v.i.* **3.** to give oneself an overdose (fol. by *on*). **4.** *(joc.)* to consume to excess; have a surfeit (fol. by *on*): *I OD'd on icecream.*

**O/D** /oʊ 'di/, **1.** on demand. **2.** overdraft. **3.** overdrawn.

**odalisque** /'ɒdəlɪsk/, *n.* a female slave or concubine in a harem, esp. in that of the Sultan of Turkey. Also, **odalisk.** [F, from Turk. *ōdalik,* from *ōdah* room]

**odd** /ɒd/, *adj.* **1.** differing in character from what is ordinary or usual: *an odd choice.* **2.** singular or peculiar in a freakish or eccentric way, as persons or their manners, etc. **3.** fantastic or bizarre, as things. **4.** out-of-the-way; secluded. **5.** (of a number) leaving a remainder of one when divided by two (opposed to **even**). **6.** additional to a whole mentioned in round numbers; being a surplus over a definite quantity; more or less: *she owed him fifty-odd dollars.* **7.** additional to what is taken into account: *ten dollars and a few odd cents.* **8.** being part of a pair, set, or series of which the rest is lacking: *an odd glove.* **9.** (of a pair) not matching: *he was wearing odd shoes.* **10.** remaining after a division into pairs, or into equal numbers or parts. **11.** left over after the rest have been consumed, used up, etc. **12.** occasional or casual: *odd jobs.* **13.** not forming part of any particular group, set, or class: *odd bits of information.* **14. odd man out,** one left over when the rest have been arranged in pairs, or in a convenient group or groups. *–n.* **15.** that which is odd. **16.** *Golf.* **a.** a stroke more than the opponent has played. **b.** a stroke taken from a player's total score for a hole in order to give him odds. See also **odds.** [ME *odde,* from Scand.; cf. Icel. *odda-tala* odd number] – **oddly,** *adv.* – **oddness,** *n.*

**oddball** /'ɒdbɔl/, *Colloq.* *–n.* **1.** one who is unusual or peculiar; an eccentric. *–adj.* **2.** unusual; eccentric.

**odd bod** /ɒd bɒd/, *n.* an eccentric person, esp. one with a particular fixation. – **odd-bod,** *adj.*

**oddish** /'ɒdɪʃ/, *adj.* rather odd; queer.

**oddity** /'ɒdəti/, *n., pl.* **-ties. 1.** the quality of being odd; singularity or strangeness. **2.** an odd characteristic or peculiarity. **3.** an odd person or thing.

**odd-job man** /ɒd-'dʒɒb mæn/, *n.* one who does odd jobs, as household repairs, gardening, etc.

**odd lot** /ˈɒd lɒt/, *n.* a number of shares which is not a marketable parcel.

**oddment** /ˈɒdmənt/, *n.* **1.** an odd article, bit, remnant, or the like. **2.** an article belonging to a broken or incomplete set. **3.** *Print.* any individual portion of a book excluding the text, as the frontispiece, index, etc.

**odd-pinnate** /ɒd-ˈpɪneɪt/, *adj.* pinnate with an odd terminal leaflet.

**odds** /ɒdz/, *n.* (*usu. construed as pl.*) **1.** an equalising allowance, as that given to a weaker side in a contest. **2.** the amount by which the bet of one party to a wager exceeds that of the other. **3.** balance of probability in favour of something occurring or being the case. **4.** advantage or superiority on the side of one of two contending parties: *to strive against odds.* **5.** difference in the way of benefit or detriment. **6.** the amount of difference. **7. at odds,** in disagreement; at variance. **8. make no odds,** not to matter; be of no importance. **9. odds and ends,** odd bits; scraps; remnants; fragments. **10. over the odds,** too much. **11. what's the odds?,** *Colloq.* what difference does it make?

**odds and sods,** *n.pl.* a miscellaneous collection of people or things.

**odds-on** /ˈɒdz-ɒn/, *adj.* (of a chance) better than even; that is more likely to win, succeed, etc.

**ode** /oʊd/, *n.* **1.** a lyric poem typically of elaborate or irregular metrical form and expressive of exalted emotion. **2.** (originally) a poem intended to be sung. **3. regular** or **Pindaric ode,** a complex poetic type, consisting of strophes and antistrophes identical in form, with contrasting epodes, the three units being repeated in the poem. **4. irregular, pseudo-Pindaric,** or **Cowleian ode,** a poetic form in the general style of the regular ode, but lacking its strict complex form and written in a series of irregular strophes. **5. Horatian** or **Sapphic ode,** an ode in which one stanzaic form is repeated. [F, from LL *ōda,* from Gk *ōidḗ,* contraction of *aoidḗ* song]

**-ode**[1], a suffix of nouns denoting something having some resemblance to what is indicated by the preceding part of the word, as in *phyllode.* [Gk *-ōdēs* like, contraction of *-oeidḗs* -OID]

**-ode**[2], a noun suffix meaning 'way', as in *anode, electrode.* [Gk *-odos,* from *hodós* way]

**odeum** /oʊˈdiəm, ˈoʊdiəm/, *n., pl.* **odea** /oʊˈdiə, ˈoʊdiə/. **1.** a hall or structure for musical or dramatic performances. **2.** (in ancient Greece and Rome) a roofed building for musical performances. [L, from Gk *ōideîon* music hall]

**odic** /ˈoʊdɪk/, *adj.* of an ode. [ODE + -IC]

**odious** /ˈoʊdiəs/, *adj.* **1.** deserving of or exciting hatred; hateful or detestable. **2.** highly offensive; disgusting. [ME, from L *odiōsus* hateful] – **odiously,** *adv.* – **odiousness,** *n.*

**odium** /ˈoʊdiəm/, *n.* **1.** hatred; dislike. **2.** the reproach, discredit, or opprobrium attaching to something hated or odious. **3.** the state of being hated. [L: hatred]

**odograph** /ˈɒdəgræf, -graf/, *n.* **1.** →**odometer. 2.** →**pedometer.** [var. of HODOGRAPH]

**odometer** /ɒˈdɒmətə, oʊ-/, *n.* an instrument for measuring distance passed over, as by a motor vehicle. Also, **hodometer.** [var. of *hodometer,* from Gk *hodó(s)* way + -METER[1]] – **odometry,** *n.*

**odont-,** variant of **odonto-** before a vowel.

**-odont,** a terminal word element equivalent to **odonto-.**

**odontalgia** /ɒdɒnˈtældʒə/, *n.* toothache. – **odontalgic,** *adj.*

**odonto-,** a word element meaning 'tooth'. Also, **odont-.** [Gk, combining form of *odoús*]

**odontoblast** /ɒˈdɒntəblæst/, *n.* one of a layer of cells which, in the development of a tooth, give rise to the dentine. – **odontoblastic** /ɒˌdɒntəˈblæstɪk/, *adj.*

**odontoglossum** /ɒˌdɒntəˈglɒsəm/, *n.* any of the epiphytic orchids constituting the genus *Odontoglossum,* natives of the mountainous regions from Bolivia to Mexico. [NL, from Gk *odonto-* ODONTO- + *glôssa* tongue]

**odontograph** /ɒˈdɒntəgræf, -graf/, *n.* an instrument for marking out the forms of geared teeth or ratchets.

**odontoid** /ɒˈdɒntɔɪd/, *adj.* **1.** denoting a toothlike process, as that of the axis, or second cervical vertebra, upon which the atlas rotates. **2.** resembling a tooth. [Gk *odontoeidḗs* toothlike]

**odontology** /ɒdɒnˈtɒlədʒi/, *n.* **1.** the science or art which treats of the study of the teeth and their surrounding tissues, and of the prevention and cure of their diseases. **2.** →**dentistry.** – **odontological** /ɒˌdɒntəˈlɒdʒɪkəl/, *adj.*

**odontophore** /ɒˈdɒntəfɔ/, *n.* a structure in the mouth of most molluscs, over which the radula is drawn backwards and forwards in the process of breaking up food. [Gk *odontophóros* bearing teeth] – **odontophoral** /ɒdɒnˈtɒfərəl/, **odontophorine** /ɒdɒnˈtɒfərin, -raɪn/, **odontophorous** /ɒdɒnˈtɒfərəs/, *adj.*

**odoriferous** /oʊdəˈrɪfərəs/, *adj.* yielding or diffusing an odour, esp. a fragrant one. [ME, from L *odōrifer* bringing odours + -OUS] – **odoriferously,** *adv.* – **odoriferousness,** *n.*

**odorous** /ˈoʊdərəs/, *adj.* having or diffusing an odour, esp. a fragrant odour. [L *odōrus* emitting a scent] – **odorously,** *adv.* – **odorousness,** *n.*

**odour** /ˈoʊdə/, *n.* **1.** that property of a substance which affects the sense of smell: *rank odours.* **2.** an agreeable scent; fragrance. **3.** a bad smell. **4.** a savour or quality characteristic or suggestive of something. **5.** repute or estimation: *in bad odour.* Also, *U.S.,* **odor.** [ME, from OF, from L] – **odourless,** *adj.*

**O.D.s** /oʊ ˈdiz/, Other Denominations.

**-odynia,** a word element meaning 'pain'. [NL, from Gk]

**odyssey** /ˈɒdəsi/, *n.* any long series of wanderings. [Gk *Odýsseia* the Odyssey, from *Odysseús* Odysseus, Ulysses, the hero of Homer's epic poem, who wandered for ten years after the Trojan War] – **odyssean** /ɒˈdɪsiən/, *adj.*

**Oe,** oersted.

**OE,** Old English. Also, **OE., O.E.**

**O.E.C.D.** /oʊ i si ˈdi/, Organisation for Economic Cooperation and Development.

**oecology** /iˈkɒlədʒi/, *n.* →**ecology.**

**oecumenical** /ikjuˈmɛnɪkəl/, *adj.* →**ecumenical.** Also, **oecumenic.**

**O.E.D.** /oʊ i ˈdi/, Oxford English Dictionary.

**oedema** /əˈdimə/, *n., pl.* **-mata** /-mətə/. effusion of serous fluid into the interstices of cells in tissue spaces or into body cavities. Also, **edema.** [NL, from Gk *oídēma* a swelling] – **oedematous** /əˈdɛmətəs/, **oedematose** /əˈdɛmətoʊs/, *adj.*

**Oedipus complex** /ˈidəpəs ˌkɒmplɛks/, *n.* **1.** the unresolved desire of a child for sexual gratification through the parent of the opposite sex. This involves, first, identification with and, later, hatred for the parent of the same sex, who is considered by the child as a rival. **2.** sexual desire of the son for the mother. Cf. **Electra complex.** [orig. with ref. to the Greek legend of *Oedipus,* who involuntarily slew his father (Laius) and unwittingly won the hand of his mother (Jocasta) in marriage. When the nature of these deeds became apparent, Jocasta hanged herself and Oedipus put out his own eyes]

**oeil-de-boeuf** /ɜjə-də-ˈbɜf/, *n., pl.* **oeils-de-boeuf** /ɜjə-də-ˈbɜf/. a comparatively small round or oval window, as in a frieze. [F: eye of ox, bull's eye]

**oenocyanin** /inoʊˈsaɪənən/, *n.* an extract from grapes consisting of tannins and colouring matter, which is sometimes added to red wine to build body. [Gk *oîno(s)* wine + *kýanos* dark blue + -IN[2]]

**oenology** /iˈnɒlədʒi/, *n.* the science of viniculture. [Gk *oîno(s)* wine + -LOGY] – **oenological** /inəˈlɒdʒɪkəl/, *adj.* – **oenologist,** *n.*

**oenomancy** /ˈinəmænsi/, *n.* the use of wine in determining omens.

**o'er** /ɔ/, *prep., adv. Poetic.* over.

**oersted** /ˈɜstəd/, *n.* a non-SI unit of measurement of magnetic field strength, approx. equal to 79.6 amperes per metre. [named after H. C. *Oersted,* 1777-1851, Danish physicist]

**oesophageal** /əsɒfəˈdʒiəl/, *adj.* pertaining to the oesophagus. Also, **esophageal.**

**oesophagus** /əˈsɒfəgəs/, *n., pl.* **-gi** /-gaɪ/. a tube connecting the mouth or pharynx with the stomach in invertebrate and vertebrate animals; gullet. Also, **esophagus.** [NL, from Gk *oisophágos*]

**oestradiol** /istrəˈdaɪəl/, *n.* the principal oestrogenic hormone, $C_{18}H_{24}O_2$, produced by the ovaries. Also, *U.S.,* **estradiol.**

**oestriol** /ˈistriɒl, ˈɛs-/, *n.* an oestrogenic hormone, $C_{18}H_{22}O_3$, occurring in the placenta and in pregnancy urine. Also, *U.S.*, **estriol.**

**oestrogen** /ˈistrədʒən, ˈɛs-/, *n.* any one of a group of female sex hormones which induce oestrus in immature or spayed mammals. Also, *U.S.*, **estrogen.** – **oestrogenic** /istrəˈdʒɛnɪk, ɛs-/, *adj.*

**oestrone** /ˈistroʊn, ˈɛs-/, *n.* an oestrogenic hormone, $C_{18}H_{22}O_2$, manufactured by the ovarian follicles and found in pregnancy urine and placental tissue. Also, *U.S.*, **estrone.**

**oestrous** /ˈistrəs, ˈɛs-/, *adj.* involving or pertaining to the oestrus. Also, *U.S.*, **estrous.**

**oestrous cycle** /ˈ– saɪkəl/, *n.* a recurrent series of physiological changes in sexual and other organs in female mammals, extending from one rutting period to the next. Also, *U.S.*, **estrus cycle.**

**oestrus** /ˈistrəs, ˈɛs-/, *n.* **1.** Also, **oestrum** /ˈistrəm, ˈɛs-/, *U.S.*, **estrus.** the oestrous cycle in mammals, esp. females. **2.** passion or passionate impulse. **3.** a stimulus. [L, from Gk *oîstros* gadfly, sting, frenzy]

**oeuvre** /ˈɜvrə/, *n., pl.* **oeuvres** /ˈɜvrə/. **1.** work, esp. a literary or artistic work. **2.** the total artistic output of a painter, writer, etc. [F]

**of** /ɒv/; *weak form* /əv/. *prep.* a particle indicating: **1.** distance or direction from, separation, deprivation, riddance, etc.: *within a metre of; to cure of.* **2.** derivation, origin, or source: *of good family; the plays of Shakespeare.* **3.** cause, occasion, or reason: *to die of hunger.* **4.** material, substance, or contents: *a packet of sugar; a suit of mohair.* **5.** a relation of identity: *the city of Sydney.* **6.** belonging or possession, connection, or association: *the queen of England; the property of all.* **7.** inclusion in a number, class, or whole: *one of us.* **8.** objective relation: *the ringing of bells.* **9.** reference or respect: *talk of peace.* **10.** qualities or attributes: *a man of tact.* **11.** time: *of an evening.* **12.** *U.S.* to or before (a designated hour of the clock): *twenty minutes of five is 4.40.* **13.** the attribution of a quality to: *it was good of you to come.* **14.** the attribution of a quality with respect to: *fleet of foot.* **15.** *Chiefly Archaic.* the agent by whom something is done: *beloved of all.* [ME and OE, c. G and L *ab*, Gk *apó*. See OFF]

**of-,** variant of **ob-**, (by assimilation) before *f*, as in *offend.*

**OF,** Old French. Also, **OF., O.F.**

**ofay** /oʊˈfeɪ/, *adj. Colloq.* →**au fait.**

**off** /ɒf/, *adv.* **1.** away from a position occupied, or from contact, connection, or attachment: *take off one's hat; the handle has come off.* **2.** to or at a distance from, or away from, a place: *to run off.* **3.** away from or out of association or relation: *to cast off.* **4.** deviating from, esp. from what is normal or regular. **5.** as a deduction: *10 per cent off on all cash purchases.* **6.** away; distant (in future time): *summer is only a week off.* **7.** out of operation or effective existence; disconnected. **8.** so as to interrupt continuity or cause discontinuance: *to break off negotiations.* **9.** away from employment or service: *we have four days off at Easter.* **10.** so as to exhaust, finish, or complete; completely: *to kill off vermin.* **11.** forthwith or immediately: *right off.* **12.** with prompt or ready performance: *to dash off a letter.* **13.** to fulfilment, or into execution or effect: *the contest came off on the day fixed.* **14.** so as to cause or undergo reduction or diminution: *to wear off.* **15.** on one's way or journey, as from a place: *to see a friend off on a journey.* **16.** *Naut.* away from the land, a ship, the wind, etc. **17. be off,** to depart; leave. **18. off and on, a.** Also, **on and off.** intermittently: *to work off and on.* **b.** *Naut.* on alternate tacks. **19. off with** (anything specified), to remove; take or cut off: *off with his head!* –*prep.* **20.** away from; so as no longer to be or rest on: *to fall off a horse.* **21.** deviating from (something normal or usual): *off one's balance.* **22.** not up to the usual standard of: *off his game.* **23.** from by subtraction or deduction: *25 per cent off the marked price.* **24.** away or disengaged from (duty, work, etc.). **25.** *Colloq.* refraining from (some food, activity, etc.): *to be off gambling.* **26.** distant from: *a waterhole a fair way off the track.* **27.** leading out of: *an alley off the main street.* **28.** *Colloq.* from, indicating source: *I bought it off him.* **29.** from, indicating material: *to make a meal off fish.* **30.** *Naut.* to seaward of. –*adj.* **31.** wide of the truth or fact; in error: *you are off on that point.* **32.** no longer in effect or operation: *the agreement is off.* **33.** as to condition, circumstances, supplies, etc.: *better off.* **34.** (of time) on which work is suspended: *pastime for one's off hours.* **35.** not so good or satisfactory as usual: *an off year for apples; off day.* **36.** off-colour; unwell. **37.** below the normal or expected standard; inferior. **38.** in bad taste; deviating from normal or accepted behaviour. **39.** (of food) tainted. **40.** of less than the ordinary activity, liveliness, or lively interest: *an off season in the woollen trade.* **41.** (of a chance) remote. **42.** (with reference to animals or vehicles) right (opposed to *near* or *left*). **43.** *Naut.* farther from the shore. **44.** *Cricket.* of pertaining to, or denoting that part of the field to the right of and behind the batsman as he faces the bowler (whether he is left-handed or right-handed). **45.** Also, **off tap.** *Prison Colloq.* convicted. **46.** (of items in a menu) not available. –*n.* **47.** the state or fact of being off. **48.** *Cricket.* the off side. –*interj.* **49.** be off! stand off! off with you! [ME and OE *of* of, off. See OF]

**off.,** **1.** office. **2.** officer. **3.** official.

**offal** /ˈɒfəl/, *n.* **1.** the inedible parts of a meat carcass after slaughter, excluding the skin. **2.** →**fancy meat. 3.** the discarded by-products of a manufacturing process. **4.** anything worthless or discarded; rubbish. [ME, from *of* off + *fal* fall]

**off-beat** /ˈɒf-bit/, *adj.* **1.** unusual; unconventional. **2.** (in jazz, etc.) having a strong accent on the second and fourth beat of a four-beat bar. –*n.* **3.** *Music.* the unaccented or less strongly accented beat of a bar.

**off break** /ˈɒf breɪk/, *n.* (in cricket) a ball bowled so as to change direction from leg to off when it pitches.

**off-centre** /ɒf-ˈsɛntə/, *adj.* **1.** having a point of rotation or equilibrium diverging from the exact centre. **2.** out of balance or alignment. **3.** of a person, unstable.

**off-chance** /ˈɒf-tʃæns, -tʃans/, *n.* **1.** a remote chance or possibility. **2. do something on the off-chance,** to embark on a course of action casually setting aside the odds against its completion.

**off-colour** /ˈɒf-kʌlə/; (*esp. in predicative use*) /ɒf-ˈkʌlə/, *adj.* **1.** defective in colour, as a gem. **2.** Also, **off.** *Colloq.* unwell. **3.** of doubtful propriety or taste: *an off-colour story.*

**off-course** /ˈɒf-kɔs/, *adj.*, /ɒfˈkɔs/, *adv.* –*adj.* **1.** of or pertaining to what is or takes place away from a racecourse, usu. betting. –*adv.* **2.** away from a racecourse.

**off-course substitute** /ɒf-kɔs ˈsʌbstətʃut/, *n.* (in doubles betting, in horseracing) the TAB replacement (usu. the on-course favourite) for a horse scratched in the second leg of a doubles after off-course bets have been laid on it.

**off-cut** /ˈɒf-kʌt/, *n.* **1.** that which is cut off, as from paper which has been reduced to a particular size. **2.** (*pl.*) small lengths of timber or other material, left over after special orders have been prepared in a hardware store, etc. –*adj.* **3.** not being of the usual or standard sizes.

**offence** /əˈfɛns/, *n.* **1.** a transgression; a wrong; a sin. **2.** any crime. **3.** a crime which is not indictable, but is punishable summarily (**summary offence**). **4.** a cause of transgression or wrong. **5.** something that offends. **6.** the act of offending or displeasing. **7.** the feeling of resentful displeasure caused: *to give offence.* **8.** the act of attacking; attack or assault: *weapons of offence.* **9.** the persons, side, etc., attacking. **10.** *Obs.* injury, harm, or hurt. Also, *U.S.*, **offense.** [ME *offens*, from L *offensus*]

**offenceless** /əˈfɛnsləs/, *adj.* **1.** without offence. **2.** incapable of offence or attack. **3.** unoffending.

**offend** /əˈfɛnd/, *v.t.* **1.** to irritate in mind or feelings; cause resentful displeasure in. **2.** to affect (the sense, taste, etc.) disagreeably. **3.** *Obs.* to violate or transgress. **4.** *Obs.* (in biblical use) to cause to sin. –*v.i.* **5.** to give offence or cause displeasure. **6.** to err in conduct; commit a sin, crime, or fault. [ME *offende(n)*, from OF *offendre*, from L *offendere* strike against, displease]

**offender** /əˈfɛndə/, *n.* **1.** one who offends. **2.** a criminal; law-breaker.

**offensive** /əˈfɛnsɪv/, *adj.* **1.** causing offence or displeasure; irritating; highly annoying. **2.** disagreeable to the sense: *an offensive odour.* **3.** repugnant to the moral sense, good taste, or the like; insulting. **4.** pertaining to offence or attack: *offensive movements.* **5.** consisting in or characterised by attack: *offensive warfare.* –*n.* **6.** the position or attitude of offence or attack: *to take the offensive.* **7.** an offensive movement: *the big Soviet offensive.* – **offensively,** *adv.* – **offensiveness,** *n.*

**offensive weapon** /– 'wɛpən/, *n.* (in law) any weapon made or adapted for use for causing injury to the person, or intended for such use by the person having it.

**offer** /'ɒfə/, *v.t.* **1.** to present for acceptance or rejection; proffer: *to offer someone a cigarette.* **2.** to put forward for consideration: *to offer a suggestion.* **3.** to make a show of intention (to do something): *we did not offer to go first.* **4.** to propose or volunteer (to do something): *she offered to accompany me.* **5.** to proffer (oneself) for marriage. **6.** to present solemnly as an act of worship or devotion, as to God, a deity, a saint, etc.; sacrifice. **7.** to present; put forward: *she offered no response.* **8.** to attempt to inflict, do, or make: *to offer battle.* **9.** to do or make (violence, resistance, etc.) actually. **10.** to present to sight or notice. **11.** to present for sale. **12.** to tender or bid as a price: *to offer fifty dollars for a radio.* **13.** to render (homage, thanks, etc.). *–v.i.* **14.** to make a proposal or suggestion. **15.** to make an offer of marriage; propose. **16.** to present itself; occur: *whenever an occasion offered.* **17.** to present something as an act of worship or devotion; sacrifice. **18.** *Obs. or Rare.* to make an attempt (fol. by *at*). *–n.* **19.** act of offering: *an offer of assistance.* **20.** a proposal of marriage. **21.** a proposal to give or accept something as a price or equivalent for something else; a bid: *an offer of $80,000 for a house.* **22.** the condition of being offered: *an offer for sale.* **23.** something offered. **24.** *Law.* a proposal which requires only acceptance in order to create a contract. **25.** an attempt or endeavour. **26.** a show of intention. [ME *offre(n)*, OE *offrian*, from L *offerre*] – **offerer,** *n.*

**offering** /'ɒfərɪŋ/, *n.* **1.** something offered in worship or devotion, as to God, a deity, etc.; an oblation; a sacrifice. **2.** a contribution given to or through the Church for a particular purpose, as at a service. **3.** anything offered; gift. **4.** the act of one who offers.

**offertory** /'ɒfətəri, -tri/, *n., pl.* **-ries. 1.** *Rom. Cath. Ch.* the oblation of the unconsecrated elements made by the celebrant in a Eucharistic service. **2.** *Eccles.* **a.** the verses, anthem, or music said, sung, or played while the offerings of the people are received at a religious service. **b.** that part of a service at which offerings are made. **c.** the offerings themselves. [ME *offertorie*, from LL *offertōrium* place to which offerings were brought, offering, oblation]

**off-form concrete** /ɒf-fɔm 'kɒŋkrit/, *n.* concrete in which the impressions left by the form-work are used as a decorative surface.

**offhand** /ɒf'hænd/, *adv.;* /'ɒfhænd/, *adj.* *–adv.* **1.** without previous thought or preparation; extempore: *to decide offhand.* **2.** cavalier, curt, or brusque. *–adj.* Also, **offhanded. 3.** done or made offhand. **4.** informal or casual.

**off-highway** /'ɒf-haɪweɪ/, *adj.* (of tractors, etc.) designed for rugged, long-distance hauling operations.

**office** /'ɒfəs/, *n.* **1.** a room or place for the transaction of business, the discharge of professional duties, or the like: *the solicitor's office.* **2.** the room or rooms in which the clerical work of an industrial or other establishment is done. **3.** a room assigned to a specific person or group of persons in a commercial or industrial organisation. **4.** a place where tickets, etc., are sold, information given, etc. **5.** the staff or body of persons carrying on work in a business or other office. **6.** a building or a set of rooms devoted to the business of a branch of a governmental organisation: *the post office.* **7.** a position of duty, trust, or authority, esp. in the government or in some company, society, or the like. **8.** the duty, function, or part of a particular person or agency: *the office of adviser.* **9.** official employment or position: *to seek office.* **10.** a service or task to be performed: *little domestic offices.* **11.** *Colloq.* (preceded by *the*) hint or signal. **12.** something (good, or occasionally, bad) done for another. **13.** *Eccles.* **a.** the prescribed order or form for a service of the Church, or for devotional use, or the services so prescribed. **b.** the prayers, readings from Scripture, and psalms that must be recited every day by all who are in major orders. **c.** a ceremony or rite, esp. for the dead. **14.** a department of government: *the Foreign Office.* **15.** *Chiefly Brit.* (*pl.*) the parts of a house, as the kitchen, pantry, etc., devoted to household work. **16.** *Chiefly Brit.* (*pl.*) the stables, barns, cowhouses, etc., of a farm. [ME, from OF, from L *officium* service, duty, ceremony]

**office-bearer** /'ɒfəs-bɛərə/, *n.* one who holds office.

**office block** /'ɒfəs blɒk/, *n.* a large office building.

**office boy** /'– bɔɪ/, *n.* a boy employed in an office for errands, etc.

**office hours** /'– aʊəz/, *n.pl.* **1.** the hours a person spends working in an office. **2.** the hours during which a professional man or an office conducts regular business.

**officer** /'ɒfəsə/, *n.* **1.** one who holds a position of rank or authority in an army, navy, airforce, or any similar organisation, esp. one who holds a commission in an army, navy, or airforce. **2.** a policeman or constable. **3.** the master or captain of a merchant vessel or pleasure vessel, or any of his chief assistants. **4.** a person appointed or elected to some position of responsibility and authority in the public service, or in some corporation, society, or the like. **5.** (in some honorary orders) a member of higher rank than the lowest. **6.** *Obs.* an agent. *–v.t.* **7.** to furnish with officers. **8.** to command or direct as an officer does. **9.** to direct, conduct, or manage. [ME, from OF *officier*, from ML *officiārius*, from L *officium* office]

**officer at arms,** *n.* →**herald.** Also, **officer of arms.**

**officer of the guard,** *n.* a junior officer detailed by rota when an officers' guard is called for, who is responsible for the guard carrying out its duties during a prescribed period.

**officer of the watch,** *n.* **1.** the deck officer who during his watch is responsible to the master for the navigation of a ship. **2.** the engineer officer who is in charge of the engine-room during his watch. **3.** *Navy.* the officer who is responsible for the upper deck when the ship is in port.

**officer's pox** /'ɒfəsəz pɒks/, *n. Mil. Colloq.* →**urethritis** (def. 2). Also, **padre's pox.**

**official** /ə'fɪʃəl/, *n.* **1.** one who holds an office or is charged with some form of official duty. *–adj.* **2.** of or pertaining to an office or position of duty, trust, or authority: *official powers.* **3.** authorised or issued authoritatively: *an official report.* **4.** holding office. **5.** appointed or authorised to act in a special capacity: *an official representative.* **6.** formal or ceremonious: *an official dinner.* **7.** *Pharm.* authorised by the pharmacopoeia. [LL *officiālis*, from L *officium* office] – **officially,** *adv.*

**officialdom** /ə'fɪʃəldəm/, *n.* **1.** the position or domain of officials. **2.** the entire body of officials.

**officialese** /əfɪʃə'liz/, *n.* a style of language found in official documents and characterised by pretentiousness, pedantry, obscurity, and the use of jargon.

**officialise** /ə'fɪʃəlaɪz/, *v.t.,* **-lised, -lising.** to make official; bring under official control. Also, **officialize.**

**officialism** /ə'fɪʃəlɪzəm/, *n.* **1.** official methods or systems. **2.** excessive attention to official routine. **3.** officials collectively.

**official receiver** /əfɪʃəl rə'sivə/, *n.* an officer of the Bankruptcy Court whose duties are to supervise the realisation and administration of the estate and the conduct of the debtor bankrupt.

**official secrets** /– 'sikrəts/, *n.pl.* classified government and esp. military information, the wrongful disclosure or improper obtaining of which are offences.

**officiant** /ə'fɪʃiənt/, *n.* one who officiates at a religious service or ceremony. [ML *officians*, ppr. of *officiāre* OFFICIATE]

**officiary** /ə'fɪʃjəri, ə'fɪʃəri/, *adj.* **1.** pertaining to or derived from an office, as a title. **2.** having a title or rank derived from an office, as a dignitary.

**officiate** /ə'fɪʃieɪt/, *v.i.,* **-ated, -ating. 1.** to perform the duties of any office or position. **2.** to perform the office of a priest or minister, as at divine worship. [ML *officiātus*, pp. of *officiāre*, from L *officium* office] – **officiation** /əfɪʃi'eɪʃən/, *n.* **officiator,** *n.*

**officinal** /ɒfə'saɪnəl, ɒ'fɪsənəl/, *adj.* **1.** kept in stock by pharmacists, as a drug. Cf. **magistral. 2.** recognised by the pharmacopoeia. *–n.* **3.** an officinal medicine. [ML *officīnālis*, from L *officīna* workshop, laboratory]

**officious** /ə'fɪʃəs/, *adj.* **1.** forward in tendering or obtruding one's services upon others. **2.** marked by or proceeding from such forwardness: *officious interference.* **3.** *Obs.* ready to serve. [L *officiōsus* obliging, dutiful] – **officiously,** *adv.* – **officiousness,** *n.*

**offie** /ˈɒfi/, *n. Cricket Colloq.* **1.** →**off break.** **2.** →**off spinner** (def. 2).

**offing** /ˈɒfɪŋ/, *n.* **1.** the more distant part of the sea as seen from the shore, beyond the anchoring ground. **2.** position at a distance from the shore. **3.** **in the offing, a.** not very distant. **b.** close enough to be seen. **c.** ready or likely to happen, appear, etc.

**offish** /ˈɒfɪʃ/, *adj. Colloq.* aloof. – **offishness,** *n.*

**off-limits** /ˈɒf-lɪməts/, *adj.* out of bounds.

**off-line** /ˈɒf-laɪn/, *adj.* **1.** of or pertaining to facilities for railway services, tickets, etc., other than at railway premises. **2.** not having direct access to a computer: *an off-line branch of the bank.*

**off-load** /ɒf-ˈloʊd/, *v.t.* **1.** to unload (goods, etc.). **2.** to get rid of. *–v.i.* **3.** to unload.

**off-peak** /ˈɒf-pik/, *adj.* **1.** of or pertaining to a period of time of less activity than the normal: *off-peak train services.* **2.** *Elect.* (of the load on a power supply system) lower than the maximum.

**offprint** /ˈɒfprɪnt/, *n.* **1.** a reprint in separate form of an article which originally appeared as part of a larger publication. *–v.t.* **2.** to reprint separately, as an article from a larger publication.

**off-putting** /ɒf-ˈpʊtɪŋ/, *adj. Colloq.* disconcerting; discouraging.

**off-road** /ˈɒf-roʊd/, *adj.* **1.** of or pertaining to the functioning, etc., of a motor vehicle when it is not being driven. **2.** designed for use on ungraded ground, as in natural bushland: *an off-road vehicle.*

**offscouring** /ˈɒfskaʊərɪŋ/, *n.* **1.** (*oft. pl.*) that which is scoured off; filth; refuse. **2.** (*pl.*) social outcasts; rabble.

**off-season** /ˈɒf-sizən/, *adj.* **1.** denoting a time of year other than the usual or most popular for a specific activity; out of season. *–n.* **2.** an off-season time of year. **3.** a time of reduced activity in business or manufacturing industry.

**offset** /ˈɒfsɛt, ɒfˈsɛt/, *v.*, **-set, -setting;** /ˈɒfsɛt/, *n., adj.* *–v.t.* **1.** to balance by something else as an equivalent: *to offset one thing by another.* **2.** to counterbalance as an equivalent does; compensate for: *the gains offset the losses.* **3.** *Print.* **a.** to make an offset of. **b.** to print by the process of offset lithography. **4.** *Archit.* to build with an offset (def. 16), as a wall. *–v.i.* **5.** to project as an offset or branch. **6.** *Print.* to make an offset. *–n.* **7.** something that offsets or counterbalances; a compensating equivalent. **8.** the start or outset. **9.** a short lateral shoot by which certain plants are propagated. **10.** any offshoot; branch. **11.** an offshoot from a family or race. **12.** a spur of a mountain range. **13.** *Print.* an impression from an inked design or the like on a lithographic stone or metal plate, made on another surface, as a rubber blanket, and then transferred to paper, instead of being made directly on the paper. **14.** *Print.* →**set-off** (def. 4). **15.** *Mach.* a more or less abrupt bend in a pipe, bar, rod, or the like, to serve some particular purpose. **16.** *Archit.* **a.** a reduction in the thickness of a wall, etc. **b.** a flat or sloping projection on a wall, buttress, or the like, below a thinner part. **17.** *Survey.* a short distance measured perpendicularly from a line. *–adj.* **18.** of, denoting, or pertaining to an offset. **19.** *Print.* pertaining to, or printed by, offset.

**off-shears** /ˈɒf-ʃɪəz/, *adj.* (of sheep) recently shorn.

**offshoot** /ˈɒfʃut/, *n.* **1.** a shoot from a main stem, as of a plant; a lateral shoot. **2.** a branch, or a descendant or scion, of a family or race. **3.** anything conceived as springing or proceeding from a main stock: *an offshoot of a mountain range, a railway, etc.*

**offshore** /ɒfˈʃɔ/, *adv.;* /ˈɒfʃɔ, ɒfˈʃɔ/, *adj.* *–adv.* **1.** off or away from the shore. **2.** at a distance from the shore. **3.** **go offshore,** (of Australian business) to have articles manufactured in an Asian cheap-labour centre, as Hong Kong, Taiwan, etc. *–adj.* **4.** moving or tending away from the shore: *an offshore wind.* **5.** being or operating at a distance from the shore: *offshore fisheries or fishermen.*

**off side** /ˈɒf saɪd/, *n.* (in cricket) that half of the field towards which the batsman's feet point as he stands ready to receive the bowling; opposed to *leg side.* Also, **off.**

**offside** /ɒfˈsaɪd, ˈɒfsaɪd/, *adj.* **1.** *Soccer, Rugby, Hockey, etc.* illegally between the ball and the opposing team's goal line and outside one's own team's half of the field when the ball is in play. **2.** of or pertaining to the right-hand side of a vehicle where traffic drives on the left. **3.** opposed; uncooperative: *I don't want him offside.* **4.** *Cricket.* of or pertaining to the off side: *an offside shot.* *–n.* **5.** the right-hand side of a vehicle (where traffic drives on the left). **6.** the right-hand side of an animal, esp. a horse or a working bullock.

**offsider** /ɒfˈsaɪdə/, *n.* **1.** a partner; friend; assistant: *the cook's offsider.* **2.** a bullock yoked on the right-hand side of a team. **3.** a bullocky's assistant, who attended to the bullocks on the offside of a team.

**off spin** /ˈɒf spɪn/, *n.* (in cricket) the spin which a bowler imparts on a ball to achieve an off break.

**off spinner** /ˈ– spɪnə/, *n. Cricket.* **1.** an off break. **2.** a bowler who specialises in such deliveries.

**offspring** /ˈɒfsprɪŋ/, *n.* **1.** children or young of a particular parent or progenitor. **2.** a child or animal in relation to its parent or parents. **3.** a descendant. **4.** descendants collectively. **5.** the product, result, or effect of something: *the offspring of delirium.* [ME and OE *ofspring.* See OFF, SPRING, *v.*]

**offstage** /ˈɒfsteɪdʒ, ɒfˈsteɪdʒ/, *adj.;* /ɒfˈsteɪdʒ/, *adv.* *–adj.* **1.** located or occurring in the region of a stage not in view of the audience; backstage. *–adv.* **2.** away from the region of a stage and not in view of the audience; in the wings.

**off-street** /ˈɒf-strit/, *adj.* away from the main street: *off-street parking.*

**off stump** /ˈɒf stʌmp/, *n.* (in cricket) the stump on the off side of the batsman.

**off-the-peg** /ˈɒf-ðə-pɛg/, *adj.* of or pertaining to clothes which are sold ready-made. Also, **off-the-rack.**

**off-the-record** /ˈɒf-ðə-rɛkɔd/, *adj.* unofficial; not intended for public quotation: *an off-the-record discussion with the prime minister.* Also (*esp. in predicative use*), **off the record.**

**off-the-road** /ˈɒf-ðə-roʊd/, *adj.* of vehicles, usu. four-wheel drive, designed for work or recreational use in rugged conditions.

**off-white** /ɒf-ˈwaɪt/, *n.* a white colour with a slight touch of grey in it.

**oft** /ɒft/, *adv. Chiefly Poetic.* often; frequently. [ME *oft(e),* OE *oft,* c. G *oft*]

**oft.,** often.

**often** /ˈɒfən, ˈɒftən/, *adv.* **1.** many times; frequently. **2.** in many cases. *–adj.* **3.** *Archaic.* frequent. [ME *oftin,* var. (before vowels) of *ofte* OFT]

**oftentimes** /ˈɒfəntaɪmz/, *adv. Archaic.* often. Also, **oft times.**

**o.g.,** a stamp with original gum; a mint stamp (having gum as issued by the post office).

**ogdoad** /ˈɒgdoʊˌæd/, *n.* **1.** the number eight. **2.** group of eight. [LL *ogdoas,* from Gk: the number eight]

**ogee** /ˈoʊdʒi/, *n.* **1.** a double curve (like the letter S) formed by the union of a concave and a convex line. **2.** *Archit., etc.* a moulding with such a curve for a profile. [var. of OGIVE]

**ogee arch** /ˈ– atʃ/, *n.* a form of pointed arch, each side of which has the curve of an ogee.

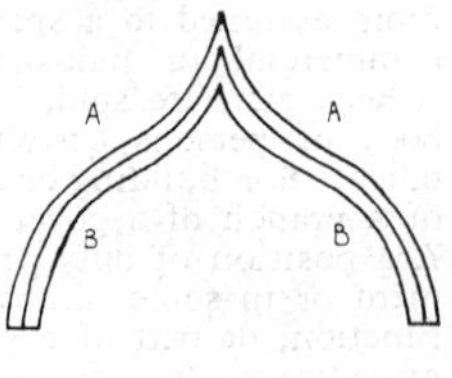

ogee arch: A, convex curve; B, concave curve

**ogham** /ˈɒgəm/, *n.* **1.** an ancient Irish alphabetical script consisting of straight lines drawn or carved perpendicularly or at an angle to a single long line or to the edge of a stone or piece of wood. **2.** a letter of this script. Also, **ogam.** [Irish]

**ogive** /ˈoʊdʒaɪv/, *n. Archit.* **1.** a diagonal groin or rib of a vault. **2.** a pointed arch. **3.** *Statistics.* a curve such that the ordinate for any given value of the abscissa represents the frequency or relative frequency of values of the ordinate less than or equal to the given value. [ME, from F, also formerly *augive;* orig. uncert.] – **ogival** /oʊˈdʒaɪvəl/, *adj.*

**ogle** /ˈoʊgəl/, *v.*, **ogled, ogling,** *n.* *–v.t.* **1.** to eye with amorous, flirtatious, ingratiating, or impertinently familiar glances. **2.** to eye; look at. *–v.i.* **3.** to cast amorous, ingratiating, or impertinently familiar glances. *–n.* **4.** an ogling glance. [apparently from a frequentative (cf. LG *oegeln,* G *äugeln*) of D *oogen* to eye, from *oog* the eye] **– ogler,** *n.*

**O'Grady says** /oʊˌgreɪdi ˈsɛz/, *n.* →**Simon says.**

**ogre** /ˈoʊgə/, *n.* **1.** a monster, commonly represented as a hideous giant, of fairy tales and popular legends, supposed to live on human flesh. **2.** a person likened to such a monster. [F] **– ogreish** /ˈoʊgərɪʃ/, **ogrish** /ˈoʊgrɪʃ/, *adj.* **– ogress** /ˈoʊgrəs/, *n. fem.*

**oh** /oʊ/, *interj., n., pl.* **oh's, ohs,** *v.* *–interj.* **1.** (an expression denoting surprise, pain, disapprobation, etc., or for attracting attention.) *–n.* **2.** the exclamation 'oh'. *–v.i.* **3.** to utter or exclaim 'oh'.

**oh boy** /oʊ ˈbɔɪ/, *interj.* **1.** (an exclamation indicating surprise, delight, etc.). **2.** (an exclamation indicating dismay, trepidation, etc.).

**OHG,** Old High German. Also, **OHG., O.H.G.**

**ohm** /oʊm/, *n.* the derived SI unit of resistance; the resistance of a conductor in which one volt produces a current of one ampere. *Symbol:* Ω [named after G. S. *Ohm,* 1787-1854, German physicist] **– ohmic** /ˈoʊmɪk/, *adj.*

**ohmage** /ˈoʊmɪdʒ/, *n.* electrical resistance expressed in ohms.

**ohmmeter** /ˈoʊmmitə/, *n.* an instrument for measuring electrical resistance in ohms.

**O.H.M.S.,** On His (or Her) Majesty's Service.

**Ohm's law** /ˈoʊmz lɔ/, *n.* the law which states that in any electric circuit the current flowing is proportional to the voltage and inversely proportional to the resistance. [named after G. S. *Ohm.* See OHM]

**o.h.v.,** overhead valve.

**OIC,** Officer in Charge.

**-oid,** a suffix used to form adjectives meaning 'like' or 'resembling', and nouns meaning 'something resembling' what is indicated by the preceding part of the word (and often implying an incomplete or imperfect resemblance), as in *alkaloid, anthropoid, cardioid, cuboid, lithoid, ovoid, planetoid.* [Gk *-oeidēs,* from *-o-* (connective vowel from preceding word element) + *-eidēs* having the form of, like, from *eîdos* form. Cf. -ODE[1]]

**-oidea,** a suffix used in naming zoological classes or entomological superfamilies. [NL, from *-oïdēs* -OID]

**oidium** /oʊˈɪdiəm/, *n.* one of a chain of spores budded off from the end of the hyphae of a fungus, which attacks the green parts of a grape vine.

**oil** /ɔɪl/, *n.* **1.** any of a large class of substances typically unctuous, viscous, combustible, liquid at ordinary temperatures, and soluble in ether or alcohol but not in water, and which is used for anointing, perfuming, lubricating, illuminating, heating, etc. **2.** →**petroleum** (def. 1). **3.** some substance of oily consistency. **4.** *Painting.* **a.** an oil colour. **b.** an oil painting. **5.** *Colloq.* flattery; bribery. **6. burn the midnight oil,** to stay up late at night to study, work, etc. **7. the good (dinkum) oil,** correct (and usu. profitable) information, often to be used in confidence; the drum. **8. the oil,** *N.Z. Colloq.* an excellent person or thing. **9. pour oil on troubled waters,** to calm; pacify. *–v.t.* **10.** to smear, lubricate, or supply with oil. **11.** to give information to; advise (fol. by *up*). **12.** to bribe. **13.** to make unctuous or smooth, as in speech. **14.** to convert (butter, etc.) into oil by melting. *–adj.* **15.** pertaining to or resembling oil. **16.** concerned with the production or use of oil. **17.** obtained from oil. **18.** using oil, esp. as a fuel. [ME *olie, oile,* from OF, from L *oleum* (olive) oil]

**oilbird** /ˈɔɪlbɜd/, *n.* →**guacharo.**

**oil-burner** /ˈɔɪl-bɜnə/, *n.* **1.** a device for atomising oil and mixing it with air so that a stable flame may be formed; used in industrial and domestic boilers. **2.** a ship, etc., that uses oil as a fuel.

**oilcake** /ˈɔɪlkeɪk/, *n.* a cake or mass of linseed, cottonseed, etc., from which the oil has been expelled used as a food for cattle or sheep, or as soil fertiliser.

**oilcan** /ˈɔɪlkæn/, *n.* a can for holding oil, with a long spout or nozzle through which the oil is squirted to lubricate machinery, etc.

**oilcloth** /ˈɔɪlklɒθ/, *n.* **1.** a cotton fabric made waterproof with oil and pigment, and used for tablecloths, etc. **2.** a piece of it.

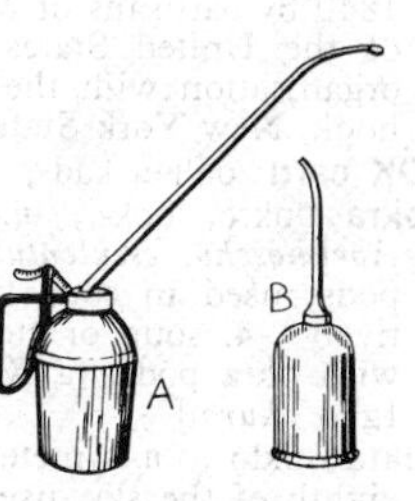

A, direct-pump oilcan; B, bench oilcan

**oil colour** /ˈɔɪl kʌlə/, *n.* a colour or paint made by grinding a pigment in oil, usu. linseed oil. Also, **oil paint.**

**oiled silk** /ɔɪld ˈsɪlk/, *n.* silk cloth treated with oil.

**oiler** /ˈɔɪlə/, *n.* **1.** one who oils; a workman employed to oil machinery. **2.** any contrivance for lubricating with oil. **3.** a can with a long spout, used for oiling machinery. **4.** *U.S.* (*oft. pl.*) an oilskin coat.

**oilfield** /ˈɔɪlfild/, *n.* a place where oil is found.

**oil-fired** /ˈɔɪl-faɪəd/, *adj.* using oil as a fuel.

**oilman** /ˈɔɪlmæn/, *n.* **1.** one who owns or operates oilwells. **2.** one who deals or trades in oils.

**oil of cloves,** *n.* an oil obtained by distillation from clove and used as a counterirritant and a mild analgesic.

**oil of turpentine,** *n.* a colourless, inflammable, volatile oil, a distillate of turpentine, having a penetrating smell and a pungent bitterish taste, which is used in paints, varnishes, and the like, and in medicine as a stimulant, diuretic, rubefacient, etc.

**oil of vitriol,** *n.* →**sulphuric acid.**

**oil painting** /ˈɔɪl peɪntɪŋ/, *n.* **1.** the art of painting with oil colours. **2.** a work executed in oil colours. **3. be no oil painting,** *Colloq.* to lack good looks.

**oil-palm** /ˈɔɪl-pam/, *n.* an African palm, *Elaeis guineensis,* whose fruits yield palm oil.

**oil-paper** /ˈɔɪl-peɪpə/, *n.* paper made transparent or waterproof by being treated with oil.

**oil-press** /ˈɔɪl-prɛs/, *n.* a machine for extracting oils from seeds, pulp, etc.

**oil rig** /ˈɔɪl rɪg/, *n.* the entire structure including all the apparatus needed in drilling for oil.

**oilseed** /ˈɔɪlsid/, *n.* any of several seeds, as linseed, rapeseed, etc., which yield oil.

**oil shale** /ˈɔɪl ʃeɪl/, *n.* shale containing such a proportion of hydrocarbons as to be capable of yielding mineral oils on slow distillation.

**oilskin** /ˈɔɪlskɪn/, *n.* **1.** a cotton fabric made waterproof by treatment with oil and used for fishermen's clothing and rain wear. **2.** a piece of this. **3.** (*oft. pl.*) a garment made of it.

**oil slick** /ˈɔɪl slɪk/, *n.* a slick or smooth place on the surface of water, caused by the presence of oil.

**oilstone** /ˈɔɪlstoʊn/, *n.* a fine-grained whetstone whose rubbing surface is lubricated with oil.

**oilstove** /ˈɔɪlstoʊv/, *n.* a stove as for cooking, heating, etc., which usu. burns paraffin oil.

**oil tanker** /ˈɔɪl tæŋkə/, *n.* a ship or motor vehicle for carrying oil in bulk.

**oilwell** /ˈɔɪlwɛl/, *n.* a well from which oil is obtained.

**oily** /ˈɔɪli/, *adj.,* **oilier, oiliest.** **1.** of or pertaining to oil. **2.** full of or containing oil. **3.** smeared or covered with oil, or greasy. **4.** of the nature of or consisting of oil; resembling oil. **5.** smooth, as in manner or speech; bland; unctuous: *an oily hypocrite.* *–adv.* **6.** in an oily manner. **– oilily,** *adv.* **– oiliness,** *n.*

**ointment** /ˈɔɪntmənt/, *n.* a soft, unctuous preparation, often medicated, for application to the skin; an unguent. [obs. *oint* (aphetic var. of ANOINT) + -MENT; replacing ME *oignement,* from OF]

**okapi** /oʊˈkapi/, *n., pl.* **-pis,** (*esp. collectively*) **-pi.** an African forest mammal, *Okapia johnstoni,* closely related to the giraffe, but smaller and with a much shorter neck. [a Central African language (Mvuba)]

**okay** /oʊˈkeɪ/, *adj., adv., v., n. Colloq. –adj.* **1.** all right; correct. *–adv.* **2.** well; effectively; correctly; acceptably. *–v.t.* **3.** to put an 'okay' on (a proposal, etc.); endorse; approve; accept. *–n.* **4.** an approval, agreement or acceptance. Also, **ok, OK, O.K., o.k.** [orig. much debated, but probably abstracted from or popularised by the 'O.K. Club', formed in 1840 by partisans of Martin Van Buren, 1782-1862, president of the United States 1837-41, who allegedly named their organisation with the initials of 'Old Kinderhook' (Kinderhook, New York State, being Van Buren's birthplace)]

**OK card** /oʊ'keɪ kad/, *n. Colloq.* →**union card.**

**okra** /'ɒkrə, 'oʊk-/, *n.* **1.** a tall plant of the mallow family, *Abelmoschus esculentus,* cultivated for its edible mucilaginous pods, used in soups, etc. **2.** the pod. **3.** the pods collectively. **4.** soup or stew, usu. containing chicken, thickened with okra pods. [a W African language (cf. Twi *ngkuruma,* Igbo *okuro*)]

**okta** /'ɒktə/, *n.* a meteorological unit, equal to the area of one eighth of the sky, used in specifying cloud amounts.

**-ol**[1], a noun suffix used in the names of chemical derivatives, pharmaceutical compounds, commercial products, etc., representing 'alcohol', as in *glycerol, naphthol, phenol,* or sometimes 'phenol' or less definitely assignable phenol derivatives. [short for ALCOHOL or PHENOL]

**-ol**[2], variant of **-ole.**

**-olatry,** a word element meaning 'worship of', as in *demonolatry.* [see LATRIA]

**old** /oʊld/, *adj.,* **older, oldest** or **elder, eldest,** *n.* *–adj.* **1.** far advanced in years or life. **2.** of or pertaining to a long life or persons advanced in years: *to live to a good old age.* **3.** having the appearance or characteristics of advanced age: *prematurely old.* **4.** having reached a specified age: *a man thirty years old.* **5.** advanced in years, in comparison with others or relatively to a scale of age. **6.** having existed long, or made long ago: *old wine.* **7.** long known or in use; familiar: *the same old excuse.* **8.** former, past, or ancient, as time, days, etc.; belonging to a past time: *old kingdoms.* **9.** formerly in use (usu. in contrast to something specified as more recent or modern): *he sold his old car in part-exchange for a new one.* **10.** having been so formerly: *the old boys of a school.* **11.** (of colours) dulled, faded or subdued. **12.** deteriorated through age or long use; worn, decayed, or dilapidated. **13.** (*cap.*) (in the history of a language) of or belonging to the earliest stage of development, preceding the period classified as Middle: *Old English.* **14.** *Phys. Geog.* (of topographical features) far advanced in reduction by erosion, etc. **15.** of long experience: *an old hand at the game.* **16.** sedate, sensible, or wise, as if from mature years: *an old head on young shoulders.* **17.** *Colloq.* (implying long acquaintance or friendly feeling): *good old Henry.* **18.** *Colloq.* carried to great lengths; great: *a fine old spree.* *–n.* **19.** old or former time, often time long past. **20.** old people collectively. **21.** *Colloq.* →**old beer.** **22.** (used in combination) a person or animal of a specified age or age-group: *a class of five-year-olds.* **23. the olds,** *Colloq.* one's parents. [ME; OE *ald, eald,* c. D *oud,* G *alt;* orig. pp., and akin to Icel. *ala* nourish, bring up, and L *alere* nourish] – **oldness,** *n.*

**old age** /– 'eɪdʒ/, *n.* the later period of life, esp. after retirement.

**old age pension,** *n.* a pension paid by the state to old people.

**old beer** /'oʊld bɪə/, *n.* beer brewed by the top fermentation method, usu. dark in colour.

**old boy** /'– bɔɪ/; *for def. 4* /– 'bɔɪ/ *n.* **1.** a former pupil of a specific school. **2.** *Chiefly Brit. Colloq.* husband; father. **3.** *Colloq.* →**penis.** **4.** a familiar or affectionate term of address to a man, or sometimes to a male animal.

**old boy network,** *n.* the system by which jobs, positions of power or influence, information, etc., are exchanged among persons having a similar background, aims, or interests, esp. among former pupils of independent schools.

**old chum** /'oʊld tʃʌm/, *n.* **1.** (formerly) one experienced in a given field, esp. life in colonial Australia. **2.** (formerly) an experienced convict.

**Old Church Slavonic,** *n.* the extinct language (South Slavic) preserved in religious texts of the Russian Orthodox Church. Also, **Old Church Slavic.**

**old country** /'oʊld kʌntri/, *n.* the country from which an immigrant or a person's ancestors came, esp. Britain.

**old Dart** /– 'dat/, *n. Colloq.* Britain, esp. England.

**old Dutch** /– 'dʌtʃ/, *n. Colloq.* **1.** wife. **2.** cleaning lady. [shortened form of DUCHESS]

**olden** /'oʊldən/, *adj. Archaic.* **1.** old. **2.** of old; ancient: *olden days.* **3.** of or pertaining to former days.

**old endemic** /oʊld ɛn'dɛmɪk/, *adj.* **1.** of or pertaining to non-marsupial mammals, chiefly rodents, indigenous in Australia from extreme antiquity. The group also includes bats and some marine mammals but excludes the dingo, certain rats, the feral cats, dogs and foxes and others that have been introduced comparatively recently. *–n.* **2.** such an animal.

**Old English** /oʊld 'ɪŋglɪʃ/, *n.* **1.** the English of periods before 1100; Anglo-Saxon. **2.** *Print.* the form of black-letter used by English printers from the 15th to the 18th century.

**Old English sheepdog,** *n.* one of an English breed of medium-sized dogs having a long, shaggy grey, blue, or blue merle coat, sometimes with white markings.

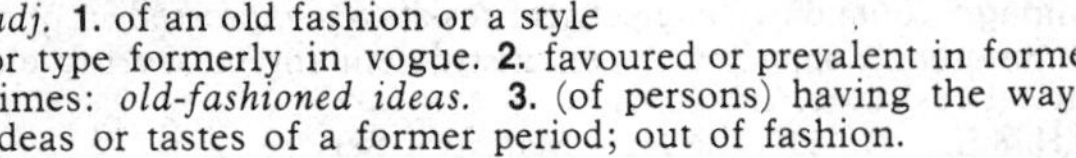

Old English sheepdog

**older** /'oʊldə/, *adj., compar. of* **old.** of greater age.

**olde-worlde** /oʊldi-'wɜldi/, *adj.* excessively quaint or old-fashioned. [pseudo ME form of *old-world*]

**old-fashioned** /'oʊld-fæʃənd/, *adj.* **1.** of an old fashion or a style or type formerly in vogue. **2.** favoured or prevalent in former times: *old-fashioned ideas.* **3.** (of persons) having the ways, ideas or tastes of a former period; out of fashion.

**old fellow** /oʊld 'fɛloʊ/, *for def. 1;* /'oʊld fɛloʊ/, *for def. 2,* *n. Colloq.* **1.** (as a term of address) friend, companion. **2.** the penis. Also, **old boy.**

**old fogy** /– 'foʊgi/, *n.* a person who is excessively conservative or tiresomely antiquated in ideas or methods. Also, **old fogey.** – **old-fogyish,** *adj.*

**Old French** /oʊld 'frɛntʃ/, *n.* the French language of periods before 1400.

**old girl** /'oʊld gɜl/ *for def. 1;* /oʊld 'gɜl/ *for defs 2 and 3,* *n.* **1.** a former pupil of a specific school. **2.** an old woman. **3.** *Chiefly Brit. Colloq.* wife; mother.

**Old Glory** /oʊld 'glɔri/, *n.* the flag of the United States.

**old gold** /oʊld 'goʊld/, *n.* a dull brownish yellow colour.

**old guard** /'– gad/, *n.* **1.** the ultra-conservative members of any group, country, etc. **2.** the members of a previous generation, or the supporters of a previous order, who survive to see their way of life or their cause go into decline. [translation of F *Vieille Garde,* Napoleon's imperial guard]

**old hand** /– 'hænd/, *n.* **1.** one experienced in some activity. **2.** (formerly) a convict who had spent some years in the colony; old chum. **3.** an ex-prisoner.

**old hat** /– 'hæt/, *adj.* old-fashioned; out-of-date; outmoded.

**Old High German,** *n.* High German of before 1100.

**Old Icelandic** /oʊld aɪs'lændɪk/, *n.* the literary language used in Iceland from *c.* 990 to 1300.

**old identity** /oʊld aɪ'dɛntəti/, *n.* **1.** anyone long identified with a place, institution, job, etc. **2.** *N.Z.* (formerly) a Scots settler of Dunedin.

**oldie** /'oʊldi/, *n. Colloq.* **1.** one regarded as old by the speaker. **2.** a parent.

**Old Irish** /oʊld 'aɪrɪʃ/, *n.* the Irish language before the 11th century.

**oldish** /'oʊldɪʃ/, *adj.* somewhat old: *an oldish man.*

**old lady** /oʊld 'leɪdi/, *n. Colloq.* **1.** a mother, usu. one's own. **2.** a wife, usu. one's own.

**old-line** /'oʊld-laɪn/, *adj. U.S.* **1.** following or supporting conservative or traditional ideas, beliefs, customs, etc. **2.** long established; traditional.

**old maid** /oʊld 'meɪd/, *n.* **1.** an elderly or confirmed spinster. **2.** *Colloq.* a person with the alleged characteristics of an old maid, such as primness, prudery, fastidiousness, etc. **3.** a game of cards in which the players draw from one another to match pairs. – **old-maidish,** *adj.*

**old man** /– 'mæn/, *n.* **1.** *Colloq.* a father, usu. one's own. **2.** *Colloq.* a husband, usu. one's own. **3.** *Colloq.* one in a position of authority, as an employer. **4.** a full-grown male kangaroo. **5.** See **snapper** (def. 1). **6.** *Colloq.* a penis.

**old-man** /'oʊld-mæn/, *adj.* strikingly large or remarkable of its kind: *old-man allotment, old-man flood.* Also, **old man.**

**old-man saltbush** /– 'sɒltbʊʃ/, *n.* a tall, shrubby, grey-green, leafy plant, *Atriplex nummularia,* of inland Australia, valuable as fodder.

**old master** /oʊld 'mastə/, *n.* **1.** an eminent painter of an earlier period, esp. during the 15th-18th centuries. **2.** a painting by such an artist.

**old moon** /'– mun/, *n.* See **moon** (def. 2d).

**Old Nick** /oʊld 'nɪk/, *n.* the devil; Satan. [contraction of *Nicholas*]

**Old Norse** /– 'nɔs/, *n.* **1.** the language of Scandinavia and Iceland up to the 15th century. **2.** →**Old Icelandic.**

**Old Persian** /– 'pɜʒən/, *n.* the ancient Iranian of the Persian cuneiforms.

**Old Prussian** /– 'prʌʃən/, *n.* a Baltic language extinct since the 17th century.

**old rose** /oʊld 'roʊz/, *n.* rose with a purplish or greyish cast.

**olds** /oʊldz/, *n. pl. Colloq.* parents.

**Old Saxon** /oʊld 'sæksən/, *n.* the Saxon dialect of Low German as spoken before 1100.

**old school** /'oʊld skul/, *n.* **1.** advocates or supporters of long-established, esp. conservative policies and practices. **2.** one's former school. *–adj.* **3.** Also, **old-school.** of or pertaining to the old school.

**old school tie,** *n.* **1.** a specific tie worn by former members of a school. **2.** (*usu. derog.*) the network of influences and associations formed among former students of independent schools.

**old soldier** /oʊld 'soʊldʒə/, *n.* **1.** a returned soldier. **2.** →**battler.**

**old squaw** /– 'skwɔ/, *n.* a lively, voluble sea-duck, *Clangula hyemalis,* of northern regions.

**old stager** /– 'steɪdʒə/, *n. Colloq.* a person of long experience; a veteran.

**oldster** /'oʊldstə/, *n.* **1.** *Colloq.* an old or older person. **2.** (in the Navy) a midshipman of four years' standing. [OLD + -STER, modelled on YOUNGSTER]

**Old Stone Age,** *n.* the Palaeolithic period.

**old style** /'oʊld staɪl/, *n.* a type style differentiated from *modern style* by the more or less uniform thickness of all strokes and the slanted serifs. – **old-style,** *adj.*

**old system** /'– sɪstəm/, *n.* a system of registration of land tenure, previous to the Torrens system.

**Old Testament** /oʊld 'tɛstəmənt/, *n.* **1.** the collection of biblical books comprising the Hebrew Scriptures of 'the old covenant', and being the first of the two main divisions of the Christian bible. **2.** the covenant between God and Israel on Mount Sinai, constituting the basis of the Hebrew religion.

**old-time** /'oʊld-taɪm/, *adj.* belonging to or characteristic of former times; old-fashioned: *old-time dancing.*

**old-timer** /oʊld-'taɪmə/, *n. Colloq.* **1.** one whose residence, membership, or experience dates from a long time ago. **2.** an old man.

**oldwife** /oʊld'waɪf/, *n.* **1.** any of various fishes as the Australian *Enoplosus armatus,* the European black sea-bream, *Cantharus lineatus,* or the menhaden of the eastern coast of the U.S. **2.** →**old squaw.**

**old wives' tale,** *n.* an erroneous idea, superstitious belief, etc., such as is traditionally ascribed to old women.

**old woman** /oʊld 'wʊmən/, *n. Colloq.* **1.** a wife, usu. one's own. **2.** a mother, usu. one's own. **3.** a fussy, silly person of any age or sex.

**old-womanish** /oʊld-'wʊmənɪʃ/, *adj.* of or like an old woman; excessively fussy.

**old-world** /'oʊld-wɜld/, *adj.* **1.** of or pertaining to the ancient world or to a former period of history; of or pertaining to past times. **2.** of or pertaining to the Old World.

**Old World, The,** *n.* **1.** that part of the world that was known before the discovery of the Americas, comprising Europe, Asia, Africa, and sometimes including Australia. **2.** the Eastern Hemisphere.

**-ole,** a noun suffix meaning 'oil'. [representing L *oleum*]

**oleaceous** /oʊli'eɪʃəs, ɒli-/, *adj.* belonging to the Oleaceae, or olive family of plants, which includes the ash, jasmine, etc. [L *olea* olive + -ACEOUS]

**oleaginous** /oʊli'ædʒənəs/, *adj.* **1.** having the nature or qualities of oil. **2.** containing oil. **3.** producing oil. **4.** oily or unctuous. [L *oleāginus* of the olive] – **oleaginousness,** *n.*

**oleander** /oʊli'ændə, ɒli-/, *n.* any plant of the genus *Nerium,* esp. *N. oleander,* a poisonous evergreen shrub with handsome rose-coloured or white flowers, or *N. odorum,* a species from India with fragrant flowers. [ML, from LL *lorandrum* (var. of L *rhododendron,* from Gk), influenced by *ole-* oil, or *olea* olive]

**olearia** /ɒli'ɛəriə/, *n.* any shrub or tree of the large genus *Olearia,* of Australia, New Guinea and New Zealand, with numerous, daisy-like, usu. white flowers; daisy-bush.

**oleaster** /oʊli'æstə, ɒli-/, *n.* an ornamental shrub or small tree, *Elaeagnus angustifolia,* of southern Europe and western Asia, with fragrant yellow flowers and an olive-like fruit. [ME, from L: the wild olive]

**oleate** /'oʊlieɪt/, *n.* an ester or a salt of oleic acid.

**olecranon** /oʊ'lɛkrənɒn, oʊlə'kreɪnən/, *n.* the part of the ulna beyond the elbow joint. [Gk *ōlékranon,* short for *ōlenókranon* the point of the elbow]

**olefine** /'oʊləfən, -fin/, *n.* any of a series of hydrocarbons homologous with ethylene, having the general formula, $C_nH_{2n}$, also known as alkenes. Also, **olefin** /'oʊləfən/. [F *oléfiant* oil-forming (from L *oleum* oil) + -INE[2]] – **olefinic** /oʊlə'fɪnɪk/, *adj.*

**oleic** /oʊ'liɪk/, *adj.* pertaining to or derived from oleic acid. [L *oleum* oil + -IC]

**oleic acid** /– 'æsəd/, *n.* an oily liquid, an unsaturated fatty acid, $CH_3(CH_2)_7CH{=}CH(CH_2)_7COOH$, present in fats and oils as the glyceride ester.

**olein** /'oʊliən/, *n.* **1.** a colourless oily compound, the glyceride of oleic acid and the component of olive oil; triolein. **2.** the oily or lower-melting fractions of a fat as distinguished from the solid or higher-melting constituents. [L *oleum* oil + -IN[2]]

**oleo-,** a word element meaning 'oil'. [L, combining form of *oleum*]

**oleograph** /'oʊliəgræf, -graf, 'ɒli-/, *n.* a kind of chromolithograph printed in oil colours. – **oleographic** /oʊliə'græfɪk/, *adj.* – **oleography** /oʊli'ɒgrəfi/, *n.*

**oleomargarine** /,oʊlioʊmadʒə'rin/, *n.* →**margarine.**

**oleo oil** /'oʊlioʊ ɔɪl/, *n.* a product obtained from beef fat, consisting mainly of a mixture of olein and palmitin; used for making butter-like foods.

**oleoresin** /oʊlioʊ'rɛzən, ɒli-/, *n.* **1.** a natural mixture of an essential oil and a resin. **2.** *Pharm.* an oil holding resin in solution, extracted from a substance (as ginger) by means of alcohol, ether, or acetone.

**oleum** /'oʊliəm/, *n.* →**fuming sulphuric acid.**

**olfaction** /ɒl'fækʃən/, *n.* **1.** the act of smelling. **2.** the sense of smell. [obs. *olfact* to smell (from L *olfactāre*) + -ION]

**olfactory** /ɒl'fæktəri/, *adj., n., pl.* **-ries.** *–adj.* **1.** of or pertaining to the sense of smell: *olfactory organs.* *–n.* **2.** (*usu. pl.*) an olfactory organ. [L *olfactōrius,* adj.]

**olibanum** /ɒ'lɪbənəm/, *n.* frankincense. [ME, from ML, var. of LL *libanus,* from Gk *líbanos,* of Semitic orig.; cf. Heb. *lĕbhonāh*]

**olig-,** variant of **oligo-** before a vowel.

**oligarch** /'ɒləgak/, *n.* one of the rulers in an oligarchy.

**oligarchic** /ɒlə'gakɪk/, *adj.* of, pertaining to, or having the form of an oligarchy. Also, **oligarchical.**

**oligarchy** /'ɒləgaki/, *n., pl.* **-chies. 1.** a form of government in which the power is vested in a few, or in a dominant class or clique. **2.** a state so governed. **3.** the ruling few collectively. [Gk *oligarchía*]

**oligo-,** a word element meaning 'few', 'little'. Also, before a vowel, **olig-.** [Gk, combining form of *olígos* small, (pl.) few]

**oligocarpous** /ɒləgoʊ'kapəs/, *adj.* (of a plant) not bearing much fruit. [OLIGO- + -CARP + -OUS]

**Oligocene** /ɒ'lɪgoʊsin/, *adj.* **1.** pertaining to an early Tertiary epoch or series. *–n.* **2.** a division of the Tertiary that follows Eocene and precedes Miocene. [OLIGO- + Gk *kainós* new]

**oligochaete** /'ɒləgoʊkit/, *n.* any of a group of annelids that have locomotory setae sunk directly in the body wall. It includes earthworms and many small freshwater annelids. – **oligochaetous** /ɒləgoʊ'kitəs/, *adj.*

**oligoclase** /'ɒləgoʊkleɪz, -eɪs/, *n.* a kind of plagioclase felspar occurring commonly in crystals of white colour, sometimes shaded with grey, green, or red. [OLIGO- + Gk *klásis* fracture]

**oligocythaemia** /ˌɒləgoʊsaɪˈθimiə/, *n.* a form of anaemia in which there is a reduction in the number of corpuscles in the blood. Also, **oligocythemia.** [OLIGO- + CYT(O)- + -(H)AEMIA]

**oligomer** /ˈɒləgəmə/, *n.* a compound containing between two and nine monomeric sub-units, particularly oligosaccharides.

**oligopoly** /ɒləˈgɒpəli/, *n.* the situation in a stock exchange market when there are only a few sellers. [OLIGO- + (MON-O)POLY]

**oligopsony** /ɒləˈgɒpsəni/, *n., pl.* **-nies.** a market situation where a small number of buyers influence the supply of a product or service. [OLIGO- + Gk *opsōnía* purchase of victuals, catering]

**oligosaccharide** /ɒləgoʊˈsækəraɪd/, *n.* a sugar containing between two and nine monosaccharides, as sucrose.

**oliguria** /ɒləˈgjuriə/, *n.* scantiness of urine due to diminished secretion. Also, **oliguresis** /ɒləgjuˈrisəs/. [OLIG- + -URIA]

**olingo** /oʊˈlɪŋgoʊ/, *n.* any of various raccoons of the genus *Bassaricyon,* living in the forests of South America.

**olio** /ˈoʊlioʊ/, *n., pl.* **olios. 1.** a dish of many ingredients. **2.** any mixture of heterogeneous elements. **3.** a medley or potpourri (musical, literary, or the like); a miscellany. [Sp. *olla* pot, stew. See OLLA]

**olivaceous** /ɒləˈveɪʃəs/, *adj.* of a deep shade of green; olive. [NL *olīvāceus.* See OLIVE]

**olivary** /ˈɒləvəri/, *adj.* **1.** shaped like an olive. **2.** *Anat.* denoting or pertaining to either of two oval bodies or prominences (**olivary bodies**), made up of nervous tissue, one on each side of the anterior surface of the medulla oblongata. [L *olīvārius* of olives]

**olive** /ˈɒləv, -lɪv/, *n.* **1.** an evergreen tree, *Olea europaea,* of Mediterranean and other warm regions, cultivated chiefly for its fruit, but yielding also a wood valued for ornamental work. **2.** the fruit, a small oval drupe, esteemed as a relish (pickled in brine when either green or ripe), and valuable as a source of oil. **3.** any of various related or similar trees. **4.** an olive branch. **5.** a wreath of it. **6.** a shade of green or yellowish green. *–adj.* **7.** of, pertaining to, or made of olives, their foliage, or their fruit. **8.** of the colour olive. **9.** tinged with this colour: *an olive complexion.* [ME, from OF, from L *olīva;* akin to Gk *elaía* olive tree]

**olive-backed oriole** /ɒləv-bækt ˈɒrioʊl/, *n.* an oriole, *Oriolus sagittatus,* with an olive-grey back, black wing quills and white underparts, found in a variety of timbered country in northern and eastern Australia.

**olive branch** /ˈɒləv bræntʃ/, *n.* **1.** a branch of the olive tree (an emblem of peace). **2.** anything offered in token of peace.

**olive drab** /– ˈdræb/, *n.* **1.** a deep yellowish green. **2.** woollen cloth of this colour used for U.S. army uniforms.

**olive green** /– ˈgrin/, *n.* green with a yellowish or brownish tinge.

**olivenite** /ɒˈlɪvənaɪt/, *n.* a mineral, basic copper arsenate, $Cu_4As_2O_8(OH)_2$, occurring in crystals and in masses, usu. olive green in colour. [G *Oliven(erz)* olive ore + -ITE[1]]

**olive oil** /ɒləv ˈɔɪl/, *n.* an oil expressed from the olive fruit, used with food, in medicine, etc.

**olive shell** /– ʃɛl/, *n.* **1.** any of various marine gastropods of the family Olividae, having an elongated, highly polished shell. **2.** the shell itself.

**olivine** /ɒləˈvin, ˈɒləvin/, *n.* a very common mineral, magnesium iron silicate, $(Mg,Fe)_2SiO_2$, occurring commonly in olive green to grey-green masses as an important constituent of basic igneous rocks; rarely, in one variety, transparent and used as a gem. [L *olīva* olive + -INE[2]]

**olla** /ˈɒlə/, *n.* (in Spanish-speaking countries) **1.** an earthen pot or jar for holding water or for cooking, etc. **2.** a dish of meat and vegetables cooked in such a pot. [Sp.: pot, stew, from LL: pot, jar]

**olla-podrida** /ɒlə-pəˈdridə/, *n.* **1.** a Spanish stew of meat and vegetables. **2.** any incongruous mixture or miscellaneous collection. [Sp.: lit., rotten pot]

**olm** /oʊlm, ɒlm/, *n.* a permanently larval form of mud puppy, *Proteus anguinus,* white in colour and about 1 metre long, living in deep caves of southern Europe.

**ology** /ˈɒlədʒi/, *n., pl.* **-gies.** *Colloq.* any science or branch of knowledge. [abstracted from words like BIOLOGY, GEOLOGY where the element -LOGY is preceded by *-o-.* See -O-]

**oloroso** /ɒləˈroʊsoʊ, oʊl-/, *adj.* (of sherry) full-flavoured. [Sp.: odoriferous]

**Olympiad** /əˈlɪmpiæd/, *n.* **1.** a period of four years reckoned from one celebration of the Olympic games to another. **2.** (*oft. l.c.*) a celebration of the modern Olympic games. [ME, from L *olympias,* from Gk]

**Olympian** /əˈlɪmpiən/, *adj.* **1.** of or pertaining to the gods of ancient Greece, who lived on Mt. Olympus. **2.** grand; imposing; superior. *–n.* **3.** one who has competed in the Olympic games.

**Olympic** /əˈlɪmpɪk/, *adj.* **1.** pertaining to the Olympic games. **2.** of a standard suitable for Olympic games: *Olympic pool.* *–n.* **3.** an Olympic game or event. **4. the Olympics,** the Olympic games.

**Olympic games** /– ˈgeɪmz/, *n.pl.* international competitions in running, jumping, swimming, shooting, etc., held every four years, each time in a different country. [named after the plain of *Olympia,* Greece, site of a Pan-Hellenic festival of athletic games held every four years, with occasional interruptions, from 776 BC to AD 393]

**om** /ɒm/, *n.* a mantric syllable indicating the supreme principle, used in mystical contemplation of ultimate reality, as in yoga. Also, **aum.** [Skt: interjection]

**O.M.** /oʊ ˈɛm/, Order of Merit.

**-oma,** *pl.* **-omas, -omata.** a suffix of nouns denoting a morbid condition of growth (tumour), as in *carcinoma, glaucoma, sarcoma.* [Gk]

**Oman** /ˈoʊmæn/, *n.* a country in south-east Arabia; a sultanate.

**omasum** /oʊˈmeɪsəm/, *n., pl.* **sa** /-sə/. the third stomach of a ruminant, between the reticulum and the abomasum; the manyplies. [NL, from L: bullock's tripe]

**ombre** /ˈɒmbə/, *n.* **1.** a card game, fashionable in the 17th and 18th centuries, played usu. by three persons with forty cards. **2.** the player who undertakes to win the pool in this game. Also, *U.S.,* **omber.** [F *(h)ombre,* from Sp. *hombre,* lit., man, from L *homo*]

**ombrometer** /ɒmˈbrɒmətə/, *n.* **1.** a rain gauge, capable of measuring very small amounts of precipitation. **2.** any rain gauge.

**ombudsman** /ˈɒmbədzmən/, *n.* an official appointed by parliament, or some other legislative body, as a city council, to investigate complaints by citizens against the government or its agencies. [Swed.: commissioner]

**omega** /ˈoʊməgə, oʊˈmigə, -ˈmeɪ-/, *n.* **1.** the last letter (Ω, ω = English long O, o) of the Greek alphabet. **2.** the last of any series; the end. [Gk *ô méga,* lit., great *o.* Cf. OMICRON]

**omegatron** /oʊˈmɛgətrɒn/, *n.* an instrument used for separating ions of different isotopes of the same element, by causing them to move in a spiral path by the application of an electric field at right angles to a constant magnetic field; used for the determination of atomic mass and isotopic and chemical analysis.

**omelette** /ˈɒmlət/, *n.* a dish consisting of eggs beaten and fried, often served folded round other ingredients, as mushrooms. Also, *Chiefly U.S.,* **omelet.** [F, earlier *amelette,* metathetic form of *alemette,* var. of *alemelle,* lit., thin plate]

**omen** /ˈoʊmən/, *n.* **1.** anything perceived or happening that is regarded as portending good or evil or giving some indication as to the future; a prophetic sign. **2.** a prognostic. **3.** prophetic significance; presage: *a bird of ill omen.* *–v.t.* **4.** to be an omen of; portend. **5.** to divine, as if from omens. [L]

**omentum** /oʊˈmɛntəm/, *n., pl.* **-ta** /tə/. a fold or duplication of the peritoneum passing between certain of the viscera, being the **great omentum,** or epiploon (attached to and hanging down from the stomach and the transverse colon), and the **lesser omentum** (between the stomach and the liver). [L] – **omental,** *adj.*

**omicron** /oʊˈmaɪkrən, -krɒn, ˈɒmɪkrɒn/, *n.* the fifteenth letter (O, o = English short O, o) of the Greek alphabet. [Gk: *ó mīkrón,* lit., small *o.* Cf. OMEGA]

**ominous** /ˈɒmənəs/, *adj.* **1.** portending evil; inauspicious; threatening: *a dull, ominous rumble.* **2.** having the significance of an omen. [L *ōminōsus* portentous] – **ominously,** *adv.* – **ominousness,** *n.*

**omissible** /oʊˈmɪsəbəl, ə-/, *adj.* that may be omitted.

**omission** /oʊˈmɪʃən, ə-/, *n.* **1.** the act of omitting. **2.** the state of being omitted. **3.** something omitted. [ME, from LL *omissio*]

**omissive** /oʊˈmɪsɪv, ə-/, *adj.* neglecting; leaving out.

**omit** /oʊˈmɪt, ə-/, *v.t.*, **omitted, omitting. 1.** to leave out: *to omit passages of a text.* **2.** to forbear or fail to do, make, use, send, etc.: *to omit a greeting.* [ME *omitte(n)*, from L *omittere* let go, neglect, omit]

**ommateum** /ɒməˈtiəm/, *n.* a compound eye of arthropods.

**ommatidium** /ɒməˈtɪdiəm/, *n., pl.* **-tidia** /-ˈtɪdiə/. one of the radial elements which make up an ommateum. [Latinisation of Gk *ommatídion*, from *ómma* eye + *-idion* (diminutive suffix)] – **ommatidial,** *adj.*

**ommatophore** /ɒˈmætəfɔ/, *n.* a tentacle or movable stalk bearing an eye, as in certain snails. [Gk *ómma* eye -O- + -PHORE] – **ommatophorous** /ɒməˈtɒfərəs/, *adj.*

**omni-**, a word element meaning 'all', used in combination as in *omniactive* (all-active, active everywhere), *omnibenevolent, omnicompetent, omnicredulous, omniprevalent,* and various other words. [L, combining form of *omnis*]

**omnibus** /ˈɒmnɪbəs, -bʌs/, *n., pl.* **-buses,** *adj.* *–n.* **1.** →**bus. 2.** a volume of reprinted works by a single author or related in interest or nature. *–adj.* **3.** pertaining to or covering numerous objects or items at once: *an omnibus clause.* [L: lit., for all (dat. pl. of *omnis*)]

**omnidirectional** /ɒmnidəˈrɛkʃənəl/, *adj.* (of an antenna) transmitting and receiving signals equally well in any direction.

**omnifarious** /ɒmnəˈfɛəriəs/, *adj.* of all forms, varieties, or kinds. [L *omnifārius* of all sorts] – **omnifariousness,** *n.*

**omnific** /ɒmˈnɪfɪk/, *adj.* creating all things.

**omnipotence** /ɒmˈnɪpətəns/, *n.* **1.** the quality of being omnipotent. **2.** (*cap.*) God.

**omnipotent** /ɒmˈnɪpətənt/, *adj.* **1.** almighty, or infinite in power, as God or a deity. **2.** having unlimited or very great authority. *–n.* **3.** an omnipotent being. **4. the Omnipotent,** God. [ME, from L *omnipotens* almighty] – **omnipotently,** *adv.*

**omnipresent** /ɒmnəˈprɛzənt/, *adj.* present everywhere at the same time: *the omnipresent God.* [ML *omnipraesens.* See OMNI-, PRESENT[1]] – **omnipresence,** *n.*

**omnirange** /ˈɒmnireɪndʒ/, *adj.* a radionavigation system in which the pilot can select any position relative to a high frequency ground transmitter, whose signal he can use to help plot his course or position.

**omniscience** /ɒmˈnɪsiəns, ɒmˈnɪʃəns/, *n.* **1.** the quality of being omniscient. **2.** infinite knowledge. **3.** (*cap.*) God.

**omniscient** /ɒmˈnɪsiənt, ɒmˈnɪʃənt/, *adj.* **1.** knowing all things, or having infinite knowledge. *–n.* **2.** an omniscient being. **3. the Omniscient,** God. [OMNI- + L *sciens*, ppr., knowing] – **omnisciently,** *adv.*

**omnium gatherum** /ˌɒmniəm ˈgæðərʊm/, *n.* a miscellaneous collection. [L *omnium* of all + *gatherum* pseudo L form of *gather*]

**omnivore** /ˈɒmnəvɔ/, *n.* an omnivorous person or animal.

**omnivorous** /ɒmˈnɪvərəs/, *adj.* **1.** eating all kinds of foods indiscriminately. **2.** eating both animal and plant foods. **3.** taking in everything, as with the mind. [L *omnivorus*] – **omnivorously,** *adv.* – **omnivorousness,** *n.*

**omophagia** /oʊməˈfeɪdʒiə/, *n.* the eating of raw flesh or raw food. [Gk] – **omophagic** /oʊməˈfædʒɪk/, **omophagous** /oʊˈmɒfəgəs/, *adj.* – **omophagist** /oʊˈmɒfədʒəst/, *n.*

**omophorion** /oʊməˈfɔriən/, *n.* a vestment, resembling a pallium, worn by bishops of the Eastern Church. [LGk *ōmophórion*, from Gk *ōmo-* (from *ômos* shoulder) LGk *-phorion* (from Gk *phérein* to bear)]

**omphalos** /ˈɒmfəlɒs/, *n.* **1.** →**navel. 2.** the central point. [Gk; orig. a rounded or conical stone in the temple of Apollo at Delphi, reputed to mark the centre of the earth]

**omphaloskepsis** /ɒmfəloʊˈskɛpsəs/, *n.* the practice of contemplating one's navel, esp. as carried out by eastern mystics as an aid to inducing a trance-like state. [Gk *omphalós* navel + *sképsis* the act of viewing]

**on** /ɒn/, *prep.* a particle expressing: **1.** position above and in contact with a supporting surface: *on the table.* **2.** contact with any surface: *the picture on the wall; the shoes on my feet.* **3.** immediate proximity: *a house on the coast; to border on absurdity.* **4.** situation, place, etc.: *a scar on the face.* **5.** support, suspension, dependence, reliance, or means of conveyance: *on foot; on wheels.* **6.** state, condition, course, process, etc.: *on the way; on strike.* **7.** ground or basis: *on good authority; a story based on fact.* **8.** risk or liability: *on pain of death.* **9.** time or occasion: *on Sunday.* **10.** with reference to something else: *on the left; on the other side.* **11.** direction or end of motion: *to march on the capital.* **12.** encounter: *to happen on a person.* **13.** object or end of action, thought, desire, etc.: *to gaze on a scene.* **14.** membership or association: *on the staff of a newspaper; to serve on a jury.* **15.** agency or means: *to speak on the telephone; we saw it on television.* **16.** manner: *on the cheap; on the sly.* **17.** subject, reference, or respect: *views on public matters.* **18.** relation of a person to an event which affects him, esp. where that person is morally responsible: *I don't want him to die on me; the apples went bad on me.* **19.** liability for expense: *drinks are on the house.* **20.** engaged in the mining of a specified resource: *on the tin.* **21.** *Colloq.* indulgence to excess: *he's on the bottle, on the turps.* **22.** direction of attention or emotion: *don't go crook on me.* *–adv.* **23.** on oneself or itself: *to put one's coat on.* **24.** fast to a thing, as for support: *to hold on.* **25.** towards a place, point, or object: *to look on.* **26.** forwards, onwards or along, as in any course or process: *further on.* **27.** with continuous procedure: *to work on.* **28.** into or in active operation or performance: *to turn the gas on.* **29. on and off,** intermittently. **30. get on to, a.** to follow up. **b.** (of a person) to consult; contact. **31. on and on,** at great length; without interruption. **32. go on at,** *Colloq.* to berate; scold. **33. have oneself on,** *Colloq.* to think oneself better, more skilled or more important, than one really is. *–adj.* **34.** operating or in use: *the heating is on; the handbrake is on.* **35.** occurring; taking place: *is there anything on tomorrow?* **36.** *Cricket.* →**leg side. 37.** (of items in a menu) available. **38. be on about,** be concerned about; to complain. **39. be on at,** to nag. **40. be on to a good thing, a.** to have hit upon a successful, esp. money-making, scheme, project, etc. **b.** (of a man) to be optimistic of having sexual intercourse with a woman. **41. not on,** *Colloq.* not a possibility; not allowable: *to buy a car now is just not on.* **42. on to,** *Colloq.* in a state of awareness; knowing or realising the true meaning, nature, etc.: *the police are already on to your little game.* *–n.* **43.** the state or fact of being on. **44.** *Cricket.* the on side. [ME *on, an, o,* OE *on, an* on, in, to, c. D *aan,* G *an,* Icel. *ā,* Goth. *ana;* akin to Gk *aná* up, upon. See ANA-]

**ON,** Old Norse. Also, **ON., O.N.**

**onager** /ˈɒnədʒə/, *n., pl.* **-gri** /-graɪ/, **-gers. 1.** *Zool.* a wild ass, *Equus hemionus,* of south-western Asia; kiang. **2.** an ancient and medieval engine of war for throwing stones. [ME, from L, from Gk *ónagros* a wild ass]

**onanism** /ˈoʊnənɪzəm/, *n.* **1.** (in sexual intercourse) withdrawal before occurrence of orgasm. **2.** →**masturbation.** [from *Onan,* son of Judah (Gen. 38:9). See -ISM] – **onanist,** *n.* – **onanistic** /oʊnəˈnɪstɪk/, *adj.*

**once** /wʌns/, *adv.* **1.** at one time in the past; formerly: *a once powerful nation.* **2.** a single time: *once a day.* **3.** even a single time; at any time; ever: *if the facts once become known.* **4.** by a single degree: *a cousin once removed.* **5. once and for all,** finally and decisively. **6. once in a while,** occasionally. **7. once upon a time,** long ago (a favourite beginning of a children's story, etc.). *–conj.* **8.** if or when at any time; if ever. **9.** whenever. *–n.* **10.** a single occasion: *once is enough.* **11. all at once, a.** suddenly. **b.** immediately. **12. at once, a.** immediately. **b.** at the same time: *don't all speak at once.* [ME *ones,* OE *ānes,* adv. (orig. genitive of *ān* ONE); replacing ME *enes,* OE *ǣnes* once, from *ǣne* once + *-es,* adv. suffix]

**once-a-month pill** /wʌns-ə-ˈmʌnθ pɪl/, *n.* a birth-control pill using prostaglandins.

**once-over** /ˈwʌns-oʊvə/, *n. Colloq.* **1.** a quick or superficial examination, inspection, treatment, etc., esp. of a person viewed as a sexual object. **2.** a beating-up; act of physical violence.

**oncer** /ˈwʌnsə/, *n.* **1.** an aberration; something which happens once only. **2.** a parliamentarian who has won a marginal seat in a landslide election and is likely to be voted out at the next election.

**oncogenesis** /ɒŋkoʊ'dʒɛnəsəs/, *n.* the production of viruses which induce tumours.

**oncology** /ɒŋ'kɒlədʒi/, *n.* the part of medical science that treats of tumours. [Gk *ónko(s)* bulk, mass + -LOGY]

**oncoming** /'ɒnkʌmɪŋ/, *adj.* **1.** approaching. *–n.* **2.** the approach: *the oncoming of winter.*

**oncost** /'ɒnkɒst/, *n.* →**burden**[1] (def. 4a).

**oncourse** /'ɒnkɔs/, *adj.;* /ɒn'kɔs/, *adv.* *–adj.* **1.** of or pertaining to facilities or activities on a racecourse: *oncourse betting.* *–adv.* **2.** on a racecourse.

**oncus** /'ɒŋkəs/, *adj. Colloq.* →**onkus.**

**ondine** /ɒn'din/, *n.* →**undine.**

**ondogram** /'ɒndəgræm/, *n.* a record made on an ondograph.

**ondograph** /'ɒndəgræf, -graf/, *n.* an instrument for graphically recording oscillatory variations, as in alternating currents. [F *onde* wave (from L *unda*) + -O- + -GRAPH]

**ondometer** /ɒn'dɒmətə/, *n.* an instrument for measuring wavelength of radio waves.

**one** /wʌn/, *adj.* **1.** being a single unit or individual, rather than two or more; a single: *one apple.* **2.** being a person, thing, or individual instance of a number of kind indicated: *one member of the party.* **3.** some (day, etc., in the future): *you will see him one day.* **4.** single through union, agreement, or harmony: *all were of one mind.* **5.** of a single kind, nature or character; the same: *all our pomp of yesterday is one with Nineveh and Tyre!* **6.** a certain (often used in naming a person otherwise unknown or undescribed): *one John Smith was chosen.* **7.** a particular (day, night, time, etc. in the past): *one evening last week.* **8.** a unique or specially remarkable person or thing: *the one man we can rely on.* **9. all one,** (*used predicatively*) all the same, as in character, meaning, consequence, etc.: *it's all one to me.* *–n.* **10.** the first and lowest whole number, or a symbol, as 1, or I, representing it; unity. **11.** a unit; a single person or thing: *to come one at a time.* **12.** an unusual person; character: *he's a one.* **13. at one,** in a state of unity, agreement, or accord: *hearts at one.* **14. get (guess), (have) it in one,** *Colloq.* to hit on the correct answer, attain a goal, etc., at one's first attempt. **15. one and all,** everybody. **16. one by one,** singly and in succession. *–pron.* **17.** a person or thing of number or kind indicated or understood: *one of the poets.* **18.** (*in certain pronominal combinations*) a person unless definitely specified otherwise: *every one.* **19.** (*with a defining clause or other qualifying words*) a person, or a personified being or agency: *the evil one.* **20.** a person indefinitely; anyone: *as good as one would desire.* **21.** a person of the speaker's kind; such as the speaker himself: *to press one's own claims.* **22.** (to avoid repetition) a person or thing of the kind just mentioned: *the portraits are fine ones.* [ME *oon, oo, o,* OE *ān,* c. G *ein*]

**-one,** a noun suffix used in the names of chemical derivatives, esp. ketones. [Gk, abstracted from fem. patronymics in *-ōnē*]

**one another** /wʌn ə'nʌðə/, *n.* (referring to each of several reciprocally): *they all began to shout at one another.*

**one-armed bandit** /wʌn-amd 'bændət/, *n. Colloq.* →**poker machine.**

**one-eyed** /'wʌn-aɪd/; (*esp. in predicative use*) /wʌn-'aɪd/, *adj.* **1.** having only one eye. **2.** having a strong bias in favour of someone or something: *he's one-eyed about his local football team.*

**one-fire stove** /wʊn-faɪə 'stoʊv/, *n.* →**fuel stove.**

**one-horse** /'wʌn-hɔs/, *adj.* using or having only a single horse: *a one-horse carriage.*

**one-horse town** /– 'taʊn/, *n. Colloq.* an insignificant, unimportant, or backward town.

**oneirocritic** /oʊˌnaɪəroʊ'krɪtɪk/, *n.* **1.** an interpreter of dreams. **2.** oneirocriticism. [Gk *oneirokritikós,* adj., of or pertaining to the interpretation of dreams] – **oneirocritical,** *adj.*

**oneirocriticism** /oʊˌnaɪəroʊ'krɪtəsɪzəm/, *n.* the art of interpreting dreams.

**oneirology** /oʊnaɪ'rɒlədʒi/, *n.* the study and interpretation of dreams.

**oneiromancy** /oʊ'naɪəroʊmænsi/, *n.* divination through dreams. [Gk *óneiro(s)* dream + -MANCY] – **oneiromancer,** *n.*

**one-man band** /wʌn-mæn 'bænd/, *n. Colloq.* **1.** a musician who alone, esp. as a street entertainer, plays many instruments, held or strapped to his body. **2.** one who undertakes alone all the tasks presented by a situation.

**one-man show** /wʌn-mæn 'ʃoʊ/, *n.* an enterprise which is dominated by the personality and wishes of one man.

**oneness** /'wʌnnəs/, *n.* **1.** the quality of being one; singleness; unity; sameness. **2.** agreement; concord; unity of thought, belief, aim, etc.

**one-night stand** /wʌn-naɪt 'stænd/, *n.* **1.** a single performance of a theatrical company, band etc., esp. on tour. **2.** *Colloq.* **a.** a chance encounter with a person, involving sexual intercourse, but not developing into a steady relationship. **b.** a person with whom one has had such an encounter.

**one-off** /'wʌn-ɒf/, *adj.* **1.** individual, unique: *an architect-designed, one-off house.* **2.** (of a book) published in one print run. – **one-off,** *n.*

**one-out** /wʌn-'aʊt/, *adj. Colloq.* alone; unaided: *the Soviet State stood one-out against the world.*

**one-piece** /'wʌn-pis/, *adj.* complete in one piece, as a garment: *a one-piece bathing costume.*

**onerous** /'oʊnərəs/, *adj.* burdensome, oppressive, or troublesome: *onerous duties.* [ME, from L *onerōsus*] – **onerously,** *adv.* – **onerousness,** *n.*

**oneself** /wʌn'sɛlf/, *pron.* **1.** a person's self (often used for emphasis or reflectively): *one hurts oneself by such methods.* **2.** one's proper or normal self; one's normal state of mind (used after *be, become,* or *come to*). Also, **one's self.**

**one-sided** /'wʌn-saɪdəd/, *adj.* **1.** considering but one side of a matter or question; partial, unjust, or unfair: *a one-sided judgment.* **2.** *Law.* unilateral, as a contract. **3.** unbalanced; unequal: *a one-sided fight.* **4.** existing or occurring on one side only. **5.** having but one side, or but one developed or finished side. **6.** having one side larger or more developed than the other. **7.** having the parts all on one side, as an inflorescence.

**onestep** /'wʌnstɛp/, *n.* **1.** (formerly) a kind of dance similar to the foxtrot. **2.** music for this dance.

**one-teacher school** /wʌn-titʃə 'skul/, *n.* a school in a country area with only one teacher and all the pupils combined in a single class; rural school.

**one-time** /'wʌn-taɪm/, *adj.* having been (as specified) at one time; former; quondam: *his one-time partner.*

**one-to-one** /'wʌn-tə-wʌn/, *adj.* **1.** having proportional amounts on each side. **2.** *Maths.* of a correspondence with an exact pairing of the elements of one set with those of another, possibly the same, set.

**one-track** /'wʌn-træk/, *adj.* **1.** with only a single track. **2.** *Colloq.* restricted; preoccupied with one idea: *a one-track mind.*

**one-up** /wʌn-'ʌp/, *v.t.,* **-upped, -upping.** to outmanoeuvre or outwit (someone), esp. in repartee.

**one-upmanship** /wʌn-'ʌpmənʃɪp/, *n.* the art or practice of achieving or demonstrating superiority over others by the acquisition of privileges, status symbols, etc.

**one-way** /'wʌn-weɪ/, *adj.* moving, or allowing motion, in one direction only: *a one-way street.*

**one-way ticket** /– 'tɪkət/, *n.* →**single** (def. 14).

**ongoing** /'ɒngoʊɪŋ/, *adj.* progressing or evolving; continuous.

**onion** /'ʌnjən/, *n.* **1.** a widely cultivated plant of the lily family *Allium cepa,* having an edible succulent bulb of pungent taste and smell. **2.** the bulb. **3.** any of the certain plants similar to the onion, as *A. fistulosum* **(Welsh onion).** **4.** *Colloq.* head. **5.** *Colloq.* a girl with whom a number of men have sexual intercourse on the one occasion. **6. know one's onions,** *Colloq.* to know one's job thoroughly; be experienced. **7. off one's onion,** *Colloq.* mad; insane. [ME *onyon,* from OF *oignon,* from L *ūnio* large pearl, onion. See UNION]

onion, A, leaves; B, bulb

**onion grass** /'– gras/, *n.* **1.** an introduced weed of lawns and pastures, *Romulea rosea,* having underground corms. **2.** →**onion weed.**

**onion orchid** /'– ɔkəd/, *n.* any of many species of the terrestrial orchid genus *Microtis,* with solitary sheathing leaves and very small, usu. green, flowers.

**onion weed** /'– wid/, *n.* **1.** a slender plant with small white flowers, *Nuthoscordum inodorum,* which seeds profusely as well as reproducing from bulbs, and which infests lawns. **2.** any of various similar bulb or corm-bearing plants, as wild onion. Also, **onion grass.**

**onka** /'ɒŋkə/, *n. Colloq.* finger. [rhyming slang, *Onkaparinga,* town in S.A.]

**onkus** /'ɒŋkəs/, *adj. Colloq.* bad; unacceptable. Also, **oncus.** [orig. uncert.]

**on-lending** /'ɒn-lɛndɪŋ/, *n.* the act of lending out, at a slightly higher rate of interest, money which has just been borrowed.

**on-line** /'ɒn-laɪn/, *adj.* **1.** of or pertaining to a computer-controlled device which is directly linked to a computer (opposed to *stand-alone*). **2.** having direct access to a computer: *an on-line branch of the bank.* Also (*esp. in predicative positions*), **on line.**

**onlooker** /'ɒnlʊkə/, *n.* a spectator.

**onlooking** /'ɒnlʊkɪŋ/, *adj.* **1.** looking on; observing; perceiving. **2.** looking onwards or foreboding.

**only** /'oʊnli/, *adv.* **1.** without others or anything further; alone; solely: *only he remained.* **2.** no more than; merely; but; just: *if you would only consent.* **3.** singly; as the only one: *the only begotten Son of God.* **4.** as recently as: *he was here only a moment ago.* **5.** exclusively: *I work here only.* **6.** **only too,** very; extremely: *she was only too pleased to come.* *–adj.* **7.** being the single one or the relatively few of the kind, or sole: *an only son.* **8.** single in superiority or distinction. *–conj.* **9.** but (introducing a single restriction, restraining circumstance, or the like): *I would have gone, only you objected.* **10.** except that; but or except for: *only for him you would not be here.* [ME *oonli(ch),* OE *ānlīc,* var. of *ǣnlīc,* from *ān* ONE + *-līc* -LY]

**o.n.o.** /oʊ ɛn 'oʊ/, or nearest offer.

**onomastic** /ɒnoʊ'mæstɪk/, *adj.* **1.** of or pertaining to proper nouns. **2.** (of a signature) written in (a script) other than that of the main document to which it is appended. [Gk *onomastikós,* from *ónoma* name]

**onomastics** /ɒnoʊ'mæstɪks/, *n.* **1.** the study of the meanings and origins of proper names, esp. of places and persons. **2.** the study of the system underlying the formation of proper names in a given language.

**onomatopoeia** /ˌɒnəmætə'piə/, *n.* **1.** the formation of a name or word by imitating sound associated with the thing designated, as in *mopoke* and *whippoorwill* which probably originated in onomatopoeia. **2.** a word so formed. **3.** the use of imitative and naturally suggestive words for rhetorical effect. [LL, from Gk *onomatopoiïa* the making of words] – **onomatopoeic, onomatopoetic** /ˌɒnəmætəpoʊ'ɛtɪk/, *adj.* – **onomatopoetically** /ˌɒnəmætəpoʊ'ɛtɪkli/, *adv.*

**on-road** /'ɒn-roʊd/, *adj.* **1.** of or pertaining to the functioning, etc., of a motor vehicle when it is being driven, esp. on public roads. **2.** suitable only for use on prepared roads: *an on-road vehicle.*

**on-road price** /– 'praɪs/, *n.* the total expenditure involved before a motor vehicle can be used on public roads, including purchase price and necessary registration and insurance fees.

**onrush** /'ɒnrʌʃ/, *n.* a strong forward rush, flow, etc.

**onset** /'ɒnsɛt/, *n.* **1.** an assault or attack: *a violent onset.* **2.** a beginning or start.

**onshore** /'ɒnʃɔ, ɒn'ʃɔ/, *adj.;* /ɒn'ʃɔ/, *adv.* *–adj.* **1.** towards or located on the shore. *–adv.* **2.** towards the shore.

**on side** /'ɒn saɪd/, *n. Cricket.* →**leg side.**

**on-side** /'ɒn-saɪd/, *adj. Cricket.* →**leg-side.**

**onside** /ɒn'saɪd/, *adj.* **1.** not offside. **2.** in agreement, acting favourably: *I'll be right now the wife's onside.*

**onslaught** /'ɒnslɔt/, *n.* an onset, assault, or attack, esp. a vigorous or furious one.

**onstage** /'ɒnsteɪdʒ, ɒn'steɪdʒ/, *adj.;* /ɒn'steɪdʒ/, *adv.* *–adj.* **1.** in view of the audience. *–adv.* **2.** on or on to the stage.

**on-stream analysis** /ˌɒn-strim ə'næləsəs/, *n.* continuous instrument analysis of a process (such as oil refining, ore separation) such that any departures from standards set for the final product can be recognised and rectified.

**on-the-job** /'ɒn-ðə-dʒɒb/, *adj.* while working: *on-the-job training.*

**onto** /'ɒntu/, *prep.* to a place or position on; upon; on: *to get onto a box.*

**ontogeny** /ɒn'tɒdʒəni/, *n.* the development of an individual organism (as contrasted with *phylogeny*). Also, **ontogenesis** /ɒntoʊ'dʒɛnəsəs/. [Gk *onto-* (combining form of *ṓn* being) + -GENY] – **ontogenetic** /ˌɒntoʊdʒə'nɛtɪk/, *adj.* – **ontogenist,** *n.*

**ontological argument** /ɒntəˌlɒdʒɪkəl 'agjəmənt/, *n.* the a priori argument for the being of God, founded on the assumption that existence is a property and one discoverable in the very concept of God, who would fall short of perfection if he had his being in intellect alone instead of in intellect and in reality.

**ontologism** /ɒn'tɒlədʒɪzəm/, *n.* the doctrine that the human intellect has an immediate cognition of God as its proper object and the principle of all its cognitions.

**ontology** /ɒn'tɒlədʒi/, *n.* **1.** the science of being, as such. **2.** the branch of metaphysics that investigates the nature of being and of the first principles, or categories, involved. [NL *ontologia,* from Gk *onto-* (combining form of *ṓn* being) + *-logia* -LOGY] – **ontological** /ɒntə'lɒdʒɪkəl/, *adj.* – **ontologist,** *n.*

**onus** /'oʊnəs/, *n.* a burden; a responsibility. [L: load, burden]

**onus probandi** /– proʊ'bændi/, *n.* the burden of proof. [L]

**onward** /'ɒnwəd/, *adj.* **1.** directed or moving onwards or forwards. *–adv.* **2.** onwards. [ME. See ON, -WARD]

**onwards** /'ɒnwədz/, *adv.* **1.** towards a point ahead or in front; forwards, as in space or time. **2.** at a position or point in advance.

**onychophoran** /ɒni'kɒfərən/, *n.* **1.** any of the caterpillar-like animals of the genus *Peripatus,* subphylum Onychophora, having both arthropod and annelid characteristics. *–adj.* **2.** of or pertaining to such an animal. [NL *Onychophora,* from Gk *onycho-* (combining form of *ónyx* claw) + *-phora* -PHORE]

**onyomancy** /'ɒniəmænsi/, *n.* an interpretation of personal characteristics from the study of the fingernails.

**onyx** /'ɒnɪks/, *n.* **1.** a quartz consisting of straight layers or bands which differ in colour, used for ornament. **2.** a nail of a finger or toe. [ME *onix,* from L *onyx,* from Gk: nail, claw, veined gem]

**oo-,** a word element meaning 'egg'. [Gk, combining form of *ōión*]

**oocyte** /'oʊəsaɪt/, *n.* a female germ cell in the maturation stage. Also, **ovocyte.**

**oodles** /'udlz/, *n.pl. Colloq.* a large quantity: *oodles of money.*

**oogamy** /oʊ'ɒgəmi/, *n.* the fusion during the process of sexual reproduction, of the relatively large female gamete with the small male gamete.

**oogenesis** /oʊə'dʒɛnəsəs/, *n.* the genesis or origin and development of the ovum.

**oogonium** /oʊə'goʊniəm/, *n., pl.* **-nia** /-niə/, **-niums.** **1.** *Biol.* one of the female germ cells at the multiplication stage, preceding the maturation or oocyte stage. **2.** *Bot.* the one-celled female reproductive organ in certain thallophytic plants, usu. a more or less spherical sac containing one or more eggs. [NL; see OO-, -GONIUM]

**oolite** /'oʊəlaɪt/, *n.* **1.** a small spherical to ellipsoidal concretion, usu. calcareous, formed in shallow water under special conditions. **2.** a limestone composed of such concretions, in some places altered to ironstone by replacement with iron oxide. **3.** (*cap.*) an upper division of the European Jurassic, largely composed of oolite limestone. [F *oolithe,* from *oo-* OO- + *-lithe* -LITE] – **oolitic** /oʊə'lɪtɪk/, *adj.*

**oology** /oʊ'ɒlədʒi/, *n.* the part of ornithology that treats of birds' eggs. – **oological** /oʊə'lɒdʒɪkəl/, *adj.* – **oologist,** *n.*

**oolong** /'ulɒŋ/, *n.* a variety of semi-fermented brown or amber tea from Taiwan. [Chinese *wu-lung,* lit., black dragon]

**oomiak** /'umiæk/, *n.* →**umiak.**

**oomph** /ʊmf/, *n. Colloq.* **1.** vitality; energy. **2.** sex appeal. – **oomphy,** *adj.*

**oondoroo** /ʊndə'ru/, *n.* an Australian plant, *Solanum simile,* often found in mallee areas. [Aboriginal]

**oophorectomy** /oʊəfə'rɛktəmi/, *n., pl.* **-mies.** *Surg.* the operation of removal of one or both ovaries. [*oophor-* (from NL, combining form of *oophoron* ovary, from Gk: lit., eggbearer) + -ECTOMY]

**oophoritis** /oʊəfə'raɪtəs/, *n.* inflammation of an ovary, usu. combined with an inflammation of the Fallopian tubes; ovaritis.

**oophyte** /ˈouəfaɪt/, *n.* the plant which produces the gametes, in flowerless plants as mosses and ferns which have both sexual and asexual phases during reproduction.

**oops** /ʊps, ups/, *interj.* (an exclamation of surprise or shock, as on bumping someone or dropping something). Cf. **whoops.**

**oorarrie** /uˈrari/, *n.* a hopping mouse, *Notomys cervinus,* of the Australian interior.

**oosphere** /ˈouəsfɪə/, *n.* an unfertilised egg within an oogonium.

**oospore** /ˈouəspɔ/, *n.* a fertilised egg within an oogonium. Also, *Obs.,* **oosperm** /ˈouəspɜm/. **–oosporic** /ouəˈspɔrɪk/, **oosporous** /ouˈɒspərəs, ouəˈspɔrəs/, *adj.*

**ootheca** /ouəˈθikə/, *n., pl.* **-cae** /-si/. a case or capsule containing eggs, as that of certain gastropods and insects. [NL, from Gk *ōo-* OO- + *thḗkē* case]

**ooze**[1] /uz/, *v.,* **oozed, oozing,** *n.* *–v.i.* **1.** (of moisture, etc.) to percolate or exude, as through pores or small openings. **2.** (of air, etc.) to pass slowly or gradually as if through pores or small openings. **3.** (of a substance) to exude moisture, etc. **4.** (of information, charm, etc.) to leak or pass (*out,* etc.) slowly or imperceptibly. *–v.t.* **5.** to make by oozing. **6.** to exude (moisture, etc.). **7.** to exude or radiate abundantly: *he oozed charm.* *–n.* **8.** the act of oozing. **9.** that which oozes. **10.** an infusion of oak bark, sumach, etc., used in tanning. [ME *wos,* OE *wōs* juice, moisture]

**ooze**[2] /uz/, *n.* **1.** a calcareous mud (chiefly the shells of small organisms) covering parts of the ocean bottom. **2.** soft mud, or slime. **3.** a marsh or bog. [ME *wose,* OE *wāse* mud]

**ooze leather** /ˈuz lɛðə/, *n.* leather, usu. of calfskin, with a soft suede finish.

**oozle** /ˈuzəl/, *v.t.,* **-zled, -zling.** *Colloq.* to steal. [var. of HOOZLE]

**oozy**[1] /ˈuzi/, *adj.,* **-zier, -ziest. 1.** exuding moisture. **2.** damp with moisture. [OOZE[1] + -Y[1]]

**oozy**[2] /ˈuzi/, *adj.,* **-zier, -ziest.** of or like ooze, soft mud, or slime. [ME *wosie,* from *wose* mud. See OOZE[2]] **–ooziness,** *n.*

**op-,** variant of **ob-,** (by assimilation) before *p,* as in *oppose.*

**op., 1.** operation. **2.** opus.

**O.P.** /ou ˈpi/, *adj.* **1.** out of print. *–n.* **2.** *Colloq.* (usu. of a cigarette) other people's. Also, **o.p.**

**opacite** /ˈoupəsaɪt/, *n.* any of certain indeterminable mineral substances (probably iron compounds) frequently observed in the microscopic examination of certain igneous rocks.

**opacity** /ouˈpæsəti/, *n., pl.* **-ties. 1.** the state of being opaque. **2.** something opaque. **3.** *Photog.* the ratio of the incident light and that emerging from a photographic density. **4.** the ability of a coat of paint to obliterate the colours of a surface to which it is applied. **5.** obscurity of meaning. **6.** mental dullness. [L *opācitas* shade]

**opah** /ˈoupə/, *n.* a large, deep-bodied, brilliantly coloured, oceanic food fish, *Lampris regius,* of Australian and other waters. Also, **moonfish.** [from a W African language (possibly Twi, Fante, or Igbo)]

**opal** /ˈoupəl/, *n.* a mineral, an amorphous form of silica, ($SiO_2$ with some water of hydration), not as hard or as heavy as quartz, found in many varieties and colours (often a milky white), certain of which are iridescent and valued as gems. [L *opalus,* from Gk *opállios*]

**opalesce** /oupəˈlɛs/, *v.i.,* **-lesced, -lescing.** to exhibit a play of colours like that of the opal.

**opalescent** /oupəˈlɛsənt/, *adj.* **1.** exhibiting a play of colours like that of the opal. **2.** having a milky iridescence. **–opalescence,** *n.*

**opal glass** /ˈoupəl glas/, *n.* a translucent or opaque glass.

**opaline** /ˈoupəlaɪn/, *adj.* of or like opal; opalescent.

**op amp** /ˈɒp æmp/, *n.* →**operational amplifier.**

**opaque** /ouˈpeɪk/, *adj., n., v.,* **opaqued, opaquing.** *–adj.* **1.** impenetrable to light; not able to transmit, or not transmitting, light. **2.** not able to transmit, or not transmitting, radiation, sound, heat, etc. **3.** not shining or bright; dark; dull. **4.** hard to understand; not clear or lucid; obscure. **5.** unintelligent; stupid. *–n.* **6.** something opaque. **7.** *Photog.* a colouring matter, usu. black or red, used to darken a part of a negative. *–v.t.* **8.** to cause to become opaque. [ME *opake,* from L *opācus* shady, darkened] **–opaquely,** *adv.* **–opaqueness,** *n.*

**op art** /ɒp ˈat/, *n.* a style of abstract art of the post 1950s which uses optical effects to give the illusion of movement, these effects themselves being the central aim.

**op. cit.** /ɒp ˈsɪt/, (in the work cited). [L *opere citātō*]

**ope** /oup/, *adj., v.t., v.i.,* **oped, oping.** *Archaic.* →**open.**

**open** /ˈoupən/, *adj.* **1.** not shut, as a door, gate, etc. **2.** not closed, covered, or shut up, as a house, box, drawer, etc. **3.** not enclosed as by barriers, as a space. **4.** that may be entered, used, shared, competed for, etc., by all: *an open session; open competition.* **5.** (of shops, etc.) ready to do business; ready to admit members of the public. **6.** (of a court hearing, etc.) able to be attended by members of the public or the press. **7.** accessible or available (oft. fol. by *to*): *the only course still open.* **8.** unfilled, as a position. **9.** not engaged, as time. **10.** without prohibition as to hunting or fishing: *open season.* **11.** *U.S. Colloq.* without legal restrictions, or not enforcing legal restrictions, as to saloons, gambling places, etc.: *an open town.* **12.** undecided, as a question. **13.** liable or subject to: *open to question.* **14.** accessible to appeals, ideas, offers, etc. (oft. fol. by *to*): *to be open to conviction.* **15.** having no cover, roof, etc.: *an open boat.* **16.** not covered or protected; exposed or bare: *to lay open internal parts with a knife.* **17.** unobstructed, as a passage, country, stretch of water, view, etc. **18.** free from ice: *open water in arctic regions.* **19.** free from frost; mild or moderate: *an open winter.* **20.** exposed to general view or knowledge; existing, carried on, etc., without concealment: *open disregard of rules.* **21.** acting publicly or without concealment, as a person. **22.** unreserved, candid, or frank, as persons or their speech, aspect, etc.: *an open face.* **23.** having openings or apertures: *open ranks.* **24.** perforated or porous: *an open texture.* **25.** expanded, extended, or spread out: *an open newspaper.* **26.** generous liberal, or bounteous: *to give with an open hand.* **27.** *Print.* **a.** (of type) in outline form. **b.** widely spaced or leaded, as printed matter. **28.** not yet balanced or adjusted, as an account. **29.** (of a cheque) uncrossed. **30.** *Music.* **a.** (of an organ pipe) not closed at the far end. **b.** (of a string) not stopped by a finger. **c.** (of a note) produced by such a pipe or string or, on a wind instrument, without the aid of a slide, key, etc. **31.** *Naut.* free from fog. **32.** not constipated, as the bowels. **33.** *Phonet.* **a.** pronounced with a relatively large opening above the tongue: *'cot' has a more open vowel than 'caught'.* **b.** (of a syllable) ending with its vowel. **34.** *Football.* of or pertaining to fast play in which the ball travels rapidly and over some distance from player to player. **35.** of or pertaining to certain gaols as prison farms, etc., in which heavy restrictions are not imposed, esp. no fences. *–v.t.* **36.** to move (a door, gate, etc.) from a shut or closed position so as to admit of passage. **37.** to make (a house, box, drawer, etc.) open (oft. fol. by *up*). **38.** to render (any enclosed space) open to passage or access. **39.** to give access to; make accessible or available, as for use. **40.** to recall or revoke, as a judgment or decree, for the purpose of allowing further contest or delay. **41.** to clear of obstructions, as a passage, etc. **42.** to make (bodily passages) clear. **43.** to uncover, lay bare, or expose to view. **44.** to disclose, reveal, or divulge: *to open one's mind.* **45.** to render accessible to knowledge, enlightenment, sympathy, etc. **46.** to expand, extend, or spread out: *to open a map.* **47.** to make less compact, less close together, or the like: *to open ranks.* **48.** to establish for the entrance or use of the public, customers, etc.: *to open an office.* **49.** to set in action, begin, start, or commence (sometimes fol. by *up*): *to open a campaign.* **50.** to cut or break into. **51.** to make an incision or opening in. **52.** to make or produce (an opening) by cutting or breaking, or by pushing aside or removing obstructions: *to open a way through a crowd.* **53.** *Naut.* to come in sight of, or get a view of, as by passing some intervening object. **54.** *Law.* to make the first statement of (a case) to the court or jury. **55.** *Cards.* to begin a hand by making (the first bid) or playing (a card or suit). *–v.i.* **56.** to become open, as a door, building, box, enclosure, etc. **57.** to afford access (into, to, etc.): *a door that opened into a garden.* **58.** (of a building, shop, etc.) to open its doors to the public. **59.** to begin a session or term, as a school. **60.** to begin a season or tour, as a theatrical company. **61.** to have an opening, passage, or outlet (into, upon, etc.): *a room that opens into a corridor.* **62.** to have its opening or outlet (fol. by *towards, to,* etc.). **63.** to come apart or asunder, or burst open, so as to admit of passage or display the interior. **64.** to become disclosed or revealed. **65.** to come into view, or become more visible or plain, as on nearer approach. **66.** to become receptive to knowledge, sympathy, etc., as the mind. **67.** to disclose or reveal one's knowledge, thoughts, feelings, etc. **68.** to spread out or expand, as the hand or a fan. **69.** to open a book, etc.: *open at page 32.* **70.** to become less compact, less close together, or the like: *the ranks opened.* **71.** to begin, start, or commence; start operations. **72.** *Hunting.* (of hounds) to begin to bark, as on the scent of game. **73.** *Law.* to make the first statement of a case to the court or jury. **74.** *Cards.* to make the first bet, bid, lead, etc. **75. open up, a.** to make accessible, as undeveloped land. **b.** to begin firing. *–n.* **76.** an open or clear space. **77.** the open air. **78.** the open water, as of the sea. **79.** the situation of one who does not use or seek concealment. **80.** an opening or aperture. **81.** an opening or opportunity. **82.** an open competition. **83. the open,** the unenclosed or unobstructed country. [ME and OE, c. G *offen*] – **openly,** *adv.* – **openness,** *n.*

**open air** /– 'ɛə/, *n.* the unconfined atmosphere; outdoor air.

**open-air** /'oupən-ɛə/, *adj.* existing in, taking place in, or characteristic of the open air; outdoor.

**open-and-shut** /'oupən-ən-ʃʌt/, *adj.* obvious; easily decided: *an open-and-shut case of fraud.*

**open book** /oupən 'bʊk/, *n.* **1.** a person whose emotions or motives can be clearly discerned. **2.** anything which can be easily understood or interpreted.

**open-book examination** /,oupən-bʊk əgzæmə'neɪʃən, ɛg-/, *n.* an examination to which it is permitted to take reference material, as text books, notes, etc.

**open-cast** /'oupən-kast/, *adj. Mining.* →**open-cut.** – **open-casting,** *n.*

**open chain** /oupən 'tʃeɪn/, *n.* a linking of atoms in an organic molecule which may be represented by a structural formula whose ends do not join to form a ring.

**open circuit** /– 'sɜkət/, *n.* an incomplete circuit, preventing the electric current from flowing.

**open city** /– 'sɪti/, *n.* a city which is officially declared to be demilitarised during a war and thus, under international law, not subject to attack.

**open classroom** /– 'klasrum/, *n.* a system of school architecture or organisation, which gives pupils the opportunity to work individually or in groups as is appropriate to their learning, and frees them from having to sit at neatly ordered rows of desks. Also, **open planning, open school.**

**open cluster** /– 'klʌstə/, *n.* a group of stars having a common motion through space in which the stars are not densely packed (as in a globular cluster) but are interspersed with gas and dust clouds.

**open cut** /– 'kʌt/, *n.* a shallow open pit allowing excavation of near surface rock layers.

**open-cut** /'oupən-kʌt/, *adj., v.,* **-cut, -cutting.** *–adj.* **1.** of or pertaining to an open cut. *–v.i.* **2.** to make an open cut.

**open day** /'oupən deɪ/, *n.* a day on which certain institutions, as schools, are open to members of the public and special activities, exhibitions, etc., are arranged for their entertainment.

**open door** /– 'dɔ/, *n.* **1.** the policy of admitting all nations to a country upon equal terms, esp. for trade. **2.** free admission or access; admission to all upon equal terms.

**open-ended** /'oupən-ɛndəd/, *adj.* organised or arranged so as to allow for various contingencies; without fixed limits.

**opener** /'oupənə/, *n.* **1.** one who or that which opens, esp. a tin-opener or a bottle opener. **2.** *Cricket.* either of the two batsmen who open their side's innings by batting first.

**open-eyed** /oupən-'aɪd/, *adj.* **1.** having the eyes open. **2.** having the eyes wide open as in wonder. **3.** watchful; alert.

**open-faced** /'oupən-feɪst/, *adj.* **1.** having a frank or ingenuous face. **2.** (of a watch) having the dial covered only by the crystal.

**open go** /oupən 'gou/, *n.* an unrestricted opportunity.

**open government** /– 'gʌvənmənt/, *n.* a system of government whereby the public has legal access to official information or documents unless otherwise determined by law, and whereby public servants are not prevented from disclosing official information except that which is protected by statute, as that relating to national security.

**open-graze** /oupən-'greɪz/, *v.t.,* **-grazed, -grazing.** to graze (cattle, etc.) freely on all the available land of a property.

**open hand** /oupən 'hænd/, *n.* (in bowls) the side of the head (def. 35) where a bowl may be played without obstruction.

**open-handed** /'oupən-hændəd/, *adj.* generous; free. – **open-handedly,** *adv.* – **open-handedness,** *n.*

**open-hearted** /'oupən-hatəd/, *adj.* **1.** unreserved, candid, or frank. **2.** kindly. – **open-heartedly,** *adv.* – **open-heartedness,** *n.*

**open-hearth** /oupən-'haθ/, *adj.* denoting a shallow-hearth reverberatory furnace for steel-making, with two openings at each end to admit fuel and air. Combustion takes place over the molten metal charge.

**open-hearth process** /'– prousɛs/, *n.* the steel-making process using an open-hearth furnace.

**open-heart surgery** /oupən-hat 'sɜdʒəri/, *n.* surgery which requires the heart to be exposed, and circulation to be maintained by artificial means.

**open house** /oupən 'haus/, *n.* **1.** a house hospitably open to all friends who may wish to visit it or enjoy its entertainment. **2. keep open house,** to offer hospitality to all; be willing to entertain visitors at any time. *–adj.* **3.** of or pertaining to an occasion when there is a general invitation to friends to call in: *it's open house at our place.*

**opening** /'oupnɪŋ, 'oupənɪŋ/, *n.* **1.** a making or becoming open. **2.** the act of one who or that which opens (in any sense). **3.** an unobstructed or unoccupied space or place. **4.** an open space in solid matter; a gap, hole, or aperture. **5.** *U.S.* a tract of land thinly wooded as compared with adjoining forest tracts. **6.** the act of beginning, starting, or commencing. **7.** the first part or initial stage of anything. **8.** a vacancy. **9.** an opportunity. **10.** a formal or official beginning. **11.** the first performance of a theatrical production; first public showing of an exhibition, etc. **12.** *Law.* the statement of the case made by counsel to the court or jury preliminary to adducing evidence. **13.** *Chess, etc.* **a.** a mode of beginning a game. **b.** the first part of a game.

**opening time** /'– taɪm/, *n.* the time at which hotels are permitted by law to start selling drinks.

**open letter** /oupən 'lɛtə/, *n.* a letter made public by radio, newspaper, or such, but written as though to a specific person.

**open-line** /oupən-'laɪn/, *n.;* /'oupən-laɪn/, *adj.* →**talkback.**

**open list** /'oupən lɪst/, *n. Colloq.* the list of drugs which can be prescribed, as a pharmaceutical benefit, without restriction.

**open market** /– 'makət/, *n.* a market (def. 5) where there is free trade, and prices are determined by supply and demand, not fixed by some outside agency.

**open-minded** /'oupən-maɪndəd/, *adj.* having or showing a mind open to new arguments or ideas; unprejudiced. – **open-mindedly,** *adv.* – **open-mindedness,** *n.*

**open-mouthed** /oupən-'mauðd/, *adj.* **1.** having the mouth open. **2.** gaping with surprise or astonishment. **3.** greedy, ravenous, or rapacious. **4.** clamouring at the sight of game or prey, as hounds. **5.** vociferous or clamorous. **6.** having a wide mouth, as a vessel.

**open order** /oupən 'ɔdə/, *n.* **1.** a military formation of troops on a ceremonial parade in which the rear rank steps back if in two ranks, or the ranks open if in three ranks, to allow more space for the inspecting officer, etc., to pass. **2.** a prescribed distance between ships in convoy or vehicles proceeding under orders.

**open plan** /– 'plæn/, *n.* an open-plan system.

**open-plan** /'oupən-plæn/, *adj.* (of the interior space of a dwelling, office, etc.) not having walls between areas designed for different uses; having few fixed partitions.

**open planning** /oupən 'plænɪŋ/, *n.* →**open classroom.**

**open policy** /– 'pɒləsi/, *n.* a form of marine policy where the value of the subject insured is not stated, and has to be proved when a loss occurs.

**open position** /'– pəzɪʃən/, *n.* arrangement of a musical chord with wide spaces between the parts.

**open-range** /'oupən-reɪndʒ/, *adj.* of or pertaining to the pasturing of livestock on unfenced land, with, as a result, no control over types and quantities of feed.

**open sandwich** /oʊpən 'sænwɪtʃ/, *n.* a thick slice of bread, garnished with meat, cheese, eggs, or the like.

**open school** /– 'skul/, *n.* →**open classroom.**

**open sea** /– 'si/, *n.* the main body of a sea or ocean, esp. that outside territorial waters or not enclosed by headlands or lying between straits.

**open season** /'– sizən/, *n.* **1.** a fixed period of time when certain animals, birds, etc. can be hunted without restriction. **2.** a concerted attack (on persons or institutions): *it was open season on politicians.*

**open secret** /– 'sikrət/, *n.* something supposedly secret but which is widely known.

**open sesame** /– 'sɛsəmi/, *n.* any very effective method for producing a desired result. [from the use of these words to open the door of the robbers' den in *Ali Baba and the Forty Thieves,* in *The Arabian Nights' Entertainments*]

**open side** /'– saɪd/, *n.* (in ice skating) that side of a skater's body which is on the outside of the curve being skated.

**open slather** /– 'slæðə/, *n. Colloq.* a situation in which there are no restraints, often becoming chaotic or rowdy; free-for-all.

**open string** /– 'strɪŋ/, *n.* an unstopped string on a stringed musical instrument.

**open university** /– junə'vɜsəti/, *n.* a university which does not have regular lectures but which teaches a variety of subjects by readily accessible means, as by television, radio, circularised notes, etc.

**open verdict** /– 'vɜdɪkt/, *n.* a finding of death by a coroner's jury without stating its cause.

**open web joint,** *n.* a metal truss with top and bottom chords parallel, in which the diagonal members are formed from one continuous rod. It is used in light frame buildings, as aeroplane hangars, etc.

**openwork** /'oʊpənwɜk/, *n.* any kind of work, esp. ornamental, as of metal, stone, wood, embroidery, lace, etc., showing openings through its substance.

**opera**[1] /'ɒprə, 'ɒpərə/, *n.* **1.** an extended dramatic composition in which music is an essential and predominant factor, consisting of recitatives, arias, choruses, etc., with orchestral accompaniment, scenery, acting, and sometimes dancing; a musical drama. See **comic opera, grand opera.** **2.** the form or branch of musical and dramatic art represented by such compositions. **3.** the score or the words of a musical drama. **4.** a performance of one. **5.** *Colloq.* an opera house. [It., from L: service, work, a work]

**opera**[2] /'ɒpərə/, *n.* plural form of **opus.**

**operable** /'ɒpərəbəl, 'ɒprə-/, *adj.* **1.** that can be put into practice. **2.** admitting of a surgical operation.

**opéra bouffe** /ɒprə 'buf/, *n.* a comic opera, esp. of farcical character. [F]

**opera-cloak** /'ɒprə-kloʊk/, *n.* a cloak for evening wear.

**opera comique** /ɒprə kɒ'mik/, *n.* →**comic opera.** [F]

**opera glasses** /'ɒprə glasəz/, *n.pl.* a small, low-power pair of binoculars for use in a theatre, etc. Also, **opera glass.**

**opera hat** /'– hæt/, *n.* a man's collapsible tall hat, held open or in shape by springs.

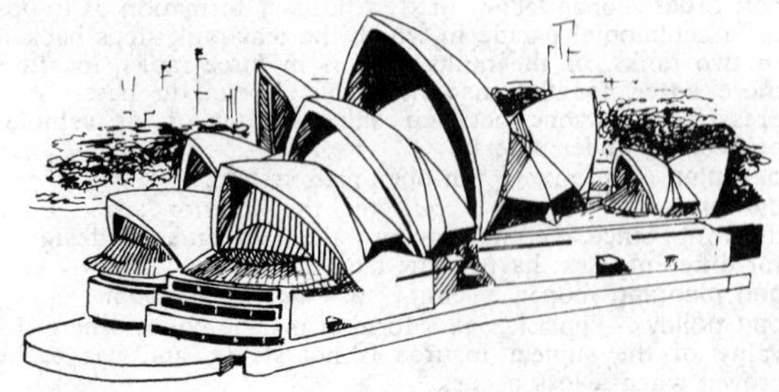

opera house (def. 1): Sydney Opera House

**opera house** /'– haʊs/, *n.* **1.** a theatre devoted chiefly to operas. **2.** *Colloq.* a hotel which is an early opener. [def. 2 ironic ref. to the Sydney Opera House which opened several years later than orig. planned]

**operand** /'ɒpərænd/, *n.* the quantity upon which a mathematical operation is performed. [L *operandum,* ger. of *operārī* work, toil]

**operant** /'ɒpərənt/, *adj.* **1.** operating; producing effects. **2.** *Psychol.* of or pertaining to behaviour elicited by an environment rather than by a specific stimulus. *–n.* **3.** one who or that which operates. [L *operans*]

opera hat

**operant conditioning** /– kən'dɪʃənɪŋ/, *n.* (in psychology) a procedure by which the probability of an organism emitting a particular response is increased by reinforcement whenever the response occurs.

**opera seria** /ɒprə 'sɪəriə/, *n.* an 18th-century style of opera with a serious subject often based on heroic or mythological plot and characterised musically by much use of aria and recitative. [It.: serious opera]

**operate** /'ɒpəreɪt/, *v.,* **-rated, -rating.** *–v.i.* **1.** to work or run, as a machine does. **2.** to work or use a machine, apparatus, or the like. **3.** to act effectively; exert force or influence (oft. fol. by *on* or *upon*): *now the same causes are operating for war.* **4.** to perform some process of work or treatment. **5.** *Surg.* to perform some manual act or series of acts upon the body of a patient, usu. with instruments, to remedy deformity, injury, or disease. **6.** (of medicines, etc.) to produce the effect intended. **7.** *Mil., Navy.* **a.** to carry on operations in war. **b.** to give orders and accomplish military acts, as distinguished from doing staff work. **8.** to carry on transactions in securities, or some commodity, esp. speculatively or on a large scale. *–v.t.* **9.** to manage or use (a machine, etc.) at work: *to operate a switchboard.* **10.** to keep (a machine, apparatus, factory, industrial system, etc.) working or in operation. **11.** to bring about, effect, or produce, as by action or the exertion of force or influence. [L *operātus,* pp., having done work, having had effect] – **operatable,** *adj.*

**operatic** /ɒpə'rætɪk/, *adj.* of or pertaining to opera: *operatic music.* – **operatically,** *adv.*

**operating** /'ɒpəreɪtɪŋ/, *adj.* used for or in surgical operations: *operating table; operating theatre.*

**operating cost** /'– kɒst/, *n.* (in the costing of services, as transport) →**unit cost.**

**operation** /ɒpə'reɪʃən/, *n.* **1.** the act, process, or manner of operating. **2.** the state of being operative: *a rule no longer in operation.* **3.** the power of operating; efficacy, influence, or virtue. **4.** exertion of force or influence; agency. **5.** a process of a practical or mechanical nature in some form of work or production: *a delicate operation in watchmaking.* **6.** a course of productive or industrial activity: *building operations.* **7.** a particular course or process: *mental operations.* **8.** a business transaction, esp. one of a speculative nature or on a large scale: *operations in oil.* **9.** *Surg.* a process or method of operating on the body of a patient, as with instruments, to remedy injury, etc. **10.** *Maths.* **a.** a process such as addition. **b.** the action of applying a mathematical process to a quantity or quantities. **11.** *Mil., Navy.* **a.** the conduct of a campaign. **b.** a campaign.

**operational** /ɒpə'reɪʃənəl/, *adj.* **1.** of or pertaining to an operation or operations. **2.** ready for use; in working order. **3.** *Mil.* of, pertaining to, required for, or involved in military operations.

**operational amplifier** /– 'æmpləfaɪə/, *n.* a basic circuit which, together with external components, can be used to add, subtract, invert, integrate, differentiate, etc., electrical signals. Also, **op amp.**

**operationalism** /ɒpə'reɪʃənəlɪzəm/, *n.* the doctrine that scientific concepts secure their meaning from the relevant set of operations involved, stimulated by the relativity theory of Einstein.

**operations branch** /ɒpə'reɪʃənz bræntʃ/, *n.* that section of a military staff which is concerned with the conduct of a campaign.

**operations research** /'– rəsɜtʃ/, *n.* the analysis, usu. involving mathematical treatment, of a process, problem, or operation to determine its purpose and effectiveness and to gain maximum efficacy. Also, **operational research.**

**operations room** /'– rum/, *n.* a room where military operations are planned.

**operative** /'ɒpərətɪv, 'ɒprə-/, *n.* **1.** a worker; one engaged, employed, or skilled in some branch of work, esp. productive or industrial work; a workman, artisan, or factory hand. **2.** *U.S.* a secret agent; detective. *–adj.* **3.** operating, or exerting force or influence. **4.** having force, or being in effect or operation: *laws operative in a community.* **5.** effective or efficacious. **6.** engaged in, concerned with, or pertaining to work or productive activity. **7.** *Med.* concerned with, involving, or pertaining to remedial operations: *operative surgery.* – **operatively,** *adv.* – **operativeness,** *n.*

**operative date** /– 'deɪt/, *n.* the date upon which the provisions of a contract, award, or agreement come into force.

**operator** /'ɒpəreɪtə/, *n.* **1.** a worker; one employed or skilled in operating a machine, apparatus, or the like: *a wireless operator; telephone operator.* **2.** one who conducts some working or industrial establishment, enterprise, or system: *the operators of a mine.* **3.** one who deals in shares, currency, etc., esp. speculatively or on a large scale. **4.** *Colloq.* one who successfully manipulates people or situations: *he's a smooth operator.*

**operculate** /ɒ'pɜkjulət, -leɪt/, *adj.* having an operculum. Also, **operculated.**

**operculum** /ɒ'pɜkjələm/, *n., pl.* **-la** /-lə/, **-lums. 1.** *Bot., Zool., etc.* a part or organ serving as a lid or cover, as a covering flap on a seed vessel. **2.** *Zool.* **a.** the gill cover of fishes and amphibians. **b.** (in many gastropods) a horny plate which closes the opening of the shell when the animal is retracted. [L: a cover, lid]

O, operculum (def. 2a)

**opere citato** /,ɒpəreɪ saɪ'tatoʊ/, See **op. cit.**

**operetta** /ɒpə'rɛtə/, *n.* a short opera, commonly of a light character. [It., diminutive of *opera* OPERA[1]]

**operose** /'ɒpəroʊs/, *adj.* **1.** industrious, as a person. **2.** done with or involving much labour. [L *operōsus*] – **operosely,** *adv.* – **operoseness,** *n.*

**ophicleide** /'ɒfəklaɪd/, *n.* a musical wind instrument, a development of the old wooden serpent, consisting of a conical metal tube bent double. [F, from Gk *óphi(s)* serpent + *kleís* key]

ophicleide

**ophidian** /ɒ'fɪdiən/, *adj.* **1.** of, pertaining to, or belonging to the snakes. *–n.* **2.** a snake. [NL *Ophidia,* pl. (from Gk *óphis* serpent) + -AN]

**ophiolatry** /ɒfi'ɒlətri, oʊ-/, *n.* the worship of snakes. [Gk *óphi(s)* snake + -OLATRY] – **ophiolatrous,** *adj.*

**ophiology** /ɒfi'ɒlədʒi, oʊ-/, *n.* the study of snakes. – **ophiological** /ɒfiə'lɒdʒɪkəl/, *adj.* – **ophiologist** /ɒfi'ɒlədʒəst/, *n.*

**ophiomancy** /'ɒfiəmænsi, 'oʊ-/, *n.* divination from serpents.

**ophite** /'ɒfit/, *n.* a greenish altered diabase. [L *ophītēs,* from Gk: serpent-like, serpentine]

**ophitic** /ɒ'fɪtɪk/, *adj.* denoting or pertaining to a rock texture exhibited by certain ophites (diabases), in which elongate felspar crystals are embedded in a matrix of pyroxenes.

**ophthalm.,** ophthalmology. Also, **ophthalmol.**

**ophthalmia** /ɒf'θælmiə/, *n.* inflammation of the eye, esp. of its membranes or external structures. [LL, from Gk: a disease of eyes]

**ophthalmic** /ɒf'θælmɪk/, *adj.* of or pertaining to the eye; ocular.

**ophthalmitis** /ɒfθæl'maɪtəs/, *n.* inflammation of the eye. [NL]

**ophthalmo-,** a word element meaning 'eye'. [Gk, combining form of *ophthalmós*]

**ophthalmologist** /ɒfθæl'mɒlədʒəst/, *n.* a doctor of medicine skilled in ophthalmology.

**ophthalmology** /ɒfθæl'mɒlədʒi/, *n.* the science dealing with the anatomy, functions, and diseases of the eye. – **ophthalmological** /ɒf,θælmə'lɒdʒɪkəl/, *adj.*

**ophthalmoscope** /ɒf'θælməskoʊp/, *n.* an instrument for viewing the interior of the eye or examining the retina. – **ophthalmoscopic** /ɒf,θælmə'skɒpɪk/, **ophthalmoscopical** /ɒf,θælmə'skɒpɪkəl/, *adj.*

**ophthalmoscopy** /ɒfθæl'mɒskəpi/, *n.* the use of an ophthalmoscope.

**-opia,** a word element of nouns denoting a condition of sight or of the visual organs, as in *amblyopia, diplopia, emmetropia, hemeralopia, myopia.* [Gk, from *ōps* eye]

**opiate** /'oʊpiət, -eɪt/, *n., adj.;* /'oʊpieɪt/ *v.,* **-ated, -ating.** *–n.* **1.** a medicine that contains opium and hence has the quality of inducing sleep; a narcotic. **2.** anything that causes dullness or inaction, or that soothes the feelings. *–adj.* **3.** mixed or prepared with opium. **4.** inducing sleep; soporific; narcotic. *–v.t.* **5.** to subject to an opiate; stupefy. **6.** to dull or deaden. [ML *opiātus,* from L *opium* OPIUM]

**opine** /oʊ'paɪn/, *v.t., v.i.,* **opined, opining.** to think; deem; hold or express an opinion, or as one's opinion. [L *opīnārī* think, deem]

**opinion** /ə'pɪnjən/, *n.* **1.** judgment or belief resting on grounds insufficient to produce certainty. **2.** a personal view, attitude, or estimation: *public opinion.* **3.** the expression of a personal view, estimation, or judgment: *to give an opinion on tariffs.* **4.** a formal or professional judgment expressed, esp. in law: *counsel's opinion.* **5.** a judgment or estimate of a person or thing with respect to character, merit, etc. **6.** a favourable estimate; esteem. [ME, from OF, from L *opīnio* supposition]

**opinionated** /ə'pɪnjəneɪtəd/, *adj.* obstinate or conceited with regard to one's opinions; conceitedly dogmatic. – **opinionatedness,** *n.*

**opinionative** /ə'pɪnjəneɪtɪv/, *adj.* **1.** of, pertaining to, or of the nature of opinion. **2.** opinionated. – **opinionatively,** *adv.* – **opinionativeness,** *n.*

**opinion poll** /ə'pɪnjən poʊl/, *n.* →**gallup poll.**

**opisthobranch** /ə'pɪsθəbræŋk/, *adj.* **1.** of or relating to the Opisthobranchia, an order of marine molluscs having the gills behind the heart and lacking an operculum. *–n.* **2.** a mollusc of the order Opisthobranchia, as the sea-hare and sea-slug.

**opium** /'oʊpiəm/, *n.* the inspissated juice of the opium poppy, containing morphine and other alkaloids, a stimulant narcotic (in sufficient quantities a powerful narcotic poison) of great value in medicine to relieve pain, induce sleep, etc. [ME, from L, from Gk *ópion,* diminutive of *opós* juice]

**opium den** /'– dɛn/, *n.* a place where opium can be bought and smoked.

**opiumism** /'oʊpiəmɪzəm/, *n.* **1.** the habit of taking opium. **2.** a morbid condition induced by the habitual use of opium.

**opium poppy** /'oʊpiəm pɒpi/, *n.* a poppy, *Papaver somniferum,* with grey-green leaves and white or red flowers which are a source of opium; mostly grown in south-western Asia.

**opossum** /ə'pɒsəm/, *n.* **1.** *N.Z.* the brush-tailed possum, *Trichosurus vulpecula,* introduced from Australia. **2. a.** a prehensile-tailed marsupial, *Didelphis virginiana,* about the size of a large cat, common in the southern U.S., which feigns death when caught. **b.** any of many neotropical genera of the same family. Also, **possum.** [Algonquian]

opossum (def. 2)

**opossum shrimp** /'– ʃrɪmp/, *n.* any of the small, shrimplike schizopod crustaceans constituting the family Mysidae, of which the females carry their eggs in a pouch between the legs.

**opp.,** opposite.

**oppilate** /'ɒpəleɪt/, *v.t.,* **-lated, -lating.** to stop up; fill with obstructing matter; obstruct. [L *oppīlātus,* pp.] – **oppilation** /ɒpə'leɪʃən/, *n.*

**opponency** /ə'poʊnənsi/, *n.* **1.** the act of opposing. **2.** the state of being an opponent.

**opponent** /ə'poʊnənt/, *n.* **1.** one who is on the opposite side in a contest, controversy or the like; an adversary. *–adj.* **2.**

being opposite, as in position. **3.** opposing; adverse. **4.** *Anat.* bringing parts into opposition, as the muscles which set the thumb and little finger against each other. [L *oppōnens,* ppr., opposing]

**opportune** /ˈɒpətjun/, *adj.* **1.** appropriate or favourable: *an opportune moment.* **2.** occurring or coming at an appropriate time; timely: *an opportune warning.* [ME, from L *opportūnus*] – **opportunely,** *adv.* – **opportuneness,** *n.*

**opportunism** /ɒpəˈtjunɪzəm, ˈɒpətʃunɪzəm/, *n.* **1.** the policy or practice, in politics or otherwise, of adapting actions, etc., to expediency or circumstances (often with implication of sacrifice of principle). **2.** an action or proceeding resulting from this policy. – **opportunist,** *n., adj.* – **opportunistic** /ɒpətʃuˈnɪstɪk/, *adj.*

**opportunity** /ɒpəˈtjunəti/, *n., pl.* **-ties.** an appropriate or favourable time or occasion.

**opportunity school** /ˈ– skul/, *n.* a school which operates with curriculums or procedures which differ from the usual and are calculated to assist special groups of children as the specially gifted, the specially handicapped, etc.

**opportunity shop** /ˈ– ʃɒp/, *n.* a shop run by a church, charity, etc., for the sale of second hand goods, esp. clothes. Also, **op-shop.**

**opposable** /əˈpoʊzəbəl/, *adj.* **1.** capable of being placed opposite to something else. **2.** that may be opposed. – **opposability** /əpoʊzəˈbɪləti/, *n.*

**oppose** /əˈpoʊz/, *v.,* **-posed, -posing.** –*v.t.* **1.** to act or contend in opposition to; drive against; resist; combat. **2.** to stand in the way of; hinder. **3.** to set as an opponent or adversary. **4.** be hostile or adverse to, as in opinion. **5.** to set as an obstacle or hindrance: *to oppose reason to force.* **6.** to set against in some relation, as of offsetting, antithesis, or contrast: *to oppose the advantages to the disadvantages.* **7.** to use or to take as being opposite or contrary: *words opposed in meaning.* **8.** to set (something) over against something else in place, or so as to face or be opposite. –*v.i.* **9.** to be or act in opposition. [ME, from OF *opposer,* b. L *oppōnere* set against and F *poser* POSE[1]] – **opposer,** *n.*

**opposite** /ˈɒpəsət/, *adj.* **1.** placed or lying over against something else or each other, or in a corresponding position from an intervening line, space, or thing: *opposite ends of a room.* **2.** contrary or diametrically different, as in nature, qualities, direction, result, or significance. **3.** *Bot.* **a.** situated on diametrically opposed sides of an axis, as leaves when there are two on one node. **b.** having one organ vertically above another; superposed. **4.** *Obs.* adverse or inimical. –*n.* **5.** one who or that which is opposite or contrary. **6.** →**antonym.** **7.** *Rare.* an opponent. –*prep.* **8.** facing: *she sat opposite me.* **9.** in a complementary role or position: *she played opposite a famous Shakespearian actor.* –*adv.* **10.** on opposite sides. [ME, from L *oppositus,* pp., put before or against, opposed] – **oppositely,** *adv.* – **oppositeness,** *n.*

opposite (def. 3a): opposite leaves

**opposite number** /– ˈnʌmbə/, *n.* a person who holds a corresponding position in another situation; counterpart.

**opposite sex** /– ˈsɛks/, *n.* men, as opposed to women, or women, as opposed to men.

**opposition** /ɒpəˈzɪʃən/, *n.* **1.** the action of resisting or combating. **2.** antagonism; hostility. **3.** an opposing group or body. **4.** (*usu. cap.*) the major political party opposed to the party in power. **5.** the act of placing opposite. **6.** the state or positon of being placed opposite. **7.** the act of opposing or the state of being opposed by way of offset, antithesis, or contrast. **8.** *Logic.* the relation with regard to truth and falsehood between two propositions which have the same subject and predicate, but which differ in quantity or quality, or in both. **9.** *Astron.* **a.** the situation of two heavenly bodies when their longitudes or right ascensions differ by 180°. **b.** the opposition of the moon or a planet and the sun, occurring when the earth is directly between them. [L *oppositio;* replacing ME *opposicioun,* from OF *opposicion*] – **oppositional,** *adj.*

**oppositionist** /ɒpəˈzɪʃənəst/, *n.* a member of an opposition.

**oppress** /əˈprɛs/, *v.t.* **1.** to lie heavily upon (the mind, a person, etc.), as care, sorrow, or any disturbing thought does. **2.** to burden with cruel or unjust impositions or restraints; to subject to a burdensome or harsh exercise of authority or power. **3.** to weigh down, as sleep or weariness does. **4.** to put down, subdue or suppress. [ME *oppresse(n),* from ML *oppressāre,* frequentative of L *opprimere* press against, bear down, subdue] – **oppressor,** *n.*

**oppression** /əˈprɛʃən/, *n.* **1.** the exercise of authority or power in a burdensome, cruel, or unjust manner. **2.** the act of oppressing. **3.** the state of being oppressed. **4.** the feeling of being oppressed by something weighing down the bodily powers or depressing the mind.

**oppressive** /əˈprɛsɪv/, *adj.* **1.** burdensome, unjustly harsh, or tyrannical, as a king, taxes, measures, etc. **2.** causing discomfort because uncomfortably great, intense, elaborate, etc.: *oppressive heat.* **3.** distressing or grievous, as sorrows. – **oppressively,** *adv.* – **oppressiveness,** *n.*

**opprobrious** /əˈproʊbriəs/, *adj.* **1.** conveying or expressing opprobrium, as language, a speaker, etc.: *opprobrious invectives.* **2.** disgraceful or shameful; contumelious. [ME, from LL *opprōbriōsus*] – **opprobriously,** *adv.* – **opprobriousness,** *n.*

**opprobrium** /əˈproʊbriəm/, *n.* **1.** the disgrace or the reproach incurred by conduct considered shameful; infamy. **2.** a cause or object of such reproach. [L]

**oppugn** /əˈpjun/, *v.t.* **1.** to assail by criticism, argument, or action. **2.** to call in question (rights, judgment, etc.); dispute (statements, etc.). [ME, from F *oppugner,* from L *oppugnāre* fight against] – **oppugner,** *n.*

**oppugnant** /əˈpʌgnənt/, *adj.* opposing; antagonistic; contrary. – **oppugnancy,** *n.*

**oppure** /ɒˈpureɪ/, *adv.* (a musical direction) to be performed as an alternative. [It: alternative]

**op-shop** /ˈɒp-ʃɒp/, *n.* →**opportunity shop.**

**-opsis,** a word element indicating apparent likeness, as in *coreopsis.* [Gk: appearance, sight]

**opsonic** /ɒpˈsɒnɪk/, *adj.* of, pertaining to, or influenced by opsonin.

**opsonic index** /– ˈɪndɛks/, *n.* the ratio of the number of bacteria taken up by phagocytes in the blood serum of a patient or test animal, to the number taken up in normal blood serum.

**opsonin** /ˈɒpsənɪn/, *n.* a constituent of normal or immune blood serum which makes invading bacteria more susceptible to the destructive action of the phagocytes. [Gk *opsṓn(ion)* provisions + -IN[2]]

**opsonise** /ˈɒpsənaɪz/, *v.t.,* **-nised, -nising.** to increase the susceptibility of (bacteria) to ingestion by phagocytes. Also, **opsonize.** – **opsonisation** /ɒpsənaɪˈzeɪʃən/, *n.*

**opt** /ɒpt/, *v.i.* **1.** to make a choice; choose. **2. opt out, a.** to decide not to participate. **b.** *Colloq.* to decide to take no part in the accepted social institutions and conventions. [F *opter,* from L *optāre* choose, wish]

**opt.,** **1.** optative. **2.** optical. **3.** optician. **4.** optics.

**Optacon** /ˈɒptəkən/, *n.* an electronic machine devised for the use of blind people, which converts the optical image of language symbols, as letters, figures, etc., into a corresponding tactile image formed by an array of rods vibrating against the fingertip. [Trademark: *op(tical -to-)ta(ctile) con-(verter)*]

**optative** /ˈɒptətɪv/, *adj.* **1.** designating or pertaining to a verb mood (as in Greek) having among its functions the expression of a wish, as Greek *íoimen* 'may we (i.e., we wish we might) go'. –*n.* **2.** the optative mood. **3.** a verb in it. [LL *optātivus* serving to express a wish] – **optatively,** *adv.*

**optic** /ˈɒptɪk/, *adj.* **1.** pertaining to or connected with the eye as the organ of sight, or sight as a function of the brain. **2.** optical. –*n.* **3.** (*usu. pl.*) the eye. **4. have an optic at,** *Colloq.* to look at. [ML *opticus,* from Gk *optikós* of sight]

**optical** /ˈɒptɪkəl/, *adj.* **1.** acting by means of sight or light, as instruments. **2.** constructed to assist the sight, as devices. **3.** pertaining to sight; visual: *an optical illusion.* **4.** pertaining to optics. **5.** dealing with or skilled in optics. – **optically,** *adv.*

**optical activity** /– æk'tɪvəti/, *n.* the property of compounds which consists of rotating the plane of vibration of polarised light.

**optical flint glass,** *n.* See **flint glass.**

**optical isomerism** /ɒptɪkəl aɪ'sɒmərɪzəm/, *n.* a form of isomerism in which the isomers differ only in their optical activity.

**optical maser** /– 'meɪzə/, *n.* →**laser.**

**optical printer** /– 'prɪntə/, *n.* an apparatus for enabling images from one film to be photographed on to another film by means of a lens; used in making reduction prints and for special effects and trick work.

**optical rotation** /– roʊ'teɪʃən/, *n.* the angle through which the plane of polarised light is rotated on passing through an optically active substance.

**optical scanner** /– 'skænə/, *n.* a photoelectric cell that scans printed data and converts it into the electric impulses fed into a computer or data-processing machine.

**optical sound** /– 'saʊnd/, *n.* the effect produced by the photographic recording and reproducing of sound pulses.

**optic axis** /ɒptɪk 'æksəs/, *n.* the direction or directions, uniaxial or biaxial respectively, in a crystal exhibiting double refraction, along which this phenomenon does not occur.

**optician** /ɒp'tɪʃən/, *n.* **1.** one who makes glasses for remedying defects of vision, in accordance with the prescriptions of oculists. **2.** a maker or seller of optical glasses and instruments. [F *opticien,* from ML *optica* OPTICS. See -ICIAN]

**optic nerve** /ɒptɪk 'nɜv/, *n.* the nerve of sight, connecting the eye with the brain.

**optics** /'ɒptɪks/, *n.* the branch of physical science that deals with the properties and phenomena of light and with vision. [pl. of OPTIC. See -ICS]

**optic thalamus** /ɒptɪk 'θæləməs/, *n.* →**thalamus** (def. 1).

**optimise** /'ɒptəmaɪz/, *v.*, **-mised, -mising.** *–v.i.* **1.** to be optimistic. *–v.t.* **2.** to make the best of; make the most effective use of. Also, **optimize.** – **optimisation** /ɒptəmaɪ'zeɪʃən/, *n.*

**optimism** /'ɒptəmɪzəm/, *n.* **1.** disposition to hope for the best; tendency to look on the bright side of things. **2.** the belief that good ultimately predominates over evil in the world. **3.** the doctrine that the existing world is the best of all possible worlds. **4.** the belief that goodness pervades reality. [NL *optimismus,* from L *optimus* best]

**optimist** /'ɒptəməst/, *n.* one given to optimism.

**optimistic** /ɒptə'mɪstɪk/, *adj.* **1.** disposed to take a favourable view of things. **2.** of, pertaining to, or characterised by optimism. Also, **optimistical.** – **optimistically,** *adv.*

**optimum** /'ɒptəməm/, *n., pl.* **-ma** /-mə/, **-mums,** *adj.* *–n.* **1.** the best or most favourable point, degree, amount, etc., for the purpose, as of temperature, light, moisture, etc., for the growth or reproduction of an organism. *–adj.* **2.** best or most favourable: *optimum conditions.* [L (neut.): best (superl. of *bonus* good)]

**option** /'ɒpʃən/, *n.* **1.** power or liberty of choosing; right of freedom of choice. **2.** something which may be or is chosen; choice. **3.** the act of choosing. **4.** a privilege acquired, as by the payment of a premium or consideration, of demanding, within a specified time, the carrying out of a transaction upon stipulated terms; the right, conferred by an agreement, to buy (or to decline to buy) a property within a certain time. **5.** *Aus. Rules.* privilege of a second kick given to a player who has scored a behind, in a case of a breach of the rules by an opponent while the ball is in flight. [L *optio* choice]

**optional** /'ɒpʃənəl/, *adj.* **1.** left to one's choice. **2.** leaving something to choice. – **optionally,** *adv.*

**optoelectronics** /,ɒptoʊɛlɛk'trɒnɪks/, *n.* the branch of electronics dealing with light sensitive and light emitting devices. – **optoelectronic,** *adj.*

**optometer** /ɒp'tɒmətə/, *n.* any of various instruments for measuring the refractive error of an eye. [OPT(IC) + -O- + -METER[1]]

**optometrist** /ɒp'tɒmətrəst/, *n.* one skilled in optometry.

**optometry** /ɒp'tɒmətri/, *n.* the practice or art of testing the eyes by means of suitable instruments or appliances, for defects of vision, in order to supply suitable glasses.

**opulence** /'ɒpjələns/, *n.* **1.** wealth, riches, or affluence. **2.** abundance, as of resources, etc. **3.** the state of being opulent. Also, **opulency.**

**opulent** /'ɒpjələnt/, *adj.* **1.** wealthy, rich, or affluent, as persons or places. **2.** richly supplied; abundant or plentiful: *opulent sunshine.* [L *opulens, opulentus* rich, wealthy] – **opulently,** *adv.*

**opuntia** /oʊ'pʌnʃiə/, *n.* any plant of the genus *Opuntia,* comprising fleshy herbs, shrubby plants, and sometimes trees, with branches usu. composed of flattened or globose joints, and usu. with yellow flowers and pear-shaped or ovoid edible fruit; prickly pear. [NL, from L *Opuntius* pertaining to *Opūs,* town in Locris, Greece]

**opus** /'oʊpəs/, *n., pl.* **opera** /'ɒpərə/. **1.** a work or composition. **2.** a musical composition. **3.** one of the compositions of a composer as numbered according to order of publication. *Abbrev.:* op. [L: work, labour, a work]

**opuscule** /ɒ'pʌskjul/, *n.* **1.** a small work. **2.** a literary or musical work of small size. [L *opusculum,* diminutive of *opus* OPUS]

**or**[1] /ɔ/, *conj.* a particle used: **1.** to connect words, phrases, or clauses representing alternatives: *to be or not to be.* **2.** to connect alternative terms: *the Hawaiian or Sandwich islands.* **3.** often in correlation: *either ... or; or ... or; whether ... or.* [ME *or,* orig. unstressed member of correlative *other ... or,* earlier *other ... other,* OE oththe ... oththe either ... or]

**or**[2] /ɔ/, *prep., conj. Archaic.* before; ere. [ME *or* before, OE *ār* soon, early (c. Icel. *ār,* Goth. *air* early); akin to OE *ǣr* soon, before, ERE]

**or**[3] /ɔ/, *n.* the tincture gold or yellow. [ME, from F, from L *aurum* gold]

**-or**[1], **1.** a suffix of nouns denoting a state or condition, a quality or property, etc., as in *error, terror.* **2.** a U.S. alternative of **-our,** as in *color, odor,* etc. [L; in some cases, esp. the U.S. variants, replacing -OUR]

**-or**[2], a suffix of nouns denoting one who or that which does something, or has some particular function or office, as in *actor, confessor, creditor, distributor, elevator, emperor, governor, juror, refractor, tailor, traitor.* This suffix occurs chiefly in nouns originally Latin, or formed from Latin stems. In some cases it is used as an alternative or a substitute for **-er**[1], esp. in legal terms (often correlative with forms in **-ee**) or with some other differentiation of use: *assignor, grantor, lessor, sailor, survivor, vendor.* [L; in some cases replacing ME *-our,* from AF *-(e)our* (= F *-eur*), from L *-or, -ātor,* etc.]

**orach** /'ɒrɪtʃ/, *n.* any of various plants of the widespread genus *Atriplex,* esp. the garden orach, *A. hortensis,* of Asia, widely naturalised in Europe, and cultivated as a leaf vegetable. Also, **orache.** [ME *orage,* from OF *arache,* from L *ātriplex,* from Gk *atráphaxis*]

**oracle** /'ɒrəkəl/, *n.* **1.** (esp. in ancient Greece) an utterance, often ambiguous or obscure, given by a priest or priestess at a shrine as the response of a god to an inquiry. **2.** the agency or medium giving such responses, or a shrine or place at which they were given: *the oracle of Apollo at Delphi.* **3.** a divine communication or revelation. **4.** (*pl.*) the Scriptures. **5.** the holy of holies in the Jewish temple. See I Kings, 6:16, 19-23. **6.** any person or thing serving as an agency of divine communication. **7.** any utterance made or received as authoritative and infallible. **8.** a person who delivers authoritative or highly regarded pronouncements. [ME, from OF, from L *ōrāculum*]

**oracular** /ə'rækjələ/, *adj.* **1.** of the nature of, resembling, or suggesting an oracle: *an oracular response.* **2.** giving forth utterances or decisions as if by special inspiration or authority. **3.** uttered or delivered as if divinely inspired or infallible; sententious. **4.** ambiguous or obscure. **5.** portentous. – **oracularly,** *adv.*

**oral** /'ɒrəl/, *adj.* **1.** uttered by the mouth; spoken: *oral testimony.* **2.** employing speech, as teachers or methods of teaching. **3.** of or pertaining to the mouth: *the oral cavity.* **4.** done, taken, or administered by the mouth: *an oral dose of medicine.* **5.** *Zool.* pertaining to that surface of polyps and marine animals which contains the mouth and tentacles. **6.** *Phonet.* articulated with none of the voice issuing through the nose; *b* and *v* are oral consonants, and the normal English vowels are oral. *–n.* **7.** an oral examination in a school, university, etc. [L *ōs* mouth + -AL[1]] – **orally,** *adv.*

i = peat ɪ = pit ɛ = pet æ = pat a = part ɒ = pot ʌ = putt ɔ = port ʊ = put u = pool ɜ = pert ə = apart aɪ = buy eɪ = bay ɔɪ = boy aʊ = how
oʊ = hoe ɪə = here ɛə = hair ʊə = tour g = give θ = thin ð = then ʃ = show ʒ = measure tʃ = choke dʒ = joke ŋ = sing j = you õ = Fr. bon

**orang** /ə'ræng/, *n.* →**orang-outang.**

**orange** /'ɒrɪndʒ/, *n.* **1.** a globose reddish yellow edible citrus fruit of which there are two principal kinds, the bitter and sweet, the latter comprising the most important of the citrus fruits. **2.** any of the white-flowered evergreen rutaceous trees yielding it, as *Citrus aurantium* (**bitter, Seville,** or **sour orange**) and *C. sinensis* (**sweet orange**), cultivated in warm countries. **3.** any of several other citrus trees, as *Poncirus trifoliata* (see **trifoliate orange**) a hardy Japanese species grown for hedges in the U.S. **4.** any of certain trees of other genera, as *Maclura pomifera* (see **Osage orange**), or the fruit. **5.** a colour between yellow and red in the spectrum; reddish yellow. *–adj.* **6.** of or pertaining to the orange. **7.** made with or prepared from oranges or having the flavour of orange. **8.** reddish yellow. [ME *orange,* from OF (b. with *or* gold), c. Sp. *naranja,* from Ar. *nāranj,* from Pers. *nārang,* from Skt *nāranja*]

**orangeade** /ɒrɪndʒ'eɪd/, *n.* an orange-flavoured drink.

**orange blossom** /'ɒrɪndʒ blɒsəm/, *n.* the flower of the orange, much worn in wreaths, etc., by brides.

**orange-blossom orchid** /ˌɒrɪndʒ-blɒsəm 'ɔkəd/, *n.* an epiphytic or rock orchid, *Sarcochilus falcatus,* found usu. in coastal ranges of eastern Australia.

**orange-breasted parrot** /ˌɒrɪndʒ-brɛstəd 'pærət/, *n.* a medium-sized flock parrot, *Neophema chrysogaster,* of coastal eastern Australia.

**Orangeism** /'ɒrɪndʒɪzəm/, *n.* the principles and practices of the Orangemen. – **Orangeist,** *n.*

**Orangeman** /'ɒrɪndʒmən/, *n., pl.* **-men.** **1.** a member of a secret society formed in the north of Ireland in 1795, having for its object the maintenance of the Protestant religion and political ascendancy. **2.** a Northern Ireland protestant.

**orange pekoe** /ɒrɪndʒ 'pikoʊ/, *n.* **1.** a superior black tea composed of only the smallest top leaves and grown in India and Ceylon. **2.** any Indian or Ceylon tea of good quality.

**orange people** /'– pipəl/, *n.pl. Colloq.* adherents of yoga who wear uniformly orange clothing.

**orangery** /'ɒrɪndʒəri/, *n., pl.* **-ries.** a place, as a greenhouse, in which orange trees are cultivated. [F *orangerie,* from *oranger* orange tree, from *orange* ORANGE]

**orange stick** /'ɒrɪndʒ stɪk/, *n.* a small stick, originally of orangewood, with one pointed and one rounded end, used in manicure.

**orange-time** /'ɒrɪndʒ-taɪm/, *n. Colloq.* a scheduled break in a game, as hockey, football, etc., during which oranges are eaten by the players as a refreshment.

**orange-winged sittella** /ˌɒrɪndʒ-wɪŋd sɪ'tɛlə/, *n.* a small Australian bird, *Neositta chrysoptera,* with orange markings on the wings, noted for its habit of running down the trunks of trees in search of insects; tree runner.

**orangewood** /'ɒrɪndʒwʊd/, *n.* the hard, fine-grained, yellowish wood of the orange tree, used in inlaid work and fine turnery.

**orang-outang** /ə'ræŋ-ətæŋ/, *n.* a large, long-armed anthropoid ape, *Pongo pygmaeus,* of arboreal habits, found in Borneo and Sumatra. Also, **orang, orang-utan** /ə'ræŋ-ətæn/. [Malay: man of the woods]

orang-outang

**orate** /ɒ'reɪt/, *v.i.,* **orated, orating.** to make an oration; hold forth. [back-formation from ORATION]

**oration** /ɒ'reɪʃən/, *n.* **1.** a formal speech, esp. one delivered on a special occasion, as on an anniversary, at a funeral, or at academic exercises. **2.** a speech characterised by an elevated style, diction, or delivery. [ME *oracion,* from L *ōrātio* speech, discourse, prayer]

**orator** /'ɒrətə/, *n.* one who delivers an oration; a public speaker, esp. one of great eloquence. [L: speaker, supplicant; replacing ME *oratour,* from AF] – **oratress** /'ɒrətrəs/, **oratrix** /'ɒrətrɪks/, *n. fem.*

**oratorical** /ɒrə'tɒrɪkəl/, *adj.* **1.** of, pertaining to, or characteristic of an orator or oratory. **2.** given to oratory. – **oratorically,** *adv.*

**oratorio** /ɒrə'tɔrioʊ/, *n., pl.* **-rios.** an extended musical composition, with a text more or less dramatic in character and usu. based upon a religious theme, for solo voices, chorus, and orchestra, and performed without action, costume, or scenery. [It., from LL *ōrātōrium* ORATORY[2]; so named from the musical services in the church of the Oratory of St Philip Neri in Rome]

**oratory**[1] /'ɒrətri/, *n.* **1.** the exercise of eloquence; eloquent speaking. **2.** the art of an orator; the art of public speaking. [L *ōrātōria,* properly fem. of *ōrātōrius* of an orator]

**oratory**[2] /'ɒrətri/, *n., pl.* **-ries.** a place of prayer, as a small chapel or a room for private devotions. [ME, from LL *ōrātōrium* place of prayer, properly neut. of L *ōrātorius* oratorical]

**orb** /ɔb/, *n.* **1.** *Chiefly Poetic.* any of the heavenly bodies: *the orb of day* (the sun). **2.** a sphere or globe. **3.** *Chiefly Poetic.* the eyeball or eye. **4.** a globe bearing a cross; the mound, or emblem of sovereignty, esp. as part of the regalia of England. **5.** *Rare.* a circle, or anything circular. **6.** *Astron. Obs.* the orbit of a heavenly body. **7.** *Astrol.* the space within which the influence of a planet, etc., is supposed to act. **8.** *Obs.* the earth. **9.** *Obs.* a range or area of action. *–v.t.* **10.** to form into a circle or a sphere. **11.** *Poetic.* to encircle; enclose. *–v.i.* **12.** to move in an orbit. **13.** *Obs.* to assume the shape of an orb. [L *orbis* circle, disc, orb]

orb (def. 4)

**orbicular** /ɔ'bɪkjələ/, *adj.* like an orb; circular; ringlike; spherical; rounded. [ME, from LL *orbiculāris,* from L *orbiculus,* diminutive of *orbis* ORB] – **orbicularity** /ɔˌbɪkjə'lærəti/, *n.* – **orbicularly,** *adv.*

**orbiculate** /ɔ'bɪkjələt, -leɪt/, *adj.* orbicular; rounded. Also, **orbiculated.** [L *orbiculātus,* from *orbiculus.* See ORBICULAR]

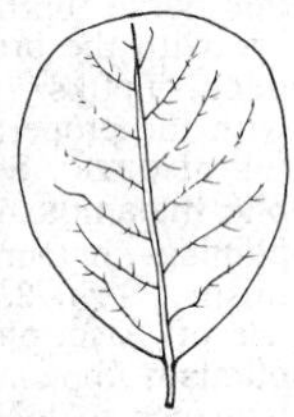

orbicular leaf

**orbit** /'ɔbət/, *n.* **1.** the elliptical or curved path described by a planet, satellite, etc., about a body, as the earth or sun. **2.** a course regularly pursued as in life. **3.** *Anat.* **a.** the bony cavity of the skull which contains the eye; the eye socket. **b.** the eye. **4.** *Zool.* the part surrounding the eye of a bird or insect. **5.** an orb or sphere. **6.** *Chem.* the path of an electron around the nucleus of an atom. *–v.t.* **7.** to move or travel in an orbital path. *–v.i.* **8.** to describe an orbit. [L *orbita* wheel track, course, circuit] – **orbital,** *adj.*

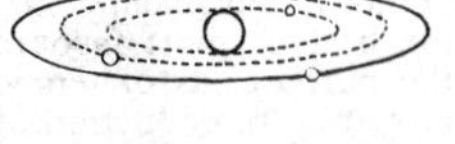
orbits of planets around a sun

**orbitale** /ɔbə'tali/, *n. Anat.* **1.** the lowermost point on the lower margin of the left orbit, located instrumentally on the skull. **2.** the lowermost point on the lower margin of the left orbit, located by palpation on the head. [L (neut.): of an orbit]

**orbital electron** /ɔbətəl ə'lɛktrɒn/, *n.* an electron contained within an atom which may be thought of as orbiting round the nucleus; a planetary electron.

**orbital engine** /– 'ɛndʒən/, *n.* a non-reciprocating engine in which a vaned piston does not rotate but moves eccentrically orbiting the combustion chamber.

**orbital index** /– 'ɪndɛks/, *n.* the ratio of the maximum breadth to the maximum height of the orbital cavity.

**orbital period** /– 'pɪəriəd/, *n.* the time taken by an orbiting object to complete one orbit.

**orbital velocity** /– və'lɒsəti/, *n.* the velocity required to overcome the earth's gravitational attraction and so maintain a satellite in orbit.

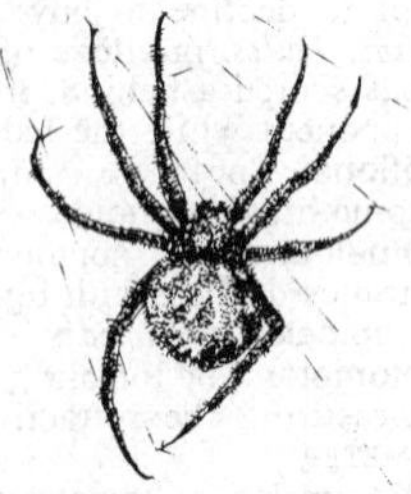
orb-weaver

**orb-weaver** /'ɔb-wivə/, *n.* any of various spiders of the genus *Araneus,* which weave an orb-shaped web each night, usu. at dusk, to catch night-flying insects.

**orby** /ˈɔbi/, *adj. Rare.* like or pertaining to an orb.

**orc** /ɔk/, *n.* **1.** a mythical monster, esp. a sea-monster. **2.** *Obs.* a whale or grampus. [L *orca* whale]

**orcein** /ˈɔsiən/, *n.* a red dye obtained by oxidising an ammoniacal solution of orcinol, and forming the principal colouring matter of cudbear and orchil. [arbitrary alteration of *orcin*. See ORCINOL]

**orch.,** orchestra.

**orchard** /ˈɔtʃəd/, *n.* **1.** a piece of ground, usu. enclosed, devoted to the cultivation of fruit trees. **2.** a collection of such trees. [ME *orch(i)ard,* OE *orceard;* replacing *ortyard,* ME *ortyerd,* OE *ortgeard* (cf. Goth. *aurtigards* garden), from *ort-* (cf. L *hortus* garden) + *geard* YARD[2]]

**orchardist** /ˈɔtʃədəst/, *n.* one who cultivates an orchard.

**orchestra** /ˈɔkəstrə/, *n.* **1. a.** any group of performers on various musical instruments chosen in accordance with the requirements of the music to be played, as a string orchestra, a gamelan orchestra, etc. **b.** such a group with instruments from the four main families (string, woodwind, brass and percussion) for the playing of concert music, as symphonies, operas and other compositions in the tradition of Western music. **2.** *Brit. and U.S.* the space in a theatre reserved for the musicians usu. the front part of the main floor. **3.** (in the ancient Greek theatre) the circular space in front of the stage, alloted to the chorus. **4.** (in the Roman theatre) a similar space reserved for persons of distinction. [L, from Gk: the space on which the chorus danced]

**orchestral** /ɔˈkɛstrəl/, *adj.* **1.** of or pertaining to an orchestra. **2.** composed for or performed by an orchestra. – **orchestrally,** *adv.*

**orchestrate** /ˈɔkəstreɪt/, *v.t.,* **-trated, -trating. 1.** to compose or arrange (music) for performance by an orchestra. **2.** to put together cohesively: *to orchestrate a policy.* – **orchestration** /ɔkəsˈtreɪʃən/, *n.*

**orchestrion** /ɔˈkɛstriən/, *n.* a mechanical musical instrument, resembling a barrel organ but more elaborate, for producing the effect of an orchestra.

**orchi-,** variant of **orchido-.**

**orchid** /ˈɔkəd/, *n.* **1.** any plant of the family Orchidaceae, comprising terrestrial and epiphytic perennial herbs of temperate and tropical regions, with flowers which are usu. beautiful and often singular in form. **2.** purple, varying from bluish to reddish. [NL *Orchideae* (later *Orchidāceae*), from L *orchis.* See ORCHIS]

**orchidaceous** /ɔkəˈdeɪʃəs/, *adj.* **1.** furnished with two tubers at the base as plants of the genus *Orchis* and its allies. **2.** pertaining to the family Orchidaceae.

**orchidectomy** /ɔkəˈdɛktəmi/, *n., pl.* **-mies.** removal of one or both testicles; castration. Also, **orchiectomy** /ɔkiˈɛktəmi/.

**orchido-,** a word element meaning 'orchid' or 'testicle'. Also, **orchi-;** (esp. before vowels), **orchid-.** [*orchid-* (wrongly supposed stem of Gk *órchis* ORCHIS) + -O-]

**orchidology** /ɔkəˈdɒlədʒi/, *n.* the branch of botany or horticulture that deals with orchids.

**orchil** /ˈɔkəl/, *n.* **1.** a violet colouring matter obtained from certain lichens, chiefly species of *Roccella.* **2.** any such lichen. Cf. **litmus.** Also, **archil.** [late ME, from OF]

**orchis** /ˈɔkəs/, *n.* **1.** any orchid. **2.** any of various terrestrial orchids (esp. of the genus *Orchis*) of temperate regions with spicate flowers. **3.** any orchid of an allied genus, esp. *Blephariglottis,* including the fringed orchis. [L, from Gk: orig., testicle; so named with reference to the shape of the root]

**orchitis** /ɔˈkaɪtəs/, *n.* inflammation of the testicle.

**orcinol** /ˈɔsənɒl/, *n.* a colourless crystalline compound, formula $CH_3C_6H_3(OH)_2$, found in many lichens, and also prepared synthetically. Also, **orcin** /ˈɔsən/. [NL *orcina* (from It. *orcello* ORCHIL) + -OL[1]]

**ord.,** **1.** order. **2.** ordinal. **3.** ordinance. **4.** ordinary.

**ordain** /ɔˈdeɪn/, *v.t.* **1.** *Eccles.* to invest with ministerial or sacerdotal functions; confer holy orders upon. **2.** to appoint authoritatively; decree; enact. **3.** *Obs.* to select or appoint for an office. **4.** (of God, fate, etc.) to destine or predestine. [ME *ordeine(n),* from OF *ordener,* from L *ordināre* order, arrange, appoint] – **ordainer,** *n.* – **ordainment,** *n.*

**ordeal** /ɔˈdil, ˈɔdil/, *n.* **1.** any severe test or trial; a trying experience. **2.** a primitive form of trial to determine guilt or innocence, as by the effect of fire, poison, or water upon the accused, the result being regarded as a divine or preternatural judgment. [ME and OE *ordāl,* var. of OE *ordēl,* c. G *Urteil* judgment]

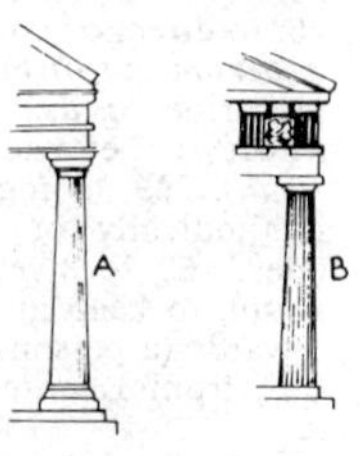

orders (def. 33): A, Tuscan; B, Doric

**order** /ˈɔdə/, *n.* **1.** an authoritative direction, injunction, command, or mandate. **2.** *Law.* a command of a court or judge. **3.** *Mil.* a command or notice issued by an army, navy, airforce, or a military commander to troops under him. **4.** the disposition of things following one after another, as in space, time, etc.; succession or sequence. **5.** a condition in which everything is in its proper place with reference to other things and to its purpose; methodical or harmonious arrangement. **6.** *Mil.* different dress, equipment, etc., for some special purpose or occasion: *full marching order.* **7.** proper or satisfactory condition: *my watch is out of order.* **8.** state or condition generally: *affairs are in good order.* **9.** *Gram.* **a.** the arrangement of the elements of a construction in a particular sequence, as the placing of *John* before and of *George* after the verb *saw* in the sentence *John saw George.* **b.** the feature of construction resulting from such an arrangement, as in the sentences *John saw George* and *George saw John* which differ only in order. **10.** any class, kind, or sort, as of persons or things, distinguished from others by nature or character: *talents of a high order.* **11.** the usual major subdivision of a class or subclass, commonly comprising a plurality of families, as the Hymenoptera (ants, bees, etc.). **12.** a rank, grade, or class of persons in the community. **13.** a body of persons of the same profession, occupation, or pursuits: *the clerical order.* **14.** a body or society of persons living by common consent under the same religious, moral, or social regulations. **15.** any of the degrees or grades of the clerical office (the number of which varies in different Churches, the Roman Catholic Church, for example, having the **major orders** of bishop, priest, deacon, and subdeacon, and the **minor orders** of acolyte, exorcist, lector, and ostiary, while the Anglican Church recognises only the three grades of bishop, priest and deacon). **16.** any of the nine grades of angels in medieval angelology (see **angel,** def. 1). **17.** a monastic society or fraternity: *the Franciscan order.* **18.** (*usu. pl.*) the rank or status of an ordained Christian minister. **19.** (*usu. pl.*) the rite or sacrament of ordination. **20.** a prescribed form of divine service, or of administration of a rite or ceremony. **21.** the service itself. **22.** *Hist.* a society or fraternity of knights, of combined military and monastic character, as in the Middle Ages as the Knights Templar, etc. **23.** a modern organisation or society more or less resembling the knightly orders: *fraternal orders.* **24.** conformity to law or established authority; absence of revolt, disturbance, turbulence, unruliness, etc. **25.** customary mode of procedure, or established usage. **26.** the customary or prescribed mode of proceeding in debates or the like, or in the conduct of deliberative or legislative bodies, public meetings, etc. **27.** conformity to this. **28.** the natural, moral, or spiritual constitution of the world; the prevailing course of things; the established system or regime: *the old order changeth.* **29.** a direction or commission to make, provide or furnish something: *shoes made to order.* **30.** a quantity of goods purchased. **31.** a written direction to pay money or deliver goods. **32.** a pass for admission to a theatre, museum, or the like. **33.** *Archit.* **a.** a series of columns with their entablature arranged in given proportions. **b.** any one of the typical variations of such an arrangement distinguished by proportion, capital types and other characteristics: *the Doric, Ionic, Corinthian, Tuscan, and Composite orders.* **34.** *Maths.* **a.** degree, as in algebra. **b.** (of a derivative) the number of times a function has been differentiated. **c.** (of a differential equation) the order of the highest derivative in the equation. **35. a tall order,** *Colloq.* a difficult task or requirement. **36. call to order,** to establish or re-establish order at a meeting. **37. in order, a.** in a proper state; correctly arranged; in a state of readiness; functioning correctly. **b.** appropriate; suitable. **c.** correct according to parliamentary procedure. **38. in order that,** to the end that. **39. in order to,** as a means to. **40. in short order,** speedily; promptly. **41. of the order of,** about, approximately. **42. on order,** ordered but not yet received. **43. out of order, a.** not functioning properly; broken. **b.** not in accordance with recognised parliamentary rules. *–v.t.* **44.** to give an order, direction, or command to. **45.** to direct or command to go or come (as specified): *to order a person out of one's house.* **46.** to give an order for. **47.** to prescribe: *a doctor orders a medicine for a patient.* **48.** to direct to be made, supplied, or furnished: *we ordered two steaks.* **49.** to regulate, conduct, or manage. **50.** to arrange methodically or suitably. **51.** to ordain, as God or fate does. **52.** to invest with clerical rank or authority. **53. order about,** to keep giving orders to; act in a domineering fashion towards (a person). *–v.i.* **54.** to issue orders. [ME *ordre,* from OF, from L *ordo* row, rank, regular arrangement] – **orderer,** *n.*

**order arms** /ɔdər 'amz/, *n.* **1.** a rifle drill position in which the rifle is held at the right side, with the butt on the ground. **2.** the command to move the rifle to this position.

**orderly** /'ɔdəli/, *adj., adv., n., pl.* **-lies.** *–adj.* **1.** arranged or disposed in order, in regular sequence, or in a tidy manner. **2.** observant of system or method, as persons, the mind, etc. **3.** characterised by or observant of order, rule, or discipline: *an orderly citizen.* **4.** charged with the communication or execution of orders. *–adv.* **5.** according to established order or rule. **6.** *Archaic.* methodically. *–n.* **7.** *Mil.* a private soldier or a non-commissioned officer attending on a superior officer to carry orders, messages, etc. **8.** Also, **medical orderly.** a person employed in a hospital to perform certain general, nonmedical duties. – **orderliness,** *n.*

**orderly marketing** /– 'makətɪŋ/, *n.* the maintenance of a level of prices of goods and services by agreement among suppliers.

**orderly officer** /'– ɒfəsə/, *n.* a junior officer detailed by rota to a 24-hour period of duty, which includes the inspection of all buildings in the camp or barracks (notably the cookhouses and dining halls at mealtimes) and of all guards, pickets, and prisoners in the guardroom.

**orderly room** /'– rum/, *n.* the office set aside in a battalion for carrying out clerical duties.

**order of the boot,** *n. Colloq.* the sack; dismissal.

**order of the day,** *n.* **1.** (in a legislative body) a program of business set down for discussion on a particular day. **2.** *Mil.* specific commands, instructions, or notices issued by a commanding officer to the men under his command. **3.** (*joc.*) a plan for the day's activities, as a family picnic, journey etc.

**order paper** /'ɔdə peɪpə/, *n.* a schedule of business to be discussed at a session of a legislative assembly.

**order statistic** /'– stəˌtɪstɪk/, *n.* one of a number of sample observations arranged in order of magnitude.

**ordinal**[1] /'ɔdənəl/, *adj.* **1.** pertaining to an order, as of animals or plants. *–n.* **2.** an ordinal number or numeral. [ME, from LL *ordinālis,* from L *ordo* order]

**ordinal**[2] /'ɔdənəl/, *n.* **1.** a directory of ecclesiastical services. **2.** a book containing the forms for the ordination of priests, consecration of bishops, etc. [ME, from ML *ordināle.* See ORDINAL[1]]

**ordinal number** /– 'nʌmbə/, *n.* any of the numbers *first, second, third, etc.,* which indicate the order in which things occur in a given set, and not the total number of things in the set (the latter is indicated by the cardinal numbers, *one, two, three,* etc.)

**ordinance** /'ɔdənəns/, *n.* **1.** an authoritative rule or law; a decree or command. **2.** a public injunction or regulation. **3.** *Eccles.* **a.** an established rite or ceremony. **b.** a sacrament. **c.** the communion. [ME *ordinaunce,* from OF *ordenance,* from *ordener* to order, from L *ordināre*]

**ordinand** /'ɔdənænd/, *n.* a candidate for ordination.

**ordinarily** /'ɔdənərəli, ɔdə'nɛərəli/, *adv.* **1.** in ordinary cases; usually. **2.** in the ordinary way. **3.** to the usual extent.

**ordinary** /'ɔdənəri, 'ɔdənri/, *adj., n., pl.* **-ries.** *–adj.* **1.** such as is commonly met with; of the usual kind. **2.** not above, but rather below, the average level of quality; somewhat inferior. **3.** customary; normal: *for all ordinary purposes.* **4.** (of jurisdiction, etc.) immediate, as contrasted with that which is delegated. **5.** (of officials, etc.) belonging to the regular staff or the fully recognised class. *–n.* **6.** the ordinary condition, degree, run, or the like: *out of the ordinary.* **7.** something regular, customary, or usual. **8.** *Eccles.* **a.** an order or form for divine service, esp. that for saying mass. **b.** the service of the mass exclusive of the canon. **9.** *Eccles. Law.* a bishop, archbishop, or other ecclesiastic or his deputy, in his capacity as an *ex officio* ecclesiastical authority. **10.** *Her.* **a.** any of the simplest and commonest heraldic charges or bearings, usu. bounded by straight lines. **b.** any of the more important of these. **11. in ordinary,** (of officials, etc.) in regular service: *a physician in ordinary to a king.* [ME, from L *ordinārius* of the usual order] – **ordinariness,** *n.*

**ordinary pay** /– 'peɪ/, *n.* remuneration for an employee's normal weekly number of hours fixed under the terms of his employment but excluding any amount payable to him for shift work, overtime, or other penalty.

**ordinary ray** /– 'reɪ/, *n.* the part of a doubly refracted ray which obeys the ordinary laws of refraction. Cf. **extraordinary ray.**

**ordinary seaman** /– 'simən/, *n.* a seaman who is not sufficiently skilled to be classed as an able-bodied seaman. *Abbrev.:* O.S.

**ordinary share** /– 'ʃɛə/, *n.* one of the series of shares into which the capital of a company is divided, which rank for dividends after preference shares and before deferred shares, if any such are in issue.

**ordinate** /'ɔdənət/, *n. Maths.* the *y* Cartesian coordinate. [L *ordinātus,* pp., ordained]

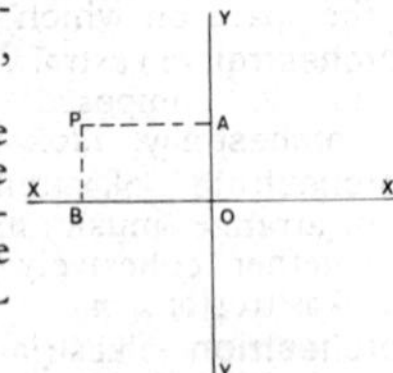

ordinate: P, any point; AO and PB, ordinate of P; YY, axis of ordinate; OB and AP, abscissa of P; XX, axis of abscissa

**ordination** /ɔdə'neɪʃən/, *n.* **1.** *Eccles.* the act or ceremony of ordaining. **2.** the fact of being ordained. **3.** a decreeing. **4.** the act of arranging. **5** the resulting state. [ME *ordinacion,* from L *ordinātio* ordainment, an ordering]

**ordn.,** ordnance.

**ordnance** /'ɔdnəns/, *n.* **1.** cannon or artillery. **2.** military weapons of all kinds with their equipment, ammunition, etc. [var. of ORDINANCE]

**ordo** /'ɔdoʊ/, *n., pl.* **ordines** /'ɔdəniz/. a booklet containing short and abbreviated directions for the contents of the office and mass of each day in the Roman Catholic church calendar. [L: row, series, order]

**ordonnance** /'ɔdənəns/, *n.* **1.** arrangement or disposition of parts, as of a building, a picture, or a literary composition. **2.** an ordinance, decree, or law. [F. See ORDINANCE]

**Ordovician** /ɔdoʊ'vɪʃən/, *adj.* **1.** pertaining to an early Palaeozoic geological period or system. *–n.* **2.** the period or system following Cambrian and preceding Silurian. [L *Ordovicēs,* pl., an ancient British tribe in N Wales + -IAN]

**ordure** /'ɔdʒʊə/, *n.* filth; dung; excrement. [ME, from OF, from *ord* filthy, from L *horridus* horrid]

**ore** /ɔ/, *n.* **1.** a metal-bearing mineral or rock, or a native metal, esp. when valuable enough to be mined. **2.** a mineral or natural product serving as a source of some non-metallic substance, as sulphur. [ME (*o*)*or* metal, ore, OE *ār* brass]

**oread** /'ɔriæd/, *n.* (in Greek mythology) a mountain nymph. [L *Orēas,* from Gk *Oreiás,* from *óros* mountain]

**ore body** /'ɔ bɒdi/, *n.* generally a solid and fairly continuous mass of ore, which may include low grade and waste as well as pay ore, but which is distinct from the surrounding country rock.

**orectic** /ɒ'rɛktɪk/, *adj.* of or pertaining to desire; appetitive. [Gk *orektikós*]

**ore dressing** /'ɔ drɛsɪŋ/, *n.* the art of separating the valuable minerals from an ore without chemical changes.

**oregano** /ɒrə'ganoʊ/, *n.* a plant of the mint family of the genus *Origanum,* related to but spicier than marjoram, and used in cookery.

**Oregon pine** /ɒrəgən 'paɪn/, *n.* See **Douglas fir.**

**oreography** /ɔri'ɒgrəfi/, *n.* →**orography.** – **oreographic** /ɔriə'græfɪk/, **oreographical** /ɒriə'græfɪkəl/, *adj.*

**oreology** /ɔri'ɒlədʒi/, *n.* →**orology.** – **oreological** /ɔriə'lɒdʒɪkəl/, *adj.* – **oreologist** /ɔri'ɒlədʒəst/, *n.*

**ore shoot** /'ɔ ʃut/, *n.* a steeply inclined vein of rich ore with well-defined boundaries.

**orfray** /ˈɔfri/, *n.* →**orphrey.**

**org.,** organic.

**organ** /ˈɔgən/, *n.* **1.** a musical instrument (**pipe organ**) consisting of one or more sets of pipes sounded by means of compressed air, played by means of keys arranged in one or more keyboards; in its full modern development, the largest and most complicated of musical instruments. **2.** a musical instrument (**electronic** or **electric organ**) resembling a pipe organ but sounded electrophonically. **3.** a reed organ or harmonium. **4.** a barrel organ or hand organ. **5.** *Obs.* any of various musical instruments, esp. wind instruments. **6.** (in an animal or a plant) a part or member, as the heart, having some specific function. **7.** an instrument or means, as of performance. **8.** a means or medium of communicating thoughts, opinions, etc., as a newspaper serving as the mouthpiece of a political party. [ME, from L *organum,* from Gk *órganon* instrument, tool, bodily organ, musical instrument]

**organdie** /ˈɔgəndi/, *n., pl.* **-dies.** a fine, thin stiff cotton fabric usu. having a durable crisp finish, and either white, dyed or printed; used for dresses, curtains, etc. Also, *U.S.,* **organdy.** [F *organdi;* orig. uncert.]

**organ-grinder** /ˈɔgən-graɪndə/, *n.* a street musician who plays a hand organ by turning the crank.

**organic** /ɔˈgænɪk/, *adj.* **1.** denoting or pertaining to a class of chemical compounds which formerly comprised only those existing in or derived from living organisms (animal or plant), but which now includes these and all other compounds of carbon except for its oxides, sulphides, and metal carbonates. **2.** characteristic of, pertaining to, or derived from living organisms: *organic remains found in rocks; organic fertiliser.* **3.** of or pertaining to an organ or the organs of an animal or plant. **4.** *Philos.* exhibiting the sort of interconnectedness characteristic of the relations of the parts of living organisms to the whole. **5.** characterised by the systematic arrangement of parts; organised; systematic. **6.** of or pertaining to the constitution or structure of a thing; constitutional; structural. **7.** *Law.* of or pertaining to the constitutional or essential law or laws organising the government of a state. [L *organicus,* from Gk *organikós*]

**organically** /ɔˈgænɪkli/, *adv.* **1.** in an organic manner; by or with organs. **2.** with reference to organic structure. **3.** by or through organisation. **4.** *Hort.* without the use of chemical fertilisers or pesticides.

**organic chemistry** /ɔˌgænɪk ˈkɛməstri/, *n.* the branch of chemistry dealing with the compounds of carbon; originally limited to substances found only in living organisms.

**organic disease** /– dəˈziz/, *n.* a disease in which there is a structural alteration (opposed to *functional disease*).

**organicism** /ɔˈgænəsɪzəm/, *n.* **1.** *Biol., Philos.* the theory that vital activities arise not from any one part of an organism but from its autonomous composition. **2.** *Neurol.* the doctrine that all or the majority of the diseases of the nervous system, including those of the mind, are organic, due to demonstrable changes in the brain or spinal cord. – **organicist** /ɔˈgænəsəst/, *n.*

**organic law** /ɔˌgænɪk ˈlɔ/, *n.* See **law** (def. 2).

**organisation** /ɔgənaɪˈzeɪʃən/, *n.* **1.** the act or process or organising. **2.** the state or manner of being organised. **3.** that which is organised. **4.** organic structure. **5.** any organised whole. **6.** a body of persons organised for some end or work. **7.** the administrative personnel or apparatus of a business. **8.** the functionaries of a political party together with the offices, committees, etc. which they hold or of which they are members. **9.** an organism. Also, **organization.** – **organisational,** *adj.*

**organise** /ˈɔgənaɪz/, *v.,* **-nised, -nising.** –*v.t.* **1.** to form as or into a whole consisting of interdependent or coordinated parts, esp. for harmonious or united action: *to organise a party.* **2.** to systematise: *to organise facts.* **3.** to give organic structure or character to. **4.** to build a trade union among: *to organise workers.* **5.** to enlist the employees of into a trade union: *to organise a factory.* **6.** to obtain; get; make: *organise me a drink.* –*v.i.* **7.** to combine in an organised company, party, or the like. **8.** to assume organic structure. Also, **organize.** [ME, from ML *organizāre,* from L *organum* ORGAN] – **organisable,** *adj.*

**organised ferment** /ɔgənaɪzd ˈfɜmɛnt/, *n.* See **ferment** (def. 1a).

**organised labour** /– ˈleɪbə/, *n.* all workers who are organised in trade unions.

**organiser** /ˈɔgənaɪzə/, *n.* **1.** one who organises. **2.** *Embryol.* any part of an embryo that influences the development and differentiation of another part. **3.** an official of a trade union whose functions include liaison between the union's executive and members of the union at their places of work. Also, **organizer.**

**organism** /ˈɔgənɪzəm/, *n.* **1.** an individual composed of mutually dependent parts constituted for subserving vital processes. **2.** any form of animal or plant life: *microscopic organisms.* **3.** any organised body or system analogous to a living being. **4.** *Philos.* any structure the parts of which function not only in terms of one another, but also in terms of the whole.

**organist** /ˈɔgənəst/, *n.* one who plays an organ.

**organo-,** word element meaning 'organ' or 'organic'. [Gk, combining form of *órganon*]

**organochlorin** /ɔˌgænəˈklɔrən/, *n.* any of a large group of compounds containing chlorine which are highly toxic to animal life and widely used as insecticides, as DDT, lindane, etc.

**organography** /ɔgəˈnɒgrəfi/, *n.* the description of the organs of animals or plants.

**organology** /ɔgəˈnɒlədʒi/, *n.* **1.** the branch of biology that deals with the structure and functions of the organs of animals or plants. **2.** →**phrenology.**

**organometallic** /ɔˌgænoʊməˈtælɪk/, *adj.* of or pertaining to an organic compound in which one or more metal atoms are linked to a carbon atom.

**organon** /ˈɔgənɒn/, *n., pl.* **-na** /-nə/, **-nons.** **1.** an instrument of thought or knowledge. **2.** *Philos.* a system of rules or principles of demonstration or investigation. [Gk. See ORGAN]

**organotherapy** /ɔgənoʊˈθɛrəpi/, *n.* that branch of therapeutics which deals with the use of remedies prepared from the organs of animals, as the thyroid gland, the suprarenal bodies, etc. Also, **organotherapeutics** /ɔgənoʊˌθɛrəˈpjutɪks/.

**organ pipe** /ˈɔgən paɪp/, *n.* **1.** one of the pipes of a pipe organ. **2.** something resembling such a pipe.

**organum** /ˈɔgənəm/, *n., pl.* **-na** /-nə/, **-nums.** **1.** →**organon. 2.** *Music.* **a.** the doubling, or simultaneous singing, of a melody at an interval of either a fourth, fifth, or octave. **b.** the second part in such singing. [L. See ORGAN]

**organza** /ɔˈgænzə/, *n.* a fabric made from a mixture of silk or nylon with cotton, similar to organdie but less fine.

**organzine** /ˈɔgənzin, ɔˈgænzin/, *n.* silk yarn used in weaving silk fabrics.

**orgasm** /ˈɔgæzəm/, *n.* **1.** *Physiol.* a complex series of responses of the genital organs and skin at the culmination of a sexual act. **2.** immoderate excitement. –*v.i.* **3.** *Colloq.* to experience an orgasm. [NL *orgasmus,* from Gk *orgasmós,* from *orgân* swell, be excited] – **orgastic** /ɔˈgæstɪk/, *adj.*

**orgeat** /ˈɔʒa/, *n.* a syrup or drink made from almonds (originally from barley), sugar, and a water prepared from orange flowers. [F, from Pr., from *orge,* from L *hordeum* barley]

**orgiastic** /ɔdʒiˈæstɪk/, *adj.* of, pertaining to, or of the nature of orgies. [Gk *orgiastikós*]

**orgy** /ˈɔdʒi/, *n., pl.* **-gies.** **1.** wild, drunken, or licentious festivities or revelry. **2.** any proceedings marked by unbridled indulgence of passions: *an orgy of killing.* **3.** (*pl.*) secret rites or ceremonies connected with the worship of certain deities of classical mythology, esp. the rites in honour of Dionysus, celebrated with wild dancing and singing, drinking, etc. [L *orgia,* pl., from Gk]

**oribi** /ˈɒrəbi/, *n., pl.* **-bis.** a small tan-coloured antelope, *Ourebia ourebi,* of southern and eastern Africa, with spikelike horns. [Afrikaans, from Hottentot]

**oriel** /ˈɔriəl/, *n.* a bay window, usu. semipolygonal, esp. in an upper storey. Also, **oriel window.** [ME, from OF *oriol* porch, passage, gallery, from L *aureolus* gilded]

**orient** /ˈɔriənt, ˈɒ-/, *n., adj.;* /ˈɔriɛnt, ˈɒ-/, *v.* –*n.* **1. the Orient, a.** the East, comprising the countries to the east (and south-east) of the Mediterranean. **b.** the countries of Asia generally, esp. eastern Asia. **2.** *Archaic.* the east; the eastern regions of the heavens or the earth. **3.** the lustre peculiar to the pearl. **4.** an orient pearl. *–adj.* **5.** *Archaic.* rising; appearing as from beneath the horizon: *the orient sun.* **6.** *Poetic.* eastern or oriental. **7.** fine or lustrous, as gems, esp. pearls. *–v.t. v.i.* **8.** →**orientate.** [ME, from L *oriens* the east, sunrise (n. use of ppr., rising)]

**oriental** /ɔri'ɛntl, ɒri-/, *adj.* **1.** (*sometimes cap.*) of, pertaining to, or characteristic of the Orient or East. **2.** (of gems) orient. **3.** designating sapphire varieties: *oriental amethyst.* *–n.* **4.** (*usu. cap.*) a native or inhabitant of the Orient, esp. one belonging to an indigenous race. [ME, from L *orientālis*]

**orientalise** /ɔri'ɛntəlaɪz, ɒri-/, *v.*, **-lised, -lising.** (*sometimes cap.*) *–v.t.* **1.** to make oriental. *–v.i.* **2.** to become or appear oriental. Also, **orientalize.**

**orientalism** /ɔri'ɛntəlɪzəm, ɒri-/, *n.* (*sometimes cap.*) **1.** a peculiarity of the oriental peoples. **2.** the character or characteristics of oriental people. **3.** the knowledge and study of oriental languages, literature, etc. – **orientalist,** *n.*

**Oriental realm** /ɔriˌɛntl 'rɛlm, ɒri-/, *n.* a biogeographical realm comprising southern Asia and the Malay Archipelago as far as and including the Philippines, Borneo and Java.

**oriental rug** /– 'rʌg/, *n.* any handmade rug or carpet usu. woven in Asia.

**orientate** /'ɒriənteɪt, 'ɔri-/, *v.*, **-tated, -tating.** *–v.t.* **1.** to place so as to face the east, esp. to build (a church) with the chief altar to the east and the chief entrance to the west. **2.** to place in any definite position with reference to the points of the compass or other points: *to orientate a building north and south.* **3.** to adjust with relation to, or bring into due relation to, surroundings, circumstances, facts, etc.: *to orientate one's ideas to new conditions.* **4.** *Survey.* to turn a map or plane table sheet so that the north direction on the map is parallel to the north direction on the ground. *–v.i.* **5.** to turn towards the east or in specified direction.

**orientation** /ˌɒriɛn'teɪʃən, ˌɔriən-/, *n.* **1.** the act or process of orientating. **2.** the state of being orientated. **3.** *Psychol.* the ability to locate oneself in one's environment with reference to time, place, and people. **4.** the ascertainment of one's true position, as in a novel situation, with reference to new ideas, etc. **5.** *Chem.* **a.** the arrangement of atoms or radicals in a particular position due to electrical charges, etc. **b.** the determination of the position of substituted atoms or radicals in a compound.

**orientation week** /'– wik/, *n.* (in a university or other tertiary institution) usu. the week before formal teaching begins, in which students are orientated to their new environment.

**orienteering** /ɒriən'tɪərɪŋ/, *n.* a sport in which competitors race on foot, skis, bicycle, etc., over a course consisting of a number of checkpoints which must be located with the aid of maps, compasses, etc.

**orifice** /'ɒrəfəs/, *n.* a mouth or aperture, as of a tube or pipe; a mouthlike opening or hole; a vent. [F, from L *ōrificium*]

**orig.,** **1.** origin. **2.** original. **3.** originally.

**origami** /ɒrə'gami/, *n.* **1.** the art of folding paper into shapes of flowers, birds, etc. **2.** an object made this way. [Jap. *ori* a folding + *-gami,* from *kami* paper]

**origan** /'ɒrɪgən/, *n.* marjoram, esp. the Old World wild marjoram, *Origanum vulgare.* [ME, from L *orĭganum,* from Gk *orĭganon*]

**origin** /'ɒrədʒən/, *n.* **1.** that from which anything arises or is derived; the source: *to follow a stream to its origin.* **2.** rise or derivation from a particular source: *these and other reports of like origin.* **3.** the first stage of existence; the beginning: *the date of origin of a sect.* **4.** birth; parentage; extraction: *Scottish origin.* **5.** *Anat.* **a.** the point of derivation. **b.** the more fixed portion of a muscle. **6.** *Maths.* the point of intersection of two or more axes in a system of Cartesian or polar coordinates; the point from which a measurement is taken. [L *orĭgo* beginning, source, rise]

**original** /ə'rɪdʒənəl/, *adj.* **1.** belonging or pertaining to the origin or beginning of something, or to a thing at its beginning: *the original binding.* **2.** new; fresh; novel: *an original way of advertising.* **3.** arising or proceeding from a thing itself, or independently of anything else. **4.** capable of or given to thinking or acting independently in self-suggested and individual ways: *an original thinker.* **5.** proceeding from a person as the inventor, maker, composer, or author: *original research.* **6.** being that from which a copy, a translation, or the like is made: *the original document is in the National Library.* **7.** *Colloq.* mentally ill; insane: *poor Dick went a bit original after that.* *–n.* **8.** a primary form or type from which varieties are derived. **9.** an original work, writing, or the like, as opposed to any copy or imitation. **10.** the person or thing represented by a picture, description, etc. **11.** one who is original in his ways of thinking or acting. **12.** an eccentric person. **13.** *Archaic.* a source of being; an author or originator.

**original gum** /– 'gʌm/, *n.* the gum on the back of a stamp as issued by the post office.

**originality** /ərɪdʒə'nælәti/, *n., pl.* **-ties.** **1.** the state or quality of being original. **2.** ability to think or act in an independent, individual manner. **3.** freshness or novelty, as of an idea, method, or performance.

**originally** /ə'rɪdʒənəli/, *adv.* **1.** with respect to origin; by origin. **2.** at the origin; at first. **3.** in the first place; primarily. **4.** from the beginning. **5.** in an original, novel, or distinctively individual manner.

**original sin** /ərɪdʒənəl 'sɪn/, *n.* **1.** *Theol.* a depravity, or tendency to evil, held to be innate in mankind and transmitted from Adam to the race in consequence of his sin. **2.** *Rom. Cath. Ch.* the privation of sanctifying grace in consequence of Adam's sin.

**originate** /ə'rɪdʒəneɪt/, *v.*, **-nated, -nating.** *–v.i.* **1.** to take its origin or rise; arise; spring. *–v.t.* **2.** to give origin or rise to; initiate; invent. – **origination** /ərɪdʒə'neɪʃən/, *n.* – **originator,** *n.*

**originating summons** /əˌrɪdʒəneɪtɪŋ 'sʌmənz/, *n. Law.* summons without the issue of a writ by which the proceedings may be commenced.

**originative** /ə'rɪdʒəneɪtɪv/, *adj.* having or characterised by the power of originating; creative. – **originatively,** *adv.*

**orinasal** /ɔrə'neɪzəl/, *Phonet.* *–adj.* **1.** sounded with the voice issuing through the mouth and nose at the same time, as the nasalised vowels in French. *–n.* **2.** an orinasal sound.

**oriole** /'ɔrioʊl/, *n.* **1.** any bird of the Old World passerine family Oriolidae, mostly bright yellow with black on the head, wings, and tail, as the olive-backed oriole. **2.** any of various brightly coloured American passerine birds of the family Iceridae, not closely related to the true orioles of the Old World, as the Baltimore oriole, *Icterus galbula.* [ML *oriolus,* var. of L *aureolus* golden]

**orison** /'ɒrəzən/, *n.* a prayer. [ME, from OF, from L *ōrātio* prayer. Cf. ORATION]

**-orium.** See **-ory**[2].

**orle** /ɔl/, *n. Her.* **1.** a narrow band within the shield and following the contour of its edge. **2.** a number of small charges set round the edge of a shield in the manner of an orle. [F, from LL *ōrulum,* diminutive of L *ōra* border]

**orlon** /'ɔlɒn/, *n.* a synthetic acrylic textile fibre of light weight and good crease resistance. [Trademark]

**orlop** /'ɔlɒp/, *n.* the lowest deck of a ship. [late ME, from D *overloop,* from *overloopen* overrun, spread over; so called because it covers the ship's hold]

**orly** /'ɔli/, *adj.* (of fish) dipped in batter, deep-fried and served with a tomato sauce. Also, **à la orly.**

**ormer** /'ɔmə/, *n.* **1.** an abalone, *Haliotis tuberculata,* a gastropod mollusc abundant in the Channel Islands. **2.** *Chiefly Brit.* any abalone. [F *ormier* (from L *auris maris* sea ear)]

**ormolu** /'ɔməlu/, *n.* **1.** an alloy of copper and zinc, used to imitate gold. **2.** **a.** gold prepared for use in gilding. **b.** gilded metal. [F *or moulu* ground gold, from *or* (from L *aurum* gold) + *moulu,* pp. of *moudre* grind (from L *molere*)]

**ornament** /'ɔnəmənt/, *n.;* /'ɔnəmɛnt/, *v.* *–n.* **1.** an accessory, article, or detail used to beautify the appearance or general effect: *architectural ornaments.* **2.** any adornment or means of adornment. **3.** a person who adds lustre, as to surroundings, society, etc. **4.** the act of adorning. **5.** the state of being adorned. **6.** mere outward display. **7.** *Chiefly Eccles.* any accessory, adjunct, or equipment. **8.** *Music.* a note or group of notes applied as decoration to a principal melody. *–v.t.* **9.** to furnish with ornaments. **10.** to be an ornament to. [L *ornāmentum* equipment, ornament; replacing ME *ornement,* from OF]

**ornamental** /ɔnə'mɛntl/, *adj.* **1.** used for ornament: *ornamen-*

*tal plants.* **2.** such as to ornament; decorative. **3.** of or pertaining to ornament. *–n.* **4.** something ornamental. **5.** a plant cultivated for decorative purposes. **– ornamentality** /ɔnəmenˈtæləti/, *n.* **– ornamentally,** *adv.*

**ornamentation** /ɔnəmɛnˈteɪʃən/, *n.* **1.** the act of ornamenting. **2.** the state of being ornamented. **3.** that with which a thing is ornamented. **4.** *Music.* the practice of decorating a musical texture or melodic line according to historical principles.

**ornate** /ɔˈneɪt/, *adj.* **1.** elaborately adorned; sumptuously or showily splendid or fine. [ME, from L *ornātus,* pp., adorned] **– ornately,** *adv.* **– ornateness,** *n.*

**ornery** /ˈɔnəri/, *adj. U.S. Colloq.* **1.** ugly in disposition or temper. **2.** stubborn. **3.** low or vile. [contraction of ORDINARY]

**ornis** /ˈɔnəs/, *n.* →**avifauna.** [G, from Gk: bird]

**ornith.,** **1.** ornithological. **2.** ornithology.

**ornithic** /ɔˈnɪθɪk/, *adj.* of or pertaining to birds. [Gk *ornithikós* birdlike]

**ornithine** /ˈɔnəθin, -aɪn/, *n.* a non-protein amino acid, $NH_2(CH_2)_3CH(NH_3^+)COO^-$, obtained by enzymic hydrolysis of arginine, an intermediate in the urea cycle.

**ornitho-,** a word element meaning 'bird'. Also, **ornith-.** [Gk, combining form of *órnis* wing]

**ornithoid** /ˈɔnəθɔɪd/, *adj.* birdlike.

**ornithol.,** **1.** ornithological. **2.** ornithology.

**ornithology** /ɔnəˈθɒlədʒi/, *n.* the branch of zoology that deals with birds. **– ornithological** /ɔnəθəˈlɒdʒɪkəl/, *adj.* **– ornithologist,** *n.*

**ornithomancy** /ˈɔnəθəmænsi/, *n.* divination by means of studying the flight of birds.

**ornithopod** /ˈɔnəθəpɒd, ɔˈnɪθəpɒd/, *n.* any of the Ornithopoda, a group of dinosaurs that walked erect on their hind feet. [NL *Ornithopoda,* pl.; or from ORNITHO- + -POD]

**ornithopter** /ˈɔnəθɒptə/, *n.* a heavier-than-air craft sustained in and propelled through the air by flapping wings. [ORNITHO- + Gk *pterón* wing]

**ornithorhynchus** /ɔnəθəˈrɪŋkəs/, *n.* →**platypus.** [NL, from Gk *ornitho-* ORNITHO- + *rhýnchos* snout, beak]

**ornithosis** /ɔnəˈθoʊsəs/, *n.* a disease of domestic pigeons and other birds, similar to psittacosis, occasionally transmitted to man.

**oro-,** a word element meaning 'mountain', as in *orography.* [Gk, combining form of *óros*]

**orogenesis** /ɒroʊˈdʒɛnəsəs/, *n. Geol.* the process of mountain-making or upheaval. Also, **orogeny** /ɒˈrɒdʒəni/. **– orogenetic** /ˌɒroʊdʒəˈnɛtɪk/, **orogenic,** *adj.*

**orographic clouds** /ˌɒrəgræfɪk ˈklaʊdz/, *n. pl.* clouds formed, under suitable conditions, by the passage of air over a mountain or ridge.

**orography** /ɒˈrɒgrəfi/, *n.* that branch of physical geography which deals with mountains. Also, **oreography.** **– orographic** /ɒroʊˈgræfɪk/, **orographical** /ɒroʊˈgræfɪkəl/, *adj.*

**oroide** /ˈɔroʊˌaɪd/, *n.* an alloy containing copper, tin, etc., used to imitate gold. [F, from *or* gold (from L *aurum*) + *-oide* -OID]

**orology** /ɒˈrɒlədʒi/, *n.* the science of mountains. Also, **oreology.** **– orological** /ɒrəˈlɒdʒɪkəl/, *adj.* **– orologist,** *n.*

**orometer** /ɒˈrɒmətə/, *n.* an aneroid barometer with a scale giving elevations above sea-level, used to determine altitudes of mountains, etc.

**oropharynx** /ɒroʊˈfærɪŋks/, *n., pl.* **-pharynges** /-fəˈrɪndʒiz/, **-pharynxes.** *Anat.* **1.** the space immediately beneath the mouth cavity. **2.** the pharynx as distinguished from the nasopharynx. [*oro-* (combining form representing L *ōs* mouth) + PHARYNX]

**orotund** /ˈɒroʊtʌnd/, *adj.* **1.** (of the voice or utterance) characterised by strength, fullness, richness, and clearness. **2.** (of a style of utterance) pompous or bombastic. [L *ōre rotundō,* lit., with round mouth]

**orphan** /ˈɔfən/, *n.* **1.** a child bereaved by death of both parents, or, less commonly, of one parent. **2.** *Print.* the opening line of a paragraph which is separated by its position on a page from the rest of the paragraph. *–adj.* **3.** of or for orphans: *an orphan institution.* **4.** bereaved of parents. *–v.t.* **5.** to bereave of parents or a parent. [late ME, from LL *orphanus,* from Gk *orphanós* without parents, bereaved] **– orphanhood,** *n.*

**orphanage** /ˈɔfənɪdʒ/, *n.* **1.** an institution for orphans. **2.** the state of being an orphan. **3.** *Archaic.* orphans collectively.

**Orphean** /ˈɔfiən/, *adj.* melodious; entrancing. [from *Orpheus,* Greek mythical poet and musician]

**Orphic** /ˈɔfɪk/, *adj.* **1.** pertaining to a religious or philosophical school maintaining a form of the cult of Dionysus: *Orphic mysteries.* **2.** (*oft. l.c.*) mystic; oracular. [Gk *orphikós.* See ORPHEAN]

**Orphism** /ˈɔfɪzəm/, *n.* **1.** the religious or philosophical system of the Orphic school. **2.** Also, **Orphic cubism.** (*oft. l.c.*) an art movement dating from 1912, asserting the importance of colour as visual communication, resulting in a form of pure abstract painting.

**orphrey** /ˈɔfri/, *n., pl.* **-phreys.** an ornamental band or border, esp. on an ecclesiastical vestment. Also, **orfray.** [ME *orfreis,* from OF, from LL *aurifrisium,* alteration of *auriphrygium* gold embroidery, from L *aurum* gold + *Phrygius* Phrygian]

**orpiment** /ˈɔpəmənt/, *n.* a mineral arsenic trisulphide, $As_2S_3$, found usu. in soft yellow foliated masses, used as a pigment, etc. [ME, from OF, from L *auripigmentum* gold pigment]

**orpine** /ˈɔpən/, *n.* a crassulaceous perennial, *Sedum telephium,* bearing purplish flowers. Also, **orpin.** [ME, from F, back-formation from *orpiment* ORPIMENT]

**Orpington** /ˈɔpɪŋtən/, *n.* one of a breed of large white-skinned domestic fowls. [from *Orpington,* town in England]

**orrery** /ˈɒrəri/, *n., pl.* **-reries.** **1.** an apparatus for representing the motions and phases of the planets, etc., in the solar system. **2.** any of certain similar machines, as a planetarium. [named after the Earl of *Orrery,* 1676-1731, for whom it was first made]

**orris**[1] /ˈɒrəs/, *n.* any of certain species of iris, as *Iris florentina,* with a fragrant rootstock. Also, **orrice.** [unexplained var. of IRIS]

**orris**[2] /ˈɒrəs/, *n.* embroidery made of gold lace; lace of various patterns of gold and silver. [? var. of ORPHREY]

**orrisroot** /ˈɒrəsrut/, *n.* the rootstock of the orris, used as a perfume, etc.

**ort** /ɔt/, *n.* (*usu. pl.*) a fragment of food left at a meal. [ME, c. LG *ort,* early mod. D *oorete,* from *oor-* rejected (lit., out, from) + *ete* food. Cf. OE *or-, ǣt*]

**Orth.,** Orthodox.

**orthicon** /ˈɔθəkɒn/, *n.* a television camera pick-up tube, in which the image is focussed on a target cathode which then emits electrons which are collected by the anode, thus establishing a charge pattern. Also, **image orthicon.**

**orthite** /ˈɔθaɪt/, *n.* a variety of allanite.

**ortho-,** **1.** a word element meaning 'straight', 'upright', 'right', 'correct', used in combination. **2.** *Chem.* **a.** a prefix indicating that acid of a series which contains most water. Cf. **meta-, pyro-.** **b.** a prefix applied to a salt of one of these acids: if the acid ends in *-ic,* the corresponding salt ends in *-ate,* as *orthoboric acid* ($H_3BO_3$) and *potassium orthoborate* ($K_3BO_3$); if the acid ends in *-ous,* the corresponding salt ends in *-ite,* as *orthoantimonous acid* ($H_3SbO_3$) and *potassium orthoantimonite* ($K_3SbO_3$). **c.** a prefix designating the 1,2 position in the benzene ring. [Gk, combining form of *orthós* straight, upright, right, correct]

**orthoboric acid** /ɔθəˌbɔrɪk ˈæsəd/, *n.* a white crystalline solid, $H_3BO_3$, occurring in nature or prepared from borates, used in aqueous solution as a mild antiseptic and in glazes; boric acid.

**orthocaine** /ˈɔθəkeɪn/, *n.* a white crystalline solid used as a local anaesthetic, $C_6H_3NH_2(OH)COOCH_3$. [ORTHO- + (CO)CAINE]

**orthocentre** /ˈɔθoʊsɛntə/, *n.* the point of intersection of the altitudes of a triangle.

**orthocephalic** /ˌɔθoʊsəˈfælɪk/, *adj.* having the relation between the height of the skull and the breadth or the length medium or intermediate. Also, **orthocephalous** /ɔθoʊˈsɛfələs/. **– orthocephaly** /ɔθoʊˈsɛfəli/, *n.*

**orthochromatic** /ɔθoʊkrəˈmætɪk/, *adj. Photog.* **1.** pertaining to or representing the correct relations of colours, as in nature. **2.** designating a film or plate sensitive to yellow and green as well as to blue and violet.

**orthoclase** /ˈɔθoʊklæs, ˈɔθəkleɪz/, *n.* a very common mineral of the felspar group, potassium aluminium silicate, $KAlSi_3O_8$, occurring as an important constituent in many igneous rocks; used in the manufacture of porcelain. [ORTHO- + Gk *klásis* cleavage]

**orthodontics** /ɔθəˈdɒntɪks/, *n.* the branch of dentistry that is concerned with the straightening of irregular teeth. Also, **orthodontia.** [NL, from Gk *orth(o)-* ORTHO- + -ODONT (stem of *odoús* tooth) + -ICS] – **orthodontic,** *adj.* – **orthodontist,** *n.*

**orthodox** /ˈɔθədɒks/, *adj.* **1.** sound or correct in opinion or doctrine, esp. theological or religious doctrine. **2.** conforming to the Christian faith as represented in the primitive ecumenical creeds. **3.** (*cap.*) of, pertaining to, or designating the Eastern Church, esp. the Greek Orthodox Church. **4.** (*cap.*) of, pertaining to, or designating Orthodox Jews or Orthodox Judaism. **5.** of, pertaining to, or conforming to the approved or accepted form of any doctrine, philosophy, ideology, etc. **6.** approved; conventional. [LL *orthodoxus,* from Gk *orthódoxos* right in opinion] – **orthodoxly,** *adv.*

**Orthodox Church** /ɔθədɒks ˈtʃɜtʃ/, *n.* the Christian Church of the countries which formerly comprised the Eastern Roman Empire, and of countries evangelised from it, as Russia; the Church or group of local and national oriental Churches in communion or doctrinal agreement with the Greek patriarchal see of Constantinople.

**orthodoxy** /ˈɔθədɒksi/, *n., pl.* **-doxies. 1.** orthodox belief or practice. **2.** orthodox character.

**orthoepy** /ˈɔθoʊɛpi/, *n.* the study of correct pronunciation. [Gk *orthoépeia* correctness of diction] – **orthoepic** /ɔθoʊˈɛpɪk/, *adj.* – **orthoepist,** *n.*

**orthogenesis** /ɔθəˈdʒɛnəsəs/, *n.* **1.** *Biol.* the evolution of species in definite lines which are predetermined by the constitution of the germ plasm. **2.** *Sociol.* a hypothetical parallelism between the stages through which any culture necessarily passes, in spite of secondary conditioning factors. – **orthogenetic** /ɔθədʒəˈnɛtɪk/, *adj.*

**orthognathous** /ɔˈθɒgnəθəs/, *adj.* straight-jawed; having the profile of the face vertical or nearly so; having a gnathic index below 98. Also, **orthognathic** /ɔθɒgˈnæθɪk/.

**orthogonal** /ɔˈθɒgənəl/, *adj.* **1.** *Maths.* pertaining to or involving right angles or perpendicular lines: *an orthogonal projection.* **2.** *Crystall.* referable to a rectangular set of axes. [obs. *orthogon(ium)* (from LL, from Gk *orthogṓnion,* neut., right-angled) + -AL[1]] – **orthogonally,** *adv.*

**orthographer** /ɔˈθɒgrəfə/, *n.* **1.** one versed in orthography or spelling. **2.** one who spells correctly. Also, **orthographist.**

**orthographic** /ɔθəˈgræfɪk/, *adj.* **1.** pertaining to orthography. **2.** →**orthogonal.** Also, **orthographical.** – **orthographically,** *adv.*

**orthography** /ɔˈθɒgrəfi/, *n., pl.* **-phies. 1.** the art of writing words with the proper letters, according to accepted usage; correct spelling. **2.** that part of grammar which treats of letters and spelling. **3.** manner of spelling. **4.** an orthogonal projection, or an elevation drawn by means of it. [ME *orthographie,* from L *orthographia,* from Gk: correct writing]

**orthohydrogen** /ɔθoʊˈhaɪdrədʒən/, *n.* molecular hydrogen in which the spins of the two constituent hydrogen nuclei are parallel.

**orthopaedic** /ɔθəˈpidɪk/, *adj.* pertaining to orthopaedics. Also, *U.S.,* **orthopedic.**

**orthopaedics** /ɔθəˈpidɪks/, *n.* (esp. of children) the correction or cure of deformities and diseases of the spine, bones, joints, muscles, or other parts of the skeletal system. Also, **orthopaedy** /ˈɔθəˌpidi/, *U.S.,* **orthopedics, orthopedy.** [ORTHO- + Gk *paîs* child + -ICS]

**orthopaedist** /ɔθəˈpidəst/, *n.* one skilled in orthopaedics. Also, *U.S.,* **orthopedist.**

**orthophosphoric acid** /ˌɔθoʊfɒsfɒrɪk ˈæsəd/, *n.* the tribasic acid of pentavalent phosphorus, $H_3PO_4$, a colourless, crystalline compound, forming phosphates which are used in fertilisers.

**orthopod** /ˈɔθəpɒd/, *n. Colloq.* an orthopaedic surgeon.

**orthopsychiatry** /ˌɔθoʊsəˈkaɪətri/, *n.* the science that concerns itself with the study and treatment of behaviour disorders, esp. of young people. – **orthopsychiatric** /ˌɔθoʊsaɪkiˈætrɪk/, **orthopsychiatrical** /ˌɔθoʊsaɪkiˈætrɪkəl/, *adj.* – **orthopsychiatrist,** *n.*

**orthopteron** /ɔˈθɒptərɒn, -tərən/, *n.* an orthopterous insect.

**orthopterous** /ɔˈθɒptərəs/, *adj.* belonging or pertaining to the Orthoptera, an order of insects that includes the crickets, grasshoppers, cockroaches, etc., characterised usu. by leathery forewings and longitudinally folded, membranous hind wings. [NL *orthopterus,* from Gk *ortho-* ORTHO- + *-pteros* winged] – **orthopteran,** *adj., n.*

**orthoptic** /ɔˈθɒptɪk/, *adj.* pertaining to or producing normal binocular vision.

**orthoptic exercises** /– ˈɛksəsaɪzəz/, *n.pl.* a method of exercising the eye and its muscles in order to cure strabismus or improve vision.

**orthorhombic** /ɔθəˈrɒmbɪk/, *adj.* denoting or pertaining to a system of crystallisation characterised by three unequal axes intersecting at right angles.

**orthoscopic** /ɔθəˈskɒpɪk/, *adj.* pertaining to, characterised by, or produced by normal vision; presenting objects correctly to the eye.

**orthostat** /ˈɔθoʊstæt/, *n. Archaeol.* a large stone or slab, set vertically.

**orthostichy** /ɔˈθɒstəki/, *n., pl.* **-chies. 1.** a vertical rank or row. **2.** an arrangement of members, as leaves, at different heights on an axis so that their median planes coincide. [ORTHO- + Gk *-stichía* alignment] – **orthostichous,** *adj.*

**orthotropic** /ɔθəˈtrɒpɪk/, *adj.* denoting, pertaining to, or exhibiting a mode of plant growth which is more or less vertical.

**orthotropism** /ɔˈθɒtrəpɪzəm/, *n.* orthotropic tendency or growth.

**orthotropous** /ɔˈθɒtrəpəs/, *adj.* (of an ovule) straight and symmetrical, with the chalaza at the evident base and the micropyle at the opposite extremity.

**ortolan** /ˈɔtələn/, *n.* **1.** an Old World bunting, *Emberiza hortulana,* esteemed as a table delicacy. **2.** →**bobolink.** [F, from Pr.: lit., gardener (i.e. frequenting gardens), from L *hortulānus* of gardens]

**-ory**[1], a suffix of adjectives meaning 'having the function or effect of', as in *compulsory, contributory, declaratory, illusory.* [L *-ōrius* (neut. *-ōrium;* see -ORY[2]), suffix of adjectives associated esp. with agent nouns in *-or.* See -OR[2]]

**-ory**[2], a suffix of nouns denoting esp. a place or an instrument or thing for some purpose, as in *directory, dormitory, purgatory.* [L *-ōrium.* See -ORY[1]]

**oryx** /ˈɒrɪks/, *n., pl.* **oryxes,** (*esp. collectively*) **oryx. 1.** a large African antelope, *Oryx beisa,* greyish with black markings, and having long, nearly straight horns. **2.** →**gemsbok.** [ME, from L, from Gk: pickaxe, oryx]

oryx

**os**[1] /ɒs/, *n., pl.* **ossa** /ˈɒsə/. a bone. [L]

**os**[2] /ɒs/, *n., pl.* **ora** /ˈɔrə/. *Anat.* a mouth, opening or entrance. [L: mouth]

**os**[3] /oʊs/, *n., pl.* **osar** /ˈoʊsa/. an esker, esp. when of great length. [Swed. *as* (pl. *asar*) ridge]

**o/s, 1.** out of stock. **2.** (in banking) outstanding.

**o.s.** /oʊ ˈɛs/, *adv.* **1.** overseas. –*adj.* **2.** overseas.

**Os,** *Chem.* osmium.

**O.S., 1.** Old Series. **2.** Out of Stock. **3.** Outsize. **4.** Old Saxon. **5.** ordinary seaman.

**Osage orange** /oʊseɪdʒ ˈɒrɪndʒ/, *n.* **1.** an ornamental tree, *Maclura pomifera,* native to the southern central U.S., used for hedges. **2.** its fruit, which resembles a warty orange.

**oscar** /ˈɒskə/, *n. Colloq.* cash, money. [rhyming slang, *Oscar Ashe* cash]

**Oscar** /ˈɒskə/, *n.* one of a group of statuettes awarded annually by the American Academy of Motion Picture Arts for outstanding achievement by a film actor, director, etc. [? from a remark made by an official on first seeing the statuette that it reminded him of his uncle Oscar]

**oscillate** /ˈɒsəleɪt/, *v.i.,* **-lated, -lating. 1.** to swing or move to and fro, as a pendulum does; vibrate. **2.** to fluctuate between states, opinions, purposes, etc. **3.** to have, produce, or generate oscillations. [L *oscillātus,* pp., swung]

**oscillation** /ɒsəˈleɪʃən/, *n.* **1.** the act or fact of oscillating. **2.** a single swing, or movement in one direction, of an oscillating body, etc. **3.** fluctuation between states, opinions, etc. **4.** *Physics.* a repetitive to and fro motion of an object; a repetitive fluctuation in amplitude of an electrical signal or electric or magnetic field.

**oscillator** /ˈɒsəleɪtə/, *n.* **1.** a device or machine producing oscillations. **2.** one who or that which oscillates.

**oscillatory** /ˈɒsəleɪtəri, -lətri/, *adj.* characterised by or involving oscillation.

**oscillogram** /ɒˈsɪləgræm/, *n.* a record, on paper, or a screen, of the movements of an oscillograph.

**oscillograph** /əˈsɪləgræf, -graf/, *n.* **1.** an instrument for recording oscillations, esp. electric oscillations. **2.** a device for recording the wave-forms of changing currents, voltages, or any other quantity which can be translated into electrical energy, as, for example, soundwaves. [L *oscillāre* swing + -O- + -GRAPH]

**oscilloscope** /əˈsɪləskoʊp/, *n.* a device which makes the shape of a voltage or current wave visible on the screen of a cathode-ray tube or other device.

**oscinine** /ˈɒsənaɪn/, *adj.* of or pertaining to the Oscines, a large group of passerine birds, containing those with the most highly developed vocal organs, and commonly termed the songbirds. Also, **oscine** /ˈɒsaɪn/. [backformation from *Oscines,* from L]

**oscitant** /ˈɒsətənt/, *adj.* **1.** gaping; yawning. **2.** drowsy; inattentive. **3.** indolent; negligent. [L *oscitans,* ppr.] – **oscitancy, oscitance,** *n.*

**osculant** /ˈɒskjələnt/, *adj.* **1.** united by certain common characteristics. **2.** *Zool.* adhering closely; embracing. [L *osculans,* ppr., kissing]

**oscular** /ˈɒskjələ/, *adj.* **1.** pertaining to an osculum. **2.** pertaining to the mouth or kissing. [L *osculum* little mouth, kiss + -AR[1]]

**osculate** /ˈɒskjəleɪt/, *v.*, **-lated, -lating.** –*v.t.* **1.** to kiss. **2.** to bring into close contact or union. **3.** *Geom.* to touch so as to have three or more points in common at the point of contact. –*v.i.* **4.** to kiss each other. **5.** to come into close contact or union. **6.** *Geom.* to osculate each other, as two curves. [L *osculātus,* pp., kissed] – **osculatory** /ˈɒskjələtri, -leɪtəri/, *adj.*

**osculating circle** /ɒskjəleɪtɪŋ ˈsɜkəl/, *n.* the circle, the arc of which best approximates a curve at a given point on that curve.

**osculation** /ɒskjəˈleɪʃən/, *n.* **1.** kissing. **2.** a kiss. **3.** close contact. **4.** *Geom.* the contact between two osculating curves or the like.

**osculum** /ˈɒskjələm/, *n.*, *pl.* **-la** /-lə/. a small mouthlike aperture, as of a sponge. [L, diminutive of *ōs* mouth]

**-ose**[1], an adjective suffix meaning 'full of', 'abounding in', 'given to', 'like', as in *frondose, globose, jocose, otiose, verbose.* [L *-ōsus.* Cf. -OUS]

**-ose**[2], a noun termination used to form chemical terms, esp. names of sugars and other carbohydrates, as *amylose, fructose, hexose, lactose,* and (rarely) of protein derivatives, as *proteose.* [abstracted from GLUCOSE]

**osier** /ˈoʊʒə/, *n.* **1.** any of various willows, as *Salix viminalis* (the common **basket osier**) and *Salix purpurea* (**red osier**), with tough flexible twigs or branches which are used for wickerwork. **2.** a twig from such a willow. [ME, from F; akin to ML *ausaria* willow bed]

**-osis,** *pl.* **-oses.** a noun suffix denoting action, process, state, condition, etc., as in *metamorphosis,* and in many pathological terms, as *tuberculosis.* [Gk, suffix forming nouns from verbs with infinitive in *-óein, -oûn*]

**-osity,** a noun suffix equivalent to **-ose**[1] (or **-ous**) plus **-ity.** [-OSE[1] + -ITY, representing stem of L *-ōsitas* and F *-osité*]

**oslo lunch** /ɒzloʊ ˈlʌntʃ/, *n.* a meal of basically wholesome foods, usu. including wholemeal bread, butter, milk, cheese, eggs, fruit and raw vegetables. [named after *Oslo,* capital of Norway]

**osmic** /ˈɒzmɪk/, *adj.* of or containing osmium in its higher valencies, esp. the tetravalent state.

**osmious** /ˈɒzmiəs/, *adj.* of or containing osmium in its lower valencies.

**osmiridium** /ɒzməˈrɪdiəm, ɒs-/, *n.* →**iridosmine.**

**osmium** /ˈɒzmiəm/, *n.* a hard, heavy, metallic element used for electric-light filaments, etc., having the greatest density of any known material, and forming octavalent compounds, such as $OsO_4$, $OsF_8$. *Symbol:* Os; *at. wt:* 190.2; *at. no.:* 76; *sp. gr.:* 22.48 at 20°C. [NL, from Gk *osmḗ* smell, odour; named from the penetrating smell of one of its oxides]

**osmometer** /ɒzˈmɒmətə/, *n.* an instrument for measuring osmotic pressures.

**osmose** /ɒzˈmoʊs/, *v.*, **-mosed, -mosing.** –*v.i.* **1.** to undergo osmosis. –*v.t.* **2.** to subject to osmosis. –*n.* **3.** →**osmosis.**

**osmosis** /ɒzˈmoʊsəs/, *n.* **1.** the tendency of a fluid to pass through a semipermeable membrane into a solution where its concentration is lower, thus equalising the conditions on either side of the membrane. **2.** the diffusion of fluids through membranes or porous partitions. **3.** a process of interchange or absorption suggestive of osmotic action. [NL, from Gk *ōsmós* a thrusting] – **osmotic** /ɒzˈmɒtɪk/, *adj.* – **osmotically** /ɒzˈmɒtɪkli/, *adv.*

**osmotic pressure** /ɒz,mɒtɪk ˈprɛʃə/, *n.* the pressure which must be applied to a solution in order to prevent the flow of solvent through a semipermeable membrane separating the solution and the pure solvent.

**osmund** /ˈɒzmənd, ˈɒs-/, *n.* any fern of the genus *Osmunda,* which includes the royal fern.

**osnaburg** /ˈɒznəbɜg/, *n.* a heavy coarse cotton in a plain weave used for grain sacks, etc.

**osprey** /ˈɒspri, ˈɒspreɪ/, *n.*, *pl.* **-preys.** **1.** a large hawk, *Pandion haliaetus,* which feeds on fish; the fish-hawk. **2.** a kind of feather used to trim hats. [ME *ospray(e),* from F *orfraie* (representing L *ossifraga*), b. with L. See OSSIFRAGE]

osprey

**ossein** /ˈɒsi,ɪn/, *n.* the organic basis of bone, mainly glycoprotein, which remains after the mineral matter has been removed by treatment with dilute acid. [L *osseus* bony + -IN[2]]

**osseous** /ˈɒsiəs/, *adj.* **1.** composed of, containing, or resembling bone; bony. **2.** →**ossiferous.** [L *osseus* bony] – **osseously,** *adv.*

**ossia** /ˈɒsiə/, *n.* an alternative, usu. simpler, version of a difficult passage in a piece of music which may be played if preferred. [It. *o sia* or let it be]

**ossicle** /ˈɒsɪkəl/, *n.* a small bone. [L *ossiculum,* diminutive of *os* bone]

**ossiferous** /ɒˈsɪfərəs/, *adj.* containing bones.

**ossification** /ɒsəfəˈkeɪʃən/, *n.* **1.** the act or process of ossifying. **2.** the resulting state. **3.** that which is ossified.

**ossifrage** /ˈɒsəfrɪdʒ/, *n.* **1.** →**osprey.** **2.** →**lammergeyer.** [L *ossifragus,* masc., *ossifraga,* fem., lit., bonebreaker]

**ossify** /ˈɒsəfaɪ/, *v.*, **-fied, -fying.** –*v.t.* **1.** to convert into, or harden like, bone. **2.** to render (attitudes, opinions, etc.) rigid or inflexible. –*v.i.* **3.** to become bone or hard like bone. **4.** to become rigid or inflexible in attitudes, opinions, etc. [L *os* bone + -IFY. Cf. F *ossifier*]

**osso buco** /,ɒsoʊ ˈbʊkoʊ/, *n.* an Italian dish in which thick slices of unboned shin of veal are stewed in white wine with tomato and herbs, and sprinkled with a mixture of grated lemon rind, chopped garlic and parsley before serving. Also, **osso bucco.** [It.: lit., bone-hole, i.e. marrow bone]

**ossuary** /ˈɒsjuəri/, *n.*, *pl.* **-aries.** a place or receptacle for the bones of the dead. [LL *ossuārium,* from L *os* bone]

**osteal** /ˈɒstiəl/, *adj.* →**osseous.** [OSTE(O)- + -AL[1]]

**osteitis** /ɒstiˈaɪtəs/, *n.* inflammation of the substance of bone. [OSTE(O)- + -ITIS]

**ostensible** /ɒsˈtɛnsəbəl/, *adj.* given out or outwardly appearing as such; professed; pretended. [F, from L *ostensus,* pp., displayed + *-ible* -IBLE] – **ostensibly,** *adv.*

**ostensive** /ɒsˈtɛnsɪv/, *adj.* **1.** manifestly demonstrative. **2.** →**ostensible.** – **ostensively,** *adv.*

**ostentation** /ɒstɛnˈteɪʃən/, *n.* **1.** pretentious show; display intended to impress others. **2.** *Obs.* a show or display. Also,

**ostentatiousness.** [ME, from L *ostentātio*]

**ostentatious** /ɒstɛn'teɪʃəs/, *adj.* **1.** characterised by or given to ostentation or pretentious show. **2.** (of actions, manner, qualities exhibited, etc.) intended to attract notice. – **ostentatiously,** *adv.*

**osteo-,** a word element meaning 'bone'. Also, before vowels, **oste-.** [Gk, combining form of *ostéon*]

**osteoarthritis** /ˌɒstioʊa'θraɪtəs/, *n.* a degenerative type of chronic arthritis.

**osteoblast** /'ɒstiəblæst/, *n.* a bone-forming cell.

**osteoclasis** /ɒsti'ɒkləsəs/, *n.* **1.** *Anat.* the breaking down or absorption of osseous tissue. **2.** *Surg.* the fracturing of a bone to correct deformity. [NL, from *osteo-* OSTEO- + Gk *klásis* fracture]

**osteoclast** /'ɒstiəklæst/, *n.* **1.** *Anat.* one of the large multinuclear cells in growing bone, and concerned in the absorption of osseous tissue, as in the formation of canals, etc. **2.** *Surg.* an instrument for effecting osteoclasis. [OSTEO- + Gk *klastós* broken]

**osteogenesis** /ɒstiə'dʒɛnəsəs/, *n.* the formation of bone.

**osteoid** /'ɒstiɔɪd/, *adj.* bonelike. [OSTE(O)- + -OID]

**osteology** /ɒsti'ɒlədʒi/, *n.* the branch of anatomy that treats of the skeleton and its parts. – **osteological** /ɒstiə'lɒdʒɪkəl/, *adj.* – **osteologist,** *n.*

**osteoma** /ɒsti'oʊmə/, *n., pl.* **-mas, -mata** /-mətə/. a tumour composed of osseous tissue. [NL. See OSTEO-, -OMA]

**osteomalacia** /ˌɒstioʊmə'leɪʃə/, *n.* a condition due to a deficiency of vitamin D and characterised by a softening of the bones leading to severe deformities, most commonly found in women and often associated with pregnancy.

**osteomyelitis** /ˌɒstioʊˌmaɪə'laɪtəs/, *n.* a purulent inflammation of the bone.

**osteopath** /'ɒstiəpæθ/, *n.* one who practises osteopathy. Also, **osteopathist** /ɒsti'ɒpəθəst/.

**osteopathy** /ɒsti'ɒpəθi/, *n.* a theory of disease and a method of treatment resting upon the supposition that most diseases are due to deformation of some part of the body and can be cured by some kind of manipulation. – **osteopathic** /ɒstiə'pæθɪk/, *adj.*

**osteophyte** /'ɒstiəfaɪt/, *n.* a small osseous excrescence or outgrowth on bone. – **osteophytic** /ɒstiə'fɪtɪk/, *adj.*

**osteoplastic** /ɒstiə'plæstɪk/, *adj.* **1.** *Surg.* pertaining to osteoplasty. **2.** *Physiol.* pertaining to bone formation.

**osteoplasty** /'ɒstiəplæsti/, *n.* the transplanting or inserting of bone, or surgical reconstruction of bone, to repair a defect or loss.

**osteotome** /'ɒstiətoʊm/, *n.* a double-bevelled chisel-like instrument for cutting or dividing bone.

**osteotomy** /ɒsti'ɒtəmi/, *n., pl.* **-mies.** the dividing of a bone, or the excision of part of it. – **osteotomist,** *n.*

**ostiary** /'ɒstiəri/, *n., pl.* **-aries. 1.** *Rom. Cath. Ch.* one ordained to the lowest of the four minor orders; a porter. **2.** a doorkeeper, as of a church. [ME, from L *ostiārius* doorkeeper]

**ostinato** /ɒstə'natoʊ/, *n., pl.* **-tos.** (in music) a constantly recurring melodic or rhythmic fragment. [It.: lit., obstinate]

**ostiole** /'ɒstioʊl/, *n.* a small opening or orifice. [L *ostiolum,* diminutive of *ostium* door] – **ostiolar** /'ɒstiələ, ɒs'ti-/, *adj.*

**ostler** /'ɒslə/, *n.* one who takes care of horses, esp. at an inn. Also, **hostler.**

**ostosis** /ɒs'toʊsəs/, *n.* the formation of bone; ossification. [NL; see OST(EO)-, -OSIS]

**ostracise** /'ɒstrəsaɪz/, *v.t.,* **-cised, -cising. 1.** to banish (a person) from his native country; expatriate. **2.** to exclude by general consent from society, privileges, etc. **3.** *Gk Antiq.* to banish (a citizen) temporarily by popular vote with ballots consisting of potsherds or tablets of earthenware. Also, **ostracize.** [Gk *ostrakízein* (def. 3), from *óstrakon* potsherd] – **ostracisable,** *adj.* – **ostraciser,** *n.*

ostrich

**ostracism** /'ɒstrəsɪzəm/, *n.* **1.** the act of ostracising. **2.** the fact or state of being ostracised. [Gk *ostrakismós*]

**ostrich** /'ɒstrɪtʃ/, *n.* **1.** a large two-toed, swift-footed, flightless bird, *Struthio camelus,* the largest of existing birds, native to Africa and Arabia, now extensively reared for the plumage. **2.** →**rhea. (American ostrich).** [ME *ostrice,* from OF *ostruce,* from LL *avi(s) strūthio,* from *avis* bird + *strūthio* ostrich, from Gk *strouthíōn*] – **ostrich-like,** *adj.*

**ot-,** variant of **oto-** before vowels.

**o/t,** overtime.

**o.t.** /oʊ 'ti/, *Colloq.* overseas. [*o(ver) t(here)*]

**O.T., 1.** Occupational Therapy. **2.** Old Testament. Also, **OT.**

**otalgia** /oʊ'tældʒə/, *n.* earache. [NL, from Gk] – **otalgic,** *adj.*

**other** /'ʌðə/, *adj.* **1.** additional or further: *he and one other person.* **2.** different or distinct from the one or ones mentioned or implied: *in some other city.* **3.** different in nature or kind: *I would not have him other than he is.* **4.** being the remaining one of two or more: *the other hand.* **5.** (with plural nouns) being the remaining ones of a number: *the other men.* **6.** former: *men of other days.* **7. every other,** every alternate: *a meeting every other week.* **8. the other day** (**night,** etc.), a day (night, etc.) or two ago. **9. the other half,** *Colloq.* either of the two classes into which society is divided, the rich or the poor (but esp. the poor): *see how the other half live.* **10. the other side, a.** *Spiritualism.* the place where the spirits of dead people reside. **b.** *N.Z. Colloq.* Australia. *–pron.* **11.** the other one: *each praises the other.* **12.** another person or thing. **13.** some person or thing else: *some day or other.* *–adv.* **14.** otherwise. [ME; OE *ōther,* c. G *ander;* akin to Skt *antara*] – **otherness,** *n.*

**other-directed** /'ʌðə-dərɛktəd/, *adj.* guided by a set of values that is derived from current trends or outward influences rather than from within oneself. – **other-directedness,** *n.* – **other-direction,** *n.*

**otherie** /'ʌðəri/, *n. Colloq.* other. Also, **othery.**

**other place** /'ʌðə pleɪs/, *n.* →**another place.**

**other ranks** /– 'ræŋks/, *n. pl.* the non-commissioned members of a military organisation, distinguished from officers, and sometimes also from non-commissioned officers.

**otherwise** /'ʌðəwaɪz/, *adv.* **1.** under other circumstances. **2.** in another manner; differently. **3.** in other respects: *an otherwise happy life.* *–adj.* **4.** other or different; of another nature or kind. [ME *other wis* (two words), OE (*on*) *ōthre wīsan* in other manner. See OTHER, WISE[2]]

**other world** /ʌðə 'wɜld/, *n.* the world of the dead; future world.

**otherworldly** /ʌðə'wɜldli/, *adj.* **1.** of, pertaining to, or devoted to another world, as the world of imagination, or the world to come. **2.** neglectful; impractical. – **otherworldliness,** *n.*

**otic** /'oʊtɪk, 'ɒtɪk/, *adj.* of or pertaining to the ear; auricular. [Gk *ōtikós*]

**-otic,** an adjective suffix meaning: **1.** 'suffering from', as in *neurotic.* **2.** 'producing', as in *hypnotic.* **3.** 'resembling', as in *Quixotic.* [Gk *-ōtikós*]

**otiose** /'oʊtioʊs/, *adj.* **1.** at leisure; idle; indolent. **2.** ineffective or futile. **3.** superfluous or useless. [L *ōtiōsus*] – **otiosely,** *adv.* – **otiosity** /oʊti'ɒsəti/, *n.*

**otitis** /oʊ'taɪtəs/, *n.* inflammation of the ear.

**oto-,** a word element meaning 'ear'. [Gk, combining form of *oûs*]

**otocyst** /'oʊtəsɪst/, *n.* the embryonic auditory vesicle.

**otolaryngology** /ˌoʊtoʊlærɪŋ'gɒlədʒi/, *n.* the branch of medicine dealing with the ear and throat.

**otolith** /'oʊtəlɪθ/, *n.* a calcareous concretion in the internal ear of vertebrates and in the balancing organ of some invertebrates.

**otologist** /oʊ'tɒlədʒəst/, *n.* a physician expert in treating diseases of the ear; an aurist.

**otology** /oʊ'tɒlədʒi/, *n.* the science of the ear and its diseases.

**otoscope** /'oʊtəskoʊp/, *n.* an instrument used by doctors to examine the external ear.

**ottava rima** /ətavə 'rimə/, *n.* an Italian stanza of eight lines, each of eleven syllables (or, in the English adaptation, of ten or eleven syllables), the first six lines rhyming alternately and the last two forming a couplet with a different rhyme (as used in Keats's *Isabella* and Byron's *Don Juan*). [It.: octave rhyme]

**otter** /'ɒtə/, *n., pl.* **-ters,** (*esp. collectively*) **-ter.** any of the various aquatic, furred, carnivorous, musteline mammals of the genus *Lutra,* and allied genera, with webbed feet adapted for swimming, and a long tail slightly flattened horizontally to act as a rudder, as *L. vulgaris,* of Europe, and *L. canadensis,* of the U.S. and Canada, and the sea-otter. [ME *oter,* OE *oter, ot(o)r,* c. D *otter,* G *Otter*]

otter

**otterhound** /ˈɒtəhaʊnd/, *n.* one of an English breed of water-dogs with a hard, crisp, oily coat and shaggy undercoat, trained to hunt otters.

**otter shrew** /ˈɒtə ʃru/, *n.* an insectivorous mammal of western Africa, *Potamogale velox,* about the size of a stoat but resembling an otter in habits and appearance, having brown fur and a flattened tail.

**ottfur hook** /ˈɒtfə hʊk/, *n.* a device on a glider to which the tow rope is attached, and which is activated by the pilot to detach his craft from the tow plane.

**ottocento** /ɒtəˈtʃɛntoʊ/, *n.* the 19th century, used commonly with reference to Italian art and literature of that period. [It.: eight hundred, short for *mille ottocento,* one thousand eight hundred]

**Otto cycle** /ˈɒtoʊ saɪkəl/, *n.* the working cycle of a four-stroke internal-combustion engine. [named after N. A. *Otto,* 1832-91, German engineer]

**ottoman** /ˈɒtəmən/, *n., pl.* **-mans.** **1.** a low-cushioned seat like a sofa without back or arms. **2.** a low chest with a padded top. **3.** a cushioned footstool. **4.** a corded silk or rayon fabric with large cotton cord for filling. [F *ottomane,* fem. of OTTOMAN]

**Ottoman** /ˈɒtəmən/, *n.* **1.** a Turk. *–adj.* **2.** Turkish. Also, **Othman.** [F, from Ar., from *Othman* Osman I, founder of the Ottoman empire]

**Ottoman Turkish** /ˈ– tɜkɪʃ/, *n.* the language of Turkey.

**ouabain** /waˈbaˌɪn/, *n.* a cardiac glucoside derived from the tree, *Strophanthus gratus.* [F, from Somali]

**oubliette** /ubliˈɛt/, *n.* a secret dungeon with an opening only at the top, as in certain old castles. [F, from *oublier* forget, from Rom. *oblītāre,* from L *oblīvīscī*]

**ouch**[1] /aʊtʃ/, *interj.* (an exclamation expressing sudden pain).

**ouch**[2] /aʊtʃ/, *Archaic.* *–n.* **1.** a clasp, buckle, or brooch, esp. one worn for ornament. **2.** the setting of a precious stone. *–v.t.* **3.** to adorn with or as with ouches. [ME *ouche,* for *nouche* (*a nouche* being taken as *an ouche*). Cf. LL *nusca,* OHG *nuscha* buckle, ultimately of Celtic orig.]

**ought**[1] /ɔt/, *v. aux.* **1.** was (were) or am (is, are) bound in duty or moral obligation: *every citizen ought to help.* **2.** was (am, etc.) bound or required on any ground, as of justice, propriety, probability, expediency, fitness, or the like (usu. fol. by an infinitive with *to* or having the infinitive omitted but understood): *he ought to be punished.* *–n.* **3.** duty or obligation. [ME *ought, aught,* etc., OE *āhte,* pret. of *āgan* OWE]

**ought**[2] /ɔt/, *n., adv.* →**aught**[2]. [var. of NOUGHT, *a nought* being taken as *an ought*]

**ouija** /ˈwidʒə, -dʒi/, *n.* a device consisting of a small board on legs, which rests on a larger board marked with words, letters of the alphabet, etc., and which, by moving over the larger board and touching the words, letters, etc., while the fingers of mediums or others rest lightly upon it, is employed to give answers, messages, etc. Also, **ouija board.** [F *oui* yes + G *ja* yes]

**ounce**[1] /aʊns/, *n.* **1.** a unit of mass in the imperial system, equal to $\frac{1}{16}$ lb. avoirdupois or 28.349 523 125 × $10^{-3}$ kg. **2. troy ounce, apothecaries ounce,** a unit of mass in the imperial system equal to 480 grains, or 31.103 4768 × $10^{-3}$ kg. **3.** →**fluid ounce.** **4.** a small quantity or portion. [ME *unce,* from OF, from L *uncia* twelfth part, inch, ounce. Cf. INCH[1]]

ounce[2]

**ounce**[2] /aʊns/, *n.* a long-haired leopard-like feline, *Panthera uncia,* inhabiting the mountain ranges of central Asia; snow leopard. [ME *once,* from OF, var. of *lonce* (taken as *l'once* the ounce), from L *lynx* LYNX]

**our** /ˈaʊə/, *pron. or adj.* the possessive form corresponding to *we* and *us,* used before a noun. Cf. **ours.** [ME *oure,* OE *ure,* gen. pl. See US]

**-our,** a suffix of nouns denoting state or condition, a quality or property, etc., as in *ardour, colour, honour, labour.* Cf. **-or**[1]. [ME, from AF (= F *-eur*), from L *-or* -OR[1]]

**ourari** /uˈrari/, *n.* →**curare.**

**ours** /ˈaʊəz/, *pron.* **1.** a form of *our* used predicatively or without a noun following: *those books are ours.* **2. of ours,** (the person(s) or thing(s)) belonging to us: *a friend of ours.*

**ourself** /aʊəˈsɛlf/, *pron.* a form corresponding to *ourselves,* used of a single person, esp. (like *we* for *I*) in the regal or formal style.

**ourselves** /aʊəˈsɛlvz/, *pron. pl.* **1.** a reflexive form of *us: we hurt ourselves.* **2.** an emphatic form of *us* or *we* used: **a.** as object: *we used it for ourselves.* **b.** in opposition to a subject or object: *we ourselves did it.*

**-ous,** **1.** an adjective suffix meaning 'full of', 'abounding in', 'given to', 'characterised by', 'having', 'of the nature of', 'like', etc.: *glorious, joyous, mucous, nervous, sonorous, wondrous.* **2.** *Chem.* a suffix used to imply the lower of two possible valencies compared to the corresponding suffix *-ic;* as *stannous chloride,* $SnCl_2$, and *stannic chloride,* $SnCl_4$. Also, **-eous, -ious.** [ME, from OF, from L *-ōsus;* often used to represent L *-us,* adj., Gk *-os,* adj.; in a few words (e.g. *wondrous*) it is attached to native stems]

**ousel** /ˈuzəl/, *n.* →**ouzel.**

**oust** /aʊst/, *v.t.* **1.** to expel from a place or position occupied. **2.** *Law.* to eject; dispossess. [AF *ouster* remove, from L *obstāre* be in the way, protect against]

**ouster** /ˈaʊstə/, *n.* **1.** *Law.* **a.** ejection; dispossession. **b.** a wrongful exclusion from real property. **2.** one who ousts. [AF, n. use of inf. See OUST]

**out** /aʊt/, *adv.* **1.** forth from, away from, or not in a place, position, state, etc.: *out of order.* **2.** away from one's home, country, etc.: *to set out on a journey.* **3.** into the open: *to go out for a walk.* **4.** to exhaustion, extinction, or conclusion; to the end; so as to finish or exhaust or be exhausted; so as to bring to naught or render useless: *to pump out a well.* **5.** to or at an end or conclusion: *to fight it out.* **6.** no longer or not burning or furnishing light; extinguished: *the lamp went out.* **7.** not in vogue or fashion: *that style has gone out.* **8.** into or in public notice or knowledge: *the book came out in May.* **9.** seeking openly and energetically to do or have: *to try out for the team.* **10.** into or in society: *a young girl who came out last season.* **11.** not in present or personal possession or use; let for hire, or placed at interest: *let out for a year.* **12.** on strike: *the miners are coming out.* **13.** so as to project or extend: *to stretch out.* **14.** into or in existence, activity, or outward manifestation: *fever broke out.* **15.** from a source, ground or cause, material, etc. (with *of*): *made out of scraps.* **16.** from a state of composure, satisfaction, or harmony: *to feel put out.* **17.** in or into a state of confusion, vexation, dispute, variance, or unfriendliness: *to fall out about trifles.* **18.** so as to deprive or be deprived (with *of*): *to cheat out of money.* **19.** having used the last (with *of*): *to run out of coal.* **20.** from a number, stock, or store: *to pick out.* **21.** aloud or loudly: *to call out.* **22.** with completeness or effectiveness: *to fit out.* **23.** thoroughly; completely; entirely. **24.** so as to make illegible or indecipherable: *to paint out, ink out.* **25. go all out,** to extend oneself; pursue an interest, goal, etc., with the utmost energy. **26. out and away,** in a pre-eminent degree; by far. *–adj.* **27.** torn or worn into holes, as clothing: *his trousers were out at the knees.* **28.** incorrect or inaccurate: *to be out in one's calculations.* **29.** at a pecuniary loss: *to be out by ten dollars.* **30.** lacking; without: *we are completely out of eggs.* **31.** unconscious; senseless: *the boxer was out for about five minutes.* **32.** not in office or employment; unemployed: *out of work.* **33.** finished; ended: *before the month is out.* **34.** *Tennis, etc.* beyond the boundary lines: *the umpire declared the ball out.* **35.** *Cricket, etc.* removed from play by being bowled, l.b.w., stumped, caught, or run out. **36.** external; exterior; outer. **37.** outlying. **38. out of it,** *Colloq.* **a.** incapacitated as a result of taking drugs or alcohol. **b.** in a dreamy or vague state of mind, as if under the influence of drugs or alcohol. **39. out to it,** *Colloq.* **a.** unconscious. **b.** asleep. *–prep.* **40.** out or forth from (now used chiefly after *from* or in certain expressions): *out the door, out the window.* **41.** outside; on the exterior of; beyond. *–interj.* **42.** begone! away! *–n.* **43.** projection, or projecting corners: *ins and outs.* **44.** a means of escaping from a place, punishment, retribution, responsibility, etc.: *he always left himself an out.* **45.** *Baseball, etc.* →**put-out. 46.** *Print.* **a.** the omission of a word or words. **b.** that which is omitted. *–v.t.* **47.** to go or come out: *murder will out.* **48.** to make known; tell; utter (fol. by *with*). *–v.t.* **49.** to put out; expel; discharge; oust. **50. out here, a.** in Australia. **b.** in a town or place thought of as being remote from the main centre. [ME; OE *ūt,* c. D *uit,* G *aus,* Icel. and Goth. *ūt*]

**out-,** prefixal use of **out**, adv., prep., or adj., occurring in various senses in compounds, as in *outcast, outcome, outside,* and serving also to form many transitive verbs denoting a going beyond, surpassing, or outdoing in the particular action indicated, as in *outbid, outdo, outgeneral, outlast, outstay, outrate,* and many other words in which the meaning is readily perceived, the more important of these being entered below.

**outact** /aʊt'ækt/, *v.t.* to outdo or surpass in acting.

**outage** /'aʊtɪdʒ/, *n.* a planned blackout (def. 2) so that maintenance, repair, etc. can be carried out.

**out-and-out** /'aʊt-ən-aʊt/, *adj.* thoroughgoing; thorough; complete; unqualified.

**outargue** /aʊt'agju/, *v.t.,* **-gued, -guing.** to outdo or defeat in arguing.

**outback** /'aʊtbæk/, *n.* **1.** (*sometimes cap.*) remote, sparsely inhabited back country. *–adj.* **2.** of, pertaining to, or located in the back country. *–adv.* **3.** in or to the back country: *to live outback.*

**outbalance** /aʊt'bæləns/, *v.t.,* **-anced, -ancing.** to outweigh.

**outbid** /aʊt'bɪd/, *v.t.,* **-bid, -bidden** or **-bid, -bidding.** to outdo in bidding.

**outboard** /'aʊtbɔd/, *adj.* **1.** on the outside, or away from the centre, of a ship, boat, aircraft, etc. – **outboard,** *adv.*

**outboard motor** /– 'moʊtə/, *n.* a petrol engine with propeller and tiller, clamped on the stern of a boat.

**outbound** /'aʊtbaʊnd/, *adj.* outward bound.

**outbox** /aʊt'bɒks/, *v.t.* to outdo in boxing.

**outbrave** /aʊt'breɪv/, *v.t.,* **-braved, -braving. 1.** to defy; stand up to. **2.** to surpass in bravery or daring. **3.** to surpass in beauty, splendour, etc.

**outbreak** /'aʊtbreɪk/, *n.* **1.** a breaking out; an outburst. **2.** a sudden and active manifestation. **3.** a public disturbance; a riot; an insurrection.

**outbreed** /aʊt'brid/, *v.t.,* **-bred, -breeding.** to breed outside the limits of the family, within a breed or variety. – **outbreeding,** *n.*

**outbuilding** /'aʊtbɪldɪŋ/, *n.* a detached building subordinate to a main building.

**outburst** /'aʊtbɜst/, *n.* **1.** a bursting forth. **2.** a sudden and violent outpouring: *an outburst of tears.*

**outcast** /'aʊtkast/, *n.* **1.** a person who is cast out, as from home or society. **2.** a vagabond; homeless wanderer. **3.** *Archaic.* rejected matter; refuse. *–adj.* **4.** cast out, as from one's home or society. **5.** pertaining to or characteristic of an outcast: *outcast misery.* **6.** rejected or discarded.

**outcaste** /'aʊtkast/, *n.* **1.** a person of no caste. **2.** (in India) one who has forfeited membership in his caste.

**outclass** /aʊt'klas/, *v.t.* to surpass in class or quality; be distinctly ahead of (a competitor, etc.).

**outcome** /'aʊtkʌm/, *n.* that which results from something; the consequence or issue.

**outcrop** /'aʊtkrɒp/, *n.;* /aʊt'krɒp/, *v.,* **-cropped, -cropping.** *–n.* **1.** a cropping out, as of a stratum or vein at the surface of the earth. **2.** the emerging part. **3.** something that occurs unexpectedly, suddenly, or violently: *an outcrop of labour unrest.* *–v.i.* **4.** to crop out, as strata.

**outcrossing** /'aʊtkrɒsɪŋ/, *n.* breeding of unrelated animals or plants within a variety or breed. Also, **outcross.**

**outcry** /'aʊtkraɪ/, *n., pl.* **-cries;** /aʊt'kraɪ/, *v.,* **-cried, -crying.** *–n.* **1.** a crying out. **2.** a cry of distress, indignation, or the like. **3.** loud clamour. **4.** widespread protest or indignation. *–v.t.* **5.** to outdo in crying; cry louder than.

**outdate** /aʊt'deɪt/, *v.t.,* **-dated, -dating.** to put out of date; make antiquated or obsolete.

**outdated** /'aʊtdeɪtəd/, *adj.* made out of date by the passage of time; old-fashioned.

**outdistance** /aʊt'dɪstəns/, *v.t.,* **-tanced, -tancing.** to distance completely; leave far behind; outstrip.

**outdo** /aʊt'du/, *v.t.,* **-did, -done, -doing.** to surpass in doing or performance; surpass.

**outdoor** /'aʊtdɔ/, *adj.* **1.** occurring or used out of doors. **2.** given or administered outside or apart from a workhouse, charitable institution, etc.: *outdoor relief.*

**outdoors** /aʊt'dɔz/, *adv.* **1.** out of doors; in the open air. *–n.* **2.** the world outside houses; open air. **3. the great outdoors,** the natural environment, esp. wilderness areas. – **outdoorsy,** *adj.*

**outer** /'aʊtə/, *adj.* **1.** farther out; external; of or pertaining to the outside. *–n.* **2.** *Colloq.* an open betting place near a racecourse. **3.** that part of a sportsground which is without shelter. **4.** *Archery, etc.* **a.** the outermost ring or part of a target. **b.** a shot which strikes this part. **c.** the score value of this part. **5. the outer,** *Prison Colloq.* the world outside prison. **6. on the outer,** *Colloq.* excluded from the group; mildly ostracised. [compar. of OUT]

**outer bar** /– 'ba/, *n.* a collective name for all barristers other than Queen's Counsel.

**outer garments** /– 'gamənts/, *n.pl.* clothes worn over ordinary dress, as overcoats, capes, etc.

**Outer Mongolia** /aʊtə mɒŋ'goʊliə/, *n.* **1.** former name of **Mongolian People's Republic. 2.** *Colloq.* any remote, isolated

---

**outbargain,** *v.t.*
**outbarter,** *v.t.*
**outbawl,** *v.t.*
**outbluff,** *v.t.*
**outbluster,** *v.t.*
**outboast,** *v.t.*
**outbrag,** *v.t.,* **-bragged, -bragging.**
**outbranch,** *v.t.*
**outbrazen,** *v.t.*
**outbribe,** *v.t.,* **-bribed, -bribing.**
**outbuild,** *v.t.*
**outcross,** *v.t.*
**outdance,** *v.t.,* **-danced, -dancing.**
**outdare,** *v.t.,* **-dared, -daring.**
**outdazzle,** *v.t.,* **-zled, -zling.**
**outdrink,** *v.t.,* **-drank, -drunk, -drinking.**
**outeat,** *v.t.,* **-ate, -eating.**
**outfight,** *v.t.,* **-fought, -fighting.**
**outflung,** *adj.*
**outgaze,** *v.t.,* **-gazed, -gazing.**
**outguess,** *v.t.*
**outjump,** *v.t.*
**outleap,** *v.t.,* **-leapt, -leaping.**
**outmarch,** *v.t.*
**outplease,** *v.t.,* **-pleased, -pleasing.**
**outprice,** *v.t.,* **-priced, -pricing.**
**outreason,** *v.t.*
**outreign,** *v.t.*
**outrig,** *v.t.,* **-rigged, -rigging.**
**outrival,** *v.t.,* **-rivalled, -rivalling.**
**outroar,** *v.t.*
**outsay,** *v.t.,* **-said, -saying.**
**outsee,** *v.t.,* **-saw, -seen, -seeing.**
**outsit,** *v.t.,* **-sat, -sitting.**
**outsleep,** *v.t.,* **-slept, -sleeping.**
**outsoar,** *v.t.*
**outsparkle,** *v.t.,* **-sparkled, -sparkling.**
**outspring,** *n.*
**outspring,** *v.,* **-sprang, -sprung, -springing.**
**outswear,** *v.t.,* **-swore, -sworn, -swearing.**
**outswim,** *v.t.,* **-swam, -swum, -swimming.**
**outtalk,** *v.t.*
**outthink,** *v.t.,* **-thought, -thinking.**
**outtell,** *v.t.,* **-told, -telling.**
**outwait,** *v.t.*
**outwalk,** *v.t.*

and therefore culturally backward place.

**outermost** /ˈaʊtəmoʊst/, *adj.* farthest out; remotest from the interior or centre. [OUTER + -MOST]

**outer space** /aʊtə ˈspeɪs/, *n.* **1.** space beyond the earth's atmosphere. **2.** space beyond the solar system. **3.** space between galaxies.

**outface** /aʊtˈfeɪs/, *v.t.*, **-faced, -facing.** **1.** to face or stare out. **2.** to face or confront boldly; defy.

**outfall** /ˈaʊtfɔl/, *n.* the outlet or place of discharge of a river, drain, sewer, etc.

**outfield** /ˈaʊtfild/, *n.* **1.** *Cricket.* the part of the field farthest from the batsman. **2.** *Baseball.* **a.** the part of the field beyond the diamond or infield. **b.** the players stationed in it. **3.** the outlying land of a farm, esp. beyond the enclosed land. **4.** an outlying region.

**outfielder** /ˈaʊtfildə/, *n.* **1.** *Baseball, Cricket, etc.* one of the players stationed in the outfield.

**outfit** /ˈaʊtfɪt/, *n., v.*, **-fitted, -fitting.** *–n.* **1.** an assemblage of articles for fitting out or equipping: *an explorer's outfit.* **2.** a set of articles for any purpose: *a model aircraft outfit.* **3.** a woman's costume, usu. including dress, coat, hat, shoes, etc., and matching accessories. **4. a.** a group associated in any undertaking, as a military body, etc. **b.** a business company engaged in a particular kind of work. **c.** a party, company, or set. **5.** the act of fitting out or equipping, as for a voyage, journey, or expedition, or for any purpose. **6.** mental or moral equipment. **7.** *Colloq.* syringe and needle used for taking drugs. *–v.t.* **8.** to furnish with an outfit; fit out; equip. *–v.i.* **9.** to furnish oneself with an outfit.

**outfitter** /ˈaʊtfɪtə/, *n.* **1.** one who provides an outfit. **2.** a shopkeeper who sells men's clothes.

**outflank** /aʊtˈflæŋk/, *v.t.* **1.** to go or extend beyond the flank of (an opposing army, etc.); outmanoeuvre by a flanking movement. **2.** to get the better of (a rival, opponent, etc.).

**outflow** /ˈaʊtfloʊ/, *n.* **1.** the act of flowing out. **2.** that which flows out. **3.** any outward movement.

**outfly** /aʊtˈflaɪ/, *v.t.*, **-flew, -flown, -flying.** **1.** to surpass or outstrip in flying. **2.** *Poetic.* to fly out or forth.

**outfoot** /aʊtˈfʊt/, *v.t.* **1.** (of one boat) to excel (another) in speed. **2.** to surpass in running, walking, dancing, etc.

**outfox** /aʊtˈfɒks/, *v.t.*, to outmanoeuvre.

**outfrown** /aʊtˈfraʊn/, *v.t.* to outdo in frowning; frown down.

**outgeneral** /aʊtˈdʒɛnərəl/, *v.t.*, **-alled, -alling** or (*U.S.*) **-aled, -aling.** to outdo in generalship.

**outgo** /ˈaʊtgoʊ/, *n., pl.*, **-goes;** /aʊtˈgoʊ/, *v.*, **-went, -gone, -going.** *–n.* **1.** a going out. **2.** expenditure. **3.** that which goes out; outflow. *–v.t.* **4.** to outstrip in going; go faster than. **5.** to go beyond or exceed. **6.** to surpass, excel, or outdo.

**outgoing** /ˈaʊtgoʊɪŋ/, *adj.* **1.** going out; departing: *outgoing trains.* **2.** interested in and responsive to others: *an outgoing personality.* *–n.* **3.** (*usu. pl.*) an amount of money expended; outlay; expenses. **4.** a going out. **5.** that which goes out; an effluence.

**out-group** /ˈaʊt-grup/, *n.* *Sociol.* everyone not belonging to an in-group.

**outgrow** /aʊtˈgroʊ/, *v.*, **-grew, -grown, -growing.** *–v.t.* **1.** to grow too large for. **2.** to leave behind or lose in the changes incident to development or the passage of time: *to outgrow a bad reputation.* **3.** to surpass in growing. *–v.i.* **4.** to grow out; protrude.

**outgrowth** /ˈaʊtgroʊθ/, *n.* **1.** a natural development, product, or result. **2.** an additional, supplementary result. **3.** a growing out or forth. **4.** that which grows out; an offshoot; an excrescence.

**outhaul** /ˈaʊthɔl/, *n.* a rope used for hauling out a sail on a boom, yard, etc.

**outhouse** /ˈaʊthaʊs/, *n.* **1.** an outbuilding. **2.** an outside toilet.

**outing** /ˈaʊtɪŋ/, *n.* **1.** an excursion or pleasure trip. **2.** the part of the sea out from the shore.

**outing flannel** /ˈ– flænəl/, *n.* a light cotton flannel with a short nap.

**outjockey** /aʊtˈdʒɒki/, *v.t.*, **-eyed, -eying.** to outmanoeuvre.

**outland** /ˈaʊtlænd/, *n.*; /ˈaʊtlænd, -lənd/, *adj.* *–n.* **1.** *Obs.* outlying land, as of an estate. *–adj.* **2.** outlying, as districts. [ME; OE *ūtland*]

**outlander** /ˈaʊtlændə/, *n.* **1.** a foreigner; an alien. **2.** *Colloq.* an outsider.

**outlandish** /aʊtˈlændɪʃ/, *adj.* **1.** freakishly or grotesquely strange or odd, as appearance, dress, objects, ideas, practices, etc.; bizarre; barbarous. **2.** foreign-looking. **3.** out-of-the-way, as places. **4.** *Archaic.* foreign. **– outlandishly,** *adv.* **– outlandishness,** *n.*

**outlast** /aʊtˈlast/, *v.t.* to last longer than.

**outlaw** /ˈaʊtlɔ/, *n.* **1.** one excluded from the benefits and protection of the law. **2.** one under sentence of outlawry. **3.** a habitual criminal. **4.** an untamed or intractable animal. *–v.t.* **5.** to deprive of the benefits and protection of the law. **6.** to prohibit. [ME *outlawe,* OE *ūtlage,* from Scand.; cf. Icel. *ūtlagi*]

**outlawry** /ˈaʊtlɔri/, *n., pl.*, **-ries.** **1.** the act or process of outlawing. **2.** the state of being outlawed. **3.** disregard or defiance of the law.

**outlay** /ˈaʊtleɪ/, *n.*; /aʊtˈleɪ/ *v.*, **-laid, -laying.** *–n.* **1.** an expending; an expenditure, as of money. **2.** an amount expended. *–v.t.* **3.** to expend, as money.

**outlet** /ˈaʊtlɛt, -lət/, *n.* **1.** an opening or passage by which anything is let out; a vent or exit. **2.** *Elect.* **a.** a point on a wiring system at which current is taken to supply electrical devices. **b. outlet box,** the metal box or receptacle designed to facilitate connections to a wiring system. **3.** *Comm.* **a.** a market for goods. **b.** (of a wholesaler or manufacturer) a shop, merchant, or agency selling one's goods: *he has many good outlets.* **4.** a means of expression; an occasion for releasing energies, etc. **5.** discharge.

**outlier** /ˈaʊtlaɪə/, *n.* **1.** one who or that which lies outside. **2.** one residing outside the place of his business, duty, etc. **3.** *Geol.* a part of a formation left detached through the removal of surrounding parts by denudation.

**outline** /ˈaʊtlaɪn/, *n., v.*, **-lined, -lining.** *–n.* **1.** the line, real or apparent, by which a figure or object is defined or bounded; the contour. **2.** a drawing or a style of drawing with merely lines of contour, without shading. **3.** a general sketch, account or report, indicating only the main features, as of a book, a subject, a project or work, facts, events, etc. **4.** (*pl.*) the essential features or chief characteristics of a subject. *–v.t.* **5.** to draw the outline of, or draw in outline, as a figure or object. **6.** to give an outline of (a subject, etc.); sketch the main features of.

**outlive** /aʊtˈlɪv/, *v.t.*, **-lived, -living.** **1.** to live longer than; survive (a person, etc.). **2.** to outlast; live or last through: *the ship outlived the storm.*

**outlook** /ˈaʊtlʊk/, *n.* **1.** the view or prospect from a place. **2.** the mental view: *one's outlook upon life.* **3.** prospect of the future: *the political outlook.* **4.** the place from which an observer looks out; a lookout. **5.** the act or state of looking out. **6.** a watch kept; watchfulness; vigilance.

**outlying** /ˈaʊtlaɪɪŋ/, *adj.* **1.** lying at a distance from the centre or the main body; remote; out-of-the-way. **2.** lying outside the boundary or limit.

**outman** /aʊtˈmæn/, *v.t.*, **-manned, -manning.** **1.** to surpass in manpower. **2.** to surpass in manliness.

**outmanoeuvre** /aʊtməˈnuvə/, *v.t.* to outdo in or get the better of by manoeuvring. Also, *U.S.*, **outmaneuver.**

**outmatch** /aʊtˈmætʃ/, *v.t.* to surpass; outdo.

**outmode** /aʊtˈmoʊd/, *v.t.*, **-moded, -moding.** to cause to be out of style or become obsolete. **– outmoded,** *adj.*

**outmost** /ˈaʊtmoʊst/, *adj.* farthest out; outermost.

**outnumber** /aʊtˈnʌmbə/, *v.t.* to exceed in number.

**out of bounds,** See **bound**[3] (def. 5).

**out-of-date** /ˈaʊt-əv-deɪt/, *adj.* of a previous style or fashion; obsolete. Also (*esp. in predicative use*), **out of date.**

**out-of-doors** /ˈaʊt-əv-dɔz, aʊt-əv-ˈdɔz/, *adj.*; /aʊt-əv-ˈdɔz/, *adv., n.* *–adj.* **1.** Also, **out-of-door;** (*esp. in predicative use*), **out of doors.** outdoor. *–adv., n.* **2.** →**outdoors.**

**out of play,** See **play** (def. 7).

**out-of-pocket** /ˈaʊt-əv-pɒkət/, *adj.* of or pertaining to what has been paid out in cash or outlay incurred: *out-of-pocket expenses.* Also (*esp. in predicative use*), **out of pocket.**

**out of print,** See **print** (def. 18).

**out-of-the-way** /ˈaʊt-əv-ðə-weɪ/, *adj.* **1.** remote from much-travelled ways or frequented or populous regions; secluded. **2.** unusual. **3.** improper. Also (*esp. in predicative use*), **out of the way.**

**outpace** /aʊt'peɪs/, *v.t.*, **-paced, -pacing.** to outstrip or outdo in walking, running, riding, etc.

**outpatient** /'aʊtpeɪʃənt/, *n.* a patient receiving treatment at a hospital but not being an inmate.

**outperform** /aʊtpə'fɔm/, *v.t.* to outdo; surpass.

**outplay** /aʊt'pleɪ/, *v.t.* to play better than; defeat.

**outpoint** /aʊt'pɔɪnt/, *v.t.* **1.** to excel in number of points, as in a competition or contest. **2.** *Naut.* to sail closer to the wind than (another vessel).

**outport** /'aʊtpɔt/, *n.* a secondary seaport, auxiliary to another seaport, and generally more accessible to larger vessels.

**outpost** /'aʊtpoʊst/, *n.* **1.** a station at a distance from the main body of an army to protect it from surprise attack. **2.** the body of troops stationed there. **3.** any remote settlement: *an outpost of civilisation.*

**outpour** /'aʊtpɔ/, *n.*; /aʊt'pɔ/, *v.* *–n.* **1.** an outflow or overflow; that which is poured out. *–v.t.* **2.** to pour out.

**outpouring** /'aʊtpɔrɪŋ/, *n.* outflow; effusion.

**output** /'aʊtpʊt/, *n.* **1.** the act of turning out; production. **2.** the quantity or amount produced, as in a given time. **3.** the product or yield, as of a mine. **4.** *Computers.* information obtained from a computer on the completion of a calculation. *–v.t.* **5.** *Computers.* to give out (results).

**outrage** /'aʊtreɪdʒ/, *n.*, *v.*, **-raged, -raging.** *–n.* **1.** an act of wanton violence; any gross violation of law or decency. **2.** anything that outrages the feelings. **3.** *Obs.* a passionate or violent outbreak. *–v.t.* **4.** to subject to grievous violence or indignity. **5.** to affect with a sense of offended right or decency; shock. **6.** to offend against (right, decency, feelings, etc.) grossly or shamelessly. **7.** to rape (a woman). [ME, from OF, from *outrer* push beyond bounds, from *outre* beyond, from L *ultrā*]

**outrageous** /aʊt'reɪdʒəs/, *adj.* **1.** of the nature of or involving gross injury or wrong: *an outrageous slander.* **2.** grossly offensive to the sense of right or decency. **3.** passing reasonable bounds; intolerable or shocking: *an outrageous price.* **4.** violent in action or temper. **– outrageously,** *adv.* **– outrageousness,** *n.*

**outrange** /aʊt'reɪndʒ/, *v.t.*, **-ranged, -ranging. 1.** to have a longer range than, as a gun. **2.** *Naut.* to outsail.

**outrank** /aʊt'ræŋk/, *v.t.* to rank above.

**outré** /'utreɪ/, *adj.* passing the bounds of what is usual and considered proper. [F, pp. of *outrer*. See OUTRAGE]

**outreach** /aʊt'ritʃ/, *v.*; /'aʊtritʃ/, *n.* *–v.t.* **1.** to reach beyond; exceed. **2.** to reach out; extend. *–v.i.* **3.** to reach out. *–n.* **4.** a reaching out. **5.** length of reach.

**outride** /aʊt'raɪd/, *v.*, **-rode, -ridden, -riding;** /'aʊtraɪd/, *n.* *–v.t.* **1.** to outdo or outstrip in riding. **2.** (of a ship) to last through a storm. *–v.i.* **3.** to act as an outrider. *–n.* **4.** *Pros.* an unaccented syllable or syllables added to a metrical foot, esp. in sprung rhythm.

**outrider** /'aʊtraɪdə/, *n.* **1.** a mounted attendant riding before or beside a carriage. **2.** a motorcyclist who rides ahead of a motor car as an escort, to clear a passage, etc. **3.** one who goes ahead as a member of a vanguard. **4.** one who rides out or forth, esp. as a scout.

**outrigger** /'aʊtrɪgə/, *n.* **1.** a framework extended outboard from the side of a boat, esp., as in South Pacific canoes, supporting a float which gives stability. **2.** a bracket extending outwards from the side of a racing shell, to support a rowlock. **3.** the shell itself. **4.** a spar rigged out from a ship's rail or the like, as for extending a sail. **5.** any of various projecting frames or parts on an aeroplane, as for supporting a rudder, etc. **6.** *Bldg Trades.* a beam projecting from a building and wedged against a ceiling inside the building, used for supporting certain kinds of scaffolding.

canoe with outrigger

**outright** /'aʊtraɪt/, *adj.* **1.** complete or total: *an outright loss.* **2.** downright or unqualified: *an outright refusal.* *–adv.* **3.** completely; entirely. **4.** without restraint, reserve, or concealment; openly. **5.** at once.

**outroot** /aʊt'rut/, *v.t.* to root out; extirpate.

**outrun**[1] /aʊt'rʌn/, *v.t.*, **-ran, -run, -running. 1.** to outstrip in running. **2.** to escape by or as by running. **3.** to exceed.

**outrun**[2] /'aʊtrʌn/, *n.* a sheep run at a considerable distance from the head station.

**outrunner** /'aʊtrʌnə/, *n.* **1.** one who or that which runs out or outside. **2.** an attendant who runs before or beside a carriage. **3.** the leader of a team of dogs. **4.** →**forerunner.**

**outsail** /aʊt'seɪl/, *v.t.* to outdo or surpass in sailing; outstrip.

**outsell** /aʊt'sɛl/, *v.t.*, **-sold, -selling. 1.** to outdo in selling; sell more than. **2.** to sell or be sold for more than. **3.** to exceed in value.

**outset** /'aʊtsɛt/, *n.* the beginning or start.

**outshine** /aʊt'ʃaɪn/, *v.*, **-shone, -shining.** *–v.t.* **1.** to surpass in shining. **2.** to surpass in splendour, excellence, etc. *–v.i.* **3.** *Rare.* to shine forth.

**outshoot** /aʊt'ʃut/, *v.*, **-shot, -shooting;** /'aʊtʃut/, *n.* *–v.t.* **1.** to surpass in shooting. **2.** to shoot beyond. **3.** to shoot or send forth. *–v.i.* **4.** to shoot forth; project. *–n.* **5.** a shooting out. **6.** something that shoots out.

**outside** /'aʊtsaɪd/, *n.*, *adj.*; /aʊt'saɪd/, *adv.*, *prep.* *–n.* **1.** the outer side, surface, or part; the exterior. **2.** the external aspect or appearance. **3.** something merely external. **4.** the space without or beyond an enclosure, boundary, etc. **5.** seaward, beyond the point where the waves break. **6.** *Rugby Football.* **a.** a back. **b.** any player other than a forward. **7. at the outside,** *Colloq.* the utmost limit: *not more than ten at the outside.* *–adj.* **8.** being, acting, done, or originating beyond an enclosure, boundary, etc.: *outside noises.* **9.** situated on or pertaining to the outside; exterior; external. **10.** not belonging to or connected with an institution, society, etc.: *outside influences.* **11.** extremely unlikely or remote: *an outside chance.* *–adv.* **12.** on or to the outside, exterior, or space without. *–prep.* **13.** on or towards the outside of. **14.** *Colloq.* with the exception of (usu. fol. by *of*).

**outside broadcast** /– 'brɔdkast/, *n.* a radio or television broadcast not made in a studio.

**outside half** /aʊtsaɪd 'haf/, *n.* *Brit.* (in rugby football) →**five-eighth.** Also, **outside half-back.**

**outside job** /aʊtsaɪd 'dʒɒb/, *n.* a job done for someone other than one's regular employer, esp. as of tradesmen.

**outside left** /aʊtsaɪd 'lɛft/, *n.* (in soccer, hockey, etc.) a player on the far left wing of the forward line. Also, **left wing.**

**outsider** /aʊt'saɪdə/, *n.* **1.** one not within an enclosure, boundary, etc. **2.** one not belonging to a particular group, set, party, etc. **3.** one unconnected or unacquainted with the matter in question. **4.** a racehorse, etc., not included among the favourites.

**outside right** /aʊtsaɪd 'raɪt/, *n.* (in soccer, hockey, etc.) a player on the far right wing of the forward line. Also, **right wing.**

**outsing** /aʊt'sɪŋ/, *v.*, **-sang, -sung, -singing.** *–v.t.* **1.** to sing better than. **2.** to sing louder than. *–v.i.* **3.** to sing out.

**out sister** /'aʊt sɪstə/, *n.* a nun, esp. in a coenobite order, who works outside the convent in its service.

**outsize** /'aʊtsaɪz/, *n.* **1.** an uncommon or irregular size. **2.** a garment of such a size, esp. when larger. *–adj.* **3.** Also, **outsized.** unusually or abnormally large; larger than average: *a display of outsize dresses.*

**outskirts** /'aʊtskɜts/, *n.pl.* outer or bordering parts or districts.

**outsmart** /aʊt'smat/, *v.t.* to prove too clever for; outwit.

**outspeak** /aʊt'spik/, *v.*, **-spoke, -spoken, -speaking.** *–v.t.* **1.** to outdo or excel in speaking. **2.** to utter frankly or boldly. *–v.i.* **3.** to speak out.

**outspoken** /'aʊtspoʊkən/, *adj.* **1.** uttered or expressed with frankness or lack of reserve: *outspoken criticism.* **2.** free or unreserved in speech: *outspoken people.* **– outspokenly,** *adv.* **– outspokenness,** *n.*

**outspread** /aʊt'sprɛd/, *v.*, **-spread, spreading;** /'aʊtsprɛd/, *adj.*, *n.* *–v.t.*, *v.i.* **1.** to spread out; extend. *–adj.* **2.** spread out; stretched out. **3.** diffused abroad. *–n.* **4.** a spreading out. **5.** that which is spread out; an expanse.

**outstand** /aʊt'stænd/, *v.*, **-stood, -standing.** *Rare.* *–v.i.* **1.** to be prominent. **2.** (of a ship) to sail out to sea. *–v.t.* **3.** to stay or remain beyond. **4.** to withstand.

**outstanding** /aʊt'stændɪŋ/, *adj.* **1.** prominent; conspicuous; striking. **2.** that continues in existence; that remains unsettled, unpaid, etc. **3.** standing out; projecting; detached. **4.** that resists or opposes.

**outstare** /aʊt'stɛə/, *v.t.*, **-stared, -staring.** **1.** to outdo in staring. **2.** to stare out of countenance.

**out-station** /'aʊt-steɪʃən/, *n.* **1.** a stock-handling depot with accommodation away from the main homestead. **2.** any remote post: *a diplomatic out-station; a military out-station.*

**outstay** /aʊt'steɪ/, *v.t.* **1.** to stay longer than. **2.** to stay beyond the time or duration of.

**outstretch** /aʊt'strɛtʃ/, *v.t.* **1.** to stretch forth; extend. **2.** to stretch beyond (a limit, etc.). **3.** to stretch out; expand. **4.** *Obs.* to strain.

**outstrip** /aʊt'strɪp/, *v.t.*, **-stripped, -stripping.** **1.** to outdo; surpass; excel. **2.** to outdo or pass in running or swift travel. **3.** to get ahead of or leave behind in a race or in any course of competition.

**outstroke** /'aʊtstroʊk/, *n.* **1.** a stroke in an outward direction. **2.** (in an engine) the stroke during which the piston rod moves outwards from the cylinder.

**outswing** /'aʊtswɪŋ/, *n.* (in cricket) the movement from leg to off of a bowled ball. Cf. **inswing.** – **outswinger,** *n.*

**outswinger** /'aʊtswɪŋə/, *n.* (in cricket) a ball bowled so as to swerve from leg to off.

**out-take** /'aʊt-teɪk/, *n.* a scene from a film or T.V. production which has been recorded but which cannot be used because of some flaw, such as the failure of a prop, wrong lines, helpless laughter, etc.

**out-tray** /'aʊt-treɪ/, *n.* a tray or other receptacle for out-going letters, files, job assignments, etc. which have received attention.

**outturn** /'aʊttɜn/, *n.* the quantity produced; output.

**outvote** /aʊt'voʊt/, *v.t.*, **-voted, -voting.** to outdo or defeat in voting.

**outward** /'aʊtwəd/, *adj.* **1.** being, or pertaining to, what is seen or apparent, as distinguished from the underlying nature, facts, etc., or from what is in the mind: *the outward looks.* **2.** pertaining to the outside of the body. **3.** pertaining to the body as opposed to the mind or spirit: *our outward eyes.* **4.** belonging or pertaining to the external world as opposed to the mind or spirit. **5.** belonging or pertaining to what is external to oneself: *a man's outward relations.* **6.** proceeding or directed towards the outside or exterior. **7.** that lies towards the outside; that is on the outer side: *my outward room.* **8.** of or pertaining to the outside, outer surface, or exterior. **9.** not directly concerned or interested. *–n.* **10.** the outward part; the outside or exterior; the external or material world. **11.** outward appearance. *–adv.* **12.** outwards. **13.** away from port: *a ship bound outward.* [ME; OE *ūtweard*]

**outward-bound** /'aʊtwəd-baʊnd/, *adj.* (of a ship) headed out to sea, esp. from a home port.

**outwardly** /'aʊtwədli/, *adv.* **1.** as regards appearance or outward manifestation. **2.** towards the outside. **3.** on the outside or outer surface.

**outwards** /'aʊtwədz/, *adv.* towards the outside; out. Also, **outward.**

**outwash** /'aʊtwɒʃ/, *n.* sheets of gravel, sand, and clay, laid down by melt-water streams at the end of a glacier or round the margin of an icesheet.

**outwatch** /aʊt'wɒtʃ/, *v.t.* **1.** to outdo in watching. **2.** to watch until the end of.

**outwear** /aʊt'wɛə/, *v.t.*, **-wore, -worn, -wearing.** **1.** to wear or last longer than; outlast. **2.** to outlive or outgrow. **3.** to wear out; consume by wearing. **4.** to exhaust in strength or endurance. **5.** to pass time.

**outweigh** /aʊt'weɪ/, *v.t.* **1.** to exceed in value, importance, influence, etc.: *the advantages of the plan outweighed its defects.* **2.** to be too heavy or burdensome for. **3.** to exceed in weight.

**outwit** /aʊt'wɪt/, *v.t.*, **-witted, -witting.** to get the better of by superior ingenuity or cleverness.

**outwork** /aʊt'wɜk/, *v.t.*, **-worked** or **-wrought, -working;** /'aʊtwɜk/, *n.* *–v.t.* **1.** to surpass in working; work harder or faster than. **2.** to work out or carry on to a conclusion; finish. *–n.* **3.** *Fort.* a part of the fortifications of a place lying outside the main work.

**outworker** /'aʊtwɜkə/, *n.* one who does work in his home, as for a central factory or organisation.

**outworn** /'aʊtwɔn/, *adj.* **1.** obsolete; out-of-date as beliefs, customs, etc. **2.** worn out, as clothes. **3.** exhausted in strength or endurance, as persons.

**ouzel** /'uzəl/, *n.* **1.** a name for members of the European thrush family, esp. the blackbird, *Turdus merula.* **2.** →**ring ouzel.** Also, **ousel, ouzel cock.** [ME *osel,* OE *ōsle,* c. G *Amsel*]

**ouzo** /'uzoʊ/, *n.* an aniseed-flavoured liqueur of Greece.

**ova** /'oʊvə/, *n.* plural of **ovum.**

**oval** /'oʊvəl/, *adj.* **1.** having the general form, shape, or outline of an egg; egg-shaped. **2.** ellipsoidal or elliptical. *–n.* **3.** any of various oval things. **4.** a body or a plane figure oval in shape or outline. **5.** a flat area (sometimes elliptical) on which sporting activities can take place. [NL *ōvālis,* from L *ōvum* egg. See OVATE] – **ovally,** *adv.* – **ovalness,** *n.*

**ovarian** /oʊ'vɛəriən/, *adj.* of or pertaining to an ovary.

**ovariotomy** /oʊ,vɛəri'ɒtəmi/, *n., pl.* **-mies.** incision into or removal of an ovary.

**ovaritis** /oʊvə'raɪtəs/, *n.* →**oophoritis.**

**ovary** /'oʊvəri/, *n., pl.* **-ries.** **1.** *Anat., Zool.* the female gonad or reproductive gland, in which the ova, or eggs, and the hormones that regulate female secondary sex characteristics develop. **2.** *Bot.* the enlarged lower part of the carpel in angiospermous flowers enclosing the ovules. [NL *ōvārium,* from L *ōvum* egg]

**ovate** /'oʊveɪt/, *adj.* **1.** eggshaped. **2.** *Bot.* **a.** having a plane figure like the longitudinal section of an egg. **b.** having such a figure with the broader end at the base, as a leaf. [L *ōvātus* egg-shaped]

ovate leaf

**ovation** /oʊ'veɪʃən/, *n.* an enthusiastic public reception of a person; enthusiastic applause. [L *ovātio* rejoicing]

**oven** /'ʌvən/, *n.* a chamber or receptacle for baking or heating, or for drying with the aid of heat. [ME; OE *ofen,* c. G *Ofen*]

**ovenproof** /'ʌvənpruf/, *adj.* not damaged by use in a hot oven.

**ovenware** /'ʌvənwɛə/, *n.* heat-resistant dishes, casseroles, etc., in which food can be baked in an oven.

**ovenwood** /'ʌvənwʊd/, *n.* brushwood; dead wood fit only for burning.

**over** /'oʊvə/, *prep.* **1.** above in place or position; higher up than: *the roof over one's head.* **2.** above and to the other side of: *to leap over a wall.* **3.** above in authority, power, etc.; so as to govern, control, or conquer. **4.** on or upon; so as to rest on or cover. **5.** on or on top of: *to hit someone over the head.* **6.** here and there on or in: *at various places over the country.* **7.** through all parts of; all through: *to look over some papers.* **8.** to and fro on or in: *to travel all over Australia.* **9.** from side to side of; to the other side of: *to go over a bridge.* **10.** on the other side of: *lands over the sea.* **11.** reaching higher than, so as to submerge. **12.** in excess of, or more than: *over a kilometre.* **13.** above in degree, etc. **14.** in preference to. **15.** throughout the extent or length of: *over a great distance.* **16.** until after the end of: *to adjourn over the holidays.* **17.** throughout the duration of: *over a long term of years.* **18.** in reference to, concerning, or about: *to quarrel over a matter.* **19.** while engaged on or concerned with: *to fall asleep over one's work.* **20.** by the agency of: *she told me over the phone; we heard the news over the radio.* **21. be all over,** *Colloq.* to show great affection towards; be excessively attentive to: *she was all over him as soon as he entered the room.* **22. over and above,** in addition to; besides. **23. over the fence,** unreasonable; unfair. *–adv.* **24.** over the top or upper surface, or edge of something. **25.** so as to cover the surface, or affect the whole surface: *to paint a thing over.* **26.** through a region, area, etc.: *to travel all over.* **27.** at some distance, as in a direction indicated: *over by the hill.* **28.** from side to side, or to the other side: *to sail over.* **29.** across any intervening space: *when are you coming over to see us?* **30.** from beginning to end, or all through: *to read a thing*

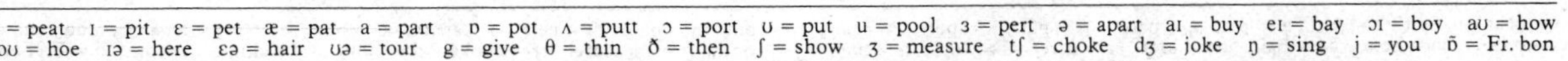
i = peat ɪ = pit ɛ = pet æ = pat a = part ɒ = pot ʌ = putt ɔ = port ʊ = put u = pool ɜ = pert ə = apart aɪ = buy eɪ = bay ɔɪ = boy aʊ = how
oʊ = hoe ɪə = here ɛə = hair ʊə = tour g = give θ = thin ð = then ʃ = show ʒ = measure tʃ = choke dʒ = joke ŋ = sing j = you õ = Fr. bon

*over.* **31.** from one person, party, etc., to another: *to make property over to others.* **32.** on the other side, as of a sea, a river, or any space: *over in Fiji.* **33.** so as to bring the upper end or side down or under: *to knock a thing over.* **34.** *Brit.* once more; again: *to do a thing over.* **35.** in repetition: *twenty times over.* **36.** in excess or addition: *to pay the full sum and something over.* **37.** remaining beyond a certain amount: *five goes into seven once, with two over.* **38.** throughout or beyond a period of time: *to stay over till Monday.* **39.** Some adverbial phrases are:
**all over, 1.** everywhere. **2.** thoroughly; entirely. **3.** done with; finished.
**all over with,** done with; finished.
**over again,** once more; with repetition.
**over against, 1.** opposite to; in front of. **2.** as contrasted with or distinguished from: *to set truth over against falsehood.*
**over and over (again),** repeatedly.
*–adj.* **40.** upper; higher up. **41.** higher in authority, station, etc. **42.** serving, or intended, as an outer covering: *outer.* **43.** in excess or addition; surplus; extra. **44.** too great; excessive. **45.** at an end; done; past: *when the war was over.* **46. all over,** *Colloq.* characteristic; typical: *that's him all over.* *–n.* **47.** an amount in excess or addition; an extra. **48.** *Mil.* a shot which strikes or bursts beyond the target. **49.** *Cricket.* **a.** the number of balls (eight in Australia and New Zealand, six in most other countries) delivered between successive changes of bowlers. **b.** the part of the game played between such changes. *–v.t.* **50.** *Rare.* to jump over; leap over. **51.** *Rare.* to get over; pass over. [ME; OE *ofer,* c. D *over,* G *über,* akin to Skt *upari*]

**over-,** prefixal use of **over,** *prep., adv.,* or *adj.,* occurring in various senses in compounds, as in *overboard, overcoat, overhang, overlap, overlord, overrun, overthrow,* and esp. employed, with the sense of 'over the limit', 'to excess', 'too much', 'too', to form verbs, adjectives, adverbs, and nouns, as *overact, overcapitalise, overcrowd, overfull, overmuch, oversupply, overweight,* and many others, mostly self-explanatory. A hyphen, commonly absent from old or well-established formations, is often used in new coinages, or in any words whose compound parts it may be desirable to set off distinctly.

**overabound** /oʊvərə'baʊnd/, *v.i.* to abound to excess.

**overabundance** /oʊvərə'bʌndəns/, *n.* excessive abundance. **– overabundant,** *adj.*

**overact** /oʊvər'ækt/, *v.t., v.i.* to act in exaggerated manner.

**overactive** /oʊvər'æktɪv/, *adj.* active to excess; too active. **– overactivity** /oʊvəræk'tɪvəti/, *n.*

**over-age** /'oʊvər-eɪdʒ/, *adj.* beyond the proper age. [OVER- + AGE, *n.*]

**overall** /'oʊvərɔl/, *adj., n.;* /oʊvər'ɔl/, *adv.* *–adj.* **1.** from one extreme limit of a thing to another: *the overall length of a bridge.* **2.** covering or including everything: *an overall estimate.* *–n.* **3. a.** a coverall or boiler suit. **b.** loose trousers of strong material, usu. with a bib and shoulder straps, worn by workmen and young children. *–adv.* **4.** covering or including everything; altogether: *the position viewed overall.*

**overanxious** /oʊvər'æŋʃəs/, *adj.* excessively anxious. **– overanxiety** /oʊvəræŋ'zaɪəti/, **overanxiousness,** *n.* **– overanxiously,** *adv.*

**overarch** /oʊvər'atʃ/, *v.t.* **1.** to span with or like an arch. *–v.i.* **2.** to form an arch over something.

**overarm** /'oʊvəram/, *adj.* **1.** performed with the arm being raised above the shoulder, as bowling. **2.** of or pertaining to a style of swimming similar to the crawl (def. 7). *–adv.* **3.** in an overarm manner.

**over-award** /'oʊvər-əwɔd/, *adj.* of or pertaining to a rate of pay which is higher than that awarded by an industrial tribunal for a particular work classification.

**overawe** /oʊvər'ɔ/, *v.t.,* **-awed, -awing.** to restrain or subdue by inspiring awe; intimidate.

**overbalance** /oʊvə'bæləns/, *v.,* **-anced, -ancing,** *n.* *–v.t.* **1.** to outweigh. **2.** to cause to lose balance or to fall or turn over. *–v.i.* **3.** to lose (one's balance). *–n.* **4.** an overbalancing weight or amount. **5.** something that more than balances.

**overbear** /oʊvə'bɛə/, *v.,* **-bore, -borne, -bearing.** *–v.t.* **1.** to bear over or down by weight or force. **2.** to overcome. **3.** to prevail over or overrule (wishes, objections, etc.). **4.** to treat in a domineering way. **5.** *Naut.* to carry more sail than (another vessel). *–v.i.* **6.** to produce fruit or progeny so abundantly as to impair the health.

**overbearing** /oʊvə'bɛərɪŋ/, *adj.* domineering; dictatorial; haughtily or rudely arrogant. **– overbearingly,** *adv.*

**overbid** /oʊvə'bɪd/, *v.,* **-bid, -bidden** or **-bid, -bidding;** /'oʊvəbɪd/, *n.* *–v.t., v.i.* **1.** to bid more than the value of (a thing). **2.** to outbid (a person, etc.). *–n.* **3.** a higher bid.

**overbite** /'oʊvəbaɪt/, *n.* occlusion in which the upper incisor teeth overlap the lower.

**overblouse** /'oʊvəblaʊz/, *n.* a blouse designed to hang loosely over a skirt, slacks, etc., and not to be tucked in at the waist.

**overblow** /oʊvə'bloʊ/, *v.,* **-blew, -blown, -blowing.** *–v.t.* **1.** to blow over the surface of, as the wind, sand, or the like does. **2.** *Music.* to increase the pressure of air in (a wind instrument), causing a higher harmonic series to sound.

**overblown** /'oʊvəbloʊn/, *adj.* **1.** more than full-blown. **2.** inflated to an excessive degree. **3.** turgid; bombastic: *an overblown prose style.*

**overboard** /'oʊvəbɔd/, *adv.* over the side of a ship or boat, esp. into or in the water: *to fall overboard.*

**overbridge** /'oʊvəbrɪdʒ/, *n.* a bridge, as for taking cars over a railway line, or pedestrians over a main road.

**overbuild** /oʊvə'bɪld/, *v.t.,* **-built, -building.** **1.** to cover or surmount with a building or structure. **2.** to erect too many buildings on (an area). **3.** to build (a structure) on too great or elaborate a scale.

**overburden** /oʊvə'bɜdn/, *v.;* /'oʊvəbɜdn/, *n.* *–v.t.* **1.** to load with too great a burden; overload. *–n.* **2.** an excessive

---

**overacidity,** *n.*
**overambitious,** *adj.*
**overambitiously,** *adv.*
**overambitiousness,** *n.*
**overassessment,** *n.*
**overattentive,** *adj.*
**overattentively,** *adv.*
**overattentiveness,** *n.*
**overballast,** *v.t.*
**overbold,** *adj.*
**overboldly,** *adv.*
**overboldness,** *n.*
**overbright,** *adj.*
**overbrightly,** *adv.*
**overbrightness,** *n.*
**overbrim,** *v.i.,* **-brimmed, -brimming.**
**overbusily,** *adv.*
**overbusy,** *adj.*
**overbusyness,** *n.*
**overcareful,** *adj.*
**overcarefully,** *adv.*
**overcarefulness,** *n.*
**overcaution,** *n., v.t.*
**overcautious,** *adj.*
**overcautiously,** *adv.*
**overcautiousness,** *n.*
**overcentralisation,** *n.*
**overcentralise,** *v.,* **-lised, -lising.**
**overcharitable,** *adj.*
**overcharitableness,** *n.*
**overcharitably,** *adv.*
**overchildish,** *adj.*
**overchildishly,** *adv.*
**overchildishness,** *n.*
**overcommercialisation,** *n.*
**overcommercialise,** *v.t.,* **-lised, -lising.**
**overconservative,** *adj.*
**overconservatively,** *adv.*
**overconservativeness,** *n.*
**overcook,** *v.*
**overcorrect,** *adj., v.*
**overcostly,** *adj.*
**overcourteous,** *adj.*
**overcourteously,** *adv.*
**overcourteousness,** *n.*
**overcredulous,** *adj.*
**overcredulously,** *adv.*
**overcredulousness,** *n.*
**overcurious,** *adj.*
**overcuriously,** *adv.*
**overcuriousness,** *n.*
**overdecorate,** *v.,* **-rated, -rating.**
**overdecorative,** *adj.*
**overdecoratively,** *adv.*
**overdecorativeness,** *n.*
**overdelicate,** *adj.*
**overdelicately,** *adv.*
**overdelicateness,** *n.*
**overdetailed,** *adj.*

burden. 3. waste material, overlying a mineral deposit.

**overburdensome** /oʊvə'bɜdnsəm/, *adj.* excessively burdensome.

**overbuy** /oʊvə'baɪ/, *v.*, **-bought, -buying.** *–v.t.* 1. to purchase in excessive quantities, esp. without regard for one's financial means. 2. *Finance.* to buy on margin in excess of one's ability to provide added security in an emergency, as in a falling market. *–v.i.* 3. to buy regardless of one's financial ability.

**overcall** /oʊvə'kɔl/, *v.t.* (in cards) to bid higher than.

**overcapitalise** /oʊvə'kæpətəlaɪz/, *v.t.*, **-lised, -lising.** 1. to fix the nominal capital (total amount of securities) of a company in excess of the limits set by law or by sound financial policy. 2. to overestimate the capital value (of a business property or enterprise). 3. to provide an excessive amount of capital (for a business enterprise). Also, **overcapitalize.** – **overcapitalisation** /,oʊvəkæpətəlaɪ'zeɪʃən/, *n.*

**overcast** /'oʊvəkast/, *adj.*, *v.*, **-cast, -casting.** *–adj.* 1. overspread with clouds, as the sky; cloudy. 2. dark; gloomy. 3. *Sewing.* sewn by overcasting. *–v.t.* 4. to overcloud, darken, or make gloomy. 5. to sew with stitches passing successively over an edge, esp. long stitches set at intervals to prevent ravelling. *–v.i.* 6. to become cloudy or dark.

**overcasting** /'oʊvəkastɪŋ/, *n.* *Sewing.* 1. the act of sewing along the edges of material with long spaced stitches to prevent ravelling. 2. the stitch used to overcast.

**overcharge** /oʊvə'tʃadʒ/, *v.*, **-charged, -charging;** /'oʊvətʃadʒ/, *n.* *–v.t.* 1. to charge (a person) too high a price. 2. to charge (an amount) in excess of what is due. 3. to overload; fill too full. 4. to exaggerate. *–v.i.* 5. to make an excessive charge; charge too much for something. *–n.* 6. a charge in excess of a just price. 7. an excessive load.

**overcheck** /'oʊvətʃɛk/, *n.* 1. a checkrein passed over a horse's head between the ears. 2. *Textiles.* a prominent check pattern superimposed on another check pattern. 3. *Textiles.* a fabric having this pattern.

**overclothes** /'oʊvəkloʊðz/, *n.pl.* clothing worn outside other garments.

**overcloud** /oʊvə'klaʊd/, *v.t.* 1. to overspread with or as with clouds. 2. to darken; obscure; make gloomy. *–v.i.* 3. to become clouded over or overcast.

**overcoat** /'oʊvəkoʊt/, *n.* 1. a coat worn over the ordinary clothing, as in cold weather; a greatcoat; topcoat. 2. an additional coat of paint applied for protection.

**overcome** /oʊvə'kʌm/, *v.*, **-came, -come, -coming.** *–v.t.* 1. to get the better of in a struggle or conflict; conquer; defeat. 2. to prevail over (opposition, objections, temptations, etc.). 3. to surmount (difficulties, etc.). 4. to overpower (a person, etc.) in body or mind, or affect in an overpowering or paralysing way, as liquor, a drug, excessive exertion, violent emotion, or the like does. *–v.i.* 5. to gain the victory; conquer. [ME; OE *ofercuman*]

**overcommit** /oʊvəkə'mɪt/, *v.t.*, **-mitted, -mitting.** to take upon oneself obligations beyond one's financial or emotional resources: *he overcommitted himself in buying goods on credit.*

**overcompensate** /oʊvə'kɒmpənseɪt/, *v.*, **-sated, -sating.** *–v.i.* 1. to strive more than required to achieve compensation. *–v.t.* 2. to compensate excessively.

**overcompensation** /,oʊvəkɒmpən'seɪʃən/, *n.* an exaggerated striving to neutralise and conceal a strong character trait by substituting for it a character trait of an opposite kind.

**overconfident** /oʊvə'kɒnfədənt/, *adj.* too confident. – **overconfidence,** *n.*

**overconscientious** /,oʊvəkɒnʃi'ɛnʃəs/, *adj.* extremely or unnecessarily conscientious.

**overcritical** /oʊvə'krɪtɪkəl/, *adj.* critical to excess; too critical; hypercritical.

**overcrop** /oʊvə'krɒp/, *v.t.*, **-cropped, -cropping.** to crop (land) to excess; exhaust the fertility of by continuous cropping.

**overcrowd** /oʊvə'kraʊd/, *v.t.*, *v.i.* to crowd to excess.

**overdamp** /'oʊvədæmp/, *v.t.* to damp (def. 12) so that no oscillations follow the initial displacement; heavily damp.

**overdamper** /'oʊvədæmpə/, *n.* (formerly) a damping mechanism for upright pianos, in which the dampers are above the hammers.

**overdevelop** /oʊvədə'vɛləp/, *v.t.* to develop to excess. – **overdevelopment,** *n.*

**overdo** /oʊvə'du/, *v.*, **-did, -done, -doing.** *–v.t.* 1. to do to excess: *to overdo exercise.* 2. to carry to excess or beyond the proper limit. 3. to overact (a part); exaggerate. 4. to overtax the strength of; fatigue; exhaust. 5. to cook too much; overcook. *–v.i.* 6. to do too much. – **overdone** /oʊvə'dʌn/, *adj.*

**overdose** /'oʊvədoʊs/, *n.;* /oʊvə'doʊs/, *v.*, **-dosed, -dosing.** *–n.* 1. an excessive dose. *–v.t.* 2. to dose to excess. *–v.i.* 3. to take an overdose of a drug.

**overdraft** /'oʊvədraft/, *n.* 1. a draft in excess of one's credit balance, or the amount of the excess. 2. an excess draft or demand made on anything. 3. the action of overdrawing an account, as at a bank. 4. →**overdraught.**

**overdraught** /'oʊvədraft/, *n.* 1. a draught made to pass over a fire, as in a furnace. 2. a draught passing downwards through a kiln. Also, **overdraft.**

**overdraw** /oʊvə'drɔ/, *v.*, **-drew, -drawn, -drawing.** *–v.t.* 1. to draw upon (an account, allowance, etc.) in excess of the balance standing to one's credit or at one's disposal. 2. to draw too far; strain, as a bow, by drawing. 3. to exaggerate in drawing, depicting, or describing. *–v.i.* 4. to overdraw an account or the like.

**overdress** /oʊvə'drɛs/, *v.*, **-dressed, -dressing;** /'oʊvədrɛs/, *n.* *–v.t.*, *v.i.* 1. to dress to excess or with too much display. *–n.* 2. a dress worn over another dress.

**overdrive** /oʊvə'draɪv/, *v.*, **-drove, -driven, -driving;** /'oʊvədraɪv/, *n.* *–v.t.* 1. to overwork; push or carry to excess. 2. to drive too hard. *–n.* 3. *Mach.* a device containing gearing that provides an extra-high ratio for motor cars when continuous high speed and low fuel consumption

---

**overdignified,** *adj.*
**overdiscriminating,** *adj.*
**overdiscriminatingly,** *adv.*
**overdramatic,** *adj.*
**overeager,** *adj.*
**overeagerly,** *adv.*
**overeagerness,** *n.*
**overearnest,** *adj.*
**overearnestly,** *adv.*
**overearnestness,** *n.*
**overeffusive,** *adj.*
**overeffusively,** *adv.*
**overeffusiveness,** *n.*
**overembellish,** *v.t.*
**overemotional,** *adj.*
**overemotionalism,** *n.*
**overemotionally,** *adv.*
**overemphasise,** *v.t.*, **-sised, -sising.**
**overenthusiastic,** *adj.*
**overenthusiastically,** *adv.*
**overexercise,** *v.*, **-cised, -cising.**
**overexpand,** *v.*
**overexpansion,** *n.*
**overexpansive,** *adj.*
**overexpansively,** *adv.*
**overexpansiveness,** *n.*
**overexplicit,** *adj.*
**overexplicitly,** *adv.*
**overfamiliar,** *adj.*
**overfamiliarly,** *adv.*
**overfanciful,** *adj.*
**overfancifully,** *adv.*
**overfancifulness,** *n.*
**overfatigue,** *v.*, **-tigued, -tiguing.**
**overfeed,** *v.*, **-fed, -feeding.**
**overfish,** *adj.*
**overfit,** *adj.*
**overfond,** *adj.*
**overfondly,** *adv.*
**overfondness,** *n.*
**overfrequent,** *adj.*
**overfrequently,** *adv.*
**overfull,** *adj.*
**overfully,** *adv.*
**overfullness,** *n.*
**overgenerous,** *adj.*
**overgenerously,** *adv.*
**overgenerousness,** *n.*
**overgentle,** *adj.*
**overgentleness,** *n.*
**overgently,** *adv.*
**overgraze,** *v.*, **-grazed, -grazing.**
**overgreedily,** *adv.*
**overgreediness,** *n.*
**overgreedy,** *adj.*
**overhastily,** *adv.*
**overhastiness,** *n.*
**overhasty,** *adj.*
**overhelpful,** *adj.*

---

are required.

**overdue** /'oʊvədju/, *adj.* past due, as a belated train or a bill not paid by the assigned date; late; long awaited.

**overdye** /oʊvə'daɪ/, *v.t.*, **-dyed, -dying. 1.** to dye too much or too long. **2.** to dye over with another colour.

**overeat** /oʊvər'it/, *v.i.*, **-ate, -eaten, -eating.** to eat too much.

**overelaborate** /oʊvərə'læbərət, -'læbrət/, *adj.*; /oʊvərə'læbəreɪt/, *v.*, **-rated, -rating.** *–adj.* **1.** excessively elaborate. *–v.t.* **2.** to fill with excessive detail. *–v.i.* **3.** to add excessive details in writing or speaking. – **overelaborately,** *adv.* – **overelaboration** /ˌoʊvərəlæbə'reɪʃən/, **overelaborateness,** *n.*

**overestimate** /oʊvər'ɛstəmeɪt/, *v.*, **-mated, -mating;** /oʊvər'ɛstəmət/, *n.* *–v.t.* **1.** to estimate at too high a value, amount, ratio, or the like. *–n.* **2.** an estimate that is too high. – **overestimation** /ˌoʊvərɛstə'meɪʃən/, *n.*

**overexcite** /oʊvərək'saɪt/, *v.t.*, **-cited, -citing.** to excite too much. – **overexcitable,** *adj.* – **overexcitement,** *n.*

**overexert** /oʊvərəg'zɜt/, *v.t.* to exert too much. – **overexertion** /oʊvərəg'zɜʃən/, *n.*

**overexpose** /oʊvərək'spoʊz/, *v.t.*, **-sposed, -sposing. 1.** to expose too much. **2.** *Photog.* to expose too long. **3.** to subject (a person) to excessive publicity in the media. – **overexposure,** *n.*

**overextend** /oʊvərəks'tɛnd/, *v.t.* to expand or push (oneself) beyond a safe or reasonable limit.

**overfall** /'oʊvəfɔl/, *n.* **1.** water made turbulent by a strong current moving over a submerged ridge or by the meeting of contrary currents. **2.** a sudden increase in the depth of the sea. **3.** a device to allow overflow of water from a canal or lock on a river when the water reaches a certain level.

**overfill** /oʊvə'fɪl/, *v.t.* **1.** to fill too full so as to cause overflowing. *–v.i.* **2.** to become too full.

**overflight** /'oʊvəflaɪt/, *n.* a flight by an aircraft that passes over a specific area or territory.

**overflow** /oʊvə'floʊ/, *v.*, **-flowed, -flown, -flowing;** /'oʊvəfloʊ/, *n.* *–v.i.* **1.** to flow or run over, as rivers, water, etc. **2.** to have the contents flowing over, as an overfull vessel. **3.** to pass from one place or part to another as if flowing from an overfull space: *the population overflowed into the adjoining territory.* **4.** to be filled or supplied in overflowing measure (fol. by *with*): *a heart overflowing with gratitude.* *–v.t.* **5.** to flow over; flood; inundate. **6.** to flow over or beyond (the brim, banks, borders, etc.). **7.** to flow over the edge or brim of (a vessel, etc.). **8.** to fill to the point of running over. **9.** to cause to flow over. *–n.* **10.** an overflowing: *the annual overflow of the Nile.* **11.** that which flows or runs over: *to carry off the overflow from a fountain.* **12.** an area of land which in time of flood is covered by the overflowing waters of a nearby watercourse. **13.** an excess or superabundance. **14.** a portion passing or crowded out from an overfilled place. **15.** an outlet for excess liquid.

**overflow lake** /'– leɪk/, *n.* a lake which is replenished by the rising floodwaters of a nearby watercourse.

**overfly** /oʊvə'flaɪ/, *v.t.*, **-flew, -flown, -flying.** to fly over a specific area, territory, etc.

**overgarment** /'oʊvəgamənt/, *n.* outer garment.

**overgild** /oʊvə'gɪld/, *v.t.*, **-gilded** or **-gilt, -gilding.** to cover with gilding.

**overglaze** /'oʊvəgleɪz/, *n.* a glaze or decoration applied over another glaze on pottery.

**overground** /'oʊvəgraʊnd/, *adj.* **1.** situated above the ground, esp. of telegraph lines, etc. *–v.t.* **2.** to place (something) above ground.

**overgrow** /oʊvə'groʊ/, *v.*, **-grew, -grown, -growing.** *–v.t.* **1.** to grow over; cover with a growth of something. **2.** to outdo in growing; choke or supplant by a more exuberant growth. **3.** to grow beyond, grow too large for, or outgrow. *–v.i.* **4.** to grow to excess; grow too large. – **overgrown,** *adj.*

**overgrowth** /'oʊvəgroʊθ/, *n.* **1.** a growth overspreading or covering something. **2.** excessive or too exuberant growth.

**overhand** /'oʊvəhænd/, *adj.* Also, **overhanded. 1.** done or delivered overhand. *–adv.* **2.** with the hand over the object. **3.** with the hand raised above the shoulder. **4.** *Sewing.* with close, shallow stitches over two selvages. *–v.t.* **5.** to sew overhand.

**overhand knot** /'– 'nɒt/, *n.* a simple knot of various uses which slips easily.

**overhang** /oʊvə'hæŋ/, *v.*, **-hung, -hanging;** /'oʊvəhæŋ/, *n.* *–v.t.* **1.** to hang or be suspended over. **2.** to extend, project, or jut over: *a dark sky overhangs the earth.* **3.** to impend over, or threaten, as danger or evil: *the sadness which overhung him.* *–v.i.* **4.** to hang over; project or jut out over something below. *–n.* **5.** an overhanging; a projection. **6.** the extent of projection, as of the bow of a vessel. **7.** *Archit.* a projecting upper part of a building as a roof or balcony. **8.** *Aeron.* the amount by which an upper wing of a biplane projects laterally beyond the corresponding lower wing. **9.** *Mountaineering.* a place on a mountain where rock, snow, or ice overhang.

**overhaul** /oʊvə'hɔl/, *v.*; /'oʊvəhɔl/, *n.* *–v.t.* **1.** to investigate or examine thoroughly, as for repair. **2.** to make necessary repairs to; restore to proper condition. **3.** to gain upon or overtake. **4.** *Naut.* **a.** to slacken (a rope) by hauling in the opposite direction to that in which it was drawn taut. **b.** to release the blocks of (a tackle). *–n.* **5.** a thorough examination.

**overhead** /oʊvə'hɛd/, *adv.*; /'oʊvəhɛd/, *adj.*, *n.* *–adv.* **1.** over one's head; aloft; up in the air or sky, esp. near the zenith: *overhead was a cloud.* *–adj.* **2.** situated, operating, or passing overhead, aloft, or above. **3.** applicable to one and all; general; average. *–n.* **4.** (*pl.*) the general cost of running a business. **5.** (*pl.*) the general cost which cannot be assigned to particular products or orders.

**overhead ball** /'– bɔl/, *n.* a type of competitive ball game in which the ball is passed overhead from one person in each team to another till it reaches the last person who runs to the beginning of the line and begins the overhead pass again.

**overhead camshaft** /– 'kæmʃaft/, *n.* a camshaft in an

---

**overhelpfully,** *adv.*
**overhelpfulness,** *n.*
**overhigh,** *adj.*
**overhighly,** *adv.*
**overimaginative,** *adj.*
**overimaginatively,** *adv.*
**overimaginativeness,** *n.*
**overindustrialisation,** *n.*
**overindustrialise,** *v.*, **-lised, -lising.**
**overjealous,** *adj.*
**overjealously,** *adv.*
**overjealousness,** *n.*
**overkind,** *adj.*
**overkindly,** *adv.*
**overkindness,** *n.*
**overlard,** *v.t.*
**overloud,** *adj.*
**overloudly,** *adv.*
**overloudness,** *n.*
**overmeasure,** *n.*
**overmerry,** *adj.*
**overmodest,** *adj.*
**overmournful,** *adj.*
**overmournfully,** *adv.*
**overmournfulness,** *n.*
**overneat,** *adj.*
**overneatly,** *adv.*
**overneatness,** *n.*
**overnegligent,** *adj.*
**overnegligently,** *adv.*
**overobedience,** *n.*
**overobedient,** *adj.*
**overobediently,** *adv.*
**overoptimism,** *n.*
**overoptimistic,** *adj.*
**overoptimistically,** *adv.*
**overplease,** *v.*, **-pleased, -pleasing.**
**overplump,** *adj.*
**overpopulous,** *adj.*
**overpopulously,** *adv.*
**overpopulousness,** *n.*
**overpowerful,** *adj.*
**overpowerfully,** *adv.*
**overpowerfulness,** *n.*
**overpraise,** *v.t.*, **-praised, -praising.**
**overprize,** *v.t.*, **-prized, -prizing.**
**overproportion,** *v.t.*, *n.*
**overpublicise,** *v.t.*
**over-rash,** *adj.*
**over-rashly,** *adv.*
**over-rashness,** *n.*
**over-religious,** *adj.*
**over-religiously,** *adv.*
**over-religiousness,** *n.*
**over-roast,** *v.*
**oversalt,** *v.t.*, *adj.*
**oversalty,** *adj.*
**oversanguine,** *adj.*
**oversanguinely,** *adv.*

---

internal-combustion engine which lies across the top of the cylinders and operates directly on to valve stems or rocker arms, rather than on to pushrods.

**overhead projector** /– prə'dʒɛktə/, *n.* a machine which can magnify and project an image by use of mirrors on to an overhead screen.

**overhead valve engine,** *n.* an internal-combustion engine in which the cylinder head contains the inlet and exhaust valves. *Abbrev.:* o.h.v. engine.

**overhear** /oʊvə'hɪə/, *v.t.,* **-heard, -hearing.** to hear (speech, etc., or a speaker) without the speaker's intention or knowledge. – **overhearer,** *n.*

**overheat** /oʊvə'hit/, *v.;* /'oʊvəhit/, *n.* *–v.t.* **1.** to heat to excess. *–v.i.* **2.** to become too hot. *–n.* **3.** excessive heat; overheated condition.

**overhung** /oʊvə'hʌŋ/, *v.;* /'oʊvəhʌŋ/, *adj.* *–v.* **1.** past tense and past participle of **overhang.** *–adj.* **2.** hung from above.

**overindulge** /oʊvərɪn'dʌldʒ/, *v.t., v.i.,* **-dulged, -dulging.** to indulge to excess. – **overindulgence,** *n.* – **overindulgent,** *adj.*

**overjoyed** /oʊvə'dʒɔɪd/, *adj.* overcome with joy; made exceedingly joyful.

**overkill** /'oʊvəkɪl/, *n.* **1.** the capacity of a nation to destroy, by nuclear weapons, more of an enemy than would be necessary for a military victory. **2.** an instance of such destruction. **3.** the use of more resources or energy than is necessary to achieve one's aim. **4.** the pursuit of a policy or campaign, as the vilification of a political opponent, to unnecessary lengths.

**overlade** /oʊvə'leɪd/, *v.t.,* **-laded, -laded** or **-laden, -lading.** to overload (now chiefly in *overladen,* pp.).

**overland** /'oʊvəlænd/, *adv.* **1.** over or across the land. **2.** by land. *–adj.* **3.** proceeding, performed, or carried on overland: *the overland route.* *–v.t., v.i.* **4.** to drive overland for long distances, as sheep or cattle.

overlanders

**overlander** /'oʊvəlændə/, *n.* a drover bringing stock overland, esp. through remote areas, as from the Northern Territory to Adelaide.

**overlap** /oʊvə'læp/, *v.,* **-lapped, -lapping;** /'oʊvəlæp/, *n.* *–v.t.* **1.** to lap over (something else or each other); extend over and cover a part of. **2.** to cover and extend beyond (something else). **3.** to coincide in part with; correspond partly with. *–v.i.* **4.** to lap over. *–n.* **5.** an overlapping. **6.** the extent or amount of overlapping. **7.** an overlapping part. **8.** the place of overlapping.

**overlay**[1] /oʊvə'leɪ/, *v.,* **-laid, -laying;** /'oʊvəleɪ/, *n.* *–v.t.* **1.** to lay or place (one thing) over or upon another. **2.** to cover, overspread, or surmount with something. **3.** to finish with a layer or applied decoration of something: *wood richly overlaid with gold.* **4.** *Print.* to put an overlay upon. *–n.* **5.** something laid over something else; a covering. **6.** a layer or decoration of something applied: *an overlay of gold.* **7.** *Print.* **a.** a shaped piece of paper, or a sheet of paper reinforced at the proper places by shaped pieces, put on the tympan of a press to increase or equalise the impression. **b.** the method of adjusting the impression thus. **c.** a method of preparing material for printing in one or more colours, in which matter to be superimposed is prepared separately on a transparent sheet which is then placed over a key plate, normally one to be printed in black. **d.** a sheet or sheets prepared in this way. **8.** a transparent sheet giving special military information not ordinarily shown on maps, used by being placed over the map on which it is based. **9. a.** (in films), one soundtrack superimposed on another in recording. **b.** (in television), one camera image combined with another during transmission. [ME, from OVER- + LAY[1]]

**overlay**[2] /oʊvə'leɪ/, *v.* past tense of **overlie.**

**overleaf** /oʊvə'lif/, *adv.* on the other side of the page or sheet: *continued overleaf.*

**overleap** /oʊvə'lip/, *v.t.,* **-leapt** or **-leaped, -leaping. 1.** to overreach (oneself) by leaping too far. **2.** to pass over or omit. **3.** to leap over or across.

**overlie** /oʊvə'laɪ/, *v.t.,* **-lay, -lain, -lying. 1.** to lie over or upon, as a covering, stratum, etc. **2.** to smother (an infant or other newborn creature) by lying upon it, as in sleep.

**overlive** /oʊvə'lɪv/, *v.,* **-lived, -living.** *Obs. –v.t.* **1.** to live longer than; outlast. *–v.i.* **2.** to survive.

**overload** /oʊvə'loʊd/, *v.;* /'oʊvəloʊd/, *n.* *–v.t.* **1.** to load to excess; overburden. *–n.* **2.** an excessive load.

**overlong** /oʊvə'lɒŋ/, *adj., adv.* too long.

**overlook** /oʊvə'lʊk/, *v.t.* **1.** to fail to notice, perceive, or consider: *to overlook a misspelt word.* **2.** to disregard or ignore indulgently, as faults, misconduct, etc. **3.** to look over, as from a higher position. **4.** to afford a view down over: *a hill overlooking the sea.* **5.** to rise above. **6.** to take no notice of; ignore. **7.** to look over in inspection, examination, or perusal. **8.** to look after, oversee, or supervise. **9.** to look upon with the evil eye; bewitch.

**overlooker** /'oʊvəlʊkə/, *n.* →**overseer.**

**overlord** /'oʊvəlɔd/, *n.* **1.** one who is lord over another or over other lords. *–v.t.* **2.** to treat in an overbearing manner. – **overlordship,** *n.*

**overly** /'oʊvəli/, *adv.* overmuch; excessively; too: *a voyage not overly dangerous.*

**overman** /'oʊvəmæn/, *n., pl.* **-men;** /oʊvə'mæn/, *v.,* **-manned, -manning.** *–n.* **1.** *Archaic.* a superman. *–v.t.* **2.** to oversupply with men, esp. for service. [ME]

**overmantel** /'oʊvəmæntl/, *n.* an ornamental structure with mirror and shelves set above a mantelpiece.

**overmast** /'oʊvəmast/, *v.t.* to provide a ship with masts that are too high or too heavy.

**overmaster** /oʊvə'mastə/, *v.t.* to overcome; overpower.

**overmatch** /oʊvə'mætʃ/, *v.t.* to outmatch; surpass; defeat.

**overmatter** /'oʊvəmætə/, *n.* *Print.* matter which has been set but cannot be fitted on any page; overset.

**overmuch** /oʊvə'mʌtʃ/, *adv.* too much. –**overmuchness,** *n.*

**overnice** /oʊvə'naɪs/, *adj.* too nice or fastidious.

**overnight** /oʊvə'naɪt/, *adv.;* /'oʊvənaɪt/, *adj., n.* *–adv.* **1.** during the night: *to stay overnight.* **2.** on the previous evening:

---

**oversanguineness,** *n.*
**oversceptical,** *adj.*
**oversceptically,** *adv.*
**overscrupulous,** *adj.*
**overscrupulously,** *adv.*
**overscrupulousness,** *n.*
**oversharp,** *adj.*
**oversimplicity,** *n.*
**oversolicitous,** *adj.*
**oversolicitously,** *adv.*
**oversolicitousness,** *n.*
**overspecialisation,** *n.*
**overspecialise,** *v.,* **-lised, -lising.**
**overstimulate,** *v.,* **-lated, -lating.**
**overstress,** *v.t.*
**overstrict,** *adj.*
**overstrictly,** *adv.*
**overstrictness,** *n.*
**oversubtlety,** *n.*
**oversubtly,** *adv.*
**oversufficient,** *adj.*
**oversufficiently,** *adv.*
**oversufficientness,** *n.*
**oversusceptible,** *adj.*
**oversusceptibleness,** *n.*
**oversusceptibly,** *adv.*
**oversuspicious,** *adj.*
**oversuspiciously,** *adv.*
**oversuspiciousness,** *n.*
**oversweet,** *adj.*
**oversweetly,** *adv.*
**oversweetness,** *n.*
**overtalkative,** *adj.*
**overtalkatively,** *adv.*
**overtalkativeness,** *n.*
**overtechnical,** *adj.*
**overtechnicality,** *n.*
**overtechnically,** *adv.*
**overtire,** *v.*
**overtrain,** *v.*
**overtwist,** *v.*
**overvehement,** *adj.*
**overvehemently,** *adv.*
**overvehementness,** *n.*
**overventuresome,** *adj.*
**overvigorous,** *adj.*
**overvigorously,** *adv.*
**overviolent,** *adj.*
**overviolently,** *adv.*
**overviolentness,** *n.*
**overwarmed,** *adj.*

---

*preparations were made overnight.* **3.** suddenly; very quickly: *new towns sprang up overnight.* *–adj.* **4.** done, occurring, or continuing during the night: *an overnight stop.* **5.** staying for one night: *overnight guests.* **6.** designed to be used one night or very few nights: *overnight bag.* **7.** of or pertaining to the previous evening. **8.** occurring suddenly or rapidly: *an overnight success.* *–n.* **9.** an overnight stopover in transit, as of planes, etc.

**overpass** /ˈoʊvəpas/, *n.;* /oʊvəˈpas/ *v.,* **-passed** or **-past, -passing.** *–n.* **1.** a bridge designed to take traffic on one road over an intersecting road. *–v.t.* **2.** to pass over or traverse (a region, space, etc.). **3.** to get over (obstacles, etc.). **4.** to go beyond, exceed, or surpass.

**overpay** /oʊvəˈpeɪ/, *v.t.,* **-paid, -paying.** **1.** to pay more than (an amount due). **2.** to pay in excess. – **overpayment,** *n.*

**overpeople** /oʊvəˈpipəl/, *v.t.,* **-pled, -pling.** to overstock with people.

**overpersuade** /oʊvəpəˈsweɪd/, *v.t.,* **-suaded, -suading.** **1.** to bring over by persuasion. **2.** to persuade (a person) against his inclination or intention.

**overpitch** /oʊvəˈpɪtʃ/, *v.t.* (in cricket) to bowl (a ball) so that it bounces too far up the wicket for the batsman to be able to play it with ease.

**overplay** /oʊvəˈpleɪ/, *v.t.* **1.** to play (a part, etc.) in an exaggerated manner; overemphasise. **2.** to defeat in playing. **3. overplay one's hand,** to overestimate one's chance of success. *–v.i.* **4.** to exaggerate one's part; overact, etc.

**overplus** /ˈoʊvəplʌs/, *n. Chiefly U.S.* an excess over a particular amount, or a surplus.

**overpopulate** /oʊvəˈpɒpjəleɪt/, *v.t.,* **-lated, -lating.** to overpeople. – **overpopulation** /ˌoʊvəpɒpjəˈleɪʃən/, *n.*

**overpower** /oʊvəˈpaʊə/, *v.t.* **1.** to overcome or overwhelm in feeling, or affect or impress excessively. **2.** to overcome, master, or subdue by superior force: *to overpower a maniac.* **3.** to overmaster the bodily powers or mental faculties of: *overpowered with wine.* **4.** to furnish or equip with excessive power.

**overpowering** /ˈoʊvəpaʊərɪŋ/, *adj.* that overpowers; overwhelming. – **overpoweringly,** *adv.*

**overprice** /oʊvəˈpraɪs/, *v.t.,* **-priced, -pricing.** to place too high a price on.

**overprint** /oʊvəˈprɪnt/, *v.;* /ˈoʊvəprɪnt/, *n.* *–v.t.* **1.** to print additional material or another colour on a forme or sheet previously printed. *–n.* **2.** a quantity of printing in excess of that desired; an overrun. **3.** *Philately.* **a.** any word, inscription or device printed across the face of a stamp altering its use or its locality, or overprinted for a special purpose. **b.** a stamp so marked.

**overproduce** /oʊvəprəˈdjus/, *v.t., v.i.,* **-duced, -ducing.** to produce excessively or in excess of demand.

**over-produced** /ˈoʊvə-prədjust/, *adj.* **1.** of recordings in which such recording techniques as echo, reverberation, etc., have been used to excess. **2.** (of any music) elaborately orchestrated.

**overproduction** /oʊvəprəˈdʌkʃən/, *n.* excessive production; production in excess of the demand.

**overproof** /ˈoʊvəpruf/, *adj.* containing a greater proportion of alcohol than proof spirit does.

**overproud** /ˈoʊvəpraʊd/, *adj.* excessively proud.

**overrate** /oʊvəˈreɪt/, *v.t.,* **-rated, -rating.** to rate too highly; overestimate: *his fortune has been overrated.*

**overreach** /oʊvəˈritʃ/, *v.t.* **1.** to reach or extend over or beyond. **2.** to reach for or aim at but go beyond, as a thing sought, a mark, etc. **3.** to stretch (the arm, etc.) to excess, as by a straining effort. **4.** to defeat (oneself) by overdoing matters, often by excessive eagerness or cunning. **5.** to strain or exert (oneself) to the point of exceeding the purpose. **6.** to get the better of (a person, etc.); cheat. *–v.i.* **7.** to reach or extend over something. **8.** to reach too far. **9.** (of horses, etc.) to strike, or strike and injure, the forefoot with the hind foot.

**overreact** /oʊvəriˈækt/, *v.i.* to react more strongly than necessary.

**overrefine** /oʊvərəˈfaɪn/, *v.t.,* **-fined, -fining.** to refine excessively.

**overrefinement** /oʊvərəˈfaɪnmənt/, *n.* excessive or unnecessary refinement.

**override** /oʊvəˈraɪd/, *v.t.,* **-rode, -ridden, -riding.** **1.** to trample underfoot; ride roughshod over. **2.** to pursue one's course in disregard of: *to override one's advisers.* **3.** to prevail over: *a decision that overrides all previous decisions.* **4.** to ride too much. **5.** to exhaust by excessive riding, as a horse. **6.** to pass or extend over. **7.** *Surg.* to overlap, as one piece of a fractured bone over another.

**overrider** /ˈoʊvəraɪdə/, *n.* **1.** one of a pair of vertical attachments to the bumper of a car, designed to protect the vehicle if in collision with a vehicle having bumpers of differing height. **2.** one who or that which overrides.

**overriding** /ˈoʊvəraɪdɪŋ/, *adj.* prevailing over all other considerations.

**overripe** /ˈoʊvəraɪp/, *adj.* too ripe; more than ripe.

**over-round system** /oʊvə-ˈraʊnd sɪstəm/, *n.* (in horseracing) a betting system where all runners in a race are backed to ensure a small percentage win, no matter which horse wins.

**overrule** /oʊvəˈrul/, *v.t.,* **-ruled, -ruling.** **1.** to rule against or disallow the arguments of (a person). **2.** to rule or decide against (a plea, argument, etc.); disallow. **3.** to prevail over so as to change the purpose or action. **4.** to exercise rule or influence over.

**overrun** /oʊvəˈrʌn/, *v.,* **-ran, -run, -running;** /ˈoʊvərʌn/, *n.* *–v.t.* **1.** to spread over rapidly and occupy (a country), as invading forces: *in 1940 German armies overran the Low Countries.* **2.** to take possession of (an enemy position, etc.): *French troops overran the German gun emplacement.* **3.** to swarm over in great numbers, as animals, esp. vermin. **4.** to spread or grow rapidly over, as plants, esp. vines, weeds, etc. **5.** to spread rapidly throughout, as a new idea, spirit, etc. **6.** to run beyond. **7.** to exceed. **8.** to run over; overflow. **9.** *Print.* to carry over (letters, words, or lines) to the next line, column, or page. **10.** *Archaic.* to outrun; overtake in running. *–v.i.* **11.** to run over; overflow. **12.** to extend beyond the proper or desired limit. **13.** (of an engine) to be driven by the object it normally drives, as the engine of a motor car when going downhill. *–n.* **14.** an overrunning. **15.** an amount overrunning or carried over; excess. **16.** the number by which the quantity manufactured exceeds the amount ordered. [OE *oferyrnan*]

**overscore** /oʊvəˈskɔ/, *v.t.,* **-scored, -scoring.** to score over, as with strokes or lines.

**overseas** /oʊvəˈsiz/, *adv.;* /ˈoʊvəsiz/, *adj.* *–adv.* **1.** over, across, or beyond the sea; abroad. *–adj.* **2.** of or pertaining to passage over the sea: *overseas travel.* **3.** situated beyond the sea: *overseas lands.* **4.** pertaining to countries beyond the sea; foreign: *overseas military service.* *–n.* **5.** (*construed as sing.*) countries or territories overseas. Also (for defs 1-4), **oversea.**

**oversee** /oʊvəˈsi/, *v.t.,* **-saw, -seen, -seeing.** **1.** to direct (work or workers); supervise; manage. **2.** to see or observe without being seen. **3.** *Obs.* to survey; watch. **4.** *Obs.* to look over; inspect. [OE *ofersēon*]

**overseer** /ˈoʊvəsɪə/, *n.* **1.** one who oversees; a supervisor. **2.** a farm manager. **3.** (formerly) the supervisor of a convict gang. **4.** Also, **overseer of the poor.** (formerly) a minor official of a parish. [ME]

**oversell** /oʊvəˈsɛl/, *v.t.,* **-sold, -selling.** **1.** to sell more of (a stock, etc.) than can be delivered. **2.** to sell to excess.

**overset** /oʊvəˈsɛt/, *v.,* **-set, -setting;** /ˈoʊvəsɛt/, *n.* *–v.t.* **1.** *Rare.* to upset or overturn; overthrow. **2.** to throw into confusion; disorder physically or mentally. *–v.i.* **3.** *Rare.* to become upset, overturned, or overthrown. **4.** *Print.* (of type or copy) **a.** to set in or to excess. **b.** (of space) to set too much type for. *–n.* **5.** the act or fact of oversetting; overturn. [OE *ofersettan*]

**oversew** /ˈoʊvəsoʊ, oʊvəˈsoʊ/, *v.t.,* **-sewed, -sewed** or **-sewn, -sewing.** to sew with stitches passing successively over an edge, esp. closely, so as to cover the edge or make a firm seam.

**oversexed** /ˈoʊvəsɛkst/, *adj.* obsessed by, or interested in sex to an abnormal or unusually high degree.

**overshade** /oʊvəˈʃeɪd/, *v.t.,* **-shaded, -shading.** **1.** to cast a shade over. **2.** to make dark or gloomy.

**overshadow** /oʊvəˈʃædoʊ/, *v.t.* **1.** to diminish the importance of, or render insignificant in comparison. **2.** to tower over so as to cast a shadow over. **3.** to cast a shadow over. **4.** to make dark or gloomy. **5.** to shelter or protect. [OE *ofersceadwian*]

**overshine** /oʊvəˈʃaɪn/, *v.t.,* **-shone, -shining. 1.** to outshine. **2.** to surpass in splendour, excellence, etc. **3.** *Archaic.* to shine over or upon. [OE *oferscīnan*]

**overshoes** /ˈoʊvəʃuz/, *n. pl. Chiefly U.S.* →**galoshes.**

**overshoot** /oʊvəˈʃut/, *v.,* **-shot, -shooting.** *–v.t.* **1.** to shoot or go over or above (something). **2.** to shoot or go beyond (a point, limit, etc.). **3.** to shoot a missile over or beyond (what is aimed at), thus missing: *to overshoot the mark.* **4.** (of an aircraft) to overrun a landing area in attempting to land. **5.** to go further in any course or matter than is intended or proper, or go too far. *–v.t.* **6.** to shoot or go beyond; fly beyond. **7.** to shoot over or too far. [ME]

**overshot** /ˈoʊvəʃɒt/, *adj.* **1.** driven by water passing over from above, as a vertical waterwheel. **2.** having the upper jaw projecting beyond the lower, as a dog; usu. considered to be a malformation.

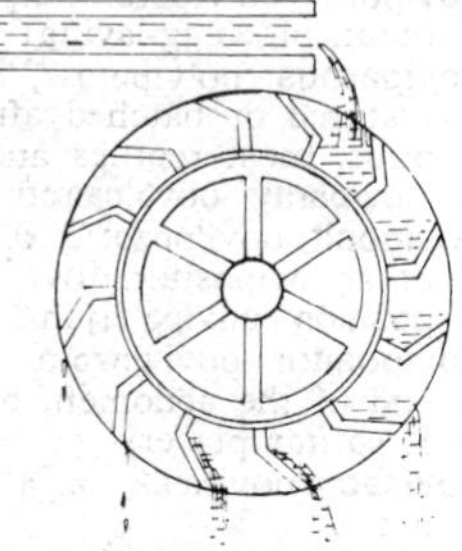
overshot waterwheel

**overside** /ˈoʊvəsaɪd/, *adv.* **1.** over the side, as of a ship. *–adj.* **2.** effected over the side of a ship. **3.** unloading or unloaded over the side.

**oversight** /ˈoʊvəsaɪt/, *n.* **1.** failure to notice or take into account. **2.** an omission or mistake due to inadvertence. **3.** supervision; watchful care. [ME]

**oversimplify** /oʊvəˈsɪmpləfaɪ/, *v.t.,* **-fied, -fying.** to present in too simple a form.

**oversize** /ˈoʊvəsaɪz/, *adj.* **1.** of excessive size. **2.** of a size larger than is necessary or required. *–n.* **3.** something that is oversize; an oversize article or object. **4.** a size larger than the proper or usual size.

**oversized** /ˈoʊvəsaɪzd/, *adj.* of excessive size; over the average size; abnormally large.

**overskirt** /ˈoʊvəskɜt/, *n.* **1.** an outer skirt. **2.** a skirt worn over the skirt of a dress.

**oversleep** /oʊvəˈslip/, *v.,* **-slept, -sleeping.** *–v.i.* **1.** to sleep beyond the proper time of waking. *–v.t.* **2.** to sleep beyond (a certain hour). [ME]

**oversleeve** /ˈoʊvəsliv/, *n.* a half sleeve, usu. of plastic, with elasticised wrist, slipped over the hand to protect the clothes.

**oversnow vehicle** /ˈoʊvəsnoʊ ˌviːkəl/, *n.* a vehicle designed to travel across the snow.

**overspend** /oʊvəˈspɛnd/, *v.,* **-spent, -spending.** *–v.i.* **1.** to spend more than one can afford. *–v.t.* **2.** to spend in excess of.

**overspill** /oʊvəˈspɪl/, *v.,* **-spilt** or **-spilled, -spilling;** /ˈoʊvəspɪl/, *n.* *–v.i.* **1.** to spill over. *–n.* **2.** that which spills out. **3.** excess or surplus population: *new towns are planned to take Sydney's overspill.*

**overspin** /ˈoʊvəspɪn/, *n.* a forward spin given to a ball, by a bowler, golfer, etc.

**overspread** /oʊvəˈsprɛd/, *v.t.,* **-spread, -spreading.** to spread or diffuse over. [OE *oferspr̄ǣdan*]

**oversquare** /ˈoʊvəskwɛə/, *adj.* of or pertaining to a motor vehicle engine in which the bore of the piston is greater than the stroke.

**overstand** /ˈoʊvəstænd/, *v.t.,* **-stood, -standing.** to sail further than necessary, usu. to windward, to reach or round (a mark or obstacle). Also, **overlay.**

**overstate** /oʊvəˈsteɪt/, *v.t.,* **-stated, -stating.** to state too strongly; exaggerate in statement: *to overstate one's case.* – **overstatement,** *n.*

**overstay** /oʊvəˈsteɪ/, *v.t.* to stay beyond the time or duration of; outstay.

**oversteer** /oʊvəˈstɪə/, *v.;* /ˈoʊvəstɪə/, *n.* *–v.i.* **1.** (of a motor vehicle) to tend to turn in a narrower circle than than indicated by the geometry of the wheels. *–n.* **2.** such a tendency.

**overstep** /oʊvəˈstɛp/, *v.t.,* **-stepped, -stepping.** to step or pass over or beyond.

**overstock** /oʊvəˈstɒk/, *v.;* /ˈoʊvəstɒk/, *n.* *–v.t.* **1.** to stock to excess. **2.** to stock with cattle in excess of the capacity of the land to provide feed. *–n.* **3.** a stock in excess of need.

**overstrain** /oʊvəˈstreɪn/, *v.;* /oʊvəˈstreɪn, ˈoʊvəstreɪn/, *n.* *–v.t., v.i.* **1.** to strain excessively. *–n.* **2.** (esp. of a person) physical or mental deterioration as a result of working too hard, worrying, etc.

**overstraiter** /ˈoʊvəstreɪtə/, *n.* (formerly) a free settler in Tasmania who travelled across Bass Strait to acquire land in the Port Phillip Bay district (Victoria).

**overstride** /oʊvəˈstraɪd/, *v.t.,* **-strode, -stridden, -striding. 1.** to stride or step over or across. **2.** to stride beyond. **3.** to surpass. **4.** to bestride. [ME]

**overstrung** /ˈoʊvəstrʌŋ/, *adj.* **1.** too highly strung. **2.** (of pianos) having two sets of strings crossing each other obliquely.

**overstudy** /oʊvəˈstʌdi/, *v.,* **-studied, -studying;** /ˈoʊvəstʌdi/, *n.* *–v.t., v.i.* **1.** to study too much or too hard. *–n.* **2.** excessive study.

**overstuff** /oʊvəˈstʌf/, *v.t.* **1.** to force too much into. **2.** *Furnit.* to envelop completely with deep upholstery.

**overstuffed** /ˈoʊvəstʌft/, *adj.* (of furniture) having the entire frame covered by stuffing and upholstery, so that only decorative woodwork or the like is exposed.

**oversubscribe** /oʊvəsəbˈskraɪb/, *v.t.,* **-scribed, -scribing.** to subscribe for in excess of what is available or required. – **oversubscription** /oʊvəsəbˈskrɪpʃən/, *n.*

**oversubscribed** /ˈoʊvəsəbskraɪbd/, *adj.* (of share issues) having applications to buy exceeding the number of shares available.

**oversubtle** /ˈoʊvəsʌtl/, *adj.* →**supersubtle.**

**oversupply** /ˈoʊvəsəplaɪ/, *n., pl.* **-plies;** /oʊvəsəˈplaɪ/, *v.,* **-plied, -plying.** *–n.* **1.** an excessive supply. *–v.t.* **2.** to supply in excess.

**overt** /ˈoʊvɜt/, *adj.* **1.** open to view or knowledge; not concealed or secret: *overt hostility.* **2.** *Her.* open, as a purse. [ME, from OF, pp. of *ovrir* open, from L *aperīre* open (changed to *o-* by association with *covrir* cover. See COVERT)]

**overtake** /oʊvəˈteɪk/, *v.,* **-took, -taken, -taking.** *–v.t.* **1.** to catch up with in travelling or in pursuit. **2.** to come up with or pass in any course of action. **3.** to come upon suddenly or unexpectedly (said esp. of night, storm, death, etc.). **4.** to pass (another vehicle). *–v.i.* **5.** to pass another vehicle. [ME]

**overtaking lane** /ˈoʊvəteɪkɪŋ leɪn/, *n.* the outside lane on a road which has more than one lane, to be used only for overtaking.

**overtask** /oʊvəˈtask/, *v.t.* to impose too heavy a task upon.

**overtax** /oʊvəˈtæks/, *v.t.* **1.** to tax too heavily. **2.** to make too great demands on: *I had overtaxed my strength.*

**over-the-counter** /ˈoʊvə-ðə-kaʊntə/, *adj.* having been dealt in at a place of business other than an exchange, esp. sale and purchase of securities.

**overthrow** /oʊvəˈθroʊ/, *v.,* **-threw, -thrown, -throwing;** /ˈoʊvəθroʊ/, *n.* *–v.t.* **1.** to depose as from a position of power; overcome, defeat, or vanquish. **2.** to put an end to by force, as governments or institutions. **3.** to throw over; upset; overturn. **4.** to knock down and demolish. **5.** to throw (something) too far. **6.** *Obs.* to destroy the sound condition of (the mind). *–n.* **7.** the act of overthrowing. **8.** the resulting state. **9.** deposition from power. **10.** defeat; destruction; ruin. **11.** *Cricket.* **a.** a ball returned by a fielder which is not caught at the wicket. **b.** a run scored as a result of this.

**overtime** /ˈoʊvətaɪm/, *n., adv., adj.;* /oʊvəˈtaɪm/, *v.,* **-timed, -timing.** *–n.* **1.** time during which one works before or after regularly scheduled working hours; extra time. **2.** pay for such time. *–adv.* **3.** during extra time: *to work overtime.* *–adj.* **4.** of or pertaining to overtime: *overtime pay.* *–v.t.* **5.** to give too much time to, as in photographic exposure.

**overtly** /ˈoʊvɜtli/, *adv.* openly; publicly.

**overtone** /ˈoʊvətoʊn/, *n.* **1.** *Acoustics, Music.* any frequency emitted by an acoustical instrument that is higher in frequency than the fundamental. **2.** (*usu. pl.*) additional meaning or implication.

**overtop** /oʊvəˈtɒp/, *v.t.,* **-topped, -topping. 1.** to rise over or above the top of. **2.** to rise above in authority; override (law, etc.). **3.** to surpass or excel.

**overtrade** /oʊvəˈtreɪd/, *v.i.,* **-traded, -trading.** to trade in excess of one's capital or the requirements of the market.

**overtrick** /ˈoʊvətrɪk/, *n.* (in bridge) a trick won in addition to the number needed to make a contract.

**overtrump** /oʊvəˈtrʌmp/, *v.t., v.i.* (in a game of cards) to trump with a higher trump than has already been played.

**overture** /ˈoʊvətʃʊə/, *n., v.,* **-tured, -turing.** *–n.* **1.** an opening of negotiations, or a formal proposal or offer. **2.** *Music.* **a.** an orchestral composition forming the prelude or introduction to an opera, oratorio, etc. **b.** an independent piece of similar character. **3.** an introductory part, as of a poem. **4.** (in Presbyterian churches) **a.** the action of an ecclesiastical court in submitting a question or proposal to other judicatories for consideration. **b.** the proposal or question so submitted. *–v.t.* **5.** to submit as an overture or proposal. **6.** to make an overture or proposal to. [ME, from OF, from L *apertūra* opening, n., with *-o-* from *overt* OVERT]

**overturn** /oʊvəˈtɜn/, *v.;* /ˈoʊvətɜn/, *n.* *–v.t.* **1.** to overthrow; destroy the power of, defeat or vanquish. **2.** to turn over on its side, face, or back; upset. **3.** to reverse (a decision, judgment, etc.): *the ruling was overturned in the High Court.* *–v.i.* **4.** to turn on its side, face, or back; upset; capsize. *–n.* **5.** the act of overturning. **6.** the state of being overturned. [ME]

**over-under** /oʊvər-ˈʌndə/, *adj.* **1.** (of double-barrelled firearms) with one barrel mounted over the other. *–n.* **2.** such a firearm.

**overuse** /oʊvəˈjuz/, *v.,* **-used, -using;** /oʊvəˈjus/, *n.* *–v.t.* **1.** to use too much. *–n.* **2.** too much use.

**overvalue** /oʊvəˈvælju/, *v.t.,* **-ued, -uing.** to value highly; put too high a value on. – **overvaluation** /ˌoʊvəvæljuˈeɪʃən/, *n.*

**overview** /ˈoʊvəvju/, *n.* a comprehensive survey.

**overwatch** /oʊvəˈwɒtʃ/, *v.t.* **1.** to watch over. **2.** to weary by watching.

**overwear** /oʊvəˈwɛə/, *v.t.,* **-wore, -worn, -wearing.** **1.** to wear or use excessively, as clothes. **2.** to tire, exhaust.

**overweary** /ˈoʊvəwɪəri/, *adj.;* /oʊvəˈwɪəri/, *v.,* **-ried, -rying.** *–adj.* **1.** excessively weary; tired out. *–v.t.* **2.** to weary to excess; overcome with weariness.

**overween** /oʊvəˈwin/, *v.i.* to be conceited or arrogant. [ME]

**overweening** /ˈoʊvəwinɪŋ/, *adj.* **1.** conceited, arrogant, self-opinionated: *an overweening person.* **2.** exaggerated, excessive: *overweening pride.* – **overweeningly,** *adv.*

**overweigh** /oʊvəˈweɪ/, *v.t.* **1.** to exceed in weight; overbalance or outweigh. **2.** to weigh down; oppress.

**overweight** /ˈoʊvəweɪt/, *n., adj.;* /oʊvəˈweɪt/, *v.* *–n.* **1.** extra weight; excess of weight. **2.** too great weight. **3.** greater weight; preponderance. *–adj.* **4.** weighing more than normally or necessarily required. *–v.t.* **5.** to overburden, overload.

**overwhelm** /oʊvəˈwɛlm/, *v.t.* **1.** to come, rest, or weigh upon overpoweringly; crush. **2.** to overcome completely in mind or feeling. **3.** to vanquish, defeat, esp. by force of numbers. **4.** to load, heap, treat or address with an overpowering or excessive amount of anything. **5.** to cover or bury beneath a mass of something, as a flood, or the like, or cover as a mass or flood does. [ME]

**overwhelming** /oʊvəˈwɛlmɪŋ/, *adj.* **1.** that overwhelms. **2.** so great as to render opposition useless: *an overwhelming majority.* – **overwhelmingly,** *adv.*

**overwind** /oʊvəˈwaɪnd/, *v.t.,* **-wound, -winding.** to wind beyond the proper limit; wind too far.

**overwork** /oʊvəˈwɜk/, *v.,* **-worked** or **-wrought, -working;** /ˈoʊvəwɜk/, *n.* *–v.t.* **1.** *(often used reflexively)* to cause to work too hard or too long; weary or exhaust with work. **2.** to fill (time) too full of work. **3.** to work up, stir up, or excite excessively. **4.** to elaborate to excess. **5.** to work or decorate all over; decorate the surface of. *–v.i.* **6.** to work too hard; work to excess. *–n.* **7.** work beyond one's strength or capacity. **8.** extra work. [OE *oferwyrcan*]

**overwrite** /oʊvəˈraɪt/, *v.,* **-wrote, -written, -writing.** *–v.t.* **1.** to cover with writing; write on top of other writing. *–v.i.* **2.** to write in a too elaborate, laboured, or diffuse style.

**overwrought** /ˈoʊvərɔt/, *adj.* **1.** wearied or exhausted by overwork. **2.** worked up or excited excessively. **3.** extremely worried; having highly strained nerves. **4.** overworked; elaborated to excess.

**overzealous** /ˈoʊvəzɛləs/, *adj.* too zealous. – **overzealously,** *adv.* – **overzealousness,** *n.*

**ovi-**[1], a word element meaning 'egg', as in *oviferous.* [L, combining form of *ōvum*]

**ovi-**[2], a word element meaning 'sheep', as in *ovine.* [L, combining form of *ovis*]

**oviduct** /ˈoʊvidʌkt/, *n.* one of a pair of ducts which lead from the body cavity to the exterior in the female and serve to transport and nourish the ova. In higher forms, the distal ends are fused to form the uterus and vagina. [NL *ōviductus,* from L *ōvi-* OVI-[1] + *ductus* DUCT] – **oviducal** /oʊviˈdjukəl/, **oviductal** /oʊviˈdʌktəl/ *adj.*

**oviferous** /oʊˈvɪfərəs/, *adj.* bearing eggs.

**oviform** /ˈoʊvifɔm/, *adj.* egg-shaped.

**ovine** /ˈoʊvaɪn/, *adj.* pertaining to, of the nature of, or like sheep. [LL *ovīnus,* from L *ovis* sheep]

**ovipara** /oʊˈvɪpərə/, *n.pl.* egg-laying animals. [NL, from L (neut. pl.): egg-laying]

**oviparous** /oʊˈvɪpərəs/, *adj.* producing ova or eggs which are matured or hatched after being expelled from the body, as birds, most reptiles and fishes, etc. [L *ōviparus* egg-laying] – **oviparity** /oʊvəˈpærəti/, *n.* – **oviparously,** *adv.*

**oviposit** /oʊviˈpɒzət/, *v.i.* to deposit or lay eggs, esp. by means of an ovipositor. [OVI-[1] + L *positus,* pp., placed, put] – **oviposition** /oʊvipəˈzɪʃən/.

**ovipositor** /oʊviˈpɒzətə/, *n.* (in certain insects) an organ at the end of the abdomen, by which eggs are deposited. [OVI-[1] + L *positor* placer]

**ovisac** /ˈoʊvisæk/, *n.* a sac or capsule containing an ovum or ova.

**ovocyte** /ˈoʊvəsaɪt/, *n.* →**oocyte.**

**ovoid** /ˈoʊvɔɪd/, *adj.* **1.** egg-shaped; having the solid form of an egg. **2.** →**ovate** (def. 2). *–n.* **3.** an ovoid body. [L *ōvum* egg + -OID]

**ovolo** /ˈoʊvəloʊ/, *n., pl.* **-li** /-li/. (in architecture) a convex moulding forming or approximating in section a quarter of a circle or ellipse. [It., var. (now obs.) of *uovolo,* diminutive of *uovo,* from L *ōvum* egg]

**ovoviviparous** /oʊvoʊvəˈvɪpərəs/, *adj.* producing eggs which are hatched within the body, so that the young are born alive but without placental attachment, as certain reptiles, fishes, etc. [*ovo-* (combining form of OVUM) + VIVIPAROUS]

**ovular** /ˈɒvjələ/, *adj.* pertaining to or of the nature of an ovule. [NL *ōvulāris*]

**ovulate** /ˈɒvjəleɪt/, *v.i.,* **-lated, -lating.** to shed eggs from an ovary or ovarian follicle. [NL *ōvulum* little egg + -ATE[1]] – **ovulation** /ɒvjəˈleɪʃən/, *n.*

**ovule** /ˈɒvjul/, *n.* **1.** *Biol.* **a.** a small egg. **2.** *Bot.* **a.** a rudimentary seed. **b.** the body which contains the embryo sac and hence the female germ cell, and which after fertilisation develops into a seed. [NL *ōvulum,* diminutive of L *ōvum* egg]

**ovum** /ˈoʊvəm/, *n., pl.* **ova** /ˈoʊvə/. **1.** *Biol.* **a.** an egg, in a broad biological sense. **b.** the female reproductive cell or gamete of plants. **c.** the female reproductive cell of animals, which (usu. only after fertilisation) is capable of developing into a new individual. **2.** *Archit.* an egg-shaped ornament. [L: egg]

human ovum (enlarged): A, nucleus; B, cytoplasm; C, vitelline membrane; D, sperm

**owe** /oʊ/, *v.,* **owed, owing.** *–v.t.* **1.** to be indebted or beholden for (usu. fol. by *to*). **2.** to be under obligation to pay or repay, or to render (oft. fol. by *to* or a simple dative): *to owe him interest on a mortgage.* **3.** (by omission of the ordinary direct object) to be in debt to: *he owes not any man.* **4.** to have or cherish (a certain feeling) towards a person: *to owe one a grudge.* *–v.i.* **5.** to be in debt. [ME *owe(n),* OE *āgan,* c. OHG *eigan.* Cf. OWN, OUGHT[1]]

**Owen gun** /ˈoʊən gʌn/, *n.* a type of light submachine gun. [named after Evelyn Ernest *Owen,* 1915-49, Australian inventor]

**owing** /ˈoʊɪŋ/, *adj.* **1.** that owes. **2.** owed or due: *to pay what is owing.* **3.** **owing to, a.** on account of; because of. **b.** attributable to.

**owl** /aʊl/, *n.* **1.** any of numerous birds of prey of the order Strigiformes, chiefly nocturnal, with a broad head and with large eyes which are usu. surrounded by discs of modified feathers and directed forwards. They feed on mice, small birds and reptiles, etc. **2.** a variety of domestic pigeons of owl-like appearance. **3.** a person of nocturnal habits. **4.** a person of owl-like solemnity or appearance. **5.** a wise person, esp. one whose knowledge is derived from book learning. [ME *oule,* OE *ūle,* c. LG *ūle;* akin to G *Eule,* Icel. *ugla*] – **owl-like,** *adj.*

barking owl

**owlet** /'aʊlət/, *n.* a young owl.

**owlet-nightjar** /aʊlət-'naɪtdʒa/, *n.* any of a small number of nocturnal, insectivorous birds of the family Aegothelidae with soft plumage and wide mouths surrounded by long bristles, as *Aegotheles cristatus,* found over much of Australia and in New Guinea.

**owlish** /'aʊlɪʃ/, *adj.* owl-like.

**own** /oʊn/, *adj.* **1.** belonging, pertaining, or relating to oneself or itself (usu. used after a possessive to emphasise the idea of ownership, interest, or relation conveyed by the possessive): *his own money.* **2.** (absolutely, with a possessive preceding) own property, relatives, etc.: *to be amongst one's own.* **3. come into one's own, a.** to receive an inheritance. **b.** to be in a situation where particular skills or attributes are evident. **4. get one's own back,** to have revenge. **5. of one's own,** belonging to oneself. **6. on one's own,** *Colloq.* on one's own account, responsibility, resources, etc. **7. be one's own master,** to be independent. [ME *owen;* OE *āgen,* orig. pp. of *āgan* have, possess. See OWE] *–v.t.* **8.** to have or hold as one's own; possess. **9.** to acknowledge or admit: *to own a fault.* **10.** to acknowledge as one's own. *–v.i.* **11.** to confess (oft. fol. by *up*): *to own to being uncertain.* [ME *ohnien,* OE *agnian,* from *āgen* OWN, *adj.*]

**owner** /'oʊnə/, *n.* one who owns; a proprietor.

**ownership** /'oʊnəʃɪp/, *n.* **1.** the state or fact of being an owner. **2.** legal right of possession; proprietorship.

**own-your-own** /'oʊn-jər-oʊn/, *n.* →**home unit.** *Abbrev.:* o.y.o.

**ox** /ɒks/, *n., pl.* **oxen. 1.** the adult castrated male of the genus *Bos,* used as a draught animal and for food. **2.** any member of the bovine family. [ME *oxe,* OE *oxa,* c. G *Ochse*] – **oxlike,** *adj.*

**oxa-,** *Chem.* a prefix meaning 'oxygen when it replaces carbon'.

**oxalate** /'ɒksəleɪt/, *n.* a salt or ester of oxalic acid. [OXAL(IC ACID) + -ATE[2]]

**oxalic acid** /ɒk,sælɪk 'æsəd/, *n.* a white, crystalline, dibasic acid, $(COOH)_2 \cdot 2H_2O$, first discovered in the juice of a species of oxalis (wood sorrel), used in textile and dye manufacturing, in bleaching, etc. [*oxalic,* from F *oxalique,* from L *oxalis* OXALIS]

oxalis

**oxalis** /ɒk'saləs/, *n.* any plant belonging to one of the numerous species of the genus *Oxalis,* as yellow wood sorrel and yellow-flowered oxalis. [L, from Gk: sorrel]

**oxaloacetic acid** /ɒksəloʊə,setɪk 'æsəd/, *n.* a dibasic carboxylic acid, $HOOCCH_2CO \cdot COOH$, a key intermediary metabolite involved in the citric acid cycle and the formation of aspartic acid.

**oxazine** /'ɒksəzin/, *n.* any of a group of thirteen compounds, $C_4H_5NO$, containing four carbon atoms, one oxygen atom, and one nitrogen atom, arranged in a six-membered ring. [OX(A)- + AZINE]

**oxbow** /'ɒksboʊ/, *n.* **1.** a bow-shaped piece of wood placed under and around the neck of an ox, with its upper ends inserted in the bar of the yoke. **2.** a former meander of a river remaining as a small bow-shaped lake after the river has straightened its course by cutting through the neck of the meander; cut-off.

**oxcart** /'ɒkskat/, *n.* an ox-drawn cart.

**oxen** /'ɒksən/, *n.* plural of **ox.**

**oxer** /'ɒksə/, *n.* an obstacle in steeplechasing, horsejumping trials, etc., consisting of a hedge bordered by rails, as a **double oxer** or **reversed oxer.**

**ox-eye** /'ɒks-aɪ/, *n.* any of various plants with flowers composed of a disc with marginal rays, as the mayweed, the ox-eye daisy, etc. [ME *oxie,* from *ox(e)* OX + *ie* EYE]

**ox-eye daisy** /– 'deɪzi/, *n.* a perennial daisy, *Chrysanthemum lencanthemum,* introduced from North America and now a weed of the northern tablelands of New South Wales.

**ox-eye herring** /– 'hɛrɪŋ/, *n.* a fast-swimming, silvery fish with large scales, *Megalops cyprinoides,* related to the Atlantic tarpon, but much smaller, and found around the northern half of the Australian coastline; tarpon.

**Oxford**[1] /'ɒksfəd/, *n.* a large English breed of sheep, hornless, with dark brown face and legs, of the mutton type, noted for its relatively large, heavy market lambs, and heavy fleece of relatively coarse wool of medium length.

**Oxford**[2] /'ɒksfəd/, *n.* **1.** a low shoe laced or buttoned over the instep. **2.** shirting of cotton or rayon in a basket weave. [named after *Oxford,* city in England]

**Oxford**[3] /'ɒksfəd/, *n. Colloq.* a dollar. [rhyming slang, *Oxford scholar* ]

**Oxford bags** /– 'bægz/, *n. pl.* very wide trousers.

**Oxford corners** /– 'kɔnəz/, *n. pl.* (in printing) ruled border lines about the text of a page, etc., that cross and project slightly at the corners.

**Oxford shoe** /– 'ʃu/, *n.* →**Oxford**[2] (def. 1).

**oxidant** /'ɒksədənt/, *n.* the substance which supplies the oxygen in an oxidation reaction, esp. for the combustion reaction in a rocket. Also, **oxidiser** /'ɒksədaɪzə/, **oxydant.**

**oxidase** /'ɒksədeɪz/, *n.* any of a group of oxidising enzymes. [OXID(E) + -ASE]

**oxidate** /'ɒksədeɪt/, *v.t., v.i.,* **-dated, -dating.** to oxidise. – **oxidation** /ɒksə'deɪʃən/, *n.* – **oxidative,** *adj.*

**oxidation number** /ɒksə'deɪʃən nʌmbə/, *n.* a number representing the electric charges that the atom would have if the electrons in a compound were assigned to the atoms in a conventional way, as $FeCl_3$, where the ferrous ion has three electric charges (Fe(+III)), and each chloride ion has one (Cl(−I)).

**oxide** /'ɒksaɪd/, *n.* a compound, usu. containing two elements only, one of which is oxygen, as *mercuric oxide.* [F (now *oxyde*), from *ox(ygène)* oxygen + *(ac)ide* acid]

**oxidimetry** /ɒksə'dɪmətri/, *n.* a technique of analytical chemistry which utilises oxidising agents for titrations.

**oxidise** /'ɒksədaɪz/, *v.,* **-dised, -dising.** *–v.t.* **1.** to convert (an element) into its oxide; to combine with oxygen. **2.** to cover with a coating of oxide, or rust. **3.** to take away hydrogen from as by the action of oxygen; to add oxygen or any non-metal to. **4.** to increase the valency of (an element) in the positive direction. **5.** to remove electrons from. **6.** (of a wine) to combine with oxygen, causing deterioration in colour, bouquet and flavour. *–v.i.* **7.** to become oxidised. Also, **oxidize.** – **oxidisable,** *adj.* – **oxidisation** /ɒksədaɪ'zeɪʃən/, *n.* – **oxidiser,** *n.*

**oxidising agent** /'ɒksədaɪzɪŋ eɪdʒənt/, *n.* any substance which brings about an oxidation process.

**oxime** /'ɒksim/, *n.* any of a group of compounds with the radical :C:NOH (**oxime group** or **radical**), prepared by the condensation of ketones or aldehydes with hydroxylamine. [OX(YGEN) + IM(ID)E]

**oxlip** /'ɒkslɪp/, *n.* a species of primrose, *Primula elatior,* with pale yellow flowers. [ME; OE *oxanslyppe,* from *oxan* ox's + *slyppe* slime. See SLIP[2], and cf. COWSLIP]

**oxonium** /ɒk'soʊniəm/, *adj. Chem.* →**hydronium.**

**oxonium compound** /– 'kɒmpaʊnd/, *n.* the product of reaction between an organic compound containing a basic oxygen atom, and a strong acid.

**oxpecker** /'ɒkspɛkə/, *n.* either of two species of African starlings of the genus *Buphagus* that feed on ticks on the hides of large animals.

**oxtail** /'ɒksteɪl/, *n.* the skinned tail of an ox used for soup, stews, etc.

**oxtongue** /ˈɒkstʌŋ/, *n.* **1.** the tongue of an ox, used as food. **2.** any perennial herb of the genus *Picris,* covered with stiff hairs, as *P. echioides.*

**oxy-**$^1$, a word element meaning 'sharp' or 'acute'. [Gk, combining form of *oxýs* sharp, keen, acid]

**oxy-**$^2$, a combining form of **oxygen**, sometimes used as an equivalent of *hydroxy-.*

**oxyacetylene** /ɒksiəˈsɛtələn/, *adj.* of or pertaining to a mixture of oxygen and acetylene.

**oxyacetylene burner** /– ˈbɜnə/, *n.* a device for obtaining a high-temperature flame (about 3300°C) for welding or cutting steel, by burning a mixture of oxygen and acetylene in a special jet.

**oxyacid** /ɒksiˈæsəd/, *n.* an inorganic acid containing oxygen. Also, **oxygen acid.**

**oxycalcium** /ɒksiˈkælsiəm/, *adj.* pertaining to or produced by oxygen and calcium: *the oxycalcium light.*

**oxygen** /ˈɒksədʒən/, *n.* a colourless, odourless gaseous element, constituting about one fifth of the volume of the atmosphere and present in a combined state throughout nature. It is the supporter of combustion in air: *weight of 1 litre at 0°C and 760 mm pressure:* 1.4290 grams. *Symbol:* O; *at. wt:* 15.9994; *at. no.:* 8. [F *oxygène,* from *oxy-* OXY-$^1$ + *-gène* -GEN]

**oxygen acid** /ˈ– æsəd/, *n.* →**oxyacid.**

**oxygenate** /ɒkˈsɪdʒəneɪt/, *v.t.,* **-nated, -nating.** to treat or combine, esp. to enrich, with oxygen. – **oxygenation** /ˌɒksidʒəˈneɪʃən/, *n.*

**oxygen effect** /ˈɒksədʒən əfɛkt/, *n.* the increased sensitivity to radiation of biological material when exposed in the presence of oxygen.

**oxygenise** /ɒkˈsɪdʒənaɪz/, *v.t.,* **-nised, -nising.** →**oxygenate.** Also, **oxygenize.**

**oxygen mask** /ˈɒksədʒən mask/, *n.* a device covering the nose and mouth used in inhaling oxygen from a cylinder or supply system.

**oxygen tent** /ˈ– tɛnt/, *n.* a small tent for delivering oxygen to a sick person at critical periods.

**oxyhaemoglobin** /ˌɒksihiməˈgloubən/, *n.* See **haemoglobin.**

**oxyhydrogen** /ɒksiˈhaɪdrədʒən/, *n.* a mixture of oxygen and hydrogen.

**oxyhydrogen burner** /ˈ– bɜnə/, *n.* a device similar to the oxyacetylene burner, except that hydrogen instead of acetylene is burnt in oxygen, and the flame temperature is about 2400°C.

**oxylobium** /ɒksəˈloubiəm/, *n.* any shrub of the endemic Australian genus *Oxylobium,* family Papilionaceae, several western Australian species of which are poisonous to stock.

**oxymoron** /ɒksiˈmɔrɒn/, *n., pl.* **-mora** /-ˈmɔrə/. a figure of speech by which a locution produces an effect by a seeming self-contradiction, as in *cruel kindness* or *to make haste slowly.* [NL, from Gk, neut. of *oxýmōros* pointedly foolish]

**oxysalt** /ˈɒksisɒlt/, *n.* any salt of an oxyacid. [OXY-$^2$ + SALT]

**oxysulphide** /ɒksiˈsʌlfaɪd/, *n.* a sulphide in which part of the sulphur is replaced by oxygen.

**oxytocic** /ɒksiˈtousɪk/, *adj.* **1.** of or causing the stimulation of the involuntary muscle of the uterus. **2.** promoting or accelerating parturition. *–n.* **3.** an oxytocic medicine or drug. [Gk *oxytókion* a medicine hastening childbirth + -IC]

**oxytocin** /ɒksiˈtousən/, *n.* a hormone produced by the pituitary gland, that stimulates contraction of the muscles of the uterus.

**oxytone** /ˈɒksitoun/, *adj.* **1.** (in Greek grammar) having an acute accent on the last syllable. *–n.* **2.** an oxytone word. [Gk *oxýtonos*]

**oyer** /ˈɔɪjə/, *n. Brit. Law.* **1.** the ancient word for assizes. **2.** the production in court of some document pleaded by one party and demanded by the other (the party pleading it is said to *make profert* and the other is said to *crave oyer*). [ME, from AF (properly inf.), var. of *oir,* from L *audīre* hear]

**oyer and terminer,** *n. Law.* **1.** (in English law) **a.** a commission or writ directing the holding of a court to try offences. **b.** the court itself. **2.** *U.S.* any of various higher criminal courts in some of the States. [ME, from AF: lit., hear and finish]

**oyez** /ouˈjɛs, ouˈjɛz/, *interj.* **1.** hear! attend! (a cry uttered, usu. thrice, by a public or court crier to command silence and attention before a proclamation, etc., is made.) *–n.* **2.** a cry of 'oyez'. Also, **oyes.** [AF: hear ye, 2nd pers. pl. impv. of *oyer.* See OYER]

**o.y.o.,** own-your-own. Also, **O.Y.O.**

**oyster** /ˈɔɪstə/, *n.* **1.** any of various edible marine bivalve molluscs, family Ostreidae, with irregularly shaped shell, found on the bottom or adhering to rocks, etc., in shallow water, some species being extensively cultivated for the market. **2.** the oyster-shaped bit of dark meat in the front hollow of the side bone of a fowl. **3.** *Colloq.* a close-mouthed person. **4.** something from which one may extract or derive advantage. *–v.i.* **5.** to dredge for or otherwise take oysters. [ME *oistre,* from OF, from L *ostrea, ostreum,* from Gk *óstreon*]

**oyster-bed** /ˈɔɪstə-bɛd/, *n.* a place where oysters breed or are cultivated.

**oyster blade** /ˈɔɪstə bleɪd/, *n.* a cut of beef from the shoulder blade, used for grilling, frying, braising, or barbecuing.

**oystercatcher** /ˈɔɪstəkætʃə/, *n.* any of several longbilled, maritime wading birds constituting the genus *Haematopus,* with a plumage chiefly of black and white, as the **pied oystercatcher,** *H. ostralegus,* of Eurasia, southern Africa and Australasia.

**oyster-crab** /ˈɔɪstə-kræb/, *n.* any of several small crabs constituting the genus *Pinnotheres,* existing commensally in the mantle cavity of oysters.

**oyster-farm** /ˈɔɪstə-fam/, *n.* an area of oyster-beds, commercially cultivated.

**oysterman** /ˈɔɪstəmən/, *n., pl.* **-men.** one who gathers, cultivates, or sells oysters.

**oyster plant** /ˈɔɪstə plænt/, *n.* the salsify, whose root tastes like oyster.

**oyster white** /– ˈwaɪt/, *n.* a greyish-white colour. Also, **oyster.**

**oz,** **1.** ounce. **2.** Also, **ozs.** ounces.

**Oz** /ɒz/, *–adj.* **1.** *Colloq.* Australian. *–n.* **2.** Australian. Also, **oz.**

**ozalid** /ˈouzəlɪd/, *n.* a cheaply-produced negative image of a printed page used in the first stages of proofing. [Trademark]

**oz apoth,** apothecaries ounce.

**ozokerite** /ouˈzoukəraɪt/, *n.* waxlike mineral resin used in the manufacture of candles. Also, **ozocerite.** [G *Ozokerit,* from Gk *ózō* I smell + *kērós* wax + *-it* -ITE$^1$]

**ozone** /ˈouzoun/, *n.* **1.** *Chem.* a form of oxygen, $O_3$, having three atoms to the molecule, with a peculiar smell suggesting that of weak chlorine, which is produced when an electric spark is passed through air, and in several other ways. It is found in the atmosphere in minute quantities, esp. after a thunderstorm, and is a powerful oxidising agent, used for bleaching, sterilising water, etc. **2.** *Colloq.* clear, invigorating, fresh air. [F, from Gk *ózein* smell + *-one* -ONE] – **ozonic** /ouˈzɒnɪk/, *adj.*

**ozone layer** /ˈ– leɪə/, *n.* a rather restricted region in the outer portion of the stratosphere at an elevation of about 30 kilometres, where much of the atmospheric ozone ($O_3$) is concentrated. Also, **ozonosphere.**

**ozoniferous** /ouzouˈnɪfərəs/, *adj.* containing ozone.

**ozonisation** /ˌouzounaɪˈzeɪʃən/, *n.* the treatment of a compound with ozone. Also, **ozonization.**

**ozonise** /ˈouzounaɪz/, *v.t.,* **-nised, -nising.** **1.** to impregnate or treat with ozone. **2.** to convert (oxygen) into ozone. Also, **ozonize.**

**ozoniser** /ˈouzounaɪzə/, *n.* an apparatus for converting oxygen into ozone. Also, **ozonizer.**

**ozonolysis** /ouzouˈnɒləsəs/, *n.* the reaction of ozone with hydrocarbons.

**ozonosphere** /ouˈzɒnəsfɪə/, *n.* →**ozone layer.**

**ozonous** /ˈouzounəs/, *adj.* of or containing ozone.

**ozs,** ounces.

**oz tr,** troy ounce.

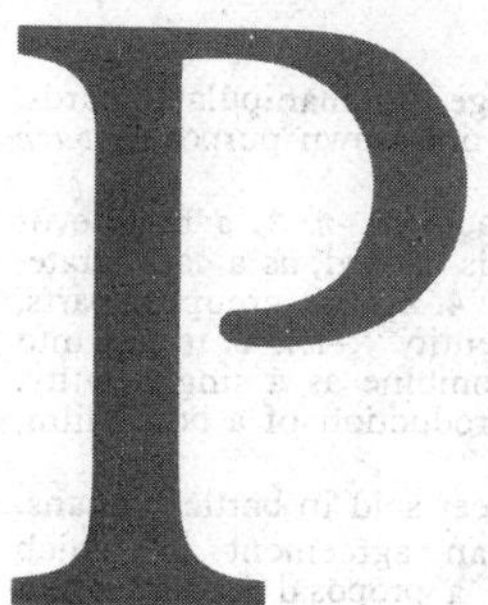

Pp Roman CASLON | Pp Sans Serif AVANT GARDE | Pp Script GILLIES | Pp Decorative NEON

*Although there are numerous typefaces in the world they can be divided into four main classifications. These are:*

*ROMAN or SERIF. This typeface came into being from the technique of the Roman masons who, working in stone, finished off each letter with a serif or small stroke projecting from the top or bottom. This was done to correct any feeling of unevenness or imbalance they may have created in cutting the characters in stone.*

*SANS SERIF (without serif). This typeface is geometric in design and has straight-edged characters and lines of a regular thickness.*

*SCRIPT. Based on the movement of the hand, this typeface is often italicised or slanted, as if drawn by a brush or quill pen.*

*DECORATIVE. Any typeface that exaggerates the characteristics of any of the other three classifications to a degree that places it outside of them.*

*The dictionary entries in this book use a SANS SERIF typeface called Helvetica (set in a bold face for the head words) and a SERIF typeface Plantin (used throughout the body of the entries).*

**P, p** /pi/, *n., pl.* **P's** or **Ps, p's** or **ps.** **1.** a consonant, the 16th letter of the English alphabet. **2.** *Genetics.* a symbol for parental generation, $P_1$ indicating parents, $P_2$ grandparents, etc. **3. mind one's p's and q's,** to heed one's behaviour.

**p-,** *Chem.* para-[1].

**p,** **1.** new penny; new pence. **2.** perch. **3.** pico-.

**p.,** **1.** page. **2.** part. **3.** particle. **4.** past. **5.** *Chess.* pawn. **6.** pence. **7.** penny. **8.** per. **9.** peseta. **10.** peso. **11.** *Music.* softly. [It. *piano*] **12.** population. **13.** *Knitting.* purl.

**P,** **1.** *Chem.* phosphorus. **2.** pressure. **3.** *Chess.* pawn. **4.** *Motor Vehicles.* parking. **5.** (of a driver's licence) provisional. **6.** poise. **7.** peta-.

**pa**[1] /pa/, *n. Colloq.* papa; father.

**pa**[2] /pa/, *n. N.Z.* **1.** a Maori settlement. **2.** (originally) a stockaded village. [Maori]

**p.a.,** per annum.

**Pa,** **1.** *Chem.* protactinium. **2.** pascal.

**PA** /pi ˈeɪ/, *n.* a public-address system.

**P.A.,** **1.** personal assistant. **2.** power of attorney.

**pabulum** /ˈpæbjələm/, *n.* **1.** that which nourishes an animal or vegetable organism; food. **2.** nourishment for the mind. [L: food, fodder]

paca

**P.A.B.X.** /ˌpi eɪ bi ˈɛks/, Private Automatic Branch Exchange.

**paca** /ˈpakə, ˈpækə/, *n.* a large, white-spotted, almost tailless, hystricomorphic rodent, *Agouti paca,* of South and Central America; the spotted cavy. [Pg. or Sp., both from Tupi]

**pace**[1] /peɪs/, *n., v.,* **paced, pacing.** *–n.* **1.** rate of stepping, or of movement in general: *a pace of ten kilometres an hour.* **2.** rate or style of doing anything: *they live at a tremendous pace.* **3.** a linear measurement of variable extent, representing the space naturally measured by the movement of the foot in walking. **4.** a single step: *she took three paces across the room.* **5.** the distance covered in a step: *stand six paces inside the gates.* **6.** manner of stepping; gait. **7.** a gait of a horse, etc., in which the feet on the same side are lifted and put down together. **8.** any of the gaits of a horse, etc. **9.** a raised step or platform. **10. put through one's paces,** to cause to perform or show ability: *the class was put through its paces when the inspector arrived.* *–v.t.* **11.** to set the pace for, as in racing: *this horse always paces the favourite.* **12.** to traverse with paces or steps: *he paced the floor.* **13.** to measure by paces. **14.** to train to a certain pace; exercise in pacing: *to pace a horse.* **15.** (of a horse) to perform as a pace. *–v.i.* **16.** to walk, esp. in a state of nervous excitement (oft. fol. by *up and down, about*): *the anxious job applicant paced about the foyer.* **17.** to take slow, regular steps. **18.** (of horses) to go at a pace (def. 7), esp. in racing; amble. [ME *pas,* from OF, from L *passus* a pace, a step, lit., a stretch (of the leg)]

**pace**[2] /ˈpeɪsi/, *prep.* with the permission of (a courteous form used to mention one who disagrees). [L, abl. of *pax* peace, pardon, leave]

**pace bowler** /ˈpeɪs boʊlə/, *n. Cricket.* →**fast bowler.**

**paced** /peɪst/, *adj.* **1.** having a specified pace: *slow-paced.* **2.** counted out or measured by paces: *a paced distance.* **3.** *Racing.* run at a pace determined by a pacemaker: *the horse did a paced work-out.*

**pacemaker** /ˈpeɪsmeɪkə/, *n.* **1.** one who sets the pace, as in racing. **2.** a person or group which is followed or imitated on account of its success: *this company is the pacemaker for the whole group.* **3.** *Physiol.* →**sinus node.** **4.** *Med.* an instrument implanted beneath the skin to control the rate of the heartbeat. – **pacemaking,** *n.*

**paceman** /ˈpeɪsmæn/, *n. Cricket.* →**fast bowler.**

**pacer** /ˈpeɪsə/, *n.* **1.** one who paces. **2.** a pacemaker. **3.** a horse that paces, or whose natural gait is a pace.

**pacesetter** /ˈpeɪssetə/, *n.* →**pacemaker** (defs 1 and 2).

**paceway** /ˈpeɪsweɪ/, *n.* a racecourse on which races are held for trotters and pacers.

**pacework** /ˈpeɪswɜk/, *n.* exercise work for racehorses.

**pacha** /ˈpaʃə/, *n.* →**pasha.**

**pachalic** /ˈpaʃəlɪk/, *n.* →**pashalik.**

**pachisi** /pəˈtʃizi, pæ-/, *n.* **1.** a game, somewhat resembling backgammon, for four players played on a cruciform board, with pieces moved according to the throw of a set of six dice. It is much played in India. **2.** →**ludo.** Also, **parcheesi.** [Hind., from *pachis* twenty-five (the highest throw in the game)]

**pachouli** /pəˈtʃuli, ˈpætʃəli/, *n.* →**patchouli.**

**pachy-,** a word element meaning 'thick', as in *pachyderm.* [Gk, combining form of *pachýs* thick]

**pachyderm** /ˈpækidɜm/, *n.* any of the thick-skinned non-ruminant ungulates, as the elephant, hippopotamus, and rhinoceros. [F *pachyderme,* from Gk *pachýdermos* thick-skinned] – **pachydermatous** /pækiˈdɜmətəs/, **pachydermous** /pækiˈdɜməs/, *adj.*

**pacific** /pəˈsɪfɪk/, *adj.* **1.** tending to make peace; conciliatory: *pacific propositions.* **2.** peaceable; not warlike: *a pacific disposition.* **3.** peaceful; at peace: *pacific state of things.* **4.** *Railways.* a steam locomotive with a particular wheel arrangement consisting of a four wheel front truck, three pairs of driving wheels and one idling wheel. Also, (defs 1-3), *Obs.,* **pacifical.** [L *pācificus* peacemaking] – **pacifically,** *adv.*

**pacificate** /pəˈsɪfəkeɪt/, *v.t.,* **-cated, -cating.** to pacify. [L *pācificātus,* pp.] – **pacification** /pæsəfəˈkeɪʃən/, *n.* – **pacificator,** *n.* – **pacificatory** /pæsəfəˈkeɪtəri/, *adj.*

**pacifier** /ˈpæsəfaɪə/, *n.* **1.** one who or that which pacifies. **2.** a baby's dummy. **3.** *U.S.* a teething ring.

**pacifism** /ˈpæsəfɪzəm/, *n.* **1.** opposition to war or violence of any kind. **2.** the principle or policy of establishing and maintaining universal peace or such relations among all nations that all differences may be adjusted without recourse to war. [PACIF(IC) + -ISM]

**pacifist** /ˈpæsəfəst/, *n.* **1.** one who opposes in principle all war or violence. **2.** a conscientious objector. *–adj.* **3.** Also, **pacifistic** /pæsəˈfɪstɪk/. of or pertaining to pacifists or pacifism.

**pacify** /ˈpæsəfaɪ/, *v.t.,* **-fied, -fying.** **1.** to bring into a state of peace; quiet; calm: *pacify an angry man.* **2.** to appease: *pacify one's appetite.* [late ME, from L *pācificāre* make peace] – **pacifiable** /pæsəˈfaɪəbəl/, *adj.*

**pack**[1] /pæk/, *n.* **1.** a quantity of anything wrapped or tied up; a parcel; a packet. **2.** a load or burden, as one carried by a person or animal; a rucksack. **3.** the quantity of anything put up or packed at one time or in one season: *last season's salmon pack.* **4.** the method, design, materials, etc., used in making a pack or parcel: *a vacuum pack.* **5.** a set or gang (of people): *a pack of thieves.* **6.** a group or unit of wolf cubs in the Boy Scout Movement. **7.** *Rugby Football.* **a.** the forwards of a team collectively, esp. acting together in rushing the ball forward or as a scrum. **b.** the forwards of two opposing teams in a scrum. **8.** a company of certain animals of the same kind: *a pack of wolves.* **9.** *Hunting.* a number of hounds used regularly for hunting together. **10.** a group of things, usu. abstract: *a pack of lies.* **11.** a complete set, as of playing cards, usu. 52 in number. **12.** a considerable area of pack-ice. **13.** *Med.* **a.** a wrapping of the body in wet or dry cloths for therapeutic purposes. **b.** the cloths so used. **14.** a paste or the like consisting of cosmetic materials applied to the skin, esp. of the face, to improve the complexion. **15. go to the pack, a.** to degenerate; collapse. **b.** to give up; admit defeat. *–v.t.* **16.** to make into a pack or bundle. **17.** to make into a group or compact mass, as animals, ice, etc. **18.** to fill with anything compactly arranged: *pack a trunk.* **19.** to press or crowd together within; cram. **20.** to put or arrange in suitable form for the market: *pack fruit.* **21.** to make airtight, steamproof, or watertight by stuffing: *pack the piston of a steam engine.* **22.** to cover or envelop with something pressed closely around. **23.** to carry, esp. as a load. **24.** to send off summarily (sometimes fol. by *off, away,* etc.): *packed off to school.* **25.** to put a load upon (a horse, etc.) **26.** *Colloq.* to be capable of (forceful blows): *he packs a mighty punch.* **27.** to treat with a therapeutic pack. **28. pack (the game, it) in,** to give up; desist from. **29. pack death (it) (shit),** *Colloq.* to be afraid. *–v.i.* **30.** to pack goods, etc., in compact form, as for transportation or storage (oft. fol. by *up*). **31. pack down,** *Rugby Football.* (in a scrum) to assume formation engaging arms and heads, and taking the strain, just prior to the ball being put in. **32.** to admit of being compactly stowed: *articles that pack well.* **33.** to crowd together, as persons, etc. **34.** to become compacted: *wet snow packs readily.* **35.** to collect into a pack: *grouse began to pack.* **36.** to leave hastily (fol. by *off, away,* etc.). **37.** *Rugby Football.* to form a scrum (oft. fol. by *down*). *–adj.* **38.** transporting, or used in transporting, a pack: *pack animals.* **39.** made up of pack animals. **40.** compressed into a pack; packed. **41.** used in or adapted for packing. **42.** in the manner of a pack of wild animals: *pack rape.* [ME *packe, pakke,* from Flem., D or LG]

**pack**[2] /pæk/, *v.t.* to collect, arrange, or manipulate (cards, persons, facts, etc.) so as to serve one's own purposes: *pack a jury.* [? var. of PACT]

**package** /ˈpækɪdʒ/, *n., v.,* **-aged, -aging.** *–n.* **1.** a bundle or parcel. **2.** that in which anything is packed, as a case, crate, etc. **3.** the packing of goods, etc. **4.** a unit, group of parts, or the like, considered as a single entity. *–v.t.* **5.** to put into wrappings or a container. **6.** to combine as a single entity. **7.** to organise the financing and production of a book, film, etc., for a publisher or producer.

**packaged beer** /pækɪdʒd ˈbɪə/, *n.* beer sold in bottles or cans.

**package deal** /ˈpækɪdʒ dil/, *n.* an agreement in which acceptance of any of the parts of a proposal is contingent upon acceptance of the whole.

**packager** /ˈpækɪdʒə/, *n.* **1.** →**packer.** **2.** one who packages a book, film, etc.

**pack drill** /ˈpæk drɪl/, *n.* a period of parade-ground marching, with a heavy pack, ordered as a military punishment.

**packer** /ˈpækə/, *n.* **1.** one whose business is packing food, etc., for the market. **2.** one who or that which packs. **3.** →**fettler.**

**packet** /ˈpækət/, *n.* **1.** a small pack or package of anything, originally of letters. **2.** a definite quantity or measure of something wrapped and retailed: *a packet of biscuits.* **3.** a ship that carries mail, passengers, and goods regularly on a fixed route. **4.** any ship. **5.** *Colloq.* a large sum of money. **6.** *Colloq.* a heavy or forceful blow, injury, setback, or the like: *he's caught a packet.* *–v.t.* **7.** to bind up in a package or parcel. [diminutive of PACK[1]]

**packet boat** /ˈ– boʊt/, *n.* →**packet** (defs 3 and 4).

**packhorse** /ˈpækhɔs/, *n.* a horse used for carrying goods, now chiefly in terrain inaccessible to wheeled vehicles.

**pack-ice** /ˈpæk-aɪs/, *n.* an area in polar seas of large blocks of ice driven together over a long period by winds, currents, etc.

**packing** /ˈpækɪŋ/, *n.* **1.** the act or work of one who or that which packs. **2.** the preparing and packaging of foodstuffs, etc. **3.** any material used for packing or making watertight, steamproof, etc., as a fibrous substance closing a joint, a metallic ring round a piston, etc.

**packing case** /ˈ– keɪs/, *n.* a large container for goods to be transported, usu. cube-shaped and made of plywood with reinforced edges.

**packing fraction** /ˈ– frækʃən/, *n.* the difference between the mass of an isotope on the physical scale of atomic weights, and its mass number, divided by the mass number; often multiplied by 10 000 for convenience.

**packing house** /ˈ– haʊs/, *n.* an establishment in which provisions, esp. beef and pork, are packed for the market.

**packman** /ˈpækmən/, *n., pl.* **-men.** **1.** a pedlar. **2.** *N.Z.* (formerly) one who carried supplies, etc., by packhorse.

**pack-rape** /pæk-ˈreɪp/, *n., v.,* **-raped, -raping.** *–n.* **1.** rape, usu. of a woman, by several men. *–v.t.* **2.** to commit pack-rape upon.

**pack rat** /ˈpæk ræt/, *n.* a large bushy-tailed rodent, *Neotoma cinerea,* of North America, noted for carrying away small articles which it keeps in its nest; wood rat.

**packsack** /ˈpæksæk/, *n. U.S.* →**knapsack.**

**pack-saddle** /ˈpæk-sædl/, *n.* a saddle specially designed for supporting the load on a pack animal.

**pack-thread** /ˈpæk-θrɛd/, *n.* a strong thread or twine for sewing or tying up packages.

**pack-track** /ˈpæk-træk/, *n. N.Z.* a track negotiable only by pack-animals.

**packtrain** /ˈpæktreɪn/, *n.* a line or group of animals, esp. horses or mules, carrying goods.

**pact** /pækt/, *n.* an agreement; a compact. [ME, from L *pactum,* properly pp. neut., agreed]

**pad**[1] /pæd/, *n., v.,* **padded, padding.** *–n.* **1.** a cushion-like mass of some soft material, for comfort, protection, or stuffing. **2.** a guard for the leg, containing padding and stiffeners, as worn by the batsmen and wicket-keeper in cricket, the goalkeeper in hockey, etc. **3.** a cushion used as a saddle; saddle of leather and padding without a tree. **4.** Also, **writing pad.** a number of sheets of paper held together at the edge to form a tablet. **5.** a soft ink-soaked block of absorbent material for inking a rubber stamp. **6.** one of the cushion-like protuberances on the underside of the feet of dogs, foxes, and some other animals. **7.** the foot of a fox or other beast of the chase. **8.** *Zool.* a pulvillus, as on the tarsus or foot of an insect. **9.** the large floating leaf of the waterlily. **10.** a device built into a road surface by which, in passing over them, vehicles actuate changes of traffic lights. **11. a.** *Aerospace.* →**launching pad. b.** *Aeron.* a smallish area set aside for helicopter or STOL use. **12.** *Colloq.* a dwelling, esp. a single room. **13.** *Colloq.* a bedroom. **14.** *Colloq.* a bed. *–v.t.* **15.** to furnish, protect, fill out, or stuff with a pad or padding. **16.** to expand (writing or speech) with unnecessary words or matter. *–v.i.* **17.** *Colloq.* to have one's dwelling (usu. fol. by *down*). [special uses of obs. *pad* bundle to lie on, ? b. PACK[1] and BED] – **padder,** *n.*

**pad**[2] /pæd/, *n., v.,* **padded, padding.** *–n.* **1.** a dull sound, as of footsteps on the ground. **2.** a road horse, distinguished from a hunter or workhorse. **3.** a highwayman. **4.** a path worn by animals, as by cattle through paddocks. *–v.t.* **5.** to travel along on foot. **6.** *Brit.* to beat down by treading. *–v.i.* **7.** to travel on foot. **8.** to go with the dull sound of footsteps. [D or LG (c. PATH); orig. beggars' and thieves' slang] – **padder,** *n.*

**padauk** /pə'daʊk, -'dɔk/, *n.* **1.** any of various trees of the genus *Pterocarpus,* family Papilionaceae, yielding a reddish wood similar to mahogany. **2.** the wood of a padauk tree.

**padded cell** /pædəd 'sɛl/, *n.* a room in a mental hospital in which a violent patient is prevented from injuring himself.

**padding** /'pædɪŋ/, *n.* **1.** material, as cotton or straw, with which to pad. **2.** unnecessary matter used to expand a speech, etc. **3.** the act of one who or that which pads.

**paddle**[1] /'pædl/, *n., v.,* **-dled, -dling.** *–n.* **1.** a short oar held in the hands (not resting in the rowlock) and used esp. for propelling canoes. **2.** one of the broad boards on the circumference of a paddlewheel; a float. **3.** a paddlewheel. **4.** one of the similar projecting blades by means of which a waterwheel is turned. **5.** an adjustable shutter that lets waters into or out of a lock, reservoir, or the like. **6.** a flipper or limb of a penguin, turtle, whale, etc. **7.** any of various implements used for beating, stirring, mixing, etc. **8.** the act of paddling. *–v.i.* **9.** to propel a canoe or the like by using a paddle. **10.** to row lightly or gently with oars. **11.** to move by means of paddlewheels, as a steamer. *–v.t.* **12.** to propel (a canoe, etc.) with a paddle. **13. paddle one's own canoe,** to act independently. **14.** to stir. **15.** *U.S. Colloq.* to beat with or as with a paddle; spank. **16.** to convey by paddling, as in a canoe. [orig. obscure] – **paddler,** *n.*

**paddle**[2] /'pædl/, *v.i.,* **-dled, -dling. 1.** to dabble or play in or as in shallow water. **2.** to toy with the fingers. **3.** to toddle. [orig. uncert.] – **paddler,** *n.*

**paddleboat** /'pædlboʊt/, *n.* **1.** a boat propelled by a paddlewheel. **2.** →**paddle-steamer.**

**paddle-box** /'pædl-bɒks/, *n.* a box or casing covering the upper part of the paddlewheel of a vessel.

**paddlefish** /'pædlfɪʃ/, *n., pl.* **-fishes,** *(esp. collectively)* **-fish.** a large ganoid fish, *Polyodon spathula,* remotely allied to the sturgeons, with a long, flat, paddle-like projection of the snout, abundant in the Mississippi and its larger tributaries.

**paddle-pop** /'pædl-pɒp/, *n.* a frozen flavoured milk-based confection on a stick. [Trademark]

**paddle-steamer** /'pædl-stimə/, *n.* a steam vessel propelled by paddlewheels. Also, **paddleboat.**

**paddlewheel** /'pædlwil/, *n.* a wheel with floats or paddles on its circumference, for propelling a vessel over the water.

**paddock** /'pædək/, *n.* **1.** an enclosed field or piece of land. **2.** *Brit.* a small field or enclosure, esp. for pasture, near a stable or house. **3.** Also, **saddling paddock.** *Horseracing.* the area in front of the members' stand in which horses are saddled prior to a race and to which the winners are brought back subsequently for the presentation of prizes. **4.** Also, **paddock enclosure.** *Horseracing.* that part of the racecourse next to the saddling paddock. **5.** *Motor Racing.* an area near the pits, in which cars are prepared for a race. **6.** *N.Z.* a football field. *–v.t.* **7.** to confine or enclose in or as in a paddock. **8.** to fence (a run) into paddocks. [var. of *parrock,* OE *pearroc* enclosure (orig. fence)]

**paddy**[1] /'pædi/, *n.* **1.** rice. **2.** rice in the husk, uncut or gathered. **3.** paddy field. [Malay *pādī*]

**paddy**[2] /'pædi/, *n. Colloq.* an intense anger; a rage. [from PADDY (the Irish being seen as quick-tempered)]

**Paddy** /'pædi/, *n., pl.* **-dies.** an Irishman. [familiar var. of Irish *Padraig* Patrick]

**paddy field** /'pædi fild/, *n.* the wet and often inundated land on which rice is grown.

**paddymelon**[1] /'pædimɛlən/, *n.* either of two southern African plants, now widely distributed in Australia: **1.** a trailing herb, *Cucumis myriocarpus,* which has small melon-like fruit, harmful to stock; prickly pear melon. **2.** a vine, *Colocynthis lanatus,* similar to the common jam melon. [? PADDY[1] (def. 3) + MELON]

**paddymelon**[2] /'pædimɛlən/, *n.* →**pademelon.**

**Paddy's lantern** /pædiz 'læntən/, *n. N.Z. Colloq.* the moon.

**Paddy's lucerne** /– 'lusən/, *n.* a perennial fibrous plant, *Sida rhombifolia,* with sharp-pointed seeds, found as a weed in arable land; named from its growth in paddy rice fields; jelly-leaf; Queensland hemp. Also, **Paddy lucerne.**

Paddy's lucerne

**paddy-wagon** /'pædi-wægən/, *n.* a police van for transporting prisoners; black maria. Also, **paddy wagon.**

**paddywhack**[1] /'pædiwæk/, *n. Colloq.* **1.** Also, **paddy.** a rage. **2.** a spanking.

**paddywhack**[2] /'pædiwæk/, *n.* **1.** *Colloq.* the back. **2.** a sinew which runs along the neck of larger quadrupeds, appearing in cuts of meat as tough yellow gristle. [rhyming slang]

**pademelon** /'pædimɛlən/, *n.* any of several species of small wallabies of the genus *Thylogale* found in areas of thick scrub or dense, moist undergrowth. Also, **paddymelon.** [alteration (by association with *melon*) of an Aboriginal word]

pademelon wallaby

**pad footing** /pæd 'fʊtɪŋ/, *n.* a box-shaped footing (def. 6) of brick or concrete supporting a column or sleeper pier.

**Padishah** /'padɪʃa/, *n.* great king; emperor (a title applied formerly to the Shah of Iran, and to the Sultan of Turkey, and in India, to the British sovereign). [Pers. (poetical form), from *pati* lord + *shāh* king]

**padlock** /'pædlɒk/, *n.* **1.** a portable or detachable lock having a pivoted or sliding hasp which passes through a staple, ring, or the like and is then made fast. *–v.t.* **2.** to fasten with or as with a padlock. [late ME, from *pad,* var. of POD[3], + LOCK[1]]

**padnag** /'pædnæg/, *n.* an ambling nag. [PAD[2] + NAG[2]]

**padre** /'padreɪ/, *n.* **1.** father (used esp. with reference to a priest). **2.** a military or naval chaplain. **3. go through on the padre's bike,** to travel at great speed. [Sp., Pg., It., from L *pater* father]

**padre's pox** /'padreɪz pɒks/, *n.* →**officer's pox.**

**padrone** /pə'droʊneɪ, -ni/, *n., pl.* **-ni** /-ni/. *U.S.* **1.** a master, as of a vessel. **2.** an innkeeper. **3.** an employer who exercises control over the private lives of his employees. [It., from *padre* father]

**paduasoy** /'pædʒusɔɪ/, *n., pl.* **-soys. 1.** a smooth, strong, rich, silk fabric. **2.** a garment made of it. [apparently alteration of F *pou-de-soie,* by association with *Padua say* serge of Padua, town in NE Italy]

**paean** /'piən/, *n.* **1.** any song of praise, joy, or triumph. **2.** a hymn of invocation or thanksgiving to Apollo or some other Greek deity. Also, **pean.** [L, from Gk *paiān* paean, *Paiān,* Homer's name for the physician of the gods, later Apollo]

**paed-,** a word element meaning 'child'. Also, **paedi-, paedo-;** *U.S.,* **ped-.** [Gk *paidi-,* combining form of *paîs*]

**paedagogue** /'pɛdəgɒg/, *n.* →**pedagogue.** – **paedagogic** /pɛdə'gɒdʒɪk/, *adj.* – **paedagogism,** *n.* – **paedagogy,** *n.*

**paederast** /'pɛdəræst/, *n.* →**pederast.**

**paederasty** /ˈpɛdəræsti/, *n.* →**pederasty.**

**paediatrician** /pidiəˈtrɪʃən/, *n.* a physician who specialises in paediatrics. Also, **paediatrist** /pidiˈætrəst/, *U.S.*, **pediatrician.**

**paediatrics** /pidiˈætrɪks/, *n.* the study and treatment of the diseases of children. Also, *U.S.*, **pediatrics.** [PAED- + Gk *iātrikós* of medicine; see -ICS] – **paediatric,** *adj.*

**paedobaptism** /pidoʊˈbæptɪzəm/, *n.* the baptism of infants. Also, *U.S.*, **pedobaptism.** [PAED(O)- + BAPTISM]

**paedogenesis** /pidoʊˈdʒɛnəsəs/, *n.* reproduction by animals in the larval state, often by parthenogenesis.

**paedology** /piˈdɒlədʒi/, *n.* **1.** the scientific study of the nature and development of children. **2.** →**paediatrics.** Also, *U.S.*, **pedology.** [PAED(O)- + -LOGY]

**paedophilia** /pidoʊˈfɪliə/, *n. Med.* sexual attraction in an adult towards children. [PAEDO- + -PHILIA]

**paella** /paɪˈɛlə/, *n.* a Spanish dish made from rice, chicken, shellfish, etc. [Sp.: orig., the large shallow pan in which it is cooked]

**paeon** /ˈpiən/, *n.* a metrical foot of four syllables, one long (in any position) and three short. [L, from Gk *paiṓn* paeon, hymn, Attic var. of *paiā́n* PAEAN]

**paeony** /ˈpiəni/, *n.* →**peony.**

**pagan** /ˈpeɪgən/, *n.* **1.** one of a people or community professing some other than the Christian religion (applied to the ancient Romans, Greeks, etc., and sometimes the Jews). **2.** one who is not a Christian, a Jew, or a Muslim. **3.** an irreligious or heathenish person. *–adj.* **4.** pertaining to the worship or worshippers of any religion which is neither Christian, Jewish, nor Muslim. **5.** of, pertaining to, or characteristic of pagans. **6.** heathen; irreligious. [ME, from L *pāgānus* civilian; so called (by the Christians) because not a soldier of Christ] – **paganish,** *adj.*

**pagandom** /ˈpeɪgəndəm/, *n.* **1.** the pagan world. **2.** pagans collectively.

**paganise** /ˈpeɪgənaɪz/, *v.,* **-nised, -nising.** *–v.t.* **1.** to make pagan. *–v.i.* **2.** to become pagan. Also, **paganize.**

**paganism** /ˈpeɪgənɪzəm/, *n.* **1.** pagan spirit or attitude in religious or moral questions. **2.** the beliefs or practices of pagans. **3.** the state of being a pagan.

**page**[1] /peɪdʒ/, *n., v.,* **paged, paging.** *–n.* **1.** one side of a leaf of a book, manuscript, letter, or the like. **2.** the entire leaf of a book, etc.: *write on both sides of the page.* **3.** any event or period regarded as an episode in history: *a glorious page in history.* **4.** *Print.* the type set and arranged for a page. *–v.t.* **5.** →**paginate.** [F, from L *pāgina*]

**page**[2] /peɪdʒ/, *n., v.,* **paged, paging.** *–n.* **1.** a boy servant or attendant. **2.** a youth in attendance on a person of rank, sometimes formerly in the course of training for knighthood. **3.** a young male attendant, usu. in uniform, in a hotel or the like; a pageboy. **4.** a summons, by means of or as by a pager. *–v.t.* **5.** to seek (a person) by calling out his name, as a hotel page does. **6.** to attend as a page. [ME, from OF, from It. *paggio*, from Gk *paídion* boy, servant]

**pageant** /ˈpædʒənt/, *n.* **1.** an elaborate public spectacle, whether processional or at some fitting spot, illustrative of the history of a place, institution, or other subject. **2.** a costumed procession, masque, allegorical tableau, or the like, in public or social festivities. **3.** a splendid or stately procession; a showy display. **4.** a specious show. **5.** *Hist.* **a.** a platform or stage, usu. moving on wheels, on which scenes from the medieval mystery plays were presented. **b.** a stage bearing any kind of spectacle. [ME *pagent, pagyn;* orig. obscure]

**pageantry** /ˈpædʒəntri/, *n., pl.* **-ries. 1.** spectacular display; pomp: *the pageantry of war.* **2.** mere show; empty display. **3.** *Obs.* pageants collectively.

**pageboy** /ˈpeɪdʒbɔɪ/, *n.* **1.** *Brit.* →**bellboy. 2.** a small boy who acts as an attendant at weddings or social occasions. **3.** a woman's hairstyle in which the hair falls straight and is rolled under at the bottom.

**page proof** /ˈpeɪdʒ pruf/, *n. Print.* a proof compiled after the work has been made up into pages.

**pager** /ˈpeɪdʒə/, *n.* a small portable device which receives, but does not transmit, audible signals, used as a means of contacting or conveying instructions to the person carrying it.

**Paget's disease** /ˈpædʒəts dəziz/, *n.* **1.** a chronic disorder, *osteitis deformans,* in which the bones are enlarged, deformed, and weakened. **2.** cancer of the breast, involving nipple and associated ducts. [named after Sir James *Paget,* 1814-99, English surgeon]

**paginal** /ˈpædʒənəl/, *adj.* **1.** of or pertaining to pages. **2.** consisting of pages. **3.** page for page: *a paginal reprint.* [LL *pāginālis,* from L *pāgina* PAGE[1]]

**paginate** /ˈpædʒəneɪt/, *v.t.,* **-nated, -nating.** to indicate the sequence of (pages) by numbers or other characters on each leaf of the book.

**pagination** /pædʒəˈneɪʃən/, *n.* **1.** the number of pages or leaves (or both) of a book identified in bibliographical description or cataloguing of the book. **2.** the figures by which pages are numbered. **3.** the act of paginating.

**pagoda** /pəˈgoʊdə/, *n.* (in India, Burma, China, etc.) a temple or sacred building, usu. more or less pyramidal or forming a tower of many storeys. Also, *Archaic,* **pagod** /ˈpægəd, pəˈgɒd/. [Pg. *pagode;* orig. uncert.] – **pagoda-like,** *adj.*

Chinese pagoda

**pagoda tree** /ˈ– tri/, *n.* a deciduous, leguminous tree of China, *Sophora japonica,* with pinnate leaves and greenish white flowers.

**pagurian** /pəˈgjuriən/, *adj.* **1.** belonging or pertaining to the hermit crab family Paguridae, esp. aquatic hermit crabs with short antennules. *–n.* **2.** a pagurian crab. [NL *Pagurus,* the typical genus (from Gk *págouros* kind of crab) + -IAN]

**pagurid** /pəˈgjurəd, ˈpægjərəd/, *n.* →**pagurian.**

**pah** /pa/, *interj.* (an exclamation of disgust or disbelief.).

**paid** /peɪd/, *v.* past tense and past participle of **pay**[1].

**paid-up** /ˈpeɪd-ʌp/, *adj.* having paid the dues, initiation fees, etc., required by any organisation or association: *the union has a paid-up membership of 6000.*

**paid-up capital** /– ˈkæpətəl/, *n.* the amount of a company's capital which has been issued to shareholders. Also, **issued capital.**

**paigle** /ˈpeɪgəl/, *n.* the cowslip, *Primula veris,* or the oxlip, *P. elatior.*

**pail** /peɪl/, *n.* a container of wood, metal, etc., nearly or quite cylindrical, with a semicircular handle, for holding liquids, etc.; a bucket. [ME *payle,* OE *pægel* wine vessel, akin to G *Pegel* water-gauge] – **pailful** /ˈpeɪlfʊl/, *n.*

**paillasse** /ˈpæliæs/, *n.* →**palliasse.** [F, from *paille* straw, from L *palea* chaff, straw]

**paillette** /pæliˈɛt/, *n.* **1.** a spangle used in ornamenting a costume. **2.** a decorative piece of foil used in enamelling. [F, diminutive of *paille* straw. See PALLET[1]]

**pain** /peɪn/, *n.* **1.** bodily or mental suffering or distress (opposed to *pleasure*). **2.** a distressing sensation in a particular part of the body. **3.** (*pl.*) laborious or careful efforts; assiduous care: *great pains have been taken.* **4.** (*pl.*) the suffering of childbirth. **5. be at pains to,** to be extremely careful to. **6. on pain of,** liable to the penalty of. **7. pain (in the neck),** *Colloq.* an irritating, tedious, or unpleasant person or thing. *–v.t.* **8.** to inflict pain on; hurt; distress. *–v.i.* **9.** to cause pain or suffering. [ME *peine,* from OF, from L *poena* penalty, pain, from Gk *poinḗ* fine]

**painful** /ˈpeɪnfəl/, *adj.* **1.** affected with or causing pain: *painful sunburn.* **2.** laborious; difficult. **3.** *Archaic.* painstaking. – **painfully,** *adv.* – **painfulness,** *n.*

**pain-killer** /ˈpeɪn-kɪlə/, *n.* something that relieves pain, esp. an analgesic.

**painless** /ˈpeɪnləs/, *adj.* without pain; causing no pain. – **painlessly,** *adv.* – **painlessness,** *n.*

**painstaking** /ˈpeɪnzteɪkɪŋ/, *adj.* **1.** assiduously careful: *painstaking work.* *–n.* **2.** careful and assiduous effort. – **painstakingly,** *adv.*

**paint** /peɪnt/, *n.* **1.** a substance composed of solid colouring matter intimately mixed with a liquid vehicle or medium, and applied as a coating. **2.** the dried surface pigment. **3.** the solid colouring matter alone; a pigment. **4.** application of colour. **5.** *Colloq.* colour, as rouge, used on the face. **6. the paint,** *Horseracing Colloq.* the rails on the edge of the track. *–v.t.* **7.** to represent (an object, etc.) in colours or pigment. **8.** to execute (a picture, design, etc.) in colours or pigment. **9.** to depict as if by painting; describe vividly in words. **10.** to describe or represent: *he's not as bad as he's painted.* **11.** to coat, cover, or decorate (something) with colour or pigment. **12.** to colour as if by painting; adorn or variegate. **13.** to apply like paint, as a liquid medicine, etc. **14. paint the town red,** *Colloq.* to have a spree; celebrate. *–v.i.* **15.** to coat or cover anything with paint. **16.** to practise painting. **17.** *Colloq.* to use artificial colours on the face. [ME *peint(en),* from OF *peint,* pp. of *peindre,* from L *pingere* paint, adorn]

**paintbox** /ˈpeɪntbɒks/, *n.* a box in which different paints, as watercolours, are kept in separate compartments.

**paintbrush** /ˈpeɪntbrʌʃ/, *n.* a brush for applying paint.

**painted applemoth** /peɪntəd ˈæpəlmɒθ/, *n.* a polyphagous moth, *Orgyia anartoides,* which infests Australian apple orchards; the female is wingless.

**painted finch** /– ˈfɪntʃ/, *n.* **→Gouldian finch.**

**painted lady** /– ˈleɪdi/, *n.* **1.** a brightly coloured butterfly, *Vanessa cardui,* of the family Nymphalidae, which inhabits Europe and North Africa. **2.** **→painted woman.**

painted lady

**painted woman** /– ˈwʊmən/, *n.* a woman of low morals or promiscuous behaviour; prostitute. Also, **painted lady.**

**painter**[1] /ˈpeɪntə/, *n.* **1.** an artist who paints pictures. **2.** one whose occupation is coating surfaces with paint. [ME *peyntour,* from AF *peintour,* from L *pictor*]

**painter**[2] /ˈpeɪntə/, *n.* a rope, usu. at the bow, for fastening a boat to a ship, stake, etc. [? var. of Brit. d. *panter* noose, from OF *pentoir* rope to hang things on, from *pendre* hang]

**painter**[3] /ˈpeɪntə/, *n. U.S.* **→puma.** [var. of PANTHER]

**painterly** /ˈpeɪntəli/, *adj.* **1.** of or pertaining to painting which is technically expert and aesthetically of the highest standard. **2.** of or pertaining to painting, sculpture and architecture in which form is defined in terms of masses of light and shade, with edges merging into one another, rather than in terms of lines and outlines.

**painter's colic** /peɪntəz ˈkɒlɪk/, *n.* lead poisoning causing intense pain in the intestines.

**pain threshold** /ˈpeɪn θrɛʃhoʊld/, *n.* the lowest limit of perceiving the sensation of pain.

**painting** /ˈpeɪntɪŋ/, *n.* **1.** a picture or design executed in paints. **2.** the act, art, or work of one who paints.

**pair** /pɛə/, *n., pl.* **pairs, pair,** *v.* *–n.* **1.** two things of a kind, matched for use together: *a pair of gloves.* **2.** a combination of two parts joined together: *a pair of scissors.* **3.** a married or engaged couple. **4.** two people, animals, etc., regarded as having a common characteristic: *a pair of fools.* **5.** two mated animals. **6.** a span or team. **7. a.** two members on opposite sides in a deliberative body who for convenience (as to permit absence) arrange together to forgo voting on a given occasion. **b.** the arrangement thus made. **8.** *Cards.* **a.** two cards of the same denomination, without regard to suit or colour. **b.** (*pl.*) two players who are matched together against different contestants. **9.** *Rowing.* a racing shell having two oarsmen, with one oar each. **10.** *Mech.* two parts or pieces so connected that they mutually constrain relative motion **(kinematic pair).** **11.** *Cricket.* **a.** a failure by a batsman to score in either innings of a match. **b. king pair,** the dismissal of a batsman by the first ball in each innings of a match. **12.** *Mining.* a party of men (usu. six) working together; a gang. **13. cancel pairs,** (in parliament) to suspend pairing, ensuring that votes are counted strictly according to the actual number of members present. *–v.t.* **14.** to arrange in pairs. **15.** to join in a pair; mate; couple. **16.** to cause to mate. *–v.i.* **17.** to separate into pairs (oft. fol. by *off*). **18.** to form a pair or pairs. **19.** (in a deliberative body) to form a pair to forgo voting. [ME, from OF *paire,* from L *pāria,* neut. pl. of *pār* equal]

**pair production** /ˈ– prədʌkʃən/, *n.* **1.** the simultaneous creation of a positron and an electron as the result of the interaction between a high-energy photon or particle and the field of an atomic nucleus. **2.** the simultaneous creation of any particle and its antiparticle.

**paisley** /ˈpeɪzli/, *n., pl.* **-leys.** **1.** a soft fabric made from wool and woven with a colourful and minutely detailed pattern. **2.** an article fashioned of paisley. **3.** any pattern similar to that woven on paisley. *–adj.* **4.** made of paisley: *a paisley shawl.* [named after *Paisley,* town in Scotland]

paisley: detail of 19th century cotton paisley shawl

**pajamas** /pəˈdʒaməz/, *n.pl. U.S.* **→pyjamas.**

**pakapoo** /pækəˈpu/, *n.* a type of Chinese lottery using slips of paper with sets of characters written on them. Also, **pakapu.** [Chinese *pai ko p'iao* white pigeon ticket]

**pakapoo ticket** /ˈ– tɪkət/, *n.* something that looks confusing or incomprehensible: *marked like a pakapoo ticket.*

**pakaru** /ˈpakəru/, *adj. N.Z. Colloq.* **1.** ruined, broken. *–v.t.* **2.** to ruin, break. Also, **puckeroo.** [Maori]

**pakeha** /ˈpakəha, ˈpakiha/, *N.Z.* *–n.* **1.** a European; white man. *–adj.* **2.** denoting or pertaining to a white man. [Maori]

**pakeha Maori** /– ˈmaʊri/, *n.* a European who adopts the Maori way of life.

**Paki** /ˈpæki/, *n. Colloq.* a Pakistani.

**pakihi** /ˈpakəhi/, *n. N.Z.* (in Westland district) patches of open, flat land, often swampy. [Maori]

**Pakistan** /pækəˈstan, pa-/, *n.* a republic in southern Asia.

**Pakistani** /pækəˈstani, pa-/, *n., pl.* **-nis,** *adj.* *–n.* **1.** a native or inhabitant of Pakistan. *–adj.* **2.** of or pertaining to, or denoting Pakistan or Pakistanis.

**pal** /pæl/, *n., v.,* **palled, palling.** *Colloq.* *–n.* **1.** a comrade; a chum. **2.** an accomplice. **3. be a pal!,** be a friend and help me! *–v.i.* **4.** to associate as pals. **5. pal up with,** to become associated or friendly with. [Gipsy, dissimilated var. of *plal, pral* brother] – **pally,** *adj.*

**PAL** /pæl/, *n.* a colour television transmission system. [*P(hase) A(lternate) L(ine)*]

**palace** /ˈpæləs/, *n.* **1.** the official residence of a sovereign, a bishop, or some other exalted personage. **2.** a stately mansion or building. **3.** a large place for exhibitions or entertainment. [ME *palais,* from OF, from L *palātium* palace, orig. the Palatine Hill in Rome (on which the emperors resided)]

**palace revolution** /– rɛvəˈluʃən/, *n.* a seizure of power by those who already hold office or positions of power under the existing government or regime.

**paladin** /ˈpælədən/, *n.* any knightly or heroic champion. [F, from It. *paladino,* from L *palātīnus* belonging to the palace; first applied to the twelve peers or knightly champions of Charlemagne, A.D. 742-814, king of the Franks]

**palae-,** variant of **palaeo-,** before most vowels, as in *palaeethnology.*

**Palaearctic** /pæliˈaktɪk, peɪ-/, *adj.* of or pertaining to a biogeographical division of the Holarctic realm comprising Europe and northern Asia together with North Africa.

**palae-ethnologic** /ˌpæli-ɛθnəˈlɒdʒɪk, ˌpeɪ-/, *adj.* of or pertaining to palae-ethnology. Also, **palae-ethnological.**

**palae-ethnology** /ˌpæli-ɛθˈnɒlədʒi, ˌpeɪ-/, *n.* the branch of ethnology that treats of the earliest or most primitive races of mankind. [PALAE- + ETHNOLOGY] – **palae-ethnologist,** *n.*

**palaeo-,** a prefix meaning 'old', 'ancient'. Also, **palae-;** *Chiefly U.S.,* **pale-, paleo-.** [Gk *palaio-,* combining form of *palaiós*]

**palaeobiology** /ˌpælioʊbaɪˈɒlədʒi, ˌpeɪ-/, *n.* that branch of palaeontology which deals with fossil plants and animals. – **palaeobiological** /ˌpælioʊbaɪəˈlɒdʒɪkəl, ˌpeɪ-/, *adj.* – **palaeobiologist,** *n.*

**palaeobotanical** /ˌpælioʊbəˈtænɪkəl, ˌpeɪ-/, *adj.* of or pertaining to palaeobotany. Also, **palaeobotanic.**

**palaeobotany** /pælioʊˈbɒtəni, peɪ-/, *n.* the branch of palaeontology that treats of fossil plants. – **palaeobotanist,** *n.*

**Palaeocene** /ˈpæliəsin, ˈpeɪ-/, *adj.* **1.** pertaining to the oldest series or epoch of the Tertiary. *–n.* **2.** a division of the Tertiary period or system that precedes Eocene. Also, **paleocene.**

**palaeoecology** /ˌpæliouiˈkɒlədʒi, ˌpeɪ-/, *n.* the study of the ecological relationships which prevailed among fossil plants and animals. – **palaeoecological** /ˌpæliouikəˈlɒdʒɪkəl, ˌpeɪ-/, *adj.* – **palaeoecologist,** *n.*

**palaeog.,** palaeography.

**Palaeogene** /ˈpæliədʒin, ˈpeɪ-/, *adj., n.* →**Eogene.** Also, **Paleogene.**

**palaeogeography** /ˌpælioudʒiˈɒgrəfi, ˌpeɪ-/, *n.* the science of representing the earth's geographic features belonging to any given period of the geological past. – **palaeogeographical** /ˌpælioudʒiəˈgræfɪkəl, ˌpeɪ-/, *adj.*

**palaeogeology** /ˌpælioudʒiˈɒlədʒi, ˌpeɪ-/, *n.* the science of representing geological conditions of some given time in past earth history. – **palaeogeological** /ˌpælioudʒiəˈlɒdʒɪkəl, ˌpeɪ-/, *adj.*

**palaeographic** /pæliəˈgræfɪk, peɪ-/, *adj.* of or pertaining to palaeography. Also, **palaeographical.** – **palaeographically,** *adv.*

**palaeography** /pæliˈɒgrəfi, peɪ-/, *n.* **1.** ancient forms of writing, as in documents and inscriptions. **2.** the study of ancient writing, including determination of origin and date, decipherment, etc. – **palaeographer,** *n.*

**palaeolith** /ˈpælioulɪθ, ˈpeɪ-/, *n.* a palaeolithic stone implement.

**Palaeolithic** /pæliəˈlɪθɪk, peɪ-/, *n.* **1.** the earliest part of the Stone Age, the Old Stone Age, characterised by implements of chipped stone; it includes the Pleistocene geological epoch and precedes the Mesolithic. *–adj.* **2.** (*sometimes l.c.*) of or pertaining to the Palaeolithic period.

**Palaeolithic man** /– ˈmæn/, *n.* any of the primitive species of man (Piltdown, Neanderthal, etc.) living in the palaeolithic period.

**palaeomagnetism** /ˌpæliouˈmægnətɪzəm, ˌpeɪ-/, *n.* **1.** the magnetism of ancient rocks. **2.** the study of the same.

**palaeontol.,** palaeontology.

**palaeontologic** /ˌpæliɒntəˈlɒdʒɪk, ˌpeɪ-/, *adj.* of or pertaining to palaeontology. Also, **palaeontological.**

**palaeontology** /ˌpæliɒnˈtɒlədʒi, ˌpeɪ-/, *n.* the science of the forms of life existing in former geological periods, as represented by fossil animals and plants. [F *paléontologie;* from PALAE- + ONTOLOGY] – **palaeontologist,** *n.*

**Palaeozoic** /ˌpæliouˈzouɪk, ˌpeɪ-/, *adj.* **1.** pertaining to the oldest geological era or rocks having abundant fossils; the age of ancient life. *–n.* **2.** the era or rocks comprising divisions from Cambrian to Permian. Also, **Paleozoic.** [PALAEO- + Gk *zōḗ* life + -IC]

**palaeozoology** /ˌpæliouzouˈɒlədʒi, ˌpeɪ-/, *n.* the branch of palaeontology that treats of fossil animals. – **palaeozoological** /ˌpæliouzouəˈlɒdʒɪkəl, ˌpeɪ-/, *adj.* – **palaeozoologist,** *n.*

**palaestra** /pəˈlɛstrə, -ˈli-/, *n.* (in ancient Greece or Rome) a public place for training or exercise in wrestling or athletics. Also, **palestra.** [ME, from L, from Gk *palaístra*]

**palais de danse** /ˌpæleɪ də ˈdæns, ˈdans/, *n., pl.* **palais de danse.** a dance hall, esp. a large and ornately decorated one. Also, **palais.** [F]

**palanquin** /ˈpælənkin, -kwin, -ən/, *n.* (in India and other Eastern countries) a covering or boxlike litter borne by means of poles resting on men's shoulders. Also, **palankeen.** [Pg. Cf. Skt *palyanka, paryanka* couch, bed; probably through Telegu]

palanquin

**palatable** /ˈpælətəbəl/, *adj.* **1.** agreeable to the palate or taste; savoury. **2.** agreeable to the mind or feelings. – **palatability** /pælətəˈbɪləti/, **palatableness,** *n.* – **palatably,** *adv.*

**palatal** /ˈpælətl/, *adj.* **1.** *Anat.* of or pertaining to the palate. **2.** *Phonet.* with the tongue held close to the hard palate. For example, the *y* of *yield* is a palatal consonant. *–n.* **3.** *Phonet.* a palatal sound. [PALAT(E) + -AL[1]] – **palatally,** *adv.*

**palatalise** /ˈpælətəlaɪz/, *v.t.,* **-lised, -lising.** *Phonet.* to pronounce with the tongue held close to the hard palate so that the sound acquires some of the quality of a *y.* For example, in *million* the *l* sound may or may not be palatalised, but is always followed by a *y* sound. Also, **palatalize.** – **palatalisation** /pælətəlaɪˈzeɪʃən/, *n.*

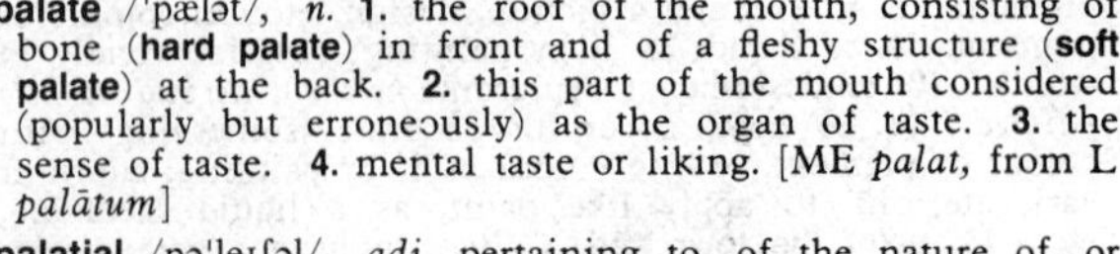

**palate** /ˈpælət/, *n.* **1.** the roof of the mouth, consisting of bone (**hard palate**) in front and of a fleshy structure (**soft palate**) at the back. **2.** this part of the mouth considered (popularly but erroneously) as the organ of taste. **3.** the sense of taste. **4.** mental taste or liking. [ME *palat,* from L *palātum*]

**palatial** /pəˈleɪʃəl/, *adj.* pertaining to, of the nature of, or befitting a palace: *palatial homes.* [L *palātium* PALACE + -AL[1]] – **palatially,** *adv.*

**palatinate** /pəˈlætənət/, *n.* a region under the rule of a court palatine.

**palatine**[1] /ˈpælətaɪn/, *adj.* **1.** possessing or characterised by royal privileges: *a count palatine.* **2.** pertaining to a count or earl palatine. **3.** of or pertaining to a palace; palatial. *–n.* **4.** (in Imperial Rome) **a.** a palace guard. **b.** a soldier in part of the army. **5.** (in late Roman and Byzantine times) an administrative official. **6.** (in Carolingian times) **a.** a vassal exercising royal privileges in a province. **b.** an imperial emissary. **7.** a shoulder cape formerly worn by women. [ME, from L *palātīnus* belonging to the palace, imperial (as n., a palace officer)]

**palatine**[2] /ˈpælətaɪn/, *adj.* palatal: *the palatine bones.* [F *palatin,* from L *palātum* PALATE]

**palatogram** /ˈpælətəgræm/, *n.* an imprint made by contact of the tongue while uttering a speech sound on an artificial hard palate.

**palaver** /pəˈlavə/, *n.* **1.** a parley or conference, esp. with much talk as between travellers and primitive natives. **2.** any conference or discussion. **3.** profuse and idle talk. **4.** cajolery or flattery. *–v.i.* **5.** to talk profusely and idly. **6.** to hold a parley or conference. *–v.t.* **7.** to cajole. [Pg. *palavra,* from L *parabola* PARABLE]

**palazzo** /pəˈlatsou/, *n., pl.* **-lazzi** /-ˈlatsi/. a palace or large building. [It.]

**pale**[1] /peɪl/, *adj.,* **paler, palest,** *v.,* **paled, paling.** *–adj.* **1.** of a whitish appearance; without intensity of colour: *pale complexion.* **2.** of a low degree of chroma, saturation, or purity; approaching white or grey: *pale yellow.* **3.** lacking in brightness; dim: *the pale moon.* **4.** faint; feeble; lacking vigour. *–v.i.* **5.** to become pale. *–v.t.* **6.** to make pale. [ME, from OF, from L *pallidus* pallid] – **palely,** *adv.* – **paleness,** *n.*

**pale**[2] /peɪl/, *n., v.,* **paled, paling.** *–n.* **1.** a stake or picket, as of a fence. **2.** any enclosing or confining barrier. **3.** limits or bounds: *outside the pale of the Church.* **4.** the area enclosed by a paling; any enclosed area. **5.** a district or region within fixed bounds. **6.** *Her.* a broad vertical stripe in the middle of an escutcheon and one third its width. **7.** **beyond the pale,** socially or morally unacceptable. *–v.t.* **8.** to enclose with pales; fence. **9.** to encircle. [ME, from F *pal,* from L *pālus* stake]

**pale-,** *Chiefly U.S.* variant of **palae-.** Also, before consonants, **paleo-.** For words beginning with **pale-,** look under **palae-.**

**palea** /ˈpeɪliə/, *n., pl.* **-leae** /-lii/. **1.** a chafflike scale or bract. **2.** the scalelike, membranous organ in the flowers of grasses which is situated upon a secondary axis in the axil of the flowering glume and envelops the stamens and pistil. [L: chaff] – **paleaceous** /peɪliˈeɪʃəs/, *adj.*

**pale ale** /peɪl ˈeɪl/, *n. Chiefly Brit.* →**light ale.**

**paleface** /ˈpeɪlfeɪs/, *n.* a white person (an expression attributed to the American Indians).

**Paleocene** /ˈpæliəsin/, *adj., n.* →**Palaeocene.**

**Paleogene** /ˈpæliədʒin/, *adj., n.* →**Palaeogene.**

**palestra** /pəˈlɛstrə, pəˈlistrə/, *n., pl.* **-tras, -trae** /-tri/. →**palaestra.**

**paletot** /ˈpæltou/, *n.* a loose outer garment or coat. [F, from OF *paltoc,* orig. uncert.]

**palette** /ˈpælət/, *n.* **1.** a thin, usu. oval or oblong, board or tablet with a thumb hole at one end, used by painters to lay and mix colours on. **2.** the range of colours used by a particular artist. **3.** Also, **pallette.** *Armour.* a small armpit plate. [F: palette, flat-bladed implement, from L *pāla* spade, shovel]

**palette knife** /ˈ– naɪf/, *n.* a thin, flexible blade set in a handle, used for mixing painters' colours, etc.

**palewise** /ˈpeɪlwaɪz/, *adv. Her.* in the manner or direction of a pale[2] (def. 6).

**palf** /pælf/, *n. Colloq.* →**palfium.**

**palfium** /ˈpælfiəm/, *n.* (*also cap.*) a powerful analgesic of the morphine type. [Trademark]

**palfrey** /ˈpɔlfri/, *n., pl.* **-freys.** *Archaic.* **1.** a riding horse, as distinguished from a warhorse. **2.** a woman's saddle horse. [ME *palefrai,* from OF *palefrei,* from LL *paraverēdus,* from Gk *pará* beside + L *verēdus* light horse (from Celtic)]

**Pali** /ˈpali/, *n.* the Prakrit language of the Buddhist scriptures. [Skt, short for *pāli-bhāsā,* lit., canon language]

**palimpsest** /ˈpæləmpsɛst/, *n.* a parchment or the like from which writing has been partially or completely erased to make room for another text. [L *palimpsestus,* from Gk *palímpsēstos* scraped again]

**palindrome** /ˈpæləndroʊm/, *n.* a word, verse, etc., reading the same backwards as forwards, as *madam, I'm Adam.* [Gk *palíndromos* running back]

**paling** /ˈpeɪlɪŋ/, *n.* **1.** a fence of pales. **2.** a pale, as in a fence. **3.** pales collectively. **4.** the act of one who builds a fence with pales. [ME, from PALE[2] + -ING[1]]

**palingenesis** /pælənˈdʒɛnəsəs/, *n.* **1.** rebirth; regeneration. **2.** *Biol.* **a.** that development of an individual which reproduces the ancestral features (opposed to *cainogenesis*). **b.** *Obs.* the supposed generation of organisms from others preformed in the germ cells. **3.** baptism in the Christian faith. **4.** the doctrine of transmigration of souls. [Gk *pálin* back, again + GENESIS]

**palinode** /ˈpælənoʊd/, *n.* **1.** a poem in which the poet retracts something said in a former poem. **2.** a recantation. [LL *palinōdia,* from Gk *palinōidía*]

**palisade** /pæləˈseɪd/, *n., v.,* **-saded, -sading.** *–n.* **1.** a fence of pales or stakes set firmly in the ground, as for enclosure or defence. **2.** one of the pales or stakes, pointed at the top, set firmly in the ground in a close row with others, for defence. **3.** *Bot.* the layer of compact cylindrical cells situated immediately beneath the adaxial epidermis of dorsiventral leaves. **4.** (*pl.*) *U.S.* a line of lofty cliffs. *–v.t.* **5.** to furnish or fortify with a palisade. [F *palissade,* from *palisser* furnish with a paling, from *palis* paling, from L *pālus* PALE[2]]

**palish** /ˈpeɪlɪʃ/, *adj.* somewhat pale.

**pall**[1] /pɔl/, *n.* **1.** a cloth, often of velvet, for spreading over a coffin, bier, or tomb. **2.** something that covers, shrouds, or overspreads, esp. with darkness or gloom. **3.** *Eccles.* **a.** a pallium (vestment). **b.** *Archaic.* a cloth spread upon the altar, esp. a corporal. **c.** a linen cloth, or now usu. a square piece of cardboard covered with linen, used to cover the chalice. **4.** *Her.* a bearing representing the front of a pallium (vestment), consisting of a Y-shaped form charged with crosses. **5.** *Obs.* a cloak. *–v.t.* **6.** to cover with or as with a pall. [ME; OE *pæll,* from L *pallium* cloak, covering]

**pall**[2] /pɔl/, *v.i.* **1.** to have a wearying effect (fol. by *on* or *upon*). **2.** to become insipid, distasteful, or wearisome. **3.** to become satiated or cloyed with something. *–v.t.* **4.** to satiate or cloy. **5.** to make vapid, insipid, or distasteful. [ME *palle(n)*; apparently aphetic var. of APPAL]

**Palladian**[1] /pəˈleɪdiən/, *adj.* of or pertaining to a type of architecture marked by a revived classic style and symmetry, esp. as introduced into England in the 18th century. [named after Andrea *Palladio,* 1508-80, Italian architect]

**Palladian**[2] /pəˈleɪdiən/, *adj.* pertaining to wisdom, knowledge, or study. [orig. with ref. to *Pallas,* a name of Athena (often *Pallas Athene*), Greek goddess of wisdom]

**Palladianism** /pəˈleɪdiənɪzəm/, *n.* Palladian architecture.

**palladic** /pəˈlædɪk, -ˈleɪdɪk/, *adj.* of or containing palladium, esp. in the tetravalent state.

**palladium**[1] /pəˈleɪdiəm/, *n., pl.* **-dia** /-diə/. anything believed to afford effectual protection or safety. [ME, from L, from Gk *Palládion* a statue of the goddess Pallas Athene in the citadel of Troy on which the safety of the city was supposed to depend]

**palladium**[2] /pəˈleɪdiəm/, *n.* a rare metallic element of the platinum group, silver-white, ductile and malleable. It is harder than platinum and fuses more readily. *Symbol:* Pd; *at. wt:* 106.4; *at. no.:* 46; *sp. gr.:* 12 at 20°C. [NL; named (1803) after the asteroid *Pallas,* then recently discovered]

**palladous** /pəˈleɪdəs, ˈpælədəs/, *adj.* containing divalent palladium.

**pallbearer** /ˈpɔlbɛərə/, *n.* one of those who carry or attend the coffin at a funeral.

**pallet**[1] /ˈpælət/, *n.* **1.** a bed or mattress of straw. **2.** a small or poor bed. [ME *pailet,* from OF, diminutive of *paille* straw, from L *palea* chaff]

**pallet**[2] /ˈpælət/, *n.* **1.** an implement consisting of a flat blade with a handle, used for shaping by potters, etc. **2.** a flat board or metal plate used to support ceramic articles during drying. **3.** *Horol.* a lever with three projections, two of which intermittently lock and receive impulses from the escape wheel, and one which transmits these impulses to the balance. **4.** a lip or projection on a pawl, that engages with the teeth of a ratchet wheel. **5.** *Gilding.* an instrument used to take up the gold leaves from the pillow, and to apply and extend them. **6.** a movable platform on which goods are placed for storage or transportation, esp. one designed to be lifted by a forklift truck. **7.** a painter's palette. [F *palette* PALETTE]

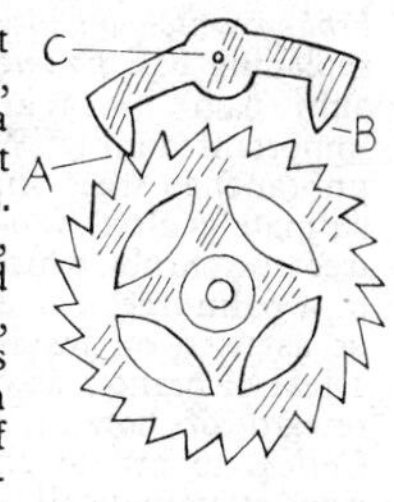


pallet[2]: A, B, pallets (def. 4); C, pivot on which pawl oscillates

**palletise** /ˈpælətaɪz/, *v.t.,* **-tised, -tising.** to place on a pallet (def. 6).

**palletiser** /ˈpælətaɪzə/, *n.* a machine that stacks cartons, as of packaged beer, on to a pallet (def. 6).

**pallet knife** /ˈpælət naɪf/, *n.* **1.** →**palette knife. 2.** a blunt, rounded, knifelike instrument, used for lifting cakes from the baking tray, mixing, etc. Also, **pallette knife.**

**pallette** /ˈpælət/, *n. Armour.* →**palette.**

**palliasse** /ˈpæliæs/, *n.* a mattress of straw or the like. Also, **paillasse.** [see PAILLASSE]

**palliate** /ˈpælieɪt/, *v.t.,* **-ated, -ating. 1.** to cause (an offence, etc.) to appear less grave or heinous; extenuate; excuse. **2.** to mitigate or alleviate: *to palliate a disease.* [L *palliātus,* pp., covered with a cloak] – **palliation** /pæliˈeɪʃən/, *n.* – **palliator,** *n.*

**palliative** /ˈpæliətɪv/, *adj.* **1.** serving to palliate. *–n.* **2.** something that palliates. – **palliatively,** *adv.*

**pallid** /ˈpæləd/, *adj.* pale; deficient in colour; wan. [L *pallidus*] – **pallidly,** *adv.* – **pallidness,** *n.*

**pallid cuckoo** /– ˈkʊku/, *n.* a medium-sized greyish-brown Australian cuckoo, *Cuculus pallidus,* having a distinctive penetrating call resembling a rising chromatic scale; semitone bird; scale bird; brain-fever bird.

**pallium** /ˈpæliəm/, *n., pl.* **pallia** /ˈpæliə/, **palliums. 1.** *Rom. Antiq.* a voluminous rectangular mantle worn by men, esp. by philosophers. **2.** *Eccles.* **a.** a woollen vestment worn by the pope and conferred by him as an honour on outstanding ecclesiastics, consisting, in its present form, of a narrow ringlike band, which rests upon the shoulders, with two dependent bands or lappets, one in front and one behind. **b.** an altar cloth; a pall. **3.** *Anat.* the entire cortex of the cerebrum. **4.** *Zool.* a mantle. [OE, from L. See PALL[1]]

**pall-mall** /pæl-ˈmæl/, *n.* **1.** a game formerly played in which a ball of boxwood was struck with a mallet, the object being to drive it through a raised iron ring at the end of an alley. **2.** an alley in which this game was played. [F (obs.) *pallemaille,* from It. *pallamaglio* the game, from *palla* ball (of Gmc orig.; akin to BALL[1]) + *maglio* mallet, from L *malleus* hammer]

**pallor** /ˈpælə/, *n.* unnatural paleness, as from fear, ill health, or death; wanness. [L]

**pally** /ˈpæli/, *adj. Colloq.* disposed to behave as a pal.

**palm**[1] /pam/, *n.* **1.** that part of the inner surface of the hand which extends from the wrist to the bases of the fingers. **2.** the corresponding part of the forefoot of an animal. **3.** the part of a glove covering the palm. **4.** a metal shield worn over the palm of the hand by sail-makers to serve instead of a thimble. **5.** a linear measure based on either the breadth of the hand (7 to 10 cm) or its length from wrist to fingertips (18 to 25 cm). **6.** the flat, expanded part of the horn or antler of some deer. **7.** a flat, widened part at the end of an armlike projection. **8.** the blade of an oar. **9.** *Naut.* the inner surface of an anchor fluke. **10. cross, grease,** or **oil someone's palm,** to bribe. *–v.t.* **11.** to conceal in the palm, as in

i = peat ɪ = pit ɛ = pet æ = pat a = part ɒ = pot ʌ = putt ɔ = port ʊ = put u = pool ɜ = pert ə = apart aɪ = buy eɪ = bay ɔɪ = boy aʊ = how
oʊ = hoe ɪə = here ɛə = hair ʊə = tour g = give θ = thin ð = then ʃ = show ʒ = measure tʃ = choke dʒ = joke ŋ = sing j = you õ = Fr. bon

cheating at cards or dice or in juggling. **12.** to touch or stroke with the palm or hand. **13.** *Aus. Rules.* at a ball-up or throw-in, to hit (the ball) with an open hand. **14.** *Obs.* to shake hands with. **15. palm off,** to impose (something) fraudulently (fol. by *on* or *upon*): *he tried to palm off the broken watch on me.* [L *palma* palm, hand, blade of an oar; replacing ME *paume,* from OF, from L]

**palm**[2] /pam/, *n.* **1.** any of the plants constituting the large and important family Palmae, the majority of which are tall, unbranched trees surmounted by a crown of large pinnate or palmately cleft (fan-shaped) leaves. **2.** any of various other trees or shrubs which resemble the palm. **3.** a leaf or branch of a palm tree, esp. as formerly borne as an emblem of victory or as used on festal occasions. **4.** a representation of such a leaf or branch, as on a decoration of honour. **5.** the victor's reward of honour. **6.** victory; triumph. **7. take the palm,** *Colloq.* to outdo; cheat. [ME and OE, from L *palma* palm tree; etymologically identical with PALM[1]] – **palmlike,** *adj.*

**palmar** /ˈpælmə/, *adj.* pertaining to the palm of the hand, or to the corresponding part of the forefoot of an animal. [L *palmāris*]

**palmate** /ˈpælmeɪt, -mət/, *adj.* **1.** shaped like an open palm, or like a hand with the fingers extended, as a leaf or an antler. **2.** *Bot.* lobed or divided so that the sinuses point to or reach the apex of the petiole, somewhat irrespective of the number of lobes. **3.** *Zool.* webfooted. Also, **palmated.** [L *palmātus*] – **palmately,** *adv.*

palmate leaf

**palmation** /pælˈmeɪʃən/, *n.* **1.** palmate state or formation. **2.** a palmate structure.

**palm butter** /pam ˈbʌtə/, *n.* palm oil in a solid state.

**palm-cabbage** /pam-ˈkæbɪdʒ/, *n.* the bud of the cabbage palm.

**palm civet** /pam ˈsɪvət/, *n.* any of various viverrine animals of south-eastern Asia, the East Indies, etc., chiefly arboreal in habit, about the size of the domestic cat, and having a spotted or striped fur and a long curled tail. Also, **palm cat.**

**palm court orchestra,** *n.* a small group of musicians, often violinist, cellist and pianist, who play light music, esp. in restaurants, etc.

**palmer**[1] /ˈpamə/, *n.* **1.** a pilgrim who had returned from the Holy Land, in token of which he bore a palm branch. **2.** any pilgrim. [ME *palmere,* from PALM[2], translating AF *palmer,* ML *palmārius,* from L *palma* PALM[2]]

**palmer**[2] /ˈpamə/, *n.* one who palms something, as in cheating at cards. [PALM[1] + -ER[1]]

**palmetto** /pælˈmɛtoʊ/, *n., pl.* **-tos, -toes.** any of various species of palm with fan-shaped leaves such as *Sabal, Serenoa, Thrinax,* and the only European palm, *Chamaerops.* [Sp. *palmito,* diminutive of *palma,* from L *palma* PALM[2]]

**palmiet** /ˈpælmiət/, *n.* an aloe-like riverside plant, *Prionium palmita,* of the family Juncaceae, of southern Africa, having fibrous leaves used for thatching. [Afrikaans, from D: palm-cabbage]

**palmistry** /ˈpaməstri/, *n.* the art or practice of telling fortunes and interpreting character by the lines and configurations of the palm of the hand. [ME *pawmestry, palmestrie,* from *palmester* chiromancer, from *palme* PALM[1] + -STER] – **palmist** /ˈpaməst/, *n.*

**palmitate** /ˈpælməteɪt/, *n.* a salt or ester of palmitic acid.

**palmitic acid** /pælˌmɪtɪk ˈæsəd/, *n.* a white crystalline acid, $C_{15}H_{31}COOH$, occurring as a glyceride in palm oil and in most solid fats.

**palmitin** /ˈpælmətən/, *n.* a colourless fatty substance, $(C_{15}H_{31}COO)_3C_3H_5$, the glyceride of palmitic acid, occurring in palm oil and solid fats, and used in soap manufacture. Also, **tripalmitin.** [F *palmitine,* from L *palma* PALM[2]]

**palm oil** /ˈpam ɔɪl/, *n.* **1.** a yellow, butter-like oil from the fruit of *Elaeis guineensis,* of western Africa, used as food and employed also for making soap, candles, etc. **2.** oil obtained from various species of palm. **3.** bribery or a bribe.

**palm sugar** /– ˈʃʊgə/, *n.* sugar from the sap of certain palm trees.

**Palm Sunday** /pam ˈsʌndeɪ/, *n.* the Sunday before Easter, celebrated in commemoration of Christ's triumphal entry into Jerusalem.

**palmy** /ˈpami/, *adj.,* **-mier, -miest.** **1.** glorious, prosperous, or flourishing. **2.** abounding in or shaded with palms: *palmy islands.* **3.** palmlike.

**palmyra** /pælˈmaɪərə/, *n.* a tropical Asian fan palm, *Borassus flabellifer.* Also, **palmyra palm.** [Pg. *palmeira,* from L *palma* PALM[2]]

**palolo worm** /pəˈloʊloʊ wɜm/, *n.* a marine, polychaete, annelid worm of the southern Pacific, *Leodice viridis,* remarkable for the constancy with which it breeds, breaking off the posterior part of the body in the process, on the day of the last quarter of the October-November moon. [*palolo* from Samoan or Tongan]

**palomino** /pæləˈminoʊ/, *n., pl.* **-nos.** a tan or cream-coloured horse with a white mane and tail. Also, **palamino.** [Sp.]

**Palomino** /pæləˈminoʊ/, *n.* a white grape variety used mainly in sherry production.

**palooka** /pəˈlukə/, *n. Colloq.* a stupid or clumsy boxer, etc.

**Palouse pony** /pəlus ˈpoʊni/, *n.* a pony distinguished by its colouring, usu. white with dark spots or dark with a white 'blanket' over the rump, and by its white sclera around the eyes, mottled skin and striped hooves. [named after the *Palouse* River, Idaho, U.S., where the Nez Perce Indians developed the breed after it was brought to America by the Spaniards]

**palp** /pælp/, *n.* **1.** →**palpus.** *–v.t.* **2.** *Obs.* to touch or feel gently; palpate. [F *palpe,* from L *palpus* a feeler]

**palpable** /ˈpælpəbəl/, *adj.* **1.** readily or plainly seen, heard, perceived, etc.; obvious: *a palpable lie.* **2.** that can be touched or felt; tangible. **3.** *Med.* perceptible by palpation. [ME, from LL *palpābilis,* from L *palpāre* touch] – **palpability** /pælpəˈbɪləti/, *n.* – **palpably,** *adv.*

**palpate**[1] /ˈpælpeɪt/, *v.t.,* **-pated, -pating.** to examine by the sense of touch, esp. in medicine. [L *palpātus,* pp., touched, stroked] – **palpation** /pælˈpeɪʃən/, *n.*

**palpate**[2] /ˈpælpeɪt/, *adj.* having a palpus or palpi. [L *palpus* a feeler + -ATE[1]]

**palpebral** /ˈpælpəbrəl/, *adj.* of or pertaining to the eyelids. [LL *palpebrālis*]

**palpebrate** /ˈpælpəbrət, -breɪt/, *adj.* having eyelids.

**palpi** /ˈpælpaɪ/, *n.* plural of **palpus.**

**palpitant** /ˈpælpətənt/, *adj.* palpitating. [L *palpitans,* ppr.]

**palpitate** /ˈpælpəteɪt/, *v.i.,* **-tated, -tating.** **1.** to pulsate with unnatural rapidity, as the heart, from exertion, emotion, disease, etc. **2.** to quiver or tremble. [L *palpitātus,* pp., moved quickly]

**palpitation** /pælpəˈteɪʃən/, *n.* **1.** an act of palpitating. **2.** rapid or violent beating of the heart.

**palpus** /ˈpælpəs/, *n., pl.* **-pi** /-paɪ/. an appendage attached to an oral part, and serving as an organ of sense, in insects, crustaceans, etc. [NL, from L: a feeler]

**palsgrave** /ˈpɔlzgreɪv/, *n.* a German count palatine. [D *paltsgrave* (now *paltsgraaf*), c. G *Pfalzgraf* palace count]

**palsgravine** /ˈpɔlzgrəvin/, *n.* the wife or widow of a palsgrave.

**palstave** /ˈpɔlsteɪv/, *n.* a bronze axe fitted into a split wooden handle. [Dan. *paalstav,* c. Icel. *pālstafr.* See PALE[2], STAVE]

**palsy** /ˈpɔlzi/, *n., pl.* **-sies,** *v.,* **-sied, -sying.** *–n.* **1.** paralysis. *–v.t.* **2.** to paralyse. [ME *parlesie,* from OF *paralisie,* from L *paralysis* PARALYSIS] – **palsied,** *adj.*

**palter** /ˈpɔltə/, *v.i.* **1.** to talk or act insincerely; equivocate; deal crookedly. **2.** to haggle. **3.** to trifle. [cf. obs. *palter* mumble, shuffle, b. PALSY and FALTER]

**paltry** /ˈpɔltri/, *adj.,* **-trier, -triest.** **1.** trifling; petty: *a paltry sum.* **2.** trashy or worthless: *paltry rags.* **3.** mean or contemptible: *a paltry coward.* [apparently from d. *palt* rubbish. Cf. LG *paltrig*] – **paltrily,** *adv.* – **paltriness,** *n.*

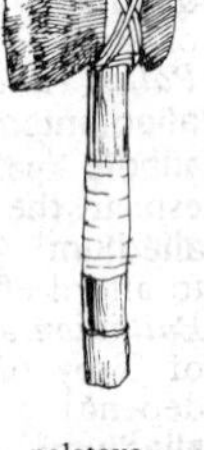
palstave

**paludal** /pəˈljudl, ˈpæljədl/, *adj.* **1.** of or pertaining to marshes. **2.** produced by marshes, as miasma or disease. [L *palus* marsh + -AL[1]]

**paludism** /ˈpæljədɪzəm/, *n.* malarial disease.

**paly**[1] /ˈpeɪli/, *adj. Archaic.* pale. [PALE[1] + -Y[1]]

**paly**[2] /'peɪli/, *adj. Her.* divided palewise, or vertically, into equal parts of alternating tinctures. [F *palé,* from *pal* PALE[2] (see def. 6)]

**palynology** /pælə'nɒlədʒi/, *n.* the study of fossil pollen in peat deposits, the stratification of which provides information about past changes in the land flora. [Gk *palýn(ein)* to scatter (akin to *pálē* dust) + -O- + -LOGY] – **palynological** /pælənə'lɒdʒɪkəl/, *adj.* – **palynologically** /pælənə'lɒdʒɪkli/, *adv.* – **palynologist,** *n.*

**pam** /pæm/, *n.* **1.** the knave of clubs, esp. in a form of the card game, loo, in which it is the best trump. **2.** this form of loo. [for F *pamphile,* orig. proper name, from Gk *Pámphilos,* lit., beloved of all]

**pampas** /'pæmpəz, -əs/, *n.pl.* the vast grassy plains lying in the rain shadow of the Andes, and south of the forested lowlands of the Amazon basin. [Sp., pl. of *pampa,* from Quechua] – **pampean** /pæm'piən, 'pæmpiən/, *adj.*

**pampas grass** /'pæmpəs gras/, *n.* any of several species of large, perennial South American grasses of the genus *Cortaderia,* esp. *C. selloana,* which has large feathery inflorescences and is frequently cultivated.

pampas grass

**pampas lily-of-the-valley** /– lɪli-əv-ðə-'væli/, *n.* a troublesome climbing weed, *Salpichroa origanifolia,* native to America.

**pamper** /'pæmpə/, *v.t.* **1.** to indulge (a person, etc.) to the full or to excess: *to pamper a child, one's appetite, etc.* **2.** to indulge with rich food, comforts, etc. [ME *pampren.* Cf. Flem. *pamperen,* G *pampen* cram] – **pamperer,** *n.*

**pamph.,** pamphlet.

**pamphlet** /'pæmflət/, *n.* **1.** a short treatise or essay, generally controversial, on some subject of temporary interest: *a political pamphlet.* **2.** a complete publication generally less than 80 pages, stitched or stapled and usu. enclosed in paper covers. **3.** →**throwaway** (def. 1). [ME *pamflet,* syncopated var. of *Pamphilet,* popular name for ML poem *Pamphilus*]

**pamphleteer** /pæmflə'tɪə/, *n.* **1.** a writer of pamphlets. *–v.i.* **2.** to write and issue pamphlets.

**pan**[1] /pæn/, *n., v.,* **panned, panning.** *–n.* **1.** a dish commonly of metal, usu. broad, shallow and open, used for culinary and other domestic purposes: *a frying pan; bed pan.* **2.** any pot or saucepan. **3.** any dishlike receptacle or part, as the scales of a balance. **4.** any of various open or closed vessels used in industrial or mechanical processes. **5.** a vessel, usu. of cast iron, in which the ores of silver are ground and amalgamated. **6.** a vessel in which gold or other heavy, valuable metals are separated from gravel, etc., by agitation with water. **7.** a depression in the ground, as a natural one containing water, mud, or mineral salts, or an artificial one for evaporating salt water to make salt. **8.** →**hardpan. 9.** (in old guns) the depressed part of the lock which holds the priming. **10.** →**brainpan. 11.** →**kneepan. 12.** *Colloq.* the face, as in *dead-pan. –v.t.* **13.** to wash (auriferous gravel, sand, etc.) in a pan, to separate the gold or other heavy valuable metal. **14.** to separate by such washing. **15.** *U.S.* to cook (oysters, etc.) in a pan. **16.** *Colloq.* to criticise or reprimand severely. *–v.i.* **17.** to wash gravel, etc., in a pan, seeking for gold. **18.** to yield gold, as gravel washed in a pan. **19. pan out,** *Colloq.* result; turn out. [ME and OE *panne,* c. G *Pfanne*]

**pan**[2] /pan/, *n.* **1.** the leaf of the betel. **2.** the masticatory of which the betel leaf comprises the wrapper. [Hind., from Skt *parna* feather, leaf]

**pan**[3] /pæn/, *v.,* **panned, panning.** *Films, Television, etc. –v.i.* **1.** (of a camera) to move continuously while shooting in order to record on film a panorama, or to keep a moving person or object in view. **2.** to operate a camera in such a manner. *–v.t.* **3.** to operate (a camera) in such a manner. [shortened form of PANORAMA]

**pan**[4] /pæn/, *n.* an international radio-television signal, indicating an urgent message follows. [*p(recautionary) a(dvisory) n(otice)*]

**pan-,** a word element or prefix meaning 'all', first occurring in words from the Greek, but now used freely as a general formative in English and other languages, esp. in terms implying the union, association, or consideration together, as forming a whole, of all the branches of a race, people, church, or other body, as in *pan-Celtic, pan-Christian,* and other like words of obvious meaning, formed at will, and tending with longer use to lose the hyphen and the capital, unless these are retained in order to set off clearly the component elements. [Gk, combining form of *pâs* (neut. *pân*)]

**panacea** /pænə'siə/, *n.* a remedy for all diseases; cure-all. [L, from Gk *panákeia*] – **panacean,** *adj.*

**panache** /pə'næʃ, -'naʃ/, *n.* **1.** a grand or flamboyant manner; swagger; verve. **2.** an ornamental plume or tuft of feathers, esp. one worn on a helmet or on a cap. [F, from It. *pennacchio,* from *penna,* from L: feather]

**panada** /pə'nadə/, *n.* a dish made of bread boiled and flavoured. [Sp., Pr., from L *pānis* bread]

**pan-African** /pæn-'æfrɪkən/, *adj.* **1.** of or pertaining to all the countries or peoples of Africa. *–n.* **2.** a believer in pan-Africanism.

**pan-Africanism** /pæn-'æfrɪkənɪzəm/, *n.* advocacy of a political alliance or union of all the countries of Africa.

**Panama** /'pænəma/, *n.* **1.** a republic in southern Central America. **2.** (*oft. l.c.*) →**Panama hat.** – **Panamanian** /pænə'meɪniən/, *adj., n.*

**Panama hat** /– 'hæt/, *n.* (*sometimes l.c.*) a fine plaited hat made of the young leaves of a palmlike plant, *Carludovica palmata,* of Central and South America. [named after PANAMA]

**pan-American** /pæn-ə'merɪkən/, *adj.* of or pertaining to all the countries or peoples of North, Central, and South America.

**pan-Americanism** /pæn-ə'merɪkənɪzəm/, *n.* the idea or advocacy of a political alliance or union of all the countries of North, Central, and South America.

**pan-Arabism** /pæn-'ærəbɪzəm/, *n.* the idea or advocacy of a political alliance or union of all Arab states. – **pan-Arab,** *n., adj.*

**panatella** /pænə'tɛlə/, *n.* a long, slender cigar, usu. tapering to a point. Also, **panetella.** [Mex. Sp.: lit., a kind of long, thin biscuit]

**pancake** /'pænkeɪk/, *n., v.,* **-caked, -caking.** *–n.* **1.** a thin flat cake made from a batter of eggs, flour, sugar, and milk, cooked in a frying pan. **2.** make-up compressed into stick form for easy application. **3.** an aeroplane landing made by pancaking. *–v.i.* **4.** (of an aeroplane, etc.) to drop flat to the ground after levelling off a few feet above it. *–v.t.* **5.** to cause (an aeroplane) to pancake.

**Pancake Day** /'pænkeɪk deɪ/, *n.* **1.** Shrove Tuesday, on which pancakes were and are traditionally eaten as the last eggs to be consumed before Lent. **2.** *Colloq.* a remote or improbable time: *she won't be back till next Pancake Day.*

**pancake ice** /'pænkeɪk aɪs/, *n.* small, thin slabs of ice which form on the surface of the sea in polar regions when it begins to freeze.

**pancake roll** /– 'roʊl/, *n.* →**spring roll.**

**panchromatic** /pænkrə'mætɪk/, *adj.* sensitive to light of all colours, as a photographic film or plate. – **panchromatism** /pæn'kroʊmətɪzəm/, *n.*

**pancreas** /'pæŋkriəs/, *n.* a gland situated near the stomach, secreting an important digestive fluid **(pancreatic juice),** discharged into the intestine by one or more ducts. Certain groups of cells **(islets of Langerhans)** also produce a hormone, insulin. [NL, from Gk *pánkreas* sweetbread] – **pancreatic** /pæŋkri'ætɪk/, *adj.*

**pancreatin** /'pæŋkriətən/, *n.* **1.** *Biochem.* a preparation containing all the enzymes of the pancreatic juice. **2.** a commercial preparation of the enzymes in the pancreas of animals, used as a digestive.

giant panda

**pancreatitis** /ˌpæŋkriə'taɪtəs/, *n.* inflammation of the pancreas.

**panda** /'pændə/, *n.* either of two mammals closely related to the bear and largely herbivorous in diet: **1.** the cat-sized

**lesser panda**, *Ailurus fulgens,* of the Himalayas, which has reddish brown fur. **2.** the bearlike **giant panda**, *Ailuropoda melanoleuca,* of central China, which is boldly marked in black and white. [F, perhaps from Nepalese]

**pandanus** /pæn'dænəs, -'deɪnəs/, *n.* any plant of the genus *Pandanus,* comprising tropical and sub-tropical trees and shrubs, esp. of the islands of the Malay Archipelago and the Indian and Pacific oceans, having a palmlike or branched stem, long, narrow, rigid, spirally arranged leaves and often aerial prop roots; screw-pine. [NL, from Malay *pandan*]

**P. & C.** /pi ən 'si/, Parents and Citizens Association.

**Pandean** /pæn'diən/, *adj.* of or pertaining to the god Pan: *Pandean pipes.*

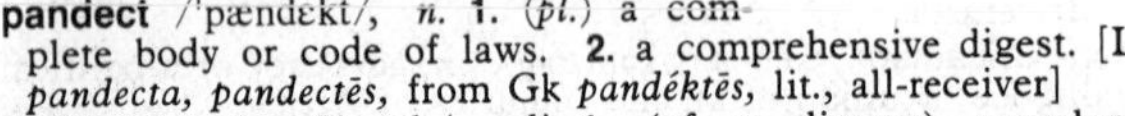

pandanus

**pandect** /'pændɛkt/, *n.* **1.** (*pl.*) a complete body or code of laws. **2.** a comprehensive digest. [L *pandecta, pandectēs,* from Gk *pandéktēs,* lit., all-receiver]

**pandemic** /pæn'dɛmɪk/, *adj.* **1.** (of a disease) prevalent throughout an entire country or continent, or the whole world. **2.** general; universal. *–n.* **3.** a pandemic disease. [Gk *pandēmos* public, common + -IC]

**pandemonium** /pændə'moʊniəm/, *n.* **1.** (*oft. cap.*) the abode of all the demons. **2.** hell. **3.** a place of riotous uproar or lawless confusion. **4.** wild lawlessness or uproar. [from *Pandaemonium,* Milton's name for the capital of hell. See PAN-, DEMON, -IUM] – **pandemoniac, pandemonic** /pændə'mɒnɪk/, *adj.*

**pander** /'pændə/, *n.* **1.** a go-between in intrigues of love. **2.** a procurer; pimp. **3.** one who ministers to the weaknesses or baser passions of others. *–v.t.* **4.** to act as a pander for. *–v.i.* **5.** to act as a pander; cater basely. **6.** to indulge (fol. by *to*): *pander to a child's whims.* [var. of *pandar,* generalised use of ME *Pandare* Pandarus, who (in works by Chaucer, Shakespeare and others) acted as procurer of Cressida for Troilus]

**pandit** /'pʌndət/, *n.* (in India) a learned man; a scholar (used as a title of respect). Cf. **pundit.** [Hind., from Skt *pandita* learned]

**pandora** /pæn'dɔrə/, *n.* →**bandore.** Also, **pandore** /pæn'dɔ, 'pændɔ/.

**Pandora's box** /pænˌdɔrəz 'bɒks/, *n.* any source of extensive troubles, esp. one expected at first to yield blessings. [in classical mythology, a box or jar given by Zeus to *Pandora,* which contained all human ills]

**pandowdy** /pæn'daʊdi/, *n. Orig. U.S.* an apple pie or pudding made in a deep dish, with a cake topping. [orig. unknown]

**p. & p.,** postage and packing.

**pandurate** /'pændʒəreɪt, -rət/, *adj.* shaped like a fiddle, as a leaf. Also, **panduriform** /pæn'djurəfɔm/. [LL *pandura* (see BANDORE) + -ATE[1]]

**pandy** /'pændi/, *n., pl.* **-dies,** *v.,* **-died, -dying.** *Chiefly Scot. –n.* **1.** a stroke on the palm with a cane or strap as a punishment in schools. *–v.t.* **2.** to strike thus. [said to be from L *pande,* impv., stretch out]

**pane** /peɪn/, *n.* **1.** one of the divisions of a window, etc., consisting of a single plate of glass in a frame. **2.** a plate of glass for such a division. **3.** a panel, as of a wainscot, ceiling, door, etc. **4.** a flat section, side, or surface, as one of the sides of a bolthead. [ME *pan,* from OF, from L *pannus* a cloth, rag]

pandurate leaf

**paned** /peɪnd/, *adj.* having panes: *a diamond-paned window.*

**panegyric** /pænə'dʒɪrɪk/, *n.* **1.** an oration, discourse, or writing in praise of a person or thing; a eulogy. **2.** a formal or elaborate encomium. [L *panēgyricus,* from Gk *panēgyrikós* festival oration, properly adj.] – **panegyrical,** *adj.* – **panegyrically,** *adv.*

**panegyrise** /'pænədʒəraɪz/, *v.,* **-rised, -rising.** *–v.t.* **1.** to pronounce or write a panegyric upon; eulogise. *–v.i.* **2.** to indulge in panegyric; bestow praises. Also, **panegyrize.**

**panegyrist** /pænə'dʒɪrəst/, *n.* one who panegyrises.

**panel** /'pænəl/, *n., v.,* **-elled, -elling** or (*U.S.*) **-eled, -eling.** *–n.* **1.** a distinct portion or division of a wainscot, ceiling, door, shutter, etc., or of any surface sunk below or raised above the general level, or enclosed by a frame or border. **2.** a pane, as in a window. **3.** a comparatively thin, flat piece of wood or the like. **4.** *Painting.* **a.** a flat piece of wood of varying kinds on which a picture is painted. **b.** a picture painted on such a piece of wood. **5.** a photograph much longer in one dimension than the other. **6.** a broad strip of the same or another material set vertically, as for ornament, in or on a woman's dress, etc. **7.** the section between two bands on the spine of a bound book. **8.** *Elect.* a division of a switchboard containing a set of related cords, jacks, relays, etc. **9.** the portion of a truss between adjacent chord joints. **10.** a surface or section of a machine on which controls, dials, etc., are mounted: *the instrument panel of a car.* **11.** *Law.* **a.** the list of persons summoned for service as jurors. **b.** the body of persons composing a jury. **12.** any list or group of persons, as one gathered to answer questions, discuss issues, etc. **13.** *Aeron.* a subdivision of the surface of an aerofoil or fuselage. **14.** *Mining.* an area of a coal seam, separated for mining purposes from adjacent areas by extra-thick masses or ribs of coal. **15.** the cushion or pad in a saddle separating the framework from the horse's back. **16.** a slip of parchment. **17.** an approximate measure of distance used in horseracing, etc., from the distance between fence posts. *–v.t.* **18.** to arrange in, or furnish with, panels. **19.** to ornament with a panel or panels. **20.** to set in a frame as a panel. **21.** to empanel. [ME *panel,* from OF: piece (of anything), from L *pannus* rag]

**panel beater** /'pænəl bitə/, *n.* one who beats sheet metal into required shapes as for the bodywork of motor vehicles, etc.

**panel game** /'– geɪm/, *n.* a quiz or the like, as on television, in which selected speakers make guesses, answer questions, etc., for public entertainment.

**panel heating** /– 'hitɪŋ/, *n.* a type of heating in which the heat is diffused through panels in walls, ceilings, etc.

**panel lighting** /– 'laɪtɪŋ/, *n.* a type of lighting in which the light is diffused through translucent panels.

**panelling** /'pænəlɪŋ/, *n.* **1.** wood or other material made into panels. **2.** panels collectively. Also, *U.S.* **paneling.**

**panellist** /'pænələst/, *n.* a member of a small group organised for public discussion, etc., as on television. Also, *U.S.,* **panelist.**

**panel pin** /'pænəl pɪn/, *n.* a short, slender nail used in joinery.

**panel saw** /'– sɔ/, *n.* a crosscut saw, smaller than a handsaw and with finer teeth, for use on thin timber.

**panel van** /'– væn/, *n.* a two-door van, similar in size and shape to a station wagon, used for the carriage of goods and sometimes fitted with sleeping accommodation.

**panentheism** /pæn'ɛnθiɪzəm/, *n.* the doctrine that all things are in God.

**panetella** /pænə'tɛlə/, *n.* →**panatella.**

**panettone** /pænə'toʊni/, *n.* a cake of Italian origin containing dried fruit and almonds and traditionally associated with Christmas. [It., from *panetto* small loaf]

**pan fry** /'pæn fraɪ/, *v.t.,* **fried, frying.** to fry in a very small amount of fat or oil. Also, **dry fry.**

**pang** /pæŋ/, *n.* **1.** a sudden feeling of mental distress. **2.** a sudden, brief, sharp pain, or a spasm or severe twinge of pain: *the pangs of hunger.* [orig. uncert.]

**panga** /'pæŋgə/, *n.* a broad, heavy African knife used as a tool and as a weapon; machete. [Swahili]

**pangenesis** /pæn'dʒɛnəsəs/, *n.* a theory advanced by Charles Darwin, 1809-82, English naturalist, according to which a reproductive cell or body contains gemmules or invisible germs which were derived from the individual cells from every part of the organism, and which are the bearers of hereditary attributes. – **pangenetic** /pændʒə'nɛtɪk/, *adj.*

**pan-Germanism** /pæn-'dʒɜmənɪzəm/, *n.* the idea or advocacy of a union of all the German peoples in one political organisation or state. – **pan-German,** *adj., n.* – **pan-Germanic** /pæn-dʒə'mænɪk/, *adj.*

**pangolin** /pæŋ'goʊlən/, *n.* any of

common pangolin

the scaly anteaters of Africa and tropical Asia, constituting an order of mammals, Pholidota, about a metre long, having a covering of broad, overlapping, horny scales. [Malay *peng-gōling* roller]

**panhandle**[1] /'pænhændl/, *n.* **1.** the handle of a pan. **2.** (*sometimes cap.*) a narrow projecting strip of land, esp. part of a nation or state: *the Panhandle of Texas, Vietnam, etc.*

**panhandle**[2] /'pænhændl/, *v.i.*, **-dled, -dling.** *U.S. Colloq.* to beg (usu. in the street). – **panhandler,** *n.*

**panhellenic** /pænhə'lɛnɪk/, *adj.* pertaining to all Greeks or to panhellenism.

**panhellenism** /pæn'hɛlənɪzəm/, *n.* the idea or principle of a union of all Greeks in one political body. – **panhellenist,** *n.* – **panhellenistic** /pænhɛlə'nɪstɪk/, *adj.*

**panic**[1] /'pænɪk/, *n., adj., v.,* **-icked, -icking.** *–n.* **1.** a sudden demoralising terror, with or without clear cause, often as affecting a group of persons or animals. **2.** an instance, outbreak, or period of such fear. **3. be at panic stations,** to be in a situation requiring extreme measures. *–adj.* **4.** (of fear, terror, etc.) suddenly destroying the self-control and impelling to some frantic action. **5.** of the nature of, due to, or showing panic: *panic haste.* *–v.t.* **6.** to affect with panic. *–v.i.* **7.** to be stricken with panic. [F *panique,* from L *pānicus,* from Gk *Pānikós* pertaining to or caused by Pan] – **panicky,** *adj.* – **panic-stricken** /'pænɪk-strɪkən/, **panic-struck** /'pænɪk-strʌk/, *adj.*

**panic**[2] /'pænɪk/, *n.* **1.** any grass of the genus *Panicum,* many species of which bear edible grain, as native millet or giant panic. **2.** the grain. **3.** any of a number of grass species of other genera which are similar. Also, **panic grass.** [OE, from L *pānicum*]

**panic bolt** /'– boʊlt/, *n.* a bolt on emergency exits, etc., opened by pressure from inside on a horizontal bar.

**panic button** /'– bʌtn/, *n. Colloq.* **1.** an imaginary device said to be pressed when one gets flustered by an emergency. **2. press** or **hit the panic button,** to react as to an emergency; overreact.

**panicle** /'pænɪkəl/, *n.* **1.** a compound raceme. **2.** any loose, diversely branching flower cluster. [L *pānicula* tuft on plants, diminutive of *pānus* swelling, ear of millet] – **panicled,** *adj.*

branch with panicles

**panic merchant** /'pænɪk mɜtʃənt/, *n.* a person who panics at the slightest untoward event.

**panic-stricken** /'pænɪk-strɪkən/, *adj.* affected by panic.

**paniculate** /pə'nɪkjəleɪt, -lət/, *adj.* arranged in panicles. – **paniculately,** *adv.*

**pan-Islamism** /pæn-'ɪzləmɪzəm/, *n.* the idea or advocacy of a union of all Muslim nations in one political body. – **pan-Islam** /pæn-'ɪzlam/, *n.* – **pan-Islamic** /pæn-ɪz'læmɪk/, *adj.*

**panjandrum** /pæn'dʒændrəm/, *n.* a mock title for any important or pretentious official. [a made-up word, with prefix PAN- and termination simulating Latin; apparently first used by Samuel Foote, 1720-77, English dramatist and actor]

**panlogism** /'pænlədʒɪzəm/, *n.* the doctrine that all that is real is intelligible and ultimately of the nature of spirit.

**panne** /pæn/, *n.* a soft, lustrous, lightweight velvet with flattened pile. [F, from L *penna* feather]

**pannier** /'pæniə/, *n.* **1.** a basket, esp. one of considerable size, for carrying provisions, etc. **2.** a basket for carrying on a person's back, or one of a pair to be slung across the back of a beast of burden. **3.** one of a pair of bags, containers, etc., attached to either side of the rear wheel of a motorcycle, used as carriers. **4.** *Obs.* a puffed arrangement of drapery about the hips. **5.** *Obs.* a framework formerly used for distending the skirt of a woman's dress at the hips. [ME *panier,* from OF, from L *pānārium* basket for bread]

**pannikin** /'pænəkən/, *n.* **1.** a small pan or metal cup. *–adj.* **2.** of or pertaining to one who acts as though his status and importance are large, when in reality they are not, as *pannikin boss, pannikin snob,* etc.

**pannikin boss** /– 'bɒs/, *n. Colloq.* an overseer of a small business or a small gang of labourers; a person of minor authority.

**pannikin snob** /– 'snɒb/, *n. Colloq.* a person of small means who affects a snobbish attitude. [modelled on PANNIKIN BOSS]

**panocha** /pə'noʊtʃə/, *n.* **1.** Also, **panoche** /pə'noʊtʃi/. a coarse grade of sugar made in Mexico. **2.** *U.S.* a sweet made of brown sugar, butter, and milk, usu. with nuts. [Mex. Sp.]

**panoply** /'pænəpli/, *n., pl.* **-plies. 1.** a complete suit of armour. **2.** a complete covering or array of something. [Gk *panoplía* complete suit of armour] – **panoplied** /'pænəplid/, *adj.*

**panoptic** /pæn'ɒptɪk/, *adj.* **1.** permitting the viewing of all parts or elements at once or from one standpoint. **2.** all-embracing; universal: *a panoptic criticism.* Also, **panoptical.** – **panoptically,** *adv.*

**panopticon** /pæn'ɒptəkən/, *n.* a prison or the like in which all parts of the interior are visible from one point. [PAN- + Gk *optikón* (adj., neut.) of or pertaining to sight; coined by Jeremy Bentham, 1748-1832, English philosopher and jurist]

**panorama** /pænə'ramə/, *n.* **1.** an unobstructed view or prospect over a wide area. **2.** an extended pictorial representation of a landscape or other scene, often exhibited a part at a time and made to pass continuously before the spectators. **3.** a continuously passing or changing scene. **4.** a comprehensive survey, as of a subject. [PAN- + Gk *hórāma* view] – **panoramic** /pænə'ræmɪk/, *adj.* – **panoramically** /pænə'ræmɪkli/, *adv.*

**panoramic sight** /ˌpænəræmɪk 'saɪt/, *n.* a sight for guns that can be swung in a complete circle.

**panpipe** /'pænpaɪp/, *n.* a primitive wind instrument consisting of a series of pipes of graduated length, the notes being produced by blowing across the upper ends. Also, **Pan's pipes.**

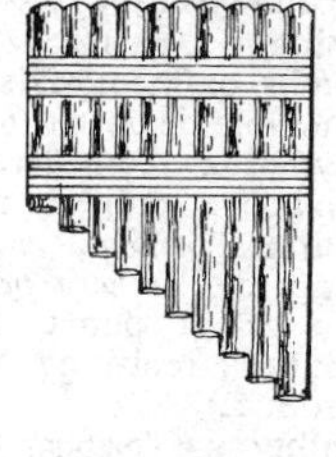
panpipe

**panplegia** /pæn'plidʒiə, -dʒə/, *n.* total paralysis.

**panpsychism** /pæn'saɪkɪzəm/, *n.* the doctrine that there is an inner, psychic nature not only to human beings, animals and plants, but to all matter.

**pan-Slavism** /pæn-'slævɪzəm/, *n.* the idea or advocacy of a union of all the Slavic races in one political body. – **pan-Slav, pan-Slavic** /pæn-'slævɪk/, *adj.*

**pansophism** /'pænsəfɪzəm/, *n.* the claim or pretension to pansophy. – **pansophist,** *n.*

**pansophy** /'pænsəfi/, *n.* universal wisdom or knowledge. [PAN- + Gk *sophía* wisdom] – **pansophic** /pæn'sɒfɪk/, **pansophical** /pæn'sɒfɪkəl/, *adj.*

**pansy** /'pænzi/, *n., pl.* **-sies,** *v.,* **pansied, pansying.** *–n.* **1.** any of several species of herbaceous plants of the genus *Viola,* esp. the **wild pansy,** *V. tricolor,* and the **garden pansy,** *V.* × *wittrockiana,* a hybrid with many cultivated varieties. **2.** its blossom. **3.** *Colloq.* **a.** an effeminate man. **b.** a male homosexual. *–v.i.* **4.** to move in an effeminate way: *he was pansying along the street.* *–v.t.* **5.** to treat something fussily or in an effeminate way: *the golfer was pansying the ball.* **6.** to overdecorate; pretty up (fol. by *up*): *to pansy up a room.* [F *pensée* pansy, lit., thought, from *penser* think. See PENSIVE]

**pant** /pænt/, *v.i.* **1.** to breathe hard and quickly, as after exertion. **2.** to emit steam or the like in loud puffs. **3.** to gasp, as for air. **4.** to long with breathless or intense eagerness: *he panted for revenge.* **5.** to throb or heave violently or rapidly; palpitate. **6.** (of a ship's hull) to vibrate when in heavy seas. *–v.t.* **7.** to breathe or utter gaspingly. *–n.* **8.** the act of panting. **9.** a short, quick, laboured effort of breathing; a gasp. **10.** a puff, as of an engine. **11.** a throb or heave, as of the breast. **12.** *Agric. Colloq.* (*pl.*) pulmonary oedema in cattle. [ME *panten;* apparently akin to OF *pantaisier,* probably (with ref. to the feeling of oppression in nightmare) from L *phantasia* phantasm, idea, FANTASY] – **pantingly,** *adv.*

**pantagruelian** /pæntəgru'eliən/, *adj.* dealing with serious matters in a spirit of broad and somewhat cynical good humour. [from *Pantagruel,* the huge son of Gargantua in *Gargantua and Pantagruel* by Francois Rabelais, c. 1490-1553, French monk, humanist, and bawdy writer] – **pantagruelism,** *n.* – **pantagruelist,** *n.*

i = peat ɪ = pit ɛ = pet æ = pat a = part ɒ = pot ʌ = putt ɔ = port ʊ = put u = pool ɜ = pert ə = apart aɪ = buy eɪ = bay ɔɪ = boy aʊ = how oʊ = hoe ɪə = here ɛə = hair ʊə = tour g = give θ = thin ð = then ʃ = show ʒ = measure tʃ = choke dʒ = joke ŋ = sing j = you õ = Fr. bon

**pantalets** /pæntə'lɛts/, *n.pl.* **1.** long drawers with a frill or other finish at the bottom of each leg, and extending below the dress, commonly worn by women and girls in the 19th century. **2.** a pair of separate frilled or trimmed pieces for attaching to the legs of women's drawers. Also, **pantalettes.** [alteration of PANTALOON, with diminutive -ET(TE) substituted for *-oon*]

**pantaloon** /pæntə'lun, 'pæntəlun/, *n.* **1.** (*pl.*) *Obs.* a man's closely fitting garment for the hips and legs, varying in form at different periods; trousers. **2.** (*oft. cap.*) (in the modern pantomime) a foolish, vicious old man, the butt and accomplice of the clown. **3.** (*usu. cap.*) (in the commedia dell'arte) a lean and foolish old Venetian wearing pantaloons and slippers. [F *pantalon,* from It. *pantalone* buffoon (see def. 3), *Pantalone* a Venetian, from St *Pantaleone* patron of Venice]

**pantechnicon** /pæn'tɛknɪkən/, *n.* **1.** a furniture van. **2.** a storage warehouse, esp. for furniture. [PAN- + Gk *technikón* (neut. of *technikós* artistic); orig. the name of a bazaar in 19th-cent. London, which became a furniture warehouse]

**pan-Teutonism** /pæn-'tjutənɪzəm/, *n.* →**pan-Germanism.**

**pantheism** /'pænθiɪzəm/, *n.* **1.** the doctrine that God is the transcendent reality of which the material universe and man are only manifestations, thereby denying God's personality, and identifying God with nature. Cf. **theism, deism. 2.** any religious belief or philosophical doctrine which identifies the universe with God. [PAN- + Gk *theós* god + -ISM] – **pantheist,** *n.* – **pantheistic** /pænθi'ɪstɪk/, **pantheistical** /pænθi'ɪstɪkəl/, *adj.* – **pantheistically** /pænθi'ɪstɪkli/, *adv.*

**pantheon** /pæn'θiən/, *n.* **1.** a public building containing tombs or memorials of the illustrious dead of a nation. **2.** a temple dedicated to all the gods. **3.** the gods of a particular mythology considered collectively. [ME, from L, from Gk *pántheion,* properly neut. of *pántheios* of all gods]

**panther** /'pænθə/, *n., pl.* **-thers,** (*esp. collectively*) **-ther. 1.** the leopard, *Panthera pardus,* esp. in its black form. **2.** *U.S.* the cougar or puma, *Felis concolor.* [L *panthēra,* from Gk *pánthēr;* replacing ME *pantere* (from OF) and OE *pandher* (from L)]

**pantheress** /'pænθərɛs/, *n.* a female panther.

**panties** /'pæntiz/, *n.pl.* underpants as worn by women and girls.

**pantihose** /'pæntihoʊz/, *n.* women's tights, usu. made out of fine-mesh material, as for stockings.

**pantile** /'pæntaɪl/, *n.* a roofing tile straight in its length but curved in its width to overlap the next tile. [PAN[1] + TILE, *n.* Cf. G *Pfannenziegel*]

pantiles

**panto** /'pæntoʊ/, *n., pl.* **-tos.** *Colloq.* →**pantomime.**

**panto-,** a word element or prefix synonymous with **pan-.** [Gk, combining form of *pâs* (stem *pant-*) all]

**pantofle** /pæn'tɒfəl, -tufəl/, *n.* →**slipper.** Also, **pantoffle** /pæn'tɒfəl/, **pantoufle.** [F *pantoufle,* from OIt. *pantufola,* var. of Sicilian *pantofola,* from Gk *pantóphellos* whole cork, through meaning of cork shoe]

**pantograph** /'pæntəgræf, -graf/, *n.* **1.** an instrument for the mechanical copying of plans, diagrams, etc., upon any desired scale. **2.** *Elect.* a roof-mounted current collector, as on a train, usu. a hinged diamond-shaped framework, sprung so as to maintain contact with an overhead wire.

**pantology** /pæn'tɒlədʒi/, *n.* a systematic view of all human knowledge. – **pantologic** /pæntə'lɒdʒɪk/, **pantological** /pæntə'lɒdʒɪkəl/, *adj.* – **pantologist,** *n.*

**pantomime** /'pæntəmaɪm/, *n., v.,* **-mimed, -miming.** –*n.* **1.** a form of theatrical entertainment common during the Christmas season, originally including a harlequinade, but now based loosely on one of several fairytales, and including stock character types. **2.** →**mime** (def. 2). **3.** an actor in dumb show, as in ancient Rome. **4.** significant gesture without speech. –*v.t.* **5.** to represent or express by pantomime. –*v.i.* **6.** to express oneself by pantomime. [L *pantomimus,* from Gk *pantómīmos,* lit., all-imitating] – **pantomimic** /pæntə'mɪmɪk/, *adj.*

**pantomime dame** /– 'deɪm/, *n.* a coarse, ludicrous female character in a pantomime, traditionally played by a man.

**pantomimist** /'pæntəmaɪməst/, *n.* **1.** one who acts in pantomime. **2.** the author of a pantomime.

**pantothenic acid** /ˌpæntəθɛnɪk 'æsəd/, *n.* an oily hydroxy acid, $HOCH_2C(CH)_2CHOHCONHCH_2CH_2COOH$, found in plant and animal tissues, rice, bran, etc., which is essential for cell growth, and is a constituent of coenzyme A.

**pantoufle** /pæn'tufəl/, *n.* →**pantofle.**

**pantry** /'pæntri/, *n., pl.* **-tries.** a room or cupboard in which bread and other provisions, or silverware, dishes, etc., are kept. [ME *panetrie,* from AF, from OF *panetier* servant in charge of bread, from L *pānis* bread]

**pants** /pænts/, *n.pl.* **1.** trousers. **2.** women's underpants. **3. get into (someone's) pants,** *Colloq.* to have sexual intercourse with. [familiar abbrev. of PANTALOONS]

**pants man** /'– mæn/, *n. Colloq.* a woman-chaser.

**pants part** /'– pat/, *n.* a role, esp. in opera, in which a woman is required to play the part of a man and dress accordingly. Also, **pants role.**

**pants-suit** /'pænts-sut/, *n.* a slacks suit.

**pantun** /pæn'tun/, *n.* a Malay verse form, usu. of four lines, the third rhyming with the first, and the fourth with the second. Also, **pantoum** /pæn'tum/. [Malay]

**panzer** /'pænzə/, *adj.* **1.** armoured: *a panzer division.* –*n.* **2.** a tank. [G]

**pap**[1] /pæp/, *n.* **1.** soft food for infants or invalids, as bread soaked in water or milk. **2.** books, ideas, talk, etc., considered as having no intellectual or permanent value; rubbish; tripe. [ME. Cf. LG *pappe,* ML *pappa*]

**pap**[2] /pæp/, *n.* **1.** a teat or nipple. **2.** something resembling a teat or nipple. [ME *pappe.* Cf. d. Norw. and Swed. *pappe*]

**papa**[1] /pə'pa/, *n.* →**father.** [F, from L. Cf. It. *pappa,* Gk *páppas*]

**papa**[2] /'papə/, *n. N.Z.* a blue clay rock. Also, **papa rock.** [Maori]

**papacy** /'peɪpəsi/, *n., pl.* **-cies. 1.** the office, dignity, or jurisdiction of the pope. **2.** the system of ecclesiastical government in which the pope is recognised as the supreme head. **3.** the time during which a pope is in office. **4.** the succession or line of the popes. [ME, from ML *pāpātia,* from *pāpa* pope, father]

**papain** /pə'peɪən/, *n.* **1.** *Biochem.* a proteolytic enzyme contained in the fruit of the papaya tree, *Carica papaya.* **2.** a commercial preparation of this, used as a digestant. [PAPA(YA) + -IN[2]]

**papal** /'peɪpəl/, *adj.* of or pertaining to the pope, the papacy, or the Roman Catholic Church. [ME, from ML *pāpālis,* from *pāpa* pope]

**papal cross** /– 'krɒs/, *n.* a cross with three horizontal crosspieces.

**papal knight** /– 'naɪt/, *n.* a member of the laity of the Roman Catholic Church who has had a pontifical order of knighthood conferred on him by the pope.

**papal nuncio** /– 'nʌnsioʊ/, *n.* →**nuncio.**

**Papanicolaou smear** /pæpə'nɪkəlaʊ smɪə/, *n.* →**Pap smear.** [from George *Papanicolaou,* 1883-1962, U.S. scientist, who invented this test]

**paparazzo** /papə'ratsoʊ/, *n., pl.* **-razzi** /-'ratsi/. a news photographer or reporter who seeks sensational but essentially trivial material with great persistence.

**papaveraceous** /pəpeɪvə'reɪʃəs/, *adj.* belonging to the Papaveraceae, or poppy family of plants. [L *papāver* poppy + -ACEOUS]

**papaverine** /pə'peɪvərin/, *n.* a fine, odourless, crystalline, white alkaloid, $C_{20}H_{21}NO_4$, derived from opium, which relaxes the involuntary muscles of the gastrointestinal tract, and other smooth muscles. Also, **papaverin** /pə'peɪvərən/.

**papaw** /'pɔpɔ/, *n.* →**pawpaw.**

**papaya** /pə'paɪə/, *n.* →**pawpaw.**

**paper** /'peɪpə/, *n.* **1.** a substance made from rags, straw, wood, or other fibrous material, usu. in thin sheets, for writing or printing on, wrapping things in, etc. **2.** something resembling this substance, as papyrus. **3.** a piece, sheet, or leaf of paper, esp. one bearing writing. **4.** a written or printed document or instrument. **5.** →**wallpaper. 6.** negotiable notes, bills, etc., collectively: *commercial paper.* **7.** (*pl.*)

documents establishing identity, status, etc. **8.** (*pl.*) the documents required to be carried by a ship for the manifestation of her ownership, nationality, destination, etc.; ship's papers. **9.** a set of questions for an examination, or an individual set of written answers to them. **10.** an essay, article, or dissertation on a particular topic. **11.** a newspaper or journal. **12. on paper, a.** confirmed in writing. **b.** in the planning or design stage. **c.** in theory rather than practice: *it seems all right on paper, but will it work?* *–v.t.* **13.** to decorate (a wall, room, etc.) with wallpaper. **14.** to line with paper: *to paper a shelf.* **15.** to fold, enclose, or put up in paper. **16.** to supply with paper. **17. paper over,** to try to hide something. **18.** to sandpaper. *–adj.* **19.** made or consisting of paper: *a paper bag.* **20.** paper-like; thin; flimsy; frail. **21.** pertaining to, or carried on by means of, letters, articles, books, etc.; *a paper war.* **22.** written or printed on paper. **23.** existing on paper only and not in reality: *paper profits.* [ME and OE, from L *papȳrus* paper, PAPYRUS] – **paper-like,** *adj.*

**paperback** /ˈpeɪpəbæk/, *n.* **1.** a book bound in a flexible paper cover, usu. cheaper than a hardback of comparable length. *–adj.* **2.** of, denoting, or pertaining to such books or the publishing of such books. *–v.t.* **3.** to publish as a paperback.

**paperbark** /ˈpeɪpəbak/, *n.* **1.** a form of bark, consisting of numerous thin layers of corky material, some parts of which peel off irregularly. **2.** a tree bearing such bark, esp. the broad-leaved tea-trees of the genus *Melaleuca.*

paperbark: flower and leaf

**paper birch** /ˈpeɪpə bɜtʃ/, *n.* the North American birch, *Betula papyrifera,* a tall tree with tough bark and valuable wood. Also, **white birch.**

**paperbound** /ˈpeɪpəbaʊnd/, *adj.* →**paperback.**

**paperboy** /ˈpeɪpəbɔɪ/, *n.* a boy employed to deliver or sell newspapers, etc.

**paperchase** /ˈpeɪpətʃeɪs/, *n.* an outdoor game in which one or more players set off in advance, laying a trail of paper for their pursuers to follow.

**paper chromatography** /ˌpeɪpə kroʊməˈtɒgrəfi/, *n.* a method of chemically analysing mixtures which depends on the different rates at which compounds in solution migrate across a sheet of porous paper specially prepared with indicators.

**paperclip** /ˈpeɪpəklɪp/, *n.* a piece of wire bent into a clip designed to hold together papers, etc.

**paperdaisy** /ˈpeɪpədeɪzi/, *n.* any of many species of daisy, esp. species of the genera *Helichrysum* and *Helipterum,* with radiating, usu. white or yellow, petal-like bracts.

**paperer** /ˈpeɪpərə/, *n.* **1.** →**paperhanger** (def. 1). **2.** one who papers.

**paperhanger** /ˈpeɪpəhæŋə/, *n.* **1.** one whose business it is to cover or decorate walls with wallpaper. **2.** *Prison Colloq.* one who passes valueless cheques. – **paperhanging,** *n.*

**paperknife** /ˈpeɪpənaɪf/, *n.* a knifelike instrument with a blade of metal, ivory, wood, or the like, for cutting open the leaves of books, folded papers, etc.

**paper money** /ˈpeɪpə mʌni/, *n.* money in the form of banknotes.

**paper mulberry** /– ˈmʌlbəri/, *n.* a small tree of eastern Asia, *Broussonetia papyrifera,* the inner bark of which was formerly used for making paper in Japan, and is still used in Polynesia for making a kind of cloth.

**paper nautilus** /– ˈnɔtələs/, *n.* any dibranchiate cephalopod of the genus *Argonauta,* characterised by the delicate shell of the female; argonaut.

**paper shop** /ˈ– ʃɒp/, *n.* a newsagent's shop.

**paperstand** /ˈpeɪpəstænd/, *n.* a booth, stall or stand, generally in a public place, where newspapers, etc., are sold.

**paper tape** /ˈpeɪpə teɪp/, *n.* a ribbon of paper through which a pattern of holes is punched to represent information in a form which can be fed into a computer.

**paper tiger** /– ˈtaɪgə/, *n.* one who or that which has the appearance of strength, power, or aggressiveness, but is in fact weak or ineffectual.

**paperweight** /ˈpeɪpəweɪt/, *n.* a small, heavy object laid on papers to keep them from being scattered.

**paperwork** /ˈpeɪpəwɜk/, *n.* written or clerical work, as the keeping of records, esp. considered as an essential but uninteresting part of some occupation.

**papery** /ˈpeɪpəri/, *adj.* like paper; thin or flimsy.

**papeterie** /ˈpæpətri/, *n.* a case or box of paper and other materials for writing. [F, from *papetier* one who makes or sells paper, from *papier* PAPER]

**papier collé** /ˌpæpieɪ ˈkɒleɪ/, *n., pl.* **papiers collés** /ˌpæpieɪ ˈkɒleɪ/. a collage made from paper. [F]

**papier-mâché** /peɪpə-ˈmæʃeɪ/, *n.* **1.** a substance made of pulped paper or paper pulp mixed with glue and other materials, or of layers of paper glued and pressed together, moulded when moist to form various articles, and becoming hard and strong when dry. *–adj.* **2.** made of papier-mâché. [F: chewed paper]

**papilionaceous** /pəˌpɪliəˈneɪʃəs/, *adj.* **1.** having an irregular corolla shaped somewhat like a butterfly, as the pea and other leguminous plants. **2.** belonging to the family Papilionaceae. [NL *pāpiliōnāceus,* from L *pāpilio* butterfly]

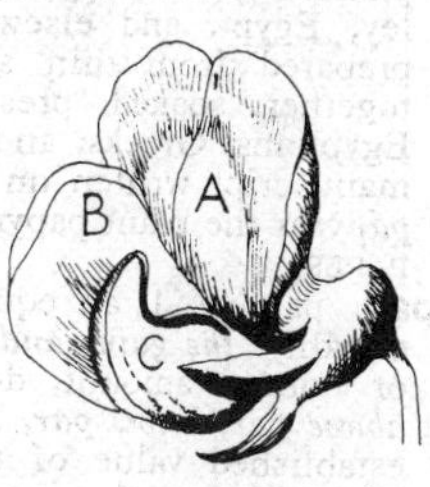

papilionaceous flower of bean: A, vexillum; B, wing; C, keel or carina

**papilla** /pəˈpɪlə/, *n., pl.* **-pillae** /-ˈpɪli/. **1.** any small nipple-like process or projection. **2.** one of certain small protuberances concerned with the senses of touch, taste, and smell: *the papillae of the tongue.* **3.** a small vascular process at the root of a hair. **4.** a papule or pimple. [L: nipple]

**papillary** /pəˈpɪləri/, *adj.* **1.** of or pertaining to, or of the nature of, a papilla or papillae. **2.** provided or furnished with papillae.

**papilloma** /pæpəˈloʊmə/, *n., pl.* **-mata** /-mətə/, **-mas.** a tumour of skin or mucous membrane, consisting of a hypertrophied papilla or group of papillae, as a wart or a corn. [PAPILL(A)· + -OMA]

**papillon** /ˈpæpəlɒn/, *n.* a variety of toy spaniel having large ears which are thought to resemble the wings of a butterfly. [F: butterfly]

**papillose** /ˈpæpəloʊs/, *adj.* full of papillae. – **papillosity** /pæpəˈlɒsəti/, *n.*

**papillote** /ˈpæpəlɒt/, *n.* a decorative curled paper, put at the end of the bone of a cutlet, chop, or the like. [F, from *papillon* butterfly, from L *pāpilio*]

**papism** /ˈpeɪpɪzəm/, *n.* (*usu. derog.*) →**Roman Catholicism.**

**papist** /ˈpeɪpəst/, *n.* **1.** an adherent of the pope. **2.** (*usu. derog.*) a member of the Roman Catholic Church. *–adj.* **3.** papistical. [NL *pāpista,* from L *pāpa* POPE[1]]

**papistical** /pəˈpɪstɪkəl/, *adj.* (*usu. derog.*) of, pertaining to, or characteristic of papists or papistry. Also, **papistic.**

**papistry** /ˈpeɪpəstri/, *n.* (*usu. derog.*) the systems, doctrines, or practices of papists.

**papoose** /pəˈpus/, *n.* **1.** a North American Indian baby or young child. **2.** *Colloq.* any baby. Also, **pappoose.** [Algonquian *papeisses,* from *peisses* child]

**pappadum** /ˈpæpədʌm/, *n.* a thin, crisp Indian wafer bread, made from spiced potato or rice flour. Also, **pappadam, poppadum.** [Hindi]

**pappose** /ˈpæpoʊs, pæˈpoʊs/, *adj.* **1.** having or forming a pappus. **2.** downy. Also, **pappous** /ˈpæpəs/.

**pappus** /ˈpæpəs/, *n., pl.* **pappi** /ˈpæpaɪ/. a downy, bristly, or tufty appendage of the achene of certain plants, as the dandelion and the thistle. [L, from Gk *páppos* down on seeds, orig. grandfather]

**pappy**[1] /ˈpæpi/, *adj.,* **-pier, -piest.** like pap; mushy.

**pappy**[2] /ˈpæpi/, *n. Chiefly Southern U.S.* father.

**paprika** /ˈpæprɪkə, pəˈprikə/, *n.* **1.** the dried fruit of a cultivated form of *Capsicum frutescens,* ground as a condiment, much less pungent than ordinary red pepper. **2.** →**capsicum** [Hung.]

**Pap smear** /ˈpæp smɪə/, *n.* a medical test in which a smear of a bodily secretion, esp. from the cervix or vagina, is used to detect cancer in an early stage or to evaluate hormonal condition; cervical smear. [abbreviated form of PAPANICOLAOU SMEAR]

**Papuan** /ˈpæpjuən/, *n.* **1.** a native or inhabitant of Papua New Guinea. **2.** any of several languages of Papua New Guinea which do not appear to belong to the Austronesian family.

**Papua New Guinea,** *n.* a country in the eastern half of the island of New Guinea; an independent member of the Commonwealth. Official name: **Independent State of Papua New Guinea.** – **Papua New Guinean,** *adj., n.*

**papule** /ˈpæpjul/, *n.* a small, somewhat pointed elevation of the skin, usu. inflammatory but not suppurative. [L *papula* pustule, pimple]

**papyraceous** /pæpəˈreɪʃəs/, *adj.* papery.

**papyrology** /pæpəˈrɒlədʒi/, *n.* the study of papyri.

**papyrus** /pəˈpaɪrəs/, *n., pl.* **-pyri** /-ˈpaɪraɪ/. **1.** a tall aquatic plant, *Cyperus papyrus,* of the sedge family, of the Nile valley, Egypt, and elsewhere. **2.** a material for writing on, prepared from thin strips of the pith of this plant laid together, soaked, pressed, and dried, used by the ancient Egyptians, Greeks, and Romans. **3.** an ancient document or manuscript written on this material. [ME, from L, from Gk *pápȳros* the plant papyrus, something made from papyrus. Cf. PAPER]

**par**[1] /pa/, *n.* **1.** an equality in value or standing; a level of equality: *the gains and the losses are on a par.* **2.** an average or normal amount, degree, quality, condition, or the like: *above par, below par, on a par with.* **3.** *Comm.* **a.** the legally established value of the monetary unit of one country in terms of that of another using the same metal as a standard of value (**mint par of exchange**). **b.** the state of the shares of any business, undertaking, loan, etc., when they may be purchased at the original price (called **issue par**) or at their face value (called **nominal par**). Such shares or bonds are said to be at par. Shares or bonds sold or acquired at a premium are said to be **above par**, and at a discount, **below par.** **4.** *Golf.* the number of strokes allowed to a hole or course as representing a target standard. *–adj.* **5.** average or expected, normal: *par for the course.* **6.** *Comm.* at or pertaining to par: *the par value of a bond.* **7.** *Bridge.* (of a bid or play) best possible. [L: equal]

**par**[2] /pa/, *n. Colloq.* a paragraph.

**par.,** parallel.

**para-**[1], **1.** a prefix meaning 'beside', 'near', 'beyond', 'aside', 'amiss', and sometimes implying alteration or modification, occurring originally in words from the Greek, but used also as a modern formative, chiefly in scientific words. **2.** *Chem.* indicating a compound containing a benzene ring substituted in the 1,4 positions. Also, before vowels, **par-.** [Gk, combining form of *pará,* prep.]

**para-**[2], a prefix of a few words meaning 'guard against', as in *parachute.* [F, from It., impv. of *parare* defend against, from L *parāre* prepare]

**para-**[3], a prefix meaning 'parachute', as in *paratroops.* [shortened form of PARACHUTE]

**para.,** paragraph.

**parabiosis** /pærəbaɪˈoʊsəs/, *n.* experimental or natural union of two individuals with exchange of blood. – **parabiotic** /pærəbaɪˈɒtɪk/, *adj.*

**parable** /ˈpærəbəl/, *n.* **1.** a short allegorical story, designed to convey some truth or moral lesson. **2.** a discourse or saying conveying the intended meaning by a comparison or under the likeness of something comparable or analogous. [ME *parabil,* from LL *parabola* comparison, parable, proverb, word, from Gk *parabolḗ* a placing beside, comparison]

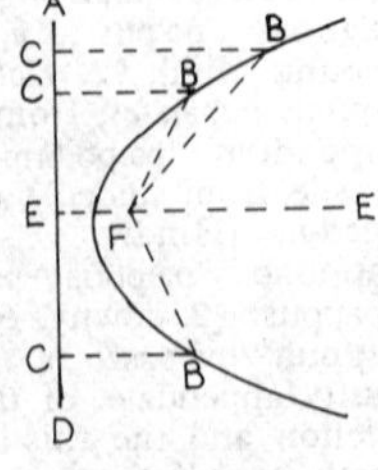


common parabola: AD, directrix; F, focus; B, point on parabola; BC, always equal to BF; EE, axis

**parabola** /pəˈræbələ/, *n. Geom.* a plane curve formed by the intersection of a right circular cone with a plane parallel to a generator of the cone. [NL, from Gk *parabolḗ.* See PARABLE]

**parabolic**[1] /pærəˈbɒlɪk/, *adj.* **1.** having the form or outline of a parabola. **2.** pertaining to or resembling a parabola. [ME, from LL *parabolicus,* from LGk *parabolikós* figurative]

**parabolic**[2] /pærəˈbɒlɪk/, *adj.* of, pertaining to, or involving a parable. Also, **parabolical.** [see PARABOLIC[1], PARABLE] – **parabolically,** *adv.*

**parabolic aerial** /– ˈɛəriəl/, *n.* an aerial used esp. in radar and radio telescopes, consisting of a large concave mirror the reflective surface of which has the shape of a paraboloid.

**parabolise**[1] /pəˈræbəlaɪz/, *v.t.,* **-lised, -lising.** to make paraboloid. Also, **parabolize.**

**parabolise**[2] /pəˈræbəlaɪz/, *v.t.,* **-lised, -lising.** to explain by means of a parable. Also, **parabolize.**

**paraboloid** /pəˈræbəlɔɪd/, *n.* a solid or surface generated by the revolution of a parabola about its axis, or one of the second degree some of whose plane sections are parabolas. – **paraboloidal** /pəræbəˈlɔɪdl/, *adj.*

**parabrake** /ˈpærəbreɪk/, *n.* →**parachute brake.**

**paracentesis** /pærəsɛnˈtisəs/, *n.* tapping of fluid from a body cavity.

**paracetamol** /pærəˈsitəmɒl/, *n.* an analgesic drug similar to phenacetin in its actions. [from *para-acetamidophenol*]

**parachute** /ˈpærəʃut/, *n., v.,* **-chuted, -chuting.** *–n.* **1.** an apparatus used in descending safely through the air, esp. from an aircraft, being umbrella-like in form and rendered effective by the resistance of the air, which expands it during the descent and then reduces the velocity of its motion. *–adj.* **2.** dropped by parachute: *parachute troops, a parachute mine.* *–v.t.* **3.** to land (troops, equipment, etc.) by parachute. *–v.i.* **4.** to descend by or as by parachute. [F, from *para-* PARA-[2] + *chute* a fall. See CHUTE[1]] – **parachutist,** *n.*

**parachute brake** /ˈ– breɪk/, *n.* a parachute which opens at the rear of an aircraft or the like to act as a brake on landing. Also, **parabrake.**

**paraclete** /ˈpærəklit/, *n.* **1.** one called in to aid; an advocate or intercessor. **2.** (*cap.*) the Holy Spirit, or Comforter. [LL *paraclētus,* from Gk *paráklētos*]

**paracymene** /pærəˈsaɪmin/, *n.* the most common form of cymene, found in several essential oils, as oil of eucalyptus.

**parade** /pəˈreɪd/, *n., v.,* **-raded, -rading.** *–n.* **1.** show, display, or ostentation: *to make a parade of one's emotions.* **2.** the orderly assembly of troops, boy scouts, or any other body, for inspection, display, or any other purpose. **3.** the troops, etc., so assembled. **4.** a military ceremony involving the marching of troop units and a mass salute at the lowering of the flag at the end of the day. **5.** a public procession for display, as to draw attention to a political party, celebrate an anniversary, etc. **6.** a promenade; a walk for pleasure or display. **7.** a body of people promenading. **8.** any street so called. **9.** a row or block of shops, etc., esp. one having a service road. **10.** *Fort.* the level space forming the interior or enclosed area of a fortification. **11.** *Fencing.* a parry. *–v.t.* **12.** to make parade of; display ostentatiously. **13.** to walk up and down on or in. **14.** to cause to march or proceed for display. **15.** to cause to assemble, as troops. *–v.i.* **16.** to march or proceed with display. **17.** to promenade in a public place to show oneself. **18.** to assemble in military order. [F, from Sp. *parada,* from *parar,* from L *parāre* prepare]

**parade ground** /ˈ– graʊnd/, *n.* a place where troops regularly assemble for parade.

**paradichlorobenzene** /ˌpærədaɪˌklɔroʊˈbɛnzin/, *n.* a white crystalline compound, $C_6H_4Cl_2$, of the benzene series, used as a moth repellent.

**paradigm** /ˈpærədaɪm/, *n.* **1.** *Gram.* **a.** the set of all forms containing a particular element, esp. the set of all inflected forms of a single root, stem, or theme. For example: *boy, boys, boy's, boys'* constitutes the paradigm of the noun *boy.* **b.** a display in fixed arrangement of such a set. **2.** a pattern; an example. [late ME, from LL *paradīgma,* from Gk *parádeigma* pattern] – **paradigmatic** /pærədɪgˈmætɪk/, **paradigmatical** /pærədɪgˈmætɪkəl/, *adj.* – **paradigmatically** /pærədɪgˈmætɪkli/, *adv.*

**paradisaical** /pærədəˈseɪəkəl/, *adj.* →**paradisiacal.** Also, **paradisaic.** – **paradisaically,** *adv.*

**paradise** /ˈpærədaɪs/, *n.* **1.** heaven, as the final abode of the righteous. **2.** (according to some) an intermediate place for the departed souls of the righteous awaiting resurrection. **3.** a place of extreme beauty or delight. **4.** supreme felicity. **5.**

See **bird of paradise.** [ME *paradis,* from LL *paradīsus,* from Gk *parádeisos* park, from OPers. *pairidaēza* enclosure]

**paradise duck** /– ˈdʌk/, *n.* a large brightly coloured duck, *Casarca variegata,* native to New Zealand.

**paradise fish** /ˈ– fɪʃ/, *n.* a beautifully coloured fish of either of two species of the genus *Macropodus,* often kept in aquariums.

**paradisiacal** /pærədəˈsaɪəkəl/, *adj.* of, like, or befitting paradise. Also, **paradisiac** /pærəˈdɪziæk/. [LL *paradīsiacus* of paradise + -AL[1]] – **paradisiacally,** *adv.*

**parados** /ˈpærədɒs/, *n.* the bank behind a trench that protects men from fire and from being seen against the skyline. [F, from *para-* PARA-[2] + *dos* back]

**paradox** /ˈpærədɒks/, *n.* **1.** a statement or proposition seemingly self-contradictory or absurd, and yet explicable as expressing a truth. **2.** a self-contradictory and false proposition. **3.** any person or thing exhibiting apparent contradictions. **4.** an opinion or statement contrary to received opinion. [L *paradoxum,* from Gk *parádoxon,* neut. of *parádoxos* contrary to received opinion, incredible] – **paradoxical** /pærəˈdɒksɪkəl/, *adj.* – **paradoxically** /pærəˈdɒksɪkli/, *adv.* – **paradoxicalness** /pærəˈdɒksɪkəlnəs/, *n.*

**paradrop** /ˈpærədrɒp/, *n.* an airdrop by means of parachute. [PARA-[3] + DROP (def. 18)]

**paraesthesia** /pærisˈθiziə, -ˈθiʒə/, *n.* abnormal sensation, as prickling, itching, etc. Also, *Chiefly U.S.,* **paresthesia.** [PAR(A)-[1] + Gk *aisthēsía* sensation] – **paraesthetic** /pærisˈθɛtɪk/, *adj.*

**paraffin** /ˈpærəfən/, *n.* **1.** *Chem.* any hydrocarbon of the methane series having general formula $C_NH_{2N+2}$. **2.** →**paraffin oil** (def. 1). **3.** *Brit.* →**kerosene.** **4.** →**paraffin wax.** [G, from L *par(um)* not enough + *affin(is)* related; so called from its lack of affinity for other substances]

**paraffine** /ˈpærəfin/, *n., v.t.,* **-fined, -fining.** →**paraffin.**

**paraffin oil** /ˈpærəfən ɔɪl/, *n.* **1.** Also, **liquid paraffin.** a thick colourless mixture of hydrocarbons obtained from petroleum used as a laxative. **2.** any oil containing hydrocarbons obtained from the distillation of petroleum; mineral oil. **3.** *Brit.* →**kerosene.**

**paraffin wax** /ˈ– wæks/, *n.* a white translucent solid with a melting point in the range 50°-60°C, consisting of the higher members of the paraffin series; used for candles, waxed papers, polishes, etc.

**paraformaldehyde** /pærəfɔˈmældəhaɪd/, *n.* a colourless non-crystalline polymer of formaldehyde, $(CH_2O)_3$, used as an antiseptic. Also, **paraform** /ˈpærəfɔm/.

**paragenesis** /pærəˈdʒɛnəsəs/, *n.* the origin and associations of a mineral or a mineral deposit. Also, **paragenesia** /pærədʒəˈniziə/. [PARA-[1] + GENESIS] – **paragenetic** /pærədʒəˈnɛtɪk/, *adj.* – **paragenetically** /pærədʒəˈnɛtɪkli/, *adv.*

**paragoge** /pærəˈgoʊdʒi/, *n.* (in linguistic change) the addition of a syllable, phoneme, or other element not originally present, at the end of a word, as the substandard pronunciation of *height* as *height-th,* the standard showing no change. [LL, from Gk: a leading past] – **paragogic** /pærəˈgɒdʒɪk/, *adj.*

**paragon** /ˈpærəgən/, *n.* **1.** a model or pattern of excellence, or of a particular excellence. **2.** *Print.* a type size (20 points). **3.** an unusually large round pearl. **4.** a perfect diamond weighing 100 carats or more. [MF, from It. *paragone* touchstone, comparison, paragon]

**paragraph** /ˈpærəgræf, -graf/, *n.* **1.** a distinct portion of written or printed matter dealing with a particular point, and usu. beginning (commonly with indention) on a new line. **2.** a character (now usu. ¶) used to indicate the beginning of a distinct or separate portion of a text, or as a mark of reference. **3.** a note, item, or brief article, as in a newspaper. *–v.t.* **4.** to divide into paragraphs. **5.** to write or publish paragraphs about. **6.** to express in a paragraph. [LL *paragraphus,* from Gk *parágraphos* line or mark in the margin]

**paragrapher** /ˈpærəgræfə/, *n.* one who writes paragraphs, as for a newspaper. Also, **paragraphist.**

**paragraphia** /pærəˈgræfiə/, *n.* a cerebral disorder marked by the writing of words or letters other than those intended, or the loss of ability to express ideas in writing. [NL, from Gk *para-* PARA-[1] + *-graphía* writing]

**paragraphic** /pærəˈgræfɪk/, *adj.* **1.** of, pertaining to, or forming a paragraph. **2.** divided into paragraphs. **3.** of or pertaining to paragraphia. Also, **paragraphical.** – **paragraphically,** *adv.*

**para grass** /ˈpærə gras/, *n.* a tropical pasture grass, *Brachiaria mutica,* native to Africa, which thrives in wet conditions.

**Paraguay** /ˈpærəgwaɪ/, *n.* a republic in central South America between Bolivia, Brazil, and Argentina. – **Paraguayan** /pærəˈgwaɪən/, *adj., n.*

**Paraguay tea** /– ˈti/, *n.* →**maté.**

**parahydrogen** /pærəˈhaɪdrədʒən/, *n.* a form of molecular hydrogen in which the spins of the two constituent atoms are antiparallel.

**parakeelya** /pærəˈkiljə/, *n.* any of several species of succulent herbs of the genus *Calandrinia* of inland Australia, with large rose-purple flowers.

**parakeet** /ˈpærəkit/, *n.* any of the numerous small, slender parrots, usu. with a long, pointed, graduated tail, as the budgerigar, *Melopsittacus undulatus.* Also, **paraquet, paroquet, parrakeet, parroket, parroquet.** [It. *parochito,* var. of *parrochetto,* diminutive of *parroco* parson]

parakeet

**paralalia** /pærəˈleɪliə/, *n.* a speech disturbance, esp. the substitution of one sound for another. [NL, from Gk *para-* PARA-[1] + *laliá* talking]

**paralanguage** /ˈpærəlæŋgwɪdʒ/, *n.* the paralinguistic aspects of language.

**paraldehyde** /pəˈrældəhaɪd/, *n.* a colourless liquid, $(CH_3CHO)_3$, formed by polymerisation of acetaldehyde, and used as a hypnotic. [PAR(A)-[1] + ALDEHYDE]

**paralegal** /pærəˈligəl/, *adj.* related to the legal profession in a supplementary capacity, often used of legal workers who are not formally qualified.

**paralexia** /pærəˈlɛksiə/, *n.* inability to read, characterised by the substitution or transposition of words or characters. – **paralexic,** *adj.*

**paralinguistic** /pærəlɪŋˈgwɪstɪk/, *adj.* of or pertaining to factors associated with but not essentially part of a language system as tone of voice, rate of utterance, overall pitch range, facial expressions, accompanying speech, etc.

**paralinguistics** /pærəlɪŋˈgwɪstɪks/, *n.* the study of paralinguistic phenomena.

**paralipsis** /pærəˈlɪpsəs/, *n., pl.* **-ses** /-siz/. a pretended ignoring, for rhetorical effect, of something actually spoken of, as in 'not to mention other faults'. Also, **paraleipsis** /pærəˈlaɪpsəs/. [NL, from Gk *paráleipsis* a passing over]

**parallax** /ˈpærəlæks/, *n.* **1.** the apparent displacement of an observed object due to a change or difference in position of the observer. **2. diurnal** or **geocentric parallax,** the apparent displacement of a heavenly body due to its being observed from the surface instead of from the centre of the earth. **3. annual** or **heliocentric parallax,** the apparent displacement of a heavenly body due to its being observed from the earth instead of from the sun. **4.** apparent change in the position of crosshairs as viewed through a telescope, when the focusing is imperfect. [Gk *parállaxis* change] – **parallactic** /pærəˈlæktɪk/, *adj.* – **parallactically** /pærəˈlæktɪkli/, *adv.*


geocentric parallax of the moon; A, parallax; B, observer; C, centre of earth; D, moon; C[1], image of C; B[1], image of B

**parallel** /ˈpærəlɛl/, *adj., n., v.,* **-leled, -leling** or **-lelled, -lelling.** *–adj.* **1.** having the same direction, course, or tendency; corresponding; similar; analogous: *parallel forces.* **2.** *Geom.* **a.** (of straight lines) lying in the same plane but never meeting no matter how far extended. **b.** (of planes) having common perpendiculars. **c.** (of a single line, plane, etc.) equidistant from another or others at all corresponding points (fol. by *to* or *with*). **3.** *Music.* **a.** (of two voice parts) progressing so that the interval between them remains the same. **b.** (of a tonality or key) having the same tonic but differing in mode. **4.** *Computers, etc.* denoting or pertaining to a system in which several activities are carried on concurrently. **5.** *Elect.* consisting of or having component parts connected in parallel. *–n.* **6.** anything parallel in direction, course, or tendency. **7.** a parallel line or plane. **8.** *Geog.* **a.** a circle on the earth's surface formed by the intersection of a plane parallel to the plane of the equator, bearing east and west and designated in degrees of latitude north or south of the equator along the arc of any meridian. **b.** the line representing this circle on a chart or map. **9.** a match or counterpart. **10.** correspondence or analogy. **11.** a comparison of things as if regarded side by side. **12.** *Print.* a pair of vertical parallel lines (||) used as a mark of reference. **13.** *Elect.* a connection of two or more circuits in which all ends having the same instantaneous polarity are electrically connected together and all ends having the opposite polarity are similarly connected. The element circuits are said to be **in parallel** (opposed to *in series*). **14.** *Fort.* a trench cut in the ground before a fortress, parallel to its defences, for the purpose of covering a besieging force. *–v.t.* **15.** to make parallel. **16.** to furnish a parallel for; find or provide a match for. **17.** to form a parallel to; be equivalent to; equal. **18.** to compare. [L *parallēlus*, from Gk *parállēlos* beside one another]

**parallel bars** /– 'baz/, *n.pl.* a gymnasium apparatus consisting of two wooden bars on uprights, adjustable in height, and used for swinging, vaulting, balancing exercises, etc.

**parallelepiped** /ˌpærəlɛlə'paɪpəd, pærələ'lɛpəpɛd/, *n.* a prism with six faces, all parallelograms. Also, **parallelepipedon** /ˌpærəlɛlə 'pɪpədən/. [Gk *parallēle pípedon* body with parallel surfaces]

parallelepiped

**parallelism** /'pærəlɛlɪzəm/, *n.* **1.** the position or relation of parallels. **2.** agreement in direction, tendency, or character. **3.** a parallel or comparison. **4.** a resemblance, or close correspondence. **5.** *Metaphys.* the doctrine that mental and bodily processes are concomitant, each varying with variation of the other, but that there is no causal relation or relation of interaction between the two series of changes.

**parallelist** /'pærəlɛləst/, *n.* **1.** a believer in the doctrine of parallelism. **2.** one who draws a parallel or comparison.

**parallelogram** /pærə'lɛləgræm/, *n.* a quadrilateral the opposite sides of which are parallel. [Gk *parallēlógrammon*, properly neut. of *parallēlógrammos* bounded by parallel lines]

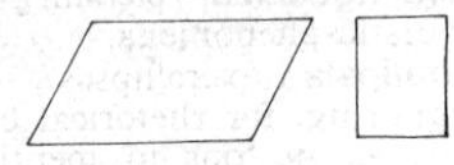

parallelograms

**parallelogram of forces,** *n.* a parallelogram drawn in such a manner that two adjacent sides represent two forces acting on a body, both in magnitude and direction; the diagonal of this parallelogram then represents the resultant of these two forces.

**paralogism** /pə'rælədʒɪzəm/, *n.* **1.** a piece of false or fallacious reasoning, esp. (as distinguished from *sophism*) one of whose falseness the reasoner is not conscious. **2.** reasoning of this kind. [Gk *paralogismós* false reasoning] – **paralogist,** *n.* – **paralogistic** /pərælə'dʒɪstɪk/, *adj.*

**paralyse** /'pærəlaɪz/, *v.t.*, **-lysed, -lysing. 1.** to affect with paralysis. **2.** to bring to a condition of helpless inactivity. Also, *U.S.*, **paralyze.** – **paralysation** /pærəlaɪ'zeɪʃən/, *n.* – **paralyser,** *n.*

**paralysis** /pə'ræləsəs/, *n.*, *pl.* **-ses** /-siz/. **1.** *Pathol.* **a.** loss of power of a voluntary muscular contraction. **b.** a disease characterised by this; palsy. **2.** a more or less complete crippling, as of powers or activities: *a paralysis of trade.* [L, from Gk: palsy]

**paralysis agitans** /– 'ædʒətænz/, *n.* →**Parkinson's disease.** [L PARALYSIS + *agitans*, ppr. of *agitare* excite]

**paralytic** /pærə'lɪtɪk/, *n.* **1.** one affected with general paralysis. *–adj.* **2.** affected with or subject to paralysis. **3.** pertaining to or of the nature of paralysis. **4.** *Colloq.* completely intoxicated with alcoholic drink; very drunk.

**paramagnetic** /pærəmæg'nɛtɪk/, *adj.* denoting or pertaining to a class of substances as liquid oxygen, which are magnetic like iron, though to a much lesser degree (distinguished from *ferromagnetic* and opposed to *diamagnetic*). [PARA-[1] + MAGNETIC]

**paramagnetism** /pærə'mægnətɪzəm/, *n.* the property of substances, as liquid oxygen, which are magnetic like iron though to a much lesser degree.

**paramatta** /pærə'mætə/, *n.* →**parramatta.**

**paramecium** /pærə'misiəm/, *n.*, *pl.* **-cia** /-siə/. a ciliate infusorian having an oval body and deep long oral groove, inhabiting fresh water and widely distributed in a number of species. [NL, from Gk *paramḗkēs* oblong]

**paramedic**[1] /pærə'mɛdɪk/, *adj.* **1.** →**paramedical.** *–n.* **2.** a person who performs paramedical services.

**paramedic**[2] /pærə'mɛdɪk/, *n. U.S.* a doctor or medical orderly who parachutes in to a place where medical supplies and attention are needed. [PARA(CHUTE) + MEDIC[2]]

**paramedical** /pærə'mɛdɪkəl/, *adj.* related to the medical profession in a supplementary capacity, as an ambulance man, etc.

**paramenstruum** /pærə'mɛnstruəm/, *n.* the period of the menstrual cycle, which includes the four days on either side of the onset of menstruation.

**parameter** /pə'ræmətə/, *n.* **1.** any constituent variable quality: *the parameters of voice quality include breathiness and degree of nasality.* **2.** *Maths.* a variable entering into the mathematical form of any distribution such that the possible values of the variable correspond to different distributions. **3.** *Maths.* one of the independent variables in a set of parametric equations. **4.** *Maths.* a variable which may be kept constant while the effect of other variables is investigated. – **parametric** /pærə'mɛtrɪk/, *adj.*

**parametric equation** /pærəˌmɛtrɪk ə'kweɪʒən/, *n.* one of two or more mathematical equations in which the coordinates of points on a curve or surface are given in terms of one or more variables (parameters, def. 3) of that curve or surface.

**paramilitary** /pærə'mɪlətri/, *adj.* of, pertaining to, or denoting an organisation having a military structure and used as a supplementary force to regular troops.

**paramo** /'pærəmoʊ/, *n.* a high plateau region in tropical South America, esp. one bare of trees. [Sp.]

**paramorph** /'pærəmɔf/, *n.* a pseudomorph formed by a change in crystal structure but not in chemical composition. – **paramorphic** /pærə'mɔfɪk/, *adj.*

**paramorphism** /pærə'mɔfɪzəm/, *n.* **1.** the process by which a paramorph is formed. **2.** the state of being a paramorph.

**paramount** /'pærəmaʊnt/, *adj.* **1.** above others in rank or authority; superior in power or jurisdiction. **2.** chief in importance; supreme; pre-eminent. *–n.* **3.** an overlord; a supreme ruler. [AF *paramont* above, from *par* by (from L *per*) + *amont* upwards, up (from L *ad montem* to the mountain). Cf. AMOUNT] – **paramountcy,** *n.*

**paramour** /'pærəmɔ/, *n.* **1.** an illicit lover, esp. of a married person. **2.** any lover. **3.** a beloved one. [ME, from OF, orig. phrase *par amour* by love, by way of (sexual) love, from *par* by (from L *per*) + *amour* love (from L *amor*)]

**parang** /'paræŋ/, *n.* a large, heavy knife used as a tool or a weapon by the Malays. [Malay]

**paranoia** /pærə'nɔɪə/, *n.* a psychotic disorder characterised by systematised delusions, usu. persecutory or grandiose in nature, outside of which personality functioning tends to be intact. Also, **paranoea** /pærə'niə/. [NL, from Gk: derangement]

**paranoiac** /pærə'nɔɪæk/, *adj.* **1.** pertaining to or affected with paranoia. *–n.* **2.** a person affected with paranoia. Also, **paranoeac** /pærə'niæk/.

**paranoid** /'pærənɔɪd/, *adj.* **1.** pertaining to or affected by paranoia. **2.** *Colloq.* emotionally hypersensitive.

**paranoid schizophrenia** /– skɪtsə'friniə/, *n.* a form of schizophrenia characterised mainly by delusions of persecution or grandeur. There are also disturbances of thinking, hallucinations and deterioration.

**paranormal** /'pærənɔməl/, *adj.* outside normal knowledge or perception; psychic.

**paranymph** /'pærənɪmf/, *n.* **1.** a best man or a bridesmaid. **2.** (in ancient Greece) **a.** a friend who accompanied the bridegroom when he went to bring home the bride. **b.** the bridesmaid who escorted the bride to the bridegroom. [Gk *paránymphos,* masc., the best man, *paranýmphē,* fem., the bridesmaid]

**parapet** /ˈpærəpət/, *n.* **1.** *Fort.* **a.** a defensive wall or elevation, as of earth or stone, in a fortification. **b.** an elevation raised above the main wall or rampart of a permanent fortification. **2.** any protective wall or barrier at the edge of a balcony, roof, bridge, or the like. [It. *parapetto,* from *para-* PARA-[2] + *petto,* from L *pectus* breast] – **parapeted,** *adj.*

**paraph** /ˈpæræf/, *n.* a flourish made after a signature, as in a document, originally as a precaution against forgery. [ME *paraf,* from ML *paraphus,* short for L *paragraphus* PARAGRAPH]

**paraphernalia** /pærəfəˈneɪliə/, *n.pl.* **1.** personal belongings. **2.** *Law.* the personal articles, apart from dower, reserved by law to a married woman. **3.** (*sometimes construed as sing.*) equipment; apparatus. **4.** (*sometimes construed as sing.*) any collection of miscellaneous articles. [ML (properly neut. pl.), from LL *parapherna,* from Gk: bride's belongings other than dowry]

**paraphilia** /pærəˈfɪliə/, *n.* preference for or addiction to unusual sexual practices. [NL, from Gk *para-* PARA-[1] + *philía* affection, fondness] – **paraphiliac,** *n., adj.*

**paraphrase** /ˈpærəfreɪz/, *n., v.,* **-phrased, -phrasing.** *–n.* **1.** a restatement of the sense of a text or passage, as for clearness; a free rendering or translation, as of a passage. **2.** the act or process of paraphrasing. *–v.t., v.i.* **3.** to restate; render in, or make, a paraphrase. [F, from L *paraphrasis,* from Gk] – **paraphrasable,** *adj.* – **paraphraser,** *n.*

**paraphrast** /ˈpærəfræst/, *n.* one who paraphrases.

**paraphrastic** /pærəˈfræstɪk/, *adj.* having the nature of a paraphrase. – **paraphrastically,** *adv.*

**paraphysis** /pəˈræfəsəs/, *n., pl.* **-ses** /-siz/. one of the sterile, usu. filamentous, outgrowths often occurring among the reproductive organs in many cryptogamous plants. [NL, from Gk: offshoot]

**paraplegia** /pærəˈplidʒə/, *n.* paralysis of both lower or upper limbs. [NL, from Gk *paraplēgíē* paralysis on one side] – **paraplegic** /pærəˈplidʒɪk/, *adj., n.*

**parapodium** /pærəˈpoʊdiəm/, *n., pl.* **-dia** /-diə/. one of the unjointed lateral locomotor processes or series of rudimentary limbs of many worms, as annelids. [NL. See PARA-[1], -PODIUM]

**parapraxis** /pærəˈpræksəs/, *n.* small deviations from normal habit or action, as spoonerisms or other slips of the tongue, supposedly the result of repressed impulses. See **Freudian slip.** [PARA-[1] + Gk *prâxis* doing, practice]

**parapsychology** /pærəsaɪˈkɒlədʒi/, *n.* a division of psychology which investigates psychic phenomena, as clairvoyance, telepathy, etc. – **parapsychological** /ˌpærəsaɪkəˈlɒdʒɪkəl/, *adj.*

**paraquet** /ˈpærəkit/, *n.* →**parakeet.**

**Pará rubber** /paˌra ˈrʌbə/, *n.* indiarubber obtained from the tree, *Hevea brasiliensis,* and other species of the same genus, of tropical South America.

**paras** /ˈpærəz/, *n.pl. Colloq.* →**paratroops.**

**paraselene** /pærəsəˈlini/, *n., pl.* **-nae** /-ni/. a bright moonlike spot on a lunar halo; a mock moon. Cf. **parhelion.** [NL, from Gk *para-* PARA-[1] + *selēnē* moon]

**parashah** /ˈpærəʃa/, *n., pl.* **parashoth** /ˈpærəʃoʊθ/, **parashioth** /pærəˈʃioʊθ/. **1.** one of the lessons from the Torah or Law read in the Jewish synagogue on Sabbaths and festivals. **2.** one of the subsections into which the weekly lessons read on Sabbaths are divided. Cf. **haphtarah.** [Heb.: division]

**parasite** /ˈpærəsaɪt/, *n.* **1.** an animal or plant which lives on or in an organism of another species (the host), from the body of which it obtains nutriment. **2.** one who lives on others or another without making any useful and fitting return, esp. one who lives on the hospitality of others. **3.** (in ancient Greece) a professional diner-out, who got free meals in return for his amusing or impudent conversation. [L *parasītus,* from Gk *parásītos* one who eats at the table of another]

**parasitic** /pærəˈsɪtɪk/, *adj.* **1.** living or growing as a parasite; pertaining to or characteristic of parasites. **2.** (of diseases) due to parasites. Also, **parasitical.** – **parasitically,** *adv.*

**parasiticide** /pærəˈsɪtəsaɪd/, *adj.* **1.** destructive to parasites. *–n.* **2.** an agent or preparation that destroys parasites.

**parasitise** /ˈpærəsətaɪz/, *v.t.,* **-tised, -tising.** to live on (a host) as a parasite. Also, **parasitize.**

**parasitism** /ˈpærəsaɪtɪzəm/, *n.* **1.** parasitic mode of life or existence. **2.** *Zool., Bot.* the vital relation which a parasite bears to its host; parasitic infestation. **3.** *Pathol.* diseased condition due to parasites.

**parasitology** /pærəsaɪˈtɒlədʒi/, *n.* a division of biology dealing with parasites and their effects. – **parasitological,** /ˌpærəsaɪtəˈlɒdʒɪkəl/, *adj.* – **parasitologist,** *n.*

**parasol** /ˈpærəsɒl/, *n.* a woman's small or light sun umbrella; a sunshade. [F, from It. *parasole,* from *para-* PARA-[2] + *sole* (from L *sōl* sun)]

parasol

**parastichy** /pəˈræstəki/, *n., pl.* **-chies** /-kiz/. (in a spiral arrangement of leaves, scales, etc., where the internodes are short and the members closely crowded, as in the houseleek and the pine cone) one of a number of secondary spirals or oblique ranks seen to wind round the stem or axis to the right and left. [PARA-[1] + Gk *-stichía* alignment]

**parasympathetic** /ˌpærəsɪmpəˈθɛtɪk/, *adj.* **1.** pertaining to that part of the autonomic nervous system which consists of nerves arising from the cranial and sacral regions, and which opposes the action of the sympathetic system, thus inhibiting heartbeat, contracting the pupil of the eye, etc. *–n.* **2.** a nerve of the parasympathetic system.

**parasynapsis** /pærəsəˈnæpsəs/, *n.* the conjugation of chromosomes side by side; synapsis. – **parasynaptic,** *adj.*

**parasynthesis** /pærəˈsɪnθəsəs/, *n.* the formation of a word by the addition of an affix to a phrase or compound, as *greathearted,* which is *great heart* plus *-ed* (not *great* plus *hearted*). [PARA-[1] + SYNTHESIS] – **parasynthetic** /pærəsɪnˈθɛtɪk/, *adj.*

**parataxic** /pærəˈtæksɪk/, *n.* (of emotions, ideas, etc.) ill-adjusted; lacking harmony.

**parataxis** /pærəˈtæksəs/, *n.* the placing together of sentences, clauses, or phrases without a conjunctive word, as *hurry up, it is getting late; I came–I saw–I conquered.* [NL, from Gk: a placing side by side] – **paratactic, paratactical,** *adj.* – **paratactically,** *adv.*

**parathyroid** /pærəˈθaɪrɔɪd/, *adj.* **1.** situated near the thyroid gland. *–n.* **2.** a parathyroid gland.

**parathyroid glands** /ˈ– glændz/, *n.pl.* several small glands or oval masses of epithelioid cells, lying near or embedded in the thyroid gland, whose internal secretion governs the calcium content of the blood.

**paratrooper** /ˈpærətrupə/, *n.* a soldier who reaches battle, esp. behind enemy lines, by landing from an aeroplane by parachute. [PARA-[3] + TROOPER]

**paratroops** /ˈpærətrups/, *n.pl.* paratroopers collectively.

**paratyphoid** /pærəˈtaɪfɔɪd/, *adj.* denoting or pertaining to paratyphoid fever.

**paratyphoid fever** /– ˈfivə/, *n.* an infectious disease similar in some ways to typhoid fever but usu. milder, and caused by different bacteria.

**paravane** /ˈpærəveɪn/, *n.* a device consisting of a pair of torpedo-shaped vanes towed at the bow of a vessel, usu. a minesweeper, at the ends of cables, that cut the cable of a moored mine, causing the mine to rise to the surface where it can be destroyed by gunfire.

**par avion** /par ˈævɪɒn/, *adv.* by aeroplane (as a designation for matter to be sent airmail). [F]

**paraxial** /pəˈræksiəl/, *adj.* (of light rays) making very small angles with, or lying close to the axis of, an optical system.

**parboil** /ˈpabɔɪl/, *v.t.* to boil partially, or for a short time; precook. [ME *parboyle(n)* boil fully (associated with PART), from OF *parbouillir,* from LL *perbullīre.* See PER-, BOIL[1]]

**parbuckle** /ˈpabʌkəl/, *n., v.,* **-led, -ling.** *–n.* **1.** a kind of tackle for raising or lowering a cask or similar object along an inclined plane or a vertical surface, consisting of a rope looped over a post or the like, with its two ends passing round the object to be moved. **2.** a kind of double sling made with a rope, as round a cask to be raised or lowered. *–v.t.* **3.** to raise, lower, or move with a parbuckle. [earlier *parbunkel;* orig. unknown]

**parcel** /ˈpasəl/, *n., v.,* **-celled, -celling,** or *(U.S.)* **-celed, -celing,** *adv.* –*n.* **1.** a quantity of something wrapped or packaged together, a package or bundle. **2.** a quantity of something, as of a commodity for sale; a lot. **3.** any group or assemblage of persons or things. **4.** a separable, separate, or distinct part or portion or section, as of land. **5.** a part or portion of anything. **6.** *Mining.* a heap of dressed ore ready for sale. **7.** *Mining.* quantity (indefinite) of fine opal. –*v.t.* **8.** to divide into or distribute in parcels or portions (usu. fol. by *out*). **9.** to make into a parcel, or put up in parcels, as goods. **10.** *Naut.* to cover or wrap (a rope etc.) with strips of canvas. –*adv.* **11.** *Archaic.* partly; in part; partially. [ME *parcelle,* from OF, from ML *particella,* diminutive of L *particula* particle]

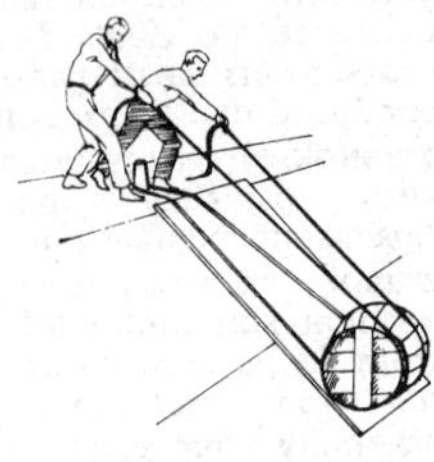
parbuckle

**parcel post** /ˈ– poʊst/, *n.* **1.** a branch of a postal service charged with conveying parcels. **2. have come up by parcel post,** *Colloq.* to be inexperienced, as of a new arrival.

**parcel-post man** /pasəl-ˈpoʊst mæn/, *n. Colloq.* an inexperienced man; new chum.

**parcenary** /ˈpasənri/, *n.* (in law) coheirship; the undivided holding of land by two or more coheirs.

**parcener** /ˈpasənə/, *n.* (in law) a joint heir; a coheir. [ME, from AF, from *parçon,* from L *partītio* partition]

**parch** /patʃ/, *v.t.* **1.** to make dry, esp. to excess, or dry up, as heat, the sun, or a hot wind does. **2.** to make (a person, the lips, throat, etc.) dry and hot, or thirsty, as heat, fever, or thirst does. **3.** *Cookery.* to brown in a dry heat. **4.** (of cold, etc.) to dry or shrivel, like heat. –*v.i.* **5.** to become parched; undergo drying by heat. **6.** to dry (fol. by *up*). **7.** to suffer from heat or thirst. [ME *parche(n), perch(en)*; orig. uncert.]

**parcheesi** /paˈtʃizi/, *n.* →**pachisi.**

**parchment** /ˈpatʃmənt/, *n.* **1.** the skin of sheep, goats, etc., prepared for use as a writing material, etc. **2.** a manuscript or document on such material. **3.** a paper resembling this material. [ME *parchemin,* from OF, b. LL *pergamēna* parchment (from *Pergamum,* city in Mysia, Asia Minor, whence parchment was brought) and L *parthica* (*pellis*) Parthian (leather)]

**parchment paper** /ˈ– peɪpə/, *n.* a waterproof and grease-resistant paper obtained by treating a paper with concentrated sulphuric acid.

**parclose** /ˈpaklouz/, *n.* a screen or railing enclosing a shrine, tomb, or chapel separating it from the main body of the church. [ME, from OF, n. use of fem. pp. of *parclore* completely enclose]

**pard**[1] /pad/, *n. Archaic.* a leopard or panther. [ME, from OF, from L *pardus,* from Gk *párdos,* earlier *párdalis;* of Eastern orig.]

**pard**[2] /pad/, *n. U.S. Colloq.* partner; friend. [alteration of PARTNER]

**pardalote** /ˈpadəlout/, *n.* any of several species of the genus *Pardalotus,* small finch-like birds conspicuously marked with brown or white diamonds, as the diamond bird.

**pardi** /paˈdi/, *adv., interj. Archaic.* verily; indeed. Also, **pardie, pardy, perdie.** [ME *parde,* from OF, from L *par Deum* by God]

**pardner** /ˈpadnə/, *n. U.S. Colloq.* partner; friend.

**pardon** /ˈpadn/, *n.* **1.** courteous indulgence or allowance, as in excusing fault or seeming rudeness: *I beg your pardon.* **2.** *Law.* **a.** a pardoning; a remission of penalty. **b.** the deed or warrant by which such remission is declared. **3.** forgiveness of an offence or offender. **4.** *Obs.* a papal indulgence. –*v.t.* **5.** to remit the penalty of (an offence): *he will not pardon your transgressions.* **6.** to release (a person) from liability for an offence. **7.** to make courteous allowance for, or excuse (an action or circumstance, or a person): *pardon me, madam.* –*interj.* **8.** (a conventional form of apology for injury or inconvenience.) **9.** (a request for the repetition of something not clearly heard.) [ME *pardone(n),* from OF *pardoner,* from LL *perdōnāre* grant, concede, from L *per-* PER- + *dōnāre* give] – **pardonable,** *adj.* – **pardonably,** *adv.*

**pardoner** /ˈpadənə/, *n.* **1.** one who pardons. **2.** *Hist.* an ecclesiastical official charged with the granting of indulgences.

**pardy** /paˈdi/, *adv., interj. Archaic.* →**pardi.**

**pare** /peə/, *v.t.,* **pared, paring. 1.** to cut off the outer coating, layer, or part of: *to pare apples.* **2.** to remove (an outer coating, layer, or part) by cutting (oft. fol. by *off* or *away*). **3.** to reduce or remove by, or as if by, cutting; diminish little by little: *to pare down one's expenses.* [ME *pare(n),* from OF *parer* prepare, trim, from L *parāre*]

**paregoric** /pærəˈgɒrɪk/, *n.* **1.** a soothing medicine; an anodyne. **2.** a camphorated tincture of opium, intended primarily to check diarrhoea in children. –*adj.* **3.** assuaging pain; soothing. [LL *parēgoricus,* from Gk *parēgorikós* encouraging, soothing]

**pareira** /pəˈreərə/, *n.* the root of a South American vine, *Chondodendron tomentosum,* used as a diuretic, etc.; a source of curare. [short for PAREIRA BRAVA]

**pareira brava** /– ˈbravə/, *n.* →**pareira.** [Pg. *parreira brava,* lit., wild vine]

**paren.,** parenthesis.

**parenchyma** /pəˈreŋkɪmə/, *n.* **1.** *Bot.* the fundamental (soft) cellular tissue of plants, as in the softer parts of leaves, the pulp of fruits, the pith of stems, etc. **2.** *Anat., Zool.* the proper tissue of an animal organ as distinguished from its connective or supporting tissue. **3.** *Zool.* a kind of jelly-like connective tissue in some lower animals. **4.** *Pathol.* the functional tissue of a morbid growth. [NL, from Gk: lit., something poured in beside] – **parenchymatous** /pæreŋˈkɪmətəs/, *adj.*

**parent** /ˈpeərənt/, *n.* **1.** a father or a mother. **2.** a progenitor. **3.** an author or source. **4.** a protector or guardian. **5.** any organism that produces or generates another. [ME, from L *parens*] – **parentless,** *adj.* – **parent-like,** *adj.*

**parentage** /ˈpeərəntɪdʒ/, *n.* **1.** derivation from parents; birth, lineage, or family; origin: *distinguished parentage.* **2.** parenthood.

**parental** /pəˈrentl/, *adj.* **1.** of or pertaining to a parent: *the parental relation.* **2.** proper to or characteristic of a parent: *parental feelings.* **3.** having the relation of a parent. **4.** *Genetics.* indicating the sequence of generations leading to a particular filial, first parental being shown as $P_1$, second parental as $P_2$, etc. – **parentally,** *adv.*

**parent award** /ˈpeərənt əwɔd/, *n.* an award which is regarded as setting the minimum standard of payment for employees in a particular calling or classification.

**parenteral** /pæˈrentərəl/, *adj.* taken into the body or administered in a manner other than through the digestive canal. [PAR(A)-[1] + Gk *énteron* intestine + -AL[1]]

**parenthesis** /pəˈrenθəsəs/, *n., pl.* **-ses** /-siz/. **1.** the upright brackets ( ) collectively, or either of them separately, used to mark off an interjected explanatory or qualifying remark, indicate groupings in mathematics, etc. **2.** *Gram.* a qualifying or explanatory word (as an appositive), phrase, clause (as a descriptive clause), sentence, or other sequence of forms which interrupts the syntactic construction without otherwise affecting it, having often a characteristic intonation, and shown in writing by commas, parentheses, or dashes. For example: *William Smith–you know him well–will be here soon.* **3.** an interval. [ML, from Gk: a putting in beside]

**parenthesise** /pəˈrenθəsaɪz/, *v.t.,* **-sised, -sising. 1.** to insert as or in a parenthesis. **2.** to put between marks of parenthesis: *parenthesise the pronunciation.* **3.** to interlard with parentheses. Also, **parenthesize.**

**parenthetic** /pærənˈθetɪk/, *adj.* **1.** of, pertaining to, or of the nature of a parenthesis: *several unnecessary parenthetic remarks.* **2.** characterised by the use of parentheses. Also, **parenthetical.** – **parenthetically,** *adv.*

**parenthood** /ˈpeərənthʊd/, *n.* the position or relation of, or state of being, a parent.

**parergon** /pəˈreəgən/, *n., pl.* **-ga** /-gə/. subordinate or secondary work, standing apart from one's main occupation. [MF, from It. *paragone* touchstone, comparison, paragon]

**paresis** /pəˈrisəs, ˈpærəsəs/, *n.* **1.** incomplete motor paralysis. **2.** See **general paralysis of the insane.** [NL, from Gk: a letting go]

**paresthesia** /pæris'θiziə, -'θiʒə/, *n. Chiefly U.S.* →**paraesthesia.** – **paresthetic** /pæris'θɛtɪk/, *adj.*
**paretic** /pə'rɛtɪk, pə'ritɪk/, *n.* **1.** one who has general paresis. *–adj.* **2.** pertaining to, or affected with, paresis.
**pareu** /'pareɪu/, *n.* a colourful rectangular cloth worn like a kilt or skirt in French-speaking islands of the South Pacific.
**pareve** /'parəvi/, *adj.* containing neither milk nor meat in any form, and therefore admissible for use with either according to the Judaic dietary laws: *pareve bread.* [Yiddish *parev*]
**par excellence** /par 'ɛksələns/, *adv.* by excellence or superiority; above all others; pre-eminently. [F]
**parfait** /pa'feɪ/, *n.* a dessert, served in a tall glass, made from layers of ice-cream, fruit, jelly, syrup, nuts, etc. [F: lit., perfect]
**pargasite** /'pagəsaɪt/, *n.* a variety of hornblende, containing fluorine, sodium, and aluminium. [named after *Pargas,* town in Finland]
**parget** /'padʒət/, *n., v.,* **-geted, -geting** or **-getted, -getting.** *–n.* **1.** gypsum or plaster stone. **2.** plaster, esp. a kind of mortar formed of lime, hair, and cow dung. **3.** plasterwork, esp. a more or less ornamental facing for exterior walls. *–v.t.* **4.** to cover or decorate with parget. [ME *pargette(n),* from OF *parjeter* throw over a surface, from *par* over + *jeter* throw]
**pargeting** /'padʒətɪŋ/, *n.* **1.** the act of one who pargets. **2.** →**parget.** Also, **pargetting.**
**parheliacal** /pahə'laɪəkəl/, *adj.* of or pertaining to or constituting a parhelion or parhelia. Also, **parhelic** /pa'hilɪk/.
**parheliacal ring** /– 'rɪŋ/, *n.* a white horizontal band passing through the sun, either incomplete or extending round the horizon, produced by the reflection of the sun's rays from the vertical faces of ice prisms in the earth's atmosphere. Also, **parhelic circle.**
**parhelion** /pa'hiliən/, *n., pl.* **-lia** /-liə/. a bright circular spot on a solar halo; a mock sun; usu. one of two or more such spots seen on opposite sides of the sun, and often accompanied by additional luminous arcs and bands. [L *parēlion* (with etymological *-h-*), from Gk, var. of *parēlios,* from *para-* PARA-[1] + *hēlios* sun]
**pariah** /pə'raɪə/, *n.* **1.** any person or animal generally despised; an outcast. **2.** (*cap.*) a member of a low caste in southern India. [Tamil *paraiyar,* pl. of *paraiyan,* lit., drummer (from a hereditary duty of the caste), from *parai* a festival drum]
**paries** /'pɛəriiz/, *n., pl.* **parietes** /pə'raɪətiz/. (*usu. pl.*) a wall, as of a hollow organ; an investing part. [L: wall]
**parietal** /pə'raɪətl/, *adj.* **1.** *Anat.* **a.** referring to the side of the skull, or to any wall or wall-like structure. **b.** denoting or pertaining to the parietal bones. **2.** *Biol.* of or pertaining to parietes or structual walls. **3.** *Bot.* pertaining to or arising from a wall, usu. applied to ovules when they proceed from or are borne on the walls or sides of the ovary. [LL *parietālis,* from L *pariēs* wall]
**parietal bones** /– 'bounz/, *n.pl.* a pair of bones of the cranium, right and left, developed in membrane, forming most of the top and sides of the skull vault, between the occipital and the frontal bones.
**parietal cell** /– 'sɛl/, *n.* a cell of the mucous membrane of the stomach that produces hydrochloric acid.
**parietal lobe** /– 'loub/, *n.* the middle lobe of the cerebrum.
**parimutuel** /pærə'mjutʃuəl/, *n. Chiefly U.S.* →**totalisator.** [F: mutual bet]
**paring** /'pɛərɪŋ/, *n.* **1.** the act of one who or that which pares. **2.** a piece or part pared off.
**pari passu** /pæri 'pæsu/, *adv.* **1.** with equal pace or progress; side by side. **2.** fairly and without bias. [L]
**paripinnate** /pærə'pɪneɪt/, *adj.* **1.** evenly pinnate. **2.** pinnate without an odd terminal leaflet.
**Paris green** /pærəs 'grin/, *n.* an emerald green pigment prepared from arsenic trioxide and acetate of copper, now used chiefly as an insecticide.
**parish** /'pærɪʃ/, *n.* **1.** an ecclesiastical district having its own church and clergyman. **2.** a local church with its field of activity. **3.** *Brit.* a civil district or administrative division. **4.** (formerly) an area of land delineated by analogy with certain British parishes for administrative convenience even though no ecclesiastical parish existed, as when setting up the early parish road trusts. **5.** the people of a parish (ecclesiastical or civil). **6.** *Brit.* **on the parish, a.** *Obs.* in receipt of poor relief. **b.** *Colloq.* poor; indigent. [ME, from OF *paroisse,* from LL *parochia,* var. of *paroecia,* from Gk *paroikía*]
**parish clerk** /– 'klak/, *n.* a lay officer of the church in a parish whose duties are to keep the register, lead the responses in services, etc.
**parish council** /– 'kaunsəl/, *n.* a body elected to manage the affairs of a parish.
**parishioner** /pə'rɪʃənə/, *n.* one of the community or inhabitants of a parish. [earlier *parishion* (from OF *parochien*) + -ER[1]]
**parish priest** /pærɪʃ 'prist/, *n.* a priest in the Roman Catholic Church who is in charge of a parish.
**parish pump** /pærɪʃ 'pʌmp/, *n.* a pump forming the common water supply for a small rural community, regarded as the gathering-place for gossip and a symbol of parochialism.
**parish-pump** /'pærɪʃ-pʌmp/, *adj.* local; parochial.
**parish register** /pærɪʃ 'rɛdʒəstə/, *n.* a record of all births, baptisms, marriages, and deaths in a parish.
**Parisian** /pə'rɪziən, -'rɪʒən/, *adj.* **1.** of or pertaining to Paris, France. **2.** (*l.c.*) Also, **à la parisienne. a.** with a sauce made of shallots, white wine and meat stock, seasoned with lemon juice. **b.** with a garnish that includes potato balls, glazed with meat jelly.
**parison** /'pærəzən/, *n.* a preliminary shape or blank, from which a glass article is to be formed. [F *paraison* preparation]
**parity**[1] /'pærəti/, *n.* **1.** equality, as in amount, status, or character. **2.** equivalence; correspondence; similarity or analogy. **3.** *Finance.* **a.** equivalence in value in the currency of another country. **b.** equivalence in value at a fixed ratio between moneys of different metals. **4.** *Maths.* (of an integer) the property of being even or odd. **5.** *Physics.* a symmetry property of a wave-function: if the parity is even (+ 1), the function is not changed by a mirror reflection of the coordinate system; if the parity is odd (−1), the function changes sign. **6.** *Computers.* a method of checking information in a computer, by counting the number of digits present in a binary number. [LL *pāritas,* from L *pār* equal]
**parity**[2] /'pærəti/, *n.* condition or fact of having borne offspring. [L *parere* bring forth + -ITY]
**parity-pricing** /pærəti-'praɪsɪŋ/, *n.* the policy of basing the local price of a commodity on an agreed international price where such exists.
**park** /pak/, *n.* **1.** an area of land within a town, often with recreational and other facilities, which is set aside for public use: *Hyde Park.* **2.** a tract of land set apart, as by a city or a nation, to be preserved in its natural state for the benefit of the public: *the Kosciusko National Park.* **3.** *Chiefly Brit.* a considerable extent of land forming the grounds of a country house. **4.** an enclosed tract of land for wild animals. **5.** *Mil.* **a.** the space occupied by the assembled guns, tanks, stores, etc., of a body of soldiers. **b.** the assemblage formed. **c.** complete equipment, as of guns, etc. **6.** a parking spot. *–v.t.* **7.** to put or leave (a car, etc.) for a time in a particular place, as at the side of the road. **8.** *Colloq.* to put or leave. **9.** to assemble (artillery, etc.) in compact arrangement. **10.** to enclose in or as in a park. *–v.i.* **11.** to park a car, bicycle, etc. [ME *parc,* from OF; of Gmc orig., akin to G *Pferch* fold, pen, and OE *pearroc* enclosure, and to PADDOCK] – **parklike,** *adj.*
**parka** /'pakə/, *n.* **1.** a strong waterproof jacket with a hood, originally for use in polar regions, now commonly used for any outdoor activity; anorak. **2.** a fur coat, cut like a shirt, worn in north-eastern Asia and Alaska. [Aleut, a language spoken by the Aleutian Indians of the Alaskan Peninsula]
**parking** /'pakɪŋ/, *n.* **1.** the act of one who or that which parks. **2.** space in which to park vehicles. **3.** permission to park vehicles. *–adj.* **4.** of, pertaining to, or used for parking.
**parking lot** /'– lɒt/, *n. Orig. U.S.* →**car park.**
**parking meter** /'– mitə/, *n.* a device for registering and collecting payment for a length of time during which a vehicle may be parked, consisting typically of a clockwork mechanism activated by a coin, mounted on a pole next to a parking space.
**parking orbit** /'– ɔbət/, *n.* a temporary orbit in which a spacecraft awaits the next phase of its planned mission.

**parking policeman** /'– pəlismən/, *n.* a police officer employed to regulate the parking of cars and use of parking meters.

**parking station** /'– steɪʃən/, *n.* a building designed and constructed for parking motor vehicles.

**Parkinson's disease** /'pakənsənz dəziz/, *n.* a form of paralysis characterised by tremor, muscular rigidity, and weakness of movement; paralysis agitans; shaking palsy. Also, **Parkinsonism.** [named after James *Parkinson,* 1755-1824, English physician who first described it]

**Parkinson's law** /– 'lɔ/, *n.* either of two ideas, stated facetiously as laws of physics, that **1.** work expands to fill the time allotted to it, and **2.** the staff of an establishment expands even while the productivity remains constant or declines. [devised by C. Northcote *Parkinson,* b. 1909, English writer]

**parkland** /'paklænd/, *n.* **1.** a grassland region with isolated or grouped trees, usu. in temperate regions. **2.** *S.A.* a public garden or park.

**parkway** /'pakweɪ/, *n.* a broad thoroughfare, often landscaped and planted with trees, or passing through attractive bushland.

**parl.,** parliamentary.

**Parl.,** Parliament.

**parlance** /'paləns/, *n.* **1.** way of speaking, or language; idiom; vocabulary: *legal parlance.* **2.** *Archaic.* talk; parley. [AF, from *parler* speak, from L *parabola.* See PARABLE]

**parlando** /pa'lændoʊ/, *adv.* (a musical direction) sung or played as though speaking or reciting. [It.] – **parlando,** *adj.*

**parley** /'pali/, *n., pl.* **-leys,** *v.,* **-leyed, -leying.** *–n.* **1.** a discussion; a conference. **2.** an informal conference between enemies under truce, to discuss terms, conditions of surrender, etc. *–v.i.* **3.** to hold an informal conference with an enemy, under a truce, as between active hostilities. **4.** to speak, talk, or confer. [F *parlée* speech]

**parliament** /'paləmənt/, *n.* **1.** (*usu. cap.*) **a.** the national assembly of elected representatives, comprising an upper and lower house, which forms with the Sovereign the legislature of the nation. **b.** a similar assembly in each State. **2.** any one of similar legislative bodies in other countries. **3.** a meeting or assembly for conference on public or national affairs. [ME *parlement,* from OF, from *parler* speak. See PARLANCE]

Parliament House, Canberra

**parliamentarian** /paləmən'tɛəriən/, *n.* **1.** a Member of Parliament. **2.** one skilled in parliamentary procedure or debate. **3.** one who supports a parliamentary system.

**parliamentarianism** /paləmən'tɛəriənɪzəm/, *n.* advocacy of a parliamentary system of government.

**parliamentary** /palə'mentəri, -tri/, *adj.* **1.** of or pertaining to a parliament. **2.** enacted or established by a parliament. **3.** characterised by the existence of a parliament. **4.** of the nature of a parliament. **5.** in accordance with the rules and usages of parliaments or deliberative bodies: *parliamentary procedure.*

**parliamentary privilege** /–'prɪvəlɪdʒ/, *n.* the sum of the special rights enjoyed by each house of parliament collectively and by the members of each house individually, necessary for the discharge of the functions of parliament without hindrance and without fear of prosecution.

**parliament hinge** /'paləmənt hɪndʒ/, *n.* a hinge with a large projection, which allows a door to open to its fullest extent.

**parlour** /'palə/, *n.* **1.** a room for the reception and entertainment of visitors; a living room. **2.** a semi-private room in a hotel, club, or the like for relaxation, conversation, etc.; a lounge. **3.** a room in a monastery or a nunnery where conversation is allowed and where visitors are received. **4.** a room fitted up for the reception of business patrons or customers: *a beauty parlour, a funeral parlour.* Also, *U.S.,* **parlor.** [ME *parlur,* from AF, from *parler* speak. See PARLANCE]

**parlour game** /'– geɪm/, *n.* any of a variety of indoor games, as consequences, quizzes, or the like, as played at parties.

**parlourmaid** /'paləmeɪd/, *n.* a maid who waits at table, etc., in a house where domestic menservants, as butlers or footmen, are not employed.

**parlour pink** /palə 'pɪŋk/, *n. Colloq.* a person who expresses enthusiasm for the philosophies of the Communist party without actively supporting it.

**parlous** /'paləs/, *adj.* **1.** perilous; dangerous. **2.** *Obs.* clever; shrewd. *–adv.* **3.** very. [ME; var. of PERILOUS] – **parlously,** *adv.*

**parl. proc.,** parliamentary procedure.

**Parlt,** Parliament.

**parma ham** /pama 'hæm/, *n.* a delicate Italian cured ham. [from *Parma,* city in N Italy]

**parma wallaby** /– 'wɒləbi/, *n.* a small wallaby, *Macropus parma,* rendered extinct in its original habitat in the coastal regions of New South Wales but since recolonised from stock taken to New Zealand last century.

**parmentier** /pa'mɛntiə/, *adj.* with potatoes.

**parmesan** /'paməzən/, *n.* a hard, dry pale yellow cheese, with a granular texture, and a range of flavours depending on maturity, often used grated. [F, from It. *parmigiano,* from *Parma,* city in N Italy]

**Parnassian** /pa'næsiən/, *adj.* **1.** pertaining to Mount Parnassus, in Greek mythology sacred to Apollo and the Muses. **2.** pertaining to poetry. **3.** denoting or pertaining to a school of French poets, of the latter half of the 19th century, characterised esp. by emphasis of form and by repression of emotion. [so called from *Le Parnasse Contemporain,* the title of their first collection of poems, published in 1866] *–n.* **4.** a member of the Parnassian school of French poets. [L *Parnās(s)ius* (from PARNAS(S)US) + -AN. Cf. F *Parnassien*]

**Parnassus** /pa'næsəs/, *n.* **1.** a collection of poems or of elegant literature. **2.** the world of poetry, esp. as part of the established literary world. [from Mount *Parnassus* in central Greece, sacred to Apollo and the Muses and symbolic of poetic inspiration and achievement]

**parochial** /pə'roʊkiəl/, *adj.* **1.** of or pertaining to a parish or parishes. **2.** confined to or interested only in one's own parish, or some particular narrow district or field. [ME, from LL *parochiālis,* from LL *parochia.* See PARISH] – **parochially,** *adv.*

**parochialism** /pə'roʊkiəlɪzəm/, *n.* parochial character, spirit, or tendency; narrowness of interests or view.

**parody** /'pærədi/, *n., pl.* **-dies,** *v.,* **-died, -dying.** *–n.* **1.** a humorous or satirical imitation of a serious piece of literature or writing. **2.** the kind of literary composition represented by such imitations. **3.** a burlesque imitation of a musical composition. **4.** a poor imitation; a travesty. *–v.t.* **5.** to imitate (a composition, author, etc.) in such a way as to ridicule. **6.** to imitate poorly. [L *parōdia,* from Gk *parōidía* burlesque poem] – **parodist,** *n.*

**paroicous** /pə'rɔɪkəs/, *adj.* (of certain mosses) having the male and female reproductive organs beside or near each other. Also, **paroecious** /pə'riʃəs/. [Gk *pároikos* dwelling beside]

**parol** /pə'roʊl/, *Law.* *–n.* **1.** *Obs.* the pleadings in a suit. *–adj.* **2.** given by word of mouth; oral; not written (opposed to *documentary,* or given by affidavit): *parol evidence.* [AF (legal) *parole.* See PAROLE]

**parole** /pə'roʊl/, *n., v.,* **-roled, -roling.** *–n.* **1. a.** the liberation of a person from prison, conditional upon good behaviour, prior to the end of the maximum sentence imposed upon that person. **b.** the temporary release of a prisoner. **c.** such release or its duration. **2.** *U.S. Mil.* **a.** the promise of a prisoner of war to refrain from trying to escape, or, if released, to return to custody or to forbear taking up arms against his captors. **b.** a password given by authorised personnel in passing through a guard. **3.** a word of honour given or pledged. **4.** *Law.* →**parol. 5.** *Linguistics.* the individual spoken utterance of members of a speech community, seen as manifestations of the commonly-held underlying language system or langue. *–v.t.* **6.** to put on parole. [F: word, from L *parabola.* See PARABLE]

**parolee** /pəroʊ'li/, *n.* one who is released on parole.

**paronomasia** /pærənoʊ'meɪziə/, *n.* **1.** a playing on words; punning. **2.** a pun. [L, from Gk] – **paronomastic,** *adj.* – **paronomastically,** *adv.*

**paronychia** /pærə'nɪkiə/, *n.* an infection of the soft tissues

around the nail bed.
**paronym** /ˈpærənɪm/, *n.* a paronymous word.
**paronymous** /pəˈrɒnəməs/, *adj.* of words having the same root or stem, as *wise* and *wisdom.* [Gk *parṓnymos* derivative]
**paroo dog** /paru ˈdɒg/, *n.* a rattle, sometimes made up of tobacco-tin lids, which, when shaken, frightens sheep into movement and prevents them from straying. [from *Paroo,* river in NW N.S.W.]
**paroo sandwich** /– ˈsænwɪtʃ/, *n.* a drink made by mixing beer and wine.
**paroquet** /ˈpærəkit/, *n.* →**parakeet.**
**parore** /pəˈrɔri/, *n. N.Z.* →**luderick.**
**parotic** /pəˈrɒtɪk/, *adj.* situated about or near the ear.
**parotid** /pəˈrɒtəd/, *n.* **1.** either of two saliva-producing glands situated one at the base of each ear. *–adj.* **2.** denoting, pertaining to, or situated near either parotid. [L *parōtis,* from Gk: tumour near the ear]
**parotitic** /pærəˈtɪtɪk/, *adj.* having the mumps.
**parotitis** /pærəˈtaɪtəs/, *n.* →**mumps.** Also, **parotiditis** /pərɒtəˈdaɪtəs/. [NL; see PAROT(ID), -ITIS]
**parotoid** /pəˈrɒtɔɪd/, *adj.* **1.** resembling a parotid gland. **2.** denoting certain cutaneous glands forming warty masses or excrescences near the ear in certain salientians, as toads. *–n.* **3.** a parotid gland. [PAROTID, -OID]
**-parous,** an adjective termination meaning 'bringing forth', 'bearing', 'producing', as in *oviparous, viviparous.* [L *-parus,* from *parere* bring forth]
**parousia** /pəˈruziə/, *n.* the return of Christ to earth at the end of the world; the Second Advent. [Gk *parousía* arrival, esp. visit of a royal or official personage, or of a god]
**paroxysm** /ˈpærəksɪzəm/, *n.* **1.** any sudden, violent outburst; a fit of violent action or emotion: *paroxysms of rage.* **2.** *Pathol.* a severe attack, or increase in violence of a disease, usu. recurring periodically. [ML *paroxysmus,* from Gk *paroxysmós* irritation] – **paroxysmal** /pærəkˈsɪzməl/, **paroxysmic** /pærəkˈsɪzmɪk/, *adj.*
**paroxytone** /pəˈrɒksətoun/, *Gk Gram. –adj.* **1.** having an acute accent on the next to the last syllable. *–n.* **2.** a paroxytone word. [Gk *paroxýtonos.* See PARA-[1], OXYTONE]
**parquet** /ˈpakeɪ, ˈpaki/, *n., v.,* **-queted** /-keɪd, -kid/, **-queting** /-keɪɪŋ, -kiɪŋ/. *–n.* **1.** composed of short pieces of wood inlaid so as to form a pattern. **2.** *U.S.* the stalls in a theatre. *–v.t.* **3.** to construct (a flooring, etc.) of parquetry. **4.** to furnish with a floor, etc., of parquetry. [F: part of a park, flooring, diminutive of *parc* PARK]
**parquet circle** /ˈ– sɜkəl/, *n. U.S.* a space with curving tiers of seats behind and around the parquet of a theatre, etc.
**parquetry** /ˈpakətri/, *n.* mosaic work of wood used for floors, wainscoting, etc. [F *parqueterie*]
**parr** /pa/, *n., pl.* **parrs,** (*esp. collectively*) **parr.** a young salmon, having dark crossbars on its sides. [orig. unknown]

parquetry

**parrakeet** /ˈpærəkit/, *n.* →**parakeet.** Also, **parroket, parroquet.**
**parramatta** /pærəˈmætə/, *n.* a light, twilled dress fabric, having a silk or cotton warp and a woollen weft. Also, **paramatta.** [named after *Parramatta,* city in N.S.W.]
**Parramatta grass** /pærəˌmætə ˈgras/, *n.* a grass, *Sporobolus africanus,* native to southern Africa but often found as a weed in temperate and sub-tropical Australia. [named after the *Parramatta* district of N.S.W., as it was erroneously thought to be a native species when found there]
**parrel** /ˈpærəl/, *n.* a sliding ring or collar of rope, metal, etc., which confines a yard or the jaws of a gaff to the mast but allows vertical movement. Also, **parral.** [ME *parail,* aphetic var. of *aparail* APPAREL]
**parricide** /ˈpærəsaɪd/, *n.* **1.** one who kills either of his parents or anyone else to whom he owes reverence. **2.** the act or crime of killing a parent or any one else to whom reverence is due. [F, from L *parricīda* (the perpetrator), *parricīdium* (the crime), apparently from *pater* father. See -CIDE, PATRICIDE] – **parricidal** /pærəˈsaɪdl/, *adj.*
**parrot** /ˈpærət/, *n.* **1.** any of numerous hook-billed, fleshy-tongued, often gaily coloured birds which constitute the order Psittaciformes, as the cockatoo, lory, macaw, parakeet, etc., esp. those of the subfamily Psittacine, valued as cagebirds because they can be taught to talk. **2.** a person who unintelligently repeats the words or imitates the actions of another. *–v.t.* **3.** to repeat or imitate like a parrot. [F *Perrot, Pierrot,* diminutive of *Pierre* Peter]
**parrot fever** /ˈ– fivə/, *n.* →**psittacosis.** Also, **parrot disease.**
**parrotfish** /ˈpærətfɪʃ/, *n.* any of various marine fishes so called because of their colouring or the shape of their jaws, mainly tropical, mostly of the family Scaridae, and certain species of the family Labridae, as the **crimson-banded parrot fish,** *Pseudolabrus gymnogenis* of Australian coastal waters.
**parrot pea** /ˈpærət pi/, *n.* →**dillwynia.**
**parrot's beak** /ˈpærəts bik/, *n.* →**kaka beak.** Also, **parrot's bill.**
**parry** /ˈpæri/, *v.,* **-ried, -rying,** *n., pl.* **-ries.** *–v.t.* **1.** to ward off (a thrust, stroke, weapon, etc.), as in fencing. **2.** to turn aside, evade, or avoid. *–v.i.* **3.** to parry a thrust, etc. *–n.* **4.** an act or mode of parrying as in fencing. **5.** a defensive movement in fencing. [probably from F *parez,* impv. of *parer,* from It. *parare* ward off, protect, from L: make ready, prepare]
**pars,** paragraphs.
**parse** /paz/, *v.t.,* **parsed, parsing.** to describe (a word or series of words) grammatically, telling the part of speech, inflectional form, syntactic relations, etc. [L *pars* part, as in *pars ōrātiōnis* part of speech] – **parser,** *n.*
**parsec** /ˈpasɛk/, *n.* a unit of measurement of length used in astronomy, equal to the distance corresponding to a heliocentric parallax of one second of arc, or $30.857 \times 10^{15}$ m. *Symbol:* pc [PAR(ALLAX) + SEC(OND)[2]]
**parsimonious** /pasəˈmouniəs/, *adj.* characterised by or showing parsimony; sparing or frugal, esp. to excess. – **parsimoniously,** *adv.*
**parsimony** /ˈpasəməni/, *n.* extreme or excessive economy or frugality; niggardliness. [ME, from L *parsimōnia, parcimōnia,* lit., sparingness]
**parsley** /ˈpasli/, *n.* **1.** a garden herb, *Petroselinum crispum,* with aromatic leaves which are much used to garnish or season food. **2.** any of certain allied or similar plants. [ME *persely,* b. OF *per(esil)* (from LL *petrosilium*) and OE *(peter)silie* (from LL)]
**parsley piert** /ˈ– piət/, *n.* a small, pale green, annual with fan-shaped leaves and minute flowers, *Aphanes arvensis,* a weed of cultivated land throughout temperate regions.
**parsnip** /ˈpasnɪp/, *n.* **1.** a plant, *Pastinaca sativa,* cultivated varieties of which have a large, whitish, edible root. **2.** the root. [ME *pasnepe* (influenced by ME *nepe* NEEP), from OF *pasnaie,* from L *pastināca*]
**parson** /ˈpasən/, *n.* **1.** a clergyman or minister. **2.** the holder or incumbent of a parochial benefice. [ME *persone,* from ML *persōna* parson, from L: person. See PERSON]
**parsonage** /ˈpasənɪdʒ/, *n.* **1.** the residence of a parson or clergyman, as provided by the parish or church. **2.** *Obs.* the benefice of a parson.
**parson-bird** /ˈpasən-bɜd/, *n.* **1.** →**grey-crowned babbler. 2.** *N.Z.* →**tui.**

parsnip

**parson's bands** /pasənz ˈbændz/, *n. pl.* a species of orchid, *Eriochilus cucullatus,* with paired lateral sepals resembling parson's bands.
**parson's nose** /– ˈnouz/, *n.* the fatty tail or rump of a fowl when cooked. Also, **pope's nose.**
**part** /pat/, *n.* **1.** a portion or division of a whole, separate in reality, or in thought only; a piece, fragment, fraction, or section; a constituent. **2.** an essential or integral attribute or quality. **3. a.** a section or major division of a work of literature. **b.** a volume. **4.** a portion, member, or organ of an animal body. **5.** each of a number of more or less equal portions composing a whole: *a third part.* **6.** *Maths.* an aliquot part or exact divisor. **7.** an allotted portion; a share. **8.**

(*usu. pl.*) a region, quarter, or district: *foreign parts.* **9.** one of the sides to a contest, question, agreement, etc. **10.** an extra piece for replacing worn out parts of a tool, machine, etc. **11.** *Music.* **a.** a voice either vocal or instrumental. **b.** the written or printed matter extracted from the score which a single performer or section uses in the performance of concerted music: *a horn part.* **12.** participation, interest, or concern in something. **13.** one's share in some action; a duty, function, or office: *nature didn't do her part.* **14.** a character sustained in a play or in real life; a role. **15.** the words or lines assigned to an actor. **16.** (*usu. pl.*) a personal or mental quality or endowment: *a man of parts.* **17.** (*pl.*) the genitals. **18.** a part of speech. **19.** a parting in the hair. **20.** Some special noun phrases are:
**for my (his, etc.) part,** so far as concerns me (him, etc.).
**for the most part,** with regard to the greatest part; mostly.
**in good part,** with favour; without offence.
**in part,** in some measure or degree; to some extent.
**part and parcel,** an essential part.
**play a part, 1.** to act deceitfully; dissemble or dissimulate. **2.** to be instrumental.
**take part,** to participate.
**take someone's part,** to support or defend.
*–v.t.* **21.** to divide (a thing) into parts; break; cleave; divide. **22.** to comb (the hair) away from a dividing line. **23.** to dissolve (a connection, etc.) by separation of the parts, persons, or things involved: *she parted company with her sisters.* **24.** to divide into shares; distribute in parts; apportion. **25.** to put or keep asunder (two or more parts, persons, etc., or one part, person, etc., from another); draw or hold apart; disunite; separate. *–v.i.* **26.** to be or become divided into parts; break or cleave: *the frigate parted amidships.* **27.** to go or come apart or asunder, or separate, as two or more things. **28.** to go apart from each other or one another, as persons: *we'll part no more.* **29.** to be or become separated from something else (usu. fol. by *from*). **30.** *Naut.* to break or rend, as a cable. **31.** to depart. **32.** to die. **33. part up,** *Colloq.* to hand over; pay (fol. by *with*). **34. part with, a.** to give up; relinquish: *I parted with my gold.* **b.** to depart from. *–adj.* **35.** in part; partial. *–adv.* **36.** in part; partly. [ME, OE, from L *pars* piece, portion]

**part.,** participle.

**partake** /pa'teɪk/, *v.*, **-took, -taken, -taking.** *–v.i.* **1.** to take or have a part or share in common with others; participate (fol. by *in*). **2.** to receive, take, or have a share (fol. by *of*). **3.** to have something of the nature or character (fol. by *of*): *feelings partaking of both joy and regret.* *–v.t.* **4.** to take or have a part in; share. [backformation from *partaking, partaker,* for *part-taking, part-taker,* translation of L *participātio, particeps*] – **partaker,** *n.*

**parted** /'patəd/, *adj.* **1.** divided into parts; cleft. **2.** put or kept apart; separated. **3.** *Bot.* (of a leaf) separated into rather distinct portions by incisions which extend nearly to the midrib or the base. **4.** *Archaic.* deceased.

**parterre** /pa'tɛə/, *n.* **1.** an ornamental arrangement of flowerbeds of different shapes and sizes. **2.** *U.S.* the part of the main floor of a theatre, etc., behind the orchestra, often under the galleries. [F, from *par* by, on (from L *per*) + *terre* earth (from L *terra*)]

**partheno-,** a word element meaning 'virgin', 'without fertilisation', as in *parthenogenesis.* [combining form of Gk *parthénos* virgin]

**parthenogenesis** /paθənoʊ'dʒɛnəsəs/, *n.* a type of reproduction characterised by the development of an egg without fertilisation. – **parthenogenetic** /ˌpaθənoʊdʒə'nɛtɪk/, *adj.* – **parthenogenetically** /ˌpaθənoʊdʒə'nɛtɪkli/, *adv.*

**Parthian shot** /paθiən 'ʃɒt/, *n.* any sharp parting remark, as though delivered in retreat. [from archers in *Parthia* (ancient NE Iran) who shot at the enemy while riding away from them]

**partial** /'paʃəl/, *adj.* **1.** pertaining to or affecting a part. **2.** being such in part only; not total or general; incomplete: *partial blindness.* **3.** *Bot.* secondary or subordinate: *a partial umbel.* **4.** being a part; component or constituent. **5.** biased or prejudiced in favour of a person, group, side, etc., as in a controversy. **6.** particularly inclined in fondness or liking (fol. by *to*): *I'm partial to chocolate.* *–n.* **7.** *Music.* a name given to each of the notes of the harmonic series, in ascending order: *first partial, second partial, etc.* [ME, from LL *partiālis,* from L *pars* PART, *n.*] – **partially,** *adv.*

**partial derivative** /– də'rɪvətɪv/, *n.* (in mathematics) a derivative of a function of several variables with respect to one of the variables, the other variables being regarded as constant.

**partial eclipse** /– i'klɪps/, *n.* an eclipse, esp. of the sun, in which part of one body remains unobscured by the other.

**partial fractions** /– 'frækʃənz/, *n. pl.* (in algebra) the simple rational functions into which a given rational function may be resolved, their sum being equal to the given rational function. The process of resolution is known as **partial fraction decomposition.**

**partiality** /paʃi'æləti/, *n., pl.* **-ties. 1.** the state or character of being partial. **2.** favourable bias or prejudice: *the partiality of parents for their own offspring.* **3.** a particular liking (oft. fol. by *for*): *a partiality for society.*

**partial pressure** /paʃəl 'prɛʃə/, *n.* the pressure that one of the gases in a mixture of gases would exert if it was present alone and occupied the same volume as the whole mixture, at the same temperature.

**partible** /'patəbəl/, *adj.* that may be parted; divisible.

**particeps criminis** /ˌpatəkɛps 'krɪmənəs/, *n.* (in law) a principal or accessory to a felony; a procurer, aider, or abettor of a misdemeanour. [L]

**participable** /pa'tɪsəpəbəl/, *adj.* capable of being participated or shared.

**participant** /pa'tɪsəpənt/, *n.* **1.** one who participates; a participator. *–adj.* **2.** participating; sharing.

**participate** /pa'tɪsəpeɪt/, *v.*, **-pated, -pating.** *–v.i.* **1.** to take or have a part or share, as with others; share (fol. by *in*): *to participate in profits.* *–v.t.* **2.** to take or have a part or share in; share. [L *participātus,* pp.] – **participator,** *n.*

**participation** /paˌtɪsə'peɪʃən/, *n.* **1.** the act or fact of participating. **2.** a taking part, as in some action or attempt. **3.** a sharing, as in benefits or profits. Also, **participance.**

**participial** /patə'sɪpiəl/, *adj.* **1.** of or pertaining to a participle. **2.** similar to or formed from a participle. *–n.* **3.** a participle. [L *participiālis*] – **participially,** *adv.*

**participle** /'patəsɪpəl/, *n.* (in many languages) an adjective form derived from verbs, which ascribes to a noun participation in the action or state of the verb, in English without specifying person or number of the subject. For example: *burning* in *a burning candle* or *devoted* in *his devoted friend.* [ME, from OF, from *participe* (b. with ending *-ple*), from L *participium* a sharing]

**particle** /'patɪkəl/, *n.* **1.** a minute portion, piece, or amount; a very small bit: *a particle of dust.* **2.** *Physics.* an elementary particle. **3.** a clause or article, as of a document. **4.** *Rom. Cath. Ch.* **a.** a little piece of the Host. **b.** the small Host given to each lay communicant. **5.** *Gram.* **a.** (in some languages) one of the major form classes, or parts of speech, consisting of words which are neither nouns nor verbs, or of all uninflected words, or the like. **b.** such a word. **c.** a small word of functional or relational use, such as an article, preposition, or conjunction, whether of a separate form class or not. [ME, from L *particula,* diminutive of *pars* PART, *n.*]

**particle accelerator** /– ək'sɛləreɪtə/, *n.* →**accelerator** (def. 5).

**particle board** /'– bɔd/, *n.* a board manufactured by bonding together particles and chips of wood. Also, **chipboard.**

**particoloured** /'patikʌləd/, *adj.* coloured differently in different parts, or variegated: *particoloured dress.* Also, **party-coloured;** *U.S.,* **particolored.**

**particular** /pə'tɪkjələ/, *adj.* **1.** pertaining to some one person thing, group, class, occasion, etc., rather than to others or all special, not general: *one's particular interests.* **2.** being a definite one, individual, or single, or considered separately *each particular item.* **3.** distinguished or different from others or from the ordinary; noteworthy; marked; unusual **4.** exceptional or especial: *to take particular pains.* **5.** being such in an exceptional degree: *a particular friend of mine.* **6** dealing with or giving details, as an account, description, etc. of a person; detailed; minute; circumstantial. **7.** attentive to or exacting about details or small points: *to be particular about one's food.* **8.** *Logic.* pertaining to a proposition that concerns one or more unspecified members of a class; 'some men are wealthy', 'some man is wealthy', are particular pro positions. Cf. **universal** (def. 9); **singular** (def. 6). **9.** *Philos.* partaking of the nature of an unspecified individual as opposed to the universal and to the singular. **10.** *Law.* **a.** denoting an estate which precedes a future or ultimate ownership, as lands devised to a widow during her lifetime, and after that to her children. **b.** denoting the tenant of such an estate. *–n.* **11.** an individual or distinct part, as an item of a list or enumeration. **12.** a point, detail, or circumstance: *a report complete in every particular.* **13.** *Logic.* an unspecified member of a class. **14. in particular,** particularly; especially: *one book in particular.* [L *particulāris* of a part, partial; replacing ME *particuler,* from OF]

**particularise** /pəˈtɪkjələraɪz/, *v.,* **-rised, -rising.** *–v.t.* **1.** to make particular (rather than general). **2.** to mention or indicate particularly. **3.** to state or treat in detail. *–v.i.* **4.** to speak or treat particularly or specifically; mention individuals. Also, **particularize.** – **particularisation** /pətɪkjələraɪˈzeɪʃən/, *n.* – **particulariser,** *n.*

**particularism** /pəˈtɪkjələrɪzəm/, *n.* **1.** exclusive attention or devotion to one's own particular interests, party, etc. **2.** the principle of leaving each state of a federation free to retain its laws and promote its interests. **3.** *Theol.* the doctrine that divine grace is provided only for the elect. – **particularist,** *n.* – **particularistic** /pətɪkjələˈrɪstɪk/, *adj.*

**particularity** /pətɪkjəˈlærəti/, *n., pl.* **-ties.** **1.** the quality or fact of being particular. **2.** special, peculiar, or individual character. **3.** detailed, minute, or circumstantial character, as of description or statement. **4.** attentiveness to details or small points, or special carefulness. **5.** fastidiousness. **6.** that which is particular; a particular or characteristic feature or trait.

**particularly** /pəˈtɪkjələli/, *adv.* **1.** in a particular or exceptional degree; especially: *he read it with particularly great interest.* **2.** in a particular manner; specially; individually. **3.** in detail; minutely.

**particulate** /pəˈtɪkjələt/, *adj.* existing as, composed of, or pertaining to particles.

**parting** /ˈpatɪŋ/, *n.* **1.** the act of one who or that which parts. **2.** division; separation. **3.** leave-taking; departure. **4.** death. **5.** a place of division or separation. **6.** something that serves to part or separate things. **7.** a dividing line formed by combing the hair so that one part falls towards the left and the other towards the right of the head. **8. parting of the ways,** a leave-taking, esp. a final one. *–adj.* **9.** given, taken, done, etc., at parting: *a parting shot.* **10.** of or pertaining to parting, leave-taking, departure, or death. **11.** departing: *the parting day.* **12.** dying. **13.** dividing; separating.

**parting strip** /ˈ– strɪp/, *n.* a strip, as of wood, used to keep two parts separated, as one in each side of the frame of a window to keep the sashes apart when lowered or raised.

**parti pris** /pati ˈpri/, *n.* decision taken; foregone conclusion. [F]

**partisan**[1] /ˈpatəzən, patəˈzæn/, *n.* **1.** an adherent or supporter of a person, party, or cause. **2.** *Mil.* a member of a party of light or irregular troops, esp. as forming the indigenous armed resistance to an invader or conqueror; a guerilla. *–adj.* **3.** pertaining to or carried on by military partisans. Also, **partizan.** [F, from It. *partigiano,* from *parte* part, n., from L *pars*] – **partisanship,** *n.*

**partisan**[2] /ˈpatəzən/, *n.* a shafted weapon with broad blade and curved basal lobes, esp. carried by bodyguards. Also, **partizan.** [F *partizane,* from It. *partigiana,* fem., n. use of *partigiano,* adj., PARTISAN[1]]

**partita** /paˈtitə/, *n.* (in music) an instrumental suite. [It., fem. of *partito* divided into parts]

**partite** /ˈpataɪt/, *adj.* **1.** divided into parts. **2.** *Bot.* parted. [L *partītus,* pp.]

**partition** /paˈtɪʃən/, *n.* **1.** division into or distribution in portions or shares. **2.** separation, as of two or more things. **3.** something that separates. **4.** the date or period of the division of a country or state into two or more new countries, or states as that of British India into India and Pakistan in 1947: *before partition.* **5.** a part, division, or section. **6.** an interior wall or barrier dividing a building, enclosure, etc. **7.** a septum or dissepiment, as in a plant or animal structure. **8.** *Law.* **a.** a division of property among joint owners or tenants in common, or a sale of such property followed by a division of the proceeds. **b.** a division of real property held in co-ownership. **9.** *Logic.* the separation of a whole into its integrant parts, in contradistinction to the division of a genus into species. **10.** *Maths.* any expression of a positive integer as a sum of positive integers: *3 + 2 + 1 + 1 is a partition of 7.* **11.** *Rhet.* (in a speech organised on classical principles) the second part, in which a speaker announces the chief lines of thought he proposes to discuss in support of his theme. *–v.t.* **12.** to divide into parts or portions. **13.** to divide or separate by a partition. **14.** *Law.* to divide property among several owners, either in specie or by sale and division of the proceeds. [ME, from L *partītio*] – **partitioner,** *n.* – **partitionist,** *n.* – **partitionment,** *n.*

**partitive** /ˈpatətɪv/, *adj.* **1.** serving to divide into parts. **2.** *Gram.* denoting part of a whole: *the Latin partitive genitive.* *–n.* **3.** *Gram.* a partitive word or formation, as *of the men* in *half of the men.* – **partitively,** *adv.*

**partizan** /ˈpatəzən, patəˈzæn/, *n., adj.* →**partisan**[1].

**partly** /ˈpatli/, *adv.* in part; in some measure; not wholly.

**partn.,** partnership.

**partner** /ˈpatnə/, *n.* **1.** a sharer or partaker; an associate. **2.** *Law.* **a.** one associated with another or others as a principal or a contributor of capital in a business or a joint venture, usu. sharing its risks and profits. **b.** See **limited partner.** **3.** See **sleeping partner.** **4.** a husband or a wife. **5.** one's companion in a dance. **6.** a player on the same side with another in a game. **7.** (*pl.*) *Naut.* fore-and-aft vertical metal plating fitted underneath a ship's deck to strengthen it where it is cut for a mast, capstan, pump, etc. *–v.t.* **8.** to associate as a partner or partners. **9.** to be, or act as, the partner of. [ME *partener,* var. of PARCENER, apparently by association with PART, *n.*] – **partnerless,** *adj.*

**partnership** /ˈpatnəʃɪp/, *n.* **1.** the state or condition of being a partner; participation; association; joint interest. **2.** *Law.* **a.** the relation subsisting between partners. **b.** the contract creating this relation. **c.** an association of persons joined as partners in business. **3.** *Cricket.* the period during which two batsmen stay at the wicket together, usu. with reference to the runs scored by them: *a last-wicket partnership of 45.*

**part of speech,** *n.* any of the mutually exclusive major form classes of a language, which taken together include the entire vocabulary. For example, in Latin, a word is either a *noun, verb, pronoun, adjective, adverb, preposition, conjunction,* or *interjection.*

**parton** /ˈpatɒn/, *n.* a hypothetical point-like object within protons, neutrons, etc.

**partook** /paˈtʊk/, *v.* past tense of **partake.**

**partridge** /ˈpatrɪdʒ/, *n., pl.* **-tridges,** (*esp. collectively*) **-tridge.** **1.** any of various gallinaceous game birds of the subfamily Perdicinae, esp. the **common partridge,** *Perdix perdix,* of Europe. **2.** any of various North American gallinaceous birds as the **ruffed grouse** (*Bonasa umbellus*); the **bobwhite quail** (*Colinus virginianus*), etc. **3.** any of various South and Central American tinamous. [ME *pertrich,* from OF *perdriz, perdiz,* from L *perdix,* from Gk]

common partridge

**partridge-wood** /ˈpatrɪdʒ-wʊd/, *n.* the hard variegated wood of a tropical American tree, *Andira inermis,* sometimes used for cabinet work.

**part-song** /ˈpat-sɒŋ/, *n.* a song with parts for several voices, esp. one meant to be sung without accompaniment. – **part-singing,** *n.*

**part time** /pat ˈtaɪm/, *n.* less than all normal working hours (opposed to *full time*).

**part-time** /ˈpat-taɪm, pat-ˈtaɪm/, *adj.;* /pat-ˈtaɪm/, *adv.* *–adj.* **1.** of, pertaining to, or occupying less than all normal working hours. **2.** not being one's chief occupation: *a part-time job.* *–adv.* **3.** during less than all normal working hours. – **part-timer,** *n.*

**parturient** /paˈtjuriənt/, *adj.* **1.** bringing forth or about to bring forth young; in labour. **2.** pertaining to parturition. **3.**

bringing forth or about to produce something, as an idea. [L *parturiens,* ppr., being in labour] – **parturiency,** *n.*

**parturifacient** /pa,tjuri'feɪʃənt/, *adj.* of a drug or other agent which stimulates uterine contractions, thereby accelerating childbirth.

**parturition** /patʃə'rɪʃən/, *n.* the act of bringing forth young; childbirth.

**party** /'pati/, *n., pl.* **-ties,** *adj. –n.* **1.** a group gathered together for some purpose, as for amusement or entertainment. **2.** a social gathering or entertainment, as of invited guests at a private house or elsewhere: *to give a party.* **3.** a detachment of troops assigned to perform some particular service. **4.** (*oft. cap.*) a number or body of persons ranged on one side, or united in purpose or opinion, in opposition to others, as in politics, etc.: *the Australian Labor Party.* **5.** the system or practice of taking sides on public questions or the like. **6.** attachment or devotion to a side or faction; partisanship. **7.** *Law.* **a.** one of the litigants in a legal proceeding; a plaintiff or defendant in a suit. **b.** a signatory to a legal instrument. **c.** one participating in or otherwise privy to a crime. **8.** *Mining.* a group of men performing geophysical work of a specific project, ordinarily using a single method. **9.** one who participates in some action or affair. **10.** the person under consideration. **11.** a person in general. **12. come to the party,** to assist, esp. with money; fall in with one's plans. *–adj.* **13.** of or pertaining to a party or faction; partisan: *party issue.* **14.** of or for a social gathering: *a party dress.* **15.** *Her.* divided into parts, usu. two parts, and a shield. *–v.i.* **16. party on,** to continue a party. [ME *parti(e),* from OF, pp. of *partir* PART, *v.*]

**party cited** /– 'saɪtəd/, *n.* the person alleged by the respondent in a divorce case to have committed adultery with the petitioner (no longer legally relevant in Australia).

**party-coloured** /'pati-kʌləd/, *adj.* →**particoloured.**

**party hack** /pati 'hæk/, *n. Colloq.* a person who is said to have given lengthy, mainly menial service to a political party.

**party ice** /'– aɪs/, *n.* ice made in small pieces and ready for use in cold drinks.

**party line** /'– laɪn/, *n.* **1.** a telephone line shared by two or more subscribers. **2.** the bounding line between adjoining premises. **3.** the authoritatively announced policies and practices of a group, usu. followed without exception: *the Communist party line.*

**party man** /'– mæn/, *n. Politics Colloq.* a person whose actions, words and associations are almost entirely directed or dictated by party considerations.

**party politics** /– 'pɒlətɪks/, *n.* politics practised with a view to the advancement of a party rather than in the public interest.

**party pooper** /'– pupə/, *n. Colloq.* a person who has a discouraging or depressing effect, esp. at a party.

**party spirit** /– 'spɪrət/, *n.* **1.** enthusiastic adherence to a political party. **2.** the mood and feeling of sociability appropriate to a party (def. 2).

**party wall** /– 'wɔl/, *n.* a wall used, or useable, as a part of contiguous structures.

**parure** /pə'ruə/, *n.* a set of jewels or ornaments. [ME, from F, from *parer* prepare, adorn. See PARE]

**parvenu** /'pavənu, -nju/, *n.* **1.** one who has risen above his class or to a position above his qualifications; an upstart. *–adj.* **2.** being or resembling a parvenu. **3.** characteristic of a parvenu. [F, properly pp. of *parvenir* arrive, from L *pervenīre*]

**parvis** /'pavəs/, *n.* **1.** a vacant enclosed area in front of a church. **2.** a colonnade or portico in front of a church. **3.** a room over a church porch. Also, **parvise** /'pavəs/. [ME *parvys,* from OF *parevis,* from LL *paradīsus* PARADISE]

**parvoline** /'pavəlin/, *n.* any of several oily isomeric, organic bases, $C_9H_{13}N$, one occurring in coal tar and another in decaying mackerel. Also, **parvolin** /'pavələn/. [L *parvus* small (with ref. to its relatively small volatility) + -OL[2] + -INE[2]; modelled on QUINOLINE]

**pas** /pa/, *n.* **1.** a step or movement in dancing, esp. in ballet. **2.** a dance. **3.** precedence; right of preceding. [see PACE[1]]

**PAS** /pi eɪ 'ɛs/, *n.* para-amino-salicylic acid, used in the treatment of tuberculosis.

**pascal** /'pæskəl, pæs'kal/, *n.* the derived SI unit of pressure, equal to 1 newton per square metre. *Symbol:* Pa [named after Blaise *Pascal,* 1623-62, French philosopher, mathematician and physicist]

**pascalia weed** /pæs'keɪliə wid/, *n.* a troublesome perennial weed, *Wedelia glauca,* family Compositae, widely naturalised in temperate regions.

**Pasch** /pæsk/, *n. Archaic.* **1.** the Passover. **2.** Easter. [ME *pasche,* from LL *pascha,* from Gk, from Heb. *pesaḥ* Passover; var. of PESACH]

**pascha** /'pæskə/, *n.* a traditional Russian Easter dessert, made with butter, egg yolks, sugar, cream cheese, cream and dried fruits, formed into a pyramidal shape and served with kulich. Also, **paskha.** [Russ.: Easter]

**paschal** /'pæskəl/, *adj.* **1.** pertaining to the Passover. **2.** pertaining to Easter. [ME *paschall,* from LL *paschālis,* from *pascha* PASCH]

**paschal flower** /'– flaʊə/, *n.* →**pasqueflower.**

**paschal lamb** /– 'læm/, *n.* **1.** (among the Jews, during the existence of the Temple) the lamb slain and eaten on the eve of the first day of the Passover. **2.** (*cap.*) Christ. **3.** (*cap.*) any of various symbolical representations of Christ. Cf. **Agnus Dei.**

**pas de deux** /pa də 'dɜ/, *n., pl.* **pas de deux.** a dance by two persons. [F]

**pash** /pæʃ/, *Colloq. –n.* **1.** a passion; infatuation. **2.** kissing or cuddling. *–v.i., v.t.* **3.** to kiss or cuddle (oft. fol. by *off*).

**pasha** /'paʃə/, *n.* a title, placed after the name, formerly borne by civil and military officials of high rank in Turkish dominions. Also, **pacha.** [Turk., var. of *bāshā,* from *bash* head, chief]

**pashalik** /'paʃəlɪk/, *n.* the territory governed by a pasha. Also, **pachalic, pashalic.** [Turk. *pāshā* PASHA + *-lik,* suffix denoting quality or condition]

**paspalum** /pæs'peɪləm/, *n.* any grass of the genus *Paspalum* but esp. *P. dilatatum,* native to southern America but now one of the most widespread grasses in the higher-rainfall areas of Australia.

**pasqueflower** /'pæskflaʊə/, *n.* **1.** an Old World plant, *Pulsatilla vulgaris,* with purple flowers blooming about Easter. **2.** any of several similar plants, as *Anemone ludoviciana.* [*Pasque* (var. spelling of PASCH) + FLOWER (so named by the herbalist Gerarde in 1597); replacing *passeflower,* from F *passefleur.* See PASS, *v.,* FLOWER]

paspalum

**pasquil** /'pæskwəl/, *n.* →**pasquinade.**

**pasquinade** /pæskwə'neɪd/, *n., v.,* **-naded, -nading.** *–n.* **1.** a publicly posted lampoon. *–v.t.* **2.** to assail in a pasquinade or pasquinades. [F, from It. *pasquinata,* from *Pasquino,* name given to an antique statue dug up in Rome (1501), which was decorated once a year and posted with verses] – **pasquinader,** *n.*

**pass** /pas/, *v.,* **passed** or (*Rare*) **past, passed** or **past, passing,** *n. –v.t.* **1.** to go by or move past (something). **2.** to go by without acting upon or noticing; leave unmentioned. **3.** to omit payment of (a dividend, etc.). **4.** to go or get through (a channel, barrier, etc.). **5.** to go across or over (a stream, threshold, etc.); cross. **6.** to undergo successfully (an examination, etc.). **7.** to undergo or get through (an obstacle, experience, ordeal, etc.). **8.** to permit to complete successfully. **9.** to go beyond (a point, degree, stage, etc.); transcend; exceed; surpass. **10.** to cause to go or move onwards: *to pass a rope through a hole.* **11.** *U.S.* to cause to go by or move past: *to pass troops in review.* **12.** to exist through; live during; spend: *to pass the time of day.* **13.** to cause to go about or circulate; give currency to. **14.** to cause to be accepted or received. **15.** to convey, transfer, or transmit; deliver. **16.** to pronounce; utter: *to pass remarks.* **17.** to pledge, as one's word. **18.** to cause or allow to go through something, as through a test, etc. **19.** to discharge or void, as excrement. **20.** to sanction or approve: *to pass a bill.* **21.** to obtain the approval or sanction of (a legislative body, etc.), as a bill. **22.** to express or pronounce, as an opinion or judgment. **23.** *Law.* to place legal title or interest in (another) by a conveyance, a will, or other transfer. **24.** *Magic.* to perform a pass (def. 62) on (cards, etc.). **25.** *Football, Hockey, etc.* to transmit (the ball, etc.) to another player. **26.** to overtake. *–v.i.* **27.** to go or move onwards; proceed; make one's, or its, way. **28.** to go away or depart. **29.** to elapse, as time. **30.** to come to an end, as a thing in time. **31.** to die. **32.** to go on or take place; happen; occur: *to learn what has passed.* **33.** to go by or move past, as a procession. **34.** to go about or circulate; be current. **35.** to be accepted or received (fol. by *for* or *as*): *material that passed for silk.* **36.** to be transferred or conveyed. **37.** to be interchanged, as between two persons: *sharp words passed between them.* **38.** to undergo transition or conversion: *to pass from a solid to a liquid state.* **39.** to go or get through something, such as a barrier, test, examination, etc., esp. without honours. **40.** to go unheeded, uncensured, or unchallenged: *but let that pass.* **41.** to express or pronounce an opinion, judgment, verdict, etc. (usu. fol. by *on* or *upon*). **42.** to be voided, as excrement. **43.** to be ratified or enacted, as a bill or law. **44.** *Law.* **a.** to vest title or other legal interest in real or personal property in a new owner. **b.** *U.S.* to adjudicate. **45.** to throw a ball from one to another; play catch. **46.** to make a pass, as in football. **47.** *Fencing.* to thrust or lunge. **48.** *Cards.* **a.** to forgo one's opportunity to bid, play, etc. **b.** to throw up one's hand. *–v.* **49.** Some special verb phrases are:

**bring to pass,** to cause to happen.

**come to pass,** to occur.

**pass away, 1.** to cease to be. **2.** to die.

**pass off, 1.** to put into circulation, or dispose of, esp. deceptively: *to pass off a counterfeit dollar.* **2.** to cause to be accepted or received in a false character: *he passed himself off as my servant.* **3.** to end gradually; to cease. **4.** to take place; occur: *the introduction passed off without incident.*

**pass on, 1.** to die. **2.** to move to another place.

**pass out, 1.** *Colloq.* to faint. **2.** to complete the course, as at a military academy.

**pass over, 1.** to disregard. **2.** to omit to notice.

**pass the buck,** to avoid responsibility by passing it to another.

**pass up,** *Colloq.* to refuse; reject.

[ME *passe(n)*, from OF *passer,* from L *passus* a step] *–n.* **50.** a narrow route across a relatively low notch or depression in a mountain barrier separating the headwaters of approaching valleys from either side. **51.** a way affording passage, as through an obstructed region. **52.** *U.S.* a navigable channel, as at the mouth or delta of a river. **53.** a permission or licence to pass, go, come, or enter. **54.** *Mil.* **a.** a military document granting the right to cross lines, or to enter or leave a military or naval reservation or other area or building. **b.** written authority given to a soldier to leave a station or duty for a few hours or days. **55.** (formerly) written authority for a convict to travel on errands. **56.** a free ticket. **57.** the passing of an examination, etc., esp. without honours. **58.** the transference of a ball, etc., from one player to another, as in football. **59.** a thrust or lunge, as in fencing. **60.** *Colloq.* a jab with the arm, esp. one that misses its mark. **61.** *Cards.* an act of not bidding or raising another bid. **62.** *Magic, etc.* **a.** a passing of the hand over, along, or before anything. **b.** the transference or changing of objects by or as by sleight of hand; a manipulation, as of a juggler; a trick. **63.** a stage in procedure or experience; a particular stage or state of affairs: *things have come to a pretty pass.* **64.** the act of passing. **65.** *Archaic.* a sally of wit. **66. make a pass,** to make an amorous overture or gesture (usu. fol. by *at*). [ME *passe;* partly n. use of PASS, *v.*; partly from F, from *passer*]

**pass., 1.** passenger. **2.** passive.

**passable** /ˈpasəbəl/, *adj.* **1.** that may be passed. **2.** that may be proceeded through or over, or traversed, penetrated, crossed, etc., as a road, forest, or stream. **3.** tolerable, fair, or moderate: *a passable knowledge of history.* **4.** that may be circulated, or has valid currency, as a coin. **5.** that may be ratified, or enacted. [ME, from F, from *passer* PASS, *v.*] **– passableness,** *n.*

**passably** /ˈpasəbli/, *adv.* fairly; moderately.

**passacaglia** /pæsəˈkaliə/, *n.* **1.** a slow dance of Spanish origin. **2.** the music for this dance, based on an ostinato figure. [Sp. *pasacalle,* lit., street-dance; with It. ending *-aglia*]

**passade** /pæˈseɪd/, *n.* a turn or course of a horse backwards or forwards on the same ground.

**passado** /pəˈsadoʊ/, *n., pl.* **-dos, -does.** *Fencing.* a forward thrust with the sword, one foot being advanced at the same time. [Sp. *pasada,* from It. *passata,* from *passare* PASS, *v.*]

**passage**[1] /ˈpæsɪdʒ/, *n., v.,* **-saged, -saging.** *–n.* **1.** an indefinite portion of a writing, speech, or the like, usu. one of no great length; a paragraph, verse, etc.: *a passage of Scripture.* **2.** *Music.* **a.** a scale- or arpeggio-like series of notes introduced as an embellishment; a run, roulade, or flourish. **b.** a phrase or other division of a piece. **3.** the act of passing. **4.** liberty, leave, or right to pass: *to refuse passage through a territory.* **5.** that by which a person or thing passes; a means of passing; a way, route, avenue, channel, etc. **6.** a corridor, or the like. **7.** movement, transit, or transition, as from one place or state to another. **8.** a voyage across the sea from one port to another: *a rough passage.* **9.** the privilege of conveyance as a passenger: *to secure a passage to Europe.* **10.** lapse, as of time. **11.** progress or course, as of events. **12.** the passing into law of a legislative measure. **13.** an interchange of communications, confidences, etc., between persons. **14.** an exchange of blows; an altercation or dispute: *a passage at arms.* **15.** the causing of something to pass; transference; transmission. **16.** an evacuation of the bowels. **17.** *Archaic.* an occurrence, incident, or event. *–v.i.* **18.** to make a passage; cross; pass; voyage. [ME, from OF, from *passer* PASS, *v.*]

**passage**[2] /ˈpæsɪdʒ/, *v.,* **-saged, -saging,** *n. –v.i.* **1.** (of a horse) to move sideways, in obedience to pressure by the rider's leg on the opposite side. **2.** (of a rider) to cause a horse to do this. *–v.t.* **3.** to cause (a horse) to passage. *–n.* **4.** the act of passaging. [F *passager,* from It. *passeggiare* to pace, walk, from *passo* pace, from L *passus* PACE[1]]

**passageway** /ˈpæsɪdʒweɪ/, *n.* a way for passage, as in a building or among buildings, etc.; a passage.

**passant** /ˈpæsənt/, *adj.* (of a beast used as a bearing in heraldry) walking with one paw raised, and looking forward to the dexter side of the escutcheon. [ME, from F, ppr. of *passer* PASS, *v.*]

**passbook** /ˈpasbʊk/, *n.* **1.** a bankbook. **2.** a customer's book in which a merchant or trader makes entries of goods sold on credit. **3.** a record of payments made to a building society.

**pass degree** /ˈpas dəgri/, *n.* (in universities) a degree conferred without honours.

**passé** /paˈseɪ/, *adj.* **1.** antiquated, or out-of-date. **2.** passed. **3.** past the prime; aged. [F, pp. of *passer* PASS, *v.*]

**passed** /past/, *adj.* **1.** that has passed or has been passed. **2.** having passed an examination or test. **3.** *Finance.* denoting a dividend not paid at the usual dividend date. **4. passed in,** of or pertaining to goods, land, etc., which, at auction, do not reach the reserve price and are withdrawn from sale.

**passementerie** /pæsˈmɛntri/, *n.* trimming made of braid, cord, beads, etc., in various forms. [F, from *passement,* from *passer* PASS, *v.*]

**passenger** /ˈpæsəndʒə/, *n.* **1.** one who travels by some form of conveyance: *the passengers of a ship.* **2.** a wayfarer. **3.** *Colloq.* a member of a team, staff, etc., who does not perform his fair share of work. [ME *passager,* from OF *passagier,* from *passage* PASSAGE[1]; for *-n-*, cf. MESSENGER, etc.]

**passe-partout** /pæs-paˈtu, pas-/, *n., pl.* **-touts** /-tuz/. **1.** a kind of ornamental mat for a picture. **2.** a frame with such a mat, to receive a photograph or other representation. **3.** a picture frame consisting of a piece of glass, under which the picture is placed, affixed to a backing by means of adhesive strips of paper or other material. **4.** that which passes, or by means of which one can pass, everywhere. **5.** a master key. [F: lit., pass-everywhere]

**passepied** /ˈpaspjeɪ/, *n.* an old French dance in 3/8 or 6/8 time rather like a fast minuet. [F]

**passer** /ˈpasə/, *n.* **1.** one that passes or causes something to pass. **2.** a passer-by.

**passer-by** /pasəˈbaɪ/, *n., pl.* **passers-by.** one who passes by.

**passeriform** /ˈpæsərəfɔm/, *adj.* belonging or pertaining to the avian order Passeriformes; passerine.

**passerine** /ˈpæsəraɪn/, *adj.* **1.** belonging or pertaining to the Passeriformes, an order of birds, typically insessorial (perching), embracing more than half of all birds, and including the finches, thrushes, warblers, swallows, crows, larks, etc. *–n.* **2.** any bird of the order Passeriformes. [L *passerīnus* of a sparrow]

**pas seul** /pa 'səl/, *n.* a dance performed by one person. [F]

**passible** /'pæsəbəl/, *adj.* capable of suffering or feeling; susceptible to sensation or emotion. [ME, from LL *passibilis*] – **passibility** /pæsə'bɪləti/, *n.*

**passim** /'pæsɪm/, *adv.* **1.** here and there, as in books or writings. **2.** throughout. [L]

**passing** /'pasɪŋ/, *adj.* **1.** going by; elapsing. **2.** fleeting or transitory. **3.** that is now happening; current. **4.** done, given, etc., in passing; cursory: *a passing mention.* **5.** surpassing, pre-eminent, or extreme. **6.** indicating that one has passed: *a passing mark on the test.* *–adv.* **7.** *Archaic.* surpassingly; exceedingly; very. *–n.* **8.** the act of one that passes or causes something to pass. **9.** a means or place of passage; passage. **10. in passing,** in the course of passing, going on, or proceeding.

**passing bell** /'– bɛl/, *n.* **1.** a bell tolled to announce a death or funeral. **2.** a portent or sign of the passing away of anything.

**passing modulation** /– ˌmɒdʒə'leɪʃən/, *n.* (in music) a modulation of a temporary nature.

**passing note** /'– noʊt/, *n.* a note foreign to the harmony, introduced between two successive chords in order to produce a melodic transition.

**passing-out** /pasɪŋ-'aʊt/, *adj.* (of a ceremony or parade) celebrating the completion of a course or training.

**passing shot** /'pasɪŋ ʃɒt/, *n.* a tennis shot which passes the opposing player or pair.

**passion** /'pæʃən/, *n.* **1.** any kind of feeling or emotion, as hope, fear, joy, grief, anger, love, desire, etc., esp. when of compelling force. **2.** strong amorous feeling or desire. **3.** passionate sexual love. **4.** an instance or experience of it. **5.** a person who is the object of such a feeling. **6.** a strong or extravagant fondness, enthusiasm, or desire for anything: *a passion for music.* **7.** the object of such a fondness or desire: *accuracy became a passion with him.* **8.** a passionate outburst: *she broke into a passion of tears.* **9.** violent anger. **10.** *Rare.* the state or fact of being acted upon or affected by something external (opposed to *action*). **11.** (*oft. cap.*) **a.** the sufferings of Christ on the Cross, or his sufferings subsequent to the Last Supper. **b.** the gospel narrative of the sufferings of Christ. **c.** a musical setting of it. **d.** a pictorial representation of Christ's sufferings. **12.** *Archaic.* the sufferings of a martyr. [ME, from OF, from L *passio* suffering]

**passional** /'pæʃənəl/, *adj.* **1.** of or pertaining to passion or the passions. **2.** due to passion: *passional crimes.* *–n.* **3.** a book containing descriptions of the sufferings of saints and martyrs, for reading on their festivals.

**passionary** /'pæʃənəri/, *n., pl.* **-ries.** →**passional.**

**passionate** /'pæʃənət/, *adj.* **1.** affected with or dominated by passion or vehement emotion: *a passionate advocate of socialism.* **2.** characterised by, expressing, or showing vehement emotion; impassioned: *passionate language.* **3.** vehement, as feelings or emotions: *passionate grief.* **4.** easily moved to anger; quick-tempered; irascible. **5.** ardently amorous; easily affected by sexual desire. [late ME *passionat,* from ML *passionātus*] – **passionately,** *adv.* – **passionateness,** *n.*

**passionflower** /'pæʃənflaʊə/, *n.* any plant of the genus *Passiflora,* or related genera, which comprise climbing vines or shrubs, mainly American, bearing showy flowers and a pulpy berry or fruit which in some species is edible, esp. the passionfruit. [so named from a supposed resemblance of the flower to the wounds, crown of thorns, etc., of Christ]

Australian passionflower

**passionfruit** /'pæʃənfrut/, *n.* **1.** Also, **passionfruit vine.** a passionflower, *Passiflora edulis.* **2.** the fruit of this plant.

**passionless** /'pæʃənləs/, *adj.* without passion; cold; unemotional.

**passion pit** /'pæʃən pɪt/, *n. Colloq.* **1.** any cinema in which petting takes place among the audience esp. a drive-in. **2.** a bedroom decorated in a vulgar and lascivious manner.

**passion play** /'– pleɪ/, *n.* a dramatic representation of the Passion of Christ, such as that given every ten years at the Bavarian village of Oberammergau.

**Passion Sunday** /pæʃən 'sʌndeɪ/, *n.* the fifth Sunday in Lent, being the second before Easter.

**Passion Week** /'– wik/, *n.* **1.** the week preceding Easter; Holy Week. **2.** the week before Holy Week, beginning with Passion Sunday.

**passivate** /'pæsəveɪt/, *v.t.,* **-vated, -vating.** (in electronics) to make passive.

**passive** /'pæsɪv, -səv/, *adj.* **1.** not acting, or not attended with or manifested in open or positive action: *passive resistance.* **2.** inactive, quiescent, or inert. **3.** suffering action, acted upon, or being the object of action (opposed to *active*). **4.** receiving or characterised by the reception of impressions from without. **5.** produced by or due to external agency. **6.** suffering, receiving, or submitting without resistance. **7.** characterised by or involving doing this: *passive obedience.* **8.** *Gram.* denoting a verb form or voice, in which the subject is represented as being acted on. For example, in the sentence *He was hit, was hit* is in the passive voice. **9.** *Electronics.* (of an electronic component, or a complete circuit) unable to amplify or switch a signal, as a resistor or capacitor (opposed to an active circuit component, as a transistor or valve). **10.** *Chem.* inactive, esp. under conditions in which chemical activity is to be expected. **11.** (of a metal) having a protective oxide film on the surface rendering it impervious to attack. **12.** (of a communications satellite) only able to reflect signals, and not retransmit them. **13.** *Med.* pertaining to certain unhealthy but insufficiently virulent conditions; inactive (opposed to *active* or *spontaneous*). *–n.* **14.** *Gram.* **a.** the passive voice. **b.** a form or construction therein. [ME, from L *passīvus* capable of feeling] – **passively,** *adv.* – **passiveness, passivity** /pæs'ɪvəti/, *n.*

**passive homing** /– 'hoʊmɪŋ/, *n.* a form of missile guidance in which the receiver in the missile utilises radiations from the target.

**passive immunity** /– ə'mjunəti/, *n.* immunity achieved by injecting immune serum from another organism.

**passive open space,** *n.* an area of land, generally in an urban context, which is landscaped, beautified and set aside for the enjoyment of the public, excluding sporting activities.

**passive resistance** /pæsɪv rə'zɪstəns/, *n.* the expression of disapproval of authority or of specific laws by various nonviolent acts, such as public demonstration, voluntary fasting, or impeding normal commercial activities and the movement of transport, police, troops, etc.

**passivism** /'pæsəvɪzəm/, *n.* **1.** the theory of passive resistance. **2.** belief in this theory or its practice.

**pass key** /'pas ki/, *n.* **1.** →**master key. 2.** →**latchkey. 3.** →**skeleton key.**

**pass out** /'– aʊt/, *n.* a card given to theatre or cinema patrons at interval, enabling them to leave the premises and return without buying another ticket.

**Passover** /'pasoʊvə/, *n.* **1.** an annual feast of the Jews, instituted to commemorate the passing over or sparing of the Hebrews in Egypt when God smote the firstborn of the Egyptians, but used in the general sense of the Feast of Unleavened Bread in commemoration of the deliverance from Egypt. **2.** (*l.c.*) →**paschal lamb. 3.** (*l.c.*) Christ. [orig. verbal phrase *pass over*]

**passport** /'paspɔt/, *n.* **1.** an official document granting permission to the person specified to visit foreign countries, and authenticating his identity, citizenship and right to protection while abroad. **2.** an authorisation to pass or go anywhere. **3.** a document issued to a ship, esp. to neutral merchant vessels in time of war, granting or requesting permission to proceed without molestation in certain waters. **4.** a certificate intended to secure admission. **5.** anything that gives admission or acceptance. [F *passeport,* from *passe(r)* PASS + *port* PORT[1] (def. 3)]

**passus** /'pæsəs/, *n., pl.* **-sus, -suses.** a section or division of a story, poem, etc.; a canto. [ML, from L: a step, PACE[1]]

**password** /'paswɜd/, *n.* a secret word, made known only to authorised persons for their use in passing through a line of guards.

**past** /past/, *v. Rare.* **1.** past participle and occasional past tense of **pass.** *–adj.* **2.** gone by in time. **3.** belonging to, or having existed or occurred in time previous to this. **4.** gone by just before the present time; just passed: *the past year.* **5.** ago. **6.** having served a term in an office: *past president.* **7.** *Gram.* designating a tense, or other verb formation or construction, which refers to events or states in time gone by. For example, in the sentence *It happened last year, happened* is in the past tense. *–n.* **8.** the time gone by: *far back in the past.* **9.** the events of that time: *to forget the past.* **10.** a past history, life, career, etc.: *a glorious past.* **11.** a past career which is kept concealed: *a woman with a past.* **12.** *Gram.* **a.** the past tense, as *he ate, he smoked.* **b.** another verb formation or construction with past meaning. **c.** a form therein. *–adv.* **13.** so as to pass by or beyond; by: *the troops marched past.* *–prep.* **14.** beyond in time; after: *past noon.* **15.** beyond in position; farther on than: *the house past the church.* **16.** beyond in amount, number, etc. **17.** beyond the reach, scope, influence, or power of: *past belief.* [see PASS, *v.*]

**pasta** /ˈpæstə, ˈpas-/, *n.* any of the several preparations made from a dough or paste of wheat flour, salt, water, and sometimes egg, such as spaghetti, macaroni, tagliatelle, etc. [It., from LL *pasta* dough, PASTE]

**paste** /peɪst/, *n., v.,* **pasted, pasting.** *–n.* **1.** a mixture of flour and water, often with starch, etc., used for causing paper, etc., to adhere. **2.** any material or preparation in a soft or plastic mass: *a toothpaste.* **3.** dough, esp. when prepared with shortening, as for making pastry. **4.** any of various sweet confections of doughlike consistency: *almond paste.* **5.** a preparation of fish, tomatoes, or some other article of food reduced to a smooth, soft mass, as for spreading on bread or for seasoning. **6.** a mixture of clay, water, etc., for making earthenware or porcelain. **7.** a brilliant, heavy glass, used for making artificial gems. **8.** an artificial gem of this material. *–v.t.* **9.** to fasten or stick with paste or the like. **10.** to cover with something applied by means of paste. **11.** *Colloq.* to strike with a smart blow, or beat soundly, as on the face or body. **12.** *Colloq.* to berate. [ME, from OF, from LL *pasta,* from Gk *pástē* barley porridge]

**pasteboard** /ˈpeɪstbɔd/, *n.* **1.** a stiff, firm board made of sheets of paper pasted or layers of paper pulp pressed together, used for book covers. *–adj.* **2.** made of pasteboard. **3.** unsubstantial or flimsy; sham.

**pastel**[1] /ˈpæstl/, *n.* **1.** a soft, subdued shade. **2.** a kind of dried paste used for crayons, made of pigments ground with chalk and compounded with gum water. **3.** a crayon made with such paste. **4.** the art of drawing with such crayons. **5.** a drawing so made. **6.** a short, slight prose study or sketch. *–adj.* **7.** having a soft, subdued shade. **8.** drawn with pastels. [F, from Pr., from LL *pasta* PASTE]

**pastel**[2] /ˈpæstl/, *n.* **1.** →**woad.** [F, from It. *pastello,* from LL *pasta* PASTE]

**pastellist** /ˈpæstələst/, *n.* an artist who draws with pastels.

**paster** /ˈpeɪstə/, *n.* **1.** a slip of paper gummed on the back, to be pasted on or over something, as over a name on a ballot. **2.** one who or that which pastes.

**pastern** /ˈpæstɜn, -tn/, *n.* **1.** that part of the foot of a horse, etc., between the fetlock and the hoof. **2.** either of two bones of this part, the upper or first phalanx **(great pastern bone)** and the lower or second phalanx **(small pastern bone),** between which is a joint **(pastern joint).** [ME *pastron,* from F *pasturon,* from *pasture* shackle for animal while pasturing]

**paste-up** /ˈpeɪst-ʌp/, *n.* (in printing) a sheet of paper on which has been pasted artwork, proofs, etc., as a guide to the page make-up.

**pasteurellosis** /pastərəˈloʊsəs/, *n.* →**haemorrhagic septicaemia.**

**pasteurise** /ˈpastʃəraɪz/, *v.t.,* **-rised, -rising. 1.** to expose (milk, etc.) to a high temperature, usu. about 60°C, in order to destroy certain micro-organisms and prevent or arrest fermentation. **2.** to subject to pasteurism in order to prevent certain diseases, esp. bovine tuberculosis. Also, **pasteurize.** – **pasteurisation** /pastʃəraɪˈzeɪʃən/, *n.*

**pasteurism** /ˈpastʃərɪzəm/, *n.* **1.** a treatment devised by Pasteur for preventing certain diseases, esp. hydrophobia, by inoculations with virus of gradually increasing strength. **2.** the act or process of pasteurising milk, etc. [named after Louis *Pasteur,* 1822-95, French chemist and microbiologist. See -ISM]

**pasticcio** /pæsˈtitʃioʊ/, *n., pl.* **-ci** /-tʃi/. **1.** →**pastiche. 2.** a pie. [It, from *pasta* PASTE]

**pastiche** /pæsˈtiʃ/, *n.* any work of art, literature, or music consisting of motifs borrowed from one or more masters or works of art. [F, from It. *pasticcio* PASTICCIO]

**pastille** /ˈpæstil, -tl/, *n.* **1.** a flavoured or a medicated lozenge. **2.** a roll or cone of paste containing aromatic substances, burned as a disinfectant, etc. **3.** pastel for crayons. **4.** a crayon made of it. Also, **pastil** /ˈpæstl/. [F, from Sp. *pastilla,* diminutive of *pasta* PASTE]

**pastime** /ˈpastaɪm/, *n.* that which serves to make time pass agreeably; amusement, or sport: *to play cards for a pastime.* [late ME, from PASS, *v.* + TIME]

**pastiness** /ˈpeɪstinəs/, *n.* pasty quality.

**pasting** /ˈpeɪstɪŋ/, *n. Colloq.* **1.** a beating or thrashing. **2.** a tirade of abuse.

**past master** /past ˈmastə/, *n.* **1.** one who has filled the office of master in a guild, lodge, etc. **2.** one who has ripe experience in any profession, art, etc.

**pastor** /ˈpastə/, *n.* **1.** a minister or clergyman with reference to his congregation. **2.** one having spiritual care of a number of persons. **3.** a bird, *Sturnus roseus,* of the starling family, found in south-eastern Europe and western Asia, and occasionally in the British Isles. [L: shepherd; replacing ME *pastour,* from AF] – **pastorship,** *n.*

**pastoral** /ˈpastərəl, -trəl/, *adj.* **1.** of or pertaining to shepherds. **2.** used for pasture, as land. **3.** having the simplicity or charm of such country, as scenery. **4.** pertaining to the country or life in the country. **5.** portraying the life of shepherds or of the country, as a work of literature, art, or music. **6.** pertaining to a minister or clergyman, or to his duties, etc. *–n.* **7.** a poem, play, or the like, dealing with the life of shepherds, commonly in a conventional or artificial manner, or with simple rural life generally; a bucolic. **8.** a picture or work of art presenting shepherd life. **9.** →**pastorale. 10.** a treatise on the duties of a minister or clergyman. **11.** a letter from a spiritual pastor to his people. **12.** a letter from a bishop to his clergy or people. **13.** a pastoral staff, or crosier. [ME, from L *pastōrālis* pertaining to a shepherd] – **pastoralism,** *n.* – **pastorally,** *adv.*

**pastorale** /pastəˈral/, *n.* **1.** a composition written in imitation of the music of shepherds. **2.** a 16th century dramatic composition which was one of the forerunners of opera. [It., from *pastore* shepherd, from L *pastor*]

**pastoralist** /ˈpastrələst/, *n.* one who grows cereal crops in addition to raising livestock, usu. on a large property.

**pastorate** /ˈpastərət/, *n.* **1.** the office, or the term of office, of a pastor. **2.** a body of pastors.

**pastorship** /ˈpastəʃɪp/, *n.* the dignity or office of a pastor.

**past participle** /past ˈpatəsɪpəl/, *n.* a participle with past or perfect meaning; perfect participle, as *fallen, sung, defeated.*

**past perfect** /– ˈpɜfəkt/, *n.* →**pluperfect.**

**pastrami** /pəsˈtrami/, *n.* a highly seasoned shoulder cut of smoked beef. [Yiddish, from Pol. from Turk.]

**pastry** /ˈpeɪstri/, *n., pl.* **-tries. 1.** food made of paste or dough, as the crust of pies, etc. **2.** articles of food of which such paste forms an essential part, as pies, tarts, etc. [PAST(E) + -RY]

**pastry-case** /ˈpeɪstri-keɪs/, *n.* a crust of pastry, baked before a pie or tart filling is added; flan-case.

**pastry-cook** /ˈpeɪstri-kʊk/, *n.* a maker or seller of pastries, cakes, etc.

**pasturable** /ˈpastʃərəbəl/, *adj.* capable of affording pasture, as land.

**pasturage** /ˈpastʃərɪdʒ/, *n.* **1.** growing grass or herbage for cattle, etc. **2.** grazing ground. **3.** the act or business of pasturing cattle, etc. [F, from *pasture* PASTURE]

**pasture** /ˈpastʃə/, *n., v.,* **-tured, -turing.** *–n.* **1.** ground covered with grass or herbage, used or suitable for the grazing of cattle, etc.; grassland. **2.** a specific piece of such ground. **3.** grass or herbage for feeding cattle, etc. *–v.t.* **4.** to feed (cattle, etc.) by putting them to graze on pasture. **5.** (of land) to furnish pasturage for (cattle, etc.). **6.** to put (cattle, etc.)

to graze upon pasture. *–v.i.* **7.** (of cattle, etc.) to graze upon pasture. [ME, from OF, from LL *pastūra,* lit., feeding, grazing]

**pasture seeds** /'– sidz/, *n.pl.* seeds sown when a pasture is established, or when a pasture is oversown or sod-seeded.

**pasty**[1] /'peɪsti/, *adj., n., pl.* **pasties.** *–adj.* **1.** of or like paste in consistency, colour, etc. *–n.* **2.** a small piece of material, usu. decorated, worn on the nipples by strip-tease dancers. [PASTE, *n.* + -Y[1]]

**pasty**[2] /'pæsti, 'pasti/, *n., pl.* **pasties.** a type of pie in which a circular piece of pastry is folded around a filling of vegetables, meat, etc. and baked. Also, **Cornish pasty.** [ME *pastee,* from OF, from *paste* PASTE]

**pasty-faced** /'peɪsti-feɪst/, *adj.* with a pale, pastelike complexion.

**pat**[1] /pæt/, *v.,* **patted, patting,** *n. –v.t.* **1.** to strike lightly with something flat, as an implement, the palm of the hand, or the foot. **2.** to stroke gently with the palm or fingers as an expression of affection, approbation, etc. **3.** to flatten or smooth into a desired shape, as butter. **4. pat (someone) on the back,** *Colloq.* to congratulate or encourage with praise. *–v.i.* **5.** to strike lightly or gently. **6.** to walk or run with lightly sounding footsteps. *–n.* **7.** a light stroke or blow with something flat. **8.** the sound of a light stroke, or of light footsteps. **9.** a small mass of something, as butter, shaped by patting or other manipulation. **10. a pat on the back,** *Colloq.* a gesture or word of encouragement or congratulation. [ME; akin to PUTT]

**pat**[2] /pæt/, *adj.* **1.** exactly to the point or purpose. **2.** apt; opportune; ready. **3.** fluently glib; readily facile. *–adv.* **4.** exactly or perfectly. **5.** aptly; opportunely. **6. off pat, a.** exactly or perfectly. **b.** unhesitatingly or without deliberation. **7. sit pat,** *Colloq.* to stick to one's decision, policy, etc. [apparently akin to PAT[1]] – **patness,** *n.* – **patter,** *n.*

**pat**[3] /pæt/, *n. in the phrase* **on one's pat,** *Colloq.* alone. Also, **Pat.** [rhyming slang, *Pat Malone* own]

**pat.,** **1.** patent. **2.** patented.

**Pat** /pæt/, *n. Colloq.* an Irishman. [shortened form of common Irish name *Patrick*]

**patagium** /pə'teɪdʒiəm/, *n., pl.* **-gia** /-dʒiə/. **1.** a wing membrane, as of a bat. **2.** the extensible fold of skin of a gliding mammal or reptile, as a flying squirrel. **3.** a membranous fold of skin on the margin of a bird's wing. [NL, from L: a gold border on a woman's tunic]

**pataka** /'patəka/, *n. N.Z.* Maori storehouse raised upon posts. [Maori]

**patch** /pætʃ/, *n.* **1.** a piece of material used to mend a hole or break, or strengthen a weak place: *a patch on a sail.* **2.** a piece of material used to cover or protect a wound, an injured part, etc.: *a patch over the eye.* **3.** any of the pieces of cloth sewn together to form patchwork. **4.** a small piece or scrap of anything. **5.** a small piece or tract of land, road, etc. **6.** a small piece of black silk or court plaster worn on the face or elsewhere to hide a defect or to heighten the complexion by contrast. **7.** a distinctive mark, an emblem, as on a soldier's uniform to identify his unit. **8.** →**flash** (def. 5). **9.** a period of time. **10. hit a bad patch,** to suffer a series of misfortunes, esp. financial. **11. not a patch on,** *Colloq.* not comparable to; not nearly as good as. **12. purple patch,** *Colloq.* a period of good fortune. *–v.t.* **13.** to mend or strengthen with or as with a patch or patches. **14.** to repair or restore, esp. in a hasty or makeshift way (usu. fol. by *up*). **15.** to make by joining patches or pieces together: *to patch a quilt.* **16.** to settle; smooth over: *they patched up their quarrel.* [ME *pacche;* orig. uncert.] – **patcher,** *n.*

**patch board** /'– bɔd/, *n.* a board containing electrical sockets so that any desired combinations of connections can be made up by inserting wires with plugs at each end.

**patch cord** /'– kɔd/, *n.* an electrical wire with plugs at each end for making connections on a patch board.

**patchouli** /pə'tʃuli, 'pætʃəli/, *n.* **1.** the East Indian plants, *Pogostemon heyneanus* and *P. cablin,* which yield a fragrant oil. **2.** a penetrating perfume derived from it. Also, **pachouli, patchouly.** [Tamil *pach-ilia,* lit., green leaf]

**patch pocket** /pætʃ 'pɒkət/, *n.* a pocket formed by sewing a piece of the material on the outside of a garment.

**patchwork** /'pætʃwɜk/, *n.* **1.** work made of pieces of cloth or leather of various colours or shapes sewn together, used esp. for covering quilts, cushions, etc. **2.** something made up of various pieces or parts put together: *a patchwork of verses.*

**patchy** /'pætʃi/, *adj.,* **-ier, -iest. 1.** marked by patches. **2.** occurring in, forming, or like patches. **3.** of unequal quality; irregular; not uniform. – **patchily,** *adv.* – **patchiness,** *n.*

**pate** /peɪt/, *n.* **1.** the head. **2.** the crown or top of the head. [ME; ? var. of PATEN]

**pâte** /pat/, *n.* porcelain paste used in ceramic work. [F: lit., paste, from OF *paste*]

**pâté** /'pæteɪ, 'pa-/, *n.* **1.** a paste or spread made of finely minced liver, meat, fish, etc., and served as an hors d'oeuvre. **2.** a small pasty, filled with forcemeat, mixed with dices or strips of the main ingredient. [F]

**pâté de foie gras** /ˌpæteɪ də ˌfwa 'gra/, *n.* a paste made with the livers of specially fattened geese.

**patella** /pə'tɛlə/, *n., pl.* **-tellae** /-'tɛli/. **1.** *Anat.* the kneecap. **2.** *Bot., Zool., etc.* a panlike or cuplike formation. **3.** *Archaeol.* a small pan or shallow vessel. [L: small pan, kneepan, diminutive of *patina.* See PATINA[2]] – **patellar,** *adj.*

**patellate** /pə'tɛlət, -eɪt/, *adj.* **1.** having a patella. **2.** →**patelliform.**

**patelliform** /pə'tɛləfɔm/, *adj.* having the form of a patella; shaped like a saucer, kneecap, or limpet shell. [L *patella* small pan + -I- + -FORM]

**paten** /'pætn/, *n.* the plate on which the bread is placed in the celebration of the Eucharist. Also, **patin, patine.** [ME *patene,* from OF, from L *patena, patina.* See PATINA[2]]

**patency** /'peɪtnsi/, *n.* **1.** the state of being patent. **2.** *Med.* the condition of not being blocked or obstructed.

**patent** /'peɪtnt/, *n.* **1.** a government grant to an inventor, his heirs, or assigns, for a stated period of time, conferring upon him a monopoly of the exclusive right to make, use, and vend an invention or discovery. **2.** an invention, process, etc., which has been patented. **3.** an official document conferring some right, privilege, or the like. **4.** *U.S.* the instrument by which the government conveys the legal fee-simple title to public land. **5.** →**patent leather.** *–adj.* **6.** of a kind specially protected by a patent: *a patent door.* **7.** endowed with a patent, as persons. **8.** belonging as if by a proprietary claim; having a trademark. **9.** conferred by a patent, as a right or privilege. **10.** appointed by a patent, as a person. **11.** open to view or knowledge; manifest; evident; plain. **12.** lying open, or not shut in or enclosed, as a place. **13.** *Chiefly Bot.* expanded or spreading. **14.** open, as a door or a passage. **15.** (of plateglass) having been ground and polished on both sides. *–v.t.* **16.** to take out a patent on; obtain the exclusive rights to (an invention) by a patent. **17.** to originate and establish as one's own. **18.** *Rare.* to grant the exclusive right to (an invention) by a patent. [ME, from L *patens,* ppr., lying open; in some senses, through OF] – **patentable,** *adj.* – **patentability** /ˌpeɪtntə'bɪləti, pæt– /, *n.* – **patently,** *adv.*

**patentee** /peɪtn'ti/, *n.* one to whom a patent is granted.

**patent leather** /peɪtnt 'lɛðə/, *n.* **1.** leather lacquered to produce a hard, glossy, smooth finish. **2.** any imitation of this. – **patent-leather,** *adj.*

**patent log** /– 'lɒg/, *n.* See **log** (def. 3c).

**patent medicine** /– 'mɛdəsən/, *n.* a medicine distributed by a company which has a patent on its manufacture.

**patentor** /peɪtn'tɔ/, *n.* one who grants a patent.

**patent right** /'peɪtnt raɪt/, *n.* the exclusive right created by a patent.

**pater** /'peɪtə/ *for def. 1;* /'patə/ *for defs 2 and 3, n.* **1.** father. **2.** the paternoster or Lord's Prayer. **3.** a recital of it. [ME, from L: father]

**paterfamilias** /peɪtəfə'mɪliəs, pa-/, *n., pl.* **patresfamilias** /peɪtreɪzfə'mɪliəs, pa-/. **1.** the head of a family. **2.** *Rom. Law.* a free male citizen who has been freed from patria potestas by death of his father or by emancipation. [L, from *pater* father + *familias,* archaic gen. of *familia* family]

**paternal** /pə'tɜnəl/, *adj.* **1.** characteristic of or befitting a father; fatherly. **2.** of or pertaining to a father. **3.** related on the father's side. **4.** derived or inherited from a father. [L *paternus* fatherly + -AL[1]] – **paternally,** *adv.*

**paternalism** /pə'tɜnəlɪzəm/, *n.* the principle or practice, on the part of a government or of any body or person in authority, of managing or regulating the affairs of a country or community, or of individuals, in the manner of a father dealing with his children. – **paternalistic** /pətɜnə'lɪstɪk/, *adj.* – **paternalistically** /pətɜnə'lɪstɪkli/, *adv.*

**paternity** /pə'tɜnəti/, *n.* **1.** derivation from a father. **2.** the state of being a father; fatherhood. **3.** origin or authorship. [ME, from LL *paternitas,* from L *paternus* fatherly]

**paternoster** /patə'nɒstə/, *n.* **1.** Also, **Pater Noster.** the Lord's Prayer, esp. in the Latin form. **2.** a recital of this prayer as an act of worship. **3.** one of certain beads in a rosary, usu. every eleventh bead, differing in size or material from the rest, and indicating the Lord's Prayer is to be said. **4.** any form of words used as a prayer or charm. **5.** fishing tackle consisting of one or more hooks spaced along a central line, the end of which is weighted. [ME and OE, from L: our father, the first words of the prayer in the Latin version]

**Paterson's curse** /pætəsənz 'kɜs/, *n.* a biennial herb, *Echium plantagineum,* native to the Mediterranean area, but widely naturalised in settled parts of Australia, having blue-purple flowers, and considered a harmful pasture weed in eastern Australia; Salvation Jane.

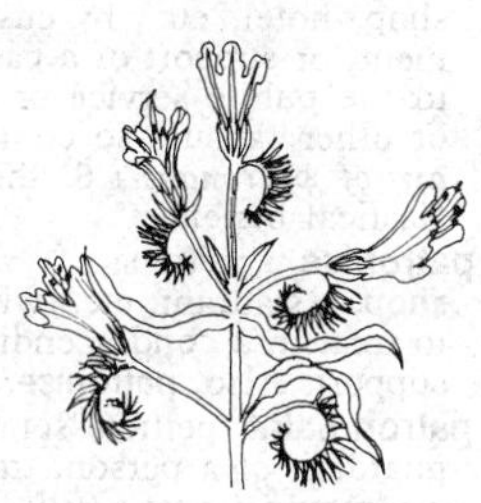

Paterson's curse

**path** /paθ/, *n.* **1.** a way beaten or trodden by the feet of men or beasts. **2.** a walk in a garden or through grounds. **3.** a route, course, or track in which something moves. **4.** a course of action, conduct, or procedure. [ME; OE *pæth,* c. G *Pfad*]

**-path,** a suffix used to form nouns denoting: **1.** a person suffering from the specified disorder, as in *neuropath.* **2.** a person who treats disorders by a particular or alternative method, as in *naturopath, osteopath.* [backformation from -PATHY]

**path.,** **1.** pathological. **2.** pathology.

**pathetic** /pə'θɛtɪk/, *adj.* **1.** exciting pity or sympathetic sadness; full of pathos. **2.** affecting or moving the feelings. **3.** pertaining or due to the feelings. **4.** *Colloq.* miserably inadequate: *her vegetables made a pathetic showing at the annual produce fair.* **5.** *Colloq.* inviting scorn or pity because of patent shortcomings, pettiness, greed, rudeness, etc. Also, **pathetical.** [LL *pathēticus,* from Gk *pathētikós* sensitive] – **pathetically,** *adv.*

**pathetic fallacy** /– 'fæləsi/, *n.* the crediting of human traits and feelings to nature.

**pathfinder** /'paθfaɪndə/, *n.* **1.** one who finds a path or way, as through a wilderness. **2.** an aircraft sent in advance of a force of bombers to drop flares, etc., to illuminate a target area.

**-pathia,** an obsolete form of **-pathy.**

**-pathic,** a word element forming adjectives from nouns ending in *-pathy,* as *psychopathic.* [see -PATHY, -IC]

**pathless** /'paθləs/, *adj.* without paths; trackless. – **pathlessness,** *n.*

**patho-,** a word element meaning 'suffering', 'disease', 'feeling'. [Gk, combining form of *páthos*]

**pathogen** /'pæθədʒən/, *n.* a pathogenic or disease-producing organism. Also, **pathogene** /'pæθədʒin/.

**pathogenesis** /pæθə'dʒɛnəsəs/, *n.* the production and development of disease. Also, **pathogeny** /pə'θɒdʒəni/. – **pathogenetic** /pæθədʒə'nɛtɪk/, *adj.*

**pathogenic** /pæθə'dʒɛnɪk/, *adj.* disease-producing.

**pathognomonic** /pæθəgnə'mɒnɪk, pæθənə'mɒnɪk/, *adj.* characteristic of a particular disease.

**pathol.,** **1.** pathological. **2.** pathology.

**pathological** /pæθə'lɒdʒɪkəl/, *adj.* **1.** of or pertaining to pathology. **2.** due to or involving disease; morbid. Also, **pathologic.** – **pathologically,** *adv.*

**pathology** /pə'θɒlədʒi/, *n., pl.* **-gies.** **1.** the science of the origin, nature, and course of diseases. **2.** the conditions and processes of a disease. **3.** the study of morbid or abnormal mental or moral conditions. – **pathologist,** *n.*

**pathos** /'peɪθɒs/, *n.* **1.** the quality or power, as in speech, music, etc., of evoking a feeling of pity or sympathetic sadness; touching or pathetic character or effect (opposed to *ethos*). **2.** *Obs.* suffering. [Gk: suffering, disease, feeling]

**pathway** /'paθweɪ/, *n.* a path.

**-pathy,** a noun element meaning 'suffering', 'feeling', as in *anthropopathy, antipathy, sympathy,* and often, esp. in words of modern formation, 'morbid affection', 'disease', as in *neuropathy, psychopathy,* and hence used also in names of systems or methods of treating disease, as in *homoeopathy, osteopathy.* [Gk *-pátheia*]

**patience** /'peɪʃəns/, *n.* **1.** calm and uncomplaining endurance, as under pain, provocation, etc. **2.** calmness in waiting: *have patience a little longer.* **3.** quiet perseverance: *to labour with patience.* **4.** a card game, usu. played by one person alone. [L *patientia;* replacing ME *pacience,* from OF]

**patient** /'peɪʃənt/, *n.* **1.** one who is under medical or surgical treatment. **2.** a person or thing that undergoes action (opposed to *agent*). *–adj.* **3.** quietly persevering or diligent: *patient workers.* **4.** enduring pain, trouble, affliction, hardship, etc., with fortitude, calmness, or quiet submission. **5.** marked by such endurance. **6.** quietly enduring strain, annoyance, etc.: *patient in a traffic jam.* **7.** disposed to or characterised by such endurance. **8.** enduring delay with calmness or equanimity, or marked by such endurance: *be patient.* **9.** having or showing the capacity for endurance (fol. by *of*). **10.** susceptible (fol. by *of*). **11.** *Rare.* undergoing the action of another (opposed to *agent*). [L *patiens,* ppr., suffering, enduring; replacing ME *pacient,* from OF] – **patiently,** *adv.*

**patiki** /'patəki/, *n. N.Z.* →**flounder**[2] (def. 1). [Maori]

**patin** /'pætn/, *n.* →**paten.** Also, **patine.**

**patina**[1] /'pætənə, pə'tinə/, *n.* **1.** a film or encrustation, usu. green, caused by oxidisation on the surface of old bronze, and esteemed as ornamental. **2.** a similar film or colouring on some other substance. **3.** a surface calcification of implements, usu. indicating great age. [It., from L: dish, through meaning tarnish (on metal dish)]

**patina**[2] /'pætənə/, *n., pl.* **-nae** /-ni/. a broad, shallow dish used by the ancient Romans. [L]

**patio** /'pætioʊ, 'peɪʃioʊ/, *n., pl.* **-tios.** **1.** a court, as of a house, esp. an inner court open to the sky. **2.** an area, usu. paved, adjoining a house, used for outdoor living. [Sp.]

**patisserie** /pə'tɪsəri/, *n.* **1.** a fancy cake, often having a cream and fruit filling. **2.** an establishment where such pastries are made and sold. [F *pâtisserie*]

**Patna rice** /pætnə 'raɪs/, *n.* long, thin, highly polished grains of rice, used for curries and savoury dishes.

**patois** /'pætwa/, *n., pl.* **patois** /'pætwaz/. any peasant or provincial form of speech. [F, from OF *patoier* handle clumsily, from *pate* paw]

**pat. pend.,** patent pending.

**patri-,** a word element meaning 'father'. [LL, combining form of *pater*]

**patrial** /'pætriəl, 'peɪtriəl/, *adj.* **1.** of or relating to one's fatherland. **2.** (of a word) derived from the name of a place or country, and used to denote a native or inhabitant of it. **3.** (of a person) having parentage deemed by the British government to be an appropriate qualification for entry to and permanent residence in the United Kingdom. *–n.* **4.** a patrial word. **5.** a patrial person. [ML *patriālis,* from L *patria* + -AL[1]]

**patria potestas** /ˌpætriə poʊ'tɛstəs/, *n. Rom. Law.* the power of a man over his children and descendants, which made all their property his and all their transactions void unless he assented. It ended only with the death of the paterfamilias or with emancipation. [L]

**patriarch** /'peɪtriak, 'pæt-/, *n.* **1.** any of the earlier biblical personages regarded as the fathers of the human race, comprising those from Adam to Noah (**antediluvian patriarchs**) and those between the Deluge and the birth of Abraham. **2.** one of the three great progenitors of the Israelites, Abraham, Isaac, or Jacob. **3.** one of the sons of Jacob (the **twelve patriarchs**), from whom the tribes of Israel were descended. **4.** (in the early church) a bishop of high rank, esp. one with jurisdiction over metropolitans. **5.** *Greek Orthodox Church.* the bishop of the ancient sees of Alexandria, Antioch, Constantinople, and Jerusalem, and in recent years of Russia,

Rumania, and Serbia. The bishop of Constantinople is the highest dignitary in the church and bears the title of **ecumenical patriarch.** **6.** a bishop of the highest rank or authority in any of the various non-Orthodox churches in the East. **7.** *Rom. Cath. Ch.* **a.** the pope (**Patriarch of Rome**). **b.** a bishop of the highest rank next after the pope. **8.** one of the highest dignitaries in the Mormon Church who pronounces the blessing of the church; Evangelist. **9.** one of the elders or leading older members of a community. **10.** a venerable old man. **11.** the male head of a family or tribal line. **12.** a person regarded as the father or founder of an order, class, etc. **13.** *Colloq.* an authoritarian man. [ME *patriarc,* from LL *patriarcha,* from Gk *patriárchēs* head of a family] – **patriarchal** /peɪtri'akəl, pæt-/, *adj.* – **patriarchally,** *adv.*

**patriarchal cross** /ˌpeɪtriakəl 'krɒs, ˌpæt-/, *n.* a cross with two crossbars.

**patriarchate** /'peɪtriakət, 'pæt-/, *n.* **1.** the office, dignity, jurisdiction, province, or residence of an ecclesiastical patriarch. **2.** →**patriarchy.**

**patriarchy** /'peɪtriaki, 'pæt-/, *n., pl.* **-archies.** **1.** a form of social organisation in which the father is head of the family, and in which descent is reckoned in the male line, the children belonging to the father's clan. **2.** a community organised and run upon such a system.

**patrician** /pə'trɪʃən/, *n.* **1.** a member of the original senatorial aristocracy in ancient Rome. **2.** (under the later Roman and Byzantine Empires) a title or dignity conferred by the emperor. **3.** a member of an influential and hereditary ruling class in certain medieval German, Swiss, and Italian free cities. **4.** any noble or aristocrat. *–adj.* **5.** of or belonging to the patrician families of ancient Rome. **6.** of high social rank or noble family. **7.** befitting an aristocrat: *patrician aloofness.* [ME, from L *patricius* of the rank of the *patrēs* senators, patricians (lit., fathers) + -AN] – **patricianly,** *adv.*

**patriciate** /pə'trɪʃiət, -eɪt/, *n.* **1.** the patrician class. **2.** patrician rank.

**patricide** /'pætrəsaɪd/, *n.* **1.** one who kills his father. **2.** the act of killing one's father. [PATRI- + -CIDE] – **patricidal** /pætrə'saɪdl/, *adj.*

**patriclinous** /pə'trɪklənəs/, *adj.* derived or inherited from the father or his line. Cf. **matriclinous.** [PATRI- + *-clinous,* from Gk *-clinēs* inclining, bending]

**patrilineal** /pætrə'lɪniəl/, *adj.* of or pertaining to associations by descent or title traced through the male line. [L *pater* father + E *lineal*]

**patrimony** /'pætrəməni/, *n., pl.* **-nies.** **1.** an estate inherited from one's father or ancestors. **2.** a heritage. **3.** the estate or endowment of a church, religious house, etc. [L *patrimōnium* paternal estate; replacing ME *patrimoygne,* from OF *patrimoine*] – **patrimonial** /pætrə'mouniəl/, *adj.*

**patriot** /'peɪtriət, 'pæt-/, *n.* a person who loves his country, zealously supporting and defending it and its interests. [LL *patriōta,* from Gk *patriōtēs* fellow countryman]

**patriotic** /peɪtri'ɒtɪk, pæt-/, *adj.* **1.** of or like a patriot. **2.** inspired by patriotism. – **patriotically,** *adv.*

**patriotism** /'peɪtriətɪzəm, 'pæt-/, *n.* the spirit or action of a patriot; devotion to one's country.

**patristic** /pə'trɪstɪk/, *adj.* of or pertaining to the Fathers of the Christian Church or their writings. Also, **patristical.** – **patristically,** *adv.*

**patrol** /pə'troul/, *v.,* **-trolled, -trolling,** *n.* *–v.i.* **1.** to go the rounds in a camp or garrison, as a guard. **2.** to traverse a particular district, as a policeman. *–v.t.* **3.** to go about in or traverse for the purpose of guarding or protecting. *–n.* **4.** a person or a body of persons charged with patrolling. **5.** a body of troops or police detailed for reconnaissance. **6.** the act of patrolling. **7.** (in the Boy Scouts and Girl Guides) a unit of about six members. [F *patrouiller* patrol, earlier paddle or dabble in mud, orig., paw over, from OF *pate* paw. Cf. PATOIS] – **patroller,** *n.*

**patrol-car** /pə'troul-ka/, *n.* a car used by police for patrolling a district.

**patrolman** /pə'troulmæn/, *n., pl.* **-men.** **1.** a man who patrols. **2.** a member of a police force patrolling a certain district.

**patrology** /pə'trɒlədʒi/, *n.* **1.** the study of the writings of the fathers of the Christian Church; patristics. **2.** a collection of the works of early ecclesiastical writers. [PATR(I)- + -O- + -LOGY]

**patrol wagon** /pə'troul wægən/, *n.* a van used by the police for the conveyance of prisoners.

**patron** /'peɪtrən/, *n.* **1.** one who supports with his patronage a shop, hotel, or the like. **2.** a protector or supporter, as of a person, cause, institution, art, or enterprise. **3.** one whose support or protection is solicited or acknowledged by the dedication of a book or other work. **4.** a patron saint. **5.** *Rom. Hist.* the protector of a dependant or client, often the ex-master of a freedman, still retaining certain rights over him. **6.** *Eccles.* one who has the right of presenting a clergyman to a benefice. [ME, from OF, from L *patrōnus* patron] – **patronal,** *adj.* – **patroness** /'peɪtrənɛs/, *n. fem.*

**patronage** /'pætrənɪdʒ/, *n.* **1.** the financial support afforded a shop, hotel, etc., by customers. **2.** the position, encouragement, or support of a patron. **3.** the control of appointments to the public service or of other political favours. **4.** offices or other favours so controlled. **5.** condescending favour: *an air of patronage.* **6.** the right of presentation to an ecclesiastical benefice.

**patronise** /'pætrənaɪz/, *v.t.,* **-nised, -nising.** **1.** to favour (a shop, restaurant, etc.) with one's patronage; to trade with. **2.** to treat in a condescending way. **3.** to act as patron towards; support. Also, **patronize.** – **patroniser,** *n.* – **patronisingly,** *adv.*

**patron saint** /peɪtrən 'seɪnt/, *n.* a saint regarded as the special guardian of a person, trade, place, etc.

**patronymic** /pætrə'nɪmɪk/, *adj.* **1.** (of names) derived from the name of a father or ancestor, esp. by the addition of a suffix or prefix indicating decent. **2.** (of a suffix or prefix) indicating such descent. *–n.* **3.** a patronymic name, such as *Williamson* (son of William) or *Macdonald* (son of Donald). **4.** a family name; surname. [LL *patrōnymicus,* from Gk *patrōnymikós* pertaining to one's father's name]

**patsy** /'pætsi/, *n. Colloq.* **1.** a scapegoat. **2.** a person who is easily deceived, swindled, ridiculed, etc. [? It. *pazzo* fool, lunatic]

**patten** /'pætn/, *n.* any of various kinds of footwear, as a wooden shoe, a shoe with a wooden sole, a chopin, etc., to protect the feet from mud or wet. [ME *paten,* from OF *patin,* from OF *pate* paw, foot. Cf. PATOIS]

**patter**[1] /'pætə/, *v.i.* **1.** to strike or move with a succession of slight tapping sounds. *–v.t.* **2.** to cause to patter. **3.** to spatter with something. *–n.* **4.** a pattering sound: *the heavy patter of the rain.* **5.** the act of pattering. [frequentative of PAT[1], *v.*]

**patter**[2] /'pætə/, *n.* **1.** the glib and rapid speech used by a salesman to praise his wares, by a magician while performing tricks, by a comedian or other entertainer, used to attract attention or amuse. **2.** rapid speech; mere chatter; gabble. **3.** the jargon or cant of any class, group, etc. **4.** *Colloq.* the words of a song. *–v.i.* **5.** to talk glibly or rapidly, esp. with little regard to matter; chatter. **6.** to repeat the paternoster or any prayer, etc., in a rapid, mechanical way. *–v.t.* **7.** to recite or repeat (prayers, etc.) in a rapid, mechanical way. **8.** to repeat or say rapidly or glibly. [var. of PATER (def. 3)] – **patterer,** *n.*

**patter**[3] /'pætə/, *n.* one who or that which pats.

**pattern** /'pætn/, *n.* **1.** a decorative design, as for china, wallpaper, textile fabrics, etc. **2.** such a design carried out on something. **3.** a style of marking of natural or chance origin: *patterns of frost on the window.* **4.** style or type in general. **5.** anything fashioned or designed to serve as a model or guide for something to be made: *a paper pattern for a dress.* **6.** *Metall.* a model or form, usu. of wood or metal, used in a foundry to make a mould. **7.** an example or instance. **8.** a sample or specimen. **9. a.** the distribution of shot in a target at which a shotgun or the like is fired. **b.** a diagram showing such distribution. *–v.i.* **10.** to model one's conduct, etc. (fol. by *by* or *after*). *–v.t.* **11.** to make after a pattern; model. **12.** to cover or mark with a pattern. **13.** *Rare.* to take as a pattern. [ME *patron,* from ML *patrōnus* model, example, from L: patron]

**patter song** /'pætə sɒŋ/, *n.* a song, usu. humorous, marked by a high rate of syllable articulation.

**patty** /'pæti/, *n., pl.* **-ies.** **1.** a little pie; a pasty: *oyster pat-*

*ties.* **2.** a savoury mixture formed into a ball or shape and cooked on a griddle or deep-fried. [F *pâté*]

**patty cake** /ˈ– keɪk/, *n.* →**cupcake.**

**patty pan** /ˈ– pæn/, *n.* **1.** a baking tray with rounded indentations for baking patties, patty cakes, etc. **2.** Also, **patty paper.** a small paper cup, often coloured, for baking cup cakes, etc.

**patu** /ˈpatu/, *n.* a Maori club of stone. [Maori]

**patulous** /ˈpætʃələs/, *adj.* **1.** open; gaping; expanded. **2.** *Bot.* **a.** spreading, as a tree or its boughs. **b.** spreading slightly, as a calyx. **c.** bearing the flowers loose or dispersed, as a peduncle. [L *patulus* lying open] – **patulously,** *adv.* – **patulousness,** *n.*

**paua** /ˈpauə/, *n.* a univalve mollusc of the abalone family, *Haliotis iris,* of New Zealand, having edible flesh and an iridescent shell used in ornaments and jewellery. [Maori]

**paucity** /ˈpɔsəti/, *n.* smallness of quantity; fewness; scantiness: *paucity of material.* [ME, from L *paucitas*]

**pauldron** /ˈpɔldrən/, *n.* a piece of armour protecting the shoulder and upper part of the arm. [late ME *paleron,* from MF *espalleron* shoulder]

**Pauline** /ˈpɔlaɪn/, *adj.* of or pertaining to the apostle Paul, or his doctrines or writings.

**Pauli's exclusion principle,** *n.* →**exclusion principle.**

**paulownia** /pɔˈlouniə/, *n.* **1.** a tree, *Paulownia tomentosa,* of Japan, bearing showy pale violet or blue flowers, which blossom in early spring. **2.** any other trees of the genus *Paulownia.* [NL; named after Anna *Paulovna,* daughter of Tsar Paul I, of Russia]

**paunch** /pɔntʃ/, *n.* **1.** the belly or abdomen. **2.** a large, prominent belly. **3.** →**rumen.** [ME *panche,* from ONF, var. of OE *pance,* from L *pantex*]

**paunchy** /ˈpɔntʃi/, *adj.* having a large, prominent belly. – **paunchiness,** *n.*

**pauper** /ˈpɔpə/, *n.* **1.** a very poor person. **2.** one without means, who is supported by a community. [L: poor (man)]

**pauperise** /ˈpɔpəraɪz/, *v.t.,* **-rised, -rising.** to make a pauper of. Also, **pauperize.** – **pauperisation** /pɔpəraɪˈzeɪʃən/, *n.*

**pauperism** /ˈpɔpərɪzəm/, *n.* utter poverty.

**paupiette** /poupiˈɛt/, *n.* a thin slice of meat, usu. veal, stuffed with forcemeat, rolled and tied, then braised. [F]

**pause** /pɔz/, *n., v.,* **paused, pausing.** *–n.* **1.** a temporary stop or rest, esp. in speech or action. **2.** a cessation proceeding from doubt or uncertainty. **3.** delay; hesitation; suspense. **4.** a break or rest in speaking or reading as depending on sense, grammatical relations, metrical divisions, etc., or in writing or printing as marked by punctuation. **5.** *Pros.* →**caesura. 6.** *Music.* the fermata symbol 𝄐 or 𝄑 placed under or over a note or rest to indicate that it is to be prolonged. **7. give pause,** to cause to hesitate. *–v.i.* **8.** to make a pause; stop; wait; hesitate. **9.** to dwell or linger (fol. by *upon*). [late ME, from L *pausa,* from Gk *paûsis* cessation] – **pausal,** *adj.* – **pauser,** *n.* – **pausingly,** *adv.*

**pav** /pæv/, *n. Colloq.* →**pavlova.**

**pavan** /pəˈvan, ˈpævən/, *n.* **1.** a stately dance in vogue in the 16th century. **2.** the music for it. Also, **pavane, pavin.** [F *pavane,* from Sp. *pavana,* from d. It.: Paduan dance]

**pave** /peɪv/, *v.t.,* **paved, paving.** **1.** to cover or lay (a road, walk, etc.) with stones, bricks, tiles, wood, concrete, etc., so as to make a firm, level surface. **2.** to prepare (the way) for. **3.** to mark (a text) with a translation or other helpful notes. [ME *pave(n),* from OF *paver,* from Rom. *pavāre,* for L *pavīre* beat down] – **paver,** *n.*

**pavé** /ˈpaveɪ/, *n.* a setting in which jewels are placed close together so as to show no metal. [orig. pp. of F *paver* PAVE]

**pavement** /ˈpeɪvmənt/, *n.* **1.** a walk or footway, esp. a paved one, at the side of a street or road. **2.** a surface, ground covering, or floor made by paving. **3.** a material used for paving. **4.** *Obs.* a paved road, etc. [ME, from OF: a floor beaten down, from *paver* PAVE]

**pavement artist** /ˈ– atəst/, *n. Brit.* one who begs for money by drawing pictures on a pavement.

**pavement light** /ˈ– laɪt/, *n.* a light formed of solid glass blocks, cast into concrete, or set in a cast-iron frame, used over a basement so as to let in daylight. Also, **vault light.**

**pavid** /ˈpævəd/, *adj.* frightened; fearful; timid. [L *pavidus*]

**pavilion** /pəˈvɪljən/, *n.* **1.** a light, more or less open structure for purposes of shelter, pleasure, etc., as in a park. **2.** a projecting element, architecturally defined, at the front or side of a building. **3.** one of a group of buildings forming a hospital. **4.** a tent. **5.** a large tent on posts. **6.** *Jewellery.* the lower part of the stone, taken from the girdle and including the culet. **7.** *Anat.* the auricle of the ear. *–v.t.* **8.** to set or place in or as in a pavilion. **9.** to furnish with pavilions. [ME *paviliоun,* from OF, from L *pāpilio* tent, orig. butterfly]

**pavin** /ˈpævən/, *n.* →**pavan.**

**paving** /ˈpeɪvɪŋ/, *n.* **1.** the act or technique of paving. **2.** a pavement. **3.** material for paving. *–adj.* **4.** of or pertaining to a pavement.

**paving stone** /ˈ– stoun/, *n.* a stone or concrete block prepared for paving.

**paviour** /ˈpeɪvjə/, *n.* **1.** one who or that which paves. **2.** a paving stone or paving tile. Also, *U.S.,* **pavior, paver.**

**pavis** /ˈpævəs/, *n.* a large medieval shield, covering the whole body. Also, **pavise.** [from *Pavia,* town in N Italy]

**paviser** /ˈpævəsə/, *n.* one armed with or bearing a pavis. Also, **pavisor.**

**pavlova** /pævˈlouvə/, *n.* a dessert made of a large soft-centred meringue, usu. roughly circular and having an indented top filled with whipped cream and often topped with fruit, esp. passionfruit. [invented in 1935 by Herbert Sachse, 1898-1974, Australian chef, and named by Harry Nairn of the Esplanade Hotel, Perth, after Anna *Pavlova,* 1885-1931, Russian ballerina]

**pavonine** /ˈpævənaɪn/, *adj.* **1.** of or like the peacock. **2.** resembling the peacock's feathers, as in colouring. [L *pāvōnīnus* pertaining to a peacock]

**paw** /pɔ/, *n.* **1.** the foot of an animal with nails or claws. **2.** the foot of any animal. **3.** *Colloq.* (*joc.*) the human hand. *–v.t.* **4.** to strike or scrape with the paws or feet. **5.** *Colloq.* to handle clumsily, rudely, or overfamiliarly. *–v.i.* **6.** to beat or scrape the ground, etc., with the paws or feet. **7.** *Colloq.* to use the hands clumsily or rudely on something. [ME *powe,* from OF, of Gmc orig.; cf. G *Pfote*]

**pawl** /pɔl/, *n.* a pivoted bar adapted to engage with the teeth of a ratchet wheel or the like so as to prevent movement or to impart motion. [? from D *pal*]

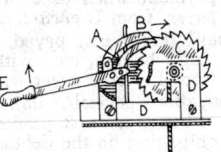

pawl in hoisting apparatus: A, B, pawls; C, ratchet wheel; D, frame; E, handle. Arrows indicate direction of motion

**pawn**[1] /pɔn/, *v.t.* **1.** to deposit as security, as for money borrowed: *to pawn a watch.* **2.** to pledge or stake: *I pawn my honour. –n.* **3.** state of being deposited or held as security: *jewels in pawn.* **4.** something given or deposited as security, as for money borrowed. **5.** any thing or person serving as security. **6.** the act of pawning. [late ME, from OF *pan.* Cf. G *Pfand*] – **pawner,** *n.*

**pawn**[2] /pɔn/, *n.* **1.** *Chess.* one of the 16 pieces of lowest value, usu. moving one square straight ahead, but capturing diagonally. **2.** an unimportant person used as the tool of another. [ME *poune,* from AF, var. of OF *peon,* from LL *pedo* foot soldier]

**pawnbroker** /ˈpɔnbroukə/, *n.* one who lends money at interest on pledged personal property. – **pawnbroking,** *n.*

**pawnshop** /ˈpɔnʃɒp/, *n.* the shop of a pawnbroker where goods can be pawned and unredeemed articles are offered for sale.

**pawnticket** /ˈpɔntɪkət/, *n.* a ticket issued by a pawnbroker as a receipt for goods pawned.

**pawpaw** /ˈpɔpɔ/, *n.* **1.** Also, **papaya.** the large yellow melon-like fruit of the shrub or small tree, *Carica papaya,* of the family Caricaceae, originally from tropical America and much prized for its palatable fruits containing a digestive principle. **2.** *U.S.* the small fleshy fruit of the temperate North American bush or small tree, *Asimina triloba.* Also, **papaw, paw-paw.** [Sp. *papaya;* of Carib orig.]

**pax** /pæks/, *n.* **1.** *Rom. Cath. Ch.* a small tablet bearing a representation of the Crucifixion or some other sacred subject, formerly kissed by the celebrating priest and the con-

i = peat ɪ = pit ɛ = pet æ = pat a = part ɒ = pot ʌ = putt ɔ = port ʊ = put u = pool ɜ = pert ə = apart aɪ = buy eɪ = bay ɔɪ = boy aʊ = how
oʊ = hoe ɪə = here ɛə = hair ʊə = tour g = give θ = thin ð = then ʃ = show ʒ = measure tʃ = choke dʒ = joke ŋ = sing j = you õ = Fr. bon

gregation at mass. *–interj.* **2.** *Brit. Schoolboy Colloq.* (a call given as a signal for a desire to cease hostilities.) [ME, from L: peace]

**pay**[1] /peɪ/, *v.*, **paid** *or* (*Obs. except for def. 1*) **payed, paying,** *n., adj.* *–v.t.* **1.** to discharge (a debt, obligation, etc.), as by giving or doing something. **2.** to give (money, etc.) as in discharge of debt or obligation. **3.** to satisfy the claims of (a person, etc.) as by giving money due. **4.** to defray (cost or expense). **5.** to give compensation for. **6.** to yield a recompense or return to; be profitable to: *it pays me to be honest.* **7.** to yield as a return: *the stock pays 4 per cent.* **8.** to requite, as for good, harm, offence, etc. **9.** to give or render (attention, regard, court, compliments, etc.) as if due or fitting. **10.** to admit the truth of; acknowledge that one has been outwitted, esp. in repartee or argument; *I'll pay that.* **11.** to make (a call, visit, etc.). **12.** *Naut., etc.* to let out (a rope, etc.) as by slackening (fol. by *out* or *away*). *–v.i.* **13.** to give money, etc., due: *to pay for goods.* **14.** to discharge debt. **15.** to yield a return or profit; be advantageous or worthwhile. **16.** to give compensation, as for damage or loss sustained. **17.** to suffer, or be punished, as for something; make amends. *–v.* **18.** Some special verb phrases are:

**pay off, 1.** to retaliate upon or punish. **2.** to discharge a debt in full. **3.** to discharge from one's employ and pay any wages, etc., due. **4.** *Colloq.* to bribe. **5.** to yield a profitable return. **6.** *Naut.* to let fall to leeward.

**pay (one's** or **its) way, 1.** to pay a fair proportion of one's expenses. **2.** to yield a profit on an investment.

**pay out, 1.** to disburse; hand out (money). **2.** to retaliate for an injury; punish in revenge. **3.** *Colloq.* to protest volubly.

**pay up, 1.** to pay upon demand, esp. as when threatened. **2.** to pay fully or promptly.

**put paid to,** put an end to; prevent.

*–n.* **19.** payment, as of wages. **20.** wages, salary, or stipend. **21.** paid employ: *in the pay of the enemy.* **22.** *Rare.* requital; reward or punishment. **23. give (someone) a pay,** to castigate or rebuke (someone). *–adj.* **24.** (of earth, etc.) containing a sufficient quantity of metal or other value to be profitably worked by the miner. **25.** having a mechanism for payment when used: *a pay telephone.* [ME *paie(n),* from F *payer,* from L *pācāre* pacify]

**pay**[2] /peɪ/, *v.t.*, **payed, paying.** to coat or cover (seams, a ship's bottom, etc.) with pitch, tar, or the like. [ONF *peier,* from L *picāre* cover with pitch]

**payable** /ˈpeɪəbəl/, *adj.* **1.** owed; to be paid; due. **2.** capable of being paid. **3.** profitable. **4.** *Law.* imposing an immediate obligation on the debtor.

**pay-as-you-earn tax** /peɪ-əz-ju-ˈɜn tæks/, *n.* a system of collection of income tax by deductions made by the employer from the employee's salary before he receives it. Also, **P.A.Y.E. tax.**

**pay card** /ˈpeɪ kad/, *n.* a card used in certain industries upon which are entered details of an employee's duty, including commencing and finishing times, periods spent on duties attracting extra or higher rates, overtime, etc.

**payday** /ˈpeɪdeɪ/, *n.* the day when payment is made, or to be made; the day on which wages are paid.

**pay-dirt** /ˈpeɪ-dɜt/, *n.* **1.** earth, rock, etc., which yields a profit to the miner. **2.** auriferous gravel rich enough to pay for washing or working. **3. strike pay-dirt,** to be successful, esp. in gaining money.

**P.A.Y.E.** /pi eɪ waɪ ˈi, peɪ/, *n.* pay as you earn. See **pay-as-you-earn tax.**

**payee** /peɪˈi/, *n.* one to whom money is paid or to be paid.

**payer** /ˈpeɪə/, *n.* **1.** one who pays. **2.** the person named in a bill or note who has to pay the holder.

**P.A.Y.E. tax** /ˈpeɪ tæks/, *n.* →**pay-as-you-earn tax.**

**paying guest** /ˌpeɪɪŋ ˈgɛst/, *n.* a lodger in a private house who pays for his accommodation and food.

**paying-in slip** /peɪɪŋ-ˈɪn slɪp/, *n.* →**deposit slip.**

**pay in hand,** *n.* the amount of pay which an employer may hold, determined by the number of days allowed to elapse between the end of the pay period and the pay day for it.

**payload** /ˈpeɪloud/, *n.* **1.** the income-producing part of a cargo. **2.** the load which a vehicle is designed to transport under specified conditions of operation in addition to its unladen weight. **3.** *Mil.* the warhead, its container and activating devices in a missile. **4.** *Astronautics.* the load carried in a rocket or satellite to obtain the results for which the vehicle has been launched.

**paymaster** /ˈpeɪmastə/, *n.* an officer or an official responsible for the payment of wages or salaries.

**payment** /ˈpeɪmənt/, *n.* **1.** the act of paying. **2.** that which is paid; compensation; recompense. **3.** →**requital.**

**payment in lieu,** *n.* payment to an employee as an alternative to his taking leave entitlements.

**paynim** /ˈpeɪnɪm/, *n. Archaic.* **1.** a pagan or heathen. **2.** →**Muslim.** [ME *painime,* from OF *paieni(s)me,* from LL *pāgānismus* heathenism]

**pay-off** /ˈpeɪ-ɒf/, *n.* **1.** the final settlement of a salary, bet, bribe, or debt. **2.** the time when such a payment is made. **3.** a settlement as in retribution. **4.** the climax, as of a joke or routine. **5.** *Colloq.* a final, sometimes unexpected consequence.

**payola** /peɪˈoulə/, *n. Orig. U.S.* a bribe, esp. for the promotion of a commercial product through the abuse of one's position or influence.

**pay-packet** /ˈpeɪ-pækət/, *n.* **1.** an envelope or packet containing wages. **2.** the wages themselves.

**pay phone** /ˈpeɪ foun/, *n. U.S.* →**public telephone.**

**payroll** /ˈpeɪroul/, *n.* **1.** a roll or list of persons to be paid, with the amounts due. **2.** the aggregate of these amounts. **3.** the money that is actually paid out. **4.** the total number of people employed by a firm.

**payroll tax** /ˈ– tæks/, *n.* a tax levied by a Government on employers, based on the salaries and wages they pay out.

**paysanne** /peɪˈzæn/, *adj.* (of cooking) in a simple country style, cooked with mixed vegetables, bacon, etc. [F fem. of *paysan* rustic]

**pay sheet** /ˈpeɪ ʃit/, *n.* a chart kept by an employer showing the names and classifications of his employees, details of hours worked by them, their rates of pay, the amounts of wages paid them together with any deductions and details of overtime worked, etc.

**pay station** /ˈ– steɪʃən/, *n. U.S.* →**telephone box.**

**Pb,** *Chem.* lead. [L *plumbum*]

**PBX** /pi bi ˈɛks/, *n.* a private telephone exchange, often with outside lines, for routing both internal and external calls in a firm, business, etc. [*P(rivate) B(ranch) (e)X(change)*]

**pc,** parsec.

**p.c.,** per cent.

**P.C., 1.** Privy Council. **2.** Privy Councillor. **3.** *Brit.* Police Constable.

**P.C.A.** /pi si ˈeɪ/, *n.* a charge made by police against a person who is driving with a proscribed concentration of alcohol in his blood. [*P(roscribed) C(oncentration of) A(lcohol)*]

**P.C. fitting** /pi ˈsi fɪtɪŋ/, *n.* →**prime-cost fitting.** Also, **P.C. item.**

**pd,** paid.

**p/d,** post dated.

**p.d., 1.** per diem. **2.** potential difference.

**Pd,** *Chem.* palladium.

**PD** /pi ˈdi/, *adj. Colloq.* of or pertaining to a police vehicle, as a police car, motorbike, paddy wagon, etc. [from the one-time numberplate of such vehicles]

**p-dichlorobenzene** /pi-daɪˌklɔrouˈbɛnzin, -bɛnˈzin/, *n.* →**paradichlorobenzene.** Also, **PDB.**

**pdl,** poundal.

**P.E., 1.** Physical Education. **2.** *Statistics.* probable error.

**pea**[1] /pi/, *n., pl.* **peas,** (*Archaic*) **pease. 1.** the round, highly nutritious seed of *Pisum sativum,* a hardy plant in wide circulation. **2.** the plant bearing such seeds. **3.** any of various related or similar plants, or their seed, as the chickpea. **4.** something small as a pea. [backformation from PEASE (orig. sing., but later taken as pl.)] – **pealike,** *adj.*

**pea**[2] /pi/, *n. Colloq.* **1.** a racehorse that seems likely to win. **2.** one who is predicted to win or succeed as a favoured applicant for a job: *Carolyn was the pea for the job as producer.*

**peace** /pis/, *n.* **1.** freedom from war or hostilities. **2.** an agreement between contending parties to abstain from further hostilities. **3.** freedom from strife or dissension. **4.** freedom from civil commotion; public order and security: *a justice of the peace.* **5.** freedom from mental disturbance: *peace of* *mind.* **6.** ease of mind or conscience. **7.** a state of being tranquil or serene. **8.** a state conducive, due to, or characterised by tranquillity or calm. **9.** quiet; stillness; silence. **10. hold one's peace,** to remain quiet; to keep silent. **11. keep the peace,** to refrain from creating a disturbance. **12. make one's peace,** to effect reconciliation for oneself, or for another person. **13. make peace,** to arrange for a stop to hostilities; to end war. [ME *pais,* from OF, from L *pax* peace]

**peaceable** /'pisəbəl/, *adj.* **1.** disposed to peace; inclined to avoid strife or dissension: *peaceable intentions.* **2.** peaceful: *a peaceable adjustment.* – **peaceableness,** *n.* – **peaceably,** *adv.*

**peaceful** /'pisfəl/, *adj.* **1.** characterised by peace; free from strife or commotion; tranquil: *a peaceful reign.* **2.** pertaining to or characteristic of a state of peace: *peaceful uses of atomic energy.* **3.** peaceable. – **peacefully,** *adv.* – **peacefulness,** *n.*

**peaceful coexistence** /– koʊəg'zɪstəns/, *n.* the simultaneous existence of two incompatible political systems, without hostilities.

**peaceful dove** /'– dʌv/, *n.* See **dove** (def. 1).

**peacekeeping** /'piskipɪŋ/, *n.* **1.** the maintenance of law and order, esp. by the presence of an armed force. *–adj.* **2.** maintaining law and order.

**peacemaker** /'pismeɪkə/, *n.* one who makes peace, as by reconciling parties at variance.

**peace-offering** /'pis-ɒfərɪŋ/, *n.* **1.** an offering or sacrifice prescribed by the Levitical law (see Lev. 3, 7) as thanksgiving to God. **2.** any offering made to procure peace.

**peace officer** /'pis ɒfəsə/, *n.* a civil officer appointed to preserve the public peace, as a sheriff or constable.

**peace-pipe** /'pis-paɪp/, *n.* the calumet or pipe smoked by the North American Indians in token or ratification of peace.

**peacetime** /'pistaɪm/, *n.* **1.** a period of peace. *–adj.* **2.** of or for such a period: *peacetime uses of atomic energy.*

**peach**[1] /pitʃ/, *n.* **1.** the juicy, drupaceous fruit of a tree, *Prunus persica,* of many varieties, widely cultivated in temperate climates. **2.** the tree itself. **3.** a light pinkish yellow, as of a peach. **4.** *Colloq.* a person or thing esp. admired or liked. *–adj.* **5.** of the colour peach. **6.** flavoured or cooked with peaches. [ME *peche,* from OF; replacing OE *persic,* from L *persicum,* from Gk *Persikón,* lit., Persian (apple)] – **peachlike,** *adj.*

**peach**[2] /pitʃ/, *v.i.* **1.** *Brit. Colloq.* to inform against an accomplice or associate. *–v.t.* **2.** *Rare.* to inform against. [aphetic var. of *appeach,* ME *apeche(n),* from AF *apecher,* var. of OF *empechier* hinder. See IMPEACH]

**peach-bloom** /'pitʃ-blum/, *n.* **1.** the powdery surface of a peach. **2.** any surface resembling this, as of human complexion, pottery, etc.

**peachblow** /'pitʃbloʊ/, *n.* a delicate purplish pink. [PEACH[1] + BLOW[3], *n.*]

**peach Melba** /pitʃ 'mɛlbə/, *n.* fresh peaches, poached in a sugar syrup, served round vanilla icecream, all topped with Melba sauce. [created in 1893 by Auguste Escoffier, 1847?-1935, French chef, for Dame Nellie *Melba* (Mrs. Nellie Mitchell Armstrong), 1861-1931, Australian soprano]

**peachy** /'pitʃi/, *adj.,* **-chier, -chiest.** **1.** peachlike, as in colour or appearance. **2.** *Colloq.* excellent; wonderful.

**peacock** /'pikɒk/, *n., pl.* **-cocks,** (*esp. collectively*) **cock.** **1.** the male of the peafowl, esp. of the common peafowl, *Pavo cristatus,* native to India but now widely domesticated, distinguished for its long, erectile, ocellated tail coverts with rich iridescent colouring of green, blue, and gold. **2.** any peafowl. **3.** a vain person. *–v.i.* **4.** to strut like a peacock; make a vainglorious display. **5.** to buy up the best portions of a piece of land, as the land around the waterholes or creeks, so that the remaining land is virtually of no value to any other buyer. *–v.t.* **6.** to pick the best portions out of. [ME *pecok,* from *pe* (OE *pea* peafowl, from L *pavo*) + *cok* COCK[1]] – **peacockish, peacocky,** *adj.*

peacock (def. 1)

**peacock blue** /– 'blu/, *n.* a lustrous greenish-blue colour, as found in certain peacock feathers.

**peacocker** /'pikɒkə/, *n. Colloq.* **1.** (formerly) a squatter who selected choice pieces of land, as around waterholes, by using dummy buyers. **2.** one who chooses the best parts, pieces, etc., of anything.

**peacock ore** /'pikɒk ɔ/, *n.* →**bornite.**

**pea crab** /'pi kræb/, *n.* a small semiparasitic crab of the family Pinnotheridae, which inhabits the branchial cavities of molluscs and tunicates.

**peafowl** /'pifaʊl/, *n.* any of the gallinaceous birds constituting the genus *Pavo:* a peacock or peahen.

**peag** /pig/, *n.* →**wampum** (def. 1).

**pea green** /pi 'grin/, *n.* a medium- or yellowish-green colour.

**peahen** /'pihɛn/, *n.* the female peafowl.

**pea jacket** /'pi dʒækət/, *n.* a short coat of thick woollen cloth worn esp. by seamen. [anglicisation of D *pij-jakker*]

**peak**[1] /pik/, *n.* **1.** the pointed top of a mountain. **2.** a mountain with a pointed summit. **3.** the pointed top of anything. **4.** the highest point: *the peak of his career.* **5.** the maximum point or degree of anything. **6.** *Elect., Mech., etc.* **a.** the maximum value of a quantity during a specified time: *a voltage peak.* **b.** the maximum power consumed or produced by a unit or group of units in a stated period of time. **7.** a projecting point: *the peak of a man's beard.* **8.** widow's peak. **9.** a projecting front piece, or visor, of a cap. **10.** *Naut.* **a.** See **after peak** and **forepeak.** **b.** the upper after-corner of a sail that is extended by a gaff. **c.** the outer extremity of a gaff. *–v.t.* **11.** *Naut.* to raise the after-end of (a yard, gaff, etc.) to or towards an angle above the horizontal. *–v.i.* **12.** to project in a peak. **13.** to reach a highest point. [b. PIKE[2] (or PICK[1]) and BEAK[1]]

**peak**[2] /pik/, *v.i.* to become weak, thin, and sickly. [orig. uncert.] – **peakily,** *adv.* – **peakiness,** *n.* – **peaky,** *adj.*

**peaked**[1] /pikt/, *adj.* having a peak. [PEAK[1], *n.* + -ED[2]]

**peaked**[2] /pikt/, *adj.* thin; emaciated. Also, **peaky.** [PEAK[2] + -ED[2]]

**peak hour** /'pik aʊə/, *n.* the period at which city traffic is at its densest. Also, **peak period, rush hour.** – **peak-hour,** *adj.*

**peak load** /'– loʊd/, *n.* the maximum load on a supply system, esp. electrical power supply.

**peal** /pil/, *n.* **1.** a loud, prolonged sound of bells. **2.** any other loud, prolonged sound as of cannon, thunder, applause, laughter, etc. **3.** a set of bells tuned to one another. **4.** a series of changes rung on a set of bells. *–v.t.* **5.** to give forth loudly and sonorously. **6.** *Obs.* to assail with loud sounds. *–v.i.* **7.** to sound forth in a peal; resound. [ME *pele;* akin to *peal, pell,* v., strike, beat]

**pean** /'piən/, *n.* →**paean.**

**peanut** /'pinʌt/, *n.* **1.** Also, **groundnut.** the fruit (pod) or the edible seed of *Arachis hypogaea,* a leguminous plant native to Brazil, the pod of which is forced underground in growing, where it ripens. **2.** the plant. **3.** (*pl.*) *Colloq.* any small amount, esp. of money. **4.** (*derog.*) an insignificant person. *–adj.* **5.** of or pertaining to the peanut or peanuts. **6.** made with or from peanuts.

**peanut brittle** /– 'brɪtl/, *n.* a hard toffee containing peanuts. Also, **peanut brickle.**

**peanut butter** /– 'bʌtə/, *n.* a smooth paste made from finely ground roasted peanuts, used as a spread, etc.

**peanut-butter sandwich** /pinʌt-bʌtə 'sænwɪtʃ/, *n. Prison Colloq.* an honest job.

**peanut paste** /pinʌt 'peɪst/, *n. Qld, S.A.* →**peanut butter.**

**peanut spread** /– 'sprɛd/, *n.* →**peanut butter.**

**pear** /pɛə/, *n.* **1.** the edible fruit, typically rounded but elongated and growing smaller towards the stem, of a tree, *Pyrus communis,* familiar in cultivation. **2.** the tree itself. [ME *peere,* OE *pere,* from LL *pirum*]

**pear drop** /'– drɒp/, *n.* **1.** a pear-shaped pendant. **2.** a fruit-flavoured sweet in the shape of a pear.

**pearl**[1] /pɜl/, *n.* **1.** a hard, smooth, often highly lustrous concretion, a mass of nacre, white or variously coloured, and rounded, pear-shaped, or irregular (baroque) in form, secreted as a morbid product within the shell of various bivalve molluscs, and often valuable as a gem. **2.** any of various man-made substances that resemble this. **3.** nacre, or mother-of-pearl. **4.** something similar in form, lustre, etc., as a dewdrop or a capsule of medicine. **5.** something precious or choice; the finest example of anything. **6.** a very pale grey approaching white but commonly with a bluish tinge. **7.** a size of type (5 point). *–v.t.* **8.** to adorn or stud with or as with pearls. **9.** to make like pearls, as in form or colour. *–v.i.* **10.** to seek for pearls. **11.** to take a pearl-like form or appearance. *–adj.* **12.** of the colour or lustre of pearl; nacreous. **13.** of, pertaining to, or inlaid with pearls or mother-of-pearl. **14.** reduced to small rounded grains: *pearl barley.* [ME *perle,* from OF, from ML *perla,* ? b. L *perna* a kind of mussel and *sphaerula* little sphere] – **pearler,** *n.*

**pearl**[2] /pɜl/, *v.t., v.i., n.* →**purl**[2].

**pearl-ash** /ˈpɜl-æʃ/, *n.* commercial carbonate of potassium.

**pearl barley** /ˈpɜl bali/, *n.* barley ground into small round grains and used in soups, etc.

**pearl blue** /– ˈblu/, *n.* a light bluish-grey colour.

**pearl button** /– ˈbʌtn/, *n.* **1.** a button made from mother-of-pearl. **2.** a button made from an artificial pearl.

**pearler** /ˈpɜlə/, *n.* **1.** a person who dives for pearls. **2.** a boat used in seeking for pearls. **3.** one who trades in pearls. **4.** →**purler** (def. 2). *–adj.* **5.** →**purler.**

**pearl grey** /– ˈgreɪ/, *n.* a very pale bluish-grey colour.

**pearling** /ˈpɜlɪŋ/, *n.* (in surfing) a situation, usu. occurring on take-off, in which the nose of the surfboard goes underwater.

**pearlite** /ˈpɜlaɪt/, *n.* **1.** *Metall.* an iron carbon alloy containing approximately 0.86 per cent carbon, and consisting of alternate layers of ferrite and cementite. **2.** *Geol.* →**perlite.** [PEARL[1] + -ITE[1]] – **pearlitic** /pɜˈlɪtɪk/, *adj.*

**pearl millet** /pɜl ˈmɪlət/, *n.* a tall grass, *Pennisetum glaucum,* cultivated widely for its edible seeds and as a forage plant.

**pearl oyster** /– ˈɔɪstə/, *n.* any of the pearl-producing bivalve molluscs of the family Ostreidae.

**pearl perch** /– ˈpɜtʃ/, *n.* a highly prized food fish, *Glaucosoma scapulare,* of the central coast of eastern Australia.

**pearl spar** /ˈ– spa/, *n.* dolomite occurring in rhombohedra and having a pearly lustre.

**pearlwort** /ˈpɜlwɜt/, *n.* any of several small herbs of the genus *Sagina,* as *S. apetala,* the common pearlwort, an annual widespread on bare soil in temperate regions.

**pearly** /ˈpɜli/, *adj.,* **-lier, -liest,** *n., pl.* **-lies.** *–adj.* **1.** like a pearl or like pearl. **2.** adorned with or abounding in pearls, pearl, or mother-of-pearl. **3.** *Colloq.* wearing pearlies. *–n.* **4.** *Colloq.* a button, esp. one of a large number sewn on to the clothes of costermongers for ornament. **5.** *Colloq.* a costermonger whose clothes are so ornamented.

**Pearly Gates** /pɜli ˈgeɪts/, *n.pl. Colloq.* **1.** the entrance to heaven. **2.** (*l.c.*) teeth.

**pearly king** /pɜli ˈkɪŋ/, *n. Brit.* a hereditary title adopted by certain costermongers, originally by a chief stall-holder who protected other traders, now entitling the possessor to dress in costumes decorated with pearl buttons. – **pearly queen,** *n. fem.*

**pearly nautilus** /– ˈnɔtələs/, *n.* →**nautilus** (def. 1).

**pear shader** /ˈpɛə ʃeɪdə/, *n.* a tool for making pear-shaped bruises on leather.

**pear-shaped** /ˈpɛə-ʃeɪpt/, *adj.* having an oval shape tapering towards one end, as a pear.

**peart** /pɪət/, *adj.* **1.** lively or brisk; cheerful. **2.** clever. [var. of PERT]

**peasant** /ˈpɛzənt/, *n.* **1.** one of a class of persons, of inferior social rank, living in the country and engaged usu. in agricultural labour. **2.** a rustic or countryman. **3.** *Colloq.* an unsophisticated person; one unable to appreciate that which is cultured and tasteful; a boor. *–adj.* **4.** of or characteristic of peasants, their crafts, traditions, etc. [late ME, from AF *paisant,* from *pais* country, from LL *pāgensis,* adj., from L *pāgus* district. Cf. PAGAN]

**peasantry** /ˈpɛzəntri/, *n.* **1.** peasants collectively. **2.** the status or character of a peasant.

**pease** /piz/, *n., pl.* **pease.** *Archaic.* **1.** a pea. **2.** (*pl.*) peas collectively. **3.** plural of **pea.** [ME *pese,* OE *peose, pise,* from LL *pīsa,* orig. pl. of *pīsum,* from Gk *píson* pulse, pea]

**peasecod** /ˈpizkɒd/, *n.* the pod of the pea. Also, **peascod.** [ME; from PEASE + COD[2]]

**pease pudding** /ˈpiz pʊdɪŋ/, *n.* split peas soaked, then boiled and sieved, and served with ham or bacon.

**peashooter** /ˈpiʃutə/, *n.* a tube through which dried peas are blown, as by children.

**pea soup** /pi ˈsup/, *n.* **1.** a thick soup made from split peas. **2.** *Colloq.* thick, dirty fog.

**pea souper** /– ˈsupə/, *n. Colloq.* an extremely thick fog.

**pea-struck** /ˈpi-strʌk/, *adj.* (of livestock) suffering from a disease induced by eating poisonous species of *Swainsona,* including the Darling Pea.

**peat** /pit/, *n.* **1.** a highly organic soil (more than fifty per cent combustible) of partially decomposed vegetable matter, in marshy or damp regions, drained and cultivated, cut out and dried for use as fuel. **2.** such vegetable matter as a substance or fuel. [ME *pete* (in Anglo-L *peta*); orig. uncert.] – **peaty,** *adj.*

**peatbog** /ˈpitbɒg/, *n.* a naturally occurring accumulation of peat or peaty matter. Also, **peatmoss.**

**peatmoss** /ˈpitmɒs/, *n.* any moss from which peat has formed or may form, as sphagnum, and used as a basis for potting mixtures.

**peat wax** /ˈpit wæks/, *n.* an organic bituminous wax extracted from some varieties of peat, used in manufacture of carbon paper, polishes, cosmetics and explosives.

**peau de soie** /poʊ də ˈswa/, *n.* a fancy reversible silk cloth made on a satin base, having a ribbed appearance. [F]

**pebble** /ˈpɛbəl/, *n., v.,* **-bled, -bling.** *–n.* **1.** a small, rounded stone, esp. one worn by the action of water. **2.** pebbled leather, or its granulated surface. **3.** a transparent, colourless rock crystal used for the lenses of spectacles. **4.** a lens made of it. **5.** *Colloq.* a man or animal which cannot be cowed or beaten. *–v.t.* **6.** to prepare (leather, etc.) so as to have a granulated surface. **7.** to pelt with or as with pebbles. [ME *puble-,* etc., OE *pæbbel* (in place-names)] – **pebbly,** *adj.*

**pebble dash** /ˈ– dæʃ/, *n.* a type of finish used on external walls, formed by throwing or pressing small stones into plaster while it is still plastic.

**pecan** /ˈpikæn, piˈkæn/, *n.* **1.** a hickory tree, *Carya illinoinensis,* indigenous to the lower Mississippi valley, southern U.S., and grown for its oval, smooth-shelled nut with a sweet, oily, edible kernel. **2.** the nut of this tree. [Algonquian *pukan, pakan* hard-shelled nut]

**peccable** /ˈpɛkəbəl/, *adj.* liable to sin or err. [ML *peccābilis*] – **peccability** /pɛkəˈbɪləti/, *n.*

**peccadillo** /pɛkəˈdɪloʊ/, *n., pl.* **-loes, -los.** a petty sin or offence; a trifling fault. [Sp. *pecadillo,* diminutive of *pecado,* from L *peccātum* a sin]

**peccant** /ˈpɛkənt/, *adj.* **1.** sinning or offending. **2.** faulty. [L *peccans,* ppr., sinning] – **peccancy,** *n.* – **peccantly,** *adv.*

**peccary** /ˈpɛkəri/, *n., pl.* **-ries** (*esp. collectively*) **-ry.** one of two species of gregarious, piglike American ungulates, of the genus *Tayassu,* the **collared peccary,** and the **white-lipped peccary,** ranging from Paraguay in South America to Texas in North America and constituting the artiodactylous family Tayassuidae, related to the pig. [Carib *pakira*]

collared peccary

**peccavi** /pɛˈkavi/, *n., pl.* **-vis.** any avowal of guilt. [L: I have sinned]

**peck**[1] /pɛk/, *n.* **1.** a dry measure in the imperial system, equal to 8 quarts or 9.092 18 × $10^{-3}$ $m^3$; the fourth part of a bushel. **2.** a container for measuring this quantity. **3.** a considerable quantity: *a peck of trouble.* [ME *pek;* orig. unknown]

**peck**[2] /pɛk/, *v.t.* **1.** to strike or indent with the beak, as a bird does, or with some pointed instrument, esp. with quick, repeated movements. **2.** to make (a hole, etc.) by such strokes. **3.** to take (food, etc.) bit by bit, with or as with the beak. **4.** to kiss in a hasty dabbing manner. *–v.i.* **5.** to make strokes with the beak or a pointed instrument. **6.** to pick or nibble at food. **7.** to carp or nag (fol. by *at*). *–n.* **8.** a pecking stroke. **9.** a hole or mark made by or as by pecking. **10.** a hasty kiss. [ME *pekke(n);* ? var. of PICK[1]]

**pecker** /ˈpɛkə/, *n.* **1.** one who or that which pecks. **2.**

→**woodpecker**. 3. **keep one's pecker up**, *Colloq.* to remain cheerful; maintain good spirits, courage, or resolution.

**pecking order** /ˈpɛkɪŋ ɔdə/, *n.* **1.** the natural hierarchy observable in a flock of poultry or in any gregarious species of birds. **2.** any order of precedence. Also, **peck order**.

**peckish** /ˈpɛkɪʃ/, *adj. Colloq.* having an appetite.

**Pecksniffian** /pɛkˈsnɪfiən/, *adj.* making a hypocritical parade of benevolence or high principle. [after Mr *Pecksniff* in *Martin Chuzzlewit* by Charles Dickens, 1812-70, English novelist]

**pecorino** /pɛkəˈrinoʊ/, *n.* a hard, granular, pale-yellow cheese, with a sharp, tangy flavour. It was originally made from ewe's milk, now often from cow's milk. [It.]

**pectate** /ˈpɛkteɪt/, *n.* a salt of pectic acid.

**pecten** /ˈpɛktən/, *n., pl.* **-tens, -tines** /-təniz/. **1.** a comblike part, process or organ of an animal. **2.** a pigmented vascular membrane with parallel folds suggesting the teeth of a comb, projecting into the vitreous humour of the eye in birds and reptiles. [ME, from L: a comb]

**pectic** /ˈpɛktɪk/, *adj.* pertaining to pectin. [Gk *pēktikós* congealing, curdling]

**pectic acid** /– ˈæsəd/, *n.* any of several water-insoluble products of the hydrolysis of pectin esters.

**pectin** /ˈpɛktən/, *n.* any of the acidic hemicelluloses which occur in ripe fruits, esp. in apples, currants, etc., and which dissolve in boiling water, forming a jelly upon subsequent evaporation. [PECT(IC) + -IN[2]]

**pectinate** /ˈpɛktəneɪt/, *adj.* comblike; formed into or with teeth like a comb. Also, **pectinated**. [L *pectinātus* comblike, pp.] – **pectination** /pɛktəˈneɪʃən/, *n.*

**pectise** /ˈpɛktaɪz/, *v.,* **-tised, -tising.** *–v.t.* **1.** to change into a jelly. *–v.i.* **2.** to jellify; gel. Also, **pectize**. [Gk *pēktós* compacted, fixed + -ISE] – **pectisation** /pɛktaɪˈzeɪʃən/, *n.*

**pectolite** /ˈpɛktəlaɪt/, *n.* a mineral silicate of calcium and sodium which crystallises in the monoclinic system.

**pectoral** /ˈpɛktərəl/, *adj.* **1.** of or pertaining to the breast or chest; thoracic. **2.** worn on the breast or chest: *the pectoral cross of a bishop.* **3.** proceeding from the heart or inner consciousness. **4.** *Phonet.* (of a vocal quality) appearing to come from resonance in the chest; full or deep. *–n.* **5.** something worn on the breast for ornament, protection, etc., as a breastplate. **6.** a pectoral fin. [late ME, from L *pectorālis* pertaining to the breast]

**pectoral arch** /– ˈatʃ/, *n.* **1.** (in vertebrates) a bony or cartilaginous arch supporting the forelimbs. **2.** (in man) the bony arch, formed by the collarbone and shoulderblade, which attaches the upper extremity to the axial skeleton. Also, **pectoral girdle**.

**pectoral fin** /– ˈfɪn/, *n.* (in fishes) either of a pair of fins situated usu. behind the head, one on each side, and corresponding to the forelimbs of higher vertebrates.

**peculate** /ˈpɛkjəleɪt/, *v.i., v.t.,* **-lated, -lating.** to embezzle (public money); appropriate dishonestly (money or goods entrusted to one's care). [L *pecūlātus,* pp., having embezzled] – **peculation** /pɛkjəˈleɪʃən/, *n.* – **peculator**, *n.*

**peculiar** /pəˈkjuliə, -ljə/, *adj.* **1.** strange, odd, or queer: *a peculiar old man.* **2.** uncommon; unusual: *a peculiar hobby.* **3.** distinguished in nature or character from others. **4.** belonging characteristically (fol. by *to*): *an expression peculiar to Australians.* **5.** belonging exclusively to a person or thing. *–n.* **6.** *Print.* →**special sort**. **7.** *Obs.* a peculiar property or privilege. **8.** a particular parish or church which is exempted from the jurisdiction of the ordinary or bishop in whose diocese it lies and is governed by another. [late ME, from L *pecūliāris* pertaining to one's own, from *pecūlium* property] – **peculiarly**, *adv.*

**peculiarity** /pəkjuliˈærəti/, *n., pl.* **-ties.** **1.** an odd trait or characteristic. **2.** singularity or oddity. **3.** peculiar or characteristic quality. **4.** a distinguishing quality or characteristic.

**peculium** /pəˈkjuliəm/, *n.* **1.** private property. **2.** *Rom. Law.* property given by a paterfamilias to those subject to him, or by a master to his slave, to be treated as though the property of the recipient. [L: property]

**pecuniary** /pəˈkjuniəri, -nəri/, *adj.* **1.** consisting of or given or exacted in money: *pecuniary penalties.* **2.** of or pertaining to money: *pecuniary affairs.* **3.** (of an offence, etc.) entailing a money penalty. [L *pecūniārius* pertaining to money] – **pecuniarily**, *adv.*

**ped-[1]**, variant of **paed-**, as in *pedagogic.*

**ped-[2]**, variant of **pedi-[1]**.

**-ped**, a word element meaning 'foot', serving to form adjectives and nouns, as *aliped, biped, quadruped.* Cf. **-pod**. [L, combining form of *pēs* foot]

**ped.**, **1.** pedal. **2.** pedestal.

**pedagogic** /pɛdəˈgɒdʒɪk/, *adj.* of or pertaining to a pedagogue or pedagogy. Also, **pedagogical**. [Gk *paidagōgikós,* from *paidagōgós* pedagogue] – **pedagogically**, *adv.*

**pedagogics** /pɛdəˈgɒdʒɪks/, *n.* the science or art of teaching or education; pedagogy.

**pedagogism** /ˈpɛdəgɒgɪzəm/, *n.* the principles, manner, or characteristics of pedagogues. Also, **pedagoguism**.

**pedagogue** /ˈpɛdəgɒg/, *n.* **1.** a teacher of children; a schoolteacher. **2.** a person who is pedantic, dogmatic, and formal. [ME *pedagoge,* from OF, from L *paedagōgus,* from Gk *paidagōgós* a teacher of boys]

**pedagogy** /ˈpɛdəgɒdʒi/, *n.* **1.** the function, work, or art of a teacher; teaching. **2.** instruction.

**pedal[1]** /ˈpɛdl/, *n., v.,* **-alled, -alling** or (*U.S.*) **-aled, -aling**, *adj.* *–n.* **1.** a lever worked by the foot, in various musical instruments, as the organ, piano, and harp, and having various functions. **2.** a keyboard attached to the organ, harpsichord, etc., operated by the feet. **3.** →**pedal point**. **4.** a lever-like part worked by the foot, in various mechanisms, as the sewing machine, bicycle, motor car, etc.; a treadle. *–v.t.* **5.** to work or use the pedals of, as in playing an organ or propelling a bicycle. *–v.i.* **6.** to operate the pedals. *–adj.* **7.** of or pertaining to a pedal or pedals. **8.** consisting of pedals: *a pedal keyboard.* [F *pédale,* from It., from L: (something) pertaining to the foot]

**pedal[2]** /ˈpidl/, *adj.* of or pertaining to a foot or the feet. [L *pedālis*]

**pedal bin** /ˈpɛdl bɪn/, *n.* a small bin for kitchen wastes, the lid of which is operated by a pedal.

**pedalfer** /pəˈdælfə/, *n.* a type of soil lacking in lime but containing accumulations of aluminium and iron components. [Gk *pedón* ground + AL(UMINIUM) + L *ferrum* iron]

**pedal point** /ˈpɛdl pɔɪnt/, *n. Music.* **1.** a note sustained by one of the parts (usu. the bass) while other parts progress without reference to it. **2.** a passage containing it.

**pedal steel guitar**, *n.* an electric guitar developed from the hawaiian guitar, consisting of a flat board horizontal to the floor, with steel strings which are played with a slide. Pitch changes can also be effected during playing by means of pedals controlling string tension. Also, **steel guitar**.

**pedal wireless** /ˈpɛdl waɪələs/, *n.* (formerly) a transceiver or two-way radio equipped with earphones or a small loudspeaker and powered by a small generator set in a box, fitted with bicycle pedals, and operated by vigorous pedalling. Also, **pedal radio**.

**pedant** /ˈpɛdnt/, *n.* **1.** one who makes an excessive or tedious show of learning or learned precision; one who possesses mere book-learning without practical wisdom. **2.** *Obs.* a schoolmaster. [It. *pedante* teacher, pedant, from *ped-, piede* foot (in meaning of servile follower)] – **pedantic** /pəˈdæntɪk/, **pedantical** /pəˈdæntɪkəl/, *adj.* – **pedantically** /pəˈdæntɪkli/, *adv.*

**pedantry** /ˈpɛdntri/, *n., pl.* **-ries.** **1.** the character or practice of a pedant; an undue display of learning. **2.** slavish attention to rules, details, etc. **3.** a pedantic expression; an instance of being pedantic.

**pedate** /ˈpɛdeɪt/, *adj.* **1.** having feet. **2.** footlike. **3.** having divisions like toes. [L *pedātus* having feet] – **pedately**, *adv.*

**pedati-**, a word element meaning 'pedate'. [combining form representing L *pedātus*]

**pedatifid** /pəˈdætəfəd, -ˈdeɪtə-/, *adj. Bot.* pedately cleft.

**peddle** /ˈpɛdl/, *v.,* **-dled, -dling.** *–v.t.* **1.** to carry about for sale at retail; hawk. **2.** to deal out in small quantities. *–v.i.* **3.** to travel about retailing small wares. **4.** to occupy oneself with trifles; trifle. [apparently a backformation from PEDLAR, and in part confused with PIDDLE]

**peddler** /ˈpɛdlə/, *n. U.S.* →**pedlar**.

**-pede**, a word element meaning 'foot', as in *centipede.* [F

-*pède,* from L -*peda,* a combining form of *pēs* foot]

**pederast** /'pɛdəræst/, *n.* one, esp. a male adult, who desires or practises pederasty. [Gk *paiderastḗs* lover of boys]

**pederasty** /'pɛdəræsti/, *n.* homosexual relations, esp. those between a male adult and a boy. – **pederastic** /pɛdə'ræstɪk/, *adj.* – **pederastically** /pɛdə'ræstɪkli/, *adv.*

**pedestal** /'pɛdəstl/, *n.*, *v.*, **-talled, -talling** or (*U.S.*) **-taled, -taling.** –*n.* **1.** an architectural support for a column, statue, vase, or the like. **2.** a supporting structure or piece; a base. **3.** one of two supports of a kneehole desk, consisting of a boxlike frame containing drawers. **4. set on a pedestal,** to idealise: *he set her on a pedestal until he discovered her true nature.* –*v.t.* **5.** to set on or supply with a pedestal. [F *piédestal,* from It. *piedestallo,* from *piè* foot (from L *pēs*) + *di* of (from L *dē*) + *stallo* (of Gmc orig. Cf. STALL[1])]

**pedestrian** /pə'dɛstriən/, *n.* **1.** one who goes or travels on foot; a walker. –*adj.* **2.** going or performed on foot; walking. **3.** pertaining to walking. **4.** commonplace; prosaic; dull. [L *pedester* on foot + -IAN]

**pedestrian crossing** /– 'krɒsɪŋ/, *n.* an area of roadway on which pedestrians have, within legally defined limits, right of way to cross the road. See **zebra crossing.**

**pedestrianism** /pə'dɛstriənɪzəm/, *n.* **1.** the exercise or practice of walking. **2.** pedestrian manner or traits.

**pedi-**[1], a word element meaning 'foot', as in *pediform.* Also, **ped-**[2]. [L, combining form of *pēs*]

**pedi-**[2], *Chiefly U.S.* variant of **paed-.**

**pediatrician** /ˌpidiə'trɪʃən/, *n. U.S.* →**paediatrician.**

**pediatrics** /pidi'ætrɪks/, *n. U.S.* →**paediatrics.** – **pediatric,** *adj.*

**pedicel** /'pɛdəsɛl/, *n.* **1.** *Bot.* **a.** a small stalk. **b.** an ultimate division of a common peduncle. **c.** one of the subordinate stalks in a branched inflorescence, bearing a single flower. **2.** *Zool., Anat.* **a.** a small stalk or stalk-like part; a peduncle. **b.** a little foot or footlike part. [NL *pedīcellus,* diminutive of L *pedīculus* PEDICLE]

A, pedicel; B, peduncle

**pedicellate** /'pɛdisɛleɪt, pɛdi'sɛleɪt, -ət/, *adj.* having a pedicel or pedicels.

**pedicle** /'pɛdɪkəl/, *n.* a small stalk or stalklike support; a pedicel or peduncle. [L *pedīculus,* diminutive of *pēs* foot]

**pedicular** /pə'dɪkjələ/, *adj.* of or pertaining to lice. [L *pedīculāris,* from *pedīculus* louse]

**pediculate** /pə'dɪkjələt, -leɪt/, *adj.* **1.** of or relating to the Pediculati, a group of teleost fishes, characterised by the elongated basis of their pectoral fins simulating an arm or penduncle. –*n.* **2.** a member of this group. [L *pedīculus* footstalk + -ATE[1]]

**pediculosis** /pədɪkjə'lousəs/, *n.* the state of being infested with lice. [NL, from L *pedīculus* louse + -*ōsis* -OSIS] – **pediculous** /pə'dɪkjələs/, *adj.*

**pedicure** /'pɛdəkjuə/, *n.* **1.** professional care or treatment of the feet. **2.** one who makes a business of caring for the feet; a chiropodist. [F, from L *pedi-* PEDI-[1] + *cūra* care. Cf. MANICURE]

**pediform** /'pɛdifɔm/, *adj.* in the form of a foot.

**pedigree** /'pɛdəgri/, *n.* **1.** an ancestral line, or line of descent, esp. as recorded; lineage. **2.** a genealogical table: *a family pedigree.* **3.** a line, family, or race. **4.** derivation, as from a source: *the pedigree of a word.* [ME *pedegru,* apparently from OF *pied de grue,* lit., foot of crane, said to refer to a mark having three branching lines, used in old genealogical tables]

**pedigreed** /'pɛdəgrid/, *adj.* having known purebred ancestry.

**pediment** /'pɛdəmənt/, *n. Archit.* **1.** a low triangular gable crowned with a projecting cornice, in the Greek, Roman, or Renaissance style, esp. over a portico or porch or at the ends of a gable-roofed building. **2.** any member of similar outline and position, as over an opening. [? from L *pedāmentum* a prop of a vine] – **pedimental** /pɛdə'mɛntl/, *adj.*

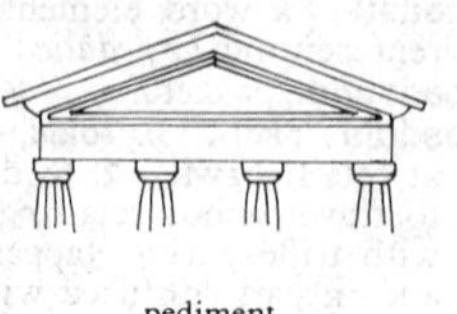

pediment

**pedipalp** /'pɛdipælp/, *n.* the second paired appendage of an arachnid, sometimes used as a weapon or as an organ of touch for feeding.

**pedlar** /'pɛdlə/, *n.* one who peddles. Also, **pedler;** *U.S.,* **peddler.** [ME *pedlere,* apparently from *pedle,* diminutive of *ped* basket]

**pedlary** /'pɛdləri/, *n.* **1.** the business of a pedlar. **2.** pedlars' wares. **3.** →**trumpery.** Also, *U.S.,* **peddlery.**

**pedobaptism** /pidou'bæptɪzəm/, *n. U.S.* →**paedobaptism.**

**pedocal** /'pɛdəkæl/, *n.* a type of soil rich in lime, having accumulations of calcium carbonate.

**pedology**[1] /pə'dɒlədʒi/, *n.* the more fundamental aspects of soil science, particularly the genesis and classification of soils. [Gk *pédo(n)* soil + -LOGY]

**pedology**[2] /pə'dɒlədʒi/, *n. U.S.* →**paedology.**

**pedometer** /pə'dɒmətə/, *n.* an instrument for recording the number of steps taken in walking, and thus showing approximately the distance travelled. [F *pédomètre,* from *pedo-* PEDI-[1] + -*mètre* -METER[1]]

**pedro** /'pidrou, 'pɛdrou/, *n., pl.* **-dros.** *U.S. Cards.* **1.** any of several varieties of seven-up in which the five of trumps counts at its face value. **2.** the five of trumps. [Sp., special use of *Pedro* Peter]

**Pedro Ximenez** /pɛdrou 'ziməneɪz/, *n.* a white grape variety used mainly in the production of sherry.

**peduncle** /pə'dʌŋkəl/, *n.* **1.** *Bot.* **a.** a flower stalk, supporting either a cluster or a solitary flower. **b.** the stalk bearing the fructification in fungi, etc. **2.** *Zool.* a stalk or stem; a stalklike part or structure. **3.** *Anat.* a stalklike part composed of white matter connecting various regions of the brain. [NL *pedunculus,* diminutive of L *pēs* foot] – **peduncled, peduncular** /pə'dʌŋkjələ/, *adj.*

P, peduncle

**pedunculate** /pə'dʌŋkjələt, -leɪt/, *adj.* **1.** having a peduncle. **2.** growing on a peduncle. Also, **pedunculated.**

**pee** /pi/, *v.,* **peed, peeing,** *n. Colloq.* –*v.i.* **1.** to urinate. –*n.* **2.** an act of urination. **3. have a pee,** to urinate.

**peek** /pik/, *v.i.* **1.** to peep; peer. –*n.* **2.** a peeking look; a peep. [ME *pike(n),* ? dissimilated var. of *kike* peep; akin to LG *kīken*]

**peekaboo** /'pikəbu/, *n.* **1.** a game played with or among children in which the player's face is alternately covered and revealed to the cry of 'peekaboo' or 'boo'. –*adj.* **2.** characterised by a partial revealing, esp. in women's clothes. [PEEK + -*a*- + BOO]

**peel**[1] /pil/, *v.t.* **1.** to strip off the skin, rind, bark, etc.; decorticate. **2.** to strip off (skin, etc.). **3.** *Croquet.* to send (another player's ball) through a hoop. **4. keep (one's) eye peeled,** *Colloq.* to keep a close watch. –*v.i.* **5.** (of skin, etc.) to come off. **6.** to lose the skin, rind, bark, etc. **7.** *Colloq.* to undress. –*n.* **8.** the skin or rind of a fruit, etc. [ME *pelen,* phonetic var. of *pilen* PILL[2]]

**peel**[2] /pil/, *n.* a shovel-like implement for putting bread, pies, etc., into the oven or taking them out. [ME *pele,* from OF: shovel, from L *pāla* spade]

**peel**[3] /pil/, *n.* one of a class of fortified towers, common in the border counties of England and Scotland in the 16th century. [ME *pel,* from OF: stake, from L *pālus* PALE[2]]

**peeler**[1] /'pilə/, *n.* one who or that which peels. [PEEL[1] + -ER[1]]

**peeler**[2] /'pilə/, *n. Obs. Colloq.* a policeman. [named after Sir Robert *Peel,* 1788-1850, British prime minister, who founded the Irish constabulary and improved it in Britain. Cf. BOBBY[1]]

**peeling** /'pilɪŋ/, *n.* **1.** the act of one who or that which peels. **2.** that which is peeled from something, as a piece of the skin or rind of a fruit peeled off.

**peen** /pin/, *n.* **1.** the sharp, spherical, or otherwise modified end of the head of a hammer, opposite to the face. –*v.t.* **2.** to treat by striking regularly all over with the peen of a hammer. [earlier *pen;* orig. uncert.]

**peep**[1] /pip/, *v.i.* **1.** to look through or as through a small aperture. **2.** to look slyly, pryingly, or furtively. **3.** to peer, as from a hiding place. **4.** to come partially into view; begin to appear. *–v.t.* **5.** to show or protrude slightly. *–n.* **6.** a peeping look or glance. **7.** the first appearance, as of dawn. **8.** an aperture for looking through. [? assimilated var. of PEEK]

**peep**[2] /pip/, *n.* **1.** a peeping cry or sound. *–v.i.* **2.** to utter the shrill little cry of a young bird, a mouse, etc.; cheep; squeak. **3.** to speak in a thin, weak voice. [ME *pēpe(n)*, also *pīpen*. Cf. OF *piper*, L *pīpāre*, D and G *piepen*, all imitative]

**peeper**[1] /ˈpipə/, *n.* the maker of a peeping sound. [PEEP[2], *v.* + -ER[1]]

**peeper**[2] /ˈpipə/, *n.* **1.** a prying or spying person. **2.** *Colloq.* (*usu. pl.*) an eye. [PEEP[1], *v.* + -ER[1]]

**peephole** /ˈpiphoʊl/, *n.* a hole through which to peep.

**peeping Tom** /pipɪŋ ˈtɒm/, *n.* a prying, furtive observer, often for sexual gratification; voyeur. [allusion to the man who peeped at Lady Godiva riding naked through Coventry]

**peepshow** /ˈpipʃoʊ/, *n.* **1.** an exhibition of objects or pictures viewed through an aperture usu. fitted with a magnifying lens. **2.** any display or spectacle arousing furtive curiosity.

**peep sight** /ˈpip saɪt/, *n.* a plate containing a small hole through which a gunner peeps in sighting.

**peep-toe** /ˈpip-toʊ/, *adj.* (of shoes) having no covering over part of the big toe and sometimes the other toes.

**peepul** /ˈpipəl/, *n.* →**pipal.**

**peer**[1] /pɪə/, *n.* **1.** a person of the same civil rank or standing; an equal before the law. **2.** one who ranks with another in respect to endowments or other qualifications; an equal in any respect. **3.** a nobleman. [ME *per*, from OF, from L *pār* equal]

**peer**[2] /pɪə/, *v.i.* **1.** to look narrowly, as in the effort to discern clearly. **2.** to peep out or appear slightly. **3.** to come into view. [late ME; orig. uncert., ? akin to PERK[1]]

**peerage** /ˈpɪərɪdʒ/, *n.* **1.** the rank or dignity of a peer. **2.** the body of peers of a country or state. **3.** a book giving a list of peers, with their genealogy, etc.

**peeress** /ˈpɪərɛs/, *n.* **1.** the wife of a peer. **2.** a woman having in her own right the rank of a peer.

**peer group** /ˈpɪə grup/, *n.* **1.** a group of people of about the same age. **2.** a group of people of the same social background, occupation, or class.

**peerless** /ˈpɪələs/, *adj.* having no peer or equal; matchless. – **peerlessly,** *adv.* – **peerlessness,** *n.*

**peetweet** /ˈpitwit/, *n. U.S.* the spotted sandpiper. See **sandpiper.** [imitative Cf. PEWIT]

**peeve** /piv/, *v.*, **peeved, peeving,** *n. Colloq. –v.t.* **1.** to render peevish. *–n.* **2.** an annoyance: *my pet peeve.* [backformation from PEEVISH]

**peevish** /ˈpivɪʃ/, *adj.* **1.** cross, querulous, or fretful, as from vexation or discontent. **2.** *Obs.* perverse. [ME *pevysh*; orig. unknown] – **peevishly,** *adv.* – **peevishness,** *n.*

**peewee** /ˈpiwi/, *n.* **1.** →**magpie lark. 2.** a black and white marble.

**peewit** /ˈpiwɪt/, *n.* →**magpie lark.**

**peg** /pɛg/, *n.*, *v.*, **pegged, pegging.** *–n.* **1.** a pin of wood or other material driven or fitted into something, as to fasten parts together, to hang things on, to make fast a rope or string on, to stop a hole, or to mark some point. **2.** *Colloq.* a leg, sometimes one of wood. **3.** an occasion; reason: *a peg to hang a grievance on.* **4.** *Colloq.* a degree: *to come down a peg.* **5.** a pin of wood or metal to which one end of a string of a musical instrument is fastened, and which may be turned in its socket to adjust the string's tension. **6.** *Colloq.* a drink usu. made of whisky or brandy and soda water. **7.** *Mountaineering.* a piton. **8.** a clothes peg. **9. off the peg,** (of a garment) available for immediate use; ready-made. **10. take down a peg,** to humble. **11. square peg in a round hole,** *Colloq.* a misfit. *–v.t.* **12.** to drive or insert a peg into. **13.** to fasten with or as with pegs. **14.** to mark with pegs (oft. fol. by *out*). **15.** to maintain (prices, wages, etc.) at a set level by laws or by manipulation. **16.** to strike or pierce with or as with a peg. **17.** *Colloq.* to aim or throw. **18.** *Baseball.* **a.** to throw (the ball) fast and low to a baseman to cause the runner to be out (def. 35). **b.** to get (someone) out in this way. *–v.i.* **19.** to work persistently, or keep on energetically (fol. by *away, along, on,* etc.). **20.** *Croquet.* to strike a peg. **21. peg out, a.** to die. **b.** to mark out a gold claim. [ME *pegge.* Cf. OE *pecg* (in a placename), d. D *peg*, LG *pigge*]

**pegboard** /ˈpɛgbɔd/, *n.* a composition board with holes for inserting pegs, hooks, etc.

**peggie** /ˈpɛgi/, *n. Colloq.* the man who acts as nipper for wharf labourers.

**peg leg** /ˈpɛg lɛg/, *n.* an artificial leg, usu. one of wood.

**pegmatite** /ˈpɛgmətaɪt/, *n.* a coarsely crystalline granite or other rock occurring in veins or dykes. [Gk *pêgma* something fastened together + -ITE[1]]

**peg top** /ˈpɛg tɒp/, *n.* **1.** a child's wooden top spinning on a metal peg. **2.** (*pl.*) peg-top trousers. **3.** a peg-top skirt.

**peg-top** /ˈpɛg-tɒp/, *adj.* shaped like a top, as men's trousers or women's skirts wide at the hips and narrowing to the ankle.

**peignoir** /ˈpeɪnwa/, *n.* **1.** a dressing-gown. **2.** a negligee. [F, from *peigner*, from L *pectināre* comb]

**pejor.,** pejorative.

**pejorate** /ˈpɛdʒəreɪt/, *v.t.*, **-rated, -rating.** to make worse; deteriorate. – **pejoration** /pɛdʒəˈreɪʃən/, *n.*

**pejorative** /pəˈdʒɒrətɪv/, *adj.* **1.** deprecatory. **2.** having a disparaging force, as certain derivative word forms. *–n.* **3.** a pejorative form or word, as *poetaster.* [L *pējōrātus*, pp., having been made worse + -IVE] – **pejoratively,** *adv.*

**peke** /pik/, *n. Colloq.* a Pekingese dog.

**Pekin** /piˈkɪn/, *n.* a hardy yellow-white duck developed in China. [named after *Peking*, traditional and present capital of China]

**Pekingese** /pikəˈniz/, *n.* **1.** small, long-haired Chinese dog prized as a pet. **2.** →**Mandarin.** Also, **Pekinese.**

Pekingese

**Peking man** /pikɪŋ ˈmæn/, *n.* a variety of *Homo erectus,* known from remains found near Peking, China.

**pekoe** /ˈpikoʊ/, *n.* a superior kind of black tea from Ceylon, India, and Java, made from leaves smaller than those used for orange pekoe. [Chinese (Amoy d.) *pek-ho* white down]

**pelage** /ˈpɛlɪdʒ/, *n.* the hair, fur, wool, or other soft covering of a mammal. [F, from *poil*, from L *pilus* hair]

**pelagic** /pəˈlædʒɪk/, *adj.* **1.** of or pertaining to the seas or oceans. **2.** living at or near the surface of the ocean, far from land, as certain animals or plants. [L *pelagicus*, from Gk *pelagikós* pertaining to the sea]

**pelargonic acid** /ˌpɛləgɒnɪk ˈæsəd/, *n.* an oily fatty acid, $CH_3(CH_2)_7COOH$, usu. made synthetically by the oxidisation of oleic acid, but which can be obtained in the form of esters, esp. from the leaves of the pelargonium; monanoic acid.

**pelargonium** /pɛləˈgoʊniəm/, *n.* any plant of the genus *Pelargonium,* the cultivated species of which are usu. called geranium. See **geranium** (def. 2). [NL, from Gk *pelargós* stork]

**pelerine** /ˈpɛlərin/, *n.* a woman's cape, esp. a narrow cape with long descending ends in front. [F: pilgrim's cape or mantle, special use of fem. of *pèlerin* pilgrim, from L *peregrīnus* wandering]

**pelf** /pɛlf/, *n.* (*derog.*) money or riches. [ME, from OF *pelfre* spoil; orig. uncert. Cf. PILFER]

**pelican** /ˈpɛlɪkən/, *n.* any of various large, totipalmate birds of the family Pelecanidae, having a large fish-catching bill with distensible pouch beneath, into which the young stick their heads when feeding. [ME and OE, from LL *pelicānus*, var. of *pelecānus*, from Gk *pelekán*]

pelican

**pelisse** /pəˈlis/, *n.* **1.** an outer garment lined or trimmed with fur. **2.** a woman's long cloak with arm openings. [F, from LL *pellicia* fur garment, properly fem. of LL *pelliceus* made of skins]

**pelite** /ˈpilaɪt/, *n.* any clay rock. Cf. **psephite** and **psammite.** [Gk *pēlós* clay, earth + -ITE¹] – **pelitic** /pəˈlɪtɪk/, *adj.*

**pellagra** /pəˈleɪgrə, pəˈlægrə/, *n.* a chronic, non-contagious disease caused by nicotinic acid deficiency, characterised by skin changes, nervous dysfunction and diarrhoea. [It., from *pelle* skin (from L *pellis*) + *-agra* (by association with PODAGRA)] – **pellagrous,** *adj.*

**pellet** /ˈpɛlət/, *n.* **1.** a round or spherical body, esp. one of small size; a little ball, as of food or medicine. **2.** a ball, usu. of stone, formerly used as a missile. **3.** a bullet or one of a charge of small shot, as for a shotgun. **4.** an imitation bullet, as of wax or paper. **5.** a boss or raised part of coins or carved ornaments. **6.** undigested remains, as of fur of the prey, which is regurgitated by certain predatory birds. *–v.t.* **7.** to form into pellets. **8.** to hit with pellets. **9.** *Agric.* to coat (seeds) with lime for sowing in acidic soils. [ME *pelet,* from OF *pelote,* from L *pila* ball]

**pelletise** /ˈpɛlətaɪz/, *v.t.,* **-tised, -tising. 1.** to roll finely divided material in a drum or inclined disc so that the particles cling together and roll up into small spherical pellets. **2.** to treat fine iron ore or coal to produce pellets.

**pellicle** /ˈpɛlɪkəl/, *n.* a thin skin or membrane; a film; a scum. [L *pellicula,* diminutive of *pellis* skin] – **pellicular** /pəˈlɪkjələ/, *adj.*

**pellitory** /ˈpɛlətri, -təri/, *n., pl.* **-ries. 1.** any of several species of herbs belonging to the genus *Parietaria,* as **pellitory-of-the-wall,** *P. diffusa,* a branched perennial often found in crevices of rocks and walls. **2.** a plant, *Anacyclus pyrethrum,* of northern Africa and southern Europe whose root is used as a local irritant (**pellitory of Spain**). [alteration with change of suffix of ME *peletre,* from AF, from L *pyrethrum* pellitory of Spain, from Gk *pýrethron* feverfew]

**pell-mell** /pɛl-ˈmɛl/, *adv.* **1.** in an indiscriminate medley; in a confused mass or crowd. **2.** in disorderly, headlong haste. *–adj.* **3.** indiscriminate; disorderly; tumultuous. *–n.* **4.** an indiscriminate medley. **5.** violent and confused disorder. Also, **pellmell.** [F *pêle-mêle,* in OF *pesle mesle,* apparently from *mesler* mix]

**pellucid** /pəˈlusəd/, *adj.* **1.** allowing the passage of light; translucent. **2.** clear or limpid, as water. **3.** clear in meaning. [L *pellūcidus* transparent] – **pellucidity** /pɛləˈsɪdəti/, **pellucidness,** *n.* – **pellucidly,** *adv.*

**pelmet** /ˈpɛlmət/, *n.* a short ornamental drapery or board, placed across the top of a window in order to hide the curtain rail.

**peloria** /pəˈlɔriə/, *n.* regularity of structure occurring abnormally in flowers normally irregular. [NL, from Gk *pélōr* monster + *-ia* -IA] – **peloric** /pɛˈlɔrɪk, -ˈlɒ-/, *adj.*

**pelorus** /pəˈlɔrəs/, *n.* a plate graduated in degrees for determining the horizontal angle between the ship's heading and the bearing of an observed object. [perhaps from L *Petorus,* a dangerous promontory on the NE tip of Sicily]

**pelota** /pəˈlɒtə/, *n.* a Basque and Spanish game played in a court with a ball and a curved wicker racquet. [Sp., augmentative of *pella,* from L *pila* ball. Cf. PELLET]

**pelt¹** /pɛlt/, *v.t.* **1.** to assail with repeated blows or with missiles; to beat or rush against. **2.** to throw (missiles). **3.** to drive, put, etc., by blows or missiles. **4.** to assail with abuse. *–v.i.* **5.** to strike blows; beat with force or violence. **6.** (of rain) to fall very heavily. **7.** to throw missiles. **8.** to cast abuse. **9.** to hurry. *–n.* **10.** the act of pelting. **11.** a vigorous stroke. **12.** a blow with something thrown. **13. full pelt,** the utmost energy or speed. [orig. uncert.; ? akin to PELLET] – **pelter,** *n.*

**pelt²** /pɛlt/, *n.* the skin of an animal with or without the hair. [ME, apparently a backformation from PELTRY]

**peltate** /ˈpɛlteɪt/, *adj.* (of a leaf, etc.) having the stalk or support attached to the lower surface at a distance from the margin; shield-shaped. [L *peltātus* armed with a light shield] – **peltately,** *adv.*

peltate leaf

**pelter** /ˈpɛltə/, *n.* a rage: *to get into a pelter.*

**Peltier effect** /ˈpɛltieɪ əˌfɛkt/, *n.* the heat evolved or absorbed when an electric current flows across the junction between two different metals or semiconductors. [named after C. A. *Peltier,* 1785-1845, French physicist]

**pelting** /ˈpɛltɪŋ/, *adj. Archaic.* paltry; petty; mean. [cf. obs. *peltry,* var. of PALTRY]

**peltry** /ˈpɛltri/, *n., pl.* **-ries. 1.** fur skins; pelts collectively. **2.** a pelt. [ME *peltre,* from OF *peleterie,* from *pel* skin, from L *pellis*]

**pelvic** /ˈpɛlvɪk/, *adj.* of or pertaining to the pelvis.

**pelvic arch** /– ˈatʃ/, *n.* **1.** (in vertebrates) a bony or cartilaginous arch supporting the hind limbs or analogous parts. **2.** (in man) the arch, formed by the innominate bones, which attaches the lower extremity to the axial skeleton. Also, **pelvic girdle.**

**pelvic fin** /– ˈfɪn/, *n.* one of the more posterior paired fins of a fish, on the lower surface of its body.

**pelvimetry** /pɛlˈvɪmətri/, *n.* measurement of the dimensions of the pelvis.

**pelvis** /ˈpɛlvəs/, *n., pl.* **-ves** /-viz/. **1.** the basin-like cavity in the lower part of the trunk of many vertebrates, formed in man by the innominate bones, sacrum, etc. **2.** the bones forming this cavity. **3.** the cavity of the kidney which receives the urine before it is passed into the ureter. [L: basin]



human pelvis (front view): A, upper base of sacrum; B, crest of ilium; C, acetabulum; D, ischium; E, pubis; F, pubic symphysis

**Pembroke** /ˈpɛmbrʊk/, *n.* the variety of the Welsh corgi breed of dogs. See **corgi.** [named after *Pembroke,* a town in Wales]

**pemmican** /ˈpɛmɪkən/, *n.* dried meat pounded into a paste with melted fat and dried fruits, pressed into cakes, originally prepared by North American Indians. Also, **pemican.** [N Amer. Ind. (Cree) *pimikan* manufactured grease, from *pimikew* he makes grease (by boiling fat)]

**pemphigus** /ˈpɛmfəgəs, pɛmˈfaɪ-/, *n.* a serious disease, commonly fatal, characterised by vesicles and bullae on the skin and mucous membranes. [NL, from Gk *pemphís* bubble + *-us* (n. ending)]

**pen¹** /pɛn/, *n., v.,* **penned, penning.** *–n.* **1.** any instrument for writing with ink. **2.** a small instrument of steel or other metal, with a split point, used, when fitted into a penholder, for writing with ink; nib. **3.** the pen and penholder together. **4.** a quill pointed and split at the nib, used for writing with ink. **5.** the pen as the instrument of writing or authorship: *the pen is mightier than the sword.* **6.** style or quality of writing. **7.** a writer or author. **8.** the profession of writing or literature: *men of the pen.* **9.** *Ornith.* **a.** a large feather of the wing or tail; a quill feather; a quill. **b.** a pin-feather of a bird. **10.** something resembling or suggesting a feather or quill. **11.** *Zool.* an internal, corneous or chitinous, feather-shaped structure in certain cephalopods, as the squid. *–v.t.* **12.** to write with a pen; set down in writing. [ME *penne,* from OF, from LL *penna* pen, from L: feather]

**pen²** /pɛn/, *n., v.,* **penned** or **pent, penning.** *–n.* **1.** an enclosure for domestic animals or livestock. **2.** animals so enclosed. **3.** any place of confinement or safekeeping. *–v.t.* **4.** to confine in or as in a pen. [ME *penne,* OE *penn;* orig. uncert.]

**pen³** /pɛn/, *n. Colloq.* prison. [short for PENITENTIARY (def. 3)]

**pen⁴** /pɛn/, *n.* a female mute swan.

**Pen.,** peninsula.

**penal** /ˈpinəl/, *adj.* **1.** of or pertaining to punishment, as for offences or crimes. **2.** prescribing punishment: *penal laws.* **3.** constituting punishment: *penal servitude.* **4.** used as a place of punishment: *a penal settlement.* **5.** subject to or incurring punishment: *a penal offence.* **6.** payable or forfeitable as penalty: *a penal sum.* [ME, from L *poenālis* pertaining to punishment]

**penal code** /ˈ– koud/, *n.* the aggregate of statutory enactments dealing with crimes and their punishment.

**penal colony** /ˈ– kɒləni/, *n.* (formerly) a colony founded to receive convicts and established in part through convict labour.

**penalise** /ˈpinəlaɪz/, *v.t.,* **-lised, -lising. 1.** to subject to a penalty, as a person. **2.** to declare penal, or punishable by law, as an action. **3.** to lay under a disadvantage. Also, **penalize.** – **penalisation** /pinəlaɪˈzeɪʃən/, *n.*

**penal settlement** /ˈ– sɛtlmənt/, *n.* a place of punishment for convicts, usu. in an isolated area remote from free settlements, as Port Arthur in Tasmania.

**penalty** /ˈpɛnəlti/, *n., pl.* **-ties.** **1.** a punishment imposed or incurred for a violation of law or rule. **2.** a loss or forfeiture to which one subjects himself by non-fulfilment of an obligation. **3.** that which is forfeited, as a sum of money. **4.** consequence or disadvantage attached to any action, condition, etc. **5.** *Sport.* **a.** a disadvantage imposed upon a competitor or side for infraction of the rules. **b.** →**penalty kick.** **6.** *Horseracing.* an additional handicap placed on a horse (for winning a race) after the original handicap weights have been issued. [PENAL + -TY[2]]

**penalty area** /ˈ– ɛəriə/, *n.* (in soccer) a space in front of each goal, within which any of various infringements by the defending team results in a penalty kick being awarded to the opposing team.

**penalty box** /ˈ– bɒks/, *n.* **1.** a box adjoining an ice-hockey rink with seating for timekeepers, scorers, and penalised players. **2.** (in other team sports) a similar area set aside for penalised players.

**penalty goal** /ˈ– goʊl/, *n.* (in soccer) a goal scored from a penalty kick.

**penalty kick** /ˈ– kɪk/, *n.* **1.** *Soccer.* a free kick taken at a prescribed distance from an opponent's goal, which is defended only by the goalkeeper. **2.** *Rugby Football.* a kick allowed to a team because of an infringement by the opposing team.

**penalty rate** /ˈ– reɪt/, *n.* a rate of pay determined by an award, higher than the usual rate, in compensation for working outside the normal spread of hours.

**penalty seconds** /ˈ– sɛkəndz/, *n.pl.* (in showjumping) a penalty in the form of seconds added to the course time, incurred for various mistakes while completing the course.

**penalty spot** /ˈ– spɒt/, *n.* (in soccer) a mark 11 metres in front of the goal on which the ball is placed for a penalty kick.

**penalty try** /ˈ– traɪ/, *n.* (in rugby football) a try which is awarded by the referee when he judges that a try would have been scored by the attacking player but for illegal interference.

**penance** /ˈpɛnəns/, *n.* **1.** punishment undergone in token of penitence for sin. **2.** a penitential discipline imposed by church authority. **3.** *Rom. Cath. Ch.* a sacrament ministered in consideration of a confession of sin with contrition and the purpose of amendment, followed by the forgiveness of sin. [ME *penaunce,* from OF *peneance,* from L *poenitentia.* See PENITENCE]

**penates** /pəˈnatiz/, *n.pl.* tutelary deities of the ancient Roman household and of the state, worshipped in close association with the lares. Also, **Penates.** [L, from *penus* innermost part of a temple. Cf. PENETRATE]

**pence** /pɛns/, *n.* plural of **penny,** used esp. when value is indicated: *he gave me twenty-one pence change out of a pound, all in pennies.*

**penchant** /ˈpɛnʃənt/, *n.* a strong inclination; a taste or liking for something. [F, orig. ppr. of *pencher* incline, lean, from L *pendēre* hang]

**pencil** /ˈpɛnsəl/, *n., v.,* **-cilled, -cilling** or (*U.S.*) **-ciled, -ciling.** *–n.* **1.** a thin tube of wood, etc., with a core of graphite, chalk, the like, for drawing or writing. **2.** style or skill in painting or delineation. **3.** a slender, pointed piece of some marking substance. **4.** a stick of cosmetic colouring material for use on the eyebrows, etc. **5.** a similarly shaped piece of some other substance, as lunar caustic. **6.** *Optics.* a set of lines, light rays, or the like, diverging from or converging to a point. **7.** *Archaic.* an artist's paintbrush, esp. for fine work. *–v.t.* **8.** to use a pencil on. **9.** to execute, draw, or write with or as with a pencil. **10.** to mark or colour with or as with a pencil. [ME *pencel,* from OF *pincel,* from VL var. of L *pēnicillum,* diminutive of *pēniculus* brush] – **penciller,** *n.*

**penciller** /ˈpɛnsələ/, *n. Horseracing Colloq.* a bookmaker's clerk, who fills in racing ledgers and betting sheets.

**pencil orchid** /ˈpɛnsəl ɔkəd/, *n.* either of two species of epiphytic orchid, *Dendrobium beckleri* and *D. teretifolium,* found on trees and rocks in forests in New South Wales and Queensland.

**pencil-sharpener** /ˈpɛnsəl-ʃapnə/, *n.* any device, usu. containing a blade, used for sharpening the point of a pencil, crayon, etc.

**pend** /pɛnd/, *v.i.* **1.** to remain undecided. **2.** to hang. **3.** *Obs.* to depend. [late ME, from L *pendēre* hang, depend]

**penda** /ˈpɛndə/, *n.* any of various rainforest trees of the genera *Xanthostemon* and *Tristania,* found mainly in northern Australia, valued for their timber.

**pendant** /ˈpɛndənt/, *n.* Also, **pendent.** **1.** a hanging ornament, as of a necklace or earring. **2.** a chandelier. **3.** a knob or other ornament suspended from the roof, vault, or ceiling. **4.** a match or parallel. **5.** *Naut.* a length of rope or wire fitted to a spar to connect it to a block of a tackle. **6.** →**pennant** (def. 1). *–adj.* **7.** →**pendent.** [ME *pendaunte,* from OF *pendant,* ppr. of *pendre* hang, from L *pendēre*]

**pendant post** /ˈ– poʊst/, *n.* a wooden member used in medieval roof framing, placed against a wall, supported by a corbel and with a hammerbeam or tie beam fixed to the top.

**pendent** /ˈpɛndənt/, *adj.* Also, **pendant.** **1.** hanging or suspended. **2.** overhanging; jutting or leaning over. **3.** impending. **4.** pending or undecided. *–n.* **5.** →**pendant.** [L *pendens,* ppr., hanging; replacing ME *penda(u)nt,* from OF *pendant,* from L] – **pendency,** *n.* – **pendently,** *adv.*

**pendentive** /pɛnˈdɛntɪv/, *n. Archit.* **1.** a triangular segment of the lower part of a hemispherical dome, between two penetrating arches. **2.** a similar segment of a groined vault, resting on a single pier or corbel. [PENDENT + -IVE, translating F *pendentif*]

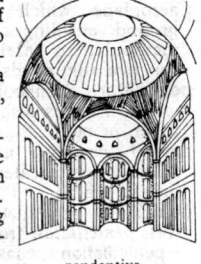

pendentive

**pending** /ˈpɛndɪŋ/, *prep.* **1.** while awaiting; until: *pending his return.* **2.** in the period before the decision or conclusion of; during: *pending the negotiations.* *–adj.* **3.** remaining undecided; awaiting decision. **4.** hanging; impending. [PEND(ENT) + -ING[2]]

**pendragon** /pɛnˈdrægən/, *n.* chief leader (a title of ancient British chiefs). [Welsh *pen* head + *dragon* dragon (used as symbol), leader] – **pendragonship,** *n.*

**pendulous** /ˈpɛndʒələs/, *adj.* **1.** hanging. **2.** swinging freely. **3.** vacillating. [L *pendulus* hanging, swinging] – **pendulously,** *adv.* – **pendulousness,** *n.*

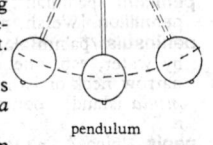

**pendulum** /ˈpɛndʒələm/, *n.* **1.** a body so suspended from a fixed point as to move to and fro by the action of gravity and acquired kinetic energy. **2.** a swinging device used for controlling the movement of clockwork. [NL, properly neut. of L *pendulus* hanging, swinging]

pendulum

**pene-,** a prefix meaning almost, as *peneplain, peninsula.* Also, *before a vowel,* **pen-.** [L *paene*]

**peneplain** /ˈpinəpleɪn, pinəˈpleɪn/, *n.* an area reduced almost to a plain by erosion. Also, **peneplane.** [L *pēne* almost + PLAIN[1]]

**penetrable** /ˈpɛnətrəbəl/, *adj.* capable of being penetrated. [ME, from L *penetrābilis*] – **penetrability** /pɛnətrəˈbɪləti/, *n.* – **penetrably,** *adv.*

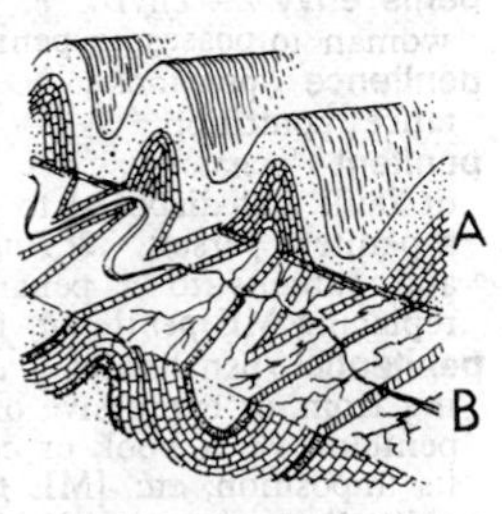


peneplain (cross-section): A, original land structures; B, peneplain

**penetralia** /pɛnəˈtreɪliə/, *n.pl.* the innermost parts or recesses of a place or thing. [L, properly neut. pl. of *penetrālis* inner, orig. penetrating]

**penetrate** /ˈpɛnətreɪt/, *v.,* **-trated, -trating.** *–v.t.* **1.** to pierce into or through. **2.** to enter the interior of. **3.** to enter and diffuse itself through; permeate. **4.** to affect or impress deeply. **5.** to arrive at the meaning of; understand. *–v.i.* **6.** to enter, reach, or pass through, as by piercing. [L *penetrātus,* pp.]

**penetrating** /ˈpɛnətreɪtɪŋ/, *adj.* **1.** that penetrates; piercing;

sharp. **2.** acute; discerning. **3.** *Surg.* denoting a wound produced by an agent or missile such that depth is its salient feature, as a wound entering a member. Also, **penetrant** /ˈpɛnətrənt/. – **penetratingly,** *adv.*

**penetration** /pɛnəˈtreɪʃən/, *n.* **1.** the act or power of penetrating. **2.** the extension, usu. peaceful, of the influence of one country on the life of another. **3.** mental acuteness, discernment, or insight. **4.** *Firearms.* the depth to which a projectile goes into the target.

**penetrative** /ˈpɛnətrətɪv/, *adj.* tending to penetrate; piercing; acute; keen. – **penetratively,** *adv.* – **penetrativeness,** *n.*

**penetrometer** /pɛnəˈtrɒmətə/, *n.* **1.** a device for measuring the hardness of a material by measuring the extent to which it is penetrated by a given force. **2.** an instrument for measuring the penetrating power of X-rays or other radiations; radiosclerometer.

**penfriend** /ˈpɛnfrɛnd/, *n.* a person, esp. one in another country, with whom a friendship is maintained through correspondence.

**penguin** /ˈpɛŋgwən, ˈpɛngwən/, *n.* **1.** any of various flightless aquatic birds of the family Spheniscidae of the Southern Hemisphere, with webbed feet, and wings reduced to flippers, as the little penguin and the Adelie penguin. **2.** *Obs.* →**great auk. 3.** *Aeron.* an aeroplane which merely rolls along the ground, enabling a beginner to learn certain manipulations safely. [cf. F *pingouin,* earlier *penguyn* auk; of disputed orig.]

emperor penguin

**penholder** /ˈpɛnhoʊldə/, *n.* **1.** a holder in which a nib is placed. **2.** a rack or stand for a pen or pens.

**penicil** /ˈpɛnəsəl/, *n.* a small brushlike tuft of hairs, as on a caterpillar. [L *pēnicillus* paintbrush, pencil]

**penicillate** /pɛnəˈsɪlət, -eɪt/, *adj.* having a penicil or penicils. [NL *pēnicillātus,* from L *pēnicillus* pencil] – **penicillately,** *adv.* – **penicillation** /pɛnəsəˈleɪʃən/, *n.*

**penicillin** /pɛnəˈsɪlən/, *n.* **1.** a powerful anti-bacterial substance produced by moulds of the genus *Penicillium.* **2.** any of a group of anti-bacterial substances made synthetically from penicillin. [PENICILL(IUM) + -IN[2]]

**penicillium** /pɛnəˈsɪliəm/, *n., pl.* **-cilliums, -cillia** /-ˈsɪliə/. any member of the fungus genus *Penicillium,* known usu. as the green moulds, embracing species used in cheese-making and species (esp. *P. notatum*) from which penicillin is extracted. [L *pēnicillus* small brush, lit., small tail + -IUM]

**penile** /ˈpinaɪl/, *adj.* of or pertaining to the penis.

**penillion** /pəˈnɪliən/, *n.* an improvisatory Welsh song. Also, **pennillion.** [Welsh, pl. of *pennill* verse]

**peninsula** /pəˈnɪnʃələ/, *n.* a piece of land almost surrounded by water, esp. one connected with the mainland by only a narrow neck or isthmus. [L *paeninsula,* from *paene* almost + *insula* island] – **peninsular,** *adj.* – **peninsularity** /pənɪnʃəˈlærəti/, *n.*

**penis** /ˈpinəs/, *n., pl.* **-nes** /-niz/, **-nises** /-nəsəz/. the male organ of copulation and urination. [L: orig., tail]

**penis envy** /ˈ– ɛnvi/, *n. Psychol.* the repressed wish of a woman to possess a penis.

**penitence** /ˈpɛnətəns/, *n.* the state of being penitent; repentance; contrition.

**penitent** /ˈpɛnətənt/, *adj.* **1.** repentant; contrite; sorry for sin or fault and disposed to atonement and amendment. *–n.* **2.** a penitent person. **3.** *Rom. Cath. Ch.* one who confesses sin and submits to a penance. [L *paenitens,* ppr., repenting; replacing ME *penitaunt,* from AF] – **penitently,** *adv.*

**penitential** /pɛnəˈtɛnʃəl/, *adj.* **1.** of or pertaining to, proceeding from, or expressive of penitence or repentance. *–n.* **2.** a penitent. **3.** a book or code of canons relating to penance, its imposition, etc. [ML *poenitentiālis*] – **penitentially,** *adv.*

**penitentiary** /pɛnəˈtɛnʃəri/, *n., pl.* **-ries,** *adj. –n.* **1.** *Rom. Cath. Ch.* **a.** an officer appointed to deal with cases of conscience reserved for a bishop or for the Holy See. **b.** an office of the Holy See (presided over by the **cardinal grand penitentiary**) having jurisdiction over such cases. **2.** a place for imprisonment and reformatory discipline. **3.** *U.S.* a prison. *–adj.* **4.** of or pertaining to penance; penitential. **5.** (of an offence) punishable by imprisonment in a penitentiary. **6** pertaining to or intended for penal confinement and discipline. [ME, from ML *poenitentiārius,* from L *paenitentia* penitence]

**penknife** /ˈpɛnnaɪf/, *n., pl.* **-knives** /-naɪvz/. a small pocket-knife, originally for making and mending quill pens.

**penman** /ˈpɛnmən/, *n., pl.* **-men. 1.** one who uses a pen. **2.** an expert in penmanship. **3.** a writer or author.

**penmanship** /ˈpɛnmənʃɪp/, *n.* **1.** the use of the pen in writing; the art of handwriting; a manner of writing. **2.** literary composition; the composing of a document.

**penna** /ˈpɛnə/, *n., pl.* **pennae** /ˈpɛni/. a contour feather, of a bird, as distinguished from a down feather, plume, etc. [L: feather]

**pen-name** /ˈpɛn-neɪm/, *n.* a name assumed to write under; an author's pseudonym; nom de plume.

**pennant** /ˈpɛnənt/, *n.* **1.** Also, **pendant, pennon.** a long triangular flag, widest next to the mast, and going almost to a point, borne on naval or other vessels or used in signalling, etc. **2.** any flag serving as an emblem, as of success in an athletic contest. **3.** *U.S. Music.* →**hook** (def. 11). [var. of PENDANT; associated also with PENNON]

**pennate** /ˈpɛneɪt/, *adj.* winged; feathered. [L *pennātus* winged]

**penner** /ˈpɛnə/, *n. N.Z.* →**sheepo.** Also, **penner-up.**

**penniless** /ˈpɛnələs/, *adj.* without a penny; destitute of money.

**pennillion** /pəˈnɪliən/, *n.* →**penillion.**

**penniveined** /ˈpɛniveɪnd/, *adj.* pinnately veined, as a leaf.

**pennon** /ˈpɛnən/, *n.* **1.** a distinctive flag in various forms (tapering, triangular, swallow-tailed, etc.), originally one borne on the lance of a knight. **2.**→**pennant** (def. 1). **3.** any flag or banner. **4.** *Poetic.* a wing or pinion. [ME *penon,* from OF, from *penne,* from L *penna* feather]

**penny** /ˈpɛni/, *n., pl.* **pennies,** (*esp. collectively*) **pence. 1.** (formerly) a bronze or copper coin equal to one twelfth of a shilling or $\frac{1}{240}$ of a pound. *Abbrev.:* d. **2.** (formerly) a similar coin of Britain. **3.** a similar coin of certain other countries. **4.** a bronze coin of the United Kingdom equal to a 100th part of a pound; new penny. *Abbrev.:* p **5.** a bronze coin of Canada, the 100th part of a dollar. **6.** a bronze coin of the U.S. the 100th part of a dollar; a cent. **7.** an unspecified sum of money: *I haven't got a penny.* **8. a bad penny,** a bad, or undesirable person or thing. **9. the penny drops,** (the explanation or remark is understood). **10. a pretty penny,** a considerable amount of money. **11. spend a penny,** go to the toilet. **12. turn an honest penny,** earn an honest living; earn money honestly. *–adj.* **13.** of the price or value of a penny. [ME *peni,* OE *penig, pening, pending,* c. Icel. *penningr,* G *Pfennig*]

**-penny,** (formerly) a suffix forming adjectives that denote price or value, as in *fourpenny, fivepenny,* etc.

**penny-a-liner** /pɛni-ə-ˈlaɪnə/, *n. Obs.* a hack writer.

**penny-ante** /pɛni-ˈænti/, *adj.* mean-minded; petty; niggardly. [PENNY + ANTE]

**penny arcade** /pɛni aˈkeɪd/, *n.* a place of amusement providing coin-operated games of chance, etc., originally at a penny per play.

**penny-cress** /ˈpɛni-krɛs/, *n.* any plant of the genus *Thlaspi* as the **field penny-cress,** *T. arvense,* a widespread annual weed of cultivated land in temperate regions.

**penny dreadful** /pɛni ˈdrɛdfəl/, *n.* a piece of cheap popular sensational literature.

**penny-farthing** /pɛni-ˈfaðɪŋ/, *n.* a high bicycle of an early type with one large wheel in front and one small wheel behind.

**penny pincher** /ˈpɛni pɪntʃə/, *n.* a mean, niggardly person. – **penny-pinching,** *adj.*

**pennyroyal** /pɛniˈrɔɪəl/, *n.* any of several herbaceous plants, as the Old World pennyroyal, *Mentha pulegium,* or the American **mock pennyroyal,** *Hedeoma pulegioides,* used medicinally and yielding a pungent aromatic oil. [*penny* (? alteration of OF *puliol,* from L *pūlegium* pennyroyal) + ROYAL]

**pennyweight** /ˈpɛniweɪt/, *n.* a unit of mass in the imperial system, equal to $\frac{1}{20}$ of an ounce, or $1.555\ 173\ 84 \times 10^{-3}$ kg. *Symbol:* dwt

**penny whistle** /ˈpɛni wɪsəl/, *n.* a simple and cheap wind instrument, usu. consisting of a tin or plastic pipe.

**penny-wise** /'pɛni-waɪz/, *adj.* wise or saving in regard to small sums: *penny-wise and pound-foolish.*

**pennywort** /'pɛniwɜt/, *n.* any of several plants with round or roundish leaves as species of the genus *Hydrocotyle,* esp. duckweed (def. 2).

**pennyworth** /'pɛnəθ, 'pɛniwɜθ/, *n.* a small quantity. [orig. as much as could be bought for a penny]

**penology** /pi'nɒlədʒi/, *n.* **1.** the science of the punishment of crime, in both its deterrent and its reformatory aspects. **2.** the science of the management of prisons. [PEN(AL) + -O- + -LOGY] – **penological** /pinə'lɒdʒɪkəl/, *adj.* – **penologist,** *n.*

**pen-pusher** /'pɛn-pʊʃə/, *n. Colloq.* one who works with his pen, esp. a clerk, considered as a menial or drudge.

**pensile** /'pɛnsaɪl/, *adj.* **1.** hanging, as the nests of certain birds. **2.** building a hanging nest. [L (neut.): hanging down] – **pensileness, pensility** /pɛn'sɪləti/, *n.*

**pension** /'pɛnʃən/, *n.* **1.** a fixed periodical payment made in consideration of past services, injury or loss sustained, merit, poverty, etc. **2.** an allowance or annuity. **3.** (in Europe) **a.** a boarding house, small hotel, or school. **b.** room and board. *–v.t.* **4.** to grant a pension to. **5.** to cause to retire on a pension (fol. by *off*). [L *pensio* payment; replacing ME *pensioun,* from OF *pensiun*] – **pensionable,** *adj.*

**pensionary** /'pɛnʃənəri/, *n., pl.* **-ries,** *adj. –n.* **1.** a pensioner. **2.** →**hireling.** *–adj.* **3.** of the nature of a pension. **4.** receiving a pension.

**pensioner** /'pɛnʃənə/, *n.* **1.** one who receives a pension, esp. old age pensioner. **2.** →**hireling.**

**pensive** /'pɛnsɪv/, *adj.* **1.** deeply, seriously, or sadly thoughtful. **2.** expressing thoughtfulness or sadness. [F (fem.), from *penser* think; replacing ME *pensif,* from F (masc.)] – **pensively,** *adv.* – **pensiveness,** *n.*

**penstock** /'pɛnstɒk/, *n.* **1.** a pipe conducting water from the head gates to a waterwheel. **2.** a conduit for conveying water to a power plant. **3.** a sluicelike contrivance used to control the flow of water.

**pent** /pɛnt/, *v.* **1.** a past tense and past participle of **pen**[2]. *–adj.* **2.** shut in. **3.** confined.

**pent-,** a word element meaning 'five'. Also, before consonants, **penta-.** [Gk, combining forms of *pénte*]

**pentaborane** /pɛntə'bɔreɪn/, *n.* a liquid, $B_5H_9$, used as a rocket propellant.

**pentacle** /'pɛntəkəl/, *n.* **1.** →**pentagram.** **2.** some more or less similar figure, as a hexagram. [probably from F, or from ML *pentaculum.* See PENT(A)-, -CLE]

**pentad** /'pɛntæd/, *n.* **1.** a period of five years. **2.** *Chem.* a pentavalent element or radical. **3.** a group of five. **4.** the number five. [Gk *pentás* a group of five]

**pentadactyl** /pɛntə'dæktl/, *adj.* having five digits on each hand or foot.

**pentagon** /'pɛntəgɒn, -gən/, *n.* a polygon having five angles and five sides. [L *pentagōnum,* from Gk *pentágōnon,* properly neut. adj. used as noun] – **pentagonal** /pɛn'tægənəl/, *adj.* – **pentagonally** /pɛn'tægənəli/, *adv.*

pentagon

**pentagram** /'pɛntəgræm/, *n.* **1.** a five-pointed, star-shaped figure made by extending the sides of a regular pentagon until they meet (a symbolical figure used by the Pythagoreans and later philosophers). **2.** a magical or talismanic symbol. **3.** a suit in the Tarot card game, in later card games stylised to diamonds. Also, **pentacle, pentalpha, pentangle.** [Gk *pentágrammon* (properly neut. of adj.) figure consisting of five lines]

**pentagrid** /'pɛntəgrɪd/, *n. Electronics.* →**heptode.**

**pentahedron** /pɛntə'hidrən/, *n., pl.* **-drons, -dra** /-drə/. a solid figure having five faces. – **pentahedral,** *adj.*

**pentalpha** /pɛnt'ælfə/, *n.* →**pentagram.**

**pentamerous** /pɛn'tæmərəs/, *adj.* consisting of or divided into five parts. [NL *pentamerus,* from Gk *pentamerḗs*]

**pentameter** /pɛn'tæmətə/, *n.* **1.** a verse of five feet. **2.** *Anc. Pros.* a verse consisting of two dactyls, one long syllable, two more dactyls, and another single syllable (**elegiac pentameter**). **3.** unrhymed iambic pentameter; heroic verse. *–adj.* **4.** consisting of five metrical feet. [L, from Gk *pentámetros*]

**pentandrous** /pɛn'tændrəs/, *adj.* **1.** (of a flower) having five stamens. **2.** (of a plant) having flowers with five stamens.

**pentane** /'pɛnteɪn/, *n.* a hydrocarbon, $C_5H_{12}$, of the methane series, existing in three isomeric forms. [Gk *pént(e)* five + -ANE]

**pentangle** /'pɛntæŋgəl/, *n.* →**pentagram.**

**pentarchy** /'pɛntaki/, *n., pl.* **-chies.** **1.** a government by five persons. **2.** a governing body of five persons. **3.** a group of five states or kingdoms, each under its own ruler. [Gk *pentarchía*]

**pentastich** /'pɛntəstɪk/, *n.* a strophe, stanza, or poem consisting of five lines or verses. [NL *pentastichus,* from Gk *pentástichos* of five lines]

pentagram

**Pentateuch** /'pɛntətjuk/, *n.* the first five books of the Old Testament, considered as a group. [L *Pentateuchus,* from Gk *pentáteuchos* consisting of five books] – **Pentateuchal** /pɛntə'tjukəl/, *adj.*

**pentathlon** /pɛn'tæθlən/, *n.* an athletic contest comprising five different exercises or events, and won by the contestant having the highest total score. [Gk]

**pentatomic** /pɛntə'tɒmɪk/, *adj. Chem.* **1.** having five atoms in the molecule. **2.** having five replaceable atoms or groups.

**pentatonic scale** /pɛntəˌtɒnɪk 'skeɪl/, *n.* **1.** a class of scales, found in most music traditions, for which the octave is divided into five tones according to numerous patterns of intervals. **2.** (in the Western chromatic system) a class of scales formed with patterns of minor seconds, major seconds, minor thirds and major thirds; the most popular is the scale corresponding to the black keys of the piano which is made up of major seconds and minor thirds only.

**pentavalent** /pɛntə'veɪlənt, pɛn'tævələnt/, *adj.* possessing a valency of 5: *pentavalent arsenic.*

**Pentecost** /'pɛntəkɒst/, *n.* **1.** a Christian festival commemorating the descent of the Holy Ghost upon the apostles on the day of the Jewish festival; Whit Sunday. **2.** a Jewish harvest festival observed on the fiftieth day from the second day of Passover. [ME *pentecoste,* OE *pentecosten,* from LL *pentecoste,* from Gk *pentekostḗ* fiftieth (day)]

**Pentecostal** /pɛntə'kɒstl/, *adj.* **1.** of or pertaining to Pentecost or the influence of the Holy Ghost. **2.** of or pertaining to any of various modern Christian organisations that lay emphasis on charismatic experience, the absolute truth of the Bible, and the possibility of direct contact with the Holy Spirit. *–n.* **3.** one who belongs to such a group.

**pentene** /'pɛntin/, *n. Chem* →**amylene.**

**penthouse** /'pɛnthaʊs/, *n., pl.* **-houses** /-haʊzəz/. **1.** a separate flat or maisonette on a roof. **2.** a structure on a roof for housing lift machinery, etc. **3.** a shed with a sloping roof, or a sloping roof, projecting from a wall or the side of a building, as to shelter a door. **4.** any roof-like shelter or overhanging part. [ME *pentis,* apparently from OF *apentis,* from L *appendere* hang to or on, append]

**pentile** /'pɛntaɪl/, *n.* **1.** *Statistics.* one of the value of a variable which divides its distribution into five groups having equal frequencies. *–adj.* **2.** of or pertaining to a pentile or a division of a distribution by pentiles. [PENT- + -ILE]

**pentimento** /pɛntə'mɛntoʊ/, *n., pl.* **-ti** /-ti/. *Art.* **1.** the reappearance, or visibility under X-ray, of forms that have been painted over in the alteration of a painting. **2.** any of such re-emergent forms. [It.: repentance]

**pentlandite** /'pɛntləndaɪt/, *n.* a mineral, a sulphide of iron and nickel, commonly associated with pyrrhotite; an important ore of nickel.

**pentobarbitone** /pɛntə'babətoʊn/, *n.* →**nembutal.**

**pentode** /'pɛntoʊd/, *n.* a radio valve containing five electrodes.

**pentosan** /'pɛntəsæn/, *n.* any of a class of polysaccharides which occur in plants, humus, etc., and form pentoses upon hydrolysis.

**pentose** /'pɛntoʊz, -oʊs/, *n.* a monosaccharide containing five atoms of carbon, and produced from pentosans by hydrolysis. [PENT- + -OSE[2]]

**pentose phosphate pathway,** *n.* an alternative series of reactions to glycolysis for oxidising glucose, important for the synthesis of pentoses, functioning in the mammary gland.

**pentothal sodium** /ˌpɛntəθæl ˈsoudiəm/, *n.* →**sodium pentothal.** [Trademark]

**pentstemon** /ˈpɛnstəmən/, *n.* any plant of the genus, *Pentstemon,* chiefly of North America, including species cultivated for their variously coloured flowers with long-tubed corolla. [NL, from Gk *pént(e)* five + *stḗmon* warp, thread]

**pent-up** /ˈpɛnt-ʌp/, *adj.* confined; restrained: *pent-up rage.*

**penuchle** /ˈpinʌkəl/, *n.* →**pinochle.** Also, **penuckle.**

**penult** /pəˈnʌlt/, *n.* the last syllable but one in a word. Also, **penultima** /pəˈnʌltəmə/. [L *paenultima* (fem.) last but one]

**penultimate** /pəˈnʌltəmət/, *adj.* **1.** next to the last. **2.** of the penult. *–n.* **3.** →**penult.**

**penumbra** /pəˈnʌmbrə/, *n., pl.* **-brae** /-bri/, **-bras. 1.** the partial or imperfect shadow outside the complete shadow (umbra) of an opaque body, as a planet, where the light from the source of illumination is only partly cut off. **2.** the greyish marginal portion of a sunspot. [NL, from L *paene* almost + *umbra* shade, shadow] – **penumbral,** *adj.*

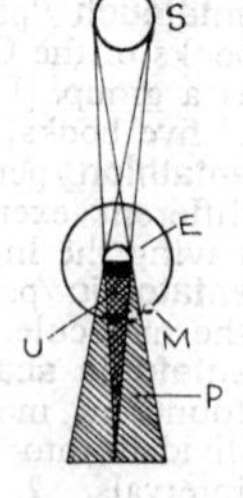

P, penumbra; U, umbra; S, sun; E, earth; M, moon

**penurious** /pəˈnjuriəs/, *adj.* **1.** meanly parsimonious; stingy. **2.** extremely poor; destitute. – **penuriously,** *adv.* – **penuriousness,** *n.*

**penury** /ˈpɛnjəri/, *n.* **1.** extreme poverty; destitution. **2.** dearth or insufficiency. [ME, from L *pēnūria* want, scarcity. Cf. Gk *penía* poverty, need]

**penwiper plant** /ˈpɛnwaɪpə plænt/, *n.* a small, fleshy, cruciferous herb, *Notothlaspi rosulatum,* endemic in New Zealand, found on screes at high altitudes.

**peon**[1] /ˈpiən/, *n.* (in Spanish America etc.) **1.** a day labourer. **2.** one who tends a horse or mule. **3.** one held in servitude to work off debts, etc., in Latin America or southern U.S. [Sp. *peón,* from L *pedo* foot soldier. See PAWN[2]]

**peon**[2] /pjun, ˈpiən/, *n. India.* **1.** a foot soldier. **2.** a messenger or attendant. **3.** a native soldier. [Pg. *peão,* and F *pion* foot soldier, pedestrian, day labourer. See PEON[1]]

**peonage** /ˈpiənɪdʒ/, *n.* **1.** the condition or service of a peon. **2.** the practice of holding persons in servitude or partial slavery, as to work off debt or (under a convict lease system) a penal sentence. Also, **peonism.**

**peony** /ˈpiəni/, *n., pl.* **-nies. 1.** any plant of the genus *Paeonia,* which comprises perennial herbs and a few shrubs with large showy flowers, familiar in gardens. **2.** the flower. [L *paeōnia,* from Gk *paiōnía,* from *Paiṓn* the physician of the gods (because the plant was used in medicine); replacing ME *pione,* from ONF, from L, from Gk; replacing OE *peonie,* from L, from Gk]

**people** /ˈpipəl/, *n., pl.* **-ple, -ples** *for def. 1, v.,* **-pled, -pling.** *–n.* **1.** the whole body of persons constituting a community, tribe, race, or nation. **2.** the persons of any particular group, company, or number: *the people of a parish.* **3.** persons in relation to a ruler, leader, etc.: *the king and his people.* **4.** one's family or relatives: *to visit one's people.* **5.** the members of any group or number to which one belongs. **6.** the body of enfranchised citizens of a state: *representatives chosen by the people.* **7.** the commonalty or populace: *a man of the people.* **8.** persons indefinitely, whether men or women: *people may say what they please.* **9.** human beings as distinguished from animals. **10.** *Chiefly Poetic.* living creatures. *–v.t.* **11.** to furnish with people; populate. **12.** to stock with animals, inanimate objects, etc. [ME *peple,* from AF *poeple,* from L *populus* people] – **peopler,** *n.*

**pep** /pɛp/, *n., v.,* **pepped, pepping.** *Colloq. –n.* **1.** spirit or animation; vigour; energy. *–v.t.* **2.** to give spirit or vigour to (fol. by *up*). [short for PEPPER]

**pepato** /pəˈpatoʊ/, *n.* a cheese, often a pecorino-type, with black peppercorns dispersed through the curd, and a spicy, sharp flavour. [It. *pepe* pepper]

**peperoni** /pɛpəˈroʊni/, *n.* →**pepperoni.**

**peplos** /ˈpɛpləs/, *n.* a voluminous outer garment worn draped in folds about the person by women in ancient Greece. Also, **peplus.** [Gk]

**peplum** /ˈpɛpləm/, *n., pl.* **-lums, -la** /-lə/. **1.** a short full flounce or an extension of the waist, covering the hips. **2.** a short skirt attached to a bodice or coat. **3.** →**peplos.** [L *peplum, peplus.* See PEPLOS]

peplum

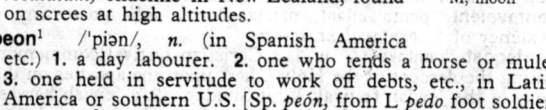

**pepo** /ˈpipoʊ/, *n., pl.* **-pos.** the characteristic fruit of plants of the family Cucurbitaceae, having a fleshy, many-seeded interior, and a hard or firm rind, as the gourd, melon, cucumber, etc. [L: melon, pumpkin, from Gk *pépōn* kind of gourd or melon eaten when ripe, orig. adj., ripe]

**pepper** /ˈpɛpə/, *n.* **1.** a pungent condiment obtained from various plants of the genus *Piper,* esp. from the dried berries, either whole or ground (affording the **black pepper** and **white pepper** of commerce), of *P. nigrum,* a tropical climbing shrub. **2.** any plant of the genus *Piper,* as the rainforest vine, *P. novaehollandiae,* which has small berries and resembles the European species *P. nigrum.* **3.** cayenne (**red pepper**), prepared from species of *Capsicum.* **4.** any species of *Capsicum,* or its fruit (green or red, hot or sweet), as the capsicum or common pepper of the garden. **5.** (*pl.*) (*in children's speech*) fast skipping. *–v.t.* **6.** to season with or as with pepper. **7.** to sprinkle as with pepper; dot; stud. **8.** to sprinkle like pepper. **9.** to pelt with shot or missiles. **10.** to discharge shot or missiles at something. [ME *peper,* OE *piper,* from L, from Gk *péperi* pepper; of Eastern orig.]

**pepper-and-salt** /pɛpər-ən-ˈsɒlt/, *adj.* **1.** composed of a fine mixture of black with white, as cloth. **2.** (of hair) streaked with grey.

**peppercorn** /ˈpɛpəkɔn/, *n.* **1.** the berry of the pepper plant, *Piper nigrum,* often dried and used in pickling. **2.** anything very small, insignificant, or trifling. [ME *pepercorn,* OE *piporcorn.* See PEPPER, CORN[1]]

**peppercorn rent** /ˈ– rɛnt/, *n.* a nominal rent.

**peppercress** /ˈpɛpəkrɛs/, *n.* any of various species of the cruciferous genus *Lepidium,* esp. *L. hyssopifolium,* a common weed.

**pepperina** /pɛpəˈrinə/, *n.* →**peppertree.**

**pepper-mill** /ˈpɛpə-mɪl/, *n.* a small, hand-operated apparatus used to crush peppercorns in order to flavour a dish.

**peppermint** /ˈpɛpəmənt/, *n.* **1.** a herb, *Mentha piperita,* cultivated for its aromatic pungent oil. **2.** any one of a group of species of *Eucalyptus* with piperitone-rich oils and characteristic bark. **3.** a lozenge or confection flavoured with peppermint.

**peppermint cod** /– ˈkɒd/, *n.* →**wirrah.** Also, **pepper cod.**

**pepperoni** /pɛpəˈroʊni/, *n.* a type of salami, much used on pizzas. Also, **peperoni.** [It., pl. of *peperone* chili]

**pepper-pot** /ˈpɛpə-pɒt/, *n.* **1.** a small, often decorated container with perforations in the top for sprinkling pepper. **2.** a West Indian stew, the principal flavouring of which is cassareep, with meat or fish and vegetables.

**pepper sauce** /pɛpə ˈsɒs/, *n.* a meat sauce made with crushed peppercorns in a white wine, vinegar, butter or cream base.

**peppertree** /ˈpɛpəˌtri/, *n.* **1.** any of several evergreen trees, members of the genus *Schinus,* mostly native of South America and cultivated in subtropical regions as ornamentals because of their evergreen foliage and bright red fruits. **2.** an aromatic shrub or tree of New Zealand *Macropiper excelsum;* kawakawa. **3.** any of certain erect aromatic shrubs of the endemic New Zealand genus *Pseudowintera;* horopito.

**peppery** /ˈpɛpəri/, *adj.* **1.** resembling pepper; full of pepper; pungent. **2.** of or pertaining to pepper. **3.** sharp or stinging, as speech. **4.** irascible or irritable, as persons or their temper. – **pepperiness,** *n.*

**pep pill** /ˈpɛp pɪl/, *n.* **1.** a pill or tablet that consists of a stimulant drug, as amphetamine. **2.** any substance taken as a stimulant.

**peppy** /ˈpɛpi/, *adj.,* **-pier, -piest.** *Colloq.* energetic. – **peppiness,** *n.*

i = peat ɪ = pit ɛ = pet æ = pat a = part ɒ = pot ʌ = putt ɔ = port ʊ = put u = pool ɜ = pert ə = apart aɪ = buy eɪ = bay ɔɪ = boy aʊ = how oʊ = hoe ɪə = here ɛə = hair ʊə = tour g = give θ = thin ð = then ʃ = show ʒ = measure tʃ = choke dʒ = joke ŋ = sing j = you õ = Fr. bon

**pepsin** /'pɛpsən/, *n.* the proteolytic enzyme produced by the stomach. Also, **pepsine.** [Gk *pépsis* digestion + -IN[2]]

**pepsinate** /'pɛpsəneɪt/, *v.t.*, **-nated, -nating.** to treat, prepare, or mix with pepsin.

**pepsinogen** /pɛp'sɪnədʒən/, *n.* the inactive form in which pepsin is synthesised and stored.

**pep talk** /'pɛp tɔk/, *n.* a vigorous talk to a person or group calculated to arouse support for a cause, increase determination to succeed, etc.

**peptic** /'pɛptɪk/, *adj.* **1.** pertaining to or concerned in digestion; digestive. **2.** promoting digestion. **3.** of pepsin. **4.** associated with the action of digestive substances: *peptic ulcer.* *–n.* **5.** a substance promoting digestion. [L *pepticus*, from Gk *peptikós* able to digest]

**peptic ulcer** /– 'ʌlsə/, *n.* an ulcer of the mucous membrane of the stomach or duodenum, caused by the digestive action of gastric juices.

**peptidase** /'pɛptədeɪz/, *n.* any of a class of enzymes which attack peptide linkages and split off amino acids.

**peptide** /'pɛptaɪd/, *n.* a compound containing two or more amino acids in which the carboxyl group of one acid is linked to the amino group of the other. [PEPT(IC) + -IDE]

**peptise** /'pɛptaɪz/, *v.t.*, **-tised, -tising.** to disperse (a substance) into colloidal form, usu. in a liquid medium. Also, **peptize.**

**peptone** /'pɛptoʊn/, *n.* any of a class of diffusible, soluble substances into which proteins are converted by hydrolysis. [G *Pepton*, from Gk (neut. adj.): cooked, digested] – **peptonic** /pɛp'tɒnɪk/, *adj.*

**peptonise** /'pɛptənaɪz/, *v.t.*, **-nised, -nising.** **1.** to convert into a peptone. **2.** to hydrolyse or dissolve by a proteolytic enzyme, such as pepsin. **3.** to subject (food) to an artificial partial digestion by pepsin or pancreatic extract, to aid digestion. Also, **peptonize.** – **peptonisation** /pɛptənaɪ'zeɪʃən/, *n.*

**per** /pɜ/; *weak form* /pə/, *prep.* through; by; for each: *per annum* (by the year), *per diem* (by the day), *per yard* (for each yard), etc. [L. Cf. PER-]

**per-**, **1.** a prefix meaning 'through', 'thoroughly', 'utterly', 'very', as in *pervert, pervade, perfect.* **2.** *Chem.* a prefix applied: **a.** to inorganic acids to indicate they possess excess of the designated element: *perboric* ($HBO_3$ or $H_2B_4O_8$), *percarbonic* ($H_2C_2O_5$), *permanganic* ($HMnO_4$), and *persulphuric* ($H_2S_2O_5$) *acids.* **b.** to salts of these acids (the name ending in *-ate*): *potassium perborate* ($K_2B_2O_8$), *potassium permanganate* ($KMnO_4$), and *potassium persulphate* ($K_2S_2O_5$). [L (in some words from OF or F), representing *per*, prep., through, by; akin to Gk *pará*]

**per.**, **1.** period. **2.** person.

**per-acid** /pɜr-'æsəd/, *n.* an acid formed by the action of hydrogen peroxide on a normal acid.

**peradventure** /pərəd'vɛntʃə/, *Archaic.* *–adv.* **1.** it may be; maybe; possibly. *–n.* **2.** chance; uncertainty. **3.** doubt or question. [ME *peraventure*, from OF *par aventure*, from *par* by (from L *per*) + *aventure* ADVENTURE]

**perambulate** /pə'ræmbjəleɪt/, *v.*, **-lated, -lating.** *–v.t.* **1.** to walk through, about, or over; travel through; traverse. **2.** to traverse and examine or inspect. *–v.i.* **3.** to walk or travel about; stroll. [L *perambulātus*, pp.] – **perambulation** /pəræmbjə'leɪʃən/, *n.* – **perambulatory** /pə'ræmbjəleɪtəri/, *adj.*

**perambulator** /pə'ræmbjəleɪtə/, *n.* →**pram.**

**per annum** /pər 'ænəm/, *adv.* by the year; yearly. [L]

**perborate** /pə'bɔreɪt/, *n.* a salt of perboric acid, containing the radicals $BO_3$ or $B_4O_8$, as *sodium perborate*, $NaBO_3 \cdot 4H_2O$, used for bleaching, disinfecting, etc. [PER- + BORATE]

**percale** /pə'keɪl, -'kal/, *n.* closely woven, smooth-finished cambric, plain or printed. [F, from Pers. *pārgālā*]

**percaline** /pɜkə'lin, 'pɜkələn/, *n.* a fine, lightweight cotton fabric, usu. finished with a gloss and dyed in one colour, used esp. for linings. [F, diminutive of *percale* PERCALE]

**per capita** /pə 'kæpətə/, *adv.* by the individual person. [L]

**perceivable** /pə'sivəbəl/, *adj.* capable of being perceived; perceptible. – **perceivably,** *adv.*

**perceive** /pə'siv/, *v.t.*, **-ceived, -ceiving.** **1.** to gain knowledge of through one of the senses; discover by seeing, hearing, etc. **2.** to apprehend with the mind; understand. [ME *perceyve(n)*, from OF *perceivre*, from L *percipere* seize, receive, understand] – **perceiver,** *n.*

**per cent** /pə 'sɛnt/, *adv.* **1.** by the hundred; for or in every hundred (used in expressing proportions, rates of interest, etc.): *to get 3 per cent interest.* *–n.* **2.** a proportion; a percentage. **3.** a stock which bears a specified rate of interest. *Symbol:* % Also, **percent.** [orig. *per cent.*, abbrev. of L *per centum* by the hundred]

**percentage** /pə'sɛntɪdʒ/, *n.* **1.** a rate or proportion per hundred. **2.** an allowance, duty, commission, or rate of interest on a hundred. **3.** a proportion in general. **4.** *Colloq.* gain; advantage.

**percentile** /pə'sɛntaɪl/, *Statistics.* *–n.* **1.** one of the values of a variable which divides the distribution of the variable into 100 groups having equal frequencies. Thus, there are 100 percentiles: *the first, second, etc., percentile.* *–adj.* **2.** of or pertaining to a percentile or a division of a distribution by percentiles. [PER CENT + *-ile*, modelled on BISSEXTILE]

**per centum** /pə 'sɛntəm/, *adv.* →**per cent.** [L]

**percept** /'pɜsɛpt/, *n.* **1.** the mental result or product of perceiving, as distinguished from the act of perceiving. **2.** that which is perceived; the object of perception. [L *perceptum*, neut. pp., (a thing) perceived]

**perceptible** /pə'sɛptəbəl/, *adj.* capable of being perceived; cognisable; appreciable: *quite a perceptible time.* – **perceptibility** /pəsɛptə'bɪləti/, **perceptibleness,** *n.* – **perceptibly,** *adv.*

**perception** /pə'sɛpʃən/, *n.* **1.** the action or faculty of perceiving; cognition; a taking cognisance, as of a sensible object. **2.** an immediate or intuitive recognition, as of a moral or aesthetic quality. **3.** the result or product of perceiving, as distinguished from the act of perceiving; a percept. **4.** *Psychol.* a single unified meaning obtained from sensory processes while a stimulus is present. [late ME, from L *perceptio* a receiving, hence apprehension] – **perceptional,** *adj.*

**perceptive** /pə'sɛptɪv/, *adj.* **1.** having the power or faculty of perceiving. **2.** of or pertaining to perception. **3.** of ready or quick perception. – **perceptively,** *adv.* – **perceptivity** /pɜsɛp'tɪvəti/, **perceptiveness,** *n.*

**perceptual** /pə'sɛptʃuəl/, *adj.* pertaining to perception.

**perceptual phonetics** /– fə'nɛtɪks/, *n.* the branch of phonetics concerned with how the brain processes and interprets speech sounds.

**perch**[1] /pɜtʃ/, *n.* **1.** a pole or rod usu. fixed horizontally to serve as a roost for birds. **2.** any thing or place serving for a bird, or for anything else, to alight or rest upon. **3.** an elevated position or station. **4.** a small elevated seat on a vehicle, for the driver. **5.** a pole connecting the fore and hind running parts of a spring carriage or other vehicle. **6.** a rod, or linear measurement in the imperial system of $5\frac{1}{2}$ yards or $16\frac{1}{2}$ feet, equal to 5.0292 m. **7.** a square rod ($30\frac{1}{4}$ sq. yds or 25.29 sq. m). **8.** a solid measure for stone, etc., formerly $16\frac{1}{2}$ feet by $1\frac{1}{2}$ feet by 1 foot. *–v.i.* **9.** to alight or rest upon a perch, as a bird. **10.** to settle or rest in some elevated position, as if on a perch. *–v.t.* **11.** to set or place on, or as if on, a perch. [ME *perche*, from OF, from L *pertica* pole, measuring rod]

**perch**[2] /pɜtʃ/, *n., pl.* **perches,** (*esp. collectively*) **perch.** *n.* **1.** any of a number of species of Australian food and sport fishes, mainly freshwater but some marine, belonging to several different families, as the golden perch, *Plectroplites ambiguus* (Serranidae) and the spangled perch, *Madigania unicolor* (Theraponidae). **2.** →**giant perch.** **3.** a spiny freshwater fish of the genus *Perca* as the European *P. fluviatilis*, which has been introduced into some rivers of south-eastern Australia, or the closely related *P. flavescens* of the U.S. **4.** any of various other similar fishes either freshwater or marine. [ME *perche*, from OF, from L *perca*, from Gk *pérkē* perch. Cf. Gk *perknós* dark-coloured]

perch[2]

**perchance** /pə'tʃæns, -'tʃans/, *adv. Poetic or Archaic.* **1.** maybe; possibly. **2.** by chance. [ME *per chance*, from AF *par chance* by chance]

**percher** /'pɜtʃə/, *n.* **1.** one who or that which perches. **2.** a bird whose feet are adapted for perching.

**Percheron** /'pɜʃərɒn/, *n.* one of a breed of draught horses, orig. raised in Perche, France. [F]

**perching bird** /'pɜtʃɪŋ bɜd/, *n.* →**passerine.**

**perchlorate** /pə'klɔreɪt/, *n.* a salt of perchloric acid, as *potassium perchlorate.*

**perchlorethylene** /pɜklɔr'ɛθəlin/, *n.* →**tetrachloroethylene.**

**perchloric acid** /pəˌklɔrɪk 'æsəd/, *n.* an acid of chlorine $HClO_4$, containing one more oxygen atom than chloric acid, and occurring as a colourless syrupy liquid. [PER- + CHLOR(INE) + -IC]

**perchloride** /pə'klɔraɪd/, *n.* that chloride of any particular element or radical with maximum proportion of chlorine. Also, **perchlorid** /pə'klɔrəd/.

**perchromic acid** /pəˌkroʊmɪk 'æsəd/, *n.* an unstable acid, $H_3CrO_8.2H_2O$, which forms stable salts called **perchromates.**

**percipient** /pə'sɪpiənt/, *adj.* **1.** perceiving. **2.** having perception. *–n.* **3.** one who or that which perceives. [L *percipiens,* ppr., perceiving] – **percipience, percipiency,** *n.*

**percoid** /'pɜkɔɪd/, *adj.* **1.** belonging to the Percoidea, a group of acanthopterygian fishes comprising the true perches and related families, and constituting one of the largest natural groups of fishes. **2.** resembling a perch. *–n.* **3.** a percoid fish. Also, **percoidean** /pə'kɔɪdiən/. [L *perca* perch + -OID]

**percolate** /'pɜkəleɪt/, *v.,* **-lated, -lating;** /'pɜkələt, -leɪt/, *n.* *–v.t.* **1.** to cause (a liquid) to pass through a porous body; filter. **2.** (of a liquid) to filter through; permeate. **3.** to make (coffee) in a percolator. *–v.i.* **4.** to pass through a porous substance; filter; ooze: *the coffee started to percolate.* **5.** gradually to become known. *–n.* **6.** a percolated liquid. [L *percolātus,* pp., strained through] – **percolation** /pɜkə'leɪʃən/, *n.*

**percolator** /'pɜkəleɪtə/, *n.* **1.** a kind of coffeepot in which boiling water is forced up a hollow stem, filters through ground coffee, and returns to the pot below. **2.** that which percolates.

**per contra** /pɜ 'kɒntrə/, *adv.* to the opposite side of an account. [L]

**percuss** /pə'kʌs/, *v.t.* **1.** to strike (something) so as to shake or cause a shock to. **2.** *Med.* to strike or tap for diagnostic or therapeutic purposes. [L *percussus,* pp., struck through]

**percussion** /pə'kʌʃən/, *n.* **1.** the striking of one body against another with some violence; impact. **2.** *Med.* the striking or tapping of a part of the body for diagnostic or therapeutic purposes. **3.** the striking of musical instruments to produce notes. **4.** a sharp light blow, esp. one for setting off a cap formerly used to discharge small arms. **5.** the act of percussing. **6.** *Music.* (collectively) the instruments in an orchestra which are played by striking.

**percussion cap** /'– kæp/, *n.* a small metallic cap or cup containing fulminating powder, formerly exploded by percussion so as to fire the charge of small arms.

**percussion instrument** /'– ɪnstrəmənt/, *n.* a musical instrument, as drum, cymbal, piano, etc., which is struck to produce a sound, as distinguished from a bowed or blown instrument.

**percussionist** /pə'kʌʃənəst/, *n.* a musician who plays a percussion instrument.

**percussion lock** /pə'kʌʃən lɒk/, *n.* a gunlock in which a hammer strikes a percussion cap.

**percussive** /pə'kʌsɪv/, *adj.* of, pertaining to, or characterised by percussion.

**percutaneous** /pɜkju'teɪniəs/, *adj.* made, done or reflected through the skin.

**Percy** /'pɜsi/, *n. Colloq.* **1.** a penis. **2. point Percy at the porcelain,** to urinate.

**per diem** /pɜ 'diəm/, *adv.* **1.** by the day. *–n.* **2.** a daily allowance, usually for living expenses while travelling in connection with one's work. [L]

**perdisulphuric acid** /pɜdaɪsʌlˌfjurɪk 'æsəd/, *n.* →**persulphuric acid** (def. 2).

**perdition** /pɜ'dɪʃən/, *n.* **1.** a condition of final spiritual ruin or damnation. **2.** the future state of the wicked. **3.** hell. **4.** utter destruction or ruin. [ME, from L *perditio* act of destroying]

**perdu** /pɜ'dju/, *adj.* **1.** hidden or concealed. *–n.* **2.** *Obs.* a soldier placed in a dangerous position. Also, **perdue.** [F, pp. of *perdre* lose, from L *perdere* lose, destroy]

**perdurable** /pɜ'djurəbəl/, *adj.* permanent; everlasting; imperishable. [ME, from LL *perdūrābilis,* from L *perdūrāre* last, hold out] – **perdurably,** *adv.*

**perdure** /pɜ'djuə/, *v.i.,* **-dured, -during.** to continue in existence; endure; last. [ME *perdure(n),* from L *perdūrāre*]

**père** /pɛə/, *n.* **1.** father. **2.** senior: *Dumas père.* [F]

**peregrinate** /'pɛrəgrəneɪt/, *v.,* **-nated, -nating.** *–v.i.* **1.** to travel or journey. *–v.t.* **2.** to travel over; traverse. [L *peregrīnātus,* pp., having travelled] – **peregrinator,** *n.*

**peregrination** /pɛrəgrə'neɪʃən/, *n.* **1.** travelling from one place to another. **2.** a course of travel; journey.

**peregrine** /'pɛrəgrən/, *adj.* **1.** foreign; alien; coming from abroad. *–n.* **2.** →**peregrine falcon.** [ME, from L *peregrīnus* coming from foreign parts; as n., a foreigner]

**peregrine falcon** /– 'fælkən/, *n.* a falcon, *Falco peregrinus,* much used in falconry.

**pereion** /pə'raɪən/, *n., pl.* **-reia** /-'raɪə/. the thorax of crustaceans.

**peremptory** /pə'rɛmptri, -təri/, *adj.* **1.** leaving no opportunity for denial or refusal; imperative: *a peremptory command.* **2.** imperious or dictatorial. **3.** *Law.* **a.** that precludes or does not admit of debate, question, etc.: *a peremptory edict.* **b.** decisive or final. **c.** in which a command is absolute: *a peremptory writ.* **4.** positive in speech, manner, etc. [L *peremptōrius* destructive, decisive] – **peremptorily,** *adv.* – **peremptoriness,** *n.*

**peremptory plea** /– 'pli/, *n. Law.* a plea which attacks the cause of and attempts to quash an action.

**perennial** /pə'rɛniəl/, *adj.* **1.** lasting for an indefinitely long time; enduring. **2.** *Bot.* having a life cycle lasting more than two years. **3.** lasting or continuing throughout the year, as a stream. **4.** perpetual; everlasting; continuing; recurrent. *–n.* **5.** a perennial plant. **6.** something continuing or recurrent. [L *perenni(s)* lasting through the year + -AL[1]] – **perennially,** *adv.*

**perennial rye** /– 'raɪ/, *n.* a tufted, frost-resistant perennial, *Lolium perenne,* extensively sown as a pasture grass in the higher rainfall countries of the world.

**perentie** /pə'rɛnti/, *n.* the largest Australian lizard, *Varanus giganteus,* dark in colour with large pale yellow spots; found in arid areas of northern and central Australia. [Aboriginal]

**perf.,** perfect.

**perfect** /'pɜfəkt/, *adj., n.;* /pɜ'fɛkt/, *v.* *–adj.* **1.** in a state proper to a thing when completed; having all essential elements, characteristics, etc.; lacking in no respect; complete. **2.** in a state of complete excellence; without blemish or defect; faultless. **3.** completely suited for a particular purpose or occasion. **4.** completely corresponding to a type or description; exact: *a perfect sphere.* **5.** correct in every detail: *a perfect copy.* **6.** thorough; complete: *perfect strangers.* **7.** pure or unmixed: *perfect yellow.* **8.** absolute; unqualified: *perfect mastery.* **9.** unmitigated or utter. **10.** *Obs.* assured or certain. **11.** *Bot.* **a.** having all parts or members present. **b.** monoclinous. **12.** *Gram.* designating a tense denoting an action or state brought to a close prior to some temporal point of reference, in contrast to imperfect or uncompleted action. For example, in the sentence *I have completed the task, have completed* is in the perfect tense, the action having been brought to a close before present time. Cf. **pluperfect, imperfect.** **13.** *Music.* **a.** applied to the consonances of unison, octave, fifth, and fourth, as distinguished from those of a third and sixth, which are called imperfect. **b.** applied to the intervals, harmonic or melodic, of an octave, fifth, and fourth in their normal form, as opposed to augmented and diminished. *–n.* **14.** *Gram.* the perfect tense. **15.** *Gram.* any verb formation or construction in the perfect tense. *–v.t.* **16.** to bring to completion, complete, or finish. **17.** to make perfect or faultless, bring to perfection. **18.** to bring nearer to perfection; improve. **19.** to make fully skilled. **20.** *Print.* to print the reverse of (a printed sheet). [L *perfectus,* pp., performed, completed; replacing ME *parfit,* from OF] – **perfecter,** *n.*

**perfect binding** /– 'baɪndɪŋ/, *n. Print.* →**thermoplastic binding.**

**perfect cadence** /– 'keɪdəns/, *n.* a musical cadence in which there is a progression from a dominant chord to a tonic chord.

**perfect gas** /– 'gæs/, *n. Physics.* →**ideal gas.**

**perfectible** /pə'fɛktəbəl/, *adj.* capable of becoming, or being made, perfect. – **perfectibility** /pəfɛktə'bɪləti/, *n.*

**perfection** /pə'fɛkʃən/, *n.* **1.** the state or quality of being perfect. **2.** the highest degree of proficiency, as in some art. **3.** a perfect embodiment of something. **4.** a quality, trait, or feature of a high degree of excellence. **5.** the highest or most perfect degree of a quality or trait. **6.** the act or fact of perfecting.

**perfectionism** /pə'fɛkʃənɪzəm/, *n.* **1.** any of various doctrines holding that religious, moral, social or political perfection is attainable. **2.** the desire or endeavour to attain perfection.

**perfectionist** /pə'fɛkʃənəst/, *n.* **1.** one who adheres to some doctrine concerning perfection. **2.** one who demands nothing less than perfection in any sphere of activity, behaviour, etc. *–adj.* **3.** of, pertaining to, or characterised by perfection or perfectionism.

**perfective** /pə'fɛktɪv/, *adj.* **1.** tending to make perfect; conducive to perfection. **2.** *Gram.* denoting an aspect of the verb rather than a tense, as in Russian, which indicates completion of the action or state of the verb prior to a temporal point of reference. *–n.* **3.** *Gram.* the perfective aspect. **4.** *Gram.* a verb in the perfective. – **perfectively,** *adv.* – **perfectiveness,** *n.*

**perfectly** /'pɜfəktli/, *adv.* **1.** in a perfect manner or degree. **2.** completely.

**perfect number** /pɜfəkt 'nʌmbə/, *n.* a number which is equal to the sum of its aliquot parts.

**perfecto** /pə'fɛktoʊ/, *n., pl.* **-tos.** a rather thick medium-sized cigar tapering towards both ends. [Sp.: lit., perfect]

**perfector** /pə'fɛktə/, *n.* a printing machine which prints both sides of a sheet of paper during one passage through the machine.

**perfect participle** /pɜfəkt 'patəsɪpəl/, *n.* →**past participle.**

**perfect pitch** /– 'pɪtʃ/, *n.* →**absolute pitch.**

**perfect rhyme** /– 'raɪm/, *n.* **1.** rhyme of two words spelt or pronounced identically but differing in meaning, as *rain, reign;* rich rhyme. **2.** correct or faultless rhyme.

**perfects** /'pɜfəkts/, *n.pl. Brit.* goods of the highest quality, without manufacturing imperfection.

**perfervid** /pɜ'fɜvəd/, *adj.* very fervid. – **perfervidity** /pɜfɜ'vɪdəti/, **perfervidness,** *n.* – **perfervidly,** *adv.* – **perfervour,** *n.*

**perfidious** /pɜ'fɪdiəs/, *adj.* guilty of perfidy; deliberately faithless; treacherous. [L *perfidiōsus*] – **perfidiously,** *adv.* – **perfidiousness,** *n.*

**perfidy** /'pɜfədi/, *n., pl.* **-dies.** a deliberate breach of faith or trust; faithlessness; treachery. [L *perfidia* faithlessness]

**perfoliate** /pə'foʊliət, -eɪt/, *adj.* having the stem apparently passing through the leaf, owing to congenital union of the basal edges of the leaf round the stem: *a perfoliate leaf.* [NL *perfoliātus,* from L *per* through + *fol-i(um)* leaf + *-ātus* -ATE[1]] – **perfoliation** /pəfoʊli'eɪʃən/, *n.*

perfoliate leaves

**perforate** /'pɜfəreɪt/, *v.,* **-rated, rating;** /'pɜfərət/, *adj.* *–v.t.* **1.** to make a hole or holes through by boring, punching or other process. **2.** to pierce through or to the interior of; penetrate. *–v.i.* **3.** to make its way through or into something; penetrate. *–adj.* **4.** →**perforated.** [L *perforātus,* pp., having been pierced through] – **perforative** /'pɜfərətɪv/, *adj.* – **perforator,** *n.*

**perforated** /'pɜfəreɪtəd/, *adj.* **1.** pierced with a hole or holes. **2.** having perforations by which one postage stamp, label, etc., can be separated from others in the sheet.

**perforation** /pɜfə'reɪʃən/, *n.* **1.** a hole, or one of a number of holes, bored or punched through something, as those between individual postage stamps of a sheet to facilitate separation. **2.** a hole made or passing through a thing. **3.** the act of perforating. **4.** the state of being perforated.

**perforce** /pə'fɔs/, *adv.* of necessity. [ME *par force,* from OF: by force, from *par* by (from L *per*) + *force* FORCE]

**perform** /pə'fɔm/, *v.t.* **1.** to carry out; execute; do: *to perform miracles.* **2.** to go through or execute in due form: *to perform a ceremony.* **3.** to carry into effect; fulfil. **4.** to act (a play, a part, etc.), as on the stage. **5.** to render (music), as by playing or singing. **6.** to execute (any skill or ability) before an audience. **7.** *Obs.* to complete. *–v.i.* **8.** to fulfil a command, promise, or undertaking. **9.** to execute or do something. **10.** to act in a play. **11.** to perform music. **12.** to go through any performance. **13.** to display anger. **14.** *Colloq.* to behave in a sexual manner: *he performs well.* [ME *parfourme(n),* from AF *parfourmer* (apparently for OF *parfournir* complete, accomplish), influenced by *fourme* form, from L *forma*] – **performable,** *adv.* – **performer,** *n.*

**performance** /pə'fɔməns/, *n.* **1.** a musical, dramatic or other entertainment. **2.** the performing of ceremonies, or of music, or of a play, part, or the like. **3.** execution or doing, as of work, acts, or feats. **4.** a particular action, deed, or proceeding. **5.** an action or proceeding of a more or less unusual or spectacular kind. **6.** the act of performing. **7.** the way in which something reacts under certain conditions or fulfils the purpose for which it was intended.

**performance test** /'– test/, *n.* a psychological test to be responded to by manual or other behavioural performance rather than verbally.

**performing arts** /pəfɔmɪŋ 'ats/, *n.pl.* drama, music and the dance, collectively.

**perfume** /'pɜfjum/, *n.;* /pə'fjum/, *v.,* **-fumed, -fuming.** *–n.* **1.** a substance, extract, or preparation for diffusing or imparting a fragrant or agreeable smell. **2.** the scent, odour, or volatile particles emitted by substances that have an agreeable smell. *–v.t.* **3.** (of substances, flowers, etc.) to impart fragrance to. **4.** to impregnate with a sweet odour; scent. [F *parfum,* from *parfumer* to scent, from *par-* PER- + *fumer* smoke]

**perfumer** /pə'fjumə/, *n.* **1.** one who or that which perfumes. **2.** a maker or seller of perfumes.

**perfumery** /pə'fjuməri/, *n., pl.* **-ries.** **1.** perfumes collectively. **2.** a perfume. **3.** the art or business of a perfumer. **4.** the place of business of a perfumer. **5.** the preparation of perfumes.

**perfunctory** /pə'fʌŋktəri/, *adj.* **1.** performed merely as an uninteresting or routine duty; mechanical; indifferent, careless, or superficial: *perfunctory courtesy.* **2.** acting merely out of duty; formal; official. [LL *perfunctōrius,* from L *perfunctus,* pp., performed] – **perfunctorily,** *adv.* – **perfunctoriness,** *n.*

**perfuse** /pə'fjuz/, *v.t.,* **-fused, -fusing.** **1.** to overspread with moisture, colour, etc. **2.** to diffuse (a liquid, etc.) through or over something. [L *perfūsus,* pp., poured through] – **perfusion,** *n.* – **perfusive,** *adj.*

**pergola** /'pɜgələ, pə'goʊlə/, *n.* **1.** an arbour formed of horizontal trelliswork supported on columns or posts, over which vines or other plants are trained. **2.** an architectural construction resembling such an arbour. [It., from L *pergula* shed, vine arbour]

**perh.,** perhaps.

**perhaps** /pə'hæps, præps/, *adv.* **1.** maybe; possibly. **2.** *Rare.* perchance. [ME *par happes* by chances]

**peri** /'pɪəri/, *n., pl.* **-ris.** **1.** one of a race of beautiful fairylike beings of Persian mythology, represented as descended from fallen angels and excluded from paradise till their penance is accomplished. **2.** any lovely, graceful creature. [Pers., from Avestan *pairika* female demon, witch]

**peri-,** a prefix meaning 'around', 'about', 'beyond', or having an intensive force, occurring in words from the Greek, and used also as a modern formative, esp. in scientific terms. [Gk, prefix and prep.]

**perianth** /'pɛriænθ/, *n.* the calyx and corolla collectively esp. where they are similar. [short for *perianthium,* from NL. See PERI-, ANTHO-, -IUM]

**periapt** /'pɛriæpt/, *n.* →**amulet.** [F *périapte,* from Gk *períapton* (neut.), lit., hung around]

**periblem** /'pɛriblɛm/, *n.* the histogen in plants which gives rise to the cortex. [Gk *períblēma* anything thrown or put around]

**pericardial** /pɛri'kadiəl/, *adj.* of or pertaining to the pericardium. Also, **pericardiac.**

**pericarditis** /ˌpɛrika'daɪtəs/, *n.* inflammation of the pericardium.

**pericardium** /pɛri'kadiəm/, *n., pl.* **-dia** /-diə/. the membranous

, sac enclosing the heart. [NL, from Gk *perikárdion*]

**pericarp** /ˈpɛrikap/, *n.* **1.** the walls of a ripened ovary or fruit, sometimes consisting of three layers, the epicarp, mesocarp, and endocarp; seed capsule; seed vessel. **2.** a membranous envelope around the cystocarp of red algae. [NL *pericarpium,* from Gk *perikárpion* pod, husk] – **pericarpial** /pɛriˈkapiəl/, *adj.*

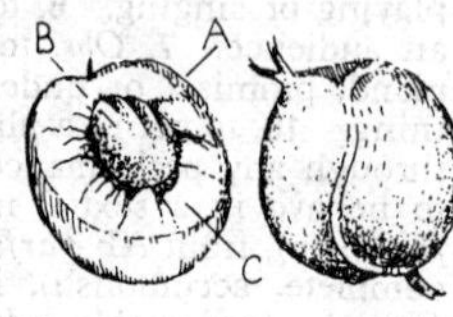


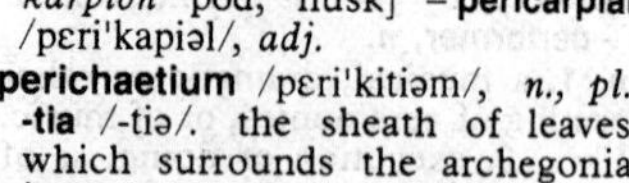

pericarps (def. 1) section and drupe of plum: A, epicarp; B, endocarp; C, mesocarp

**perichaetium** /pɛriˈkitiəm/, *n., pl.* **-tia** /-tiə/. the sheath of leaves which surrounds the archegonia in mosses.

**perichondrium** /pɛriˈkɒndriəm/, *n., pl.* **-dria** /-driə/. the membrane of fibrous connective tissue covering the surface of cartilages except at the joints. [PERI- + Gk *chóndros* cartilage + -IUM] – **perichondrial,** *adj.*

**periclase** /ˈpɛrikleɪz, -eɪs/, *n.* naturally occurring magnesium oxide.

**periclinal** /pɛriˈklaɪnəl/, *adj.* parallel to the outer surface of a plant part.

**pericline** /ˈpɛriklaɪn/, *n. Geol.* a dome shaped structure in which strata dip away from a central point. [Gk *periklīnḗs* sloping on all sides]

**pericope** /pəˈrɪkəpi/, *n.* an extract or passage from a work, esp. one selected for reading in church. – **pericopic** /pɛriˈkɒpɪk/, *adj.*

**pericranium** /pɛriˈkreɪniəm/, *n., pl.* **-nia** /-niə/. **1.** *Anat.* the external periosteum of the cranium. **2.** *Obs.* the skull or brain. [NL, from Gk *perikránion* (neut.) around the skull] – **pericranial,** *adj.*

**pericycle** /ˈpɛrisaɪkəl/, *n. Bot.* the outmost cell layer of the stele frequently becoming a multilayered zone. [Gk *períkyklos* all around, used as n.]

**pericynthion** /pɛriˈsɪnθiən/, *n.* the point of a satellite's orbit about the moon closest to the moon (opposed to *apocynthion*).

**periderm** /ˈpɛridɜm/, *n.* the cork-producing tissue of plant stems together with the cork layers and other tissues derived from it.

**peridium** /pəˈrɪdiəm/, *n., pl.* **-ridia** /-ˈrɪdiə/. the outer enveloping coat of the fruit body in many fungi, sometimes itself differentiated into outer and inner layers, exoperidium and endoperidium respectively. [NL, from Gk *pērídion,* diminutive of *pḗra* leather pouch, wallet] – **peridial,** *adj.*

**peridot** /ˈpɛridɒt/, *n.* a green variety of olivine used as a gem. [ME, from F; orig. uncert.] – **peridotic** /pɛriˈdɒtɪk/, *adj.*

**peridotite** /pɛriˈdoutaɪt/, *n.* any of a group of igneous rocks of granitic texture, composed chiefly of olivine with an admixture of various other minerals, but nearly or wholly free from felspar.

**perigee** /ˈpɛrədʒi/, *n.* **1.** *Astron.* the point in an orbit round the earth that is nearest to the earth (opp. to *apogee*). **2.** *Astronautics.* the point at which a satellite orbit is the least distance from the centre of the gravitational field of the controlling body or bodies. [F, from NL *perigēum,* from Gk *perígeion* (neut.) close around the earth] – **perigeal** /pɛrəˈdʒiəl/, **perigean** /pɛrəˈdʒiən/, *adj.*

**perigynous** /pəˈrɪdʒənəs/, *adj.* **1.** situated around the pistil on the edge of a cuplike receptacle, as stamens, etc. **2.** having stamens, etc., so arranged, as a flower. [NL *perigynus,* from Gk *peri-* PERI- + *gynḗ* woman, female]

**perigyny** /pəˈrɪdʒəni/, *n.* perigynous condition.

**perihelion** /pɛriˈhiliən/, *n., pl.* **-lia** /-liə/. the point of the orbit of a planet, comet, or artificial satellite which is nearest to the sun (opp. to *aphelion*). [NL *perihēlium,* from Gk *peri-* PERI- + *hḗlios* sun]

perigynous flower (section)

**peril** /ˈpɛrəl/, *n., v.,* **-rilled, -rilling.** *–n.* **1.** exposure to injury, loss, or destruction; risk; jeopardy; danger. *–v.t.* **2.** to imperil. [ME, from F, from L *perīculum*]

**perilous** /ˈpɛrələs/, *adj.* full of or attended with peril; hazardous; dangerous. [ME, from AF *perillous,* from L *perīculōsus*] – **perilously,** *adv.* – **perilousness,** *n.*

**perilune** /ˈpɛrilun/, *n.* the lowest point in the orbit of a body around the moon, measured from the moon's centre.

**perilymph** /ˈpɛrilɪmf/, *n.* the fluid filling the bony labyrinth of the ear and separating it from the membranous labyrinth.

**perimeter** /pəˈrɪmətə/, *n.* **1.** the circumference, border, or outer boundary of a two-dimensional figure. **2.** the length of such a boundary. **3.** *Ophthalm.* an instrument for determining the extent and defects of the visual field. **4.** *Colloq.* any boundary. [L *perimetros,* from Gk] – **perimetric** /pɛriˈmɛtrɪk/, **perimetrical** /pɛriˈmɛtrɪkəl/, *adj.* – **perimetrically** /pɛriˈmɛtrɪkli/, *adv.* – **perimetry,** *n.*

**perimorph** /ˈpɛrimɔf/, *n.* a mineral enclosing another mineral (opp. to *endomorph* (def. 1)). [PERI- + Gk *morphḗ* form] – **perimorphic** /pɛriˈmɔfɪk/, **perimorphous** /pɛriˈmɔfəs/, *adj.*

**peri-natal** /ˈpɛri-neɪtl/, *adj.* of or pertaining to the period closest to the time of birth.

**perinephrium** /pɛriˈnɛfriəm/, *n.* the capsule of connective tissue which envelopes the kidney. [PERI- + Gk *nephrós* kidney + -IUM]

**perineum** /pɛrəˈniəm/, *n., pl.* **-nea** /-ˈniə/. **1.** the urogenital triangle in front of the anus which is bounded by the rami of the pubis, including the vulva or the roots of the penis. **2.** the diamond-shaped area corresponding to the outlet of the pelvis, containing the anus and vulva or the roots of the penis. [NL, from Gk *perínaion*] – **perineal,** *adj.*

**perineuritis** /ˌpɛrinjuˈraɪtəs/, *n.* inflammation of the perineurium.

**perineurium** /pɛriˈnjuriəm/, *n., pl.* **-neuria** /-ˈnjuriə/. the sheath of connective tissue which encloses a bundle of nerve fibres. [NL, from *peri-* PERI- + Gk *neûron* nerve + *-ium* -IUM]

**period** /ˈpɪəriəd/, *n.* **1.** an indefinite portion of time, or of history, life, etc., characterised by certain features or conditions. **2.** any specified division or portion of time. **3.** *Educ.* a specific length of time in a school timetable devoted to a single subject. **4.** *Sport, etc.* a definite, timed part of a game: *a rest between periods.* **5.** *Music.* a division of a composition, usu. a passage of eight or sixteen bars, complete or satisfactory in itself, commonly consisting of two or more contrasted or complementary phrases ending with a conclusive cadence. **6.** *Geol.* a main division of a geological era, represented in the earth's crust by systems of rocks laid down during it; it is divided into epochs. **7.** *Physics.* the time of one complete oscillation or cycle of a periodic quantity or motion; the time between a given phase and its next recurrence. **8.** *Astron.* the time in which a planet or satellite revolves about its primary. **9.** *Chem.* a group of elements forming a horizontal row in the periodic table. **10.** a round of time or series of years by which time is measured. **11.** a round of time marked by the recurrence of some phenomenon or occupied by some recurring process of action. **12.** the time during which anything runs its course. **13.** the present time. **14.** the point of completion of a round of time or course of duration or action. **15.** →**menstruation.** **16.** →**full stop.** **17.** a full pause such as is made at the end of a complete sentence. **18.** a complete sentence, esp. an elaborately constructed one. **19.** (*pl.*) rhetorical language. **20.** *Class. Pros.* a group of two or more cola. *–adj.* **21.** pertaining to, denoting, characteristic of, imitating, or representing a past period or the fashions current during a specific period of history: *period costumes.* [ME *peryod,* from L *periodus,* from Gk *períodos* a going around, cycle, period]

**periodate** /pɜˈraɪədeɪt/, *n.* a salt of periodic acid.

**periodic** /pɪəriˈɒdɪk/, *adj.* **1.** characterised by periods or rounds of recurrence. **2.** occurring or appearing at regular intervals. **3.** intermittent. **4.** *Physics.* recurring after equal intervals of time. **5.** *Astron.* **a.** characterised by a series of successive circuits or revolutions, as the motion of a planet or satellite. **b.** of or pertaining to a period, as of the revolution of a heavenly body. **6.** pertaining to or characterised by rhetorical periods or periodic sentences. **7.** (of a sentence) having the sense incomplete until the end is reached. [L *periodicus,* from Gk *periodikós*] – **periodically,** *adv.*

**periodic acid** /pɜraɪˌɒdɪk ˈæsəd/, *n.* any of a series of acids derived from $I_2O_7$ by the addition of *n* molecules of water, where *n* has values from 1 to 7. [PER- + IODIC]

**periodical** /pɪəriˈɒdɪkəl/, *n.* **1.** a magazine, journal, etc., issued at regularly recurring intervals. *–adj.* **2.** issued at regularly recurring intervals. **3.** of or pertaining to such publications. **4.** →**periodic.**

**periodic detainee** /pɪəriˌɒdɪk ˌditeɪˈni/, *n.* one who is sentenced to spend each weekend in gaol for a certain length of time.

**periodicity** /pɪəriəˈdɪsəti/, *n., pl.* **-ties.** periodic character; tendency to recur at regular intervals.

**periodic sentence** /pɪəriˌɒdɪk ˈsɛntəns/, *n.* a sentence in which the completion of the main clause is left to the end, with subsidiary clauses interspersed.

**periodic table** /– ˈteɪbəl/, *n.* a table in which the chemical elements are arranged in rows and columns so that elements with similar chemical properties lie in the same column.

**periodide** /pɜˈraɪədaɪd/, *n.* an iodide with the maximum proportion of iodine.

**periodising** /ˈpɪəriədaɪzɪŋ/, *n.* an accounting procedure by which items of income and expenditure relating to time periods which do not coincide with the financial year, are segregated in the final accounts into one portion which affects the result of the financial year under review, and another portion which is transferred to one or more subsequent financial years.

**periodontics** /ˌpɛrioʊˈdɒntɪks/, *n.* the study of periodontal tissue and its diseases.

**periodontitis** /ˌpɛrioʊdɒnˈtaɪtəs/, *n.* inflammation of the periodontium.

**periodontium** /ˌpɛrioʊˈdɒntiəm/, *n.* the tissues surrounding the tooth, including the periodontal membrane, the gums, and bone. – **periodontal, periodontic,** *adj.*

**periosteum** /pɛriˈɒstiəm/, *n., pl.* **-tea** /-tiə/. the normal investment of bone, made up of a dense outer fibrous tissue layer and a more delicate inner layer which is the layer of bone regeneration. [NL, var. of LL *periosteon,* from Gk (neut.): around the bones] – **periosteal,** *adj.*

**periostitis** /ˌpɛriɒsˈtaɪtəs/, *n.* inflammation of the periosteum. [PERIOST(EUM) + -ITIS] – **periostitic** /ˌpɛriɒsˈtɪtɪk/, *adj.*

**periotic** /pɛriˈɒtɪk/, *adj.* **1.** surrounding the ear. **2.** denoting or pertaining to certain bones or bony elements which form or help to form a protective capsule for the internal ear, being usually confluent or fused, and in man constituting part of the temporal bone. [Gk *peri-* PERI- + *ōtikós* of the ear]

**peripatetic** /ˌpɛripəˈtɛtɪk/, *adj.* **1.** walking or travelling about; itinerant. *–n.* **2.** one who walks or travels about. [orig. with ref. to the philosophy or the followers of Aristotle, 384-322 B.C., who taught while walking in the Lyceum of ancient Athens; ME, from L *peripatēticus,* from Gk *peripatētikós* walking about]

**peripatus** /pəˈrɪpətəs/, *n.* →**onychophoran.**

**peripeteia** /ˌpɛripəˈtaɪə, -ˈtiə/, *n.* a sudden reversal or change of fortune, esp. in a dramatic work. [Gk]

**peripheral** /pəˈrɪfərəl/, *adj.* **1.** pertaining to, situated in, or constituting the periphery. **2.** of minor importance; not essential; superficial. **3.** *Anat.* outside of; external (as distinguished from *central*). *–n.* **4.** →**peripheral device.** – **peripherally,** *adv.*

**peripheral device** /– dəˈvaɪs/, *n.* a device attached to a computer which transfers information into or out of the computer; peripheral.

**periphery** /pəˈrɪfəri/, *n., pl.* **-ries.** **1.** the external boundary of any surface or area. **2.** the external surface, or outside, of a body. [LL *peripherīa,* from Gk *periphéreia*]

**periphrasis** /pəˈrɪfrəsəs/, *n., pl.* **-ses** /-siz/. **1.** a roundabout way of speaking; circumlocution. **2.** a roundabout expression. Also, **periphrase** /ˈpɛrifreɪz/. [L, from Gk]

**periphrastic** /pɛriˈfræstɪk/, *adj.* **1.** circumlocutory; roundabout. **2.** *Gram.* **a.** denoting a construction of two or more words with a class meaning which in other languages or in other forms of the same language is expressed by inflectional modification of a single word. For example: *The son of Mr Smith* is periphrastic; *Mr Smith's son* is inflectional. **b.** denoting a class meaning expressed by a construction of two or more words. – **periphrastically,** *adv.*

**periplus** /ˈpɛripləs/, *n.* **1.** a circumnavigation; voyage round a coast. **2.** a narrative of this. [L, from Gk *períplous*]

**perique** /pəˈrik/, *n.* a rich-flavoured tobacco produced in Louisiana. [Louisiana F]

**perisarc** /ˈpɛrisak/, *n.* the horny or chitinous outer case or covering with which the soft parts of hydrozoans are often protected. [PERI- + Gk *sárx* flesh]

**periscope** /ˈpɛrəskoʊp/, *n.* an optical instrument consisting essentially of a tube with an arrangement of prisms or mirrors by which a view at the surface of water, the top of a parapet, etc., may be seen from below or behind. [Gk *periskopeîn* look around]

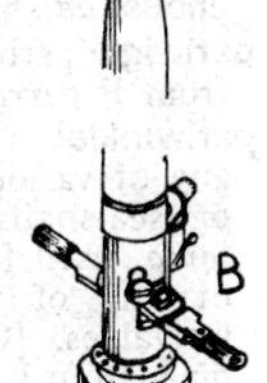

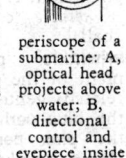

periscope of a submarine: A, optical head projects above water; B, directional control and eyepiece inside ship

**periscopic** /pɛrəˈskɒpɪk/, *adj.* **1.** (of certain lenses in special microscopes, cameras, etc.) giving distinct vision obliquely, or all around, as well as, or instead of, in a direct line. **2.** pertaining to periscopes or their use. Also, **periscopical.**

**perish** /ˈpɛrɪʃ/, *v.i.* **1.** to suffer death, or lose life, through violence, privation, etc.: *to perish in battle.* **2.** to pass away; decay and disappear. **3.** to rot: *rubber perishes.* **4.** to suffer destruction: *whole cities perish in an earthquake.* **5.** to suffer spiritual death. *–n.* **6. do a perish,** *Colloq.* **a.** to die. **b.** to suffer greatly from cold, hunger, etc. [ME *perisse(n),* from OF *periss-,* stem of *perir,* from L *perīre* pass away, perish]

**perishable** /ˈpɛrɪʃəbəl/, *adj.* **1.** liable to perish; subject to decay or destruction. *–n.* **2.** (*usu. pl.*) a perishable thing, as food. – **perishableness, perishability** /ˌpɛrɪʃəˈbɪləti/, *n.*

**perished** /ˈpɛrɪʃt/, *adj. Colloq.* weakened or exhausted by cold or hunger.

**perisher** /ˈpɛrɪʃə/, *n. Colloq.* **1.** a bitterly cold day. **2.** an annoying or mischievous child.

**perishing** /ˈpɛrɪʃɪŋ/, *Colloq. –adj.* **1.** bitterly cold. **2.** unpleasant; objectionable. *–adv.* **3.** very; extremely. – **perishingly,** *adv.*

**perisperm** /ˈpɛrispɜm/, *n.* nutritive tissue which surrounds the embryo in some seeds.

**perispore** /ˈpɛrispɔ/, *n.* a membrane surrounding a spore.

**perissodactyl** /pəˌrɪsoʊˈdæktl/, *adj.* **1.** having an uneven number of toes or digits on each foot. *–n.* **2.** any animal of the mammalian order Perissodactyla, which comprises the odd-toed hoofed quadrupeds as the tapirs, the rhinoceroses, and horses (Equidae), sometimes classified as a suborder of ungulates. Also, **perissodactyle.** [NL *perissodactylus,* from Gk *perissó(s)* odd, uneven + *dáktylos* finger or toe] – **perissodactylous,** *adj.*

**peristalsis** /pɛrəˈstælsəs/, *n., pl.* **-ses** /-siz/. peristaltic movement. [NL, from Gk *peri-* PERI- + *stálsis* compression]

**peristaltic** /pɛrəˈstæltɪk/, *adj.* denoting or pertaining to the alternate waves of constriction and dilation of a tubular muscle system or cylindrical structure, as the wavelike circular contractions of the alimentary canal. [Gk *peristaltikós* compressing]

**peristome** /ˈpɛristoʊm/, *n.* **1.** *Bot.* the one or two circles of small, pointed, toothlike appendages around the orifice of the capsule or urn of mosses, appearing when the lid is removed. **2.** *Zool.* any of various structures or sets of parts which surround, or form the walls, etc., of a mouth or mouthlike opening. [NL *peristoma,* from Gk *peri-* PERI- + *stóma* mouth]

**peristyle** /ˈpɛristaɪl/, *n.* **1.** a range or ranges of columns surrounding a building, court, or the like. **2.** a space or court so enclosed. [F, from L *peristȳlum,* from Gk *perístȳlon,* neut. of *perístȳlos* having columns all around] – **peristylar** /pɛriˈstaɪlə/, *adj.*

peristyle

**perithecium** /pɛriˈθisiəm/, *n., pl.* **-cia** /-siə/. the fructification of certain fungi, typically a minute, more or less completely closed, globose or flask-shaped body enclosing the asci. [NL, from Gk *peri-* PERI- + *thēkíon,* diminutive of *thḗkē* case]

**peritoneum** /pɛrətəˈniəm/, *n., pl.* **-nea** /-ˈniə/. the serous membrane lining the abdominal cavity and investing its viscera. Also, **peritonaeum.** [LL, from Gk *peritónaion,* lit., stretched over] – **peritoneal,** *adj.*

**peritonitis** /pɛrətə'naɪtəs/, *n.* inflammation of the peritoneum. [NL, from Gk *perítonos* stretched round or over + *-ītis* -ITIS. See PERITONEUM]

**peritricha** /pə'rɪtrəkə/, *n.pl.* **1.** any of various protozoans of the order Peritrichida, which have a spiral of cilia around the mouth. **2.** bacteria having the organs of locomotion all round the cell surface. Cf. **monotricha, amphitricha.** – **peritrichous,** *adj.*

**periwig** /'pɛriwɪg/, *n.* a peruke or wig. [alteration of *perruck,* from F *perruque.* See PERUKE]

**periwinkle**[1] /'pɛriwɪŋkəl/, *n.* **1.** any of various marine gastropods or sea-snails, esp. *Littorina littorea,* used for food. **2.** the shell of any of various other small univalves. [OE *pīnewincle,* from *pīne* (from L *pīna* kind of mussel) + *wincle* (c. Dan. *vinkel* snail shell)]

periwinkle[1]

**periwinkle**[2] /'pɛriwɪŋkəl/, *n.* any plant of the genus *Vinca,* or the related genus *Catharanthus,* as the **blue periwinkle,** *V. major,* or the **pink periwinkle,** *C. roseus.* [ME *perwynke,* OE *perwince,* from L *pervinca*]

**perjure** /'pɜdʒə/, *v.t.,* **-jured, -juring.** to render (oneself) guilty of swearing falsely, or of wilfully making a false statement under oath or solemn affirmation. [late ME, from L *perjūrāre*] – **perjurer,** *n.*

**perjured** /'pɜdʒəd/, *adj.* **1.** guilty of perjury. **2.** characterised by or involving perjury: *perjured testimony.*

**perjury** /'pɜdʒəri/, *n., pl.* **-ries.** the wilful utterance of a false statement under oath or affirmation, before a competent tribunal, upon a point material to a legal inquiry. [ME, from AF *perjurie,* from L *perjūrium*]

**perk**[1] /pɜk/, *v.i.* **1.** to carry oneself, lift the head, or act in a jaunty manner. **2.** to become lively or vigorous, as after depression or sickness (fol. by *up*). **3.** to put oneself forward briskly or presumptuously. *–v.t.* **4.** to raise smartly or briskly (oft. fol. by *up*). **5.** to dress smartly, or deck (sometimes fol. by *up* or *out*). [ME *perke(n)*; ? akin to PEER[2]]

**perk**[2] /pɜk/, *v.i., v.t. Colloq.* →**percolate.**

**perk**[3] /pɜk/, *n.* →**perquisite** (def. 2).

**perk**[4] /pɜk/, *v.i., v.t. Colloq.* to vomit (fol. by *up*).

**perky** /'pɜki/, *adj.,* **-kier, -kiest.** jaunty; brisk; pert.

**perlite** /'pɜlaɪt/, *n.* a glassy form of rhyolite, obsidian or other vitreous rock, usu. appearing as a mass of enamel-like globules; used in lightweight aggregates. Also, **pearlite.** – **perlitic** /pɜ'lɪtɪk/, *adj.*

**perm** /pɜm/, *n.* **1.** →**permanent wave.** *–v.t.* **2.** to give (the hair) a permanent wave.

**perm.,** permanent.

**permafrost** /'pɜməfrɒst/, *n.* ground that is permanently frozen, as in arctic regions.

**permalloy** /pɜm'ælɔɪ/, *n.* one of a class of alloys of high magnetic permeability, containing 30-90 per cent nickel. [PERM(EABLE) + ALLOY; Trademark]

**permanence** /'pɜmənəns/, *n.* the condition or quality of being permanent; continued existence.

**permanency** /'pɜmənənsi/, *n., pl.* **-cies. 1.** →**permanence. 2.** a permanent person, thing, or position.

**permanent** /'pɜmənənt/, *adj.* lasting or intended to last indefinitely; remaining unchanged; not temporary; enduring; abiding. [ME, from L *permanens,* ppr., remaining throughout] – **permanently,** *adv.*

**permanent building society,** *n.* an organisation which accepts money on deposit and channels it into housing loans, the repayments from which constantly renew the society's funds.

**permanent gas** /pɜmənənt 'gæs/, *n.* a gas which cannot be liquefied by pressure alone.

**permanent hardness** /– 'hadnəs/, *n.* hardness of water which is not destroyed by boiling.

**permanent loan** /'– loʊn/, *n.* a loan to a permanent building society.

**permanent magnet** /– 'mægnət/, *n.* a magnet which retains its magnetism without the presence of an external magnetic field.

**permanent-press** /'pɜmənənt-prɛs/, *adj.* of or pertaining to a garment which is treated so that it does not lose its creases in washing or wearing.

**permanent wave** /pɜmənənt 'weɪv/, *n.* a wave set into the hair by a special technique and remaining for a number of months.

**permanent way** /– 'weɪ/, *n.* the ballast, sleepers, and rails which constitute the main running track of a railway.

**permanent-way man** /pɜmənənt-'weɪ mæn/, *n.* →**fettler.**

**permanganate** /pə'mæŋgəneɪt, -nət/, *n.* a salt of permanganic acid.

**permanganic acid** /ˌpɜmæŋgænɪk 'æsəd/, *n.* an acid, $HMnO_4$, containing manganese.

**permeability** /ˌpɜmiə'bɪləti/, *n.* **1.** the property or state of being permeable. **2.** *Physics.* **a.** the ratio of flux density in a material to the magnetising force producing it (**absolute magnetic permeability**). **b.** the ratio of flux density produced in a material to that which would be produced in a vacuum by the same magnetising force (**relative magnetic permeability**). **3.** *Aeron.* the rate at which gas is lost through the envelope of a balloon or airship, usually expressed as the number of litres thus diffused in one day through a square metre.

**permeable** /'pɜmiəbəl/, *adj.* capable of being permeated. [L *permeābilis*]

**permeance** /'pɜmiəns/, *n.* **1.** the act of permeating. **2.** the conducting power of a magnetic circuit for magnetic flux, or the reciprocal of magnetic reluctance.

**permeant** /'pɜmiənt/, *adj.* permeating; pervading.

**permeate** /'pɜmieɪt/, *v.,* **-ated, -ating.** *–v.t.* **1.** to pass through the substance or mass of. **2.** to penetrate through the pores, interstices, etc., of. **3.** to be diffused through; pervade; saturate. *–v.i.* **4.** to penetrate; become diffused. [L *permeātus,* pp., passed through] – **permeation** /pɜmi'eɪʃən/, *n.* – **permeative,** *adj.*

**per mensem** /pɜ 'mɛnsəm/, *adv.* by the month. [L]

**Permian** /'pɜmiən/, *adj.* **1.** pertaining to the latest Palaeozoic geological period or system. *–n.* **2.** the period or system following Carboniferous and preceding Triassic, characterised by prominence of salt deposits and, in the Southern Hemisphere, by extensive glaciation. **3.** a subgroup of certain closely related Finno-Ugric languages of Russia, esp. Zyrian and Votyak. [named after *Perm,* a town in European Russia (where such strata occur) + -IAN]

**per mill,** per thousand. Also, **per mil.**

**permissible** /pə'mɪsəbəl/, *adj.* →**allowable.** – **permissibility** /pəmɪsə'bɪləti/, *n.* – **permissibly,** *adv.*

**permission** /pə'mɪʃən/, *n.* **1.** the act of permitting; formal or express allowance or consent. **2.** liberty or licence granted to do something. [ME, from L *permissio*]

**permissive** /pə'mɪsɪv/, *adj.* **1.** granting permission. **2.** permitted or allowed; optional. **3.** tolerant. **4.** sexually and morally tolerant: *we are living in a permissive society.* – **permissively,** *adv.* – **permissiveness,** *n.*

**permissive society** /– sə'saɪəti/, *n.* a society in which the restraints of traditional morality operate weakly, esp. with regard to sexual behaviour.

**permit** /pə'mɪt/, *v.,* **-mitted, -mitting;** /'pɜmɪt/, *n.* *–v.t.* **1.** to allow (a person, etc.) to do something: *permit me to explain.* **2.** to let (something) be done or occur: *the law permits the sale of such drugs.* **3.** to tolerate; agree to. **4.** to afford opportunity for, or admit of: *vents permitting the escape of gases.* *–v.i.* **5.** to grant permission; allow liberty to do something. **6.** to afford opportunity or possibility: *write when time permits.* **7.** to allow or admit (fol. by *of*): *statements that permit of no denial.* *–n.* **8.** a written order granting leave to do something. **9.** an authoritative or official certificate of permission; a licence. **10.** permission. [late ME, from L *permittere* to let go through] – **permitter,** *n.*

**permittivity** /pɜmə'tɪvəti/, *n.* **1.** **absolute permittivity,** the ratio of electric displacement to electric field strength in a dielectric medium. **2. relative permittivity,** the ratio of the absolute permittivity of a medium to the absolute permittivity of a vacuum; dielectric constant.

**permonosulphuric acid** /pɜˌmɒnoʊsʌlˌfjurɪk ˈæsəd/, *n.* →**persulphuric acid** (def. 1).

**permutate** /ˈpɜmjəteɪt/, *v.t.*, **-tated, -tating. 1.** to subject (something) to permutation. **2.** to arrange (items) in a different sequence.

**permutation** /pɜmjəˈteɪʃən/, *n.* **1.** *Maths.* **a.** the act of changing the order of elements arranged in a particular order (as, *abc* into *acb, bac,* etc.), or of arranging a number of elements in groups made up of equal numbers of the elements in different orders (as, *a* and *b* in *ab* and *ba*). **b.** any of the resulting arrangements or groups. **2.** the act of permuting; alteration.

**permute** /pəˈmjut/, *v.t.*, **-muted, -muting. 1.** to alter. **2.** *Maths.* to subject to permutation. [ME *permute(n)*, from L *permūtāre*] – **permutable,** *adj.*

**pernicious** /pəˈnɪʃəs/, *adj.* **1.** ruinous; highly hurtful: *pernicious teachings.* **2.** deadly; fatal. **3.** evil or wicked. [L *perniciōsus*] – **perniciously,** *adv.* – **perniciousness,** *n.*

**pernicious anaemia** /– əˈnimiə/, *n.* a macrocytic anaemia produced by deficient maturation of the red blood cells, and associated with subacute degenerative lesions in the posterior and lateral columns of the spinal cord, glossitis, gastric disturbances, and atrophy of the gastric mucosa.

**pernickety** /pəˈnɪkəti/, *adj. Colloq.* **1.** fastidious; fussy. **2.** requiring painstaking care. [orig. Scot.]

**pernod** /ˈpɜnoʊ/, *n.* a French aperitif based on aniseed. [Trademark]

**peroneal** /pɛrəˈniəl/, *adj.* pertaining or proximate to the fibula. [NL *peronē* fibula (from Gk: pin, brooch) + -AL[1]]

**peroneus** /pɛrəˈniəs/, *n.* any of several fibular muscles on the outer side of the leg.

**perorate** /ˈpɛrəreɪt/, *v.i.*, **-rated, -rating. 1.** to speak at length; make a speech. **2.** to bring a speech to a close with a formal conclusion. [L *perōrātus,* pp., spoken at length]

**peroration** /pɛrəˈreɪʃən/, *n.* the concluding part of a speech or discourse, in which the speaker or writer recapitulates the principal points and urges them with greater earnestness and force. [late ME, from L *perōrātio*]

**perosis** /pəˈroʊsəs/, *n.* a condition of poultry caused by manganese deficiency leading to malformed young birds and poor egg production in older ones; spraddle legs.

**peroxidase** /pəˈrɒksədeɪz/, *n.* any of a class of enzymes which are capable of catalysing the oxidation of a compound by the decomposition of hydrogen peroxide or any other peroxide.

**peroxide** /pəˈrɒksaɪd/, *adj., v.*, **-ided, -iding.** *–n.* **1.** *Chem.* **a.** an oxide derived from hydrogen peroxide which contains the -O-O- group; generally that oxide of an element or radical which contains an unusually large amount of oxygen. **b.** hydrogen peroxide, $H_2O_2$. *–adj.* **2.** (of the hair) bleached by peroxide (def. 1b): *she's a peroxide blonde.* *–v.t.* **3.** to use peroxide (def. 1b) on (the hair) as a bleach.

**peroxidise** /pəˈrɒksədaɪz/, *v.t., v.i.*, **-dised, -dising.** to convert into a peroxide. Also, **peroxidize.**

**peroxyacid** /pərɒksiˈæsəd/, *n.* an acid derived from hydrogen peroxide which contains the -O-O group.

**peroxyboric acid** /pəˌrɒksibɔrɪk ˈæsəd/, *n.* the hypothetical acid, $HBO_3$, known by its salts (perborates).

**peroxydisulphuric acid** /pəˌrɒksidaɪsʌlˌfjurɪk ˈæsəd/, *n. Chem.* →**persulphuric acid** (def. 2).

**peroxymonosulphuric acid** /pəˌrɒksiˌmɒnoʊsʌlˌfjurɪk ˈæsəd/, *n. Chem.* →**persulphuric acid** (def. 1).

**perp.,** perpendicular.

**perpend**[1] /ˈpɜpɛnd/, *n.* **1.** *Bldg Trades.* a vertical joint in brickwork or masonry. **2.** *Masonry.* a large stone passing through the entire thickness of a wall so as to show on both sides, and forming a border. Also, **perpend stone, perpent.** [OF *perpain,* from LL *perpannius* extending to the visible portion of the wall, influenced by PEND]

**perpend**[2] /pəˈpɛnd/, *Archaic.* *–v.t.* **1.** to consider. *–v.i.* **2.** to ponder; deliberate. [L *perpendere*]

**perpendicular** /pɜpənˈdɪkjələ/, *adj.* **1.** vertical; upright. **2.** *Geom.* meeting a given line or surface at right angles. **3.** (*cap.*) *Archit.* denoting or pertaining to a style of architecture, the last stage of English Gothic, in which a large proportion of the chief lines of the tracery intersect at right angles. *–n.* **4.** a perpendicular line or plane. **5.** an instrument for indicating the vertical line from any point. **6.** upright position. **7.** →**rectitude.** [L *perpendiculāris;* replacing ME *perpendiculer,* from OF] – **perpendicularity** /ˌpɜpəndɪkjəˈlærəti/, *n.* – **perpendicularly,** *adv.*

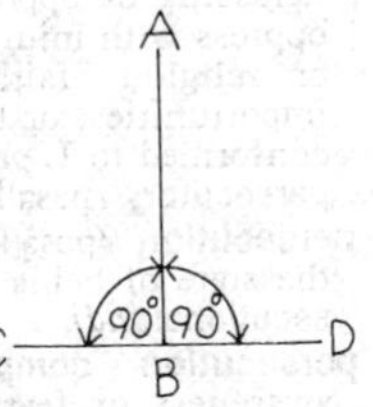

AB, perpendicular to CD

**perpend stone** /ˈpɜpɛnd stoʊn/, *n.* →**perpend**[1].

**perpent** /ˈpɜpənt/, *n. Masonry.* →**perpend**[1].

**perpetrate** /ˈpɜpətreɪt/, *v.t.*, **-trated, -trating.** to perform, execute, or commit (a crime, deception, etc.). [L *perpetrātus,* pp.] – **perpetration** /pɜpəˈtreɪʃən/, *n.* – **perpetrator,** *n.*

**perpetual** /pəˈpɛtʃuəl/, *adj.* **1.** continuing or enduring for ever or indefinitely: *perpetual snows.* **2.** continuing or continued without intermission or interruption: *a perpetual stream of visitors.* **3.** *Hort.* blooming more or less continuously throughout the season or the year. *–n.* **4.** a hybrid rose that is perpetual. [ME *perpetuall,* from L *perpetuālis*] – **perpetuality** /pəpɛtʃuˈæləti/, *n.* – **perpetually,** *adv.*

**perpetual motion** /– ˈmoʊʃən/, *n.* **1.** the motion of a theoretical machine that would continue to operate for ever without loss of energy and without receiving any energy from outside. **2.** *Music.* a rapid and brilliant piece of music with many repetitions. Also, **perpetuo moto.**

**perpetuate** /pəˈpɛtʃueɪt/, *v.t.*, **-ated, -ating.** to make perpetual; preserve from oblivion. [L *perpetuātus,* pp.] – **perpetuation** /pəˌpɛtʃuˈeɪʃən/, **perpetuance,** *n.* – **perpetuator,** *n.*

**perpetuity** /pɜpəˈtjuəti/, *n., pl.* **-ties. 1.** endless or indefinitely long duration or existence. **2.** something that is perpetual. **3.** an annuity paid for life. **4.** *Law.* (of property) an interest under which property is less than completely alienable for longer than the law allows. **5. in perpetuity,** for ever. [ME *perpetuite,* from F, from L *perpetuitas*]

**perpetuo moto** /pəˌpɛtʃuoʊ ˈmoʊtoʊ/, *n.* →**perpetual motion.**

**perplex** /pəˈplɛks/, *v.t.* **1.** to cause to be puzzled over what is not understood or certain; bewilder; confuse mentally. **2.** to make complicated or confused, as a matter, question, etc. **3.** to hamper with complications, confusion, or uncertainty. [backformation from PERPLEXED] – **perplexing,** *adj.* – **perplexingly,** *adv.*

**perplexed** /pəˈplɛkst/, *adj.* **1.** bewildered or puzzled. **2.** tangled; involved. [ME *perplex* intricate, bewildered (from L *perplexus* involved) + -ED[2]] – **perplexedly** /pəˈplɛksədli/, *adv.*

**perplexity** /pəˈplɛksəti/, *n., pl.* **-ties. 1.** a perplexed or puzzled condition; uncertainty as to what to think or do. **2.** something that perplexes. **3.** tangled, involved, or confused condition.

**perquisite** /ˈpɜkwəzət/, *n.* **1.** an incidental emolument, fee, or profit over and above fixed income, salary, or wages. **2.** Also, **perk. a.** anything customarily supposed to be allowed or left to an employee or servant as an incidental advantage of the position held. **b.** any fringe benefit, bonus, etc., attaching to a particular post which an employee receives in addition to his normal salary. **3.** something regarded as due by right. [late ME, from ML *perquīsītum,* neut. pp., sought for]

**perron** /ˈpɛrən/, *n.* an outside platform upon which the entrance door of a building opens, with steps leading to it. [ME *peroun,* from OF *perron,* from *pierre* rock, from L *petra*]

**perry** /ˈpɛri/, *n.* a fermented beverage, similar to cider, made from the juice of pears. [ME *pereye,* from OF, from L *pirum.* See PEAR]

**pers.,** **1.** person. **2.** personal.

**Pers.,** **1.** Persia. **2.** Persian.

**per-salt** /ˈpɜ-sɒlt/, *n.* (in a series of salts of a given metal or radical) that salt in which the metal or radical has a high, or the highest apparent, valency; a salt corresponding to a per-acid.

**per se** /pɜ ˈseɪ/, *adv.* by or in itself; intrinsically. [L]

**perse** /pɜs/, *adj.* of a very deep shade of blue or purple. [ME *pers,* from OF, from LL *persus;* orig. uncert.]

**persecute** /ˈpɜsəkjut/, *v.t.*, **-cuted, -cuting. 1.** to pursue with harassing or oppressive treatment; harass persistently. **2.** to oppress with injury or punishment for adherence to principles or religious faith. **3.** to annoy by persistent attentions, importunities, or the like. [backformation from PERSECUTION, conformed to L *persecūtus,* pp., having pursued] – **persecutive, persecutory** /pɜsəˈkjutəri/, *adj.* – **persecutor,** *n.*

**persecution** /pɜsəˈkjuʃən/, *n.* **1.** the act of persecuting. **2.** the state of being persecuted. [ME, from L *persecūtio*] – **persecutional,** *adj.*

**persecution complex** /ˈ– ˌkɒmplɛks/, *n.* an exaggerated awareness or fear that others are acting against one's best interests.

**perseverance** /pɜsəˈvɪərəns/, *n.* **1.** steady persistence in a course of action, a purpose, a state, etc. **2.** *Theol.* continuance in a state of grace to the end, leading to eternal salvation. – **perseverant,** *adj.*

**persevere** /pɜsəˈvɪə/, *v.i.,* **-vered, -vering.** to persist in anything undertaken; maintain a purpose in spite of difficulty or obstacles; continue steadfastly. [ME *persevere(n),* from F *persévérer,* from L *persevērāre* continue steadfastly]

**persevering** /pɜsəˈvɪərɪŋ/, *adj.* showing perseverance; steadfast; persistent. – **perseveringly,** *adv.*

**Persia** /ˈpɜʒə/, *n.* **1.** an ancient empire situated in western and south-western Asia. **2.** former official name (until 1935) of **Iran.**

**Persian** /ˈpɜʒən/, *adj.* **1.** of or pertaining to Iran, its people, or their language. –*n.* **2.** a member of the native race of Iran, now a mixed race descended in part from the ancient Iranians. **3.** a citizen of ancient Persia. **4.** an Iranian language, the principal language of Iran, in its historical (Old Persian, Avestan, and Pahlavi) and modern forms.

**Persian carpet** /– ˈkapət/, *n.* a large one-piece carpet having a pile of wool, sometimes of silk, twisted by hand with a special knot over the warp.

**Persian cat** /– ˈkæt/, *n.* a variety of domestic cat with long, silky hair and bushy tail, probably originating in Persia.

**Persian lamb** /– ˈlæm/, *n.* **1.** the lamb of the karakul sheep. **2.** the fur of this animal, having closely curled lustrous hairs, and usually dyed black; caracul.

**persiennes** /pɜziˈɛnz/, *n.pl.* (*construed as sing.*) a fabric, usu. cotton or silk, with a printed or painted pattern. [F, pl. of fem. adj.: Persian]

**persiflage** /ˈpɜsəflaʒ/, *n.* **1.** light, bantering talk. **2.** a frivolous style of treating a subject. [F, from *persifler* banter lightly, from *per-* PER- + *siffler* whistle, hiss, from L *sifilāre, sibilāre*]

**persimmon** /ˈpɜsəmən, pəˈsɪmən/, *n.* **1.** any of various trees of the genus *Diospyros,* esp. D. *virginiana* of North America, with astringent plumlike fruit becoming sweet and edible when thoroughly ripe, and *D. kaki* of Japan and China, with soft, rich red or orange fruits. **2.** the fruit. [Algonquian *pasimenan* (artificially) dried fruit]

persimmon

**persist** /pəˈsɪst/, *v.i.* **1.** to continue steadily or firmly in some state, purpose, course of action, or the like, esp. in spite of opposition, remonstrance, etc. **2.** to last or endure. **3.** to be insistent in a statement or question. [L *persistere* to continue steadfastly]

**persistence** /pəˈsɪstəns/, *n.* **1.** the action or fact of persisting. **2.** the quality of being persistent. **3.** continued existence or occurrence. **4.** the continuance of an effect after its cause is removed, esp. the short-term tendency of a cathode ray tube picture to remain visible after its original production. Also, **persistency.**

**persistent** /pəˈsɪstənt/, *adj.* **1.** persisting, esp. in spite of opposition, etc.; persevering. **2.** lasting or enduring. **3.** continued; constantly repeated. **4.** *Biol.* continuing or permanent. **5.** *Zool.* perennial; holding to morphological character, or continuing in function or activity. – **persistently,** *adv.*

**person** /ˈpɜsən/, *n.* **1.** a human being, whether man, woman, or child: *the only person in sight.* **2.** a human being as distinguished from an animal or a thing. **3.** *Philos.* a self-conscious or rational being. **4.** the actual self or individual personality of a human being: *to assume a duty in one's own person.* **5.** the living body of a human being, often including the clothes worn. **6.** the body in its external aspect. **7.** a character, part, or role, in a play, story, or in real life, etc. **8.** an individual of distinction or importance. **9.** *Colloq.* one not entitled to social recognition or respect: *that person!* **10.** *Law.* any human being or artificial body of people, having rights and duties before the law. **11.** *Gram.* **a.** (in some languages) a category of verb inflection and of pronoun classification, distinguishing between the speaker (**first person**), the one addressed (**second person**), and anyone or anything else (**third person**), sometimes with further subdivisions of the third; as *I* and *we* (first person), *you* (second person), and *he, she, it* and *they* (third person). **b.** any of these three (or more) divisions. **12.** *Theol.* any of the three hypostases or modes of being in the Trinity (Father, Son, and Holy Ghost). **13. in person, a.** in one's own bodily presence: *to apply in person.* **b.** *Law.* of a plaintiff or defendant, conducting his own court case. [ME *persone,* from OF, from L *persōna* actor's mask, character acted, personage, being]

**-person,** a noun suffix used to avoid the specification or implication of sex, as in *chairman, salesman;* hence *chairperson, salesperson.*

**persona** /pɜˈsoʊnə/, *n., pl.* **-nae** /-ni/. **1.** a person. **2.** (in the psychology of C. G. Jung) the outer or public personality, which is presented to the world and does not represent the inner personality of the individual (contrasted with *anima*). [L: mask]

**personable** /ˈpɜsənəbəl/, *adj.* of pleasing personal appearance; comely; presentable.

**personage** /ˈpɜsənɪdʒ/, *n.* **1.** a person of distinction or importance. **2.** any person. **3.** a character in a play, story, etc. [late ME, from OF]

**persona grata** /pɜˌsoʊnə ˈgratə/, *n.* **1.** an acceptable person. **2.** a diplomatic representative acceptable to the government to which he is accredited. [LL]

**personal** /ˈpɜsənəl/, *adj.* **1.** of or pertaining to a particular person; individual; private: *a personal matter.* **2.** relating to, directed to, or aimed at, a particular person: *a personal favour.* **3.** referring or directed to a particular person in a disparaging or offensive sense or manner: *personal remarks.* **4.** making personal remarks or attacks: *to become personal in a dispute.* **5.** done, affected, held, etc., in person: *a personal conference, personal service.* **6.** pertaining to or characteristic of a person or self-conscious being. **7.** of the nature of an individual rational being: *a personal God.* **8.** pertaining to the person, body, or bodily aspect: *personal cleanliness.* **9.** *Gram.* **a.** denoting grammatical person. For example, in Latin *portō* 'I carry', *portās* 'you carry', *portat* 'he, she or it carries', *-ō, -s* and *-t* are said to be personal endings. **b.** denoting a class of pronouns classified as referring to the speaker, the one addressed, and anyone or anything else. **10.** *Law.* denoting or pertaining to estate or property consisting of moveable chattels, money, securities and choses in action (distinguished from *real*). **11. be personal,** to make disparaging remarks about a person rather than directing oneself to an argument. **12. get personal,** to touch on intimate or private matters. –*n.* **13.** *U.S.* **a.** a short news paragraph in a newspaper, concerning a particular person or particular persons. **b.** a short, confidential notice in a newspaper, often addressed to a particular individual. [ME, from L *persōnalis*]

**personal action** /– ˈækʃən/, *n. Law.* **1.** action in person. **2.** action for a tort affecting personal rights.

**personal column** /ˈ– kɒləm/, *n.* a part of a newspaper devoted to advertisements of a personal nature.

**personal effects** /– əˈfɛkts/, *n.pl.* a person's moveable and more intimate property as clothing, toilet articles, keys, etc.

**personal equation** /– əˈkweɪʒən/, *n.* personal tendency to deviation or error, for which allowance must be made.

**personalise** /ˈpɜsənəlaɪz/, *v.t.,* **-lised, -lising.** **1.** to make personal. **2.** to mark in some way so as to identify as the property of a particular person. **3.** to personify. Also, **personalize.**

**personalism** /ˈpɜsənəlɪzəm/, *n.* a philosophical movement which finds ultimate value and reality in persons, human or divine, usu. favouring democracy, self-psychology, theism, and idealism, while opposing naturalism, dualism, and irrationalism. **–personalist,** *n.* **–personalistic** /pɜsənəˈlɪstɪk/, *adj.*

**personality** /pɜsəˈnæləti/, *n., pl.* **-ties. 1.** distinctive or notable personal character: *a man with personality.* **2.** a person as an embodiment of an assemblage of qualities. **3.** *Psychol.* **a.** all the constitutional, mental, emotional, social, etc., characteristics of an individual. **b.** an organised pattern of all the characteristics of an individual. **c.** a pattern of characteristics consisting of two or more usu. opposing types of behaviour: *multiple personality.* **4.** the quality of being a person; existence as a self-conscious being; personal identity. **5.** the essential character of a person as distinguished from a thing. **6.** application or reference to a particular person or particular persons, often in disparagement or hostility. **7.** a disparaging or offensive statement referring to a particular person. **8.** a well-known or prominent person; celebrity. **9.** *Geog.* the distinguishing or peculiar characteristics of a region.

**personality cult** /ˈ– kʌlt/, *n.* excessive adulation of an individual, esp. a political leader.

**personally** /ˈpɜsənəli/, *adv.* **1.** as regards onself: *personally I don't care to go.* **2.** as an individual person: *he hates me personally.* **3.** in person. **4.** as if intended for one's own person: *don't take his bluntness personally.*

**personal page** /pɜsənəl ˈpeɪdʒ/, *n.* →**pager.**

**personal pronoun** /– ˈproʊnaʊn/, *n.* any one of the pronouns which indicate grammatical person (*I, we, thou, you, he, she, it, they*).

**personalty** /ˈpɜsənəlti/, *n., pl.* **-ties.** (in law) personal estate or property.

**persona non grata** /pɜˌsoʊnə nɒn ˈgratə/, *n.* an unacceptable or unwelcome person, esp. a diplomatic representative. [L]

**personate**[1] /ˈpɜsəneɪt/, *v.,* **-nated, -nating.** *–v.t.* **1.** to act or present (a character in a play, etc.). **2.** to assume the character or appearance of; pass oneself off as, esp. for fraudulent purposes. **3.** (in the arts) to represent in terms of personal properties. *–v.i.* **4.** to act or play a part. [LL *persōnātus,* pp.] **–personation** /pɜsəˈneɪʃən/, *n.* **– personative,** *adj.* **– personator,** *n.*

**personate**[2] /ˈpɜsənət, -neɪt/, *adj.* **1.** (of a bilabiate corolla) masklike. **2.** having the lower lip pushed upwards so as to close the hiatus between the lips, as in the snap-dragon. [L *persōnātus* masked]

**personification** /pəsɒnəfəˈkeɪʃən/, *n.* **1.** the attribution of personal nature or character to inanimate objects or abstract notions, esp. as a rhetorical figure. **2.** the representation of a thing or abstraction in the form of a person, as in art. **3.** the person or thing embodying a quality or the like; an embodiment. **4.** an imaginary person or creature conceived or figured to represent a thing or abstraction. **5.** the act of personifying.

**personify** /pəˈsɒnəfaɪ/, *v.t.,* **-fied, -fying. 1.** to attribute personal nature or character to (an inanimate object or an abstraction), as in speech or writing. **2.** to represent (a thing or abstraction) in the form of a person, as in art. **3.** to embody (a quality, idea, etc.) in a real person or a concrete thing. **4.** to be an embodiment of; typify. **5.** →**personate**[1]. [PERSON + -(I)FY, apparently modelled on F *personnifier*] **– personifier,** *n.*

**personnel** /pɜsəˈnɛl/, *n.* the body of persons employed in any work, undertaking, or service (distinguished from *matériel*). [F, n. use of adj.]

**person-to-person** /ˌpɜsən-tə-ˈpɜsən/, *adj.* **1.** of or pertaining to a telephone call over a long distance for which timed charging begins when the required person has been connected. *–n.* **2.** such a call.

**persorption** /pəˈsɔpʃən/, *n.* (of a substance) adsorption in pores only slightly wider than the diameter of the adsorbed molecule.

**persp.,** perspective.

**perspective** /pəˈspɛktɪv/, *n.* **1.** the art of depicting on a flat surface, various objects, architecture, landscape, etc., in such a way as to express dimensions and spatial relations. **2.** the relation of parts to one another and to the whole, in a mental view or prospect. **3.** a visible scene, esp. one extending to a distance; a vista. **4.** the appearance of objects with reference to relative position, distance, etc. **5.** a mental view or prospect. **6.** *Obs.* an optical glass. **7. in perspective, a.** according to the laws of perspective. **b.** in true proportion. *–adj.* **8.** of or pertaining to the art of perspective, or represented according to its laws. [ME, from ML *perspectīva* (*ars*) science of optics, from L *perspicere* see through] **– perspectively,** *adv.*

**perspex** /ˈpɜspɛks/, *n.* an optically clear thermoplastic resin, polymethyl methacrylate, used as a substitute for glass in certain applications. [Trademark]

**perspicacious** /pɜspəˈkeɪʃəs/, *adj.* **1.** having keen mental perception; discerning. **2.** *Archaic.* having keen sight. [PERSPICACI(TY) + -OUS] **– perspicaciously,** *adv.*

**perspicacity** /pɜspəˈkæsəti/, *n.* **1.** keenness of mental perception; discernment; penetration. **2.** *Archaic.* keenness of sight. [L *perspicācitas*]

**perspicuity** /pɜspəˈkjuəti/, *n.* **1.** clearness or lucidity, as of a statement. **2.** the quality of being perspicuous. **3.** →**perspicacity.** [late ME, from L *perspicuitas*]

**perspicuous** /pəˈspɪkjuəs/, *adj.* **1.** clear to the understanding. **2.** clear in expression or statement; lucid. **3.** →**perspicacious.** [late ME, from L *perspicuus*] **– perspicuously,** *adv.* **– perspicuousness,** *n.*

**perspiration** /pɜspəˈreɪʃən/, *n.* **1.** the act or process of perspiring. **2.** that which is perspired; sweat.

**perspiratory** /pəˈspaɪrətri, -ˈspɪr-, ˈpɜspərətri/, *adj.* of, pertaining to or stimulating perspiration.

**perspire** /pəˈspaɪə/, *v.,* **-spired, -spiring.** *–v.i.* **1.** to excrete watery fluid through the pores; sweat. *–v.t.* **2.** to emit through pores; exude. [L *perspīrāre,* lit., breathe through]

**persuade** /pəˈsweɪd/, *v.t.,* **-suaded, -suading. 1.** to prevail on (a person, etc.), by advice, urging, reasons, inducements, etc., to do something: *we could not persuade him to wait.* **2.** to induce to believe; convince. [L *persuādēre*] **– persuadable,** *adj.* **– persuader,** *n.*

**persuado** /pəˈsweɪdoʊ/, *adj., n.* (*joc.*) →**pseudo.**

**persuasible** /pəˈsweɪzəbəl/, *adj.* open to persuasion. **– persuasibility** /pəsweɪzəˈbɪləti/, *n.*

**persuasion** /pəˈsweɪʒən/, *n.* **1.** the act of persuading or seeking to persuade. **2.** power of persuading; persuasive force. **3.** the state or fact of being persuaded or convinced. **4.** a conviction or belief. **5.** a form or system of belief, esp. religious belief, or the body of persons adhering to it. **6.** sect or denomination. **7.** *Colloq.* kind or sort: *of the heathen persuasion.* [ME, from L *persuāsio*]

**persuasive** /pəˈsweɪsɪv, -zɪv/, *adj.* **1.** able, fitted, or intended to persuade. *–n.* **2.** something that persuades. **– persuasively,** *adv.* **– persuasiveness,** *n.*

**persulphate** /pɜˈsʌlfeɪt/, *n.* a salt of persulphuric acid.

**persulphuric acid** /ˌpɜsʌlfjurɪk ˈæsəd/, *n.* **1.** Also, **Caro's acid, permonosulphuric acid, peroxymonosulphuric acid.** a white crystalline solid, $H_2SO_5$, used as an oxidising agent. **2.** Also, **perdisulphuric acid, peroxydisulphuric acid.** a white hygroscopic crystalline solid, $H_2S_2O_8$, used in the manufacture of hydrogen peroxide.

**pert** /pɜt/, *adj.* **1.** bold; forward; impertinent; impudent; saucy. **2.** lively; sprightly; in good health. [ME, aphetic var. of *apert,* apparently b. OF *apert* open (from L *apertus*) and OF *a(s)pert* skilled (from L *expertus*)] **– pertly,** *adv.* **– pertness,** *n.*

**pertain** /pəˈteɪn/, *v.i.* **1.** to have reference or relation; relate: *documents pertaining to the case.* **2.** to belong or be connected as a part, adjunct, possession, attribute, etc. **3.** to belong properly or fittingly; be appropriate. [ME *partene(n),* from OF *partenir,* from L *pertinēre* extend, reach, relate]

**Perthes' disease** /ˈpɜθiz dəziz/, *n.* aseptic necrosis of the head of the femur, most common in boys aged five to ten years. [named after Georg Clemens *Perthes,* 1869-1927, German physician]

**Perthite** /ˈpɜθaɪt/, *n.* **1.** one who was born in Perth, the capital city of Western Australia, or who has come to regard it as his home. *–adj.* **2.** of or pertaining to the city of Perth.

**pertinacious** /pɜtəˈneɪʃəs/, *adj.* **1.** holding tenaciously to a purpose, course of action, or opinion. **2.** extremely persistent: *pertinacious efforts.* [L *pertinācia* + -OUS] **– pertinaciously,** *adv.* **– pertinaciousness,** *n.*

**pertinacity** /pɜtəˈnæsəti/, *n.* the quality of being pertinacious.

**pertinent** /ˈpɜtənənt/, *adj.* pertaining or relating to the matter in hand; relevant; apposite: *pertinent details.* [ME, from L *pertinens,* ppr.] – **pertinence, pertinency,** *n.* – **pertinently,** *adv.*

**perturb** /pə'tɜb/, *v.t.* **1.** to disturb or disquiet greatly in mind; agitate. **2.** to disturb greatly; throw into disorder; derange. **3.** *Astron.* to induce perturbation of. [ME, from L *perturbāre*] – **perturbable,** *adj.*

**perturbation** /pɜtə'beɪʃən/, *n.* **1.** the act of perturbing. **2.** the state of being perturbed. **3.** mental disquiet or agitation. **4.** a cause of mental disquiet. **5.** *Astron.* deviation of a celestial body from regular motion around its primary due to some force other than the gravitational attraction of a spherical primary.

**pertussis** /pə'tʌsəs/, *n.* →**whooping cough.** [NL, from PER- + L *tussis* cough] – **pertussal,** *adj.*

**Peru** /pə'ru/, *n.* a republic in western South America. – **Peruvian,** *adj., n.*

**peruke** /pə'ruk/, *n.* a wig, esp. of the kind worn by men in the 17th and 18th centuries; a periwig. [F *perruque,* from It. *perrucca*]

man wearing a peruke

**perusal** /pə'ruzəl/, *n.* **1.** a reading. **2.** the act of perusing; survey or scrutiny.

**peruse** /pə'ruz/, *v.t.,* **-rused, -rusing.** **1.** to read through, as with thoroughness or care. **2.** to read. **3.** *Archaic.* to survey or examine in detail. [late ME; orig., use up, from PER- + USE, *v.*] – **perusable,** *adj.* – **peruser,** *n.*

**Peruvian bark** /pə,ruviən 'bak/, *n.* →**cinchona** (def. 2).

**perv** /pɜv/, *Colloq.* –*n.* **1.** a pervert. **2.** **have a perv,** to perv. –*v.i.* **3.** to look at lustfully (fol. by *on*). Also, **perve.**

**pervade** /pə'veɪd/, *v.t.,* **-vaded, -vading.** **1.** to extend its presence, activities, influence, etc., throughout: *spring pervaded the air.* **2.** to go, pass, or spread through. **3.** *Rare.* to go everywhere throughout (a place), as a person. [L *pervādere*] – **pervader,** *n.* – **pervasion,** *n.* – **pervasive** /pə'veɪsɪv, -zɪv/, *adj.* – **pervasively,** *adv.* – **pervasiveness,** *n.*

**perverse** /pə'vɜs/, *adj.* **1.** wilfully determined or disposed to go counter to what is expected or desired; contrary. **2.** characterised by or proceeding from such a determination: *a perverse mood.* **3.** wayward; cantankerous. **4.** persistent or obstinate in what is wrong. **5.** turned away from what is right, good, or proper; wicked. [ME, from L *perversus,* pp., turned the wrong way, awry] – **perversely,** *adv.* – **perverseness,** *n.*

**perverse verdict** /– 'vɜdɪkt/, *n.* a verdict by a jury which has refused to follow a judicial direction on a point of law.

**perversion** /pə'vɜʒən/, *n.* **1.** the act of perverting. **2.** the state of being perverted. **3.** a perverted form of something. **4.** *Psychol.* unnatural or abnormal condition of the sexual instincts (**sexual perversion**). **5.** *Pathol.* change to what is unnatural or abnormal: *a perversion of function, taste, etc.*

**perversity** /pə'vɜsəti/, *n., pl.* **-ties.** **1.** the quality of being perverse. **2.** an instance of it.

**perversive** /pə'vɜsɪv/, *adj.* tending to pervert.

**pervert** /pə'vɜt/, *v.;* /'pɜvɜt/, *n.* –*v.t.* **1.** to turn away from the right course. **2.** to lead astray morally. **3.** to lead into mental error or false judgment. **4.** to bring over to a religious belief regarded as false or wrong. **5.** to turn to an improper use; misapply. **6.** to distort. **7.** to bring to a less excellent state, vitiate, or debase. **8.** *Pathol.* to change to what is unnatural or abnormal. **9.** to affect with perversion. –*n.* **10.** *Psychol., Pathol.* one affected with perversion. **11.** one who has been perverted. [ME, from L *pervertere*] – **perverter,** *n.* – **pervertible,** *adj.*

**perverted** /pə'vɜtəd/, *adj.* **1.** *Pathol.* changed to or being of an unnatural or abnormal kind: *a perverted appetite.* **2.** turned from what is right; wicked; misguided; misapplied; distorted. **3.** affected with or due to perversion. – **pervertedly,** *adv.*

**pervious** /'pɜviəs/, *adj.* **1.** admitting of passage or entrance; permeable: *pervious soil.* **2.** accessible to reason, feeling, etc. [L *pervius*] – **perviousness,** *n.*

**per-way** /'pɜ-weɪ/, *n.* →**permanent way.**

**Pesach** /'peɪsak/, *n.* →**Passover.** Also, **Pesah.** [Heb. *pesah*]

**pesante** /pə'zænti/, *adv.* (a musical direction) heavily. [It.]

**peseta** /pə'sɛtə, -'seɪ-/, *n.* the monetary unit of Spain. *Abbrev.:* pta

**pesky** /'pɛski/, *adj.,* **-kier, -kiest.** *Chiefly U.S. Colloq.* troublesome; annoying. [b. *pesty* (from PEST) and RISKY]

**peso** /'peɪsoʊ/, *n.* **1.** the basic monetary unit of Mexico, Cuba, and the Philippines. **2.** a note or coin of this denomination. **3.** any of various monetary units or coins of Spanish America. **4.** any of certain former Spanish gold or silver coins. *Abbrev.:* p. [Sp.: lit., weight, from L *pensum,* pp., weighed]

**pessary** /'pɛsəri/, *n., pl.* **-ries.** *Med.* **1.** an instrument worn in the vagina to remedy uterine displacement. **2.** a vaginal suppository. **3.** →**diaphragm** (def. 4). [ME, from LL *pessārium,* from L *pessus,* from Gk *pessós,* orig., oval stone used in a game]

**pessimism** /'pɛsəmɪzəm, 'pɛz-/, *n.* **1.** disposition to take the gloomiest possible view. **2.** the doctrine that the existing world is the worst of all possible worlds, or that all things naturally tend to evil. **3.** the belief that the evil and pain in the world are not compensated for by the good and happiness. [L *pessimus* worst + -ISM, modelled on OPTIMISM]

**pessimist** /'pɛsəməst, 'pɛz-/, *n.* **1.** one who looks on the gloomy side of things. **2.** an adherent of pessimism.

**pessimistic** /pɛsə'mɪstɪk, pɛz-/, *adj.* pertaining to or characterised by pessimism. – **pessimistically,** *adv.*

**pessomancy** /'pɛsəmænsi/, *n.* divination from pebbles.

**pest** /pɛst/, *n.* **1.** a noxious, destructive, or troublesome thing or person; nuisance. **2.** a deadly epidemic disease; a pestilence. **3.** a disease produced by the plague bacillus. **4.** an organism harmful to agriculture. [L *pestis* plague, disease]

**pester** /'pɛstə/, *v.t.* to harass with petty annoyances, vexing importunities, or the like; torment. [? OF *empestrer* hobble (a horse); later associated with PEST]

**pest fence** /'pɛst fɛns/, *n.* a fence erected to keep out animal pests, as a rabbit fence.

**pesticide** /'pɛstəsaɪd/, *n.* a chemical substance for destroying pests, such as mosquitoes, flies, etc.

**pestiferous** /pɛs'tɪfərəs/, *adj.* **1.** carrying or producing plague. **2.** →**pestilential.** **3.** pernicious in any way. **4.** *Colloq.* mischievous, troublesome, or annoying. [L *pestifer* plague-bringing + -OUS] – **pestiferously,** *adv.*

**pestilence** /'pɛstələns/, *n.* **1.** a deadly epidemic disease. **2.** that which produces or tends to produce epidemic disease. **3.** →**bubonic plague.**

**pestilent** /'pɛstələnt/, *adj.* **1.** infectious, as a disease; pestilential. **2.** producing or tending to produce infectious disease. **3.** destructive to life; deadly; poisonous. **4.** injurious to peace, morals, etc. **5.** troublesome or annoying. **6.** pernicious or mischievous. [ME, from L *pestilens,* ppr.] – **pestilently,** *adv.*

**pestilential** /pɛstə'lɛnʃəl/, *adj.* **1.** producing or tending to produce pestilence. **2.** pertaining to or of the nature of pestilence, esp. bubonic plague. **3.** pernicious; harmful. [ME, from ML *pestilentiālis*]

**pestle** /'pɛsəl/, *n., v.,* **-tled, -tling.** –*n.* **1.** an instrument for breaking up and grinding substances in a mortar. **2.** any of various appliances for pounding, stamping, etc. –*v.t.* **3.** to pound or triturate with or as with a pestle. –*v.i.* **4.** to work with a pestle. [ME, from OF *pestel,* from L *pistum,* pp., pounded]

**pesto** /'pɛstoʊ/, *n.* a thick, uncooked sauce consisting of a puree of nuts, garlic, basil, and cheese, with oil. [It.]

**pest pear** /'pɛst pɛə/, *n.* →**prickly pear** (def. 2).

**pet**[1] /pɛt/, *n., adj., v.,* **petted, petting.** –*n.* **1.** any domesticated or tamed animal that is cared for affectionately. **2.** a person especially cherished or indulged; a favourite. **3.** a thing particularly cherished. –*adj.* **4.** treated as a pet, as an animal. **5.** especially cherished or indulged, as a child or other person. **6.** favourite: *a pet theory.* **7.** principal; most important: *pet aversion.* **8.** showing affection: *a pet name.* –*v.t.* **9.** to treat as a pet; fondle; indulge. **10.** to fondle or caress one of the opposite sex. [? backformation from *pet lamb* cade lamb, itself ? syncopated var. of *petty lamb* little lamb, where *petty* marks affection. Cf. PETCOCK]

**pet**[2] /pɛt/, *n., v.,* **petted, petting.** *–n.* **1.** a fit of peevishness: *to be in a pet.* *–v.i.* **2.** to be peevish; sulk. [apparently backformation from PETTISH]

**Pet.,** *Bible.* Peter.

**peta-** /'pitə-/, a prefix denoting $10^{15}$ of a given unit, as in *petaherty. Symbol:* P

**petal** /'pɛtl/, *n.* one of the members of a corolla. [NL *petalum* petal, from Gk *pétalon* leaf, properly neut. adj., outspread] – **petalled,** *adj.*

**petaliferous** /pɛtə'lɪfərəs/, *adj.* bearing petals.

**petaline** /'pɛtəlaɪn/, *adj.* pertaining to or resembling a petal.

**petalody** /'pɛtəloudi/, *n.* a condition in flowers, in which certain organs, as the stamens in most double flowers, assume the appearance of, or become metamorphosed into, petals. [Gk *petalṓdēs* leaf-like + -Y[3]]

**petaloid** /'pɛtəlɔɪd/, *adj.* having the form or appearance of a petal.

**petalous** /'pɛtələs/, *adj.* having petals.

**petard** /pə'tad/, *n.* **1.** an engine of war or an explosive device formerly used to blow in a door or gate, form a breach in a wall, etc. **2.** a kind of firework. **3. hoist with one's own petard,** caught in one's own trap. [F, from *péter* break wind, explode, from *pet* fart, from L *pēditum,* from *pēdere* break wind]

**petasus** /'pɛtəsəs/, *n.* a low-crowned, broad-brimmed hat worn by ancient Greeks and Romans, often represented as worn by Hermes or Mercury. [L, from Gk *pétasos*]

**petcock** /'pɛtkɒk/, *n.* a small valve or tap, as for draining off excess or waste material from the cylinder of a steam-engine or for checking the water-level in a boiler. [PET(TY) + COCK[1]]

**peter**[1] /'pitə/, *v.i.* to diminish gradually and then disappear or cease (fol. by *out*). [orig. unknown]

**peter**[2] /'pitə/, *v.i.* (in whist) to signal or call for trumps. [from the blue *Peter,* flag displayed by vessel about to sail]

**peter**[3] /'pitə/, *n. Colloq.* **1.** a till; cash register. **2.** a prison cell. **3. black peter,** a punishment cell devoid of light or furniture. **4. tickle (rat) the peter,** to ring up false amounts on a cash register, so as to pocket the extra money. [Brit. obs. *peter* portmanteau, box, parcel of any kind]

**peter**[4] /'pitə/, *n.* (formerly) a stone demijohn; now a glass flagon for beer.

**Peter Pan** /pitə 'pæn/, *n.* a man who, though ageing, still thinks of himself and behaves like a young man. [after *Peter Pan,* the boy who didn't want to grow up, hero of a play (1904) by J. M. Barrie, 1860-1937, Scottish writer]

**peter pan collar,** *n.* a small, rounded collar on a high, closefitting neckline, worn by women and children.

**Peter principle** /'pitə prɪnsəpəl/, *n.* the theory that in a hierarchy every employee tends to rise to a level just beyond his level of competence. [from *The Peter Principle* (1969) by Dr Laurence J. *Peter* and Raymond Hull]

**petersham** /'pitəʃəm/, *n.* **1.** a kind of heavy woollen cloth used for overcoats, etc. **2.** a kind of heavy overcoat formerly in fashion. **3.** a thick ribbed or corded ribbon used for belts, hatbands, etc. [named after Viscount *Petersham,* 1780-1851, English army officer]

**Peter's pence** /'pitəz pɛns/, *n.* **1.** an annual tax or tribute, originally of a penny from each householder, formerly paid by the people of certain countries to the papal see at Rome. **2.** a voluntary contribution to the pope, made by Roman Catholics everywhere.

**peter thief** /'pitə θif/, *n. Prison Colloq.* a prisoner who steals from other prisoners' cells. [PETER[3] + THIEF]

**peth** /pɛθ/, *n. Colloq.* →**pethidine.**

**pethidine** /'pɛθədin, -dən/, *n.* an analgesic similar to morphine, administered esp. in childbirth.

**petillant** /'pɛtələnt/, *adj.* →**spritzig.** [F *pétillant* sparkling]

**petiolar** /'pɛtiələ/, *adj.* (in botany) of, pertaining to, or growing from a petiole.

**petiolate** /'pɛtiəleɪt, -lət/, *adj. Bot., Zool.* having a petiole or peduncle. Also, **petiolated.**

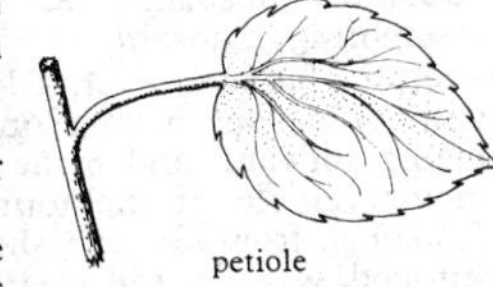
petiole

**petiole** /'pɛtioul/, *n.* **1.** *Bot.* the slender stalk by which a leaf is attached to the stem; a leafstalk. **2.** *Zool.* a stalk or peduncle, as that connecting the abdomen and thorax in wasps, etc. [F, from L *petiolus* little foot, stem, stalk, diminutive of *pēs* foot]

**petit** /'pɛti/, *adj. Chiefly Law.* small; petty; minor. [ME, from F, from Rom. stem *pit-* small]

**petit bourgeois** /– 'buʒwa, 'buə-/, *n.* a member of the petite bourgeoisie. [F; see PETTY, BURGESS] – **petit-bourgeois,** *adj.*

**petite** /pə'tit/, *adj.* (of women) little; of small size; tiny. [F]

**petite bourgeoisie** /– buʒwa'zi, -buə-/, *n.* the section of the bourgeoisie having least wealth, status, etc., as shopkeepers, clerks, etc.

**petit four** /pɛti 'fɔ/, *n.* a dainty, small, iced cake. [F: lit., little oven]

**petition** /pə'tɪʃən/, *n.* **1.** a formally drawn-up request addressed to a person or a body of persons in authority or power, soliciting some favour, right, mercy, or other benefit. **2.** a request made for something desired, esp. a respectful or humble request, as to a superior or to one or those in authority: *a petition for aid.* **3.** that which is sought by request or entreaty. **4.** *Law.* an application for an order of court or for some judicial action. **5.** a supplication or prayer, as to God. *–v.t.* **6.** to entreat, supplicate, or beg, as for something desired. **7.** to address a formal petition to (a sovereign, a legislative body, etc.). **8.** to ask by petition for (something) (fol. by *that*). *–v.i.* **9.** to present a petition. **10.** to address a formal petition. [ME, from L *petītio*] – **petitioner,** *n.*

**petitionary** /pə'tɪʃənəri/, *adj.* **1.** of the nature of or expressing a petition. **2.** *Obs. or Archaic.* (of a person) petitioning or suppliant.

**petitioning creditor** /pəˌtɪʃənɪŋ 'krɛdətə/, *n.* (in law) a creditor who applies to have the debtor adjudged bankrupt.

**petitio principii** /pəˌtɪʃiou prɪn'kɪpiaɪ/, *n.* (in logic) a fallacy in reasoning resulting from the assumption of that which in the beginning was set forth to be proved; begging the question. [L, translation of Gk *tò en archeî aiteîsthai* an assumption at the outset]

**petit jury** /pɛti 'dʒuəri/, *n.* →**petty jury.** – **petit juror,** *n.*

**petit larcency** /– 'lasəni/, *n.* →**petty larceny.**

**petit mal** /'– mæl/, *n.* a mild epilepsy in which the sufferer may lose consciousness or normal function for up to thirty seconds. Cf. **grand mal.** [F: little illness]

**petit point** /– 'pɔɪnt/, *n.* a tent stitch in embroidery worked over a single-thread canvas. [F: small point]

**petits pois** /pɛti 'pwa/, *n.pl.* small green peas. [F]

**petrel** /'pɛtrəl/, *n.* **1.** any of numerous sea-birds of the family Procellariidae, as the mutton-bird. **2.** →**storm-petrel. 3.** →**diving petrel.** [F, earlier *pétérel,* from *péter* break wind. See PETARD]

**Petri dish** /'pitri dɪʃ/, *n.* a shallow, circular dish, usu. of glass, used esp. for growing bacteria, etc. [named after J. R. *Petri,* died 1921, German biologist]

**petrifaction** /pɛtrə'fækʃən/, *n.* **1.** the act or process of petrifying. **2.** the state of being petrified. **3.** something petrified. Also, **petrification** /pɛtrəfə'keɪʃən/. – **petrifactive,** *adj.*

**petrify** /'pɛtrəfaɪ/, *v.,* **-fied, -fying.** *–v.t.* **1.** to convert into stone or a stony substance. **2.** to make rigid, stiffen, or benumb; deaden; make inert. **3.** to stupefy or paralyse with astonishment, horror, fear, or other strong emotion. *–v.i.* **4.** to become petrified. [F *pétrifier,* from *pétri-* (representing L *petra* rock, stone, from Gk) + *-fier* -FY]

**petrifying liquid** /pɛtrəfaɪɪŋ 'lɪkwəd/, *n.* a sealing coat applied to a porous surface before applying an oil-bound water paint, usu. consisting of an emulsion of drying oil and/or resin in water.

**petro-,** a word element meaning 'stone' or 'rock'. [Gk, combining form of *pétra* rock, *pétros* stone]

**petrochemical** /pɛtrou'kɛmɪkəl/, *n.* a chemical made from petroleum. [PETRO(LEUM) + CHEMICAL]

**petrodollars** /'pɛtroudɒləz/, *n.pl.* surplus trading funds of the Organisation of Petroleum Exporting Countries for investment abroad, usu. in U.S. dollars.

**petrogenesis** /pɛtrou'dʒɛnəsəs/, *n.* the mode of formation of rocks, esp. of igneous rocks. – **petrogenetic** /ˌpɛtroudʒə'nɛtɪk/, *adj.*

**petroglyph** /'pɛtrəglɪf/, *n.* a drawing or carving on rock made by prehistoric or primitive people. [F *pétroglyphe,* from Gk *petro-* PETRO- + *glyphḗ* carving]

**petrography** /pəˈtrɒgrəfi/, *n.* the scientific description and classification of rocks. – **petrographer,** *n.* – **petrographic** /pɛtroʊˈgræfɪk/, **petrographical** /pɛtroʊˈgræfɪkəl/, *adj.* – **petrographically** /pɛtroʊˈgræfɪkli/, *adv.*

**petrol** /ˈpɛtrəl/, *n.* **1.** a mixture of volatile liquid hydrocarbons, as hexane, heptane, and octane, used as a solvent and extensively as a fuel in internal-combustion engines; gasoline. **2.** *Obs.* petroleum. [F *pétrole,* from ML *petroleum* PETROLEUM]

**petrolatum** /pɛtrəˈleɪtəm/, *n.* →**petroleum jelly.** [NL. See PETROL, -ATE[2]]

**petroleum** /pəˈtroʊliəm/, *n.* **1.** Also, **rock-oil.** an oily, usu. dark-coloured liquid (a form of bitumen or mixture of various hydrocarbons), occurring naturally in various parts of the world, and commonly obtained by boring. It is used (in its natural state or after certain treatment) as a fuel, or separated by distillation into petrol, naphtha, benzine, lubricating oil, paraffin oil, paraffin wax, etc. **2.** →**petrol.** [ML, from *petro-* PETRO- + L *oleum* oil (from Gk *élaion*)]

**petroleum ether** /– ˈiθə/, *n.* an inflammable low-boiling hydrocarbon mixture produced by the fractional distillation of petroleum, used as a solvent.

**petroleum jelly** /– ˈdʒɛli/, *n.* a soft or semi-solid unctuous substance obtained from petroleum, used as a basis for ointments and as a protective dressing. Also, **petrolatum.**

**petrolic** /pəˈtrɒlɪk/, *adj.* relating to, resembling, or produced from petroleum: *petrolic ether.*

**petrology** /pəˈtrɒlədʒi/, *n., pl.* **-gies.** the scientific study of rocks, including their origin, structure, changes, etc. – **petrologic** /pɛtrəˈlɒdʒɪk/, **petrological** /pɛtrəˈlɒdʒɪkəl/, *adj.* – **petrologically** /pɛtrəˈlɒdʒɪkli/, *adv.* – **petrologist,** *n.*

**petrol pump** /ˈpɛtrəl pʌmp/, *n.* **1.** a pump at a petrol station; bowser. **2.** a pump, electrically or mechanically driven, which delivers petrol to the carburettor of an internal-combustion engine.

**petrol station** /ˈ– steɪʃən/, *n.* →**service station.**

**petronel** /ˈpɛtrənɛl/, *n.* a 16th-century firearm which was fired with the butt resting against the breast. [F *petrinal,* orig. adj., for the breast, from L *pectus* chest]

**petronella** /pɛtrəˈnɛlə/, *n.* a Scottish country dance.

**petrosal** /pəˈtroʊsəl/, *adj. Anat.* **1.** →**petrous.** *–n.* **2.** a bone forming the pyramidal part of the temporal bone. [L *petrōsus* stony, rocky + -AL[1]. See PETROUS]

**petrous** /ˈpɛtrəs, ˈpitrəs/, *adj.* **1.** *Anat.* denoting or pertaining to the hard, dense portion of the temporal bone, containing the internal auditory organs; petrosal. **2.** like stone in hardness; stony; rocky. [L *petrōsus,* from *petra* rock, from Gk]

**petticoat** /ˈpɛtikoʊt/, *n.* **1.** a skirt, esp. an underskirt, worn by women and girls; a slip. **2.** any skirtlike part or covering. **3.** *Colloq.* a woman or girl. **4.** *Elect.* the skirt-shaped portion of an insulator. *–adj.* **5.** female or feminine. **6.** wearing petticoats. [ME; see PETTY, COAT]

**pettifog** /ˈpɛtifɒg/, *v.i.,* **-fogged, -fogging. 1.** to quibble over petty details. **2.** to carry on a petty or shifty law business. **3.** to practise chicanery of any sort. [backformation from *pettifogger,* from PETTY + *fogger* (of obscure orig.)] – **pettifogger,** *n.* – **pettifoggery,** *n.*

**pettifogging** /ˈpɛtifɒgɪŋ/, *adj.* **1.** petty; mean; paltry. **2.** dishonest.

**pettish** /ˈpɛtɪʃ/, *adj.* peevish; petulant: *a pettish refusal.* [PET[1] + -ISH[1], orig., like a spoiled child] – **pettishly,** *adv.* – **pettishness,** *n.*

**pettitoes** /ˈpɛtitoʊz/, *n.pl.* **1.** the feet of a pig, esp. as food. **2.** the human feet, esp. those of a child.

**petty** /ˈpɛti/, *adj.,* **-tier, -tiest. 1.** of small importance; trifling; trivial: *petty grievances.* **2.** of lesser or secondary importance, merit, etc. **3.** having or showing narrow ideas, interests, etc.: *petty minds.* **4.** mean or ungenerous in small or trifling things: *a petty revenge.* [ME *pety,* from OF *petit.* See PETIT] – **pettily,** *adv.* – **pettiness,** *n.*

**petty cash** /– ˈkæʃ/, *n.* a small cash fund set aside to meet incidental expenses, as for office supplies.

**petty jury** /– ˈdʒʊəri/, *n.* a jury, usu. of 12 persons, empanelled to determine the facts and render a verdict pursuant to the court's instructions on the law. Also, **petit jury.** – **petty juror,** *n.*

**petty larceny** /– ˈlasəni/, *n. Law.* **1.** (formerly) the stealing of a sum of value up to one shilling. **2.** *Colloq.* a minor theft.

**petty officer** /– ˈɒfəsə/, *n.* a naval officer who does not hold a commission.

**petty patent** /– ˈpeɪtnt/, *n.* (in law) a special patent which may be more readily obtained but which may be protective for a shorter time.

**petty sessions** /ˈ– sɛʃənz/, *n.* See **court of petty sessions.**

**petulance** /ˈpɛtʃələns/, *n.* **1.** petulant spirit or behaviour. **2.** the state or quality of being petulant. **3.** a petulant speech or action.

**petulancy** /ˈpɛtʃələnsi/, *n., pl.* **-cies.** →**petulance.**

**petulant** /ˈpɛtʃələnt/, *adj.* moved to or showing sudden, impatient irritation, esp. over some trifling annoyance: *a petulant toss of the head.* [L *petulans* forward, pert, wanton, from *petere* fall on, assail] – **petulantly,** *adv.*

**petunia** /pəˈtjunjə/, *n.* **1.** any of the herbs constituting the genus *Petunia,* native to tropical America but cultivated elsewhere, bearing funnel-shaped flowers of various colours. **2.** a deep reddish purple. [NL, from Guarani *petun* tobacco + *-ia* -IA]

**petuntse** /pəˈtʊntsi/, *n.* a Chinese rock reduced mechanically to a fine powder and used as one of the ingredients of certain kinds of porcelain. Also, **petuntze.** [Chinese, from *pe* (d. var. of *pai*) white + *tun* mound, stone + *tze* (a formative element)]

**pew** /pju/, *n.* **1.** (in a church) one of an assemblage of fixed benchlike seats (with backs), accessible by aisles, for the use of the congregation. **2.** an enclosed seat in a church, or an enclosure with seats, appropriated to the use of a family or other worshippers. **3.** *Colloq.* any chair; any place to sit down: *take a pew.* [ME *puwe,* from OF *puie* balcony, from L *podia,* pl. of *podium* elevated place, balcony. See PODIUM]

**pewit** /ˈpiwɪt/, *n.* the lapwing or green plover, *Vanellus vanellus.* Also, **peewit.** [imitative of its cry]

**pewter** /ˈpjutə/, *n.* **1.** any of various alloys in which tin is the chief constituent, originally one of tin and lead. **2.** a vessel or utensil made of such an alloy. **3.** such utensils collectively. *–adj.* **4.** consisting or made of pewter: *a pewter mug.* [ME *peutre,* from OF; orig. uncert.]

**pewterer** /ˈpjutərə/, *n.* a maker of pewter utensils.

**peyote** /peɪˈoʊti, piˈoʊti/, *n.* **1.** the mescal, *Lophophora williamsii.* **2.** any of several related or unrelated cacti which grow in Mexico. [Amer. Sp., from Nahuatl *peyotl* caterpillar (referring to the downy centre of the peyote button)]

**p.f.,** *Music.* louder. [It. *più forte*]

**Pf.,** *Elect.* pico-farad.

**pfennig** /ˈpfɛnɪg, ˈfɛn-/, *n., pl.* **-igs, -ige** /-ɪgə/. a small copper-coated coin of West Germany, the hundredth part of a mark. [G. See PENNY]

**pg.,** page.

**Pg.,** **1.** Portugal. **2.** Portuguese.

**ph,** phot.

**ph.,** telephone.

**pH** /pi ˈeɪtʃ/, *n.* a measure of acidity or alkalinity, as of soil, water, etc., on a scale, running from 1 (extreme acidity) to 14 (extreme alkalinity), numerically equal to the negative logarithm of the concentration of the hydrogen ion in gram atoms per litre. Thus pH of 5 indicates a concentration of $10^{-5}$ gram atoms of hydrogen ions in one litre.

phaeton (def. 1)

**Ph,** *Chem.* phenyl.

**phacolite** /ˈfækəlaɪt/, *n.* a mineral of the zeolite group resembling chabazite.

**phaeton** /ˈfeɪtən/, *n.* **1.** a light four-wheeled carriage, with or without a top, having one or (more commonly) two seats facing forward, and made in various forms. **2.** (formerly) a motor vehicle of the touring-car type. [F *phaéton,* from L *Phaëthon,* from Gk: lit., shining. Phaethon, son of Helios, the sun-god, was allowed to drive his father's chariot for one day, but could not control the horses, and would have set the earth on fire had not Zeus killed him with a thunderbolt]

**-phage,** a word element meaning 'eating', 'devouring', used in biology to refer to phagocytes, as in *bacteriophage.* [F, from L *-phagus,* from Gk *-phagos.* See -PHAGOUS]

**phagedaena** /fædʒə'dinə/, *n.* a severe destructive eroding ulcer. Also, **phagedena.** [L, from Gk *phagédaina* an eating ulcer]

**phago-,** a word element corresponding to **-phage.** [Gk]

**phagocyte** /'fægəsaɪt/, *n.* a cell which ingests and destroys foreign particles, bacteria and other cells, found mainly in blood and lymphatic tissue. – **phagocytic** /fægə'sɪtɪk/, *adj.*

**phagocytosis** /fægəsaɪ'tousəs/, *n.* the ingestion of particle-like matter by cells, in contrast to the entrance of dissolved substance. [NL. See PHAGOCYTE, -OSIS]

**-phagous,** a word element used as an adjective termination meaning 'eating', 'feeding on', 'devouring', as in *creophagous, hylophagous, rhizophagous.* [L *-phagus,* from Gk *-phagos*]

**-phagy,** a word element used as a noun termination meaning 'eating', 'devouring', esp. as a practice or habit, as in *allotriophagy, anthropophagy.* [Gk *-phagia,* from *-phagos* -PHAGOUS]

**phalange** /'fælændʒ/, *n.* →**phalanx.** [backformation from PHALANGES]

**phalangeal** /fə'lændʒiəl/, *adj.* pertaining to, or of the nature of, a phalanx or phalanges.

**phalanger** /fə'lændʒə/, *n.* any of numerous arboreal marsupials constituting the family Phalangeridae, of the Australian region, esp. those of the genus *Phalanger* (or *Cuscus*), as *P. maculatus* (**spotted cuscus**). The group also includes the brush-tailed possums of the genus *Trichosurus.* [NL, from Gk *phálanx* bone of finger or toe; with reference to the webbed digits of the hind feet]

**phalanges** /fə'lændʒiz/, *n.* plural of **phalanx.**

**phalanx** /'fælæŋks/, *n., pl.* **phalanxes** /'fælæŋksəz/, **phalanges** /fə'lændʒiz/. **1.** (in ancient Greece) a body of heavily armed infantry formed in ranks and files close and deep, with shields joined and long spears overlapping. **2.** any body of troops in close array. **3.** a compact or closely massed body of persons, animals, or things. **4.** a number of persons, etc., united for a common purpose. **5.** (in Fourierism) a group of about 1800 persons, living together and holding their property in common. **6.** *Anat., Zool.* any of the bones of the fingers or toes. **7.** *Bot.* a bundle of stamens, joined by their filaments. [L, from Gk (defs 1, 2, 6)]

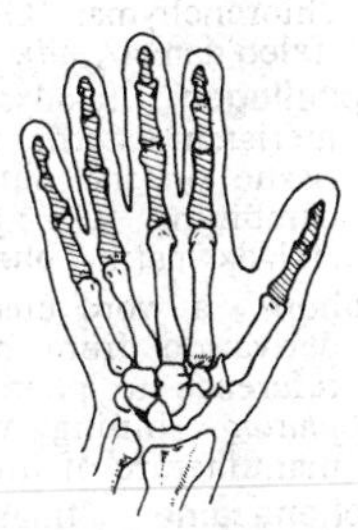

phalanx (def. 6): phalanxes of the hand

**phalaris** /fə'larəs/, *n.* any grass of the Northern Hemisphere genus *Phalaris,* esp. *P. tuberosa,* a useful fodder species.

**phalarope** /'fælərOUp/, *n.* any of three species of small aquatic birds constituting the family Phalaropodidae, resembling sandpipers but having lobate toes, as *Phalaropus lobatus* of both Old and New Worlds. [F, from NL *Phalaropūs* (genus name), from *phalaro-* (combining form representing Gk *phalāris* coot) + *-pūs* (from Gk *poús* foot)]

**phallic** /'fælɪk/, *adj.* of or pertaining to the phallus or phallicism. Also, **phallical.** [Gk *phallikós*]

**phallicism** /'fæləsɪzəm/, *n.* worship of the phallus. Also, **phallism,** *n.* – **phallicist,** *n.*

**phallus** /'fæləs/, *n., pl.* **phalluses, phalli** /'fælaɪ/. **1.** an image of the erect male reproductive organ, symbolising in certain religious systems the generative power in nature. **2.** *Anat.* the penis, clitoris, or the sexually undifferentiated embryonic organ out of which each develops. [L, from Gk *phallós*]

**-phane,** a word element indicating apparent similarity to some particular substance. [Gk *phan-,* stem of *phaínein* shine, (in pass.) appear]

**phanerogam** /'fænərougæm/, *n.* **1.** any of the Phanerogamia, an old primary division of plants comprising those having reproductive organs (stamens and pistils). **2.** a flowering plant or seed plant (opposed to *cryptogam*). [NL *phanerogamus,* from Gk *phaneró(s)* visible + *gámos* marriage] – **phanerogamic** /fænərou'gæmɪk/, **phanerogamous** /fænə'rɒgəməs/, *adj.*

**phantasm** /'fæntæzəm/, *n.* **1.** an apparition or spectre. **2.** a creation of the imagination or fancy. **3.** an illusive likeness of something. **4.** a mental image or representation of a real object. Also, **fantasm.** [LL *phantasma,* from Gk. Cf. PHANTOM]

**phantasma** /fæn'tæzmə/, *n., pl.* **-mata** /-mətə/. →**phantasm.**

**phantasmagoria** /fæn,tæzmə'gɔriə/, *n.* **1.** a shifting series of phantasms, illusions, or deceptive appearances, as in a dream or as created by the imagination. **2.** a changing scene made up of many elements. **3.** an exhibition of optical illusions produced by a magic lantern or the like, as one in which figures increase or diminish in size, dissolve, pass into each other, etc. [NL, from Gk *phántasma* phantasm + (apparently) *agorá* assembly] – **phantasmagorial, phantasmagoric** /fæntæzmə'gɒrɪk/, **phantasmagorical,** *adj.*

**phantasmagory** /fæn'tæzməgəri/, *n., pl.* **-ries.** →**phantasmagoria.**

**phantasmal** /fæn'tæzməl/, *adj.* pertaining to or of the nature of a phantasm; unreal; illusive; spectral. Also, **phantasmic.**

**phantasy** /'fæntəsi/, *n., pl.* **-sies.** →**fantasy.**

**phantom** /'fæntəm/, *n.* **1.** an image appearing in a dream or formed in the mind. **2.** an apparition or spectre. **3.** a thing or person that is little more than an appearance or show. **4.** an appearance without material substance. *–adj.* **5.** of the nature of a phantom; unreal; illusive; spectral. [ME *fantosme,* from OF, var. of *fantasme,* from LL *phantasma* PHANTASM]

**phantom limb pains,** *n.pl.* pains seemingly occurring in part of a limb which has been amputated.

**phantom pregnancy** /fæntəm 'prɛgnənsi/, *n.* a psychosomatic condition, in which a female, who is not in fact pregnant, manifests, sometimes for several months, many of the symptoms of pregnancy. Also, **hysterical pregnancy.**

**-phany,** a noun termination meaning 'appearance', 'manifestation', as of deity or a supernatural being, as in *angelophany, Christophany, epiphany, satanophany.* [Gk *-pháneia* (sometimes *-phánia*). See -PHANE]

**Pharaoh** /'fɛərou/, *n.* a title of the ancient Egyptian kings. [ME *Pharao,* OE *Pharaon,* from L, from Gk, from Heb. *Phar'ōh,* from Egyptian *per-'o* great house] – **Pharaonic** /fɛə'rɒnɪk/, *adj.*

**pharisaic** /færə'seɪɪk/, *adj.* practising or advocating strict observance of external forms and ceremonies of religion without regard to its spirit; self-righteous; hypocritical. Also, **pharisaical.**

**pharisaism** /'færəseɪ,ɪzəm/, *n.* **1.** pharisaic doctrine and practice. **2.** rigid observance of external forms of religion without genuine piety; hypocrisy. Also, **phariseeism** /'færəsi,ɪzəm/.

**pharisee** /'færəsi/, *n.* a pharisaic, self-righteous, or hypocritical person. [from the *Pharisees,* members of an ancient Jewish sect which observed strictly religious traditions and the written law. ME *Pharise,* ME and OE *farisē,* from L *Pharisēus,* from Gk *pharisaîos,* from Aram. *p'rīshāiyā* separated]

**pharm.,** **1.** pharmaceutic. **2.** pharmacopoeia. **3.** pharmacy. Also, **pharm.**

**pharmaceutical** /famə'sjutɪkəl/, *adj.* pertaining to pharmacy. Also, **pharmaceutic.** [L *pharmaceuticus,* from Gk *pharmakeutikós*] – **pharmaceutically,** *adv.*

**pharmaceutics** /famə'sjutɪks/, *n.* →**pharmacy** (def. 1). [pl. of *pharmaceutic.* See -ICS]

**pharmacist** /'faməsəst/, *n.* one skilled in pharmacy; a druggist or pharmaceutical chemist. Also, **pharmaceutist** /famə'sjutəst/.

**pharmacology** /famə'kɒlədʒi/, *n.* the science of drugs, their preparation, uses, and effects. [NL *pharmacologia,* from Gk *phármako(n)* drug + *-logia* -LOGY] – **pharmacological** /faməkə'lɒdʒɪkəl/, *adj.* – **pharmacologist,** *n.*

**pharmacopoeia** /faməkə'piə/, *n.* **1.** a book, esp. one published by authority, containing a list of drugs and medicines and describing their preparation, properties, uses, etc. **2.** a stock of drugs. [NL, from Gk *pharmakopoiía* art of preparing drugs] – **pharmacopoeial,** *adj.*

**pharmacy** /'faməsi/, *n., pl.* **-cies.** **1.** the art or practice of preparing and dispensing drugs and medicines. **2.** the occupation of a druggist. **3.** a dispensary; chemist's shop. [LL *pharmacīa,* from Gk *pharmakeía* the practice of a druggist; replacing ME *fermacie,* from OF]

**pharmocol** /'faməkɒl/, *n. Chem.* (*also cap.*) →**phenazocine hydrobromide.** [Trademark]

**pharos** /'fɛərɒs/, *n.* any lighthouse or beacon to direct seamen. [from the lighthouse, one of the seven ancient wonders of the world, on an island off Alexandria, in Egypt]

**pharyngeal** /færən'dʒiəl, fə'rɪndʒiəl/, *adj.* of, pertaining to, or connected with the pharynx. Also, **pharyngal** /fə'rɪŋgəl/.

**pharyngitis** /færən'dʒaɪtəs/, *n.* inflammation of the mucous membrane of the pharynx. [NL, from Gk *phárynx* throat + *-ītis* -ITIS]

**pharyngo-**, a word element meaning 'pharynx'. [Gk, combining form of *phárynx* throat]

**pharyngology** /færəŋ'gɒlədʒi/, *n.* the science of the pharynx and its diseases.

**pharyngoscope** /fə'rɪŋgəskoʊp/, *n.* an instrument for inspecting the pharynx.

**pharynx** /'færɪŋks/, *n., pl.* **pharynges** /fə'rɪndʒiz/, **pharynxes.** the tube or cavity, with its surrounding membrane and muscles, which connects the mouth and nasal passages with the oesophagus. [NL, from Gk: throat]

**phascogale** /'fæskəgeɪl, fæs'kagəli/, *n.* →**tuan.**

**phase** /feɪz/, *n., v.,* **phased, phasing.** *–n.* **1.** any of the appearances or aspects in which a thing of varying modes or conditions manifests itself to the eye or mind. **2.** a stage of change or development. **3.** *Astron.* **a.** the particular appearance presented by a planet, etc., at a given time. **b.** one of the recurring appearances or states of the moon or a planet in respect to the form, or the absence, of its illuminated disc: *the phases of the moon.* **4.** *Biol.* an aspect of or stage in meiosis or mitosis. **5.** *Zool.* any of the stages of development of certain animals which take on a different colour according to the breeding condition. **6.** *Chem., Physics.* a mechanically separate, homogeneous part of a heterogeneous system: *the solid, liquid, and gaseous phases of a substance.* **7.** *Physics, Electronics.* a particular stage or point of advancement in a cycle; the fractional part of the period through which the time has advanced, measured from some arbitrary origin. **8. in (out of) phase,** having (not having) the same part of one cycle elapsed at a given point of time. *–v.t.* **9.** to plan or order (services, materials, etc.) to be available when required. **10.** to introduce (into a system or the like) in stages. **11.** to adjust or synchronise (with another element in a system). **12. phase in,** to introduce gradually and synchronise into a system, or the like. **13. phase out,** to withdraw gradually from a system. [backformation from *phases,* pl. of PHASIS]

**phase contrast microscope,** *n.* a type of microscope for examining colourless transparent objects, which depends on phase differences of the transmitted light rays.

**phase modulation** /feɪz mɒdʒə'leɪʃən/, *n.* radio transmission in which the carrier wave is modulated by changing its phase to transmit the amplitude and pitch of the signal.

**phase-out** /'feɪz-aʊt/, *n.* a gradual elimination or withdrawal.

**phaser** /'feɪzə/, *n.* a device for phasing.

**phase rule** /'feɪz rul/, *n.* a law which states that for a heterogenous system in equilibrium, the sum of the number of phases and the number of degrees of freedom is equal to the number of components plus 2.

**phase shift** /'– ʃɪft/, *n.* **1.** a change of phase in a wave form. **2.** that part of one cycle of a wave form by which the wave form has been delayed.

**phase velocity** /– və'lɒsəti/, *n. Physics.* (of a wave) the velocity of the wavefronts.

**-phasia,** a word element referring to disordered speech, as in *aphasia.* Also, **-phasy.** [Gk, from *phánai* speak]

**phasing** /'feɪzɪŋ/, *n.* a musical effect caused by mixing a sound with a delayed version of the same sound, and varying delay slowly.

**phasis** /'feɪsəs/, *n., pl.* **-ses** /-siz/. a phase; an appearance; a manner, stage, or aspect of being. [L, from Gk]

**phatic** /'fætɪk/, *adj.* of speech used to make social contact, without necessarily conveying a particular meaning: *phatic communication.* [Gk *phatós* spoken + -IC]

**Ph.D.** /pi eɪtʃ 'di/, Doctor of Philosophy. [L *Philosophiae Doctor*]

**pheasant** /'fɛzənt/, *n.* **1.** any of various large, long-tailed, gallinaceous birds of the genus *Phasianus* and allied genera, originally native to Asia, esp. the **ring-necked pheasant,** *P. colchicus,* introduced and now established in a number of localities in Australia. **2.** any of various other gallinaceous birds, as, in the southern U.S., the ruffed grouse. [ME *fesant,* from AF, var. of OF *faisan,* from Pr., from L *phāsiānus,* from Gk *phāsiānós* Phasian (bird)]

common pheasant

**pheasant coucal** /– 'kukəl/, *n.* a large cuckoo, *Centropus phasianinus,* with a long, pheasant-like tail and a deep booming voice, found in damp, heavily grassed, mainly coastal areas of the northern half of Australia; swamp pheasant.

**pheasant's-eye** /'fɛzənts-aɪ/, *n.* **1.** an annual herb with bright red flowers, *Adonis annua,* native to southern Europe and south-western Asia but sometimes found as a weed elsewhere. **2.** a subspecies of a variable bulbous plant, *Narcissus poeticus,* formerly cultivated but now replaced by other forms and hybrids.

**phellem** /'fɛləm/, *n.* the layer of dead cork cells produced on the outside of a plant by the phellogen.

pheasant coucal

**phelloderm** /'fɛloʊdɜm/, *n.* a layer of tissue in certain plants, formed from the inner cells of phellogen, and consisting usu. of chlorenchyma. [Gk *phelló(s)* cork + -DERM] – **phellodermal** /fɛloʊ'dɜməl/, *adj.*

**phellogen** /'fɛlədʒən/, *n.* a layer of tissue or secondary meristem external to the true cambium and giving rise to cork tissue on the outside and phelloderm on the inside; cork cambium. [Gk *phelló(s)* cork + -GEN] – **phellogenetic** /fɛlədʒə'nɛtɪk/, **phellogenic** /fɛlə'dʒɛnɪk/, *adj.*

**phen-,** a word element used in chemical terms to indicate derivation from benzene, sometimes used with particular reference to phenol. Also, before consonants, **pheno-.** [Gk *phaino-* shining; with reference orig. to products from the manufacture of illuminating gas]

**phenacaine** /'finəkeɪn, 'fɛnə-/, *n.* a local anaesthetic, $C_{18}H_{22}N_2O_2HCl$, resembling cocaine in its action, and used chiefly for the eye. [PHEN- + A(CET)- + (CO)CAINE]

**phenacetin** /fə'næsətən/, *n.* a crystalline organic compound used as an antipyretic, etc.

**phenacite** /'fɛnəsaɪt/, *n.* a vitreous mineral, beryllium silicate, $Be_2SiO_4$, occurring in crystals, sometimes used as a gem. Also, **phenakite** /'fɛnəkaɪt/. [Gk *phénax* cheat, imposter + -ITE[1]]

**phenanthrene** /fə'nænθrin/, *n.* a colourless shiny crystalline isomer of anthracene, $C_{14}H_{10}$, derived from coal tar, and used in the dye and drug industries. [PHEN- + ANTHR(ACITE) + -ENE]

**phenazine** /'fɛnəzin/, *n.* a yellowish crystalline organic compound, $C_{12}H_8N_2$, some derivatives of which are important dyes. [PHEN- + AZ(O)- + -INE[2]]

**phenazocine hydrobromide** /fɛnə,zoʊsin haɪdrə'broʊmaɪd/, *n.* a narcotic analgesic, $C_{22}H_{25}NO \cdot HBr$. Cf. **morphine.**

**phenetidine** /fə'nɛtədin/, *n.* a liquid organic compound, $C_8H_{11}NO$, a derivative of phenetole, used in making phenacetin, etc. [PHENET(OLE) + -ID[2] + -INE[2]]

**phenetole** /'fɛnətoʊl, -tɒl/, *n.* the ethyl ether of phenol, $C_6H_5OC_2H_5$, a colourless volatile aromatic liquid. [PHEN(YL) + ET(HYL) + -OLE]

**pheno-,** variant of **phen-,** before consonants.

**phenobarbitone** /fɛnə'babətoʊn/, *n.* a hypnotic, $C_{12}H_{12}N_2O_3$, a white, odourless powder. Also, **phenobarbital** /fɛnə'babətl/.

**phenocryst** /'finəkrɪst, 'fɛnə-/, *n.* any of the relatively large and ordinarily conspicuous crystals in a porphyritic rock. [PHENO- + CRYST(AL)]

**phenol** /'finɒl/, *n.* **1.** carbolic acid, $C_6H_5OH$, a hydroxyl derivative of benzene used as a disinfectant, antiseptic, and in organic synthesis. **2.** any analogous hydroxyl derivative of benzene. [PHEN- + -OL[1]] – **phenolic** /fəˈnɒlɪk/, *adj.*

**phenolate** /ˈfinəleɪt/, *n.* a salt of phenol.

**phenolic resin** /fəˌnɒlɪk ˈrɛzən/, *n.* any of a class of synthetic thermosetting resins produced by the condensation of phenol or its derivatives with formaldehyde, used in paints, varnishes, adhesives, and plastics.

**phenology** /fəˈnɒlədʒi/, *n.* the science dealing with the influence of climate on the recurrence of such annual phenomena of animal and plant life as bird migrations, budding, etc. [short for PHENOMENOLOGY] – **phenological** /finəˈlɒdʒɪkəl/, *adj.* – **phenologically** /finəˈlɒdʒɪkli/, *adv.* – **phenologist,** *n.*

**phenolphthalein** /ˌfinəlˈθælin, ˌfinəlˈfθælin, -θeɪl-, -iən/, *n.* a white crystalline compound, $C_{20}H_{14}O_4$, used as an indicator in acid-base titration and as a laxative.

**phenomena** /fəˈnɒmənə/, *n.* plural of **phenomenon.**

**phenomenal** /fəˈnɒmənəl/, *adj.* **1.** extraordinary or prodigious: *phenomenal speed.* **2.** of or pertaining to a phenomenon or phenomena. **3.** of the nature of a phenomenon; cognisable by the senses. – **phenomenally,** *adv.*

**phenomenalism** /fəˈnɒmənəlɪzəm/, *n. Philos.* **1.** the manner of thinking that considers things as phenomena only. Cf. **positivism. 2.** the philosophical doctrine that phenomena are the only objects of knowledge, or that phenomena are the only realities. – **phenomenalist,** *n.* – **phenomenalistic** /fənɒmənəˈlɪstɪk/, *adj.*

**phenomenology** /fənɒməˈnɒlədʒi/, *n.* **1.** the science of phenomena, as distinguished from ontology or the science of being. **2.** the school of the German philosopher Edmund Husserl, 1859-1938, which stresses the careful description of phenomena in all domains of experience without regard to traditional epistemological questions.

**phenomenon** /fəˈnɒmənən/, *n., pl.* **-na** /-nə/. **1.** a fact, occurrence, or circumstance observed or observable: *the phenomena of nature.* **2.** something that impresses the observer as extraordinary; a remarkable thing or person. **3.** *Philos.* **a.** an appearance or immediate object of awareness in experience. **b.** (in Kantian philosophy) a thing as it appears to, and is constructed by, us, as distinguished from a noumenon, or thing in itself. [LL *phaenomenon,* from Gk *phainómenon,* properly neut. ppr. (that which is) appearing]

**phenotype** /ˈfinoʊtaɪp/, *n.* the observable hereditary characters arising from the interaction of the genotype with its environment. Organisms with the same phenotype look alike but may breed differently because of dominance. [PHENO(MENON) + TYPE]

**phenoxide** /fəˈnɒksaɪd/, *n.* →**phenolate.**

**phenyl** /ˈfɛnəl, ˈfinəl/, *n.* a univalent radical, $C_6H_5$, from benzene. [F *phényle.* See PHEN, -YL]

**phenyl acetate** /- ˈæsəteɪt/, *n.* a colourless liquid, $C_6H_5OOCCH_3$ or $CH_3COOC_6H_5$, used as a solvent.

**phenylalanine** /fɛnəlˈælənin/, *n.* an essential amino acid, $C_6H_5CH_2CH(NH_3^+)COO^-$, occurring in proteins.

**phenylbutazone** /fɛnəlˈbjutəzoʊn/, *n.* a synthetic pyrazolone derivative, $C_{19}H_{20}N_2O_2$, used as an anti-inflammatory drug.

**phenylene** /ˈfɛnəlin, ˈfinə-/, *n.* a bivalent organic radical, $C_6H_4$, derived from benzene by removal of two of its hydrogen atoms.

**phenylephrine** /fɛnəlˈɛfrin, finəl-, -frən/, *n.* a drug used to constrict blood vessels to reduce nasal congestion arising from the common cold or hayfever. Also, **neo-synephrine.**

**phenylketonuria** /ˌfinəlkitəˈnjuriə, ˌfɛnəl-/, *n.* the excretion of large amounts of alpha-keto acids and related compounds derived from phenylalanine, caused by inability to utilise phenylalanine; a congenital metabolic disease resulting in mental retardation. *Abbrev.:* P.K.U.

**pheromone** /ˈfɛrəmoʊn/, *n.* any of a large group of compounds secreted by animals esp. insects, in response to a stimulus, as sex, food, etc., and used as a chemical means of communication. [Gk *phérein* carry + -O- + (HOR)MONE]

**phew** /fju/, *interj.* (an exclamation of disgust, impatience, exhaustion, surprise, relief, etc.).

**phi** /faɪ/, *n.* the twenty-first letter (Φ, φ) of the Greek alphabet.

**phial** /ˈfaɪəl/, *n., v.,* **-alled, -alling.** *–n.* **1.** a small vessel as of glass, for liquids. *–v.t.* **2.** to put into or keep in a phial. [ME *fiole,* from OF, from LL *fiola,* L *phiala,* from Gk *phiálē* saucer-like drinking vessel]

**phil-,** a word element meaning 'loving', as in *philanthropy.* Also, **philo-.** [Gk, combining form of *phílos* loving, dear]

**-phil,** a word element meaning 'loving', 'friendly', or 'lover', 'friend', serving to form adjectives and nouns, as *Anglophil, bibliophil.* Also, **-phile.** [L *-philus, -phila,* from Gk *-phīlos* dear, beloved, occurring in proper names. Cf. F *-phile*]

**phil.,** **1.** philosophical. **2.** philosophy.

**Phil.,** **1.** *Bible.* Philippians. **2.** Philippine.

**philadelphia** /fɪləˈdɛlfiə/, *n.* a cream cheese with a soft, rich, moist texture. [Trademark]

**philadelphus** /fɪləˈdɛlfəs/, *n.* →**mock orange.**

**philander** /fəˈlændə/, *v.i.* (of a man) to make love, esp. without serious intentions; carry on a flirtation. [Gk *phílandros* man-loving (person), later used in fiction as proper name, given to a lover] – **philanderer,** *n.*

**philanthropic** /fɪlənˈθrɒpɪk/, *adj.* of, pertaining to, or characterised by philanthropy; benevolent. Also, **philanthropical.** – **philanthropically,** *adv.*

**philanthropist** /fəˈlænθrəpəst/, *n.* one who practises philanthropy. [PHILANTHROP(Y) + -IST]

**philanthropy** /fəˈlænθrəpi/, *n., pl.* **-pies.** **1.** love of mankind, esp. as manifested in deeds of practical beneficence. **2.** a philanthropic action, work, institution, or the like. [LL *philanthrōpia,* from Gk]

**philately** /fəˈlætəli/, *n.* the collecting and study of postage stamps, impressed stamps, stamped envelopes, postmarks, postcards, covers and similar material. [F *philatélie,* from *phil-* PHIL- + Gk *atéleia* exemption from charge] – **philatelic** /fɪləˈtɛlɪk/, **philatelical** /fɪləˈtɛlɪkəl/, *adj.* – **philatelically** /fɪləˈtɛlɪkli/, *adv.* – **philatelist,** *n.*

**-phile,** variant of **-phil.**

**Philem.,** *Bible.* Philemon.

**philharmonic** /fɪlhaˈmɒnɪk, ˈfɪləmɒnɪk/, *adj.* fond of music; music-loving, used esp. in the name of certain musical societies (**Philharmonic Societies**) and hence applied to their concerts (**philharmonic concerts**). [F *philharmonique.* See PHIL-, HARMONIC]

**philhellene** /ˈfɪlhɛlin/, *n.* a friend or supporter of the Greeks. Also, **philhellenist** /fɪlˈhɛlənəst/. – **philhellenic** /fɪlhəˈlɛnɪk/, *adj.* – **philhellenism** /fɪlˈhɛlənɪzəm/, *n.*

**-philia,** a word element used as a noun termination meaning 'fondness', 'craving' or 'affinity for'. [NL, from Gk *phílos* loving]

**philibeg** /ˈfɪlibɛg/, *n.* →**filibeg.**

**philippic** /fəˈlɪpɪk/, *n.* any discourse or speech of bitter denunciation. [from the speeches of Demosthenes, 384-322 B.C., Athenian orator, attacking *Philip,* King of Macedon; L *Philippicus,* from Gk *Philippikós* pertaining to Philip]

**Philippine** /ˈfɪləpin/, *adj.* of or pertaining to the Philippines or their inhabitants. Also, **Filipine.** [Sp. *Filipino*]

**Philippines** /ˈfɪləpinz/, **The,** *n. pl.* a republic comprising an archipelago of islands in the Pacific, south-east of China. Official name: **Republic of the Philippines.**

**philistine** /ˈfɪləstaɪn/, *n.* **1.** one looked down upon as lacking in and indifferent to culture, aesthetic refinement, etc., or contentedly commonplace in ideas and tastes. *–adj.* **2.** lacking in culture; commonplace. [named after a native or inhabitant of *Philistia,* an ancient country on the east coast of the Mediterranean; ME, from LL *Philistīnī,* pl., from LGk *Philistīnoi,* from Heb. *p'lishtīm*] – **philistinism,** *n.*

**phillumenist** /fəˈlumənəst/, *n.* a collector of matchboxes. [PHIL- + L *lūmen* light + -IST] – **phillumenistic** /fəluməˈnɪstɪk/, *adj.*

**philo-,** variant of **phil-,** before consonants, as in *philosopher.*

**philodendron** /fɪləˈdɛndrən/, *n.* a tropical American climbing plant of the family Araceae, usu. with smooth, shiny, evergreen leaves, often used as an ornamental house plant. [NL. See PHILO-, -DENDRON]

**philogyny** /fəˈlɒdʒəni/, *n.* love of women. [Gk *philogynía*] – **philogynist,** *n.* – **philogynous,** *adj.*

**philol.,** **1.** philological. **2.** philology.

**philologian** /fɪləˈloʊdʒiən/, *n.* →**philologist.**

**philologic** /fɪləˈlɒdʒɪk/, *adj.* of or pertaining to philology.

Also, **philological**. – **philologically**, *adv.*

**philology** /fəˈlɒlədʒi/, *n.* **1.** the study of written records, the establishment of their authenticity and their original form, and the determination of their meaning. **2.** linguistics. [ME *philologie*, from L *philologia*, from Gk: love of learning and literature] – **philologist, philologer**, *n.*

**philomel** /ˈfɪləmɛl/, *n. Poetic.* →**nightingale.** Also, **Philomela** /fɪləˈmɛlə/. [named after *Philomela*, daughter of a king of Athens, who was turned into a nightingale; ME, from L *philomēla*, from Gk]

**philoprogenitive** /ˌfɪloupraˈdʒɛnətɪv/, *adj.* **1.** fond of young children, esp. one's own. **2.** inclined towards having offspring.

**philos.**, **1.** philosopher. **2.** philosophical. **3.** philosophy.

**philosophe** /fɪləˈsɒf, -ˈsouf/, *n.* **1.** a philosopher of the 18th-century French Enlightenment. **2.** one who imagines himself to be an intellectual. [F]

**philosopher** /fəˈlɒsəfə/, *n.* **1.** one versed in philosophy. **2.** a person who regulates his life, actions, judgments, utterances, etc., by the light of philosophy or reason. **3.** one who is philosophic, esp. in trying circumstances. **4.** *Obs.* an alchemist or occult scientist. [ME *philosophre*, from AF; replacing OE *philosoph*, from L *philosophus*, Gk *philósophos* lover of wisdom]

**philosopher's stone** /fəˈlɒsəfəz stoun/, *n.* an imaginary substance or preparation believed capable of transmuting baser metals into gold or silver, and of prolonging life.

**philosophical** /fɪləˈsɒfɪkəl/, *adj.* **1.** of or pertaining to philosophy: *philosophical studies.* **2.** versed in or occupied with philosophy, as persons. **3.** proper to or befitting a philosopher. **4.** rationally or sensibly calm in trying circumstances: *a philosophical acceptance of necessity.* **5.** (formerly) of or pertaining to natural philosophy or physical science. Also, **philosophic**. – **philosophically**, *adv.*

**philosophise** /fəˈlɒsəfaɪz/, *v.i.*, **-phised, -phising.** **1.** to speculate or theorise; moralise. **2.** to think or reason as a philosopher. Also, **philosophize.** – **philosophiser**, *n.*

**philosophism** /fəˈlɒsəfɪzəm/, *n.* **1.** philosophising. **2.** the affectation of philosophy; spurious philosophy.

**philosophy** /fəˈlɒsəfi/, *n., pl.* **-phies.** **1.** the study or science of the truths or principles underlying all knowledge and being (or reality). **2.** any one of the three branches (natural philosophy, moral philosophy, and metaphysical philosophy) accepted as composing this science. **3.** a system of philosophical doctrine: *the philosophy of Spinoza.* **4.** metaphysical science; metaphysics. **5.** the study or science of the principles of a particular branch or subject of knowledge: *the philosophy of history.* **6.** a system of principles for guidance in practical affairs. **7.** philosophical spirit or attitude; wise composure throughout the vicissitudes of life. [ME *philosophie*, from L *philosophia*, from Gk: lit., love of wisdom]

**-philous**, a word element used as an adjective termination meaning 'loving', as in *anthophilous, dendrophilous, heliophilous.* [L *-philus*, from Gk *-philos*]

**philtre** /ˈfɪltə/, *n., v.*, **-tred, -tring.** *–n.* **1.** a potion, drug, or the like, supposed to induce love. **2.** a magic potion for any purpose. *–v.t.* **3.** to charm with a philtre. Also, *esp. U.S.*, **philter.** [F *philtre*, from L *philtrum*, from Gk *phíltron* love charm]

**phiz** /fɪz/, *n. Colloq.* a face. [short for PHYSIOGNOMY]

**phlebitis** /fləˈbaɪtəs/, *n.* inflammation of a vein. [NL, from Gk *phléps* vein + *-ītis* -ITIS] – **phlebitic** /fləˈbɪtɪk/, *adj.*

**phlebo-**, a word element meaning 'vein', as in *phlebotomy.* Also, *before a vowel*, **phleb-**. [Gk *phléps* vein]

**phlebosclerosis** /ˌflɛbouskləˈrousəs/, *n.* sclerosis or hardening of the walls of veins. [*phlebo-* (from Gk, combining form of *phléps* vein) + SCLEROSIS]

**phlebotomise** /fləˈbɒtəmaɪz/, *v.t.*, **-mised, -mising.** to subject to phlebotomy; bleed. Also, **phlebotomize.**

**phlebotomy** /fləˈbɒtəmi/, *n., pl.* **-mies.** the act or practice of opening a vein for letting blood; bleeding. [ME *flebotomie*, from LL *phlebotomia*, from Gk] – **phlebotomist**, *n.*

**phlegethon** /ˈflɛgəθɒn/, *n.* a stream of fire or fiery light. [from a fabled river of fire in Hades; Gk: lit., burning, blazing]

**phlegm** /flɛm/, *n.* **1.** *Physiol.* the thick mucus secreted in the respiratory passages and discharged by coughing, etc., esp. that occurring in the lungs and throat passages during a cold, etc. **2.** (in old physiology) that one of the four humours supposed when predominant to cause sluggishness or apathy. **3.** *Obs.* sluggishness or apathy. **4.** *Obs.* coolness or self-possession. [ME *fleume*, from OF, from LL *phlegma*, from Gk: flame, clammy humour] – **phlegmy**, *adj.*

**phlegmatic** /flɛgˈmætɪk/, *adj.* **1.** not easily excited to action or feeling; sluggish or apathetic. **2.** cool or self-possessed. **3.** of the nature of or abounding in phlegm. Also, **phlegmatical.** [LL *phlegmaticus*, from Gk *phlegmatikós*] – **phlegmatically**, *adv.*

**phloem** /ˈflouəm/, *n.* that part of a vascular bundle not included in the xylem, including sieve tubes and companion cells, parenchyma, secretory cells, etc.; bast; liber. [G, from Gk *phlóos* bark + *-ēm(a)* (passive suffix)]

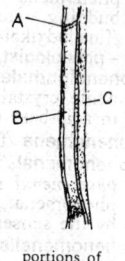

portions of phloem, showing oblique and transverse striation of the cell walls: A, sieve plate; B, sieve tube segment; C, companion cell

**phlogistic** /fləˈdʒɪstɪk/, *adj.* **1.** *Pathol.* inflammatory. **2.** *Chem. Obs.* pertaining to or consisting of phlogiston.

**phlogiston** /fləˈdʒɪstən/, *n.* a non-existent chemical which, previous to the discovery of oxygen, was thought to be released during combustion. [NL, from Gk (neut.): inflammable]

**phlogopite** /ˈflɒgəpaɪt/, *n.* a mica, $KMg_3AlSi_3O_{10}(OH)_2$, usu. yellowish brown, but sometimes reddish brown. [Gk *phlogōpós* fiery-looking + -ITE[1]]

**phlorizin** /ˈflɔrəzən, ˈflɒ-, fləˈraɪzən/, *n.* a bitter, crystalline glucoside, $C_{21}H_{24}O_{10}$, obtained from the root bark of the apple, pear, cherry, etc., and at one time used as a tonic and antiperiodic. Also, **phlorhizin, phlorrhizin, phloridzin** /fləˈrɪdzən/. [Gk *phlóos* bark + *rhíza* root + -IN[2]]

**phlox** /flɒks/, *n.* **1.** any of the herbs constituting the genus *Phlox*, native to North America, many of which are cultivated for their showy flowers of various colours. **2.** the flower of these plants. [L, from Gk: kind of plant, orig., flame]

**phlyctena** /flɪkˈtinə/, *n., pl.* **-nae** /-ni/. *Pathol.* a small vesicle, blister, or pustule. Also, **phlyctaena.** [NL, from Gk *phlýktaina*]

**-phobe**, a word element used as a noun termination meaning 'one who fears or dreads', and often implying aversion or hatred, as in *Anglophobe, Russophobe.* [F, from L *-phobus* fearing, from Gk *-phobos*]

**phobia** /ˈfoubiə/, *n.* any obsessing or morbid fear or dread. [independent use of -PHOBIA] – **phobic**, *adj.*

**-phobia**, a word element used as a noun termination meaning 'fear' or 'dread', often morbid, or with implication of aversion or hatred, as in *agoraphobia, Anglophobia, hydrophobia, monophobia.* [L, from Gk]

**phocine** /ˈfousaɪn/, *adj.* **1.** of or pertaining to the seals. **2.** belonging to the Phocinae, the pinniped subfamily that includes the typical seals. [L *phōca* (from Gk *phṓkē* seal) + -INE[1]]

**Phoebe** /ˈfibi/, *n. Poetic.* the moon personified. [in classical mythology identified with Artemis (Diana), goddess of the moon; L, from Gk *Phoíbē*, properly fem. of *Phoîbos* PHOEBUS]

**Phoebus** /ˈfibəs/, *n. Poetic.* the Sun personified. [in Greek mythology, Apollo, the Sun-god; ME *Phebus*, from L *Phoebus*, from Gk *Phoîbos*, lit., bright]

**Phoenician** /fəˈniʃən/, *n.* **1.** a native or inhabitant of Phoenicia, an ancient maritime country on the east coast of the Mediterranean. **2.** the extinct Semitic language of the Phoenicians. *–adj.* **3.** of or pertaining to Phoenicia.

**phoenix** /ˈfinɪks/, *n.* **1.** Also, **Phoenix.** a mythical bird of great beauty, the only one of its kind, fabled to live 500 or 600 years in the Arabian wilderness, to burn itself on a funeral pile, and to rise from its ashes in the freshness of youth and live through another cycle of years (often an emblem of immortality). **2.** a person or thing that is restored after death or destruction. **3.** a person or thing of peerless beauty or excellence; a paragon. Also, *U.S.*, **phenix.** [ME and OE *fēnix*, from ML *phēnix*, L *phoenix*, from Gk *phoînix*]

**phon** /fɒn/, *n.* a unit of loudness such that the number of phons of a given sound is equal to the number of decibels in a 1000 herz pure tone judged to be as loud as the sound

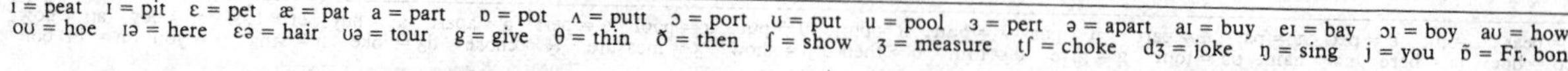

being assessed.

**phon-,** a word element meaning 'voice', 'sound'. Also, **phono-**. [Gk, combining form of *phōnē*]

**phon.,** phonetics.

**phonate** /'foʊneɪt/, *v.,* **-nated, -nating.** *–v.i.* **1.** to produce speech sounds by vibration of the vocal bands; vocalise. *–v.t.* **2.** to utter (a sound). – **phonation** /foʊ'neɪʃən/, *n.* – **phonatory,** *adj.*

**phonautograph** /fə'nɔtəgræf, -graf/, *n.* an early mechanical apparatus for recording soundwaves, consisting of a horn for collecting the sound energy which operates on a diaphragm attached to which is a needle arranged so that it makes a trace upon a smoked rotating cylinder. – **phonautographic** /foʊnɔtə'græfɪk/, *adj.* – **phonautographically** /foʊnɔtə'græfɪkli/, *adv.*

**phone**[1] /foʊn/, *n., v.t., v.i.,* **phoned, phoning.** *Colloq.* →**telephone.** [short for TELEPHONE]

**phone**[2] /foʊn/, *n.* an individual speech sound. [Gk. See PHON-] – **phonal,** *adj.*

**-phone,** a word element meaning 'sound', esp. used in names of instruments, as in *xylophone, megaphone, telephone.* [combining form representing Gk *phōnē*]

**phone freak** /'foʊn frik/, *n.* a person who makes a hobby of discovering ways to use the telephone without paying, as cracking codes, inventing devices which will bypass switchboard operators, etc.

**phone-in** /'foʊn-ɪn/, *n.* **1.** *T.V., Radio.* a program on which people are invited by a radio or television personality to ring the station and express their views on a specific subject. **2.** a large number of phone calls received by the media, a politician, etc., made by people who are expressing opinions and attempting to exercise influence in a matter of public debate. *–adj.* **3.** *T.V., Radio.* of or pertaining to a phone-in.

**phoneme** /'foʊnim/, *n.* the smallest distinctive group or class of phones in a language. The phonemes of a language contrast with one another; e.g., in English, *pip* differs from *nip, pin, tip, pit, bib,* etc., and *rumple* from *rumble,* by contrast of a phoneme (p) with other phonemes. In writing, the same symbol can be used for all the phones belonging to one phoneme without causing confusion between words, for example, the (r) consonant phoneme includes the voiceless fricative *r* phone of *tree,* the voiced *r* phone of *red,* etc. [Gk *phṓnēma* a sound]

**phonemic** /fə'nimɪk/, *adj.* **1.** of or pertaining to phonemes: *a phonemic system.* **2.** of or pertaining to phonemics; concerning or involving the discrimination of distinctive speech sounds: *a phonemic contrast.* – **phonemically,** *adv.*

**phonemics** /fə'nimɪks/, *n.* the science of phonemic systems and contrasts. – **phonemicist,** *n.*

**phonet.,** phonetics.

**phonetic** /fə'nɛtɪk/, *adj.* **1.** of or pertaining to speech sounds and their production. **2.** agreeing with or corresponding to pronunciation: *phonetic transcription.* Also, **phonetical.** [NL *phoneticus,* from Gk *phōnētikós*] – **phonetically,** *adv.*

**phonetic alphabet** /–'ælfəbɛt/, *n.* **1.** a set of symbols for transcribing speech sounds, in which each symbol represents one distinct sound or sound unit. **2.** a list of words used in certain communication channels to identify unambiguously the letters of the alphabet, as Alpha for A, Dog for D.

**phonetics** /fə'nɛtɪks/, *n.* **1.** the science of speech sounds and their production. **2.** the phonetic system, or the body of phonetic facts, of a particular language. – **phonetician** /foʊnə'tɪʃən/, *n.*

**phonetist** /'foʊnətəst/, *n.* one who uses or advocates phonetic spelling.

**phone tree** /'foʊn tri/, *n.* a group of people urged to ring and petition an MP, alderman, etc., such having been requested to do so by another member of the tree and undertaking to solicit similar action from a number of others.

**phoney** /'foʊni/, *adj.,* **-nier, -niest,** *n., pl.* **-nies** or **-neys.** *Colloq.* *–adj.* **1.** not genuine; spurious, counterfeit, or bogus; fraudulent. *–n.* **2.** a counterfeit or fake. **3.** a faker. Also, **phony.** [var. of *fawney* ring (used in confidence trick), from Irish *fáinne*]

**phonic** /'fɒnɪk/, *adj.* of or pertaining to speech sounds.

**phonics** /'fɒnɪks/, *n.* **1.** a method of teaching reading, pronunciation, and spelling based upon the phonetic interpretation of ordinary spelling. **2.** *Obs.* →**phonetics.**

**phono-,** variant of **phon-,** before consonants, as in *phonogram.*

**phonogram** /'foʊnəgræm/, *n.* **1.** a unit symbol of a phonetic writing system, standing for a speech sound, syllable, or other sequence of speech sounds, without reference to meaning. **2.** a telegram phoned to the recipient. – **phonogramic** /foʊnə'græmɪk/, *adj.*

**phonograph** /'foʊnəgræf, -graf/, *n.* *Obs. except U.S.* →**record-player.** – **phonographic** /foʊnə'græfɪk/, *adj.* – **phonographically** /foʊnə'græfɪkli/, *adv.*

**phonography** /foʊ'nɒgrəfi/, *n.* **1.** phonetic spelling, writing, or shorthand. **2.** a system of phonetic shorthand invented in 1837 by the Englishman Sir Isaac Pitman, 1813-97.

**phonol.,** phonology.

**phonolite** /'foʊnəlaɪt/, *n.* a fine-grained volcanic rock composed chiefly of orthoclase and nepheline, some nepheline varieties of which split into pieces which give a ringing sound on being struck. – **phonolitic** /foʊnə'lɪtɪk/, *adj.*

**phonologist** /fə'nɒlədʒəst/, *n.* a phonetician or phonemicist.

**phonology** /fə'nɒlədʒi/, *n.* **1.** phonetics or phonemics, or both together. **2.** the phonetic and phonemic system, or the body of phonetic and phonemic facts, of a language. – **phonologic** /foʊnə'lɒdʒɪk/, **phonological** /foʊnə'lɒdʒɪkəl/, *adj.* – **phonologically** /foʊnə'lɒdʒɪkli/, *adv.*

**phonon** /'foʊnɒn/, *n.* a quantum of energy in a solid body.

**phonoscope** /'foʊnəskoʊp/, *n.* **1.** a device by which sound is indicated by the optical phenomena it is made to produce. **2.** a device for testing the quality of strings for musical instruments.

**phonotype** /'foʊnətaɪp/, *n.* **1.** a type bearing a phonetic character or symbol. **2.** phonetic type or print.

**phony** /'foʊni/, *adj.,* **-nier, -niest,** *n., pl.* **-nies.** →**phoney.**

**-phony,** a word element used in abstract nouns related to **-phone,** as in *telephony.* [Gk *-phōnía*]

**phooey** /'fui/, *interj.* *Orig. U.S. Colloq.* an exclamation denoting contempt, disbelief, rejection, etc. [var. of PHEW]

**-phore,** a word element used as a noun termination meaning 'bearer', 'thing or part bearing (something)', as in *anthophore, gonophore, ommatophore.* [NL *-phorus,* from Gk *-phoros* bearing. Cf. F *-phore*]

**-phorous,** a word element used as an adjective termination meaning 'bearing', 'having', as in *anthrophorous.* [NL *-phorus,* from Gk *-phoros* bearing]

**phosgene** /'fɒzdʒin/, *n.* carbonyl chloride, $COCl_2$, a poisonous gas used in chemical warfare and in organic synthesis. [Gk *phôs* light + GENE]

**phosph-,** variant of **phospho-,** before vowels, as in *phosphate.*

**phosphagen** /'fɒsfədʒən/, *n.* one of the compounds (creatine phosphate in vertebrates and some invertebrates, arginine phosphate in most invertebrates), widely distributed in animal tissues, in which they act as a store of chemical energy. [PHOSPHA(TE) + -GEN]

**phosphatase** /'fɒsfəteɪz/, *n.* any of a group of enzymes that catalyses the hydrolysis of organic phosphates with the production of inorganic phosphate. [PHOSPHAT(E) + -ASE]

**phosphate** /'fɒsfeɪt/, *n.* **1.** *Chem.* **a.** (loosely) a salt or ester of phosphoric acid. **b.** the tertiary salt of orthophosphoric acid: *sodium phosphate.* **2.** *Agric.* a fertiliser containing compounds of phosphorus. [F. See PHOSPH-, -ATE[2]]

**phosphate rock** /'– rɒk/, *n.* a sedimentary rock containing calcium phosphate.

**phosphatic** /fɒs'fætɪk/, *adj.* pertaining to, of the nature of, or containing phosphates: *phosphatic slag.*

**phosphatide** /'fɒsfətaɪd/, *n.* a derivative of phosphatidic acid; phospholipid.

**phosphatidic acid** /fɒsfə,taɪdɪk 'æsəd/, *n.* the parent acid for many phospholipids, containing laevoglycerol esterified with two fatty acid residues and phosphoric acid.

**phosphatidyl choline** /fɒsfə,taɪdl 'koʊlin/, *n.* an ester of phosphatidic acid and choline, important in membranes; lecithin.

**phosphatise** /'fɒsfətaɪz/, *v.t.,* **-tised, -tising.** **1.** to treat with phosphates. **2.** to change to phosphate. Also, **phosphatize.**

**phosphaturia** /fɒsfə'tjuriə/, *n.* the presence of an excessive quantity of phosphates in the urine. [NL *phōsphātum* phosphate + -URIA] – **phosphaturic,** *adj.*

**phosphene** /ˈfɒsfin/, *n.* a luminous image produced by mechanical stimulation of the retina, as by pressing the eyeball with the finger when the lid is closed. [F, from Gk *phôs* light + *phaínein* show, shine]

**phosphide** /ˈfɒsfaɪd/, *n.* a compound of phosphorus with a basic element or radical.

**phosphine** /ˈfɒsfin/, *n.* **1.** a colourless, poisonous, ill-smelling gas, $PH_3$, which is spontaneously inflammable. **2.** any of certain organic derivatives of this compound.

**phosphite** /ˈfɒsfaɪt/, *n.* **1.** (loosely) a salt of phosphorous acid. **2.** the tertiary salt of orthophosphorous acid.

**phospho-,** a word element representing **phosphorus,** as in *phosphoprotein.* Also, **phosph-.**

**phosphofructokinase** /fɒsfəfrʌktəˈkaɪneɪz/, *n.* the controlling enzyme for the utilisation of glucose.

**phospholipid** /fɒsfəˈlɪpəd/, *n.* →**phosphatide.**

**phosphonium** /fɒsˈfoʊniəm/, *n.* the positively charged radical $PH_4^+$–, analogous to ammonium ($NH_4^+$–). [PHOSPH(OROUS) + (AMM)ONIUM]

**phosphoprotein** /fɒsfoʊˈproʊtin/, *n.* a protein composed of a molecule of protein linked with a substance other than nucleic acid or phosphatide and containing phosphorus.

**phosphor** /ˈfɒsfə/, *n.* a substance which is capable of storing energy imparted from ultra-violet or other ionising radiations, and releasing it later as light; any substance which exhibits luminescence. [see PHOSPHORUS]

**phosphorate** /ˈfɒsfəreɪt/, *v.t.,* **-rated, -rating.** to combine or impregnate with phosphorus.

**phosphor bronze** /fɒsfə ˈbrɒnz/, *n.* an alloy of copper, tin, and phosphorus, sometimes also nickel, antimony or lead; a hard, elastic metal with high corrosive resistance.

**phosphoresce** /fɒsfəˈrɛs/, *v.i.,* **-resced, -rescing.** to be luminous without sensible heat, as phosphorus. [PHOSPHOR(US) + -ESCE]

**phosphorescence** /fɒsfəˈrɛsəns/, *n.* **1.** the property of being luminous at temperatures below incandescence, as from slow oxidation, in the case of phosphorus, or after exposure to light or other radiation. **2.** this luminous appearance. **3.** any radiation emitted by a substance after the removal of the exciting agent.

**phosphorescent** /fɒsfəˈrɛsənt/, *adj.* exhibiting phosphorescence.

**phosphoretted** /ˈfɒsfərɛtəd/, *adj.* →**phosphuretted.** Also, *U.S.,* **phosphoreted.**

**phosphoric** /fɒsˈfɒrɪk/, *adj.* pertaining to or containing phosphorus, esp. in its pentavalent state.

**phosphoric acid** /– ˈæsəd/, *n.* any of three acids, orthophosphoric acid, $H_3PO_4$, metaphosphoric acid, $HPO_3$, or pyrophosphoric acid, $H_4P_2O_7$, derived from phosphorus pentoxide, $P_2O_5$, with various amounts of water.

**phosphorism** /ˈfɒsfərɪzəm/, *n.* condition of chronic phosphorus poisoning.

**phosphorite** /ˈfɒsfəraɪt/, *n.* **1.** a massive form of the mineral apatite, which is the principal source of phosphate for fertilisers. **2.** any of various compact or earthy, more or less impure varieties of calcium phosphate.

**phosphoroscope** /fɒsˈfɒrəskoʊp/, *n.* an instrument for measuring the duration of evanescent phosphorescence in different substances. [PHOSPHOR(US) + -O- + -SCOPE]

**phosphorous** /ˈfɒsfərəs, -frəs/, *adj.* containing trivalent phosphorus.

**phosphorous acid** /– ˈæsəd/, *n.* a colourless, water-soluble, crystalline acid of phosphorus, $H_3PO_3$, from which phosphites are derived.

**phosphorus** /ˈfɒsfərəs/, *n. pl.* **-ri** /-raɪ/. **1.** *Chem.* a solid non-metallic element existing in three main allotropic forms; white or yellow (poisonous, flammable, exhibits phosphorescence at room temperature); red (less reactive and less poisonous); black (electrically conducting, insoluble in most solvents). *Symbol:* P; *at. wt.:* 30.9738; *at. no.* 15; *sp.gr:* (white) 1.82 at 20°C, (red) 2.34 at 20°C, (black) 2.70 at 20°C. The element is used in forming smokescreens; its compounds are used in matches and in phosphate fertilisers. It is a necessary constituent in plant and animal life, in bones, nerves, and embryos. The radioactive isotope, **phosphorus-32,** is used as a chemotherapeutic agent. **2.** *Rare.* any phosphorescent substance. [NL, special use of L *Phōsphorus,* the morning star, from Gk *Phōsphóros,* lit., light-bringer]

**phosphorus pentoxide** /– pɛntˈɒksaɪd/, *n.* a deliquescent, colourless crystalline solid, $P_2O_5$, more correctly $P_4O_{10}$, used as a drying agent and in organic synthesis.

**phosphorylase** /fɒsˈfɒrəleɪz/, *n.* an enzyme that catalyses the breakdown of polysaccharides and polynucleotides with the formation of phosphate compounds.

**phosphorylate** /fɒsˈfɒrəleɪt/, *v.t.,* **-lated, -lating.** to break down (a polysaccharide) with addition of a phosphate group by the action of a phosphorylase. – **phosphorylation** /fɒsˌfɒrəˈleɪʃən/, *n.*

**phosphuretted** /ˈfɒsfjurɛtəd/, *adj.* combined with phosphorus, esp. in its lowest valency state. Also, **phosphoretted;** *U.S.,* **phosphoreted, phosphureted.** [*phosphuret* phosphide (from NL *phosphorētum,* with *-u-* from *phosphure*) + -ED[3]]

**phot** /fɒt, foʊt/, *n.* a non-SI unit of illuminance, equal to 10 000 lux. *Symbol:* ph [Gk *phôs* light]

**photic** /ˈfoʊtɪk/, *adj.* **1.** of or pertaining to light. **2.** pertaining to the generation of light by organisms, or their excitation by means of light.

**photinia** /fəˈtɪniə/, *n.* any deciduous or evergreen tree or shrub of the genus *Photinia* of southern and eastern Asia many of which, as a variety of *P. glabra* with bright-red immature leaves, are cultivated as ornamentals.

**photo** /ˈfoʊtoʊ/, *n., pl.* **-tos.** →**photograph.**

**photo-,** **1.** a word element meaning 'light' (sometimes used to represent 'photographic' or 'photograph'). **2.** a word element meaning liberated by light or higher energy electromagnetic radiation, as *photoelectron.* [Gk, combining form of *phôs* light]

**photoactinic** /ˌfoʊtoʊækˈtɪnɪk/, *adj.* emitting radiation having the chemical effects of light and ultraviolet rays, as on a photographic film.

**photoactive** /foʊtoʊˈæktɪv/, *adj.* capable of responding to light or other radiant energy.

**photoallergy** /foʊtoʊˈælədʒi/, *n.* abnormal sensitivity to ultraviolet light induced by specific allergens in predisposed people.

**photobathic** /foʊtoʊˈbæθɪk/, *adj.* in or relating to the stratum of ocean depth penetrated by sunlight.

**photocell** /ˈfoʊtoʊsɛl/, *n.* **1.** →**photoelectric cell. 2.** →**phototube. 3.** →**photoconductive cell.**

**photochemistry** /foʊtoʊˈkɛməstri/, *n.* the branch of chemistry that deals with the chemical action of light. – **photochemical** /foʊtoʊˈkɛmɪkəl/, *adj.*

**photochromism** /foʊtəˈkroʊmɪzəm/, *n.* a reversible process in which a solid changes colour on exposure to light and reverts to the original in the dark.

**photochromy** /ˈfoʊtoʊkroʊmi/, *n.* the art of producing photographs showing objects in natural colours.

**photochronograph** /foʊtoʊˈkrɒnəgræf, -graf/, *n.* **1.** a device for taking instantaneous photographs at regular and generally short intervals of time, as of a bird, a horse, a projectile, etc., in motion. **2.** a picture taken by such a device. **3.** a chronograph in which the tracing or record is made by a pencil of light on a sensitised surface. **4.** an instrument for measuring small intervals of time by the photographic trace of a pencil of light.

**photocomposition** /ˌfoʊtoʊkɒmpəˈzɪʃən/, *n.* a method of typesetting by photographic means; filmsetting. Also, **phototypesetting.**

**photoconduction** /ˌfoʊtoʊkənˈdʌkʃən/, *n.* conduction in certain materials stimulated by light.

**photoconductive** /ˌfoʊtoʊkənˈdʌktɪv/, *adj.* of or pertaining to a material or device which conducts electricity if exposed to light.

**photoconductive cell** /– ˈsɛl/, *n.* a photoelectric cell which uses a photoconductive material, as selenium, to register an increase in light exposure, thereby causing a greater discharge of electrical current.

**photoconductive effect** /– əˈfɛkt/, *n.* an increase in electrical conductivity when illuminated (usu. of crystals which are normally poor conductors).

**photocopier** /ˈfoʊtoʊkɒpiə/, *n.* a photostat machine.

**photocopy** /ˈfoʊtoʊkɒpi/, *n., pl.* **-copies;** *v.t.,* **-copied, -copy-**

ing. →**photostat** (defs 2 and 3).

**photodisintegration** /ˌfoutoudɪsɪntəˈgreɪʃən/, *n.* any nuclear reaction caused by a photon which results in the emission of charged fragments or neutrons.

**photodynamics** /ˌfoutoudaɪˈnæmɪks/, *n.* the science dealing with light in its relation to movement in plants.

**photoelasticity** /foutouˌilæsˈtɪsəti/, *n.* change in optical properties of transparent materials when subjected to stresses.

**photoelectric** /ˌfoutouəˈlɛktrɪk/, *adj.* pertaining to the electronic or other electrical effects produced by light. Also, **photoelectrical.**

**photoelectric cell** /– ˈsɛl/, *n.* a device used for the detection of light. Its operation may depend on the photoelectric effect (def. 1), the photovoltaic effect or photoconductive effect. Also, **photocell.**

**photoelectric effect** /– əˈfɛkt/, *n.* **1.** the emission of photoelectrons from a substance subjected to ultraviolet, X-ray or gamma ray; electromagnetic radiation. **2.** any effect whereby electrons in a substance gain energy from incident electromagnetic radiation (esp. light).

**photoelectric meter** /– ˈmitə/, *n.* an exposure meter using a photoelectric cell for the measurement of light intensity.

**photoelectron** /ˌfoutouəˈlɛktrɒn/, *n.* an electron liberated from a substance as a result of the photoelectric effect.

**photoelectrotype** /ˌfoutouəˈlɛktrətaɪp/, *n.* an electrotype made by the aid of photography.

**photoengrave** /ˌfoutouənˈgreɪv/, *v.t.*, **-graved, -graving.** to make a photoengraving of. – **photoengraver,** *n.*

**photoengraving** /ˌfoutouənˈgreɪvɪŋ/, *n.* **1.** a process of preparing printing plates for letterpress printing. **2.** a process of photographic reproduction by which a relief-printing surface is obtained for letterpress printing. **3.** a plate so produced.

**photo finish** /foutou ˈfɪnɪʃ/, *n.* a close race in which the decision is made from a photograph of the contestants as they cross the finishing line.

**photofission** /foutouˈfɪʃən/, *n.* nuclear fission caused by a high-energy photon.

**photoflash lamp** /ˈfoutouflæʃ læmp/, *n.* →**flashbulb.**

**photoflood lamp** /ˈfoutouflʌd læmp/, *n.* an incandescent tungsten lamp, in which high intensity is obtained by overloading the voltage.

**photog.,** **1.** photographic. **2.** photography.

**photogene** /ˈfoutoudʒin/, *n.* an after-image on the retina.

**photogenic** /foutəˈdʒɛnɪk, -ˈdʒinɪk/, *adj.* **1.** *Photog.* **a.** (of a person) suitable for being photographed for artistic purposes, etc. **b.** a good subject for photography; beautiful. **2.** *Biol.* producing or emitting light as certain bacteria; luminiferous; phosphorescent. **3.** *Rare.* produced by light. – **photogenically,** *adv.*

**photogeology** /ˌfoutoudʒiˈɒlədʒi/, *n.* interpretation of the geology of an area by study of aerial photographs, usu. with the aid of a stereoscope.

**photogram** /ˈfoutəgræm/, *n.* a photograph made without a camera, by exposing to light an object placed on sensitised paper.

**photogrammetry** /foutouˈgræmətri/, *n.* the process of making surveys and maps utilising photographs. [PHOTO- + -GRAM[1] (for -GRAPH) + -METRY] – **photogrammetrist,** *n.* – **photogrammetric** /ˌfoutougrəˈmɛtrɪk/, *adj.*

**photograph** /ˈfoutəgræf, -graf/, *n.* **1.** a picture produced by photography. *–v.t.* **2.** to take a photograph of. *–v.i.* **3.** to practise photography.

**photographer** /fəˈtɒgrəfə/, *n.* one who takes photographs or practises photography.

**photographic** /foutəˈgræfɪk/, *adj.* **1.** of or pertaining to photography. **2.** used in or produced by photography. **3.** suggestive of a photograph; extremely realistic and detailed: *photographic accuracy; photographic memory.* **4.** mechanically imitative, with lack of artistic feeling. Also, **photographical.** – **photographically,** *adv.*

**photography** /fəˈtɒgrəfi/, *n.* the process or art of producing images of objects on sensitised surfaces by the chemical action of light or of other forms of radiant energy, as X-rays, gamma rays, cosmic rays, etc.

**photogravure** /foutəgrəˈvjuə/, *n.* **1.** any of various processes, based on photography, by which an intaglio engraving is formed on a metal plate, from which ink reproductions are made. **2.** the plate. **3.** a print made from it. [F, from *photo-* PHOTO- + *gravure* engraving]

**photojournalism** /foutouˈdʒɜnəlɪzəm/, *n.* journalism using photographs rather than words as the principal mode of communication.

**photojournalist** /foutouˈdʒɜnələst/, *n.* a photographer who researches a particular subject, place, etc., and documents it with photographs. – **photojournalism,** *n.*

**photokinesis** /ˌfoutoukəˈnisəs, -kaɪ-/, *n.* movement occurring upon exposure to light. – **photokinetic,** *adj.*

**photolithograph** /foutouˈlɪθəgræf, -graf/, *n.* **1.** a lithograph printed from a stone, etc., upon which a picture or design has been formed by photography. *–v.t.* **2.** to make a photolithograph of.

**photolithography** /ˌfoutoulɪˈθɒgrəfi/, *n.* the technique or art of making photolithographs. – **photolithographic** /ˌfoutoulɪθəˈgræfɪk/, *adj.*

**photoluminescence** /ˌfoutouluməˈnɛsəns/, *n.* luminescence caused by absorption of the energy of light or of infra-red or ultraviolet radiation.

**photolysis** /fouˈtɒləsəs/, *n.* the breakdown of materials under the influence of light. [NL, from Gk *phōto-* PHOTO- + *lýsis* a loosing] – **photolytic** /foutouˈlɪtɪk/, *adj.*

**photom.,** **1.** photometry. **2.** photometrical.

**photomechanical** /ˌfoutouməˈkænɪkəl/, *adj.* denoting or pertaining to any of various processes for printing in ink from plates or surfaces prepared by the aid of photography. – **photomechanically,** *adv.*

**photomeson** /foutouˈmizɒn/, *n.* a meson produced by the interaction between a photon and an atomic nucleus.

**photometer** /fouˈtɒmətə/, *n.* an instrument for measuring the intensity of light or the relative illuminating power of different lights.

**photometry** /fouˈtɒmətri/, *n.* **1.** the measurement of the intensity of light or of relative illuminating power. **2.** the science dealing with this. – **photometric** /foutəˈmɛtrɪk/, **photometrical** /foutəˈmɛtrɪkəl/, *adj.* – **photometrist,** *n.*

**photomicrograph** /foutouˈmaɪkrəgræf, -graf/, *n.* **1.** a photograph of a microscopic object, taken through a microscope. **2.** →**microphotograph.** – **photomicrography** /foutoumaɪˈkrɒgrəfi/, *n.*

**photomontage** /ˌfoutoumɒnˈtaʒ/, *n.* a combination of several photographs joined together for artistic effect or to show more of the subject than can be disclosed in a single photograph.

**photomultiplier** /foutouˈmʌltəplaɪə/, *n.* a sensitive instrument which detects light by means of the photoelectric effect.

**photomural** /foutouˈmjurəl/, *n.* a very large photograph covering most of a wall as decoration.

**photon** /ˈfoutɒn/, *n.* a quantum of light energy, the energy being proportional to the frequency of the radiation. [PHOTO-; modelled on ELECTRON, PROTON]

**photonasty** /ˈfoutounæsti/, *n.* the movement of plant parts in response to changes in light intensity, as the diurnal opening of leaves and flowers.

**photoneutron** /foutouˈnjutrɒn/, *n.* a neutron resulting from photodisintegration.

**photo-offset** /foutou-ˈɒfsɛt/, *n.* a method of printing similar to offset lithography (see **offset** def. 13), in which the text or designs are impressed on metal plates by photography.

**photophilous** /fouˈtɒfələs/, *adj.* thriving in strong light, as a plant.

**photophobia** /foutouˈfoubiə/, *n.* a morbid dread or intolerance of light, as in iritis. [NL. See PHOTO-, -PHOBIA]

**photopia** /fouˈtoupiə/, *n.* the ability to see in light of an intensity sufficient to permit colour differentiation; day vision. [NL, from PHOTO- + -OPIA] – **photopic** /fouˈtɒpɪk/, *adj.*

**photoplay** /ˈfoutoupleɪ/, *n. Obs.* →**film** (def. 4b).

**photoproton** /foutouˈproutɒn/, *n.* a proton resulting from photo disintegration.

**photo relief** /ˌfoutou rəˈlif/, *n.* a process in which a model depicting the relief of a tract of country is illuminated by a light situated at the north-west corner, and photographed vertically to produce a map in which the distribution of light and shadow gives a representation of the configuration of hills and valleys.

**photoresearch** /ˌfoutouərəˈsɜtʃ, -ˈrisɜtʃ/, *n.* the acquisition of photographs for a specific purpose, esp. the illustration of a book, together usu. with the clearance of their copyright, etc.

**photoresearcher** /ˌfoutourəˈsɜtʃə/, *n.* a person engaged in photoresearch.

**photosensitive** /foutouˈsɛnsətɪv/, *adj.* sensitive to light or similar radiation.

**photospectroscope** /foutouˈspɛktrəskoup/, *n.* →**spectrograph** (def. 2).

**photosphere** /ˈfoutousfɪə/, *n.* **1.** a sphere of light. **2.** *Astron.* the luminous envelope of gas surrounding the sun. – **photospheric** /foutouˈsfɛrɪk/, *adj.*

**photostat** /ˈfoutəstæt/, *n.* **1.** a special camera for making facsimile copies of maps, drawings, pages of books or manuscripts, etc., which photographs directly as a positive on sensitised paper. **2.** Also, **photocopy.** a copy or photograph made with such a camera. *–v.t.* **3.** Also, **photocopy.** to make a photostatic copy or copies (of). *–adj.* **4.** Also, **photostatic.** denoting or pertaining to such a camera or copy. [Trademark]

**photosynthesis** /foutouˈsɪnθəsəs/, *n.* the synthesis of complex organic materials by plants from carbon dioxide, water, and inorganic salts using sunlight as the source of energy and with the aid of a catalyst such as chlorophyll; commonly used in the more restricted sense of the synthesis of carbohydrates. [NL. See PHOTO-, SYNTHESIS] – **photosynthetic** /ˌfoutousɪnˈθɛtɪk/, *adj.*

**phototaxis** /foutouˈtæksəs/, *n.* a movement of an organism towards or away from a source of light. Also, **phototaxy.** [NL. See PHOTO-, -TAXIS]

**phototelegraphy** /ˌfoutoutəˈlɛgrəfi/, *n.* the electric transmission of facsimiles of photographs, etc.; telephotography. – **phototelegraphic** /ˌfoutoutɛləˈgræfɪk/, *adj.*

**phototherapeutics** /ˌfoutouθɛrəˈpjutɪks/, *n.* that branch of therapeutics which deals with the curative use of light rays. – **phototherapeutic,** *adj.*

**phototherapy** /foutouˈθɛrəpi/, *n.* treatment of disease by means of light rays.

**photothermic** /foutouˈθɜmɪk/, *adj.* **1.** pertaining to the thermal effects of light. **2.** pertaining to or involving both light and heat.

**phototonus** /fouˈtɒtənəs/, *n.* **1.** the normal condition of sensitiveness to light in leaves, etc. **2.** the irritability exhibited by protoplasm when exposed to light of a certain intensity. [NL, from Gk *phōto-* PHOTO- + *tónos* tension] – **phototonic** /foutouˈtɒnɪk/, *adj.*

**phototopography** /ˌfoutoutəˈpɒgrəfi/, *n.* →**photogrammetry.**

**phototransistor** /ˌfoutoutrænˈzɪstə/, *n.* a transistor in which carriers are produced by absorption of light.

**phototropic** /foutouˈtrɒpɪk/, *adj.* **1.** taking a particular direction under the influence of light. **2.** growing towards or away from the light. – **phototropically,** *adv.*

**phototropism** /fouˈtɒtrəpɪzəm/, *n.* phototropic tendency or growth.

**phototube** /ˈfoutoutjub/, *n.* →**photoelectric cell.**

**phototype** /ˈfoutoutaɪp/, *n., v.,* **-typed, -typing.** *Print. Obs.* *–n.* **1.** a plate with a (relief) printing surface produced by photography. **2.** any process for making such a plate. **3.** a print made from it. *–v.t.* **4.** to reproduce by phototypy.

**phototypesetting** /foutouˈtaɪpsɛtɪŋ/, *n.* →**filmsetting.**

**phototypography** /ˌfoutoutaɪpˈɒgrəfi/, *n. Print. Obs.* the art of making printing surfaces by light or photography, by any of a large number of processes.

**phototypy** /ˈfoutoutaɪpi/, *n.* the art or process of producing phototypes.

**photovoltaic** /ˌfoutouvɒlˈteɪɪk/, *adj.* providing a source of electric current under the influence of light or similar radiation.

**photovoltaic cell** /– ˈsɛl/, *n.* any type of cell in which an electromotive force is produced as a result of the photovoltaic effect.

**photovoltaic effect** /– əˈfɛkt/, *n.* the production of an electromotive force by the incidence of light on a junction of two dissimilar materials (esp. a p-n junction or a metal-semiconductor junction).

**phr.,** phrase.

**phrasal** /ˈfreɪzəl/, *adj.* of the nature of, or consisting of, a phrase.

**phrasal verb** /– ˈvɜb/, *n.* a verb phrase consisting of a verb and a particle which together have a unitary meaning; in *How much did he put in?,* the words *put* and *in* together make a phrasal verb with the sense of *contribute.*

**phrase** /freɪz/, *n., v.,* **phrased, phrasing.** *–n.* **1.** *Gram.* **a.** a sequence of two or more words arranged in a grammatical construction and acting as a unit in the sentence. **b.** (in English) such a sequence which is smaller than a clause, as one consisting of preposition plus noun or pronoun, adjective plus noun, adverb plus verb, etc. (but not a verb and its subject). **2.** *Speech.* a word or group of spoken words which the mind focuses on momentarily as a meaningful unit and which is preceded and followed by pauses. **3.** way of speaking, mode of expression, or phraseology. **4.** a characteristic, current, or proverbial expression. **5.** a brief utterance or remark. **6.** *Music.* a group of notes forming a recognisable entity. **7.** *Dance.* a sequence of motions making up a choreographic pattern. *–v.t.* **8.** to express or word in a particular way. **9.** to express in words. **10.** *Music.* **a.** to mark off or bring out the phrases of (a piece), esp. in execution. **b.** to group (notes) into a phrase. [backformation from *phrases,* pl. of LL *phrasis,* from Gk: speech, phraseology, expression]

**phrasebook** /ˈfreɪzbʊk/, *n.* a book of phrases in foreign languages with translations.

**phrase marker** /ˈfreɪz makə/, *n.* (in linguistics) a representation, usu. in the form of a tree diagram, of the constituent structure of a sentence.

**phrasemonger** /ˈfreɪzmʌŋgə/, *n.* one who constantly uses important sounding but often meaningless phrases, usu. not of his own invention. – **phrasemongering,** *n.*

**phraseogram** /ˈfreɪziəgræm/, *n.* a written symbol, as in shorthand, representing a phrase. [PHRASEO(LOGY) + -GRAM[1]]

**phraseograph** /ˈfreɪziəgræf, -graf/, *n.* a phrase for which there is a phraseogram.

**phraseologist** /freɪziˈɒləgəst/, *n.* **1.** one who treats of phraseology. **2.** one who affects a particular phraseology.

**phraseology** /freɪziˈɒlədʒi/, *n.* **1.** manner or style of verbal expression; characteristic language: *the phraseology of lawyers.* **2.** phrases or expressions: *medical phraseology.* [NL *phraseologia,* from Gk] – **phraseological** /freɪziəˈlɒdʒɪkəl/, *adj.*

**phratry** /ˈfreɪtri/, *n., pl.* **-tries.** a grouping of clans or other social units within a tribe. [Gk *phratría*]

**phren.,** **1.** phrenological. **2.** phrenology.

**phrenetic** /frəˈnɛtɪk/, *adj.* **1.** delirious; insane; frantic; frenzied. **2.** filled with extreme emotion, esp. in religious matters. *–n.* **3.** a phrenetic individual. Also, **frenetic.** [ME *frenetike,* from OF, from L *phrenēticus,* from LGk *phrenētikós*] – **phrenetically,** *adv.*

**phrenic** /ˈfrɛnɪk/, *adj.* **1.** *Anat.* of or pertaining to the diaphragm. **2.** *Physiol.* relating to the mind or mental activity. [NL *phrenicus,* from Gk *phrḗn* diaphragm, mind + *-icus* -IC]

**phrenol.,** **1.** phrenological. **2.** phrenology.

**phrenology** /frəˈnɒlədʒi/, *n.* the theory that one's mental powers are indicated by the shape of the skull. [*phreno-* (combining form representing Gk *phrḗn* mind) + -LOGY] – **phrenologic** /frɛnəˈlɒdʒɪk/, **phrenological** /frɛnəˈlɒdʒɪkəl/, *adj.* – **phrenologist,** *n.*

**phrensy** /ˈfrɛnzi/, *n., pl.* **-sies,** *v.t.,* **-sied, -sying.** →**frenzy.**

**Phrygian mode** /ˈfrɪdʒiən moud/, *n.* (in music) a mode which can be represented by a scale of an octave of white keys on the piano from E to E.

**phthalein** /ˈθælin, ˈfθælin, -eɪ-, -iən/, *n.* any of a group of compounds (certain of whose derivatives are important dyes) formed by treating phthalic anhydride with phenols. [(NA)PHTHALE(NE) + -IN[2]]

**phthalic** /ˈθælɪk, ˈfθælɪk, -eɪ-/, *adj.* **1.** denoting or pertaining to any of three isomeric acids, $C_6H_4(COOH)_2$, derived from benzene, esp. one which is prepared by oxidising naphthalene, which forms an anhydride. **2.** denoting this anhydride. [(NA)PHTHAL(ENE) + -IC]

**phthalin** /ˈθælən, ˈfθælən/, *n.* any of a group of compounds obtained by reduction of the phthaleins.

**phthiocol** /ˈθaɪəkɒl, ˈfθaɪ-/, *n.* a yellow pigment, the vitamin K properties of which counteract haemorrhage. [PHTHI(SIS) +

-O- + -C- + -OL[1]]

**phthisic** /'θɪsɪk, 'fθɪ-/, *n.* of the phthisis. [ME *tisike,* from OF, from L *phthisica,* fem. of *phthisicus,* from Gk *phthisikós* consumptive]

**phthisical** /'θɪsəkəl, 'fθɪ-/, *adj.* pertaining to, of the nature of, or affected by phthisis. Also, **phthisicky.**

**phthisis** /'θɪsəs, 'fθɪ-/, *n.* **1.** a wasting away. **2.** tuberculosis of the lungs; consumption. [L, from Gk]

**phut** /fʌt/, *Colloq.* *–adv.* **1. go phut,** to collapse, become ruined. *–interj.* **2.** (an exclamation of annoyance, etc.) Also, **fut.** [Hind. *phatnā* to explode]

**-phyceae,** a combining form used in names of algae. [NL, from Gk *phŷkos* seaweed]

**phycology** /faɪ'kɒlədʒi/, *n.* the branch of botany that deals with algae. [Gk *phŷko(s)* seaweed + -LOGY] – **phycologist,** *n.*

**phycomycetous** /ˌfaɪkoʊmaɪ'sitəs/, *adj.* belonging or pertaining to the Phycomycetes, the simplest of the three primary subdivisions of the fungi, whose members more closely resemble algae than do the higher fungi. [NL *Phycomycētes,* pl., (from Gk *phŷko(s)* seaweed + pl. of *mýkēs* fungus) + -OUS]

**phylactery** /fə'læktəri/, *n., pl.* **-teries. 1.** either of two small leather cases containing slips inscribed with certain texts from the Pentateuch, worn by Jews, one on the head and one on the left arm during prayer to remind them to keep the law. **2.** (in early Christianity) a receptacle containing a holy relic. **3.** *Archaic.* a reminder. **4.** *Archaic.* an amulet, charm, or safeguard. [LL *phylactērium,* from Gk *phylaktḗrion* outpost, safeguard, amulet; replacing ME *philaterie,* from OF]

**phyletic** /faɪ'lɛtɪk/, *adj.* pertaining to race or species; phylogenic; racial. [Gk *phyletikós*]

**-phyll,** a word element used as a noun termination meaning 'leaf', as in *chlorophyll, cladophyll, lithophyll.* Also, **-phyl.** [Gk *phýllon*]

**phyllite** /'fɪlaɪt/, *n.* a slaty rock intermediate in metamorphic grade between slate and schist, with lustrous cleavage planes due to minute scales of mica. [PHYLL(O)- + -ITE[1]]

**phyllo-,** a word element meaning 'leaf'. Also, before vowels, **phyll-.** [Gk, combining form of *phýllon*]

**phylloclade** /'fɪloʊkleɪd/, *n.* **1.** a flattened stem or branch having the function of a leaf. **2.** →**cladode.** [PHYLLO- + Gk *kládos* branch]

**phyllode** /'fɪloʊd/, *n.* an expanded petiole resembling, and having the function of, a leaf. [F, from NL *phyllōdium,* from Gk *phyllṓdēs* leaf-like. See -ODE[1]]

P, phyllode

**phylloid** /'fɪlɔɪd/, *adj.* leaf-like.

**phyllome** /'fɪloʊm/, *n.* **1.** a leaf of a plant. **2.** a structure corresponding to it. [NL *phyllōma,* from Gk] – **phyllomic** /fə'lɒmɪk/, *adj.*

**phyllopod** /'fɪləpɒd/, *n.* **1.** any of the Phyllopoda, an order of crustaceans characterised by leaf-like swimming appendages. *–adj.* **2.** pertaining to the phyllopods. **3.** belonging to the Phyllopoda. Also, **phyllopodan** /fə'lɒpədən/. [NL *Phyllopoda,* pl. See PHYLLO-, -POD]

**phyllotaxis** /fɪloʊ'tæksəs/, *n.* **1.** the arrangement of leaves on a stem or axis. **2.** the principles governing such arrangement. Also, **phyllotaxy** /'fɪloʊtæksi/. [NL. See PHYLLO-, -TAXIS]

**-phyllous,** a word element used as an adjective termination meaning 'having leaves', 'leaved', or implying some connection with a leaf, as in *diphyllous, epiphyllous, monophyllous, polyphyllous.* [Gk *-phyllos* pertaining to a leaf]

**phylloxera** /fə'lɒksərə/, *n., pl.* **phylloxerae** /fə'lɒksəri/. any of the plant lice constituting the genus *Phylloxera,* esp. *P. vastatrix,* very destructive to grapevines. [NL, from Gk *phyllo-* PHYLLO- + *xērós* dry]

**phylo-,** a word element meaning 'tribe'. [Gk, combining form of *phŷlon* race, tribe]

**phylogeny** /faɪ'lɒdʒəni/, *n., pl.* **-nies.** the development or evolution of a kind or type of animal or plant; racial history. Cf. **ontogeny.** Also, **phylogenesis** /faɪloʊ'dʒɛnəsəs/. – **phylogenetic** /ˌfaɪloʊdʒə'nɛtɪk/, **phylogenic** /faɪloʊ'dʒɛnɪk/, *adj.* – **phylogenetically** /ˌfaɪloʊdʒə'nɛtɪkli/, *adv.*

**phylum** /'faɪləm/, *n., pl.* **-la** /-lə/. **1.** *Biol.* a primary division of the animal or vegetable kingdom, as the arthropods, the molluscs, the spermatophytes. **2.** (in the classification of languages) a group of linguistic stocks or families having no known congeners outside the group. [NL, from Gk *phŷlon* race, tribe]

**-phyre,** a word element used to form names of porphyritic rocks, as in *granophyre.* [Gk *-phyr,* meaning porphyry]

**phys., 1.** physical. **2.** physics. **3.** physiological. **4.** physiology.

**phys. chem.,** physical chemistry.

**phys. ed.,** physical education.

**physeptone** /faɪ'sɛptoʊn/, *n.* (*also cap.*) →**methadone.** [Trademark]

**phys. geog.,** physical geography.

**physic** /'fɪzɪk/, *n., v.,* **-icked, -icking.** *–n.* **1.** a medicine that purges; a cathartic. **2.** any medicine; a drug or medicament. **3.** *Archaic.* the medical art or profession. **4.** *Obs.* natural science. *–v.t.* **5.** to treat with physic or medicine. **6.** to treat with or to act upon as a cathartic; purge. **7.** to work upon as a medicine does; relieve or cure. [ME *fisyke,* from ML medical (L natural) science, from Gk *physikḗ* science of nature, properly fem. adj., pertaining to nature]

**physical** /'fɪzəkəl, 'fɪzɪkəl/, *adj.* **1.** pertaining to the body; bodily: *physical exercise.* **2.** of or pertaining to material nature; material. **3.** denoting or pertaining to the properties of matter and energy other than those that are chemical or peculiar to living matter; pertaining to physics. **4.** denoting or pertaining to the properties of matter and energy other than those peculiar to living matter; pertaining to physical science. [ME, from ML *physicālis,* from *physica* PHYSIC] – **physically,** *adv.*

**physical anthropology** /– ænθrə'pɒlədʒi/, *n.* the science concerned with evolutionary changes in man's bodily structure and the classification of modern races, in which mensurational and descriptive techniques are employed.

**physical chemistry** /– 'kɛməstri/, *n.* that branch of chemistry which deals with the relations between the physical (i.e. electrical, optical, etc.) properties of substances and their chemical composition and transformations.

**physical education** /– ɛdʒə'keɪʃən/, *n.* instruction given in exercises, gymnastics, sports, etc., for the development and health of the body. Also, **physical training.**

**physical examination** /– əgzæmə'neɪʃən, ɛg-/, *n.* an examination of the various parts of a person's body, to determine state of health, esp. as made by a physician.

**physical geography** /– dʒi'ɒgrəfi/, *n.* that part of geography concerned with natural features and phenomena of the earth's surface, as land forms, drainage features, climates, ocean currents, soils, vegetation, and animal life.

**physicality** /fɪzə'kæləti/, *n.* physical character or presence, esp. when causing a strong awareness of physical strength or of the body as an object of sexual desire: *she sensed his closeness, his physicality.*

**physical jerks** /fɪzəkəl 'dʒɜks/, *n.pl. Colloq.* physical exercises, usu. performed without apparatus, to improve the health of the body. Also, **jerks.**

**physical science** /–'saɪəns/, *n.* the study of natural laws and processes other than those peculiar to living matter, as in physics, chemistry, astronomy, etc.

**physical therapy** /– 'θɛrəpi/, *n.*→*U.S.* **physiotherapy.**

**physical training** /– 'treɪnɪŋ/, *n.*→**physical education.**

**physician** /fə'zɪʃən/, *n.* **1.** one legally qualified to practise medicine. **2.** one engaged in general medical practice as distinguished from one specialising in surgery. **3.** one who is skilled in the art of healing. [ME *fisicien,* from OF, from ML *physica* PHYSIC. See -IAN]

**physicist** /'fɪzəsəst/, *n.* a person versed in physics and its methods.

**physics** /'fɪzɪks/, *n.* the science dealing with natural laws and processes, and the states and properties of matter and energy, other than those restricted to living matter and to chemical changes. [pl. of PHYSIC. See -ICS]

**physio** /'fɪzioʊ/, *n. Colloq.* **1.** →**physiotherapy. 2.** →**physiotherapist.**

**physio-**, a word element representing **physical, physics.** [Gk, combining form of *phýsis* nature]

**physiocrat** /'fɪziəkræt/, *n.* one of a school of political economists, followers of François Quesnay, 1694-1774, French economist and physician, who recognised an inherent natural order as properly governing society, regarded land as the basis of wealth and taxation, and advocated freedom of industry and trade. [F *physiocrate.* See PHYSIO-, -CRAT] – **physiocratic** /fɪziə'krætɪk/, *adj.*

**physiognomy** /fɪzi'ɒnəmi/, *n., pl.* **-mies. 1.** the face or countenance, esp. as considered as an index to the character. **2.** the art of determining character or personal characteristics from the features of the face or the form of the body. **3.** the general or characteristic appearance of anything. [Gk *physiognōmonía* the judging of one's nature; replacing ME *fisonomie,* from ML *phisonomia*] – **physiognomic** /fɪziə'nɒmɪk/, **physiognomical** /fɪziə'nɒmɪkəl/, *adj.* – **physiognomically** /fɪziə'nɒmɪkli/, *adv.* – **physiognomist** /fɪzi'ɒnəməst/, *n.*

**physiography** /fɪzi'ɒgrəfi/, *n.* **1.** →**physical geography. 2.** the systematic description of nature in general. – **physiographer,** *n.* – **physiographic** /fɪziə'græfɪk/, **physiographical** /fɪziə'græfɪkəl/, *adj.*

**physiol.,** physiology.

**physiological** /fɪziə'lɒdʒɪkəl/, *adj.* **1.** of or relating to physiology. **2.** consistent with the normal functioning of an organism. Also, **physiologic.** – **physiologically,** *adv.*

**physiology** /fɪzi'ɒlədʒi/, *n.* the science dealing with the functioning of living organisms or their parts. [L *physiologia,* from Gk] – **physiologist,** *n.*

**physiotherapy** /ˌfɪzioʊ'θɛrəpi/, *n.* the treatment of disease or bodily weaknesses or defects by physical remedies, such as massage, gymnastics, etc. Also, **physio.** – **physiotherapist,** *n.*

**physique** /fə'zik/, *n.* **1.** human bodily structure or type: *a good muscular physique.* **2.** the structure or type of a given geographic region. [F, properly adj., physical, from L *physicus,* from Gk *physikós*]

**physoclistous** /faɪsoʊ'klɪstəs/, *adj.* having the air-bladder closed off from the mouth. [NL *Physōclīstī,* genus name (from *physō-* (combining form representing Gk *phŷsa* bladder) + Gk *kleistoí* (pl.) shut) + -OUS]

**physostigmine** /faɪsoʊ'stɪgmin/, *n.* a poisonous alkaloid, $C_{15}H_{21}N_3O_2$, constituting the active principle of the Calabar bean, used in medicine as a miotic, etc. [NL *Phȳsostigma* (from Gk *phŷsa* bellows + *stígma* stigma) + -INE[2]]

**physostomous** /faɪ'sɒstəməs/, *adj.* having the mouth and air-bladder connected by an air-duct. [NL *Phȳsostomī,* a genus name (from Gk *phŷsa* bladder + *-stomos* mouthed) + -OUS]

**-phyte,** a word element used as a noun termination meaning 'a growth', 'plant', as in *epiphyte, halophyte, lithophyte, osteophyte.* [combining form representing Gk *phytón*]

**phytin** /'faɪtən/, *n.* an organic compound containing phosphorus, occurring in seeds, tubers, and rhizomes as a reserve material. [Trademark; PHYT(O)- + -IN[2]]

**phyto-,** a word element meaning 'plant'. Also (before vowels), **phyt-.** [Gk, combining form of *phytón* plant]

**phytobezoar** /faɪtoʊ'bizoʊə/, *n.* a concentration of fibrous matter found in the stomachs of some animals, chiefly ruminants. [PHYTO- + Ar. *bezoar* poison]

**phytogenesis** /faɪtoʊ'dʒɛnəsəs/, *n.* the origin and development of plants. Also, **phytogeny** /faɪ'tɒdʒəni/. – **phytogenetic** /ˌfaɪtoʊdʒə'nɛtɪk/, **phytogenetical** /ˌfaɪtoʊdʒə'nɛtɪkəl/, *adj.* – **phytogenetically** /ˌfaɪtoʊdʒə'nɛtɪkli/, *adv.*

**phytogenic** /faɪtoʊ'dʒɛnɪk, -'dʒɪnɪk/, *adj.* of plant origin.

**phytogeography** /ˌfaɪtoʊdʒi'ɒgrəfi/, *n.* the science treating of the geographical relationships of plants.

**phytography** /faɪ'tɒgrəfi/, *n.* that branch of botany which deals with the description of plants.

**phytology** /faɪ'tɒlədʒi/, *n. Obs.* →**botany.**

**phyton** /'faɪtɒn/, *n.* the smallest part of a plant, capable of growth on its own. [Gk *phytón* plant]

**phytopathology** /ˌfaɪtoʊpə'θɒlədʒi/, *n.* the study of plant diseases.

**phytophagous** /faɪ'tɒfəgəs/, *adj.* →**herbivorous.**

**phytophthora** /faɪ'tɒfθərə/, *n.* **1.** a genus of destructive parasitic fungi which attack the roots of plants and trees. **2.** the disease caused by such a fungus. [NL, from PHYT(O)- + Gk *phthórios* destructive]

**pi**[1] /paɪ/, *n., pl.* **pis. 1.** the sixteenth letter (Π, π) of the Greek alphabet. **2.** *Maths.* **a.** the letter π, used as the symbol for the ratio (3.141 592+) of the circumference of a circle to its diameter. **b.** the ratio itself. [Gk; in def. 2 the initial letter of *periphéreia* PERIPHERY]

**pi**[2] /paɪ/, *n., v.t.,* **pied, piing.** *Chiefly U.S.* →**pie**[3].

**pi**[3] /paɪ/, *adj. Brit. Colloq.* pious, esp. hypocritically or smugly so.

**piacevole** /piatʃə'voʊleɪ/, *adv.* **1.** (a musical direction) pleasantly; agreeably. *–adj.* **2.** pleasant; agreeable. [It.]

**piacular** /paɪ'ækjələ/, *adj.* **1.** →**expiatory. 2.** requiring expiation; sinful; wicked. [L *piāculāris*]

**piaffe** /pi'æf/, *v.i.,* **piaffed, piaffing. 1.** (of a horse) to lift each pair of diagonally opposite legs in succession, as in the trot, but without going forwards, backwards, or sideways. **2.** to move slowly forwards, backwards, or sideways in this manner. [F. See PIAFFER]

**piaffer** /pi'æfə/, *n.* the act of piaffing. Also, **piaffe.** [F (inf.), from Pr. *piafá* prance, make merry, b. with *pialhà* scream (from L *pīca* magpie) and *pifrá* play the bagpipes, of Gmc orig.]

**pia mater** /paɪə 'meɪtə, piə 'matə/, *n.* the delicate, fibrous, and highly vascular membrane forming the innermost of the three meninges enveloping the brain and spinal cord. [ME, from ML: tender mother, an inexact rendering of Ar. *umm raqīqah* thin or tender mother. Cf. DURA MATER]

**pianism** /'piənɪzəm/, *n.* the set of skills and qualities of mind involved in performance on the piano, esp. in advanced players.

**pianissimo** /piə'nɪsəmoʊ/, *adv., adj., n., pl.* **-mos, -mi** /-mi/. *–adv.* **1.** (a musical direction) very softly. *–adj.* **2.** very soft. *–n.* **3.** a passage or movement played in this way. *Abbrev.:* pp [It., superl. of *piano,* from L *plānus.* See PIANO[2]]

**pianist** /'piənəst/, *n.* a performer on the piano.

**pianistic** /piə'nɪstɪk/, *adj.* suitable to or written for the piano.

**pianna** /pi'ænə/, *n. Colloq.* **1.** a piano. **2. play the pianna,** to ring up false amounts on a cash register, so as to pocket the extra money.

**piano**[1] /pi'ænoʊ, pi'anoʊ/, *n.* **1.** a musical instrument in which hammers, operated from a keyboard, strike upon metal strings. **2. grand piano,** a piano with a harpshaped body supported horizontally, called **concert grand piano** in the largest size, and **baby grand** in the smallest. **3. upright piano,** a piano with a rectangular body placed vertically. **4. square piano,** a piano with a rectangular body supported horizontally. [It., short for *pianoforte* or *fortepiano* PIANOFORTE]

**piano**[2] /pi'anoʊ/, *adv.* **1.** (a musical direction) softly. *–adj.* **2.** soft; subdued (opposed to *forte*). *Abbrev.:* p [It., from L *plānus* PLAIN[1]]

**piano accordion** /piænoʊ ə'kɔdiən/, *n.* an accordion having a piano-like keyboard for the right hand.

**pianoforte** /piænoʊ'fɔteɪ, pianoʊ-/, *n.* →**piano**[1]. [It., from *piano* soft + *forte* loud, strong]

**pianola** /piə'noʊlə/, *n.* **1.** →**player piano. 2.** *Cards.* a very good hand (one so good it plays itself). [Trademark]

**piano nobile** /pianoʊ 'noʊbəleɪ/, *n.* the principal storey of a house. [It.]

**piano roll** /pi'ænoʊ roʊl/, *n.* a roll of paper prepared for use on a player piano.

piano accordion

**piano score** /'– skɔ/, *n.* the score of a vocal work such as an opera, an oratorio etc. in which the orchestral parts have been transcribed for piano.

**piano trio** /– 'trioʊ/, *n.* **1.** an ensemble of musical instruments including a piano and, usu., a violin and a cello. **2.** a piece of music, usu. in sonata form, written for such an ensemble.

**piano wire** /'– waɪə/, *n.* wire of high tensile strength and even thickness, as used in pianos.

**piassava** /piə'savə/, *n.* **1.** a coarse, woody fibre obtained from the palms *Leopoldinia piassaba* and *Attalea funifera* of South America, used in making brooms, etc. **2.** either of these trees. Also, **piassaba.** [Pg., from Tupi *piaçaba*]

**piastre** /pi'æstə/, *n.* **1.** any of various other monetary units, as of Libya and (formerly) of South Vietnam. **2.** the old Spanish peso or dollar. Also, **piaster.** [F *piastre,* from It. *piastra* metal plate (coin), from L *emplastrum* a plaster. See PLASTER]

**piazza** /pi'ætsə, -a-/, *n., pl.* **piazzas. 1.** an open square or public place in a city or town. **2.** an arcade or covered walk or gallery, as around a public square or in front of a building. **3.** *U.S.* a veranda of a house. [It., from L *platēa,* from Gk *plateía* broad street. See PLACE]

**pibroch** /'pibrɒk/, *n.* (in the Scottish Highlands) a kind of musical piece performed on the bagpipe, comprising a series of variations on a theme, usu. martial in character, but sometimes used as a dirge or otherwise. [Gaelic *piobaireachd* pipe music, the art of playing a bagpipe, from *piobair* PIPER]

**pic** /pɪk/, *n. Colloq.* picture.

**pica**[1] /'paɪkə/, *n. Print.* **1.** a type (12 point) of a size between small pica and English. **2.** the depth of this type size (4.217 517 6 mm) as a unit of linear measurement for type, etc. [AL: book of rules for church services, apparently the same word as L *pīca* magpie. See PIE[2]]

**pica**[2] /'paɪkə/, *n.* depraved or perverted appetite or craving for unnatural food, as chalk, clay, etc., common in chlorosis, pregnancy, etc. [NL or ML, from L: magpie, with reference to its omnivorous feeding]

**picador** /'pɪkədɔ/, *n.* one of the horsemen who open a bullfight by irritating and enraging the bull with pricks of lances, without disabling him. [Sp., from *picar* prick, pierce]

**picaresque** /pɪkə'rɛsk/, *adj.* of or pertaining to rogues; applied to a type of episodic fiction, of Spanish origin, with a rogue or rogues for hero(es). [F, from Sp. *picaresco,* from *picaro* rogue, from F *Picard* native of Picardy]

**picaroon** /pɪkə'run/, *n.* **1.** a rogue, thief, or brigand. **2.** a pirate or corsair. *–v.i.* **3.** to act or cruise as a brigand or pirate. [Sp. *picarón,* augmentative of *picaro* rogue. See PICARESQUE]

**picayune** /pɪkeɪ'jun/, *n.* **1.** *Colloq.* an insignificant person or thing. **2.** *U.S.* any small coin, as a five-cent piece. *–adj.* **3.** Also, **picayunish.** *Colloq.* of little value or account; small; petty. [from *picayune,* a Spanish coin, formerly used in some southern states of the USA, from F *picaillon,* from Pr. *picaioun,* old copper coin of Piedmont, Italy, from L *pecūnia* money]

**piccabeen** /'pɪkəbin/, *n. Chiefly Qld.* →**bangalow.**

**Piccadilly bushman** /pɪkədɪli 'bʊʃmən/, *n.* (formerly) a grazier living away from his property, esp. in London's West End.

**piccalilli** /'pɪkəlɪli/, *n., pl.* **-lis.** a highly seasoned pickle, of East Indian origin, made of chopped vegetables.

**piccaninny** /'pɪkənɪni/, *n., pl.* **-nies. 1.** a Negro or coloured child. **2.** an aboriginal child. **3.** a small child. Also, **pickaninny.** [Negro pidgin E: child, from Pg. *pequenino* very little]

**piccaninny daylight** /– 'deɪlaɪt/, *n.* the time immediately before dawn breaks.

**piccie** /'pɪki/, *n.* →**pickie.**

**piccolo** /'pɪkəloʊ/, *n., pl.* **-los.** a small flute, sounding an octave higher than the ordinary flute. [It.: small]

**piceous** /'pɪsiəs, 'pisiəs/, *adj.* **1.** of, pertaining to, or resembling pitch. **2.** inflammable or combustible. **3.** *Zool.* black or nearly black as pitch. [L *piceus*]

**pichiciago** /ˌpɪtʃəsi'agoʊ, -'eɪgoʊ/, *n., pl.* **-gos.** the smallest of the armadillos, of the genera *Chlamyphorus* and *Burmeisteria* of southern South America. [S Amer. Sp. *pichiciego,* from Guarani *pichey* small armadillo + Sp. *ciego* blind (from L *caecus*)]

**pick**[1] /pɪk/, *v.t.* **1.** to choose or select carefully. **2.** to choose (one's way or steps), as over rough ground or through a crowd. **3.** to seek and find occasion for: *to pick a quarrel.* **4.** to seek or find (flaws) in a spirit of faultfinding. **5.** to steal the contents of (a person's pocket, purse, etc.). **6.** to open (a lock) with a pointed instrument, a wire, or the like, as for robbery. **7.** to pierce, indent, dig into, or break up (something) with a pointed instrument. **8.** to form (a hole, etc.) by such action. **9.** to use a pointed instrument, the fingers, the teeth, the beak, etc., on (a thing), in order to remove something. **10.** to clear (a thing) of something by such action: *to pick one's teeth.* **11.** to prepare for use by removing feathers, hulls, or other parts: *to pick a fowl.* **12.** to detach or remove with the fingers, the beak, or the like. **13.** to pluck or gather: *to pick flowers.* **14.** (of birds or other animals) to take up (small bits of food) with the bill or teeth. **15.** to eat in small morsels or daintily. **16.** to separate, pull apart, or pull to pieces (fibres, etc.). **17.** *Music.* **a.** to pluck (the strings of an instrument). **b.** to play (a stringed instrument) by plucking. **18.** *Mining.* to select good ore out of a heap. *–v.i.* **19.** to strike with or use a pointed instrument or the like on something. **20.** to eat with dainty bites. **21.** to choose; make careful or fastidious selection. **22.** to pilfer. *–v.* **23.** Some special verb phrases are:

**pick and choose,** to choose with great care, esp. fussily.

**pick at,** *Colloq.* **1.** to find fault with, in a petty way. **2.** to eat very little of: *the child picked at her food.*

**pick holes in,** to criticise; find fault with.

**pick off,** to single out and shoot.

**pick on,** *Colloq.* **1.** to annoy; tease; criticise or blame. **2.** to choose (a person) indiscriminately, esp. for an unpleasant task.

**pick out, 1.** to choose. **2.** to distinguish (a thing) from surrounding or accompanying things. **3.** to make out (sense or meaning). **4.** to extract by picking.

**pick (someone's) brains,** to find out as much as one can, from someone else's knowledge of a subject.

**pick to pieces,** to criticise, esp. in petty detail.

**pick up, 1.** to take up: *to pick up a stone.* **2.** to remove fleeces from the shearing floor. **3.** to pluck up, recover, or regain (health, courage, etc.). **4.** to learn by occasional opportunity or without special teaching. **5.** to get casually. **6.** to become acquainted with informally or casually. **7.** to take (a person or thing) into a car, ship, etc., or along with one. **8.** to bring into the range of reception, observation, etc.: *to pick up New Zealand on one's radio.* **9.** to accelerate, esp. in speed. **10.** *Colloq.* to improve. **11.** *Colloq.* to arrest.

*–n.* **24.** choice or selection. **25.** that which is selected. **26.** the choicest or most desirable part, example, or examples. **27.** the right of selection. **28.** an act of picking. **29.** the quantity of a crop picked at a particular time. **30.** *Print.* a speck of dirt, hardened ink, or extra metal on set type or a plate. **31.** *Mining.* (*pl.*) steel cutting points used on a coal cutter chain. **32.** a stroke with something pointed. **33.** →**plectrum. 34.** *Colloq.* a hypodermic needle used for taking drugs. [ME *picke* (c. G *picken*), var. of *pike,* v. (now d.), ME *piken.* Cf. OE *pīcung* pricking]

**pick**[2] /pɪk/, *n.* **1.** a hand tool consisting of an iron bar, usu. curved, tapering to a point at one or both ends, mounted on a wooden handle, and used for loosening and breaking up soil, rock, etc. **2.** any pointed or other tool or instrument for picking. **3.** *Colloq.* →**anchor.** [ME *pikk(e),* OE *pīc*]

pick[2]

**pick**[3] /pɪk/, *Weaving. –v.t.* **1.** to cast (a shuttle). *–n.* **2.** (in a loom) one passage of the shuttle. **3.** a single filling yarn. [var. of PITCH[1]]

**pick**[4] /pɪk/, *n.* **1.** a sparse covering of new fodder appearing after light rain, insufficient for prolonged grazing. **2.** **good pick,** an area where stock can graze: *a good pick in the netted paddock.*

**pickaback** /'pɪkəbæk/, *n.* →**piggyback.**

**pickaninny** /'pɪkənɪni/, *n., pl.* **-nies.** →**piccaninny.**

**pickaxe** /'pɪkæks/, *n., v.,* **-axed, -axing.** *–n.* **1.** a pick, esp. a mattock. *–v.t.* **2.** to cut or clear away with a pickaxe. *–v.i.* **3.** to use a pickaxe. Also, *U.S.,* **pickax.** [PICK[2] + AXE; replacing ME *picois,* from OF (cf. OF *pic,* OE *pīc* PIKE[3])]

**picked** /pɪkt/, *adj.* **1.** specially chosen or selected: *a crew of picked men.* **2.** cleared or cleaned, as of refuse parts, by picking. [PICK[1], *v.* + -ED[2]]

**picker**[1] /'pɪkə/, *n.* **1.** one who picks. **2.** one who plucks or gathers fruit, flowers, etc. **3.** *Mining.* a person who picks out the low-grade coal as it moves along a belt. **4.** →**picker-up.** [PICK[1], *v.* + -ER[1]]

**picker**[2] /ˈpɪkə/, *n. Weaving.* **1.** a tool or instrument for picking. **2.** the piece that throws the shuttle of the loom through the warp. **3.** one who works a picker. [PICK[3], *v.* + -er[1]]

**pickerel** /ˈpɪkərəl/, *n., pl.* **-rels,** (*esp. collectively*) **-rel.** any of various species of pike, esp. one of the smaller species, as the **chain pickerel,** *Esox niger,* and the **mud pickerel,** *Esox vermiculatus.* [ME *pykerel,* from PIKE[1] + -REL]

**pickerelweed** /ˈpɪkərəlwid/, *n.* any plant of the American genus *Pontederia,* esp. *P. cordata,* a blue-flowered herb common in shallow fresh water.

**picker-up** /pɪkər-ˈʌp/, *n.* **1.** Also, **picker.** a shearing hand who gathers the fleece from the floor and puts it on the sorting table. **2.** →**sweeper** (def. 2).

**picket** /ˈpɪkət/, *n.* **1.** a pointed post, stake, pale, or peg, as for driving into the ground in making a stockade, for placing vertically to form the main part of a fence (**picket fence**), for driving into the ground to fasten something to, etc. **2.** a person or a body of persons stationed by a trade union or the like before a place of work and attempting to dissuade or prevent workers from entering the building during a strike. **3.** *Mil.* a small detached body of troops, posted out from a force to warn against an enemy's approach. *–v.t.* **4.** to enclose, fence, or make secure with pickets. **5.** to fasten or tether to a picket. **6.** to place pickets at, as during a strike. **7.** *Mil.* **a.** to guard, as a camp, by or as pickets. **b.** *Obs.* to post as a picket. *–v.i.* **8.** to stand or march by a place of employment as a picket. [F *piquet* pointed stake, military picket, diminutive of *pic* a pick; in other senses connected with *piquer* prick, pierce, with diminutive suffix. See -ET] – **picketer,** *n.*

**picket fence** /– ˈfɛns/, *n.* a fence made of wooden slats, close-set vertically, and attached to horizontal timbers fixed to posts in the ground.

**picket line** /ˈ– laɪn/, *n.* a line of persons forming a picket (def. 2).

**pickie** /ˈpɪki/, *n. Colloq.* **1.** picture, as a photograph, illustration, etc. **2.** →**film** (def. 4b). **3.** (*pl.*) →**cinema.** Also, **piccie, pikkie.**

**picking** /ˈpɪkɪŋ/, *n.* **1.** the act of one who or that which picks. **2.** that which is or may be picked or picked up. **3.** the amount picked. **4.** (*pl.*) things, portions, or scraps remaining and worth picking up or appropriating. **5.** (*pl.*) pilferings, or perquisites obtained by means not strictly honest. [PICK[1] + -ING[1]]

**pickle** /ˈpɪkəl/, *n., v.,* **-led, -ling.** *–n.* **1.** (*oft. pl.*) vegetables, as cucumbers, onions, cauliflowers, etc., preserved in vinegar, brine, etc., and eaten as a relish. **2.** anything preserved in a pickling liquid. **3.** a liquid or marinade prepared with salt or vinegar for the preservation of fish, meat, vegetables, etc., or for the hardening of wood, leather, etc. **4.** a pickled article of food, esp. cucumber. **5.** *Metall.* an acid or other chemical solution in which metal objects are dipped to remove oxide scale or other adhering substances. **6.** *Colloq.* a predicament. **7.** a mischievous child. **8. have a rod in pickle,** have a punishment ready. *–v.t.* **9.** to preserve or steep in pickle. **10.** to clean or treat (objects) in a chemical pickle. [ME *pekille, pykyl,* from MD or MLG *pekel*(*e*). Cf. G *Pökel* brine]

**pickled** /ˈpɪkəld/, *adj.* **1.** preserved or hardened in pickle. **2.** *Colloq.* drunk.

**picklock** /ˈpɪklɒk/, *n.* **1.** a person who picks locks. **2.** a thief. **3.** an instrument for picking locks.

**pick-me-up** /ˈpɪk-mi-ʌp/, *n. Colloq.* **1.** a stimulating or refreshing drink, esp. alcoholic. **2.** any restorative, such as a meal or drink.

**pickpocket** /ˈpɪkpɒkət/, *n.* one who steals from the pockets, handbags, etc., of people in public places.

**pickthank** /ˈpɪkθæŋk/, *n.* one who curries favour by sycophancy or tale-bearing.

**pick-up** /ˈpɪk-ʌp/, *n.* **1.** *Colloq.* an informal or casual acquaintance, esp. one made in the hope of sexual adventure. **2.** Also, **pick-up truck.** a small, open-bodied delivery lorry, built on a chassis comparable to that of a passenger car. **3.** *Sport.* the act of fielding a ball after it hits the ground. **4.** *Radio.* **a.** the process of receiving soundwaves in the transmitting set in order to change them into electrical waves. **b.** a receiving or recording device as in a tape-recorder; a microphone. **c.** the place at which a broadcast is being transmitted. **d.** interference. **5.** *Television.* **a.** the change of light energy into electrical energy in the transmitting set. **b.** the device used. **6.** Also, **cartridge.** a device which generates electric or acoustic impulses in accordance with the mechanical variations impressed upon a gramophone record (**gramophone pick-up**). **7.** *Motor Vehicles.* a capacity for rapid acceleration. **8.** a stop made to collect a passenger or item of freight, as by a taxi, bus, etc. **9.** the passenger or item so collected. **10.** *Colloq.* a free lift in a motor vehicle. **11.** *Colloq.* **a.** improvement. **b.** →**pick-me-up.**

**pick-up arm** /ˈ– am/, *n.* the free-swinging arm of a gramophone which contains the pick-up.

**pick-up baler** /ˈ– beɪlə/, *n.* an automatic hay-baler used to bale winnowed hay.

**pick-up tube** /ˈ– tjub/, *n.* a tube in a television camera in which an image is focused by means of a lens system, then scanned to produce an electrical representation of the picture.

**Pickwickian** /pɪkˈwɪkiən/, *adj.* (of the use or interpretation of an expression) unusual, or intended to be understood in an unusual sense; recondite. [from Samuel *Pickwick,* the benevolent, naive founder of the Pickwick Club, in *The Pickwick Papers* by Charles Dickens, 1812-70, English novelist]

**picky** /ˈpɪki/, *adj.* petty; mean-minded; obsessed with detail.

**picloran** /pɪˈklɔrən/, *n.* a herbicide, 4-amino-3, 5, 6-trichloro-picolinic acid, used for the control of woody vegetation and noxious weeds.

**picnic** /ˈpɪknɪk/, *n., v.,* **-nicked, -nicking.** *–n.* **1.** an outing or excursion, typically one in which those taking part carry food with them and share a meal in the open air. **2.** the meal eaten on such an outing. **3.** *Colloq.* an enjoyable experience or time. **4.** *Colloq.* an easy undertaking. **5.** *Colloq.* an awkward situation; a hullaballoo. **6. be no picnic,** (of an event, chore, etc.) to be difficult or unpleasant: *compiling a dictionary is no picnic.* *–v.i.* **7.** to hold, or take part in, a picnic. [F *pique-nique;* orig. unknown] – **picknicker,** *n.*

**picnic races** /– ˈreɪsəz/, *n. pl.* horseraces held in the country, usu. for amateurs.

**pico-** /ˈpikoʊ-/, a prefix denoting $10^{-12}$ of a given unit, as in *picofarad. Symbol:* p [Sp. *pico* odd number, peak]

**picoline** /ˈpɪkəlin, -laɪn/, *n.* any of three isomeric derivatives of pyridine, $CH_3C_5H_4N$, obtained from coal tar as colourless oily liquids with a strong smell. [L *pix* pitch + *ol*(*eum*) oil + -INE[2]]

**picolinic acid** /pɪkəˌlɪnɪk ˈæsəd/, *n.* a crystalline acid, $C_5H_4N(COOH)$, obtained by oxidation from an isomer of picoline.

**picot** /ˈpikoʊ/, *n., v.,* **picoted** /ˈpikoʊd/, **picoting** /ˈpikoʊɪŋ/. *–n.* **1.** one of a number of ornamental loops in embroidery, or along the edge of lace, ribbon, etc. *–v.t.* **2.** to make or ornament with picots. [F, diminutive of *pic* a pick, something pointed. See PIKE[2]]

**picotee** /pɪkəˈti/, *n.* a variety of carnation whose petals have an outer margin of another colour, usu. red. [F *picoté,* pp. of *picoter* mark with pricks or spots. See PICOT]

**picrate** /ˈpɪkreɪt, ˈpɪkrət/, *n.* a salt or ester of picric acid.

**picric acid** /pɪkrɪk ˈæsəd/, *n.* an intensely bitter yellow acid, $C_6H_2OH(NO_2)_3$ used as a dye and an explosive. [Gk *pikrós* bitter + -IC]

**picrite** /ˈpɪkraɪt/, *n.* a granular igneous rock composed chiefly of olivine and augite, but containing small amounts of felspar. [Gk *pikrós* bitter + -ITE[1]]

**pictograph** /ˈpɪktəgræf, -graf/, *n.* **1.** a record consisting of pictorial symbols. **2.** a pictorial sign or symbol. [L *pictus,* pp., painted, represented pictorially + -O- + -GRAPH] – **pictographic** /pɪktəˈgræfɪk/, *adj.* – **pictographically** /pɪktəˈgræfɪkli/, *adv.*

**pictography** /pɪkˈtɒgrəfi/, *n.* the use of pictographs; picture writing.

**pictorella mannikin** /ˌpɪktərelə ˈmænəkən/, *n.* a species of finch, *Lonchura pectoralis,* adapted to arid country and found in northern Australia; white-breasted finch. Also, **pictorella, pictorella finch, pictorella munia.**

**pictorial** /pɪkˈtɔriəl/, *adj.* **1.** pertaining to, expressed in, or of the nature of, a picture or pictures: *pictorial writing.* **2.** illustrated by or containing pictures: *a pictorial history.* **3.** of or pertaining to a painter or maker of pictures. **4.** suggestive of, or representing as if by, a picture; graphic. *–n.* **5.** a periodical in which pictures are the leading feature. [LL *pictōrius* (from L *pictor* painter) + -AL[1]] – **pictorially,** *adv.*

**picture** /ˈpɪktʃə/, *n., v.,* **-tured, -turing.** *–n.* **1.** a representation, upon a surface, usu. flat, as a painting, drawing or photograph, etc. **2.** any visible image, however produced: *the pictures in the fire, the pictures made by reflections in a pool of water.* **3.** a mental image: *a picture of what would happen.* **4.** a verbal description intended to be or taken as informative: *Gibbon's picture of ancient Rome.* **5.** a tableau, as in theatrical representation. **6.** a very beautiful object, esp. a person: *she looks a picture in her new dress.* **7.** →**film** (def. 4b). **8. the pictures,** a cinema. **9.** the image or counterpart (of someone else). **10.** an object or person possessing a quality in such a high degree as to seem to embody that quality: *she is a picture of health.* **11.** a situation or set of circumstances: *the employment picture.* **12. get the picture, be in the picture,** to understand the situation. **13. put in the picture,** make fully cognisant; inform. **14.** Also, **clinical picture.** *Pathol.* the overall view of a case. *–v.t.* **15.** to form a mental image of: *he couldn't picture himself doing such a thing.* **16.** to describe, verbally and, usually, plausibly. [MF, from L *pictūra*]

**picture card** /ˈ– kad/, *n.* →**court card.**

**picture hat** /ˈ– hæt/, *n.* a woman's hat having a broad flexible brim, often decorated with ostrich feathers, flowers, etc.

**picture house** /ˈ– haʊs/, *n. Obs.* →**cinema.**

**picture mould** /ˈ– moʊld/, *n. Chiefly U.S.* →**picture rail.** Also, **picture mold, picture moulding, picture molding.**

**picture palace** /ˈ– pæləs/, *n. Obs.* →**picture theatre.**

**picture plane** /ˈ– pleɪn/, *n.* **1.** the surface on which a picture is painted. **2.** the extreme front edge of the imaginary space in a two-dimensional painting.

**picture rail** /ˈ– reɪl/, *n.* a moulding on a wall near the ceiling from which pictures can be hung. See **dado.**

**picture show** /ˈ– ʃoʊ/, *n.* a screening of a film or films.

**picturesque** /pɪktʃəˈrɛsk/, *adj.* **1.** visually charming or quaint, as resembling or suitable for a picture. **2.** (of written or spoken language) strikingly vivid or graphic. **3.** having pleasing or interesting qualities; strikingly effective in appearance. [PICTURE + -ESQUE, modelled on F *pittoresque,* from It. *pittoresco,* from *pittore* painter, from L *pictor*] – **picturesquely,** *adv.* – **picturesqueness,** *n.*

**picture theatre** /ˈpɪktʃə θɪətə/, *n.* an auditorium where films are shown; a cinema.

**picture tube** /ˈ– tjub/, *n.* →**cathode-ray tube.**

**picture window** /ˈ– wɪndoʊ/, *n.* a large window in a house, usu. dominating the room, and sometimes designed to focus attention on the view through it.

**picture writing** /ˈ– raɪtɪŋ/, *n.* **1.** the art of recording events or expressing ideas by pictures or pictorial symbols, as practised by preliterate peoples. **2.** pictorial symbols forming a record or communication.

**piculet** /ˈpɪkjələt/, *n.* any of several small short-billed woodpeckers, chiefly of the genus *Picumnus,* lacking stiffened shafts in the tail feathers. [L *pīcu(s)* woodpecker + -LET]

**piddle** /ˈpɪdl/, *v.i.,* **-dled, -dling. 1.** *Colloq.* →**urinate. 2.** to do anything in a trifling or ineffective way; dawdle. [cf. Norw. *pydla* pout]

**piddling** /ˈpɪdlɪŋ/, *adj.* trifling; petty. Also, **piddly.**

**piddock** /ˈpɪdək/, *n.* any of the bivalve molluscs of the genus *Pholas* or the family Pholadidae, mostly marine, with long ovate shell, and burrowing in soft rock, wood, etc. [cf. OE *puduc* wart]

**pidgin** /ˈpɪdʒən/, *n.* a language used for communication between groups having different first languages, usu. European traders or colonisers and native peoples, and which typically has features deriving from those languages, together with elements which are common to all pidgins and suggest some degree of common ancestory for them all. Also, **pigeon.** [? Chinese pronunciation of BUSINESS]

**pidgin English** /– ˈɪŋglɪʃ/, *n.* a pidgin much influenced by English as that formerly much used for commerce in Chinese ports, or in Melanesia, West Africa, etc. Also, **pigeon English.**

**pi-dog** /ˈpaɪ-dɒg/, *n.* →**pye-dog.**

**pie**[1] /paɪ/, *n.* **1.** a baked dish consisting of a sweet (fruit, etc.) or savoury filling (meat, fish, etc.), enclosed in or covered by pastry, or sometimes other topping as mashed potatoes. **2.** *U.S.* →**tart**[2]. **3.** a group of bidders at an auction who secretly agree not to bid against each other. **4.** Also, **pie-heap.** (in a freezing works) a mass of sheepskin, flesh, etc., from which wool is plucked. **5. have a finger in every pie,** to have an interest in or play a part in many affairs. **6. pie in the sky,** the illusory prospect of future benefits. [ME; orig. uncert.] – **pielike,** *adj.*

**pie**[2] /paɪ/, *n.* →**magpie.** [ME, from OF, from L *pīca* magpie]

**pie**[3] /paɪ/, *n., v.,* **pied, pieing.** *–n.* **1.** printing types mixed together indiscriminately. *–v.t.* **2.** to reduce (printing types) to a state of confusion. Also, *Chiefly U.S.,* **pi.** [orig. uncert.]

**pie**[4] /paɪ/, *n. Eccles.* (in England before the Reformation) a book of rules for finding the particulars of the service for the day. Also, **pye.** [translation of L *pīca* magpie; see PICA[1]]

**pie**[5] /paɪ/, *N.Z. –adj.* **1.** good; straight. **2. be pie on,** to be good at or keen on. *–interj.* **3.** (an exclamation indicating delight, approval, etc.). [Maori *(e) pai ana*]

**piebald** /ˈpaɪbɔld/, *adj.* **1.** having patches of black and white or of other colours; particoloured. **2.** (of a horse) white with black patches. *–n.* **3.** a piebald animal, esp. a horse. [PIE[2] (see PIED) + BALD]

**pie-cart** /ˈpaɪ-kat/, *n.* a mobile food-shop, orig. selling mainly pies.

**piece** /pis/, *n., v.,* **pieced, piecing.** *–n.* **1.** a limited portion or quantity, of something: *a piece of land.* **2.** a quantity of some substance or material forming a mass or body. **3.** one of the more or less definite parts or portions into which something may be divided: *a piece of chocolate.* **4.** one of the parts, fragments, or shreds into which something may be divided or broken: *to tear a letter into pieces.* **5.** one of the parts which, when assembled, form a combined whole: *the pieces of a machine.* **6.** an individual article of a set or collection: *a dinner service of 36 pieces.* **7.** (*pl.*) inferior wool from the skirtings but not containing necks, bellies, stains or locks. **8.** any of the counters, discs, blocks, or the like, of wood, ivory, or other material, used in any of a number of board games, as draughts, backgammon, or chess. **9.** *Chess.* a superior man, as distinguished from a pawn. **10.** a particular length, as of certain goods prepared for sale: *cloth sold by the piece.* **11.** an amount of work forming a single job: *to work by the piece.* **12.** a specimen of workmanship, esp. of artistic production, as a picture or statue. **13.** a literary composition, in prose or verse, usu. short. **14.** a play; drama. **15.** a situation or episode: *the villain of the piece.* **16.** a passage of verse, music, or the like, prepared for recitation or performance on a particular occasion. **17.** a musical composition, usu. a short one. **18.** an individual musical instrument in an ensemble: *a three-piece band.* **19.** an individual thing of a particular class or kind: *a piece of furniture.* **20.** an example, instance, or specimen of something: *a fine piece of workmanship.* **21.** (*derog.*) a woman: *she's a nice little piece.* **22. a.** *Mil.* an item of ordnance. **b.** a firearm: *a fowling piece.* **c.** *Prison Colloq.* a concealable firearm. **23.** a coin: *a threepenny piece.* **24.** *U.S.* a distance, esp. a short one. **25. a piece of cake,** *Colloq.* an easily achieved enterprise or undertaking. **26. a piece of one's mind,** outspoken criticism or reproach. **27. go to pieces,** to lose emotional or physical control of oneself. **28. of a piece,** of the same kind; consistent. **29. piece of work, a.** an example or instance of workmanship; something produced. **b.** a person, considered as an example of a specified quality: *a nasty piece of work.* **30. say one's piece,** to express an opinion; speak one's mind. **31. take a piece out of,** to reprimand severely. *–v.t.* **32.** to mend (something broken); reassemble (usu. fol. by *together*). **33.** to fit together, as pieces or parts. **34.** to make up or form into a whole by or as if by joining pieces (usu. fol. by *together*): *to piece together a picture of the situation.* **35.** to patch; to mend (a garment, etc.) by applying a piece or pieces (usu. fol. by *up*). **36.** to complete, enlarge, or extend by making additions (usu. fol. by *out*). **37.** to add as a piece or part (fol. by *into, onto*): *to piece new palings into a fence.* See **part.** [ME *pece,* from OF, from Rom. *pettia* broken piece, piece of land, of Celtic orig.]

**pièce de résistance** /pi,ɛs də rəˈzɪstəns/, *n.* **1.** the principal dish of a meal. **2.** the principal event, incident, article, etc., of a series. [F]

**piece-dyed** /ˈpis-daɪd/, *adj.* dyed after weaving (opposed to *yarn-dyed*).

**piece goods** /ˈpis gʊdz/, *n.pl.* goods or fabrics woven in lengths suitable for retail sale by the usual linear measure.

**piecemeal** /ˈpismil/, *adv.* **1.** piece by piece; gradually. **2.** into pieces or fragments. *–adj.* **3.** done piece by piece; fragmentary. [ME *pecemele* (replacing OE *styccemǣlum*). See PIECE]

**piece of eight,** *n.* the old Spanish dollar or peso, of the value of 8 reals.

**piece-picker** /ˈpis-pɪkə/, *n.* a woolshed hand who takes skirtings from the roller and sorts it into varieties defined by the classer. Also, **fleece-picker.**

**piecer** /ˈpisə/, *n.* **1.** Also, **piecener.** *Textiles.* one who joins the ends of threads which break on a mechanical loom. **2.** one who mends, patches, or assembles something. [PIECE + -ER[1]]

**piece rate** /ˈpis reɪt/, *n.* compensation based on output or production, usu. a fixed sum per piece of work turned out.

**piecework** /ˈpiswɜk/, *n.* work done and paid for by the piece. **– pieceworker,** *n.*

**piecrust** /ˈpaɪkrʌst/, *n.* **1.** the pastry covering of a pie. **2.** the pastry of which the covering of a pie is made. [PIE[1] + CRUST]

**pied** /paɪd/, *adj.* **1.** having patches of two or more colours, as various birds and other animals. **2.** wearing particoloured clothes. [PIE[2] (with reference to the black-and-white plumage of the magpie) + -ED[3]]

**pied-à-terre** /pieɪd-a-ˈtɛə/, *n.* a lodging for occasional or temporary use. [F: lit., foot (footing) on ground]

**pied goose** /paɪd ˈgus/, *n.* a large, noisy, black and white goose, *Anseranas semipalmata,* with a conspicuous knob on its head, found on the coastal plains of northern Australia.

**pie-dish beetle** /,paɪ-dɪʃ ˈbitl/, *n.* any of several large dark beetles of the Australian sub-family Helaeinae, found in arid inland areas, having a dish-shaped body with a characteristic flange around the outer margin.

**piedmont** /ˈpidmɒnt/, *n.* **1.** a district lying along or near the foot of a mountain range. *–adj.* **2.** lying along or near the foot of a mountain range. [It. *Piemonte,* lit., foothill (region), a region in NW Italy]

**piedmontite** /ˈpidmɒntaɪt, -mən-/, *n.* a mineral silicate of calcium, aluminium, manganese, and hydrogen crystallising in the monoclinic system. Also, **manganepidote, manganese epidote.**

**Pied Piper** /paɪd ˈpaɪpə/, *n.* (*sometimes l.c.*) one who causes others to follow him, esp. on some foolish venture. [from the *Pied Piper,* the hero of a legend from Hamelin, NW Germany, popularised by Robert Browning, 1812-89, English poet]

**pie-eater** /ˈpaɪ-itə/, *n. Colloq.* (*sometimes derog.*) an Australian. [from a supposed preference for meat pies, seen as a characteristic Australian dish] **– pie-eating,** *adj.*

**pie-eyed** /ˈpaɪ-aɪd/, *adj. Colloq.* drunk.

**pie-heap** /ˈpaɪ-hip/, *n. N.Z.* →**pie**[1] (def. 4).

**pie-picker** /ˈpaɪ-pɪkə/, *n.* one who plucks wool from a mass of sheepskin, flesh, etc., in a freezing works.

**pie piece** /ˈpaɪ pis/, *n.* a piece of skin with wool adhering to it, which has been cut from skins during fellmongering.

**pier** /pɪə/, *n.* **1.** a structure built out into the water to serve as a landing place for ships, and, sometimes, protect a harbour, a breakwater or a jetty. **2.** such a structure used as a pleasure promenade. **3.** one of the supports of a span of a bridge or of two adjacent spans. **4.** a square pillar. **5.** a portion of wall between doors, windows, etc. **6.** a pillar or post on which a gate or door is hung. **7.** a support of masonry or the like for sustaining vertical pressure. [ME *per(e),* from ML *pera*]

**pierce** /pɪəs/, *v.,* **pierced, piercing.** *–v.t.* **1.** to penetrate or run into or through (something), as a sharp-pointed instrument does; puncture. **2.** to make a hole or opening in. **3.** to bore into or through; tunnel. **4.** to perforate. **5.** to make (a hole, etc.) by or as by boring or perforating. **6.** to force or make a way into or through: *to pierce a wilderness.* **7.** to penetrate with the eye or mind; see into or through. **8.** to affect sharply with some sensation or emotion, as of cold, pain, grief, etc. **9.** to sound sharply through (the air, stillness, etc.) as a cry. *–v.i.* **10.** to force or make a way into or through something; penetrate. [ME *perce(n), persche(n),* from OF *percier,* from L *pertūsus,* pp. pierced] **– piercer,** *n.* **– piercingly,** *adv.*

**pier glass** /ˈpɪə glas/, *n.* **1.** a tall mirror such as is used to fill the pier or space between two windows. **2.** any tall window.

**pieridine** /paɪˈɛrədaɪn, -din/, *adj.* of or denoting a butterfly of the large and almost cosmopolitan family Pieridae, which includes various white, yellow, and orange species. [NL *Pīeridinae,* pl., from *Pīeris,* the typical genus, from Gk: a Muse]

**Pierrette** /pɪəˈrɛt/, *n.* female counterpart of Pierrot.

**Pierrot** /pɪəˈroʊ/, *n.* a masquerader or buffoon, with whitened face and wearing a loose white fancy costume. [after a male character in certain French pantomime; F, diminutive of *Pierre,* man's name]

**pier table** /ˈpɪə teɪbəl/, *n.* a table or low bracket for occupying the space against a pier between two windows, often used under a pier glass.

**pietà** /piˈeɪtə/, *n.* a representation of the Virgin Mary mourning over the body of the dead Christ. [It.: pity, from L *pietās* PIETY]

**pietism** /ˈpaɪətɪzəm/, *n.* **1.** depth of religious feeling; godliness of life. **2.** exaggeration or affectation of piety. [from a movement originating during the latter part of the 17th century in the Lutheran churches in Germany, that stressed personal piety over religious formality and orthodoxy; NL (G) *Pietismus*] **– pietist,** *n.* **– pietistic** /paɪəˈtɪstɪk/, *adj.*

**piety** /ˈpaɪəti/, *n., pl.* **-ties. 1.** reverence for God, or regard for religious obligations. **2.** the quality or fact of being pious. **3.** dutiful respect or regard for parents or others. **4.** a pious act, remark, belief, or the like. [ME, from L *pietās*]

**pie-wool** /ˈpaɪ-wʊl/, *n.* wool plucked from the pie in a freezing works.

**piezoelectricity** /paɪ,izoʊəlɛkˈtrɪsəti/, *n.* electricity produced by pressure, as in a crystal subjected to compression along a certain axis. [*piezo-* (combining form representing Gk *piézein* press, squeeze) + ELECTRICITY] **– piezoelectric** /paɪ,izoʊəˈlɛktrɪk/, *adj.* **– piezoelectrically** /paɪ,izoʊəˈlɛktrɪkli/, *adv.*

**piezometer** /paɪəˈzɒmətə/, *n.* any of various instruments for measuring pressure. **– piezometric** /,paɪəzoʊˈmɛtrɪk/, **piezometrical** /,paɪəzoʊˈmɛtrɪkəl/, *adj.*

**piezometry** /paɪəˈzɒmətri/, *n.* the measurement of pressure or compressibility.

**piffle** /ˈpɪfəl/, *n., v.,* **-fled, -fling.** *Colloq. –n.* **1.** nonsense; idle talk. *–v.i.* **2.** to talk nonsense. [cf. OE *pyff* PUFF] **– piffler,** *n.*

**piffling** /ˈpɪflɪŋ/, *adj. Colloq.* trivial; petty; nonsensical.

**pig**[1] /pɪg/, *n., v.,* **pigged, pigging.** *–n.* **1.** an omnivorous non-ruminant mammal of the family Suidae, suborder Artiodactyla and order Ungulata; a sow, hog, or boar; a swine. Cf. **hog. 2.** a young swine, of either sex, bred for slaughter. **3.** the flesh of swine; pork. **4.** *Colloq.* a person or animal of piggish character or habit. **5.** *Colloq.* (*derog.*) a policeman. **6.** *Rugby Union Colloq.* a forward. **7.** *Metall.* **a.** an oblong mass of metal that has been run while still molten into a mould of sand or the like, esp. such a mass of iron from a blast furnace; an ingot. **b.** one of the moulds for such masses of metal. **c.** metal in the form of such masses. **8. a pig in a poke,** something purchased without inspection. **9. make a pig of oneself,** to over-indulge oneself, as by eating too much. **10. home on the pig's back,** *Colloq.* successful by an easy margin. **11. pigs!** Also, **pig's arse, pig's bum.** *Colloq.* (an exclamation of contempt, derision, denial, etc.). *–v.i.* **12.** to bring forth pigs. **13.** Also, **pig it.** to live, lie, etc., as if in a pigsty; live in squalor. [ME *pigge,* OE *picg* (in *pic(g)-bred* pig-bread, mast). Cf. D *big* young pig]

**pig**[2] /pɪg/, *n. N.Z. Colloq.* a demijohn or flagon of beer.

**pig-bed** /ˈpɪg-bɛd/, *n.* a bed of sand for moulding pigs, into which molten metal is poured.

**pig-bucket** /ˈpɪg-bʌkət/, *n.* a container for the collection of kitchen refuse which is given to pigs. Also, **pig-bin.**

**pig-dog** /ˈpɪg-dɒg/, *n.* a dog trained to seek and hold wild pigs.

**pig drummer** /ˈpɪg drʌmə/, *n.* →**drummer** (def. 5).

**pigeon**[1] /ˈpɪdʒən/, *n.* **1.** any bird of the family Columbidae, having a compact body and short legs, of which there are several species distributed throughout the world; esp. the larger varieties with square or rounded tails. Cf. **dove** (def. 1). **2.** any domesticated member of this family, as bred for racing, exhibiting, etc. **3.** *Colloq.* responsibility; concern: *that's his pigeon.* **4.** *Colloq.* a dupe. [ME *pejon,* from OF *pijon,* from LL *pīpio* squab]

**pigeon**[2] /ˈpɪdʒən/, *n.* →**pidgin.**

**pigeonberry** /ˈpɪdʒənbɛri/, *n.* →**native mulberry.**

**pigeon breast** /ˈpɪdʒən brɛst/, *n.* a malformation of the chest in which there is abnormal projection of the sternum and sternal region, often associated with rickets. Also, **pigeon chest.** – **pigeon-breasted,** *adj.* – **pigeon-breastedness,** *n.*

**pigeon English** /– ˈɪŋglɪʃ/, *n.* →**pidgin English.**

**pigeon-fancier** /ˈpɪdʒən-fænsiə/, *n.* one who keeps, breeds, and sometimes trains domestic pigeons. – **pigeon-fancying,** *n.*

**pigeon grass** /ˈpɪdʒən gras/, *n.* any species of the common grass genus *Setaria* found in nearly all temperate countries.

**pigeon-hawk** /ˈpɪdʒən-hɔk/, *n.* **1.** a hawk that preys on pigeons, as the goshawk. **2.** *U.S.* the American merlin, *Falco columbarius.*

**pigeon-hearted** /ˈpɪdʒən-hatəd/, *adj.* timid; meek.

**pigeonhole** /ˈpɪdʒənhoʊl/, *n., v.,* **-holed, -holing.** *–n.* **1.** one of a series of small compartments in a desk, cabinet, or the like, used for papers, etc. **2.** a hole or recess, or one of a series of recesses, for pigeons to nest in. **3.** any series or set of small holes or recesses, as cutaway parts in a boat's superstructure to lead rigging through. *–v.t.* **4.** to put away for reference at some indefinite future time. **5.** to assign a definite place in some orderly system. **6.** to put aside for the present, esp. with the intention of ignoring or forgetting. **7.** to place in a pigeonhole or pigeonholes. **8.** to furnish (a desk, etc.) with pigeonholes.

**pigeon-livered** /ˈpɪdʒən-lɪvəd/, *adj.* meek; spiritless.

**pigeon pair** /pɪdʒən ˈpɛə/, *n. Colloq.* a son and a daughter.

**pigeon pea** /– ˈpi/, *n.* a perennial shrub, *Cajanus cajan,* family Papilionaceae, widely cultivated as a food crop, esp. in India.

**pigeon post** /ˈ– poʊst/, *n.* a system of sending messages by attaching them to the legs of homing pigeons.

**pigeonpox** /ˈpɪdʒənpɒks/, *n.* a disease affecting pigeons, similar to fowl pox.

**pigeon-toed** /ˈpɪdʒən-toʊd/, *adj.* having the toes or feet turned inwards.

**pigeonwing** /ˈpɪdʒənwɪŋ/, *n.* **1.** a fancy step or evolution in dancing. **2.** *U.S.* a particular figure in skating, outlining the spread wing of a pigeon.

**pigeonwood** /ˈpɪdʒənwʊd/, *n.* a forest tree of New Zealand, *Hedycarya arborea,* which bears bright red fruit.

**pigface** /ˈpɪgfeɪs/, *n.* any succulent herb of the family Ficoidaceae, esp. species of the genus Carpobrotus, which have large showy daisy-like purple, pink or white flowers and succulent fruit.

**pig fern** /ˈpɪg fɜn/, *n. N.Z.* →**bracken.**

**pigfish** /ˈpɪgfɪʃ/, *n., pl.* **-fishes** (*esp. collectively*) **-fish. 1.** →**rock blackfish. 2.** any of various fishes, as the grunt, *Orthopristis chrysopterus,* a food fish of the South Atlantic coast of the U.S.

**pig-footed bandicoot** /ˌpɪg-fʊtəd ˈbændikut/, *n.* a small, graceful, eastern Australian bandicoot, *Chaeropus ecaudatus,* rare or possibly extinct, having the second and third digits of the forelimb strongly clawed and resembling a cloven hoof.

**piggery** /ˈpɪgəri/, *n., pl.* **-geries. 1.** a place where pigs are kept. **2.** piggishness.

**piggie** /ˈpɪgi/, *n.* **1.** (*in children's speech*) a pig. **2.** a small pig. Also, **piggy.**

**piggin** /ˈpɪgən/, *n.* a small wooden pail or tub of staves and hoops with a handle formed by continuing one of the staves above the rim. [? from *pig* pot, jar]

**piggish** /ˈpɪgɪʃ/, *adj.* **1.** like or befitting a pig; greedy or filthy. **2.** mean or stubborn. – **piggishly,** *adv.* – **piggishness,** *n.*

**piggyback** /ˈpɪgibæk/, *adv.* **1.** on the back or shoulders: *to ride piggyback.* *–n.* **2.** a method of transportation in which truck trailers are carried on trains, or cars on specially designed trucks. **3.** a piggyback ride. *–v.t.* **4.** to attach or join (something extra) to a basic piece of equipment, system, etc.

**piggybacking** /ˈpɪgibækɪŋ/, *n.* the transporting of loaded lorry trailers, esp. on flat railway trucks.

**piggy bank** /ˈpɪgi bæŋk/, *n.* a moneybox shaped like a pig, usu. made of china, in which a child might keep his savings; any small money-box.

**pig-headed** /ˈpɪg-hɛdəd/, *adj.* stupidly obstinate.

**pig-iron** /ˈpɪg-aɪən/, *n.* **1.** iron produced in a blast furnace, poured into special moulds in preparation for making wrought iron, cast iron, or steel. **2.** iron in the unrefined state, before conversion into steel, alloys, etc.

**pig island** /ˈpɪg aɪlənd/, *n. Colloq.* →**New Zealand.** [from the wild pigs said to have been released there by Captain James Cook, 1728-79, English navigator and explorer] – **pig islander,** *n.*

**pigjump** /ˈpɪgdʒʌmp/, *v.i.* →**pigroot.**

**pig Latin** /ˈpɪg lætn/, *n.* spoken language distorted in one of various ways to make it unintelligible to overhearers.

**pig-lead** /ˈpɪg-lɛd/, *n.* lead moulded in pigs.

**piglet** /ˈpɪglət/, *n.* a little pig.

**pigling** /ˈpɪglɪŋ/, *n.* a young or small pig.

**pigment** /ˈpɪgmənt/, *n.* **1.** a colouring matter or substance. **2.** a dry substance, usu. pulverised, which when mixed with a liquid vehicle in which it is insoluble becomes a paint, ink, etc. **3.** *Biol.* any substance whose presence in the tissues or cells of animals or plants colours them. [ME, from L *pigmentum*]

**pigmentary** /ˈpɪgməntəri, -tri/, *adj.* of pigment. Also, **pigmental** /pɪgˈmɛntl/.

**pigmentation** /pɪgmɛnˈteɪʃən/, *n. Biol.* colouration with or deposition of pigment.

**pigmy** /ˈpɪgmi/, *n., pl.* **-mies,** *adj.* →**pygmy.**

**pignut** /ˈpɪgnʌt/, *n.* **1.** the nut of the brown hickory, *Carya glabra,* of North America. **2.** the tree itself. **3.** the tuber of a European plant, *Conopodium majus,* a kind of earthnut.

**pigpen** /ˈpɪgpɛn/, *n.* **1.** a pigsty. **2.** a dirty place.

**pig-rat** /ˈpɪg-ræt/, *n.* →**bandicoot.**

**pigroot** /ˈpɪgrut/, *v.i.* to plant the forelegs stiffly down and kick up with the hind legs (of a horse). Also, **pigjump.**

**pigs'-feet** /ˈpɪgz-fit/, *n.* a heavy claw-hammer used to pull out dog-spikes.

**pigskin** /ˈpɪgskɪn/, *n.* **1.** leather made from the skin of a pig. **2.** any piece of a pig's skin, whether tanned or not. **3.** leather, made from the skins of capybaras, peccaries, etc. **4.** *Colloq.* a saddle. *–adj.* **5.** made of pigskin.

**pigstick** /ˈpɪgstɪk/, *v.i.* to hunt wild boar with a spear, on foot or on horseback. – **pigsticking,** *n.*

**pigsticker** /ˈpɪgstɪkə/, *n.* **1.** one who hunts wild boar. **2.** a longish sheath-knife. **3.** a thin, sharp attachment to a penknife.

**pigsty** /ˈpɪgstaɪ/, *n., pl.* **-sties. 1.** a sty or pen for pigs. **2.** *Railways.* the criss-crossed sleepers beneath the rails replacing temporarily the earthworks which have been washed away.

**pig-swill** /ˈpɪg-swɪl/, *n.* **1.** waste food given to pigs. **2.** *Colloq.* inferior or unpleasant food.

**pigtail** /ˈpɪgteɪl/, *n.* **1.** a braid of hair hanging down the back of the head. **2.** tobacco in a thin twisted roll. **3.** *Elect.* a short flexible wire.

**pig-tucker** /ˈpɪg-tʌkə/, *n. N.Z. Colloq.* →**pig-swill.**

**pigwash** /ˈpɪgwɒʃ/, *n.* →**pig-swill.**

**pigweed** /ˈpɪgwid/, *n.* →**purslane.**

**pihoihoi** /piˈhoʊiˌhoʊi/, *n. N.Z.* →**pipit.**

**pika** /ˈpaɪkə, ˈpikə/, *n.* any of various small mammals allied to the rabbits and inhabiting alpine regions of the Northern Hemisphere, as *Ochotona princeps* of North America. [Tungusic (of Siberia) *piika*]

**pikau** /ˈpikaʊ/, *n. N.Z.* **1.** a knapsack burden; swag. *–v.t.* **2.** to carry on the back. [Maori]

**pike**[1] /paɪk/, *n., pl.* **pikes,** (*esp. collectively*) **pike. 1.** →**sea pike. 2.** any of various large, slender, fierce, voracious freshwater fishes of the Northern Hemisphere, of the genus *Esox,* having a long snout, esp. the **northern pike,** *E. lucius.*

3. any of various superficially similar fishes, as the **American pike,** *Stizostedion vitreum.* [ME, short for *pikefish,* so called from its pointed snout. See PIKE[2]] – **pikelike,** *adj.*

**pike**[2] /paɪk/, *n., v.,* **piked, piking.** *–n.* **1.** *Hist.* an infantry weapon with long shaft and comparatively small metal head. *–v.t.* **2.** to pierce, wound, or kill with or as with a pike. [F *pique,* akin to *pic* a pick (cf. PIKE[3]) and *piquer* prick (see PIQUE, *v.*)]

**pike**[3] /paɪk/, *n.* **1.** a sharp point; a spike. **2.** the pointed end of anything, as of an arrow or a spear. [ME *pīk,* OE *pīc* a pick or pickaxe, a point. See PIKE[2]]

**pike**[4] /paɪk/, *n. U.S.* →**turnpike.**

**pike**[5] /paɪk/, *v.i.,* **piked, piking.** *Colloq.* **1.** to let down; abandon (fol. by *on*): *don't pike on me.* **2. pike out,** to go back on an arrangement; to opt out (fol. by *on*): *he piked out on the deal.*

**pike**[6] /paɪk/, *v.i.,* **piked, piking.** *Colloq.* to go quickly. [orig. uncert.]

**pike**[7] /paɪk/, *n.* →**jackknife dive.**

**piked hang** /ˈpaɪkt hæŋ/, *n. Gymnastics.* a position of the body in which the hips are vertically above the shoulders and the legs together parallel to the ground.

**pike dive** /ˈpaɪk daɪv/, *n.* →**jackknife dive.**

**pike eel** /ˈ– il/, *n.* a long, greyish eel, related to the conger, found in northern Australian waters and elsewhere.

**pikelet** /ˈpaɪklət/, *n.* a small thick, sweet pancake, cooked on a flat heated surface, as a frypan or griddle; drop scone; scotch pancake.

**pikeman** /ˈpaɪkmən/, *n., pl.* **-men.** a soldier armed with a pike.

**pike-perch** /ˈpaɪk-pɜtʃ/, *n.* any of several pikelike fishes of the perch family, as the walleye, *Stizostedion vitreum,* of North America.

**piker**[1] /ˈpaɪkə/, *n. Colloq.* **1.** one who gambles, speculates, etc., in a small, cautious way. **2.** one who, from lack of courage or from diffidence, does anything in a contemptibly small or cheap way. **3.** one who opts out of an arrangement or challenge or does not do his fair share.

**piker**[2] /ˈpaɪkə/, *n. Colloq.* a wild bullock.

**pikestaff** /ˈpaɪkstaf/, *n., pl.* **-staffs** /-stafs/. **1.** the staff or shaft of a pike (weapon). **2. as plain as a pikestaff,** extremely, unmistakably clear.

**pikkie** /ˈpɪki/, *n. Colloq.* →**pickie.**

**pilaf** /ˈpilæf/, *n.* a rice dish of Central Asian origin consisting of rice, pre-cooked or raw, fried in butter or other fat with stock, meats, vegetables, nuts, etc., depending on the particular recipe. Also, **pilaff, pilau, pulao, pilaw.** [Pers. *pilāw*]

**pilaster** /pəˈlæstə/, *n.* a square or rectangular pillar, with capital and base, engaged in a wall from which it projects. [F *pilastre,* from It. *pilastro,* from L *pīla* pillar]

pilaster

**pilau** /ˈpilaʊ/, *n.* →**pilaf.** Also, **pilaw.**

**pilchard** /ˈpɪltʃəd/, *n.* **1.** a small abundant fish, *Sardinops neopilchardus,* occurring in shoals around the southern half of the Australian coast. **2.** a related marine food fish, *Sardina pilchardus,* of the eastern Atlantic and western Mediterranean. **3.** any of numerous similar fishes found elsewhere. [earlier *pilcher,* orig. uncert.]

**pilchers** /ˈpɪltʃəz/, *n. pl.* flannel or plastic pants or a plastic wrapper worn by an infant over a nappy. [ME *pilche,* OE *pylce, pylece,* from LL *pellīcia,* from L *pellis,* skin]

**pile**[1] /paɪl/, *n., v.,* **piled, piling.** *–n.* **1.** an assemblage of things laid or lying one upon another in a more or less orderly fashion: *a pile of boxes.* **2.** *Colloq.* a large number, quantity, or amount of anything: *a pile of things to do.* **3.** a heap of wood on which a dead body, a living person, or a sacrifice is burnt. **4.** a lofty or large building or mass of buildings. **5.** *Colloq.* a large accumulation of money. **6.** *Metall.* a bundle of pieces of iron ready to be welded and drawn out into bars; faggot. **7.** *Physics.* a latticework of uranium and various moderating substances used to produce plutonium in the original harnessing of atomic energy, essentially a means of controlling the nuclear chain reaction; atomic pile; nuclear reactor. **8.** →**voltaic pile.** **9.** *Mil.* arms arranged systematically. *–v.t.* **10.** to lay or dispose in a pile (oft. fol. by *up* or *on*). **11.** to accumulate (fol. by *up*). **12.** to cover or load, with a pile or piles. **13. pile arms,** to prop (usu. four) rifles, muskets, etc., in the form of a pyramid, with the muzzles pointing upwards. **14. pile on the agony, pile it on,** *Colloq.* to exaggerate. *–v.i.* **15.** to accumulate, as money, debts, evidence, etc. (fol. by *up*). **16.** *Colloq.* to get somewhere (fol. by *in, into, out, off, down,* etc.) in a body and more or less confusedly. **17.** to gather or rise in a pile or piles, as snow, etc. **18.** *Colloq.* (of a vehicle, driver, etc.) to crash (fol. by *up*). [ME, from OF, from L *pīla* pillar, pier, mole]

**pile**[2] /paɪl/, *n., v.,* **piled, piling.** *–n.* **1.** a heavy timber, stake or pole, sometimes pointed at the lower end, driven vertically into the ground or the bed of a river, etc., to support a superstructure or form part of a wall. **2.** any steel or concrete member similarly used. **3.** *Archery.* the tip of an arrow. **4.** *Her.* a bearing in the form of a wedge, usu. with its point downwards. *–v.t.* **5.** to furnish, strengthen, or support with piles. **6.** drive piles into. [ME and OE *pīl* shaft, stake, from L *pīlum* javelin]

**pile**[3] /paɪl/, *n.* **1.** hair, esp. soft, fine hair or down. **2.** wool, esp. of a carpet, fur, or pelage. **3.** a raised surface on cloth, composed of upright cut or looped yarns, as velvet, Turkish towelling, etc. **4.** one of the strands in such a surface. [ME *pilus,* from L: hair]

**pile**[4] /paɪl/, *n.* (*usu. pl.*) →**haemorrhoid.** [ME *pyle*]

**pileate** /ˈpɪlieɪt, -iət/, *adj.* capped, as a mushroom. [L *pīleātus* capped. See PILEUS]

**pileated** /ˈpɪlieɪtəd/, *adj. Ornith.* →**crested.**

**pileated woodpecker** /– ˈwʊdpɛkə/, *n.* a large black-and-white North American woodpecker, *Ceophloeus pileatus,* with prominent red crest.

**piled** /paɪld/, *adj.* having a pile, as velvet and other fabrics. [PILE[3] + -ED[3]]

**pile-driver** /ˈpaɪl-draɪvə/, *n.* **1.** a machine for driving down piles, usu. a tall framework in which a heavy weight of iron is raised between guides to a height, as by steam, and then allowed to fall upon the head of the pile. **2.** *Colloq.* a powerful blow of the fist, kick, stroke, etc.

**pile-dwelling** /ˈpaɪl-dwɛlɪŋ/, *n.* a dwelling supported on piles so as to be raised above the ground or water; a lake-dwelling.

**pileous** /ˈpaɪliəs/, *adj.* **1.** of or pertaining to hair. **2.** hairy. [PILE[3] + -OUS]

**pileum** /ˈpaɪliəm, ˈpɪl-/, *n., pl.* **pilea** /ˈpaɪliə/. the top of the head of a bird, from the base of the bill to the nape. [NL, from L, var. of *pilleum.* See PILEUS]

**pile-up** /ˈpaɪl-ʌp/, *n. Colloq.* **1.** a crash or collision, usu. involving more than one vehicle. **2.** an accumulation; backlog.

**pileus** /ˈpaɪliəs, ˈpɪliəs/, *n., pl.* **pilei** /ˈpaɪliaɪ, ˈpɪliaɪ/. **1.** *Bot.* the horizontal portion of a mushroom, bearing gills, tubes, etc., on its underside; a cap. **2.** *Zool.* the disc-shaped part of a coelenterate which takes the form of a medusa. [L, more correctly *pilleus,* also *pilleum* felt cap; akin to L *pilus* hair, Gk *pîlos* felt, felt cap]

**pilfer** /ˈpɪlfə/, *v.t.* **1.** to steal (a small amount or object). *–v.i.* **2.** to practise petty theft. [apparently from AF or OF *pelfrer* pillage, rob. Cf. PELF] – **pilferer,** *n.*

**pilferage** /ˈpɪlfərɪdʒ/, *n.* **1.** the act or practice of pilfering; petty theft. **2.** *Archaic.* that which is pilfered.

**pilgrim** /ˈpɪlgrəm/, *n.* **1.** one who journeys, esp. a long distance, to some sacred place as an act of devotion. **2.** *Poetic.* a traveller or wanderer. [ME *pelegrim,* from AF (unrecorded), from ML *peregrīnus* pilgrim, L foreigner. See PEREGRINE]

**pilgrimage** /ˈpɪlgrəmɪdʒ/, *n.* **1.** a journey, esp. a long one, made to some sacred place, as an act of devotion. **2.** any long journey. [ME, from AF *pilgrymage,* var. of OF *peligrinage.* See PILGRIM]

**pili** /pɪˈli/, *n., pl.* **-lis.** **1.** a Philippine tree, *Canarium ovatum,* the seeds of which are edible, resembling a sweet almond. **2.** its seeds (**pili-nuts**). [Tagalog]

**piliferous** /paɪˈlɪfərəs/, *adj.* having hair. [*pili-* (combining form representing L *pilus* hair) + -FEROUS]

**piliform** /ˈpaɪləfɔm/, *adj.* having the form of a hair.

**piling** /ˈpaɪlɪŋ/, *n.* **1.** piles collectively. See **pile**[2]. **2.** a structure composed of piles. [PILE[2] + -ING[1]]

i = peat ɪ = pit ɛ = pet æ = pat a = part ɒ = pot ʌ = putt ɔ = port ʊ = put u = pool ɜ = pert ə = apart aɪ = buy eɪ = bay ɔɪ = boy aʊ = how
oʊ = hoe ɪə = here ɛə = hair ʊə = tour g = give θ = thin ð = then ʃ = show ʒ = measure tʃ = choke dʒ = joke ŋ = sing j = you

**pill**[1] /pɪl/, *n.* **1.** a small globular or rounded mass of medicinal substance, to be swallowed whole; tablet. **2.** something unpleasant that has to be accepted or endured: *a bitter pill to swallow.* **3.** *Colloq.* a disagreeable, insipid person. **4.** *Sports Colloq.* a ball, esp. in football, tennis, etc. **5.** (*pl.*) *Colloq.* billiards, football, tennis, etc. **6. sugar the pill,** to make bearable some unpleasant experience. **7. the pill,** *Colloq.* oral contraceptive. **8.** *Textiles.* a small ball of fibre formed by friction. *–v.i.* **9.** (of woollen, and other fabrics, esp. knitted) to form into small balls of fibres because of rubbing. [late ME, probably from MD or MLG *pille,* from L *pilula,* diminutive of *pila* ball]

**pill**[2] /pɪl/, *v.t., v.i.* **1.** *Archaic.* to peel. **2.** *Obs.* to make or become bald. [partly ME *pilen,* OE *pilian* peel, skin, from L *pilāre* deprive of hair; also ME *pille(n), pylle(n),* from OF *piller* plunder, mishandle, from L *pilleāre* flay]

**pill**[3] /pɪl/, *v.t. Archaic.* to rob, plunder, or pillage. [ME, probably akin to PILL[2]]

**pillage** /ˈpɪlɪdʒ/, *v.,* **-laged, -laging,** *n.* *–v.t.* **1.** to strip of money or goods by open violence, as in war; plunder. **2.** to take as booty. *–v.i.* **3.** to rob with open violence; take booty. *–n.* **4.** the act of plundering, esp. in war. **5.** booty or spoil. [ME *pilage,* from OF *pillage,* from *piller* PILL[3]] – **pillager,** *n.*

**pillar** /ˈpɪlə/, *n.* **1.** an upright shaft or structure, of stone, brick, or other material, relatively slender in proportion to its height, and of any shape in section, used as a support, or standing alone, as for a monument. **2.** an upright supporting part. **3.** any natural or accidental object resembling or serving as such a support. **4.** *Horol.* a supporting strut for the framework of a watch or clock. **5.** a person who is a chief support of a state, institution, etc.: *a pillar of society.* **6. from pillar to post, a.** from one predicament or difficulty to another. **b.** aimlessly from place to place. *–v.t.* **7.** to provide or support with pillars. [ME *pylere,* from OF *piler,* from L *pīla* pillar, PILE[1]]

**pillar-box** /ˈpɪlə-bɒks/, *n.* a large letter-box, usu. of cast-iron, usu. roughly cylindrical.

**pillar cock** /ˈpɪlə kɒk/, *n.* a faucet or tap in which the pipe carrying the water supply is vertical and the nozzle horizontal to it.

**pillbox** /ˈpɪlbɒks/, *n.* **1.** a box, usu. shallow and often round, for holding pills. **2.** a small cylindrical hat of similar shape. **3.** a small, low structure of reinforced concrete, enclosing machine-guns, and employed as a minor fortress in warfare.

**pill-bug** /ˈpɪl-bʌg/, *n.* a terrestrial isopod or woodlouse (genus *Armadillidium*) of Britain and Europe, capable of rolling itself into a ball.

**pillie** /ˈpɪli/, *n. Colloq.* →**pilchard** (def. 1).

**pillion** /ˈpɪljən/, *n.* **1.** a pad or cushion attached behind a saddle, esp. as a seat for a woman. **2.** an extra saddle behind the driver's seat on a motorcycle. *–adj.* **3.** riding on a pillion: *a pillion passenger.* *–adv.* **4.** on a pillion: *to ride pillion.* [apparently from Gaelic *pillean, pillin,* diminutive of *pell* cushion, from L *pellis* skin, pelt]

**pillory** /ˈpɪləri/, *n., pl.* **-ries,** *v.,* **-ried, -rying.** *–n.* **1.** a wooden framework erected on a post, with holes for securing the head and hands, used to expose an offender to public derision. *–v.t.* **2.** to set in the pillory. **3.** to expose to public ridicule or abuse. [ME *pillori,* from OF, from Pr. *espi(ng)lóri,* ? from ML, alteration of *speculum in glōriam Deī* court (lit., mirror) to the glory of God]

pillory

**pillow** /ˈpɪloʊ/, *n.* **1.** a bag or case filled with feathers, down, or other soft material, commonly used as a support for the head during sleep or rest. **2.** anything used to support the head; a headrest. **3.** a cushion or pad, as the cushion on which pillow lace is made. **4.** a supporting piece or part, as the block on which the inner end of a bowsprit rests. *–v.t.* **5.** to rest on or as on a pillow. **6.** to support with pillows. **7.** to serve as a pillow for. *–v.i.* **8.** to rest as on a pillow. [ME *pilwe,* OE *pyle, pylu,* pre-E **pulwī(n),* from L *pulvīnus*] – **pillow-like,** *adj.*

**pillow block** /ˈ– blɒk/, *n.* a metal box or case for supporting the end of a revolving shaft or journal.

**pillow book** /ˈ– bʊk/, *n.* a book depicting various positions of sexual intercourse, and kept under the pillow, as in Japan.

**pillowcase** /ˈpɪloʊkeɪs/, *n.* a removable cover, usu. of cotton, linen or nylon, drawn over a pillow. Also, **pillowslip** /ˈpɪloʊslɪp/.

**pillow-fight** /ˈpɪloʊ-faɪt/, *n.* a children's game, in which pillows are used as weapons.

**pillow lace** /ˈpɪloʊ leɪs/, *n.* lace made on a padded board with threads wound on bobbins.

**pillow sham** /ˈ– ʃæm/, *n.* an ornamental cover laid over a bed pillow.

**pillowslip** /ˈpɪloʊslɪp/, *n.* →**pillowcase.**

**pillowy** /ˈpɪloʊi/, *adj.* pillow-like; soft; yielding: *a pillowy clump of sod.*

**pill popper** /ˈpɪl pɒpə/, *n.* a person who is addicted to pills, esp. analgesics.

**pillwort** /ˈpɪlwɜt/, *n.* any small aquatic pteridophyte of the genus *Pilularia,* as *P. novae-hollandiae* of coastal swamps of Australia.

**pilocarpine** /paɪloʊˈkapin, -pən/, *n.* an alkaloid, $C_{11}H_{16}N_2O_2$, obtained from the leaflets of a South American shrub, *Pilocarpus* (jaborandi), used as a diaphoretic and diuretic. Also, **pilocarpin** /paɪloʊˈkapən/. [NL *Pilocarpus* (from Gk *pîlo(s)* cap + *karpós* fruit) + -INE[2]]

**pilonidal sinus** /ˌpaɪlənaɪdl ˈsaɪnəs/, *n.* a pouch in the sacrococcygeal area caused by the ingrowth of a hair and prone to infection.

**pilose** /ˈpaɪloʊs/, *adj.* covered with hair, esp. soft hair; furry. [L *pilōsus*] – **pilosity** /paɪˈlɒsəti/, *n.*

**pilot** /ˈpaɪlət/, *n.* **1.** one duly qualified to steer ships into or out of a harbour or through certain difficult waters. **2.** the steersman of a ship. **3.** *Aeron.* one who controls an aeroplane, balloon, or other aircraft. **4.** a guide or leader. **5.** →**pilot light.** **6.** a sample episode for a television series. *–v.t.* **7.** to steer. **8.** to guide or conduct, as through unknown places, intricate affairs, etc. **9.** to act as pilot on, in or over. *–adj.* **10.** experimental; denoting investigation on a small scale designed to assess the practicability of a major commitment, as a pilot film. **11.** of or pertaining to pilots. **12.** acting as a guide. [F *pilote,* from It. *pilota,* from MGk **pēdṓtēs,* from *pēdá,* pl., rudder]

**pilotage** /ˈpaɪlətɪdʒ/, *n.* **1.** the act of piloting. **2.** the fee paid to a pilot for his services. [F]

**pilot ball** /ˈpaɪlət bɔl/, *n.* (in croquet) a ball struck by a player's ball, thus enabling the player to keep his turn and reach a position from which to hit the ball through a hoop.

**pilot balloon** /ˈ– bəlun/, *n.* a balloon used for the visual observation of upper-air wind currents, etc.

**pilot bird** /ˈ– bɜd/, *n.* a mottled reddish-brown, finch-like bird, *Pycnoptilus floccosus,* with a melodious call, found in damp forest areas of south-eastern Australia, often accompanying ('piloting') the lyrebird.

**pilot burner** /ˈ– bɜnə/, *n.* →**pilot light.**

**pilot-cloth** /ˈpaɪlət-klɒθ/, *n.* a heavy, dark blue, woollen cloth used for overcoats, seamen's clothing, etc.

**pilot film** /ˈpaɪlət fɪlm/, *n.* a film, esp. television film, shown to test the likely success of a projected series. Also, **pilot.**

**pilot fish** /ˈ– fɪʃ/, *n.* any of various species of carangoid marine fishes which accompany and were once thought to act as guides to sharks, as *Naucrates angeli* of Australian and New Zealand waters.

**pilot flag** /ˈ– flæg/, *n.* **1.** a square flag bearing three blue and three yellow vertical stripes, flown to request an official pilot for navigating a harbour, river, etc. **2.** a rectangular flag with its upper half white and its lower half red, or a square flag halved red and white with the white portion next to the mast indicating that the vessel has a pilot on board, or is a pilot boat.

**pilot house** /ˈ– haʊs/, *n.* an enclosed place on the deck of a vessel, for the steering gear and the pilot; a wheelhouse.

**piloti** /pɪləˈti/, *n. Archit.* a heavy column or stilt used to carry a structure above ground level. Also, **pilotis.** [F *piloti(s),* equiv. to *pilot* (augmentative of *pile* PILE[1]) + *-is* collective suffix]

**pilot lamp** /ˈpaɪlət læmp/, *n.* an electric lamp, used in association with a control, which by means of position or colour indicates the functioning of the control; an indicator light or a control light. Also, **pilot light.**

**pilot light** /ˈ– laɪt/, *n.* **1.** a small light kept burning continuously, as beside a large gas burner, to relight a main light whenever desired. **2.** →**pilot lamp.** Also, **pilot burner.**

**pilot officer** /– ˈɒfəsə/, *n.* the junior commissioned rank in the Royal Australian Air Force.

**pilot plant** /ˈ– plænt/, *n.* a small industrial plant in which processes planned for full-scale operation are tested in advance to eliminate problems, etc.

**pilot study** /ˈ– stʌdi/, *n.* a limited research undertaking designed as a preliminary test of the hypotheses and methods of a subsequent major project.

**pilot whale** /ˈ– weɪl/, *n.* any of the cetaceans constituting the genus *Globicephala* (family Delphinidae), up to 8.50 metres long, esp. *G. melaena,* of the Atlantic and Pacific oceans.

**pilous** /ˈpaɪləs/, *adj.* hairlike. [L *pilōsus*]

**pilsener** /ˈpɪlsənə/, *n.* a light pale lager. Also, **pilsner.** [G, adj. from *Pilsen,* a city in Czechoslovakia where it was originally made]

**Piltdown man** /ˈpɪltdaʊn mæn/, *n.* a supposedly very early form of man, *Eoanthropus,* whose existence was inferred from bone fragments found at Piltdown, Sussex, England in 1912; these were shown in 1953 to have been assembled as a hoax.

**pilular** /ˈpɪljulə/, *adj.* of, pertaining to, or characteristic of pills. [L *pilula* pill + -AR[1]]

**pilule** /ˈpɪljul/, *n.* a pill, esp. a little one. [ME, from L *pilula* pill, diminutive of *pila* ball]

**pimento** /pəˈmɛntoʊ/, *n., pl.* **-tos. 1.** the dried fruits of the tree *Pimenta dioica;* allspice. **2.** the tropical American tree yielding this. **3.** →**bayberry.** [Sp. *pimienta* pepper, allspice, from LL *pigmenta,* pl. of *pigmentum* plant juice, pigment]

**pimeson** /ˈpaɪˌmizɒn/, *n.* a meson, which may have positive, negative, or zero charge, and a mass of between 264 and 273 electron masses. Also, **pion.**

**pimiento** /pɪˈmjɛntoʊ/, *n., pl.* **-tos.** a red pepper, originally of Spain, with a sweet, pungent flavour, also eaten less ripe, when it is green or yellow. See **pepper** (def. 4). [Sp. See PIMENTO]

**pimp** /pɪmp/, *n.* **1.** one who solicits for a prostitute, or brothel; a procurer. **2.** a contemptible person. **3.** an informer; a tale-bearer. *–v.i.* **4.** to procure; pander. **5.** to inform; tell tales. [cf. OE *Pimpern* (place name)]

**pimpernel** /ˈpɪmpənɛl/, *n.* a herb of the genus *Anagallis,* esp. the scarlet pimpernel, *A. arvensis,* a species with scarlet, purplish or white flowers that close at the approach of bad weather. [ME, from OF *pimprenele,* earlier *piprenelle,* from L *piperīnus* consisting of peppercorns; replacing OE *pipeneale,* of Rom. orig.]

**pimping** /ˈpɪmpɪŋ/, *adj.* **1.** petty. **2.** weak; sickly.

**pimple** /ˈpɪmpəl/, *n.* a small, usu. inflammatory swelling or elevation of the skin; a papule or pustule. [ME; cf. OE *piplian* be pimpled]

**pimply** /ˈpɪmpli/, *adj.,* **-plier, -pliest.** having many pimples. Also, **pimpled** /ˈpɪmpəld/.

**pin** /pɪn/, *n., v.,* **pinned, pinning.** *–n.* **1.** a small, slender, sometimes tapered or pointed piece of wood, metal, etc., used to fasten, or hold things together, to hang things upon, to stop up holes, or to convey or check motion; a bolt; peg. **2.** a short, slender piece of wire with a point at one end and a head at the other, for fastening things together, as cloth or paper. **3.** any of various forms of fastening or ornament consisting essentially or in part of a pointed penetrating bar: *a safety pin.* **4.** a badge or brooch having a pointed bar or pin attached, by which it is fastened to the clothing. **5.** a linchpin, serving to keep a wheel on its axle. **6.** that part of the stem of a key which enters the lock. **7.** a rolling pin. **8.** →**hairpin. 9.** a peg, nail, or stud marking the centre of a target. **10.** one of the bottle-shaped pieces of wood knocked down in ninepins, tenpins, etc. **11.** a surfboard with wide sides. **12.** (in quoits) the peg over which quoits are thrown. **13.** *Golf.* the flagpole which identifies a hole. **14.** *Colloq.* a leg. **15.** *Music.* a peg. **16.** *Naut.* any of various pegs, fixing devices and axles, as a belaying pin, thole, etc. **17.** *Carp.* →**dovetail. 18.** (in the imperial system) a cask containing $4\frac{1}{2}$ gallons (20.4 litres). **19.** a very small amount; a trifle. **20.** See **pins and needles.** *–v.t.* **21.** to fasten or attach with a pin or pins, or as if with a pin. **22.** to hold (a man, etc.) fast in a spot or position: *the debris pinned him down.* **23.** to bind or hold to a course of action, a promise, etc. (oft. fol. by *down*). **24.** to transfix with a pin or the like. **25.** *Chess, Draughts, etc.* to effectively confine your opponent's men. **26.** *Bldg Trades.* Also, **underpin.** to support (masonry, etc.), as by wedges driven in over a beam. [ME; OE *pinn* peg (c. G *Pinne*)]

**piña cloth** /ˈpinjə klɒθ/, *n.* a fine, sheer fabric, made from the fibre of pineapple leaves. [*piña,* from S Amer. Sp., formerly *pinna,* from L *pīnea* pine cone]

**pinacoid** /ˈpɪnəkɔɪd/, *n. Crystall.* a form whose faces are parallel to two of the axes. [Gk *pínax* slab + -OID]

**pina colada** /pinə kəˈladə/, *n.* a drink made from pineapple and coconut juice with milk or cream, often with white rum. [S. Amer. Sp.]

**pinafore** /ˈpɪnəfɔ/, *n.* **1.** an apron, usu. one large enough to cover most of the dress, esp. a child's. **2.** a loose dress worn over clothing to protect it during housework, etc. **3.** a dress, sleeveless with low neck, worn with a jumper particularly in winter. Also, **pinny.** [PIN, *v.,* + AFORE, *adv.*]

**pinafore frock** /– ˈfrɒk/, *n.* a sleeveless dress worn over a jumper or blouse.

**pinball** /ˈpɪnbɔl/, *n.* any of various games played on a sloping board, the object usu. being either to shoot a ball, driven by a spring, up a side passage and cause it to roll back down against pins or bumpers and through channels which electrically record the score, or to shoot a ball into pockets at the back of the board.

**pin bullock** /ˈpɪn bʊlək/, *n.* the bullock harnessed next to the poler in a bullock team.

**pince-nez** /ˈpæns-neɪ, ˈpɪns-neɪ/, *n.* a pair of spectacles kept in place by a spring which pinches the nose. [F: pinch nose]

**pincer movement** /ˈpɪnsə muvmənt/, *n.* a military manoeuvre in which both of the enemy's flanks are attacked simultaneously, as if by a pair of pincers.

**pincers** /ˈpɪnsəz/, *n.pl. or sing.* **1.** a gripping tool consisting of two pivoted limbs forming a pair of jaws and a pair of handles (often called a **pair of pincers**). **2.** *Zool.* a grasping organ or pair of organs resembling this. [ME *pynceours,* from OF, from *pincier* PINCH]

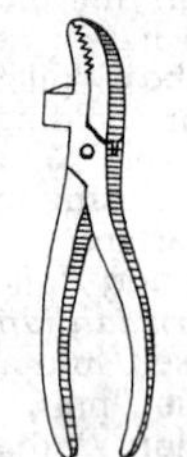
pincers

**pinch** /pɪntʃ/, *v.t.* **1.** to compress between the finger and thumb, the jaws of an instrument, or any two opposed surfaces. **2.** to compress, constrict, or squeeze painfully, as a tight shoe does. **3.** to cramp within narrow bounds or quarters. **4.** to render (the face, etc.) unnaturally thin and drawn, as pain or distress does. **5.** to nip (plants) injuriously, as frost does. **6.** to affect with sharp discomfort or distress, as cold, hunger, or need does. **7.** to straiten in means or circumstances. **8.** to stint in allowance of money, food, or the like. **9.** to hamper or inconvenience by lack of something specified. **10.** to stint the supply or amount of (a thing). **11.** to put a pinch or small quantity of (a powder, etc.) into something. **12.** *Colloq.* to steal. **13.** *Colloq.* to arrest. **14.** to move (a heavy object) by means of a pinch or pinch-bar. **15.** *Naut.* to sail (a vessel) so close to the wind that her sails shake slightly and her speed is reduced. **16.** *Hort.* to snip off (part of a shoot, bud, etc.) to improve the shape, quality, etc., of a plant (oft. fol. by *out, off,* or *back*). *–v.i.* **17.** to exert a sharp or painful compressing force. **18.** to cause sharp discomfort or distress: *when hunger pinches.* **19.** to stint oneself; economise unduly; be stingy or miserly. **20.** *Mining.* (of a vein of ore, etc.) to become narrower or smaller, or to give (*out*) altogether. *–n.* **21.** the act of pinching; nip; squeeze. **22.** as much of anything as can be taken up between the finger and thumb: *a pinch of salt.* **23.** a very small quantity of anything. **24.** sharp or painful stress, as of hunger, need, or any trying circumstances. **25.** a situation or time of special stress; an emergency: *any help is useful in a pinch.* **26.** a section of tramway track which veers to the side of the road, as at a stop. **27.** a pinch-bar.

**28.** *Colloq.* an arrest. **29.** *Colloq.* a theft. **30. pinch of salt.** See **grain** (def. 7). **31. at a pinch,** in an emergency, crisis, etc.; if necessary. [ME *pinche(n)*, from OF *pincier,* from LL *punctiāre* (from *punctio* act of pricking), b. with stem *pic-* PIKE[2]]

**pinch-bar** /ˈpɪntʃ-ba/, *n.* a kind of crowbar or lever with a projection which serves as a fulcrum.

**pinchbeck** /ˈpɪntʃbɛk/, *n.* **1.** an alloy of copper and zinc, used in imitation of gold. **2.** something spurious. *–adj.* **3.** made of pinchbeck. **4.** sham or spurious. [named after the inventor, Christopher *Pinchbeck* (died 1732), a London clockmaker]

**pinchcock** /ˈpɪntʃkɒk/, *n.* a clamp for compressing a flexible pipe, as a rubber tube, in order to regulate or stop the flow of a fluid.

**pinch effect** /ˈpɪntʃ əfɛkt/, *n.* the constriction of a stream of charged particles resulting from the magnetic field associated with the current carried by the particles.

**pincher** /ˈpɪntʃə/, *n.* **1.** one who or that which pinches. **2.** (*pl.*) →**pincers.**

**pinch-hit** /pɪntʃ-ˈhɪt/, *v.i.*, **-hit, -hitting. 1.** *Baseball.* to serve as a pinch-hitter. **2.** *U.S.* to substitute for someone.

**pinch-hitter** /pɪntʃ-ˈhɪtə/, *n.* **1.** *Baseball.* a substitute who, usu. at some critical moment of the game, bats for another. **2.** any substitute for another, esp. in an emergency.

**pinchpenny** /ˈpɪntʃpɛni/, *n., pl.* **-nies,** *adj. –n.* **1.** a very mean person. *–adj.* **2.** miserly.

**pinch test** /ˈpɪntʃ tɛst/, *n.* a method of gauging excess body fat by pinching a piece of skin usu. near the ribs, between thumb and forefinger.

**pin-curl** /ˈpɪn-kɜl/, *n.* a curl which is pinned into place by a bobby pin while the hair sets.

**pincushion** /ˈpɪnkʊʃən/, *n.* a small cushion in which pins are stuck, in readiness for use.

**pindan** /ˈpɪndæn/, *n.* semi-arid country; scrub.

**Pindaric** /pɪnˈdærɪk/, *adj.* **1.** of, pertaining to, or after the manner of Pindar, 518-438 B.C., lyric poet. **2.** *Class. Pros.* of elaborate and regular metrical structure. **3.** *Pros.* having an irregular metrical structure, supposedly in imitation of Pindar. *–n.* **4.** an ode or other poem by or in imitation of Pindar. See **ode** (def. 3).

**pine**[1] /paɪn/, *n.* **1.** any member of the genus *Pinus,* comprising evergreen coniferous trees varying greatly in size, with long needle-shaped leaves, including many species of economic importance for their timber and as a source of turpentine, tar, pitch, etc. **2.** any of various more or less similar coniferous trees. **3.** the wood of the pine tree. **4.** *Colloq.* →**pineapple.** [ME; OE *pīn,* from L *pīnus*] – **pinelike,** *adj.*

**pine**[2] /paɪn/, *v.,* **pined, pining,** *n. –v.i.* **1.** to suffer with longing, or long painfully (fol. by *for*). **2.** to fail gradually in health or vitality from grief, regret, or longing. **3.** to languish, droop, or waste away. **4.** to repine or fret. *–v.t.* **5.** *Archaic.* to suffer grief or regret over. *–n.* **6.** *Obs. or Archaic.* painful longing. [ME; OE *pīnian* to torture, from *pīn,* n., torture, from VL *pēna,* L *poena* punishment]

**pineal** /ˈpɪniəl/, *adj.* **1.** pertaining to the pineal body. **2.** resembling a pine cone in shape. [NL *pīneālis,* from L *pīnea* pine cone]

**pineal body** /– ˈbɒdi/, *n.* a body of unknown function present in the brain of all vertebrates having a cranium, believed to be a vestigial sense organ. Also, **pineal gland.**

**pineapple** /ˈpaɪnæpəl/, *n.* **1.** the edible juicy fruit (somewhat resembling a pine cone) of a tropical plant, *Ananas comosus,* being a large collective fruit developed from a spike or head of flowers, and surmounted by a crown of leaves. **2.** the plant itself, native to tropical South America and now widely cultivated throughout the tropics, having a short stem and rigid, spiny-margined, recurved leaves. **3.** *Mil. Colloq.* a bomb or hand grenade esp. of the fragmentation type, resembling a pineapple in appearance. **4. rough end of the pineapple,** *Colloq.* a raw deal; the worst part of a bargain.

**pineapple guava** /– ˈgwavə/, *n.* →**feijoa.**

**pine cone** /ˈpaɪn koʊn/, *n.* the cone or strobilus of a pine tree.

**pine-cone lizard** /paɪn-koʊn ˈlɪzəd/, *n.* →**stump-tailed skink.**

**pine marten** /ˈpaɪn matn/, *n.* a slender carnivore, *Martes martes,* belonging to the weasel family and inhabiting Britain, much of Europe and part of Asia, and having fine brown fur.

**pinene** /ˈpaɪnin/, *n.* a terpene, $C_{10}H_{16}$, forming the principal constituent of oil of turpentine and occurring also in other essential oils. [PIN(E)[1] + -ENE]

**pine needle** /ˈpaɪn nidl/, *n.* the needle-like leaf of the pine tree.

**pinery** /ˈpaɪnəri/, *n., pl.* **-eries. 1.** a place in which pineapples are grown. **2.** a forest or grove of pine trees.

**pine-tar** /ˈpaɪn-ta/, *n.* the residue left after the destructive distillation of pine wood, used medicinally.

**pinetum** /paɪˈneɪtəm/, *n., pl.* **-ta** /-tə/. an arboretum of pines and coniferous trees. [L: pine grove]

**piney** /ˈpaɪni/, *adj.,* **-nier, -niest.** →**piny.**

**pinfall** /ˈpɪnfɔl/, *n. Wrestling.* the fact of being thrown on one's back by an opponent and held down with both shoulder-blades touching the canvas for a count of three. In professional wrestling the first contestant to win the best of three pinfalls, three submissions, or a knockout is declared the winner.

**pin-feather** /ˈpɪn-fɛðə/, *n.* **1.** an undeveloped feather, before the web portions have expanded. **2.** a feather just coming through the skin.

**pinfold** /ˈpɪnfoʊld/, *n.* **1.** a pound for stray animals. **2.** a fold, as for sheep or cattle. *–v.t.* **3.** to confine in or as in a pinfold. [*pin(d),* v., impound + FOLD[2]; replacing ME *pondfold,* OE *pundfald.* Cf. POUND[3]]

**ping** /pɪŋ/, *v.i.* **1.** to produce a sharp, ringing, high-pitched sound like that of a bullet striking an object, or of a small bell. **2.** *Motor Vehicles.* →**knock** (def. 2). *–n.* **3.** a pinging sound. [imitative]

**pingao** /ˈpɪŋaʊ/, *n.* a New Zealand sand or sea-shore plant, *Desmoschoenus spiralis.* [Maori]

**pinger** /ˈpɪŋə/, *n.* a bell, as on a timer.

**ping-pong** /ˈpɪŋ-pɒŋ/, *n.* →**table tennis.** [PING, *n.,* on model of *ding-dong,* etc.]

**pinguid** /ˈpɪŋgwəd/, *adj.* **1.** fat; oily; unctuous. **2.** (of soil) fertile. [L *pinguis* fat + -ID[4]] – **pinguidity** /pɪŋˈgwɪdəti/, *n.*

**pinhead** /ˈpɪnhɛd/, *n.* **1.** the head of a pin. **2.** something very small or insignificant. **3.** *Colloq.* a stupid person.

**pinhole** /ˈpɪnhoʊl/, *n.* a small hole made by, for, or as by a pin.

**pinie** /ˈpaɪni/, *n. Colloq.* pineapple.

**pinion**[1] /ˈpɪnjən/, *n. Mach.* **1.** a small cogwheel engaging with a larger cogwheel or with a rack. **2.** an arbor or spindle with teeth which engage with a cogwheel. [F *pignon* pinion, from OF: battlement, from L *pinna* pinnacle]

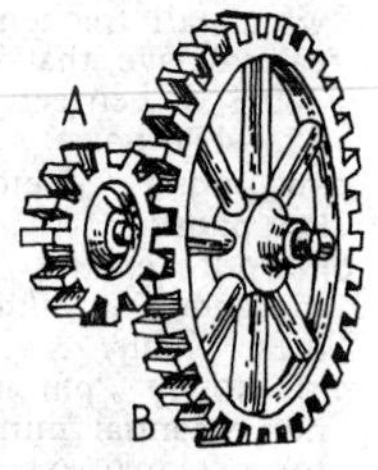

A, pinion[1] (def. 1); B, cogwheel

**pinion**[2] /ˈpɪnjən/, *n.* **1.** the distal or terminal segment of a bird's wing (the carpus, metacarpus, and phalanges). **2.** the wing of a bird. **3.** a feather. **4.** *Chiefly Poetic.* the flight feathers collectively. *–v.t.* **5.** to cut off the pinion of (a wing) or bind (the wings), as in order to prevent a bird from flying. **6.** to disable or restrain (a bird) thus. **7.** to bind (a person's arms or hands) so as to deprive him of the use of them. **8.** to disable thus; shackle. **9.** to bind or hold fast, as to a thing. [ME, from OF *pignon* feather, from L *pinna*]

**pinite** /ˈpɪnaɪt, ˈpaɪn-/, *n.* a mica-like material, essentially a hydrous silicate of aluminium and potassium. [G *Pinit;* named after the *Pini* mine in Saxony. See -ITE[1]]

**pink**[1] /pɪŋk/, *n.* **1.** a light tint of crimson; pale reddish purple. **2.** any plant of the genus *Dianthus,* as *D. plumarius* (the common **garden pink**), *D. sinensis* (**China pink**), or *D. caryophyllus* (**clove pink,** or carnation). **3.** the flower of such a plant; a carnation. **4.** the highest type or example of excellence. **5.** the highest form of degree: *in the pink of condition.* **6.** (*oft. cap.*) a person with moderately left-wing or radical political opinions. **7.** scarlet, or scarlet cloth, as worn by foxhunters. **8.** a fox-hunter. *–adj.* **9.** of the colour pink. **10.** having moderately left-wing or radical political opinions. **11.** flushed, pink in the face: *she turned pink with excitement.* [orig. uncert.]

**pink**[2] /pɪŋk/, *v.t.* **1.** to pierce with a rapier or the like; stab.

**2.** to finish at the edge with a scalloped, notched, or other ornamental pattern. **3.** to punch (cloth, leather, etc.) with small holes or figures for ornament. **4.** *Chiefly Brit.* to deck or adorn (oft. fol. by *out* or *up*). **5.** *Agric.* to shear so closely that the skin of the sheep is exposed. [ME *pynke(n)* make points (marks) or holes (with a sharp instrument). Cf. OE *pynca* point, from *pyng-* (stem of *pyngan* to prick)]

**pink**[3] /pɪŋk/, *n.* a kind of vessel with a narrow stern. [ME *pinck,* from MD *pincke* fishing boat]

**pink**[4] /pɪŋk/, *v.i. Motor Vehicles.* →**knock** (def. 2).

**pink bollworm** /– ˈboulwɜm/, *n.* the larva of a Queensland moth, *Pectinophora scutigera,* which usu. feeds on a native hibiscus but also attacks cotton.

**pink champagne** /– ʃæmˈpeɪn/, *n.* **1.** champagne in which the black grapeskins have been left during part of the fermentation period, the drink having as a consequence a pinkish tinge. **2.** a carbonated soft drink alleged to resemble this.

**pink elephant** /– ˈɛləfənt/, *n.* **1.** a hallucination, esp. as reputedly experienced by alcoholics. **2.** *(pl.) Obs.* →**delirium tremens.**

**pinkeye** /ˈpɪŋkaɪ/, *n.* **1.** a contagious form of conjunctivitis, so called, because of the colour of the inflamed eye. **2.** *Colloq.* ophthalmia suffered by travelling sheep.

**pink fit** /pɪŋk ˈfɪt/, *n.* a hypothetical frenzied state of mind in which discrimination is impaired: *I wouldn't do it in a pink fit.*

**pink gin** /– ˈdʒɪn/, *n.* a cocktail made from gin and angostura bitters.

**pink heath** /– ˈhiθ/, *n.* the pink-flowered form of the southern Australian heath species *Epacris impressa,* which has long tubular flowers, which may vary in colour from white through pink to deep red, hanging from vertical stems; the floral emblem of Victoria.

**pinkie** /ˈpɪŋki/, *n. Colloq.* **1.** a communist sympathiser. **2.** *Vic.* a parking ticket. **3.** the little finger or toe.

**pinking shears** /ˈpɪŋkɪŋ ʃɪəz/, *n.pl.* shears with notched blades, used for giving a scalloped or notched edge to fabrics to prevent them fraying.

**pinkish** /ˈpɪŋkɪʃ/, *adj.* somewhat pink.

**pink noise** /pɪŋk ˈnɔɪz/, *n.* an electronically produced noise used for experimental purposes such as sound machinery, etc., in which all frequencies are represented with equal energy in each octave, that is with as much energy between $100H_z$ and $200H_z$ as between $200H_z$ and $400H_z$, $1000H_z$ and $2000H_z$, etc. Cf. **white noise.**

**pink pages** /– ˈpeɪdʒəz/, *n.pl. (construed as sing.) Obs.* →**yellow pages.**

**pinkroot** /ˈpɪŋkrut/, *n.* **1.** the root of any of various plants of the genus *Spigelia,* which is used as a vermifuge. **2.** any of these plants.

**pin money** /ˈpɪn mʌni/, *n.* **1.** any small sum set aside for non-essential minor expenditures. **2.** money a woman has for personal expenditure, esp. an allowance from her husband.

**pinna** /ˈpɪnə/, *n., pl.* **pinnae** /ˈpɪni/, **pinnas. 1.** *Bot.* one of the primary divisions of a pinnate leaf. **2.** *Zool.* **a.** a feather, wing, or winglike part. **b.** a fin or flipper. **3.** *Physiol.* the auricle of the ear. [L: feather (pl. wing), fin] – **pinnal,** *adj.*

**pinnace** /ˈpɪnəs/, *n.* **1.** a light sailing ship, esp. one formerly used in attendance on a larger vessel. **2.** any of various kinds of ship's boats. [F *pinace,* from It. *pinaccia,* or from Sp. *pinaza,* from L *pīnus* pine tree]

**pinnacle** /ˈpɪnəkəl/, *n., v.,* **-cled, -cling.** *–n.* **1.** a lofty peak. **2.** a lofty eminence or position. **3.** the highest or culminating point: *the pinnacle of fame.* **4.** any pointed, towering part or formation, as of rock. **5.** *Archit.* a relatively small upright structure, commonly terminating in a gable, a pyramid, or a cone, rising above the roof or coping of a building or capping a tower, buttress, or other projecting architectural member. *–v.t.* **6.** to place on or as on a pinnacle. **7.** to form a pinnacle on; crown. [ME *pinacle,* from OF, from LL *pinnāculum,* diminutive of L *pinna* pinnacle, usu. identified with *pinna* PINNA]

**pinnate** /ˈpɪneɪt, -ət/, *adj.* **1.** resembling a feather. **2.** having parts arranged on each side of a common axis. **3.** *Bot.* (of a leaf) having leaflets or primary divisions arranged on each side of a common petiole. Also, **pinnated.** [L *pinnātus* feathered, pinnate] – **pinnately,** *adv.*

pinnate leaf

**pinnati-,** a word element meaning 'pinnate'. [combining form representing L *pinnātus*]

**pinnatifid** /pɪˈnætəfɪd/, *adj. Bot.* (of a leaf) pinnately cleft, with clefts reaching halfway or more to the midrib. [NL *pinnātifidus,* from *pinnāti-* PINNATI- + *-fidus* cleft]

**pinnatilobate** /pɪˌnætəˈloubeɪt/, *adj.* (of a leaf) pinnately lobed, with the divisions extending less than halfway to the midrib. Also, **pinnatilobed** /pɪˈnætəloubd/.

**pinnation** /pɪˈneɪʃən/, *n.* pinnate condition or formation.

**pinnatiped** /pɪˈnætəpɛd/, *adj. Ornith.* having lobate feet.

**pinnatisect** /pɪˈnætəsɛkt/, *adj.* (of a leaf) divided in a pinnate manner almost to the midrib.

**pinner** /ˈpɪnə/, *n.* **1.** one who or that which pins. **2.** a headdress with a long hanging flap pinned on at each side.

**pinnie** /ˈpɪni/, *n. Colloq.* a pinball machine.

**pinnigrade** /ˈpɪnəgreɪd/, *adj.* **1.** moving by means of finlike parts or flippers, as the seals and walruses. *–n.* **2.** a pinnigrade animal.

**pinniped** /ˈpɪnəpɛd/, *adj.* belonging to the Pinnipedia, a suborder of carnivores with limbs adapted to an aquatic life, including the seals and walruses. [*pinni-* (from L, combining form of *pinna* feather, fin) + -PED] – **pinnipedian** /pɪnəˈpidiən/, *adj., n.*

pinnatifid leaf

**pinnula** /ˈpɪnjulə/, *n., pl.* **-lae** /-li/. **1.** →**pinnule. 2.** barb of a feather. [L, diminutive of *pinna* feather, fin]

**pinnulate** /ˈpɪnjuleɪt, -lət/, *adj.* having pinnules. Also, **pinnulated.**

**pinnule** /ˈpɪnjul/, *n.* **1.** *Zool.* **a.** a part or organ resembling the barb of a feather, or a fin or the like. **b.** →**finlet. c.** one of the lateral branchlets of the arms of a crinoid. **2.** *Bot.* a secondary pinna, one of the pinnately disposed divisions of a bipinnate leaf. [L *pinnula* PINNULA] – **pinnular,** *adj.*

**pinny** /ˈpɪni/, *n. Colloq.* a pinafore.

**pinochle** /ˈpinʌkəl/, *n.* **1.** a card game resembling bezique played by two, three, or four persons, with a 48-card pack. **2.** the combination of the queen of spades and the jack of diamonds in this game. Also, **penuchle, penuckle, pinocle.** See **bezique.** [orig. uncert.]

**pinole** /pəˈnouli/, *n.* **1.** maize or wheat flour, sweetened with the flour of mesquite beans or with sugar and spice and used as food in Mexico, California, etc. **2.** any of various mixtures or aromatic powders, used as flavouring. [Sp., from Aztec *pinolli*]

**pinpoint** /ˈpɪnpɔɪnt/, *n.* **1.** the point of a pin. **2.** a trifle. *–v.t.* **3.** to locate or describe exactly as on the ground or on a map. *–adj.* **4.** exact, precise.

**pinprick** /ˈpɪnprɪk/, *n.* **1.** any small puncture made by or as by a pin. **2.** any petty annoyance. – **pinpricking,** *n.* – **pin-prick,** *v.*

**pins and needles,** *n.pl.* a tingling sensation in the limbs, as that which accompanies the return of feeling after numbness; a form of paraesthesia.

**pinstripe** /ˈpɪnstraɪp/, *n. Textiles.* **1.** a very narrow stripe. **2.** any material having a regular pattern of such stripes.

**pint** /paɪnt/, *n.* **1.** a liquid measure of capacity in the imperial system equal to $\frac{1}{8}$ gallon, or 0.568 261 litres or, in the U.S., to 0.104 085 gallon, or 0.473 176 litres. **2.** a liquid or dry measure in the imperial system, varying in different periods and places. **3.** *Brit. Colloq.* a pint of beer. [ME *pynte,* from F *pinte,* from MD: plug]

**pinta** /ˈpɪntə/, *n.* a disease prevalent in Mexico, Central and South America, and elsewhere, marked by spots of various colours on the skin. [Sp.: spot, from L *pi(n)cta,* fem. pp., painted]

**pintable** /ˈpɪnteɪbəl/, *n.* a table or board on which pinball is played.

**pintail** /ˈpɪnteɪl/, *n.* **1.** a long-necked duck, *Anas acuta,* of the

Old and New Worlds, having long narrow middle tail feathers. **2.** the pin-tailed sand-grouse, *Pterocles alchata.* **3.** the American ruddy duck, *Erismatura jamaicensis rubida.* **4.** the sharp-tailed grouse, *Pedioecetes phasianellus,* of North America. **5.** *Colloq.* a surfboard with a pointed tail.

**pintle** /'pɪntl/, *n.* **1.** a pin or bolt, esp. one upon which something turns, as in a hinge. **2.** a pin, bolt, or hook on the rear of a towing vehicle. **3.** *Naut.* a pin on which a ship's or boat's rudder pivots. [ME and OE *pintel* penis, from *pint* (c. D *pint* and G *Pint*) + *-el,* diminutive suffix]

**pinto** /'pɪntoʊ/, *adj., n., pl.* **-tos.** *U.S. –adj.* **1.** piebald; mottled; spotted: *a pinto horse.* *–n.* **2.** a pinto horse. [Sp.: painted, short for *pintado,* pp. of *pintar* paint. See PINTA]

**pin tooth** /'pɪn tuθ/, *n.* a sharp baby tooth of a young pig.

**pint-pot** /'paɪnt-pɒt/, *n.* a pot or vessel holding a pint, esp. one of pewter made to hold beer.

**Pintsch gas** /'pɪntʃ gæs/, *n.* gas with high illuminating power made from shale oil or petroleum, once widely used in floating buoys, lighthouses, and railway carriages. [named after Richard *Pintsch,* 1840-1919, German inventor]

**pint-size** /'paɪnt-saɪz/, *adj. Colloq.* (of a person, etc.) small or insignificant.

**Pintubi** /'pɪntəbi/, *n.* an Australian Aboriginal language spoken in the region near the western border of the Northern Territory.

**pintuck** /'pɪntʌk/, *n.* **1.** a fine tuck used esp. as a decorative feature on a garment. *–v.t.* **2.** to make such a tuck in a garment.

**pin-up** /'pɪn-ʌp/, *Colloq. –n.* **1.** a picture, typically pinned to the wall by a personally unknown admirer, of an attractive member of the opposite sex, esp. a film star, or a nude or nearly nude girl. **2.** the girl or man depicted. *–adj.* **3.** of or in such a picture: *a pin-up girl.*

**pinwale corduroy** /pɪnweɪl 'kɔdʒərɔɪ/, *n.* fine, narrowly-ridged corduroy. Also, **pinwale cord.**

**pinwheel** /'pɪnwil/, *n.* **1.** a small catherine-wheel. **2.** *Mach.* a wheel with pins, usu. on the periphery as cogs. **3.** *Horol.* such a wheel, its pins projecting at right angles to the face, used in an escapement. Also, **pin wheel.**

**pinworm** /'pɪnwɜm/, *n.* a small nematode worm, *Enterobius vermicularis,* infesting the intestine and migrating to the rectum and anus, esp. in children; threadworm.

**piny** /'paɪni/, *adj.,* **-nier, -niest. 1.** abounding in or covered with pine trees. **2.** consisting of pine trees. **3.** pertaining to or suggestive of pine trees. Also, **piney.**

**pion** /'paɪən/, *n. Physics.* →**pimeson.**

**pioneer** /paɪə'nɪə/, *n.* **1.** one of those who first enter or settle a region, thus opening it for occupation and development by others. **2.** one of those who are first or earliest in any field of inquiry, enterprise, or progress: *pioneers in cancer research.* **3.** one of a body of foot soldiers detailed to make roads, dig entrenchments, etc., in advance of the main body. **4.** *Ecol.* a plant or animal which successfully invades and becomes established in a bare area. *–v.i.* **5.** to act as a pioneer. *–v.t.* **6.** to open or prepare (a way, etc.), as a pioneer does. **7.** to open a way for. **8.** to be a pioneer in. [F *pionnier* pioneer, from OF *peon* foot soldier. See PEON[1], PAWN[2]]

**pioneer ball** /'– bɔl/, *n.* (in croquet) a ball waiting for the player at the next hoop but one.

**piopio** /'pioʊˌpioʊ/, *n.* the native thrush of New Zealand, *Turnagra capensis.* [Maori]

**pious** /'paɪəs/, *adj.* **1.** having or displaying religious fervour or conscientiousness in religious observance. **2.** practised or used from religious motives (real or pretended), or for some good object: *a pious deception.* **3.** sacred as distinguished from secular: *pious literature.* **4.** heartfelt. **5.** respectful or dutiful. **6.** sanctimonious. [L *pius*] **– piously,** *adv.* **– piousness,** *n.*

**pip[1]** /pɪp/, *n.* **1.** one of the spots on dice, playing cards, or dominoes. **2.** each of the small segments into which the surface of a pineapple is divided. **3.** *Mil. Colloq.* a badge of rank worn on the shoulders of certain commissioned officers. [earlier *peep;* orig. unknown]

**pip[2]** /pɪp/, *v.,* **pipped, pipping.** *–n.* **1.** a contagious disease of birds, esp. poultry, characterised by the secretion of a thick mucus in the mouth and throat. **2.** (*joc.*) any minor ailment in a person. **3. give (someone) the pip,** *Colloq.* to annoy; irritate, esp. without intention: *his stupidity gives me the pip.* *–v.t.* **4.** to annoy. [ME *pippe,* apparently from MD, from VL *pipita,* for L *pītuīta* phlegm, pip]

**pip[3]** /pɪp/, *n.* a small seed, esp. of a fleshy fruit, as an apple or orange. [short for PIPPIN]

**pip[4]** /pɪp/, *v.,* **pipped, pipping.** *–v.i.* **1.** to peep or chirp. *–v.t.* **2.** (of a young bird) to crack or chip a hole through (the shell). [var. of PEEP[2]]

**pip[5]** /pɪp/, *v.t.,* **pipped, pipping.** *Colloq.* **1.** to beat in a race, etc., esp. by a small margin: *the favourite was pipped at the post.* **2.** to hit with a missile, as by shooting.

**pip[6]** /pɪp/, *n.* **1.** a brief high-pitched sound made by a radio receiver, echo-sounder, or the like. **2.** the signal on the screen of a radar set or the like.

**pipa** /pɪ'pa, 'pipə/, *n.* a tongueless, flat-bodied frog, *Pipa pipa,* found in the Amazon and Orinoco basins, and noted for its unique practice of hatching its young in pockets in the skin of its back; Surinam toad.

**pipage** /'paɪpɪdʒ/, *n.* **1.** conveyance, as of water, gas, or oil, by means of pipes. **2.** the pipes so used. **3.** the sum charged for the conveyance.

**pipal** /'pipəl/, *n.* a species of fig tree, *Ficus religiosa,* of India, somewhat resembling the banyan. Also, **pipul, peepul.** Cf. **bo tree.** [Hind., from Skt *pippala*]

**pipe[1]** /paɪp/, *n., v.,* **piped, piping.** *–n.* **1.** a hollow cylinder of metal, wood, or other material, for the conveyance of water, gas, steam, etc., or for some other purpose; a tube. **2.** any of various tubular or cylindrical objects, parts, or formations. **3.** a tube of wood, clay, hard rubber, or other material, with a small bowl at one end, used for smoking tobacco, opium, etc. **4.** a quantity, as of tobacco, that fills the bowl. **5.** *Music.* **a.** a tube used as, or to form an essential part of, a musical wind instrument. **b.** a musical wind instrument consisting of a single tube of straw, reed, wood, or other material, as a flute, clarinet, or oboe. **c.** one of the wooden or metal tubes from which the sounds of an organ are produced. **d.** (*pl.*) any musical wind instrument. **e.** (*pl.*) any woodwind instrument. **f.** (*usu. pl.*) →**bagpipe. g.** (*usu. pl.*) a set of flutes, as panpipes. **h.** a small primitive type of flute, played with one hand and usu. accompanied by a drum which is struck by the other hand (called a tabor). **6.** *Naut.* **a.** a boatswain's whistle. **b.** the sounding of it as a call. **7.** the note or call of a bird, etc. **8.** *Obs.* the voice, esp. as used in singing. **9.** a tubular organ or passage in an animal body. **10.** (*pl.*) *Colloq.* the respiratory passages. **11.** *Mining.* **a.** a cylindrical vein or body of ore. **b.** one of the vertical cylindrical masses of bluish rock, of eruption origin, found in southern Africa, in which diamonds are found embedded. **12.** *Bot.* the hollow stem of a plant. *–v.i.* **13.** to play on a pipe. **14.** *Naut.* to announce orders, etc., by a boatswain's pipe or other signal. **15.** to speak shrilly. **16.** to make or utter a shrill sound like that of a pipe. **17.** *Mining.* to carve forming a cylindrical cavity. **18.** to form cylindrical or conical holes during moulding, as in casting steel ingots. **19. pipe down,** *Colloq.* to become or keep quiet. **20. pipe up,** *Colloq.* **a.** to begin to talk, esp. unexpectedly. **b.** to make oneself heard. **c.** to speak up, as to assert oneself. *–v.t.* **21.** to convey by means of pipes. **22.** to supply with pipes. **23.** to play (music) on a pipe or pipes. **24.** to summon, order, etc., by sounding the boatswain's pipe or whistle: *all hands were piped on deck.* **25.** to bring, lead, etc., by playing on a pipe. **26.** to utter in a shrill tone. **27.** to trim or finish (a garment, etc.) with piping. [ME and OE *pipe* (c. LG *pipe,* G *Pfeife*), from L *pīpāre* chirp] **– pipelike,** *adj.*

**pipe[2]** /paɪp/, *n.* **1.** a large cask, of varying capacity, for wine, etc. **2.** such a cask as a measure of capacity for wine, etc., equal to 4 barrels, 2 hogsheads, or half a tun, and containing 126 wine gallons (105 imperial gallons or 477 litres). **3.** such a cask with its contents. [OF, ultimately same as PIPE[1]]

**pipeclay** /'paɪpkleɪ/, *n.* a fine white clay used for making tobacco pipes, whitening parts of military or other dress, etc.

**pipe-cleaner** /'paɪp-klinə/, *n.* any of various devices used for cleaning the inside of the stem of a tobacco pipe, as one consisting of a short, flexible piece of wire encased in tufted fabric.

**piped music** /paɪpt 'mjuzɪk/, *n.* recorded background music played, usu. continuously, through loudspeakers in places of work, hotels, restaurants, etc.

**pipedream** /ˈpaɪpdrim/, *n.* a futile hope, far-fetched fancy, or fantastic story.

**pipefish** /ˈpaɪpfɪʃ/, *n., pl.* **-fishes,** (*esp. collectively*) **-fish.** an elongate fish belonging to the Syngnathidae, a family of lophobranch fishes with an elongated tubular snout and a slender body of angular section, encased in bony armour; needlefish.

**pipeful** /ˈpaɪpfʊl/, *n., pl.* **-fuls.** a quantity sufficient to fill the bowl of a pipe.

**pipeline** /ˈpaɪplaɪn/, *n.* **1.** a pipe or several pipes together forming a conduit for the transportation of petroleum, petroleum products, natural gas, etc. **2.** a channel of information, usu. confidential, direct or privileged. **3. in the pipeline,** on the way; in preparation.

**pipe major** /paɪp ˈmeɪdʒə/, *n.* the chief player in a pipe band.

**pipe of peace,** *n.* →**calumet.**

pipefish

**pipe-opener** /ˈpaɪp-oʊpənə/, *n. Colloq.* →**heart-starter.**

**pipe organ** /ˈpaɪp ɔgən/, *n.* an organ with pipes, as distinguished from a reed organ. See **organ** (def. 1).

**piper** /ˈpaɪpə/, *n.* **1.** one who plays on a pipe. **2.** →**bagpiper. 3. pay the piper,** to bear an expense or disadvantage, and so have rights over a corresponding advantage: *he who pays the piper calls the tune.*

**piperade** /pipəˈrad/, *n.* a French dish of tomatoes, peppers, and eggs combined in a fluffy puree.

**piperidine** /pəˈpɛrədin, -daɪn/, *n.* a volatile liquid, $C_5H_{11}N$, with the smell of an amine, obtained from the alkaloid piperine or from pyridine. [L *piper* pepper + ID(E) + -INE[2]]

**piperine** /ˈpɪpəraɪn, -rin/, *n.* a white crystalline alkaloid, $C_{17}H_{19}NO_3$, obtained from pepper and other piperaceous plants, and also prepared synthetically. [F, from It. *peperino* a cement of volcanic ashes, from L *piper* pepper]

**piperonal** /ˈpɪpəroʊnəl/, *n.* a white crystalline aldehyde, $C_8H_6O_3$, a benzene derivative, with a smell resembling that of heliotrope, used in perfumery.

**pipestem** /ˈpaɪpstɛm/, *n.* the stem of a tobacco pipe.

**pipestone** /ˈpaɪpstoʊn/, *n.* a reddish argillaceous stone, used by North American Indians for making tobacco pipes.

**pipette** /pɪˈpɛt/, *n.* a slender graduated tube for measuring and transferring liquids from one vessel to another. Also, **pipet.** [F, diminutive of *pipe* PIPE[1]]

**pipewort** /ˈpaɪpwɜt/, *n.* a monocotyledonous plant, *Eriocaulon septangulare,* with narrow, tufted leaves and small unisexual flowers, occurring only in wet situations in western Scotland and Ireland.

**pipe wrench** /ˈpaɪp rɛntʃ/, *n.* a wrench for gripping and turning a pipe, and usu. having serrated jaws to exert purchase in one direction only.

**pipi** /ˈpɪpi/, *n.* any of several edible, smooth-shelled burrowing, bivalve molluscs as the eastern Australian *Plebidonax deltoides* and the *Mesodesma* species of New Zealand. [Maori]

pipis

**piping** /ˈpaɪpɪŋ/, *n.* **1.** pipes collectively. **2.** material formed into a pipe or pipes. **3.** the act of one who or that which pipes. **4.** the sound of pipes. **5.** shrill sound. **6.** the music of pipes. **7.** a cord-like ornamentation made of icing, used on cakes, pastry, etc. **8.** a tubular band of material, sometimes containing a cord, for trimming garments, etc., as along edges and seams. *–adj.* **9.** playing on a musical pipe. **10.** that pipes. **11.** emitting a shrill sound: *a piping voice.* **12.** *Archaic.* characterised by the music of the peaceful pipe (rather than the martial fife or trumpet). **13. piping hot, a.** very hot. **b.** freshly arrived; brand-new.

**pipistrelle** /pɪpəˈstrɛl/, *n.* the commonest and smallest of the species of bats which inhabits Britain, *Pipistrellus pipistrellus,* the range of which also includes much of Europe and Asia.

**pipit** /ˈpɪpət/, *n.* any of various small passerine birds of the family Motacillidae, esp. the genus Anthus, bearing a superficial resemblance to the larks, as the Australian pipit. [imitative of its note]

**pipkin** /ˈpɪpkən/, *n.* **1.** a small earthen pot. **2.** *U.S.* →**piggin.** [? PIPE[2] + -KIN]

**pippin** /ˈpɪpən/, *n.* **1.** any of numerous varieties of apple, generally characterised by substantial roundish, oblate fruit. **2.** *Bot.* a seed. [ME *pipyn,* from OF *pepin* fruit seed, pip; orig. uncert.]

**pippy** /ˈpɪpi/, *n.* →**pipi.**

**pipsqueak** /ˈpɪpskwik/, *n. Colloq.* a small or insignificant person or thing.

**pipul** /ˈpipəl/, *n.* →**pipal.**

**pipy** /ˈpaɪpi/, *adj.,* **-pier, -piest. 1.** pipelike; tubular. **2.** piping; shrill.

**piquant** /ˈpikənt/, *adj.* **1.** agreeably pungent or sharp in taste or flavour; biting; tart. **2.** agreeably stimulating, interesting, or attractive. **3.** of a smart or racy character: *piquant wit.* **4.** *Archaic.* sharp or stinging, esp. to the feelings. [F: pricking, pungent, ppr. of *piquer.* See PIQUE, *v.*] **– piquancy,** *n.* **– piquantly,** *adv.*

**pique** /pik/, *v.,* **piqued, piquing,** *n. –v.t.* **1.** to affect with sharp irritation and resentment, esp. by some wound to pride: *to be piqued at a refusal.* **2.** to wound (the pride, vanity, etc.). **3.** to excite (interest, curiosity, etc.). **4.** to affect with a lively interest or curiosity. **5.** to pride or plume (oneself). *–n.* **6.** anger, resentment, or ill feeling, as resulting from a slight or injury, esp. to pride or vanity; offence taken. [F *piquer* prick, sting]

**piqué** /ˈpikeɪ/, *n.* **1.** a fabric, having a corded or similar texture. **2.** fine inlaid work of gold, silver, etc., esp. in points, on tortoiseshell or ivory. *–adj.* **3.** (of glove seams and gloves) stitched through lapping edges. [F: stitched, quilted, pp. of *piquer.* See PIQUE]

**piquet** /pɪˈkɛt/, *n.* a card game played by two persons with a pack of 32 cards, the cards from two to six in each suit being excluded. [F, orig. uncert.]

**piracy** /ˈpaɪrəsi/, *n., pl.* **-cies. 1.** robbery or illegal violence at sea or on the shores of the sea. **2.** the unauthorised appropriation or use of a copyrighted or patented work, idea, etc. **3.** the act of operating a pirate bus service, pirate radio station, or the like. [ML *pirātia,* from Gk *peirāteía*]

**piragua** /pɪˈragwə, -ˈrægwə/, *n.* →**pirogue.** [Sp., from Carib: a dugout. Cf. PIROGUE]

**piranha** /pəˈranə/, *n.* any small (hand-sized) South American characin fish of the subfamily Serraosalminae, noted for voracious habits, and despite their small size, dangerous even to men and large animals. [Pg.]

**pirate** /ˈpaɪrət/, *n., v.,* **-rated, -rating.** *–n.* **1.** one who robs or commits illegal violence at sea or on the shores of the sea. **2.** a vessel employed by such persons. **3.** any plunderer. **4.** one who appropriates and reproduces, without authorisation as for his own profit, the literary, artistic, or other work or any invention of another. **5.** Also, **pirate radio.** a radio station broadcasting on an unauthorised wavelength, and often operating outside territorial waters or in a foreign country so as to avoid payment of copyright fees or other legal restrictions. *–v.t.* **6.** to commit piracy upon; rob or plunder as a pirate does. **7.** to take by piracy. **8.** to appropriate and reproduce (literary work, etc.) without authorisation or legal right. *–v.i.* **9.** to commit or practise piracy. [ME, from L *pīrāta,* from Gk *peirātḗs*] **– piratical** /pɪˈrætɪkəl/, *adj.* **– piratically,** *adv.*

**piriform** /ˈpɪrəfɔm/, *adj.* shaped like a pear.

**piripiri** /ˈpɪripɪri/, *n. N.Z.* →**biddy-biddy.**

**pirn** /pɜn/, *n.* **1.** a bobbin, spool or reel used in weaving. **2.** a fishing reel. [ME *pirne*]

**pirogue** /pəˈroʊg/, *n.* a canoe or open boat hollowed from the trunk of a tree, as the outrigger canoes of Polynesia. Also **piragua.** [F, probably from Galibi. Cf. PIRAGUA]

**pirouette** /pɪruˈɛt/, *n., v.,* **-etted, -etting.** *–n.* **1.** a whirling about on one foot or on the points of the toes, as in dancing. *–v.i.* **2.** to perform a pirouette, whirl as on the toes. [F: top, whirligig, whirl, b. *pivot* pivot and *girouette* weathervane (from *girer* to turn)]

**pirri point** /ˈpɪri pɔɪnt/, *n.* an early Aboriginal implement consisting of a pointed stone trimmed to a functional shape on one side.

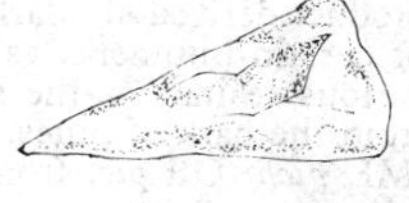
pirri point

**pis aller** /ˌpiz aˈleɪ/, *n.* the last resort. [F: lit., to go worst]

**piscary** /ˈpɪskəri/, *n., pl.* **-ries.** **1.** *Law.* the right or privilege of fishing in particular waters. **2.** a fishing place. [late ME, from ML *piscāria,* properly fem. of L *piscārius* pertaining to fish]

**piscatorial** /pɪskəˈtɔriəl/, *adj.* **1.** of or pertaining to fishermen or fishing. **2.** given or devoted to fishing. Also, **piscatory** /ˈpɪskətəri, -tri/. [L *piscātorius* + -AL[1]]

**Piscean** /ˈpaɪsiən/, *n.* **1.** a person born under the sign of Pisces, and (according to tradition) exhibiting the typical Piscean personality traits to some degree. *–adj.* **2.** of or pertaining to Pisces. **3.** of or pertaining to such a person or such a personality trait.

**Pisces** /ˈpaɪsiz/, *n.pl.* **1.** the Fishes, a constellation and sign of the zodiac. **2.** →**Piscean.** **3.** *Zool.* the class of vertebrates that includes the fishes (teleosts), exclusive of elasmobranchs, dipnoans, and marsipobranchs. [L, pl. of *piscis* fish]

**pisci-**, a word element meaning 'fish'. [L, combining form of *piscis*]

**pisciculture** /ˈpɪsɪkʌltʃə/, *n.* the breeding, rearing, and transplantation of fish by artificial means.

**piscina** /pəˈʃinə, pəˈʃaɪnə/, *n., pl.* **-nas, -nae** /-ni/. *Eccles.* a basin with a drain used for certain ablutions, specifically to receive the water with which the vessels have been cleansed after the celebration of the Eucharist. Also, **piscine.** [L: orig., fishpond] – **piscinal,** *adj.*

**piscine** /ˈpɪsin/, *adj.* **1.** of or pertaining to fish. *–n.* **2.** →**piscina.** [L *piscis* fish + -INE[1]]

**piscivorous** /pəˈsɪvərəs/, *adj.* fish-eating.

**pish** /pɪʃ, pʃ/, *interj.* (an exclamation of contempt or impatience.)

**pisiform** /ˈpɪsəfɔm/, *adj.* **1.** having the shape of a pea. **2.** *Anat., Zool.* pertaining to the pealike bone on the ulnar side of the carpus. [NL *pīsiformis,* from *pīsi-* (combining form representing L *pīsum* pea) + *-formis* -FORM]

**pisolite** /ˈpaɪzəlaɪt/, *n.* a sedimentary rock containing spherical or subspherical concretions more than 2 mm in diameter. [NL *pisolithus,* from Gk *píso(s)* pea + *-lithos* -LITE] – **pisolitic** /paɪzəˈlɪtɪk/, *adj.*

**piss** /pɪs/, *Colloq.* *–v.i.* **1.** to urinate. **2.** to rain heavily: *it was pissing down.* **3. piss on,** to drink considerable quantities of liquor, esp. beer. **4. piss about (around),** to mess about. **5. piss (all) over,** to beat or confound utterly. **6. piss in (someone's) pocket,** to behave obsequiously towards (someone). **7. piss into the wind,** to embark on a futile course of action. **8. piss off,** (*sometimes offensive*) to go away. *–v.t.* **9. piss (someone) off, a.** to send (someone) away. **b.** to annoy (someone) intensely. *–n.* **10.** urine. **11.** an act of passing water; urination. **12.** beer. **13. all piss 'n' wind,** loquacious, but insincere. *–adv.* **14.** (an intensifier) very: *piss-awful.* [OF *pisser,* from Rom. **pissare* of echoic orig.]

**pissant** /ˈpɪsænt/, *n. in the phrases* **a. game as a pissant,** very brave. **b. drunk as a pissant,** very drunk.

**pissed** /pɪst/, *adj. Colloq.* drunk.

**pissed-off** /pɪst-ˈɒf/, *adj. Colloq.* disgruntled; fed up; thoroughly discontent.

**piss-elegant** /ˈpɪs-ɛləgənt/, *adj. Colloq.* with pretensions to elegance. – **piss-elegance,** *n.*

**pisser** /ˈpɪsə/, *n. Colloq.* **1.** a pub. **2.** a urinal. **3.** →**pisswhacker.**

**pisspot** /ˈpɪspɒt/, *n. Colloq.* a drunkard. Also, **pisshead.**

**piss-up** /ˈpɪs-ʌp/, *n. Colloq.* an occasion on which a large quantity of alcohol is consumed by a group of people, as at a party, etc.

**piss-weak** /ˈpɪs-wik/, *adj.* **1.** inadequate; disappointing; not up to standard. **2.** of weak character; cowardly; irresolute. Also, **piss-poor.**

**pisswhacker** /ˈpɪswækə/, *n.* a female cicada which makes no sound but squirts a noisome fluid when disturbed. Also, **pisser.**

**pissy** /ˈpɪsi/, *adj. Colloq.* **1.** unpleasant. **2.** mildly drunk.

**pistachio** /pɪsˈtaʃioʊ/, *n., pl.* **-chios.** **1.** the stone (nut) of the fruit of a small anacardiaceous tree, *Pistacia vera,* of southern Europe and Asia Minor. **2.** its edible greenish kernel, used for flavouring. **3.** the tree itself. **4.** pistachio nut flavour. **5.** light yellowish green. Also, **pistache** /pɪsˈtæʃ/. [It. *pistacchio,* from L *pistācium,* from Gk *pistákion*]

**piste** /pist/, *n.* (in fencing) a striplike area of specified size upon which bouts take place. [F: path]

**pistil** /ˈpɪstl/, *n. Bot.* **1.** the ovule-bearing or seed-bearing organ of a flower, consisting when complete of ovary, style and stigma. **2.** such organs collectively, where there are more than one in a flower. **3.** →**gynoecium.** [NL *pistillum* pistil, from L: pestle]

pistil of lily: A, stigma; B, style; C, ovary

**pistillate** /ˈpɪstələt, -leɪt/, *adj. Bot.* **1.** having a pistil or pistils. **2.** having a pistil or pistils but no stamens.

**pistol** /ˈpɪstl/, *n., v.,* **-tolled, -tolling** or (*U.S.*) **-toled, -toling.** *–n.* **1.** a short firearm intended to be held and fired with one hand. *–v.t.* **2.** to shoot with a pistol. [F *pistole* pistol, from G, from Czech *pist'al*]

**pistoleer** /pɪstəˈlɪə/, *n.* one who is armed with or uses a pistol. [F *pistolier*]

**pistol-grip** /ˈpɪstl-grɪp/, *n.* a handle or a saw, rifle, electric drill, etc., perpendicular to the main axis and thus resembling the stock of a pistol.

**pistol-whip** /ˈpɪstl-wɪp/, *v.t.,* **-whipped, -whipping.** to beat about the head with a revolver.

pistol: early 19th-century

**piston** /ˈpɪstən/, *n.* **1.** a movable disc or cylinder fitting closely within a tube or hollow cylinder, and capable of being driven alternately forwards and backwards in the tube by pressure, as in an internal-combustion engine, thus imparting reciprocating motion to a rod **(piston rod)** attached to it on one side, or of being driven thus by the rod, as in a pump. **2.** a pumplike valve used to change the pitch in a cornet or the like. [F, from It. *pistone,* from *pistare* pound, from L *pistus,* pp., pounded]

**piston ring** /ˈ– rɪŋ/, *n.* a metallic ring, usu. one of a series, and split so as to be expansible, placed around a piston in order to maintain a tight fit, as inside the cylinder of an internal-combustion engine.

**piston rod** /ˈ– rɒd/, *n.* the rod which connects the piston of a reciprocating steam-engine to the crosshead.

**pit**[1] /pɪt/, *n., v.,* **pitted, pitting.** *–n.* **1.** a hole or cavity in the ground. **2.** a covered or concealed excavation in the ground to serve as a trap; pitfall. **3.** *Mining.* **a.** an excavation made in digging for some mineral deposit. **b.** the shaft of a coalmine. **c.** the mine itself. **4.** a sunken area in the floor of a garage used for the inspection of vehicles from below. **5.** a hole in the ground used for any of various purposes, as disposal of waste, burning charcoal, making silage, etc. **6.** the abode of evil spirits and lost souls; hell, or a part of it. **7.** a hollow or indentation in a surface. **8.** a natural hollow or depression in the body: *the pit of the stomach.* **9.** a small depressed scar such as one of those left on the skin after smallpox. **10.** an enclosure for combats, as of dogs or cocks. **11.** *U.S.* that part of the floor of an exchange devoted to a special kind of business: *the grain pit.* **12.** (in a theatre) **a.** the ground floor of the auditorium. **b.** the part of the ground floor behind the stalls. **c.** the persons occupying this section. **13.** *Athletics.* an area, typically slightly sunken and filled with sand, which softens the fall of a long jumper, high jumper, etc. **14.** any of the stalls beside the motor-racing track in which competing cars undergo running repairs, are refuelled, etc., during a race. **15.** *Bot.* a thin place in a cell wall affording communication with another cell. **16. the pits,** *Colloq.* the most unpleasant or most obnoxious (place, circumstance, condition, etc.). *–v.t.* **17.** to mark with pits or depressions. **18.** to place or bury in a pit. **19.** to set in active opposition, as one against another. **20.** to set (animals) in a pit or enclosure to fight. *–v.i.* **21.** to become marked with pits or depressions. **22.** *Pathol.* to retain for a time the mark of pressure by the finger, etc., as the skin. [ME and OE *pytt,* from L *puteus* well, pit, shaft]

**pit**[2] /pɪt/, *n., v.,* **pitted, pitting.** *U.S.* *–n.* **1.** the stone of a fruit, as of a cherry, peach, or plum. *–v.t.* **2.** to take out the stone from (a fruit, etc.). [D: kernel]

**pita** /ˈpitə/, *n.* **1.** a fibre obtained from species of *Agave, Aechmea,* or related genera, used for cordage, etc. **2.** one of these plants. [Sp., from Quechua]

**pitapat** /pɪtəˈpæt/, *adv., n., v.,* **-patted, -patting.** *–adv.* **1.** with a quick succession of beats or taps. *–n.* **2.** the movement or the sound of something going pitapat. *–v.i.* **3.** to go pitapat. [imitative]

**pitch**[1] /pɪtʃ/, *v.t.* **1.** to set up or erect (a tent, camp, etc.). **2.** to put, set, or plant in a fixed or definite place or position (as cricket stumps, etc.). **3.** to set or aim at a certain point, degree, level, etc.: *he pitched his hopes too high.* **4.** *Music.* to set at a particular pitch, or determine the key or keynote of (a tune, etc.). **5.** to throw, fling or toss. **6.** *Baseball.* to deliver (the ball) to the batter. **7.** *Golf.* to hit (the ball) so that it rises steeply and rolls little on landing. **8.** *Cards.* **a.** to lead (a card of a particular suit), thereby fixing that suit as trumps. **b.** to determine (trumps) thus. **9.** *Bldg Trades.* to dress, work, or place (masonry, etc.). **10.** *Archit.* to build a roof with a certain slope or steepness: *to pitch a roof steeply.* **11. pitch a line,** to attempt to impress by boastful and sometimes untruthful speech often as a means of winning sexual favours from a woman. *–v.i.* **12. pitch a tale (yarn, etc.),** to tell a story, esp. one that is exaggerated or untrue. **13.** to plunge or fall forward or headlong. **14.** to lurch. **15.** to throw, fling or toss. **16.** to slope downwards; dip. **17.** to plunge with alternate fall and rise of bow and stern, as a ship, aeroplane, etc. (opposed to *roll*). **18.** *Aeron.* to change the angle which the longitudinal axis makes relative to the horizontal. **19.** to fix a tent or temporary habitation; encamp. **20.** *Rare.* to settle. **21.** to fix or decide (oft. fol. by *on* or *upon*), often casually or without particular consideration. **22.** *Golf.* to hit the ball so that it rises steeply and does not roll much on landing. **23.** *Baseball.* **a.** to deliver the ball to the batter. **b.** to fill the position of pitcher. **24. pitch in,** *Colloq.* **a.** to contribute or join in. **b.** to begin vigorously. **25. pitch into, a.** to attack verbally or physically. **b.** to begin to do or work on (something). *–n.* **26.** relative point, position, or degree. **27.** height (now chiefly in certain specific uses): *pitch of an arch.* **28.** the highest point or greatest height: *the pitch of perfection.* **29.** *Acoustics, Music.* the apparent predominant frequency of a sound from an acoustical source, musical instrument, etc. **30.** a particular tonal standard with which given notes may be compared in respect to their relative level. **31.** the act or manner of pitching. **32.** a throw or toss. **33.** the pitching movement, or the plunge forward of a ship, aeroplane or the like. **34.** inclination or slope. **35.** degree of inclination or slope; angle. **36.** a sloping part or place. **37.** a quantity of something pitched or placed somewhere. **38. a.** *Sport.* the whole area of play, usu. of grass, of cricket, football, hockey, etc. **b.** *Cricket.* the area between the wickets. **39.** a spot where a person or thing is placed or stationed esp. the established location of a stall in a street market or of a street pedlar, singer, etc. **40.** a sales talk. **41.** specific plan of action; way of approaching a problem. **42.** *Geol., Mining.* **a.** the angle that a line in the plane makes with a horizontal line in that plane. **b.** in ore deposits, the angle between the axis of the ore shoot and the strike of the vein. **43.** *Mining.* **a.** the defined section of a lode assigned to a tributer. **b.** working place in a slope. **44.** *Archit.* the slope or steepness of a roof. **45.** *Mach.* **a.** the distance between corresponding surfaces of adjacent teeth of a gearwheel or the like. **b.** the distance between two things in a regular series, as between threads of a screw, rivets, etc. **46.** the distance which a propeller would advance in one revolution, assuming no slip. **47.** *Cards.* a game in which trumps are determined for any one round by the first card led. **48. queer someone's pitch,** *Colloq.* to upset someone's plans. [ME *picche(n)*; ? akin to PICK[1]]

**pitch**[2] /pɪtʃ/, *n.* **1.** any of various dark-coloured tenacious or viscous substances used for covering the seams of vessels after caulking, for making pavements, etc., as the residuum left after the distillation of coal tar (coal-tar pitch), or a product derived similarly from wood tar (wood pitch). **2.** any of certain bitumens, as *mineral pitch* (asphaltum). **3.** any of various resins. **4.** the sap or crude turpentine which exudes from the bark of pines. *–v.t.* **5.** to smear or cover with pitch. [ME *pich,* OE *pic,* from L *pix;* akin to Gk *píssa*] **– pitchlike,** *adj.*

**pitch-and-toss** /pɪtʃ-ən-ˈtɒs/, *n.* a game in which players throw coins at a mark, the most accurate player then being allowed to toss all the coins and keep those which come down heads up.

**pitch-black** /ˈpɪtʃ-blæk/, *adj.* very black or dark.

**pitchblende** /ˈpɪtʃblɛnd/, *n.* an impure uraninite, occurring in black pitchlike masses; the principal ore of uranium and radium. [half translation, half adoption of G *Pechblende.* See PITCH[2], BLENDE]

**pitch circle** /ˈpɪtʃ sɜkəl/, *n.* an imaginary circle concentric with the axis of a toothed wheel, at such a distance from the base of the teeth that it is in contact with and rolls upon a similar circle of another toothed wheel engaging with the first.

**pitch-dark** /ˈpɪtʃ-dak/, *adj.* black or dark as pitch. Also, **pitch-black.**

**pitched battle** /pɪtʃt ˈbætl/, *n.* **1.** a battle following the deliberate choice of time and place, and the orderly arrangement of forces (opposed to a *skirmish*). **2.** a battle fully engaging the resources of the opposing armies. **3.** *Colloq.* any violent fight involving many people.

**pitcher**[1] /ˈpɪtʃə/, *n.* **1.** a container, usu. with a handle and spout or lip, for holding and pouring liquids. **2.** *Bot.* **a.** a pitcher-like modification of the leaf of certain plants. **b.** →**ascidium.** [ME *picher,* from OF *pichier;* ? akin to BEAKER] **– pitcher-like,** *adj.*

**pitcher**[2] /ˈpɪtʃə/, *n.* **1.** one who pitches. **2.** *Baseball.* the player who delivers or throws the ball to the batter. **3.** *Golf.* a lightweight iron golf club (number 7 iron) with a broad, sloping face. [PITCH[1], *v.* + -ER[1]]

**pitcher plant** /ˈ– plænt/, *n.* any of various, often insectivorous, plants with leaves modified into a pitcher-like receptacle or ascidium, as in some species of *Nepenthes* and *Cephalotus.*

pitcher plant

**pitch-faced** /ˈpɪtʃ-feɪst/, *adj. Bldg Trades.* (of masonry) composed of stones roughly squared with the pitching tool.

**pitchfork** /ˈpɪtʃfɔk/, *n.* **1.** a fork for lifting and pitching hay, etc. *–v.t.* **2.** to pitch or throw with or as with a pitchfork.

**pitchi** /ˈpɪtʃi/, *n.* a large, shallow, wooden vessel used by Aboriginal women as a container for food or water and sometimes for carrying infants. [Aboriginal]

**pitching** /ˈpɪtʃɪŋ/, *n.* a stone facing laid on an earth slope, as on a dam, to prevent erosion.

**pitching tool** /ˈ– tul/, *n. Bldg Trades.* a chisel for roughly squaring stones.

**pitchi-pitchi** /ˌpɪtʃi-ˈpɪtʃi/, *n.* a small, carnivorous marsupial mouse, *Antechinomys spenceri;* wuhl-wuhl. [Aboriginal]

**pitch line** /ˈpɪtʃ laɪn/, *n.* **1.** →**pitch circle. 2.** a corresponding straight line on a toothed rack.

**pitchman** /ˈpɪtʃmən/, *n. U.S.* **1.** an itinerant salesman of small wares which are usu. carried in a case with collapsible legs, allowing it to be set up or removed quickly. **2.** any high-pressure salesman, usu. of goods of dubious quality. [PITCH[1] + MAN]

pitchfork

**pitch pine** /ˈpɪtʃ paɪn/, *n.* any of several species of pine from which pitch or turpentine is obtained.

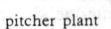

**pitchpipe** /ˈpɪtʃpaɪp/, *n.* a small pipe, sounded to give the pitch for singing, tuning an instrument, etc.

**pitch shot** /ˈpɪtʃ ʃɒt/, *n.* (in golf) a shot, used to approach the green, that lifts the ball steeply up, often with backspin applied, to prevent it rolling when it lands.

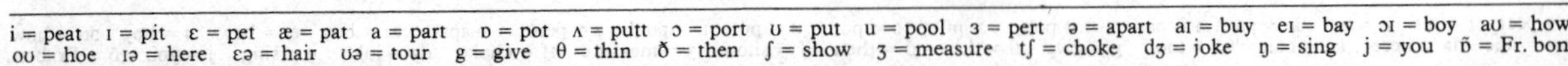

**pitchstone** /ˈpɪtʃstoʊn/, *n.* a glassy igneous rock having a resinous lustre and resembling hardened pitch. [PITCH[2], *n.,* + STONE, translation of G *Pechstein*]

**pitchy** /ˈpɪtʃi/, *adj.,* **-ier, -iest.** **1.** full of or abounding in pitch. **2.** smeared with pitch. **3.** of the nature of pitch; resembling pitch. **4.** black; dark as pitch. – **pitchiness,** *n.*

**piteous** /ˈpɪtiəs/, *adj.* **1.** such as to excite or deserve pity, or appealing strongly for pity; pathetic. **2.** *Archaic.* compassionate. [*pite* PITY + -OUS; replacing ME *pitous,* from AF, from L *pietas* piety] – **piteously,** *adv.* – **piteousness,** *n.*

**pitfall** /ˈpɪtfɔl/, *n.* **1.** a concealed pit prepared as a trap for animals or men to fall into. **2.** any trap or danger for the unwary.

**pith** /pɪθ/, *n.* **1.** any soft, spongy tissue or substance: *the pith of an orange.* **2.** *Bot.* the central cylinder of parenchymatous tissue in the stems of dicotyledonous plants. **3.** any of various analogous inner parts of substances, as the centre of a log, a feather, etc. **4.** the important or essential part; essence. **5.** strength, force, or vigour. *–v.t.* **6.** to take the pith from (plants, etc.). **7.** to destroy the spinal cord or brain of. **8.** to slaughter, as cattle, by severing the spinal cord. [ME; OE *pitha* pith. Cf. D *pit* pith, PIT[2]]

**pithead** /ˈpɪthɛd/, *n.* **1.** the top of a mine shaft. **2.** the machinery, offices, etc., on the surface associated with the running of a mine.

**pithecanthrope** /pɪθiˈkænθroʊp/, *n.* a member of the genus *Pithecanthropus.*

**Pithecanthropus** /pɪθiˈkænθrəpəs/, *n., pl.* **-pi** /-paɪ/. an extinct genus of apelike man, now classified under the genus Homo, as *homo erectus.* [NL, from Gk: *píthēkos* ape + *ánthrōpos* man] – **pithecanthropoid,** *adj.*

**pith helmet** /ˈpɪθ hɛlmət/, *n.* a sun-hat, usu. domed with a sloping brim, made of spongewood, and formerly much worn by Europeans in tropical countries; topee.

**pithos** /ˈpɪθɒs/, *n., pl.* **pithoi** /ˈpɪθɔɪ/. a large pottery jar for the storage of oil or grain. [Gk]

**pithy** /ˈpɪθi/, *adj.,* **-ier, -iest.** **1.** full of vigour, substance, or meaning; terse; forcible: *a pithy criticism.* **2.** of, like, or abounding in pith. – **pithily,** *adv.* – **pithiness,** *n.*

**pitiable** /ˈpɪtiəbəl/, *adj.* **1.** deserving to be pitied; such as justly to excite pity; lamentable; deplorable. **2.** such as to excite a contemptuous pity; miserable; contemptible. – **pitiableness,** *n.* – **pitiably,** *adv.*

**pitier** /ˈpɪtiə/, *n.* one who pities.

**pitiful** /ˈpɪtəfəl/, *adj.* **1.** such as to excite or deserve pity: *a pitiful fate.* **2.** such as to excite contempt by smallness, poor quality, etc.: *pitiful attempts.* **3.** full of pity or compassion; compassionate. – **pitifully,** *adv.* – **pitifulness,** *n.*

**pitiless** /ˈpɪtələs/, *adj.* feeling or showing no pity; merciless. – **pitilessly,** *adv.* – **pitilessness,** *n.*

**Pitjantjatjara** /pɪtʃəntʃəˈtʃærə/, *n.* an Australian Aboriginal language of the desert area, near Ernabella, South Australia, still in extensive use. Also, **Pitjantjara** /pɪtʃənˈdʒærə/.

**pitman** /ˈpɪtmən/, *n., pl.* **-men** *for def. 1,* **-mans** *for def. 2.* **1.** one who works in a pit, as in coal-mining. **2.** *Mach., Chiefly U.S.* →**connecting rod.** [PIT[1] + MAN]

**pitocin** /ˈpɪtəsən/, *n.* an aqueous solution containing the oxytocic principle of the posterior lobe of the pituitary gland, used to induce labour. [PIT(UITARY) + (OXYT)OCIN]

**piton** /ˈpitɒn/, *n.* (in mountaineering) a metal spike with an eye through which a rope may be passed. Also, **peg.** [F]

**Pitot tube** /ˈpitoʊ tjub/, *n.* an instrument for measuring fluid velocity. [named after H. *Pitot,* 1695-1771, French physicist and engineer]

**pit pony** /ˈpɪt poʊni/, *n.* a small pony, formerly used for haulage in coalmines, etc.

**pitsaw** /ˈpɪtsɔ/, *n.* a saw operated by two men, one above the log and the other below it, in a pit.

**pit silo** /ˈpɪt saɪloʊ/, *n.* →**silo** (def. 3).

**pit stop** /ˈ– stɒp/, *n.* a stop made at the pits by a racing car during a race.

**pitta** /ˈpɪtə/, *n.* any of several species of small, brightly coloured, ground-dwelling birds of the genus *Pitta* of northern and eastern Australia, as the noisy pitta.

**pittance** /ˈpɪtns/, *n.* **1.** a small allowance or sum for living expenses. **2.** a scanty income or remuneration. **3.** any small portion or amount. [ME *pita(u)nce,* from OF, from *pitie* pity. See PIETY, PITY]

**pitter-patter** /ˈpɪtə-pætə/, *n.* **1.** a rapid succession of light beats or taps, as of rain. *–adv.* **2.** with a rapid succession of light beats or taps, as of rain.

**pittosporum** /pəˈtɒspərəm/, *n.* any tree or shrub of the large genus *Pittosporum* of Asia, Africa and Australasia, as the sweet-scented *P. undulatum* of eastern Australia which has white bell shaped flowers and orange fruit.

**Pitt Street farmer,** *n.* (in New South Wales) one who owns a country property, often for tax loss purposes, but who lives and works in Sydney. Cf. **Collin's street cocky, Queens Street bushie.**

**pituitary** /pəˈtjuətri, -təri/, *n., pl.* **-taries,** *adj.* *–n.* **1.** *Anat.* →**pituitary gland.** **2.** *Med.* the extract obtained from either the anterior or posterior lobes of the pituitary. The anterior lobe substance regulates growth of the skeleton; that of the posterior lobe increases blood pressure, contracts the smooth muscles, etc. *–adj. Anat.* **3.** of the pituitary gland. **4.** denoting a physical type of abnormal size with overgrown extremities resulting from excessive pituitary secretion. [L *pītuītārius* pertaining to, or secreting phlegm]

**pituitary gland** /ˈ– glænd/, *n.* a small, oval, endocrine gland attached to the base of the brain and situated in a depression of the sphenoid bone, which secretes several hormones, and was formerly supposed to secrete mucus. Also, **pituitary body.**

**pituri** /ˈpɪtʃəri/, *n.* a shrub, *Duboisia hopwoodii,* of Australia, the leaves and twigs of which are used by Aborigines as a narcotic. [Aboriginal]

**pit viper** /ˈpɪt vaɪpə/, *n.* any of the snakes of the subfamily Crotalinae, with a wide distribution in the Old and New Worlds, having a pit on each side of the head in front of the eye.

**pity** /ˈpɪti/, *n., pl.* **pities,** *v.,* **pitied, pitying.** *–n.* **1.** sympathetic or kindly sorrow excited by the suffering or misfortune of another, often leading one to give relief or aid or to show mercy: *to weep from pity, to take pity on a person.* **2.** a cause or reason for pity, sorrow, or regret: *What a pity you could not go!* *–v.t.* **3.** to feel pity or compassion for; be sorry for; commiserate. *–v.i.* **4.** *Obs.* to feel pity. [ME *pite,* from OF, from L *pietas* piety] – **pityingly,** *adv.*

**pityriasis** /pɪtəˈraɪəsəs/, *n.* **1.** *Pathol.* any of various skin diseases marked by the shedding of branlike scales of epidermis. **2.** *Vet. Sci.* a skin disease in various domestic animals marked by dry scales. [NL, from Gk: branlike eruption]

**più** /pju/, *adv.* (a musical direction) more; somewhat. [It.]

**piupiu** /ˈpiu,piu/, *n. N.Z.* a Maori flax skirt. [Maori]

**pivot** /ˈpɪvət/, *n.* **1.** a pin or short shaft on the end of which something rests and turns, or upon and about which something rotates or oscillates. **2.** the end of a shaft or arbor, resting and turning in a bearing. **3.** that on which something turns, hinges, or depends. **4.** the person upon whom a line, as of troops, wheels about. **5.** *Aus. Rules.* →**centre** (def. 8). **6.** *Rugby Union.* a half-back. *–v.i.* **7.** to turn on or as on a pivot. *–v.t.* **8.** to mount on, attach by, or provide with a pivot or pivots. [F; orig. uncert.]

**pivotal** /ˈpɪvətl/, *adj.* **1.** of, pertaining to, or serving as a pivot. **2.** of critical importance. – **pivotally,** *adv.*

**pivot bridge** /ˈpɪvət brɪdʒ/, *n.* →**swing bridge.**

**pivot punch** /ˈ– pʌntʃ/, *n. Boxing.* →**backhander.**

**piwakawaka** /piˈwɒkəwɒkə/, *n.* the fantail of New Zealand. [Maori]

**pix** /pɪks/, *n.* →**pyx.**

**pixilated** /ˈpɪksəleɪtəd/, *adj. Colloq.* amusingly eccentric. [from PIXY, modelled on TITILLATED]

**pixy** /ˈpɪksi/, *n., pl.* **pixies.** a fairy or sprite. Also, **pixie.** [orig. uncert.]

**pizz.,** *Music.* pizzicato.

**pizza** /ˈpitsə, ˈpɪtsə/, *n.* an Italian dish made from yeast dough covered with tomato, grated cheese, anchovies, olives, etc.

**pizzazz** /pəˈzæz/, *n. Orig. U.S.* panache; zest; verve.

**pizzeria** /pɪtsəˈriə/, *n.* a cafe, shop, restaurant, etc., where pizzas are made and sold. [It.]

**pizzicato** /pɪtsəˈkatoʊ/, *adj.* **1.** played by plucking the strings with the finger instead of using the bow, as on a violin. *–n.* **2.** a note or passage so played. [It., pp. of *pizzicare* pick, twang (a stringed instrument)]

**pizzle** /ˈpɪzəl/, *n.* an animal's penis, esp. of a ram or bull.

**pizzle rot** /ˈ– rɒt/, *n.* a disease which affects the inside of the penis sheath and the orifice of wethers and, more rarely, rams; sheath rot; balanitis.

**P.J.s** /pi ˈdʒeɪz/, *n.pl. Colloq.* pyjamas.

**P.J.T.** /pi dʒeɪ ˈti/, Prices Justification Tribunal.

**Pk,** Park.

**pkt,** packet.

**P.K.U.** /pi keɪ ˈju/, phenylketonuria.

**P.K.U. test** /pi keɪ ˈju tɛst/, *n.* →**Guthrie test.**

**pl.,** plural.

**Pl.,** Place (in street names, etc.)

**placable** /ˈplækəbəl/, *adj.* capable of being placated or appeased; forgiving: *he seemed mild and placable.* [ME, from L *plācābilis*] – **placability** /plækəˈbɪləti/, **placableness,** *n.* – **placably,** *adv.*

**placard** /ˈplækad/, *n.* **1.** a written or printed notice to be posted in a public place; a poster. *–v.t.* **2.** to post placards on or in. **3.** to give notice of by means of placards. **4.** to post as a placard. [F, from *plaque,* from D *plak* flat board] – **placarder,** *n.*

**placate** /pləˈkeɪt/, *v.t.,* **-cated, -cating.** to appease; pacify. [L *plācātus,* pp.] – **placation,** *n.*

**placatory** /pləˈkeɪtəri, ˈplækətəri/, *adj.* tending or intending to placate. [L *plācātōrius*]

**place** /pleɪs/, *n., v.,* **placed, placing.** *–n.* **1.** a particular portion of space, of definite or indefinite extent. **2.** space in general (chiefly in connection with *time*). **3.** the portion of space occupied by anything. **4.** a space or spot, set apart or used for a particular purpose: *a place of worship.* **5.** any part or spot in a body or surface: *a decayed place in a tooth.* **6.** a particular passage in a book or writing. **7.** a space or seat for a person, as in a theatre, train, etc. **8.** the space or position customarily or previously occupied by a person or thing. **9.** position, situation, or circumstances: *if I were in your place.* **10.** a proper or appropriate location or position. **11.** a short street, a court, etc.: *Martin Place.* **12.** a job, post, or office. **13.** a function or duty. **14.** position or standing in the social scale, or in any order of merit, estimation, etc. **15.** high position or rank. **16.** official employment or position. **17.** a region. **18.** an open space, or square, in a city or town. **19.** an area, esp. one regarded as an entity and identifiable by name, used for habitation, as a city, town, or village. **20.** a building. **21.** a part of a building. **22.** a residence, dwelling, or house. **23.** stead or lieu: *use water in place of milk.* **24.** a step or point in order of proceeding: *in the first place.* **25.** a fitting opportunity. **26.** a reasonable ground or occasion. **27.** *Arith.* **a.** the position of a figure in a series, as in decimal notation. **b.** (*pl.*) the figures of the series. **28.** *Drama.* one of three unities. See **unity** (def. 10). **29.** *Astron.* the position of a heavenly body at any instant. **30.** *Sport.* **a.** a position among the leading competitors, usu. the first three, at the finish of a race. **b.** the position of the second or third (opposed to *win*). **31.** Some special noun phrases are:

**give place, 1.** to make room. **2.** be superseded.

**go places,** *Colloq.* to be successful in one's career.

**know one's place,** to recognise one's (low) social rank and behave accordingly.

**out of place, 1.** not in the proper position. **2.** inappropriate; unsuitable.

**pride of place,** the highest or most important position.

**put in one's place,** to humble (an arrogant person, etc.).

**take one's place,** to sit down, or take up a position, as of right.

**take place,** to happen.

**take the place of,** to be a substitute for; oust.

*–v.t.* **32.** to put in a particular place; set. **33.** to put in an appropriate position or order. **34.** to put into a suitable or desirable place for some purpose, as money for investment, an order or contract, etc. **35.** to fix (confidence, esteem, etc.) in a person or thing. **36.** to appoint (a person) to a post or office. **37.** to find a place, situation, etc., for (a person). **38.** to determine or indicate the place of. **39.** to assign a certain position or rank to. **40.** to direct or aim with precision. **41.** to assign a position to (a horse, etc.) among the leading competitors, usu. the first three, at the finish of a race, competition, etc. **42.** to put or set in a particular place, position, situation, or relation. **43.** to identify by connecting with the proper place, circumstances, etc.: *to be unable to place a person.* **44.** to sing or speak with consciousness of the bodily point of emphasis of resonance of each note or register. *–v.i.* **45.** *U.S. Racing.* to finish among the three placegetters, usu. second; to be placed. [ME; OE *plætse, plæce,* from L *platēa* street, area, from Gk *plateîa* broad way, properly fem. of *platýs* broad]

**placebo** /pləˈsiboʊ/, *n., pl.* **-bos, -boes. 1.** *Med.* a medicine which performs no physiological function but may benefit the patient psychologically. **2.** *Rom. Cath. Ch.* the vespers of the office for the dead, so called from the initial word of the first antiphon, taken from Psalm 114:9 of the Vulgate. [ME, from L: I shall be pleasing, acceptable]

**placebo effect** /ˈ– əfɛkt/, *n.* a beneficial effect asserted by a patient after taking a placebo.

**place-card** /ˈpleɪs-kad/, *n.* a card put by each place at a dinner table, etc., indicating who is to sit there.

**placed man** /pleɪst ˈmæn/, *n. Aus. Rules.* a player in a fixed position as opposed to a follower.

**placegetter** /ˈpleɪsgɛtə/, *n.* a winner of a position among the leaders in a competition.

**placekick** /ˈpleɪskɪk/, *n.* (in rugby football, etc.) a kick made when the ball has been placed on the ground, at a predetermined spot.

**placeman** /ˈpleɪsmən/, *n., pl.* **-men.** *Brit.* (*usu. derog.*) one who holds a place or office, esp. under a government.

**placemat** /ˈpleɪsmæt/, *n.* →**tablemat.**

**placement** /ˈpleɪsmənt/, *n.* **1.** the act of placing. **2.** the act of an employment exchange or employer in filling a position. **3.** the state of being placed. **4.** location; arrangement.

**placename** /ˈpleɪsneɪm/, *n.* the name of a place.

**placenta** /pləˈsɛntə/, *n., pl.* **-tas, -tae** /-ti/. **1.** *Zool., Anat.* the organ formed in the lining of the mammalian uterus by the union of the uterine mucous membrane with the membranes of the foetus to provide for the nourishment of the foetus and the elimination of its waste products. **2.** *Bot.* **a.** that part of the ovary of flowering plants which bears the ovules. **b.** (in ferns, etc.) the tissue giving rise to sporangia. [NL: something having a flat circular form, from L: a cake, from Gk *plakoûnta,* acc. of *plakoûs* flat cake] – **placental,** *adj.*

**placental** /pləˈsɛntl/, *adj.* **1.** of or pertaining to a placenta. **2.** *Zool.* of or pertaining to an animal which undergoes substantial development as a foetus attached to a placenta before birth. Cf. **marsupial.**

**placenta praevia** /pləsɛntə ˈpriviə/, *n.* a condition in pregnancy in which the placenta is superimposed on the exit of the uterus.

**placentate** /pləˈsɛnteɪt/, *adj.* having a placenta.

**placentation** /plæsənˈteɪʃən/, *n.* **1.** *Zool., Anat.* **a.** the formation of a placenta. **b.** the manner of the disposition or construction of a placenta. **2.** *Bot.* the disposition or arrangement of a placenta or placentas.

**placentography** /plæsənˈtɒgrəfi/, *n.* an X-ray examination to show the site of the placenta in the uterus.

**placer**[1] /ˈpleɪsə/, *n. Mining.* **1.** a superficial gravel or similar deposit containing particles of gold or the like (distinguished from *lode*). **2.** a place where such a deposit is washed for gold, etc. [Amer. Sp.: sandbank; akin to *plaza.* See PLACE]

**placer**[2] /ˈpleɪsə/, *n.* one who places. [PLACE, *v.* + -ER[1]]

**placet** /ˈpleɪsət/, *n.* (an expression or vote of assent or sanction). [L *placet* it pleases]

**placid** /ˈplæsəd/, *adj.* pleasantly calm or peaceful; unruffled; tranquil; serene. [L *placidus*] – **placidity** /pləˈsɪdəti/, **placidness,** *n.* – **placidly,** *adv.*

**placket** /ˈplækət/, *n.* an opening at the top of a skirt, or in a dress or blouse, to facilitate putting it on and off.

**placoid** /ˈplækɔɪd/, *adj.* **1.** platelike, as the scales or dermal investments of sharks. **2.** relating to the Placoidae. *–n.* **3.** a member of the Placoidae, a group of fishes including the sharks and rays, and distinguished by irregular bony scales. [Gk *pláx* something flat, tablet + -OID]

**plafond** /plæˈfɒnd/, *n.* a ceiling, whether flat or arched, esp. one of decorative character. [F, from *plat* flat + *fond* bottom. See PLATE[1], FUND]

**plagal** /ˈpleɪgəl/, *adj. Music.* (of a church mode) having the final in the middle of the compass. [ML *plagālis,* from *plaga* plagal mode, apparently backformation from *plagius,* from MGk *plágios,* from Gk: oblique]

**plagal cadence** /- 'keɪdəns/, *n.* (in music) a cadence in which there is a progression from a subdominant chord to a tonic chord.

**plagiarise** /'pleɪdʒəraɪz/, *v.,* **-rised, -rising.** *–v.t.* **1.** to appropriate by plagiarism. **2.** to appropriate ideas, passages, etc., from by plagiarism. *–v.i.* **3.** to commit plagiarism. Also, **plagiarize.** – **plagiariser,** *n.*

**plagiarism** /'pleɪdʒərɪzəm/, *n.* **1.** the appropriation or imitation of another's ideas and manner of expressing them, as in art, literature, etc., to be passed off as one's own. **2.** something appropriated and passed off as one's own in this manner. – **plagiarist,** *n.* – **plagiaristic** /pleɪdʒə'rɪstɪk/, *adj.*

**plagiary** /'pleɪdʒəri/, *n., pl.* **-ries. 1.** →**plagiarism. 2.** a plagiarist. [L *plagiārius* one who abducts the child or slave of another]

**plagioclase** /'pleɪdʒioʊˌkleɪz, -ˌkleɪs/, *n.* any of the felspar minerals varying in composition from $NaAlSi_3O_8$ to $CaAl_2Si_2O_8$, important constituents of many igneous rocks. [Gk *plágio(s)* oblique + *klásis* fracture]

**plagioclimax** /ˌpleɪdʒioʊ'klaɪmæks/, *n.* a climax (def. 4) in a plant community which is affected by introduced factors, as a grassland area under pasture.

**plagiotropic** /ˌpleɪdʒioʊ'trɒpɪk/, *adj.* denoting, pertaining to, or exhibiting a mode of plant growth which is more or less divergent from the vertical. [Gk *plágio(s)* oblique + *tropikós* inclined] – **plagiotropically,** *adv.*

**plagiotropism** /pleɪdʒi'ɒtrəpɪzəm/, *n.* plagiotropic tendency or growth.

**plagon** /'plægən/, *n. Colloq.* →**flagon.** [Aboriginal pidgin for FLAGON]

**plagon wagon** /'– wægən/, *n. Colloq. (derog.)* a car full of Aborigines.

**plague** /pleɪg/, *n., v.,* **plagued, plaguing.** *–n.* **1.** an epidemic disease of high mortality; a pestilence. **2.** an infectious, epidemic disease, occurring in several forms (**bubonic, pneumonic,** and **septicaemic**), known in history as the **Black Death** of the 14th century, the **Great Plague of London** in 1664-65, and the **Oriental Plague** in the 1890s. **3.** an affliction, calamity, or evil, esp. one regarded as a visitation from God: *the ten plagues.* **4.** any cause of trouble or vexation. *–v.t.* **5.** to trouble or torment in any manner. **6.** to annoy, bother, or pester. **7.** to smite with a plague. **8.** to infect with a plague. **9.** to afflict with any evil. [ME *plage,* from LL *plāga* affliction, pestilence, from L: blow, wound; akin to Gk *plēgḗ* stroke] – **plaguer,** *n.*

**plague locust** /– 'loʊkəst/, *n.* **1.** the Australian migratory grasshopper, *Chortoicetes terminifera.* **2.** the migratory phase of the Old World grasshopper, *Locusta migratoria.*

**plaguy** /'pleɪgi/, *Archaic.* *–adj.* **1.** such as to plague, torment, or annoy; vexatious. *–adv.* **2.** vexatiously or excessively. – **plaguily,** *adv.*

**plaice** /pleɪs/, *n., pl.* **plaice. 1.** a European flatfish, *Pleuronectes platessa,* an important food fish. **2.** any of various American flatfishes or flounders. [ME *plais,* from OF, from LL *platessa* flatfish, from Gk *platýs* flat]

**plaid** /plæd/, *n.* **1.** any fabric woven of different coloured yarns in a cross-barred pattern. **2.** a pattern of this kind. **3.** a long, rectangular piece of cloth, usu. with such a pattern, worn about the shoulders by Scottish Highlanders. *–adj.* **4.** having the pattern of a plaid. [Gaelic *plaide* blanket, plaid]

**plaided** /'plædəd/, *adj.* **1.** wearing a plaid. **2.** made of plaid, or having a similar pattern.

**plain**[1] /pleɪn/, *adj.* **1.** clear or distinct to the eye or ear: *leaving a plain trail.* **2.** clear to the mind; evident, manifest, or obvious: *to make one's meaning plain.* **3.** conveying the meaning clearly or simply; easily understood: *plain talk.* **4.** downright; sheer: *plain folly.* **5.** free from ambiguity or evasion; candid; outspoken; honest. **6.** without special pretensions, superiority, elegance, etc.: *plain people.* **7.** not beautiful; unattractive: *a plain face.* **8.** without intricacies or difficulties. **9.** ordinary, simple, or unostentatious. **10.** with little or no embellishment, decoration, or enhancing elaboration: *plain clothes.* **11.** without pattern, device, or colouring. **12.** unruled, as paper. **13.** not rich, highly seasoned, or elaborately prepared, as food. **14.** flat or level: *plain country.* **15.** unobstructed, clear, or open, as ground, a space, etc. **16.** *Cards.* **a.** not a court card. **b.** not a trump. **17.** (of knitting) consisting of plain stitches. *–adv.* **18.** simply; absolutely. **19.** clearly or intelligibly. *–n.* **20.** an area of land not significantly higher than adjacent areas and with relatively minor differences in elevation within the area. **21.** the simplest stitch in knitting. [ME, from OF, from L *plānus* flat, level, plane] – **plainly,** *adv.* – **plainness,** *n.*

**plain**[2] /pleɪn/, *v.i. Archaic.* →**complain.** [ME *plei(g)ne,* from OF *plaindre,* from L *plangere* beat (the breast, etc.), lament]

**plainchant** /'pleɪntʃænt/, *n.* →**plainsong.**

**plain-clothes** /'pleɪn-kloʊðz/, *adj.* wearing civilian clothes rather than a uniform, as a detective.

**plain dealing** /pleɪn 'dilɪŋ/, *n.* honesty; straightforwardness. – **plain-dealer,** *n.*

**plain flour** /'– flaʊə/, *n.* white wheat flour that does not contain a raising agent.

**plain-laid** /'pleɪn-leɪd/, *adj.* (of a rope) made by laying three strands together with a right-handed twist.

**plain sailing** /pleɪn 'seɪlɪŋ/, *n.* **1.** sailing on a plain course, free from obstruction or difficulty. **2.** an easy and unhindered course of action. Also, **plane sailing.**

**plains grass** /'pleɪnz gras/, *n.* a spear grass, *Stipa aristiglumis,* widespread in the eastern states.

**plains kangaroo** /– kæŋgə'ru/, *n.* →**red kangaroo.**

**plainsman** /'pleɪnzmən/, *n., pl.* **-men.** a man or inhabitant of the plains.

**plainsong** /'pleɪnsɒŋ/, *n.* the unisonal liturgical music used in the Christian Church from the earliest times; Gregorian chant. Also, **plainchant.** [translation of ML *cantus plānus*]

**plain-spoken** /'pleɪn-spoʊkən/, *adj.* candid; blunt.

**plains wanderer** /'pleɪnz wɒndərə/, *n.* a small, shy, brownish bird, *Pedionomus torquatus,* which prefers to run rather than fly, once common but now infrequently seen in open plains and grasslands of eastern Australia; turkey quail.

plains wanderer

**plaint** /pleɪnt/, *n.* **1.** →**complaint. 2.** *Law.* a statement of grievance made to a court for the purpose of asking redress. **3.** *Archaic and Poetic.* lament. [ME *plainte,* from OF, from L *planctus* lamentation. See PLAIN[2]]

**plaintiff** /'pleɪntəf/, *n. Law.* one who brings an action in a civil case. [ME *plaintif* complaining, from OF. See PLAINTIVE]

**plaintive** /'pleɪntɪv/, *adj.* expressing sorrow or melancholy discontent; mournful: *plaintive music.* [ME *plaintif,* from OF. See PLAINT] – **plaintively,** *adv.* – **plaintiveness,** *n.*

**plain turkey** /'pleɪn tɜki/, *n.* →**bustard** (def. 1).

**plaister** /'pleɪstə/, *n., v.t. Obs.* →**plaster.**

**plait** /plæt/, *n.* **1.** a braid, as of hair or straw. **2.** a pleat or fold, as of cloth. *–v.t.* **3.** to braid (hair, etc.). **4.** to make (a mat, etc.) by braiding. **5.** to pleat (cloth, etc.). Also, **plat.** [ME *pleyt,* from OF *pleit,* from L *plicitum,* pp. neut., folded. See PLY[2]]

**plan** /plæn/, *n., v.,* **planned, planning.** *–n.* **1.** a scheme of action or procedure: *a plan of operations.* **2.** a design or scheme of arrangement. **3.** a project or definite purpose: *plans for the future.* **4.** a drawing made to scale to represent the top view or a horizontal cut of a structure or a machine, as a floor plan of a building. **5.** a representation of a thing drawn on a plane, as a map or diagram: *a town plan.* **6.** one of several planes in front of a represented object, and perpendicular to the line between the object and the eye. *–v.t.* **7.** to arrange a plan or scheme for (any work, enterprise, or proceeding). **8.** to form a plan, project, or purpose of: *to plan a visit.* **9.** to draw or make a plan of (a building, etc.). *–v.i.* **10.** to make plans. [F, n. use of *plan* flat, plane, from L *plānus.* See PLANE[1], PLAIN[1]]

**plan-,** variant of **plano-,** before vowels, as in *planarian.*

**planarian** /plə'nɛəriən/, *n.* a free-living turbellarian flatworm having a trifid intestine. [NL *Plānāria,* the typical genus (properly fem. of LL *plānārius* level, flat, from L *plānus*) + -AN]

**planch** /plæntʃ/, *n.* a flat piece of metal, stone, or baked clay, used as a tray in an enamelling oven. [ME *plaunche,* from OF *planche.* See PLANK]

**planchet** /ˈplæntʃət/, *n.* a flat piece of metal for stamping, as a coin; a coin blank. [PLANCH + -ET]

**planchette** /plænˈʃɛt/, *n.* a small board on two castors and a vertical pencil, said to write messages without conscious effort by persons whose fingers rest lightly on the board. [F, diminutive of *planche* PLANCH]

A, planarian; B, diagram showing branched digestive tract; C, pharynx; D, mouth

**Planck's constant** /ˈplæŋks kɒnstənt/, *n. Physics.* a universal constant (approx. $6.626 \times 10^{-34}$ joule seconds; *Symbol: h*) expressing the proportion of the energy of any form of wavelike radiation to its frequency. [named after M. *Planck,* 1858-1947, German physicist]

**plane**[1] /pleɪn/, *n., adj., v.,* **planed, planing.** *–n.* **1.** a flat or level surface. **2.** *Maths.* a surface such that the straight line joining any two distinct points in it lies entirely within it. **3.** a level of dignity, character, existence, development, or the like: *a high moral plane.* **4.** an aeroplane or a hydroplane. **5.** *Aeron.* a thin, flat, or curved, extended member of an aeroplane or a hydroplane, affording a supporting surface. *–adj.* **6.** flat or level, as a surface. **7.** of plane figures: *plane geometry.* *–v.i.* **8.** to glide. **9.** to lift partly out of water when running at high speed, as a racing boat does. [L *plānum* level ground. See PLAIN[1]] **– planeness,** *n.*

**plane**[2] /pleɪn/, *n., v.,* **planed, planing.** *–n.* **1.** a tool with an adjustable blade for paring, truing, smoothing, or finishing the surface of wood, etc. **2.** a tool resembling a trowel for smoothing the surface of the clay in a brick mould. *–v.t.* **3.** to smooth or dress with or as with a plane or a planer. **4.** to remove by or as by means of a plane (fol. by *away* or *off*). *–v.i.* **5.** to work with a plane. **6.** to function as a plane. [ME, from F, from LL *plāna*]

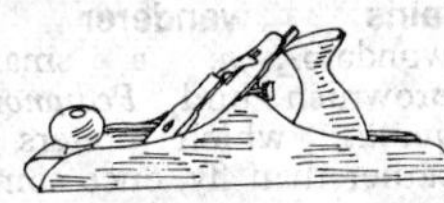

plane[2]: iron jack plane

**plane**[3] /pleɪn/, *n.* →**plane tree.** [ME, from F, from L *platanus,* from Gk *plátanos,* from *platýs* broad (with reference to the leaves)]

**plane angle** /'– æŋgəl/, *n.* an angle between two intersecting lines.

**plane figure** /'– fɪgə/, *n.* a figure whose parts all lie in one plane.

**plane geometry** /– dʒiˈɒmətri/, *n.* the geometry of figures whose parts all lie in one plane.

**planer** /ˈpleɪnə/, *n.* **1.** one who or that which planes. **2.** *Carp.* a power machine for removing the rough or excess surface from a board. **3.** *Print.* a flat piece of wood laid on top of printing type which is in a chase, and tapped with a wooden mallet to ensure that the type stands level.

**planer saw** /'– sɔ/, *n.* a type of circular saw which saws so smoothly that planing is unnecessary.

**plane sailing** /pleɪn ˈseɪlɪŋ/, *n.* →**plain sailing.**

**planet** /ˈplænət/, *n.* **1.** *Astron.* **a.** a solid body revolving around the sun, or a similar body revolving around a star other than the sun; planets are only visible by reflected light. Around the sun (in the solar system) there are nine **major planets** (Mercury, Venus, Earth, Mars, Jupiter, Saturn, Uranus, Neptune, and Pluto, in their order from the sun) and thousands of **minor planets** or asteroids between the orbit of Mars and Jupiter. **Inferior planets** are those nearer to the sun than the earth is; **superior planets** are those farther from the sun than the earth is. **b.** (originally) a celestial body moving in the sky, as distinguished from a fixed star, formerly applied also to the sun and moon. **2.** *Astrol.* a heavenly body regarded as exerting influence on mankind and events. [ME *planete,* from LL *planēta,* from Gk *planḗtēs,* lit., wanderer]

**plane table** /ˈpleɪn teɪbəl/, *n.* a drawing-board mounted on a tripod by means of which survey data may be obtained and plotted in the field.

**plane-table** /ˈpleɪn-teɪbəl/, *v.i., v.t.,* **-bled, -bling.** to survey with a plane table.

**planetarium** /plænəˈtɛəriəm/, *n., pl.* **-tariums, -taria** /-ˈtɛəriə/. **1.** an apparatus or model representing the planetary system. **2.** an optical device which projects a representation of the heavens upon a dome through the use of many stereopticons in motion. **3.** the structure in which such a planetarium is housed. [NL, properly neut. of L *planētārius* planetary]

**planetary** /ˈplænətəri, -tri/, *adj.* **1.** of, pertaining to, of the nature of, or resembling a planet or the planets. **2.** wandering or erratic. **3.** terrestrial or mundane. **4.** *Mach.* denoting or pertaining to a form of transmission (consisting of an epicyclic train of gears) for varying the speed in motor vehicles. [L *planētārius*]

**planetary nebula** /– ˈnɛbjələ/, *n.* shells of gas ejected from certain very hot stars.

**planetesimal** /plænəˈtɛsəməl/, *adj.* **1.** of or pertaining to minute bodies in the solar system or in similar systems, which, according to the **planetesimal hypothesis,** move in planetary orbits and gradually unite to form the planets and satellites of the system. *–n.* **2.** one of the minute bodies of the planetesimal hypothesis. [from PLANET, modelled on INFINITESIMAL]

**planetoid** /ˈplænətɔɪd/, *n.* a minor planet; an asteroid. **– planetoidal** /plænəˈtɔɪdl/, *adj.*

**plane tree** /ˈpleɪn tri/, *n.* any tree of the genus *Platanus,* esp. the southern European *P. orientalis,* the North American *P. occidentalis,* and the widely planted hybrid between these two species.

**planet wheel** /ˈplænət wil/, *n.* any of the wheels in an epicyclic train, whose axes revolve round the common centre.

**plangent** /ˈplændʒənt/, *adj.* **1.** beating or dashing, as waves. **2.** resounding loudly. [L *plangens,* ppr., beating, lamenting. Cf. PLAIN[2]] **– plangency,** *n.*

**plani-,** variant of **plano-,** as in *planimeter.*

**planigale** /ˈplænəgeɪl/, *n.* any of the flat-skulled marsupial mice of the genus *Planigale,* which includes the smallest known marsupials.

**planimeter** /pləˈnɪmətə/, *n.* an instrument for measuring mechanically the area of plane figures.

**planimetry** /pləˈnɪmətri/, *n.* the measurement of plane areas. **– planimetric** /plænəˈmɛtrɪk/, **planimetrical** /plænəˈmɛtrɪkəl/, *adj.*

**planish** /ˈplænɪʃ/, *v.t.* **1.** to flatten or smooth (metal) by hammering, rolling, etc. **2.** to finish off (metal, paper, etc.) with a polished surface. [ME, from F (obs.) *planiss-,* stem of *planir,* for *planner.* See PLANE[2], *v.*] **– planisher,** *n.*

**planisphere** /ˈplænəsfɪə/, *n.* **1.** a map of half or more of the celestial sphere with a device for indicating the part visible at a given time. **2.** a projection or representation of the whole or a part of a sphere on a plane. [PLANI- + SPHERE; replacing ME *planisperie,* from ML *plānisphaerium*]

**plank** /plæŋk/, *n.* **1.** a long, flat piece of timber thicker than a board. **2.** timber in such pieces. **3.** something to stand on or to cling to for support. **4.** *U.S.* a principle of a party expressed on a political platform. **5. to walk the plank,** to be compelled, as by pirates, to walk to one's death by stepping off a plank extending from a ship's side over the water. *–v.t.* **6.** to lay, cover, or furnish with planks. **7.** *Colloq.* to lay, put, or pay (fol. by *down,* etc.). **8.** *U.S.* to cook (and usu. to serve) meat or fish on a special wooden board of well-seasoned hardwood, of long or oval shape. [ME *planke,* from ONF, from L *planca.* Cf. PLANCH]

**planking** /ˈplæŋkɪŋ/, *n.* **1.** planks collectively, as in a floor. **2.** the act of laying or covering with planks.

**plank-sheer** /ˈplænk-ʃɪə/, *n.* a timber around a vessel's hull at the deck line.

**plankton** /ˈplæŋktən/, *n.* the small animal and plant organisms that float or drift in the water, esp. at or near the surface. [G, from Gk (neut.): wandering] **– planktonic** /plæŋkˈtɒnɪk/, *adj.*

**planned obsolescence** /ˌplænd ɒbsəˈlɛsəns/, *n.* the deliberate policy of making a product become rapidly out of date or unserviceable, as by changing minor characteristics of a model, in order to ensure continued sales of new goods.

**planner** /'plænə/, *n.* one who plans.

**planning permission** /'plænɪŋ pəmɪʃən/, *n.* permission which must be given by a government authority before property may be developed.

**plano-,** a word element meaning 'flat', 'plane'. Also, **plan-, plani-.** [combining form representing L *plānus*]

**plano-concave** /pleɪnoʊ-'kɒnkeɪv/, *adj.* (of lenses) plane on one side and concave on the other.

**plano-convex** /pleɪnoʊ-'kɒnvɛks/, *adj.* (of lenses) plane on one side and convex on the other.

**planogamete** /'plænəgəmit/, *n.* a motile gamete.

**planography** /plə'nɒgrəfi/, *n.* one of the basic printing processes in which the printing areas are in the same plane as the non-printing areas. The areas to print are ink-attracting and the remaining areas are ink-repellent.

**planometer** /plə'nɒmətə/, *n.* a flat plate, usu. of cast iron, used as a gauge for plane surfaces. – **planometric** /plænə'mɛtrɪk/, *adj.*

**plant** /plænt, plant/, *n.* **1.** any member of the vegetable group of living organisms. **2.** a herb or other small vegetable growth, in contrast to a tree or a shrub. **3.** a seedling or a growing slip, esp. one ready for transplanting. **4.** the equipment, including the fixtures, machinery, tools, etc., and often the buildings, necessary to carry on any industrial business: *a manufacturing plant.* **5.** the complete equipment or apparatus for a particular mechanical process or operation: *the power plant of a factory.* **6.** a stockman's horses, equipment, etc. **7.** *U.S.* the buildings, equipment, etc., of an institution: *the sprawling plant of the university.* **8.** *Colloq.* **a.** something or someone intended to trap, decoy, or lure, as criminals. **b.** a spy. **9.** *Colloq.* something hidden, often illegally. **10.** place where stolen goods are hidden. **11.** a miner's hiding place for his opals, etc. **12.** *Colloq.* a scheme to trap, trick, swindle, or defraud. *–v.t.* **13.** to put or set in the ground for growth, as seeds, young trees, etc. **14.** to furnish or stock (land) with plants. **15.** to implant (ideas, sentiments, etc.); introduce and establish (principles, doctrines, etc.) **16.** to introduce (a breed of animals) into a country. **17.** to deposit (young fish, or spawn) in a river, lake, etc. **18.** to bed (oysters). **19.** to insert or set firmly in or on the ground or some other body or surface. **20.** to put or place. **21.** *Colloq.* to deliver (a blow, etc.). **22.** to post or station. **23.** to locate or situate. **24.** to establish or set up (a colony, city, etc.); found. **25.** to settle (persons), as in a colony. **26.** *Colloq.* to hide or conceal, as stolen goods. **27.** to place (evidence) so that it will be discovered and incriminate an innocent person. **28.** *Colloq.* to put (gold dust, ore, etc.) in a mine or the like to create a false impression of the value of the property. *–v.i.* **29.** to plant trees, colonies, etc. [ME and OE *plante,* from L *planta* sprout, slip, graft]

**plantain**[1] /'plæntən/, *n.* **1.** a tropical herbaceous plant, *Musa paradisiaca.* **2.** its fruit, very similar to the banana, usu. requiring cooking. [Sp. *plántano* plantain, also plane tree, from L *pla(n)tanus.* See PLANE[3]]

**plantain**[2] /'plæntən/, *n.* any plant of the widespread genus *Plantago,* esp. *P. lanceolata,* a common weed with leaves close to the ground and long, slender spikes of small flowers. [ME *planteine,* from OF *plantain,* from L *plantāgo*]

**plantain-eater** /'plæntən-itə/, *n.* any of several African birds of the family Musophagidae, as the **blue-crested plantain-eater,** *Tauraco hartlaubi,* related to the cuckoos.

**plantar** /'plæntə/, *adj.* of or pertaining to the sole of the foot. [L *plantāris*]

**plantation** /plæn'teɪʃən/, *n.* **1.** a farm or estate, esp. in a tropical or semitropical country, on which cotton, tobacco, coffee, sugar, or the like is cultivated, usu. by resident labourers. **2.** a group of planted trees or plants. **3.** *Hist.* **a.** a colony. **b.** the establishment of a colony, etc. **4.** *Rare.* the planting of seeds, etc. [late ME, from L *plantātio* a planting]

**planter** /'plæntə, 'plantə/, *n.* **1.** one who plants. **2.** an implement or machine for planting seeds in the ground. **3.** the owner or occupant of a plantation. **4.** *Hist.* a colonist. **5.** *U.S.* →**planter box.**

**planter box** /'plæntə bɒks/, *n.* a decorative container, often of polished wood, of a variety of sizes and shapes for plants, ferns, etc.

**plant hormone** /plænt 'hɔmoʊn/, *n.* **1.** an organic substance produced by a plant to regulate physiological activities, as an auxin which regulates growth. **2.** a synthetic substance having the same effect.

**plantigrade** /'plæntəgreɪd/, *adj.* **1.** walking on the whole sole of the foot, as man, the bears, etc. *–n.* **2.** a plantigrade animal. [NL *plantigradus,* from L *planta* sole + *-gradus* walking]

**plant kingdom** /'plænt kɪŋdəm/, *n.* the plants of the world collectively (distinguished from *animal kingdom*). Also, **vegetable kingdom.**

**plant-louse** /'plænt-laʊs/, *n., pl.* **-lice.** →**aphid.**

**planula** /'plænjələ/, *n., pl.* **-lae** /-li/. the ciliate, free-swimming larva of a coelenterate, characterised by the solid interior. [NL, diminutive of L *plānus* flat, plane] – **planular,** *adj.*

**plaque** /plak, plæk/, *n.* **1.** a thin, flat plate or tablet of metal, porcelain, etc., intended for ornament, as on a wall, or set in a piece of furniture. **2.** a platelike brooch or ornament, esp. one worn as the badge of an honorary order. **3.** *Anat., Zool.* a small flat, rounded formation or area, as a deposit of fibrous matter in the wall of a blood vessel, or localised patch of skin disease. **4.** a film on teeth harbouring bacteria. [F, from D *plak* flat board]

**plash**[1] /plæʃ/, *n.* **1.** a splash. **2.** a pool or puddle. *–v.t., v.i.* **3.** to splash. [ME *plasch,* OE *plæsc,* c. D and LG *plas,* probably of imitative orig.]

**plash**[2] /plæʃ/, *v.t.* **1.** to interweave (branches, etc., bent over and often cut partly through), as for a hedge or an arbour. **2.** to make or renew (a hedge, etc.) by such interweaving. [ME, from OF *plaissier,* from L *plectere* plait. Cf. PLEACH]

**plashy** /'plæʃi/, *adj.,* **-ier, -iest. 1.** marshy; wet. **2.** splashing.

**-plasia,** a word element meaning 'biological cellular growth', as in *hypoplasia.* Also, **-plasy.** [NL, from Gk *plásis* a moulding]

**-plasm,** a word element used as a noun termination meaning 'something formed or moulded' in biological and other scientific terms, as in *bioplasm, metaplasm, neoplasm, protoplasm.* [combining form representing Gk *plásma*]

**plasma** /'plæzmə/, *n.* **1.** *Anat., Physiol.* the liquid part of blood or lymph, as distinguished from the corpuscles. **2.** *Biol.* →**protoplasm. 3.** →**whey. 4.** a green, faintly translucent chalcedony. **5.** *Physics.* a highly ionised gas which, because it contains an approximately equal number of positive ions and electrons, is electrically neutral and highly conducting. Also, **plasm** /'plæzəm/. [LL, from Gk: something formed or moulded] – **plasmatic** /plæz'mætɪk/, **plasmic,** *adj.*

**plasma engine** /'– ɛndʒən/, *n.* a rocket engine, the propelling force of which is obtained by the discharge at the rear of a jet of plasma (def. 5). Cf. **ion engine.**

**plasmagene** /'plæzmədʒin/, *n.* a protein particle in the cytoplasm of a cell; believed to affect heredity.

**plasmalogen** /plæz'mælədʒən/, *n.* any of a group of phospholipids found in the brain and heart; a component of cell membranes.

**plasmodium** /plæz'moʊdiəm/, *n., pl.* **-dia** /-diə/. **1.** *Biol.* a mass or sheet of protoplasm formed by the fusion or contact of a number of amoeboid bodies. **2.** *Zool.* a parasitic protozoan organism of the genus *Plasmodium* (malaria parasites). [NL, from *plasma* PLASMA + *-ōdium* -ODE[1]]

A B C D E

plasmodium (def. 2): A, young form with a red corpuscle; B, developing pigmented form; C, full-grown body; D, segmenting body; E, degenerating form undergoing vacuolation

**plasmolysis** /plæz'mɒləsəs/, *n.* contraction of the protoplasm in a living cell when water is removed by exosmosis. [*plasmo-* (combining form representing Gk *plásma* PLASMA) + -LYSIS]

**plasmoquin** /'plæzməkwɪn/, *n.* a synthetic antimalarial drug, $C_{19}H_{29}N_3O$.

**plasmosome** /'plæzməsoʊm/, *n.* a true nucleolus which is stained by cytoplasmic dyes. Cf. **karyosome.** [*plasmo-* (combining form representing Gk *plásma* PLASMA) + Gk *sôma* body]

**-plast,** a word element used as a noun termination, meaning 'formed', 'moulded', esp. in biological and botanical terms, as in *bioplast, chloroplast, mesoplast, protoplast.* [combining form representing Gk *plastós*]

**plaster** /'plastə/, *n.* **1.** a pasty composition, as of lime, sand, water, and often hair, used for covering walls, ceilings, etc., where it hardens in drying. **2.** gypsum powdered but not calcined. **3.** calcined gypsum (**plaster of Paris**), a white powdery material which swells when mixed with water and sets rapidly, used for making casts, moulds, etc. **4.** a solid or semisolid preparation for spreading upon cloth or the like and applying to the body for some remedial or other purpose. **5.** →**sticking plaster.** *–v.t.* **6.** to cover (walls, etc.) with plaster. **7.** to treat with gypsum or plaster of Paris. **8.** to lay flat like a layer of plaster. **9.** to daub or fill with plaster or something similar. **10.** to apply a plaster to (the body, etc.). **11.** to overspread with anything, esp. thickly or to excess: *a wall plastered with posters.* **12.** *Colloq.* to hit hard and often. **13.** *Colloq.* to bomb heavily. [ME and OE, from VL and ML *plastrum* plaster (both medical and builder's senses), from L *emplastrum,* from Gk *émplastron* salve] **– plasterer,** *n.* **– plastering,** *n.* **– plastery,** *adj.*

**plasterboard** /'plastəbɔd/, *n.* plaster in paper-covered sheets, used for walls.

**plaster cast** /plastə 'kast/, *n.* **1.** any piece of sculpture cast in plaster of Paris. **2.** *Surg.* See **cast** (def. 47).

**plastered** /'plastəd/, *adj. Colloq.* drunk.

**plastic** /'plæstɪk/, *adj.* **1.** concerned with or pertaining to moulding or modelling: *plastic arts.* **2.** capable of being moulded or of receiving form: *plastic substances.* **3.** produced by moulding: *plastic figures.* **4.** having the power of moulding or shaping formless or yielding material. **5.** *Biol., Pathol.* →**formative. 6.** Also, **anaplastic.** *Surg.* concerned with or pertaining to the remedying or restoring of malformed, injured, or lost parts: *plastic surgery.* **7.** pliable; impressionable: *the plastic mind of youth.* **8.** made of or consisting of plastic: *a plastic bag.* **9. a.** characterised by artificiality: *she's a plastic lady.* **b.** (of food) synthetic and tasteless. *–n.* **10.** any of a group of synthetic or natural organic materials which may be shaped when soft and then hardened, including many types of resins, resinoids, polymers, cellulose derivatives, casein materials, and proteins. Plastics are used in place of such other materials as glass, wood, and metals in construction and decoration, for making many articles, as coatings, and, drawn into filaments, for weaving. [L *plasticus* that may be moulded, from Gk *plastikós*] **– plastically,** *adv.*

**-plastic,** a word element forming adjectives related to *-plast, -plasty,* as in *protoplastic.* [see PLASTIC]

**plastic art** /plæstɪk 'at/, *n.* **1.** three-dimensional art created from modelling, moulding, etc., as sculpture, as distinct from painting and drawing. **2.** (*usu. pl.*) any of the creative visual arts, including sculpture, painting, drawing, architecture and the graphic arts, as distinct from literature and music.

**plastic bomb** /– 'bɒm/, *n.* a bomb, often home-made, consisting of a plastic putty-like explosive, as cyclonite, manually moulded around a detonator and used, either by direct adhesion (without a container) or in any rudimentary form of container, esp. in guerrilla warfare, by commandos, or in civil disturbances.

**plastic bronze** /– 'brɒnz/, *n.* a bronze containing a high proportion of lead (8-20 per cent) in addition to copper, tin, and sometimes zinc, nickel, or phosphorus.

**plastic curd** /– 'kɜd/, *n.* (of cheese) soft, but with a resilient texture like plastic, as mozzarella.

**plastic deformation** /– ˌdifɔ'meɪʃən/, *n.* a permanent change in the shape of a piece of metal as a result of a mechanical stress.

**plasticine** /'plæstəsin/, *n.* a plastic modelling compound, in various colours. [Trademark]

**plasticise** /'plæstəsaɪz/, *v.t., v.i.,* **-cised, -cising.** to make or become plastic. Also, **plasticize. – plasticisation** /plæstəsaɪ'zeɪʃən/, *n.*

**plasticiser** /'plæstəsaɪzə/, *n.* **1.** any of a group of substances which are used in plastics, mortar, or the like, to impart softness and viscous quality to the finished product. **2.** a non-volatile substance added to paints, etc., to prevent brittleness when dry. Also, **plasticizer.**

**plasticity** /plæs'tɪsəti/, *n.* **1.** the quality of being plastic. **2.** capability of being moulded, receiving shape, or being brought to a definite form.

**plastic paint** /plæstɪk 'peɪnt/, *n.* **1.** a paint based on polyvinyl acetate, which can be thinned with water. **2.** *Colloq.* any paint which can be thinned with water.

**plastic range** /'– reɪndʒ/, *n.* the stress range in which a material will not fail when subjected to the action of a force, but will not recover completely, so that a permanent deformation results when the force is removed.

**plastic surgeon** /– 'sɜdʒən/, *n.* a doctor specialising in plastic surgery.

**plastic surgery** /– 'sɜdʒəri/, *n.* surgery which attempts to remodel malformed or damaged parts of the body.

**plastic welder** /– 'wɛldə/, *n.* a machine which welds plastic.

**plastid** /'plæstəd/, *n. Biol.* **1.** a morphological unit consisting of a single cell. **2.** any of certain small specialised masses of protoplasm (as chloroplasts, chromoplasts, etc.) in certain cells. [G, short for *plastidion,* from Gk *plast(ós)* formed + *-idion,* diminutive suffix]

**plastral** /'plæstrəl/, *adj. Zool.* relating to the plastron.

**plastron** /'plæstrən/, *n.* **1.** *Armour.* a medieval metal breastplate worn under the hauberk. **2.** a protective shield of leather for the breast of a fencer. **3.** an ornamental front piece of a woman's bodice. **4.** the starched front of a shirt. **5.** *Zool.* the ventral part of the shell of a tortoise or turtle. [F, from It. *piastrone,* augmentative of *piastra* metal plate. See PLASTER. Cf. PIASTRE]

**-plasty,** a word element used as a noun termination meaning 'formation', occurring in the names of processes of plastic surgery, as *autoplasty, cranioplasty, dermatoplasty, neoplasty, rhinoplasty,* and occasionally in other words, as *galvanoplasty.* [Gk *-plastía,* combining form from *plastós* formed]

**-plasy,** variant of **-plasia.**

**plat**[1] /plæt/, *n., v.,* **platted, platting.** *–n.* **1.** a plot of ground, usu. small. **2.** *U.S.* a plan or map, as of land. *–v.t.* **3.** *U.S.* to make a plat of; plot. [ME (in place-names), c. Goth. *plat* patch]

**plat**[2] /plæt/, *n.* a plait or braid. [var. of PLAIT]

**platan** /'plætən/, *n.* →**plane tree.**

**platanna** /plə'tænə/, *n.* a frog, *Xenopus laevis,* of southern Africa, having clawed feet; used in pregnancy testing. [Afrikaans, said to be alteration of *plathander,* lit., flat-hander]

**plat du jour** /pla də 'ʒʊə/, *n.* a dish recommended or specially available on a certain day in a restaurant. [F: dish of the day]

**plate**[1] /pleɪt/, *n., v.,* **plated, plating.** *–n.* **1.** a shallow, usu. circular dish, now usu. of earthenware or porcelain, from which food is eaten. **2.** a service of food for one person at the table. **3.** an entire course: *a cold plate.* **4.** a plate of sandwiches, cakes, etc., prepared and brought by women to a party or similar social occasion: *Entrance: Gents–$1.00, Ladies–a plate.* **5.** domestic dishes, utensils, etc., of gold or silver. **6.** a dish, as of metal or wood, used for collecting offerings in a church, etc. **7.** a thin, flat sheet or piece of metal or other material, esp. of uniform thickness. **8.** metal in such sheets. **9.** a flat, polished piece of metal on which something may be or is engraved. **10.** a sheet of metal for printing from, formed by stereotyping or electrotyping a page of type, or metal or plastic formed by moulding, etching, or photographic development. **11.** a printed impression from such a piece, or from some similar piece, as a woodcut. **12.** such a piece engraved to print from. **13.** a full-page inserted illustration forming part of a book. **14.** plated metallic ware. **15.** wrought metal, or a piece of it, used in making armour. **16.** armour composed of such pieces. **17.** *Dentistry.* a piece of metal, vulcanite, or plastic substance, with artificial teeth attached, to replace lost or missing natural teeth. **18.** *Baseball.* the home base, at which the batter stands and which he must return to and touch, after running round the bases, in order to score a run. **19.** →**plate glass. 20.** *Photog.* a sensitised sheet of glass, metal, film, etc., on which to take a photograph or make a reproduction by photography. **21.** *Anat., Zool., etc.* a platelike part, structure, or organ. **22.** *U.S. Electronics.* the anode of a radio valve. **23.** *Elect.* an electrode in an accumulator. **24.** *Archit.* a timber laid horizontally, as in a wall, to receive the ends of other timbers. **25.** *Geol.* one of a number of major areas of the earth's crust, the boundaries of which are generally ocean ridges or deep trenches; each plate is capable of moving as a rigid unit. **26.**

a gold or silver cup or the like, or guaranteed prize money, awarded as a prize in horseracing, etc. **27.** a horserace or other contest for such a prize. **28.** a light metal shoe, as worn by a horse in a race. **29.** →**plate rail. 30. on a plate,** (of something offered) capable of being taken without effort. **31. on one's plate,** waiting to be dealt with; pending. *–v.t.* **32.** to coat (metal) with a thin film of gold, silver, nickel, etc., by mechanical or chemical means. **33.** to cover or overlay with metal plates for protection, etc. **34.** *Print.* to make a stereotype or electrotype plate from (type). **35.** to iron leather at a certain heat, giving it a smooth, shiny surface. [ME, from OF: flat piece, plate, probably from OF *plat* flat, from LL *plattus,* from Gk *platýs* broad, flat] – **platelike,** *adj.*

**plate**[2] /pleɪt/, *n. Obs.* a coin, esp. of silver. [ME, from OF; etymologically same as PLATE[1]]

**plateau** /'plætoʊ/, *n., pl.* **-eaus, -eaux** /-oʊz/. **1.** a tabular surface of high elevation, often of considerable extent. **2.** *Psychol.* a period of little or no progress in an individual's learning, marked by temporary constancy in speed, number of errors committed, etc., and indicated by a flat stretch on a graph. **3.** any period of minimal growth or decline. [F, from OF: flat object, from *plat* flat]

**plateau indexation** /– ɪndɛk'seɪʃən/, *n.* a form of indexation in which wages below a certain value are increased on a proportional basis, and wages above that value, by a fixed amount.

**plated** /'pleɪtəd/, *adj.* (of a knitted fabric) made of two yarns, as wool on the face and cotton on the back.

**plateful** /'pleɪtfʊl/, *n., pl.* **-fuls.** as much as a plate will hold.

**plate glass** /pleɪt 'glas/, *n.* a soda-lime-silica glass formed by rolling the hot glass into a plate which is subsequently ground and polished; used in large windows, mirrors, etc.

**platelayer** /'pleɪtleɪə/, *n.* one who lays and maintains the rails of a railway track.

**platelet** /'pleɪtlət/, *n.* a microscopic disc occurring in profusion in the blood, and acting as an important aid in coagulation. [PLATE[1] + -LET]

**platemaker** /'pleɪtmeɪkə/, *n.* **1.** a tradesman who produces metal sheets by passing the metal between rollers. **2.** *Print.* a tradesman who makes a plate (def. 10).

**plate-mark** /'pleɪt-mak/, *n.* →**hallmark.**

**platen** /'plætən/, *n.* **1.** a variety of printing press in which the sheet of paper to be printed is held on a flat metal surface and pressed against the inked type or plates which are also held on a flat surface. **2.** the surface on which the paper is held. **3.** *Mach.* the work-table of a machine tool, which may be slotted to allow the use of clamping bolts. **4.** the roller of a typewriter. [ME *plateyne,* from OF *platine* flat piece of metal, also popular alteration of *patene* PATEN, from its form]

**plater** /'pleɪtə/, *n.* one who or that which plates.

**plate rack** /'pleɪt ræk/, *n.* →**dish rack.**

**plate rail** /'– reɪl/, *n.* (formerly) a flanged wheel track, as used for colliery tracks. Also, **plate.**

**plateresque** /plætə'rɛsk/, *adj.* denoting an ornate style of architecture much used in 16th-century Spain, characterised by many ornamental motifs. [*plater-* (stem of Sp. *platero* silversmith) + -ESQUE]

**platform** /'plætfɔm/, *n.* **1.** a raised flooring or structure, as in a hall or meeting place, for use by public speakers, performers, etc. **2.** the raised area between or alongside the tracks of a railway station, from which the train is entered. **3.** the open entrance area at the end of a bus or the like. **4.** a level place for mounting guns, as in a fort. **5.** a flat elevated piece of ground. **6.** a body of principles on which a party or the like takes its stand in appealing to the public. **7.** a public statement of the principles and policy of a political party, esp. as put forth by the representatives of the party. **8.** a plan or set of principles. **9. a.** a sole several centimetres thick on a shoe. **b.** the shoe itself. **10.** *Rare.* a scheme of religious principles or doctrines. [F *plateforme,* lit., flat form, plan, flat area, terrace. See PLATE[1]]

**platform ticket** /'– tɪkət/, *n.* a ticket allowing the purchaser to go beyond the barrier on to a railway platform.

**platina** /'plætənə, plə'tinə/, *n.* a native alloy of platinum with palladium, iridium, osmium, etc. [NL or Sp. See PLATINUM]

**plating** /'pleɪtɪŋ/, *n.* **1.** a thin coating of gold, silver, etc. **2.** an external layer of metal plates. **3.** the act of one who or that which plates.

**platinic** /plə'tɪnɪk/, *adj.* of or containing platinum, esp. in its tetravalent state.

**platiniridium** /plætənə'rɪdiəm/, *n.* a natural alloy composed chiefly of platinum and iridium. [PLATIN(UM) + IRIDIUM]

**platinise** /'plætənaɪz/, *v.t.,* **-nised, -nising.** to coat or plate with metallic platinum. Also, **platinize.**

**platinised asbestos** /ˌplætənaɪzd æs'bɛstəs/, *n.* asbestos which has been treated with finely divided platinum, used as a catalyst.

**platino-,** a combining form of **platinum.**

**platinocyanic acid** /ˌplætənoʊsaɪˌænɪk 'æsəd/, *n.* an acid containing platinum and the radical cyanogen.

**platinocyanide** /ˌplætənoʊ'saɪənaɪd/, *n.* a salt of platinocyanic acid.

**platinoid** /'plætənɔɪd/, *adj.* **1.** resembling platinum: *the platinoid elements.* *–n* **2.** any of the metals (palladium, iridium, etc.) with which platinum is usu. associated. **3.** an alloy of copper, zinc, and nickel, to which small quantities of such elements as tungsten or aluminium have been added; used in electrical work, etc.

**platinotype** /'plætənoʊtaɪp/, *n. Photog.* **1.** a process of printing in which a platinum salt is employed yielding more permanent prints than those obtainable with silver salts. **2.** a print made by such a process.

**platinous** /'plætənəs/, *adj.* containing divalent platinum.

**platinum** /'plætənəm/, *n.* **1.** *Chem.* a heavy, greyish white, highly malleable and ductile metallic element, resistant to most chemicals, practically unoxidisable save in the presence of bases, and fusible only at extremely high temperatures, used esp. for making chemical and scientific apparatus, as a catalyst in the oxidation of ammonia to nitric acid, and in jewellery. *Symbol:* Pt; *at. wt:* 195.09; *at. no.:* 78; *sp. gr.:* 21.5 at 20°C. **2.** a light metallic grey with very slight bluish tinge when compared with silver. [NL, earlier *platina,* from Sp., from *plata* silver]

**platinum black** /– 'blæk/, *n.* a black powder consisting of very finely divided metallic platinum, used as a catalyst, esp. in organic synthesis.

**platinum blonde** /– 'blɒnd/, *adj.* **1.** (of hair) silvery blonde. *–n.* **2.** a person with hair of this colour. – **platinum blond,** *n. masc.*

**platinum record** /– 'rɛkɔd/, *n.* a platinum-coated record made by a recording company when a certain number of copies of the record have been sold (in Australia, 50 000), and presented by it to artists and other people involved in its production and promotion.

**platinum thermometer** /– θə'mɒmətə/, *n.* an instrument for measuring temperatures up to about 1200°C which consists of a coil of platinum wire enclosed within a protective tube, changes of temperature being indicated by a change in the resistance of the platinum wire.

**platitude** /'plætətjud/, *n.* **1.** a flat, dull, or trite remark, esp. one uttered as if it were fresh and profound. **2.** flatness, dullness, or triteness. [F, from *plat* flat. Cf. F and E *latitude, altitude.* See PLATE[1], -TUDE]

**platitudinise** /plætə'tjudənaɪz/, *v.i.,* **-nised, -nising.** to utter platitudes. Also, **platitudinize.**

**platitudinous** /plætə'tjudənəs/, *adj.* **1.** characterised by or given to platitudes. **2.** of the nature of a platitude.

**Platonic** /plə'tɒnɪk/, *adj.* **1.** (*l.c.*) purely spiritual; free from sensual desire: *platonic love.* **2.** of or pertaining to Plato, 427? - 347 B.C., Greek philosopher, or his doctrines: *the Platonic philosophy.* **3.** of or pertaining to love which, in Platonic philosophy, transcends the feeling for the individual and rises to a contemplation of the ideal. – **Platonically,** *adv.*

**Platonise** /'pleɪtənaɪz/, *v.,* **-nised, -nising.** *–v.i.* **1.** to follow the opinions or doctrines of Plato. **2.** to reason like Plato. *–v.t.* **3.** to give a Platonic character to. **4.** to explain in accordance with Platonic principles. Also, **Platonize.**

**Platonism** /'pleɪtənɪzəm/, *n.* **1.** the philosophy or doctrines of Plato, 427?-347 B.C., philosopher, or his followers. **2.** a Platonic doctrine or saying. **3.** the belief that physical objects are but impermanent representations of unchanging ideas, and that these ideas alone give true knowledge as they are known by the mind. **4.** (*l.c. or cap.*) the doctrine or the practice of platonic love. – **Platonist,** *n., adj.*

**platoon** /plə'tun/, *n.* **1.** a military sub-unit consisting of two or more sections, being part of a company. **2.** a company or group of persons. [F *peloton* little ball, group, platoon, diminutive of *pelote* ball. See PELLET]

**Plattdeutsch** /plat'dɔɪtʃ/, *n.* →**Low German.**

**platter** /'plætə/, *n.* **1.** a large, shallow dish, commonly oval, for holding or serving meat, etc. **2. on a platter,** (of something offered) capable of being taken without effort. [ME *plater,* from AF, from OF *plat* plate, dish]

**platyhelminth** /plæti'hɛlmɪnθ/, *n.* a member of the Platyhelminthes, a phylum of worms, the flatworms, having bilateral symmetry and a soft, solid, usu. flattened body, including the planarians, flukes, tapeworms, and others. [NL *Platyhelmintha,* from Gk *platýs* broad, flat + *hélmins* worm]

**platypus** /'plætəpʊs/, *n., pl.* **-puses, -pi** /paɪ/. an amphibious, egg-laying monotreme, *Ornithorhynchus anatinus,* of Australia and Tasmania, 45-60 cm in total length, having webbed feet and a muzzle like the bill of a duck; duckbill. [NL, from Gk *platýpous* flat-footed]

platypus

**platyrrhine** /'plætəraɪn/, *adj.* having a broad, flat-bridged nose; belonging to one of the two divisions of primates (opposed to *catarrhine*). [*platy-* (from Gk, combining form of *platýs* broad) + Gk *rhís* nose]

**plaudit** /'plɔdət/, *n.* (*usu. pl.*) **1.** a demonstration or round of applause, as for some approved or admired performance. **2.** any enthusiastic expression of approval. [L, alteration of *plaudite,* impv., APPLAUD]

**plausible** /'plɔzəbəl/, *adj.* **1.** having an appearance of truth or reason; seemingly worthy of approval or acceptance: *a plausible story.* **2.** fair-spoken and apparently worthy of confidence: *a plausible adventurer.* [L *plausibilis*] – **plausibility** /plɔzə'bɪləti/, **plaisibleness,** *n.* – **plausibly,** *adv.*

**plausive** /'plɔsɪv/, *adj.* **1.** *Rare.* applauding. **2.** *Obs.* →**plausible.**

**play** /pleɪ/, *n.* **1.** a dramatic composition or piece; a drama. **2.** a dramatic performance, as on the stage. **3.** exercise or action by way of amusement or recreation. **4.** fun, jest, or trifling, as opposed to earnest: *he said it merely in play.* **5.** the playing, or carrying on, of a game. **6.** manner or style of playing. **7.** the state, as of a ball, of being played with or in use in the active playing of a game: *in play, out of play.* **8.** a playing for stakes; gambling. **9.** *Obs.* (except in *fair play,* etc.) action, conduct, or dealing of a specified kind. **10.** action, activity, or operation: *the play of fancy.* **11.** brisk movement or action: *a fountain with a leaping play of water.* **12.** elusive change, as of light or colours. **13.** a space in which a thing, as a piece of mechanism, can move. **14.** freedom of movement, as within a space, as of a part of a mechanism. **15.** freedom for action, or scope for activity: *full play of the mind.* **16.** an act or performance in playing: *a stupid play.* **17.** turn to play: *it is your play.* –*v.t.* **18.** to act the part of (a person or character) in a dramatic performance: *to play Lady Macbeth.* **19.** to perform (a drama, etc.) on or as on the stage. **20.** to act or sustain (a part) in a dramatic performance or in real life. **21.** to sustain the part or character of in real life: *to play the fool.* **22.** to give performances in, as a theatrical company does: *to play the larger cities.* **23.** to engage in (a game, pastime, etc.). **24.** to contend against in a game. **25.** to employ (a player, etc.) in a game. **26.** to move or throw (an object) in a game: *he played the card reluctantly.* **27.** to use as if in playing a game, as for one's own advantage: *play off one person against another.* **28.** to play an extra game or round in order to settle (a tie) (fol. by *off*). **29.** to stake or wager, as in playing. **30.** to lay a wager or wagers on (something). **31.** to represent or imitate in sport: *to play school.* **32.** to perform on (a musical instrument). **33.** to perform (music) on an instrument. **34.** to do, perform, bring about, or execute: *to play tricks.* **35.** to cause to move or change lightly or quickly: *play coloured lights on a fountain.* **36.** to operate, or cause to operate, esp. continuously or with repeated action: *to play a hose on a fire.* **37.** to allow (a hooked fish) to exhaust itself by pulling on the line. **38.** to bring to an end; use up (fol. by *out*). –*v.i.* **39.** to exercise or employ oneself in diversion, amusement, or recreation. **40.** to do something only in sport, which is not to be taken seriously. **41.** to amuse oneself or toy; trifle (fol. by *with*). **42.** to take part or engage in a game. **43.** to take part in a game for stakes; gamble. **44.** to act, or conduct oneself, in a specified way: *to play fair.* **45.** to act on or as on the stage; perform. **46.** to perform on a musical instrument. **47.** (of the instrument or the music) to sound in performance. **48.** to move freely, as within a space, as a part of a mechanism. **49.** to move about lightly or quickly. **50.** to present the effect of such motion, as light or the changing colours of an iridescent substance. **51.** to operate continuously or with repeated action, often on something: *the noise played on his nerves.* **52.** to function during play: *the wicket played well at first.* **53.** to work on (the feelings, weaknesses, etc., of another) for one's own purposes (fol. by *on* or *upon*): *to play on one's emotions.* –*v.* **54.** Some special verb phrases are:

**play around,** to philander.

**play at,** to take part in (a game, hobby, etc.), often without serious attention.

**play back,** to reproduce sound, music, etc., which has just been recorded.

**play ball,** to cooperate.

**play cat and mouse, a.** to delay the inevitable defeat of an opponent so as to enjoy observing his struggles and discomfiture. **b.** (in racing) to speed up and slow down as a tactic to gain an advantage over the rest of the field.

**play down,** to minimise.

**play for time,** to gain time for one's own purposes by prolonging something unduly.

**play into the hands of,** to act in such a way as to give an advantage to.

**play (it) cool,** to act cautiously.

**play on, 1.** *Cricket.* **a.** (of a batsman) to hit his own wicket with the ball and thus be dismissed. **b.** (of a team) to play a second innings immediately after a bad first innings. **2.** *Aus. Rules.* to kick, handball, or run with the ball, without either waiting for the umpire's decision, or going back to take a free kick.

**play out,** (in a game when no result appears possible or one side is convincingly ahead) to play without attempting to score: *to play out time.*

**play silly buggers,** to act the fool.

**play the ball,** *Rugby League.* to restart the play after being tackled by tapping the ball back with one's foot to the dummy half.

**play the field, a.** to have as many flirtations as possible. **b.** to keep oneself open to advantage from a number of sources.

**play the game,** *Colloq.* **a.** to play in accordance with the rules. **b.** to play one's part.

**play through,** *Golf.* (of a group of players) to catch up to the group of players in front and with their permission to pass them and play ahead.

**play up, a.** to behave naughtily or annoyingly. **b.** to philander.

**play up to,** to attempt to get into the favour of. [ME *pleye(n),* OE *plegan,* c. MD *pleyen* dance, leap for joy]

**playa** /'plajə/, *n.* **1.** the sandy, salty, or mud-caked floor of a desert basin with interior drainage, usu. occupied by a shallow lake during the rainy season or after prolonged, heavy rains. **2.** the lake itself. [Sp.: shore, beach, from LL *plăgia,* from Gk *plágios* oblique, sloping]

**playable** /'pleɪəbəl/, *adj.* **1.** capable of or suitable for being played. **2.** (of ground) fit to be played on.

**play-act** /'pleɪ-ækt/, *v.i.* to pretend; to behave theatrically or melodramatically. – **play-acting,** *n.*

**playback** /'pleɪbæk/, *n.* **1.** the reproduction of sound, music, etc., which has just been recorded. –*adj.* **2.** of or pertaining to a device used in reproducing such a recording: *a hi-fi playback system.*

**playbill** /'pleɪbɪl/, *n.* a program or announcement of a play.

**playboy** /'pleɪbɔɪ/, *n.* a wealthy, carefree man who spends most of his time at parties, nightclubs, etc.

**play centre** /'pleɪ sɛntə/, *n.* a place, usu. a school and its grounds, where organised activities as games, classes in handicrafts, etc., are conducted during school vacations for children who wish to attend.

**played-out** /pleɪd-'aʊt/, *adj. Colloq.* exhausted; used up.

**player** /'pleɪə/, *n.* **1.** one who or that which plays. **2.** one who takes part or is skilled in some game. **3.** a person engaged in playing a game professionally. **4.** one who plays parts on the stage; an actor. **5.** one who plays a musical instrument. **6.** a gambler.

**player piano** /– pi'ænoʊ/, *n.* a piano played by machinery controlled by two pedals which, when operated by the performer, pump a pneumatic mechanism that turns a paper roll provided with perforations which cause air pressure to move the piano keys in a predetermined order and combination.

**playfellow** /'pleɪfɛloʊ/, *n.* →**playmate.**

**playful** /'pleɪfəl/, *adj.* **1.** full of play; sportive; frolicsome. **2.** pleasantly humorous: *a playful remark.* – **playfully,** *adv.* – **playfulness,** *n.*

**playgoer** /'pleɪgoʊə/, *n.* one who often or habitually attends the theatre.

**playground** /'pleɪgraʊnd/, *n.* **1.** ground used specifically for open-air recreation, as one attached to a school. **2.** any place of open-air recreation. **3.** an area where swings, etc., are provided for children.

**playgroup** /'pleɪgrup/, *n.* an informal gathering of preschool children with their parents, organised by families within a community to provide social contact and play experience for the children.

**playhouse** /'pleɪhaʊs/, *n.* **1.** a theatre. **2.** a cubbyhouse. [OE *pleghūs* theatre]

**playing card** /'pleɪɪŋ kad/, *n.* **1.** one of the conventional set of 52 cards, in 4 suits (diamonds, hearts, spades, and clubs), used in playing various games of chance and skill. **2.** one of any set or pack of cards used in playing games.

playing card

**playing field** /'– fild/, *n.* a field or open space used for sports, athletics, etc., esp. by schools.

**playlet** /'pleɪlət/, *n.* a short play.

**playlunch** /'pleɪlʌntʃ/, *n.* **1.** a snack eaten during the mid-morning recess at school. **2.** such a break; playtime.

**playmate** /'pleɪmeɪt/, *n.* a companion in play.

**play-off** /'pleɪ-ɒf/, *n.* the playing off of a tie, as in games or sports.

**play-on** /'pleɪ-ɒn/, *adj.* (in Australian Rules) of the style of play in which a team or an individual attempts to keep the ball moving at all times, even when entitled to take a free kick.

**play on words,** *n.* →**pun.**

**playpen** /'pleɪpɛn/, *n.* a small enclosure in which a young child can play safely without constant supervision.

**playroom** /'pleɪrum/, *n.* a room in a house set aside for children to play in.

**playsuit** /'pleɪsut/, *n.* an outfit worn by women and children for sports and leisure wear, consisting of shorts with a top.

**plaything** /'pleɪθɪŋ/, *n.* **1.** a thing to play with; a toy. **2.** a person used without consideration for the gratification of another.

**playtime** /'pleɪtaɪm/, *n.* **1.** time for play or recreation. **2.** a mid-morning break between school classes; recess. Also, **playlunch.**

**playwright** /'pleɪraɪt/, *n.* a writer of plays; a dramatist. [PLAY + WRIGHT]

**plaza** /'plazə/, *n.* a public square or open space in a city or town. [Sp., from L *platēa.* See PLACE]

**plea** /pli/, *n.* **1.** that which is alleged, urged, or pleaded in defence or justification. **2.** an excuse; a pretext. **3.** *Law.* **a.** an allegation made by, or on behalf of, a party to a legal suit, in support of his claim or defence. **b.** (in courts of equity) a plea which admits the truth of the declaration, but alleges special or new matter in avoidance. **c.** a suit or action at law: *to hold pleas (to try actions at law).* **d.** *Archaic.* statement of defence. **4.** an appeal or entreaty: *a plea for mercy.*

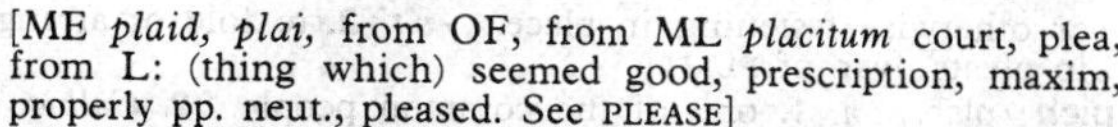

[ME *plaid, plai,* from OF, from ML *placitum* court, plea, from L: (thing which) seemed good, prescription, maxim, properly pp. neut., pleased. See PLEASE]

**plea bargaining** /'– bagənɪŋ/, *n.* the negotiation for an agreement between the prosecution and the defence in a law suit that the accused will face only specified charges or reduced penalties if a plea of guilty is entered.

**pleach** /plitʃ/, *v.t.* **1.** to plash or interweave (growing branches, vines, etc.), as for a hedge or arbour. **2.** to interlace or entwine. [ME *pleche(n),* var. of PLASH[2]]

**plead** /plid/, *v.,* **pleaded** or **plead** /plɛd/, **pleading.** –*v.i.* **1.** to make earnest appeal or entreaty: *to plead for help.* **2.** to use arguments or persuasions, as with a person, for or against something. **3.** to afford an argument or appeal: *his youth pleads for him.* **4.** *Law.* **a.** to make any allegation or plea in an action at law. **b.** to address a court as an advocate. **c.** *Obs.* to prosecute a suit or action at law. –*v.t.* **5.** to allege or urge in defence, justification, or excuse: *to plead ignorance.* **6.** *Law.* **a.** to maintain (a cause, etc.) by argument before a court. **b.** to allege or set forth (something) formally in an action at law. **c.** to allege or cite in legal defence: *to plead a statute of limitations.* [ME *plaide(n),* from OF *plaidier* go to law, plead, from VL *placitāre,* from L *placitum* thing which pleases]

**pleadable** /'plidəbəl/, *adj.* capable of being pleaded.

**pleader** /'plidə/, *n.* one who pleads, esp. at law.

**pleading** /'plidɪŋ/, *n.* **1.** the act of one who pleads. **2.** *Law.* **a.** the advocating of a cause in a court of law. **b.** the art or science of setting forth or drawing pleas in legal causes. **c.** a formal statement (now usu. written) setting forth the cause of action or the defence of a case at law. **d.** (*pl.*) the successive statements delivered alternately by plaintiff and defendant until issue is joined. – **pleadingly,** *adv.*

**pleasance** /'plɛzəns/, *n.* **1.** a space laid out with trees, walks, etc. **2.** *Archaic.* pleasure. [ME, from OF *plaisance,* from *plaisant* PLEASANT]

**pleasant** /'plɛzənt/, *adj.* **1.** pleasing, agreeable, or affording enjoyment; pleasurable: *pleasant news.* **2.** (of persons, manners, disposition, etc.) agreeable socially. **3.** (of weather, etc.) fair. **4.** gay, sprightly, or merry. **5.** jocular or facetious. [ME *pleasaunt,* from OF *plaisant,* ppr. of *plaisir* PLEASE] – **pleasantly,** *adv.* – **pleasantness,** *n.*

**pleasantry** /'plɛzəntri/, *n., pl.* **-tries. 1.** good-humoured raillery; pleasant humour in conversation. **2.** a humorous or jesting remark. **3.** a humorous action.

**pleasant Sunday afternoon,** *n.* (formerly) a meeting conducted by a Methodist Church.

**please** /pliz/, *v.,* **pleased, pleasing.** –*v.t.* **1.** to act to the pleasure or satisfaction of: *to please the public.* **2.** to be the pleasure or will of; seem good to: *may it please God.* **3.** (as a polite addition to requests, etc.) if you are willing: *please come here.* **4.** to find something agreeable; like, wish, or choose: *go where you please.* –*v.i.* **5.** to be agreeable; give pleasure or satisfaction. **6. if you please, a.** if you like; if it be your pleasure. **b.** (in stating some surprising fact): *in his pocket, if you please, was the letter.* [ME *plese,* from OF *plaisir,* from L *placēre* please, seem good]

**pleasing** /'plizɪŋ/, *adj.* that pleases; giving pleasure; agreeable; gratifying; likeable. – **pleasingly,** *adv.* – **pleasingness,** *n.*

**pleasurable** /'plɛʒərəbəl/, *adj.* such as to give pleasure; agreeable; pleasant. – **pleasurableness,** *n.* – **pleasurably,** *adv.*

**pleasure** /'plɛʒə/, *n., v.,* **-ured, -uring.** –*n.* **1.** the state or feeling of being pleased. **2.** enjoyment or satisfaction derived from what is to one's liking; gratification; delight. **3.** worldly or frivolous enjoyment: *the pursuit of pleasure.* **4.** sensual gratification. **5.** a cause or source of enjoyment or delight: *it was a pleasure to see you.* **6.** pleasurable quality. **7.** one's will, desire, or choice: *to make known one's pleasure.* –*v.t.* **8.** to give pleasure to; gratify; please. –*v.i.* **9.** to take pleasure; delight. **10.** *Colloq.* to seek pleasure, as by taking a holiday. [ME *plesir,* from OF *plaisir* PLEASE]

**pleasure principle** /'– prɪnsəpəl/, *n.* an automatic mental drive or instinct seeking to avoid pain and to obtain pleasure. Also, **pleasure-pain principle.**

**pleat** /plit/, *n.* **1.** a fold of definite even width made by doubling cloth or the like upon itself, and pressing, stitching, or otherwise fastening in place. *–v.t.* **2.** to fold or arrange in pleats. [var. of PLAIT]

**pleb** /plɛb/, *n.* **1.** one of the common people. **2.** *Colloq.* a commonplace or vulgar person. *–adj.* **3.** *Colloq.* vulgar, commonplace. [shortened form of PLEBEIAN]

**plebeian** /plə'biən/, *adj.* **1.** belonging or pertaining to the ancient Roman plebs. **2.** belonging or pertaining to the common people. **3.** common, commonplace, or vulgar. *–n.* **4.** a member of the Roman plebs. **5.** a plebeian person. [L *plēbēius* belonging to the plebs + -AN] – **plebeianism,** *n.*

**plebiscite** /'plɛbəsaɪt, -sət/, *n.* **1.** a direct vote of the qualified electors of a state in regard to some important public question. **2.** the vote by which the people of a political unit determine autonomy or affiliation with another country. [L *plēbiscītum*]

**plebs** /plɛbz/, *n.* **1.** *Colloq.* the common people; the populace. **2.** (in ancient Rome) the commons as contrasted with the patricians, the later senatorial nobility, or the equestrian order. [L]

**plectognath** /'plɛktɒgnæθ/, *adj.* belonging to the Plectognathi, a group of teleost fishes having the jaws extensively ankylosed and including the filefish, globefish, etc. [NL *Plectognathī,* pl., from Gk *plektó(s)* plaited, twisted + *gnáthos* jaw]

**plectron** /'plɛktrən/, *n., pl.* **-tra** /-trə/. →**plectrum.**

**plectrum** /'plɛktrəm/, *n., pl.* **-tra** /-trə/, **-trums.** a small piece of wood, metal, ivory, etc., for plucking strings of a lyre, mandolin, guitar, etc. [L, from Gk *plêktron*]

**pledge** /plɛdʒ/, *n., v.,* **pledged, pledging.** *–n.* **1.** a solemn promise of something, or to do or refrain from doing something: *a pledge of aid.* **2.** a piece of personal property delivered as security for the payment of a debt or the discharge of some obligation, and liable to forfeiture. **3.** the state of being given or held as security: *to put a thing in pledge.* **4.** *Law.* **a.** the act of delivering goods, etc., to another for security. **b.** the resulting legal relationship. **5.** anything given or regarded as a security of something. **6.** *Obs.* **a.** a hostage. **b.** one who becomes bail or surety for another. **7.** an assurance of support or goodwill conveyed by drinking a person's health; a toast. **8.** the solemn, formal vow to abstain from intoxicating drink: *to take the pledge.* *–v.t.* **9.** to bind by or as by a pledge: *to pledge hearers to secrecy.* **10.** to promise solemnly, or engage to give, maintain, etc.: *to pledge one's support.* **11.** to give or deposit as a pledge; pawn. **12.** to plight or stake, as one's honour, etc. **13.** to secure by a pledge; give a pledge for. **14.** to drink a health or toast to. [ME *plege,* from OF, from ML *plevium, plebium;* of Gmc orig.] – **pledger,** *n.*

**pledgee** /plɛ'dʒi/, *n.* the person with whom something is deposited as a pledge.

**pledget** /'plɛdʒət/, *n.* a small, flat mass of lint, absorbent cotton, or the like, for use on a wound, sore, etc.

**pledgor** /plɛ'dʒɔ/, *n. Law.* one who deposits personal property as a pledge.

**-plegia,** a word element used as a noun termination in pathological terms denoting forms of paralysis, as in *paraplegia.* [Gk, combining form from *plēgē* blow, stroke]

**plein-air** /plæn-'ɛə/, *adj.* pertaining to an art movement, originating in France about 1865 and concerned with rendering the effects of outdoor light and atmosphere on to a canvas so that the finished painting gives the impression of the open air. [F *plein air* open air]

**Pleiocene** /'plaɪousin/, *adj., n. Geol.* →**Pliocene.**

**Pleistocene** /'plaɪstousin/, *adj.* **1.** pertaining to the earlier division of the Quaternary period or system (the glacial epoch or ice age). *–n.* **2.** the epoch or series of the Quaternary that follows Pliocene and precedes Recent. [Gk *pleîsto(s)* most (superl. of *polýs* much) + -CENE]

**plenary** /'plinəri/, *adj.* **1.** full; complete; entire; absolute; unqualified. **2.** attended by all qualified members, as a council; fully constituted. [late ME, from LL *plēnārius*] – **plenarily,** *adv.*

**plenary indulgence** /– ɪn'dʌldʒəns/, *n. Rom. Cath. Ch.* remission of the total temporal punishment which is still due to sin after sacramental absolution. See **indulgence** (def. 5).

**plenipotent** /plɛ'nɪpətənt/, *adj.* invested with or possessing full power. [LL *plēnipotens,* from L *plēni-* full + *potens* potent]

**plenipotentiary** /ˌplɛnəpə'tɛnʃəri/, *n., pl.* **-ries,** *adj.* *–n.* **1.** a person, esp. a diplomatic agent, invested with full power or authority to transact business. *–adj.* **2.** invested with full power or authority, as a diplomatic agent. **3.** bestowing full power, as a commission. **4.** absolute or full, as power. [ML *plēnipotentiārius,* from LL *plēnipotens*]

**plenish** /'plɛnɪʃ/, *v.t. Chiefly Scot.* to fill up; stock; furnish. [late ME *plenyss,* from OF *pleniss-,* stem of *plenir,* from *plen-,* from L *plēnus* full]

**plenitude** /'plɛnətjud/, *n.* **1.** fullness in quantity, measure, or degree; abundance. **2.** the condition of being full. [L *plēnitūdo*]

**plenteous** /'plɛntiəs/, *adj.* **1.** plentiful; copious; abundant: *a plenteous supply of corn.* **2.** yielding abundantly. – **plenteously,** *adv.* – **plenteousness,** *n.*

**plentiful** /'plɛntəfəl/, *adj.* **1.** existing in great plenty. **2.** amply supplied with something. **3.** yielding abundantly. – **plentifully,** *adv.* – **plentifulness,** *n.*

**plenty** /'plɛnti/, *n., pl.* **-ties,** *adj., adv.* *–n.* **1.** a full or abundant supply: *there is plenty of time.* **2.** abundance: resources in plenty. **3.** a time of abundance. *–adj.* **4.** *Chiefly Colloq.* existing in ample quantity or number (usu. in the predicate): *this is plenty.* *–adv.* **5.** *Colloq.* fully: *plenty good enough.* [ME *plente(th),* from OF *plente(t),* from L *plēnitas* fullness, abundance]

**plenum** /'plinəm/, *n., pl.* **-nums, -na** /-nə/. **1.** a container of air, or other gas, under greater than the surrounding pressure. **2.** the whole of space regarded as being filled with matter. **3.** a full assembly, as a joint legislative assembly. [L, properly neut. of *plēnus* full, filled, complete, abundant]

**pleochroic** /pliou'krouɪk/, *adj.* (of a biaxial crystal) exhibiting different colours in three different directions when viewed by transmitted polarised light. [Gk *pleíōn* more + *chrô(s)* colour + -IC] – **pleochroism** /pli'ɒkrouɪzəm/, *n.*

**pleonasm** /'pliənæzəm/, *n.* **1.** the use of more words than are necessary to express an idea; redundancy. **2.** an instance of this. **3.** a redundant word or expression. [L *pleonasmus,* from Gk *pleonasmós*] – **pleonastic** /pliə'næstɪk/, *adj.* – **pleonastically** /pliə'næstɪkli/, *adv.*

**pleopod** /'pliəpɒd/, *n. Zool.* →**swimmeret.** [Gk *pléō(n),* ppr., swimming + -POD]

**plesiosaur** /'plisiəsɔ/, *n.* any member of the extinct genus *Plesiosaurus* (and of the order Sauropterygia) which existed in the Jurassic and Cretaceous periods, comprising marine reptiles with small head, very long neck, short tail, and four large flippers. Also, **plesiosaurus** /ˌplisiə'sɔrəs/. [NL *plēsiosaurus,* from Gk *plēsío(s)* near + *saûros* lizard]

**plessor** /'plɛsɔ/, *n.* →**plexor.**

**plethora** /'plɛθərə/, *n.* **1.** overfullness; superabundance. **2.** *Pathol., Obs.* a morbid condition due to excess of red corpuscles in the blood or increase in the quantity of blood. [NL, from Gk *plēthṓrē* fullness]

**plethoric** /plə'θɒrɪk/, *adj.* **1.** overfull; turgid; inflated. **2.** characterised by plethora. – **plethorically,** *adv.*

**pleur-,** a word element meaning 'side', 'pleura', sometimes 'rib'. Also, before consonants, **pleuro-.** [Gk, combining form of *pleurá* side, rib, or *pleurón* rib; or abstracted from PLEURA]

**pleura** /'plurə/, *n., pl.* **pleurae** /'pluri/. a delicate serous membrane investing each lung in mammals and folded back as a lining of the corresponding side of the thorax. [NL, from Gk: rib, side] – **pleural,** *adj.*

**pleurisy** /'plurəsi/, *n.* inflammation of the pleura, with or without a liquid effusion. [ME, from OF *pleurisie,* from LL *pleurisis,* for L *pleurītis,* from Gk] – **pleuritic** /plu'rɪtɪk/, *adj.*

**pleuro** /'plurou/, *n. Colloq.* →**pleuropneumonia.**

**pleurodont** /'plurədɒnt/, *adj.* **1.** ankylosed or attached to the inner edge of the jaw, as a tooth. **2.** having teeth so ankylosed, as certain lizards. *–n.* **3.** a pleurodont animal. [PLEUR- + -ODONT]

**pleuron** /'plurɒn/, *n., pl.* **pleura** /'plurə/. the lateral plate or plates of a thoracic segment of an insect. [Gk: side]

**pleuropneumonia** /ˌplurounju'mounjə/, *n.* **1.** *Pathol.* pleurisy conjoined with pneumonia. **2.** *Vet. Sci.* a contagious bovine disease prevalent in northern Australia, and occasionally found in the south.

**plexiform** /'plɛksəfɔm/, *adj.* in the form of a plexus. [PLEX(US)

+ -I- + -FORM]

**plexiglas** /ˈplɛksiglas/, *n.* a thermoplastic notable for its permanent transparency, light weight, and resistance to weathering. It can be bent to any shape when hot, but returns to its original shape when reheated. Also, **plexiglass.** [Trademark]

**pleximeter** /plɛkˈsɪmətə/, *n. Med.* a small, thin plate, as of ivory, to receive the blow of a plexor. [Gk *plêxi(s)* stroke, percussion + -METER[1]]

**plexor** /ˈplɛksə/, *n. Med.* a small hammer with a soft rubber head or the like, used in percussion for diagnostic purposes. Also, **plessor.** [Gk *plêx(is)* stroke, percussion + -OR[2]]

**plexus** /ˈplɛksəs/, *n., pl.* **plexuses, plexus.** a network, as of nerves or blood vessels. [L: an interweaving, twining] – **plexal,** *adj.*

**plf,** plaintiff.

**pliable** /ˈplaɪəbəl/, *adj.* **1.** easily bent; flexible; supple. **2.** easily influenced; yielding; adaptable. [F, from *plier* fold, bend. See PLY[2]] – **pliability** /plaɪəˈbɪləti/, **pliableness,** *n.* – **pliably,** *adv.*

**pliant** /ˈplaɪənt/, *adj.* **1.** bending readily; flexible; supple. **2.** easily inclined or influenced; yielding; compliant. [ME, from OF, ppr. of *plier* fold, bend. See PLY[2]] – **pliancy, pliantness,** *n.* – **pliantly,** *adv.*

**plica** /ˈplaɪkə/, *n., pl.* **plicae** /ˈplaɪsi/. **1.** *Zool., Anat.* a fold or folding. **2.** *Pathol.* a matted, filthy condition of the hair, caused by disease, etc. [ML: a fold, from L *plicāre* fold]

**plicate** /ˈplaɪkeɪt/, *adj.* folded like a fan; pleated. Also, **plicated.** [L *plicātus,* pp., folded] – **plicately,** *adv.*

plicate leaf

**plication** /plaɪˈkeɪʃən, plə-/, *n.* **1.** a folding or fold. **2.** plicate form or condition. Also, **plicature** /ˈplɪkətʃə/.

**plié** /ˈplieɪ/, *n.* a ballet position in which the knees are bent and the back kept straight. [F, pp. of *plier* bend]

**pliers** /ˈplaɪəz/, *n.pl.* small pincers with long jaws, for bending wire, holding small objects, etc.

**plight**[1] /plaɪt/, *n.* condition, state, or situation (usu. bad). [ME *plit,* from AF, var. of OF *pleit* fold, manner of folding, condition (see PLAIT); ? influenced by PLIGHT[2] in archaic sense of danger]

**plight**[2] /plaɪt/, *v.t.* **1.** to pledge (one's troth) in engagement to marry. **2.** to bind by a pledge, now esp. of marriage. **3.** to give in pledge; pledge (one's honour, etc.). *–n.* **4.** *Rare.* pledge. [ME; OE *pliht* danger, risk, c. G *Pflicht* duty, obligation] – **plighter,** *n.*

**plimsoll** /ˈplɪmsəl/, *n. Brit.* →**sandshoe.** [probably from supposed resemblence between a PLIMSOLL LINE and the line of rubber binding the sole to the side of the shoe]

**Plimsoll line** /ˈplɪmsəl laɪn/, *n.* a line or mark required to be placed on the hull of all British merchant vessels, showing the depth to which they may be submerged through loading. Also, **Plimsoll mark.** [named after Samuel *Plimsoll,* 1824-98, politician and social reformer]

**plinth** /plɪnθ/, *n. Archit.* **1.** the lower square part of the base of a column. **2.** a square base or a lower block, as of a pedestal. **3.** a course of stones, as at the base of a wall, forming a continuous plinthlike projection. [L *plinthus,* from Gk *plínthos* plinth, squared stone] – **plinthlike,** *adj.*

**Pliocene** /ˈplaɪoʊsin/, *adj.* **1.** pertaining to the latest principal division of the Tertiary period or system. *–n.* **2.** the epoch or series of the Tertiary that follows Miocene and precedes Pleistocene. Also, **Pleiocene.** [Gk *pleíon* more (compar. of *polýs* much) + -CENE]

**plod** /plɒd/, *v.,* **plodded, plodding,** *n. –v.i.* **1.** to walk heavily; trudge; move laboriously. **2.** to work with dull perseverence; drudge. *–v.t.* **3.** to walk heavily over or along. *–n.* **4.** the act or a course of plodding. **5.** a sound of or as of a heavy tread. **6.** *Colloq.* a time sheet. [? imitative] – **plodder,** *n.* – **ploddingly,** *adv.*

**plodder** /ˈplɒdə/, *n.* **1.** one who achieves results by working laboriously. **2.** one who moves slowly and with effort.

**-ploid,** a word element used in cytology and genetics referring to the number of chromosomes as *diploid.* [Gk *-ploos* (equivalent to E suffix *-fold*) + -(O)ID]

**plonk**[1] /plɒŋk/, *v.t.* **1.** to place or drop heavily or suddenly (oft. fol. by *down*). *–v.i.* **2.** to drop heavily or suddenly (oft. fol. by *down*). *–n.* **3.** the act or sound of plonking. *–adv.* **4.** with a plonking sound. **5.** *Colloq.* exactly. [imitative]

**plonk**[2] /plɒŋk/, *n. Colloq.* any alcoholic liquor, esp. cheap wine. [? var. of F (*vin*) *blanc* white (wine)]

**plonko** /ˈplɒŋkoʊ/, *n. Colloq.* a wine addict. Also, **plonkie.**

**plop** /plɒp/, *v.,* **plopped, plopping,** *n. –v.i.* **1.** to make a sound like that of a flat object striking water without a splash. **2.** to fall plump with such a sound. *–n.* **3.** a plopping sound or fall. **4.** the act of plopping. *–adv.* **5.** with a plop. [imitative]

**plosion** /ˈploʊʒən/, *n.* the audible end of a stop consonant at break of closure.

**plosive** /ˈploʊsɪv, -zɪv/, *adj., n. Phonet.* a stop consonant that ends with an explosion.

**plot**[1] /plɒt/, *n., v.,* **plotted, plotting.** *–n.* **1.** a secret plan or scheme to accomplish some purpose, esp. a hostile, unlawful, or evil purpose. **2.** the plan, scheme, or main story of a play, novel, poem, or the like. **3.** *Artillery.* the position of a target and the fall of shot correctly indicated on a map or graph. *–v.t.* **4.** to plan secretly (something hostile or evil): *to plot mutiny.* **5.** to mark on a plan, map, or chart, as a ship's course, etc. **6.** to make a plan or map of, as a tract of land, a building, etc. **7.** to determine and mark (points), as on graph paper, by means of measurements or co-ordinates. **8.** to draw (a curve) by means of points so marked. **9.** to represent by means of such a curve. **10.** to make (a calculation) by graph. *–v.i.* **11.** to form secret plots; conspire. [aphetic var. of COMPLOT] – **plotter,** *n.*

**plot**[2] /plɒt/, *n., v.,* **plotted, plotting.** *–n.* **1.** a small piece or area of ground: *a garden plot.* **2.** *Chiefly U.S.* a plan, map, or diagram, as of land, a building, etc. *–v.t.* **3.** to divide (land) into plots. [ME and OE; orig. uncert.]

**plot ratio** /ˈ– reɪʃioʊ/, *n.* →**floorspace index.**

**plotting paper** /ˈplɒtɪŋ peɪpə/, *n.* →**graph paper.**

**plough** /plaʊ/, *n.* **1.** an agricultural implement for cutting and turning over the soil. **2.** any of various implements resembling this, as a plane for cutting grooves or a device for snow clearance. **3.** a device on a tram, formerly used for collecting current from a conductor in a conduit. **4.** *Colloq.* ploughed land. **5.** *Brit. Colloq.* an examination failure. *–v.t.* **6.** to make furrows in or turn up (the soil) with a plough. **7.** to make (a furrow, etc.) with a plough. **8.** to furrow, remove, etc., or make (a furrow, groove, etc.) with or as with a plough. **9.** *Naut.* **a.** to cleave the surface of (the water). **b.** to make (a way) or follow (a course) thus. **10.** *Brit. Colloq.* **a.** to fail (someone) in an examination. **b.** to fail (an examination). **11. plough back,** to reinvest (profits of a business) in that business. *–v.i.* **12.** to till the soil with a plough; work with a plough. **13.** to take ploughing in a specified way: *land that ploughs easily.* **14.** to move through anything in the manner of a plough. **15.** to work at something slowly and with perseverance (usu. fol. by *through*). **16.** to move through water by cleaving the surface. **17.** *Brit. Colloq.* to fail an examination. **18. plough into,** to attack energetically, to throw oneself into. Also, *Chiefly U.S.,* **plow.** [ME; OE *plōh* ploughland, c. G *Pflug* plough] – **plougher,** *n.*

**ploughboy** /ˈplaʊbɔɪ/, *n.* **1.** a boy who leads or guides a team drawing a plough. **2.** a country boy. Also, *Chiefly U.S.,* **plowboy.**

**ploughman** /ˈplaʊmən/, *n., pl.* **-men. 1.** a man who ploughs. **2.** a farm labourer or a rustic. Also, *Chiefly U.S.,* **plowman.**

**ploughman's spikenard** /plaʊmənz ˈspaɪknad/, *n.* an erect composite herb with dull yellow capitula, *Inula conyza,* found on calcareous soils in England and Wales, central and south-eastern Europe.

**ploughshare** /ˈplaʊʃɛə/, *n.* the share of a plough which cuts the slice of earth and raises it to the mouldboard. Also, *Chiefly U.S.,* **plowshare.**

**plover** /ˈplʌvə/, *n.* any of various small to medium-sized limicoline birds of the family Charadriidae, with a short, straight bill characteristically thickened at the end, as the **banded plover,** *Vanellus tricolor,* of southern Australia and

Tasmania. [ME, from AF, from L *pluvia* rain (cf. PLUVIAL[1]); the connection of the bird with rain being uncert.]

masked plover

**plow** /plaʊ/, *n., v.t., v.i. Chiefly U.S.* →**plough.**

**plowboy** /ˈplaʊbɔɪ/, *n. U.S.* →**ploughboy.**

**plowman** /ˈplaʊmən/, *n. U.S.* →**ploughman.**

**plowshare** /ˈplaʊʃɛə/, *n. U.S.* →**ploughshare.**

**ploy** /plɔɪ/, *n.* a manoeuvre or stratagem, as in conversation, to gain the advantage. [F *ployer,* from L *plicāre* fold]

**pluck** /plʌk/, *v.t.* **1.** to pull off or out from the place of growth, as fruit, flowers, feathers, etc. **2.** to give a pull at. **3.** to pull with sudden force or with a jerk. **4.** to pull by force (fol. by *away, off, out,* etc.). **5.** to pull off the feathers, hair, etc., from. **6.** *Colloq.* to rob, plunder, or fleece. **7.** to sound (the strings of a musical instrument) by pulling at them with the fingers or a plectrum. **8.** *Brit. Colloq.* to reject, as after an examination. **9. pluck up, a.** to pull up; uproot; eradicate. **b.** to rouse (courage, spirit, etc.) *–v.i.* **10.** to pull sharply; tug (*at*). **11.** to snatch (*at*). *–n.* **12.** the act of plucking; a pull, tug, or jerk. **13.** the heart, liver, and lungs, esp. of an animal used for food. **14.** courage or resolution in the face of difficulties. [ME *plukke,* OE *pluccian,* c. MLG *plucken;* akin to G *pflücken*] – **plucker,** *n.*

**plucked wool** /plʌkt ˈwʊl/, *n.* wool removed from the carcass of dead sheep as soon as the fibres become loose in the skin; a superior grade of dead wool.

**plucky** /ˈplʌki/, *adj.,* **-ier, -iest.** having or showing pluck or courage; brave. – **pluckily,** *adv.* – **pluckiness,** *n.*

**plug** /plʌg/, *n., v.,* **plugged, plugging.** *–n.* **1.** a piece of rubber or plastic for stopping the flow of water from a basin, bath (def. 3) or sink (def. 33). **2.** a piece of wood or other material used to stop up a hole or aperture, to fill a gap, or to act as a wedge. **3.** *Elect.* **a.** a tapering piece of conducting material designed to be inserted between contact surfaces and so establish connection between elements of an electric current connected to the respective surfaces. **b.** a device, usu. with three prongs, which by insertion in a socket establishes contact between an electrical appliance and a power supply. **4.** →**spark plug. 5.** *U.S.* →**fire hydrant. 6.** a cake of pressed tobacco. **7.** a piece of tobacco cut off for chewing, etc. **8.** *Colloq.* the favourable mention of a product or the like on radio, television, etc.; an advertisement, esp. unsolicited. **9.** *U.S. Colloq.* a worn-out or unsaleable article. **10.** *Colloq.* a punch. **11.** *Colloq.* a worn-out or inferior horse. **12.** *Orig. U.S. Angling.* an artificial bait with hooks attached. **13.** *U.S. Colloq.* a man's tall silk hat. *–v.t.* **14.** to stop or fill with or as with a plug. **15.** to insert or drive a plug into: *to plug a wall for the hanging of a picture.* **16.** to secure by a plug. **17.** to insert (something) as a plug. **18.** *Colloq.* to mention (a publication, product or the like) favourably and, often, repetitively as in a lecture, radio show, etc. **19.** *Colloq.* to punch. **20.** *Colloq.* to shoot. **21.** to connect (an electrical device) with an outlet (fol. by *in*). *–v.i.* **22.** *Colloq.* to work steadily or doggedly (usu. fol. by *on*). **23.** *Colloq.* to strike; shoot. [MD *plugge* (D *plug*) plug, peg; akin to G *Pflock*] – **plugger,** *n.*

**plug board** /ˈ– bɔd/, *n. Elect.* →**patch board.**

**plug-in** /ˈplʌg-ɪn/, *adj.* electrically powered but not having any fixed connection to the mains supply: *plug-in stove.*

**plug-ugly** /ˈplʌg-ʌgli/, *n., pl.* **-lies,** *adj. U.S. Colloq. –n.* **1.** a ruffian; a rowdy; a tough. *–adj.* **2.** characteristic of or pertaining to ruffians or the like.

**plum**[1] /plʌm/, *n.* **1.** the drupaceous fruit of any of various trees of the rosaceous genus *Prunus,* closely related to the cherry but with an oblong stone. **2.** a tree bearing such fruit. **3.** any of various other trees with a plum-like fruit. **4.** the fruit itself. **5.** →**sugarplum. 6.** a raisin as in a cake or pudding. **7.** anything resembling a plum, as in taste or shape. **8.** a deep purple varying from bluish to reddish. **9.** a good or choice thing, as one of the best parts of anything, a fine situation or appointment, etc. [ME; OE *plūme* (c. G *Pflaume*), from Gk *proûmnon*] – **plumlike,** *adj.*

**plum**[2] /plʌm/, *adj., adv.* →**plumb** (defs 4-8).

**plumage** /ˈplumɪdʒ/, *n.* **1.** the entire feathery covering of a bird. **2.** feathers collectively. [late ME, from OF, from *plume* feather + *-age* -AGE]

**plumate** /ˈplumeɪt/, *adj.* resembling a feather, as a hair or bristle which bears smaller hairs. [L *plūmātus,* pp., covered with feathers]

**plumb** /plʌm/, *n.* **1.** a small mass of lead or heavy material, used for various purposes. **2.** the position of a plumbline when freely suspended; the perpendicular. **3. out of plumb, a.** not perpendicular. **b.** not functioning properly. *–adj.* **4.** true according to a plumbline; perpendicular. **5.** *Colloq.* downright or absolute. *–adv.* **6.** in a perpendicular or vertical direction. **7.** exactly, precisely, or directly: *plumb in the middle.* **8.** *Colloq.* completely or absolutely. *–v.t.* **9.** to test or adjust by a plumbline. **10.** to make vertical. **11.** to sound (the ocean, etc.) with, or as with, a plumbline. **12.** to measure (depth) by sounding. **13.** to sound the depths of, or penetrate to the bottom of. **14.** to seal with lead. *–v.i.* **15.** *Colloq.* to work as a plumber. Also, **plum** for defs 4-8. [ME *plumbe,* from OF *plomb,* from L *plumbum* lead]

**plumbago**[1] /plʌmˈbeɪgoʊ/, *n.* a genus of annual or perennial plants from warm regions, with blue, white, or pink flowers, including the frequently cultivated southern African climbing shrub *P. capensis.*

**plumbago**[2] /plʌmˈbeɪgoʊ/, *n., pl.* **-gos. 1.** graphite. **2.** *Obs.* a drawing made by an instrument with a lead point. [L: lead, ore]

**plumb-bob** /ˈplʌm-bɒb/, *n.* →**plummet** (def. 1).

**plumbeous** /ˈplʌmbiəs/, *adj.* →**leaden.** [L *plumbeus*]

**plumber** /ˈplʌmə/, *n.* **1.** one who installs and repairs piping, fixtures, appliances, and appurtenances in connection with the water supply, drainage systems, etc., both in and out of buildings. **2.** a worker in lead or similar metals. [ME, from OF *plombier,* from LL *plumbārius,* from L *plumbum* lead]

**plumbery** /ˈplʌməri/, *n., pl.* **ries. 1.** a plumber's workshop. **2.** a plumber's work.

**plumbic** /ˈplʌmbɪk/, *adj.* containing lead, esp. in the tetravalent state. [L *plumbum* lead + -IC]

**plumbicon** /ˈplʌmbɪkɒn/, *n.* a television camera pick-up tube in which the image is focused on a photoconductive lead oxide plate.

**plumbiferous** /plʌmˈbɪfərəs/, *adj.* yielding or containing lead. [L *plumbum* lead + -I- + -FEROUS]

**plumbing** /ˈplʌmɪŋ/, *n.* **1.** the system of pipes and other apparatus for conveying water, liquid wastes, etc., as in a building. **2.** the work or trade of a plumber. **3.** the act of one who plumbs, as in ascertaining depth.

**plumbism** /ˈplʌmbɪzəm/, *n.* chronic lead poisoning.

**plumbline** /ˈplʌmlaɪn/, *n.* **1.** a string to one end of which is attached a metal bob, used to determine perpendicularity, find the depth of water, etc. **2.** →**plumb-rule.**

**plumbous** /ˈplʌmbəs/, *adj.* containing divalent lead. [L *plumbōsus*]

**plumb-rule** /ˈplʌm-rul/, *n.* a device used by builders, etc., for determining perpendicularity, consisting of a narrow board fitted with a plumbline and bob.

**plumbum** /ˈplʌmbəm/, *n. Chem.* →**lead**[2]. *Symbol:* Pb [L]

**plum duff** /plʌm ˈdʌf/, *n.* a kind of flour pudding containing raisins or currants, steamed, or boiled in a cloth. Also, **plumduff.**

**plume** /plum/, *n., v.,* **plumed, pluming.** *–n.* **1.** a feather. **2.** a large, long, or conspicuous feather: *the plume of an ostrich.* **3.** a soft, fluffy feather. **4.** any plumose part or formation. **5.** a feather, a tuft of feathers, or some substitute, worn as an ornament on the hat, helmet, etc. **6.** an ornament; a token of honour or distinction. **7.** *Chiefly Poetic.* plumage. *–v.t.* **8.** to furnish, cover, or adorn with plumes or feathers. **9.** (of a bird) to preen (itself or its feathers). **10.** to display or feel satisfaction with or pride in (oneself); pride (oneself) complacently (fol. by *on* or *upon*). [OF, from L *plūma* feather; replacing OE *plūm,* from L *plūma*] – **plumelike,** *adj.*

**plumelet** /ˈplumlət/, *n.* a small plume.

**plummet** /ˈplʌmət/, *n.* **1.** Also, **plumb-bob.** a piece of lead or some other weight attached to a line, used for determining perpendicularity, for sounding, etc.; the bob of a plumb-line. **2.** →**plumb-rule.** **3.** *Angling.* an apparatus consisting of a weight attached to a line, used to determine the depth of water. **4.** something that weighs down or depresses. *–v.i.* **5.** to plunge. [ME *plomet,* from OF *plommet, plombet,* diminutive of *plomb* lead]

**plummy** /ˈplʌmi/, *adj.* **1.** full of or resembling plums. **2.** *Colloq.* choice, good, or desirable. **3.** (of a voice) deep or vibrant, esp. excessively or affectedly so.

**plumose** /ˈplumoʊs/, *adj.* **1.** having feathers or plumes; feathered. **2.** feathery or plumelike. [L *plūmōsus*] – **plumosity** /pluˈmɒsəti/, *n.*

**plump**[1] /plʌmp/, *adj.* **1.** well filled out or rounded in form; somewhat fleshy or fat; chubby. *–v.i.* **2.** to become plump (oft. fol. by *up* or *out*). *–v.t.* **3.** to make plump (fol. by *up* or *out*). [ME *plompe* dull, rude, c. MLG *plump* blunt, thick, rude] – **plumply,** *adv.* – **plumpness,** *n.*

**plump**[2] /plʌmp/, *v.i.* **1.** to fall heavily or suddenly and directly; drop, sink, or come abruptly, or with direct impact. **2.** to vote exclusively for or choose one out of a number (oft. fol. by *for*): *to plump for oil rather than gas heating.* *–v.t.* **3.** to drop or throw heavily or suddenly. **4.** *Brit.* to utter or say bluntly (oft. fol. by *out*). *–n.* **5.** a heavy or sudden fall. *–adv.* **6.** with a heavy or sudden fall or drop. **7.** *Brit.* directly or bluntly, as in speaking. **8.** straight. **9.** with sudden encounter. **10.** with direct impact. *–adj.* **11.** direct; downright; blunt. [ME *plumpen,* c. D *plompen;* probably imitative]

**plumper**[1] /ˈplʌmpə/, *n.* **1.** a plumping or falling heavily. **2.** the vote of one who plumps. **3.** a voter who plumps. [PLUMP[2], *v.* + -ER[1]]

**plumper**[2] /ˈplʌmpə/, *n.* **1.** something that plumps, or makes plump. **2.** something carried in the mouth to fill out hollow cheeks. [PLUMP[1], *v.* + -ER[1]]

**plum pine** /plʌm ˈpaɪn/, *n.* →**brown pine.**

**plum pudding** /– ˈpʊdɪŋ/, *n.* →**Christmas pudding.**

**plumule** /ˈplumjul/, *n.* **1.** *Bot.* the bud of the ascending axis of a plant while still in the embryo. **2.** *Ornith.* a down feather. [L *plūmula,* diminutive of *plūma* feather]

**plumy** /ˈplumi/, *adj.* **1.** having plumes or feathers. **2.** adorned with a plume or plumes: *a plumy helmet.* **3.** plumelike or feathery.

P

P, plumule in rhubarb

**plunder** /ˈplʌndə/, *v.t.* **1.** to rob of goods or valuables by open force, as in war, hostile raids, brigandage, etc: *to plunder a town.* **2.** to rob, despoil, or fleece: *to plunder the public treasury.* **3.** to take by pillage or robbery. *–v.i.* **4.** to take plunder; pillage. *–n.* **5.** plundering, pillage, or spoliation. **6.** that which is taken in plundering; loot. **7.** anything taken by robbery, theft, or fraud. [G *plündern*] – **plunderer,** *n.*

**plunderage** /ˈplʌndərɪdʒ/, *n.* **1.** the act of plundering; pillage. **2.** *Marine Law.* **a.** the embezzlement of goods on board ship. **b.** the goods embezzled.

**plunge** /plʌndʒ/, *v.,* **plunged, plunging,** *n.* *–v.t.* **1.** to cast or thrust forcibly or suddenly into a liquid, a penetrable substance, a place, etc.; immerse; submerge: *to plunge a dagger into one's heart.* **2.** to bring into some condition, situation, etc.: *to plunge a country into war.* **3.** to immerse mentally, as in thought. *–v.i.* **4.** to cast oneself, or fall as if cast, into water, a deep place, etc. **5.** *Swimming.* to dive headfirst into the water. **6.** to rush or dash with headlong haste: *to plunge through a doorway.* **7.** *Colloq.* to bet or speculate recklessly. **8.** to throw oneself impetuously or abruptly into some condition, situation, matter, etc.: *to plunge into war.* **9.** to descend abruptly or precipitously, as a cliff, a road, etc. **10.** to pitch violently forward, esp. with the head downwards, as a horse, ship, etc. *–n.* **11.** the act of plunging. **12.** a leap or dive into water or the like. **13.** a headlong or impetuous rush or dash. **14.** a sudden, violent pitching movement. **15.** *U.S.* a place for plunging or diving, as a swimming pool. **16. take the plunge,** to resolve to do something (usu. unpleasant) and to act straightaway. [ME, from OF *plungier,* from L *plumbum* lead]

**plunge dip** /ˈ– dɪp/, *n.* a long narrow trough through which sheep are swum in a chemical solution to destroy external parasites.

**plunger** /ˈplʌndʒə/, *n.* **1.** *Mach.* a device or a part of a machine which acts with a plunging or thrusting motion; a piston; a ram. **2.** one who or that which plunges; a diver. **3.** *Colloq.* a reckless punter or speculator.

**plunging** /ˈplʌndʒɪŋ/, *adj.* **1.** that plunges. **2.** *Mil.* (of fire) directed downwards from pieces situated above the plane of the object fired at.

**plunk** /plʌŋk/, *v.t.* **1.** to pluck (a stringed instrument or its strings); twang. **2.** to throw, push, put etc., heavily or suddenly. **3.** *Colloq.* to shoot at. *–v.i.* **4.** to give forth a twanging sound. **5.** to drop down heavily or suddenly; plump. *–n.* **6.** the act or sound of plunking. **7.** a direct, forcible blow. **8.** *U.S. Colloq.* a dollar. *–adv.* **9.** with a plunking sound. Also (for defs 2, 5, 6, 7, 9) **plonk.** [imitative]

**Plunket** /plʌŋkət/, *adj.* of or pertaining to a nurse trained to care for mothers and newborn children according to the principles of the Plunket Society, now the Royal New Zealand Society for the Health of Women and Children. [from Lady *Plunket,* wife of the governor-general, the Society's first president]

**plup.,** pluperfect.

**pluperfect** /pluˈpɜfəkt/, *Gram.* *–adj.* **1.** perfect with respect to a temporal point of reference in the past. For example: In *'He had done it when I came', had done* is pluperfect in relation to *came* since the action was brought to a close before I came. Cf. **perfect, imperfect.** **2.** designating a tense with such meaning. Latin *portāveram* 'I had carried' etc., is in the pluperfect tense. *–n.* **3.** the pluperfect tense. **4.** a form therein. [L, contraction of *plūs quam perfectum* more than perfect]

**plur.,** **1.** plural. **2.** plurality.

**plural** /ˈplurəl/, *adj.* **1.** consisting of, containing, or pertaining to more than one. **2.** pertaining to or involving a plurality of persons or things. **3.** being one of such a plurality: *a plural candidate.* **4.** *Gram.* (in many languages) designating the number category that normally implies more than one person, thing, or collection, as English, *men, things, they.* *–n.* **5.** *Gram.* the plural number. **6.** a form therein. [ME, from L *plūrālis*]

**pluralise** /ˈplurəlaɪz/, *v.t.,* **-lised, -lising.** **1.** to make plural. **2.** to express in the plural form. Also, **pluralize.**

**pluralism** /ˈplurəlɪzəm/, *n.* **1.** *Philos.* a theory or system that recognises more than one ultimate substance or principle. Cf. **monism, dualism.** **2.** the holding by one person of two or more offices, esp. ecclesiastical benefices, at the same time. **3.** the character of being plural. **4.** →**multiculturalism.**

**pluralist** /ˈplurələst/, *adj.* **1.** of or pertaining to pluralism. **2.** →**multicultural.** Also, **pluralistic** /plurəˈlɪstɪk/.

**plurality** /pluˈræləti/, *n., pl.* **-ties.** **1.** more than half of the whole; the majority. **2.** *U.S.* →**majority** (def. 3). **3.** a number greater than unity. **4.** the fact of being numerous. **5.** a large number, or a multitude. **6.** the state or fact of being plural. **7.** →**pluralism** (def. 2). **8.** any of the offices or benefices so held.

**plurally** /ˈplurəli/, *adv.* as a plural; in a plural sense.

**plural voting** /plurəl ˈvoʊtɪŋ/, *n.* a system by which a person is allowed to vote more than once in an election.

**pluri-,** a word element meaning 'several', 'many'. [L, combining form of *plūrēs,* pl.]

**plurry** /ˈplʌri/, *adj.* bloody. [alteration of BLOODY]

**plus** /plʌs/, *prep.* **1.** more by the addition of; increased by: *ten plus two.* **2.** with the addition of; with. *–adj.* **3.** involving or denoting addition. **4.** positive: *a plus quantity.* **5.** *Colloq.* with something in addition. **6.** more (by a certain amount). **7.** *Elect.* positive or to be connected to the positive: *the plus terminal.* **8.** *Bot.* designating, in the absence of morphological difference, one of the two strains or mycelia in fungi which must unite in the sexual process. *–n.* **9.** a plus quantity. **10.** the plus sign (+). **11.** something additional. **12.** a surplus or gain. [L: more]

**plus-fours** /plʌs-ˈfɔz/, *n.pl.* baggy trousers, covering the knee and strapping below it.

**plush** /plʌʃ/, *n.* **1.** a fabric of silk, cotton, wool, etc., having

i = peat ɪ = pit ɛ = pet æ = pat a = part ɒ = pot ʌ = putt ɔ = port ʊ = put u = pool ɜ = pert ə = apart aɪ = buy eɪ = bay ɔɪ = boy aʊ = how
oʊ = hoe ɪə = here ɛə = hair ʊə = tour g = give θ = thin ð = then ʃ = show ʒ = measure tʃ = choke dʒ = joke ŋ = sing j = you õ = Fr. bon

a longer pile than that of velvet. *–adj.* **2.** Also, **plushy.** denoting something, esp. a room, furnishings, or the like, luxurious and costly. [F *pluche, peluche,* from L *pilus* hair]

**plus sign** /'plʌs saɪn/, *n.* the symbol (+) indicating summation or a positive quantity.

**Pluto** /'plutoʊ/, *n.* the ninth and outermost planet from the sun, discovered in 1930. [from *Pluto,* Greek god, the ruler of HADES; L, from Gk *Ploútōn*]

**plutocracy** /plu'tɒkrəsi/, *n., pl.* **-cies. 1.** the rule or power of wealth or of the wealthy. **2.** a government or state in which the wealthy class rules. **3.** a class or group ruling, or exercising power or influence, by virtue of its wealth. [Gk *ploutokratía.* See -CRACY]

**plutocrat** /'plutəkræt/, *n.* a member of a plutocracy.

**plutocratic** /plutə'krætɪk/, *adj.* of, pertaining to, or indicative of a plutocracy or plutocrats. Also, **plutocratical.**

**pluton** /'plutɒn/, *n.* any body of igneous rock that solidified far below the earth's surface. [named after *Pluto.* See PLUTO]

**plutonian** /plu'toʊniən/, *adj.* (*sometimes cap.*) **1.** gloomy; harsh. **2.** pertaining to the theory that the present condition of the earth's crust is mainly due to igneous action.

**plutonic** /plu'tɒnɪk/, *adj.* **1.** *Geol.* denoting a class of igneous rocks which have solidified far below the earth's surface. **2.** (*sometimes cap.*) →**plutonian.**

**plutonium** /plu'toʊniəm/, *n. Chem.* a radioactive element, capable of self-maintained explosive fission, isolated during research on the atomic bomb in 1940. It is formed by deuteron bombardment of neptunium, and has an isotope of major importance, $^{239}_{94}$Pu, which is fissionable and can be produced in chain-reacting units from uranium-238, by neutron capture followed by the spontaneous emission of two beta particles. *Symbol:* Pu; *at. no.:* 94. [Gk *Ploútōn* Pluto + -IUM. See PLUTON]

**pluvial**[1] /'pluviəl/, *adj.* **1.** of or pertaining to rain; rainy. **2.** *Geol.* due to rain. [L *pluviālis*]

**pluvial**[2] /'pluviəl/, *n.* →**cope**[2] (def. 1).

**pluviometer** /pluvi'ɒmətə/, *n.* an instrument for measuring rainfall. [L *pluvia* rain + -O- + -METER[1]] – **pluviometric** /pluviə'mɛtrɪk/, **pluviometrical** /pluviə'mɛtrɪkəl/, *adj.* – **pluviometry,** *n.*

**pluvious** /'pluviəs/, *adj.* **1.** rainy. **2.** pertaining to rain. [L *pluviōsus*]

**ply**[1] /plaɪ/, *v.,* **plied, plying.** *–v.t.* **1.** to use; employ busily, or work with or at: *to ply the needle.* **2.** to carry on, practise, or pursue: *to ply a trade.* **3.** to treat with something repeatedly applied: *I plied the fire with fresh fuel.* **4.** to assail persistently: *to ply horses with a whip.* **5.** to supply with something pressingly offered: *to ply a person with drink.* **6.** to address persistently or importunately, as with questions, solicitations, etc.; importune. **7.** to traverse (a river, etc.), esp. on regular trips. *–v.i.* **8.** to travel or run regularly over a fixed course or between certain places, as a boat, a stage, etc. **9.** to perform one's or its work or office busily or steadily: *to ply with the oars.* **10.** to pursue or direct the course, on the water or otherwise. **11.** *Naut.* to make way windward by tacking. **12.** *Naut.* to make regular voyages between certain ports. [ME *plye(n),* aphetic var. of ME *aplye(n)* APPLY]

**ply**[2] /plaɪ/, *n., pl.* **plies,** *v.,* **plied, plying.** *–n.* **1.** a fold; a thickness. **2.** a strand of yarn: *single ply.* **3.** bent, bias, or inclination. *–v.t.* **4.** to bend, fold, or mould. *–v.i.* **5.** *Obs.* to bend, incline, or yield. [ME *plien,* from OF *plier* fold, bend, from L *plicāre* fold]

**-ply,** suffixal use of **ply**[2] (strand, thickness), as in *three-ply, fourteen-ply,* etc., as of wool, wood, etc.

**plygr.,** playground.

**Plymouth Rock** /plɪməθ 'rɒk/, *n.* one of a North American breed of medium-sized domestic fowls.

**plywood** /'plaɪwʊd/, *n.* a material consisting of an odd number of thin sheets or strips of wood glued together with the grains (usu.) at right angles, used in building, cabinetwork, and aeroplane construction.

**p.m.** /pi 'ɛm/, **1.** after noon. [L *post meridiem*] **2.** the period from 12 noon to 12 midnight. **3.** post-mortem.

**P.M.** /pi 'ɛm/, **1.** Police Magistrate. **2.** Postmaster. **3.** post-mortem. **4.** Prime Minster. **5.** Provost Marshal.

**PMG** /pi ɛm 'dʒi/, Post Master General.

**PMT** /pi ɛm 'ti/, premenstrual tension.

**pneuma** /'njumə/, *n. Gk Philos., etc.* the vital spirit; the soul. [Gk]

**pneumatic** /nju'mætɪk/, *adj.* **1.** of or pertaining to air, or gases in general. **2.** pertaining to pneumatics. **3.** operated by air, or by pressure or exhaustion of air. **4.** containing air; filled with compressed air, as a tyre. **5.** of or pertaining to an unusually shapely woman. **6.** *Theol.* of or pertaining to the spirit; spiritual. **7.** *Zool.* containing air or air cavities. [L *pneumaticus,* from Gk *pneumatikós*] – **pneumatically,** *adv.*

**pneumatic brake** /– 'breɪk/, *n.* a system of braking used on some railway trains in which compressed air is used to operate brake cylinders throughout the train simultaneously.

**pneumatic drill** /– 'drɪl/, *n.* a hard rock, or road, drill which is operated by compressed air.

**pneumatics** /nju'mætɪks/, *n.* the branch of physics that deals with the mechanical properties of air and other gases. [pl. of PNEUMATIC, *adj.* See -ICS]

**pneumatic trough** /nju,mætɪk 'trɒf/, *n.* a vessel used in laboratories for the collection of gases.

**pneumatic tyre** /– 'taɪə/, *n.* a rubber tyre filled with air under pressure.

**pneumato-,** a word element, used chiefly in scientific terms, referring to air, breath, spirit. [Gk, combining form of *pneûma*]

**pneumatology** /njumə'tɒlədʒi/, *n.* **1.** *Theol.* **a.** the doctrine of the Holy Spirit. **b.** the belief in intermediary spirits between men and God. **2.** the doctrine or theory of spiritual beings. **3.** *Archaic.* →**psychology. 4.** *Obs.* →**pneumatics.**

**pneumatolysis** /njumə'tɒləsəs/, *n.* the process by which minerals and ores are formed by the action of vapours given off from solidifying igneous rocks.

**pneumatolytic** /njumətoʊ'lɪtɪk/, *adj.* pertaining to or formed by pneumatolysis.

**pneumatometer** /njumə'tɒmətə/, *n.* an instrument for measuring the quantity of air inhaled or exhaled during a single inspiration or expiration, or the force of inspiration or expiration.

**pneumatophore** /'njumətoʊfɔ/, *n.* **1.** *Bot.* a specialised structure developed from the root in certain plants growing in swamps and marshes and serving as a respiratory organ. **2.** *Zool.* the air-sac of a siphonophore, serving as a float.

**pneumatotherapy** /njumətoʊ'θɛrəpi/, *n.* the use of compressed or rarefied air in treating disease.

**pneumo-,** a word element referring to the lungs or to respiration. [combining form representing Gk *pneúmōn* lung, or, less often, *pneûma* wind, air, breath]

**pneumobacillus** /,njumoʊbə'sɪləs/, *n., pl.* **-cilli** /-'sɪlaɪ/. a bacillus *Klebsiella pneumoniae,* the causative agent of certain respiratory diseases, esp. pneumonia. [NL. See PNEUMO-, BACILLUS]

**pneumococcus** /njumoʊ'kɒkəs/, *n., pl.* **-cocci** /-'kɒksaɪ/. a bacterium, *Micrococcus lanceolatus,* a rather large pear-shaped coccus, occurring in pairs and surrounded by a wide capsule, the cause of acute lobar pneumonia and **pneumococcal meningitis.** [NL. See PNEUMO-, COCCUS]

**pneumoconiosis** /,njumoʊkɒni'oʊsəs/, *n.* a disease of the lungs caused by the inhalation of dust. [NL, from *pneumo-* PNEUMO- + Gk *kónis* dust + *-osis* -OSIS]

**pneumodynamics** /,njumoʊdaɪ'næmɪks/, *n.* →**pneumatics.**

**pneumogastric** /njumoʊ'gæstrɪk/, *adj.* of or pertaining to the lungs and stomach.

**pneumogastric nerve** /– 'nɜv/, *n.* →**vagus nerve.**

**pneumonectomy** /njumə'nɛktəmi/, *n., pl.* **-mies.** the total or partial removal of lung tissue by surgery. [Gk *pneúmōn* lung + -ECTOMY]

**pneumonia** /nju'moʊnjə/, *n.* **1.** inflammation of the lungs. **2.** an acute affection of the lungs, **croupous pneumonia** or **lobar pneumonia,** regarded as due to the pneumococcus. [NL, from Gk]

**pneumonic** /nju'mɒnɪk/, *adj.* **1.** of, pertaining to, or affecting the lungs; pulmonary. **2.** pertaining to or affected with pneumonia.

**pneumothorax** /njumoʊ'θɔræks/, *n.* the presence of air or gas in the pleural cavity.

**PNG** /pi ɛn 'dʒi/, Papua New Guinea. Also, **P.N.G.**

**p-n junction** /pi-ˈɛn dʒʌŋkʃən/, *n.* the junction between semiconductor material with acceptor impurities (p-type semiconductor) and semiconductor material with donor impurities (n-type semiconductor). A diode has one such junction, a transistor has two.

**po** /poʊ/, *n.* →**chamber-pot.**

**Po,** *Chem.* polonium.

**P.O.** /pi ˈoʊ/, **1.** petty officer. **2.** pilot officer. **3.** postal order. **4.** post office.

**poach**[1] /poʊtʃ/, *v.i.* **1.** to trespass on another's land, etc., esp. in order to steal game. **2.** to take game or fish illegally. **3.** to encroach on another's rights; take something belonging to another. **4.** *Tennis.* when playing doubles to intercept a shot which should have been played by one's partner. **5.** (of land) to become broken up or slushy by being trampled. *–v.t.* **6.** to trample. **7.** to mix with water and reduce to a uniform consistency, as clay. [MF *pocher* thrust or put out (eyes), dig out with the fingers, probably from Gmc; akin to POKE[1]]

**poach**[2] /poʊtʃ/, *v.t.* to simmer in liquid in a shallow pan. [F *pocher;* cf. *poche* cooking spoon, from LL *popia,* of Gaelic orig.; ultimately c. L *coquere* to cook]

**poacher**[1] /ˈpoʊtʃə/, *n.* one who trespasses on another's land, to steal game.

**poacher**[2] /ˈpoʊtʃə/, *n.* a pan or the like for poaching eggs.

**P.O. Box** /ˈpi oʊ bɒks/, post office box.

**pochette** /pɒˈʃɛt/, *n.* **1.** a small handbag, without handles, clutched in the hand. **2.** →**kit**[2]. [F, diminutive of *poche* pocket]

**pock** /pɒk/, *n.* **1.** a pustule on the body in an eruptive disease, as smallpox. **2.** a mark or spot left by or resembling such a pustule. [ME *pokke,* OE *poc,* c. G *Pocke;* ? akin to OE *pocca* bag. See POKE[2]]

**pocket** /ˈpɒkət/, *n.* **1.** a small bag inserted in a garment, for carrying a purse or other small articles. **2.** a bag or pouch. **3.** money, means, or financial resources. **4.** any pouchlike receptacle, hollow, or cavity. **5.** *Tas.* a sack of potatoes. **6.** a small isolated area: *a pocket of resistance.* **7.** *Mining.* **a.** a small body of ore. **b.** an enlargement of a lode or vein. **c.** an irregular cavity containing ore. **d.** a small ore body or mass of ore, frequently isolated. **8.** a cavity in the earth, esp. one containing gold or other ore. **9.** *Mining.* **a.** a bin for ore or rock storage. **b.** a raise or small stope fitted with chute gates. **10.** a small bag or net at the corner or side of a billiard table. **11.** *Racing.* a position in which a contestant is so hemmed in by others that his progress is impeded. **12.** *Aus. Rules.* a side position: *the back pocket.* **13.** See **air-pocket. 14. in one's pocket,** under one's control. **15. in pocket,** having money or a profit, esp. after some transaction. **16. line one's pockets,** to gain, esp. financially, at the expense of others. **17. out of pocket,** without money or having made a loss, esp. after some transaction. *–adj.* **18.** suitable for carrying in the pocket: *a pocket edition of a novel.* **19.** small enough to go in the pocket; diminutive. *–v.t.* **20.** to put into one's pocket. **21.** to take possession of as one's own, often dishonestly. **22.** to submit to or endure without protest or open resentment. **23.** to conceal or suppress: *to pocket one's pride.* **24.** to enclose or confine as in a pocket. **25.** to drive (a ball) into a pocket, as in billiards. **26.** *U.S.* (of the President or a legislative executive) to retain (a bill) without action on it and thus prevent it from becoming a law. **27.** to hem in (a contestant) so as to impede progress, as in racing. [ME *pocket,* from AF *pokete,* diminutive of ONF *poke,* var. of F *poche* bag. See POKE[2], POUCH]

**pocket battleship** /– ˈbætlʃɪp/, *n.* a small, heavily armed and armoured warship serving as a battleship because of limitations imposed by treaty.

**pocket billiards** /– ˈbɪljədz/, *n.* See **pool**[2] (def. 8).

**pocket-book** /ˈpɒkət-bʊk/, *n.* **1.** →**wallet. 2.** a small notebook.

**pocketful** /ˈpɒkətfʊl/, *n., pl.* **-fuls.** as much as a pocket will hold.

**pocket gopher** /ˈpɒkət goʊfə/, *n.* →**gopher**[1] (def. 2).

**pocket-handkerchief** /pɒkət-ˈhæŋkətʃif/, *n.* a handkerchief carried in the pocket.

**pocket-knife** /ˈpɒkət-naɪf/, *n., pl.* **-knives** /-naɪvz/. a knife with one or more blades which fold into the handle, suitable for carrying in the pocket.

**pocket-money** /ˈpɒkət-mʌni/, *n.* a small weekly allowance of money, as given to a child by his parents.

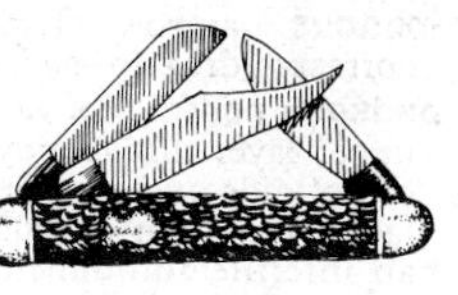
pocket-knife

**pocket veto** /ˈpɒkət vitoʊ/, *n. U.S.* **1.** the retaining, without action, past the time of the adjournment of Congress, by the President of the U.S., of a bill presented to him for signature within ten days of the end of a session, which is equivalent to a veto. **2.** a similar action on the part of any legislative executive.

**pockmark** /ˈpɒkmak/, *n.* a mark or pit left by a pustule in smallpox or the like. – **pockmarked,** *adj.*

**pocky** /ˈpɒki/, *adj.* having pocks; marked by pocks.

**poco** /ˈpoʊkoʊ/, *adv.* (a musical direction) somewhat: *poco presto (somewhat fast).* [It.: little, from L *paucus* few]

**poco a poco** /ˌpoʊkoʊ a ˈpoʊkoʊ/, *adv.* (a musical direction) gradually. [It.]

**pococurante** /poʊkoʊkjuˈrænti/, *n.* **1.** a careless or indifferent person. *–adj.* **2.** caring little; indifferent; nonchalant. [It. *poco* little + *curante* caring, from L *curans,* ppr.] – **pococurantism,** *n.*

**pod**[1] /pɒd/, *n., v.,* **podded, podding.** *–n.* **1.** a more or less elongated, two-valved seed vessel, as that of the pea or bean. **2.** a dehiscent fruit or pericarp with several seeds. **3.** *Aeron.* a streamlined structure suspended under the wing of an aircraft for housing a jet engine, cargo, missiles, or other weapons. **4.** a protective housing for a nuclear reactor. **5. in pod,** *Colloq.* pregnant. *–v.i.* **6.** to produce pods. **7.** to swell out like a pod. *–v.t.* **8.** to remove the shell from. [apparently backformation from *podder* peasecod-gatherer. Cf. *podder,* var. of *podware,* unexplained var. of *codware* podded vegetables (from COD[2] pod, bag + *-ware* crops, vegetables)]

**pod**[2] /pɒd/, *n.* **1.** a small herd or school, esp. of seals or whales. **2.** a small flock of birds. [orig. uncert.]

**pod**[3] /pɒd/, *n.* the straight groove or channel in the body of certain augers or bits. [cf. OE *pād* covering, cloak]

**pod-,** a word element meaning 'foot', as in *podiatry.* Also, before consonants, **podo-.** [Gk, combining form of *poús*]

**-pod,** a word element meaning 'footed', as in *cephalopod.* Cf. **-poda.** [Gk *-podos,* from *poús* foot]

**-poda,** plural of **-pod,** as in *Cephalopoda.*

**podagra** /pəˈdægrə/, *n.* gout in the foot. [L, from Gk: lit., a trap for the feet]

**poddy** /ˈpɒdi/, *n.* **1.** Also, **poddy-calf.** a handfed calf. *–adj.* **2.** (of a small animal, esp. a lamb or calf) requiring to be handfed. **3.** *Brit. Colloq.* pot-bellied. [? Brit. d. *poddy* fat]

**poddy-dodger** /ˈpɒdi-dɒdʒə/, *n. Colloq.* one who steals unbranded calves. – **poddy-dodging,** *n.*

**poddy mullet** /pɒdi ˈmʌlət/, *n., pl.* **poddy mullet.** a very young mullet, not large enough for human consumption, but used for fishing bait; fingerling.

**podge** /pɒdʒ/, *n. Colloq.* a podgy person.

**podgy** /ˈpɒdʒi/, *adj.,* **-ier, -iest.** short and fat; plump. Also, **pudgy.** [orig. obscure] – **podgily,** *adv.* – **podginess,** *n.*

**podiatry** /pɒˈdaɪətri/, *n.* the investigation and treatment of foot disorders. [POD- + -IATRY] – **podiatrist,** *n.*

**podium** /ˈpoʊdiəm/, *n., pl.* **-dia** /-diə/. **1.** a small platform for the conductor of an orchestra, for a public speaker, etc. **2.** *Archit.* **a.** a continuous projecting base of a building forming the front of the basement of the foundation behind it. **b.** a low continuous structure serving as a base or terrace wall. **c.** the stylobate or the structure under the stylobate of a temple. **d.** a raised platform surrounding the arena of an ancient amphitheatre. **3.** *Zool., Anat.* a foot. **4.** *Bot.* a footstalk or stipe. [L: elevated place, balcony, from Gk *pódion,* diminutive of *poús* foot. Cf. PEW]

**-podium,** a word element meaning 'footlike', used in nouns. [NL. See PODIUM]

**podophyllin** /pɒdoʊˈfɪlən/, *n.* a resin obtained from podophyllum and used as a cathartic and in the treatment of some skin diseases.

**podophyllum** /pɒdoʊˈfɪləm/, *n.* the dried rhizome of the May apple, *Podophyllum peltatum,* used in the treatment of warts.

[NL, from Gk *podo-* (see POD-) + *phýllon* leaf]

**-podous,** a word element used as an adjective termination, corresponding to *-pod.* [Gk *-podos* footed, from *poús* foot]

**podsol** /ˈpɒdsɒl/, *n.* a forest soil, notably acidic, having an upper layer that is greyish white or ash-coloured and depleted of colloids and iron and aluminium compounds, and a lower layer, brownish in colour, in which these have accumulated; an infertile soil difficult to cultivate, found over vast areas in northern North America and Eurasia and common in eastern Australia. Also, **podzol.** [Russ., adj.: resembling ashes] – **podsolic** /pɒdˈsɒlɪk/, *adj.*

**podsolise** /ˈpɒdsəlaɪz/, *v.t., v.i.,* **-lised, -lising.** to form podsol. Also, **podzolise, podzolize, podsolize.**

**poem** /ˈpoʊəm/, *n.* **1.** a composition in verse, esp. one characterised by artistic construction and imaginative or elevated thought: *a lyric poem.* **2.** a composition which, though not in verse, is characterised by beauty of language or thought: *a prose poem.* **3.** a work in poetry rather than prose. **4.** something having qualities suggestive of or likened to those of poetry. [L *poēma,* from Gk *poíēma* poem, something made]

**poenology** /piˈnɒlədʒi/, *n.* →**penology.**

**poesy** /ˈpoʊəzi/, *n., pl.* **-sies. 1.** *Poetic.* poetry in general. **2.** *Archaic.* the work or the art of poetic composition. **3.** *Archaic.* poetry or verse. **4.** *Obs.* a verse or poetry or the like used as a motto. See **posy** (def. 2). **5.** *Obs.* a poem. [ME *poesie,* from OF, from L *poēsis,* from Gk *poíēsis* poetic composition, poetry, a making]

**poet** /ˈpoʊət/, *n.* **1.** one who composes poetry. **2.** one having the gift of poetic thought, imagination, and creation, together with eloquence of expression. [ME *poete,* from L *poēta,* from Gk *po(i)ētḗs* poet, maker]

**poet., 1.** poetic. **2.** poetical. **3.** poetry.

**poetaster** /poʊəˈtæstə/, *n.* an inferior poet; a writer of indifferent verse. [ML or NL. See POET, -ASTER[1]]

**poetess** /ˈpoʊətɛs/, *n.* a female poet. .

**poetic** /poʊˈɛtɪk/, *adj.* Also, **poetical. 1.** possessing the qualities or the charm of poetry: *poetic descriptions of nature.* **2.** of or pertaining to a poet or poets. **3.** characteristic of or befitting a poet: *poetic feeling.* **4.** endowed with the faculty or feeling of a poet, as a person. **5.** having or showing the sensibility of a poet. **6.** of or pertaining to poetry: *poetic licence.* **7.** of the nature of poetry: *a poetic composition.* **8.** celebrated in poetry, as a place. **9.** affording a subject for poetry. **10.** of or pertaining to literature in verse form. *–n.* **11.** →**poetics.** [L *poēticus,* from Gk *po(i)ētikós*] – **poetically,** *adv.*

**poetic justice** /– ˈdʒʌstəs/, *n.* an ideal distribution of rewards and punishments such as is common in poetry and fiction.

**poetic licence** /– ˈlaɪsəns/, *n.* licence or liberty taken by a poet in deviating from rule, conventional form, logic, or fact, in order to produce a desired effect.

**poetics** /poʊˈɛtɪks/, *n.* **1.** literary criticism treating of the nature and laws of poetry. **2.** a treatise on poetry: *the 'Poetics' of Aristotle.*

**poetise** /ˈpoʊətaɪz/, *v.,* **-tised -tising.** *–v.i.* **1.** to compose poetry. *–v.t.* **2.** to write about in poetry; express in poetic form. **3.** to make poetic: *he poetised his letter to her.* Also, **poetize.**

**poet laureate** /poʊət ˈlɒriət/, *n., pl.* **poets laureate. 1.** (in Britain) an officer of the royal household, of whom no special duty is required, but who formerly was expected to write odes, etc., in celebration of court and national events. **2.** (formerly) a title given to any eminent poet.

**poetry** /ˈpoʊətri/, *n.* **1.** the art of rhythmical composition, written or spoken, for exciting pleasure by beautiful, imaginative, or elevated thoughts. **2.** literary work in metrical form; verse. **3.** prose with poetic qualities. **4.** poetic qualities however manifested. **5.** poetic spirit or feeling. **6.** something suggestive of or likened to poetry. [ME *poetrie,* from LL *poētria*]

**poet's day** /ˈpoʊəts deɪ/, *n. Colloq. (joc.)* Friday, the day on which people often leave work a little early. [*p(iss) o(ff) e(arly) t(omorrow's) s(aturday)*]

**po faced** /ˈpoʊ feɪst/, *adj. Colloq.* expressionless.

**pogge** /pɒg/, *n.* a common small fish of the North Atlantic, *Agonus cataphractus;* the armed bullhead.

**pogonophora** /pɒgəˈnɒfərə, poʊgə-/, *n.* a phylum of wormlike sedentary invertebrates which have no alimentary canal and which live on the seabed.

**pogo stick** /ˈpoʊgoʊ stɪk/, *n.* a metal stick on a spring, with handles at the top and footrests near the base, on which children jump up and down.

**pogrom** /ˈpɒgrəm/, *n.* an organised massacre, esp. of Jews. [Russ.: devastation, destruction]

**pohutukawa** /poʊˌhutəˈkawə/, *n.* the New Zealand Christmas tree, *Metrosideros excelsa,* having brilliant red flowers in summer. [Maori]

**poi**[1] /pɔɪ, ˈpoʊi/, *n.* a Hawaiian dish made of the root of the taro baked, pounded, moistened, and fermented.

**poi**[2] /pɔɪ/, *n. N.Z.* a small light ball on a string, used by Maori women in ceremonial dances as the **Poi dance.** [Maori]

**-poiesis,** a word element meaning 'making', 'creation', 'genesis', as in *erythropoiesis.* [Gk *poíēsis* act of making]

**-poietic,** a word element meaning 'productive', as in *haematopoietic.* [Gk *poiētikós* creative, active]

**poignant** /ˈpɔɪnjənt, ˈpɔɪnənt/, *adj.* **1.** keenly distressing to the mental or physical feelings: *poignant regret, poignant suffering.* **2.** keen or strong in mental appeal: *a subject of poignant interest.* **3.** pungent to the taste or smell. [ME *poynaunt,* from OF *poignant,* ppr. of *poindre,* from L *pungere* prick, pierce. Cf. PUNGENT] – **poignancy,** *n.* – **poignantly,** *adv.*

**poikilothermal** /pɔɪkəloʊˈθɜməl/, *adj.* having a body temperature that fluctuates with the temperature of the environment. [Gk *poikílo(s)* various + THERMAL]

**poinciana** /pɔɪnsiˈanə, -ˈænə/, *n.* **1.** a plant of the genus *Poinciana,* of the warmer parts of the world, comprising trees or shrubs with showy orange or scarlet flowers. **2.** a closely related tree, *Delonix regia,* native to Madagasgar but now widely cultivated, remarkable for its showy scarlet flowers. [NL, named after M. de *Poinci,* governor of the French West Indies in the 17th century]

**poinsettia** /pɔɪnˈsɛtiə/, *n.* a perennial, *Euphorbia (Poinsettia) pulcherrima,* native to Mexico and Central America, with variously lobed leaves and brilliant usu. scarlet bracts. [NL, named after J.R. *Poinsett,* 1779-1851, U.S. minister to Mexico, who discovered the plant there in 1828]

**point** /pɔɪnt/, *n.* **1.** a sharp or tapering end, as of a dagger. **2.** projecting part of anything. **3.** a tapering extremity, as a cape. **4.** something having a sharp or tapering end. **5.** a pointed tool or instrument, as an etching needle. **6.** a mark made as with a sharp end of something. **7.** a mark of punctuation. **8.** →**full stop. 9.** a decimal point, etc. **10.** *Phonet., etc.* a diacritical mark indicating a modification of a sound. **11.** one of the embossed dots used in certain systems of writing and printing for the blind. **12.** something that has position but not extension, as the intersection of two lines. **13.** a place of which the position alone is considered; a spot. **14.** any definite position, as in a scale, course, etc.: *the boiling point.* **15. a.** each of the 32 positions indicating direction marked at the circumference of the card of a compass. **b.** the interval of 11° 15′ between any two adjacent positions. **16.** a degree or stage: *frankness to the point of insult.* **17.** a particular instant of time. **18.** critical position in a course of affairs. **19.** a decisive state of circumstances. **20.** the important or essential thing: *the point of the matter.* **21.** the salient feature of a story, epigram, joke, etc. **22.** a particular aim, end, or purpose: *he carried his point.* **23.** *(pl.)* hints or suggestions: *points on getting a job.* **24.** a single or separate article or item, as in an extended whole; a detail or particular. **25.** an individual part or element of something: *noble points in her character.* **26.** the coloured markings of a Siamese cat: *seal point, chocolate point.* **27.** a distinguishing mark or quality, esp. one of an animal, used as a standard in stockbreeding, etc. **28.** →**blocked shoe. 29.** *(pl.)* the extremities of a horse, pig, etc. **30.** a single unit, as in counting, measuring rations allowed, etc. **31.** a unit of count in the score of a game. **32.** *Cricket.* **a.** the position of the fielder who stands a short distance in front and to the offside of the batsman. **b.** the player himself. **33.** *Aus. Rules* →**behind** (def. 13). **34.** *Boxing.* the tip of the chin. **35.** *Hunting.* the position taken by a pointer or setter when it finds game. **36.** a branch of an antler of a deer. **37.** one of the narrow tapering spaces marked on a backgammon board. **38.** *Elect.* **a.** either of a pair of contacts tipped with tungsten or platinum that makes or breaks current flow in a distributor. **b.** →**power point.** **39.** *Comm.* a unit of price quotation in share transactions on the stock exchange: *copper advanced two points yesterday.* **40.** *Mil.* **a.** the stroke in bayonet drill or battle. **b.** a patrol or reconnaissance unit that goes ahead of the advance party of an advance guard, or follows the rear party of the rear-guard. **c.** a target which requires the accurate placement of bombs or fire. **41.** *Print.* a unit of measurement equal to $0.351 \times 10^{-3}$ m, or $\frac{1}{72}$ inch. **42.** a unit of measurement of rainfall in the imperial system, equal to $\frac{1}{100}$ of an inch or $0.254 \times 10^{-3}$ m. **43.** →**vaccine point.** **44.** →**point lace.** **45.** (*usu. pl.*) *Railways.* a device for shifting moving trains, etc., from one track to another, commonly consisting of a pair of movable rails. **46.** the act of pointing. **47.** *Obs. or Rare.* an end or conclusion. **48.** any lace made by hand. **49.** *Archaic.* a tagged ribbon or cord, formerly much used in dress, as for tying or fastening parts. **50.** Some special noun phrases are:

**at, on,** or **upon the point of,** close to; on the verge of.

**give points,** to acknowledge the value of; praise.

**in point,** pertinent; relevant: *the case in point.*

**in point of,** as regards: *in point of fact.*

**make a point of,** to consider as important; insist upon.

**off the point,** not relevant.

**on points,** (of a ballerina wearing blocked shoes) dancing on her toes.

**stretch a point,** to make a special concession; depart from the normal procedure.

**to the point,** pertinent; relevant.

[ME, from OF *point* dot, mark, place, moment (from L *punctum*) and OF *pointe* sharp end (from L *puncta*); both L words properly pp. forms of *pungere* prick, stab]

*–v.t.* **51.** to direct (the finger, a weapon, the attention, etc.) at, to, or upon something. **52.** to indicate the presence or position of, as with the finger (usu. fol. by *out*). **53.** to direct attention to (fol. by *out*). **54.** to furnish with a point or points; sharpen. **55. a.** to mark with one or more points, dots, or the like. **b.** to mark psalms with signs indicating how they are to be chanted. **56.** to punctuate, as writing. **57.** *Phonet., etc.* to mark (letters) with points. **58.** to separate (figures) by dots or points (usu. fol. by *off*). **59.** to give point or force to (speech, action, etc.). **60.** *Hunting.* (of a pointer or setter) to indicate game by standing rigid, with the muzzle usu. directed towards it. **61.** to fill the joints of (brickwork, etc.) with mortar or cement, smoothed with the point of the trowel. **62.** →**hotpoint.** **63. point the bone.** See **bone** (def. 15). *–v.i.* **64.** to indicate position or direction, or direct attention, with or as with the finger. **65.** to direct the mind or thought in some direction: *everything points to his guilt.* **66.** to aim. **67.** to have a tendency, as towards something. **68.** to have a specified direction. **69.** to face in a particular direction, as a building. **70.** *Hunting.* (of a pointer or setter) to point game. **71.** *Naut.* to sail close to the wind. **72.** (of an abscess) to come to a head. [ME, from OF *pointer*, from *point(e)*, n.]

**point-blank** /pɔɪnt-ˈblæŋk/, *adj.* **1.** aimed or fired straight at the mark at close range; direct. **2.** straight-forward, plain, or explicit. *–adv.* **3.** with a direct aim at close range; directly; straight. **4.** bluntly. [POINT, *v.* + BLANK (def. 17)]

**point-device** /pɔɪnt-dəˈvaɪs/, *Archaic.* *–adv.* **1.** completely; perfectly; exactly. *–adj.* **2.** perfect; precise; scrupulously nice or neat. [ME *at poynt devys* (cf. OF or AF *devis* devised, arranged). See POINT, DEVISE]

**point distant** /pɔɪnt ˈdɪstənt/, *n.* a place of work to which a council worker, labourer, etc., is required to go which is not a headquarters or temporary headquarters, and which has no amenities.

**point duty** /ˈ– djuti/, *n.* traffic control by a policeman at a road junction, etc.

**pointe** /pɔɪnt/, *n.* (in ballet) the tip of the toe: *on pointes.* [F]

**pointed** /ˈpɔɪntəd/, *adj.* **1.** having a point or points: *a pointed arch.* **2.** sharp or piercing: *pointed wit.* **3.** having point or force: *pointed comment.* **4.** directed; aimed. **5.** directed particularly, as at a person. **6.** marked; emphasised. **– pointedly,** *adv.* **– pointedness,** *n.*

**pointed fox** /– ˈfɒks/, *n.* a red fox fur having badger hairs glued to the fur near the skin, in order to simulate silver fox.

**pointer** /ˈpɔɪntə/, *n.* **1.** one who or that which points. **2.** a long, tapering stick used by teachers, lecturers, etc., in pointing things out on a map, blackboard, or the like. **3.** the hand on a watch, machine, or instrument. **4.** one of a breed of short-haired hunting dogs trained to point game. **5.** →**poler.** **6.** a hint or suggestion; piece of advice. **7.** *U.S. Mil. and Navy.* one whose function is to control the aim, elevation, etc., of a gun.

pointer (def. 4)

**pointillism** /ˈpwæntəlɪzəm, ˈpɔɪntəlɪzəm/, *n.* a method of painting in which luminosity is produced by laying on the colours in points or small dots of unmixed colour in close proximity, which are then fused by the eye into an optical mixture of their constituents. [F *pointillisme,* from *pointiller* mark with points] **– pointillist,** *n.*

**pointing** /ˈpɔɪntɪŋ/, *n.* **1.** (in psalm-singing) a method of showing how to fit irregular lines to a regular tune. **2.** the treatment of mortar joints in brickwork or masonry, as to render them waterproof, etc.

**point lace** /ˈpɔɪnt leɪs/, *n.* lace made with a needle rather than with bobbins; needle point.

**pointless** /ˈpɔɪntləs/, *adj.* **1.** without a point. **2.** blunt, as an instrument. **3.** without force, meaning, or relevance, as a remark. **4.** without a point scored, as in a game. **– pointlessly,** *adv.* **– pointlessness,** *n.*

**point of honour,** *n.* something that affects one's honour, reputation, etc.

**point of order,** *n.* a question raised as to whether proceedings are in order, esp. in the conduct of a meeting.

**point of view,** *n.* **1.** a point from which things are viewed. **2.** a mental position or viewpoint.

**point post** /ˈpɔɪnt poʊst/, *n.* →**behind post.**

**point shoe** /ˈ– ʃu/, *n.* →**blocked shoe.**

**pointsman** /ˈpɔɪntsmən/, *n. N.Z.* a policeman on traffic control duty at an intersection.

**point source** /ˈpɔɪnt sɔs/, *n.* the theoretical concept of a source of radiation which emanates from a point.

**point system** /ˈ– sɪstəm/, *n.* **1.** *Print.* a system for grading the sizes of type bodies, leads, etc., which employs the point as a unit of measurement. See **point** (def. 41). **2.** any of certain systems of writing and printing for the blind which employ embossed symbols for letters, etc.

**point-to-point** /pɔɪnt-tə-ˈpɔɪnt/, *n.* a cross-country horserace from one specified place to another.

**poise**[1] /pɔɪz/, *n., v.,* **poised, poising.** *–n.* **1.** a state of balance or equilibrium, as from equality or equal distribution of weight; equipoise. **2.** composure; self-possession. **3.** steadiness; stability. **4.** suspense or indecision. **5.** the way of being poised, held, or carried. **6.** a state or position of hovering: *the poise of a bird in the air.* *–v.t.* **7.** to balance evenly; adjust, hold, or carry in equilibrium. **8.** to hold supported or raised, as in position for casting, using, etc.: *to poise a spear.* **9.** to hold or carry in a particular manner. **10.** *Obs.* to weigh. *–v.i.* **11.** to be balanced; rest in equilibrium. **12.** to hang supported or suspended. **13.** to hover, as a bird in the air. [late ME, from OF *peser* (OF 3rd pers. sing. pres. ind. *poise*), from L *pensāre,* frequentative of *pendere* weigh]

**poise**[2] /pɔɪz/, *n.* a non-SI unit of viscosity equal to 0.1 pascal seconds. [named after J. L. M. *Poiseuille,* 1799-1869, French physician]

**poised** /pɔɪzd/, *adj.* **1.** self-possessed; self-assured; confident; dignified. **2.** in a state of balance or equilibrium. **3.** wavering. **4.** hovering; suspended.

**poison** /ˈpɔɪzən/, *n.* **1.** any substance (liquid, solid, or gaseous) which by reason of an inherent deleterious property tends to destroy life or impair health. **2.** anything harmful, fatal, baneful, or highly pernicious, as to character, happiness, or well-being: *the poison of slander.* **3.** a substance which absorbs neutrons in a nuclear reactor, either added deliberately or formed as a fission product. **4.** a substance which weakens a catalyst or enzyme. *–v.t.* **5.** to administer poison to (a person or animal). **6.** to affect with poison, or as poison does. **7.** to put poison into or upon; impregnate with poison: *to poison food.* **8.** to ruin, vitiate, or corrupt: *to poison the mind.* **9.** to destroy or diminish the activity of (a catalyst, enzyme, etc.). **10.** to absorb neutrons in a nuclear reactor, thus destroying the reaction. *–adj.* **11.** poisonous; causing poisoning. [ME, from OF: potion, draught, poison, from L *pōtio.* See POTION]

**poison-bush** /ˈpɔɪzən-bʊʃ/, *n.* any poisonous shrub; in Australia esp. the genus *Gastrolobium* which has many species poisonous to stock.

**poison cart** /ˈpɔɪzən kat/, *n.* a cart carrying a machine which leaves a trail of poisoned food for rabbits to eat.

**poisoner** /ˈpɔɪzənə/, *n.* **1.** one who administers poison. **2.** *Colloq.* a cook.

**poison gas** /ˈpɔɪzən gæs/, *n.* any of various toxic gases, esp. those used in warfare, as chlorine, phosgene, etc.

**poison ivy** /– ˈaɪvi/, *n.* any of several North American shrubs of the genus *Toxicodendron,* poisonous to the touch, with shiny leaves, green flowers, and whitish berries, esp. a climbing species, *T. radicans,* growing on fences, rocks, trees, etc.

**poison oak** /– ˈoʊk/, *n.* **1.** any of several shrubs of the genus *Toxicodendron.* **2.** →**poison sumach.** **3.** common poison ivy.

**poisonous** /ˈpɔɪzənəs/, *adj.* **1.** full of or containing poison. **2.** having the properties or effects of a poison. **3.** unpleasant; offensive. **4.** characterised by malice or ill feeling: *poisonous gossip.* – **poisonously,** *adv.* – **poisonousness,** *n.*

**poison-pen** /pɔɪzən-ˈpɛn/, *adj.* of or pertaining to a letter, note, etc., usu. anonymous, and sent with malicious intent.

**poison sumach** /pɔɪzən ˈsumæk, ˈʃumæk/, *n.* a highly poisonous North American shrub or small tree, *Toxicodendron vernix,* a sumach with pinnate leaves and whitish berries, growing in swamps.

**poison-tree** /ˈpɔɪzən-tri/, *n.* any poisonous tree; in Australia esp. species of the genus *Excoecaria* with irritant milky sap.

**Poisson distribution** /ˌpwʌsɒn dɪstrəˈbjuʃən/, *n.* a limiting form of the binomial probability distribution for small values of the probability of success and for large numbers of trials. It is particularly useful in industrial quality-control work and in radiation and bacteriological problems. [named after Siméon Denis *Poisson,* 1781-1840, French mathematician]

**Poisson's ratio** /ˌpwʌsɒnz ˈreɪʃioʊ/, *n.* an elastic constant of a material, defined as the ratio of lateral strain to the longitudinal strain.

**poke**[1] /poʊk/, *v.,* **poked, poking,** *n.* *–v.t.* **1.** to thrust against or into (something) with the finger or arm, a stick, etc.; prod: *to poke a person in the ribs.* **2.** to make (a hole, one's way, etc.) by or as by thrusting. **3.** to thrust or push: *he poked his head through the door.* **4.** to force or drive (*away, in, out,* etc.) by or as by thrusting or pushing. **5.** to thrust obtrusively. **6.** *Colloq.* to have sexual intercourse with. *–v.i.* **7.** to make a thrusting or pushing movement with the finger, a stick, etc. **8.** to extend or project; protrude (oft. fol. by *out*). **9.** to thrust oneself obtrusively. **10.** to pry; search curiously (oft. fol. by *about* or *around*). **11. more than one can poke a stick at,** *Colloq.* a lot of; many; much. **12. poke fun (mullock, borak) at,** *Colloq.* to ridicule or mock, esp. covertly or slyly. **13. poke one's nose into,** to interfere; pry; show too much curiosity. *–n.* **14.** to thrust or push. **15.** *Colloq.* a blow with the fist. **16.** *Colloq.* the act of sexual intercourse. **17. take a poke at,** *Colloq.* to aim a blow at. [ME *poken,* c. LG and D *poken.* Cf. POACH[1]]

**poke**[2] /poʊk/, *n.* **1.** *Obs.* a bag or sack. **2.** *Archaic.* a pocket. **3. to buy a pig in a poke.** See **pig**[1] (def. 8). [ME *poke,* c. MD *poke;* akin to OE *pocca, pohha* pocket, bag. Cf. ONF *poke* (from D) and *pouche* POUCH]

poke[3] (def. 2)

**poke**[3] /poʊk/, *n.* **1.** a projecting brim at the front of a woman's bonnet or hat. **2.** a bonnet (**poke bonnet**) or hat with such a brim. [apparently special use of POKE[1]]

**poke**[4] /poʊk/, *n.* →**pokeweed.** [Algonquian *puccoon* plant used in dyeing]

**poker**[1] /ˈpoʊkə/, *n.* **1.** one who or that which pokes. **2.** a metal rod for poking or stirring a fire. [POKE[1], *v.* + -ER[1]]

**poker**[2] /ˈpoʊkə/, *n.* a card game played by two or more persons, in which the players bet on the value of their hands, the winner taking the pool. [orig. uncert. Cf. G *Pochspiel,* a similar game, from *pochen* POKE[1]]

**poker dice** /ˈ– daɪs/, *n.pl.* **1.** dice marked on their faces with symbols representing the six highest playing cards instead of spots. **2.** any of various gambling games played with such dice.

**poker face** /ˈ– feɪs/, *n. Colloq.* an expressionless face. – **poker-faced** /ˈpoʊkə-feɪst/, *adj.*

**poker machine** /ˈ– məʃin/, *n.* a coin-operated gambling machine, usu. operated by pulling a handle, the score being usu. shown in the form of replicas of three or four playing cards, pictures of fruit etc. Also, **fruit machine, slot machine.**

**pokerwork** /ˈpoʊkəwɜk/, *n.* ornamentation of wood by burning a design into it with a heated point.

**pokeweed** /ˈpoʊkwid/, *n.* a tall herb, *Phytolacca americana,* of North America, having juicy purple berries and a purple root used in medicine, and young edible shoots resembling asparagus. Also, **pokeroot** /ˈpoʊkrut/, **poke.** [POKE[4] + WEED[1]]

**pokey** /ˈpoʊki/, *n. Colloq.* →**gaol.** [from *pogie* workhouse; ult. orig. uncert.]

**pokies** /ˈpoʊkiz/, *n. pl. Colloq.* poker machines.

**poky** /ˈpoʊki/, *adj.,* **-kier, -kiest.** **1.** (of a person) pottering; concerned with petty matters. **2.** (of a place) small and cramped. [POKE[1] + -Y[1]]

**pol.,** **1.** political. **2.** politics.

**Pol.,** **1.** Poland. **2.** Polish.

**polacca**[1] /pəˈlækə/, *n.* any of various three-masted sailing vessels, formerly used in the Mediterranean. Also, **polacre.**

**polacca**[2] /pəˈlækə/, *n.* a Polish dance in 3/4 time; a polonaise.

**Polack** /ˈpoʊlæk/, *n.* **1.** *Chiefly U.S.* (*derog.*) a person of Polish descent. **2.** *Archaic.* a Pole.

**Poland** /ˈpoʊlənd/, *n.* a republic in central Europe.

**polar** /ˈpoʊlə/, *adj.* **1.** of or pertaining to a pole, as of the earth, a magnet, an electric cell, etc. **2.** opposite in character or action. **3.** existing as ions; ionised. **4.** central. **5.** analogous to the Pole Star as a guide; guiding. [ML *polāris,* from L *polus* POLE[2]]

**polar axis** /poʊlər ˈæksəs/, *n.* a line about which a body rotates, or about which a rotation is measured.

**polar bear** /poʊlə ˈbɛə/, *n.* a large white bear, *Thalarctos maritimus,* of the arctic regions.

polar bear

**polar body** /– ˈbɒdi/, *n.* one of the minute cells arising by the very unequal meiotic divisions of the ovum at or near the time of fertilisation.

**polar bond** /– ˈbɒnd/, *n.* →**electrovalent bond.**

**polar circles** /– ˈsɜkəlz/, *n.pl.* the Arctic and Antarctic circles.

**polar coordinates** /– koʊˈɔdənəts/, *n.pl.* a system of plane coordinates in which the position of a point is determined by the length of its radius vector from a fixed origin and the angle this vector makes with a fixed line.

polar coordinate: r, radius vector; θ, polar angle; P, a point in the X-Y plane; O, origin or pole

**polar distance** /– ˈdɪstns/, *n.* →**codeclination.**

**polar front** /– ˈfrʌnt/, *n.* the transition region, or belt, between the cold polar easterly winds and the relatively warm south-westerly winds of the middle latitudes.

**polarimeter** /poʊləˈrɪmətə/, *n.* **1.** an instrument for measuring the amount of polarised light, or the extent of polarisation, in the light received from a given source. **2.** a form of polariscope for measuring the angular rotation of the plane of polarisation. [ML *polāri(s)* polar + -METER[1]]

**Polaris** /pəˈlarəs/, *n.* a U.S. intermediate-range ballistic missile developed for firing from a submarine. [short for ML *stella polāris* polar star]

**polarisation** /poʊləraɪ'zeɪʃən/, *n.* **1.** *Optics.* a state, or the production of a state, in which rays of light, or similar radiation, exhibit different properties in different directions, as when they are passed through a crystal of tourmaline, which transmits rays in which the vibrations are confined to a single plane. **2.** *Elect.* the process by which gases produced during electrolysis are deposited on the electrodes of a cell. **3.** *Chem.* the separation of a molecule into positive and negative ions. **4.** the production or acquisition of polarity. **5.** *Physics.* the electric flux due to electric charges induced on the surface of a dielectric. Also, **polarization.**

**polariscope** /poʊ'lærəskoʊp/, *n.* an instrument for exhibiting or measuring the polarisation of light, or for examining substances in polarised light.

**polarise** /'poʊləraɪz/, *v.,* **-rised, -rising.** *–v.t.* **1.** to cause polarisation in. **2.** to give polarity to. *–v.i.* **3.** to become polarised. Also, **polarize.** [POLAR + -ISE[1]] – **polarisable,** *adj.* – **polariser,** *n.*

**polarity** /poʊ'lærəti/, *n.* **1.** *Physics.* **a.** the possession of an axis with reference to which certain physical properties are determined; the possession of two poles. **b.** the power or tendency of a magnetised bar, etc., to orientate itself along the lines of force. **c.** positive or negative polar condition. **2.** the possession or exhibition of two opposite or contrasted principles or tendencies.

**polar lights** /poʊlə 'laɪts/, *n.pl.* the aurora borealis or the aurora australis.

**polar molecule** /– 'mɒləkjul/, *n.* a molecule which has a permanent electric dipole as a result of the configuration of the electric charges within it.

**polarograph** /poʊ'lærəgræf, -graf/, *n.* an instrument that automatically measures and records the concentration, solubility, constituents, equilibrium, etc., of an electrolytic solution.

**polaroid** /'poʊlərɔɪd/, *n.* a material which polarises light, consisting of a pane compounded of a sheet of plastic holding orientated iodo-quinine crystals between two panes of protecting glass, thus allowing only light polarised in a particular direction to pass. [Trademark]

**polaroid camera** /– 'kæmrə/, *n.* a type of camera which takes instant, self-developing pictures. [Trademark]

**polaroids** /'poʊlərɔɪdz/, *n.pl. Colloq.* →**sunglasses.**

**polar regions** /'poʊlə ridʒənz/, *n.pl.* the regions within the Arctic and Antarctic circles.

**polder** /'poʊldə, 'pɒldə/, *n.* a tract of low land, esp. in the Netherlands, reclaimed from the sea or other body of water and protected by dykes. [D]

**pole**[1] /poʊl/, *n., v.,* **poled, poling.** *–n.* **1.** a long, rounded, usu. slender piece of wood, metal, etc. **2.** the long tapering piece of wood extending from the front axle of a vehicle, between the animals drawing it. **3.** *Naut.* a light spar. **4.** a unit of length in the imperial system equal to $16\frac{1}{2}$ ft or 5.0292 m; a rod. **5.** a square rod, $30\frac{1}{4}$ sq. yds or 25.29 m$^2$. **6.** the lane of a race track, nearest the inner boundary. **7.** →**ski-pole. 8. pitch pole,** *Naut.* to turn over end on end. **9. under bare poles,** *Naut.* (of a sailing ship) having all sails furled. **10. up the pole,** *Colloq.* **a.** in a predicament. **b.** slightly mad. **c.** completely wrong. *–v.t.* **11.** to furnish with poles. **12.** to push, strike, propel, etc., with a pole. **13.** *Metall.* to stir (as molten copper) with green wood poles, thus introducing carbon which reacts with the oxygen present and reduces the amount of copper oxide in the copper. *–v.i.* **14.** to propel a boat, etc., with a pole. **15. pole on,** to impose on by loafing or cadging (originally of a horse, bullock, etc. which had the position of poler). [ME; OE *pāl,* from L *pālus* stake. Cf. PALE[2]]

**pole**[2] /poʊl/, *n.* **1.** each of the extremities of the axis of the earth or of any more or less spherical body. **2.** each of the two points in which the extended axis of the earth cuts the celestial sphere, about which the stars seem to revolve **(celestial pole). 3.** *Physics.* each of the two regions or parts of a magnet, electric battery, etc., at which certain opposite forces are manifested or appear to be concentrated. **4.** *Biol.* **a.** either end of an ideal axis in a nucleus, cell, or ovum, about which parts are more or less symmetrically arranged. **b.** either end of a spindle-shaped figure formed in a cell during mitosis. **5.** *Anat.* the point in a nerve cell where a process forming an axis cylinder begins. **6.** one of two completely opposed or contrasted principles, tendencies, etc. **7. poles apart,** having completely opposite or widely divergent views, interests, etc. [ME *pol,* from L *polus,* from Gk *pólos* pivot, axis, pole]

**Pole** /poʊl/, *n.* a native or inhabitant of Poland. [G, sing. of *Polen,* from Pol. *Poljane* Poles, lit., field-dwellers, from *pole* field]

**poleaxe** /'poʊlæks/, *n., v.,* **-axed, -axing.** *–n.* **1.** a medieval shafted weapon with blade combining axe, hammer, and apical spike, used for fighting on foot. **2.** an axe, usu. with a hammer opposite the cutting edge, used in felling or stunning animals. **3.** an axe formerly much used in naval warfare, to help in boarding vessels, cutting rigging, etc. *–v.t.* **4.** to fell with a poleaxe. Also, *U.S.,* **poleax.** [ME *pollax,* lit., head-axe. Cf. MLG *polexe* and see POLL[1] (def. 10)]

**polecat** /'poʊlkæt/, *n.* **1.** a European mammal, *Mustela putorius,* of the weasel family, having blackish brown fur, and giving off an offensive smell. **2.** any of various North American skunks. [ME *polcat; pol-* of uncert. orig.]

polecat

**pole horse** /'poʊl hɔs/, *n.* a horse harnessed alongside the pole of a vehicle; a poler; wheeler.

**polemic** /pə'lɛmɪk/, *n.* **1.** a controversial argument; argumentation against some opinion, doctrine, etc. **2.** one who argues in opposition to another; a controversialist. *–adj.* **3.** Also, **polemical.** of or pertaining to disputation or controversy; controversial. [Gk *polemikós* of or for war] – **polemically,** *adv.*

**polemicist** /pə'lɛməsəst/, *n.* one engaged or versed in polemics. Also, **polemist** /pə'lɛməst/.

**polemics** /pə'lɛmɪks/, *n.* the art or practice of disputation or controversy, esp. in theology.

**polenta** /pɒ'lɛntə/, *n.* a thick porridge eaten in Italy, usu. made from maize. [It., from L: pearl barley]

**poler** /'poʊlə/, *n.* **1.** one of the two bullocks or horses nearest in the team to the wagon and harnessed to the pole; the polers do not take as much weight as the leaders, but are important in steering the wagon. **2.** *Colloq.* a lazy person; loafer.

**pole star** /'poʊl sta/, *n.* a guiding principle. [from the *Pole Star,* a star of the second magnitude situated close to the north celestial pole]

**pole vault** /'– vɔlt/, *n.* a leap over a horizontal bar with the help of a long pole.

**poley** /'poʊli/, *Colloq. –n.* **1.** a dehorned or hornless animal; a polled beast. **2.** a saddle without kneepads. *–adj.* **3.** (of a cup) having lost its handle: *a poley cup.* **4.** (of an animal) dehorned or hornless. **5.** (of a saddle) without kneepads.

**police** /pə'lis/, *n., v.,* **-liced, -licing.** *–n.* **1.** an organised civil force for maintaining order, preventing and detecting crime, and enforcing the laws. **2.** (*construed as pl.*) the members of such a force. **3.** the regulation and control of a community, esp. with reference to the maintenance of public order, safety, health, morals, etc. **4.** the department of the government concerned with this, esp. with the maintenance of order. **5.** any body of men officially maintained or employed to keep order, enforce regulations, etc. **6.** *Mil.* (in the U.S. Army) **a.** the cleaning and keeping clean of a camp, post, station, etc. **b.** the condition of a camp, post, station, etc., with reference to cleanliness. *–v.t.* **7.** to regulate, control, or keep in order by police or as a police force does. **8.** *U.S. Mil.* to clean and keep clean (a camp, etc.). [F: government, civil administration, police, from ML *polītia,* var. of L *polītīa* POLITY. Cf. POLICY[1]]

**police constable** /'– kʌnstəbəl/, *n.* a policeman of the lowest regular rank.

**police court** /'– kɔt/, *n.* →**court of petty sessions.**

**police dog** /'– dɒg/, *n.* any dog used or trained to assist the police.

**police line-up** / – 'laɪn-ʌp/, *n.* an identification parade run by the police.

**policeman** /pə'lismən/, *n., pl.* **-men.** a member of a body or force of police. – **policewoman,** *n. fem.*

**policeman bird** /'– bɜd/, *n.* →**jabiru** (def. 1).

**policeman fly** /'– flaɪ/, *n.* a small wasp of the families Nyssonidae, Arpactidae and Stizidae, which hunts the small bush-fly.

**police officer** /pə'lis ɒfəsə/, *n.* →**policeman.**

**police state** /'– steɪt/, *n.* a country in which the police, esp. the secret police, are employed to detect and suppress any form of opposition to the government in power.

**police station** /'– steɪʃən/, *n.* the headquarters of a police force, or branch of a police force.

**policy**[1] /'pɒləsi/, *n., pl.* **-cies. 1.** a definite course of action adopted as expedient or from other considerations: *a business policy.* **2.** a course or line of action adopted and pursued by a government, ruler, political party, or the like: *the foreign policy of a country.* **3.** action or procedure conforming to, or considered with reference to, prudence or expediency: *it was good policy to consent.* **4.** prudence, practical wisdom, or expediency. **5.** sagacity; shrewdness. **6.** *Rare.* government; polity. [ME *policie,* from OF: government, civil administration, from L *polītīa* POLITY. Cf. POLICE]

**policy**[2] /'pɒləsi/, *n., pl.* **-cies. 1.** a document embodying a contract of insurance. **2.** *U.S.* a method of gambling in which bets are made on numbers to be drawn by lottery. [F *police,* from It. *polizza,* from ML *apodixa,* from Gk *apódeixis* a showing or setting forth]

**policyholder** /'pɒləsi,houldə/, *n.* the person in whose name an insurance policy is written; the insured.

**polio** /'pouliou/, *n.* →**poliomyelitis.**

**poliomyelitis** /,poulioumaɪə'laɪtəs/, *n.* an acute viral disease, most common in infants but often attacking older children and even adults, characterised by inflammation of the nerve cells, mainly of the anterior horns of the spinal cord, and resulting in motor paralysis, followed by muscular atrophy, and often by permanent deformities; infantile paralysis. [NL, from Gk *poliό(s)* grey + *myelós* marrow + *-ītis* -ITIS]

**-polis,** a word element meaning 'city', as in *metropolis* (lit., 'the mother city'). [Gk, combining form of *pólis*]

**polish** /'pɒlɪʃ/, *v.t.* **1.** to make smooth and glossy, esp. by friction: *to polish metal.* **2.** to render finished, refined or elegant: *his speech needs polishing.* **3.** to take or bring to a different state by smoothing or refining (oft. fol. by *away, off, out,* etc.). **4.** *Colloq.* to finish, or dispose of quickly (fol. by *off*): *to polish off an opponent.* **5.** *Colloq.* to improve (fol. by *up*). **6.** *Colloq.* to praise. *–v.i.* **7.** to become smooth and glossy; take on a polish. **8.** *Archaic.* to become refined or elegant. *–n.* **9.** a substance used to give smoothness or gloss: *shoe polish.* **10.** the act of polishing. **11.** the state of being polished. **12.** smoothness and gloss of surface. **13.** superior or elegant finish imparted; refinement; elegance: *the polish of literary style.* [ME *polische(n),* from F *poliss-,* stem of *polir,* from L *polīre*] – **polisher,** *n.*

**Polish** /'poulɪʃ/, *adj.* **1.** of or pertaining to Poland, its inhabitants, or their language. *–n.* **2.** a Slavic language, the principal language of Poland.

**polished** /'pɒlɪʃt/, *adj.* **1.** made smooth and glossy. **2.** naturally smooth and glossy. **3.** refined, cultured, or elegant. **4.** flawless or excellent. **5.** (of rice) milled, so that the husk, etc., is removed.

**polit.,** **1.** political. **2.** politics.

**politburo** /pɒ'lɪtbjurou, 'pɒlɪt-/, *n.* **1.** the chief policy-making and executive committee of a Communist party. **2.** a group said to resemble a Communist politburo because of its absolute control. [Russ. *Polit(icheskoe) Byuro* political bureau]

**polite** /pə'laɪt/, *adj.* **1.** showing good manners towards others, as in behaviour, speech, etc.; courteous; civil: *a polite reply.* **2.** refined or cultured: *polite society.* **3.** of a refined or elegant kind: *polite learning.* [late ME, from L *polītus,* pp., polished] – **politely,** *adv.* – **politeness,** *n.*

**polit. econ.,** political economy.

**politesse** /pɒlə'tɛs/, *n.* politeness. [F, from It. *pulitezza,* from *pulito* polished, pp. of *pulire,* from L *polīre*]

**politic** /'pɒlətɪk/, *adj.* **1.** sagacious; prudent. **2.** shrewd; artful. **3.** expedient; judicious. **4.** political (now chiefly in *body politic,* which see). [ME, from L *polīticus,* from Gk *polītikós* pertaining to citizens or to the state] – **politicly,** *adv.*

**political** /pə'lɪtɪkəl/, *adj.* **1.** pertaining to or dealing with the science of art of politics: *political writers.* **2.** pertaining to or connected with a political party, or its principles, aims, activities, etc.: *a political campaign.* **3.** exercising or seeking power in the governmental or public affairs of a state, municipality, or the like: *a political party.* **4.** of or pertaining to the state or its government: *political measures.* **5.** affecting or involving the state of government: *a political offence.* **6.** engaged in or connected with civil administration: *political office.* **7.** having a definite policy or system of government: *a political community.* **8.** of or pertaining to citizens: *political rights.* **9.** *Colloq.* interested in politics: *Sheila is not political.* **10. political animal,** a person, often a politician, whose whole life involves the conniving, dissembling tactics commonly believed to be essential for political success. – **politically,** *adv.*

**political economy** /– ə'kɒnəmi/, *n.* **1.** a social science dealing with the relationship between political and economic policies and their influence on social institutions. **2.** (in the 17th and 18th centuries) the control of society, esp. with regard to the wealth of a government. **3.** (in the 19th century) a social science similiar to modern economics, but concerned mainly with social policy.

**political science** /– 'saɪəns/, *n.* the science of politics, or of the principles and conduct of government.

**politician** /pɒlə'tɪʃən/, *n.* **1.** one who is active in party politics. **2.** one skilled in political government or administration; a statesman. **3.** one who holds a political office. **4.** a seeker or holder of public office who is more concerned to win favour or to retain power than to maintain principles. **5.** one who seeks power or advancement within an organisation by unscrupulous or dishonest means. **6.** *Rare.* an expert in politics or political government.

**politicise** /pə'lɪtəsaɪz/, *v.,* **-cised, -cising.** *–v.t.* **1.** to make political. *–v.i.* **2.** to engage in, or talk about politics. Also, **politicize.**

**politicking** /pə'lɪtəkɪŋ/, *n.* political campaigning or agitating, esp. in an attempt to gain publicity and win votes.

**politico** /pə'lɪtɪkou/, *n., pl.* **-cos.** *Chiefly U.S.* a politician. [It. or Sp.]

**politico-,** a word element meaning 'political', used in combination, as in *politico-military* (political and military), *politico-religious, politico-social.* [combining form representing Gk *polītikós*]

**politics** /'pɒlətɪks/, *n.* (*construed as sing. or pl.*) **1.** the science or art of political government. **2.** the practice or profession of conducting political affairs. **3.** political affairs. **4.** political methods or manoeuvres. **5.** political principles or opinions. **6.** the use of underhand or unscrupulous methods in obtaining power or advancement within an organisation.

**polity** /'pɒləti/, *n., pl.* **-ties. 1.** a particular form or system of government (civil, ecclesiastical, or other). **2.** the condition of being constituted as a state or other organised community or body. **3.** government or administrative regulation. **4.** a state or other organised community or body. [F (obs.) *politie,* from L *polītīa,* from Gk *polīteía* citizenship, government, form of government, commonwealth]

**polje** /'pɒlji/, *n., pl.* **polja** /'pɒljə/. (in limestone country or karst regions) an extensive elliptical depression, usu. flat-floored and sometimes having a small lake or marsh. [Serbo-Croat: lit., field]

**polka** /'pɒlkə/, *n., v.,* **-kaed, -kaing.** *–n.* **1.** a lively round dance of Bohemian origin, with music in duple time. **2.** a piece of music for such a dance or in its rhythm. *–v.i.* **3.** to dance the polka. [F and G, from Czech *pulka* half-step]

**polka dot** /'– dɒt/, *n.* **1.** a dot or round spot (printed, woven, or embroidered) repeated to form a pattern on a textile fabric. **2.** a pattern of, or a fabric with such dots.

**poll**[1] /poul/, *n.* **1.** the registering of votes, as at an election. **2.** the voting at an election. **3.** the number of votes cast. **4.** the numerical result of the voting. **5.** an enumeration or a list of individuals, as for purposes of taxing or voting. **6.** (*usu. pl.*) the place where votes are taken. **7.** →**poll tax. 8.** a person or individual in a number or list. **9.** an analysis of public opinion on a subject, usu. by selective sampling. **10.** the head, esp. the part of it on which the hair grows. **11.** the back of the head. **12.** the broad end or face of a hammer. **13. go to the polls, a.** to call an election, esp. as a means of resolving a political issue. **b.** to vote at an election. *–v.t.* **14.** to receive at the polls, as votes. **15.** to enrol in a list or register, as for purposes of taxing or voting. **16.** to take or register the votes of, as persons. **17.** to deposit or cast at the polls, as a vote. **18.** to bring to the polls, as voters. **19.** to cut off or cut short the hair, etc., of (a person, etc.); crop; clip; shear. **20.** to cut off or cut short (hair, etc.). **21.** to cut off the top of (a tree, etc.); pollard. **22.** to cut off or cut short the horns of (cattle). *–v.i.* **23.** to vote at the polls; give one's vote. *–adj.* **24.** (of cattle) bred to have no horns. [ME *pol(le),* c. MD and LG *polle.* Cf. d. Swed. *pull* crown of the head, Dan. *puld*] – **pollable,** *adj.*

**poll**[2] /pɒl/, *n.* →**parrot.**

**pollack** /ˈpɒlək/, *n., pl.* **-acks,** (*esp. collectively*) **-ack.** a darkly coloured North Atlantic food fish, *Pollachius virens,* of the cod family; coalfish. Also, **pollock.** [Scot. d. *podlock,* of unknown orig.]

**pollard** /ˈpɒləd/, *n.* **1.** a tree cut back nearly to the trunk, so as to produce a dense mass of branches. **2.** an animal, as a stag, ox, or sheep, without horns. **3.** a by-product of the process of the milling of wheat, used esp. for feeding domestic fowls. *–v.t.* **4.** to convert into a pollard. [apparently from POLL[1], *v.* + -ARD]

**polled** /poʊld/, *adj.* **1.** hornless, as a breed of cattle. **2.** of a beast whose horns have been removed.

**pollen** /ˈpɒlən/, *n.* **1.** the fertilising element of flowering plants, consisting of fine, powdery, yellowish grains or spores, sometimes in masses. *–v.t.* **2.** to pollinate. [L: fine flour, dust]

A

B

pollen: A, chicory; B, passionflower

**pollen analysis** /ˈ– ənæləsəs/, *n.* →**palynology.**

**pollen basket** /ˈ– baskət/, *n.* an area on the leg of a bee adapted for carrying pollen.

**pollen count** /ˈ– kaʊnt/, *n.* a measure of pollen in the air published as a guide to sufferers from hay fever.

**pollenosis** /pɒləˈnoʊsəs/, *n.* →**pollinosis.**

**pollex** /ˈpɒlɛks/, *n., pl.* **-lices** /-ləsiz/. the innermost digit of the forelimb; the thumb. [L: thumb]

**pollie** /ˈpɒli/, *n. Colloq.* a politician.

**pollinate** /ˈpɒləneɪt/, *v.t.,* **-nated, -nating.** to convey pollen for fertilisation to; shed pollen on.

**pollination** /pɒləˈneɪʃən/, *n.* the transfer of pollen from the anther to the stigma.

**polling booth** /ˈpoʊlɪŋ buð/, *n.* **1.** a small cubicle with a writing bench provided for a voter at elections, esp. to ensure privacy. **2.** a place, often a school, town hall, etc., where voters go to record their votes in an election. Also, **booth.**

**polling day** /ˈ– deɪ/, *n.* the day appointed for the recording of votes in an election.

**polliniferous** /pɒləˈnɪfərəs/, *adj.* **1.** *Bot.* producing or bearing pollen. **2.** *Zool.* fitted for carrying pollen. [L *pollen* dust + -I- + -FEROUS]

**pollinium** /pəˈlɪniəm/, *n., pl.* **-linia** /-ˈlɪniə/. *Bot.* an agglutinated mass or body of pollen grains, characteristic of the orchid family. [NL, from L *pollen* dust + *-ium* -IUM]

**pollinosis** /pɒləˈnoʊsəs/, *n.* →**hay fever.** Also, **pollenosis.** [NL, from L *pollen* dust + *-osis* -OSIS]

**polliwog** /ˈpɒliwɒg/, *n.* →**tadpole.** Also, **pollywog.** [cf. ME *polwygle,* from POLL[1] (def. 10) + WIGGLE]

**pollock** /ˈpɒlək/, *n.* →**pollack.**

**pollster** /ˈpoʊlstə/, *n.* one whose occupation is the taking of public opinion polls.

**poll tax** /ˈpoʊl tæks/, *n.* a capitation tax, the payment of which is often a prerequisite to exercise of the right of suffrage.

**poll-taxer** /ˈpoʊl-tæksə/, *n. U.S. Colloq.* **1.** an advocate of the poll tax. **2.** a congressman from a state having a poll tax.

**pollutant** /pəˈlutnt/, *n.* that which pollutes; a polluting agent.

**pollute** /pəˈlut/, *v.t.,* **-luted, -luting.** **1.** to make foul or unclean; dirty. **2.** to make morally unclean; defile. **3.** to render ceremonially impure; desecrate. [L *pollūtus,* pp.] – **polluter,** *n.* – **pollution** /pəˈluʃən/, *n.*

**polluted** /pəˈlutəd/, *adj.* made impure or unclean; tainted; contaminated.

**pollyanna** /pɒliˈænə/, *n. Colloq.* a girl of unreasonable optimism, cheerfulness and goodwill. [after the chief character in *Pollyanna* (1913), a novel by Eleanor Porter, 1868-1920, American writer]

**pollywog** /ˈpɒliwɒg/, *n.* →**polliwog.**

**polo** /ˈpoʊloʊ/, *n.* **1.** a game resembling hockey, played on horseback with long-handled mallets and a wooden ball. **2.** some game more or less resembling this, as water polo. [Baltī (language of Kashmir), c. Tibetan *pulu* ball] – **poloist,** *n.*

**polocrosse** /ˈpoʊloʊkrɒs/, *n.* a game combining elements of polo and lacrosse, played by two teams each of six players on horseback, their equipment consisting of a rubber ball and sticks with heads like a crosse and a shaft like a polo stick, and their aim being to shoot goals through the opposing team's goalposts.

polocrosse

**polonaise** /pɒləˈneɪz/, *n.* **1.** a slow dance of Polish origin, in triple time, consisting chiefly of a march or promenade in couples. **2.** a piece of music for, or in the rhythm of, such a dance. **3.** a woman's overdress combining a bodice and a cutaway overskirt. [F (fem.): Polish]

**polo-neck** /ˈpoʊloʊ-nɛk/, *adj.* **1.** of or denoting a sweater, etc., having a closely fitting, doubled-over collar. *–n.* **2.** such a collar. **3.** a garment having such a collar.

**polonium** /pəˈloʊniəm/, *n.* a radioactive element forming the last stage before lead in the decay of radium; radium F. *Symbol:* Po; *at. no.:* 84; *at. wt of most stable isotope:* 210. [ML *Polon(ia)* Poland (birthplace of Marie Curie, 1867-1934, chemist, who discovered it in 1898) + -IUM]

**polony** /pəˈloʊni/, *n. Colloq.* →**bologna sausage.**

**poltergeist** /ˈpɒltəgaɪst/, *n.* a ghost or spirit which manifests its presence by noises, knockings, movement of physical objects, etc. [G: lit., noise-ghost]

**poltroon** /pɒlˈtrun/, *n.* a wretched coward; a craven. [F *poltron,* from It. *poltrone,* from *poltro* lazy (as n., bed; cf. *poltrire* lie lazily in bed), from Gmc; cf. OHG *polstar* BOLSTER]

**poltroonery** /pɒlˈtrunəri/, *n.* cowardice.

**Polwarth** /ˈpɒlwəθ/, *n.* one of a breed of sheep evolved in Victoria from a Lincoln-Merino cross and used widely in the production of comeback ewes on mixed farms. [from *Polwarth,* a region in Victoria]

**poly** /ˈpɒli/, *n. Brit., U.S. Colloq.* →**polytechnic.**

**poly-,** a word element or prefix, meaning 'much', 'many', first occurring in words from the Greek (as *polyandrous*), but now used freely as a general formative, esp. in scientific or technical words. Cf. **mono-.** [Gk, combining form of *polýs* much, many; akin to L *plēnum* full, and to FULL[1]]

**polyadelphous** /pɒliəˈdɛlfəs/, *adj.* (of stamens) united by their filaments into three or more bundles or sets.

**polyamide** /pɒliˈæmaɪd, -əd/, *n.* any polymer in which the units are linked by amide or thio-amide groups.

**polyandrous** /pɒliˈændrəs/, *adj.* of, pertaining to, or characterised by polyandry.

**polyandry** /pɒliˈændri/, *n.* the practice or the condition of having more than one husband at one time. [Gk *polyandría*]

**polyanthus** /pɒliˈænθəs/, *n.* **1.** a hybrid primrose, *Primula polyantha.* **2.** a narcissus, *Narcissus tazetta,* in many varieties, bearing small white or yellow flowers. [NL, from Gk *polýanthos* having many flowers]

**polybasic** /pɒliˈbeɪsɪk/, *adj.* (of an acid) having two or more atoms of replaceable hydrogen.

**polybeef** /ˈpɒlibif/, *n.* beef with a high level of polyunsaturated fat, as a result of giving cattle a special diet of sunflower seed and casein.

**polycarpic** /pɒliˈkapɪk/, *adj.* producing fruit many times a year or year after year. Also, **polycarpous.** [Gk *polýkarpos*]

**polychaete** /ˈpɒlikit/, *n.* **1.** any of the Polychaeta, a group or division of annelids having unsegmented swimming appendages with many chaetae or bristles, and including most of the common marine worms. *–adj.* **2.** Also, **polychaetous** /pɒləˈkitəs/, pertaining to the polychaetes. [NL *Polychaeta,* from Gk *polychaítēs* having much hair]

**polychasium** /pɒliˈkeɪziəm/, *n., pl.* **-sia** /-ziə/. a form of cymose inflorescence on a plant, in which each axis produces more than two lateral axes. [NL, from *poly-* POLY- + Gk *chásis* separation + *-ium* -IUM]

**polychromatic** /pɒlikrəˈmætɪk/, *adj.* having many colours; exhibiting a variety of colours. Also, **polychromic** /pɒliˈkroumɪk/. – **polychromatism** /pɒliˈkroumətɪzəm/, *n.*

**polychrome** /ˈpɒlikroum/, *adj.* **1.** being of many or various colours. **2.** decorated or executed in many colours, as a statue, a vase, a mural painting, a printed work, etc. [F, from Gk *polýchrōmos* many-coloured]

**polychromy** /ˈpɒlikroumi/, *n.* polychrome colouring; decoration or execution in many colours.

**polyclinic** /pɒliˈklɪnɪk/, *n. Brit.* a clinic or a hospital dealing with various diseases; a general hospital.

**polyconic projection** /ˌpɒlikɒnɪk prəˈdʒɛkʃən/, *n.* in cartography, a conic projection in which the parallels are arcs of circles that are not concentric but are equally spaced along the central straight meridian, all other meridians being curves equally spaced along the parallels.

**polycyclic** /pɒliˈsaɪklɪk/, *adj.* of or pertaining to a molecule which contains more than one ring.

**polycyesis** /pɒlisaɪˈisəs/, *n.* multiple pregnancy.

**polydactyl** /pɒliˈdæktəl/, *adj.* **1.** having many or several digits. **2.** having more than the normal number of fingers or toes. *–n.* **3.** a polydactyl animal. – **polydactylism,** *n.*

**polydipsia** /pɒliˈdɪpsiə/, *n.* excessive thirst.

**polyembryony** /pɒliˈɛmbriəni/, *n.* the production of more than one embryo from one egg.

**polyester** /ˈpɒliɛstə/, *n.* a synthetic polymer in which the structural units are linked by ester groups, formed by condensing carboxylic acids with alcohols.

**polyethylene** /pɒliˈɛθəlin/, *n.* →**polythene.**

**polyfoil** /ˈpɒlifɔɪl/, *Archit. –adj.* **1.** having many, esp. more than five, foils: *a polyfoil window.* *–n.* **2.** a polyfoil ornament or decorative feature.

**polygala** /pəˈlɪgələ/, *n.* any of the herbs and shrubs, commonly known as milkworts, which constitute the genus *Polygala.* [Gk, pl. of *polýgalon* milkwort]

**polygamist** /pəˈlɪgəməst/, *n.* one who practises or favours polygamy.

**polygamous** /pəˈlɪgəməs/, *adj.* **1.** of, pertaining to, characterised by, or practising polygamy. **2.** *Bot.* bearing both unisexual and hermaphrodite flowers on the same or on different plants. [Gk *polýgamos*] – **polygamously,** *adv.*

**polygamy** /pəˈlɪgəmi/, *n.* **1.** the practice or condition of having many or several spouses, esp. wives, at one time. **2.** *Zool.* the habit of mating with more than one of the opposite sex.

**polygenesis** /pɒliˈdʒɛnəsəs/, *n.* the descent of a species or race from more than one ancestral species.

**polygenetic** /pɒlidʒəˈnɛtɪk/, *adj.* **1.** *Biol.* relating to or exhibiting polygenesis. **2.** formed by several different causes, in several different ways, or of several different parts. Also, **polygenic** /pɒliˈdʒɛnɪk/.

**polygenic inheritance** /pɒlidʒɛnɪk ɪnˈhɛrətəns/, *n.* the heredity of complex characters based on their development from a large number of genes, each one ordinarily with a relatively small effect.

**polyglot** /ˈpɒliglɒt/, *adj.* **1.** knowing many or several languages, as a person. **2.** containing, made up of, or in several languages, as a book. **3.** heterogeneous; impure. *–n.* **4.** a mixture or confusion of languages. **5.** a person with a command of a number of languages, whether as to reading or speaking, or both. **6.** a book or writing, esp. a Bible, containing the same text in several languages. [ML *polyglōttus,* from Gk *polýglōttos* many-tongued]

**polygon** /ˈpɒligɒn, -gən/, *n.* a figure, esp. a closed plane figure, having many (more than four) angles and sides. [L *polygōnum,* from Gk *polýgōnon* (neut.) many-angled] – **polygonal** /pəˈlɪgənəl/, *adj.* – **polygonally** /pəˈlɪgənəli/, *adv.*

**polygonaceous** /ˌpɒlɪgəˈneɪʃəs, pəˌlɪgə-/, *adj.* belonging to the Polygonaceae, or polygonum family of plants, including the knotgrass, dock, etc.

**polygonum** /pəˈlɪgənəm/, *n.* a plant of the genus *Polygonum,* which consists chiefly of herbs, often with knotty, jointed stems, and which includes the knotgrass, bistort, etc. [NL, from Gk *polýgōnon* knotgrass]

**polygraph** /ˈpɒligræf, -graf/, *n.* **1.** an apparatus for producing copies of a drawing or writing. **2.** *Med.* an instrument for recording certain bodily activities, as pulse beats, respiratory movements, etc., sometimes used in lie detection. [Gk *polygráphos* writing much] – **polygraphic** /pɒliˈgræfɪk/, *adj.*

**polygynous** /pəˈlɪdʒənəs/, *adj.* **1.** of, pertaining to, characterised by, or practising polygyny. **2.** characterised by plurality of wives for one husband.

**polygyny** /pəˈlɪdʒəni/, *n.* **1.** the practice or the condition of having more than one wife at one time. **2.** the habit or condition of mating with more than one female. [Gk *polygýn(aios)* having many wives + -Y[3]]

**polyhedral** /pɒliˈhidrəl/, *adj.* many-faced.

**polyhedron** /pɒliˈhidrən/, *n., pl.* **-drons, -dra** /-drə/. a solid figure having many faces. [Gk *polýedron* (neut.) having many bases. See -HEDRON]

**polyhistor** /pɒliˈhɪstə/, *n.* a person of great and varied learning. [Gk] – **polyhistoric** /ˌpɒlihɪsˈtɒrɪk/, *adj.*

**polyhouse** /ˈpɒlihaus/, *n.* a greenhouse made from polythene supported on a frame.

**polyhydric alcohol** /ˌpɒlihaɪdrɪk ˈælkəhɒl/, *n.* an alcohol which contains two or more hydroxyl groups in the molecule.

**polyhydroxy** /ˌpɒlihaɪˈdrɒksi/, *adj.* containing a number of hydroxyl groups.

**polyisoprene** /pɒliˈaɪsəprin/, *n.* a polymer of isoprene which is the primary constituent of natural rubber.

**polymath** /ˈpɒlimæθ/, *n.* a person of great and varied learning. [Gk *polymathḗs*]

**polymeat** /ˈpɒlimit/, *n.* meat from animals which have been specially fed to raise the level of polyunsaturated fat in the meat.

**polymer** /ˈpɒləmə/, *n.* **1.** a compound of high molecular weight derived either by the combination of many smaller molecules or by the condensation of many smaller molecules eliminating water, alcohol, etc. **2.** any of two or more polymeric compounds. **3.** a product of polymerisation. [Gk *polymerḗs* of many parts]

**polymer colour** /ˈ– kʌlə/, *n.* →**acrylic colour.**

**polymeric** /pɒləˈmɛrɪk/, *adj.* (of compounds, or of one compound in relation to another) having the same elements combined in the same proportions by weight, but differing in molecular weight, more recently extended to include high molecular weight substances resulting from condensation.

**polymerisation** /pəˌlɪməraɪˈzeɪʃən, ˈpɒləməraɪ-/, *n.* **1.** the act or process of forming a polymer or polymeric compound. **2.** the union of two or more molecules of a compound to form a more complex compound with a higher molecular weight. **3.** the conversion of one compound into another by such a process. Also, **polymerization.**

**polymerise** /pəˈlɪməraɪz, ˈpɒləməraɪz/, *v.t., v.i.,* **-rised, -rising. 1.** to combine so as to form a polymer. **2.** to subject to or undergo polymerisation. Also, **polymerize.**

**polymerism** /pəˈlɪmərɪzəm, ˈpɒləmə-/, *n.* **1.** *Chem.* polymeric state. **2.** *Biol.* polymerous state.

**polymerous** /pəˈlɪmərəs/, *adj. Biol.* composed of many parts.

**polymethyl methacrylate** /pɒliˌmɛθəl məˈθækrəleɪt/, *n.* →**perspex.**

**polymilk** /ˈpɒlimɪlk/, *n.* milk with a high polyunsaturated fat content.

**polymorph** /ˈpɒlimɔf/, *n.* **1.** *Zool., etc.* a polymorphous organism or substance. **2.** *Crystall.* one of the forms assumed by a polymorphous substance. **3.** *Anat.* a type of white blood cell. [Gk *polýmorphos,* adj., multiform]

**polymorphism** /pɒliˈmɔfɪzəm/, *n.* **1.** polymorphous state or condition. **2.** *Crystall.* crystallisation into two or more chemically identical but crystallographically distinct forms. **3.** *Zool., Bot.* existence of an animal or plant in several form or colour varieties.

**polymorphous** /pɒli'mɔfəs/, *adj.* having, assuming, or passing through many or various forms, stages, or the like. Also, **polymorphic.**

**Polynesia** /pɒlə'niʒə/, *n.* one of the three principal divisions of Oceania, comprising those island groups in the Pacific lying east of Melanesia and Micronesia, and extending from the Hawaiian Islands south to New Zealand. [NL, from F *Polynésie,* from *poly-* POLY- + *-nésie,* from Gk *nêsos* island]

**Polynesian** /pɒlə'niʒən/, *adj.* **1.** of or pertaining to Polynesia, its inhabitants, or their languages. *–n.* **2.** a member of any of a number of brown-skinned peoples, variously classified as to race, of distinctive customs, speaking closely related Austronesian languages, and inhabiting Polynesia. **3.** the easternmost group of the Austronesian languages, including Maori, Tahitian, Samoan, Hawaiian, and the language of Easter Island.

**Polynesian realm** /– 'rɛlm/, *n.* a biogeographical realm including New Caledonia, New Hebrides, Fiji, Samoa and most of the tropical islands of the central Pacific, all of which are of volcanic origin and lack endemic mammals.

**polynomial** /pɒli'noʊmiəl/, *adj.* **1.** consisting of or characterised by many or several names or terms. *–n.* **2.** a polynomial name or the like. **3.** *Alg.* an expression consisting of a number of terms each of which has the form of a coefficient times a non-negative integral power of the variable, as $1 + 3x^2 + 4x^3$; any similar expression in more variables, as $x + xy + 5x^2y^3$. **4.** *Zool., Bot.* a species name containing more than two terms. [POLY- + *-nomial* as in BINOMIAL]

**polynuclear** /pɒli'njukliə/, *adj.* →**multinuclear.**

**polynucleotide** /pɒli'njukliətaɪd/, *n.* any polymer formed from a nucleotide.

**polyp** /'pɒlɪp/, *n.* **1.** *Zool.* **a.** a sedentary type of animal form characterised by a more or less fixed base, columnar body, and free end with mouth and tentacles, esp. as applied to coelenterates. **b.** an individual zooid of a compound or colonial organism. **2.** *Pathol.* a projecting growth from a mucous surface, as of the nose, being either a tumour or a hypertrophy of the mucous membrane. [F *polype,* from L *polypus,* from Gk *polýpous* octopus, also polyp (def. 2)]

**polypary** /'pɒləpəri/, *n., pl.* **-ries.** the common supporting structure of a colony of polyps, as corals.

**polypeptide** /pɒli'pɛptaɪd/, *n.* one of a group of compounds having two or more amino acids and one or more peptide radicals. See **peptide.**

**polypetalous** /pɒli'pɛtələs/, *adj.* having many or (commonly) separate petals.

**polyphagia** /pɒli'feɪdʒiə/, *n.* **1.** *Pathol.* excessive desire to eat. **2.** *Zool.* the habit of subsisting on many different kinds of food. [NL, from Gk] – **polyphagous** /pə'lɪfəgəs/, *adj.*

**polyphase** /'pɒlifeɪz/, *adj. Elect.* **1.** having more than one phase. **2.** denoting or pertaining to a system combining two or more alternating currents which differ from one another in phase.

**polyphone** /'pɒlifoʊn/, *n.* a polyphonic letter or symbol.

**polyphonic** /pɒlə'fɒnɪk/, *adj.* **1.** consisting of many voices or sounds. **2.** *Music.* **a.** having two or more voices or parts, each with an independent melody, but all harmonising; contrapuntal (opposed to *homophonic*). **b.** of or pertaining to music of this kind. **c.** capable of producing more than one note at a time, as an organ or a harp. **3.** *Phonet.* having more than one phonetic value, as a letter. [Gk *polýphōnos* having many tones + -IC]

**polyphony** /pə'lɪfəni/, *n.* **1.** *Music.* polyphonic composition; counterpoint. **2.** *Phonet.* representation of different sounds by the same letter or symbol. [Gk *polyphōnía* variety of tones or speech] – **polyphonous,** *adj.*

**polyphyletic** /ˌpɒlifaɪ'lɛtɪk/, *adj.* developed from more than one ancestral type, as a group of animals. [POLY- + Gk *phyletikós* of the same tribe]

**polyploid** /'pɒliplɔɪd/, *adj.* **1.** having or being a chromosome number that is a multiple greater than two of the monoploid number. *–n.* **2.** a cell or organism which is polyploid. – **polyploidy,** *n.*

**polypody** /'pɒliˌpoʊdi/, *n., pl.* **-dies.** any fern of the genus *Polypodium,* as *P. vulgare,* a common species with creeping rootstocks, deeply pinnatifid evergreen fronds, and round, naked sori. [L *polypodium,* from Gk *polypódion*]

**polypoid** /'pɒlipɔɪd/, *adj.* of, pertaining to, or resembling a polyp.

**polypropylene** /pɒli'proʊpəlin/, *n.* a plastic polymer of propylene, similar to polythene but of greater strength; used as a substitute for jute in making bags, etc.

**polyptych** /'pɒlɪptɪk/, *n.* a painted or sculptured ensemble, usu. an altarpiece, composed of several connected panels. Cf. **diptych.** [LL *polyptycha* (neut. pl.) account books, from Gk: having many folds]

**polypus** /'pɒləpəs/, *n., pl.* **-pi** /-paɪ/. →**polyp.** [L. See POLYP]

**polyrhythm** /'pɒlirɪðəm/, *n.* the simultaneous use of contrasting rhythmic patterns in a musical composition.

**polysaccharide** /pɒli'sækəraɪd, -rəd/, *n.* a carbohydrate, as starch, inulin, cellulose, etc., containing more than three monosaccharide units per molecule, the units being attached to each other in the manner of acetals, and therefore capable of hydrolysis by acids or enzymes to monosaccharides.

**polysaturated** /pɒli'sætʃəreɪtəd/, *adj.* **1.** of or pertaining to, fats based wholly on saturated fatty acids such as stearic and lauric acids. **2.** of or pertaining to foodstuffs, as meat, rich in polysaturated fat; believed to be associated with cardiac disease.

**polysemy** /pə'lɪsəmi/, *n.* the acquisition and retention of many meanings by one word, as in the case of the word *tank* which referred to a receptacle for liquids and then additionally to a military vehicle. – **polysemous,** *adj.*

**polysepalous** /pɒli'sɛpələs/, *adj.* having the sepals separate from one another.

**polysome** /'pɒlisoʊm/, *n.* a group of ribosomes attached to messenger RNA, involved in protein synthesis.

**polystyle** /'pɒlistaɪl/, *adj.* having many columns.

**polystyrene** /pɒli'staɪrin/, *n.* a clear, plastic polymer of styrene easily coloured and moulded and used as an insulating material.

**polysulphide** /pɒli'sʌlfaɪd/, *n.* a sulphide containing more than the ordinary quantity of sulphur.

**polysyllabic** /ˌpɒlisə'læbɪk/, *adj.* **1.** consisting of many, or more than three, syllables, as a word. **2.** characterised by such words, as language, etc. Also, **polysyllabical.** [ML *polysyllabus* (from Gk *polysýllabos* of many syllables) + -IC]

**polysyllable** /pɒli'sɪləbəl/, *n.* a polysyllabic word.

**polysyllogism** /pɒli'sɪlədʒɪzəm/, *n.* a number of syllogisms arranged in a series, so that the conclusion of one (a **prosyllogism**) serves as the premise of another (an **episyllogism**).

**polysyndeton** /pɒli'sɪndətən/, *n.* the rhetorical use of a number of conjunctions in close succession. Cf. **asyndeton.** [NL, from Gk *poly-* POLY- + *sýndeton* (neut.) bound together]

**polysynthesism** /pɒli'sɪnθəsɪzəm/, *n.* **1.** the synthesis of various elements. **2.** the combining of several words in a sentence into a single word.

**polysynthetic** /ˌpɒlisɪn'θɛtɪk/, *adj.* (of a language) having many word elements in a sentence combined into one word, as in a number of American Indian languages.

**polytechnic** /pɒli'tɛknɪk/, *adj.* **1.** of, pertaining to, or dealing with scientific or technical subjects. *–n.* **2.** *Brit., U.S.* an institute of higher education in which instruction is given chiefly in scientific and technical subjects. [F *polytechnique,* from Gk *polýtechnos* + *-ique* -IC]

**polytetrafluoroethylene** /ˌpɒlitɛtrəˌfluroʊ'ɛθəlin/, *n.* the plastic produced by the polymerisation of tetrafluoroethylene, with a very low coefficient of friction and good resistance to temperature; noted for non-stick properties. *Abbrev.:* PTFE

**polytheism** /'pɒliθiˌɪzəm/, *n.* the doctrine of, or belief in, many gods or more gods than one. [F *polythéisme,* from Gk *polýtheos* of many gods + *-isme* -ISM] – **polytheist,** *n.* – **polytheistic** /ˌpɒliθi'ɪstɪk/, *adj.*

**polythene** /'pɒləθin/, *n.* a plastic polymer of ethylene used for containers, electrical insulation, packaging, etc. Also, **polyethylene.**

**polytonality** /ˌpɒlitoʊ'næləti/, *n. Music.* the use of more than one key at the same time.

**polytypic** /pɒli'tɪpɪk/, *adj.* having or involving many or several types. Also, **polytypical.**

**polyunsaturated** /ˌpɒliʌn'sætʃəreɪtəd/, *adj. Chem.* **1.** of or pertaining to, a fat or oil based at least partly on fatty acids which have two or more double bonds per molecule, such as linolenic and linoleic acids. **2.** of or pertaining to foodstuffs based on polyunsaturated fat, as safflower oil, etc. or margarines based on such vegetable oils and believed not to increase cholesterol levels in the blood.

**polyurethane** /pɒliˈjurəθeɪn/, *n.* a polymer of urethane used in making rigid foam products for insulation, decoration, etc.

**polyuria** /pɒliˈjuriə/, *n.* the passing of an excessive quantity of urine, as in diabetes, certain nervous diseases, etc. [NL. See POLY, -URIA] – **polyuric,** *adj.*

**polyvalent** /pɒliˈveɪlənt, pəˈlɪvələnt/, *adj.* **1.** *Chem.* having more than one valency. **2.** *Bacteriol.* denoting a serum which contains antibodies against a group of similar diseases and is capable of attacking their different antigens. [POLY- + -VALENT] – **polyvalence,** *n.*

**polyvinyl acetate** /pɒliˌvaɪnəl ˈæsəteɪt/, *n.* a transparent thermoplastic resin, produced by the polymerisation of vinyl acetate, used as an adhesive, in inks and lacquers, etc. *Abbrev.:* PVA

**polyvinyl chloride** /– ˈklɔraɪd/, *n.* a colourless thermoplastic resin, produced by the polymerisation of vinyl chloride, with good resistance to water, acids, and alkalis, used in a wide variety of manufactured products, including rainwear, garden hoses, gramophone records, and floor tiles. *Abbrev.:* PVC

**polyvinylidene chloride** /ˌpɒlivaɪˌnɪlədin ˈklɔraɪd/, *n.* a white thermoplastic material, produced by the polymerisation of vinylidene chloride, used alone or as a copolymer with vinyl chloride for a variety of purposes.

**polyzoan** /pɒliˈzouən/, *adj., n.* →**bryozoan.** [POLY- + -ZO(A) + -AN]

**polyzoarium** /ˌpɒlizouˈɛəriəm/, *n., pl.* **-aria** /-ˈɛəriə/. a bryozoan colony, or its supporting skeleton.

**polyzoic** /pɒliˈzouɪk/, *adj.* **1.** (of a bryozoan colony) composed of many zooids. **2.** (of a spore) producing many sporozoites.

**pom** /pɒm/, *n.* →**pommy.**

**Pom** /pɒm/, *n.* a Pomeranian dog.

**poma** /ˈpɒmə/, *n.* a ski-lift consisting of small circular plates, suspended from the towing cable, which skiers straddle to be towed uphill. [Trademark]

**pomace** /ˈpʌməs/, *n.* **1.** the pulpy residue from apples or similar fruit after crushing and pressing, as in cider-making. **2.** any crushed or ground pulpy substance. [ME, from ML *pōmācium* cider, from L *pōmum* fruit]

**pomaceous** /pɒˈmeɪʃəs/, *adj.* pertaining to pomes, as the apple, pear, and quince. [NL *pōmāceus,* from L *pōmum* fruit]

**pomade** /pəˈmeɪd, -ˈmad/, *n., v.,* **-maded, -mading.** *–n.* **1.** a scented ointment, used for the scalp and hair. *–v.t.* **2.** to anoint or dress with pomade. [F *pommade,* from It. *pomata* (so called because orig. made with apples), from L *pōmum* fruit. Cf. POMATUM]

**pomander** /pəˈmændə/, *n.* **1.** a mixture of aromatic substances, often in the form of a ball, formerly carried on the person for perfume or as a guard against infection. **2.** the container in which it is carried. [earlier *pomeamber,* from POME + AMBER]

**pomatum** /pəˈmeɪtəm/, *n.* →**pomade.** [NL, from L *pōmum* fruit]

**pome** /poum/, *n.* the characteristic fruit of the apple family, as an apple, pear, quince, etc. [ME, from OF, from LL *pōma* (neut. pl.) fruit] – **pomelike,** *adj.*

**pomegranate** /ˈpɒməgrænət/, *n.* **1.** a several-chambered, many-seeded, globose fruit of medium size, with a tough rind (usu. red) and surmounted by a crown of calyx lobes, the edible portion consisting of pleasantly acid flesh developed from the outer seed coat. **2.** the shrub or small tree, *Punica granatum,* which yields it, native to south-western Asia but widely cultivated in warm regions. [ME *pomegarnet,* from OF *pome grenate* (from *pome* apple, fruit + *grenate,* from L *grānāta* (fem.) having grains or seeds). See POME, GRAIN]

A B

pomegranate: A, fruit; B, transverse section

**pomelo** /ˈpɒməlou/, *n., pl.* **-los. 1.** →**grapefruit. 2.** →**shaddock.** [D (along pseudo-Spanish lines) *pompelmoes*]

**Pomeranian** /pɒməˈreɪniən/, *n.* one of a breed of small dogs with erect ears, and long, thick silky hair. [originating in *Pomerania,* a region of N central Europe, now largely in Poland]

Pomeranian

**pomiculture** /ˈpɒməkʌltʃə/, *n.* the cultivation or growing of fruit. [*pōmi-* (combining form of L *pōmum* fruit) + CULTURE] – **pomiculturist** /pɒməˈkʌltʃərəst/, *n.*

**pomiferous** /pɒˈmɪfərəs/, *adj.* bearing pomes or pomelike fruits. [L *pōmifer* fruit-bearing + -OUS]

**pommel** /ˈpʌməl, ˈpɒməl/, *n., v.,* **-melled, -melling** or (*U.S.*) **-meled, -meling.** *–n.* Also, **pummel. 1.** a terminating knob, as on the top of a tower, hilt of a sword, etc. **2.** the protuberant part at the front and top of a saddle. *–v.t.* **3.** →**pummel.** [ME *pomel,* from OF, from L *pōmum* fruit]

**pommy** /ˈpɒmi/, *n., pl.* **-mies.** *Colloq.* **1.** an Englishman. *–adj.* **2.** English. Also, **pom.** [orig. uncert.]

**pommy wash** /ˈ– wɒʃ/, *n.* (*joc.*) →**sponge bath.**

**pomology** /pəˈmɒlədʒi/, *n.* the science that deals with fruits and fruit-growing. [NL *pōmologia.* See POME, -LOGY] – **pomological** /pɒməˈlɒdʒɪkəl/, *adj.* – **pomologist,** *n.*

**pomp** /pɒmp/, *n.* **1.** stately or splendid display; splendour; magnificence. **2.** ostentatious or vain display, esp. of dignity or importance. **3.** (*pl.*) pompous displays or things. **4.** *Obs.* a stately or splendid procession; pageant. [ME *pompe,* from OF, from L *pompa,* from Gk *pompḗ,* orig., a sending]

**pompadour** /ˈpɒmpədɔ/, *n.* **1.** an arrangement of a woman's hair, popular in the early 18th century, in which it is raised above the forehead, often over a pad. **2.** a shade of pink or of crimson. **3.** *Textiles.* **a.** a fabric, esp. silk, often in red, having a small floral design. **b.** the design. [named after the Marquise de *Pompadour,* 1721-64, mistress of Louis XV of France]

**pompano** /ˈpɒmpənou/, *n., pl.* **-nos. 1.** a deep-bodied Atlantic food fish of the genus *Trachinotus.* **2.** a prized food fish, *Palometus simillimus,* of California. [Sp. *pampano,* from L *pampinus*]

**Pompeian red** /pɒmˌpeɪən ˈred/, *n.* greyish-yellow red.

**pompom**[1] /ˈpɒmpɒm/, *n.* **1.** an ornamental tuft or ball of feathers, wool, or the like, used in millinery, etc. **2.** a tuft of wool or the like worn on a shako, a sailor's cap, etc. **3.** *Hort.* a form of small, globe-shaped flower head that characterises a class or type of various flowering plants, esp. chrysanthemums and dahlias. Also, **pompon.** [F, from *pompe* POMP]

**pompom**[2] /ˈpɒmpɒm/, *n.* an automatic anti-aircraft cannon. [imitative]

**pomposity** /pɒmˈpɒsəti/, *n., pl.* **-ties. 1.** the quality of being pompous. **2.** pompous parade of dignity or importance. **3.** ostentatious loftiness of language, style, behaviour, etc. [ME, from ML *pompōsitas*]

**pompous** /ˈpɒmpəs/, *adj.* **1.** characterised by an ostentatious parade of dignity or importance: *a pompous bow.* **2.** (of language, style, etc.) ostentatiously lofty. **3.** characterised by pomp, stately splendour, or magnificence. [ME, from LL *pompōsus*] – **pompously,** *adv.* – **pompousness,** *n.*

**ponce** /pɒns/, *n., v.,* **ponced, poncing.** *Colloq.* *–n.* **1.** →**pimp. 2.** a dandy, often effeminate. **3. all ponced up,** spruced up. *–v.i.* **4.** to act as a pimp. **5.** to flounce; behave in a foolishly effeminate fashion (fol. by *about*). [orig. uncert.]

poncho

**poncho** /ˈpɒntʃou/, *n., pl.* **-chos. 1.** a blanket-like cloak with a hole in the centre to put over the head. **2.** a similar woman's fashion garment. [S Amer. Sp., from Araucanian *pontho* woollen fabric]

**poncy** /ˈpɒnsi/, *adj.* in the manner of a dandy.

**pond** /pɒnd/, *n.* a body of water smaller than a lake, often one artificially formed. [ME, anomalous var. of POUND[3]]

**pondage** /ˈpɒndɪdʒ/, *n.* water in excess of normal levels temporarily trapped behind an embankment.

**ponder** /ˈpɒndə/, *v.i.* **1.** to consider deeply; meditate. *–v.t.* **2.** to weigh carefully in the mind, or consider carefully. [ME *pondre(n)*, from OF *ponderer*, from L *ponderāre* ponder, weigh]

**ponderable** /ˈpɒndərəbəl/, *adj.* capable of being weighed; having appreciable weight. – **ponderability** /pɒndərəˈbɪləti/, *n.*

**ponderous** /ˈpɒndərəs, -drəs/, *adj.* **1.** of great weight; heavy; massive: *a ponderous mass of iron.* **2.** without graceful lightness or ease; dull: *a ponderous dissertation.* [ME, from *ponderōsus*] – **ponderously,** *adv.* – **ponderousness, ponderosity** /pɒndəˈrɒsəti/, *n.*

**ponding board** /ˈpɒndɪŋ bɔd/, *n.* a piece of sheet material placed under the sarking or at the edge of a roof to direct water off the sarking into the gutter.

**pond scum** /ˈpɒnd skʌm/, *n.* any free-floating freshwater alga that forms a green scum on water.

**pond-skater** /ˈpɒnd-skeɪtə/, *n.* →**water-strider.**

**pondweed** /ˈpɒndwid/, *n.* any of the aquatic plants constituting the genus *Potamogeton*, most of which grow in ponds and quiet streams.

**pone**[1] /poun/, *n. U.S.* **1.** Also, **pone bread.** baked or fried bread made of maize. **2.** an oval-shaped loaf or cake of it. [Algonquian *äpan* something baked]

**pone**[2] /ˈpouni/, *n.* the player in a card game on the dealer's right.

**pong** /pɒŋ/, *Colloq.* *–n.* **1.** a stink; unpleasant smell. *–v.i.* **2.** to stink.

**ponga** /ˈpɒŋə/, *n.* a tall tree fern with large, leathery bipinnate or tripinnate leaves, *Cyathea dealbata,* native to New Zealand. Also, **bunger, bungie, punga.** [Maori]

**pongee** /pɒnˈdʒi, ˈpɒndʒi/, *n.* **1.** silk of a plain weave made from filaments of wild silk woven in natural tan colour. **2.** a cotton or rayon fabric imitating it. [? North Chinese *pun-chī,* Mandarin *pun-kī* own loom]

**pongid** /ˈpɒndʒɪd/, *n.* **1.** one of the great apes of the family Pongidae, which includes the chimpanzee, gorilla, and orang-utan. *–adj.* **2.** belonging or pertaining to the Pongidae. [NL *Pongidae,* the family, equivalent to *Pongo,* the typical genus (from Kongo *mpungu* ape) + *-idae* -IDAE]

**pongo**[1] /ˈpɒŋgou/, *n.* →**gliding possum.** [Aboriginal]

**pongo**[2] /ˈpɒŋgou/, *n.* **1.** (*cap.*) a genus of anthropoid apes comprising the orangutans. **2.** an anthropoid ape. [NL, from Kongo *mpongi, mpungu*]

**pongo**[3] /ˈpɒŋgou/, *N.Z. Colloq.* *–n.* **1.** a British soldier. **2.** an Englishman. *–adj.* **3.** English. [orig. uncert.]

**pongo**[4] /ˈpɒŋou/, *adj. Colloq.* smelly. [PONG + -O]

**Pongolia** /pɒŋˈgouliə/, *n. N.Z. Colloq.* Britain. [from PONGO[3] modelled on Mongolia] – **Pongolian,** *n., adj.*

**pongy** /ˈpɒŋi/, *adj. Colloq.* smelly. [PONG + -Y[1]]

**poniard** /ˈpɒnjəd, -ad/, *n.* **1.** a dagger. *–v.t.* **2.** to stab with a poniard. [F *poignard,* from *poing,* from L *pugnus* fist]

**pons** /pɒnz/, *n., pl.* **pontes** /ˈpɒntiz/. *Anat.* a connecting part. [L: bridge]

**pons asinorum** /– æsəˈnɔrəm/, *n.* the geometrical proposition (Euclid, 1:5) that if a triangle has two of its sides equal, the angles opposite these sides are also equal; so named from the difficulty experienced by beginners in mastering it. [L: bridge of asses]

**pons Varolii** /– vəˈrouliaɪ/, *n.* a band of nerve fibres in the brain connecting the lobes of the cerebellum, as well as the medulla and cerebrum. [named after Costanzo *Varolio,* 1543-75, Italian anatomist]

**pontiff** /ˈpɒntɪf/, *n.* **1.** a high or chief priest. **2.** *Eccles.* **a.** a bishop. **b.** the bishop of Rome (the pope). [L *pontifex*]

**pontifical** /pɒnˈtɪfɪkəl/, *adj.* **1.** of, pertaining to, or characteristic of a pontiff; papal. *–n.* **2.** (in the Western Church) a book containing the forms for the sacraments and other rites and ceremonies to be performed by a bishop. **3.** (*pl.*) the vestments and insignia of a bishop, proper to his liturgical functions. [ME, from L *pontificālis*] – **pontifically,** *adv.*

**Pontifical College** /pɒnˌtɪfɪkəl ˈkɒlɪdʒ/, *n.* **1.** the chief body of priests in ancient Rome. **2.** the chief hieratic body of the Roman Catholic Church.

**pontificate** /pɒnˈtɪfəkət/, *n.;* /pɒnˈtɪfəkeɪt/, *v.,* **-cated, -cating.** *–n.* **1.** the office, or term of office, of a pontiff. *–v.i.* **2.** to speak in a pompous manner. **3.** to serve as a pontiff or bishop, esp. in a Pontifical Mass. [ML *pontificātus,* pp.]

**pontil** /ˈpɒntɪl/, *n.* →**punty.**

**pontlevis** /pɒntˈlɛvəs/, *n.* →**drawbridge.**

**pontoon**[1] /pɒnˈtun/, *n.* **1.** a boat, or some other floating structure, used as one of the supports for a temporary bridge over a river. **2.** a floating construction serving as a temporary dock or a floating bridge. **3.** a watertight box or cylinder used in raising a submerged vessel, etc. **4.** a seaplane float. Also, **ponton** /ˈpɒntən/. [F *ponton,* from L *ponto* bridge, pontoon, punt]

**pontoon**[2] /pɒnˈtun/, *n.* a gambling game, the object of which is to obtain from the dealer cards whose total values add up to, or nearly add up to, 21, but do not exceed it. [(? humorous) mispronunciation of F *vingt-et-un* twenty-one]

**pontoon bridge** /– ˈbrɪdʒ/, *n.* a bridge supported by pontoons.

**pony** /ˈpouni/, *n., pl.* **-nies,** *v.,* **-nied, -nying.** *–n.* **1.** a horse of a small type, usu. not more than 13 or 14 hands high. **2.** a horse of any small type or breed. **3.** *U.S. Colloq.* →**crib** (def. 13). **4.** a small glass for beer or spirits. **5.** *Colloq.* **a.** (formerly) the sum of £25. **b.** the sum of $25. *–v.t. U.S. Colloq.* **6.** to prepare (lessons) by means of a crib. **7.** to pay (money), as in settling an account (fol. by *up*). [var. of *powney,* from F *poulenet,* from L *pullus* young animal. See FOAL]

**ponytail** /ˈpouniteɪl/, *n.* a woman's hairstyle in which the hair is drawn back tightly and tied at the back of the head and then hangs loose.

**poo** /pu/, *n.* **1.** *Colloq.* (*euph.*) →**faeces.** **2. in the poo,** *Colloq.* in trouble or bad favour (fol. by *with*). Also, **pooh.**

**pooch** /putʃ/, *n. Colloq.* a dog.

**poodle** /ˈpudl/, *n.* one of a breed of intelligent pet dogs, of several varieties, with thick curly hair often trimmed in an elaborate manner. [short for *poodle dog,* half adoption, half translation of G *Pudelhund,* lit., splash-dog (because the poodle is a water-dog). Cf. PUDDLE]

poodle

**poof** /pʊf/, *n.* →**poofter.**

**poofter** /ˈpʊftə/, *n. Colloq.* **1.** a male homosexual. **2.** (*derog.*) a person, esp. one who is weak or cowardly. Also, **poof.**

**poofter-basher** /ˈpʊftə-bæʃə/, *n. Colloq.* one who participates in poofter-bashing.

**poofter-bashing** /ˈpʊftə-bæʃɪŋ/, *n. Colloq.* **1.** assault on male homosexuals. **2.** verbal attacks on men in public life reputed to be homosexuals.

**poofter-rorter** /ˈpʊftə-rɔtə/, *n. Colloq.* **1.** a procurer of male homosexuals. **2.** one who assaults and robs homosexuals.

**pooh** /pu/, *interj.* **1.** (an exclamation of disdain or contempt.) *–n.* **2.** an exclamation of 'pooh'. **3.** →**poo.**

**Pooh-Bah** /ˈpu-ba/, *n. Colloq.* a pompous person, esp. an official. [from *Pooh-Bah,* the Lord-High-Everything-Else, in Gilbert and Sullivan's opera, *The Mikado*]

**poohey** /ˈpui/, *adj.* disagreeable; unpleasant.

**pooh-pooh** /pu-ˈpu/, *v.t.* to express disdain or contempt for; make light of; dismiss as unworthy of consideration.

**pool**[1] /pul/, *n.* **1.** a small body of standing water; pond. **2.** a puddle. **3.** any small collection of liquid on a surface: *a pool of blood.* **4.** a still, deep place in a stream. **5.** a swimming pool. [ME and OE *pōl,* c. G *Pfuhl*]

**pool**[2] /pul/, *n.* **1.** an association of competitors who agree to control the production, market, and price of a commodity for mutual benefit, although they appear to be rivals. **2.** *Chiefly U.S. Finance.* a combination of persons to manipulate one or more securities. **3.** a combination of interests, funds, etc., for common advantage. **4.** the combined interests or funds. **5.** a facility or service that is shared by a number of people: *a typing pool.* **6.** the persons or parties involved. **7.** the stakes in certain games. **8.** Also, **pocket billiards.** any of various games played on a billiard table in which the object is to drive all the balls into the pockets with the cue ball. **9.** the total amount staked by a combination of betters, as on a race, to be awarded to the successful better or betters. **10.**

the combination of such betters. **11.** *Fencing.* a match in which each team-mate successively plays against each member of the opposite team. *–v.t.* **12.** to put (interests, money, etc.) into a pool, or common stock or fund, as for a financial venture, according to agreement. **13.** to form a pool of. **14.** to make a common interest of. *–v.i.* **15.** to enter into or form a pool. [F *poule,* lit., hen; probably at first slang for booty]

**poolroom** /ˈpulrum/, *n.* **1.** an establishment or room in which pool or billiards is played. **2.** a place in which betting is carried on.

**pools** /pulz/, *n.pl.* →**football pools.**

**poolside** /ˈpulsaɪd/, *adj.* at the side of a swimming pool: *poolside party.*

**pool table** /ˈpul teɪbəl/, *n.* a billiard table with six pockets, on which pool is played.

**poon**[1] /pun/, *n.* **1.** any of several East Indian trees of the tropical genus *Calophyllum,* which yield a light, hard wood used for masts, spars, etc. **2.** the wood. [Singhalese *pūna,* probably from Tamil *punnai*]

**poon**[2] /pun/, *n. Colloq. (derog.)* **1.** a stupid, useless person; an idiot; fool. **2.** an eccentric or weird person. [Brit. d. *poind* fool, simpleton]

**poonce** /pʊns/, *n. Colloq. (derog).* a male homosexual. [var. of PONCE]

**pooncey** /ˈpʊnsi/, *adj. Colloq.* effeminate.

**poop**[1] /pup/, *n.* **1.** the enclosed space in the aftermost part of a ship, above the main deck. **2.** a deck above the ordinary deck in that part, often forming the roof of a cabin, etc. *–v.t.* **3.** (of a wave) to break over the stern of (a ship). **4.** to take (seas) over the stern. [ME *pouppe,* from OF *poupe,* from It. *poppa,* from L *puppis*]

**poop**[2] /pup/, *v.t. Colloq.* to tire or exhaust. [ME *poupe(n),* lit., blow]

**poop**[3] /pʊp/, *Colloq. n.* excrement.

**poop deck** /ˈpup dɛk/, *n.* a raised deck built on the stern of a ship above the main deck.

**pooped** /pupt/, *adj. Colloq.* exhausted.

**poor** /pɔ/, *adj.* **1.** having little or nothing in the way of wealth, goods, or means of subsistence. **2.** (of a country, institution, etc.) meagrely supplied or endowed with resources or funds. **3.** (of the circumstances, life, home, dress, etc.) characterised by or showing poverty. **4.** deficient or lacking in something specified: *a region poor in mineral deposits.* **5.** faulty or inferior, as in construction. **6.** deficient in desirable ingredients, qualities, or the like: *poor soil.* **7.** lean or emaciated, as cattle. **8.** of an inferior, inadequate, or unsatisfactory kind; not good: *poor health.* **9.** deficient in aptitude or ability: *a poor cook.* **10.** deficient in moral excellence; cowardly, abject, or mean. **11.** scanty, meagre, or paltry in amount or number: *a poor pittance.* **12.** humble: *deign to visit our poor house.* **13.** unfortunate or hapless (much used to express pity): *the poor mother was in despair.* *–n.* **14.** poor persons collectively (usu. prec. by *the*). [ME *povere,* from OF *povre,* from L *pauper.* Cf. PAUPER] – **poorness,** *n.*

**poor-box** /ˈpɔ-bɒks/, *n.* a box in which money may be placed for distribution to the poor.

**poorhouse** /ˈpɔhaʊs/, *n.* a house in which paupers are maintained at the public expense.

**poorly** /ˈpɔli/, *adv.* **1.** in a poor manner or way. *–adj.* **2.** in poor health; somewhat ill.

**poor-man's orange** /pɔ-mænz ˈɒrɪndʒ/, *n.* **1.** a bitter orange used for marmalade. **2.** any of various other bitter citrus fruits used in this way.

**poor-man's orchid** /– ˈɔkəd/, *n.* →**schizanthus.**

**poor relation** /pɔ rəˈleɪʃən/, *n.* something or somebody considered inferior to another in the same broad field or class.

**poor-spirited** /pɔ-ˈspɪrətəd/, *adj.* having or showing a poor, cowardly, or abject spirit.

**poor white** /pɔ ˈwaɪt/, *n.* (*usu. collective or pl.*) *Orig. U.S.* (*oft. derog.*) an ignorant, shiftless, poverty-stricken white, in multi-racial areas of a low socio-economic level.

**poor white trash,** *n.* (*derog.*) poor whites collectively.

**poove** /puv/, *n.* →**poofter.** Also, **pouf, pouffe.**

**pop**[1] /pɒp/, *v.,* **popped, popping,** *n., adv.* *–v.i.* **1.** to make a short, quick, explosive sound or report: *the cork popped.* **2.** to burst open with such a sound, as chestnuts or corn in roasting. **3.** to come or go quickly, suddenly or unexpectedly (fol. by *in, into, out,* etc.). **4.** to shoot with a firearm: *to pop at a mark.* **5. pop off,** *Colloq.* **a.** to depart, esp. abruptly. **b.** to die, esp. suddenly. *–v.t.* **6.** to cause to make a sudden, explosive sound. **7.** to cause to burst open with such a sound, as a blister, balloon, champagne bottle, etc. **8.** to put or thrust quickly, suddenly or unexpectedly. **9.** *Colloq.* to fire (a gun, etc.). **10.** to shoot (fol. by *off,* etc.). **11.** *Colloq.* to pawn. **12. pop the question,** *Colloq.* to propose marriage. *–n.* **13.** a short, quick, explosive sound. **14.** a popping. **15.** a shot with a firearm. **16.** an attempt: *to have a pop at something.* **17.** *Colloq.* each: *they cost five dollars a pop.* **18.** an effervescent beverage, esp. a non-alcoholic one. *–adv.* **19.** with a pop or explosive sound. **20.** quickly, suddenly, or unexpectedly. [ME; imitative]

**pop**[2] /pɒp/, *Colloq. –adj.* **1.** popular. **2.** denoting or pertaining to a type of tune or song having great but ephemeral popularity, esp. among the young, and usu. characterised by an insistent rhythmic beat. **3.** denoting or pertaining to a singer or player of such music. *–n.* **4.** a pop tune or song. [short for POPULAR]

**pop**[3] /pɒp/, *n. Colloq.* father, or grandfather.

**pop.,** **1.** popular. **2.** population.

**popadum** /ˈpɒpədəm/, *n.* →**pappadum.**

**pop art** /pɒp ˈat/, *n.* modern art, including painting, sculpture, serigraphy and collage, which rejects any distinction between good and bad taste, and which draws images and materials from popular culture and industry, esp. mass production.

**popcorn** /ˈpɒpkɔn/, *n.* **1.** any of several varieties of maize whose kernels burst open and puff out when subjected to dry heat. **2.** popped corn.

**pope**[1] /poʊp/, *n.* **1.** (*oft. cap.*) the bishop of Rome as head of the Roman Catholic Church. **2.** one considered as having or assuming a similar position or authority. [ME; OE *pāpa,* from ML: bishop, pope, orig. father, from Gk *pápas,* var. of *páppas* father]

**pope**[2] /poʊp/, *n.* a rough-skinned freshwater fish of the genus *Acerina,* found in northern Europe and southern Britain; ruffe.

**popedom** /ˈpoʊpdəm/, *n.* **1.** the office or dignity of a pope. **2.** the tenure of office of a pope. **3.** the papal government. **4.** a system resembling the papacy.

**popery** /ˈpoʊpəri/, *n.* (*usu. derog.*) the doctrines, customs, etc., of the Roman Catholic Church.

**pope's nose** /poʊps ˈnoʊz/, *n.* →**parson's nose.**

**popeyed** /ˈpɒpaɪd/, *adj.* having prominent, bulging, or staring eyes.

**pop group** /ˈpɒp grup/, *n.* a number, usu. small, of musicians, who perform pop music.

**popgun** /ˈpɒpgʌn/, *n.* a child's toy gun from which a pellet is shot with a loud pop by compressed air.

**popinjay** /ˈpɒpəndʒeɪ/, *n.* **1.** a vain, chattering person; a coxcomb; a fop. **2.** a figure of a parrot formerly used as a target. **3.** a woodpecker, esp. the green woodpecker, *Picus viridis,* of Europe. **4.** *Archaic.* a parrot. [ME *papejay,* from OF *papegai* parrot, from Sp. *papagayo,* from Ar. *babbaghā',* from Pers.]

**popish** /ˈpoʊpɪʃ/, *adj.* (*usu. derog.*) of or pertaining to the Roman Catholic Church. – **popishly,** *adv.* – **popishness,** *n.*

**poplar** /ˈpɒplə/, *n.* **1.** any of various rapidly growing trees constituting the genus *Populus,* yielding a useful, light, soft wood, as *P. nivra* var. *italica* **(Lombardy poplar),** a tall tree of striking columnar or spire-shaped outline due to the fastigiate habit of its branches. **2.** the wood itself. **3.** the wood of any such tree. [ME *popler,* from OF *poplier;* replacing OE *pōpul,* from L *pōpulus*]

**poplin** /ˈpɒplən/, *n.* a strong, finely ribbed, mercerised cotton material, used for dresses, blouses, children's wear, etc. [F *popeline,* from It. *papalina,* fem. of *papalino* papal; so called from being made at the papal city of Avignon]

**popliteal** /pɒpˈlɪtiəl, pɒpləˈtiəl/, *adj.* of or pertaining to the ham, or part of the leg behind the knee. [NL *popliteus* (from L *poples* the ham) + -AL[1]]

**pop music** /ˈpɒp mjuzɪk/, *n.* a type of commercial tune or song having great but ephemeral popularity, esp. among the young, and often characterised by an insistent rhythmic beat

i = peat ɪ = pit ɛ = pet æ = pat a = part ɒ = pot ʌ = putt ɔ = port ʊ = put u = pool ɜ = pert ə = apart aɪ = buy eɪ = bay ɔɪ = boy aʊ = how oʊ = hoe ɪə = here ɛə = hair ʊə = tour g = give θ = thin ð = then ʃ = show ʒ = measure tʃ = choke dʒ = joke ŋ = sing j = you õ = Fr. bon

in the style of unsophisticated rock music.

**pop-out** /ˈpɒp-aʊt/, *n. Colloq.* a mass-produced surfboard.

**popover** /ˈpɒpoʊvə/, *n.* an individual batter pudding served with roast beef.

**poppa** /ˈpɒpə/, *n. Colloq.* father.

**poppadum** /ˈpɒpədʌm/, *n.* →**pappadum.** Also, **poppadom.**

**popper** /ˈpɒpə/, *n.* **1.** one who or that which pops. **2.** a utensil for popping maize. **3.** *Colloq.* a press-stud.

**poppet** /ˈpɒpət/, *n.* **1.** Also, **poppet valve.** a valve which in opening is lifted bodily from its seat instead of being hinged at one side. **2.** *Naut.* a piece of shaped wood fitted to close up the slot cut in a boat's gunwhale and top strake for shipping an oar. **3.** a term of endearment for a girl or child. [earlier form of PUPPET]

**poppet head** /ˈ– hɛd/, *n.* headframe of a mine.

**poppied** /ˈpɒpid/, *adj.* **1.** covered or adorned with poppies. **2.** affected by or as by opium; listless.

**popping crease** /ˈpɒpɪŋ kris/, *n.* See **crease**[1] (def. 3b).

**popple** /ˈpɒpəl/, *v.*, **-pled, -pling,** *n.* –*v.i.* **1.** to move in a tumbling, irregular manner, as boiling water. –*n.* **2.** a poppling motion. [ME *pople(n)*; probably imitative]

**poppy** /ˈpɒpi/, *n., pl.* **-pies. 1.** any plant of the family Papaveraceae, esp. species of the genus *Papaver,* comprising herbs with showy flowers of various colours, as *P. somniferum,* the source of opium. **2.** an extract, as opium, from such a plant. **3.** an orangeish-red; scarlet. **4.** *Archit.* →**poppyhead** (def. 2). **5. tall poppy,** a person who is pre-eminent in a particular field; a person with outstanding ability, wealth, status. [ME; OE *popæg, papig,* from VL *papāvum,* for L *papāver*]

**poppycock** /ˈpɒpikɒk/, *n. Colloq.* nonsense; bosh. [Dutch d. *pappekak* soft dung]

**poppyhead** /ˈpɒpihɛd/, *n.* **1.** the seed capsule of the poppy. **2.** Also, **poppy.** *Archit.* a finial or other ornament, often richly carved, as at the top of the upright end of a bench or pew.

**poppy seed** /ˈpɒpi sid/, *n.* seed of the poppy plant, used as a topping for breads, rolls, and biscuits.

**poppyseed loaf** /ˌpɒpisid ˈloʊf/, *n.* a crusty loaf of white bread sprinkled with poppy seeds on the top before baking.

**poppy show** /ˈpɒpi ʃoʊ/, *n. Colloq.* an indecorous showing of a girl's or woman's upper legs and underwear.

**pop-shop** /ˈpɒp-ʃɒp/, *n. Colloq.* →**pawnshop.**

**popsy** /ˈpɒpsi/, *n. Colloq.* a girl, esp. a sexually attractive one.

**populace** /ˈpɒpjələs/, *n.* the common people of a community, as distinguished from the higher classes. [F, from It. *popolaccio,* pejorative of *popolo* PEOPLE]

**popular** /ˈpɒpjələ/, *adj.* **1.** regarded with favour or approval by associates, acquaintances, the general public, etc.: *a popular preacher.* **2.** of, pertaining to, or representing the people, or the common people: *popular discontent.* **3.** prevailing among the people generally: *a popular superstition.* **4.** suited to or intended for the general mass of people: *popular music.* **5.** adapted to the ordinary intelligence or taste: *popular lectures on science.* **6.** suited to the means of ordinary people: *popular prices.* [L *populāris*]

**popular front** /– ˈfrʌnt/, *n.* an alliance of left-wing or progressive political parties, often formed against a common opponent, as against fascism.

**popularise** /ˈpɒpjələraɪz/, *v.t.,* **-rised, -rising.** to make popular. Also, **popularize.** – **popularisation** /pɒpjələraɪˈzeɪʃən/, *n.* – **populariser,** *n.*

**popularity** /pɒpjəˈlærəti/, *n.* **1.** the quality or fact of being popular. **2.** favour enjoyed with the people, the public generally, or a particular set of people.

**popularly** /ˈpɒpjələli/, *adv.* **1.** by the people as a whole; generally. **2.** in a popular manner.

**populate** /ˈpɒpjəleɪt/, *v.t.,* **-lated, -lating. 1.** to inhabit. **2.** to furnish with inhabitants, as by colonisation; people. [ML *populātus,* pp., inhabited]

**population** /pɒpjəˈleɪʃən/, *n.* **1.** the total number of persons inhabiting a country, town, or any district or area. **2.** the body of inhabitants of a place. **3.** the number or body of inhabitants of a particular race or class in a place. **4.** *Statistics.* an aggregate of statistical items. **5.** *Ecol.* **a.** all the individuals of one species in a given area. **b.** the assemblage of plants or animals living in a given area. **6.** the act or process of populating.

**population parameter** /– pəˈræmətə/, *n. Statistics.* a variable entering into the mathematical form of the distribution of a population such that the possible values of the variable correspond to different distributions: *the mean and variance of a population are population parameters.*

**population pyramid** /– ˈpɪrəmɪd/, *n.* a graph showing the distribution of a population in terms of sex, age, etc.

**populous** /ˈpɒpjələs/, *adj.* full of people or inhabitants, as a region; well populated. [L *populōsus*] – **populously,** *adv.* – **populousness,** *n.*

**p.o.q.** /pi oʊ ˈkju/, *v.i.* to depart in a hurry. Also, **P.O.Q.** [*p(iss) o(ff) q(uick)*]

**porae** /ˈpɔreɪ/, *n. N.Z.* →**morwong.** [Maori]

**porangi** /ˈpoʊrʌŋi, -ˈræŋi/, *adj. N.Z. Colloq.* mad, crazy. [Maori]

**porbeagle** /ˈpɔbigəl/, *n.* **1.** a large voracious shark, *Lamna nasus,* of the North Atlantic and Pacific oceans, often found in New Zealand waters and occasionally off the Australian coastline; mackerel shark. **2.** any other species of the genus *Lamna.* [Cornish]

**porcelain** /ˈpɔsələn, ˈpɔslən/, *n.* **1.** a vitreous, more or less translucent, ceramic material; china. **2.** a vessel or object made of this material. [F *porcelaine,* from It. *porcellana,* orig., a kind of shell, from *porcella,* diminutive of *porca* sow, of uncert. orig. (? akin to PORK)]

**porcelain enamel** /– əˈnæməl/, *n. U.S.* →**vitreous enamel.**

**porch** /pɔtʃ/, *n.* **1.** an exterior appendage to a building, forming a covered approach or vestibule to a doorway. **2.** *U.S.* →**veranda. 3.** →**portico.** [ME *porche,* from OF, from L *porticus* porch, portico]

**porch light** /ˈ– laɪt/, *n.* an exterior light near an entrance door of a house.

**porcine** /ˈpɔsaɪn/, *adj.* **1.** of or resembling swine. **2.** swinish, hoggish, or piggish. [L *porcīnus*]

**porcupine** /ˈpɔkjəpaɪn/, *n.* **1.** any of various rodents covered with stout, erectile spines or quills, as the **crested porcupine,** *Hystrix cristata,* of southern Europe and northern Africa, with long spines, and the common porcupine of North America, *Erethizon dorsatum,* with short spines or quills partially concealed by the fur. **2.** *Obs.* →**echidna.** [ME *porkepyn,* from OF *porcespin,* lit., spine-pig. See PORK, SPINE]

porcupine

**porcupine fish** /ˈ– fɪʃ/, *n.* any of various species of spiny, self-inflating fishes of the family Diodontidae, poisonous to eat, and found in Australian and New Zealand waters.

**porcupine grass** /ˈ– gras/, *n.* any species of the genus *Triodia,* comprising spiny-leaved, tussock-forming grasses of inland Australia, and the western U.S.

**pore**[1] /pɔ/, *v.t.,* **pored, poring. 1.** to meditate or ponder intently (usu. fol. by *over, on,* or *upon*). **2.** to gaze earnestly or steadily. **3.** to read or study with steady attention or application. [ME *pouren, puren;* orig. uncert.]

**pore**[2] /pɔ/, *n.* **1.** a minute opening or orifice, as in the skin or a leaf, for perspiration, absorption, etc. **2.** a minute interstice in a rock, etc. [ME, from F, from L *porus,* from Gk *póros* passage]

**poriferan** /pɔˈrɪfərən/, *n.* **1.** any animal of the phylum Porifera, comprising the sponges. –*adj.* **2.** belonging to or pertaining to the Porifera.

**poriferous** /pɔˈrɪfərəs/, *adj.* bearing or having pores. [L *porus* pore + -I- + -FEROUS]

**porion** /ˈpɔriən/, *n., pl.* **poria** /ˈpɔriə/. the most lateral point in the roof of the bony external auditory meatus (or earhole). [NL, from Gk *póros* passage, way]

**pork** /pɔk/, *n.* **1.** the flesh of pigs used as food. **2.** *U.S. Colloq.* appropriations, appointments, etc., by the government for political reasons rather than for public necessity, as for public buildings, river improvements, etc. [ME *porc,* from OF, from L *porcus* hog, pig. See FARROW[1]] – **pork-like,** *adj.*

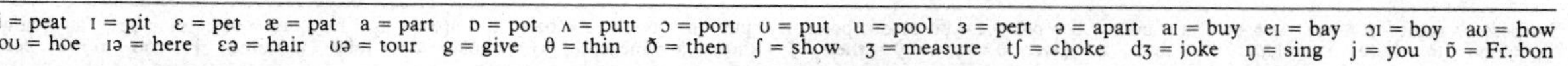
i = peat ɪ = pit ɛ = pet æ = pat a = part ɒ = pot ʌ = putt ɔ = port ʊ = put u = pool ɜ = pert ə = apart aɪ = buy eɪ = bay ɔɪ = boy aʊ = how
oʊ = hoe ɪə = here ɛə = hair ʊə = tour g = give θ = thin ð = then ʃ = show ʒ = measure tʃ = choke dʒ = joke ŋ = sing j = you õ = Fr. bon

**pork barrel** /'– bærəl/, *n. Colloq.* a government appropriation, bill, or policy which supplies funds for local improvements designed to ingratiate legislators with their constituents.

**pork-barrelling** /'pɔk-bærəlɪŋ/, *n.* the use of patronage for political advantage.

**porker** /'pɔkə/, *n.* a pig, esp. one fattened for killing, for pork.

**pork fillet** /pɔk 'fɪlət/, *n.* a tenderloin of pork; fillet (def. 6b).

**pork fritz** /– 'frɪts/, *n.* →**fritz** (def. 3).

**pork-pie** /pɔk-'paɪ/, *n.* a pie made of minced, seasoned pork.

**pork-pie hat** /– 'hæt/, *n.* a felt hat with a snap brim and a crown moulded to a roughly circular depression, the centre of which is elevated so as to fit the head.

**porky** /'pɔki/, *adj.* **1.** pork-like. **2.** *Colloq.* fat.

**porno** /'pɔnoʊ/, *Colloq.* *–n.* **1.** Also, **porn.** pornography. **2.** one who delights in pornography. *–adj.* **3.** pornographic: *a porno film.*

**pornographer** /pɔ'nɒgrəfə/, *n.* one who writes or sells pornography.

**pornography** /pɔ'nɒgrəfi/, *n.* obscene literature, art, or photography, designed to excite sexual desire. [Gk *pornográphos* writing of prostitutes + -Y³] – **pornographic** /pɔnə'græfɪk/, *adj.*

**porn shop** /'pɔn ʃɒp/, *n. Colloq.* →**sex shop.**

**poroporo** /'pɒroʊ,pɒroʊ/, *n. N.Z.* any of various shrubs or small trees of the genus *Solanum,* some species of which have berries which are used as a drug base; bull-a-bull. [Maori]

**porosity** /pɔ'rɒsəti/, *n.* state or quality of being porous. [ME, from ML *porōsitas*]

**porous** /'pɔrəs/, *adj.* **1.** full of pores. **2.** permeable by water, air, or the like. – **porousness,** *n.*

**porphyria** /pɔ'fɪriə/, *n.* a metabolic disorder associated with excess porphyrin in the blood and urine.

**porphyrin** /'pɔfərən/, *n.* any of a group of cyclic compounds formed from four pyrrole units, which combined with iron or magnesium and a protein are found in all cells, such as haemoglobin and chlorophyll.

**porphyritic** /pɔfə'rɪtɪk/, *adj.* **1.** of, pertaining to, containing, or resembling porphyry. **2.** denoting, pertaining to, or resembling the texture or structure characteristic of porphyry.

**porphyroid** /'pɔfərɔɪd/, *n.* **1.** a rock resembling porphyry. **2.** a sedimentary rock which has been altered by some metamorphic agency so as to take on a slaty and more or less perfectly developed porphyritic structure.

**porphyry** /'pɔfəri/, *n., pl.* **-ries. 1.** any igneous rock containing conspicuous phenocrysts in a finegrained or aphanitic groundmass. **2.** a very hard rock, quarried in ancient Egypt, having a dark, purplish red groundmass containing small crystals of felspar. **3.** a sweet variety of white wine. [ME *porfirie,* from AF, from ML *porphyreum,* for L *porphyrītes,* from Gk, from *pórphyros* PURPLE]

**porpoise** /'pɔpəs/, *n., pl.* **-poises,** (*esp. collectively*) **-poise. 1.** any of the gregarious cetaceans constituting the genus *Phocaena* (family Delphinidae), 1.5 to 2.4 metres long, usu. blackish above and paler beneath, and having a blunt, rounded snout, esp. the common porpoise, *P. phocaena,* of both the North Atlantic and Pacific. **2.** a name used erroneously for other cetaceans. [ME *porpeys,* from OF *porpeis,* from LL *porcus piscis* hogfish, for L *porcus marīnus*]

porpoise

**porridge** /'pɒrɪdʒ/, *n.* **1.** a breakfast dish, originating in Scotland, consisting of oatmeal, or the like, water, or milk. **2. stir the porridge,** *Colloq.* to take one's turn relatively late in a pack-rape, etc. [var. of POTTAGE]

**porringer** /'pɒrɪndʒə/, *n.* a dish or basin from which soup, porridge, etc., may be eaten. [alteration of earlier *potager,* from OF, from *potage* POTTAGE]

**port¹** /pɔt/, *n.* **1.** a town or place where ships load or unload. **2.** a place along the coast where ships may take refuge from storms. **3.** *Law.* any place where persons and merchandise are allowed to pass (by water or land) into and out of a country and where customs officers are stationed to inspect or appraise imported goods; port of entry. [ME and OE, from L *portus* harbour, haven]

**port²** /pɔt/, *Naut.* *–n.* **1.** the left-hand side of a ship or aircraft facing forward (opposed to *starboard*). *–adj.* **2.** pertaining to the port. **3.** on the left side of a ship or aircraft. *–v.t.* **4.** to turn (a ship) to the port or left side. [orig. uncert.; perhaps because the larboard side was customarily next to the shore in port]

**port³** /pɔt/, *n.* **1.** any of a class of very sweet, fortified wines, mostly dark red, made in Portugal. **2.** a similar wine made elsewhere. [from *Oporto* (from Pg. *o porto* the port), city in Portugal]

**port⁴** /pɔt/, *n.* **1.** *Naut.* a porthole. **2.** a steel door in the side of a ship for loading and discharging cargo and baggage. **3.** *Mech.* an aperture in the surface of a cylinder, for the passage of steam, air, water, etc. **4.** *Mil.* →**gunport. 5.** *Elect.* a point in a circuit where an external connection is made. **6.** the curved mouthpiece of certain bits. **7.** *Chiefly Scot.* a gate or portal, as of a town or fortress. [ME and OE, from L *porta* gate]

**port⁵** /pɔt/, *v.t.* **1.** *Mil.* to carry (a rifle, etc.) with both hands, in a slanting direction across the front of the body with the barrel or like part near the left shoulder. **2.** to carry (something). *–n.* **3.** *Mil.* the position of a rifle or other weapon when ported. **4.** manner of bearing oneself; carriage or bearing. [F *porter,* from L *portāre* carry; ultimately akin to FARE]

**port⁶** /pɔt/, *n.* **1.** a portmanteau; suitcase. **2.** *Qld.* a school bag, esp. one slung on the back; satchel. **3.** *Qld.* a shopping bag.

**portable** /'pɔtəbəl/, *adj.* **1.** capable of being transported or conveyed. **2.** easily carried or conveyed by hand. **3.** (of a building) able to be removed from its foundations and relocated. **4.** (of benefits, superannuation, etc.) capable of being transferred with a change in job, esp. from one department of the public service to another. **5.** *Obs.* endurable. *–n.* **6.** something that is portable. [ME, from LL *portābilis*] – **portability,** *n.*

**portage** /'pɔtɪdʒ/, *n.* **1.** the act of carrying; carriage. **2.** the carrying of boats, goods, etc., overland from one navigable water to another. **3.** place or course over which this is done. **4.** cost of carriage. [ME, from F, from *porter* carry]

**portal¹** /'pɔtl/, *n.* **1.** a door, gate, or entrance, esp. one of imposing appearance, as in a palace. **2.** Also, **portal frame.** a stiff, rectangular frame used as the skeleton for buildings and other structures. [ME *portale,* from ML, from L *porta* gate]

**portal²** /'pɔtl/, *adj.* **1.** denoting or pertaining to the transverse fissure of the liver. *–n.* **2.** portal vein. [ML *portālis* of a gate]

**portal vein** /'– veɪn/, *n.* the large vein conveying blood to the liver from the veins of the stomach, intestine, spleen, and pancreas.

**portamento** /pɔtə'mɛntoʊ/, *n., pl.* **-ti** /-ti/. *Music.* a passing or gliding from one pitch to another with a smooth progression. [It.: a bearing, carrying, from *portare* carry, from L]

**portative** /'pɔtətɪv/, *adj.* **1.** portable. **2.** having or pertaining to the power or function of carrying. *–n.* **3.** Also, **portative organ.** (formerly) a small, portable organ. [ME *portatif,* from OF, from *porter* carry. See -IVE]

**portcullis** /pɔt'kʌləs/, *n.* a strong grating, as of iron, made to slide in vertical grooves at the sides of a gateway of a fortified place, and let down to prevent passage. [ME *portcullise,* from OF *porte coleice,* from *porte* PORT⁴ (def. 7) + *coleice,* fem. of *coleis* flowing, sliding, from L *cōlātus,* pp., filtered]

portcullis

**Port du Salut,** *n.* →**Port-salut.**

**porte-cochere** /pɔt-kɒ'ʃɛə/, *n.* **1.** a covered carriage entrance, leading into a courtyard. **2.** a porch at the door of a building for sheltering persons entering and leaving carriages. [F: gate for coaches]

**portend** /pɔ'tɛnd/, *v.t.* **1.** to indicate beforehand, or presage, as an omen does. **2.** *Obs.* to signify; mean. [ME, from L *portendere* point out, indicate, portend]

**portent** /'pɔtɛnt/, *n.* **1.** an indication or omen of something about to happen, esp. something momentous. **2.** ominous significance: *an occurrence of dire portent.* **3.** a prodigy or marvel. [L *portentum,* properly neut. pp., presaged]

**portentous** /pɔ'tɛntəs/, *adj.* **1.** of the nature of a portent; momentous. **2.** ominous; ominously indicative. **3.** marvellous; amazing; prodigious. – **portentously,** *adv.* – **portentousness,** *n.*

**porter**[1] /'pɔtə/, *n.* **1.** one employed to carry burdens or luggage, as at a railway station, hotel, etc. **2.** *U.S.* a railway carriage attendant. [ME *portour,* from OF *porteour,* from L *portāre* carry]

**porter**[2] /'pɔtə/, *n.* **1.** one who has charge of a door or gate; a doorkeeper; a janitor. **2.** *Rom. Cath. Ch.* →**ostiary.** [ME, from AF, from LL *portārius,* from L *porta* gate]

**porter**[3] /'pɔtə/, *n.* a heavy, dark brown beer made with malt browned by drying at a high temperature. [short for *porter's ale,* apparently orig. brewed for porters]

**porterage** /'pɔtərɪdʒ/, *n.* **1.** the work of a porter or carrier. **2.** the charge for such work.

**portergaff** /'pɔtəgæf/, *n.* a mixed drink of porter with ginger beer or lemonade. [PORTER[3] + (SHANDY)GAFF]

**porterhouse** /'pɔtəhaus/, *n.* **1.** Also, **porterhouse steak.** a thick cut T-bone steak from the rump end of the loin. **2.** *Archaic.* a house where porter and other liquors are retailed. **3.** *Archaic.* →**steakhouse.**

**portfolio** /pɔt'fouliou/, *n., pl.* **-lios. 1.** a portable case for loose papers, prints, etc. **2.** such a case for carrying documents of a state department. **3.** the office or post of a minister of state or member of a cabinet. **4.** an itemised account or list of financial assets, as securities, shares, discount paper, etc., of an investment organisation, bank or other investor. [It. *portafoglio,* from *porta,* impv. of *portare* carry (from L) + *foglio* leaf, sheet (from L *folium*)]

**porthole** /'pɔthoul/, *n.* an aperture in the side of a ship, for admitting light and air.

**portico** /'pɔtəkou/, *n., pl.* **-coes, -cos.** a structure consisting of a roof supported by columns or piers, forming the entrance to a temple, church, house, etc. [It., from L *porticus* porch, portico]

**portiere** /pɔti'ɛə/, *n.* a curtain hung at a doorway, either to replace the door or merely for decoration. [F]

**porting** /'pɔtɪŋ/, *n.* the ports of a machine collectively. See **port**[4] (def. 3).

**portion** /'pɔʃən/, *n.* **1.** a part of any whole, whether actually separated from it or not: *a portion of the manuscript is illegible.* **2.** the part of a whole allotted to or belonging to a person or group; a share. **3.** a quantity of food served for one person. **4.** the part of an estate that goes to an heir or next of kin. **5.** the money, goods, or estate which a woman brings to her husband at marriage; a dowry. **6.** that which is allotted to a person by God or fate. *–v.t.* **7.** to divide into or distribute in portions or shares; parcel (oft. fol. by *out*). **8.** to furnish with a portion, inheritance, or dowry. **9.** to provide with a lot or fate. [ME *porcion,* from OF, from L *portio* share, part; akin to L *pars* part] – **portionless,** *adj.*

**Port Jackson fig,** *n.* a large umbrageous tree, *Ficus rubiginosa,* of coastal areas of New South Wales, characterised by the rust colour of the lower surface of the leaves; rusty fig. [named after *Port Jackson,* N.S.W.]

**Port Jackson pine,** *n.* a cypress pine, *Callitris rhomboidia,* found in south-eastern Australia. [named after *Port Jackson,* N.S.W.]

**Port Jackson rose,** *n.* →**native rose.** [named after *Port Jackson,* N.S.W.]

**Port Jackson shark,** *n.* a primitive mollusc-eating shark, *Heterodontus portusjacksoni,* of eastern and southern Australian waters. [named after *Port Jackson,* N.S.W.]

**Portland cement** /pɔtlənd sə'mɛnt/, *n.* a kind of hydraulic cement usu. made by burning a mixture of limestone and clay in a kiln. [named after the Isle of *Portland,* Dorset, England]

**Portland stone** /– 'stoun/, *n.* a type of limestone, used in building. [quarried on the Isle of *Portland,* Dorset, England]

**portly** /'pɔtli/, *adj.,* **-lier, -liest. 1.** large in person; stout; corpulent. **2.** stately, dignified, or imposing. [PORT[5], *n.* + -LY] – **portliness,** *n.*

**portmanteau** /pɔt'mæntou/, *n., pl.* **-teaus, -teaux.** a case or bag to carry clothing, etc., while travelling, esp. a leather case which opens into two halves. Also, **port.** [F *portemanteau* cloak-carrier. See PORT[5], MANTLE]

**portmanteau word** /'– wɜd/, *n.* a word made by telescoping or blending two other words, as *brunch* for *breakfast* and *lunch.* See **blend** (def. 8).

**port of call,** *n.* a port where ships stop briefly to take on stores or undergo repairs.

**port of entry,** *n.* →**port**[1] (def. 3).

**portrait** /'pɔtrət, 'pɔtreɪt/, *n.* **1.** a likeness of a person, esp. of the face, usu. made from life. **2.** a verbal picture, usu. of a person. **3.** *Print.* a page or illustration larger in depth than width. [F, orig. pp. of *portraire,* from LL *prōtrahere* portray, from L: bring forward]

**portraitist** /'pɔtrətəst/, *n.* a portrait painter.

**portraiture** /'pɔtrətʃə/, *n.* **1.** the art of portraying. **2.** a pictorial representation; a portrait. **3.** a verbal picture. [ME *purtreyture,* from OF *portraiture,* from *portrait* PORTRAIT]

**portray** /pɔ'treɪ/, *v.t.* **1.** to represent by a drawing, painting, carving, or the like. **2.** to represent dramatically, as on the stage. **3.** to depict in words; describe graphically. [ME, from OF *portraire,* from LL *prōtrahere* depict, from L: draw forth] – **portrayable,** *adj.* – **portrayer,** *n.*

**portrayal** /pɔ'treɪəl/, *n.* **1.** the act of portraying. **2.** a representation portraying something.

**portress** /'pɔtrəs/, *n.* a female porter or doorkeeper.

**Port-salut** /pɔt-sə'lu/, *n.* a semi-hard, cow's milk cheese, mild in flavour but with a strong and pungent odour, usu. made in flat, round shapes weighing about 1.5 kg. [made orig. in 1865, in the Trappist Abbey, *Port du Salut,* France]

**portugaise sauce** /ˌpɔtʃugeɪz 'sɔs/, *n.* a sauce for meat dishes made with tomatoes and butter or oil and flavoured with onion and garlic. [F *Portugaise* Portugese]

**Portugal** /'pɔtʃəgəl/, *n.* a republic in south-western Europe, on the Iberian peninsula west of Spain.

**Portuguese** /pɔtʃə'giz/, *adj.* **1.** of or pertaining to Portugal, its people, or their language. *–n.* **2.** a native or inhabitant of Portugal. **3.** the Romance language of Portugal and Brazil.

**Portuguese man-of-war** /– mæn-əv-'wɔ/, *n.* **1.** *Brit., U.S.* →**bluebottle** (def. 1). **2.** →**jellyfish.**

**portulaca** /pɔtʃə'lækə/, *n.* any plant of the genus *Portulaca,* which comprises herbs with thick, succulent leaves and variously coloured flowers, as *P. grandiflora,* cultivated in gardens, and *P. oleracea,* the common purslane. [NL, from L: purslane]

**portulacaceous** /pɔtʃələ'keɪʃəs/, *adj.* belonging to the Portulacaceae, or portulaca family of plants.

**port wine magnolia,** *n.* **1.** a large evergreen shrub, *Michelia figo,* native to China, with glossy leaves, and small red and creamy flowers with a heavy fragrance. **2.** →**magnolia** (def. 2).

**pos.,** **1.** positive. **2.** possessive.

**pose**[1] /pouz/, *v.,* **posed, posing,** *n.* *–v.i.* **1.** to affect a particular character as with a view to the impression made on others. **2.** to present oneself before others: *to pose as a judge of literature.* **3.** to assume or hold a position or attitude for some artistic purpose. *–v.t.* **4.** to place in a suitable position or attitude for a picture, tableau, or the like: *to pose a group for a photograph.* **5.** to assert, state, or propound: *to pose a hard problem.* **6.** *Archaic.* to put or place. *–n.* **7.** attitude or posture of body: *her pose had a kind of defiance in it.* **8.** attitude assumed in thought or conduct. **9.** the act or period of posing, as for a picture. **10.** a position or attitude assumed in posing, or exhibited by a figure in a picture, sculptural work, tableau, or the like. **11.** a studied attitude or mere affectation, as of some character, quality, sentiment, or course: *his liberalism is all a pose.* [ME, from OF *poser,* from LL *pausāre* lay down (a sense due to confusion with L *pōnere* place, put), from L: halt, cease]

**pose**[2] /pouz/, *v.t.,* **posed, posing. 1.** to embarrass by a difficult question or problem. **2.** *Obs.* to examine by putting questions. [aphetic var. of obs. *appose,* var. of OPPOSE, used in sense of L *appōnere* put to]

**poser**[1] /'pouzə/, *n.* one who poses. [POSE[1] + -ER[1]]

**poser**[2] /'pouzə/, *n.* a question or problem that puzzles. [POSE[2] + -ER[1]]

**poseur** /poʊ'zɜ/, *n.* one who affects a particular pose (def. 11) to impress others. [F, from *poser* POSE[1]]

**posh** /pɒʃ/, *Colloq.* –*adj.* **1.** elegant; luxurious; smart; first-class. –*v.t.* **2.** to make smart or elegant (fol. by *up*). [? *p*(*ort*) *o*(*ut*), *s*(*tarboard*) *h*(*ome*), orig. with ref. to the better (i.e. cooler) accommodation on vessels sailing from Britain to India, Australia, etc.] – **poshly,** *adv.* – **poshness,** *n.*

**posigrade rocket** /poʊzəgreɪd 'rɒkət/, *n.* a small rocket which fires in the direction of flight, often used to separate an expended stage from a multistage rocket.

**posit** /'pɒzət/, *v.t.* **1.** to place, put, or set. **2.** to lay down or assume as a fact or principle; affirm; postulate. [L *positus,* pp., placed]

**position** /pə'zɪʃən/, *n.* **1.** condition with reference to place; location. **2.** a place occupied or to be occupied; site: *a fortified position.* **3.** proper or appropriate place: *out of position.* **4.** situation or condition, esp. with relation to circumstances: *to be in an awkward position.* **5.** status or standing. **6.** high standing, as in society. **7.** a post of employment: *a position in a bank.* **8.** manner of being placed, disposed, or arranged: *the relative position of the hands of a clock.* **9.** posture or attitude of body. **10.** mental attitude; way of viewing a matter; stand: *one's position on a public question.* **11.** condition (of affairs, etc.). **12.** the act of positing. **13.** that which is posited. **14.** *Class. Pros.* the situation of a short vowel before two or more consonants or their equivalent, making the syllable metrically long. **15.** *Music.* **a.** one of the points on the fingerboard of a stringed instrument. **b.** a shift of the slide of a trombone. –*v.t.* **16.** to put in a particular or appropriate position; place. **17.** to determine the position of; locate. [ME, from L *positio.* Cf. POSIT, POSE[1]] – **positional,** *adj.*

**positive** /'pɒzətɪv/, *adj.* **1.** explicitly laid down or expressed: *a positive declaration.* **2.** arbitrarily laid down; determined by enactment or convention (opposed to *natural*): *positive law.* **3.** admitting of no question: *positive proof.* **4.** stated; express; emphatic. **5.** confident in opinion or assertion, as a person; fully assured. **6.** overconfident or dogmatic. **7.** without relation to or comparison with other things; absolute (opposed to *relative* and *comparative*). **8.** *Colloq.* downright; out-and-out. **9.** possessing an actual force, being, existence, etc. **10.** *Philos.* concerned with or based on matters of experience: *positive philosophy.* See **positivism** (def. 2). **11.** practical; not speculative or theoretical. **12.** characterised by optimism or hopefulness: *a positive attitude.* **13.** consisting in or characterised by the presence or possession of distinguishing or marked qualities or features (opposed to *negative*): *light is positive, darkness negative.* **14.** denoting the presence of such qualities, as a term. **15.** measured or proceeding in a direction assumed as that of increase, progress, or onward motion. **16.** *Elect.* denoting or pertaining to the kind of electricity developed on glass when rubbed with silk, or the kind of electricity present at that pole where electrons enter, or return to, an electric generator; having a deficiency of electrons. **17.** *Chem.* (of an element or radical) basic. **18.** *Photog.* showing the lights and shades as seen in the original, as a print from a negative. **19.** *Gram.* being, denoting, or pertaining to the initial degree of the comparison of adjectives and adverbs, as English *smooth* in contrast to *smoother* and *smoothest.* **20.** *Maths.* denoting a quantity greater than zero. **21.** *Biol.* orientated or moving towards the focus of excitation: *a positive tropism.* **22.** *Bacteriol.* (of blood, affected tissue, etc.) showing the presence of an organism which causes a disease. **23.** *Mach.* denoting or pertaining to a process or machine part having a fixed or certain operation, esp. as the result of elimination of play, free motion, etc.: *positive lubrication.* –*n.* **24.** something positive. **25.** a positive quality or characteristic. **26.** a positive quantity or symbol. **27.** *Photog.* a positive picture. **28.** *Gram.* **a.** the positive degree. **b.** a form in it. [L *positīvus;* replacing ME *positif,* from OF] – **positiveness,** *n.*

**positive feedback** /– 'fidbæk/, *n.* See **feedback** (def. 2).

**positive geotropism** /– dʒi'ɒtrəpɪzəm/, *n.* geotropism orientated towards gravity. See **negative geotropism.**

**positively** /'pɒzətɪvli/, *adv.* absolutely; decidedly; definitely; undoubtedly.

**positive organ** /pɒsətɪv 'ɔgən/, *n.* (formerly) a kind of small fixed organ (opposed to *portative organ*).

**positivism** /'pɒzətɪvɪzəm/, *n.* **1.** the state or quality of being positive; definiteness; assurance. **2.** a philosophical system founded by Comte, concerned with positive facts and phenomena, and excluding speculation upon ultimate causes or origins. – **positivist,** *adj., n.* – **positivistic** /pɒzətə'vɪstɪk/, *adj.*

**positron** /'pɒzətrɒn/, *n.* an elementary particle with positive charge and mass equal to that of the electron; the antiparticle corresponding to the electron. [POSIT(IVE) + (ELECT)RON]

**positronium** /pɒzə'troʊniəm/, *n.* an unstable unit, resembling an atom of hydrogen, except that it consists of a positron and an electron.

**posology** /pə'sɒlədʒi/, *n.* the branch of medicine dealing with the determination of dosage. [Gk *póso(s)* how much + -LOGY]

**poss.,** **1.** possession. **2.** possessive. **3.** possible.

**posse** /'pɒsi/, *n. Chiefly U.S.* **1.** →**posse comitatus. 2.** a body or force armed with legal authority. [ML: power, force, n. use of L inf., to be able, have power. See POTENT]

**posse comitatus** /– kɒmə'tatəs/, *n.* **1.** the body of men that a sheriff is empowered to call to assist him in preserving the peace, making arrests, and serving writs. **2.** a body of men so called into service. [ML: force of the county]

**posser** /'pɒsə/, *n.* **1.** a pestle, as in goldmining. **2.** a stick or other similar device for stirring clothes in the wash; dolly. [Brit. d. *poss* to pound + -ER[1]]

**possess** /pə'zɛs/, *v.t.* **1.** to have as property; to have belonging to one. **2.** to have as a faculty, quality, or the like: *to possess courage.* **3.** to have knowledge of. **4.** to impart; inform; familiarise. **5.** to keep or maintain (oneself, one's mind, etc.) in a certain state, as of peace, patience, etc. **6.** to maintain control over (oneself, one's mind, etc.). **7.** (of a spirit, esp. an evil one) to occupy and control, or dominate from within, as a person. **8.** (of a feeling, idea, etc.) to dominate or actuate after the manner of such a spirit. **9.** to make (one) owner, holder, or master, as of property, information, etc. **10.** to cause to be dominated or influenced, as by a feeling, idea, etc.; imbue (*with*). **11.** (of a man) to have sexual intercourse with. **12.** *Obs.* to occupy or hold. **13.** *Archaic.* to seize or take. **14.** *Archaic.* to gain or win. [backformation from *possessor,* ME *possessour,* from L *possessor*] – **possessor,** *n.* – **possessorship,** *n.*

**possessed** /pə'zɛst/, *adj.* **1.** moved by a strong feeling, madness, or some supernatural agency; frenzied (oft. fol. by *by, of,* or *with*). **2.** self-possessed; calm; poised. **3. possessed of,** having; possessing.

**possession** /pə'zɛʃən/, *n.* **1.** the act or fact of possessing. **2.** the state of being possessed. **3.** ownership. **4.** *Law.* actual holding or occupancy, either with or without rights of ownership. **5.** a thing possessed. **6.** (*pl.*) property or wealth. **7.** a territorial dominion of a state. **8.** control over oneself, one's mind, etc. **9.** domination or actuation by a feeling, idea, etc. **10.** the feeling or idea itself. [ME, from L *possessio*]

**possessive** /pə'zɛsɪv/, *adj.* **1.** of or pertaining to possession or ownership. **2.** exerting or seeking to exert excessive influence on the affections, behaviour, etc., of others: *a possessive wife.* **3.** *Gram.* **a.** indicating possession, ownership, origin, etc. **b.** denoting a case that indicates possession, ownership, origin, etc. –*n. Gram.* **4.** the possessive case. **5.** a form in the possessive. – **possessively,** *adv.* – **possessiveness,** *n.*

**possessory** /pə'zɛsəri/, *adj.* **1.** pertaining to a possessor or to possession. **2.** arising from possession: *a possessory interest.* **3.** having possession.

**posset** /'pɒsət/, *n.* **1.** a drink made of hot milk curdled with ale, wine, or the like, often sweetened and spiced. **2.** a cold or frozen dessert made with lemon rind and juice, whipped cream and egg whites. [late ME *poshote, possot,* ? OE **poswǣt* drink good for cold, from *pos* cold in the head + *wǣt* drink]

**possibility** /pɒsə'bɪləti/, *n., pl.* **-ties. 1.** the state or fact of being possible: *the possibility of error.* **2.** a possible thing or person.

**possible** /'pɒsəbəl/, *adj.* **1.** that may or can be, exist, happen, be done, be used, etc.: *no possible cure.* **2.** that may be true or a fact, or may perhaps be the case, as something concerning which one has no knowledge to the contrary: *it is possible that he went.* [ME, from L *possibilis*]

**possibly** /ˈpɒsəbli/, *adv.* **1.** perhaps or maybe. **2.** in a possible manner. **3.** by any possibility.

**possie** /ˈpɒzi/, *n. Colloq.* a place; position.

**possum** /ˈpɒsəm/, *n.* **1.** Also, **opossum.** any of many herbivorous, largely arboreal, Australian marsupials, esp. of the genera *Trichosurus, Pseudochirus* and *Petaurus,* ranging in size from the mouse-like pigmy possum to the cat-sized brush-tailed possum, having both pairs of limbs well-developed for climbing and grasping, and a long, often prehensile, tail. **2.** *Colloq.* →**opossum. 3. play possum,** *Colloq.* to dissemble; feign illness or death.

possum: brush-tailed possum

**post**[1] /poʊst/, *n.* **1.** a strong piece of timber, metal, or the like, set upright as a support, a point of attachment, a mark, a place for displaying notices, etc. **2.** *Horseracing.* a pole on a racecourse marking a specific distance, or the starting or finishing points for races. *–v.t.* **3.** to affix (a notice, etc.) to a post, wall, or the like. **4.** to bring to public notice by or as by a placard: *to post a reward.* **5.** to denounce by a public notice or declaration: *to post a person as a coward.* **6.** to enter the name of in a published list. **7.** to publish the name of (a ship) as missing or lost. **8.** to placard (a wall, etc.) with notices or bills. [ME and OE, from L *postis*]

**post**[2] /poʊst/, *n.* **1.** a position of duty, employment, or trust to which one is assigned or appointed: *a diplomatic post.* **2.** the station, or round of a soldier, sentry, or other person on duty. **3.** a military station with permanent buildings. **4.** *U.S.* the body of troops occupying a military station. **5.** →**trading post. 6.** *Mil.* either of two bugle calls (**first post** and **last post**) giving notice of the hour for retiring, as for the night. *–v.t.* **7.** to station at a post or place as a sentry or for some other purpose. **8.** *Mil.* to transfer away to another unit or command. [F *poste,* from It. *posto,* from L *positus,* pp., placed, put. Cf. POSITION]

**post**[3] /poʊst/, *n.* **1.** a single collection or delivery of letters, packages, etc. **2.** the letters, packages, etc., themselves; mail. **3.** an established service or system for the conveyance of letters, etc., esp. under government authority. **4.** →**post office. 5.** →**post-box. 6.** (formerly) one of a series of stations along a route, for furnishing relays of men and horses for carrying letters, etc. **7.** one who travels express, esp. over a fixed route with letters, etc. **8.** any of three sizes of paper, most commonly in use before metrication: **large post,** $16\frac{1}{2} \times 21$ inches, **small post,** $15\frac{1}{4} \times 19$ inches, and **pinched post,** $14\frac{1}{2} \times 18\frac{1}{2}$ inches. *–v.t.* **9.** to place (a letter, etc.) in a post-box, post office, etc., for transmission. **10.** *Bookkeeping.* **a.** to transfer (an entry or item), as from the journal to the ledger. **b.** to enter (an item) in due place and form. **c.** to make all the requisite entries in (the ledger, etc.). **11.** to supply with up-to-date information; inform: *please keep me posted about the financial developments. –v.i.* **12.** to travel with relays of horses. **13.** to travel with speed; go or pass rapidly; hasten. *–adv.* **14.** by post or courier. **15.** with post-horses, or by posting. **16.** with speed or haste; posthaste. [F *poste,* from It. *posta,* from *posita,* pp. fem., placed, put. Cf. POST[2]]

**post**[4] /poʊst/, *n.* an examination held after the main examination for those who were absent from the first one or whose result in the first needs confirmation by a second. [? shortened form of POSTPONE]

**post-,** a prefix meaning 'behind', 'after', occurring originally in words from the Latin, but now freely used as an English formative: *post-Elizabethan, postfix, postgraduate.* Cf. **ante-** and **pre-**. [L, representing *post,* adv. and prep.]

**postage** /ˈpoʊstɪdʒ/, *n.* the charge for the conveyance of a letter or other matter sent by post, usu. prepaid by means of a stamp or stamps.

**postage stamp** /ˈ– stæmp/, *n.* an official stamp on an envelope, postcard, etc., in the form of a printed, adhesive label, as evidence of prepayment of a designated postage.

**postal** /ˈpoʊstl/, *adj.* **1.** of or pertaining to the post office or the carriage of mails. *–n.* **2.** *U.S. Colloq.* a postal card.

**postal card** /ˈ– kad/, *n. U.S.* **1.** →**lettercard. 2.** →**postcard.**

**postal chess** /ˈ– tʃɛs/, *n.* →**correspondence chess.**

**postal order** /ˈ– ɔdə/, *n.* an order for the payment of a small amount of money, bought from and generally cashed at a post office. Also, **postal note.** Cf. **money order.**

**postal shoot** /ˈ– ʃut/, *n.* a match or series of matches in which competitors shoot on their home ranges, and send the scores to other competitors by mail.

**postal union** /ˈ– junjən/, *n.* an agreement among governments of many countries for the regulation of international post office business.

**postal vote** /ˈ– voʊt/, *n.* a vote recorded on a ballot paper which is then sent by post to an electoral office.

**post-and-beam construction** /poʊst-ən-ˈbim kənstrʌkʃən/, *n.* a constructional system in which the load is borne by the posts and beams, and not by the walls. Also, **post-and-lintel construction.**

**post-and-rail fence** /ˌpoʊst-ən-reɪl ˈfɛns/, *n.* a wooden fence constructed from posts with connecting rails slotted into them.

post-and-rail fence

**post-and-rail tea** /– ˈti/, *n. Colloq.* strong bush tea.

**postaxial** /poʊstˈæksiəl/, *adj.* behind the body axis, as the posterior part of the limb axis.

**post-bag** /ˈpoʊst-bæg/, *n.* **1.** →**mailbag. 2.** (considered collectively) letters received.

**post bellum** /poʊst ˈbɛləm/, *adv.* after the war. [L]

**post-bellum** /poʊst-ˈbɛləm/, *adj.* occurring after the war, esp. the American Civil War.

**post-box** /ˈpoʊst-bɒks/, *n.* a letterbox (def. 1), esp. one on a public thoroughfare.

**postboy** /ˈpoʊstbɔɪ/, *n.* **1.** a boy or man who rides post or carries letters. **2.** →**postilion.**

**postcard** /ˈpoʊstkad/, *n.* a card of standard size, often having a photograph, picture, etc., on one side, on which a message may be written and sent by post.

**post-chaise** /ˈpoʊst-ʃeɪz/, *n.* a hired coach drawn by horses changed at each stage, used for rapid travelling in the 18th and early 19th centuries.

**postcibal** /poʊstˈsaɪbəl/, *adj.* occurring after the taking of food. [POST- + L *cibus* food + -AL[1]]

**postclassical** /poʊstˈklæsɪkəl/, *adj.* denoting, or occurring during, a period after a classical period, as of literature, language, etc.

**postcode** /ˈpoʊstkoʊd/, *n.* a group of numbers or letters added as part of the address and intended to facilitate the delivery of mail.

**postdate** /poʊstˈdeɪt/, *v.t.,* **-dated, -dating. 1.** to date (a document, cheque, invoice, etc.) with a date later than the current date. **2.** to follow in time.

**postdiluvian** /poʊstdəˈluviən/, *adj.* **1.** existing or occurring after the Flood, the universal deluge recorded as having occurred in the days of Noah. *–n.* **2.** one who has lived since the Flood. [POST- + *diluvian.* See DILUVIAL]

**postdoctoral** /poʊstˈdɒktərəl/, *adj.* of or pertaining to studies or research work undertaken above the level of a doctorate.

**poster**[1] /ˈpoʊstə/, *n.* **1.** a large placard or bill, often incorporating photographs or illustrations, and posted for advertisement or publicity or for decorative purposes. **2.** Also, **newsposter.** a sheet of paper advertising the headlines of the day, used for display by vendors of newspapers. **3.** →**billposter.** [POST[1], *v.* + -ER[1]]

**poster**[2] /ˈpoʊstə/, *n. Aus. Rules. Colloq.* a kick which hits one of the goalposts, scoring a point. [POST[1], *n.* + -ER[1]]

**poster colour** /ˈ– kʌlə/, *n.* opaque watercolour paint. Also, **poster paint.**

**poste restante** /poʊst rəsˈtɒnt/, *n.* a department in a post office where letters may be kept until they are called for. [F: standing post]

**posterior** /pɒsˈtɪəriə/, *adj.* **1.** situated behind, or hinder (opposed to *anterior*). **2.** coming after in order, as in a series. **3.** coming after in time; later; subsequent (sometimes fol. by *to*). **4.** *Zool.* pertaining to the caudal end of the body. **5.** *Anat.* of or pertaining to the dorsal side of man. **6.** *Bot.* (of an axillary flower) on the side next to the main axis. *–n.* **7.** (*sometimes pl.*) the hinder parts of the body; the buttocks. [L, compar. of *posterus* coming after] – **posteriorly,** *adv.*

**posteriority** /pɒsˌtɪəri'ɒrəti/, *n.* posterior position or date.

**posterity** /pɒ'stɛrəti/, *n.* **1.** succeeding generations collectively. **2.** descendants collectively. [ME *posterite,* from L *posteritas*]

**postern** /'pɒstən/, *n.* **1.** a back door or gate. **2.** any lesser or private entrance. *–adj.* **3.** like or pertaining to a postern. [ME, from OF *posterne,* for *posterle,* from LL *posterula,* diminutive of L *posterus* behind]

**poster paint** /'poustə peɪnt/, *n.* →**poster colour.**

**postfix** /'poustfɪks/, *v.t.* **1.** to affix at the end of something; append; suffix. *–n.* **2.** something postfixed. **3.** *Rare.* a suffix. [POST- + FIX, modelled on PREFIX]

**post-free** /'poust-fri/, *adj.* exempt from postal charges.

**postglacial** /poust'gleɪʃəl/, *adj.* denoting or occurring during a period following a glacial epoch.

**postgraduate** /poust'grædʒuət/, *n.* **1.** one studying at a university for a higher degree. *–adj.* **2.** of or pertaining to courses of study offered for a higher degree. Also, **post-graduate.**

**posthaste** /poust'heɪst/, *adv.* **1.** with all possible speed or promptness: *to come posthaste.* *–n.* **2.** *Archaic.* great haste. [POST[3] + HASTE]

**post-hole digger** /'poust-houl dɪgə/, *n.* a power driven auger on a vertical shaft or spindle, for digging holes in which to set posts, esp. for a fence.

**post-horn** /'poust-hɔn/, *n.* a simple brass instrument without keys, formerly used by coachmen on post-chaises.

**post-horse** /'poust-hɔs/, *n.* a horse kept for the use of persons riding post or for hire by travellers.

**posthum.,** **1.** posthumous. **2.** posthumously.

**posthumous** /'pɒstʃəməs/, *adj.* **1.** (of books, music, medals, etc.) published or awarded after a person's death. **2.** born after the death of the father. **3.** arising, existing, or continuing after one's death. [L *posthumus,* alteration (by erroneous association with *humus* earth, ground, as if referring to burial) of *postumus* last] – **posthumously,** *adv.*

**posthypnotic** /pousthɪp'nɒtɪk/, *adj.* **1.** of or pertaining to the period following a hypnotic trance. **2.** (of a suggestion) made during a hypnotic trance so as to be effective when the subject awakes.

**postiche** /pɒs'tiʃ/, *adj.* **1.** superadded, esp. inappropriately, as a sculptural or architectural ornament. **2.** artificial, counterfeit, or false. *–n.* **3.** an imitation or substitute. **4.** pretence. **5.** →**hairpiece.** [F, from It. *(ap)posticcio,* from L *appositīcius* put on, factitious, false]

**posticous** /pɒs'tikəs, -'taɪ-/, *adj. Bot.* hinder; posterior. [L *postīcus*]

**postie** /'pousti/, *n. Colloq.* a postman.

**postilion** /pɒs'tɪljən/, *n.* one who rides the near horse of the leaders when four or more horses are used to draw a carriage, or who rides the near horse when only one pair is used. Also, **postillion.** [F *postillon,* from It. *postiglione,* from *posta* POST[3]]

**post-impressionism** /poust-ɪm'prɛʃənɪzəm/, *n.* a movement in modern painting about 1870-1920, which rejected the impressionists' imitation of natural forms in favour of other forms, but accepted their use of pure colour as a means of intensifying permanence and solidity, movement, pattern, etc.

**posting** /'poustɪŋ/, *n.* the transfer of service personnel away to another unit or command.

**postliminy** /poust'lɪməni/, *n.* the right by which persons and things taken in war are restored to their former status when coming again under the power of the nation to which they belonged. [L *postlīminium*]

**postlude** /'poustlud/, *n.* **1.** a concluding piece of music. **2.** a voluntary at the end of a church service. [POST- + L *lūdus* game; modelled on PRELUDE]

**postman** /'poustmən/, *n., pl.* **-men.** **1.** a postal employee who sorts and delivers letters and parcels, or collects letters from postboxes. **2.** *Obs.* courier.

**postmark** /'poustmak/, *n.* **1.** an official mark stamped on letters or other mail, to cancel the postage stamp, indicate the place and date of sending or of receipt, etc. *–v.t.* **2.** to stamp with a postmark.

**postmaster** /'poustmastə/, *n.* **1.** a man in charge of a post office. **2.** *Obs.* the master of a station for furnishing post-horses for travellers. – **postmastership,** *n.*

**postmaster general** /– 'dʒɛnrəl/, *n., pl.* **postmasters general.** the minister at the head of the postal system of a country.

**postmedieval** /poustmɛdi'ivəl/, *adj.* after the Middle Ages. Also, **postmediaeval.**

**postmeridian** /poustmə'rɪdiən/, *adj.* **1.** occurring after noon. **2.** of or pertaining to the afternoon.

**post meridiem** /poust mə'rɪdiəm/, *adv.* after noon; used in specifying the hour, usu. in the abbreviated form *p.m.* [L]

**postmillennial** /poustmə'lɛniəl/, *adj.* of or pertaining to the period following the millennium.

**postmillennialism** /poustmə'lɛniəlɪzəm/, *n.* the doctrine or belief that the second coming of Christ will follow the millennium. – **postmillennialist,** *n.*

**postmistress** /'poustmɪstrəs/, *n.* a woman in charge of a post office.

**post-mortem** /'poust-mɔtəm/, *adj.;* /poust-'mɔtəm/, *n.* *–adj.* **1.** subsequent to death, as an examination of the body. *–n.* **2.** a post-mortem examination. **3.** an examination of the causes of failure of a plan, project, or the like. **4.** an evaluation of a party, concert, holiday, etc., after the event. [L: after death]

**post-mortem examination** /– əgzæmə'neɪʃən/, *n.* →**autopsy.**

**postnatal** /'poustneɪtl/, *adj.;* /poust'neɪtl/, *n.* *–adj.* **1.** subsequent to birth. *–n.* **2.** a postnatal examination (of the mother).

**postnuptial** /poust'nʌpʃəl/, *adj.* of or pertaining to the period after marriage.

**post-obit** /poust-'oubət, -'ɒbət/, *adj.* effective after a particular person's death. [short for POST OBITUM]

**post-obit bond** /'– bɒnd/, *n.* a bond paying a sum of money after the death of some specified person, from whose estate the giver of the bond expects to inherit.

**post obitum** /poust 'ɒbətəm/, *adv.* after death. [L]

**post-object art** /poust-ˌɒbdʒɛkt 'at/, *n.* art not concerned with producing a material object but with sharing the intellectual and emotional process involved in creating something.

**post office** /'poust ɒfəs/, *n.* **1.** a department of government responsible for a country's postal and telecommunications services. **2.** a local office of this department for receiving, distributing, and transmitting mail, selling postage stamps, providing telecommunications services, etc. – **post-office,** *adj.*

**post-office box** /'poust-ɒfəs bɒks/, *n.* **1.** (in a post office) a numbered compartment into which letters addressed to a particular individual or firm are put until called for. *Abbrev.:* P.O. Box. **2.** *Elect.* a portable type of Wheatstone bridge in which the resistances are contained in a box and variations in the resistance of the arms are made by inserting and removing plugs.

**post-operative** /poust-'ɒpərətɪv/, *adj.* of or pertaining to the period of time following a surgical operation.

**postorbital** /poust'ɔbətl/, *adj.* situated behind the orbit or socket of the eye.

**post-paid** /'poust-peɪd/, *adj.* with the postage prepaid.

**post-partum** /'poust-patəm/, *adj.* occurring after childbirth. [L]

**postpone** /poust'poun, pous'poun/, *v.,* **-poned, -poning.** *–v.t.* **1.** to put off to a later time; defer: *he postponed his departure an hour.* **2.** to place after in order of importance or estimation; subordinate: *to postpone private ambitions to the public welfare.* [L *postpōnere*] – **postponable,** *adj.* – **postponement,** *n.* – **postponer,** *n.*

**postposition** /poustpə'zɪʃən/, *n.* **1.** the act of placing after. **2.** the state of being so placed. **3.** *Gram.* a word placed after another as a modifier or to show its relation to other parts of the sentence, as in *attorney general, the man afloat.* [POST- + POSITION. Cf. PREPOSITION]

**postpositive** /poust'pɒzətɪv/, *Gram.* *–adj.* **1.** placed after. *–n.* **2.** a postposition. – **postpositively,** *adv.*

**post-prandial** /poust-'prændiəl/, *adj.* after a meal. [POST- + L *prandium* meal + -AL[1]]

**postrevolutionary** /poustrɛvə'luʃənri/, *adj.* after a revolution.

**postrider** /'poustraɪdə/, *n.* one who rides post; a mounted mail carrier.

**postroad** /'poustroud/, *n.* **1.** (formerly) a road with stations for furnishing horses for postriders, mail coaches, or travellers. **2.** a road or route over which mail is carried.

**postscript** /ˈpoʊstskrɪpt/, *n.* **1.** a paragraph, sentence, etc., added to a letter which has already been concluded and signed by the writer. *Abbrev.:* P.S. **2.** any supplementary part. [L *postscriptum,* pp. neut., written after]

**post-tensioned** /poʊst-ˈtɛnʃənd/, *adj.* (in prestressed concrete) having the reinforcement stretched after the concrete is cast. Cf. **pre-tensioned.**

**postulancy** /ˈpɒstʃələnsi/, *n.* the period or condition of being a postulant, esp. in a religious order.

**postulant** /ˈpɒstʃələnt/, *n.* **1.** one who asks or applies for something. **2.** a candidate, esp. for admission into a religious order. [L *postulans,* ppr., demanding]

**postulate** /ˈpɒstʃəleɪt/, *v.,* **-lated, -lating;** /ˈpɒstʃələt/, *n.* *–v.t.* **1.** to ask, demand, or claim. **2.** to claim or assume the existence or truth of, esp. as a basis for reasoning. **3.** to assume without proof, or as self-evident; take for granted. **4.** *Geom.* to assume; to take as an axiom. **5.** *Eccles.* to nominate to a position, subject to the approval of a higher authority. *–n.* **6.** something postulated or assumed without proof as a basis for reasoning or as self-evident. **7.** a fundamental principle. **8.** a necessary condition; a prerequisite. [L *postulātum,* properly pp. neut., thing requested] – **postulation,** *n.*

**posture** /ˈpɒstʃə/, *n., v.,* **-tured, -turing.** *–n.* **1.** the relative disposition of the various parts of anything. **2.** the position of the body and limbs as a whole: *a change in posture, a sitting posture.* **3.** an affected or unnatural attitude, or a contortion of the body: *antic postures and gestures.* **4.** mental or spiritual attitude. **5.** position, condition, or state, esp. of affairs. *–v.t.* **6.** to place in a particular posture or attitude; dispose in postures. *–v.i.* **7.** to assume a particular posture. **8.** to assume affected or unnatural postures; bend or contort the body in various ways, esp. in public performing. **9.** to act in an affected or artificial way, as if for show; pose for effect. [F, from L *positūra*] – **postural,** *adj.* – **posturer,** *n.*

**posturise** /ˈpɒstʃəraɪz/, *v.i.,* **-rised, -rising.** to posture; pose. Also, **posturize.**

**postvocalic** /poʊstvoʊˈkælɪk/, *adj. Phonet.* occurring after a vowel.

**postwar** /ˈpoʊstwɔ/, *adj.* of or pertaining to the period following a war, esp. World War II: *postwar trade.*

**posy** /ˈpoʊzi/, *n., pl.* **-sies.** **1.** a flower; a nosegay or bouquet. **2.** *Archaic.* a brief motto or the like, such as is inscribed within a ring. [syncopated var. of POESY]

**pot**[1] /pɒt/, *n., v.,* **potted, potting.** *–n.* **1.** an earthen, metallic, or other container, usu. round and deep, used for domestic or other purposes. **2.** such a vessel with its contents. **3.** a potful. **4.** a potful of liquor. **5.** liquor or other drink. **6.** a wicker vessel for trapping fish or crustaceans. **7.** a round or oval refractory container in which glass is melted. **8.** *Colloq.* a large sum of money. **9.** the aggregate of bets at stake at one time, as in card games, esp. poker. **10.** *Colloq.* (in horseracing) a heavily backed horse; favourite. **11.** →**pot shot.** **12. a.** a medium sized beer glass; middy. **b.** the contents of such a glass. **13.** *Colloq.* an important person: *a big pot.* **14.** *Colloq.* →**potbelly.** **15.** a chamber-pot; potty. **16.** *Colloq.* a trophy or prize in a contest, esp. a silver cup. **17.** (*pl.*) *Colloq.* a large quantity. **18.** *Colloq.* →**marijuana.** **19. go to pot,** to deteriorate. **20. put (someone's) pot on,** *Colloq.* to inform against. *–v.t.* **21.** to put into a pot. **22.** to preserve (food) in a pot. **23.** to cook in a pot. **24.** to plant in a pot of soil. **25.** *Hunting.* **a.** to shoot (game birds) on the ground or water, or (game animals) at rest, instead of in flight or running. **b.** to shoot for food, not for sport. **26.** *Colloq.* to capture, secure, or win. **27.** *Billiards.* to pocket. **28.** *Colloq.* to put (a young child) on a potty. **29.** to make pregnant. *–v.i.* **30.** *Colloq.* to take a pot shot; shoot. [ME and OE *pott,* c. MLG *pot.* Cf. F *pot* (? from G)]

**pot**[2] /pɒt/, *n. Scot.* a deep hole; a pit. [ME; ? same as POT[1]]

**pot.,** **1.** potential. **2.** potentiometer.

**potable** /ˈpoʊtəbəl/, *adj.* **1.** fit or suitable for drinking. *–n.* **2.** (*usu. pl.*) anything drinkable. [LL *pōtābilis,* from L *pōtāre* drink]

**potage** /pɒˈtaʒ/, *n.* soup. [F, from L *pōtāre* to drink]

**potamic** /pɒˈtæmɪk/, *adj.* of or pertaining to rivers. [Gk *potamós* + -IC]

**potash** /ˈpɒtæʃ/, *n.* **1.** potassium carbonate, esp. the crude impure form obtained from wood ashes. **2.** →**caustic potash.** **3.** the oxide of potassium, $K_2O$. **4.** potassium: *carbonate of potash.* [earlier *pot-ashes,* pl., translation of early D *potasschen*]

**potassic** /pəˈtæsɪk/, *adj.* of, pertaining to, or containing potassium.

**potassium** /pəˈtæsiəm/, *n.* a silvery white metallic element, which oxidises rapidly in the air, and whose compounds are used as fertiliser and in special hard glasses. *Symbol:* K; *at. wt:* 39.102; *at. no.:* 19; *sp. gr:* 0.86 at 20°C. [NL *potassa* (from F *potasse,* a former equivalent of POTASH) + -IUM]

**potassium-argon dating** /pəˌtæsiəm-ˈagɒn deɪtɪŋ/, *n.* a method of dating rocks which depends on the ratio of potassium-40 to radiogenic argon-40 which they contain.

**potassium bicarbonate** /pəˌtæsiəm baɪˈkabənət/, *n.* a white powder, $KHCO_3$, used in cookery and medicine. Also, **potassium hydrogencarbonate.**

**potassium bromide** /– ˈbroʊmaɪd/, *n.* a white crystalline compound, KBr, used in photography and medicinally as a sedative.

**potassium carbonate** /– ˈkabəneɪt/, *n.* a white solid, $K_2CO_3$, used in the manufacture of glass, etc.

**potassium cyanide** /– ˈsaɪənaɪd/, *n.* a white, crystalline, poisonous compound, KCN, used in metallurgy and photography.

**potassium dichromate** /– daɪˈkroʊmeɪt/, *n.* an orange-red crystalline compound, $K_2Cr_2O_7$, used in dyeing, photography, etc.

**potassium ferricyanide** /– fɛriˈsaɪənaɪd/, *n.* a red crystalline solid, $K_3Fe(CN)_6$, used in the manufacture of pigments.

**potassium ferrocyanide** /– fɛroʊˈsaɪənaɪd/, *n.* a yellow crystalline solid, $K_4Fe(CN)_6 \cdot H_2O$, used in dyeing and metallurgy.

**potassium hydrogencarbonate** /– haɪdrədʒənˈkabənət/, *n.* →**potassium bicarbonate.**

**potassium hydroxide** /– haɪˈdrɒksaɪd/, *n.* a white caustic solid, KOH, used in making soft soap, etc.

**potassium nitrate** /– ˈnaɪtreɪt/, *n.* a crystalline compound, $KNO_3$, used in gunpowder, fertilisers, preservatives, and medicinally as a diaphoretic, and produced by nitrification in soil; saltpetre.

**potassium permanganate** /– pɜˈmæŋgənət/, *n.* a nearly black crystalline compound, $KMnO_4$, forming red-purple solution in water, and used as an oxidising agent, disinfectant, etc.

**potation** /poʊˈteɪʃən/, *n.* **1.** the act of drinking. **2.** a drink or draught, esp. of an alcoholic beverage. [L *pōtātio;* replacing ME *potacioun,* from OF]

**potato** /pəˈteɪtoʊ/, *n., pl.* **-toes.** **1.** the edible tuber **(white potato** or **Irish potato)** of a cultivated plant, *Solanum tuberosum.* **2.** the plant itself. **3.** →**sweet potato.** [Sp. *patata* white potato, var. of *batata* sweet potato, from Haitian]

B

A

potato: A, plant with root system and tubers; B, flowers

**potato beetle** /ˈ– bitl/, *n.* →**Colorado beetle.** Also, *Chiefly U.S.,* **potato bug.**

**potato chip** /ˈ– tʃɪp/, *n.* **1.** a deep-fried finger of potato. **2.** a wafer of potato, fried and served cold; a crisp.

**potato crisp** /– ˈkrɪsp/, *n.* →**crisp** (def. 11).

**potato orchid** /ˈ– ɔkəd/, *n.* a leafless saprophytic herb, *Gastrodia sesamoides,* family Orchidaceae, with bell-shaped, brownish-white flowers, found in cool moist forests in southern Australia and New Zealand.

**potato peeler**[1] /ˈ– pilə/, *n.* a small kitchen implement with a double blade which cannot penetrate beyond a certain depth, used for peeling vegetables, fruit, etc.

**potato peeler**[2] /ˈ– pilə/, *n.* a girlfriend. [rhyming slang, *potato peeler* SHEILA]

**potatory** /ˈpoʊtətəri, -tri/, *adj.* **1.** of, pertaining to, or given to drinking. **2.** *Rare.* potable. [L *pōtātōrius*]

**potato scallop** /pəˌteɪtoʊ ˈskɒləp/, *n.* a thin slice of potato dipped in batter and deep-fried. Also, *Vic.*, **potato cake.**

**pot-au-feu** /pɒt-oʊ-'fɜ/, *n.* a traditional French dish of meat and vegetables. [F: lit., pot on the fire]

**potbelly** /'pɒtbɛli/, *n., pl.* **-lies.** a distended or protuberant belly. – **potbellied,** *adj.*

**pot-belly stove** /pɒt-bɛli 'stoʊv/, *n.* a barrel-shaped fuel stove which is enlarged slightly at or below the middle.

**potboiler** /'pɒtbɔɪlə/, *n. Colloq.* an inferior work of literature, piece of music, film, etc., produced merely for financial gain.

**pot-bound** /'pɒt-baʊnd/, *adj.* (of the roots of a pot plant) having grown to the point where further growth is impossible without re-potting.

**potch** /pɒtʃ/, *n.* an opal which may have colour, but lacks the fine play of colour which distinguishes gem-quality opal; it is commonly the matrix stone in which precious opal is found.

**poteen** /pɒ'tin/, *n.* (in Ireland) illicitly distilled whiskey. Also, **potheen.** [Irish *poitīn* small pot, diminutive of *pota* pot]

**potence** /'poʊtns/, *n.* potency.

**potency** /'poʊtnsi/, *n., pl.* **-cies. 1.** the quality of being potent. **2.** power or authority. **3.** powerfulness or effectiveness. **4.** strength or efficacy, as of a drug. **5.** a person or thing exerting power or influence. **6.** *Obs.* capability of development, or potentiality. Also, **potence.** [L *potentia*]

**potent** /'poʊtnt/, *adj.* **1.** powerful; mighty. **2.** cogent, as reasons, motives, etc. **3.** producing powerful physical or chemical effects, as a drug. **4.** possessed of great power or authority. **5.** exercising great moral influence. **6.** having sexual power. [L *potens,* ppr., being able, powerful] – **potently,** *adv.* – **potentness,** *n.*

**potentate** /'poʊtnteɪt/, *n.* one who possesses great power; a sovereign, monarch, or ruler. [LL *potentātus* potentate, from L: power, dominion]

**potential** /pə'tɛnʃəl/, *adj.* **1.** possible as opposed to actual. **2.** capable of being or becoming; latent. **3.** *Gram.* expressing possibility, as of a mode or modal construction, as 'I *can* go'. **4.** *Physics.* potential energy. **5.** *Rare.* potent. *–n.* **6.** a possibility or potentiality. **7.** *Gram.* a potential mode or construction, or a form therein. **8.** Also, **electric potential.** a measure of the potential energy at a point of an electric charge relative to its potential energy at an infinite distance from that point, or relative to some other reference point such as the earth. **9.** *Maths., Physics.* a type of function from which the intensity of a field may be derived, usu. by differentiation. [ME, from ML *potentiālis*]

**potential difference** /– 'dɪfrəns/, *n.* the difference in potential between two points, defined as the work performed when unit positive charge is moved from one point to the other; voltage drop. *Abbrev.:* p.d.

**potential divider** /– də'vaɪdə/, *n.* →**voltage divider.**

**potential energy** /– 'ɛnədʒi/, *n.* energy which is due to position rather than motion, as a coiled spring or a raised weight (opposed to *kinetic energy*).

**potentiality** /pətɛnʃi'æləti/, *n., pl.* **-ties. 1.** potential state or quality; possibility; latent power or capacity. **2.** something potential. [ML *potentiālitas*]

**potentially** /pə'tɛnʃəli/, *adv.* not actually, but possibly.

**potentilla** /poʊtən'tɪlə/, *n.* any plant of the genus *Potentilla,* comprising herbs, or small shrubs, abundant in north temperate regions. [NL, from L *potens* potent + *-illa* (diminutive suffix)]

**potentiometer** /pətɛnʃi'ɒmətə/, *n.* **1.** an instrument for measuring electromotive force or difference in potential. **2.** →**voltage divider.** [POTENTI(AL), *n.,* + -O- + -METER[1]] – **potentiometric** /pəˌtɛnʃiə'mɛtrɪk/, *adj.*

**potful** /'pɒtfʊl/, *n.* the amount that can be carried in a pot.

**pot glass** /'pɒt glas/, *n.* glass melted in a pot rather than a tank furnace.

**pothead** /'pɒthɛd/, *n. Colloq.* a person who smokes marijuana frequently.

**potheen** /pɒ'θin/, *n.* →**poteen.**

**pother** /'pɒðə/, *n.* **1.** commotion; uproar. **2.** a disturbance or fuss. **3.** a choking or suffocating cloud, as of smoke or dust. *–v.t., v.i.* **4.** to worry; bother. [orig. uncert.]

**potherb** /'pɒthɜb/, *n.* any herb prepared as food by cooking in a pot, or added as seasoning in cookery, as thyme.

**pothole** /'pɒthoʊl/, *n.* **1.** a deep hole; a pit. **2.** a more or less cylindrical hole formed in rock by the grinding action of the detrital material in eddying water. **3.** Also, **sinkhole.** a hole formed in soluble rock by the action of water, serving to conduct water to an underground passage. **4.** a hole in the surface of a road.

**potholing** /'pɒthoʊlɪŋ/, *n.* the exploration of potholes and underground passages. – **potholer,** *n.*

**pothook** /'pɒthʊk/, *n.* **1.** a hook for suspending a pot or kettle over an open fire. **2.** an iron rod, usu. curved, with a hook at the end, used to lift hot pots, irons, stove lids, etc. **3.** a stroke in writing, in the shape of a pothook, esp. as made by children in learning to write.

**pothunter** /'pɒthʌntə/, *n.* **1.** one who hunts merely for food or profit, regardless of the rules of sport. **2.** one who takes part in contests merely to win prizes.

**potiche** /pɒ'tiʃ/, *n., pl.* **-tiches** /-'tiʃ/. a vase or jar, as of porcelain, with rounded or polygonal body narrowing at the top. [F, from *pot* POT[1]]

**potion** /'poʊʃən/, *n.* **1.** a drink or draught, esp. one of a medicinal, poisonous, or magical kind. **2.** *Rare.* a beverage. [L *pōtio;* replacing ME *pocioun,* from OF]

**potlatch** /'pɒtlætʃ/, *n.* **1.** (among some American Indians of the northern Pacific coast) a ceremonial festival at which gifts are bestowed on the guests and property destroyed in a competitive show of wealth. **2.** a celebration; party. [N Amer. Ind. (Chinook, from Nootka *patshatl* a giving, present]

**potline** /'pɒtlaɪn/, *n.* a succession of electrolytic reduction cells used to make such metals as aluminium from a fused electrolyte.

**potluck** /pɒt'lʌk/, *n. Colloq.* **1.** whatever food happens to be at hand without special preparation or buying. **2.** a random or haphazard choice.

**pot marigold** /pɒt 'mærigoʊld/, *n.* the common marigold, *Calendula officinalis,* the flower heads of which are sometimes used in cookery for seasoning.

**pot metal** /'– mɛtl/, *n.* **1.** an alloy of copper and lead formerly used in plumbing fixtures. **2.** *Glassmaking.* glass coloured while it is being fused.

**potoroo** /poʊtə'ru/, *n.* any of several species of rat-kangaroo of the genus *Potorous,* having pointed heads and living in dense grass and low, thick scrub in various parts of Australia. [Aboriginal]

potoroo

**pot-plant** /'pɒt-plænt/, *n.* a plant grown in a flowerpot.

**potpourri** /pɒt'pʊəri, poʊpʊ'ri/, *n., pl.* **-ris. 1.** a mixture of dried petals of roses or other flowers with spices, etc., kept in a jar for the fragrance. **2.** a musical medley. **3.** a collection of miscellaneous literary extracts. **4.** any mixture of unrelated things. [F: rotten pot, translation of Sp. *olla podrida* OLLA-PODRIDA]

**pot roast** /'pɒt roʊst/, *n.* meat which is browned, then cooked slowly in a covered pot, with very little water.

**potsherd** /'pɒtˌʃɜd/, *n.* a fragment or broken piece of pottery. [POT[1] + *sherd,* var. of SHARD]

**pot shot** /'pɒt ʃɒt/, *n.* **1.** a shot fired at game merely for food, with little regard to skill or the rules of sport. **2.** a shot at an animal or person within easy range, as from ambush. **3.** a random or aimless shot.

**pot still** /'– stɪl/, *n.* an apparatus resembling a large pot which is used in the distillation of spirits. – **pot-still,** *adj.*

**potstone** /'pɒtstoʊn/, *n.* a kind of soapstone, sometimes used for making pots and other household utensils.

**pottage** /'pɒtɪdʒ/, *n.* **1.** a thick soup made of vegetables, without or with meat. **2. mess of pottage,** a small and contemptible portion, reward, etc. [ME *potage,* from OF, from *pot* pot]

**potted** /'pɒtəd/, *adj.* **1.** placed in a pot. **2.** preserved or cooked in a pot. **3.** *Colloq.* abridged, summarised, or condensed. **4.** *U.S. Colloq.* drunk.

**potter**[1] /ˈpɒtə/, *n.* one who makes earthen pots or other vessels. [ME; OE *pottere,* from *pott* POT[1] + *-ere* -ER[1]]

**potter**[2] /ˈpɒtə/, *v.i.* **1.** to busy or occupy oneself in an ineffective manner. **2.** to move or go with ineffective action or little energy or purpose (fol. by *about, along,* etc.). **3.** to move or go slowly or aimlessly; loiter. *–n.* **4.** pottering or ineffective action; dawdling. Also, *U.S.,* **putter.** [apparently frequentative of obs. *pote* push, poke, OE *potian* push, thrust. See PUT] – **potterer,** *n.* – **potteringly,** *adv.*

**potter's field** /pɒtəz ˈfild/, *n.* a piece of ground reserved as a burial place for strangers and the friendless poor.

**potter's wheel** /ˈ– wil/, *n.* a device with a rotating horizontal disc upon which clay is moulded by a potter.

**pottery** /ˈpɒtəri/, *n., pl.* **-teries. 1.** ware fashioned from clay or other earthy material and hardened by heat. **2.** a place where earthen pots or vessels are made. **3.** the art or business of a potter; ceramics. [late ME, from F *poterie,* from *potier* potter, from *pot* pot]

**potting mixture** /ˈpɒtɪŋ mɪkstʃə/, *n.* an amalgam of elements providing a good growing medium for plants in pots, usu. including moisture-retaining substances, fertilisers, sand and soil.

**pottle** /ˈpɒtl/, *n.* **1.** a former liquid measure equal to two quarts (approx. 2.25 litres). **2.** a pot or tankard of this capacity. **3.** the wine, etc., in it. **4.** alcoholic beverages. **5. a.** a small container or basket, as for fruit or the like. **b.** *N.Z.* a cardboard cup, in which hot chips are sold. [ME *potel,* from OF, diminutive of *pot* POT[1]]

**potto** /ˈpɒtoʊ/, *n.* a member of the loris family, *Perodicticus potto,* with nocturnal habits, living in the forest belt of central Africa. [a West African language]

**Pott's disease** /ˈpɒts dəziz/, *n.* caries of the bodies of the vertebrae, often resulting in marked curvature of the spine, and usu. associated with a tuberculosis infection. [named after Percival *Pott,* 1714-88, English surgeon, who described it]

**potty**[1] /ˈpɒti/, *adj. Colloq.* **1.** foolish; crazy. **2.** *Brit.* paltry; petty.

**potty**[2] /ˈpɒti/, *n. Colloq.* a chamber-pot, esp. one for a child. Also, **pottie.**

**potty-training** /ˈpɒti-treɪnɪŋ/, *n. Colloq.* →**toilet-training.**

**pot-valiant** /ˈpɒt-væljənt/, *adj.* brave only when drunk.

**pot-walloper** /ˈpɒt-wɒləpə/, *n. Colloq.* a heavy drinker.

**pouch** /paʊtʃ/, *n.* **1.** a bag, sack, or similar receptacle, esp. one for small articles. **2.** a small moneybag. **3.** a bag or case of canvas, leather, etc., used by soldiers for carrying ammunition. **4.** a bag for carrying mail. **5.** something shaped like or resembling a bag or pocket. **6.** *Chiefly Scot.* a pocket in a garment. **7.** a baggy fold of flesh under the eye. **8.** *Zool.* a baglike or pocket-like part; a sac or cyst, as the sac beneath the bill of pelicans, the saclike dilation of the cheeks of gophers, or (esp.) the receptacle for the young of marsupials. **9.** *Bot.* a baglike cavity. *–v.t.* **10.** to put into or enclose in a pouch, bag, or pocket; pocket. **11.** to arrange (something) in the form of a pouch. **12.** (of a fish or bird) to swallow. *–v.i.* **13.** to form a pouch or a cavity resembling a pouch. [ME *pouche,* from ONF, var. of OF *poche,* also *poque, poke* bag. Cf. POKE[2]] – **pouchy,** *adj.*

**pouf** /puf, pʊf/, *n.* **1.** a kind of headdress worn by women in the latter part of the 18th century. **2.** an arrangement of the hair over a pad. **3.** a puff of material as an ornament in a dress or headdress. **4.** a stuffed cushion of thick material forming a low seat. **5.** →**poof.** Also, **pouffe.** [F. Cf. PUFF]

**poulard** /ˈpulad/, *n.* **1.** a hen spayed to improve the flesh for use as food. **2.** a fatted hen. [F, from *poule* hen. See PULLET]

**poult** /ˈpoʊlt/, *n.* the young of the domestic fowl, the turkey, the pheasant, or a similar bird. [ME *pult(e),* syncopated var. of PULLET]

**poulterer** /ˈpoʊltərə/, *n.* a dealer in poultry, game, etc. [*poulter* poultry dealer (from F *pouletier*) + -ER[1]]

**poultice** /ˈpoʊltəs/, *n., v.,* **-ticed, -ticing.** *–n.* **1.** a soft, moist mass of bread, meal, linseed, etc., applied as a medicament to the body. **2.** *Colloq.* a large amount: *he has a poultice of money.* **3.** *Colloq.* a mortgage. *–v.t.* **4.** to apply a poultice to. [orig. *pultes,* apparently pl. of L *puls* thick pap]

**poultry** /ˈpoʊltri/, *n.* domestic fowls collectively, as chickens, turkeys, guineafowls, ducks, and geese. [ME *pult(e)rie,* from OF *pouleterie,* from *poulet* PULLET]

**pounamu** /ˈpunəmu/, *n.* →**greenstone** (def. 2). [Maori]

**pounce**[1] /paʊns/, *v.,* **pounced, pouncing,** *n. –v.i.* **1.** to swoop down suddenly and lay hold, as a bird does on its prey. **2.** to spring, dash, or come suddenly. *–v.t.* **3.** to seize with the talons. **4.** to swoop down upon and seize suddenly, as a bird of prey does. *–n.* **5.** the claw or talon of a bird of prey. **6.** a sudden swoop, as on prey. [orig. uncert.]

**pounce**[2] /paʊns/, *v.t.,* **pounced, pouncing.** to emboss (metal) by hammering on an instrument applied on the reverse side. [probably same as POUNCE[1]]

**pounce**[3] /paʊns/, *n., v.,* **pounced, pouncing.** *–n.* **1.** a fine powder, as of cuttlebone, formerly used to prevent ink from spreading in writing, as over an erasure or an unsized paper, or to prepare parchment for writing. **2.** a fine powder, usu. charcoal, rubbed through a perforated pattern, for transferring a design. *–v.t.* **3.** to sprinkle, smooth, or prepare with pounce. **4.** to trace (a design) with pounce. **5.** to finish the surface of (hats) by rubbing with sandpaper or the like. [F *ponce,* from L *pūmex* PUMICE] – **pouncer,** *n.*

**pounce box** /ˈ– bɒks/, *n.* a small box with perforated lid for holding pounce powder for transferring designs, or for use in writing.

**pouncet box** /ˈpaʊnsət bɒks/, *n. Archaic.* a small perfume box with a perforated lid. [POUNCE[2] or POUNCE[3]]

**pound**[1] /paʊnd/, *v.t.* **1.** to strike repeatedly and with great force, as with an instrument, the fist, heavy missiles, etc. **2.** to produce (sound) by striking or thumping, or with an effect of thumping (oft. fol. by *out*): *to pound out a tune on a piano.* **3.** to force (a way) by battering. **4.** to crush by beating, as with an instrument; pulverise. *–v.i.* **5.** to strike heavy blows repeatedly: *to pound on a door.* **6.** to beat or throb violently, as the heart. **7.** to give forth a sound of or as of thumps: *the drums pounded loudly.* **8.** to walk or go with heavy steps; move along with force or vigour. *–n.* **9.** the act of pounding. **10.** a heavy or forcible blow. **11.** a thump. [ME *pounen,* OE *pūnian;* akin to D *puin* rubbish, LG *pün* fragments]

**pound**[2] /paʊnd/, *n., pl.* **pounds,** (*collectively*) **pound. 1.** a unit of mass, varying in different periods and different countries. **2.** either of two units in imperial measure, the **pound avoirdupois** (of 7000 grains, divided into 16 ounces, and equal to 0.453 592 37 kg) used for ordinary commodities, or the **pound troy** (of 5760 grains, divided into 12 ounces, equal to 0.373 241 721 6 kg) used for gold, silver, etc., and also serving as the basis of apothecaries' weight. **3.** →**pound-force. 4.** a British money of account **(pound sterling)** of the value of 100 new pence. **5.** a former unit of currency in Australia of the value of 240 pence. **6.** the monetary unit of various countries. **7.** a note or coin of any of these denominations. [ME and OE *pund,* from L *pondo* a pound, orig. *lībra pondō* a pound in weight]

**pound**[3] /paʊnd/, *n.* **1.** an enclosure maintained by public authorities for confining stray or homeless animals. **2.** an enclosure for sheltering, keeping, confining, or trapping animals. **3.** an enclosure or trap for fish. **4.** a place of confinement or imprisonment. **5.** a punishment cell in a prison; black peter. *–v.t.* **6.** to shut up in or as in pound; impound; imprison. [ME and OE *pund-.* Cf. obs. *pind,* v., enclose, OE *pyndan*]

**poundage**[1] /ˈpaʊndɪdʒ/, *n.* **1.** a tax, commission, rate, etc., of so much per pound sterling or per pound weight. **2.** weight measured in pounds. [POUND[2] + -AGE]

**poundage**[2] /ˈpaʊndɪdʒ/, *n.* **1.** confinement within an enclosure or within certain limits. **2.** the fee demanded to free animals from a pound. [POUND[3] + -AGE]

**poundal** /ˈpaʊndl/, *n.* a unit of force in the f.p.s. system, equal to the force which will accelerate a mass of one pound by $1 ft/s^2$ in the direction of that force, approx. equal to 0.14 newton. *Symbol:* pdl

**poundbreach** /ˈpaʊndbritʃ/, *n.* the retaking, from the custody of the law, of a chattel which has been impounded.

**poundcake** /ˈpaʊndkeɪk/, *n.* a rich, sweet cake originally made with a pound each of butter, sugar, and flour.

**pounder**[1] /ˈpaʊndə/, *n.* one who or that which pounds, pulverises, or beats. [POUND[1] + -ER[1]]

**pounder**[2] /ˈpaʊndə/, *n.* **1.** a person or thing having, or associated with, a weight or value of a pound or a specified number of pounds. **2.** a gun that discharges a missile of a specified weight in pounds. **3.** a person possessing, receiving an income of, or paying a specified number of pounds. [POUND[2] + -ER[1]]

**pound-foolish** /paʊnd-ˈfulɪʃ/, *adj.* foolish in regard to large sums. Cf. **penny-wise.**

**pound-force** /paʊnd-ˈfɔs/, *n.* a unit of force in the f.p.s. system, equal to the gravitational force acting on a mass of one pound, approx. equal to 32.174 pdl or 4.45 newtons. *Symbol:* lbf

**pound net** /ˈpaʊnd nɛt/, *n.* a trap for catching fish consisting of an arrangement of netting having a pound or enclosure with a contracted opening.

**pour** /pɔ/, *v.t.* **1.** to send (a liquid or fluid, or anything in loose particles) flowing or falling, as from a container or into, over, or on something. **2.** to emit or discharge, esp. continuously or rapidly. **3.** to send forth (words, etc.) as in a stream or flood (oft. fol. by *out* or *forth*). *–v.i.* **4.** to issue, move, or proceed in great quantity or number. **5.** to flow forth or along. **6.** to rain heavily. *–n.* **7. a.** the act or process of pouring molten metal, concrete, etc., into a mould. **b.** the amount poured. **8.** an abundant or continuous flow or stream. **9.** a heavy fall of rain; downpour. [ME *poure(n)*; orig. uncert.] – **pourer,** *n.* – **pouringly,** *adv.*

**pourboire** /pɔˈbwa/, *n.* a tip or gratuity. [F: lit., for drinking]

**pourparler** /pɔpaˈleɪ/, *n.* an informal preliminary conference. [F, n. use of OF *pourparler* discuss, from *pour-* for, before (from L *prō*) + *parler* speak]

**pourpresture** /ˈpɔprɛstʃə/, *n.* →**purpresture.**

**poussette** /puˈsɛt/, *n., v.,* **-setted, -setting.** *–n.* **1.** a dance step in which a couple or several couples dance around the ballroom, holding hands, used in country dances. *–v.i.* **2.** to perform a poussette, as a couple in a country dance. [F, from *pousser* push]

**poussin** /ˈpusən/, *n.* a chicken killed when young to preserve its flavour and tenderness. [F]

**pout**[1] /paʊt/, *v.i.* **1.** to thrust out or protrude the lips, esp. in displeasure or sullenness. **2.** to look sullen. **3.** to swell out or protrude, as lips. *–v.t.* **4.** to protrude (lips, etc.). **5.** to utter with a pout. *–n.* **6.** a protrusion of the lips, as in pouting. **7.** a fit of sullenness. [ME *poute(n)*, c. d. Swed. *puta* be inflated]

**pout**[2] /paʊt/, *n., pl.* **pouts,** (*esp. collectively*) **pout. 1.** →**eelpout. 2.** →**bib** (def. 3). [OE *-pūte* in *ælepūte* eelpout, c. D *puit* frog]

**pouter** /ˈpaʊtə/, *n.* **1.** one who pouts. **2.** one of a breed of long-legged domestic pigeons characterised by the habit of puffing out the crop.

pouter (def. 2)

**poverty** /ˈpɒvəti/, *n.* **1.** the condition of being poor with respect to money, goods, or means of subsistence. **2.** deficiency or lack of something specified: *poverty of ideas.* **3.** deficiency of desirable ingredients, qualities, etc.: *poverty of soil.* **4.** scantiness; scanty amount. [ME *poverte,* from OF, from L *paupertas.* Cf. POOR, PAUPER]

**poverty-stricken** /ˈpɒvəti-ˌstrɪkən/, *adj.* suffering from poverty; very poor: *poverty-striken exiles.*

**POW** /pi oʊ ˈdʌbəlju/, prisoner of war. Also, **P.O.W.**

**powan** /ˈpoʊən/, *n.* a freshwater fish resembling a herring, *Coregonus clupeoides,* found in some Scottish lochs.

**powder** /ˈpaʊdə/, *n.* **1.** any solid substance in the state of fine, loose particles, as produced by crushing, grinding, or disintegration; dust. **2.** a preparation in this form for some special purpose, as gunpowder, a medicinal powder, a cosmetic or toilet powder, etc. **3. take a powder,** *Colloq.* to depart; disappear. *–v.t.* **4.** to reduce to powder; pulverise. **5.** to sprinkle or cover with powder. **6.** to apply powder to (the face, skin, etc.) as a cosmetic. **7.** to sprinkle or strew as with powder. **8.** to ornament with small objects scattered over a surface. *–v.i.* **9.** to use powder as a cosmetic. **10.** to become pulverised. [ME *poudre,* from OF, from L *pulvis* dust] – **powderer,** *n.*

**powder blue** /– ˈblu/, *n.* pale blue diluted with grey.

**powdered milk** /paʊdəd ˈmɪlk/, *n.* dehydrated milk.

**powdered sugar** /– ˈʃʊgə/, *n. U.S.* →**icing sugar.**

**powder flask** /ˈpaʊdə flask/, *n.* a flask or case for gunpowder.

**powder horn** /ˈ– hɔn/, *n.* a powder flask made of horn.

**powder magazine** /ˈ– mægəzin/, *n.* a compartment for the storage of ammunition and explosives.

**powder metallurgy** /ˈ– ˌmɛtələdʒi/, *n.* the art or science of manufacturing useful articles by compacting metal and other powders in a die, followed by sintering.

**powder monkey** /ˈ– mʌŋki/, *n.* **1.** a boy formerly employed on warships, etc., to carry powder. **2.** a man in charge of explosives in any operation requiring their use.

**powder puff** /ˈ– pʌf/, *n.* a soft, feathery ball or pad, as of down, for applying powder to the skin.

**powder room** /ˈ– rum/, *n.* a women's lavatory in a restaurant or other public building.

**powdery** /ˈpaʊdəri/, *adj.* **1.** of the nature of, or consisting of, powder. **2.** easily reduced to powder. **3.** sprinkled or covered with powder.

**power** /ˈpaʊə/, *n.* **1.** ability to do or act; capability of doing or effecting something. **2.** (*usu. pl.*) a particular faculty of body or mind. **3.** political or national strength: *the balance of power in Europe.* **4.** great or marked ability to do or act; strength; might; force. **5.** the possession of control or command over others; dominion; authority; ascendancy or influence. **6.** political ascendancy or control in the government of a country, etc.: *the party in power.* **7.** legal ability, capacity, or authority. **8.** delegated authority; authority vested in a person or persons in a particular capacity. **9.** a written statement, or document, conferring legal authority. **10.** one who or that which possesses or exercises authority or influence. **11.** a state or nation having international authority or influence: *the great powers of the world.* **12.** a military or naval force. **13.** (*oft. pl.*) a deity or divinity. **14.** (*pl.*) *Theol.* an order of angels. **15.** *Colloq.* a large number or amount. **16.** *Physics, Elect.* the time rate of transferring or transforming energy; work done, or energy transferred, per unit of time. **17.** *Mech.* energy or force available for application to work. **18.** mechanical energy as distinguished from hand labour. **19.** a particular form of mechanical energy. **20.** *Maths.* the product obtained by multiplying a quantity by itself one or more times: *4 is the second, 8 the third, power of 2.* **21.** *Optics.* the magnifying capacity of a microscope, telescope, etc., expressed as ratio of diameter of image to object. **22. the powers that be,** those in authority. *–v.t.* **23.** to supply with electricity or other means of power. **24.** (of an engine, etc.) to provide the force or motive power to operate (a machine). [ME *poër* from AF, properly inf., be able, from VL *potēre,* for L *posse*]

**powerboat** /ˈpaʊəboʊt/, *n.* **1.** a boat propelled by mechanical power. **2.** →**motor boat.**

**power cable** /ˈpaʊə keɪbəl/, *n.* a cable for conducting electricity, esp. high-voltage electricity.

**power cut** /ˈ– kʌt/, *n.* an interruption or reduction, either planned or accidental, to the local supply of electricity. Cf. **blackout.**

**power-dive** /ˈpaʊə-daɪv/, *n., v.,* **-dived, -diving.** *Aeron. –n.* **1.** a steep dive by an aircraft with engines at full power. *–v.i.* **2.** to perform a power-dive.

**power drill** /ˈpaʊə drɪl/, *n.* a drill operated by a motor.

**powered** /ˈpaʊəd/, *adj.* having, exerting or producing, or propelled by, mechanical energy.

**power factor** /ˈpaʊə fæktə/, *n.* the ratio of the power dissipated in an electrical circuit to the product of the E.M.F. and the current. In single- and three-phase circuits it is equal to the cosine of the phase angle between the E.M.F. and the current.

**powerful** /ˈpaʊəfəl/, *adj.* **1.** having or exerting great power or force. **2.** strong physically, as a person. **3.** producing great physical effects, as a machine or a blow. **4.** potent, as a drug. **5.** having great influence, as a speech, speaker, description, reason, etc. **6.** having great power, authority, or influence, as a nation; mighty. **7.** *Colloq.* great in number or amount: *a powerful lot of money.* – **powerfully,** *adv.* – **powerfulness,** *n.*

**powerhouse** /ˈpaʊəhaʊs/, *n.* →**generating station.**

**powerless** /ˈpaʊələs/, *adj.* **1.** lacking power or ability; unable to produce any effect. **2.** lacking power to act; helpless. – **powerlessly,** *adv.* – **powerlessness,** *n.*

**powerlines** /ˈpaʊəlaɪnz/, *n.pl.* high or relatively low voltage electrical wires carrying power for industrial or domestic use, etc.

**power-loading** /ˈpaʊə-loʊdɪŋ/, *n.* See **loading** (def. 4).

**power loom** /ˈpaʊə lum/, *n.* a loom worked by mechanical power.

**power of appointment,** *n.* the right granted by one person (the donor) to another (the donee or appointer) to dispose of the donor's property or create rights therein.

**power of attorney,** *n.* a written document given by one person or party to another authorising the latter to act for the former.

**power pack** /ˈpaʊə pæk/, *n.* the unit in an electronic device which supplies power at the required voltages to the rest of the circuit.

**power plant** /ˈ– plænt/, *n.* **1.** a plant (including engines, dynamos, etc., with the building or buildings) for the generation of power. **2.** the apparatus for supplying power for a particular mechanical process or operation.

**power point** /ˈ– pɔɪnt/, *n.* a socket, connected to a power supply, usu. made of plastic and set in a wall, into which the plug of an electrical appliance may be inserted.

**power politics** /– ˈpɒlətɪks/, *n.* international diplomacy based on the use, or threatened use, of military power.

**power reactor** /ˈ– riˌæktə/, *n.* a nuclear reactor designed to produce electric power.

**power serve** /ˈ– sɜv/, *n.* a very fast and accurate service in tennis.

**power station** /ˈ– steɪʃən/, *n.* an industrial building in which electricity is generated.

**power steering** /– ˈstɪərɪŋ/, *n.* a steering mechanism in a motor vehicle that provides mechanical or hydraulic aid in turning the wheels.

**power structure** /ˈ– strʌktʃə/, *n.* the pattern of distribution of power in a social, political, or business group.

**power take-off** /– ˈteɪk-ɒf/, *n.* a supplementary mechanism on a truck or tractor which enables the engine power to be used to operate non-automotive apparatus, as winches, pumps, saws, cement-mixers, etc.

**powwow** /ˈpaʊwaʊ/, *n.* **1.** (among North American Indians) a ceremony, esp. one accompanied by magic, feasting, and dancing, performed for the cure of disease, success in a hunt, etc. **2.** a council or conference of or with Indians. **3.** *Colloq.* any conference or meeting. *–v.i.* **4.** to hold a powwow. **5.** *Colloq.* to confer. [Algonquian *pow wah* or *po-wah*]

**pox** /pɒks/, *n.* **1.** a disease characterised by multiple skin pustules, as smallpox. **2.** Also, **great (French) pox.** →**syphilis. 3.** *Colloq.* any venereal disease. [for *pocks,* pl. of POCK]

**pozzie** /ˈpɒzi/, *n.* →**possie.**

**pozzuolana** /pɒtswəˈlanə/, *n.* a porous variety of volcanic tuft or ash used in making hydraulic cement. Also, **pozzolana** /pɒtsəˈlanə/. [It., n. use of adj., belonging to *Pozzuoli,* seaport in Italy, (L *Puteolī,* lit., little springs)]

**pp.,** **1.** pages. **2.** past participle. **3.** pianissimo.

**p.p.,** past participle.

**P.P.,** **1.** Parish Priest. **2.** Progress Party.

**P.P.** /pi ˈpi/, *n. Colloq.* (usu. among school teachers) a proud parent.

**ppl.,** participle.

**P-plate** /ˈpi-pleɪt/, *n.* one of a pair of identification plates which by law must be displayed (at the front and rear) on any motor vehicle driven by a driver with a provisional licence.

**P-plater** /ˈpi-pleɪtə/, *n.* a person who has obtained a provisional driver's licence and must display P plates on his car.

**P.P.M.,** *Chem.* parts per million. Also, **p.p.m.**

**ppr.,** present participle. Also, **p.pr.**

**P.PS.,** a second postscript. [L *post postscriptum*]

**pr,** **1.** pair. **2.** pairs. **3.** present. **4.** price. **5.** pronoun.

**p.r.,** *Med.* taken through the rectum, as a suppository. [L *per rectum*]

**Pr,** *Chem.* praseodymium.

**Pr.,** **1.** preferred (stock). **2.** Priest. **3.** Prince. **4.** Provençal.

**PR** /pi ˈa/, *n.* →**public relations.**

**P.R.,** proportional representation.

**prac**[1] /præk/, *adj. Colloq.* practice: *prac teaching.*

**prac**[2] /præk/, *n., adj.* →**practical.**

**practicable** /ˈpræktɪkəbəl/, *adj.* **1.** capable of being put into practice, done, or effected, esp. with the available means or with reason or prudence; feasible. **2.** capable of being used or traversed, or admitting of passage: *a practicable road.* [ML *practicāre* PRACTISE + -ABLE] – **practicability** /ˌpræktɪkəˈbɪləti/, **practicableness,** *n.* – **practicably,** *adv.*

**practical** /ˈpræktɪkəl/, *adj.* **1.** pertaining or relating to practice or action: *practical mathematics.* **2.** consisting of, involving, or resulting from practice or action: *a practical application of a rule.* **3.** pertaining to or connected with the ordinary activities, business, or work of the world: *practical affairs.* **4.** adapted for actual use: *a practical method.* **5.** engaged or experienced in actual practice or work: *a practical politician.* **6.** inclined towards or fitted for actual work or useful activities: *a practical man.* **7.** mindful of the results, usefulness, advantages or disadvantages, etc., of action or procedure. **8.** matter-of-fact; prosaic. **9.** being such in practice or effect; virtual: *a practical certainty.* **10.** of or pertaining to a practical. *–n.* **11.** that part of a course of study which is designed to develop practical skills or to demonstrate the practical foundation of a theory. [PRACTIC(E) + -AL[1]] – **practicality** /præktəˈkæləti/, **practicalness,** *n.*

**practical joke** /– ˈdʒoʊk/, *n.* a trick played upon a person, often involving some physical action. – **practical joker,** *n.*

**practically** /ˈpræktɪkli/, *adv.* **1.** in effect; virtually. **2.** in a practical manner. **3.** from a practical point of view. **4.** nearly; almost.

**practice** /ˈpræktəs/, *n., v.,* **-ticed, -ticing,** *adj.* *–n.* **1.** habitual or customary performance: *normal business practice.* **2.** a habit or custom. **3.** repeated performance or systematic exercise for the purpose of acquiring skill or proficiency: *practice makes perfect.* **4.** skill gained by experience or exercise. **5.** the action or process of performing or doing something (opposed to *theory* or *speculation*). **6.** the exercise of a profession or occupation, esp. law or medicine. **7.** the business of a professional man: *a doctor with a large practice.* **8.** *Law.* the established method of conducting legal proceedings. **9.** deceitful or dishonest dealing or procedure; trickery: *sharp practice.* **10.** (*usu. pl.*) *Archaic.* a plot or intrigue. **11. make a practice of,** to do (something) habitually or usually. *–v.t., v.i.* **12.** *U.S.* →**practise.** *–adj.* **13.** of or pertaining to an attempt which is undertaken merely to develop skill, refresh one's memory, etc: *a practice shot.* [n. use of PRACTISE, *v.,* substituted for earlier *practic,* n.]

**practice range** /ˈ– reɪndʒ/, *n.* **1.** a short golf course for practising golf. **2.** →**rifle range.**

**practician** /prækˈtɪʃən/, *n.* one who works at a profession or occupation; practitioner.

**practise** /ˈpræktəs/, *v.,* **-tised, -tising.** *–v.t.* **1.** to carry out, perform, or do habitually or usually. **2.** to follow, observe, or use habitually or in customary practice. **3.** to exercise or pursue as a profession, art, or occupation: *to practise law.* **4.** to perform or do repeatedly in order to acquire skill or proficiency. **5.** to exercise (a person, etc.) in something in order to give proficiency; train or drill. *–v.i.* **6.** to act habitually; do something habitually or as a practice. **7.** to pursue a profession, esp. law or medicine. **8.** to exercise oneself by performance tending to give proficiency: *to practise shooting.* **9.** *Archaic.* to plot or conspire. Also, *U.S.,* **practice.** [ME, from OF *pra(c)tiser,* from LL *practicus* PRACTICAL] – **practiser,** *n.*

**practised** /ˈpræktəst/, *adj.* **1.** experienced; expert; proficient. **2.** acquired or perfected through practice.

**practitioner** /prækˈtɪʃənə/, *n.* **1.** one engaged in the practice of a profession or the like: *a medical practitioner.* **2.** one who practises something specified. [modified form of *practician* (from obs. *practic* + -IAN) + -ER[1]]

**prad** /præd/, *n. Colloq.* a horse.

**prae-,** variant of **pre-.**

**praecipe** /ˈprɛsəpi/, *n.* a document filed in a court to inform it that a matter is ready for trial, supplying details such as the length of the trial, witnesses to be called and whether all interlocutory proceedings are completed. [L: principally]

**praedial** /'pridiəl/, *adj.* **1.** of, pertaining to, or consisting of land or its products; real; landed. **2.** arising from or consequent upon the occupation of land. **3.** attached to land. Also, **predial.** [ML *praediālis,* from L *praedium* farm, estate]

**praefect** /'prifɛkt/, *n.* →**prefect.**

**praeludium** /pri'ljudiəm/, *n.* →**prelude** (def. 3). [L]

**praemunire** /primjə'naɪəri/, *n. Brit. Law.* **1.** a writ charging the offence of resorting to a foreign court or authority, as that of the pope, and thus calling in question the supremacy of the English Crown. **2.** the offence. **3.** the penalty of forfeiture, imprisonment, outlawry, etc., incurred. [ML, a word used in the writ (by confusion with L *praemūnīre* fortify, protect) for L *praemonēre* forewarn, admonish. See PREMONISH]

**praenomen** /pri'noʊmən/, *n., pl.* **-nomina** /-'nɒmənə/. **1.** the first or personal name of a Roman citizen, as 'Gaius' in 'Gaius Julius Caesar'. **2.** any first or given name. [L, from *prae* before + *nōmen* name] – **praenominal,** *adj.*

**pragmatic** /præg'mætɪk/, *adj.* Also, **pragmatical** (*for defs 3, 5, 6, 7*). **1.** treating historical phenomena with special reference to their causes, antecedent conditions, and results. **2.** *Philos.* of or pertaining to pragmatism. **3.** concerned with practical consequences or values. **4.** pertaining to the affairs of a state or community. **5.** busy or active. **6.** officiously busy; meddlesome. **7.** conceited; opinionated; dogmatic. *–n.* **8.** a pragmatic sanction. [L *pragmaticus,* from Gk *pragmatikós* active, versed in state affairs; as n., a man of business or action] – **pragmatically,** *adv.*

**pragmatism** /'prægmətɪzəm/, *n.* **1.** character or conduct which emphasises practical values or attention to facts; practicality. **2.** *Philos.* the doctrine of C. S. Peirce, 1839-1914, U.S. logician, that difference of meaning depends on difference of practice. It has been interpreted by some as the doctrine that both truth and conduct are to be judged by practical consequences. – **pragmatist,** *n., adj.*

**prairie** /'prɛəri/, *n.* **1.** an extensive or slightly undulating treeless tract of land, characterised by highly fertile soil and originally grassland, which occurs in the interior of continents in temperate latitudes, as that of the upper Mississippi valley, U.S., and in Canada. **2.** a meadow. **3.** (in the southern U.S.) a tract of grassland often covered with water; marshland. [F, from *pré* field, from L *prātum* meadow]

**prairie chicken** /'– 'tʃɪkən/, *n.* a North American gallinaceous bird, *Tympanuchus cupido,* inhabiting prairies and valued as game. Also, **prairie hen.**

**prairie dog** /'– dɒg/, *n.* any of certain gregarious burrowing rodents (genus *Cynomys*) of North American prairies, which utter a barklike cry.

prairie dog

**prairie grass** /'– gras/, *n.* an annual and biennial grass species, *Bromus unioloides,* native to South America, and widespread in many countries.

**prairie oyster** /'– 'ɔɪstə/, *n.* a drink made primarily from a raw egg, the yolk of which remains unbroken and is thought to resemble an oyster, given to invalids and those suffering from a hangover.

**prairie schooner** /'– 'skunə/, *n. U.S.* a small covered wagon used by pioneers in crossing the prairies and plains of North America.

**prairie wolf** /'– wʊlf/, *n.* →**coyote.**

**praise** /preɪz/, *n., v.,* **praised, praising.** *–n.* **1.** the act of expressing approval or admiration; commendation; laudation. **2.** the offering of grateful homage in words or song, as an act of worship. **3.** state of being approved or admired. **4.** *Archaic.* a ground for praise, or a merit. **5.** *Obs.* an object of praise. **6. sing (someone's) praises,** to be highly complimentary to (someone). *–v.t.* **7.** to express approval or admiration of; commend; extol. **8.** to offer grateful homage to (God or a deity), as in words or song. [ME *preise(n),* from OF *preisier* value, prize, from L *pretium* price. Cf. PRIZE[2]] – **praiser,** *n.*

**praiseworthy** /'preɪzwɜði/, *adj.* deserving of praise; laudable. – **praiseworthily,** *adv.* – **praiseworthiness,** *n.*

**Prakrit** /'prakrɪt/, *n.* any of the vernacular Indic languages of the ancient and medieval periods, as distinguished from Sanskrit. [Skt *prākrta* natural, common, vulgar. Cf. SANSKRIT]

**praline** /'pralin, 'preɪ-/, *n.* **1.** a confection of nuts and caramelised sugar, often used as a centre for chocolates and to decorate puddings. **2.** a French sweet consisting of an almond encased in sugar. [F; named after Comte de Plessis-*Praslin,* 1598-1675, whose cook invented them]

**pralltriller** /'praltrɪlə/, *n.* See **inverted mordent.** [G: lit., rebounding quaver]

**pram** /præm/, *n.* a small, four-wheeled vehicle used for carrying a baby, pushed from behind. [shortened form of PERAMBULATOR]

**prana** /'pranə/, *n.* **1.** a life breath or vital principle in Vedic and Hindu religion. **2.** the principle of life moving in the human body. [Skt *prāna,* lit., breath]

**prance** /præns, prans/, *v.,* **pranced, prancing,** *n. –v.i.* **1.** to spring, or move by springing, from the hind legs, as a horse. **2.** to ride on a horse doing this. **3.** to ride gaily, proudly, or insolently. **4.** to move or go in an elated manner; swagger. **5.** to caper or dance. *–v.t.* **6.** to cause to prance. *–n.* **7.** the act of prancing; a prancing movement. [ME *pra(u)nce,* ? alliterative alteration of DANCE. Cf. *prick and prance* (Gower)] – **prancer,** *n.* – **prancingly,** *adv.*

**prandial** /'prændiəl/, *adj.* of or pertaining to a meal, esp. dinner. [L *prandium* luncheon, meal + -AL[1]] – **prandially,** *adv.*

**prang** /præŋ/, *Colloq. –v.t.* **1.** to crash-land (an aircraft); damage; destroy. **2.** to bomb or damage by bombing (a town, etc.). **3.** to crash (a car or the like). *–v.i.* **4.** to have a crash. *–n.* **5.** an aircraft crash. **6.** a bombing raid by aircraft. **7.** a crash, esp. a minor one, in a motor vehicle or the like.

**prank**[1] /præŋk/, *n.* **1.** a trick of a playful nature. **2.** a trick of a malicious nature. [orig. uncert.] – **prankery,** *n.*

**prank**[2] /præŋk/, *v.t.* **1.** to dress or deck in a showy manner; adorn. *–v.i.* **2.** to make an ostentatious show or display. [cf. D *pronk* show, finery, MLG *prank* pomp]

**prankish** /'præŋkɪʃ/, *adj.* **1.** of the nature of a prank. **2.** full of pranks.

**prankster** /'præŋkstə/, *n.* a practical joker; mischievous or malicious person.

**prase** /preɪz/, *n.* a leek-green cryptocrystalline variety of chalcedony. [ME, from F, from L *prasius* a leek-green stone, from Gk *prásios* leek-green]

**praseodymium** /ˌpreɪzioʊ'dɪmiəm/, *n.* a rare-earth, metallic, trivalent element, so named from its green salts. *Symbol:* Pr; *at. wt:* 140.907; *at. no.:* 59; *sp. gr.:* 6.5 at 20°C. [*praseo-* (combining form representing PRASE) + (DI)DYMIUM]

**prasine** /preɪ'zin/, *n.* **1.** a green coloured mineral, similar to malachite. *–adj.* **2.** having a leek-green colour. [L. *prasinus,* from Gk *prásinos* leek-green]

**prate** /preɪt/, *v.,* **prated, prating,** *n. –v.i.* **1.** to talk too much; talk foolishly or pointlessly; chatter; babble. *–v.t.* **2.** to utter in empty or foolish talk. *–n.* **3.** the act of prating. **4.** empty or foolish talk. [late ME *prate,* c. D and LG *praten*] – **prater,** *n.* – **pratingly,** *adv.*

**pratfall** /'prætfɔl/, *n. U.S.* an undignified fall on the buttocks.

**pratie** /'preɪti/, *n. Irish.* a potato.

**pratincole** /'prætɪŋkoʊl, 'preɪtɪŋ-/, *n.* **1.** →**Australian courser.** **2.** any bird of the Old World family Glareolidae, somewhat resembling swallows in appearance and habits. [NL *prātincola,* from L *prātum* meadow + *incola* inhabitant]

**pratique** /'prætɪk/, *n.* licence or permission to use a port, given to a ship after quarantine or on showing a clean bill of health. [F: lit., practice, from ML *practica*]

**prattle** /'prætl/, *v.,* **-tled, -tling,** *n. –v.i.* **1.** to talk or chatter in a simple-minded or foolish way; babble. *–v.t.* **2.** to utter by chattering or babbling. *–n.* **3.** the act of prattling. **4.** chatter; babble. **5.** a babbling sound. [frequentative and diminutive of PRATE] – **prattler,** *n.* – **prattlingly,** *adv.*

**prau** /praʊ/, *n.* →**proa.**

**prawn** /prɔn/, *n.* **1.** any of various shrimplike decapod crustaceans of the genera *Palaemon, Penaeus,* etc. (suborder Macrura), certain of which are used as food. **2. come the raw prawn,** *Colloq.* to try to deceive; delude (fol. by *with*). *–v.i.* **3.** to catch prawns, as for food. [ME *pra(y)ne;* orig. unknown] – **prawner,** *n.*

**prawn crisp** /'– 'krɪsp/, *n.* a Chinese cracker (def. 1) made from rice flour and prawn flavouring.

**prawn cutlet** /– 'kʌtlət/, *n.* a large prawn, usu. a king prawn, boiled, shelled, flattened to a cutlet shape, coated in egg and breadcrumbs, and deep fried.

**prawnie** /'prɔni/, *n. Colloq.* a prawn fisherman.

**prawn night** /'prɔn naɪt/, *n. Colloq.* a social function at a club at which prawns and beer are served.

**praxis** /'præksəs/, *n.* **1.** practice, esp. as opposed to theory. **2.** habit; custom. **3.** a set of examples for practice. [ML, from Gk]

**pray** /preɪ/, *v.t.* **1.** to make earnest petition to (a person, etc.). **2.** to make devout petition to (God or an object of worship). **3.** to make petition or entreaty for; crave. **4.** to offer (a prayer). **5.** to bring, put, etc., by praying. *–v.i.* **6.** to make entreaty or supplication, as to a person or for a thing. **7.** to make devout petition to God or to an object of worship. **8.** to enter into spiritual communion with God or an object of worship through prayer. [ME *preie(n)*, from OF *preier*, from L *precārī* beg, pray; akin to OE *fricgan*, G *fragen* ask]

**prayer**[1] /prɛə/, *n.* **1.** a devout petition to, or any form of spiritual communion with, God or an object of worship. **2.** the act, action, or practice of praying to God or an object of worship, as in supplication, thanksgiving, adoration, or confession. **3.** a form of words used in or appointed for praying: *the Lord's Prayer.* **4.** a religious observance, either public or private, consisting wholly or mainly of prayer. **5.** that which is prayed for. **6.** a petition or entreaty. **7.** the section of a bill in equity, or of a petition, setting forth the complaint or the action desired. [ME *preiere*, from OF, from Rom. *precāria*, orig. neut. pl. of L *precārius* obtained by entreaty]

**prayer**[2] /'preɪə/, *n.* one who prays. [PRAY + -ER[1]]

**prayer book** /'prɛə bʊk/, *n.* a book of forms of prayer.

**prayerful** /'prɛəfəl/, *adj.* given to, characterised by, or expressive of prayer. – **prayerfully,** *adv.* – **prayerfulness,** *n.*

**prayer meeting** /'prɛə mitɪŋ/, *n.* (in some Protestant churches) a meeting at which those present offer up individual prayers to God.

**prayer rug** /'– rʌg/, *n.* a small rug on which Muslims kneel and prostrate themselves during prayer. Also, **prayer mat.**

**prayer wheel** /'– wil/, *n.* a wheel or cylinder inscribed with or containing prayers, used chiefly by Buddhists of Tibet as a mechanical aid to continual praying, each revolution counting as an uttered prayer.

**praying mantis** /preɪɪŋ 'mæntəs/, *n.* →**mantis.**

**praying virgin** /– 'vɜdʒən/, *n.* a terrestrial orchid, *Drakaea elastica*, endemic in south-western Australia.

**pre-,** a prefix applied freely to mean 'prior to', 'in advance of' (*prewar*), also 'early', 'beforehand' (*prepay*), 'before', 'in front of' (*preoral, prefrontal*), and in many figurative meanings, often attached to stems not used alone (*prevent, preclude, preference, precedent*). [L *prae-*, representing *prae*, prep. and adv.]

**preach** /pritʃ/, *v.t.* **1.** to advocate or inculcate (religious or moral truth, right conduct, etc.) in speech or writing. **2.** to proclaim or make known by sermon (the gospel, good tidings, etc.). **3.** to deliver (a sermon or the like). *–v.i.* **4.** to deliver a sermon. **5.** to give earnest advice, as on religious subjects. **6.** to do this in an obtrusive or tedious way. [ME *preche(n)*, from OF *preëchier*, from LL *praedicāre.* See PREDICATE]

**preacher** /'pritʃə/, *n.* **1.** one whose occupation or function it is to preach the gospel. **2.** one who preaches.

**preachify** /'pritʃəfaɪ/, *v.i.*, **-fied, -fying.** *Chiefly U.S.* (*usu. derog.*) to preach in an obtrusive or tedious way. [PREACH + -(I)FY]

**preaching** /'pritʃɪŋ/, *n.* **1.** the act or practice of one who preaches. **2.** the art of delivering sermons. **3.** a sermon. **4.** a public religious service with a sermon. – **preachingly,** *adv.*

**preachment** /'pritʃmənt/, *n.* **1.** the act of preaching. **2.** a sermon or other discourse, esp. when obtrusive or tedious.

**preadamite** /pri'ædəmaɪt/, *n.* **1.** a person supposed to have existed before Adam. **2.** a person who believes that there were men in existence before Adam. *–adj.* **3.** existing before Adam. **4.** of the preadamites.

**preadolescence** /priædə'lɛsəns/, *n.* the period immediately preceding adolescence.

**preadolescent** /priædə'lɛsənt/, *adj.* pertaining to the period just before adolescence.

**preadult** /pri'ædʌlt/, *adj.* of or pertaining to the period before adulthood.

**preallotment** /priə'lɒtmənt/, *n.* an allotment given in advance.

**prealtar** /pri'ɔltə/, *adj.* in front of the altar.

**preamble** /pri'æmbəl/, *n.* **1.** an introductory statement; a preface; an introduction. **2.** the introductory part of a statute, deed, or the like, stating the reasons and intent of what follows. **3.** a preliminary or introductory fact or circumstance. [ME, from F *préambule*, from ML *praeambulum*, properly neut. of LL *praeambulus* walking before]

**preamplifier** /pri'æmpləfaɪə/, *n.* a device in the amplifier circuit of a radio or gramophone which increases the strength of a weak signal for detection and amplification. Also, **preamp** /pri'æmp/, **preselector.**

**prearrange** /priə'reɪndʒ/, *v.t.*, **-ranged, -ranging.** to arrange beforehand. – **prearrangement,** *n.*

**preaxial** /pri'æksiəl/, *adj.* situated before the body axis; pertaining to the radial side of the upper limb and the tibial side of the lower limb.

**prebend** /'prɛbənd/, *n.* **1.** a stipend allotted from the revenues of a cathedral or a collegiate church to a canon or member of the chapter. **2.** the land yielding such a stipend. **3.** →**prebendary.** [ME *prebende*, from ML *prēbenda*, var. of *praebenda* prebend, in LL allowance, properly neut. pl. ger. of L *prae(hi)bēre* offer, furnish] – **prebendal** /prə'bɛndl/, *adj.*

**prebendary** /'prɛbəndəri, -dri/, *n., pl.* **-daries.** a canon or clergyman who for special services at a cathedral or collegiate church is entitled to a prebend.

**prec.,** **1.** preceded. **2.** preceding.

**Pre-Cambrian** /ˌpri-'kæmbriən/, *adj.* **1.** pertaining to time or systems of rocks older than the Cambrian. *–n.* **2.** geological period, era, or systems of rocks older than the Cambrian, characterised by almost complete lack of fossils.

**precancel** /ˌpri'kænsəl/, *v.*, **-celled, -celling** or (*U.S.*) **-celed, -celing,** *n.* *–v.t.* **1.** to cancel a stamp before placing it on postal matter. *–n.* **2.** a precancelled stamp.

**precarious** /prə'kɛəriəs/, *adj.* **1.** dependent on circumstances beyond one's control; uncertain; unstable; insecure: *a precarious livelihood.* **2.** dependent on the will or pleasure of another; liable to be withdrawn or lost at the will of another: *precarious tenure.* **3.** exposed to or involving danger; dangerous; perilous; risky: *a precarious life.* **4.** having insufficient, little, or no foundation: *a precarious assumption.* [L *precārius* obtained by entreaty or by mere favour, hence uncertain, precarious] – **precariously,** *adv.* – **precariousness,** *n.*

**precast** /'prikast/, *adj.*; /ˌpri'kast/, *v.*, **-cast, -casting.** *Bldg Trades.* *–adj.* **1.** (of concrete parts) cast before being put into position in a structure. *–v.t.* **2.** to cast (concrete parts) before putting them into position in a structure.

**precatory** /'prɛkətəri, -tri/, *adj.* pertaining to, or of the nature of, or expressing entreaty or supplication. Also, **precative** /'prɛkətɪv/. [LL *precātōrius*]

**precatory trust** /– 'trʌst/, *n. Law.* construed from the use of precatory words if these can be regarded as an intention to impose a trust and not merely expressing a wish.

**precaution** /prə'kɔʃən/, *n.* **1.** a measure taken beforehand to ward off possible evil or secure good results. **2.** caution employed beforehand; prudent foresight. [LL *praecautio*, from L *praecavēre* guard against]

**precautionary** /prə'kɔʃənəri/, *adj.* **1.** pertaining to or of the nature of precaution or a precaution. **2.** expressing or advising precaution. Also, **precautional.**

**precautious** /prə'kɔʃəs/, *adj.* using or displaying precaution.

**precede** /pri'sid/, *v.*, **-ceded, -ceding.** *–v.t.* **1.** to go before, as in place, order, rank, importance, or time. **2.** to introduce by something preliminary; preface. *–v.i.* **3.** to go or come before. [ME *precede(n)*, from L *praecēdere*]

**precedence** /'prɛsədəns, pri'sidəns/, *n.* **1.** the act or fact of preceding. **2.** priority in order, rank, importance, etc. **3.** priority in time. **4.** the right to precede others in ceremonies or social formalities. **5.** the order to be observed ceremonially by persons of different ranks. Also, **precedency** /'prɛsədənsi, pri'sidənsi/.

**precedent**[1] /ˈprisədənt, ˈprɛ-/, *n.* **1.** a preceding instance or case which may serve as an example for or a justification in subsequent cases. **2.** *Law.* a legal decision or form of proceeding serving as an authoritative rule or pattern in future similar or analogous cases. [n. use. of PRECEDENT[2]]

**precedent**[2] /priˈsidənt, ˈprɛsədənt/, *adj.* →**preceding.** [ME, from L *praecēdens,* ppr., going before]

**precedential** /prɛsəˈdɛnʃəl/, *adj.* **1.** of the nature of or constituting a precedent. **2.** having precedence.

**preceding** /priˈsidɪŋ/, *adj.* that precedes; previous.

**precent** /prəˈsɛnt/, *v.t.* **1.** to lead as a precentor in singing. *–v.i.* **2.** to act as precentor. [backformation from PRECENTOR]

**precentor** /prəˈsɛntə/, *n.* **1.** one who leads a church choir or congregation in singing. **2.** the member of a cathedral chapter in charge of the music. [LL *praecentor* leader in music, from L *praecinere* sing before] – **precentorial** /prisɛnˈtɔriəl/, *adj.* – **precentorship,** *n.*

**precept** /ˈprisɛpt/, *n.* **1.** a commandment or direction given as a rule of action or conduct. **2.** an injunction as to moral conduct; a maxim. **3.** a rule, as for the performance of some technical operation. **4.** *Law.* **a.** a writ or warrant. **b.** *Brit.* a written order issued pursuant to law, as a sheriff's order for an election. **5.** an order for the collection of money under a rate. [ME, from L *praeceptum,* properly neut. pp., instructed]

**preceptive** /prəˈsɛptɪv/, *adj.* **1.** of the nature of or expressing a precept; mandatory. **2.** giving instructions; instructive. – **preceptively,** *adv.*

**preceptor** /prəˈsɛptə/, *n.* an instructor; a teacher; a tutor. [L *praeceptor*]

**precession** /priˈsɛʃən/, *n.* **1.** the act or fact of preceding; precedence. **2.** *Astron.* **a.** the precession of the equinoxes. **b.** the related motion of the earth's axis of rotation. **3.** the motion of a rotating body which, as a result of an applied couple whose axis is perpendicular to the axis of rotation, also involves rotation about a third mutually perpendicular axis. [ME, from LL *praecessio,* from L *praecessus,* pp., gone before]

**precessional** /priˈsɛʃənəl/, *adj.* of, pertaining to, characterised by, or resulting from precession.

**precession of the equinoxes,** *n.* the earlier occurrence of the equinoxes in each successive sidereal year because of a slow retrograde motion of the equinoctial points along the ecliptic, caused by the combined action of the sun and moon on the mass of matter accumulated about the earth's equator. A complete revolution of the equinoxes requires about 26 000 years.

**pre-Christian** /ˌpri-ˈkrɪstʃən/, *adj.* of, pertaining to, or belonging to a period of time before the Christian era.

**precinct** /ˈprisɪŋkt/, *n.* **1.** a place or space of definite or understood limits. **2.** (*oft. pl.*) an enclosing boundary or limit. **3.** (*pl.*) the parts or regions immediately about any place; the environs: *the precincts of a town.* **4.** the ground immediately surrounding a church, temple, or the like. **5.** a walled or otherwise bounded or limited space within which a building or place is situated. **6.** an area in a town, etc., whose use is in some way restricted: *a shopping precinct, a pedestrian precinct.* **7.** *U.S.* a district, as of a town, defined for governmental, administrative, or other purposes: *a police precinct.* **8.** *U.S.* one of a number of districts, each containing a polling place, into which a town is divided for electoral purposes. [ME, from ML *praecinctum,* properly neut. of L *praecinctus,* pp., girded about, surrounded]

**preciosity** /prɛʃiˈɒsəti, prɛs-/, *n., pl.* **-ties.** fastidious or carefully affected refinement, as in language, style, or taste. [ME *preciosite,* from OF, from L *pretiōsitas*]

**precious** /ˈprɛʃəs/, *adj.* **1.** of great price or value; valuable; costly: *precious metals.* **2.** of great moral or spiritual worth. **3.** dear or beloved. **4.** egregious; arrant, or gross. **5.** affectedly or excessively delicate, refined, or nice. *–n.* **6.** precious one; darling. *–adv.* **7.** *Colloq.* extremely; very. [ME, from OF *precios,* from L *pretiōsus* costly] – **preciously,** *adv.* – **preciousness,** *n.*

**precious stone** /– ˈstoʊn/, *n.* a gem distinguished for its beauty and rarity, used in jewellery, etc.

**precipice** /ˈprɛsəpəs/, *n.* **1.** a cliff with a vertical, or nearly vertical, or overhanging face. **2.** a situation of great peril. [F, from L *praecipitium*]

**precipitancy** /prəˈsɪpətənsi/, *n., pl.* **-cies. 1.** the quality or fact of being precipitant. **2.** headlong or rash haste. **3.** (*pl.*) hasty or rash acts. Also, **precipitance.**

**precipitant** /prəˈsɪpətənt/, *adj.* **1.** falling headlong. **2.** rushing headlong, rapidly, or hastily onwards. **3.** hasty; rash. **4.** unduly sudden or abrupt. *–n.* **5.** *Chem.* anything that causes precipitation. [L *praecipitans,* ppr., falling headlong] – **precipitantly,** *adv.*

**precipitate** /prəˈsɪpəteɪt/, *v.,* **-tated, -tating;** /prəˈsɪpətət/, *adj., n.* *–v.t.* **1.** to hasten the occurrence of; bring about in haste or suddenly: *to precipitate a quarrel.* **2.** *Chem.* to separate (a substance) in solid form from a solution, as by means of a reagent. **3.** *Physics, Meteorol.* to condense (moisture) from a state of vapour in the form of rain, dew, etc. **4.** to cast down headlong; fling or hurl down. **5.** to cast, plunge, or send, violently or abruptly: *to precipitate oneself into a struggle.* *–v.i.* **6.** to separate from a solution as a precipitate. **7.** *Physics, Meteorol.* to be condensed as rain, dew, etc. **8.** to be cast down or falling headlong. *–adj.* **9.** headlong. **10.** rushing headlong or rapidly onwards. **11.** proceeding rapidly or with great haste: *a precipitate retreat.* **12.** exceedingly sudden or abrupt. **13.** acting, or done or made, in sudden haste, or without due deliberation; overhasty; rash. *–n.* **14.** *Chem.* a substance precipitated from a solution. **15.** *Physics, Meteorol.* moisture condensed in the form of rain, dew, etc. [L *praecipitātus,* pp., cast headlong] – **precipitately,** *adv.* – **precipitateness,** *n.* – **precipitative,** *adj.* – **precipitator,** *n.*

**precipitation** /prəsɪpəˈteɪʃən/, *n.* **1.** the act of precipitating. **2.** the state of being precipitated. **3.** a casting down or falling headlong. **4.** a hastening or hurrying in movement, procedure, or action. **5.** sudden haste. **6.** unwise or rash rapidity. **7.** *Chem., Physics.* the precipitating of a substance from a solution. **8.** *Meteorol.* **a.** falling products of condensation in the atmosphere, as rain, snow, hail. **b.** the amount precipitated at a given place within a given period, usu. expressed in millimetres (rain) or centimetres (snow). **9.** *Spiritualism.* →**materialisation.**

**precipitin** /prəˈsɪpətən/, *n.* a substance developed in certain blood serums, capable of precipitating proteinaceous substances, etc. [PRECIPIT(ATE) + -IN[2]]

**precipitous** /prəˈsɪpətəs/, *adj.* **1.** of the nature of a precipice, or characterised by precipices: *a precipitous wall of rock.* **2.** extremely or impassably steep. **3.** precipitate. [PRECIPIT(ATE), *adj.,* + -OUS] – **precipitously,** *adv.,* – **precipitousness,** *n.*

**precis** /ˈpreɪsi/, *n., pl.* **-cis,** *v.* *–n.* **1.** an abstract or summary. *–v.t.* **2.** to make a precis of. Also, **précis.** [F, n. use of adj., cut short, PRECISE]

**precise** /prəˈsaɪs/, *adj.* **1.** definite or exact; definitely or strictly stated, defined, or fixed: *precise directions.* **2.** being exactly that, and neither more nor less: *the precise amount.* **3.** being just that, and not some other. **4.** definite or exact in statement, as a person. **5.** carefully distinct, as the voice. **6.** exact in measuring, recording, etc., as an instrument. **7.** excessively or rigidly particular; puritanical. [L *praecīsus,* pp., cut short, brief] – **precisely,** *adv.* – **preciseness,** *n.*

**precision** /prəˈsɪʒən/, *n.* **1.** the quality or state of being precise. **2.** accuracy; exactness. **3.** mechanical exactness. **4.** exact observance of forms in conduct or actions; punctiliousness. *–adj.* **5.** of, pertaining to, or characterised by precision or accuracy; adapted for fine measurement: *precision instruments, precision tools.* – **precisionist,** *n.*

**precision bombing** /– ˈbɒmɪŋ/, *n.* aerial bombing in which bombs are dropped as accurately as possible on a narrowly defined target area.

**preclassical** /ˌpriˈklæsɪkəl/, *adj.* of, pertaining to, or characteristic of a time preceding the classical era.

**preclinical** /ˌpriˈklɪnɪkəl/, *adj.* **1.** pertaining to the period prior to the appearance of the symptoms. *–n.* **2.** a preliminary course in anatomy and physiology taken by medical students before actual medical or surgical work in a hospital.

**preclude** /priˈklud/, *v.t.,* **-cluded, -cluding. 1.** to shut out or exclude; prevent the presence, existence, or occurrence of; make impossible. **2.** to shut out, debar, or prevent (a person, etc.) from something. [L *praeclūdere* shut off, close] – **pre-**

clusion /pri'kluʒən/, *n.* – **preclusive** /pri'klusɪv/, *adj.* – **preclusively,** *adv.*

**precocial** /pri'kouʃəl/, *adj.* (of birds) active, down-covered, and able to move about freely when hatched. [PRECOCI(OUS) + -AL[1]]

**precocious** /prə'kouʃəs/, *adj.* **1.** forward in development, esp. mental development, as a child. **2.** prematurely developed, as the mind, faculties, etc. **3.** pertaining to or showing premature development. **4.** *Bot.* **a.** flowering, fruiting, or ripening early, as plants or fruit. **b.** bearing blossoms before leaves, as plants. **c.** appearing before leaves, as flowers. [PRECOCI(TY) (from F *précocité* early maturity) + -OUS] – **precociously,** *adv.* – **precociousness, precocity** /prə'kɒsəti/, *n.*

**precognition** /ˌprikɒg'nɪʃən/, *n.* foreknowledge; knowledge of future events, esp. through extrasensory means. – **precognitive** /pri'kɒgnətɪv/, *adj.*

**pre-Columbian** /ˌpri-kə'lʌmbiən/, *adj.* of, pertaining to, or belonging to the period before the discovery of America by Columbus: *pre-Columbian civilisations.* [from Christopher *Columbus,* 1446?-1506, Italian navigator in Spanish service]

**preconceive** /prikən'siv/, *v.t.,* **-ceived, -ceiving.** to conceive beforehand; form an idea of in advance.

**preconception** /prikən'sɛpʃən/, *n.* **1.** a conception or opinion formed beforehand. **2.** bias; predilection.

**preconcert** /prikən'sɜt/, *v.t.* to arrange beforehand.

**precondemn** /prikən'dɛm/, *v.t.* to condemn beforehand, esp. before a fair and objective trial.

**precondition** /prikən'dɪʃən/, *n.* a prior or pre-existing condition; a condition necessary to a subsequent result; prerequisite.

**preconise** /'prikənaɪz/, *v.t.,* **-nised, -nising. 1.** to proclaim; commend publicly. **2.** to summon publicly. **3.** *Rom. Cath. Ch.* (of the pope) to declare solemnly in consistory the appointment of (a new bishop). Also, **preconize.** [ME, from ML *praecōnīzāre,* from L *praeco* crier, herald]

**preconscious** /ˌpri'kɒnʃəs/, *adj.* **1.** *Psychoanal.* absent from the conscious mind but capable of being easily recalled to it. **2.** of or pertaining to a state before the development of consciousness. *–n.* **3.** the preconscious part of the mind. – **preconsciously,** *adv.* – **preconsciousness,** *n.*

**precontract** /ˌpri'kɒntrækt/, *n.;* /prikən'trækt/, *v.* *–n.* **1.** a pre-existing contract, esp. of marriage. *–v.t.* **2.** to engage (a person) beforehand, esp. in a contract of marriage. **3.** to establish (an agreement) by prior contract. *–v.i.* **4.** to enter into a contract in advance.

**precook** /ˌpri'kʊk/, *v.t.* to cook partly or wholly beforehand.

**precritical** /ˌpri'krɪtɪkəl/, *adj. Med.* anteceding a crisis.

**pre-crumple** /ˌpri-'krʌmpəl/, *adj.* of or pertaining to the section of the bodies of certain motor cars which are expressly designed to crumple in collision as a protection to the more rigid central passenger compartment.

**precursor** /ˌpri'kɜsə/, *n.* **1.** one who or that which precedes; a predecessor. **2.** one who or that which indicates the approach of another or something else. **3.** *Biochem.* a metabolite which can be converted into another metabolite by one or more enzymic reactions. [L *praecursor*]

**precursory** /ˌpri'kɜsəri/, *adj.* **1.** of the nature of a precursor; introductory. **2.** indicative of something to follow. Also, **precursive** /pri'kɜsɪv/.

**pred.,** predicate.

**predacious** /prə'deɪʃəs/, *adj.* →**predatory.** Also, **predaceous.** [L *praedārī* take booty + -ACIOUS] – **predaciousness, predacity** /prə'dæsəti/, *n.*

**predate** /ˌpri'deɪt/, *v.t.,* **-dated, -dating. 1.** to date before the actual time: *he predated the cheque by three days.* **2.** to precede in date.

**predator** /'prɛdətə/, *n.* a predatory person, organism, or thing. [L *praedātor*]

**predatory** /'prɛdətəri, -tri/, *adj.* **1.** of, pertaining to, or characterised by plundering, pillaging, or robbery. **2.** addicted to or living by plundering or robbery: *predatory bands.* **3.** *Zool.* habitually preying upon other animals. [L *praedātōrius*] – **predatorily,** *adv.* – **predatoriness,** *n.*

**predecease** /ˌpridə'sis/, *v.t.,* **-ceased, -ceasing.** to die before (a person or an event).

**predecessor** /'pridəsɛsə/, *n.* **1.** one who precedes another in an office, position, etc. **2.** anything succeeded or replaced by something else. **3.** an ancestor or forefather. [ME *predecessour,* from LL *praedēcessor*]

**predefine** /ˌpridə'faɪn/, *v.t.,* **-fined, -fining.** to define or delimit beforehand.

**predella** /pri'dɛlə/, *n.* **1.** *Archit.* the base step of an altar. **2.** *Painting.* a long, narrow, painted panel, at the base of an altarpiece. [It.: slab, from Gmc]

**predesignate** /ˌpri'dɛzɪgneɪt/, *v.t.,* **-nated, -nating.** to designate beforehand. – **predesignation** /priˌdɛzɪg'neɪʃən/, *n.*

**predestinarian** /pridɛstə'nɛəriən/, *adj.* **1.** of or pertaining to predestination. **2.** believing in predestination. *–n.* **3.** one who holds the doctrine of predestination. – **predestinarianism,** *n.*

**predestinate** /pri'dɛstəneɪt/, *v.,* **-nated, -nating;** /pri'dɛstənət, -eɪt/, *adj.* *–v.t.* **1.** to foreordain; predetermine. **2.** *Theol.* to foreordain by divine decree or purpose. *–adj.* **3.** foreordained. [ME, from L *praedestinātus,* pp., appointed beforehand]

**predestination** /priˌdɛstə'neɪʃən/, *n.* **1.** the act of predestinating or predestining. **2.** the resulting state. **3.** fate or destiny. **4.** *Theol.* **a.** the action of God in foreordaining from eternity whatever comes to pass. **b.** the decree of God by which men are foreordained to everlasting happiness (election) or misery.

**predestine** /pri'dɛstən/, *v.t.,* **-tined, -tining.** to destine beforehand; foreordain; predetermine: *he seemed almost predestined for the ministry.*

**predeterminate** /pridə'tɜmənət/, *adj.* determined beforehand.

**predetermine** /pridə'tɜmən/, *v.t.,* **-mined, -mining. 1.** to determine or decide beforehand. **2.** to ordain beforehand; predestine. **3.** to direct or impel beforehand to something. – **predetermination** /pridəˌtɜmə'neɪʃən/, *n.* – **predeterminative,** *adj.*

**predial** /'pridiəl/, *adj.* →**praedial.**

**predicable** /'prɛdɪkəbəl/, *adj.* **1.** that may be predicated or affirmed; assertable. *–n.* **2.** that which may be predicated; an attribute. **3.** *Logic.* any one of the various kinds of predicate that may be used of a subject (in Aristotelian logic: genus, species, difference, property, and accident). – **predicability** /prɛdɪkə'bɪləti/, **predicableness,** *n.* – **predicably,** *adv.*

**predicament** /prə'dɪkəmənt/, *n.* **1.** an unpleasant, trying, or dangerous situation. **2.** a particular state, condition, or situation. **3.** one of the classes or categories of logical predications. [ME, from LL *praedicāmentum,* from L *praedicāre* proclaim] – **predicamental** /prədɪkə'mɛntl/, *adj.*

**predicant** /'prɛdɪkənt/, *adj.* **1.** preaching. *–n.* **2.** *Obs.* a preacher, esp. a member of a predicant order.

**predicate** /'prɛdɪkeɪt/, *v.,* **-cated, -cating;** /'prɛdɪkət/, *adj., n.* *–v.t.* **1.** to proclaim; declare; affirm or assert. **2.** to affirm or assert (something) of the subject of a proposition. **3.** to connote or imply. **4.** *U.S.* to found or base (a statement, action, etc.) on something. *–v.i.* **5.** to make an affirmation or assertion. *–adj.* **6.** predicated. **7.** *Gram.* belonging to the predicate: *a predicate noun.* *–n.* **8.** *Gram.* (in many languages) the active verb in a sentence or clause together with all the words it governs and those which modify it, as *is here* in *Jack is here.* **9.** *Logic.* that which is predicated or said of the subject in a proposition. [L *praedicātus,* pp., declared publicly, asserted, in LL preached] – **predication** /prɛdə'keɪʃən/, *n.* – **predicative** /prə'dɪkətɪv/, *adj.* – **predicatively** /prə'dɪkətɪvli/, *adv.*

**predicate noun** /– 'naʊn/, *n.* (in English and some other languages) a noun following one of a certain group of verbs and designating the same entity as the subject (he is *the king*) or the direct object (they made him *king*).

**predicative adjective** /prəˌdɪkətɪv 'ædʒəktɪv/, *n.* (in English and certain other languages, when one of a particular group of verbs is used) an adjective of the predicate bearing a kind of attributive relation to the subject (he is *dead*) or to the direct object (it made him *sick*).

**predicatory** /'prɛdɪkətri, prɛdə'keɪtəri/, *adj.* pertaining to preaching.

**predict** /prə'dɪkt/, *v.t.* **1.** to foretell; prophesy. *–v.i.* **2.** to foretell the future. [L *praedictus,* pp.] – **predictable,** *adj.* – **predictive,** *adj.* – **predictively,** *adv.*

**prediction** /prə'dɪkʃən/, *n.* **1.** the act of predicting. **2.** an instance of this; a prophecy.

**predictive** /prə'dɪktɪv/, *adj.* having the character or quality of predicting or indicating the future. – **predictively,** *adv.* – **predictiveness,** *n.*

**predictor** /prə'dɪktə/, *n.* **1.** one who or that which predicts. **2.** *Mil.* a machine used to range anti-aircraft guns against hostile aircraft.

**predigest** /pridə'dʒɛst, -daɪ-/, *v.t.* to treat (food) by an artificial process similar to digestion, in order to make it more easily digestible. – **predigestion,** *n.*

**predilection** /pridə'lɛkʃən/, *n.* a predisposition of the mind in favour of something; a partiality; preference. [PRE- + L *dīlectio* love, choice]

**predispose** /pridəs'pouz/, *v.,* **-posed, -posing.** *–v.t.* **1.** to give a previous inclination or tendency to. **2.** to render subject, susceptible, or liable: *poor health predisposed them to infection.* **3.** to dispose beforehand. *–v.i.* **4.** to give or furnish a tendency or inclination.

**predisposition** /ˌpridɪspə'zɪʃən/, *n.* **1.** the condition of being predisposed. **2.** *Pathol.* the condition of being particularly susceptible to a certain disease.

**prednisone** /'prɛdnəsoun/, *n.* a hydrogenated product of cortisone having the basic steroid structure.

**predominance** /prə'dɒmənəns/, *n.* the quality of being predominant; prevalence over others. Also, **predominancy.**

**predominant** /prə'dɒmənənt/, *adj.* **1.** having ascendancy, power, authority, or influence over others; ascendant. **2.** prevailing. – **predominantly,** *adv.*

**predominate** /prə'dɒməneɪt/, *v.,* **-nated, -nating.** *–v.i.* **1.** to be the stronger or leading element; preponderate; prevail. **2.** to have or exert controlling power (oft. fol. by *over*). **3.** to surpass others in authority or influence. **4.** to be more noticeable or imposing than something else. *–v.t.* **5.** to dominate or prevail over. [PRE- + L *dominātus,* pp., ruled, dominated] – **predominatingly,** *adv.* – **predomination** /prəˌdɒmə'neɪʃən/, *n.* – **predominator,** *n.*

**predynastic** /pridə'næstɪk, -daɪ-/, *adj.* of or pertaining to the period in Egypt before the first dynasty, generally taken as before 3200 B.C.

**pre-election** /'pri-əlɛkʃən/, *adj.* occurring before an election.

**pre-eminence** /pri-'ɛmənəns/, *n.* the state or character of being pre-eminent.

**pre-eminent** /pri-'ɛmənənt/, *adj.* eminent before or above others; superior to or surpassing others; distinguished beyond others. [ME, from L *praeēminens,* ppr., standing out, rising above] – **pre-eminently,** *adv.*

**pre-empt** /pri-'ɛmpt/, *v.t.* **1.** to occupy (land) in order to establish a prior right to buy. **2.** to acquire or appropriate beforehand. **3.** to anticipate. *–v.i.* **4.** *Bridge.* to make a pre-emptive bid. [backformation from PRE-EMPTION] – **pre-emptory,** *adj.* – **pre-emptor,** *n.*

**pre-emption** /pri-'ɛmpʃən/, *n.* the act or right of purchasing before or in preference to others. [PRE- + L *emptio* a buying]

**pre-emptive** /pri-'ɛmptɪv/, *adj.* **1.** of or pertaining to pre-emption. **2.** *Bridge.* of or pertaining to an unnecessarily high bid, made to deter one's opponents from bidding.

**preen** /prin/, *v.t.* **1.** to trim or dress with the beak, as a bird does its feathers. **2.** to prepare, dress, or array (oneself) carefully in making one's toilet. **3.** to pride (oneself) on an achievement, etc. [probably var. of obs. *prune* to preen, from ME *prune(n)*] – **preener,** *n.*

**pre-engage** /pri-ən'geɪdʒ/, *v.t., v.i.,* **-gaged, -gaging.** to engage beforehand. – **pre-engagement,** *n.*

**pre-English** /pri-'ɪŋglɪʃ/, *n.* **1.** the ancient Germanic dialect which by differentiation from its sister dialects eventually became English. **2.** the languages current in Britain before the English settlement. *–adj.* **3.** pertaining to the ancestral Germanic dialect from which English grew, and to its speakers. **4.** pertaining to the languages and peoples of Britain before the English settlement.

**pre-establish** /pri-əs'tæblɪʃ/, *v.t.* to establish beforehand. – **pre-establishment,** *n.*

**pre-European** /ˌpri-jurə'piən/, *adj.* before discovery or colonisation by Europeans.

**pre-examination** /pri-əgzæmə'neɪʃən/, *adj.* before an examination: *pre-examination nerves.* Also, *Colloq.,* **pre-exam.**

**pre-exilian** /pri-ɛg'zɪljən/, *adj.* before the Babylonian exile or captivity of the Jews. Also, **pre-exilic.** [PRE- + L *exilium* exile + -AN]

**pre-exist** /pri-əg'zɪst, pri-ɛg-, pri-ɪg-/, *v.i.* **1.** to exist beforehand. **2.** to exist in a previous state. – **pre-existence,** *n.* – **pre-existent,** *adj.*

**pref.,** **1.** preface. **2.** prefaced. **3.** preference. **4.** preferred. **5.** prefix. **6.** prefixed.

**prefab** /'prifæb/, *n.* a prefabricated house.

**prefabricate** /pri'fæbrəkeɪt/, *v.t.,* **-cated, -cating. 1.** to fabricate or construct beforehand. **2.** to manufacture (houses, etc.) in standardised parts or sections ready for rapid assembly and erection. – **prefabricated,** *adj.* – **prefabrication** /priˌfæbrə'keɪʃən/, *n.*

**preface** /'prɛfəs/, *n., v.,* **-aced, -acing.** *–n.* **1.** a preliminary statement by the author or editor of a book, setting forth its purpose and scope, expressing acknowledgment of assistance from others, etc. **2.** an introductory part, as of a speech. **3.** something preliminary or introductory. **4.** *Eccles.* a prayer of thanksgiving, the introduction to the canon of the mass, ending with the Sanctus. *–v.t.* **5.** to provide with or introduce by a preface. **6.** to serve as a preface to. [ME, from OF, from ML *prēfātia,* replacing L *praefātio* a saying beforehand]

**prefatory** /'prɛfətəri, -tri/, *adj.* of the nature of a preface; preliminary. – **prefatorily,** *adv.*

**prefect** /'prifɛkt/, *n.* **1.** a person appointed to any of various positions of command, authority, or superintendence, as a chief magistrate in ancient Rome, or the chief administrative official of a department of France and Italy. **2.** (in many schools) one of a body of senior pupils with authority for maintaining order and discipline. **3.** the dean in a Jesuit school or college. Also, **praefect.** [ME, from L *praefactus* overseer, director, properly pp., appointed as a superior]

**prefectorial** /prifɛk'tɔriəl/, *adj.* of, pertaining to, or characteristic of a prefect.

**prefecture** /'prifɛktʃə/, *n.* **1.** the office, jurisdiction, territory, or official residence of a prefect. **2.** the administrative centre of a French region. [L *praefectūra*] – **prefectural** /pri'fɛktʃərəl/, *adj.*

**prefer** /prə'fɜ/, *v.t.,* **-ferred, -ferring. 1.** to set or hold before or above other persons or things in estimation; like better; choose rather: *to prefer Dickens to Thackeray.* **2.** *Law.* to give priority, as to one creditor over another. **3.** to put forward or present (a statement, suit, charge, etc.) for consideration or sanction. **4.** to put forward or advance, as in rank or office. [ME *preferre,* from L *praeferre* bear before, set before, prefer] – **preferrer,** *n.*

**preferable** /'prɛfərəbəl, 'prɛfrəbəl/, *adj.* **1.** worthy to be preferred. **2.** more desirable. – **preferability** /prɛfərə'bɪləti/, **preferableness,** *n.* – **preferably** /'prɛfrəbli, prə'fɜrəbli/, *adv.*

**preference** /'prɛfərəns, 'prɛfrəns/, *n.* **1.** the act of preferring; estimation of one thing above another; prior favour or choice. **2.** the state of being preferred. **3.** that which is preferred; the object of prior favour or choice. **4.** a practical advantage given to one over others. **5.** a prior right or claim, as to payment of dividends, or to assets upon dissolution. **6.** the favouring of one country or group of countries by granting special advantages over others in international trade.

**preference shares** /'– ʃɛəz/, *n.pl.* shares which rank before ordinary shares in the entitlement to dividends, usu. at a fixed rate of interest. Also, *U.S.,* **preferred stock.**

**preference stock** /'– stɒk/, *n.* stock in a company which entitles the holder to preferential rights in respect of dividends over holders of other classes of stock or shares, as ordinary or deferred.

**preferential** /prɛfə'rɛnʃəl/, *adj.* **1.** pertaining to or of the nature of preference. **2.** showing or giving preference. **3.** receiving or enjoying preference. – **preferentialism,** *n.* – **preferentialist,** *n.* – **preferentially,** *adv.*

**preferential voting** /– 'voutɪŋ/, *n.* a system of voting which enables the voter to indicate his order of preference for candidates in the ballot. If no candidate achieves an absolute majority, the candidate with fewest first preferences is eliminated and the second preferences on the relevant ballot papers are distributed and so on until one candidate has an absolute majority. See **absolute majority.**

**preferment** /prə'fɜmənt/, *n.* **1.** the act of preferring. **2.** the state of being preferred. **3.** advancement or promotion, as in rank. **4.** a position or office giving social or pecuniary advancement.

**preferred stock** /prəfɜd 'stɒk/, *n. U.S.* →**preference shares.**

**prefiguration** /ˌprifɪgjə'reɪʃən/, *n.* **1.** the act of prefiguring. **2.** that in which something is prefigured.

**prefigure** /pri'fɪgə/, *v.t.,* **-ured, -uring.** **1.** to represent beforehand by figure or type; foreshow; foreshadow. **2.** to figure or represent to oneself beforehand. [late ME, from LL *praefigūrāre.* See PRE-, FIGURE, *v.*] – **prefigurative** /pri'fɪgjərətɪv/, *adj.* – **prefigurement,** *n.*

**prefix** /'prifɪks/, *n.;* /pri'fɪks, 'prifɪks/, *v.* *–n.* **1.** *Gram.* an affix which is put before a word, stem, or word element to add to or qualify its meaning (as *un-* in *unkind*), strictly speaking an inseparable form, but usu. applied to prepositions and adverbs also, as in German *mitgehen.* **2.** something prefixed, as a title before a person's name. *–v.t.* **3.** to fix or put before or in front. **4.** *Gram.* to add as a prefix. **5.** *Rare.* to fix, settle, or appoint beforehand. [ME, from L *praefixus,* pp., fixed before] – **prefixal** /'prifɪksəl, pri'fɪksəl/, *adj.* – **prefixally,** *adv.*

**preform** /ˌpri'fɔm/, *v.t.* to form beforehand.

**preformation** /prifɔ'meɪʃən/, *n.* **1.** previous formation. **2.** *Biol.* a theoretical concept according to which the individual, with all its parts, pre-exists in the germ and grows from microscopic to normal proportions during embryogenesis (opposed to *epigenesis*).

**prefrontal** /ˌpri'frʌntl/, *adj.* **1.** in front of the frontal bone or gyrus. *–n.* **2.** the middle portion of the ethmoid bone.

**preggers** /'prɛgəz/, *adj. Colloq.* →**pregnant** (def. 1). Also, **preggie, preggies, preggo.**

**preglacial** /ˌpri'gleɪʃəl, -'gleɪsiəl/, *adj.* existing or occurring before a glacial epoch, esp. the Pleistocene.

**pregnable** /'prɛgnəbəl/, *adj.* **1.** capable of being taken or won by force, as a fortress. **2.** open to attack; assailable. [late ME *prenable,* from OF, from *prendre,* from L *pre(he)ndere* seize, take] – **pregnability** /prɛgnə'bɪləti/, *n.*

**pregnancy** /'prɛgnənsi/, *n., pl.* **-cies.** the condition or quality of being pregnant.

**pregnant** /'prɛgnənt/, *adj.* **1.** being with child or young, as a woman or female mammal; having a foetus in the womb. **2.** fraught, filled, or abounding (fol. by *with*): *words pregnant with meaning.* **3.** fertile or rich (fol. by *in*): *a mind pregnant in ideas.* **4.** full of meaning; highly significant: *a pregnant utterance.* **5.** full of possibilities, involving important issues or results, or momentous. **6.** teeming with ideas or imagination: *a pregnant wit.* [ME, from L *praegnans*] – **pregnantly,** *adv.*

**preheat** /ˌpri'hit/, *v.t.* to heat before using or before submitting to some process.

**prehensile** /pri'hɛnsaɪl/, *adj.* **1.** adapted for seizing, grasping, or laying hold of anything. **2.** fitted for grasping by folding or wrapping round an object. [F, from L *prehensus,* pp., seized + *-ile* -ILE] – **prehensility** /prihɛn'sɪləti/, *n.*

**prehension** /pri'hɛnʃən/, *n.* **1.** the act of seizing, grasping, or taking hold. **2.** mental apprehension. [L *prehensio*]

**prehistoric** /ˌprihɪs'tɒrɪk/, *adj.* of or belonging to a period prior to that of recorded history. Also, **prehistorical.** – **prehistorically,** *adv.*

**prehistory** /ˌpri'hɪstəri/, *n.* **1.** the history of man in the period before recorded events, known mainly through archaeological research; an account or study of prehistoric man. **2.** a history of events leading up to a particular incident, situation, etc.

**prehuman** /ˌpri'hjumən/, *adj.* before the advent or evolution of man.

**pre-ignition** /pri-ɪg'nɪʃən/, *n.* ignition of the charge in an internal-combustion engine earlier in the cycle than is compatible with proper operation.

**pre-industrial** /pri-ɪn'dʌstriəl/, *adj.* before the growth of modern industrial processes; before the Industrial Revolution.

**prejudge** /ˌpri'dʒʌdʒ/, *v.t.,* **-judged, -judging.** **1.** to judge beforehand. **2.** to pass judgment on prematurely or in advance of due investigation. – **prejudger,** *n.* – **prejudgment,** *n.*

**prejudice** /'prɛdʒədəs/, *n., v.,* **-diced, -dicing.** *–n.* **1.** an unfavourable opinion or feeling formed beforehand or without knowledge, thought, or reason. **2.** any preconceived opinion or feeling, favourable or unfavourable. **3.** disadvantage resulting from some judgment or action of another. **4.** resulting injury or detriment. **5. without prejudice,** *Law.* without dismissing, damaging, or otherwise affecting a legal interest or demand. *–v.t.* **6.** to affect with a prejudice, favourable or unfavourable: *these facts prejudiced us in his favour.* **7.** to affect disadvantageously or detrimentally. [ME, from F, from L *praejūdicium*]

**prejudicial** /prɛdʒə'dɪʃəl/, *adj.* causing prejudice or disadvantage; detrimental. – **prejudicially,** *adv.*

**pre-labour** /ˌpri-'leɪbə/, *n.* →**false labour.**

**prelacy** /'prɛləsi/, *n., pl.* **-cies.** **1.** the office or dignity of a prelate. **2.** the order of prelates. **3.** the body of prelates collectively. **4.** (*oft. derog.*) the system of church government by prelates.

**prelate** /'prɛlət/, *n.* an ecclesiastic of a high order, as an archbishop, bishop, etc.; a church dignitary. [ME *prelat,* from ML *praelātus* a civil or ecclesiastical dignitary; in L, pp., set before, preferred] – **prelateship,** *n.* – **prelatic** /prə'lætɪk/, *adj.*

**prelatism** /'prɛlətɪzəm/, *n.* prelacy or episcopacy. – **prelatist,** *n.*

**prelature** /'prɛlətʃə/, *n.* **1.** the office of a prelate. **2.** the order of prelates. **3.** prelates collectively. [ML *praelātūra,* from L *praelātus.* See PRELATE]

**prelibation** /ˌprilaɪ'beɪʃən/, *n.* →**foretaste.** [LL *praelībātio,* from L *praelībāre* taste beforehand]

**prelim** /'prilɪm/, *n.* **1.** any event, as an examination or sporting contest, which is preliminary to the main event. **2.** (*pl.*) the preliminary pages preceding the main text of a work. [abbrev. of PRELIMINARY]

**prelim.,** preliminary.

**preliminary** /prə'lɪmənəri/, *adj., n., pl.* **-naries.** *–adj.* **1.** preceding and leading up to the main matter or business; introductory; preparatory. *–n.* **2.** something preliminary; introductory or preparatory step, measure, sporting contest, or the like. [NL *praelīmināris,* from L *prae-* PRE- + *līmināris* of a threshold] – **preliminarily,** *adv.*

**preliminary final** /– 'faɪnəl/, *n.* (in a sporting competition, etc., where the winner is not decided on a simple knockout basis) a match to determine which of two teams or contestants will play in the grand final against the team or contestant already qualified. Also, **final.**

**preliterate** /ˌpri'lɪtərət/, *adj.* not leaving or having written records: *a preliterate culture.*

**prelude** /'prɛljud/, *n., v.,* **-uded, -uding.** *–n.* **1.** a preliminary to an action, event, condition, or work of broader scope and higher importance. **2.** preliminary action, remarks, etc. **3.** *Music.* **a.** a relatively short, independent instrumental composition, free in form and of an improvised character. **b.** a piece which precedes a more important movement. **c.** the overture to an opera. **d.** an independent piece, of moderate length, sometimes used as an introduction to a fugue. **e.** music opening a church service; an introductory voluntary. *–v.t.* **4.** to serve as a prelude or introduction to. **5.** to introduce by a prelude. **6.** to play as a prelude. *–v.i.* **7.** to serve as a prelude. **8.** to give a prelude. **9.** to play a prelude. [F, from ML *praelūdium,* from L *praelūdere* play beforehand] – **preluder,** *n.*

**prelusive** /prə'lusɪv/, *adj.* introductory. Also, **prelusory** /prə'lusəri/. – **prelusively,** *adv.*

**prem** /prɛm/, *n.* →**premmie.** Also, **premie.**

**premarital** /ˌpri'mærətl/, *adj.* before marriage.

**premature** /'prɛmətʃə, prɛmə'tjuə/, *adj.* **1.** coming into existence or occurring too soon. **2.** mature or ripe before the proper time. **3.** overhasty, as in action. [L *praemātūrus*] – **prematurely,** *adv.* – **prematureness, prematurity,** *n.*

**premaxilla** /ˌprimæk'sɪlə/, *n., pl.* **-maxillae** /-mæk'sɪli/. one of a pair of bones of the upper jaw of vertebrates, situated in front of and between the maxillary bones. [NL *praemaxilla,* from L *prae-* PRE- + *maxilla* jawbone] – **premaxillary,** *adj.*

**premed** /ˌpri'mɛd/, *n. Colloq.* **1.** →**premedication.** **2.** →**premedical.**

**premedical** /ˌpri'mɛdɪkəl/, *adj.* **1.** pertaining to the preparation for the study of medicine. *–n.* **2.** (in medical training) a course of study in basic sciences to be completed prior to the preclinical studies.

**premedication** /ˌprimɛdə'keɪʃən/, *n.* the giving of drugs prior to an operation, to sedate and prepare a patient.

**premeditate** /priˈmɛdəteɪt/, *v.t., v.i.,* **-tated, -tating.** to meditate, consider, or plan beforehand. [L *praemeditātus,* pp., meditated beforehand] – **premeditatedly,** *adv.* – **premeditative,** *adj.* – **premeditator,** *n.*

**premeditation** /ˌprimɛdəˈteɪʃən, prəˌmɛd-/, *n.* **1.** the act of premeditating. **2.** *Law.* sufficient forethought to impute deliberation and intent to commit the act.

**premenstrual tension** /ˌpriˌmɛnstruəl ˈtɛnʃən/, *n.* symptoms of physiological and emotional upset, as headache, pelvic discomfort, and breast enlargement, experienced by women in the week prior to menstruation.

**premier** /ˈprɛmiə/, *n.* **1.** the leader of a State government. **2.** (*pl.*) (in sport) the team which wins the season's competition. **3.** *Brit.* the prime minister, or first minister of state. *–adj.* **4.** first in rank; chief; leading. **5.** winning: *the premier team.* **6.** earliest. [F: first, from L *prīmārius* of the first rank]

**premiere** /prɛmiˈɛə/, *n., v.,* **premiered, premiering.** *–n.* **1.** a first public performance of a play, etc. **2.** the leading woman, as in a drama. *–v.t.* **3.** to present to the public for the first time. *–v.i.* **4.** to have the first public showing of a film, play, etc. [F: lit., first (fem.)]

**premiership** /ˈprɛmiəʃɪp/, *n.* **1.** the office of premier of a State. **2.** a sporting competition, esp. football.

**premillenarian** /ˌprimɪləˈnɛəriən/, *adj.* **1.** of or pertaining to premillennialism. *–n.* **2.** a believer in premillennialism.

**premillennial** /priməˈlɛniəl/, *adj.* of or pertaining to the period preceding the millennium.

**premillennialism** /priməˈlɛniəlɪzəm/, *n.* the doctrine or belief that the second coming of Christ will precede the millennium. – **premillennialist,** *n.*

**premise** /ˈprɛməs/, *n., v.,* **-ised, -ising.** *–n.* **1.** (*pl.*) **a.** the property forming the subject of a conveyance. **b.** a tract of land. **c.** a house or building with the grounds, etc., belonging to it. **2.** Also, **premiss.** *Logic.* a proposition (or one of several) from which a conclusion is drawn. **3.** *Law.* **a.** a basis, stated or assumed, on which reasoning proceeds. **b.** an earlier statement in a document. **c.** (in a bill in equity) the statement of facts upon which the complaint is based, the parties, etc. *–v.t.* **4.** to set forth beforehand, as by way of introduction or explanation. **5.** to assume, whether explicitly or implicitly, a proposition as a premise for some conclusion. *–v.i.* **6.** to set down, as a preface. **7.** to state or assume as a premise. [ME *premiss,* from ML *praemissa,* properly fem. pp., sent before]

**premium** /ˈprimiəm/, *n.* **1.** a prize to be won in a competition. **2.** a bonus, gift, or sum additional to price, wages, interest, or the like. **3.** a bonus, prize, or the like, offered as an inducement to buy a product. **4.** the amount paid or agreed to be paid, in one sum or periodically, as the consideration for a contract of insurance. **5.** *Econ.* the excess value of one form of money over another of the same nominal value. **6.** a sum above the nominal or par value of a thing. **7.** *Stock Exchange.* the amount that a buyer is prepared to pay for the right to subscribe for a new or rights issue of stocks or shares in a company. **8.** a fee paid for instruction in a trade or profession. **9. at a premium, a.** in high esteem; in demand. **b.** at a high price. *–adj.* **10.** highly regarded, special. **11.** of highest quality; best. [L *praemium* profit]

**premmie** /ˈprɛmi/, *Colloq.* *–n.* **1.** an infant born prematurely. *–adj.* **2.** of or pertaining to such an infant. Also, **prem, premie.**

**premolar** /ˌpriˈmoʊlə/, *adj.* **1.** denoting or pertaining to certain of the permanent teeth in mammals (in man, usu. called bicuspid teeth) in front of the molar teeth. *–n.* **2.** a premolar tooth. **3.** →**bicuspid.**

**premonish** /priˈmɒnɪʃ/, *v.t.* to forewarn. [L *praemonēre* forewarn + -ISH², modelled on ADMONISH]

**premonition** /prɛməˈnɪʃən, pri-/, *n.* **1.** a forewarning. **2.** →**presentiment.** [F (obs.), from LL *praemonitio*]

**premonitory** /priˈmɒnətəri, -tri/, *adj.* giving premonition; serving to warn beforehand.

**premorse** /priˈmɔs/, *adj. Biol.* having the end irregularly truncate, as if bitten or broken off. [L *praemorsus,* pp., bitten off in front]

**prenatal** /ˌpriˈneɪtl/, *adj.* →**antenatal.** – **prenatally,** *adv.*

**prenominate** /prəˈnɒmənət/, *adj. Archaic* forementioned. [L *praenōminātus,* pp., named before]

**prenotion** /ˌpriˈnoʊʃən/, *n.* →**preconception.** [L *praenōtio*]

**prentice** /ˈprɛntəs/, *n.* **1.** *Archaic.* apprentice. *–adj.* **2.** of or pertaining to juvenilia: *prentice piece.*

**preoccupancy** /priˈɒkjəpənsi/, *n.* **1.** previous occupancy. **2.** the state of being preoccupied; engrossed in thought.

**preoccupation** /priɒkjəˈpeɪʃən/, *n.* **1.** the state of being preoccupied. **2.** the act of preoccupying. **3.** that with which one is preoccupied.

**preoccupied** /priˈɒkjəpaɪd/, *adj.* **1.** completely engrossed in thought; absorbed. **2.** occupied previously. **3.** *Biol.* already used as a name for some species, genus, etc., and not available as a designation for any other.

**preoccupy** /priˈɒkjəpaɪ/, *v.t.,* **-pied, -pying.** **1.** to absorb or engross to the exclusion of other things. **2.** to occupy or take possession of beforehand or before others. – **preoccupant, preoccupier,** *n.*

**preoral** /priˈɒrəl/, *adj.* situated in front of or before the mouth. – **preorally,** *adv.*

**preordain** /priɔˈdeɪn/, *v.t.* to ordain beforehand; foreordain. – **preordainment, preordination** /priˌɔdəˈneɪʃən/, *n.*

**pre-owned** /ˈpri-oʊnd/, *adj.* second-hand; used: *a pre-owned Mercedes-Benz.*

**prep** /prɛp/, *adj., n., v.,* **prepped, prepping.** *Colloq.* *–adj.* **1.** preparatory: *a prep school.* *–n.* **2.** a preparatory school. **3.** →**preparation** (def. 3). *–v.t.* **4.** to prepare (a patient) for an operation.

**prep.,** **1.** preparation. **2.** preparatory. **3.** preposition.

**prepacked** /ˈpripækt/, *adj.* (of goods, esp. foodstuffs) packed for sale.

**preparation** /prɛpəˈreɪʃən/, *n.* **1.** a proceeding, measure, or provision by which one prepares for something: *preparations for a journey.* **2.** any proceeding, experience, or the like considered as a mode of preparing for the future. **3.** homework, or, esp. in a boarding school, individual work supervised by a teacher. **4.** the act of preparing. **5.** the state of being prepared. **6.** something prepared, manufactured, or compounded. **7.** a specimen, as an animal body, prepared for scientific examination, dissection, etc. **8.** *Music.* **a.** the preparing of a dissonance, by introducing the dissonant note as a consonant note in the preceding chord. **b.** the note so introduced. **9.** the day before the Jewish Sabbath, or any other major Jewish festival. **10.** (in the Eastern European and Orthodox churches) the day before the Christian Sabbath.

**preparative** /prəˈpærətɪv/, *adj.* **1.** preparatory. *–n.* **2.** something that prepares. **3.** a preparation.

**preparatory** /prəˈpærətri/, *adj.* **1.** serving or designed to prepare or make ready: *preparatory arrangements.* **2.** preliminary or introductory. **3.** of or pertaining to education which prepares a child for public school, etc. – **preparatorily,** *adv.*

**preparatory school** /ˈ– skul/, *n.* an independent school, often boarding, for pupils under about 13 years of age, before entering a public school (def. 2).

**prepare** /prəˈpɛə/, *v.,* **-pared, -paring.** *–v.t.* **1.** to make ready, or put in due condition, for something. **2.** to get ready for eating, as a meal, by due assembling, dressing, or cooking. **3.** to manufacture, compound, or compose. **4.** *Music.* to lead up to (a discord, an embellishment, etc.) by some preliminary note or notes. *–v.i.* **5.** to put things or oneself in readiness; get ready: *to prepare for war.* [L *praeparāre* make ready beforehand] – **preparedly** /prəˈpɛərədli, -ˈpɛədli/, *adv.* – **preparer,** *n.*

**preparedness** /prəˈpɛərədnəs, -ˈpɛədnəs/, *n.* the state of being prepared; readiness.

**prepared piano** /prəˌpɛəd piˈænoʊ/, *n.* a piano whose natural sound is altered by the application of objects such as screws, glass and rubber bands to the strings.

**prepay** /ˌpriˈpeɪ/, *v.t.,* **-paid, -paying.** **1.** to pay beforehand. **2.** to pay the charge upon in advance. – **prepayable,** *adj.* – **prepayment,** *n.*

**prepense** /prəˈpɛns/, *adj.* premeditated: *malice prepense.* [earlier *prepenst, prepensed,* pp. of obs. *prepense* meditate beforehand; replacing ME *purpense,* from OF]

**preponderance** /prəˈpɒndərəns, pri-, -drəns/, *n.* the quality or fact of being preponderant; superiority in weight, power, number, etc. Also, **preponderancy.**

**preponderant** /prə'pɒndərənt, pri-, -drənt/, *adj.* superior in weight, force, influence, number, etc.; preponderating; predominant. – **preponderantly,** *adv.*

**preponderate** /prə'pɒndəreɪt, pri-/, *v.i.*, **-rated, -rating.** **1.** to exceed something else in weight; be the heavier. **2.** to incline downwards or descend, as one scale or end of a balance, because of greater weight; be weighed down. **3.** to be superior in power, force, influence, number, amount, etc.; predominate. [L *praeponderātus,* pp. See PONDER] – **preponderating,** *adj.* – **preponderatingly,** *adv.* – **preponderation** /prə,pɒndə'reɪʃən/, *n.*

**preposition** /prɛpə'zɪʃən/, *n.* **1.** (in some languages) one of the major form-classes, or parts of speech, comprising words placed before nouns to indicate their relation to other words or their function in the sentence. *By, to, in, from* are prepositions in English. **2.** any such word, as *by, to, in, from.* **3.** any word or construction of similar function or meaning, as *on top of* (=*on*). [ME, from L *praepositio*] – **prepositional,** *adj.* – **prepositionally,** *adv.*

**prepositive** /pri'pɒzətɪv/, *adj.* **1.** put before; prefixed. –*n.* **2.** *Gram.* a word placed before another as a modifier or to show its relation to other parts of the sentence. *Red* in *red book* is a prepositive adjective. *John's* in *John's book* is a prepositive genitive.

**prepossess** /pripə'zɛs/, *v.t.* **1.** to possess or dominate mentally beforehand, as a prejudice does. **2.** to prejudice or bias, esp. favourably. **3.** to impress favourably beforehand or at the outset.

**prepossessing** /pripə'zɛsɪŋ/, *adj.* that prepossesses, esp. favourably. – **prepossessingly,** *adv.*

**prepossession** /pripə'zɛʃən/, *n.* **1.** the state of being prepossessed. **2.** a prejudice, esp. in favour of a person or thing.

**preposterous** /prə'pɒstərəs/, *adj.* directly contrary to nature, reason, or common sense; absurd, senseless, or utterly foolish. [L *praeposterus* with the hinder part foremost] – **preposterously,** *adv.* – **preposterousness,** *n.*

**prepotency** /pri'poʊtnsi/, *n.* the ability of one parent to impress its hereditary characters on its progeny because it possesses more homozygous, dominant, or epistatic genes.

**prepotent** /pri'poʊtnt/, *adj.* **1.** pre-eminent in power, authority, or influence; predominant. **2.** *Genetics.* denoting, pertaining to, or having prepotency. [L *praepotens,* ppr., having superior power. See POTENT] – **prepotently,** *adv.*

**pre-prandial** /,pri-'prændiəl/, *adj.* before a meal, esp. of drinks.

**preprint** /'priprɪnt/, *n.* an advance printing, usu. of a portion of a book or of an article in a periodical.

**prepublication** /,pripʌblə'keɪʃən/, *adj.* before publication, as a specially reduced price of a book before the official date of publication.

**prepuce** /'pripjus/, *n.* the fold of skin which covers the head of the penis or clitoris; foreskin. [ME, from F, from L *praepūtium*] – **preputial** /pri'pjuʃəl/, *adj.*

**Pre-Raphaelite** /,pri-'ræfəlaɪt/, *adj.* of, pertaining to, or characteristic of the Pre-Raphaelites, a group of English artists (the Pre-Raphaelite brotherhood), formed in 1848, and including Holman Hunt, John Everett Millars and Dante Gabriel Rossetti, who aimed to revive the style and spirit of the Italian artists before the time of Raphael (1483-1520), by producing work delicate in colour and finish and imbued with poetic sentiment.

**prerecord** /prirə'kɔd/, *v.t.* to record beforehand, for playing back at a subsequent date.

**prerelease** /prirə'lis/, *n.* the release of something before the scheduled date, as a film, record, etc.

**prerequisite** /pri'rɛkwəzət/, *adj.* **1.** required beforehand; requisite as an antecedent condition. –*n.* **2.** something prerequisite: *a knowledge of French was the only prerequisite for admission to the course.*

**prerogative** /prə'rɒgətɪv/, *n.* **1.** an exclusive right or privilege attaching to an office or position. **2.** a right or privilege attached to a specific person or group of persons. **3.** royal prerogative. **4.** a prior, peculiar, or exclusive right or privilege. **5.** *Obs.* precedence; pre-eminence. –*adj.* **6.** having or exercising a prerogative. **7.** pertaining to, characteristic of, or existing by virtue of, a prerogative. [ME, from L *praerogātīva,* properly fem. adj., voting first]

**prerogative order** /– 'ɔdə/, *n.* process issued from extraordinary occasions on proper cause, being shown as writ of mandamus, habeas corpus, etc. Also, **prerogative writ.**

**Pres.,** President.

**presa** /'prɛsə/, *n., pl.* **prese** /'prɛseɪ/. a mark used in music, as :S:, +, or ※, used in a canon, round, etc., to indicate where the successive voice parts are to take up the theme. [It.: a taking, fem. of *preso,* pp. of *prendere* take, from L *prehendere*]

**presage** /'prɛsɪdʒ/, *n.;* /'prɛsɪdʒ, prə'seɪdʒ/, *v.,* **-saged, -saging.** –*n.* **1.** a presentiment or foreboding. **2.** a prophetic impression. **3.** something that portends or foreshadows a future event; an omen, prognostic, or warning indication. **4.** prophetic significance; augury. **5.** a forecast or prediction. –*v.t.* **6.** to have a presentiment of. **7.** to portend, foreshadow. **8.** to forecast; predict. –*v.i.* **9.** to have a presentiment. **10.** to make a prediction. [ME, from L *praesāgium*] – **presager,** *n.*

**Presb.,** Presbyterian.

**Presbo** /'prɛzboʊ/, *n. Colloq.* a Presbyterian.

**presbyopia** /,prɛzbi'oʊpiə/, *n.* a defect of vision incident to advancing age, in which near objects are seen with difficulty. [*presby-* (from Gk, combining form of *présbys* old man) + -OPIA] – **presbyopic** /prɛzbi'ɒpɪk/, *adj.*

**presbyter** /'prɛzbətə, 'prɛspətə/, *n.* **1.** (in the early Christian church) an office-bearer exercising teaching, priestly, and administrative functions. **2.** (in hierarchical churches) a priest. **3.** an elder of the church. [LL, from Gk *presbýteros,* properly adj., older] – **presbyteral** /prɛz'bɪtərəl/, *adj.*

**presbyterate** /prɛz'bɪtərət/, *n.* **1.** the office of presbyter or elder. **2.** a body of presbyters.

**presbyterial** /prɛzbə'tɪəriəl/, *adj.* **1.** of or pertaining to a presbytery. **2.** →**presbyterian** (def. 1).

**presbyterian** /prɛzbə'tɪəriən, prɛspə-/, *adj.* **1.** pertaining to or based on the principle of ecclesiastical government by an elected body of lay elders. **2.** (*cap.*) designating or pertaining to various churches having this form of government and holding more or less modified forms of Calvinism. –*n.* **3.** (*cap.*) a member or adherent of a Presbyterian church. [L *presbyterium* presbytery + -AN]

**Presbyterianism** /prɛzbə'tɪəriənɪzəm, prɛspə-/, *n.* **1.** church government by presbyters, or elders, who are equal in rank, consisting of ministers (teaching elders) and laymen (ruling elders). **2.** the doctrines of Presbyterian churches.

**presbytery** /'prɛzbətri, 'prɛspə-/, *n., pl.* **-teries.** **1.** a body of presbyters or elders. **2.** (in Presbyterian churches) a judicatory consisting of all the ministers (teaching elders) and representative lay or ruling elders from the congregations within a district. **3.** the churches under the jurisdiction of a presbytery. **4.** the part of a church, east of the choir, in which the high altar is situated. **5.** (now only in Roman Catholic use) a clergyman's or priest's house. [ME, from LL *presbyterium,* from Gk *presbytérion.* See PRESBYTER]

**preschool** /'priskul/, *adj.* **1.** denoting, pertaining to, or taught prior to compulsory school age. –*n.* **2.** →**kindergarten.** – **preschooler,** *n.*

**prescience** /'prɛsiəns/, *n.* knowledge of things before they exist or happen; foreknowledge; foresight. [ME, from LL *praescientia,* from L *praesciens,* ppr., knowing before] – **prescient,** *adj.* – **presciently,** *adv.*

**prescientific** /,prisaɪən'tɪfɪk/, *adj.* before the widespread development of a scientific culture.

**prescind** /prə'sɪnd/, *v.t.* **1.** to separate in thought; abstract. **2.** to remove. –*v.i.* **3.** to withdraw the attention (*from*). **4.** to turn aside in thought. [L *praescindere* cut off in front]

**prescribe** /prə'skraɪb/, *v.,* **-scribed, -scribing.** –*v.t.* **1.** to lay down, in writing or otherwise, as a rule or a course to be followed; appoint, ordain, or enjoin. **2.** *Med.* to designate or order for use, as a remedy or treatment. –*v.i.* **3.** to lay down rules, direct, or dictate. **4.** *Med.* to designate remedies or treatment to be used. **5.** *Law.* to claim a right or title by virtue of long use and enjoyment (esp. with *for* or *to*). [L *praescribere* write before, direct] – **prescriber,** *n.*

**prescript** /prə'skrɪpt, 'pri-/, *adj.;* /'priskrɪpt/, *n.* –*adj.* **1.** prescribed. –*n.* **2.** that which is prescribed; a rule; a regulation. [L *praescriptum,* n. use of pp., (thing) prescribed]

**prescriptible** /prə'skrɪptəbəl/, *adj.* **1.** subject to effective prescription. **2.** depending on or derived from prescription, as a claim or right.

**prescription** /prə'skrɪpʃən/, *n.* **1.** *Med.* **a.** a direction (usu. written) by the doctor to the pharmacist for the preparation and use of a medicine or remedy. **b.** the medicine prescribed. **2.** the act of prescribing. **3.** that which is prescribed. **4.** *Law.* **a.** a long or immemorial use of some right with respect to a thing so as to give a right to continue such use. **b.** the process of acquiring rights by uninterrupted assertion of the right over a long period of time. [ME, from L *praescriptio*]

**prescriptive** /prə'skrɪptɪv/, *adj.* **1.** that prescribes; giving directions or injunctions. **2.** depending on or arising from effective prescription, as a right or title. – **prescriptively,** *adv.*

**prescriptive grammar** /– 'græmə/, *n.* a grammar which seeks to establish rules for correct usage (opposed to *descriptive grammar*).

**preselect** /prisə'lɛkt/, *v.t.* **1.** to select in advance. *–v.i.* **2.** to use or be used as a preselector.

**preselection** /'prisəlɛkʃən/, *n.* the process within a political party of choosing candidates to stand for election.

**preselector** /prisə'lɛktə/, *n.* **1.** *Radio.* →**preamplifier. 2.** *Mach.* a type of gearbox for motor vehicles in which the gear ratio is selected before it is actually required. *–adj.* **3.** denoting or pertaining to a preselector.

**presence** /'prɛzəns/, *n.* **1.** the state or fact of being present, as with others or in a place. **2.** attendance or company. **3.** immediate vicinity; close proximity: *in the presence of witnesses.* **4.** the immediate personal vicinity of a great personage giving audience or reception. **5.** personal appearance or bearing, esp. of a dignified or imposing kind: *a man of fine presence.* **6.** a person, esp. of dignified or fine appearance. **7.** a divine or spiritual being. **8.** a supernatural influence felt to be close at hand. [ME, from OF, from L *praesentia*]

**presence of mind,** *n.* alert, calm state of mind enabling one to act quickly in emergencies.

**present**[1] /'prɛzənt/, *adj.* **1.** being, existing, or occurring at this time or now: *the present ruler.* **2.** for the time being: *articles for present use.* **3.** *Gram.* designating a tense denoting an action or state in process at the moment of speaking. For example: *'knows' is a present form in 'he knows that'.* **4.** being with one or others, or in the specified or understood place (opposed to *absent*): *to be present at a wedding.* **5.** being here or there, rather than elsewhere. **6.** existing in a place, thing, combination, or the like: *carbon is present in many minerals.* **7.** being actually here or under consideration. **8.** being before the mind. **9.** *Obs.* mentally alert or calm, esp. in emergencies. **10.** *Obs.* immediate or instant. *–n.* **11.** the present time. **12.** *Gram.* the present tense or a form therein. **13.** (*pl.*) *Law.* the present writings, or this document, used in a deed of conveyance, a lease, etc., to denote the document itself: *know all men by these presents.* **14.** *Obs.* the matter in hand. [ME, from L *praesens,* ppr., lit., being before (one)]

**present**[2] /prə'zɛnt/, *v.;* /'prɛzənt/, *n.* *–v.t.* **1.** to furnish or endow with a gift or the like, esp. by formal act: *to present someone with a gold watch.* **2.** to bring, offer, or give, often in a formal or ceremonious way: *to present a message, one's card, etc.* **3.** afford or furnish (an opportunity, possibility, etc.). **4.** to hand or send in, as a bill or a cheque for payment. **5.** to bring (a person, etc.) before, or into the presence of another, esp. a superior. **6.** to introduce (a person) to another. **7.** to bring before or introduce to the public: *to present a new play.* **8.** to come to show (oneself) before a person, in or at a place, etc. **9.** to show or exhibit. **10.** to bring before the mind; offer for consideration. **11.** to set forth in words: *to present arguments.* **12.** to represent, impersonate, or act, as on the stage. **13.** to direct, point, or turn to something or in a particular way. **14.** to level or aim (a weapon, esp. a firearm). *–v.i.* **15.** (of a medical, dental, or veterinary patient) to exhibit or complain of a disability, illness, malfunction, etc. (usu. fol. by *with*). *–n.* **16.** a thing presented as a gift; a gift: *Christmas presents.* [ME *presente(n),* from OF *presenter,* from L *praesentāre*] – **presenter,** *n.*

**presentable** /prə'zɛntəbəl/, *adj.* **1.** that may be presented. **2.** suitable as in appearance, dress, manners, etc., for being introduced into society or company. **3.** of sufficiently good appearance, or fit to be seen. – **presentability** /prə,zɛntə'bɪləti/, **presentableness,** *n.* – **presentably,** *adv.*

**present arms** /prəzɛnt 'amz/, *n.* position in which the rifle is held in both hands vertically in front of the body, with the muzzle up and the trigger side of the gun forward.

**presentation** /prɛzən'teɪʃən/, *n.* **1.** the act of presenting. **2.** the state of being presented. **3.** *Brit.* introduction, as of a person at court. **4.** exhibition or representation, as of a play. **5.** offering, delivering, or bestowal, as of a gift. **6.** a gift. **7.** *Comm.* the presentment of a bill, note, or the like. **8.** *Med.* the appearance of a particular part of the foetus at the mouth of the uterus during labour.

**presentational** /prɛzən'teɪʃənəl/, *adj.* **1.** of or pertaining to presentation. **2.** →**presentive.**

**presentationism** /prɛzən'teɪʃənɪzəm/, *n.* the doctrine that perception is an immedite cognition of ideas. – **presentationist,** *n., adj.*

**presentative** /prə'zɛntətɪv/, *adj.* having the power of presenting a notion to the mind.

**present-day** /'prɛzənt-deɪ/, *adj.* current.

**presentee** /prɛzən'ti/, *n.* **1.** one to whom something is presented. **2.** one who is presented.

**presentiment** /prə'zɛntəmənt/, *n.* a feeling or impression of something about to happen, esp. something evil; a foreboding. [F (obs.), from L *praesentīre* perceive beforehand] – **presentimental** /prəzɛntə'mɛntl/, *adj.*

**presentive** /prə'zɛntɪv/, *adj.* (esp. formerly) belonging to a class of words which express clear concepts, as distinct from *symbolic* words, which express relations between concepts; notional. – **presentively,** *adv.* – **presentiveness,** *n.*

**presently** /'prɛzəntli/, *adv.* **1.** in a little while or soon. **2.** at this time, currently. **3.** *Archaic.* immediately.

**presentment** /pri'zɛntmənt/, *n.* **1.** the act of presenting. **2.** the state of being presented. **3.** presentation. **4.** a representation, pictures, or likeness. **5.** *Comm.* the presenting of a bill, note, or the like, as for acceptance or payment. **6.** *Law.* the written statement of an offence by a jury, of their own knowledge or observation, when no indictment has been laid before them, sometimes used to refer to an indictment. [ME, from OF *presentement,* from *presenter* PRESENT[2]]

**present participle** /prɛzənt 'patəsɪpəl/, *n.* a participle with present meaning, as *growing* in 'a growing boy'.

**present perfect** /– 'pɜfəkt/, *n.* **1.** (in English) the tense form constructed by using the present tense of *have* with a past participle, and denoting that the action of the verb was completed prior to the present, as *I have finished.* **2.** (in some other languages) a tense form of similar construction. **3.** a verb in this tense.

**preservative** /prə'zɜvətɪv/, *n.* **1.** something that preserves or tends to preserve. **2.** a chemical substance used to preserve foods, etc., from decomposition or fermentation. **3.** a medicine that preserves health or prevents disease. *–adj.* **4.** tending to preserve.

**preserve** /prə'zɜv/, *v.,* **-served, -serving,** *n.* *–v.t.* **1.** to keep alive or in existence; make lasting. **2.** to keep safe from harm or injury; save. **3.** to keep up; maintain. **4.** to keep possession of; retain: *to preserve one's composure.* **5.** to prepare (food or any perishable substance) so as to resist decomposition or fermentation. **6.** to prepare (fruit, etc.) by cooking with sugar. **7.** to keep (game, etc.) undisturbed for personal use in hunting or fishing. *–v.i.* **8.** to preserve fruit, etc.; make preserves. **9.** to maintain a preserve for game animals. *–n.* **10.** something that preserves. **11.** that which is preserved. **12.** (*usu. pl.*) fruit, etc., prepared by cooking with sugar. **13.** a place set apart for the protection and propagation of game or fish for sport, etc. [ME *preserve(n),* from LL *praeservāre,* from L *prae-* PRE- + *servāre* keep] – **preservable,** *adj.* – **preservation** /prɛzə'veɪʃən/, *n.* – **preserver,** *n.*

**preset** /,pri'sɛt/, *v.,* **-set, -setting;** /'prisɛt/, *adj.* *–v.t.* **1.** to set in advance: *to preset an oven to roast a joint four hours later.* *–adj.* **2.** determined in advance to follow a certain course or the like: *a preset ICBM.*

**preshrunk** /'priʃrʌŋk/, *adj.* (of a fabric or garment) having been subjected to a shrinking process so that it will not shrink further when washed.

**preside** /prə'zaɪd/, *v.i.*, **-sided, -siding.** **1.** to occupy the place of authority or control, as in an assembly; act as chairman or president. **2.** to exercise superintendence or control. [L *praesidēre* sit before, guard, preside over] – **presider,** *n.*

**presidency** /'prɛzədənsi/, *n., pl.* **-cies.** the office, function, or term of office of a president.

**president** /'prɛzədənt/, *n.* **1.** (*oft. cap.*) the highest official in a republic. **2.** an officer appointed or elected to preside over an organised body of persons, as a council, society, etc. **3.** the chief officer of a college or university, or the chairman of a company, etc. **4.** one who presides over a meeting, conference, or the like. [ME, from L *praesidens*, ppr., presiding, ruling]

**president-elect** /prɛzədənt-ə'lɛkt/, *n.* a president after election but before induction into office.

**presidential** /prɛzə'dɛnʃəl/, *adj.* **1.** of or pertaining to a president or presidency. **2.** of the nature of a president. [ML *praesidentiālis*]

**presidential primary** /– 'praɪmri/, *n. U.S.* a direct primary for the choice of State delegates to a national party convention and the expression of preference for a presidential nominee.

**presidentship** /'prɛzədəntʃɪp/, *n.* →**presidency.**

**presidio** /prə'sɪdioʊ/, *n., pl.* **-sidios** /-'sɪdioʊz/. **1.** a garrisoned fort; a military post. **2.** →**penal settlement.** [Sp., from L *praesidium* guard, garrison, post] – **presidial, presidiary,** *adj.*

**presidium** /prə'sɪdiəm/, *n.* (in countries in the eastern bloc) an administrative committee, usu. permanent and governmental. [Russ. *prezidium*, from L *praesidium* a sitting before]

**presignify** /pri'sɪgnəfaɪ/, *v.t.*, **-fied, -fying.** to signify or indicate beforehand; foretell. [L *praesignificāre*]

**press**[1] /prɛs/, *v.t.* **1.** to act upon with weight or force. **2.** to move by weight or force in a certain direction or into a certain position. **3.** to compress or squeeze, as to alter in shape or size. **4.** to weigh heavily upon; to subject to pressure. **5.** to subject to heavy weights, as a method of fatal punishment. **6.** to make flat by subjecting to weight: *she pressed the flowers between the pages of a book.* **7.** to hold closely, as in an embrace; clasp. **8.** to iron (clothes, etc.). **9.** to extract juice, etc., from by pressure. **10.** to squeeze out or express, as juice. **11.** to form hot glass into ware (**pressed ware**) by means of iron mould and plunger, operated by hand or mechanically. **12.** to beset or harass. **13.** to oppress or trouble; to put to straits, as by lack of something: *they were pressed for time.* **14.** to urge or impel, as to a particular course; constrain or compel. **15.** to urge onwards; hurry; hasten. **16.** to urge (a person, etc.), importune, beseech, or entreat. **17.** to insist on: *to press the payment of a debt, to press one's theories.* **18.** to plead with insistence: *to press a claim.* **19.** to push forward. **20.** *Archaic.* to crowd upon or throng. *–v.i.* **21.** to exert weight, force, or pressure. **22.** to iron clothes, etc. **23.** to bear heavily, as upon the mind. **24.** to compel haste: *time presses.* **25.** to demand immediate attention. **26.** to use urgent entreaty: *to press for an answer.* **27.** to push forward with force, eagerness, or haste. **28.** to crowd or throng. [ME *pressen*, v., from *presse*, n.; but cf. OF *presser*, from L *pressāre*, frequentative of *premere* press] *–n.* **29.** printed publications collectively, esp. newspapers and periodicals. **30. a.** Also, **printed press.** the body or class of persons engaged in writing for or editing newspapers or periodicals. **b.** the news media generally, including the electronic media. **31.** the critical comment of newspapers, etc., on some matter of current public interest. **32.** *Print.* **a.** machine used for printing, as a **flat-bed cylinder press,** one in which a flat bed holding the printing forme moves against a revolving cylinder which carries the paper. **b. rotary press,** one in which the types or plates to be printed are fastened upon a rotating cylinder and are impressed on a continuous roll of paper. **33.** an establishment for printing books, etc. **34.** the process or art of printing. **35.** any of various instruments or machines for exerting pressure. **36.** the act of pressing; pressure. **37.** a pressing or pushing forward. **38.** a pressing together in a crowd, or a crowding or thronging. **39.** a crowd, throng, or multitude. **40.** pressed state. **41.** pressure or urgency, as of affairs or business. **42.** an upright case, or piece of furniture, for holding clothes, books, etc. **43.** a framework secured by screws for holding tennis racquets, and the like, when not in use. **44.** *Weight-lifting.* a lift where the barbell is raised first to the shoulders, then slowly and smoothly above the head with the arms held straight. **45.** *Obs.* a crease caused by pressing. **46. go to press, a.** to begin to be printed. **b.** *Prison Colloq.* to put a statement in writing incriminating oneself or others. [ME *presse*, OE *press*, from ML *pressa*]

**press**[2] /prɛs/, *v.t.* **1.** to force into service, esp. naval or military service; to impress. **2.** to make use of in a manner different from that intended or desired. *–n.* **3.** impressment into service, esp. naval or military service. [backformation from *prest*, pp. of obs. *prest*, v., take (men) for military service, v. use of obs. *prest*, n., enlistment, loan, from OF, from *prester* furnish, lend, from L *praestāre* perform, vouch for, excel]

**press agency** /'– eɪdʒənsi/, *n.* an organisation that collects news for distribution to the newspapers, radio, etc.

**press agent** /'– eɪdʒənt/, *n.* a person employed to attend to the advertising and publicity of a theatre, performer, etc., through advertisements and other notices in the press.

**press-box** /'prɛs-bɒks/, *n.* a shelter or stand for reporters at sports matches, etc.

**press conference** /'prɛs kɒnfərəns/, *n.* an interview of a famous person, public official, etc., with the press, often to make an important announcement or to answer questions.

**press-cutting** /'prɛs-kʌtɪŋ/, *n.* an article or the like cut from a newspaper. Also, **press-clipping.**

**pressed steel** /prɛst 'stil/, *n.* sheet steel, pressed hot or cold into various shapes as car bodies, doorframes, etc.

**presser** /'prɛsə/, *n.* one who or that which presses, or applies pressure, as one who irons clothes, presses wool into bales, etc.

**press gallery** /'prɛs gæləri/, *n.* **1.** a gallery or area reserved for the press, esp. in the legislative chamber of a house of parliament. **2.** the group or corps of reporters eligible to enter such a gallery: *the Canberra press gallery.*

**press-gang** /'prɛs-gæŋ/, *n.* a body of men under the command of an officer, formerly employed to impress other men for service, esp. in the navy or army. [PRESS[2] + GANG[1]]

**pressie** /'prɛzi/, *n. Colloq.* a present.

**pressing** /'prɛsɪŋ/, *adj.* **1.** urgent; demanding immediate attention: *a pressing need.* *–n.* **2.** an act or instance of one who or that which presses. **3. a.** a run of gramophone records produced at one time. **b.** →**record** (def. 17). – **pressingly,** *adv.*

**pressing board** /'– bɔd/, *n.* a wooden board with a metal edge used to give books a pronounced groove when they dry under pressure after binding.

**pressman** /'prɛsmən/, *n., pl.* **-men. 1.** a man who operates or has charge of a printing press. **2.** a newspaper reporter.

**pressmark** /'prɛsmak/, *n.* a mark put upon a volume to indicate its place in a library, etc.

**press office** /'prɛs ɒfəs/, *n.* an office maintained by government departments, institutions, large companies, etc., which releases information about its activities to the press. – **press officer,** *n.*

**press of sail,** *n.* as much sail as the wind, etc., will permit a ship to carry. Also, **press of canvas.**

**pressor** /'prɛsə/, *adj.* increasing pressure, as in the circulatory system.

**pressor nerve** /'– nɜv/, *n.* a nerve whose stimulation causes an increase of blood pressure.

**press proof** /'prɛs pruf/, *n.* the final proof (def. 14) before printing.

**press release** /'– rəlis/, *n.* an item of news prepared for and distributed to the press.

**pressroom** /'prɛsrum/, *n.* the room in a printing establishment containing the presses.

**press secretary** /'prɛs sɛkrətri/, *n.* one who arranges the release of information to the press and public for a public figure, esp. a politician.

**press-stud** /'prɛs-stʌd/, *n.* a metal fastener, used esp. on clothing, in which two parts are pressed together.

**press-up** /'prɛs-ʌp/, *n.* →**push-up.**

**pressure** /'prɛʃə/, *n.* **1.** the exertion of force upon a body by another body in contact with it; compression. **2.** *Physics.* the force per unit area exerted at a given point. The SI unit of pressure is the pascal. One pascal is equal to one newton per square metre. **3.** *Elect.* electromotive force. **4.** the act of pressing. **5.** the state of being pressed. **6.** harassment; oppression. **7.** a state of trouble or embarrassment. **8.** a constraining or compelling force or influence. **9.** urgency, as of affairs or business. **10.** *Obs.* that which is impressed. [ME, from F (obs.), from L *pressūra*]

**pressure contour** /– 'kɒntɔ/, *n.* a line drawn on a chart indicating the altitude at which a specified pressure occurs in the atmosphere.

**pressure cooker** /'– kʊkə/, *n.* a strong, closed vessel in which stews, meats, vegetables, etc., may be cooked above the normal boiling point under pressure.

**pressure drag** /'– dræg/, *n.* that part of the drag due to the resolved component of the pressure normal to the surface of a moving body.

**pressure gauge** /'– geɪdʒ/, *n.* **1.** an apparatus for measuring the pressure of gases or liquids, as of steam in a boiler. **2.** an instrument used to determine the pressure in the bore or chamber of a gun when the charge explodes.

**pressure gradient** /'– greɪdiənt/, *n.* the decrease in atmospheric pressure per unit of horizontal distance in the direction in which pressure decreases most rapidly.

**pressure group** /'– grup/, *n.* a group, in politics, business, etc., which attempts to protect or advance its own interests.

**pressure head** /'– hɛd/, *n.* the pressure of a fluid at a given point in a system divided by the unit weight of the fluid.

**pressure pack** /'– pæk/, *n.* a container from which a liquid is dispersed as a gas or under pressure of a gas; aerosol.

**pressure point** /'– pɔɪnt/, *n.* any of the points in the body at which pressure applied with the fingers, a tourniquet, etc., will control bleeding from an artery at a point further away from the heart.

**pressure suit** /'– sut/, *n.* a garment designed to provide body pressure and air, for use in conditions, as in high-flying aircraft and spacecraft, where the ambient pressure is low. Also, **pressurised suit.**

**pressurise** /'prɛʃəraɪz/, *v.t., v.i.*, **-rised, -rising. 1.** to maintain normal air pressure in (the cockpit or cabin of) an aeroplane designed to fly at high altitudes. **2.** to compress (a gas or liquid) to a pressure greater than normal. Also, **pressurize.** – **pressurisation** /prɛʃəraɪ'zeɪʃən/, *n.*

**pressurised water reactor,** *n.* a type of nuclear reactor in which water under high pressure is used as both coolant and moderator. *Abbrev.:* P.W.R.

**presswork** /'prɛswɜk/, *n.* **1.** the working or management of a printing press. **2.** the work done by it.

**prestidigitation** /ˌprɛstədɪdʒə'teɪʃən/, *n.* sleight of hand; legerdemain. [F, from L *praestīgiātor* juggler, b. with *preste* lively (from It. *presto,* from L *praestō*) and with L *digitus* finger] – **prestidigitator** /prɛstə'dɪdʒəteɪtə/, *n.*

**prestige** /prɛs'tiʒ/, *n.* **1.** reputation or influence arising from success, achievement, rank, or other circumstances. **2.** distinction or reputation attaching to a person or thing and dominating the mind of others or of the public. *–adj.* **3.** characteristic of one who has attained success, wealth, etc. [F: illusion, glamour, from L *praestīgium* illusion, from *praestīgiae,* pl., jugglers' tricks] – **prestigious** /prɛs'tɪdʒəs/, *adj.*

**prestige form** /'– fɔm/, *n.* that form of the speech of a nation which, in comparison with others, is considered the most cultivated.

**prestissimo** /prɛs'tɪsimoʊ/, *adv.* (in musical direction) in the most rapid tempo. [It., superl. of *presto* PRESTO]

**presto** /'prɛstoʊ/, *adv., adj., n., pl.* **-tos.** *–adv.* **1.** quickly, rapidly, or immediately. **2.** *Music.* in quick tempo; to be played very fast. *–adj.* **3.** quick or rapid. **4.** *Music.* in quick tempo. *–n.* **5.** *Music.* a movement or piece in quick tempo. [It.: quick, quickly, from LL *praestus,* adj., ready, L *praestō,* adv., at hand]

**prestress** /ˌpri'strɛs/, *v.t.* to induce an initial stress, as in concrete, to cancel out stresses resulting from applied loads. – **prestressed,** *adj.*

**prestressed concrete** /ˌpristrɛst 'kɒŋkrit/, *n.* compressed concrete strengthened with tensioned wires to increase its efficiency.

**presumable** /prə'zjuməbəl/, *adj.* capable of being taken for granted; probable. – **presumably,** *adv.*

**presume** /prə'zjum/, *v.,* **-sumed, -suming.** *–v.t.* **1.** to take for granted, assume, or suppose: *I presume you're tired.* **2.** *Law.* to assume as true in the absence of proof to the contrary. **3.** to undertake, with unwarrantable boldness. **4.** to undertake or venture (to do something) as by taking a liberty: *to presume to speak for another.* *–v.i.* **5.** to take something for granted; suppose. **6.** to act or proceed with unwarrantable or impertinent boldness. **7.** to rely (*on* or *upon*) in acting unwarrantably or taking liberties. [ME, from L *praesūmere* take beforehand, venture] – **presumedly,** *adv.* – **presumer,** *n.*

**presumption** /prə'zʌmpʃən/, *n.* **1.** the act of presuming. **2.** assumption of something as true. **3.** belief on reasonable grounds or probable evidence. **4.** that which is presumed; an assumption. **5.** a ground or reason for presuming or believing. **6.** *Law.* an inference required or permitted by law as to the existence of one fact from proof of the existence of other facts. **7.** unwarrantable, unbecoming, or impertinent boldness.

**presumptive** /prə'zʌmptɪv/, *adj.* **1.** affording ground for presumption. **2.** based on presumption: *a presumptive title.* **3.** regarded as such by presumption: *an heir presumptive.* – **presumptively,** *adv.*

**presumptuous** /prə'zʌmptʃuəs/, *adj.* **1.** full of, characterised by, or showing presumption or readiness to presume in conduct or thought. **2.** unwarrantedly or impertinently bold; forward. **3.** *Obs.* →**presumptive.** [ME *presumptuose,* from LL *praesumptuōsus,* var. of *praesumptiōsus*] – **presumptuously,** *adv.* – **presumptuousness,** *n.*

**presuppose** /prisə'poʊz/, *v.t.,* **-posed, -posing. 1.** to suppose or assume beforehand; to take for granted in advance. **2.** (of a thing) to require or imply as an antecedent condition: *an effect presupposes a cause.* – **presupposition** /ˌprisʌpə'zɪʃən/, *n.*

**presurmise** /prisə'maɪz/, *n.* a surmise previously formed.

**pret.,** preterite.

**pretence** /prə'tɛns/, *n.* **1.** pretending or feigning; make-believe: *my sleepiness was all pretence.* **2.** a false show of something: *a pretence of friendship.* **3.** a piece of make-believe. **4.** the act of pretending or alleging, now esp. falsely. **5.** an alleged or pretended reason or excuse, or a pretext. **6.** insincere or false profession. **7.** the putting forth of a claim. **8.** the claim itself. **9.** pretension (fol. by *to*): *destitute of any pretence to wit.* **10.** →**pretentiousness.** Also, *U.S.,* **pretense.** [ME, from AF *pretensse,* from ML *praetensa,* properly fem. (replacing L *praetenta*) of pp. of *praetendere* pretend]

**pretend** /prə'tɛnd/, *v.t.* **1.** to put forward a false appearance of; feign: *to pretend illness.* **2.** to venture or attempt falsely (to do something). **3.** to allege or profess, esp. insincerely or falsely. *–v.i.* **4.** to make believe. **5.** to lay claim (fol. by *to*). **6.** to make pretensions (fol. by *to*). **7.** to aspire, as a suitor or candidate (fol. by *to*). [ME *pretende(n),* from L *praetendere* stretch forth, put forward, pretend]

**pretended** /prə'tɛndəd/, *adj.* **1.** insincerely or falsely professed. **2.** feigned, fictitious, or counterfeit. **3.** alleged or asserted; reputed. – **pretendedly,** *adv.*

**pretender** /prə'tɛndə/, *n.* **1.** one who pretends; one who makes false professions. **2.** an aspirant or candidate. **3.** a claimant to a throne.

**pretense** /prə'tɛns/, *n. U.S.* →**pretence.**

**pretension** /prə'tɛnʃən/, *n.* **1.** a laying claim to something. **2.** a claim or title to something. **3.** (*oft. pl.*) a claim made, esp. indirectly or by implication, or right to some quality, merit, or the like: *pretensions to superior judgment.* **4.** claim to dignity, importance, or merit. **5.** pretentiousness. **6.** the act of pretending or alleging. **7.** →**allegation. 8.** →**pretext.**

**pre-tensioned** /'pri-tɛnʃənd/, *adj.* (in prestressed concrete) having the reinforcement stretched before the concrete is cast. Cf. **post-tensioned.**

**pretentious** /prə'tɛnʃəs/, *adj.* **1.** full of pretension. **2.** characterised by assumption of dignity or importance. **3.** making an exaggerated outward show; ostentatious. [L *praetenti(o)* pretension + -OUS] – **pretentiously,** *adv.* – **pretentiousness,** *n.*

**preter-,** a prefix meaning 'beyond', 'more than'. [L *praeter-,* representing *praeter,* adv. and prep.]

**preterhuman** /pritə'hjumən/, *adj.* beyond what is human.

**preterite** /ˈprɛtərət, ˈprɛtrət/, *adj.* **1.** *Gram.* designating a tense usu. denoting an action or state which was completed in the past. For example, in the sentence *John hit Jack, hit* could be said to be in the preterite tense, though in English grammar such verbs are more commonly said to be in the past tense. **2.** bygone; past. Also, **preterit.** *–n.* **3.** *Gram.* **a.** the preterite tense. **b.** a form therein. [ME, from L *praeteritus,* pp., gone by]

**preterition** /prɛtəˈrɪʃən/, *n.* **1.** the act of passing by or over; omission; neglect. **2.** *Law.* the passing over by a testator of an heir otherwise entitled to a portion. **3.** *Calvinistic Theol.* the passing over by God of those not elected to salvation or eternal life. [LL *praeteritio* a passing over. See PRETERITE]

**preteritive** /ˈprɛtərətɪv/, *adj.* **1.** preterite. **2.** (of verbs) limited to past tenses.

**pretermit** /pritəˈmɪt/, *v.t.*, **-mitted, -mitting.** **1.** to let pass without notice; disregard. **2.** to leave undone; neglect; omit. **3.** to leave off for a short time. [L *praetermittere* let pass] – **pretermission** /pritəˈmɪʃən/, *n.*

**preternatural** /pritəˈnætʃərəl/, *adj.* **1.** out of the ordinary course of nature; abnormal. **2.** →**supernatural.** – **preternaturalism,** *n.* – **preternaturally,** *adv.*

**pretext** /ˈpritɛkst/, *n.* **1.** that which is put forward to conceal a true purpose or object; an ostensible reason. **2.** an excuse; a pretence. [L *praetextus*]

**prettify** /ˈprɪtəfaɪ/, *v.t.*, **-fied, -fying.** (*oft. derog.*) to make pretty. [PRETT(Y) + -IFY]

**pretty** /ˈprɪti/, *adj.*, **-tier, -tiest,** *n., pl.* **-ties,** *adv.* *–adj.* **1.** fair or attractive to the eye in a feminine or childish way: *a pretty face.* **2.** (of things, places, etc.) pleasing to the eye, esp. without grandeur. **3.** pleasing to the ear: *a pretty tune.* **4.** pleasing to the mind or aesthetic taste: *some pretty little story.* **5.** *Obs.* fine, pleasant, or excellent. **6.** (*ironic*) dreadful: *a pretty mess.* **7.** *Colloq.* considerable; fairly great. **8.** *Archaic or Scot.* brave; hardy. **9.** *Archaic.* smart; elegant. **10. pretty penny,** a considerable sum of money. *–n.* **11.** (*usu. pl.*) a pretty thing, as a trinket or ornament. **12.** a pretty one (used esp. in address). *–adv.* **13.** moderately: *her work was pretty good.* **14.** quite; very: *the wind blew pretty hard.* **15. sitting pretty,** in a satisfactory and unchallenged position. *–v.t.* **16.** to make pretty: *she prettied herself up for her boyfriend.* [ME *prety, praty,* OE *prættig* cunning, wily, from OE *prætt,* n., wile, trick; akin to D *part* trick, prank, Icel. *prettr* trick, *prettugr* tricky] – **prettily,** *adv.* – **prettiness,** *n.* – **prettyish,** *adj.*

**pretty-face wallaby** /ˌprɪti-feɪs ˈwɒləbi/, *n.* →**whiptail wallaby.**

**pretty-pretty** /ˈprɪti-ˌprɪti/, *adj.* pretty but lacking character or style.

**pretypify** /ˌpriˈtɪpəfaɪ/, *v.t.*, **-fied, -fying.** to typify beforehand; prefigure.

**pretzel** /ˈprɛtzəl/, *n.* a crisp, dry biscuit, usu. in the form of a knot or stick, salted on the outside. [G, var. of *Bretzel.* Cf. ML *bracellus* bracelet]

**prevail** /prəˈveɪl/, *v.i.* **1.** to be widespread or current; to exist everywhere or generally: *dead silence prevailed.* **2.** to appear or occur as the more important or frequent feature or element; predominate: *green tints prevail in the picture.* **3.** to be or prove superior in strength, power, or influence. **4.** to operate effectually; to be efficacious. **5.** to use persuasion or inducement successfully (fol. by *on, upon,* or *with*). [ME *prevaylle(n),* from L *praevalēre* be more able]

**prevailing** /prəˈveɪlɪŋ/, *adj.* **1.** predominant. **2.** generally current. **3.** having superior power or influence. **4.** effectual. – **prevailingly,** *adv.* – **prevailingness,** *n.*

**prevalent** /ˈprɛvələnt/, *adj.* **1.** widespread; of wide extent or occurrence; in general use or acceptance. **2.** *Rare.* having the superiority or ascendancy. **3.** *Rare.* effectual or efficacious. [L *praevalens,* ppr., prevailing] – **prevalence,** *n.* – **prevalently,** *adv.*

**prevaricate** /prəˈværəkeɪt/, *v.i.*, **-cated, -cating.** to act or speak evasively; equivocate; quibble. [L *praevāricātus,* pp., walked crookedly, deviated] – **prevarication** /prəværəˈkeɪʃən/, *n.* – **prevaricator,** *n.*

**prevenient** /prəˈvinjənt/, *adj.* **1.** coming before; antecedent. **2.** anticipatory. [L *praeveniens,* ppr.] – **prevenance** /ˈprɛvənəns/, **prevenience** /prəˈvinjəns/, *n.*

**prevent** /prəˈvɛnt/, *v.t.* **1.** to keep from occurring; hinder. **2.** to hinder (a person, etc.), as from doing something: *there is nothing to prevent us from going.* **3.** *Rare.* to cut off beforehand or debar (a person, etc.), as from something. **4.** *Obs.* to precede. **5.** *Obs.* to anticipate. *–v.i.* **6.** to interpose a hindrance: *he will come if nothing prevents.* [ME, from L *praeventus,* pp., lit., come before] – **preventable, preventible,** *adj.*

**preventer** /prəˈvɛntə/, *n.* **1.** one who or that which prevents. **2.** *Naut.* a supplementary rope or stay, supporting a mast.

**prevention** /prəˈvɛnʃən/, *n.* **1.** the act of preventing; effectual hindrance. **2.** a preventive.

**preventive** /prəˈvɛntɪv/, *adj.* **1.** *Med.* warding off disease. **2.** serving to prevent or hinder. **3.** of or pertaining to the customs and excise service: *a preventive officer.* *–n.* **4.** *Med.* a drug, etc., for preventing disease. **5.** a preventive agent or measure. **6.** a contraceptive. Also, **preventative** /prəˈvɛntətɪv/. – **preventively,** *adv.* – **preventiveness,** *n.*

**preview** /ˈprivju/, *n.* **1.** a previous view; a view in advance, as of a film. *–v.t.* **2.** to view beforehand or in advance.

**previous** /ˈpriviəs/, *adj.* **1.** coming or occurring before something else; prior. **2.** *Colloq.* done, occurring, etc., before the proper time; premature. [L *praevius*] – **previously,** *adv.* – **previousness,** *n.*

**previous question** /– ˈkwɛstʃən/, *n. Parl. Proc.* the question whether a vote shall be taken on a main question, moved before the main question is put in order to cut off debate.

**previse** /ˌpriˈvaɪz/, *v.t.*, **-vised, -vising.** **1.** to foresee. **2.** to forewarn. [L *praevīsus,* pp., foreseen]

**prevision** /ˌpriˈvɪʒən/, *n.* **1.** foresight, foreknowledge, or prescience. **2.** an anticipatory vision or perception. [PRE- + VISION] – **previsional,** *adj.*

**prevocalic** /privoʊˈkælɪk/, *adj. Phonet.* occurring before a vowel.

**prewar** /ˈpriwɔ/, *adj.* before a war, esp. World War II.

**prey** /preɪ/, *n.* **1.** an animal hunted or seized for food, esp. by a carnivorous animal. **2.** a person or thing that falls a victim to an enemy, a disease, or any adverse agency. **3.** the action or habit of preying: *beast of prey.* **4.** *Rare.* booty or plunder. *–v.i.* **5.** to seek for and seize prey, as an animal does. **6.** to take booty or plunder. **7.** to make profit by activities on a victim. **8.** to exert a harmful or destructive influence: *these worries preyed upon his mind.* [ME *preye,* from OF, from L *praeda* booty, prey] – **preyer,** *n.*

**prezzie** /ˈprɛzi/, *n. Colloq.* a gift. [shortened form of PRESENT[2]]

**Prezzie** /ˈprɛzi/, *n. Colloq.* a Presbyterian.

**priapism** /ˈpraɪəpɪzəm/, *n.* persistent painful erection of the penis. [from *Priapus* Greek and Roman god of procreation + -ISM]

**price** /praɪs/, *n., v.*, **priced, pricing.** *–n.* **1.** the sum or amount of money or its equivalent for which anything is bought, sold, or offered for sale. **2.** a sum offered for the capture of a person alive or dead: *a price on a man's head.* **3.** the sum of money, or other consideration, for which a person's support, consent, etc., may be obtained: *he has his price.* **4.** that which must be given, done, or undergone in order to obtain a thing: *to gain a victory at a heavy price.* **5.** *Archaic.* value; worth. **6.** betting odds. **7. at a price,** at a somewhat high price. **8. at any price,** at any cost, no matter how great. **9. beyond** or **without price,** unobtainable; priceless. **10. what price,** *Colloq.* **a.** what is the chance of. **b.** what do you think. *–v.t.* **11.** to fix the price of. **12.** *Colloq.* to ask the price of. [ME, from OF *pris,* from L *pretium* price, value, worth]

**price control** /ˈ– kəntroʊl/, *n.* the setting of maximum prices for nominated goods and services by a government, as an economic policy.

**price-cutting** /ˈpraɪs-kʌtɪŋ/, *n.* the act of selling an article at a price under the usual or advertised price.

**price discrimination** /ˈpraɪs dɪskrɪməˌneɪʃən/, *n.* the selling of identical goods to different buyers at different prices.

**price earnings ratio,** *n.* a figure calculated by dividing the price of a share by its earnings per share.

**price index** /ˈpraɪs ɪndɛks/, *n.* an indicator used to show the general level of prices.

**priceless** /ˈpraɪsləs/, *adj.* **1.** having a value beyond all price;

invaluable: *she was a priceless help to him.* **2.** *Colloq.* delightfully amusing; absurd.

**price-list** /ˈpraɪs-lɪst/, *n.* a list of articles for sale, with prices.

**price ring** /ˈpraɪs rɪŋ/, *n.* an agreement whereby suppliers of goods or services agree to charge uniform prices.

**price-tag** /ˈpraɪs-tæg/, *n.* a label attached to an item offered for sale, showing its price.

**price war** /ˈpraɪs wɔ/, *n.* a fiercely competitive price-cutting battle, usu. among retailers.

**pricey** /ˈpraɪsi/, *adj. Colloq.* expensive.

**prick** /prɪk/, *n.* **1.** a puncture made by a needle, thorn, or the like. **2.** the act of pricking: *the prick of a needle.* **3.** the state or sensation of being pricked. **4.** *Obs.* a small or minute mark; a dot or a point. **5.** *Archaic.* a goad for oxen. **6.** *Obs.* any pointed instrument or weapon. **7.** *Colloq.* **a.** the penis. **b.** an unpleasant or despicable person. **8. kick against the pricks,** to hurt oneself by vain resistance. [ME *prike,* OE *prica* dot, c. LG *prik* point] *–v.t.* **9.** to pierce with a sharp point; puncture. **10.** to affect with sharp pain, as from piercing. **11.** to cause sharp mental pain to; sting, as with remorse or sorrow: *his conscience pricked him suddenly.* **12.** to urge on with, or as with, a goad or spur: *my duty pricks me on.* **13.** to mark (a surface) with pricks or dots in tracing something. **14.** to mark or trace (something) on a surface by pricks or dots. **15.** to cause to stand erect or point upwards: *to prick up one's ears.* **16.** *Farriery.* **a.** to lame (a horse) by driving a nail improperly into its hoof. **b.** to nick: *to prick a horse's tail.* **17.** to measure (distance, etc.) on a chart with dividers (fol. by *off*). **18.** to transplant (seedlings, etc.) from their original beds to larger boxes (fol. by *out*). *–v.i.* **19.** to perform the action of piercing or puncturing something. **20.** to have a sensation of being pricked. **21.** to rise erect or point upwards, as the ears of an animal (fol. by *up*). **22.** *Archaic.* to spur or urge a horse on; ride rapidly. **23. prick up one's ears,** to listen, esp. at something unexpected or of particular interest. [ME *priken,* OE *prician,* from *prica* puncture] – **prickingly,** *adv.*

**pricked** /prɪkt/, *adj.* of wine which has become acetified through exposure to the air, or through age.

**pricket** /ˈprɪkət/, *n.* **1.** a sharp metal point on which to stick a candle. **2.** a candlestick with one or more such points. **3.** a buck in his second year. [ME, from PRICK + -ET]

**pricking coat** /ˈprɪkɪŋ koʊt/, *n.* the first coat of plaster, usu. on laths, used as a key (def. 18).

**prickle** /ˈprɪkəl/, *n., v.,* **-led, -ling.** *–n.* **1.** a sharp point. **2.** a small, pointed process growing from the bark of a plant; a thorn. **3.** *Colloq.* a pricking sensation. **4.** (of wine) slight gassiness produced naturally by secondary fermentation in the bottle. *–v.t.* **5.** to prick. **6.** to cause a pricking sensation in. *–v.i.* **7.** to rise or stand erect like prickles. **8.** to tingle as if pricked. [ME *prykel,* OE *pricel,* from *pric(a)* prick + *-el,* n. suffix]

**prickly** /ˈprɪkli/, *adj.,* **-lier, -liest.** **1.** full of or armed with prickles. **2.** full of troublesome points. **3.** prickling; smarting. **4.** sensitive; easily angered. – **prickliness,** *n.*

**prickly ash** /– ˈæʃ/, *n.* **1.** a shrub or small tree, *Zanthoxylum americanum,* of North America, with aromatic leaves and branches usu. armed with strong prickles. **2.** an Australian tree, *Orites excelsa,* with useful and attractive timber.

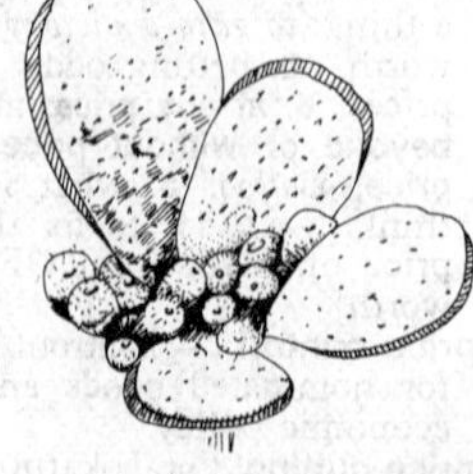
prickly pear

**prickly heat** /– ˈhit/, *n.* a cutaneous eruption accompanied by a prickling and itching sensation, due to an inflammation of the sweat glands.

**prickly Moses** /– ˈmoʊzəz/, *n.* a spreading, densely-branched shrub, *Acacia farnesiana,* with globular yellow flower-heads from which a perfume is made, found in dry inland areas. [corruption of *prickly mimosa* (*mimosa* obs. name for wattle)]

**prickly pear** /– ˈpɛə/, *n.* **1.** the pear-shaped or ovoid, often prickly, and sometimes edible fruit of any of certain species of cactus (genus *Opuntia*). **2.** any of a number of species of *Opuntia,* as *O. stricta,* native to Mexico, which has become a serious pest in Australia.

**prickly pear melon,** *n.* →**paddymelon**[1] (def. 1).

**prickly poppy** /prɪkli ˈpɒpi/, *n.* **1.** a tropical American herb, *Argemone mexicana,* having spiny leaves and yellow flowers, now naturalised in other warm parts of the world and believed to have medicinal properties. **2.** a native poppy of Australia, *Papaver aculeatum.*

**prick-song** /ˈprɪk-sɒŋ/, *n. Archaic or Hist.* written music, esp. a descant.

**prickteaser** /ˈprɪktizə/, *n. Colloq.* one who withholds sexual favours from a man after having encouraged expectation of them. Also, **cockteaser.**

**pride** /praɪd/, *n., v.,* **prided, priding.** *–n.* **1.** high or inordinate opinion of one's own dignity, importance, merit, or superiority, whether as cherished in the mind or as displayed in bearing, conduct, etc. **2.** the state or feeling of being proud. **3.** becoming or dignified sense of what is due to oneself or one's position or character; self-respect; self-esteem. **4.** pleasure or satisfaction taken in something done by or belonging to oneself or conceived as reflecting credit upon oneself: *civic pride.* **5.** that of which a person or a body of persons is proud: *he was the pride of the family.* **6.** the best or most admired part of anything. **7.** the most flourishing state or period: *in the pride of manhood.* **8.** a company of lions. **9.** mettle in a horse. **10.** *Archaic.* splendour, magnificence, or pomp. **11.** *Archaic.* ornament or adornment. **12.** *Obs.* sexual desire, esp. in a female animal. *–v.t.* **13.** to indulge or plume (oneself) in a feeling of pride (usu. fol. by *on* or *upon*). [ME; OE *prȳde* (c. Icel. *prȳdhi* bravery), from *prūd* proud] – **prideful,** *adj.* – **pridefully,** *adv.*

**pride of place,** *n.* the highest or most important position.

**prie-dieu** /ˈpri-djɜ/, *n.* a piece of furniture for kneeling on during prayer, having a rest above, as for a book. [F: pray God]

prie-dieu

**prier** /ˈpraɪə/, *n.* one who looks or searches curiously or inquisitively into something. Also, **pryer.** [PRY[1] + -ER[1]]

**priest** /prist/, *n.* **1.** one whose office it is to perform religious rites, and esp. to make sacrificial offerings. **2.** (in Christian use) **a.** one ordained to the sacerdotal or pastoral office; a clergyman; a minister. **b.** (in hierarchal churches) a clergyman of the order next below that of bishop, authorised to carry out the Christian ministry. **3.** a minister of any religion. **4.** a club or mallet used for killing fish. [ME *preest,* OE *prēost,* from L *presbyter.* See PRESBYTER]

**priestcraft** /ˈpristkraft/, *n.* priestly arts.

**priestess** /ˈpristes/, *n.* a woman who officiates in sacred rites.

**priest-hole** /ˈprist-hoʊl/, *n.* a hiding-place for a priest in a house, as when Roman Catholic priests were proscribed in England.

**priesthood** /ˈpristhʊd/, *n.* **1.** the condition or office of a priest. **2.** priests collectively. [ME; OE *prēosthād.* See PRIEST, -HOOD]

**priestly** /ˈpristli/, *adj.,* **-lier, -liest.** **1.** of or pertaining to a priest; sacerdotal. **2.** characteristic of or befitting a priest. – **priestliness,** *n.*

**priest-ridden** /ˈprist-rɪdn/, *adj.* managed or governed by priests; dominated by priestly influence.

**prig** /prɪg/, *n.* **1.** one who is precise to an extreme in attention to principle or duty, esp. in a self-righteous way. **2.** *Archaic.* a coxcomb. [? akin to PRINK]

**priggery** /ˈprɪgəri/, *n., pl.* **-geries.** the conduct or character of a prig.

**priggish** /ˈprɪgɪʃ/, *adj.* excessively precise, esp. in an affectedly superior or high-minded way. – **priggishly,** *adv.* – **priggishness,** *n.*

**prim** /prɪm/, *adj.* **primmer, primmest,** *v.,* **primmed, primming.** *–adj.* **1.** affectedly precise or proper, as persons, behaviour, etc.; stiffly neat. *–v.i.* **2.** to draw up the mouth in an affectedly nice or precise way. *–v.t.* **3.** to make prim, as in appearance. **4.** to purse (the mouth, etc.) into a prim expression. [orig. obscure] – **primly,** *adv.* – **primness,** *n.*

**prim.**, **1.** primary. **2.** primate. **3.** primitive.

**primacy** /'praɪməsi/, *n., pl.* **-cies.** **1.** the state of being first in order, rank, importance, etc. **2.** *Eccles.* the office, rank, or dignity of a primate. **3.** *Rom. Cath. Ch.* the jurisdiction of the pope as supreme bishop. [ME, from ML *prīmātia,* from L *prīmas* PRIMATE]

**prima donna** /primə 'dɒnə, prɪmə/, *n., pl.* **prima donnas.** **1.** a first or principal female singer of an operatic company. **2.** *Colloq.* a temperamental, petulant person. [It.: first lady]

**prima facie** /praɪmə 'feɪʃi/, *adv.* at first appearance; at first view, before investigation. [L]

**prima-facie evidence** /ˌpraɪmə-feɪʃi 'ɛvədəns/, *n.* (in law) evidence sufficient to establish a fact, or to raise a presumption of fact, unless rebutted.

**primage** /'praɪmɪdʒ/, *n.* **1.** a small allowance formerly paid by a shipper to the master and crew of a vessel for the loading and care of the goods; now charged with the freight and retained by the shipowner. **2.** a primary ad valorem revenue placed by the government on imports. [PRIME, *v.,* load + -AGE]

**primal** /'praɪməl/, *adj.* **1.** first; original; primeval. **2.** of first importance; fundamental. [ML *prīmālis,* from L *prīmus* first]

**primarily** /'praɪmrəli, 'praɪmərəli/; *Chiefly U.S.* /praɪ'mɛrəli/, *adv.* **1.** in the first place; chiefly; principally. **2.** in the first instance; at first; originally.

**primary** /'praɪməri, 'praɪmri/, *adj., n., pl.* **-ries.** *–adj.* **1.** first or highest in rank or importance; chief; principal. **2.** first in order in any series, sequence, etc. **3.** first in time; earliest; primitive. **4.** constituting, or belonging to, the first stage in any process. **5.** of or pertaining to the production of naturally occurring foods as meat, grains, fish, etc., or of naturally occurring things as wool, cotton, etc.: *a primary industry.* (Cf. **secondary**). **6.** of the nature of the ultimate or simpler constituents of which something complex is made up. **7.** original, not derived or subordinate; fundamental; basic. **8.** immediate or direct, or not involving intermediate agency. **9.** *Ornith.* pertaining to any of the set of flight feathers situated on the distal segment of a bird's wing. **10.** *Elect.* denoting or pertaining to the inducing circuit, coil, or current in an induction coil or the like. **11.** *Chem.* **a.** involving, or obtained by replacement of one atom or radical. **b.** denoting or containing a carbon atom united to no other or to only one other carbon atom in a molecule. **12.** *Gram.* **a.** (of derivation) with a root or other unanalysable element as underlying form. **b.** (of Latin, Greek, Sanskrit tenses) having reference to present or future time. **13.** *Educ.* denoting or pertaining to the education given in primary schools. *–n.* **14.** that which is first in order, rank, or importance. **15.** *U.S. Politics.* **a.** a meeting of the voters of a political party in an election district for nominating candidates for office, choosing delegates for a convention, etc. **b.** a preliminary election in which voters of each party nominate candidates for office, party officers, etc. **16.** one of any set of primary colours. See **primary colours.** **17.** *Ornith.* a primary feather. **18.** *Elect.* a primary circuit or coil. **19.** *Astron.* a body in relation to a smaller body or smaller bodies revolving round it, as a planet in relation to its satellites. **20.** *Chem.* a substance obtained directly from natural or crude raw materials by extraction and purification. [late ME, from L *prīmārius* of the first rank. See PRIME, -ARY[1]]

**primary accent** /– 'æksɛnt/, *n.* →**primary stress.**

**primary cell** /– 'sɛl/, *n.* a cell designed to produce electric current through an electrochemical reaction which is not efficiently reversible and hence the cell, when discharged, cannot efficiently be recharged by an electric current.

**primary colour** /– 'kʌlə/, *n.* a colour belonging to a group of colours which is regarded as generating all colours. **Additive colours** are red, green and blue since light of these wavelengths, properly selected and mixed, can produce any hue, even white. In mixing dyes and pigments the colours act subtractively; the **subtractive primary colours** are loosely named as red, yellow, and blue, but properly the red must be a purple and the blue must be a blue-green. More than 100 different hues have been detected in the spectrum, but only four of them (red, yellow, green, and blue) contain no suggestion of another hue. From the viewpoint of sensation, therefore, these four may be considered primary colours. To these, white and black may be added for the same reason.

**primary education** /– ɛdʒə'keɪʃən/, *n.* education for children aged six to eleven years.

**primary election** /– ə'lɛkʃən/, *n.* →**primary** (def. 15b).

**primary flow** /– 'floʊ/, *n.* the input of irrigation water into a furrow until it reaches the far end.

**primary group** /– 'grup/, *n. Sociol.* a group of individuals living in close, intimate, and personal relationship, considered as a sociological unit.

**primary industry** /– 'ɪndəstri/, *n.* any industry such as dairy farming, forestry, mining, etc., which is involved in the growing, producing, extracting, etc., of natural resources.

**primary producer** /– prə'djusə/, *n.* **1.** one who works in a primary industry as a farmer, a fisherman, etc. **2.** a business or industry devoted to primary production.

**primary school** /'– skul/, *n.* a school for full-time elementary instruction of children from the age of six to about eleven years.

**primary stress** /– 'strɛs/, *n.* the principal or strongest accent of a word. Also, **primary accent.**

**primate** /'praɪmət/ *for defs 1 and 3;* /'praɪmeɪt/ *for def. 2, n.* **1.** *Eccles.* an archbishop or bishop ranking first among the bishops of a province, country, etc. **2.** any mammal of the order Primates, that includes man, the apes, the monkeys, the lemurs, etc. **3.** *Rare.* a chief or leader. [ME, from ML *prīmas* chief bishop, in LL chief, head, n. use of L *prīmas,* adj., of first rank] – **primateship,** *n.* – **primatial** /praɪ'meɪʃəl/, *adj.*

**prime** /praɪm/, *adj., n., v.,* **primed, priming.** *–adj.* **1.** first in importance, excellence, or value. **2.** first or highest in rank, dignity, or authority; chief; principal; main: *the prime minister.* **3.** first in comparison with others. **4.** of the first grade or best quality: *prime ribs of beef.* **5.** first in order of time, existence, or development; earliest; primitive. **6.** original; fundamental. **7.** *Maths.* **a.** of a number which has itself and unity as its only factors. **b.** having no common divisor except unity: *2 is prime to 9.* [late ME, from L *prīmus* first (superl. of *prior* PRIOR[1]] *–n.* **8.** the most flourishing stage or state. **9.** the time of early manhood or womanhood: *prime of youth.* **10.** the period or state of greatest perfection or vigour of human life: *in the prime of life.* **11.** the choicest or best part of anything. **12.** the beginning or earliest stage of any period. **13.** the spring of the year. **14.** the first hour or period of the day, after sunrise. **15.** *Eccles.* the second of the seven canonical hours or the service for it, originally fixed for the first hour of the day. **16.** *Maths.* **a.** →**prime number.** **b.** one of the equal parts into which a unit is primarily divided. **c.** the mark (′) indicating such a division (also variously used as a distinguishing mark). **17.** *Fencing.* the first of eight defensive positions. **18.** *Music.* (in a scale) the tonic or keynote. **19.** *Cycling.* a section of a race which carries points, or prizes. [ME; OE *prīm* (def. 15), from L *prīma (hōra)* first (hour). Cf. F *prime*] *–v.t.* **20.** to prepare or make ready for a particular purpose or operation. **21.** to supply (a firearm) with powder for communicating fire to a charge. **22.** to lay a train of powder to (any charge, a mine, etc.). **23.** to pour water into (a pump) so as to swell the sucker and so act as a seal, making it work effectively. **24.** to cover (a surface) with a preparatory coat or colour, as in painting. **25.** to supply or equip with information, words, etc., for use. **26.** (of a boiler or a steam-engine) to operate so that water is carried over into the cylinder with the steam. [orig. uncert.] – **primeness,** *n.*

**prime cost** /– 'kɒst/, *n.* that part of the cost of a commodity deriving from the labour, materials, and expense directly involved in its construction.

**prime-cost fitting** /praɪm-'kɒst fɪtɪŋ/, *n.* an item in a building contract for which the price is known before tendering, such as bathroom fittings, air conditioning, etc. Also, **P.C. fitting.**

**primed** /praɪmd/, *adj. Colloq.* drunk.

**prime lamb** /praɪm 'læm/, *n.* →**fat lamb** (def. 1).

**prime meridian** /– mə'rɪdiən/, *n.* a meridian from which longitude east and west is reckoned, usu. that of Greenwich, England.

**prime minister** /– 'mɪnəstə/, *n.* (*oft. cap.*) the first or principal minister of certain governments; the chief of the cabinet or ministry. – **prime ministry,** *n.*

**prime mover** /– 'muvə/, *n.* **1.** *Mech.* **a.** the initial agent which puts a machine in motion, as wind, electricity, etc. **b.** a machine, as a waterwheel or steam-engine, which receives and modifies energy as supplied by some natural source. **2.** a powerful motor vehicle designed to draw a trailer, as in a semi-trailer. **3.** (in Aristotelian philosophy) that which is the first cause of all movement and does not itself move. **4.** a person who is the prime organiser or creative force in an enterprise.

**prime number** /'– nʌmbə/, *n.* a positive integer not exactly divisible by any integer except itself and unity: *5 is a prime number.*

**primer**[1] /'praɪmə/, *n.* **1.** an elementary book for teaching children to read. **2.** any small book of elementary principles: *a primer of phonetics.* [ME, from ML *prīmārium,* properly neut. adj., PRIMARY]

**primer**[2] /'praɪmə/, *n.* **1.** one who or that which primes. **2.** a cap, cylinder, etc., containing a compound which may be exploded by percussion or other means, used for firing a charge of powder. **3.** the first complete coat of paint applied to an unpainted surface. **4.** any preliminary coating or preparation applied before a final surface finish. [PRIME, *v.* + -ER[1]]

**prime time** /praɪm 'taɪm/, *n.* the peak viewing hours on television, characterised by the highest advertising rates, and the most popular programs.

**primeval** /praɪ'mivəl/, *adj.* of or pertaining to the first age or ages, esp. of the world: *primeval forms of life.* Also, **primaeval.** [L *prīmaevus* young + -AL[1]] – **primevally,** *adv.*

**primigenial** /praɪmə'dʒiniəl/, *adj.* **1.** of a primitive type; primordial. **2.** *Obs.* first generated or produced. [L *prīmigenius* original + -AL[1]]

**primigravida** /praɪmə'grævədə/, *n.* a woman who is having her first pregnancy. [L *prīmi-* (combining form of *prīmus* first) + *gravida* (fem.) pregnant]

**priming** /'praɪmɪŋ/, *n.* **1.** the powder or other material used to ignite a charge. **2.** the act of one who or that which primes. **3.** →**primer**[2] (def. 3). [see PRIME, *v.*]

**primipara** /praɪ'mɪpərə/, *n.* **1.** a woman who has given birth once. **2.** a woman parturient for the first time. [L, from *prīmi-* (combining form of *prīmus* first) + *-para* (fem.) -PAROUS] – **primiparity** /praɪmə'pærəti/, *n.* – **primiparous,** *adj.*

**primitive** /'prɪmətɪv/, *adj.* **1.** being the first or earliest of the kind or in existence, esp. in an early age of the world: *primitive forms of life.* **2.** early in the history of the world or of mankind. **3.** characteristic of early ages or of an early state of human development: *primitive art.* **4.** *Anthrop.* of or pertaining to a race, group, etc., having cultural or physical similarities with their early ancestors. **5.** unaffected or little affected by civilising influences. **6.** being in its or the earliest period; early. **7.** old-fashioned. **8.** original or radical (as opposed to *derivative*): *a primitive word.* **9.** primary (as opposed to *secondary*). **10.** *Biol.* **a.** rudimentary; primordial. **b.** denoting species, etc., only slightly evolved from early antecedent types. **c.** of early formation and temporary, as a part that subsequently disappears. **11.** *Theol.* belonging to a minority group detached from one of the protestant sects which seeks to return to the original simplicity of the gospel message: *primitive Baptist, primitive Methodist.* –*n.* **12.** something primitive. **13.** *Art.* **a.** an artist, esp. a painter, belonging to an early period in the development of a style, esp. that preceding the Renaissance. **b.** a provincial or naive painter. **c.** a work of art by such an artist. **14.** *Maths.* **a.** a geometrical or algebraic form or expression from which another is derived. **b.** a function whose derivative is equal to a given function. **15.** the form from which a given word or other linguistic form has been derived, by either morphological or historical processes, as *take* in *undertake.* [L *prīmitīvus* first of its kind; replacing ME *primitif,* from OF] – **primitively,** *adv.* – **primitiveness,** *n.*

**primitivism** /'prɪmətəvɪzəm/, *n.* a recurrent theory or belief, as in philosophy, art, etc., that the qualities of primitive or chronologically early cultures are superior to those of contemporary civilisation. – **primitivist,** *n.*

**primogenitor** /praɪmoʊ'dʒɛnətə/, *n.* **1.** a first parent or earliest ancestor. **2.** a forefather or ancestor. [ML, from L *prīmō* at first + *genitor* male parent]

**primogeniture** /praɪmoʊ'dʒɛnətʃə/, *n.* **1.** the state or fact of being the firstborn among the children of the same parents. **2.** *Law.* the principle of inheritance or succession by the firstborn, specifically the eldest son. [ML *prīmōgenitūra,* from L *prīmōgenitus* firstborn]

**primordial** /praɪ'mɔdiəl/, *adj.* **1.** constituting a beginning; giving origin to something derived or developed; original; elementary. **2.** *Biol.* primitive; initial; first. **3.** pertaining to or existing at or from the very beginning: *primordial matter.* [ME, from LL *prīmordiālis,* from L *prīmordium* beginning] – **primordially,** *adv.*

**primordium** /praɪ'mɔdiəm/, *n., pl.* **-dia** /-diə/. the first recognisable, histologically undifferentiated stage in the development of an organ. [L, properly neut. of *prīmordius* original]

**primp** /prɪmp/, *v.t.* **1.** to dress or deck with nicety. –*v.i.* **2.** *Colloq.* to primp oneself; to prink. [akin to PRIM, *v.*]

**primrose** /'prɪmroʊz/, *n.* **1.** any plant of the genus *Primula* (family Primulaceae), comprising perennial herbs with variously coloured flowers, as *P. vulgaris,* a common yellow-flowered European species. **2.** →**evening primrose.** **3.** pale yellow. –*adj.* **4.** pertaining to the primrose. **5.** pleasant; being that of ease and pleasure: *the primrose path.* **6.** of a pale yellow. [ME *primerose,* from ML *prīma rosa* first rose]

**primula** /'prɪmjələ/, *n.* →**primrose** (def. 1). [ML: kind of flower; short for *prīmula vēris,* lit., first (flower) of spring]

**primulaceous** /prɪmjə'leɪʃəs/, *adj.* belonging to the Primulaceae, a family of plants which includes the primrose. [PRIMUL(A) + -ACEOUS]

**primum mobile** /primәm 'moʊbәleɪ/, *n.* **1.** (in Ptolemaic astronomy) the outermost of the ten concentric spheres of the universe, making a complete revolution every twenty-four hours and causing all the others to do likewise. **2.** a prime mover. [L: lit., first moving thing]

**primus** /'praɪməs/, *n.* a portable cooking stove burning kerosene. [Trademark]

**prin.,** principal.

**prince** /prɪns/, *n.* **1.** a non-reigning male member of a royal family. **2.** a sovereign or monarch; a king. **3.** (in Britain) a son, or a grandson (if the child of a son), of a king or queen. **4.** the English equivalent of certain titles of nobility of varying importance or rank in certain continental European (or other) countries. **5.** the holder of such a title. **6.** the ruler of a small state, as one actually or nominally subordinate to a suzerain. **7.** one who or that which is chief or pre-eminent in any class, group, etc.: *a merchant prince.* [ME, from OF, from L *princeps* principal person, properly adj., first, principal] – **princeliness,** *n.*

**Prince Albert** /prɪns 'ælbət/, *n.* **1.** a double-breasted, long frockcoat. **2.** (*pl.*) →**alberts.**

**prince consort** /prɪns 'kɒnsɔt/, *n.* a prince who is the husband of a reigning female sovereign.

**princedom** /'prɪnsdəm/, *n.* **1.** the position, rank, or dignity of a prince. **2.** a principality (territory). **3.** (*pl.*) the principalities (angels).

**prince imperial** /prɪns ɪm'pɪəriəl/, *n.* the eldest son of an emperor.

**princeling** /'prɪnslɪŋ/, *n.* a young or minor prince.

**princely** /'prɪnsli/, *adj.,* **-lier, -liest.** **1.** greatly liberal; lavish. **2.** like or befitting a prince; magnificent. **3.** of or pertaining to a prince; royal; noble; magnificent. – **princeliness,** *n.*

**Prince of Darkness,** *n.* the devil; Satan.

**Prince of Peace,** *n.* Christ.

**Prince of Wales feather,** *n.* a New Zealand fern of the genus *Todea,* thought to resemble the feathers of the Prince of Wales' heraldic device.

**prince regent** /prɪns 'ridʒənt/, *n.* a prince who is regent of a country.

**prince royal** /– 'rɔɪəl/, *n.* the eldest son of a king or queen.

**prince's-feather** /prɪnsəz-'fɛðə/, *n.* **1.** a tall, showy, garden annual, a variety of *Amaranthus hybridus,* bearing thick crowded spikes of small red flowers. **2.** any of certain related plants. **3.** a tall, tropical annual, *Polygonum orientale,* with long pendulous inflorescences.

**princess** /'prɪnsɛs/, *n.* **1.** a non-reigning female member of a royal family. **2.** a female sovereign. **3.** the consort of a prince. **4.** (in Britain) a daughter, or a grand-daughter (if the child of a son), of a king or queen. [ME *princesse,* from F, fem. of *prince* PRINCE]

**princess line** /'– laɪn/, *n.* a style of woman's dress which is cut in an unbroken line from shoulder to hem, usu. close-fitting down to the hips then flaring out.

**princess royal** /– 'rɔɪəl/, *n.* a title which may be conferred on the eldest daughter of the British sovereign.

**principal** /'prɪnsəpəl/, *adj.* **1.** first or highest in rank, importance, value, etc.; chief; foremost. **2.** of the nature of principal, or a capital sum. *–n.* **3.** a chief or head. **4.** a governing or presiding officer, as of a school or college. **5.** one who takes a leading part; a chief actor or doer. **6.** the first player of a division of instruments in an orchestra (excepting the leader of the first violins). **7.** something of principal or chief importance. **8.** *Law.* **a.** a person authorising another (an agent) to represent him. **b.** a person directly responsible for a crime, either as actual perpetrator or as abetter present at its commission. Cf. **accessory** (def. 3). **9.** a person primarily liable for an obligation (opposed to an *endorser*). **10.** the main body of an estate, etc., as distinguished from income. **11.** *Comm.* a capital sum, as distinguished from interest or profit. **12.** *Music.* **a.** an organ stop otherwise called diapason. **b.** the subject of a fugue (opposed to *answer*). **13.** the central structure of a roof which determines its shape and supports it. **14.** each of the combatants in a duel, as distinguished from the seconds. [ME, from L *principālis* first, chief] – **principalship,** *n.*

**principal axis** /– 'æksəs/, *n.* the straight line passing through both the centre of the surface of a lens or mirror and its centre of curvature.

**principal boy** /– 'bɔɪ/, *n.* the hero of a pantomime, a part traditionally played by a woman dressed as a boy.

**principal clause** /– 'klɔz/, *n.* →**main clause.**

**principal focus** /– 'foʊkəs/, *n.* →**focal point.**

**principality** /prɪnsə'pæləti/, *n., pl.* **-ties. 1.** a state ruled by a prince, usu. a relatively small state or a state that falls within a larger state such as an empire. **2.** the position or authority of a prince or chief ruler; sovereignty; supreme power. **3.** the rule of a prince of a small or subordinate state. **4.** (*pl.*) *Theol.* an order of angels. See **angel** (def. 1). **5.** *Obs.* pre-eminence.

**principally** /'prɪnsəpli/, *adv.* chiefly; mainly.

**principal parts** /prɪnsəpəl 'pats/, *n.pl.* a set of inflected forms of a verb from which all the other inflected forms can be inferred (theoretically, the smallest such set) as *sing, sang, sung; smoke, smoked.*

**principal points** /– 'pɔɪnts/, *n.pl.* two points on the principal axis of a thick lens or lens system, such that if the object distance is measured from one and the image distance from the other, the equations relating object-image distance and focal length are similar to those for a simple thin lens.

**principate** /'prɪnsəpət/, *n.* chief place or authority.

**principle** /'prɪnsəpəl/, *n.* **1.** an accepted or professed rule of action or conduct: *a man of good principles.* **2.** a fundamental, primary, or general truth, on which other truths depend: *the principles of government.* **3.** a fundamental doctrine or tenet; a distinctive ruling opinion: *the principles of the Stoics.* **4.** (*pl.*) right rules of conduct. **5.** guiding sense of the requirements and obligations of right conduct: *a man of principle.* **6.** fixed rule or adopted method as to action. **7.** a rule or law exemplified in natural phenomena, in the construction or operation of a machine, the working of a system, or the like: *the principle of capillary attraction.* **8.** the method of formation, operation, or procedure exhibited in a given case: *a community organised on the principle of one great family.* **9.** a determining characteristic of something; essential quality of character. **10.** an originating or actuating agency or force. **11.** an actuating agency in the mind or character, as an instinct, faculty, or natural tendency. **12.** *Chem.* a constituent of a substance, esp. one giving to it some distinctive quality or effect. **13.** *Obs.* beginning or commencement. **14. in principle,** according to the rule generally followed. **15. on principle, a.** according to fixed rule, method, or practice. **b.** according to the personal rule for right conduct, as a matter of moral principle. [ME, from F *principe* (from L *principium*) + *-le,* n. suffix (cf. SYLLABLE, etc.)]

**principled** /'prɪnsəpəld/, *adj.* imbued with or having principles: *high-principled.*

**principle of equivalence,** *n.* the principle that no experiment can distinguish between a gravitational field and an accelerating frame of reference; the basis of Einstein's general theory of relativity.

**prink** /prɪŋk/, *v.t.* **1.** to deck or dress for show. *–v.i.* **2.** to deck oneself out. **3.** to fuss over one's dress, esp. before the looking glass. [apparently akin to PRANK[2], *v.*] – **prinker,** *n.*

**print** /prɪnt/, *v.t.* **1.** to produce (a text, a picture, etc.) by applying inked types, plates, blocks, or the like, with direct pressure to paper or other material. **2.** to cause (a manuscript, etc.) to be reproduced in print. **3.** to write in letters like those commonly used in print. **4.** to indent or mark (a surface, etc.) by pressing something into or on it. **5.** to produce or fix (an indentation, mark, etc.) as by pressure. **6.** to impress on the mind, memory, etc. **7.** to apply (a thing) with pressure so as to leave an indentation, mark, etc. **8.** *Photog.* to produce a positive picture from (a negative) by the transmission of light. **9.** *Computers.* to produce (a result, data, etc.) in a legible form on paper (oft. fol. by *out*). *–v.i.* **10.** to take impressions from type, etc., as in a press. **11.** to produce books, etc., by means of a press. **12.** to give an impression on paper, etc., as types, plates, etc. **13.** to write in characters such as are used in print. **14.** to follow the craft of a printer. **15.** *Computers.* to produce results in a legible form on paper (oft. fol. by *out*). *–n.* **16.** the state of being printed. **17. in print, a.** in printed form; published. **b.** (of a book, etc.) still available for purchase from the publisher. **18. out of print,** (of a book, etc.) no longer available for purchase from the publisher; sold out by the publisher. **19.** printed lettering, esp. with reference to character, style, or size. **20.** printed matter. **21.** a printed publication, as a newspaper. **22.** newsprint. **23.** a picture, design, or the like, printed from an engraved or otherwise prepared block, plate, etc. **24.** an indentation, mark, etc., made by the pressure of one body or thing on another. **25.** something with which an impression is made; a stamp or die. **26.** a design, usu. in colour, pressed on woven cotton with engraved rollers. **27.** the cloth so treated. **28.** something that has been subjected to impression, as a pat of butter. **29.** *Photog.* a picture made from a negative. *–adj.* **30.** made of printed material, esp. cotton. [ME *priente,* from OF: impression, print, pp. of *preindre,* from L *premere* press] – **printable,** *adj.*

**print.,** printing.

**printanier** /prɪn'tanieɪ/, *n.* a mixture of vegetables scooped into small balls, or cut into small dice, cooked and served with butter. [F, from *printemps* spring + *-ier* -IER]

**printed circuit** /prɪntəd 'səkət/, *n.* a circuit forming part of electronic equipment in which the wiring between components, and some components themselves, are printed, or etched, on to an insulating board.

**printed press** /'– prɛs/, *n.* →**print media.** Also, **print press.**

**printer** /'prɪntə/, *n.* **1.** one who or that which prints. **2.** a person or a firm engaged in the printing industry. **3.** *Computers.* a machine that prints on paper information sent by means of electrical or mechanical signals.

**printer's devil** /prɪntəz 'dɛvəl/, *n.* →**devil** (def. 5).

**printer's ream** /– 'rim/, *n.* →**ream**[1] (def. 1).

**printery** /'prɪntəri/, *n., pl.* **-ries. 1.** an establishment for typographic printing. **2.** an establishment for the printing of calico or the like.

**printing** /'prɪntɪŋ/, *n.* **1.** the art, process, or business of producing books, newspapers, etc., by impression from movable types, plates, etc.; typography. **2.** the act of one who or that which prints. **3.** words, etc., in printed form. **4.** printed matter. **5.** the whole number of copies of a book, etc., printed at one time. **6.** writing in which the letters are like those commonly used in print.

**printing press** /'– prɛs/, *n.* a machine for printing on paper or the like from type, plates, etc. Cf. **press** (def. 32).

**printless** /'prɪntləs/, *adj.* making, retaining, or showing no print or impression.

**print media** /'prɪnt midiə/, *n.* that section of the media which appears in print (opposed to *electronic media*).

**print-out** /'prɪnt-aʊt/, *n.* results, data, or the like printed automatically by a computer in legible form.

**print press** /'prɪnt prɛs/, *n.* →**printed press.**

**print run** /'– rʌn/, *n.* one uninterrupted printing of a book, magazine, etc.

**print-through** /'prɪnt-θru/, *n.* the unwanted transfer of sound from one part of a recording tape to another when the tape is stored on reels and successive layers are in contact with each other.

**prion** /'praɪɒn/, *n.* any of various seabirds of the genus *Pachyptila,* pale blue above and pure white underneath, with a slightly wedge-shaped tail, which feed by collecting planktonic organisms, esp. crustaceans and squid, from the surface of the sea, and which migrate to Australia.

**prior**[1] /'praɪə/, *adj.* **1.** preceding in time, or in order; earlier or former; anterior or antecedent: *a prior agreement.* **2.** prior to, preceding: *prior to that time.* *–adv.* **3.** previously (fol. by *to*). [L: former, earlier]

**prior**[2] /'praɪə/, *n.* **1.** an officer in a monastic order or religious house, sometimes next in rank below an abbot. **2.** the superior of certain monastic orders and houses. **3.** a chief magistrate, as in the medieval republic of Florence. [ME and OE, from ML: superior, head] – **priorship,** *n.*

**priorate** /'praɪərət/, *n.* **1.** the office, rank, or term of office of a prior. **2.** a priory.

**prioress** /'praɪərɛs/, *n.* a woman holding a position corresponding to that of a prior, sometimes ranking next below an abbess.

**priority** /praɪ'ɒrəti/, *n., pl.* **-ties. 1.** the state of being earlier in time, or of preceding something else. **2.** precedence in order, rank, etc. **3.** the having of certain rights before another. **4.** *Computers.* the position in rank of an interrupt system in gaining the attention of the computer when there is more than one interrupt system.

**priority-paid** /praɪˌɒrəti-'peɪd/, *adj.* of or pertaining to mail, the delivery of which is guaranteed within a specified time.

**priority road** /praɪ'ɒrəti roʊd/, *n.* a road on which traffic has right of way over traffic from crossroads.

**priory** /'praɪəri/, *n., pl.* **-ries.** a religious house governed by a prior or prioress, often dependent upon an abbey. [ME *priorie,* from ML *priōria*]

**prise** /praɪz/, *v.,* **prised, prising,** *n.* *–v.t.* **1.** to raise, move, or force with or as with a lever. *–n.* **2.** leverage. Also, **prize;** *Chiefly U.S.,* **pry.** [ME *prise,* from F: a taking hold, from L *pre(he)nsa,* fem. pp., seized]

**prism** /'prɪzəm/, *n.* **1.** *Optics.* a transparent prismatic body (esp. one with triangular bases) used for decomposing light into its spectrum or for reflecting light beams. **2.** *Geom.* a solid whose bases or ends are any congruent and parallel polygons, and whose sides are parallelograms. **3.** *Crystall.* **a.** a form consisting of faces which are parallel to the vertical axis and intersect the horizontal axes. **b.** a dome **(horizontal prism).** [LL *prisma,* from Gk: lit., something sawed]

prisms

**prismatic** /prɪz'mætɪk/, *adj.* **1.** of, pertaining to, or like a prism. **2.** formed by, or as if by, a transparent prism. **3.** varied in colour; brilliant. Also, **prismatical.** – **prismatically,** *adv.*

**prismatic colours** /– 'kʌləz/, *n.pl.* the components of ordinary white or near-white light as separated by a prism.

**prismatic instrument** /– 'ɪnstrəmənt/, *n.* an instrument, as binoculars, in which a right-angled prism is used to invert the inverted image produced by the objective.

**prison** /'prɪzən/, *n.* **1.** a public building for the confinement or safe custody of criminals and others committed by law. **2.** a place of confinement or involuntary restraint. **3.** imprisonment. [ME, from OF, from L *pre(he)nsio* seizure, arrest]

**prison-camp** /'prɪzən-kæmp/, *n.* a camp for prisoners of war, political prisoners, etc.

**prisoner** /'prɪzənə, 'prɪznə/, *n.* **1.** one who is confined in prison or kept in custody, esp. as the result of legal process. **2.** one who or something that is deprived of liberty or kept in restraint.

**prisoner constable** /– 'kʌnstəbəl/, *n.* →**convict constable.**

**prisoner of the crown,** *n.* (formerly) a convict.

**prisoner of war,** *n.* one taken by an enemy in war. *Abbrev:* P.O.W.

**prisoner servant** /prɪzənə 'sɜvənt/, *n.* (formerly) a convict working as a servant under the assignment system.

**prison farm** /'prɪzən fam/, *n.* a farm on which prisoners serving out their sentence supply the labour.

**prissy** /'prɪsi/, *adj.,* **-sier, -siest.** *Colloq.* precise; prim; affectedly nice. [b. PRIM and SISSY]

**pristine** /'prɪstin/, *adj.* **1.** of or pertaining to the earliest period or state; original; primitive. **2.** having its original purity. [L *pristinus* early]

**prithee** /'prɪði/, *interj. Archaic.* (I) pray thee.

**privacy** /'praɪvəsi, 'prɪvəsi/, *n., pl.* **-cies. 1.** the state of being private; retirement or seclusion. **2.** secrecy. **3.** *Rare.* a private place. [PRIV(ATE) + -ACY]

**private** /'praɪvət/, *adj.* **1.** belonging to some particular person or persons; belonging to oneself; being one's own: *private property.* **2.** pertaining to or affecting a particular person or a small group of persons; individual; personal: *for your private satisfaction.* **3.** confined to or intended only for the person or persons immediately concerned; confidential: *a private communication.* **4.** not holding public office employment, as a person. **5.** not of an official or public character: *to retire to private life.* **6.** (of a school) non-government. **7.** (of a company) having the right to transfer its shares restricted, the number of its members limited to 50, and prohibited from using public subscription for its shares or debentures. **8.** removed from or out of public view of knowledge; secret. **9.** not open or accessible to people in general: *a private road.* **10.** without the presence of others; alone; secluded. **11.** (of a member of parliament) not holding a government post. **12.** of lowest military rank. *–n.* **13.** a private soldier. **14.** *U.S.* a soldier of one of the three lowest ranks **(private 1, private 2, private first class). 15. in private,** in secret; not publicly. [ME, from L *prīvātus,* pp., lit., separated] – **privately,** *adv.* – **privateness,** *n.*

**private act** /'– ækt/, *n.* a statute passed in the interests of individuals, local authorities, etc., rather than the general public.

**Private Automatic Branch Exchange,** *n.* a fully automatic telephone exchange by means of which it is possible to dial direct from one extension to another in the same establishment. *Abbrev.:* P.A.B.X.

**private bar** /praɪvət 'ba/, *n.* a small room in a hotel, originally mainly used for private parties. Cf. **public bar, saloon bar.**

**private bill** /'– bɪl/, *n.* a parliamentary bill for the particular interest or benefit of some person or body of persons.

**private branch exchange,** *n.* a telephone exchange by means of which it is possible for an operator to connect any two extensions in the same establishment.

**private company** /praɪvət 'kʌmpəni/, *n.* →**proprietary limited company.**

**private enterprise** /– 'ɛntəpraɪz/, *n.* **1.** business or commercial activities independent of state ownership or control. **2.** the principle of free enterprise or laissez-faire capitalism.

**privateer** /praɪvə'tɪə/, *n.* **1.** a privately owned and manned armed vessel, commissioned by a government in time of war to fight the enemy, esp. his commercial shipping. **2.** the commander, or one of the crew, of such a vessel. *–v.i.* **3.** to cruise as a privateer. [PRIVATE + -EER, modelled on VOLUNTEER]

**private eye** /praɪvət 'aɪ/, *n. Colloq.* →**private investigator.**

**private hospital** /– 'hɒspɪtl/, *n.* a hospital, privately or corporately owned, run for profit.

**private hotel** /– hoʊ'tɛl/, *n.* a hotel or boarding house, usu. unlicensed and often residential, where guests are accepted at the proprietor's discretion.

**private investigator** /– ɪn'vɛstəgeɪtə/, *n.* a detective working under private contract, as opposed to one employed by a public police force; shamus. Also, **private eye.**

**private means** /– 'minz/, *n.pl.* an income which does not depend on a salary or the like. Also, **independent means.**

**private member's bill,** *n.* a bill introduced by a backbench member of parliament or (rarely) by a minister in his capacity as a member, rather than by the government.

**private parts** /praɪvət 'pats/, *n.pl.* the external sex organs.

Also, **privy parts, privates.**

**private patient** /– 'peɪʃənt/, *n.* **1.** a patient in a hospital who pays extra for choice of doctor and accommodation. **2.** a patient in a private hospital. **3.** a patient in a private ward.

**private practice** /– 'præktəs/, *n.* **1.** medical practice involving care for the health of private patients, for which charges are made to the individual. **2.** self-employment.

**private school** /'– skul/, *n.* a school which is privately financed and managed, and is outside the state system of education.

**private secretary** /– 'sɛkrətri/, *n.* a person who handles the individual or confidential correspondence, etc., of a person or business organisation.

**private sector** /'– sɛktə/, *n.* that sector of the community which controls private enterprise.

**private ward** /'– wɔd/, *n.* a section containing single rooms, or a single room in a hospital, for the accommodation of private patients.

**privation** /praɪ'veɪʃən/, *n.* **1.** lack of the usual comforts or necessaries of life, or an instance of this: *to lead a life of privation.* **2.** a depriving. **3.** the state of being deprived. [ME *privacion,* from L *prīvātio*]

**privative** /'prɪvətɪv/, *adj.* **1.** having the quality of depriving. **2.** consisting in or characterised by the taking away of something, or the loss or lack of something properly present. **3.** *Gram.* indicating negation or absence. *–n.* **4.** *Gram.* a privative element, as *a-* in *asymmetric* (without symmetry). **5.** that which is privative. [L *prīvātīvus*] **– privately,** *adv.*

**privet** /'prɪvət/, *n.* **1.** a European shrub, *Ligustrum vulgare,* with evergreen leaves and small, heavily perfumed, white flowers, now considered a noxious plant. **2.** any of various other species of the genus *Ligustrum.* [orig. uncert.]

**privilege** /'prɪvəlɪdʒ/, *n., v.,* **-leged, -leging.** *–n.* **1.** a right or immunity enjoyed by a person or persons beyond the common advantages of others. **2.** a special right or immunity granted to persons in authority or office; a prerogative. **3.** a prerogative, advantage, or opportunity enjoyed by anyone in a favoured position (as distinct from a right). **4.** a grant to an individual, a company, etc., of a special right or immunity, sometimes in derogation of the common right. **5.** the principle or condition of enjoying special rights or immunities. **6.** any of the more sacred and vital rights common to all citizens under a modern constitution. *–v.t.* **7.** to grant a privilege to. **8.** to free or exempt (fol. by *from*). **9.** to authorise or to license (something otherwise forbidden). [ME *privileg(i)e,* from L *prīvilēgium,* orig., a law in favour of or against an individual]

**privily** /'prɪvəli/, *adv. Archaic.* in a privy manner; secretly.

**privity** /'prɪvəti/, *n., pl.* **-ties 1.** participation in the knowledge of something private or secret, esp. as implying concurrence or consent. **2.** *Law.* the relation between privies. **3.** *Obs.* privacy. [ME *privete, privite,* from OF, from L *prīvus* private. See PRIVATE, -ITY]

**privy** /'prɪvi/, *adj., n., pl.* **privies.** *–adj.* **1.** participating in the knowledge of something private or secret (usu. fol. by *to*): *many persons were privy to the plot.* **2.** private; assigned to private uses: *the privy purse.* **3.** belonging or pertaining to some particular person or persons, now esp. with reference to a sovereign. **4.** *Archaic.* secret, concealed, hidden, or secluded. **5.** *Archaic.* acting or done in secret. *–n.* **6.** an outhouse serving as a toilet. **7.** *Law.* one participating directly in a legal transaction, or claiming through or under such a one. [ME, from OF *prive,* adj. and n., from L *prīvātus,* pp., separated, private]

**Privy Council** /prɪvi 'kaʊnsəl/, *n.* (in Britain) a body of advisers, selected theoretically by the sovereign, whose function of advising the Crown in matters of state is, except in a formal sense, now discharged by the cabinet, committees, etc. **– Privy Councillor,** *n.*

**privy parts** /prɪvi 'pats/, *n.* →**private parts.**

**privy purse** /– 'pɜs/, *n.* (*sometimes cap.*) (in Britain) a sum of money voted by parliament for the private expenses of the sovereign.

**prize**[1] /praɪz/, *n.* **1.** a reward of victory or superiority, as in a contest or competition. **2.** that which is won in a lottery or the like. **3.** anything striven for, worth striving for, or much valued. **4.** a taking or capturing at sea. **5.** a capturing. **6.** something seized or captured, esp. an enemy's ship with the property in it taken at sea under the law of war. **7.** *Archaic.* a contest or match. *–adj.* **8.** that has gained a prize; prize-winning. **9.** worthy of a prize. **10.** given or awarded as a prize. [ME *prise,* from OF: a taking, pp. of *prendre* take, capture, from L *pre(he)ndere;* influenced by ME *pris, prise* reward, prize, PRICE]

**prize**[2] /praɪz/, *v.t.,* **prized, prizing. 1.** to value or esteem highly. **2.** to estimate the worth or value of. [ME *prise(n),* from OF *prisier* praise, from L *pretiāre* prize]

**prize**[3] /praɪz/, *v.t.,* **prized, prizing,** *n.* →**prise.**

**prize fight** /'– faɪt/, *n.* a contest between professional boxers for a money prize. **– prize-fighter,** *n.* **– prize-fighting,** *n., adj.*

**prize money** /'– mʌni/, *n.* **1.** money won as a prize in a competition. **2.** *Archaic.* a portion of the money from the sale of a prize, esp. an enemy's vessel, divided among the captors.

**prize ring** /'– rɪŋ/, *n.* a ring or enclosed square area for prize-fighting.

**p.r.n.,** (used in prescriptions) as and when needed. [L *prō rē nāta*]

**pro**[1] /proʊ/, *adv., n., pl.* **pros.** *–adv.* **1.** in favour of a proposition, opinion, etc. (opposed to *con*). *–n.* **2.** a proponent of an issue; one who upholds the affirmative in a debate. **3.** an argument, consideration, vote, etc., for something. [L, prep.: in favour of, for]

**pro**[2] /proʊ/, *n., pl.* **pros,** *adj. Colloq.* professional.

**pro**[3] /proʊ/, *n., pl.* **pros.** *Colloq.* →**prostitute.**

**pro-**[1], **1.** a prefix indicating favour for some party, system, idea, etc., usu. without identity with the group, as *pro-British, pro-communist, pro-slavery,* having *anti-* as its opposite. **2.** a prefix of priority in space or time having esp. a meaning of advancing or projecting forwards or outwards, having also extended figuration meanings, including substitution, and attached widely to stems not used as words, as *provision, prologue, proceed, produce, protract, procathedral, proconsul.* [L, representing *prō,* prep., before, for, in favour of, on behalf of]

**pro-**[2], a prefix identical in meaning with **pro-**[1], occurring in words taken from Greek (as *prodrome*) or formed of Greek (and occasionally Latin) elements. [Gk, representing *pró* for, before, in favour of]

**proa** /'proʊə/, *n.* **1.** any of various types of South Pacific boat. **2.** a swift Malay sailing boat built with the leeside flat and balanced by a single outrigger. Also, **prau.** [Malay *prāū*]

**prob., 1.** probably. **2.** problem.

**probabilism** /'prɒbəbəlɪzəm/, *n.* **1.** *Philos.* the doctrine that certainty is impossible, and that probability suffices to govern faith and practice. **2.** *Rom. Cath. Theol.* a theory that in cases of doubt as to the lawfulness or unlawfulness of an action, it is permissible to follow a soundly probable opinion favouring its lawfulness. **– probabilist,** *n., adj.*

**probabilistic machine** /prɒbəbə'lɪstɪk mə,ʃin/, *n.* a model of a physically realisable machine simulated by a digital computer in order to exercise a limited number of states of the machine in an apparently random sequence.

**probability** /prɒbə'bɪləti/, *n., pl.* **-ties. 1.** the quality or fact of being probable. **2.** a likelihood or chance of something: *there is a probability of his coming.* **3.** a probable event, circumstance, etc.: *to regard a thing as a probability.* **4.** *Statistics.* the relative frequency of the occurrence of an event as measured by the ratio of the number of cases or alternatives favourable to the event to the total number of cases or alternatives. **5. in all probability,** likely; very probably.

**probability curve** /'– kɜv/, *n. Statistics.* **1.** a curve which describes the distribution of probability over the values of a variable. **2.** →**normal curve.**

**probable** /'prɒbəbəl/, *adj.* **1.** likely to occur or prove true. **2.** having more evidence for than against, or evidence which inclines the mind to belief but leaves some room for doubt. **3.** affording ground for belief: *probable evidence.* [ME, from L *probābilis*]

**probable cause** /– 'kɔz/, *n.* reasonable ground for a belief, esp. as a defence to an action for malicious prosecution.

**probable error** /– 'ɛrə/, *n. Statistics.* a value such that the error in an error distribution is equally likely to be greater or smaller than it.

**probably** /ˈprɒbəbli/, *adv.* in a probable manner; with probability; in all likelihood.

**probang** /ˈproʊbæŋ/, *n.* a long, slender, elastic rod with a sponge, ball, or the like, at the end, formerly introduced into the oesophagus, etc., as for removing foreign bodies, or for introducing medication. [orig. *provang,* b. obs. *prov(et)* probe and (F)ANG[1], *n.* or *v.*]

**probate** /ˈproʊbeɪt/, *n., adj., v.,* **-bated, -bating.** *–n.* **1.** *Law.* the official proving of a will as authentic or valid. **2.** *Law.* an officially certified copy of a will so proved. *–adj.* **3.** of or pertaining to probate or a court of probate. *–v.t.* **4.** *U.S.* to establish the authenticity or validity of (a will). [ME, from L *probātum,* neut. pp., (a thing) proved]

**probate court** /ˈ– kɔt/, *n.* a special court limited to the administration of estates of deceased persons, the probate of wills, etc.

**probate duty** /ˈ– djuti/, *n.* a tax on the gross value of the property of the deceased testator.

**probation** /prəˈbeɪʃən/, *n.* **1.** the act of testing. **2.** the testing or trial of a person's conduct, character, qualifications, or the like. **3.** the state or period of such testing or trial. **4.** *Law.* **a.** a method of dealing with offenders, esp. young persons guilty of minor crimes or first offences, by allowing them to go at large conditionally under supervision, as that of a person (**probation officer**) appointed for such duty. **b.** the state of having been conditionally released. **5.** a trial period in which a person can redeem failures, misconduct, etc. **6.** the testing or trial of a candidate for membership in a religious body or order, for holy orders, etc. **7.** *Rare.* proof. [ME *probacion,* from L *probātio*] – **probational, probationary,** *adj.*

**probationer** /prəˈbeɪʃənə/, *n.* one undergoing probation or trial. – **probationership,** *n.*

**probation officer** /prəˈbeɪʃən ɒfəsə/, *n.* a person appointed to advise and supervise offenders under probation.

**probation pass-holder** /– ˈpas-hoʊldə/, *n.* (formerly) a convict working under the probation system.

**probation system** /ˈ– sɪstəm/, *n.* (formerly) a system which replaced the assignment scheme, under which convicts worked in restricted freedom, initially in gangs for the government and then for private employers for wages.

**probative** /ˈproʊbətɪv/, *adj.* **1.** serving or designed for testing or trial. **2.** affording proof or evidence. Also, **probatory** /proʊˈbeɪtəri, ˈproʊbətri/.

**probe** /proʊb/, *v.,* **probed, probing,** *n.* *–v.t.* **1.** to search into or examine thoroughly; question closely. **2.** to examine or explore as with a probe. *–v.i.* **3.** to penetrate or examine with or as with a probe. *–n.* **4.** the act of probing. **5.** a slender surgical instrument for exploring the depth or direction of a wound, sinus, or the like. **6.** *Electronics.* an electronic circuit connected to a long thin rod, used for monitoring otherwise inaccessible points in an electronic system. **7.** *Aeron.* a spacecraft capable of exploring, examining and testing conditions in space and radioing back the results. **8.** *U.S.* an investigation or inquiry, esp. by a legislative committee, of suspected illegal activity. [ML *proba* test, in LL proof. See PROOF] – **prober,** *n.*

**probity** /ˈproʊbəti/, *n.* integrity; uprightness; honesty. [L *probitas*]

**problem** /ˈprɒbləm/, *n.* **1.** any question or matter involving doubt, uncertainty, or difficulty. **2.** a question proposed for solution or discussion. *–adj.* **3.** difficult to train or guide; unruly: *a problem child.* **4.** *Lit.* dealing with choices of action difficult either for an individual or for society at large: *a problem play.* [ME *probleme,* from L *problēma,* from Gk]

**problematic** /prɒbləˈmætɪk/, *adj.* **1.** of the nature of a problem; doubtful; uncertain; questionable. **2.** *Logic.* denoting a proposition or judgment which claims that it may or may not be true. See **modality** (def. 3b). Also, **problematical.** – **problematically,** *adv.*

**proboscidean** /proʊbəˈsɪdiən/, *adj.* **1.** pertaining to or resembling a proboscis. **2.** having a proboscis. **3.** belonging or pertaining to the Proboscidea, the order of mammals that consists of the elephants and their extinct allies. Also, **proboscidian.** [NL *Proboscidea,* pl. (see PROBOSCIS) + -AN]

**proboscis** /prəˈbɒskəs, prəˈboʊsəs/, *n., pl.* **-boscises** /-ˈbɒskəsəz, -ˈbɒsəsəz/, **-boscides** /-ˈbɒskədiz, -ˈbɒsədiz/. **1.** an elephant's trunk. **2.** any long flexible snout, as of the tapir. **3.** *Entomol.* **a.** an elongate but not rigid feeding organ of certain insects formed of the mouthparts, as in the Lepidoptera and Diptera. **b.** any elongate or snoutlike feeding organ. **4.** (*joc.*) the human nose. [L, from Gk *proboskís*]

**proboscis monkey** /– ˈmʌŋki/, *n.* a powerfully built monkey, *Nasalis larvatus,* of Borneo, having a long, bulbous nose.

**proc.,** **1.** procedure. **2.** proceedings. **3.** process.

**procaine** /proʊˈkeɪn, ˈproʊkeɪn/, *n.* →**novocaine.** [PRO-[1] + (CO)CAINE]

**procaine penicillin** /– pɛnəˈsɪlən/, *n.* penicillin that has a slow absorption rate.

**procambium** /proʊˈkæmbiəm/, *n.* the meristem from which vascular bundles are developed. [NL. See PRO-[1], CAMBIUM] – **procambial,** *adj.*

**procarp** /ˈproʊkap/, *n.* a carpogonium plus certain cells intimately associated with it.

**procathedral** /proʊkəˈθidrəl/, *n.* a church used temporarily as a cathedral.

**procedure** /prəˈsidʒə/, *n.* **1.** the act or manner of proceeding in any action or process; conduct. **2.** a particular course or mode of action. **3.** mode of conducting legal, parliamentary, or other business, esp. litigation and judicial proceedings. [F, from *procéder* PROCEED] – **procedural,** *adj.*

**proceed** /prəˈsid/, *v.;* /ˈproʊsid/, *n.* *–v.i.* **1.** to move or go forwards or onwards, esp. after stopping. **2.** to go on with or carry on any action or process. **3.** to go on (to do something). **4.** to continue one's discourse. **5.** *Law.* **a.** to begin and carry on a legal action. **b.** to take legal proceedings (fol. by *against*). **6.** to be carried on, as an action, process, etc. **7.** to go or come forth; issue. **8.** to arise, originate, or result. *–n.* **9.** (*usu. pl.*) the sum derived from a sale or other transaction. **10.** that which results or accrues. [ME *procede(n),* from L *prōcēdere*]

**proceeding** /prəˈsidɪŋ/, *n.* **1.** a particular action or course of action. **2.** action, course of action, or conduct. **3.** the act of one who or that which proceeds. **4.** (*pl.*) records of the doings of a society. **5.** *Law.* **a.** the instituting or carrying on of an action at law. **b.** a legal step or measure: *to institute proceedings against a person.*

**proceleusmatic** /proʊsəlusˈmætɪk/, *adj.* **1.** inciting, animating, or inspiriting. **2.** *Pros.* **a.** denoting a metrical foot of four short syllables. **b.** pertaining to or consisting of feet of this kind. *–n.* **3.** *Pros.* a proceleusmatic foot. [LL *proceleusmaticus,* from Gk *prokeleusmatikós*]

**process** /ˈproʊsɛs/, *n.* **1.** a systematic series of actions directed to some end: *the process of making butter.* **2.** a continuous action, operation, or series of changes taking place in a definite manner: *the process of decay.* **3.** *Law.* **a.** the summons, mandate, or writ by which a defendant or thing is brought before court for litigation. **b.** the total of such summoning writs. **c.** the whole course of the proceedings in an action at law. **4.** *Photog.* **a.** photomechanical or photoengraving methods collectively. **b.** a system of superimposing background in a film, or otherwise creating a picture by combining elements not ordinarily united: *a process shot.* **5.** *Biol.* a natural outgrowth, projection, or appendage: *a process of a bone.* **6.** a prominence or protuberance. **7.** the action of going forward or on. **8.** the condition of being carried on. **9.** course or lapse, as of time. **10. in (the) process of,** during the course of; in the middle of. *–v.t.* **11.** to treat or prepare by some particular process, as in manufacturing. **12.** to convert (an agricultural commodity) into marketable form by some special process. **13.** to institute a legal process against. **14.** to serve a process or summons on. **15.** *Computers.* (of data) to manipulate in order to abstract the required information. *–adj.* **16.** prepared or modified by an artificial process. **17.** pertaining to, made by or using, or used in, photomechanical or photoengraving methods. [ME *proces,* from F, from L *prōcessus* a going forward]

**process control** /– kənˈtroʊl/, *n.* the control of a complex industrial or chemical process usu. by electronic means.

**process costing** /– ˈkɒstɪŋ/, *n.* a method of costing used to ascertain the cost of the product at each stage of manufacture.

**processed cheese** /proʊsɛst ˈtʃiz/, *n.* a medium soft cheese, usu. a cheddar, with a mild flavour, treated to prevent maturing and to give consistent flavour, texture, etc.

**procession** /prəˈsɛʃən/, *n.* **1.** the proceeding or moving along in orderly succession, in a formal or ceremonious manner, of a line or body of persons, animals, vehicles, etc. **2.** the line or body of persons, animals, etc., moving along. **3.** *Eccles.* an office, litany, etc., said or sung in a religious procession. **4.** *Theol.* the relation of the Holy Spirit to the Father and later, in the Western Church, to the Son; distinguished from the 'generation' of the Son and the 'unbegottenness' of the Father. **5.** the act of proceeding forth from a source. *–v.i.* **6.** to go in procession. [early ME, from ML *prōcessio* a religious procession, in L a marching on]

**processional** /prəˈsɛʃənəl/, *adj.* **1.** of or pertaining to a procession. **2.** of the nature of a procession. **3.** characterised by processions. **4.** sung or recited in procession, as a hymn. *–n.* **5.** a processional hymn. **6.** an office book containing hymns, litanies, etc., for use in religious processions.

**processor** /ˈprousɛsə/, *n.* **1.** a machine which processes information, as a telephone. **2.** →**digital computer.**

**process printing** /prousɛs ˈprɪntɪŋ/, *n.* a method of printing practically any colour by using four separate halftone plates for red, yellow, blue, and black ink.

**process-server** /ˈprousɛs-sɜvə/, *n.* one who serves legal documents such as a subpoena, writ, or warrant, etc., requiring appearance in court or before a notary public, etc.

**process worker** /ˈprousɛs wɜkə/, *n.* a person engaged on a production line in a manufacturing process who is not required to make adjustments to machinery or to exercise skills of fitting or adjustment.

**proclaim** /prəˈkleɪm/, *v.t.* **1.** to announce or declare publicly or officiously: *to proclaim one's opinions.* **2.** to announce or declare, publicly and officially: *to proclaim war.* **3.** (of things) to indicate or make known. **4.** to declare (a district, etc.) subject to particular legal restrictions. **5.** to declare to be an outlaw, evildoer, or the like. **6.** to denounce or prohibit publicly. *–v.i.* **7.** to make proclamation. [ME *proclame(n)*, from L *proclāmāre*] – **proclaimer,** *n.*

**proclamation** /prɒkləˈmeɪʃən/, *n.* **1.** that which is proclaimed; a public and official announcement. **2.** the act of proclaiming.

**proclitic** /prouˈklɪtɪk/, *Gram. –n.* **1.** an element similar to a prefix but of more independent status, approaching that of a separate word. *–adj.* **2.** having the nature of a proclitic. [NL *procliticus,* from Gk *proklī́nein* lean forward. Cf. ENCLITIC]

**proclivity** /prəˈklɪvəti/, *n., pl.* **-ties.** natural or habitual inclination or tendency; propensity; predisposition: *a proclivity to fault-finding.* [L *prōclīvitas* tendency, propensity. Cf. F *proclivité*]

**proconsul** /prouˈkɒnsəl/, *n.* any appointed administrator over a dependency or an occupied area. [ME, from L] – **proconsular,** *adj.*

**procrastinate** /prouˈkræstəneɪt/, *v.,* **-nated, -nating. 1.** to defer action; delay: *to procrastinate until an opportunity is lost. –v.t.* **2.** to put off till another day or time; defer; delay. [L *prōcrastinātus,* pp., put off till the morrow] – **procrastination** /prəkræstəˈneɪʃən/, *n.* – **procrastinator,** *n.*

**procreant** /ˈproukriənt/, *adj.* **1.** procreating; generating. **2.** pertaining to procreation. [L *prōcreans,* ppr.]

**procreate** /ˈproukrieɪt/, *v.t.,* **-ated, -ating. 1.** to beget or generate (offspring). **2.** to produce; bring into being. [L *prōcreātus,* pp.] – **procreation** /proukriˈeɪʃən/, *n.* – **procreative,** *adj.* – **procreator,** *n.*

**procrustean** /prouˈkrʌstiən/, *adj.* (*also cap.*) **1.** tending to produce conformity by violent or arbitrary means. **2. procrustean bed,** an arbitrary standard to which strict conformity is forced. [from *Procrustes,* a brigand in Greek legend, who stretched or mutilated his victims to make them conform to the length of his bed]

**proctitis** /prɒkˈtaɪtəs/, *n.* inflammation situated around or about the rectum or anus.

**proctology** /prɒkˈtɒlədʒi/, *n.* the branch of medicine dealing with the rectum and anus. [*procto-* (combining form representing Gk *prōktós* anus) + -LOGY] – **proctological** /prɒktəˈlɒdʒɪkəl/, *adj.* – **proctologist,** *n.*

**proctor** /ˈprɒktə/, *n.* **1.** (in certain universities) an official charged with various duties, esp. with the maintenance of discipline among undergraduates. **2.** *Law.* (formerly) a person employed to manage another's cause in a court of civil or ecclesiastical law, or to collect tithes for the owner of them. **3.** *C. of E.* a representative of the clergy in convocation. [contracted var. of PROCURATOR] – **proctorial** /prɒkˈtɔriəl/, *adj.* – **proctorship,** *n.*

**proctoscope** /ˈprɒktəskoup/, *n.* an instrument for examining the interior of the rectum. [*procto-* (from Gk *prōkto-,* combining form of *prōktós* anus) + -SCOPE]

**procumbent** /prouˈkʌmbənt/, *adj.* **1.** lying on the face; prone; prostrate. **2.** *Bot.* (of a plant or stem) lying along the ground, but without putting forth roots. [L *prōcumbens,* ppr., falling forward]

**procurable** /prəˈkjurəbəl/, *adj.* obtainable.

**procurance** /prəˈkjurəns/, *n.* the act of bringing something about; agency.

**procuration** /prɒkjəˈreɪʃən/, *n.* **1.** the appointment of a procurator, agent, or attorney. **2.** the authority given. **3.** a document whereby the authority is given. **4.** the act of obtaining or getting; procurement. **5.** the act of procuring for the gratification of lust or purposes of prostitution. **6.** *Obs.* management for another; agency.

**procuration fee** /ˈ– fi/, *n.* commission to brokers, etc., for procuring a loan of money (as on mortgage).

**procurator** /ˈprɒkjəreɪtə/, *n.* (in Presbyterian Churches) the lawyer appointed to advise the Church Courts on the interpretation of law and to appear in civil courts for the church. [ME *procuratour,* from L *prōcūrātor*]

**procure** /prəˈkjuə/, *v.,* **-cured, -curing.** *–v.t.* **1.** to obtain or get by care, effort, or the use of special means: *to procure evidence.* **2.** to effect; cause; bring about, esp. by unscrupulous or indirect means: *to procure a person's death.* **3.** to obtain for the gratification of lust or purposes of prostitution. *–v.i.* **4.** to act as a procurer or pimp. [ME, from L *prōcūrāre* take care of, manage] – **procurement,** *n.*

**procurer** /prəˈkjuərə/, *n.* one who procures, esp. a pander or pimp. – **procuress,** *n. fem.*

**prod** /prɒd/, *v.,* **prodded, prodding,** *n. –v.t.* **1.** to poke or jab with something pointed: *to prod an animal with a stick.* **2.** to seek to rouse or incite as if by poking. *–n.* **3.** the act of prodding; a poke or jab. **4.** any of various pointed instruments, as a goad. [cf. OE *prod-* in *prodbor* auger] – **prodder,** *n.*

**prod.,** **1.** produce. **2.** produced. **3.** product.

**Prod** /prɒd/, *Colloq. –n.* **1.** a Protestant. *–adj.* **2.** Protestant.

**Proddie** /ˈprɒdi/, *n. Colloq.* a Protestant. Also, **Proddy.**

**prodgie** /ˈprɒdʒi/, *n. Colloq.* a produce store.

**prodigal** /ˈprɒdɪgəl/, *adj.* **1.** wastefully or recklessly extravagant: *prodigal expenditure.* **2.** giving or yielding profusely; lavish (fol. by *of*): *prodigal of smiles.* **3.** lavishly abundant; profuse. *–n.* **4.** one who spends, or has spent, his money or substance with wasteful extravagance; a spendthrift. [backformation from PRODIGALITY] – **prodigally,** *adv.*

**prodigality** /prɒdəˈgæləti/, *n., pl.* **-ties. 1.** quality or fact of being prodigal; wasteful extravagance in spending. **2.** an instance of it. **3.** lavish abundance. [ME *prodigalite,* from ML *prōdigālitas*]

**prodigious** /prəˈdɪdʒəs/, *adj.* **1.** extraordinary in size, amount, extent, degree, force, etc.: *a prodigious noise.* **2.** wonderful or marvellous: *a prodigious feat.* **3.** abnormal; monstrous. [L *prōdigiōsus*] – **prodigiously,** *adv.* – **prodigiousness,** *n.*

**prodigy** /ˈprɒdədʒi/, *n., pl.* **-gies. 1.** a person, esp. a child, endowed with extraordinary gifts or powers: *a musical prodigy.* **2.** a marvellous example (fol. by *of*): *that prodigy of learning.* **3.** something wonderful or marvellous; a wonder. **4.** something abnormal or monstrous. **5.** *Rare.* something extraordinary regarded as of prophetic significance. [L *prōdigium* prophetic sign]

**prodrome** /ˈprɒdroum/, *n.* a premonitory symptom. [F, from NL *prodromus,* from Gk *pródromos* running before] – **prodromal,** *adj.*

**produce** /prəˈdjus/, *v.,* **-duced, -ducing;** /ˈprɒdʒus/, *n. –v.t.* **1.** to bring into existence; give rise to; cause: *to produce steam.* **2.** to bring into being by mental or physical labour, as a work of literature or art. **3.** *Econ.* to create (something having an exchangeable value). **4.** to bring forth; bear; give birth to. **5.** to yield; provide, furnish, or supply: *a mine producing silver.* **6.** to cause to accrue: *money producing interest.* **7.** to bring forward; present to view or notice; exhibit. **8.** to bring (a play, film, etc.) before the public. **9.** to extend or prolong, as a line. *–v.i.* **10.** to bring forth or yield offspring, products, etc. **11.** *Econ.* to create value; bring crops, goods, etc., into a state in which they will command a price. *–n.* **12.** that which is produced; yield; product. **13.** agricultural or natural products collectively. [L *prōdūcere* lead or bring forward, extend, prolong, bring forth, produce] – **producible,** *adj.*

**producer** /prə'djusə/, *n.* **1.** one who produces. **2.** *Econ.* one who creates value, or produces goods and services (opposed to *consumer*). **3.** a person who exercises general supervision over a film production, having particular responsibility for all administrative and financial aspects of the production. **4.** the person who is responsible for a film, television, or radio production, or a music recording, who controls the performers, and who is final arbiter on artistic matters. Cf. **director.** **5.** *Theat.* a person responsible for the presentation of a play, including the interpretation of the author's script, the direction of actors at rehearsals, the use of costumes, etc. **6.** an apparatus for making producer gas.

**producer gas** /'– gæs/, *n.* a vaporous fuel produced by gasifying cheap solid fuel with steam, used in the place of petrol, natural gas, etc. The chief constituents are carbon monoxide, hydrogen, and nitrogen.

**producer goods** /'– gʊdz/, *n.pl.* goods that are used in the process of creating final consumer goods, as machinery, raw materials, etc.

**produce stakes** /'prɒdʒus steɪks/, *n.* a set-weight race for three-year old horses of recognised breeding, for which the contestant's size is nominated and the breeder of the winning horse takes the prize.

**produce store** /'– stɔ/, *n.* a store, esp. in a country town, selling grain, fodder, etc.

**product** /'prɒdʌkt/, *n.* **1.** a thing produced by any action or operation, or by labour; an effect or result. **2.** something produced; a thing produced by nature or by a natural process. **3.** *Chem.* a substance obtained from another substance through chemical change. **4.** *Maths.* the result obtained by multiplying two or more quantities together. [ME, from L *prōductum,* neut. pp., (thing) produced]

**production** /prə'dʌkʃən/, *n.* **1.** the act of producing; creation; manufacture. **2.** that which is produced; a product. **3.** *Econ.* the creation of value; the producing of articles having an exchangeable value. **4.** the total amount produced. **5.** a work of literature or art. **6.** the act of exhibiting or displaying. **7.** the artistic direction and interpretation of a play. [ME, from L *prōductio*]

**production reactor** /'– riæktə/, *n.* a nuclear reactor whose main function is the production of fissile material.

**productive** /prə'dʌktɪv/, *adj.* **1.** having the power of producing; generative; creative. **2.** producing readily or abundantly; fertile; prolific. **3.** *Econ.* producing or tending to produce goods and services having exchangeable value. – **productively,** *adv.* – **productivity** /prɒdʌk'tɪvəti/, **productiveness,** *n.*

**productivity bargaining** /'– bagənɪŋ/, *n.* a negotiation between employers and employees in which the employees agree to certain changes in work practices, thus resulting in increased productivity, in exchange for better wages, etc.

**proem** /'proʊɛm/, *n.* an introductory discourse; an introduction; a preface; a preamble. [L *prooemium,* from Gk *prooímion;* replacing ME *proheme,* from OF] – **proemial** /proʊ'imiəl/, *adj.*

**proembryo** /proʊ'ɛmbrioʊ/, *n.* the group of cells produced by division of a zygote before differentiation of the embryo proper.

**prof** /prɒf/, *n. Colloq.* professor.

**Prof.,** Professor.

**profanation** /prɒfə'neɪʃən/, *n.* the act of profaning; desecration; defilement; debasement.

**profanatory** /prə'fænətri/, *adj.* tending to desecrate; profaning.

**profane** /prə'feɪn/, *adj., v.,* **-faned, -faning.** *–adj.* **1.** characterised by irreverence or contempt for God or sacred things; irreligious, esp. speaking or spoken in manifest or implied contempt for sacred things. **2.** not sacred, or not devoted to sacred purposes; unconsecrated; secular: *profane history.* **3.** unholy; heathen; pagan. **4.** not initiated into religious rites or mysteries, as persons. **5.** common or vulgar. *–v.t.* **6.** to misuse (anything that should be held in reverence or respect); defile; debase; employ basely or unworthily. **7.** to treat (anything sacred) with irreverence or contempt. [ME *prophane,* from F, from L *profānus,* lit., before (outside) the temple] – **profanely,** *adv.* – **profaneness,** *n.* – **profaner,** *n.*

**profanity** /prə'fænəti/, *n., pl.* **-ties.** **1.** the quality of being profane; irreverence. **2.** profane conduct or language; a profane act or utterance.

**profert** /'proʊfət/, *n.* an exhibition of a record or paper in open court. [L: he brings forward]

**profess** /prə'fɛs/, *v.t.* **1.** to lay claim to (a feeling, etc.), often insincerely; pretend to: *he professed extreme regret.* **2.** to declare openly; announce or affirm; avow or acknowledge: *to profess one's satisfaction.* **3.** to affirm faith in or allegiance to (a religion, God, etc.). **4.** to declare oneself skilled or expert in; claim to have knowledge of; make (a thing) one's profession or business. **5.** to receive or admit into a religious order. *–v.i.* **6.** to make profession. **7.** to take the vows of a religious order. [backformation from PROFESSED]

**professed** /prə'fɛst/, *adj.* **1.** alleged; pretended. **2.** avowed; acknowledged. **3.** professing to be qualified; professional (rather than amateur). **4.** having taken vows of or been received into a religious order. [ME (def. 4), from L *professus,* pp., + -ED[2]]

**professedly** /prə'fɛsədli/, *adv.* **1.** allegedly. **2.** avowedly. **3.** ostensibly.

**profession** /prə'fɛʃən/, *n.* **1.** a vocation requiring knowledge of some department of learning or science, esp. one of the three vocations of theology, law, and medicine (formerly known specifically as **the professions** or **the learned professions**): *a lawyer by profession.* **2.** any vocation, occupation, etc. **3.** the body of persons engaged in an occupation or calling: *to be respected by the medical profession.* **4.** the act of professing; avowal; a declaration, whether true or false: *professions of love.* **5.** the declaration of belief in or acceptance of religion or a faith: *the profession of Christianity.* **6.** a religion or faith professed. **7.** the declaration made on entering a religious order. [ME, from L *professio*]

**professional** /prə'fɛʃnəl, -ʃənəl/, *adj.* **1.** following an occupation as a means of livelihood or for gain: *a professional actor.* **2.** pertaining or appropriate to a profession: *professional studies.* **3.** engaged in one of the learned professions: *a professional man.* **4.** following as a business an occupation ordinarily engaged in as a pastime: *a professional golfer.* **5.** making a business of something not properly to be regarded as a business: *a professional politician.* **6.** undertaken or engaged in as a means of livelihood or for gain: *professional football.* *–n.* **7.** one belonging to one of the learned or skilled professions. **8.** one who makes a business of an occupation, etc., esp. of an art or sport, in which amateurs engage for amusement or recreation. **9.** an expert in a game or sport, hired by a sports club to instruct members. – **professionally,** *adv.*

**professional foul** /–'faʊl/, *n.* (in soccer) a deliberate infringement committed in order to prevent a goal being scored by the opposing team.

**professionalise** /prə'fɛʃnəlaɪz, -ʃən-/, *v.,* **-lised, -lising.** *–v.t.* **1.** to give a professional status or character to. *–v.i.* **2.** to become professional. Also, **professionalize.**

**professionalism** /prə'fɛʃnəlɪzəm, -ʃən-/, *n.* **1.** professional character, spirit, or methods. **2.** the standing, practice, or methods of a professional as distinguished from an amateur.

**professor** /prə'fɛsə/, *n.* **1.** a teacher of the highest rank, usu. holding a chair in a particular branch of learning, in a university or college. **2.** a teacher. **3.** an instructor in some popular art, as singing, etc. **4.** one who professes his sentiments, beliefs, etc. [ME, from L] – **professorial** /prɒfə'sɔriəl/, *adj.* – **professorially,** *adv.*

**professoriate** /prɒfə'sɔriət/, *n.* **1.** a group of professors. **2.** the office or post of professor.

**professorship** /prə'fɛsəʃɪp/, *n.* the office or post of a professor.

**proffer** /'prɒfə/, *v.t.* **1.** to put before a person for acceptance;

offer. *–n.* **2.** the act of proffering. **3.** an offer. [ME *profre(n)*, from AF *profrer*, var. of OF *poroffrir*, from *por-* PRO-[1] + *offrir* (from LL *offerīre*, var. of L *offerre* offer)]

**proficiency** /prəˈfɪʃənsi/, *n., pl.* **-cies.** the state of being proficient; skill; expertness: *proficiency in music.*

**proficient** /prəˈfɪʃənt/, *adj.* **1.** well advanced or expert in any art, science, or subject; skilled. *–n.* **2.** an expert. [L *prōficiens*, ppr., making progress. See PROFIT] – **proficiently,** *adv.*

**profile** /ˈproʊfaɪl/, *n., v.,* **-filed, -filing.** *–n.* **1.** the outline or contour of the human face, esp. as seen from the side. **2.** a drawing, painting, etc., of the side view of the head. **3.** the outline of something seen against a background. **4.** *Archit., Engineering.* a drawing of a section, esp. a vertical section, through something. **5.** a vivid and concise sketch of the biography and personality of an individual. **6. keep (maintain) a low (high) profile,** *Colloq.* to act so as to be inconspicuous (conspicuous); maintain an unobtrusive (obtrusive) level of activity. *–v.t.* **7.** to draw a profile of. **8.** to shape as to profile. [It. *profilo*, from *profilare* draw in outline, from L *pro-* PRO-[1] + LL *filāre* spin]

**profile drag** /ˈ– dræg/, *n.* the drag of a body, excluding that due to lift, comprising the sum of the form drag (which depends on the shape of the body) and the skin friction (which depends on the nature of its surface); head resistance.

**profit** /ˈprɒfət/, *n.* **1.** (*oft. pl.*) pecuniary gain resulting from the employment of capital in any transaction: **a. gross profit,** gross receipts less the immediate costs of production. **b. net profit,** amount remaining after deducting all costs from gross receipts. **c.** the ratio of such pecuniary gain to the amount of capital invested. **2.** (*oft. pl.*) returns, proceeds, or revenue, as from property or investments. **3.** *Econ.* the surplus left to the producer or employer after deducting wages, rent, cost of raw materials, etc. **4.** (*usu. pl.*) such additional benefits as interest on capital, insurance, etc. **5.** advantage; benefit; gain. *–v.i.* **6.** to gain advantage or benefit. **7.** to make profit. **8.** to be of advantage or benefit. **9.** to take advantage. **10.** *Obs.* to make progress. *–v.t.* **11.** to be of advantage or profit to. [ME, from OF, from L *prōfectus* progress, profit] – **profitless,** *adj.*

**profitable** /ˈprɒfətəbəl/, *adj.* **1.** yielding profit; remunerative. **2.** beneficial or useful. – **profitableness,** *n.* – **profitably,** *adv.*

**profit and loss,** *n.* the gain and loss arising from commercial or other transactions, applied esp. to an account in bookkeeping showing gains and losses in business. – **profit-and-loss,** *adj.*

**profit a prendre** /prɒfət a ˈprɒndrə/, *n., pl.* **profits a prendre.** *n.* right to enter upon the land of another and take away soil or its produce. Also, **profit à prendre.** [F]

**profiteer** /prɒfəˈtɪə/, *n.* **1.** one who seeks or exacts exorbitant profits, as by taking advantage of public necessity. *–v.i.* **2.** to act as a profiteer. – **profiteering,** *n.*

**profiterole** /prəˈfɪtəroʊl/, *n.* a small ball of choux pastry cooked, then filled with cream, jam, cheese, or the like. [F]

**profit sharing** /ˈprɒfət ʃɛərɪŋ/, *n.* the sharing of profits, as between employer and employee, esp. in such a way that the employee receives, in addition to his wages, a share in the profits of the business. – **profit-sharing,** *adj.*

**profit taker** /ˈ– teɪkə/, *n.* a trader who sells shares or commodities in the market following a rise in price.

**profligacy** /ˈprɒfləgəsi/, *n.* **1.** shameless dissoluteness. **2.** reckless extravagance. **3.** great abundance.

**profligate** /ˈprɒfləgət/, *adj.* **1.** utterly and shamelessly immoral; thoroughly dissolute. **2.** recklessly prodigal or extravagant. *–n.* **3.** a profligate person. [L *prōflīgātus*, pp., overthrown, ruined] – **profligately,** *adv.* – **profligateness,** *n.*

**profluent** /ˈprɒfluənt/, *adj.* flowing smoothly along. [ME, from L *prōfluens*, ppr., flowing forth]

**pro forma** /proʊ ˈfɔmə/, *adv.* according to form; as a matter of form. [L]

**pro-forma** /proʊ-ˈfɔmə/, *adj.* done for the sake of an established form or procedure.

**profound** /prəˈfaʊnd/, *adj.* **1.** penetrating or entering deeply into subjects of thought or knowledge: *a profound thinker.* **2.** intense; extreme: *profound sleep.* **3.** being or going far beneath what is superficial, external, or obvious: *profound insight.* **4.** of deep meaning; abstruse: *a profound book.* **5.** extending, situated, or originating far down, or far beneath the surface. **6.** low: *a profound bow.* **7.** deep. *–n. Poetic.* **8.** that which is profound. **9.** the deep sea; ocean. **10.** depth; abyss. [ME, from OF *profond*, from L *profundus*] – **profoundly,** *adv.* – **profoundness,** *n.*

**profundity** /prəˈfʌndəti/, *n., pl.* **-ties. 1.** quality of being profound; depth. **2.** a profoundly deep place; an abyss. **3.** (*pl.*) profound or deep matters. [ME *profundite*, from LL *profunditas*]

**profuse** /prəˈfjus/, *adj.* **1.** spending or giving freely and in large amount, often to excess; extravagant (oft. fol. by *in*). **2.** made or done freely and abundantly: *profuse apologies.* **3.** abundant; in great amount. [ME, from L *profūsus*, pp., poured forth] – **profusely,** *adv.* – **profuseness,** *n.*

**profusion** /prəˈfjuʒən/, *n.* **1.** abundance; abundant quantity. **2.** a great quantity or amount (oft. fol. by *of*). **3.** lavish spending; extravagance.

**prog.,** progressive.

**progenitive** /prəˈdʒɛnətɪv/, *adj.* producing offspring; reproductive.

**progenitor** /prəˈdʒɛnətə/, *n.* **1.** a direct ancestor; forefather. **2.** an originator, as of an artistic movement. [ME *progenitour*, from L *prōgenitor*]

**progeny** /ˈprɒdʒəni/, *n., pl.* **-nies.** offspring; issue; descendants. [ME *progenie*, from OF, from L *prōgenies*]

**progesterone** /prəˈdʒɛstəroʊn/, *n.* a hormone of the corpus luteum of the ovary, which prepares the uterus for the fertilised ovum and helps to maintain pregnancy. [PRO-[1] + GE(STATION) + STER(OL) + -ONE]

**progestin** /proʊˈdʒɛstən/, *n.* →**progestogen.**

**progestogen** /proʊˈdʒɛstədʒən/, *n.* any of a class of steroid hormones that have functions similar to those of progesterone. Also, **progestin.**

**proglottis** /proʊˈglɒtəs/, *n., pl.* **-glottides** /-ˈglɒtədiz/. one of the segments or joints of a tapeworm, containing complete reproductive systems, usu. both male and female. Also, **proglottid** /proʊˈglɒtəd/. [NL, from Gk *proglōssís* point of the tongue (with reference to shape)] – **proglottic,** *adj.*

**prognathous** /prɒgˈneɪθəs/, *adj.* **1.** (of a jaw) protruding; with a gnathic index over 103. **2.** (of a skull or a person) having protrusive jaws. Also, **prognathic.** [PRO-[2] + Gk *gnáthos* jaw + -OUS] – **prognathism** /ˈprɒgnəθɪzəm/, **prognathy,** *n.*

**prognosis** /prɒgˈnoʊsəs/, *n., pl.* **-noses** /-ˈnoʊsiz/. **1.** a forecasting of the probable course and termination of a disease. **2.** a particular forecast made. [LL, from Gk: foreknowledge]

**prognostic** /prɒgˈnɒstɪk/, *adj.* **1.** of or pertaining to prognosis. **2.** indicating something in the future. *–n.* **3.** a forecast or prediction. **4.** a portent or omen. [L *prognōsticon*, from Gk *prognōstikón* a prognostic; replacing ME *pronostike*, from F]

**prognosticate** /prɒgˈnɒstəkeɪt/, *v.,* **-cated, -cating.** *–v.t.* **1.** to forecast or predict (something future) from present indications or signs; to prophesy. *–v.i.* **2.** to make a forecast; to prophesy. – **prognosticative,** *adj.* – **prognosticator,** *n.*

**prognostication** /prɒgˌnɒstəˈkeɪʃən/, *n.* **1.** the act of prognosticating. **2.** a forecast or prediction.

**program** /ˈproʊgræm/, *n., v.,* **-grammed, -gramming.** *–n.* **1.** a plan or policy to be followed. **2.** a list of things to be done; agenda. **3.** a list of items, pieces, performers, etc., in a musical, theatrical, or other entertainment; playbill. **4.** an entertainment with reference to its pieces or numbers. **5.** *Radio, T.V.* a particular item or production. **6.** a prospectus or syllabus. **7.** →**computer program.** *–v.t.* **8.** *Computers.* to organise and arrange (data, etc.) relevant to a problem so that it can be solved by a computer. *–v.i.* **9.** to plan a program. Also, **programme.** [LL *programma*, from Gk: public notice in writing]

**programmable** /ˈproʊgræməbəl/, *adj.* capable of being programmed. Also, **programable.**

**programmed art** /ˈproʊgræmd ˈat/, *n.* →**computer art.**

**programme music** /ˈproʊgræm mjuzɪk/, *n.* music intended to convey an impression of a definite series of images, scenes, or events (opposed to *absolute music*).

**programmer** /ˈproʊgræmə/, *n.* one who prepares data, etc., for a computer.

**progress** /ˈproʊgrɛs/, *n.*; /prəˈgrɛs/, *v.* *–n.* **1.** a proceeding to a further or higher stage, or through such stages successively:

*the progress of a scholar in his studies.* **2.** advancement in general. **3.** growth or development; continuous improvement. **4.** *Sociol.* the development of an individual or group in a direction considered as beneficial and to a degree greater than that yet attained. **5.** *Biol.* increasing differentiation and perfection in the course of ontogeny or phylogeny. **6.** forward or onward movement. **7.** course of action, of events, of time, etc. **8. in progress,** taking place; under way; happening. *–v.i.* **9.** to advance. **10.** to go forwards or onwards. [ME, from L *prōgressus* a going forward]

**progression** /prəˈgrɛʃən/, *n.* **1.** the act of progressing; forward or onward movement. **2.** a passing successively from one member of a series to the next; succession; sequence. **3.** *Astron.* (of a planet) direct, as opposed to retrograde, motion. **4.** *Maths.* a sequence of numbers in which there is a constant relation between each number and its successor. Cf. **arithmetical progression** and **geometric progression. 5.** *Music.* the manner in which notes or chords follow one another. – **progressional,** *adj.*

**progressionist** /prəˈgrɛʃənəst/, *n.* one who believes in or advocates progress, as of mankind, society, etc. – **progressionism,** *n.*

**progressive** /prəˈgrɛsɪv/, *adj.* **1.** favouring or advocating progress, improvement, or reform, esp. in political matters. **2.** progressing or advancing; making progress towards better conditions, more enlightened or liberal ideas, the use of new and advantageous methods, etc.: *a progressive community, a progressive school.* **3.** characterised by such progress, or by continuous improvement. **4.** going forwards or onwards; passing successively from one member of a series to the next; proceeding step by step. **5.** denoting or pertaining to a form of taxation in which the rate increases with certain increases in the taxable income. **6.** *Gram.* continuous (def. 3). **7.** *Med.* continuously increasing in extent or severity, as a disease. *–n.* **8.** one who is progressive, or who favours progress or reform, esp. in political matters. **9.** *Gram.* the progressive aspect of a verb. **10.** →**progressive handicap. 11.** →**progressive horse.** – **progressively,** *adv.* – **progressiveness,** *n.*

**progressive dinner** /– ˈdɪnə/, *n.* a dinner party, usu. to raise funds for charity, where each course is served at a different house.

**progressive handicap** /– ˈhændikæp/, *n.* a restricted race for horses which are specified as being in the progressive class in accordance with the rules operating in each State.

**progressive horse** /– ˈhɔs/, *n.* a horse eligible to run in a progressive handicap. Also, **progressive-class horse.**

**progressive jazz** /– ˈdʒæz/, *n.* any style of modern jazz which is marked by progressive characteristics, either in its use of unconventional instrumentation, harmony, or rhythm, or in a combination of these elements.

**progressivism** /prəˈgrɛsəvɪzəm/, *n.* the principles and practices of progressives.

**prohibit** /prəˈhɪbət/, *v.t.* **1.** to forbid (an action, a thing) by authority: *smoking is prohibited.* **2.** to forbid (a person) from doing something. **3.** to prevent; to hinder. [ME, from L *prohibitus,* pp., held back, restrained]

**prohibition** /prouəˈbɪʃən/, *n.* **1.** the act of prohibiting. **2.** a law or decree that forbids. **3.** (*oft. cap.*) the interdiction by law of the manufacture and sale of alcoholic drinks for common consumption, esp. in the U.S. between 1919 and 1933.

**prohibitionist** /prouəˈbɪʃənəst/, *n.* one who favours or advocates the prohibition of the manufacture and sale of alcoholic drinks for common consumption. – **prohibitionism,** *n.*

**prohibition order** /prouəˈbɪʃən ɔdə/, *n. N.Z.* a court order taken out against, or by, an habitual drunkard to prevent his drinking alcoholic liquor.

**prohibitive** /prəˈhɪbətɪv/, *adj.* **1.** that prohibits or forbids something. **2.** serving to prevent the use, purchase, etc., of something: *the prohibitive price of meat.* Also, **prohibitory.** – **prohibitively,** *adv.*

**proinsulin** /prouˈɪnʃələn/, *n.* the inactive form in which insulin is synthesised and stored in the pancreas.

**project** /ˈproudʒɛkt, ˈprɒ-/, *n.;* /prəˈdʒɛkt/, *v.* *–n.* **1.** something that is contemplated, devised, or planned; a plan; a scheme; an undertaking. *–v.t.* **2.** to propose, contemplate, or plan. **3.** to throw, cast, or impel forwards or onwards. **4.** to set forth; present. **5.** to communicate; convey; make known (an idea, impression, etc.). **6.** to throw or cause to fall upon a surface or into space, as a ray of light, a shadow, etc. **7.** to cause (a figure or image) to appear as on a background. **8.** to visualise and regard (an idea, etc.) as an objective reality. **9.** to cause to jut out or protrude. **10.** to throw forwards (a figure, etc.) by straight lines or rays (parallel or from a centre) which pass through all points of it and reproduce it on a surface or other figure. **11.** to delineate by any system of correspondence between points. **12.** to transform the points of (one figure) into those of another by any correspondence between points. *–v.i.* **13.** to extend or protrude beyond something else. **14.** to communicate or convey an idea or impression. [ME, from L *prōjectum,* pp. neut., (thing) thrown out]

**project house** /ˈ– haus/, *n.* a house of a standard design built as one of a series. Also, **exhibition house.**

**projectile** /prəˈdʒɛktaɪl/, *n.* **1.** *Mil.* an object fired from a gun with an explosive propelling charge, such as a bullet, shell, rocket, or grenade. **2.** an object set in motion by an exterior force which then continues to move by virtue of its own inertia. *–adj.* **3.** impelling or driving forwards, as a force. **4.** caused by impulse, as motion. **5.** capable of being impelled forwards, as a missile. **6.** *Zool.* protrusile, as the jaws of a fish. [NL, neut. of *prōjectilis,* adj., projecting]

**projection** /prəˈdʒɛkʃən/, *n.* **1.** a projecting or protruding part. **2.** the state or fact of jutting out or protruding. **3.** a causing to jut out or protrude. **4.** *Geom., etc.* the act, process, or result of projecting. **5.** Also, **map projection.** *Cartog.* a systematic drawing of lines representing the meridians of longitude and parallels of latitude on a plane surface; the earth's surface (or celestial sphere) or some portion of it may be drawn on the grid so produced. **6.** *Photog.* **a.** the projection of an image by optical means, as in the projection of slides or films on to a screen or the making of enlargements. **b.** the image so formed. **7.** the act of visualising and regarding an idea or the like as an objective reality. **8.** that which is so visualised and regarded. **9.** *Psychol.* **a.** the tendency to attribute to another person, or to the environment, what is actually within oneself. **b.** *Psychoanal.* (usu.) such an attribution relieving the ego of guilt feelings. **10.** the act of planning or scheming. **11.** *Alchemy.* the casting of the powder of the philosopher's stone upon metal in fusion, to transmute it into gold or silver. [L *prōjectio*]

**projectionist** /prəˈdʒɛkʃənəst/, *n.* one who operates a cinema projector.

**projective** /prəˈdʒɛktɪv/, *adj.* **1.** of or pertaining to projection. **2.** produced, or capable of being produced, by projection. **3.** *Psychol.* **a.** pertaining to projection. **b.** of, pertaining to, or denoting a technique for revealing the hidden motives or underlying personality structure of an individual by using certain test materials that allow him to express himself freely. – **projectivity** /prɒdʒɛkˈtɪvəti/, *n.*

**projective geometry** /– dʒiˈɒmətri/, *n.* the geometric study of projective properties.

**projective property** /– ˈprɒpəti/, *n.* a geometric property which is unaltered by projection.

**projector** /prəˈdʒɛktə/, *n.* **1.** an apparatus for throwing an image on a screen, as of a slide; a film projector, etc. **2.** a device for projecting a beam of light. **3.** one who forms projects or plans; a schemer.

**prolactin** /prouˈlæktən/, *n.* an anterior pituitary hormone which regulates milk secretion in mammals and the activity of the crop glands in birds.

**prolamine** /ˈprouləmin/, *n.* one of a group of proteins which are soluble in relatively strong alcohol, but insoluble in water, pure alcohol, and neutral solvents.

**prolapse** /ˈproulæps/, *n.;* /prəˈlæps/, *v.,* **-lapsed, -lapsing.** *–n.* Also, **prolapsus. 1.** *Pathol.* a falling down of an organ or part, as the uterus, from its normal position. *–v.i.* **2.** *Chiefly Pathol.* to fall or slip down or out of place. [LL *prōlapsus* a falling down]

**prolate** /ˈprouleɪt/, *adj.* elongated along the polar diameter, as a spheroid generated by the revolution of an ellipse about its longer

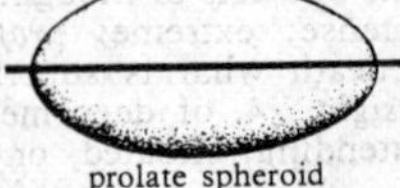
prolate spheroid

axis (opposed to *oblate*). [L *prōlātus,* pp., brought forward, extended]

**prole** /proʊl/, *n. Colloq.* a member of the proletariat. Also, **prol.**

**proleg** /'proʊlɛg/, *n.* one of the abdominal ambulatory processes of caterpillars and other larvae, as distinct from the true or thoracic legs. [PRO-[1] + LEG]

**prolegomenon** /proʊlə'gɒmənən/, *n., pl.* **-gomena** /-'gɒmənə/. a preliminary observation, as on the subject of a book (usu. pl., as applied to an introduction to a book). [NL, from Gk (neut. ppr. pass.): being said beforehand]

**prolegomenous** /proʊlə'gɒmənəs/, *adj.* **1.** prefatory; preliminary. **2.** characterised by unnecessary or lengthy prologuising.

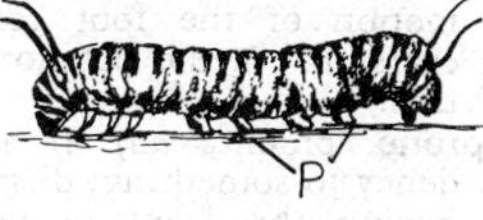

P, prolegs of larva of monarch butterfly

**prolepsis** /proʊ'lɛpsəs/, *n., pl.* **-ses** /-siz/. **1.** *Rhet.* an anticipation of objections in order to answer them in advance. **2.** the assigning of an event, etc., to a period earlier than its actual date. **3.** the use of an epithet in anticipation of its becoming applicable. [L, from Gk: anticipation, preconception] – **proleptic,** *adj.*

**proletarian** /proʊlə'tɛəriən/, *adj.* **1.** pertaining or belonging to the proletariat. **2.** (in ancient Rome) belonging to the lowest or poorest class of people. *–n.* **3.** a member of the proletariat. Also, **proletary.** [L *prōlētārius* a Roman citizen of the lowest class + -AN]

**proletariat** /proʊlə'tɛəriət/, *n.* **1.** the unpropertied class; that class which is dependent for support on the sale of its labour. **2.** the working class, or wage-earners in general. [F, from L *prōlētārius* a Roman citizen of the lowest class + *-at* -ATE[3]]

**proliferate** /prə'lɪfəreɪt/, *v.i., v.t.,* **-rated, -rating.** to grow or produce by multiplication of parts, as in budding or cell division. – **proliferation** /prəlɪfə'reɪʃən/, *n.*

**proliferous** /prə'lɪfərəs/, *adj.* **1.** proliferating. **2.** *Bot.* **a.** producing new individuals by budding or the like. **b.** producing an organ or shoot from an organ which is itself normally the last, as a shoot or a new flower from the midst of a flower. [ML *prōlifer* (from L *prōli-* offspring + *-fer* bearing) + -OUS]

**prolific** /prə'lɪfɪk/, *adj.* **1.** producing offspring, young, fruit, etc., esp. abundantly; fruitful. **2.** producing much or abundantly: *a prolific writer.* **3.** abundantly productive of or fruitful in something specified. **4.** characterised by, involving, or causing abundant production. [ML *prōlificus,* from L *prōli-* offspring + *-ficus* -FIC] – **prolificacy, prolificness,** *n.* – **prolifically,** *adv.*

**proline** /'proʊlin/, *n.* an amino acid, $C_5H_9NO_2$, found in all proteins, particularly collagen. [contraction of *pyrroline,* from PYRROLE + -INE[2]]

**prolix** /'proʊlɪks/, *adj.* **1.** extended to great, unnecessary, or tedious length; long and wordy. **2.** speaking or writing at great or tedious length. [ME, from L *prōlixus* extended, long] – **prolixity** /prə'lɪksəti/, **prolixness,** *n.* – **prolixly,** *adv.*

**prolocutor** /proʊ'lɒkjətə/, *n.* **1.** a presiding officer of an assembly; a chairman. **2.** *C. of E.* the chairman of the lower house of a convocation. [L] – **prolocutorship,** *n.*

**prologue** /'proʊlɒg/, *n., v.,* **-logued, -loguing.** *–n.* **1.** an introductory speech, often in verse, calling attention to the theme of a play. **2.** the actor who delivers it. **3.** an introductory act of a dramatic performance. **4.** a preliminary discourse; a preface or introductory part of a discourse, poem, or novel. **5.** any introductory proceeding, event, etc. *–v.t.* **6.** to introduce with, or as with, a prologue. [ME *prolog,* from L *prōlogus,* from Gk *prólogos*]

**prologuise** /'proʊlɒgaɪz/, *v.i.,* **-gised, -gising.** to compose or deliver a prologue. Also, **prologise, prologuize.** – **prologuiser,** *n.*

**prolong** /prə'lɒŋ/, *v.t.* **1.** to lengthen out in time; to extend the duration of; to cause to continue longer: *to prolong one's life.* **2.** to make longer in spatial extent: *to prolong a line.* [late ME *prolonge(n),* from LL *prolongāre*] – **prolonger,** *n.* – **prolongment,** *n.*

**prolongate** /'proʊlɒŋgeɪt/, *v.t.,* **-gated, -gating.** *Rare.* to prolong.

**prolongation** /proʊlɒŋ'geɪʃən/, *n.* **1.** the act of prolonging: *the prolongation of a line.* **2.** the state of being prolonged. **3.** a prolonged or extended form. **4.** an added part.

**prolusion** /prə'luʒən/, *n.* **1.** a preliminary written article. **2.** an essay preliminary to a more profound work, or of an introductory or slight nature. [L *prōlūsio* preliminary exercise]

**prolusory** /prə'luzəri/, *adj.* **1.** serving for prolusion. **2.** of the nature of a prolusion.

**prom** /prɒm/, *n.* **1.** →**prom concert.** **2.** *U.S. Colloq.* a formal dance, esp. at a school or college. [short for PROMENADE]

**prom.,** promontory.

**prom concert** /'prɒm kɒnsət/, *n.* a concert at which part of the audience have no formal seating arrangements, patronised often by young people and offering programs usu. more adventurous that those of subscription concerts. [shortened form of *promenade concert*]

**pro memoria** /proʊ mə'mɔriə/, *adv.* for memory (used in diplomacy to recall rights which have lapsed for a long time). [L]

**promenade** /prɒmə'nad/; /prɒmə'neɪd/ *for defs 3, 5, and 8, n., v.,* **-naded, -nading.** *–n.* **1.** a walk, esp. in a public place, as for pleasure or display. **2.** an area suitable for leisurely walking, esp. one along the seafront at a seaside resort; esplanade. **3.** a march of dancers in folk or square-dancing. *–v.i.* **4.** to take a promenade. **5.** to dance a promenade. *–v.t.* **6.** to take a promenade through or about. **7.** to take or conduct on or as on a promenade; parade. **8.** to dance (a promenade). [F, from *promener* lead out, take for a walk or airing] – **promenader,** *n.*

**promenade concert** /prɒmə'nad kɒnsət/, *n.* →**prom concert.**

**promenade deck** /'– dɛk/, *n.* a deck on a liner for use as a promenade by the passengers.

**Promethean** /prə'miθiən/, *adj.* **1.** creative; boldly original. *–n.* **2.** one who dares to exceed the bounds which others accept. [from *Prometheus,* who, in Greek myth, made men from clay, stole fire for them from Mount Olympus, and taught them various arts, in punishment for which he was chained by Zeus' order to a rock where his liver was daily gnawed by an eagle]

**promethium** /prə'miθiəm/, *n.* a radioactive, rare-earth, metallic, trivalent element. *Symbol:* Pm; *at. no.:* 61.

**prominence** /'prɒmənəns/, *n.* **1.** Also, **prominency.** the state of being prominent; conspicuousness. **2.** that which is prominent; a projection or protuberance: *the prominence of a rock or cliff, the prominences of a face.* **3.** *Astron.* a cloud of gas high above the surface of the sun, esp. when seen in silhouette at the sun's edge.

**prominent** /'prɒmənənt/, *adj.* **1.** standing out so as to be easily seen; conspicuous; esp. noticeable: *a prominent feature.* **2.** standing out beyond the adjacent surface or line; projecting. **3.** important; leading; well-known: *a prominent citizen.* [L *prōminens,* ppr., jutting out] – **prominently,** *adv.*

**promiscuity** /prɒməs'kjuəti/, *n., pl.* **-ties.** **1.** the state of being promiscuous. **2.** promiscuous sexual union. **3.** indiscriminate mixture.

**promiscuous** /prə'mɪskjuəs/, *adj.* **1.** characterised by or involving indiscriminate mingling or association, esp. indulging in sexual intercourse with a number of partners. **2.** consisting of parts, elements, or individuals of different kinds brought together without order. **3.** indiscriminate; without discrimination. **4.** casual; without particular plan or reason. [L *prōmiscuus*] – **promiscuously,** *adv.* – **promiscuousness,** *n.*

**promise** /'prɒməs/, *n., v.,* **-ised, -ising.** *–n.* **1.** a declaration made, as to another person, with respect to the future, giving assurance that one will do, not do, give, not give, etc., something. **2.** an express assurance on which expectation is to be based. **3.** something that has the effect of an express assurance; indication of what may be expected. **4.** indication of future excellence or achievement: *a writer that shows promise.* **5.** that which is promised. **6. be on a promise,** *Colloq.* (of a man) to be assured of a particular sexual partner: *he was on a promise in every second house.* *–v.t.* **7.** to engage or undertake by promise (with an infinitive or clause): *to promise not to interfere.* **8.** to make a promise of: *to promise help.* **9.** to make a promise of (something) to. **10.** to afford ground for expecting. **11.** to engage to join in marriage. **12.** to assure (used in emphatic declarations). *–v.i.* **13.** to afford ground for expectation (oft. fol. by *well* or *fair*). **14.** to make a promise. [ME, from L *prōmissum* a promise, properly neut. pp. of *prōmittere* to promise] – **promiser;** *Law,* **promisor** /prɒmə'sɔ/, *n.*

**promisee** /prɒmə'si/, *n. Law.* one to whom a promise is made.

**promising** /'prɒməsɪŋ/, *adj.* giving promise; likely to turn out well: *a promising young man.* – **promisingly,** *adv.*

**promissory** /'prɒməsəri/, *adj.* **1.** containing or implying a promise. **2.** of the nature of a promise. **3.** *Insurance.* of or denoting preliminary agreements and representations, made in drawing up a contract of insurance. [ML *prōmissōrius,* from L *prōmissor*]

**promissory note** /'– noʊt/, *n.* a written promise to pay a specified sum of money to a person designated or to his order, or to the bearer, at a time fixed or on demand.

**promo** /'proʊmoʊ/, *n.* an advertisement for a coming television or radio program, consisting of extracts from it with commentary.

**promontory** /'prɒməntri/, *n., pl.* **-ries.** **1.** a high point of land or rock projecting into the sea or other water beyond the line of coast; a headland. **2.** *Anat.* a prominent or protuberant part. [ML *prōmontōrium,* for L *prōmunturium*]

**promote** /prə'moʊt/, *v.t.,* **-moted, -moting.** **1.** to advance in rank, dignity, position, etc. **2.** to further the growth, development, progress, etc., of; encourage. **3.** to help to found; originate; organise; launch (a financial undertaking, publicity campaign, etc.). [ME, from L *prōmōtus,* pp., moved forward, advanced]

**promoter** /prə'moʊtə/, *n.* **1.** one who initiates or takes part in the organising of a company, development of a project, etc. **2.** one who or that which promotes. **3.** *Chem.* a substance which increases the activity of a catalyst. **4.** *Obs.* an informer.

**promotion** /prə'moʊʃən/, *n.* **1.** advancement in rank or position. **2.** furtherance or encouragement. **3.** the act of promoting. **4.** the state of being promoted.

**promotive** /prə'moʊtɪv/, *adj.* tending to promote.

**prompt** /prɒmpt/, *adj.* **1.** done, performed, delivered, etc., at once or without delay: *a prompt reply.* **2.** ready in action; quick to act as occasion demands. **3.** ready and willing. *–v.t.* **4.** to move or incite to action. **5.** to suggest or induce (action, etc.); inspire or occasion. **6.** to assist (a person speaking) by suggesting something to be said. **7.** *Theat.* to supply (an actor or reciter) with his cue from offstage if he has missed it, or his line if he has forgotten it. *–v.i.* **8.** *Theat.* to supply offstage cues and effects. *–n.* **9.** *Comm.* **a.** a limit of time given for payment for merchandise purchased, the limit being stated on a note of reminder called a **prompt note. b.** the contract setting the time limit. **10.** the act of prompting. **11.** something that prompts. [ME, from L *promptus,* pp., taken out, at hand] – **promptly,** *adv.* – **promptness,** *n.*

**prompt-book** /'prɒmpt-bʊk/, *n.* the script of a play, containing cues, etc., used by a prompter. Also, **prompt-copy.**

**prompt-box** /'prɒmpt-bɒks/, *n.* the place in a theatre where a prompter sits.

**prompter** /'prɒmptə/, *n.* **1.** *Theat.* one who follows offstage a play in progress from the book, to repeat missed cues and supply actors with forgotten lines. **2.** one who or that which prompts.

**promptitude** /'prɒmptətjud/, *n.* promptness. [late ME, from LL *promptitūdō*]

**prompt neutron** /prɒmpt 'njutrɒn/, *n.* a neutron emitted during a nuclear fission process without measurable delay, i.e., in less than a millionth of a second.

**prompt-side** /'prɒmpt-saɪd/, *n.* that part of the stage to the actor's left as he faces the audience.

**promulgate** /'prɒməlgeɪt/, *v.t.,* **-gated, -gating.** **1.** to make known by open declaration; to publish; to proclaim formerly or put into operation (a law or rule of court or decree). **2.** to set forth or teach publicly (a creed, doctrine, etc.). [L *prōmulgātus,* pp., made publicly known, published] – **promulgation** /prɒməl'geɪʃən/, *n.* – **promulgator,** *n.*

**promycelium** /proʊmaɪ'siliəm/, *n., pl.* **-lia** /-liə/. a short filament produced in the germination of a spore, which bears small spores and then dies. – **promycelial,** *adj.*

**pron.,** **1.** pronominal. **2.** pronoun. **3.** pronounced. **4.** pronunciation.

**pronate** /proʊ'neɪt/, *v.,* **-nated, -nating.** *–v.t.* **1.** to render prone; to rotate or place (the hand or forearm) so that the surface of the palm is downward when the limb is stretched forward horizontally. Cf. **supinate.** *–v.i.* **2.** to become pronated. [LL *prōnātus,* pp., bent forward, from L *prōnus* PRONE] – **pronator,** *n.*

**pronation** /proʊ'neɪʃən/, *n.* **1.** a rotation of the hand which leaves the palm facing downwards and the bones of the forearm crossed (opposed to *supination*). **2.** a comparable motion of the foot consisting of abduction followed by eversion. **3.** the position assumed as the result of this rotation.

**prone** /proʊn/, *adj.* **1.** having a natural inclination or tendency to something; disposed; liable: *to be prone to anger.* **2.** having the front or ventral part downwards; lying face downwards. **3.** lying flat; prostrate. **4.** having a downward direction or slope. **5.** having the palm downwards, as the hand. [ME, from L *prōnus* turned or leaning forwards, inclined downwards, disposed, prone] – **pronely,** *adv.* – **proneness,** *n.*

**pronephros** /proʊ'nɛfrɒs/, *n.* a primitive kidney functioning in lower vertebrates but vestigial in higher vertebrates and man. Cf. **mesonephros.** [NL, from Gk *pro-* PRO-[2] + *nephrós* kidney]

**prong** /prɒŋ/, *n.* **1.** one of the pointed divisions or tines of a fork. **2.** any pointed projecting part, as of an antler. *–v.t.* **3.** to pierce or stab with a prong. **4.** to supply with prongs. [ME *prang(e),* c. MLG *prange* pinching instrument; cf. MLG *pfrengen* press, Goth. *anaprangan* oppress]

**pronged** /prɒŋd/, *adj.* having prongs.

**pronghorn** /'prɒŋhɔn/, *n.* a fleet, antelope-like ruminant, *Antilocapra americana,* of the plains of western North America.

**pronominal** /proʊ'nɒmənəl/, *adj.* pertaining to or having the nature of a pronoun. [LL *prōnōminālis,* from L *prōnōmen* pronoun] – **pronominally,** *adv.*

**pronominalise** /proʊ'nɒmənəlaɪz/, *v.t.,* **-lised, -lising.** to make into a pronoun. – **pronominalisation** /proʊˌnɒmənəlaɪ'zeɪʃən/, *n.*

**pronoun** /'proʊnaʊn/, *n.* **1.** (in many languages) one of the major form classes, or parts of speech, comprising words used as substitutes for nouns. **2.** any such word, as *I, you, he, this, who, what.* **3.** a word of similar function or meaning, whether member of a special form class or not. [F *pronom,* from L *prōnōmen*]

**pronounce** /prə'naʊns/, *v.,* **-nounced, -nouncing.** *–v.t.* **1.** to enunciate or articulate (words, etc.). **2.** to utter or sound in a particular manner in speaking. **3.** to declare (a person or thing) to be as specified. **4.** to utter or deliver formally or solemnly. **5.** to announce authoritatively or officially. *–v.i.* **6.** to pronounce words, etc. **7.** to make a statement or assertion, esp. an authoritative statement (oft. fol. by *on*). **8.** to give an opinion or decision (usu. fol. by *on*). [ME, from OF *prononcier,* from L *prōnuntiāre* proclaim, announce, recite, utter] – **pronounceable,** *adj.* – **pronouncer,** *n.*

**pronounced** /prə'naʊnst/, *adj.* **1.** strongly marked. **2.** clearly indicated. **3.** decided; definite: *to have very pronounced views.* – **pronouncedly** /prə'naʊnsədli/, *adv.*

**pronouncement** /prə'naʊnsmənt/, *n.* **1.** a formal or authoritative statement. **2.** an opinion or decision. **3.** the act of pronouncing.

**pronto** /'prɒntoʊ/, *adv. Colloq.* promptly; quickly. [Sp. (adj. and adv.), from L *promptus.* See PROMPT]

**pronucleus** /proʊ'njukliəs/, *n., pl.* **-clei** /-klii/. *Embryol.* either of the gametic nuclei which after fertilisation unite and form a double nucleus.

**pronunc.,** pronunciation.

**pronunciation** /prənʌnsi'eɪʃən/, *n.* the act or the result of producing the sounds of speech including articulation, vowel and consonant formation, accent, inflection, and intonation, often with reference to the correctness or acceptability of the speech sounds. [ME, from L *prōnuntiātio*] – **pronunciational,** *adj.*

**proof** /pruf/, *n.* **1.** evidence sufficient to establish a thing as true, or to produce belief in its truth. **2.** anything serving as such evidence. **3.** the act of testing or making trial of anything; test; a trial: *to put a thing to the proof.* **4.** the establishment of the truth of anything; demonstration. **5.** a logical presentation of the way in which given assumptions imply a certain result. **6.** *Law.* (in judicial proceedings) evidence having probative weight. **7.** the effect of evidence in convincing the mind. **8.** an arithmetical operation serving to check the correctness of a calculation. **9.** a test to determine the quality, etc., of materials used in manufacture. **10.** the state of having been tested and approved. **11.** proved strength, as of armour. **12. a.** the arbitrary standard strength, as of alcoholic liquors. **b.** strength with reference to this standard, indicated on a scale on which '100 proof' signifies a proof spirit. **13.** *Photog.* a trial print from a negative. **14.** *Print.* **a.** a trial impression as of composed type, taken to correct errors and make alterations. **b.** one of a number of early and superior impressions taken before the printing of the ordinary issue. **15.** *Engraving, etc.* an impression taken from a plate or the like to show its state during the process of execution. *–adj.* **16.** impenetrable, impervious, or invulnerable: *proof against temptation.* **17.** of tested or proved strength or quality: *proof armour.* **18.** used for testing or proving; serving as proof. **19.** of standard strength, as an alcoholic liquor. *–v.t.* **20.** to treat or coat (a material) in order to make it resistant to deterioration or damage, impervious to water, etc. **21.** *Print., etc.* to take a trial impression of (type, etc.). [ME *preove,* from OF *prueve,* from LL *proba* proof, from L *probāre* PROVE]

**-proof,** a suffix meaning 'insulated from', 'impervious to', 'not affected by', etc., as in *waterproof.*

**proofing** /ˈprufɪŋ/, *n.* **1.** the act or process of making a thing resistant to deterioration, damage, etc. **2.** a chemical used in manufacture to make materials waterproof.

**proofread** /ˈprufrid/, *v.t., v.i.,* **-read, -reading.** to read (printers' proofs, etc.) in order to detect and mark errors to be corrected. – **proofreader,** *n.* – **proofreading,** *n.*

**proof sheet** /ˈpruf ʃit/, *n.* a printer's proof.

**proof spirit** /– ˈspɪrət/, *n.* **1.** an alcoholic liquor, or a mixture of alcohol and water, containing 57.06 per cent alcohol by volume at a specific temperature. **2.** *U.S.* one having 50 per cent alcohol by volume.

**prop**[1] /prɒp/, *v.,* **propped, propping,** *n.* *–v.t.* **1.** to support, or prevent from falling, with or as with a prop (oft. fol. by *up*): *to prop a roof.* **2.** to rest (a thing) against support. **3.** to support or sustain. *–v.i.* **4.** (of horses) to stop suddenly with all four legs stiff, jolting the rider. **5.** to stop suddenly and change direction. *–n.* **6.** a stick, rod, pole, beam, or other rigid support. **7.** a person or thing serving as a support or stay. **8.** (*pl.*) *Colloq.* the legs. **9.** Also, **prop-forward.** *Rugby Football.* either of the two forwards outermost in the front row of the scrum. **10.** a sudden stop. [ME *proppe,* c. MD *proppe* prop, support; orig. uncert.]

**prop**[2] /prɒp/, *n.* →**property** (def. 9).

**prop**[3] /prɒp/, *n.* *Colloq.* →**propeller.**

**prop.,** proprietor.

**propaedeutic** /proupiˈdjutɪk/, *adj.* Also, **propaedeutical. 1.** pertaining to or of the nature of preliminary instruction. **2.** introductory to some art or science. *–n.* **3.** a propaedeutic subject or study. **4.** (*pl.*) the preliminary body of knowledge and rules necessary for the study of some art or science. [PRO-[2] beforehand + Gk *paideutikós* pertaining to teaching]

**propagable** /ˈprɒpəgəbəl/, *adj.* capable of being propagated.

**propaganda** /prɒpəˈgændə/, *n.* **1.** the systematic propagation of a given doctrine. **2.** the particular doctrines or principles propagated by an organisation or movement. **3.** dissemination of ideas, information or rumour for the purpose of injuring or helping an institution, a cause or a person. **4.** doctrines, arguments, facts spread by deliberate effort through any medium in order to further one's cause or to damage an opposing cause. **5.** a public action or display aimed at furthering or hindering a cause. [It., from use of L *propāgandā* in NL title, *Sacra Congregatio de Propaganda Fide,* a committee of cardinals established in 1622 by Pope Gregory XV for the propagation of the faith]

**propagandise** /prɒpəˈgændaɪz/, *v.,* **-dised, -dising.** *–v.t.* **1.** to propagate or spread (principles, etc.) by propaganda. *–v.i.* **2.** to spread propaganda. Also, **propagandize.**

**propagandism** /prɒpəˈgændɪzəm/, *n.* zealous propagation of particular doctrines or principles.

**propagandist** /prɒpəˈgændəst/, *n.* **1.** one devoted to the propagation of particular doctrines or principles. *–adj.* **2.** pertaining to propaganda or propagandists.

**propagate** /ˈprɒpəgeɪt/, *v.,* **-gated, -gating.** *–v.t.* **1.** to cause (plants, animals, etc.) to multiply by any process of natural reproducing from the parent stock. **2.** to reproduce (itself, its kind, etc.), as a plant or an animal does. **3.** to transmit (traits, etc.) in reproduction, or through offspring. **4.** to spread (a report, doctrine, practice, etc.) from person to person; disseminate. **5.** to cause to increase in number or amounts. **6.** to cause to extend to a greater distance, or transmit through space or a medium: *to propagate sound.* *–v.i.* **7.** to multiply by any process of natural reproduction, as plants or animals; to breed. [L *propāgātus,* pp., propagated (orig. referring to plants by layers or slips)] – **propagative,** *adj.* – **propagator,** *n.*

**propagation** /prɒpəˈgeɪʃən/, *n.* **1.** the act of propagating. **2.** the fact of being propagated. **3.** multiplication by natural reproduction. **4.** transmission; dissemination.

**propane** /ˈproupeɪn/, *n.* a gaseous hydrocarbon, $C_3H_8$, of the methane series, found in petroleum. [PROP(IONIC ACID) + -ANE]

**propanoate** /proupəˈnoueɪt/, *n.* →**propionate.**

**propanoic acid** /ˌproupənouɪk ˈæsəd/, *n.* →**propionic acid.**

**propanol** /ˈproupənɒl/, *n.* →**propyl alcohol.**

**proparoxytone** /proupəˈrɒksətoun/, *Class. Gk Gram.* *–adj.* **1.** having an acute accent on the antepenultimate syllable. *–n.* **2.** a proparoxytone word. [Gk *proparoxýtonos*] – **proparoxytonic** /ˌproupərɒksəˈtɒnɪk/, *adj.*

**pro patria** /prou ˈpætriə/, *adv.* for one's country. [L]

**propel** /prəˈpɛl/, *v.t.,* **-pelled, -pelling. 1.** to drive, or cause to move, forwards: *a boat propelled by oars.* **2.** to impel or urge onwards. [L *prōpellere*]

**propellant** /prəˈpɛlənt/, *n.* **1.** a propelling agent. **2.** *Mil.* the charges of explosive used in a gun to fire the projectile. **3.** *Aeron.* one or more substances used in rocket motors for the chemical generation of gas at the controlled rates required to provide thrust. **4.** the compressed gas used in an aerosol container to expel the liquid product through a fine jet, in the form of a spray.

**propellent** /prəˈpɛlənt/, *adj.* **1.** propelling; driving forward. *–n.* **2.** a propelling agent.

**propeller** /prəˈpɛlə/, *n.* **1.** a device having a revolving hub with radiating blades, for propelling a ship, aircraft, etc. **2.** one who or that which propels.

aircraft propeller

**propeller shaft** /ˈ– ʃaft/, *n.* the shaft which transmits power from an engine to a propeller, etc.

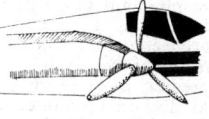

**propend** /prouˈpɛnd/, *v.i.* to incline or tend. [L *prōpendēre*]

**propene** /ˈproupin/, *n.* →**propylene.**

**propenol** /ˈproupənɒl/, *n.* →**allyl alcohol.**

**propensity** /prəˈpɛnsəti/, *n., pl.* **-ties. 1.** natural or habitual inclination or tendency: *a propensity to find fault.* **2.** *Obs.* favourable disposition or partiality. Also, *Rare,* **propension.**

**proper** /ˈprɒpə/, *adj.* **1.** adapted or appropriate to the purpose or circumstances; fit; suitable: *the proper time to plant.* **2.** conforming to established standards of behaviour or manners; correct or decorous. **3.** fitting; right. **4.** strictly belonging or applicable: *the proper place for a stove.* **5.** belonging or pertaining exclusively or distinctly to a person or thing. **6.** strict; accurate. **7.** strictly so-called; in the strict sense of the word (now usu. following the noun): *shellfish do not belong to the fishes proper.* **8.** *Gram.* **a.** (of a name, noun, or adjective) designating a particular person or thing, written in English with an initial capital letter: *John, Hobart, Monday, French.* **b.** having the force or function of a proper name: *a proper adjective.* **9.** normal or regular. **10.** *Her.* (of an object used as a bearing) represented in its natural colour or colours: *an eagle proper.* **11.** *Eccles.* used only on a particular day or festival: *the proper introit.* **12.** *Colloq.* complete or thorough: *a proper thrashing.* **13.** *Archaic.* **a.** excellent; capital; fine. **b.** good-looking or handsome. **14.** *Archaic.* belonging to oneself or itself; own. **15.** *Archaic.* of good character; respectable. *–n.* **16.** *Eccles.* a special office or special parts of an office appointed for a particular day or time. [ME *propre,* from OF, from L *proprius* one's own]

**proper fraction** /– 'frækʃən/, *n.* a fraction having the numerator less than the denominator.

**properly** /'prɒpəli/, *adv.* **1.** in a proper manner. **2.** correctly. **3.** appropriately. **4.** decorously. **5.** accurately. **6.** justifiably. **7.** *Colloq.* completely.

**proper motion** /prɒpə 'mouʃən/, *n.* the component of a star's motion in space which is perpendicular to the line of sight.

**proper name** /– 'neɪm/, *n.* See **name** (def. 9).

**proper noun** /– 'naʊn/, *n.* a noun that is not usu. preceded by an article or other limiting modifier, in meaning applicable only to a single person or thing, or to several persons or things which constitute a unique class only by virtue of having the same name: *Whitlam, Perth* in contrast to *man, city.* See **common noun.**

**propertied** /'prɒpətid/, *adj.* owning property.

**property** /'prɒpəti/, *n., pl.* **-ties. 1.** that which one owns; the possession or possessions of a particular owner. **2.** goods, lands, etc., owned: *a man of property.* **3.** a piece of land owned: *property near Bondi.* **4.** ownership; right of possession, enjoyment, or disposal of anything, esp. of something tangible: *to have property in land.* **5.** Also, **country property.** a farm, station, orchard, etc. **6.** (formerly) supplies obtained by a landholder for his employees. **7.** something at the disposal of a person, a group of persons, or the community or public: *the secret became common property.* **8.** an essential or distinctive attribute or quality of a thing. **9.** *Logic.* **a.** any attribute or characteristic. **b.** (according to Aristotelian usage) one of the five ways in which a predicate can be related to a subject. **10.** *Theat.* Also, **prop.** an item of furniture, ornament, or decoration in a stage setting; any object handled or used by an actor in performance. [ME *proprete,* from *propre* PROPER (defs 5 and 14) + *-te* -TY[2]]

**property man** /'– mæn/, *n.* a man in charge of stage properties in a theatre.

**prop-forward** /prɒp-'fɔwəd/, *n.* →**prop** (def. 9).

**prophase** /'proufeɪz/, *n.* the first stage of mitosis during which the chromosomes progressively contract and become thicker and the nuclear membrane begins to disappear.

**prophecy** /'prɒfəsi/, *n., pl.* **-cies. 1.** foretelling or prediction (originally by divine inspiration) of what is to come. **2.** that which is declared by a prophet; a prediction. **3.** divinely inspired utterance or revelation. **4.** the action, function, or faculty of a prophet. [ME *prophecie,* from OF, from LL *prophētia,* from Gk *prophēteía*]

**prophesy** /'prɒfəsaɪ/, *v.,* **-sied, -sying.** *–v.t.* **1.** to foretell or predict: *to prophesy a storm.* **2.** to indicate beforehand. **3.** to declare or foretell by or as by divine inspiration. **4.** to utter in prophecy or as a prophet. *–v.i.* **5.** to make predictions. **6.** to make inspired declarations of what is to come. **7.** to speak as a mediator between God and man or in God's stead. **8.** to teach religious subjects or material. [v. use of and var. of PROPHECY] – **prophesier,** *n.*

**prophet** /'prɒfət/, *n.* **1.** one who speaks for God or a deity, or by divine inspiration. **2.** one regarded as, or claiming to be, an inspired teacher or leader. **3.** one who foretells or predicts what is to come: *a weather prophet.* **4.** a spokesman or proclaimer of some doctrine, cause, or the like. [ME *prophete,* from L *prophēta,* from Gk *prophḗtēs* spokesman, interpreter, prophet] – **prophetess** /'prɒfətes/, *n. fem.* – **prophethood,** *n.*

**prophetic** /prə'fɛtɪk/, *adj.* **1.** of or pertaining to a prophet: *prophetic inspiration.* **2.** of the nature of or containing prophecy: *prophetic writings.* **3.** having the function or powers of a prophet, as a person. **4.** predictive; presageful; ominous. Also, **prophetical.** – **prophetically,** *adv.*

**prophylactic** /prɒfə'læktɪk/, *adj.* **1.** defending or protecting from disease, as a drug. **2.** preventive; preservative; protective. *–n.* **3.** a prophylactic medicine or measure. **4.** →**contraceptive.** [Gk *prophylaktikós*]

**prophylaxis** /prɒfə'læksəs/, *n.* **1.** the preventing of disease. **2.** the prevention of a specific disease, as by studying the biological behaviour, transmission, etc., of its causative agent and applying a series of measures against it. **3.** prophylactic treatment. [NL, from Gk *pro-* PRO-[2] + *phýlaxis* a watching, guarding]

**propinquity** /prə'pɪŋkwəti/, *n.* **1.** nearness in place; proximity. **2.** nearness of relation; kinship. **3.** affinity of nature; similarity. **4.** nearness in time. [ME *propinquite,* from L *propinquitas*]

**propionate** /'proupiənət, -eɪt/, *n.* an ester or salt of propionic acid. Also, **propanoate.**

**propionic acid** /ˌproupiɒnɪk 'æsəd/, *n.* a liquid organic acid, $C_2H_5COOH$. Also, **propanoic acid.** [PRO-[2] + Gk *píōn* fat + -IC]

**propitiate** /prə'pɪʃieɪt/, *v.t.,* **-ated, -ating.** to make favourably inclined; appease; conciliate. [L *propitiātus,* pp.] – **propitiable,** *adj.* – **propitiative,** *adj.* – **propitiator,** *n.*

**propitiation** /prəpɪʃi'eɪʃən/, *n.* **1.** the act of propitiating; conciliation. **2.** that which propitiates.

**propitiatory** /prə'pɪʃiətri/, *adj.* **1.** serving or intended to propitiate. **2.** making propitiation; conciliatory. *–n.* **3.** →**mercy seat.**

**propitious** /prə'pɪʃəs/, *adj.* **1.** presenting favourable conditions; favourable: *propitious weather.* **2.** indicative of favour: *propitious omens.* **3.** favourably inclined; disposed to bestow favours or forgive. [late ME *propicius,* from L *propitius*] – **propitiously,** *adv.* – **propitiousness,** *n.*

**propjet** /'prɒpdʒɛt/, *n.* →**turboprop.**

**propl,** proportional.

**Prop. Ltd.,** proprietary limited.

**propn,** proportion.

**propolis** /'prɒpələs/, *n.* a reddish resinous cement collected by bees from the buds of trees, used to stop up crevices in the hives, strengthen the cells, etc. [L, from Gk]

**proponent** /prə'pounənt/, *n.* **1.** one who puts forward a proposition or proposal. **2.** *Law.* one who argues in favour of; specifically, one who seeks to obtain probate of a will. **3.** one who supports a cause or doctrine.

**proportion** /prə'pɔʃən/, *n.* **1.** comparative relation between things or magnitudes as to size, quantity, number, etc.; ratio: *a house tall in proportion to its width.* **2.** proper relation between things or parts. **3.** relative size or extent. **4.** (*pl.*) dimensions: *a rock of gigantic proportions.* **5.** a portion or part in its relation to the whole: *a large proportion of the total.* **6.** a portion or part. **7.** symmetry; harmony; balanced relationship. **8.** *Maths.* a relation of four quantities such that the first divided by the second is equal to the third divided by the fourth; the equality of ratios. **9.** *Archaic.* comparison; analogy. *–v.t.* **10.** to adjust in proper proportion or relation, as to size, quantity, etc. **11.** to adjust the proportions of. [ME *proporcioun,* from L *prōportio*] – **proportioner,** *n.*

**proportionable** /prə'pɔʃənəbəl/, *adj.* being in due proportion; proportional. – **proportionably,** *adv.*

**proportional** /prə'pɔʃənəl/, *adj.* **1.** having due proportion; corresponding. **2.** being in or characterised by proportion. **3.** of or pertaining to proportion; relative. **4.** *Maths.* having the same or a constant ratio. – **proportionality** /prəpɔʃə'næləti/, *n.* – **proportionally,** *adv.*

**proportional representation** /– reprəzɛn'teɪʃən/, *n.* **1.** a system of electing representatives to a legislative assembly in which there is a number of members representing any one electorate. The number of successful candidates from each party is directly proportional to the percentage of the total vote won by the party. **2.** a similar arrangement for the representation of factions within a group, as a political party.

**proportionate** /prə'pɔʃənət/, *adj.;* /prə'pɔʃəneɪt/, *v.,* **-nated, -nating.** *–adj.* **1.** proportioned; being in due proportion; proportional. *–v.t.* **2.** to make proportionate. – **proportionately,** *adv.* – **proportionateness,** *n.*

**proportionment** /prə'pɔʃənmənt/, *n.* **1.** the act of proportioning. **2.** the state of being proportioned.

**proposal** /prə'pouzəl/, *n.* **1.** the act of proposing for acceptance, adoption, or performance. **2.** a plan or scheme proposed. **3.** an offer, esp. of marriage.

**propose** /prə'pouz/, *v.,* **-posed, -posing.** *–v.t.* **1.** to put forward (a matter, subject, case, etc.) for consideration, acceptance, or action: *to propose a new method; to propose a* *toast.* **2.** to put forward or suggest as something to be done: *he proposed that a messenger be sent.* **3.** to present (a person) for some position, office, membership, etc. **4.** to put before oneself as something to be done; to design; to intend. **5.** to present to the mind or attention; state. **6.** to propound (a question, riddle, etc.). *–v.i.* **7.** to make a proposal, esp. of marriage. **8.** to form or entertain a purpose or design. [ME, from F *proposer,* from *pro-* PRO-[1] + *poser* put (see POSE[1]), but associated with derivatives of L *prōpōnere* set forth] – **proposer,** *n.*

**proposition** /prɒpəˈzɪʃən/, *n.* **1.** the act of proposing, or a proposal of, something to be considered, accepted, adopted, or done. **2.** a plan or scheme proposed. **3.** an offer of terms for a transaction, as in business. **4.** a thing, matter, or person considered as something to be dealt with or encountered. **5.** anything stated or affirmed for discussion or illustration. **6.** *Logic.* a statement in which something (a predicate) is affirmed or denied of a subject, or in which membership of a class is affirmed or denied of something, or in which a relation is affirmed or denied to hold between two or more things. **7.** *Maths.* a formal statement of a result to be proved; theorem. **8.** a proposal for sexual intercourse. **9.** *Archaic.* a statement of the subject of a discourse or argument; the introductory part of a speech, literary work, etc. *–v.t.* **10.** to propose a plan, deal, etc., to. **11.** to propose sexual intercourse to. [ME *proposicioun,* from L *prōpositio* a setting forth] – **propositional,** *adj.* – **propositionally,** *adv.*

**propositional calculus** /prɒpəˌzɪʃənəl ˈkælkjələs/, *n.* that part of modern logic which systematises the relations between unanalysed propositions.

**propound** /prəˈpaʊnd/, *v.t.* **1.** to put forward for consideration, acceptance, or adoption. **2.** to demand probate of (a will) in solemn form. [later var. of ME *propone,* from L *prōpōnere* set forth. Cf. COMPOUND[1], EXPOUND] – **propounder,** *n.*

**propr.,** **1.** proprietory. **2.** proprietor.

**proprietary** /prəˈpraɪətri/, *adj., n., pl.* **-taries.** *–adj.* **1.** belonging to a proprietor or proprietors. **2.** being a proprietor or proprietors; holding property: *the proprietary class.* **3.** pertaining to property or ownership: *proprietary rights.* **4.** belonging or controlled as property. **5.** manufactured and sold only by the owner of the patent, formula, brand name, or trademark associated with the product: *proprietary medicine.* *–n.* **6.** an owner or proprietor. **7.** a body of proprietors. **8.** ownership. See **proprietary limited company.** **9.** something owned. **10.** a proprietary medicine. [ME, from LL *proprietārius,* from L *proprietas* ownership]

**proprietary limited company,** *n.* a company with a limit of fifty shareholders, which cannot issue shares for public conscription and which is not listed on the stock exchange; shareholders enjoy limited liability, on liquidation. Also, **proprietary company.**

**proprietor** /prəˈpraɪətə/, *n.* **1.** the owner of a business establishment, a hotel, newspaper, etc. **2.** one who has the exclusive right or title to something; an owner, as of property. **3.** →**proprietary** (def. 7). [PROPRIET(Y) (in obs. sense of property) + -OR[2]] – **proprietorship,** *n.*

**proprietress** /prəˈpraɪətrəs, -trɛs/, *n.* a female proprietor.

**propriety** /prəˈpraɪəti/, *n., pl.* **-ties.** **1.** conformity to established standards of behaviour or manners. **2.** appropriateness to the purpose or circumstances; suitability. **3.** rightness or justness. **4. the proprieties,** the conventional standards or requirements of proper behaviour. [ME *propriete,* from L *proprietas* peculiarity, ownership]

**proprioceptive** /ˌproʊpriəˈsɛptɪv/, *adj.* pertaining to sensory excitations originating in muscles, tendons and joints. [*proprio-* (combining form of L *proprius* one's own) + (RE)CEPTIVE]

**proprioceptor** /ˌproʊpriəˈsɛptə/, *n.* the sensory end organ in muscles, tendons and joints responding to certain activities of these parts. [PROPRIOCEPT(IVE) + -OR[2]]

**prop root** /ˈprɒp rut/, *n.* a root that supports the plant, as the aerial roots of the pandanus tree or of maize.

**proptosis** /prɒpˈtoʊsəs/, *n.* forward displacement of the eyeball. [NL, from Gk: a fall forward]

**propulsion** /prəˈpʌlʃən/, *n.* **1.** the act of propelling or driving forward or onward. **2.** the state of being propelled. **3.** propulsive force; impulse given. [L *prōpulsus,* pp., driven forward + -ION] – **propulsive,** *adj.*

**propulsion reactor** /ˈ– riæktə/, *n.* a nuclear reactor designed to provide energy for propulsion, as in a ship or submarine.

**propyl** /ˈproʊpəl/, *n.* the univalent radical, $C_3H_7$, derived from propane. [PROP(IONIC ACID) + -YL]

**propylaeum** /prɒpəˈliəm/, *n., pl.* **-laea** /-ˈliə/. (*usu. pl.*) a vestibule or entrance to a temple area or other enclosure, esp. when elaborate or of architectural importance. Also, **propylon.** [L, from Gk *propýlaion* (neut.) before the gate]

**propyl alcohol** /proʊpəl ˈælkəhɒl/, *n.* a colourless liquid alcohol, $C_3H_7OH$, used in organic synthesis and as a solvent. Also, **propanol.**

**propylene** /ˈproʊpəlin/, *n.* a colourless, unsaturated, gaseous hydrocarbon gas, $C_3H_6$. Also, **propene.**

**propylite** /ˈprɒpəlaɪt/, *n.* an altered form of andesite or some allied rock, usu. containing secondary minerals such as chlorite and calcite. [Gk *própylon* gateway + -ITE[1]; so named because supposed to open the tertiary volcanic epoch]

**propylon** /ˈprɒpəlɒn/, *n., pl.* **-la** /-lə/. →**propylaeum.**

**pro rata** /proʊ ˈratə/, *adv.;* /ˈproʊ ratə/, *adj.* *–adv.* **1.** in proportion; according to a certain rate. *–adj.* **2.** proportionate. [ML: according to rate]

**prorogation** /proʊrəˈgeɪʃən/, *n.* **1.** the act of proroguing. **2.** the time during which a legislative body is prorogued.

**prorogue** /prəˈroʊg/, *v.t.,* **-rogued, -roguing.** **1.** to discontinue meetings of (parliament or similar legislative body) until the next session. **2.** *Rare.* to defer; postpone. [late ME *proroge,* from F *proroguer,* from L *prōrogāre* prolong, protract, defer]

**pros.,** prosody.

**prosaic** /proʊˈzeɪɪk, prə-/, *adj.* **1.** commonplace or dull; matter-of-fact or unimaginative: *a prosaic mind.* **2.** having the character or spirit of prose as opposed to poetry, as verse or writing. Also, **prosaical.** [ML *prōsaicus,* from L *prōsa* PROSE] – **prosaically,** *adv.* – **prosaicness,** *n.*

**prosaism** /ˈproʊzeɪˌɪzəm/, *n.* **1.** prosaic character. **2.** a prosaic expression. Also, **prosaicism** /proʊˈzeɪəsɪzəm/, *n.*

**proscenium** /prəˈsiniəm/, *n., pl.* **-nia** /-niə/. **1.** (in the modern theatre) the decorative arch or opening between the stage and the auditorium. **2.** (in the ancient theatre) the stage. Also, **proscenium arch.** [L, from Gk *proskḗnion*]

**prosciutto** /prəˈʃutoʊ/, *n.* a dry-cured, spiced ham, originally made in Italy. [It.: ham]

**proscribe** /proʊˈskraɪb/, *v.t.,* **-scribed, -scribing.** **1.** to denounce or condemn (a thing) as dangerous; to prohibit. **2.** to put outside the protection of the law; to outlaw. **3.** to banish or exile. **4.** to announce the name of (a person) as condemned to death and subject to confiscation of property. [L *prōscrībere* write before, publish, proscribe] – **proscriber,** *n.*

**proscription** /proʊˈskrɪpʃən/, *n.* **1.** the act of proscribing. **2.** the state of being proscribed. **3.** outlawry; interdiction. – **proscriptive,** *adj.* – **proscriptively,** *adv.*

**prose** /proʊz/, *n., adj., v.,* **prosed, prosing.** *–n.* **1.** the ordinary form of spoken or written language, without metrical structure (as distinguished from poetry or verse). **2.** matter-of-fact, commonplace, or dull expression, quality, discourse, etc. **3.** *Liturgy.* a hymn in rhythmic prose or verse sung or said after the gradual and before the gospel; a sequence. *–adj.* **4.** consisting of or pertaining to prose. **5.** prosaic. *–v.t.* **6.** to turn into prose. *–v.i.* **7.** to write or talk in a dull or prosy manner. [ME, from F, from L *prōsa* (*ōrātio*), lit., straightforward (speech), fem. of *pro(r)sus,* for *prōversus,* pp., turned forward]

**prosect** /proʊˈsɛkt/, *v.t.* to dissect (a cadaver) for anatomical demonstration.

**prosector** /proʊˈsɛktə/, *n.* one who dissects cadavers for the illustration of anatomical lectures or the like. [LL: anatomist, from L *prōsectus,* pp., cut off]

**prosecute** /ˈprɒsəkjut/, *v.,* **-cuted, -cuting.** *–v.t.* **1.** *Law.* **a.** to institute legal proceedings against (a person, etc.). **b.** to seek to enforce or obtain by legal process. **c.** to conduct criminal proceedings in court against. **2.** to follow up or go on with something undertaken or begun: *to prosecute an inquiry.* **3.** to carry on or practice. *–v.i.* **4.** *Law.* **a.** to institute and carry on a legal prosecution. **b.** to act as prosecutor. [ME, from L *prōsecūtus,* pp., pursued, continued]

**prosecution** /prɒsəˈkjuʃən/, *n.* **1.** *Law.* **a.** the institution and carrying on of legal proceedings against a person. **b.** the body of persons by whom such proceedings are instituted and carried on. **2.** the following up of any matter in hand; pursuit.

**prosecutor** /ˈprɒsəkjutə/, *n.* **1.** *Law.* **a.** one who institutes and carries on legal proceedings in a court of justice, esp. in a criminal court. **b.** an officer charged with the conduct of criminal prosecution in the interest of the public: *public prosecutor.* **2.** one who prosecutes.

**proselyte** /ˈprɒsəlaɪt/, *n., v.,* **-lyted, -lyting.** *–n.* **1.** one who has come over or changed from one opinion, religious belief, sect, or the like to another; a convert. *–v.i., v.t.* **2.** →**proselytise.** [ME, from LL *prosēlytus,* from Gk *prosḗlytos* newcomer, proselyte]

**proselytise** /ˈprɒsələtaɪz/, *v.,* **-tised, -tising.** *–v.t.* **1.** to make a proselyte of; convert. *–v.i.* **2.** to make proselytes. Also, **proselytize.**

**proselytism** /ˈprɒsələtɪzəm/, *n.* **1.** the state or condition of a proselyte. **2.** the practice of making proselytes.

**prosencephalon** /ˌprɒsɛnˈsɛfəlɒn/, *n., pl.* **-la** /-lə/. **1.** the anterior segment of the brain, consisting of the cerebral hemispheres (or their equivalent) and certain adjacent parts. **2.** the forebrain. [NL, from Gk *prós* before + *enképhalon* brain] – **prosencephalic** /ˌprɒsɛnsəˈfælɪk/, *adj.*

**prosenchyma** /prɒsˈɛŋkəmə/, *n.* the tissue characteristic of the woody and bast portions of plants, consisting typically of long, narrow cells with pointed ends. [NL, from Gk *prós* towards, to + *énchyma* infusion; modelled on PARENCHYMA] – **prosenchymatous** /prɒsɛŋˈkɪmətəs/, *adj.*

**prose poem** /ˈproʊz poʊəm/, *n.* a composition written as prose but having many of the characteristics of poetry.

**prosodic** /prəˈsɒdɪk, -ˈzɒd-/, *adj.* **1.** of prosody, conforming to the rules of metre. **2.** *Phonet.* of or pertaining to features of speech, like rhythm, intonation, etc., which are tied to units made up of numbers of sounds, as the syllable, the phrase, etc. – **prosodical,** *adj.* – **prosodically,** *adv.*

**prosodist** /ˈprɒsədəst, ˈprɒz-/, *n.* one versed in prosody.

**prosody** /ˈprɒsədi, ˈprɒz-/, *n.* **1.** the science or study of poetic metres and versification. **2.** a particular or distinctive system of metrics and versification: *Milton's prosody.* [late ME, from L *prosōdia,* from Gk *prosōidía* tone or accent, modulation of voice, song sung to music]

**prosopopoeia** /prɒsəpəˈpiə/, *n. Rhet.* **1.** personification, as of inanimate things. **2.** representation of an imaginary or absent person as speaking or acting. Also, **prosopopeia.** [L *prosōpopoeia,* from Gk *prosōpopoiía*]

**prospect** /ˈprɒspɛkt/, *n.* **1.** (*usu. pl.*) an apparent probability of advancement, success, profit, etc. **2.** a mental looking forward, or contemplation of something future or expected. **3.** the outlook for the future: *good business prospects.* **4.** something in view as a source of profit. **5.** a prospective customer, as in business. **6.** a view or scene presented to the eye, esp. of scenery. **7.** outlook or view over a region or in a particular direction. **8.** a mental view or survey, as of a subject or situation. **9.** *Mining.* **a.** an apparent indication of metal, etc. **b.** a spot giving such indications. **c.** excavation or workings in search of ore. **10.** *Sport.* a new recruit to a club; a young player of whom much is expected. **11.** *Archaic.* sight; range of vision. **12. in prospect,** in view; under consideration. *–v.t.* **13.** to search or explore (a region), as for gold. **14.** to work (a mine or claim) experimentally in order to test its value. *–v.i.* **15.** to search or explore a region for gold or the like. [ME, from L *prōspectus* outlook, view]

prospecting (def. 9c): miner panning for gold

**prospective** /prəˈspɛktɪv/, *adj.* **1.** of or in the future. **2.** potential; likely; expected. – **prospectively,** *adv.*

**prospector** /ˈprɒspɛktə/, *n.* a person who prospects for gold and other minerals.

**prospectus** /prəˈspɛktəs/, *n.* **1.** a circular or advertisement inviting applications from the public to subscribe for securities of a corporation or proposed corporation. **2.** a statement which describes or advertises a forthcoming literary work, a new enterprise, or the like. **3.** a pamphlet issued by a school or other institution giving details about itself. [L: outlook, view]

**prosper** /ˈprɒspə/, *v.i.* **1.** to be prosperous or successful; to thrive. *–v.t.* **2.** to make prosperous or successful. [late ME, from L *prosperāre* make prosperous]

**prosperity** /prɒsˈpɛrəti/, *n., pl.* **-ties.** **1.** prosperous, flourishing, or thriving condition; good fortune; success.

**prosperous** /ˈprɒspərəs, -prəs/, *adj.* **1.** having or characterised by continued good fortune; flourishing; successful: *a prosperous business.* **2.** well-to-do or well-off: *a prosperous family.* **3.** favourable or propitious. [late ME, from L *prosperus*] – **prosperously,** *adv.* – **prosperousness,** *n.*

**prossie** /ˈprɒsi/, *n. Colloq.* a prostitute.

**prostaglandin** /prɒstəˈglændən/, *n.* any of a large group of modified fatty acids, widely distributed in animal tissue and playing a part in the control of lipid metabolism and the induction of labour; one of the group, prostaglandin $E_2$ is an important abortifacient.

**prostate** /ˈprɒsteɪt/, *n.* **1.** the prostate gland. *–adj.* **2.** designating or pertaining to the prostate gland. [ML *prostata,* from Gk *prostátēs* one standing before] – **prostatic** /prɒsˈtætɪk/, *adj.*

**prostatectomy** /prɒstəˈtɛktəmi/, *n.* removal of the prostate gland.

**prostate gland** /ˈprɒsteɪt glænd/, *n.* the composite gland which surrounds the urethra of males at the base of the bladder.

**prostatitis** /prɒstəˈtaɪtəs/, *n.* inflammation of the prostate gland.

**prosthesis** /prɒsˈθisəs, prəs-/, *n., pl.* **-ses** /-siz/. the addition of an artificial part to supply a defect of the body. [LL, from Gk: a putting to, addition] – **prosthetic,** *adj.*

**prosthetic group** /prɒsˌθɛtɪk ˈgrup/, *n.* a non-protein molecule which is combined with a protein, as the haem group in haemoglobin.

**prosthion** /ˈprɒsθiɒn/, *n.* the most forward projecting point of the anterior surface of the upper jaw (maxilla), in the midsagittal plane. [Gk *prosthéōn* running forward]

**prosthodontics** /prɒsθəˈdɒntɪks/, *n.* the branch of dentistry concerned with the reconstruction and replacement of missing teeth. Also, **prosthodontia.** [PROSTH(ESIS) + -ODONT + -ICS] – **prosthodontist,** *n.*

**prostitute** /ˈprɒstətjut/, *n., v.,* **-tuted, -tuting.** *–n.* **1.** a person, esp. a woman, who engages in sexual intercourse for money as a livelihood. **2.** one who debases himself or allows his talents to be used in an unworthy way, usu. for financial gain. *–v.t.* **3.** to submit to sexual intercourse for money as a livelihood. **4.** to put to any base or unworthy use. [L *prōstitūtus,* pp., placed before, exposed publicly, prostituted] – **prostitutor,** *n.*

**prostitution** /prɒstəˈtjuʃən/, *n.* **1.** the act or practice of engaging in sexual intercourse for money. **2.** any base or unworthy use of talent, ability, etc.

**prostrate** /prɒsˈtreɪt/, *v.,* **-trated, -trating;** /ˈprɒstreɪt/, *adj.* *–v.t.* **1.** to cast (oneself) down in humility, submission, or adoration. **2.** to lay flat, as on the ground. **3.** to throw down level with the ground. **4.** to overthrow, overcome, or reduce to helplessness. **5.** to reduce to physical weakness or exhaustion. *–adj.* **6.** lying flat or at full length, as on the ground. **7.** lying with the face to the ground, as in token of submission or humility. **8.** overthrown, overcome, or helpless: *a prostrate country.* **9.** in a state of physical weakness or exhaustion. **10.** submissive. **11.** disconsolate; depressed; dejected. **12.** *Bot.* (of a plant or stem) lying flat on the ground. [ME *prostrat,* from L *prōstrātus,* pp., spread out]

**prostration** /prɒsˈtreɪʃən/, *n.* **1.** the act of prostrating. **2.** the state of being prostrated. **3.** extreme mental depression or dejection. **4.** extreme physical weakness or exhaustion: *nervous prostration.*

**prostyle** /ˈproʊstaɪl/, *adj.* **1.** having a portico in front, standing out from the walls of the building, as a temple. *–n.* **2.** a prostyle building. [L, from Gk *próstylos,* adj., equivalent to *pro-* PRO-[2] + *stŷlos* pillar]

**prosy** /ˈproʊzi/, *adj.,* **-sier, -siest.** **1.** of the nature of or resembling prose. **2.** prosaic; commonplace, dull, or wearisome. – **prosily,** *adv.* – **prosiness,** *n.*

**prot-,** variant of **proto-**, before some vowels, as in *protamine.*

**Prot.,** Protestant.

**protactinium** /proʊtæk'tɪniəm/, *n.* a radioactive, metallic element. *Symbol:* Pa; *at. no.:* 91. Formerly, **protoactinium.** [PROT(O)- + ACTINIUM]

**protagonist** /prə'tægənəst/, *n.* **1.** the leading character in a play, novel, etc. **2.** any leading character or personage in a movement, cause, etc. **3.** a champion, or supporter of a movement, cause, idea, etc.; advocate; spokesman. [Gk *prōtagōnistḗs*]

**protamine** /'proʊtəmin/, *n.* any of a group of basic, simple proteins, usu. associated with nucleic acids. [PROT- + AMINE]

**protandry** /proʊ'tændri/, *n.* (in a hermaphrodite animal or plant) a condition in which the development and maturation of the male organs takes place before that of the female organs. – **protandrous,** *adj.* – **protandrously,** *adv.*

**protanopia** /proʊtə'noʊpiə/, *n.* a form of dichromatic vision in which colours can be matched by a mixture of yellow and blue stimuli, but in which red and orange vision is much less than normal; red-blindness.

**protasis** /'prɒtəsəs/, *n.* **1.** the clause expressing the condition in a conditional sentence, in English usu. beginning with *if.* Cf. **apodosis.** **2.** (in ancient drama) the first part of the play, in which the characters are introduced and the subject is proposed. [L, from Gk]

**protea** /'proʊtiə/, *n.* any of the shrubs or trees of the southern African genus *Protea,* which exhibits a wide variety of forms, as the giant protea, *Protea cynaroides,* which has large showy flowers. [NL, from Gk; named after *Proteus,* a sea-god of classical mythology, who was able to assume different shapes at will]

**proteaceous** /proʊti'eɪʃəs/, *adj.* **1.** belonging to the plant family Proteaceae which includes the waratah and banksia. **2.** resembling the genus *Protea.*

**protean** /prə'tiən, 'proʊtiən/, *adj.* readily assuming different forms or characters; exceedingly variable. [from *Proteus* (see PROTEA) + -AN]

**protease** /'proʊtieɪz/, *n.* any enzyme that acts upon proteins. [PROTE(IN) + -ASE]

**protect** /prə'tɛkt/, *v.t.* **1.** to defend or guard from attack, invasion, annoyance, insult, etc.; cover or shield from injury or danger. **2.** *Econ.* to guard (a country's industry) from foreign competition by imposing import duties. *–v.i.* **3.** to provide, or be capable of providing protection. [L *prōtectus,* pp., covered over]

**protection** /prə'tɛkʃən/, *n.* **1.** the act of protecting. **2.** the state of being protected. **3.** preservation from injury or harm. **4.** something that protects. **5.** *Insurance.* coverage. **6.** immunity from prosecution or harassment obtained by a person involved in illegal activities by means of bribes to appropriate officials. **7.** *Econ.* the system or theory of fostering or developing home industries by protecting them from foreign competition through duties imposed on imports from foreign countries. **8.** a treaty, safe-conduct, passport, or other writing which secures from molestation the person, persons, or property specified in it. **9.** patronage. *–adj.* **10.** of or pertaining to money, organisations, etc., involved in protection (def. 6): *protection racket; protection money.*

**protectionism** /prə'tɛkʃənɪzəm/, *n.* the economic system or theory of protection. – **protectionist,** *n.*

**protective** /prə'tɛktɪv/, *adj.* **1.** having the quality of protecting. **2.** tending to or designed to protect. **3.** of, pertaining to, or designed for economic protection. – **protectively,** *adv.*

**protective colouring** /– 'kʌlərɪŋ/, *n.* colouring assumed by various animals in their natural surroundings, rendering them inconspicuous to their enemies.

**protective custody** /– 'kʌstədi/, *n.* the state of being under police guard as protection against threats, violence, etc.

**protective tariff** /– 'tærəf/, *n.* a tariff for the protection of domestic production, rather than for revenue.

**protective trust** /– 'trʌst/, *n.* a trust for life or any less period of the beneficiary, which is to be determined in certain events such as bankruptcy of the beneficiary, whereupon the trust income is to be applied for the maintenance of the beneficiary and his family at the absolute discretion of the trustee.

**protector** /prə'tɛktə/, *n.* **1.** one who or that which protects; a defender; a guardian. **2.** *Hist.* one in charge of a kingdom during the sovereign's minority, incapacity, or absence. – **protectoral,** *adj.* – **protectorship,** *n.*

**protectorate** /prə'tɛktərət, -trət/, *n.* **1.** the relation of a strong state towards a weaker state or territory which it protects and partly controls. **2.** a state or territory so protected. **3.** the office or position, or the term of office, of a protector. **4.** the government of a protector.

**protectress** /prə'tɛktrəs/, *n.* a female who gives protection.

**protégé** /'proʊtəʒeɪ/, *n.* one who is under the protection or friendly patronage of another. [F, pp. of *protéger* protect, from L *prōtegere*]

**protein** /'proʊtin/, *n.* **1.** *Biochem.* any of the polymers formed from amino acids, which are found in all cells and which include enzymes, plasma proteins, and structural proteins such as collagen. **2.** (formerly) a substance thought to be the essential nitrogenous component of all organic bodies. Also, **proteid** /'proʊtid/. [G, from Gk *prōteîos* primary + *-in* -IN[2]]

**proteinase** /'proʊtəneɪz, -eɪs/, *n.* any of several enzymes which are capable of hydrolysing proteins.

**proteinuria** /proʊtə'njuriə/, *n.* a condition marked by the presence of protein in the urine.

**pro tem** /proʊ 'tɛm/, *adv., adj.* →**pro tempore.**

**pro tempore** /proʊ 'tɛmpəreɪ/, *adv.* **1.** temporarily; for the time being. *adj.* **2.** temporary. [L]

**proteolysis** /proʊti'ɒləsəs/, *n.* the hydrolysis or breaking down of proteins into amino acids and peptides, as in digestion. [*proteo-* (combining form representing PROTEIN) + -LYSIS] – **proteolytic** /ˌproʊtiə'lɪtɪk/, *adj.*

**proteose** /'proʊtioʊz, -oʊs/, *n.* any of a class of soluble compounds derived from proteins by the action of gastric juice, etc. [PROTE(IN) + -OSE[2]]

**Proterozoic** /ˌproʊtəroʊ'zoʊɪk, -rə-/, *adj.* **1.** of or pertaining to a geological era or rocks preceding the Palaeozoic; the late Pre-Cambrian. *–n.* **2.** the era or rocks intervening between Archaeozoic and Palaeozoic, presumed to be characterised by relative prominence of sedimentary rocks in a few of which fossils of early primitive organisms occur. Also, **Proterzoic.** [Gk *prótero(s)* being before + *zōḗ* life + -IC]

**protest** /'proʊtɛst/, *n.*; /prə'tɛst, proʊ-/, *v.* *–n.* **1.** a formal expression or declaration of objection or disapproval, often in opposition to something which one is powerless to prevent or avoid: *to submit under protest.* **2.** *Comm.* **a.** a formal notarial certificate attesting the fact that a cheque, note, or bill of exchange has been presented for acceptance or payment and that it has been refused. **b.** the action taken to fix the liability for a dishonoured bill of exchange or note. **3.** *Law.* **a.** (upon one's payment of a sum of money) a formal statement disputing the legality of the demand. **b.** a written and attested declaration made by the master of a ship stating the circumstances in which some injury has happened to the ship or cargo, or other circumstances involving the liability of the officers, crew, etc. **4.** *Sport.* a formal expression of objection or complaint placed with an official. **5.** *Colloq.* a demonstration or meeting of people protesting against something. [ME, from ML *prōtestum* declaration] *–v.i.* **6.** to give formal expression to objection or disapproval; remonstrate. **7.** to make solemn declaration. *–v.t.* **8.** to make a protest or remonstrance against. **9.** to say in protest or remonstrance. **10.** to declare solemnly or formally; affirm; assert. **11.** to make a formal declaration of the non-acceptance or non-payment of (a bill of exchange or note). [late ME, from F *protester,* from L *prōtestārī* declare publicly] – **protester,** *n.* – **protestingly,** *adv.*

**Protestant** /'prɒtəstənt/, *n.* **1.** an adherent of any of those Christian bodies which separated from the Church of Rome at the Reformation, or of any group descended from them. **2.** (*l.c.*) one who protests. *–adj.* **3.** belonging or pertaining to Protestants or their religion. **4.** (*l.c.*) protesting. [sing. of *protestants* for L *prōtestantes,* pl. ppr. of *prōtestārī* protest; from the German princes who protested against the Diet of Speyer in 1529, which had denounced the Reformation]

**Protestant Episcopal Church,** *n.* the church in the U.S. which inherited the doctrine, discipline, and worship of the Church of England and which became an independent body within the Anglican communion.

**Protestantism** /ˈprɒtəstəntɪzəm/, *n.* **1.** the religion of Protestants. **2.** the Protestant churches, collectively. **3.** adherence to Protestant principles.

**protestation** /prɒtəsˈteɪʃən, proʊ-/, *n.* **1.** the act of protesting or affirming. **2.** a solemn declaration or affirmation. **3.** the formal expression of objection or disapproval; protest.

**prothalamion** /proʊθəˈleɪmiən/, *n., pl.* **-mia** /-miə/. a song or poem written to celebrate a marriage. Also, **prothalamium** /proʊθəˈleɪmiəm/. [PRO-² + Gk *thálamos* bridal chamber + -ION; coined by Spenser, after Gk *epithalámion* EPITHALAMIUM]

**prothallium** /proʊˈθæliəm/, *n., pl.* **-thallia** /-ˈθæliə/. **1.** the gametophyte of ferns, etc. **2.** the analogous rudimentary gametophyte of seed-bearing plants. [NL, from Gk *pro-* PRO-² + *thallíon,* diminutive of *thallós* young shoot] – **prothallial,** *adj.*

**prothesis** /ˈprɒθəsəs/, *n.* **1.** the addition of a phoneme or syllable at the beginning of a word, as in Spanish *escala* (ladder) from Latin *scala.* **2.** *Gk Orth. Ch.* **a.** the preparation and preliminary oblation of the eucharistic elements. **b.** the table on which this is done. **c.** the part of the bema or sanctuary where this table stands. [LL, from Gk: a putting before] – **prothetic** /prɒˈθɛtɪk/, *adj.* – **prothetically** /prɒˈθɛtɪkli/, *adv.*

**prothonotary** /proʊθəˈnoʊtəri, proʊˈθɒnətri/, *n., pl.* **-ries. 1.** one of the principal officials of a Supreme Court, who has a responsibility to issue writs, and also has some judicial powers. **2.** Also, **prothonotary apostolic(al).** *Rom. Cath. Ch.* a member of the college of twelve prelates which records papal acts, canonisations, beatifications, etc. **3.** the principal ecclesiastical secretary of a patriarch of the Eastern Church. Also, **protonotary.** [ML *prōthonotārius,* LL *prōtonotārius,* from Gk *prōtonotários*] – **prothonotarial** /ˌprɒθənoʊˈtɛəriəl/, *adj.*

**prothorax** /proʊˈθɔræks/, *n., pl.* **-thoraxes, -thoraces** /-ˈθɔrəsiz/. the anterior division of an insect's thorax, bearing the first pair of legs. – **prothoracic** /proʊθɔˈræsɪk/, *adj.*

**prothrombin** /proʊˈθrɒmbən/, *n.* one of the clotting factors in blood, the forerunner of thrombin.

**protist** /ˈproʊtəst/, *n.* any of the single-celled organisms, including all the unicellular animals and plants. [NL *protista,* pl., from Gk *prṓtistos* the very first, superl. of *prôtos* first] – **protistan** /proʊˈtɪstən/, *adj., n.* – **protistic** /proʊˈtɪstɪk/, *adj.*

**protium** /ˈproʊtiəm/, *n.* the common isotope of hydrogen, of atomic weight 1.008. *Symbol:* $H^1$

**proto-,** a word element meaning: **1.** first, earliest form of, as *prototype.* **2.** *Chem.* **a.** the first of a series of compounds. **b.** that one of a series of compounds which contains the minimum amount of an element. **3.** (*usu. cap.*) *Linguistics.* the reconstructed earliest form of a language: *Proto-Australian.* [Gk, combining form of *prôtos* first]

**protoactinium** /ˌproʊtoʊækˈtɪniəm/, *n. Obs.* →**protactinium.**

**protochordate** /proʊtoʊˈkɔdeɪt/, *n.* any of the non-vertebrate chordates, as the tunicates, cephalochordates, and hemichordates.

**protocol** /ˈproʊtəkɒl/, *n.* **1.** the customs and regulations dealing with the ceremonies and etiquette of the diplomatic corps and others at a court or capital. **2.** an original draft, minute, or record from which a document, esp. a treaty, is prepared. **3.** a supplementary international agreement. **4.** an agreement between states. **5.** an annex to a treaty giving data relating to it. *–v.i.* **6.** to issue a protocol. *–v.t.* **7.** to record in a protocol. [earlier *protocoll,* from ML *prōtocollum,* from LGk *prōtókollon,* orig., a first leaf glued to the front of a manuscript containing notes as to contents]

**protogyny** /proʊˈtɒdʒəni/, *n.* (in a hermaphrodite animal or plant) a condition in which the development and maturation of the female organs takes place before that of the male organs. – **protogynous** /proʊˈtɒdʒənəs/, *adj.*

**protohistory** /ˈproʊtoʊˌhɪstri/, *n.* the study of a culture just prior to its earliest recorded history. [PROTO- + HISTORY]

**protolanguage** /ˈproʊtoʊˌlæŋgwɪdʒ/, *n.* a recorded or reconstructed language which is believed to be the ancestor of another language or group of languages.

**protolithic** /proʊtoʊˈlɪθɪk/, *adj.* denoting or pertaining to stone implements characteristic of the early Stone Age, selected according to fitness of form, and shaped by wear without definite shaping on the part of the user.

**protomartyr** /proʊtoʊˈmatə/, *n.* the first martyr in any cause, esp. St Stephen, the first Christian martyr.

**protomorphic** /proʊtoʊˈmɔfɪk/, *adj.* (of animals and plants) having a primitive character or structure. – **protomorph,** *n.*

**proton** /ˈproʊtɒn/, *n.* an elementary particle present in every atomic nucleus, the number of protons being different for each element, which has an electric charge equal in magnitude to that of the electron but of opposite sign and a mass of $1.7 \times 10^{-27}$ kg; hydrogen ion. [Gk, neut. of *prôtos* first]

**protonema** /proʊtəˈnimə/, *n., pl.* **-mata** /-mətə/. a primary, usu. filamentous structure produced by the germination of the spore in mosses and certain related plants, and upon which the leafy plant which bears the sexual organs arises as a lateral or terminal shoot. [NL, from Gk *prōto-* PROTO- + *nêma* thread]

**protonotary** /proʊtəˈnoʊtəri, proʊˈtɒnətri/, *n., pl.* **-teries.** →**prothonotary.**

**protopathic** /proʊtəˈpæθɪk/, *adj. Physiol.* **1.** denoting general non-discriminating sensory reception (opposed to *epicritic*). **2.** primitive; primary.

**protoplasm** /ˈproʊtəplæzəm/, *n.* **1.** a complex substance (typically colourless and semifluid) regarded as the physical basis of life, having the power of spontaneous motion, reproduction, etc.; the living matter of all vegetable and animal cells and tissues. **2.** (formerly) cytoplasm. [G *protoplasma,* from Gk *prōto-* PROTO- + *plásma* something formed] – **protoplasmic** /proʊtəˈplæzmɪk/, *adj.*

**protoplast** /ˈproʊtəplæst/, *n.* **1.** *Biol.* **a.** the protoplasm within a cell considered as a fundamental entity. **b.** the primordial living unit or cell. **2.** one who or that which is first formed; the original. **3.** the hypothetical first individual or one of the supposed first pair of a species or the like. [LL *prōtoplastus* the first man, from Gk *prōtóplastos* formed first] – **protoplastic** /proʊtəˈplæstɪk/, *adj.*

**protostar** /ˈproʊtoʊstə/, *n.* a developing star consisting of condensing interstellar gas and dust.

**protostele** /ˈproʊtəstili, -stil/, *n.* the solid stele of most roots, having a central core of xylem enclosed by phloem. – **protostelic** /proʊtəˈstilɪk/, *adj.*

**prototrophic** /proʊtəˈtrɒfɪk/, *adj.* (of certain micro-organisms) having no specific nutritional requirements for growth. [PROTO- + Gk *trophḗ* nourishment + -IC]

**prototype** /ˈproʊtətaɪp/, *n.* **1.** the original or model after which anything is formed. **2.** *Biol.* an archetype; a primitive form regarded as the basis of a group. [NL *prōtotypon,* from Gk (neut.): original, primitive] – **prototypal** /ˈproʊtətaɪpəl/, **prototypic** /proʊtəˈtɪpɪk/, *adj.*

**protoxide** /proʊˈtɒksaɪd/, *n.* the oxide of an element which contains the least number of oxygen atoms, when that element forms more than one oxide.

**protoxylem** /proʊtəˈzaɪləm/, *n.* the part of the primary xylem that develops first, consisting of narrow, thin-walled cells. [PROTO- + XYLEM]

**protozoan** /proʊtəˈzoʊən/, *adj.* **1.** Also, **protozoic.** belonging to or pertaining to the phylum Protozoa, comprising animals consisting of one cell or of a colony of like or similar cells. *–n.* **2.** any of the Protozoa. [NL *prōtozōa* (pl. of *prōtozōon,* from Gk *prōto-* PROTO- + *zôion* animal) + -AN]

**protract** /prəˈtrækt/, *v.t.* **1.** to draw out or lengthen in time; extend the duration of; prolong. **2.** *Anat., etc.* to extend or protrude. **3.** *Survey., etc.* to plot; to draw by means of a scale and protractor. [L *prōtractus,* pp., drawn forth, drawn out] – **protractive,** *adj.*

**protractile** /prəˈtræktaɪl/, *adj.* capable of being protracted, lengthened, or protruded.

**protraction** /prəˈtrækʃən/, *n.* **1.** the act of protracting. **2.** extension in time or space. **3.** that which is protracted.

**protractor** /prəˈtræktə/, *n.* **1.** one who or that which protracts. **2.** a flat semicircular instrument, graduated around the circular edge, used to measure or mark off angles.

**protrude** /prəˈtrud/, *v.,* **-truded, -truding.** *–v.i.* **1.** to project. *–v.t.* **2.** to thrust forward; cause to project. [L *prōtrūdere*] – **protrudent,** *adj.* – **protrusible** /prəˈtruzəbəl/, *adj.*

**protrusile** /prəˈtrusaɪl, -zaɪl/, *adj.* capable of being thrust forth or extended, as a limb, etc. [L *prōtrūsus,* pp., thrust forth + -ILE]

**protrusion** /prəˈtruʒən/, *n.* **1.** the act of protruding. **2.** the state of being protruded. **3.** that which protrudes.

**protrusive** /prəˈtrusɪv, -zɪv/, *adj.* **1.** thrusting forward. **2.** obtrusive. **3.** projecting. – **protrusively,** *adv.*

**protuberance** /prəˈtjubərəns, -brəns/, *n.* **1.** protuberant state or form. **2.** a protuberant part; a rounded projection.

**protuberancy** /prəˈtjubərənsi, -brənsi/, *n., pl.* **-cies.** →**protuberance.**

**protuberant** /prəˈtjubərənt, -brənt/, *adj.* bulging out beyond the surrounding surface. [LL *prōtūberans,* ppr., swelling] – **protuberantly,** *adv.*

**proud** /praʊd/, *adj.* **1.** feeling pleasure or satisfaction over something conceived as highly honourable or creditable to oneself (oft. fol. by *of,* an infinitive, or a clause). **2.** having or cherishing, or proceeding from or showing, a high, esp. an inordinately high, opinion of one's own dignity, importance, or superiority. **3.** having or showing self-respect or self-esteem. **4.** highly gratifying to the feelings or self-esteem. **5.** highly honourable or creditable: *a proud achievement.* **6.** (of things) stately, majestic, or magnificent: *proud cities.* **7.** of lofty dignity or distinction: *a proud name, proud nobles.* **8.** *Poetic.* full of vigour or spirit. **9.** *Bldg Trades.* projecting beyond the surrounding elements or objects: *to stand proud.* **10.** *Obs.* brave. *–adv.* **11. do (someone) proud, a.** to be a source of credit to (a person). **b.** to entertain (someone) generously or lavishly. [ME; late OE *prūd,* c. Icel. *prūdhr* magnificent, stately, gallant, apparently from VL. Cf. OF *prud, prod* gallant, from L *prōd-* in *prōdesse* be of worth] – **proudly,** *adv.*

**proud flesh** /– ˈflɛʃ/, *n.* →**granulation tissue.**

**proustite** /ˈprustaɪt/, *n.* a mineral, silver arsenic sulphide, $Ag_3AsS_3$, which occurs in scarlet crystals and masses, and is a minor ore of silver; ruby silver. [named after J. L. *Proust,* 1754-1826, French chemist. See -ITE[1]]

**Prov.,** *Bible.* Proverbs.

**prove** /pruv/, *v.,* **proved, proved** or **proven, proving.** *–v.t.* **1.** to establish the truth or genuineness of, as by evidence or argument: *to prove one's contention.* **2.** *Law.* to establish the authenticity or validity of (a will or testament). **3.** to give demonstration of by action. **4.** to put to the test; try or test. **5.** to show (oneself) to have the character, ability, courage, etc., expected of one, esp. through one's actions. **6.** to show (oneself) to be as specified. **7.** *Maths.* to give a proof (def. 5). **8.** →**proof** (def. 20). **9.** to determine the characteristics of by scientific analysis: *to prove ore.* **10.** *Cookery.* to cause (dough) to rise in a warm place before baking. **11.** *Archaic.* to experience. *–v.i.* **12.** to turn out: *the report proved to be false.* **13.** to be found by trial or experience, or in the event, to be. **14.** (of dough) to rise in a warm place before baking. [ME, from OF *prover,* from L *probāre* try, test, prove, approve] – **provable,** *adj.* – **prover,** *n.*

**provenance** /ˈprɒvənəns/, *n.* **1.** the place of origin, as of a work of art, etc. **2.** the record of ownership of a work of art. [F, from *provenir,* from L *prōvenīre* come forth]

**Provençal** /prɒvɒnˈsal/, *adj.* **1.** of or pertaining to Provence, a province of France, its people, or their language. *–n.* **2.** a native or inhabitant of Provence. **3.** a Romance language, formerly widely spoken and written, of south-eastern France. [F, from *Provence,* from L *prōvincia* province]

**Provençale** /prɒvɒnˈsal/, *adj.* characterised by the use of a mixture of tomato and garlic, or sometimes garlic alone. Also, **Provencale.** [F, from PROVENÇAL]

**provender** /ˈprɒvəndə/, *n.* **1.** dry food for livestock, as hay; fodder. **2.** food or provisions. [ME *provendre,* from OF, var. of *provende* prebend, provender, from LL *prōbenda,* b. *praebenda* prebend and *prōvidēre* look out for]

**provenience** /prəˈviniəns/, *n.* provenance; origin. [*provenient,* from L *prōveniens,* ppr., coming forth]

**proverb** /ˈprɒvɜb/, *n.* **1.** a short popular saying, long current, embodying some familiar truth or useful thought in expressive language. **2.** a wise saying or precept; a didactic sentence. **3.** a person or thing that is commonly regarded as the embodiment of some quality; byword. **4.** *Bible.* a profound saying or oracular utterance requiring interpretation. *–v.t.* **5.** to utter in the form of a proverb. **6.** to make (something) the subject of a proverb. **7.** to make a byword of. [ME *proverbe,* from OF, from L *prōverbium*]

**proverbial** /prəˈvɜbiəl/, *adj.* **1.** pertaining to or characteristic of a proverb: *proverbial brevity.* **2.** expressed in a proverb or proverbs: *proverbial wisdom.* **3.** of the nature of or resembling a proverb: *proverbial sayings.* **4.** having been made the subject of a proverb. **5.** having become an object of common mention or reference: *clean and fresh as the proverbial daisy.* – **proverbially,** *adv.*

**provide** /prəˈvaɪd/, *v.,* **-vided, -viding.** *–v.t.* **1.** to furnish or supply. **2.** to afford or yield. **3.** *Law.* to arrange for or stipulate beforehand, as by a provision or proviso. **4.** *Archaic.* to get ready, prepare, or procure beforehand. *–v.i.* **5.** to take measures with due foresight (usu. fol. by *for* or *against*). **6.** to make arrangements for supplying means of support, money, etc. (usu. fol. by *for*). **7.** to supply means of support, etc. (oft. fol. by *for*). [ME, from L *prōvidēre* foresee, look after, provide for] – **provider,** *n.*

**provided** /prəˈvaɪdəd/, *conj.* it being stipulated or understood (that); on the condition or supposition (that): *to consent, provided* (or *provided that*) *all the others agree.*

**providence** /ˈprɒvədəns/, *n.* **1.** the foreseeing care and guardianship of God over His creatures. **2.** (*cap.*) God. **3.** a manifestation of the divine care or direction. **4.** provident or prudent management of resources; economy. **5.** *Rare.* foresight; provident care.

**provident** /ˈprɒvədənt/, *adj.* **1.** having or showing foresight; careful in providing for the future. **2.** characterised by or proceeding from foresight: *provident care.* **3.** mindful in making provision (usu. fol. by *of*). **4.** economical or frugal. [ME, from L *prōvidens,* ppr., looking for, providing] – **providently,** *adv.*

**provident fund** /ˈ– fʌnd/, *n.* →**superannuation fund.**

**providential** /prɒvəˈdɛnʃəl/, *adj.* **1.** of, pertaining to, or proceeding from divine providence: *providential care.* **2.** opportune, fortunate, or lucky: *a providential occurrence.* – **providentially,** *adv.*

**provident society** /ˈprɒvədənt səsaɪəti/, *n.* →**friendly society.**

**providing** /prəˈvaɪdɪŋ/, *conj.* provided.

**province** /ˈprɒvəns/, *n.* **1.** an administrative division or unit of a country: *the provinces of Spain.* **2. the provinces,** the parts of a country outside the capital or the largest cities. **3.** a country, territory, district, or region. **4.** *Geog.* an area lower in rank than a region. **5.** a department or branch of learning or activity: *the province of mathematics.* **6.** the sphere or field of action of a person, etc.; one's office, function, or business. **7.** an ecclesiastical territorial division, as that within which an archbishop or a metropolitan exercises jurisdiction. [ME, from F, from L *prōvincia* province, official charge]

**provincial** /prəˈvɪnʃəl/, *adj.* **1.** belonging or peculiar to some particular province or provinces; local: *provincial customs.* **2.** of or pertaining to the provinces: *the provincial press.* **3.** having or showing the manners characteristic of inhabitants of a province or the provinces; countrified; rustic; unsophisticated; narrow or illiberal. *–n.* **4.** one who lives in or comes from the provinces. **5.** a countrified, unsophisticated, or narrow-minded person. **6.** *Eccles.* **a.** the head of an ecclesiastical province. **b.** a member of a religious order presiding over his order in a given district or province. – **provincially,** *adv.*

**provincialism** /prəˈvɪnʃəlɪzəm/, *n.* **1.** narrowness of outlook or interests resulting from provincial life. **2.** manner, habit of thought, etc., characteristic of a province or the provinces. **3.** a word, expression, or mode of pronunciation peculiar to a province. **4.** devotion to one's own province before the nation as a whole.

**provinciality** /prəvɪnʃiˈæləti/, *n., pl.* **-ties. 1.** provincial character. **2.** a provincial characteristic.

**proving ground** /ˈpruvɪŋ graʊnd/, *n.* any place or area for conducting experiments or testing something, as a piece of scientific equipment, a new theory, etc.

**proving stand** /ˈ– stænd/, *n.* an apparatus for testing reaction engines, as rocket engines.

**proving time** /ˈ– taɪm/, *n.* the time taken for dough to prove (def. 14).

**provision** /prəˈvɪʒən/, *n.* **1.** a clause in a legal instrument, a law, etc., providing for a particular matter; stipulation; proviso. **2.** the providing or supplying of something, as of food or other necessities. **3.** arrangement or preparation beforehand, as for the doing of something, the meeting of needs, the supplying of means, etc. **4.** something provided; a measure or other means for meeting a need. **5.** a supply or stock of something provided. **6.** (*pl.*) supplies of food. **7.** *Eccles.* **a.** appointment to an ecclesiastical office. **b.** appointment by the pope to a see or benefice not yet vacant. *–v.t.* **8.** to supply with provisions, or stores of food. [ME, from L *prōvīsio*] – **provisioner,** *n.*

**provisional** /prəˈvɪʒənəl/, *adj.* Also, **provisionary. 1.** serving for the time being only; existing until permanently replaced; temporary; conditional; tentative: *a provisional agreement.* *–n.* **2.** *Philately.* a stamp which serves temporarily pending the appearance of the regular issue, or during a temporary shortage of the regular stamps. – **provisionally,** *adv.*

**provisional licence** /– ˈlaɪsəns/, *n.* a licence to drive a motor vehicle, obtained after passing a driving test, which stipulates a restricted speed and the use of P-plates, usu. for one year.

**provisional tax** /– ˈtæks/, *n.* tax paid in advance on income to be earned in the next financial year from sources other than salary and wages.

**proviso** /prəˈvaɪzoʊ/, *n., pl.* **-sos, -soes. 1.** a clause in a statute, contract, or the like, by which a condition is introduced. **2.** a stipulation or condition. [late ME, from ML *prōvīsō (quod)* it being provided that]

**provisory** /prəˈvaɪzəri/, *adj.* **1.** provisional. **2.** containing a proviso or condition; conditional.

**provitamin** /proʊˈvaɪtəmən, -ˈvɪt-/, *n.* a substance which an organism can transform into a vitamin, as carotene, which is converted into vitamin A in the liver.

**provocation** /prɒvəˈkeɪʃən/, *n.* **1.** the act of provoking. **2.** something that incites, instigates, angers, or irritates. **3.** *Law.* words or conduct leading to a killing in hot passion and without deliberation. [ME, from L *prōvocātio* a calling forth]

**provocative** /prəˈvɒkətɪv/, *adj.* **1.** tending or serving to provoke; inciting, stimulating, irritating, or vexing. *–n.* **2.** something provocative. – **provocatively,** *adv.* – **provocativeness,** *n.*

**provoke** /prəˈvoʊk/, *v.t.,* **-voked, -voking. 1.** to anger, enrage, exasperate, or vex. **2.** to stir up, arouse, or call forth. **3.** to incite or stimulate (a person, etc.) to action. **4.** to give rise to, induce, or bring about. [ME, from L *prōvocāre* call forth, challenge, provoke] – **provoker,** *n.* – **provoking,** *adj.* – **provokingly,** *adv.*

**provolone** /prɒvəˈloʊni/, *n.* a soft ripened cheese with a plastic curd and a firm, smooth texture, moulded in various forms and hung in a net to cure. [It., from *provola,* from ML *probula* cheese made from buffalo milk]

**provost** /ˈprɒvəst/, *n.* **1.** a person appointed to superintend or preside. **2.** an officer in a Scottish burgh corresponding to mayor. **3.** *Eccles.* **a.** the head officer of a chapter or governing body, esp. of a religious foundation. **b.** (formerly) the official next in dignity to the abbot of a monastery. **4.** the head of certain colleges, schools, etc. **5.** *U.S.* an administrative officer in a university having responsibility for curriculum, faculty appointments, etc. **6.** *Hist.* a feudal overseer. **7.** *Obs.* a prison warder. [ME; OE *profost,* from ML *prōpositus,* lit., one placed before, president] – **provostship,** *n.*

**provost marshal** /proʊvoʊ ˈmaʃəl/, *n.* **1.** (in the army) an officer acting as head of military police in a camp or area, and charged with the maintenance of order, etc. **2.** (in the navy) head of the police.

**prow** /praʊ/, *n.* **1.** the forepart of a ship or boat above the waterline; the bow. **2.** *Poetic.* a ship. [F *proue,* from d. It. (Genoese) *proa,* from L *prōra,* from Gk *prôira*]

**prowess** /ˈpraʊɛs, praʊˈɛs/, *n.* **1.** valour; bravery. **2.** outstanding ability: *prowess at shooting.* [ME *prowesse,* from OF *proec(c)e,* from *proue* good, valiant, from L *prōd-* in *prōdesse* be useful]

**prowl** /praʊl/, *v.i.* **1.** to rove or go about stealthily in search of prey, plunder, etc. *–v.t.* **2.** to rove over or through in search of what may be found. *–n.* **3.** the act of prowling. [ME *proll(en)*; orig. uncert.] – **prowler,** *n.*

**prowl car** /ˈ– ka/, *n. U.S.* a police patrol car.

**prox.,** next month; proximo. [L *proximō (mense)*]

**proximal** /ˈprɒksəməl/, *adj.* situated towards the point of origin or attachment, as of a limb or bone (opposed to *distal*). [L *proximus* next + -AL[1]] – **proximally,** *adv.*

**proximate** /ˈprɒksəmət/, *adj.* **1.** next; nearest. **2.** closely adjacent; very near. **3.** fairly accurate; approximate. **4.** next in a chain of relation. [LL *proximātus,* pp., approached] – **proximately,** *adv.*

**proximity** /prɒkˈsɪməti/, *n.* nearness in place, time, or relation. [late ME, from L *proximitas*]

**proximity fuse** /ˈ– fjuz/, *n.* a fuse designed to detonate a projectile, bomb, mine, or charge when activated by some external influence, as light, heat, etc., which is emitted by its target; variable time fuse.

**proximo** /ˈprɒksɪmoʊ/, *adv.* in or of the next or coming month: *on the 1st proximo.* Cf. **ultimo.** *Abbrev.:* prox. [L: in the next (month), abl. of *proximus* next. See PROXIMAL]

**proxy** /ˈprɒksi/, *n., pl.* **proxies. 1.** the agency of a person deputed to act for another. **2.** the person so deputed; an agent; a substitute. **3.** a written authorisation empowering another to vote or act for the signer. [ME *prokecye,* contraction of *procuracy* (see PROCURATOR)]

**proxyholder** /ˈprɒksihoʊldə/, *n.* one who is authorised by a person having a right to attend or vote at a meeting, to exercise that right on that person's behalf.

**prs,** pairs.

**prude** /prud/, *n.* a person who affects extreme modesty or propriety. [F: a prude, as adj., prudish, backformation from OF *preudefeme, prodefeme* worthy or respectable woman]

**prudence** /ˈprudns/, *n.* **1.** cautious practical wisdom; good judgment; discretion. **2.** the quality or fact of being prudent. **3.** regard for one's own interests. **4.** provident care in management; economy or frugality.

**prudent** /ˈprudnt/, *adj.* **1.** wise, judicious, or wisely cautious in practical affairs, as a person; sagacious or judicious; discreet or circumspect. **2.** careful of one's own interests; provident, or careful in providing for the future. **3.** characterised by or proceeding from prudence, as conduct, action, etc. [ME, from L *prūdens* foreseeing, knowing, contraction of *prōvidens* PROVIDENT] – **prudently,** *adv.*

**prudential** /pruˈdɛnʃəl/, *adj.* **1.** of, pertaining to, or characterised by prudence. **2.** exercising prudence. **3.** *U.S.* having discretionary charge of certain matters. – **prudentially,** *adv.*

**prudery** /ˈprudəri/, *n., pl.* **-ries. 1.** extreme modesty or propriety. **2.** prudish action or speech.

**prudish** /ˈprudɪʃ/, *adj.* **1.** extremely modest or proper. **2.** characteristic of a prude. – **prudishly,** *adv.* – **prudishness,** *n.*

**pruinose** /ˈpruənoʊs/, *adj.* covered with a frostlike bloom or powdery secretion, as a plant surface. [L *pruīnōsus* frosty]

**prune**[1] /prun/, *n.* **1.** the purplish black dried fruit of any of several varieties of plum tree, used for eating, cooked or uncooked. **2.** such a fruit, whether dried or not. **3.** a variety of plum tree bearing such fruit. **4.** *Obs.* any plum. [late ME, from F, from LL *prūna,* for L *prūnum* plum (*prūnus* plum tree), from Gk *proûnon* plum]

**prune**[2] /prun/, *v.t.,* **pruned, pruning. 1.** to cut or lop off (twigs, branches, or roots). **2.** to cut or lop superfluous or undesired twigs, branches, or roots from; to trim. **3.** to rid or clear of (anything superfluous or undesirable). **4.** to remove (superfluities, etc.). [ME *prouyne(n),* from OF *proignier* prune (vines), from L *prōvīneāre,* from *vīnea* a vine] – **pruner,** *n.*

**pruning hook** /ˈprunɪŋ hʊk/, *n.* an implement with a hooked blade, used for pruning vines, etc.

**pruning knife** /ˈ– naɪf/, *n.* a short knife with a curved blade used for pruning.

**pruning shears** /ˈ– ʃɪəz/, *n.pl.* →**secateurs.**

**prunus** /ˈprunəs/, *n.* any shrub or tree of the genus *Prunus,* widespread in horticulture and including the many varieties of plum, esp. garden varieties with dark purplish-red leaves.

**prurient** /ˈpruriənt/, *adj.* **1.** inclined to or characterised by lascivious thought. **2.** morbidly uneasy, as desire or longing. **3.** itching. **4.** *Bot.* causing itching. [L *prūriens,* ppr., itching] – **prurience, pruriency,** *n.* – **pruriently,** *adv.*

**pruriginous** /prəˈrɪdʒənəs/, *adj.* itching. [LL *prūrīginōsus*]

**prurigo** /prəˈraɪgoʊ/, *n.* a skin affection characterised by itching papules. [L: an itching]

**pruritus** /prəˈraɪtəs/, *n.* itching. [L: an itching. See PRURIENT]

– **pruritic** /prəˈrɪtɪk/, *adj.*

**Prussian blue** /prʌʃən ˈblu/, *n.* a dark blue, crystalline, insoluble pigment, $Fe_4[Fe(CN)_6]_3 \cdot 10H_2O$, formed in testing for the ferric ion, and produced by ageing **soluble Prussian blue,** $KFe_2(CN)_6$.

**prussiate** /ˈprʌʃiət, ˈprʌs-, -eɪt/, *n.* a salt of prussic acid; a cyanide. [PRUSSI(C ACID) + -ATE[2]]

**prussic acid** /prʌsɪk ˈæsəd/, *n.* →**hydrocyanic acid.** [*prussic,* from F *prussique,* from *Prusse* Prussia]

**pry**[1] /praɪ/, *v.,* **pried, prying,** *n., pl.* **pries.** *–v.i.* **1.** to look closely or curiously, peer, or peep. **2.** to search or inquire curiously or inquisitively into something: *to pry into the affairs of others.* *–v.t.* **3.** to ferret or find (*out*) by curious searching or inquiry. *–n.* **4.** the act of prying; a prying glance. **5.** an inquisitive person. [ME *prye(n), prie(n);* orig. uncert.]

**pry**[2] /praɪ/, *v.t.,* **pried, prying,** *n., pl.* **pries.** *Chiefly U.S.* →**prise.** [backformation from PRISE, *n.* (taken as pl.)]

**pryer** /ˈpraɪə/, *n.* →**prier.**

**prying** /ˈpraɪɪŋ/, *adj.* **1.** that pries; looking or searching curiously. **2.** unduly curious; inquisitive. – **pryingly,** *adv.*

**Ps.,** *Bible.* **1.** Psalm. **2.** Psalms.

**P.S.,** Also, **p.s.** postscript.

**psalm** /sam/, *n.* **1.** a sacred or solemn song, or hymn. **2.** a metric version or paraphrase of any of these. **3.** a poem of like character. *–v.t.* **4.** to celebrate in psalms; hymn. [ME *psalme,* OE *ps(e)alm, sealm,* from LL *psalmus,* from Gk *psalmós* song sung to the harp, orig., a plucking, as of strings]

**psalmist** /ˈsaməst/, *n.* the author of a psalm or psalms.

**psalmody** /ˈsamədi, ˈsælmədi/, *n., pl.* **-dies. 1.** the arrangement of psalms for singing. **2.** psalms or hymns collectively. **3.** the act, practice, or art of singing psalms or hymns. [ME, from LL *psalmōdia,* from Gk *psalmōidía* singing to the harp] – **psalmodist,** *n.*

**Psalter** /ˈsɔltə/, *n.* (*sometimes l.c.*) a book containing psalms for liturgical or devotional use. [LL *psaltērium* the Psalter, from L: a psaltery, from Gk *psaltḗrion* a stringed instrument; replacing ME *sauter* (from AF) and OE *saltere* (from LL *psaltērium*)]

**psalterium** /sɔlˈtɪəriəm/, *n., pl.* **-teria** /-ˈtɪəriə/. the omasum or manyplies. [LL: the Psalter (the folds of the omasum being likened to the leaves of a book), from Gk *psaltḗrion*]

**psaltery** /ˈsɔltəri/, *n., pl.* **-teries. 1.** an ancient musical instrument consisting of a flat sounding box with numerous strings which were plucked with the fingers or struck with a plectrum. [L *psaltērium,* from Gk *psaltḗrion* psaltery, later the Psalter; replacing ME *sautrie,* from OF]

psaltery

**psammite** /ˈsæmaɪt/, *n.* any sandstone (contrasted with *psephite* and *pelite*). [Gk *psámmos* sand + -ITE[1]] – **psammitic** /sæˈmɪtɪk/, *adj.*

**p's and q's** /piz ən ˈkjuz/, *n.* behaviour; manners: *mind one's p's and q's.* [perhaps from children's difficulty in distinguishing *p* and *q*]

**psephite** /ˈsifaɪt/, *n.* a coarse fragmental rock composed of rounded pebbles and conglomerate. Cf. **psammite** and **pelite.** [Gk *psêphos* pebble + -ITE[1]] – **psephitic** /səˈfɪtɪk/, *adj.*

**psephology** /səˈfɒlədʒi/, *n.* the study of elections by analysing their results, trends, etc. [Gk *psêpho-* (combining form of *psêphos* a pebble (used in ancient Athens for voting) + -LOGY] – **psephological** /sɛfəˈlɒdʒɪkəl/, *adj.* – **psephologically** /sɛfəˈlɒdʒɪkli/, *adv.* – **psephologist,** *n.*

**pseud** /sjud/, *n. Chiefly Brit. Colloq.* a person who pretends to be what he is not.

**pseud.,** pseudonym.

**pseudaxis** /sjuˈdæksəs/, *n.* →**sympodium.** [PSEUD(O)- + AXIS[1]]

**pseudepigrapha** /sjudəˈpɪgrəfə/, *n.pl.* certain writings (other than the canonical books and the Apocrypha) professing to be biblical in character, but not considered canonical or divinely inspired. [NL, from Gk, neut. pl. of *pseudepígraphos* falsely inscribed, bearing a false title] – **pseudepigraphic** /sjudəpəˈgræfɪk/, **pseudepigraphous,** *adj.*

**pseudo** /ˈsjudoʊ/; (*oft. joc.*) /pəˈsweɪdoʊ/, *adj.* **1.** false; counterfeit; spurious; sham; pretended. *–n.* **2.** a person who pretends to be what he is not, esp. one who affects a knowledge of cultural matters or superiority in general. [ME; independent use of PSEUDO-]

**pseudo-,** a word element meaning 'false', 'pretended', freely used as a formative; in scientific use, denoting close or deceptive resemblance to the following element, used sometimes in chemical names of isomers. Also, before vowels, **pseud-.** [Gk, combining form of *pseudḗs* false]

**pseudoaquatic** /ˌsjudoʊəˈkwɒtɪk/, *adj.* not aquatic but indigenous to moist regions.

**pseudocarp** /ˈsjudoʊkap/, *n.* a fruit which includes other parts besides the mature ovary and its contents, as the apple, pineapple, etc. – **pseudocarpous** /sjudoʊˈkapəs/, *adj.*

**pseudoclassic** /sjudoʊˈklæsɪk/, *adj.* falsely or spuriously classic. – **pseudoclassicism,** *n.*

**pseudocopulation** /ˌsjudoʊkɒpjəˈleɪʃən/, *n.* the pollination of those species of orchid whose flowers resemble female wasps by the male ichneumon wasp.

**pseudoforce** /ˈsjudoʊfɔs/, *n.* a fictitious force introduced to make Newton's laws of motion work in an accelerative frame of reference, as Coriolis force.

**pseudolearned** /sjudoʊˈlɜnəd/, *adj.* **1.** characterised by erroneous or defective learning. **2.** exhibiting unnecessary or misguided antiquarianism, as in adding *b* in the spelling of *debt* after the Latin source *debitum,* for Middle English *det.*

**pseudomorph** /ˈsjudoʊmɔf/, *n.* **1.** a false or deceptive form. **2.** *Mineral.* a mineral which takes its external appearance from another mineral which it has replaced in chemical action. – **pseudomorphic** /sjudoʊˈmɔfɪk/, **pseudomorphous** /sjudoʊˈmɔfəs/, *adj.* – **pseudomorphism** /sjudoʊˈmɔfɪzəm/, *n.*

**pseudonym** /ˈsjudənɪm/, *n.* an assumed name adopted by an author to conceal his identity; pen-name. [Gk *pseudṓnymon* false name]

**pseudonymity** /sjudəˈnɪməti/, *n.* **1.** pseudonymous character. **2.** the use of a pseudonym.

**pseudonymous** /sjuˈdɒnəməs/, *adj.* **1.** bearing a false name. **2.** writing or written under an assumed name. [Gk *pseudṓnymos*] – **pseudonymously,** *adv.*

**pseudopodium** /sjudoʊˈpoʊdiəm/, *n., pl.* **-dia** /-diə/. a temporary protrusion of the protoplasm of a protozoan, serving as an organ of locomotion, prehension, etc. Also, **pseudopod** /ˈsjudoʊpɒd/. [NL, from Gk *pseudo-* PSEUDO- + *pódion,* diminutive of *poús* foot]

**pseudoscalar** /sjudoʊˈskeɪlə/, *adj.* describing a scalar quantity which changes sign in the transition from a right-handed to a left-handed system of coordinates.

**pseudoscorpion** /sjudoʊˈskɔpiən/, *n.* any of a number of widely distributed small arthropods belonging to the order Chelonethida, which superficially resemble scorpions but are more closely related to the mites.

**pshaw** /pʃɔ/, *interj.* (an exclamation expressing impatience, contempt, etc.)

**psi** /psaɪ/, *n.* the twenty-third letter (Ψ, ψ) of the Greek alphabet.

**psilomelane** /saɪloʊˈmɛleɪn/, *n.* **1.** a common mineral, a hydrated barium manganate, occurring in smooth, black to steel-grey, botryoidal or stalactitic forms and in masses; an ore of manganese. **2.** any hard massive manganese oxide. [Gk *psiló(s)* bare + *mélan* (neut. adj.) black]

**psilosis** /saɪˈloʊsəs/, *n.* →**sprue**[2]. [NL, from Gk]

**psittacosis** /psɪtəˈkoʊsəs, sɪtə-/, *n.* a severe infectious disease of parrots characterised by high fever and pneumonia, which is also known to affect other species of birds, and is easily transmissible to man; parrot fever. [NL, from Gk *psittakós* parrot + *-ōsis* -OSIS]

**psoas** /ˈsoʊəs/, *n.* a muscle of the loin, arising internally from the sides of the spinal column and fitting into the upper end of the thighbone. [NL, from Gk, acc. pl. of *psóa* a muscle of the loins]

**psoralea** /sɒˈreɪljə/, *n.* any plant of the leguminous genus *Psoralea.* [NL, from Gk (neut. pl.): scabby; with reference to the glandular dots on the plant]

**psoriasis** /səˈraɪəsəs/, *n.* a common chronic skin disease characterised by scaly patches. [NL, from Gk]

– **psoriatic** /sɔri'ætɪk/, *adj.*

**psych** /saɪk/, *v.t. Colloq.* **1.** to persuade by the application of psychological knowledge and techniques rather than overtly by argument, esp. when leading others to perform better in a race, competition, etc. (oft. fol. by *up*): *the coach psyched them into a brilliant display of tennis.* **2.** to persuade (oneself) by similar techniques to perform better (oft. fol. by *up*): *he psyched himself up to go into the exam.* **3.** to gain an advantage over (an opponent) by employing similar techniques, as by making him nervous or unsure.

**psych-,** variant of **psycho-,** before some vowels, as in *psychasthenia.*

**psych.,** **1.** psychological. **2.** psychology.

**psychasthenia** /saɪkəs'θiniə, -θə'niə/, *n.* **1.** *Psychiatry.* a neurosis marked by fear, anxiety, phobias, etc. **2.** *Pathol.* mental weakness or exhaustion. [NL. See PSYCH-, ASTHENIA] – **psychasthenic** /saɪkəs'θɛnɪk/, *adj.*

**psyche** /'saɪki/, *n.* **1.** the human soul, spirit, or mind. **2.** *Philos.* by Homer, identified with life itself; by Plato, as immortal and akin to the gods; and by neoplatonism, as the animating principle of the body, but inferior to the nous and the logos. [L, from Gk: lit., breath]

**psychedelic** /saɪkə'dɛlɪk/, *adj.* **1.** denoting or pertaining to a mental state of enlarged consciousness, involving a sense of aesthetic joy and increased perception transcending verbal concepts. **2.** denoting or pertaining to any of a group of drugs inducing such a state, esp. LSD. **3.** *Colloq.* intensely pleasurable or fashionable. **4.** *Colloq.* having bright colours and imaginative patterns, as materials. **5.** of or pertaining to music which is played very loud and accompanied by a lightshow. [PSYCHE + *-delic* (from Gk *dēlóein* to show, reveal)]

**psychiatric hospital** /saɪki,ætrɪk 'hɒspɪtl/, *n.* a hospital for the treatment and care of people suffering from mental illness. Also, **mental hospital.**

**psychiatrist** /sə'kaɪətrəst, saɪ-/, *n.* one who is versed in or practises psychiatry. Also, *Obs.,* **psychiater** /sə'kaɪətə, saɪ-/.

**psychiatry** /sə'kaɪətri, saɪ-/, *n.* the practice or the science of treating mental diseases. [PSYCH- + Gk *iatreía* healing] – **psychiatric** /saɪki'ætrɪk/, **psychiatrical** /saɪki'ætrɪkəl/, *adj.* – **psychiatrically** /saɪki'ætrɪkli/, *adv.*

**psychic** /'saɪkɪk/, *adj.* Also, **psychical.** **1.** of or pertaining to the human soul or mind; mental (opposed to *physical*). **2.** *Psychol.* pertaining to super- or extra-sensory mental functioning, such as clairvoyance, telepathy. See **parapsychology.** **3.** exerted by or proceeding from non-physical agency. **4.** of the nature of such an agency. **5.** associated with or attributed to such agencies, as phenomena, etc. **6.** of or pertaining to the class of phenomena associated with such agencies: *psychic research.* **7.** specially susceptible to psychic influences. *–n.* **8.** a person specially susceptible to psychic influences. [Gk *psȳchikós* of the soul] – **psychically,** *adv.*

**psychic bid** /'– bɪd/, *n.* (in bridge) a bid based on intuition rather than on the strength of one's hand.

**psycho** /'saɪkoʊ/, *Colloq.* *–n.* **1.** an insane person. **2.** →**psychopath.** *–adj.* **3.** insane, obsessional. **4.** psychopathic.

**psycho-,** a word element representing 'psyche' (as in *psychological*) and 'psychological' (as in *psychoanalysis*). Also, **psych-.** [Gk, combining form of *psȳchē* breath, spirit, soul, mind]

**psychoacoustics** /,saɪkoʊə'kustɪks/, *n.* the study of sounds in relation to their physiological and psychological effects.

**psychoanal.,** psychoanalysis.

**psychoanalyse** /saɪkoʊ'ænəlaɪz/, *v.t.,* **-lysed, -lysing.** to investigate or treat by psychoanalysis. Also, *U.S.,* **psychoanalyze.** – **psychoanalyser,** *n.*

**psychoanalysis** /,saɪkoʊə'næləsəs/, *n.* **1.** a systematic structure of theories concerning the relation of conscious and unconscious psychological processes. **2.** a technical procedure for investigating unconscious mental processes, and for treating neuroses. – **psychoanalytic** /,saɪkoʊænə'lɪtɪk/, **psychoanalytical** /,saɪkoʊænə'lɪtɪkəl/, *adj.* – **psychoanalytically** /,saɪkoʊænə'lɪtɪkli/, *adv.*

**psychoanalyst** /saɪkoʊ'ænələst/, *n.* one who is versed in or practises psychoanalysis.

**psychobiology** /,saɪkoʊbaɪ'ɒlədʒi/, *n.* **1.** that branch of biology which treats of the relations or interactions between body and mind, esp. as exhibited in the nervous system, receptors, effectors, or the like. **2.** psychology as studied by biological methods or in terms of biology. – **psychobiological** /,saɪkoʊbaɪə'lɒdʒɪkəl/, *adj.* – **psychobiologist,** *n.*

**psychodrama** /'saɪkoʊdramə/, *n.* **1.** a type of group therapy used in treating patients in a mental hospital, in which the patients act out a theme of their own choosing, thereby having an opportunity to express and resolve their own personal conflicts. **2.** the drama itself. – **psychodramatic** /,saɪkoʊdrə'mætɪk/, *adj.*

**psychogenesis** /saɪkoʊ'dʒɛnəsəs/, *n.* **1.** genesis of the psyche. **2.** the study of the origin of physical or psychological states, normal or abnormal, out of the interplay of conscious and unconscious psychological forces. – **psychogenetic** /,saɪkoʊdʒə'nɛtɪk/, *adj.* – **psychogenetically,** *adv.*

**psychogenic** /saɪkoʊ'dʒɛnɪk/, *adj.* of psychic origin, or dependent on psychic conditions or processes, as a mental disorder.

**psychognosis** /saɪ'kɒgnəsəs/, *n.* *Psychiatry.* a complete examination of the mind.

**psychograph** /'saɪkəgræf, -graf/, *n.* **1.** *Psychol.* the graphic representation of the relative strength of the various traits of a personality. **2.** a character analysis. **3.** an instrument for recording psychic processes, esp. for spirit writing. – **psychographic** /saɪkə'græfɪk/, *adj.* – **psychographically** /saɪkə'græfɪkli/, *adv.*

**psychography** /saɪ'kɒgrəfi/, *n.* **1.** writing thought to be guided by a spiritual being. **2.** a manifestation of a spiritual being on a photographic plate, without the use of a camera. [PSYCHO- + -GRAPHY]

**psychokinesis** /,saɪkoʊkə'nisəs/, *n.* the moving of objects by the power of the mind. – **psychokinetic,** *adj.* – **psychokinetics,** *n.*

**psychol.,** **1.** psychological. **2.** psychology.

**psycholinguistics** /,saɪkoʊlɪŋ'gwɪstɪks/, *n.* the study of relations between linguistic events and mental processes. – **psycholinguistic,** *adj.* – **psycholinguist** /saɪkoʊ'lɪŋgwəst/, *n.*

**psychological** /saɪkə'lɒdʒɪkəl/, *adj.* **1.** of or pertaining to psychology. **2.** pertaining to the mind or to mental phenomena, esp. as the subject matter of psychology. Also, **psychologic.** – **psychologically,** *adv.*

**psychological moment** /– 'moʊmənt/, *n.* the most appropriate moment for effect on the mind; the critical moment: *at the psychological moment he announced his resignation.*

**psychological warfare** /– 'wɔfɛə/, *n.* the use of propaganda and tactics in a hostile situation to influence people to accept a particular belief, undertake a course of action, weaken their will to resist, etc.

**psychologise** /saɪ'kɒlədʒaɪz/, *v.i.,* **-gised, -gising.** to make psychological investigations or speculations. Also, **psychologize.**

**psychologism** /saɪ'kɒlədʒɪzəm/, *n.* a tendency to attach preponderating importance to the psychological aspect of things and affairs.

**psychologist** /saɪ'kɒlədʒəst/, *n.* one trained in psychology.

**psychology** /saɪ'kɒlədʒi/, *n., pl.* **-gies.** **1.** the science of mind, or of mental states and processes; the science of human nature. **2.** the science of human and animal behaviour. **3.** the mental states and processes of a person or of a number of persons, esp. as determining action: *the psychology of the fighting man in war.* [NL *psȳchologia,* from Gk *psȳcho-* PSYCHO- + *-logía* -LOGY]

**psychomancy** /'saɪkoʊmænsi/, *n.* occult communication between souls or with spirits.

**psychometry** /saɪ'kɒmətri/, *n.* **1.** Also, **psychometrics** /saɪkə'mɛtrɪks/. *Psychol.* the measurement of mental states, mental processes, and their relationships. **2.** the alleged art or faculty of divining the properties of an object, or matters associated with it, through contact with or proximity to it. – **psychometer,** *n.* – **psychometric** /saɪkə'mɛtrɪk/, *adj.* – **psychometrically** /saɪkə'mɛtrɪkli/, *adv.*

**psychomotor** /'saɪkoʊmoʊtə/, *adj.* of or pertaining to voluntary movement.

**psychoneurosis** /,saɪkoʊnju'roʊsəs/, *n., pl.* **-ses** /-siz/. →**neurosis.** – **psychoneurotic** /,saɪkoʊnju'rɒtɪk/, *adj.*

**psychopath** /ˈsaɪkəpæθ/, *n.* one affected with psychopathy or a psychopathic personality.

**psychopathic** /saɪkəˈpæθɪk/, *adj.* **1.** denoting a personality outwardly normal but characterised by a diminished sense of social responsibility, inability to establish deep human relationships, and sometimes, abnormal or dangerous acts. **2.** pertaining to or of the nature of, affected with, or engaged in treating psychopathy. **3.** pertaining to a psychosis or neurosis, or to any other mental disorder.

**psychopathology** /ˌsaɪkoʊpəˈθɒlədʒi/, *n.* mental pathology; the science of diseases of the mind. – **psychopathological** /ˌsaɪkoʊpæθəˈlɒdʒɪkəl/, *adj.* – **psychopathologist,** *n.*

**psychopathy** /saɪˈkɒpəθi/, *n.* **1.** mental disease or disorder. **2.** a psychopathic personality. **3.** the treatment of disease by mental or psychological influence.

**psychophysics** /saɪkoʊˈfɪzɪks/, *n.* that department of psychology which deals with the measurement of relationships between attributes of the stimulus and of the sensation. – **psychophysical** /saɪkoʊˈfɪzɪkəl/, *adj.* – **psychophysically,** *adv.* – **psychophysicist** /saɪkoʊˈfɪzəsəst/, *n.*

**psychophysiology** /ˌsaɪkoʊfɪziˈɒlədʒi/, *n.* the branch of physiology which deals with the mind and its functions. – **psychophysiological** /ˌsaɪkoʊfɪziəˈlɒdʒɪkəl/, *adj.* – **psychophysiologist,** *n.*

**psychopomp** /ˈsaɪkoʊpɒmp/, *n.* one who conducts spirits or souls to the other world, as Hermes or Charon. [PSYCHO- + Gk *pompós* conductor]

**psychoprophylaxis** /ˌsaɪkoʊprɒfəˈlæksəs/, *n.* a method of conditioning pregnant women for child-bearing by training in labour technique, breathing control, etc. [PSYCHO- + PROPHYLAXIS] – **psychoprophylactic,** *adj.*

**psychosis** /saɪˈkoʊsəs/, *n., pl.* **-ses** /-siz/. **1.** *Pathol.* any major, severe form of mental affection or disease. **2.** *Rare.* the state of consciousness at a given time. [NL, from LGk] – **psychotic** /saɪˈkɒtɪk/, *adj., n.*

**psychosomatic** /ˌsaɪkoʊsəˈmætɪk/, *adj.* denoting a physical disorder which is caused by or notably influenced by the emotional state of the patient.

**psychosomatic medicine** /– ˈmɛdəsən/, *n.* the application of the principles of psychology in the study and treatment of physical diseases.

**psychotherapeutics** /ˌsaɪkoʊθɛrəˈpjutɪks/, *n.* therapeutics concerned with the treatment of disease by psychological influence, as by mental suggestion. – **psychotherapeutic,** *adj.* – **psychotherapeutically,** *adv.* – **psychotherapeutist,** *n.*

**psychotherapy** /saɪkoʊˈθɛrəpi/, *n.* the science or art of curing psychological abnormalities and disorders by psychological techniques. – **psychotherapist,** *n.*

**psychotic** /saɪˈkɒtɪk/, *adj.* **1.** of or pertaining to psychosis. –*n.* **2.** a person suffering from a psychosis.

**psychotropic** /saɪkoʊˈtrɒpɪk/, *adj. Med.* affecting the psyche; applied specifically to drugs used to treat mental illness.

**psychrometer** /saɪˈkrɒmətə/, *n.* an instrument used to determine atmospheric humidity by the reading of two thermometers, the bulb of one of which is kept moistened and ventilated; wet-and-dry bulb hygrometer. [*psychro-* (from Gk, combining form of *psȳchrós* cold) + -METER[1]] – **psychrometric** /saɪkroʊˈmɛtrɪk/, *adj.*

**psychrometry** /saɪˈkrɒmətri/, *n.* the measurement of the humidity of the atmosphere.

**psychrophile** /ˈsaɪkrəfaɪl, -fil/, *n.* an organism which flourishes at low temperatures. Cf. **mesophile, thermophile.** – **psychrophilic,** *adj.*

**psyllid** /ˈsɪləd/, *n.* a member of an insect family, Psyllidae, comprising the jumping plant lice, having long antennaes, thick, feathery forewings, and hind legs adapted for jumping.

**psylocibin** /saɪləˈsaɪbən/, *n.* a hallucinogenic substance obtained from the mushroom, *Psylociba cubensis;* a tryptamine derivative.

**pt,** **1.** point. **2.** port. **3.** pint. **4.** part.

**pt.,** preterite.

**p.t.,** **1.** past tense. **2.** part time.

**Pt,** *Chem.* platinum.

**P.T.,** Physical Training.

**pta,** peseta.

**ptarmigan** /ˈtaməgən/, *n.* any of various species of grouse of the genus *Lagopus,* characterised by feathered feet, and found in mountainous and cold regions. [Gaelic *tarmachan;* orig. unknown]

**Pte,** Private.

**pteridology** /tɛrəˈdɒlədʒi/, *n.* the branch of botany that treats of ferns. [*pterido-* (combining form representing Gk *pterís* fern) + -LOGY] – **pteridological** /tɛrədoʊˈlɒdʒɪkəl/, *adj.* – **pteridologist,** *n.*

**pteridophyte** /ˈtɛrədoʊfaɪt/, *n.* any of the Pteridophyta, a primary division of the vegetable kingdom comprising plants (as the ferns and fern allies) which are without seeds, have vascular tissue, and are differentiated into root, stem, and leaf. It includes ferns, horsetails, and club mosses. [NL *Pteridophyta,* pl., from Gk *pterido-* (combining form representing Gk *pterís* fern) + *phytá* plants] – **pteridophytic** /tɛrədoʊˈfɪtɪk/, **pteridophytous** /tɛrəˈdɒfətəs/, *adj.*

**pterion** /ˈtɪəriən, ˈtɛriən/, *n.* the craniometric point at the side of the sphenoidal fontanelle.

**ptero-,** a word element meaning 'wing', as in *pterodactyl.* [Gk, combining form of *pterón*]

**pterocarpous** /tɛroʊˈkapəs/, *adj.* having a winged fruit.

**pterodactyl** /tɛrəˈdæktl/, *n.* any member of the Pterosauria, an order of extinct (Jurassic to Cretaceous) flying reptiles, having the outside digit of the forelimb greatly elongated and supporting a wing membrane. [NL *Pterodactylus,* genus name, from Gk *pteró(n)* wing + *dáktylos* digit]

pterodactyl

**pteropod** /ˈtɛrəpɒd/, *adj.* belonging or pertaining to the Pteropoda, a group of molluscs which have the lateral portions of the foot expanded into winglike lobes. [NL *Pteropoda,* pl., from Gk, neut. pl. of *pterópous* wingfooted]

**-pterous,** an adjectival word element meaning 'winged', as in *dipterous.* [Gk *-pteros,* combining form from *pterón* feather, wing]

**pterygoid** /ˈtɛrəgɔɪd/, *adj.* **1.** winglike. **2.** *Anat.* denoting or pertaining to the pterygoid process. –*n.* **3.** *Anat.* the muscles, nerves, blood vessels, etc., of the pterygoid process. [Gk *pterygoeidḗs* winglike]

**pterygoid process** /–ˈproʊsɛs/, *n.* **1.** either of two processes descending, one on each side, from the point where the body of the sphenoid bone joins a bone of a temporal wing within the skull, each process consisting of two plates (**external pterygoid plate** and **internal pterygoid plate**) separated by a notch. **2.** either of these two plates.

**PTFE,** polytetrafluoroethylene.

**ptisan** /təˈsan/, *n.* a nourishing decoction, often having a slight medicinal quality, originally one made from barley. [L *ptisana,* from Gk *ptisánē* peeled barley, barley water: replacing ME *tisane,* from F]

**p.t.o.** /pi ti ˈoʊ/, please turn over. Also, **P.T.O.**

**Ptolemaic system** /tɒləˈmeɪɪk ˌsɪstəm/, *n.* a system elaborated by Ptolemy and subsequently modified by others, according to which the earth was the fixed centre of the universe, with the heavenly bodies moving about it. [named after *Ptolemy,* (Claudius Ptolemaeus), fl. A.D. 127-151, Greek mathematician, astronomer, and geographer]

**Ptolemaist** /tɒləˈmeɪəst/, *n.* a believer in the Ptolemaic system of astronomy.

**ptomaine** /təˈmeɪn/, *n.* any of a class of basic nitrogenous substances, some of them very poisonous, produced during putrefaction of animal or plant proteins. Also, **ptomain.** [It. *ptomaina,* from Gk *ptôma* dead body + *-ina* -INE[2]]

**ptomaine poisoning** /– ˈpɔɪzənɪŋ/, *n.* **1.** a toxic condition caused by the consumption of ptomaines. **2.** (formerly) food poisoning.

**ptosis** /ˈtoʊsəs/, *n.* a dropping of the upper eyelid. [NL, from Gk: a falling] – **ptotic** /ˈtoʊtɪk/, *adj.*

**P trap** /ˈpi træp/, *n.* a trap[1] (def. 5) shaped like a P.

**pts,** **1.** payments. **2.** points. **3.** ports.

**Pty,** Proprietary.

**ptyalin** /ˈtaɪələn/, *n.* an enzyme in the saliva of man and

i = peat ɪ = pit ɛ = pet æ = pat a = part ɒ = pot ʌ = putt ɔ = port ʊ = put u = pool ɜ = pert ə = apart aɪ = buy eɪ = bay ɔɪ = boy aʊ = how oʊ = hoe ɪə = here ɛə = hair ʊə = tour g = give θ = thin ð = then ʃ = show ʒ = measure tʃ = choke dʒ = joke ŋ = sing j = you ɒ̃ = Fr. bon

certain of the lower animals, possessing the property of converting starch into dextrin and maltose; salivary amylase. [Gk *ptýalon* spittle, saliva + -IN[2]]

**ptyalism** /ˈtaɪəlɪzəm/, *n.* excessive secretion of saliva. [Gk *ptyalismós* expectoration]

**p-type** /ˈpi-taɪp/, *adj.* pertaining to a semiconductor material dosed with electron-absorbing impurities to create conduction properties.

**pub** /pʌb/, *n. Colloq.* a hotel. [short for PUBLIC HOUSE]

**pub crawl** /ˈ– krɔl/, *n. Colloq.* drinking at a series of hotels in succession either alone or in company with others.

**puberty** /ˈpjubəti/, *n.* sexual maturity; the earliest age at which a person is capable of procreating offspring. [ME *puberte,* from L *pūbertas*]

**pubes** /ˈpjubiz/, *n., pl.* **-bes** /-biz/. **1.** the lower part of the abdomen, esp. the region between the right and left iliac regions. **2.** the hair appearing on the lower part of the abdomen at puberty. [L: pubic hair, groin]

**pubescent** /pjuˈbɛsənt/, *adj.* **1.** arriving or arrived at puberty. **2.** *Bot., Zool.* covered with down or fine short hair. [L *pūbescens,* ppr., reaching puberty, becoming hairy or downy] – **pubescence,** *n.*

**pubic** /ˈpjubɪk/, *adj.* pertaining to the pubes or pubis.

**pubis** /ˈpjubəs/, *n., pl.* **-bes** /-biz/, **-bises** /-bəsiz/. that part of either innominate bone which, with the corresponding part of the other, forms the front of the pelvis. [short for NL *os pūbis* bone of the pubes]

**public** /ˈpʌblɪk/, *adj.* **1.** of, pertaining to, or affecting the people as a whole or the community, state, or nation: *public affairs.* **2.** done, made, acting, etc., for the people or community as a whole: *a public prosecutor.* **3.** open to all the people: *a public meeting.* **4.** pertaining to or engaged in the affairs or service of the community or nation: *a public official.* **5.** maintained at the public expense, under public control, and open to the public generally: *a public library.* **6.** open to the view or knowledge of all; existing, done, etc., in public: *the fact became public.* **7.** having relations with or being known to the public generally: *a public character.* **8.** **go public, a.** (of a proprietary limited company) to sell part or all of its capital to the public at large. **b.** (of a company) to seek listing on the stock exchange. *–n.* **9.** the people constituting a community, state, or nation. **10.** a particular section of the people: *the novel-reading public.* **11.** public view or access: *in public.* [L *pūblicus;* replacing ME *publique,* from F (fem.)]

**public accountant** /– əˈkaʊntənt/, *n.* an accountant in commerce, in private practice, or in the public service who is a member of the Australian Society of Accountants.

**public-address system** /pʌblɪk-əˈdrɛs sɪstəm/, *n.* an electronic system consisting of microphone, amplifier, and a loudspeaker, or a number of each of these units, which serves to amplify sound, as for use in a public hall, for speech or music.

**publican** /ˈpʌblɪkən/, *n.* **1.** the owner or manager of a hotel. **2.** (in Roman times) a contractor for public revenues; a tax collector, generally execrated but especially so by Jews if he was Jewish and working for Rome: *publicans and sinners.* [L *pūblicānus*]

**publication** /pʌbləˈkeɪʃən/, *n.* **1.** the publishing of a book, periodical, map, piece of music, engraving, or the like. **2.** the act of publishing. **3.** the state or fact of being published. **4.** that which is published, as a book or the like. [ME, from L *pūblicātio*]

**public bar** /pʌblɪk ˈba/, *n.* (in a hotel) the bar which is least comfortably furnished and where drinks are cheaper than at other bars. Cf. **lounge, saloon bar.**

**public bed** /– ˈbɛd/, *n. Obs.* a hospital bed in a public ward.

**public bill** /ˈ– bɪl/, *n.* a parliamentary bill which relates to matters of public policy and usu. has general application over the entire nation.

**public company** /ˈ– kʌmpəni/, *n.* →**limited company.**

**public convenience** /– kənˈviniəns/, *n.* a room, building, etc., having toilets, washbasins, etc., for public use.

**public domain** /– dəˈmeɪn/, *n.* **1.** the status of a writing in which no copyright subsists. **2.** the status of an invention which has not been patented or where the patent has expired.

**public enemy** /– ˈɛnəmi/, *n.* **1.** a person who is a danger or menace to the public, usu. as shown by his criminal record. **2.** a nation or government at war with one's own.

**public figure** /– ˈfɪgə/, *n.* a person, as a politician, community leader, etc., who is generally known and usu. respected and admired.

**public holiday** /– ˈhɒlədeɪ/, *n.* an official holiday for members of the public generally throughout Australia, or throughout the whole of a particular State.

**public hospital** /– ˈhɒspɪtl/, *n.* a hospital owned and run by the government.

**public house** /ˈ– haʊs/, *n.* a hotel.

**publicise** /ˈpʌbləsaɪz/, *v.t.,* **-cised, -cising.** to give publicity to; bring to public notice; advertise: *they publicised the meeting as best they could.* Also, **publicize.**

**publicist** /ˈpʌbləsəst/, *n.* **1.** one who is expert in or writes on current public or political affairs. **2.** an expert in public or international law. **3.** a press agent or public relations officer.

**publicity** /pʌbˈlɪsəti/, *n.* **1.** the state of being public, or open to general observation or knowledge. **2.** public notice as the result of advertising or other special measures. **3.** the state of being brought to public notice by announcements (apart from advertisements), by mention in the mass media, or by any other means serving to effect the purpose. **4.** the measures, process, or business of securing public notice. **5.** advertisement matter, as leaflets, films, etc., intended to attract public notice.

**public lending right,** *n.* the right under which an author and publisher may receive payments on their books available in public libraries.

**public liability insurance,** *n.* insurance which protects the policyholder against risks involving liability to the public for legal damages occasioned by negligence.

**publicly** /ˈpʌblɪkli/, *adv.* **1.** in a public or open manner. **2.** by the public. **3.** in the name of the community. **4.** by public action or consent.

**public opinion** /pʌblɪk əˈpɪnjən/, *n.* an opinion held by a wide section of a community: *public opinion was against disarmament.*

**public opinion poll,** *n.* a poll by sampling to predict election results or to estimate public attitudes on issues.

**public patient** /pʌblɪk ˈpeɪʃənt/, *n.* a patient in a public ward.

**public prosecutor** /– ˈprɒsəkjutə/, *n.* an officer of the state who is required to prosecute in certain important legal cases and who is also appointed to defend criminal actions.

**public relations** /– rəˈleɪʃənz/, *n.* **1.** the practice of promoting goodwill among the public for a company, government body, individual or the like; the practice of working to present a favourable image. **2.** the techniques used.

**public school** /ˈ– skul/, *n.* **1.** →**state school.** **2.** (in some States) →**private school.** **3.** *Brit.* a private school of the type on which Australian private schools were modelled.

**public servant** /– ˈsɜvənt/, *n.* a member of the public service.

**public service** /– ˈsɜvəs/, *n.* the structure of departments and personnel responsible for the administration of government policy and legislation.

**public-spirited** /pʌblɪk-ˈspɪrətəd/, *adj.* having or showing an unselfish desire for the public good: *a public-spirited citizen.*

**public telephone** /pʌblɪk ˈtɛləfoʊn/, *n.* a telephone, usu. in a telephone box or booth, which is available to the public, each caller paying for his call by inserting the appropriate number of coins in the phone.

**public trustee** /– trʌsˈti/, *n.* a government-appointed official who acts as executor or trustee if required, thus ensuring continuity of service.

**public utility** /– juˈtɪləti/, *n.* an organisation performing an essential public service, as supplying gas, electricity or transport, and operated or regulated either by a company, the state, or local government.

**public ward** /ˈ– wɔd/, *n.* (formerly) a hospital ward, usu. containing a large number of beds, for which low fees, or no fees at all, are charged.

**public works** /– ˈwɜks/, *n.* constructions as roads, dams, post offices, etc., out of government funds for public use.

**publish** /ˈpʌblɪʃ/, *v.t.* **1.** to issue, or cause to be issued, in copies made by printing or other processes, for sale or distribution to the public, as a book, periodical, map, piece of music, engraving, or the like. **2.** to issue to the public the works of (an author). **3.** to announce formally or officially; proclaim; promulgate. **4.** to make publicly or generally known. **5.** *Law.* (in the law of defamation) to communicate (the defamatory statement in some form) to some person or persons other than the person defamed. *–v.i.* **6.** to issue a periodical or the like, esp. regularly: *they publish on Fridays.* **7.** to have one's writing published by a particular publishing house: *with whom does he publish?* [ME, from F *publ(ier)* + -ISH[2]] – **publishable,** *adj.*

**publisher** /ˈpʌblɪʃə/, *n.* one whose business is the publishing of books, periodicals, engravings, or the like.

**publishing** /ˈpʌblɪʃɪŋ/, *n.* the business of a publisher.

**publishment** /ˈpʌblɪʃmənt/, *n.* →**publication.**

**pub lunch** /ˈpʌb lʌntʃ/, *n.* →**counter lunch.**

**pub TAB** /ˈpʌb tæb/, *n.* an unofficial and illegal service provided by a publican in which he lays bets through his TAB telephone account on behalf of the drinkers in his hotel.

**puccoon** /pəˈkun/, *n.* **1.** any of certain plants which yield a red dye, as the bloodroot and certain herbs of the genus *Lithospermum.* **2.** the dye itself. [Algonquian]

**puce** /pjus/, *adj.* **1.** of a dark or purplish brown. *–n.* **2.** dark or purplish brown. [F: lit., flea, from L *pūlex*]

**puck**[1] /pʌk/, *n.* a malicious or mischievous demon or spirit; a goblin. [ME *pouke,* OE *pūca,* c. Icel. *pūki* a mischievous demon]

**puck**[2] /pʌk/, *n.* a flat rubber disc used in place of a ball in ice hockey. [var. of POKE[1]]

**pucka** /ˈpʌkə/, *n.* →**pukka.**

**pucker** /ˈpʌkə/, *v.t., v.i.* **1.** to draw or gather into wrinkles or irregular folds. *–n.* **2.** a wrinkle; an irregular fold. **3.** a puckered part, as of cloth tightly or crookedly sewn. [apparently a frequentative form connected with POKE[2] (bag). Cf. PURSE, *v.*]

**puckeroo** /ˈpʌkəru/, *N.Z. n.* →**pakaru.** Also, **pukaru.**

**puckery** /ˈpʌkəri/, *adj.* **1.** puckered. **2.** puckering. **3.** tending to pucker.

**puckish** /ˈpʌkɪʃ/, *adj.* (*also cap.*) mischievous; impish. – **puckishly,** *adv.*

**pud** /pʊd/, *n. Colloq.* pudding. Also, **pudden.**

**pudding** /ˈpʊdɪŋ/, *n.* **1.** a sweet or savoury dish made in many forms and of various ingredients, as flour (or rice, tapioca, or the like), milk, and eggs, with fruit, meat, or other ingredients. **2.** a course in a meal following the main or meat course; dessert; sweet. **3.** a skin filled with seasoned minced meat, oatmeal, blood, etc., and cooked; a kind of sausage. **4.** anything resembling a pudding (def. 1), as in texture, etc. **5.** *Colloq.* a small, fat person. **6.** *Colloq.* a stupid person. **7. in the pudding club,** pregnant. [ME *puddyng, poding;* orig. uncert. Cf. LG *puddewurst* black pudding]

**pudding face** /ˈ– feɪs/, *n. Colloq.* a round, fat, smooth face. – **pudding-faced,** *adj.*

**pudding fender** /ˈ– fɛndə/, *n.* a spherical or cylindrical canvas bag covered with coir matting, filled with small pieces of cork or other soft material, used as a fender (def. 4) on the side of a boat.

**pudding head** /ˈ– hɛd/, *n. Colloq.* a stupid person. – **pudding-headed,** *adj.*

**pudding stone** /ˈ– stoʊn/, *n.* →**conglomerate.**

**puddle** /ˈpʌdl/, *n., v., -***dled, -dling.** *–n.* **1.** a small pool of water, esp. dirty water, as in a road after rain. **2.** a small pool of any liquid. **3.** clay, or a similar material, which has been mixed with water and tempered, used as a watertight canal lining, etc. **4.** *Rowing.* the swirl of water left by the blade of an oar or all the oars, after a stroke. *–v.t.* **5.** to mark or fill with puddles. **6.** to wet with dirty water, etc. **7.** to make (water) muddy or dirty. **8.** to muddle or confuse. **9.** to make (clay, etc.) into puddle. **10.** to cover with pasty clay or puddle. **11.** *Mining.* to work together water and earth rich in clay so as to separate out any gold, opal, etc. **12.** to subject (molten iron) to the process of puddling. **13.** *Hort.* to dip (the roots of a tree, shrub, etc.) into a mixture of loam and water to retard drying out during transplanting. [ME *puddel, podel,* apparently from OE *pudd* ditch] – **puddler,** *n.* – **puddly,** *adj.*

**puddling** /ˈpʌdlɪŋ/, *n.* **1.** the act of one who puddles. **2.** the conversion of pig-iron into wrought iron by heating and stirring the molten metal in a reverberatory furnace, with an oxidising agent. **3.** the act or method of making puddle of clay or a similar material. **4.** →**puddle** (def. 3).

**puddling machine** /ˈ– məʃin/, *n.* a machine, usu. operated by horse, steam, or other power, used to puddle earth containing ores, gemstones, etc.

**puddling tank** /ˈ– tæŋk/, *n.* (in mining) a dam at which earth is puddled.

**puddling tub** /ˈ– tʌb/, *n.* (in mining) the vessel in which earth is puddled. Also, **puddling box.**

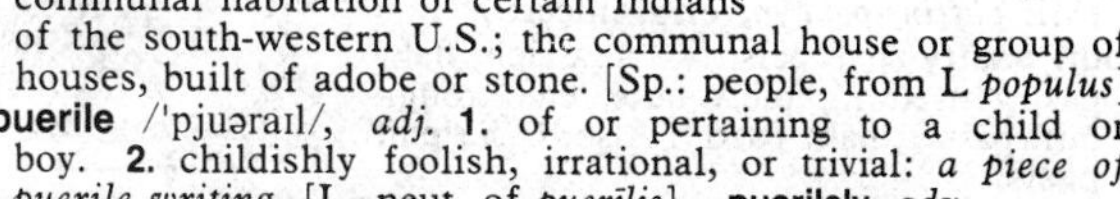
puddling tub

**pudency** /ˈpjudnsi/, *n.* shamefacedness; modesty. [LL *pudentia*]

**pudendum** /pjuˈdɛndəm/, *n., pl.* **-da** /-də/. (*also pl.*) the external genital organs, esp. those of a woman; the vulva. [L: that of which one ought to be ashamed]

**pudgy** /ˈpʌdʒi/, *adj.,* **pudgier, pudgiest.** →**podgy.** [orig. obscure] – **pudgily,** *adv.* – **pudginess,** *n.*

**pueblo** /ˈpwɛbloʊ/, *n., pl.* **-los.** *U.S.* a communal habitation of certain Indians of the south-western U.S.; the communal house or group of houses, built of adobe or stone. [Sp.: people, from L *populus*]

**puerile** /ˈpjuəraɪl/, *adj.* **1.** of or pertaining to a child or boy. **2.** childishly foolish, irrational, or trivial: *a piece of puerile writing.* [L, neut. of *puerīlis*] – **puerilely,** *adv.*

**puerilism** /ˈpjuərəlɪzəm/, *n.* childishness (the stage following infantilism).

**puerility** /pjuəˈrɪləti/, *n., pl.* **-ties. 1.** the quality of being puerile; childish foolishness or triviality. **2.** something puerile; a puerile act, idea, remark, etc.: *an inexcusable puerility.*

**puerperal** /pjuˈɜpərəl/, *adj.* **1.** of or pertaining to a woman in childbirth. **2.** pertaining to or consequent on childbirth. [NL *puerperālis,* from L *puerperus* bringing forth children]

**puerperal fever** /– ˈfivə/, *n.* an infection occurring during the puerperium; childbed fever.

**puerperium** /pjuəˈpɪəriəm/, *n.* the period following childbirth during which the organs of reproduction are returning to normal, usu. lasting 6 weeks. [L]

**puff** /pʌf/, *n.* **1.** a short, quick blast, as of wind or breath. **2.** an abrupt emission of air, vapour, etc. **3.** a single inhalation and exhalation, as of a cigarette. **4.** the sound of an abrupt emission of air, etc. **5.** a small quantity of vapour, smoke, etc., emitted at one blast. **6.** an inflated or distended part of a thing; a swelling; a protuberance. **7.** a commendation, esp. an exaggerated one, of a book, an actor's performance, etc. **8.** inflated or exaggerated praise, esp. as uttered or written from interested motives. **9.** →**powder puff. 10.** a form of light pastry with a filling of cream, jam, or the like. **11.** a portion of material gathered and held down at the edges but left full in the middle, as in a dress, etc. **12.** a cylindrical roll of hair. **13.** *Vet. Sci.* a disease of animals caused by transferring from a temperate to a tropical climate and associated with excessive loss of chloride from persistent sweating. *–v.i.* **14.** to blow with short, quick blasts, as the wind. **15.** to be emitted in a puff. **16.** to emit a puff or puffs; to breathe quick and hard, as after violent exertion. **17.** to go with puffing or panting. **18.** to emit puffs or whiffs of vapour or smoke. **19.** to move with such puffs. **20.** to take puffs at a cigar, etc. **21.** to become inflated or distended (usu. fol. by *up*). **22.** (of an auctioneer's accomplice) to make artificial bids at an auction in order to inflate the price of an object. *–v.t.* **23.** to send forth (air, vapour, etc.) in short quick blasts. **24.** to drive or impel by puffing, or with a short quick blast. **25.** to extinguish with a puff; blow out (fol. by *out*): *to puff out a light.* **26.** to smoke (a cigar, etc.). **27.** to inflate or distend, esp. with air. **28.** to inflate with pride, etc. **29.** to praise in exaggerated language. **30.** to advertise with exaggerated commendation. **31.** to apply (powder) with a powder puff. **32.** to arrange in puffs, as the hair. **33.** to artificially inflate the price of (an object being auctioned), as by having an accomplice in the audience who makes false bids. [ME, OE *pyff;* of imitative orig.]

**puff adder** /'– ædə/, *n.* a large, venomous African snake, *Bitis arietans,* which puffs up its body when irritated.

**puffball** /'pʌfbɔl/, *n.* any of various basidiomycetous fungi, esp. genus *Lycoperdon* and allied genera, characterised by a ball-like fruit body which emits a cloud of spores when broken.

**puffed** /pʌft/, *adj.* **1.** distended or inflated. **2.** *Colloq.* out of breath.

**puffed-up** /'pʌft-ʌp/, *adj. Colloq.* self-important.

**puffer** /'pʌfə/, *n.* **1.** one who or that which puffs. **2.** any of various fishes of the family Tetraodontidae, capable of inflating the body with water or air until it resembles a globe, with the spines in the skin erected. **3.** an auctioneer's accomplice who makes false bids in order to inflate prices artificially. **4.** (*in children's speech*) a steam locomotive.

**puffery** /'pʌfəri/, *n., pl.* **-eries.** **1.** act of praising unduly. **2.** exaggerated commendation.

**puffin** /'pʌfən/, *n.* any of various seabirds (genera *Fratercula* and *Lunda*) of the auk family, with a curious bill, as *F. arctica,* the common species, which abounds on the coasts of the northern Atlantic, nesting in holes in the ground. [ME *poffin, pophyn;* orig. uncert.]

common puffin

**puff pastry** /pʌf 'peɪstri/, *n.* a rich, flaky pastry used for pies, tarts, etc.; rough puff pastry; flaky pastry. Also, *U.S.,* **puff paste.**

**puffy** /'pʌfi/, *adj.,* **puffier, puffiest.** **1.** gusty. **2.** short-winded. **3.** inflated or distended. **4.** fat. **5.** conceited. **6.** bombastic. – **puffiness,** *n.*

**puftaloon** /pʌftə'lun/, *n.* a scone made from plain damper dough fried in fat. Also, **puftalooner.**

**pug**[1] /pʌg/, *n.* **1.** Also, **pugdog.** one of a breed of dogs, having a short, smooth coat of silver, fawn, or black, a deeply wrinkled face and a tightly curled tail. **2.** →**pug nose.** [orig. unknown]

pug[1]

**pug**[2] /pʌg/, *v.t.,* **pugged, pugging.** **1.** to knead (clay, etc.) with water to make it plastic, as in brick-making. **2.** to stop or fill in with clay or the like. **3.** to pack or cover with mortar, etc., to deaden sound. **4.** to mix with water, forming a paste. **5.** *Agric.* to compact soil by trampling it down, usu. during very wet conditions. [orig. uncert.] – **puggy,** *adj.*

**pug**[3] /pʌg/, *n. Colloq.* →**pugilist.** [short for PUGILIST]

**pug**[4] /pʌg/, *n., v.,* **pugged, pugging.** –*n.* **1.** a footprint, as of an animal. –*v.t.* **2.** to track (game, etc.) by following footprints. [Hind. *pag*]

**puggaree** /'pʌgəri/, *n.* **1.** a light turban worn by natives in India. **2.** a scarf of silk or cotton wound round a hat or helmet and falling down behind, as a protection against the sun. Also, **pugaree, puggree, pugree.** [Hind. *pagrī* turban]

**puggim** /'pʌgɪm/, *adj. Colloq.* →**fucking.** [Aboriginal pidgin for *fucking*]

**pugilism** /'pjudʒəlɪzəm/, *n.* the art or practice of fighting with the fists; boxing. [L *pugil* boxer (akin to *pugnus* fist, and *pugnāre* fight) + -ISM]

**pugilist** /'pjudʒələst/, *n.* one who fights with the fists; a boxer, usu. a professional. – **pugilistic** /pjudʒə'lɪstɪk/, *adj.* – **pugilistically** /pjudʒə'lɪstɪkli/, *adv.*

**pugnacious** /pʌg'neɪʃəs/, *adj.* given to fighting; quarrelsome; aggressive. [*pugnaci(ty)* (from L *pugnācitas* combativeness) + -OUS] – **pugnaciously,** *adv.* – **pugnacity** /pʌg'næsəti/, **pugnaciousness,** *n.*

**pug nose** /pʌg 'noʊz/, *n.* a short nose turning abruptly up at the tip. – **pug-nosed,** *adj.*

**puha** /'puha/, *n.* a vegetable, esp. the sow-thistle of the genus *Sonchus* used by the Maori as a green vegetable; Maori cabbage. Also, **puwha.** [Maori]

**puisne** /'pwini, 'pjuni/, *adj. Law.* younger; inferior in rank; junior, as in appointment. [archaic form of PUNY, from OF *puis* after (from var. of L *posteā*) + *ne* born, pp. of *naistre* come into existence (from L *nascere*)]

**puissance** /'pwisəns, 'pjusəns/, *n. Archaic.* power, might, or force. [ME, from OF, from *puissant* PUISSANT]

**puissant** /'pwisənt, 'pjusənt/, *adj. Archaic.* powerful; mighty; potent. [ME, from OF, from var. of L *potens,* ppr., being able, having power] – **puissantly,** *adv.*

**pukatea** /pʊkə'tiə/, *n.* an aromatic timber tree, *Laurelia novae-zelandiae,* found in lowland and gully forests of New Zealand. [Maori]

**puke** /pjuk/, *v.i., v.t.,* **puked, puking,** *n.* →**vomit.** [orig. uncert.]

**pukeko** /'pʊkəkoʊ/, *n. N.Z.* the swamphen, *Porphyrio melanotus.* Also, **pukako** /'pukækə/. [Maori]

**pukka** /'pʌkə/, *adj. Colloq.* of colonial, esp. Anglo-Indian, origin, behaviour, etc. Also, **pucka.** [Anglo-Indian: reliable, genuine, from Hind. *pakkā* cooked, ripe, mature]

**puku**[1] /'puku/, *n.* a medium-sized foxy-red antelope, *Cobus vardoni* or *Adenota vardonii,* of southern Africa, now rare except in Zambia. [Tonga (a language of Zambia) *mpuku*]

**puku**[2] /'pʊku/, *n. N.Z.* a belly. [Maori]

**pukunui** /pʊku'nui/, *n. N.Z. Colloq.* a big belly. [Maori]

**pulao** /'pulaʊ/, *n.* →**pilaf.**

**pulchritude** /'pʌlkrətjud, 'pʊl-/, *n.* beauty; comeliness. [ME, from L *pulchritūdo*]

**pulchritudinous** /pʌlkrə'tjudənəs, pʊl-/, *adj.* beautiful.

**pule** /pjul/, *v.i.,* **puled, puling.** to cry in a thin voice, as a child; whimper; whine. [? imitative]

**puling** /'pjulɪŋ/, *adj.* whining: *a puling child.* – **pulingly,** *adv.*

**pull** /pʊl/, *v.t.* **1.** to draw or haul towards oneself or itself, in a particular direction, or into a particular position: *to pull a sledge up a hill.* **2.** to draw or tug at with force: *to pull a person's hair.* **3.** to draw, rend, or tear (apart, to pieces, etc.). **4.** to draw or pluck away from a place of growth, attachment, etc.: *to pull a tooth.* **5.** to strip of feathers, hair, etc., as a bird, a hide, etc. **6.** *Colloq.* to draw out for use, as a knife or a pistol. **7.** *Colloq.* to put or carry through (something attempted): *to pull a fast one.* **8.** to cause to form, as a grimace: *to pull a face.* **9.** *Golf.* to play (the ball) with a curve to the left (or, if a left-handed player, to the right). **10.** *Print.* to take (an impression or proof) from type, etc. **11.** to propel by rowing, as a boat. **12.** to be provided with, or rowed with (a certain number of oars), as a boat: *a racing shell pulls eight oars.* **13.** to strain, as a ligament. **14.** *Racing.* to hold in or check (a horse), esp. so as to keep it from winning. **15.** *Boxing.* to deliver (a punch) without full force; check or restrain. **16.** *Cricket.* to hit (a ball pitched on the wicket or on the off side) to the on side. **17.** *Colloq.* to have sexual intercourse with. –*v.i.* **18.** to exert a drawing, tugging, or hauling force (oft. fol. by *at*). **19.** to inhale through a pipe, cigarette, etc. **20.** to become or come as specified, by pulling: *a rope pulls apart.* **21.** to row. **22.** to proceed by rowing. **23.** *Cricket, Golf.* to pull the ball. **24.** *Colloq.* to have sexual intercourse. –*v.* **25.** Some special verb phrases are:

**pull a fast one** or **swiftie,** *Colloq.* to deceive; to play a sly trick.

**pull ahead,** to move towards the front, or begin to win in a race or other contest.

**pull apart,** **1.** to rend in pieces. **2.** to analyse critically in detail.

**pull down,** **1.** to lower; draw downwards: *to pull down the blinds.* **2.** to demolish. **3.** to reduce or make lower: *to pull down prices in a sale.*

**pull in,** **1.** (of a vehicle, driver, etc.) to move to the side of the road in order to stop. **2.** to arrive at a destination, stopping place, etc.: *the train pulled in to Central.* **3.** *Colloq.* to arrest (a person). **4.** to earn (as a wage or salary).

**pull off,** *Colloq.* to succeed in achieving or performing something.

**pull oneself off,** *Colloq.* to masturbate.

**pull one's finger out,** *Colloq.* to attack (a job, task, etc.) with energy after a period of inertia or laziness.

**pull one's head in,** *Colloq.* to withdraw; to mind one's own business.

**pull one's punches,** 1. *Boxing.* to deliver punches without full force. 2. to act with more show than effect, as by failing to follow through an initial move.

**pull oneself together,** to recover one's self-control.

**pull one's weight,** to make a full and fair contribution to a task or undertaking, as in rowing or any other activity.

**pull out,** 1. to leave; depart: *a train pulling out of a station.* 2. (of a vehicle, driver, etc.) to move out of a lane or stream of traffic, as in preparing to overtake. 3. *Colloq.* to withdraw, as from an agreement or enterprise. 4. (of an aircraft) to return to level flight after a dive.

**pull over,** (of a vehicle, driver, etc.) to move towards the side of the road, or in some other direction as specified.

**pull rank** or **the braid,** to invoke senior privileges or powers.

**pull round,** *Colloq.* to recover, as from an illness, period of adversity, or the like.

**pull someone's leg,** *Colloq.* to tease a person.

**pull strings,** *Colloq.* to seek the advancement of oneself or another by using social contacts and other means not directly connected with one's ability or suitability.

**pull the rug from under someone's feet,** *Colloq.* to place someone in a position of disadvantage.

**pull the wool over someone's eyes,** *Colloq.* to deceive; hoodwink.

**pull through,** *Colloq.* 1. to recover, as from an illness, period of adversity, or the like. 2. to make one's way through, as by a pull or effort.

**pull together,** to cooperate, as in a team.

**pull to pieces,** 1. to rend in pieces; destroy completely. 2. to analyse critically in detail.

**pull up,** 1. to stop. 2. to cause to stop. 3. to correct or rebuke. 4. to improve; bring to a higher or required standard. 5. to uproot or pull out of the ground. 6. *Colloq.* to gain ground, as a horse in a race.

*–n.* 26. the act of pulling or drawing. 27. force used in pulling; pulling power. 28. a drawing of a liquid into the mouth: *he took a long pull at his glass of beer.* 29. an inhalation of tobacco, as from a pipe or cigarette. 30. a part or thing to be pulled, as a handle or the like. 31. an instrument or device for pulling something. 32. a spell at rowing. 33. a stroke of an oar. 34. a pulling of the ball in cricket or golf. 35. *Colloq.* an advantage over another or others. 36. *Colloq.* influence, as with persons able to grant favours. 37. *Colloq.* the ability to attract or draw audiences, followers, etc.: *an actor with box office pull.* [ME *pulle(n),* OE *pullian* pull, pluck. Cf. MLG *pūlen* strip off husks, pick, Icel. *pūla* work hard] – **puller,** *n.*

**pullback** /ˈpʊlbæk/, *n.* a device for pulling a moving part back to its original position.

**pull date** /ˈpʊl deɪt/, *n.* the date after which a consumer commodity should no longer be sold.

**pullet** /ˈpʊlət/, *n.* a young hen, less than one year old. [ME *poullet,* from OF *poulette* young hen, diminutive of *poule* hen, from LL *pulla* young animal, chicken]

**pulley** /ˈpʊli/, *n., pl.* **-leys.** 1. a wheel with a grooved rim for carrying a line, turning in a frame or block and serving to change the direction of or transmit power, as in pulling at one end of the line to raise a weight at the other end. 2. a combination of such wheels in a block, or of such wheels or blocks in a tackle, to increase the power applied. 3. a wheel driven by or driving a belt or the like, as in the transmission of power. [ME, from OF *poulie,* from a derivative of Gk *pólos* axle]

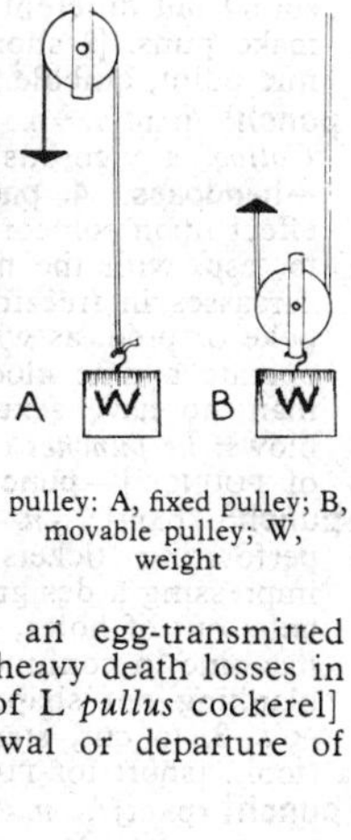

pulley: A, fixed pulley; B, movable pulley; W, weight

**pullie** /ˈpʊli/, *n. Colloq.* pullover.

**pull-in** /ˈpʊl-ɪn/, *n.* 1. a place by the roadside where vehicles may pull in and stop. 2. *Brit.* a roadside cafe.

**pullorum disease** /pʊˈlɔrəm dəziz/, *n.* an egg-transmitted bacterial disease, frequently a cause of heavy death losses in very young poultry. [*pullorum,* gen. pl. of L *pullus* cockerel]

**pullout** /ˈpʊlaʊt/, *n.* a military withdrawal or departure of troops.

**pullover** /ˈpʊloʊvə/, *n.* →**jumper**[2].

**pull-through** /ˈpʊl-θru/, *n.* a cord used to pull a piece of cloth or a brush through the barrel of a rifle or other firearm in order to clean or oil it.

**pullulate** /ˈpʌljəleɪt/, *v.i.,* **-lated, -lating.** 1. to come forth in growth; sprout. 2. to send forth sprouts, buds, etc. 3. to spring up abundantly. 4. to breed; multiply; teem. 5. to be produced as offspring. [L *pullulātus,* pp., sprouted] – **pullulation** /pʌljəˈleɪʃən/, *n.*

**pulmonary** /ˈpʌlmənri/, *adj.* 1. of or pertaining to the lungs. 2. of the nature of a lung; lunglike. 3. affecting the lungs. 4. having lungs or lunglike organs. 5. pertaining to or affected with disease of the lungs. [L *pulmōnārius,* from *pulmo* lung, akin to Gk *pleúmōn,* later *pneúmōn* lung]

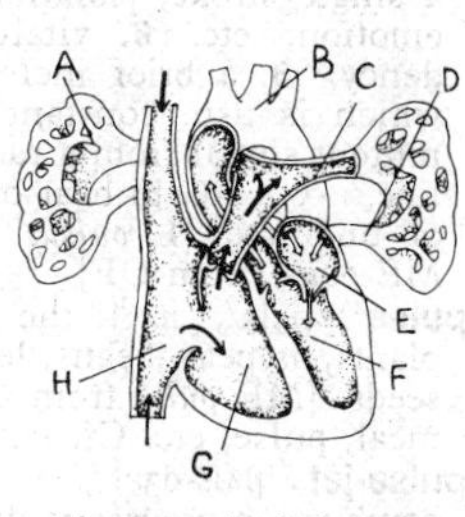

pulmonary circulation: A, pulmonary vessels of lung; B, aorta; C, pulmonary artery; D, pulmonary vein; E, left atrium; F, left ventricle; G, right ventricle; H, right atrium

**pulmonary artery** /– ˈatəri/, *n.* an artery conveying (venous) blood from the right ventricle of the heart to the lungs.

**pulmonary vein** /– ˈveɪn/, *n.* a vein conveying (arterial) blood from the lungs to the left auricle of the heart.

**pulmonate** /ˈpʌlmənət/, *adj.* 1. having lungs or lunglike organs. 2. belonging to the Pulmonata, an order or group of gastropod molluscs usu. breathing by means of a lunglike sac, and including most of the terrestrial snails and the slugs and certain aquatic snails. *–n.* 3. a pulmonate gastropod. [NL *pulmōnātus,* from L *pulmo* lung]

**pulmonic** /pʌlˈmɒnɪk/, *adj.* 1. →**pulmonary.** 2. →**pneumonic.** [F *pulmonique,* from L *pulmo* lung]

**pulp** /pʌlp/, *n.* 1. the succulent part of a fruit. 2. the pith of the stem of a plant. 3. a soft or fleshy part of an animal body. 4. the inner substance of the tooth containing arteries, veins, and lymphatic and nerve tissue which communicate with their respective vascular and lymph and nerve systems of the body. 5. any soft, moist, slightly cohering mass, as that into which linen, wood, etc., are converted in the making of paper. 6. anything worthless, as a magazine containing sensational and lurid stories, articles, etc.; trash. 7. *Mining.* **a.** ore pulverised and mixed with water. **b.** dry crushed ore. *–v.t.* 8. to reduce to pulp. 9. to remove the pulp from. *–v.i.* 10. to become reduced to pulp. [L *pulpa*]

**pulpit** /ˈpʊlpət/, *n.* 1. a platform or raised structure in a church, from which the priest delivers a sermon, etc. 2. **the pulpit, a.** the clergy collectively. **b.** the Christian ministry. 3. preaching. [ME, from ML *pulpitum,* from L: stage, platform]

**pulpiteer** /pʊlpəˈtɪə/, *n.* (*derog.*) a preacher by profession. Also, **pulpiter** /ˈpʊlpətə/.

**pulpwood** /ˈpʌlpwʊd/, *n.* spruce or other soft wood suitable for making paper.

**pulpy** /ˈpʌlpi/, *adj.,* **pulpier, pulpiest.** of the nature of or resembling pulp; fleshy; soft. – **pulpiness,** *n.*

**pulpy kidney** /– ˈkɪdni/, *n.* →**enterotoxaemia.**

**pulque** /ˈpʊlki/, *n.* a Mexican fermented milky drink made from the juice of the agave. [Mex. Sp.]

**pulsar** /ˈpʌlsa/, *n.* one of a number of sources of pulsed radio signals detected within the galaxy but outside the solar system. [*puls(ating st)ar*]

**pulsate** /pʌlˈseɪt/, *v.i.,* **-sated, -sating.** 1. to expand and contract rhythmically, as the heart; beat; throb. 2. to vibrate; quiver. [L *pulsātus,* pp., pushed, struck, beaten. See PULSE[1]]

**pulsatile** /ˈpʌlsətaɪl/, *adj.* pulsating; throbbing.

**pulsatilla** /pʌlsəˈtɪlə/, *n.* a small group of perennial herbs belonging to the genus *Pulsatilla,* differing from the related genus *Anemone* in having persistent, feathery styles, as *P. vulgaris,* the pasque flower.

**pulsation** /pʌlˈseɪʃən/, *n.* 1. the act of pulsating; beating or throbbing. 2. a beat or throb, as of the pulse. 3. vibration or undulation. 4. a single vibration.

**pulsative** /ˈpʌlsətɪv/, *adj.* pulsating.

**pulsator** /pʌl'seɪtə/, *n.* **1.** something that pulsates, beats, or strikes. **2.** →**vacuum pump.** [L: striker]

**pulsatory** /pʌl'seɪtəri/, *adj.* pulsating; throbbing.

**pulse**[1] /pʌls/, *n., v.,* **pulsed, pulsing.** *–n.* **1.** the regular throbbing of the arteries caused by the successive contractions of the heart, esp. as felt in an artery at the wrist. **2.** a single beat or throb of the arteries or the heart. **3.** the rhythmic recurrence of strokes, vibrations, or undulations. **4.** a single stroke, vibration, or undulation. **5.** a throb of life, emotion, etc. **6.** vitality. **7.** feeling, sentiment, or tendency. **8.** a brief increase in the magnitude of a quantity which is usu. constant as current or voltage. **9.** an intermittent signal from a radio transmitter, radar apparatus or the like. *–v.i.* **10.** to beat or throb; pulsate. **11.** to beat, vibrate, or undulate. [L *pulsus* a pushing, beating, pulse; replacing ME *pous,* from OF]

**pulse**[2] /pʌls/, *n.* **1.** the edible seeds of certain leguminous plants, as peas, beans, lentils, etc. **2.** a plant producing such seeds. [ME *puls,* from OF *po(u)ls,* from L *puls* thick pap of meal, pulse, etc. Cf. POULTICE]

**pulse-jet** /'pʌls-dʒɛt/, *n.* a type of ramjet engine in which the combustion process is discontinuous and is arranged to occur at intervals between which the pressure in the combustion chamber is allowed to build up, as used in the flying bombs of World War II. Also, **pulse jet.**

**pulse-time modulation** /ˌpʌls-taɪm mɒdʒə'leɪʃən/, *n.* radio transmission in which the carrier is modulated to produce a series of pulses timed to transmit amplitude and pitch of the signal.

**pulse-train** /'pʌls-treɪn/, *n.* a finite sequence of regular electrical pulses.

**pulse-wave** /'pʌls-weɪv/, *n.* the wave of blood flowing along an artery as the result of a heartbeat.

**pulsimeter** /pʌl'sɪmətə/, *n.* an instrument for measuring the strength or quickness of the pulse. [*pulsi-* (combining form representing PULSE[1]) + -METER[1]]

**pulsometer** /pʌl'sɒmətə/, *n.* **1.** →**pulsimeter. 2.** →**vacuum pump.** [*pulso-* (combining form representing PULSE[1]) + -METER[1]]

**pulverable** /'pʌlvərəbəl/, *adj.* pulverisable.

**pulverise** /'pʌlvəraɪz/, *v.,* **-rised, -rising.** *–v.t.* **1.** to reduce to dust or powder, as by pounding, grinding, etc. **2.** to demolish. **3.** *Colloq.* to defeat overwhelmingly, as a fighter. *–v.i.* **4.** to become reduced to dust. Also, **pulverize.** [ME, from LL *pulverizāre,* from L *pulvis* dust] – **pulverisable,** *adj.* – **pulverisation** /pʌlvəraɪ'zeɪʃən/, *n.* – **pulveriser,** *n.*

**pulverulent** /pʌl'vɛrələnt/, *adj.* **1.** consisting of dust or fine powder. **2.** crumbling to dust. **3.** covered with dust or powder. [L *pulverulentus* dusty]

**pulvillus** /pʌl'vɪləs/, *n., pl.* **-villi** /-'vɪlaɪ/. a cushion-like pad or process on an insect's foot. [L, diminutive of *pulvīnus* cushion]

**pulvinar** /pʌl'vaɪnə/, *adj., n., pl.* **-nars, -naria** /pʌlvə'nɛəriə/. *–adj.* **1.** cushion-like. **2.** of or pertaining to a pulvinus. *–n.* **3.** *Rom. Antiq.* **a.** a cushioned couch, as one kept in readiness for a visitation by a god. **b.** a cushioned seat at a circus. **c.** any cushioned seat or sofa. [L: couch]

puma

**pulvinate** /'pʌlvəneɪt/, *adj.* **1.** cushion-shaped. **2.** having a pulvinus. Also, **pulvinated.** [L *pulvīnātus* made into or like a cushion]

**pulvinus** /pʌl'vaɪnəs/, *n., pl.* **-ni** /-naɪ/. a cushion-like swelling at the base of a leaf or leaflet, at the point of junction with the axis. [L: cushion]

**puma** /'pjumə/, *n.* **1.** a large tawny feline, *Felis concolor,* of North and South America; cougar; mountain lion. **2.** its fur. [Sp., from Quechua]

**pumice** /'pʌməs/, *n., v.,* **-iced, -icing.** *–n.* **1.** Also, **pumice stone.** a porous or spongy form of volcanic glass, used, esp. when powdered, as an abrasive, etc. *–v.t.* **2.** to rub, smooth, clean, etc., with pumice. [ME *pomis,* from OF, from L

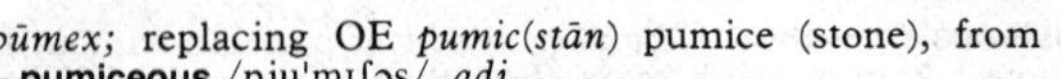
*pūmex;* replacing OE *pumic(stān)* pumice (stone), from L] – **pumiceous** /pju'mɪʃəs/, *adj.*

**pummel** /'pʌməl/, *v.,* **-melled, -melling** or (*U.S.*) **-meled, -meling,** *n.* *–v.t.* Also, *Chiefly U.S.,* **pommel. 1.** to beat or thrash with rapid blows, as with the fists or, originally, a pommel. *–n.* **2.** →**pommel.**

**pump**[1] /pʌmp/, *n.* **1.** an apparatus or machine for raising, driving, exhausting, or compressing fluids, as by means of a piston, plunger, or rotating vanes. *–v.t.* **2.** to raise, drive, etc., with a pump. **3.** to free from water, etc., by means of a pump (sometimes fol. by *out*). **4.** to inflate by pumping (oft. fol. by *up*): *to pump up a tyre.* **5.** to operate by action like that on a pump handle. **6.** to supply with air, as an organ, by means of a pumplike device. **7.** to drive, force, etc., as if from a pump: *they pumped ten bullets into him.* **8.** to seek to elicit information from, as by artful questioning. **9.** to elicit (information) by questioning. **10.** to shake (someone's hand) vigorously. *–v.i.* **11.** to work a pump; raise or move water, etc., with a pump. **12.** to operate as a pump does. **13.** to gush out in spurts, as if driven by a pump: *blood pumping from a wound.* **14.** to move up and down like a pump-handle. **15.** to exert oneself in a manner likened to pumping. **16.** to seek to elicit information from a person. [ME *pumpe,* c. G *Pumpe;* orig. uncert.] – **pumpable,** *adj.* – **pumper,** *n.*

**pump**[2] /pʌmp/, *n.* **1.** a low, light, black, patent-leather shoe worn by men for ballroom dancing, with formal dress, etc. **2.** a low, slipper-like shoe worn by women, as for dancing. [orig. uncert.]

**pump action** /'– ækʃən/, *n.* the sliding action of certain rifles and shotguns which reloads the weapon without the need to break the breech.

**pumpernickel** /'pʌmpənɪkəl/, *n.* a coarse, slightly sour bread made with wholemeal rye. [G]

**pump gun** /'pʌmp gʌn/, *n.* a repeating shotgun, operated by sliding a handle backwards and forwards along the magazine.

**pumpkin** /'pʌmpkən/, *n.* **1.** the large edible fruits of species of coarse plants, esp. *Cucurbita maxima* in Europe and Australia, and *C. pepo* and its varieties in the U.S. **2.** the plants. [alteration of *pumpion,* from F *pompon* a melon, from L *pepo,* from Gk *pépōn*]

**pumpkin-seed** /'pʌmpkən-sid/, *n.* **1.** the seed of the pumpkin. **2.** a freshwater sunfish, *Lepomis gibbosus,* of eastern North America.

**pumpman** /'pʌmpmən/, *n., pl.* **-men.** a man who operates a power-driven pump.

**pump-out septic** /pʌmp-aʊt 'sɛptɪk/, *n.* a septic tank designed to be pumped out at regular intervals. Also, **pump-out.**

**pumproom** /'pʌmprum/, *n.* a room in a spa where medicinal water is dispensed.

**pump worm** /'pʌmp wɜm/, *n.* →**sandworm.**

**pun** /pʌn/, *n., v.,* **punned, punning.** *–n.* **1.** the humorous use of a word in such a manner as to bring out different meanings or applications, or of words alike or nearly alike in sound but different in meaning; a play on words. *–v.i.* **2.** to make puns. [? short for obs. *pundigrion,* from It. *puntiglio,* fine point, quibble. See PUNCTILIO]

**punch**[1] /pʌntʃ/, *n.* **1.** a thrusting blow, esp. with the fist. **2.** *Colloq.* a vigorous, telling effect or force. **3.** *Aus. Rules.* →**handpass. 4. pack a punch,** *Colloq.* to have an extreme effect upon someone. *–v.t.* **5.** to give a sharp thrust or blow to, esp. with the fist. **6.** *N.Z.* to punch or strip pelts from carcasses in freezing works. **7.** *Obs.* to drive (cattle). **8.** to poke or prod, as with a stick. **9. punch the bundy,** *Colloq.* to operate a time clock. **10. punch one through,** *Colloq.* (of a man) to have sexual intercourse with. *–v.i.* **11.** to deliver blows: *he punches cleanly.* **12.** *Aus. Rules.* →**handpass.** [? var. of POUNCE[1]] – **puncher,** *n.*

**punch**[2] /pʌntʃ/, *n.* **1.** a tool or apparatus for piercing, or perforating tickets, leather, etc., or stamping materials, impressing a design, forcing nails beneath a surface, driving bolts out of holes, etc. **2.** the solid tool used in a punching machine in conjunction with a corresponding hollow die for blanking out shaped pieces of sheet metal; the upper die. *–v.t.* **3.** to cut, stamp, pierce, form, or drive with a punch (tool). [short for PUNCHEON[2] (def. 3)]

**punch**[3] /pʌntʃ/, *n.* **1.** a beverage consisting of wine or spirits mixed with water, fruit juice, etc., and flavoured with sugar, lemon, spices, etc. **2.** a beverage of two or more fruit juices, sugar and water, often carbonated. [? short for PUNCHEON[1]; if so, a metonymic use]

**Punch** /pʌntʃ/, *n.* **1.** the chief character in the puppet show called 'Punch and Judy', a grotesque, hook-nosed, hunchbacked figure who strangles his child, beats his wife (Judy) to death, etc. **2. pleased as Punch,** delighted; highly pleased. [short for PUNCHINELLO]

**punchball** /'pʌntʃbɔl/, *n.* →**punching bag.**

**punchbowl** /'pʌntʃboʊl/, *n.* **1.** a bowl in which punch is mixed, and from which it is served by means of a ladle. **2.** →**devil's punchbowl.**

**punch card** /'pʌntʃ kad/, *n.* a standard-sized card through which a pattern of holes is punched to represent information in a form which can be read by a computer or business machine. Also, **punched card.**

**punch-drunk** /'pʌntʃ-drʌŋk/, *adj.* **1.** having cerebral concussion so that one's movements resemble those of a drunken person, a condition sometimes found in boxers. **2.** *Colloq.* dull-witted; stupid or dazed.

**punched paper tape,** *n.* See **paper tape.**

**puncheon**[1] /'pʌntʃən/, *n.* a large cask of varying capacity, but usu. about 500 litres. [F, ultimately identical with PUNCHEON[2]]

**puncheon**[2] /'pʌntʃən/, *n.* **1.** a slab of timber, or a piece of a split log, with the face roughly dressed, used for flooring, etc. **2.** a short upright timber in a framing. **3.** (in goldsmith work) **a.** any of various pointed instruments; a punch. **b.** a stamping tool. [ME *punchon,* from OF *po(i)nchon,* from L *punctus,* pp., pricked, pierced. Cf. PUNGENT]

**punch graft** /'pʌntʃ graft/, *n.* a surgical skin graft using a very small, punched-out piece of skin.

**Punchinello** /pʌntʃə'nɛloʊ/, *n., pl.* **-los, -loes.** any grotesque or absurd person or thing similar to Punchinello, the chief character in a puppet show of Italian origin. [It. *Pulcinella,* probably orig. diminutive of *pulcino* chicken, from L *pullus* young animal]

**punching bag** /'pʌntʃɪŋ bæg/, *n.* **1.** Also, **punching ball.** an inflated or stuffed ball or bag, usu. suspended, punched with the fists as exercise or training. **2.** *U.S.* a game resembling baseball in which a rubber ball is thrown in the air and punched rather than hit with a bat.

**punching machine** /'– məʃin/, *n.* a power-driven machine used to cut, draw, or otherwise shape material, esp. metal sheets, with dies, under pressure or by heavy blows. Also, **punching press;** *U.S.,* **punch press.**

**punch line** /'pʌntʃ laɪn/, *n.* the culminating sentence, line, phrase, or the like of a joke, esp. that on which the whole joke depends.

**punch-up** /'pʌntʃ-ʌp/, *n. Colloq.* a fight.

**punchy** /'pʌntʃi/, *adj.,* **-chier, -chiest.** *Colloq.* **1.** punch-drunk. **2.** forceful; vigorously effective.

**punctate** /'pʌŋkteɪt/, *adj.* marked with points or dots; having minute spots or depressions. Also, **punctated** /pʌŋk'teɪtəd/. [NL *punctātus,* from L *punctum* point]

**punctation** /pʌŋk'teɪʃən/, *n.* **1.** punctate condition or marking. **2.** one of the marks or depressions.

**punctilio** /pʌŋk'tɪlioʊ/, *n., pl.* **-tilios. 1.** a fine point, particular, or detail, as of conduct, ceremony, or procedure. **2.** strictness or exactness in the observance of forms. [It. *puntiglio,* from Sp. *puntillo,* diminutive of *punto* point, from L *punctum*]

**punctilious** /pʌŋk'tɪliəs/, *adj.* attentive to punctilios; strict or exact in the observance of forms in conduct or actions. – **punctiliously,** *adv.* – **punctiliousness,** *n.*

**punctual** /'pʌŋktʃuəl/, *adj.* **1.** strictly observant of an appointed or regular time; not late. **2.** prompt, as an action; made at an appointed or regular time: *punctual payment.* **3.** of or pertaining to a point: *punctual coordinates* (the coordinates of a point). **4.** *Obs.* punctilious. [ME, from ML *punctuālis,* from L *punctus* a pricking, a point] – **punctually,** *adv.* – **punctualness,** *n.*

**punctuality** /pʌŋktʃu'æləti/, *n.* **1.** the quality or state of being punctual. **2.** strict observance in keeping engagements, etc.; promptness.

**punctuate** /'pʌŋktʃueɪt/, *v.,* **-ated, -ating.** *–v.t.* **1.** to mark or divide with punctuation marks, as a sentence, etc., in order to make the meaning clear. **2.** to interrupt at intervals, as a speech by cheers. **3.** to give point or emphasis to. *–v.i.* **4.** to insert or use marks of punctuation. [ML *punctuātus,* pp., pointed, from L *punctus* a point] – **punctuator,** *n.*

**punctuation** /pʌŋktʃu'eɪʃən/, *n.* **1.** the practice, art, or system of inserting marks or points in writing or printing in order to make the meaning clear; the punctuating of written or printed matter with commas, semicolons, colons, full stops, etc. (**punctuation marks**). **2.** the act of punctuating.

**puncture** /'pʌŋktʃə/, *n., v.,* **-tured, -turing.** *–n.* **1.** the act of pricking or perforating as with a pointed instrument or object. **2.** a mark or hole so made. **3.** *Zool.* a small point-like depression. *–v.t.* **4.** to prick, pierce, or perforate: *to puncture the skin with a pin.* **5.** to make (a hole, etc.) by pricking or perforating. **6.** to make a puncture in: *to puncture a tyre.* *–v.i.* **7.** to admit of being punctured. [L *punctūra*] – **puncturable,** *adj.*

**pundit** /'pʌndət/, *n.* **1.** *Colloq.* one who sets up as an expert. **2.** →**pandit.** [see PANDIT]

**punga** /'pʌŋə/, *n.* →**ponga.**

**pungent** /'pʌndʒənt/, *adj.* **1.** sharply affecting the organs of taste, as if by a penetrating power; biting; acrid. **2.** acutely distressing to the feelings or mind; poignant. **3.** caustic, biting, or sharply expressive, as speech, etc. **4.** mentally stimulating or appealing. **5.** *Biol.* piercing or sharp-pointed. [L *pungens,* ppr., pricking. Cf. POIGNANT, POINT, PUNCHEON[2], etc.] – **pungency,** *n.* – **pungently,** *adv.*

**punish** /'pʌnɪʃ/, *v.t.* **1.** to subject to a penalty, or to pain, loss, confinement, death, etc., for some offence, transgression, or fault: *to punish a criminal.* **2.** to inflict a penalty for (an offence, fault, etc.): *to punish theft.* **3.** to handle severely or roughly, as in a fight. **4.** to put to painful exertion, as a horse in racing. **5.** *Colloq.* to make a heavy inroad on (a supply, etc.). *–v.i.* **6.** to inflict punishment. [ME *punische(n),* from OF *puniss-,* stem of *punir,* from L *pūnīre*] – **punisher,** *n.*

**punishable** /'pʌnɪʃəbəl/, *adj.* liable to or deserving punishment. – **punishability** /ˌpʌnɪʃə'bɪləti/, *n.*

**punishing** /'pʌnɪʃɪŋ/, *adj.* disagreeable; unpleasant; boring: *I found the long, hot trip to Yass very punishing.*

**punishment** /'pʌnɪʃmənt/, *n.* **1.** the act of punishing. **2.** the fact of being punished, as for an offence or fault. **3.** that which is inflicted as a penalty in punishing. **4.** severe handling or treatment.

**punitive** /'pjunətɪv/, *adj.* serving for, concerned with, or inflicting punishment: *punitive laws.* Also, **punitory** /'pjunətəri, -tri/.

**punk**[1] /pʌŋk/, *n. Chiefly U.S.* **1.** a preparation that will smoulder, used in sticks, as for lighting fireworks. **2.** decayed wood used as tinder. [orig. uncert.]

**punk**[2] /pʌŋk/, *Colloq. –n.* **1.** something or someone worthless, degraded, or bad. **2.** a petty criminal. **3.** a catamite. **4.** *Archaic.* a prostitute. *–adj.* **5.** worthless, degraded, or of poor quality. [orig. unknown]

**punk**[3] /pʌŋk/, *adj.* **1.** of or pertaining to punk rock and an associated style of dress and behaviour. *–n.* **2.** →**punk rock.**

**punkah** /'pʌŋkə/, *n.* (in India and elsewhere) a fan, esp. a large, swinging, screenlike fan hung from the ceiling and kept in motion by a servant or by machinery. Also, **punka.** [Hind. *pankhā* a fan, from Skt *pakshaka*]

**punkah wallah** /'– wɒlə/, *n.* a servant employed to operate a punkah.

**punk rock** /pʌŋk 'rɒk/, *n.* a type of rock music usu. with a fast, energetic beat reminiscent of early rock, which is associated with rebelliousness, great aggressiveness, violence and sexuality.

**punnet** /'pʌnət/, *n.* a small, shallow basket, as for strawberries. [diminutive of Brit. d. *pun* POUND[2]]

**punster** /'pʌnstə/, *n.* one given to making puns.

**punt**[1] /pʌnt/, *n.* **1.** *Football.* a kick given to a dropped ball before it touches the ground. **2.** *Soccer.* a light, rising shot. **3. have a punt at,** to make an attempt at. *–v.t.* **4.** *Football.* to kick (a dropped ball) before it touches the ground. **5.** *Soccer.* to kick the ball so that it rises. [Brit. d. *bunt, punt* push with force] – **punter,** *n.*

**punt**[2] /pʌnt/, *n.* **1.** a shallow, flat-bottomed, square-ended boat, usu. propelled by thrusting with a pole against the bottom of the river, etc. **2.** a ferry for carrying vehicles across rivers, etc. *–v.t.* **3.** to propel (a punt or other boat) by thrusting with a pole against the bottom. **4.** to convey a person in, or as in, a punt. *–v.i.* **5.** to propel, or travel in, a punt. [OE *punt,* from L *ponto* punt, PONTOON[1]] – **punter,** *n.*

**punt**[3] /pʌnt/, *v.i.* **1.** to lay a stake against the bank, as at faro. **2.** to gamble; wager; lay bets. *–n.* **3.** one who lays such stake. **4.** a wager; bet: *to take a punt.* [F *ponter,* from *ponte* punter, from Sp. *punto* point, from L *punctum*]

**punt**[4] /pʌnt/, *n.* the hollow found in the bottom of some wine bottles, particularly, champagne bottles. [It. *ponte* bridge]

**punter** /'pʌntə/, *n.* one who lays bets on contestants, esp. horses or dogs, in races. [PUNT[3] + -ER[1]]

**punty** /'pʌnti/, *n., pl.* **-ties.** an iron rod used in glass-making for handling the hot glass. Also, **pontil.** [It. *ponte* bridge]

**puny** /'pjuni/, *adj.,* **-nier, -niest. 1.** of less than normal size and strength; weakly. **2.** petty; insignificant. **3.** *Obs.* puisne. [var. of PUISNE] – **punily,** *adv.* – **puniness,** *n.*

**P.U.O.,** *Med.* pyrexia of unknown origin.

**pup** /pʌp/, *n., v.,* **pupped, pupping.** *–n.* **1.** a young dog, under one year; a puppy. **2.** a young seal. **3.** a conceited or empty-headed boy or young man. **4. be sold a pup,** *Colloq.* to be the victim of some deception. *–v.i.* **5.** to bring forth pups. [apocopated var. of PUPPY]

**pupa** /'pjupə/, *n., pl.* **-pae** /-pi/. an insect in the non-feeding, usu. immobile, transformation stage between the larva and the imago. [NL, from L: girl, doll, puppet. Cf. PUPIL[1], PUPPET] – **pupal,** *adj.*

**puparium** /pju'pɛəriəm/, *n.* a pupal case formed of the cuticula of a preceding larval instar. [NL, from L *pupa* PUPA + *-ārium;* modelled on HERBARIUM]

**pupate** /pju'peɪt/, *v.i.,* **-pated, -pating.** to become a pupa. – **pupation** /pju'peɪʃən/, *n.*

**pupil**[1] /'pjupəl/, *n.* **1.** one who is under an instructor or teacher; a student. **2.** *Civil Law.* a person under a specified age (in Roman law, under puberty), orphaned or emancipated, and under the care of a guardian. [ME *pupille,* from OF, from L *pūpillus* (masc.) *pūpilla* (fem.) orphan, ward, diminutives of *pūpus* boy, *pūpa* girl]

**pupil**[2] /'pjupəl/, *n.* the expanding and contracting opening in the iris of the eye, through which light passes to the retina. [L *pūpilla,* lit., little doll. See PUPA]

**pupillage** /'pjupəlɪdʒ/, *n.* the state or period of being a pupil. Also, *Chiefly U.S.,* **pupilage.**

**pupillary**[1] /'pjupələri/, *adj.* pertaining to a pupil or student. Also, **pupilary.** [L *pūpillāris*]

**pupillary**[2] /'pjupələri/, *adj.* pertaining to the pupil of the eye. Also, **pupilary.** [L *pūpilla* PUPIL[2] + -ARY[1]]

**pupiparous** /pju'pɪpərəs/, *adj.* bringing forth young which are already developed to the pupal phase, as in certain parasitic insects. [NL *pūpiparus,* from *pūpi-* PUPA + *-parus* -PAROUS]

**puppet** /'pʌpət/, *n.* **1.** a doll. **2.** an artificial figure with jointed limbs, moved by wires, etc., as on a miniature stage; a marionette. **3.** a person or group whose actions are prompted and controlled by another or others. *–adj.* **4.** controlled by external forces: *a puppet government.* [earlier *poppet,* ME *popet,* apparently from MLG *poppe* doll, of Rom. orig.; cf. LL *puppa*]

**puppeteer** /pʌpə'tɪə/, *n.* one who manipulates puppets. Also, **puppet-master.**

**puppetry** /'pʌpətri/, *n., pl.* **-ries. 1.** the art of making puppets perform. **2.** the action of puppets. **3.** a mummery; mere show. **4.** puppets collectively.

**puppet state** /'pʌpət steɪt/, *n.* a state whose government is more or less controlled by a more powerful state.

**puppy** /'pʌpi/, *n., pl.* **-pies. 1.** a young dog. **2.** the young of certain other animals, as the shark. **3.** a presuming, conceited, or empty-headed young man. [F *poupée* doll, from LL *puppa.* See PUPPET]

**puppy fat** /'– fæt/, *n.* plumpness during adolescence.

**puppy love** /'– lʌv/, *n.* temporary infatuation of a young boy or girl for another person of the opposite sex.

**pur** /pɜ/, *v.i., v.t.,* **purred, purring,** *n.* →**purr.**

**purblind** /'pɜblaɪnd/, *adj.* **1.** nearly blind; partially blind; dim-sighted. **2.** dull in discernment or understanding. **3.** *Obs.* totally blind. [ME *pur blind* completely blind. See PURE, formerly used as adv., entirely] – **purblindly,** *adv.* – **purblindness,** *n.*

**purchasable** /'pɜtʃəsəbəl/, *adj.* **1.** capable of being bought. **2.** that may be won over by bribery; venal. – **purchasability** /pɜtʃəsə'bɪləti/, *n.*

**purchase** /'pɜtʃəs/, *v.,* **-chased, -chasing,** *n.* *–v.t.* **1.** to acquire by the payment of money or its equivalent; buy. **2.** to acquire by effort, sacrifice, flattery, etc. **3.** to win over by a bribe. **4.** (of things) to be sufficient to buy. **5.** *Law.* to acquire, as an estate in lands, otherwise than by inheritance. **6.** to haul, draw, or raise, esp. by the aid of a mechanical power. **7.** to get a leverage on. **8.** *Obs.* to procure, acquire, or obtain. *–n.* **9.** acquisition by the payment of money or its equivalent; buying, or a single act of buying. **10.** something which is purchased or bought. **11.** a (good, bad, etc.) bargain. **12.** *Law.* the acquisition of an estate in lands, etc., otherwise than by inheritance. **13.** acquisition by means of effort, sacrifice, etc. **14.** a means of increasing power or influence. **15.** the annual return or rent from land. **16.** a tackle, lever, or other device to increase power in raising or moving a heavy object. **17.** an effective hold or position for applying leverage. **18.** a firm grasp or foothold. **19.** *Obs.* booty. [ME, from AF *purchacer* seek to obtain, procure, from *pur-* PRO-[1] + *chacer* CHASE[1]] – **purchaser,** *n.*

**purchase tax** /'– tæks/, *n. Brit.* →**sales tax.**

**purdah** /'pɜdə/, *n.* (in India, Pakistan, and elsewhere). **1.** a screen hiding women from the sight of men or strangers. **2.** the system of such seclusion. [Urdu: curtain, from Pers. *pardah*]

**pure** /'pjuə, pjʊə/, *adj.,* **purer, purest. 1.** free from extraneous matter, or from mixture with anything of a different, inferior, or contaminating kind: *pure gold.* **2.** unmodified by an admixture; simple or homogeneous: *a pure colour.* **3.** of unmixed descent. **4.** free from foreign or inappropriate elements: *pure Attic Greek.* **5.** (of language) idiomatic, and unmixed with foreign elements. **6.** (of literary style) straightforward; unaffected. **7.** abstract or theoretical (opposed to *applied*): *pure science.* **8.** without discordant quality; clear and true. **9.** *Phonet.* monophthongal. **10.** unqualified; absolute; utter; sheer: *pure ignorance.* **11.** being that and nothing else; mere: *a pure accident.* **12.** clean, spotless, or unsullied: *pure hands.* **13.** clear; free from blemish: *a pure complexion.* **14.** untainted with evil; innocent. **15.** inexperienced or uninterested in sexual matters; virginal. **16.** ceremonially clean. **17.** free or without guilt; guiltless. **18.** independent of sense or experience: *pure knowledge.* **19.** *Biol., Genetics.* **a.** homozygous. **b.** containing but one characteristic for a trait. [ME *pur,* from OF, from L *pūrus* clean, unmixed, plain, pure] – **pureness,** *n.*

**purebred** /'pjuəbrɛd/, *adj.* **1.** denoting an animal the ancestors of which are all of the same standard breed over many generations. *–n.* **2.** such an animal.

**pure culture** /pjuə 'kʌltʃə/, *n.* a nutrient medium and a single bacterial or other species cultivated on it.

**puree** /'pjureɪ/, *n., v.,* **-reed, -reeing.** *–n.* **1.** a cooked and sieved vegetable or fruit used for soups or other foods. *–v.t.* **2.** to make a puree of. Also, **purée.** [F, from *purer* strain, from *pur* PURE]

**pure line** /pjuə 'laɪn/, *n.* a uniform strain of organisms which is relatively pure genetically because of continued inbreeding coupled with selection.

**purely** /'pjuəli/, *adv.* **1.** in a pure manner; without admixture. **2.** merely; entirely: *purely accidental.* **3.** exclusively. **4.** cleanly; innocently; chastely.

**pure Merino** /pjuə mə'rinoʊ/, *n. Colloq.* **1.** (formerly) a free settler of substance who opposed the social advancement of the emancipists. **2.** a member of an old and established Australian family of free, not convict, descent.

**pure tone** /– 'toʊn/, *n.* a sound consisting of a wave of a single frequency.

**purfle** /'pɜfəl/, *v.,* **-fled, -fling.** *n.* *–v.t.* **1.** to finish with an ornamental border. *–n.* **2.** Also, **purfling.** an ornamental border, as one of inlaid wood around the edge of a violin table. [ME *purfile(n),* from OF *porfiler,* from *por-* PRO-[1] +

*filer* spin, from *fil* thread, from L *filum*]

**purgation** /pɜ'geɪʃən/, *n.* the act of purging.

**purgative** /'pɜgətɪv/, *adj.* **1.** purging; cleansing; specifically, causing evacuation of the bowels. *–n.* **2.** a purgative medicine or agent. [ME, from LL *purgātīvus,* pp., cleansed] – **purgatively,** *adv.*

**purgatorial** /pɜgə'tɔriəl/, *adj.* **1.** removing sin; purifying. **2.** of, pertaining to, or like purgatory.

**purgatory** /'pɜgətri/, *n., pl.* **-ries,** *adj.* *–n.* **1.** (*also cap.*) (in the belief of Roman Catholics and others) a condition or place in which the souls of those dying penitent are purified from venial sins, or undergo the temporal punishment which, after the guilt of mortal sin has been remitted, still remains to be endured by the sinner. **2.** any condition, situation, or place of temporary suffering, expiation, or the like. *–adj.* **3.** serving to purge, cleanse, or purify; expiatory. [ME *purgatorye,* from LL *purgātōrius,* adj., from *purgāre* cleanse]

**purge** /pɜdʒ/, *v.,* **purged, purging,** *n.* *–v.t.* **1.** to cleanse; rid of whatever is impure or undesirable; purify. **2.** to rid or clear (fol. by *of*) or free (fol. by *from*): *to purge a party of undesirable members.* **3.** to eliminate, as by killing, an unwanted person, as a political opponent or potential opponent. **4.** to clear (a person, etc.) of imputed guilt. **5.** to clear away or wipe out legally (an offence, accusation, etc.) by atonement or other suitable action. **6.** to remove by cleansing or purifying (oft. fol. by *away, off,* or *out*). **7.** to clear or empty (the bowels, etc.) by causing evacuation. **8.** to cause evacuation of the bowels of (a person). *–v.i.* **9.** to become cleansed or purified. **10.** to undergo or cause purging of the bowels. *–n.* **11.** the act or process of purging. **12.** something that purges, as a purgative medicine or dose. **13.** the elimination from political activity, as by killing, of political opponents and others. **14.** the period when such an elimination takes place: *he disappeared in Stalin's great purge of 1936-38.* **15.** *N.Z. Colloq.* any alcoholic beverage. [ME, from OF *purgier,* from L *purgāre* cleanse] – **purger,** *n.*

**purificator** /'pjurəfəkeɪtə/, *n.* a cloth used at Holy Communion to wipe the chalice and paten, and also the celebrant's fingers and lips.

**purify** /'pjurəfaɪ/, *v.,* **-fied, -fying.** *–v.t.* **1.** to make pure; free from extraneous matter, or from anything that debases, pollutes, or contaminates: *to purify metals.* **2.** to free from foreign or objectionable elements: *to purify a language.* **3.** to free from whatever is evil or base. **4.** to clear or purge (fol. by *of* or *from*). **5.** to make ceremonially clean. *–v.i.* **6.** to become pure. [ME *puryfie(n),* from OF *purifier,* from L *pūrificāre*] – **purification** /pjurəfə'keɪʃən/, *n.* – **purificatory** /pjurəfə'keɪtəri/, *adj.* – **purifier,** *n.*

**purine** /'pjurin, -raɪn/, *n.* a white crystalline compound, $C_5H_4N_4$, regarded as the parent substance of a group of compounds including uric acid, xanthine, caffeine, etc. Also, **purin** /'pjurən/. [b. PURE and URINE, modelled on G *Purin*]

**purine base** /'– beɪs/, *n.* any of several compounds related to purine present in combined form in nucleic acids.

**puriri** /pu'riri/, *n.* a New Zealand forest tree, *Vitex lucens,* with white trunk, glossy green leaves, dull red flowers and crimson berries, often cultivated as an ornamental and yielding hard, durable timber. [Maori]

**purism** /'pjurɪzəm/, *n.* **1.** scrupulous or excessive observance of or insistence on purity in language, style, etc. **2.** an instance of this. **3.** a theory and practice in art, originated in 1918, which reduces all natural appearances to a geometric simplicity characteristic of machines. [PURE + -ISM] – **purist,** *n.* – **puristic** /pju'rɪstɪk/, *adj.*

**puritan** /'pjurətən/, *n.* **1.** one who aspires to great purity or strictness of life in moral and religious matters. *–adj.* **2.** of or pertaining to puritans. [from a class of Protestants who arose in the 16th century within the Church of England, demanding further reforms in doctrine and worship, and greater strictness in religious discipline; LL *pūrit(ās)* purity + -AN]

**puritanical** /pjurə'tænɪkəl/, *adj.* **1.** having the character of a puritan; excessively strict, rigid, or austere. **2.** of, pertaining to, or characteristic of puritans. Also, **puritanic.** – **puritanically,** *adv.* – **puritanicalness,** *n.*

**puritanism** /'pjurətənɪzəm/, *n.* strictness in matters of conduct or religion; puritanical austerity.

**purity** /'pjurəti/, *n.* **1.** the condition or quality of being pure; freedom from extraneous matter or from anything that debases or contaminates: *the purity of drinking water.* **2.** freedom from any admixture or modifying addition. **3.** freedom from foreign or inappropriate elements; careful correctness: *purity of language.* **4.** (of colour) chroma; saturation; degree of freedom from white. **5.** cleanness or spotlessness, as of garments. **6.** ceremonial cleanness. **7.** freedom from evil or guilt; innocence; chastity. [LL *pūritas;* replacing ME *pur(e)te,* from OF]

**purl**[1] /pɜl/, *v.i.* **1.** to flow with curling or rippling motions, as a shallow stream does over stones. **2.** to flow with a murmuring sound. **3.** to pass in a manner or with a sound likened to this. *–n.* **4.** the action or sound of purling. **5.** a circle or curl made by the motion of water; a ripple; eddy. [cf. Norw. *purla* bubble up, gush]

**purl**[2] /pɜl/, *v.t., v.i.* **1.** to knit with inversion of the stitch. **2.** to finish with loops or a looped edging. *–n.* **3.** a stitch used in hand knitting to make a rib effect. **4.** one of a series of small loops along the edge of lace braid. **5.** thread made of twisted gold or silver wire. Also, **pearl.** [orig. uncert. Cf. obs. or d. *pirl* twist (threads, etc.) into a cord]

**purler** /'pɜlə/, *n.* **1.** a headlong or heavy fall or throw. **2.** anything or anyone of top quality. *–adj.* **3.** excellent; superior. [Brit. d. *purl* whirl round, turn head over heels + -ER[1]]

**purlieu** /'pɜlju/, *n.* **1.** a piece of land on the border of a forest. **2.** any bordering, neighbouring, or outlying region or district. **3.** (*pl.*) neighbourhood. **4.** a place where one may range at large; one's bounds. **5.** one's haunt or resort. [alteration (simulating F *lieu* place) of earlier *purlewe, purley, puraley* purlieu of a forest, from AF *purale(e)* a going through]

**purlin** /'pɜlən/, *n.* a timber or piece laid horizontally on the principal rafters of a roof to support the common rafters. Also, **purline.** [orig. uncert.]

**purloin** /pɜ'lɔɪn/, *v.t.* **1.** to take dishonestly or steal. *–v.i.* **2.** to commit theft. [ME *purloyne(n),* from AF *purloigner* put off, remove, from *pur-* PRO-[1] + *loin* far off (from L *longē*)] – **purloiner,** *n.*

**purple** /'pɜpəl/, *n., adj., v.,* **-pled, -pling.** *–n.* **1.** any colour having components of both red and blue, esp. a dark shade of such a colour. **2.** *Hist.* crimson. **3.** cloth or clothing of this hue, esp. as formerly worn distinctively by persons of imperial, royal, or other high rank: *born to the purple.* **4.** the rank or office of a cardinal, in allusion to his scarlet official dress. **5.** the office of a bishop. **6.** imperial or lofty rank or position. *–adj.* **7.** of the colour of purple. **8.** imperial or regal. **9.** brilliant or gorgeous. **10.** full of elaborate literary devices and pretentious effects: *a purple passage.* *–v.t.* **11.** to make purple. *–v.i.* **12.** to become purple. [ME *purpel,* OE (Northumbrian) *purpl(e),* var. of OE *purpur(e),* from L *purpura,* from Gk *porphýra* kind of shellfish yielding purple dye]

**purple-breasted finch** /ˌpɜpəl-brɛstəd 'fɪntʃ/, *n.* →**Gouldian finch.**

**purple heart** /pɜpəl 'hat/, *n.* **1.** a heart-shaped purple pill containing an addictive drug consisting of dexamphetamine and amylobarbitone. **2.** the drug. **3.** (*caps*) *U.S.* a medal awarded to anyone wounded by enemy action while in service.

**purple of Cassius,** *n.* a purple pigment consisting of a mixture of colloidal gold and stannic acid; used for making ruby glass and ceramic glazes. [named after A. *Cassius,* 17th-cent. German physician]

**purple patch** /'pɜpəl pætʃ/, *n.* →**patch** (def. 12).

**purple top** /'pɜpəl tɒp/, *n.* a perennial, *Verbena bonariensis,* native to South America, with narrow stems and clustered purplish flowers, and found in high rainfall areas; blue top.

**purplish** /'pɜplɪʃ/, *adj.* of a somewhat purple hue. Also, **purply.**

**purport** /pɜ'pɔt, 'pɜpɔt/, *v.;* /'pɜpɔt, -pət/, *n.* *–v.t.* **1.** to profess or claim: *a document purporting to be official.* **2.** to convey to the mind as the meaning or thing intended; express; imply. *–n.* **3.** tenor, import, or meaning. **4.** purpose or object. [late ME, from AF *purporter* convey, from *pur-* PRO-[1] + *porter* (from L *portāre*) carry]

**purpose** /'pɜpəs/, *n., v.,* **-posed, -posing.** *–n.* **1.** the object for which anything exists or is done, made, used, etc. **2.** an intended or desired result; end or aim. **3.** intention or determination. **4.** that which one puts before oneself as something to be done or accomplished. **5.** the subject in hand; the point at issue: *to the purpose.* **6.** practical result, effect, or advantage: *to good purpose.* **7. on purpose, a.** by design; intentionally. **b.** with the particular purpose specified. *–v.t.* **8.** to put before oneself as something to be done or accomplished; propose. **9.** to determine on the performance of; design; intend. **10.** to be resolved. [ME *purpos,* from OF, from *purposer,* var. of *proposer* PROPOSE] – **purposeless,** *adj.* – **purposelessly,** *adv.* – **purposelessness,** *n.*

**purposeful** /ˈpɜpəsfəl/, *adj.* **1.** having a purpose. **2.** determined; resolute. – **purposefully,** *adv.* – **purposefulness,** *n.*

**purposely** /ˈpɜpəsli/, *adv.* **1.** intentionally: *to do a thing purposely.* **2.** with the particular purpose specified; expressly.

**purposive** /ˈpɜpəsɪv/, *adj.* **1.** acting with, characterised by, or showing a purpose, intention, or design. **2.** adapted to a purpose or end. **3.** serving some purpose. **4.** characterised by purpose, determination, or resolution. **5.** of or of the nature of purpose. – **purposively,** *adv.* – **purposiveness,** *n.*

**purpresture** /pɜˈprɛstʃə/, *n. Brit.* anything done to the nuisance or hurt of the monarch's demesnes, or the highways, by enclosure or building. Also, **pourpresture.**

**purpura** /ˈpɜpjurə/, *n.* a disease characterised by purple or livid spots on the skin or mucous membrane, caused by the extravasation of blood. [NL, special use of L *purpura.* See PURPLE]

**purpure** /ˈpɜpjuə, -pjʊə/, *n., adj. Her.* purple. [OE, from L *purpura.* See PURPLE]

**purpurin** /pɜˈpjurən/, *n.* a reddish crystalline dye, $C_{14}H_8O_5$ (isomeric with flavopurpurin).

**purr** /pɜ/, *v.i.* **1.** to utter a low, continuous murmuring sound expressive of satisfaction, as a cat does. **2.** (of things) to make a sound suggestive of the purring of a cat. *–v.t.* **3.** to express by, or as if by, purring. *–n.* **4.** the act of purring. **5.** the sound of purring. Also, **pur.** [imitative]

**purse** /pɜs/, *n., v.,* **pursed, pursing.** *–n.* **1.** a small bag, pouch, or case for carrying money on the person. **2.** *Chiefly U.S.* a handbag. **3.** a purse with its contents. **4.** money, resources, or wealth. **5.** a sum of money collected as a present or the like. **6.** a sum of money offered as a prize. **7.** any baglike receptacle. **8.** the scrotum, esp. of an animal. *–v.t.* **9.** to contract into folds or wrinkles; pucker. **10.** *Rare.* to put into a purse. [ME and OE *purs,* b. *pusa* bag and *burs,* from LL *bursa* bag, from Gk *býrsa* hide, leather]

**purse-proud** /ˈpɜs-praʊd/, *adj.* proud of one's wealth.

**purser** /ˈpɜsə/, *n.* an officer, esp. on board a ship, charged with keeping accounts, etc.

**purse seine** /ˈpɜs seɪn/, *n. U.S.* a large seine, generally drawn by two boats, which can be closed into a baglike net around a school of fish.

**purse strings** /ˈ– strɪŋz/, *n.pl.* **1.** the strings by which a purse is closed. **2.** the power to spend or withhold money.

**purslane** /ˈpɜslən/, *n.* **1.** a widely distributed, yellow-flowered species of portulaca, *Portulaca oleracea,* used as a salad plant and potherb; pigweed. **2.** any other plant of the genus *Portulaca.* [ME *purcelan(e),* from OF *porcelaine,* apparently b. L *porcilāca* (for *portulāca* purslane) and It. *porcellana* porcelain]

**pursuance** /pəˈsjuəns/, *n.* the following or carrying out of some plan, course, injunction, or the like.

**pursuant** /pəˈsjuənt/, *adj.* **1.** proceeding conformably (fol. by *to*). **2.** pursuing. *–adv.* Also, **pursuantly. 3.** according (fol. by *to*): *to do something pursuant to an agreement.* **3.** in a manner conformable (fol. by *to*).

**pursue** /pəˈsju/, *v.,* **-sued, -suing.** *–v.t.* **1.** to follow with the view of overtaking, capturing, killing, etc.; chase. **2.** to follow close upon; go with; attend: *bad luck pursued him.* **3.** to strive to gain; seek to attain or accomplish (an end, object, purpose, etc.). **4.** to proceed in accordance with (a method, plan, etc.). **5.** to carry on (a course of action, train of thoughts, etc.). **6.** to prosecute (inquiries, studies, etc.). **7.** to practise (an occupation, pastime, etc.). **8.** to continue to discuss (a subject, topic, etc.). **9.** to follow (a path, etc.). **10.** to continue on (one's way, course, etc.); go on with or continue (a journey, etc.). *–v.i.* **11.** to follow in pursuit. **12.** to continue. [ME *pursue(n),* from AF *pursuer,* from L *prōsequī* follow, continue. Cf. PROSECUTE] – **pursuable,** *adj.* – **pursuer,** *n.*

**pursuit** /pəˈsjut/, *n.* **1.** the act of pursuing: *in pursuit of the fox.* **2.** the effort to secure; quest: *the pursuit of happiness.* **3.** any occupation, pastime, or the like, regularly or customarily pursued: *literary pursuits.* **4.** *Cycling.* a race in which competitors try to catch each other after starting from various points of the course or circuit. [ME *pursuit,* from AF *purseute,* from *pursuer* PURSUE]

**pursuivant** /ˈpɜsəvənt/, *n.* **1.** a heraldic officer of the lowest class, ranking below a herald. **2.** an official attendant on heralds. **3.** any attendant. [ME *purs(ev)aunt,* from OF *poursuivant,* properly ppr. of *poursuivre* PURSUE]

**pursy** /ˈpɜsi/, *adj.,* **-sier, -siest. 1.** short-winded, esp. from corpulence or fatness. **2.** corpulent or fat. [earlier *pursive,* ME *pursif,* from AF *porsif,* var. of OF *polsif,* from *polser* pant, heave. See PUSH] – **pursiness,** *n.*

**purtenance** /ˈpɜtənəns/, *n. Archaic.* the heart, liver, and lungs of an animal. [ME; aphetic var. of APPURTENANCE]

**purulence** /ˈpjurələns/, *n.* **1.** the condition of containing or forming pus. **2.** pus. Also, **purulency.**

**purulent** /ˈpjurələnt/, *adj.* **1.** full of, containing, forming, or discharging pus; suppurating: *a purulent sore.* **2.** attended with suppuration: *purulent appendicitis.* **3.** of the nature of or like pus: *purulent matter.* [L *pūrulentus*] – **purulently,** *adv.*

**purvey** /pəˈveɪ/, *v.t.* to provide, furnish, or supply (esp. food or provisions). [ME *porveie(n),* from AF *porveier,* from L *prōvidēre* foresee, provide for] – **purveyor,** *n.*

**purveyance** /pəˈveɪəns/, *n.* **1.** the act of purveying. **2.** that which is purveyed, as provisions.

**purview** /ˈpɜvju/, *n.* **1.** range of operation, activity, concern, etc. **2.** range of vision; view. **3.** that which is provided or enacted in a statute, as distinguished from the preamble. **4.** the full scope or compass of a statute or law, or of any document, statement, book, subject, etc. [ME *purveu,* from AF: provided, pp. of *porveier* PURVEY]

**pus** /pʌs/, *n.* a yellow-white, more or less viscid substance produced by suppuration and found in abscesses, sores, etc., consisting of a liquid plasma in which leucocytes, etc., are suspended. [L; akin to Gk *pýon* pus. See PYIN, FOUL] – **puslike,** *adj.*

**Puseyism** /ˈpjusiɪzəm/, *n.* (*usu. pejor.*) the principles or movement of a party of nineteenth-century religious reformers who sought to revive Catholic doctrine and observance in the Church of England. See **Tractarianism.** [from Dr. E.B. *Pusey,* 1800-82, professor of Hebrew and Canon of Christ Church at Oxford, England] – **Puseyite,** *n.*

**push** /pʊʃ/, *v.t.* **1.** to exert force upon or against (a thing) in order to move it away. **2.** to move (*away, off,* etc.) by exerting force thus; shove; thrust; drive. **3.** to make by thrusting obstacles aside: *to push one's way through the crowd.* **4.** to press or urge (a person, etc.) to some action or course. **5.** to press (an action, etc.) with energy and insistence. **6.** to carry (an action or thing) further, to a conclusion or extreme, too far, etc. **7.** to press the adoption, use, sale, etc., of. **8.** to peddle (narcotics). **9.** to press or bear hard upon (a person, etc.) as in dealings. **10.** *Colloq.* to place excessive or dangerous strain on: *you're pushing your luck.* *–v.i.* **11.** to exert a thrusting force upon something. **12.** to use steady force in moving a thing away; shove. **13.** to make one's way with effort or persistence, as against difficulty or opposition. **14.** to put forth vigorous or persistent efforts. *–v.* **15.** Some special verb phrases are:

**push it,** *Colloq.* **1.** to work harder than normal, as to meet a deadline. **2.** to be exorbitant in one's demands.

**push off, 1.** to move away from the shore, etc., as the result of a push. **2.** *Colloq.* to leave; go away.

**push on,** to continue; proceed.

**push shit uphill,** *Colloq.* to attempt the impossible.

**push up daisies,** *Colloq.* to be dead and buried.

*–n.* **16.** the act of pushing; a shove or thrust. **17.** a contrivance or part to be pushed in order to operate a mechanism. **18.** a vigorous onset or effort. **19.** a determined pushing forward or advance. **20.** the pressure of circumstances. **21.** an emergency. **22.** *Colloq.* persevering energy; enterprise. **23.** *Colloq.* a group or set of people who have a common interest or background. **24.** (formerly) a gang of

vicious city hooligans, as the Rocks push in Sydney. **25.** *Colloq.* influence; power. **26. the push,** *Colloq.* dismissal; rejection; the sack: *she gave him the push.* [ME *posshe(n),* from OF *poulser,* from L *pulsāre.* See PULSATE]

**pushball** /ˈpʊʃbɔl/, *n.* **1.** a game played with a large, heavy ball, usu. about two metres in diameter, which two sides of players endeavour to push towards opposite goals. **2.** the ball used in this game.

**pushbike** /ˈpʊʃbaɪk/, *n.* →**bicycle.**

**push-button** /ˈpʊʃ-bʌtn/, *n.* **1.** a device designed to close or open an electric circuit when a button or knob is depressed, and to return to a normal position when it is released. *–adj.* **2.** operated by, or as by, push-buttons.

**pushcart** /ˈpʊʃkat/, *n.* a light cart pushed by hand.

**pushchair** /ˈpʊʃtʃɛə/, *n.* →**stroller** (def. 3).

**pushed** /pʊʃt/, *v.* **1.** past participle of **push.** *–adj.* **2.** in difficulties with; lacking (fol. by *for*): *we're pushed for time.*

**pusher** /ˈpʊʃə/, *n.* **1.** one who or that which pushes. **2.** a small child's table implement for pushing food on to a spoon. **3.** *Brit.* →**stroller** (def. 3). **4.** an aggressively ambitious person. **5.** a pedlar of narcotics or drugs. **6.** *Aeron.* **a.** a former type of aeroplane which had its propeller behind the main supporting planes. **b.** the propeller.

**pushing** /ˈpʊʃɪŋ/, *adj.* **1.** energetic; unusually active in the pursuit of an aim. *–adv.* **2.** nearly; almost (a specified age, etc.): *pushing forty.*

**pushover** /ˈpʊʃoʊvə/, *n. Colloq.* **1.** anything done easily. **2.** an easily defeated person or team. **3.** *Canoeing.* a paddle stroke used to move the canoe sideways, away from the paddle.

**push-pull** /pʊʃ-ˈpʊl/, *Electronics.* *–n.* **1.** a two-valve symmetrical arrangement in which the grid excitation voltages are opposite in phase. *–adj.* **2.** denoting or pertaining to such an arrangement or a device having such an arrangement.

**pushrod** /ˈpʊʃrɒd/, *n.* a rod which operates a rocker from a tappet of an internal-combustion engine when the camshaft is in the crankcase.

**push-start** /ˈpʊʃ-stat/, *v.t.* **1.** →**clutch-start** (def. 1). *–n.* **2.** →**clutch-start** (def. 3).

**push-up** /ˈpʊʃ-ʌp/, *n.* an exercise in which one raises one's body from a prone position to the full extent of the arms and then lowers it, the feet remaining on the ground and the body and legs in a straight line. Also, **press-up.**

**pushy** /ˈpʊʃi/, *adj.* aggressive; presuming.

**pusillanimity** /pjusəˈlænəməti/, *n.* the state or condition of being pusillanimous; timidity; cowardliness.

**pusillanimous** /pjusəˈlænəməs/, *adj.* **1.** lacking strength of mind or courage; faint-hearted; cowardly. **2.** proceeding from or indicating a cowardly spirit. [LL *pusillanimis,* from L *pusillus* very small, petty + *-animis* -spirited] – **pusillanimously,** *adv.*

**puss**[1] /pʊs/, *n.* **1.** a cat. **2.** a hare. **3.** *Colloq.* a girl or woman. [cf. D *poes,* LG *puus-katte,* d. Swed. *katte-pus*]

**puss**[2] /pʊs/, *n. Colloq.* **1.** face. **2.** mouth. [orig. uncert.]

**pussy**[1] /ˈpʊsi/, *n., pl.* **pussies.** **1.** a cat. **2.** →**tipcat.** [diminutive of PUSS[1]]

**pussy**[2] /ˈpʌsi/, *adj.* puslike. [PUS + -S- + -Y[1]]

**pussy**[3] /ˈpʊsi/, *n. Colloq.* the vulva. [? Swed. d. *pusa,* akin to Icel. *pūss* mare's vulva]

**pussyfoot** /ˈpʊsifʊt/, *v.i.* **1.** to go with a soft, stealthy tread like that of a cat. **2.** to act cautiously or timidly, as if afraid to commit oneself on a point at issue. *–n.* **3.** a person with a catlike, or soft and stealthy tread. **4.** one who pussyfoots.

**pussy-footer** /ˈpʊsi-fʊtə/, *n. Colloq.* a sneak thief.

**pussy willow** /pʊsi ˈwɪloʊ, ˈpʊsi wɪloʊ/, *n.* **1.** a small tree or shrub, *Salix caprea,* with silky catkins. **2.** any of various similar willows.

**pustulant** /ˈpʌstʃələnt/, *adj.* **1.** causing the formation of pustules. *–n.* **2.** a medicament or agent causing pustulation. [LL *pustulans,* ppr.]

**pustular** /ˈpʌstʃələ/, *adj.* **1.** of, pertaining to, or of the nature of pustules. **2.** characterised by pustules. [NL *pustulāris*]

**pustulation** /pʌstʃəˈleɪʃən/, *n.* the formation or breaking out of pustules.

**pustule** /ˈpʌstjul/, *n.* **1.** *Pathol.* a small elevation of the skin containing pus. **2.** any pimple-like or blister-like swelling or elevation. [ME, from L *pustula*]

**put** /pʊt/, *v.,* **put, putting,** *n.* *–v.t.* **1.** to move or place (anything) so as to get it into or out of some place or position: *to put money in one's purse.* **2.** to bring into some relation, state, etc.: *put everything in order.* **3.** to place in the charge or power of a person, etc.: *to put oneself under a doctor's care.* **4.** to subject to the endurance or suffering of something: *to put a person to death.* **5.** to set to a duty, task, action, etc.: *to put one to work.* **6.** to force or drive to some course or action: *to put an army to flight.* **7.** to render or translate, as into another language. **8.** to assign or attribute: *to put a certain construction upon an action.* **9.** to set at a particular place, point, amount, etc., in a scale of estimation: *he puts the distance at ten metres.* **10.** to wager; bet. **11.** to express or state: *to put a thing in writing.* **12.** to apply, as to a use or purpose. **13.** to set, give, or make: *to put an end to a practice.* **14.** to propose or submit for answer, consideration, deliberation, etc.: *to put a question.* **15.** to impose, as a burden, charge, or the like: *to put a tax on an article.* **16.** to lay the blame of (fol. by *on, to,* etc.). **17.** to invest: *to put $1000 into Commonwealth Bonds.* **18.** to throw or cast, esp. with a forward motion of the hand when raised close to the shoulder: *to put the shot.* *–v.i.* **19.** to go, move, or proceed: *to put to sea.* **20.** *U.S. Colloq.* to make off: *to put for home.* *–v.* **21.** Some special verb phrases are:

**put about, 1.** to propagate; disseminate (a rumour, etc.). **2.** to inconvenience; upset. **3.** *Naut.* to change direction, as on a course.

**put across, a.** to communicate; cause to be understood; explain effectively. **b.** to perform a song, monologue, etc., effectively so as to involve and win the approval of members of the audience.

**put aside,** to save or store up. Also, **put away** or **by.**

**put away, 1.** to eat and drink. **2.** to gaol. **3.** (*euph.*) to kill (an animal), usu. because of sickness, old age, etc.

**put down, 1.** to write down. **2.** to repress or suppress. **3.** to ascribe or attribute (usu. fol. by *to*). **4.** to pay as a lump sum, esp. the down payment on an article to be bought by hire-purchase. **5.** to land an aircraft or in an aircraft. **6.** to destroy (an animal) esp. mercifully, as for reasons of old age, disease, etc.

**put forth, 1.** to bring out or bear: *a plant puts forth new shoots.* **2.** to set out: *to put forth from the shore.*

**put forward, 1.** to suggest or propose. **2.** to nominate.

**put in, 1.** *Naut.* to enter a port or harbour, esp. in turning aside from the regular course for shelter, repairs, provisions, etc. **2.** to interpose; say as an intervention. **3.** to apply (oft. fol. by *for*). **4.** to devote, as time, work, etc.: *I have put in a great deal of work on this project.* **5.** *Colloq.* to betray, report (someone) as for a misdemeanour. **6** *Colloq.* to nominate (someone absent) for an unpleasant task.

**put in the boot,** *Colloq.* **1.** to attack savagely by kicking. **2.** to attack without restraint. **3.** to take unfair advantage.

**put in the fangs (hooks) (nips) (screws),** *Colloq.* to borrow.

**put it across (someone),** *Colloq.* to deceive or outwit.

**put it on (someone),** *Colloq.* to confront (someone) directly on an issue.

**put off, 1.** to postpone. **2.** to bid or cause to wait until later. **3.** to get rid of (a person, demand, etc.) by delay or evasive shifts. **4.** to lay aside. **5.** to set down, as from a bus. **6.** to disconcert or distract (from): *to put someone off his work.* **7.** to disgust or cause to dislike: *the smell puts me off curry.* **8.** *Naut.* to start out, as on a voyage.

**put on, 1.** to assume: *to put on airs.* **2.** to assume insincerely or falsely: *his sorrow is only put on.* **3.** to don; dress in (clothing). **4.** to impose on or take advantage of. **5.** to produce; stage. **6.** to cause to speak on the telephone: *she asked them to put on the manager.*

**put on an act,** to make a show of anger, aggrievedness, etc., in order to impress someone.

**put one over,** *Colloq.* to deceive; outwit; defraud.

**put out, 1.** to extinguish (fire, etc.). **2.** to confuse or embarrass. **3.** to distract, disturb, or interrupt. **4.** to subject to inconvenience. **5.** to annoy, irritate, or vex. **6.** (of a woman) to be free with sexual favours. **7. a.** *Cricket.* to dismiss (a batsman). **b.** *Baseball.* to retire (a player). **8.** *Naut.* to go out to sea.

**put over, 1.** to put across. **2.** *U.S.* to postpone. **3.** *U.S.* to

accomplish.
**put paid to,** *Colloq.* to destroy finally: *bankruptcy put paid to his hopes of becoming a millionaire.*
**put (someone) down,** to humiliate or rebuke (someone).
**put the acid on,** *Colloq.* to put pressure on (someone), for a favour, esp. a loan.
**put the hard word on,** *Colloq.* to ask favours of, esp. in a sexual context.
**put through, 1.** to connect by telephone. **2.** to organise or carry into effect.
**put up, 1.** to erect. **2.** to preserve (jam, etc.). **3.** to arrange (hair) in some style so that it does not hang down. **4.** to provide (money, etc.). **5.** to lodge. **6.** to give lodging to. **7.** to show. **8.** to stand as a candidate. **9.** to nominate as a candidate. **10.** to persuade to do (fol. by *to*). **11.** *Archaic.* to sheathe one's sword; stop fighting.
**put upon,** to impose on or take advantage.
**put up or shut up,** *Colloq.* to be prepared to support what one says or else remain silent.
**put up the shutters,** to fail in business.
**put up with,** to endure; tolerate; bear.
*–n.* **22.** a throw or cast, esp. one made with a forward motion of the hand when raised close to the shoulder. **23.** *Finance.* the privilege of delivering a certain amount of stock, at a specified price, within a specified time to the maker of the contract. [ME *putten, puten* push, thrust, put. Cf. OE *putung* an impelling, inciting, *potian* push, thrust, also Dan. *putte* put, put in]

**putamen** /pju'teɪmən/, *n., pl.* **-tamina** /-'tæmənə/. a hard or stony endocarp, as a peach stone. [L: that which is removed in pruning]

**putative** /'pjutətɪv/, *adj.* commonly regarded as such; reputed; supposed. [late ME, from LL *putātīvus,* from L *putāre* think] – **putatively,** *adv.*

**put-down** /'pʊt-daʊn/, *n.* rebuke; insult; humiliation.

**putlog** /'pʌtlɒg/, *n.* one of the short horizontal timbers or pipes that support the floor of a scaffolding. Also, **putlock.**

**put-on** /'pʊt-ɒn/, *n. Colloq.* a bluff; pretence.

**put option** /'pʊt ˌɒpʃən/, *n. Stock Exchange.* the right to sell a parcel of shares at an agreed price within a specified period.

**put-out** /'pʊt-aʊt/, *n.* (in baseball) an act or instance of putting out a batter.

**putrefaction** /pjutrə'fækʃən/, *n.* the act or process of putrefying; rotting. – **putrefactive,** *adj.*

**putrefy** /'pjutrəfaɪ/, *v.,* **-fied, -fying.** *–v.t.* **1.** to render putrid; cause to rot or decay with an offensive smell. *–v.i.* **2.** to become putrid; rot. **3.** to become gangrenous. [ME *putrefie(n),* from OF *putrefier,* from L *putrefierī* rot]

**putrescent** /pju'trɛsənt/, *adj.* becoming putrid; in process of putrefaction. [L *putrescens,* ppr., growing rotten] – **putrescence,** *n.*

**putrescible** /pju'trɛsəbəl/, *adj.* **1.** liable to become putrid. *–n.* **2.** a putrescible substance. – **putrescibility** /pjuˌtrɛsə'bɪləti/, *n.*

**putrescine** /'pjutrəsin/, *n.* a colourless, liquid ptomaine, $NH_2(CH_2)_4NH_2$, with a disagreeable smell, derived from decayed animal tissue.

**putrid** /'pjutrəd/, *adj.* **1.** in a state of foul decay or decomposition, as animal or vegetable matter; rotten. **2.** attended with or pertaining to putrefaction. **3.** having the smell of decaying flesh. **4.** thoroughly corrupt, depraved, or bad. **5.** offensively or disgustingly objectionable or bad. [L *putridus*] – **putridity** /pju'trɪdəti/, **putridness,** *n.* – **putridly,** *adv.*

**putrilage** /'pjutrəlɪdʒ/, *n.* putrid matter. [L *putrilāgo* putrefaction] – **putrilaginous** /pjutrə'lædʒənəs/, *adj.*

**putsch** /pʊtʃ/, *n.* a revolt or uprising. [G]

**putt** /pʌt/, *Golf. –v.t.* **1.** to strike (the ball) gently and carefully so as to make it roll along the putting green into the hole. *–v.i.* **2.** to putt the ball. *–n.* **3.** an act of putting. **4.** a stroke made in putting. [var. of PUT]

**puttee** /'pʌti/, *n.* **1.** a long strip of cloth wound spirally round the leg from ankle to knee, formerly worn by sportsmen, soldiers, etc., as a protection or support. **2.** a kind of gaiter or legging of leather or other material, worn by soldiers, riders, etc. Also, **putty.** [Hind. *paṭṭī* bandage. Cf. Skt *paṭṭa* strip of cloth, bandage]

**putter**[1] /'pʌtə/, *v.i., n. U.S.* →**potter**[2].

**putter**[2] /'pʌtə/, *n. Golf.* **1.** one who putts. **2.** a club with a relatively short, stiff shaft and a wooden or iron head, used in putting. [PUTT + -ER[1]]

**putter**[3] /'pʊtə/, *n.* **1.** one who puts. **2.** an athlete who puts the shot; shot-putter.

**puttier** /'pʌtiə/, *n.* one who putties, as a glazier.

**putting green** /'pʌtɪŋ grin/, *n. Golf.* **1.** the area at the end of the fairway which surrounds the hole, and is marked by green, close-cropped grass, suitable for putting. **2.** a practice area for putting.

puttee

**putty**[1] /'pʌti/, *n., pl.* **-ties,** *v.,* **-tied, -tying.** *–n.* **1.** a kind of cement, of doughlike consistency, made of whiting and linseed oil and used for securing panes of glass, stopping up holes in woodwork, etc. **2.** any of various more or less similar preparations, prepared from other ingredients and used for the same or other purposes. **3.** a substance consisting of linseed oil and various other materials (as ferric oxide and red and white lead), employed in sealing the joints of tubes, pipes, etc. **4.** *Plastering, etc.* a very fine cement made of lime only. **5.** any person or thing easily moulded, influenced, etc. **6.** light brownish or yellowish grey. **7. up to putty,** worthless. *–adj.* **8.** of a yellowish or light brownish grey colour. *–v.t.* **9.** to secure, cover, etc., with putty. [F *potée,* properly, a potful]

**putty**[2] /'pʌti/, *n., pl.* **-ties.** →**puttee.**

**putty knife** /'– naɪf/, *n.* a tool having a thin, flexible blade for laying on putty.

**putty powder** /'– paʊdə/, *n.* stannic oxide used for glass-polishing.

**put-up** /'pʊt-ʌp/, *adj. Colloq.* planned beforehand in a secret or crafty manner: *a put-up job.*

**put-upon** /'pʊt-əpɒn/, *adj.* much subject to impositions; ill-used.

**puwha** /'puha/, *n.* →**puha.**

**puzzle** /'pʌzəl/, *n., v.,* **-zled, -zling.** *–n.* **1.** a toy or other contrivance designed to amuse by presenting difficulties to be solved by ingenuity or patient effort. **2.** something puzzling; a puzzling matter or person. **3.** puzzled or perplexed condition. *–v.t.* **4.** to cause to be at a loss; bewilder; confuse. **5.** to perplex or confound, as the understanding. **6.** to exercise (oneself, one's brain, etc.) over some problem or matter. **7.** to make, as something obscure, by careful study or effort (fol. by *out*): *to puzzle out the meaning of a sentence. –v.i.* **8.** to be in perplexity. **9.** to ponder or study over some perplexing problem or matter. [? ME *poselet* puzzled, confused; orig. obscure]

**puzzlement** /'pʌzəlmənt/, *n.* **1.** puzzled state; perplexity. **2.** something puzzling.

**puzzler** /'pʌzlə/, *n.* **1.** a person who puzzles. **2.** a baffling question or problem.

**p.v.,** taken through the vagina, as a suppository. [L *per vāgīnam*]

**PVA** /pi vi 'eɪ/, *n. Chem.* →**polyvinyl acetate.**

**PVC** /pi vi 'si/, *n. Chem.* →**polyvinyl chloride.**

**p.w.,** per week.

**pyaemia** /paɪ'imiə/, *n.* the growth, in different tissues, of multiple metastatic abscesses, developing from emboli disseminated in the bloodstream as fragments of a disintegrating thrombus. Also, **pyemia.** [NL. See PYO-, -AEMIA]

**pyalla** /paɪ'ælə/, *Colloq. –v.i.* **1.** to talk. *–n.* **2.** talk. [Aboriginal]

**pycnidium** /pɪk'nɪdiəm/, *n., pl.* **-nidia** /-'nɪdiə/. (in certain ascomycetes and *Fungi imperfecti*) an asexual (imperfect) fruit body, commonly globose or flask-shaped and bearing conidia on conidiophores. [NL, from PYCN(O)- + Gk *-idion* (diminutive suffix)]

**pycno-,** a word element meaning 'dense', 'close', 'thick', as in *pycnometer.* Also, **pykno-;** before vowels, **pych-.** [NL, combining form representing Gk *pyknós*]

**pycnometer** /pɪk'nɒmətə/, *n.* a flask holding a definite volume, used in determining relative density or specific gravity. Also, **pyknometer.** [PYCNO- + -METER[1]]

i = peat ɪ = pit ɛ = pet æ = pat a = part ɒ = pot ʌ = putt ɔ = port ʊ = put u = pool ɜ = pert ə = apart aɪ = buy eɪ = bay ɔɪ = boy aʊ = how
oʊ = hoe ɪə = here ɛə = hair ʊə = tour g = give θ = thin ð = then ʃ = show ʒ = measure tʃ = choke dʒ = joke ŋ = sing j = you õ = Fr. bon

**pycnostyle** /ˈpɪknəstaɪl/, *adj.* (of a building) having columns set $1\frac{1}{2}$ diameters apart.

**pye** /paɪ/, *n.* →**pie**[4].

**pye-dog** /ˈpaɪ-dɒg/, *n.* **1.** a half-wild dog common in villages throughout much of southern and eastern Asia. **2.** any mongrel dog. Also, **pi-dog.** [Anglo-Indian, ? alteration of *pariah dog*]

**pyelitis** /paɪəˈlaɪtəs/, *n.* inflammation of the pelvis or outlet of the kidney. [NL, from Gk. See PYELO-, -ITIS] – **pyelitic** /paɪəˈlɪtɪk/, *adj.*

**pyelo-,** a word element used with the meaning 'pelvis' in the formation of compound words, as in *pyelogram.* Also, before vowels, **pyel-.** [NL, combining form representing Gk *pýelos* basin. Cf. L *pelvis* basin, PELVIS]

**pyelogram** /ˈpaɪələgræm/, *n.* an X-ray produced by pyelography. Also, **pyelograph** /ˈpaɪələgræf, -graf/.

**pyelography** /paɪəˈlɒgrəfi/, *n.* the art of making photographs of the kidneys and ureter by means of X-rays, after the injection of an opaque solution or of a radiopaque dye. – **pyelographic** /paɪələˈgræfɪk/, *adj.*

**pyelonephritis** /ˌpaɪəloʊnəˈfraɪtəs/, *n.* inflammation of the kidney and the pelvis of the ureter.

**pyemia** /paɪˈimiə/, *n.* →**pyaemia.**

**pygal** /ˈpaɪgəl/, *adj.* of or pertaining to the posterior or rump of an animal. [Gk *pȳgḗ* rump + -AL[1]]

**pygidium** /paɪˈdʒɪdiəm, paɪˈgɪd-/, *n., pl.* **-gidia** /-ˈdʒɪdiə, -ˈgɪd-/. the posterior part of the body in certain invertebrates. [NL, from Gk *pȳg(ḗ)* rump + *-idion,* diminutive suffix]

**pygmaean** /pɪgˈmiən, ˈpɪgmiən/, *adj.* →**pygmy.** Also, **pygmean.**

**pygmy** /ˈpɪgmi/, *n., pl.* **-mies. 1.** a small or dwarfish person. **2.** anything very small of its kind. **3.** one who is of small importance, or who has some quality, etc., in very small measure. **4.** one of a race of dwarfs in ancient history and tradition. *–adj.* **5.** of or pertaining to small or dwarfish persons. **6.** of very small size, capacity, power, etc. Also, **pigmy.** [ME *pigmeis* the Pygmies, from L *Pygmaeī,* pl., from Gk *Pygmaîoi,* properly pl. of *pygmaîos* dwarfish]

**pygmy glider** /– ˈglaɪdə/, *n.* the smallest of the gliding possums, *Acrobates pygmaeus,* of eastern Australia; feather-tail glider; flying mouse.

**pygopod** /ˈpɪgəpɒd/, *adj.* of or characteristic of the Pygopodidae, a family of Australian lizards having no forelimbs and only rudimentary hind limbs, as the common scaly foot.

**pyin** /ˈpaɪən/, *n.* an albuminous constituent of pus. [Gk *pýon* pus + -IN[2]]

**pyjama party** /pəˈdʒamə pati/, *n.* a party which one attends dressed in one's night attire and intending to stay the night. Also, **slumber party.**

**pyjamas** /pəˈdʒaməz/, *n.* (*construed as pl.*) **1.** nightclothes consisting of loose trousers and jacket. **2.** loose trousers, usu. of silk or cotton, worn by both sexes in oriental countries. Also, *U.S.,* **pajamas.** [Hind., from Pers. *pāejāmah,* lit., leg garment] – **pyjama,** *adj.*

**pyknic** /ˈpɪknɪk/, *adj.* **1.** (of a physical type) characterised by stocky build, with a large chest and abdomen, and a tendency to obesity. *–n.* **2.** a person of the pyknic type. [Gk *pyknós* thick + -IC]

**pykno-,** →**pycno-.**

**pyknometer** /pɪkˈnɒmətə/, *n.* →**pycnometer.**

**pylon** /ˈpaɪlɒn/, *n.* **1.** a steel tower or mast carrying high-tension, telephonic or other cables and lines. **2.** a relatively tall structure at either side of a gate, bridge, or avenue, marking an entrance or approach. **3.** an architectural form of a projecting nature which flanks an entrance. **4.** a marking post or tower for guiding pilots, frequently used in races. **5.** *Aeron.* a structure supporting an engine or fuel tank. [Gk: gateway]

**pylorectomy** /paɪlɔˈrɛktəmi/, *n., pl.* **-mies.** removal of the pylorus. [PYLOR(US) + -ECTOMY]

**pylorus** /paɪˈlɔrəs/, *n., pl.* **-lori** /-ˈlɔraɪ/. the opening between the stomach and the intestine. [LL, from Gk *pylōrós,* lit., gatekeeper] – **pyloric** /paɪˈlɒrɪk/, *adj.*

**pyo-,** a word element meaning 'pus'. [Gk, combining form of *pýon*]

**pyogenesis** /paɪəˈdʒɛnəsəs/, *n.* the generation of pus; the process of the formation of pus.

**pyogenic** /paɪəˈdʒɛnɪk, -ˈdʒinɪk/, *adj.* **1.** producing or generating pus. **2.** pertaining to the formation of pus.

**pyoid** /ˈpaɪɔɪd/, *adj.* pertaining to pus; puslike. [Gk *pyoeidḗs* puslike]

**pyorrhoea** /paɪəˈriə/, *n.* a disease occurring in various forms and degrees of severity, characterised in its severe forms by the formation of pus in the pockets between the root of the tooth and its surrounding tissues, and frequently accompained by the loss of the teeth; Riggs' disease. Also, **pyorrhea.** [NL. See PYO-, -(R)RHOEA] – **pyorrhoeal,** *adj.*

**pyosis** /paɪˈoʊsəs/, *n.* the formation of pus; suppuration. [NL, from Gk]

**pyr-,** variant of **pyro-,** used occasionally before vowels or *h,* as in *pyran.*

**pyracantha** /paɪərəˈkænθə/, *n.* any evergreen shrub of the genus *Pyracantha,* family Rosaceae, as *P. coccinea,* the firethorn with clusters of bright red fruits.

**pyralid** /ˈpɪrəlɪd/, *n.* **1.** any of numerous slender-bodied, long-legged moths of the family Pyralidae. *–adj.* **2.** of, pertaining to, or belonging to the family Pyralidae.

**pyramid** /ˈpɪrəmɪd/, *n.* **1.** *Archit.* a massive structure built of stone, with square (or polygonal) base, and sloping sides meeting at an apex, such as those built by the ancient Egyptians as royal tombs or by the Mayas as platforms for their sanctuaries. **2.** anything of such form. **3.** a number of things heaped up or arranged in this form. **4.** *Geom.* a solid having a triangular, square, or polygonal base, and triangular sides which meet in a point. **5.** *Crystall.* any form the planes of which intersect all three of the axes. **6.** *Anat., Zool.* any of various parts or structures of pyramidal form. **7.** a tree pruned, or trained to grow, in pyramidal form. **8.** *Econ.* a multi-company structure in which one company controls two or more companies, each of which may itself control a number of companies, and so on. **9.** (*pl.*) a form of billiards played with 15 coloured balls, initially arranged in the form of a triangle, and one cue ball. *–v.i.* **10.** to be disposed in the form or shape of a pyramid. *–v.t.* **11.** to arrange in the form of a pyramid. **12.** to raise or increase (costs, wages, etc.) by increasing additions, as if building up a pyramid. [L *pyramis,* from Gk, of Egypt. orig.; replacing ME *pyramis,* from L] – **pyramid-like,** *adj.*

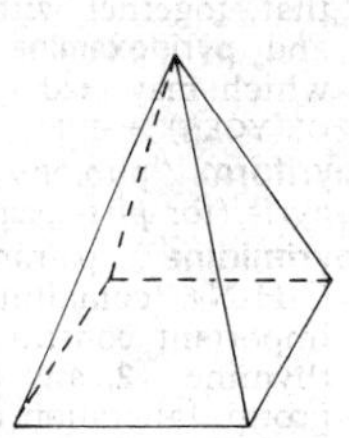
pyramid (def. 4)

**pyramidal** /pəˈræmədl, ˈpɪrəmɪdl/, *adj.* **1.** of or pertaining to a pyramid: *the pyramidal form.* **2.** of the nature of a pyramid; pyramid-like. – **pyramidally,** *adv.*

**pyramidical** /pɪrəˈmɪdɪkəl/, *adj.* →**pyramidal.** Also, **pyramidic.** [Gk *pyramidikós* + -AL[1]] – **pyramidically,** *adv.*

**pyramid selling** /ˈpɪrəmɪd sɛlɪŋ/, *n.* a scheme whereby one person, the man at the top of the pyramid, sells agencies to others, who sell them in turn to others. The people at the bottom of the pyramid are those actually selling goods, whilst everyone else in the organisation is merely selling agencies.

**pyran** /ˈpaɪræn, paɪˈræn/, *n.* either of two compounds, $C_5H_6O$, containing one oxygen and five carbon atoms arranged in a six-membered ring. [PYR- + -AN. Cf. PYRONE]

**pyrargyrite** /paɪˈradʒəraɪt/, *n.* a blackish mineral, silver antimony sulphide ($AgSbS_3$), showing (when transparent) a deep ruby red colour by transmitted light; an ore of silver. [G *Pyrargyrit,* from Gk *pŷr* fire + Gk *árgyron* silver + *-it* -ITE[1]]

**pyrazalone** /pəˈræzəloʊn/, *n.* any of a group of hydroxylated derivatives of pyrazoles.

**pyrazole** /ˈpɪrəzɒl/, *n.* **1.** a colourless crystalline solid, $C_3H_4N_2$, serving as the parent substance of important dyestuffs. **2.** *Chem.* any of a group of monocyclic organic compounds containing two adjacent nitrogen atoms in a five-membered ring.

**pyre** /ˈpaɪə/, *n.* **1.** a pile or heap of wood or other combustible material. **2.** such a pile for burning a dead body. [L *pyra,* from Gk]

**pyrene** /ˈpaɪrin/, *n.* **1.** *Bot.* a putamen or stone, esp. when there are several in a single fruit. **2.** *Chem.* a yellow crystalline tetracyclic hydrocarbon, $C_{16}H_{10}$, found in coal tar. [NL *pȳrēna,* from Gk *pȳrḗn* fruit stone]

**pyrethrin** /paɪ'riθrən/, *n.* either of two compounds, $C_{21}H_{28}O_3$ **(pyrethrin-1)**, or $C_{22}H_{28}O_5$ **(pyrethrin-2)**, which are obtained from pyrethrum flowers and are used as contact insecticides.

**pyrethrum** /paɪ'riθrəm/, *n.* **1.** a name given by horticulturalists to certain species of the genus *Chrysanthemum,* esp. *C. coccineum* and its many cultivated varieties. **2.** an insecticide prepared from the dried heads of *C. coccineum.*

**pyretic** /paɪ'rɛtɪk/, *adj.* of, pertaining to, affected by, or producing fever. [NL *pyreticus,* from Gk *pyretós* fever]

**pyretology** /pɪrə'tɒlədʒi, paɪrə-/, *n.* the branch of medicine that treats of fevers. [Gk *pyretó(s)* fever + -LOGY]

**pyrex** /'paɪrɛks/, *n.* a heat-resistant glassware for baking, frying, etc. [Trademark]

**pyrexia** /paɪ'rɛksiə/, *n.* **1.** fever. **2.** feverish condition. [NL, from Gk *pýrexis* feverishness] – **pyrexial, pyrexic,** *adj.*

**pyrheliometer** /pəˌhili'ɒmətə/, *n.* an instrument for measuring the total intensity of the sun's energy radiation. [Gk *pŷr* fire + HELIO- + -METER[1]]

**pyridine** /'paɪrədin/, *n.* a liquid organic base, $C_5H_5N$, with a pungent smell, found in coal tar, bone oil, etc., and the parent substance of many compounds, and which is used as a solvent and as an amine. [Gk *pŷr* fire + -ID[2] + -INE[2]] – **pyridic** /paɪ'rɪdɪk/, *adj.*

**pyridoxine** /paɪrə'dɒksin/, *n. Biochem.* a derivative of pyridine that, together with the closely related compounds **pyridoxal** and **pyridoxamine,** is known as vitamin $B_6$, deficiency of which may lead to dermatitis and anaemia. [PYR- + -ID[2] + OX(YGEN) + -INE[2]]

**pyriform** /'pɪrəfɔm/, *adj.* pear-shaped. [NL *pyriformis,* from *pyri-* (for *piri-* pear) + *-formis* -FORM]

**pyrimidine** /'paɪrəmədin/, *n.* **1.** a heterocyclic compound, $C_4H_4N_2$, containing two nitrogen atoms in the ring, an important constituent of several biochemical substances, as thymine. **2.** any of a group of compounds containing this group. [alteration of PYRIDINE]

**pyrimidine base** /'– beɪs/, *n.* any of several compounds related to pyrimidine present in combined form in nucleic acids.

**pyrite** /'paɪraɪt/, *n.* a very common brass-yellow mineral, iron disulphide ($FeS_2$), with a metallic lustre, burnt to sulphur dioxide in the manufacture of sulphuric acid; fool's gold. Also, **pyrites, iron pyrites.** [L *pyrītēs.* See PYRITES] – **pyritic** /paɪ'rɪtɪk/, **pyritical** /paɪ'rɪtɪkəl/, *adj.*

**pyrites** /paɪ'raɪtiz/, *n.* **1.** pyrite (sometimes called **iron pyrites**). **2.** →**marcasite. 3.** any of various other sulphides, as of copper, tin, etc. [L, from Gk, orig. adj., of or in fire]

**pyro-,** a word element used: **1.** *Chem.* **a.** before the name of an inorganic acid, indicating that its water content is intermediate between that of the corresponding ortho- (more water) and meta- (least water) acids: *pyroantimonic,* $H_4Sb_2O_7$, *pyroarsenic,* $H_4As_2O_7$, and *pyrosulphuric,* $H_2S_2O_7$, *acids.* **b.** applied to salts of these acids. If the acid ends in *-ic,* the corresponding salt ends in *-ate,* as *pyroboric acid,* $H_2B_4O_7$ and *potassium pyroborate,* $K_2B_4O_7$. If the acid ends in *-ous,* the corresponding salt ends in *-ite: pyrophosphorous acid,* $H_4P_2O_5$, *potassium pyrophosphite,* $K_4P_2O_5$. **2.** *Geol.* in the names of minerals, rocks, etc., indicating a quality produced by the action of fire. **3.** to mean 'of, relating to, or concerned with fire'. Also, before vowels, **pyr-.** [Gk, combining form of *pŷr* fire]

**pyrocatechol** /paɪroʊ'kætəkɒl/, *n.* →**catechol.** Also, **pyrocatechin** /paɪroʊ'kætəkən/.

**pyrochemical** /paɪroʊ'kɛmɪkəl/, *adj.* pertaining to or producing chemical change at high temperatures. – **pyrochemically,** *adv.*

**pyrochroite** /paɪroʊ'kroʊaɪt/, *n.* a mineral hydroxide of manganese crystallising in the trigonal system.

**pyroclastic** /paɪroʊ'klæstɪk/, *adj.* composed chiefly of fragments of volcanic origin, as agglomerate, tuff, and certain other rocks.

**pyroelectric** /ˌpaɪroʊə'lɛktrɪk/, *adj.* of, subject to, or manifesting, pyroelectricity.

**pyroelectricity** /ˌpaɪroʊəlɛk'trɪsəti/, *n.* the electrified state, or electric polarity, in some crystals produced by and changing with temperature.

**pyrogallate** /paɪroʊ'gæleɪt/, *n.* a salt or ester of pyrogallol.

**pyrogallol** /paɪroʊ'gælɒl/, *n.* a white crystalline phenolic compound, $C_6H_3(OH)_3$, obtained by heating gallic acid, and used as a photographic developer. Also, **pyrogallic acid.** – **pyrogallic,** *adj.*

**pyrogen** /'paɪroʊdʒɛn/, *n.* a substance which produces a rise of temperature in an animal body.

**pyrogenic** /paɪroʊ'dʒɛnɪk/, *adj.* **1.** producing heat or fever. **2.** produced by fire, as igneous rocks.

**pyrogenous** /paɪ'rɒdʒənəs/, *adj.* produced by the action of heat or fire.

**pyrognostics** /paɪrɒg'nɒstɪks/, *n.pl.* those properties of a mineral which it exhibits when heated, alone or with fluxes, in the blowpipe flame, as the fusibility, intumescence, or other phenomena of fusion, flame colouration, etc. [pl. of *pyrognostic,* from PYRO- + Gk *gnōstikós* pertaining to knowledge. See -ICS]

**pyrography** /paɪ'rɒgrəfi/, *n.* the process of burning designs on wood, leather, etc., with a heated tool. – **pyrographer,** *n.* – **pyrographic** /paɪrə'græfɪk/, *adj.*

**pyroligneous** /paɪroʊ'lɪgniəs/, *adj.* produced by the distillation of wood. Also, **pyrolignic.** [PYRO- + L *ligneus* of wood]

**pyroligneous acid** /– 'æsəd/, *n.* an acidic distillate obtained from wood and containing about 10 per cent acetic acid; wood vinegar.

**pyroligneous alcohol** /– 'ælkəhɒl/, *n.* →**methyl alcohol.**

**pyrolusite** /paɪroʊ'lusaɪt/, *n.* a common mineral, manganese dioxide, $MnO_2$, the principal ore of manganese, used in various manufactures, as a decolouriser of brown or green tints in glass, as a depolariser in dry-cell batteries, etc. [PYRO- + Gk *loûsis* washing + -ITE[1]]

**pyrolysis** /paɪ'rɒləsəs/, *n.* the subjection of organic compounds to very high temperatures and the resulting decomposition. – **pyrolytic** /paɪroʊ'lɪtɪk/, *adj.*

**pyromagnetic** /ˌpaɪroʊmæg'nɛtɪk/, *adj.* **1.** pertaining to or depending upon the combined action of heat and magnetism. **2.** relating to magnetic properties as changing with the temperature.

**pyromancy** /'paɪrəmænsi/, *n.* divination by fire or by forms appearing in fire. [ME *piromancie,* from ML *pyromantia,* from Gk *pyromanteía*]

**pyromania** /paɪrə'meɪniə/, *n.* a mania for setting things on fire. – **pyromaniac,** *n.* – **pyromaniacal** /ˌpaɪroʊmə'naɪəkəl/, *adj.*

**pyrometallurgy** /paɪroʊ'mɛtələdʒi/, *n.* the practice of refining ores by the use of heat which serves to accelerate chemical reactions or to melt the metallic or non-metallic content.

**pyrometer** /paɪ'rɒmətə/, *n.* an apparatus for determining high temperatures which depends commonly on observation of colour or measurement of electric current produced by heating of dissimilar metals. – **pyrometric** /paɪroʊ'mɛtrɪk/, **pyrometrical** /paɪroʊ'mɛtrɪkəl/, *adj.*

**pyrometric cone equivalent,** *n.* a measure of the melting point of refractory materials, based on the use of Seger cones. *Abbrev.:* p.c.e.

**pyromorphite** /paɪroʊ'mɔfaɪt/, *n.* a mineral, lead chlorophosphate, $Pb_5P_3O_{12}Cl$, occurring in crystalline and massive forms and of a green yellow, or brown colour; a minor ore of lead. [G *Pyromorphit.* See PYRO-, MORPH-, -ITE[1]]

**pyrone** /'paɪroʊn, paɪ'roʊn/, *n.* either of two heterocyclic ketones, $C_5H_4O_2$. [PYR- + -ONE]

**pyrope** /'paɪroʊp/, *n.* a mineral, magnesium-aluminium garnet, $Mg_3Al_2Si_3O_{12}$, occurring in crystals of varying shades of red, and frequently used as a gem. [ME *pirope,* from OF, from L *pyrōpus* gold-bronze, from Gk *pyrōpós* fiery (eyed), gold-bronze. Cf. G *Pyrop*]

**pyrophoric alloy** /paɪroʊˌfɒrɪk 'ælɔɪ/, *n.* an alloy which emits sparks when scraped or struck, and used as a flint in automatic lighters.

**pyrophosphoric acid** /ˌpaɪroʊfɒsfɒrɪk 'æsəd/, *n.* the acid $H_4P_2O_7$, formed by the union of one molecule of phosphorus pentoxide with two molecules of water. It is a water-soluble, crystalline powder.

**pyrophotometer** /ˌpaɪroʊfoʊ'tɒmətə/, *n.* a form of pyrometer which measures temperature by optical or photometric means.

**pyrophyllite** /paɪroʊ'fɪlaɪt/, *n.* a mineral, hydrous aluminium silicate, $AlSi_2O_5(OH)_4$, usu. having a white or greenish colour, and occurring commonly in soft radiated aggregates resembling talc, or compact masses, the latter variety being used like soapstone. [G *Pyrophyllit;* so called from its exfoliating when heated. See PYRO-, PHYLL(O)-, -ITE[1]]

**pyrostat** /ˈpaɪrəstæt/, *n.* a thermostat for high temperatures.

**pyrosulphate** /paɪroʊˈsʌlfeɪt/, *n.* a salt of pyrosulphuric acid.

**pyrosulphuric acid** /ˌpaɪroʊsʌlfjurɪk ˈæsəd/, *n.* →**fuming sulphuric acid.**

**pyrotechnic** /paɪroʊˈtɛknɪk/, *adj.* **1.** of or pertaining to pyrotechnics. **2.** pertaining to, resembling, or suggesting fireworks. Also, **pyrotechnical.**

**pyrotechnics** /paɪroʊˈtɛknɪks/, *n.* **1.** the art of making fireworks. **2.** the making and use of fireworks for display, military purposes, etc. **3.** a brilliant or sensational display, as of rhetoric, etc. Also, **pyrotechny** /ˈpaɪroʊtɛkni/ *for defs 1 and 2.*

**pyrotechnist** /paɪroʊˈtɛknəst/, *n.* one skilled in pyrotechnics.

**pyroxene** /ˈpaɪrɒksin/, *n.* a very common group of minerals of many varieties, silicates of magnesium, iron, calcium, and other elements, occurring as important constituents of many kinds of rocks, chiefly igneous. [F, from Gk *pyro-* PYRO- + *xénos* stranger; orig. supposed to be a foreign substance when found in igneous rocks] – **pyroxenic** /paɪrɒkˈsɛnɪk/, *adj.*

**pyroxenite** /paɪˈrɒksənaɪt/, *n.* an igneous rock composed essentially, or in large part, of pyroxene of any kind.

**pyroxylin** /paɪˈrɒksələn/, *n.* a nitrocellulose compound containing fewer nitro groups than guncotton and used as collodion, and in the artificial silk, leather, oilcloth industries, etc. Also, **pyroxyline.** [PYRO- + Gk *xýlon* wood + -IN[2]]

**pyrrhic**[1] /ˈpɪrɪk/, *adj.* **1.** of a metrical foot consisting of two short or unaccented syllables. **2.** composed of or pertaining to pyrrhics. *–n.* **3.** a pyrrhic foot. [L *pyrrhichius,* from Gk *pyrrhíchios* pertaining to the *pyrrhíchē* PYRRHIC[2]]

**pyrrhic**[2] /ˈpɪrɪk/, *n.* **1.** an ancient Grecian warlike dance in which the motions of actual warfare were imitated. *–adj.* **2.** of or pertaining to this dance. [L *pyrrhicha,* from Gk *pyrríchē* a dance; said to be named after *Pyrrhichus,* the inventor]

**Pyrrhic victory** /pɪrɪk ˈvɪktəri/, *n.* a victory gained at too great a cost. [from *Pyrrhus,* 319-272 B.C., king of Epirus, who won such a victory over the Romans at Asculum in 279 B.C.]

**pyrrhotite** /ˈpɪrətaɪt/, *n.* a common mineral, iron sulphide (nearly FeS), occurring in crystalline and massive forms, of a bronze colour and metallic lustre, and generally slightly magnetic. Also, **pyrrhotine** /ˈpɪrətaɪn/. [for earlier *pyrrhotine,* from Gk *pyrrhótēs* redness + -INE[2]]

**pyrrhuloxia** /pɪrəˈlɒksiə/, *n.* a cardinal-like grosbeak, *Pyrrhuloxia sinuata,* inhabiting the south-western U.S. and Mexico, and having a bill superficially resembling that of a parrot.

**pyrrole** /ˈpɪroʊl, pəˈroʊl/, *n.* a five-membered ring system, $C_4H_5N$, containing four carbon atoms and a nitrogen atom. Chlorophyll, haemin, and many other important naturally occurring substances are built up of pyrrole rings. [Gk *pyrr(hós)* red + -OLE]

**pyrrolidine** /pəˈrɒlədin/, *n.* a compound, $C_4H_9N$, derived from proline and some alkaloids, and present in tobacco.

**pyrroline** /ˈpɪrəlaɪn, -lən/, *n.* a colourless liquid, $C_4H_7N$, derived from pyrrole.

**pyruvic acid** /paɪˌruvɪk ˈæsəd/, *n.* an alpha-keto acid, $CH_3COCOOH$, important in many biochemical processes. [PYR(O)- + L *ūv(a)* grape + -IC]

**pyruvic aldehyde** /– ˈældəhaɪd/, *n.* an organic compound, $CH_3COCHO$, containing both an aldehyde and a ketone group, usu. obtained in a polymeric form.

**Pythagoras's theorem** /paɪˌθægərəsəz ˈθɪərəm/, *n.* the geometrical theorem which states that, in a right-angled triangle, the square on the hypotenuse is equal to the sum of the squares on the other two sides. [see PYTHAGOREAN]

**Pythagorean** /ˌpaɪθægəˈriən/, *adj.* **1.** of or pertaining to Pythagoras, *c.*582-*c.*500 B.C., Greek philosopher, mathematician, and religious reformer, who is thought to have viewed philosophy more as a means to a way of life than solely as a search for knowledge, and to have formulated theories of metempsychosis, the eternal recurrence of things, and the mystical significance of numbers. *–n.* **2.** a follower of Pythagoras. – **Pythagoreanism,** *n.*

**python** /ˈpaɪθən/, *n.* any of various non-venomous snakes, generally large and with vestiges of hind limbs, which kill by constriction. [L, from Gk]

**pythoness** /ˈpaɪθənɛs/, *n.* **1.** a woman supposed to be possessed by a soothsaying spirit, as the priestess of Apollo at Delphi. **2.** a woman with power of divination; a witch. [L Gk *pýthōn* familiar spirit, demon + -ESS; replacing ME *phitonesse,* from OF]

python

**pythonic**[1] /paɪˈθɒnɪk/, *adj.* prophetic; oracular. [L *pythōnicus,* from Gk *pythōnikós* prophetic]

**pythonic**[2] /paɪˈθɒnɪk/, *adj.* python-like. [PYTHON + -IC]

**pyuria** /paɪˈjuriə/, *n.* the presence of pus in the urine. [PY(O)- + -URIA]

**pyx** /pɪks/, *n.* **1.** *Eccles.* **a.** the box or vessel in which the reserved Eucharist or Host is kept. **b.** a watch-shaped container for carrying the Eucharist to the sick. **c.** a box for storing relics. **2.** a box or chest at a mint, in which specimen coins are deposited and reserved for trial by weight and assay. Also, **pix.** [ME, from L *pyxis,* from Gk: a box, orig., made of boxwood]

**pyxidium** /pɪkˈsɪdiəm/, *n., pl.* **pyxidia** /pɪkˈsɪdiə/. a seed vessel which dehisces transversely, the top part acting as a lid, as in the purslane. [NL, from Gk *pyxídion,* diminutive of *pyxís* box]

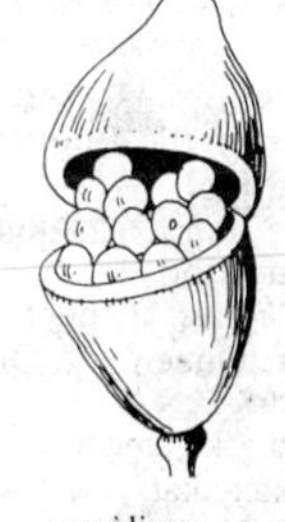
pyxidium

**pyxis** /ˈpɪksəs/, *n., pl.* **pyxides** /ˈpɪksədiz/. **1.** a small box or boxlike vase. **2.** a casket. **3.** →**pyxidium.** [ME, from L. See PYX]

**P.Z.I.,** protamine zinc insulin, a type of insulin used in the treatment of diabetes mellitus.

Qq Roman CENTURY Qq Sans Serif EUROSTYLE Qq Script CRAYONETTE

Qq Decorative BROADWAY

*Although there are numerous typefaces in the world they can be divided into four main classifications. These are:*

*ROMAN or SERIF. This typeface came into being from the technique of the Roman masons who, working in stone, finished off each letter with a serif or small stroke projecting from the top or bottom. This was done to correct any feeling of unevenness or imbalance they may have created in cutting the characters in stone.*

*SANS SERIF (without serif). This typeface is geometric in design and has straight-edged characters and lines of a regular thickness.*

*SCRIPT. Based on the movement of the hand, this typeface is often italicised or slanted, as if drawn by a brush or quill pen.*

*DECORATIVE. Any typeface that exaggerates the characteristics of any of the other three classifications to a degree that places it outside of them.*

*The dictionary entries in this book use a SANS SERIF typeface called Helvetica (set in a bold face for the head words) and a SERIF typeface Plantin (used throughout the body of the entries).*

**Q, q** /kju/, *n., pl.* **Q's** or **Qs, q's** or **qs.** a consonant, the 17th letter of the English alphabet.

**q,** quintal.

**q.,** **1.** quart. **2.** quarter. **3.** quarterly. **4.** quarto. **5.** queen. **6.** question.

**Q,** *Physics.* **1.** heat. **2.** Q-value.

**Q.,** **1.** Queen. **2.** Queensland. **3.** Question. **4.** Quotient. **5.** quarto.

**qango** /ˈkwæŋgoʊ/, *n.* →**quango.**

**qat** /kæt, kat/, *n.* →**kat.**

**Qatar** /kəˈta/, *n.* a country in eastern Arabia, on the peninsula of Qatar extending into the south-western Persian Gulf.

**QB,** Queen's Bishop.

**Q.C.** /kju ˈsi/, Queen's Counsel.

**q.e.,** which is. [L *quod est*]

**Q.E.D.** /kju i ˈdi/, which was to be shown or proved. [L *quod erat dēmonstrandum*]

**Q.E.F.** /kju i ˈɛf/, which was to be done. [L *quod erat faciendum*]

**Q-fever** /ˈkju-fivə/, *n.* a fever exhibiting pneumonia-like symptoms, and caused by *Rickettsia burnetii.*

**QKt,** Queen's Knight.

**q.l.,** (in pharmaceutical prescriptions) as much as you like. [L *quantum libet*]

**Qld,** Queensland.

**Q.M.,** Quartermaster. Also, **QM.**

**Q.M.S.,** Quartermaster-Sergeant. Also, **QMS.**

**QP,** Queen's Pawn.

**q. pl.,** as much as you please. [L *quantum placet*]

**qq.,** questions.

**qq. v.,** which (words, etc.) see. [L *quae vidē*]

**qr,** quarter.

**QR,** Queen's Rook.

**q.s.,** as much as suffices; enough. [L *quantum sufficit*]

**Q.S.,** quarter sessions.

**Q-ship** /ˈkju-ʃɪp/, *n.* (in World War I) a naval vessel disguised as a merchant ship or fishing boat in order to lure enemy submarines within range of its guns. Also, **Q-boat** /ˈkju-boʊt/.

**qt,** quart.

**qt.,** quantity.

**q.t.** /kju ˈti/, *Colloq. –adj.* **1.** quiet. *–n.* **2. on the q.t.,** secretly.

**qto,** quarto.

**qtr,** **1.** quarter. **2.** quarterly.

**qts,** quarts.

**qua** /kweɪ, kwa/, *adv.* as; as being; in the character or capacity of. [L, orig. abl. fem. of *qui* who]

**quack**[1] /kwæk/, *v.i.* **1.** to utter the cry of a duck, or a sound resembling it. *–n.* **2.** the cry of a duck, or some similar sound. [imitative. Cf. D *kwaken,* G *quacken*]

**quack**[2] /kwæk/, *n.* **1.** an ignorant or fraudulent pretender to medical skill. **2.** one who pretends professionally or publicly to skill, knowledge, or qualifications which he does not possess; a charlatan. **3.** *Colloq.* any medical practitioner. **4.** of, pertaining to, befitting or characteristic of a quack: *a quack doctor. –adj.* **5.** falsely claiming curative powers: *quack medicine.* **6.** involving quackery: *quack methods. –v.i.* **7.** to play the quack. *–v.t.* **8.** to treat in the manner of a quack. [short for QUACKSALVER]

**quackery** /ˈkwækəri/, *n., pl.* **-eries.** **1.** the practice or methods of a quack. **2.** an instance of this.

**quack grass** /ˈkwæk gras/, *n.* →**couch**[2]. [var. of QUITCH GRASS]

**quacksalver** /ˈkwæksælvə/, *n.* **1.** a quack in medicine. **2.** *Archaic.* a charlatan. [early mod. D. Cf. QUACK[1], SALVE[1]]

**quad**[1] /kwɒd/, *n. Colloq.* a quadrangle, originally of a college. [short for QUADRANGLE; orig. university slang]

**quad**[2] /kwɒd/, *n.* a piece of type metal of less height than the lettered types, serving to cause a blank in printed matter, used for spacing, etc. [short for QUADRAT]

**quad**[3] /kwɒd/, *n. Colloq.* →**quod.**

**quad**[4] /kwɒd/, *n. Colloq.* →**quadruplet.**

**quad**[5] /kwɒd/, *adj.* denoting a size of printing paper having four times the area of the size specified: *quad crown.* [short for QUADRUPLE]

**quad**[6] /kwɒd/, *n.* →**section car.** [short for *quadracycle*]

**quad**[7] /kwɒd/, *n.* →**quadrant moulding.**

**quad.,** quadrangle.

**quadr-,** variant of **quadri-,** before vowels, as in *quadrangle.*

**quadracycle** /ˈkwɒdrəsaɪkəl/, *n.* →**section car.** Also, **quad.**

quadrangle

**quadradisc** /ˈkwɒdrədɪsk/, *n.* a record made to be played on a quadraphonic sound system.

**quadrangle** /ˈkwɒdræŋgəl/, *n.* **1.** a plane figure having four angles and four sides, as a square. **2.** a quadrangular space or court wholly or nearly surrounded by a building or buildings, as in a college, etc. **3.** the building or buildings about such a space or court. [ME, from LL *quadrangulum* (neut.), lit., four-cornered (thing)] – **quadrangular** /kwɒd'ræŋgjələ/, *adj.*

**quadrant** /'kwɒdrənt/, *n.* **1.** the quarter of a circle; an arc of 90°. **2.** the area included between such an arc and two radii drawn one to each extremity. **3.** something shaped like a quarter of a circle, as a part of a machine. **4.** *Geom.* one of the four parts into which a plane is divided by two perpendicular lines. **5.** an instrument, usu. containing a graduated arc of 90°, used in astronomy, navigation, etc., for measuring altitudes. [ME, from L *quadrans* fourth part] – **quadrantal** /kwɒd'ræntl/, *adj.*

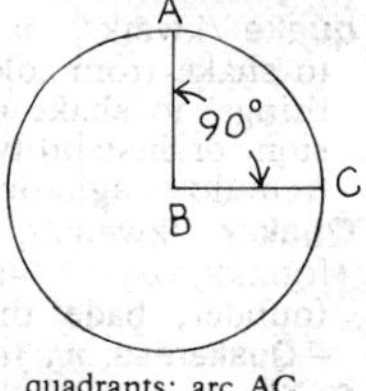

quadrants: arc AC (def. 1); segment ABC (def. 2)

**quadrant moulding** /– 'mouldɪŋ/, *n.* a moulding whose section is in the shape of a quadrant of a circle. Also, **quad.**

**quadraphonic** /kwɒdrə'fɒnɪk/, *adj.* of or pertaining to four-channel sound reproduction. Cf. **stereophonic.** Also, **quadrasonic.**

**quadraphonics** /kwɒdrəfɒnɪks/, *n.* →**quadrophony.**

**quadraplegic** /kwɒdrə'plidʒɪk/, *n., adj.* →**quadriplegic.**

**quadrasonic** /kwɒdrəsɒnɪk/, *adj.* →**quadraphonic.** Also, **quadrisonic.**

**quadrat** /'kwɒdrət/, *n.* **1.** *Print.* →**quad**². **2.** *Ecol.* a rectangular plot of land selected at random for the study of plants and animals within it. [var. of QUADRATE]

**quadrate** /'kwɒdrət/, *adj., n.;* /kwɒd'reɪt/, *v.,* **-rated, -rating.** *–adj.* **1.** square; rectangular. **2.** *Zool.* of or pertaining to the quadrate. *–n.* **3.** a square, or something square or rectangular. **4.** *Zool.* one of a pair of bones in the skulls of many lower vertebrates, to which the lower jaw is articulated. *–v.t.* **5.** to cause to conform; adapt. *–v.i.* **6.** to agree; conform. [ME *quadrat,* from L *quadrātus,* pp., made square]

**quadratic** /kwɒd'rætɪk/, *adj.* **1.** square. **2.** *Alg.* involving the square and no higher power of the unknown quantity; the second degree: *a quadratic equation.* *–n.* **3.** *Alg.* a quadratic polynomial or equation.

**quadratics** /kwɒd'rætɪks/, *n.* (*construed as sing.*) the branch of algebra that treats of quadratic equations.

**quadrature** /'kwɒdrətʃə/, *n.* **1.** the act of squaring. **2.** the act or process of finding a square equal in area to a given surface, esp. a surface bounded by a curve. **3.** *Astron.* **a.** the situation of two heavenly bodies when their longitudes differ by 90°. **b.** either of the two points in the orbit of a body, as the moon, midway between the syzygies. **c.** (of the moon) one of the points or moments at which a half-moon is visible. **4.** *Electronics.* the relationship between two waves which are out of phase by 90°. [L *quadrātūra*]

**quadrature of the circle,** *n.* the mathematical problem of constructing, subject to certain conditions, a square equal in area to a given circle.

**quadrella** /kwɒd'rɛlə/, *n.* four horseraces, usu. the last four in a race meeting, at which off-course jackpot betting on the TAB is conducted.

**quadrennial** /kwɒd'rɛniəl/, *adj.* **1.** occurring every four years. **2.** of or for four years. [earlier *quadriennial,* from L *quadrienni(s)* + -AL[1]] – **quadrennially,** *adv.*

**quadrennium** /kwɒd'rɛniəm/, *n., pl.* **-renniums, -rennia** /-'rɛniə/. a period of four years. [NL, alteration of L *quadriennium*]

**quadri-,** a word element meaning 'four'. Also, *before vowels,* **quadr-.** [L; cf. L *quattuor* four]

**quadric** /'kwɒdrɪk/, *Maths. –adj.* **1.** of the second degree, said esp. of functions with more than two variables. *–n.* **2.** a surface such as an ellipsoid or paraboloid as defined by a second degree equation in three real variables. [L *quadra* a square + -IC]

**quadricentennial** /kwɒdrəsɛn'tɛniəl/, *adj.* **1.** pertaining to, consisting of, or marking the completion of, a period of 400 years. *–n.* **2.** *U.S.* →**quatercentenary.**

**quadriceps** /'kwɒdrəsɛps/, *n.* the great muscle of the front of the thigh, which extends the leg and is considered as having four heads or origins. [NL, from L *quadri-* QUADRI- + *-ceps* headed. Cf. BICEPS]

**quadricycle** /'kwɒdrəsaɪkəl/, *n.* a vehicle similar to the bicycle and tricycle but having four wheels.

**quadrifid** /'kwɒdrəfɪd/, *adj.* cleft into four parts or lobes. [L *quadrifidus.* See QUADRI-, -FID]

**quadrilateral** /kwɒdrə'lætrəl, -'lætərəl/, *adj.* **1.** having four sides. *–n.* **2.** a plane figure having four sides and four angles. **3.** something of this form. **4.** the space enclosed between and defended by four fortresses. [L *quadrilaterus* four-sided + -AL[1]]

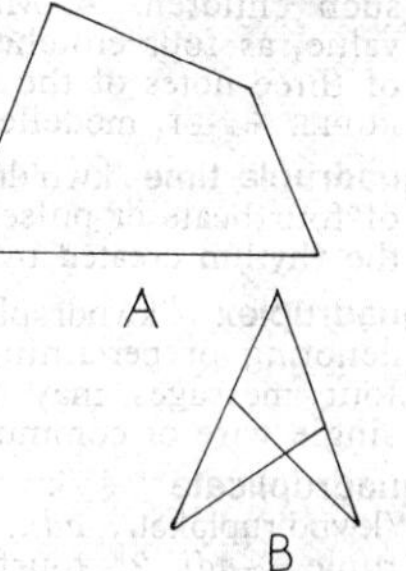

quadrilaterals: A, simple; B, complete

**quadrilingual** /kwɒdrə'lɪŋgwəl/, *adj.* using or involving four languages. [QUADRI- + L *lingua* tongue + -AL[1]]

**quadrille**[1] /kwə'drɪl/, *n.* **1.** a square dance for four couples, consisting of five parts or movements, each complete in itself. **2.** the music for such a dance. [F, from Sp. *cuadrilla* company, troop, diminutive of *cuadra* square, from L *quadra*]

**quadrille**[2] /kwə'drɪl/, *n.* a card game played by four persons. [F, from Sp. *cuartillo,* from *cuarto* fourth, from L *quartus*]

**quadrillion** /kwɒ'drɪljən/, *n.* **1.** a million times a trillion, or $10^{24}$. **2.** *U.S.* a million times a U.S. billion, or $10^{15}$. *–adj.* **3.** amounting to a quadrillion in number. [QUADR(I)- + (M)ILLION]

**quadrinomial** /kwɒdrə'noumiəl/, *Alg. –adj.* **1.** consisting of four terms. *–n.* **2.** a quadrinomial expression.

**quadripartite** /kwɒdrə'pataɪt/, *adj.* **1.** divided into or consisting of four parts. **2.** involving four participants: *a quadripartite treaty.* [L *quadripartītus*]

**quadriplegia** /kwɒdrə'plidʒə/, *n.* a condition in which the arms and legs are paralysed. [QUADRI- + (PARA)PLEGIA]

**quadriplegic** /kwɒdrə'plidʒɪk/, *n.* **1.** a person whose arms and legs are paralysed. *–adj.* **2.** of or pertaining to quadriplegia.

**quadrisonic** /kwɒdrə'sɒnɪk/, *adj.* →**quadraphonic.**

**quadrisyllable** /'kwɒdrəsɪləbəl/, *n.* a word of four syllables. – **quadrisyllabic** /kwɒdrəsə'læbɪk/, *adj.*

**quadrivalent** /kwɒdrə'veɪlənt, kwɒ'drɪvələnt/, *adj. Chem.* **1.** having a valency of four; tetravalent. **2.** exercising four different valencies, as antimony with valencies 5, 4, 3, and –3. – **quadrivalency, quadrivalence,** *n.*

**quadrivial** /kwɒ'drɪviəl/, *adj.* **1.** having four ways or roads meeting in a point. **2.** (of ways or roads) leading in four directions. [ME, from ML *quadriviālis,* from L *quadrivium.* See QUADRIVIUM]

**quadrivium** /kwɒ'drɪviəm/, *n.* (during the Middle Ages) the more advanced division of the seven liberal arts, comprising arithmetic, geometry, astronomy, and music. Cf. **trivium.** [LL, special use of L *quadrivium* place where four ways meet]

**quadroon** /kwɒ'drun/, *n.* a person who is one-fourth Negro; the offspring of a mulatto and white. [Sp. *cuarterón,* from *cuarto* fourth, from L *quartus*]

**quadrophony** /kwɒ'drɒfəni/, *n.* quadraphonic sound reproduction, as **a. discrete system quadrophony,** a system in which the signals for the rear speakers derive ultimately from separate microphones and there are at least four truly separate sound sources. **b. matrix system quadrophony,** a system in which the signals for the rear speakers are not truly separate, but derive from those for the front speakers. Also, **quadraphonics.**

**quadrumane** /'kwɒdrəmeɪn/, *n.* a quadrumanous animal, as a monkey.

**quadrumanous** /kwɒ'drumənəs/, *adj.* four-handed; having all four feet adapted for use as hands, as animals of the monkey kind. [NL *quadrumanus*]

**quadruped** /'kwɒdrəpɛd/, *adj.* **1.** four-footed. *–n.* **2.** an animal, esp. a mammal, having four feet. [L *quadrupēs*] – **quadrupedal** /kwɒ'drupədəl, 'kwɒdrəpidəl/, *adj.*

**quadruple** /kwɒ'drupəl, 'kwɒdrəpəl/, *adj., n., v.,* **-pled, -pling.** *–adj.* **1.** fourfold; consisting of four parts: *a quadruple alliance.* **2.** four times as great. *–n.* **3.** a number, amount, etc., four times as great as another. *–v.t.* **4.** to make four times as great. *–v.i.* **5.** to become four times as great. [ME, from L *quadruplus*]

**quadruplet** /kwɒ'druplət/, *n.* **1.** any group or combination of four. **2.** (*pl.*) four children born at one birth. **3.** one of four such children. **4.** *Music.* a group of four notes of equal value, as four crotchets, which are to be played in the time of three notes of the same value, i.e. three crotchets. [QUADRUPLE + -ET, modelled on TRIPLET]

**quadruple time** /kwɒ'drupəl taɪm/, *n.* **1.** a measure consisting of four beats or pulses with accent on the first and third. **2.** the rhythm created by use of this measure.

**quadruplex** /'kwɒdrəplɛks/, *adj.* **1.** fourfold; quadruple. **2.** denoting or pertaining to a system of telegraphy by which four messages may be transmitted simultaneously over a single wire or communications channel. [L]

**quadruplicate** /kwɒ'drupləkeɪt/, *v.*, **-cated, -cating;** /kwɒd'ruplәkət/, *adj.*, *n.* *–v.t.* **1.** to make fourfold; quadruple. *–adj.* **2.** fourfold; quadruple. *–n.* **3.** one of four identical things. [L *quadruplicātus*, pp., quadrupled] – **quadruplication** /kwɒˌdruplə'keɪʃən/, *n.*

**quaff** /kwɒf/, *v.i.* **1.** to drink a beverage, esp. an alcoholic one in large draughts, as with hearty enjoyment. *–v.t.* **2.** to drink (a beverage, etc.), copiously and heartily. *–n.* **3.** a quaffing. [earlier *quaft*, b. QUENCH and DRAUGHT] – **quaffer,** *n.*

**quaffing wine** /'kwɒfɪŋ waɪn/, *n.* a cheap wine for drinking in large quantities.

**quagga** /'kwægə/, *n.* an equine mammal of southern Africa, *Equus quagga*, extinct since about 1875, related to the zebra, but striped only on the forepart of the body and the head. [probably from Hottentot; akin to Xhosa *iqwara*]

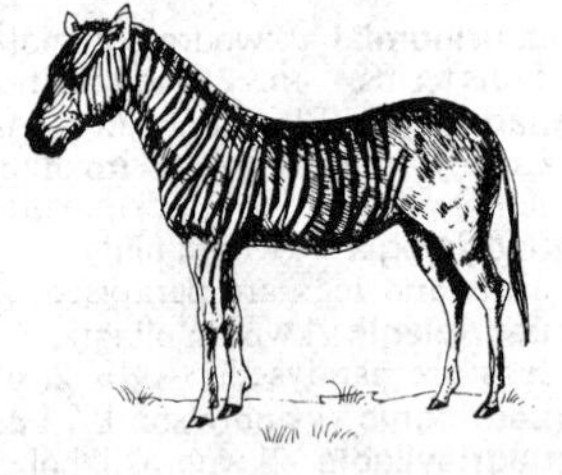

quagga

**quaggy** /'kwɒgi, 'kwægi/, *adj.*, **-gier, -giest.** of the nature of or resembling a quagmire; boggy.

**quagmire** /'kwɒgmaɪə, 'kwæg-/, *n.* **1.** a piece of miry or boggy ground whose surface yields under the tread; a bog. **2.** a situation from which extrication is difficult. [*quag-* (? b. QUAKE and SAG) + MIRE]

**quahog** /'kwahɒg/, *n.* an edible clam with a hard heavy, rounded shell, native to the Atlantic coast of North America.

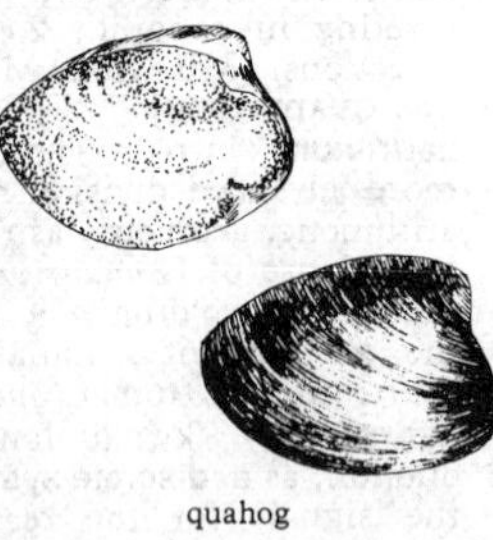

quahog

**quail**[1] /kweɪl/, *n.*, *pl.* **quails,** (*esp. collectively*) **quail. 1.** in Australia, **a.** any of several small ground-dwelling birds of the family Phasianidae, heavy-bodied with small heads, short legs and rounded wings, as the **stubble quail,** *Coturnix pectoralis.* **b.** →**bustard quail. c.** →**plains wanderer. 2.** elsewhere, **a.** a small migratory Old World gallinaceous game bird, *Coturnix coturnix.* **b.** any of several other birds of the genus *Coturnix* and allied genera. [ME *quaille*, from OF; of Gmc orig. Cf. D *kwakkel* quail, and MD, MLG *quackele*, akin to QUACK[1]]

**quail**[2] /kweɪl/, *v.i.* to lose heart or courage in difficulty or danger; shrink with fear. [ME; orig. uncert.]

**quail-thrush** /'kweɪl-θrʌʃ/, *n.* any of various ground-dwelling birds of the family Timalidae, which have a limited, jerky, undulating flight.

quail[1]

**quaint** /kweɪnt/, *adj.* **1.** strange or odd in an interesting, pleasing, or amusing way: *the quaint streets of an old English village.* **2.** oddly picturesque; having an old-fashioned attractiveness or charm: *a quaint old house.* **3.** strange; odd; whimsical. **4.** *Archaic.* wise; skilled. [ME *queinte*, from OF, var. of *cointe* pretty, pleasing, from L *cognitus*, pp., known] – **quaintly,** *adv.* – **quaintness,** *n.*

**quake** /kweɪk/, *v.*, **quaked, quaking,** *n.* *–v.i.* **1.** (of persons) to shake from cold, weakness, fear, anger, or the like. **2.** (of things) to shake or tremble, as from shock, internal convulsion, or instability. *–n.* **3.** an earthquake. **4.** a trembling or tremulous agitation. [ME; OE *cwacian* shake, tremble]

**Quaker** /'kweɪkə/, *n.* a member of the Society of Friends. [QUAKE, *v.*, + -ER[1]; first used because George Fox, the founder, bade them 'tremble at the word of the Lord'] – **Quakeress,** *n., fem.* – **Quakerish,** *adj.*

**Quakerism** /'kweɪkərɪzəm/, *n.* the beliefs, principles, and customs of the Quakers.

**Quakerly** /'kweɪkəli/, *adj.* **1.** like a Quaker. *–adv.* **2.** in the manner of the Quakers.

**quaking grass** /'kweɪkɪŋ gras/, *n.* any grass of the genus *Briza*, esp. *B. maxima*, an erect perennial with slender, spreading inflorescences which are readily shaken by the wind.

**quaky** /'kweɪki/, *adj.* inclined to quake; shaky.

**qual.,** **1.** qualified. **2.** qualify. **3.** quality.

**qualification** /kwɒləfə'keɪʃən/, *n.* **1.** a quality, accomplishment, etc., which fits for some function, office, etc. **2.** a required circumstance or condition for acquiring or exercising a right, holding an office, or the like. **3.** the act of qualifying. **4.** the state of being qualified. **5.** modification, limitation, or restriction; an instance of this: *to assert a thing without any qualification.*

**qualified** /'kwɒləfaɪd/, *adj.* **1.** possessed of qualities or accomplishments which fit one for some function or office. **2.** having qualifications required by law or custom. **3.** modified, limited, or restricted in some way: *a qualified statement.* – **qualifiedly,** *adv.*

**qualifier** /'kwɒləfaɪə/, *n.* **1.** one who or that which qualifies. **2.** *Gram.* a word which qualifies the meaning of another, as an adjective or adverb.

**qualify** /'kwɒləfaɪ/, *v.*, **-fied, -fying.** *–v.t.* **1.** to invest with proper or necessary qualities, skills, etc.; make competent. **2.** to attribute some quality or qualities to; characterise, call, or name. **3.** to modify in some way; limit; make less strong or positive: *to qualify a statement.* **4.** *Gram.* to modify. **5.** to make less violent, severe, or unpleasant; moderate; mitigate. **6.** to modify or alter the strength or flavour of. *–v.i.* **7.** to make or show oneself competent for something. **8.** to obtain authority, licence, power, etc., as by fulfilling necessary conditions or taking an oath. **9.** *Sport.* to demonstrate the necessary ability in an initial contest. **10.** *Mil.* to pass a test in one's branch of the service to achieve a higher standard of efficiency. [ML *quālificāre.* See -FY]

**qualitative** /'kwɒləˌteɪtɪv, 'kwɒlətətɪv/, *adj.* pertaining to or concerned with quality or qualities. – **qualitatively,** *adv.*

**qualitative analysis** /– ə'næləsəs/, *n.* the chemical analysis of a substance in order to ascertain the nature of its constituents.

**quality** /'kwɒləti/, *n.*, *pl.* **-ties. 1.** a characteristic, property, or attribute. **2.** character or nature, as belonging to or distinguishing a thing. **3.** character with respect to excellence, fineness, etc., or grade of excellence: *food of poor quality, silk of the finest quality.* **4.** high grade; superior excellence: *goods of quality.* **5.** native excellence or superiority. **6.** an accomplishment or attainment. **7.** good or high social position: *a man of quality.* **8.** the superiority or distinction associated with high social position. **9.** *Acoustics.* the texture of a note, dependent on its overtone content, which distinguishes it from others of the same pitch and loudness. **10.** *Phonet.* the timbre or tonal colour of a speech sound. **11.** *Logic.* the character of a proposition as affirmative or negative. **12.** *Archaic.* social status or position. **13.** *Archaic.* persons of high social position. [ME *qualite*, from L *quālitas*]

**quality control** /'– kəntroʊl/, *n.* a method of sampling the output of an industrial process, based on the theory of probability, with the object of detecting and controlling any variations in quality.

**quality number** /'– nʌmbə/, *n.* one of a series of numbers used to indicate the spinning capacity of wool, which is determined mainly by fibre fineness.

**qualm** /kwam/, *n.* **1.** an uneasy feeling or a pang of conscience as to conduct. **2.** a sudden misgiving, or feeling of apprehensive uneasiness. **3.** a sudden sensation of faintness or illness, esp. of nausea. [OE *cwealm* torment, pain, plague]

**qualmish** /ˈkwamɪʃ/, *adj.* **1.** inclined to have, or having, qualms, esp. of nausea. **2.** characterised by qualms. **3.** of the nature of a qualm. **4.** apt to cause qualms. – **qualmishly,** *adv.* – **qualmishness,** *n.*

**qualup bell** /ˈkwɒləp bɛl/, *n.* a species of *Darwinia* with a small head of flowers surrounded by large bell-shaped colourful bracts, found in south-western Australia. [from *Qualup,* the name of a property in W.A.]

**quandary** /ˈkwɒndri/, *n., pl.* **-ries.** a state of embarrassing perplexity or uncertainty, esp. as to what to do; a dilemma. [orig. obscure]

**quandong** /ˈkwɒndɒŋ/, *n.* **1.** a tree, *Santalum acuminatum,* of Australia, yielding an edible drupaceous fruit whose seed (**quandong nut**) has an edible kernel. **2.** the fruit, or the seed or nut. **3.** any of several other Australian trees as the brush quandong, *Elaeocarpus grandis.* Also, **quandang.** [Aboriginal]

quandong

**quango** /ˈkwæŋgoʊ/, *n. Orig. Brit.* a government body or organisation with independent powers; statutory authority. Also, **qango.** [*qu(asi)-a(utonomous) n(ational) g(overnment) o(rganisation)*]

**quanta** /ˈkwɒntə/, *n.* plural of **quantum.**

**quantic** /ˈkwɒntɪk/, *n.* (in mathematics) a rational, integral, homogeneous function of two or more variables. [L *quantus* how great + -IC]

**quantifiable** /ˈkwɒntəfaɪəbəl/, *adj.* able to be measured or quantified.

**quantifier** /ˈkwɒntəfaɪə/, *n.* (in logic) an expression, such as 'all' or 'some', which indicates the quantity of a proposition.

**quantify** /ˈkwɒntəfaɪ/, *v.t.,* **-fied, -fying.** **1.** to determine the quantity of; measure. **2.** *Logic.* to make explicit the quantity of. [ML *quantificāre.* See -FY] – **quantification** /kwɒntəfəˈkeɪʃən/, *n.*

**quantise** /ˈkwɒntaɪz/, *v.t.,* **-tised, -tising.** *Physics.* **1.** to restrict (a variable) to a discrete value rather than a set of continuous values. **2.** to assign (a discrete value), as a quantum, to the energy content or level of a system. **3.** *Electronics.* to convert a continuous signal waveform into a waveform which can have only a finite number (usu. two) of values. Also, **quantize.** – **quantisation** /kwɒntaɪˈzeɪʃən/, *n.*

**quantitative** /ˈkwɒntəˌteɪtɪv, ˈkwɒntətətɪvi/, *adj.* **1.** that is or may be estimated by quantity. **2.** of or pertaining to the describing or measuring of quantity. **3.** of or pertaining to the metrical system in classical poetry based on feet of long and short, rather than accented and unaccented, syllables. **4.** of or pertaining to the length or quantity of a vowel. – **quantitatively,** *adv.* – **quantitativeness,** *n.*

**quantitative analysis** /– əˈnæləsəs/, *n.* the chemical analysis of a substance in order to determine the amounts and proportions of its constituents.

**quantity** /ˈkwɒntəti/, *n., pl.* **-ties.** **1.** a particular, indefinite, or considerable amount of anything: *a small quantity of water.* **2.** amount or measure: *to mix the ingredients in the right quantities.* **3.** considerable or great amount: *to extract ore in quantity.* **4.** *Maths.* **a.** an entity subject to treatment in accordance with a set of consistent rules. **b.** the property of magnitude involving comparability with other magnitudes. **c.** something having magnitude, or size, extent, amount, or the like. **d.** magnitude, size, volume, area, or length. **5.** *Music.* the length or duration of a note. **6.** *Logic.* the character of a proposition as either universal, or particular, or (with Kant) singular. **7.** *Philos.* that which can be augmented or diminished, and the augmentation or diminution of which is directly measurable either in terms of its own kind (as length, duration, weight) or, if at all, in terms of something else (as pain, pleasure, beauty, loudness, brightness). **8.** *Pros., Phonet.* (of sounds or syllables) character as to being longer or shorter, with reference to the time required in uttering them. **9.** *Law.* the duration of an estate, or interest. [ME *quantite,* from L *quantitas*]

**quantity surveyor** /ˈ– səveɪə/, *n.* one who estimates the materials and labour required for the construction of a building, etc., in order to prepare a bill of quantities. – **quantity survey,** *n.*

**quantum** /ˈkwɒntəm/, *n., pl.* **-ta.** **1.** quantity or amount. **2.** a particular amount. **3.** a share or portion. **4.** *Physics.* **a.** one of the discrete quantities of energy or momentum of an atomic system which are characteristic of the quantum theory. **b.** this amount of energy regarded as a unit. [L (neut.): how great, how much]

**quantum electrodynamics** /– əˌlɛktroʊdaɪˈnæmɪks/, *n.* the study of the interaction between electrons, positrons and electromagnetic radiation based on quantised theories of the electron and of radiation.

**quantum mechanics** /– məˈkænɪks/, *n.* the dynamics of atomic and subatomic systems based on the earlier quantum theory and wave mechanics. Also, **quantum theory.**

**quantum meruit** /– ˈmɛruət/, *n.* a form of action in contract in which a person engaged to do work sues for payment for the work done on an implied promise to pay. [L: for as much as he has earned]

**quantum number** /ˈ– nʌmbə/, *n.* one of a set of integers or half-integers which defines the energy state of a system, or its components, in quantum mechanics.

**quantum theory** /ˈ– θɪəri/, *n.* **1.** →**quantum mechanics.** **2.** an early development of quantum mechanics where energetic electromagnetic radiation is described in terms of quanta.

**quar.,** **1.** quarter. **2.** quarterly.

**quarantine** /ˈkwɒrəntin/, *n., v.,* **-tined, -tining.** *–n.* **1.** a strict isolation designed to prevent the spread of disease. **2.** a period, originally forty days, of detention or isolation imposed upon ships, persons, etc., on arrival at a port or place, when liable or suspected to be bringing some infectious or contagious disease. **3.** a system of measures maintained by public authority at ports, on frontiers, etc., for preventing the spread of disease. **4.** a place or station at which such measures are carried out. **5.** the detention or isolation enforced. **6.** the port or place where the ships are detained. **7.** the place (esp. a hospital) where people are detained. **8.** a period of forty days. *–v.t.* **9.** to put in or subject to quarantine. **10.** to isolate politically and commercially. [It. *quarantina,* from *quaranta,* from L *quadrāgintā* forty]

**quark**[1] /kwak/, *n.* (used in cables, etc.) a question mark. [b. QU(ESTION M)ARK]

**quark**[2] /kwak/, *n.* one of three hypothetical particles with three corresponding antiparticles which have been postulated as the basis of all other particles in the universe. [special use of *quark* in 'Three quarks for Muster Mark', from *Finnegan's Wake* by James Joyce, 1882-1941, Irish novelist]

**quarrel**[1] /ˈkwɒrəl/, *n., v.,* **-relled, -relling** or (*U.S.*) **-reled, -reling.** *–n.* **1.** an angry dispute or altercation; a disagreement marked by a break in friendly relations. **2.** a cause of complaint or hostile feeling against a person, etc. *–v.i.* **3.** to disagree angrily, squabble, or fall out. **4.** to dispute angrily; wrangle. **5.** to raise a complaint, or find fault. [ME *querele,* from OF, from L *querēl(l)a* complaint] – **quarreller,** *n.*

**quarrel**[2] /ˈkwɒrəl/, *n.* **1.** a square-headed bolt or arrow, formerly used with a cross-bow. **2.** a small square or diamond-shaped pane of glass, as used in latticed windows. **3.** any of certain tools, as a stonemason's chisel. [ME *quarel,* from OF, from ML *quadrellus,* diminutive of L *quadrus* square]

quarrel[2] (def. 2)

**quarrelsome** /ˈkwɒrəlsəm/, *adj.* inclined to quarrel. – **quarrelsomely,** *adv.* – **quarrelsomeness,** *n.*

**quarrier** /ˈkwɒriə/, *n.* →**quarryman.**

**quarrion** /ˈkwɒriən/, *n.* →**cockatiel.** Also, **kwarrion.** [Aboriginal]

**quarry**[1] /ˈkwɒri/, *n., pl.* **-ries,** *v.,* **-ried, -rying.** *–n.* **1.** an excavation or pit, usu. open to the air, from which building stone, slate, or the like is obtained by cutting, blasting, etc. *–v.t.* **2.** to obtain (stone, etc.) from, or as from, a quarry. **3.** to make a quarry in. [ME *quarey,* from ML *quareia,* var. of *quareria,* VL *quadrāria* place where stone is squared, from L *quadrāre* to square]

**quarry**[2] /'kwɒri/, *n., pl.* **-ries.** **1.** an animal or bird hunted or pursued. **2.** game, esp. game hunted with hounds or hawks. **3.** any object of pursuit or attack. [ME *querre,* from OF *cuiree,* from *cuir* skin, hide, from L *corium*]

**quarry**[3] /'kwɒri/, *n., pl.* **-ries.** **1.** a square stone or tile. **2.** →**quarrel**[2] (def. 2). [n. use of obs. *quarry,* adj., square, from OF *quarre*]

**quarryman** /'kwɒrimən/, *n.* one who quarries stone. Also, **quarrier.**

**quarry tile** /'kwɒri taɪl/, *n.* a baked clay paving or wall tile, usu. square and unglazed. [see QUARRY[3]]

**quart**[1] /kwɔt/, *n.* **1.** a liquid measure of capacity in the imperial system, equal to a quarter of a gallon, or 1.136 5225 litres. **2.** a vessel or measure holding a quart. [ME, from F *quarte,* from ML *quarta* (fem.) fourth]

**quart**[2] /kat/, *n.* **1.** *Cards.* (in piquet) **a.** a sequence of four cards. **b. quart major,** the sequence of the highest four cards in any suit. **2.** *Fencing.* →**quarte.** [F *quarte* (fem.) fourth, from L *quarta*]

**quart.,** **1.** quarter. **2.** quarterly.

**quartal harmony** /kwɔtl 'hamənі/, *n.* harmony based on chords constructed of fourths instead of thirds.

**quartan** /'kwɔtn/, *adj. Archaic.* **1.** (of a fever, ague, etc.) characterised by paroxysms which recur every fourth day, both days of consecutive occurrence being counted. *–n.* **2.** a quartan fever or ague. [ME *quartaine,* from F, from L (*febris*) *quartāna* quartan fever, (fever) of the fourth]

**quarte** /kat/, *n.* (in fencing) the fourth of eight defensive positions. Also, **carte, quart.** [F, from It. *quarta* fourth]

**quarter** /'kwɔtə/, *n.* **1.** one of the four equal or equivalent parts into which anything is or may be divided: *a quarter of an apple.* **2.** *U.S. and Canada.* one fourth of a dollar (25 cents). **3.** a silver coin of this value. **4.** one fourth of an hour (15 minutes). **5.** the moment marking this period. **6.** one fourth of a year. **7.** *Astron.* **a.** a fourth of the moon's period or monthly revolution, being that portion of its period or orbital course between a quadrature and a syzygy. **b.** either quadrature of the moon. **c. first quarter,** that fourth of the moon's period coming between the new moon and the last half-moon. **d. last quarter,** that fourth of the moon's period coming between the second half-moon and the new moon. **8.** *Sport.* any one of the four periods that make up certain games, as Australian Rules, baseball, etc. **9.** a unit of weight in the imperial system, the fourth part of a hundredweight, or approx. 12.7 kg. **10.** a measure in the imperial system of capacity of grain, etc., equal to 8 bushels, or approx. 0.3 $m^3$. **11.** the region of any of the four principal points of the compass or divisions of the horizon. **12.** such a point or division. **13.** any point or direction of the compass. **14.** a region, district, or place. **15.** a particular district of a city or town, esp. one appropriated to or occupied by a particular class or group of people. **16.** (*usu. pl.*). **a.** a place of stay; lodgings; residence. **b.** *Mil.* the buildings, houses, barracks, or rooms occupied by military personnel or their families. **17.** a part or member of a community, government, etc., which is not specified: *information from a high quarter.* **18.** mercy or indulgence, esp. as shown to a vanquished enemy in sparing his life and accepting his surrender. **19.** one of the four parts, each including a leg, of the body or carcass of a quadruped. **20.** *Vet. Sci.* either side of a horse's hoof, between heel and toe. **21.** *Shoemaking.* the part of a boot or shoe on either side of the foot, from the middle of the back to the vamp. **22.** *Naut.* **a.** the after part of a ship's side, usu. from about the aftermost mast to the stern. **b.** the general horizontal direction 45° from the stern of a ship on either side: *land in sight on the port quarter.* **c.** one of the stations to which crew members are called for battle, emergencies, or drills. **d.** the part of a yard between the slings and the yardarm. **23.** *Her.* **a.** one of the four (or more) parts into which a shield may be divided by horizontal and vertical lines. **b.** a charge occupying one fourth of the shield, placed in chief. **c.** a quartering, or one of various coats of arms marshalled upon one shield. **24.** *Football.* the space between the quarter-line and the back-line: *the ball was in Manly's quarter.* *–v.t.* **25.** to divide into four equal or equivalent parts. **26.** to divide into parts fewer or more than four. **27.** to cut the body of (a person) into quarters, esp. in executing for treason or the like. **28.** *Mach.* to make holes in, fix, etc., a quarter of a circle apart. **29.** to provide with lodgings in a particular place. **30.** to impose (soldiers) on persons, etc., to be lodged and fed. **31.** to assign to a particular position for living purposes, action, etc., as on a ship. **32.** to traverse (the ground) from left to right and right to left while advancing, as dogs in search of game. **33.** *Her.* **a.** to divide a shield into four (or more) parts by horizontal and vertical lines. **b.** to place or bear quarterly upon a shield, as different coats of arms. **c.** to add (a coat of arms) thus to one's own. *–v.i.* **34.** to take up or be in quarters; lodge. **35.** to range to and fro, as dogs in search of game. **36.** *Naut.* to sail so as to have the wind or the sea on the quarter. *–adj.* **37.** being one of the four equal (or approximately equal) parts into which anything is or may be divided. **38.** being equal to only about one fourth of the full measure. [ME, from OF, from L *quartārius* fourth part]

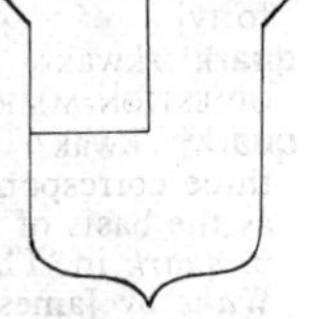
heraldic quarter (def. 23b)

**quarterage** /'kwɔtərɪdʒ/, *n.* a quarterly payment, charge, or allowance. [ME, from OF]

**quarter cask** /'kwɔtə kask/, *n.* a cask used in wine storage having a capacity varying between 100-127 litres.

**quarter-caste** /'kwɔtə-kast/, *n.* **1.** a person having a grandparent of a different race, esp. where the races are of different colours. *–adj.* **2.** of or pertaining to such a person.

**quarter-day** /'kwɔtə-deɪ/, *n.* one of the four days, regarded as marking off the quarters of the year, on which tenancies begin and end, quarterly payments fall due, etc.

**quarterdeck** /'kwɔtədɛk/, *n.* the upper deck between the mainmast and the poop or stern.

quarterdeck

**quartered** /'kwɔtəd/, *adj.* **1.** divided into quarters. **2.** furnished with quarters or lodging. **3.** (of timber) quartersawn. **4.** *Her.* **a.** divided or arranged quarterly. **b.** (of a cross) having a square piece missing in the centre.

**quarterfinal** /kwɔtə'faɪnəl/, *Sport.* *–adj.* **1.** of or pertaining to the contests preceding the semi-finals in a tournament. *–n.* **2.** such a contest. – **quarterfinalist,** *n.*

**quarter horse** /'kwɔtə hɔs/, *n.* a small horse with well developed hind quarters and chest, bred for speed over short distances, originally a quarter of a mile, and used for roping and cutting out cattle.

**quartering** /'kwɔtərɪŋ/, *n.* **1.** the act of one who or that which quarters. **2.** the assigning of quarters or lodgings. **3.** *Her.* **a.** the division of a shield into (four or more) quarters. **b.** the marshalling of various coats of arms upon one shield, as to indicate family alliances. **c.** (*usu. pl.*) one of the coats so marshalled. *–adj.* **4.** that quarters. **5.** lying at right angles. **6.** *Naut.* (of a wind) blowing on a ship's quarter.

quartered arms (def. 4a)

**quarterly** /'kwɔtəli/, *adj., n., pl.* **-lies,** *adv.* *–adj.* **1.** occurring, done, etc., at the end of every quarter of a year. **2.** pertaining to or consisting of a quarter. *–n.* **3.** a periodical issued every three months. *–adv.* **4.** by quarters; once in a quarter of a year. **5.** *Her.* **a.** with division into quarters. **b.** in the quarters of a shield.

**quartermaster** /'kwɔtəmastə/, *n.* **1.** *Mil.* a regimental officer in charge of quarters, rations, clothing, equipment, and transport. **2.** *Navy.* a petty officer having charge of signals, navigating apparatus, etc. *Abbrev.:* Q.M.

**quartermaster-sergeant** /ˌkwɔtəmastə-'sadʒənt/, *n.* a regimental non-commissioned officer assisting the quartermaster and ranking as a staff sergeant; colour sergeant. *Abbrev.:* Q.M.S.

**quartern** /ˈkwɔtn/, *n. Obs.* a quarter, or fourth part, esp. of certain former weights and measures. [ME *quarteroun,* from OF *quarteron,* from *quart* fourth. See QUART[1]]

**quarter note** /ˈkwɔtə noʊt/, *n.* →**crotchet** (def. 5).

**quarter-phase** /ˈkwɔtə-feɪz/, *adj.* denoting a combination of circuits energised by alternating electromotive forces which differ in phase by a quarter of a cycle; diphase.

**quarter point** /ˈkwɔtə pɔɪnt/, *n.* the fourth part of the distance between any two adjacent points of the 32 marked on a compass, being 2° 48′ 45″.

**quartersaw** /ˈkwɔtəsɔ/, *v.t.,* **-sawed, -sawn** or **-sawed, -sawing.** to saw (timber) into quarters so that the faces coincide with radii of the log.

**quarter sessions** /ˈkwɔtə sɛʃənz/, *n.* **1.** a criminal court which tries certain indictable offences and hears appeals from the magistrates' court (petty sessions). **2.** *U.S.* a court having limited criminal jurisdiction.

**quarterstaff** /ˈkwɔtəstaf/, *n., pl.* **-staves** /-steɪvz, -stavz/. **1.** a former weapon consisting of a stout pole 2 to 2.5 metres long, tipped with iron. **2.** exercise or fighting with this weapon.

**quarter time** /kwɔtə ˈtaɪm/, *n.* the interval between the first and second quarters of certain games, as Australian Rules, basketball, etc.

**quarter tone** /ˈ– toʊn/, *n.* an interval equivalent to half a semitone.

**quarter-vent window** /ˌkwɔtə-vɛnt ˈwɪndoʊ/, *n.* a small window at the front of each of the front doors in some cars.

**quarter-wave plate** /ˈkwɔtə-weɪv ˌpleɪt/, *n.* a plate of doubly refracting material cut parallel to the optic axis of the crystal, of such a thickness that a phase difference of a quarter of a period is introduced between the ordinary and extraordinary rays travelling normally through the plate.

**quartet** /kwɔˈtɛt/, *n.* **1.** any group of four persons or things. **2.** a group of four singers or players. **3.** a musical composition for four voices or instruments. Also, **quartette.** [F *quartette,* from It. *quartetto,* from *quarto* fourth, from L *quartus*]

**quartile** /ˈkwɔtaɪl/, *adj.* **1.** *Astrol.* denoting or pertaining to the aspect of two heavenly bodies when their longitudes differ by 90°. *–n.* **2.** *Astrol.* a quartile aspect. **3.** *Statistics.* (in a frequency distribution) one of the values of a variable which divides the distribution of the variable into four groups having equal frequencies. [ML, neut. of *quartīlis,* from L *quartus* fourth]

**quarto** /ˈkwɔtoʊ/, *n., pl.* **-tos,** *adj. –n.* **1.** a volume printed from sheets folded twice to form four leaves or eight pages; *Abbrev.:* 4to or 4°. *–adj.* **2.** in quarto. [short for NL *in quartō* in fourth]

**quart pot** /ˈkwɔt pɒt/, *n.* a tin vessel holding a quart of liquid, used for drinking and for cooking.

**quartz** /kwɔts/, *n.* **1.** one of the commonest minerals, silicon dioxide, $SiO_2$, having many varieties which differ in colour, lustre, etc., occurring in crystals (rock crystal, amethyst, citrine, etc.) or massive (agate, bloodstone, chalcedony, jasper, etc.), an important constituent of many rocks. It is piezoelectric and is cut into wafers used to control the frequencies of radio transmitters. *–adj.* **2.** →**quartz-crystal.** [G *Quarz;* orig. uncert.]

**quartz-crushing** /ˈkwɔts-krʌʃɪŋ/, *n.* the process of crushing quartz to a fine powder, from which gold may be extracted by washing or amalgamation.

**quartz crystal** /ˈkwɔts krɪstəl/, *n.* a piece of piezoelectric quartz ground so as to vibrate at a particular frequency.

**quartz-crystal** /ˈkwɔts-krɪstəl/, *adj.* (of a watch, clock, etc.) having the function of the hairspring of a traditional clock performed by a quartz crystal, which gives great accuracy. Also, **quartz.**

**quartz glass** /ˈkwɔts glas/, *n.* a glass composed entirely of silica.

**quartziferous** /kwɔtsˈɪfərəs/, *adj.* containing quartz; consisting of quartz. [QUARTZ + -I- + -FEROUS]

**quartz-iodine lamp** /kwɔts-ˈaɪədaɪn ˌlæmp/, *n.* an incandescent lamp made of quartz and containing iodine vapour and tungsten filament, used esp. in car headlights.

**quartzite** /ˈkwɔtsaɪt/, *n.* a granular rock consisting essentially of quartz in interlocking grains.

**quartz plate** /ˈkwɔts pleɪt/, *n.* a carefully cut quartz crystal which is piezoelectrically active. See **crystal** (def. 11).

**quartz-reef** /ˈkwɔts-rif/, *n.* a vein of auriferous quartz.

**quasar** /ˈkweɪsa/, *n.* one of many extragalactic, very massive sources of high-energy, radio-frequency, electromagnetic radiation of unknown constitution or structure. [short for *qua(si-stell)ar (source)*]

**quash**[1] /kwɒʃ/, *v.t.* to put down or suppress completely; subdue. [ME *quasche(n),* from OF *quasser,* from L *quassāre* shake, frequentative of *quatere*]

**quash**[2] /kwɒʃ/, *v.t.* to make void, annul, or set aside (a law, indictment, decision, etc.). [ME *quasche(n),* from OF *quasser,* from L *quassāre* shake, but influenced by LL *cassāre* annul, from L *cassus* empty, void]

**quasi** /ˈkwazi/, *adj.* **1.** resembling; as it were. *–adv.* **2.** seemingly, but not actually. [ME, from L]

**quasi-,** a prefix form of 'quasi', *adj.* and *adv.,* as in **quasi-official, quasi-deify.**

**quasi contract** /kwazi ˈkɒntrækt/, *n.* an obligation imposed by law in the absence of a contract to prevent unjust enrichment; an implied contract.

**quasi-judicial** /kwazi-dʒuˈdɪʃəl/, *adj.* having characteristics of a judicial act but performed by an administrative agency.

**quasistatic** /kwaziˈstætɪk/, *adj.* of a thermodynamic process in which the system remains infinitesimally close to equilibrium throughout.

**quass** /kfas/, *n.* →**kvass.**

**quassia** /ˈkwɒʃə/, *n.* **1.** a plant of the genus *Quassia,* esp. *Q. amara,* a tree of tropical America. **2.** the bitter wood of this tree and certain other trees. **3.** a medicinal preparation made from it. [NL; named after *Quassi,* a Surinam Negro, who (c. 1730) used the bark as a fever remedy]

**quatercentenary** /kwætəsɛnˈtinəri, kwɒ-/, *adj., n., pl.* **-naries.** *–adj.* **1.** of or pertaining to a 400th anniversary. *–n.* **2.** a 400th anniversary. **3.** its celebration. **4.** a period of 400 years.

**quaternary** /kwɒˈtɜnəri/, *adj., n., pl.* **-ries.** *–adj.* **1.** consisting of four. **2.** arranged in fours. **3.** (*cap.*) *Geol.* pertaining to the most recent geological epoch or succession of strata, which constitutes the last principal division of the Cainozoic era. *–n.* **4.** a group of four. **5.** the number four. **6.** (*cap.*) *Geol.* the epoch following the Tertiary. [ME, from L *quaternārius*]

**quaternary ammonium compound,** *n.* any of a class of compounds with the general formula, $NR_4OH$, theoretically derived from ammonium hydroxide.

**quaternion** /kwəˈtɜniən/, *n.* **1.** a group or set of four persons or things. **2.** *Maths.* **a.** a quantity analogous to a vector, having four components, and obeying certain rules of combination. **b.** (*pl.*) the calculus of such quantities. [ME, from LL *quaternio* the number four, a group of four, from L *quaternī* four together]

**quatrain** /ˈkwɒtreɪn/, *n.* a grouping, stanza, or poem, of four lines of verse. [F, from *quatre* four]

**quatrefoil** /ˈkætrəfɔɪl/, *n.* **1.** a leaf composed of four leaflets, as sometimes a leaf of clover. **2.** *Archit.* an ornament or decorative feature having four foils or lobes. [late ME *quater foyl(e),* from MF. See FOIL[2]]

quatrefoils (def. 2)

**quattrocento** /kwætroʊˈtʃɛntoʊ, kwɒt-/, *n.* the 15th century, used in reference to Italian art of that time. [It.: four hundred, short for *mille quattrocento* one thousand four hundred]

**quaver** /ˈkweɪvə/, *v.i.* **1.** to shake tremulously, quiver, or tremble (now said usu. of the voice). **2.** to sound, speak, or sing tremulously. **3.** to perform quavers, shakes, or trills in singing or on a musical instrument. *–v.t.* **4.** to utter, say, or sing with a quavering or tremulous voice. *–n.* **5.** a quavering or tremulous shake, esp. in the voice. **6.** a quavering tone or utterance. **7.** *Music.* a note equal in length to half a crotchet. [ME; b. QUAKE and WAVER] – **quavery,** *adj.*

**quay** /ki/, *n.* an artificial landing place, as of masonry built along navigable water, for vessels unloading or loading cargo, etc. [later spelling (after F *quai*) of earlier *kay,* also *key* (whence the mod. pronunciation), from OF *kay, cay;* akin to Sp. *cayo* shoal. See KEY[2]]

**quayage** /ˈkiidʒ/, *n.* **1.** quays collectively. **2.** space appropriated to quays. **3.** a charge for the use of a quay or quays. [F, from *quai* QUAY]

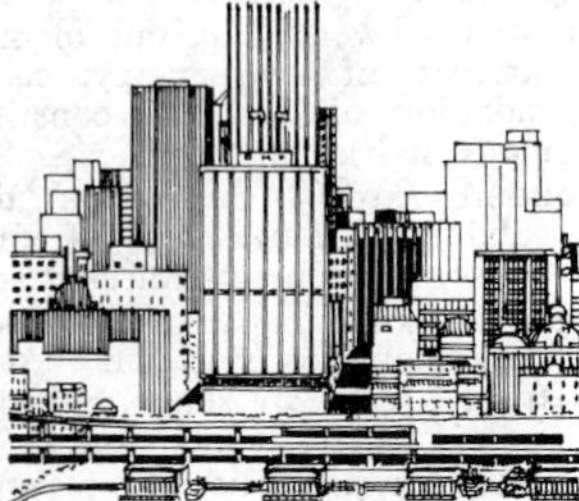
quay: Circular Quay, Sydney

**quean** /kwin/, *n.* **1.** a bold, impudent woman; a shrew; a hussy. **2.** a prostitute. **3.** *Scot.* a girl or young woman, esp. one of robust appearance. **4.** *Obs. Colloq.* a male homosexual. [ME *quene,* OE *cwene,* c. OHG *quena* woman; akin to Gk *gynḗ* woman. Cf. QUEEN]

**queasy** /ˈkwizi/, *adj.,* **-sier, -siest.** **1.** inclined to nausea, as the stomach, a person, etc. **2.** tending to cause nausea, as articles of food. **3.** uneasy or uncomfortable, as feelings, the conscience, etc. **4.** squeamish; excessively fastidious. [late ME; orig. obscure] – **queasily,** *adv.* – **queasiness,** *n.*

**quebracho** /keɪˈbratʃoʊ/, *n.* **1.** any of several trees of the genus *Schinopsis,* the wood and bark of which are important in tanning and dyeing. **2.** the tree *Aspidosperma quebrachoblanco,* yielding a medicinal bark. **3.** any of several hard-wooded South American trees. **4.** the wood or bark of any of these trees. [Sp., from *quebrar* break, from L *crepāre* burst]

**Quechua** /ˈkɛtʃwə/, *n.* **1.** a language spoken by Indians in Peru, Bolivia, and Ecuador, formerly the language of the Incas. **2.** a member of an Indian people of Peru speaking Quechua. Also, **Kechua.** – **Quechuan,** *adj., n.*

**queen** /kwin/, *n.* **1.** the wife or consort of a king. **2.** a female sovereign or monarch. **3.** a woman, or something personified as a woman, that is chief or pre-eminent in any respect: *a beauty queen.* **4.** a playing card bearing the formalised picture of a queen, in most games counting as next below the king in its suit. **5.** *Chess.* the most powerful piece, moving any distance in any straight or diagonal line. **6.** a fertile female of ants, bees, wasps, or termites. **7.** *Colloq.* a male homosexual. *–v.i.* **8.** to reign as queen. **9.** to have queenly pre-eminence; behave in an overbearing or pretentious manner (usu. fol. by indefinite *it*). **10. queen (it) up,** *Colloq.* to adopt effeminate dress or manner. *–adj.* **11.** (of a bed, mattress, etc.) slightly smaller than king-size. [ME *quene,* OE *cwēn* wife, queen, c. OS *quān,* Goth. *qēns* woman, wife; akin to QUEAN]

**Queen Anne** /kwin ˈæn/, *adj.* denoting or pertaining to a style of architecture which obtained in England in the reign of Queen Anne (1702-14), combining classical designs and plans with baroque decorative motifs.

**Queen Anne's lace,** *n.* an umbelliferous plant, *Daucus carota,* with large lacy umbels of minute, white flowers, the central one usu. dark purple; wild carrot.

**queen cake** /ˈkwin keɪk/, *n.* a small, light, rich cake containing dried fruit and cooked in patty tins or paper cases.

**queen consort** /– ˈkɒnsɔt/, *n.* the wife of a reigning king.

**queendom** /ˈkwindəm/, *n.* **1.** the position or dignity of a queen. **2.** the realm of a queen.

**queen dowager** /kwin ˈdaʊədʒə/, *n.* the widow of a king.

**queenhood** /ˈkwinhʊd/, *n.* the rank or dignity of a queen.

**Queenie** /ˈkwini/, *n.* a children's game in which a ball is hidden on the person of one child and must be located by ritual procedures of calling, etc. Also, **Queeny.**

**queenly** /ˈkwinli/, *adj.,* **-lier, -liest,** *adv.* *–adj.* **1.** belonging or proper to a queen: *queenly rank.* **2.** befitting, or suggestive of, a queen: *queenly dignity.* *–adv.* **3.** in a queenly manner. – **queenliness,** *n.*

**queen mother** /kwin ˈmʌðə/, *n.* a queen dowager who is also mother of a reigning sovereign.

**queen post** /ˈ– poʊst/, *n.* one of a pair of timbers or posts extending vertically upwards from the tie beam of a roof truss or the like, one on each side of the centre.

**queen pudding** /– ˈpʊdɪŋ/, *n.* a pudding made in layers of custard, bread and butter, jam, and topped by meringue.

**queen regent** /– ˈridʒənt/, *n.* a queen who rules on behalf of another.

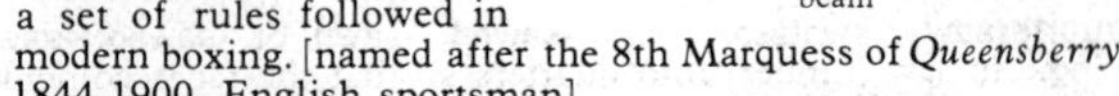

queen post roof: A, queen post; B, tie beam; C, strut; D, straining beam

**queen regnant** /– ˈrɛgnənt/, *n.* a queen who reigns in her own right.

**Queensberry rules** /ˈkwinzbəri rulz, -bri/, *n.pl.* a set of rules followed in modern boxing. [named after the 8th Marquess of *Queensberry,* 1844-1900, English sportsman]

**Queen's Counsel** /kwinz ˈkaʊnsəl/, *n.* a senior barrister who has received a commission to act as adviser to the Crown as a form of recognition of his eminence. Also, **Q.C.**

**queen's English** /kwinz ˈɪŋglɪʃ/, *n.* (when the reigning monarch is a woman) →**king's English.**

**queen's evidence** /– ˈɛvədəns/, *n.* evidence given by an accomplice in a crime on behalf of the Crown against the other defendants. Cf. **king's evidence.**

**queen's highway** /– ˈhaɪweɪ/, *n. Brit.* any portion of land or passage which every subject of the kingdom has a right to use. Cf. **king's highway.**

**Queensland** /ˈkwinzlænd, -lənd/, *n.* a State in north-eastern Australia, one of the six States of Australia. *Abbrev.* Qld., QLD.

**Queensland bean** /–ˈbin/, *n.* **1.** →**Leichhardt bean.** **2.** →**matchbox bean.**

Queensland: coat of arms

**Queensland blue** /– ˈblu/, *n.* a hardy native blue grass, *Dicanthium sericeum,* with long white silky hairs on the seed spikes, used widely for pasture and esp. plentiful in Queensland.

**Queensland blue couch,** *n.* a creeping grass resembling couch, *Digitaria didactyla,* with blue-green foliage, often planted as lawns in mild coastal regions.

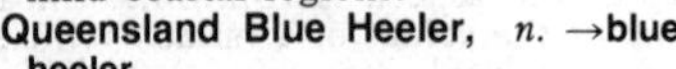

**Queensland Blue Heeler,** *n.* →**blue heeler.**

**Queenslander** /ˈkwinzlændə/, *n.* one who was born in Queensland or who has come to regard it as his home.

**Queensland halibut** /kwinzlænd ˈhæləbət/, *n.* a dusky-brown flatfish of fine edible quality, *Psettodes erumei,* found in tropical waters of Australia and elsewhere.

**Queensland hemp** /– ˈhɛmp/, *n.* →**Paddy's lucerne.**

**Queensland kauri** /– ˈkaʊri/, *n.* a large and valuable softwood timber tree, *Agathis robusta,* found in Queensland rainforests.

**Queensland kingfish** /– ˈkɪŋfɪʃ/, *n.* →**Spanish mackerel** (def. 1).

**Queensland lungfish** /– ˈlʌŋfɪʃ/, *n.* a large, primitive, freshwater fish with a paddle-shaped tail and limblike fins, *Neoceratodus forsteri,* which usu. breathes through its gills but can also rise to the surface and gulp air into a lung-like sac.

**Queensland maple** /– ˈmeɪpəl/, *n.* an evergreen tree of Australia, *Flindersia brayleyana,* having small flowers and a conelike fruit, the timber of which is widely used for furniture.

**Queensland nut** /– ˈnʌt/, *n.* →**macadamia nut.**

**Queensland silver wattle,** *n.* an attractive small tree, *Acacia podalyriifolia,* with silvery foliage and bright yellow flowers, often planted as an ornamental.

**Queensland trumpeter** /kwinzlænd ˈtrʌmpətə/, *n.* →**javelin fish.**

**queen's scout** /kwinz ˈskaʊt/, *n.* a boy scout who has achieved the greatest degree of proficiency in scouting. Cf. **king's scout.**

**queen's shilling** /– ˈʃɪlɪŋ/, *n.* (when the reigning monarch was a woman) (until 1879) →**king's shilling.**

**Queen's speech** /kwinz ˈspitʃ/, *n.* a speech read by the sovereign to the assembled members of both houses of Parliament at the beginning of a new parliamentary session, reviewing the nation's affairs and outlining the government's program of legislation for the new session. Cf. **King's speech.**

**Queen Street bushie,** *n.* (in Queensland) one who owns a country property, often for tax loss purposes, but who lives and works in Brisbane. Cf. **Collins Street cocky, Pitt Street farmer.** [from *Queen Street,* a major street in the city of Brisbane]

**queeny** /ˈkwini/, *adj. Colloq.* effeminate.

**queer** /ˈkwɪə/, *adj.* **1.** strange from a conventional point of view; singular or odd: *a queer notion.* **2.** *Colloq.* of questionable character; suspicious; shady. **3.** out of the normal state of feeling physically; giddy, faint, or qualmish: *to feel queer.* **4.** *Colloq.* mentally unbalanced or deranged. **5.** *Colloq.* bad, worthless, or counterfeit. **6.** *Colloq.* homosexual. **7. queer for,** *Chiefly Brit. Colloq.* having an inordinate craving for. *–v.t.* **8.** *Colloq.* to spoil; jeopardise; ruin. *–n.* **9.** *Colloq.* a male homosexual. [G *quer* oblique, cross, adverse] – **queerly,** *adv.* – **queerness,** *n.*

**queer street** /ˈ– strit/, *n.* (*oft. caps.*) *Colloq.* a state of financial embarrassment.

**quell** /kwɛl/, *v.t.* **1.** to suppress (disorder, mutiny, etc.); put an end to; extinguish. **2.** to vanquish; subdue. **3.** to quiet or allay (feelings, etc.). [ME; OE *cwellan* kill, causative of *cwelan* die; akin to D *kwellen,* G *quälen*] – **queller,** *n.*

**quench** /kwɛntʃ/, *v.t.* **1.** to slake, as thirst; allay; satisfy. **2.** to put out or extinguish (fire, flames, etc.). **3.** to cool suddenly, as by plunging into water, as steel in tempering it. **4.** to suppress; stifle; subdue; overcome. **5.** *Electronics.* to suppress (an oscillation) in a circuit, or (a discharge) in a valve or counter tube. **6.** *Physics.* to reduce (the duration of phosphorescence) in a luminescent material by the addition of a suitable substance. [ME *quench(en),* OE *-cwencan,* causative of *-cwincan.* Cf. Fris. *kwinka* be put out] – **quenchable,** *adj.* – **quencher,** *n.*

**quenchless** /ˈkwɛntʃləs/, *adj.* that cannot be quenched; inextinguishable.

**quenda** /ˈkwɛndə/, *n.* a short-nosed, brown bandicoot, *Isoodon obesulus,* generally distributed in Australian woodlands and heaths. [Aboriginal]

**quenelle** /kəˈnɛl/, *n.* a preparation of fish, meat, or poultry, cooked and sieved, blended with egg, and cooked in stock or fried as croquettes. [F, from G *Knödel*]

**quercetin** /ˈkwɜsətən/, *n.* a yellow crystalline powder, $C_{15}H_{10}O_7$, obtained from the bark of the quercitron and from other vegetable substances, used as a yellow dye. [apparently from L *quercētum* oak wood + -IN[2]] – **quercetic** /kwɜˈsɛtɪk, -ˈsitɪk/, *adj.*

**quercine** /ˈkwɜsaɪn/, *adj.* of or pertaining to the oak. [LL *quercīnus,* from L *quercus* oak]

**quercitol** /ˈkwɜsətɒl/, *n.* a colourless crystalline solid, $C_6H_7(OH)_5$, found in oak wood and acorns.

**quercitron** /ˈkwɜsɪtrən/, *n.* **1.** a species of oak, *Quercus velutina,* of eastern North America, whose inner bark yields a yellow dye. **2.** the bark itself. **3.** the dye obtained from it. [abbrev. for *querci-citron,* from *querci-* (combining form representing L *quercus* oak) + CITRON]

**querist** /ˈkwɪərəst/, *n.* one who puts a query. [L *quaerere* ask + -IST]

**quern** /kwɜn/, *n.* a hand mill for grinding corn. [ME; OE *cweorn,* c. OHG *quirn,* Icel. *kvern*]

**querulous** /ˈkwɛrələs/, *adj.* **1.** full of complaints; complaining. **2.** characterised by, or uttered in, complaint; peevish: *a querulous tone.* [L *querulus*] – **querulously,** *adv.* – **querulousness,** *n.*

**query** /ˈkwɪəri/, *n., pl.* **-ries,** *v.,* **-ried, -rying.** *–n.* **1.** a question; an enquiry. **2.** doubt; uncertainty. **3.** *Print.* a question or interrogation mark (?), esp. as added on a manuscript, proofs or the like, with reference to some point in the text. *–v.t.* **4.** to ask or enquire about. **5.** to question (a statement, etc.) as doubtful or obscure. **6.** *Print.* to mark with a query. **7.** to ask questions of. [earlier *quere,* from ML, for L *quaere,* impv. of *quaerere* ask]

**quest** /kwɛst/, *n.* **1.** a search or pursuit made in order to find or obtain something: *a quest for gold.* **2.** (in medieval legend) a knightly expedition undertaken to secure or achieve something: *the quest of the Holy Grail.* **3.** those engaged in such an expedition. **4.** a jury of inquest. *–v.i.* **5.** to search; seek (usu. fol. by *for* or *after*). **6.** to go on a quest. **7.** *Hunting.* (of dogs, etc.) **a.** to search for game. **b.** to bay or give tongue in pursuit of game. *–v.t.* **8.** to search or seek for; pursue. [ME *queste,* from OF, from L *quaesītus,* pp., sought, asked] – **quester,** *n.*

**question** /ˈkwɛstʃən/, *n.* **1.** a sentence in an interrogative form, addressed to someone in order to elicit information. **2.** a problem for discussion or under discussion; a matter for investigation. **3.** a matter or point of uncertainty or difficulty; a case (fol. by *of*): *to be a question of time.* **4.** a subject of dispute or controversy. **5.** a proposal to be debated or voted on, as in a meeting or a deliberative assembly. **6.** *Law.* **a.** a controversy which is submitted to a judicial tribunal or administrative agency for decision. **b.** the interrogation by which information is secured. **c.** *Obs.* judicial examination or trial. **7.** the act of asking or enquiring; interrogation; query. **8.** enquiry into or discussion of, some problem or doubtful matter. **9. beyond question,** beyond dispute; indisputably. **10. call in** or **into question, a.** to dispute; challenge. **b.** to cast doubt upon. **11. in question, a.** under consideration. **b.** in dispute. **12. out of the question,** not to be considered; impossible. *–v.t.* **13.** to ask a question or questions of; interrogate. **14.** to ask or enquire. **15.** to make a question of; doubt. **16.** to challenge; dispute. *–v.i.* **17.** to ask a question or questions. [ME *questiun,* from AF, from L *quaestio*] – **questioner,** *n.*

**questionable** /ˈkwɛstʃənəbəl/, *adj.* **1.** of doubtful propriety, honesty, morality, respectability, etc. **2.** open to question or dispute; doubtful or uncertain: *whether this is true is questionable.* **3.** open to question as being such: *a questionable privilege.*

**questionary** /ˈkwɛstʃənəri/, *n., pl.* **-aries.** →**questionnaire.**

**questioning** /ˈkwɛstʃənɪŋ/, *adj.* **1.** expressing or implying a question. **2.** characterised by curiosity; enquiring; inquisitive. – **questioningly,** *adv.*

**questionless** /ˈkwɛstʃənləs/, *adj.* **1.** unquestionable. **2.** unquestioning. *–adv.* **3.** without question.

**question mark** /ˈkwɛstʃən mak/, *n.* a mark indicating a question as, in English, the mark (?) placed after the question; interrogation mark.

**question-master** /ˈkwɛstʃən-mastə/, *n.* one who puts questions to the members of a brains trust, contestants in a quiz game, etc.

**questionnaire** /kwɛstʃənˈɛə, kɛs-/, *n.* a list of questions, usu. printed on a form as for statistical purposes, or to obtain opinions on some subject. [F]

**question on notice,** *n.* a question asked of a minister or a chairman of a parliamentary committee, usu. submitted and answered in writing.

**question time** /ˈkwɛstʃən taɪm/, *n.* (in parliament) a period during which ministers reply to questions submitted by members.

**question without notice,** *n.* an oral question asked of a minister or a chairman of a parliamentary committee without prior warning, concerning a matter falling within the minister's responsibilities or committee's term of reference.

**quetzal** /ˈkɛtsəl/, *n.* a Central American bird, *Pharomachrus mocinno,* having golden-green and scarlet plumage, and, in the male, long flowing upper tail coverts (the national bird of Guatemala). Also, **quezal.** [Sp., from Aztec *quetzalli* tail-feather of the bird *quetzaltototl*]

**queue** /kju/, *n., v.,* **queued, queuing.** *–n.* **1.** a file or line of people, vehicles, etc., waiting in turn to obtain something, enter a place, proceed along a road, etc. **2.** a braid of hair worn hanging down behind. *–v.i.* **3.** to form in a line while waiting; line up (oft. fol. by *up*). [F, from L *cōda* tail, replacing *cauda*] – **queuer,** *n.*

**quia timet** /kwiə ˈtɪmɛt/, *n.* action to prevent a threatened injury to property which could cause substantial or irreparable damage if it occurred. [L: because he fears]

**quibble** /ˈkwɪbəl/, *n., v.,* **-bled, -bling.** *–n.* **1.** a use of ambiguous, prevaricating, or irrelevant language or arguments to evade a point at issue. **2.** the use of such arguments. **3.** trivial, petty, or carping criticism. *–v.i.* **4.** to use a quibble or quibbles; evade the point or the truth by a quibble. [? from *quib* gibe, apparently var. of QUIP] – **quibbler,** *n.*

**quibbling** /ˈkwɪblɪŋ/, *adj.* **1.** characterised by quibbles; petty;

carping. –*n.* **2.** an instance of quibbling.

**quica** /ˈkwikə/, *n.* →**cuica.**

**quiche** /kiʃ/, *n.* a savoury custard tart, a speciality of Alsace and Lorraine, regions in north-eastern France. [F (Alsace d.), from G *Kuchen* cake]

**quick** /kwɪk/, *adj.* **1.** done, proceeding, or occurring with promptness or rapidity, as an action, process, etc.; prompt; immediate: *a quick answer.* **2.** that is over or completed within a short space of time. **3.** moving with speed. **4.** swift or rapid, as motion. **5.** hasty; impatient: *a quick temper.* **6.** lively or keen, as feelings. **7.** prompt in action; acting with swiftness or rapidity. **8.** prompt or swift (to do something): *quick to respond.* **9.** prompt to perceive: *a quick eye.* **10.** prompt to understand, learn, etc.; of ready intelligence. **11.** consisting of living plants: *a quick hedge.* **12.** brisk, as fire, flames, heat, etc. **13.** *Finance.* readily convertible into cash; liquid, as assets. **14.** *Mining.* containing ore, or productive, as veins. **15.** *Archaic.* endowed with life. **16.** *Archaic.* living, as persons, animals, plants, etc. **17.** *Rare.* having a high degree of vigour, energy, or activity. –*n.* **18.** living persons: *the quick and the dead.* **19.** living plants (esp. hawthorn) as set to form a hedge. **20.** a single such plant. **21.** the tender sensitive flesh of the living body, esp. that under the nails: *nails bitten down to the quick.* **22.** the vital or most important part. **23. cut to the quick,** to hurt deeply the feelings of. –*adv.* **24.** quickly. [ME; OE *cwic, cwicu* living, c. OS *quik,* G *queck, keck,* Icel. *kvikr;* akin to L *vīvus* living] – **quickness,** *n.*

**quick assets** /– ˈæsɛts/, *n.pl.* liquid assets including cash, receivables and marketable securities.

**quick bread** /ˈ– brɛd/, *n.* a bread leavened with baking powder instead of yeast. Also, **hot bread.**

**quick-change** /kwɪk-ˈtʃeɪndʒ/, *adj.* quickly changing from one thing to another, as an entertainer, actor, etc., who changes costumes, etc., during a performance: *quick-change artist.*

**quicken** /ˈkwɪkən/, *v.t.* **1.** to make more rapid; accelerate; hasten: *she quickened her pace.* **2.** to make quick or alive; restore life to. **3.** to give or restore vigour or activity to; stir up, rouse, or stimulate: *to quicken the imagination.* –*v.i.* **4.** to become more active, sensitive, etc. **5.** to become alive; receive life. **6.** (of the mother) to enter that stage of pregnancy in which the child gives indications of life. **7.** (of a child in the womb) to begin to manifest signs of life. – **quickener,** *n.*

**quick fire** /kwɪk ˈfaɪə/, *n.* →**rapid fire.**

**quick-firing** /ˈkwɪk-faɪərɪŋ/, *adj.* shooting, or capable of shooting, rapidly.

**quick-freeze** /kwɪk-ˈfriz/, *v.t.,* **-froze, -frozen, -freezing.** to subject (cooked or uncooked food) to rapid refrigeration, permitting it to be stored almost indefinitely at freezing temperatures. – **quick-frozen** /ˈkwɪk-froʊzən/, *adj.*

**quick grass** /ˈkwɪk gras/, *n.* →**couch**[2]. [*quick,* var. of QUITCH (GRASS)]

**quickie** /ˈkwɪki/, *n. Colloq.* **1.** something produced in a short space of time on a low budget and therefore of inferior quality. **2.** anything taken or done quickly, as a drink, sexual intercourse, etc. **3.** *Cricket.* a fast bowler.

**quicklime** /ˈkwɪklaɪm/, *n.* unslaked lime. See **lime**[1].

**quickly** /ˈkwɪkli/, *adv.* with speed; rapidly; very soon.

**quick march** /ˈkwɪk matʃ/, *n.* a march in quick time.

**quicksand** /ˈkwɪksænd/, *n.* an area of soft or loose wet sand of considerable depth, as on a coast or inland, yielding under weight and hence apt to engulf persons, animals, etc., coming upon it.

**quickset** /ˈkwɪksɛt/, *n.* **1.** a plant or cutting (esp. of hawthorn) set to grow, as in a hedge. **2.** such plants collectively. **3.** a hedge of such plants. –*adj.* **4.** formed of quickset, or of growing plants.

**quick-setting** /ˈkwɪk-sɛtɪŋ/, *adj.* made so as to set more quickly than usual, as cement, paint, etc.

**quick shift** /ˈkwɪk ʃɪft/, *n.* a shift which an employee is called upon to work, with less than sixteen hours break since a previous shift.

**quicksilver** /ˈkwɪksɪlvə/, *n.* **1.** the metallic element mercury. –*adj.* **2.** mercurial; changing rapidly. [ME *qwyksilver,* OE *cwicseolfor* living silver, c. G *Quecksilber,* after L *argentum vīvum* living silver]

**quicksilver cradle** /– ˈkreɪdl/, *n.* a cradle in which crushed quartz and gold are rocked together with mercury (quicksilver) which causes the gold to amalgamate; amalgam is then placed in a retort and the gold and mercury separated.

**quick smart** /kwɪk ˈsmat/, *adv.* promptly; quickly.

**quickstep** /ˈkwɪkstɛp/, *n.* **1.** (formerly) a lively step used in marching. **2.** music adapted to such a march, or in a brisk march rhythm. **3.** a rapid ballroom dance step.

**quick-tempered** /ˈkwɪk-tɛmpəd/, *adj.* easily moved to anger.

**quick time** /ˈkwɪk taɪm/, *n.* **1.** a quick rate of marching. **2.** *Mil.* a normal rate of marching in which 116 paces are taken in a minute (as opposed to the ceremonial *slow march*).

**quick trick** /– ˈtrɪk/, *n.* (in bridge) a card, or group of cards, that will probably win the first or second trick in a suit, regardless of who plays it or at what declaration.

**quick-witted** /ˈkwɪk-wɪtəd/, *adj.* having a nimble, alert mind. – **quick-wittedly,** *adv.* – **quick-wittedness,** *n.*

**quid**[1] /kwɪd/, *n.* a portion of something, esp. tobacco, for holding in the mouth and chewing. [OE *cwidu* CUD]

**quid**[2] /kwɪd/, *n., pl.* **quid, quids.** *Colloq.* **1.** (formerly) a pound in money, esp. £1 as a pound note. **2.** (*pl.*) money, esp. a large amount: *I'll bet that cost quids and quids.* **3. a quick quid,** money earned with little effort, often by dishonest means. **4. earn (make) a quid,** to earn some money. **5. have a quid,** to be wealthy. **6. not for quids,** never; for no inducement at all. **7. not get (be) the full quid,** not to obtain (be) the full value for one's money. **8. not the full quid,** mentally retarded; dull-witted. **9. turn an honest quid,** to earn money by honest means. [orig. uncert.]

**quiddity** /ˈkwɪdəti/, *n., pl.* **-ties.** **1.** that which makes a thing what it is; the essential nature. **2.** a trifling nicety or subtle distinction, as in argument. [ML *quidditas,* from L *quid* what]

**quidnunc** /ˈkwɪdnʌŋk/, *n.* one who is curious to know all the news and gossip. [L *quid nunc* ? what now?]

**quid pro quo** /kwɪd proʊ ˈkwoʊ/, *n.* **1.** one thing in return for another. **2.** *Law.* compensation, consideration. [L: something for something]

**quiescent** /kwiˈɛsənt/, *adj.* being at rest, quiet, or still; inactive or motionless. [L *quiescens,* ppr., keeping quiet] – **quiescently,** *adv.* – **quiescence, quiescency,** *n.*

**quiet** /ˈkwaɪət/, *n.* **1.** freedom from disturbance or tumult; tranquillity; rest; repose: *to live in quiet.* **2.** peace; peaceful condition of affairs. –*adj.* **3.** making no disturbance or trouble; not turbulent; peaceable. **4.** free from disturbance or tumult; tranquil; peaceful: *a quiet life.* **5.** free from disturbing emotions, etc.; mentally peaceful. **6.** being at rest. **7.** refraining or free from activity, esp. busy or vigorous activity: *a quiet evening at home.* **8.** motionless or still; moving gently: *quiet waters.* **9.** making no noise or sound, esp. no disturbing sound: *quiet neighbours.* **10.** free, or comparatively free, from noise: *a quiet street.* **11.** silent: *be quiet!* **12.** restrained in speech, manner, etc.; saying little. **13.** said, expressed, done, etc., in a restrained or unobtrusive way. **14.** of an inconspicuous kind; not showy; subdued. **15.** *Comm.* commercially inactive. **16. on the quiet,** *Colloq.* secretly. –*v.t.* **17.** to make quiet. **18.** to make tranquil or peaceful; pacify. **19.** to calm mentally, as a person. **20.** to allay, as tumult, doubt, fear, etc. **21.** to silence. –*v.i.* **22.** to become quiet. [ME *quiet(e),* from L *quiētus,* pp., rested, from *quies* rest, repose, quiet] – **quieter,** *n.* – **quietly,** *adv.* – **quietness,** *n.*

**quieten** /ˈkwaɪətn/, *v.i.* **1.** to become quiet. –*v.t.* **2.** to make quiet.

**quietism** /ˈkwaɪətɪzəm/, *n.* **1.** quietness of mind or life. **2.** a form of religious mysticism requiring extinction of the will. [It. *quietismo*] – **quietist,** *n.*

**quietude** /ˈkwaɪətʃud/, *n.* the state of being quiet; tranquillity; calmness; stillness; quiet. [LL *quiētūdo,* from L *quiētus*]

**quietus** /kwaɪˈitəs/, *n.* **1.** a finishing stroke; anything that effectually ends or settles: *to give a quietus to a rumour.* **2.** discharge or release from life. [ML: quit (in *quiētus est* he is quit, a formula of acquittance), from L: quiet, at rest. See QUIET, *adj.* Cf. QUIT, *adj.*]

**quiff** /kwɪf/, *n.* a lock or curl of hair on the forehead. [orig. uncert.]

**quill** /kwɪl/, *n.* **1.** one of the large feathers of the wing or tail of a bird. **2.** the hard, tube-like part of a feather of a bird, nearest the body, extending to the superior umbilicus. **3.** a feather, as of a goose, formed into a pen for writing. **4.** one of the hollow spines on a porcupine or hedgehog. **5.** a device for plucking the strings of a musical instrument (as of a harpsichord), made from the quill of a feather. **6.** a roll of bark, as of cinnamon, as formed in drying. **7.** a reed or other hollow stem on which yarn is wound. **8.** a bobbin or spool. **9.** *Archaic.* a musical pipe, esp. one made from a hollow stem. **10.** *Mach.* any object that resembles the quill of a bird, as a **quill bit** for boring in wood or a quill shaft. **11. drive a quill.** *Colloq.* to work in an office. *–v.i.* **12.** *Textiles.* to form work into the shape of a quill. [ME *quil.* Cf. LG *quiele,* G *Kiel*]

quill

**quillai bark** /ˈkwɪlaɪ bak/, *n.* →**soapbark** (def. 2).

**quillet** /ˈkwɪlət/, *n. Archaic.* a subtlety; a quibble.

**quillon** /ˈkijɒn/, *n.* either of the two arms forming the cross-guard of a sword.

**quill shaft** /ˈkwɪl ʃaft/, *n.* a hollow shaft revolving on an inner spindle.

**quillwort** /ˈkwɪlwɜt/, *n.* any of the aquatic and paludal pteridophytic plants constituting the genus *Isoëtes,* characterised by clustered, quill-like leaves bearing sporangia in their bases.

**quilt** /kwɪlt/, *n.* **1.** a coverlet for a bed, made by stitching together two thicknesses of fabric with a padding of some soft substance, as wool, down, etc., between them, the padding being kept in place by stitching passing through both thicknesses. **2.** anything quilted or resembling a quilt. **3.** a bedspread or counterpane. **4.** *Obs.* a kind of mattress. *–v.t.* **5.** to stitch together (two pieces of cloth with a soft interlining), usu. in an ornamental pattern. **6.** to sew up between pieces of material. **7.** to pad or line with some material. *–v.i.* **8.** to make quilts or quilted work. [ME *quilte,* from OF *cuilte,* from L *culcita* mattress, cushion] – **quilter,** *n.*

**quilted** /ˈkwɪltəd/, *adj.* **1.** resembling a quilt, as in texture, design, etc. **2.** filled or padded like a quilt.

**quilting** /ˈkwɪltɪŋ/, *n.* **1.** the act of one who quilts. **2.** material for making quilts.

**quim** /kwɪm/, *n. Colloq.* the female genitalia. [Scot. var. of OE *queme* pleasure]

**quin** /kwɪn/, *n. Colloq.* one of five children born at one birth.

**quin.** /kwɪn/, quintuplet.

**quinacrine** /ˈkwɪnəkrin/, *n.* →**atabrine.**

**quinary** /ˈkwaɪnəri/, *adj.* **1.** pertaining to or consisting of five. **2.** arranged in fives. **3.** of, pertaining to, or denoting a numeral system based on the number 5. *–n.* **4.** a number in a quinary system. [L *quīnārius* containing five]

**quince** /kwɪns/, *n.* **1.** the hard, yellowish, acid fruit of a small, hardy tree, *Cydonia oblonga.* **2.** the tree itself. **3.** *Colloq.* a homosexual who is both active and passive. **4. get on one's quince.** *Colloq.* to annoy, irritate. [ME *qwince,* apparently orig. pl., taken as sing., of ME *quyne, coyn,* from OF *cooin,* from L *cotōneum,* for *cydōnium,* from Gk *kydṓnion* quince, lit., (apple) of *Cydonia* (ancient city of Crete)]

**quincentenary** /kwɪnsɛnˈtinəri/, *adj., n., pl.* **-naries.** *–adj.* **1.** of or pertaining to a 500th anniversary. *–n.* **2.** a 500th anniversary. **3.** its celebration. **4.** a period of 500 years.

**quincentennial** /kwɪnsɛnˈtɛniəl/, *adj.* →**quincentenary.**

**quincuncial** /kwɪnˈkʌnʃəl/, *adj.* **1.** consisting of or resembling a quincunx. **2.** *Bot.* denoting a five-ranked arrangement of leaves or petals in the bud.

**quincunx** /ˈkwɪnkʌŋks/, *n.* **1.** an arrangement of five objects (as trees) in a square or rectangle, one at each corner and one in the middle. **2.** *Bot.* an imbricated arrangement of five petals or leaves, in which two are interior, two are exterior, and one is partly interior and partly exterior. [L: orig., five twelfths (the Roman coin worth five twelfths of the as was marked with a quincunx of spots)]

**quindecagon** /kwɪnˈdɛkəgən/, *n.* a polygon with fifteen angles and fifteen sides. [L *quindec(im)* fifteen + *-agon* (abstracted from DECAGON)]

**quindecennial** /kwɪndəˈsɛniəl/, *adj.* **1.** of or pertaining to a period of fifteen years or the fifteenth occurrence of a series, as an anniversary. *–n.* **2.** a fifteenth anniversary. [L *quindec(im)* fifteen + *-ennial,* as in DECENNIAL]

**quinella** /kwəˈnɛlə/, *n.* **1.** a form of betting where bets are laid on the first and second place-getters in any order in the one race. **2. forecast quinella,** a form of betting in which first and second place-getters must be nominated in correct order. [Amer. Sp. *quiniela* a game of chance]

**quinic acid** /kwɪnɪk ˈæsəd/, *n.* a white crystalline organic acid, $C_6H_7(OH)_4COOH \cdot H_2O$, present in cinchona bark, coffee beans, and the leaves of many plants. [Sp. *quin(a)* (from Quechua *kina* bark) + -IC]

**quinidine** /ˈkwɪnədin/, *n.* a colourless crystalline alkaloid isomeric with quinine, $C_{20}H_{24}N_2O_2$, derived from the bark of species of *Cinchona* which is used to regulate the heart rhythm, and to treat malaria.

**quinine** /ˈkwɪnin, kwəˈnin/, *n.* **1.** a bitter colourless alkaloid, $C_{20}H_{24}N_2O_2 \cdot 3H_2O$, having needle-like crystals, which is used in medicine as a stimulant and to treat malaria, and which was originally derived from the bark of species of the genus *Cinchona.* **2.** a salt of this alkaloid, esp. the sulphate. [Sp. *quin(a)* (from Quechua *kina* bark) + -INE[2]]

**quinoid** /ˈkwɪnɔɪd/, *n.* a quinonoid substance.

**quinol** /ˈkwɪnɒl/, *n.* →**hydroquinone.**

**quinoline** /ˈkwɪnəlin, -lən/, *n.* a nitrogenous organic base, $C_9H_7N$, a colourless liquid with a pungent odour, occurring in coal tar, and obtained by oxidation of a mixture of aniline and glycerol, and used in preparing other compounds. Also, **quinolin** /ˈkwɪnələn/. [*quinole* (from Sp. *quin(a)* quinine bark + -OLE) + -INE[2]]

**quinone** /kwɪˈnoun, ˈkwɪnoun/, *n.* **1.** Also, **benzoquinone.** a yellow crystalline unsaturated cyclic diketone, $C_6H_4O_2$, formed by oxidising aniline or hydroquinone, and used in tanning leather. **2.** any of a class of compounds based on this structure. [Sp. *quin(a)* quinine bark + -ONE]

**quinonoid** /ˈkwɪnənɔɪd, kwəˈnounɔɪd/, *adj.* of or resembling quinone. [QUINON(E) + -OID]

**quinoxaline** /kwɪnˈɒksəlin/, *n.* **1.** a colourless, crystalline solid, $C_8H_6N_2$, consisting of a benzene ring condensed with a diazine ring. **2.** any of a class of compounds based on this structure.

**quinquagenarian** /kwɪŋkwədʒəˈnɛəriən/, *adj.* **1.** of the age of 50 years. **2.** between 50 and 60 years old. *–n.* **3.** a quinquagenarian person. [L *quinquāgēnārius* consisting of fifty + -AN]

**Quinquagesima** /kwɪŋkwəˈdʒɛsəmə/, *n.* the Sunday before Lent (more fully, **Quinquagesima Sunday**), being the fiftieth day before Easter (reckoning inclusively); Shrove Sunday. [ME, from ML, short for L *quinquāgēsima dies* fiftieth day]

**quinque-,** a word element meaning 'five'. [L, combining form of *quinque*]

**quinquefoliolate** /kwɪŋkwəˈfouliələt/, *adj.* having five leaflets.

**quinquennial** /kwɪŋˈkwɛniəl/, *adj.* **1.** of or for five years. **2.** occurring every five years. *–n.* **3.** something that occurs every five years. **4.** a fifth anniversary. **5.** a five-year term in office. [late ME, from L *quinquenni(s)* of five years + -AL[1]]

**quinquennium** /kwɪŋˈkwɛniəm/, *n., pl.* **-quenniums, -quennia** /-ˈkwɛniə/. a period of five years. Also, **quinquenniad.** [L]

**quinquepartite** /kwɪŋkwəˈpataɪt/, *adj.* divided into or consisting of five parts.

**quinquereme** /ˈkwɪŋkwərim/, *n.* an ancient ship having five banks of oars.

**quinquevalent** /kwɪŋkwəˈveɪlənt, kwɪŋˈkwɛvələnt/, *adj.* **1.** →**pentavalent.** **2.** exercising five different valencies, as phosphorus with valencies 5, 4, 3, 1, and -3. – **quinquevalence, quinquevalency,** *n.*

**quinsy** /ˈkwɪnzi/, *n., pl.* **-sies.** a suppurative inflammation of the tonsils; suppurative tonsillitis. [ME *qwinaci,* from ML *quinancia,* from LL *cynanchē,* from Gk *kynánchē* sore throat]

**quint** /kwɪnt/ *for def. 1;* /kɪnt/ *for def. 2, n.* **1.** an organ stop sounding a fifth higher than the corresponding digitals. **2.** *Piquet.* a series of five cards, all of the same suit. [F *quinte* (fem.), from L *quinta* fifth]

**quintain** /ˈkwɪntən/, *n.* **1.** (during the Middle Ages and later) a post, or an object mounted on a post, for tilting at as a knightly or other exercise. **2.** such exercise or sport. [ME *quyntain,* from OF *quintaine,* from ML *quintāna* quintain (in L: market of a camp)]

**quintal** /ˈkwɪntl/, *n.* a unit of mass equal to 100 kg. *Symbol:* q [late ME, from ML *quintāle,* from Ar. *qinṭār* weight of a hundred pounds, probably from L *centēnārius,* from *centum* hundred. Cf. KANTAR]

**quintan** /ˈkwɪntən/, *Archaic.* –*adj.* **1.** (of a fever, ague, etc.) characterised by paroxysms which recur every fifth day, both days of consecutive occurrence being counted. –*n.* **2.** a quintan fever or ague. [L *quintāna (febris)* (fever) belonging to the fifth]

**quinte** /kant/, *n.* (in fencing) the fifth of eight defensive positions. [F]

**quintessence** /kwɪnˈtɛsəns/, *n.* **1.** the pure and concentrated essence of a substance. **2.** the most perfect embodiment of something. **3.** the fifth essence or element of ancient and medieval philosophy (in addition to earth, water, air, and fire), supposed to constitute the heavenly bodies, to permeate the material world, and to be capable of extraction. [ME, from ML, alteration of *quinta essentia* fifth essence] – **quintessential** /kwɪntəˈsɛnʃəl/, *adj.*

**quintet** /kwɪnˈtɛt/, *n.* **1.** any set or group of five persons or things. **2.** a set of five singers or players. **3.** a musical composition for five voices or instruments. Also, **quintette.** [F *quintette,* from It. *quintetto,* from *quinto* fifth, from L *quintus* fifth]

**quintic** /ˈkwɪntɪk/, *Maths.* –*adj.* **1.** of the fifth degree or order. –*n.* **2.** a quantity of the fifth degree.

**quintile** /ˈkwɪntəl/, *adj.* **1.** pertaining to the aspect of two heavenly bodies distant from each other the fifth part of the zodiac, or 72°. –*n.* **2.** a quintile aspect. [L, neut. of *quintīlis* fifth]

**quintillion** /kwɪnˈtɪljən/, *n.* **1.** a cardinal number represented by one followed by 30 zeros. **2.** in the U.S. and France a cardinal number represented by one followed by 15 zeros. –*adj.* **3.** amounting to one quintillion in number. [L *quintus* fifth + (M)ILLION]

**quintuple** /ˈkwɪntəpəl, kwɪnˈtjupəl/, *adj., n., v.,* **-pled, -pling.** –*adj.* **1.** fivefold; consisting of five parts. **2.** five times as great. –*n.* **3.** a number, amount, etc., five times as great as another. –*v.t.* **4.** to make five times as great. –*v.i.* **5.** to become five times as great. [F, from *quint* fifth + *-uple* (abstracted from *quadruple* QUADRUPLE)]

**quintuplet** /kwɪnˈtʌplət/, *n.* **1.** any group or combination of five. **2.** (*pl.*) five offspring born at one birth. **3.** one of five children born at one birth. **4.** *Music.* a group of five notes of equal length in a beat of different tempo.

**quintuplicate** /kwɪnˈtjuplɪkət/, *adj., n.;* /kwɪnˈtjupləkeɪt/, *v.,* **-cated, -cating.** –*adj.* **1.** fivefold; quintuple. –*n.* **2.** one of five things; five copies of a document. –*v.t.* **3.** to make fivefold; to multiply by five. – **quintuplication** /kwɪnˌtjupləˈkeɪʃən/, *n.*

**quip** /kwɪp/, *n., v.,* **quipped, quipping.** –*n.* **1.** a sharp, sarcastic remark; a cutting jest. **2.** a clever or witty saying. **3.** a quibble. **4.** an odd or fantastic action or thing. –*v.i.* **5.** to utter quips. [backformation from *quippy* quip, from L *quippe* indeed]

**quipster** /ˈkwɪpstə/, *n.* one given to making quips.

**quipu** /ˈkipu, ˈkwɪpu/, *n.* (among the ancient Peruvians) a device consisting of a cord with knotted strings of various colours attached, for recording events, keeping accounts, etc. [Quechua: lit., knot]

**quire**[1] /ˈkwaɪə/, *n.* **1.** a set of 24 uniform sheets of paper. **2.** *Bookbinding.* the section of leaves or pages in proper sequence after the printed sheet or sheets have been folded; a gathering. [ME *quayer,* from OF *quaier,* from VL **quaternum* set of four sheets, from L *quaternī* four each]

**quire**[2] /ˈkwaɪə/, *n., v.i., v.t.,* **quired, quiring.** *Archaic.* →**choir.**

**Quirinal** /ˈkwɪrənəl/, *n.* **1.** the Italian civil authority or government (as distinguished from the *Vatican*). –*adj.* **2.** denoting or pertaining to the Quirinal. [L *Quirīnālis* name of one of the Seven Hills on which Rome was built, frcm *Quirīnus* an ancient Italian war god identified by the Romans with Romulus]

**quirk** /kwɜk/, *n.* **1.** a trick or peculiarity. **2.** a shift or evasion; a quibble. **3.** a sudden twist, turn, or curve. **4.** a flourish, as in writing. **5.** an acute angle or a channel, as one separating a convex part of a moulding from a fillet. –*adj.* **6.** formed with a quirk or channel, as a moulding. [orig. obscure] – **quirky,** *adj.*

**quirt** /kwɜt/, *U.S.* –*n.* **1.** a riding whip consisting of a short, stout stock and a lash of braided leather. –*v.t.* **2.** to strike with a quirt. [Sp. *cuerda* cord]

quirt

**quisling** /ˈkwɪzlɪŋ/, *n.* a person who betrays his own country by helping an occupying enemy force; a fifth columnist. [from Vidkun *Quisling,* 1887-1945, pro-Nazi Norwegian leader]

**quit** /kwɪt/, *v.,* **quitted** or **quit, quitting,** *adj.* –*v.t.* **1.** to stop, cease, or discontinue. **2.** to depart from; leave. **3.** to give up; let go; relinquish. **4.** to let go one's hold of (something grasped). **5.** *Archaic.* to acquit (oneself). –*v.i.* **6.** to cease from doing something; stop. **7.** to depart or leave. **8.** to give up one's job or position; resign. –*adj.* **9.** released from obligation, penalty, etc.; free, clear, or rid (usu. fol. by *of*). [ME *quitte(n), quite(n),* from OF *quit(t)er.* from ML *quittāre, quiētāre* release, discharge, from LL: QUIET, *v.*]

**quitch grass** /ˈkwɪtʃ gras/, *n.* →**couch**[2]. [OE *cwice,* c. D *kweek,* Norw. *kvike;* akin to QUICK, *adj.*]

**quit claim** /ˈkwɪt kleɪm/, *n.* **1.** a transfer of all one's interest, as in a parcel of real estate. –*v.t.* **2.** to quit or give up claim to (a possession, etc.). [ME *quitclayme,* from AF *quiteclame,* from *quiteclamer* declare quit. See QUIT, *adj.,* CLAIM]

**quit claim deed,** *n.* the legal instrument effecting a quit claim (as distinguished from a *warranty deed*). Cf. **warranty.**

**quite** /kwaɪt/, *adv.* **1.** completely, wholly, or entirely: *quite the reverse.* **2.** actually, really, or truly: *quite a sudden change.* **3.** *Colloq.* to a considerable extent or degree: *quite pretty.* –*interj.* **4.** (an expression of agreement, etc.). [ME; adv. use of ME *quite,* adj., QUIT]

**quitrent** /ˈkwɪtrɛnt/, *n.* rent paid by a freeholder or copyholder in lieu of services which might otherwise have been required of him. Also, **quit-rent.** [QUIT, *adj.,* + RENT[1]]

**quits** /kwɪts/, *adj.* **1.** on equal terms by repayment or retaliation. **2. call it quits, a.** to abandon an activity, esp. temporarily. **b.** to give up a quarrel, rivalry, etc.; agree to end a dispute, competition, etc. –*adv.* **3. bet double or quits,** to make a bet, usu. to cover a preceding lost bet, so that if the better loses he forfeits twice the stake, but if he wins he pays nothing. [cf. QUIT, *adj.;* -s of uncert. orig.]

**quittance** /ˈkwɪtns/, *n.* **1.** recompense or requital. **2.** →**acquittance.**

**quitter** /ˈkwɪtə/, *n. Colloq.* one who quits or gives up easily.

**quittor** /ˈkwɪtə/, *n.* any of various infections of the foot in which tissues degenerate and form a slough, possibly involving tendons and bone as well as skin. [ME, from OF *cuiture* cooking]

**quiver**[1] /ˈkwɪvə/, *v.i., v.t.* **1.** to shake with a slight but rapid motion; vibrate tremulously; tremble. –*n.* **2.** the act or state of quivering; a tremble; a tremor. [ME; c. MD *quiveren* tremble] – **quivery,** *adj.*

**quiver**[2] /ˈkwɪvə/, *n.* **1.** a case for holding arrows. **2.** the contents of such a case. **3. a full quiver,** *Colloq.* a large family. [ME, from AF *quiveir,* var. of OF *quivre;* ? of Gmc orig.; cf. OE *cocer* quiver]

**quiverful** /ˈkwɪvəfʊl/, *n.* **1.** as much as a quiver can hold. **2.** a sizable quantity or number.

**quiver tree** /ˈ– tri/, *n.* a tall, multi-branched aloe, *Aloe dichotoma,* of southern Africa, the hollowed stems of which were used by the Bushmen as quivers.

**qui vive** /ki ˈviv/, *n. in the phrase* **on the qui vive,** on the alert. [F: (long) live who? – as if calling for such a reply as *Vive le roi!* Long live the king!]

**quixotic** /kwɪkˈsɒtɪk/, *adj.* extravagantly chivalrous or romantic; visionary; impracticable. [orig. with ref. to Don *Quixote,* the hero of a romance by Miguel de Cervantes, 1547-1616, Spanish novelist]

**quixotism** /ˈkwɪksətɪzəm/, *n.* **1.** (*sometimes cap.*) quixotic character or practice. **2.** a quixotic idea or act.

**quiz** /kwɪz/, *v.,* **quizzed, quizzing,** *n., pl.* **quizzes.** –*v.t.* **1.** to question closely. **2.** to examine or test (a student or class) informally by questions. **3.** *Obs.* to make fun of; ridicule; chaff. **4.** *Obs.* to look at or stare at mockingly or impudently. *–n.* **5.** a general knowledge test, esp. as an entertainment on radio, television, etc. **6.** a questioning. **7.** an informal examination or test of a student or class. **8.** *Obs.* a practical joke; hoax. [orig. uncert.] – **quizzer,** *n.*

**quizmaster** /ˈkwɪzmastə/, *n.* one who puts questions to competitors in a quiz, esp. in radio or television programs.

**quizzical** /ˈkwɪzɪkəl/, *adj.* **1.** odd, queer, or comical. **2.** quizzing, ridiculing, or chaffing: *a quizzical smile.* – **quizzically,** *adv.*

**quod** /kwɒd/, *n. Colloq.* a prison. [orig. uncert.]

**quodlibet** /ˈkwɒdlɪbɛt/, *n.* **1.** a sophisticated or complex problem or point of argument, esp. one which arises in the study of philosophy or theology. **2.** a thesis or debate devoted to a problem of this type. **3.** *Music.* a composition, often lighthearted in character, consisting of a combination of well-known tunes blended together melodically. [ME, from L *quod libet* what pleases] – **quodlibetical** /kwɒdləˈbɛtɪkəl/, *adj.* – **quodlibetically** /kwɒdləˈbɛtɪkli/, *adv.*

**quoin** /kɔɪn/, *n.* **1.** an external solid angle of a wall or the like. **2.** one of the stones forming it; a cornerstone. **3.** a wedge-shaped piece of wood, stone, or other material used for any of various purposes. **4.** *Print.* a wedge of wood or metal for securing type in a chase, etc. *–v.t.* **5.** to provide with quoins, as a corner of a wall. **6.** to secure or raise with a quoin or wedge. [var. of COIN]

**quoit** /kɔɪt/, *n.* **1.** Also, **deck quoit.** a flattish ring of iron or some other material thrown in play to encircle a peg stuck in the ground or to come as close to it as possible. **2.** (*pl., construed as sing.*) the game so played. **3.** Also, **coit.** *Colloq.* the anus. **4.** Also, **coit.** *Colloq.* the buttocks. *–v.t.* **5.** to throw as or like a quoit. [ME *coyte;* orig. unknown]

**quokka** /ˈkwɒkə/, *n.* a small wallaby, *Setonix brachyurus,* found in considerable numbers on Rottnest and Bald Islands, off Western Australia, and as small colonies in south-western mainland Western Australia. [Aboriginal]

quokka

**quoll** /kwɒl/, *n.* the eastern marsupial native cat, *Dasyurus viverrinus,* distinguished from the tiger cat in lacking the spot marks on the tail.

**quondam** /ˈkwɒndæm/, *adj.* that formerly was or existed; former: *his quondam partner.* [L: formerly]

**quondong** /ˈkwɒndɒŋ/, *n.* →**quandong.**

**quonset hut** /ˈkwɒnsət hʌt/, *n. U.S.* a type of temporary prefabricated shed of corrugated metal, consisting of a half-cylinder with its ends closed, used for storage or for housing soldiers. [Trademark]

**quorum** /ˈkwɔrəm/, *n.* **1.** the number of members of a body required to be present to transact business legally. **2.** a particularly chosen group. [L: of whom; from a use of the word in commissions written in Latin]

**quot.,** **1.** quotation. **2.** quotient.

**quota** /ˈkwoʊtə/, *n.* **1.** the proportional part or share of a total which is due from, or is due or belongs to, a particular district, area, person, etc. **2.** a proportional part or share of a fixed total amount or quantity. **3.** the number of persons of a particular group allowed to immigrate to a country, join an institution, etc. **4.** the maximum amount of a commodity which one is allowed to produce in an orderly marketing system. [ML, short for L *quota pars* how great a part?]

**quotable** /ˈkwoʊtəbəl/, *adj.* **1.** able to be quoted; easily or effectively quoted. **2.** suitable or appropriate for quotation.

**quotation** /kwoʊˈteɪʃən/, *n.* **1.** that which is quoted; a passage quoted from a book, speech, etc. **2.** the act or practice of quoting. **3.** *Comm.* **a.** the statement of the current or market price of a commodity or security. **b.** the price so stated. **4.** the statement of the current odds being offered in betting.

**quotation mark** /ˈ– mak/, *n.* one of the marks used to indicate the beginning and end of a quotation, in English usu. consisting of an inverted comma (‘) at the beginning and an apostrophe (’) at the end, or, for a quotation within a quotation, of double marks of this kind: *‘He said, “I will go”.’* Double marks are still sometimes used instead of single, the latter then being used for a quotation within a quotation.

**quote** /kwoʊt/, *v.,* **quoted, quoting,** *n.* *–v.t.* **1.** to repeat (a passage, etc.) from a book, speech, etc., as the words of another, as by way of authority, illustration, etc. **2.** to repeat words from (a book, author, etc.). **3.** to bring forward, adduce, or cite. **4.** to enclose (words) within quotation marks. **5.** *Comm.* **a.** to state (a price). **b.** to state the current price of. *–v.i.* **6.** to make a quotation or quotations, as from a book or author. *–n.* **7.** a quotation. **8.** →**quotation mark.** [ME, from ML *quotāre* divide into chapters and verses, from L *quot* how many] – **quotable,** *adj.*

**quoth** /kwoʊθ/, *v.t. Archaic.* said (used with nouns, and with first and third person pronouns, and always placed before the subject): *quoth the raven, ‘Never more’.* [pret. of *quethe* (otherwise obs.), OE *cwethan* say. Cf. BEQUEATH]

**quotha** /ˈkwoʊθə/, *interj. Archaic.* indeed! (used ironically or contemptuously in quoting another). [for *quoth a* quoth he]

**quotidian** /kwəˈtɪdiən/, *adj. Archaic.* **1.** daily. **2.** everyday; ordinary. **3.** (of a fever, ague, etc.) characterised by paroxysms which recur daily. *–n.* **4.** something recurring daily. **5.** a quotidian fever or ague. [L *quotīdiānus* daily; replacing ME *cotidien,* from OF]

**quotient** /ˈkwoʊʃənt/, *n.* (in mathematics) the result of division; the number of times one quantity is contained in another. [ME. from L *quotiens* how many times]

**quo warranto** /kwoʊ ˈwɒrəntoʊ/, *n.* **1.** (formerly) a writ calling upon a person to show by what warrant he claims an office, privilege, franchise, or liberty. **2.** a similar proceeding upon an information of this nature of quo warranto or under statutory provisions. [ML: by what warrant]

**q.v.** /kju ˈvi/, which see. [L *quod vide*]

**Q-value** /ˈkju-vælju/, *n.* the net energy released in a nuclear reaction, usu. expressed in millions of electron volts. *Abbrev.:* Q

**Qy,** Quay.

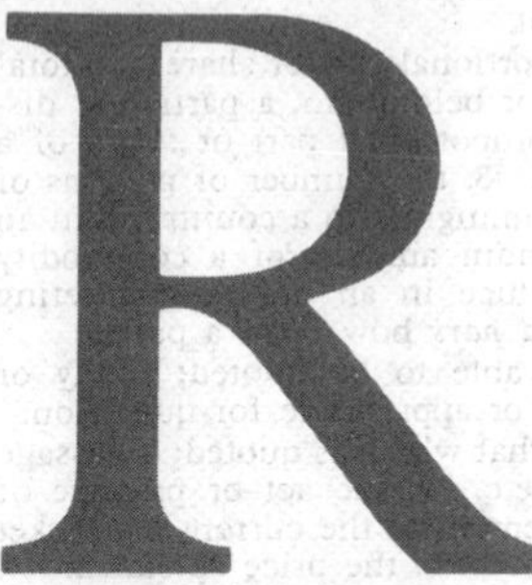

**Rr** Roman CLARENDON **Rr** Sans Serif FRUTIGER *Rr* Script TRAFTON **Rr** Decorative HOBO

*Although there are numerous typefaces in the world they can be divided into four main classifications. These are:*

*ROMAN or SERIF. This typeface came into being from the technique of the Roman masons who, working in stone, finished off each letter with a serif or small stroke projecting from the top or bottom. This was done to correct any feeling of unevenness or imbalance they may have created in cutting the characters in stone.*

*SANS SERIF (without serif). This typeface is geometric in design and has straight-edged characters and lines of a regular thickness.*

*SCRIPT. Based on the movement of the hand, this typeface is often italicised or slanted, as if drawn by a brush or quill pen.*

*DECORATIVE. Any typeface that exaggerates the characteristics of any of the other three classifications to a degree that places it outside of them.*

*The dictionary entries in this book use a SANS SERIF typeface called Helvetica (set in a bold face for the head words) and a SERIF typeface Plantin (used throughout the body of the entries).*

**R, r** /a/, *n., pl.* **R's** or **Rs, r's** or **rs.** **1.** the 18th letter of the English alphabet. **2.** See **three R's.**

**r,** *Elect.* resistance.

**r.,** **1.** radius. **2.** rare. **3.** *Comm.* received. **4.** replacing. **5.** right. **6.** river. **7.** rod. **8.** rouble. **9.** rule(d). **10.** *Cricket, Baseball, etc.* runs. **11.** (*pl.* **rs**) rupee. **12.** ratio.

**R,** **1.** *Physics, Chem.* gas constant. **2.** *Chem.* radical. **3.** *Maths.* ratio. **4.** *Elect.* resistance. **5.** (*pl.* **Rs**) rupee. **6.** rand. **7.** Rankine. **8.** Reaumur. **9.** roentgen.

**R** /a/, *adj.* denoting a film considered unsuitable for people under 18 years of age. [*r(estricted exhibition)*]

**R-,** a prefix used to indicate that a substance has right-handed chirality. [L *rectus* right]

**R.,** **1.** rabbi. **2.** rector. **3.** radius. **4.** railway. **5.** Regina (the Queen) or Rex (the King). **6.** *Theat.* stage right. **7.** River. **8.** rouble. **9.** Royal. **10.** resistance. **11.** Rook.

**Ra,** *Chem.* radium.

**R.A.,** **1.** Rear Admiral. **2.** *Astron.* right ascension.

**R.A.A.F.** /a dʌbəl eɪ 'ɛf, ræf/, Royal Australian Air Force. Also, **RAAF.**

**rabbet** /'ræbət/, *n., v.t., v.i.,* **-beted, -beting.** →**rebate**[2].

**rabbi** /'ræbaɪ/, *n., pl.* **-bis.** **1.** the principal religious official of a synagogue, equivalent to the Christian minister of religion; the spiritual leader of a Jewish community. **2.** a Jewish scholar; an expounder of the Jewish law. **3.** (*cap.*) a title of respect accorded to such an official or scholar. **4.** any of the early Jewish scholars who contributed to the formation of the Talmud. [ME and OE, from L, from Heb.: my master]

**rabbin** /'ræbən/, *n.* →**rabbi.** [ML *rabbinus*]

**rabbinate** /'ræbənət/, *n.* **1.** the status or tenure of office of a rabbi. **2.** rabbis collectively, esp. the rabbis of a particular place or region.

**Rabbinic** /rə'bɪnɪk/, *n.* the Hebrew language as used by the rabbis in their writings; the later Hebrew.

**rabbinical** /rə'bɪnɪkəl/, *adj.* of or pertaining to the rabbis or their learning, writings, etc. Also, **rabbinic.**

**rabbinist** /'ræbənəst/, *n.* (among the Jews) one who accepts the teaching of the Talmud and the tradition of the rabbis. Also, **rabbinite.** – **rabbinism,** *n.* – **rabbinistic** /ræbə'nɪstɪk/, **rabbinistical** /ræbə'nɪstɪkəl/, *adj.*

**rabbit**[1] /'ræbət/, *n., v.,* **-bited, -biting.** –*n.* **1.** a small, long-eared, burrowing lagomorph, *Oryctolagus cuniculus,* of the hare family. **2.** any of various rodent-like lagomorph mammals, as *Sylvilagus floridanus,* the eastern cottontail rabbit of North America. **3.** the skin of any member of the rabbit family. **4.** its flesh, used as food. **5.** *Colloq.* a bottle of beer. **6.** *Cricket.* a poor batsman. Cf. **ferret**[1] (def. 2). **7.** *Colloq.* a fool. –*v.i.* **8.** to hunt rabbits. **9.** *Colloq.* talk nonsense, usu. at length (fol. by *on*). [ME *rabet.* Cf. Walloon *robett,* Flem. *robbe*]

rabbit[1]

**rabbit**[2] /'ræbət/, *n.* a small container in which samples are passed through a nuclear reactor for irradiation. [orig. uncert.]

**rabbit-eared bandicoot** /ˌræbət-ɪəd 'bændikut/, *n.* →**long-eared bandicoot.** Also, **rabbit bandicoot.**

**rabbit ears** /'ræbət ɪəz/, *n.pl. Colloq.* an indoor television antenna with two adjustable arms. Also, **rabbit's ears.**

**rabbiter** /'ræbətə/, *n.* a person who catches rabbits, esp. on a rural property.

**rabbit fence** /'ræbət fɛns/, *n.* a wire fence of a suitable gauge, in which the wire extends into the ground so that rabbits cannot dig under it. Also, **rabbit-proof fence.**

**rabbit fever** /– 'fivə/, *n.* →**tularaemia.**

**rabbit-fish** /'ræbət-fɪʃ/, *n.* **1.** →**spinefoot.** **2.** a deep-water fish of the Atlantic, *Chimaera monstrosa,* whose large cutting teeth resemble those of a rabbit; angel shark; ghost shark. **3.** any of various other fishes said to resemble a rabbit.

**rabbit-killer** /'ræbət-kɪlə/, *n.* a short sharp blow to the nape of the neck or the lower part of the skull. Also, **rabbit-punch.**

**rabbit-oh** /'ræbət-oʊ/, *n. Colloq.* a street vendor selling rabbits. Also, **rabbito.** [from the vendor's cry *rabbit-oh*]

**rabbitry** /'ræbətri/, *n., pl.* **-tries.** **1.** a collection of rabbits. **2.** a place where rabbits are kept.

**rabbit-warren** /'ræbət-wɒrən/, *n.* →**warren.**

**rabble**[1] /'ræbəl/, *n., v.,* **-bled, -bling.** –*n.* **1.** a disorderly crowd; a mob. **2.** (*derog.*) the lowest class of people (prec. by *the*). –*v.t.* **3.** to beset as a rabble does; mob. –*v.i.* **4.** *Colloq.* to create an uproar: *the class is rabbling.* [ME *rabel;* ? akin to Brit. d. *rabble,* v., utter in a rapid confused manner]

**rabble**[2] /'ræbəl/, *n., v.,* **-bled, -bling.** –*n.* **1.** a tool or mechanically operated device used for stirring or mixing a charge in a roasting furnace. –*v.t.* **2.** to stir (the charge) in a roasting furnace. Also, **ribble.** [F *râble,* from L *rutābulum* fire-shovel] – **rabbler,** *n.*

**rabblerouser** /'ræbəlraʊzə/, *n.* **1.** a trouble maker. **2.**

→**demagogue.**

**Rabelaisian** /ræbəˈleɪziən, -ʒən/, *adj.* **1.** of, pertaining to, or suggesting François Rabelais, c. 1494-1553, whose work is characterised by broad, coarse humour and keen satire. *–n.* **2.** one who admires or studies the works of Rabelais. **3.** a person resembling in some way, esp. in coarse humour or grossness, a character created by Rabelais.

**rabid** /ˈræbəd/, *adj.* **1.** irrationally extreme in opinion or practice: *a rabid isolationist.* **2.** furious or raging; violently intense: *rabid hunger.* **3.** affected with or pertaining to rabies; mad. [L *rabidus* raving, mad] – **rabidity** /rəˈbɪdəti/, **rabidness,** *n.* – **rabidly,** *adv.*

**rabies** /ˈreɪbiz/, *n.* a fatal, infectious disease of the brain which occurs in all warm-blooded animals including man, and is due to a specific virus which occurs in saliva and is transmitted to new victims by the bite of an afflicted animal, generally the dog; hydrophobia. [L: madness, rage]

**raccoon** /rəˈkun/, *n.* **1.** any of several small nocturnal carnivores of the genus *Procyon,* esp. the North American *P. lotor,* arboreal in habit, and having a sharp snout and a bushy ringed tail. **2.** the thick grey to brown underfur of the raccoon, with silver-grey guard hairs tipped with black. Also, **racoon.** [Algonquian *ärähkunem* he scratches with the hands]

raccoon

**raccoon dog** /ˈ– dɒg/, *n.* a small wild dog of eastern Asia, of the genus *Nyctereutes* having dark marks around the eyes that give it some resemblance to a raccoon.

**race**[1] /reɪs/, *n., v.,* **raced, racing.** *–n.* **1.** a contest of speed, as in running, riding, driving, sailing, etc. **2.** (*pl.*) a series of races, esp. horseraces or greyhound races run at a set time over a regular course. **3.** any contest or competition: *an armaments race, the race for the presidency.* **4.** *Geol.* **a.** a strong or rapid current of water, as in the sea or a river. **b.** the channel or bed of such a current, or of any stream. **5.** an artificial channel, leading water to or from a place where its energy is utilised. **6.** the current of water in such a channel. **7. a.** a narrow passageway for livestock, as one leading to a sheep dip. **b.** any similar passageway, as through a cafeteria: *a food race.* **8.** *Mach.* a channel, groove, or the like, for a sliding or rolling part, as for ball-bearings. **9.** *Archaic.* onward movement; an onward or regular course. **10.** *Archaic.* the course of time. **11.** *Archaic.* the course of life, or of a part of life. **12. not in the race,** having no chance at all. *–v.i.* **13.** to engage in a contest of speed; run a race. **14.** to run horses in races; engage in or practise horseracing. **15.** to run, move, or go swiftly. **16.** (of an engine, wheel, etc.) to run with undue or uncontrolled speed when the load is diminished without corresponding reduction of fuel, power, etc. **17. race off with,** *Colloq.* to steal. *–v.t.* **18.** to run a race with; try to beat in a contest of speed. **19.** to cause to run in a race or races. **20.** to cause to run, move, or go swiftly: *to race a motor.* **21.** *Colloq.* to seduce (fol. by *off.*). [ME *ras(e),* from Scand.; cf. Icel. *rās* a running, race, rush of liquid, c. OE *rǣs* a running, rush]

**race**[2] /reɪs/, *n.* **1.** a group of persons connected by common descent, blood, or heredity. **2.** a population so connected. **3.** *Ethnol.* a subdivision of a stock, characterised by a more or less unique combination of physical traits which are transmitted in descent. **4.** a group of tribes or peoples forming an ethnic stock. **5.** the state of belonging to a certain ethnic stock. **6.** the distinguishing characteristics of special ethnic stocks. **7.** the human race or family, or mankind. **8.** *Zool.* a variety; a subspecies. **9.** a natural kind of living creature: *the human race, the race of fishes.* **10.** any group, class, or kind, esp. of persons. **11.** *Archaic.* (of speech, writing, etc.) characteristic quality, esp. liveliness or piquancy; raciness. **12.** the characteristic taste or flavour of wine. [F, from It. *razza* race, breed, lineage; orig. uncert.]

**race**[3] /reɪs/, *n.* a root (of ginger). [ME, from OF *rais,* from L *rādix* root]

**race caller** /ˈ– kɔlə/, *n.* one whose verbal description of a race is broadcast over the public address system to those present, or by means of radio or television to a wider audience.

**race-card** /ˈreɪs-kad/, *n.* the program for a race meeting. Also, **card.**

**racecourse** /ˈreɪskɔs/, *n.* **1.** a piece of ground on which horseraces are held for public entertainment. **2.** any place where races are held. **3.** a millrace or the like.

**race ginger** /ˈreɪs dʒɪndʒə/, *n.* →**gingerroot.**

**racegoer** /ˈreɪsgouə/, *n.* one who attends or is going to a race meeting; one who goes often to the races.

**race-hatred** /reɪs-ˈheɪtrəd/, *n.* animosity engendered by racial differences.

**racehorse** /ˈreɪshɔs/, *n.* **1.** a horse bred or kept for racing. **2.** *Colloq.* a thinly rolled cigarette. **3.** a swag rolled in a long thin roll, like a cigarette.

**racemase** /ˈræsəmeɪz/, *n.* any enzyme which will catalyse the conversion of an optically active compound into its racemic mixture.

**raceme** /rəˈsim, ˈreɪsim/, *n.* **1.** a simple indeterminate inflorescence in which the flowers are borne on short pedicels lying along a common axis, as in the lily-of-the-valley. **2.** a compound inflorescence in which the short pedicels with single flowers of the simple raceme are replaced by racemes (**compound raceme**). [L *racēmus* cluster of grapes. See RAISIN] – **racemiferous** /ræsəˈmɪfərəs/, *adj.*

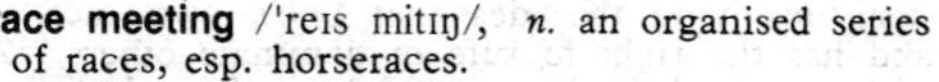
raceme of lily-of-the-valley

**race meeting** /ˈreɪs mitɪŋ/, *n.* an organised series of races, esp. horseraces.

**racemic** /rəˈsimɪk, -ˈsɛmɪk/, *adj.* denoting or pertaining to any of various organic compounds in which racemism occurs. [L *racēmus* cluster of grapes + -IC]

**racemic acid** /– ˈæsəd/, *n.* an isomeric modification of tartaric acid, which is sometimes found in the juice of grapes in conjunction with the common dextrorotatory form, and which is optically inactive, but can be separated into the two usual isomeric forms, dextrorotatory and laevorotatory.

**racemisation** /ræsəmaɪˈzeɪʃən/, *n.* the conversion of substances which are optically active into ones which are optically inactive. Also, **racemization.**

**racemism** /ˈræsəmɪzəm, rəˈsimɪzəm/, *n.* the character of an optically inactive substance (as racemic acid) separable into two other substances, of the same chemical composition as the original substance, one of which is dextrorotatory and the other laevorotatory.

**racemose** /ˈræsəmous/, *adj.* **1.** having the form of a raceme. **2.** arranged in racemes. [L *racēmōsus* clustering]

**racer** /ˈreɪsə/, *n.* **1.** one who or that which races, or takes part in a race, as a racehorse, or a bicycle, yacht, etc., used for racing. **2.** anything having great speed. **3.** a mounting on which a heavy gun is turned.

**race relations** /ˈreɪs rəleɪʃənz/, *n.pl.* the reciprocal behaviour of two or more races of people, esp. in a single society.

**race riot** /ˈ– raɪət/, *n.* an act of mob violence resulting from racial animosity.

**race suicide** /– ˈsuəsaɪd/, *n.* the extinction of a race or people which tends to result when, through the unwillingness or forbearance of its members to have children, the birthrate falls below the death rate.

**racetrack** /ˈreɪstræk/, *n.* **1.** a track on which races, esp. motor races, are held. **2.** a racecourse.

**raceway** /ˈreɪsweɪ/, *n.* a passage or channel for water, as a millrace.

**rachilla** /rəˈkɪlə/, *n.* the axis within the spikelet of a grass; a small or secondary rachis. Also, **rhachilla.**

**rachis** /ˈreɪkəs/, *n., pl.* **rachises** /ˈreɪkəsiz/, **rachides** /ˈrækədiz, ˈreɪkə-/ **1.** *Bot.* **a.** the axis of an inflorescence when somewhat elongated, as in a raceme. **b.** (in a pinnately compound leaf or frond) the prolongation of the petiole along which the leaflets are disposed. **c.** any of various axial structures. **2.** *Zool.* the shaft of a feather, esp. that part, anterior to the superior umbilicus,

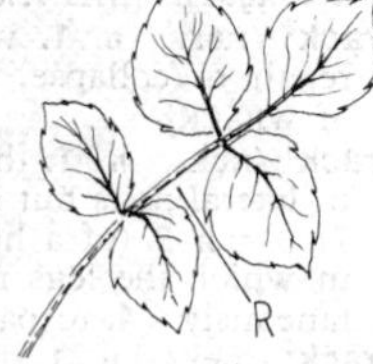

R, rachis (def. 1b)

i = peat ɪ = pit ɛ = pet æ = pat a = part ɒ = pot ʌ = putt ɔ = port ʊ = put u = pool ɜ = pert ə = apart aɪ = buy eɪ = bay ɔɪ = boy aʊ = how oʊ = hoe ɪə = here ɛə = hair ʊə = tour g = give θ = thin ð = then ʃ = show ʒ = measure tʃ = choke dʒ = joke ŋ = sing j = you õ = Fr. bon

bearing the web, as distinguished from the quill. **3.** *Anat.* the spinal column. Also, **rhachis.** [NL, from Gk]

**rachitis** /rəˈkaɪtəs/, *n.* →**rickets.** [NL, from Gk: disease of the spine] – **rachitic** /rəˈkɪtɪk/, *adj.*

**Rachmanism** /ˈrækmənɪzəm/, *n.* unscrupulous practices by landlords, esp. the extortion of high rents from tenants in slum properties. [from Perec *Rachman,* 1920-62, a London landlord]

**racial** /ˈreɪʃəl/, *adj.* **1.** pertaining to or characteristic of race or extraction, or a race or races. **2.** pertaining to the relations between people of different races. – **racially,** *adv.*

**racialism** /ˈreɪʃəlɪzəm/, *n.* →**racism.** – **racialist,** *n., adj.*

**racing** /ˈreɪsɪŋ/, *adj.* **1.** of, pertaining to, designed for, or used in races, speed tests, etc.: *a racing car.* –*n.* **2.** the act of taking part in or attending races, esp. horseraces.

**racing calendar** /ˈ– kæləndə/, *n.* the official publication of the controlling body of horseracing in each State.

**racing colours** /ˈ– kʌləz/, *n.pl.* registered colours exclusive to an owner and worn by jockeys riding his horses.

**racing commentator** /ˈ– kɒmənteɪtə/, *n.* one who offers opinions and commentary on horseracing and greyhound racing, etc., as in a newspaper, on radio, etc.

**racing stripes** /ˈ– straɪps/, *n.pl.* stripes, sometimes representing team colours, on articles of clothing as swimsuits, tracksuits, etc., worn by athletes.

**racism** /ˈreɪsɪzəm/, *n.* **1.** the belief that human races have distinctive characteristics which determine their respective cultures, usu. involving the idea that one's own race is superior and has the right to rule or dominate others. **2.** offensive or aggressive behaviour to members of another race stemming from such a belief. **3.** a policy or system of government and society based upon it. Also, **racialism.** – **racist,** *n., adj.*

**rack**[1] /ræk/, *n.* **1.** a framework of bars, wires, or pegs on which articles are arranged or deposited (used esp. in composition): *a shoe rack, wine rack.* **2.** a spreading framework, fixed or movable, for carrying hay, straw, or the like in large loads, esp. for fodder. **3.** *Print.* an upright framework with side cleats or other supports for the storing of cases or galleys of type, etc. **4.** *Mach.* **a.** a bar with teeth on one of its sides, adapted to engage with the teeth of a pinion or the like, as for converting circular into rectilinear motion or vice versa. **b.** a similar bar with notches over which the projections of such devices as pawls operate. **5.** an apparatus or instrument formerly in use for torturing persons by stretching the body. **6.** a cause or state of intense suffering of body or mind. **7.** torment, anguish. **8.** violent strain. **9. on the rack, a.** in great pain, distress, or anxiety. **b.** under the strain of great effort. –*v.t.* **10.** to torture; distress acutely; torment. **11.** to strain in mental effort: *to rack one's brains.* **12.** to strain by physical force or violence; shake violently. **13.** to strain beyond what is normal or usual. **14.** to stretch the joints of (a person) in torture by means of a rack. **15.** to furnish with, or put on or in a rack. **16.** *Bldg Trades.* to leave (a wall) with unfinished ends for later additions. **17.** to score, as in a game (fol. by *up*): *she had racked up many a conquest.* [ME *rekke, rakke,* from MD or MLG]

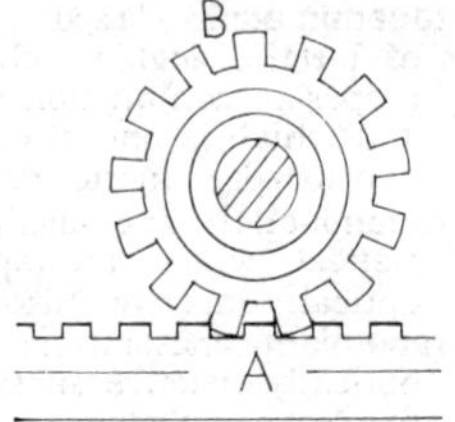

A, rack[1] (def. 4); B, pinion gear

**rack**[2] /ræk/, *n.* **1.** wreck; destruction. **2. rack and ruin,** disrepair or collapse, esp. owing to neglect; dilapidation. [var. of WRACK]

**rack**[3] /ræk/, *n.* **1.** the gait of a horse in which the legs move in lateral pairs but not quite simultaneously. **2.** →**pace**[1] (def. 7). –*v.i.* **3.** (of a horse) to go with a gait, similar to a pace, in which the legs move in lateral pairs but not quite simultaneously. **4.** to pace. [? var. of ROCK[2], *v.*]

**rack**[4] /ræk/, *n.* **1.** flying, broken clouds; a mass of clouds driven by the wind. –*v.i.* **2.** to drive or move, esp. before the wind. [ME *rak, rakke,* probably from Scand.; cf. Icel. *reki* drift, wreckage, *reka* drive]

**rack**[5] /ræk/, *v.t.* to draw off (wine, cider, etc.) from the lees. [late ME; cf. obs. F *raqué* (of wine) pressed from the marc of grapes, Pr. *arracar* to rack, *raca* dregs]

**rack**[6] /ræk/, *n.* **1.** the neck portion of mutton, pork, or veal. **2. rack of lamb,** trimmed ribs or cutlets prepared for roasting in one piece. [cf. G *Rachen* throat]

**rack**[7] /ræk/, *v.i. Colloq.* to leave; go (fol. by *off*): *he racked off ages ago; rack off, hairy legs!*

**rack-and-pinion** /ræk-ən-ˈpɪnjən/, *n.* **1.** a system for the conversion of rotary to linear motion and vice versa, consisting of a pinion and a mated rack (def. 4). –*adj.* **2.** of, using, or comprising such a system.

**racket**[1] /ˈrækət/, *n.* **1.** a loud noise, esp. of a disturbing or confusing kind; din; uproar; clamour or noisy fuss. **2.** social excitement, gaiety, or dissipation. **3.** *Colloq.* an organised illegal activity such as the extortion of money by threat or violence from legitimate businessmen: *the protection racket.* **4.** *Colloq.* a dishonest scheme, trick, etc. **5.** *Colloq.* one's legitimate business or occupation: *he's in the advertising racket.* –*v.i.* **6.** to make a racket or noise. **7.** to indulge in social gaiety or dissipation. [metathetic var. of d. *rattick.* See RATTLE[1]]

**racket**[2] /ˈrækət/, *n.* →**racquet.**

**racketeer** /rækəˈtɪə/, *n.* **1.** one engaged in a racket. –*v.i.* **2.** to engage in a racket. [RACKET[1] (defs 3 and 4) + -EER] – **racketeering,** *n., adj.*

**rackett** /ˈrækət/, *n.* →**racquet.**

**rackety** /ˈrækəti/, *adj.* **1.** making or causing a racket; noisy. **2.** fond of excitement or dissipation.

**rack-rail** /ˈræk-reɪl/, *n.* (in an inclined-plane or mountain-climbing railway) a rail between the running rails having cogs or teeth with which cogwheels on the locomotive engage.

**rack-railway** /ræk-ˈreɪlweɪ/, *n.* a steep railway fitted with a rack-rail.

**rack-rent** /ˈræk-rɛnt/, *n.* **1.** a rent for land equal or nearly equal to its full annual value. **2.** an exorbitant rent. –*v.t.* **3.** to exact the highest possible rent for. **4.** to demand rack-rent from. [RACK[1], *v.* + RENT[1]] – **rack-renter,** *n.*

**rackwork** /ˈrækwɜk/, *n.* a mechanism in which a rack is used; a rack and pinion or the like.

**racon** /ˈreɪkɒn/, *n.* →**radio beacon.** [b. RA(DIO BEA)CON]

**raconteur** /rækɒnˈtɜ/, *n.* a person skilled in relating stories and anecdotes. [F. See RECOUNT]

**racoon** /rəˈkun/, *n.* →**raccoon.**

**racquet** /ˈrækət/, *n.* **1.** a light bat having a network of cord or catgut stretched in a more or less elliptical frame, used in tennis, etc. **2.** (*pl. construed as sing.*) a game of ball, played in a walled court, in which such bats are used. **3.** a snowshoe made in the manner of a tennis racquet. –*v.t.* **4.** to strike with a racket. Also, **racket, rackett.** [F *raquette;* orig. uncert.]

**racy** /ˈreɪsi/, *adj.,* **-cier, -ciest.** **1.** vigorous; lively; spirited. **2.** sprightly; piquant; pungent: *a racy style.* **3.** having an agreeably peculiar taste or flavour, as wine, fruits, etc. **4.** suggestive; risqué: *a racy story.* [RACE[1] + -Y[1]] – **racily,** *adv.* – **raciness,** *n.*

**rad,** radian.

**rad** /ræd/, *n.* a non-SI unit of absorbed dose of ionising radiation equal to 0.01 grams. [short for RADIATION]

**rad.,** **1.** *Maths.* radical. **2.** radix.

**radar** /ˈreɪda/, *n.* a device to determine the presence and location of an object by measuring the time for the echo of a radio wave to return from it, and the direction from which it returns. [short for *ra(dio) d(etecting) a(nd) r(anging)*]

**radar scanner** /ˈ– skænə/, *n.* the revolving transmitter-receiver antenna of a radar unit.

**radarscope** /ˈreɪdaskoʊp/, *n.* the oscilloscope viewing screen of radar equipment.

**radar trap** /ˈreɪda træp/, *n.* a place beside a road where police have set up radar equipment to detect speeding motorists.

**Radburn planning** /ˌrædbɜn ˈplænɪŋ/, *n.* a style of housing development in which houses front on to a communally shared parkland area, and vehicular access is from the rear. [named after *Radburn,* U.S. town, built c. 1930, and the first example of this style of town-planning]

**raddle** /ˈrædl/, *n., v.t.,* **-dled, dling.** –*n.* **1.** a red variety of

i = peat ɪ = pit ɛ = pet æ = pat a = part ɒ = pot ʌ = putt ɔ = port ʊ = put u = pool ɜ = pert ə = apart aɪ = buy eɪ = bay ɔɪ = boy aʊ = how
oʊ = hoe ɪə = here ɛə = hair ʊə = tour g = give θ = thin ð = then ʃ = show ʒ = measure tʃ = choke dʒ = joke ŋ = sing j = you õ = Fr. bon

ochre. **2.** a coloured mark, often red, placed upon sheep for identification or to indicate a badly shorn sheep. *–v.t.* **3.** to mark a sheep for identification. [var. of RUDDLE]

**raddle harness** /'– hanəs/, *n.* a harness placed on a ram's brisket containing raddle, to identify ewes tupped.

**raddle-marked** /'rædl-makt/, *adj.* **1.** of an animal, marked by raddle for identification purposes. **2.** *Colloq.* of a shearer, due for early dismissal because his sheep were badly shorn and thus marked with raddle.

**radial** /'reɪdiəl/, *adj.* **1.** arranged like radii or rays. **2.** having spokes, bars, lines, etc., arranged like radii, as a machine. **3.** *Zool.* pertaining to structures that radiate from a central point, as the arms of a starfish. **4.** of, like, or pertaining to a radius or a ray. **5.** *Anat.* referring to the radius or more lateral of the two bones of the forearm. *–n.* **6.** →**radial-ply tyre.** [ML *radiālis,* from L *radius* RADIUS + *-ālis* -AL[1]] – **radially,** *adv.*

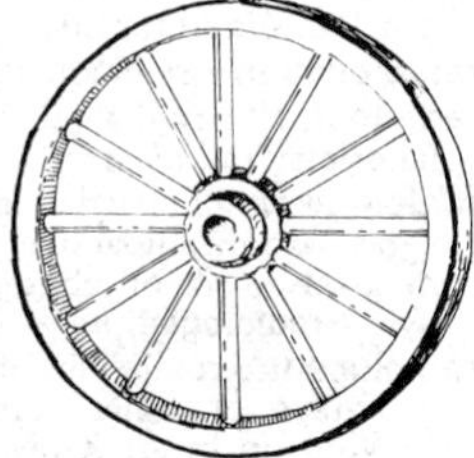
radial arrangement of spokes of a wheel

**radial engine** /– 'ɛndʒən/, *n.* an engine having cylinders grouped so that they resemble equally spaced radii of a circle, or spokes of a wheel, esp. where the cylinders are stationary, and the crankshaft revolves.

**radial-ply tyre** /ˌreɪdiəl-plaɪ 'taɪə/, *n.* a pneumatic tyre with flexible walls achieved by having the casing cords running radially and with additional plies strengthening the tread only.

**radial velocity** /reɪdiəl və'lɒsəti/, *n.* the velocity, usu. expressed in kilometres per second, with which a celestial body approaches or recedes from the observer. Also, **line-of-sight velocity.**

**radian** /'reɪdiən/, *n.* the supplementary SI unit of measurement of plane angle, being the plane angle between two radii of a circle which cut off on the circumference an arc equal to the length of the radius. *Symbol:* rad

**radiance** /'reɪdiəns/, *n.* **1.** radiant brightness or light: *radiance of the tropical sun, radiance lit her face.* **2.** →**radiation.** Also, **radiancy.**

**radiant** /'reɪdiənt/, *adj.* **1.** emitting rays of light; shining; bright: *the radiant sun, radiant colours.* **2.** bright with joy, hope, etc.: *radiant smiles.* **3.** *Physics.* emitted in rays, or by radiation. *–n.* **4.** a point or object from which rays proceed. **5.** *Astron.* the point in the heavens from which a shower of meteors appears to radiate. [late ME, from L *radians,* ppr., emitting rays] – **radiantly,** *adv.*

**radiata pine** /ˌreɪdiatə 'paɪn/, *n.* a valuable softwood timber tree, *Pinus radiata,* native to California but widely cultivated in Australia; Monterey pine; insignis pine.

**radiate** /'reɪdieɪt/, *v.,* **-ated, -ating,** *adj.* *–v.i.* **1.** to spread or move like rays or radii from a centre. **2.** to emit rays, as of light or heat; irradiate. **3.** to issue or proceed in rays. *–v.t.* **4.** to emit in rays; disseminate as from a centre. **5.** (of persons) to exhibit abundantly (good humour, benevolence, etc.). *–adj.* **6.** radiating from a centre. **7.** represented with rays proceeding from it, as a head on a coin, in art, etc. [L *radiātus,* pp.]

**radiation** /reɪdi'eɪʃən/, *n.* **1.** *Physics.* the emission and propagation of particles or waves such as by a radioactive substance, a source of electromagnetic waves or a source of sound waves. **2.** the act or process of radiating. **3.** that which is radiated; a ray or rays. **4.** radial arrangement of parts.

**radiation sickness** /'– sɪknəs/, *n.* illness caused by exposure to ionising radiations or the consumption of radioactive materials.

**radiative** /'reɪdiətɪv/, *adj.* **1.** emitting radiation. **2.** of or pertaining to that which radiates.

**radiator** /'reɪdieɪtə/, *n.* **1.** one who or that which radiates. **2.** a device for heating a room in which a cylindrical rod, heated red-hot electrically, radiates heat directly and sometimes via a reflector placed behind it. **3.** any of various heating devices, as a series or coil of pipes through which steam or hot water passes. **4.** a device constructed from thin-walled tubes and metal fins, used for cooling circulating water, as in the cooling system of a motor-car engine, etc. **5.** *Radio.* a type of aerial.

**radical** /'rædɪkəl/, *adj.* **1.** going to the root or origin; fundamental: *a radical change.* **2.** thoroughgoing or extreme, esp. towards reform. **3.** (*oft. cap.*) **a.** favouring drastic political, social or other reforms. **b.** belonging or pertaining to a political party holding such views. **4.** forming the basis or foundation. **5.** existing inherently in a thing or person: *radical defects of character.* **6.** *Maths.* **a.** pertaining to or forming a root. **b.** denoting or pertaining to the radical sign. **7.** *Gram.* of or pertaining to a root. **8.** *Bot.* of or arising from the root or the base of the stem. *–n.* **9.** one who holds or follows extreme principles, esp. left-wing political principles; an extremist. **10.** (*oft. cap.*) **a.** one who advocates fundamental and drastic political reforms or changes. **b.** a member of a radical (political) party. **11.** *Maths.* **a.** a quantity expressed as a root of another quantity. **b.** a radical sign. **12.** *Chem.* an atom or group of atoms regarded as an important constituent of a molecule, which remains unchanged and behaves as a unit in many reactions. **13.** *Gram.* →**root**[1] (def. 13). [ME, from LL *rādīcālis,* from L *rādix* root] – **radicalness,** *n.*

**radical axis** /– 'æksəs/, *n.* (of two circles) the line such that tangents drawn from any point of the line to the two circles are equal in length.

**radicalise** /'rædɪkəlaɪz/, *v.,* **-lised, -lising.** *–v.t.* **1.** to make radical. *–v.i.* **2.** to become radical. – **radicalisation** /ˌrædɪkəlaɪ'zeɪʃən/, *n.*

**radicalism** /'rædɪkəlɪzəm/, *n.* **1.** the holding or following of radical or extreme views or principles, esp. leftwing political principles. **2.** the principles or practices of radicals.

**radically** /'rædɪkli/, *adv.* **1.** with regard to origin or root. **2.** in a complete or fundamental manner.

**radical sign** /ˌrædɪkəl 'saɪn/, *n.* the symbol √ or $\sqrt{\phantom{x}}$ (initially the first letter of *radix*) indicating extraction of a root of the following quantity: $\sqrt{a^2} = \pm a$, $\sqrt[3]{a^3 b^3} = ab$.

**radicel** /'rædəsɛl/, *n.* (in botany) a minute root; a rootlet. [NL *rādicella,* diminutive of L *rādix* root]

**radicle** /'rædɪkəl/, *n.* **1.** (of plants) the lower part of the axis of an embryo; the primary root. **2.** a rudimentary root; a radicel or rootlet. **3.** *U.S. Chem.* →**radical.** **4.** *Anat.* a small rootlike part, as the beginning of a nerve fibre. [L *rādicula,* diminutive of *rādix* root]

**radii** /'reɪdiaɪ, -dii/, *n.* plural of **radius.**

**radio** /'reɪdioʊ/, *n., v.,* **-dios,** *adj., v.,* **-dioed, -dioing.** *–n.* **1.** wireless telegraphy or telephony: *speeches broadcast by radio.* **2.** an apparatus for receiving radio broadcasts; a wireless. **3.** a message transmitted by radio. *–adj.* **4.** pertaining to, used in, or sent by radio. **5.** pertaining to or employing radiations, as of electrical energy. *–v.t.* **6.** to transmit (a message, etc.) by radio. **7.** to send a message to (a person) by radio. *–v.i.* **8.** to transmit a message, etc., by radio. [short for *radiotelegraphic* (or *-telephonic*) *instrument, message,* or *transmission*]

**radio-,** a word element meaning: **1.** radio. **2.** radial. **3.** radium, radioactive, or radiant energy. [orig. combining form of RADIUS]

**radioactivate** /ˌreɪdioʊ'æktəveɪt/, *v.t.,* **-vated, -vating.** to make radioactive. – **radioactivation** /ˌreɪdioʊˌæktə'veɪʃən/, *n.*

**radioactive** /ˌreɪdioʊ'æktɪv/, *adj.* possessing, pertaining to, or caused by radioactivity.

**radioactive age** /– 'eɪdʒ/, *n.* the age of a mineral, fossil, or wooden object as estimated from its content of radioactive isotopes.

**radioactive series** /– 'sɪəriz/, *n.* the series of isotopes of various elements through which a radioactive substance decays before it reaches a stable state. The three known spontaneous series start with thorium and two different isotopes of uranium and each ends at a stable isotope of lead.

**radioactive tracer** /– 'treɪsə/, *n.* See **tracer** (def. 5).

**radioactivity** /ˌreɪdioʊæk'tɪvəti/, *n.* the property of spontaneous disintegration possessed by certain elements due to changes in their atomic nuclei. The disintegration is accompanied by the emission of alpha, beta, or gamma radiation.

**radio altimeter** /ˌreɪdioʊ ˈæltəmitə/, *n.* an electronic altimeter which indicates the height of an aircraft by measuring the time taken for an emitted radio wave to travel to the ground and back again.

**radioastronomy** /ˌreɪdioʊəˈstrɒnəmi/, *n.* the branch of astronomy based on the radio-frequency radiation (as distinct from light) which is received on the earth. – **radioastronomical** /ˌreɪdioʊˌæstrəˈnɒmɪkəl/, *adj.*

**radioautograph** /ˌreɪdioʊˈɔtəgræf/, *n.* →**autoradiograph.**

**radio beacon** /ˈreɪdioʊ bikən/, *n.* a radio transmitter emitting a characteristic signal so as to enable ships or aircraft to determine their position or bearing by a receiving instrument (**radio compass**).

**radio beam** /ˈ– bim/, *n.* →**beam** (def. 13).

**radiobiology** /ˌreɪdioʊbaɪˈɒlədʒi/, *n.* the branch of biology concerned with the effects of radiation on living organisms and the behaviour of radioactive materials, or the use of radioactive tracers, in biological systems.

**radiocarbon dating** /ˌreɪdioʊkabən ˈdeɪtɪŋ/, *n.* the determination of the age of objects of plant or animal origin by means of their content of radioactive carbon (${}^{14}_{6}C$). Also, **carbon dating.**

**radiochemistry** /ˌreɪdioʊˈkɛməstri/, *n.* the chemical study of radioactive elements, both natural and artificial, and their use in the study of other chemical processes.

**radio-compass** /ˌreɪdioʊ-ˈkʌmpəs/, *n.* any device, as a radio receiver with a directional aerial, which can be used for position-finding.

**radio control** /ˌreɪdioʊ kənˈtroʊl/, *n.* **1.** the remote control of an apparatus, as a pilotless aircraft or the like, by means of signals from a radio transmitter. **2.** the direction of a vehicle, as a police car or taxi, by instructions from a radio transmitter. – **radio-controlled,** *adj.*

**radio direction-finder** /– dəˈrɛkʃən-faɪndə/, *n.* See **direction-finder.**

**radio doctor** /ˈ– dɒktə/, *n.* **1.** a doctor in the outback who works in conjunction with the flying doctor service and who gives diagnosis and assistance over the pedal wireless. **2.** a doctor employed to do night and weekend calls for other doctors, and who works from a car in radio contact with a central control.

**radioelement** /ˌreɪdioʊˈɛləmənt/, *n.* **1.** an element which is naturally radioactive. **2.** →**radioisotope.**

**radiofrequency** /ˌreɪdioʊˈfrikwənsi/, *n., pl.* **-cies. 1.** the frequency of the transmitting waves of a given radio message or broadcast. **2.** a frequency within the range of radio transmission. –*adj.* **3.** pertaining to, denoting, or operating at a radiofrequency. Also, **radio frequency.**

**radiofrequency heating** /– ˈhitɪŋ/, *n.* industrial dielectric or induction heating.

**radiofrequency welding** /– ˈwɛldɪŋ/, *n.* a method of welding thermoplastic materials in which the necessary heat is generated by the application of a radiofrequency field to the material.

**radio galaxy** /ˌreɪdioʊ ˈgæləksi/, *n.* a galaxy which is observed to emit electromagnetic radiation of radiofrequencies.

**radiogenic** /ˌreɪdioʊˈdʒɛnɪk, -ˈdʒinɪk/, *adj.* resulting from radioactive decay.

**radiogram** /ˈreɪdioʊˌgræm/, *n.* **1.** a combined radio and gramophone. **2.** a message transmitted by radiotelegraphy. **3.** →**radiograph.**

**radiograph** /ˈreɪdioʊgræf, -graf/, *n.* **1.** an image or picture produced by the action of X-rays, usu. on a photographic plate (def. 20). –*v.t.* **2.** to make a radiograph of.

**radiography** /reɪdiˈɒgrəfi/, *n.* the production of images or pictures produced by the action of X-rays, or other rays, (as from radioactive substances) on a photographic plate, esp. as used in medicine; X-ray photography. – **radiographer,** *n.* – **radiographic** /ˌreɪdioʊˈgræfɪk/, *adj.*

**radio interferometer** /ˌreɪdioʊ ɪntəfəˈrɒmətə/, *n.* a type of radio telescope, based on the principle of the optical interferometer but operating on radiofrequencies. It consists of two or more aerials all receiving electromagnetic radiation from the same source and connected to the same receiver, thus producing an analysable interference pattern.

**radioisotope** /ˌreɪdioʊˈaɪsətoʊp/, *n.* a radioactive isotope, usu. artificially produced, of a normally inert chemical element, used in physical and biological research, therapeutics, etc.

**radiol.,** radiology.

**radiolarian** /ˌreɪdioʊˈlɛəriən/, *n.* any of the Radiolaria, an extensive group or order of minute marine protozoans, having amoeba-like bodies with fine radiating pseudopodia, and usu. elaborate skeletons. [NL *Radiolāria,* pl., (from L *radiolus,* diminutive of *radius* ray) + -AN]

**radio link** /ˈreɪdioʊ lɪŋk/, *n.* a radio communication circuit, comprising transmitters, receivers, and aerials, often used to join land-line circuits.

**radiolocation** /ˌreɪdioʊləˈkeɪʃən/, *n. Elect.* →**radar.**

**radiological** /reɪdiəˈlɒdʒɪkəl/, *adj.* **1.** involving radioactive materials: *radiological warfare.* **2.** pertaining to radiology.

**radiology** /reɪdiˈɒlədʒi/, *n.* **1.** the science dealing with X-rays or rays from radioactive substances, esp. for medical uses. **2.** the examining or photographing of organs, etc., with such rays. – **radiologist,** *n.*

**radiolucent** /ˌreɪdioʊˈlusənt/, *adj.* partly or wholly permeable to X-rays or other forms of radiation, and therefore not showing up in an X-ray photograph. Cf. **radiopaque.**

**radioluminescence** /ˌreɪdioʊˌluməˈnɛsəns/, *n.* luminescence caused by radiation from a radioactive material.

**radiolysis** /reɪdiˈɒləsəs/, *n.* the chemical decomposition of a substance as a result of irradiation.

**radio magnetic indicator,** *n.* a flight instrument combining a remote indicating compass and one or more radio navaids.

**radiometeorograph** /ˌreɪdioʊˈmitiərəgræf/, *n.* →**radiosonde.**

**radiometer** /reɪdiˈɒmətə/, *n.* **1.** an instrument for indicating the transformation of radiant energy into mechanical work, consisting of an exhausted glass vessel containing vanes which revolve about an axis when exposed to radiant energy. **2.** an instrument based on the same principle, but used for detecting and measuring small amounts of radiant energy. – **radiometric** /ˌreɪdioʊˈmɛtrɪk/, *adj.* – **radiometry,** *n.*

radiometer (def. 1)

**radiometric dating** /ˌreɪdioʊˌmɛtrɪk ˈdeɪtɪŋ/, *n.* determining the age of a rock or mineral by measuring the ratios of certain radioactive isotopes contained in the specimen.

**radiomicrometer** /ˌreɪdioʊmaɪˈkrɒmətə/, *n.* a sensitive instrument for measuring heat radiation, consisting of a thermocouple connected directly into a single copper loop which forms the coil of a galvanometer.

**radionavigation** /reɪdioʊˌnævəˈgeɪʃən/, *n.* the use of radio techniques as an aid to navigation.

**radionuclide** /ˌreɪdioʊˈnjuklaɪd/, *n.* a radioactive nuclide.

**radiopaque** /ˌreɪdioʊˈpeɪk/, *adj.* opaque to radiation, hence, visible in X-ray photographs and under fluoroscopy. – **radiopacity** /ˌreɪdioʊˈpæsəti/, *n.*

**radioparent** /ˌreɪdioʊˈpærənt/, *adj.* permitting the passage of X-rays without hindrance.

**radiophone** /ˈreɪdioʊfoʊn/, *n.* **1.** any of various devices for producing sound by the action of radiant energy. Thus, light falling on a phototube will vary an electric current which can actuate a loudspeaker. **2.** →**radiotelephone.**

**radio receiver** /ˈreɪdioʊ rəsivə/, *n.* a device which converts the information conveyed by radio waves into soundwaves.

**radio relay** /– ˈrileɪ/, *n.* a system which receives radio signals and retransmits them, thus establishing radio communication between two points which could not otherwise communicate directly.

**radiosclerometer** /ˌreɪdioʊskləˈrɒmətə/, *n.* →**penetrometer** (def. 2).

**radioscopy** /reɪdiˈɒskəpi/, *n.* the examination of opaque objects by means of the X-rays or rays emitted by radioactive substances. – **radioscopic** /ˌreɪdioʊˈskɒpɪk/, **radioscopical** /ˌreɪdioʊˈskɒpɪkəl/, *adj.*

**radio set** /ˈreɪdioʊ sɛt/, *n.* a radio receiver or transceiver.

**radio signal** /ˈ– sɪgnəl/, *n.* any electromagnetic wave emitted by a radio transmitter.

**radiosonde** /ˈreɪdioʊsɒnd/, *n.* an instrument carried aloft by a balloon and sending back information, by means of a small radio transmitter, about the atmospheric temperature, pressure, and humidity encountered. [RADIO- + SONDE]

**radio source** /ˌreɪdioʊ ˈsɔs/, *n.* a powerful mass of energy, such as a quasar or supernova remnant, as a source of radio waves. Formerly, **radio star.**

**radio star** /ˈ– sta/, *n. Obs.* →**radio source.**

**radio station** /ˈ– steɪʃən/, *n.* **1.** a combination of devices for radio transmitting and/or receiving. **2.** a complete installation for radio broadcasting, including transmitting apparatus, broadcasting studios, etc. **3.** an organisation engaged in broadcasting, on a fixed frequency or frequencies, programs of news, entertainment, propaganda, etc.

**radiotelegram** /ˌreɪdioʊˈtɛləgræm/, *n.* a message transmitted by radiotelegraphy.

**radiotelegraph** /ˌreɪdioʊˈtɛləgræf, -graf/, *n.* **1.** →**radiotelegram.** *–v.t., v.i.* **2.** to telegraph by radiotelegraphy. **– radiotelegraphic** /ˌreɪdioʊˌtɛləˈgræfɪk/, *adj.*

**radiotelegraphy** /ˌreɪdioʊtəˈlɛgrəfi/, *n.* telegraphy without wires or cables, in which messages are transmitted through space by means of the radiated energy of electromagnetic waves; wireless telegraphy.

**radiotelemetry** /ˌreɪdioʊtəˈlɛmətri/, *n.* the transmission of measurements from a distant or inaccessible point to a recording device by the use of radio waves.

**radiotelephone** /ˌreɪdioʊˈtɛləfoʊn/, *n., v.,* **-phoned, -phoning.** *–n.* **1.** a telephone in which the signal is transmitted by radiotelephony; wireless telephone. *–v.t., v.i.* **2.** to telephone using the process of radiotelephony. **– radiotelephonic** /ˌreɪdioʊˌtɛləˈfɒnɪk/, *adj.*

**radiotelephony** /ˌreɪdioʊtəˈlɛfəni/, *n.* a system of transmitting and receiving voice messages by means of radio; wireless telephony.

**radio telescope** /ˌreɪdioʊ ˈtɛləskoʊp/, *n.* a large parabolic reflector, or a radio interferometer, used to gather radio signals emitted by celestial bodies or spacecraft and focus them for reception by a receiver. See **radioastronomy.**

radio telescope, Parkes, N.S.W.

**radiotherapy** /ˌreɪdioʊˈθɛrəpi/, *n.* treatment of disease by means of X-rays or of radioactive substances.

**radiothermy** /ˈreɪdioʊˌθɜmi/, *n.* therapy which utilises the heat from a short-wave radio apparatus or diathermy machine.

**radiothorium** /ˌreɪdioʊˈθɔriəm/, *n.* a disintegration product of thorium. [NL. See RADIO-, THORIUM]

**radio transmitter** /ˌreɪdioʊ trænzˈmɪtə/, *n.* an apparatus which emits electromagnetic radiation modulated by signals.

**radio valve** /ˈ– vælv/, *n.* →**valve** (def. 7). Also, **radio tube.**

**radio wave** /ˈ– weɪv/, *n.* an electromagnetic wave of radio-frequency.

**radish** /ˈrædɪʃ/, *n.* **1.** the crisp, pungent, edible root of a plant, *Raphanus sativus.* **2.** the plant. [late ME; OE *rædic,* from L *rādix* root, radish]

**radium** /ˈreɪdiəm/, *n.* a naturally occurring radioactive metallic element with chemical properties resembling those of barium. *Symbol:* Ra; *at. wt. of most stable isotope:* 226; *at. no.:* 88. [NL, from L *radius* ray]

**radium A** /– ˈeɪ/, *n.* a substance, formed from radon by disintegration, which gives rise to radium B.

**radium B** /– ˈbi/, *n.* an isotope of lead, formed from radium A by disintegration, which gives rise to an isotope of bismuth called **radium C,** from which **radium D, radium E,** and **radium F** (polonium) are derived.

**radium emanation** /– ɛməˈneɪʃən/, *n.* →**radon.**

**radium-228** /ˌreɪdiəm-tu tu ˈeɪt/, *n.* an isotope of radium (though far more radioactive), used in pigments and in medicines.

**radius** /ˈreɪdiəs/, *n., pl.* **-dii** /-diaɪ/, **-diuses.** **1.** a straight line extending from the centre of a circle or sphere to the circumference or surface. **2.** the length of such a line. **3.** any radial or radiating part. **4.** a circular area of an extent indicated by the length of the radius of its circumscribing circle: *every house within a radius of fifty kilometres.* **5.** field

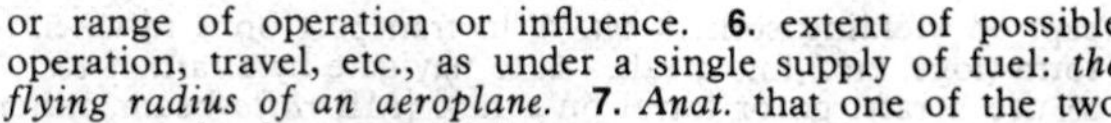

or range of operation or influence. **6.** extent of possible operation, travel, etc., as under a single supply of fuel: *the flying radius of an aeroplane.* **7.** *Anat.* that one of the two bones of the forearm which is on the thumb side. **8.** *Zool.* a corresponding bone in the forelimb of other vertebrates. **9.** *Mach.* the throw of an eccentric wheel or cam. [L: staff, rod, spoke of a wheel, radius, ray or beam of light]

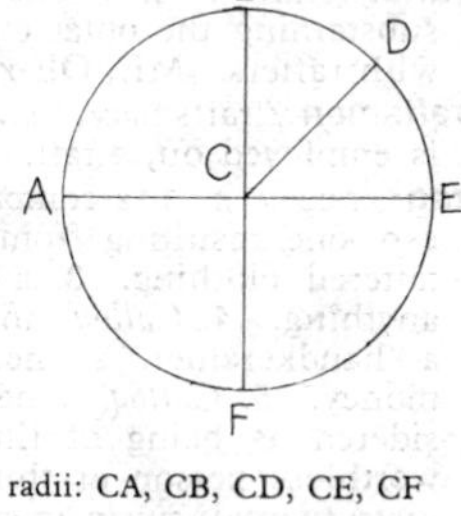


radii: CA, CB, CD, CE, CF

**radius of curvature,** *n.* the radius of that circle (called the osculating circle) whose arc best approximates a curve in the vicinity of a point on the curve.

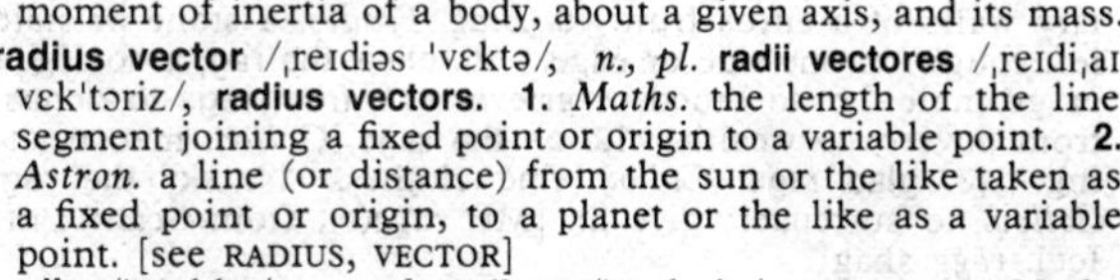

**radius of gyration,** *n.* the square root of the quotient of the moment of inertia of a body, about a given axis, and its mass.

**radius vector** /ˌreɪdiəs ˈvɛktə/, *n., pl.* **radii vectores** /ˌreɪdiˌaɪ vɛkˈtɔriz/, **radius vectors.** **1.** *Maths.* the length of the line segment joining a fixed point or origin to a variable point. **2.** *Astron.* a line (or distance) from the sun or the like taken as a fixed point or origin, to a planet or the like as a variable point. [see RADIUS, VECTOR]

**radix** /ˈreɪdɪks/, *n., pl.* **radices** /ˈreɪdəsiz/, **radixes.** **1.** *Maths.* a number taken as the base of a system of numbers, logarithms, or the like. **2.** *Bot.* a root; a radical. **3.** *Gram.* →**root**[1] (def. 13). [L: root]

**radome** /ˈreɪdoʊm/, *n.* a domed cover over an aerial system designed to allow the free passage of radio waves.

**radon** /ˈreɪdɒn/, *n.* a rare, chemically inert, radioactive gaseous element produced in the disintegration of radium. *Symbol.:* Rn; *at. no.:* 86; *at. wt:* 222. Also, **radium emanation.** [RAD(IUM) + *-on,* modelled on ARGON, NEON]

**radula** /ˈrædʒələ/, *n., pl.* **-lae** /-li/. a chitinous band in the mouth of most molluscs, set with numerous minute horny teeth, and drawn backwards and forwards over the odontophore in the process of breaking up food. [L: a scraper] **– radular,** *adj.*

**raff** /ræf/, *n.* the riffraff; the rabble. [apparently abstracted from RIFFRAFF]

**rafferty** /ˈræfəti/, *adj. N.Z. Colloq.* rough, ragged. [Brit. d.]

**Rafferty's rules** /ˈræfətiz rulz/, *n. pl.* no rules at all, as of a contest or organisation run in a slipshod fashion. Also, **Rafferty rules.** [Brit. d. *rafferty* irregular; cf. *raff* a confused heap and *raffy* drunken, wild; linked by association with the Irish surname *Rafferty*]

**raffia** /ˈræfiə/, *n.* **1.** a species of palm, *Raphia farinifera,* of Madagascar, bearing long, plume-like, pinnate leaves, the leafstalks of which yield an important fibre. **2.** the fibre, much used for tying plants, cut flowers, small parcels, etc., and for making matting, baskets, hats, and the like. **3.** some other palm of the same genus. **4.** its fibre. [Malagasy]

**raffinose** /ˈræfənoʊz, -oʊs/, *n.* a colourless crystalline trisaccharide, $C_{18}H_{32}O_{16} \cdot 5H_2O$, with little or no sweetness, occurring in the sugar beet, cottonseed, etc., and breaking down to fructose, glucose, and galactose on hydrolysis. [F *raffiner* refine + -OSE[2]]

**raffish** /ˈræfɪʃ/, *adj.* **1.** disreputable, rakish. **2.** vulgar, tawdry. [RAFF + -ISH[1]] **– raffishly,** *adv.* **– raffishness,** *n.*

**raffle** /ˈræfəl/, *n., v.,* **-fled, -fling.** *–n.* **1.** a lottery in which the prizes are usu. goods rather than money. *–v.t.* **2.** to dispose of by a raffle (sometimes fol. by *off*): *to raffle off a watch.* *–v.i.* **3.** to take part in a raffle. [ME *rafle,* from OF *raffle* kind of game at dice, net, plundering, from *rafler* scratch, from D *rafelen* ravel] **– raffler,** *n.*

**rafflesia** /ræˈfliʒiə, -ziə/, *n.* one of the genus *Rafflesia* of Malaysian parasitic plants, as *R. arnoldii,* which has fleshy flowers 45 cm across. [named after Sir Thomas *Raffles,* 1781-1826, English colonial administrator]

**raft** /raft/, *n.* **1.** a more or less rigid floating platform made of buoyant materials, assembled for ease of transport or for the conveyance of people, their possessions, etc. **2.** such a platform for use in an emergency, often collapsible. **3.** a slab of reinforced concrete extending entirely under a building used to spread the weight of the building over the whole area, esp. on yielding soils. *–v.t.* **4.** to transport on a raft. **5.** to form (logs, etc.) into a raft. **6.** to navigate by a raft. *–v.i.* **7.** to use a raft; go or travel on a raft. [ME *rafte* beam, rafter, from Scand.; cf. Icel. *raptr* log]

**rafter** /ˈraftə/, *n.* **1.** one of the sloping timbers or members substaining the outer covering of a roof. *–v.t.* **2.** to furnish with rafters. [ME; OE *ræfter,* c. MLG *rafter.* See RAFT]

**raftsman** /ˈraftsmən/, *n., pl.* **-men.** a man who manages, or is employed on, a raft.

**rag**[1] /ræg/, *n.* **1.** a comparatively worthless fragment of cloth, esp. one resulting from tearing or wear. **2.** (*pl.*) ragged or tattered clothing. **3.** a shred, scrap, or fragmentary bit of anything. **4.** *Colloq.* an article of cloth, paper, etc., such as a handkerchief, a theatre curtain, or a piece of paper money. **5.** *Colloq.* a newspaper or magazine, esp. one considered as being of little value. **6.** *Colloq.* a wretched or worthless person or thing. **7.** *Colloq.* a song or a piece of instrumental music in ragtime. **8.** *Bot.* the axis and carpellary walls of a citrus fruit. **9.** *Bldg Trades.* a stone or slate left rough on one side or edge. **10. chew the rag, a.** to argue or grumble. **b.** to brood or grieve. **11. from rags to riches,** from poverty to wealth. **12. on the rags,** *Colloq.* menstruating. **13. glad rags,** *Colloq.* fine clothes. **14. sky the rag,** *Colloq.* to surrender; give in. [ME *ragg(e),* from Scand.; cf. Icel. *rögg* shag]

**rag**[2] /ræg/, *v.,* **ragged, ragging,** *n. Colloq. –v.t.* **1.** to scold. **2.** to tease; torment. **3.** to play rough jokes on. *–n.* **4.** any disorderly or high-spirited conduct, esp. by a group of young people. **5.** (in certain student communities) an organised display of grotesque or absurd behaviour publicising a collection of money for charity, or the like. [cf. Icel. *ragna* curse, swear]

**raga** /ˈragə, rag/, *n.* (in Indian music) a scale of specified character often associated with a particular time of the day, a special mood, etc. [Indian]

**ragamuffin** /ˈrægəmʌfən/, *n.* **1.** a ragged, disreputable person; a tatterdemalion. **2.** a ragged child.

**rag-and-bone man** /ræg-ən-ˈboʊn mæn/, *n.* a dealer in discarded clothing, furniture, household articles, etc. Also, **rag-and-bone merchant.**

**ragbag** /ˈrægbæg/, *n.* **1.** a bag for scraps of fabric. **2.** a slovenly or unkempt person.

**rag bolt** /ˈræg boʊlt/, *n.* a foundation bolt with a long, tapered, jagged head around which molten lead or concrete can be poured to provide an anchorage.

**rage** /reɪdʒ/, *n., v.,* **raged, raging.** *–n.* **1.** angry fury; violent anger: *to fall into a rage.* **2.** fury or violence of wind, waves, fire, disease, etc. **3.** violence of feeling, desire, or appetite: *the rage of thirst.* **4.** a violent desire or passion. **5.** ardour; fervour; enthusiasm: *poetic rage.* **6.** the object of widespread enthusiasm: *chess became all the rage.* **7.** *Colloq.* an exciting or entertaining event: *that party was a rage.* **8.** *Obs.* insanity. *–v.i.* **9.** to act or speak with fury; show or feel violent anger. **10.** to move, rush, dash, or surge furiously. **11.** to proceed, continue, or prevail with great violence: *the battle raged ten days.* **12.** (of feelings, etc.) to hold sway with unabated violence. **13.** *Colloq.* to set about enjoying oneself: *let's go raging.* [ME, from OF, from VL *rabia,* for L *rabies* madness, rage. See RABIES]

**ragged** /ˈrægəd/, *adj.* **1.** clothed in tattered garments. **2.** torn or worn to rags; tattered: *ragged clothing.* **3.** shaggy, as an animal, its coat, etc. **4.** having loose or hanging shreds or fragmentary bits: *a ragged wound.* **5.** full of rough or sharp projections; jagged: *ragged stones.* **6.** in a wild or neglected state: *a ragged garden.* **7.** rough, imperfect, or faulty: *a ragged piece of work.* **8.** irregular: *a ragged volley of shots.* **9.** harsh, as sound, the voice, etc. **– raggedly,** *adv.* **– raggedness,** *n.*

**ragged robin** /– ˈrɒbən/, *n.* a plant, *Lychnis flos-cuculi,* bearing pink or white flowers with dissected petals, widespread in Europe and Asia.

**ragged school** /ˈ– skul/, *n. Brit.* (formerly) a charity school for poor children.

**raggle-taggle** /ˈrægəl-tægəl/, *adj.* motley; unkempt.

**ragi** /ˈrægi/, *n.* a cereal grass, *Eleusine coracana,* cultivated in Asia, etc., for its grain. Also, **raggee, raggy.** [Hind. *rāgī*]

**raglan** /ˈræglən/, *n.* **1.** a loose overcoat the sleeves of which are cut so as to continue up to the collar. *–adj.* **2.** (of a coat or sleeve) tailored in such a manner. [named after Lord *Raglan,* 1788-1855, British field marshal]

**ragman** /ˈrægmæn/, *n., pl.* **-men.** a man who gathers, or deals in, rags.

**ragnit** /ˈrægnət/, *n.* →**tilsit.**

**ragout** /ˈrægu/, *n., v.,* **-gouted** /ˈrægud/, **-gouting** /ˈræguɪŋ/. *–n.* **1.** a highly seasoned stew of poultry or meat and vegetables, usu. flavoured with mushrooms, tomatoes, port wine, etc. *–v.t.* **2.** to make into a ragout. Also, **ragoust, ragu.** [F, from *ragoûter* restore the appetite of, from *re-* RE- + *à* to (from L *ad*) + *goût* taste (from L *gustus*)]

**rag-picker** /ˈræg-pɪkə/, *n.* one who picks up rags and other waste material from the streets, refuse heaps, etc., for a livelihood.

**ragtag and bobtail,** *n.* riffraff or rabble.

**ragtime** /ˈrægtaɪm/, *n. Music.* **1.** rhythm marked by frequent syncopation, such as is common in early American Negro piano music. **2.** music in this rhythm. [probably alteration of *ragged time*]

**rag trade** /ˈræg treɪd/, *n. Colloq.* the clothes-manufacturing trade.

**ragweed** /ˈrægwid/, *n.* **1.** any of the herbs constituting the genus *Ambrosia,* whose airborne pollen is a cause of hay fever, as the common ragweed, *A. artemisiifolia.* **2.** →**ragwort.**

**ragwort** /ˈrægwɜt/, *n.* any of various plants of the genus *Senecio,* as *S. jacobaea,* a yellow-flowered herb with irregularly lobed leaves.

**rah** /ra/, *interj.* (an exclamation). [short for HURRAH]

**raid** /reɪd/, *n.* **1.** a sudden onset or attack, as upon something to be seized or suppressed: *a police raid on a gambling house.* **2.** *Mil.* a sudden attack on the enemy, esp. by air or by a small force. *–v.t.* **3.** to make a raid on. *–v.i.* **4.** to engage in a raid. [ME *raide,* OE *rād* expedition, lit., riding. See ROAD] **– raider,** *n.*

**rail**[1] /reɪl/, *n.* **1.** a bar of wood or metal fixed more or less horizontally for any of various purposes, as for a support, barrier, fence, railing, etc. **2.** a fence; a railing, esp. (*pl.*) at a racecourse. **3.** one of a pair of steel bars that provide a guide and running surface for the wheels of vehicles. **4.** the railway, as a means of transportation: *to travel by rail.* **5.** (*pl.*) *Stock Exchange.* stocks, shares, etc., of railways. **6.** *Naut.* the upper part of the bulwarks of a ship. **7.** the edge of a surfboard. **8.** a horizontal timber or piece in a framework or in panelling. **9. off the rails,** in an abnormal condition; insane; out of control. *–v.t.* **10.** to furnish with a rail or rails. **11.** to enclose with a fence, rail or rails (usu. fol. by *in* or *off*). *–v.i.* **12.** (of horses, dogs etc.) to run close to the rails. [ME *raylle,* from OF *reille,* from L *rēgula* rule, straight stick, bar. See RULE]

**rail**[2] /reɪl/, *v.i.* **1.** to utter bitter complaint or vehement denunciation (oft. fol. by *at* or *against*): *to rail at fate.* *–v.t.* **2.** to bring, force, etc., by railing. [late ME, from F *railler* deride, from Pr. *ralhar* chatter, from L *ragere* shriek] **– railer,** *n.*

**rail**[3] /reɪl/, *n.* any of numerous wading birds constituting the subfamily Rallinae (family Rallidae), characterised by short wings, a narrow body, strong legs, long toes, and a harsh cry, and abounding in marshes in most parts of the world, as the **water rail,** *Rallus pectoralis.* [late ME, from OF *raale,* c. Pr. *rascla,* probably from L *rādere* scratch]

rail[3]: waterrail

**railcar** /ˈreɪlka/, *n.* →**railmotor.**

**railcarriage** /ˈreɪlkærɪdʒ/, *n.* →**railmotor.**

**railcoach** /ˈreɪlkoʊtʃ/, *n.* →**railmotor.**

**railhead** /ˈreɪlhɛd/, *n.* **1.** the farthest point to which a railway has been laid. **2.** *Chiefly Mil.* a railway depot at which supplies are unloaded to be distributed or forwarded by other means.

**railing** /ˈreɪlɪŋ/, *n.* **1.** (*oft. pl.*) a barrier made of rails, rails and supports, etc. **2.** rails collectively.

**raillery** /ˈreɪləri/, *n., pl.* **-ries.** **1.** good-humoured ridicule; banter. **2.** a bantering remark. [F *raillerie.* See RAIL[2]]

**railman** /ˈreɪlmən, -mæn/, *n., pl.* **-men** /-mən/. a railway worker.

**railmotor** /ˈreɪlmoʊtə/, *n.* a diesel powered self-propelled railway carriage.

**railroad** /ˈreɪlroʊd/, *U.S. –n.* **1.** a railway. *–v.t.* **2.** to transport by means of a railway. **3.** to supply with railways. **4.** *Colloq.* to send or push forward with great or undue speed: *to railroad a bill through parliament.* **5.** to force or compel, esp. by unfair means: *he was railroaded out of office.* **6.** *Colloq.* to convict (a person) unjustly or with undue haste.

**rails bookmaker** /reɪlz ˈbʊkmeɪkə/, *n.* a bookmaker working on the dividing fence between public and members enclosures, betting with both the members and public.

**railway** /ˈreɪlweɪ/, *n.* **1.** a permanent road or way, laid or provided with rails of steel, iron, etc., commonly in one or more pairs of continuous lines forming a track or tracks, on which vehicles run for the transporting of passengers, goods, and mail. **2.** such a road together with its rolling stock, buildings, etc.; the entire railway plant, including fixed and movable property. **3.** the company of persons owning or operating it. **4.** any line or lines of rails forming a track for flanged-wheel equipment.

**railway curve** /ˈ– kɜv/, *n.* →**French curve.**

**railwayman** /ˈreɪlweɪmən/, *n., pl.* **-men** /-mən/. one who works on a railway.

**raiment** /ˈreɪmənt/, *n. Archaic or Poetic.* clothing; apparel; attire. [ME *rayment,* aphetic var. of *arrayment.* See ARRAY]

**rain** /reɪn/, *n.* **1.** water in drops falling from the sky to the earth, being condensed from the aqueous vapour in the atmosphere. **2.** a rainfall, rainstorm, or shower. **3.** (*pl.*) the seasonal rainfalls, or the rainy or wet season, in some regions, as India. **4.** a large quantity of anything falling thickly: *a rain of blows.* **5. right as rain,** perfectly all right. *–v.i.* **6.** (of rain) to fall: *it rained all night.* **7.** to fall like rain: *tears rained from her eyes.* **8.** to send down or let fall rain (said of God, the sky, the clouds, etc.). *–v.t.* **9.** to send down, scatter, or sprinkle (rain, etc.). **10.** to offer, bestow, or give abundantly: *to rain blows upon a person.* **11. rain cats and dogs,** to rain heavily. [ME *rein,* OE *regn,* c. D *regen,* G *Regen,* Icel. *regn*]

**rainband** /ˈreɪnbænd/, *n.* a dark band in the solar spectrum, due to water-vapour in the atmosphere.

**rainbird** /ˈreɪnbɜd/, *n.* any of various birds whose call is thought to presage rain as, in Australia, the channel-billed cuckoo or the grey currawong and, in New Zealand, the riroriro.

**rainbow** /ˈreɪnboʊ/, *n.* **1.** a bow or arc of prismatic colours appearing in the sky opposite the sun, due to the refraction and reflection of the sun's rays in drops of rain. **2.** a similar bow of colours, esp. one appearing in the spray of cataracts, etc. **3.** any array of many bright colours. **4.** the spectrum. *–adj.* **5.** multicoloured. [ME *reinbowe,* OE *regnboga,* c. OHG *reginbogo,* Icel. *regnbogi*]

**rainbow ball** /ˈ– bɔl/, *n.* a small, round, very hard lolly, built up in layers of different colours.

**rainbow bee-eater** /– ˈbi-itə/, *n.* a small, multi-coloured insectivorous bird, *Merops ornatus,* which has broad black bands through the eye and below the throat, and which makes a constant high-pitched chattering sound, esp. in flight; found throughout Australia and New Guinea; berrin-berrin.

**rainbow lorikeet** /– lɒrəˈkit/, *n.* a gaudy parrot, *Trichoglossus haematodus,* orange and green with a bright blue head, found in timbered areas from Cape York to southern Australia.

**rainbow trout** /ˈ– traʊt/, *n.* a trout, *Salmo gairdnerii,* native to North America in the coastal waters and streams from lower California to Alaska but introduced elsewhere.

**raincheck** /ˈreɪntʃɛk/, *n. U.S.* **1.** a ticket for future use given to spectators at a baseball game, sports meeting etc., stopped by rain. **2.** *Colloq.* a postponement (as of an invitation, etc.). **3. take a raincheck,** to accept an invitation or make an agreement for which the specific details, as time and place, have not yet been fixed.

**rain cloud** /ˈreɪn klaʊd/, *n.* →**nimbus** (def. 4).

**raincoat** /ˈreɪnkoʊt/, *n.* **1.** a waterproof coat, worn as a protection from rain. **2.** *Colloq.* a contraceptive sheath.

**raindrop** /ˈreɪndrɒp/, *n.* a drop of rain.

**rained off** /reɪnd ˈɒf/, *adj.* **1.** (of a sporting match) interrupted or cancelled because of rain. **2.** (of the competitors in such a match) forced to suspend play because of rain.

**rainfall** /ˈreɪnfɔl/, *n.* **1.** a fall or shower of rain. **2.** the amount of water falling as rain, snow, etc., within a given time and area, ordinarily expressed as a hypothetical depth of coverage: *a rainfall of 1210 mm a year.*

**rainforest** /ˈreɪnfɒrəst/, *n.* dense forest found in tropical and temperate areas with high humidity and heavy rainfall occurring throughout the year.

**rain gauge** /ˈreɪn geɪdʒ/, *n.* an instrument for measuring rainfall. Also, *U.S.,* **rain gage.**

**rainmaker** /ˈreɪnmeɪkə/, *n.* **1.** (in certain societies) one who is believed to make it rain by performing certain ceremonies, rites, etc. **2.** *Aus. Rules Colloq.* a very high kick.

**rainout** /ˈreɪnaʊt/, *n.* radioactive material in the atmosphere brought down by precipitation.

**rainproof** /ˈreɪnpruf/, *adj.* **1.** proof against rain; impervious to rain. *–v.t.* **2.** to make impervious to rain.

**rain shadow** /ˈreɪn ʃædoʊ/, *n.* a drier area to the lee of a mountain range in the path of rain-bearing winds.

**rainstorm** /ˈreɪnstɔm/, *n.* a storm accompanied by heavy rain.

**rainwater** /ˈreɪnwɔtə/, *n.* water fallen as rain, and thus relatively free of impurities.

**rainwater goods** /ˈ– gʊdz/, *n.pl.* gutters, downpipes, and their attachments, used for the disposal of rainwater.

**rainy** /ˈreɪni/, *adj.,* **-nier, -niest. 1.** characterised by rain: *rainy weather, a rainy region.* **2.** wet with rain: *rainy streets.* **3.** bringing rain: *rainy clouds.* **4. a rainy day,** a time of need or emergency in the future. **– raininess,** *n.*

**raise** /reɪz/, *v.,* **raised, raising,** *n. –v.t.* **1.** to move to a higher position; lift up; elevate: *to raise one's hand.* **2.** to set upright; lift up. **3.** to cause to rise or stand up. **4.** *Archaic.* to rouse. **5.** to build; erect: *to raise a monument.* **6.** *U.S.* to set up the framework of (a house, etc.). **7.** to cause to project; bring into relief. **8.** to cause to be or appear: *to raise a tempest.* **9.** to cultivate, produce, breed (crops, plants, animals, etc.). **10.** to bring up; rear (children, etc.). **11.** to give rise to; bring up or about (a question, issue, etc.); put forward (an objection, etc.). **12.** *Law.* to institute (a lawsuit, etc.). **13.** to restore to life: *to raise the dead.* **14.** to stir up: *to raise a rebellion.* **15.** to give vigour to; animate (the mind, spirits, hopes). **16.** to advance in rank, dignity, etc.: *to raise someone to Chief Justice.* **17.** to gather together; collect: *to raise an army, raise funds.* **18.** to increase in height or thickness. **19.** to cause (dough, etc.) to rise and become light, as by the addition of yeast. **20.** to increase in degree, intensity, pitch, or force. **21.** to utter (a cry, etc.) esp. in a loud voice. **22.** to make (the voice) louder. **23.** to express, as in protest, agreement, or the like. **24.** to increase in amount, as rent, prices, wages, etc. **25.** to increase the price of (a commodity, stock, etc.). **26.** *Poker, etc.* to bet more than (another player, or previous bet). **27.** *Mil.* to end (a siege or blockade), by withdrawing or repelling the besieging forces. **28.** to remove (a prohibition, etc.). **29.** *Naut.* to come in sight of (an object) (as by its rising above the horizon in coming nearer); sight. **30.** *Maths.* to multiply (a number) by itself for a stated number of times: *100 is 10 raised to the power of 2.* **31.** *Colloq.* to establish communication with, as by two-way radio: *we tried in vain to raise headquarters.* **32.** to contact by telephone. **33. raise Cain** or **hell,** to create a disturbance, nuisance, or trouble. **34. raise the roof,** *Colloq.* to cause a great noise, excitement, etc. *–n.* **35.** a rise (in wages). **36.** the amount of such an increase. **37.** a raising, lifting, etc. [ME *reise(n),* from Scand.; cf. Icel. *reisa,* c. OE *rǣran* raise, causative of OE *rīsan* RISE. See REAR[2]] **– raiseable,** *n.* **– raiser,** *n.*

**raised beach** /reɪzd ˈbitʃ/, *n.* an ancient wave-cut platform cut into a cliff, and now above sea-level as a result of a relative fall in sea-level.

**raised pie** /– ˈpaɪ/, *n.* a pie made with hot-water crust pastry which becomes firm during baking and retains its shape, usu. served cold, filled with stock which sets into a jelly.

**raisin** /ˈreɪzən/, *n.* **1.** a grape of any of various sweet varieties dried in the sun or artificially. **2.** dark bluish purple. [ME *razin,* from OF, from L *racēmus* cluster of grapes]

**raisin bread** /'– brɛd/, *n.* a sweet milk bread containing raisins, sultanas or currants.

**raisin toast** /'– toʊst/, *n.* toasted raisin bread.

**raison d'être** /reɪzɒn 'dɛtrə/, *n.* reason or justification for being or existence. [F]

**raj** /radʒ/, *n.* (in India) rule; dominion: *the British raj.*

**Rajah** /'radʒə, 'radʒa/, *n.* **1.** (in India) **a.** a king or prince. **b.** a chief or dignitary. **c.** an honorary title conferred on Hindus in India. **2.** a title of rulers, princes, or chiefs in Java, Borneo, etc. Also, **Raja.** [Hind. *rājā,* c. L *rex* king]

**rake**[1] /reɪk/, *n., v.,* **raked, raking.** *–n.* **1.** a long-handled tool with teeth or tines for gathering together hay or the like, breaking and smoothing the surface of ground, etc. **2.** a similar implement used in agriculture, esp. one drawn by a tractor. **3.** any of various implements having a similar form or function, as a croupier's implement for gathering in money on a gaming table. **4.** a long, forcible sweep or onset. **5.** *Colloq.* a comb. *–v.t.* **6.** to gather together, draw, or remove with a rake: *to rake dead leaves from a lawn.* **7.** to clear, smooth, or prepare with a rake: *to rake a garden bed.* **8.** to clear (a fire, etc.) by stirring with a poker or the like. **9.** to gather or collect abundantly (oft. fol. by *in*): *to rake in the money.* **10.** to collect, esp. with difficulty (oft. fol. by *up*). **11.** to reveal, as to discredit someone (usu. fol. by *up*): *to rake up an old scandal.* **12.** to search thoroughly through. **13.** to scrape; scratch; graze. **14.** to traverse with gunfire, the length of (a place, ship, a body of troops, etc.). **15.** to sweep with the eyes. *–v.i.* **16.** to use a rake. **17.** to search as with a rake. **18.** to scrape or sweep (fol. by *against, over,* etc.). [ME; OE *raca*]

**rake**[2] /reɪk/, *n.* a profligate or dissolute man, esp. one in fashionable society; a roué. [short for RAKEHELL]

**rake**[3] /reɪk/, *v.,* **raked, raking,** *n.* *–v.i.* **1.** to incline from the vertical (as a mast, funnel, stem or keel of a vessel) or from the horizontal (as a stage). *–n.* **2.** inclination or slope away from the perpendicular or the horizontal, as of a ships's mast, funnel, stem or keel. **3.** *Aeron.* the angle measured between the tip edge of an aerofoil and the plane of symmetry. **4.** *Mach.* the angle between the cutting face of a tool and a plane perpendicular to the surface of the work at the cutting point. **5.** *Theat.* the slope of a stage down to the footlights. [orig. uncert.]

**rake**[4] /reɪk/, *v.i.,* **raked, raking.** **1.** (of a hawk) to fly along after the game, or to fly wide of it. **2.** (of a dog) to hunt with the nose close to the ground. [OE *racian* go, proceed, hasten, c. Swed. *raka* run, rush]

**raked-back** /'reɪkt-bæk/, *adj.* (of brickwork) sloped back by one brick at each course to allow for future work to continue. Cf. **toothed.** Also, **racked-back** /'rækt-bæk/.

**raked floor** /'reɪkt flɔ/, *n.* (of auditoriums) a floor, usu. with fixed seating, sloping down towards the stage. See **stepped floor, flat floor.**

**rakehell** /'reɪkhɛl/, *n. Archaic.* a roué; a rake. [RAKE[1] (def. 12) + HELL; replacing ME *rakel,* adj., rash, rough, coarse, hasty, from RAKE[4]]

**rakehelly** /'reɪkhɛli/, *adj. Archaic.* →**profligate.**

**rake-off** /'reɪk-ɒf/, *n. Colloq.* **1.** a share or portion, as of a sum involved or of profits. **2.** a share or amount taken or received illicitly.

**raki** /'raki, 'ræki/, *n.* an alcoholic spirit drink in south-eastern Europe and the Near East distilled from grain, grapes, plums, etc., flavoured with aniseed and mastic. [Turk. *rāqī*]

**raking** /'reɪkɪŋ/, *adj.* going swiftly, as a horse, or its stride.

**raking shore** /'– ʃɔ/, *n.* one of a set of sloping timbers used to support a wall that is bulging or a ship on the stocks.

**rakish**[1] /'reɪkɪʃ/, *adj.* **1.** smart; jaunty; dashing. **2.** like a rake; dissolute. [RAKE[2] + -ISH[1]] – **rakishly,** *adv.* – **rakishness,** *n.*

**rakish**[2] /'reɪkɪʃ/, *adj.* (of ships) having an appearance suggestive of speed and dash. [RAKE[3] + -ISH[1]]

**raku** /'raku/, *n.* a low-fired glazed pottery enabling variations of colours to be achieved on cooling, finally sealed by oil, grease or tea. [Jap. *raku* ease, enjoyment; from the ideograph engraved on a gold seal with which the original ware was stamped in the 16th C]

**râle** /ral/, *n.* an abnormal sound accompanying the normal respiratory murmur, as in pulmonary diseases. [F, from *râler* rattle when breathing, from *râle* RAIL[3]]

**rall.,** rallentando.

**rallentando** /rælən'tændoʊ/, *adv.* **1.** (a musical direction) more and more slowly. *–n.* **2.** such a passage. [It., ppr. of *rallentare* abate]

**ralliform** /'rælǝfɔm/, *adj.* rail-like in shape, anatomy, etc. [NL *ralliformis.* See RAIL[3]]

**ralline** /'rælaɪn, -ən/, *adj.* belonging or pertaining to the subfamily Rallinae, or the family Rallidae, which includes the rails and their near relatives. [NL *Rallus,* typical genus of rails + -INE[1]]

**rally**[1] /'ræli/, *v.,* **-lied, -lying,** *n., pl.* **-lies.** *–v.t.* **1.** to bring together or into order again: *to rally an army.* **2.** to draw or call (persons) together for common action. **3.** to concentrate or revive, as one's strength, spirits, etc. *–v.i.* **4.** to come together for common action. **5.** to come together or into order again. **6.** to come to the assistance of a person, party, or cause. **7.** to recover partially from illness. **8.** to acquire fresh strength or vigour: *the stock market rallied today.* **9.** *Tennis, etc.* to engage in a rally. *–n.* **10.** a recovery from dispersion or disorder, as of troops. **11.** a renewal or recovery of strength, activity, etc. **12.** a partial recovery of strength during illness. **13.** a drawing or coming together of persons, as for common action, as in a mass meeting. **14.** *Finance.* a sharp rise in price and active trading, after a declining market. **15.** *Tennis, etc.* the return of the ball by both sides a number of times consecutively. **16.** *Boxing.* an exchange of blows. **17.** a motor-car competition, mainly over public roads, in which speed is less important than skill and consistency in adhering to specified rules and schedules. **18.** *Theat.* to quicken the pace of a performance. [F *rallier.* See RE- ALLY]

**rally**[2] /'ræli/, *v.t.,* **-lied, -lying.** to ridicule (someone) good-humouredly; banter. [F *railler* RAIL[2]]

**rallycross** /'rælikrɒs/, *n.* a motor race or a series of races on a closed circuit on different types of road surfaces as dirt, clay or bitumen.

**ram**[1] /ræm/, *n., v.,* **rammed, ramming.** *–n.* **1.** an uncastrated male sheep. **2.** (*cap.*) the zodiacal constellation or sign Aries. **3.** any of various devices for battering, crushing, driving, or forcing something. **4.** a battering ram. **5.** a heavy beak or spur projecting from the bow of a warship, for penetrating an enemy's ship. **6.** a vessel so equipped. **7.** the heavy weight which strikes the blow in a pile-driver or the like. **8.** a piston, as on a hydraulic press. **9.** a hydraulic ram. *–v.t.* **10.** to drive or force by heavy blows. **11.** to strike with great force; dash violently against. **12.** to cram; stuff. **13.** to push firmly. **14.** to force (a charge) into a firearm, as with a ramrod. [ME and OE, c. D and LG *ram,* G *Ramm*]

**ram**[2] /ræm/, *n., v.,* **rammed, ramming.** *–n.* **1.** a trickster's confederate. *–v.i.* **2.** to act as a trickster's confederate. [var. of RAMP (def. 5)]

**ram-,** an intensive prefix, as in *ramshackle.* [cf. Icel. *ram-* very, special use of *rammr* strong, akin to RAM[1]]

**RAM** /ræm/, *n.* a computer memory which is so structured that each item can be accessed equally quickly. [*R*(*andom*)-*A*(*ccess*) *M*(*emory*)]

**Ramadan** /ræmə'dan/, *n.* **1.** the ninth month of the Muslim year. **2.** the daily fast which is rigidly enjoined from dawn until sunset during this month. [Ar. *Ramadān*]

**Raman effect** /'ramən əfɛkt/, *n.* a phenomenon occurring in the scattering of light from the molecules of transparent gases, liquids and solids, in which some of the incident light undergoes a change in frequency. [named after Sir C.V. *Raman,* b. 1888, Indian physicist]

**ramarama** /'ramərama/, *n.* a shrub or small tree, *Lophomyrtus bullata,* found in lowland forests of New Zealand. [Maori]

**ramble** /'ræmbəl/, *v.,* **-bled, -bling,** *n.* *–v.i.* **1.** to wander about in a leisurely manner, without definite aim or direction; walk for pleasure. **2.** to have an aimless or meandering course, as a stream or path. **3.** to grow or extend in an unsystematic fashion, as a plant or building. **4.** to talk or write discursively, without sequence of ideas, or incoherently. *–n.* **5.** a walk without a definite route, taken for pleasure. [? frequentative of ROAM, but cf. Icel. *ramba* sway to and fro]

**rambler** /ˈræmblə/, *n.* **1.** one who or that which rambles. **2.** any of various climbing roses, esp. the many cultivated hybrids, as *Rosa wichuraiana* and *Rosa multiflora.*

**rambling** /ˈræmblɪŋ/, *adj.* **1.** wandering about aimlessly. **2.** taking an irregular course; straggling. **3.** spread out irregularly in various directions: *a rambling mansion.* **4.** straying from one subject to another.

**Rambouillet** /ˈrɒmbujeɪ, ˈræmbəleɪ/, *n.* a variety of Merino sheep yielding good mutton and wool, esp. common in the western U.S. [named after *Rambouillet,* town in France]

**rambunctious** /ræmˈbʌŋkʃəs/, *adj. U.S. Colloq.* **1.** boisterous; noisy. **2.** obstreperous; perverse; unruly. [var. of RUMBUSTIOUS]

**rambutan** /ræmˈbutn/, *n.* **1.** the bright red, oval, edible fruit of a Malayan tree, *Nephelium lappaceum,* covered with soft spines or hairs. **2.** the tree. [Malay]

**ramekin** /ˈræməkən/, *n.* **1.** a small, separately cooked portion of some savoury preparation, or other food mixture, baked in a small dish. **2.** the dish. Also, **ramequin.** [F *ramequin,* from D. Cf. G *Rahm* cream]

**rami** /ˈreɪmaɪ/, *n.* plural of **ramus.**

**ramie** /ˈræmi/, *n.* **1.** an Asiatic shrub, *Boehmeria nivea,* yielding a fibre used in making textiles, etc. **2.** the fibre itself. [Malay *rāmī*]

**ramification** /ræməfəˈkeɪʃən/, *n.* **1.** the act, process, or manner of ramifying. **2.** a branch: *the ramifications of a nerve.* **3.** a division or subdivision springing or derived from a main stem or source: *to pursue a subject in all its ramifications.* **4.** *Bot.* **a.** a structure formed of branches. **b.** a configuration of branching parts.

**ramiform** /ˈræməfɔm/, *adj.* **1.** having the form of a branch; branchlike. **2.** branched. [*rami-* (from L, combining form of *rāmus* branch) + -FORM]

**ramify** /ˈræməfaɪ/, *v.t., v.i.,* **-fied, -fying.** to divide or spread out into branches or branchlike parts. [F *ramifier,* from ML *rāmificāre,* from L *rāmi-* (combining form of *rāmus* branch) + *-ficāre* make]

**ramjet** /ˈræmdʒɛt/, *n.* a jet-propulsion engine operated by the injection of fuel into a stream of air compressed by the forward speed of the aircraft.

**ramkie** /ˈræmki/, *n.* a hybrid lutelike musical instrument of the Hottentots of southern Africa, having three to six plucked strings stretched over a body made of calabash, wood, or an empty tincan. [Pg. *rabequinha* a little violin]

**rammer** /ˈræmə/, *n.* one who or that which rams.

**rammish** /ˈræmɪʃ/, *adj.* **1.** like a ram. **2.** →**rank**[2] (def. 3).

**ramose** /ˈreɪmoʊs, ræˈmoʊs/, *adj.* **1.** having many branches. **2.** branching. [L *rāmōsus*]

**ramous** /ˈreɪməs/, *adj.* **1.** →**ramose. 2.** like branches.

**ramp** /ræmp/, *n.* **1.** a sloping surface connecting two different levels. **2.** a short concave slope or bend, as one connecting the higher and lower parts of a bannister at a landing or of the top of a wall. **3.** any extensive sloping walk or passageway. **4.** the act of ramping. **5.** a swindle, esp. one depending on a rise in prices. **6.** →**cattlegrid. 7.** *Prison Colloq.* a search, esp. of a prisoner's cell. [F *rampe*] *–v.i.* **8.** to rise or stand on the hind legs, as a quadruped, esp. a lion (often one represented in heraldry or sculpture). **9.** to rear as if to spring. **10.** to leap or dash with fury (fol. by *about,* etc.). **11.** to act violently; rage; storm. [ME, from F *ramper* creep, crawl, climb]

**rampage** /ˈræmpeɪdʒ/, *n.;* /ræmˈpeɪdʒ/, *v.,* **-paged, -paging.** *–n.* **1.** violent or furious behaviour. **2.** an instance of this: *to go on the rampage. –v.i.* **3.** to rush, move, or act furiously or violently. [orig. Scot.; apparently dissimilated var. of *ramp-rage.* See RAMP (def. 10), RAGE (def. 11)]

**rampageous** /ræmˈpeɪdʒəs/, *adj.* violent; unruly; boisterous. – **rampageousness,** *n.*

**rampancy** /ˈræmpənsi/, *n.* rampant condition or position.

**rampant** /ˈræmpənt/, *adj.* **1.** violent in action, spirit, opinion, etc.; raging; furious. **2.** in full sway; unchecked: *the rampant growth of anarchy.* **3.** luxurious, as a plant. **4.** lustful. **5.** standing on the hind legs; ramping. **6.** *Her.* (of a lion, bear, etc.) standing on its left hind leg with the forelegs elevated, the right higher than the left, and, unless otherwise specified, with the head in profile. **7.** *Archit.* (of an arch or vault) springing at one side from one level of support and resting at the other on a higher level. [ME *rampaunt,* from OF *rampant,* ppr. of *ramper* climb, RAMP] – **rampantly,** *adv.*

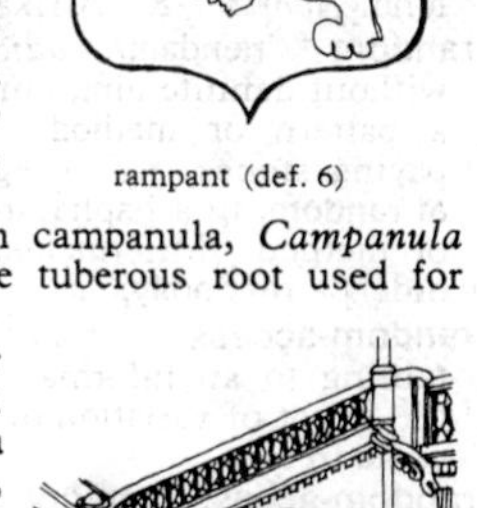

rampant (def. 6)

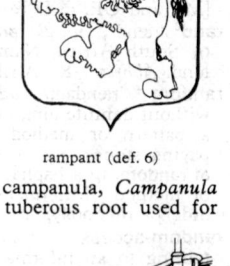

**rampart** /ˈræmpat/, *n.* **1.** *Fort.* **a.** a broad elevation or mound of earth raised as a fortification about a place, and usu. having a stone or earth parapet built upon it. **b.** such an elevation together with the parapet. **2.** anything serving as a bulwark or defence. *–v.t.* **3.** to furnish with or as with a rampart. [F *rempart,* from *remparer* fortify]

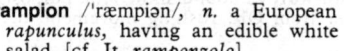

**rampion** /ˈræmpiən/, *n.* a European campanula, *Campanula rapunculus,* having an edible white tuberous root used for salad. [cf. It. *ramponzolo*]

**ramrod** /ˈræmrɒd/, *n.* **1.** a rod for ramming down the charge of a muzzle-loading firearm. **2.** a cleaning rod for the barrel of a rifle, etc. **3.** any person or thing considered as exemplifying or exercising stiffness or unyielding rigidity.

**ramset** /ˈræmsɛt/, *n.* an explosive powered fixing tool which shoots nails, etc., into any surface, as timber, masonry, etc. [Trademark]

rampant arch in staircase

**ramshackle** /ˈræmʃækəl/, *adj.* loosely made or held together; rickety; shaky: *a ramshackle house.* [earlier *ramshackled,* from RAM- + *shackled,* pp. of *shackle,* frequentative of SHAKE, *v.*]

**ramson** /ˈræmsən, -zən/, *n.* **1.** a species of garlic, *Allium ursinum,* with broad leaves. **2.** (*usu. pl.*) its bulbous root, used as a relish. [orig. pl. taken as sing.; ME *ramsyn,* OE *hramsan,* pl. of *hramsa* kind of garlic]

**ramulose** /ˈræmjəloʊs/, *adj.* having many small branches. Also, **ramulous** /ˈræmjələs/. [L *rāmulōsus*]

**ramus** /ˈreɪməs/, *n., pl.* **-mi** /-maɪ/. a branch, as of a plant, a vein, a bone, etc. [L]

**ran**[1] /ræn/, *v.* past tense of **run.**

**ran**[2] /ræn/, *n.* (formerly) a measure of twine or netting. [orig. unknown]

**R.A.N.** /ar eɪ ˈɛn/, Royal Australian Navy. Also, **RAN.**

**rana** /ˈreɪnə/, *n.* any of the family of the true frogs, Ranidae, having approximately 2500 species with worldwide distribution. [NL, genus name]

**ranch** /ræntʃ/, *n.* **1.** a farm for cattle, horses, or the like, generally having extensive grazing land. **2.** *U.S.* such a farm for sheep. **3.** the establishment, staff, buildings, etc., of such. **4.** *U.S.* any farm or farming establishment. *–v.i.* **5.** to own, manage, or work on, a ranch. [Sp. *rancho.* See RANCHO]

**rancher** /ˈræntʃə/, *n.* one who owns or works on a ranch.

**ranchero** /rænˈtʃɛəroʊ/, *n., pl.* **-cheros.** (in Spanish America and the south-western U.S.) a rancher. [Sp.]

**ranch house** /ˈræntʃ haʊs/, *n.* **1.** the main building on a ranch, where the owner lives. **2.** a long, single-storey house, often having an open-plan interior layout.

**ranchman** /ˈræntʃmən/, *n., pl.* **-men.** *U.S.* →**rancher.**

**rancho** /ˈræntʃoʊ/, *n., pl.* **-choes** /-tʃoʊz/. (in Spanish America and the south-western U.S.) **1.** a hut or collection of huts for herdsmen, labourers, or travellers. **2.** a ranch. [Sp.: mess, group of persons who eat together, in Sp. Amer. applied to the huts occupied by herdsmen and labourers]

**rancid** /ˈrænsəd/, *adj.* **1.** having a rank, unpleasant, stale smell or taste: *rancid butter.* **2.** rank in this manner: *a rancid smell.* [L *rancidus*] – **rancidness,** *n.*

**rancidity** /rænˈsɪdəti/, *n.* **1.** rancid state or quality. **2.** a rancid smell or taste.

**rancio** /ˈransioʊ/, *adj.* (of wine) having attained great age and concentration of flavour from long storage in wood. [Sp.: choice, old]

**rancorous** /ˈræŋkərəs/, *adj.* full of or showing rancour. – **rancorously,** *adv.* – **rancorousness,** *n.*

**rancour** /'ræŋkə/, *n.* bitter, rankling resentment or ill will; hatred; malice. Also, *U.S.,* **rancor.** [ME, from OF, from LL *rancor* rank smell or taste, from L *rancere* to be rank]

**rand**[1] /rænd/, *n.* **1.** *Shoemaking.* a strip of leather, for levelling, set in a shoe at the heel before the lifts are attached. **2.** *Scot.* a border, margin, or strip. **3.** *S. African.* a rocky ridge. [ME and OE, c. D *rand,* G *Rand* border, margin]

**rand**[2] /rænd/, *n., pl.* **rand.** the monetary unit of the Republic of South Africa, Namibia, Lesotho, Botswana, and Swaziland. *Abbrev.:* R. [Afrikaans, special use of *rand* RAND[1]]

**random** /'rændəm/, *adj.* **1.** going, made, occurring, etc., without definite aim, purpose, or reason. **2.** not according to a pattern or method. **3.** *Bldg Trades.* (of slates, blocks, paving stones, etc.) irregular in size or arrangement. *–n.* **4. at random,** in a haphazard way; without definite aim, purpose, or method. [ME *randon,* from OF: rushing movement, disorder] – **randomly,** *adv.*

**random-access** /rændəm-'æksɛs/, *adj.* denoting or pertaining to an information-storage device designed to reduce the effect of variation of access time for an arbitrary sequence of addresses.

**random-access memory** /rændəm-'æksɛs mɛmri/, *n.* →**RAM.**

**randomise** /'rændəmaɪz/, *v.t.,* **-mised, -mising.** to arrange or sort items, actions, etc., in a deliberately random way, esp. in order to secure statistical validity in a survey or experiment.

**random sampling** /rændəm 'sæmplɪŋ/, *n.* the drawing of a sample from a statistical population in which all members of the population have equal probabilities of being included in the sample.

**random walk** /– 'wɔk/, *n. Statistics.* the path traversed by a particle which moves in steps, each step being determined by chance either in regard to direction or in regard to magnitude or both.

**R and R** /ar ən 'a/, *n. U.S. Mil.* rest and recreation.

**randy** /'rændi/, *adj.* **1.** *Colloq.* →**lecherous. 2.** sexually aroused. [*rand* (var. of RANT) + -Y[1]]

**rang** /ræŋ/, *v.* past tense of **ring**[2].

**rangatira** /rʌŋgə'tɪərə, ræŋ-/, *n. N.Z.* **1.** a Maori noble leader. **2.** *Colloq.* a chief, a boss, superior of any kind. [Maori]

**range** /reɪndʒ/, *n., adj., v.,* **ranged, ranging.** *–n.* **1.** the extent to which, or the limits between which, variation is possible: *the range of prices for a commodity.* **2.** the extent or scope of the operation or efficacy of something: *within range of vision.* **3.** the distance to which a projectile is or may be sent by a weapon, etc. **4.** the distance of the target from the weapon. **5.** an area in which shooting at targets is practised either with guns or with missiles. **6.** the distance which an aircraft, ship, or land vehicle can travel without refuelling. **7.** the distance of something to be located from some point of operation, as in sound-ranging. **8.** *Statistics.* the difference between the smallest and largest varieties in a statistical distribution. **9.** the compass of a musical instrument or a voice. **10.** *Survey.* **a.** the extension or prolongation of a line to intersect a transit line usu. employed for location of physical features. **b.** a line established by markers on shore for the location of soundings. **11.** a rank, class, or order. **12.** a row or line, as of persons or things. **13.** a set or series. **14.** the act of ranging, or moving about, as over an area or region. **15.** an area or tract that is or may be ranged over. **16.** the region over which something is distributed, is found, or occurs: *the range of a plant.* **17.** a chain of mountains: *a mountain range.* **18.** a form of large stove, portable or stationary, for cooking, now usu. having one or more ovens, and openings on the top for heating various articles at once. [ME, from OF, from *ranger* RANGE, *v.*] *–v.t.* **19.** to draw up or dispose (persons or things) in a row or line, in rows or lines, or in a particular position, company, or group (oft. fol. by *in, among, alongside,* etc.). **20.** to dispose systematically; set in order; arrange. **21.** to place in a particular class; classify. **22.** to make straight, level, or even, as lines of type. **23.** to pass over or through (an area or region) in all directions, as in exploring or searching. **24.** to pasture (cattle) on a range. **25.** to train, as a telescope, upon an object. **26.** to obtain the range of (something aimed at or to be located). **27.** *Naut.* to lay out (an anchor cable) so that the anchor may descend smoothly. *–v.i.* **28.** to vary within certain limits: *prices ranging from $5 to $10.* **29.** to have range of operation. **30.** to have a particular range, as a gun or a projectile. **31.** to find the range, as of something aimed at or to be located. **32.** to stretch out or extend in a line. **33.** to extend, run or go in a certain direction: *a boundary ranging east and west.* **34.** to lie or extend in the same line, or the same plane, as one thing with another or others. **35.** to take up a position in a line or in order. **36.** to take up or occupy a particular place or position. **37.** to move about or through a region in all directions, as persons, animals, etc. **38.** to rove, roam, or wander: *the talk ranged over a variety of matters.* **39.** to extend, be found, or occur over an area or throughout a period, as animals, plants, etc.: *a plant which ranges from Queensland to New South Wales.* [ME *range(n),* v., from OF *ranger* arrange in line, from *reng* line. See RANK[1]]

**rangefinder** /'reɪndʒfaɪndə/, *n.* any of various instruments for determining the range or distance of an object, as in order that a gun may be accurately sighted when firing at it, or to focus a camera.

**ranger** /'reɪndʒə/, *n.* **1.** one who or that which ranges. **2.** a person employed to patrol a public reserve, wild-life park, etc. **3.** (*cap.*) a member of the senior division of the Girl Guides. – **rangership,** *n.*

**rangiora** /rʌŋi'ɔrə/, *n.* a shrub or tree of New Zealand, *Brachyglottis repanda,* with densely tomentose branches. [Maori]

**rangy** /'reɪndʒi/, *adj.,* **-gier, -giest. 1.** slender and longlimbed, as animals or persons. **2.** given to or fitted for ranging or moving about, as animals. **3.** having a mountain range; mountainous.

**rani** /'rani, ra'ni/, *n., pl.* **-nis.** (in India and elsewhere) **1.** the wife of a raja, king, or prince. **2.** a reigning queen or princess. Also, **ranee.** [Hind. *rānī*]

**rank**[1] /ræŋk/, *n.* **1.** a number of persons forming a separate class in the social scale or in any graded body: *men of every rank and station.* **2.** position or standing in the social scale or in any graded body: *the rank of colonel.* **3.** high position or station in the social or some similar scale: *pride of rank.* **4.** a class in any scale of comparison. **5.** relative position or standing: *a writer of the highest rank.* **6.** a row, line, or series of things or persons. **7.** a set of organ pipes of the same kind which is controlled by a stop. **8.** (*pl.*) the lines or body of an army or other force or organisation. **9.** the general body of any party, society, or organisation apart from the officers or leaders. **10.** orderly arrangement; array. **11.** a line of persons, esp. soldiers, standing abreast (distinguished from *file*). **12.** (*pl.*) the members of an army, etc., other than and distinguished from commissioned officers; other ranks: *to rise from the ranks.* **13.** *Chess.* one of the horizontal lines of squares on a chessboard. **14. pull (one's) rank (on),** to resort to use of a position of authority, esp. military authority, to compel some action or behaviour. *–v.t.* **15.** to arrange in a rank or row, or in ranks, as things or persons. **16.** to dispose in suitable order; arrange; classify. **17.** to assign to a particular position, station, class, etc. *–v.i.* **18.** to form a rank or ranks. **19.** to stand in rank. **20.** to take up or occupy a place in a particular rank, class, etc. **21.** *U.S.* to be the senior in rank: *the major ranks here.* [F (obs.) *ranc,* OF *renc, reng,* of Gmc orig.; cf. OE *hring* RING[1]]

**rank**[2] /ræŋk/, *adj.* **1.** growing with excessive luxuriance; vigorous and tall of growth: *tall rank grass.* **2.** producing an excessive and coarse growth, as land. **3.** having an offensively strong smell or taste: *a rank cigar.* **4.** offensively strong, as smell or taste. **5.** utter; unmistakable: *a rank outsider, rank treachery.* **6.** highly offensive; disgusting. **7.** grossly coarse or indecent. [ME; OE *ranc* proud, bold. c. Icel. *rakkr* erect] – **rankly,** *adv.* – **rankness,** *n.*

**rank and file,** *n.* the body of an army, or any other organisation or group, apart from officers or leaders.

**ranker** /'ræŋkə/, *n.* **1.** a soldier in the ranks. **2.** a commissioned officer promoted from the ranks. **3.** one who ranks. [RANK[1], *n.,* + -ER[1]]

**Rankine** /'ræŋkən/, *adj.* **1.** denoting or pertaining to an absolute scale of temperature based on the Fahrenheit degree. One degree Rankine equals 5/9 Kelvin. *–n.* **2.** the Rankine scale. Symbol: R [named after W.J.M. *Rankine,* 1820-70,

Scottish physicist]

**ranking** /'ræŋkɪŋ/, *adj.* **1.** *U.S.* of high rank; leading; foremost. *–n.* **2.** standing; position on a scale.

**rankle** /'ræŋkəl/, *v.i.*, **-kled, -kling.** (of unpleasant feelings, experiences, etc.) to produce or continue to produce within the mind keen irritation or bitter resentment; fester; be painful. [ME *rancle(n)*, from OF *(d)raoncler,* from ML *dracunculus* ulcer, diminutive of L *draco* serpent, DRAGON]

**ransack** /'rænsæk/, *v.t.* **1.** to search thoroughly or vigorously through (a house, receptacle, etc.). **2.** to search (a place, etc.) for plunder; pillage. [ME *ransake(n)*, from Scand.; cf. Icel. *rannsaka* search (a house), from *rann* house + *-saka,* akin to *sœkja* SEEK] – **ransacker,** *n.*

**ransom** /'rænsəm/, *n.* **1.** the redemption of a prisoner, slave, kidnapped person, captured goods, etc., for a price. **2.** the sum or price paid or demanded. **3.** a means of delivering or rescuing, esp., in religious use, from sin and its consequences. **4. hold to ransom, a.** to confine (a person or thing) until redeemed at a price. **b.** to attempt to compel (someone) to accede to one's demands. **5. king's ransom,** any very large sum of money or valuables. *–v.t.* **6.** to redeem from captivity, bondage, detention, etc., by paying a price demanded. **7.** to release or restore on receipt of a ransom. **8.** to deliver or redeem from sin and its consequences. [ME *ransome,* from OF *rancon,* from L *redemptio* REDEMPTION] – **ransomer,** *n.*

**rant** /rænt/, *v.i.* **1.** to speak or declaim extravagantly or violently; talk in a wild or vehement way: *a ranting actor.* *–v.t.* **2.** to utter or declaim in a ranting manner. *–n.* **3.** ranting, extravagant, or violent declamation. **4.** a ranting utterance. [MD *ranten* rave, c. G *ranzen* frolic] – **ranter,** *n.* – **ranting,** *adj.*

**ran-tan** /'ræn-tæn/, *n. in the phrase* **on the ran-tan,** on a drinking bout.

**ranunculaceous** /rənʌŋkjə'leɪʃəs/, *adj.* belonging to the Ranunculaceae, or buttercup family of plants, which includes also the anemone, clematis, larkspur, etc. [RANUNCUL(US) + -ACEOUS]

**ranunculus** /rə'nʌŋkjələs/, *n., pl.* **-luses, -li** /-laɪ/. any plant of the large and widely distributed genus *Ranunculus,* comprising herbs with leaves mostly divided, and flowers, commonly yellow, with five petals; crowfoot; buttercup. [L, orig., diminutive of *rana* frog]

**rap**[1] /ræp/, *v.,* **rapped, rapping,** *n.* *–v.t.* **1.** to strike, esp. with a quick, smart, or light blow, as to attract attention, communicate in code, etc. **2.** to produce or announce by raps (fol. by *out,* and used esp. of communications ascribed to spirits). **3.** to utter sharply or vigorously (usu. fol. by *out*): *to rap out an oath.* **4.** *Colloq.* to accelerate (a motor vehicle). **5. rap over** or **on the knuckles,** *Colloq.* to reprimand sharply; reprove. *–v.i.* **6.** to knock smartly or lightly, esp. so as to make a noise: *to rap on a door.* *–n.* **7.** a quick, smart, or light blow. **8.** the sound so produced. **9.** *Colloq.* punishment or blame, esp. of one who accepts punishment for a crime he did not commit: *to take the rap.* **10.** *Colloq.* a criminal charge: *a housebreaking rap.* **11. give (a motor vehicle) a rap,** *Colloq.* to accelerate (a motor vehicle) and travel at full speed for a short period. **12.** (in modern spiritualism) a sound as of knocking, ascribed to the agency of disembodied spirits. [ME; cf. Swed. *rappa* beat, drub, G *rappeln* rattle]

**rap**[2] /ræp/, *n.* **1.** a counterfeit coin used in Ireland in the 18th century for a halfpenny. **2.** the least bit: *I don't care a rap.* [short for Irish-Gaelic *ropaire*]

**rap**[3] /ræp/, *n., v.,* **rapped, rapping.** *Colloq.* *–n.* **1.** a conversation. *–v.i.* **2.** to talk discursively (fol. by *on*) [? RAP(PORT)]

**rapacious** /rə'peɪʃəs/, *adj.* **1.** given to seizing for plunder or the satisfaction of greed. **2.** inordinately greedy; predatory; extortionate: *a rapacious disposition.* **3.** (of animals) subsisting by the capture of living prey; predacious. [RAPACI(TY) (from L: *rāpācitas* greediness) + -OUS] – **rapaciously,** *adv.* – **rapacity** /rə'pæsəti/, **rapaciousness,** *n.*

**rape**[1] /reɪp/, *n., v.,* **raped, raping.** *–n.* **1.** the crime of having sexual intercourse with a woman against her will. **2.** the act of having sexual intercourse with any other person against his or her will. **3.** the act of forcing someone to consent to anything against his or her will. **4.** an act of aggression by which one state seizes the territory of another. *–v.t.* **5.** to commit the crime or act of rape on. **6.** to seize, take, or carry off by force. **7.** to plunder (a place). **8.** to despoil or lay waste (land). *–v.i.* **9.** to commit rape. [ME *rape(n)*, from L *rapere* seize, carry off] – **rapist,** *n.*

**rape**[2] /reɪp/, *n.* a variable herb, *Brassica napus,* widely cultivated as a fodder plant and for the seeds, which yield rapeseed oil. [ME, from L *rāpum, rāpa* turnip]

**rape**[3] /reɪp/, *n.* the refuse of grapes, after the juice has been extracted, used as a filter in making vinegar. [F, from LL *raspa,* from *raspāre* grate, from Gmc; cf. OHG *raspōn*]

**rape-cake** /'reɪp-keɪk/, *n.* cattle food made of the husks of rapeseed remaining after the extraction of the oil.

**rapeseed** /'reɪpsid/, *n.* **1.** the seed of the rape. **2.** the plant itself.

**rapeseed oil** /– 'ɔɪl/, *n.* a brownish yellow oil obtained from rapeseed, used as a lubricant, etc.; colza oil. Also, **rape oil.**

**raphe** /'reɪfi/, *n., pl.* **-phae** /-fi/. **1.** *Anat.* a seamlike union between two parts or halves of an organ or the like. **2.** *Bot.* **a.** (in certain ovules) a ridge connecting the hilum with the chalaza. **b.** a median line or slot on a cell wall of a diatom. [NL, from Gk: seam, suture]

**raphides** /'ræfədiz/, *n.pl.* acicular crystals, usu. composed of calcium oxalate, which occur in bundles in the cells of many plants. [NL (pl.), from Gk: needles]

**rapid** /'ræpəd/, *adj.* **1.** occurring with speed; coming about within a short time: *rapid growth.* **2.** moving or acting with great speed; swift: *a rapid worker.* **3.** characterised by speed, as motion. *–n.* **4.** (*usu. pl.*) a part of a river where the current runs very swiftly, as over a steep slope in the bed. [L *rapidus*] – **rapidly,** *adv.*

**rapid eye movement,** *n.* the frequent and rapid movement of the eyes while the eyelids are closed in sleep, occurring during a dreaming period. Also, **REM**

**rapid fire** /– 'faɪə/, *n.* fast firing, as used against a moving target.

**rapid-fire** /'ræpəd-faɪə/, *adj.* **1.** characterised by or delivered or occurring in rapid procedure, esp. in speech: *rapid-fire questions.* **2.** *Ordn.* denoting or pertaining to any of various mounted guns of moderate calibre which can be fired rapidly. **3.** *Mil.* firing shots in rapid succession. Also, **rapid-firing.** – **rapid-firer,** *n.*

**rapidity** /rə'pɪdəti/, *n.* rapid state or quality.

**rapid-transit** /'ræpəd-trænzət/, *adj.* (of a transport system) involving or pertaining to high-speed urban railways.

**rapier** /'reɪpiə/, *n.* **1.** a sword, with elaborate hilt, and long, slender, pointed blade, used only for thrusting. **2.** (originally) a long, narrow, two-edged sword, used chiefly for thrusting. [F: *rapière,* orig. adj., from *râpe* grater. See RAPE[3]]

rapier: late 16th century

**rapine** /ræ'pin/, *n.* the violent seizure and carrying off of property of others; plunder. [ME from L *rapīna*]

**rappee** /ræ'pi/, *n.* a strong snuff made by rasping the darker and ranker kinds of tobacco leaves. [F *râpé* grated, pp. of *râper.* See RAPE[3], RASP]

**rappel** /ræ'pɛl/, *n., v.,* **-pelled, -pelling.** *–n.* **1.** *Mountaineering.* →**abseil.** **2.** a beat of a drum formerly used to call soldiers to arms. *–v.i.* **3.** *Mountaineering.* to descend by rappel. [F: lit., a recall]

**rapper** /'ræpə/, *n.* one who or that which performs the act or produces the sound of rapping or knocking. [RAP[1] + -ER[1]]

**rapport** /ræ'pɔ/, *n.* relation; connection, esp. harmonious or sympathetic relation. See **en rapport.** [F, *rapporter* bring back, refer, from *re-* RE- + *apporter* (from L *apportāre* bring to)]

**rapporteur** /rapɔ'tɜ/, *n.* a person who is a member of a committee, conference, etc., appointed to record the proceedings and to prepare reports. [F: recorder, reporter]

**rapprochement** /rə'prɒʃmɒ̃, -mənt/, *n.* an establishment or re-establishment of harmonious relations. [F, from *rapprocher* bring near. See APPROACH]

**rapscallion** /ræp'skæljən/, *n. Obs.* a rascal; rogue; scamp. [RASCAL]

**rapt** /ræpt/, *adj.* **1.** deeply engrossed or absorbed: *rapt in thought.* **2.** transported with emotion; enraptured: *rapt with* *joy.* **3.** showing or proceeding from rapture: *a rapt smile.* **4.** carried off to another place, sphere of existence, etc. [first used as pp., ME, from L *raptus,* pp., seized, transported. See RAPE[1]]

**raptor** /ˈræptə/, *n.* a bird of the order Raptores, consisting of birds of prey, as the eagles, hawks, etc. [L: robber, plunderer]

**raptorial** /ræpˈtɔriəl/, *adj.* **1.** preying upon other animals; predatory. **2.** adapted for seizing prey, as the beak or claws of a bird. **3.** belonging or pertaining to the raptors. [NL *Raptōrēs* (pl. of L *raptor* robber, plunderer) + -(I)AL]

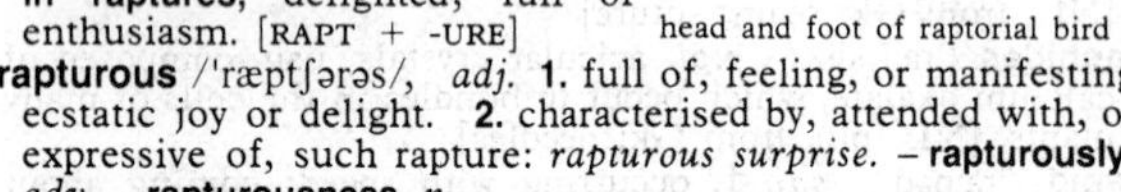

head and foot of raptorial bird

**rapture** /ˈræptʃə/, *n.* **1.** ecstatic joy or delight; joyful ecstasy. **2.** (*oft. pl.*) an utterance or expression of ecstatic delight. **3.** the carrying of a person to another place or sphere of existence. **4. in raptures,** delighted; full of enthusiasm. [RAPT + -URE]

**rapturous** /ˈræptʃərəs/, *adj.* **1.** full of, feeling, or manifesting ecstatic joy or delight. **2.** characterised by, attended with, or expressive of, such rapture: *rapturous surprise.* – **rapturously,** *adv.* – **rapturousness,** *n.*

**rara avis** /rɛərə ˈeɪvəs/, *n., pl.* **rarae aves** /rɛəri ˈeɪviz/. a rare person or thing. [L: a rare bird]

**rare**[1] /rɛə/, *adj.,* **rarer, rarest. 1.** coming or occurring far apart in space or time; unusual; uncommon: *rare occasions, a rare smile, a rare disease.* **2.** few in number. **3.** thinly distributed over an area, or few and widely separated: *rare lighthouses.* **4.** having the component parts not closely compacted; of low density or pressure: *rare mountain air.* **5.** remarkable or unusual, esp. in excellence or greatness: *rare tact, a rare find; sympathetic to a rare degree.* [ME, from L *rārus* thin, not dense] – **rareness,** *n.*

**rare**[2] /rɛə/, *adj.,* **rarer, rarest.** (of meat) not thoroughly cooked; underdone. [ME *rere,* OE *hrēr* lightly boiled (said of eggs)]

**rarebit** /ˈrɛəbət/, *n.* →**Welsh rarebit.**

**rare book** /rɛə ˈbʊk/, *n.* a book which is distinctive by virtue of its early printing date, limited copies, special character of the edition, binding, historical interest, or the like.

**rare earth** /rɛər ˈɜθ/, *n.* the oxide of any of the rare-earth elements contained in various minerals.

**rare-earth elements** /rɛər-ɜθ ˈɛləmənts/, *n.pl.* **1.** a group of closely related metallic elements of atomic number 57 to 71 inclusive, often divided into three groups: **cerium metals** (lanthanum, cerium, praseodymium, neodymium, promethium, and samarium), **terbium metals** (europium, gadolinium, and terbium), and **yttrium metals** (dysprosium, holmium, erbium, thulium, yttrium, ytterbium, and lutetium); lanthanides. **2.** this group of fifteen elements together with the element scandium.

**rarefaction** /rɛərəˈfækʃən/, *n.* **1.** the act or process of rarefying. **2.** the state of being rarefied. – **rarefactive,** *adj.*

**rarefy** /ˈrɛərəfaɪ/, *v.,* **-fied, -fying.** *–v.t.* **1.** to make rare, more rare, or less dense. **2.** to make less gross; refine. *–v.i.* **3.** to become rare or less dense; become thinned. [L *rārēfacere*]

**rare gas** /rɛə ˈgæs/, *n.* any of the gases, helium, neon, argon, krypton, xenon or radon; chemically inactive, although some compounds have been reported. Also, **inert gas, noble gas.**

**rarely** /ˈrɛəli/, *adv.* **1.** on rare occasions; infrequently; in few instances: *he is rarely late.* **2.** exceptionally; in an unusual degree. **3.** unusually or remarkably well or excellent.

**raring** /ˈrɛərɪŋ/, *adj.* ready; eager: *he was raring to go.* [ppr. of d. *rare,* var. of REAR[2]]

**rarity** /ˈrɛərəti/, *n., pl.* **-ties. 1.** something rare, unusual, or uncommon. **2.** something esteemed or interesting being rare, uncommon, or curious. **3.** rare state or quality. **4.** rare occurrence; infrequency. **5.** unusual excellence. **6.** thinness, as of air or a gas.

**R.A.S.,** Royal Agricultural Society.

**rascal** /ˈraskəl/, *n.* **1.** a base, dishonest person. **2.** (mildly or affectionately reproving) any child or young animal: *you little rascal.* [ME *rascayl,* from OF *rascaille* rabble, from L *rādere* scratch]

**rascality** /ræsˈkæləti/, *n., pl.* **-ties. 1.** rascally or knavish character or conduct. **2.** a rascally act.

**rascally** /ˈraskəli/, *adj.* **1.** being, characteristic of, or befitting a rascal or knave; dishonest; mean: *a rascally trick.* **2.** (of places, etc.) wretchedly bad or unpleasant. *–adv.* **3.** in a rascally manner.

**rase** /reɪz/, *v.t.,* **rased, rasing.** →**raze.**

**rash**[1] /ræʃ/, *adj.* **1.** acting too hastily or without due consideration. **2.** characterised by or showing too great haste or lack of consideration: *rash promises.* [ME *rasch,* c. D and G *rasch* quick, brisk] – **rashly,** *adv.* – **rashness,** *n.*

**rash**[2] /ræʃ/, *n.* **1.** an eruption or efflorescence on the skin. **2.** a proliferation: *a rash of complaints.* [F *rache,* from L *rādere* scratch]

**rasher** /ˈræʃə/, *n.* a thin slice of bacon. [cf. OE *ræscettan* crackle]

**rasorial** /rəˈsɔriəl/, *adj.* given to scratching the ground for food, as poultry; gallinaceous. [NL *Rasōrēs* (pl.) lit., scratchers, from L *rāsus* scratched + -(I)AL]

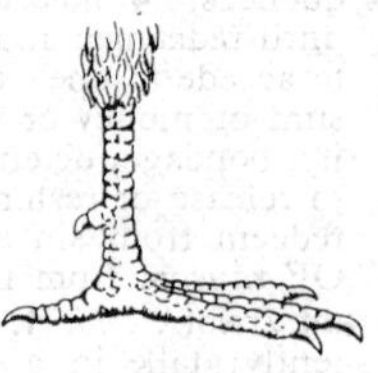

foot of rasorial bird

**rasp** /rasp, ræsp/, *v.t.* **1.** to scrape or abrade with a rough instrument. **2.** to scrape or rub roughly. **3.** to grate upon or irritate (the nerves, feelings, etc.). **4.** to utter with a grating sound. *–v.i.* **5.** to scrape or grate. **6.** to make a grating sound. *–n.* **7.** the act of rasping. **8.** a rasping sound. **9.** a coarse form of file, having separate pointlike teeth. **10.** any similar surface. [ME *raspe(n),* from OF *rasper* scrape, grate, from Gmc; cf. obs. G *raspen* grate]

**raspberry**[1] /ˈrazbəri, -bri/, *n., pl.* **-ries. 1.** the fruit of several shrubs of the rosaceous genus *Rubus,* consisting of small juicy drupelets, red, black, or pale yellow, forming a detachable cap about a convex receptacle, being thus distinguished from the blackberry. **2.** one of these plants, as the **red raspberry,** *R. idaeus,* of Europe. **3.** dark reddish purple. [*rasp(is)* raspberry (orig. uncert.) + BERRY]

**raspberry**[2] /ˈrazbəri, -bri/, *n., pl.* **-ries,** *v.,* **-ried, -rying.** *Colloq.* *–n.* **1.** a sound expressing derision or contempt made with the tongue and lips. *–v.i.* **2.** to make such a sound. [rhyming slang, *raspberry tart* fart]

**raspberry jam** /– ˈdʒæm/, *n.* jam prepared from raspberries.

**raspberry-jam tree** /ˌrazbəri-ˈdʒæm tri/, *n.* **1.** a wattle, *Acacia acuminata,* of western Australia, with long narrow leaves and timber which smells like raspberry jam. **2.** any of various plants with wood smelling of raspberries. Also, **jam tree.**

**rasper** /ˈraspə/, *n.* one who or that which rasps, as a machine for rasping sugar cane.

**rasp fern** /ˈrasp fɜn/, *n.* a terrestrial fern, *Doodia aspera,* found among rocks in forests.

**rasping** /ˈraspɪŋ/, *adj.* harsh: *a rasping voice.*

**raspy-root** /ˈraspi-rut/, *n.* an epiphytic orchid, *Rhinerrhiza divitiflora,* of coastal ranges of northern New South Wales and Queensland, characterised by thick, tuberculate, rasp-like roots.

**Rasta** /ˈrastə/, *n.* →**Rastafarian.**

**Rastafarian** /rastəˈfɛəriən/, *adj.* **1.** of or pertaining to Rastafarianism. *–n.* **2.** a member of the Rastafarian cult.

**Rastafarianism** /rastəˈfɛəriənɪzəm/, *n.* a Jamaican cult, the members of which believe in black supremacy and the back-to-Africa movement. [after *Ras Tafari,* the name of Haile Selassie before he was crowned emperor of Ethiopia in 1930; regarded by followers of the cult as a god]

**raster** /ˈræstə/, *n.* a series of parallel sweeps by an electronic scanning device. [G, from L *rastrum* a rake]

**rat** /ræt/, *n., v.,* **ratted, ratting.** *–n.* **1.** any of certain long-tailed rodents of the genus *Rattus* and allied genera (family Muridae), resembling but larger than the mouse, as the **brown rat,** *R. norvegicus.* **2.** any rodent of the same family, or any of various similar animals. **3.** →**desert rat. 4.** *Colloq.* one who abandons his friends or associates, esp. in time of trouble. **5.** *Colloq.* a person considered as wretched or despicable. **6. smell a rat,** *Colloq.* to be suspicious. *–interj.* **7.** (*pl.*) *Colloq.* (an exclamation of annoyance, incredulity, denial, or disappointment). *–v.i.* **8.** *Colloq.* to desert one's party or associates, esp. in time of trouble: *a man who would rat on his friends.* **9.** *Colloq.* to work as a scab (def. 4). **10.** *Colloq.* to inform (on); betray. **11.** *Colloq.* to go back on a statement, agreement, etc. (fol. by *on*). **12.** *Mining. Colloq.* **a.** to pilfer opal from a miner's hiding place. **b.** enter someone's mine and take out opal rock. **13.** to hunt or catch rats. **14. rat through,** to sort through in a careless or hasty manner. [ME *ratte,* OE *rat,* c. G *Ratz, Ratte*]

rat

**rata** /ˈratə/, *n.* any large usu. red-flowered New Zealand tree or vine of the genus *Metrosideros.* [Maori]

**ratable** /ˈreɪtəbəl/, *adj.* →**rateable.** – **ratability** /reɪtəˈbɪləti/, **ratableness,** *n.* – **ratably,** *adv.*

**ratafia** /rætəˈfiə/, *n.* **1.** a cordial or liqueur flavoured with fruit-kernels, fruit, or the like. **2.** a flavouring essence made with the essential oil of almonds. **3.** an almond biscuit or cake. Also, **ratafee** /rætəˈfi/. [F]

**ratafia biscuit** /– ˈbɪskət/, *n.* a type of sweet biscuit usu. flavoured with ratafia essence, similar to a macaroon, but smaller.

**ratal** /ˈreɪtl/, *n.* the amount on which rates or taxes are assessed. [RAT(E)[1] + -AL[1]]

**rataplan** /rætəˈplæn/, *n., v.,* **-planned, -planning.** *–n.* **1.** a sound of or as of the beating of a drum; a rub-a-dub. *–v.t., v.i.* **2.** to play by or play a rataplan. [F]

**ratatouille** /rætəˈtui/, *n.* a type of vegetable casserole or stew. [F]

**ratbag** /ˈrætbæg/, *n. Colloq.* **1.** a rascal; rogue. **2.** a person of eccentric or noncomforming ideas or behaviour. – **ratbaggery,** *n.* – **ratbaggy,** *adj.*

**ratbite fever** /rætbaɪt ˈfivə/, *n.* a relapsing fever, widely distributed geographically, caused by infection with a spirillum transmitted by rats. Also, **ratbite disease.**

**ratcatcher** /ˈrætkætʃə/, *n.* one who catches and destroys rats, esp. as a profession.

**ratch** /rætʃ/, *n.* →**ratchet.** [var. of RATCHET. Cf. G *Ratsche*]

**ratchet** /ˈrætʃət/, *n.* **1.** a toothed bar with which a pawl engages. **2.** the pawl used with such a device. **3.** a mechanism consisting of such a bar or wheel with the pawl. **4.** a ratchet wheel. [F *rochet* ratchet, bobbin, from It. *rocchetto,* from *rocca* distaff, from Gmc; cf. obs. E *rock* distaff]

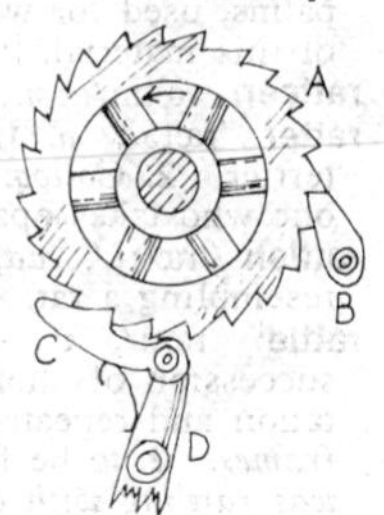

ratchet wheel: A, wheel; B, pawl preventing reversal of motion; C, pawl conveying motion to wheel; D, reciprocating lever

**ratchet wheel** /ˈ– wil/, *n.* a wheel with teeth on the edge, in which a pawl catches, as to prevent reversal of motion or convert reciprocating into rotatory motion.

**rate**[1] /reɪt/, *n., v.,* **rated, rating.** *–n.* **1.** a certain quantity or amount of one thing considered in relation to a unit of another thing and used as a standard or measure: *at the rate of 60 kilometres an hour.* **2.** a fixed charge per unit of quantity: *a rate of 10 cents in the dollar.* **3.** the amount of a charge or payment with reference to some basis of calculation: *the rate of interest.* **4.** price: *to cut rates.* **5.** degree of speed, of travelling, working, etc.: *to work at a rapid rate.* **6.** degree or relative amount of action or procedure: *the rate of increase.* **7.** relative condition or quality; grade, class, or sort. **8.** assigned position in any of a series of graded classes; rating. **9.** (*usu. pl.*) a tax on property, imposed by a local authority and used for the maintenance of local services, etc. **10. at any rate, a.** under any circumstances; in any case; at all events. **b.** at least. **11. at this rate,** if the present circumstances continue. *–v.t.* **12.** to estimate the value or worth of; appraise. **13.** to esteem, consider, or account: *he was rated one of the rich men of the city.* **14.** to fix at a certain rate, as of charge or payment. **15.** to value for purposes of taxation, etc. **16.** to make subject to the payment of a certain rate or tax. **17.** to deserve. **18.** *Chiefly Naut.* to place in a certain class, etc., as a ship or a seaman; give a certain rating to. **19.** *U.S.* to arrange for the conveyance of (goods) at a certain rate. *–v.i.* **20.** to have value, standing, etc. **21.** to have position in a certain class. [ME, from ML *rata* fixed amount or portion, rate, prop. fem. of L *ratus,* pp., fixed by calculation, determined. See RATIO]

**rate**[2] /reɪt/, *v.t., v.i.,* **rated, rating.** to chide vehemently; scold. [ME; apparently c. Swed. *rata* find fault]

**rateable** /ˈreɪtəbəl/, *adj.* **1.** capable of being rated or appraised. **2.** proportional. **3.** liable to payment of rates or local taxes. Also, **ratable.** – **rateability** /reɪtəˈbɪləti/, **rateableness,** *n.* – **rateably,** *adv.*

**rateable value** /– ˈvælju/, *n.* the value of a property assessed by a local authority on which the amount of rate charged is based.

**rateen** /rəˈtin/, *n.* **1.** an all-wool lining serge, similar to frieze. **2.** →**ratine.** [F *ratine.* See RATINE]

**ratel** /ˈreɪtl/, *n.* a badger-like carnivore, *Mellivora capensis,* of Africa and India. [Afrikaans]

**rate of exchange,** *n.* the ratio at which the unit of currency of one country can be exchanged for the unit of currency of another country. Also, **exchange rate.**

**ratepayer** /ˈreɪtpeɪə/, *n.* one who pays rates on property, esp. a householder.

**rat factory** /ˈræt fæktri/, *n. N.Z. Colloq.* →**psychiatric hospital.**

**rat-fink** /ˈræt-fɪŋk/, *n. Orig. U.S.* a despicable person.

**ratguard** /ˈrætgad/, *n.* a large, thin circular piece of metal fitted round a ship's mooring ropes to prevent rats climbing up them to get on board.

**rathe** /reɪð/, *adj.* **1.** *Archaic and Poetic.* growing, blooming, or ripening early in the year or season. *–adv.* **2.** *Archaic.* quickly. **3.** *Archaic.* early. [ME; OE *hræth,* c. OHG *hrad,* Icel. *hradhr* quick]

**rather** /ˈraðə/; *def. 8 sometimes* /raˈðɜ/, *adv.* **1.** more so than not; to a certain extent; somewhat: *rather good.* **2.** (with verbs) in some degree (used either literally to modify a statement, or ironically to lend emphasis). **3.** more properly or justly; with better reason: *the contrary is rather to be supposed.* **4.** sooner or more readily or willingly: *to die rather than yield, I would rather go today.* **5.** in preference; as a preferred or accepted alternative. **6.** more properly or correctly speaking; more truly. **7.** on the contrary. **8.** *Chiefly Brit.* (as a response, a colloquial equivalent of an emphatic affirmative): *Is it worth going to? Rather!* [ME; OE *hrathor,* compar. of *hrathe* quickly]

**ratification** /rætəfəˈkeɪʃən/, *n.* **1.** the act of ratifying; confirmation; sanction. **2.** the state of being ratified. **3.** *Law.* the adoption of a contract or the like by one not initially bound by it.

**ratify** /ˈrætəfaɪ/, *v.t.,* **-fied, -fying.** **1.** to confirm by expressing consent, approval, or formal sanction. **2.** to confirm (something done or arranged by an agent or by representatives) by such action. [ME *ratifie(n),* from OF *ratifier,* from ML *ratificāre,* from *rati-* (combining form representing L *ratus* fixed; see RATE[1]) + L *-ficāre* make] – **ratifier,** *n.*

**ratine** /rəˈtin/, *n.* **1.** a rough woollen cloth, formerly in use chiefly for travelling coats. **2.** a coarse fabric made from fine warp-yarn cotton. **3.** →**rateen** (def. 1). Also, **rateen, ratiné** /ˈrætəneɪ/. [F]

**rating**[1] /ˈreɪtɪŋ/, *n.* **1.** classification according to grade or rank. **2.** *Naut.* **a.** assigned position in a particular class or grade, or relative standing, as of a ship or a seaman. **b.** *Navy.* a sailor who has no commissioned rank. **3.** a person's or firm's credit standing. **4.** an amount fixed as a municipal rate; the act of assessing this. **5.** a proportion of one dollar or some other monetary unit payable in tax. **6.** *Elect.* (of a machine, apparatus, etc.) a designated limit of operating characteristics, as voltage, amperes, frequency, etc., based on definite conditions. **7.** a measure of success, as of a television program, based on an assessment of audience size. **8.** *Rowing.* the rate of striking, usu. in strokes per minute. [RATE[1] + -ING[1]]

**rating**[2] /ˈreɪtɪŋ/, *n.* angry reprimand or rebuke; a scolding. [RATE[2] + -ING[1]]

**ratio** /ˈreɪʃioʊ/, *n., pl.* **-tios.** **1.** the relation between two similar magnitudes in respect to the number of times the first contains the second: *the ratio of 5 to 2, which may be written 5: 2, or 5/2.* **2.** proportional relation; rate; quotient of two numbers. **3.** *Finance.* the relative value of gold and silver in a bimetallic currency system, fixed by the government of a country. [L: reckoning, relation, reason]

**ratiocinate** /ræti'oʊsəneɪt/, *v.i.*, **-nated, -nating.** to reason; carry on a process of reasoning; think logically. [L *ratiōcinātus,* pp., calculated] – **ratiocinator,** *n.*

**ratiocination** /ˌrætiˌoʊsə'neɪʃən/, *n.* reasoning, or a process of reasoning; logical thought or thinking. – **ratiocinative,** *adj.*

**ratio decidendi** /ˌreɪʃioʊ disə'dɛndaɪ/, *n. Law.* **1.** the decision in a case and the facts material to it. **2.** the principle upon which a case is decided. [L: reason for deciding]

**ration** /'ræʃən/, *n.* **1.** a fixed allowance of provisions or food: *rations of coal and coffee.* **2.** (*usu. pl.*) a fixed allowance of food, clothing, etc., supplied to a soldier, sailor, shearer, seaman, etc. *–v.t.* **3.** to apportion or distribute as rations or by some method of allowance. **4.** to put on, or restrict to, rations. **5.** to supply with rations, as of food: *to ration an army.* [F, from ML *ratio* allowance of provisions, L account. See RATIO] – **rationing,** *n.*

**rational** /'ræʃnəl, 'ræʃənəl/, *adj.* **1.** agreeable to reason; reasonable; sensible. **2.** having or exercising reason, sound judgment, or good sense. **3.** being in or characterised by full possession of one's reason; sane; lucid: *the patient appeared perfectly rational.* **4.** endowed with the faculty of reason: *man is a rational animal.* **5.** of or pertaining to reason: *the rational faculty.* **6.** proceeding or derived from reason, or based on reasoning: *a rational explanation.* **7.** *Maths.* **a.** expressible as the quotient of two integers. **b.** (of functions) expressible as the quotient of two polynomials. **8.** *Gk and Lat. Pros.* capable of measurement in terms of the metrical unit (mora). [L *ratiōnālis*] – **rationally,** *adv.*

**rationale** /ræʃə'nal/, *n.* **1.** a statement of reasons. **2.** a reasoned exposition of principles. **3.** the fundamental reasons serving to account for something. [L, neut. of *ratiōnālis* rational]

**rationalise** /'ræʃnəlaɪz/, *v.*, **-lised, -lising.** *–v.t.* **1.** *Psychol.* to invent a rational, acceptable explanation for behaviour which has its origin in the unconscious; to justify unconscious behaviour. **2.** to remove unreasonable elements from. **3.** to make rational or conformable to reason. **4.** *Maths.* to remove radicals from part of an expression without altering its value. **5.** to treat or explain in a rational or rationalistic manner. **6.** to reorganise (resources, the components of a business, etc.) to promote efficiency, economy, etc. *–v.i.* **7.** to employ reason; think in a rational or rationalistic manner. **8.** to reorganise and integrate (an industry). **9.** to justify one's behaviour by plausible explanations, as to deceive oneself or others. Also, **rationalize.** – **rationalisation** /ræʃnəlaɪ'zeɪʃən/, *n.* – **rationaliser,** *n.*

**rationalism** /'ræʃnəlɪzəm/, *n.* **1.** the principle or habit of accepting reason as the supreme authority in matters of opinion, beliefs, or conduct. **2.** *Philos.* **a.** the theory that reason is in itself a source of knowledge independently of the senses (distinguished from *empiricism,* def. 2). **b.** the theory that even sense experience is possible only because of a rational element supplied by reason (distinguished from *sensationalism,* def. 5). **3.** *Theol.* the doctrine that revelation and scriptural tradition are to be accepted only so far as, in principle, they conform with reason. – **rationalistic** /ræʃnə'lɪstɪk/, **rationalistical** /ræʃnə'lɪstɪkəl/, *adj.* – **rationalistically** /ræʃnə'lɪstɪkli/, *adv.*

**rationality** /ræʃə'nælәti/, *n.*, *pl.* **-ties.** **1.** the quality of being rational. **2.** the possession of reason. **3.** reasonableness. **4.** the exercise of reason. **5.** a rational or reasonable view, practice, etc.

**rational number** /ræʃnəl 'nʌmbə/, *n.* a number which can be expressed as the quotient of two integers.

**ration-book** /'ræʃən-bʊk/, *n.* a book of coupons or vouchers for rationed goods.

**ration-card** /'ræʃən-kad/, *n.* a card entitling the holder to receive rations.

**ratite** /'rætaɪt/, *adj.* **1.** without a carina, as a breastbone. **2.** having a flat breastbone, as the ostrich, cassowary, emu, moa, etc. (contrasted with *carinate*). [L *ratis* raft + -ITE[2]]

**rat-kangaroo** /ˌræt-kæŋgə'ru/, *n.* any of various kangaroos of the *Bettongia, Potorous* and related genera, cat-sized or smaller, and resembling small wallabies.

**ratline** /'rætlən/, *n. Naut.* **1.** any of the small ropes or lines which traverse the shrouds horizontally, serving as steps for going aloft. **2.** the kind of rope or line from which these are made. Also, **ratlin.** [late ME *ratling, radelyng;* orig. uncert.]

rat-kangaroo

**ratoon** /rə'tun/, *n.* **1.** a sprout or shoot from the root of a plant (esp. a sugar cane) after it has been cropped. *–v.i., v.t.* **2.** to put forth or cause to put forth ratoons. Also, **rattoon.** [Sp. *retoño,* from Hind. *ratun*]

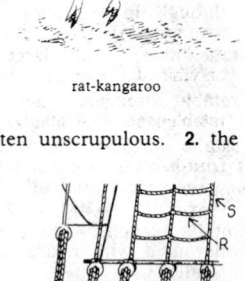

**rat-race** /'ræt-reɪs/, *n.* **1.** the struggle for success, esp. in career, fiercely competitive and often unscrupulous. **2.** the frantic pace of city life.

**ratsbane** /'rætsbeɪn/, *n.* **1.** rat poison. **2.** the trioxide of arsenic. [earlier *rats bane.* See RAT, BANE]

R, ratline; S, shroud

**ratshit** /'rætˌʃɪt/, *adj. Colloq.* **1.** useless; broken. **2.** depressed or unwell. **3.** no good: *that exam was ratshit.* Also, **R.S.**

**rat's-tail fescue** /ˌræts-teɪl 'fɛskju/, *n.* a weed introduced into Australia, *Vulpia myuros,* which has a hairy inflorescence.

**rat's-tail orchid** /– 'ɔkəd/, *n.* an epiphytic orchid, *Dendrobium teretifolium,* found on trees, esp. swamp oak, and rocks of eastern New South Wales and Queensland.

**rat-tail grass** /'ræt-teɪl gras/, *n.* any grass with an inflorescence thought to resemble a rat's tail, as the grasses of the genus *Sporobulus.* Also, **rat's-tail grass.**

**rattan** /rə'tæn/, *n.* **1.** any of various climbing palms of the genus *Calamus,* or allied genera. **2.** the tough stems of such palms, used for wickerwork, canes, etc. **3.** a stick or switch of this material. [var. of *rotang,* from Malay *rōtan*]

**ratteen** /rə'tin/, *n. Obs.* →**ratine.**

**ratter** /'rætə/, *n.* **1.** one who or that which catches rats, as a terrier. **2.** *Colloq.* a deserter or betrayer. **3.** *Mining Colloq.* one who takes opal from someone else's mine.

**rattish** /'rætɪʃ/, *adj.* **1.** of, pertaining to, characteristic of, or resembling a rat. **2.** infested with rats.

**rattle**[1] /'rætl/, *v.*, **-tled, -tling,** *n.* *–v.i.* **1.** to give out a rapid succession of short sharp sounds, as in consequence of agitation and repeated concussions: *the windows rattled in their frames.* **2.** to be filled with such sounds, as a place: *the hall was rattling with excitement.* **3.** to move or go, esp. rapidly, with such sounds. **4.** to talk rapidly; chatter. *–v.t.* **5.** to cause to rattle: *he rattled the doorknob violently.* **6.** to drive, send, bring, etc., esp. rapidly, with rattling. **7.** to utter or perform in a rapid or lively manner: *to rattle off a speech.* **8.** *Colloq.* to disconcert or confuse (a person). **9.** *Hunting.* to stir up (a cover). *–n.* **10.** a rapid succession of short, sharp sounds, as from the collision of hard bodies. **11.** an instrument contrived to make a rattling sound, as a child's toy. **12.** a device consisting of a wooden frame with a wheel and clapper, which, when swung round, emits a loud clacking noise, as used by football fans to encourage players, express emotions, etc. **13.** any plant with a dry capsule in which seeds rattle, as the **rattlepod** of the genus *Crotalaria,* and the **red-rattle,** *Pedicularis palustris.* **14.** the series of horny pieces or rings at the end of a rattlesnake's tail, with which it produces a rattling sound. **15.** a rattling sound in the throat, as the death rattle. [ME *ratele(n),* c. D *ratelen,* G *rasseln;* imitative]

**rattle**[2] /'rætl/, *v.t.*, **-tled, -tling.** *Naut.* to furnish with ratlines (usu. fol. by *down*). [backformation from RATLINE, taken as a verbal n.]

**rattlebrain** /'rætlbreɪn/, *n.* a giddy, empty-headed chatterer.

Also, **rattlehead** /ˈrætlhɛd/, **rattlepate** /ˈrætlpeɪt/.

**rattlepod** /ˈrætlpɒd/, *n.* →**crotalaria.**

**rattler** /ˈrætlə/, *n.* **1.** a rattlesnake. **2.** one who or that which rattles. **3.** *Colloq.* a person regarded as extremely good or extremely bad. **4.** *Chiefly U.S. Colloq.* a freight train. **5.** **jump (scale) the rattler,** *Colloq.* board a train illegally.

**rattlesnake** /ˈrætlsneɪk/, *n.* any of various venomous American snakes of the genera *Crotalus* and *Sistrurus,* having several loosely articulated horny pieces or rings at the end of the tail, which produce a rattling or whirring sound when shaken.

rattlesnake

**rattletrap** /ˈrætltræp/, *n.* **1.** a shaky, rattling object, as a rickety vehicle. **2.** *Colloq.* a garrulous person. **3.** *Colloq.* the mouth.

**rattling** /ˈrætlɪŋ/, *adv., adj. Colloq.* extremely (good).

**rattly** /ˈrætli/, *adj.* **1.** apt to rattle. **2.** making or having a rattling sound.

**rattoon** /rəˈtun/, *n., v.i., v.t.* →**ratoon.**

**rat-trap** /ˈræt-træp/, *n.* **1.** a device for catching rats. **2.** a difficult and involved set of circumstances. **3.** a bicycle pedal having deep serrations to prevent the foot slipping.

**ratty** /ˈræti/, *adj.,* **-tier, -tiest. 1.** full of rats. **2.** of or characteristic of a rat. **3.** wretched; shabby. **4.** annoyed; irritable. **5.** *Colloq.* slightly eccentric.

**raucous** /ˈrɔkəs/, *adj.* hoarse; harsh-sounding, as a voice. [L *raucus*] – **raucously,** *adv.* – **raucousness, raucity** /ˈrɔsəti/, *n.*

**raunchy** /ˈrɔntʃi/, *adj.* **1.** (usu. of a man) randy. **2.** stimulating sexual desire; bawdy. **3.** coarse; earthy; lusty.

**raupo** /ˈraʊpoʊ/, *n.* the giant bulrush, *Typha orientalis,* of New Zealand; cooper's flag. [Maori]

**rauriki** /ˈraʊrəki/, *n. N.Z.* →**puha.** [Maori]

**rauwolfia** /rɔˈwʊlfiə, raʊ-/, *n.* **1.** *Bot.* any tree or shrub of the genus *Rauwolfia,* family Apocynaceae, esp. *R. vomitoria,* a species of tropical Africa. **2.** *Pharm.* an extract from the roots of the rauwolfia with many medicinal uses in its various purified forms. [named after Leonhart *Rauwolf,* 16th C German botanist and physician]

**ravage** /ˈrævɪdʒ/, *n., v.,* **-aged, -aging.** *–n.* **1.** devastating or destructive action. **2.** havoc; ruinous damage: *the ravages of war.* *–v.t.* **3.** to work havoc upon; damage or mar by ravages: *a face ravaged by grief.* *–v.i.* **4.** to work havoc; do ruinous damage. [F, from *ravir.* See RAVISH] – **ravager,** *n.*

**rave** /reɪv/, *v.,* **raved, raving,** *n., adj.* *–v.i.* **1.** to talk wildly, as in delirium. **2.** (of wind, water, storms, etc.) to make a wild or furious sound; rage. **3.** *Colloq.* to talk or write with extravagant enthusiasm. **4.** *Colloq.* to act boisterously or enthusiastically. *–v.t.* **5.** to utter as if in madness. *–n.* **6.** an act of raving. **7.** extravagantly enthusiastic praise. **8.** *Colloq.* a wild or hectic party or the like. *–adj.* **9.** praising with extravagant enthusiasm: *a rave review.* [ME, probably from OF *raver* wander, be delirious]

**ravel** /ˈrævəl/, *v.,* **-elled, -elling** or (*U.S.*) **-eled, -eling,** *n.* *–v.t.* **1.** to tangle or entangle. **2.** to involve; confuse; perplex. **3.** to disengage the threads or fibres of (a woven or knitted fabric, a rope, etc.). **4.** to make plain or clear (oft. fol. by *out*). *–v.i.* **5.** to become disjoined thread by thread or fibre by fibre; fray. **6.** to become tangled. **7.** to become confused or perplexed. **8.** *Civ. Eng.* (of a road surface) to lose aggregate because of wear. *–n.* **9.** a tangle or complication. [apparently from MD *ravelen* entangle] – **raveller,** *n.*

**ravelin** /ˈrævlən/, *n.* a triangular fortification, outside the main ditch, having two embankments forming a projecting angle. [F, earlier *revellin,* from D *regeling* framework]

**ravelling** /ˈrævəlɪŋ/, *n.* something ravelled out, as a thread drawn from a knitted or woven fabric. Also, *Chiefly U.S.,* **raveling.**

**ravelment** /ˈrævəlmənt/, *n.* entanglement; confusion.

**raven**[1] /ˈreɪvən/, *n.* **1.** either of two large, glossy black, omnivorous and somewhat predacious birds with loud harsh calls, the **Australian raven,** *Corvus coronoides,* or the **little raven,** *C. mellori.* **2.** any of a number of similar birds of the family Corvidae found elsewhere, esp. *C. corax,* often considered a bird of ill-omen *–adj.* **3.** lustrous black: *raven locks.* [ME, OE *hræfn,* c. OHG *hraban,* MD *rāven*]

**raven**[2] /ˈrævən/, *v.i. Obs.* **1.** to seek plunder or prey. **2.** to eat or feed voraciously or greedily. **3.** to have a ravenous appetite. *–v.t.* **4.** to seize as spoil or prey. **5.** to devour voraciously. *–n.* **6.** rapine; robbery. **7.** plunder or prey. Also, **ravin.** [ME *ravine,* from F, from L *rapīna* RAPINE]

raven[1] (def. 2)

**ravening** /ˈrævənɪŋ/, *adj. Obs.* **1.** rapacious; voracious. *–n.* **2.** rapacity.

**ravenous** /ˈrævənəs/, *adj.* **1.** extremely hungry. **2.** extremely rapacious. **3.** voracious or gluttonous. **4.** given to seizing prey in order to devour, as animals. [ME, from OF *ravinos.* See RAVEN[2]] – **ravenously,** *adv.* – **ravenousness,** *n.*

**raver** /ˈreɪvə/, *n.* **1.** one who or that which raves. **2.** *Colloq.* an enthusiastic person, usu. a young one, as a fan of a pop singer.

**ravine** /rəˈvin/, *n.* a long, deep, narrow valley, esp. one worn by water. [F: torrent of water, ravine]

**raving** /ˈreɪvɪŋ/, *adj.* **1.** that raves; delirious; frenzied. **2.** *Colloq.* extraordinary or remarkable: *she's no raving beauty.* *–n.* **3.** irrational, incoherent talk.

**ravioli** /ræviˈoʊli/, *n. pl.* small pieces of pasta, cut square or otherwise, enclosing forcemeat (and often spinach), cooked, and served in a tomato sauce. [It., from d. It. *rava,* from L *rāpum* turnip, beet]

**ravish** /ˈrævɪʃ/, *v.t.* **1.** to fill with strong emotion, esp. joy. **2.** to seize and carry off by force. **3.** to carry off (a woman) by force. **4.** to rape (a woman). [ME *ravisshe(n),* from OF *ravir,* from L *rapere* seize, carry off. Cf. RAPE[1], RAPTURE] – **ravisher,** *n.*

**ravishing** /ˈrævəʃɪŋ/, *adj.* entrancing; enchanting. – **ravishingly,** *adv.*

**ravishment** /ˈrævɪʃmənt/, *n.* **1.** rapture or ecstasy. **2.** violent removal. **3.** the forcible abduction of a woman. **4.** →**rape**[1].

**raw** /rɔ/, *adj.* **1.** uncooked, as articles of food. **2.** (of foods, textiles, etc.) not having undergone processes of preparing, dressing, finishing, refining, or manufacture. **3.** unnaturally or painfully exposed, as flesh, etc., by removal of the skin or natural integument. **4.** painfully open, as a sore, wound, etc. **5.** crude in quality or character; not tempered or refined by art or taste. **6.** ignorant, inexperienced, or untrained: *a raw recruit.* **7.** brutally or grossly frank: *a raw portrayal of human passions.* **8.** *Educ.* denoting a score, level of achievement, etc., as in a test, before adjustments for age, etc., have been made. **9.** *Colloq.* harsh or unfair: *a raw deal.* **10.** disagreeably damp and chilly, as the weather, air, etc. **11.** not diluted, as spirits. **12.** **the raw, a.** a crude, uncultured state: *the play portrayed life in the raw.* **b.** naked; nude: *she sunbakes in the raw.* **c.** a particularly sensitive place, point, topic or the like: *her remark touched him on the raw.*

**raw-boned** /ˈrɔ-boʊnd/, *adj.* having little flesh; gaunt.

**rawhide** /ˈrɔhaɪd/, *n., adj. v.,* **-hided, -hiding.** *–n.* **1.** →**greenhide. 2.** a rope or whip made of this. *–adj.* **3.** →**greenhide.** *–v.t.* **4.** to whip with a rawhide.

**rawlplug** /ˈrɔlplʌg/, *n.* a small drilled plug, usu. of wood fibre, inserted into a hole in a wall as a fixing for a nail or screw. [Trademark]

**raw material** /rɔ məˈtɪəriəl/, *n.* **1.** material before it is made in a final form. **2.** an untrained recruit or a group of such recruits.

**raw score** /ˈ– skɔ/, *n.* the initial mark given by an examiner to an individual test paper (opposed to the *scaled score*).

**raw sienna** /– siˈɛnə/, *n.* See **sienna.**

**raw silk** /– ˈsɪlk/, *n.* **1.** silk as reeled from the cocoons. **2.** material woven from this silk.

**raw stock** /ˈ– stɒk/, *n. Films, T.V., etc.* unused film.

**ray**[1] /reɪ/, *n.* **1.** a narrow beam of light. **2.** a gleam, or slight manifestation, of intelligence, comfort, etc.: *a ray of hope.* **3.**

a raylike line or stretch of something. **4.** *Poetic.* light or radiance. **5.** a line of sight. **6.** *Physics.* **a.** any of the lines or streams in which light or radiant energy appears to issue from a luminous object. **b.** the straight line perpendicular to the wavefront in the propagation of radiant energy. **c.** a stream of material particles moving in the same line. **7.** *Maths.* one of a system of straight lines emanating from a point. **8.** any of a system of parts radially arranged. **9.** *Zool.* **a.** one of the branches or arms of a starfish or other radiate animal. **b.** one of the jointed supports of the soft fins of fishes. **10.** *Bot.* **a.** a ray flower. **b.** one of the branches of an umbel. **c.** →**medullary ray. d.** (in certain plants of the family Compositae) the marginal part of the flower head. **11.** *Astron.* one of many long bright streaks radiating from the large lunar craters. *–v.i.* **12.** to emit rays. **13.** to issue in rays. *–v.t.* **14.** to send forth in rays. **15.** to throw rays upon; irradiate. **16.** to subject to the action of rays, as in radiotherapy. **17.** to furnish with rays or radiating lines. [ME *raye* from OF *rai,* from L *radius.* See RADIUS]

**ray**[2] /reɪ/, *n.* an elasmobranch fish, with flat (depressed) body fitted for life on the sea bottom, distinguished by having the gill openings on the lower surface. [ME *raye,* from F *raie,* from L *raia*]

**ray**[3] /reɪ/, *n.* the syllable used for the second note of the scale in solfa. Also, **re.** See **solfa.**

**ray flower** /'– flaʊə/, *n.* one of the marginal florets surrounding the disc of the family Compositae. Also, **ray floret.**

**ray gun** /'– gʌn/, *n.* any of the guns of science fiction said to shoot out radioactive rays.

**Rayleigh criterion** /'reɪli kraɪˌtɪəriən/, *n.* (of optical instruments) a criterion for determining whether two point sources of light will produce two distinct images in spite of diffraction effects. [named after Baron J.W.S. *Rayleigh,* 1842-1919, English physicist]

**Rayleigh disc** /'– dɪsk/, *n.* a small disc hung by a fine thread in the path of a soundwave so that the extent to which the disc is deflected is a measure of the intensity of the soundwave. [see RAYLEIGH CRITERION]

**rayless** /'reɪləs/, *adj.* **1.** without rays. **2.** unillumined, dark, or gloomy.

**Raynaud's disease** /'reɪnoʊz dəziz/, *n.* a syndrome characterised by pallor and cyanosis of the digits, usu. precipitated by cold, with subsequent engorgement and pain. [named after Maurice *Raynaud,* 1834-81, French physician]

**rayon** /'reɪɒn/, *n.* **1.** any textile made from cellulose by passing an appropriate solution of it through spinnerets to form filaments which are used in yarns for making cloth; artificial silk. **2.** fabric made with the product. [F: ray, from OF *rai* RAY[1]]

**raze** /reɪz/, *v.t.,* **razed, razing. 1.** to tear down, demolish, or level to the ground. **2.** *Obs.* to scratch or graze. Also, **rase.** [ME *rase(n),* from F *raser,* from VL *rāsāre,* from L *rāsus,* pp., scraped] – **razer,** *n.*

**razee** /reɪ'zi/, *n., v.,* **-zeed, -zeeing.** *Obs. –n.* **1.** a ship, esp. a warship, reduced in height by the removal of the upper deck. *–v.t.* **2.** to cut down (a ship) by removing the upper deck. [F *rasé,* pp. of *raser* RAZE]

**raznici** /ræz'nɪtʃi/, *n.* a dish consisting of meat on a skewer cooked on a charcoal grill. [Serbo-Croat]

**razoo** /ra'zu/, *n. Colloq.* **1.** a gambling chip. **2. not have a brass razoo,** to have no money at all. [orig. uncert.]

**razor** /'reɪzə/, *n.* **1.** a sharp-edged instrument used esp. for shaving hair from the skin. **2.** an electrically powered device, as one having rotating or reciprocating blades behind a foil, used for the same purpose. *–v.t.* **3.** to apply a razor to. **4.** to shave. [ME *rasour,* from OF *rasor,* from *raser* scrape, shave, RAZE]

**razorback** /'reɪzəbæk/, *n.* **1.** a sharp ridge. **2.** →**finback. 3.** a bullock, or cow, etc., in poor condition. **4.** a wild pig with long legs, sharp snout and lean body.

**razorbill** /'reɪzəbɪl/, *n.* a shorebird, *Alca torda,* of rocky coasts of the North Atlantic, having a flattened, slightly hooked bill.

**razor cut** /'reɪzə kʌt/, *n.* **1.** a haircut done with a razor, not scissors. **2.** a short, layered haircut, tapering at the back, common in the 1970s.

**razorshell** /'reɪzəʃɛl/, *n.* an elongated marine bivalve mollusc of the family Solenidae, as *Ensis ensis,* common on sandy shores in Europe.

**razz** /ræz/, *Colloq. –v.t.* **1.** to deride; make fun of; chiack. *–n.* **2.** severe criticism; derision. [short for RASPBERRY[2]]

**razza** /'ræzə/, *n. Colloq.* an RSL club.

**razzamatazz** /'ræzmətæz/, *n. Colloq.* **1.** noisy and showy activity. **2.** any traditional style of jazz. Also, **razzmatazz.**

**razzle-dazzle** /'ræzəl-dæzəl/, *n. Colloq.* noisy and showy activity; razzamatazz.

**Rb,** *Chem.* rubidium.

**R.C.** /a 'si/, **1.** Red Cross. **2.** Roman Catholic.

**r-coloured** /'a-kʌləd/, *adj.* (as of vowels) pronounced with a special articulation, usu. retroflex, which produces an *r* quality. – **r-colour,** *n.*

**rd, 1.** road. **2.** rod; rods. **3.** road.

**Rd,** Road.

**R.D.F.** /a di 'ɛf/, radio direction-finder.

**RDX,** *Chem.* cyclonite.

**re**[1] /reɪ, ri/, *n.* **1.** (in music) the syllable used for the second degree of the scale in solfege. See **solfège. 2.** →**ray**[3]. [See GAMUT]

**re**[2] /ri, reɪ/, *prep.* in the case of; with reference to. [L, abl. of *rēs* thing, matter]

**'re,** *v.* a contracted form of *are:* **we're** /'wiə, wɪə, wɛə/, **you're** /'juə, jʊə, jɔ/, **they're** /'ðeɪə, ðɛə/.

**re-, 1.** a prefix indicating repetition, as in *reprint, rebirth.* **2.** a prefix indicating withdrawal or backward motion, often figurative like 'back', applied often to stems not used as words, as in *revert, retract.* [L]

**Re, 1.** *Chem.* rhenium. **2.** Also, **re.** rupee.

**reach** /ritʃ/, *v.t.* **1.** to get to, or get as far as, in moving, going, travelling, etc.: *the boat reached the shore.* **2.** to come to or arrive at in some course of progress, action, etc.: *his letter reached me.* **3.** to succeed in touching or seizing with an outstretched hand, a pole, etc.: *to reach a book on a high shelf.* **4.** to stretch or hold out; extend. **5.** to stretch or extend so as to touch or meet: *the bookcase reaches the ceiling.* **6.** to establish communication with. **7.** to amount to, as in the sum or total: *the cost will reach millions.* **8.** to penetrate to (a point, etc.). **9.** to succeed in striking or hitting, as with a weapon or missile. **10.** to succeed in influencing, impressing, interesting, convincing, etc. *–v.i.* **11.** to make a stretch, as with the hand or arm. **12.** to become outstretched, as the hand or arm. **13.** to make a movement or effort as if to touch or seize something: *to reach for a weapon.* **14.** to extend in operation or effect: *power that reaches throughout the land.* **15.** to stretch in space; extend in direction, length, distance, etc.: *a coat reaching to the knee.* **16.** to extend or continue in time. **17.** to get or come to a specified place, person, condition, etc. (oft. fol. by *to*). **18.** to amount (fol. by *to*): *sums reaching to a considerable total.* **19.** to penetrate. **20.** *Naut.* **a.** to sail on a reach. **b.** to sail with the wind from somewhere near abeam, i.e., neither ahead nor dead astern. *–n.* **21.** the act of reaching: *to make a reach for a weapon.* **22.** the extent or distance of reaching: *within reach of his voice.* **23.** range of effective action, power, or capacity. **24. a.** the length of the arm from the armpit to the finger tips. **b.** *Boxing.* the distance between the finger tips of the outstretched arm, across the chest to the finger tips of the other arm. **25.** a continuous stretch or extent of something: *a reach of woodland.* **26.** a level portion of a canal, between locks. **27.** a portion of a river between bends. **28.** *Naut.* a point of sailing where the wind is coming from within a few points of abeam. In a **close reach** the wind is forward of the beam; in a **broad reach** it is abaft the beam; in a **beam reach** it is abeam or nearly so; in a **head reach** it is very nearly dead ahead. **29.** the pole connecting the rear axle of a wagon to the transverse bar or bolster over the front axle supporting the wagon bed. [ME *reche,* OE *rǣcan,* c. G *reichen*] – **reacher,** *n.*

**reach-me-down** /'ritʃ-mi-daʊn/, *n.* →**hand-me-down.**

**re-act** /ri-'ækt/, *v.t.* to act or perform again; re-enact. [RE- (def. 1) + ACT, *v.*]

**react** /ri'ækt/, *v.i.* **1.** to act in return on an agent or influence; act reciprocally upon each other, as two things. **2.** to act in a reverse direction or manner. **3.** to act in opposition, as against some force. **4.** to respond to a stimulus in a particular manner. [RE- (def. 2) + ACT, *v.*]

**reactance** /ri'æktəns/, *n.* that part of the impedance of an alternating-current circuit which is due to inductance and capacity. [ REACT + -ANCE]

**reactant** /ri'æktənt/, *n.* a substance which takes part in a chemical reaction.

**reaction** /ri'ækʃən/, *n.* **1.** a reverse movement or tendency. **2.** action in a reverse direction or manner. **3.** action in response to some influence, event, etc.: *his reaction to the president's speech.* **4.** a political tendency or movement in the direction of extreme conservatism, esp. in opposition to radical or socialist policies. **5.** *Physiol.* action in response to a stimulus, as of the system, or of a nerve, muscle, etc. **6.** *Med.* **a.** the action caused by the resistance to another action. **b.** a return to the opposite physical condition, as after shock, exhaustion, or chill. **7.** *Bacteriol., Immunol.* the specific cellular effect produced by a foreign matter, as in testing for allergies. **8.** *Chem.* the reciprocal action of chemical agents upon each other; a chemical change. **9.** →**nuclear reaction. 10.** *Physics.* See **Newton's laws. 11.** *Mech.* a force called into existence together with another force, being equal and opposite to it. **12.** *Comm.* a drop in the market after an advance in prices.

**reactionary** /ri'ækʃənəri, -ʃənri/, *adj., n., pl.* **-aries.** *–adj.* **1.** of, pertaining to, marked by, or favouring reaction, as in politics. *–n.* **2.** one who favours or inclines to reaction (def. 4). Also, **reactionist.**

**reaction engine** /ri'ækʃən ɛndʒən/, *n.* an engine that develops thrust by reaction to the ejection of a substance from it, esp. an engine that ejects a stream of gases created by the burning of fuel within itself as a rocket or jet engine. Also, **reaction motor.**

**reaction product** /'– prɒdʌkt/, *n.* a substance formed as the result of a chemical or nuclear reaction.

**reaction propulsion** /'– prəpʌlʃən/, *n.* →**jet propulsion.**

**reaction turbine** /'– tɜbaɪn/, *n.* See **turbine.**

**reactivate** /ri'æktəveɪt/, *v.t.*, **-vated, -vating.** to cause something to be active again.

**reactive** /ri'æktɪv/, *adj.* **1.** tending to react. **2.** *Chem.* chemically active; readily entering into a chemical reaction. **3.** pertaining to or characterised by reaction. **4.** *Elect.* characterised by or pertaining to reactance.

**reactive dye** /– 'daɪ/, *n.* dye which adheres to fibre by means of chemical interaction.

**reactor** /ri'æktə/, *n.* **1.** a substance or person undergoing a reaction. **2.** *Elect.* a device, the primary purpose of which is to introduce reactance into a circuit. **3.** *Immunol., Vet. Sci.* a patient or animal that reacts positively towards a foreign matter. **4.** *Physics.* →**nuclear reactor.**

**read**[1] /rid/, *v.,* **read** /rɛd/, **reading** /'ridɪŋ/, *n.* *–v.t.* **1.** to observe, and apprehend the meaning of (something written, printed, etc.): *to read a book.* **2.** to utter aloud; render in speech (something written, printed, etc.). **3.** to have such knowledge of (a language) as to be able to understand things written in it: *to be able to read French.* **4.** to apprehend the meaning of (signs, characters, etc.) otherwise than with the eyes, as by means of the fingers. **5.** to make out the significance of, by scrutiny or observation: *to read the sky.* **6.** to foresee, foretell, or predict: *to read a person's fortune.* **7.** to make out the character, etc., of (a person, etc.), as by the interpretation of outward signs. **8.** to understand or take (something read or observed) in a particular way. **9.** to introduce (something not expressed or directly indicated) into what is read or considered. **10.** to adopt or give as a reading in a particular passage: *for 'one thousand' another version reads 'ten thousand'.* **11.** to register or indicate, as a thermometer or other instrument. **12.** (of a computer) to take (information) from a peripheral device, as a set of punched cards, into the central computer. **13.** to study, as by perusing books: *to read law.* **14.** to learn by, or as if by, perusal: *to read a person's thoughts.* **15.** to bring, put, etc., by reading: *to read oneself to sleep.* **16.** to give one (a lecture or lesson) by way of admonition or rebuke. **17.** to discover or explain the meaning of (a riddle, a dream, etc.). *–v.i.* **18.** to read or peruse writing, printing, etc., or papers, books, etc. **19.** to utter aloud, or render in speech, written or printed words that one is perusing: *to read to a person.* **20.** to give a public reading or recital. **21.** to inspect and apprehend the meaning of written or other signs or characters. **22.** to occupy oneself seriously with reading or study, esp. in a specific course of study: *to read for holy orders.* **23.** to obtain knowledge or learn of something by reading. **24.** to admit of being read, esp. properly or well. **25.** to have a certain wording. **26.** to admit of being read or interpreted (as stated): *a rule that reads two different ways.* **27.** (of a computer) to take in information. **28. read between the lines,** to perceive the truth of a situation, regardless of its appearances. **29. read oneself in,** *C. of E.* to take possession of a benefice by publicly reading the Thirty-nine Articles. **30. you wouldn't read about it!** (an exclamation of astonishment, sometimes ironic). *–n.* **31.** the act or process of reading: *I just lay in bed and had a good read.* [ME *rede(n)*, OE *rǣdan* counsel, consider, read, c. D *raden,* G *raten,* Icel. *rādha*]

**read**[2] /rɛd/, *adj.* having knowledge gained by reading: *a widely read person.* [properly pp. of READ[1]]

**readable** /'ridəbəl/, *adj.* **1.** easy or interesting to read. **2.** capable of being read; legible. – **readability** /ridə'bɪləti/, **readableness,** *n.* – **readably,** *adv.*

**reader** /'ridə/, *n.* **1.** one who reads. **2.** a book intended for instruction and practice in reading. **3.** one employed to read and report on manuscripts, etc., submitted for publication. **4.** one who reads or recites before an audience. **5.** one authorised to read the lessons, etc., in a church service. **6.** a university teacher ranking next below a professor, being a recognised authority on some subject but not normally in charge of a department. **7.** *U.S.* an assistant to a professor. **8.** a proofreader.

**readership** /'ridəʃɪp/, *n.* **1.** the readers collectively of a pub-

---

**reabsorb,** *v.t.*
**reabsorption,** *n.*
**reaccede,** *v.t.,* **-ceded, -ceding.**
**reaccelerate,** *v.,* **-rated, -rating.**
**reaccept,** *v.t.*
**reaccession,** *n.*
**reaccommodate,** *v.t.,* **-dated, -dating.**
**reaccompanying,** *v.t.,* **-nied, -nying.**
**reaccuse,** *v.t.,* **-cused, -cusing.**
**reaccustom,** *v.t.*
**reacknowledge,** *v.t.,* **-ledged, -ledging.**
**reacquire,** *v.t.,* **-quired, -quiring.**
**reactivate,** *v.t.,* **-vated, -vating.**
**readapt,** *v.t.*
**readaptation,** *n.*
**readdress,** *v.t.*
**readjourn,** *v.*
**readjournment,** *n.*
**readminister,** *v.t.*
**readmission,** *n.*
**readmit,** *v.,* **-mitted, -mitting.**
**readmittance,** *n.*
**readopt,** *v.t.*
**readoption,** *n.*
**readorn,** *v.t.*
**readvance,** *v.,* **-vanced, -vancing.**
**readvertise,** *v.,* **-tised, -tising.**
**reaffirm,** *v.t.*
**reaffirmation,** *n.*
**realign,** *v.*
**realignment,** *n.*
**reallocate,** *v.t.,* **-cated, -cating.**
**reallot,** *v.t.,* **-lotted, -lotting.**
**reanalyse,** *v.t.,* **-lysed, -lysing.**
**reanalysis,** *n.*
**reappeal,** *v.t.*
**reappear,** *v.i.*
**reappearance,** *n.*
**reapplication,** *n.*
**reapply,** *v.,* **-plied, -plying.**
**reappoint,** *v.t.*
**reappointment,** *n.*
**reappraisal,** *n.*
**reapprehend,** *v.t.*
**reapprehension,** *n.*
**reapproach,** *v.*
**reappropriate,** *v.t.,* **-ated, -ating.**
**reappropriation,** *n.*
**reargue,** *v.t.,* **-gued, -guing.**
**rearrange,** *v.t.,* **-ranged, -ranging.**

---

lication, esp. a newspaper or periodical. **2.** the position, duty, or profession of a university or other reader. **3.** the fact or state of being a reader.

**readily** /ˈrɛdəli/, *adv.* **1.** promptly; quickly; easily. **2.** in a ready manner; willingly.

**readiness** /ˈrɛdinəs/, *n.* **1.** the condition of being ready. **2.** ready action or movement; promptness; quickness; ease; facility. **3.** willingness; inclination; cheerful consent: *a readiness to help others.*

**reading** /ˈridɪŋ/, *n.* **1.** the action or practice of one who reads. **2.** ability to read; the oral interpretation of written language. **3.** the rendering given to a dramatic part, musical composition, etc., by a particular person. **4.** the extent to which one has read; literary knowledge: *a man of wide reading.* **5.** matter read or for reading: *a novel that makes good reading.* **6.** the form or version of a given passage in a particular text: *the various readings of a line in Shakespeare.* **7.** an interpretation given to anything: *what is your reading of the situation?* **8.** the indication of a graduated instrument. **9.** *Parl. Proc.* the formal presentation of a bill to a legislative body. *–adj.* **10.** pertaining to, or used for, reading. **11.** given to reading: *the reading public.*

**reading desk** /ˈ– dɛsk/, *n.* **1.** a desk for use in reading, esp. by a person standing. **2.** →**lectern.**

**reading room** /ˈ– rum/, *n.* a room appropriated to reading, as in a library or a club.

**readjust** /riəˈdʒʌst/, *v.t.* to adjust again or anew; rearrange. – **readjuster,** *n.*

**readjustment** /riəˈdʒʌstmənt/, *n.* **1.** a readjusting or state of being readjusted. **2.** *Finance.* important changes in the financial structure of a company (often less drastic than in *reorganisation*).

**readout** /ˈridaʊt/, *n.* →**digital display.**

**read-write** /rid-ˈraɪt/, *adj.* of or pertaining to a computer, etc., which reads and then restores memory data.

**ready** /ˈrɛdi/, *adj.,* **readier, readiest,** *v.,* **readied, readying,** *n.* *–adj.* **1.** completely prepared or in due condition for immediate action or use: *troops ready for battle, dinner is ready.* **2.** duly equipped, completed, adjusted, or arranged, as for the occasion or purpose. **3.** willing: *ready to forgive.* **4.** prompt or quick in perceiving, comprehending, speaking, writing, etc. **5.** proceeding from or showing such quickness: *a ready reply.* **6.** prompt or quick in action, performance, manifestation, etc. **7.** inclined, disposed, or apt: *too ready to criticise others.* **8.** in such a condition as to be about; likely or liable at any moment (to do something): *a tree ready to fall.* **9.** immediately available for use: *ready money.* **10.** pertaining to prompt payment. **11.** present or convenient (to hand, to the hand, etc.): *to lie ready to one's hand.* *–v.t.* **12.** to make ready; prepare. *–n.* **13.** *Colloq.* ready money. **14.** the condition or position of being ready: *to bring a rifle to the ready.* **15.** *Colloq.* scheme; racket; lurk. **16. work a ready,** *Colloq.* to adopt a scheme or racket, usu. dishonest or illegal. [ME *redy,* early ME *rædig,* from OE *rǣde* ready + *-ig* -Y[1]]

**ready-made** /ˈrɛdi-meɪd/, *adj.* **1.** made for sale to any purchaser, rather than to order: *ready-made shoes.* **2.** made for immediate use. **3.** perfectly suited; apt. **4.** unoriginal; conventional. *–n.* **5.** a ready-made article, esp. a tailor-made cigarette. **6.** a found object, typically functional and mass-produced, displayed in isolation from its normal environment as a work of art.

**ready-mix** /ˈrɛdi-mɪks/, *n.* **1.** any preparation, as food, in which the ingredients are already mixed for immediate use. **2.** concrete mixed and delivered in wet form to a site. *–adj.* **3.** of or pertaining to a preparation in which the contents are already mixed.

**ready reckoner** /rɛdi ˈrɛkənə/, *n.* a collection of mathematical and other tables for rapid calculation.

**ready-to-wear** /ˌrɛdi-tə-ˈwɛə/, *adj.* (of clothing) made in standard sizes to fit a large number of people.

**ready-witted** /rɛdi-ˈwɪtəd/, *adj.* having a quick wit or intelligence.

**reafforest** /riəˈfɒrəst/, *v.t.* to replant with forest trees. Also, **reforest.** – **reafforestation** /ˌriəfɒrəˈsteɪʃən/, *n.*

**reagent** /riˈeɪdʒənt/, *n.* a substance which, on account of the reactions it causes, is used in chemical analysis.

**real**[1] /ril/, *adj.* **1.** true (rather than merely ostensible, nominal, or apparent): *the real reason for an act.* **2.** existing or occurring as fact; actual (rather than imaginary, ideal, or fictitious): *a story taken from real life.* **3.** being an actual thing, with objective existence (rather than merely imaginary). **4.** being actually such (rather than merely so called): *a real victory.* **5.** genuine; not counterfeit, artificial, or imitation: *a real antique, a real diamond, real silk.* **6.** unfeigned or sincere: *real sympathy.* **7.** *Philos.* **a.** existent or pertaining to the existent as opposed to the non-existent. **b.** actual as opposed to possible or potential. **c.** independent of experience as opposed to phenomenal or apparent. **8.** *Law.* denoting or pertaining to immoveable property of a freehold type, as lands and tenements excluding leaseholds (opposed to *personal*). **9.** *Optics.* (of an image) formed by the actual convergence of rays, as the image produced in a camera (opposed to *virtual*). **10.** *Maths.* of or pertaining to a real number. *–adv.* **11.** *Colloq.* very. **12. for real, a.** actual, definite: *that overseas trip is for real.* **b.** genuine, sincere: *he's for real.* *–n.* **13. the real, a.** that which is real or actually exists. **b.** reality in general. **14. the real McCoy** or **thing,** the genuine article. [ME, from LL *reālis,* from L *rēs* thing, matter] – **realness,** *n.*

**real**[2] /reɪˈal/, *n., pl.* **reals, reales** /reɪˈalz/. a former silver coin of Spain and certain Spanish-American countries. [Sp.: lit., royal, from L *rēgālis* regal]

**real estate** /ˈril əsteɪt/, *n.* land and whatever by nature or artificial annexation is part of it or is the means of its enjoyment, as minerals, trees, buildings, fences, etc. Also, **real property.**

**realgar** /riˈælgə/, *n.* arsenic disulphide, $As_2S_2$, found native as

---

**rearrangement,** *n.*
**rearrest,** *v.t., n.*
**rearticulate,** *v.,* **-lated, -lating.**
**rearticulation,** *n.*
**reascend,** *v.*
**reascent,** *n.*
**reassemble,** *v.,* **-sembled, -sembling.**
**reassembly,** *n.*
**reassert,** *v.t.*
**reassertion,** *n.*
**reassess,** *v.t.*
**reassessment,** *n.*
**reassign,** *v.t.*
**reassignment,** *n.*
**reassimilate,** *v.,* **-lated, -lating.**
**reassimilation,** *n.*
**reassociate,** *v.,* **-ated, -ating.**
**reassume,** *v.t.,* **-sumed, -suming.**
**reassumption,** *n.*
**reattach,** *v.t.*
**reattachment,** *n.*
**reattain,** *v.t.*
**reattainment,** *n.*
**reattempt,** *v.t.*
**reaudit,** *v., n.*
**reaudition,** *v., n.*
**reauthorise,** *v.t.,* **-rised, -rising.**
**reawaken,** *v.*
**reawakening,** *n.*
**rebait,** *v.t.*
**rebaptism,** *n.*
**rebaptise,** *v.t.,* **-tised, -tising.**
**rebid,** *v.,* **-bade** or **-bid, -bidding.**
**rebind,** *v.t.,* **-bound, -binding.**
**reboard,** *v.t.*
**rebroadcast,** *v.t.,* **-cast** or **-casted, -casting,** *n.*
**rebuild,** *v.,* **-built, -building.**
**rebury,** *v.t.,* **-buried, -burying.**
**recalculate,** *v.*
**recalk,** *v.t.*
**recarpet,** *v.t.*
**recarry,** *v.t.,* **-carried, -carrying.**
**recelebrate,** *v.,* **-rated, -rating.**
**recelebration,** *n.*
**recertify,** *v.t.,* **-fied, -fying.**
**rechallenge,** *v.t.,* **-lenged, -lenging.**
**rechannel,** *v.t.,* **-nelled, -nelling.**
**recharge,** *v.,* **-charged, -charging.**
**rechargeable,** *adj.*
**recharger,** *n.*
**rechart,** *v.t.*
**recharter,** *v.t., n.*

an orange-red mineral and used in pyrotechnics. [ME, from ML, from Ar. *rehj alghār* powder of the mine]

**realia** /ri'eɪliə/, *n. pl.* **1.** *Philos.* realities; real things. **2.** objects, as artefacts, costumes, models, etc., used in teaching to relate classroom learning to the daily life of peoples studied.

**realisation** /riəlaɪ'zeɪʃən/, *n.* **1.** the making or being made real of something imagined, planned, etc. **2.** the result of such a process: *the realisation of a project.* **3.** the act of realising. **4.** the state of being realised. **5.** an instance or result of realising. **6.** *Music.* **a.** the act of realising a piece of music. **b.** the work so realised. Also, **realization.**

**realise** /'riəlaɪz/, *v.*, **-lised, -lising.** *–v.t.* **1.** to grasp or understand clearly. **2.** to make real, or give reality to (a hope, fear, plan, etc.). **3.** to bring vividly before the mind. **4.** to convert into cash or money: *to realise securities.* **5.** to obtain as a profit or income for oneself by trade, labour, or investment. **6.** to bring as proceeds, as from a sale: *the goods realised $1000.* **7.** *Music.* **a.** to create, as an orchestral work, from parts or a part left by a composer. **b.** to create a complete work from. *–v.i.* **8.** to convert property or goods into cash or money. **9.** to realise a profit. Also, **realize.** – **realisable,** *adj.* – **realiser,** *n.*

**realism** /'riəlɪzəm/, *n.* **1.** interest in or concern for the actual or real as distinguished from the abstract, speculative, etc. **2.** the taking of a practical rather than a moral view in human problems, etc. **3.** the tendency to view or represent things as they really are. **4.** the treatment of subjects in literature with fidelity to nature or to real life (opposed to *idealism*). **5. a.** deliberate depiction of ugly things or people in art. **b.** art not reduced into abstract forms. **c.** art which faithfully represents natural appearances, without stylising or idealising its subjects. **6.** *Philos.* **a.** the doctrine that universals have a real objective existence (**medieval realism**). **b.** the doctrine that objects of sense perception have an existence independent of the act of perception.

**realist** /'riələst/, *n.* **1.** one, esp. a writer or artist, who tends to view or represent things as they are rather than idealising or romanticising them. **2.** one who takes a practical rather than a moral view in human problems, etc. **3.** an adherent of philosophical or literary or artistic realism. *–adj.* **4.** of, pertaining to, denoting, or characteristic of artistic or literary realism.

**realistic** /riə'lɪstɪk/, *adj.* **1.** interested in or concerned with what is real or practical. **2.** taking a practical rather than a moral view in human problems, etc. **3.** pertaining to, characterised by, or given to the representation in literature or art of things as they really are: *a realistic novel.* **4.** of or pertaining to realists or realism in philosophy. – **realistically,** *adv.*

**reality** /ri'æləti/, *n., pl.* **-ties. 1.** the state or fact of being real. **2.** resemblance to what is real. **3.** a real thing or fact. **4.** *Philos.* **a.** that which exists independently of ideas concerning it. **b.** that which exists independently of all other things; an ultimate thing which produces derivatives. **5.** that which is real. **6.** that which constitutes the real or actual thing, as distinguished from that which is merely apparent. **7. in reality,** really; actually; in fact or truth.

**really** /'rɪəli/, *adv.* **1.** in reality; actually: *to see things as they really are.* **2.** genuinely or truly: *a really honest man.* **3.** indeed: *really, this is too much.*

**realm** /rɛlm/, *n.* **1.** a royal domain; kingdom: *the realm of England.* **2.** the region, sphere, or domain within which anything rules or prevails: *the realm of dreams.* **3.** the special province or field of something: *the realm of physics.* [ME *realme,* from OF *reialme,* from *reial* regal, from L *rēgālis*]

**real number** /ril 'nʌmbə/, *n.* **1.** a number which can be the result of a measurement (opposed to *complex number*). **2.** →**decimal number.**

**Realpolitik** /reɪˌalpɒlə'tik/, *n.* political realism, esp. policy based on power rather than on ideals. [G]

**Real Presence** /ril 'prɛzəns/, *n.* the doctrine of the Roman Catholic and Orthodox Churches that in the liturgy, under the semblance of bread and wine, the actual body and blood of the Saviour are present on the altar.

**real property** /ril 'prɒpəti/, *n.* →**real estate.**

**real tennis** /– 'tɛnɪs/, *n.* →**royal tennis.** [ME *real* royal (OF) + TENNIS]

**real-time** /'ril-taɪm/, *adj.*, /ril-'taɪm/, *n.* *–adj.* **1.** of or pertaining to an analytical or computing device which processes information and outputs results at the same rate at which the original information is presented. *–n.* **2.** a method using real-time processing: *this machine processes in real-time.*

**realtor** /'riəltə, -tɔ/, *n.* →**estate agent.** [REALT(Y) + -OR[2]]

**realty** /'riəlti/, *n.* →**real estate.** [REAL[1] (def. 8) + -TY[2]]

**real wages** /ril 'weɪdʒəz/, *n.pl.* wages paid for work done, expressed in terms of purchasing power (opposed to *money wages.*).

**ream**[1] /rim/, *n.* **1.** Also, **printer's ream.** a standard quantity among paper dealers meaning 20 quires or 500 sheets (formerly 480 sheets. **2.** (*pl.*) *Colloq.* a large quantity: *to write reams and reams of poetry.* [ME *rem.* from OF *rayme,* through Sp., from Ar. *razmah, rizmah* bundle or bale]

**ream**[2] /rim/, *v.t.* to enlarge (a hole or opening) to size by means of a reamer. [ME *reme,* OE *rēman* open up]

**reamer** /'rimə/, *n.* one of many rotating finishing tools with spiral or straight fluted cutting edges for finishing a hole to size and shape. [REAM[2] + -ER[1]]

head of machinist's reamer

**reanimate** /ri'ænəmeɪt/, *v.t.*, **-mated, -mating. 1.** to restore to life; resuscitate. **2.** to give fresh vigour, spirit, or courage to. **3.** to stimulate to renewed activity. – **reanimation** /ˌriænə'meɪʃən/, *n.*

**reap** /rip/, *v.t.* **1.** to cut (grain, etc.) with a sickle or other implement or a machine, as in harvest. **2.** to gather or take (a crop, harvest, etc.). **3.** to get as a return, recompense, or

---

**recheck,** *v.*
**recheck,** *n.*
**rechoose,** *v.t.*, **-chose, -chosen, -choosing.**
**rechristen,** *v.t.*
**recircle,** *v.*, **-circled, -circling.**
**recirculate,** *v.t.*, **-lated, -lating.**
**recirculation,** *n.*
**reclasp,** *v.t.*
**reclass,** *v.t.*
**reclothe,** *v.t.*, **-clothed** or **-clad, -clothing.**
**recodification,** *n.*
**recodify,** *v.t.*, **-fied, -fying.**
**recoin,** *v.t.*
**recoinage,** *n.*
**recolonise,** *v.t.*, **-nised, -nising.**
**recolour,** *v.t.*
**recombination,** *n.*
**recombine,** *v.*, **-bined, -bining.**
**recommence,** *v.*, **-menced, -mencing.**
**recommencement,** *n.*
**recommission,** *v.t.*
**recomplicate,** *v.t.*, **-cated, -cating.**
**recompute,** *v.t.*, **-puted, -puting.**
**reconceal,** *v.t.*
**reconcentrate,** *v.*, **-trated, -trating.**
**reconcentration,** *n.*
**recondensation,** *n.*
**recondense,** *v.*, **-densed, -densing.**
**reconfirm,** *v.t.*
**reconfront,** *v.t.*
**reconnect,** *v.t.*
**reconnection,** *n.*
**reconquer,** *v.t.*
**reconquest,** *n.*
**reconsecrate,** *v.t.*, **-crated, -crating.**
**reconsecration,** *n.*
**reconsolidate,** *v.*, **-dated, -dating.**
**reconsolidation,** *n.*
**recontact,** *v., n.*
**recontend,** *v.i.*
**recontest,** *v.t.*
**recontract,** *v.*
**recontraction,** *n.*
**reconvene,** *v.*, **-vened, -vening.**
**reconverge,** *v.t.*, **-verged, -verging.**
**reconvergence,** *n.*
**reconversion,** *n.*
**reconvert,** *v.t.*

---

result: *to reap large profits.* *–v.i.* **4.** to reap grain, etc. [ME *repe(n)*, OE *repan*, c. MLG *repen* ripple (flax); akin to RIPE]

**reaper** /ˈripə/, *n.* **1.** a machine for cutting standing grain; a reaping machine. **2.** one who reaps. **3. the grim reaper,** Death personified.

**reaping machine** /ˈripɪŋ məʃin/, *n.* a machine for reaping corn.

**rear**[1] /rɪə/, *n.* **1.** the back of anything, as opposed to the front. **2.** the space or position behind anything. **3.** the behind; buttocks. **4.** the hindmost portion of an army, fleet, etc. *–adj.* **5.** situated at or pertaining to the rear: *the rear door.* [aphetic var. of ARREAR, *n.*]

**rear**[2] /rɪə/, *v.t.* **1.** to care for and support up to maturity: *to rear a child.* **2.** to raise by building; erect. **3.** to raise to an upright position: *to rear a ladder.* **4.** to lift or hold up; elevate; raise. *–v.i.* **5.** to rise on the hind legs, as a horse or other animal. **6.** (of persons) to start up in angry excitement, hot resentment, or the like (commonly fol. by *up*). **7.** to rise high or tower aloft, as a building. [ME *rere(n)*, OE *rǣran* RAISE, c. Goth. *-raisjan,* Icel. *reisa*]

**rear admiral** /rɪər ˈædmərəl/, *n.* a naval officer next in rank below a vice-admiral.

**rear area** /ˈ– ɛəriə/, *n.* a rest and recreational area during wartime: *Sydney was a rear area for the troops fighting in Vietnam.*

**rearguard** /ˈrɪəgad/, *n.* a part of an army or military force detached from the main body to bring up and guard the rear from surprise attack, esp. in a retreat.

**rearm** /riˈam/, *v.t.* **1.** to arm again. **2.** to furnish with new or better weapons: *they rearmed the troops as soon as possible.* *–v.i.* **3.** to arm oneself again. **–rearmament** /riˈaməmənt/, *n.*

**rearmost** /ˈrɪəmoust/, *adj.* farthest in the rear; last.

**rear sight** /ˈrɪə saɪt/, *n.* the sight nearest the breech of a firearm.

**rear-vision mirror** /rɪə-ˈvɪʒən mɪrə/, *n.* a mirror on a motor vehicle placed so that the driver can see traffic approaching from behind. Also, **rear-view mirror.**

**rearward** /ˈrɪəwəd/, *adj.* **1.** directed toward or located in the rear. *–adv.* **2.** Also, **rearwards.** towards or in the rear.

**reason** /ˈrizən/, *n.* **1.** a ground or cause, as for a belief, action, fact, event, etc.: *the reason for declaring war.* **2.** a statement in justification or explanation of belief or action. **3.** the mental powers concerned with drawing conclusions or inferences. **4.** sound judgment or good sense. **5.** normal or sound powers of mind; sanity. **6.** *Logic.* a premise of an argument. **7.** *Philos.* intellect as opposed to sensibility. **8. by reason of,** on account of; because of. **9. in** or **within reason,** in accordance with reason; justifiable or proper. **10. it stands to reason,** it is obvious or logical. *–v.i.* **11.** to think or argue in a logical manner. **12.** to draw conclusions or inferences from facts or premises. **13.** to urge reasons which should determine belief or action. *–v.t.* **14.** to think out (a problem, etc.) logically (oft. fol. by *out*). **15.** to conclude or infer (fol. by *that*). **16.** to bring, persuade, etc., by reasoning. **17.** to support with reasons. [ME *reisun*, from OF *raison*, from L *ratio* reckoning, account] **–reasoner,** *n.*

**reasonable** /ˈrizənəbəl/, *adj.* **1.** endowed with reason. **2.** agreeable to reason or sound judgment: *a reasonable choice.* **3.** not exceeding the limit prescribed by reason; not excessive: *reasonable terms.* **4.** moderate, or moderate in price: *the coat was reasonable but not cheap.* **–reasonableness, reasonability** /rizənəˈbɪləti/, *n.* **–reasonably,** *adv.*

**reasoned** /ˈrizənd/, *adj.* **1.** guided by reason: *a carefully reasoned decision.* **2.** logically thought out and presented: *a reasoned reply.*

**reasoning** /ˈrizənɪŋ, ˈriznɪŋ/, *n.* **1.** the act or process of one who reasons. **2.** the process of drawing conclusions or inferences from facts or premises. **3.** the reasons, arguments, proofs, etc., resulting from this process.

**reasonless** /ˈrizənləs/, *adj.* **1.** not according to reason: *an utterly reasonless display of temper.* **2.** not endowed with reason. **–reasonlessly,** *adv.* **–reasonlessness,** *n.*

**reassure** /riəˈʃɔ/, *v.t.*, **-sured, -suring.** **1.** to restore (a person, etc.) to assurance or confidence: *his remarks reassured me.* **2.** to assure again. **3.** →**reinsure.** **–reassurance,** *n.* **–reassurer,** *n.* **–reassuring,** *adj.* **–reassuringly,** *adv.*

**Reaumur** /ˈreɪoumjuə/, *adj.* designating, or in accordance with, the thermometric scale in which the freezing point of water is at 0°, and the boiling point at 80°. *Abbrev.:* R, Reaum. Also, **Réamur.** [introduced by René Antoine Ferehault de *Réaumur,* 1683-1757, French physicist and inventor]

rebates[2]

**reave**[1] /riv/, *v.t.*, **reaved** or **reft, reaving.** *Archaic.* to deprive forcibly, strip, or rob. [ME *reve(n)*, OE *rēafian*, c. G *rauben* ROB]

**reave**[2] /riv/, *v.t., v.i.*, **reaved** or **reft, reaving.** *Archaic.* to rend; break; tear. [apparently special use of REAVE[1] by association with RIVE]

**rebarbative** /rəˈbabətɪv/, *adj.* unattractive; fearsome or repellent. [F *rébarbatif*, from *rébarber*, equivalent to *ré-* RE- + *barbe* beard + *-atif* -ATIVE]

**rebate**[1] /ˈribeɪt/, *n., v.*, **-bated, -bating.** *–n.* **1.** a return of part of an original amount paid for some service or merchandise; repayment, as of a part of charges. *–v.t.* **2.** to allow as a discount. **3.** to deduct (a certain amount), as from a total. [ME, from OF *rabatre* beat or put down, from *re-* RE- + *abatre* ABATE]

**rebate**[2] /ˈribeɪt/, *n., v.*, **-bated, -bating.** *–n.* **1.** a cut, groove, or recess made on the edge or surface of a board or the like, as to receive the end or edge of another board or the like similarly shaped. **2.** a joint so made. *–v.t.* **3.** to cut or form a rebate in (a board, etc). **4.** to join by rebates. *–v.i.* **5.** to join by a rebate (fol. by *on* or *over*). Also, **rabbet.** [ME *rabit,*

---

**reconvey,** *v.t.*
**reconveyance,** *n.*
**recopy,** *v.t.*, **-copied, -copying.**
**recoronation,** *n.*
**recorrect,** *v.t.*
**recrate,** *v.t.*, **-crated, -crating.**
**recross,** *v.*
**recrown,** *v.t.*
**recrystallise,** *v.*, **-lised, -lising.**
**recultivate,** *v.t.*, **-vated, -vating.**
**recultivation,** *n.*
**recut,** *v.t.*, **-cut, -cutting.**
**redarn,** *v.t.*
**redate,** *v.t.*, **-dated, -dating.**
**redebate,** *n., v.t.*, **-bated, -bating.**
**redecorate,** *v.t.*, **-rated, -rating.**
**redecoration,** *n.*
**rededicate,** *v.t.*, **-cated, -cating.**
**rededication,** *n.*
**redefeat,** *v.t., n.*
**redefend,** *v.t*
**redefine,** *v.t.*, **-fined, -fining.**
**redefinition,** *n.*
**redefy,** *v.t.*, **-fied, -fying.**
**redeliberate,** *v.t.*, **-rated, -rating.**
**redeliberation,** *n.*
**redemonstrate,** *v.t.*, **-strated, -strating.**
**redemonstration,** *n.*
**redenial,** *n.*
**redeny,** *v.t.*, **-nied, -nying.**
**redeposit,** *v., n.*
**redescend,** *v.*
**redescent,** *n.*
**redescribe,** *v.t.*, **-scribed, -scribing.**
**redescription,** *n.*
**redesign,** *v.t.*
**redesignate,** *v.t.*, **-nated, -nating.**
**redesignation,** *n.*
**redetermine,** *v.*, **-mined, -mining.**
**rediffuse,** *v.*, **-fused, -fusing.**
**rediffusion,** *n.*
**redigest,** *v.t.*
**rediscipline,** *v.t.*, **-plined, -plining.**
**rediscover,** *v.t.*
**rediscovery,** *n.*
**rediscuss,** *v.t.*
**redispersal,** *n.*
**redisperse,** *v.*, **-persed, -persing.**
**redisplay,** *v.t.*
**redissolve,** *v.*, **-solved, -solving.**

probably from OF *rabat* a beating down, or *rabot* a joiner's plane]

**rebate plane** /'– pleɪn/, *n.* a plane for cutting rebates having its blade either at right angles or diagonal to the direction of motion.

**rebec** /'ribɛk/, *n.* a small medieval fiddle having commonly a pear-shaped body and three strings, and played with a bow. Also, **rebeck.** [F; replacing ME *ribibe*, from Ar. *rabāb* primitive one- or two-stringed viol]

rebec

**rebel** /'rɛbəl/, *n., adj.;* /rə'bɛl/, *v.,* **-belled, -belling.** *–n.* **1.** one who refuses allegiance to, resists, or rises in arms against, the established government or ruler. **2.** one who or that which resists any authority or control. **3.** one who rejects traditional or established customs, culture, etc. *–adj.* **4.** rebellious. **5.** of or pertaining to rebels. *–v.i.* **6.** to rise in arms or active resistance against one's government or ruler. **7.** to resist any authority. **8.** to manifest or feel utter repugnance: *her very soul rebelled at going back.* [ME *rebell(en)*, from OF *rebeller*, from L *rebellāre* wage war again (as conquered people)]

**rebeldom** /'rɛbəldəm/, *n.* **1.** a region controlled by rebels. **2.** rebels collectively. **3.** rebellious conduct.

**rebellion** /rə'bɛljən/, *n.* **1.** open, organised, and armed resistance to one's government or ruler. **2.** resistance against or defiance of any authority or control. **3.** rejection of traditional or established customs, culture, etc. **4.** the act of rebelling. [ME, from L *rebellio*]

**rebellious** /rə'bɛljəs/, *adj.* **1.** defying lawful authority; insubordinate; disposed to rebel. **2.** pertaining to or characteristic of rebels or rebellion. **3.** (of things) resisting treatment; refractory. [ME, from REBELLI(ON) + -OUS] **– rebelliously,** *adv.* **– rebelliousness,** *n.*

**rebirth** /ˌri'bɜθ/, *n.* **1.** being born again; a second birth. **2.** a renaissance; a new activity or growth.

**reboant** /'rɛboʊənt/, *adj.* resounding loudly. [L *reboans*, ppr., bellowing in return]

**rebop** /'ribɒp/, *n. Jazz.* →**bebop.**

**rebore** /ˌri'bɔ/, *v.,* **-bored, -boring,** *n.* *–v.t.* **1.** to bore again. **2.** to bore out (the cylinders of an internal-combustion engine). *–n.* **3.** the process of reboring or being rebored.

**reborn** /ˌri'bɔn/, *adj.* born again.

**rebound** /rə'baʊnd/, *v.;* /'ribaʊnd, rə'baʊnd/, *n.* *–v.i.* **1.** to bound or spring back from force of impact. *–v.t.* **2.** to cause to bound back; cast back. *–n.* **3.** the act of rebounding; recoil. **4. on the rebound, a.** in the act of bouncing back. **b.** during a period of reaction, as after being rejected: *she married him on the rebound after an unhappy love affair.* [ME, from OF *rebondir*]

**rebreathing apparatus** /riˌbriðɪŋ æpə'ratəs/, *n.* a breathing apparatus in which exhaled gases are passed through a carbon dioxide filter and breathed again.

**rebuff** /rə'bʌf/, *n.* **1.** a blunt or abrupt check, as to one making advances. **2.** a peremptory refusal of a request, offer, etc.; a snub. **3.** a check to action or progress. *–v.t.* **4.** to give a rebuff to; check; repel; refuse; drive away. [F (obs.) *rebuffe*, from It. *ribuffo*]

**rebuke** /rə'bjuk/, *v.,* **-buked, -buking,** *n.* *–v.t.* **1.** to reprove or reprimand. *–n.* **2.** a reproof; a reprimand. [ME, from AF *rebuker*, var. of OF *rebuchier* beat back] **– rebukeable,** *adj.* **– rebuker,** *n.*

**rebus** /'ribəs/, *n.* an enigmatical representation of a word or phrase by pictures, symbols, etc., suggesting the word elements or words: *two gates and a head is a rebus for Gateshead.* [L, abl. pl. of *rēs* thing]

**rebut** /rə'bʌt/, *v.t.,* **-butted, -butting. 1.** to refute by evidence or argument. **2.** to oppose by contrary proof. [ME *rebute(n)*, from AF *reboter*, from *re-* RE- + *boter* BUTT[3], *v.*] **– rebuttable,** *adj.*

**rebuttal** /rə'bʌtl/, *n.* the act of rebutting, esp. in law.

**rebutter**[1] /rə'bʌtə/, *n.* one who or that which rebuts. [REBUT + -ER[1]]

**rebutter**[2] /rə'bʌtə/, *n. Law.* a defendant's answer to a plaintiff's surrejoinder. [AF *rebuter*, inf. used as noun]

**rec** /rɛk/, *n. N.Z.* (*sometimes cap.*) recreation or sports ground.

**rec., 1.** receipt. **2.** recipe. **3.** record.

**recalcitrant** /rə'kælsətrənt/, *adj.* **1.** resisting authority or control; not obedient or compliant; refractory. *–n.* **2.** a recalcitrant person. [L *recalcitrans*, ppr., lit., kicking back] **– recalcitrance, recalcitrancy,** *n.*

**recalcitrate** /rə'kælsətreɪt/, *v.i.,* **-trated, -trating.** to make resistance or opposition; show strong objection or repugnance. **– recalcitration** /rəkælsə'treɪʃən/, *n.*

**recalesce** /rikə'lɛs/, *v.i.,* **-lesced, -lescing.** to become hot again (said esp. of cooling iron, which glows with increased brilliancy upon passing certain temperatures). [L *recalescere*] **– recalescence,** *n.* **– recalescent,** *adj.*

**recall** /rə'kɔl/, *v.;* /'rikɔl/, *n.* *–v.t.* **1.** to recollect or remember. **2.** to call back; summon to return. **3.** to bring back in thought or attention, as to present circumstances. **4.** to revoke, take back, or withdraw: *to recall a promise.* **5.** to deprive (a public official) of office. **6.** *Poetic.* to revive. *–n.* **7.** the act of recalling. **8.** memory; recollection. **9.** the act or possibility of revoking something. **10.** a signal flag used to recall a boat to a ship, etc. **– recallable,** *adj.*

**recant** /rə'kænt/, *v.t.* **1.** to withdraw or disavow (a statement, etc.), esp. formally; retract. *–v.i.* **2.** to disavow an opinion, etc., esp. formally. [L *recantāre*] **– recantation** /rikæn'teɪʃən/, *n.* **– recanter,** *n.*

**recap**[1] /'rikæp/, *n., v.,* **-capped, -capping.** *Colloq.* *–n.* **1.** →**recapitulation.** *–v.t., v.i.* **2.** →**recapitulate.**

**recap**[2] /ri'kæp/, *v.,* **-capped, -capping;** /'rikæp/, *n.* *–v.t.* **1.** →**retread.** *–n.* **2.** a retreaded tyre.

**recapitalisation** /riˌkæpətəlaɪ'zeɪʃən/, *n.* a revision of a company's capital structure by an exchange of securities. Also, **recapitalization.**

---

**redistil,** *v.t.,* **-tilled, -tilling.**
**redistillation,** *n.*
**redistribute,** *v.t.,* **-buted, -buting.**
**redistribution,** *n.*
**redivide,** *v.,* **-vided, -viding.**
**redo,** *v.t.,* **-did, -done, -doing.**
**redrain,** *v.t.*
**redraw,** *v.t.,* **-drew, -drawn, -drawing.**
**redrill,** *v.t.*
**redrop,** *v.,* **-dropped, -dropping.**
**redry,** *v.,* **-dried, -drying.**
**redye,** *v.t.,* **-dyed, -dying.**
**re-earn,** *v.*
**re-edify,** *v.t.,* **-fied, -fying.**
**re-edit,** *v.t.*
**re-eject,** *v.t.*
**re-elect,** *v.t.*
**re-election,** *n.*
**re-elevate,** *v.t.,* **-vated, -vating.**
**re-elevation,** *n.*
**re-embark,** *v.*
**re-embellish,** *v.t.*
**re-embrace,** *v.,* **-braced, -bracing.**
**re-emerge,** *v.i.,* **-merged, -merging.**
**re-emergence,** *n.*
**re-emergent,** *adj.*
**re-emigrate,** *v.i.,* **-grated, -grating.**
**re-emigration,** *n.*
**re-emission,** *n.*
**re-emit,** *v.t.,* **-mitted, -mitting.**
**re-emphasis,** *n., pl.,* **-ses.**
**re-emphasise,** *v.t.,* **-sised, -sising.**
**re-employ,** *v.t.*
**re-employment,** *n.*
**re-enact,** *v.t.*
**re-enactment,** *n.*
**re-enclose,** *v.t.,* **-closed, -closing.**
**re-encounter,** *v.t., n.*
**re-encourage,** *v.t.,* **-raged, -raging.**
**re-encouragement,** *n.*
**re-endorse,** *v.t.,* **-dorsed, -dorsing.**
**re-endorsement,** *n.*
**re-endow,** *v.t.*
**re-endowment,** *n.*
**re-energise,** *v.t.,* **-gised, -gising.**
**re-engage,** *v.,* **-gaged, -gaging.**
**re-engagement,** *n.*
**re-engrave,** *v.t.,* **-graved, -graving.**

**recapitalise** /riˈkæpətəlaɪz/, *v.t.*, **-lised, -lising.** to renew or change the capital of. Also, **recapitalize.**

**recapitulate** /rikəˈpɪtʃəleɪt/, *v.*, **-lated, -lating.** *–v.t.* **1.** to review by way of an orderly summary, as at the end of a speech or discourse. **2.** *Zool.* (of a young animal) to repeat (ancestral evolutionary stages) in its development. **3.** *Music.* to restate (an original musical argument) in a sonata-form movement. *–v.i.* **4.** to sum up statements or matters. [LL *recapitulātus,* pp]

**recapitulation** /ˌrikəpɪtʃəˈleɪʃən/, *n.* **1.** the act of recapitulating. **2.** the state or fact of being recapitulated. **3.** a review or summary, as at the end of a speech or discourse. **4.** *Zool.* the repetition of ancestral evolutionary stages in the development of an individual. **5.** the theory that such repetition takes place, as in the embryonic development of an individual. **6.** *Music.* (in a sonata-form movement) the restatement of the original musical argument. **–recapitulative** /rikəˈpɪtʃələtɪv/, **recapitulatory** /rikəˈpɪtʃələtri, ˌrikəpɪtʃəˈleɪtəri/, *adj.*

**recaption** /riˈkæpʃən/, *n. Law.* the remedy of retaking one's goods, wife, child, or servant, without a breach of the peace, from one who has taken them.

**recapture** /riˈkæptʃə/, *v.*, **-tured, -turing,** *n.* *–v.t.* **1.** to capture again; recover by capture; retake. **2.** *U.S.* (of the government) to take by recapture. **3.** to evoke anew or repeat (an experience, sensation, achievement, or the like). *–n.* **4.** recovery or retaking by capture. **5.** *U.S.* the taking by the government of a fixed part of all earnings in excess of a certain percentage of property value, as in the case of a railway. **6.** the fact of being recaptured.

**recast** /ˌriˈkast/, *v.*, **-cast, -casting;** /ˌriˈkast, ˈrikast/, *n.* *–v.t.* **1.** to cast again or anew. **2.** to provide a new or altered cast for (a play, etc.). **3.** to form, fashion, or arrange again. **4.** to remodel or reconstruct (a literary work, a document, a sentence, etc.). *–n.* **5.** a recasting. **6.** a new form produced by recasting. **– recaster,** *n.*

**recce** /ˈrɛki/, *n. Colloq.* **1.** →**reconnaissance. 2.** *Films, T.V.* research work for location shots or background material. Also, **reccy.**

**recd,** received. Also, **rec'd.**

**re-cede** /ˌri-ˈsid/, *v.t.*, **-ceded, -ceding.** to cede back; yield or grant to a former possessor. [RE- + CEDE]

**recede** /rəˈsid/, *v.i.*, **-ceded, -ceding. 1.** to go or move back, to or towards a more distant point. **2.** to become more distant. **3.** to slope backwards: *a receding chin.* **4.** to draw back or withdraw from a position taken in a matter, or from an undertaking, promise, etc. [ME, from L *recēdere* go back]

**receipt** /rəˈsit/, *n.* **1.** a written acknowledgment of having received money, goods, etc., specified. **2.** (*pl.*) the amount or quantity received. **3.** the act of receiving. **4.** the state of being received. **5.** that which is received. **6.** a recipe. *–v.t.* **7.** to acknowledge in writing the payment of (a bill). **8.** to give a receipt for (money, goods, etc.). *–v.i.* **9.** to give a receipt, as for money or goods. [ME *receite,* from AF, from L *recepta,* fem. pp., received]

**receivable** /rəˈsivəbəl/, *adj.* **1.** fit for acceptance. **2.** awaiting receipt of payment: *accounts receivable.* **3.** capable of being received.

**receive** /rəˈsiv/, *v.*, **-ceived, -ceiving.** *–v.t.* **1.** to take into one's hand or one's possession (something offered or delivered). **2.** to have (something) bestowed, conferred, etc.: *to receive an honorary degree.* **3.** to have delivered or brought to oneself: *to receive a letter.* **4.** to get or learn: *to receive notice, to receive news.* **5.** to become the support of; sustain. **6.** to hold or contain. **7.** to take into the mind; apprehend mentally. **8.** to take from another by hearing or listening: *a priest received his confession.* **9.** to meet with; experience: *to receive attention.* **10.** to suffer or undergo: *to receive an affront.* **11.** to have inflicted upon one: *to receive a broken arm.* **12.** to be at home to (visitors). **13.** to greet or welcome (guests, etc.) upon arriving. **14.** to admit (a person) to a place. **15.** to admit to a state or condition, a privilege, membership, etc.: *to receive someone into the Church.* **16.** to accept as authoritative, valid, true, or approved: *a principle universally received.* *–v.i.* **17.** to receive something. **18.** to receive visitors or guests. **19.** *Radio.* to convert incoming electromagnetic waves into the original signal, as soundwaves or light on a television screen. **20.** to receive the Eucharist. [ME *receve,* from ONF *receivre,* from L *recipere* take back, take to one's self, receive]

**Received Standard English,** *n.* the dialect of English which has won general acceptance in England and certain other places as 'correct'; the speech of the southern middle classes, the B.B.C., and the universities, historically deriving chiefly from the south-east Midland dialect of Middle English.

**receiver** /rəˈsivə/, *n.* **1.** one who or that which receives. **2.** a device or apparatus which receives electrical signals, waves, or the like, and renders them perceptible to the senses, as the part of a telephone held to the ear, a radio receiving set, or a television receiving set. **3.** *Law.* a person appointed, usu. by a court, to take charge of a business or property of others, pending litigation. **4.** *Comm.* one appointed to receive money due. **5.** one who, for purposes of profit or concealment, knowingly receives stolen goods. **6.** a receptacle; a device or apparatus for receiving or holding something. **7.** *Chem. Obs.* a vessel for collecting and containing a distillate. **8.** *Tennis.* the player who receives the ball from the server; striker.

**receivership** /rəˈsivəʃɪp/, *n.* **1.** *Law.* the condition of being in the hands of a receiver. **2.** the position or function of being a receiver in charge of administering the property of others.

**receiving home** /rəˈsivɪŋ houm/, *n.* a home where a child may be temporarily accommodated while waiting for a place in a foster home or some other establishment.

**receiving set** /ˈ– sɛt/, *n.* a mechanism for the reception of electromagnetic waves.

**recension** /rəˈsɛnʃən/, *n.* **1.** a revision of an early work on the basis of critical examination of the text and the sources used. **2.** a version of a text resulting from such revision. [L *recensio*]

---

**re-engross,** *v.t.*
**re-enjoin,** *v.t.*
**re-enlarge,** *v.t.*, **-larged, -larging.**
**re-enlargement,** *n.*
**re-enlist,** *v.*
**re-enlistment,** *n.*
**re-enslave,** *v.t.*, **-slaved, slaving.**
**re-enunciate,** *v.t.*, **-ated, -ating.**
**re-equip,** *v.t.*, **-quipped, -quipping.**
**re-erect,** *v.t.*
**re-erection,** *n.*
**re-erupt,** *v.i.*
**re-establish,** *v.t.*
**re-establishment,** *n.*
**re-estimate,** *v.t.*, **-mated, -mating.**
**re-estimate,** *n.*
**re-evacuate,** *v.*, **-ated, -ating.**
**re-evacuation,** *n.*
**re-evaluate,** *v.t.*, **-ated, -ating.**
**re-evaluation,** *n.*
**re-excavate,** *v.t.*, **-vated, -vating.**
**re-excavation,** *n.*
**re-execute,** *v.t.*, **-cuted, -cuting.**
**re-exhibit,** *v.t.*
**re-expand,** *v.*
**re-expansion,** *n.*
**re-expel,** *v.t.*, **-pelled, -pelling.**
**re-explain,** *v.t.*
**re-explanation,** *n.*
**re-exploration,** *n.*
**re-explore,** *v.t.*, **-plored, -ploring.**
**re-expose,** *v.t.*, **-posed, -posing.**
**re-exposition,** *n.*
**re-exposure,** *n.*
**re-express,** *v.t.*
**re-expulsion,** *n.*
**re-fashion,** *v.t.*
**re-fasten,** *v.t.*
**re-fertilise,** *v.t.*, **-lised, -lising.**
**refile,** *v.t.*, **-filed, -filing.**
**refilm,** *v.t.*
**refilter,** *v.t.*
**refire,** *v.t.*, **-fired, -firing.**
**refix,** *v.t.*
**refloat,** *v.t.*
**reflorescence,** *n.*
**reflow,** *v.i.*
**refocus,** *v.*, **-focussed, -focussing.**
**refold,** *v.*
**reforge,** *v.t.*, **-forged, -forging.**
**reformulate,** *v.t.*, **-lated, -lating.**

**recent** /ˈrisənt/, *adj.* **1.** of late occurrence, appearance, or origin; lately happening, done, made, etc.: *recent events.* **2.** not long past, as a period. **3.** belonging to such a period; not remote or primitive. **4.** (*oft. cap.*) *Geol.* pertaining to the later division of the Quaternary period or system, succeeding the Pleistocene, and regarded as the present or existing geological division. [L *recens*] – **recency, recentness,** *n.* – **recently,** *adv.*

**recept** /ˈrisɛpt/, *n.* (in psychology) an idea formed by the repetition of similar percepts, as successive percepts of the same object. [L *receptum,* neut. pp., taken back]

R, receptacle (def. 2): longitudinal section

**receptacle** /rəˈsɛptəkəl/, *n.* **1.** that which serves to receive or hold something; a repository; a container. **2.** *Bot.* the modified or expanded portion of an axis, which bears the organs of a single flower or the florets of a flower head. **3.** *Elect., U.S.* a socket outlet. [late ME, from L *receptāculum*]

**reception** /rəˈsɛpʃən/, *n.* **1.** the act of receiving. **2.** the fact of being received. **3.** a manner of being received: *the book met with a favourable reception.* **4.** a function or occasion when people are formally received. **5.** a place, office, desk, or the like where callers are received, as in an office or hotel. **6.** *Radio.* the quality or fidelity attained in receiving under given circumstances. [ME *recepcion,* from L *receptio*]

**receptionist** /rəˈsɛpʃənəst/, *n.* a person employed to receive and direct callers, as in an office or hotel.

**reception room** /rəˈsɛpʃən rum/, *n.* a room for receiving visitors, clients, etc.

**receptive** /rəˈsɛptɪv/, *adj.* **1.** having the quality of receiving, taking in, or admitting. **2.** able or quick to receive ideas, etc.: *a receptive mind.* **3.** having, or characterised by, a disposition to receive a suggestion, offer, or the like with favour: *a receptive person.* **4.** of or pertaining to reception or receptors. – **receptively,** *adv.* – **receptivity** /risɛpˈtɪvəti/, **receptiveness,** *n.*

**receptor** /rəˈsɛptə/, *n.* one of or a group of the end organs of sensory or afferent neurons, specialised to be sensitive to stimulating agents. [L: a receiver]

**recess** /rəˈsɛs, ˈrisɛs/, *n.;* /rəˈsɛs/, *v.* –*n.* **1.** a part or space that is set back or recedes, as a bay or an alcove in a room. **2.** an indentation in a line or extent of coast, hills, forest, etc. **3.** (*usu. pl.*) a secluded inner area or part: *in the recesses of the palace.* **4.** withdrawal or cessation for a time from the usual occupation, work, or activity. **5.** a period of such withdrawal, as the midmorning break between school classes. –*v.t.* **6.** to place or set in a recess. **7.** to set or form as or like a recess; make a recess or recesses in: *to recess a wall.* –*v.i.* **8.** to take a recess. [L *recessus* a going back]

**recession**[1] /rəˈsɛʃən/, *n.* **1.** the act of receding or withdrawing. **2.** a receding part of a wall, etc. **3.** a procession at the end of a church service. **4.** a decline in business. **5.** a period of adverse economic circumstances, usu. less severe than a depression.

**recession**[2] /riˈsɛʃən/, *n.* the returning of ownership to a former possessor. [RE- + CESSION]

**recessional** /rəˈsɛʃənəl/, *adj.* **1.** of or pertaining to a recession of the clergy and choir after a church service. **2.** of or pertaining to a recess, as of a legislative body. –*n.* **3.** a recessional hymn, or music for it.

**recessional hymn** /– ˈhɪm/, *n.* a hymn sung at the close of a church service while the clergy and choir retire from the chancel to the vestry.

**recessive** /rəˈsɛsɪv/, *adj.* **1.** tending to recede; receding. **2.** *Biol.* pertaining to or exhibiting a recessive, as opposed to a dominant. **3.** (of accent) showing a tendency to recede from the end towards the beginning of a word. –*n. Biol.* **4.** a hereditary character resulting from a gene which possesses less biochemical activity than another termed the dominant, and hence is suppressed more or less completely by it when in a heterozygous condition. **5.** an individual exhibiting such character. – **recessively,** *adv.* – **recessiveness,** *n.*

**réchauffé** /reɪʃoʊˈfeɪ/, *n., pl.* **-fés. 1.** a warmed-up dish of food. **2.** anything old or stale brought out again. [F: lit., warmed again]

**recherché** /rəˈʃɛəʃeɪ/, *adj.* **1.** sought out with care. **2.** rare or choice. **3.** of studied refinement or elegance. [F, pp. of *rechercher.* See RESEARCH, *v.*]

**recidivism** /rəˈsɪdəvɪzəm/, *n.* **1.** repeated or habitual relapse into crime. **2.** *Psychol.* the chronic tendency towards repetition of criminal or antisocial behaviour patterns. [L *recidīvus* relapsing + -ISM] – **recidivist,** *n.* – **recidivistic** /rəsɪdəˈvɪstɪk/, **recidivous,** *adj.*

**recipe** /ˈrɛsəpi/, *n.* **1.** any formula, esp. one for preparing a dish in cookery. **2.** a method to attain a desired end. [ME, from L: take, impv. of *recipere* (see RECEIVE), as used at the head of prescriptions]

**recipience** /rəˈsɪpiəns/, *n.* **1.** the act of receiving; reception. **2.** the state or quality of being receptive; receptiveness. Also, **recipiency.**

**recipient** /rəˈsɪpiənt/, *n.* **1.** one who or that which receives; a receiver. –*adj.* **2.** receiving or capable of receiving. [L *recipiens,* ppr., receiving]

**reciprocal** /rəˈsɪprəkəl/, *adj.* **1.** given, felt, etc., by each to or towards each; mutual: *reciprocal affection.* **2.** given, performed, felt, etc., in return: *reciprocal aid.* **3.** *Gram.* expressing mutual relation, as *each other, one another,* etc. (sometimes opposed to, but often including, *reflexive* when referring to plural subjects). **4.** *Maths.* denoting or pertaining to relations or functions which involve reciprocals. –*n.* **5.** a thing that is reciprocal to something else; an equivalent; a counterpart; a complement. **6.** *Maths.* that by which a given quantity is multiplied to produce unity. [L

---

**refortify,** *v.t.,* **-fied, -fying.**
**reforward,** *v.t.*
**refracture,** *v.,* **-tured, -turing.**
**reframe,** *v.t.,* **-framed, -framing.**
**refreeze,** *v.,* **-froze, -frozen, -freezing.**
**refunction,** *v.i.*
**refurl,** *v.t.*
**refurnish,** *v.t.*
**regalvanise,** *v.t.,* **-nised, -nising.**
**regarrison,** *v.t.*
**regather,** *v.*
**regauge,** *v.t.,* **-gauged, -gauging.**
**regear,** *v.t.*
**regel,** *v.i.,* **-gelled, -gelling.**
**regerminate,** *v.t.,* **-nated, -nating.**
**regermination,** *n.*
**regild,** *v.t.,* **-gilded, -gilt, -gilding.**
**regird,** *v.t.,* **-girt** or **-girded, -girding.**
**reglaze,** *v.t.,* **-glazed, -glazing.**
**reglorify,** *v.t.,* **-fied, -fying.**
**reglue,** *v.t.,* **-glued, -gluing.**
**regrade,** *v.t.,* **-graded, -grading.**
**regraft,** *v.t.*
**regrant,** *v.t.*
**regrease,** *v.t.,* **-greased, -greasing.**
**regrind,** *v.t.,* **-ground, -grinding.**
**regroup,** *v.*
**regrow,** *v.,* **-grew, -grown, -growing.**
**rehandle,** *v.t.,* **-dled, -dling.**
**rehang,** *v.t.,* **-hung, -hanged, -hanging.**
**reharden,** *v.*
**reharness,** *v.t.*
**reheel,** *v.t.*
**rehem,** *v.t.,* **-hemmed, -hemming.**
**re-ice,** *v.,* **-iced, -icing.**
**re-identify,** *v.t.,* **-fied, -fying.**
**reignite,** *v.t.,* **-nited, -niting.**
**reilluminate,** *v.t.,* **-nated, -nating.**
**reimplant,** *v.t.*
**reimpose,** *v.,* **-posed, -posing.**
**reimposition,** *n.*
**reimpregnate,** *v.t.,* **-nated, -nating.**
**reimpress,** *v.t.*
**reimprint,** *v.t.*
**reimprison,** *v.t.*

*reciprocus* returning, reciprocal + -AL[1]] **–reciprocality** /rəsɪprəˈkæləti/, *n.* **–reciprocally,** *adv.*

**reciprocal translocation** /– trænzləˈkeɪʃən/, *n.* an atypical interchange of parts of two or more pairs of non-homologous chromosomes, ordinarily giving a ring of such chromosomes.

**reciprocate** /rəˈsɪprəkeɪt/, *v.*, **-cated, -cating.** *–v.t.* **1.** to give, feel, etc., in return. **2.** to give and receive reciprocally; interchange: *to reciprocate favours.* **3.** to cause to move alternately backwards and forwards. *–v.i.* **4.** to make return, as for something given. **5.** to make interchange. **6.** to be correspondent. **7.** to move alternately backwards and forwards. [L *reciprocātus,* pp.] **–reciprocative,** *adj.* **–reciprocator,** *n.*

**reciprocating engine** /rəˌsɪprəkeɪtɪŋ ˈɛndʒən/, *n.* an engine characterised by the movement of the pistons in the cylinders back and forth in a straight line.

**reciprocation** /rəsɪprəˈkeɪʃən/, *n.* **1.** the act or fact of reciprocating. **2.** a making return for something. **3.** a mutual giving and receiving. **4.** the state of being reciprocal or corresponding.

**reciprocity** /rɛsəˈprɒsəti/, *n.* **1.** reciprocal state or relation. **2.** reciprocation; mutual exchange. **3.** that relation or policy in commercial dealings between countries by which corresponding advantages or privileges are granted by each country to the citizens of the other.

**recision** /rəˈsɪʒən/, *n.* an invalidating or rescinding. [L *recīsio*]

**recit.,** *Music.* recitative.

**recital** /rəˈsaɪtl/, *n.* **1.** a musical or other entertainment given usu. by a single performer, or consisting of selections from a single composer. **2.** the act of reciting. **3.** a detailed statement. **4.** an account, narrative, or description. **5.** (*usu. pl.*) *Law.* introductory and explanatory part (beginning 'whereas') in a deed leading up to the operative part.

**recitation** /rɛsəˈteɪʃən/, *n.* **1.** the act of reciting. **2.** a reciting or repeating of something from memory, esp. formally or publicly. **3.** an elocutionary delivery of a piece of poetry or prose, without the text, before an audience. **4.** a piece so delivered or for such delivery. [L *recitātio*]

**recitative**[1] /rəˈsaɪtətɪv, ˈrɛsəˌteɪtɪv/, *adj.* pertaining to or of the nature of recital, as of facts. [RECITE + -ATIVE]

**recitative**[2] /rɛsətəˈtiv/, *adj.* **1.** of the nature of or resembling recitation or declamation. *–n.* **2.** a style of vocal music intermediate between speaking and singing. **3.** a passage, part, or piece in this style. [It. *recitativo,* from *recitare* RECITE]

**recitativo** /rɛsətəˈtivoʊ/, *adj., n., pl.* **-vi** /-vi/, **-vos.** →**recitative**[2]. [It.]

**recitativo secco** /– ˈsɛkoʊ/, *n.* recitative not accompanied by the orchestra but usu. by a keyboard instrument, as the harpsichord. [It: dry recitative]

**recite** /rəˈsaɪt/, *v.*, **-cited, -citing.** *–v.t.* **1.** to repeat the words of, as from memory, esp. in a formal manner: *to recite a lesson.* **2.** to repeat (a piece of poetry or prose) before an audience, as for entertainment. **3.** to give an account of: *to recite one's adventures.* **4.** to enumerate. *–v.i.* **5.** to recite or repeat something from memory. [late ME, from L *recitāre* read aloud, repeat] **–reciter,** *n.*

**reck** /rɛk/, *v.i.* **1.** to have care, concern, or regard (oft. fol. by *of, with,* or a clause). **2.** to take heed. **3.** *Archaic.* to be of concern or importance, or matter: *it recks not.* *–v.t.* **4.** to have regard for; mind; heed. [ME *rekke(n),* OE *reccan,* var. of *rēcan,* c. G *(ge)ruhen* deign]

**reckless** /ˈrɛkləs/, *adj.* **1.** utterly careless of the consequences of action; without caution (fol. by *of*). **2.** characterised by or proceeding from such carelessness: *reckless extravagance.* [ME *rekles,* OE *recceléas,* var of *rēceléas* careless (c. G *ruchlos*)] **–recklessly,** *adv.* **–recklessness,** *n.*

**reckon** /ˈrɛkən/, *v.t.* **1.** to count, compute, or calculate as to number or amount. **2.** to esteem or consider (as stated): *to be reckoned a wit.* **3.** *Colloq.* to think or suppose. *–v.i.* **4.** to count; make a computation or calculation. **5.** to settle accounts, as with a person. **6.** to count, depend, or rely (*on*), as in expectation. **7.** to deal (*with*), as with something to be taken into account or entering into a case. **8.** to think; suppose. **9. reckon without,** to fail to take into account: *they reckoned without his strong sense of duty when they tried to bribe him.* [ME *reken(e),* OE *(ge)recenian,* c. G *rechnen*]

**reckoner** /ˈrɛkənə/, *n.* **1.** one who reckons. **2.** →**ready reckoner.**

**reckoning** /ˈrɛkənɪŋ/, *n.* **1.** count, computation, or calculation. **2.** the settlement of accounts, as between parties. **3.** a statement of an amount due; bill. **4.** an accounting, as for things received or done: *a day of reckoning.* **5.** →**dead reckoning.**

**re-claim** /ri-ˈkleɪm/, *v.t.* to claim or demand the return or restoration of (something, someone). [RE- + CLAIM]

**reclaim** /rəˈkleɪm/, *v.t.* **1.** to bring (wild, waste, or marshy land) into a condition for cultivation or other use. **2.** to recover (substances) in a pure or usable form from refuse matter, articles, etc. **3.** to bring back to more socially, morally, or religiously acceptable courses, living, principles, ideas, etc. *–n.* **4.** reclamation: *beyond reclaim.* [ME *reclaime(n),* from OF *reclaimer,* from L *reclāmāre* cry out against] **–reclaimable,** *adj.* **–reclaimant, reclaimer,** *n.*

**reclamation** /rɛkləˈmeɪʃən/, *n.* **1.** the reclaiming of waste, desert, marshy, or submerged land for cultivation or other use. **2.** the act or process of reclaiming. **3.** the state of being reclaimed. **4.** the process or industry of deriving usable materials from waste products. [L *reclāmātio*]

**reclassify** /ˌriˈklæsəfaɪ/, *v.t.*, **-fied, -fying.** **1.** to put into a new or another category. **2.** to classify again; reassess. **–reclassification** /ˌriklæsəfəˈkeɪʃən/, *n.*

**rec leave** /ˈrɛk liv/, *n.* recreation leave.

**recline** /rəˈklaɪn, ri-/, *v.*, **-clined, -clining.** *–v.i.* **1.** to lean or lie back; rest in a recumbent position. *–v.t.* **2.** to cause to lean back on something; place in a recumbent position. [late ME, from L *reclīnāre*] **–reclinable,** *adj.* **–recliner,** *n.* **–reclination** /rɛkləˈneɪʃən/, *n.*

**recluse** /rəˈklus/, *n.* **1.** a person who lives in seclusion or

---

**reimprisonment,** *n.*
**reinaugurate,** *v.t.*, **-rated, -rating.**
**reinauguration,** *n.*
**reincite,** *v.t.*, **-cited, -citing.**
**reincorporate,** *v.t.*, **-rated, -rating.**
**reincur,** *v.t.*, **-curred, -curring.**
**reindex,** *v.t.*
**reindicate,** *v.t.*, **-cated, -cating.**
**reindict,** *v.t.*
**reindoctrinate,** *v.t.*, **-nated, -nating.**
**reindorse,** *v.t.*, **-dorsed, -dorsing.**
**reindorsement,** *n.*
**reinduce,** *v.t.*, **-duced, -ducing.**
**reindustrialisation,** *n.*
**reindustrialise,** *v.t.*, **-lised, -lising.**
**reinfect,** *v.t.*
**reinfection,** *n.*
**reinfiltrate,** *v.*, **-trated, -trating.**
**reinflame,** *v.t.*, **-flamed, -flaming.**
**reinflatable,** *adj.*
**reinflate,** *v.t.*, **-flated, -flating.**
**reinflation,** *n.*
**reinform,** *v.t.*
**reinfuse,** *v.t.*, **-fused, -fusing.**
**reinhabit,** *v.t.*
**reinject,** *v.t.*
**re-ink,** *v.t.*
**reinoculate,** *v.t.*, **-lated, -lating.**
**reinscribe,** *v.t.*, **-scribed, -scribing.**
**reinsert,** *v.t.*
**reinsertion,** *n.*
**reinspect,** *v.t.*
**reinspection,** *n.*
**reinspire,** *v.t.*, **-spired, -spiring.**
**reinstall,** *v.t.*
**reinstallation,** *n.*
**reinstalment,** *n.*
**reinstitute,** *v.t.*, **-tuted, -tuting.**
**reinstitution,** *n.*
**reinstruct,** *v.t.*
**reinstruction,** *n.*
**reintegrate,** *v.*, **-grated, -grating.**
**reintegration,** *n.*
**reinter,** *v.t.*, **-terred, -terring.**
**reinterest,** *v.t.*
**reinterment,** *n.*
**reinterpret,** *v.t.*
**reinterpretation,** *n.*
**reinterrogate,** *v.*, **-gated, -gating.**
**reinterrogation,** *n.*

apart from society, often for religious meditation. **2.** a religious voluntarily immured or remaining for life within a cell; incluse. *–adj.* **3.** shut off or apart from the world, or living in seclusion, often for religious reasons. **4.** characterised by seclusion. [ME *reclus,* from OF, from LL *reclūsus,* pp., shut up] – **reclusive,** *adj.*

**reclusion** /rəˈkluʒən/, *n.* **1.** the condition or life of a recluse. **2.** a shutting or a being shut up in seclusion.

**recognisance** /rəˈkɒgnəzəns/, *n.* **1.** the act of recognising; recognition. **2.** *Law.* **a.** a bond or obligation of record entered into before a court of record or a magistrate, binding a person to do a particular act. **b.** the sum pledged as surety on such a bond. Also, **recognizance.** [ME *reconissance,* from OF. See RECOGNISE]

**recognise** /ˈrɛkəgnaɪz/, *v.t.,* **-nised, -nising. 1.** to know again; perceive to be identical with something previously known: *he had changed so much that one could scarcely recognise him.* **2.** to identify from knowledge of appearance or character. **3.** to perceive as existing or true; realise: *to be the first to recognise a fact.* **4.** to acknowledge formally as existing or as entitled to consideration: *one government recognises another.* **5.** to acknowledge or accept formally as being something stated: *to recognise a government as a belligerent.* **6.** to acknowledge or treat as valid: *to recognise a claim.* **7.** to acknowledge acquaintance with (a person, etc.) as by a salute. **8.** to show appreciation of (kindness, service, merit, etc.) as by some reward or tribute. Also, **recognize.** [apparently from *recogn(ition)* + -ISE[1]; replacing late ME (Scot.) *racunnys,* from OF] – **recognisable,** *adj.* – **recognisably,** *adv.*

**recognisee** /rəkɒgnəˈzi/, *n. Law.* one to whom a person who enters into a recognisance is bound. Also, **recognizee.**

**recognisor** /ˈrɛkəgnaɪzə/, *n.* **1.** one who or that which recognises. **2.** *Law.* one who enters into a recognisance.

**recognition** /rɛkəgˈnɪʃən/, *n.* **1.** the act of recognising. **2.** the state of being recognised. **3.** the perception of something as identical with something previously known or in the mind. **4.** the perception of something as existing or true; realisation. **5.** the acknowledgment of something as valid or as entitled to consideration: *the recognition of a claim.* **6.** the acknowledgment of kindness, service, merit, etc. **7.** the expression of this by some token of appreciation. **8.** formal acknowledgment conveying approval or sanction. **9.** *Internat. Law.* an official act by which one state acknowledges the existence of another state or government, or of belligerency or insurgency. [late ME, from L *recognitio*] – **recognitive** /rəˈkɒgnətɪv/, **recognitory** /rəˈkɒgnətri/, *adj.*

**recoil** /rəˈkɔɪl/ *for defs 1-4;* /rəˈkɔɪl, ˈrikɔɪl/ *for defs 5-7. v.i.* **1.** to draw back; start or shrink back, as in alarm, horror, or disgust. **2.** to spring or fly back, as in consequence of force of impact or the force of the discharge, as a firearm. **3.** to spring or come back; react (fol. by *on* or *upon*). **4.** *Physics.* (of an atom, nucleus, or particle) to undergo a change of momentum as a result of ejection of another particle or photon. *–n.* **5.** the act of recoiling. **6.** the length through which a weapon moves backwards after its discharge. **7.** *Physics.* the motion acquired by an atom, nucleus or particle through ejecting another particle or photon. [ME *recuyel(l)e(n),* from OF *reculer,* from L *re-* RE- + *cūlus* the buttocks]

**recoilless** /rəˈkɔɪlləs/, *adj.* without recoil: *recoilless artillery.*

**re-collect** /ri-kəˈlɛkt/, *v.t.* **1.** to collect, gather together, or assemble again (what is scattered). **2.** to rally (one's faculties, powers, spirits, etc.); recover or compose (oneself). [orig. from L *recollectus,* pp., collected again, but later taken as from RE- + COLLECT]

**recollect** /rɛkəˈlɛkt/, *v.t.* **1.** to recall to mind, or recover knowledge of by an act or effort of memory; remember. **2.** to concentrate or absorb (the mind, etc.), as in preparation for mystical contemplation. *–v.i.* **3.** to have a recollection; remember. [from the same source as RE-COLLECT, but distinguished in sense and pronunciation] – **recollective,** *adj.* – **recollectively,** *adv.*

**re-collection** /ri-kəˈlɛkʃən/, *n.* **1.** the act of re-collecting, or gathering together again. **2.** the state of being re-collected. [RE-COLLECT + -ION]

**recollection** /rɛkəˈlɛkʃən/, *n.* **1.** the act or power of recollecting, or recalling to mind; remembrance. **2.** that which is recollected: *recollections of one's childhood.* [RECOLLECT + -ION]

**recommend** /rɛkəˈmɛnd/, *v.t.* **1.** to commend by favourable representations; present as worthy of confidence, acceptance, use, etc.: *to recommend a book.* **2.** to represent or urge as advisable or expedient: *to recommend caution.* **3.** to advise (a person, etc., to do something): *to recommend one to wait.* **4.** to make acceptable or pleasing: *a plan that has very little to recommend it.* [ME *recommende(n),* from ML *recommendāre,* from L *re-* RE- + *commendāre* commend] – **recommendable,** *adj.* – **recommender,** *n.*

**recommendation** /ˌrɛkəmɛnˈdeɪʃən/, *n.* **1.** the act of recommending. **2.** a letter or the like recommending a person or thing. **3.** representation in favour of a person or thing. **4.** anything that serves to recommend a person or thing or induce acceptance or favour.

**recommendatory** /rɛkəˈmɛndətəri, -tri/, *adj.* **1.** serving to recommend; recommending. **2.** serving as, or of the nature of, a recommendation.

**recommit** /rikəˈmɪt/, *v.t.,* **-mitted, -mitting. 1.** to commit again. **2.** to refer again to a committee. – **recommitment, recommittal,** *n.*

**recompense** /ˈrɛkəmpɛns/, *v.,* **-pensed, -pensing,** *n. –v.t.* **1.** to make compensation to (a person, etc.); repay, remunerate, reward, or requite for service, aid, etc. **2.** to make compensation for; make a return or requital for. *–v.i.* **3.** to make compensation for something; repay or reward a person for service, aid, etc. *–n.* **4.** compensation made, as for loss, injury, or wrong: *to make recompense.* **5.** repayment or requital. **6.** remuneration or a reward. [ME, from LL *recompensāre,* from L *re-* RE- + *compensāre* compensate]

**recompose** /rikəmˈpoʊz/, *v.t.,* **-posed, -posing. 1.** to compose

---

**reintervene,** *v.i.,* **-vened, -vening.**
**reintervention,** *n.*
**reinterview,** *v.t.*
**reintroduce,** *v.t.,* **-duced, -ducing.**
**reintroduction,** *n.*
**reinvade,** *v.t.,* **-vaded, -vading.**
**reinvasion,** *n.*
**reinvent,** *v.t.*
**reinvest,** *v.t.*
**reinvestigate,** *v.t.,* **-gated, -gating.**
**reinvestigation,** *n.*
**reinvestment,** *n.*
**reinvigorate,** *v.t.,* **-rated, -rating.**
**reinvite,** *v.t.,* **-vited, -viting.**
**reinvoke,** *v.t.,* **-voked, -voking.**
**reinvolve,** *v.t.,* **-volved, -volving.**
**reinvolvement,** *n.*
**reisolate,** *v.t.,* **-lated, -lating.**
**rejudge,** *v.t.,* **-judged, -judging.**
**rekindle,** *v.,* **-dled, -dling.**
**reknot,** *v.t.,* **-knotted, -knotting.**
**relabel,** *v.t.,* **-belled, -belling.**
**relace,** *v.t.,* **-laced, -lacing.**
**relacquer,** *v.t.*
**relance,** *v.t.,* **-lanced, -lancing.**
**relatch,** *v.t.*
**relaunch,** *v.t.*
**relaunder,** *v.t.*
**relearn,** *v.*
**relet,** *v.,* **-let, -letting.**
**relight,** *v.t.,* **-lit** or **-lighted, -lighting.**
**reline,** *v.t.,* **-lined, -lining.**
**reliquefy,** *v.,* **-fied, -fying.**
**reliquidate,** *v.t.,* **-dated, -dating.**
**relive,** *v.,* **-lived, -living.**
**reload,** *v.t.*
**reloan,** *v.t., n.*
**relocate,** *v.t.,* **-cated, -cating.**
**relocation,** *n.*
**relower,** *v.t.*
**relubricate,** *v.t.,* **-cated, -cating.**
**remagnetisation,** *n.*
**remagnetise,** *v.t.,* **-tised, -tising.**
**remagnify,** *v.t.,* **-fied, -fying.**
**remanifest,** *v.t.*
**remap,** *v.t.,* **-mapped, -mapping.**
**remarriage,** *n.*
**remarry,** *v.,* **-ried, -rying.**
**remarshal,** *v.t.,* **-shalled, -shalling.**

---

again; reconstitute; rearrange. **2.** to restore to composure or calmness. – **recomposition** /rikɒmpəˈzɪʃən/, *n.*

**recompression chamber** /rikəmˈprɛʃən tʃeɪmbə/, *n.* a room in which a diver suffering from the bends may be placed, in which the air pressure is increased to minimise the effects of the disorder, and then gradually brought to normal.

**reconcilable** /ˈrɛkənsaɪləbəl/, *adj.* that can be reconciled; capable of reconciliation. – **reconcilability** /ˌrɛkənsaɪləˈbɪləti/, **reconcilableness,** *n.* – **reconcilably,** *adv.*

**reconcile** /ˈrɛkənsaɪl/, *v.t.,* **-ciled, -ciling.** **1.** to render no longer opposed; bring to acquiescence (fol. by *to*): *to reconcile someone to his fate.* **2.** to win over to friendliness: *to reconcile a hostile person.* **3.** to compose or settle (a quarrel, difference, etc.). **4.** to bring into agreement or harmony; make compatible or consistent: *to reconcile differing statements.* [ME, from L *reconciliāre*] – **reconcilement,** *n.* – **reconciler,** *n.*

**reconciliation** /ˌrɛkənsɪliˈeɪʃən/, *n.* **1.** the act of reconciling. **2.** the state of being reconciled. **3.** the process of making consistent or compatible.

**reconciliatory** /rɛkənˈsɪliətri/, *adj.* tending to reconcile.

**recondite** /rəˈkɒndaɪt, ˈrɛkəndaɪt/, *adj.* **1.** dealing with abstruse or profound matters: *a recondite treatise.* **2.** removed from ordinary knowledge or understanding; abstruse; profound: *recondite principles.* **3.** little known; obscure. [earlier *recondit,* from L *reconditus,* pp., put away, hidden] – **reconditely,** *adv.* – **reconditeness,** *n.*

**recondition** /rikənˈdɪʃən/, *v.t.* to restore to a good or satisfactory condition; repair; overhaul.

**reconnaissance** /rəˈkɒnəsəns/, *n.* **1.** the act of reconnoitring. **2.** *Mil.* a search made for useful military information in the field, esp. by examining the ground. **3.** *Civ. Eng.* a preliminary examination of a region as to its general natural features, before a more exact survey for triangulation, etc. **4.** *Geol.* an examination or survey of the general geological characteristics of a region. [F. See RECOGNISANCE]

**reconnoitre** /rɛkəˈnɔɪtə/, *v.,* **-tred, -tring,** *n.* –*v.t.* **1.** to inspect, observe, or survey (the enemy, the enemy's strength or position, a region, etc.) in order to gain information for military purposes. **2.** to examine or survey (a region, etc.) for engineering, geological, or other purposes. –*v.i.* **3.** to make a reconnaissance. –*n.* **4.** the act of reconnoitring; a reconnaissance. Also, *U.S.,* **reconnoiter.** [F *reconnoitre,* earlier form of *reconnaître* reconnoitre, RECOGNISE] – **reconnoitrer,** *n.*

**reconsider** /rikənˈsɪdə/, *v.t.* **1.** to consider again. **2.** to consider again with a view to a change of decision or action: *to reconsider a refusal.* –*v.i.* **3.** to reconsider a matter. – **reconsideration** /ˌrikənsɪdəˈreɪʃən/, *n.*

**reconsign** /rikənˈsaɪn/, *v.t.* to consign again.

**reconsignment** /rikənˈsaɪnmənt/, *n.* a consigning again.

**reconstitute** /riˈkɒnstətjut/, *v.t.,* **-tuted, -tuting.** to constitute again; reconstruct; recompose: *reconstituted milk, a reconstituted committee.* – **reconstitution** /rikɒnstəˈtjuʃən/, *n.*

**reconstruct** /rikənˈstrʌkt/, *v.t.* **1.** to construct again; rebuild. **2.** to re-create or re-enact past events or another place: *to reconstruct a crime, the scene of a crime.* **3.** *Linguistics.* to suggest hypothetical forms for (a language, or parts of a language, for which no documentary evidence survives) by comparison of related languages or forms for which such evidence is available.

**reconstruction** /rikənˈstrʌkʃən/, *n.* **1.** the act of reconstructing. **2.** something reconstructed, as a model or a re-enactment of past events.

**reconstructive** /rikənˈstrʌktɪv/, *adj.* tending to reconstruct.

**record** /rəˈkɔd/, *v.;* /ˈrɛkɔd/, *n., adj.* –*v.t.* **1.** to set down in writing or the like, as for the purpose of preserving evidence. **2.** to cause to be set down or registered: *to record one's vote.* **3.** to indicate or state: *they recorded a protest by sitting down in the streets.* **4.** to serve to relate or to tell of, as a written statement. **5.** to set down or register in some permanent form, as instruments. **6.** to set down, register, or fix by characteristic marks, incisions, magnetism, etc., for the purpose of reproduction by a gramophone or tape-recorder. **7.** to play or read for the purposes of making a recording: *the orchestra recorded a symphony.* –*v.i.* **8.** to record something. –*n.* **9.** the act of recording. **10.** the state or fact of being recorded, as in writing. **11.** an account in writing or the like preserving the memory or knowledge of facts or events. **12.** information or knowledge preserved in writing or the like. **13.** *Computers.* a self-contained group of data, as a punched card or a line of print. **14.** a report, list, or aggregate of actions or achievements, as in the case of a person, an organisation, a horse, a ship, etc.: *to have a good record.* **15.** any thing or person serving as a memorial. **16.** the tracing, marking, or the like made by recording instrument. **17.** a disc or, formerly, a cylinder, or other device having characteristic markings for reproducing sound, esp. for use with a record-player or a gramophone; gramophone record. **18.** the highest or farthest recorded degree attained; the best rate, amount, etc., attained, as in some form of sport: *to break the record in the high jump.* **19.** an official writing intended to be preserved. **20.** *Law.* **a.** the commitment to writing, as authentic evidence, of something having legal importance, esp. as evidence of the proceedings or verdict of a court. **b.** evidence preserved in this manner. **c.** an authentic or official written report of proceedings of a court of justice. **21. off the record,** unofficially; without intending to be quoted. **22. on record,** recorded in a publicly available document: *he is on record as having said that he would launch a war against China.* –*adj.* **23.** making or affording a record. **24.** notable in the degree of attainment; surpassing all others: *a record year for sales.* [ME *recorde(n),* from OF *recorder,* from L *recordāri* call to mind, remember]

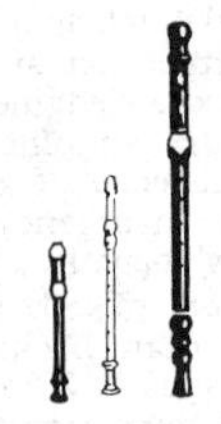

recorders: 18th century German

**record-changer** /ˈrɛkɔd-tʃeɪndʒə/, *n.* a device which auto-

**remaster,** *v.t.*
**rematch,** *v.t.*
**rematerialise,** *v.t.,* **-lised, -lising.**
**rematriculate,** *v.i.,* **-lated, -lating.**
**remeasure,** *v.t.,* **-ured, -uring.**
**remelt,** *v.*
**rememorise,** *v.t.,* **-rised, -rising.**
**remerge,** *v.,* **-merged, -merging.**
**remigrate,** *v.i.,* **-grated, -grating.**
**remigration,** *n.*
**remilitarisation,** *n.*
**remilitarise,** *v.t.,* **-rised, rising.**
**remix,** *v.t.*
**remobilisation,** *n.*
**remobilise,** *v.,* **-lised, -lising.**
**remodification,** *n.*
**remodify,** *v.t.,* **-fied, -fying.**
**remodulate,** *v.t.,* **-lated, -lating.**
**remonetisation,** *n.*
**remonetise,** *v.t.,* **-tised, -tising.**
**remortgage,** *v.t.,* **-gaged, -gaging.**
**remultiplication,** *n.*
**remultiply,** *v.,* **-plied, -plying.**
**rename,** *v.t.,* **-named, -naming.**
**renationalise,** *v.,* **-lised, -lising.**
**renavigate,** *v.t.,* **-gated, -gating.**
**renegotiate,** *v.,* **-ated, -ating.**
**renegotiation,** *n.*
**renominate,** *v.t.,* **-nated, -nating.**
**renormalise,** *v.,* **-lised, -lising.**
**renotify,** *v.t.,* **-fied, -fying.**
**renourish,** *v.t.*
**renourishment,** *n.*
**renumber,** *v.t.*
**renumerate,** *v.t.,* **-rated, -rating.**
**reobtain,** *v.t.*
**reobtainable,** *adj.*
**reoccupation,** *n.*
**reoccupy,** *v.t.,* **-pied, -pying.**
**reoperate,** *v.,* **-rated, -rating.**
**reoppose,** *v.t.,* **-posed, -posing.**
**reorchestrate,** *v.,* **-trated, -trating.**
**reorchestration,** *n.*
**reoutline,** *v.t.,* **-lined, -lining.**
**repacify,** *v.t.,* **-fied, -fying.**
**repack,** *v.*
**repad,** *v.t.,* **-padded, -padding.**

matically changes the records on a record-player.

**recorder** /rəˈkɔdə/, *n.* **1.** one who records, esp. as an official duty. **2.** a recording or registering apparatus or device. **3.** →**tape-recorder.** **4.** a soft-toned flute with a plug in the mouthpiece, played in vertical position. – **recordership,** *n.*

**recording** /rəˈkɔdɪŋ/, *n.* **1.** the act or practice of making a record. **2.** *Electronics.* a record of music, speech or the like made on magnetic tape or similar medium for purposes of reproduction; a record or tape.

**recording head** /ˈ– hɛd/, *n.* **1.** (in the manufacture of gramophone records) an electromagnetic device which cuts the original track in the master wax record from which the stampers are made. **2.** an inductance coil in a tape-recorder for recording the signal on a magnetic tape.

**recording instrument** /ˈ– ɪnstrəmənt/, *n.* any measuring instrument which is so constructed that it makes a permanent record of the measurements it makes, as a recording barograph.

**record-player** /ˈrɛkɔd-pleɪə/, *n.* a machine that reproduces sound from a record; gramophone; phonograph.

**re-count** /ˌri-ˈkaʊnt/, *v.;* /ˈri-kaʊnt/, *n.* –*v.t.* **1.** to count again. –*n.* **2.** a second or additional count, as of votes in an election. [RE- + COUNT[1]]

**recount** /rəˈkaʊnt/, *v.t.* **1.** to relate or narrate; tell in detail; give the facts or particulars of. **2.** to narrate in order. **3.** to tell one by one; enumerate. [late ME *recompte(n),* from AF *reconter* repeat, relate, from *re-* RE- + *conter* tell, COUNT[1]]

**recountal** /rəˈkaʊntl/, *n.* the act of recounting.

**recoup** /rəˈkup/, *v.;* /ˈrikup/, *n.* –*v.t.* **1.** to obtain an equivalent for; compensate for: *to recoup one's losses.* **2.** to regain or recover. **3.** to yield in return; return an amount equal to. **4.** to reimburse or indemnify: *to recoup a person for expenses.* **5.** *Law.* to withhold (a portion of something due) having some rightful claim to do so. –*v.i.* **6.** to obtain an equivalent, as for something lost. –*n.* **7.** the act of recouping. [ME, from F *recouper* cut again, from *re-* RE- + *couper* cut] – **recoupment,** *n.*

**recourse** /rəˈkɔs/, *n.* **1.** resort or application to a person or thing for help or protection, as when in difficulty: *to have recourse to someone.* **2.** a person or thing resorted to for help or protection. **3.** *Comm.* the right to resort to a person for pecuniary compensation. An endorsement **without recourse** is one by which a payee or holder of a negotiable instrument, by writing 'without recourse' with his name, merely transfers the instrument without assuming any liability upon it. [ME *recours,* from OF, from L *recursus* a running back]

**re-cover** /ˌri-ˈkʌvə/, *v.t.* to cover again or anew.

**recover** /rəˈkʌvə/, *v.t.* **1.** to get again, or regain (something lost or taken away): *to recover lost property.* **2.** to make up for or make good (loss, damage, etc., to oneself). **3.** to regain the strength, composure, balance, etc., of (oneself). **4.** *Law.* **a.** to obtain by judgment in a court of law, or by legal proceedings: *to recover damages for a wrong.* **b.** to acquire title to through judicial process: *to recover land.* **5.** to reclaim from a bad state, practice, etc. **6.** to regain (a substance) in usable form, as from refuse material or from a waste product or by-product of manufacture; reclaim. **7.** *Mil.* **a.** to bring back (a weapon) to a certain position, as after use. **b.** to bring back (equipment, etc.) from a battlefield after an action. –*v.i.* **8.** to regain health after sickness, a wound, etc. (oft. fol. by *from*): *to recover from an illness.* **9.** to regain a former (and better) state or condition: *the city soon recovered from the effects of the explosion.* **10.** to regain one's composure, balance, etc. **11.** *Law.* to obtain a favourable judgment in a suit. **12.** *Fencing, Rowing, etc.* to make a recovery. **13.** *Swimming.* to move the arm back to its position ready for the next stroke. [ME *recovere,* from AF *recoverer,* from L *recuperāre* recuperate] – **recoverable,** *adj.* – **recoverer,** *n.*

**recovery** /rəˈkʌvəri, rəˈkʌvri/, *n., pl.* **-eries.** **1.** the act of recovering. **2.** the regaining of something lost or taken away, or the possibility of this. **3.** restoration or return to health from sickness. **4.** restoration or return to a former (and better) state or condition. **5.** the overcoming of a mistake, setback or difficulty: *after trailing badly at half-time, the team made a good recovery and won the game.* **6.** time required for recovery. **7.** that which is gained in recovering. **8.** the regaining of substances in usable form, as from refuse material or waste products. **9.** *Law.* the obtaining of right to something by verdict or judgment of a court of law. **10.** *Fencing.* the movement to the position of guard after a lunge. **11.** *Rowing.* a return to a former position for making the next stroke. **12.** *Athletics.* the movement in running of the leg when it is not touching the ground.

**recreant** /ˈrɛkriənt/, *adj.* **1.** cowardly or craven. **2.** unfaithful, disloyal, or false. –*n.* **3.** a coward or craven. **4.** an apostate; a traitor. [ME, from OF, from *recreire,* yield in a contest, from *re-* back + *creire,* from L *crēdere* believe] – **recreance, recreancy,** *n.* – **recreantly,** *adv.*

**re-create** /ri-kriˈeɪt/, *v.t.,* **-ated, -ating.** to create anew. [RE- + CREATE]

**recreate** /ˈrɛkrieɪt/, *v.,* **-ated, -ating.** –*v.t.* **1.** to refresh by means of relaxation and enjoyment, as after work. **2.** to restore or refresh physically or mentally. –*v.i.* **3.** to take recreation. [late ME, from L *recreātus,* pp. of *recreāre* restore, from *re-* RE- + *creāre* create]

**re-creation** /ri-kriˈeɪʃən/, *n.* **1.** the act of creating anew. **2.** a thing created anew. [RE- + CREATION]

**recreation** /rɛkriˈeɪʃən/, *n.* **1.** refreshment by means of some pastime, agreeable exercise, or the like. **2.** a pastime, diversion, exercise, or other resource affording relaxation and enjoyment. **3.** the act of recreating. **4.** the state of being recreated. –*adj.* **5.** of or pertaining to an area, room, etc., set aside for recreation. [ME, from L *recreātio*] – **recreational,** *adj.*

**recrement** /ˈrɛkrəmənt/, *n.* a secretion which, after having been separated from the blood, is returned to it, as the saliva. – **recremental** /rɛkrəˈmɛntl/, *adj.*

**recriminate** /rəˈkrɪməneɪt/, *v.,* **-nated, -nating.** –*v.i.* **1.** to

---

**repaginate,** *v.t.,* **-nated, -nating.**
**repagination,** *n.*
**repanel,** *v.t.,* **-nelled, -nelling.**
**repaper,** *v.t.*
**repark,** *v.t.*
**repatch,** *v.t.*
**repave,** *v.t.,* **-paved, -paving.**
**repeddle,** *v.t.,* **-dled, -dling.**
**repenalise,** *v.t.,* **-lised, -lising.**
**rephotograph,** *v.t.*
**replan,** *v.t.,* **-planned, -planning.**
**replant,** *v.t.*
**replaster,** *v.t.*
**replate,** *v.t.,* **-plated, -plating.**
**replay,** *v.t.*
**replay,** *n.*
**repledge,** *v.t.,* **-pledged, -pledging.**
**replot,** *v.t.,* **-plotted, plotting.**
**replunge,** *v.,* **-plunged, -plunging.**
**repolarisation,** *n.*
**repolarise,** *v.t.,* **-rised, -rising.**
**repolish,** *v.*
**repopularise,** *v.t.,* **-lised, -lising.**
**repopulate,** *v.t.,* **-lated, -lating.**
**repopulation,** *n.*
**reportion,** *v.t.*
**repostpone,** *v.t.,* **-poned, -poning.**
**repostulate,** *v.t.,* **-lated, -lating.**
**repour,** *v.t.*
**reprepare,** *v.t.,* **-pared, -paring.**
**reprice,** *v.t.,* **-priced, -pricing.**
**reprime,** *v.t.,* **-primed, -priming.**
**reprocess,** *v.t.*
**reproclaim,** *v.t.*
**reprogram,** *v.t.,* **-grammed, -gramming.**
**reproject,** *v.t.*
**repromulgate,** *v.t.,* **-gated, -gating.**
**repromulgation,** *n.*
**repropose,** *v.,* **-posed, -posing.**
**reprovision,** *v.t.*
**republish,** *v.t.*
**repunctuate,** *v.t.,* **-ated, -ating.**
**repunish,** *v.t.*
**repurification,** *n.*
**repurify,** *v.t.,* **-fied, -fying.**
**repursue,** *v.t.,* **-sued, -suing.**
**requalify,** *v.,* **-fied, -fying.**
**requestion,** *v.t.*
**requicken,** *v.*

bring a countercharge against an accuser. –*v.t.* **2.** to accuse in return. [ML *recrīminātus,* pp.] – **recrimination** /rəkrɪmə'neɪʃən/, *n.* – **recriminative, recriminatory,** *adj.* – **recriminator,** *n.*

**recrudesce** /rikru'dɛs/, *v.i.,* **-desced, -descing.** to break out afresh, as a sore or as a disease, or anything that has been quiescent. [L *recrūdescere*]

**recrudescence** /rikru'dɛsəns/, *n.* a breaking out afresh, or into renewed activity; revival or reappearance in active existence. Also, **recrudescency.** – **recrudescent,** *adj.*

**recruit** /rə'krut/, *n.* **1.** a newly enlisted member of the armed forces. **2.** a newly secured member of any body or class. –*v.t.* **3.** to enlist (men) for service in the armed forces. **4.** to raise (a force) by enlistment. **5.** to strengthen or supply (an army, etc.) with new men. **6.** to furnish or replenish with a fresh supply; renew. **7.** to renew or restore (the health, strength, etc.). –*v.i.* **8.** to enlist or raise men for service in the armed forces. **9.** to recover health, strength, etc. **10.** to gain new supplies of anything lost or wasted. [F *recruter,* from *recrue* a new growth, properly pp. of *recroître* grow again, from *re-* RE- + *croître* (from L *crescere*) grow] – **recruitable,** *adj.* – **recruiter,** *n.* – **recruitment,** *n.*

**recta** /'rɛktə/, *n.* plural of **rectum.**

**rectal** /'rɛktl/, *adj.* of or pertaining to the rectum. – **rectally,** *adv.*

**rectangle** /'rɛktæŋgəl/, *n.* a parallelogram with all its angles right angles. [LL *rectangulum,* neut. of *rectangulus* right-angled]

**rectangular** /rɛk'tæŋgjələ/, *adj.* **1.** shaped like a rectangle. **2.** having the base or section in the form of a rectangle. **3.** having right angles or a right angle. **4.** forming a right angle. – **rectangularity** /rɛkˌtæŋgjə'lærəti/, *n.* – **rectangularly,** *adv.*

**recti** /'rɛktaɪ/, *n.* plural of **rectus.**

**recti-,** a word element meaning 'straight', 'right'. Also, before vowels, **rect-.** [L, combining form of *rectus*]

**rectifier** /'rɛktəfaɪə/, *n.* **1.** one who or that which rectifies. **2.** *Elect.* an apparatus or contrivance which changes an alternating current into a direct current, without an intermediate transformation of energy. **3.** *Chem.* an apparatus used in chemical rectifying for collecting the most volatile distillate. **4.** *Elect.* **a.** a vacuum tube or semiconductor diode used to convert an alternating current into a direct current. **b.** a device using the above.

**rectify** /'rɛktəfaɪ/, *v.t.,* **-fied, -fying. 1.** to make, put, or set right; remedy; correct. **2.** to put right by adjustment or calculation, as an instrument or a course at sea. **3.** *Chem.* to purify (esp. a spirit or liquor) by repeated distillation. **4.** *Elect.* to change (an alternating current) into a direct current. **5.** to determine the length of (a curve). **6.** *Astron., Geog.* to adjust (a globe) for the solution of any proposed problem. [ME, from LL *rectificāre.* See RECTI-, -FY] – **rectifiable,** *adj.* – **rectification** /rɛktəfə'keɪʃən/, *n.*

**rectilinear** /rɛktə'lɪniə/, *adj.* **1.** forming a straight line. **2.** formed by straight lines. **3.** characterised by straight lines. **4.** moving in a straight line. Also, **rectilineal.** – **rectilinearly,** *adv.*

**rectitude** /'rɛktətjud/, *n.* **1.** rightness of principle or practice: *the rectitude of one's motives.* **2.** correctness: *rectitude of judgment.* **3.** *Rare.* straightness. [ME, from LL *rectitūdo,* from L *rectus.* See RECTI-, -TUDE]

**recto** /'rɛktoʊ/, *n., pl.* **-tos.** *Print.* a right-hand page of an open book or manuscript; the front of a leaf (opposed to *verso*). [L, short for *rectō* (*foliō*) on right-hand (leaf)]

**rectocele** /'rɛktəsil/, *n.* a hernia of the rectum into the vagina. [*recto-* (combining form of RECTUM) + -CELE[1]]

**rector** /'rɛktə/, *n.* **1.** *Rom. Cath. Ch.* an ecclesiastic in charge of a college, religious house, or congregation. **2.** *C. of E.* a clergyman who has the charge of a parish. **3.** the permanent head in certain universities, colleges, and schools. **4.** *U.S.* a clergyman in charge of a parish in the Protestant Episcopal Church. [ME, from L: ruler] – **rectorial** /rɛk'tɔriəl/, *adj.*

**rectorate** /'rɛktərət/, *n.* the office, dignity, or term of a rector.

**rectory** /'rɛktəri/, *n., pl.* **-ries.** a rector's house; a parsonage.

**rectrix** /'rɛktrɪks/, *n., pl.* **rectrices** /rɛk'traɪsiz/. a large tail feather of a bird. [L: fem. of *rector* director]

**rectum** /'rɛktəm/, *n., pl.* **-ta** /-tə/. the comparatively straight terminal section of the intestine, ending in the anus. [NL, short for L *rectum intestīnum* straight intestine]

**rectus** /'rɛktəs/, *n., pl.* **-ti** /-taɪ/. any of several straight muscles, as of the abdomen, thigh, eye, etc. [NL, short for L *rectus musculus* straight muscle]

**recumbent** /rə'kʌmbənt/, *adj.* **1.** lying down; reclining; leaning. **2.** inactive; idle. **3.** *Zool., Bot.* denoting a part that leans or reposes upon anything. –*n.* **4.** a recumbent person, animal, plant, etc. [L *recumbens,* ppr.] – **recumbency,** *n.* – **recumbently,** *adv.*

**recuperate** /rə'kupəreɪt/, *v.,* **-rated, -rating.** –*v.i.* **1.** to recover from sickness or exhaustion; regain health or strength. **2.** to recover from pecuniary loss. –*v.t.* **3.** to restore to health, vigour, etc. [L *recuperātus,* pp., regained, recovered] – **recuperation** /rəkupə'reɪʃən/, *n.*

**recuperative** /rə'kuprətɪv, -pərətɪv/, *adj.* **1.** that recuperates. **2.** having the power of recuperating. **3.** pertaining to recuperation: *recuperative powers.* Also, **recuperatory** /rə'kupərətri/. – **recuperativeness,** *n.*

**recuperator** /rə'kupəreɪtə/, *n.* **1.** one who or that which recuperates. **2.** a system of thin-walled refractory ducts for exchange of heat between gases, esp. for heating the incoming air required by a furnace with the exhaust gases.

**recur** /ri'kɜ, rə-/, *v.i.,* **-curred, -curring. 1.** to occur again, as an event, experience, etc. **2.** to return to the mind: *recurring ideas.* **3.** to come up again for consideration, as a question. **4.** to return in action, thought, etc.: *to recur to a subject.* **5.** *Maths.* to repeat a fixed set of one or more digits in a decimal. **6.** *Rare.* to have recourse. [late ME, from L *recurrere* run back]

**recurrence** /rə'kʌrəns/, *n.* **1.** the act or fact of recurring. **2.**

---

**requote,** *v.t.,* **-quoted, -quoting.**
**re-radiate,** *v.,* **-ated, -ating.**
**re-rate,** *v.t.,* **-rated, -rating.**
**re-read,** *v.t.,* **-read, -reading.**
**re-record,** *v.t.*
**re-reel,** *v.*
**re-register,** *v.*
**re-registration,** *n.*
**re-regulate,** *v.t.,* **-lated, -lating.**
**re-root,** *v.t.*
**re-route,** *v.t.,* **-routed, -routeing.**
**resaddle,** *v.,* **-dled, -dling.**
**resalt,** *v.t.*
**reschedule,** *v.t.,* **-uled, -uling.**
**rescrutinise,** *v.t.,* **-nised, -nising.**
**reseal,** *v.t.*
**resecure,** *v.t.,* **-cured, -curing.**
**reseed,** *v.*
**resegregate,** *v.,* **-gated, -gating.**
**resegregation,** *n.*
**reseize,** *v.t.,* **-seized, -seizing.**
**reseizure,** *n.*
**resell,** *v.,* **-sold, -selling.**
**reseparate,** *v.,* **-rated, -rating.**
**reseparation,** *n.*
**resettle,** *v.,* **-tled, -tling.**
**resettlement,** *n.*
**resew,** *v.t.,* **-sewed, -sewn, -sewing.**
**resharpen,** *v.t.*
**reshine,** *v.,* **-shone, -shining.**
**reshoe,** *v.t.,* **-shoed, -shoeing.**
**reshorten,** *v.t.*
**reshoulder,** *v.t.*
**reshuffle,** *v.,* **-fled, -fling.**
**resift,** *v.t.*
**resight,** *v.t.*
**resilver,** *v.t.*
**resite,** *v.t.,* **-sited, -siting.**
**resmooth,** *v.t.*
**resoak,** *v.t.*
**resoften,** *v.t.*
**resolder,** *v.t.*
**resolicit,** *v.t.*
**resolidify,** *v.,* **-fied, -fying.**
**respecify,** *v.t.,* **-fied, -fying.**
**resplice,** *v.t.,* **-spliced, -splicing.**
**respread,** *v.t.,* **-spread, -spreading.**
**resprinkle,** *v.t.,* **-kled, -kling.**
**restabilise,** *v.t.,* **-lised, -lising.**
**restable,** *v.t.,* **-bled, -bling.**
**restack,** *v.t.*
**restaff,** *v.t.*
**restage,** *v.t.,* **-ged, -ging.**

return to a state, habit, subject, etc. **3.** →**recourse.**

**recurrent** /rə'kʌrənt/, *adj.* **1.** that recurs; occurring or appearing again, esp. repeatedly or periodically. **2.** *Anat., etc.* turned back so as to run in a reverse direction, as a nerve, artery, branch, etc. [L *recurrens*] – **recurrently,** *adv.*

**recurring decimal** /rə,kɜrɪŋ 'dɛsəməl/, *n. Maths.* a decimal which eventually recurs. The recurring digits are indicated by a bar or dots above them, as in 0.21532 = 0.21532 = 0.21532532.

**recurring fraction** /– 'frækʃən/, *n. Maths.* →**continued fraction.**

**recursion** /rə'kɜʒən/, *n.* the operation of a rule or formula to determine a succession of terms, the rule being derived by analysis of the preceding terms.

**recursive** /rə'kɜsɪv/, *adj.* **1.** of or pertaining to recursion. **2.** permitting or relating to an operation that may be repeated indefinitely, as a rule in generative grammar.

**recurvate** /ri'kɜvət, -veɪt/, *adj.* recurved. [L *recurvātus,* pp.]

**recurve** /ri'kɜv/, *v.t., v.i.,* **-curved, -curving.** to curve or bend back or backwards.

**recusancy** /'rɛkjəzənsi/, *n.* **1.** the state of being recusant. **2.** obstinate refusal or opposition. [RECUSANT. See -CY]

**recusant** /'rɛkjəzənt/, *adj.* **1.** refusing to submit, comply, etc. **2.** obstinate in refusal. [L *recūsans,* ppr., refusing]

**recyclable** /ri'saɪkləbəl/, *adj.* of or pertaining to products which can be broken down after use to serve as the raw material for new manufactured products.

**recycle** /ri'saɪkəl/, *v.t.,* **-cycled, -cycling.** to treat (waste, empty bottles, old tins, etc.) so that new products can be manufactured from them.

**red** /rɛd/, *adj.,* **redder, reddest,** *n.* *–adj.* **1.** of a spectral hue beyond orange in the spectrum. **2.** distinguished by being red, wearing red, having red clothing, etc. **3.** (*oft. cap.*) ultraradical politically, esp. communist. *–n.* **4.** any of the hues adjacent to orange in the spectrum, such as scarlet, vermilion, cherry. **5.** something red. **6.** red wine, as opposed to white (def. 34). **7.** (*oft. cap.*) an ultraradical in politics, esp. a communist. **8.** *Archery.* a ring on a target coloured red, scoring seven points. **9. paint the town red,** *Colloq.* to celebrate, esp. wildly and extravagantly. **10. see red,** *Colloq.* to become angry or infuriated. **11. the red, a.** red ink as used in bookkeeping and accounting practice for recording losses and deficits in financial statements. **b.** loss or deficit: *to be in or out of the red.* [ME *red(e),* OE *rēad,* c. G *rot,* akin to L *rūfus, ruber*]

**-red,** a noun suffix denoting condition, as in *hatred, kindred.* [ME *-rede,* OE *-rǣden*]

**redact** /ri'dækt/, *v.t.* **1.** to bring into presentable literary form; revise; edit. **2.** to draw up or frame (a statement, etc.). [L *redactus,* pp., brought back, reduced] – **redaction,** *n.* – **redactor,** *n.*

**red admiral** /rɛd 'ædmərəl/, *n.* a common butterfly, *Vanessa atalanta,* having wings bearing reddish bands.

**red algae** /– 'ældʒi/, *n.* algae of the class Rhodophyceae, in which the chlorophyll is masked by a red or purplish pigment.

**redan** /ri'dæn/, *n.* a work consisting of two parapets forming a salient angle. [F, var. of *redent,* a double notching or jagging, from *re-* RE- + *dent* tooth, L *dens*]

**red-arse** /'rɛd-as/, *n. N.Z. Mil. Colloq.* raw recruit; rookie

**red-backed sandpiper** /rɛd-bækt 'sændpaɪpə/, *n.* →**dunlin.**

**red-back spider** /rɛd-bæk 'spaɪdə/, *n.* a small, highly venomous, Australian spider, *Latrodectus hasseltii,* glossy dark brown to black, usu. with a red or orange streak on the body, closely related to the katipo of New Zealand and the black widow spider of America.

red-back spider

**red-baiting** /'rɛd-beɪtɪŋ/, *n. Colloq.* the act of denouncing or deprecating political opponents who are radical or left-wing. – **red-baiter,** *n.*

**red bean** /rɛd 'bin/, *n.* **1.** the edible red seed of some varities of French bean, esp. when dried; haricot rouge. **2.** a tree, *Dysoxylum muelleri,* family Meliaceae, of eastern Australia, which has red timber.

**red beech** /– 'bitʃ/, *n.* a New Zealand forest tree of the genus, *Nothofagus,* esp. *N. fusca* with dark red wood.

**red beet** /– 'bit/, *n.* See **beet** (def. 1).

**red-bellied black snake,** *n.* a venomous snake of eastern Australian forests and scrubs, *Pseudechis porphyriacus,* glossy black above and pale pink to red below, growing to two metres or more in length.

**red belt** /rɛd 'bɛlt/, *n. Judo.* **1.** a belt worn by an experienced contestant ranking from the ninth to the eleventh Dan. **2.** a contestant entitled to wear this.

**redbill** /'rɛdbɪl/, *n.* any of various birds having a red bill, as the swamp hen and the sooty oystercatcher.

**red-blindness** /'rɛd-blaɪndnəs/, *n.* →**protanopia.**

**red blood cell,** *n.* →**erythrocyte.**

**red-blooded** /'rɛd-blʌdəd/, *adj.* vigorous; virile. – **red-bloodedness,** *n.*

**red brass** /rɛd 'bras/, *n.* an alloy of zinc and copper containing less than 15 per cent zinc.

**red bream** /– 'brɪm/, *n.* See **snapper** (def. 1).

**redbreast** /'rɛdbrɛst/, *n.* the European robin, *Erithacus rubecula,* so called from the colour of the breast feathers.

**redbrick** /'rɛdbrɪk/, *adj. Chiefly Brit.* denoting or pertaining to universities of comparatively recent foundation, esp. those which emphasise technical subjects, as opposed to older-established and more traditional universities, as Oxford and Cambridge.

**redbud** /'rɛdbʌd/, *n.* the leguminous American Judas tree, *Cercis canadensis,* bearing small, budlike, pink flowers.

**redbug** /'rɛdbʌg/, *n. U.S.* →**chigger.**

**red cabbage** /rɛd 'kæbɪdʒ/, *n.* a purplish variety of cabbage,

---

**restamp,** *v.t.*
**restart,** *v.*
**restation,** *v.t.*
**resterilise,** *v.t.,* **-lised, -lising.**
**restimulate,** *v.t.,* **-lated, -lating.**
**restir,** *v.t.,* **-stirred, stirring.**
**restitch,** *v.t.*
**restraighten,** *v.*
**restrengthen,** *v.t.*
**restress,** *v.t.*
**restrike,** *v.t.,* **-struck, -striking.**
**restring,** *v.t.,* **-strung, -stringing.**
**restudy,** *v.t.,* **-studied, -studying.**
**restuff,** *v.t.*
**restyle,** *v.t.,* **-styled, -styling.**
**resubject,** *v.t.*
**resubmerge,** *v.,* **-merged, -merging.**
**resubmit,** *v.,* **-mitted, -mitting.**
**resubscribe,** *v.i.,* **-scribed, -scribing.**
**resummon,** *v.t.*
**resupply,** *v.t.,* **-plied, -plying.**
**resuppress,** *v.t.*
**resurvey,** *v.t.*
**resurvey,** *n.*
**resuspend,** *v.t.*
**resweep,** *v.t.,* **-swept, -sweeping.**
**resweeten,** *v.t.*
**resynthesis,** *n., pl.* **-ses.**
**resynthesise,** *v.t.,* **-sised, -sising.**
**retabulate,** *v.t.,* **-lated, -lating.**
**retack,** *v.t.*
**retape,** *v.t.,* **-taped, -taping.**
**retar,** *v.t.,* **-tarred, -tarring.**
**retaste,** *v.t.,* **-tasted, -tasting.**
**retax,** *v.t.*
**reteach,** *v.t.,* **-taught, -teaching.**
**retell,** *v.t.,* **-told, -telling.**
**retemper,** *v.t.*
**retest,** *v.t.*
**retest,** *n.*
**retestify,** *v.,* **-fied, -fying.**
**retexture,** *v.t.,* **-tured, -turing.**
**rethatch,** *v.t.*
**rethicken,** *v.*
**rethread,** *v.t.*
**rethreaten,** *v.t.*
**retie,** *v.t.,* **-tied, -tying.**

used for cooking, pickling, etc.

**red carpet** /– 'kapət/, *n.* **1.** a red strip of carpet laid for important persons to walk on when entering or leaving a building, etc. **2.** highly favoured or deferential treatment.

**red cedar** /– 'sidə/, *n.* **1.** a tree, *Toona australis,* native to New Guinea and eastern Australia, with easily worked red timber valued for cabinet work. **2.** any of several coniferous trees, esp. a juniper, *Juniperus virginiana,* with a fragrant reddish wood used for making pencils, etc., and an arbor vitae, *Thuja plicata,* both of North America. **3.** the wood of these trees.

**red clover** /– 'klouvə/, *n.* the common clover, *Trifolium pratense,* a leguminous plant with red flowers, widely cultivated as a forage plant.

**redcoat** /'rɛdkout/, *n.* (formerly) a British soldier.

**red cooking** /rɛd 'kukɪŋ/, *n.* a Chinese method of stewing meat or poultry in water, soya sauce, and seasonings.

**Red Cross** /rɛd 'krɒs/, *n.* **1.** an international philanthropic organisation (**Red Cross Society**) formed, in consequence of the Geneva Convention of 1864, to care for the sick and wounded in war, and secure the neutrality of nurses, hospitals, etc., and active also in relieving suffering occasioned by a pestilence, floods, fire, and other calamities. **2.** a branch of it: *the British Red Cross.* **3.** the English national emblem of St George's cross, which was also the emblem of the crusaders. **4.** →**Geneva cross.**

**redcurrant** /rɛd'kʌrənt/, *n.* **1.** the small, red, edible fruit of the shrub *Ribes sativum.* **2.** the shrub itself.

**red deer** /rɛd 'dɪə/, *n.* a species of deer, *Cervus elaphus,* native to the forests of Europe and Asia, and formerly very abundant in England.

**redden** /'rɛdn/, *v.t.* **1.** to make or cause to become red. *–v.i.* **2.** to become red. **3.** to blush; flush.

**reddendum** /rə'dɛndəm/, *n.* a clause specifying the rent in a lease. [L: gerund of *reddere* return]

**reddish** /'rɛdɪʃ/, *adj.* somewhat red; tending to red; tinged with red. – **reddishness,** *n.*

**reddle** /'rɛdl/, *n., v.,* **-led, -ling.** *–n.* **1.** →**raddle.** *–v.t.* **2.** to colour coarsely. **3.** →**raddle.** [var. of RUDDLE]

**red earth** /rɛd 'ɜθ/, *n.* a clayey, tropical soil formed by intensive chemical weathering, and usu. highly leached and coloured red by iron compounds.

**redeem** /rə'dim/, *v.t.* **1.** to buy or pay off; clear by payment: *to redeem a mortgage.* **2.** to buy back, as after a tax sale or a mortgage foreclosure. **3.** to recover (something pledged or mortgaged) by payment or other satisfaction: *to redeem a pawned watch.* **4.** to convert (paper money) into specie. **5.** to discharge or fulfil (a pledge, promise, etc.). **6.** to make up for; make amends for: *a redeeming feature.* **7.** to obtain the release or restoration of, as from captivity, by paying a ransom. **8.** *Theol.* to deliver from sin and its consequences by means of a sacrifice offered for the sinner. [late ME, from L *redēm-,* perfect of *redimere* buy back]

**redeemable** /rə'dimәbəl/, *adj.* **1.** capable of being redeemed. **2.** that is to be redeemed: *bonds redeemable in five years' time.* Also, **redemptible** /rə'dɛmptəbəl/. **–redeemably,** *adv.*

**redeemer** /rə'dimə/, *n.* **1.** one who redeems. **2.** (*cap.*) Jesus Christ.

**red emperor** /rɛd 'ɛmpərə/, *n.* a strikingly coloured bream-like fish, *Lutjanus sebae,* of the Great Barrier Reef waters, highly prized as a catch for eating.

**redemption** /rə'dɛmpʃən/, *n.* **1.** the act of redeeming. **2.** the state of being redeemed. **3.** deliverance; rescue. **4.** *Theol.* deliverance from sin and its penalties; salvation. **5.** repurchase, as of something sold. **6.** paying off, as of a mortgage, bond, or note. **7.** recovery by payment, as of something pledged. **8.** convertibility of paper money into specie. [ME *redempcio(u)n,* from L *redemptio,* from *redemptus,* pp. of *redimere* buy back]

**redemptive** /rə'dɛmptɪv/, *adj.* **1.** serving to redeem. **2.** denoting or pertaining to religions of which redemption is a major doctrine.

**redemptory** /rə'dɛmptəri/, *adj.* **1.** of or pertaining to redemption. **2.** →**redemptive.**

**red ensign** /rɛd 'ɛnsən/, *n.* **1.** the flag borne by all Australian-registered merchant vessels, consisting of five white stars of the Southern Cross and the white Commonwealth star on a red background with a Union Jack in canton. **2.** *Brit.* a flag borne by British-registered merchant ships consisting of a Union Jack in canton on a red background.

**redeploy** /ridə'plɔɪ/, *v.t.* **1.** to rearrange, reorganise, or transfer (a person, department, military unit, or the like), as in order to promote greater efficiency. *–v.i.* **2.** to carry out a reorganisation or rearrangement. – **redeployment,** *n.*

**redevelop** /ridə'vɛləp/, *v.t.* **1.** to develop (something) again. **2.** *Photog.* to intensify or tone by a second developing process. *–v.i.* **3.** to develop again. – **redeveloper,** *n.* – **redevelopment,** *n.*

**redevelopment area** /ridə'vɛləpmənt ˌɛəriə/, *n.* an urban area designated as being below certain sanitary and other standards and scheduled for improvement but not demolition.

**red-eye** /'rɛd-aɪ/, *n. Colloq.* a black cicada of eastern Australia, *Psaltoda moerens,* having ruby red eyes.

**red-faced** /'rɛd-feɪst/, *adj.* **1.** having a naturally red face. **2.** having a face reddened with embarrassment, anger, etc. – **red-facedly,** *adv.*

**redfed** /'rɛdfɛd/, *n. Colloq.* a socialist, leftist, unionist, etc. [from *red* a communist + *Fed(eration* of Labour) an early Australian trade union congress]

**Redfern** /'rɛdfən/, *n. in the phrase* **get off at Redfern,** *Colloq.* to practise coitus interruptus. [from *Redfern,* a railway station immediately before Central Railway Station, Sydney]

**redfin** /'rɛdfɪn/, *n.* **1.** (in Australia) the introduced English perch, *Perca fluviatilis.* **2.** (elsewhere) any of various small freshwater minnows with red fins, esp. a shiner, *Natropis umbratilis,* of eastern and central North America.

**red fir** /rɛd 'fɜ/, *n.* **1.** any of certain coniferous trees of the Northern Hemisphere as *Abies magnifica* and *Pseudotsuga*

---

**retile,** *v.t.,* **-tiled, -tiling.**
**retime,** *v.t.,* **-timed, -timing.**
**retint,** *v.t.*
**retitle,** *v.t.,* **-tled, -tling.**
**retool,** *v.*
**retotal,** *v.t.,* **-talled, -talling.**
**retrain,** *v.*
**retransfer,** *v.t.,* **-ferred, -ferring.**
**retranslate,** *v.t.,* **-lated, -lating.**
**retransmit,** *v.t.,* **-mitted, -mitting.**
**retransplant,** *v.t.*
**retrial,** *n.*
**retry,** *v.t.,* **-tried, -trying.**
**retune,** *v.t.*
**returf,** *v.t.*
**retwine,** *v.,* **-twined, -twining.**
**retwist,** *v.*
**retype,** *v.t.,* **-typed, -typing.**
**reunification,** *n.*
**reunify,** *v.t.,* **-fied, -fying.**
**reupholster,** *v.t.*
**reusable,** *adj.*
**reuse,** *v.t.,* **-used, -using.**
**reutilise,** *v.t.,* **-lised, -lising.**
**revaccinate,** *v.t.,* **-nated, -nating.**
**revaporise,** *v.,* **-rised, -rising.**
**revarnish,** *v.t.*
**revend,** *v.t.*
**reverify,** *v.t.,* **-fied, -fying.**
**reveto,** *v.,* **-toed, -toing.**
**revibrate,** *v.,* **-brated, -brating.**
**revictual,** *v.,* **-ualled, -ualling.**
**revindicate,** *v.t.,* **-cated, -cating.**
**reviolate,** *v.t.,* **-lated, -lating.**
**reviolation,** *n.*
**revisit,** *v.t.*
**revisitation,** *n.*
**revitalisation,** *n.*
**revitalise,** *v.t.,* **-lised, -lising.**
**revote,** *v.,* **-voted, -voting.**
**rewarm,** *v.t.*
**rewash,** *v.t.*
**rewater,** *v.t.*
**reweigh,** *v.t.*
**rewind,** *v.t.,* **-wound, -winding.**
**rework,** *v.t.,* **-worked** or **-wrought, -working.**
**rewrap,** *v.t.,* **-wrapped, -wrapping.**
**reyoke,** *v.t.,* **-yoked, -yoking.**

*taxifolia* of North America and *Larix potaninii* of China. **2.** their wood. **3.** →**Douglas fir.**

**red fire** /– 'faɪə/, *n.* any of various combustible preparations (as one containing strontium nitrate) burning with a vivid red light, used in pyrotechnic displays, signalling, etc.

**redfish** /'rɛdfɪʃ/, *n.* **1.** →**nannygai.** **2.** →**sockeye.**

**red flag** /rɛd 'flæg/, *n.* **1.** the recognised symbol of a socialist or revolutionary party. **2.** a socialist revolutionary song. **3.** a danger signal. **4.** something certain to arouse anger, etc.

**red giant** /– 'dʒaɪənt/, *n.* one of a class of stars in an intermediate stage of stellar evolution, characterised by a large volume and a low surface temperature.

**red goshawk** /– 'gɒshɔk/, *n.* a large hawk, *Erythrotriorchis radiatus,* brown tinged with cream, with cream head, throat, and red-brown underparts, found throughout northern and eastern Australia, and feeding on other birds and small ground animals. Also, **red buzzard, rufous-bellied buzzard.**

**red grouse** /– 'graʊs/, *n.* See **grouse**[1].

**red gum** /'– gʌm/, *n.* **1.** any tree of a group of species of the genus *Eucalyptus* with characteristic hard red timber as *E. tereticornis,* forest red gum of eastern Australia. **2.** a flowering gum of western Australia, *E. calophylla.*

**red-handed** /rɛd-'hændəd/, *adj., adv.* in the very act of a crime or other deed: *catch a thief red-handed.*

**red hat** /rɛd 'hæt/, *n.* **1.** the official hat of a cardinal. **2.** the office or dignity of a cardinal. **3.** →**cardinal.** **4.** *Mil. Colloq.* an officer of the rank of colonel and above.

**redhead** /'rɛdhɛd/, *n.* **1.** a person having red hair. **2.** the red-capped robin. See **robin.**

**red-headed** /'rɛd-hɛdəd/, *adj.* **1.** having red hair, as a person. **2.** having a red head, as a bird.

**red heat** /rɛd 'hit/, *n.* **1.** the temperature of a red-hot body. **2.** the condition of being red-hot.

**red herring** /– 'hɛrɪŋ/, *n.* **1.** something to divert attention; a false clue. **2.** a smoked herring.

**red-hot** /'rɛd-hɒt/, *adj.* **1.** red with heat; very hot. **2.** very excited or enthusiastic. **3.** violent; furious: *red-hot anger.* **4.** fresh; new; most recent: *a red-hot tip for a horserace.*

**red-hot poker** /– 'poʊkə/, *n.* any plant of the genus *Kniphofia,* frequently cultivated handsome perennial herbs from southern and eastern Africa, with rosettes of long leaves and tall erect spikes of colourful flowers.

**red hots** /rɛd 'hɒts/, *n.pl. Horseracing Colloq.* the trots. See **trot** (def. 10). [rhyming slang]

**redia** /'ridiə/, *n., pl.* **-diae** /-di,i/. larva produced asexually by previous larval stage of trematodes. Rediae reproduce giving rise to cercariae or to more rediae.

**Red Indian** /rɛd 'ɪndiən/, *n.* an aborigine of North America; Amerindian.

**redingote** /'rɛdɪŋgoʊt/, *n.* **1.** a full-length double-breasted coat with skirts sometimes cut away in front. **2.** a man's outer coat of similar cut, worn in the 18th century. [F, from E *riding coat*]

redingote

**redintegrate** /rə'dɪntəgreɪt/, *v.t.,* **-grated, -grating.** to make whole again; restore to a perfect state; renew; re-establish. [L *redintegrātus,* pp. See REINTEGRATE] – **redintegrative** /rə'dɪntəgreɪtɪv, -grətɪv/, *adj.*

**redintegration** /rədɪntə'greɪʃən/, *n.* **1.** the act or process of redintegrating. **2.** *Psychol.* the tendency, when a response has occurred to a complex stimulus, to make that same response later to any part of that stimulus.

**redirect** /ridə'rɛkt/, *v.t.* **1.** to direct again. **2.** to readdress. *–adj.* **3.** *U.S. Law.* →**re-examine** (def. 2). – **redirection,** *n.*

**rediscount** /,ri'dɪskaʊnt/, *v.t.* **1.** to discount again. *–n.* **2.** an act of rediscounting. **3.** (*usu. pl.*) commercial paper which is discounted a second time.

**redistribute** /ridə'strɪbjut/, *v.t.,* **-buted, -buting. 1.** to distribute again in a different way. **2.** to change the shape and size of an electorate thereby changing the number of electors in it and surrounding electorates; ideally it is the means used to ensure that electorates are drawn so as to reflect the principle that all votes have equal value. – **redistribution** /,ridɪstrə'bjuʃən/, *n.*

**red kangaroo** /rɛd kæŋgə'ru/, *n.* a large, slender-bodied kangaroo, *Megaleia rufa,* widely distributed throughout the plains and grasslands of inland Australia. The males may be up to 1.80 metres in height and measure 2.5 metres from muzzle to tail tip. Also, **plains kangaroo.**

**red lead** /– 'lɛd/, *n.* a heavy, earthy substance, $Pb_3O_4$, orange to red in colour, used as a paint pigment and in the manufacture of glass and glazes; minium.

**red-lead ore** /rɛd-lɛd 'ɔ/, *n.* →**crocoite.**

**red-letter day** /rɛd-'lɛtə deɪ/, *n.* **1.** a day marked by red letters in the Church calendar, on which judges wear red robes. **2.** a memorable or especially happy occasion: *a red-letter day for someone.*

**red light** /rɛd 'laɪt/, *n.* **1.** a red lamp, used as a signal to mean 'stop'. **2.** an order to stop. **3.** a warning signal. **4.** the symbol of a brothel.

**red-light district** /rɛd-'laɪt dɪstrɪkt/, *n.* a neighbourhood with many brothels, sometimes, esp. formerly, indicated by red lights.

**red man** /'rɛd mæn/, *n.* a North American Indian.

**red meat** /'– mit/, *n.* meat that is dark-coloured, as beef, lamb, venison, etc. (distinguished from *white meat*).

**red mite** /– 'maɪt/, *n.* a common mite, *Dermanyssus gallinae,* of domestic and wild birds in temperate regions.

**red mullet** /– 'mʌlət/, *n.* a common food fish, *Mullus surmuletus,* of European waters, esp. the Mediterranean.

**redneck** /'rɛdnɛk/, *n. U.S. Colloq.* (*derog.*) a southern U.S. white farm labourer, esp. one who is ill-educated or ignorant.

**red-necked avocet** /rɛd-nɛkt 'ævəsɛt/, *n.* an avocet native to Australia, *Recurvirostra novaehollandiae,* with a bright chestnut head and neck, white body and black wing tips, found in salty or brackish marshes or tidal inlets. Also, **Australian avocet.**

**red-necked stint** /– 'stɪnt/, *n.* a small migratory shorebird, *Calidris ruficollis,* mottled grey to brown, with white underparts and black tail, beak and legs, and marked with a deep salmon pink in its breeding plumage.

**red-necked wallaby** /– 'wɒləbi/, *n.* →**red wallaby.**

**red ned** /rɛd 'nɛd/, *n. Colloq.* cheap red wine.

**redness** /'rɛdnəs/, *n.* the quality or state of being red.

**red oak** /rɛd 'oʊk/, *n.* **1.** any of several oak trees, as *Quercus borealis,* common to North America. **2.** the hard cross-grained wood of these trees.

**red ochre** /– 'oʊkə/, *n.* any of the red natural earths, mixtures of haematites, which are used as pigments.

**redolent** /'rɛdələnt/, *adj.* **1.** having a pleasant smell; fragrant. **2.** odorous or smelling (fol. by *of*). **3.** suggestive; reminiscent (fol. by *of*): *stories redolent of mystery.* [ME, from L *redolens,* ppr., giving back a smell] – **redolence,** *n.* – **redolently,** *adv.*

**redouble** /ri'dʌbəl/, *v.,* **-led, -ling,** *n. –v.t.* **1.** to double or increase greatly: *to redouble one's efforts.* **2.** to repeat: *to redouble an attack.* **3.** to echo or re-echo. **4.** *Bridge.* to double the double of (an opponent). *–v.i.* **5.** to be doubled; become greatly increased. **6.** to be echoed; resound. **7.** *Bridge.* to double the double of an opponent. *–n.* **8.** *Bridge.* the act of doubling one's opponent's double. [late ME, from F *redoubler*]

**redoublement** /ri'dʌbəlmənt/, *n.* (in fencing) an attack immediately following one that has failed but which has not brought a riposte.

**redoubt** /rə'daʊt/, *n.* **1.** an isolated work forming a complete enclosure of any form used to defend a prominent point. **2.** an independent earthwork built within a permanent fortification to reinforce it. [F *redoute,* from It. *ridotto,* from LL *reductus* a refuge, L, pp., retired; with intrusive *-b-* due to association with REDOUBTABLE]

**redoubtable** /rə'daʊtəbəl/, *adj.* **1.** that is to be feared; formidable. **2.** commanding respect. [ME *redoutable,* from OF, from *redouter* fear, from *douter* DOUBT] – **redoubtableness,** *n.* – **redoubtably,** *adv.*

**redoubted** /rə'daʊtəd/, *adj.* **1.** dreaded; formidable. **2.** respected; renowned.

**redound** /rə'daʊnd/, *v.i.* **1.** to have an effect or result, as to the advantage, disadvantage, credit, or discredit of a person or thing. **2.** to result or accrue, as to a person. **3.** to come back or recoil, as upon a person. **4.** to proceed, issue, or arise. *–v.t.* **5.** *Archaic.* to reflect; cast: *to redound dishonour on someone's head.* *–n.* **6.** the fact of redounding or resulting. [ME *redounde,* from OF *redonder,* from L *redundāre* overflow]

**redowa** /ˈrɛdəvə, -wə/, *n.* a Bohemian dance in two forms, the more common resembling the waltz or the mazurka, the other resembling the polka. [G, from Czech *reydovák,* from *reydovati* turn or whirl round]

**redox** /ˈridɒks/, *adj.* →**reduction-oxidation.**

**red pencil** /rɛd ˈpɛnsəl/, *n.* a pencil with red lead.

**red-pencil** /rɛd-ˈpɛnsəl/, *v.t.*, **-cilled, -cilling** or (*U.S.*) **-ciled, -ciling.** to correct or edit manuscript or typescript with or as with a red pencil.

**red pepper** /rɛd ˈpɛpə/, *n.* **1.** the condiment cayenne. **2.** any of the hot peppers, *Capsicum frutescens* and botanical varieties, the yellow or red pods of which are used for flavouring, sauces, etc.

**red peril** /– ˈpɛrəl/, *n. Colloq.* the threatened expansion of communism.

**red phone** /ˈ– foun/, *n.* a public telephone, always coloured red, located in shops, arcades, etc.

**red pine** /– ˈpaɪn/, *n.* →**rimu.**

**redpoll** /ˈrɛdpoul/, *n.* **1.** any of various small fringilline birds of the genus *Acanthis,* the adults of which usu. have a crimson crown patch, such as the **lesser redpoll,** *A. flammea,* of Europe, including Britain. **2.** (*cap.*) one of a breed of polled red, good-quality beef and milk cattle, having a coat of short hair.

**redraft** /ˈridraft/, *n.;* /ˌriˈdraft/, *v.* *–n.* **1.** a second draft or drawing. **2.** *Comm.* a draft on the drawer or endorser of a dishonoured and protested bill of exchange for the amount of the bill plus the costs and charges. *–v.t.* **3.** to make a second draft of.

**red rag** /rɛd ˈræg/, *n.* something that excites a person's anger or passion: *like a red rag to a bull.*

**re-dress** /ˌri-ˈdrɛs/, *v.t., v.i.* to dress again.

**redress** /rəˈdrɛs/, *n.* **1.** the setting right of what is wrong: *redress of abuses.* **2.** relief from wrong or injury. **3.** compensation for wrong or injury. *–v.t.* **4.** to set right; remedy or repair (wrongs, injuries, etc.). **5.** to correct or reform (abuses, evils, etc.). **6.** to remedy or relieve (suffering, want, etc.). **7.** to adjust evenly again, as a balance. [ME *redresse,* from F. See RE-, DRESS] – **redresser, redressor,** *n.*

**red rock cod,** *n.* a common scorpaenid fish, *Scorpaena cardinalis,* occurring on rocky and weedy foreshores of the east coast of Australia.

**Red Sea** /rɛd ˈsi/, *n.* a long narrow arm of the Indian Ocean, between Africa and Arabia.

**red setter** /rɛd ˈsɛtə/, *n.* a variety of Irish setter.

**redshank** /ˈrɛdʃæŋk/, *n.* either of two wading birds of the genus *Tringa,* as the **common redshank,** *T. totanus,* or **spotted redshank,** *T. erythio.*

**red shift** /ˈrɛd ʃɪft/, *n.* a shift of spectral lines toward the red end of the visible spectrum in the light emitted by a receding celestial body; thought to be a consequence of the Doppler effect. Cf. **blue shift.**

**red shirt** /– ˈʃɜt/, *n.* (formerly) a flogged back: *to give a convict a red shirt.*

**red-short** /ˈrɛd-ʃɔt/, *adj.* brittle when at a red heat, as iron or steel containing too much sulphur. [Swed. *rödskört* neut. of *rödskör,* from *röd* red + *skör* brittle]

**redskin** /ˈrɛdskɪn/, *n., adj.* North American Indian.

**red squirrel** /rɛd ˈskwɪrəl/, *n.* a reddish arboreal rodent, *Sciurus vulgaris* (family Sciuridae), of Europe and northern and central Asia.

**redstart** /ˈrɛdstat/, *n.* a small European bird, *Phoenicurus phoenicurus,* with reddish brown tail. [RED + *start* tail, OE *steort*]

**red steer** /rɛd ˈstɪə/, *n. Colloq.* a bushfire.

**red tape** /– ˈteɪp/, *n.* **1.** tape of a reddish colour, much used for tying up official papers. **2.** excessive attention to formality and routine. – **red-tape,** *adj.*

**red throat** /ˈ– θrout/, *n.* a wren-like bird, *Pyrrholaemus brunneus,* of central Australia, the male of the species being olive-brown with grey underparts and a pale chestnut or cinnamon brown throat.

**reduce** /rəˈdjus/, *v.*, **-duced, -ducing.** *–v.t.* **1.** to bring down to a smaller extent, size, amount, number, etc. **2.** to lower in degree, intensity, etc.: *to reduce speed.* **3.** to bring down to a lower rank, dignity, etc. **4.** to lower in price. **5.** to bring to a certain state, condition, arrangement, etc.: *to reduce glass to powder, reduce a person to tears.* **6.** to bring under control or authority; subdue. **7.** *Photog.* to treat so as to make less dense, as a negative. **8.** to adjust or correct by making allowances, as an astronomical observation. **9.** *Maths.* to change the denomination or form of. **10.** *Chem.* **a.** →**deoxidise. b.** to add hydrogen to. **c.** to change (a compound) so that the valency of the positive element is lower. **11.** *Chem., Metall.* to bring into the metallic state by separating from non-metallic constituents; smelt. **12.** to lower the proof of wines or spirits by adding water. **13.** to thin (paints, etc.) with oil or turpentine. **14.** *Biol.* to cause (a cell) to undergo meiotic division. **15.** *Surg.* to restore to the normal place, relations, or condition, as a dislocated organ or a fractured bone with separation of the fragment ends. *–v.i.* **16.** to become reduced. [ME, from L *redūcere* bring back, restore, replace] – **reducible,** *adj.* – **reducibility** /rədjusəˈbɪləti/, *n.* – **reducibly,** *adv.*

**reduced** /rəˈdjust/, *adj.* that is or has been reduced.

**reducer** /rəˈdjusə/, *n.* **1.** one who or that which reduces. **2.** *Photog.* **a.** an oxidising solution used to reduce a negative in density. **b.** a developing agent. **3.** *Bldg Trades.* a special fitting for connecting pipes of varying diameter.

**reducing agent** /rəˈdjusɪŋ eɪdʒənt/, *n.* a substance that causes another substance to undergo reduction and is oxidised in the process.

**reductase** /rəˈdʌkteɪz, -teɪs/, *n.* any enzyme that catalyses a chemical reaction. [REDUCT(ION) + -ASE]

**reductio ad absurdum,** *n.* a reduction to an absurdity; the refutation of a proposition by demonstrating the absurd inevitable conclusion to which it would logically lead. [L]

**reduction** /rəˈdʌkʃən/, *n.* **1.** the act of reducing. **2.** the state of being reduced. **3.** the amount by which something is reduced or diminished. **4.** a form produced by reducing; a copy on a smaller scale. **5.** →**meiosis. 6.** *Chem.* the converse of oxidation. [L *reductio*] – **reductional,** *adj.* – **reductive,** *adj.*

**reductionism** /rəˈdʌkʃənɪzəm/, *n.* the tendency to make supposedly comprehensive explanations of complex phenomena simply by analysing and describing their parts. – **reductionist,** *n.*

**reduction-oxidation** /rəˌdʌkʃən-ɒksəˈdeɪʃən/, *n.* **1.** a reaction in which one substance is reduced (def. 10) and another is oxidised (def. 4). *–adj.* **2.** of or pertaining to such a reaction.

**reduction print** /rəˈdʌkʃən prɪnt/, *n.* (in filming) a print of narrower gauge than the master copy from which it is made.

**reduction sale** /ˈ– seɪl/, *n.* a special sale held on a property, usu. to sell surplus stock and plant.

**reductor** /rəˈdʌktə/, *n.* a tube with a stopcock at one end, filled with granulated zinc, for reducing iron to a ferrous state for analysis.

**redundancy** /rəˈdʌndənsi/, *n., pl.* **-cies. 1.** the state of being redundant. **2.** a redundant thing, part, or amount; a superfluity. **3.** the payment made to a redundant employee. Also, **redundance.**

**redundant** /rəˈdʌndənt/, *adj.* **1.** being in excess; exceeding what is usual or natural: *a redundant part.* **2.** characterised by or using too many words to express ideas: *a redundant style.* **3.** denoting or pertaining to an employee who is or becomes superfluous to the needs of his employer. **4.** having some unusual or extra part or feature. **5.** characterised by superabundance or superfluity. **6.** *Electronics.* of or pertaining to elements in a system which are not normally used, but come into operation if an active element fails. **7.** *Engineering.* (of a structure) having members which do not have a force acting through them. [L *redundans,* ppr., overflowing] – **redundantly,** *adv.*

**reduplicate** /riˈdjupləkeɪt/, *v.*, **-cated, -cating;** /rəˈdjupləkət/, *adj.* *–v.t.* **1.** to double; repeat. **2.** *Gram.* to form (a derivative or inflected form) by doubling a specified syllable or other portion of the primitive, sometimes with fixed modifications, as in Greek *léloipa* 'I have left'; *leípo* 'I leave'.

–*v.i.* **3.** to become doubled. **4.** *Gram.* to become reduplicated. –*adj.* **5.** doubled. **6.** *Bot.* valvate, with the edges folded back so as to project outwards. [LL *reduplicātus,* pp., doubled]

**reduplication** /rədjupləˈkeɪʃən/, *n.* **1.** the act of reduplicating. **2.** the state of being reduplicated. **3.** something resulting from reduplicating. **4.** *Gram.* **a.** reduplicating as a grammatical pattern. **b.** the added element in a reduplicated form. **c.** a form containing a reduplicated element.

**reduplicative** /rəˈdjupləkeɪtɪv, -kətɪv/, *adj.* **1.** tending to reduplicate. **2.** pertaining to or marked by reduplication. **3.** →**reduplicate.**

**red valerian** /rɛd vəˈlɪəriən/, *n.* an erect perennial herb with dense heads of small, spurred, red (rarely pink or white) flowers, *Centranthus ruber,* native to southern Europe and Asia Minor, but widely naturalised elsewhere.

**red wallaby** /– ˈwɒləbi/, *n.* an eastern Australian wallaby, *Macropus rufogriseus,* greyish in colour, with red-tinged shoulders and rump and a whitish face-stripe; brush kangaroo. Also, **red-necked wallaby, rufous wallaby.**

**redwater fever** /ˌrɛdwɔtə ˈfivə/, *n.* →**tick fever.**

**redwing** /ˈrɛdwɪŋ/, *n.* a European thrush, *Turdus musicus,* having chestnut-red flank and axillary feathers.

**redwood** /ˈrɛdwʊd/, *n.* **1.** a coniferous tree, *Sequoia sempervirens,* of the south-western U.S., esp. California, remarkable for its height. **2.** its valuable brownish red timber. **3.** a red-coloured wood. **4.** any of various trees with a reddish wood. **5.** any tree whose wood produces a red dyestuff. **6.** the wood of such a tree.

**re-echo** /ri-ˈɛkoʊ/, *v.,* **-echoed, -echoing,** *n., pl.* **-echoes.** –*v.i.* **1.** to echo back, as a sound. **2.** to give back an echo; resound. –*v.t.* **3.** to echo back. **4.** to repeat like an echo. –*n.* **5.** a repeated echo.

**reed** /rid/, *n.* **1.** the straight stalk of any of various tall grasses, esp. of the genera *Phragmites* and *Arundo,* growing in marshy places. **2.** the stalk of *Phragmites.* **3.** any of the plants themselves. **4.** such stalks or plants collectively. **5.** anything made from such a stalk or from something similar, as an arrow. **6.** *Music.* **a.** a pastoral or rustic musical pipe made from a reed or from the hollow stalk of some other plant. **b.** a small flexible piece of cane of metal which, attached to the mouths of some wind instruments **(reed instruments),** is set into vibration by a stream of air and, in turn, sets into vibration the air column enclosed in the tube of the instrument. **c.** any instrument with such a device, as the oboe, clarinet, etc. **7.** *Archit., Carp., etc.* a small convex moulding. **8.** (in a loom) the series of parallel strips of wires which force the weft up to the web and separate the threads of the warp. **9. broken reed,** one who is too weak to be relied upon. –*v.t.* **10.** to decorate with reed. **11.** to thatch with or as with reed. [ME; OE *hrēod,* c. D *riet* and G *Riet*]

**reedbird** /ˈridbɜd/, *n.* the American bobolink.

**reedbuck** /ˈridbʌk/, *n., pl.* **-bucks,** (*esp. collectively*) **-buck.** any of various yellowish African antelopes, genus *Redunca,* about the size of a small deer. The males have short, forward-curving horns. [translation of Afrikaans *rietbok*]

**reed grass** /ˈrid gras/, *n.* a widespread, waterside grass, *Phalaris arundinacea,* with flowers in dense cylindrical clusters. Also, **reed canary grass.**

**reeding** /ˈridɪŋ/, *n.* **1.** a small convex or semicylindrical moulding, resembling a reed. **2.** a set of such mouldings, as on a column, where they resemble small convex fluting. **3.** ornamentation consisting of such mouldings. **4.** vertical grooves on the edge of a coin. [REED, *v.* + -ING[1]]

**reedling** /ˈridlɪŋ/, *n.* a small European bird, *Panurus biarmicus,* frequenting reedy places, and characterised in the male by a tuft of black feathers on each side of the chin; bearded tit. [REED, *n.* + -LING[1]]

**reed mace** /ˈrid meɪs/, *n.* any species of plant of the genus *Typha;* cumbungi.

**reed organ** /ˈ– ɔgən/, *n.* a musical keyboard instrument resembling the pipe organ but having the notes produced by small metal reeds.

**reed pipes** /ˈ– paɪps/, *n.pl.* the pipes of a reed organ.

**reedstop** /ˈridstɒp/, *n.* a set of reed pipes (opposed to *flue-stop*).

**re-educate** /ri-ˈɛdʒəkeɪt/, *v.t.,* **-cated, -cating.** **1.** to educate again. **2.** to educate for resumption of normal activities, as a person handicapped by accident or disease; rehabilitate. – **re-education** /ri-ˌɛdʒəˈkeɪʃən/, *n.*

**reedwarbler** /ˈridwɔblə/, *n.* **1.** a small warbler of the family Sylviidae, *Acrocephalus stentoreus,* inhabiting freshwater reedy areas throughout Australia, New Guinea and islands to the north. **2.** a small old world warbler, *A. scirpaceus,* inhabiting marshy places.

**reedy** /ˈridi/, *adj.,* **reedier, reediest.** **1.** full of reeds. **2.** consisting or made of a reed or reeds: *a reedy pipe.* **3.** like a reed or reeds: *reedy grass.* **4.** denoting or having a tone like that of a reed instrument. – **reediness,** *n.*

**reef**[1] /rif/, *n.* **1.** a narrow ridge of rocks or sand, often of coral debris, at or near the surface of water. **2.** *Mining.* a lode or vein. [earlier *riff(e),* from D or LG *rif,* from Scand.; cf. Icel. *rif* rib, reef]

reef[1]: Great Barrier Reef

**reef**[2] /rif/, *n.* **1.** a part of a sail which is rolled and tied down to reduce the area exposed to the wind. –*v.t.* **2.** to shorten (sail) by tying in one or more reefs. **3.** to reduce the length of (a topmast, a bowsprit, etc.), as by lowering, sliding inboard, or the like. –*v.i.* **4.** (of a horse) to throw its head up, thereby pulling against the reins. [ME *riff,* from Scand.; cf. Icel. *rif* rib, reef]

**reef**[3] /rif/, *v.t. Colloq.* **1.** to remove, usu. by force (fol. by *out*). **2.** to steal (fol. by *off*).

**reef band** /ˈ– bænd/, *n.* a strip of canvas stitched over a sail to strengthen it where the reef points are secured.

**reef claim** /ˈ– kleɪm/, *n.* a mining claim on a quartz reef.

**reefer**[1] /ˈrifə/, *n.* **1.** *Naut.* one who reefs. **2.** Also, **reefer jacket.** a short coat or jacket of thick cloth. [REEF[2] + -ER[1]]

**reefer**[2] /ˈrifə/, *n. Colloq.* a marijuana cigarette. [same as REEF[2], in generalised sense of rolled object]

**reefer**[3] /ˈrifə/, *n.* a miner working a reef. [REEF[1] (def. 2) + -ER[1]]

**reefer**[4] /ˈrifə/, *n.* **1.** a refrigerator. **2.** a motor vehicle, railroad freight car, shop, aircraft, or other conveyance, so constructed and insulated as to protect commodities from either heat or cold. [short for REFRIGERATOR]

**reef knot** /ˈrif nɒt/, *n.* a kind of knot, so called because it is used in tying reef points.

**reef point** /ˈ– pɔɪnt/, *n.* a short piece of line fastened through a sail, used to tie in a reef.

**reek** /rik/, *n.* **1.** a strong, unpleasant smell. **2.** vapour or steam. –*v.i.* **3.** to smell strongly and unpleasantly. **4.** to be strongly pervaded with something unpleasant or offensive. **5.** to give off steam, smoke, etc. **6.** to be wet with sweat, blood, etc. –*v.t.* **7.** to expose to or treat with smoke. **8.** to emit (smoke, fumes, etc.). [ME *rek(e),* OE *rēc,* c. G *Rauch*] – **reeker,** *n.* – **reeky,** *adj.*

**reel**[1] /ril/, *n.* **1.** a cylinder, frame, or other device, turning on an axis, on which to wind something. **2.** a rotatory device attached to a fishing rod at the butt, for winding up or letting out the line. **3.** a small cylinder of wood or other material, now typically expanded at each end and having a hole lengthwise through the centre, on which thread is wound. **4.** a quantity of something wound on a reel. **5. a.** the spool, usu. metal, on which film is wound. **b.** a roll of celluloid bearing a series of photographs to be exhibited with a film projector. **c.** the standard length of cinema film for projection (about 300 metres). **6.** a rotatory spool of line used by surf-lifesavers. –*v.t.* **7.** to wind on a reel, as thread, yarn, etc. **8.** to draw with a reel, or by winding: *to reel in a fish.* **9.** to say, write, or produce in an easy, continuous way (fol. by *off*). [ME *rele,* OE *hrēol*] – **reeler,** *n.*

**reel**[2] /ril/, *v.i.* **1.** to sway or rock under a blow, shock, etc.: *to reel under a heavy blow.* **2.** to fall back; waver, as troops. **3.** to sway about in standing or walking, as from dizziness, intoxication, etc.; stagger. **4.** to turn round and round; whirl. **5.** to have a sensation of whirling: *his brain reeled.* –*v.t.* **6.** to cause to reel. –*n.* **7.** the act of reeling; a reeling or staggering movement. [ME *rele(n)*, from *rele* REEL[1]]

**reel**[3] /ril/, *n.* **1.** a lively dance popular in Scotland. **2.** music for this. [special use of REEL[2] (def. 7)]

**reelman** /ˈrilmən/, *n.* the member of a surf-lifesaving team who handles the reel.

**reel-to-reel** /ril-tə-ˈril/, *n.* **1.** a tape recorder which uses reels of tape rather than cassettes or cartridges. *–adj.* **2.** of or pertaining to such a system of recording.

**re-enforce** /ri-ənˈfɔs/, *v.t.*, **-forced, -forcing.** to enforce again.

**re-enter** /ri-ˈɛntə/, *v.t.* **1.** to come or go into again. **2.** to record again, as in a list or account. *–v.i.* **3.** to come or go into again. **– re-entrance,** *n.*

**re-entrant** /ri-ˈɛntrənt/, *adj.* **1.** pointing inwards: *a re-entrant angle.* *–n.* **2.** a re-entrant angle or part.

**re-entrant angle** /– ˈæŋgəl/, *n.* an angle directed back inwards, rather than extending outwards, as an exterior angle of less than 180° in a closed polygon.

R, re-entrant angle

**re-entrant polygon** /– ˈpɒlɪgɒn/, *n.* a polygon having one or more re-entrant angles.

**re-entry** /ri-ˈɛntri/, *n., pl.* **-tries.** **1.** the act of re-entering. **2.** *Law.* the retaking of possession under a right reserved in a prior conveyance. **3.** Also, **re-entry card.** *Whist and Bridge.* a card which will win a trick and thereby permit one to take the lead once again. **4.** *Aeron.* the return of a spacecraft, rocket, etc., into the earth's atmosphere. **5.** *Print., esp. Philatelic Printing.* the rectifying of an unsatisfactory plate by re-entering the appropriate section of the design. **6.** a surfing manoeuvre in which the surfer heads up into, and comes over with, the breaking part of the wave. *–adj.* **7.** of or pertaining to re-entry.

**re-entry vehicle** /ˈ– ˌviɪkəl/, *n.* that part of a space vehicle designed to re-enter the earth's atmosphere.

**reeve**[1] /riv/, *n.* **1.** *Hist.* an administrative officer of a town or district. **2.** *Hist.* one of high rank representing the crown. **3.** a bailiff, steward, or overseer. [ME *ireve*, OE *gerēfa* high official, lit., head of a *rōf* array, number (of soldiers)]

**reeve**[2] /riv/, *v.t.*, **reeved** or **rove, reeving.** **1.** to pass (a rope, etc.) through a hole, ring, or the like. **2.** to fasten by placing through or around something. **3.** to pass a rope through (a block, etc.). [? D *rēven* REEF[2]]

**reeve**[3] /riv/, *n.* the female of the European ruff, *Philomachus pugnax.*

**re-examine** /ri-əgˈzæmən/, *v.t.*, **-ined, -ining.** **1.** to examine again. **2.** *Law.* to examine (a witness) again after he has been cross-examined by the other party's advocate. **– re-examination** /ri-əgˌzæməˈneɪʃən/, *n.* **– re-examiner,** *n.*

**re-export** /ri-əksˈpɔt/, *v.*; /ri-ˈɛkspɔt/, *n.* *–v.t.* **1.** to export again, as imported goods. *–n.* **2.** a re-exporting. **3.** that which is re-exported. **– re-exportation** /ˌriɛkspɔˈteɪʃən/, *n.*

**ref** /rɛf/, *n. Colloq.* referee.

**ref.,** reference.

**reface** /ˌriˈfeɪs/, *v.t.*, **-faced, -facing.** **1.** to renew, restore, or repair the face or surface of (buildings, stone, etc.). **2.** to provide (a garment, etc.) with a new facing.

**refection** /rəˈfɛkʃən/, *n.* **1.** refreshment, esp. with food or drink. **2.** a portion of food or drink; repast. [ME, from L *refectio*]

**refectory** /rəˈfɛktri/, *n., pl.* **-ries.** a dining hall in a religious house, a university or other institution. [ML *refectōrium*, from L *reficere* restore]

**refectory table** /ˈ– teɪbəl/, *n.* a long, narrow, wooden dining table supported on two pillar-like legs.

**refer** /rəˈfɜ/, *v.*, **-ferred, -ferring.** *–v.t.* **1.** to direct the attention or thoughts of: *the asterisk refers the reader to a footnote.* **2.** to direct for information or for anything required: *to refer students to books on a subject.* **3.** to return (a thesis, examination paper or the like) to a candidate in order that he may improve the thesis, retake the examination, etc., in order to reach the required standard. **4.** to allow (a candidate) who did not reach the required standard in an examination, etc., to take it again. **5.** to hand over or submit for information, consideration, decision, etc.: *to refer a cause to arbitration.* **6.** to assign to a class, period, etc.; regard as belonging or related. *–v.i.* **7.** to direct attention, as a reference mark does. **8.** to direct anyone for information, esp. about one's character, abilities, etc.: *to refer to a former employer.* **9.** to have relation; relate; apply. **10.** to have recourse or resort; turn, as for aid or information: *to refer to one's notes.* **11.** to direct a remark or mention; make reference or allusion, as a speaker or writer does. [ME *referre*, from L: lit., carry back] **– referable,** *adj.* **– referral,** *n.* **– referrer,** *n.*

**referee** /rɛfəˈri/, *n., v.*, **-reed, -reeing.** *–n.* **1.** one to whom something is referred, esp. for decision or settlement; arbitrator; umpire. **2.** a judge in certain games having functions fixed by the rules. **3.** *Law.* **a.** a person selected by a court to take testimony in a case and return it to the court with recommendations as to the decision. **b.** a person selected to hear and decide controversies pending before administrative agencies. **4.** →**reference** (def. 8). *–v.t.* **5.** to preside over as referee; act as referee in. *–v.i.* **6.** to act as referee.

**reference** /ˈrɛfrəns/, *n.* **1.** the act or fact of referring. **2.** direction of the attention: *marks of reference.* **3.** a mention; allusion. **4.** a direction in a book or writing to some book, passage, etc.: *to look up a reference.* **5.** a note indicating this. **6.** direction or a direction to some source of information. **7.** use or recourse for purposes of information: *a library for public reference.* **8.** a person to whom one refers for testimony as to one's character, abilities, etc. **9.** a written testimonial as to character, abilities, etc. **10.** relation, regard, or respect: *all persons, without reference to age.* **11.** *Law.* **a.** the proceedings before a referee. **b.** the act of submitting a matter to a referee for investigation or judgment. **12.** See **frame of reference.** **13. terms of reference,** the scope allowed to an investigating body. **14. with reference to,** concerning; with regard to.

**reference book** /ˈ– bʊk/, *n.* a publication consulted to identify certain facts or for background information, as an encyclopaedia, dictionary, atlas, etc.

**reference group** /ˈ– grup/, *n.* **1.** a group or class of persons with which an individual wishes to conform and which sanctions attitudes and standards of behaviour. **2.** a group which is used as a standard for the purposes of self-perception.

**reference library** /ˈ– laɪbri/, *n.* a library of reference books which may be consulted but generally not borrowed or taken away.

**reference mark** /ˈ– mak/, *n.* a sign as *, †, etc., used in a publication to direct the reader's attention from the text to a footnote.

**referendum** /rɛfəˈrɛndəm/, *n., pl.* **-da** /-də/, **-dums.** **1.** the principle or procedure of referring or submitting measures proposed or passed by a legislative body to the vote of the electorate for approval or rejection. **2.** an instance of this procedure. [L, gerund (or neut. gerundive) of *referre* refer]

**referent** /ˈrɛfərənt/, *n.* **1.** *Rhet., Semantics.* **a.** the object to which a term of discourse refers. **b.** the object of thought, alternatively as viewed by the thinker or by a supposedly all-knowing mind. **2.** *Logic.* any related term from which the relation proceeds. For example, in 'John loves Mary', *John* is the referent.

**referred pain** /rəfɜd ˈpeɪn/, *n.* pain felt in some part of the body other than the part actually affected or irritated.

**reffo** /ˈrɛfoʊ/, *n. Colloq.* a refugee, esp. one arriving in Australia before World War II. Also, **refo.** [shortened form of REFUGEE]

**refill** /ˌriˈfɪl/, *v.*; /ˈrifɪl/, *n.* *–v.t.* **1.** to fill again. *–n.* **2.** the material replacing a used-up product which was in an original purchase: *a refill for a lipstick.* **3.** any instance of filling again: *give me your glass and I'll get you a refill.* **– refillable** /ˌriˈfɪləbəl/, *adj.*

**re-finance** /ˌri-ˈfaɪnæns/, *v.*, **-nanced, -nancing.** *–v.i.* **1.** to borrow money in order to meet maturing liabilities. *–v.t.* **2.** to provide (a company, enterprise, etc.) with money borrowed in order to meet its maturing liabilities.

**refine** /rəˈfaɪn/, *v.*, **-fined, -fining.** *–v.t.* **1.** to bring to a fine or a pure state; free from impurities: *to refine metal, sugar, petroleum, etc.* **2.** to purify from what is coarse, vulgar, or debasing; make elegant or cultured. **3.** to bring by purifying, as to a finer state or form. **4.** to make more fine, nice, subtle, or minutely precise. *–v.i.* **5.** to become pure. **6.** to become more fine, elegant, or polished. **7.** to make fine distinctions in thought or language. **8. refine on** or **upon, a.** to reason or discourse on with subtlety. **b.** to improve on by superior fineness, excellence, etc. [RE- + FINE[1], *v.*] – **refiner,** *n.*

**refined** /rə'faɪnd/, *adj.* **1.** imbued with or showing nice feeling, taste, etc.: *refined people.* **2.** freed or free from coarseness, vulgarity, etc.: *refined taste.* **3.** freed from impurities: *refined sugar.* **4.** subtle: *refined distinctions.* **5.** minutely precise; exact.

**refinement** /rə'faɪnmənt/, *n.* **1.** fineness of feeling, taste, etc. **2.** elegance of manners or language. **3.** an instance of refined feeling, manners, etc. **4.** the act of refining. **5.** the state of being refined. **6.** improvement on something else. **7.** an instance or result of this. **8.** a subtle point or distinction. **9.** subtle reasoning. **10.** an improved, higher, or extreme form of something.

**refinery** /rə'faɪnəri/, *n., pl.* **-eries.** an establishment for refining something, as metal, sugar, petroleum, etc.

**refit** /ri'fɪt/, *v.,* **-fitted, -fitting;** /'rifɪt/, *n.* *–v.t.* **1.** to fit, prepare, or equip again. *–v.i.* **2.** to renew supplies or equipment. **3.** to get refitted. *–n.* **4.** the act of refitting.

**refl.,** **1.** reflection. **2.** reflective. **3.** reflex. **4.** reflexive.

**reflate** /ri'fleɪt/, *v.,* **-flated, -flating.** *–v.i.* **1.** to increase the amount of money and credit in circulation by relaxing government controls over economic restriction. *–v.t.* **2.** to increase (money and credit) again by relaxing government controls over restrictions.

**reflation** /ri'fleɪʃən/, *n.* the relaxation of government controls over economic restrictions, with a view to improving a country's economy.

**reflect** /rə'flɛkt/, *v.t.* **1.** to cast back (light, heat, sound, etc.) after incidence. **2.** to give back or show an image of; mirror. **3.** to throw or cast back; cause to return or rebound. **4.** to reproduce; show: *followers reflecting the views of the leader.* **5.** to serve to cast or bring (credit, discredit, etc.). **6.** to think carefully; meditate on. *–v.i.* **7.** to be turned or cast back, as light. **8.** to cast back light, heat, etc. **9.** to be reflected or mirrored. **10.** to give back or show an image. **11.** to serve or tend to bring reproach or discredit. **12.** to serve to give a particular aspect or impression: *his speech reflects badly on his candidacy.* **13.** to think, ponder, or meditate. [late ME, from L *reflectere* bend back]

**reflectance** /rə'flɛktəns/, *n.* the ratio of the luminous flux reflected by a surface to the incident luminous flux. Also, **reflection factor.**

**reflecting telescope** /rə,flɛktɪŋ 'tɛləskoʊp/, *n.* a telescope using a mirror instead of a lens to form the principal image.

**reflection** /rə'flɛkʃən/, *n.* **1.** the act of reflecting. **2.** the state of being reflected. **3.** an image; representation; counterpart. **4.** a fixing of the thoughts on something; careful consideration. **5.** a thought occurring in consideration or meditation. **6.** an unfavourable remark or observation. **7.** the casting of some imputation or reproach. **8.** *Physics.* **a.** the casting back, or the change of direction, of light, heat, sound, etc., after striking a surface. **b.** something so reflected, as heat, or esp., light. Also, **reflexion.** – **reflectional,** *adj.*

**reflective** /rə'flɛktɪv/, *adj.* **1.** that reflects; reflecting. **2.** of or pertaining to reflection. **3.** cast by reflection. **4.** given to or concerned with meditation. – **reflectively,** *adv.*

**reflector** /rə'flɛktə/, *n.* **1.** one who or that which reflects. **2.** a body, surface, or device that reflects light, heat, sound, or the like. **3.** a reflecting telescope. **4.** *Physics.* a layer of material surrounding the core of a nuclear reactor which reflects back into the core some of the neutrons which would otherwise escape. **5.** a piece of red glass or metal attached to the rear of a cycle or motor vehicle, or used to mark the edge of a road near road hazards.

**reflet** /rə'fleɪ/, *n.* an effect of lustre, colour, or iridescence on an object (as a piece of pottery) due to reflection of light. [F: reflection]

**reflex** /'riflɛks/, *adj., n.;* /rə'flɛks/, *v.* *–adj.* **1.** *Physiol.* denoting or pertaining to an involuntary response in which an impulse evoked by a stimulus is transmitted along an afferent nerve to a nerve centre, and from there through one or more synapses to an efferent nerve, calling into play muscular or other activity. **2.** occurring in reaction; responsive. **3.** designating a radio apparatus in which the same part performs two functions, as in a **reflex klystron,** in which one resonator acts as buncher and catcher. **4.** cast back; reflected, as light, etc. **5.** bent or turned back. *–n.* **6.** *Physiol.* a reflex action or movement. **7.** *Psychol.* an immediate response to a stimulus, inborn and often unaccompanied by consciousness, as blinking, perspiring, sneezing, etc. **8.** the reflection or image of an object, as exhibited by a mirror or the like. **9.** a reproduction as if in a mirror. **10.** a copy; adaptation. **11.** reflected light, colour, etc. **12.** a reflex radio receiving apparatus or set. *–v.t.* **13.** to bend, turn, or fold back. [L *reflexus,* pp., reflected, bent back]

**reflex angle** /– 'æŋgəl/, *n.* an angle greater than 180° but less than 360°.

**reflex arc** /– 'ak/, *n.* the path taken by neural impulses within the body from stimulus to reflex action.

**reflex camera** /– 'kæmrə/, *n.* a camera containing a pivoted mirror which allows the image of the object which is to be photographed to be viewed and focused on a ground-glass screen up to the moment of exposure.

**reflexion** /rə'flɛkʃən/, *n.* **1.** *Chiefly Anat.* the bending or folding back of a thing upon itself. **2.** reflection.

**reflexive** /rə'flɛksɪv/, *adj.* **1.** (of a verb) having identical subject and object, as *shave* in *he shaved himself.* **2.** (of a pronoun) indicating identity of object with subject, as *himself* in the example above. *–n.* **3.** a reflexive verb or pronoun, as *himself* in *he deceived himself.* – **reflexively,** *adv.* – **reflexiveness, reflexivity** /riflɛk'sɪvəti/, *n.*

**reflexive relation** /– rə'leɪʃən/, *n. Logic, Maths.* a relation on a set such that every element is related to itself, as the equality relation, which satisfies $x = x$ for every $x$.

**refluent** /'rɛfluənt/, *adj.* flowing back; ebbing, as the waters of a tide. [ME, from L *refluens,* ppr.] – **refluence,** *n.*

**reflux** /'riflʌks/, *n.* a flowing back; ebb. [RE- + FLUX. Cf. F *reflux*]

**reflux condenser** /– kən'dɛnsə/, *n.* a condenser attached to a vessel containing a boiling liquid so that the condensed vapour flows back into the vessel, thus preventing it from boiling dry.

**refo** /'rɛfoʊ/, *n.* →**reffo.**

**reforest** /,ri'fɒrəst/, *v.t.* →**reafforest.** – **reforestation** /,rifɒrəs'teɪʃən/, *n.*

**re-form** /,ri-'fɔm/, *v.t., v.i.* to form again.

**reform** /rə'fɔm/, *n.* **1.** the improvement or amendment of what is wrong, corrupt, etc.: *social reform.* **2.** an instance of this. **3.** the amendment of conduct, etc. *–v.t.* **4.** to restore to a former and better state; improve by alteration, substitution, abolition, etc. **5.** to cause (a person) to abandon wrong or evil ways of life or conduct. **6.** to put an end to (abuses, disorders, etc.). *–v.i.* **7.** to abandon evil conduct or error. [ME *reforme,* from L *reformāre*] – **reformable,** *adj.* – **reformative,** *adj.* – **reformer,** *n.*

**re-format** /,ri-'fɔmæt/, *v.t.* to give a new format to (an index, magazine, etc.).

**reformation** /rɛfə'meɪʃən/, *n.* **1.** the act of reforming. **2.** the state of being reformed. **3.** (*cap.*) the great religious movement in the 16th century which had for its object the reform of the Roman Catholic Church, and which led to the establishment of the Protestant Churches. – **reformational,** *adj.*

**reformatory** /rə'fɔmətri/, *adj., n., pl.* **-ries.** *–adj.* **1.** serving or designed to reform: *reformatory schools.* *–n.* **2.** Also, **reform school.** a penal institution for the reformation of young offenders.

**reformed** /rə'fɔmd/, *adj.* **1.** amended by removal of faults, abuses, etc. **2.** improved in conduct, morals, etc. **3.** (*cap.*) denoting or pertaining to Protestant Churches, esp. Calvinist as distinguished from Lutheran.

**reformism** /rə'fɔmɪzəm, 'rɛfəmɪzəm/, *n.* the policy of bringing about reform within the means and limitations of the existing system of government, usu. without radically changing the current political system.

**reformist** /rə'fɔməst, 'rɛfəməst/, *adj.* **1.** of or pertaining to a doctrine or movement of reform. *–n.* **2.** a person who pursues reformist policies.

**refract** /rə'frækt/, *v.t.* **1.** to subject to refraction. **2.** to determine the refractive condition of (an eye, a lens). [L *refractus,* pp., broken up]

**refracting telescope** /rə,fræktɪŋ 'tɛləskoʊp/, *n.* a telescope consisting essentially of a lens for forming an image and an eyepiece for viewing it. See **telescope** (def. 1).

**refraction** /rəˈfrækʃən/, *n.* **1.** *Physics.* the change of direction of a ray of light, heat, or the like, in passing obliquely from one medium into another in which its speed is different. **2.** *Optics.* **a.** the ability of the eye to refract light which enters it so as to form an image on the retina. **b.** the determining of the refractive condition of the eye. – **refractional,** *adj.*

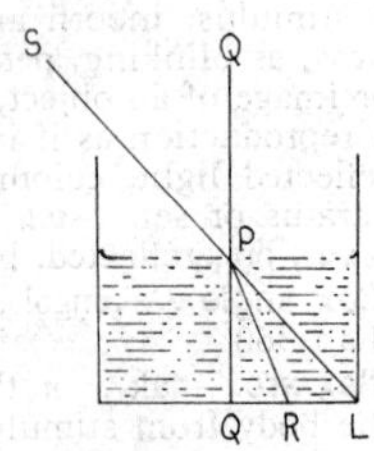

refraction: SP, ray of light; SPL, original direction; SPR, refracted ray; QQ, perpendicular

**refraction correction** /ˈ– kərɛkʃən/, *n.* the small correction which has to be made to the observed altitude of a celestial body due to the refraction by the earth's atmosphere of the light which it emits or reflects.

**refractive** /rəˈfræktɪv/, *adj.* **1.** of or pertaining to refraction. **2.** having power to refract. **3.** refracting. – **refractively,** *adv.* – **refractiveness,** *n.*

**refractive index** /– ˈɪndɛks/, *n.* a specific property of a material equal to the ratio of the velocity of light (or other electromagnetic vibration) in a vacuum to its velocity in that material.

**refractivity** /rifrækˈtɪvəti/, *n.* **1.** the difference between the refractive index of a material and unity. **2.** this difference divided by the density of the material (**specific refractivity**). **3.** the specific refractivity multiplied by the molecular weight of the material (**molecular refractivity**).

**refractometer** /rifrækˈtɒmətə/, *n.* an instrument for determining the refractive index of a material. [REFRACT + -O- + -METER[1]]

**refractor** /riˈfræktə/, *n.* **1.** something that refracts. **2.** →**refracting telescope.**

**refractory** /rəˈfræktəri/, *adj., n., pl.* **-ries.** –*adj.* **1.** stubborn; unmanageable: *a refractory child.* **2.** resisting ordinary methods of treatment. **3.** difficult to fuse, reduce, or work, as an ore or metal. –*n.* **4.** a material having the ability to retain its physical shape and chemical identity when subjected to high temperatures. **5.** (*pl.*) bricks of various shapes used in lining furnaces. **6.** *Physiol.* a momentary state of reduced excitability following a response: *the refractory period of a nerve.* – **refractorily,** *adv.* – **refractoriness,** *n.*

**refrain**[1] /rəˈfreɪn/, *v.i.* **1.** to forbear; keep oneself back (oft. fol. by *from*). –*v.t.* **2.** *Rare.* to curb. [ME *refreyne(n)*, from OF *refrener,* from L *refrēnāre* to bridle] – **refrainer,** *n.*

**refrain**[2] /rəˈfreɪn/, *n.* **1.** a phrase or verse recurring at intervals in a song or poem, esp. at the end of each stanza; chorus. **2.** a musical setting for the refrain of a poem. [ME *refreyne,* from OF *refrain,* from *refraindre,* from VL *refrangere,* replacing L *refringere* refract]

**refrangible** /rəˈfrændʒəbəl/, *adj.* capable of being refracted, as rays of light. [RE- + L *frangere* break + -IBLE] – **refrangibleness, refrangibility** /rəfrændʒəˈbɪləti/, *n.*

**refresh** /rəˈfrɛʃ/, *v.t.* **1.** (*oft. reflexive*) to reinvigorate by rest, food, etc. **2.** to stimulate (the memory). **3.** to make fresh again; reinvigorate or cheer (a person, the mind, spirits, etc.). **4.** to freshen in appearance, colour, etc., as by a restorative. –*v.i.* **5.** to take refreshment, esp. food or drink. **6.** to become fresh or vigorous again; revive. [ME, from OF *refrescher,* from *re-* RE- + *fresche* FRESH] – **refreshing,** *adj.* – **refreshingly,** *adv.*

**refresher** /rəˈfrɛʃə/, *adj.* **1.** serving as a review of material previously studied: *a refresher course.* –*n.* **2.** one who or that which refreshes. **3.** a fee paid to a counsel in addition to that marked on his brief.

**refresher course** /ˈ– kɔs/, *n.* a short course of study provided to renew or update one's knowledge of a subject, technique, etc.

**refreshing** /rəˈfrɛʃɪŋ/, *adj.* **1.** capable of reinvigorating, cooling, restoring energy, etc. **2.** interesting because of unique or unusual qualities.

**refreshment** /rəˈfrɛʃmənt/, *n.* **1.** that which refreshes, esp. food or drink. **2.** (*pl.*) articles or portions of food or drink, esp. for a light meal. **3.** the act of refreshing. **4.** the state of being refreshed.

**refrigerant** /rəˈfrɪdʒərənt/, *adj.* **1.** refrigerating; cooling. **2.** reducing bodily heat or fever. –*n.* **3.** a refrigerant agent, as in a drug. **4.** a liquid capable of vaporising at a low temperature, as ammonia, used in mechanical refrigeration. **5.** a cooling substance, as ice, solid carbon dioxide, etc., used in a refrigerator.

**refrigerate** /rəˈfrɪdʒəreɪt/, *v.t.,* **-rated, -rating. 1.** to make or keep cold or cool. **2.** to freeze (food, etc.) for preservation. [L *refrīgerātus,* pp., made cool again] – **refrigerative, refrigeratory,** *adj.*

**refrigeration** /rəfrɪdʒəˈreɪʃən/, *n.* **1.** the process of producing low temperatures, usu. throughout an appreciable volume. **2.** the resulting state.

**refrigerator** /rəˈfrɪdʒəreɪtə/, *n.* **1.** a box, room, or cabinet in which food, drink, etc., are kept cool, as by means of ice or mechanical refrigeration. **2.** the element of a refrigerating system consisting of the space or medium to be cooled.

**refrigerator biscuit** /ˈ– bɪskət/, *n.* an uncooked type of biscuit, of various flavours, made with a shortening agent which solidifies on refrigeration.

**refringence** /rəˈfrɪndʒəns/, *n.* →**refraction.** [L *refringens,* ppr.] – **refringent,** *adj.*

**reft** /rɛft/, *v.* past tense and past participle of **reave.**

**refuel** /riˈfjuəl/, *v.,* **-elled, -elling** or (*U.S.*) **-eled, -eling.** –*v.t.* **1.** to supply again with fuel: *to refuel an aeroplane.* –*v.i.* **2.** to take on a fresh supply of fuel: *they refuelled at Paris and flew on.*

**refuge** /ˈrɛfjudʒ/, *n.* **1.** shelter or protection from danger, trouble, etc.: *to take refuge from a storm.* **2.** a place of shelter, protection, or safety. **3.** anything to which one has recourse for aid, relief, or escape. **4.** a platform in the centre of a street for the use of pedestrians in crossing; island (def. 5). [ME, from OF, from L *refugium*]

**refugee** /rɛfjuˈdʒi/, *n.* one who flees for refuge or safety, esp. to a foreign country, as in time of political upheaval, war, etc. [F *refugié,* pp. of *refugier* take refuge, from *refuge* REFUGE]

**refulgent** /rəˈfʌldʒənt/, *adj.* shining; radiant; glowing. [L *refulgens,* ppr.] – **refulgence,** *n.* – **refulgently,** *adv.*

**refund**[1] /rəˈfʌnd/, *v.;* /ˈrifʌnd/, *n.* –*v.t.* **1.** to give back or restore (esp. money); repay. **2.** to make repayment to; reimburse. –*v.i.* **3.** to make repayment. –*n.* **4.** a repayment. [ME, from L *refundere,* lit., pour back]

**refund**[2] /riˈfʌnd/, *v.t.* **1.** to fund anew. **2.** *Finance.* **a.** to meet (a matured debt structure) by new borrowing, esp. through issuance of bonds. **b.** to replace (an old issue) with a new, esp. with one bearing a lower rate of interest. [RE- + FUND]

**refurbish** /riˈfɜbɪʃ/, *v.t.* to furbish again; renovate; polish up again; brighten.

**refusal** /rəˈfjuzəl/, *n.* **1.** the act of refusing. **2.** priority in refusing or taking something; option.

**refuse**[1] /rəˈfjuz/, *v.,* **-fused, -fusing.** –*v.t.* **1.** to decline to accept (something offered): *to refuse an office.* **2.** to decline to give; deny (a request, demand, etc.). **3.** to express a determination not (to do something): *to refuse to discuss the question.* **4.** to decline to submit to. **5.** (of a horse) to decline to leap over (a fence, water, etc.). **6.** *Obs.* to renounce. –*v.i.* **7.** to decline acceptance, consent, or compliance. [ME, from OF *refuser,* from VL *refusāre,* from L *refusus,* pp., lit., poured back] – **refuser,** *n.*

**refuse**[2] /ˈrɛfjus/, *n.* **1.** that which is discarded as worthless or useless; rubbish. –*adj.* **2.** rejected as worthless; discarded: *refuse matter.* [ME, from OF *refus,* pp., refused. See REFUSE[1]]

**refutation** /rɛfjuˈteɪʃən/, *n.* the act of refuting a statement, charge, etc.; disproof. Also, **refutal** /rəˈfjutl/.

**refute** /rəˈfjut/, *v.t.,* **-futed, -futing. 1.** to prove to be false or erroneous, as an opinion, charge, etc. **2.** to prove (a person) to be in error. [L *refūtāre* repel, refute] – **refutable** /ˈrɛfjətəbəl, rəˈfjutəbəl/, *adj.* – **refutably** /ˈrɛfjətəbli/, *adv.* – **refuter,** *n.*

**reg.,** **1.** registration. **2.** registered. **3.** regulation.

**Reg.,** **1.** Regina. **2.** Regiment.

**regain** /rəˈgeɪn/ *v.;* /ˈrigeɪn/, *n.* –*v.t.* **1.** to get again; recover. **2.** to succeed in reaching again; get back to: *to regain the shore.* –*n.* **3.** *Textiles.* the amount of moisture in a material expressed as a percentage of the clean dry weight.

**regal**[1] /ˈrigəl/, *adj.* **1.** of or pertaining to a king; royal: *the* *regal power.* **2.** befitting or resembling a king. **3.** stately; splendid. **4.** (of a woman) tall, dignified, and elegant. [ME, from L *rēgālis*] – **regally,** *adv.*

**regal**[2] /ˈrigəl/, *n.* a small portable reed organ, of the 16th and 17th centuries. [MF *régale;* connection with REGAL[1] obscure]

**regale** /rəˈgeɪl/, *v.,* **-galed, -galing,** *n.* *–v.t.* **1.** to entertain agreeably; delight. **2.** to entertain with choice food or drink. *–v.i.* **3.** to feast. *–n.* **4.** a choice feast. **5.** a choice article of food or drink. **6.** refreshment. [F *régaler,* from OF *regale* feast, from *gale* pleasure, from MD *wale* wealth] – **regalement,** *n.*

**regalia** /rəˈgeɪljə/, *n.pl.* **1.** the rights and privileges of a king. **2.** the ensigns or emblems of royalty, as the crown, sceptre, etc. **3.** the decorations or insignia of any office or order. [ML, properly neut. pl. of L *rēgālis* regal]

**regality** /rəˈgæləti/, *n., pl.* **-ties. 1.** royalty, sovereignty, or kingship. **2.** a right or privilege pertaining to a king. **3.** a kingdom.

**regard** /rəˈgad/, *v.t.* **1.** to look upon or think of with a particular feeling: *to regard a person with favour.* **2.** to have or show respect or concern for. **3.** to think highly of. **4.** to take into account; consider. **5.** to look at; observe. **6.** to relate to; concern. *–v.i.* **7.** to pay attention. **8.** to look or gaze. *–n.* **9.** reference; relation: *to err in regard to facts.* **10.** a point or particular: *quite satisfactory in this regard.* **11.** thought; attention; concern. **12.** look; gaze. **13.** respect; deference: *due regard to authority.* **14.** kindly feeling; liking. **15.** (*pl.*) sentiments of esteem or affection: *give them my regards.* **16. as regards,** in relation to. **17. with regard to,** concerning. [ME *regard,* n., from F, from *regarder,* v., from *re-* RE- + *garder* GUARD]

**regardant** /rəˈgadənt/, *adj.* looking backwards. [F, ppr. of *regarder* REGARD]

**regardful** /rəˈgadfəl/, *adj.* **1.** observant; attentive; heedful (oft. fol. by *of*). **2.** considerate or thoughtful; respectful. – **regardfully,** *adv.* – **regardfulness,** *n.*

**regarding** /rəˈgadɪŋ/, *prep.* with regard to; respecting; concerning: *he knew nothing regarding the lost watch.*

**regardless** /rəˈgadləs/, *adj.* **1.** having or showing no regard; heedless; unmindful; careless (oft. fol. by *of*). **2.** without regard to expense, danger, etc. *–adv.* **3.** anyway. **4.** without regard for. – **regardlessly,** *adv.* – **regardlessness,** *n.*

**regatta** /rəˈgætə/, *n.* **1.** a boat race, as of rowing boats, yachts, or other vessels. **2.** an organised series of such races. **3.** (originally) a gondola race in Venice. **4.** a coloured, striped cotton cloth with a twill weave. [It. (Venetian) *regata,* from *regatare* complete]

**regelate** /ˈrɛdʒəleɪt/, *v.i.,* **-lated, -lating.** to freeze together, as two pieces of ice pressed together near the freezing point. [L *regelātus*] – **regelation** /rɛdʒəˈleɪʃən/, *n.*

**regency** /ˈridʒənsi/, *n., pl.* **-cies,** *adj.* *–n.* **1.** the office, jurisdiction, or control of a regent or body of regents exercising the ruling power during the minority, absence, or disability of a sovereign. **2.** a body of regents. **3.** a government consisting of regents. **4.** a territory under the control of a regent or regents. **5.** the term of office of a regent. **6.** (*cap.*) (in Britain) the period (1811-20) during which George (later, George IV) was regent. **7.** the office or function of a regent or ruler. *–adj.* **8.** pertaining to a regency. **9.** (*cap.*) of or pertaining to the Regency or to the styles popular at that time.

**regeneracy** /rəˈdʒɛnərəsi/, *n.* regenerate state.

**regenerate** /rəˈdʒɛnəreɪt/, *v.,* **-rated, -rating;** /rəˈdʒɛnərət/, *adj.* *–v.t.* **1.** to effect a complete moral reform in. **2.** to re-create, reconstitute, or make over, esp. in a better form or condition. **3.** to generate or produce anew; bring into existence again. **4.** *Physics.* to restore (a substance) periodically to a favourable thermal state or physical condition from which it later departs while performing a desired function. **5.** *Electronics.* to magnify the amplification of, by relaying part of the output circuit power into the input circuit. **6.** *Theol.* to cause to be born again spiritually. *–v.i.* **7.** to come into existence or be formed again. **8.** to reform; become regenerate. **9.** to produce a regenerative effect. *–adj.* **10.** reconstituted in a better form. **11.** reformed. **12.** *Theol.* born again spiritually. [late ME, from L *regenerātus,* pp., made over, produced anew]

**regeneration** /rədʒɛnəˈreɪʃən/, *n.* **1.** the act of regenerating. **2.** the state of being regenerated. **3.** *Electronics.* a feedback process in which energy fed back to the control electrode reinforces the input. **4.** *Biol.* the restitution of a lost part by an organism. **5.** *Theol.* spiritual rebirth.

**regeneration burn** /– bɜn/, *n.* the controlled burning of bushland to encourage new growth.

**regenerative** /rəˈdʒɛnərətɪv/, *adj.* **1.** pertaining to regeneration. **2.** tending to regenerate. – **regeneratively,** *adv.*

**regenerative braking** /– ˈbreɪkɪŋ/, *n.* a method of braking electric motors in which they are operated as generators, the power produced being returned to the supply source.

**regenerative cooling** /– ˈkulɪŋ/, *n.* **1.** *Aeron.* the cooling of a rocket combustion chamber wall by the circulation of a propellant before its injection into the chamber. **2.** *Chem.* the cooling of a gas by allowing a portion of it to expand rapidly.

**regenerative furnace** /– ˈfɜnəs/, *n.* a furnace in which the hot combustion products pass into a chamber containing a lattice structure of firebricks (the regenerator). The direction of the gas flow is periodically reversed so that the hot bricks in the regenerator can be used to preheat the incoming cold gas.

**regenerator** /rəˈdʒɛnəreɪtə/, *n.* **1.** one who or that which regenerates. **2.** *Mech.* (in a regenerative furnace, etc.) a device for heating the incoming air or fuel gas.

**regent** /ˈridʒənt/, *n.* **1.** one who exercises the ruling power in a kingdom during the minority, absence, or disability of the sovereign. **2.** (formerly in some universities) a member of certain governing and teaching bodies. **3.** *U.S.* a member of the governing board of certain universities and other institutions. **4.** *U.S.* a university officer who exercises a general supervision over the conduct and welfare of the students. **5.** a ruler or governor. *–adj.* **6.** acting as regent of a country. **7.** exercising vicarious ruling authority: *a prince regent.* **8.** *U.S.* holding the position of a regent in a university. **9.** *Rare.* ruling. [ME, from L *regens,* ppr., ruling] – **regentship,** *n.*

**regent bower-bird** /– ˈbaʊə-bɜd/, *n.* the second largest of the Australian bower-birds, *Sericulus chrysocephalus,* the male being jet black and golden in colour. Also, **regent-bird.**

**regent honeyeater** /– ˈhʌniˌitə/, *n.* one of the larger and most strikingly marked of the Australian honeyeaters, *Zanthomiza phrygia;* flying coachman.

**regent parrot** /– ˈpærət/, *n.* a bright yellow parrot, *Polytelis anthopeplus,* found in large flocks in south-western Australia; rock pebbler.

**reggae** /ˈrɛgeɪ/, *n.* music of the Rastafarian cult of Jamaica which, in the 1970s, developed into a highly stylised and influential pop music idiom with international appeal. [West Indian]

**regicide** /ˈrɛdʒəsaɪd/, *n.* **1.** one who kills a king; one responsible for the death of a king. **2.** the killing of a king. [*regi-* (combining form representing L *rex* king) + -CIDE] – **regicidal** /rɛdʒəˈsaɪdl/, *adj.*

**regime** /reɪˈʒim/, *n.* **1.** a mode or system of rule or government. **2.** a ruling or prevailing system. **3.** →**regimen. 4.** the variation in the volume of a river with the season. **5.** the seasonal pattern of a climate. Also, **régime.** [F, from L *regimen* direction, government]

**regimen** /ˈrɛdʒəmən/, *n.* **1.** *Med.* a regulated course of diet, exercise, or manner of living, intended to preserve or restore health or to attain some result. **2.** rule or government. **3.** a particular form or system of government. **4.** a prevailing system. [ME, from L]

**regiment** /ˈrɛdʒəmənt/, *n.;* /ˈrɛdʒəmɛnt/, *v.* *–n.* **1.** *Mil.* a unit of ground forces, commanded by a lieutenant colonel, consisting of two or more battalions, a headquarters unit, and certain supporting units. *–v.t.* **2.** to form into a regiment or regiments. **3.** to assign to a regiment or group. **4.** to form into an organised body or group; organise or systematise. **5.** to group together and treat in a uniform manner; subject to strict discipline. [ME, from LL *regimentum* rule] – **regimentation** /rɛdʒəmɛnˈteɪʃən/, *n.*

**regimental** /rɛdʒəˈmɛntl/, *adj.* **1.** of or pertaining to a regiment. *–n.* **2.** (*pl.*) the uniform of a regiment.

**regina** /rəˈdʒinə/, *n.* (*oft. cap.*) reigning queen. [L]

**region** /ˈridʒən/, *n.* **1.** any more or less extensive, continuous part of a surface or space. **2.** a part of the earth's surface (land or sea) of considerable and usu. indefinite extent: *tropical regions.* **3.** a district without respect to boundaries or extent. **4.** a part or division of the universe, as the heavens: *celestial regions.* **5.** one of the administrative divisions into which a territory or country, as Italy, is divided. **6.** *Geog.* a large faunal area of the earth's surface, sometimes one regarded as a division of a larger area. **7.** *Anat.* a place in, or a divison of, the body or a part of the body: *the abdominal region.* [ME, from L *regio* line, district]

**regional** /ˈridʒənəl/, *adj.* **1.** of or pertaining to a region of considerable extent; not merely local. **2.** of or pertaining to a particular region, district, area, or part; sectional; local. – **regionally,** *adv.*

**regionalism** /ˈridʒənəlɪzəm/, *n.* **1.** *Politics.* the theory, principles, and practice of dividing a country into administrative regions. **2.** regional patriotism.

**register** /ˈrɛdʒəstə/, *n.* **1.** a book in which entries of acts, occurrences, names, or the like are made for record. **2.** any list of such entries; a record of acts, occurrences, etc. **3.** an entry in such a book, record, or list. **4.** *Comm.* a ship's official document of identification which must be produced when a ship is entering or leaving a port. **5.** registration or registry. **6.** a mechanical device by which certain data are automatically recorded, as a cash register. **7.** *Music.* **a.** the compass or range of a voice or an instrument. **b.** a particular series of tones, esp. of the human voice, produced in the same way and having the same quality: *the head register.* **c.** (in an organ) a stop. **8.** *Linguistics.* a section of the vocabulary of a language according to the cultural or occupational area in which the words are used; occupational dialect. **9.** a contrivance for regulating the passage of warm air, or the like, esp. a closable perforated plate in a duct of a heating or ventilating system. **10.** *Photog.* the proper relationship between two plane surfaces in photography, as corresponding plates in photoengraving, etc. **11.** *Print., etc.* **a.** a precise adjustment or correspondence, as of lines, columns, etc., esp. on the two sides of a leaf. **b.** correct relation or exact superimposition, as of colours in colour printing. **12.** *Computers.* a device capable of holding digital information until it is required. *–v.t.* **13.** to enter or have entered formally in a register. **14.** to have a motor vehicle, which has been assessed as roadworthy and on which the appropriate tax has been paid, entered in the register of motor vehicles kept by a public authority. **15.** to cause to be recorded for purposes of safety, as letters or parcels at a post office, for security in transmission, by payment of a special fee. **16.** to indicate by a record, as instruments do. **17.** to indicate or show, as on a scale. **18.** *Print. etc.* to adjust so as to secure exact correspondence; cause to be in register. **19.** *Mil.* to adjust (fire) on a known point. **20.** to show (surprise, joy, anger, etc.), as by facial expression or by actions. **21.** *Music.* to select the stops appropriate for (a piece of music for the organ). *–v.i.* **22.** to enter one's name, or cause it to be entered, in an electoral or other register; enrol. **23.** *Print., etc.* to be in register. **24.** to show surprise, joy, etc. **25.** *Colloq.* to make an impression. [ME *registre,* from ML *registrum,* for *regestum,* neut. of L *regestus,* pp., recorded] – **registerer,** *n.* – **registrable,** *adj.*

**registered** /ˈrɛdʒəstəd/, *adj.* **1.** recorded, as in a register or book; enrolled. **2.** *Comm.* officially listing the owner's name with the issuing company and suitably inscribing the certificate, as with bonds to evidence title. **3.** officially or legally certified by a government officer or board: *a registered patent.* **4.** denoting cattle, horses, dogs, etc., having pedigrees verified and filed by authorised associations of breeders.

**registered mail** /– ˈmeɪl/, *n.* a pre-paid postal service by which a letter or parcel is handled apart from the general mail, and delivered only after signature of a receipt by the addressee, the customer having proof of mailing date and guarantee of compensation if the article is lost in the post.

**registered post** /– ˈpoʊst/, *n.* a postal service in which post offices offer greater security in transmission of mail and compensation for loss or damage, in return for a registration fee.

**registered publications post,** *n.* an arrangement for the conveyance of books and other publications at cheaper rates than other parcels.

**register tonnage** /ˈrɛdʒəstə tʌnɪdʒ/, *n.* a measure of volume of earning space on a ship, consisting of the gross tonnage less the volume of the master's cabin, crew accommodation, wheelhouse, galley, etc., measured in gross tons.

**registrar** /ˈrɛdʒəstra/, *n.* **1.** one who keeps a record; an official recorder. **2.** the chief administrative official in a university. **3.** a doctor in a hospital next below a consultant, who is training to be a specialist. **4.** *Law.* an official in a court, subordinate to a judge, who deals with interlocutory matters, but who may also hear certain cases. **5.** an employee of a limited company who is responsible for registering the issues of securities. [REGISTER, *v.* + -AR[3]]

**Registrar-General** /ˌrɛdʒəstra-ˈdʒɛnrəl/, *n.* an official responsible for the registration of all births, deaths, and marriages.

**registration** /rɛdʒəˈstreɪʃən/, *n.* **1.** the act of registering. **2.** an instance of this as of motor vehicles: *registration number.* **3.** an entry in a register. **4.** *Music.* the selection of stops used in playing the organ.

**registration plate** /ˈ– pleɪt/, *n.* →**numberplate.**

**registry** /ˈrɛdʒəstri/, *n., pl.* **-tries. 1.** the act of registering; registration. **2.** a place where a register is kept; an office of registration.

**registry office** /ˈ– ɒfəs/, *n.* **1.** an office where births, marriages and deaths are recorded, and civil marriages take place. **2.** *Obs.* an employment bureau, esp. of domestic staff.

**regius** /ˈridʒiəs/, *adj.* **1.** of or belonging to a king. **2.** (of a professor in a British university) holding a chair founded by the sovereign. [L]

**reglet** /ˈrɛglət/, *n.* **1.** *Archit.* a narrow, flat moulding. **2.** *Print.* **a.** a thin strip, usu. of wood, less than type-high, used to produce a blank in or about a page of type. **b.** such strips collectively. [F, diminutive of *regle,* from L *rēgula* rule]

**regma** /ˈrɛgmə/, *n., pl.* **-mata** /-mətə/. a dry fruit consisting of three or more carpels which separate from the axis at maturity. [NL, from Gk *rhêgma* rupture]

**regnal** /ˈrɛgnəl/, *adj.* of or pertaining to reigning, sovereignty, or a reign: *the second regnal year.* [ML *regnālis,* from L *regnum* kingdom]

**regnant** /ˈrɛgnənt/, *adj.* **1.** reigning; ruling: *a queen regnant.* **2.** exercising sway or influence; predominant. **3.** prevalent; widespread. [L *regnans,* ppr., ruling] – **regnancy,** *n.*

**rego** /ˈrɛdʒoʊ/, *n. Colloq.* →**registration** (def. 2).

**regolith** /ˈrɛgəlɪθ/, *n.* →**mantle rock.** [Gk *rhêgo(s)* blanket covering + -LITH]

**regorge** /riˈgɔdʒ/, *v.,* **-gorged, -gorging.** *–v.t.* **1.** to disgorge; cast up again. *–v.i.* **2.** to rush back again; gush: *the waters regorged.* [F *regorger,* or from RE- + GORGE, *v.,* after L *regurgitāre* regurgitate]

**regrate** /riˈgreɪt/, *v.t.,* **-grated, -grating. 1.** to buy up (grain, provisions, etc.) in order to sell again at a profit in or near the same market. **2.** to sell again (commodities so bought); retail. [ME, from OF *regrater,* ? from *grater* GRATE[2]] – **regrater,** *n.*

**regress** /riˈgrɛs/, *v.;* /ˈrigrɛs/, *n.* *–v.i.* **1.** to move in a backward direction; go back. *–n.* **2.** the act of going back; return. **3.** backward movement or course; retrogression. [ME, from L *regressus* a going back] – **regressive,** *adj.* – **regressively,** *adv.*

**regression** /riˈgrɛʃən/, *n.* **1.** the act of going back; return; backward movement. **2.** retrogradation; retrogression. **3.** *Biol.* reversion to an earlier or less advanced state or form or to a common or general type. **4.** *Psychol.* the reversion to a chronologically earlier or less adapted pattern of behaviour and feeling. **5.** the disappearance of the symptoms or signs of a disease.

**regression coefficient** /– koʊəˈfɪʃənt/, *n.* a constant by which a given value of a variable may be multiplied to obtain the best estimate of the value of a second variable corresponding to this value.

**regret** /rəˈgrɛt/, *v.,* **-gretted, -gretting,** *n.* *–v.t.* **1.** to feel sorry about (anything disappointing, unpleasant, etc.). **2.** to think of with a sense of loss: *to regret one's vanished youth.* *–n.* **3.** a sense of loss, disappointment, dissatisfaction, etc. **4.** the feeling of being sorry for some fault, act, omission, etc., of one's own. **5.** (*pl.*) feelings of sorrow over what is lost, gone, done, etc. **6.** (*pl. or sing.*) a polite and formal expression of regretful feelings. [ME *regrette,* from OF *regretter,* from Gmc **grētan;* cf. OE *grǣtan* lament, grieve] – **regrettable,** *adj.* – **regrettably,** *adv.* – **regretter,** *n.*

**regretful** /rəˈgrɛtfəl/, *adj.* full of regret; sorrowful because of what is lost, gone, done, etc. – **regretfully,** *adv.* – **regretfulness,** *n.*

**Regt, 1.** regent. **2.** regiment.

**regular** /ˈrɛgjələ/, *adj.* **1.** usual; normal; customary: *to put something in its regular place.* **2.** conforming in form or arrangement; symmetrical: *regular teeth.* **3.** characterised by fixed principle, uniform procedure, etc.: *regular breathing.* **4.** recurring at fixed times; periodic: *regular meals.* **5.** adhering to rule or procedure: *to be regular in one's diet.* **6.** observing fixed times or habits: *regular customer.* **7.** orderly; well-ordered: *a regular life.* **8.** conforming to some accepted rule, discipline, etc. **9.** carried out in accordance with an accepted principle; formally correct. **10.** properly qualified for or engaged in an occupation. **11.** *Colloq.* complete; thorough: *a regular rascal.* **12.** (of a flower) having the members of each of its floral circles or whorls normally alike in form and size. **13.** *Gram.* conforming to the most prevalent pattern of formation, inflection, construction, etc. **14.** *Maths.* governed by one law throughout: *a regular polygon has all its angles and sides equal.* **15.** *Mil.* denoting or belonging to the permanently organised or standing army of a state. **16.** *Eccles.* subject to a religious rule, or belonging to a religious or monastic order (opposed to *secular*): *regular clergy.* **17.** *U.S. Politics.* of, pertaining to, or selected by the recognised agents of a political party: *the regular ticket.* –*n.* **18.** *Eccles.* a member of a duly constituted religious order under a rule. **19.** a soldier in a regular army. **20.** *Colloq.* a regular customer. [L *rēgulāris;* replacing ME *reguler,* from OF] – **regularity** /rɛgjəˈlærəti/, *n.*

**regular army** /rɛgjələr ˈami/, *n.* a permanent army maintained in peace as well as in war; standing army.

**regularise** /ˈrɛgjələraɪz/, *v.t.,* **-rised, -rising.** to make regular. Also, **regularize.** – **regularisation** /ˌrɛgjələraɪˈzeɪʃən/, *n.*

**regularly** /ˈrɛgjələli/, *adv.* **1.** at regular times or intervals. **2.** according to plan, custom, etc.

**regulate** /ˈrɛgjəleɪt/, *v.t.,* **-lated, -lating. 1.** to control or direct by rule, principle, method, etc. **2.** to adjust to some standard or requirement, as amount, degree, etc.: *to regulate the temperature.* **3.** to adjust so as to ensure accuracy of operation: *to regulate a watch.* **4.** to put in good order: *to regulate the digestion.* [LL *rēgulātus,* pp., from L *rēgula* rule] – **regulative, regulatory,** *adj.*

**regulation** /rɛgjəˈleɪʃən/, *n.* **1.** a rule or order, as for conduct, prescribed by authority; a governing direction or law. **2.** the act of regulating. **3.** the state of being regulated. –*adj.* **4.** according to or prescribed by regulation: *regulation shoes had to be worn.*

**regulator** /ˈrɛgjəleɪtə/, *n.* **1.** one who or that which regulates. **2.** *Horol.* **a.** a device in a clock or a watch for causing it to go faster or slower. **b.** a master clock, esp. one of great accuracy, against which other clocks are checked. **3.** *Mach.* **a.** a governor. **b.** a governor employed to control the closing of the port opening for admission of steam to the cylinder of a steam engine. **c.** a reducing valve for regulating steam pressure. **4.** *Elect.* a device which functions to maintain a designated characteristic, as voltage or current, at a predetermined value, or to vary it according to a predetermined plan.

**regulus** /ˈrɛgjələs/, *n., pl.* **-luses, -li** /-laɪ/. *Metall.* **a.** the metallic mass which forms beneath the slag at the bottom of the crucible or furnace in smelting ores. **b.** an impure intermediate product obtained in smelting ores. [L: a little king, diminutive of *rex* king; in early chemistry, antimony, so called because it readily combines with gold (the king of metals)]

**regulus of antimony,** *n.* commercially pure metallic antimony.

**regur** /ˈrɛgə, ˈreɪgə/, *n.* a rich soil formed from basalt, occurring in tropical regions, notably in the Deccan, in India, its titanium content giving it a dark colouration; black cotton soil; tropical black earth. [Hind. *regar*]

**regurgitate** /rəˈgɜdʒəteɪt/, *v.,* **-tated, -tating.** –*v.i.* **1.** to surge or rush back, as liquids, gases, undigested food, etc. –*v.t.* **2.** to cause to surge or rush back. [ML *regurgitātus,* pp.] – **regurgitant,** *n., adj.*

**regurgitation** /rəgɜdʒəˈteɪʃən/, *n.* **1.** the act of regurgitating. **2.** *Med.* voluntary or involuntary return of partly digested food from the stomach to the mouth. **3.** *Physiol.* the reflux of blood through leaking heart valves.

**rehab** /ˈrihæb/, *n.* →**rehabilitation** (def. 3).

**rehabilitate** /rihəˈbɪləteɪt/, *v.t.,* **-tated, -tating. 1.** to restore to a good condition, esp. in a medical sense, of persons; regenerate, or alter to an improved form. **2.** to educate for resumption of normal activities, as a person handicapped by accident or disease. **3.** to re-establish in good repute or accepted respectability, as a person or the character, name, etc., after disrepute. **4.** to restore formally to a former capacity or standing, or to rank, rights, or privileges lost or forfeited. [ML *rehabilitātus,* pp., restored]

**rehabilitation** /rihəbɪləˈteɪʃən/, *n.* **1.** restoration to former health. **2.** restoration of rights, privileges or reputation. **3.** *N.Z.* →**repatriation** (def. 2).

**rehash** /riˈhæʃ/, *v.;* /ˈrihæʃ/, *n.* –*v.t.* **1.** to work up (old material) in a new form. –*n.* **2.** the act of rehashing. **3.** something rehashed.

**rehearsal** /rəˈhɜsəl/, *n.* **1.** a performance beforehand by way of practice or drill. **2.** the act of going through a dramatic, musical, or other performance in private, for practice, before going through it publicly or on some formal occasion. **3.** a repeating or relating: *a rehearsal of grievances.*

**rehearse** /rəˈhɜs/, *v.,* **-hearsed, -hearsing.** –*v.t.* **1.** to perform (a play, part, piece of music, etc.) in private by way of practice, before a public performance. **2.** to drill or train (a person, etc.) by rehearsal, as for some performance or part. **3.** to relate the facts or particulars of; enumerate. –*v.i.* **4.** to rehearse a play, part, etc. [ME *reherce(n),* from OF *rehercier,* apparently from *re-* RE- + *hercier* harrow] – **rehearser,** *n.*

**reheat** /ˌriˈhit/, *v.t.* **1.** to heat again. –*n.* **2.** Also, **reheating.** the process of injecting fuel into the jet pipe of a turbojet engine in order to obtain extra thrust by combustion with the unburnt air in the turbine exhaust gases; afterburning.

**rehoboam** /riəˈbouəm/, *n.* a large wine bottle with a capacity equal to 6 normal bottles. [named after *Rehoboam,* reigned ?922-?915 B.C., first king of Judah; modelled on JEROBOAM]

**rehouse** /ˌriˈhauz/, *v.t.,* **-housed, -housing.** to provide with a new house or houses. – **rehousing,** *n.*

**Reid's baseline** /ridz ˈbeɪslaɪn/, *n.* a line passing through the lower margin of the orbital opening and the auricular point. [named after Robert William *Reid,* 1851-1939, Scottish anatomist]

**reify** /ˈriəfaɪ/, *v.t.,* **-fied, -fying.** to convert into or regard as a concrete thing: *to reify an abstract concept.* [L *rē(s)* thing + -(I)FY]

**reign** /reɪn/, *n.* **1.** the period or term of ruling, as of a sovereign. **2.** royal rule or sway. **3.** dominating power or influence: *the reign of law.* –*v.i.* **4.** to possess or exercise sovereign power or authority. **5.** to hold the position and name of sovereign without exercising the ruling power. **6.** to have ascendancy; predominate. [ME *reyne,* from OF *regne,* from L *regnum*]

**reimburse** /riɪmˈbɜs/, *v.t.,* **-bursed, -bursing. 1.** to make repayment to for expense or loss incurred. **2.** to pay back; refund; repay. [RE- + *imburse* (from ML *imbursāre,* from L *in-* IN-[2] + ML *bursa* purse, bag)] – **reimbursement,** *n.*

**reimport** /riɪmˈpɔt/, *v.t.* to import back into the country of exportation. – **reimportation** /ˌriɪmpɔˈteɪʃən/, *n.*

**reimpression** /riɪmˈprɛʃən/, *n.* **1.** a second or repeated impression. **2.** a reprinting or a reprint.

**rein** /reɪn/, *n.* **1.** a long, narrow strap or thong, fastened to the bridle or bit, by which a rider or driver restrains and guides a horse or other animal. **2.** any of certain other straps or thongs forming part of a harness, as a bearing rein. **3.** any means of curbing, controlling, or directing; a check; restraint. **4.** complete licence; free scope: *to give free rein to one's imagination.* **5.** (*pl.*) the controlling influence and power. **6. rein back,** (of a horse) a step backwards. –*v.t.* **7.** to furnish with a rein or reins, as a horse. **8.** to check or guide (a horse, etc.) by pulling at the reins (oft. fol. by *back* or *in*). **9.** to curb; restrain; control. –*v.i.* **10.** to obey the reins: *a horse that reins well.* **11.** to rein a horse (fol. by *in* or *up* or *back*). [ME *rene,* from OF, var. of *resne* (AF *redne*), from L *retinēre* hold back]

**reincarnate** /riɪn'kaneɪt/, *v.t.,* **-nated, -nating.** to give another body to; incarnate again.

**reincarnation** /,riɪnka'neɪʃən/, *n.* **1.** the belief that the soul, upon death of the body, moves to another body or form. **2.** rebirth of the soul in a new body. **3.** a new incarnation or embodiment, as of a person. – **reincarnationist,** *n.*

**reindeer** /'reɪndɪə/, *n., pl.* **-deer,** (*occasionally*) **-deers.** any of various species of large deer of the genus *Rangifer,* with branched antlers in both males and females, found in northern or arctic regions, and often domesticated. See **caribou.** [ME *raynedere,* from Scand.; cf. Icel. *hreindȳri*]

reindeer

**reindeer moss** /'– mɒs/, *n.* a grey, branched lichen, *Cladonia rangiferina,* widespread in arctic regions, where it is eaten during the winter by reindeer.

**reinforce** /riɪn'fɔs/, *v.t.,* **-forced, -forcing.** **1.** to strengthen with some added piece, support, or material: *to reinforce a wall.* **2.** to strengthen with additional men or ships for military or naval purposes: *to reinforce a garrison.* **3.** to strengthen; make more forcible or effective: *to reinforce efforts.* **4.** to augment; increase: *to reinforce a supply.* [RE- + *inforce,* var. of ENFORCE]

**reinforced concrete** /,riɪnfɔst 'kɒŋkrit/, *n.* concrete embodying steel bars to give tensile strength.

**reinforcement** /riɪn'fɔsmənt/, *n.* **1.** the act of reinforcing. **2.** the state of being reinforced. **3.** something that reinforces or strengthens. **4.** (*oft. pl.*) an additional supply of men, ships, etc., for a military or naval force. **5.** *Psychol.* the process of following the conditioned stimulus with the unconditioned stimulus in establishing conditioned responses; in operant conditioning, the rewarding of acceptable responses. **6.** *Colloq.* any reward which encourages learning.

**reins** /reɪnz/, *n.pl. Archaic.* **1.** the kidneys. **2.** the region of the kidneys, or the lower part of the back. **3.** the seat of the feelings or affections, formerly identified with the kidneys (esp. in biblical use). [ME, from OF; replacing ME *reenes,* OE *rēnys,* from L *rēnēs,* pl. kidneys, loins]

**reinsman** /'reɪnzmən/, *n.* (in trotting and pacing) the driver of a gig. – **reinswoman,** *n.*

**reinstate** /riɪn'steɪt/, *v.t.,* **-stated, -stating.** to put back or establish again, as in a former position or state. – **reinstatement,** *n.*

**reinsure** /riɪn'ʃɔ, -'ʃʊə/, *v.t.,* **-sured, -suring.** **1.** to insure again. **2.** to insure under a contract by which a first insurer relieves himself from a part or from all of the risk and devolves it upon another insurer. – **reinsurance,** *n.* – **reinsurer,** *n.*

**reissue** /ri'ɪʃʊ, ri'ɪsju/, *v.t.* **1.** to issue again, esp. in a different form, at a different price, etc. *–n.* **2.** that which is reissued.

**reiterant** /ri'ɪtərənt/, *adj.* repetitive and constant: *his reiterant chatter was very annoying.*

**reiterate** /ri'ɪtəreɪt/, *v.t.,* **-rated, -rating.** to repeat; say or do again or repeatedly. [*reiterātus,* pp.] – **reiteration** /ri,ɪtə'reɪʃən/, *n.* – **reiterative,** *adj.*

**reject** /rə'dʒɛkt/, *v.;* /'ridʒɛkt/, *n. –v.t.* **1.** to refuse to have, take, recognise, etc. **2.** to refuse to grant (a demand, etc.). **3.** to refuse to accept (a person); rebuff. **4.** to throw away, discard, or refuse as useless or unsatisfactory. **5.** to cast out or eject; vomit. **6.** to cast out or off. *–n.* **7.** something rejected, as an imperfect article. [L *rejectus,* pp., thrown back] – **rejecter,** *n.*

**rejectamenta** /ri,dʒɛktə'mɛntə/, *n.pl.* **1.** things or matter rejected as useless or worthless. **2.** refuse; excrement. [NL, pl. of *rejectāmentum,* from L *rejectus,* pp., thrown away. See -MENT]

**rejection** /rə'dʒɛkʃən/, *n.* **1.** the act of rejecting. **2.** the state of being rejected. **3.** that which is rejected.

**rejoice** /rə'dʒɔɪs/, *v.,* **-joiced, -joicing.** *–v.i.* **1.** to be glad; take delight (*in*). *–v.t.* **2.** to make joyful; gladden. [ME, from OF *rejoiss-,* stem of *rejoir,* from *re-* RE- + *joir* joy] – **rejoicer,** *n.*

**rejoicing** /rə'dʒɔɪsɪŋ/, *n.* **1.** the act of one who rejoices. **2.** the feeling or the expression of joy. **3.** (*oft. pl.*) an occasion for expressing joy.

**rejoin**[1] /rə'dʒɔɪn/, *v.t.* **1.** to come again into the company of: *to rejoin a party after a brief absence.* **2.** to join together again; reunite. *–v.i.* **3.** to become joined together again. [RE- + JOIN]

**rejoin**[2] /rə'dʒɔɪn/, *v.t.* **1.** to say in answer. *–v.i.* **2.** to answer. **3.** *Law.* to answer the plaintiff's replication. [late ME *rejoyne,* from AF *rejoyner,* F *rejoindre,* from *re-* RE- + *joindre* JOIN]

**rejoinder** /rə'dʒɔɪndə/, *n.* **1.** an answer to a reply; response. **2.** *Law.* the defendant's answer to the plaintiff's replication. Cf. **replication.** [late ME *rejoyner,* from AF, inf. used as n.; cf. F *rejoindre*]

**rejuvenate** /rə'dʒuvəneɪt/, *v.t.,* **-nated, -nating.** **1.** to make young again; restore to youthful vigour, appearance, etc. **2.** *Phys. Geog.* **a.** to renew the activity, erosive power, etc., of (a stream) by the uplifting of the region it drains, or by removal of a barrier in the bed of the stream. **b.** to impress again the characters of youthful topography on (a region) by the action of rejuvenated streams. [LL *rejuven(escere)* become young again + -ATE[1]] – **rejuvenation** /rədʒuvə'neɪʃən/, *n.* – **rejuvenator,** *n.*

**rejuvenescent** /rədʒuvə'nɛsənt/, *adj.* **1.** becoming young again. **2.** making young again; rejuvenating. – **rejuvenescence,** *n.*

**rejuvenise** /rə'dʒuvənaɪz/, *v.t.,* **-nised, -nising.** →**rejuvenate.** Also, **rejuvenize.**

**-rel,** a noun suffix having a diminutive or pejorative force, as in *wastrel.* Also, **-erel.** [ME, from OF *-erel, -erelle*]

**relapse** /rə'læps/, *v.,* **-lapsed, -lapsing,** *n. –v.i.* **1.** to fall or slip back into a former state, practice, etc.: *to relapse into silence.* **2.** to fall back into illness after convalescence or apparent recovery. **3.** to fall back into wrongdoing or error; backslide. *–n.* **4.** the act of relapsing. **5.** a return of a disease or illness after partial recovery. [L *relapsus,* pp., slipped back] – **relapser,** *n.*

**relapsing fever** /rəlæpsɪŋ 'fivə/, *n.* one of a group of fevers characterised by relapses, occurring in many tropical countries, and caused by several species of spirochaetes transmitted by several species of lice and ticks.

**relate** /rə'leɪt/, *v.,* **-lated, -lating.** *–v.t.* **1.** to tell. **2.** to bring into or establish association, connection, or relation. *–v.i.* **3.** to have reference (*to*). **4.** to have some relation (*to*). [L *relātus,* pp., reported, carried back] – **relater,** *n.*

**related** /rə'leɪtəd/, *adj.* **1.** associated; connected. **2.** allied by nature, origin, kinship, marriage, etc. **3.** narrated. **4.** (in diatonic music) of notes belonging to keys which have several notes in common.

**relation** /rə'leɪʃən/, *n.* **1.** an existing connection; a particular way of being related: *the relation between cause and effect.* **2.** (*pl.*) the various connections between peoples, countries, etc.: *commercial or foreign relations.* **3.** (*pl.*) the various connections in which persons are brought together, as by common interests. **4.** the mode or kind of connection between one person and another, between man and God, etc. **5.** connection between persons by blood or marriage. **6.** a relative. **7.** reference; regard; respect: *to plan with relation to the future.* **8.** the action of relating, narrating, or telling; narration. **9.** a narrative; account. **10.** *Maths.* a property which associates two or more quantities or functions. **11. have relations,** *Colloq.* to have sexual intercourse. [ME, from L *relātio* a bringing back, report]

**relational** /rə'leɪʃənəl/, *adj.* **1.** of or pertaining to relations. **2.** indicating or specifying some relation. **3.** *Gram.* serving to indicate relations between other elements in a sentence, as prepositions, conjunctions, etc. Cf. **notional.**

**relationism** /rə'leɪʃənɪzəm/, *n.* **1.** the theory that relations exist in their own right. **2.** the theory that knowledge is relative, as opposed to being absolute.

**relationship** /rə'leɪʃənʃɪp/, *n.* **1.** connection; a particular connection. **2.** connection by blood or marriage. **3.** an emotional connection between people, sometimes involving sexual relations.

**relative** /ˈrɛlətɪv/, *n.* **1.** one who is connected with another or others by blood or marriage. **2.** something having, or standing in, some relation to something else; esp., in scientific usage, as opposed to *absolute.* **3.** *Gram.* a relative pronoun, adjective, or adverb. *–adj.* **4.** considered in relation to something else; comparative: *the relative merits of a republic and a monarchy.* **5.** existing only by relation to something else; not absolute or independent. **6.** having relation or connection: *relative phenomena.* **7.** having reference or regard; relevant; pertinent (fol. by *to*). **8.** correspondent; proportionate: *value is relative to demand.* **9.** (of a term, name, etc.) depending for significance upon something else: *better is a relative term.* **10.** *Gram.* **a.** designating words which introduce subordinate clauses and refer to some element of the principal clause (the antecedent), as *who* in 'He's the man *who saw you*'. **b.** (of a clause) introduced by such a word. [ME, from LL *relātīvus,* from L *relātus* carried back] – **relativeness,** *n.*

**relative density** /– ˈdɛnsəti/, *n.* **1.** →**specific gravity.** **2.** the ratio of the density of a gas to that of hydrogen under the same conditions.

**relative frequency** /– ˈfrikwənsi/, *n.* **1.** *Maths.* the ratio of the number of times an event occurs to the number of occasions on which it might occur in the same period. **2.** *Statistics.* the number of items of a certain type divided by the number of all the items considered.

**relative humidity** /– hjuˈmɪdəti/, *n.* See **humidity** (def. 2).

**relatively** /ˈrɛlətɪvli/, *adv.* in a relative manner; comparatively: *a relatively small difference.*

**relative major** /rɛlətɪv ˈmeɪdʒə/, *n.* the major musical key whose tonic is the third degree of a given minor key.

**relative minor** /– ˈmaɪnə/, *n.* the minor musical key whose tonic is the sixth degree of a given major key.

**relative pitch** /– ˈpɪtʃ/, *n.* a listening skill which enables a musician, given a pitch reference, to be able to name changes in pitch.

**relative pronoun** /– ˈprounaun/, *n.* a pronoun with a relative function. See **relative** (def. 10a).

**relativism** /ˈrɛlətɪvɪzəm/, *n.* the theory of knowledge or ethics which holds that criteria of judgment are relative, varying with the individual, time, and circumstance. – **relativist,** *n.*

**relativistic** /rɛlətəˈvɪstɪk/, *adj.* **1.** of or pertaining to relativity or relativism. **2.** *Physics.* having, or pertaining to an entity which has a velocity comparable to that of light: *a relativistic particle or mass.*

**relativity** /rɛləˈtɪvəti/, *n.* **1.** the state or fact of being relative. **2. a. special theory of relativity,** the theory formed by Albert Einstein, 1879-1955, physicist, of how the observed motion of objects changes from one frame of reference to another moving at constant velocity relative to it, based on the hypothesis that the observed velocity of light remains the same in all such frames of reference. **b. general theory of relativity,** Einstein's geometrical theory of gravitation based on the principle of equivalence. **3.** (*pl.*) the relative differences in wages between groups of workers.

**relativity of knowledge,** *n.* the doctrine that all human knowledge is relative to the human mind, or that the mind can know concerning things only the effects which they produce upon it and not what the things themselves are.

**relator** /rəˈleɪtə/, *n.* **1.** one who relates or narrates. **2.** *Law.* the person responsible for costs on whose complaint an action is commenced by the attorney general. [L. Cf. F *relateur*]

**relax** /rəˈlæks/, *v.t.* **1.** to make lax, or less tense, rigid, or firm: *to relax the muscles.* **2.** to diminish the force of. **3.** to slacken or abate, as effort, attention, etc. **4.** to make less strict or severe, as rules, discipline, etc. *–v.i.* **5.** to become less tense, rigid, or firm. **6.** to become less strict or severe; grow milder. **7.** to slacken in effort, application, etc.; take relaxation. [ME, from L *relaxāre*] – **relaxer,** *n.*

**relaxation** /rilækˈseɪʃən/, *n.* **1.** abatement or relief of bodily or mental effort or application. **2.** something affording such relief; a diversion or entertainment. **3.** a loosening or slackening. **4.** diminution or remission of strictness or severity. **5.** *Maths.* a method of solving complex groups of simultaneous equations by successive approximations.

**relaxed** /rəˈlækst/, *adj.* **1.** freed from tension; relieved of fatigue, strain, etc. **2.** made less strict and rigid, as rules. **3.** slackened; rendered more pliable.

**relaxed throat** /– ˈθrout/, *n.* a form of sore throat.

**re-lay** /ˌriˈleɪ/, *v.t.* to lay again.

**relay** /ˈrileɪ/, *n.*; /rəˈleɪ, ˈrileɪ/, *v.* *–n.* **1.** a set of persons relieving others or taking turns; a shift. **2.** a fresh set of dogs or horses posted in readiness for use in a hunt, on a journey, etc. **3.** *Athletics.* **a.** a relay race. **b.** one of the lengths, or legs, of a relay race. **4.** an automatic device for operating the controls of a larger piece of equipment. **5.** *Elect.* **a.** a device by means of which a change of current or voltage in one circuit can be made to produce a change in the electrical condition of another circuit. **b.** a device that is operative by a variation in the conditions of one electric circuit to effect the operation of other devices in the same or another electric circuit. *–v.t.* **6.** to carry forward by or as by relays: *to relay a message.* **7.** to provide with or replace by fresh relays. **8.** *Elect.* to retransmit by means of a telegraphic relay, or as such a relay does. *–v.i.* **9.** *Elect.* to relay a message. [ME, from OF *relais,* orig., hounds in reserve along the line of the hunt, from *relaier* leave behind]

**relay race** /ˈ– reɪs/, *n.* a race of two or more teams of contestants, each contestant running part of the distance and being relieved by a team-mate.

**relay station** /ˈ– steɪʃən/, *n.* a place from which radio and television programs, etc., are broadcast, after being received from another station.

**re-lease** /ˌriˈlis/, *v.t.,* **-leased, -leasing.** **1.** to lease again. **2.** *Law.* to make over (land, etc.), as to another.

**release** /rəˈlis/, *v.,* **-leased, -leasing,** *n.* *–v.t.* **1.** to free from confinement, bondage, obligation, pain, etc.; let go. **2.** to free from anything that restrains, fastens, etc. **3.** to allow to become known, be issued or exhibited: *to release an article for publication.* **4.** *Law.* give up, relinquish, or surrender (a right, claim, etc.). *–n.* **5.** a freeing or releasing from confinement, obligation, pain, etc. **6.** liberation from anything that restrains or fastens. **7.** some device for effecting such liberation. **8.** the releasing of something for public exhibition or sale, as a film, record, or the like. **9.** the releasing of an article, statement, etc., to the radio, press, or the like, for publication. **10.** the article so released. **11.** *Law.* **a.** the surrender of a right or the like to another. **b.** a document embodying such a surrender. **12.** *Obs. or Law.* a remission, as of a debt, tax, or tribute. **13.** *Mach.* a control mechanism for starting or stopping a machine, esp. by removing some restrictive apparatus. **14.** *Mach.* **a.** (in a steam-engine) the opening of the exhaust port of the cylinder at or near the end of the working stroke of the piston. **b.** the moment at which the exhaust port is opened. [ME *relesse(n),* from OF *relesser,* from L *relaxāre* relax]

**release binding** /ˈ– baɪndɪŋ/, *n.* →**safety binding.**

**relegate** /ˈrɛləgeɪt/, *v.t.,* **-gated, -gating.** **1.** to send or consign to some obscure position, place, or condition. **2.** to consign or commit (a matter, task, etc.), as to a person. **3.** to assign or refer (something) to a particular class or kind. **4.** to send into exile; banish. **5.** *Sport.* to transfer (the lowest scoring team) to a lower division, as a team in a football league. [L *relēgātus,* pp., sent back] – **relegation** /rɛləˈgeɪʃən/, *n.*

**relent** /rəˈlɛnt/, *v.i.* **1.** to soften in feeling, temper, or determination; become more mild, compassionate, or forgiving. *–v.t.* **2.** *Obs.* to cause to relent. [ME *relente* melt, apparently from L *relentescere* grow slack or soft]

**relentless** /rəˈlɛntləs/, *adj.* that does not relent; unrelenting: *a relentless enemy.* – **relentlessly,** *adv.* – **relentlessness,** *n.*

**relevant** /ˈrɛləvənt/, *adj.* bearing upon or connected with the matter in hand; to the purpose; pertinent: *a relevant remark.* [ML *relevans,* properly ppr. of L *relevāre* raise up] – **relevance, relevancy,** *n.* – **relevantly,** *adv.*

**reliable** /rəˈlaɪəbəl/, *adj.* that may be relied on; trustworthy: *reliable sources of information.* – **reliability** /rəlaɪəˈbɪləti/, **reliableness,** *n.* – **reliably,** *adv.*

**reliant** /rəˈlaɪənt/, *adj.* **1.** having or showing reliance. **2.** confident; trustful. – **reliance,** *n.*

**relic** /ˈrɛlɪk/, *n.* **1.** a surviving memorial of something past. **2.** an object having interest by reason of its age or its association with the past: *a museum of historical relics.* **3.** a

Q-R ↔

surviving trace of something: *a custom which is a relic of paganism.* **4.** (*pl.*) remaining parts or fragments. **5.** something kept in remembrance. **6.** *Eccles.* (esp. in Roman Catholic and Greek churches) the body, a part of the body, or some personal memorial of a saint, martyr, or other sacred persons, preserved as worthy of veneration. **7.** (*pl.*) the remains of a deceased person. [ME *relik,* OE *relic,* short for *reliquium,* from L]

**relict** /ˈrɛlɪkt/, *n.* **1.** *Ecol.* a plant or animal species living in an environment which has changed from that which is typical for it. **2.** a survivor. **3.** (*pl.*) remains; remnants; residue. **4.** *Archaic or Rare.* a widow. [late ME, from ML *relicta* widow, properly fem. of L *relictus,* pp., left behind]

**relief** /rəˈlif/, *n.* **1.** deliverance, alleviation, or ease through the removal of pain, distress, oppression, etc. **2.** a means of relieving, or a thing that relieves pain, distress, anxiety, etc. **3.** help or assistance given, as to those in poverty or need. **4.** something affording a pleasing change, as from monotony. **5.** release from a post of duty, as by the coming of a substitute or replacement. **6.** the person or persons thus bringing release. **7.** the deliverance of a besieged town, etc., from an attacking force. **8.** prominence, distinctness, or vividness due to contrast. **9.** the projection of a figure or part from the ground or plane on which it is formed, in sculpture or similar work. **10.** a piece or work in such projection: *high relief.* **11.** an apparent projection of parts in a painting, drawing, etc., giving the appearance of the third dimension. **12.** *Phys. Geog.* the departure of the land surface in any area from that of a level surface. **13.** *Engraving.* any printing process by which the printing ink is transferred to paper, etc., from areas that are higher than the rest of the block, as letterpress printing. **14.** a receipt of some state or charitable financial assistance. **15. on relief,** in the situation of being a relief worker. [ME *relef,* from OF, from *relever* RELIEVE; defs 8-13 from F, from It. *rilievo*]

**relief map** /ˈ– mæp/, *n.* a map showing the relief of an area, usu. by generalised contour lines.

**relief teacher** /ˈ– titʃə/, *n.* a schoolteacher who temporarily replaces regular teachers who are absent.

**relief work** /ˈ– wɜk/, *n.* **1.** work provided by the government for the unemployed as a temporary means of relief. **2.** work carried out by military or civilian organisations in times of natural disaster to feed, clothe, and house victims.

**relieve** /rəˈliv/, *v.t.,* **-lieved, -lieving. 1.** to ease or alleviate (pain, distress, anxiety, need, etc.). **2.** to free from anxiety, fear, pain, etc. **3.** to deliver from poverty, need, etc. **4.** to bring efficient aid to (a besieged town, etc.). **5.** to ease (a person) of any burden, wrong, or oppression, as by legal means. **6.** to make less tedious, unpleasant, or monotonous; break or vary the sameness of. **7.** to bring into relief or prominence; heighten the effect of. **8.** to release (one on duty) by coming as or providing a substitute. **9. relieve oneself,** to empty the bowels or bladder. [ME *releve,* from OF *relever,* from L *relevāre* raise again, assist] – **relievable,** *adj.* – **reliever,** *n.*

**relievo** /rəˈlivoʊ/, *n., pl.* **-vos, -vi** /-vi/. →**relief** (defs 9, 10). Also, **rilievo.** [It., from *rilevare* raise, modelled on F *relief*]

**relig.,** religion.

**religion** /rəˈlɪdʒən/, *n.* **1.** the quest for the values of the ideal life, involving three phases, the ideal, the practices for attaining the values of the ideal, and the theology or world view relating the quest to the environing universe. **2.** a particular system in which the quest for the ideal life has been embodied: *the Christian religion.* **3.** recognition on the part of man of a controlling superhuman power entitled to obedience, reverence, and worship. **4.** the feeling or the spiritual attitude of those recognising such a controlling power. **5.** the manifestation of such feeling in conduct or life. **6.** a point or matter of conscience, esp. when zealously or obsessively observed: *to make a religion of doing something.* **7.** *Obs.* the practice of sacred rites or observances. **8.** (*pl.*) *Obs.* religious rites. [ME, from L *religio* fear of the gods, religious awe, sacredness, scrupulousness]

**religionism** /rəˈlɪdʒənɪzəm/, *n.* **1.** excessive or exaggerated religious zeal. **2.** affected or pretended religious zeal. – **religionist,** *n.*

**religiosity** /rəlɪdʒiˈɒsəti/, *n.* **1.** the quality of being religious; piety; devoutness. **2.** affected or excessive devotion to religion.

**religious** /rəˈlɪdʒəs/, *adj.* **1.** of, pertaining to, or concerned with religion. **2.** imbued with or exhibiting religion; pious; devout; godly. **3.** scrupulously faithful; conscientious: *religious care.* **4.** belonging to a religious order, as persons. **5.** pertaining to or connected with a monastic or religious order. **6.** appropriate to religion or to sacred rites or observances. –*n.* **7.** a member of a religious order, congregation, etc.; a monk, friar, or nun. **8.** (*construed as pl.*) such persons collectively. [ME, from L *religiōsus*] – **religiously,** *adv.* – **religiousness,** *n.*

**relinquish** /rəˈlɪŋkwɪʃ/, *v.t.* **1.** to renounce or surrender (a possession, right, etc.). **2.** to give up; put aside or desist from: *to relinquish a plan.* **3.** to let go: *to relinquish one's hold.* [ME, from OF *relinquiss-,* stem of *relinquir,* from L *relinquere*] – **relinquisher,** *n.* – **relinquishment,** *n.*

**reliquary** /ˈrɛləkwəri/, *n., pl.* **-quaries.** a repository or receptacle for a relic or relics. [ML *reliquiārium,* from L *reliquiae,* pl., remains. See RELIC]

**reliquiae** /rəˈlɪkwi,i/, *n.pl.* remains, as those of fossil organisms. [L]

**relish** /ˈrɛlɪʃ/, *n.* **1.** liking for the taste of something, or enjoyment of something eaten. **2.** pleasurable appreciation of anything; liking: *no relish for such jokes.* **3.** something appetising or savoury added to a meal, as chutney. **4.** a pleasing or appetising flavour. **5.** a pleasing or enjoyable quality. **6.** a taste or flavour. **7.** a smack, trace, or touch of something. –*v.t.* **8.** to take pleasure in; like; enjoy. **9.** to make pleasing to the taste. **10.** to like the taste or flavour of. –*v.i.* **11.** to have taste or flavour. **12.** to be agreeable or pleasant. [ME *reles,* from OF: what is left, remainder, from *relaisser* leave behind] – **relishable,** *adj.*

**relive** /ˌriˈlɪv/, *v.t.,* **-lived, -living.** to repeat former experiences or rehearse the memory of them.

**rellie** /ˈrɛli/, *n. Colloq.* a relative.

**relocatable home** /ˌriloʊkeɪtəbəl ˈhoʊm/, *n.* a house which is designed for easy transferal from one location to another.

**relocate** /ˌriloʊˈkeɪt/, *v.t.,* **-cated, -cating.** to move (a firm, factory, etc.) to a different place.

**rel. pron.,** relative pronoun.

**relucent** /rəˈlusənt/, *adj.* shining; bright. [L *relūcens,* ppr., shining back; replacing ME *relusant,* from OF]

**reluct** /rəˈlʌkt/, *v.i. Archaic or Rare.* **1.** to struggle against something; resist. **2.** to object; show reluctance. [backformation from RELUCTANCE, RELUCTANT]

**reluctance** /rəˈlʌktəns/, *n.* **1.** unwillingness; disinclination: *reluctance to speak.* **2.** *Elect.* the resistance offered to the passage of magnetic lines of force, being numerically equal to the magnetomotive force divided by the magnetic flux. Also **reluctancy.**

**reluctant** /rəˈlʌktənt/, *adj.* **1.** unwilling; disinclined. **2.** *Rare.* struggling in opposition. [L *reluctans,* ppr., struggling against] – **reluctantly,** *adv.*

**reluctivity** /rɛlʌkˈtɪvəti/, *n.* the magnetic reluctance of a material compared with that of air.

**relume** /rəˈlum/, *v.t.,* **-lumed, -luming.** to light or illuminate again. [LL *relūmināre.* See RE-, ILLUMINE]

**rely** /rəˈlaɪ/, *v.i.,* **-lied, -lying.** to depend confidently; put trust in (fol. by *on* or *upon*). [ME *relie,* from OF *relier* bind together, from L *religāre* bind back]

**rem** /rɛm/, *n.* the quantity of ionising radiation whose biological effect is equal to that produced by one roentgen of X-rays. [*r(oentgen) e(quivalent in) m(an)*]

**REM** /ˌar i ˈɛm, rɛm/, *n.* →**rapid eye movement.**

**remain** /rəˈmeɪn/, *v.i.* **1.** to continue in the same state; continue to be (as specified): *to remain at peace.* **2.** to stay in a place: *to remain at home.* **3.** to be left after the removal, departure, loss, etc., of another or others. **4.** to be left to be done, told, etc. –*n.* (*always pl.*) **5.** that which remains or is left; a remnant. **6.** miscellaneous, fragmentary, or other writings collected after the author's death. **7.** traces of some quality, condition, etc. **8.** that which remains of a person after death; a dead body. **9.** parts or substances remaining from animal or plant life, occurring in the earth's crust or strata: *fossil remains, organic remains.* [ME *remayn,* from AF *remaindre,* from L *remanēre*]

**remainder** /rə'meɪndə/, *n.* **1.** that which remains or is left: *the remainder of the day.* **2.** a remaining part. **3.** *Arith.* the quantity that remains after subtraction or division. **4.** *Law.* a future interest so created as to take effect at the end of another estate, as when property is conveyed to A for life and then to B. **5.** (*pl.*) *Philately.* the quantities of stamps on hand after they have been demonetised or otherwise voided for postal use. **6.** a copy of a book remaining in the publisher's stock when the sale has practically ceased, frequently sold at a reduced price. *–adj.* **7.** remaining; left. *–v.t.* **8.** to dispose of or sell as a publisher's remainder. [late ME *remaindre,* from AF, properly inf. See REMAIN]

**remainderman** /rə'meɪndəmæn/, *n.* a person entitled to an estate in expectancy.

**remake** /ri'meɪk/, *v.t.,* **-made, -making;** /'rimeɪk/, *n.* *–v.t.* **1.** to make again. *–n.* **2.** a remade version of something, esp. a film.

**reman** /ri'mæn/, *v.t.,* **-manned, -manning. 1.** to man again; furnish with a fresh supply of men. **2.** to restore the manliness or courage of.

**remand** /rə'mænd, -'mand/, *v.t.* **1.** to send back, remit, or consign again. **2.** *Law.* (of a court or magistrate) to send back (a prisoner or accused person) into custody, as to await further proceedings. *–n.* **3.** the act of remanding. **4.** the state of being remanded. **5.** a person remanded. [late ME *remaund(en),* from LL *remandāre* to send back word, repeat a command]

**remanence** /'rɛmənəns/, *n.* the residual magnetisation of a ferromagnetic substance after the magnetising force has been removed; retentivity.

**remanent** /'rɛmənənt/, *adj. Rare.* remaining; left behind. [late ME, from L *remanens*]

**remanet** /'rɛmənɛt/, *n. Law.* an action which remains to be heard after a sitting. [L: it remains]

**re-mark** /,ri-'mak/, *v.;* /'ri-mak/, *n.* *–v.t.* **1.** to mark (an essay, examination paper, etc.) again. *–n.* **2.** a second or additional marking of a paper.

**remark** /rə'mak/, *v.t.* **1.** to say casually, as in making a comment. **2.** to note; perceive. *–v.i.* **3.** to make a remark or observation (fol. by *on* or *upon*). *–n.* **4.** the act of remarking; notice. **5.** comment: *to let a thing pass without remark.* **6.** a casual or brief expression of thought or opinion. **7.** *Engraving.* →**remarque.** [F *remarquer* note, heed, from *re-* RE- + *marquer* mark]

**remarkable** /rə'makəbəl/, *adj.* **1.** notably or conspicuously unusual, or extraordinary: *a remarkable change.* **2.** worthy of remark or notice. – **remarkableness,** *n.* – **remarkably,** *adv.*

**remarque** /rə'mak/, *n. Engraving.* **1.** a distinguishing mark or peculiarity indicating a particular stage of a plate. **2.** a small sketch engraved on the margin of a plate, and usually removed after a number of early proofs have been printed. **3.** a plate so marked. Also, **remark.** [F]

**remediable** /rə'midiəbəl/, *adj.* capable of being remedied. – **remediably,** *adv.*

**remedial** /rə'midiəl/, *adj.* **1.** affording remedy; tending to remedy something. **2.** of or pertaining to the treatment of physical defects with exercises, etc., rather than by medical or surgical means. **3.** (of teaching) designed to meet the needs of retarded, backward, or maladjusted children. [L *remediālis*] – **remedially,** *adv.*

**remedial teacher** /'– titʃə/, *n.* a teacher who is trained in special methods for the teaching of mentally retarded children or children with particular learning problems as aphasia, dyslexia, etc.

**remediless** /'rɛmədiləs/, *adj.* not admitting of remedy, as disease, trouble, damage, etc.

**remedy** /'rɛmədi/, *n., pl.* **-dies,** *v.,* **-died, -dying.** *–n.* **1.** something that cures or relieves a disease or bodily disorder; a healing medicine, application, or treatment. **2.** something that corrects or removes an evil of any kind. **3.** *Law.* legal redress; the legal means of enforcing a right or redressing a wrong. **4.** *Coining.* a certain allowance at the mint for deviation from the standard weight and fineness of coins; tolerance. *–v.t.* **5.** to cure or heal. **6.** to put right, or restore to the natural or proper condition: *to remedy a matter.* **7.** to counteract or remove: *to remedy an evil.* [ME, from L *remedium*]

**remember** /rə'mɛmbə/, *v.t.* **1.** to recall to the mind by an act or effort of memory. **2.** to retain in the memory; bear in mind. **3.** to have (something) come into the mind again. **4.** to bear (a person) in mind as deserving a gift, reward, or fee. **5.** to reward; tip. **6.** to mention to another as sending kindly greetings. **7.** *Archaic.* to remind. *–v.i.* **8.** to possess or exercise the faculty of memory. **9.** *Archaic or Scot.* to have memory or recollection (fol. by *of*). [ME *remembre(n),* from OF *remembrer,* from LL *rememorārī,* from L *re-* RE- + *memorāre* call to mind] – **rememberer,** *n.*

**remembrance** /rə'mɛmbrəns/, *n.* **1.** a mental impression retained. **2.** the act or fact of remembering. **3.** the power or faculty of remembering. **4.** *Obs.* the length of time over which recollection or memory extends. **5.** the state of being remembered; commemoration. **6.** something that serves to bring to or keep in mind, as a gift. **7.** (*pl.*) greetings.

**remembrancer** /rə'mɛmbrənsə/, *n.* **1.** one who reminds another of something. **2.** one engaged to do this. **3.** a reminder; memento; souvenir.

**remex** /'rimɛks/, *n., pl.* **remiges** /'rɛmədʒiz/. →**flight feather.** [L: lit., oarsman (pl. *rēmigēs*), from *rēmus* oar] – **remigial** /rə'mɪdʒiəl/, *adj.*

**remind** /rə'maɪnd/, *v.t.* **1.** to cause (one) to remember. **2. remind of,** to look like: *you remind me of Winston Churchill.* [RE- + MIND, *v.*] – **reminder,** *n.*

**remindful** /rə'maɪndfəl/, *adj.* **1.** reviving memory of something; reminiscent. **2.** retaining memory of something; mindful.

**reminisce** /rɛmə'nɪs/, *v.i.,* **-nisced, -niscing.** to indulge in reminiscence; recall past experiences. [backformation from REMINISCENCE]

**reminiscence** /rɛmə'nɪsəns/, *n.* **1.** the act or process of remembering one's past. **2.** a mental impression retained and revived. **3.** (*oft. pl.*) a recollection narrated or told. **4.** something that recalls or suggests something else. **5.** (in Platonic philosophy) the doctrine that, on occasion of perception, the mind can educe from itself universal ideas which are really memories of what it knew in a former state. [L *reminiscentia*]

**reminiscent** /rɛmə'nɪsənt/, *adj.* **1.** awakening memories of something else; suggestive (fol. by *of*). **2.** characterised by or of the nature of reminiscence or reminiscences. **3.** given to reminiscence, as a person. [L *reminiscens,* ppr., remembering] – **reminiscently,** *adv.*

**remise**[1] /rə'maɪz/, *v.t.,* **-mised, -mising.** *Law.* to give up a claim to; surrender by deed. [OF, pp. (fem.) of *remettre* put back, deliver, from *re-* RE- + *mettre* put (from L *mittere* send)]

**remise**[2] /rə'miz/, *n.* (in fencing) renewal of an attack delivered while on the same lunge. [special use of REMISE[1]]

**remiss** /rə'mɪs/, *adj.* **1.** not diligent, careful, or prompt in duty, business, etc. **2.** characterised by negligence or carelessness. **3.** lacking force or energy; languid; sluggish. [ME, from L *remissus,* pp., lit., sent back]

**remissible** /rə'mɪsəbəl/, *adj.* that may be remitted. – **remissibility** /rəmɪsə'bɪləti/, *n.*

**remission** /rə'mɪʃən/, *n.* **1.** the act of remitting. **2.** pardon; forgiveness, as of sins or offences. **3.** *Law.* a pardon from the Crown; a release. **4.** abatement or diminution, as of diligence, labour, intensity, etc. **5.** the relinquishment of a payment, obligation, etc. **6.** a temporary decrease or subsidence of manifestations of a disease.

**remissness** /rə'mɪsnəs/, *n.* the state or character of being remiss; slackness.

**remit** /rə'mɪt/, *v.,* **-mitted, -mitting,** *n.* *–v.t.* **1.** to transmit or send (money, etc.) to a person or place. **2.** to refrain from inflicting or enforcing, as a punishment, sentence, etc. **3.** to refrain from exacting, as a payment or service. **4.** to pardon or forgive (a sin, offence, etc.). **5.** to slacken; abate: *to remit watchfulness.* **6.** to give back: *to remit a fine.* **7.** *Law.* to send back (a case) to an inferior court for further action. **8.** to put back into a previous position or condition. **9.** to put off; postpone. **10.** *Obs.* to set free; release. **11.** *Obs.* to send back to prison or custody. **12.** *Obs.* to give up; surrender. *–v.i.* **13.** to transmit money, etc., as in payment. **14.** to abate for a time or at intervals, as a fever. **15.** to slacken; abate. *–n.* **16.** *Law.* a transfer of the record of an action from one tribunal to another, particularly from an appellate court to the court of original jurisdiction. **17.** *N.Z.* a recommendation from a branch of an organisation to the main body or annual conference for possible adoption. [ME, from L *remittere* send back] – **remittable,** *adj.*

**remittal** /rəˈmɪtl/, *n.* →**remission.**

**remittance** /rəˈmɪtns/, *n.* **1.** the remitting of money, etc., to a recipient at a distance. **2.** money or its equivalent sent from one place to another.

**remittance man** /ˈ– mæn/, *n.* (formerly) an Englishman in Australia whose presence was no longer acceptable in England and who was supported by remittance from his family.

**remittent** /rəˈmɪtnt/, *adj.* **1.** abating for a time or at intervals, used esp. of a fever in which the symptoms diminish considerably at intervals without disappearing entirely. *–n.* **2.** a remittent fever. – **remittence, remittency,** *n.* – **remittently,** *adv.*

**remitter** /rəˈmɪtə/, *n.* **1.** one who makes a remittance. **2.** *Law.* the principle or operation by which a person who enters on an estate by a defective title, and who previously had an earlier and more valid title to it, is adjudged to hold it by the earlier and more valid one. **3.** *Law.* the act of remitting a case to another court for decision. **4.** restoration, as to a former right or condition.

**remnant** /ˈrɛmnənt/, *n.* **1.** a part, quantity, or number (usu. small) remaining. **2.** a fragment or scrap, esp. an odd piece of cloth, lace, etc., unsold or unused. **3.** a trace; vestige: *remnants of former greatness.* *–adj.* **4.** remaining. [ME; syncopated var. of ME *remenant,* from OF, ppr. of *remenoir* remain]

**remodel** /riˈmɒdl/, *v.t.,* **-elled, -elling** or (*U.S.*) **-eled, -eling.** **1.** to model again. **2.** to reconstruct; make in an improved form.

**remonstrance** /rəˈmɒnstrəns/, *n.* **1.** the act of remonstrating; expostulation. **2.** a protest: *deaf to remonstrances.* **3.** *Parl. Proc.* a written petition of grievance listing complaints and requesting redress, addressed by the governed to their government or parliament. [late ME, from ML *remonstrantia*]

**remonstrant** /rəˈmɒnstrənt/, *adj.* **1.** remonstrating; expostulatory. *–n.* **2.** one who remonstrates.

**remonstrate** /ˈrɛmənstreɪt/, *v.,* **-strated, -strating.** *–v.t.* **1.** to say in remonstrance; protest. *–v.i.* **2.** to present reasons in complaint; plead in protest (fol. by *with*). [ML *remonstrātus,* pp., exhibited] – **remonstration** /rɛmənˈstreɪʃən/, *n.* – **remonstrative** /rəˈmɒnstrətɪv/, *adj.* – **remonstrator,** *n.*

**remontant** /rəˈmɒntənt/, *adj.* **1.** (of certain roses) blooming more than once in a season. *–n.* **2.** a remontant rose. [F, ppr. of *remonter* REMOUNT]

**remora** /ˈrɛmərə/, *n.* **1.** any of various fishes (family Echeneididae) having on the top of the head a sucking disc by which they can attach themselves to sharks, turtles, ships, and other moving objects. **2.** *Archaic.* an obstacle, hindrance, or obstruction. [L: name of a fish, lit., delay, hindrance]

remora

**remorse** /rəˈmɔs/, *n.* **1.** deep and painful regret for wrong-doing; compunction. **2.** *Obs.* pity; compassion. [ME *remors,* from L *remorsus* a biting back]

**remorseful** /rəˈmɔsfəl/, *adj.* **1.** full of remorse. **2.** characterised by or due to remorse: *a remorseful mood.* – **remorsefully,** *adv.* – **remorsefulness,** *n.*

**remorseless** /rəˈmɔsləs/, *adj.* without remorse; relentless; pitiless. – **remorselessly,** *adv.* – **remorselessness,** *n.*

**remote** /rəˈmoʊt/, *adj.,* **-moter, -motest.** **1.** far apart; far distant in space. **2.** out-of-the-way; retired; secluded: *a remote village.* **3.** distant in time: *remote antiquity.* **4.** distant in relationship or connection: *a remote ancestor.* **5.** far removed; alien: *remote from common experience.* **6.** far off; removed: *principles remote from actions.* **7.** by intervention; not proximate: *remote control.* **8.** slight or faint: *not the remotest idea.* **9.** abstracted; cold and aloof: *she seemed very remote at their first meeting.* [ME, from L *remōtus,* pp., removed] – **remotely,** *adv.* – **remoteness,** *n.*

**remote control** /– kənˈtroʊl/, *n.* the control of a system by means of electrical, radio, or mechanical signals from a point outside the system.

**remotion** /rəˈmoʊʃən/, *n.* the act of removing; removal.

**remoulade** /rɛməˈleɪd/, *n.* a dressing for salads, asparagus, cold fish or meat, etc., made from a highly spiced mayonnaise and hard-boiled egg yolks. [F, from It. *remolata*]

**remould** /riˈmoʊld/, *v.;* /ˈrimoʊld/, *n.* *–v.t.* **1.** to recondition (a used motor-vehicle tyre which has a sound fabric casing) by moulding on to it new rubber walls and tread. *–n.* **2.** a tyre which has been subjected to this process.

**remount** /riˈmaʊnt/, *v.i., v.t.* **1.** to mount again; reascend. *–n.* **2.** a fresh horse, or a supply of fresh horses. [ME, from OF *remonter.* See RE-, MOUNT[1]]

**removable** /rəˈmuvəbəl/, *adj.* that may be removed. – **removability** /rəmuvəˈbɪləti/, **removableness,** *n.* – **removably,** *adv.*

**removal** /rəˈmuvəl/, *n.* **1.** the act of removing. **2.** a change of residence, position, etc. **3.** dismissal, as from an office.

**removalist** /rəˈmuvələst/, *n.* a person or firm engaged in moving household and office furniture, etc.

**remove** /rəˈmuv/, *v.,* **-moved, -moving,** *n.* *–v.t.* **1.** to move from a place or position; take away; take off: *to remove a book from a desk, remove one's tie.* **2.** to move or shift to another place or position. **3.** to put out; send away: *to remove a tenant.* **4.** to displace from a position or office. **5.** to take, withdraw, or separate (from). **6.** to do away with; put an end to: *to remove a stain.* **7.** to kill; assassinate. *–v.i.* **8.** to move from one place to another, esp. to another locality or residence. **9.** *Poetic.* to go away; depart; disappear. *–n.* **10.** the act of removing. **11.** a removal from one place, as of residence, to another. **12.** the distance by which one person, place, or thing is separated from another. **13.** a step or degree, as in a graded scale. **14.** a degree of relationship: *he is my cousin at two removes.* **15.** *Brit.* (in certain schools) **a.** a form or class intermediate between ordinary yearly stages, as between fourth and fifth form. **b.** a stream of a yearly stage from which pupils may be removed either to a higher or to a lower stage. [ME, from OF *remouvoir,* from L *removēre*] – **remover,** *n.*

**removed** /rəˈmuvd/, *adj.* **1.** remote; separate; not connected with; distinct from. **2.** distant, used in expressing degrees of relationship: *a first cousin twice removed is a cousin's grandchild.*

**remunerate** /rəˈmjunəreɪt/, *v.t.,* **-rated, -rating.** **1.** to pay, recompense, or reward for work, trouble, etc. **2.** to yield a recompense for (work, services, etc.). [L *remūnerātus,* pp., given back]

**remuneration** /rəmjunəˈreɪʃən/, *n.* **1.** the act of remunerating. **2.** that which remunerates; reward; pay: *little remuneration for his services.*

**remunerative** /rəˈmjunərətɪv/, *adj.* **1.** affording remuneration; profitable: *remunerative work.* **2.** that remunerates. – **remuneratively,** *adv.*

**renaissance** /rəˈneɪsəns, rəˈnæsəns/, *n.* **1.** a new birth; a revival. **2.** (*cap.*) **a.** the activity, spirit, or time of the great revival of art, letters, and learning in Europe during the 14th, 15th, and 16th centuries, marking the transition from the medieval to the modern world. **b.** the forms and treatments in art used during this period. **c.** any similar revival in the world of art and learning. *–adj.* **3.** (*cap.*) of, pertaining to, or denoting the European Renaissance. **4.** (*cap.*) denoting or pertaining to the style of building and decoration succeeding the medieval, originating in Italy in the early 15th century and based upon clarity and mathematical relationship of plan and design, and employing to this end the forms and ornaments of classical Roman art. Also, **renascence.** [F, from *renaître* be born again. See RENASCENT]

**renal** /ˈrinəl/, *adj.* of or pertaining to the kidneys or the surrounding regions. [LL *rēnālis,* from L *rēn* kidney]

**renascence** /rəˈnæsəns/, *n.* →**renaissance.**

**renascent** /rəˈnæsənt/, *adj.* being reborn; springing again into being or vigour: *a renascent interest in Henry James.* [L *renascens,* ppr.]

**rencounter** /rɛnˈkaʊntə/, *v.t., v.i.* **1.** to meet hostilely. **2.** to encounter casually. *–n.* Also, **rencontre** /rɛnˈkɒntə/. **3.** a hostile meeting; a battle. **4.** a contest. **5.** a casual meeting. [F *rencontrer,* from *re-* RE- + *encontrer* ENCOUNTER]

**rend** /rɛnd/, *v.*, **rent, rending.** *–v.t.* **1.** to separate into parts with force or violence: *rent to pieces.* **2.** to tear apart, split, or divide. **3.** to pull or tear violently (fol. by *away, off, up,* etc.). **4.** to tear (one's garments or hair) in grief, rage, etc. **5.** to disturb (the air) sharply with loud noise. **6.** to harrow or distress (the heart, etc.) with painful feelings. *–v.i.* **7.** to render or tear something. **8.** to become rent or torn. [ME *rende(n),* OE *rendan,* c. OFris. *renda*]

**render** /ˈrɛndə/, *v.t.* **1.** to make, or cause, to be or become: *to render someone helpless.* **2.** to do; perform: *to render a service.* **3.** to furnish: *to render aid.* **4.** to exhibit or show (obedience, attention, etc.). **5.** to present for consideration, approval, payment, action, etc., as an account. **6.** *Law.* to return; to make a payment in money, kind, or service, as by a tenant to his superior. **7.** to pay as due (a tax, tribute, etc.). **8.** to deliver officially, as judgment. **9.** to reproduce in another language; translate. **10.** to represent; depict, as in painting. **11.** to represent (a perspective view of a projected building) in drawing or painting. **12.** to bring out the meaning of by performance or execution, or interpret, as a part in a drama, a piece of music, a subject in representational art, etc. **13.** to give in return or requital. **14.** to give back; restore (oft. fol. by *back*). **15.** to give up; surrender. **16.** to cover (brickwork, stone, etc.) with a first coat of plaster. **17.** to extract (fat, etc.) from meat trimmings by melting. *–n.* **18.** *Naut.* to slacken or pay out (rope) slowly, as when there is a heavy weight or strain on it. **19.** →**rendering** (def. 3). **20.** the mixture of sand, cement, etc. used to render (def. 16). [ME *rendre(n),* from OF, from Rom. *rendere* give back (b. *prendere,* L *prehendere* take and L *reddere* give back)] – **renderable,** *adj.* – **renderer,** *n.*

**rendering** /ˈrɛndərɪŋ/, *n.* **1.** an act or instance of performance, execution, or interpretation of a drama, piece of music, subject, etc. **2.** a translation. **3.** the first coat of plaster applied to brickwork or stone.

**rendezvous** /ˈrɒndeɪvu, rɒndeɪˈvu/, *n., pl.* **-vous** /-vuz/, *v.,* **-voused** /-vud/, **-vousing** /-vuɪŋ/. *–n.* **1.** an appointment or engagement made between two or more persons to meet at a fixed place and time. **2.** a place for meeting or assembling, esp. of troops, ships, or spacecraft. *–v.i., v.t.* **3.** to assemble at a place previously appointed. [F, n. use of *rendez vous* present or betake yourself (yourselves)]

**rendition** /rɛnˈdɪʃən/, *n.* **1.** the act of rendering. **2.** translation. **3.** interpretation, as of a role or a piece of music. [obs. F, from L *redditio,* with *-n-* from *rendre* RENDER]

**rendzina** /rɛndˈzinə/, *n.* soil developed from relatively soft calcareous material under grass or mixed grass and forest in humid to semiarid regions, which generally consists of black to brown friable topsoil underlain by light grey to yellowish limy material.

**renegade** /ˈrɛnəgeɪd/, *n.* **1.** one who deserts a party or cause for another. **2.** an apostate from a religious faith. *–adj.* **3.** of or like a renegade; traitorous. *–v.i.* **4.** to turn renegade. [Sp. *renegado,* from *renegar* renounce, from ML *renegāre,* from L *negāre* deny]

**renege** /rəˈnɛg, -ˈnɪg/, *v.,* **-neged, -neging,** *n.* *–v.i.* **1.** *Cards.* to revoke. **2.** *Colloq.* to go back on one's word. *–v.t.* **3.** *Archaic.* to deny; disown; renounce. *–n.* **4.** *Cards.* a revoke. Also, **renegue.** [ML *renegāre,* from L *re-* RE- + *negāre* deny] – **reneger,** *n.*

**renew** /rəˈnju/, *v.t.* **1.** to begin or take up again, as acquaintance, conversation, etc. **2.** to make effective for an additional period: *to renew a lease.* **3.** to restore or replenish: *to renew a stock of goods.* **4.** to make, say, or do again. **5.** to revive; re-establish. **6.** to recover (youth, strength, etc.). **7.** to make new, or as if new, again; restore to a former state. *–v.i.* **8.** to begin again; recommence. **9.** to renew a lease, note, etc. **10.** to become new, or as if new, again. – **renewable,** *adj.*

**renewal** /rəˈnjuəl/, *n.* **1.** the act of renewing. **2.** the state of being renewed. **3.** an instance of this.

**reniform** /ˈrɛnəfɔm/, *adj.* kidney-shaped: *a reniform leaf, haematite in reniform masses.* [*reni-* (combining form representing L *rēn* kidney) + -FORM]

**renin** /ˈrinən/, *n.* an enzyme secreted by the kidneys. [L *rēn* kidney + -IN²]

**renitent** /rəˈnaɪtənt, ˈrɛnə-/, *adj.* **1.** resisting pressure; resistant. **2.** persistently opposing; recalcitrant. [L *renītens,* ppr., struggling, resisting] – **renitency** /ˈrɛnətənsi/, *n.*

**rennet**¹ /ˈrɛnət/, *n.* **1.** the lining membrane of the fourth stomach of a calf, or of the stomach of certain other young animals. **2.** *Biochem.* the substance from the stomach of the calf which contains rennin. **3.** a preparation or extract of the rennet membrane, used to curdle milk, as in making cheese, junket, etc. [ME, from *renne* run + *-et* (OE *-et*), n. suffix]

reniform leaf

**rennet**² /ˈrɛnət/, *n.* a sweet kind of apple.

**rennin** /ˈrɛnən/, *n.* a coagulating enzyme occurring in the gastric juice of the calf, forming the active principle of rennet, and able to curdle milk.

**renounce** /rəˈnaʊns/, *v.,* **-nounced, -nouncing,** *n.* *–v.t.* **1.** to give up or put aside voluntarily. **2.** to give up by formal declaration: *to renounce a claim.* **3.** to repudiate; disown. *–v.i.* **4.** *Cards.* **a.** to play a card of a different suit from that led. **b.** to renounce a suit led. *–n.* **5.** *Cards.* an act or instance of renouncing. [ME, from F *renoncer,* from L *renuntiāre* make known, report] – **renouncement,** *n.*

**renovate** /ˈrɛnəveɪt/, *v.t.,* **-vated, -vating.** **1.** to make new or as if new again; restore to good condition; repair. **2.** to reinvigorate; refresh; revive. [L *renovātus,* pp.] – **renovation** /rɛnəˈveɪʃən/, *n.* – **renovator,** *n.*

**renown** /rəˈnaʊn/, *n.* **1.** widespread and high repute; fame. **2.** *Obs.* report or rumour. [ME, from AF *renoun,* from OF *renommer* name over again (frequently), from *nommer* name, from L *nōmināre*]

**renowned** /rəˈnaʊnd/, *adj.* celebrated; famous.

**rent**¹ /rɛnt/, *n.* **1.** a return or payment made periodically by a tenant to an owner or landlord for the use of land or building. **2.** a similar return or payment for the use of property of any kind. **3.** *Econ.* the excess of the produce or return yielded by a given piece of cultivated land over the cost (labour, capital, etc.) of production; the yield from a piece of land or property. **4.** profit or return derived from any differential advantage in production. **5.** *Obs.* revenue or income. *–v.t.* **6.** to grant the possession and enjoyment of (property) in return for payments to be made at agreed times. **7.** to take and hold (property) in return for payments to be made at agreed times. *–v.i.* **8.** to be leased or let for rent. [ME, from OF *rente,* from Rom. *rendita,* from L *reddita* (*pecūnia*) paid (money), with *-n-* from *pre(he)ndere* take] – **rentable,** *adj.*

**rent**² /rɛnt/, *n.* **1.** an opening made by rending or tearing; slit; fissure. **2.** a breach of relations or union. *–v.* **3.** past tense and past participle of **rend.** [n. use of *rent,* v., var. of REND]

**rental** /ˈrɛntl/, *n.* **1.** an amount received or paid as rent. **2.** an income arising from rents received. *–adj.* **3.** pertaining to rent. **4.** available for rent: *rental accommodation.* [ME *rentall,* from AF *rental,* or from Anglo-L *rentale.* See RENT¹, -AL²]

**rent-collector** /ˈrɛnt-kəlɛktə/, *n.* an agent employed to collect rents from tenants.

**rent control** /ˈrɛnt kəntroʊl/, *n.* a regulatory system for assessing and controlling the rent which a landlord may charge under a lease.

**renter** /ˈrɛntə/, *n.* **1.** one who rents. **2.** one who holds, or has the use of, property by payment of rent. **3.** a wholesaler in the film trade; a theatre shareholder.

**rent-free** /rɛnt-ˈfri/, *adv.;* /ˈrɛnt-fri/, *adj.* *–adv.* **1.** without payment of rent. *–adj.* **2.** not subject to payment of rent: *a rent-free flat.*

**rentier** /ˈrɒnti,eɪ/, *n.* one who has a fixed income, as from lands, bonds, etc. [F *rente* revenue, income]

**renunciation** /rənʌnsiˈeɪʃən/, *n.* **1.** the formal abandoning of a right, title, etc. **2.** a voluntary giving up, esp. as a sacrifice. – **renunciative** /rəˈnʌnsiətɪv/, **renunciatory** /rəˈnʌnsiətri/, *adj.*

**renvoi** /rɛnˈvɔɪ/, *n.* *Internat. Law.* the referring of a legal matter to the law of a legal system outside the jurisdiction where it arose.

**reopen** /ri'oupən/, *v.t.* **1.** to open again. **2.** to start again; resume: *to reopen an argument, an attack, etc.* *–v.i.* **3.** to open or begin again.

**reorder** /ri'ɔdə/, *v.t.* **1.** to put in order again. **2.** *Comm.* to give a reorder for. *–n.* **3.** *Comm.* a second or repeated order for the same goods from the same dealer.

**reorganisation** /riˌɔgənaɪ'zeɪʃən/, *n.* **1.** the act or process of reorganising. **2.** the state of being reorganised. **3.** *Finance.* a thorough or drastic reconstruction of a business company, including a marked change in capital structure, often following a failure and receivership or bankruptcy trusteeship. Also, **reorganization.**

**reorganise** /ri'ɔgənaɪz/, *v.t., v.i.,* **-nised, -nising.** to organise again. Also, **reorganize.** – **reorganiser,** *n.*

**reorientate** /ri'ɒrɪənteɪt, -'ɔri-/, *v.t.* to orientate afresh or anew. Also, **reorient.** – **reorientation** /riˌɒriən'teɪʃən, -ˌɔri-/, *n.*

**rep**[1] /rɛp/, *n.* a transversely corded fabric of wool, silk, rayon, or cotton. Also, **repp.** [F *reps*]

**rep**[2] /rɛp/, *n. Colloq.* repertory theatre. [shortened form]

**rep**[3] /rɛp/, *n. Colloq.* **1.** a travelling salesman. **2.** *Colloq.* a sportsman who is selected to represent his area in sport: *a hockey rep.* **3.** a union representative. *–adj.* **4.** *Colloq.* of or pertaining to such a sportsman: *a rep swimmer.*

**rep**[4] /rɛp/, *n. U.S. Colloq.* →**reputation.** [shortened form]

**rep.,** **1.** report. **2.** reporter. **3.** repeat. **4.** representative.

**Rep.,** Republic.

**repaint** /ˌri'peɪnt/, *v.t.* **1.** to paint again. *–n.* **2.** a part repainted, esp. a part of a picture by a restorer.

**repair**[1] /rə'pɛə/, *v.t.* **1.** to restore to a good or sound condition after decay or damage; mend: *to repair a clock.* **2.** to restore or renew by any process of making good, strengthening, etc.: *repair a broken constitution.* **3.** to remedy; make good; make up for: *to repair damage, a loss, a deficiency, etc.* **4.** to make amends for: *repair a wrong done.* *–n.* **5.** the act, process, or work of repairing: *repair of a building.* **6.** (*esp. pl.*) an instance or operation of repairing: *to carry out repairs.* **7.** a part that has been repaired or an addition made in repairing. **8.** the good condition resulting from repairing: *to keep in repair.* **9.** (*usu. pl.*) *Accounting.* the cost of making repairs. [ME *repaire(n),* from L *reparāre* put in order] – **repairable,** *adj.* – **repairer,** *n.*

**repair**[2] /rə'pɛə/, *v.i.* **1.** to betake oneself or go, as to a place: *he soon repaired in person to Bathurst.* **2.** to go frequently or customarily. *–n.* **3.** the act of repairing or going: *to make repair to Bathurst.* **4.** *Archaic.* a resort or haunt. [ME *repaire(n),* from OF *repairer* return, from LL *repatriāre* return to one's country]

**repairer** /rə'pɛərə/, *n.* →**fettler.**

**repairman** /rə'pɛəmæn/, *n., pl.* **-men.** one whose occupation is repairing things.

**repand** /rə'pænd/, *adj. Bot.* **1.** having the margin slightly wavy, as a leaf. **2.** slightly wavy. [L *repandus* bent back]

repand leaf

**reparable** /'rɛpərəbəl, 'rɛprəbəl/, *adj.* capable of being repaired or remedied. Also, **repairable** /rə'pɛərəbəl/. [L *reparābilis*] – **reparably,** *adv.*

**reparation** /rɛpə'reɪʃən/, *n.* **1.** the making of amends for wrong or injury done: *a wrong which admits of no reparation.* **2.** (*usu. pl.*) compensation in money, material, labour, etc., paid by a defeated nation (as by Germany and her allies after World War I) for damage to civilian population and property during war. **3.** restoration to good condition. **4.** repairs. [ME *reparacion,* from L *reparātio*]

**reparative** /rə'pærətɪv/, *adj.* **1.** tending to repair. **2.** pertaining to or involving reparation. Also, **reparatory** /rə'pærətri/.

**repartee** /rɛpa'ti/, *n., v.,* **-teed, -teeing.** *–n.* **1.** a ready and witty reply. **2.** speech or talk characterised by quickness and wittiness of reply. **3.** skill in making witty replies. *–v.i.* **4.** *Obs.* to make witty replies. [F *repartie* an answering thrust, properly pp. of *repartir* reply promptly, from *re-* RE- + *partir* divide (cf. F *jeu parti* question-and-answer poem or contest)]

**repartition** /ripa'tɪʃən/, *n.* **1.** distribution; partition. **2.** redistribution. *–v.t.* **3.** to divide up.

**repass** /ˌri'pas/, *v.t., v.i.* to pass back or again. – **repassage** /ri'pæsɪdʒ/, *n.*

**repast** /rə'past/, *n.* **1.** a quantity of food taken at or provided for one occasion of eating: *to eat a light repast.* **2.** a taking of food; a meal: *the evening repast.* **3.** *Obs.* food. [ME, from OF, from LL *repastus,* properly pp. of *repascere* feed regularly]

**repat** /'ripæt/, *n. Colloq.* →**repatriation.**

**repatriate** /ri'pætrieɪt/, *v.t.,* **-ated, -ating;** /ri'pætriət/, *n.* *–v.t.* **1.** to bring or send back (a person) to his own country, esp. (prisoners of war, refugees, etc.) to the land of citizenship. *–n.* **2.** one who has been repatriated. [LL *repatriātus,* pp.]

**repatriation** /ˌripætri'eɪʃən/, *n.* **1.** the act of returning to one's native land. **2.** assistance given to ex-servicemen returning to a civilian life, in the form of pensions, medical care, allowances for dependents, etc.

**repay** /ri'peɪ/, *v.,* **-paid, -paying.** *–v.t.* **1.** to pay back or refund (money, etc.). **2.** to make return for: *repaid with thanks.* **3.** to make return to in any way: *feel repaid for sacrifices made.* **4.** to return: *repay a visit.* *–v.i.* **5.** to make repayment or return. – **repayable,** *adj.* – **repayment,** *n.*

**repeal** /rə'pil/, *v.t.* **1.** to revoke or withdraw formally or officially: *to repeal a grant.* **2.** to revoke or annul (a law, tax, duty, etc.) by express legislative enactment; abrogate. *–n.* **3.** the act of repealing; revocation; abrogation. [ME *repele(n),* from AF *repel(l)er,* from *re-* RE- + *apeler* APPEAL] – **repealable,** *adj.* – **repealer,** *n.*

**repeat** /rə'pit/, *v.t.* **1.** to say or utter again (something one has already said): *to repeat a word for emphasis.* **2.** to say or utter in reproducing the words, etc., of another: *repeat a sentence after the teacher.* **3.** to reproduce (utterances, sounds, etc.) as an echo, a gramophone or the like does. **4.** to tell (something heard) to another or others. **5.** to do, make, perform, etc., again: *to repeat an action, a ceremony, a passage of music, etc.* **6.** to go through or undergo again: *to repeat an experience.* *–v.i.* **7.** to do or say something again. **8.** (of food eaten) to rise from the stomach so as to be tasted: *that meat is repeating on me.* **9.** to belch lightly. **10.** (of a firearm) to fire several times without reloading. **11.** (of a watch, clock, etc.) to strike the hour (and sometimes the quarter-hour) last past, when required. **12.** *U.S.* to vote more than once at the same election (a form of fraud). *–n.* **13.** an act of repeating. **14.** something repeated. **15.** an order for goods identical to a previous order. **16.** a radio or television program that has been broadcast at least once before. **17.** a duplicate or reproduction of something. **18.** *Music.* **a.** a passage to be repeated. **b.** a sign, as a vertical arrangement of dots, calling for the repetition of a passage. [ME *repete(n),* from L *repetere* do or say again] – **repeatable,** *adj.*

**repeated** /rə'pitəd/, *adj.* done, made, or said again and again: *repeated attempts.* – **repeatedly,** *adv.*

**repeater** /rə'pitə/, *n.* **1.** one who or that which repeats. **2.** a repeating firearm. **3.** a watch or clock, esp. a watch, which may be made to strike the hour (and sometimes the quarter-hour, etc.) last past. **4.** *Elect.* an amplifier used in telephone circuits to make good losses of power. **5.** an instrument for automatically retransmitting telegraphic messages. **6.** a recurring decimal. **7.** a student who repeats a course or group of courses, in which he has previously failed. **8.** *U.S.* one who fraudulently votes more than once at an election.

**repeating** /rə'pitɪŋ/, *adj.* of or pertaining to a rifle or firearm capable of discharging a number of shots without reloading.

**repeating decimal** /rəˌpitɪŋ 'dɛsəməl/, *n. Maths.* →**recurring decimal.**

**repechage** /'rɛpəʃaʒ/, *Rowing, etc.* *–n.* **1.** a race in which contestants eliminated in earlier heats contest for a place in the final. *–adj.* **2.** of, pertaining to, or denoting such a race. [F *repêchage* lit., act of fishing out again]

**repel** /rə'pɛl/, *v.,* **-pelled, -pelling.** *–v.t.* **1.** to drive or force back (an assailant, invader, etc.). **2.** to thrust back or away; reject: *he repelled several useless suggestions.* **3.** to resist effectually (an attack, onslaught): *repel the invader's attack.* **4.** to keep off or out; fail to mix with: *water and oil repel each other.* **5.** to put away from one; refuse to have to do with: *repel temptation.* **6.** to refuse to accept or admit; reject: *to* *repel a suggestion.* **7.** to discourage the advances of (a person): *he repelled her with his harshness.* **8.** to excite feelings of distaste or aversion: *her slatternly appearance repels me.* **9.** *Mech.* to push back or away by a force, as one body acting upon another (opposed to *attract*). *–v.i.* **10.** to act with a force that drives or keeps away something. **11.** to cause distaste or aversion. [ME *repelle,* from L *repellere* drive back] **– repellence, repellency,** *n.* **– repeller,** *n.*

**repellent** /rə'pɛlənt/, *adj.* **1.** causing distaste or aversion; repulsive. **2.** repelling; driving back. *–n.* **3.** something that repels. **4.** a medicine that serves to prevent or reduce swellings, tumours, etc. **5.** any of various solutions applied to fabrics to make them water-repellent. **– repellently,** *adv.*

**repent**[1] /rə'pɛnt/, *v.i.* **1.** to feel self-reproach, compunction, or contrition for past conduct; change one's mind with regard to past action in consequence of dissatisfaction with it or its results (oft. fol. by *of*). **2.** to feel such sorrow for sin or fault as to be disposed to change one's life for the better; be penitent (oft. fol. by *of*). *–v.t.* **3.** to remember or regard with self-reproach or contrition: *to repent one's injustice to another.* **4.** to feel sorry for; regret: *to repent one's words.* [ME *repenten,* from OF *repentir,* from *re-* RE- + Rom. *penitīre* (replacing L *poenitēre*)] **– repenter,** *n.*

**repent**[2] /'ripənt/, *adj.* creeping. Also, **reptant.** [L *rēpens,* ppr., creeping]

**repentance** /rə'pɛntəns/, *n.* **1.** compunction or contrition for wrongdoing or sin. **2.** regret for any past action.

**repentant** /rə'pɛntənt/, *adj.* **1.** repenting; experiencing repentance. **2.** characterised by or showing repentance: *a repentant mood.* [ME, from OF, ppr. of *repentir* REPENT[1]] **– repentantly,** *adv.*

**repeople** /ˌri'pipəl/, *v.t.,* **-pled, -pling.** **1.** to furnish again with people. **2.** to restock with animals. [OF *repeupler.* See RE-, PEOPLE, *v.*]

**repercussion** /ripə'kʌʃən/, *n.* **1.** an after-effect, often an indirect result, of some event or action: *the repercussions of the wool marketing plan were very widely felt.* **2.** the state of being driven back by a resisting body. **3.** a rebounding or recoil of something after impact. **4.** reverberation; echo. **5.** *Music.* (in a fugue) the point after the development of an episode at which the subject and answer appear again. [ME, from L *repercussio*]

**repercussive** /ripə'kʌsɪv/, *adj.* **1.** causing repercussion; reverberating. **2.** reflected; reverberated.

**repertoire** /'rɛpətwa/, *n.* **1.** the list of dramas, operas, parts, pieces, etc., which a company, actor, singer or the like, is prepared to perform. **2.** all the works of a particular kind considered collectively. [F, from L *repertōrium* inventory, catalogue]

**repertory** /'rɛpətri/, *n., pl.* **-ries.** **1.** →**repertoire.** **2.** a type of theatrical company, usu. based on a particular theatre, which prepares several plays, operas, or the like, and produces them alternately or in succession, for a limited run only. **3.** a store or stock of things available. **4.** →**storehouse.** [L *repertōrium*]

**repetend** /'rɛpətɛnd, rɛpə'tɛnd/, *n.* **1.** *Maths.* that part of a recurring decimal repeated indefinitely. **2.** *Music.* a phrase or sound which is repeated. [L *repetendum,* neut. ger., (that) which is to be repeated]

**répétiteur** /rəpɛtə'tɜ/, *n.* one who rehearses and prompts opera singers. [F]

**re-petition** /ri-pə'tɪʃən/, *v.t.* to petition again.

**repetition** /rɛpə'tɪʃən/, *n.* **1.** the act of repeating; repeated action, performance, production, or presentation. **2.** repeated utterance; reiteration. **3.** something made by or resulting from repeating. **4.** a reproduction, copy, or replica. **5.** *Civil Law.* an action for recovery of a payment or delivery made by error or upon failure to fulfil a condition. [L *repetītio*]

**repetitious** /rɛpə'tɪʃəs/, *adj.* abounding in repetition; characterised by undue and tedious repetition. **– repetitiously,** *adv.* **– repetitiousness,** *n.*

**repetitive** /rə'pɛtətɪv/, *adj.* pertaining to or characterised by repetition.

**rephrase** /ˌri'freɪz/, *v.t.,* **-phrased, -phrasing.** to phrase again or differently: *he rephrased the statement to give it greater clarity.*

**repine** /rə'paɪn/, *v.i.,* **-pined, -pining.** to be fretfully discontented; fret; complain. [apparently RE- + PINE[2], *v.*]

**replace** /rə'pleɪs/, *v.t.,* **-placed, -placing.** **1.** to fill or take the place of; substitute for (a person or thing): *electricity has replaced gas as a means of illumination.* **2.** to provide a substitute or equivalent in the place of: *to replace a broken vase or dish.* **3.** to restore; return; make good: *to replace a sum of money borrowed.* **4.** to restore to a former or the proper place: *the stolen paintings were replaced in the museum.* **– replaceable,** *adj.* **– replacer,** *n.*

**replacement** /rə'pleɪsmənt/, *n.* **1.** the act of replacing. **2.** one who or that which replaces another. **3.** *Mil.* a reinforcement. **4.** *Geol.* the process of practically simultaneous removal and deposition by which a new mineral of partly or wholly differing chemical composition grows in the body of an old mineral or mineral aggregate. **5.** *Crystall.* the replacing of an angle or edge by one face or more.

**replacement part** /'– pat/, *n.* →**spare part.**

**replay** /'ripleɪ/, *n.;* /ˌri'pleɪ/, *v.* *–n.* **1.** (in sport) a match, contest etc. which is played again because of some difficulty or disagreement. **2.** (in television coverage of sport by the electronic media) the playing again of some highlight of a game, often immediately after it has happened. **3.** →**playback.** *–v.t.* **4.** to repeat (a sporting event, match, etc. or a sequence from it) on radio or television.

**repleader** /ri'plidə/, *n. Law.* **1.** a second pleading. **2.** the right or privilege of pleading again. [RE- + PLEAD + -ER[3]. Cf. OF *repledoier,* F *replaider*]

**replenish** /rə'plɛnɪʃ/, *v.t.* **1.** to bring back to a state of fullness or completeness, as by supplying what is lacking: *to replenish a stock of goods.* **2.** to supply (a fire, stove, etc.) with fresh fuel. **3.** to fill again or anew. [ME *replenys,* from OF *repleniss-,* stem of *replenir* fill up again, from *re-* RE- + *plenir* fill, from *plein* full, from L *plēnus*] **– replenisher,** *n.* **– replenishment,** *n.*

**replete** /rə'plit/, *adj.* **1.** abundantly supplied or provided (fol. by *with*). **2.** stuffed or gorged with food and drink. [ME, from L *replētus,* pp., filled] **– repleteness,** *n.*

**repletion** /rə'pliʃən/, *n.* **1.** the condition of being replete; fullness. **2.** overfullness resulting from eating or drinking to excess.

**replevin** /rə'plɛvən/, *Law. –n.* **1. a.** the recovery of goods or chattels wrongfully taken or detained, on security given that the issue shall be tried at law and the goods returned in case of an adverse decision. **b.** the common law action or writ by which goods are replevied. *–v.t.* **2.** to replevy. [late ME, from AF, from OF *replevir;* whence also Anglo-L *replevina*]

**replevy** /rə'plɛvi/, *v.,* **-plevied, -plevying,** *n., pl.* **-plevies.** *Law. –v.t.* **1.** to recover possession of by an action of replevin. *–v.i.* **2.** to take possession of goods or chattels under a replevin order. *–n.* **3.** a seizure in replevin. [late ME, from OF *replevir,* AF *replever,* from *re-* RE- + *plevir* PLEDGE]

**replica** /'rɛplɪkə/, *n.* **1.** a copy or reproduction of a work of art by the maker of the original. **2.** any copy or reproduction. [It., *replicare.* See REPLY, *v.*]

**replicate** /'rɛpləkət/, *adj.* folded; bent back on itself. Also, **replicated** /'rɛpləkeɪtəd/. [L *replicātus,* pp.]

**replication** /rɛplə'keɪʃən/, *n.* **1.** a reply. **2.** a reply to an answer. **3.** *Law.* the reply of the plaintiff or complainant to the defendant's plea or answer. **4.** *Biochem.* the process whereby new DNA is synthesised, by the exact copying of DNA already present within the cell. **5.** reverberation; echo. **6.** a reproduction, copy, or duplication.

**replum** /'rɛpləm/, *n., pl.* **-lums, -la** /-lə/. a septum formed in a fruit by the ingrowth of the placentas, as in the siliqua of the Cruciferae. [L: bolt for a door]

**reply** /rə'plaɪ/, *v.,* **-plied, -plying,** *n., pl.* **-plies.** *–v.i.* **1.** to make answer in words or writing; answer; respond: *I must reply to his letter at once.* **2.** to respond by some action, performance, etc.: *reply to the enemy's fire.* **3.** to return a sound; echo. **4.** *Law.* to answer a defendant's plea. *–v.t.* **5.** to return as an answer: *he replied that no consideration would induce him to accept.* *–n.* **6.** an answer or response in words or writing. **7.** a response made by some action, performance, etc. **8.** *Music.* →**answer** (def. 8). [ME *replye(n),* from OF *replier* fold again, turn back, reply, from L *replicāre* unfold, reply] **– replier,** *n.*

**répondez s'il vous plaît** /rə'pɒndeɪ sɪl vu ˌpleɪ/, please reply. *Abbrev.:* R.S.V.P. [F]

**report** /rə'pɔt/, *n.* **1.** an account brought back or presented; a statement submitted in reply to enquiry as the result of investigation, or by a person authorised to examine and bring or send information. **2.** an account of a speech, debate, meeting, etc., esp. as taken down for publication. **3.** a statement or account of a judicial opinion or decision, or of a case argued and determined in a court of justice. **4.** a statement prepared at the end of every term by a school for each pupil to inform his parents of his work and progress. **5.** a statement or announcement. **6.** a statement generally circulated; rumour. **7.** repute; reputation. **8.** a loud noise, as from an explosion. *–v.t.* **9.** to carry and repeat as an answer or message; repeat as what one has heard. **10.** to relate as what has been learned by observation or investigation. **11.** to give or render a formal account or statement of: *to report a deficit.* **12.** to make a formal report on (a bill, etc., officially referred). **13.** to lay a charge against (a person), as to a superior. **14.** to make known the presence or whereabouts of. **15.** to present (oneself) to a person in authority, as in accordance with requirements. **16.** to take down (a speech, etc.) in writing. **17.** to write an account of (an event, situation, etc.), as for publication in a newspaper. **18.** to relate or tell. *–v.i.* **19.** to make a report; draw up or submit a formal report. **20.** to act as a reporter, as for a newspaper. **21.** to present or give an account of oneself, as to one in authority: *to report to one's boss; report sick.* **22.** to present oneself duly, as at a place. [ME *reporte(n),* from OF *reporter,* from L *reportāre*] **– reportable,** *adj.*

**reportage** /rə'pɔtɪdʒ, rɛpɔ'taʒ/, *n.* **1.** the style, manner, or act of reporting news. **2.** journalistic writing in general.

**report card** /rə'pɔt kad/, *n.* a written assessment of a pupil's progress in all aspects of his school life, as academic achievement, attitudes, attendance, etc., sent to his parents or guardians.

**reported speech** /rəpɔtəd 'spitʃ/, *n.* the speech or writing of another not quoted verbatim, but modified as to person, tense, etc., so that the hearer or reader is aware that the statements made are at second hand; indirect speech (opposed to *direct speech*).

**reporter** /rə'pɔtə/, *n.* **1.** one who reports. **2.** one employed to gather and report news for a newspaper, news agency, or broadcasting organisation. **3.** one who prepares official reports, as of legal or legislative proceedings.

**report stage** /rə'pɔt steɪdʒ/, *n.* the stage at which a parliamentary bill as amended in committee is reported to the legislative body before the third reading.

**reposal** /rə'poʊzəl/, *n.* the act of reposing.

**re-pose** /ˌri-'poʊz/, *v.t.,* **-posed, -posing.** to pose again: *he re-posed the question.*

**repose**[1] /rə'poʊz/, *n., v.,* **-posed, -posing.** *–n.* **1.** the state of reposing or resting; rest; sleep. **2.** peace or tranquillity. **3.** dignified calmness, as of manner or demeanour. **4.** absence of movement, animation, etc. *–v.i.* **5.** to lie at rest; take rest. **6.** to be at peace or in tranquillity; lie in quiet. **7.** to lie or rest on something. **8.** to lie dead. **9.** to depend or rely on a person or thing. *–v.t.* **10.** (*oft. used reflexively*) to lay to rest; rest; refresh by rest. [late ME, from F *reposer,* from L *repausāre*]

**repose**[2] /rə'poʊz/, *v.t.,* **-posed, -posing. 1.** to put (confidence, trust, etc.) in a person or thing. **2.** *Obs. or Rare.* to deposit. [L *repos-* (in *reposuī, repositus,* forms of *repōnere* replace), modelled on DISPOSE, etc.]

**reposeful** /rə'poʊzfəl/, *adj.* full of repose; calm; quiet. **– reposefully,** *adv.* **– reposefulness,** *n.*

**reposit** /rə'pɒzət/, *v.t.* **1.** to put back; replace. **2.** to lay up or store; deposit. [L *repositus,* pp., put back in place]

**re-position** /ri-pə'zɪʃən/, *v.t.* to place in a new position.

**reposition** /ripə'zɪʃən, 'rɛpə-/, *n.* **1.** the act of depositioning or storing. **2.** replacement, as of a bone.

**repository** /rə'pɒzətri/, *n., pl.* **-tories. 1.** a receptacle or place where things are deposited, stored, or offered for sale, as a warehouse. **2.** a place in which a dead body is deposited. **3.** a person to whom something is entrusted or confided. [L *repositōrium*]

**repossess** /ripə'zɛs/, *v.t.* **1.** to possess again; regain possession of. **2.** to put again in possession of something. **– repossession** /ripə'zɛʃən/, *n.*

**repoussé** /rə'puseɪ/, *adj.* **1.** (of a design) raised in relief by hammering on the reverse side. **2.** ornamented or made in this kind of raised work. [F, pp. of *repousser,* from *re-* RE- + *pousser* PUSH, *v.*]

**repp** /rɛp/, *n.* →**rep**[1].

**reprehend** /rɛprə'hɛnd/, *v.t.* to reprove or find fault with; rebuke; censure; blame. [ME, from L *reprehendere*]

**reprehensible** /rɛprə'hɛnsəbəl/, *adj.* deserving to be reprehended; blameworthy: *reprehensible conduct.* **– reprehensibility** /ˌrɛprəhɛnsə'bɪləti/, **reprehensibleness,** *n.* **– reprehensibly,** *adv.*

**reprehension** /rɛprə'hɛnʃən/, *n.* the act of reprehending; reproof; censure. **– reprehensive,** *adj.* **– reprehensively,** *adv.*

**re-present** /ri-prə'zɛnt/, *v.t.* to present again or anew. **– re-presentation** /ˌri-prɛzən'teɪʃən/, *n.*

**represent** /rɛprə'zɛnt/, *v.t.* **1.** to serve to express, designate, stand for, or denote, as a word, symbol, or the like; symbolise. **2.** to express or designate by some term, character, symbol, or the like: *to represent musical sounds by notes.* **3.** to stand or act in the place of, as a substitute, proxy, or agent. **4.** to speak and act for by delegated authority: *to represent one's government in a foreign country.* **5.** to act for (a constituency, etc.) by deputed right in exercising a voice in legislation or government. **6.** to portray, depict, or figure; present the likeness or semblance of, as a picture, image, or the like. **7.** to present to the mind; place clearly before or picture to the mind. **8.** to present in words; set forth; describe; state. **9.** to set forth or describe as having a particular character (fol. by *as, to be,* etc.). **10.** to set forth clearly or earnestly with a view to influencing opinion or action or making protest. **11.** to present, produce, or perform (a play, etc.), as on the stage. **12.** to impersonate (a character, etc.), as in acting. **13.** to serve as an example or specimen of; exemplify: *a genus represented by two species.* **14.** to be the equivalent of; correspond to: *the llama represents the camel in the New World.* [ME *represente(n),* from L *repraesentāre*] **– representable,** *adj.*

**representation** /ˌrɛprəzɛn'teɪʃən/, *n.* **1.** the act of representing. **2.** the state of being represented. **3.** the expression or designation by some term, character, symbol, or the like. **4.** speech or action on behalf of a person, body, business house, district, or the like by an agent, deputy, or representative. **5.** the state or fact of being so represented: *to demand representation on a board of directors.* **6.** *Govt.* the state, fact, or right of being represented by delegates having a voice in legislation or government. **7.** the body or number of representatives, as of a constituency. **8.** *Diplomacy.* **a.** the fact or process of speaking and acting for a state. **b.** an utterance on behalf of a state. **9.** presentation to the mind. **10.** a mental image or idea presented to the mind; concept. **11.** the act of portrayal, picturing, or other rendering in visible form. **12.** a picture, figure, statue, etc. **13.** the production, or performance, of a play or the like, as on the stage. **14.** (*oft. pl.*) a description or statement, as of things true or alleged. **15.** a statement of facts, reasons, etc., made in appealing or protesting; a protest or remonstrance. **16.** *Law.* a statement of fact to which legal liability may attach if material: *a representation of authority.* **– representational,** *adj.*

**representationalism** /rɛprəzɛn'teɪʃənəlɪzəm/, *n.* →**representationism. – representationalist,** *n., adj.*

**representationism** /rɛprəzɛn'teɪʃənɪzəm/, *n.* a theory of knowledge (one form of which was advocated by Locke) according to which percepts stand for things other than themselves, of which things the mind then obtains knowledge by inference. Cf. **phenomenalism** (def. 2). **– representationist,** *n., adj.*

**representative** /rɛprə'zɛntətɪv/, *adj.* **1.** serving to represent; representing. **2.** standing or acting for another or others. **3.** exemplifying a class; typical: *a representative selection of Australian verse.* **4.** representing a constituency or community or the people generally in legislation or government: *a representative assembly.* **5.** characterised by, founded on, or pertaining to representation of the people in government: *representative of government.* **6.** corresponding to or replacing some other species or the like, as in a different locality. *–n.* **7.** one who or that which represents another or others. **8.** an example or specimen; type; typical embodiment, as of some quality. **9.** a commercial traveller; a travelling salesman. **10.** an agent or deputy: *a legal representative.* **11.** one who represents a constituency or community in a legislative body, esp. a member of the lower house in parliament or in a state legislature. – **representatively,** *adv.* – **representativeness,** *n.*

**re-press** /ˌri-ˈprɛs/, *v.t.* to press again.

**repress** /rəˈprɛs/, *v.t.* **1.** to keep under control, check, or suppress (desires, feelings, action, tears, etc.). **2.** to keep down or suppress (anything objectionable). **3.** to put down or quell (sedition, disorder, etc.). **4.** to reduce (persons) to subjection. **5.** *Psychol.* to reject from consciousness, as thoughts, feelings, memories, or impulses not acceptable to the ego. [ME, from L *repressus,* pp.] – **repressed** /rəˈprɛst/, *adj.* – **represser,** *n.* – **repressible,** *adj.*

**repression** /rəˈprɛʃən/, *n.* **1.** the act of repressing. **2.** the state of being repressed. **3.** *Psychol.* the rejection from consciousness of painful or disagreeable ideas, memories, feelings, and impulses.

**repressive** /rəˈprɛsɪv/, *adj.* tending or serving to repress. – **repressively,** *adv.* – **repressiveness,** *n.*

**reprieve** /rəˈpriv/, *v.,* **-prieved, -prieving,** *n.* –*v.t.* **1.** to respite (a person) from impending punishment, esp. to grant a delay of the execution of (a condemned person). **2.** to relieve temporarily from any evil. –*n.* **3.** respite from impending punishment, esp. from execution of a sentence of death. **4.** a warrant authorising this. **5.** any respite or temporary relief. [ME *repreven* REPROVE, apparently taken in literal sense of test again (involving postponement)]

**reprimand** /ˈrɛprəmand, -mænd/, *n.* **1.** a severe reproof, esp. a formal one by a person in authority. –*v.t.* **2.** to reprove severely, esp. in a formal way. [F *réprimande,* from *réprimer* repress, reprove]

**reprint** /riˈprɪnt/, *v.;* /ˈriprɪnt/, *n.* –*v.t.* **1.** to print again; print a new impression of. –*n.* **2.** a reproduction in print of matter already printed. **3.** a new impression, without alteration, of any printed work. **4.** *Philately.* an impression from the original plate after issue of the stamps has ceased and their use for postage voided. – **reprinter,** *n.*

**reprisal** /rəˈpraɪzəl/, *n.* **1.** the infliction of similar or greater injury on the enemy in warfare, in retaliation for some injury, as by the punishment or execution of prisoners of war. **2.** an instance of this. **3.** the act or practice of using force, short of war, against another nation, to secure redress of a grievance. **4.** retaliation, or an act of retaliation. **5.** (orig.) the forcible seizing of property or subjects in retaliation. [ME *reprisail,* from AF *reprisaille,* from *repris(e),* pp., taken back]

**reprise** /rəˈpraɪz/ *for def. 1;* /rəˈpraɪz, -ˈpriz/ *for def. 2;* /rəˈpriz/ *for def. 3, n.* **1.** *Law.* (*usu. pl.*) an annual deduction, duty, or payment out of an estate, as an annuity or the like. **2.** *Music.* **a.** a repetition. **b.** a return to the first theme or subject. **3.** *Fencing.* a renewal of action. [ME, from F, fem. pp. of *reprendre* take back, from L *reprehendere*]

**repro** /ˈriproʊ/, *n., pl.* **-pros.** *Colloq.* →**reproduction** (def. 3). [shortened form]

**reproach** /rəˈproʊtʃ/, *v.t.* **1.** to find fault with (a person, etc.); blame; censure. **2.** to upbraid (fol. by *with*). **3.** to be a cause of blame or discredit to. –*n.* **4.** blame or censure conveyed by reproaching: *a term of reproach.* **5.** an expression of upbraiding, censure or reproof. **6.** disgrace, discredit, or blame incurred: *to bring reproach on one's family.* **7.** a cause or occasion of disgrace or discredit. **8.** an object of scorn or contempt. [late ME *reproche,* from F *reprocher,* from L *reprobāre* REPROVE] – **reproachable,** *adj.* – **reproachableness,** *n.* – **reproachably,** *adv.* – **reproacher,** *n.*

**reproachful** /rəˈproʊtʃfəl/, *adj.* **1.** full of or expressing reproach or censure; upbraiding: *a reproachful look.* **2.** *Obs.* deserving reproach; shameful. – **reproachfully,** *adv.* – **reproachfulness,** *n.*

**reproachless** /rəˈproʊtʃləs/, *adj.* →**irreproachable.**

**reprobate** /ˈrɛprəbeɪt/, *n., adj., v.,* **-bated, -bating.** –*n.* **1.** an abandoned, unprincipled, or reprehensible person: *a penniless drunken reprobate.* **2.** a person rejected by God or beyond hope of salvation. –*adj.* **3.** morally depraved; unprincipled; bad. **4.** rejected by God; excluded from the number of the elect. –*v.t.* **5.** to disapprove, condemn, or censure. **6.** (of God) to reject (a person), as for sin; exclude from the number of the elect or from salvation. **7.** *Law.* See **approbate** (def. 2). [ME, from LL *reprobātus,* pp., reproved]

**reprobation** /rɛprəˈbeɪʃən/, *n.* **1.** disapproval, condemnation, or censure. **2.** rejection. **3.** *Theol.* rejection by God, as of persons excluded from the number of the elect or from salvation.

**reprobative** /ˈrɛprəbeɪtɪv/, *adj.* reprobating; expressing reprobation. – **reprobatively,** *adv.*

**re-processed wool** /ˌri-proʊsɛst ˈwʊl/, *n.* wool which has been recovered from a manufactured fabric, as torn-up cloth, trade waste, tailors' clippings, etc., before being re-used.

**reproduce** /riprəˈdjus/, *v.,* **-duced, -ducing.** –*v.t.* **1.** to make a copy, representation, duplicate, or close imitation of: *to reproduce a picture, voice, etc.* **2.** to produce again or anew by natural process: *to reproduce a broken claw.* **3.** to produce another or more individuals of (some animal or plant kind) by some process of generation or propagation, sexual or asexual. **4.** to cause or foster the reproduction of (animals or plants). **5.** to produce, form, make, or bring about again or anew in any manner. **6.** to call up again before the mind or represent mentally (a past scene, etc.) as by the aid of memory or imagination. **7.** to produce again (a play, etc., produced at an earlier time). –*v.i.* **8.** to reproduce its kind, as an animal or plant; propagate. **9.** to turn out (well, etc.) when copied. – **reproducible,** *adj.*

**reproducer** /riprəˈdjusə/, *n.* **1.** one who or that which reproduces. **2.** *Computers.* a machine which duplicates punched cards.

**reproduction** /riprəˈdʌkʃən/, *n.* **1.** the act or process of reproducing. **2.** the state of being reproduced. **3.** that which is made by reproducing; a copy or duplicate, esp. of a picture or the like made by photoengraving or some similar process. **4.** the natural process among animals and plants by which new individuals are generated and the species perpetuated.

**reproduction proof** /ˈ– pruf/, *n.* a proof which is produced by inking composed matter and transferring the ink image to a sheet of opaque or transparent material; it is then either photographed or used directly for exposure in photomechanical plate making.

**reproductive** /riprəˈdʌktɪv/, *adj.* **1.** serving to reproduce. **2.** concerned with or pertaining to reproduction. – **reproductively,** *adv.* – **reproductiveness,** *n.*

**reprography** /riˈprɒgrəfi/, *n.* **1.** reproduction by photography. **2.** any duplicating or copying process.

**reproof** /rəˈpruf/, *n.* **1.** the act of reproving, censuring, or rebuking. **2.** an expression of censure or rebuke.

**reprovable** /rəˈpruvəbəl/, *adj.* deserving of reproof.

**reproval** /rəˈpruvəl/, *n.* **1.** the act of reproving. **2.** a reproof.

**re-prove** /ˌri-ˈpruv/, *v.t.* **-proved, -proving.** to prove anew.

**reprove** /rəˈpruv/, *v.,* **-proved, -proving.** –*v.t.* **1.** to address words of disapproval to (a person, etc.); rebuke; blame. **2.** to express disapproval of (actions, words, etc.). **3.** *Obs.* to disprove or refute. –*v.i.* **4.** to speak in reproof; administer a reproof. [ME, from OF *reprover,* from L *reprobāre*] – **reprover,** *n.* – **reprovingly,** *adv.*

**Reps** /rɛps/, *n. Colloq.* House of Representatives.

**reptant** /ˈrɛptənt/, *adj.* →**repent**[2]. [L *rēptans,* ppr., creeping]

**reptile** /ˈrɛptaɪl/, *n.* **1.** any of the Reptilia, a class of cold-blooded vertebrates, including the lizards, snakes, turtles, alligators, and rhynchocephalians, together with various extinct types. Reptiles are now relatively unimportant, but before the development of birds and mammals they were the dominant class of land animals, and appear as fossils in a great variety of forms. They are distinguished from amphibians chiefly by adaptations to a more completely terrestrial life, without the further elaborations characteristic of the birds and mammals. **2.** any of various creeping or crawling animals, as the lizards, snakes, etc. **3.** a grovelling, mean, or despicable person. –*adj.* **4.** creeping or crawling. **5.** grovelling, mean, or malignant. [ME, from LL *reptilis,* adj.]

**reptilian** /rɛpˈtɪliən/, *adj.* **1.** belonging or pertaining to the reptiles or Reptilia. **2.** reptile-like. **3.** mean; base; malignant. –*n.* **4.** any of the Reptilia; a reptile.

**Repub.,** Republic.

**republic** /rəˈpʌblɪk/, *n.* **1.** a state in which the supreme power rests in the body of citizens entitled to vote and is exercised by representatives chosen directly or indirectly by them. **2.** any body of persons, etc., viewed as a commonwealth. **3.** a state, especially a democratic state, in which the head of the government is an elected or nominated president, not a hereditary monarch. [L *rēspublica* (abl. *rēpublicā*) state, lit., public matter]

**republican** /rə'pʌblɪkən/, *adj.* **1.** of, pertaining to, or of the nature of a republic. **2.** favouring a republic. *–n.* **3.** one who favours a republican form of government.

**republicanise** /rə'pʌblɪkənaɪz/, *v.t.*, **-nised, -nising.** *Chiefly U.S.* to make republican. Also, **republicanize.** – **republicanisation** /rə,pʌbləkənaɪ'zeɪʃən/, *n.*

**republicanism** /rə'pʌblɪkənɪzəm/, *n.* **1.** republican government. **2.** republican principles or adherence to them.

**republication** /,ripʌblə'keɪʃən/, *n.* **1.** publication anew. **2.** a book or the like published again.

**Republic of Belaw** /bə'laʊ/, *n.* a group of islands formerly called the Palau Islands, in the western Pacific Ocean.

**Republic of Korea,** *n.* Official name of **South Korea.**

**republic of letters,** *n.* **1.** the collective body of literary people. **2.** literature.

**repudiate** /rə'pjudieɪt/, *v.t.*, **-ated, -ating.** **1.** to reject as having no authority or binding force, as a claim, etc. **2.** to cast off or disown: *to repudiate a son.* **3.** to reject with disapproval or condemnation, as a doctrine, etc. **4.** to reject with denial, as a charge, etc. **5.** to refuse to acknowledge and pay, as a debt (said specifically of a state, municipality, etc.). [LL *repudiātus,* pp., rejected, divorced] – **repudiable,** *adj.* – **repudiative,** *adj.* – **repudiator,** *n.*

**repudiation** /rəpjudi'eɪʃən/, *n.* **1.** the act of repudiating. **2.** the state of being repudiated. **3.** refusal, as by a state of municipality, to pay a debt lawfully contracted.

**repugn** /rə'pjun/, *v.t, v.i. Obs.* to resist. [ME *repugne(n),* from OF *repugner,* from L *repugnāre* fight against]

**repugnance** /rə'pʌgnəns/, *n.* **1.** the state of being repugnant. **2.** objection, distaste, or aversion. **3.** contradictoriness or inconsistency. Also, **repugnancy.**

**repugnant** /rə'pʌgnənt/, *adj.* **1.** distasteful or objectionable. **2.** making opposition; objecting; averse. **3.** opposed or contrary, as in nature or character. [L *repugnans,* ppr., fighting against] – **repugnantly,** *adv.*

**repulp** /,ri'pʌlp/, *v.t.* to make into pulp again (something, as paper, which was originally made from pulp).

**repulse** /rə'pʌls/, *v.*, **-pulsed, -pulsing.** *–v.t.* **1.** to drive back, or repel, as an assailant, etc. **2.** to repel with denial, discourtesy, or the like; refuse or reject. *–n.* **3.** the act of repelling. **4.** the act of being repelled, as in hostile encounter. **5.** refusal or rejection. [L *repulsus,* pp., repelled] – **repulser,** *n.*

**repulsion** /rə'pʌlʃən/, *n.* **1.** the act of repelling or driving back. **2.** the state of being repelled. **3.** the feeling of being repelled; distaste, repugnance, or aversion. **4.** *Physics.* a situation in which bodies are forced apart (opposed to *attraction*).

**repulsive** /rə'pʌlsɪv/, *adj.* **1.** causing repugnance or aversion. **2.** tending to repel by denial, discourtesy, or the like. **3.** *Physics.* of the nature of or characterised by physical repulsion; tending to repel or drive back. – **repulsively,** *adv.* – **repulsiveness,** *n.*

**repurchase** /,ri'pɜtʃəs/, *v.*, **-chased, -chasing,** *n.* *–v.t.* **1.** to buy again; regain by purchase. *–n.* **2.** the act of repurchasing. – **repurchaser,** *n.*

**reputable** /'rɛpjətəbəl/, *adj.* held in good repute; honourable; respectable; estimable. – **reputability** /rɛpjətə'bɪləti/, *n.* – **reputably,** *adv.*

**reputation** /rɛpjə'teɪʃən/, *n.* **1.** the estimation in which a person or thing is held, esp. by the community or the public generally; repute: *a man of good reputation.* **2.** favourable repute; good name: *to ruin one's reputation by misconduct.* **3.** a favourable and publicly recognised name or standing for merit, achievement, etc.: *to build up a reputation.* **4.** the estimation or name of being, having, having done, etc., something specified.

**repute** /rə'pjut/, *n., v.*, **-puted, -puting.** *–n.* **1.** estimation in the view of others; reputation: *persons of good repute.* **2.** favourable reputation; good name; credit or note. *–v.t.* **3.** to consider or esteem (a person or thing) to be as specified; account or regard (commonly in the passive): *he was reputed to be a millionaire.* [late ME, from L *reputāre* reckon, think]

**reputed** /rə'pjutəd/, *adj.* accounted or supposed to be such: *the reputed author of a book.* – **reputedly,** *adv.*

**request** /rə'kwɛst/, *n.* **1.** the act of asking for something to be given, or done, esp. as a favour or courtesy; solicitation or petition: *a dying request.* **2.** that which is asked for: *to obtain one's request.* **3.** the state of being much asked for; demand: *to be in great request as an after-dinner speaker.* *–v.t.* **4.** to ask for, solicit (something), esp. politely or formally. **5.** to ask or beg (used with a clause or an infinitive): *to request that he leave, to request to be excused.* **6.** to make request to, ask, or beg (a person, etc.) to do something: *he requested me to go.* [ME *requeste,* from OF, from Gallo-Rom. *requaesita,* pp., (things) asked for, from LL *requaerere* seek, replacing L *requīrere*]

**requiem** /'rɛkwiəm/, *n.* (*oft. cap.*) **1.** *Rom. Cath. Ch.* **a.** the mass celebrated for the repose of the souls of the dead. **b.** a celebration of this mass **(Requiem Mass).** **c.** a musical setting of this mass. **2.** any musical service, hymn, or dirge for the repose of the dead. [ME, from L, acc. of *requies* rest, the first word of the introit of the Latin mass for the dead]

**requiescat** /rɛkwi'ɛskæt/, *n.* a wish or prayer for the repose of the dead. [L: short for *requiescat in pāce* may he (or she) rest in peace]

**requiescat in pace** /rɛkwi,ɛskæt ɪn 'patʃeɪ/, (rest in peace). [L]

**require** /rə'kwaɪə/, *v.*, **-quired, -quiring.** *–v.t.* **1.** to have need of; need: *he requires medical care.* **2.** to call on authoritatively, order, or enjoin (a person, etc.) to do something: *to require an agent to account for money spent.* **3.** to ask for authoritatively or imperatively; demand. **4.** to impose need or occasion for; make necessary or indispensable: *the work required infinite patience.* **5.** to call for or exact as obligatory: *the law requires annual income-tax returns.* **6.** to place under an obligation or necessity. **7.** to wish to have: *will you require tea at four o'clock?* *–v.i.* **8.** to make demand; impose obligation or need: *to do as the law requires.* [ME, from L *requīrere* search for, require]

**requirement** /rə'kwaɪəmənt/, *n.* **1.** that which is required; a thing demanded or obligatory: *a knowledge of Spanish is among the requirements.* **2.** the act or an instance of requiring. **3.** a need: *to meet the requirements of daily life.*

**requisite** /'rɛkwəzət/, *adj.* **1.** required by the nature of things or by circumstances; indispensable: *he has the requisite qualifications.* *–n.* **2.** something requisite; a necessary thing. [late ME, from L *requīsītus,* pp., sought for] – **requisitely,** *adv.* – **requisiteness,** *n.*

**requisition** /rɛkwə'zɪʃən/, *n.* **1.** the act of requiring or demanding. **2.** a demand made. **3.** the demanding authoritatively or formally of something to be done, given, furnished, etc. **4.** an authoritative or official demand. **5.** the form on which such a demand is written. **6.** the state of being required for use or called into service. **7.** a requirement, or essential condition. *–v.t.* **8.** to require or take for use; press into service. **9.** to demand or take, as by authority, for military purposes, public needs, etc.: *to requisition supplies.*

**requisitions on title,** *n. pl. Law.* written inquiries made by the solicitor of the intending purchaser of land, etc., to the vendor's solicitor for the purpose of ascertaining any defects in the title and obtaining information as to rates, rents, etc.

**requital** /rə'kwaɪtl/, *n.* **1.** the act of requiting. **2.** a return or reward for service, kindness, etc. **3.** retaliation for a wrong, injury, etc. **4.** repayment; something given or serving to requite.

**requite** /rə'kwaɪt/, *v.t.*, **-quited, -quiting.** **1.** to make repayment or return for (service, benefits, etc.). **2.** to make retaliation for (a wrong, injury, etc.). **3.** to make return to (a person) for service, etc. **4.** to make retaliation on (a person) for a wrong, etc. **5.** to give or do in return. [RE- + *quite,* obs. var. of QUIT, *v.*] – **requitable,** *adj.* – **requitement,** *n.* – **requiter,** *n.*

**re-radiation** /,ri-reɪdi'eɪʃən/, *n.* radiation emitted as a consequence of a previous absorption of radiation.

**re-rail** /ˌri-ˈreɪl/, *v.t.* to replace on the rails.

**rerebrace** /ˈrɪəbreɪs/, *n.* a piece of armour for the upper arm; upper cannon. [ME, from AF (cf. BRACE) *rerebras,* from *rere* back + *bras* arm]

**rerecord** /ˌrirəˈkɔd/, *v.t.* to record again, esp. to transfer sound from a record or tape to another record or tape.

**reredos** /ˈrɪədɒs/, *n.* a screen or a decorated part of the wall behind an altar in a church. [ME, from AF, aphetic var. of *areredos,* from *arere* REAR[1] + *dos* back]

**re-run** /ˌri-ˈrʌn/, *v.,* **-ran, -run, -running;** /ˈri-rʌn/, *n.* *–v.t.* **1.** to run again. *–n.* **2.** the act of re-running. **3.** a re-showing of a cinema film.

**res.,** **1.** reserve. **2.** residence. **3.** resigned. **4.** research.

**resail** /ˌriˈseɪl/, *v.i.* to sail back or again.

**resale** /ˈriseɪl, riˈseɪl/, *n.* the act of reselling. – **resaleable,** *adj.*

**resale price maintenance,** *n.* the establishment of a fixed or minimum retail price for branded products, by agreement between manufacturer and retailer.

**rescind** /rəˈsɪnd/, *v.t.* **1.** to abrogate; annul, revoke; repeal. **2.** to invalidate (an act, measure, etc.) by a later action or a higher authority. [L *rēscindere* cut off, annul] – **rescindable,** *adj.* – **rescinder,** *n.*

**rescissible** /rəˈsɪsəbəl/, *adj.* able to be rescinded.

**rescission** /rəˈsɪʒən/, *n.* the act of rescinding.

**rescissory** /rəˈsɪsəri/, *adj.* serving to rescind. [LL *rescissōrius,* from L *rescissus,* pp., annulled]

**rescript** /ˈriskrɪpt/, *n.* **1.** a written answer, as of a Roman emperor or a pope, to a query or petition in writing. **2.** any edict, decree, or official announcement. **3.** the act, or the product, of rewriting. *–v.t.* **4.** to rewrite (a script). [L *rēscriptum,* properly neut. pp., rescribed, written back. Cf. OF *rescrit*]

**rescue** /ˈrɛskju/, *v.,* **-cued, -cuing,** *n.* *–v.t.* **1.** to free or deliver from confinement, violence, danger, or evil. **2.** *Law.* to liberate or take by forcible or illegal means from lawful custody. *–n.* **3.** the act of rescuing. [ME *rescoue,* from OF *rescoure,* from L *re-* RE- + *excutere* shake out or off] – **rescuer,** *n.*

**research** /rəˈsɜtʃ, ˈrisɜtʃ/, *n.* **1.** diligent and systematic enquiry or investigation into a subject in order to discover facts or principles: *research in nuclear physics.* *–v.i.* **2.** to make researches; investigate carefully. *–v.t.* **3.** to investigate carefully: *to research a subject exhaustively.* *–adj.* **4.** of or pertaining to research. [F (obs.) *recerche.* See RE-, SEARCH, *v.*] – **researcher,** *n.*

**research assistant** /ˈ– əsɪstənt/, *n.* one who assists another in research.

**research library** /ˈ– laɪbri/, *n.* a library which concentrates on materials for specialists and scholars in certain fields.

**reseat** /ˌriˈsit/, *v.t.* **1.** to provide with a new seat or new seats. **2.** to seat again.

**reseau** /ˈrɛzoʊ, rɛˈzoʊ/, *n., pl.* **-seaux** /-zoʊ, -ˈzoʊ/. **1.** a network. **2.** a netted or meshed ground in lace. **3.** *Astron.* a network of fine lines on a glass plate, used in a photographic telescope in order to produce a corresponding network (for measuring purposes) on photographs of the stars. [F, diminutive of OF *roiz,* from L *rēte* net]

**resect** /rəˈsɛkt/, *v.t. Surg.* to cut away or pare off; excise a portion of. [L *resectus,* pp., cut back, cut off] – **resection,** *n.*

**reseda** /ˈrɛsədə/, *n.* **1.** any plant of the genus *Reseda,* esp. *R. odorata,* the garden mignonette. **2.** a greyish-green colour. *–adj.* **3.** greyish-green, like the flowers of the mignonette plant. [L: plant name; said to be special use of impv. of *resēdāre* heal]

**reseller** /ˈrisɛlə/, *n.* a retailer.

**resemblance** /rəˈzɛmbləns/, *n.* **1.** the state or fact of resembling; similarity. **2.** a degree, kind, or point of likeness. **3.** the likeness, appearance, or semblance of something. [ME, from AF; see RESEMBLE, -ANCE]

**resemblant** /rəˈzɛmblənt/, *adj. Archaic.* resembling; similar; having a likeness (*to*).

**resemble** /rəˈzɛmbəl/, *v.t.,* **-bled, -bling. 1.** to be like or similar to. **2.** *Archaic.* to liken or compare. [ME, from OF *resembler,* from *re-* RE- + *sembler* be like, from L *simulāre* simulate, imitate, copy] – **resembler,** *n.*

**resend** /ˌriˈsɛnd/, *v.t.,* **-sent, -sending. 1.** to send again. **2.** to send back.

**resent** /rəˈzɛnt/, *v.t.* to feel or show displeasure or indignation at, from a sense of injury or insult. [F *ressentire,* from *re-* RE- + *sentire,* from L *sentīre* feel]

**resentful** /rəˈzɛntfəl/, *adj.* full of, or marked by, resentment. – **resentfully,** *adv.* – **resentfulness,** *n.*

**resentment** /rəˈzɛntmənt/, *n.* the feeling of displeasure or indignation at something regarded as an injury or insult, or against the author or source of it.

**reserpine** /ˈrɛsəpin/, *n.* originally, a purified extract from the root of *Rauwolfia serpentina,* but now a substance made synthetically. It is widely used as a tranquilliser and in the treatment of hypertension and various psychogenic illnesses. [G *Reserpin,* probably from L *serpentīna* (see specific name of the plant)]

**reservation** /rɛzəˈveɪʃən/, *n.* **1.** a keeping back, withholding, or setting apart. **2.** the making of some exception or qualification. **3.** an exception or qualification made, expressly or tacitly: *a mental reservation.* **4.** a tract of public land set apart for a special purpose, as (in the U.S.) for the use of an Indian tribe. **5.** the allotting or the securing of accommodation at a hotel, on a train or boat, etc., as for a traveller: *to write for reservations.* **6.** the record or assurance of such an arrangement.

**re-serve** /ˌri-ˈsɜv/, *v.t.* to serve again.

**reserve** /rəˈzɜv/, *v.,* **-served, -serving,** *n., adj.* *–v.t.* **1.** to keep back or save for future use, disposal, treatment, etc. **2.** to retain or secure by express stipulation. **3.** to secure or book in advance as accommodation, theatre seats, etc. **4.** to set apart for a particular use, purpose, service, etc.: *ground reserved for gardening.* **5.** to keep for some fate, lot, experience, etc. **6.** *Eccles.* to save or set aside (the Eucharistic Hosts) to be administered outside the mass or communion service or at subsequent masses. **7.** *Law.* to delay handing down (a judgment or decision), esp. to give time for better consideration of the issues involved. *–n.* **8.** an amount of capital retained by a company to meet contingencies, or for any other purpose to which the profits of the company may be profitably applied. **9.** something reserved, as for some purpose or contingency; a store or stock. **10.** *Sport.* **a.** a player kept in readiness to take the place of a team member who may drop out through injury or the like. **b.** (*pl.*) a club's second team. **11.** a tract of public land set apart for recreation, as public reserve, or for a special purpose, as a nature reserve. **12.** a tract of public land for the habitation and use of the aboriginal people of a country, allowing them to retain their traditional lifestyle. **13.** a reservation, exception, or qualification. **14.** the act of reserving. **15.** the state of being reserved, as for future use or for some purpose or person: *money in reserve.* **16.** *Mil.* **a.** a fraction of a military force held in readiness to sustain the attack or defence made by the rest of the force. **b.** the part of a country's fighting force not in active service, but used as a further means of defence in case of necessity. **17.** avoidance of familiarity in social relationships; self-restraint in action or speech. **18.** reticence or silence. **19.** →**reserve price.** *–adj.* **20.** kept in reserve; forming a reserve: *a reserve fund or supply.* [ME, from L *reservāre* keep back]

**reserve bank** /– ˈbæŋk/, *n.* the national banking organisation of a country which administers the monetary policy of a government, receives revenue, pays government expenditure and issues money, both paper and coin, as legal tender.

**reserved** /rəˈzɜvd/, *adj.* **1.** kept in reserve; set apart for a particular use or purpose. **2.** kept by special arrangement for some person or persons: *a reserved seat.* **3.** self-restrained in action or speech; disposed to keep one's feelings, thoughts, or affairs to oneself. **4.** characterised by reserve, as the disposition, manner, etc. **5.** denoting an occupation of national importance which carries exemption from service in the armed forces in times of conscription. – **reservedly** /rəˈzɜvədli/, *adv.* – **reservedness,** *n.*

**reserve grade** /rəˈzɜv greɪd/, *n. Sport.* the second grade.

**reserve price** /– ˈpraɪs/, *n.* the lowest price at which a person is willing that his property shall be sold at auction. Also, **reserve.**

**reservist** /rəˈzɜvəst/, *n.* one who belongs to a reserve military force of a country.

**reservoir** /ˈrɛzəvwa/, *n.* **1.** a natural or artificial place where water is collected and stored for use, esp. water for supplying a community, irrigating land, furnishing power, etc. **2.** a receptacle or chamber for holding a liquid or fluid, as oil or gas. **3.** *Biol.* a cavity or part which holds some fluid or secretion. **4.** a place where anything is collected or accumulated in great amount. **5.** a great supply, store, or reserve of something. [F, from *reserver* keep, reserve]

**reset** /ˌriˈsɛt/, *v.*, **-set, -setting;** /ˈrisɛt/, *n.* *–v.t., v.i.* **1.** to set again. *–n.* **2.** the act of resetting. **3.** that which is reset. **4.** a plant which is replanted.

**res gestae** /reɪz ˈdʒɛstaɪ/, *n.pl.* **1.** achievements. **2.** *Law.* facts forming part of a transaction which is in issue; facts (esp. statements) accompanying and explaining the facts in issue. [L: the things done]

**reshape** /ˌriˈʃeɪp/, *v.t.*, **-shaped, -shaping.** to shape again or into different form.

**reship** /ˌriˈʃɪp/, *v.*, **-shipped, -shipping.** *–v.t.* **1.** to ship again. **2.** to transfer from one ship to another. *–v.i.* **3.** to go on a ship again. **4.** (of a member of a ship's crew) to sign up for another voyage. **– reshipment,** *n.*

**reshuffle** /ˌriˈʃʌfəl/, *v.*, **-fled, -fling,** *n.* *–v.t.* **1.** to shuffle again. **2.** to make a new allocation of jobs, esp. within a government or cabinet. *–n.* **3.** a rearrangement or reorganisation; a shake-up.

**reside** /rəˈzaɪd/, *v.i.*, **-sided, -siding.** **1.** to dwell permanently or for a considerable time; have one's abode for a time: *he resided in Box Hill.* **2.** (of things, qualities, etc.) to abide, lie, or be present habitually; exist or be inherent (fol. by *in*). **3.** to rest or be vested, as powers, rights, etc. (fol. by *in*). [late ME, from L *residēre*]

**residence** /ˈrɛzədəns/, *n.* **1.** the place, esp. the house, in which one resides; dwelling place; dwelling. **2.** a large house. **3.** the act or fact of residing. **4.** living or staying in a place of official or other duty. **5.** the time during which one resides in a place.

**residency** /ˈrɛzədənsi/, *n., pl.* **-cies. 1.** →**residence. 2.** the dwelling place of officials or diplomats representing the heads of state of foreign countries.

**resident** /ˈrɛzədənt/, *n.* **1.** one who resides in a place. **2.** *Brit.* a resident ambassador. **3.** a bird, animal, etc., that does not migrate. *–adj.* **4.** residing; dwelling in a place. **5.** living or staying at a place in discharge of duty: *resident representative, resident engineer.* **6.** (of qualities) existing; intrinsic. **7.** (of birds, etc.) not migratory. [ME, from L *residens*]

**residential** /rɛzəˈdɛnʃəl/, *adj.* **1.** of or pertaining to residence or residences. **2.** adapted or used for residence: *a residential district.* **3.** (of a hotel, etc.) catering for guests who stay permanently or for extended periods.

**residentiary** /rɛsəˈdɛnʃəri/, *adj., n., pl.* **-aries.** *–adj.* **1.** residing; resident. **2.** bound to or involving official residence. *–n.* **3.** a resident. **4.** an ecclesiastic bound to official residence.

**resident medical officer,** *n.* a medical officer who has graduated recently and who is appointed to and resident in a hospital. *Abbrev.:* **R.M.O.**

**residual** /rəˈzɪdʒuəl/, *adj.* **1.** pertaining to or constituting a residuum; remaining; left over. **2.** formed by the subtraction of one quantity from another: *a residual quantity.* *–n.* **3.** a residual quantity; a remainder. **4.** *Maths.* **a.** the deviation of one of a set of observations or numbers from the mean of the set. **b.** the deviation between an empirical and a theoretical result (in all experimental sciences). [RESIDU(E) + -AL[1]] **– residually,** *adv.*

**residuary** /rəˈzɪdʒuəri/, *adj.* **1.** entitled to the residue of an estate: *a residuary legatee.* **2.** pertaining to or of the nature of a residue, remainder, or residuum. [RESIDU(UM) + -ARY[1]]

**residue** /ˈrɛzədʒu/, *n.* **1.** that which remains after a part is taken, disposed of, or gone; remainder; rest. **2.** *Chem.* **a.** a quantity of matter remaining after evaporation, combustion, or some other process; a residuum. **b.** an atom or group of atoms considered as a radical or part of a molecule. **c.** that part remaining as a solid on a filter paper after a liquid passes through in the filtration procedure. **3.** *Law.* that which remains of a testator's or intestate's estate when all his liabilities have been discharged. [ME, from F *residu,* from L *residuum*]

**residuum** /rəˈzɪdʒuəm/, *n., pl.* **-sidua** /-ˈzɪdʒuə/. **1.** the residue, remainder, or rest of something. **2.** *Chem.* a quantity or body of matter remaining after evaporation, combustion, distillation, or the like. **3.** any residual product. **4.** *Law.* the residue of an estate. [L]

**re-sign** /ˌriˈsaɪn/, *v.i., v.t.* to sign again.

**resign** /rəˈzaɪn/, *v.i.* **1.** to give up an office or position (oft. fol. by *from*). **2.** to submit; yield. *–v.t.* **3.** to give up (an office, position, etc.) formally. **4.** to relinquish, as a right or claim. **5.** to submit (oneself, one's mind, etc.) without resistance. **6.** to hand or sign over; surrender, as to the care or control of another: *to resign a child to foster-parents.* [ME *resignen,* from OF *resigner,* from L *resignāre* unseal, annul]

**resignation** /rɛzɪgˈneɪʃən/, *n.* **1.** the act of resigning. **2.** the formal statement, document, etc., stating that one resigns an office, position, etc. **3.** the state of being submissive; submission; unresisting acquiescence. [ME, from ML *resignātio*]

**resigned** /rəˈzaɪnd/, *adj.* **1.** submissive or acquiescent. **2.** characterised by or indicative of resignation. **– resignedly** /rəˈzaɪnədli/, *adv.* **– resignedness** /rəˈzaɪnədnəs/, *n.*

**resile** /rəˈzaɪl/, *v.i.*, **-siled, -siling. 1.** to spring back; rebound; resume the original form or position, as an elastic body. **2.** to shrink back; recoil. [L *resilīre*]

**resilience** /rəˈzɪliəns, -ˈzɪljəns/, *n.* **1.** resilient power; elasticity. **2.** resilient action; rebound; recoil. **3.** power of ready recovery from sickness, depression, or the like; buoyancy; cheerfulness. Also, **resiliency.**

**resilient** /rəˈzɪliənt, -ˈzɪljənt/, *adj.* **1.** springing back; rebounding. **2.** returning to the original form or position after being bent, compressed, or stretched. **3.** readily recovering, as from sickness, depression, or the like; buoyant; cheerful. [L *resiliens,* ppr., rebounding] **– resiliently,** *adv.*

**resin** /ˈrɛzən/, *n.* **1.** any of a class of non-volatile, solid or semisolid organic substances (copal, mastic, etc.) obtained directly from certain plants as exudations or prepared by polymerisation of simple molecules, and used in medicine and in the making of varnishes and plastics. **2.** (not in scientific usage) a substance of this type obtained from certain pines; rosin. *–v.t.* **3.** to treat or rub with resin. [ME *resyn,* from L *rēsīna,* c. Gk *rhētínē*] **– resin-like,** *adj.*

**resinate** /ˈrɛzəneɪt/, *v.t.*, **-nated, -nating.** to treat with resin, as by impregnation.

**resiniferous** /rɛzəˈnɪfərəs/, *adj.* yielding resin.

**resinoid** /ˈrɛzənɔɪd/, *adj.* **1.** resin-like. *–n.* **2.** a resinoid substance. **3.** a resinous substance synthetically compounded. **4.** →**gum resin.**

**resinous** /ˈrɛzənəs/, *adj.* **1.** full of or containing resin. **2.** of the nature of or resembling resin. **3.** pertaining to or characteristic of resin. Also, **resiny** /ˈrɛzəni/. [L *rēsīnōsus*]

**res ipsa loquitur** /ˌreɪz ɪpsə ˈlɒkwətə/, *n.* the legal doctrine that when a thing is exclusively under the control of the defendant or his servant, and damage or injury occurs which would not ordinarily happen without negligence being present, negligence of the defendant is presumed from the mere fact of its happening. [L: the thing speaks for itself]

**resist** /rəˈzɪst/, *v.t.* **1.** to withstand, strive against, or oppose: *to resist infection.* **2.** to withstand the action or effect of: *gold resists corrosion.* **3.** to refrain or abstain from: *to resist a smile.* *–v.i.* **4.** to make a stand or make efforts in opposition; act in opposition; offer resistance. *–n.* **5.** a substance applied to a surface to enable it to resist corrosion or the like. [ME *resisten,* from L *resistere* withstand] **– resister,** *n.*

**resistance** /rəˈzɪstəns/, *n.* **1.** the act or power of resisting, opposing, or withstanding. **2.** the opposition offered by one thing, force, etc., to another. **3.** *Elect.* **a.** the property of a device which opposes the flow of an electric current. **b.** a measure of the ability of a device to oppose the flow of an electric current. The derived SI unit of resistance is the ohm. **c.** a device opposing the flow of an electric current; a resistor. **4.** (*oft. cap.*) a secret organisation in an enemy-occupied country working to maintain hostilities unofficially after a formal capitulation. [late ME, from F; replacing ME *resistence,* from OF, from LL *resistentia*]

**resistance thermometer** /– θəˈmɒmətə/, *n.* a form of thermometer in which the temperature is deduced from the resistance of a spiral of wire (usu. platinum).

**resistance welding** /– ˈwɛldɪŋ/, *n.* a form of welding in which the heat required to fuse the metal surfaces to be welded is produced by a current flowing across the contact resistance between them.

**resistant** /rəˈzɪstənt/, *adj.* **1.** resisting. *–n.* **2.** one who or that which resists.

**resistible** /rəˈzɪstəbəl/, *adj.* that may be resisted. – **resistibility** /rəzɪstəˈbɪləti/, *n.*

**resistive** /rəˈzɪstɪv/, *adj.* resisting; capable of or characterised by resistance.

**resistivity** /rizɪsˈtɪvəti/, *n.* **1.** the power or property of resistance. **2.** *Elect.* a measure of the ability of a material to oppose the flows of an electric current (the reciprocal of *conductivity*).

**resistless** /rəˈzɪstləs/, *adj.* **1.** irresistible. **2.** unresisting. – **resistlessly,** *adv.* – **resistlessness,** *n.*

**resistor** /rəˈzɪstə/, *n.* a device, the primary purpose of which is to introduce resistance into an electric circuit.

**resit** /ˌriˈsɪt/, *v.t., v.i.* to sit (an examination) again after having failed it.

**res nullius** /reɪz ˈnʊliəs/, *n. Law.* a thing which has no owner. [L]

**resole** /ˌriˈsoʊl/, *v.t.* **-soled, -soling.** to put a new sole on (a shoe, etc.).

**re-soluble** /ˌri-ˈsɒljəbəl/, *adj.* capable of being dissolved again.

**resoluble** /rəˈzɒljəbəl/, *adj.* capable of being resolved. [LL *resolūbilis*] – **resolubility** /rəzɒljəˈbɪləti/, *n.* – **resolubleness,** *n.*

**resolute** /ˈrɛzəlut/, *adj.* **1.** firmly resolved or determined; set in purpose or opinion. **2.** characterised by firmness and determination, as the temper, spirit, actions, etc. [ME, from L *resolūtus*, pp., resolved] – **resolutely,** *adv.* – **resoluteness,** *n.*

**resolution** /rɛzəˈluʃən/, *n.* **1.** a formal determination, or expression of opinion, of a deliberative assembly or other body of persons. **2.** a resolve or determination: *to make a firm resolution to do something.* **3.** the act of resolving or determining as to action, etc. **4.** the mental state or quality of being resolved or resolute; firmness of purpose. **5.** the act or process of resolving or separating into constituent or elementary parts. **6.** the resulting state. **7.** solution or explanation, as of a problem, a doubtful point, etc. **8.** *Music.* **a.** progression of a voice part or of the harmony as a whole from a dissonance to a consonance, or sometimes to another less violent dissonance. **b.** the note or chord to which this is effected. **9.** reduction to a simpler form; conversion. **10.** *Med.* the reduction or disappearance of a swelling or inflammation without suppuration. **11.** *Optics.* **a.** the act or process of distinguishing between the individual parts of an image. **b.** resolving power. [ME *resolucion*, from L *resolūtio*]

**resolutioner** /rɛzəˈluʃənə/, *n.* one joining in or subscribing to a resolution. Also, **resolutionist.**

**resolvable** /rəˈzɒlvəbəl/, *adj.* that may be resolved. – **resolvability** /rəzɒlvəˈbɪləti/, **resolvableness,** *n.*

**resolve** /rəˈzɒlv/, *v.,* **-solved, -solving,** *n. –v.t.* **1.** to fix or settle on by deliberate choice and will; determine (to do something). **2.** to separate into constituent or elementary parts, break up, or disintegrate; separate or break up (fol. by *into*). **3.** *Physics.* (of forces, velocities, etc.) to divide into components. **4.** to reduce or convert by or as by breaking up or disintegration (fol. by *into* or *to*). **5.** to convert or transform by any process (often reflexive). **6.** to reduce by logical analysis (fol. by *into*). **7.** to settle, determine, or state formally in a vote or resolution, as of a deliberative assembly. **8.** to deal with (a question, a matter of uncertainty, etc.) conclusively; explain; solve (a problem). **9.** to clear away or dispel (doubts, etc.), as by explanation. **10.** *Chem.* to separate (a racemic mixture) into its optically active components. **11.** *Music.* to cause (a voice part or the harmony as a whole) to progress from a dissonance to a consonance. **12.** *Optics.* to separate and make visible the individual parts of (an image); to distinguish between. **13.** *Med.* to cause (swellings, inflammation, etc.) to disappear without suppuration. *–v.i.* **14.** to come to a determination; make up one's mind; determine (oft. fol. by *on* or *upon*). **15.** to break up or disintegrate. **16.** to be reduced or changed by breaking up or otherwise (fol. by *into* or *to*). **17.** *Music.* to progress from a dissonance to a consonance. *–n.* **18.** a resolution or determination made, as to follow some course of action. **19.** determination; firmness of purpose. [ME, from L *resolvere* loosen, dissolve] – **resolver,** *n.*

**resolved** /rəˈzɒlvd/, *adj.* determined; firm in purpose; resolute. – **resolvedly** /rəˈzɒlvədli/, *adv.*

**resolvent** /rəˈzɒlvənt/, *adj.* **1.** resolving; causing solution; solvent. *–n.* **2.** something resolvent. **3.** *Med.* a remedy that causes resolution, as of swellings, etc. [L *resolvens*, ppr., resolving]

**resolving power** /rəˈzɒlvɪŋ paʊə/, *n.* the ability of an optical device to produce separate images of close objects. Also, **resolution.**

**resonance** /ˈrɛzənəns/, *n.* **1.** the state or quality of being resonant. **2.** the prolongation of sound by reflection; reverberation. **3.** the amplification of vocal tone by the bones of the head and upper chest and by the air cavities of the pharynx, mouth, and nasal passages. **4.** *Physics.* (of a physical system) the state of having large amplitude vibrations excited by an external periodic impulse having a frequency near a natural frequency of the system (as in the reinforcement of sound by induced vibration, the increase in the amplitude of alternating current in an electric circuit when the frequency of the electromotive force has a particular value, etc.) **5.** *Physics.* the excitation of an atomic or subatomic system from one energy state to another by an incident light, or an incident particle, which has exactly the requisite energy. **6.** *Chem.* the condition exhibited by a molecule when the actual arrangement of its valency electrons is intermediate between two or more arrangements having nearly the same energy, and the positions of the atomic nuclei are identical. **7.** *Med.* a sound produced when air is present (in percussing for diagnostic purposes).

**resonant** /ˈrɛzənənt/, *adj.* **1.** resounding or re-echoing, as sounds, places, etc. **2.** deep and full of resonance: *a resonant voice.* **3.** pertaining to resonance. **4.** having the property of increasing the intensity of sound by sympathetic vibration. [L *resonans*, ppr., resounding] – **resonantly,** *adv.*

**resonant cavity** /– ˈkævəti/, *n.* →**resonator** (def. 4a).

**resonant circuit** /– ˈsɜkət/, *n.* an electronic circuit containing both an inductance and a capacitance which is capable of resonance.

**resonate** /ˈrɛzəneɪt/, *v.i.,* **-nated, -nating.** **1.** to resound. **2.** to act as a resonator; exhibit resonance. **3.** *Electronics.* to reinforce oscillations because the natural frequency of the device is the same as the frequency of the source. **4.** to amplify vocal sound by the sympathetic vibration of air in certain cavities and bony structures. *–v.t.* **5.** to cause to resound. [L *resonātus*, pp., resounded] – **resonation** /rɛzəˈneɪʃən/, *n.*

**resonator** /ˈrɛzəneɪtə/, *n.* **1.** anything that resonates. **2.** an appliance for increasing sound by resonance. **3.** an instrument for detecting the presence of a particular frequency by means of resonance. **4.** *Electronics.* **a.** Also, **cavity resonator.** a hollow enclosure made of conducting material of such dimensions that electromagnetic radiation of a certain frequency will resonate. **b.** any circuit having this frequency characteristic. [NL. See RESONATE, -OR[2]]

**resonator guitar** /– gəˈta/, *n.* a steel guitar in which the strings pass over a bridge which is connected to the centre of a large, metal, cone-shaped resonator.

**resorb** /riˈsɔb/, *v.t.* to absorb again, as an exudation. [L *resorbēre* suck back] – **resorption,** *n.* – **resorptive,** *adj.*

**resorcinol** /rəˈzɔsənɒl/, *n.* a colourless crystalline benzene derivative, $C_6H_4(OH)_2$, originally obtained from certain resins, used in medicine and in making dyes. Also, **resorcin.** [RES(IN) + ORCINOL]

**re-sort** /ˌri-ˈsɔt/, *v.t.* to sort again.

**resort** /rəˈzɔt/, *v.i.* **1.** to have recourse for use, service, or help: *to resort to war.* **2.** to go, esp. frequently or customarily: *a beach to which many people resort.* *–n.* **3.** a place frequented, esp. by the public generally: *a summer resort.* **4.** a habitual or general going, as to a place or person. **5.** a resorting to some person or thing for aid, service, etc.; recourse: *to have resort to force.* **6.** a person or thing resorted to for aid, service, etc. **7. last resort,** the expedient to which one turns when all others have failed. [ME *resorte(n)*, from OF *resortir*, from *re-* RE- + *sortir* issue, go out]

**re-sound** /ˌri-ˈsaʊnd/, *v.t., v.i.* to sound again. [RE- + SOUND[1]]

**resound** /rəˈzaʊnd/, *v.i.* **1.** to re-echo or ring with sound, as a place. **2.** to make an echoing sound, or sound loudly, as a thing. **3.** to be echoed, or ring, as sounds. **4.** to be famed or celebrated. *–v.t.* **5.** to re-echo (a sound). **6.** to proclaim loudly (praises, etc.). **7.** *Rare.* to give forth or utter loudly. [ME *resoun(en)*, from *re-* RE- + *soun(en)* SOUND[1], after L *resonāre*] – **resoundingly,** *adv.*

**resounding** /rə'zaʊndɪŋ/, *adj.* **1.** ringing, re-echoing, or reverberating, as a sound or its cause or location. **2.** thoroughgoing; outstanding; great: *a resounding success.* **3.** (of actions) firmly executed and often noisy: *a resounding blow.*

**resource** /rə'zɔs, rə'sɔs/, *n.* **1.** a source of supply, support, or aid. **2.** (*pl.*) the collective wealth of a country, or its means of producing wealth. **3.** (*oft. pl.*) money, or any property which can be converted into money; assets. **4.** available means afforded by the mind or the personal capabilities. **5.** an action or measure to which one may have recourse in an emergency; expedient. **6.** capability in dealing with a situation or in meeting difficulties. [F *ressource,* from OF *res(s)-sourdre* (from *re-* RE- + *sourdre*), from L *resurgere* rise again]

**resourceful** /rə'zɔsfəl, rə'sɔsfəl/, *adj.* full of resource; ingenious; skilful in overcoming difficulties. – **resourcefully,** *adv.* – **resourcefulness,** *n.*

**resources boom** /rə'zɔsəz ˌbum/, *n.* an upsurge in the economic activity and general prosperity of a country as a result of the widespread development of mineral resources, as coal, nickel, etc.

**respect** /rə'spɛkt/, *n.* **1.** a particular, detail, or point (in phrases prec. by *in*): *to be defective in some respect.* **2.** relation or reference (prec. by *in* or *with*): *enquiries with respect to a route.* **3.** esteem or deferential regard felt or shown. **4.** the condition of being esteemed or honoured. **5.** (*pl.*) deferential, respectful, or friendly compliments, as paid by making a call on a person or otherwise: *to pay one's respects.* **6.** consideration or regard, as to something that might influence a choice. **7.** *Archaic.* consideration. *–v.t.* **8.** to hold in esteem or honour: *to respect one's elders.* **9.** to show esteem, regard, or consideration for: *to respect someone's wishes.* **10.** to treat with consideration; refrain from interfering with: *to respect a person's privacy.* **11.** *Obs.* to relate or have reference to. [ME, from L *respectus,* pp., having been regarded] – **respecter,** *n.*

**respectability** /rəspɛktə'bɪləti/, *n., pl.* **-ties.** **1.** the state or quality of being respectable. **2.** respectable social standing, character, or reputation. **3.** respectable people. **4.** (*pl.*) things accepted as respectable.

**respectable** /rə'spɛktəbəl/, *adj.* **1.** worthy of respect or esteem; estimable; worthy: *a respectable citizen.* **2.** of good social standing, reputation, etc.: *a respectable neighbourhood.* **3.** pertaining or appropriate to such standing; proper or decent: *respectable language.* **4.** having socially accepted standards of moral behaviour; virtuous: *a respectable girl.* **5.** of presentable appearance; decently clothed. **6.** of moderate excellence; fairly good; fair: *a respectable performance.* **7.** considerable in size, number, or amount: *a respectable navy.* – **respectableness,** *n.* – **respectably,** *adv.*

**respecter of persons,** *n.* one who is unduly influenced in his dealings by the social standing, importance, etc., of persons.

**respectful** /rə'spɛktfəl/, *adj.* full of, characterised by, or showing respect: *a respectful reply.* – **respectfully,** *adv.* – **respectfulness,** *n.*

**respecting** /rə'spɛktɪŋ/, *prep.* regarding; concerning.

**respective** /rə'spɛktɪv/, *adj.* pertaining individually or severally to each of a number of persons, things, etc.; particular: *the respective merits of the candidates.*

**respectively** /rə'spɛktɪvli/, *adv.* with respect to each of a number in the stated or corresponding order: *labelled respectively A, B, and C.*

**respell** /ri'spɛl/, *v.t.* to spell again or anew.

**respirable** /'rɛspərəbəl/, *adj.* **1.** capable of being respired. **2.** capable of respiring.

**respiration** /rɛspə'reɪʃən/, *n.* **1.** the act of respiring; inhalation and exhalation of air; breathing. **2.** (in living organisms) the process by which oxygen and carbohydrates are assimilated into the system and the oxidation products (carbon dioxide and water) are given off.

**respirator** /'rɛspəreɪtə/, *n.* **1.** a device worn over the mouth, or nose and mouth, to prevent the inhalation of noxious substances, etc., as a gasmask. **2.** an apparatus to induce artificial respiration.

**respiratory** /'rɛsprətri, rɛs'pɪrətri/, *adj.* pertaining to or serving for respiration: *the respiratory system of mammals.*

**respire** /rə'spaɪə/, *v.,* **-spired, -spiring.** *–v.i.* **1.** to inhale and exhale air for the purpose of maintaining life; breathe. **2.** to breathe freely again, after anxiety, trouble, exertion, etc. *–v.t.* **3.** to breathe; inhale and exhale. **4.** *Rare.* to exhale or exude. [ME, from L *respīrāre*]

**respite** /'rɛspət, 'rɛspaɪt/, *n., v.,* **-pited, -piting.** *–n.* **1.** a delay or cessation for a time, esp. of anything distressing or trying; an interval of relief: *to toil without respite.* **2.** temporary suspension of the execution of a person condemned to death; a reprieve. *–v.t.* **3.** to relieve temporarily, esp. from anything distressing or trying; give an interval of relief from. **4.** to grant delay in the carrying out of (a punishment, obligation, etc.). [ME *respit,* from OF, from LL *respectus* delay, from L *respectāre* look for, wait for]

**resplendence** /rə'splɛndəns/, *n.* resplendent state; splendour. Also, **resplendency.**

**resplendent** /rə'splɛndənt/, *adj.* shining brilliantly; gleaming; splendid: *resplendent in white uniforms.* [L *resplendens,* ppr., shining] – **resplendently,** *adv.*

**respond** /rə'spɒnd/, *v.i.* **1.** to answer; give a reply in words: *to respond briefly to a question.* **2.** to make a return by some action as if in answer: *to respond generously to a charitable appeal.* **3.** *Physiol.* to exhibit some action or effect as if in answer; react: *nerves respond to a stimulus.* **4.** to correspond (fol. by *to*). *–v.t.* **5.** to say in answer; reply. *–n.* **6.** *Archit.* a half-pillar or the like engaged in a wall to support an arch. **7.** *Eccles.* **a.** a short anthem chanted at intervals during the reading of a lection. **b.** →**responsory.** **c.** →**response** (def. 4a). [ME, from L *respondēre*]

**respondence** /rə'spɒndəns/, *n.* **1.** the act of responding; response: *respondence to a stimulus.* **2.** agreement; correspondence. Also, **respondency.**

**respondent** /rə'spɒndənt/, *n.* **1.** *Law.* a defendant, esp. in appellate and divorce cases. **2.** *Biol.* one who responds or makes reply. *–adj.* **3.** answering; responsive. [L *respondens,* ppr., answering]

**response** /rə'spɒns/, *n.* **1.** answer or reply, whether in words, in some action, etc. **2.** *Biol.* any behaviour of a living organism which results from stimulation. **3.** *Elect.* the ratio of the output level to the input level of an electrical device or transmission line, at a given frequency. **4.** *Eccles.* **a.** a verse, sentence, phrase, or word said or sung by the choir or congregation in reply to the officiant during public worship. **b.** →**responsory.** [L *responsum,* neut. of *responsus,* pp., answered; replacing ME *respouns(e),* from OF *respuns, respons* (masc.), *response* (fem.)]

**response time** /'– taɪm/, *n.* the time between the initiating of a computer operation and the receipt of the results at a terminal.

**responsibility** /rəspɒnsə'bɪləti/, *n., pl.* **-ties.** **1.** the state or fact of being responsible. **2.** an instance of being responsible. **3.** a particular burden of obligation upon one who is responsible: *to feel the responsibilities of one's position.* **4.** something for which one is responsible: *a child is a responsibility to its parents.* **5.** ability to meet debts or payments. **6. on one's own responsibility,** on one's own initiative or authority.

**responsible** /rə'spɒnsəbəl/, *adj.* **1.** answerable or accountable, as for something within one's power, control, or management (oft. fol. by *to* or *for*). **2.** involving accountability or responsibility: *a responsible position.* **3.** chargeable with being the author, cause, or occasion of something (fol. by *for*). **4.** having a capacity for moral decisions and therefore accountable; capable of rational thought or action. **5.** able to discharge obligations or pay debts. **6.** reliable in business or other dealings; showing reliability. – **responsibleness,** *n.* – **responsibly,** *adv.*

**responsible government** /– 'gʌvənmənt/, *n.* a system under which the government must account for its actions to some representative assembly of the people.

**responsive** /rə'spɒnsɪv/, *adj.* **1.** making answer or reply, esp. responding readily to influences, appeals, efforts, etc. **2.** *Physiol.* acting in response, as to some stimulus. – **respon-**

**sively,** *adv.* – **responsiveness,** *n.*

**responsory** /rəˈspɒnsəri/, *n., pl.* **-ries.** *Eccles.* an anthem sung after a lection by a soloist and choir alternately. [ME, from LL *responsoria,* pl.]

**respray** /ˌriˈspreɪ/, *v.;* /ˈrispreɪ/, *n.* –*v.t.* **1.** to spray again. **2.** to paint (a motor vehicle or the like) again by spraying. –*n.* **3.** the act, process, or fact of (a motor vehicle or the like) being or having been repainted in this manner. [RE- + SPRAY[1]]

**respring** /ˌriˈsprɪŋ/, *v.t.,* **-sprang** or **-sprung, -springing.** to replace the springs of (a mattress, or upholstered piece of furniture).

**respublica** /reɪsˈpʊblɪkə/, *n.* the state; republic; commonwealth. [L]

**rest**[1] /rɛst/, *n.* **1.** the refreshing quiet or repose of sleep: *a good night's rest.* **2.** refreshing ease or inactivity after exertion or labour: *to allow an hour for rest.* **3.** relief or freedom, esp. from anything that wearies, troubles, or disturbs. **4.** mental or spiritual calm; tranquillity: *to set one's mind at rest.* **5.** the repose of death: *to lay the dead to rest.* **6.** cessation or absence of motion: *to bring a machine to rest.* **7.** a pause or interval. **8.** *Music.* **a.** an interval of silence between notes. **b.** a mark or sign indicating this. **9.** *Pros.* a short pause in reading; a caesura. **10.** an establishment for providing shelter or lodging for some class of persons. **11.** a piece or thing for something to rest on: *an elbow rest.* **12.** a support, or supporting device. **13.** *Billiards.* →**bridge**[1] (def. 10). **14.** *Prison Colloq.* a period of imprisonment of one year. **15. at rest, a.** dead. **b.** quiescent, inactive, or motionless, as something formerly in motion. **c.** tranquil; unworried. **d.** in a state of rest, as asleep. –*v.i.* **16.** to refresh oneself, as by sleeping, lying down, or relaxing. **17.** to relieve weariness by cessation of exertion or labour. **18.** to be at ease; have tranquillity or peace. **19.** to repose in death. **20.** to be quiet or still. **21.** to cease from motion, come to rest, or stop. **22.** to become or remain inactive. **23.** to remain without further action or notice: *to let a matter rest.* **24.** to lie, sit, lean, or be set (fol. by *in, on, against,* etc.): *his arm rested on the table.* **25.** *Agric.* to lie fallow or unworked: *to let land rest.* **26.** to be imposed as a burden or responsibility (fol. by *on* or *upon*). **27.** to rely (fol. by *on* or *upon*). **28.** to be based or founded (fol. by *on* or *upon*). **29.** to be found or be (where specified): *the blame rests with them.* **30.** to be present; dwell; linger (fol. by *on* or *upon*): *the moonlight rests upon the floor.* **31.** to be a responsibility, as something to be done (fol. by *in* or *with*): *it rests with you to complete the job.* **32.** to be fixed or directed on something, as the gaze, eyes, etc. **33.** *Law.* to terminate voluntarily the introduction of evidence in a case. **34.** *Theat. Colloq.* to be unemployed, as an actor. **35. rest on one's laurels,** to allow one's reputation to rely on past achievements, and make no further effort. **36. rest on one's oars, a.** *Rowing.* to stop rowing. **b.** to suspend any activity for a time. –*v.t.* **37.** to give rest to; refresh with rest: *to rest oneself.* **38.** to lay or place for rest, ease, or support: *to rest one's back against a tree.* **39.** to direct (the eyes, etc.): *to rest one's eyes on someone.* **40.** to base, or let depend, as on some ground of reliance. **41.** to bring to rest; halt; stop. **42.** *Law.* to terminate voluntarily the introduction of evidence on: *to rest one's case.* [ME *resten,* OE *restan,* c. OHG *restan,* akin to G *rasten*]

A B C D E F G H

rests (def. 8): A, breve; B, semibreve; C, minim; D, crotchet; E, quaver; F, semiquaver; G, demisemiquaver; H, hemidemisemiquaver

**rest**[2] /rɛst/, *n.* **1.** that which is left or remains; the remainder: *the rest of the money is his.* **2.** the others; those who are left; everyone else: *all the rest are going.* [late ME *reste,* from F, from *rester,* v. (see below)] –*v.i.* **3.** to continue to be; remain (as specified): *rest assured.* [late ME, from F *rester,* from L *restāre* remain]

**rest**[3] /rɛst/, *n.* →**lance rest.** [ME, aphetic var. of *arest* ARREST, *n.*]

**rest area** /ˈ– ɛəriə/, *n.* a parking spot at the side of the road, sometimes with cooking and toilet facilities.

**restate** /ˌriˈsteɪt/, *v.t.,* **-stated, -stating.** to state again or in a new way. – **restatement,** *n.*

**restaurant** /ˈrɛstərɒnt/, *n.* an establishment where meals are served to customers. [F, special use of ppr. of *restaurer* RESTORE]

**restaurant car** /ˈ– ka/, *n.* →**dining car.**

**restauranteur** /rɛstərɒnˈtɜ/, *n.* the keeper of a restaurant. [alteration of RESTAURATEUR]

**restaurateur** /rɛstərəˈtɜ/, *n.* →**restauranteur.** [F, from *restaurer* RESTORE]

**rest cure** /ˈrɛst kjuə/, *n.* a treatment for nervous disorders, consisting of a complete rest, usu. combined with systematic diet, massage, etc.

**restful** /ˈrɛstfəl/, *adj.* **1.** full of, or giving, rest. **2.** being at rest; quiet; tranquil; peaceful. – **restfully,** *adv.* – **restfulness,** *n.*

**rest-harrow** /ˈrɛst-hæroʊ/, *n.* any of several European plants of the leguminous genus *Ononis,* esp. *O. repens* and *O. spinosa,* which have tough stems and roots that hinder the plough. [REST[1] + HARROW]

**rest home** /ˈrɛst hoʊm/, *n.* a place where old people are cared for.

**restiform bodies** /ˈrɛstəfɔm ˌbɒdiz/, *n.pl.* a pair of cordlike bundles of nerve fibres lying one on each side of the medulla oblongata and connecting it with the cerebellum. [*restiform* from NL *restiformis,* from L *resti(s)* rope, cord + *-formis* -FORM]

**resting** /ˈrɛstɪŋ/, *adj.* **1.** that rests. **2.** *Bot.* dormant (applied esp. to spores or seeds which germinate after a period of dormancy).

**resting paddock** /ˈ– pædək/, *n.* a paddock adjacent to saleyards or along a stockroute.

**resting place** /ˈ– pleɪs/, *n.* **1.** a place where a person may rest. **2.** a place of burial; the grave.

**restionaceous** /ˌrɛstiəˈneɪʃəs/, *adj.* of or pertaining to rushlike plants belonging to the family Restionaceae.

**restitute** /ˈrɛstətjut/, *v.t., v.i.* to make restitution (of).

**restitutio in integrum** /rɛstəˌtjutsioʊ ɪn ˈɪntəgrəm/, *n.* the rescinding of a contract when the parties can be put back into their original positions, entailing a giving back and taking back on each side. [L: restoration to the original position]

**restitution** /rɛstəˈtjuʃən/, *n.* **1.** reparation made by giving an equivalent or compensation for loss, damage, or injury caused; indemnification. **2.** the restoration of property or rights previously taken away, conveyed, or surrendered. **3.** restoration to the former or original state or position. **4.** *Physics.* the return of an elastic material to its original form when released from strain. [ME *restitucion,* from L *restitūtio* a restoring]

**restive** /ˈrɛstɪv/, *adj.* **1.** restless; uneasy; impatient of control, restraint, or delay, as persons. **2.** →**refractory. 3.** refusing to go forward, as a horse. [REST[2] (def. 3) + -IVE; replacing ME *restif* stationary, balking, from OF *restif* inert] – **restively,** *adv.* – **restiveness,** *n.*

**restless** /ˈrɛstləs/, *adj.* **1.** characterised by or showing inability to remain at rest: *a restless mood.* **2.** unquiet or uneasy, as a person, the mind, heart, etc. **3.** never at rest, motionless, or still; never ceasing. **4.** without rest; without restful sleep: *a restless night.* **5.** characterised by unceasing activity; averse to quiet or inaction, as persons. – **restlessly,** *adv.* – **restlessness,** *n.*

**restless flycatcher** /– ˈflaɪkætʃə/, *n.* a black and white flycatcher, *Myiagra inquieta,* which hovers a metre or so above the ground when feeding, and which has a call resembling the sound a grindstone makes; scissors grinder.

**rest mass** /ˈrɛst mæs/, *n.* the mass of a body which is at rest relative to the observer.

**restock** /ˌriˈstɒk/, *v.t., v.i.* to stock again; replenish.

**restoration** /rɛstəˈreɪʃən/, *n.* **1.** the act of restoring; renewal, revival, or re-establishment. **2.** the state or fact of being restored. **3.** a bringing back to a former, original, normal, or unimpaired condition. **4.** restitution of something taken away or lost. **5.** something which is restored. **6.** a representation or reconstruction of an ancient building, extinct animal, or the like, showing it in its original state. **7.** a putting back into a former position, dignity, etc. **8. the Restoration, a.** the re-establishment of the monarchy in England with the return of Charles II in 1660. **b.** the period of the reign of Charles II (1660-85), sometimes extended to include the reign of James II (1685-88). *–adj.* **9.** (*cap.*) denoting, pertaining to, or produced during the period of the Restoration, esp. a form of drama: *Restoration comedy.*

**restorative** /rəˈstɔrətɪv/, *adj.* **1.** serving to restore; pertaining to restoration. **2.** capable of renewing health or strength. *–n.* **3.** a restorative agent. **4.** a means of restoring a person to consciousness.

**restore** /rəˈstɔ/, *v.t.*, **-stored, -storing.** **1.** to bring back into existence, use, or the like; re-establish: *to restore order.* **2.** to bring back to a former, original, or normal condition, as a building, statue, or painting. **3.** bring back to a state of health, soundness, or vigour. **4.** to put back to a former place, or to a former position, rank, etc. **5.** to give back; make return or restitution of (anything taken away or lost). **6.** to reproduce, reconstruct, or represent (an ancient building, extinct animal, etc.) in the original state. [ME, from OF *restorer,* from L *restaurāre* restore, repair] – **restorer,** *n.*

**restrain** /rəˈstreɪn/, *v.t.* **1.** to hold back from action; keep in check or under control; keep down; repress. **2.** to deprive of liberty, as a person. [ME *restreyn(en),* OF *restrei(g)n-,* stem of *restreindre,* from L *restringere*] – **restrainable,** *adj.* – **restrainedly,** *adv.*

**restrainer** /rəˈstreɪnə/, *n.* **1.** one who or that which restrains. **2.** a chemical, as potassium bromide, added to a photographic developer to retard its action.

**restraining order** /rəˈstreɪnɪŋ ɔdə/, *n.* an injunction made by a court, as one to prevent a husband from visiting his wife during divorce proceedings.

**restraint** /rəˈstreɪnt/, *n.* **1.** restraining action or influence: *freedom from restraint.* **2.** a means of restraining. **3.** the act of restraining, or holding back, controlling, or checking. **4.** →**child restraint.** **5.** the state or fact of being restrained; deprivation of liberty; confinement. **6.** constraint or reserve in feelings. [ME *restraynte,* from OF *restraint(e),* n. use of pp. of *restraindre* restrain]

**restraint of trade,** *n.* the restriction of business activity and freedom to compete.

**restrict** /rəˈstrɪkt/, *v.t.* to confine or keep within limits, as of space, action, choice, quantity, etc. [L *restrictus,* pp., restrained, restricted] – **restricted,** *adj.* – **restrictedly,** *adv.*

**restricted** /rəˈstrɪktəd/, *adj.* **1.** *Mil.* limited to persons authorised to have access, as to information, etc. **2.** limited; confined. **3.** admitting only members of certain groups, as a restricted club. **4.** of or pertaining to a horse which is eligible to compete in certain races by complying with the conditions of that race.

**restricted area** /– ˈɛəriə/, *n.* **1.** an area in which traffic is not permitted to exceed a certain speed. **2.** any area from which certain groups or races of people are excluded.

**restricted exhibition** /– ɛksəˈbɪʃən/, *n.* of or pertaining to a film considered suitable for adult viewing only. *Abbrev.:* R.

**restricted race** /– ˈreɪs/, *n.* a horserace in which entry is restricted to horses who have not previously entered in other specified races or won specified amounts of prize money.

**restricted title** /– ˈtaɪtl/, *n.* the statement at the beginning of a parliamentary bill of its scope, which delimits the debate and the amendments which can be moved.

**restriction** /rəˈstrɪkʃən/, *n.* **1.** something that restricts; a restrictive condition or regulation; a limitation. **2.** the act of restricting. **3.** the state of being restricted.

**restrictive** /rəˈstrɪktɪv/, *adj.* **1.** tending or serving to restrict. **2.** of the nature of a restriction. **3.** expressing or implying restriction or limitation of application, as terms, expressions, etc. – **restrictively,** *adv.*

**restrictive clause** /– ˈklɔz/, *n.* a relative clause, usu. not set off by commas, which identifies the person or object named by the antecedent (opposed to *descriptive clause*).

**restrictive covenant** /– ˈkʌvənənt/, *n.* a negative covenant entered into by the purchaser of land, as a promise to the vendor not to build a factory on it.

**restrictive practice** /– ˈpræktəs/, *n.* **1.** a practice on the part of the members of an association such as a trade union, tending to limit the freedom of choice of their coworkers or employers. **2.** →**restrictive trade practice.**

**restrictive trade practice,** *n.* an agreement between trading companies which is contrary to the public interest, as resale price maintenance, exclusive dealing, price discrimination, etc.

**rest room** /ˈrɛst rum/, *n.* **1.** a room set aside for people to rest in, as in an office, factory, etc. **2.** a lavatory, or similar room having washing facilities, etc.

**restump** /ˌriˈstʌmp/, *v.t.* to replace the stump foundations of (a house).

**result** /rəˈzʌlt/, *n.* **1.** that which results; the outcome, consequence, or effect. **2.** *Maths.* a quantity, value, etc., obtained by calculation. *–v.i.* **3.** to spring, arise, or proceed as a consequence from actions, circumstances, premises, etc.; be the outcome. **4.** to terminate or end in a specified manner or thing. **5.** →**revert** (def. 4). [late ME, from L *resultāre* spring back]

**resultant** /rəˈzʌltənt/, *adj.* **1.** that results; following as a result or consequence. **2.** resulting from the combination of two or more agents: *a resultant force.* *–n.* **3.** *Physics.* a force, velocity, etc., equal in result or effect to two or more other forces, velocities, etc. **4.** that which results.

**resultant note** /ˈ– noʊt/, *n.* an effect in which the vibrations of two notes, fairly close in pitch and sounded simultaneously, give rise to a further set of vibrations which may be heard as a third note. The principle is sometimes used by organ-builders to provide an inexpensive equivalent of a deep register. Also, **resultant tone.**

**resume** /rəˈzjum/, *v.*, **-sumed, -suming.** *–v.t.* **1.** to take up or go on with again after interruption: *to resume a journey.* **2.** to take or occupy again: *to resume one's seat.* **3.** to take, or take on, again: *to resume one's maiden name.* **4.** to take back. *–v.i.* **5.** to go on or continue after interruption. **6.** to begin again. [late ME, from L *resūmere* take up again] – **resumable,** *adj.* – **resumer,** *n.*

**résumé** /ˈrɛzjəmeɪ/, *n.* a summing up; a summary. [F, properly pp. of *résumer* RESUME]

**resumption** /rəˈzʌmpʃən/, *n.* **1.** the act of resuming; a taking back, as of something previously granted. **2.** a taking up or going on with again, as of something interrupted. **3.** a taking, or taking on, again, as of something given up or lost. [late ME, from L *resumptio*]

**resumptive** /rəˈzʌmptɪv/, *adj.* **1.** summarising. **2.** repeating; repetitive.

**resupinate** /rəˈsjupənət/, *adj.* **1.** bent backwards. **2.** *Bot.* inverted; appearing as if upside down. [L *resupīnātus,* pp., bent back]

**resupination** /rəsjupəˈneɪʃən/, *n.* resupinate condition.

**resupine** /rəˈsjupaɪn/, *adj.* lying on the back; supine. [L *resupīnus*]

**resurface** /ˌriˈsɜfəs/, *v.*, **-faced, -facing.** *–v.t.* **1.** to give a new surface to. *–v.i.* **2.** to come to the surface again.

**resurge** /riˈsɜdʒ/, *v.i.*, **-surged, -surging.** to rise again, as from the dead. [L *resurgere* rise again]

**resurgent** /rəˈsɜdʒənt/, *adj.* **1.** rising or tending to rise again. *–n.* **2.** one who has risen again. – **resurgence,** *n.*

**resurrect** /rɛzəˈrɛkt/, *v.t.* **1.** to raise from the dead; bring to life again. **2.** to bring back into use, practice, etc.: *to resurrect an ancient custom.* *–v.i.* **3.** to rise from the dead. [backformation from RESURRECTION]

**resurrection** /rɛzəˈrɛkʃən/, *n.* **1.** the act of rising again from the dead. **2.** (*cap.*) the rising again of Christ after His death and burial. **3.** (*cap.*) the rising again of men on the judgment day. **4.** the state of those risen from the dead. **5.** a rising again, as from decay, disuse, etc.; revival. [ME *resur(r)ectioun,* from LL *resurrectio*] – **resurrectional,** *adj.*

**resurrectionary** /rɛzəˈrɛkʃənəri/, *adj.* **1.** pertaining to or of the nature of resurrection. **2.** pertaining to resurrectionism.

**resurrectionism** /rɛzəˈrɛkʃənɪzəm/, *n.* **1.** belief in resurrection. **2.** *Hist.* exhuming and stealing of dead bodies, esp. for dissection; body-snatching.

**resurrectionist** /rɛzəˈrɛkʃənəst/, *n.* **1.** one who brings something to life or view again. **2.** a believer in resurrection. **3.** *Hist.* one who exhumes and steals dead bodies, esp. for dissection; body-snatcher.

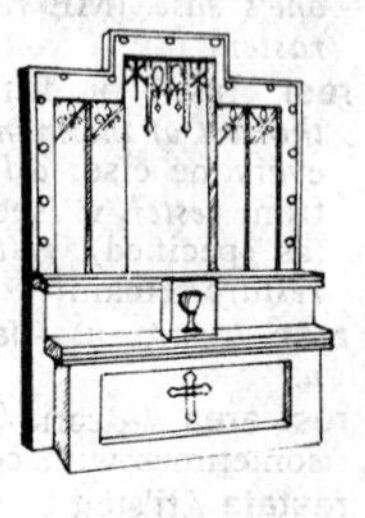
retable

**resuscitate** /rə'sʌsəteɪt/, *v.t., v.i.*, **-tated, -tating.** to revive, esp. from apparent death or from unconsciousness. [L *resuscitātus*, pp., revived] – **resuscitable,** *adj.* – **resuscitation** /rəsʌsə'teɪʃən/, *n.* – **resuscitative,** *adj.* – **resuscitator,** *n.*

**ret** /rɛt/, *v.t.*, **retted, retting.** to expose to moisture or soak in water, as flax, in order to soften by partial rotting. [ME *retten, reten*, akin to D *reten*. Cf. also D *roten*, c. d. E *rait*, from Scand.; cf. Swed. *röta* ret]

**ret.,** retired.

**retable** /rə'teɪbəl/, *n.* a decorative structure raised above an altar at the back, often forming a frame for a picture, bas-relief, or the like, and sometimes including a shelf or shelves, as for ornaments. [F, from OF *rere* at the back (from L *retrō*) + *table* TABLE]

**retail** /'riteɪl/ *for defs 1-4, 6;* /ri'teɪl/ *for def. 5, n.* **1.** the sale of commodities to household or ultimate consumers, usu. in small quantities (opposed to *wholesale*). *–adj.* **2.** pertaining to, connected with, or engaged in sale at retail: *the retail price.* *–adv.* **3.** at a retail price or in a retail quantity; at retail. *–v.t.* **4.** to sell at retail; to sell directly to the consumer. **5.** to relate or repeat in detail to others: *to retail scandal.* *–v.i.* **6.** to be sold at retail: *it retails at a dollar.* [late ME, from AF: a cutting, from *retailler* cut, clip, pare, from *re-* RE- + *tailler* cut] – **retailer,** *n.*

**retain** /rə'teɪn/, *v.t.* **1.** to keep possession of. **2.** to continue to use, practise, etc.: *to retain an old custom.* **3.** to continue to hold or have: *this cloth retains its colour.* **4.** to keep in mind; remember. **5.** to hold in place or position. **6.** to engage, esp. by the payment of a preliminary fee, as a barrister. [ME *reteyne*, from OF *retenir*, from Rom. *retenēre*, replacing L *retinēre* hold back, keep. Cf. CONTAIN, DETAIN] – **retainable,** *adj.* – **retainment,** *n.*

**retained object** /rəteɪnd 'ɒbdʒɛkt/, *n.* an object in a passive construction identical with the direct or indirect object in the corresponding active construction, as *me* in *the picture was shown me* (corresponding active construction: *they showed me the picture*).

**retainer**[1] /rə'teɪnə/, *n.* **1.** one who or that which retains. **2.** *Hist.* one attached to a noble household or owing it service. **3.** any servant, esp. a personal or family servant of long standing. **4.** *Mach.* the groove or frame in which roller-bearings operate. [RETAIN + -ER[1]]

**retainer**[2] /rə'teɪnə/, *n.* **1.** the act of retaining in one's service. **2.** the fact of being so retained. **3.** a fee paid to secure services, as of a barrister. **4.** a reduced rent paid during absence for a flat or lodging as an indication of future requirement. [F *retenir*, inf. used as n. See RETAIN]

**retaining fee** /rə'teɪnɪŋ fi/, *n.* →**retainer**[2] (def. 3).

**retaining wall** /'– wɔl/, *n.* **1.** a wall built to hold back a mass of earth, etc. **2.** →**revetment.**

**retake** /ˌri'teɪk/, *v.*, **-took, -taken, -taking;** /'riteɪk/, *n.* *–v.t.* **1.** to take again; take back. **2.** to recapture. **3.** *Films.* to film again. *–n.* **4.** a retaking, as of a picture. **5.** a scene, sequence, etc., which is to be or has been filmed again. – **retaker,** *n.*

**retaliate** /rə'tælieɪt/, *v.*, **-ated, -ating.** *–v.i.* **1.** to return like for like, esp. evil for evil or requital (esp. for an injury); take reprisals: *to retaliate for an injury.* *–v.t.* **2.** to make return for or requite (now usu. wrong, injury, etc.) [LL *retāliātus*, pp., requited]

**retaliation** /rətæli'eɪʃən/, *n.* the act of retaliating; return of like for like; reprisal.

**retard** /rə'tad/, *v.t.* **1.** to make slow; delay the progress of (an action, process, etc.); hinder or impede. **2.** to delay or limit (a person's intellectual or emotional development). *–v.i.* **3.** to be delayed. *–n.* **4.** retardation; delay. **5. in retard,** *Obs.* delayed. [L *retardāre*] – **retarder,** *n.*

**retardation** /rita'deɪʃən/, *n.* **1.** the act of retarding. **2.** the state of being retarded. **3.** that which retards; a hindrance. **4.** *Physics.* deceleration; rate of decrease of velocity; negative acceleration. Also, **retardment** /rə'tadmənt/. – **retardative** /rə'tadətɪv/, **retardatory** /rə'tadətri/, *adj.*

**retarded** /rə'tadəd/, *adj.* (of a child) **1.** slow in mental development, esp. having an IQ of 70-85; backward. **2.** seriously delayed in school work, as due to protracted absence through illness; behind.

**retarder** /rə'tadə/, *n.* **1.** that which or one who retards. **2.** *Chem.* a substance added to a composition, as paint, plaster, cement, etc., to slow down chemical or physical changes.

**retarding basin** /rə'tadɪŋ beɪsən/, *n.* an extensive man-made depression in the ground used in conditions of torrential rain to hold back water and hence prevent local flooding; often used under normal weather conditions as a sports ground.

**retch** /rɛtʃ/, *v.i.* **1.** to make efforts to vomit. *–n.* **2.** the act or an instance of retching. [OE *hrǣcan* clear the throat (from *hrāca* clearing of the throat), c. Icel. *hrækja* hawk, spit]

**retd,** **1.** retired. **2.** returned.

**rete** /'riti/, *n., pl.* **retia** /'ritiə, 'riʃiə/. a network, as of fibres, nerves, or blood vessels. [ME *riet*, from L *rēte* net]

**retene** /'ritin, 'rɛtin/, *n.* a crystalline hydrocarbon, $C_{18}H_{18}$, obtained from the tar of resinous woods, certain fossil resins, etc. [Gk *rhētínē* resin. See -ENE]

**retention** /rə'tɛnʃən/, *n.* **1.** the act of retaining. **2.** the state of being retained. **3.** power to retain; capacity for retaining. **4.** the act or power of remembering things; memory. [ME, from L *retentio*]

**retentive** /rə'tɛntɪv/, *adj.* **1.** tending or serving to retain something. **2.** having power or capacity to retain. **3.** having power or ability to remember; having a good memory. – **retentiveness,** *n.*

**retentivity** /ritɛn'tɪvəti/, *n.* **1.** power to retain; retentiveness. **2.** →**remanence.**

**retepore** /'ritəpɔ/, *n.* any bryozoan of the family Reteporidae, which forms colonies with a network-like structure. [NL *Rētepora*, the typical genus, from L *rēte* net + *-pora* (from Gk *póros* PORE[2])]

**rethink** /ri'θɪŋk/, *v.*, **-thought, -thinking.** *–v.t.* **1.** to review or alter one's ideas on (a matter, one's plans, etc.). *–v.i.* **2.** to think again; reflect. [RE- + THINK[1]]

**R. et I.,** **1.** King and Emperor. [L *Rex et Imperator*] **2.** Queen and Empress. [L *Regina et Imperatrix*]

**retiarius spider** /rɛti'ɛəriəs ˌspaɪdə/, *n.* a nocturnal spider, *Dinopis subrupta*, which builds a rectangular web to throw over its prey. [L *rētiārius* gladiator equipped with a net, from *rēte* net]

**retiary** /'ritiəri, 'riʃjəri/, *adj.* **1.** using a net or any entangling device. **2.** netlike. **3.** making a net or web, as a spider.

**reticent** /'rɛtəsənt/, *adj.* disposed to be silent; not inclined to speak freely; reserved. [L *reticens*, ppr., keeping silent] – **reticence,** *n.* – **reticently,** *adv.*

**reticle** /'rɛtɪkəl/, *n.* a network of fine lines, wires, or the like, placed in the focus of the objective of a telescope. [L *rēticulum*, diminutive of *rēte* net. Cf. RETICULE]

**reticular** /rə'tɪkjələ/, *adj.* **1.** having the form of a net; netlike. **2.** intricate or entangled. [NL *rēticulāris*, from L *rēticulum* small net]

**reticulate** /rə'tɪkjələt/, *adj.;* /rə'tɪkjəleɪt/ *v.*, **-lated, -lating.** *–adj.* **1.** netted; covered with a network. **2.** netlike. **3.** *Bot.* (of leaves, etc.) having the veins or nerves disposed like the threads of a net. *–v.t.* **4.** to form into a network. **5.** to cover or mark with a network. **6.** to cause (water, etc.) to pass through a system of pipes. *–v.i.* **7.** to form a network. [L *rēticulātus* made like a net]

**reticulation** /rətɪkjə'leɪʃən/, *n.* **1.** reticulated formation, arrangement, or appearance; a network. **2.** *Bldg Trades.* the wires, pipes or ducts which convey services through a building.

**reticule** /'rɛtəkjul/, *n.* **1.** a small purse or bag, originally of network but later of silk, etc. **2.** →**reticle.** [F, from L *rēticulum*, diminutive of *rēte* net]

**reticulum** /rə'tɪkjələm/, *n., pl.* **-la** /-lə/. **1.** a network; any reticulated system or structure. **2.** *Anat.* reticular endothelial tissue. **3.** *Zool.* the second stomach of ruminating animals, between the rumen and the omasum. [L: little net]

**retiform** /'rɛtəfɔm/, *adj.* netlike; reticulate. [NL *rētiformis*, from L *rēti-* (combining form of *rēte* net) + *-formis* -FORM]

**retina** /'rɛtənə/, *n., pl.* **-nas, -nae** /-ni/. the innermost coat of the posterior part of the eyeball, consisting of a layer of light-sensitive cells connecting with the optic nerve by way of a record layer of nerve cells, and serving to receive the image. [ME, from ML, ? from L *rēte* net] – **retinal,** *adj.*

**retinene** /'rɛtənin/, *n.* the aldehyde of vitamin A, which combines with protein in the substance visual purple. [RETIN(A) + -ENE]

**retinite** /ˈrɛtənaɪt/, *n.* any of various fossil resins, esp. one of those derived from brown coal. [F, from Gk *rhētínē* resin + *-ite* -ITE[1]]

**retinitis** /rɛtəˈnaɪtəs/, *n.* inflammation of the retina. [NL. See RETINA, -ITIS]

**retinol** /ˈrɛtənɒl/, *n.* a yellowish oil obtained by the distillation of resin, used as a solvent, a mild antiseptic, etc. [*retin-* (stem of Gk *rhētínē* resin) + -OL[2]]

**retinoscope** /ˈrɛtənəskoʊp/, *n.* →**skiascope.**

**retinoscopy** /rɛtəˈnɒskəpi/, *n.* an objective method of determining the refractive error of an eye. [*retino-* (combining form representing RETINA) + -SCOPY] – **retinoscopic** /rɛtənəˈskɒpɪk/, *adj.*

**retinue** /ˈrɛtənju/, *n.* a body of retainers in attendance upon an important personage; a suite. [ME, from OF *retenue,* fem. pp. of *retenir* RETAIN]

**retire** /rəˈtaɪə/, *v.,* **-tired, -tiring.** *–v.i.* **1.** to withdraw, or go away or apart, to a place of abode, shelter, or seclusion. **2.** to go to bed. **3.** to withdraw from office, business, or active life: *to retire at the age of sixty.* **4.** to fall back or retreat, as from battle or danger. **5.** to withdraw, go away, or remove oneself. **6.** *Sport.* to leave the field, ring, etc. before completion of the contest, usu. because of injury. *–v.t.* **7.** to withdraw from circulation by taking up and paying, as bonds, bills, etc. **8.** to withdraw or lead back (troops, etc.), as from battle or danger; retreat. **9.** to remove from active service or the usual field of activity, as an officer in the army or the navy. [F *retirer* withdraw, from *re-* RE- + *tirer* draw]

**retired** /rəˈtaɪəd/, *adj.* **1.** withdrawn from or no longer occupied with one's business or profession: *a retired sea-captain.* **2.** due or given a retired person: *retired pay.* **3.** withdrawn; secluded or sequestered.

**retired list** /ˈ– lɪst/, *n.* a list of officers who are retired from active service and who may draw a pension.

**retirement** /rəˈtaɪəmənt/, *n.* **1.** the act of retiring. **2.** the state of being retired. **3.** removal or retiring from service, office, or business. **4.** withdrawal into privacy or seclusion. **5.** privacy or seclusion. **6.** a private or secluded place. **7.** retreat of a military force. **8.** repurchase of its own securities by a company.

**retirement village** /ˈ– vɪlɪdʒ/, *n.* an establishment for the aged in which they live in communal or semi-communal dwellings.

**retiring** /rəˈtaɪərɪŋ/, *adj.* **1.** that retires. **2.** withdrawing from contact with others; reserved; shy.

**retool** /ˌriˈtul/, *v.t.* to change the tools, machinery, or procedures, in (a factory), esp. as part of a new development.

**retorsion** /rəˈtɔʃən/, *n. Internat. Law.* retaliation or reprisal by one state identical or similar to an act by an offending state, such as high tariffs or discriminating duties. Also, **retortion.** [ML *retorsio,* var. of *retortio* RETORTION]

**retort**[1] /rəˈtɔt/, *v.t.* **1.** to reply in retaliation; make a retort or retorts, often quickly and sharply; reply in kind to. **2.** to return (an accusation, epithet, etc.) upon the person uttering it. **3.** to answer (an argument or the like) by another to the contrary. *–n.* **4.** a severe, incisive, or witty reply, esp. one that counters a first speaker's statement, argument, etc. **5.** the act of retorting. [L *retortus,* pp., twisted back]

**retort**[2] /rəˈtɔt/, *n.* **1.** *Chem.* a vessel, commonly a glass bulb with a long neck bent downwards, used for distilling or decomposing substances by heat. **2.** *Metall.* a vessel, generally cylindrically shaped, within which an ore is heated so that the metal may be removed by distillation or sublimation. **3.** a large autoclave for sterilising sealed food tins with superheated steam under pressure. [ML *retorta,* properly fem. pp., twisted back. See RETORT[1], *v.*]

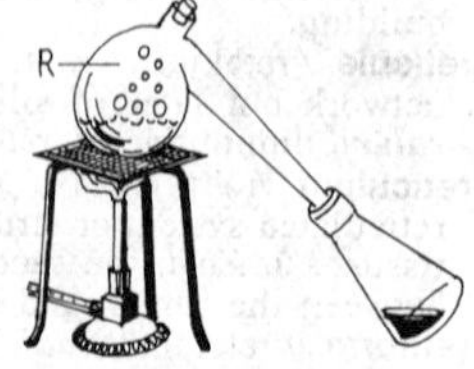

R, retort[2] (def. 1)

**retortion** /rəˈtɔʃən/, *n.* **1.** the act of turning or bending back. **2.** →**retaliation. 3.** *Internat. Law.* →**retorsion.** [ML *retortio,* from L *retortus,* pp., twisted back]

**retouch** /riˈtʌtʃ/, *v.;* /ˈritʌtʃ/, *n.* *–v.t.* **1.** to improve by new touches or the like, as a painting, make-up, etc. **2.** *Photog.* to correct or improve (a negative or print) by the use of a pencil, scraping knife, etc. *–n.* **3.** an added touch to a painting, etc., by way of improvement or alteration. – **retoucher,** *n.*

**re-trace** /ˌriˈtreɪs/, *v.t.,* **-traced, -tracing.** to trace again, as lines in writing or drawing. [RE- + TRACE[1] (defs 18 and 19)]

**retrace** /rəˈtreɪs/, *v.t.,* **-traced, -tracing. 1.** to trace back; go back over: *to retrace one's steps.* **2.** to go back over with the memory. **3.** to go over again with the sight or attention. [F *retracer,* from *re-* RE- + *tracer* TRACE[1]] – **retraceable,** *adj.*

**retract**[1] /rəˈtrækt/, *v.t.* to draw back or in. [late ME, from L *retractus,* pp., drawn back]

**retract**[2] /rəˈtrækt/, *v.t.* **1.** to withdraw (a statement, opinion, etc.) as unjustified. **2.** to withdraw or revoke (a decree, promise, etc.). *–v.i.* **3.** to draw or shrink back. **4.** to withdraw a promise, etc. **5.** to make disavowal of a statement, opinion, etc., or recant. [L *retractāre* recall] – **retractable,** *adj.* – **retractation** /ritrækˈteɪʃən/, *n.*

**retractile** /rəˈtræktaɪl/, *adj.* capable of being drawn back or in, as the head of a tortoise; exhibiting the power of retraction. – **retractility** /ritrækˈtɪləti/, *n.*

**retraction** /rəˈtrækʃən/, *n.* **1.** the act of retracting. **2.** the state of being retracted. **3.** withdrawal of a promise, statement, opinion, etc.: *his retraction of the libel came too late.* **4.** retractile power.

**retractive** /rəˈtræktɪv/, *adj.* tending or serving to retract.

**retractor** /rəˈtræktə/, *n.* **1.** one who or that which retracts. **2.** *Anat.* a muscle that retracts an organ or protruded part, etc. **3.** *Surg.* an instrument or appliance for drawing back an impeding part.

**re-tread** /ˌriˈtrɛd/, *v.t., v.i.,* **-trod, -trodden** or **-trod, -treading.** to tread again. [RE- + TREAD]

**retread** /ˌriˈtrɛd/, *v.,* **-treaded, -treading;** /ˈritrɛd/, *n.* *–v.t.* **1.** to recondition (a worn motor-vehicle tyre) by moulding a fresh tread (on to it) and vulcanising by subjecting to heat and pressure. *–n.* **2.** a retreaded tyre. **3.** *Colloq.* a person who has come out of retirement to take up work again. [RE- + TREAD (def. 18)]

**retreat** /rəˈtrit/, *n.* **1.** the forced or strategic retirement of an armed force before an enemy, or the withdrawing of a ship or fleet from action. **2.** the act of withdrawing, as into safety or privacy; retirement; seclusion. **3.** a place of refuge, seclusion, or privacy. **4.** an asylum, as for the insane. **5.** a retirement, or a period of retirement, for religious exercises and meditation. **6.** a signal given in the army or navy by drum, bugle, or trumpet, at sunset. *–v.i.* **7.** to withdraw, retire, or draw back, esp. for shelter or seclusion. **8.** to make a retreat, as an army. **9.** to slope backwards; recede: *a retreating forehead.* *–v.t.* **10.** to draw or lead back. [ME *retrete(n),* from *retret,* n., retreat]

**retrench** /rəˈtrɛntʃ/, *v.t.* **1.** to cut down, reduce, or diminish; curtail (expenses). **2.** to sack or dismiss, as part of an effort to economise. **3.** to cut off or remove. **4.** *Mil.* to protect by a retrenchment. *–v.i.* **5.** to economise: reduce expenses: *they retrenched by cutting down staff.* [F (obs.) *retrencher.* See RE-, TRENCH]

**retrenchment** /rəˈtrɛntʃmənt/, *n.* **1.** the act of retrenching; a cutting down or off; reduction of expenses. **2.** *Fort.* **a.** an interior work which cuts off a part of a fortification from the rest, and to which a garrison may retreat. **b.** →**entrenchment.**

**retrial** /ˌriˈtraɪəl/, *n.* a second or new trial.

**retribution** /rɛtrəˈbjuʃən/, *n.* **1.** requital according to merits or deserts, esp. for evil. **2.** something given or inflicted in such requital. **3.** *Theol.* the distribution of rewards and punishments in a future life. [ME, from L *retribūtio*]

**retributive** /rəˈtrɪbjətɪv/, *adj.* characterised by or involving retribution. Also, **retributory.**

**retrieval** /rəˈtrivəl/, *n.* **1.** the act of retrieving. **2.** chance of recovery or restoration: *lost beyond retrieval.*

**retrieve** /rəˈtriv/, *v.,* **-trieved, -trieving,** *n.* *–v.t.* **1.** to recover or regain. **2.** to bring back to a former and better state; restore: *to retrieve one's fortunes.* **3.** to make amends for (an error, etc.). **4.** to make good; repair (a loss, etc.). **5.** *Hunting.* (of dogs) to find and fetch (killed or wounded game). **6.** to rescue or save. *–v.i.* **7.** *Hunting.* to retrieve game. *–n.* **8.**

i = peat ɪ = pit ɛ = pet æ = pat a = part ɒ = pot ʌ = putt ɔ = port ʊ = put u = pool ɜ = pert ə = apart aɪ = buy eɪ = bay ɔɪ = boy aʊ = how
oʊ = hoe ɪə = here ɛə = hair ʊə = tour g = give θ = thin ð = then ʃ = show ʒ = measure tʃ = choke dʒ = joke ŋ = sing j = you õ = Fr. bon

the act of retrieving; recovery. **9.** possibility of recovery. [ME *retreve,* from OF *retroev-* stressed stem of *retrouver,* from *re-* RE- + *trouver* find. See TROVER] – **retrievable,** *adj.*

**retriever** /rə'trivə/, *n.* **1.** one who or that which retrieves. **2.** any of several breeds of dog for retrieving game, as the golden retriever. **3.** any dog trained to retrieve game.

Labrador retriever

**retro-,** a prefix meaning 'backwards' in space or time, as *retrogression, retrospect.* [L, prefix representing *retrō,* adv., backward, back, behind]

**retroaction** /rɛtrou'ækʃən/, *n.* action which is opposed or contrary to the preceding action.

**retroactive** /rɛtrou'æktɪv/, *adj.* operative with respect to past occurrences, as a statute; retrospective. – **retroactively,** *adv.* – **retroactivity** /ˌrɛtrouæk'tɪvəti/, *n.*

**retrobulbar** /rɛtrou'bʌlbə/, *adj.* behind the eyeball.

**retrocaecal** /rɛtrou'sikəl/, *adj.* of an appendix which does not lie in its normal position but is twisted back behind the intestine.

**retrocede**[1] /rɛtrə'sid/, *v.i.,* **-ceded, -ceding.** to go back; recede; retire. [L *retrōcēdere* yield, go back] – **retrocession** /rɛtrə'sɛʃən/, *n.*

**retrocede**[2] /rɛtrə'sid/, *v.t.,* **-ceded, -ceding.** to cede back (territory, etc.). [RETRO- + CEDE] – **retrocession** /rɛtrə'sɛʃən/, *n.*

**retrochoir** /'rɛtroukwaɪə/, *n.* that part of a church behind the choir or the high altar. [RETRO- + CHOIR, after ML *retrōchorus*]

**retroflex** /'rɛtrəflɛks/, *adj.* **1.** bent backwards; exhibiting retroflexion. **2.** *Phonet.* **a.** (of vowels) pronounced with the tip of the tongue raised or tilted upwards, as the vowel in *burn* in a common American pronunciation. **b.** (of consonants) pronounced with the tip of the tongue curled back to touch the roof of the mouth; cacuminal; cerebral. [L *retrōflexus,* pp., bent back. See FLEX[1]]

**retroflexion** /rɛtrə'flɛkʃən/, *n.* **1.** a bending backwards. **2.** *Pathol.* a bending backwards of the body of the uterus. **3.** *Phonet.* **a.** retroflex articulation. **b.** the acoustic quality resulting from retroflex articulation; r-colour.

**retrogradation** /ˌrɛtrougrə'deɪʃən/, *n.* **1.** backward movement. **2.** decline or deterioration.

**retrograde** /'rɛtrəgreɪd/, *adj., v.,* **-graded, -grading.** *–adj.* **1.** moving backwards; having a backward motion or direction; retiring or retreating. **2.** returning to an earlier and inferior state: *a retrograde step.* **3.** inverse or reversed, as order. **4.** *Chiefly Biol.* exhibiting degeneration or deterioration. **5.** *Astron.* **a.** denoting an apparent or actual motion in a direction opposite to the order of the signs of the zodiac, or from east to west. **b.** moving in an orbit in the direction opposite to that of the earth in its revolution round the sun. **6.** *Music.* of or pertaining to a tone row read from the end to the beginning. *–v.i.* **7.** to move or go backwards; retire or retreat. **8.** *Chiefly Biol.* to decline to a worse condition; degenerate. **9.** *Astron.* to have a retrograde motion. [ME *retrograd,* from L *retrōgradus* going backwards]

**retrograde inversion** /– ɪn'vɜʒən/, *n.* (in twelve-tone composition) a tone row which has been inverted and made retrograde.

**retrograde rocket** /– 'rɒkət/, *n. Aeron.* →**retro-rocket.**

**retrogress** /rɛtrə'grɛs/, *v.i.* **1.** to go backwards into a worse or earlier condition. **2.** to move backwards.

**retrogression** /rɛtrə'grɛʃən/, *n.* **1.** the act of retrogressing; backward movement. **2.** *Biol.* degeneration; retrograde metamorphosis; passing from a more complex to a simpler structure.

**retrogressive** /rɛtrə'grɛsɪv/, *adj.* characterised by retrogression; degenerating. – **retrogressively,** *adv.*

**retrolental fibroplasia** /rɛtrəˌlɛntl faɪbrə'pleɪziə/, *n.* the formation of fibrous tissue behind the lens of the eye due to the administration of too high concentrations of oxygen to premature babies, causing blindness. [*retrolental* from RETRO- + *lent-* (stem of L *lens* LENS) + -AL[1]]

**retro-rocket** /'rɛtrou-rɒkət/, *n.* **1.** a braking rocket used for slowing down a spacecraft and preparing it for re-entry. **2.** a rocket used to retard one part of a spacecraft from another. Cf. **posigrade rocket.** Also, **retrograde rocket.**

**retrorse** /rə'trɔs/, *adj.* turned backwards. [L *retrōrsus,* contraction of *retrōversus* bent or turned backwards] – **retrorsely,** *adv.*

**retrospect** /'rɛtrəspɛkt/, *n.* **1.** contemplation of the past; a survey of past time, events, etc. **2. in retrospect,** looking backwards in time. *–v.i. Rare.* **3.** to look back in thought. **4.** to refer back (fol. by *to*). *–v.t.* **5.** *Rare.* to look back upon, contemplate, or think of (something past). [backformation from RETROSPECTION]

**retrospection** /rɛtrə'spɛkʃən/, *n.* action or faculty of looking back on things past; a survey of past events or experiences. [L *retrōspectus* (pp. of *retrōspicere* look back at) + -ION]

**retrospective** /rɛtrə'spɛktɪv/, *adj.* **1.** directed to the past; contemplative of past events, etc. **2.** looking or directed backwards. **3.** retroactive, as a statute. *–n.* **4.** an exhibition of an entire phase or representative examples of an artist's lifework. – **retrospectively,** *adv.*

**retrospectivity** /ˌrɛtrouspɛk'tɪvəti/, *n.* **1.** the quality of being retrospective. **2. a.** (in union or other agreements) the dating of the effectiveness of the agreement to a time prior to the date of the discussion concerning the agreement. **b.** such monies as come to those who benefit from retrospectivity.

**retroussé** /rə'truseɪ/, *adj.* (esp. of the nose) turned up. [F, pp. of *retrousser,* from *re-* RE- + *trousser* TRUSS]

**retroversion** /rɛtrə'vɜʒən/, *n.* **1.** a looking or turning back. **2.** the resulting state or condition. **3.** *Pathol.* a tilting or turning backwards of an organ or part: *retroversion of the uterus.* [L *retrōversus* turned back + -ION]

**retsina** /rɛt'sinə/, *n.* a white or red Greek wine flavoured with resin from the pine tree while still in the cask. [NGk, from It. *resina* RESIN]

**return** /rə'tɜn/, *v.i.* **1.** to go or come back, as to a former place, position, state, etc. **2.** to revert to a former owner. **3.** to revert or recur in thought or discourse. **4.** to make reply; retort. *–v.t.* **5.** to put, bring, take, give, or send back: *return a book to its shelf.* **6.** to send or give back in reciprocation, recompense, or requital: *return shot for shot.* **7.** to reciprocate, repay, or requite (something sent, given, done, etc.) with something similar: *return the enemy's fire.* **8.** to answer; retort. **9.** *Law.* to render (a verdict, etc.). **10.** to reflect (light, sound, etc.). **11.** to yield (a profit, revenue, etc.), as in return for labour, expenditure, or investment. **12.** to report or announce officially. **13.** to elect, as to a legislative body. **14.** *Mil.* to put (a weapon) back into its holder. **15.** *Cards.* to respond to (a suit led) by a similar lead. **16.** to turn back or in the reverse direction. **17.** *Chiefly Archit.* to turn away from, or at an angle, to the previous line of direction. *–n.* **18.** the act or fact of returning; a going or coming back; a bringing, sending, or giving back. **19.** a recurrence: *many happy returns of the day.* **20.** reciprocation, repayment, or requital: *profits in return for outlay.* **21.** response or reply. **22.** one who or that which is returned. **23.** a ticket which is returned to a theatre box office by the original purchaser for resale. **24.** the gain realised on an exchange of goods. **25.** (*oft. pl.*). a yield or profit, as from labour, land, business, investment, etc. **26.** a report, esp. a formal or official report: *tax returns; election returns.* **27.** the report or statement of financial condition. **28.** *Golf.* a player's score for a round, handed in for competition purposes. **29.** a return ticket. **30.** *Archit.* **a.** the continuation of a moulding, projection, etc., in a different direction. **b.** a side or part which falls away from the front of any straight work. **31.** *Sport.* **a.** the process of returning a ball. **b.** the ball which is returned. **32.** *Econ.* yield per unit as compared to the cost per unit involved in a specific industrial process. **33.** *Law.* **a.** the bringing or sending back of various documents, such as a writ, summons or subpoena, with a brief written report usu. endorsed upon it, by a sheriff, etc., to the court from which it issued. **b.** a certified return by a great variety of officers, such as assessors, collectors, and election officers. **c.** the report or certificate endorsed on such documents. **34.** *Cards.* a lead which responds to a partner's lead. **35.** →**return ticket. 36. by return,** by the next post. *–adj.* **37.** of or pertaining to return or returning: *a return trip.* **38.** sent, given, or done in return: *a return shot.* **39.** done or occurring again: *a return engagement of the opera.* **40.** (of a game) played so that the loser of a previous game played between the same two players or teams has a second chance to win. **41.** denoting a person or thing which is returned or returning to a place: *return cargo.* **42.** changing in direction; doubling or returning on itself: *return bend in the road.* [ME *retorne(n),* from OF *retorner.* See RE-, TURN, *v.*]

**returnable** /rə'tɜnəbəl/, *adj.* **1.** that may be returned. **2.** required to be returned.

**return crease** /rə'tɜn kris/, *n.* See **crease**[1] (def. 3c).

**returned soldier** /rətɜnd 'souldʒə/, *n.* a soldier who has served in wars abroad.

**returning officer** /rə'tɜnɪŋ ɒfəsə/, *n.* an official responsible for the organisation of an election, the accuracy of the count, the reading of the results, etc.

**return pipe** /rə'tɜn paɪp/, *n.* the pipe in hot-water systems by which the water that has lost heat returns to the boiler.

**return ticket** /– 'tɪkət/, *n.* a ticket entitling the holder to travel to a destination and, within a specified period, to return to the point of departure.

**retuse** /rə'tjus/, *adj.* (of a leaf, etc.) having an obtuse or rounded apex with a shallow notch. [L *retūsus,* pp., blunted]

retuse leaf

**reunion** /ri'junjən/, *n.* **1.** the act of uniting again. **2.** the state of being united again. **3.** a gathering of relatives, friends, or associates after separation: *a family reunion.*

**reunionist** /ri'junjənəst/, *n.* one who advocates the reunion of the Anglican Church with the Roman Catholic Church. – **reunionism,** *n.* – **reunionistic** /ˌrijunjə'nɪstɪk/, *adj.*

**reunite** /riju'naɪt/, *v.t., v.i.,* **-nited, -niting.** to unite again, as after separation. – **reunitable,** *adj.* – **reuniter,** *n.*

**rev** /rɛv/, *n., v.,* **-revved, revving.** *–n.* **1.** a revolution (in an engine or the like). *–v.t.* **2.** to change, esp. to increase the speed of (in a specified way): *to rev a motor up.* *–v.i.* **3.** to undergo revving. [short for REVOLUTION]

**rev.,** **1.** revenue. **2.** reverse. **3.** review. **4.** revise. **5.** revised. **6.** revision. **7.** revolution. **8.** revolving.

**Rev.,** **1.** *Bible.* Revelation. **2.** Reverend.

**revalue** /ri'vælju/, *v.t.,* **-ued, -uing.** **1.** to value again, esp. to raise the legal value of (a currency). **2.** to reassess; review. See **devalue.** *–v.i.* **3.** of a currency, to increase in legal value. – **revaluation** /rivælju'eɪʃən/, *n.*

**revamp** /ri'væmp/, *v.t.* to vamp afresh; renovate.

**reveal** /rə'vil/, *v.t.* **1.** to make known; disclose; divulge: *to reveal a secret.* **2.** to lay open to view; display; exhibit. *–n.* **3.** a revealing; revelation; disclosure. **4.** *Archit.* **a.** that part of a jamb, or vertical face of an opening for a window or door, included between the face of the wall and that of the frame containing the window or door. **b.** the whole jamb or vertical face of an opening. [ME *revele,* from L *revēlāre* unveil, reveal] – **revealable,** *adj.* – **revealer,** *n.*

**revealed religion** /rəvild rə'lɪdʒən/, *n.* religion based upon divine revelation of concepts of God which could not have been reached by man's efforts alone.

**revealment** /rə'vilmənt/, *n.* the act of revealing; revelation.

**revegetate** /ri'vɛdʒəteɪt/, *v.i.,* **-tated, -tating.** **1.** to grow again, as plants. **2.** to put forth vegetation again, as plants. *–v.t.* **3.** to provide with vegetation again. – **revegetation** /rivɛdʒə'teɪʃən/, *n.*

**reveille** /rə'væli/, *n.* a signal, as of a drum or bugle, sounded at a prescribed hour, to waken soldiers or sailors for the day's duties. [F *réveillez,* impv. pl. of *réveiller* awaken, from *re-* RE- + *veiller,* from L *vigilāre* keep watch]

**revel** /'rɛvəl/, *v.,* **-elled, -elling** or (*U.S.*) **-eled, -eling,** *n.* *–v.i.* **1.** to take great pleasure or delight (fol. by *in*). **2.** to make merry; indulge in boisterous festivities. *–n.* **3.** boisterous merrymaking or festivity; revelry. **4.** (*oft. pl.*). an occasion of merrymaking or noisy festivity with dancing, etc. [ME *revel(en),* from OF *reveler,* orig., to make noise, rebel, from L *rebellāre.* See REBEL] – **reveller,** *n.*

**revelation** /rɛvə'leɪʃən/, *n.* **1.** the act of revealing or disclosing; disclosure. **2.** something revealed or disclosed, esp. a striking disclosure, as of something not before realised. **3.** *Theol.* **a.** God's disclosure of Himself and of His will to His creatures. **b.** an instance of such communication or disclosure. **c.** something thus communicated or disclosed. **d.** that which contains such disclosure, as the Bible. [ME, from L *revēlātio*]

**revelationist** /rɛvə'leɪʃənəst/, *n.* one who believes in divine revelation.

**revelator** /'rɛvəleɪtə/, *n.* one who makes a revelation.

**revelry** /'rɛvəlri/, *n., pl.* **-ries.** revelling; boisterous festivity: *the sound of their revelry could be heard across the river.*

**revenant** /'rɛvənənt/, *n.* **1.** one who returns. **2.** one who returns as a spirit after death; a ghost. [F, properly ppr. of *revenir* return, from *re-* RE- + *venir* come, from L *venīre*]

**revenge** /rə'vɛndʒ/, *n., v.,* **-venged, -venging.** *–n.* **1.** the act of revenging; retaliation for injuries or wrongs; vengeance. **2.** something done in revenging. **3.** the desire to revenge; vindictiveness. **4.** an opportunity of retaliation or satisfaction. *–v.t.* **5.** to take vengeance or exact expiation on behalf of (a person, etc.) or for (a wrong, etc.) esp. in a resentful or vindictive spirit. *–v.i.* **6.** *Obs.* to take revenge. [ME, from OF *revengier,* from *re-* RE- + *vengier* VENGE] – **revenger,** *n.*

**revengeful** /rə'vɛndʒfəl/, *adj.* full of revenge; vindictive. – **revengefully,** *adv.* – **revengefulness,** *n.*

**revenue** /'rɛvənju/, *n.* **1.** the income of a government from taxation, excise duties, customs, or other sources, appropriated to the payment of the public expenses. **2.** the government department charged with the collection of such income. **3.** (*pl.*) the collective items or amounts of income of a person, a state, etc. **4.** the return or yield from any kind of property; income. **5.** an amount of money regularly coming in. **6.** a particular item or source of income. [late ME, from F, orig. fem. pp. of *revenir* return, from *re-* RE- + *venir* come]

**revenue cutter** /– 'kʌtə/, *n. Brit.* See **cutter** (def. 4).

**reverb** /rə'vɜb/, *n.* **1.** →**reverberation unit.** **2.** reverberation (in electronically produced music).

**reverberant** /rə'vɜbərənt/, *adj.* reverberating; re-echoing.

**reverberate** /rə'vɜbəreɪt/, *v.,* **-rated, -rating.** *–v.i.* **1.** to re-echo or resound. **2.** *Physics.* to be reflected many times, as soundwaves from the walls, etc., of a confined space. **3.** to rebound or recoil. **4.** to be deflected, as flame in a reverberatory furnace. *–v.t.* **5.** to echo back or re-echo (sound). **6.** to cast back or reflect (light, etc.). **7.** to treat (a substance) in a reverberatory furnace or the like. **8.** to deflect (flame or heat) on something, as in a reverberatory furnace. [L *reverberātus,* pp., beaten back] – **reverberative,** *adj.* – **reverberator,** *n.*

**reverberation** /rəvɜbə'reɪʃən/, *n.* **1.** a re-echoed sound. **2.** the fact of being reverberated or reflected. **3.** that which is reverberated. **4.** an act or instance of reverberating. **5.** *Physics.* multiple reflection of sound in a room, causing a sound to persist after the stopping of the source. **6.** the action or process of subjecting something to reflected heat as in a reverberatory furnace. [ME, from L *reverberātio*]

**reverberation time** /– taɪm/, *n.* the time taken, in seconds, for a sound made in a room or auditorium to diminish by 60 decibels. Also, **reverberation period.**

**reverberation unit** /– junət/, *n.* an electronic device for adding reverberation to amplified music.

**reverberatory** /rə'vɜbərətri/, *adj., n., pl.* **-ries.** *–adj.* **1.** characterised by or produced by reverberation. **2.** denoting a furnace, kiln, or the like, in which the fuel is not in direct contact with the ore, metal, etc., to be heated, but furnishes a flame that plays over the material, esp. by being deflected downwards from the roof. **3.** deflected, as flame. *–n.* **4.** any device, as a furnace, embodying reverberation.

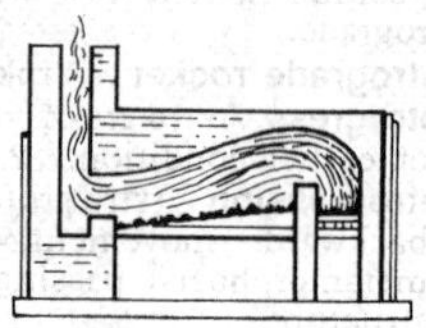
reverberatory furnace (section)

**revere** /rə'vɪə/, *v.t.,* **-vered, -vering.** to regard with respect tinged with awe; venerate. [L *reverērī* feel awe of, fear, revere]

**reverence** /'rɛvərəns, 'rɛvrəns/, *n., v.,* **-renced, -rencing.** *–n.*

1. the feeling or attitude of deep respect tinged with awe; veneration. 2. the outward manifestation of this feeling: *to pay reverence.* 3. a gesture indicative of deep respect; an obeisance, bow, or curtsy. 4. the state of being revered. 5. (*cap.*) a title used in addressing or mentioning a clergyman (prec. by *your* or *his*). –*v.t.* 6. to regard or treat with reverence; venerate. [ME, from L *reverentia*]

**reverend** /ˈrɛvrənd, ˈrɛvərənd/, *adj.* 1. (*oft. cap.*) an epithet of respect applied to, or prefixed to the name of, a clergyman. 2. worthy to be revered; entitled to reverence. 3. pertaining to or characteristic of the clergy. –*n.* 4. *Colloq.* a clergyman. [L *reverendus,* ger. of *reverērī* revere]

**Reverend Mother** /rɛvrənd ˈmʌðə/, *n.* the title of respect accorded the abbess or presiding nun of a convent.

**reverent** /ˈrɛvrənt, ˈrɛvərənt/, *adj.* feeling, exhibiting, or characterised by reverence; deeply respectful. [L *reverens,* ppr., feeling awe of] – **reverently,** *adv.*

**reverential** /rɛvəˈrɛnʃəl/, *adj.* of the nature of or characterised by reverence; reverent: *reverential awe.* – **reverentially,** *adv.*

**reverie** /ˈrɛvəri/, *n.* 1. a state of dreamy meditation or fanciful musing: *lost in reverie.* 2. a daydream. 3. a fantastic, visionary, or unpractical idea. 4. *Music.* an instrumental composition of a vague and dreamy character. Also, **revery.** [F *rêver* to dream]

**revers** /rəˈvɪə/, *n., pl.* **-vers** /-ˈvɪəz/. 1. a part of a garment turned back to show the lining or facing, as a lapel. 2. a trimming simulating such a part. 3. the facing used. [F. See REVERSE]

**reversal** /rəˈvɜsəl/, *n.* 1. the act of reversing. 2. an instance of this. 3. the state of being reversed. 4. *Law.* the revocation of a lower court's decision by an appellate court.

**reverse** /rəˈvɜs/, *adj., n., v.,* **-versed, -versing.** –*adj.* 1. opposite or contrary in position, direction, order, or character: *an impression reverse to what was intended.* 2. acting in a manner opposite or contrary to that which is usual, as an appliance or apparatus. 3. with the rear part towards one: *reverse side of a coin.* 4. producing a rearward motion: *reverse gear.* 5. *Motor Vehicles.* of or pertaining to reverse (gear ratio). 6. *Print.* of or pertaining to a type matter which appears white on a solid or screened background. –*n.* 7. the opposite or contrary of something. 8. the back or rear of anything. 9. *Coining.* that side of a coin, medal, etc., which does not bear the principal design (opposed to *obverse*). 10. an adverse change of fortune; a misfortune, check, or defeat: *to meet with an unexpected reverse.* 11. *Motor Vehicles.* a transmission gear ratio driving a car backwards. 12. *Mach.* a reversing mechanism, etc. 13. *Print.* type matter produced in reverse printing. –*v.t.* 14. to turn in an opposite position; transpose. 15. to turn inside out or upside down. 16. to turn in the opposite direction; send on the opposite course. 17. to turn in the opposite order: *to reverse the usual order.* 18. to alter to the opposite in character or tendency, or change completely. 19. to revoke or annul (a decree, judgment, etc.). 20. *Law.* to overrule a judgment on appeal. 21. *Mach.* to cause to revolve or act in an opposite or contrary direction or manner. 22. **to drive (a motor vehicle) backwards:** *he reversed the car into a parking space.* 23. *Print.* to produce in reverse printing. (oft. fol. by *out*) 24. **reverse arms,** *Mil.* to carry out a drill manoeuvre in which the rifle is turned muzzle downwards. 25. **reverse stick,** *Hockey.* to strike the ball with the face of the stick on the left side of the body if a right-handed player, and on the right side of the body if a left-handed player. 26. **reverse charges,** to make a telephone call or send a telegram for which the receiver pays. –*v.i.* 27. to turn or move in the opposite or contrary direction, as in dancing. 28. (of an engine) to reverse the action of the mechanism. 29. to drive a vehicle backwards: *he reversed into the garage.* [ME *revers,* from L *reversus,* pp., turned about] – **reversely,** *adv.* – **reverser,** *n.*

**reverse-charge** /rəˈvɜs-tʃadʒ/, *adj.* referring to a telephone call paid for by the person receiving the call.

**reverse gazump** /rəvɜs gəˈzʌmp/, *v.t.* (of a buyer before entering upon a binding contract) to force a vendor to accept a price lower than that previously agreed upon.

**reversible** /rəˈvɜsəbəl/, *adj.* 1. capable of being reversed or of reversing. 2. capable of re-establishing the original condition after a change by the reversal of that change. 3. (of a fabric, garment, etc.) woven or printed so that either side may be exposed. –*n.* 4. a garment, esp. a coat, that may be worn with either side exposed. – **reversibility** /rəvɜsəˈbɪləti, ri-/, **reversibleness,** *n.* – **reversibly,** *adv.*

**reversible reaction** /– riˈækʃən/, *n.* a chemical reaction which, under suitable conditions, may be made to proceed in either direction.

**reversing light** /rəˈvɜsɪŋ laɪt/, *n.* a tail-light which is automatically switched on when the vehicle is put in reverse gear.

**reversion** /rəˈvɜʒən/, *n.* 1. the act of turning something the reverse way. 2. the state of being so turned; reversal. 3. the act of reverting; return to a former practice, belief, condition, etc. 4. *Biol.* **a.** reappearance of ancestral characters that have been absent in intervening generations. **b.** return to an earlier or primitive type; atavism. 5. Also, **reverter,** *Law.* **a.** the returning of an estate to the grantor or his heirs after the interest granted expires. **b.** an estate which so returns. **c.** the right of succeeding to an estate, etc. [ME, from L *reversio* a turning about]

**reversionary** /rəˈvɜʒənəri, -ʒənri/, *adj.* of, pertaining to, or involving a reversion. Also, **reversional.**

**reversionary bonus** /– ˈbounəs/, *n.* free annual additions to the sum assured on a life insurance policy, and payable when the policy matures. See **terminal bonus.**

**reversioner** /rəˈvɜʒənə, -ʃənə/, *n. Law.* one who possesses a reversion.

**reverso** /rəˈvɜsou/, *n.* →**verso.**

**revert** /rəˈvɜt/, *v.i.* 1. to return to a former habit, practice, belief, condition, etc. 2. to go back in thought or discourse, as to a subject. 3. *Biol.* to return to an earlier or primitive type. 4. *Law.* to go back or to return to the former owner or his heirs. [ME *reverte(n),* from OF *revertir,* from LL *revertīre,* replacing L *revertere*] – **revertible,** *adj.*

**reverter** /rəˈvɜtə/, *n.* →**reversion** (def. 5).

**revery** /ˈrɛvəri/, *n., pl.* **-eries.** →**reverie.**

**revest** /ˌriˈvɛst/, *v.t.* 1. to vest (a person, etc.) again, as with ownership or office; reinvest; reinstate. 2. to vest (powers, etc.) again. –*v.i.* 3. to become vested again in a person; go back again to a former owner.

**revet** /rəˈvɛt/, *v.t.,* **-vetted, -vetting.** to face, as an embankment, with masonry or other material. [F *revêtir,* lit., clothe. See REVEST]

**revetment** /rəˈvɛtmənt/, *n.* 1. a facing of masonry or the like, esp. for protecting an embankment. 2. a barricade against bombs or other explosives. 3. →**retaining wall.**

**review** /rəˈvju/, *n.* 1. a critical article or report, as in a periodical, on some literary work, commonly some work of recent appearance; a critique. 2. a periodical publication containing articles on current events or affairs, books, art, etc.: *a literary review.* 3. a viewing again; a second or repeated view of something. 4. an inspection, or examination by viewing, esp. a formal inspection of any military or naval force, parade, or the like. 5. a viewing of the past; contemplation or consideration of past events, circumstances, or facts. 6. a general survey of something, esp. in words; a report or account of something. 7. a judicial re-examination, as by a higher court, of the decision or proceedings in a case. [F *revue,* orig. pp. fem. of *revoir* see again, from L *revidēre*] –*v.t.* 8. to view, look at, or look over again. 9. to inspect, esp. formally or officially. 10. to look back upon; view retrospectively. 11. to survey mentally; take a survey of: *to review the situation.* 12. to present a survey of in speech or writing. 13. to discuss (a book, etc.) in a critical review; write a critical report upon. 14. *Law.* to re-examine judicially. –*v.i.* 15. to write reviews; review books, etc., as for some periodical. [v. use of REVIEW, *n.*] – **reviewable,** *adj.*

**reviewal** /rəˈvjuəl/, *n.* the act of reviewing.

**reviewer** /rəˈvjuə/, *n.* 1. one who reviews. 2. one who writes reviews of new books, films, plays, etc.

**revile** /rəˈvaɪl/, *v.,* **-viled, -viling.** –*v.t.* 1. to assail with contemptuous or opprobrious language; address, or speak of, abusively. –*v.i.* 2. to speak abusively. [ME *revile(n),* from OF *reviler* treat or regard as vile, from *re-* RE- + *vil* VILE] – **revilement,** *n.* – **reviler,** *n.* – **revilingly,** *adv.*

**revisal** /rəˈvaɪzəl/, *n.* the act of revising; revision.

**revise** /rəˈvaɪz/, *v.,* **-vised, -vising,** *n.* –*v.t.* 1. to amend or alter: *to revise one's opinion.* 2. to alter after one or more typings or printings: *to revise a manuscript, proof, or book.* **3.** to go over (a subject, book, etc.) again or study in order to fix it in the memory, as before an examination. *–v.i.* **4.** to go over a subject or the like again to fix it in the memory. *–n.* **5.** a revising. **6.** a revised form of something. **7.** *Print.* a proof sheet taken after alterations have been made, for further examination or correction. [F *reviser,* from L *revīsere* go to see again, look back on] – **reviser,** *n.*

**revision** /rəˈvɪʒən/, *n.* **1.** the act or work of revising. **2.** a process of revising. **3.** the process of going over a subject or the like again to fix it in the memory. **4.** a revised form or version, as of a book. [LL *revīsio*] – **revisional, revisionary,** *adj.*

**revisionism** /rəˈvɪʒənɪzəm/, *n.* the advocacy or act of revising, esp. some political or religious doctrine, practice, or the like.

**revisionist** /rəˈvɪʒənəst/, *n.* **1.** an advocate of revision, esp. of some political or religious doctrine. **2.** a reviser.

**revisory** /rəˈvaɪzəri/, *adj.* pertaining to or for the purpose of revision.

**revival** /rəˈvaɪvəl/, *n.* **1.** the act of reviving. **2.** the state of being revived. **3.** restoration to life, consciousness, vigour, strength, etc. **4.** restoration to use, acceptance, or currency: *the revival of old customs.* **5.** a renewing of interest in a theory, practice, etc., of the past. **6.** the production anew of an old play. **7.** an awakening, in a church or a community, of interest in and care for matters relating to personal religion. **8.** a service or a series of services for the purpose of effecting a religious awakening: *to hold a revival, a revival meeting.* **9.** *Law.* the re-establishment of legal force and effect. **10.** a new recorded version of an old song.

**revivalism** /rəˈvaɪvəlɪzəm/, *n.* **1.** the tendency to revive what belongs to the past. **2.** that form of religious activity which manifests itself in revivals.

**revivalist** /rəˈvaɪvələst/, *n.* **1.** one who revives former customs or methods. **2.** one who promotes or holds religious revivals. – **revivalistic** /rəvaɪvəˈlɪstɪk/, *adj.*

**revive** /rəˈvaɪv/, *v.,* **-vived, -viving.** *–v.t.* **1.** to set going or in activity again: *to revive old feuds.* **2.** to make operative or valid again. **3.** to bring back into notice, use, or currency: *to revive a subject of discussion.* **4.** to produce (an old play) again. **5.** to restore to life or consciousness. **6.** to reanimate or cheer (the spirit, heart, etc., or a person). **7.** to quicken or renew in the mind; bring back: *to revive memories.* **8.** *Chem.* to restore or reduce to its natural or uncombined state, as a metal. *–v.i.* **9.** to return to life, consciousness, vigour, strength, or a flourishing condition. **10.** to recover from depression. **11.** to be quickened, restored, or renewed, as hope, confidence, suspicions, memories, etc. **12.** to return to notice, use, or currency, as a subject, practice, doctrine, etc. **13.** to become operative or valid again. **14.** *Chem.* to recover its natural or uncombined state, as a metal. [ME, from L *revīvere* live again]

**reviver** /rəˈvaɪvə/, *n.* **1.** one who or that which revives. **2.** *Colloq.* an intoxicating drink; a stimulant.

**revivify** /riˈvɪvəfaɪ/, *v.t.,* **-fied, -fying.** to restore to life; give new life to; revive; animate anew. – **revivification** /riˌvɪvəfəˈkeɪʃən/, *n.*

**reviviscence** /rɛvəˈvɪsəns/, *n.* the act or state of being revived; revival; reanimation. Also, **reviviscency.** – **reviviscent,** *adj.*

**revocable** /ˈrɛvəkəbəl/, *adj.* that may be revoked. Also, **revokable** /rəˈvoʊkəbəl/. [late ME, from L *revocābilis*] – **revocability** /rɛvəkəˈbɪləti/, *n.* – **revocably,** *adv.*

**revocation** /rɛvəˈkeɪʃən/, *n.* **1.** the act of revoking; annulment. **2.** *Law.* nullification or withdrawal, as of an offer to contract, a will, or a right of agency. [late ME, from L *revocātio*] – **revocatory** /ˈrɛvəkeɪtəri/, *adj.*

**revoice** /ˌriˈvɔɪs/, *v.t.,* **-voiced, -voicing.** **1.** to voice again or in return; echo. **2.** to readjust the tone of.

**revoke** /rəˈvoʊk/, *v.,* **-voked, -voking,** *n.* *–v.t.* **1.** to take back or withdraw; annul, cancel, or reverse; rescind or repeal: *to revoke a decree.* *–v.i.* **2.** *Cards.* to fail to follow suit when one can and should do so; renege. *–n.* **3.** *Cards.* an act or instance of revoking; renege. [ME, from L *revocāre* call back] – **revoker,** *n.*

**revolt** /rəˈvoʊlt/, *v.i.* **1.** to break away from or rise against constituted authority, as by open rebellion; cast off allegiance or subjection to those in authority; rebel; mutiny. **2.** to turn away in mental rebellion, utter disgust, or abhorrence (fol. by *from*); rebel in feeling (fol. by *against*); feel disgust or horror (fol. by *at*). *–v.t.* **3.** to affect with disgust or abhorrence. *–n.* **4.** the act of revolting; an insurrection or rebellion. **5.** aversion, disgust, or loathing. **6.** the state of those revolting: *to be in revolt.* [F *révolte,* from It. *rivolta* revolt, turning, from *rivoltare* turn, from Rom. *revolvitāre,* from L *revolvere* overturn, revolve] – **revolter,** *n.*

**revolting** /rəˈvoʊltɪŋ/, *adj.* **1.** rebellious. **2.** disgusting; repulsive. – **revoltingly,** *adv.*

**revolute** /ˈrɛvəlut/, *adj.* rolled backwards or downwards; rolled backwards at the tip or margin, as a leaf. [L *revolūtus,* pp., revolved]

A, revolute margined leaf; B, transverse section

**revolution** /rɛvəˈluʃən/, *n.* **1.** a complete overthrow of an established government or political system. **2.** a complete or marked change in something. **3.** procedure or course as if in a circuit, as back to a starting point in time. **4.** a single turn of this kind. **5.** *Mech.* **a.** a turning round or rotating, as on an axis. **b.** a moving in a circular or curving course, as about a central point. **c.** a single cycle in such a course. **6.** *Astron.* **a.** (of a heavenly body) the action or fact of going round in an orbit. **b.** a single course of such movement. **c.** an apparent movement round the earth. **7.** round or cycle of events in time, or a recurring period of time. [ME *revolucion,* from L *revolūtio*]

**revolutionary** /rɛvəˈluʃənəri, -ʃənri/, *adj., n., pl.* **-ries.** *–adj.* **1.** pertaining to, characterised by, or of the nature of a revolution, or complete or marked change. **2.** subversive to established procedure, principles, etc. **3.** revolving. *–n.* **4.** one who advocates or takes part in a revolution; revolutionist.

**revolution counter** /rɛvəˈluʃən kaʊntə/, *n.* an instrument which indicates the number of revolutions made by a rotating shaft.

**revolutionise** /rɛvəˈluʃənaɪz/, *v.t.,* **-nised, -nising.** **1.** to bring about a revolution in; effect a radical change in. **2.** to subject to a political revolution. Also, **revolutionize.**

**revolutionist** /rɛvəˈluʃənəst/, *n. U.S.* →**revolutionary.**

**revolve** /rəˈvɒlv/, *v.,* **-volved, -volving.** *–v.i.* **1.** to turn round or rotate, as on an axis. **2.** to move in a circular or curving course, or orbit. **3.** to proceed in a round or cycle. **4.** to come round in the process of time. **5.** to be revolved in the mind. *–v.t.* **6.** to cause to turn round, as on an axis. **7.** to cause to move in a circular or curving course, as about a central point. **8.** to think about; consider. [ME, from L *revolvere* roll, turn] – **revolvable,** *adj.*

**revolver** /rəˈvɒlvə/, *n.* **1.** a pistol having a revolving chambered cylinder for holding a number of cartridges which may be discharged in succession without reloading. **2.** one who or that which revolves.

revolver

**revolving** /rəˈvɒlvɪŋ/, *adj.* **1.** that revolves. **2.** *Mach.* denoting or pertaining to a radial engine, whose cylinders revolve about a stationary crankshaft, such as a helicopter motor, or the blades of a propeller.

**revolving door** /– ˈdɔ/, *n.* a series of doors arranged radially round a pivot, which revolve as people pass through, in order to prevent draughts.

**revolving fund** /ˈ– fʌnd/, *n.* any loan fund intended to be maintained by the repayment of past loans.

**revue** /rəˈvju/, *n.* **1.** a form of theatrical entertainment in which recent events, popular fads, etc., are parodied. **2.** any group of skits, dances, and songs. [F. See REVIEW, *n.*]

**revulsion** /rəˈvʌlʃən/, *n.* **1.** a sudden and violent change of feeling or reaction in sentiment. **2.** a violent dislike or aversion for something. **3.** *Med.* the diminution of morbid action in one part of the body by irritation in another. **4.** the act of drawing something back or away. **5.** the fact of being so drawn. [L *revulsio* a plucking away]

**revulsive** /rəˈvʌlsɪv/, *adj.* tending to alter the distribution of blood by causing congestion, esp. in the intestine.

i = peat ɪ = pit ɛ = pet æ = pat a = part ɒ = pot ʌ = putt ɔ = port ʊ = put u = pool ɜ = pert ə = apart aɪ = buy eɪ = bay ɔɪ = boy aʊ = how
oʊ = hoe ɪə = here ɛə = hair ʊə = tour g = give θ = thin ð = then ʃ = show ʒ = measure tʃ = choke dʒ = joke ŋ = sing j = you õ = Fr. bon

**reward** /rəˈwɔd/, *n.* **1.** something given or received in return or recompense for service, merit, hardship, etc. **2.** a sum of money offered for the detection or capture of a criminal, the recovery of lost or stolen property, etc. *–v.t.* **3.** to recompense or requite (a person, etc.) for service, merit, achievement, etc. **4.** to make return for or requite (service, merit, etc.); recompense. [ME *rewarde,* from ONF *rewarder,* var. of OF *regarder.* See REGARD] – **rewarder,** *n.*

**reward claim** /ˈ– kleɪm/, *n.* (formerly) a claim granted to a miner in reward for his discovery of gold in a new district.

**rewarding** /rəˈwɔdɪŋ/, *adj.* giving satisfaction that the effort made was worth while: *looking after handicapped children is very rewarding.*

**rewarewa** /riwəˈriwə, reɪwəˈreɪwə/, *n. N.Z.* →**honeysuckle** (def. 4). [Maori]

**rewind** /riˈwaɪnd/, *v.,* **-wound, -winding.** *–v.t.* **1.** to wind again. *–v.i.* **2.** (of film or tape) to wind back onto its original reel.

**rewire** /ˌriˈwaɪə/, *v.t.,* **-wired, -wiring.** to provide with new wiring: *to rewire a house, radio, lamp, etc.*

**reword** /ˌriˈwɜd/, *v.t.* **1.** to put into other words. **2.** to repeat.

**rewrite** /ˌriˈraɪt/, *v.,* **-wrote, -written, -writing;** /ˈriraɪt/, *n.* *–v.t.* **1.** to write again or in a different form. **2.** *U.S.* to subedit (the news submitted by a reporter). *–n.* **3.** reworded version. **4.** *U.S.* subedited copy.

**rex** /rɛks/, *n., pl.* **reges** /ˈridʒiz/. king. [L]

**Reynold's number** /ˈrɛnəldz nʌmbə/, *n.* a dimensionless number which determines whether the fluid flow in a particular situation will be viscous or turbulent. It is important in hydrodynamics and aeronautics since models with the same Reynold's number as full scale situations can be used to predict full scale results. [named after O. *Reynolds,* b. 1912, English physicist]

**r.f.,** radio frequency.

**r.h.,** right hand.

**Rh,** **1.** *Chem.* rhodium. **2.** See **Rh factor.**

**R.H.,** Royal Highness.

**rhabdomancy** /ˈræbdəmænsi/, *n.* divination by means of a rod or wand, esp. in discovering ores, springs of water, etc. [LL *rhabdomantīa,* from Gk *rhabdomanteía*] – **rhabdomantist,** *n.*

**rhabdomyoma** /ˌræbdoumaɪˈoumə/, *n., pl.* **-mata** /-mətə/, **-mas.** a tumour made up of striate muscular tissue. Cf. **leiomyoma.** [NL, from Gk *rhábdo(s)* rod + NL *myoma* MYOMA]

**rhachilla** /ræˈkɪlə/, *n.* →**rachilla.**

**rhachis** /ˈreɪkəs/, *n., pl.* **rhachises, rhachides** /ˈrækədiz, ˈreɪkə-/. →**rachis.**

**Rhaetic** /ˈritɪk/, *adj.* pertaining to certain geological strata, extensively developed in the Rhaetian Alps (eastern Switzerland), having features of the Triassic and Jurassic but generally classed as belonging to the former. Also, **Rhetic.**

**Rhaeto-Romanic** /ˌritou-rəˈmænɪk/, *n.* **1.** a group of closely related Romance languages, spoken in certain valleys of the Swiss Alps. *–adj.* **2.** denoting or pertaining to these languages.

**-rhagia,** a word element meaning 'bursting forth'. Also, **-rhage, -rhagy, -rrhagia, -rrhage, -rrhagy.** [Gk *-rrhagia*]

**rhamnaceous** /ræmˈneɪʃəs/, *adj.* belonging to the Rhamnaceae, or buckthorn family of plants. [NL *Rhamnus,* the typical genus (Gk *rhámnos* a prickly shrub) + -ACEOUS]

**rhapsodical** /ræpˈsɒdɪkəl/, *adj.* **1.** pertaining to, characteristic of, or of the nature of rhapsody. **2.** extravagantly enthusiastic; ecstatic. Also, **rhapsodic.** – **rhapsodically,** *adv.*

**rhapsodise** /ˈræpsədaɪz/, *v.,* **-dised, -dising.** *–v.i.* **1.** to speak or write rhapsodies. **2.** to talk rhapsodically. *–v.t.* **3.** to recite as a rhapsody. Also, **rhapsodize.**

**rhapsodist** /ˈræpsədəst/, *n.* **1.** one who rhapsodises. **2.** a reciter of epic poetry among the ancient Greeks, esp. a professional reciter of the Homeric poems.

**rhapsody** /ˈræpsədi/, *n., pl.* **-dies.** **1.** an exalted or exaggerated expression of feeling or enthusiasm. **2.** an epic poem, or a part of such a poem, as a book of the *Iliad,* suitable for recitation at one time. **3.** a similar piece of modern literature. **4.** an unusually intense or irregular poem or piece of prose. **5.** *Music.* an instrumental composition irregular in form and suggestive of improvisation: *Liszt's Hungarian Rhapsodies.* **6.** *Archaic.* a collection of miscellaneous items; medley; jumble. [L *rhapsōdia,* from Gk *rhapsōidía* epic recital]

**rhatany** /ˈrætəni/, *n., pl.* **-nies.** **1.** a procumbent leguminous shrub, *Krameria triandra,* from Peru, the root of which is used as an astringent and tonic in medicine and also to colour port wine. **2.** some other plant of this genus, esp. *K. argentea.* **3.** the roots of these plants. [Pg. *rhatanhia,* or from Sp. *ratania;* from Quechua]

**rhea** /ˈriə/, *n.* a bird of the genus *Rhea* which consists of South American native birds resembling the African ostrich but smaller and having three toes instead of two. [L, from Gk]

**-rhea,** *Chiefly U.S.* variant of **-rhoea.** Also, **-rrhea.**

**rhematic** /riˈmætɪk/, *adj.* **1.** pertaining to the formation of words. **2.** pertaining to or derived from a verb. [Gk *rhēmatikós* belonging to a verb, a word]

**rhenic** /ˈrinɪk/, *adj.* of or containing rhenium.

**rhenium** /ˈriniəm/, *n.* a rare metallic element of the manganese subgroup, with a high melting point, used in platinum-rhenium thermocouples. *Symbol:* Re; *at. no.:* 75; *at. wt:* 186.20. [L *Rhēnus* the Rhine + -IUM]

**rheo-,** a word element meaning 'something flowing', 'a stream', 'current'. [combining form representing Gk *rhéos*]

**rheo.,** rheostat.

**rheology** /riˈɒlədʒi/, *n.* the study of the deformation and flow of matter. [RHEO- + -LOGY] – **rheological** /riəˈlɒdʒɪkəl/, *adj.*

**rheometer** /riˈɒmətə/, *n.* an instrument for measuring the velocity of flow of fluids, as blood flow.

**rheoscope** /ˈriəskoup/, *n.* an instrument which indicates the presence of an electric current. – **rheoscopic** /riəˈskɒpɪk/, *adj.*

**rheostat** /ˈriəstæt/, *n.* a variable electrical resistor. – **rheostatic** /riəˈstætɪk/, *adj.*

**rheotaxis** /riəˈtæksəs/, *n.* the property in a cell or organism of responding by movement to the stimulus of a current of water.

**rheotropism** /riˈɒtrəpɪzəm/, *n.* the effect of a current of water upon the direction of plant growth.

**rhesus** /ˈrisəs/, *n.* a macaque monkey, *Macacus rhesus,* common in India, much used in experimental medicine. [L, from Gk *Rhêsos,* mythological king of Thrace]

**Rhesus factor** /ˈrisəs fæktə/, *n.* →**Rh factor.**

**rhet.,** rhetoric.

**Rhetic** /ˈritɪk/, *adj. Geol.* →**Rhaetic.**

**rhetor** /ˈritə/, *n.* **1.** a master or teacher of rhetoric. **2.** an orator. [L, from Gk; replacing ME *rethor,* from ML]

**rhetoric** /ˈrɛtərɪk/, *n.* **1.** the art or science of all specially literary uses of language in prose or verse, including the figures of speech. **2.** the art of prose in general as opposed to verse. **3.** (in prose or verse) the use of exaggeration or display, in an unfavourable sense. **4.** (originally) the art of oratory. **5.** (in classical oratory) the art of influencing the thought of one's hearers. [ME *retorik,* from L *rhētorica,* from Gk *rhētorikḗ* (*téchnē*) the rhetorical (art)]

**rhetorical** /rəˈtɒrɪkəl/, *adj.* **1.** belonging to or concerned with mere style or effect. **2.** having the nature of rhetoric. **3.** overelaborate, bombastic in style. – **rhetorically,** *adv.*

**rhetorical question** /– ˈkwɛstʃən/, *n.* a question designed to produce an effect and not to draw an answer.

**rhetorician** /rɛtəˈrɪʃən/, *n.* **1.** one versed in the art of rhetoric. **2.** one given to display in language. **3.** a person who teaches rhetoric.

**rheum** /rum/, *n.* **1.** *Pathol.* a thin serous or catarrhal discharge. **2.** catarrh; a cold. [ME *rewme,* from OF *reume,* from L *rheuma,* from Gk: a flow, rheum]

**rheumatic** /ruˈmætɪk/, *adj.* **1.** pertaining to or of the nature of rheumatism. **2.** affected with or subject to rheumatism. *–n.* **3.** one affected with or subject to rheumatism. **4.** (*pl.*) rheumatic pains. [ME *r(e)umatyk(e),* from L *rheumaticus,* from Gk *rheumatikós*]

**rheumatic fever** /– ˈfivə/, *n.* a disease usu. afflicting children and marked by fever, inflammation of the joints, generalised muscle pains, and frequently associated with pathological changes in the heart and the different serous membranes.

**rheumaticky** /ruˈmætɪki/, *adj.* having aches or pains as those likely to occur in rheumatism.

**rheumatism** /ˈrumətɪzəm/, *n.* **1.** *Pathol.* a disease commonly affecting the joints and accompanied by constitutional disturbances, now usu. thought to be due to a micro-organism. **2.** (in a growing child) rheumatic fever. **3.** any of various ailments of the joints or muscles, as certain chronic disabilities of the joints (**chronic rheumatism**) and certain painful affections of the muscles (**muscular rheumatism**). [LL *rheumatismus,* from Gk *rheumatismós* liability to rheum]

**rheumatoid** /ˈrumətɔɪd/, *adj.* **1.** resembling rheumatism. **2.** →**rheumatic.** Also, **rheumatoidal** /ruməˈtɔɪdl/.

**rheumatoid arthritis** /– aθˈraɪtəs/, *n.* a chronic disease marked by inflammation of the joints, frequently accompanied by marked deformities, and ordinarily associated with manifestations of a general or systemic affliction.

**Rh factor** /arˈeɪtʃ fæktə/, *n.* an agglutinogen often present in human blood. Blood containing this factor (**Rh positive**) may cause haemolytic reactions, esp. during pregnancy or after repeated transfusions with blood lacking it (**Rh negative**). In infants it may cause haemolytic anaemias. In full, **Rhesus factor.** [so called because first found in the blood of the RHESUS]

**rhigolene** /ˈrɪdʒəlin/, *n.* an extremely volatile liquid obtained from petroleum, used to produce local anaesthesia by freezing. [Gk *rhîgos* cold + -OL² + -ENE]

**rhin-,** variant of **rhino-,** before vowels, as in *rhinencephalon.*

**rhinal** /ˈraɪnəl/, *adj.* of or pertaining to the nose; nasal. [RHIN- + -AL¹]

**rhinencephalon** /raɪnənˈsɛfəlɒn/, *n., pl.* **-la** /-lə/. the olfactory portion of the brain. [RHIN- + ENCEPHALON] – **rhinencephalic** /raɪnənsəˈfælɪk/, *adj.*

**Rhine riesling** /raɪn ˈrizlɪŋ/, *n.* →**riesling.**

**rhinestone** /ˈraɪnstoʊn/, *n.* an artificial gem made of paste. [translation of F *caillou du Rhin* pebble of the Rhine]

**rhinitis** /raɪˈnaɪtəs/, *n.* inflammation of the nose or its mucous membrane.

**rhino** /ˈraɪnoʊ/, *n., pl.* **-nos.** →**rhinoceros.**

**rhino-,** a word element meaning 'nose'. Also, **rhin-.** [Gk, combining form of *rhîs*]

**rhinoceros** /raɪˈnɒsərəs, raɪˈnɒsrəs/, *n., pl.* **-roses,** (*esp. collectively*) **-ros.** any of various large, ungainly, thick-skinned, perissodactyl mammals, found in Asia and Africa, family Rhinocerotidae, with one or two upright horns on the snout. Five species are still extant. [ME *rinoceros,* from LL, from Gk *rhīnókerōs,* from *rhīno-* RHINO- + *-kerōs* horned] – **rhinocerotic** /ˌraɪnoʊsəˈrɒtɪk/, *adj.*

Indian rhinoceros

**rhinoceros beetle** /ˈ– bitl/, *n.* any of various large, scarabaeid beetles of the sub-family Dynastinae, having prominent horns on head and prothorax.

**rhinolalia** /raɪnoʊˈleɪliə/, *n.* speech characterised by abnormal nasal resonance. [NL, from Gk *rhîs* RHINO- + *laliá* talking]

**rhinology** /raɪˈnɒlədʒi/, *n.* the science dealing with the nose and its diseases. – **rhinologist,** *n.*

**rhinoplasty** /ˈraɪnoʊˌplæsti/, *n.* plastic surgery of the nose. – **rhinoplastic** /raɪnoʊˈplæstɪk/, *adj.*

**rhinoscope** /ˈraɪnəskoʊp/, *n.* an instrument for examining the nasal passages.

**rhinoscopy** /raɪˈnɒskəpi/, *n.* the investigation of the nasal passages.

**rhizanthous** /raɪˈzænθəs, rəˈzæn-/, *adj.* producing flowers from the root, or appearing to do so.

**rhizo-,** a word element meaning 'root'. [Gk, combining form of *rhíza*]

**rhizobium** /raɪˈzoʊbiəm/, *n., pl.* **-bia** /-biə/. any bacterium of a genus *Rhizobium,* characterised by a rodlike shape, found as nitrogen fixers in nodules on the roots of the bean, clover, etc. [NL, from *rhizo-* RHIZO- + Gk *bíos* life]

**rhizocarpous** /raɪzoʊˈkapəs/, *adj.* **1.** bearing subterranean flowers and fruits. **2.** having the root perennial but the stem annual, as perennial herbs.

**rhizocephalous** /raɪzoʊˈsɛfələs/, *adj.* belonging to the Rhizocephala, a group of degenerate hermaphrodite crustaceans which are parasitic chiefly on crabs. [NL *Rhizocephala,* pl. (from *rhizo-* RHIZO- + Gk *kephalḗ* head) + -OUS]

**rhizogenic** /raɪzoʊˈdʒɛnɪk/, *adj.* producing roots, as certain cells. Also, **rhizogenous** /raɪˈzɒdʒənəs/.

**rhizoid** /ˈraɪzɔɪd/, *adj.* **1.** rootlike. *–n.* **2.** (in mosses, etc.) one of the rootlike filaments by which the plant is attached to the substratum. [RHIZ(O)- + -OID] – **rhizoidal** /raɪˈzɔɪdl/, *adj.*

**rhizome** /ˈraɪzoʊm/, *n.* a rootlike subterranean stem, commonly horizontal in position, which usu. produces roots below and sends up shoots progressively from the upper surface. [Gk *rhízōma* mass of roots] – **rhizomatous** /raɪˈzɒmətəs, -ˈzoʊmə-/, *adj.*

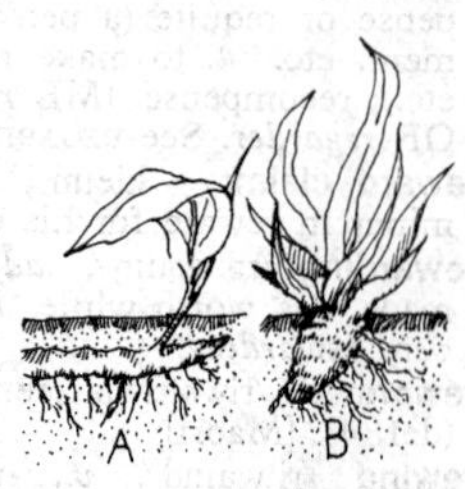

forms of rhizome: A, solomon's seal; B, iris

**rhizomorph** /ˈraɪzoʊmɔf/, *n.* a long strandlike structure composed of parallel fungal hyphae, as produced by the honey fungus, *Armillaria mellea.*

**rhizomorphous** /raɪzoʊˈmɔfəs/, *adj.* rootlike in form.

**rhizophagous** /raɪˈzɒfəgəs/, *adj.* feeding on roots.

**rhizophore** /ˈraɪzoʊfɔ/, *n.* a branch borne on the aerial stem in the pteridophyte genus *Selaginella* which has no leaves but produces roots when in contact with the soil.

**rhizopod** /ˈraɪzəpɒd/, *n.* any of the Rhizopoda, a class of protozoans having pseudopodia. [NL *Rhizopoda,* pl. See RHIZO-, -POD] – **rhizopodan** /raɪˈzɒpədən/, *adj., n.* – **rhizopodous,** *adj.*

**rhizopus** /ˈraɪzəpəs/, *n.* any fungus of the phycomycetous genus *Rhizopus,* of which the bread mould, *R. nigricans,* is best known. [NL, from *rhizo-* RHIZO- + Gk *poús* foot]

**rhizosphere** /ˈraɪzoʊsfɪə/, *n.* the soil in contact with a living root which usu. contains more micro-organisms than the rest of the soil.

**rhizotomy** /raɪˈzɒtəmi/, *n., pl.* **-mies.** the surgical section or cutting of the spinal nerve roots, usu. posterior or sensory roots, to eliminate pain or paralysis.

**Rh negative** /ˌareɪtʃ ˈnɛgətɪv/, *adj.* See **Rh factor.**

**rho** /roʊ/, *n.* the 17th letter (Ρ, ρ) of the Greek alphabet.

**rhod-,** variant of **rhodo-,** before vowels, as in *rhodamine.*

**rhodamine** /ˈrɒdəmin, -mən/, *n.* **1.** a red dye obtained by heating an alkyl aminophenol with phthalic anhydride. **2.** any of various related dyes. [RHOD- + AMINE]

**Rhode Island Red** /ˌroʊd aɪlənd ˈrɛd/, *n.* one of a variety of the domestic fowl originating in North America and having dark reddish brown feathers.

Rhode Island Red: rooster

**rhodes grass** /ˈroʊdz gras/, *n.* a species of pasture grass, *Chloris gayana,* native to southern Africa but widespread in warmer parts of Australia; often used to prevent soil erosion.

**Rhodesia** /roʊˈdiʒə/, *n.* former name of **Zimbabwe.** – **Rhodesian,** *adj., n.*

**Rhodesian ridgeback** /roʊˌdiʒən ˈrɪdʒbæk/, *n.* a hunting dog with a short reddish coat, and a characteristic ridge of hair along the back.

Rhodesian ridgeback

**Rhodes scholarship** /roʊdz ˈskɒləʃɪp/, *n.* one of a number of scholarships at Oxford University established by the will of Cecil Rhodes, for selected students (**Rhodes scholars**) from the countries of the British Commonwealth, and from the U.S. [named after Cecil *Rhodes,* 1853-1902, British colonial government administrator in Africa]

**rhodic** /ˈroudɪk/, *adj.* of or containing rhodium, esp. in the tetravalent state.

**rhodium** /ˈroudiəm/, *n.* a silvery white metallic element of the platinum family, forming salts which give rose-coloured solutions and used to electroplate microscopes and instrument parts to prevent corrosion. *Symbol:* Rh; *at. wt:* 102.905; *at. no.:* 45; *sp. gr.:* 12.4 at 20°C. [NL. See RHOD-, -IUM]

**rhodo-**, a word element meaning 'rose'. Also, **rhod-**. [Gk, combining form of *rhódon*]

**rhodochrosite** /roudəˈkrousaɪt/, *n.* a mineral, manganese carbonate, $MnCO_3$, commonly containing some iron and calcium and usu. rose red in colour; a minor ore of manganese. [G *Rhodochrosit,* from Gk *rhodóchrōs* rose-coloured + *-it* -ITE[1]]

**rhododendron** /roudəˈdɛndrən/, *n.* any plant of the genus *Rhododendron,* comprising evergreen and deciduous shrubs and trees with handsome pink, purple, or white flowers, and oval or oblong leaves, as *R. ponticum,* much cultivated for ornament. [NL, from Gk: lit., rose tree]

**rhodolite** /ˈrɒdəlaɪt/, *n.* a rose red variety of pyrope garnet, with a brilliant lustre, sometimes used as a gem.

**rhodonite** /ˈrɒdənaɪt/, *n.* a mineral, manganese metasilicate, $MnSiO_3$, occurring usu. in rose red masses, sometimes used as an ornamental stone. [G *Rhodonit,* from Gk *rhódon* rose + *-it* -ITE[1]]

**rhodopsin** /rouˈdɒpsən/, *n.* →**visual purple.**

**rhodora** /rouˈdɔrə/, *n.* a low shrub, *Rhododendron canadense,* of North America, with rose-coloured flowers which appear before the leaves. [L: kind of plant]

**-rhoea,** a word element meaning 'flow', 'discharge', as in *gonorrhoea.* Also, **-rrhoea,** *Chiefly U.S.,* **-rhea.** [Gk *-(r)rhoia,* from *rhéein* to flow]

**rhomb** /rɒm/, *n.* →**rhombus.**

**rhombencephalon** /rɒmbənˈsɛfəlɒn/, *n.* the part of the brain made up of the cerebellum, the pons, and the medulla oblongata; the hindbrain. [RHOMB + ENCEPHALON]

**rhombic** /ˈrɒmbɪk/, *adj.* **1.** having the form of a rhombus. **2.** having a rhombus as base or cross-section. **3.** bounded by rhombs, as a solid. **4.** *Crystall.* →**orthorhombic.** Also, **rhombical.**

**rhombohedron** /rɒmbəˈhidrən/, *n., pl.* **-drons, -dra** /-drə/. a solid bounded by six rhombic planes. [*rhombo-* (combining form representing Gk *rhómbos* rhombus) + -HEDRON] – **rhombohedral,** *adj.*

**rhomboid** /ˈrɒmbɔɪd/, *n.* **1.** an oblique-angled parallelogram with only the opposite sides equal. *–adj.* **2.** Also, **rhomboidal** /rɒmˈbɔɪdl/. having a form like, or approaching that of, a rhombus; shaped like a rhomboid. [LL *rhomboīdes,* from Gk *rhomboeidḗs*]

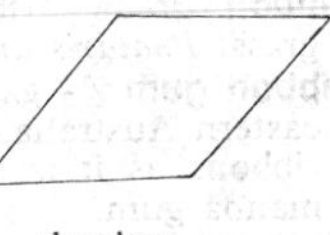

rhombus

**rhombus** /ˈrɒmbəs/, *n., pl.* **-buses, -bi** /-baɪ/. **1.** an oblique-angled equilateral parallelogram. **2.** →**rhombohedron.** [L, from Gk *rhómbos*]

**rhonchus** /ˈrɒŋkəs/, *n., pl.* **-chi** /-kaɪ/. a râle, esp. when produced in the bronchial tubes. [L, from Gk (unrecorded) *rhónchos,* var. of *rhénchos* snoring] – **rhonchal, rhonchial,** *adj.*

**rhotacism** /ˈroutəsɪzəm/, *n.* the defective pronunciation of *r,* excessive trilling, or some other pronunciational peculiarity. [NL *rhōtacismus,* from Gk *rhōtakízein* use *rhō* (sound or letter) to excess]

**rhotic** /ˈroutɪk/, *adj.* **1.** of or pertaining to a dialect in which a postvocalic written *r* is evident in the pronunciation as in the word *hard* in American and Scottish English (compared with the r-less pronunciations of dialects like Australian English). **2.** of or pertaining to speech showing rhotacism.

**Rh positive** /ˌareɪtʃ ˈpɒzətɪv/, *adj.* See **Rh factor.**

**r.h.s.,** right hand side.

**rhubarb** /ˈrubab/, *n.* **1.** any of the herbs constituting the polygonaceous genus *Rheum,* as *R. officinale,* a plant with a medicinal rhizome, and *R. rhaponticum,* a garden plant with edible leafstalks. **2.** the rhizome of any medicinal species of this plant, forming a combined cathartic and astringent. **3.** the edible fleshy leafstalks of any of the garden species, used in making pies, etc. **4.** the word supposedly spoken by actors to simulate noisy conversation in the background. **5.** *Colloq.* confused noise, argument, etc., as in a quarrel. **6.** *Colloq.* a quarrel or squabble; commotion. **7.** nonsense; empty conversation: *they're talking rhubarb.* [ME *rubarbe,* from OF *reubarbe,* from ML *reubarbarum.* from Gk *rhéon bárbaron* foreign rhubarb]

**rhumb** /rʌm/, *n.* **1.** →**rhumb line. 2.** a point of the compass. [Sp. *rumbo,* from L *rhombus* RHOMBUS]

**rhumbatron** /ˈrʌmbətrɒn/, *n. Electronics.* See **resonator** (def. 4a).

**rhumb line** /ˈrʌm laɪn/, *n.* a loxodromic curve; a curve on the surface of a sphere which cuts all meridians at the same angle. It is the path taken by a ship which maintains a constant compass direction.

**rhus** /rʊs, rʌs/, *n.* any plant of the genus *Rhus,* native to temperate regions and having simple or pinnate leaves and small flowers producing a small one-seeded drupe, as poison ivy; sumach.

**rhus tree** /ˈ– tri/, *n.* a small deciduous tree, *Toxicodendron succedaneum,* originating in the Chinese Himalayas, with pinnate leaves, slightly waxy on the underside, which turn deep red in autumn; wax tree.

**rhyacolite** /raɪˈækəlaɪt/, *n.* a glassy type of orthoclase found in lava.

**rhyme** /raɪm/, *n., v.,* **rhymed, rhyming.** *–n.* **1.** agreement in the terminal sounds of lines of verse, or of words. **2.** a word agreeing with another in terminal sound. **3.** verse or poetry having correspondence in the terminal sounds of the line. **4.** a poem or piece of verse having such correspondence. **5. rhyme or reason,** logic; explanation; meaning: *there was no rhyme or reason for her behaviour.* *–v.t.* **6.** to treat in rhyme, as a subject; turn into rhyme, as something in prose. **7.** to compose (verse, etc) in metrical form with rhymes. **8.** to use (a word) as a rhyme to another word; use (words) as rhymes. *–v.i.* **9.** to make rhyme or verse; versify. **10.** to use rhyme in writing verse. **11.** to form a rhyme, as one word or line with another. **12.** to be composed in metrical form with rhymes, as verse. Also, **rime.** [ME *rime,* from OF, from *rimer* to rhyme, from Gallo-Rom. *rimāre* put in a row, from OHG *rīm* series, row; probably not connected with L *rhythmus* rhythm] – **rhymer,** *n.*

**rhyme royal** /– ˈrɔɪəl/, *n.* a form of verse introduced into English by Chaucer, consisting of seven-line stanzas of iambic pentameter in which there are three rhymes, the first line rhyming with the third, the second with the fourth and fifth, and the sixth with the seventh.

**rhyme scheme** /ˈ– skim/, *n.* the pattern of rhymes used in a poem, usu. marked by letters, as rhyme royal, *ababbcc.*

**rhymester** /ˈraɪmstə/, *n.* a maker of rhyme or verse, esp. of an inferior order; a poetaster. Also, **rimester, rhymist.**

**rhyming slang** /raɪmɪŋ ˈslæŋ/, *n.* a form of slang, extensively used in Australia and elsewhere, esp. among men in groups, (army, sporting clubs, etc.) in which the last of two or more words is a rhyme of the word to be represented, *as plates of meat* (= feet). An elliptical form is also found in which the rhyming word is omitted, as *China* (= mate, the word *plate* being omitted). Some examples are: *babbling* (*brook*), cook; *elephant's* (*trunk*), drunk; *John* (*Hop*), cop, policeman; *Khyber* (*Pass*) arse; *Oxford* (*scholar*), dollar; *septic* (*tank*), Yank. Local and nonce forms occur frequently, as *Werris* (*Creek*), Greek; *Ballarat,* cat; *Sydney* (*Harbour*), barber; *leg of pork,* walk; *ginger ale,* bail.

**rhynchocephalian** /ˌrɪŋkousəˈfeɪliən/, *adj.* **1.** belonging to the Rhynchocephalia, an order of lizard-shaped reptiles, now extinct except for the tuatora of New Zealand. *–n.* **2.** a rhynchocephalian reptile. [NL, *Rhynchocephalia,* n. pl. (from Gk *rhyncho-,* combining form of *rhýnchos* snout + *kephalḗ* head) + -AN]

**rhyolite** /ˈraɪəlaɪt/, *n.* a kind of acid volcanic rock containing at least 66 per cent of silica, similar to granite but having solidified rapidly from a lava flow, and as a result fine-grained. [*rhyo-* (irregular combining form of Gk *rhýax* stream) + -LITE] – **rhyoletic,** *adj.*

**rhythm** /ˈrɪðəm/, *n.* **1.** movement or procedure with uniform recurrence of a beat, accent, or the like. **2.** measured movement, as in dancing. **3.** *Music.* **a.** the pattern of regular or irregular pulses caused in music by the occurrence of strong and weak melodic and harmonic beats. **b.** a particular form of this: *duple rhythm, triple rhythm.* **4.** the pattern of recurring stress, vowel length, vocalising, etc., in any utterance in any language. **5.** *Pros.* **a.** a metrical or rhythmical form; metre. **b.** a particular kind of metrical form. **c.** metrical movement. **6.** *Art.* a proper relation and interdependence of parts with reference to one another and to an artistic whole. **7.** procedure marked by the regular recurrence of particular elements, phases, etc. **8.** regular recurrence of elements in a system of motion. **9.** *Physiol.* the regular occurrence of a physiological function. [L *rhythmus,* from Gk *rhythmós*]

**rhythm and blues,** *n.* a commercialised style of popular music in vogue in the early 1960s, using both vocal and instrumental elements, based on the guitar and derived ultimately from the Negro blues style but with a quicker tempo and more complex rhythms.

**rhythm guitar** /ˌrɪðəm gəˈta/, *n.* **1.** an electric guitar in a rock group, used for playing chords rhythmically (opposed to *lead guitar*). **2.** the person who plays the rhythm guitar.

**rhythmic** /ˈrɪðmɪk/, *adj.* **1.** →**rhythmical.** *–n.* **2.** →**rhythmics.**

**rhythmical** /ˈrɪðmɪkəl/, *adj.* **1.** periodic, as motion, etc. **2.** having a flowing rhythm. **3.** of or pertaining to rhythm: *an excellent rhythmical sense.* – **rhythmically,** *adv.*

**rhythmics** /ˈrɪðmɪks/, *n.* the science of rhythm and rhythmic forms.

**rhythmist** /ˈrɪðməst/, *n.* **1.** one versed in, or having a fine sense of, rhythm. **2.** one who uses rhythm in a certain way: *a good rhythmist.*

**rhythm machine** /ˈrɪðəm məʃin/, *n.* an electronic device which synthesises a variety of standard rhythmic drum patterns.

**rhythm method** /ˈ– mɛθəd/, *n.* a method of avoiding conception by confining sexual intercourse to the infertile phases of the menstrual cycle.

**rhythm section** /ˈ– sɛkʃən/, *n.* the instruments in a dance band, such as piano, bass, guitar, and percussion, responsible for maintaining a regular beat.

**rhythm sticks** /ˈ– stɪks/, *n.pl. Music.* →**claves.**

**rhyton** /ˈraɪtɒn/, *n.* an ancient Greek drinking cup or horn. [Gk]

**ria** /riə/, *n.* a wedge-shaped indentation of the sea caused by submergence of the edges of the land where hill ranges and rivers are at right angles to the coastline. [Sp.]

**rialto** /riˈæltoʊ/, *n., pl.* **-tos.** an exchange or mart. [from *Rialto,* island and district in Venice, Italy, in which the exchange was situated]

**riant** /ˈraɪənt/, *adj.* laughing; smiling; cheerful; gay. [F, ppr. of *rire,* from L *rīdēre* laugh] – **riantly,** *adv.*

**rib**[1] /rɪb/, *n., v.,* **ribbed, ribbing.** *–n.* **1.** one of a series of long, slender, curved bones, occurring in pairs, more or less enclosing the thoracic cavity, and articulated with the vertebrae. **2.** a cut of meat, as beef, containing a rib. **3.** some thing or part resembling a rib in form, position, or use, as a supporting or strengthening part. **4.** an arch or arched member, plain or moulded, forming a support of a vault, or a merely decorative feature of like appearance on the surface of a vault or ceiling. **5.** a structural member which supports the shape of something: *an umbrella rib.* **6.** one of the curved timbers or members in a ship's frame which spring upwards and outwards from the keel. **7.** a primary vein of a leaf. **8.** a ridge, as in poplin or rep, caused by heavy yarn. **9.** *Knitting.* a pattern in which plain and purl stitches are alternated. **10.** a wife (in humorous allusion to the creation of Eve. Gen. 2:21-22). **11.** a strip of metal joining the barrel of a double-barrelled shotgun, which acts as a guide to aligning the sights. **12.** *Bookbinding.* **a.** one of the raised lines where the stitching runs across the spine of a book. **b.** such a line used ornamentally. *–v.t.* **13.** to furnish or strengthen with ribs. **14.** to enclose as with ribs. **15.** to mark with riblike ridges or markings. **16.** to knit (an article) in a rib. *–v.i.* **17.** to knit in a rib. [ME and OE, c. G *Rippe*] – **ribbed,** *adj.*

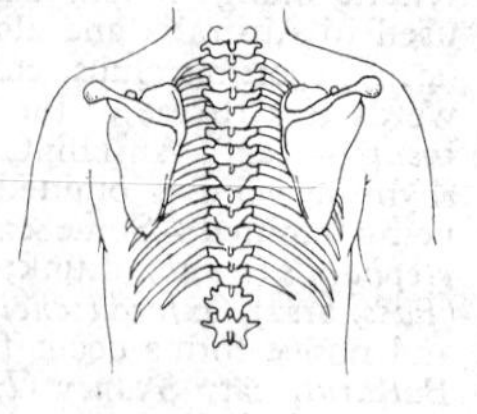
human ribs viewed from behind

**rib**[2] /rɪb/, *v.t.,* **ribbed, ribbing.** *Colloq.* to tease; ridicule; make fun of. [apparently short for *rib-tickle,* v.]

**ribald** /ˈrɪbəld, ˈraɪ-/, *adj.* **1.** offensive or scurrilous in speech, language, etc.; coarsely mocking or abusive; wantonly irreverent. *–n.* **2.** a ribald person. [ME *ribaut,* from OF, from *riber* dissipate, from MHG *rīben* be on heat, copulate, or from MD *ribe* whore]

**ribaldry** /ˈrɪbəldri, ˈraɪ-/, *n.* **1.** ribald character, as of language; scurrility. **2.** ribald speech.

**riband** /ˈrɪbənd/, *n.* **1.** Also, **ribbon.** *Carp.* a horizontal member fixed to uprights, in strutting, shoring, etc. **2.** *Archaic.* a ribbon. [ME, var. of RIBBON]

**ribband** /ˈrɪbənd/, *n.* a lengthwise timber or the like used to secure a ship's ribs in position while the outside planking or plating is being put on. [apparently from RIB[1] + BAND[2]]

**ribbing** /ˈrɪbɪŋ/, *n.* **1.** ribs collectively. **2.** an assemblage or arrangement of ribs. **3.** *Knitting.* →**rib**[1] (def. 9).

**ribble** /ˈrɪbəl/, *n., v.t.,* **-bled, -bling.** →**rabble**[2].

**ribbon** /ˈrɪbən/, *n.* **1.** a woven strip or band of fine material, as silk, rayon, etc., finished off at the edges, and varying in width, used for ornament, tying, etc. **2.** material in such strips. **3.** anything resembling or suggesting a ribbon or woven band. **4.** (*pl.*) torn or ragged strips; shreds: *clothes torn to ribbons.* **5.** a long, thin, flexible band of metal, as for a spring, bandsaw, tape measure, etc. **6.** a band of material charged with ink, or supplying ink, for the impression in a typewriter. **7.** *Shipbuilding.* →**ribband.** **8.** a badge of an order of knighthood or other distinction: *the red ribbon of the French Legion of Honour.* **9.** (*pl.*) *Colloq.* reins for driving. *–v.t.* **10.** to adorn with ribbon. **11.** to mark with something suggesting ribbon. **12.** to separate into or reduce to ribbon-like strips. *–v.i.* **13.** to form in ribbon-like strips. [ME *riban,* from OF, var. of *r(e)uban,* ? from Gmc; see RUDDY, BAND[2]] – **ribbon-like,** *adj.*

**ribbon development** /ˈ– dəvɛləpmənt/, *n.* the unplanned building of houses, etc., along main roads leading out of large towns.

**ribbonfish** /ˈrɪbənfɪʃ/, *n., pl.* **-fishes,** (*esp. collectively*) **-fish.** any of various deep-sea fishes belonging to the family Trachipteridae, characterised by a long, compressed tape-like body, as *Desmodema arawatae,* occasionally found along the eastern coast of Australia and in New Zealand waters.

**ribbon grass** /ˈrɪbən gras/, *n.* a tall, perennial variegated grass, *Phalaris arundinacea* var. *variegata.*

**ribbon gum** /ˈ– gʌm/, *n.* a tall tree, *Eucalyptus viminalis,* of eastern Australia with white smooth bark tending to hang in ribbons as it is shed, and from which manna is collected; manna gum.

**ribbonwood** /ˈrɪbənwʊd/, *n.* a small evergreen tree, *Hoheria populnea,* native to New Zealand.

**ribbon worm** /ˈrɪbən wɜm/, *n.* →**nemertean** (def. 2).

**rib eye** /ˈrɪb aɪ/, *n.* a cut of beef consisting of some of the best muscle meat near the ribs, cooked as a full roast or cut into steaks; scotch fillet; cube roll.

**rib loin** /ˈ– lɔɪn/, *n.* a standard cut of lamb or pork which is the remaining loin after the removal of the mid loin.

**riboflavin** /raɪboʊˈfleɪvən/, *n.* one of the vitamins included in the vitamin B complex found in green vegetables, fish, milk, etc. Also, **riboflavine** /raɪboʊˈfleɪvin/. [RIBO(SE) + FLAVIN]

**ribonuclease** /raɪboʊˈnjuklieɪz/, *n.* an enzyme which catalyses the hydrolysis of ribonucleic acid into nucleotides.

**ribonucleic acid** /raɪboʊˌnjukliɪk ˈæsəd/, *n.* any polymer of ribonucleotides found in all living cells and some viruses, the main function of which is the translation of the genetic code in protein synthesis. *Abbrev.:* RNA

**ribose** /ˈraɪboʊz, -oʊs/, *n.* a pentose sugar, $C_5H_{10}O_5$; dextroribose is present in combined form in RNA.

**ribosome** /ˈraɪbəsoʊm/, *n.* one of the minute granules present in living cells, containing ribonucleic acid and protein. They are the site of protein synthesis. – **ribosomal** /raɪbəˈsoʊməl/, *adj.*

**rib steak** /rɪb ˈsteɪk/, *n.* →**entrecote.**

**ribuck** /ˈraɪbʌk/, *adj. Obs. Colloq.* very good, genuine. Also, **ryebuck.** [orig. uncert.]

**ribwort** /ˈrɪbwɜt/, *n.* **1.** a plantain, *Plantago lanceolata,* having narrow leaves with prominent ribs. **2.** any of various similar plantains.

**rice** /raɪs/, *n.* **1.** the starchy seeds or grain of a species of grass, *Oryza sativa,* cultivated in warm climates and constituting an important food. **2.** the plant itself. [ME *rys,* from OF *ris,* from It. *riso,* (through MGk) from Gk *óryza;* of Eastern orig.]

**rice bowl** /ˈ– boʊl/, *n.* **1.** a small bowl in which cooked rice is served. **2.** an area or country in which rice is cultivated extensively.

**rice bubbles** /ˈ– bʌbəlz/, *n.pl.* a breakfast cereal made from toasted rice flour and served with milk, sugar, etc. [Trademark]

**rice-flower** /ˈraɪs-flaʊə/, *n.* any one of many species of the Australian genus *Pimelea,* family Thymeleaceae.

**rice paper** /ˈraɪs peɪpə/, *n.* **1.** a thin, edible paper made from the straw of rice. **2.** a Chinese paper consisting of the pith of certain plants cut and pressed into thin sheets.

**rice pudding** /– ˈpʊdɪŋ/, *n.* a hot or cold sweet dish made with milk and whole or ground rice and sugar.

**ricercare** /ritʃəˈkareɪ/, *n.* (originally) a piece of contrapuntal music for instruments, using elaborate imitation, later used by composers of elaborate figures. Also, **ricercar.** [It.]

**rich** /rɪtʃ/, *adj.* **1.** having wealth or great possessions; abundantly supplied with resources, means, or funds: *a rich man or nation.* **2.** abounding in natural resources: *a rich territory.* **3.** having wealth or valuable resources (fol. by *in*): *a tract rich in minerals.* **4.** abounding (fol. by *in* or *with*): *a country rich in traditions.* **5.** of great value or worth; valuable: *a rich harvest.* **6.** costly; expensively elegant or fine, as dress, jewels, etc. **7.** sumptuous, as a feast. **8.** of valuable materials or elaborate workmanship, as buildings, furniture, etc. **9.** abounding in desirable elements or qualities. **10.** (of food) containing good, nutritious, or choice ingredients, as butter, cream, sugar, etc. **11.** (of wine, gravy, etc.) strong and full flavoured. **12.** (of colour) deep, strong, or vivid. **13.** (of sound, the voice, etc.) full and mellow in tone. **14.** (of smell) strongly scented. **15.** producing or yielding abundantly: *a rich soil.* **16.** abundant, plentiful, or ample: *a rich supply.* **17.** *Colloq.* highly amusing. **18.** *Colloq.* ridiculous, absurd, or preposterous. *–n.* **19.** rich people collectively (usu. prec. by *the*). [ME; OE *rīce,* c. G *reich,* of Celtic orig.; akin to L *rex* king] – **richly,** *adv.* – **richness,** *n.*

**Richard's pipit** /rɪtʃədz ˈpɪpət/, *n.* →**Australian pipit.**

**riches** /ˈrɪtʃəz/, *n.pl.* abundant and valuable possessions; wealth. [ME, from OF *richesse* wealth, from *riche* (of Gmc orig.) RICH]

**rich rhyme** /rɪtʃ ˈraɪm/, *n.* complete identity in sound but not in sense, of the rhyming syllables, as *bare, bear* or *mind, mined.*

**Richter scale** /ˈrɪktə skeɪl/, *n.* an open ended logarithmic scale used to express the magnitude or total energy of a seismic disturbance (as an earthquake). In this scale an increase of 1 indicates a thirty-fold increase in energy. [named after Charles F. *Richter,* b. 1900, U.S. seismologist]

**ricin** /ˈraɪsən, ˈrɪsən/, *n.* a white, toxic protein from the bean of the castor-oil plant. [NL *ricinus* a genus of plants, from L]

**ricinoleic acid** /ˌrɪsənoʊˌliɪk ˈæsəd, -əˌnoʊliɪk/, *n.* an unsaturated hydroxy acid, $C_{17}H_{32}(OH)COOH$, occurring in castor oil in the form of the glyceride. [RICIN + -OLE + -IC]

**ricinolein** /rɪsəˈnoʊliən/, *n.* the glyceride of ricinoleic acid, the chief constituent of castor oil.

**rick**[1] /rɪk/, *n.* **1.** a stack of hay, straw, or the like, esp. one thatched or covered for protection. *–v.t.* **2.** to pile in ricks. [ME *rek(e),* OE *hrēac,* c. D *rook*]

**rick**[2] /rɪk/, *v.t.* to sprain or strain as one's neck, back, etc. [var. of WRICK]

**ricker** /ˈrɪkə/, *n. N.Z.* a kauri sapling. Also, **rika.** [orig. uncert.; ? Naut.]

**rickets** /ˈrɪkəts/, *n.* **1.** *Pathol.* a disease of childhood, characterised by softening of the bones as a result of malnutrition (ordinarily lack of vitamin D), or insufficient ingestion of calcium, or both, and often resulting in deformities. **2.** an insidious and incurable disease of cattle caused by eating certain poisonous plants prevalent in Queensland cattle country. [orig. uncert.]

**rickettsia** /rɪˈkɛtsiə/, *n.pl.* bacteria-like micro-organisms, apparently members of a single group or genus, which are found living as parasites in arthropods and are the cause of certain human diseases. [named after Howard T *Ricketts,* 1871-1910, U.S. pathologist] – **rickettsial,** *adj.*

**rickety** /ˈrɪkəti/, *adj.* **1.** liable to fall or collapse; shaky: *a rickety chair.* **2.** feeble in the joints; tottering; infirm. **3.** irregular, as motion or action. **4.** affected with or suffering from rickets. **5.** pertaining to or of the nature of rickets. [RICKET(S) + -Y[1]]

**rickrack** /ˈrɪkræk/, *n.* a narrow zigzag braid used to trim clothing, etc. Also, **ricrac.** [dissimilated reduplication of RACK[1]]

**rickshaw** /ˈrɪkʃɔ/, *n.* a small two-wheeled hooded vehicle drawn by one or more men, used in the Orient; jinrikisha. Also, **ricksha.**

rickshaw

**ricochet** /ˈrɪkəʃeɪ/, *n., v.,* **-cheted, -chetted** /-ʃeɪd/, **-cheting, -chetting** /-ʃeɪɪŋ/. *–n.* **1.** the motion of an object or projectile which rebounds one or more times from a flat surface over which it is passing. *–v.i.* **2.** to move in this way, as a projectile. [F; orig. uncert.]

**ricotta** /rəˈkɒtə/, *n.* a soft cottage cheese with a fresh bland flavour, made from the whey obtained in the manufacture of other cheeses. [It.]

**ricrac** /ˈrɪkræk/, *n.* →**rickrack.**

**rictus** /ˈrɪktəs/, *n.* **1.** *Zool.* the gape of an animal and particularly of a bird. **2.** *Bot.* the opening of the lipped petals of a flower. [L: gape] – **rictal,** *adj.*

**rid**[1] /rɪd/, *v.t.,* **rid** or **ridded, ridding.** **1.** to clear, disencumber, or free of something objectionable (fol. by *of*). **2.** to disembarrass or relieve (fol. by *of*): *to rid the mind of doubt.* **3. get rid of, a.** to get free, or relieved of. **b.** to get (a thing or person) off one's hands. **c.** to do away with. [ME *rydde,* OE *geryddan* clear (land), c. Icel. *rydhja* clear, empty] – **ridder,** *n.*

**rid**[2] /rɪd/, *v. Archaic.* past tense and past participle of **ride.**

**ridable** /ˈraɪdəbəl/, *adj.* →**rideable.**

**riddance** /ˈrɪdns/, *n.* **1.** a clearing away or out, as of anything undesirable. **2.** a relieving or deliverance from something. **3. good riddance,** a welcome deliverance.

**ridden** /ˈrɪdn/, *v.* past participle of **ride.**

**riddle**[1] /ˈrɪdl/, *n., v.,* **-dled, -dling.** *–n.* **1.** a question or statement so framed as to exercise one's ingenuity in answering it or discovering its meaning; conundrum. **2.** a puzzling question, problem, or matter. **3.** a puzzling thing or person. **4.** any enigmatic or dark saying or speech. *–v.i.* **5.** to propound riddles; to speak enigmatically. [ME *redele,* OE *rǣdelle,* var. of *rǣdels(e)* enigma (c. G *Rätsel*), from *rǣdan* READ[1]]

**riddle**[2] /ˈrɪdl/, *v.,* **-dled, -dling,** *n.* *–v.t.* **1.** to pierce with many holes suggesting those of a sieve. **2.** to sift through a riddle, as gravel. **3.** to fill with (esp. something undesirable). **4.** to impair or refute completely by persistent verbal attacks: *to riddle a person's reputation.* *–n.* **5.** a coarse sieve, as one for sifting sand in the foundry. [ME *riddil,* OE *hriddel,* dissimilated var. of *hridder,* akin to L *cribrum* sieve]

**ride** /raɪd/, *v.,* **rode** or (*Archaic*) **rid; ridden** or (*Archaic*) **rid; riding;** *n.* *–v.i.* **1.** to sit on and manage a horse or other animal in motion; be carried on the back of an animal. **2.** to be carried on something as if on horseback. **3.** to be borne along on or in a vehicle or any kind of conveyance. **4.** to move along in any way; be carried or supported: *distress riding among the people.* **5.** to move or float on the water. **6.** to lie at anchor, as a ship. **7.** to appear to float in space, as a heavenly body. **8.** to turn or rest on something. **9.** to extend or project over something, as the edge of one thing over the edge of another thing. **10.** to work or move (*up*) from the proper position, as a skirt, or the like. **11.** to have a specified character for riding purposes: *the train rides smoothly.* **12. ride for a fall, a.** to ride (a horse) recklessly. **b.**

to act in a way which will inevitably bring disaster. *–v.t.* **13.** to sit on and manage (a horse or other animal, or a bicycle or the like) so as to be carried along. **14.** to sit or be mounted on (something) as if on horseback; be carried or borne along on. **15.** to rest on, esp. by overlapping. **16.** to control, dominate or tyrannise over: *a land that was king-ridden.* **17.** *Colloq.* to harass or torment. **18.** to ride over, along or through (a road, boundary, region, etc.). **19.** to execute by riding: *to ride a race.* **20.** to keep (a vessel) at anchor or moored. **21. ride down, a.** to trample under a horse's hooves. **b.** to pursue and catch up with. **22. ride out, a.** to sustain (a gale, etc.) without damage, as while riding at anchor. **b.** to sustain or endure successfully. *–n.* **23.** a journey or excursion on a horse, etc., or on or in a vehicle. **24.** a way, road, etc., made esp. for riding. **25. take for a ride,** *Colloq.* **a.** to kidnap and murder. **b.** to deceive and wilfully mislead. [ME *ride(n),* OE *rīdan,* c. D *rijden,* G *reiten,* Dan. *ride*]

**rideable** /ˈraɪdəbəl/, *adj.* **1.** capable of being ridden, as a horse. **2.** capable of being ridden over, through, etc., as a road or a stream. Also, **ridable.**

**ride cymbal** /raɪd ˈsɪmbəl/, *n.* a cymbal whose resonance is controlled so that when it is struck rapidly many times in succession each attack is clearly distinguishable.

**rident** /ˈraɪdnt/, *adj.* laughing; smiling; cheerful. [L *rīdens,* ppr.]

**rider** /ˈraɪdə/, *n.* **1.** one who rides a horse or other animal, or a bicycle or the like. **2.** one who or that which rides. **3.** any of various objects or devices straddling, mounted on, or attached to something else. **4.** *Chem.* a small piece of platinum wire used on a chemical balance arm to make the final adjustment. **5.** an additional clause usu. unrelated to the main body, attached to a legislative bill in passing it. **6.** an addition or amendment to a document, etc. **7.** *Law.* an addition, of no legal effect, made by a jury to their verdict, usu. explaining or seeking to qualify it. **8.** *Maths.* a problem arising out of a proposition.

**ridge**[1] /rɪdʒ/, *n., v.,* **ridged, ridging.** *–n.* **1.** a long, narrow elevation of land, or a chain of hills or mountains. **2.** the long and narrow upper part or crest of something, as of an animal's back, a hill, a wave, etc. **3.** *Obs.* the back of an animal. **4.** any raised narrow strip, as on cloth, etc. **5.** the horizontal line in which the tops of the rafters of a roof meet. **6.** *Meteorol.* **a.** a band of relatively high pressure usu. joining two anticyclones. **b.** an elongated wedge (def. 3). **7.** the earth thrown up by a plough between furrows. **8.** a strip of arable land, usu. between furrows. *–v.t.* **9.** to provide with or form into a ridge or ridges. **10.** to mark with or as with ridges. *–v.i.* **11.** to form ridges. [ME *rigge,* OE *hrycg* spine, crest, ridge, c. D *rug*]

**ridge**[2] /rɪdʒ/, *adj. Colloq.* true; correct; genuine. Also, **ridgy-didge.**

**ridge lift** /ˈ– lɪft/, *n.* a lifting action to a glider produced by strong winds blowing against a hill, or other obstruction.

**ridgeling** /ˈrɪdʒlɪŋ/, *n.* a colt with undescended testicles. Also, **ridgel** /ˈrɪdʒəl/.

**ridgepole** /ˈrɪdʒpoʊl/, *n.* **1.** the horizontal timber or member at the top of a roof, to which the upper ends of the rafters are fastened. **2.** the horizontal pole at the top of a tent.

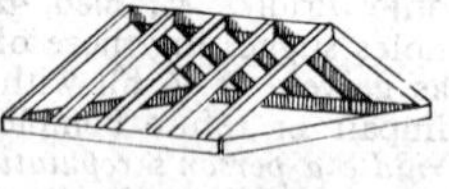

ridgepole

**ridge rope** /ˈrɪdʒ roʊp/, *n.* a centre line rope or wire over which a canvas awning is spread.

**ridge tile** /ˈ– taɪl/, *n.* a special angle tile made to cap the apex of a pitched roof.

**ridgeway** /ˈrɪdʒweɪ/, *n.* a path or road along a ridge.

**ridgy** /ˈrɪdʒi/, *adj.* rising in a ridge or ridges.

**ridgy-didge** /ˈrɪdʒi-ˌdɪdʒ/, *adj.* →**ridge**[2]. Also, **ridgie-didge.**

**ridicule** /ˈrɪdəkjul/, *n., v.,* **-culed, -culing.** *–n.* **1.** words or actions intended to excite contemptuous laughter at a person or thing; derision. *–v.t.* **2.** to deride; make fun of. [F, from L *ridiculum* laughable (thing), properly neut. adj.] – **ridiculer,** *n.*

**ridiculous** /rəˈdɪkjələs/, *adj.* **1.** such as to excite ridicule or derision; absurd, preposterous, or laughable. *–n.* **2.** that which is ridiculous (prec. by *the*). – **ridiculously,** *adv.* – **ridiculousness,** *n.*

**riding**[1] /ˈraɪdɪŋ/, *n.* **1.** the act of one who or that which rides. *–adj.* **2.** used in travelling or in riding. [RIDE + -ING[1]]

**riding**[2] /ˈraɪdɪŋ/, *n.* **1.** (*usu. cap*) an area division within a shire. **2.** *Brit.* (*cap.*) one of the three administrative divisions into which the northern county of Yorkshire was formerly divided. [ME *triding,* from Scand.; cf. Icel. *thridhjungr* third part; *t-* for *th-* by assimilation to *-t* in *east* and *west;* later *-t t-* simplified to *-t*]

**riding boot** /ˈ– but/, *n.* a close-fitting leather boot, worn as part of a riding habit.

**riding breeches** /ˈ– brɪtʃəz/, *n. pl.* calf-length trousers flaring at the sides of the thighs and closely-fitting just below the knee, worn with riding boots.

**riding crop** /ˈ– krɒp/, *n.* →**crop** (def. 7).

**riding light** /ˈ– laɪt/, *n.* →**anchor light.**

**riding master** /ˈ– mastə/, *n.* a man who teaches horse-riding.

**riding school** /ˈ– skul/, *n.* a place where horse-riding is taught.

**riding stables** /ˈ– steɪbəlz/, *n. pl.* stables for the housing of saddle horses.

**ridotto** /rəˈdɒtoʊ/, *n., pl.* **-tos.** a public ball or social gathering, often in masquerade (common in the 18th century). [It.: a retreat, resort. See REDOUBT]

**Riesling** /ˈrizlɪŋ, ˈrislɪŋ/, *n.* **1.** a wine grape of Alsace, the Rhine region, and elsewhere. **2.** (*oft. l.c.*) the wine made from this.

**rifacimento** /rəfatʃəˈmɛntoʊ/, *n., pl.* **-ti** /-ti/. a recast or adaptation, as of a literary or musical work. [It.: a remaking, from *rifare* make over, from *ri-* RE- + *fare* make, from L *facere*]

**rife** /raɪf/, *adj.* **1.** of common or frequent occurrence; prevalent; in widespread existence, activity, or use. **2.** current in speech or report. **3.** abundant, plentiful, or numerous. **4.** abounding (fol. by *with,* formerly *in*). [ME; late OE *rȳfe,* c. MD *riif*]

**riff** /rɪf/, *n.* (in jazz and rock music) a short repeated melodic phrase, usu. for guitar or piano, which is intended to give a strong rhythmic impetus. [short for REFRAIN[2]]

**riffle** /ˈrɪfəl/, *n., v.,* **-fled, -fling.** *–n.* **1.** *Mining.* **a.** the lining at the bottom of a sluice or the like, made of blocks or slats of wood, or of stones, arranged in such a manner that grooves or openings are left between them for catching and collecting particles of gold. **b.** one of the slats of wood or the like so used. **c.** one of the grooves or openings formed. **2.** the method of riffling cards. *–v.t., v.i.* **3.** to cause or become a riffle. **4.** to flutter and shift, as pages. **5.** to shuffle (cards) by dividing the pack in two, raising the corners slightly, and allowing them to fall alternately together. [b. RIPPLE[1] and RUFFLE[1]]

**riffler** /ˈrɪflə/, *n.* a curved file for shaping concave surfaces.

**riffraff** /ˈrɪfræf/, *n.* **1.** the worthless or disreputable element of society; the rabble: *the riffraff of the city.* **2.** worthless or low persons. [ME *rif and raf* every particle, things of small value, from OF *rif et raf, rifle rafle,* from OF *rifler* spoil, *raffler* ravage, snatch away]

**rifle**[1] /ˈraɪfəl/, *n., v.,* **-fled, -fling.** *–n.* **1.** a shoulder firearm with spiral grooves cut in the inner surface of the gun barrel to give the bullet a rotatory motion and thus render its flight more accurate. **2.** one of the grooves. **3.** a cannon with such grooves. **4.** (*pl.*) certain military units or bodies equipped with rifles. *–v.t.* **5.** to cut spiral grooves within (a gun barrel, etc.). [LG *rīfeln* to groove, from *rīve, riefe* groove, flute, furrow; akin to OE *rifelede* wrinkled, *rīf* violent]

rifle[1]: A, Winchester 66: B, M-16

**rifle**[2] /ˈraɪfəl/, *v.t.,* **-fled, -fling. 1.** to ransack and rob (a place, receptacle, etc.). **2.** to search and rob (a person). **3.** to plunder or strip bare of. **4.** to steal or take away. [ME *rifel,* from OF *rifler* scrape, graze, plunder, from D *riffelen* scrape, c. RIFLE[1], *v.*] – **rifler,** *n.*

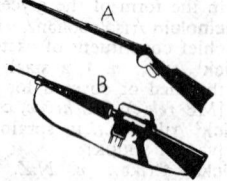

**riflebird** /ˈraɪfəlbɜd/, *n.* any bird of paradise of the family Paradisaeidae, of the genera *Ptiloris* and *Craspedophora,* of Australia and New Guinea.

**rifle grenade** /raɪfəl grəˈneɪd/, *n.* a hand grenade mounted on a round steel rod which is then fired from the barrel of a rifle.

**rifleman** /ˈraɪfəlmən/, *n., pl.* **-men. 1.** a soldier armed with a rifle. **2.** one skilled in the use of a rifle. **3.** a small New Zealand bush wren, *Acanthisitta chloris.*

**rifle range** /ˈraɪfəl reɪndʒ/, *n.* **1.** a target practice ground. **2.** the distance covered by the bullet discharged from a rifle.

**rifling** /ˈraɪflɪŋ/, *n.* **1.** the act or process of cutting spiral grooves in a gun barrel, etc. **2.** the system of spiral grooves so cut.

**rift** /rɪft/, *n.* **1.** an opening made by riving or splitting; a fissure; a cleft; a chink. **2.** a break in the friendly relations between two people, countries, etc. *–v.t.* **3.** to burst open. *–v.i.* **4.** to split. [ME, from Scand.; cf. Dan. *rift* cleft; akin to RIVE, *v.*]

**rift valley** /ˈ– væli/, *n.* a portion of the earth's crust, bounded on at least two sides by faults, that has been moved downwards in relation to the adjacent portions; graben.

**rig** /rɪg/, *v.,* **rigged, rigging,** *n. –v.t.* **1.** *Chiefly Naut.* **a.** to put in proper order for working or use. **b.** to fit (a vessel, a mast, etc.) with the necessary shrouds, stays, etc. **c.** to fit (shrouds, stays, sails, etc.) to the mast, yard, or the like. **2.** *Aeron.* to obtain the correct relative positions of the different components of an aircraft. **3.** to furnish or provide with equipment, etc.; fit (usu. fol. by *out* or *up*). **4.** to prepare or put together, esp. as a makeshift (oft. fol. by *up*). **5.** *Colloq.* to fit or deck with clothes, etc. (oft. fol. by *out* or *up*). **6.** to manipulate fraudulently: *to rig an election, prices, etc. –n.* **7.** the arrangement of the masts, spars, sails, etc., on a boat or ship. **8.** apparatus for some purpose; equipment; outfit. **9.** *Colloq.* a vehicle with a horse or horses, as for driving. **10.** the equipment used in drilling an oil or gas well. **11.** Also, **rig-out.** *Colloq.* costume or dress, esp. when odd or conspicuous. **12.** a male sheep, horse, etc., not properly castrated. **13.** →**semitrailer.** [probably from Scand.; cf. d. Swed. *rigga på* to harness] – **rigged,** *adj.*

**rigadoon** /rɪgəˈdun/, *n.* **1.** a lively dance, formerly popular, for one couple, characterised by a peculiar jumping step, and usu. in quick duple rhythm. **2.** a piece of music for this dance, or in its rhythm. [F *rigaudon;* named after *Rigaud,* the originator]

**rigatoni** /rɪgəˈtoʊni/, *n.pl.* ridged, cut macaroni, sometimes curved. [It.]

**rigger** /ˈrɪgə/, *n.* **1.** one who rigs. **2.** an erector of steel frame work esp. in high building. **3.** →**dogman. 4.** one whose occupation is the fitting of the rigging of ships. **5.** one who works with hoisting tackle, etc. **6.** one of the metal stays which support the rowlock away from the boat's side. **7.** this stay together with the rowlock. **8.** *Aeron.* a mechanic skilled at assembling and repairing aeroplane wings, fuselages, and sometimes control mechanisms.

**rigging** /ˈrɪgɪŋ/, *n.* **1.** the ropes, chains, etc., employed to support and work the masts, yards, sails, etc., on a ship. **2.** a system of wires used to obtain the correct angles of incidence and dihedral, or the relative positions, of different components in an aircraft. **3.** a system of wires by which loads are distributed over the hull of an airship. **4.** tackle in general.

**rigging batten** /ˈ– bætn/, *n.* a long narrow strip of wood or metal fastened to a shroud or the like of a ship's rigging as a protection against chafing.

**rigging plan** /ˈ– plæn/, *n.* an architectural plan of the rigging of a ship's mast.

**Riggs' disease** /ˈrɪgz dəziz/, *n.* →**pyorrhoea.** [named after John M. *Riggs,* 1810-85, U.S. dentist]

**right** /raɪt/, *adj.* **1.** in accordance with what is just or good: *right conduct.* **2.** in conformity with fact, reason, or some standard or principle; correct: *the right solution.* **3.** correct in judgment, opinion, or action. **4.** sound or normal, as the mind, etc.; sane, as persons. **5.** in good health or spirits, as persons: *he is all right again.* **6.** in a satisfactory state; in good order: *to put things right.* **7.** adequately supplied with (fol. by *for*): *are you right for supplies?* **8.** principal, front, or upper: *the right side of the cloth.* **9.** most convenient, desirable, or favourable. **10.** all right, okay. **11.** fitting or appropriate: *to say the right thing.* **12.** genuine; legitimate: *the right owner.* **13.** belonging or pertaining to the side of a person or thing which is turned towards the east when the face is towards the north (opposed to *left*). **14.** belonging or pertaining to the political right. **15.** straight: *a right line.* **16.** formed by, or with reference to, a line or a plane extending to another line or a surface by the shortest course: *a right angle.* **17.** *Geom.* having the axis perpendicular to the base: *a right cone.* **18.** *Colloq.* unquestionable; unmistakeable; true: *he's a right idiot.* **19. right as rain,** *Colloq.* safe, okay, in good health. **20. she'll be right.** Also, **she's right,** *Colloq.* an expression of confidence that everything will go well. **21. too right,** an emphatic expression of agreement. *–n.* **22.** a just claim or title, whether legal, prescriptive, or moral. **23.** that which is due to anyone by just claim: *to give one his right or his rights.* **24.** *Finance.* **a.** the privilege, usu. pre-emptive, which accrues to the owners of the stock of a company to subscribe for additional stock or shares at an advantageous price. **b.** (*oft. pl.*) a privilege of subscribing for a stock or bond. **25.** that which is ethically good and proper and in conformity with the moral law. **26.** that which accords with fact, reason, or propriety. **27.** the right or proper way of thinking: *to be in the right.* **28.** the right side or what is on the right side: *to turn to the right.* **29.** a punch with the right hand, as in boxing. **30. the Right,** (*oft. l.c.*) **a.** that part of a legislative assembly in continental Europe which sits on the right of the president, a position customarily assigned to the conservatives. **b.** a body of persons, political party, etc., holding conservative views. **31. by rights,** in all fairness; rightfully. **32. dead to rights,** *Prison Colloq.* →**red-handed. 33. to rights,** into proper condition: *to set a room to rights. –adv.* **34.** in a right or straight line; straight; directly (fol. by *to, into, through,* etc.): *right to the bottom.* **35.** quite or completely: *his hat was knocked right off.* **36.** immediately: *right after dinner.* **37.** exactly, precisely, or just: *right here.* **38.** uprightly or righteously. **39.** correctly or accurately: *to guess right.* **40.** properly or fittingly: *to behave right, it serves you right.* **41.** advantageously, favourably, or well: *to turn out right.* **42.** towards the right hand; to the right. **43.** very (used in certain titles): *the right reverend.* **44.** *Colloq.* very; really; extraordinarily: *he's right stupid. –v.t.* **45.** to bring or restore to an upright or the proper position. **46.** to set in order or put right. **47.** to bring into conformity with fact, or correct. **48.** to do justice to. **49.** to redress (wrong, etc.). *–v.i.* **50.** to resume an upright or the proper position. [ME; OE *reht, riht,* c. D and G *recht,* Icel. *rēttr,* Goth. *raihts;* akin to L *rectus*]

**rightabout** /ˈraɪtəbaut/, *n.* the opposite direction as faced after turning about to the right.

**right about turn,** *interj.* **1.** (a military command to turn so as to face in the opposite direction). *–n.* **2.** the action itself.

**right angle** /ˈraɪt æŋgəl/, *n.* an angle formed at the interception of two perpendicular lines, and equal to half a straight angle, or approx. 1.57 radians; an angle of 90°.

**right-angled triangle** /ˌraɪt-æŋgəld ˈtraɪæŋgəl/, *n.* a triangle in which one of the angles is a right angle. Also, **right triangle.**

**right ascension** /raɪt əˈsɛnʃən/, *n. Astron.* **1.** the rising of a star or point above the horizon on the celestial sphere. **2.** the arc of the celestial equator measured eastwards from the vernal equinox to the foot of the great circle passing through the celestial poles and the point on the celestial sphere in question, and expressed in degrees or time.

**right away** /– əˈweɪ/, *adv.* directly; immediately: *I'll do it right away.*

**right back** /– ˈbæk/, *n.* (in soccer, hockey, etc.) the full-back on the right side of the field of play.

**right-branching** /ˈraɪt-bræntʃɪŋ/, *adj.* (of a grammatical construction) having most of its constituents on the right of its node on a tree diagram (def. 2).

**right centre** /raɪt ˈsɛntə/, *n. Brit., S. African.* (in rugby football) the centre who is the right-hand member of the two centres, when looking ahead, for a particular disposition of the back line.

**righteous** /ˈraɪtʃəs/, *adj.* **1.** characterised by uprightness or morality: *a righteous act.* **2.** morally right or justifiable: *righteous indignation.* **3.** in accordance with right; upright or virtuous: *a righteous and godly man.* –*n.* **4.** righteous people collectively (prec. by *the*). [earlier *rightwos(e), rightwis(e),* OE *rihtwīs,* from *riht* RIGHT + *wīs* WISE²] – **righteously,** *adv.* – **righteousness,** *n.*

**right-footer** /raɪt-ˈfʊtə/, *n. Colloq.* a Protestant. – **right-footed,** *adj.*

**rightful** /ˈraɪtfəl/, *adj.* **1.** having a right, or just claim, as to some possession or position: *the rightful owner.* **2.** belonging by right, or just claim: *one's rightful property.* **3.** equitable or just, as actions, etc.: *a rightful cause.* – **rightfully,** *adv.* – **rightfulness,** *n.*

**right half** /raɪt ˈhaf/, *n.* (in soccer, hockey etc.) the right of the three players in the half-back line.

**right hand** /– ˈhænd/, *n.* the most efficient help or resource.

**right-hand** /ˈraɪt-hænd/, *adj.* **1.** on or to the right: *right-hand drive.* **2.** of, for, or with the right hand. **3.** most efficient or useful as a helper: *one's right-hand man.*

**right-handed** /raɪt-ˈhændəd/, *adj.* **1.** having the right hand or arm more serviceable than the left; preferring to use the right hand. **2.** adapted to or performed by the right hand. **3.** situated on the side of the right hand. **4.** moving or rotating from left to right, or in the same direction as the hands of a clock. **5.** (of a rope) having the strands forming a spiral to the right. **6. right-handed helix** or **spiral,** one that is turned in this way and runs upwards from left to right when viewed from the side with the axis vertical, as the thread of a right-handed screw.

**right inner** /raɪt ˈɪnə/, *n. Hockey.* →**inside right.**

**rightist** /ˈraɪtəst/, *n.* **1.** a member of a conservative or reactionary party or a person sympathising with their views. –*adj.* **2.** having conservative or reactionary political ideas. [RIGHT (def. 30) + -IST]

**rightly** /ˈraɪtli/, *adv.* **1.** in accordance with truth or fact; correctly. **2.** in accordance with morality or equity; uprightly. **3.** properly, fitly, or suitably. **4.** *Colloq.* positively, certainly: *I don't rightly know.* [ME; OE *rihtlīce.* See RIGHT, -LY]

**right-minded** /ˈraɪt-maɪndəd/, *adj.* having right opinions or principles. – **right-mindedness,** *n.*

**rightness** /ˈraɪtnəs/, *n.* **1.** correctness or accuracy. **2.** propriety or fitness. **3.** straightness or directness.

**righto** /raɪtˈoʊ/, *interj. Colloq.* (an expression indicating agreement). Also, **rightio, rightoh, righty-ho.**

**right of search,** *n. Law.* a privilege of a nation at war to search neutral ships on the high seas for contraband or other matters in violation of neutrality which may subject the ship to seizure.

**right of way,** *n.* **1.** the legal or customary right of a person, motor car or vessel to proceed ahead of another. **2.** a path or route which may lawfully be used. **3.** a right of passage, as over another's land. **4.** the strip of land acquired for use by a railway for its tracks. **5.** land covered by a public road. **6.** land over which a power line passes.

**rights issue** /ˈraɪts ɪʃu/, *n.* an issue of stocks or shares offered to members of a company at a preferential price.

**right-to-life** /raɪt-tə-ˈlaɪf/, *adj.* of or pertaining to an organisation, demonstration, etc., which is against abortion and euthanasia.

**right-to-lifer** /raɪt-tə-ˈlaɪfə/, *n. Colloq.* a person who supports anti-abortion policies.

**right triangle** /raɪt ˈtraɪæŋgəl/, *n.* →**right-angled triangle.**

**right turn** /– ˈtɜn/, *interj.* **1.** (a military command to face to the right in a prescribed manner while standing). –*n.* **2.** the action itself.

**rightward** /ˈraɪtwəd/, *adv.* **1.** Also, **rightwards.** towards or on the right. –*adj.* **2.** situated on the right. **3.** directed towards the right.

**right whale** /ˈraɪt weɪl/, *n.* any of various large toothless whales, family Balaenidae, including those hunted commercially.

**right wing** /– ˈwɪŋ/, *n.* **1.** the members of a conservative or reactionary political party or section of a party, generally those opposing extensive political reform. **2.** such a group, party, or a group of such parties. **3.** *Sport.* that part of the field of play which forms the right flank of the area being attacked by either team. **4.** *Sport.* a player positioned on the right flank, as the outside right in soccer, the right of the wing-three-quarters in rugby football, etc. – **right-wing,** *adj.* – **right-winger,** *n.*

**rigid** /ˈrɪdʒəd/, *adj.* **1.** stiff or unyielding; not pliant or flexible; hard. **2.** firmly fixed, set, or not moving. **3.** inflexible, strict, or severe: *a rigid discipline or disciplinarian.* **4.** rigorously strict regarding opinion or observance. **5.** severely exact; rigorous: *a rigid examination.* **6.** *Aeron.* **a.** (of an airship or dirigible) having its form maintained by a rigid structure contained within the envelope. **b.** pertaining to a helicopter rotor which is fixedly held at its root. [L *rigidus*] – **rigidity** /rəˈdʒɪdəti/, **rigidness,** *n.* – **rigidly,** *adv.*

**rigmarole** /ˈrɪgməroʊl/, *n.* **1.** a succession of confused or foolish statements; incoherent or rambling discourse. **2.** a long and complicated process. [alteration of obs. *ragman roll* a roll, list, or catalogue, from *ragman,* in same sense (of obscure orig.) + ROLL]

**rigor** /ˈrɪgə/, *n. U.S.* →**rigour.**

**rigorism** /ˈrɪgərɪzəm/, *n.* **1.** extreme strictness. **2.** *Rom. Cath. Theol.* the theory that in doubtful cases of conscience the strict course is always to be followed. – **rigorist,** *n.* – **rigoristic** /rɪgəˈrɪstɪk/, *adj.*

**rigor mortis** /rɪgə ˈmɔtəs/, *n.* the stiffening of the body after death. [L: lit., stiffness of death]

**rigorous** /ˈrɪgərəs/, *adj.* **1.** characterised by rigour; rigidly severe or harsh, as persons, rules, discipline, etc.: *rigorous laws.* **2.** severely exact or rigidly accurate: *rigorous accuracy.* **3.** severe or sharp, as weather or climate. – **rigorously,** *adv.* – **rigorousness,** *n.*

**rigour** /ˈrɪgə/, *n.* **1.** strictness, severity, or harshness, as in dealing with persons. **2.** the full or extreme severity of laws, rules, etc.: *the rigour of the law.* **3.** severity of life; hardship. **4.** a severe or harsh act, circumstance, etc. **5.** severity of weather or climate, or an instance of this: *the rigours of winter.* **6.** *Pathol.* a sudden coldness, as that preceding certain fevers; a chill. **7.** stiffness or rigidity. Also, *U.S.,* **rigor.** [ME *rigour,* from OF, from L *rigor*]

**rig-out** /ˈrɪg-aʊt/, *n.* **1.** apparatus; equipment. **2.** dress; clothes, esp. when conspicuous.

**Rig-Veda** /rɪg-ˈveɪdə/, *n. Hinduism.* the Veda of Verses, or Psalms (totalling 1028), the oldest document among the sacred scriptures of the world's living religions dating not later than the second millennium B.C. See **Veda.** [Skt, from *ric* praise + *veda* knowledge]

**rika** /ˈrɪkə/, *n. N.Z.* →**ricker.**

**Riksmål** /ˈriksmoʊl/, *n.* Former name of **Bokmål.** [Norw.: state's speech]

**rile** /raɪl/, *v.t.,* **riled, riling.** *Colloq.* **1.** to irritate or vex. **2.** *U.S.* →**roil.** [var. of ROIL]

**rilievo** /rɪliˈeɪvoʊ/, *n., pl.* **-vi** /-vi/. →**relief** (defs 9 and 10). [It.: relief]

**rill¹** /rɪl/, *n.* a small rivulet or brook. [cf. D, Fris., and LG *ril,* G *Rille*]

**rill²** /rɪl/, *n.* any of certain long, narrow trenches or valleys observed on the surface of the moon. Also, **rille.** [G. See RILL¹]

**rillettes** /riˈjɛt/, *n. pl.* a preparation of small pieces of pork, cooked, cooled and pounded in a mortar. [F]

**rim** /rɪm/, *n., v.,* **rimmed, rimming.** –*n.* **1.** the outer edge, border, or margin, esp. of a circular object. **2.** any edge or margin, often a raised one. **3.** the circular part of a wheel, farthest from the axle. **4.** a circular strip of metal forming the connection between the wheel and tyre of a motor vehicle, and either permanently attached to or removable from the wheel. **5.** *Basketball.* the metal ring in front of the backboard from which the goal net is suspended. –*v.t.* **6.** to furnish with a rim, border, or margin. **7.** (of a ball) to roll round the edge of (a hole). [ME; OE *rima,* c. Icel. *rimi* raised strip of land, ridge]

**rime¹** /raɪm/, *n., v.t., v.i.,* **rimed, riming.** →**rhyme.**

**rime²** /raɪm/, *n., v.,* **rimed, riming.** –*n.* **1.** a rough, white icy covering deposited on trees, etc., somewhat resembling white frost, but formed only from fog or vapour-bearing air. –*v.t.* **2.** to cover with rime or hoar-frost. [ME; OE *hrīm,* c. D *rijm*]

**rimester** /ˈraɪmstə/, *n.* →**rhymester.**

**rim-fire** /ˈrɪm-faɪə/, *adj.* **1.** of or pertaining to a cartridge which has the explosive in a rim around the base. **2.** of or pertaining to a rifle designed to fire such cartridges.

**rimose** /raɪˈmoʊs/, *adj.* full of chinks or crevices. [L *rīmōsus* full of fissures]

**rimu** /ˈrimu/, *n.* a tall conifer, *Dacrydium cupressinum,* of New Zealand, having awl-shaped leaves; red pine. [Maori]

**rimy** /ˈraɪmi/, *adj.*, **rimier, rimiest.** covered with rime.

**rind** /raɪnd/, *n.* a thick and firm coat or covering, as of animals, plants, fruits, cheeses, etc. [ME and OE *rind(e),* c. G *Rinde*]

**rinderpest** /ˈrɪndəpɛst/, *n.* an acute, usu. fatal, infectious virus disease of cattle, sheep, etc., characterised by high fever, diarrhoea, lesions of the skin and mucous membranes, etc. [G: cattle pest]

**rinforzando** /ˌrɪnfɔtˈsændoʊ/, *adv.* **1.** (a musical direction) suddenly more loudly. *–adj.* **2.** suddenly louder. [It]

**ring**[1] /rɪŋ/, *n., v.,* **ringed, ringing.** *–n.* **1.** a circular band of metal or other material, esp. one of gold or other precious metal, often set with gems, for wearing on the finger as an ornament, a token of betrothal or marriage, etc. **2.** anything having the form of a circular band. **3.** a circular line or mark. **4.** a circular course: *to dance in a ring.* **5.** the outside edge of a circular body, as a wheel. **6.** a single turn in a spiral or helix or in a spiral course. **7.** *Geom.* the area or space between two concentric circles. **8.** one of the concentric layers of wood produced yearly in the trunks of exogenous trees. **9.** a circle of bark cut from around a tree. **10.** a number of persons or things placed in a circle. **11.** an enclosed circular or other area, as one in which some sport or exhibition takes place: *the ring of a circus.* **12.** an enclosure in which boxing and wrestling matches take place (usu. a square area marked off by stakes and ropes). **13.** the sport of boxing. **14.** a space devoted to betting at a racecourse, not necessarily circular in shape: *betting ring, ledger ring, paddock ring.* **15.** competition; contest: *to toss one's hat in the ring.* **16.** a group of persons cooperating for selfish or illegal purposes, as to control a business, monopolise a particular market, etc. **17.** *Chem.* a number of atoms so united that they may be graphically represented in cyclic form. **18.** **run rings round,** *Colloq.* to be markedly superior to; easily surpass. **19.** *Colloq.* anus. *–v.t.* **20.** to surround with a ring; encircle. **21.** to form into a ring. **22.** to put a ring in the nose of (an animal). **23.** to hem in (animals) by riding or circling about them. **24.** *Agric.* to remove wool from around the prepuce of rams and wethers to prevent fouling. **25.** to ringbark. **26.** to cut away the bark in a ring about (a tree, branch, etc.). **27.** (in ring toss games) to hurl a ring over (a stake or peg). **28.** **ring the board (shed),** to shear more sheep than anyone else in the shearing shed. *–v.i.* **29.** to form a ring or rings. **30.** to move in a ring or a constantly curving course. [ME; OE *hring,* c. D *ring,* G *Ring,* Icel. *hringr.* Cf. RANK[1]] – **ringlike,** *adj.*

**ring**[2] /rɪŋ/, *v.,* **rang, rung, ringing,** *n.* *–v.i.* **1.** to give forth a clear, resonant sound when set in sudden vibration by a blow or otherwise, as a bell, glass, etc. **2.** to seem (true, false, etc.) in the effect produced on the mind: *his words ring true.* **3.** to cause a bell or bells to sound, esp. as a summons: *ring for a messenger.* **4.** to sound loudly; be loud or resonant; resound. **5.** to be filled with sound; re-echo with sound, as a place. **6.** (of the ears) to have the sensation of a continued humming sound. *–v.t.* **7.** to cause to ring, as a bell, etc. **8.** to produce (sound) by or as if by ringing. **9.** to proclaim, usher in or out, summon, signal, etc., by or as by the sound of a bell. **10.** to test (coin, etc.) by the sound produced in striking on something. **11.** to telephone. *–v.* **12.** Some special verb phrases are:

**ring a bell,** to arouse a memory; sound familiar.

**ring down the curtain,** to give a direction to lower a theatre curtain, as at the end of a performance.

**ring down the curtain on,** to bring to an end.

**ring for,** to summon by ringing a bell.

**ring in, 1.** to announce the arrival of by ringing bells. **2.** to insert or substitute, often dishonestly.

**ring off,** to end a telephone conversation.

**ring out, 1.** to make a loud, resounding noise. **2.** to announce the departure of by ringing.

**ring the changes,** to vary the manner of performing an action; repeat in varying order.

**ring true,** to appear to be true, sincere, genuine, etc.

**ring up, 1.** to telephone. **2.** to record (the cost of an item) on a cash register.

**ring up the curtain,** to give a direction to raise a theatre curtain, as at the beginning of a performance.

**ring up the curtain on,** to begin; inaugurate.

*–n.* **13.** a ringing sound, as of a bell, etc.: *the ring of sleigh-bells.* **14.** a resonant sound or note: *there was a ring in his voice.* **15.** any loud sound; sound continued, repeated, or reverberated. **16.** a set or peal of bells. **17.** a telephone call: *give me a ring tomorrow.* **18.** an act of ringing a bell. **19.** a characteristic sound, as of a coin. **20.** a characteristic or inherent quality: *his words had the ring of truth.* [ME; OE *hringan,* c. Icel. *hringja,* G *ringen*]

**ringbark** /ˈrɪŋbak/, *v.t.* **1.** to cut away the bark in a ring around a tree trunk or branch, in order to kill the tree or the affected part. *–n.* **2.** a mark on a tree made by ringbarking. Also, **bark.** – **ringbarked,** *adj.*

**ringbolt** /ˈrɪŋboʊlt/, *n.* **1.** a bolt with a ring fitted in an eye at its head. *–v.i.* **2.** *N.Z. Colloq.* to stow away on a ship with the connivance of the crew.

**ringbone** /ˈrɪŋboʊn/, *n.* a morbid bony growth on the pastern bones of a horse, often resulting in lameness.

**ringcraft** /ˈrɪŋkraft/, *n.* a boxer's skill, particularly in moving around the ring.

**ring dollar** /ˈrɪŋ dɒlə/, *n.* →**holey dollar.**

**ringdove** /ˈrɪŋdʌv/, *n.* **1.** the European woodpigeon, *Columba palumbus,* with two whitish patches on the neck. **2.** Also, **ringed turtledove.** a small Old World pigeon, *Streptopelia risoria,* with a black half-ring around the neck.

**ringed** /rɪŋd/, *adj.* **1.** having or wearing a ring or rings. **2.** marked or decorated with a ring or rings. **3.** surrounded by a ring or rings. **4.** formed of or with rings; ringlike or annular.

**ringed sea-snake** /– ˈsi-sneɪk/, *n.* →**banded sea-snake.**

**ringent** /ˈrɪndʒənt/, *adj.* gaping. [L *ringens,* ppr.]

**ringer**[1] /ˈrɪŋə/, *n.* **1.** one who or that which rings, encircles, etc. **2.** a quoit or horseshoe so thrown as to encircle a peg. **3.** the throw itself. **4.** →**boxer. 5.** a station hand, esp. a stockman or drover. [RING[1] + -ER[1]]

**ringer**[2] /ˈrɪŋə/, *n.* **1.** one who or that which rings a bell, etc. **2.** *Colloq.* an athlete, horse, etc., entered in a competition under false representations as to identity or ability. **3.** Also, **dead ringer, dead ring.** a person or thing that closely resembles another: *he was a dead ringer for the local policeman.* [RING[2] + -ER[1]]

**ringer**[3] /ˈrɪŋə/, *n.* **1.** the fastest shearer of a group. **2.** any person of outstanding competence. [Brit. d. *ringer* anything superlatively good]

**ring finger** /ˈrɪŋ fɪŋgə/, *n.* the third finger of the left hand, on which engagement rings, wedding rings, etc., are usu. worn.

**ringgit** /ˈrɪŋgət/, *n.* the monetary unit of Malaysia, divided into 100 sens. [Malay]

**ringhals** /ˈrɪŋhæls/, *n.* a poisonous snake of southern Africa, *Hemachatus haemachutus,* characterised by the ability to spit its venom at its victim's eyes; spitting snake. Also, **ringhals cobra.**

**ringie** /ˈrɪŋi/, *n.* →**boxer** (def. 5). [RING(KEEPER) + -IE]

**ring-in** /ˈrɪŋ-ɪn/, *n. Colloq.* **1.** a person or thing substituted for another at the last moment. **2.** one belonging to a group only in appearance.

**ringing tone** /ˈrɪŋɪŋ toʊn/, *n.* a tone made by a telephone, indicating to the subscriber that the called number is ringing.

**ringkeeper** /ˈrɪŋkipə/, *n.* →**boxer** (def. 5).

**ringleader** /ˈrɪŋlidə/, *n.* one who leads others in opposition to authority, law, etc. [from phrase *to lead the ring* to be first]

**ringlet** /ˈrɪŋlət/, *n.* **1.** a small ring or circle. **2.** a curled lock of hair. – **ringleted** /ˈrɪŋlətəd/, *adj.*

**ring main** /ˈrɪŋ meɪn/, *n.* **1.** a method of distributing electricity in which the supply cables form a closed ring, thus localising supply failure. **2.** a similar system applied to the wiring of a house, factory, etc.

**ringmaster** /ˈrɪŋmastə/, *n.* one in charge of the performances in the ring of a circus.

**ringneck** /ˈrɪŋnɛk/, *n.* any of various birds having a ring of distinctive colour about the neck, as the ring-necked pheasant, the mallard, etc.

**ring-necked pheasant** /ˌrɪŋ-nɛkt ˈfɛzənt/, *n.* a gallinaceous Asiatic bird, *Phasianus colchicus,* now acclimatised esp. in Britain and the U.S.

**ringneck parrot** /ˌrɪŋnɛk ˈpærət/, *n.* a medium-sized parrot *Barnardius barnardi,* predominantly green with dark blue back, red forehead and a narrow yellow band at the neck, found in open inland areas of south-eastern Australia; buln buln.

**ring ouzel** /ˈrɪŋ uzəl/, *n.* an ouzel cock, *Turdus torquatus,* which breeds in northern Europe and migrates to Africa.

**ring-pull can** /ˌrɪŋ-pʊl ˈkæn/, *n.* a can or tin, frequently one containing a drink, which is opened by pulling a ring set into the top of the can.

**ring-road** /ˈrɪŋ-roʊd/, *n.* a road skirting a town or urban centre, used to relieve traffic congestion.

**ringside** /ˈrɪŋsaɪd/, *n.* **1.** the space immediately surrounding an arena, as the first row of seats round a boxing or wrestling ring. **2.** any place providing a close view. *–adj.* **3.** of or pertaining to the area immediately surrounding a ring or arena. **4.** close to the scene of action, or providing a close view.

ringtail possum

**ring-streaked** /ˈrɪŋ-strikt/, *adj.* having streaks or bands of colour round the body.

**ringtail** /ˈrɪŋteɪl/, *n.* **1.** →**ringtail possum.** **2.** *Naut.* a small sail, an extension to the spanker, set abaft it on an extended spanker boom.

**ringtail possum** /rɪŋteɪl ˈpɒsəm/, *n.* any of various species of possums, esp. of the genera *Pseudocheirus* and *Hemibelideus,* with a long tail, the prehensile tip of which is curled into a ring; found throughout Australia. Also, **ring-tailed possum.**

**ring tank** /ˈrɪŋ tæŋk/, *n.* a circular excavated tank in which the water is partly above, partly below the natural surface.

**ring-the-tin boycott** /ˌrɪŋ-ðə-tɪn ˈbɔɪkɒt/, *n.* a boycott imposed by trade-unionists whereby the victim of the boycott is ostracised both at work and in places of recreation.

**ring tin** /ˈrɪŋ tɪn/, *n.* a round pan with a tube-shaped centre for baking ring or angel food cakes.

**ringworm** /ˈrɪŋwɜm/, *n.* any of certain contagious skin diseases due to fungi and characterised by the formation of ring-shaped eruptive patches.

**rink** /rɪŋk/, *n.* **1.** a sheet of ice for skating, often one artificially prepared and under cover. **2.** a smooth floor for roller-skating. **3.** a building or enclosure containing a surface prepared for skating. **4.** an area of ice marked off for the game of curling. **5.** a section of a bowling green where a match can be played. **6.** a set of players on one side in bowling or curling. [orig. Scot.; ME *renk,* apparently from OF *renc* RANK[1]]

**rinse** /rɪns/, *v.,* **rinsed, rinsing,** *n.* *–v.t.* **1.** to wash lightly, as by pouring water into or over or by dipping in water. **2.** to put through clean water, as a final stage in cleansing. **3.** to remove (impurities, etc.) thus. *–n.* **4.** an act or instance of rinsing. **5.** a final application of water to remove impurities, unwanted substances, etc. **6.** the water or the like used. **7.** any liquid preparation used for impermanently tinting the hair. [ME *rynce* from OF *reincer,* from Rom. *recentiāre* make fresh, from L *recens* fresh, recent] – **rinser,** *n.*

**rinsing** /ˈrɪnsɪŋ/, *n.* **1.** the act of one who rinses. **2.** (*chiefly pl.*) the liquid with which anything has been rinsed.

**riot** /ˈraɪət/, *n.* **1.** any disturbance of the peace by an assembly of persons. **2.** *Law.* the execution of a violent and unlawful purpose by three or more persons acting together, to the terror of the people. **3.** violent or wild disorder or confusion. **4.** loose or wanton living; unrestrained revelry. **5.** an unbridled outbreak, as of emotions, passions, etc. **6.** a brilliant display: *a riot of colour.* **7.** *Colloq.* one who or that which causes great amusement, enthusiasm, etc. **8. run riot, a.** to act without control or restraint; disregard all limits. **b.** to grow luxuriantly or wildly. *–v.i.* **9.** to take part in a riot or disorderly public outbreak. **10.** to live in a loose or wanton manner; indulge in unrestrained revelry. **11.** to indulge unrestrainedly; run riot. **12.** *Hunting.* (of a hound) to follow the scent of an animal other than the intended quarry. *–v.t.* **13.** to spend (money, etc.) or pass (time, etc.) in riotous living (fol. by *away* or *out*). [ME, from OF *riote* debate, dispute, quarrel, from *r(u)ihoter* to quarrel, diminutive of *ruir* make an uproar, from L *rugīre* roar] – **rioter,** *n.*

**riotous** /ˈraɪətəs/, *adj.* **1.** characterised by or of the nature of rioting, or disturbance of the peace, as actions. **2.** inciting to or taking part in a riot, as persons. **3.** given to or marked by unrestrained revelry; loose; wanton. **4.** boisterous or uproarious: *riotous laughter.* – **riotously,** *adv.* – **riotousness,** *n.*

**rip**[1] /rɪp/, *v.,* **ripped, ripping,** *n.* *–v.t.* **1.** to cut or tear apart in a rough or vigorous manner; slash; slit. **2.** to cut or tear away in a rough or vigorous manner. **3.** to saw (wood) in the direction of the grain. **4.** Also, **rip up.** to scarify or scratch (the soil) without turning it over. *–v.i.* **5.** to become torn apart or split open. **6.** *Colloq.* to move along with violence or great speed. *–v.* **7.** Some special verb phrases are:

**let it rip,** to allow an engine, etc., to go as fast as possible by ceasing to check or control its speed.

**let rip, 1.** to give free rein to anger, passion, etc. **2.** to utter oaths; swear.

**rip in(to),** begin rapidly, eagerly: *let's rip into the housework.*

**rip off, 1.** to tear off violently. **2.** to overcharge; swindle.

**rip out, 1.** to remove forcibly or violently; wrench. **2.** to utter angrily; shout.

*–n.* **8.** a rent made by ripping; a tear. [late ME; c. Fris. *rippe,* Flem. *rippen* rip; akin to d. E *ripple,* v., scratch]

**rip**[2] /rɪp/, *n.* **1.** a disturbance in the sea caused by opposing currents or by a fast current passing over an uneven bottom. **2.** a fast current, esp. one at a beach which can take swimmers out to sea. **3.** →**rip-tide.** [see RIP[1], *v.,* RIPPLE[1]]

**rip**[3] /rɪp/, *n.* *Colloq.* **1.** a dissolute or worthless person. **2.** a worthless or worn-out horse. **3.** anything of little or no value. [OE *rypa,* var. of *reopa* bundle of corn, sheaf, akin to *rīpan* reap]

**R.I.P.** /ar aɪ ˈpi/, may he or she (or they) rest in peace. [L *requiescat* (or *requiescant*) *in pace*]

**riparian** /raɪˈpɛəriən/, *adj.* **1.** of, pertaining to, or situated or dwelling on the bank of a river or other body of water. *–n.* **2.** *Law.* one who owns land on the bank of a natural watercourse or body of water. [L *rīpārius* belonging to a river bank or shore + -AN]

**riparian right** /– ˈraɪt/, *n.* (*usu. pl.*) a right, as fishing or use of water for irrigation or power, enjoyed by one who owns riparian property.

**ripcord** /ˈrɪpkɔd/, *n.* **1.** a cord or ring which opens a parachute during a descent. **2.** a cord fastened in the bag of a balloon or dirigible so that a sharp pull upon it will rip or open the bag and let the gas escape, thus causing the balloon to descend rapidly.

**ripe** /raɪp/, *adj.,* **riper, ripest.** **1.** ready for reaping or gathering, as grain, fruits, etc.; complete in natural growth or development, as when arrived at the stage most fit for eating or use. **2.** resembling ripe fruit, as in ruddiness and fullness. **3.** fully grown or developed, as animals when ready to be killed and used for food. **4.** advanced to the point of being in the best condition for use, as cheese, beer, etc. **5.** malodorous: *a ripe old pipe.* **6.** arrived at the highest or a high point of development or excellence; mature. **7.** of mature judgment or knowledge. **8.** characterised by full development of body or mind: *of ripe years.* **9.** advanced in years: *a ripe old age.* **10.** ready for action, execution, etc. **11.** fully prepared or ready to do or undergo something, or for some action, purpose, or end. **12.** ready for some operation or process: *a ripe abscess.* **13.** (of time) fully or sufficiently advanced. **14.** *Colloq.* →**drunk.** **15.** *Colloq.* obscene or pertaining to obscenity. [ME and OE; c. D *riip,* G *reif;* akin to OE *ripan* reap] – **ripely,** *adv.* – **ripeness,** *n.*

**ripen** /ˈraɪpən/, *v.i.* **1.** to become ripe. **2.** to come to maturity, the proper condition, etc.; mature. *–v.t.* **3.** to make ripe. **4.** to bring to maturity. [ME *ripe(n),* OE *rīpian* (c. D *rijpen*), from *rīpe* RIPE] – **ripener,** *n.*

**ripieno** /rɪˈpjeɪnoʊ/, *n.* (in old use) the tutti of an orchestra as opposed to the soloists. [It.: full]

**rip-off** /ˈrɪp-ɒf/, *n.* an excessive charge or price; swindle.

**riposte** /rəˈpɒst/, *n., v.,* **-posted, -posting.** *–n.* **1.** *Fencing.* a quick thrust given after parrying a lunge. **2.** a quick, sharp return in speech or action. *–v.i.* **3.** to make a riposte. **4.** to reply or retaliate. Also, **ripost.** [F, from It. *risposta* response, from *rispondere* answer, from L *rēspondēre*]

**ripped** /rɪpt/, *adj.* **1.** torn. **2.** *Colloq.* heavily under the influence of drugs or alcohol; stoned.

**ripper** /ˈrɪpə/, *n.* **1.** one who or that which rips. **2.** an excavating device, usu. on the back of a bulldozer, used for breaking up rock. **3.** *Colloq.* something or someone exciting extreme admiration.

**ripping** /ˈrɪpɪŋ/, *adj.* **1.** that rips. **2.** *Colloq.* excellent, splendid, or fine.

**ripple**[1] /ˈrɪpəl/, *v.,* **-pled, -pling,** *n.* *–v.i.* **1.** to form small waves or undulations on the surface, as water when agitated by a gentle breeze or by running over a rocky bottom. **2.** to flow with a light ruffling of the surface. **3.** to form or have small undulations. **4.** (of sound) to go on or proceed with an effect like that of water flowing in ripples. *–v.t.* **5.** to form small waves or undulations on; agitate lightly. **6.** to mark as with ripples; give a wavy form to. *–n.* **7.** a small wave or undulation, as on water. **8.** any similar movement or appearance; a small undulation, as in hair. **9.** a ripple mark. **10.** a sound as of water flowing in ripples: *a ripple of laughter.* [orig. uncert.] – **ripplingly,** *adv.*

**ripple**[2] /ˈrɪpəl/, *n., v.,* **-pled, -pling.** *–n.* **1.** a toothed or comblike device for removing seeds or capsules from flax, etc. *–v.t.* **2.** to remove the seeds or capsules from (flax, etc.) with a ripple. [ME *rypel;* akin to G *Riffel*]

**ripple current** /ˈ– kʌrənt/, *n.* a variation in a direct current which has arisen from the fact that the current was derived from an alternating current.

**ripple mark** /ˈ– mak/, *n.* one of the wavy lines or ridges produced on sand, etc., by waves, wind, or the like.

**rippler** /ˈrɪplə/, *n.* **1.** one who ripples flax, etc. **2.** an instrument for rippling; ripple.

**ripplet** /ˈrɪplət/, *n.* a little ripple.

**ripply** /ˈrɪpli/, *adj.* **1.** characterised by ripples; rippling. **2.** sounding as rippling water.

**riprap** /ˈrɪpræp/, *n., v.,* **-rapped, -rapping.** *–n.* **1.** broken stones used for foundations, revetments, etc. **2.** a foundation or wall of stones thrown together irregularly. *–v.t.* **3.** to construct with or strengthen by stones, either loose or fastened with mortar. [varied reduplication of RAP[1]]

**rip-roaring** /ˈrɪp-rɔrɪŋ/, *adj. Colloq.* boisterous; riotous; wild and noisy: *to have a rip-roaring time.*

**ripsaw** /ˈrɪpsɔ/, *n.* a saw used for sawing timber with the grain. [RIP[1], *v.* + SAW[1]]

**ripsnorter** /ˈrɪpsnɔtə/, *n. Colloq.* a person or thing made remarkable by some outstanding characteristic, as great strength, excellence, liveliness, beauty, etc.

**rip-tide** /ˈrɪp-taɪd/, *n.* a fast-flowing tide such as might be associated with the formation of a rip. Also, **rip-current.**

**riroriro** /ˈrirouˌrirou/, *n.* the New Zealand grey warbler, *Gerygone igata;* rainbird. [Maori]

**rise** /raɪz/, *v.,* **rose, risen, rising,** *n.* *–v.i.* **1.** to get up from a lying, sitting, or kneeling posture; assume a standing position. **2.** to get up from bed: *to rise early.* **3.** to become erect and stiff, as the hair. **4.** to get up after falling or being thrown down. **5.** to become active in opposition or resistance; revolt or rebel. **6.** to be built up, erected, or constructed. **7.** to spring up or grow, as plants. **8.** to become prominent on a surface, as a blister. **9.** to come into existence; appear. **10.** to come into action, as a wind, storm, etc. **11.** to occur: *a quarrel rose between them.* **12.** to originate, issue, or be derived; to have its spring or source. **13.** to move from a lower to a higher position; move upwards; ascend: *a bird rises in the air.* **14.** to come above the horizon, as a heavenly body. **15.** to extend directly upwards: *the tower rises to the height of 20 metres.* **16.** to have an upward slant or curve: *the path rises as it approaches the house.* **17.** *Angling.* (of a fish) to come to the surface of the water to take bait, etc. **18.** to attain higher rank, importance, etc. **19.** to advance to a higher level of action, thought, feeling, expression, etc. **20.** to prove oneself equal to a demand, emergency, etc.: *to rise to the occasion.* **21.** to become animated or cheerful, as the spirits. **22.** to become stirred or roused: *to feel one's temper rising.* **23.** to increase in height, as water: *the river sometimes rose 10 metres in eight hours.* **24.** to swell or puff up, as dough from the action of yeast. **25.** to increase in amount, as prices, etc. **26.** to increase in price or value, as commodities. **27.** to increase in degree, intensity, or force, as colour, fever, etc. **28.** to become louder or of higher pitch, as the voice. **29.** to adjourn, or close a session, as a deliberative body or court. **30.** to return from the dead. *–v.t.* **31.** to cause to rise. **32.** *Naut.* to cause (something) to rise above the visible horizon by approaching nearer to (it); raise. *–n.* **33.** the act of rising; upward movement or ascent. **34.** appearance above the horizon, as of the sun or moon. **35.** elevation or advance in rank, position, fortune, etc.: *the rise and fall of ancient Rome.* **36.** an increase in height, as of water. **37.** the amount of such increase. **38.** an increase in amount, as of prices. **39.** an increase in price or value, as of commodities. **40.** an increase in amount, as of wages, salary, etc. **41.** the amount of such an increase. **42.** an increase in degree of intensity, as of temperature. **43.** an increase in loudness or in pitch, as of the voice. **44.** the vertical height of any of various things as a stair step, a flight of steps, a roof, an arch, the crown of a road, etc. **45.** origin, source, or beginning: *the rise of a stream in a mountain.* **46.** a coming into existence or notice. **47.** extension upwards. **48.** the amount of this. **49.** upward slope, as of ground or a road. **50.** a piece of rising or high ground. **51.** *Angling.* the movement of a fish to the surface of the water to take a bait. **52. get** or **take a rise out of,** to provoke to anger, annoyance, etc., by banter, mockery, deception, etc. **53. give rise to,** cause, produce. **54. make a rise,** *Colloq.* to be successful; gain prosperity. [ME; OE *rīsan,* c. D *rijzen,* G *reisen.* Cf. RAISE]

**riser** /ˈraɪzə/, *n.* **1.** one who rises, esp. from bed: *to be an early riser.* **2.** the vertical face of a stair step.

**risibility** /rɪzəˈbɪləti/, *n., pl.* **-ties.** **1.** ability or disposition to laugh. **2.** →**laughter.**

**risible** /ˈrɪzəbəl/, *adj.* **1.** having the faculty or power of laughing; inclined to laughter. **2.** pertaining to or connected with laughing. **3.** capable of exciting laughter; laughable or ludicrous. [LL *rīsibilis,* from L *rīsus,* pp., laughed at]

**rising** /ˈraɪzɪŋ/, *adj.* **1.** that rises; advancing, ascending, or mounting. **2.** growing, or advancing to adult years: *the rising generation.* *–adv.* **3.** almost; nearly; approaching the age of. *–n.* **4.** the act of one who or that which rises. **5.** an insurrection or revolt. **6.** something that rises; a projection or prominence. **7.** a period of leavening of dough preceding baking.

**rising damp** /– ˈdæmp/, *n.* dampness in the walls of a house seeping up from the foundations.

**risk** /rɪsk/, *n.* **1.** exposure to the chance of injury or loss; a hazard or dangerous chance: *to run risks.* **2.** *Insurance.* **a.** the hazard or chance of loss. **b.** the degree of probability of such loss. **c.** the amount which the insurance company may lose. **d.** a person or thing with reference to the risk involved in insuring him or it. **e.** the type of loss, as life, fire, marine, disaster, earthquake, etc., against which insurance policies are drawn. **3. no risk!** (an exclamation of reassurance or approval). *–v.t.* **4.** to expose to the chance of injury or loss, or hazard: *to risk one's life to save another.* **5.** to venture upon; take or run the risk of: *to risk a fall in climbing, to risk a battle.* [F *risque,* from It. *risc(hi)o,* from *risicare* to risk, dare, ? from Gk *rhīza* cliff, root (through meaning of to sail around a cliff)]

**risk capital** /ˈ– kæpətl/, *n.* capital invested or available for investment in an enterprise, esp. a speculative one.

**risky** /ˈrɪski/, *adj.,* **riskier, riskiest.** **1.** attended with or involving risk; hazardous: *a risky undertaking.* **2.** →**risqué.**

**risoluto** /rɪzəˈlutou/, *adv.* **1.** (a musical direction) in a resolute or determined manner. *–adj.* **2.** resolute. [It.]

**risotto** /rəˈsɒtou/, *n.* an Italian dish of rice fried in butter with onion, steamed in bouillon, flavoured with Parmesan cheese, and other flavourings. [It.]

**risqué** /ˈrɪskeɪ, rɪsˈkeɪ/, *adj.* daringly close to indelicacy or impropriety: *a risqué story.* [F, pp. of *risquer* RISK]

**rissole** /ˈrɪsoul/, *n.* a small fried ball, roll, or cake of minced meat or fish mixed with breadcrumbs, egg, etc., formerly enclosed in a thin envelope of pastry before frying. [F, ? from VL *russeola* (fem. adj.) reddish]

**rit.**, ritardando. Also, **ritard.**

**ritardando** /rɪtəˈdændoʊ/, *adv.* **1.** (a musical direction) gradually more slowly. *–adj.* **2.** becoming gradually slower. [It., gerund of *ritardare* RETARD]

**Ritchie board** /ˈrɪtʃi bɔd/, *n.* a notice board on which one forms words with detachable letters, often used as a room directory, etc. [Trademark]

**rite** /raɪt/, *n.* **1.** a formal or ceremonial act or procedure prescribed or customary in religious or other solemn use: *rites of baptism, sacrificial rites.* **2.** a particular form or system of religious or other ceremonial practice: *the Roman rite.* **3.** (*oft. cap.*) (historically) one of the versions of the Eucharistic service: *the Anglican rite.* **4.** (*oft. cap.*) →**liturgy.** **5.** (*sometimes cap.*) a division or differentiation of Eastern and Western Churches according to liturgy. **6.** any customary observance or practice. [ME, from L *rītus* ceremony]

**ritenuto** /rɪtəˈnjutoʊ/, *adv.* **1.** (a musical direction) more slowly. *–adj.* **2.** slower; held back. [It.]

**rite of passage,** *n.* a ritualised ceremony whereby a society marks a change in the status of a member, as at puberty, marriage, etc.

**ritornello** /rɪtɔˈnɛloʊ/, *n.* **1.** an orchestral interlude between sung sections of a song or aria, or between certain larger sections of a baroque opera. **2.** a passage for the full orchestra in a baroque concerto grosso. **3.** the recurring refrain of a rondo. [It., diminutive of *ritorno* a return]

**ritual** /ˈrɪtʃuəl/, *n.* **1.** an established or prescribed procedure, code, etc., for a religious or other rite. **2.** a form or system of religious or other rites. **3.** observance of set forms in public worship. **4.** a book of rites or ceremonies. **5.** a book containing the offices to be used by priests in administering the sacraments and for visitation of the sick, burial of the dead, etc. **6.** a ritual proceeding or service: *the ritual of the dead.* **7.** ritual acts or features collectively, as in religious services. **8.** any solemn or customary action, code of behaviour, etc., regulating social conduct. *–adj.* **9.** of the nature of, or practised as, a rite or rites: *a ritual dance.* **10.** of or pertaining to rites: *ritual laws.* [L *rītuālis*, adj.] – **ritually,** *adv.*

**ritualise** /ˈrɪtʃuəlaɪz/, *v.*, **-lised, -lising.** *–v.i.* **1.** to practise ritualism. *–v.t.* **2.** to convert or make into a ritual. **3.** to convert to ritualism. Also, **ritualize.**

**ritualism** /ˈrɪtʃuəlɪzəm/, *n.* **1.** adherence to or insistence on ritual. **2.** the study of ritual practices or religious rites. **3.** fondness for ritual.

**ritualist** /ˈrɪtʃuələst/, *n.* **1.** a student of or authority on ritual practices or religious rites. **2.** one who practises or advocates observance of ritual, as in religious services. – **ritualistic** /ˌrɪtʃuəˈlɪstɪk/, *adj.* – **ritualistically** /ˌrɪtʃuəˈlɪstɪkli/, *adv.*

**ritzy** /ˈrɪtsi/, *adj. Colloq.* luxurious, elegant. [after the *Ritz* Hotel, London, a luxurious hotel. See -Y[1]]

**riv.**, river.

**rivage** /ˈrɪvɪdʒ/, *n. Archaic.* a bank, shore, or coast. [ME, from OF, from *rive* bank, from L *rīpa.* See -AGE]

**rival** /ˈraɪvəl/, *n., adj., v.,* **-valled, -valling** or (*U.S.*) **-valed, -valing.** *–n.* **1.** one who is in pursuit of the same object as another, or strives to equal or outdo another; a competitor. **2.** one who or that which is in a position to dispute preeminence or superiority with another: *a theatre without a rival.* *–adj.* **3.** being a rival; competing or standing in rivalry: *rival suitors, rival business houses.* *–v.t.* **4.** to compete with in rivalry; strive to equal or outdo. **5.** to prove to be a worthy rival of: *he soon rivalled the others in skill.* **6.** to equal (something) as if in rivalry. *–v.i.* **7.** *Archaic.* to engage in rivalry; compete (*with*). [L *rīvālis*, orig., one living by or using the same stream as another]

**rivalry** /ˈraɪvəlri/, *n., pl.* **-ries.** the action, position, or relation of a rival or rivals; competition; emulation: *rivalry between Sydney and Melbourne.*

**rive** /raɪv/, *v.*, **rived, rived** or **riven, riving.** *–v.t.* **1.** to tear or rend apart. **2.** to strike asunder; split; cleave. **3.** to rend, harrow, or distress (the heart, etc.). *–v.i.* **4.** to become rent or split apart. [ME *rive(n)*, from Scand.; cf. Icel. *rīfa.* See RIFT]

**riven** /ˈrɪvən/, *v.* **1.** past participle of **rive.** *–adj.* **2.** rent or split apart.

**river**[1] /ˈrɪvə/, *n.* **1.** a considerable natural stream of water flowing in a definite course or channel or series of diverging and converging channels. **2.** a similar stream of something other than water. **3.** any abundant stream or copious flow: *rivers of lava, blood, etc.* **4. sell down the river,** *Colloq.* to betray; deceive. [ME, from OF *riv(i)ere,* from L *rīpa* bank]

**river**[2] /ˈraɪvə/, *n.* a person who rives. [RIVE + -ER[1]]

**river basin** /ˈrɪvə beɪsən/, *n.* the area drained by a river and its branches.

**riverbed** /ˈrɪvəbɛd/, *n.* the channel in which a river flows.

**river blackfish** /rɪvə ˈblækfɪʃ/, *n.* a medium-sized fish, *Gadopsis marmoratus,* found mainly in the Murray-Darling river system, which together with its Tasmanian relative, *G. tasmanicus,* constitute a family of fish unique to Australia.

**riverfront** /ˈrɪvəfrʌnt/, *n.* the bank of a river, esp. at a town site.

**rivergum** /ˈrɪvəgʌm/, *n.* →**river red gum.**

**riverhead** /ˈrɪvəhɛd/, *n.* the spring or source of a river.

**river-horse** /ˈrɪvə-hɔs/, *n.* →**hippopotamus.**

**riverine** /ˈrɪvəraɪn/, *adj.* **1.** of or pertaining to a river. **2.** situated or dwelling beside a river.

**river oak** /ˈrɪvər oʊk/, *n.* a tree, *Casuarina cunninghamiana,* found in eastern Australia where it lines river banks on the tablelands and western slopes.

**river red gum,** *n.* a large tree, *Eucalyptus camaldulensis,* with white smooth bark on the upper trunk and branches, found lining the banks of Australian inland rivers. Also, **rivergum.**

**riverside** /ˈrɪvəsaɪd/, *n.* **1.** the bank of a river. *–adj.* **2.** on the bank of a river.

**river wallaby** /ˈrɪvə ˌwɒləbi/, *n.* →**agile wallaby.**

**rivet** /ˈrɪvət/, *n.* **1.** a metal pin or bolt for passing through holes in two or more plates or pieces to hold them together, usu. made with a head at one end, the other end being hammered into a head after insertion. *–v.t.* **2.** to fasten with a rivet or rivets. **3.** to hammer or spread out the end of (a pin, etc.), in order to form a head and secure something; clinch. **4.** to fasten or fix firmly: *to stand riveted to the spot.* **5.** to hold (the eye, attention, etc.) firmly. [ME *ryvette,* from OF *rivet,* from *river* fix, clinch, from Rom. *rīpāre* make firm, come to shore, from L *rīpa* shore] – **riveter,** *n.*

**rivière** /rɪviˈɛə/, *n.* a necklace of diamonds or other gems, esp. in more than one string. [F: lit., river]

**rivulet** /ˈrɪvjələt/, *n.* a small stream; a streamlet; a brook. [earlier *rivolet,* from It. *rivoletto,* diminutive of *rivolo,* from L *rīvulus* small stream]

**riyal** /riˈjal/, *n.* a unit of currency in Saudi Arabia, Yemen and Dubai. [Ar., from Sp. *real* REAL[2]]

**RL,** Rugby League.

**rm,** room.

**R.M.,** Royal Mail.

**R.M.I.,** radio magnetic indicator.

**R.M.O.** /ar ɛm ˈoʊ/, resident medical officer.

**r.m.s.** /ar ɛm ˈɛs/, root mean square.

**Rn,** *Chem.* radon.

**RNA** /ar ɛn ˈeɪ/, *Biochem.* ribonucleic acid.

**R'n'B** /ar ən ˈbi/, rhythm and blues.

**RNZAF** /ar ɛn zɛd eɪ ˈɛf/, Royal New Zealand Air Force.

**R.N.Z.N.** /ar ɛn zɛd ˈɛn/, Royal New Zealand Navy.

**roach**[1] /roʊtʃ/, *n., pl.* **roaches,** (*esp. collectively*) **roach.** **1.** a European freshwater fish, *Rutilus rutilus,* of the carp family, introduced into Australia. **2.** any of various similar fishes, as the **golden shiner,** *Notemigonus crysoleucas,* of eastern North America. **3.** a freshwater sunfish, genus *Lepomis,* of eastern North America. [ME *roche,* from OF; orig. uncert.]

**roach**[2] /roʊtʃ/, *n.* →**cockroach.**

**roach**[3] /roʊtʃ/, *n. Colloq.* the butt of a marihuana cigarette. [orig. uncert.]

**roach**[4] /roʊtʃ/, *n.* the curvature at the foot or bottom of a square sail to give a clearance for the fore and aft stay which passes underneath it. [orig. uncert.]

**roach back** /ˈ– bæk/, *n.* an arched back.

**road** /roʊd/, *n.* **1.** a way, usu. open to the public for the passage of vehicles, persons, and animals. **2.** any street so called. **3.** the track on which vehicles, etc., pass, as opposed to the pavement. **4. a.** *U.S.* →**railway. b.** *Railways.* one of the tracks of a railway: *the train took the wrong road.* **5.** a way or course: *the road to peace.* **6.** (*oft. pl.*) a protected place near the shore where ships may ride at anchor. **7. one for the road,** *Colloq.* a final alcoholic drink consumed before setting out on a journey, returning home from a public house, etc. **8. on the road, a.** travelling, esp. as a salesman. **b.** on tour, as a theatrical company. **c.** (formerly of convicts) employed in road building. **9. take the road,** to set out (fol. by *for*). **10. take to the road, a.** to begin a journey. **b.** to become a tramp. **c.** *Obs.* to become a highwayman. [ME *rode,* OE *rād* a riding, journey on horseback (akin to *ridan* ride), c. G *Reede*]

**roadability** /roudəˈbɪləti/, *n.* a car's performance on roads.

**roadbed** /ˈroudbɛd/, *n.* **1.** the bed or foundation structure for the track of a railway. **2.** a layer of ballast directly beneath the sleepers of a railway track. **3.** the material of which a road is composed.

**roadblock** /ˈroudblɒk/, *n.* an obstruction placed across a road by police, soldiers, etc., to halt or slow down traffic for control or inspection, impede the progress of an enemy, etc.

**roadbook** /ˈroudbʊk/, *n.* a guide book for motorists, issued by motoring organisations, etc.

**road gang** /ˈroud gæŋ/, *n.* (formerly) a party of convicts, usu. in irons, employed in roadmaking.

**road-hog** /ˈroud-hɒg/, *n.* a motorist who drives without consideration for other road users.

**roadholding** /ˈroudhouldɪŋ/, *n.* **1.** the ability of a motor vehicle to grip the road esp. when driven fast or under difficult conditions. *–adj.* **2.** of or pertaining to this ability.

**roadhouse** /ˈroudhaus/, *n.* an inn, hotel, restaurant, etc., on a main road, esp. in a country district.

**roadie** /ˈroudi/, *n. Colloq.* a person associated with a pop group who arranges road transportation, sets up equipment, etc. Also, **road manager.**

**roadman** /ˈroudmæn/, *n.* one who repairs roads. Also, **road-mender** /ˈroudmɛndə/.

**road metal** /ˈroud mɛtl/, *n.* broken stone, etc., used for making roads.

**road party** /ˈ– pati/, *n.* (formerly) a party of convicts employed in road-making and paid for their labour.

**road rider** /ˈ– raɪdə/, *n.* a cyclist who races on ordinary roads.

**road-roller** /ˈroud-roulə/, *n.* a power-driven roller used for compacting roads.

**roadrunner** /ˈroudrʌnə/, *n.* →**chaparral cock.**

**road-sense** /ˈroud-sɛns/, *n.* the ability to use roads safely, as a motorist, pedestrian, dog, etc.

**road show** /ˈroud ʃou/, *n.* a public entertainment, esp. a popular band, which travels from town to town.

**roadside** /ˈroudsaɪd/, *n.* **1.** the side or border of the road; the wayside. *–adj.* **2.** on the side of a road.

**roadstead** /ˈroudstɛd/, *n. Naut.* →**road** (def. 6). [ROAD + STEAD]

**roadster** /ˈroudstə/, *n.* **1.** an open sports car, usu. for two persons. **2.** a horse for riding or driving on the road.

**road test** /ˈroud tɛst/, *n.* a test on a motor vehicle to gauge its performance on the open road.

**road-test** /ˈroud-tɛst/, *v.t.* to give (a vehicle) a road test.

**road toll** /ˈroud toul/, *n.* the tally of traffic accident deaths.

**road train** /ˈ– treɪn/, *n.* a group of articulated motor vehicles, used for transportation, esp. of cattle, and consisting of a prime mover and one or more trailers.

**roadway** /ˈroudweɪ/, *n.* **1.** a way used as a road; a road. **2.** the part of a road used by vehicles, etc.

**roadworthy** /ˈroudwɜði/, *adj.* (of a vehicle) fit for use on the roads. – **roadworthiness,** *n.*

**roam** /roum/, *v.i.* **1.** to walk, go, or travel about without fixed purpose or direction; ramble; wander; rove. *–v.t.* **2.** to wander over or through: *to roam the bush.* *–n.* **3.** the act of roaming; a ramble. [ME *romen;* orig. obscure] – **roamer,** *n.*

**roan** /roun/, *adj.* **1.** (chiefly of horses) of a sorrel, chestnut, or bay colour sprinkled with grey or white. **2.** prepared from roan (def. 4). *–n.* **3.** a roan horse or other animal. **4.** a soft, flexible sheepskin leather, used in bookbinding, often made in imitation of morocco. [ME, from F, from Sp. *roano,* from L *rāvidus* yellow-grey]

**roar** /rɔ/, *v.i.* **1.** to utter a loud, deep sound, esp. of excitement, distress, or anger. **2.** to laugh loudly or boisterously. **3.** to make a loud noise in breathing, as a horse. **4.** to make a loud noise or din, as thunder, cannon, waves, wind, etc. **5.** to function or move with a roar, as a vehicle: *the sports car roared away.* *–v.t.* **6.** to utter or express in a roar. **7.** to bring, put, make, etc. by roaring: *to roar oneself hoarse.* **8. roar (someone) up,** *Colloq.* to scold angrily or abuse. *–n.* **9.** the sound of roaring; a loud, deep sound, as of a person or persons, or of a lion or other large animal. **10.** a loud outburst of laughter. **11.** a loud noise, as of thunder, waves, etc.: *the roar of the surf.* [ME *rore(n),* OE *rārian,* c. G *röhren;* ult. orig. obscure] – **roarer,** *n.*

**roaring** /ˈrɔrɪŋ/, *n.* **1.** the act of one who or that which roars. **2.** a loud, deep cry or sound. **3.** *Vet. Sci.* a disease of horses causing them to make a loud noise in breathing under exertion. *–adj.* **4.** that roars, as a person, thunder, etc. **5.** *Colloq.* brisk or highly successful, as trade. **6.** characterised by noisy or boisterous behaviour; riotous.

**roaring forties** /– ˈfɔtiz/, *n.pl.* **1.** prevailing westerly winds of temperate latitudes (below 40°S) in oceans of the Southern Hemisphere. **2.** (*construed as sing.*) an area of ocean characterised by these winds.

**roast** /roust/, *v.t.* **1.** to bake (meat or other food) by dry heat, as in an oven. **2.** to prepare (meat or other food) for eating by direct exposure to dry heat, as on a spit. **3.** to brown by exposure to heat, as coffee. **4.** to embed in hot coals, embers, etc.; to cook. **5.** to heat (any material) more or less violently. **6.** to heat (an ore, etc.) with access of air, as to cause oxidation. **7.** to warm (oneself, etc.) at a hot fire. **8.** *Colloq.* to criticise, rebuke or ridicule severely. *–v.i.* **9.** to roast meat, etc. **10.** to undergo the process of becoming roasted. *–n.* **11.** a piece of roasted meat; roasted meat. **12.** a piece of meat for roasting. **13.** something that is roasted. **14.** the act or operation of roasting. **15.** *Colloq.* a severe criticism or rebuke. *–adj.* **16.** roasted: *roast beef.* [ME *roste(n),* from OF *rostir,* from Gmc; cf. D *roosten*]

**roaster** /ˈroustə/, *n.* **1.** a contrivance for roasting something. **2.** a pig, chicken, or other animal or article fit for roasting. **3.** one who or that which roasts.

**roasting** /ˈroustɪŋ/, *adj.* **1.** that roasts. **2.** exceedingly hot; scorching. *–n.* **3.** severe criticism.

**rob** /rɒb/, *v.,* **robbed, robbing.** *–v.t.* **1.** to deprive of something by unlawful force or threat of violence; steal from. **2.** to deprive of something legally belonging or due. **3.** to plunder or rifle (a house, etc.). **4.** to deprive of something unjustly or injuriously: *the shock robbed him of speech.* **5. rob Peter to pay Paul,** to benefit one person at the expense of another. *–v.i.* **6.** to commit or practise robbery. [ME *robbe(n),* from OF *robber,* from OHG *roubōn,* c. REAVE[1]]

**robalo** /ˈrɒbəlou, ˈroubə-/, *n., pl.* **-los,** (*esp. collectively*) **-lo.** any of the marine fishes constituting the family Centropomidae, esp. *Centropomus undecimalis,* a valuable food fish of warm and tropical waters. [Pg., from Catalan *elobarro,* from L *lupus* wolf]

**roband** /ˈrɒbənd, ˈroubənd/, *n.* a short piece of spun yarn or other material, used to secure a sail to a yard, gaff, or the like. Also, **robbin, robin.** [southern form answering to northern E *raband,* from D *rā* sailyard + *band* BAND[2]]

**robber** /ˈrɒbə/, *n.* one who robs.

**robber baron** /– ˈbærən/, *n.* a noble who robbed travellers passing through his lands.

**robber crab** /ˈ– kræb/, *n.* a large anomuran crab, *Birgus latro,* of the Indo-Pacific tropics, highly specialised to climb coconut palms for the meat of the nuts; coconut crab.

**robber fly** /ˈ– flaɪ/, *n.* any of the swift, often large, flies constituting the family Asilidae, that prey on other insects.

**robbery** /ˈrɒbəri/, *n., pl.* **-ries. 1.** the action or practice, or an instance, of robbing. **2.** *Law.* the felonious taking of the property of another from his person or in his immediate presence, against his will, by violence or intimidation. [ME *roberie,* from OF, from *rober* ROB]

**robbin** /ˈrɒbən/, *n. Naut.* →**roband.**

**robby** /ˈrɒbi/, *n.* a handsome tree of the Tweed and Richmond Rivers area of northern New South Wales, *Eugenia moorei,* with showy red flowers and large, rounded, cream-coloured fruit. Also, **durobby.**

**robe**[1] /roub/, *n., v.,* **robed, robing.** *–n.* **1.** a long, loose or flowing gown or outer garment worn by men or women, esp. for formal occasions; an official vestment, as of a judge. **2.** any long, loose garment: *a bathrobe.* **3.** a woman's gown or dress, esp. of a more elaborate kind. **4.** (*pl.*) apparel in general; dress; costume. *–v.t.* **5.** to clothe or invest in a robe or robes; dress or apparel. *–v.i.* **6.** to put on a robe. [ME, from OF: orig., spoil, booty. See ROB]

**robe**[2] /roub/, *n.* →**wardrobe.**

**robin** /ˈrɒbən/, *n.* **1.** any of various small Australian birds of the family Muscicapidae resembling European robins but more brightly and variously coloured as the **red-capped robin,** *Petroica goodenovii,* or the **yellow robin,** *Eopsaltria australis.* **2.** any of several small Old World birds having a red or reddish breast, esp. *Erithacus rubecula,* of Europe. **3.** a large American thrush, *Turdus migratorius,* with a chestnut-red breast and abdomen. **4.** *Naut.* →**roband.** [ME *Robyn,* from OF *Robin,* diminutive of *Robert* Robert]

**Robin Hood** /rɒbən ˈhʊd/, *n.* one who champions the poor or oppressed. [from *Robin Hood,* English outlaw of the 12th century, a popular hero in many ballads, who robbed the rich to give to the poor]

**robin redbreast** /rɒbən ˈrɛdbrɛst/, *n.* **1.** the scarlet robin of Australia, *Petroica multicolor.* **2.** →**robin** (defs 2 and 3).

**roble** /ˈroubleɪ/, *n.* **1.** a Californian white oak, *Quercus lobata.* **2.** any of several other trees, esp. of the oak and beech families. [Sp. and Pg., from L *rōbur* oak tree]

**roborant** /ˈrɒbərənt/, *Med.* *–adj.* **1.** strengthening. *–n.* **2.** →**tonic.** [L *rōborans,* ppr., strengthening]

**robot** /ˈroubɒt/, *n.* **1.** a manufactured or machine-made man. **2.** a merely mechanical being; an automaton. [first used in the play *R.U.R.* by Karel Capek, 1890-1938, Czech dramatist and novelist; apparently backformation from Czech *robotnik* serf] **– robotism,** *n.* **– robotistic** /roubəˈtɪstɪk/, *adj.*

**robust** /ˈroubʌst, rəˈbʌst/, *adj.* **1.** strong and healthy, hardy, or vigorous. **2.** strongly or stoutly built: *his robust frame.* **3.** suited to or requiring bodily strength or endurance. **4.** rough, rude, or boisterous. [L *rōbustus*] **– robustly,** *adv.* **– robustness,** *n.*

**robustious** /rəˈbʌstʃəs/, *adj.* **1.** rough, rude, or boisterous. **2.** robust, strong, or stout. **– robustiously,** *adv.*

**roc** /rɒk/, *n.* (in Arabian mythology) a bird of enormous size and strength. [Ar. *rukhkh,* probably from Pers.]

**rocaille** /rɒˈkaɪ/, *n.* a style of ornamentation based on the forms of shells and rocks characteristic of the rococo period. [F]

**rocambole** /ˈrɒkəmboul/, *n.* a European plant, *Allium scorodoprasum,* used like garlic. [F, from G *Rockenbolle,* lit., distaff bulb (from its shape)]

**Rochelle powder** /rəˈʃɛl paudə/, *n.* →**Seidlitz powder.**

**Rochelle salt** /ˈ– sɒlt/, *n.* a tartrate of sodium and potassium, used as a laxative. [named after (*La*) *Rochelle,* seaport in SW France]

Aboriginal rock engraving, Sydney area

**roche moutonnée** /rɒʃ mutəˈneɪ/, *n., pl.* **roches moutonnées** /rɒʃ mutəˈneɪ/. a knob or rock rounded and smoothed by glacial action. [F]

**rochet** /ˈrɒtʃət/, *n.* a vestment of linen or lawn, resembling a surplice, worn esp. by bishops and abbots. [ME, from OF, from *roc* outer garment, from Gmc; cf. OE *rocc* outer garment]

**rock**[1] /rɒk/, *n.* **1.** a large mass of stone forming an eminence, cliff, or the like. **2.** *Geol.* **a.** mineral matter of various composition, consolidated or unconsolidated, assembled in masses or considerable quantities in nature, as by the action of heat **(igneous rock)** or of water, air, or ice **(sedimentary rock),** or by the structural alteration of either of these two types by natural agencies of pressure and heat **(metamorphic rock).** **b.** a particular kind of such matter. **3.** stone in the mass. **4.** something resembling or suggesting a rock. **5.** a firm foundation or support: *the Lord is my rock.* **6.** a hard sweet made in various flavours, as peppermint, usu. long and cylindrical in shape. **7.** (*oft. cap.*) *Colloq.* a jewel, esp. a diamond. **8.** a stone of any size. **9. on the rocks, a.** on rocks, as a shipwrecked vessel. **b.** *Colloq.* into or in a state of disaster or ruin. **c.** (of drinks) with ice-cubes: *Scotch on the rocks.* **10. the Rock, a.** Ayers Rock. **b.** Gibraltar. [ME *rokk(e),* OE *-rocc,* from ML *rocca*] **– rocklike,** *adj.*

**rock**[2] /rɒk/, *v.i.* **1.** to move or sway to and fro or from side to side. **2.** to be moved or swayed powerfully with emotion, etc. **3.** *Mining.* to be rocked or panned with a rocker: *this ore rocks slowly.* **4.** to dance to rock'n'roll music. *–v.t.* **5.** to move or sway to and fro or from side to side, esp. gently and soothingly. **6.** to lull in security, hope, etc. **7.** to move or sway powerfully with emotion, etc. **8.** to shake or disturb violently. **9.** *Engraving.* to roughen the surface of (a copperplate) with a rocker preparatory to scraping a mezzotint. **10.** *Mining.* to pan with a cradle: *to rock gravel for gold.* **11. rock the boat,** *Colloq.* to cause a disturbance; make difficulties; raise awkward questions; threaten the status quo. *–n.* **12.** →**rock music.** **13.** →**rock'n'roll** (defs 1 and 2). *–adj.* **14.** of or pertaining to rock music. [ME *rocken,* OE *roccian,* c. MD *rocken;* akin to Icel. *rykkja* jerk]

**rock-and-roll** /rɒk-ən-ˈroul/, *n.* →**rock'n'roll.**

**rock-ape** /ˈrɒk-eɪp/, *n. Colloq.* (*derog.*) an oaf; idiot.

**rock-bass** /ˈrɒk-bæs/, *n.* an eastern North American fresh-water food fish, *Ambloplites rupestris,* of the sunfish family, Centrarchidae.

**rock beat** /ˈrɒk bit/, *n.* a musical rhythm on the second and fourth beats of a four beat measure.

**rock blackfish** /– ˈblækfɪʃ/, *n.* a fine sport fish, *Girella elevata,* found around rocks in estuaries and along the coast of south-eastern Australia; black drummer; pigfish.

**rock bottom** /– ˈbɒtəm/, *n.* the lowest level, esp. of fortune: *to touch rock bottom.*

**rock-bottom** /ˈrɒk-bɒtəm/, *adj.* at the lowest limit; extreme lowest: *rock-bottom prices.*

**rock-bound** /ˈrɒk-baund/, *adj.* hemmed in by rocks; rocky: *a rock-bound coast.*

**rock-cake** /ˈrɒk-keɪk/, *n.* a small cake with a rough surface, containing fruit and spice.

**rock chopper** /ˈrɒk tʃɒpə/, *n. Colloq.* a Roman Catholic. [from the initials *R.C.*]

**rock cod** /ˈ– kɒd/, *n.* **1.** a common marine fish, *Physiculus barbatus,* of southern Australian waters. **2.** any of a number of fishes of various families, usu. distinctively coloured or marked, inhabiting rocky offshore areas around the northern half of Australia, as the **black rock cod,** *Epinephelus damellii,* and the **red rock cod,** *Scorpaena cardinalis.*

**rock college** /– ˈkɒlɪdʒ/, *n. Colloq.* prison.

**rock-cress** /ˈrɒk-krɛs/, *n.* any of several small herbs of the genus *Arabis,* as the **alpine rock-cress,** *A. alpina,* a widespread arctic-alpine plant of the Northern Hemisphere.

**rock-crystal** /ˈrɒk-krɪstl/, *n.* transparent quartz, esp. of the colourless kind.

**rock-dove** /ˈrɒk-dʌv/, *n.* a European pigeon, *Columba livia,* from which most domestic pigeons have developed.

**rock engraving** /ˈrɒk ɛngreɪvɪŋ/, *n.* a figure, design, etc., engraved into a rock, usu. primitive in style and often of religious significance; petroglyph.

**rocker** /ˈrɒkə/, *n.* **1.** one of the curved pieces on which a cradle or a rocking chair rocks. **2.** a rocking chair. **3.** any of various devices that operate with a rocking motion. **4.** *Engraving.* a small steel plate with one curved and toothed edge for roughening a copperplate to make a mezzotint. **5.** *Mining.* →**cradle** (def. 9). **6.** the curve in an ice-skate blade. **7.** *Colloq.* a young person of the early 1960s, characterised by rough, unruly behaviour, who usu. wore leather clothing, had greased-back hair and rode a motorcycle. Cf. **mod** (def. 3). **8. off one's rocker,** *Colloq.* crazy; mad; demented: *you must be off your rocker to suggest such a thing.*

**rocker arm** /ˈrɒkər am/, *n.* a lever, usu. pivoted near its midpoint, used to transmit motion to a valve stem from a cam.

**rockery** /ˈrɒkəri/, *n., pl.* **-ries.** a mound of rocks and earth for growing ferns or other plants.

**rocket**[1] /ˈrɒkət/, *n.* **1.** *Aeron.* a structure propelled by a rocket engine, used for pyrotechnic effect, signalling, carrying a lifeline, propelling a warhead, launching spacecraft, etc. **2.** *Colloq.* a severe reprimand; reproof. **3.** a type of firework which shoots into the air and explodes forming coloured stars of light. *–v.i.* **4.** to move like a rocket. **5.** (of gamebirds) to fly straight up rapidly when flushed. **6.** to increase rapidly as prices, rents or the like. **7. go like a rocket,** *Colloq.* **a.** to move fast. **b.** (of a machine) to function well. [F *roquet,* or It *rocchetta,* apparently a diminutive of *rocca* ROCK[1] with reference to its shape]

**rocket**[2] /ˈrɒkət/, *n.* any of numerous plants of the family Cruciferae, esp. those belonging to the genera *Barbarea* and *Sisymbrium.* [F *roquette,* from Pr. *rouquetto,* from L *ērūca* kind of colewort]

**rocket base** /ˈ- beɪs/, *n.* an area in which military rockets are prepared for firing.

**rocket bomb** /ˈ- bɒm/, *n.* **1.** a bomb equipped with a rocket engine which increases its velocity after it has been dropped from an aircraft. **2.** any rocket-propelled explosive missile.

**rocket engine** /ˈ- ɛndʒən/, *n.* a reaction engine containing all the substances necessary for its operation and the combustion of its fuel. Also, **rocket motor.**

**rocket gun** /ˈ- gʌn/, *n.* any weapon which uses a rocket as a projectile, as a rocket launcher or bazooka.

**rocket-launcher** /ˈrɒkət-lɔntʃə/, *n.* a cylindrical weapon used by infantrymen to fire rockets capable of penetrating several centimetres of armour-plate.

**rocket propulsion** /ˈrɒkət prəpʌlʃən/, *n.* a type of reaction propulsion in which the thrust is generated by discharging matter contained within the vehicle.

**rocket range** /ˈ- reɪndʒ/, *n.* an area containing various instruments and equipment, over which rockets are flown for testing.

**rocketry** /ˈrɒkətri/, *n.* the science of rocket design, development, and flight.

**rock-fern** /ˈrɒk-fɜn/, *n.* a small fern, *Cheilanthes tenuifolia,* which has a very wide distribution in Australia, and is poisonous to stock.

**rockfest** /ˈrɒkfɛst/, *n.* a rock concert usu. given by several rock groups and lasting two or three days.

**Rock fever** /ˈrɒk fivə/, *n.* →**undulant fever.** [named after the *Rock* of Gibraltar, where it is prevalent]

**rockfish** /ˈrɒkfɪʃ/, *n., pl.* **-fishes,** *(esp. collectively)* **-fish. 1.** any of various fishes found about rocks. **2.** the striped bass, *Roccus saxatilis.* **3.** any of the shallow-water marine fish of the genus *Clinus* of southern Africa. **4.** any of the North Pacific marine fishes of the genus *Sebastodes.* **5.** any fish of the family Scorpaenidae.

**rock-flour** /ˈrɒk-flauə/, *n.* finely ground rock material produced when a glacier containing rocks abrades its bed. Also, **glacial meal.**

**rock-garden** /ˈrɒk-gadən/, *n.* **1.** a garden on rocky ground or among rocks, for the growing of alpine or other plants. **2.** a garden decorated with rocks of different varieties, colours, shapes, etc.

**rock group** /ˈrɒk grup/, *n.* a group (def. 10) which plays rock music.

**rock-hop** /ˈrɒk-hɒp/, *v.i.* **-hopped, -hopping.** *Colloq.* **1.** (in a sailing race) to sail very close inshore, risking running aground, to gain advantage. **2.** to fish from coastal rocks. **– rock-hopper,** *n.*

**rock hopper** /ˈrɒk hɒpə/, *n.* a small penguin, *Eudyptes crestatus,* with a short beak and a yellow crest on both sides of the head, found in New Zealand and the Antarctic.

**rock-hound** /ˈrɒk-haund/, *n. Colloq.* a geologist.

**rocking chair** /ˈrɒkɪŋ tʃɛə/, *n.* a chair mounted on rockers, or on springs, so as to permit a rocking back and forth.

**rocking horse** /ˈ- hɔs/, *n.* a toy horse, as of wood, mounted on rockers, on which children play.

**rockjumper** /ˈrɒkdʒʌmpə/, *n.* a bird found in rocky areas of southern Africa, *Chaetops frenatus,* which has black and white plumage, and is about the size of a thrush.

**rock lily** /ˈrɒk lɪli/, *n.* a widely cultivated epiphytic or rock orchid, *Dendrobium speciosum,* of eastern Australia, with numerous many-flowered racemes. Also, **rock orchid.**

**rockling** /ˈrɒklɪŋ/, *n.* **1.** a long, slim, marine fish, *Genypterus microstomus,* belonging to the family Ophidiidae, found in southern Australian waters. **2.** a related larger species *G. blacodes* of New Zealand. **3.** any species of fish of the genus *Mottella,* having barbels on their jaws.

**rockmelon** /ˈrɒkmɛlən/, *n.* **1.** the edible fruit of the melon *Cucumis melo* var. *cantalupensis,* having a hard, usu. ribbed and netted rind, and orange-coloured flesh; cantaloupe. **2.** any of several similar melons.

**rock music** /ˈrɒk mjuzɪk/, *n.* contemporary music which is derived basically from the blues, but which has incorporated aspects of country and western, jazz, gospel music and blue grass.

**rock'n'roll** /rɒk ən ˈroul/, *n.* **1.** a form of pop music of the 1950s which has a twelve bar blues form, and a heavily accented rhythm. **2.** a dance performed to this music, usu. with vigorous, exaggerated movements. *–adj.* **3.** of or pertaining to this music. Also, **rock-and-roll, rock-'n'-roll.**

**rock-oil** /ˈrɒk-ɔɪl/, *n.* →**petroleum** (def. 1).

**rock opera** /ˈrɒk ɒprə/, *n.* a form of opera, the music of which is in the rock idiom.

**rock orchid** /ˈ- ɔkəd/, *n.* →**rock lily.**

**rock oyster** /ˈ- ɔɪstə/, *n.* the oyster *Crassostrea commercialis,* which grows in clusters on rocks in estuaries and bays of the eastern Australian central coast.

**rock parakeet** /ˈ- ˌpærəkit/, *n.* one of the smaller Australian parrots, *Neophema petrophila,* which nests in rocky cliff faces.

**rock pebbler** /ˈ- pɛblə/, *n.* →**regent parrot.**

**rock-plant** /ˈrɒk-plænt/, *n.* any plant which grows among rocks, on rockeries, etc.

**rock possum** /ˈrɒk pɒsəm/, *n.* →**wogoit.**

**rock python** /ˈ- paɪθən/, *n.* →**amethystine python.**

**rock-rat** /ˈrɒk-ræt/, *n.* **1.** any of several Australian endemic rodents of genus *Zyzomys* found only in areas of rocky outcrops. **2.** a small rodent, *Petronys typicus,* of rocky areas of southern Africa.

**rockrose** /ˈrɒkrouz/, *n.* **1.** any plant of the genus *Cistus* or some allied genus, as *Helianthemum.* **2.** any plant of the family Cistaceae.

**rock-salt** /ˈrɒk-sɒlt/, *n.* a common salt (sodium chloride), occurring in extensive, irregular beds in rocklike masses.

**rockshaft** /ˈrɒkʃaft/, *n.* a shaft that rocks or oscillates on its journals instead of revolving, as the shaft of a bell or a pendulum, or a shaft operating the valves of a steam-engine.

**rock thrush** /ˈrɒk θrʌʃ/, *n.* **1.** a bird of the thrush family, *Monticola saxatilis,* of Europe. **2.** any other member of this genus.

**rock-wallaby** /ˈrɒk-wɒləbi/, *n.* any of a number of small wallabies of the genera *Petrogale* and *Peradorcas,* having long, cylindrical, hairy tails and thickly padded and roughened feet adapted for rocky environments.

**rock weed** /ˈrɒk wid/, *n.* any of the seaweeds which attach themselves to the rocks exposed at low tide.

**rock whiting** /ˈrɒk waɪtɪŋ/, *n.* →**herring cale.**

**rock-wool** /ˈrɒk-wul/, *n.* an insulating material consisting of wool-like fibres made from molten rock or slag by forcing a blast of steam through the liquid.

**rocky**[1] /ˈrɒki/, *adj.,* **rockier, rockiest. 1.** full of or abounding in rocks. **2.** consisting of rock. **3.** rocklike. **4.** firm as a rock. **5.** (of the heart, etc.) hard or unfeeling. [ROCK[1] + -Y[1]] **– rockiness,** *n.*

**rocky**[2] /ˈrɒki/, *adj.,* **rockier, rockiest. 1.** inclined to rock; tottering or shaky. **2.** unpleasantly uncertain. **3.** *Colloq.* weak; shaky; dizzy. [ROCK[2] + -Y[1]]

**Rocky Mountain goat,** *n.* a long-haired, white, goat-like, bovid ruminant, *Oreamnos montanus,* of the western North American mountains, having short black horns.

**Rocky Mountain spotted fever,** *n.* a disease of the typhus-rickettsia group characterised by high fever, pains in joints, bones, and muscles, and a cutaneous eruption, and caused by rickettsia transmitted by ticks. It was first found in the Rocky Mountains area, North America, but is now more widely distributed.

rococo

**rococo** /rəˈkoukou/, *n.* **1.** a style of art, architecture and decoration of the 18th century, popular esp. in France, evolved from baroque types and distinguished by its ornate use of scrolls and curves to achieve charming and pretty effects in ornamentation. *–adj.* **2.** in the rococo style. **3.** tastelessly or clumsily florid. **4.** antiquated. [F, said to be from *rocaille* rockwork, pebblework or shellwork, from *roc* ROCK[1]]

**rod** /rɒd/, *n.* **1.** a stick, wand, staff, shaft, or the like, of wood, metal, or other material. **2.** a straight, slender shoot or stem of any woody plant, whether growing upon or cut from the plant. **3.** a pole used in angling or fishing. **4.** a stick used to measure with. **5.** a linear measure in the imperial system, of $5\frac{1}{2}$ yards or $16\frac{1}{2}$ feet, equal to 5.0292 m. **6.** a square rod ($30\frac{1}{4}$ square yards or 25.29 $m^2$); a square perch or pole. **7.** *Bldg Trades.* a standard measure of brickwork, 272 square feet of a standard thickness of $1\frac{1}{2}$ bricks, or 306 cubic feet (approx. 8.66 $m^3$). **8.** a stick, or a bundle of sticks or switches bound together, used as an instrument of punishment. **9.** punishment or chastisement. **10.** a wand or staff carried as a symbol of office, authority, power, etc. **11.** authority; sway; tyrannical rule. **12.** *Colloq.* revolver; pistol. **13.** (in biblical use) an offshoot or branch of a family; a scion; a tribe. **14.** *Anat.* one of the rodlike cells in the retina of the eye which respond to dim light. **15.** *Bacteriol.* any microorganism which is neither spherical nor spiral, but elongated. **16.** an electrode, as in arc welding. **17.** a car. **18.** *Colloq.* the erect penis. [ME and OE *rodd;* appar. akin to Icel. *rudda* kind of club]

**rode** /roʊd/, *v.* past tense of **ride.**

**rodent** /ˈroʊdnt/, *adj.* **1.** belonging or pertaining to the Rodentia, the order of gnawing or nibbling mammals, that includes the mice, squirrels, beavers, etc. **2.** gnawing. *–n.* **3.** a rodent mammal. [L *rōdens,* ppr., gnawing]

**rodeo** /roʊˈdeɪoʊ, ˈroʊdioʊ/, *n., pl.* **-deos.** an exhibition of the skills of cowboys, riding horses, steers, etc., for public entertainment. [Sp.: cattle ring, from *rodear* go round, from *rueda* wheel, from L *rota*]

**rodomontade** /ˌrɒdəmɒnˈteɪd, -ˈtad/, *n., adj., v.,* **-taded, -tading.** *–n.* **1.** vainglorious boasting or bragging; pretentious, blustering talk. *–adj.* **2.** bragging. *–v.i.* **3.** to boast; brag; rant. [F, from It. *rodomontata*]

**rod pruning** /ˈrɒd prunɪŋ/, *n.* the pruning of the lateral growth of a grape vine to encourage heavier fruiting next season.

**rod-walloper** /ˈrɒd-wɒləpə/, *n. Colloq.* a male who masturbates.

**roe**[1] /roʊ/, *n.* **1.** the mass of eggs, or spawn, within the ovarian membrane of the female fish (**hard roe**). **2.** the milt or sperm of the male fish (**soft roe**). [ME *row(e),* c. OHG *rogo*]

**roe**[2] /roʊ/, *n., pl.* **roes,** (*esp. collectively*) **roe.** →**roedeer.** [ME *roo,* OE *rā,* earlier *rāha,* c. G *Reh*]

**roebuck** /ˈroʊbʌk/, *n.* a male roedeer.

**roedeer** /ˈroʊdɪə/, *n.* a small, agile deer, *Capreolus capreolus,* of Europe and parts of Asia, the mature male of which has three-pointed antlers. [OE *rāhdēor.* See ROE[2], DEER]

roedeer

**roentgen** /ˈrɜntgən/, *n.* a non-SI unit of measurement of exposure to ionising radiation equal to $0.258 \times 10^{-3}$ coulombs per kilogram. *Symbol:* R [named after W. K. *Roentgen,* 1845-1923, German physicist who discovered X-rays in 1895]

**roentgenise** /ˈrɜntgənaɪz/, *v.t.,* **-nised, -nising.** to subject to the action of roentgen rays. Also, **roentgenize.**

**roentgenogram** /ˈrɜntgənəgræm/, *n.* →**radiograph.** Also, **roentgenograph** /ˈrɜntgənəgræf, -graf/.

**roentgenology** /rɜntgəˈnɒlədʒi/, *n.* →**radiology.**

**roentgenoparent** /ˌrɜntgənoʊˈpærənt/, *adj.* visible in roentgen rays.

**roentgen ray** /ˈrɜntgən reɪ/, *n.* →**X-ray.**

**rogation** /roʊˈgeɪʃən/, *n.* (*usu. pl.*) *Eccles.* solemn supplication, esp. as chanted during procession on the three days **(Rogation Days)** before Ascension Day. [ME *rogacio(u)n,* from L *rogātio*]

**rogatory** /ˈrɒgətəri, -tri/, *adj.* pertaining to asking or requesting: *a rogatory commission.* [ML *rogātōrius,* from L *rogātor* asker, solicitor]

**roger**[1] /ˈrɒdʒə/, *interj.* **1.** message received and understood (used in signalling and telecommunications). **2.** (an expression of agreement, comprehension, etc.). *–v.i.* **3.** to express assent or agreement to (fol. by *on*). [*Roger* (personal name) used in telecommunications as a name for *r,* used as an abbrev. for *received*]

**roger**[2] /ˈrɒdʒə/, *Colloq. –n.* **1.** (*sometimes cap.*) the penis, esp. when erect. *–v.t.* **2.** (of a man) to have sexual intercourse with. [? from *Roger* (personal name)]

**rogue** /roʊg/, *n., v.,* **rogued, roguing.** *–n.* **1.** a dishonest person. **2.** a playfully mischievous person; rascal; scamp. **3.** a vagrant or vagabond. **4.** an elephant or other animal of savage disposition and solitary life. **5.** *Biol.* an individual varying markedly from the normal, usu. inferior. *–v.i.* **6.** to live or act like a rogue. *–v.t.* **7.** to cheat. **8.** to uproot or destroy, as plants which do not conform to a desired standard. **9.** to perform this operation upon: *to rogue a field.* [apparently short for obs. *roger* begging vagabond, b. ROAMER and BEGGAR]

**roguery** /ˈroʊgəri/, *n., pl.* **-gueries.** **1.** roguish conduct; rascality. **2.** a rascally act; playful mischief.

**rogues' gallery** /roʊgz ˈgæləri/, *n.* **1.** a collection of portraits of criminals, as at a police station. **2.** *Colloq.* any collection of portraits resembling this.

**rogue's march** /– ˈmatʃ/, *n.* derisive music played to accompany a person's expulsion from a regiment, community, etc.

**roguish** /ˈroʊgɪʃ/, *adj.* **1.** pertaining to, characteristic of, or acting like a rogue; knavish or rascally. **2.** playfully mischievous: *a roguish smile.* – **roguishly,** *adv.* – **roguishness,** *n.*

**roil** /rɔɪl/, *v.t.* **1.** to render (water, etc.) turbid by stirring up sediment. **2.** to disturb or disquiet; irritate; vex. [obs. F *ruiler* mix up mortar, from OF *rieule* mason's formboard, from L *rēgula* rule]

**roily** /ˈrɔɪli/, *adj.* turbid; muddy.

**roister** /ˈrɔɪstə/, *v.i.* **1.** to act in a swaggering, boisterous, or uproarious manner. **2.** to revel noisily or without restraint. [v. use of *roister,* n., from F *ru(i)stre* ruffian, boor, from *ru(i)ste* RUSTIC, *n.*] – **roisterer,** *n.* – **roisterous,** *adj.*

**role** /roʊl/, *n.* **1.** the part or character which an actor presents in a play. **2.** proper or customary function: *the teacher's role in society.* Also, **rôle.** [F: properly, the roll (as of paper) containing an actor's part]

**role-playing** /ˈroʊl-pleɪɪŋ/, *n.* **1.** the subconscious adoption of attitudes manifested in behaviour patterns commonly associated with a certain status or function in a social unit. **2.** the deliberate assumption of such behaviour patterns, either in an informal context, or in teaching, counselling, etc.

**roll** /roʊl/, *v.i.* **1.** to move along a surface by turning over and over, as a ball or a wheel. **2.** to move or be moved on wheels, as a vehicle or its occupants (oft. fol. by *along*). **3.** to move onwards or advance in a stream or with an undulating motion, as water, waves, or smoke. **4.** to extend in undulations, as land. **5.** to move (fol. by *on,* etc.) or pass (oft. fol. by *away,* etc.), as time. **6.** to move (fol. by *round*) as in a cycle, as seasons. **7.** to perform a periodical revolution in an orbit, as a heavenly body. **8.** to continue with or have a deep, prolonged sound, as thunder, etc. **9.** to turn over, or over and over, as a person or animal lying down. **10.** *Colloq.* to luxuriate or abound (in wealth, etc.). **11.** to turn round in different directions, as the eyes in their sockets. **12.** to sway or rock from side to side, as a ship (opposed to *pitch*). **13.** to sail with a rolling motion. **14.** to walk with a rolling or swaying gait. **15.** (of a rocket or guided missile) to rotate about its longitudinal axis in flight. **16.** to form into a roll, or curl up from itself. **17.** to admit of being rolled up, as a material. **18.** to spread out from being rolled up; unroll (fol. by *out,* etc.). **19.** to spread out as under a roller. **20.** *Colloq.* to cast dice. *–v.t.* **21.** to cause to move along a surface by turning over and over, as a cask, a ball, or a hoop. **22.** to move along on wheels or rollers; to convey in a wheeled vehicle. **23.** to drive, impel, or cause to flow onwards with a sweeping motion. **24.** to utter or give forth with a full, flowing, continuous sound. **25.** to trill: *to roll one's r's.* **26.**

to cause to turn over, or over and over. **27.** to cause to turn round in different directions, as the eyes. **28.** to cause to sway or rock from side to side, as a ship. **29.** to wrap round an axis, round upon itself, or into a roll, ball, or the like. **30.** to make by forming a roll: *to roll a cigarette.* **31.** to spread out from being rolled up; unroll (fol. by *out*, etc.). **32.** to wrap, enfold, or envelope, as in some covering. **33.** to operate upon with a roller or rollers, as to spread out, level, compact, or the like, with a rolling pin, etc. **34.** to beat (a drum) with rapid, continuous strokes. **35.** to cast (dice). **36.** *Print.* to apply ink to with a roller or series of rollers. **37.** *Colloq.* to rob a person, often with violence. **38.** to defeat; overcome. **39. roll up, a.** to form a roll. **b.** *Colloq.* to arrive. **c.** *Colloq.* to gather round. **40. roll in, a.** to arrive. **b.** *Colloq.* to retire to bed. **c.** *Hockey.* to return the ball to play after it has crossed the sideline by rolling it back on to the pitch. **41. roll over,** *Colloq.* (of a politician) to resign gracefully. *–n.* **42.** a piece of parchment, paper, or the like, as for writing, etc., which is or may be rolled up; a scroll. **43.** a list, register, or catalogue. **44.** a list containing the names of the persons belonging to any company, class, society, etc. **45.** anything rolled up in cylindrical form. **46.** a number of papers or the like rolled up together. **47.** a quantity of cloth, wallpaper, or the like, rolled up in cylindrical form (often forming a definite measure). **48.** a cylindrical or rounded mass of something: *rolls of fat.* **49.** some article of cylindrical or rounded form, as a moulding. **50.** a cylindrical piece upon which something is rolled along to facilitate moving. **51.** a cylinder upon which something is rolled up, as plastic food wrap, etc. **52.** a roller with which something is spread out, levelled, crushed, compacted, or the like. **53.** thin sponge spread with jam, cream, or the like and rolled up. **54.** a small cake of bread, originally and still often rolled or doubled on itself before baking. **55.** pastry spread with apple, jam, etc., and doubled on itself before baking. **56.** food which is rolled up. **57.** meat rolled up and cooked. **58.** the act or an instance of rolling. **59.** undulation of surface: *the roll of a prairie.* **60.** sonorous or rhythmical flow of words. **61.** a deep, prolonged sound, as of thunder, etc.: *the deep roll of a breaking wave.* **62.** the trill of certain birds. **63.** the continuous sound of a drum rapidly beaten. **64.** a rolling motion, as of a ship. **65.** a rolling or swaying gait. **66.** *Aeron.* a single complete rotation of an aeroplane around the axis of the fuselage with little loss of altitude or change of direction. **67.** the rotation of a rocket or guided missile or the like about its longitudinal axis. **68.** *Athletics.* a style used by competitors in the high jump and pole vault where the body is rolled over the bar in a near horizontal position. **69.** a single throw of dice. **70.** *Colloq.* a wad of paper currency. **71.** *Colloq.* any amount of money. **72.** *Colloq.* the sexual act. [ME *roll(en)*, from OF *roller*, from L *rotula*, diminutive of *rota* wheel] – **rollable,** *adj.*

**roll bar** /'– ba/, *n.* a metal bar fastened as a safety feature over the top of some vehicles, as a sports car, for protection in the event of the car's overturning.

**roll cage** /'– keɪdʒ/, *n.* a simple framework made from metal tubing and built into a car, preventing the occupants from being crushed in the event of the car's turning over.

**rollcall** /'roʊlkɔl/, *n.* **1.** the calling of a list of names, as of soldiers or students, to find out who is absent. **2.** a military signal for this, as one given by a drum.

**roll-collar** /roʊl-'kɒlə/, *n.* **1.** a coat collar that rolls over in a continuous fold to the front fastening. **2.** a loose collar on a woman's garment doubled over and fastening at the back. **3.** a soft collar on a man's shirt which forms a roll over the tie instead of lying flat.

**rolled beef** /roʊld 'bif/, *n.* any flat section of boneless meat rolled and tied so as to be suitable for roasting.

**rolled gold** /– 'goʊld/, *n.* metal covered with a thin coating of gold.

**rolled oats** /– 'oʊts/, *n.* a breakfast cereal made from oat grains that have been treated with heat while passing them through rollers.

**rolled roast** /– 'roʊst/, *n.* a piece of beef, or other meat, boned, rolled, and tied, for roasting.

**rolled steel joist,** *n.* a steel bar rolled into one of various cross-sections in standard sizes for structural use. *Abbrev.:* R.S.J.

**roller** /'roʊlə/, *n.* **1.** one who or that which rolls. **2.** a cylinder, wheel, or the like, upon which something is rolled along. **3.** a cylindrical body, revolving on a fixed axis, esp. one to facilitate the movement of something passed over or around it. **4.** a cylindrical body upon which cloth or other material is rolled up. **5.** a cylinder of plastic, wire, etc., around which hair is rolled to set it. **6.** a cylindrical body for rolling over something to be spread out, levelled, crushed, compacted, impressed, linked, etc. **7.** a device used for applying paint, consisting of a cylinder covered with lamb's wool, felt, or the like, and having a handle. **8.** any of various other revolving cylindrical bodies, as the barrel of a musical box. **9.** *Cycling.* a device consisting of two sets of rollers, usu. linked to a time or distance recorder, on which a cyclist may pedal his machine without its moving forward. **10.** a long, swelling wave advancing steadily. **11.** *Shearing.* a shed hand who skirts and rolls fleeces. **12.** a rolled bandage. **13.** *Ornith.* **a.** Also, **broad-billed roller.** →**dollar bird. b.** any of the non-passerine birds constituting the family Coraciidae, esp. the common roller, *Coracias garrulus.* **c.** a variety of canary, remarkable for rolling or trilling.

**roller-bearing** /roʊlə-'bɛərɪŋ/, *n.* a bearing in which the shaft or journal turns upon a number of steel rollers running in an annular track.

**roller-coaster** /'roʊlə-koʊstə/, *n.* **1.** →**big dipper.** *–adj.* **2.** experiencing severe fluctuations in direction or momentum, and apparently proceeding without control: *a roller-coaster economy.* Also, *U.S.,* **coaster.**

**roller derby** /'roʊlə dabi/, *n.* a race on roller skates around a short closed circuit in which aggression between contestants is usu. tolerated.

**roller-mill** /'roʊlə-mɪl/, *n.* any mill which pulverises or otherwise changes material by passing it between rollers.

**roller race** /'roʊlə reɪs/, *n.* a race in which cyclists ride against each other on rollers.

**roller-skate** /'roʊlə-skeɪt/, *n., v.,* **-skated, -skating.** *–n.* **1.** a form of skate running on small wheels or rollers, for use on a smooth floor, footpath, etc. *–v.i.* **2.** to move on roller-skates.

**roller-towel** /roʊlə-'taʊəl/, *n.* a long towel sewn together at the ends and hung on a roller.

**roll film** /'roʊl fɪlm/, *n.* a rolled strip of sensitised film for taking successive still pictures.

**rollick** /'rɒlɪk/, *v.i.* to move or act in a careless, frolicsome manner; behave in a free, hearty, gay, or jovial way. [b. ROMP and FROLIC]

**rollicking** /'rɒlɪkɪŋ/, *adj.* swaggering and jolly: *a pair of rollicking drunken sailors.* Also, **rollicksome** /'rɒlɪksəm/.

**rollie** /'roʊli/, *n.* →**roll-your-own.**

**roll-in** /'roʊl-ɪn/, *n.* (in hockey) the act of rolling in.

**rolling** /'roʊlɪŋ/, *n.* **1.** the action, motion, or sound of anything that rolls. *–adj.* **2.** that rolls. **3.** rising and falling in gentle slopes, as land. **4.** moving in undulating billows, as clouds or waves. **5.** rocking or swaying from side to side. **6.** turning or folding over, as a collar. **7.** producing a deep, continuous sound. **8.** *Colloq.* drunk. **9.** Also, **rolling in money, rolling in it.** *Colloq.* very rich.

**rolling ban** /– 'bæn/, *n.* a rolling strike in which the employees refuse to use or handle certain materials or goods.

**rolling hitch** /'– hɪtʃ/, *n.* a kind of hitch which is made round a spar or the like with the end of a rope, and which jams when the rope is pulled.

**rolling mill** /'– mɪl/, *n.* **1.** a mill or establishment where (heated) iron or other metal is rolled into sheets, bars, or the like. **2.** a machine or set of rollers for rolling out or shaping metal, etc.

**rolling pin** /'– pɪn/, *n.* a cylinder of wood or other material for rolling out pastry, etc.

**rolling stock** /'– stɒk/, *n.* the wheeled vehicles of a railway, including engines and carriages.

**rolling stone** /– 'stoʊn/, *n.* a wanderer; an itinerant; a person without ties or fixed address.

**rolling strike** /– 'straɪk/, *n.* industrial action by employees against their employer in which groups of employees go on strike consecutively.

**rollmop** /'roʊlmɒp/, *n.* a marinated fillet of herring wrapped around a gherkin, pickled cucumber or onion, and served as an hors d'oeuvre. [G *rollmops,* from *rollen* to roll + *mops* simpleton, pugnosed dog]

**rollneck** /'roʊlnɛk/, *adj.* →**polo-neck.**

**roll of honour,** *n.* the list of those who are in some way distinguished and honoured, esp. those who have fought for their country. Also, **honour roll.**

**roll-on** /'roʊl-ɒn/, *n.* **1.** a woman's elastic foundation garment without fastenings; a girdle; step-in. *–adj.* **2.** of or pertaining to a liquid deodorant, perfume, etc., applied from a bottle which has a rotating ball in the neck opening.

**roll-on roll-off** /ˌroʊl-ɒn 'roʊl-ɒf/, *adj.* **1.** of or pertaining to cargo, usu. containerised, and designed to be driven onto ships, trains, etc., and driven off on arrival without the use of cranes. **2.** of or pertaining to systems of transport which offer this facility.

**roll-ons** /'roʊl-ɒns/, *n. Colloq.* →**step-ins.**

**roll-over provision** /'roʊl-oʊvə prəˌvɪʒən/, *n.* an agreement made between a borrower and lender in which each guarantees to renew a loan, when it matures, at a rate of interest based on the ruling rate of interest at the time of renewal.

**Rolls Royce** /roʊlz 'rɔɪs/, *n.* the best of its type: *this is the Rolls Royce of tape recorders.* [Trademark of a car noted for its excellence in design and performance]

**roll stationery** /'roʊl steɪʃənri/, *n.* continuous stationery in the form of rolls of paper.

**roll-top** /'roʊl-tɒp/, *adj.* fitted with a slatted cover, that rolls up: *a roll-top desk.*

**roll-up** /'roʊl-ʌp/, *n.* **1.** an assembly, gathering. **2.** the number of people attending such a meeting.

**rollway** /'roʊlweɪ/, *n. U.S.* **1.** a place on which things are rolled or moved on rollers. **2.** a place where logs are rolled into a stream for transportation. **3.** a pile of logs at the side of a stream awaiting transportation.

**roll-your-own** /'roʊl-jər-oʊn/, *n.* **1.** Also, **rollie.** a hand rolled cigarette. *–adj.* **2.** of or pertaining to a hand-rolled cigarette.

**roly-poly** /ˌroʊli-'poʊli/, *adj., n., pl.* **-lies.** *–adj.* **1.** plump and podgy, as a person, a young animal, etc. *–n.* **2.** a roly-poly person or thing. **3.** a strip of suet-crust pastry spread with jam, fruit, or the like, or sometimes with a savoury mixture, rolled up, wrapped in greaseproof paper, and steamed or boiled as a pudding. **4.** any of several bushy plants, as *Salsola kali,* which break loose and roll in the wind. [earlier *rowle powle,* by reduplication]

**rom.,** roman type.

**Rom.,** **1.** Roman. **2.** Romance. **3.** Romanic. **4.** *Bible.* Romans.

**Romaic** /roʊ'meɪɪk/, *n.* **1.** Modern Greek. *–adj.* **2.** of or pertaining to modern Greece, its inhabitants, or their language. [Gk *Rhōmaïkós* Roman, used of the Eastern empire]

**romaine** /roʊ'meɪn/, *n.* a fine woven fabric in plain dyes used as a lining or, when printed, used for dress goods.

**roman** /roʊ'mɒn/, *n.* **1.** a metrical narrative, esp. in medieval French literature. **2.** a novel. [F]

**Roman** /'roʊmən/, *adj.* **1.** of or pertaining to Rome, ancient or modern, or its inhabitants. **2.** of a kind or character regarded as typical of the ancient Romans. **3.** (*usu. l.c.*) designating or pertaining to the upright style of printing types most commonly used in modern books, etc. **4.** denoting or pertaining to the alphabet employed by the Romans for the writing of Latin and since adopted with modifications and additions for writing western European and other languages. **5.** denoting or pertaining to the Roman numerals. **6.** of, pertaining to, or resembling the Roman architecture. **7.** of or pertaining to the Roman Catholic Church. *–n.* **8.** a native, inhabitant, or citizen of ancient or modern Rome. **9.** the dialect of Italian spoken in Rome. **10.** (*usu. l.c.*) roman type or letters. **11.** *Colloq.* a member of the Roman Catholic Church. [OE, from L *Rōmānus;* replacing ME *Romain,* from OF]

**roman à clef** /roʊˌmɒn a 'kleɪ/, *n.* a novel in which actual persons and events are disguised as fiction. [F: lit., novel with a key]

**Roman arch** /roʊmən 'atʃ/, *n.* a semicircular arch.

**Roman architecture** /– 'akətɛktʃə/, *n.* the architecture of the ancient Romans, characterised by rational design and planning, the use of vaulting and concrete masonry, and the use of the classical orders only sporadically for purposes of architectural articulation and decoration.

**Roman calendar** /– 'kæləndə/, *n.* the ancient Roman calendar, the ancestor of present-day calendars.

**Roman candle** /– 'kændl/, *n.* a kind of firework consisting of a tube which sends out a shower of sparks.

**Roman Catholic** /– 'kæθlɪk/, *adj.* **1.** of or pertaining to the Roman Catholic Church. *–n.* **2.** a member of the Roman Catholic Church.

**Roman Catholic Church,** *n.* the Christian Church of which the pope, or bishop of Rome, is the supreme head.

**Roman Catholicism** /roʊmən kə'θɒləsɪzəm/, *n.* the faith, practice, membership, and government of the Roman Catholic Church.

**romance**[1] /rə'mæns, 'roʊmæns/, *n.;* /rə'mæns/, *v.,* **-manced, -mancing,** *adj.* *–n.* **1.** a tale depicting heroic or marvellous achievements, colourful events or scenes, chivalrous devotion, unusual, even supernatural, experiences, or other matters of a kind to appeal to the imagination. **2.** the world, life, or conditions depicted in such tales. **3.** a medieval tale, originally one in verse and in some Romance dialect, treating of heroic personages or events: *the Arthurian romances.* **4.** a made-up story; fanciful or extravagant invention or exaggeration. **5.** romantic spirit or sentiment. **6.** romantic character or quality. **7.** a romantic affair or experience; a love affair. *–v.i.* **8.** to invent or relate romances; indulge in fanciful or extravagant stories. **9.** to think or talk romantically. *–adj.* **10.** (*cap.*) pertaining to the Romance languages. [ME *romanz,* from OF, from VL *Rōmānicē,* adv., in Romance (i.e., in one of the Romance languages), from L *rōmānicus* Romanic] **– romancer,** *n.*

**romance**[2] /rə'mæns/, *n.* **1.** *Music.* a short, simple melody, vocal or instrumental, of tender character. **2.** *Spanish Lit.* a short epic narrative poem; historical ballad. [F, from Sp.: kind of poem, ballad, from OF *romanz.* See ROMANCE[1]]

**Romance language** /'– læŋgwɪdʒ/, *n.* any of the group of languages which have developed out of Latin, in their historical or modern forms, principally, Sardinian, Dalmatian (extinct), Rumanian, Italian, Rhaeto-Romanic, French, Provençal, Catalan, Spanish, and Portuguese. [OF: from the phrase *langue romance* (now *langue romane*), lit., Romantic language]

**Roman Empire** /roʊmən 'ɛmpaɪə/, *n.* **1.** the lands and peoples subject to the authority of ancient Rome. **2.** the form of government established in ancient Rome in 27 B.C., comprising the Principate or Early Empire (27 B.C. to A.D. 284) and the Autocracy or Later Empire (A.D. 284-476). **3.** a later empire, as that of Charlemagne or the Byzantine Empire, regarded as a restoration or continuation of the ancient Roman empire or one of its branches.

**Romanesque** /roʊmə'nɛsk/, *adj.* **1.** denoting or pertaining to the style of architecture which, developing from earlier medieval and Near Eastern types, prevailed in western and southern Europe from the late 10th until the 12th and 13th centuries, characterised by the rich outline of the exterior (towers), the clear organisation of the interior (bays), heavy walls, small windows, and the use of open timber roofs and groin, barrel, or rib vaults. **2.** denoting or pertaining to the corresponding styles of sculpture, ornament, and painting. **3.** (*l.c.*) of or pertaining to fanciful or extravagant literature, as romance or fable; fanciful. *–n.* **4.** the Romanesque style of art or architecture. [ROMAN + -ESQUE. Cf. F *romanesque* romantic]

**Romania** /rə'meɪniə/, *n.* a republic in south-eastern Europe, bordering on the Black Sea. Also, **Rumania.**

**Romanian** /roʊ'meɪniən, rə-/, *adj.* **1.** of Romania, its inhabitants, or their language. *–n.* **2.** a native or inhabitant of Romania. **3.** the language of Romania (a Romance language). Also, **Rumanian.**

**Romanic** /roʊ'mænɪk, rə-/, *adj.* **1.** derived from the Romans. **2.** pertaining to the Romance languages. *–n.* **3.** Romance language. [L *Rōmānicus* (def. 1)]

**Romanise** /'roʊmənaɪz/, *v.,* **-nised, -nising.** *–v.t.* **1.** to render Roman Catholic. **2.** to make Roman in character. *–v.i.* **3.** to conform to Roman Catholic doctrine, etc.; become Roman

Catholic. **4.** to follow Roman practices. Also, **Romanize.** – **Romanisation** /ˌroʊmənaɪˈzeɪʃən/, *n.*

**Romanism** /ˈroʊmənɪzəm/, *n.* (*usu. derog.*) Roman Catholicism.

**Romanist** /ˈroʊmənəst/, *n.* **1.** a member of the Roman Catholic Church. **2.** one versed in Roman institutions, law, etc. **3.** (*usu. derog.*) a member of a Church, esp. the Church of England, who has a liking for the ritual of the Roman Catholic Church.

**Roman law** /roʊmən ˈlɔ/, *n.* the system of jurisprudence elaborated by the ancient Romans, forming the basis of civil law in many countries.

**Roman nettle** /– ˈnɛtl/, *n.* an annual or biennial herb, *Urtica pilulifera,* with minute green female flowers in dense spherical heads.

**Roman nose** /– ˈnoʊz/, *n.* a nose having a prominent upper part or bridge. – **Roman-nosed,** *adj.*

**Roman numerals** /– ˈnjumərəlz/, *n.pl.* the numerals in the ancient Roman system of notation, still used for certain limited purposes. The common basic symbols are I(=1), V(=5), X(=10), L(=50), C(=100), D(=500), and M(=1000). Integers are written according to these two rules: if a letter is immediately followed by one of equal or lesser value, the two values are added, thus, XX equals 20, XV equals 15, VI equals 6; if a letter is immediately followed by one of greater value, however, the first is subtracted from the second, thus IV equals 4, XL equals 40, CM equals 900. Examples: XLVII(= 47), CXVI(= 116), MCXX(= 1120), MCMXIV(= 1914). The Roman numerals for one to nine are: I, II, III, IV, V, VI, VII, VIII, IX. Roman numerals are usu. written in capital letters, but may be in lower case. A bar over a letter multiplies it by 1000, thus $\overline{X}$ equals 10 000.

**romano** /rəˈmanoʊ/, *n.* a hard, pale yellow cheese, with a dry and granular texture, and a full, sharp flavour, made in cylindrical shapes of about 20 kg in weight. [It.: Roman]

**Roman rite** /roʊmən ˈraɪt/, *n.* the form in which mass is today most generally said and sung in the Roman Catholic Church, originating in the liturgy of the early Church at Rome.

**Romansh** /roʊˈmænʃ/, *n.* **1.** a Rhaeto-Romanic language spoken in the Swiss canton Grisons. It has equal standing with German, French, and Italian as one of the official languages of Switzerland. **2.** Rhaeto-Romanic in general. *–adj.* **3.** of or pertaining to Romansh. Also, **Romansch.** [Rhaeto-Romanic: ROMANIC]

**romantic** /rəˈmæntɪk/, *adj.* **1.** of, pertaining to, or of the nature of romance; characteristic or suggestive of the world of romance: *a romantic adventure.* **2.** proper to romance rather than to real or practical life; fanciful; unpractical; quixotic: *romantic ideas.* **3.** imbued with or dominated by the ideas, spirit, or sentiment prevailing in romance. **4.** displaying or expressing love, emotion, strong affection, etc. **5.** (*sometimes cap.*) of or pertaining to a style of literature, art, and music of the late 18th and the 19th centuries characterised by freedom of treatment, subordination of form to matter, imagination, experimentation with form, picturesqueness, etc. (opposed to *classical*). **6.** imaginary, fictitious, or fabulous. *–n.* **7.** a romantic person. **8.** a romanticist. **9.** (*pl.*) romantic ideas, ways, etc. [F *romantique,* from *romant* older form of *roman* romance, novel. See ROMANCE[1]] – **romantically,** *adv.*

**romanticise** /rəˈmæntəsaɪz/, *v.,* **-cised, -cising.** *–v.t.* **1.** to make romantic; invest with a romantic character: *she romanticised her work as an actress.* *–v.i.* **2.** to have romantic ideas; indulge in romance. Also, **romanticize.**

**romanticism** /rəˈmæntəsɪzəm/, *n.* **1.** romantic spirit or tendency. **2.** the romantic style or movement in literature and art, or adherence to its principles (as contrasted with *classicism*).

**romanticist** /rəˈmæntəsəst/, *n.* an adherent of romanticism in literature, art, etc.

**Romany** /ˈrɒməni/, *n., pl.* **-nies,** *adj.* *–n.* **1.** a Gipsy. **2.** Gipsies collectively. **3.** the Indic language of the Gipsies, its various forms differing greatly because of local influences. *–adj.* **4.** pertaining to Gipsies, their language, or customs. Also, **Rommany.** [Gipsy *Romain,* fem. and pl. of *Romano,* adj., from *Rom* Gipsy, man, husband]

**romaunt** /rəˈmɒnt/, *n. Archaic.* a romance, or romantic poem or tale. [AF, var. of OF *romant* ROMANCE[1]]

**Rom. Cath.,** Roman Catholic.

**Rom. Cath. Ch.,** Roman Catholic Church.

**Romeo** /ˈroʊmioʊ/, *n.* any man who behaves amorously or romantically. [from *Romeo,* the romantic hero in the play *Romeo and Juliet* by William Shakespeare, 1564-1616, English poet and dramatist]

**Romish** /ˈroʊmɪʃ/, *adj.* (*oft. derog.*) of or pertaining to Rome as the centre of the Roman Catholic Church; Roman Catholic.

**Rommany** /ˈrɒməni/, *n., pl.* **-nies,** *adj.* →**Romany.**

**Romney** /ˈrɒmni/, *n.* a breed of sheep suitable for high rainfall areas, having long wool, and developed as a dual-purpose sheep. Also, **Romney Marsh.** [from *Romney Marsh,* district in SW England]

**romp** /rɒmp/, *v.i.* **1.** to play or frolic in a lively or boisterous manner. **2.** to run or go rapidly and without effort, as in racing. **3. romp home** or **in,** to win easily. *–n.* **4.** a romping frolic. **5.** a swift, effortless pace. [var. of obs. *ramp* rough woman, lit., one who ramps. See RAMP, *v.*]

**rompers** /ˈrɒmpəz/, *n.pl.* a one-piece loose outer garment for a baby combining a sleeveless top and short or long trousers; crawlers. Also, **romper suit.**

**romper suit** /ˈrɒmpə sut/, *n.* →**rompers.**

**rompish** /ˈrɒmpɪʃ/, *adj.* given to romping. – **rompishness,** *n.*

**rondavel** /ˈrɒndəvɛl/, *n.* a circular one-roomed building or dwelling, usu. having a thatched roof, common in southern Africa. [Afrikaans *rondawel;* orig. obscure]

**ronde** /rɒnd/, *n.* a typeface imitative of upright angular handwriting. [F: n. use of fem. of *rond* ROUND]

**rondeau** /ˈrɒndoʊ/, *n., pl.* **-deaux** /-doʊ, -doʊz/. a short poem of fixed form, consisting of thirteen (or ten) lines on two rhymes and having the opening words or phrase used in two places as an unrhymed refrain. [see RONDEL]

**rondel** /ˈrɒndl/, *n.* a short poem of fixed form, consisting usually of fourteen lines on two rhymes, of which four are made up of the initial couplet repeated in the middle and at the end (the second line of the couplet sometimes being omitted at the end). [ME *rondeal,* from OF *rondel, rondeau,* diminutive of *rond* round]

**rondo** /ˈrɒndoʊ/, *n., pl.* **-dos.** a musical work or movement, often the last movement of a sonata, having one principal subject which is stated at least three times in the same key and to which return is made after the introduction of each subordinate theme. [It., from F *rondeau.* See RONDEL]

**roneo** /ˈroʊnioʊ/, *v.t.* to make a copy or copies of by cutting a stencil and duplicating it on a fluid-containing copier. [Trademark]

**roo** /ru/, *n. Colloq.* →**kangaroo**[1].

**roo bar** /ˈ– ba/, *n.* →**bull-bar.**

**rood** /rud/, *n.* **1.** a crucifix, esp. a large one at the entrance to the choir or chancel of a medieval church, often supported on a rood beam or rood screen. **2.** *Archaic.* the cross on which Christ died. **3.** a cross as used in crucifixion. **4.** a unit of length in the imperial system varying locally from $5\frac{1}{2}$ to 8 yards. **5.** a unit of land measure in the imperial system, equal to 40 square rods or $\frac{1}{4}$ acre (approx. 1011.714 $m^2$). *Symbol:* rd **6.** a unit of 1 square rod, or thereabouts. [ME; OE *rōd,* akin to G *Rute.* See ROD]

**rood beam** /ˈ– bim/, *n.* a beam extending across the entrance to the choir or chancel of a church to support the rood, and usu. forming the head of a rood screen.

**rood loft** /ˈ– lɒft/, *n.* a loft or gallery over a rood screen.

**rood screen** /ˈ– skrin/, *n.* a screen, often of elaborate design, and properly surmounted by a rood, separating the nave from the choir or chancel of a church.

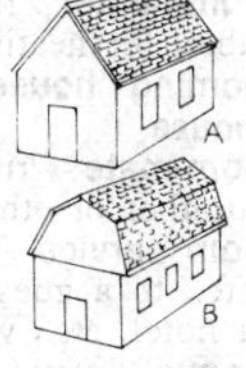

types of roofs: A, saddle or ridge; B, gambrel

**roof** /ruf/, *n., pl.* **roofs** /rufs, ruvz/. **1.** the external upper covering of a house or other building. **2.** a house. **3.** the highest part or summit. **4.** something which in form or position resembles the roof of a house, as the top of a car, the upper part of the mouth etc. **5. hit the roof,** *Colloq.* become very

i = peat ɪ = pit ɛ = pet æ = pat a = part ɒ = pot ʌ = putt ɔ = port ʊ = put u = pool ɜ = pert ə = apart aɪ = buy eɪ = bay ɔɪ = boy aʊ = how oʊ = hoe ɪə = here ɛə = hair ʊə = tour g = give θ = thin ð = then ʃ = show ʒ = measure tʃ = choke dʒ = joke ŋ = sing j = you õ = Fr. bon

angry; lose one's temper. **6. raise the roof, a.** to create a loud noise. **b.** to make loud protests or complaints. **7. under one's roof,** in one's family circle; in one's home. **8. without a roof,** without shelter of any kind. *–v.t.* **9.** to provide or cover with a roof. **10.** *Colloq.* to kick or punch in the mouth. [ME; OE *hrōf,* c. D *roef* cover, cabin]

**roofboard** /ˈrufbɔd/, *n.* a board forming part of a layer sometimes used to cover the rafters of a house under the tiles.

**roofer** /ˈrufə/, *n.* one who makes or repairs roofs.

**roof garden** /ˈruf ˌgadn/, *n.* **1.** a garden on the flat roof of a house or other building. **2.** the top, or top storey, of a building, having a garden, restaurant, or the like. Also, **rooftop garden.**

**roofguard** /ˈrufgad/, *n.* a guard of boards fixed just above the eaves of a roof to prevent snow sliding off. Also, **snowguard.**

**roofing** /ˈrufɪŋ/, *n.* **1.** the act of covering with a roof. **2.** material for roofs. **3.** a roof.

**roofing felt** /ˈ– fɛlt/, *n.* sheets of matted fibres as asbestos, flax, etc., treated with coal tar, bitumen, or pitch, and generally used for waterproofing roofs.

**roofless** /ˈrufləs/, *adj.* **1.** having no roof. **2.** without the shelter of a house; homeless.

**roof-rack** /ˈruf-ræk/, *n.* a system of bars attached to the roof of a car and used for the carriage of luggage, etc. Also, **luggage-rack.**

**rooftop** /ˈruftɒp/, *n.* the outer part of the roof of a building.

**rooftop garden** /ˈ– gadn/, *n.* →**roof garden.**

**rooftree** /ˈruftri/, *n.* **1.** the ridgepole of a roof. **2.** the roof itself.

**rook**[1] /rʊk/, *n.* **1.** a black European crow, *Corvus frugilegus,* of a gregarious disposition and given to nesting in colonies in trees about buildings. **2.** a sharper, as at cards or dice; a swindler. *–v.t.* **3.** to cheat; fleece; swindle. [ME *roke,* OE *hrōc,* c. D *roek,* Icel. *hrōkr*]

**rook**[2] /rʊk/, *n.* a chess piece having the power to move any unobstructed distance in a straight line forwards, backwards, or sideways; a castle. [ME *rok,* from OF, from Pers. *rukhkh*]

**rookery** /ˈrʊkəri/, *n., pl.* **-ries. 1.** a colony of rooks. **2.** a place where rooks congregate to breed. **3.** a breeding place or colony of other birds or animals, as penguins, seals, etc. **4.** any instance of cheating, sharp practice, exorbitant prices, etc.

**rookie** /ˈrʊki/, *n. Colloq.* a raw recruit, originally in the army, and hence in any service, sporting team, etc. Also, **rooky.**

**room** /rum/, *n.* **1.** a portion of space within a building or other structure, separated by walls or partitions from other parts: *a dining room.* **2.** (*pl.*) lodgings or quarters, as in a house or building. **3.** the persons present in a room: *the whole room laughed.* **4.** space, or extent of space, occupied by or available for something: *the desk takes up too much room.* **5.** opportunity or scope for or to do something: *room for improvement.* **6. no room to swing a cat,** *Colloq.* confined, cramped or cluttered place. **7. room to move,** scope to manoeuvre; options or choices. **8. the smallest room,** *Colloq.* a toilet or bathroom. *–v.i.* **9.** to occupy a room or rooms; to share a room; lodge. **10. room in,** of a mother in a maternity hospital, to sleep in the same room as her baby. [ME *roume,* OE *rum,* c. D *ruim,* G *Raum*]

**roomer** /ˈrumə/, *n. U.S.* →**lodger.**

**roomette** /ruˈmɛt/, *n. U.S.* a private sleeping compartment on a train.

**roomful** /ˈrumfʊl/, *n., pl.* **-fuls.** an amount or number sufficient to fill a room.

**room-heater** /ˈrum-hitə/, *n.* any device, often small and portable, for heating a room.

**rooming house** /ˈrumɪŋ haʊs/, *n. Chiefly U.S.* →**lodging house.**

**room-mate** /ˈrum-meɪt/, *n.* one who shares a room with another or others.

**room service** /ˈrum sɜvəs/, *n.* **1.** the serving of food, drinks, etc., to a guest at a hotel, etc., in his room. **2.** the staff at a hotel, etc., which renders this service.

**roomy** /ˈrumi/, *adj.,* **-mier, -miest.** affording ample room; spacious; large. **– roomily,** *adv.* **– roominess,** *n.*

**roop** /rup/, *n. Vet. Sci.* →**roup.**

**roost** /rust/, *n.* **1.** a perch upon which domestic fowls rest at night. **2.** a house or place for fowls or birds to roost in. **3.** a place for sitting, resting, or staying. **4. rule the roost,** to be in charge; dominate. *–v.i.* **5.** to sit or rest on a roost, perch, etc. **6.** to settle or stay, esp. for the night. **7. come home to roost,** to come back upon the originator; recoil. [ME *rooste,* OE *hrōst,* c. MD and Flem. *roest*]

**rooster** /ˈrustə/, *n.* a domestic cock. [ROOST + -ER[1]]

**root**[1] /rut/, *n.* **1.** a part of the body of a plant which, typically, develops from the radicle, and grows downwards into the soil, fixing the plant and absorbing nutriment and moisture. **2.** a similar organ developed from some other part of the plant, as one of those by which ivy clings to its support. **3.** any underground part of a plant, as a rhizome. **4.** something resembling or suggesting the root of a plant in position or function. **5.** the embedded or basal portion of a hair, tooth, nail, etc. **6.** the fundamental or essential part: *the root of a matter.* **7.** the source or origin of a thing: *love of money is the root of all evil.* **8.** the base or point of origin of something. **9.** a person or family as the source of offspring or descendants. **10.** an offshoot or scion. **11.** (*pl.*) **a.** a person's real home and environment: *though he's lived in the city for ten years his roots are still in the country.* **b.** those elements, as personal relationships, a liking for the area, customs, etc., which make a place one's true home: *he lived in Darwin for five years but never established any roots there.* **12.** *Maths.* **a.** a quantity which, when multiplied by itself a certain number of times, produces a given quantity: *2 is the square root of 4, the cube root of 8, and the fourth root of 16.* **b.** a quantity which, when substituted for the unknown quantity in an algebraic equation, satisfies the equation. **13.** *Gram.* **a.** a morpheme which underlies an inflectional paradigm or is used itself as a word or element of a compound. Thus, *dance* is the root of *dancer, dancing.* In German, *seh* is the root of *gesehen.* **b.** such a morpheme as posited for a parent language, such as proto-Indo-European, on the basis of comparison of extant forms in daughter languages. **14.** *Music.* **a.** the fundamental note of a chord or of a series of harmonies. **b.** the lowest note of a chord when arranged as a series of thirds; the fundamental. **15.** *Mach.* that part of a screw thread which connects adjacent flanks at the bottom of the groove. **16.** *Colloq.* the act of sexual intercourse. **17. root and branch,** entirely; completely: *we destroyed them root and branch.* **18. take (or strike) root, a.** to send out roots and begin to grow. **b.** to become fixed or established. *–v.i.* **19.** to send out roots and begin to grow. **20.** to become fixed or established. *–v.t.* **21.** to fix by, or as if by, roots. **22.** to implant or establish deeply. **23.** to pull, tear, or dig (fol. by *up, out,* etc.) by the roots. **24.** to extirpate; exterminate (with *up, out,* etc.). **25.** *Colloq.* to have sexual intercourse with. **26.** *Colloq.* **a.** to exhaust. **b.** to break; ruin. [ME; OE *rōt,* from Scand.; cf. Icel. *rōt*] **– rootless,** *adj.*

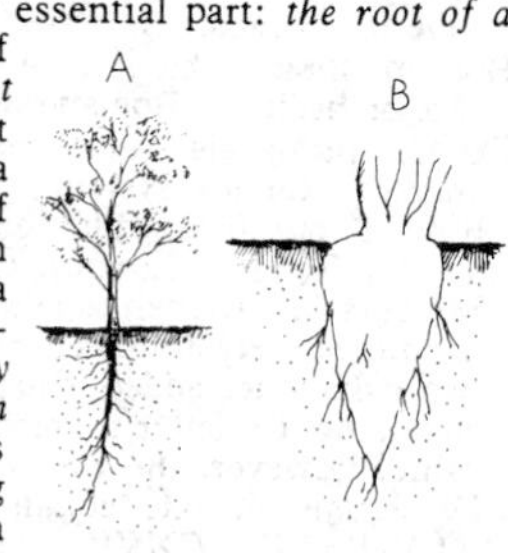

types of roots: A, tap; B, fleshy

**root**[2] /rut/, *v.i.* **1.** to turn up the soil with the snout, as swine. **2.** to poke, pry, or search, as if to find something (fol. by *around*). *–v.t.* **3.** to turn over with the snout (oft. fol. by *up*). **4.** to unearth; bring to light (fol. by *up,* etc.). [var. of obs. *wroot,* OE *wrōtan,* akin to *wrōt* snout] **– rooter,** *n.*

**root**[3] /rut/, *v.i. U.S. Colloq.* to give encouragement to, or applaud, a contestant, etc. [? var. of *rout* make a loud noise. Cf. Norw. *ruta*] **– rooter,** *n.*

**rootage** /ˈrutɪdʒ/, *n.* **1.** the act of taking root. **2.** firm fixture by means of roots.

**root beer** /ˈrut bɪə/, *n. U.S.* a drink containing the extracted juices of various roots, as of dandelion, sarsaparilla, sassafras, etc.

**root-bound** /ˈrut-baʊnd/, *adj.* of a plant, the roots of which have outgrown the space and nourishment available.

**root cap** /ˈrut kæp/, *n.* a sheath of cells at the end of a root.

**root crop** /ˈ– krɒp/, *n.* a crop such as beets, carrots, turnips, etc., grown for its edible roots.

**rooted** /ˈrutəd/, *adj. Colloq.* **1.** exhausted. **2.** frustrated; thwarted. **3.** broken; ruined. **4. get rooted,** (*derog.*) go away.

**root hair** /'rut hɛə/, *n.* an elongated tubular extension of an epidermal cell of the root serving to absorb water and minerals from the soil.

**rootlet** /'rutlət/, *n.* **1.** a little root. **2.** a small or fine branch of a root. **3.** one of the adventitious roots by which ivy or the like clings to rocks, etc.

**root mean square,** *n.* the square root of the arithmetic mean of the squares of a set of values. *Abbrev.:* r.m.s.

**rootrot** /'rutrɒt/, *n.* the damage or decay of roots caused by many plant diseases.

**rootstock** /'rutstɒk/; *n.* **1.** *Hort.* a root used as a stock in plant propagation. **2.** *Bot.* the basal persistent part of the stems of erect herbacious perennials from which new roots and aerial shoots arise in the next growing season. **3.** a source from which offshoots have originated; ancestral form.

**rooty** /'ruti/, *adj.*, **rootier, rootiest.** abounding in roots. – **rootiness,** *n.*

**roove** /ruv/, *n., v.,* **rooved, rooving.** –*n.* **1.** *Shipbuilding.* a small copper washer used when copper nails are being clinched. –*v.t.* **2.** to secure (a nail) with a roove. [orig. obscure]

**rope** /roup/, *n., v.,* **roped, roping.** –*n.* **1.** a strong, thick line or cord, commonly one composed of twisted or braided strands of hemp, flax, or the like, or of wire or other material. **2.** (*pl.*) the cords used to enclose a boxing ring or other space. **3.** a hangman's noose. **4.** death by hanging as a punishment. **5.** a quantity of material or a number of things twisted or strung together in the form of a thick cord: *a rope of beads.* **6.** *U.S.* →**lasso. 7.** a stringy, viscid, or glutinous formation in a liquid. **8.** (*pl.*) methods; procedure; operations of a business, etc.: *know the ropes; learn the ropes.* **9.** *Mil.* a long piece of metal foil used as chaff to confuse the low-frequency radar spectrum. **10. give someone enough rope to hang himself,** *Colloq.* allow freedom to someone to prove his (her) unworthiness. **11. on the ropes, a.** *Boxing.* driven against the ropes by one's opponent. **b.** in a hopeless position; near to failure. –*v.t.* **12.** to tie, bind, or fasten with a rope. **13.** to enclose or mark off with a rope. **14.** to catch with a lasso. **15.** *Colloq.* to draw, entice, or inveigle into something (fol. by *in*). –*v.i.* **16.** to be drawn out into a filament of thread; become ropy. [ME; OE *rāp,* c. D *reep,* G *Reif*]

**ropeable** /'roupəbəl/, *adj.* **1.** capable of being roped. **2.** (of animals) wild; intractable. **3.** *Colloq.* angry; bad-tempered. Also, **ropable.**

**rope-dance** /'roup-dæns/, *n.* a performance as of dancing, walking, etc., on a tightrope. – **rope-dancer,** *n.*

**rope-ladder** /'roup-lædə/, *n.* a ladder made of two long pieces of strong rope connected at regular intervals by short pieces of rope, wood, metal, etc.

**ropemaking** /'roupmeɪkɪŋ/, *n.* the art, act, or process of making rope.

**rope's end** /'roups ɛnd/, *n.* **1.** (formerly) a short length of rope, often knotted, used to flog sailors. **2.** a hangman's noose.

**ropewalk** /'roupwɔk/, *n.* **1.** a long, usu. covered, course. **2.** a long, low building, where ropes are made.

**rope-walker** /'roup-wɔkə/, *n.* a tightrope performer.

**ropeway** /'roupweɪ/, *n.* a system of overhead cables, etc., used for transporting goods or passengers.

**rope yarn** /'roup jan/, *n.* See **yarn** (def. 2).

**roping-in award** /roupɪŋ-'ɪn əˌwɔd/, *n.* an industrial award made for the purpose of extending the provisions of an existing award to respondent employers to ensure that they do not remain award-free.

**roping pole** /'roupɪŋ poul/, *n.* →**catching pole.**

**ropy** /'roupi/, *adj.,* **ropier, ropiest. 1.** resembling a rope or ropes. **2.** forming viscid or glutinous threads, as a liquid. **3.** *Colloq.* worn; deteriorated; below the desired standard. Also, **ropey.** – **ropiness,** *n.*

**roquefort** /'roukfət/, *n.* a semi-soft ripened cheese, with a strong flavour, veined with mould. [orig. made at *Roquefort,* town in S France]

**roquet** /'rouki/, *v.,* **-queted** /-kid/, **-queting** /kiˌɪŋ/, *n. Croquet.* –*v.t.* **1.** to cause one's ball to strike (another player's ball). **2.** (of a ball) to strike (another ball). –*v.i.* **3.** to roquet a ball. –*n.* **4.** the act of roqueting. [? alteration of CROQUET]

**rorqual** /'rɔkəl/, *n.* any of the whalebone whales, some being very large, that constitute the genus *Balaenoptera,* having a dorsal fin; a finback. [F, from Norw. *röyrkval* finner-whale]

**Rorschach test** /'rɔʃak tɛst/, *n.* a test devised for the analysis of personality, calling for responses to ink blots and drawings. [named after Hermann *Rorschach,* 1884-1922, Swiss psychiatrist]

common rorqual

**rort** /rɔt/, *n. Colloq.* **1.** a trick; lurk; scheme. **2.** a wild party. –*v.t.* **3.** to gain control over (an organisation, as a branch of a political party) esp. by falsifying records. [orig. uncert.] – **rorty,** *adj.*

**rorter** /'rɔtə/, *n. Colloq.* a con man operating on a small scale, as with worthless goods.

**rosaceous** /rou'zeɪʃəs/, *adj.* **1.** belonging to the Rosaceae, or rose family of plants, which includes also the blackberry, strawberry, spiraea, etc. **2.** having a corolla of five broad petals, like that of a rose. **3.** roselike. **4.** rose-coloured; rosy. [L *rosāceus*]

**rosaniline** /rou'zænələn, -lin, -laɪn/, *n.* **1.** a red dye, $C_{20}H_{19}N_3 \cdot HCl$, derived from aniline and orthotoluidine; a constituent of fuchsine. **2.** the base, $C_{20}H_{21}N_3O$, which with hydrochloric acid forms this dye. [ROSE[1] + ANILINE]

**rosarian** /rou'zɛəriən/, *n.* one who grows roses, for pleasure or profit. [ROSE[1] + -ARIAN]

**rosary** /'rouzəri/, *n., pl.* **-ries. 1.** *Rom. Cath. Ch.* **a.** a series of prayers consisting (in the usual form) of fifteen decades of Ave Marias, each decade being preceded by a paternoster and followed by a gloria (Gloria Patri), one of the mysteries or events in the life of Christ and of the Virgin Mary being recalled at each decade. **b.** a string of beads used for counting these prayers in reciting them. **2.** (among other religious bodies) a string of beads similarly used in praying. **3.** a rose garden; a bed of roses. [ME, from L *rosārium* rose garden, ML rosary, properly neut. of *rosārius* of roses]

**roscoe** /'rɒskou/, *n. Prison Colloq.* a gun. [? from the name *Roscoe*]

**roscoelite** /'rɒskouˌlaɪt/, *n.* a greenish brown mineral, similar to muscovite, in which the aluminium is partly replaced by vanadium. [named after Sir Henry *Roscoe,* 1833-1915, English chemist. See -LITE]

**rose**[1] /rouz/, *n., v.,* **rosed, rosing.** –*n.* **1.** any of the wild or cultivated, usu. prickly-stemmed, showy-flowered shrubs constituting the genus *Rosa,* having in the wild state a corolla of five roundish petals. **2.** any of various related or similar plants. **3.** the flower of any such shrubs, usu. of a red, pink, white, or yellow colour, and often fragrant. **4.** an ornament shaped like or suggesting a rose; a rosette of ribbon or the like. **5.** the traditional reddish colour of the rose, varying from a purplish red through different shades to a pale pink. **6.** a pinkish red colour in the cheek. **7.** a rose window. **8.** an ornamental plate or socket which surrounds a doorknob on the face of a door, an electric or gas light fitting, on a ceiling, etc. **9.** the compass card of the mariners' compass as printed on charts. **10.** a form of cut gem formerly much used with a triangularly faceted top and flat underside: *a rose diamond.* **11.** a perforated cap or plate at the end of a water pipe or the spout of a watering-can, etc., to break a flow of water into a spray. **12. bed of roses,** a situation of luxurious ease; an easy and highly agreeable position. **13. under the rose,** secretly; privately. –*adj.* **14.** of the colour rose. –*v.t.* **15.** to make rose-coloured. **16.** to flush (the cheeks, face, etc.). [ME and OE, from L *rosa*] – **roselike,** *adj.*

**rose**[2] /rouz/, *v.* past tense of **rise.**

**rosé** /rou'zeɪ/, *n.* a light wine of a translucent pale red colour. [F]

**rose acacia** /rouz ə'keɪʃə/, *n.* a small tree, *Robinia hispida,* of the north-eastern U.S., having large, dark rose-coloured scentless flowers in racemes.

**rose-apple** /'rouz-æpəl/, *n.* a small, evergreen tree, *Syzygium jambos,* native to the East Indies, with an edible fruit much used in the tropics in confectionery.

**roseate** /'rouziət/, *adj.* **1.** tinged with rose; rosy. **2.** bright or promising. **3.** optimistic. [L *roseus* rosy + -ATE[1]] – **roseately,** *adv.*

**rosebay willowherb** /ˌroʊzbeɪ ˈwɪloʊhɜb/, *n.* a tall perennial herb with handsome spikes of deep pink flowers, *Chamaenerion angustifolium,* widespread in open places throughout northern temperate regions.

**rosebud** /ˈroʊzbʌd/, *n.* the bud of a rose.

**rosebush** /ˈroʊzbʊʃ/, *n.* a shrub which bears roses.

**rose campion** /roʊz ˈkæmpiən/, *n.* a frequently cultivated herb with red or white flowers, *Lychnis coronaria.*

**rose-coloured** /ˈroʊz-kʌləd/, *adj.* **1.** of rose colour; rosy; rosaceous. **2.** promising, cheerful, or optimistic. **3. look at through rose-coloured glasses,** to have an overly-optimistic attitude towards.

**rose-comb** /ˈroʊz-koʊm/, *n.* a comb, characteristic of some breeds of the domestic fowl, having numerous low, rounded crests not necessarily arranged in line.

**rose hip** /ˈroʊz hɪp/, *n.* →**hip**².

**rosella**¹ /roʊˈzɛlə/, *n.* a plant of southern Europe, *Hibiscus sabdariffa,* used in jams and preserves. Also, **rozelle.**

**rosella**² /roʊˈzɛlə/, *n.* **1.** any of a number of brilliantly coloured parrots of the genus *Platycercus,* as the eastern rosella, *P. eximius,* a common bird of eastern Australia. **2.** *Colloq.* a sheep that has lost wool, esp. from disease and is showing patches of bare skin. **3.** *Colloq.* a shearer who is stripped to the waist while he is working. [from *Rosehill,* an early settlement in N.S.W.]

rosella²

**rosella bush** /ˈ– bʊʃ/, *n.* an annual shrub, *Hibiscus sabdariffa,* with large lobed leaves and yellow hibiscus-like flowers producing a fruit comprised of a green seed surrounded by dark red fleshy leaves, the latter being picked when young and used to make jam. Also, **rosella.**

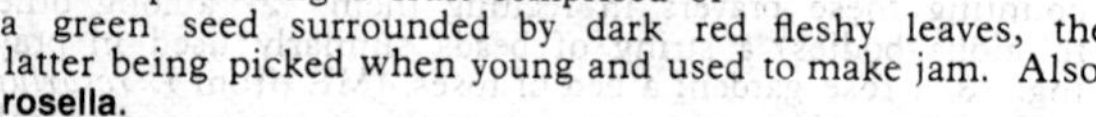

**rose mallow** /roʊz ˈmæloʊ/, *n.* **1.** any of various plants of the genus *Hibiscus,* bearing rose-coloured flowers. **2.** the hollyhock, *Althaea rosea.*

**rosemary** /ˈroʊzməri/, *n., pl.* **-maries.** an evergreen shrub, *Rosmarinus officinalis,* native to the Mediterranean region, used as a herb in cooking and yielding a fragrant essential oil. It is a traditional symbol of remembrance. [ME *rose mary,* from L *rōs maris,* lit., dew of the sea; in E the final -s mistaken for pl. sign]

**rose of Jericho** /roʊz əv ˈdʒɛrɪkoʊ/, *n.* an Asiatic plant, *Anastatica hierochuntica,* which, after drying and curling up, expands when moistened.

**rose of Sharon** /roʊz əv ˈʃærən/, *n.* **1.** a plant mentioned in the Bible (see Cant. 2:1). **2.** a name given to several garden plants, as the yellow-flowered species of the genus *Hypericum* and *Hibiscus mutabilis,* the flowers of which are white and pink.

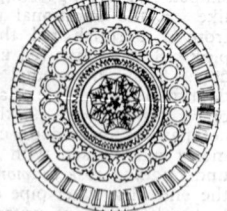

**roseola** /roʊˈziələ/, *n.* a kind of rose-coloured rash. [NL, from L *rose(us)* rosy + diminutive suffix -*ola*]

architectural rosette

**Rose's metal** /ˈroʊzəz mɛtl/, *n.* an alloy of bismuth (approx. 50 per cent) with 25 per cent each of tin and lead.

**rosette** /roʊˈzɛt/, *n.* **1.** any arrangement, part, object, or formation more or less resembling a rose. **2.** a rose-shaped arrangement of ribbon or other material, used as an ornament or badge. **3.** an architectural ornament resembling a rose or having a generally circular combination of parts. **4.** *Bot.* a circular cluster of leaves or other organs. [F, diminutive of *rose* ROSE¹]

**rosewater** /ˈroʊzwɔtə/, *n.* **1.** distilled water tinctured with the essential oil of roses. *–adj.* **2.** having the scent of rosewater. **3.** affectedly delicate, nice, or fine; sentimental.

**rose window** /roʊz ˈwɪndoʊ/, *n.* a circular window with roselike tracery or radiating mullions.

**rosewood** /ˈroʊzwʊd/, *n.* **1.** any of various reddish cabinet woods (sometimes with a roselike odour) yielded by trees such as *Dysoxylum fraserianum* of Australia and tropical species of the genus *Dalbergia* of India and Brazil. **2.** a tree yielding such wood.

**Rosh Hashana** /rɒʃ həˈʃanə/, *n.* the two-day Jewish holiday celebrated at the start of the Jewish New Year, when the shophar is blown. Also, **Rosh Hashona** /rɒʃ həˈʃoʊnə/. [Heb. *rōsh* head + *hash-shānāh* the year]

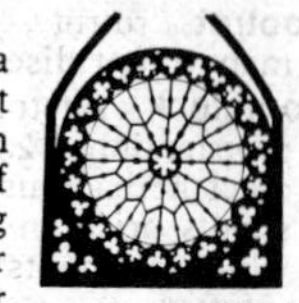

rose window

**Rosicrucian** /roʊzəˈkruʃən/, *n.* **1.** one of a number or body of persons (an alleged secret society) prominent in the 17th and 18th centuries, laying claim to various forms of occult knowledge and power and professing esoteric principles of religion. **2.** a member of any of several later or modern bodies or societies professing principles derived from or attributed to the earlier Rosicrucians. *–adj.* **3.** of, pertaining to, or characteristic of the Rosicrucians. [*Rosicruc-* (Latinised form of G *Rosenkreuz,* name of supposed founder) + -IAN] – **Rosicrucianism,** *n.*

**rosily** /ˈroʊzəli/, *adv.* **1.** with a rosy colour. **2.** in a rosy manner.

**rosin** /ˈrɒzən/, *n.* **1.** the hard, brittle resin left after distilling off the oil of turpentine from the crude oleoresin of the pine, used in making varnish, for rubbing on violin bows, etc.; colophony. **2.** (not in scientific usage) resin. *–v.t.* **3.** to cover or rub with rosin. [ME, from OF *rosine,* var. of *resine* RESIN]

**rosiner** /ˈrɒzənə/, *n.* *Colloq.* a strong alcoholic drink. Also, **rosner, roziner.** [from obs. Brit. *rosin* to make drunk (from the resin applied to violin strings)]

**rostellate** /rɒsˈtɛlət/, *adj.* having a rostellum.

**rostellum** /rɒsˈtɛləm/, *n., pl.* **-la** /-lə/. **1.** any small, beaklike process. **2.** a modification of the stigma in many orchids. [L, diminutive of *rōstrum* beak]

**roster** /ˈrɒstə/, *n.* **1.** a list of persons or groups with their turns or periods of duty. **2.** any list, roll, or register. *–v.t.* **3.** to put on a roster; to list. [D *rooster* list, orig., gridiron (from *roosten* roast), from the ruled paper used]

**rostral** /ˈrɒstrəl/, *adj.* of or pertaining to a rostrum. [LL *rostrālis,* from L *rōstrum* beak + *-ālis* -AL¹]

**rostrate** /ˈrɒstreɪt/, *adj.* furnished with a rostrum or beak.

**rostrum** /ˈrɒstrəm/, *n., pl.* **-trums, -tra** /-trə/. **1.** any platform, stage, or the like, for public speaking. **2.** a platform for musicians or their conductor, or the like. **3.** →**pulpit. 4.** a beaklike projection from the prow of a ship, esp. one on an ancient warship for ramming an enemy ship. **5.** the platform or elevated place (adorned with the beaks of captured warships) in the ancient Roman forum, from which orations, pleadings, etc., were delivered. **6.** *Biol.* a beaklike process or extension of some part. **7.** *Theat.* a portable platform placed on the stage as part of the scenery. [L: beak, in pl., speakers' platform (cf. def. 5)]

**rosy** /ˈroʊzi/, *adj.,* **rosier, rosiest. 1.** pink or pinkish red; roseate. **2.** (of persons, the cheeks, lips, etc.) having a fresh, healthy redness. **3.** bright or promising: *a rosy future.* **4.** cheerful or optimistic: *rosy anticipations.* **5.** made or consisting of roses. – **rosily,** *adv.* – **rosiness,** *n.*

**rot** /rɒt/, *v.,* **rotted, rotting,** *n., interj.* *–v.i.* **1.** to undergo decomposition; decay. **2.** to fall or become weak due to decay (fol. by *away, off,* etc.). **3.** to become morally corrupt or offensive. *–v.t.* **4.** to cause to rot. **5.** →**ret.** *–n.* **6.** the process of rotting. **7.** the state of being rotten; decay; putrefaction. **8.** rotting or rotten matter. **9.** any of various diseases characterised by decomposition. **10.** any of various plant diseases or forms of decay produced by fungi or bacteria. **11.** *Colloq.* nonsense. *–interj.* **12.** (an exclamation of dissent, distaste, or disgust. [ME, from Scand.; cf. Icel. *rot,* n., akin to OE *rotian* to rot]

**rota** /ˈroʊtə/, *n.* **1.** a round, as of duty. **2.** →**roster.** [L: wheel]

**rotary** /ˈroʊtəri/, *adj.* **1.** turning round as on an axis, as an object. **2.** taking place round an axis, as motion. **3.** having a part or parts that rotate, as a machine. **4.** of or pertaining to a rotary engine. **5.** *Agric.* denoting various implements having rotating blades, scrapers, or the like: *rotary hoe.* [LL *rotārius*, from L *rota* wheel. See -ARY[1]]

**rotary beater** /– 'bitə/, *n.* →**egg-beater.**

**rotary convertor** /– kən'vɜtə/, *n.* a device for converting alternating current into direct current, or vice-versa by mechanically coupling an a.c. electric motor to a d.c. generator; synchronous connector.

**rotary engine** /– 'ɛndʒən/, *n.* an internal combustion engine whose operating action is non-reciprocal, its piston, usu. three-faced, rotating about the crankshaft to which it may be geared, in an irregularly shaped combustion chamber.

**rotary hoe** /– 'hoʊ/, *n.* an implement with many finger-like wheels, pulled over the ground for early crop cultivation and destruction of weeds.

**rotary hoist** /– 'hɔɪst/, *n.* →**clothes hoist.**

**rotary plough** /– 'plaʊ/, *n.* a series of swinging knives mounted on a horizontal power-driven shaft which pulverise unploughed soil, for planting, in one operation. Also, **rotary tiller.**

**rotary press** /– 'prɛs/, *n.* See **press**[1] (def. 32b).

**rotary wing aircraft,** *n.* an aircraft wholly or partly supported in flight by rotors. Also, **rotorcraft.**

**rotate**[1] /roʊ'teɪt/, *v.*, **-tated, -tating.** *–v.t.* **1.** to cause to turn round like a wheel on its axis. **2.** to cause to go through a round of changes; cause to pass or follow in a fixed routine of succession: *to rotate crops.* *–v.i.* **3.** to turn round as on an axis. **4.** to proceed in a fixed routine of succession. [L *rotātus*, pp., swung round, revolved] – **rotatable,** *adj.*

**rotate**[2] /'roʊteɪt/, *adj.* wheel-shaped (applied esp. to a gamopetalous short-tubed corolla with a spreading limb). [L *rota* wheel + -ATE[1]]

rotate[2] corolla of potato

**rotation** /roʊ'teɪʃən/, *n.* **1.** the act of rotating; a turning round as on an axis. **2. a.** the turning of the earth or other celestial body about its own axis. **b.** one complete revolution of such a body. **3.** regularly recurring succession, as of governments. **4.** *Agric.* the process or method of varying, in a definite order, the crops grown on the same ground. – **rotational,** *adj.*

**rotational grazing** /roʊ,teɪʃənəl 'greɪzɪŋ/, *n.* a planned system of paddock usage where animals graze for a limited period of time in each paddock.

**rotative** /'roʊtətɪv/, *adj.* **1.** rotating; pertaining to rotation. **2.** producing rotation. **3.** happening in regular succession.

**rotator** /roʊ'teɪtə/, *n.*, *pl.* **rotators** *for def. 1*, **rotatores** /roʊtə'toriz/ *for def. 2.* **1.** one who or that which rotates. **2.** *Anat.* a muscle serving to rotate a part of the body. [L]

**rotatory** /'roʊtətri, roʊ'teɪtəri/, *adj.* **1.** pertaining to or of the nature of rotation: *rotatory motion.* **2.** rotating, as an object. **3.** passing or following in rotation or succession. **4.** causing rotation, as a muscle, etc.

**rote**[1] /roʊt/, *n.* **1.** *Obs.* routine; fixed or mechanical course of procedure. **2. by rote,** in a mechanical way without thought of the meaning. [ME; orig. uncert.]

**rote**[2] /roʊt/, *n.* a kind of medieval musical stringed instrument. [ME, from OF; of Celtic orig.]

**rote learning** /– 'lɜnɪŋ/, *n.* memorisation by repetition without explanation of principles.

**rotenone** /'roʊtənoʊn/, *n.* a crystalline heterocyclic compound, $C_{23}H_{22}O_6$, possessing ketone, olefine, and ether functional groups; the poisonous principle of certain insecticides, derived from the tropical derris plant.

**rotgut** /'rɒtgʌt/, *n. Colloq.* alcoholic liquor of inferior quality.

**rotifer** /'roʊtəfə/, *n.* any of the animalcules constituting the phylum Rotifera, found in fresh and salt water, and characterised by a ciliary apparatus on the anterior end; a wheel animalcule. [NL, from *roti-* (combining form representing L *rota* wheel) + *-fer* bearing] – **rotiferal** /roʊ'tɪfərəl/, **rotiferous** /roʊ'tɪfərəs/, *adj.*

rotifer (greatly magnified)

**rotisserie** /roʊ'tɪsəri/, *n.* **1.** Also, **roasting spit.** a spit, driven by clockwork mechanism or electricity, on which meat, poultry, and game can be cooked. **2.** a restaurant, cafe, etc., where such a spit is used. [F: roasting place]

**rotogravure** /,roʊtoʊgrə'vjuə/, *n.* **1.** a photomechanical intaglio process in which pictures, letters, etc., are printed from an engraved copper cylinder, the ink-bearing lines being depressed (etched in) instead of raised as in ordinary metal type. **2.** a print made by this process. [*roto-* (combining form of L *rota* wheel) + F *gravure* engraving]

**rotor** /'roʊtə/, *n.* **1.** *Elect.* the rotating member of a machine (opposed to *stator*). **2.** *Aeron.* a system of rotating aerofoils, usu. horizontal, as those of a helicopter. **3.** *Mach.* the rotating assembly of blades in a turbine. **4.** *Naut.* a high, tower-like, cylindrical structure of metal, rising above the deck and rotated by a small motor, which so operates in connection with the wind that it propels the ship **(rotor ship).** [short for ROTATOR]

**rotorcraft** /'roʊtəkraft/, *n.* →**rotary wing aircraft.**

**rotten** /'rɒtn/, *adj.* **1.** in a state of decomposition or decay; putrid; tainted, foul, or ill-smelling. **2.** corrupt or offensive morally, politically, or otherwise. **3.** *Colloq.* wretchedly bad, unsatisfactory, or unpleasant: *to feel rotten, rotten work.* **4.** contemptible: *a rotten little snob.* **5.** (of soil, rocks, etc.) soft, yielding, or friable as the result of decomposition. **6.** *Colloq.* extremely drunk. [ME *roten*, from Scand.; cf. Icel. *rotinn*] – **rottenly,** *adv.* – **rottenness,** *n.*

**rottenstone** /'rɒtnstoʊn/, *n.* a friable stone resulting from the decomposition of a siliceous limestone, used as a powder for polishing metals.

**rotter** /'rɒtə/, *n. Chiefly Brit. Colloq.* a thoroughly bad, worthless, and objectionable person.

**Rottweiler** /'rɒtwaɪlə/, *n.* one of a breed of large, smooth-coated black dogs, originally bred in Germany. [G, named after *Rottweil*, town in S Germany]

**rotund** /roʊ'tʌnd/, *adj.* **1.** rounded; plump. **2.** full-toned or sonorous: *rotund speeches.* [L *rotundus*] – **rotundity, rotundness,** *n.* – **rotundly,** *adv.*

**rotunda** /rə'tʌndə/, *n.* **1.** a round building, esp. one with a dome. **2.** a large and high circular hall or room in a building, esp. one surmounted by a dome. [L, fem. of *rotundus* rotund]

**rouble** /'rubəl/, *n.* the monetary unit of the Soviet Union. Also, **ruble.** [Russ.; orig. uncert.]

**roué** /'rueɪ/, *n.* a debauchee or rake. [F, pp. of *rouer* break on the wheel; first applied to the profligate companions of the Duc d'Orléans (*c.* 1720)]

**rouge** /ruʒ/, *n.*, *v.*, **rouged, rouging.** *–n.* **1.** any of various red cosmetics for colouring the cheeks or lips. **2.** a reddish powder, chiefly ferric oxide, used for polishing metal, etc. *–v.t.* **3.** to colour with rouge. *–v.i.* **4.** to use rouge. [F: properly adj., red, from L *rubeus*]

**rouge et noir** /ruʒ eɪ 'nwa/, *n.* a gambling game at cards, played on a table marked with two red and two black diamond-shaped spots on which the players place their stakes; trente et quarante. [F: red and black]

**rough** /rʌf/, *adj.* **1.** uneven from projections, irregularities, or breaks of surface; not smooth: *rough boards, a rough road.* **2.** (of ground) wild; broken; covered with scrub, boulders, etc. **3.** shaggy: *a dog with a rough coat.* **4.** acting with or characterised by violence. **5.** violently disturbed or agitated, as the sea, water, etc. **6.** violently irregular, as motion. **7.** stormy or tempestuous, as wind, weather, etc. **8.** sharp or harsh: *a rough temper.* **9.** unmannerly or rude. **10.** disorderly or riotous. **11.** *Colloq.* severe, hard, or unpleasant: *to have a rough time of it.* **12.** harsh to the ear, grating, or jarring, as sounds. **13.** harsh to the taste, sharp, or astringent, as wines: *rough cider.* **14.** coarse, as food, cloth, materials, etc. **15.** (of people or their behaviour) lacking culture or refinement: *rough as bags.* **16.** without refinements, luxuries, or ordinary comforts or conveniences. **17.** requiring exertion or strength rather than intelligence or skill, as work. **18.** unpolished, as language, verse, style, etc.; not elaborated, perfected, or corrected: *a rough draft.* **19.** made or done without any attempt at exactness, completeness, or thoroughness: *a rough guess.* **20.** crude, unwrought, undressed, or unprepared: *a rough diamond, rough rice.* **21.** *Phonet.* with aspiration; having the sound of *h.* **22.** of or pertaining to the back of a racquet (from the texture of the strings on that side). **23. cut up rough,** to behave angrily or violently; be upset. **24. rough on, a.** severe towards. **b.** unfortunate for (someone). *–n.* **25.** that which is rough; rough ground. **26.** any piece of work, esp. a work of art, in an unfinished or preliminary condition. **27.** *Golf.* any part of the course bordering the fairway on which the grass, weeds, etc., are not trimmed. **28.** the rough, hard, or unpleasant side or part of anything. **29.** the rough side of a racquet. **30.** *Colloq.* a rough person; rowdy. **31. in the rough,** in a rough, crude, unwrought, or unfinished state. *–adv.* **32.** in a rough manner; roughly. **33.** *Colloq.* **a bit rough,** unfair, unreasonable. *–v.t.* **34.** to make rough; roughen. **35.** to treat roughly or harshly (oft. fol. by *up*). **36.** to subject to some rough preliminary process of working or preparation. (oft. fol. by *up*). **37.** to cut, shape, or sketch roughly (fol. by *in* or *out*): *to rough out a plan, to rough in the outlines of a face.* *–v.i.* **38. rough it,** to live without even the ordinary comforts or conveniences: *we roughed it all month long.* [ME; OE *ruh,* c. D *ruig,* G *rauh*] – **roughly,** *adv.*

**roughage** /ˈrʌfɪdʒ/, *n.* **1.** rough or coarse material. **2.** the coarser kinds or parts of fodder or food, of less nutritive value, esp. those which assist digestion, as distinguished from those affording more concentrated nutriment.

**rough-and-ready** /rʌf-ən-ˈrɛdi/, *adj.* **1.** rough, rude, or crude, but good enough for the purpose: *in a rough-and-ready fashion.* **2.** exhibiting or showing rough vigour rather than refinement or delicacy: *a rough-and-ready person.*

**rough-and-tumble** /rʌf-ən-ˈtʌmbəl/, *adj.* **1.** characterised by violent, disorganised, unconstrained behaviour: *a rough-and-tumble fight.* **2.** given to such action.

**rough breathing** /rʌf ˈbriðɪŋ/, *n.* an aspirate mark (ʽ) placed over initial vowels to indicate a preceding *h* sound. Cf. **smooth breathing.** [translation of L *spiritus asper*]

**roughcast** /ˈrʌfkast/, *n., adj., v.,* **-cast, -casting.** *–n.* **1.** a coarse plaster mixed with gravel, shells, or the like, for outside surfaces, usu. thrown against the wall. **2.** a crudely formed pattern or model; a rough. *–adj.* **3.** made of or covered with roughcast; crudely formed. *–v.t.* **4.** to cover or coat with roughcast. **5.** to make, shape, or prepare in a rough form: *to roughcast a story.* – **roughcaster,** *n.*

**rough cut** /rʌf ˈkʌt/, *n.* the first assembly of a film which the editor makes by roughly trimming the selected takes and joining them together in the order planned in the script.

**rough diamond** /– ˈdaɪmənd/, *n.* **1.** an uncut diamond. **2.** a person without refinement of manner but having an essentially good or likeable personality.

**rough-dry** /rʌf-ˈdraɪ/, *v.,* **-dried, -drying,** *adj.* *–v.t.* **1.** to dry (clothes, etc.) after washing, without smoothing, ironing, etc. *–adj.* **2.** dry but unironed.

**roughen** /ˈrʌfən/, *v.t.* **1.** to make rough. *–v.i.* **2.** to become rough.

**rough-hew** /rʌf-ˈhju/, *v.t.,* **-hewed, -hewed** or **hewn, -hewing.** **1.** to hew (timber, stone, etc.) roughly or without smoothing or finishing. **2.** to shape roughly; give crude form to.

**rough-house** /ˈrʌf-haʊs/, *n., v.,* **-housed, -housing.** *Colloq.* *–n.* **1.** noisy, disorderly behaviour or play; rowdy conduct; a brawl. *–v.i.* **2.** to engage or take part in a rough-house. *–v.t.* **3.** to disturb or harass by a rough-house.

**roughie**[1] /ˈrʌfi/, *n.* →**tommy ruff.**

**roughie**[2] /ˈrʌfi/, *n. Colloq.* **1.** one who is rough or crude. **2.** a shrewd trick; a cunning act. **3.** *Horseracing.* a horse with little chance of ever winning a race.

**roughish** /ˈrʌfɪʃ/, *adj.* rather rough: *a roughish sea.*

**rough lemon** /rʌf ˈlɛmən/, *n.* a species of citrus, *Citrus jambhiri,* related to the lemon but probably of hybrid origin, often used as stock for other citrus fruits.

**roughly** /ˈrʌfli/, *adv.* **1.** in a crude, harsh or violent manner. **2.** inexactly; without precision. **3.** approximately; about.

**roughneck** /ˈrʌfnɛk/, *n. Colloq.* **1.** a rough, coarse person. **2.** *Chiefly U.S.* a member of an oil-drilling crew.

**rough puff pastry,** *n.* →**puff pastry.**

**roughrider** /ˈrʌfraɪdə/, *n.* **1.** one who breaks horses to the saddle. **2.** one accustomed to rough or hard riding.

**roughshod** /ˈrʌfʃɒd/, *adj.* **1.** shod with horseshoes having projecting nails or points. **2. ride roughshod over,** to override harshly or domineeringly; treat without consideration.

**rough-spoken** /rʌf-ˈspoʊkən/, *adj.* having an uncouth or rude manner of speech.

**rough stuff** /ˈrʌf stʌf/, *n.* violence, esp. more than the situation seems to require.

**rough-up** /ˈrʌf-ʌp/, *n. Colloq.* a brawl, fight.

**roulade** /ruˈlad/, *n.* **1.** a meat roll or galantine. **2.** *Music.* a vocal or instrumental flourish, usu. consisting of brilliant and rapid runs. [F, from *rouler* roll]

**rouleau** /ˈruloʊ/, *n., pl.* **-leaux, -leaus** /-loʊz/. **1.** a cylindrical pile or roll of something. **2.** a number of coins put up in cylindrical form in a paper wrapping. **3.** *Med.* a number of red cells in a cylindrical configuration. [F, from *rôle* roll]

**roulette** /ruˈlɛt/, *n., v.,* **-letted, -letting.** *–n.* **1.** a game of chance played at a table, in which an unlimited number of players bet on which of the compartments of a revolving disc or wheel will be the resting-place of a ball circling it in the opposite direction. **2.** the wheel or disc used in this game. **3.** a small wheel, esp. one with sharp teeth, mounted in a handle, for making lines of marks, dots, or perforations: *engravers' roulettes, a roulette for perforating sheets of postage stamps.* **4.** *Philately.* short consecutive cuts in the paper between the individual stamps of the sheet so that they may be readily separated from each other. It differs from perforation in that no paper is removed. *–v.t.* **5.** to mark, impress, or perforate with a roulette. [F, diminutive of *rouelle* round slice. See ROWEL]

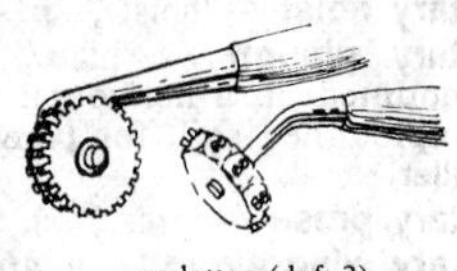
roulettes (def. 3)

**round** /raʊnd/, *adj.* **1.** circular, as a disc. **2.** ring-shaped, as a hoop. **3.** curved like part of a circle, as an outline. **4.** having a circular cross-section, as a cylinder. **5.** spherical or globular, as a ball. **6.** rounded more or less like a part of a sphere. **7.** free from angularity; curved, as parts of the body. **8.** executed with or involving circular motion: *a round dance.* **9.** completed by passing through a course which finally returns to the place of starting: *a round trip.* **10.** full, complete, or entire: *a round dozen.* **11.** forming, or expressed by, an integer or whole number (with no fraction). **12.** expressed in tens, hundreds, thousands, or the like: *in round numbers.* **13.** roughly correct: *a round guess.* **14.** considerable in amount: *a good round sum of money.* **15.** portrayed in depth, rather than in stylised or stereotyped fashion as a literary character. **16.** full and sonorous, as sound. **17.** vigorous, brisk, or smart: *a round trot.* **18.** plain, honest, or straightforward. **19.** candid or outspoken. **20.** unmodified, as an oath; positive or unqualified, as an assertion. **21.** (of paint) of good consistency (opposed to *thin*). *–n.* **22.** something round; a circle, ring, curve, etc.; a circular, ring-shaped, or curved object; a rounded form. **23.** something circular in cross-section, as a rung of a ladder. **24.** a completed course of time, a series of events, operations, etc. **25.** any complete course, series, or succession. **26.** (*sometimes pl.*) a circuit of any place, series of places, etc., covered in a customary or predetermined way: *the postman on his rounds.* **27.** a series (of visits, etc.) **28.** a completed course or spell of activity, commonly one of a series, in some game, sport, competition, or the like. **29.** a recurring period or time, succession of events, duties, etc.: *the daily round.* **30.** a single outburst, as of applause, cheers, etc. **31.** a single discharge of shot by each of a number of guns, rifles, etc., or by a single piece. **32.** a charge of ammunition for a single shot. **33.** a distribution of drink, etc., to all the members of a company. **34.** *Obs.* a dance with the dancers arranged or moving in a circle or ring. **35.** movement in a circle or about an axis. **36.** a form of sculpture in which figures are executed apart from any background (contrasted with *relief*). **37.** a standard cut of beef from the lower part of the butt, used for roasting or as steaks. **38. a.** (of bread) a slice. **b.** a sandwich. **39.** *Archery.* a specified number of arrows shot from a specified distance from the target in accordance with the rules. **40.** one of a series of periods (separated by rests) making up a boxing or wrestling match, etc. **41.** *Music.* **a.** a partsong in which the several voices follow one another at equal intervals of time, and at the same pitch as the octave. **b.** (*pl.*) the order followed in ringing a peal of bells in diatonic sequence from the highest to the lowest. **42.** *Golf.* a complete circuit of a prearranged series of holes, usu. the whole course of eighteen holes. **43.** *Cards.* a single turn of play by each player. **44. go the rounds, a.** (of people) to make a series of visits. **b.** (of gossip, information, etc.) to become generally known. **45. in the round,** (of a play, concert, etc.) with the audience seated all around the stage. *–adv.* **46.** in a circle, ring, or the like, or so as to surround something. **47.** on all sides, or about, whether circularly or otherwise. **48.** in all directions from a centre. **49.** *Chiefly U.S.* in the region about a place: *the country round.* **50.** in circumference: *a tree 40 centimetres round.* **51.** in a circular or rounded course: *to fly round and round.* **52.** through a round, circuit, or series, as of places or persons: *to show a person round.* **53.** through a round, or recurring period, of time, esp. to the present or a particular time: *when the time rolls round.* **54.** throughout, or from beginning to end of, a recurring period of time: *all the year round.* **55.** by a circuitous or roundabout course. **56.** to a place or point as by a circuit or circuitous course: *to get round into the navigable channel.* **57.** *Chiefly. U.S.* in circulation, action, etc.; about. **58.** with a rotating course or movement: *the wheels went round.* **59.** with change to another or opposite direction, course, opinion, etc.: *to sit still without looking round.* *–prep.* **60.** so as to encircle, surround, or envelop: *to tie paper round a parcel.* **61.** on the circuit, border, or outer part of it. **62.** around; about. **63.** in or from all or various directions from: *to look round one.* **64.** in the vicinity of: *the country round Geelong.* **65.** in a round, circuit, or course through. **66.** to all or various parts of: *to wander round the country.* **67.** throughout (a period of time): *a resort visited all round the year.* **68.** here and there in: *people standing round a room.* **69.** so as to make a turn or partial circuit about or to the other side of: *to sail round a cape.* **70.** reached by making a turn or partial circuit about (something): *the church round the corner.* **71.** so as to revolve or rotate about (a centre or axis): *the earth's motion round its axis.* **72. round the bend** or **twist,** *Colloq.* insane. *–v.t.* **73.** to make round. **74.** to free from angularity or flatness; fill out symmetrically; make plump. **75.** to bring to completeness or perfection; finish (oft. fol. by *off*). **76.** to frame or form neatly, as a sentence, etc. **77.** to end (a sentence, etc.) with something specified. **78.** to encircle or surround. **79.** to make a turn or partial circuit about, as to get to the other side of: *to round a cape.* **80.** to cause to move in a circle or turn round. **81.** *Phonet.* to pronounce with the lips forming an approximately oval opening: *'boot' has a rounded vowel.* **82. round up,** to collect (cattle, people, etc.) in a particular place or for a particular purpose. *–v.i.* **83.** to become round. **84.** to become free from angularity; become plump. **85.** to develop to completeness or perfection. **86.** to take a circular course; make a circuit; go the round, as a guard. **87.** to make a turn or partial circuit about something. **88.** to turn round as on an axis: *to round on one's heels.* **89. round on** or **upon,** to attack, usu. verbally, with sudden and often unexpected vigour. **90. round out,** add in more detail; give finishing touches. [ME, from OF *rond,* from L *rotundus* wheel-shaped] – **roundish,** *adj.* – **roundness,** *n.*

**roundabout** /ˈraʊndəbaʊt/, *n.* **1.** →**merry-go-round.** **2.** a road junction at which the flow of traffic is facilitated by moving in one direction only round a circular arrangement. *–adj.* **3.** circuitous or indirect, as a road, journey, method, statement, person, etc.

**round-arm** /ˈraʊnd-am/, *Cricket.* *–adj.* **1.** denoting a manner of bowling in which the arm was held more or less horizontal, now no longer allowed. *–adv.* **2.** employing such a style of bowling.

**round dance** /ˈraʊnd dæns/, *n.* **1.** a dance performed by couples and characterised by circular or revolving movement, as the waltz. **2.** (originally) a dance with the dancers arranged in or moving about in a circle or ring.

**rounded** /ˈraʊndəd/, *adj.* **1.** curved or convex; reduced to simple curves; made round. **2.** (of wine) full and soft. **3.** *Phonet.* labialised. **4.** Also, **well-rounded.** complete; mature; brought to perfection, as a character in a play, etc.

**roundel** /ˈraʊndl/, *n.* **1.** something round or circular. **2.** a small round pane or window. **3.** a decorative plate, panel, tablet, or the like, round in form. **4.** *Armour.* **a.** a disc of metal which protects the armpit. **b.** a disc of metal on a hafted weapon or a dagger to protect the hand. **5.** *Pros.* **a.** a rondel or rondeau. **b.** a modification of the rondeau consisting of nine lines with two refrains. **6.** a dance in a circle or ring. [ME *roundele,* from OF *rondel,* from *rond* ROUND, *adj.*]

**roundelay** /ˈraʊndəleɪ/, *n.* **1.** a song in which a phrase, line, or the like is continually repeated. **2.** the music for such a song. **3.** a dance in a circle. [ROUNDEL (def. 5) + LAY[4]]

**rounder** /ˈraʊndə/, *n.* **1.** one who or that which rounds something. **2.** one who makes a round. **3.** (*pl. construed as sing.*) a game played with bat and ball, in which points are scored by running between bases, as in baseball. **4.** a complete run round all the bases in this game.

**round game** /ˈraʊnd geɪm/, *n.* any game in which each participant plays on his own account.

**roundhand** /ˈraʊndhænd/, *n.* **1.** a style of handwriting in which the letters are round, full, and distinct. *–adj.* **2.** denoting or written in this style of handwriting.

**roundhouse** /ˈraʊndhaʊs/, *n.* **1.** a circular-shaped building. **2.** *Naut.* **a.** the captain's accommodation on the quarterdeck of an Indiaman. **b.** the house on the afterdecks of later sailing ships, occupied by apprentices. **c.** the toilets on the forward top deck in the old ships of the Royal Navy. **3.** →**running shed.** **4.** *Obs.* a gaol.

**roundlet** /ˈraʊndlət/, *n.* a small circle or circular object. [ME *rondlet,* from OF *rondelet,* diminutive of *rondel.* See ROUNDEL]

**roundly** /ˈraʊndli/, *adv.* in a round manner; vigorously or briskly; outspokenly, severely, or unsparingly.

**round-off error** /raʊnd-ɒf ˈɛrə/, *n.* any computational error resulting from calculations being carried out only to a specified number of decimal (or binary) digits.

**round robin** /raʊnd ˈrɒbən/, *n.* **1.** a petition, remonstrance, or other letter or paper, having the signatures arranged in circular form, so as to conceal the order of signing. **2.** any petition, etc., signed by a number of people. **3.** a notice or memorandum addressed to a number of persons, each of whom note it and send it to the next on the list of addressees.

**round-shot** /ˈraʊnd-ʃɒt/, *n.* →**cannonball.**

**round-shouldered** /raʊnd-ˈʃoʊldəd/, *adj.* having the shoulders bent forwards, giving a rounded form to the upper part of the back.

**roundsman** /ˈraʊndzmən/, *n., pl.* **-men.** **1.** one who makes rounds, calling on customers to make deliveries, as of milk, bread, etc., or to take orders; a deliveryman. **2.** *U.S.* one who makes rounds of inspection, as, formerly, a police officer who inspects policemen on duty. **3.** a newspaper reporter covering a specific area: *police roundsman, industrial roundsman.*

**round steak** /raʊnd ˈsteɪk/, *n.* the beef cut directly above the hind leg.

**round table** /– ˈteɪbl/, *n.* a number of persons assembled for conference or discussion of some subject, and considered as meeting on equal terms. [from the celebrated table in Arthurian legend, about which King Arthur and his knights sat, made round to avoid quarrels as to precedence]

**round-the-clock** /ˈraʊnd-ðə-klɒk/, *adj.* continuous throughout the day and night: *the police kept up a round-the-clock watch for the suspect.* Also, *esp. in predicative use,* **round the clock.**

**round trip** /raʊnd ˈtrɪp/, *n.* **1.** a tour, as of a city, etc., viewing the main places of interest, and finishing at the point of departure. **2.** →**return trip.**

**round-trip ticket** /raʊnd-trɪp ˈtɪkət/, *n. U.S.* →**return ticket.**

**round-up** /ˈraʊnd-ʌp/, *n.* **1.** the driving together of cattle, etc., for inspection, branding, or the like. **2.** the men and horses who do this. **3.** the herd so collected. **4.** any similar driving or bringing together, as of people, facts, etc.

**roundworm** /ˈraʊndwɜm/, *n.* any nematode, esp. *Ascaris lumbricoides,* infesting the human intestine, or other ascarids in other animals.

**roup** /rup/, *n.* **1.** *Vet. Sci.* any kind of catarrhal inflammation of the eyes and nasal passages of poultry. **2.** hoarseness or huskiness. Also, **roop.** [orig. uncert.]

**roupy** /ˈrupi/, *adj.* **1.** affected with the disease roup. **2.** hoarse or husky.

**rouse**[1] /raʊz/, *v.,* **roused, rousing,** *n.* *–v.t.* **1.** to bring out of a state of sleep, unconsciousness, inactivity, fancied security, apathy, depression, etc. **2.** to stir to strong indignation or anger. **3.** to cause (game) to start from a covert or lair. *–v.i.* **4.** to come out of a state of sleep, unconsciousness, inaction, apathy, depression, etc. **5. rouse away,** *Naut.* pull heavily on a rope. *–n.* **6.** a rousing. **7.** *Obs.* a signal for rousing; the reveille. [orig. uncert.] – **rouser,** *n.*

**rouse**[2] /raʊs/, *v.i.* scold, upbraid (fol. by *on, at*). [Scot. *roust* to shout; roar. Cf. Norw. *rausta, rousta*]

**rouseabout** /ˈraʊsəbaʊt/, *n.* a handyman on a station, in a hotel, etc; blue-tongue. [ROUSE[1] + ABOUT]

**rouser** /ˈraʊsə/, *n. Colloq.* →**rouseabout.** Also, **rousie.**

**Roushians** /ˈruʃiənz/, *n.pl. Colloq.* →**Russians.**

**rousing** /ˈraʊzɪŋ/, *adj.* **1.** that rouses; stirring: *a rousing song.* **2.** vigorous: *a rousing fire.* **3.** brisk; lively: *a rousing trade.* **4.** *Colloq.* great, extraordinary, or outrageous: *a rousing lie.*

rouseabouts in a shearing shed

**roust** /raʊst/, *v.t.* to rout out; incite to activity: *he rousted them out of bed to do the dishes.* [? from ROUSE[1]]

**roustabout** /ˈraʊstəbaʊt/, *n.* →**rouseabout.** [ROUST + ABOUT]

**rout**[1] /raʊt/, *n.* **1.** a defeat attended with disorderly flight; dispersal of a defeated force in complete disorder: *to put an army to rout.* **2.** a defeated and dispersing army. **3.** a tumultuous or disorderly crowd of persons. **4.** a clamour or fuss. **5.** *Law.* an assembly of three or more persons doing some act towards a violent and unlawful purpose, to the terror of the people. **6.** *Archaic.* a troop, company, or band. **7.** (formerly) a large evening party or social gathering. *–v.t.* **8.** to disperse in defeat and disorderly flight: *to rout an army.* **9.** to defeat utterly. [ME, from AF *rute,* from L *rupta,* pp. (fem.), broken]

**rout**[2] /raʊt/, *v.i.* **1.** to poke, search or rummage. **2.** to root, as swine. *–v.t.* **3.** to turn over or dig up with the snout, as swine. **4.** to bring or get in poking about, searching, etc. (fol. by *out*). **5.** to cause to get from bed (fol. by *up* or *out*). **6.** to force or drive out. **7.** to hollow out or furrow, as with a scoop, gouge, or machine. [see ROOT[2], and cf. MD *ruten* root out]

**route** /rut/, *n., v.,* **routed, routeing** or **routing.** *–n.* **1.** a way or road taken or planned for passage or travel. **2.** a customary or regular line of passage or travel. **3.** *Med.* the area of the body through which a curative is introduced: *the digestive route.* *–v.t.* **4.** to fix the route of. **5.** to send or forward by a particular route. [ME, from F, from L *rupta (via)* broken (road)]

**route-march** /ˈrut-matʃ/, *n.* a march, often long or arduous, as taken by soldiers in the course of training.

**router** /ˈrautə/, *n.* **1.** any of various tools or machines for routing, hollowing out, or furrowing. **2.** a carpentry plane designed for working out the bottom of a rectangular cavity. **3.** a tool or machine for routing out parts of an etched plate, electrotype, etc.

**routine** /ruˈtin/, *n.* **1.** a customary or regular course of procedure: *the routine of an office.* **2.** regular, unvarying, or mechanical procedure. **3.** *Computers.* a set of orders which cause a digital computer to perform some simple function. **4.** (in modern dancing, ballet) etc., a piece of choreography. **5.** a rehearsed or habitual persuasive patter: *a salesman's routine.* **6.** *Poker.* →**straight flush.** **7.** of the nature of, proceeding by, or adhering to routine: *routine duties.* [F, from *route* ROUTE]

**roux** /ru/, *n.* a mixture of fat and flour which forms the foundation of most sauces. [F: browned, reddish, from L *russus*]

**rove**[1] /roʊv/, *v.,* **roved, roving.** *–v.i.* **1.** to wander about without definite destination; move hither and thither at random, esp. over a wide area. **2.** to wander, as the eyes, mind, etc. *–v.t.* **3.** to wander over or through; traverse: *to rove the woods.* [ME, from Scand.; cf. Icel. *rāfa*]

**rove**[2] /roʊv/, *v.* a past tense and past participle of **reeve**[2].

**rove**[3] /roʊv/, *n., v.,* **roved, roving.** *–n.* **1.** slivers of wool, cotton, etc., formed into slightly twisted strands in a preparatory process of spinning. *–v.t.* **2.** to form (slivers of wool, cotton, etc.) into such roves. [orig. uncert.]

**rove-beetle** /ˈroʊv-bitl/, *n.* any beetle of the family Staphylinidae, which comprises numerous insects which have long, slender bodies and very short elytra, and which run swiftly.

**rove-over** /ˈroʊv-oʊvə/, *adj.* (in sprung rhythm) of or pertaining to the completion of a metrical foot, incomplete at the end of one line, completed with a syllable or syllables from the beginning of the next line.

**rover**[1] /ˈroʊvə/, *n.* **1.** one who roves; a wanderer. **2.** *Archery.* **a.** a mark selected at random. **b.** any of a group of set marks at a long distance. **c.** one who starts from a distance. **3.** *Croquet.* a ball that has gone through all the arches and needs only to strike the winning peg to be out of the game. **4.** a senior boy scout, of eighteen years or above. **5.** *Aus. Rules.* a player, usu. small, who specialises in ground play, esp. taking and clearing the ball after ruck duels. [ROVE[1] + -ER[1]]

**rover**[2] /ˈroʊvə/, *n. Archaic.* **1.** a sea-robber or pirate. **2.** a pirate ship. [MD or MLG, from *roven* rob]

**roving** /ˈroʊvɪŋ/, *n.* **1.** a strand of loosely assembled fibres, wool, cotton, etc., preparatory to spinning. **2.** *Archery.* shooting at random objects at unknown distances. **3.** *Aus. Rules.* the tasks and activities of a rover.

**roving commission** /ˈ– kəmɪʃən/, *n.* authority to act which is valid in a loosely defined area.

**row**[1] /roʊ/, *n.* **1.** a number of persons or things arranged in a line, esp. a straight line. **2.** a line of adjacent seats facing the same way, as in a theatre. **3.** a street, esp. a narrow one, formed by two continuous lines of buildings. **4.** *Music.* →**tone row.** [ME *row(e),* OE *rāw,* akin to Lithuanian *raiwe* stripe]

**row**[2] /roʊ/, *v.i.* **1.** to use oars or the like for propelling a boat. **2.** to be moved by oars, as a boat. *–v.t.* **3.** to propel (a boat, etc.) by or as by the use of oars. **4.** to convey in a boat, etc., so propelled. **5.** to employ (a number of oars): *the captain's barge rowed twenty oars.* **6.** to use (oars or oarsmen) for rowing. **7.** to perform (a race, etc.) by rowing. **8.** to row against in a race. **9.** to convey or propel (something) in a manner suggestive of rowing. *–n.* **10.** an act of rowing; a turn at the oars. **11.** an excursion in a rowing boat: *to go for a row.* [ME; OE *rōwan,* c. Icel. *rōa;* akin to L *rēmus,* Gk *eretmón.* Cf. RUDDER] – **rower,** *n.*

**row**[3] /raʊ/, *n.* **1.** a noisy dispute or quarrel; commotion. **2.** *Colloq.* noise or clamour. *–v.i.* **3.** *Colloq.* to make or engage in a noisy quarrel. *–v.t.* **4.** *Obs. Colloq.* to assail roughly; upbraid severely. [orig. uncert.]

**R.O.W.,** right of way.

**rowan** /ˈroʊən, ˈraʊ-/, *n.* **1.** the European mountain ash, *Sorbus aucuparia,* a tree with red berries. **2.** either of two American mountain ashes, *S. americana* and *S. sambucifolia.* **3.** the berry of any of these trees. [Scand.; cf. Norw. *raun*]

**rowboat** /ˈroʊboʊt/, *n.* →**rowing boat.**

**rowdy** /ˈraʊdi/, *adj.,* **-dier, -diest,** *n., pl.* **-dies.** *–adj.* **1.** of the nature of or characteristic of a rowdy; rough and disorderly. *–n.* **2.** a rough, disorderly person. [orig. obscure] – **rowdily,** *adv.* – **rowdiness,** *n.* – **rowdyish,** *adj.*

**rowdyism** /ˈraʊdiɪzəm/, *n.* rowdy conduct.

**rowel** /ˈraʊəl/, *n., v.,* **-elled, -elling** or (*U.S.*) **-eled, -eling.** *–n.* **1.** a small wheel with radiating points, forming the extremity of a horseman's spur. **2.** *Vet. Sci.* a piece of leather or the like inserted beneath the skin of a horse or other animal, to cause a discharge. *–v.t.* **3.** to prick, or urge, with a rowel. **4.** *Vet. Sci.* to insert a rowel in. [ME, from OF *roel,* diminutive of *roe, roue,* from L *rota* wheel]

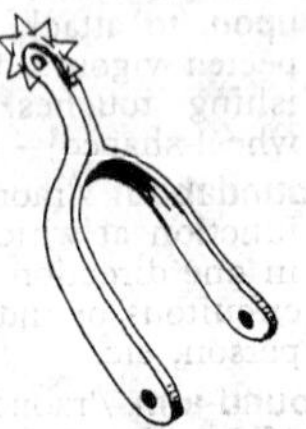

spur with rowel

**rowing boat** /ˈroʊɪŋ boʊt/, *n.* a boat propelled by oars.

**rowlock** /ˈrɒlək/, *n.* a device on or attached by a rigger to a boat's gunwale in or on which

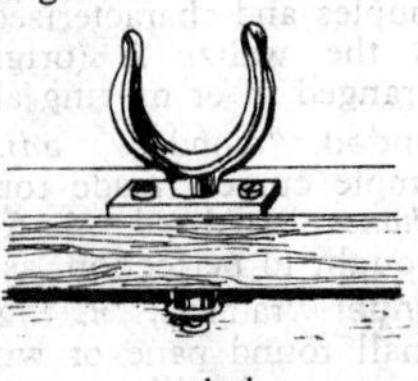

rowlock

the oar rests and swings. Also, *Chiefly U.S.*, **oarlock.** [var. of OARLOCK, by association with ROW[2]]

**Roy** /rɔɪ/, *n.* the archetype of the young, status-conscious Australian (opposed to *Alf*).

**royal** /ˈrɔɪəl/, *adj.* **1.** of or pertaining to a sovereign, king, queen, or the like, or sovereignty: *royal power, a royal palace, the royal family.* **2.** belonging to the royal family: *a royal prince.* **3.** having the rank of a king or queen. **4.** established or chartered by, or existing under the patronage of, a sovereign: *a royal society.* **5.** proceeding from or performed by a sovereign: *a royal warrant.* **6.** befitting, or appropriate to, a sovereign; kinglike or princely; magnificent; splendid: *royal splendour.* **7.** *Obs. Colloq.* fine, first-rate, or excellent: *in royal spirits.* **8.** having a character befitting a sovereign, as noble, generous, brave, etc. **9.** beyond the common or ordinary in size, quality, etc. **10.** (*usu. cap.*) pertaining to the sovereign as civil or military head of state. *–n.* **11.** *Naut.* a sail set on the royal mast, the highest except for the skysail. **12.** a stag having twelve or more points to his antlers. **13.** a traditional size of printing paper in the imperial systems, 20 × 25 in., or of writing paper, 19 × 24 in. **14.** any of various former coins. **15.** *Colloq.* a member of a royal family, esp. the British royal family. [ME, from OF *roial*, from L *rēgālis*] – **royally**, *adv.*

**Royal assent** /rɔɪəl əˈsɛnt/, *n.* →**assent** (def. 3).

**royal blue** /rɔɪəl ˈblu/, *n.*; /ˈrɔɪəl blu/, *adj.* *–n.* **1.** a rich deep blue, often with a faint reddish tinge. *–adj.* **2.** of or pertaining to the colour royal blue.

**Royal Commission** /rɔɪəl kəˈmɪʃən/, *n.* a person or persons, usu. judicial, appointed by the government to enquire into and report on some aspect of public affairs.

**royal fern** /rɔɪəl ˈfɜn/, *n.* a fern, *Osmunda regalis*, with tall fronds.

**royal flush** /– ˈflʌʃ/, *n.* (in poker) the five highest cards of a suit; royal routine.

**royal icing** /– ˈaɪsɪŋ/, *n.* cake icing made from icing sugar and egg-whites, chiefly used for wedding and Christmas cakes, as it hardens and keeps well.

**royalist** /ˈrɔɪələst/, *n.* **1.** a supporter or adherent of a king or a royal government, esp. in times of rebellion or civil war. *–adj.* **2.** of or pertaining to royalists. – **royalism**, *n.* – **royalistic** /rɔɪəˈlɪstɪk/, *adj.*

**royal jelly** /rɔɪəl ˈdʒɛli/, *n.* a substance, secreted from the pharyngeal glands of worker honeybees, and fed to very young larvae and to those selected as queens.

**royal lifesaving** /– ˈlaɪfseɪvɪŋ/, *n.* lifesaving practised in still water (opposed to *surf-lifesaving*).

**royal mast** /– ˈmast/, *n.* the mast next above the topgallant mast.

**royal palm** /– ˈpam/, *n.* any of various tall decorative feather palms of the genus *Roystonea*, including *R. regia* and others.

**royal prerogative** /– prəˈrɒgətɪv/, *n.* the rights of a sovereign, which in theory are unrestricted.

**royal purple** /– ˈpɜpəl/, *n.* a deep bluish-purple colour.

**royal routine** /– ruˈtin/, *n.* →**royal flush.**

**royal tennis** /– ˈtɛnəs/, *n.* an ancient form of tennis played in a walled court, points being scored by hitting the ball so that it lands between certain lines marked on the walls, or in certain openings in the walls. Also, **real tennis;** *Chiefly U.S.*, **court tennis.**

**royalty** /ˈrɔɪəlti/, *n., pl.* **-ties.** **1.** royal persons collectively. **2.** royal status, dignity, or power; sovereignty. **3.** a prerogative or right belonging to a king or sovereign. **4.** a royal domain; a kingdom; a realm. **5.** character or quality proper to or befitting a sovereign; kingliness; nobility; generosity. **6.** a compensation or portion of proceeds paid to the owner of a right, as a patent, for the use of it. **7.** an agreed portion of the proceeds from his work, paid to an author, composer, etc. **8.** a royal right, as over minerals, granted by a sovereign to a person or company. **9.** any such rights granted by their owner to another. **10.** the payment made for such a right. [ME *roialte*, from OF. See ROYAL]

**rozzer** /ˈrɒzə/, *n. Colloq.* a policeman.

**r.p.m.** /a pi ˈɛm/, revolutions per minute.

**r.p.s.** /a pi ˈɛs/, revolutions per second.

**-rrhagia,** variant of **-rhagia.** Also, **-rrhage, -rrhagy.**

**-rrhoea,** variant of **-rhoea.** Also, *Chiefly U.S.*, **-rrhea.**

**R.S.** /ar ˈɛs/, *adj.* **1.** defeated; disgraced. **2.** exhausted; ill. **3.** broken; beyond repair. [abbrev. for RATSHIT]

**RSA** /ar ɛs ˈeɪ/, *N.Z.* Returned Services Association.

**R.S.J.** /ar ɛs ˈdʒeɪ/, rolled steel joist.

**RSL** /ar ɛs ˈɛl/, Returned Services League of Australia.

**R.S.M.** /ar ɛs ˈɛm/, Regimental Sergeant-Major.

**RSPCA** /ˌar ɛs pi si ˈeɪ/, Royal Society for the Prevention of Cruelty to Animals.

**R.S.V.P.** /ˌar ɛs vi ˈpi/, please reply. [F *répondez s'il vous plaît*]

**rt,** right.

**Rt Hon.,** Right Honourable.

**Rt Rev.,** Right Reverend.

**Ru,** *Chem.* ruthenium.

**R.U.,** Rugby Union.

**ruakura round farrowing house** /ruəˈkurə/, *n.* a type of farrowing house developed in New Zealand, which prevents the sow from overlying her piglets, by having a central heat lamp to attract the suckers out of reach of the sow. [from the *Ruakura* Agricultural Research Centre, Hamilton, N.Z.]

**rub** /rʌb/, *v.*, **rubbed, rubbing,** *n.* *–v.t.* **1.** to subject (an object) to pressure and friction, esp. in order to clean, smooth, polish, etc. **2.** to move, spread, or apply (something) with pressure and friction over something else. **3.** to move (things) with pressure and friction over each other (fol. by *together*, etc.). **4.** to force, etc., by rubbing (fol. by *over, in, into*, etc.). **5.** to remove or erase by rubbing (fol. by *off, out*, etc.): *to rub off rust.* **6.** to chafe or abrade. **7. rub down, a.** to rub (the surface of something) as to smooth, reduce, clean, etc. **b.** to massage, dry or clean (an animal, athlete, etc.) by rubbing, as with a towel after exercise, etc. **8. rub noses,** *N.Z.* to touch noses in the Maori welcoming act of hongi. **9. rub out, a.** to erase. **b.** *Colloq.* to kill. **10. rub shoulders** or **elbows,** to come into social contact. **11. rub (up) the right way,** to please. **12. rub (up) the wrong way,** to annoy. **13. rub up, a.** to polish or smooth. **b.** to refresh or revive one's memory (fol. by *on*). **14. rub it in,** to remind someone repeatedly of his mistakes, failures or short comings. *–v.i.* **15.** to exert pressure and friction on something. **16.** to move with pressure along the surface of something. **17.** to proceed, continue in a course, or keep going, with a little effort or difficulty (fol. by *on, along, through*, etc.). **18.** to admit of being rubbed (*off*, etc.): *that stain will rub off.* **19. rub off,** to be transferred, esp. as a result of repeated close contact: *his vulgarity rubbed off on her.* *–n.* **20.** the act of rubbing. **21.** something irritating to the feelings; a reproof, gibe, sarcasm, or the like. **22.** an annoying experience or circumstance. **23.** a difficulty; source of doubt or difficulty: *there's the rub.* **24. rub of the green,** *Golf.* an accidental influence on the ball which may or may not be in the player's favour. **25.** *Archaic.* any difficulty or obstacle. [ME *rubbe*, c. LG *rubben*, of uncert. orig.]

**rub-a-dub** /ˈrʌb-ə-dʌb/, *n.* the sound of a drum when beaten. [imitative]

**rubato** /ruˈbatoʊ/, *n.* **1.** the technique of varying the tempo within a bar of music without either lengthening or shortening the bar. *–adj.* **2.** of music played in this manner. [It., short for *tempo rubato* stolen time]

**rubber**[1] /ˈrʌbə/, *n.* **1.** an elastic material, derived from the latex of species of the genera *Hevea* and *Ficus;* caoutchouc; indiarubber (**natural rubber**). **2.** a class of elastomers made from polymers or copolymers of simple molecules with properties resembling those of natural rubber (**synthetic rubber**). **3.** a piece of indiarubber for erasing pencil marks, etc. **4.** an instrument, tool, etc., used for rubbing something. **5.** a coarse file. **6.** one who rubs, as in order to smooth or polish something. **7.** a cloth, pad or the like, used for polishing, buffing, etc. **8.** *U.S.* (*pl.*) rubber or rubberised waterproof clothes or shoes, as wellington boots or a mackintosh. **9.** *U.S. Colloq.* →**contraceptive sheath.** **10.** *Colloq.* →**thong** (def. 3). [RUB + -ER[1]]

**rubber**[2] /ˈrʌbə/, *n.* **1.** *Bridge, Whist, etc.*, a set of games, usu. three or five, a majority of which decides the overall winner. **2.** a series of games on this pattern in various other sports, as cricket, bowls, croquet, etc.

**rubber band** /– 'bænd/, *n.* a thin, continuous loop of highly elastic rubber, used for holding small objects, etc., together; elastic band.

**rubber bullet** /– 'bʊlət/, *n.* a bullet made of rubber, used in controlling riots, etc., which inflicts pain but rarely causes serious injury.

**rubber cheque** /'– tʃɛk/, *n. (joc.)* a cheque which is dishonoured and so bounces back from the bank.

**rubber duckie** /– 'dʌki/, *n. Colloq.* a small inflated rubber boat usu. with a powerful outboard motor and often used for surf rescue.

**rubberdy** /'rʌbədi/, *n. Colloq.* →**rubbidy.**

**rubberise** /'rʌbəraɪz/, *v.t.*, **-rised, -rising.** to coat or impregnate with rubber or some preparation of it. Also, **rubberize.**

**rubberneck** /'rʌbənɛk/, *Colloq. –n.* **1.** an extremely or excessively curious person. **2.** a tourist. *–adj.* **3.** pertaining to or for such people. *–v.i.* **4.** to look at things in an excessively curious manner.

**rubber plant** /'rʌbə plænt/, *n.* **1.** a plant, *Ficus elastica,* with oblong, shining, leathery leaves, growing native as a tall tree in India, the Malay Archipelago, etc., and much cultivated as an ornamental house plant. **2.** any plant yielding caoutchouc.

**rubber ring** /– 'rɪŋ/, *n.* an inflatable ring-shaped, rubber tube worn round the waist as an aid to swimming.

**rubber stamp** /– 'stæmp/, *n.* **1.** a device of rubber for printing dates, etc., by hand. **2.** *Colloq.* one who gives approval without consideration, or without demur.

**rubber-stamp** /rʌbə-'stæmp/, *v.t.* **1.** to imprint with a rubber stamp. **2.** *Colloq.* to give approval without consideration.

**rubber tree** /'rʌbə tri/, *n.* **1.** a large shrub, native to Asia and northern Africa, *Calotropis procera,* which has been used for fibre and for mattress-filling. **2.** a tree from which rubber is obtained. See **rubber**[1].

**rubbery** /'rʌbəri/, *adj.* like rubber; elastic; tough.

**rubbidy** /'rʌbədi/, *n. Colloq.* a pub. Also, **rubbity, rubbidy-dub.** [rhyming slang, *rub-a-dub,* pub]

**rubbing** /'rʌbɪŋ/, *n.* **1.** the act of one who or that which rubs. **2.** a reproduction of an incised or sculptured surface made by laying paper or the like upon it and rubbing with some marking substance.

**rubbish** /'rʌbɪʃ/, *n.* **1.** waste or refuse material; debris; litter. **2.** worthless stuff; trash. **3.** nonsense. *–v.t.* **4.** to speak of scornfully; criticise; denigrate. [ME *robous, robys;* orig. obscure. Cf. RUBBLE] – **rubbishy,** *adj.*

**rubbish tin** /'– tɪn/, *n.* →**garbage bin.**

**rubble** /'rʌbəl/, *n.* **1.** rough fragments of broken stone, formed by geological action, in quarrying, etc., and sometimes used in masonry. **2.** rough fragments of brick, concrete, or any other building material, esp. when reused for building or foundation. **3.** masonry built of rough fragments of broken stone. **4.** any solid substance, as ice, in irregularly broken pieces. [ME *robyl, robel;* orig. obscure. Cf. RUBBISH] – **rubbly,** *adj.*

**rubble drain** /'– dreɪn/, *n.* a trench with rubble at the bottom and filled with porous soil such that effluents, liquids, etc., may filter through it and be dispersed into the soil below.

**rubblework** /'rʌbəlwɜk/, *n.* masonry built of rubble or roughly dressed stones.

**rub-down** /'rʌb-daʊn/, *n.* →**massage.**

**rube**[1] /rub/, *n. U.S. Colloq.* an unsophisticated countryman. [short for *Reuben,* man's name]

**rube**[2] /rub/, *n, adj. N.Z. Colloq.* →**ruby-dazzler.**

**rubefacient** /rubə'feɪʃənt/, *adj.* **1.** producing redness of the skin, as a medicinal application. *–n.* **2** *Med.* a rubefacient application, as a mustard plaster. [L *rubefaciens,* ppr., making red]

**rubefaction** /rubə'fækʃən/, *n.* **1.** a making red, esp. with a rubefacient. **2.** redness of the skin produced by a rubefacient.

**rubella** /ru'bɛlə/, *n.* →**German measles.** [NL, properly neut. pl. of L *rubellus* reddish]

**rubellite** /'rubəlaɪt/, *n.* a deep red variety of tourmaline, used as a gem. [L *rubellus* reddish + -ITE[1]]

**Rubenism** /'rubənɪzəm/, *n.* a French art movement of the late 17th century which defended the importance of colour in painting. [named after Peter Paul *Rubens,* 1577-1640, Flemish painter]

**rubeola** /ru'biələ/, *n.* **1.** →**measles. 2.** →**German measles.** [NL, diminutive (neut. pl.) of L *rubeus* red] – **rubeolar,** *adj.*

**rubescent** /ru'bɛsənt/, *adj.* becoming red; blushing. [L *rubescens,* ppr.] – **rubescence,** *n.*

**rubiaceous** /rubi'eɪʃəs/, *adj.* belonging to the Rubiaceae, or madder family of plants, including also the coffee, cinchona, ipecacuanha, gardenia, bedstraw, etc. [NL *Rubiaceae* (from L *rubia* madder) + -OUS]

**Rubicon** /'rubəkɒn/, *n.* **1.** a boundary or limitation. **2. pass (cross) the Rubicon,** to take a decisive, irrevocable step. [from *Rubicon,* river in N Italy forming the S boundary of Julius Caesar's province of Cisalpine Gaul, by crossing which, in 49 B.C., he began a civil war with Pompey]

**rubicund** /'rubəkənd/, *adj.* **1.** red or reddish. **2.** of a high colour, as from good living. [L *rubicundus*] – **rubicundity** /rubə'kʌndəti/, *n.*

**rubidium** /ru'bɪdiəm/, *n.* a silvery white metallic, active element resembling potassium, with no commercial uses. *Symbol:* Rb; *at. wt:* 85.47; *at. no.:* 37; *sp. gr.:* 1.53 at 20°C. [NL, from L *rubidus* red (in allusion to the two red lines in its spectrum) + *-ium* -IUM]

**rubiginous** /ru'bɪdʒənəs/, *adj.* rusty; rust-coloured; brownish red. [L *rūbīgo* rust + -OUS]

**rubric** /'rubrɪk/, *n.* **1.** a title, heading, direction, or the like, in a manuscript, book, etc., written or printed in red or otherwise distinguished from the rest of the text. **2.** the title or a heading of a statute, etc. (originally written in red). **3.** a direction for the conduct of divine service or the administration of the sacraments, inserted in liturgical books. **4.** the instructions to the candidate printed at the top of an examination paper. **5.** anything important or worthy of note. [L *rubrīca* red earth; replacing ME *rubriche,* from OF]

**rubrical** /'rubrɪkəl/, *adj.* **1.** of, pertaining to, or enjoined by liturgical rubrics. **2.** *Obs.* reddish; marked with red. – **rubrically,** *adv.*

**rubricate** /'rubrəkeɪt/, *v.t.*, **-cated, -cating. 1.** to mark or colour with red. **2.** to furnish with or regulate by rubrics. [L *rubrīcātus,* pp.] – **rubrication** /rubrə'keɪʃən/, *n.* – **rubricator,** *n.*

**rubricated** /'rubrəkeɪtəd/, *adj.* (in ancient manuscripts, early printed books, etc.) having titles, catchwords, etc., distinctively coloured.

**rubrician** /ru'brɪʃən/, *n.* an expert in rubrics.

**ruby** /'rubi/, *n., pl.* **-bies. 1.** a red variety of corundum, highly prized as a gem **(true ruby** or **oriental ruby). 2.** a piece of this stone. **3.** any of various similar stones, as the spinel ruby, balas ruby, etc. **4.** deep red; carmine. **5.** a printing type (about 5½ point) of a size between pearl and nonpareil. *–adj.* **6.** ruby-coloured: *ruby lips.* **7.** made from or containing a ruby. [ME, from OF *rubi(s),* from L *rubeus* red]

**ruby-dazzler** /rubi-'dæzlə/, *Colloq. –n.* **1.** Also, **bobby-dazzler.** an excellent thing or person. *–adj.* **2.** excellent.

**ruby glass** /'rubi glas/, *n.* glass coloured red by colloidal suspensions of elemental gold, copper, or selenium.

**ruby port** /– 'pɔt/, *n.* a port wine of a deep red colour, younger and fresher than tawny port.

**ruby saltbush** /– 'sɒltbʊʃ/, *n.* a low, spreading shrub, *Enchylaena tomentosa,* family Chenopodiaceae, of mainland Australia, usu. having red, succulent, shiny fruits.

**ruby silver** /'– sɪlvə/, *n.* **1.** →**proustite. 2.** →**pyrargyrite.**

**ruche** /ruʃ/, *n.* a full pleating or frilling of lace, net, muslin, ribbon, etc., used as a trimming or finish. [F: lit., beehive, from LL *rūsca*]

**ruching** /'ruʃɪŋ/, *n.* **1.** material made into a ruche. **2.** ruches collectively.

**ruck**[1] /rʌk/, *n.* **1.** the great mass of undistinguished or inferior persons or things. **2.** a large number or quantity; a crowd or throng. **3.** *Aus. Rules.* **a.** a group of three players, a rover and two ruckmen, who do not have fixed positions but follow the play with the purpose of winning possession of the ball. **b.** the two ruckmen only. **c.** a member of either of these groups. **4.** *Rugby Football.* a group of players struggling for the ball in no set pattern of play; scrimmage.

*–v.i.* **5.** to play as a member of a ruck. **6.** to form a ruck (def. 4). [ME *ruke,* probably from Scand.; cf. Norw. *ruka* in same senses; akin to RICK[1], *n.*]

**ruck**[2] /rʌk/, *n., v.t., v.i.* fold, crease, or wrinkle. [Scand.; cf. Icel. *hrukka*]

**ruckman** /ˈrʌkmæn, -mən/, *n., pl.* **-men** /-mən/. (in Australian Rules) one who plays in the ruck.

**ruck-rover** /rʌk-ˈroʊvə/, *n.* (in Australian Rules) one who follows the play as a ruckman, but does not generally contest hit-outs, being given his role for his ability in general play.

**rucksack** /ˈrʌksæk/, *n.* a kind of knapsack carried by hikers, etc. [G: lit., back sack]

**ruckus** /ˈrʌkəs/, *n. Chiefly U.S. Colloq.* **1.** a commotion; rumpus. **2.** a violent disagreement.

**ruckwork** /ˈrʌkwɜk/, *n.* the tasks assigned to a ruckman, esp. contesting hit-outs.

**ruction** /ˈrʌkʃən/, *n. Colloq.* a disturbance, quarrel or row. [cf. obs. *ructation* belching, vomiting, aphetic var. of ERUCTATION]

**rudbeckia** /rʌdˈbɛkiə/, *n.* any of the showy-flowered herbs constituting the genus *Rudbeckia,* as the tall, frequently cultivated *R. laciniata,* which has a large capitulum with a conical green disc, and golden yellow rays; coneflower. [NL; named after O. *Rudbeck,* 1630-1702, Swedish botanist]

**rudd** /rʌd/, *n.* a European freshwater fish, *Scardinius erythrophthalmus,* of the carp family. [apparently special use of *rud* (now d.), OE *rudu* redness]

**rudder** /ˈrʌdə/, *n.* **1.** a board or plate of wood or metal hinged vertically at the stern of a boat or ship as a means of steering. **2.** a device like a ship's rudder for steering an aeroplane, etc., hinged vertically (for right-and-left steering). [ME *roder, rother,* OE *rōthor,* c. G *Ruder.* See ROW[2]]

R, rudder

**rudderhead** /ˈrʌdəhɛd/, *n.* the upper end of the rudderpost which is connected to the quadrant or tiller and controlled by the wheel.

**rudderpost** /ˈrʌdəpoʊst/, *n.* **1.** Also, **rudderstock** /ˈrʌdəstɒk/. the vertical member at the forward end of a rudder which is hinged to the sternpost and attached to the helm or steering gear. **2.** the vertical member abaft the screw, in single-screw vessels, which holds the rudder.

**ruddle** /ˈrʌdl/, *n., v.,* **-dled, -dling.** →**raddle.** [OE *rudu* a red cosmetic]

**ruddy** /ˈrʌdi/, *adj.,* **-dier, -diest,** *adv.* *–adj.* **1.** of or having a fresh, healthy red colour. **2.** reddish. *–adv.* **3.** *Colloq.* extremely: *I've a ruddy good mind to hit him.* [ME *rudi,* OE *rudig,* from *rudu* redness] – **ruddiness,** *n.*

**rude** /rud/, *adj.,* **ruder, rudest. 1.** discourteous or impolite: *a rude reply.* **2.** without culture, learning, or refinement. **3.** rough in manners or behaviour; unmannerly. **4.** rough, harsh, or ungentle: *rude hands.* **5.** roughly wrought, built, or formed; of a crude make or kind. **6.** unwrought, raw, or crude. **7.** harsh to the ear, as sounds. **8.** without artistic elegance; of a primitive simplicity. **9.** violent or tempestuous, as the waves. **10.** robust, sturdy, or vigorous: *rude strength.* [ME, from L *rudis*] – **rudely,** *adv.* – **rudeness,** *n.*

**ruderal** /ˈrudərəl/, *adj.* growing near human habitations in waste places.

**rudiment** /ˈrudəmənt/, *n.* **1.** the elements or first principles of a subject: *the rudiments of grammar.* **2.** (*usu. pl.*) a mere beginning, first slight appearance, or undeveloped or imperfect form of something. **3.** *Biol.* an organ or part incompletely developed in size or structure, as one in an embryonic stage, one arrested in growth, or one with no functional activity, as a vestige. [L *rudīmentum* beginning]

**rudimentary** /rudəˈmɛntəri, -tri/, *adj.* **1.** pertaining to rudiments or first principles; elementary. **2.** of the nature of a rudiment; undeveloped. **3.** vestigial; abortive. Also, **rudimental.** – **rudimentarily,** *adv.* – **rudimentariness,** *n.*

**rue**[1] /ru/, *v.,* **rued, ruing,** *n.* *–v.t.* **1.** to feel sorrow over; repent of; regret bitterly. **2.** to wish (that something might never have been done, taken place, etc.): *to rue the day one was born.* *–v.i.* **3.** to feel sorrow; be repentant. **4.** to feel regret. *–n. Archaic.* **5.** sorrow; repentance; regret. **6.** pity or compassion. [ME *rue, rewe,* OE *hrēowan,* c. G *reuen*]

**rue**[2] /ru/, *n.* any of the strongly scented plants constituting the genus *Ruta,* esp. *R. graveolens,* a yellow-flowered herb with decompound leaves formerly much used in medicine. [ME from OF and F, from L *rūta,* from Gk *rhȳtḗ*]

**rueful** /ˈrufəl/, *adj.* **1.** such as to cause sorrow or pity; deplorable; pitiable: *a rueful plight.* **2.** feeling, showing, or expressing sorrow or pity; wry; mournful; doleful. – **ruefully,** *adv.* – **ruefulness,** *n.*

**rufescent** /ruˈfɛsənt/, *adj.* somewhat reddish; tinged with red; rufous. [L *rūfescens,* ppr., becoming reddish] – **rufescence,** *n.*

**ruff**[1] /rʌf/, *n.* **1.** a neckpiece or collar of lace, lawn, etc., gathered or drawn into deep, full, regular folds, much worn in the 16th century by both men and women. **2.** something resembling such a piece in form or position. **3.** a collar, or set of lengthened or specially marked hairs or feathers, on the neck of an animal. **4.** a shorebird, *Philomachus pugnax,* the male of which has an enormous frill of feathers on the neck during the breeding season. The female is called a *reeve.* [? n. use of ROUGH *adj.*] – **ruffed,** *adj.*

ruff[1]

**ruff**[2] /rʌf/, *n.* **1.** *Cards.* the act of trumping when one cannot follow suit. **2.** *Obs.* an old game at cards, resembling whist. *–v.t., v.i.* **3.** *Cards.* to trump when unable to follow suit. [probably from F *ro(u)ffle,* c. It. *ronfa* a card game]

**ruff**[3] /rʌf/, *n.* →**tommy ruff.**

**ruffe** /rʌf/, *n.* →**pope**[2]. [ME *ruf, roffe;* ? special use of ROUGH, *adj.*]

**ruffian** /ˈrʌfiən/, *n.* **1.** a violent, lawless man; a rough brute. *–adj.* **2.** Also, **ruffianly.** pertaining to or characteristic of a ruffian; lawless; brutal. [earlier *rufian,* from F]

**ruffianism** /ˈrʌfiənɪzəm/, *n.* **1.** conduct befitting a ruffian. **2.** ruffianly character.

**ruffle**[1] /ˈrʌfəl/, *v.,* **-fled, -fling,** *n.* *–v.t.* **1.** to destroy the smoothness or evenness of: *the wind ruffled the sand.* **2.** to erect (the feathers), as in anger, as a bird. **3.** to annoy, disturb, discompose, or irritate. **4.** to turn over (the pages of a book) rapidly. **5.** to pass (cards) through the fingers rapidly. **6.** to draw up (cloth, lace, etc.) into a ruffle by gathering along one edge. *–v.i.* **7.** to be or become ruffled. *–n.* **8.** a break in the smoothness or evenness of some surface. **9.** a strip of cloth, lace, etc., drawn up by gathering along one edge, and used as a trimming on dress, etc. **10.** some object resembling this, as the ruff of a bird. **11.** a disturbing experience; an annoyance or vexation. **12.** a disturbed state of the mind; perturbation. [ME; c. LG *ruffelen* crumple, rumple; cf. Icel. *hrufla* scratch]

**ruffle**[2] /ˈrʌfəl/, *n., v.,* **-fled, -fling.** *–n.* **1.** a low, continuous beating of a drum, less loud than a roll. *–v.t.* **2.** to beat (a drum) in this manner. [from *ruff* in same sense; ? imitative]

**rufous** /ˈrufəs/, *adj.* reddish; rufescent; tinged with red; brownish red. [L *rūfus* red, reddish]

**rufous-bellied buzzard** /ˌrufəs-bɛlid ˈbʌzəd/, *n.* →**red goshawk.**

**rufous rat-kangaroo** /rufəs ˈræt-kæŋgəru/, *n.* a large rat-kangaroo, *Aepyprymnus rufescens,* of eastern Australia, having a reddish fur.

**rufous wallaby** /– ˈwɒləbi/, *n.* →**red wallaby.**

**rug** /rʌg/, *n.* **1.** a small, often thick, carpet, used as a floor covering or a hanging, and made of woven or tufted wool, cotton, or the like, fur, etc. **2.** a thick, warm blanket used as a coverlet, etc., or wrap, to keep travellers warm. **3. cut a rug,** *Chiefly U.S. Colloq.* to dance, esp. with verve, as to jazz. *–v.t.* **4. rug (oneself) up,** to make or keep (oneself) warm by wrapping (oneself) up in thick clothing or covering, as coats, scarves, socks, rugs, etc. [Scand.; cf. d. Norw. *rugga* coarse covering (for bed or body)]

**ruga** /ˈrugə/, *n., pl.* **-gae** /-dʒi/. a wrinkle, fold, or ridge. [L]

**rugate** /ˈrugeɪt, -gət/, *adj.* wrinkled; rugose.

**Rugby football** /ˌrʌgbi ˈfʊtbɔl/, *n.* **1.** →**Rugby Union.** **2.** →**Rugby League.**

**Rugby League** /– ˈlig/, *n.* **1.** one of the two forms of Rugby football, played by teams of thirteen players each, differing from Rugby Union in certain details of the rules and in permitting professionalism. **2.** the organisation that regulates conditions of the game. Also, **League.**

**Rugby Union** /– ˈjunjən/, *n.* one of the two forms of Rugby football, played by teams of fifteen players each, differing from Rugby League in certain details of the rules and restricted to amateurs. Also, **Union.**

**rugged** /ˈrʌgəd/, *adj.* **1.** roughly broken, rocky, hilly, or otherwise difficult of passage: *rugged ground.* **2.** wrinkled or furrowed: *a rugged face.* **3.** roughly irregular, heavy, or hard in outline or form: *Lincoln's rugged features.* **4.** rough, harsh, or stern, as persons, their nature, etc. **5.** severe, hard, or trying: *a rugged life.* **6.** *Obs.* tempestuous, as weather. **7.** harsh to the ear, as sounds. **8.** rude, uncultivated, or unrefined, but sturdy or strong: *rugged individualism.* **9.** *U.S.* robust or vigorous. **10.** *Colloq.* uncomfortable; entailing hardship. [ME, from Scand.; cf. Swed. *rugga* roughen. See RUG] – **ruggedly,** *adv.* – **ruggedness,** *n.*

**rugger** /ˈrʌgə/, *n.* →**Rugby Union.**

**rugger-bugger** /ˈrʌgə-bʌgə/, *n. Colloq.* (*derog.*) **1.** a fanatical Rugby Union supporter. **2.** an aggressively self-confident man, often of good social standing and reactionary views, given to loud displays and larrikin behaviour.

**rugose** /ˈrugoʊs, ruˈgoʊs/, *adj.* **1.** having wrinkles; wrinkled; ridged. **2.** *Bot.* rough and wrinkled (applied to leaves in which the reticulate venation is very prominent beneath with corresponding creases on the upper side). [L *rūgōsus* wrinkled] – **rugosely,** *adv.* – **rugosity** /ruˈgɒsəti/, *n.*

**ruin** /ˈruən/, *n.* **1.** (*pl.*) the remains of a fallen building, town, etc., or of anything in a state of destruction or decay: *the ruins of an ancient city.* **2.** a ruined building, town, etc. **3.** fallen and wrecked or decayed state; ruinous condition: *a building falls to ruin.* **4.** the downfall, decay, or destruction of anything. **5.** the complete loss of means, position, or the like. **6.** something that causes downfall or destruction. **7.** the downfall of a person. **8.** a person as the wreck of his former self. **9.** the seduction of a woman. *–v.t.* **10.** to reduce to ruin. **11.** to bring (a person, etc.) to financial ruin. **12.** to injure (a thing) irretrievably. **13.** to seduce. *–v.i.* **14.** to fall into ruins. **15.** to come to ruin. [ME *ruine,* from OF, from L *ruīna* overthrow, ruin] – **ruinable,** *adj.* – **ruined,** *adj.* – **ruiner,** *n.*

**ruination** /ruəˈneɪʃən/, *n.* **1.** the act of ruining. **2.** the state of being ruined. **3.** something that ruins.

**ruinous** /ˈruənəs/, *adj.* **1.** bringing or tending to bring ruin; destructive; disastrous: *a ruinous war.* **2.** fallen into ruin; dilapidated. **3.** consisting of ruins. – **ruinously,** *adv.* – **ruinousness,** *n.*

**rule** /rul/, *n., v.,* **ruled, ruling.** *–n.* **1.** a principle or regulation governing conduct, action, procedure, arrangement, etc. **2.** the code of regulations observed by a religious order or congregation. **3.** that which customarily or normally occurs or holds good: *the rule rather than the exception.* **4.** control, government, or dominion. **5.** tenure or conduct of reign or office. **6.** a prescribed mathematical method for performing a calculation or solving a problem. **7.** →**ruler** (def. 2). **8.** *Print.* **a.** a thin, type-high strip of metal, usu. brass, for printing a line or lines. **b.** (in photocomposition) a black tape in various widths and designs. **c.** a printed line. **9.** *Law.* **a.** a formal order or direction made by a court and limited in application to the case for which it is given (**special rule**). **b.** an order or regulation governing the procedure of a court (**general rule**). **c.** a proposition of law. **10.** (*pl.*) *Brit.* **a.** a fixed area in the neighbourhood of certain prisons, within which certain prisoners were allowed to live on giving security. **b.** the freedom of such an area. **11. as a rule,** usually. **12. bend the rules,** *Colloq.* to make an exception to the rules. *–v.t.* **13.** to control or direct; exercise dominating power or influence over. **14.** to exercise authority or dominion over; govern. **15.** to decide or declare judicially or authoritatively; decree. **16.** to mark with lines, esp. parallel straight lines, with the aid of a ruler or the like. **17.** to mark out or form (a line) by this method. **18. rule off,** to mark the end (of something written) by ruling a line beneath. **19. rule out,** to exclude, refuse to admit, declare (something) out of the question. *–v.i.* **20.** to exercise dominating power or influence. **21.** to exercise authority, dominion, or sovereignty. **22.** to make a formal decision or ruling, as on a point at law. **23.** to prevail or be current, as prices. [ME, from OF *riule,* from L *rēgula* straight stick, pattern]

**rule nisi** /– ˈnaɪsaɪ/, *n.* an order made by the court calling on the party against whom it is made to show cause why the rule should not be made absolute.

**rule of law,** *n.* **1.** the doctrine that all men are equal before the law, and that the government is subject to the law. **2.** the absence of arbitrary executive power.

**rule of the road,** *n.* a code or custom regulating movement of ships, vehicles, etc., for their mutual convenience and safety.

**rule of three,** *n.* the method of finding the fourth term in a proportion when three terms are given; golden rule.

**rule of thumb,** *n.* **1.** a rule based on experience or practice rather than on scientific knowledge. **2.** a rough, practical method of procedure.

**ruler** /ˈrulə/, *n.* **1.** one who or that which rules or governs; a sovereign. **2.** a strip of wood, metal, or other material with a graduated straight edge, used in drawing lines, measuring, etc. **3.** one who or that which rules paper, etc. – **rulership,** *n.*

**Rules** /rulz/, *n. Colloq.* →**Australian Rules.**

**ruling** /ˈrulɪŋ/, *n.* **1.** an authoritative decision, as by a judge on a point at law. **2.** the act of drawing straight lines with a rule. **3.** ruled lines. *–adj.* **4.** that rules; governing. **5.** →**predominating.** **6.** →**prevalent.**

**rum**[1] /rʌm/, *n.* **1.** an alcoholic spirit distilled from molasses or some other sugar-cane product. **2.** *U.S.* alcoholic drink in general; intoxicating liquor. [? short for obs. *rumbullion.* Cf. F *rebouillir* boil again]

**rum**[2] /rʌm/, *adj. Colloq.* **1.** odd, strange, or queer. **2.** *Archaic.* good or fine. **3. rum go,** *Colloq.* harsh or unfair treatment. Also, **rummy.** [earlier *rome, room,* great, of unknown orig.]

**Rumania** /ruˈmeɪniə/, *n.* →**Romania.**

**Rumanian** /ruˈmeɪniən/, *adj.* →**Rumanian.**

**rumba** /ˈrʌmbə/, *n.* **1.** a dance, Cuban in origin and complex in rhythm (in 8 time). **2.** an imitation or adaptation of this dance. **3.** the music for this dance or in its rhythm. [Sp., probably of Afr. orig.]

**rum baba** /rʌm ˈbabə/, *n.* →**baba.**

**rumball** /ˈrʌmbɔl/, *n.* a small ball of rum and chocolate flavoured cake, esp. one made with biscuit or cake crumbs held together with shortening and rolled in coconut, crushed nuts, etc.

**rumble** /ˈrʌmbəl/, *v.,* **-bled, -bling,** *n.* *–v.i.* **1.** to make a deep, heavy, continuous, resonant sound, as thunder, etc. **2.** to move, travel or be conveyed with such a sound: *the train rumbled on.* **3.** *Colloq.* to take part in a fight, as between gangs. *–v.t.* **4.** to give forth or utter with a rumbling sound. **5.** to cause to make or move with a rumbling sound. **6.** to subject to the action of a rumble or tumbling box, as for the purpose of polishing. **7.** *Colloq.* to detect or become suspicious of, as a fraud. **8. a.** to fight. **b.** to get the better of, as in a contest. *–n.* **9.** a rumbling sound, as of thunder or a heavy vehicle. **10.** *U.S.* a dicky; rumble seat. **11.** a rear part of a carriage containing seating accommodation as for servants or space for baggage. **12.** a tumbling box. **13.** *Colloq.* a fight, esp. between teenage gangs. **14.** *Colloq.* a prank, usu. undertaken by a group, sometimes involving violence. [ME. Cf. D *rommelen,* probably of imitative orig.]

**rumbled brick** /rʌmbəld ˈbrɪk/, *n.* a brick, usu. not of the first quality, which has been tumbled in a drum to round off its corners and arrises, and which is used for special effects in building.

**rumble seat** /ˈ– sit/, *n. U.S.* →**dicky**[1] (def. 4).

**rumble strip** /ˈ– strɪp/, *n.* one of several strips of concrete or other such material fixed to a road to discourage vehicle encroachment by producing a loud noise when a car travels over them.

**rumbly** /ˈrʌmbli/, *adj.* **1.** rumbling. **2.** attended with, making, or causing a rumbling sound.

**rumbustious** /rʌmˈbʌstʃəs/, *adj.* boisterous, noisy. [probably var. of ROBUSTIOUS]

**rumen** /ˈrumən/, *n., pl.* **-mina** /-mənə/. **1.** the first stomach of ruminating animals, lying next to the reticulum. **2.** the cud of a ruminant. [L: throat, gullet]

**ruminant** /ˈrumənənt/, *n.* **1.** any animal of the artiodactyl suborder or division, Ruminantia, which comprises the various 'cloven-hoofed' and cud-chewing quadrupeds, as cattle, bison, buffalo, sheep, goats, chamois, deer, antelopes, giraffes, camels, chevrotains, etc. *–adj.* **2.** ruminating; chewing the cud. **3.** given to or characterised by meditation; meditative. [L. *rūminans*, ppr., ruminating]

ruminant stomach: A, duodenum; B, abomasum; C, omasum; D, oesophagus; E, reticulum; F, rumen

**ruminate** /ˈruməneɪt/, *v.,* **-nated, -nating.** *–v.i.* **1.** to chew the cud, as a ruminant. **2.** to meditate or muse; ponder. *–v.t.* **3.** to chew again. **4.** to meditate on; ponder. [L *rūminātus*, pp.] **– ruminatingly,** *adv.* **– rumination** /ruməˈneɪʃən/, *n.* **– ruminative** /ˈrumənətɪv/, *adj.* **– ruminator,** *n.*

**rummage** /ˈrʌmɪdʒ/, *v.,* **-maged, -maging,** *n.* *–v.t.* **1.** to search thoroughly or actively through (a place, receptacle, etc.), esp. by moving about, turning over, or looking through contents. **2.** to find (fol. by *out* or *up*) by searching. *–v.i.* **3.** to search actively, as in a place or receptacle, or among contents, etc. *–n.* **4.** miscellaneous articles; odds and ends. **5.** a rummaging search. [F *arrumage*, n., from *arrumer* stow goods in hold of ship; orig. uncert.] **– rummager,** *n.*

**rummage sale** /ˈ– seɪl/, *n.* →**jumble sale.**

**rummer** /ˈrʌmə/, *n.* a large drinking glass or cup typically of a heavy goblet shape. [cf. Flem. *rummer,* G *Romer;* orig. uncert.]

**rummy**[1] /ˈrʌmi/, *n.* a card game in which the object is to match cards into sets and sequences. [orig. uncert.]

**rummy**[2] /ˈrʌmi/, *adj.,* **-mier, -miest.** *Colloq.* odd; queer. [RUM[2] + -Y[1]]

**rumour** /ˈrumə/, *n.* **1.** a story or statement in general circulation without confirmation or certainty as to facts. **2.** unconfirmed gossip. *–v.t.* **3.** to circulate, report, or assert by a rumour. Also, *U.S.,* **rumor.** [ME, from OF, from L *rūmor*]

**rump** /rʌmp/, *n.* **1.** the hinder part of the body of an animal. **2.** a cut of beef from this part of the animal, behind the loin and above the round, as chump of lamb, fillet of pork, etc. **3.** →**buttocks. 4.** any remnant; the last and unimportant or inferior part; fag-end. [ME *rumpe,* from Scand.; cf. Dan. *rumpe* rump, c. G *Rumpf* trunk]

**rumper** /ˈrʌmpə/, *n.* a domestic fowl with peculiar feather growth due to lack of a tail bone.

**rumple** /ˈrʌmpəl/, *v.,* **-pled, -pling,** *n.* *–v.t.* **1.** to draw or crush into wrinkles; crumple: *a rumpled sheet.* **2.** to ruffle; tousle (oft. fol. by *up*). *–v.i.* **3.** to become wrinkled or crumpled. *–n.* **4.** a wrinkle or irregular fold; crease. [MD *rompel,* n., or from MLG *rumpel*]

**rumpus** /ˈrʌmpəs/, *n. Colloq.* **1.** disturbing noise; uproar. **2.** a noisy or violent disturbance or commotion.

**rumpus room** /ˈ– rum/, *n.* **1.** a playroom. **2.** a room in a house for informal recreation and entertainment.

**run** /rʌn/, *v.,* **ran, run, running,** *n., adj.* *–v.i.* **1.** to move quickly on foot, so as to go more rapidly than in walking (in bipedal locomotion, so that for an instant in each step neither foot is on the ground). **2.** to do this for exercise, as a sport, etc. **3.** to hurry; go quickly. **4.** to move swiftly by rolling on wheels or in various other ways: *the train ran along the track.* **5.** to make a quick succession of movements, as with the fingers: *the pianist ran up the scale.* **6.** to move easily or swiftly, as a vehicle, on wheels, a vessel, etc. **7.** to make off quickly, take to flight. **8.** to make a short, quick, or casual journey, as for a visit, etc. (oft. fol. by *up, over, round,* etc.). **9.** *Racing.* **a.** to take part in a race. **b.** to finish a race in a certain (numerical) position: *he ran second.* **10.** *U.S.* to stand as a candidate for election: *he is running for president.* **11.** *Colloq.* to migrate, as fish: *to run in huge shoals.* **12.** to pass upstream or inshore from deep water to spawn. **13.** to sail or be driven (ashore, into a channel, etc.), as a vessel or those on board. **14.** *Naut.* to sail before the wind. **15.** to ply between places, as a vessel. **16.** to traverse a route, as a public conveyance: *the buses run every hour.* **17.** to roam without restraint (oft. fol. by *about*): *children running about in the park.* **18.** to have recourse to, as for consolation: *he's always running to his mother.* **19.** to move, revolve, slide, etc., esp. easily, freely, or smoothly: *a rope runs in a pulley.* **20.** to flow, as a liquid or a body of liquid, or as sand, grain, or the like. **21.** to flow along, esp. strongly, as a stream, the sea, etc.: *with a strong tide running.* **22.** to melt and flow, as solder, varnish, etc. **23.** to spread or diffuse when exposed to moisture, as dyestuffs: *the colours in a fabric run.* **24.** to flow, stream, or be wet with a liquid. **25.** to discharge or give passage to a liquid. **26.** to overflow or leak, as a vessel (oft. fol. by *over*). **27.** to creep, trail, or climb, as vines, etc. **28.** to pass quickly: *a thought ran across his mind.* **29.** to continue in or return to the mind persistently: *a tune running through one's head.* **30.** to recur or be inherent: *madness runs in the family.* **31.** to come undone, as stitches or a fabric; ladder. **32.** to be in operation or continue operating, as a machine. **33.** *Comm.* **a.** to accumulate, or become payable in due couse, as interest on a debt. **b.** to make many withdrawals in rapid succession. **34.** *Law.* **a.** to have legal force or effect, as a writ. **b.** to continue to operate. **c.** to go along with or accompany: *the easement runs with the land.* **35.** to pass or go by, as time. **36.** to continue to be performed, as a play, over a period. **37.** to be disseminated, spread rapidly, as news. **38.** to spread or pass quickly from point to point: *a shout ran through the crowd.* **39.** to be in a certain form or expression: *so the story runs.* **40.** to extend or stretch. **41.** to have a specified quality, character, form, etc. **42.** to be or tend to be of a specified size or number: *potatoes running large.* **43.** to exist or occur within a specified range of variation. **44.** to pass into a certain state or condition; become: *to run wild.* *–v.t.* **45.** to cause (an animal, etc.) to move quickly on foot. **46.** to cause (a vehicle, etc.) to move: *I'll just run the car into the garage.* **47.** to traverse (a distance or course) in running: *he ran a kilometre.* **48.** to perform by or as by running: *to run a race, run an errand.* **49. a.** to compete with in a race. **b.** to lead in a chase; outrun. **50.** to enter a horse, etc., in a race. **51.** to run along: *to run the streets.* **52.** to run or get past or through: *to run a blockade.* **53.** to bring into a certain state by running: *to run oneself out of breath.* **54.** to pursue or hunt (game, etc.). **55.** to drive (livestock), esp. to pasture. **56.** to keep (livestock), as on pasture. **57.** to cause to move, esp. quickly or cursorily: *to run one's fingers through one's hair, to run one's eyes over a letter.* **58.** to cause to ply between places, as a vessel, conveyance, or system of transport: *to run a train service between two cities.* **59.** to convey or transport, as in a vessel or vehicle. **60.** to keep operating or in service, as a machine. **61.** to possess and use, as a car. **62.** to expose oneself to or be exposed to (a risk, etc.). **63.** to sew, esp. with quick, even stitches in a line. **64.** (in some games, as billiards) to complete a series of successful strokes, shots, etc. **65.** to bring, lead, or force into some state, action, etc.: *to run oneself into debt.* **66.** to cause (a liquid) to flow. **67.** to give forth or flow with (a liquid). **68.** to pour forth or discharge. **69.** to cause (a bath, etc.) to contain water; fill. **70.** to cause to move easily, freely, or smoothly: *to run a sail up the mast.* **71.** to drive, force, or thrust. **72.** to extend or build, as in a particular direction: *to run a road through the forest.* **73.** to draw or trace, as a line. **74.** to conduct, administer, or manage, as a business, an experiment, or the like. **75.** (of a newspaper) to publish (a story). **76.** *U.S.* to put up (a candidate) for election. **77.** to melt, fuse, or smelt, as ore. **78.** →**smuggle. 79. run a book,** *Colloq.* to accept bets. *–v.* **80.** Some special verb phrases are:

**cut and run,** to take to flight.

**run across,** to meet or find unexpectedly.

**run after,** to seek to attract.

**run around,** to behave promiscuously.

**run (around) with,** to keep company with.

**run away, 1.** to take a flight. **2.** to depart: *run away, I'm busy; he ran away to sea.*

**run away with, 1.** to elope with. **2.** to steal. **3.** to win easily:

*he ran away with the election.* **4.** to use up (money, etc.) quickly. **5.** to get out of control, as a horse, a vehicle, one's emotions or ideas, etc. **6.** *Colloq.* to accept (an idea), esp. erroneously or with insufficient justification: *don't run away with the idea that you can go on behaving so badly.*
**run close,** to press severely, as a competitor.
**run down, 1.** to slow up before stopping, as a clock or other mechanism. **2.** to knock down and injure, as a vehicle or driver; run over. **3.** *Naut.* to collide with and cause to sink, as a smaller vessel. **4.** to denigrate; make adverse criticism of. **5.** to reduce, as stocks. **6.** to find, esp. after extensive searching. **7.** to pass quickly over or review: *to run down a list of possibilities.*
**run hard,** to press severely, as a competitor.
**run in, 1.** to cause (new machinery, esp. a motor vehicle) to run at reduced load and speed for an initial period, so that stiffness, etc., is reduced gradually and the machine becomes ready for full operation without damage. **2.** *Colloq.* →**arrest. 3.** *Print.* to add (new text matter) without indentation. **4.** *Aeron.* to approach a landing.
**run into, 1.** to encounter unexpectedly. **2.** to collide with. **3.** to amount to: *an income running into five figures.*
**run off, 1.** to depart or retreat quickly. **2.** to produce by a printing or similar process. **3.** to write or otherwise create quickly. **4.** to steal (fol. by *with*). **5.** →**elope. 6.** to determine the result of (a tied contest, etc.) by a run-off.
**run on, 1.** to have as a topic: *the conversation ran on politics.* **2.** to continue, as talking, at length and without interruption. **3.** (of handwritten lettering) to be linked up. **4.** *Print.* to print as continuous unindented text.
**run out, 1.** to depart, as from a room, quickly. **2.** to be completely used up: *the food has run out, time is running out.* **3.** *Cricket.* to put (a batsman) out by hitting the wicket with the ball while neither he nor his bat are touching the ground within the popping crease. **4.** *Naut.* to pass or pay out (a rope). **5.** *Showjumping.* (of a horse) to refuse by running outside the jump. **6.** *U.S.* to drive out; expel.
**run out on,** to desert; abandon.
**run over, 1.** to knock down and injure, as a vehicle or driver. **2.** to exceed (a time-limit or the like). **3.** to review, rehearse, or recapitulate.
**run rings (a)round (someone),** to perform with far greater success.
**run short,** to become scarce or nearly used up.
**run through, 1.** to rehearse or review. **2.** to exhaust or use up (money, etc.). **3.** to pass a sword or the like through (somebody).
**run to, 1.** to be sufficient for: *the money doesn't run to caviar.* **2.** to include: *his books don't run to descriptions.* **3.** to become as specified: *to run to fat.*
**run up, 1.** to climb quickly: *a sailor ran up the mast.* **2.** to hoist (a sail, flag, etc.). **3.** to amass or incur, as a bill. **4.** to make, esp. quickly, as something sewn.
**run up against, 1.** to meet unexpectedly. **2.** to be impeded by.
**run upon, 1.** to have as a topic, as thoughts or a conversation. **2.** (of a ship) to go aground upon.
*–n.* **81.** an act, instance, or spell of running: *to go for a run.* **82.** a running pace. **83.** an act or instance of escaping, running away, etc. **84.** an act or spell of moving rapidly, as in a boat or vehicle. **85.** the distance covered. **86.** a period or act of travelling, esp. a scheduled journey: *an uneventful run to Paris.* **87.** a quick, short trip. **88.** a spell of driving in a car, riding a horse, etc. **89.** a spell or period of causing something, as a machine, to run or continue operating. **90.** the amount of something produced in any uninterrupted period of operation. **91.** a continuous course of performances, as of a play. **92.** a line or place in knitted or sewn work where a series of stitches have slipped or come undone; a ladder. **93.** the direction of something fixed: *the run of the grain of a piece of timber.* **94.** *Mining.* a direction of secondary or minor cleavage grain; rift. **95.** onward movement, progression, course, etc. **96.** the particular course or tendency of something: *in the normal run of events, the general run of the voting.* **97.** freedom to range over, go through, or use: *the run of the house.* **98.** any rapid or easy course or progress. **99.** a continuous course of some condition of affairs, etc.: *a run of bad luck.* **100.** a continuous extent of something, as a vein of ore. **101.** *Mining.* a ribbonlike, irregular ore body, lying nearly flat and following the stratification. **102.** a continuous series of something. **103.** a set of things in regular order, as a sequence of cards. **104.** any continued or extensive demand, call, or the like. **105.** a spell of being in demand or favour with the public. **106.** a series of sudden and urgent demands for payment, as on a bank. **107.** a spell of causing some liquid to flow. **108.** a flow or rush of water, etc. **109.** *U.S.* a small stream; brook; rivulet. **110.** a kind or class, as of goods. **111.** the ordinary or average kind. **112.** that in or on which something runs or may run. **113.** an enclosure within which domestic animals may range about. **114.** a way, track, or the like, along which something runs or moves. **115.** the habitual track or route taken by certain animals, as mice, rabbits, etc. **116.** a course for a particular purpose or activity, as an inclined course for skiing. **117.** the area and habitual route covered by a vendor who delivers goods to houses, etc.: *milk run, paper run.* **118.** a large area of grazing land; a rural property. **119.** *Mil.* the movement in a straight line up to the point of the launching of a bomb, torpedo, or the like, by an aeroplane, submarine, etc. **120.** *Aeron.* the period during which an aeroplane moves along the ground or water under its own power preceding take-off and following touchdown. **121.** a trough or pipe through which water, etc., runs. **122.** the movement of a number of fish upstream or inshore from deep water. **123.** large numbers of fish in motion, esp. inshore from deep water or upstream for spawning. **124.** a number of animals moving together. **125.** *Music.* a rapid succession of notes; a roulade. **126.** *Cricket.* **a.** the score unit, made by the successful running of both batsmen from one popping crease to the other. **b.** a performance of such a running. **127.** *Baseball.* **a.** the score unit, made by successfully running round all the bases and reaching the home plate. **b.** a successful performance of this. **128.** *Naut.* the curved afterpart of a ship's hull below the waterline. **129. at a run,** (of some action) performed while running, or by means of running; without stopping. **130. by the run,** *Naut.* without checking, as in letting go a rope in a tackle. **131. on the run,** escaped or hiding from pursuit, esp. by the police. **132. in the long run,** ultimately. **133. in the short run,** ignoring possible future developments; considering only immediate effects, etc. **134. the runs,** *Colloq.* →**diarrhoea.** *–adj.* **135.** melted or liquefied. **136.** poured in a melted state; run into a cast in a mould. [ME *rinne(n)*, OE *rinnan*, c. G *rinnen*, Icel. *rinna*. Form *run* orig. pp., later extended to present tense]

**runabout** /ˈrʌnəbaʊt/, *n.* **1.** a small car used to make short trips, usu. around the city and suburbs. **2.** a small boat, usu. with an outboard motor, used mainly for short trips and recreational purposes.

runcinate leaf

**run-around** /ˈrʌn-əraʊnd/, *n.* **1.** *Colloq.* equivocation; evasion. **2.** *Print.* an arrangement of type using a column width narrower than the body of the text, as around an illustration. **3. give (someone) the run-around,** *Colloq.* to fob (someone) off with evasions and subterfuges. Also, **runround.**

**runaway** /ˈrʌnəweɪ/, *n.* **1.** one who runs away; a fugitive; a deserter. **2.** a horse or vehicle which has broken away from control. **3.** the act of running away. *–adj.* **4.** having run away; escaped; fugitive. **5.** (of a horse, etc.) having escaped from the control of the rider, or driver. **6.** pertaining to or accomplished by running away or eloping: *a runaway marriage.* **7.** easily won, as a race. **8.** *Comm.* uncontrolled.

**runcible spoon** /rʌnsəbəl ˈspun/, *n.* a utensil with two broad prongs (like a fork) and one sharp, curved prong (like a spoon), or other similar implement. [coined in 1871 by Edward Lear, 1812-88, English humorist and painter]

**runcinate** /ˈrʌnsənət, -neɪt/, *adj.* (of a leaf, etc.) pinnately incised, with the lobes or teeth curved backwards. [NL *runcīnātus*, from L *runcīna* plane (once thought to mean saw)]

**rundle** /ˈrʌndl/, *n.* **1.** a rung of a ladder. **2.** a wheel or similar rotating object. [var. of ROUNDEL]

**run-down** /rʌn-ˈdaʊn/, *adj.*; /ˈrʌn-daʊn/, *n.* *–adj.* **1.** in a poor or deteriorated state of health; depressed, sick or tired. **2.** fallen into disrepair. **3.** (of a spring-operated watch or clock) not running because not wound. *–n.* **4.** a cursory review or summary of points of information: *this brief run-down of past events will bring you up to date.*

**rune**[1] /run/, *n.* **1.** any of the characters of an alphabet used by the ancient Germanic-speaking peoples, esp. the Scandinavians. **2.** something written or inscribed in such characters. [Icel. *rūn*]

**rune**[2] /run/, *n. Poetic.* a poem, song, or verse. [Finnish *runo* poem or canto, from Scand. See RUNE[1]]

**rung**[1] /rʌŋ/, *v.* past tense and past participle of **ring**[2].

**rung**[2] /rʌŋ/, *n.* **1.** one of the rounded crosspieces forming the steps of a ladder. **2.** a rounded or shaped piece fixed horizontally, for strengthening purposes, as between the legs of a chair. **3.** a stout stick, rod, or bar, esp. one of rounded section, forming a piece in something framed or constructed: *the rungs of a wheel.* **4.** a stage in a progress or ascent: *the next rung of the ladder to success.* [ME; OE *hrung*, c. G *Runge*]

**run-holder** /ˈrʌn-houldə/, *n.* one who controls or owns a country property.

**runic**[1] /ˈrunɪk/, *adj.* **1.** consisting of or set down in runes: *runic inscriptions.* **2.** (of ornamental knots, figures, etc.) of an interlaced form seen on ancient monuments, metalwork, etc., of the northern European peoples. **3.** mysterious or magical. *–n.* **4.** *Print.* a condensed form of bold typeface. [RUNE[1] + -IC]

**runic**[2] /ˈrunɪk/, *adj.* of the ancient Scandinavian class or type, as literature, poetry, etc. [RUNE[2] + IC]

**run-in** /ˈrʌn-ɪn/, *n.* **1.** *Colloq.* disagreement; argument; quarrel. **2.** *Print.* matter that is added to a text, esp. without indenting or making a new paragraph. **3.** an approach, as of an aeroplane. **4.** the final stretch of a race.

f u þ o r c g w h
n i j ė p x s t b
e ng d l m oe a ae y ea

rune[1]: runic alphabet, 9th century

**run-in groove** /ˈ– gruv/, *n.* a groove preceding the soundtrack on a gramophone record on which the pick-up is placed.

**runlet** /ˈrʌnlət/, *n.* →**runnel.** [RUN, *n.*, + -LET]

**runnel** /ˈrʌnəl/, *n.* **1.** a small stream or brook, or a rivulet. **2.** a small channel, as for water. [OE *rynel(e)*, var. of *rinelle* diminutive of RUN, *n.*]

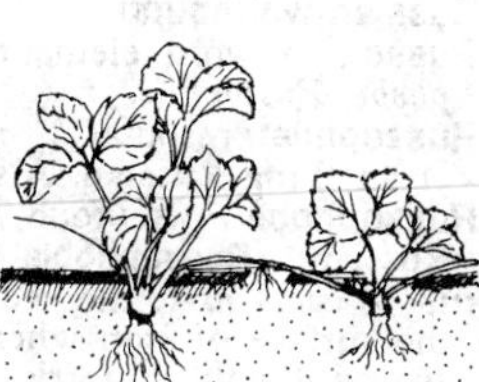

runner (def. 16) of strawberry

**runner** /ˈrʌnə/, *n.* **1.** one who or that which runs. **2.** a competitor in a race. **3.** a messenger. **4.** a messenger of a bank, broker, etc. **5.** one acting as collector, agent, or the like for a bank, broker, etc. **6.** one whose business it is to solicit patronage or trade. **7.** something in or on which something else runs or moves, as the strips of wood that guide a drawer, the rails supporting the sliding seat of a rowing boat, etc. **8.** either of the long pieces of wood or metal on which a sledge or the like slides. **9.** the blade of a skate. **10.** a sharp curved blade used to open a furrow for placing seed. **11.** the rotating system of blades driven by the fluid passing through a reaction turbine. **12.** a roller on which something moves along. **13.** an operator or manager, as of a machine. **14.** a long, narrow rug, suitable for a hall or staircase. **15.** a long, narrow strip of linen, embroidery, lace, or the like, for placing across a table. **16.** *Bot.* **a.** a slender, prostrate stem which throws out roots at its nodes or end, thus producing new plants. **b.** a plant that spreads by such stems. **17.** *Foundry.* →**gate**[1] (def. 14). **18.** →**runner bean. 19.** →**sandshoe.**

**runner bean** /ˈ– bin/, *n.* a climbing perennial leguminous herb, *Phaseolus multiflorus,* commonly cultivated as an annual for the long green edible pods; string bean; green bean. Also, **scarlet runner.**

**runner-up** /rʌnər-ˈʌp/, *n.* the competitor, player, or team finishing in second place.

**running** /ˈrʌnɪŋ/, *n.* **1.** the act of one who or that which runs. **2.** competition, as in a race: *to be out of the running.* **3.** smuggling: *gun-running.* **4.** managing or directing: *the running of a business.* **5. in the running,** having a chance of success. **6. make the running,** to set the pace, as of a competition. *–adj.* **7.** that runs; moving or passing rapidly. **8.** creeping or climbing, as plants. **9.** moving or proceeding easily or smoothly. **10.** moving when pulled or hauled, as a rope. **11.** slipping or sliding easily, as a knot or a noose. **12.** operating, as a machine. **13.** (of measurement) linear; straight-line. **14.** cursive, as handwriting. **15.** flowing, as a stream. **16.** liquid or fluid. **17.** current: *the running month.* **18.** prevalent, as a condition, etc. **19.** going or carried on continuously; sustained: *a running commentary.* **20.** extending or repeated continuously, as a pattern. **21.** following in succession (placed after the noun): *for three nights running.* **22.** performed with, by means of, or during a run: *a running jump.* **23.** discharging matter, esp. fluid, as a sore. **24. running battle,** a battle between pursuer and pursued. **25. running fire, a.** sustained discharge of firearms. **b.** anything resembling this.

**running board** /ˈ– bɔd/, *n.* (esp. formerly) a small ledge, step, or footboard, beneath the doors of a car, to assist passengers entering or leaving.

**running head** /ˈ– hɛd/, *n.* a descriptive heading repeated at the top of (usu.) each page. Also, **running title.**

**running knot** /ˈ– nɒt/, *n.* a knot made round and so as to slide along a part of the same rope, thus forming a noose (**running noose**) which tightens as the rope is pulled.

**running mate** /ˈ– meɪt/, *n.* **1.** a horse used to establish the pace for another horse in a race. **2.** *U.S.* a candidate for an office linked with another and more important office, as the vice-presidency.

**running postman** /– ˈpoustmən/, *n.* a prostrate plant, *Kennedia prostrata,* bearing red, pea-shaped flowers.

**running race** /ˈ– reɪs/, *n.* a race in which the winner is the one who runs the fastest.

**running rigging** /ˈ– rɪgɪŋ/, *n.* the working ropes of a sailing ship used for hauling round the yards and setting or making fast the sails.

**running shed** /ˈ– ʃɛd/, *n.* a building for railway engines built over a turntable.

**running spikes** /ˈ– spaɪks/, *n.pl.* (used in athletics) footwear with metal spikes on the soles to give increased grip on the track.

**running stitch** /ˈ– stɪtʃ/, *n.* a small, even stitch made by passing the thread up and down through the cloth at small intervals; used for seams, gathering, quilting, etc.

**running writing** /ˈ– raɪtɪŋ/, *n.* (*in children's speech*) cursive script.

**runny** /ˈrʌni/, *adj.* **1.** (of matter) fluid or tending to flow. **2.** tending to discharge liquid: *a runny nose.*

**run-off** /ˈrʌn-ɒf/, *n.* **1.** a deciding final contest held after a principal one. **2.** a deciding race held after a dead heat. **3.** something which runs off, as rain which flows off from the land in streams. **4.** *N.Z.* pasture not adjacent to the farm.

**run-of-the-mill** /ˈrʌn-əv-ðə-mɪl/, *adj.* ordinary; mediocre; commonplace.

**run-on** /ˈrʌn-ɒn/, *adj.* **1.** designating text which is run on without indentation: *a run-on entry in a dictionary.* *–n.* **2.** text matter which is run on without indentation.

**runout campaign** /ˈrʌnaut kæmˌpeɪn/, *n.* a vigorous program to sell previous model cars before the release of the latest model.

**runround** /ˈrʌnraund/, *n.* →**run-around.**

**runt** /rʌnt/, *n.* **1.** an undersized, stunted animal, person, or thing, esp. one that is small as compared with others of its kind. **2.** the smallest in a litter, as of pigs. **3.** a term of opprobrium for a person. [OE **hrunta* (in *Hrunting* name of sword in Beowulf), from *hrung* RUNG[2]]

**run-through** /ˈrʌn-θru/, *n.* **1.** the performing of a sequence of designated actions, esp. as a trial prior to their official performance; rehearsal. **2.** *Bowls.* a bowl played with enough force to displace other bowls and reach the jack.

**run time** /ˈrʌn taɪm/, *n.* the time required for a computer to complete a single, continuous program.

**runty** /ˈrʌnti/, *adj.*, **runtier, runtiest.** stunted; dwarfish.

**runway** /ˈrʌnweɪ/, *n.* **1.** a way along which something runs.

2. a paved or cleared strip on which aeroplanes land and take off; airstrip. 3. the beaten track of deer or other animals. 4. *U.S.* the bed of a stream.

**rupe** /rup/, *n. Colloq.* 1. a rupee. 2. a rupiah.

**rupee** /ru'pi/, *n.* 1. the monetary unit of India. 2. any of various similar units as the currencies of Pakistan, Ceylon, Mauritius, and Muscat and Oman. 3. a note or coin of any of these denominations. *Abbrev.:* R, Re. [Hind. (Urdu) *rupiyah,* from Skt *rūpya* wrought silver]

**rupiah** /'rupiə/, *n.* 1. the monetary unit of Indonesia. [Malay, from Hind. *rupiyah* RUPEE]

**rupture** /'rʌptʃə/, *n., v.,* **-tured, -turing.** *-n.* 1. the act of breaking or bursting. 2. the state of being broken or burst. 3. a breach of harmonious, friendly, or peaceful relations. 4. *Pathol.* hernia, esp. abdominal hernia. *-v.t.* 5. to break or burst (a blood vessel, etc.). 6. to cause a breach of (relations, etc.). 7. *Pathol.* to affect with hernia. *-v.i.* 8. to suffer a break or rupture. [L *ruptūra*]

**rural** /'rurəl/, *adj.* 1. of, pertaining to, or characteristic of the country (as distinguished from towns or cities), country life, or country people; rustic. 2. living in the country. 3. of or pertaining to agriculture: *rural economy.* [ME, from L *rūrālis*] – **ruralism,** *n.* – **ruralist,** *n.* – **rurally,** *adv.*

**ruralise** /'rurəlaɪz/, *v.,* **-lised, -lising.** *-v.t.* 1. to make rural. *-v.i.* 2. to rusticate. Also, **ruralize.** – **ruralisation** /rurəlaɪ'zeɪʃən/, *n.*

**rurality** /ru'rælәti/, *n., pl.* **-ties.** 1. rural character. 2. a rural characteristic, matter, or scene.

**rural school** /'rurəl skul/, *n.* →**one-teacher school.**

**ruru** /'ruru/, *n. N.Z.* →**mopoke.** [Maori]

**rusa deer** /'rusə dɪə/, *n.* →**Javan rusa deer.**

**ruse** /ruz/, *n.* a trick, stratagem, or artifice. [ME, n. use of obs. *ruse* to detour, from F *ruser.* See RUSH[1]]

**rush**[1] /rʌʃ/, *v.i.* 1. to move or go with speed, impetuosity, or violence. 2. to dash; dash forward for an attack or onslaught. 3. to go or plunge with headlong or rash haste. 4. to go, come, pass, etc., rapidly: *tears rushed to her eyes.* *-v.t.* 5. to send or drive with speed or violence. 6. to carry or convey with haste: *to rush an injured person to the hospital.* 7. to perform, complete, or organise (some process or activity) with special haste. 8. to send, push, force, etc., with unusual speed or undue haste: *to rush a bill through Parliament.* 9. to attack with a rush. 10. to overcome or take (a person, force, place, etc.). 11. *Colloq.* to heap attentions on. 12. put pressure on someone. 13. *Rugby Football.* (of a pack of forwards, etc.) to move (the ball) rapidly forwards by short kicks. 14. *Croquet.* to strike or drive a ball hard with the mallet swung from the shoulders, rather than with the wrists. *-n.* 15. the act of rushing; a rapid, impetuous, or headlong onward movement. 16. a hostile attack. 17. a. a sudden concerted movement, as in a particular direction. b. an eager rushing of numbers of persons to some region to be occupied or exploited, esp. to a new goldfield. 18. a sudden coming or access: *a rush of blood to his face.* 19. hurried activity; busy haste: *the rush of city life.* 20. a hurried state, as from pressure of affairs: *to be in a rush.* 21. press of work, business, traffic, etc., requiring extraordinary effort or haste. 22. a period of intense activity: *the Christmas rush.* 23. a great demand for a commodity, etc. (fol. by *on*): *there was a rush on gold.* 24. *Rugby Football.* the act by a pack of forwards, etc., of moving the ball rapidly forward by short kicks. 25. *Croquet.* a drive or hard stroke with the mallet. 26. (*pl.*) *Films.* the first prints made after shooting a scene or scenes. *-adj.* 27. requiring or performed with haste: *a rush order.* 28. characterised by rush or press of work, traffic, etc. [ME *rusche(n),* from AF *russher, russer,* var. of *re(h)usser, re(h)user, ruser,* from LL *recūsāre* push back, L refuse] – **rusher,** *n.*

**rush**[2] /rʌʃ/, *n.* 1. any plant of the genus *Juncus* (family Juncaceae), which comprises grasslike herbs with pithy or hollow stems, found in wet or marshy places. 2. any plant of the same family. 3. any of various similar plants of other families as, bog-rush, or spike-rush. 4. a stem of such a plant, used for making chair bottoms, mats, baskets, etc. 5. a former type of floor covering, consisting of such plants scattered on the floor. 6. something of little or no value: *not worth a rush.* [ME *russhe,* OE *rysc(e),* c. D *rusch* and G *Rusch*] – **rushlike,** *adj.*

**rush hour** /'– aʊə/, *n.* →**peak hour.**

**rushy** /'rʌʃi/, *adj.,* **rushier, rushiest.** 1. abounding with rushes. 2. covered or strewn with rushes. 3. consisting or made of rushes. 4. rushlike.

**rusk** /rʌsk/, *n.* 1. a type of sweetened tea biscuit. 2. a piece of bread or cake crisped in the oven. 3. a similar commercially made product, given esp. to babies when teething, and invalids. [Sp. or Pg. *rosca* twist of bread, lit., screw]

**Russ.,** 1. Russia. 2. Russian.

**russet** /'rʌsət/, *n.* 1. reddish brown; light brown; yellowish brown. 2. a coarse reddish brown or brownish homespun cloth formerly in use. 3. a winter apple with a rough brownish skin. *-adj.* 4. reddish brown; light brown; yellowish brown. [ME, from OF *rousset,* diminutive of *rous* red, from L *russus*]

**Russia** /'rʌʃə/, *n.* →**Soviet Union.**

**Russian** /'rʌʃən/, *adj.* 1. of or pertaining to Russia, its people, or their language. *-n.* 2. a native or inhabitant of Russia. 3. a member of the dominant, Slavic race of Russia. 4. the principal Slavic language, belonging to the East Slavic subgroup, and the predominant language of the Soviet Union. See **Great Russian, Little Russian, White Russian.**

**Russian blue** /– 'blu/, *n.* one of a breed of slender, large-eared, domestic cats with short, bluish-grey fur.

**Russian Church** /– 'tʃɜtʃ/, *n.* the national church of Russia (before 1918), a branch of the Orthodox Eastern Church.

**Russian dressing** /– 'drɛsɪŋ/, *n.* a sharp-tasting mayonnaise dressing prepared by the addition of chopped pickles, chilli sauce, pimentos, etc.

**Russian Orthodox Church,** *n.* →**Russian Church.**

**Russian roulette** /rʌʃən ru'lɛt/, *n.* a macabre game of chance, as formerly played by Russian army officers, in which each player in turn spins the cylinder of a revolver containing only one bullet, points it at his head, and pulls the trigger.

**Russians** /'rʌʃənz/, *n. pl. Colloq.* wild cattle. Also, **Rooshians.** [? pun on *rush'uns*]

**Russian salad** /rʌʃən 'sæləd/, *n.* a salad of cold cooked vegetables made with Russian dressing, mayonnaise or sour cream.

**Russian wolfhound** /– 'wʊlfhaʊnd/, *n.* →**borzoi.**

**Russo-,** a word element representing Russia, as in *Russophobe, Russophile.*

**Russophile** /'rʌsoʊfaɪl/, *n.* one who admires or favours Russia or anything Russian. Also, **Russophil** /'rʌsoʊfɪl/.

**Russophobe** /'rʌsoʊfoʊb/, *n.* one who fears or hates anything Russian. – **Russophobia** /rʌsoʊ'foʊbiə/, *n.*

**rust** /rʌst/, *n.* 1. the red or orange coating which forms on the surface of iron when exposed to air and moisture, consisting chiefly of ferric hydroxide and ferric oxide. 2. any film or coating on metal due to oxidation, etc. 3. a stain resembling iron rust. 4. any growth, habit, influence, or agency tending to injure the mind, character, abilities, usefulness, etc. 5. *Bot.* a. any of the various plant diseases caused by fungi, esp. members of the order Uredinales, in which the leaves and stems become spotted and acquire a red to brown colour. b. Also, **rust fungus.** a fungus producing such a disease. 6. rust colour; reddish brown or orange. *-v.i.* 7. to grow rusty, as iron does; corrode. 8. to contract rust. 9. to deteriorate or become impaired, as through inaction or disuse. 10. to become rust-coloured. *-v.t.* 11. to affect with rust. 12. to impair as if with rust. 13. to make rust-coloured. [ME and OE, c. G *Rost*] – **rustable,** *adj.*

**rust bucket** /'– bʌkət/, *n. Colloq.* a badly rusted motor vehicle.

**rustic** /'rʌstɪk/, *adj.* 1. of, pertaining to, or living in the country as distinguished from towns or cities; rural. 2. simple, artless, or unsophisticated. 3. uncouth, rude, or boorish. 4. made of roughly dressed limbs or roots of trees, as garden seats, etc. 5. *Masonry.* having the surface rough or irregular, or the joints deeply sunk or chamfered. *-n.* 6. a country person. 7. an unsophisticated country person. [late ME, from L *rusticus*] – **rustically,** *adv.*

**rusticate** /'rʌstəkeɪt/, *v.,* **-cated, -cating.** *-v.i.* 1. to go to the country. 2. to stay or sojourn in the country. *-v.t.* 3. to send to or domicile in the country. 4. to make rustic, as persons, manners, etc. 5. to construct or finish (masonry, etc.) in the rustic manner. **6.** *Brit.* to suspend (a student) from a university as punishment. [L *rusticātus,* pp., having lived in the country] – **rustication** /rʌstə'keɪʃən/, *n.* – **rusticator,** *n.*

**rusticity** /rʌs'tɪsəti/, *n., pl.* **-ties. 1.** the state or quality of being rustic. **2.** rural character or life.

**rustle** /'rʌsəl/, *v.,* **-tled, -tling,** *n.* –*v.t.* **1.** to make a succession of slight, soft sounds, as of parts rubbing gently one on another, as leaves, silks, papers, etc. **2.** to cause such sounds by moving or stirring something. –*v.t.* **3.** to move or stir so as to cause a rustling sound. **4.** to steal (cattle, etc.). **5.** *Colloq.* to move, bring, get, etc., by energetic action (oft. fol. by *up*): *rustle up breakfast.* –*n.* **6.** the sound made by anything that rustles. [ME; OE *hrūxlian* make a noise] – **rustlingly,** *adv.*

**rustler** /'rʌslə/, *n.* **1.** one who or that which rustles. **2.** a cattle thief.

**rustless** /'rʌstləs/, *adj.* **1.** free from rust. **2.** →**rustproof.**

**rustproof** /'rʌstpruf/, *adj.* protected from rust; rustless.

**rusty** /'rʌsti/, *adj.,* **-tier, -tiest. 1.** covered or affected with rust. **2.** consisting of or produced by rust. **3.** of the colour of rust; rust-coloured; tending towards rust. **4.** faded or shabby; impaired by time or wear, as clothes, etc. **5.** impaired through disuse or neglect: *my Latin is rusty.* **6.** having lost agility or alertness; out of practice. **7.** (of plants) affected with the rust disease. [ME; OE *rustig,* c. G *rostig*] – **rustily,** *adv.* – **rustiness,** *n.*

**rusty fig** /– 'fɪg/, *n.* →**Port Jackson fig.**

**rut**[1] /rʌt/, *n., v.,* **rutted, rutting.** –*n.* **1.** a furrow or track in the ground, esp. one made by the passage of a vehicle or vehicles. **2.** any furrow, groove, etc. **3.** a fixed or established way of life: *to get into a rut.* –*v.t.* **4.** to make a rut or ruts in; furrow. [orig. uncert.; ? var. of ROUTE]

**rut**[2] /rʌt/, *n., v.,* **rutted, rutting.** –*n.* **1.** the periodically recurring sexual excitement of the deer, goat, sheep, etc. –*v.i.* **2.** to be in the condition of rut. [ME *rutte,* from OF *rut,* var. of *ruit,* from L *rugītus* a roaring]

**rutabaga** /rutə'beɪgə, -'bɛgə/, *n. U.S.* the Swedish or yellow turnip, *Brassica napobrassica.* [Swed. *rotabagge*]

**rutaceous** /ru'teɪʃəs/, *adj.* **1.** of or like the plant rue. **2.** belonging to the Rutaceae, a family of plants including the boronia, orange, lemon, kumquat, etc., having pellucid dotted leaves. [L *rūtāceus*]

**ruth**[1] /ruθ/, *n. Archaic.* **1.** pity or compassion. **2.** sorrow or grief. [ME *r(e)uthe,* from *rewe* RUE[1], or *rewe,* n., pity, OE *hrēow*]

**ruth**[2] /ruθ/, *n. in the phrase* **cry ruth,** to vomit. [onomatopoeic]

**ruthenic** /ru'θɛnɪk/, *adj.* containing ruthenium in a higher valency state than the corresponding ruthenious compound.

**ruthenious** /ru'θiniəs/, *adj.* containing divalent ruthenium.

**ruthenium** /ru'θiniəm/, *n.* a steel-grey, rare metallic element, difficult to fuse, belonging to the platinum group of metals, and very little acted on by aqua regia. *Symbol:*Ru; *at. wt:* 101.07; *at. no.:* 44; *sp. gr.:* 12.2 at 20°C. [NL, from ML *Ruthenia* Russia (so named because it was first found in ores from the Ural Mountains) + *-ium* -IUM]

**Rutherford-Bohr atom** /ˌrʌðəfəd-'bɔr ætəm/, *n.* See **Bohr theory.**

**Rutherfordium** /rʌðə'fɔdiəm/, *n. Chem.* a synthetic, radioactive element; (formerly) eka-hafnium. *Symbol:* Rf; *at. no.:* 104. [named after Ernest *Rutherford,* 1st Baron, 1871-1937, British physicist, born in New Zealand]

**Rutherglen bug** /rʌðəglən 'bʌg/, *n.* a chinch bug, *Nysius vinitor,* destructive of crops and orchards.

**ruthful** /'ruθfəl/, *adj. Archaic.* **1.** compassionate or sorrowful. **2.** such as to excite sorrow or pity. – **ruthfully,** *adv.* – **ruthfulness,** *n.*

**ruthless** /'ruθləs/, *adj.* without pity or compassion; pitiless; merciless. – **ruthlessly,** *adv.* – **ruthlessness,** *n.*

**rutilant** /'rutələnt/, *adj. Rare.* glowing, shining, or glittering with a red or gold light. [L *rutilans,* ppr.]

**rutile** /'rutaɪl/, *n.* a common mineral, titanium dioxide, $TiO_2$, having a brilliant metallic-adamantine lustre and usu. of a reddish brown colour. It occurs usu. in crystals and is used to coat welding rods. [F, from G *Rutil,* from L *rutilus* red]

**ruttish** /'rʌtɪʃ/, *adj. Obs.* lustful. [RUT[2] + -ISH[1]]

**rutty** /'rʌti/, *adj.,* **-tier, -tiest.** full of or abounding in ruts, as a road. – **ruttiness,** *n.*

**Rwanda** /ru'ændə/, *n.* a republic in central Africa, east of the Congo.

**-ry,** a suffix of abstract nouns of condition, practice (*heraldry, husbandry, dentistry*), and of collectives (*peasantry, Jewry*). [short form of -ERY]

**rye**[1] /raɪ/, *n.* **1.** a widely cultivated cereal grass, *Secale cereale,* with one-nerved glumes (differing from wheat which is many-nerved) and two- or three-flowered spikelets. **2.** the seeds or grain of this plant, used for making wholemeal flour, for livestock feed, and for a type of whisky. **3.** an American whisky distilled from a mash containing 51 per cent or more rye grain. [ME; OE *ryge,* c. Icel. *rugr,* akin to D *rogge,* G *Roggen*]

**rye**[2] /raɪ/, *n.* a gentleman: *Romany rye.* [Gipsy]

**ryebread** /'raɪbrɛd/, *n.* bread made from rye flour.

**ryebuck** /'raɪbʌk/, *adj. Colloq. Obs.* →**ribuck.**

**rye-grass** /'raɪ-gras/, *n.* any of a number of plants of the genus *Lolium,* many of which are valuable pasture grasses as perennial rye, Wimmera rye, and Italian rye.

**Ryeland** /'raɪlænd/, *n.* one of a British breed of short wool sheep, noted for the quality of its mutton and fat lambs. [from *Ryelands,* district in Herefordshire, England]

**ryot** /'raɪət/, *n.* (in India) **1.** a peasant. **2.** one who holds land as a cultivator of the soil. [Urdu *raiyat*]

Ss Roman JANSON Ss Sans Serif STANDARD Ss Script CORONET Ss Decorative FANTASIE ROC

*Although there are numerous typefaces in the world they can be divided into four main classifications. These are:*

*ROMAN or SERIF. This typeface came into being from the technique of the Roman masons who, working in stone, finished off each letter with a serif or small stroke projecting from the top or bottom. This was done to correct any feeling of unevenness or imbalance they may have created in cutting the characters in stone.*

*SANS SERIF (without serif). This typeface is geometric in design and has straight-edged characters and lines of a regular thickness.*

*SCRIPT. Based on the movement of the hand, this typeface is often italicised or slanted, as if drawn by a brush or quill pen.*

*DECORATIVE. Any typeface that exaggerates the characteristics of any of the other three classifications to a degree that places it outside of them.*

*The dictionary entries in this book use a SANS SERIF typeface called Helvetica (set in a bold face for the head words) and a SERIF typeface Piantin (used throughout the body of the entries).*

**S, s** /ɛs/, *n., pl.* **S's** or **Ss, s's** or **ss.** **1.** a consonant, the 19th letter of the English alphabet. **2.** something resembling the letter S in shape.

**'s**[1], an ending which marks the possessive singular of nouns, as in *man's.* [ME and OE *-es*]

**'s**[2], an ending which marks the possessive plural of nouns, as in *men's.* [pl. use of poss. sing. ending]

**'s**[3], colloquial reduction of: **1.** is: *he's here.* **2.** has: *he's just gone.* **3.** does: *what's he do now?* **4.** us: *let's go.*

**-s**[1], a suffix serving to form adverbs, as *always, evenings, needs, unawares.* Cf. **-ways.** [ME and OE *-es,* orig. gen. sing. ending]

**-s**[2], an ending which marks the third person sing. indicative active of verbs, as in *hits.* [northern ME and OE *-(e)s* (orig. ending of second person, as in L and Gk); replacing ME and OE *-(e)th*]

**-s**[3], **1.** an ending which marks the regular plural of nouns, as in *dogs.* **2.** a quasi-plural ending occurring in nouns for which there is no proper singular, as *trousers, shorts, scissors.* [ME *-es,* OE *-as,* nom. and acc. pl. of certain classes of strong nouns]

**s.,** **1.** second. **2.** shilling [L *solidus*]; shillings [L *solidi*]. **3.** singular. **4.** son. **5.** substantive. **6.** south. **7.** southern.

**S,** **1.** Saxon. **2.** South. **3.** Southern. **4.** *Chem.* sulphur. **5.** *Physics.* entropy. **6.** Sea. **7.** Saturday. **8.** Sunday. **9.** siemens.

**S-,** a prefix used to denote that a substance has left-handed chirality. [L *sinister* left]

**S.,** **1.** Saint. **2.** Saturday. **3.** Sea. **4.** September. **5.** South. **6.** Southern. **7.** Sunday. **8.** School. **9.** Society. **10.** Soprano. **11.** Summer.

**s.a.,** **1.** semiannual. **2.** without year or date [L *sine anno*]. **3.** subject to approval. **4.** sex appeal.

**Sa,** *Chem. Obs.* samarium.

**S.A.,** **1.** South Australia. **2.** South Africa. **3.** South America. **4.** Salvation Army.

**Saanen** /ˈseɪnən/, *n.* one of a breed of white or light coloured, usu. hornless, dairy goats. [from *Saanen,* an area in SW switzerland]

**Sab.,** Sabbath.

**sabadilla** /sæbəˈdɪlə/, *n.* **1.** a plant of Mexico, *Schoenocaulon officinale,* with long grasslike leaves and bitter seeds. **2.** the seeds, which are used medicinally and as a source of veratrine and veratridine. [Sp. *cebadilla,* diminutive of *cebada* barley]

**Sabaoth** /sæˈbeɪɒθ, ˈsabaoʊθ/, *n. pl.* (in the Bible, etc.) armies; hosts. [L, from Gk, from Heb. *ç'bhāōth,* pl. of *cābhā* army]

**sabayon** /sæbaɪˈjɒn/, *n.* a sweet sauce served with a rich sponge or fruit pudding.

**sabbat** /ˈsæbæt, ˈsæbət/, *n.* →**sabbath** (def. 3).

**Sabbatarian** /sæbəˈtɛəriən/, *n.* **1.** one who observes the seventh day of the week (Saturday) as the Sabbath. **2.** one who adheres to or favours a strict observance of Sunday. [obs. *Sabbatary* (from L *sabbatārius* pertaining to the Sabbath) + -AN] – **Sabbatarianism,** *n.*

**Sabbath** /ˈsæbəθ/, *n.* **1.** the seventh day of the week (Saturday) as the day of rest and religious observance among the Jews and certain Christian sects. **2.** the first day of the week (Sunday), similarly observed by most Christians in commemoration of the resurrection of Christ. **3.** (*l.c.*) Also, **sabbat.** a secret nocturnal meeting of witches. [ME *sabath,* var. of ME and OE *sabat,* from L *sabbatum,* from Gk *sábbaton,* from Heb. *shabbāth*]

**Sabbath school** /ˈ– skul/, *n.* **1.** →**Sunday school.** **2.** (among Seventh-Day Adventists) such a school held on Saturday, their holy day.

**sabbatic** /səˈbætɪk/, *adj., n.* →**sabbatical.** [Gk *sabbatikós*]

**sabbatical** /səˈbætɪkəl/, *adj.* **1.** of, pertaining to, or appropriate to the Sabbath. **2.** bringing a period of rest. **3.** of, denoting, or pertaining to a sabbatical. *–n.* **4.** Also, **sabbatical leave.** (in certain universities, etc.) a year, term, or other period, of freedom from teaching granted to a teacher, as for study or travel. [SABBATIC + -AL[1]] – **sabbatically,** *adv.*

**sabbatical year** /ˈ– jɪə/, *n.* (among ancient Jews) every seventh year, during which fields were to be left untilled, debtors were to be released, etc.

**saber** /ˈseɪbə/, *n., v.t. U.S.* →**sabre.**

**Sabin vaccine** /ˈseɪbən ˌvæksin/, *n.* a vaccine taken orally which immunises against poliomyelitis. [from Albert B. *Sabin,* b. 1906, U.S. virologist, who developed it]

**sable** /ˈseɪbəl/, *n.* **1.** a weasel-like mammal, *Mustela zibellina,* of cold regions, valued for its dark brown fur. **2.** a marten, esp. *Mustela americana.* **3.** the fur of the sable. **4.** some similar fur, used as a substitute. **5.** the colour black, often one of the heraldic colours. **6.** (*pl.*) mourning garments. *–adj.* **7.** made of the

sable

fur or hair of the sable. **8.** *Poetic.* black; very dark. [ME, from OF, from Slavic; cf. Russ. *sobol*]

**sable antelope** /– 'æntəloup/, *n.* a large antelope, *Hippotragus niger,* of Africa, with long, sabre-like horns.

**sabot** /'sæbou/, *n.* **1.** a wooden shoe made of a single piece of wood hollowed out, worn by peasants in France, Belgium, etc. **2.** a shoe with a thick wooden sole and sides, and top of coarse leather. **3.** *Mil.* a soft metal shoe fitted to the base of a shell before firing in order to increase its muzzle velocity. **4.** a class of small sailing boats, intended for children. [F, in OF *çabot,* from *savate* old shoe (from Ar. *sabbât* sandal), b. with *botte* boot]

**sabotage** /'sæbətaʒ/, *n., v.,* **-taged, -taging.** *–n.* **1.** malicious injury to work, tools, machinery, etc., or any underhand interference with production or business, by enemy agents during wartime, by employees during a trade dispute, etc. **2.** any malicious attack on or undermining of a cause. *–v.t.* **3.** to injure or attack by sabotage. [F, from *saboter* make a noise with sabots, do work badly, from *sabot* SABOT]

**saboteur** /sæbə'tɜ/, *n.* one who commits or practises sabotage. [F]

**sabre** /'seɪbə/, *n., v.,* **-bred, -bring.** *–n.* **1.** a heavy one-edged sword, usu. slightly curved, used esp. by cavalry. **2.** a soldier armed with such a sword. **3.** a light sword for fencing and duelling, with a tapering flexible blade and a semicircular guard. *–v.t.* **4.** to strike, wound, or kill with a sabre. Also, *U.S.,* **saber.** [F *sabre, sable,* from G *Sabel,* (now *Säbel*), from Hung. *szàblya*] – **sabre-like,** *adj.*

sabre

**sabretache** /'sæbətæʃ/, *n.* a case, as of leather, suspended by long straps from the sword-belt of a cavalryman and hanging beside the sabre. [F, from G *Säbeltasche* sabre pocket]

**sabre-toothed** /'seɪbə-tuθt/, *adj.* having sabre-like teeth, as some extinct feline mammals whose long upper canine teeth sometimes extended below the margin of the lower jaw, as the sabre-toothed tiger.

**sabulous** /'sæbjələs/, *adj.* sandy; gritty. [L *sabulōsus*] – **sabulosity** /sæbjə'lɒsəti/, *n.*

**sac** /sæk/, *n.* a baglike structure in an animal or plant, as one containing fluid. [L *saccus.* See SACK[1]] – **saclike,** *adj.*

**saccate** /'sækət, -eɪt/, *adj.* in the form of, or having a sac. [ML *saccātus,* from L *saccus.* See SAC]

**sacchar-,** a word element referring to sugar or saccharine. Also, **saccharo-.** [combining form representing Gk *sákchar, sákcharon,* etc., sugar]

sabre-toothed tiger

**saccharate** /'sækəreɪt/, *n.* **1.** a salt of saccharic acid. **2.** a compound formed by interaction of sucrose with a metallic oxide, usu. lime, and useful in the purification of sugar.

**saccharic acid** /sə,kærɪk 'æsəd/, *n.* a white crystalline dicarboxylic acid, $COOH(CHOH)_4COOH$, made by the oxidisation of glucose.

**saccharide** /'sækəraɪd/, *n.* any sugar or other carbohydrate, esp. a simple sugar.

**saccharify** /sə'kærəfaɪ/, *v.t.,* **-fied. -fying.** to convert (starch, etc.) into sugar. – **saccharification** /sə,kærəfə'keɪʃən/, *n.*

**saccharimeter** /sækə'rɪmətə/, *n.* an optical instrument for determining the strength of sugar solutions by measuring polarisation of light through them. [F *saccharimètre.* See SACCHAR-, -I-, -METER[1]]

**saccharimetry** /sækə'rɪmətri/, *n.* the measuring of the amount of sugar in a solution, as with a saccharimeter.

**saccharin** /'sækərən, -krən/, *n.* a crystalline compound, $C_6H_4SO_2CONH$, obtained from toluene. It is some 400 times as sweet as cane sugar and is used as a sweetening agent in cases of diabetes and obesity. Also, **saccharine.**

**saccharine** /'sækərən, -krən/, *adj.* **1.** of a sugary sweetness: *a saccharine smile.* **2.** pertaining to, of the nature of, or containing sugar. *–n.* **3.** →**saccharin.** – **saccharinity** /sækə'rɪnəti/, *n.*

**saccharise** /'sækəraɪz/, *v.t.,* **-rised, -rising.** **1.** to convert into sugar; saccharify. **2.** to convert (the starches in grain) to fermentable sugars during mashing. Also, **saccharize.** – **saccharisation** /,sækəraɪ'zeɪʃən/, *n.*

**saccharo-,** variant of **sacchar-,** before consonants.

**saccharoid** /'sækərɔɪd/, *adj. Geol.* having a granular texture like that of loaf sugar. Also, **saccharoidal** /sækə'rɔɪdl/.

**saccharolytic** /sækərə'lɪtɪk/, *adj.* **1.** *Chem.* of, or causing, the hydrolysis of sugars. **2.** (of bacteria) using simple carbohydrates and starches as a source of energy.

**saccharometer** /sækə'rɒmətə/, *n.* a type of hydrometer used for determining the concentration of a sugar solution by measuring its specific gravity; usu. calibrated to read the percentage of sugar direct.

**saccharose** /'sækərouz, -ous/, *n.* →**sucrose.**

**sacculate** /'sækjələt, -leɪt/, *adj.* formed into or with a saccule, sac, or saclike dilatations. Also, **sacculated.** – **sacculation** /sækjə'leɪʃən/, *n.*

**saccule** /'sækjul/, *n.* **1.** *Anat.* the smaller of two sacs in the membranous labyrinth of the internal ear. **2.** a little sac. [L *sacculus,* diminutive of *saccus* SAC]

**sacculus** /'sækjələs/, *n., pl.* **-li** /-laɪ/. →**saccule.** [L. See SACCULE]

**sacerdotal** /sæsə'doutl, sækə-, sætʃə-/, *adj.* of priests; priestly. [L *sacerdōtālis*] – **sacerdotally,** *adv.*

**sacerdotalism** /sæsə'doutəlɪzəm, sækə-, sætʃə-/, *n.* **1.** the system, spirit, or methods of the priesthood. **2.** the belief that the priest has the power to offer sacrifice in offering the Eucharist. **3.** the belief that the priest has supernatural powers of consecration, absolution, etc., vested in him by virtue of his ordination. **4.** (*derog.*) priestcraft.

**sachet** /'sæʃeɪ/, *n.* **1.** a small sealed bag used for packaging a variety of goods, as foodstuffs, cosmetics, etc. **2.** a small bag, case, pad, etc., containing perfumed powder or the like for placing among articles of clothing. **3.** the powder. [F, diminutive of *sac,* from L *saccus.* See SACK[1]]

**sack[1]** /sæk/, *n.* **1.** a large bag of stout woven material, as for grain, potatoes, coal, etc. **2.** the amount which a sack will hold, a varying unit of measure. **3.** a woman's loose-fitting, unbelted dress. **4.** Also, **sacque.** a loose-fitting coat or jacket, esp. for women and children. **5.** *Colloq.* dismissal or discharge, as from employment. **6.** *Colloq.* a bed. **7. hit the sack,** *Colloq.* to go to bed. *–v.t.* **8.** to put into a sack or sacks. **9.** *Colloq.* to dismiss or discharge, as from employment. [ME *sak,* OE *sacc,* from L *saccus* bag, sackcloth, from Gk *sákkos,* from Heb. *saq*]

**sack[2]** /sæk/, *v.t.* **1.** to pillage or loot after capture; plunder: *to sack a city.* *–n.* **2.** the plundering of a captured place; pillage: *the sack of Troy.* [F *sac,* from It. *sacco,* special use of *sacco* SACK[1]] – **sacker,** *n.*

**sack[3]** /sæk/, *n.* any of various strong light-coloured wines formerly brought from Spain, the Canary Islands, etc. [F (*vin*) *sec* dry (wine), from L *siccus* dry]

**sackbut** /'sækbʌt/, *n.* **1.** a medieval form of the trombone. **2.** (in biblical usage) an ancient stringed musical instrument. [F *saquebute,* ONF *saqueboute,* lit., pull-push]

**sackcloth** /'sækklɒθ/, *n.* **1.** sacking. **2.** coarse cloth worn as a sign of mourning or penitence.

**sack coat** /'sæk kout/, *n.* →**sack[1]** (def. 4).

**sackful** /'sækful/, *n., pl.* **-fuls.** the amount that fills a sack.

**sacking** /'sækɪŋ/, *n.* stout or coarse woven material of hemp, jute, or the like, used for making sacks, etc.

**sack-race** /'sæk-reɪs/, *n.* a race in which each competitor jumps forward while his legs are confined in a sack.

**sacque** /sæk/, *n.* →**sack[1]** (def. 4).

**sacral[1]** /'seɪkrəl/, *adj.* of or pertaining to sacred rites or observations. [L *sacrum* sacred rite (properly neut. adj.) + -AL[1]]

**sacral[2]** /'seɪkrəl/, *adj.* of or pertaining to the sacrum. [NL *sacrālis.* See SACRUM]

**sacrament** /'sækrəmənt/, *n.* **1.** *Eccles.* a visible sign divinely instituted to confer grace or Divine Life on those who worthily receive it. In the various Christian denominations, the sacraments include some or all of the following: baptism; confirmation; the Eucharist or Lord's Supper; matrimony; penance; holy orders; and extreme unction. **2.** (*oft. cap.*) the

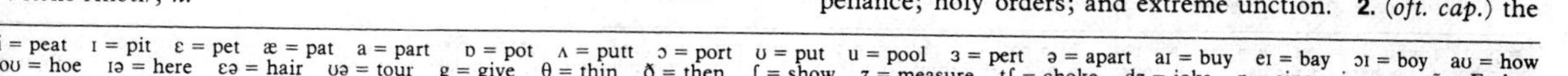
i = peat ɪ = pit ɛ = pet æ = pat a = part ɒ = pot ʌ = putt ɔ = port ʊ = put u = pool ɜ = pert ə = apart aɪ = buy eɪ = bay ɔɪ = boy aʊ = how
oʊ = hoe ɪə = here ɛə = hair ʊə = tour g = give θ = thin ð = then ʃ = show ʒ = measure tʃ = choke dʒ = joke ŋ = sing j = you õ = Fr. bon

Eucharist, or Lord's Supper. **3.** the consecrated elements of the Eucharist, esp. the bread (the **Blessed Sacrament**). **4.** something regarded as possessing a sacred character or a mysterious significance. **5.** a sign, token, or symbol. **6.** an oath; solemn pledge. [ME, from L *sacrāmentum* oath, solemn engagement]

**sacramental** /sækrəˈmɛntl/, *adj.* **1.** of, pertaining to, or of the nature of a sacrament, esp. the sacrament of the Eucharist. **2.** peculiarly sacred: *a sacramental obligation.* *–n.* **3.** *Rom. Cath. Ch.* a sacrament-like ritual, object, etc., which the church institutes and uses for obtaining a spiritual effect, such as the sign of the cross, the use of holy water, etc. – **sacramentally,** *adv.* – **sacramentality** /sækrəmɛnˈtæləti/, *n.*

**sacramentalist** /sækrəˈmɛntələst/, *n.* one who holds strong convictions about the importance and efficacy of the sacrament.

**sacrarium** /sæˈkrɛəriəm/, *n., pl.* **-craria** /-ˈkrɛəriə/. **1.** *Eccles.* the sanctuary or chancel. **2.** *Rom. Hist.* a shrine; a sanctuary. [L]

**sacred** /ˈseɪkrəd/, *adj.* **1.** appropriated or dedicated to a deity or to some religious purpose; consecrated. **2.** entitled to veneration or religious respect by association with divinity or divine things; holy. **3.** pertaining to or connected with religion (opposed to *profane* and *secular*): *sacred music.* **4.** reverently dedicated to some person or object: *a monument sacred to her memory.* **5.** regarded with reverence: *the sacred memory of a dead hero.* **6.** secured against violation, infringement, etc., by reverence, sense of right, etc.: *sacred oaths, sacred rights.* **7.** properly immune from violence, interference, etc., as a person or his office. [ME, pp. of *sacren* render holy, from L *sacrāre*] – **sacredly,** *adv.* – **sacredness,** *n.*

**sacred cow** /– ˈkaʊ/, *n.* something or somebody that escapes critical examination by virtue of popular esteem, high repute, etc.

**sacred fig tree,** *n.* →**bo tree.**

**sacred ibis** /seɪkrəd ˈaɪbəs/, *n.* an ibis, *Threskiornis aethiopica,* about 60 cm long with black-and-white plumage, venerated by the ancient Egyptians but now most common south of the Sahara.

**sacred kingfisher** /– ˈkɪŋfɪʃə/, *n.* a small, greenish-blue migratory kingfisher, *Halcyon sanctus,* widely distributed in wooded areas throughout Australia, New Zealand and islands to the north.

**sacrifice** /ˈsækrəfaɪs/, *n., v.,* **-ficed, -ficing.** *–n.* **1.** the offering of life (animal, plant, or human) or some material possession, etc., to a deity, as in propitiation or homage. **2.** that which is so offered. **3.** the surrender or destruction of something prized or desirable for the sake of something considered as having a higher or more pressing claim. **4.** the thing so surrendered or devoted. **5.** a loss incurred in selling something below its value. **6.** *Theol.* **a.** Christ's offering of His death to God on behalf of sinful mankind; exemplified in the concept of the Lamb of God taking away the sins of the world. **b.** *Rom. Cath. Ch.* the offering of mass by a priest as a re-representation of the sacrifice of Christ on Calvary. *–v.t.* **7.** to make a sacrifice or offering of. **8.** to surrender or give up, or permit injury or disadvantage to, for the sake of something else. **9.** to dispose of (goods, etc.) regardless of profit. *–v.i.* **10.** to offer or make a sacrifice. [ME, from F, from L *sacrificium*] – **sacrificer,** *n.*

**sacrificial** /sækrəˈfɪʃəl/, *adj.* pertaining to or concerned with sacrifice. – **sacrificially,** *adv.*

**sacrilege** /ˈsækrəlɪdʒ/, *n.* **1.** the violation or profanation of anything sacred or held sacred. **2.** an instance of this. **3.** the stealing of anything consecrated to the service of God. [ME, from OF, from L *sacrilegium*]

**sacrilegious** /sækrəˈlɪdʒəs/, *adj.* **1.** guilty of sacrilege: *a sacrilegious person.* **2.** involving sacrilege: *sacrilegious practices.* [L *sacrilegium* sacrilege + -OUS] – **sacrilegiously,** *adv.* – **sacrilegiousness,** *n.*

**sacring bell** /ˈseɪkrɪŋ bɛl/, *n.* (in the Roman Catholic Church) a small bell rung during mass at the Elevation.

**sacristan** /ˈsækrəstən/, *n.* **1.** an official in charge of the sacred vessels, vestments, etc., of a church or a religious house. **2.** *Obs.* a sexton. [ME, from ML *sacristānus*]

**sacristy** /ˈsækrəsti/, *n., pl.* **-ties.** an apartment in or a building connected with a church or a religious house, in which the sacred vessels, vestments, etc., are kept. [ML *sacristia*]

**sacro-,** a word element: **1.** meaning 'holy'. **2.** referring to the sacrum. [L, combining form of *sacer* (neut. *sacrum*) holy]

**sacroiliac** /sækroʊˈɪliæk/, *Anat.* *–n.* **1.** the joint where the sacrum and ilium meet. *–adj.* **2.** pertaining to this joint. [SACRO- + ILIAC]

**sacrosanct** /ˈsækrəsæŋkt/, *adj.* especially or superlatively sacred or inviolable. [L *sacrōsanctus*] – **sacrosanctity** /sækrəˈsæŋktəti/, *n.*

**sacrosciatic** /ˌsækroʊsaɪˈætɪk/, *adj.* pertaining to the sacrum and the ischium: *the sacrosciatic ligament.*

**sacrum** /ˈseɪkrəm/, *n., pl.* **-cra** /-krə/. a bone resulting from the ankylosis of two or more vertebrae between the lumbar and the coccygeal regions, in man composed (usu.) of five fused vertebrae and forming the posterior wall of the pelvis. [NL, short for L (*os*) *sacrum,* lit., sacred (bone); so called because used in sacrifices]

**sad** /sæd/, *adj.,* **sadder, saddest.** **1.** sorrowful or mournful: *to feel sad.* **2.** expressive of or characterised by sorrow: *sad looks.* **3.** causing sorrow: *a sad disappointment.* **4.** (of colour) sombre, dark, or dull. **5.** deplorable; shocking: *a sad attempt.* **6.** *Colloq.* (of bread, cake, etc.) soggy, not having risen. [ME; OE *sæd,* c. G *satt,* Goth. *saths* sated; akin to L *sat, satis* enough, *satur* sated, Gk *hádēn* enough] – **sadly,** *adv.*

**sadden** /ˈsædn/, *v.t.* **1.** to make sad. *–v.i.* **2.** to become sad.

**saddle** /ˈsædl/, *n., v.,* **-dled, -dling.** *–n.* **1.** a seat for a rider on the back of a horse or other animal. **2.** a similar seat on a bicycle, machine, etc. **3.** a part of a harness laid across the back of an animal and girded under the belly. **4.** that part of an animal's back on which the saddle is placed. **5.** something resembling a saddle in shape or position. **6.** (of mutton, venison, etc.) a cut including part of the backbone and both loins. **7.** (of poultry) the posterior part of the back. **8.** the saddle of an animal prepared for food. **9.** a ridge connecting two higher elevations. **10.** *Naut.* a hollowed-out piece of wood which provides a resting place for the end of a spar. **11.** the clitellum of an earthworm. **12.** *Ordn.* the support for the trunnion on some guncarriages. **13. in the saddle,** in a position of authority; in control. *–v.t.* **14.** to put a saddle upon (a horse, etc.). **15.** to load or charge, as with a burden. **16.** to impose as a burden or responsibility. *–v.i.* **17.** to put a saddle on a horse (oft. fol. by *up*). [ME *sadel,* OE *sadol,* c. G *Sattel*]

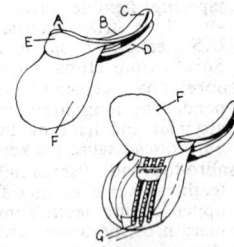

saddle: A, pommel; B, seat; C, cantle; D, panel; E, skirt; F, flap; G, girth straps

**saddleback** /ˈsædlbæk/, *n.* **1.** a rare New Zealand bird, *Philesturnus carunculatus,* with a saddle-shaped area of plumage across its back and wings. **2.** any of various other animals or birds having marks on the back resembling a saddle. **3.** a saddle-shaped surface, as a ridge between two peaks. *–adj.* **4.** having a shape like a saddle.

**saddle-backed** /ˈsædl-bækt/, *adj.* **1.** having the back or upper surface curved like a saddle. **2.** having a saddle-like marking on the back, as certain birds.

**saddlebag** /ˈsædlbæg/, *n.* a large bag, often one of a pair, hung from or laid over a saddle.

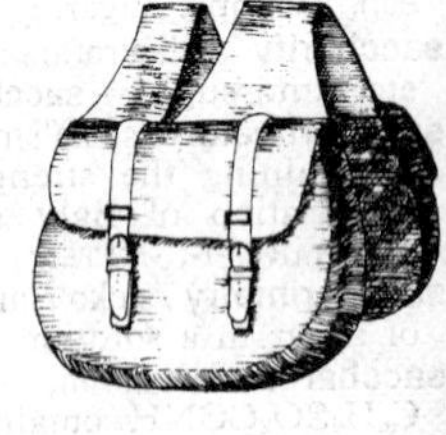

saddlebag

**saddlebill** /ˈsædlbɪl/, *n.* a tall, handsome stork of tropical Africa, *Ephippiorhynchus senegalensis,* having a saddle-like shield on its large, pointed bill.

**saddlebow** /ˈsædlboʊ/, *n.* the arched front part of a saddle or saddletree.

**saddlecloth** /ˈsædlklɒθ/, *n.* a cloth placed between a horse's back and the saddle.

**saddle graft** /ˈsædl graft/, *n.* a type of graft in which a chisel-shaped projection at the top of the stock is inserted in a groove cut in the base of the scion.

**saddle-horse** /ˈsædl-hɔs/, *n.* any type of horse which has a strong back and trained gait and is therefore used for riding.

**saddler** /ˈsædlə/, *n.* one who makes or deals in saddlery.

**saddle reef** /ˈsædl rif/, *n.* an ore deposit shaped like a saddle, with a distinct cap branching symmetrically outwards and downwards on each side.

**saddle roof** /ˈ– ruf/, *n.* a roof having two gables.

**saddlery** /ˈsædləri/, *n., pl.* **-ries.** **1.** saddles and other articles pertaining to the equipment of horses, etc. **2.** the work, business, or shop of a saddler.

**saddle-soap** /ˈsædl-soʊp/, *n.* a soap, usu. consisting of a mild soap and neat's-foot oil, used for cleaning and preserving leather.

**saddle-sore** /ˈsædl-sɔ/, *adj.* **1.** sore after horse-riding. **2.** (of a horse) having sores produced by a saddle.

**saddle stitch** /ˈsædl stɪtʃ/, *n.* **1.** a running stitch usu. set in from an edge that is used as a decorative trimming on clothing and leather articles. **2.** *Bookbinding.* a stitch used to secure pages at the centrefold, with thread or wire.

**saddle-stitch** /ˈsædl-stɪtʃ/, *v.t.* to sew (a garment, book, etc.) with a saddle stitch.

**saddletree** /ˈsædlˌtri/, *n.* the frame of a saddle.

**saddling paddock** /ˈsædlɪŋ pædək/, *n.* →**paddock** (def. 3).

**sadie** /ˈseɪdi/, *n. Colloq.* a cleaning woman. [from the song '*Sadie,* the cleaning lady']

**sadism** /ˈsædɪzəm, ˈseɪ-/, *n.* **1.** sexual gratification gained through causing physical pain and humiliation. **2.** any morbid enjoyment in inflicting mental or physical pain. [F *sadisme,* from the Marquis de *Sade,* 1740-1814, French soldier and novelist, notorious for the mixture of sex and cruelty in his books] – **sadist,** *n., adj.* – **sadistic** /səˈdɪstɪk/, *adj.* – **sadistically** /səˈdɪstɪkli/, *adv.*

**sadness** /ˈsædnəs/, *n.* **1.** the quality of being sad; unhappiness. **2.** the state of being sad; grief.

**sadomasochism** /ˌseɪdoʊˈmæsəkɪzəm, ˌsædoʊ-/, *n.* a disturbed condition of the mind marked by the presence of sadistic and masochistic tendencies. – **sadomasochist,** *n.*

**sad sack** /ˈsæd sæk/, *n. Colloq.* **1.** a habitually (and often demonstratively) sad person. **2.** an ineffective person who always blunders despite good intentions, esp. a soldier.

**s.a.e.,** stamped addressed envelope.

**safari** /səˈfari/, *n., pl.* **-ris.** **1.** a journey; an expedition, esp. for hunting. **2.** the persons, animals, etc., forming such an expedition. [Swahili, from Ar.]

**safari park** /ˈ– pak/, *n.* a large park where wild animals are kept, uncaged, to be viewed by the public from cars, etc.

**safari suit** /ˈ– sut/, *n.* a suit consisting of trousers and jacket, usu. made from white or light coloured cloth, and resembling the clothes originally worn on safari.

**safe** /seɪf/, *adj.,* **safer, safest,** *n., adv.* –*adj.* **1.** secure from liability to harm, injury, danger, or risk: *a safe place.* **2.** free from hurt, injury, danger, or risk: *to arrive safe and sound.* **3.** involving no risk of mishap, error, etc.: *a safe estimate.* **4.** dependable or trustworthy: *a safe guide.* **5.** cautious in avoiding danger: *a safe player.* **6.** placed beyond the power of doing harm; in secure custody: *a criminal safe in gaol.* **7.** **be on the safe side,** *Colloq.* to take every precaution. –*n.* **8.** a steel or iron box or repository for money, jewels, papers, etc. **9.** any receptacle or structure for the storage or preservation of articles: *a meat safe.* –*adv.* **10.** **play safe,** to act cautiously. [ME *sauf,* from OF, from L *salvus* uninjured] – **safely,** *adv.* – **safeness,** *n.*

**safeblower** /ˈseɪfbloʊə/, *n.* a burglar who breaks open safes by means of explosives.

**safebreaker** /ˈseɪfbreɪkə/, *n.* a burglar who robs safes.

**safe-conduct** /seɪf-ˈkɒndʌkt/, *n.* **1.** a document securing a safe passage through a region, esp. in time of war. **2.** this privilege. **3.** a conducting in safety.

**safe-deposit** /ˈseɪf-dəpɒzət/, *n.* **1.** a building containing safes, strongrooms, etc., where valuables may be stored. –*adj.* **2.** providing safekeeping for valuables: *a safe-deposit vault or box.*

**safeguard** /ˈseɪfgad/, *n.* **1.** something serving as a protection or defence, or ensuring safety. **2.** a permit for safe passage. **3.** a guard or convoy. **4.** a mechanical device for ensuring safety. –*v.t.* **5.** to guard; protect; secure. [ME *saufegard,* from OF *sauvegarde,* from *sauve* (fem. of *sauf*) + *garde.* See SAFE, GUARD]

**safekeeping** /seɪfˈkipɪŋ/, *n.* protection; care.

**safelight** /ˈseɪflaɪt/, *n.* a light used in a darkroom, fitted with filters which can be adjusted to prevent the passage of light of a frequency which could affect the emulsion and fog the film.

**safe period** /ˈseɪf pɪəriəd/, *n.* the infertile phase of a woman's menstrual cycle.

**safety** /ˈseɪfti/, *n., pl.* **-ties.** **1.** the state of being safe; freedom from injury or danger. **2.** the quality of insuring against hurt, injury, danger, or risk. **3.** a contrivance or device to prevent injury or avert danger. **4.** the action of keeping safe. **5.** *Obs.* close confinement or custody.

**safety belt** /ˈ– bɛlt/, *n.* **1.** Also, **seat belt.** a belt attached to the seat of an aeroplane, for securing a passenger or pilot against sudden turns, stops, turbulence, etc. **2.** a belt or strap fastening a person working at a height to a fixed object, to prevent him from falling. **3.** →**seat belt** (def. 1).

**safety bicycle** /ˈ– baɪsəkəl/, *n.* a bicycle with two equal-sized wheels.

**safety binding** /ˈ– baɪndɪŋ/, *n.* a mechanism, part of a ski binding, which automatically opens to release the boot, under a heavy forward or rotary strain. Also, **release binding.**

**safety catch** /ˈ– kætʃ/, *n.* a locking or cut-off device, as one that prevents a gun from being fired accidentally.

**safety curtain** /ˈ– kɜtn/, *n.* a fireproof curtain between the stage and the auditorium in a theatre, etc.

**safety film** /ˈ– fɪlm/, *n.* non-flammable photographic film.

**safety fuse** /ˈ– fjuz/, *n.* **1.** a fuse in an electrical circuit which prevents overloading which might cause damage or fire in the circuit. **2.** a fuse for igniting explosives which burns slowly, allowing those who have lit it to move safely away.

**safety glass** /ˈ– glas/, *n.* **1.** →**laminated glass.** **2.** →**shatterproof glass** (def. 2). **3.** glass which is reinforced with a wire mesh within its body; wired glass.

**safety helmet** /ˈ– hɛlmət/, *n.* a metal or plastic protective hat having a reinforced crown, and worn on construction sites.

**safety lamp** /ˈ– læmp/, *n.* a miner's lamp in which the flame is protected by wire gauze, thus preventing immediate ignition of explosive gases.

**safety match** /ˈ– mætʃ/, *n.* a match designed to ignite only when rubbed on a specially prepared surface.

**safety net** /ˈ– nɛt/, *n.* **1.** a net intended to catch and prevent injury to acrobats, construction workers, etc., in case of a fall. **2.** →**shark net.**

**safety pin** /ˈ– pɪn/, *n.* **1.** a pin bent back on itself to form a spring, with a guard to cover the point. **2.** a locking device on grenades, mines, etc., to keep them safe until required for use.

safety pin

**safety ramp** /ˈ– ræmp/, *n.* a sharply rising side track leading off a roadway with a steep downgrade, and intended to be used to bring a vehicle to an emergency stop in the event of brake failure.

**safety razor** /ˈ– reɪzə/, *n.* a razor provided with a guard or guards to prevent cutting the skin.

**safety valve** /ˈ– vælv/, *n.* **1.** a valve in a steam boiler or the like, which, when the pressure becomes abnormal or dangerous, opens and allows the steam or fluid to escape. **2.** a harmless outlet for emotion, nervousness, etc.

**safflower** /ˈsæflaʊə/, *n.* **1.** a thistle-like herb, *Carthamus tinctorius,* native to the Old World, bearing large orange-red flower heads, and cultivated for seed-oil. **2.** its dried florets, used medicinally or as a dyestuff. [D *saffloer,* from OF *saffleur,* from It. *saffiore;* ult. orig. uncert.]

**safflower oil** /ˈ– ɔɪl/, *n.* an edible oil, high in polyunsaturated fats, yielded from the seeds of the safflower, and used in cookery, cosmetics, paints and medicines.

**saffron** /ˈsæfrən/, *n.* **1.** a crocus, *Crocus sativus,* with handsome purple flowers. **2.** an orange-coloured product consisting of its dried stigmas, used to colour confectionery, for flavouring, etc., in rolls and buns and in rice dishes. **3.** Also,

**saffron yellow**. yellow-orange. [ME, from F *safran,* from Ar. *za'farān*]

**saffron thistle** /– 'θɪsəl/, *n.* a prickly annual herb with yellow flowers, *Carthamus lanatus,* family Compositae, native to Mediterranean regions, now a troublesome weed in Australia and other warm temperate regions.

**safing** /'seɪfɪŋ/, *n.* the changing of a weapon or ammunition from a state of readiness back to a safe condition.

**S. Afr.**, **1.** South Africa. **2.** South African.

**safranine** /'sæfrənin, -ən/, *n.* **1.** any of a class of (chiefly red) organic dyes, phenazine derivatives, used for dyeing wool, silk, etc. **2.** a dye, $C_{18}H_{14}N_4$. [var. of *safranin,* from G, from *Safran* saffron + *-in* -INE[2]]

**safrole** /'sæfroʊl/, *n.* a colourless or faintly yellow liquid, $C_{10}H_{10}O_2$, obtained from oil of sassafras, etc., and used for flavouring and in perfumery. Also, **safrol** /'sæfrɒl/. [(SAS)SAF-R(AS) + -OLE]

**sag** /sæg/, *v.,* **sagged, sagging,** *n.* *–v.i.* **1.** to sink or bend downwards by weight or pressure, esp. in the middle. **2.** to droop; hang loosely: *sagging shoulders.* **3.** to yield through weakness, lack of effort, or the like. **4.** to decline, as in price. **5.** *Naut.* to drift out of the intended course. **6.** *Naut.* of a ship, to bend down in the middle, esp. when loading. *–n.* **7.** the act of sagging. **8.** the degree of sagging. **9.** a place where anything sags; a depression. **10.** moderate decline in prices. **11.** *Naut.* leeway. **12.** *Chiefly Tas.* →**rush**[2]. [ME *sagge;* probably akin to D *zakken* subside]

**saga** /'sagə/, *n.* **1.** a medieval Icelandic or Norse prose narrative of achievements and events in the history of a personage, family, etc. **2.** a form of novel, characteristically French **(roman-fleuve)** but also written in English, in which the members or generations of a family or social group are chronicled in a long and leisurely narrative. **3.** any narrative or legend of heroic exploits. [Icel.: story, history; c. SAW[3]]

**sagacious** /sə'geɪʃəs/, *adj.* having acute mental discernment and keen practical sense; shrewd: *a sagacious author.* [SAGACI(TY) + -OUS] – **sagaciously,** *adv.* – **sagaciousness,** *n.*

**sagacity** /sə'gæsəti/, *n., pl.* **-ties.** acuteness of mental discernment and soundness of judgment. [L *sagācitas*]

**sage**[1] /seɪdʒ/, *n., adj.,* **sager, sagest.** *–n.* **1.** a profoundly wise man; a man famed for wisdom. **2.** a man venerated for his wisdom, judgment, and experience: *the seven sages of ancient Greece.* *–adj.* **3.** wise, judicious, or prudent: *sage conduct.* [ME, from OF, from L *-sapius* wise] – **sagely,** *adv.* – **sageness,** *n.*

**sage**[2] /seɪdʒ/, *n.* **1.** a perennial plant, *Salvia officinalis,* whose greenish grey leaves are used for seasoning in cookery. **2.** the leaves themselves. **3.** any of various related plants. **4.** sagebrush. [ME *sauge,* from OF, from L *salvia*]

**sagebrush** /'seɪdʒbrʌʃ/, *n.* any of various sagelike bushy plants of the genus *Artemisia,* common on the dry plains of the western U.S.

**sage-green** /seɪdʒ-'grin/, *n.* **1.** a greyish-green colour. *–adj.* **2.** greyish-green.

**saggar** /'sægə/, *n.* **1.** a box or case made of refractory baked clay in which the finer ceramic wares are enclosed and protected while baking. *–v.t.* **2.** to place in or upon a saggar. Also, **saggard, sagger.** [probably contraction of SAFEGUARD]

**sagittal** /'sædʒətl/, *adj.* **1.** *Anat.* **a.** denoting or pertaining to the suture between the parietal bones of the skull, or to a venous channel within the skull and parallel to this suture. **b.** (in direction or location) from front to back in the median plane, or in a plane parallel to the median. **2.** pertaining to or resembling an arrow or arrowhead. [NL *sagittālis,* from L *sagitta* arrow]

sagittate leaf

**Sagittarian** /sædʒə'teəriən/, *n.* **1.** a person born under the sign of Sagittarius, and (according to tradition) exhibiting some of the typical Sagittarian personality traits to some degree. *–adj.* **2.** of or pertaining to Sagittarius. **3.** of or pertaining to such a person or such a personality trait.

**Sagittarius** /sædʒə'teəriəs/, *n.* **1.** the Archer (a centaur drawing a bow), a constellation and sign of the zodiac. **2.** →**Sagittarian.** [L]

**sagittate** /'sædʒəteɪt/, *adj.* shaped like an arrowhead: *a sagittate leaf.* Also, **sagittiform** /'sædʒətəfɔm, sə'dʒɪtəfɔm/. [NL *sagittātus,* from L *sagitta* arrow]

**sago** /'seɪgoʊ/, *n.* **1.** a starchy foodstuff derived from the soft interior of the trunk of various palms and cycads, used in making puddings, and other dishes. **2.** any of various plants from which this foodstuff may be obtained. [Malay *sāgū*]

**sago grass** /'– gras/, *n.* **1.** →**shot grass. 2.** →**small burr grass.**

**saguaro** /sə'gwaroʊ, sə'waroʊ/, *n., pl.* **-ros.** an extremely tall cactus, *Carnegiea gigantea,* of the south-western U.S., yielding a useful wood and an edible fruit. [Sp.; of Amer. Ind. orig.]

saguaro

**sag wagon** /'sæg wægən/, *n.* →**bonk wagon.**

**Sahara** /sə'harə/, *n.* **1.** a desert in northern Africa, extending from the Atlantic to the Nile valley. **2.** any arid waste.

**sahib** /sab, 'sa-ɪb/, *n.* (in India) a term of respect which follows a man's name. [Hind., from Ar. *çāḥib* master, lit., friend]

**said** /sɛd/, *v.* **1.** past tense and past participle of **say.** *–adj.* **2.** named or mentioned before: *said witness, said sum.*

**saiga** /'saɪgə/, *n.* an antelope, *Saiga tartarica,* of western Asia. [Russ.]

**Saigon rose** /saɪgɒn 'roʊz/, *n.* a form of venereal disease, thought to have been introduced by returned soldiers from Vietnam.

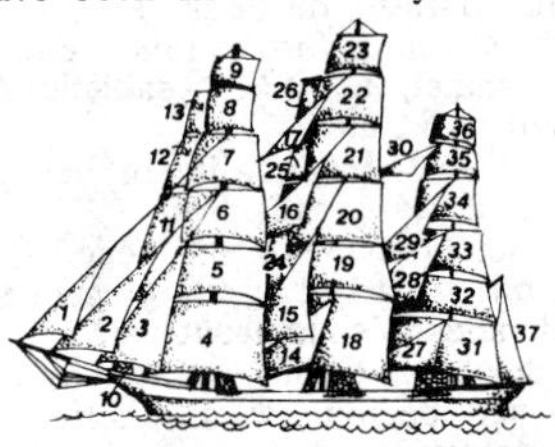
sailing ship under all plain sail (def. 9)

1. flying jib
2. jib
3. fore-topmast staysail
4. foresail
5. lower fore-topsail
6. upper fore-topsail
7. fore-topgallant sail
8. fore-royal
9. fore-skysail
10. lower studding sail
11. fore-topmast studding sail
12. fore-topgallant sail
13. fore-royal studding sail
14. main staysail
15. main-topmast staysail
16. main-topgallant staysail
17. main-royal staysail
18. main sail
19. lower main topsail
20. upper main topsail
21. main-topgallant sail
22. main royal
23. main skysail
24. main-topmast studding sail
25. main-topgallant studding sail
26. main-royal studding sail
27. mizzen staysail
28. mizzen-topmast staysail
29. mizzen-topgallant staysail
30. mizzen-royal staysail
31. mizzen sail
32. lower mizzen topsail
33. upper mizzen topsail
34. mizzen-topgallant sail
35. mizzen royal
36. mizzen skysail
37. spanker

**sail** /seɪl/, *n.* **1.** an expanse of canvas or similar material spread to the wind to make a vessel move through the water. It is called a **square sail** when quadrilateral and extended by a yard, usu. at right angles to the masts, and a **fore-and-aft sail** when set on a mast, boom, gaff, or stay, more or less in line with the keel. **2.** some similar piece or apparatus, as the part of an arm of a windmill which catches the wind. **3.** a voyage or excursion, esp. in a sailing vessel. **4.** a sailing vessel or ship. **5.** sailing vessels collectively: *the fleet numbered thirty sail.* **6.** sails for a vessel or vessels, collectively. **7. make sail,** *Naut.* **a.** to set the sail or sails of a boat, or increase the amount of sail already set. **b.** to set out on a voyage. **8. set sail,** to start a voyage. **9. under sail,** with sails set. *–v.i.* **10.** to travel in a vessel conveyed by the action of wind, steam, etc. **11.** to move along or be conveyed by wind, steam, etc.: *steamships sailing to Fremantle.* **12.** to manage a boat, esp. for sport. **13.** to begin a journey by water: *sailing at dawn.* **14.** to move along in a manner suggestive of a sailing vessel: *clouds sailing overhead.* **15.** to travel through the air, as a balloon. **16.** to move along with dignity: *to sail into a room.* **17.** *Colloq.* to go boldly into action (fol. by *in*). *–v.t.* **18.** to sail upon, over, or through: *to sail the seven seas.* **19.** to navigate (a ship, etc.). **20.** to cause to sail (a toy boat or the like). [ME; OE *segl,* c. G *Segel*] – **sailable,** *adj.* – **sailless,** *adj.*

**sailboard** /ˈseɪlbɔd/, *n.* **1.** a lightweight, polyurethane surfboard, equipped with a mast and sail, on which the rider stands to manoeuvre the sail. *–v.i.* **2.** to ride on a sailboard. – **sailboarding,** *n.*

**sailboat** /ˈseɪlboʊt/, *n.* a sailing boat.

**sailcloth** /ˈseɪlklɒθ/, *n.* **1.** a strong canvas or other material such as is used for making sails. **2.** a lightweight canvas material used for making clothing, curtains, etc.

**sailer** /ˈseɪlə/, *n.* **1.** a vessel propelled by a sail or sails. **2.** a vessel with reference to its powers or manner of sailing. **3.** *N.Z. Colloq.* a falling tree-branch.

**sailfish** /ˈseɪlfɪʃ/, *n., pl.* **-fishes,** (*esp. collectively*) **-fish.** any of the large marine fishes constituting the genus *Istiophorus,* characterised by a very large dorsal fin likened to a sail, and related to the swordfishes, as *I. ludibundus* of north Australian and Pacific waters.

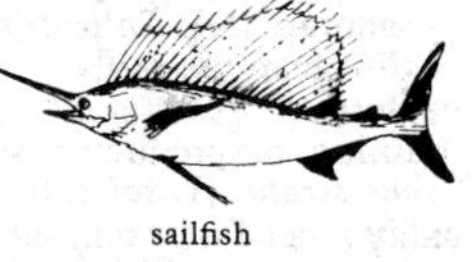
sailfish

**sailing** /ˈseɪlɪŋ/, *n.* **1.** the act of one who or that which sails. **2.** the procedure of solving problems of courses, distances, and positions in navigating a ship, without the use of celestial observations.

**sailing boat** /ˈ– boʊt/, *n.* a boat propelled by sails. Also, **sailing ship.**

**sailor** /ˈseɪlə/, *n.* **1.** one whose occupation is sailing or navigation; a mariner; a seaman. **2.** a seaman below the rank of officer. **3.** a person, with reference to susceptibility to seasickness: *a bad sailor.* **4.** a sailor-hat. [ME *sailer* one who sails]

**sailor-hat** /ˈseɪlə-hæt/, *n.* **1.** a hat worn by a sailor. **2.** a soft flat-brimmed straw hat with a low flat crown.

**sailorly** /ˈseɪləli/, *adj.* like or befitting a sailor.

**sailor suit** /ˈseɪlə sut/, *n.* a suit in imitation of a sailor's uniform, formerly much worn by children.

**sailplane** /ˈseɪlpleɪn/, *n.* **1.** a glider designed esp. for sustained flight using ascending air currents. *–v.i.* **2.** to soar in a sailplane.

**sailyard** /ˈseɪljad/, *n.* a spar on which sails are extended.

**sain** /seɪn/, *v.t. Archaic.* **1.** to make the sign of the cross on as to protect against evil influences. **2.** to safeguard by prayer. **3.** to bless. [ME; OE *segnian* (c. G *segnen*), from L *signāre*]

**sainfoin** /ˈsænfɔɪn/, *n.* **1.** a European herb, *Onobrychis viciifolia,* family Papilionaceae, cultivated as a forage plant. **2.** any of various related herbs of Eurasia or North America cultivated for fodder. [F, from *sain* wholesome (or *saint* holy) + *foin* hay, from L *faenum*]

**saint** /seɪnt/, *n.* **1.** one of certain persons of exceptional holiness of life formally recognised by the Christian Church as having attained an exalted position in heaven and as being entitled to veneration on earth; a canonised person. **2.** (in certain religious bodies) a designation applied by the members to themselves. **3.** a person of great holiness. **4.** a sanctimonious person. *–v.t.* **5.** to enrol formally among the saints recognised by the church. **6.** to give the name of saint to; reckon as a saint. [ME, from OF, from L *sanctus,* pp., consecrated]

**Saint** /seɪnt/, *n.* see **St** for entries more commonly written in the abbreviated form.

**Saint Andrew's Cross,** *n.* an X-shaped cross.

**Saint Anthony's Cross,** *n.* a T-shaped cross.

**Saint Barnaby's thistle,** *n.* an annual or biennial plant with yellow flowers and long yellow spines, *Centaurea solstitialis,* native to south-eastern Europe, found as a weed of arable fields elsewhere.

**Saint Bernard** /sənt ˈbɜnəd/, *n.* one of a breed of large dogs with a massive head, noted for their intelligence. [named after the hospice of *St Bernard,* on the pass of the Great St Bernard in the Alps, between Switzerland and Italy, where they are kept by the monks for rescuing travellers from the snow]

Saint Bernard

**sainted** /ˈseɪntəd/, *adj.* **1.** enrolled among the saints. **2.** being a saint in heaven. **3.** sacred or hallowed. **4.** saintly.

**Saint George's Cross,** *n.* the Greek cross.

**sainthood** /ˈseɪnthʊd/, *n.* **1.** the character or status of a saint. **2.** saints collectively.

**saintly** /ˈseɪntli/, *adj.,* **-lier, -liest.** like, proper to, or befitting a saint: *saintly lives.* – **saintliness,** *n.*

**Saint's day** /ˈseɪnts deɪ/, *n.* a day in the church calendar set apart for the commemoration of a saint.

**saintship** /ˈseɪntʃɪp/, *n.* the qualities of a saint.

**Saint Valentine's Day,** *n.* 14 February, when tokens of affection or valentines are given.

**saith** /sɛθ/, *v. Archaic or Poetic.* third person singular present of **say.**

**saithe** /seɪθ/, *n.* →**coalfish.** [Scot., from Scand.; cf. Icel. *seithr,* Norw. *seid*]

**sake**[1] /seɪk/, *n.* **1.** cause, account, or interest: *for my sake.* **2.** purpose or end: *for the sake of appearances.* [ME; OE *sacu* lawsuit, cause, c. G *Sache*]

**sake**[2] /ˈsaki/, *n.* a Japanese fermented alcoholic drink made from rice. [Jap.]

**saker** /ˈseɪkə/, *n.* an Old World falcon, *Falco sacer cherrug,* used in falconry. [F *sacre,* from Ar. *çaqr*]

**saki** /ˈsaki/, *n.* any of several small monkeys of the family Cebidae, living in the Amazon basin.

**sal** /sæl/, *n. Chiefly Pharm.* salt. [L]

**Sal** /sæl/, *n. Colloq.* →**Sallie.**

**salaam** /səˈlam/, *n.* **1.** (in the Orient) a salutation meaning 'peace'. **2.** a very low bow or obeisance, esp. with the palm of the right hand placed on the forehead. *–v.i.* **3.** to salute with a salaam. **4.** to perform a salaam. *–v.t.* **5.** to salute (someone) with a salaam. [Ar. *salām* peace]

**salable** /ˈseɪləbəl/, *adj.* →**saleable.** – **salability** /seɪləˈbɪləti/, *n.* – **salably,** *adv.*

**salacious** /səˈleɪʃəs/, *adj.* **1.** lustful or lecherous. **2.** (of writings, etc.) obscene; titillating. [*salaci(ty)* (from L *salācitas* lust) + -OUS] – **salaciously,** *adv.* – **salaciousness, salacity** /səˈlæsəti/, *n.*

**salad** /ˈsæləd/, *n.* **1.** a dish of uncooked vegetables, typically served with a savoury dressing. **2.** any of various raw or cooked foods served cold, usu. cut up and mixed with a dressing: *fruit salad, potato salad.* **3.** any of various herbs used for such a dish or commonly eaten raw. *–adj.* **4.** of or pertaining to a salad. [ME *salade,* from OF, from OPr. *salada,* from *salar* to salt, from L *sal* salt]

**salad burnet** /– bɜˈnɛt/, *n.* a perennial herb, *Poterium sanguisorba,* family Rosaceae, of Britain, Europe, western Asia and northern Africa, having leaves which can be used as a salad vegetable.

**salad days** /ˈ– deɪz/, *n. pl.* days of youthful inexperience. [from 'my *salad days* when I was green in judgment, cold in blood' (Shakespeare, *Antony and Cleopatra*)]

**salad dressing** /ˈ– drɛsɪŋ/, *n.* a dressing for a salad, as French dressing, mayonnaise, etc.

**salad oil** /ˈ– ɔɪl/, *n.* any edible vegetable oil prepared for use in salads, for cooking, etc.

**salamander** /ˈsæləmændə/, *n.* **1.** any of various tailed amphibians, most of which have an aquatic larval stage but are terrestrial as adults, such as *Salamandra salamandra,* the **European** or **fire salamander** of central and southern Europe. **2.** a mythical lizard or other reptile, or a being supposed to be able to live in fire. **3.** any person or thing able to survive great heat. **4.**

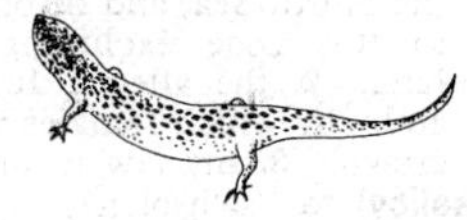
salamander

*Metall.* a mass of slag or metal remaining on the walls of a blast furnace. **5.** a small portable stove used on building sites to keep materials dry. [ME *salamandre,* from OF, from L *salamandra,* from Gk] – **salamandrine** /sælə'mændrən/, *adj.*

**salami** /sə'lami/, *n.* a kind of sausage, originally Italian, often flavoured with garlic. [It. (pl.), from L *salāre* to salt]

**sal ammoniac** /sæl ə'mouniæk/, *n.* →**ammonium chloride.**

**salaried** /'sælərid/, *adj.* **1.** receiving a salary. **2.** having a salary attached.

**salary** /'sæləri/, *n., pl.* **-ries.** a fixed periodical payment, usu. monthly, paid to a person for regular work or services, esp. work other than that of a manual, mechanical, or menial kind. [ME *salarie,* from AF, from L *salārium,* orig., money allowed to soldiers for the purchase of salt]

**salbutamol** /sæl'bjutəmɒl/, *n.* a bronchodilator used by inhalation for the treatment of respiratory diseases, which assists breathing without affecting the heart rate; ventolin.

**sale** /seɪl/, *n.* **1.** the act of selling. **2.** the quantity sold. **3.** opportunity to sell; demand: *slow sale.* **4.** a special disposal of goods, as at reduced prices. **5.** transfer of property for money or credit. **6. for sale** or **on sale,** offered to be sold; offered to purchasers. **7. have (make) a sale,** *N.Z. Colloq.* to vomit. [ME; late OE *sala,* c. Icel. and OHG *sala.* See SELL]

**saleable** /'seɪləbəl/, *adj.* **1.** subject to or suitable for sale. **2.** attractive to the prospective buyer; easily sold. Also, **salable.** – **saleability** /seɪlə'bɪləti/, *n.* – **saleably,** *adv.*

**salep** /'sæləp/, *n.* a starchy Asian drug or foodstuff consisting of the dried tubers of certain orchids. [Turk., from d. Ar. *sa'leb,* var. of *tha'leb,* short for *khasyu'th-tha'lab,* lit., fox's testicles]

**saleratus** /sælə'reɪtəs/, *n. U.S.* potassium or sodium bicarbonate, used as an ingredient in baking powder. [NL *sal ǣrātus* aerated salt]

**saleroom** /'seɪlrum/, *n.* →**salesroom.**

**salesclerk** /'seɪlzklak/, *n. U.S.* one who sells goods in a shop or store.

**salesgirl** /'seɪlzgɜl/, *n.* a girl engaged to sell goods, in a shop, store, etc.

**saleslady** /'seɪlzleɪdi/, *n., pl.* **-dies.** a saleswoman.

**salesman** /'seɪlzmən/, *n., pl.* **-men.** a man engaged in selling.

**salesmanship** /'seɪlzmənʃɪp/, *n.* **1.** the art of selling. **2.** skill in persuading people to buy, through attractive presentation of goods, convincing talk, etc.

**sales promotion** /'seɪlz prəmouʃən/, *n.* any activity which is calculated to increase the sale of a particular commodity or service.

**sales resistance** /'– rəzɪstəns/, *n.* unwillingness or refusal to buy.

**salesroom** /'seɪlzrum/, *n.* **1.** a room in which goods are sold or displayed. **2.** an auction room.

**sales talk** /'seɪlz tɔk/, *n.* **1.** a line of reasoning or argument intended to effect a sale. **2.** any persuasive argument.

**sales tax** /'– tæks/, *n.* a tax added to the retail price of goods.

**saleswoman** /'seɪlzwʊmən/, *n., pl.* **-women.** a woman engaged in selling.

**saleyard** /'seɪljad/, *n.* a yard from which livestock, motor vehicles, etc., are sold.

**salicaceous** /sælə'keɪʃəs/, *adj.* belonging to the Salicaceae, a family of trees and shrubs containing the willows and poplars. [L *salix* willow + -ACEOUS]

**salicin** /'sæləsən/, *n.* a colourless, crystalline glucoside, $C_{13}H_{18}O_7$, obtained from the American aspen bark and used as an antipyretic. [F *salicine,* from L *salix* willow + *-ine* -INE[2]]

**Salic law** /'sælɪk lɔ, 'seɪlɪk/, *n.* **1.** a code of laws of the Salian Franks, a tribe who dwelt in the regions of the Rhine near the North Sea, and of other Germanic tribes, esp. a provision in this code excluding females from the inheritance of land. **2.** the alleged fundamental law of the French monarchy by which females were excluded from succession to the crown. **3.** any law to the same effect.

**salicylate** /sə'lɪsəleɪt/, *n.* a salt or ester of salicylic acid. [SALIC(IN) + -YL + -ATE[2]]

**salicylic acid** /ˌsæləsɪlɪk 'æsəd/, *n.* an acid, $HOC_6H_4COOH$, prepared from salicin or from phenol, and used as an antiseptic, in the manufacture of aspirin, and medically as a remedy for rheumatic and gouty affections, usu. in the form of a salicylate.

**salience** /'seɪliəns/, *n.* **1.** the state or condition of being salient. **2.** a salient or projecting object, part, or feature.

**saliency** /'seɪliənsi/, *n., pl.* **-cies.** →**salience.**

**salient** /'seɪliənt/, *adj.* **1.** prominent or conspicuous: *salient features.* **2.** projecting or pointing outwards, as an angle. **3.** leaping or jumping. *–n.* **4.** *Fort.* a salient angle or part, as the central outward projecting angle of a bastion or an outward projection in a battle line. [L *saliens,* ppr., leaping forth] – **saliently,** *adv.*

S
S
S
R
S
S

S, salient angle; R, re-entrant angle

**salientian** /seɪli'ɛnʃiən/, *adj., n.* →**anuran.** [NL *Salienti(a)* (from L *salīre* leap) + -AN]

**saliferous** /sə'lɪfərəs/, *adj.* containing or producing salt: *saliferous strata.* [L *sal* salt + -I- + -FEROUS]

**salify** /'sæləfaɪ/, *v.t.,* **-fied, -fying.** **1.** to form into a salt, as by chemical combination. **2.** to mix or combine with a salt. [NL *salificāre,* from L *sal* salt. See -FY]

**salina** /sə'laɪnə/, *n.* **1.** a saline marsh, spring, or the like. **2.** a saltworks. [Sp., from L (found in pl. only)]

**saline** /'seɪlaɪn, -lin/, *adj.* **1.** salty or saltlike; containing or tasting like common table salt: *a saline solution.* **2.** of or pertaining to a chemical salt, of sodium, potassium, magnesium, etc., as used as a cathartic. *–n.* **3.** a saline health drink or medicine. [L *salīnus* (found in neut. only), from *sal* salt] – **salinity** /sə'lɪnəti/, *n.*

**salinometer** /sælə'nɒmətə/, *n.* a hydrometer used for determining the concentration of salt solutions.

**Salishan** /'seɪləʃən, 'sæl-/, *n.* **1.** an American Indian linguistic stock of south-western Canada and the north-western U.S. *–adj.* **2.** of this linguistic family.

**saliva** /sə'laɪvə/, *n.* a fluid consisting of the secretions produced by glands which discharge into the mouth, containing ptyalin in man and certain other animals; spittle. [ME, from L] – **salivary,** *adj.*

**salivate** /'sæləveɪt/, *v.,* **-vated, -vating.** *–v.i.* **1.** *Physiol.* to produce saliva. *–v.t.* **2.** to produce an excessive secretion of saliva in, as by the use of mercury. [L *salīvātus,* pp., spat out, salivated]

**salivation** /sælə'veɪʃən/, *n.* **1.** the act or process of salivating. **2.** an abnormally abundant flow of saliva. **3.** mercurial poisoning.

**sallee** /'sæli/, *n.* →**sally**[2].

**sallee rover** /– 'rouvə/, *n.* →**velella.**

**sallet** /'sælət/, *n.* a light medieval helmet, usu. with a vision slit or a movable visor. [late ME, from F *salade,* from It. *celata,* from L *caelāta,* pp. fem., engraved]

**Sallie** /'sæli/, *n. Colloq.* **1.** a member of the Salvation Army. **2. the Sallies,** the Salvation Army. Also, **Sal, Sally, Salvo.**

**sallow**[1] /'sælou/, *adj.* **1.** of a yellowish, sickly hue or complexion: *sallow cheeks.* *–v.t.* **2.** to make sallow. [ME *salowe,* OE *salo,* c. Icel. *sölr* yellow] – **sallowish,** *adj.* – **sallowness,** *n.*

**sallow**[2] /'sælou/, *n.* any of several tall shrubby willows with elliptical or ovate leaves, as the common sallow, *Salix cinerea,* of Europe, temperate western Asia, and northern Africa. [ME; OE *sealh,* c. OHG *salaha,* Icel. *selja,* L *salix*]

**sally**[1] /'sæli/, *n., pl.* **-lies,** *v.,* **-lied, -lying.** *–n.* **1.** a sortie of troops from a besieged place upon an enemy. **2.** a sudden rushing forth or activity. **3.** an excursion or expedition. **4.** an outburst or flight of passion, fancy, etc.: *sally of anger.* **5.** a sprightly or brilliant utterance or remark. *–v.i.* **6.** to make a sally, as a body of troops from a besieged place. **7.** to set out on an excursion or expedition. **8.** to set out briskly or energetically. **9.** (of things) to issue forth. *–v.t.* **10.** *Naut.* to force (a ship that is icebound or has run aground) to free herself by making her roll from side to side. **11.** *N.Z.* to berate, stir up (fol. by *up*). [F *saillie* issuing forth, outrush, from *saillir* leap, from L *salīre*]

**sally**[2] /'sæli/, *n., pl.* **-lies. 1.** any of various Australian trees thought to resemble the willow, esp. wattles and gums, as the **black sally,** *Eucalyptus stellulata,* family Myrtaceae, of New South Wales and Victoria. **2.** *Brit.* →**sallow**[2]. Also, **sallee.**

**Sally** /'sæli/, *n.* →**Sallie.**

**salmagundi** /sælmə'gʌndi/, *n.* **1.** a mixed dish consisting of minced meat, anchovies, eggs, onions, oil, etc. **2.** any mixture or miscellany. [F *salmigondis,* from It. *salami conditi* pickled sausages]

**salmi** /'sælmi/, *n.* a ragout of roasted game, fowl, or the like, stewed in wine. Also, **salmis** /'sælmi/. [F, probably short for *salmigondis.* See SALMAGUNDI]

**salmon** /'sæmən/, *n., pl.* **-mons,** (*esp. collectively*) **-mon,** *adj.* *–n.* **1.** →**Australian salmon 2.** a marine and freshwater food fish, introduced into Australia, *Salmo salar* (family Salmonidae), with pink flesh, common in the northern Atlantic Ocean near the mouths of large rivers, which it ascends to spawn. **3.** a variety of this species confined to lakes, etc. (**landlocked salmon**). **4.** any of several important food fishes of the North Pacific salmonoid genus *Oncorhynchus,* as the **chinook, king,** or **quinnat, salmon,** *O. tschwaytscha;* the **red, sockeye,** or **blueback, salmon,** *O. nerka;* or the **pink** or **humpback salmon,** *O. gorbuscha.* **5.** Also, **salmon pink.** light yellowish-pink. *–adj.* **6.** Also, **salmon pink.** of the colour salmon. [ME, from AF *salmun,* from L *salmo*]

**salmon catfish** /– 'kætfɪʃ/, *n.* the fork-tailed catfish, *Hexamematichthys leptaspis,* of northern Australian rivers.

**salmonella** /sælmə'nɛlə/, *n., pl.* **-nellae** /-'nɛli/. any of several facultatively anaerobic bacteria (genus *Salmonella*), pathogenic for man and warmblooded animals. [named after Daniel E. *Salmon,* 1850-1914, U.S. pathologist]

**salmon gum** /'sæmən gʌm/, *n.* a smooth-barked eucalypt, *Eucalyptus salmonophloia,* family Myrtaceae, with dense, hard, fine-grained salmon-coloured wood, which forms forests in western Australia.

**salmonoid** /'sælmənɔɪd/, *adj.* **1.** resembling a salmon. **2.** belonging or pertaining to the suborder Salmonoidea, to which the salmon family belongs. *–n.* **3.** a member of the salmon family, Salmonidae. **4.** a salmonoid fish.

**salmon trout** /'sæmən traʊt/, *n.* **1.** →**Australian salmon. 2.** a European trout, *Salmo trutta.* **3.** any large trout.

**salol** /'sælɒl/, *n.* a white crystalline substance, $C_{13}H_{10}O_3$, prepared by the interaction of salicylic acid and phenol, and used as an antipyretic, antiseptic, etc. [*sal(icyl)* (see SALICYLATE) + -OL[1]]

**salon** /'sælɒn/, *n.* **1.** a drawing room or reception room in a large house. **2.** an assembly of guests in such a room, esp. such an assembly consisting of leaders in fashion, art, politics, etc. (common during the 17th and 18th centuries). **3.** a hall or place used for the exhibition of works of art. **4.** a fashionable business establishment or shop: *beauty salon, hairdressing salon.* [F, from It. *salone,* augmentative of *sala* hall, from Gmc; cf. OE *sæl* hall]

**saloon** /sə'lun/, *n.* **1.** a room or place for general use for a specific purpose: *a dining saloon on a ship.* **2.** a large cabin for the common use of passengers on a passenger vessel. **3.** →**saloon bar. 4.** *U.S.* any place where alcoholic drinks are sold to be consumed on the premises. **5.** a saloon car or carriage. [F *salon* SALON]

**saloon bar** /'– ba/, *n.* in a hotel, a bar with better appointments and higher prices than those in the public bar. Cf. **lounge.**

**saloon car** /'– ka/, *n.* **1.** →**sedan. 2.** →**buffet car.**

**saloop** /sə'lup/, *n.* a hot drink prepared from salep, or, later, from sassafras or other herbs. [var. of SALEP]

**salpa** /'sælpə/, *n.* any of the pelagic oceanic tunicates constituting the genus *Salpa,* common in warm regions, and having a transparent, more or less fusiform body. Also, **salp.** [NL, special use of L *salpa* stockfish] – **salpiform** /'sælpəfɔm/, *adj.*

**salpingitis** /sælpɪn'dʒaɪtəs/, *n.* inflammation of the uterine or Eustachian tubes.

**salpinx** /'sælpɪŋks/, *n., pl.* **salpinges** /sæl'pɪndʒiz/. a trumpet-shaped tube, as the Fallopian (uterine) and Eustachian (auditory) tubes. [NL, from Gk: trumpet]

**salsify** /'sælsəfi/, *n., pl.* **-fies.** a herb, *Tragopogon porrifolius,* family Compositae, of the Mediterranean area, having purple flowers and an edible taproot thought to resemble the oyster in flavour when cooked; oyster plant. [F *salsifis,* from It. *sassefrica;* ult. orig. uncert.]

**sal soda** /sæl 'soʊdə/, *n.* →**sodium carbonate.**

**salt** /sɒlt, sɔlt/, *n.* **1.** a crystalline compound, sodium chloride, NaC1, occurring as a mineral, a constituent of sea water, etc., and used for seasoning food, as a preservative, etc. **2.** *Chem.* a compound which upon dissociation yields cations (positively charged) of a metal, and anions (negatively charged) of an acid radical. **3.** (*pl.*) any of various salts used as purgatives: *Epsom salts.* **4.** →**saltcellar. 5.** →**salt marsh. 6.** that which gives liveliness, piquancy, or pungency to anything. **7.** wit; pungency. **8.** *Colloq.* a sailor, esp. an experienced one: *old salt.* **9. below the salt,** of an inferior status. **10.** (*pl.*) **go through like a dose (packet) of salts,** *Colloq.* **a.** to have the same effect as a purgative. **b.** to make a brief visit causing great disturbance. **11. rub salt into the wound,** to make things worse; add insult to injury. **12. salt of the earth,** the best kind of people. **13. take with a grain of salt,** to believe with reservations. **14. worth one's salt,** capable; efficient; deserving one's pay. *–v.t.* **15.** to season with salt. **16.** to cure, preserve, or treat with salt. **17.** to furnish with salt: *to salt cattle.* **18.** *Chem.* **a.** to treat with common salt or with any chemical salt. **b.** to add common salt to (a solution) in order to separate a dissolved substance (usu. with *out*). **19.** to introduce rich ore or other valuable matter, information, etc., to create a false impression of value: *to salt a mine, a sample, etc.* **20. salt away** or **down, a.** to preserve by adding quantities of salt. **b.** *Colloq.* to lay or store away in reserve: *to salt a lot of money away.* *–adj.* **21.** containing salt; having the taste of salt: *salt water.* **22.** cured or preserved with salt: *salt cod.* **23.** overflowed with or growing in salt water: *salt marsh.* **24.** pungent or sharp: *salt speech.* [ME; OE *sealt,* c. G *Salz,* Icel. and Goth. *salt;* akin to Gk *háls,* L *sal*] – **saltlike,** *adj.*

**saltant** /'sæltənt/, *adj.* dancing; leaping; jumping. [L *saltans,* ppr.]

**saltarello** /sɒltə'rɛloʊ/, *n., pl.* **-relli** /-'rɛli/. **1.** a lively Italian dance for one person or a couple. **2.** the music for it. [It., from L *saltāre* dance]

**saltation** /sæl'teɪʃən/, *n.* **1.** dancing; leaping. **2.** an abrupt movement or transition. **3.** movement of particles of sand or the like by wind or water in short intermittent leaps or waves. **4.** →**mutation.**

**saltatorial** /sæltə'tɔriəl/, *adj.* **1.** pertaining to saltation. **2.** characterised by or adapted for leaping.

**saltatory** /sæl'teɪtəri/, *adj.* **1.** pertaining to or adapted for saltation. **2.** proceeding by abrupt movements.

**saltbush** /'sɒltbʊʃ/, *n.* **1.** any of various drought-resistant plants of the family Chenopodiaceae, esp. the Australian and New Zealand genus *Rhagodia* and the widespread genus *Atriplex,* used as grazing plants in arid, saline and alkaline parts of Australia, North America and southern Africa. **2. the saltbush,** regions where saltbush is the predominant vegetation.

**salt-bush snake** /'sɒlt-bʊʃ sneɪk/, *n.* →**myall snake.**

**saltcake** /'sɒltkeɪk/, *n.* an impure form of sodium sulphate.

**saltcellar** /'sɒltsɛlə/, *n.* **1.** a shaker or vessel for salt. **2.** *Colloq.* either of the hollows above the collarbone of thin people. [ME *saltsaler,* from SALT + (now obs.) *saler* saltceller, from OF *saliere,* from *sel* salt, from L *sal*]

**salt dome** /'sɒlt doʊm/, *n.* (in sedimentary rocks) a domelike anticline having a core of rock-salt which was forced upwards from an underlying bed of salt when in the plastic state under pressure. Also, **salt plug.**

**salted** /'sɒltəd, 'sɔltəd/, *adj.* **1.** seasoned, cured, or otherwise treated with salt. **2.** *Colloq.* experienced in some occupation, etc.

**salted weapon** /– 'wɛpən/, *n.* a nuclear weapon which has, in addition to its normal components, certain elements or isotopes which capture neutrons at the time of the explosion and produce radioactive products over and above the usual radioactive weapon debris.

**salter** /'sɒltə, 'sɔltə/, *n.* **1.** one who makes or deals in salt. **2.** one who salts meat, fish, etc.

**saltern** /'sɒltən, 'sɔltən/, *n.* **1.** →**saltworks. 2.** a plot of land laid out in pools for the evaporation of sea water to produce salt. [OE *sealtærn* saltworks, from *sealt* SALT + *ærn* house. Cf. BARN[1]]

**salt flat** /'sɒlt flæt/, *n.* **1.** a wide expanse of flat country in which the soil is very salty. **2.** →**saltpan.**

**salt glaze** /'sɒlt gleɪz/, *n.* a glaze formed on stoneware when salt is introduced into the kiln during firing.

**saltigrade** /'sæltəgreɪd/, *adj.* **1.** moving by leaping. **2.** belonging to the Saltigradae, a group of saltatorial spiders. [*salti-* (combining form of L *saltus* leap) + -GRADE]

**saltimbocca** /sɒltɪm'bɒkə/, *n.* an Italian dish consisting of thin slices of veal and ham rolled with a sage leaf inside and braised in butter and Marsala or white wine. [It.]

**saltire** /'sɔltaɪə/, *n. Her.* an ordinary in the form of a Saint Andrew's Cross. Also, **saltier.** [ME *sawtire,* from OF *sautoir,* orig., saddle cord for aid in mounting, from *sauter* leap, from L *saltāre*]

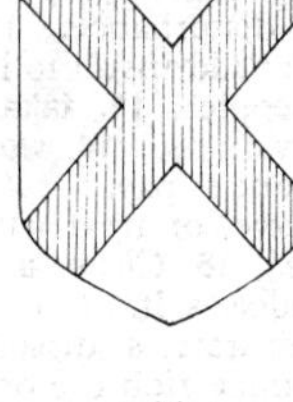
saltire

**saltish** /'sɒltɪʃ, 'sɔltɪʃ/, *adj.* somewhat salt; salty.

**salt lake** /sɒlt 'leɪk/, *n.* an inland sheet of water with high salinity.

**salt-lick** /'sɒlt-lɪk/, *n.* **1.** a place to which wild animals resort to lick salt occurring naturally there. **2.** *Agric.* rock salt or compressed salt in blocks with or without minerals and other additives placed in the paddock for animals grazing there.

**salt marsh** /'sɒlt maʃ/, *n.* a marshy tract, wet with salt water or flooded by the sea.

**salt mine** /'– maɪn/, *n.* **1.** a mine from which salt is excavated. **2.** (*usu. pl.*) *Colloq.* (*joc.*) a place of habitual confinement and drudgery.

**saltpan** /'sɒltpæn/, *n.* a small basin flooded by salt deposits, the remains of an evaporated salt lake which may have entirely disappeared.

**saltpetre** /sɒlt'pitə/, *n.* →**nitre.** Also, *U.S.,* **saltpeter.** [alteration (after SALT) of ME *salpetre,* from ML *sal petrae* salt of the rock]

**saltpit** /'sɒltpɪt/, *n.* a pit where salt is obtained.

**salt plug** /'sɒlt plʌg/, *n.* →**salt dome.**

**salt pork** /'– pɔk/, *n.* pork cured with salt.

**salts of lemon,** *n.pl.* a white water-soluble salt, $KHC_2O_4$, formed from oxalic acid and used for removing ink and rust stains.

**salt tablet** /'sɒlt tæblət/, *n.* a tablet of common salt, sodium chloride, used to prevent development of muscular cramps when working in a hot atmosphere.

**salt water** /– 'wɔtə/, *n.* water containing a high proportion of salt, esp. sea water.

**salt-water** /'sɒlt-wɔtə/, *adj.* **1.** of or pertaining to salt water. **2.** inhabiting salt water.

**saltworks** /'sɒltwɜks/, *n. sing. and pl.* a building or place where salt is made.

**saltwort** /'sɒltwɜt/, *n.* any of various plants of sea beaches, salt marshes, and alkaline regions, esp. of the genus *Salsola,* as *S. kali,* a bushy plant with prickly leaves.

**salty** /'sɒlti/, *adj.,* **saltier, saltiest. 1.** containing, or tasting of, salt. **2.** piquant; sharp; witty; racy. – **saltily,** *adv.* – **saltiness,** *n.*

**salubrious** /sə'lubriəs/, *adj.* (esp. of air, climate, etc.) favourable to health; promoting health. [*salubri(ty)* (from L *salūbritas* healthfulness) + -OUS] – **salubriously,** *adv.* – **salubriousness, salubrity** /sə'lubrəti/, *n.*

**saluki** /sə'luki/, *n.* a smooth silky-coated hunting dog, a member of the greyhound family, with long ears, legs, and tail. [Ar. *salūqī,* named after *Salūq* ancient city in Arabia]

**salutary** /'sæljətri/, *adj.* **1.** conducive to health; healthful. **2.** promoting or conducive to some beneficial purpose; wholesome. [L *salūtāris,* from *Salus,* Roman goddess of health and prosperity] – **salutarily,** *adv.* – **salutariness,** *n.*

**salutation** /sæljə'teɪʃən/, *n.* **1.** the act of saluting. **2.** something uttered, written, or done by way of saluting. **3.** the opening of a letter or of a speech as 'Dear Sir', 'Ladies and Gentlemen'.

**salutatory** /sæljə'teɪtəri, -tri/, *adj., n., pl.* **-ries.** *–adj.* **1.** pertaining to or of the nature of a salutation. *–n.* **2.** an address of welcome, esp. one given by a member of the graduating class in an American college.

**salute** /sə'lut/, *v.,* **-luted, -luting,** *n. –v.t.* **1.** to address with expressions of goodwill, respect, etc.; greet. **2.** to make a bow, gesture, or the like to in greeting, farewell, respect, etc. **3.** *Mil., Navy.* to pay respect to or honour by some formal act, as by raising the right hand to the side of the headgear, presenting arms, firing cannon, dipping colours, etc. *–v.i.* **4.** to perform a salutation. **5.** *Mil., Navy.* to give a salute. *–n.* **6.** an act of saluting; salutation; greeting. **7.** *Mil., Navy.* **a.** the special act of respect paid in saluting. **b.** the position of the hand or rifle in saluting: *at the salute.* **8.** Also, **Australian salute, Barcoo salute.** (*joc.*) the movement of hand and arm to brush away flies from one's face. [ME, from L *salūtāre* greet] – **saluter,** *n.*

**salutiferous** /sælju'tɪfərəs/, *adj.* →**salutary.**

**Salvador** /'sælvədɔ/, *n.* →**El Salvador.**

**salvage** /'sælvɪdʒ/, *n., v.,* **-vaged, -vaging.** *–n.* **1.** the act of saving a ship or its cargo from perils of the seas. **2.** the property so saved. **3.** compensation given to those who voluntarily save a ship or its cargo. **4.** the saving of anything from fire, danger, etc., or the property so saved. **5.** the value or proceeds upon sale of goods recovered from a shipwreck, fire, danger, or the like. *–v.t.* **6.** to save from shipwreck, fire, etc. **7.** to recover or save as salvage. [ML *salvāgium,* from L *salvāre* save] – **salvager,** *n.*

**salvarsan** /'sælvəsæn/, *n.* →**arsphenamine.** [Trademark; L *salvus* well + ARS(ENIC) + -AN]

**salvation** /sæl'veɪʃən/, *n.* **1.** the act of saving or delivering. **2.** the state of being saved or delivered. **3.** a source, cause, or means of deliverance: *to be the salvation of a friend.* **4.** *Theol.* deliverance from the power and penalty of sin; redemption. [ME, from LL *salvātio*]

**Salvation Army** /sæl,veɪʃən 'ami/, *n.* a quasi-military organisation, founded in 1865 by William Booth to revive religion among the masses; renowned for its charitable work among the poor and homeless.

**Salvationism** /sæl'veɪʃənɪzəm/, *n.* **1.** religious teaching stressing the salvation of the soul. **2.** the principles of the Salvation Army.

**Salvationist** /sæl'veɪʃənəst/, *n.* **1.** a member of the Salvation Army. **2.** a member of any other evangelical movement.

**salvation Jane** /sæl,veɪʃən 'dʒeɪn/, *n.* →**Paterson's curse.**

**salve**[1] /sav, sælv/, *n., v.,* **salved, salving.** *–n.* **1.** a healing ointment to be applied to wounds and sores for relief or healing. **2.** anything that soothes or mollifies. *–v.t.* **3.** to soothe as if with salve: *to salve one's conscience.* **4.** *Obs.* to apply salve to. [ME; OE *sealf,* c. G *Salbe*]

**salve**[2] /sælv/, *v.i., v.t.,* **salved, salving.** to save from loss or destruction; to salvage. [backformation from SALVAGE]

**salver** /'sælvə/, *n.* a tray. [Sp. *salv(a)* foretasting, hence tray (from *salvar* protect, save, from L *salvāre*) + *-er,* modelled on *platter* or the like]

**salvia** /'sælviə/, *n.* any of the herbs or shrubs constituting the genus *Salvia,* as *S. splendens,* the scarlet salvia, an ornamental garden plant. [L]

**sal vital** /sæl 'vaɪtl/, *n.* an effervescent powder taken in water as a restorative.

**salvo**[1] /'sælvoʊ/, *n., pl.* **-vos, -voes. 1.** a discharge of artillery or other firearms, in regular succession, often intended as a salute. **2.** a round of cheers, applause, etc. [earlier *salva,* from It., from OF *salve,* from L *salvē, impv. of salvēre* be in good health]

**salvo**[2] /'sælvoʊ/, *n., pl.* **-vos.** *Rare.* **1.** an excuse or quibbling evasion. **2.** something to save a person's reputation, feelings, etc. [L, abl. of *salvus* safe, used in legal phrases, as *salvō jurē* the right being safe]

**Salvo** /'sælvoʊ/, *n.* **1.** a member of the Salvation Army. **2. the Salvos,** the Salvation Army.

**sal volatile** /sæl və'lætəli/, *n.* **1.** →**ammonium carbonate. 2.** an aromatic alcoholic solution of this salt used as a restorative for fainting, dizziness, etc., by inhalation.

**salvor** /'sælvə/, *n.* one who salvages or helps to salvage a ship, cargo, etc.

**Sam.,** *Bible.* Samuel.

**S. Am.,** **1.** South America. **2.** South American.

**SAM** /sæm/, surface-to-air missile.

**samadhi** /sæ'madi/, *n.* (in yoga) a state of deep, meditative concentration. [Skt *samādhi,* lit., application, concentration]

**samara** /'sæmərə/, *n.* an indehiscent, usu. one-seeded, winged fruit, as of the elm. [NL, special use of L *samara* seed of the elm]

**samarium** /sə'mɛəriəm/, *n.* a rare-earth metallic element discovered in samarskite. *Symbol:* Sm; *at. wt:* 150.35; *at. no.:* 62. [SAMAR(SKITE) + -IUM]

**samarskite** /sə'maskaɪt/, *n.* a velvet-black mineral, a complex of columbium and tantalum compounds with uranium, cerium, etc., occurring in masses; a minor source of uranium. [G *Samarskit,* named after Col. von *Samarski,* 19th-cent. Russian mine official. See -ITE[1]]

A B C

samara: A, ash; B, elm; C, birch

**Sama-Veda** /samə-'veɪdə/, *n.* See **Veda.**

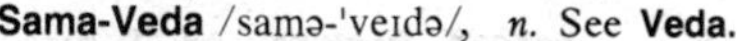

**samba** /'sæmbə/, *n.* a ballroom dance of Brazilian (ultimately African) origin.

**sambal** /'sæmbəl, -bal/, *n.* a condiment based on hot chillies used in southern Indian, Malay and Indonesian food. [Bahasa Indonesia]

**sambal goreng** /– 'gɒrɛŋ/, *n.* an Indonesian dish in which meat, fish, game, vegetable or eggs are first fried and then stewed in a hot, thick, and spicy sauce. [Bahasa Indonesia]

**sambar** /'sæmbə/, *n.* a medium-to-large deer of the subgenus *Rusa,* having three-pointed antlers, found in south-eastern Asia. Also, **sambur.** [Hind.]

**sambo** /'sæmboʊ/, *n., pl.* **-bos. 1.** the offspring of Negro and Indian (or mulatto) parents. **2.** (*usu. cap.*) (*derog.*) a Negro. [probably from Sp. *zambo*]

**Sam Browne belt,** *n.* a military belt having a supporting strap over the right shoulder, worn by officers. [designed after the sword belt invented by Sir *Samuel* James *Browne,* 1824-1901, British general]

**sambuca** /sæm'bukə/, *n.* an ancient stringed musical instrument used in Greece and the Near East. [L, from Gk *sambýkē.* Cf. Aramaic *sabbeka*]

**same** /seɪm/, *adj.* **1.** identical with what is about to be or has just been mentioned: *the very same man.* **2.** being one or identical, though having different names, aspects, etc.: *these are one and the same thing.* **3.** agreeing in kind, amount, etc.; corresponding: *two boxes of the same dimensions.* **4.** unchanged in character, condition, etc. *–pron.* **5.** the same person or thing. **6. the same,** with the same manner (used adverbially). **7. all the same, a.** notwithstanding; nevertheless. **b.** immaterial; unimportant. **8. just the same, a.** in the same manner. **b.** nevertheless. [ME and OE, c. Icel. *sami, sama, samr;* in OE used only as adv.]

**sameness** /'seɪmnəs/, *n.* **1.** the state of being the same; identity; uniformity. **2.** lack of variety; monotony.

**S. Amer.,** **1.** South America. **2.** South American.

**samiel** /'sæmjəl/, *n.* →**simoom.** [Turk. *samyel,* from *sam* (from Ar. *samma* to poison) + *yel* wind]

**samisen** /'sæməsɛn/, *n.* a Japanese guitar-like musical instrument, having an extremely long neck and three strings, played with a plectrum. [Jap., from Chinese *san-hsien* three-stringed (instrument)]

**samite** /'sæmaɪt, 'seɪmaɪt/, *n.* a heavy silk fabric, sometimes interwoven with gold, worn in the Middle Ages. [ME, from OF *samit,* from MGk *hexámiton,* lit., six-threaded]

samisen

**samlet** /'sæmlət/, *n.* a young salmon. [syncopated and dissimilated var. of *salmonet,* from SALMON + -ET]

**sammie** /'sæmi/, *n. Colloq.* a sandwich.

**Samoa** /sə'moʊə/, *n.* a group of islands in the southern Pacific, divided into **German Samoa** and **American Samoa** in the mid 19th century. The former was mandated to New Zealand in 1916 and, as **Western Samoa,** became fully independent in 1962.

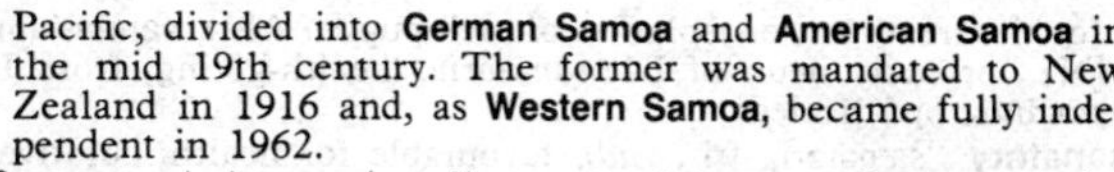

**Samoan** /sə'moʊən/, *adj.* **1.** pertaining to Samoa or its (Polynesian) people. *–n.* **2.** a native or inhabitant of Samoa. **3.** the Polynesian language of Samoa.

**samousa** /sə'musə/, *n.* a savoury pastry with curried meat or vegetable filling, usu. triangular in shape. [? Malay, from Swahili *sambusa*]

**samovar** /'sæməva/, *n.* a metal urn, commonly of copper, used in the Soviet Union and elsewhere for heating the water for making tea. [Russ.: self-boiler]

samovar

**Samoyed** /'sæmɔɪˌɛd/ *for defs 1 and 2;* /'sæmɔɪd/ *for def. 3, n.* **1.** a member of a Ural-Altaic people dwelling in north-western Siberia and along the north-eastern coast of the Soviet Union in Europe. **2.** a family of five closely related Uralian languages scattered over a large area of the north-western Asiatic and north-eastern European Soviet Union. **3.** one of a breed of Russian dogs, medium in size, with a coat of long, dense, white hair. [Russ.: self-eater]

**Samoyedic** /sæmɔɪ'ɛdɪk/, *adj.* of or pertaining to the Samoyeds.

**sampan** /'sæmpæn/, *n.* any of various small boats of China, etc., as one propelled by a single scull over the stern, and provided with a roofing of mats. [Chinese *san-pan,* lit., three boards]

sampan

**samphire** /'sæmfaɪə/, *n.* **1.** a succulent herb, *Crithmum maritimum,* of Europe, growing in clefts of rock near the sea; its fleshy leaves are used in pickles. **2.** →**glasswort. 3.** other salt-tolerating plant species. [earlier *sampere, sampire,* alteration of F (*herb de*) *Saint Pierre* St Peter's herb]

**sample** /'sæmpəl/, *n., adj., v.,* **-pled, -pling.** *–n.* **1.** a small part of anything or one of a number, intended to show the quality, style, etc., of the whole; a specimen. *–adj.* **2.** serving as a specimen: *a sample copy. –v.t.* **3.** to take a sample or samples of; test or judge by a sample. [ME, aphetic var. of *essample,* var. of EXAMPLE]

**sample bag** /'– bæg/, *n.* a bag distributed by a manufacturer to people attending a show (def. 32), originally containing free samples of the manufacturer's products.

**sampler** /'sæmplə/, *n.* **1.** one who samples. **2.** a piece of cloth embroidered with various devices, serving to show a beginner's skill in needlework. [ME *samplere,* from OF *essamplaire,* from LL *exemplārium,* from L *exemplum* EXAMPLE]

**samsoe** /'sæmsoʊ/, *n.* a Swiss cheese with a smooth, close texture and many holes, and a sweet, nutty flavour. [named after *Samsoe,* an island off the coast of Denmark]

**Samson** /'sæmsən/, *n.* any man of extraordinary strength. [from *Samson,* a man of great strength, the fifteenth of the 'judges' of Israel (see Judges 13-16)]

**samson fish** /'sæmsən fɪʃ/, *n.* a fine sporting fish of temperate eastern and western Australian waters; trevally.

**samson post** /'– poʊst/, *n.* a short, strong mast fitted with a derrick for the handling of cargoes.

**samurai** /'sæmjəraɪ/, *n., pl.* **-rai.** (in feudal Japan) **1.** a member of the military class. **2.** a retainer of a Japanese feudal noble, holding land or receiving a stipend in rice or money. [Jap.]

**san** /sæn/, *n. Colloq.* →**sanatorium.**

**san.,** sanitation.

**sanative** /'sænətɪv/, *adj.* having the power to heal; curative. [ML *sānātīvus*]

**sanatorium** /sænə'tɔriəm/, *n., pl.* **-toriums, -toria** /-'tɔriə/. **1.** an establishment for the treatment of invalids, convalescents, etc., esp. in a favourable climate: *a tuberculosis sanatorium.* **2.** a health resort. **3.** that part of a boarding school set apart for the treatment or isolation of sick pupils. Also, **sanitarium.** [NL, properly neut. of LL *sānātōrius* health-giving, from L *sānātus,* pp., healed]

**sanatory** /'sænətəri, -tri/, *adj.* favourable for health; curative; healing. [LL *sānātōrius*]

**sanbenito** /sænbə'nitoʊ/, *n., pl.* **-tos.** (under the Spanish Inquisition) **1.** a black garment ornamented with flames, devils, etc., worn by a condemned heretic at an auto-da-fé. **2.** a yellow penitential garment worn by a confessed heretic. [Sp., named after *San Benito* St Benedict, from its resemblance to the scapular introduced by him]

**sanctified** /'sæŋktəfaɪd/, *adj.* **1.** made holy; consecrated: *sanctified wine.* **2.** →**sanctimonious.**

**sanctify** /'sæŋktəfaɪ/, *v.t.,* **-fied, -fying. 1.** to make holy; set apart as sacred; consecrate. **2.** to purify or free from sin: *sanctify your hearts.* **3.** to impart religious sanction to; render legitimate or binding: *to sanctify a vow.* **4.** to make productive of or conducive to spiritual blessing. **5.** *Obs.* to entitle to reverence or respect. [Eccles. L *sanctificāre* make holy; replacing ME *seintefie,* from OF] – **sanctification** /sæŋktəfə'keɪʃən/, *n.* – **sanctifier,** *n.* – **sanctifiable,** *adj.*

**sanctimonious** /sæŋktə'moʊniəs/, *adj.* **1.** making a show of holiness; affecting sanctity. **2.** *Obs.* holy; sacred. [SANCTIMONY + -OUS] – **sanctimoniously,** *adv.* – **sanctimoniousness,** *n.*

**sanctimony** /'sæŋktəməni/, *n.* **1.** pretended, affected, or hypocritical holiness or devoutness. **2.** *Obs.* sanctity; sacredness. [L *sanctimōnia*]

**sanction** /'sæŋkʃən/, *n.* **1.** authoritative permission; countenance or support given to an action, etc.; solemn ratification. **2.** something serving to support an action, etc. **3.** binding force given, or something which gives binding force, as to an oath, rule of conduct, etc. **4.** *Law.* **a.** a provision of a law enacting a penalty for disobedience. **b.** the penalty. **5.** *Internat. Law.* action by one or more states towards another state calculated to force it to comply with legal obligations. *–v.t.* **6.** to authorise, countenance, or approve: *sanctioned by usage.* **7.** to ratify or confirm: *to sanction a law.* [L *sanctio*]

**sanctity** /'sæŋktəti/, *n., pl.* **-ties. 1.** holiness, saintliness, or godliness. **2.** sacred or hallowed character: *inviolable sanctity of the temple.* **3.** a sacred thing. [L *sanctitas;* replacing ME *saintite,* from OF]

**sanctuary** /'sæŋktʃəri, 'sæŋktʃuəri/, *n., pl.* **-ries. 1.** a sacred or holy place. **2.** an especially holy place in a temple or church. **3.** the part of a church about the altar; the chancel. **4.** a church or other sacred place where fugitives were formerly entitled to immunity from arrest; asylum. **5.** immunity afforded by refuge in such a place. **6.** a place protected by law where flora and fauna are left undisturbed; flora and fauna reserve. [ME, from L *sanctuārium*]

**sanctum** /'sæŋktəm/, *n., pl.* **-tums, -ta** /-tə/. **1.** a sacred or holy place. **2.** an especially private place or retreat: *the inner sanctum.* [L (neut.): holy]

**sanctum sanctorum** /– sæŋk'tɔrəm/, *n.* **1.** the holy of holies of the Jewish tabernacle and temple. **2.** any especially private place or retreat. [L (Vulgate), translated from Gk (Septuagint), itself translating Heb. *qōdhesh haqqodhāshīm* holy of holies]

**Sanctus** /'sæŋktəs/, *n.* **1.** *Liturgy.* the hymn beginning 'Holy, holy, holy, Lord God of hosts', with which the Eucharistic preface culminates. **2.** a musical setting for this hymn. [L: holy, the first word of the hymn]

**Sanctus bell** /'– bɛl/, *n.* a bell rung during the celebration of mass to give notification of the more solemn portions.

**sand** /sænd/, *n.* **1.** the more or less fine debris of rocks, consisting of small, loose grains, often of quartz. **2.** (*usu. pl.*) a tract or region composed principally of sand. **3.** the sand in an hourglass, or a grain of this. **4.** (*pl.*) moments of time or of one's life. **5.** a dull reddish yellow colour. *–v.t.* **6.** to smooth or polish with sand or sandpaper. **7.** to sprinkle with, or as with, sand. **8.** to fill up with sand, as a harbour. **9.** to add sand to: *to sand sugar.* [ME and OE, c. G *Sand*]

**sandal**[1] /'sændl/, *n., v.,* **-dalled, -dalling.** *–n.* **1.** a kind of shoe, consisting of a sole of leather or other material fastened to the foot by thongs or straps. **2.** any of various kinds of low shoes or slippers. **3.** a band for fastening a low shoe or slipper on, by passing over the instep or round the ankle. *–v.t.* **4.** to furnish with sandals. [F *sandale;* replacing ME *sandalie,* from L *sandalium,* from Gk *sandálion,* lit., little sandal] – **sandalled,** *adj.*

**sandal**[2] /'sændl/, *n.* →**sandalwood.**

**sandalwood** /'sændlwʊd/, *n.* **1.** the fragrant heartwood of any of certain Asiatic and Australian trees of the genus *Santalum* (family Santalaceae), used for ornamental carving and burnt as incense. **2.** any of these trees, esp. *S. album* (**white sandalwood**), an evergreen of India. **3.** any of various related or similar trees or their woods, esp. an East Indian tree, *Pterocarpus santalinus* **(red sandalwood),** or its heavy dark red wood, which is used as a dyestuff. [*sandal* (from ML *sandalum,* from Skt *čandana*) + WOOD[1]]

**sandarac** /'sændəræk/, *n.* **1.** a brittle, usu. pale yellow, more or less transparent, faintly aromatic resin exuding from the bark of the sandarac tree and used chiefly as incense and in making varnish. **2.** a tree, *Tetraclinis articulata* (*Callitris quadrivalvis*), native to north-western Africa, yielding the resin sandarac, and having a fragrant, hard, dark-coloured wood much used in building. Also, **sandarach.** [L *sandaraca,* from Gk *sandarákē*]

**sandbag** /'sændbæg/, *n., v.,* **-bagged, -bagging.** *–n.* **1.** a bag filled with sand, used in fortifications, levees, as ballast, etc. **2.** such a bag used as a weapon. *–v.t.* **3.** to furnish with sandbags. **4.** to hit or stun with a sandbag.

**sandbank** /'sændbæŋk/, *n.* a bank of sand in the sea or a river, formed by currents and often exposed at low tide.

**sandbar** /'sændba/, *n.* a bar of sand formed in a river or sea by the action of tides or currents.

**sand-binder** /'sænd-baɪndə/, *n.* any plant which can successfully grow in and stabilise loose sand, as the marram grass, *Ammophila arenaria.*

**sandblast** /'sændblast/, *n.* **1.** a blast of air or steam laden with sand, used to clean, grind, cut, or decorate hard surfaces, as of glass, stone, or metal. **2.** the apparatus used to apply such a blast. *–v.t.* **3.** to clean, smooth, etc., with a sandblast.

**sand-blind** /'sænd-blaɪnd/, *adj. Archaic.* partially blind; dim-sighted. [ME; for **samblind,* from OE *sām-* half (c. L *sēmi-*) + blind]

**sand blow** /'sænd bloʊ/, *n.* a large unstable dune of sand which is slowly driven forward over a period of years by a prevailing wind.

**sandbox** /'sændbɒks/, *n.* a box or receptacle for holding sand, esp. for dropping from a locomotive or a tram on to slippery rails.

**sandbox tree** /'– tri/, *n.* a tree, *Hura crepitans,* of tropical America, bearing a furrowed roundish fruit about the size of an orange which when ripe and dry bursts with a sharp report and scatters the seeds.

**sand-cake** /'sænd-keɪk/, *n.* a Madeira-type cake containing cornflour, ground rice, or potato flour.

**sand-cast** /'sænd-kast/, *v.t.* to produce (a casting) by pouring molten metal, wax, etc., into sand moulds.

**sandcastle** /'sændkasəl/, *n.* a model of a castle made by or for children from damp sand.

**sand crab** /'sænd kræb/, *n.* →**blue swimmer.**

**sand-crack** /'sænd-kræk/, *n.* **1.** any fine crack or fissure. **2.** a crack or fissure in the hoof of a horse, extending from the coronet downwards towards the sole, occurring on any part of the wall of the hoof, caused by a dryness of horn and liable to cause lameness.

**sand-dab** /'sænd-dæb/, *n.* any of several flatfishes used as food.

**sand-dollar** /'sænd-dɒlə/, *n.* any of various flat, disclike urchins, esp. *Echinarachnius parma,* which live on sandy bottoms off the coast of North America.

**sand-dune** /'sænd-djun/, *n.* →**dune.**

**sand-eel** /'sænd-il/, *n.* an elongate fish of the family Ammodytidae, which burrows in sand. Also, **sandlaunce.**

**sander** /'sændə/, *n.* **1.** one who or that which sands or sandpapers. **2.** →**sanding machine.**

**sanderling** /'sændəlɪŋ/, *n.* a widespread small shorebird, *Calidris alba,* found on sandy beaches.

**sandfill** /'sændfɪl/, *n.* a mining technique whereby sand is used to fill stopes from which ore has been mined.

**sandflea** /'sændfli/, *n.* **1.** →**beach flea. 2.** →**chigoe.**

**sandfly** /ˈsændflaɪ/, *n., pl.* **-flies. 1.** a small bloodsucking dipterous fly of the genus *Phlebotomus,* carrier of several human diseases. **2.** a small bloodsucking dipterous fly of the genus *Calicoides.*

**sand-glass** /ˈsænd-glas/, *n.* →**hourglass.**

**sand goanna** /sænd goʊˈænə/, *n.* →**Gould's goanna.**

**sandgroper** /ˈsændgroʊpə/, *n. Colloq.* →**West Australian.**

**sand-grouse** /ˈsænd-graʊs/, *n.* any of certain birds inhabiting sandy tracts of the Old World, which constitute the family Pteroclidae, structurally allied to the pigeons.

**sandhi form** /ˈsændi fɔm/, *n.* the phonetic or phonemic form of a word or phrase occurring in a context of other (preceding and following) forms, when different from the absolute form. For example, in *Jack's at home* the *'s* is a sandhi form corresponding to the absolute form *is.* [*sandhi,* from Skt: putting together]

**sandhill** /ˈsændhɪl/, *n.* →**dune.**

**sandhopper** /ˈsændhɒpə/, *n.* →**beach flea.**

**sandie** /ˈsændi/, *n. Colloq.* **1.** →**sandfly. 2.** →**sand crab. 3.** a girl who frequents the beach.

**sanding machine** /ˈsændɪŋ məʃin/, *n.* one of several machines, as drum sander, belt sander, orbital sander, rotary sander, with a powered abrasive-covered drum, belt or disc, used for smoothing or polishing. Also, **sander.**

**sand-launce** /ˈsænd-lɔns/, *n.* →**sand-eel.** Also, **sand-lance.**

**sand-lizard** /ˈsænd-lɪzəd/, *n.* a small lizard, *Lacerta agilis,* which occurs throughout Europe from England (rarely) to western Russia.

**sandman** /ˈsændmæn/, *n.* the man who, in the fairytale, makes children sleepy by putting sand in their eyes.

**sand-martin** /ˈsænd-matn/, *n.* a small bird, *Riparia riparia,* of the swallow family (Hirundinidae), which has a widespread distribution and nests in tunnels in banks of sand.

**sandpaper** /ˈsændpeɪpə/, *n.* **1.** strong paper coated with a layer of sand or the like, used for smoothing or polishing. *–v.t.* **2.** to smooth or polish with or as with sandpaper.

**sandpiper** /ˈsændpaɪpə/, *n.* any of a number of shorebirds of the family Scolopacidae that breed in the Northern Hemisphere and are seen in Australia as non-breeding migrants, as the **sharp-tailed sandpiper,** *Calidris acuminata,* common in Australasia.

sharp-tailed sandpiper

**sandpit** /ˈsændpɪt/, *n.* a container for holding sand for children to play in.

**sandshoe** /ˈsænʃu, ˈsændʃu/, *n.* a rubber-soled canvas shoe, laced to fit the foot, worn esp. for gymnastics, sports, etc.

**sandsoap** /ˈsændsoʊp/, *n.* a soap with mildly abrasive power used esp. to remove stubborn stains.

**sand spurry** /ˈsænd spʌri/, *n.* a spreading annual, sometimes biennial herb, *Spergularia rubra,* with narrow leaves and small pink flowers, introduced from Europe and now common in sandy, open wasteland.

**sandstock brick** /ˈsændstɒk brɪk/, *n.* **1.** (formerly) a handpressed brick, with sand dusted on the surface of the clay to allow for easy release from the wooden form. **2.** a machine-made brick using the same technique but which is fired at a higher temperature producing a glassy effect from the burnt sand. [SAND + STOCK (def. 28)]

**sandstone** /ˈsændstoʊn/, *n.* a rock formed by the consolidation of sand, the grains being held together by a cement of silica, lime, gypsum, or iron salts.

**sandstorm** /ˈsændstɔm/, *n.* a windstorm that bears along clouds of sand.

**sand-table** /ˈsænd-teɪbəl/, *n.* a large, shallow wooden tray filled with sand on which can be modelled, in scale, tracts of land, towns, etc., and used for gunnery and tactics.

**sandtrack** /ˈsændtræk/, *n.* a racetrack with a sand surface.

**sand-trap** /ˈsænd-træp/, *n.* →**bunker**[1].

**sand trout** /ˈsænd traʊt/, *n.* →**congolli.**

**sand wedge** /ˈ– wɛdʒ/, *n.* a golf club used for playing a ball which has landed in a bunker; blaster. Also, **wedge.**

**sandwich** /ˈsænwɪtʃ, -wɪdʒ/, *n.* **1.** two slices of bread (or toast), plain or buttered, with a layer of meat, fish, cheese, or the like between. **2.** something formed by a similar combination. **3. the meat in the sandwich,** *Colloq.* a person caught between two opposing parties, with each of whom he has some connection, but over whose actions he has no control. *–v.t.* **4.** to put into a sandwich. **5.** to insert or hem in between two other things: *the child was sandwiched between two adults in the crush.* [named after the 4th Earl of *Sandwich,* 1718-92]

**sandwich board** /ˈ– bɔd/, *n.* one of the advertising boards carried by a sandwich man.

**sandwich cake** /ˈ– keɪk/, *n.* →**layer cake.**

**sandwich course** /ˈ– kɔs/, *n.* an educational course combining industrial training and academic studies, as one in which a student spends alternating periods of full-time work in industry, and full-time attendance at a college.

**sandwich loaf** /ˈ– loʊf/, *n.* a rectangular shaped loaf of bread, esp. suited to making sandwiches.

**sandwich man** /ˈ– mæn/, *n.* a man who walks about the streets carrying advertising boards hung before and behind him from straps over the shoulders.

**sandworm** /ˈsændwɜm/, *n.* a polychaete of the family Nereididae, esp. *Australonereis ehlersi,* found in the sandy mud in estuaries or brackish waters of Australia.

**sandwort** /ˈsændwɜt/, *n.* any of the plants constituting the genus *Arenaria,* many of which grow in sandy soil.

**sandy** /ˈsændi/, *adj.,* **-dier, -diest. 1.** of the nature of or consisting of sand; containing or covered with sand. **2.** of a yellowish red colour: *sandy hair.* **3.** having such hair. **4.** shifting or unstable, like sand. – **sandiness,** *n.*

**sandyacht** /ˈsændjɒt/, *n.* a boatlike structure built on wheels and fitted with sails, used for sailing over large areas of sand.

**sandy blight** /sændi ˈblaɪt/, *n.* →**trachoma.**

**sandy cobbler** /– ˈkɒblə/, *n.* →**cobbler**[2].

**sandy wallaby** /– ˈwɒləbi/, *n.* →**agile wallaby.**

**sane** /seɪn/, *adj.,* **saner, sanest. 1.** free from mental derangement: *a sane person.* **2.** having or showing reason, sound judgment, or good sense: *a sane approach to the problem.* **3.** *Obs.* sound; healthy. [L *sānus* sound, healthy] – **sanely,** *adv.* – **saneness,** *n.*

**san fairy Ann** /ˌsæn fɛəri ˈæn/, *Colloq.* it doesn't matter. [F *ça ne fait rien*]

**sanforise** /ˈsænfəraɪz/, *v.t.,* **-rised, -rising.** to shrink (cotton or linen fabrics) mechanically by a patented process before tailoring. Also, **sanforize.** [Trademark]

**sang** /sæŋ/, *v.* past tense of **sing.**

**sangaree** /sæŋgəˈri/, *n.* a drink composed of wine, diluted, sweetened, and spiced. [Sp. *sangría* SANGRIA]

**sanger** /ˈsæŋə/, *n. Colloq.* a sandwich. [shortened form of SANDWICH]

**sangfroid** /sõŋˈfrwa/, *n.* coolness of mind; calmness; composure. [F: cold blood]

**sangria** /ˈsæŋgriə/, *n.* a cold drink made of red or white wine, with brandy and sugar, and slices of orange and lemon. [Sp. *sangría* bleeding, from *sangre* blood, from L *sanguis*]

**sanguiferous** /sæŋˈgwɪfərəs/, *adj.* conveying blood, as a blood vessel. [*sangui-* (combining form representing L *sanguis* blood) + -FEROUS]

**sanguinaria** /sæŋgwəˈnɛəriə/, *n.* **1.** →**bloodroot** (def. 3). **2.** its medicinal rhizome. [short for L *herba sanguināria* bloody plant (in NL applied to bloodroot)]

**sanguinary** /ˈsæŋgwənəri/, *adj.* **1.** attended with or characterised by bloodshed; bloody: *a sanguinary struggle.* **2.** bloodthirsty: *a sanguinary person.* **3.** inflicting the death penalty freely. [L *sanguinārius*] – **sanguinarily,** *adv.* – **sanguinariness,** *n.*

**sanguine** /ˈsæŋgwən/, *adj.* **1.** naturally cheerful and hopeful: *a sanguine disposition.* **2.** hopeful or confident: *sanguine expectations.* **3.** ruddy: *a sanguine complexion.* **4.** (in the old physiology) having blood as the predominating humour, and hence ruddy-faced, cheerful, etc. **5.** →**sanguinary. 6.** blood red; red. *–n.* **7.** a red iron oxide crayon used in making drawings. [ME, from L *sanguineus,* from *sanguis* blood] – **sanguinely,** *adv.* – **sanguineness,** *n.*

**sanguineous** /sæŋˈgwɪniəs/, *adj.* **1.** of, pertaining to, or containing blood. **2.** of the colour of blood. **3.** abounding with blood. **4.** sanguine; confident.

**sanguinolent** /sæŋ'gwɪnələnt/, *adj.* **1.** of or pertaining to blood. **2.** containing or tinged with blood; bloody. [L *sanguinolentus*]

**Sanhedrin** /sæn'hidrən, 'sænədrən/, *n.* **1.** the supreme council and highest ecclesiastical and judicial tribunal of the ancient Jewish nation, with seventy-one members. **2.** a similar lower tribunal, with twenty-three members. Also, **Sanhedrim** /'sænədrəm/. [LHeb., from Gk *synédrion,* from *syn-* SYN- + *hédrion,* from *hédra* seat]

**sanicle** /'sænɪkəl/, *n.* any of the umbelliferous herbs constituting the genus *Sanicula,* as *S. europaea,* widespread in woodlands of temperate regions and tropical mountains.

**sanidine** /'sænədin/, *n.* a mineral form of potash felspar, similar to orthoclase and occurring in some lavas.

**sanies** /'seɪni,iz/, *n.* a thin serous fluid, often greenish, discharged from ulcers, wounds, etc. [L]

**sanious** /'seɪniəs/, *adj.* characterised by the discharge of a thin fluid, as from an ulcer. [L *saniōsus* pertaining to or yielding sanies]

**sanitarian** /sænə'tɛəriən/, *adj.* **1.** sanitary. *–n.* **2.** one expert or engaged in sanitary work.

**sanitarium** /sænə'tɛəriəm/, *n., pl.* **-tariums, -taria** /-'tɛəriə/. →**sanatorium.** [NL, from L *sānit(as)* health + *-ārium* -ARY[1]]

**sanitary** /'sænətri/, *adj.* **1.** of or pertaining to health or the conditions affecting health, esp. with reference to cleanliness, precautions against disease, etc. **2.** favourable to health; free from dirt, germs, etc. [L *sānit(as)* health + -ARY[1]] – **sanitarily,** *adv.* – **sanitariness,** *n.*

**sanitary belt** /'– bɛlt/, *n.* a narrow elastic belt for holding a sanitary napkin in place.

**sanitary can** /'– kæn/, *n.* a tarred can or tin, usu. placed under a seat in an outside toilet used to hold excreta for collection and disposal.

**sanitary cart** /'– kat/, *n.* a truck used to collect and dispose of full sanitary cans. Also, **sanitary wagon.**

**sanitary inspector** /'– ɪn,spɛktə/, *n.* an official appointed by a local authority to inspect the condition of sewage and drainage systems, etc.

**sanitary man** /'– mæn/, *n.* a man who is employed to collect sanitary cans.

**sanitary napkin** /'– næpkən/, *n.* a soft, absorbent, disposable pad worn during menstruation to absorb the discharge from the uterus. Also, **sanitary pad.**

**sanitation** /sænə'teɪʃən/, *n.* **1.** the study and practical application of sanitary measures. **2.** a drainage system.

**sanitise** /'sænətaɪz/, *v.t.,* **-tised, -tising.** to make sanitary: *sanitised for your convenience.* – **sanitiser,** *n.*

**sanity** /'sænəti/, *n.* **1.** the state of being sane; soundness of mind. **2.** soundness of judgment. [L *sānitas*]

**sank** /sæŋk/, *v.* past tense of **sink.**

**San Marino** /sæn mə'rinoʊ/, *n.* a small republic in eastern Italy; the oldest independent country in Europe.

**sanny cart** /'sæni kat/, *n. Colloq.* →**sanitary cart.**

**sanny man** /'– mæn/, *n. Colloq.* →**sanitary man.**

**sans** /sænz/, *prep. Archaic.* without. [ME, from OF, from L *absentiā* in the absence of, b. with *sine* without]

**Sanscrit** /'sænskrɪt/, *n.* →**Sanskrit.**

**sanserif** /sæn'sɛrəf/, *n. Print.* a style of type without serifs.

**sansevieria** /sænsə'vɪəriə/, *n.* any plant of the genus *Sansevieria,* grown as a house plant for its stiff sword-shaped leaves. [NL, named after Raimondo di Sangro, prince of *San Seviero,* 1710-71, Italian scholar]

**Sansk.,** Sanskrit.

**Sanskrit** /'sænskrɪt/, *n.* an extinct Indic language, the ancient classical literary language of India, with a voluminous literature extending over several centuries. It is one of the oldest recorded Indo-European languages. Also, **Sanscrit.** [Skt *samskrita* prepared, cultivated] – **Sanskritic** /sæns'krɪtɪk/, *adj.* – **Sanskritist,** *n.*

**Santa Claus** /'sæntə klɔz/, *n.* the patron saint of children, dispenser of gifts on Christmas Eve; Father Christmas; Saint Nicholas. [d. D *Sante Klaas* St Nicholas]

**Santa Gertrudis** /– gə'trudəs/, *n., pl.* **-dis** /-dəz/. one of a breed of beef cattle developed on King Ranch, Texas, in the U.S., from crossbreeding Brahmans and Shorthorns, said to be esp. tolerant of sub-tropical conditions. [named after *Santa Gertrudis,* an area on which King Ranch was established]

**santal** /'sæntl/, *n.* →**sandalwood.**

**santalaceous** /sæntə'leɪʃəs/, *adj.* belonging to the Santalaceae, or sandalwood family of plants. [NL *Santalāceae* (from *santalum* sandalwood) + -OUS]

**santir** /'sæntɪə/, *n.* a musical instrument somewhat like a dulcimer, used by the Arabs and Persians. Also, **santur, santour.**

**Santo Domingo** /sæntoʊ də'mɪŋgoʊ/, *n.* →**Dominican Republic.**

**santonica** /sæn'tɒnɪkə/, *n.* **1.** a wormwood, *Artemisia cina.* **2.** the dried flower heads of this plant, used as a vermifuge. [L, properly fem. of *Santonicus* pertaining to the Santoni, tribe of ancient Gaul]

**santonin** /'sæntənən/, *n.* a crystalline compound, $C_{15}H_{18}O_3$, the active principle of santonica.

**Sao Tome and Principe** /saʊ ,tumɛ ænd 'prɪntʃəpeɪ/, *n.* a country in the Gulf of Guinea off the west coast of Africa.

**sap**[1] /sæp/, *n.* **1.** the juice or vital circulating fluid, esp. of a woody plant. **2.** →**sapwood.** **3.** *Colloq.* a fool or weak person; a saphead. [ME; OE *sæp,* c. D *sap,* akin to G *Saft,* Icel. *safi*]

**sap**[2] /sæp/, *n., v.,* **sapped, sapping.** *–n.* **1.** *Fort.* a deep narrow trench constructed to approach a besieged place or an enemy's position. *–v.t.* **2.** *Fort.* **a.** to approach (a besieged place, etc.) with deep narrow trenches protected by gabions or parapets. **b.** to dig such trenches in (ground). **3.** to undermine; weaken or destroy insidiously. *–v.i.* **4.** *Fort.* to dig a sap. [earlier *zappe,* from It. *zappa* spade, hoe]

**sapajou** /'sæpədʒu/, *n.* →**capuchin** (defs 1 and 2). [F; of S Amer. orig.]

**sapanwood** /'sæpənwʊd/, *n.* →**sappanwood.**

**saphead** /'sæphɛd/, *n. Colloq.* a simpleton; a fool.

**sapheaded** /'sæphɛdəd/, *adj. Colloq.* silly; foolish.

**saphena** /sæ'finə/, *n., pl.* **-nae** /-ni/. either of two large superficial veins of the leg, one (**long** or **internal saphena**) on the inner side, and the other (**short, external,** or **posterior saphena**) on the outer and posterior sides. [ML, from Ar. *çāfin*] – **saphenous,** *adj.*

**sapid** /'sæpəd/, *adj.* **1.** having taste or flavour. **2.** palatable. **3.** to one's liking; agreeable. [L *sapidus* savoury] – **sapidity** /sə'pɪdəti/, *n.*

**sapient** /'seɪpiənt/, *adj.* (*oft. ironic*) wise or sage. [late ME, from L *sapiens,* ppr., being wise] – **sapience, sapiency,** *n.* – **sapiently,** *adv.*

**sapiential** /seɪpi'ɛnʃəl, sæpi-/, *adj.* containing, exhibiting, or affording wisdom; characterised by wisdom. [LL *sapientiālis*] – **sapientially,** *adv.*

**sapindaceous** /sæpɪn'deɪʃəs/, *adj.* belonging to the Sapindaceae, or soapberry family of plants. [NL *Sapindāceae* (from *sapindus* soapberry) + -OUS]

**sapless** /'sæpləs/, *adj.* **1.** destitute of sap; withered: *sapless plants.* **2.** lacking vitality; insipid.

**sapling** /'sæplɪŋ/, *n.* **1.** a young tree. **2.** a young person.

**sapodilla** /sæpə'dɪlə/, *n.* **1.** a large evergreen tree, *Achras zapota,* of tropical America, bearing an edible fruit (**sapodilla plum**) and yielding chicle. **2.** the fruit. [Sp. *zapotillo,* diminutive of *zapote*]

**saponaceous** /sæpə'neɪʃəs/, *adj.* soaplike; soapy. [NL *sāpōnāceus,* from L *sāpo* soap]

**saponification number** /sə,pɒnəfə'keɪʃən ,nʌmbə/, *n.* the number of milligrams of potassium hydroxide required to completely saponify one gram of a fat or oil.

**saponify** /sə'pɒnəfaɪ/, *v.,* **-fied, -fying.** *Chem. –v.t.* **1.** to convert (a fat) into soap by treating with an alkali. **2.** to decompose (any ester), forming the corresponding alcohol and acid or salt. *–v.i.* **3.** to become converted into soap. [NL *sāpōnificāre,* from L *sāpo* soap + *-(i)ficāre* make] – **saponifiable,** *adj.* – **saponification** /səpɒnəfə'keɪʃən/, *n.* – **saponifier,** *n.*

**saponin** /'sæpənən/, *n.* any of a group of amorphous glucosidal compounds of steroid structure obtainable from many plants. Their aqueous solutions foam like soap on shaking and are used as detergents. [F *saponine,* from L *sāpo* soap + *-ine* -INE[2]]

**saponite** /'sæpənaɪt/, *n.* a soft amorphous mineral found in certain rock cavities consisting of a silicate of magnesium and aluminium.

**sapor** /ˈseɪpɔ, -pə/, *n.* that quality in a substance which affects the sense of taste; savour; flavour. [L] – **saporous** /ˈsæpərəs/, *adj.*

**sapotaceous** /sæpəˈteɪʃəs/, *adj.* belonging to the Sapotaceae, or sapodilla family of plants.

**sappanwood** /ˈsæpənwʊd/, *n.* **1.** a dyewood yielding a red colour, produced by a small East Indian tree, *Caesalpinia sappan.* **2.** the tree itself. Also, **sapanwood.** [*sapan* (from Malay *sapang*) + WOOD[1]]

**sapper** /ˈsæpə/, *n. Colloq.* a private in the Royal Australian Engineers. [SAP[2] + -ER[1]]

**Sapphic** /ˈsæfɪk/, *adj.* **1.** pertaining to Sappho, lyric poetess of Lesbos, Greece, fl. c. 600 B.C., or to certain metres or a form of strophe or stanza used by or named after her. *–n.* **2.** a Sapphic verse. [L *sapphicus,* from Gk *sapphikós*]

**Sapphic ode** /– ˈoʊd/, *n.* See **ode** (def. 5).

**sapphire** /ˈsæfaɪə/, *n.* **1.** a variety of corundum, esp. a transparent blue kind valued as a gem. **2.** a gem of this kind. **3.** the colour of the gem, a deep blue. *–adj.* **4.** resembling sapphire; deep blue: *a sapphire sky.* [L *sapphīrus,* from Gk *sáppheiros;* replacing ME *saphyr,* from OF]

**sapphirine** /ˈsæfəraɪn, -rən/, *adj.* **1.** consisting of sapphire; like sapphire, esp. in colour. *–n.* **2.** a pale blue or greenish, usu. granular mineral, a silicate of magnesium and aluminium. **3.** a blue variety of spinel.

**sapphism** /ˈsæfɪzəm/, *n.* →**lesbianism.** [*Sappho* + -ISM. See SAPPHIC]

**sappy** /ˈsæpi/, *adj.* **1.** abounding in sap, as a plant. **2.** full of vitality and energy. **3.** *Colloq.* silly or foolish.

**sapraemia** /sæˈprimiə/, *n.* a form of blood-poisoning, esp. that due to the toxins produced by certain micro-organisms. Also, *U.S.,* **sapremia.** [SAPR(O)- + -AEMIA] – **sapraemic,** *adj.*

**sapro-,** a word element meaning 'rotten', or 'saprophytic', as in *saprolite.* Also, before vowels, **sapr-.** [Gk, combining form of *saprós* putrid]

**saprogenic** /sæprəˈdʒɛnɪk/, *adj.* **1.** producing putrefaction or decay, as certain bacteria. **2.** formed by putrefaction. Also, **saprogenous** /sæˈprɒdʒənəs/.

**saprolegnia** /sæproʊˈlɛgniə/, *n.* any of a group of aquatic fungi of the genus *Saprolegnia,* which feed on animal matter including diseased fish.

**saprolite** /ˈsæprəlaɪt/, *n.* soft, disintegrated, usu. more or less decomposed rock, remaining in its original place.

**saprophyte** /ˈsæprəfaɪt/, *n.* any vegetable organism that lives on dead organic matter, as certain fungi and bacteria. – **saprophytic** /sæprəˈfɪtɪk/, *adj.*

**sapsago** /ˈsæpsəgoʊ/, *n.* a hard greenish cheese flavoured with melilot, made in Switzerland. [G *Schabziger,* from *schaben* to grate + d. *Ziger* a kind of cheese]

**sapwood** /ˈsæpwʊd/, *n.* in a woody plant, the softer part of the wood between the inner bark and the heartwood.

**saraband** /ˈsærəbænd/, *n.* **1.** a popular and vigorous Spanish castanet dance. **2.** a slow, stately Spanish dance in triple rhythm derived from this. **3.** a piece of music for, or in the rhythm of, this dance, usu. forming one of the movements in the classical suite, following the courante. [F *sarabande,* from Sp. *zarabanda;* probably of Oriental orig.]

**Saracen** /ˈsærəsən/, *n.* **1.** (among the later Romans and Greeks) a member of the nomadic tribes on the Syrian borders of the Roman Empire. **2.** (in later use) an Arab. **3.** any Muslim or Mohammedan, esp. with reference to the Crusades. [mod. E and OE, from LL *Saracēnus,* from LGk *Sarakēnós;* replacing ME *Sarezin,* from OF] – **Saracenic** /særəˈsɛnɪk/, **Saracenical** /særəˈsɛnɪkəl/, *adj.*

**saran** /səˈræn/, *n.* any of various thermoplastic resins derived from vinyl compounds and used to make corrosion-resistant pipes, fittings and bristles, wrapping plastics and as a fibre in carpets, curtain materials and other heavy fabrics. [Trademark]

**saratoda** /særəˈtoʊdə/, *n.* →**barramundi** (def. 2). Also, **saratoga.**

**sarc-,** a word element meaning 'flesh', as in *sarcous.* Also, before consonants, **sarco-.** [Gk *sark-,* combining form of *sárx*]

**sarcasm** /ˈsakæzəm/, *n.* **1.** harsh or bitter derision or irony. **2.** an ironical taunt or gibe; a sneering or cutting remark. [LL *sarcasmus,* from LGk *sarkasmós* sneer]

**sarcastic** /saˈkæstɪk/, *adj.* **1.** characterised by, of the nature of, or pertaining to sarcasm: *a sarcastic reply.* **2.** using, or given to the use of, sarcasm. – **sarcastically,** *adv.*

**sarcenet** /ˈsasnət/, *n.* a very fine, soft, silk fabric, used esp. for linings. Also, **sarsenet.** [ME, from AF *sarzinett,* diminutive of *Sarzin* Saracen. Cf. OF *drap sarrasinois* Saracen cloth]

**sarco** /ˈsakoʊ/, *n. Colloq.* →**sarcosporidiosis.**

**sarcocarp** /ˈsakoʊkap/, *n.* **1.** the fleshy part surrounding the stone in some fruits, as the peach. **2.** any fruit of fleshy consistency.

**sarcoma** /saˈkoʊmə/, *n., pl.* **-mata** /-mətə/. any of various malignant tumours originating in the connective tissue, attacking esp. the bones. [NL, from Gk *sárkōma*] – **sarcomatoid, sarcomatous,** *adj.*

**sarcomatosis** /saˌkoʊməˈtoʊsəs/, *n.* a condition marked by the production of an overwhelming number of sarcomata throughout the body. [NL, from Gk *sárkōma* SARCOMA + *-ōsis* -OSIS]

**sarcophagus** /saˈkɒfəgəs/, *n., pl.* **-gi** /-gaɪ/, **-guses. 1.** a stone coffin, esp. one bearing sculpture or inscriptions, etc., often displayed as a monument. **2.** (among the ancient Greeks) a kind of stone supposed to consume the flesh of corpses, used for coffins. [L, from Gk *sarkophágos,* orig. adj., flesh-eating]

**sarcosporidiosis** /ˌsakoʊspərɪdiˈoʊsəs/, *n.* an infestation with or disease caused by a parasitic protozoan of the order Sarcosporidia which attacks the muscles of vertebrates.

**sarcous** /ˈsakəs/, *adj.* consisting of or pertaining to flesh or skeletal muscle. [Gk *sárx* flesh + -OUS]

**sard** /sad/, *n.* a brownish red chalcedony, or a piece of it, used in jewellery, etc. [ME *saarde,* from L *sarda* SARDIUS]

**sardine** /saˈdin/, *n., pl.* **-dines,** (*esp. collectively*) **-dine. 1.** the young of the common pilchard, often preserved in oil and canned for food. **2.** any of various allied or similar fishes used in this way, esp. the **California sardine,** *Sardinops caeruleus.* [ME *sardyn,* from It. *sardina,* from L *sardīna,* from *sarda* kind of fish]

**Sardinian** /saˈdɪniən/, *n.* a Romance language spoken in Sardinia, a large island in the Mediterranean, west of Italy.

**sardius** /ˈsadiəs/, *n.* **1.** →**sard. 2.** the precious stone in the breastplate of the Jewish high priest, thought to have been a ruby. [ME, from L (Vulgate), from Gk *sárdios* (stone) of Sardis]

**sardonic** /saˈdɒnɪk/, *adj.* bitterly ironical; sarcastic; sneering: *a sardonic grin.* [F *sardonique,* from L *Sardonius,* from Gk *Sardónios* Sardinian, for earlier *sardánios* bitter, scornful, from the notion of a Sardinian plant said to bring on convulsions resembling laughter] – **sardonically,** *adv.*

**sardonyx** /ˈsadənɪks/, *n.* a kind of onyx containing layers or bands of sard. [ME, from L, from Gk. See SARD, ONYX]

**sargasso** /saˈgæsoʊ/, *n.* →**gulfweed.** [Pg. *sargaço*]

**sargassum** /saˈgæsəm/, *n.* any seaweed of the genus *Sargassum,* widely distributed in warmer waters, as the pelagic species *S. natans* and *S. fluitans.* [NL, from Pg. *sargaço*]

**sari** /ˈsari/, *n., pl.* **-ris.** a long piece of cotton or silk, the principal outer garment of Hindu women, worn round the body with one end over the head or shoulder. [Hind.]

sari

**Sarich engine** /ˈsærɪtʃ ɛndʒən/, *n.* an improved rotary motor smaller and lighter than the normal piston engine, with the same power output. [invented by Tony Ralph *Sarich,* b. 1940, W.A. inventor]

**sark** /sak/, *n. Scot. or Archaic.* a shirt or chemise. [ME, from Scand.; cf. Icel. *serkr,* c. OE *serc*]

**sarking** /ˈsakɪŋ/, *n.* **1.** a layer of boarding, sometimes used to cover the rafters of a house under the tiles. **2.** sheet material laid under tiles, shingles or slates for reflective insulation or additional waterproofing.

**sarky** /ˈsaki/, *adj. Colloq.* sarcastic.

**sarmentose** /saˈmɛntoʊs/, *adj.* **1.** (of a plant) having runners. **2.** (of a plant part) like a runner. [L *sarmentōsus*]

**sarong** /səˈrɒŋ/, *n.* **1.** the principal garment for both sexes in the Malay Archipelago, etc., consisting of a piece of cloth enveloping the lower part of the body like a skirt. **2.** a kind of cloth for such garments. [Malay *sārung.* Cf. Skt *sāranga* variegated]

**saros** /ˈseɪrɒs/, *n.* the interval between two similar solar eclipses, equal to 18 years and 10-12 days. [Gk]

**sarracenia** /særəˈsiniə/, *n.* any plant of the genus *Sarracenia,* comprising American marsh plants with hollow leaves of a pitcher-like form in which insects are trapped and digested, as *S. purpurea,* a common pitcher plant. [NL; named after D. *Sarrazin* of Quebec, who first sent samples of the plant to Europe]

**sarsaparilla** /saspəˈrɪlə/, *n.* **1.** any of various climbing or trailing plants of the genus *Smilax,* having a root which has been much used in medicine as an alterant. **2.** any similar species as **false sarsaparilla,** *Hardenbergia violacea.* **3.** the root of any plant of the genus *Smilax.* **4.** an extract or other preparation made of it. **5.** *U.S.* a soft drink flavoured with it. [Sp. *zarzaparilla,* from *zarza* bramble + *-parilla* (? diminutive of *parsa* vine)]

**sarsenet** /ˈsasnət/, *n.* →**sarcenet.**

**sartorial** /saˈtɔriəl/, *adj.* **1.** of or pertaining to clothes or dress, generally men's: *sartorial splendour.* **2.** *Anat.* pertaining to the sartorius. [L *sartōrius* of a tailor + -AL[1]]

**sartorius** /saˈtɔriəs/, *n.* a flat, narrow muscle, the longest in the human body, running from the hip to the inner side of the shinbone, and crossing the thigh obliquely in front. [NL: lit., pertaining to a tailor]

**sash**[1] /sæʃ/, *n.* a long band or scarf of silk, etc., worn over one shoulder or round the waist, as by military officers as a part of the costume, or by women and children for ornament. [dissimilated var. of *shash,* from Ar.: turban]

**sash**[2] /sæʃ/, *n.* **1.** a movable framework in which panes of glass are set, as in a window or the like. **2.** the part of a window which moves. **3.** such frameworks collectively. *–v.t.* **4.** to furnish with sashes or with windows having sashes. [ME; alteration of CHASSIS]

**sashay** /ˈsæʃeɪ/, *v.i. Colloq.* to strut, move exaggeratedly. [var. of CHASSÉ]

**sashcord** /ˈsæʃkɔd/, *n.* a cord passing over a pulley and attaching a vertically sliding sash to counterweights so that it may be raised or lowered.

**sashcutter** /ˈsæʃkʌtə/, *n.* a paintbrush with long, supple bristles.

**sashimi** /sæˈʃimi/, *n.* a Japanese dish of raw fish. [Jap., from *sasu* pierce, stab + *mi* flesh, meat]

**sash-window** /ˈsæʃ-wɪndoʊ/, *n.* a window which opens by sliding sashes up or down.

**sasin** /ˈsæsɪn/, *n.* the common Indian antelope. [Nepalese]

**saskatoon** /sæskəˈtun/, *n.* **1.** any of several species of *Amelanchier,* esp. the serviceberry. **2.** the berry of this bush. [Algonquian (Cree) *misáskwatomin* serviceberry, lit., fruit of *misâskwat* the tree of much wood]

**sasquatch** /ˈsæskwætʃ/, *n.* an abominable snowman associated with certain Canadian wastelands.

**sassaby** /ˈsæsəbi/, *n., pl.* **-bies.** a large, blackish red antelope, *Damaliscus lunatus,* of southern Africa. [Bantu *tsessébe*]

**sassafras** /ˈsæsəfræs/, *n.* **1.** an American tree, *Sassafras albidum.* **2.** the aromatic bark of its root, used medicinally and esp. for flavouring beverages, confectionery, etc. **3.** any of several Australian trees with fragrant bark, as the canary sassafras, or the southern sassafras. [Sp. *sasafras;* orig. uncert.]

**sassafras oil** /ˈ– ɔɪl/, *n.* a volatile oil derived from the root of the sassafras tree, consisting of camphor, pinene, etc.

**Sassenach** /ˈsæsənæk/, *n.* an Englishman (a name applied by the Scottish inhabitants of the British Isles). [Gaelic *Sasunnach* Englishman, from *Sasunn* Saxon + *-ach* (adj. suffix)]

**sassy**[1] /ˈsæsi/, *adj.,* **-sier, -siest.** *Colloq.* saucy. [d. var. of SAUCY]

**sassy**[2] /ˈsæsi/, *n.* →**sassy bark.** [W African; said to be from E. See SASSY[1]]

**sassy bark** /ˈ– bak/, *n.* **1.** the bark of a large African tree, *Erythrophloeum guineense,* used by the natives as a poison in ordeals. **2.** Also, **sassywood.** the tree itself. [see SASSY[2]]

**sat** /sæt/, *v.* past tense and past participle of **sit.**

**sat.,** saturated.

**Sat.,** **1.** Saturday. **2.** Saturn.

**Satan** /ˈseɪtn/, *n.* the chief evil spirit; the great adversary of man; the devil. Cf. **Lucifer.** [ME and OE, from L, from Gk, from Heb.: adversary]

**satanellus** /sætəˈnɛləs/, *n.* →**northern native cat.** [NL: little devil]

**satanic** /səˈtænɪk/, *adj.* **1.** of Satan. **2.** characteristic of or befitting Satan; extremely wicked; diabolical. Also, **satanical.** **– satanically,** *adv.*

**Satanism** /ˈseɪtənɪzəm/, *n.* **1.** the worship of Satan. **2.** a form of such worship which travesties Christian rites. **3.** satanic disposition or practice. **– Satanist,** *n.*

**satay** /ˈsateɪ/, *n.* cubes of spiced meat grilled on a skewer and covered with a hot peanut or soya-based sauce. [Malay]

**satchel** /ˈsætʃəl/, *n.* a bag, made of leather, canvas, or the like, usu. with a shoulder-strap, used for carrying schoolbooks. [ME, from OF *sachel,* from *sac* sack, from L *saccus.* See SACK[1]]

**sate**[1] /seɪt/, *v.t.,* **sated, sating.** **1.** to satisfy (any appetite or desire) to the full. **2.** to surfeit; glut. [b. obs. *sade* satiate (OE *sadian*) and L *sat* enough. See SAD]

**sate**[2] /sæt, seɪt/, *v. Archaic.* past tense and past participle of **sit.**

**sateen** /sæˈtin/, *n.* a cotton fabric woven in satin weave and resembling satin in gloss. [var. of SATIN, by association with VELVETEEN]

**satellite** /ˈsætəlaɪt/, *n.* **1.** a small body which revolves round a planet; a moon. **2.** an attendant upon a person of importance. **3.** a subservient or obsequious follower. **4.** a country under the domination or influence of another. **5.** a man-made device, usu. containing recording and transmitting instruments, for launching into orbit round the earth, another planet, or the sun, for purposes of communication, research, etc. See **communication satellite.** *–v.t.* **6.** to send (pictures, messages) by satellite. [L *satelles* attendant, guard]

**satellite town** /ˈ– taʊn/, *n.* **1.** a small town or city dependent on local industry but having economic linkages with a large city from which it is separated by open country. **2.** an extensive collection of commuters' dwellings, physically separate from but associated with a large town. Also, **satellite city.**

**satem** /ˈsatəm/, *adj.* pertaining to those Indo-European languages which changed primitive Indo-European [*k*] to [*s*], in contrast to those which retained the [*k*]. Cf. **centum.** [from Avestan *satem* hundred (an example of this change, where initial /s/ represents Indo-European /k/)]

**satiable** /ˈseɪʃəbəl/, *adj.* that can be satiated. **– satiability** /seɪʃəˈbɪləti/, **satiableness,** *n.* **– satiably,** *adv.*

**satiate** /ˈseɪʃieɪt/, *v.,* **-ated, -ating;** /ˈseɪʃiət, -ieɪt/, *adj.* *–v.t.* **1.** to supply with anything to excess, so as to disgust or weary; surfeit; cloy. **2.** to satisfy to the full. *–adj.* **3.** *Archaic or Poetic.* satiated. [L *satiātus,* pp., filled full] **– satiation** /seɪʃiˈeɪʃən/, *n.*

**satiety** /səˈtaɪəti, -ˈti-/, *n.* the state of being satiated; surfeit. [L *satietas* abundance]

**satin** /ˈsætn/, *n.* **1.** a very smooth, glossy fabric made in a warp-face weave, usu. rayon or silk. *–adj.* **2.** of or like satin; smooth; glossy. [ME *satine,* from OF, from It. *setino, from L *sēta* silk] **– satin-like,** *adj.*

**satin bower-bird** /– ˈbaʊə-bɜd/, *n.* the largest of the Australian bower-birds, *Ptilonorhynchus violaceus,* the adult male being a lustrous blue in colour.

**satinet** /sætəˈnɛt/, *n.* **1.** an inferior kind of satin containing cotton. **2.** *Obs.* a thin light satin. Also, **satinette.** [F. See SATIN, -ET]

**satin flycatcher** /sætn ˈflaɪkætʃə/, *n.* a small darting bird, *Myiagra cyanoleuca,* the male of the species being glossy black with white underparts, and the female brown with white underparts and rufous throat; found along the east coast of Australia and in Tasmania and the island of New Guinea. Also, **satin sparrow.**

**satin sparrow** /– ˈspæroʊ/, *n.* →**satin flycatcher.**

**satin stitch** /ˈ– stɪtʃ/, *n.* an embroidery stitch in close parallel lines, which gives a satiny finish.

**satin top** /ˈ– tɒp/, *n.* a dry-country pasture grass, *Bothriochloa* *erianthoides,* with long flowering stalks.

**satinwood** /'sætnwʊd/, *n.* **1.** the satiny wood of an East Indian tree, *Chloroxylon swietenia,* used for cabinetwork, etc. **2.** the tree itself. **3.** any of several Australian trees, as the scented satinwood, *Ceratopetalum apetalum.*

**satiny** /'sætəni/, *adj.* satin-like; smooth; glossy.

**satire** /'sætaɪə/, *n.* **1.** the use of irony, sarcasm, ridicule, etc., in exposing, denouncing, or deriding vice, folly, etc. **2.** a literary composition, in verse or prose, in which vices, abuses, follies, etc., are held up to scorn, derision, or ridicule. **3.** the species of literature constituted by such composition. [L *satira,* var. of *satura* medley, properly fem. of *satur* full, sated]

**satirical** /sə'tɪrɪkəl/, *adj.* **1.** of or pertaining to satire; of the nature of satire: *satirical novels.* **2.** indulging in or given to satire: *a satirical poet.* Also, **satiric.** – **satirically,** *adv.* – **satiricalness,** *n.*

**satirise** /'sætəraɪz/, *v.,* **-rised, -rising.** *–v.t.* **1.** to make the object of satire. *–v.i.* **2.** to write or perform a satire or satires. Also, **satirize.** – **satiriser,** *n.*

**satirist** /'sætərəst/, *n.* **1.** a writer of satires. **2.** one who indulges in satire.

**satisfaction** /sætəs'fækʃən/, *n.* **1.** the act of satisfying. **2.** the state of being satisfied. **3.** the cause of being satisfied. **4.** reparation, as of a wrong or injury. **5.** the opportunity of repairing a supposed wrong, as by a duel. **6.** payment, as for debt; discharge, as of obligations. **7.** *Eccles.* the performance by a penitent of the penal acts enjoined by church authority for injury done to another or to God. [ME, from L *satisfactio*]

**satisfactory** /sætəs'fæktəri, -tri/, *adj.* **1.** affording satisfaction; fulfilling all demands or requirements: *a satisfactory answer.* **2.** *Theol.* atoning or expiating. – **satisfactorily,** *adv.* – **satisfactoriness,** *n.*

**satisfy** /'sætəsfaɪ/, *v.,* **-fied, -fying.** *–v.t.* **1.** to fulfil the desires, expectations, needs, or demands of, or content (a person, the mind, etc.); supply fully the needs of (a person, etc.). **2.** to fulfil (a desire, expectation, want, etc.). **3.** to give assurance to; convince: *to satisfy oneself by investigation.* **4.** to answer sufficiently (an objection, etc.); solve (a doubt, etc.). **5.** to discharge fully (a debt, etc.). **6.** to make reparation to (a person, etc.) or for (a wrong, etc.). **7.** to pay (a creditor). **8.** to fulfil the requirements or conditions of: *to satisfy an algebraic equation.* *–v.i.* **9.** to give satisfaction. [ME *satisfye,* from OF *satisfier,* from L *satisfacere* do enough] – **satisfier,** *n.* – **satisfyingly,** *adv.*

**satrap** /'sætræp/, *n.* **1.** a governor of a province under the ancient Persian monarchy. **2.** a subordinate ruler, often a despotic one. [ME, from L *satrapa,* from Gk *satrápēs,* from OPers.: lit., country-protector]

**satrapy** /'sætrəpi/, *n., pl.* **-trapies.** the province or jurisdiction of a satrap.

**Satsuma pottery** /sæt,sumə 'pɒtəri/, *n.* Japanese hand-made pottery, noted for its crackle glaze and scenes of birds combined with floral designs.

**saturable** /'sætʃərəbəl/, *adj.* that may be saturated. – **saturability** /sætʃərə'bɪləti/, *n.*

**saturate** /'sætʃəreɪt/, *v.,* **-rated, -rating;** /'sætʃərət, -reɪt/, *adj.* *–v.t.* **1.** to cause (a substance) to unite with the greatest possible amount of another substance, through solution, chemical combination, or the like. **2.** to charge to the utmost, as with magnetism. **3.** to soak, impregnate, or imbue thoroughly or completely. **4.** *Mil.* to bomb or shell (an enemy position) so thoroughly that the enemy defences are powerless. **5.** *Mil.* to send so many planes over (a target area) that the enemy electronic tracking equipment is neutralised. *–adj.* **6.** *Chiefly Poetic.* saturated. [L *saturātus,* pp., satisfied, saturated]

**saturated** /'sætʃəreɪtəd/, *adj.* **1.** soaked, impregnated, or imbued thoroughly; charged thoroughly or completely; brought to a state of saturation. **2.** (of colours) of maximum chroma or purity; of the highest intensity of hue; free from admixture of white.

**saturated compound** /– 'kɒmpaʊnd/, *n.* **1.** a compound which does not form addition compounds, the molecules of which contain no double or triple bonds. **2.** a compound which has no free valency electrons.

**saturated solution** /– sə'luʃən/, *n.* a solution which contains as much solute as can be dissolved under any particular set of conditions.

**saturated vapour** /– 'veɪpə/, *n.* a vapour which is sufficiently concentrated to exist in equilibrium with its liquid.

**saturation** /sætʃə'reɪʃən/, *n.* **1.** the act or process of saturating. **2.** the resulting state. **3.** *Meteorol.* a condition in the atmosphere corresponding to 100 per cent relative humidity. **4.** (of colours) the degree of purity or chroma; degree of freedom from admixture with white.

**saturation point** /'– pɔɪnt/, *n.* the point at which a substance will receive no more of another substance in solution, chemical combination, etc.

**Saturday** /'sætədeɪ, -di/, *n.* the seventh day of the week, following Friday. [ME; OE *Sæterdæg, Sætern(es)dæg,* c. D *zaterdag,* LG *Saterdag,* half translation, half adoption of L *Sāturnī dies* day of Saturn (the planet)]

**Saturn** /'sætən/, *n.* the second largest planet, the sixth in order from the sun. [from *Saturn,* the Roman god of agriculture]

**saturnalia** /sætə'neɪljə/, *n. pl.* any period of unrestrained revelry. [from *Saturnalia,* the festival of Saturn, Roman god of agriculture, celebrated in ancient Rome in December, and observed as a time of general feasting and unrestrained merrymaking] – **saturnalian,** *adj.*

**Saturnian** /sə'tɜniən/, *adj.* prosperous, happy, or peaceful: *Saturnian days.* [from *Saturn,* Roman god of agriculture and vegetation, whose reign was characterised by happiness and virtue and was referred to as 'the golden age']

**saturniid** /sə'tɜniɪd/, *n.* **1.** any of the large moths of the family Saturniidae, including many of the most strikingly coloured species. *–adj.* **2.** denoting or pertaining to these moths. [NL *Sāturniidae,* from L *Sāturnius* of Saturn]

**saturnine** /'sætənaɪn/, *adj.* **1.** having or showing a sluggish, gloomy temperament; gloomy; taciturn. **2.** suffering from lead poisoning, as a person. **3.** due to absorption of lead, as disorders. [SATURN + -INE[1]; the planet being supposed to give a gloomy nature to those born under its sign] – **saturninely,** *adv.*

**saturnism** /'sætənɪzəm/, *n.* lead poisoning; plumbism.

**Satyagraha** /'sʌtjəgrʌhə/, *n.* the principle of non-violent resistance, as enunciated in India by Mahatma Gandhi, 1869-1948, Indian nationalist leader, as a means of political reform. [Hind., from Skt *satyāgraha* truth-grasping]

**satyr** /'sætə, 'seɪtə/, *n.* **1.** *Class. Myth.* one of a class of woodland deities attendant on the god of wine, Bacchus, represented as part human and part goat, and noted for riot and lasciviousness. **2.** a lascivious man. **3.** a man affected with satyriasis. **4.** any of the rather sombre butterflies that constitute the family Satyridae. [ME, from L *satyrus,* from Gk *sátyros*] – **satyric** /sə'tɪrɪk/, *adj.*

**satyriasis** /sætə'raɪəsəs/, *n.* morbid and uncontrollable sexual desire in men. [NL, from Gk]

**sauce** /sɔs/, *n., v.,* **sauced, saucing.** *–n.* **1.** any preparation, usu. liquid or soft, eaten as a relish or appetising accompaniment to food. **2.** something that adds piquance. **3.** *Colloq.* impertinence; impudence. *–v.t.* **4.** to dress or prepare with sauce; season: *meat well sauced.* **5.** to give zest to. **6.** to make agreeable or less harsh. **7.** *Colloq.* to speak impertinently to. [ME, from OF, from VL *salsa,* fem. of *salsus* salted]

**sauce bearnaise** /– beə'neɪz/, *n.* →**bearnaise sauce.**

**sauce bechamel** /– beʃə'mel/, *n.* →**bechamel sauce.**

**sauce boat** /'– boʊt/, *n.* a low boat-shaped vessel in which sauce is served at table.

**sauce noire** /– 'nwa/, *n.* →**black butter sauce.**

**saucepan** /'sɔspən/, *n.* a metal container of moderate depth, usu. having a long handle and a lid, for boiling, stewing, etc.

**saucer** /'sɔsə/, *n.* **1.** a small, round, shallow dish to hold a cup. **2.** any similar dish, plate, or the like. **3.** any saucer-shaped thing: *a flying saucer.* [ME, from OF *saucier(e)* vessel for holding sauce, from *sauce* SAUCE]

**saucy** /'sɔsi/, *adj.,* **-cier, -ciest. 1.** impertinent; insolent: *a saucy remark or child.* **2.** piquantly pert; smart: *saucy hat.* – **saucily,** *adv.* – **sauciness,** *n.*

**Saudi Arabia** /saʊdi ə'reɪbiə/, *n.* a kingdom in northern and central Arabia.

**sauerkraut** /'saʊəkraʊt/, *n.* cabbage cut fine, salted, and allowed to ferment until sour. [G, from *sauer* sour + *Kraut* cabbage]

**sauger** /ˈsɔgə/, *n.* a freshwater North American pike-perch, *Stizostedion canadense.*

**sauna** /ˈsɔnə/, *n.* **1.** a type of steam bath, originally Finnish, in which the bather sits in a steam-filled room or cabinet and is cleansed through the process of perspiration, usu. following this treatment with immersion in cold water and sometimes a light beating with birch twigs. **2.** a room or device for taking such a bath. [Finnish]

**Saunder's case moth,** *n.* a very large moth, *Metura elongata,* having an elongate, tough, silken case to the outside of which are attached short lengths of twigs and sticks.

**saunter** /ˈsɔntə/, *v.i.* **1.** to walk with a leisurely gait; stroll. *–n.* **2.** a leisurely walk or ramble; a stroll. **3.** a leisurely gait. [late ME; orig. uncert.] – **saunterer,** *n.*

**-saur,** a word element meaning 'lizard'. [see SAURO-]

**saurian** /ˈsɔriən/, *adj.* **1.** belonging or pertaining to the Sauria, a group of reptiles originally including the lizards, crocodiles, etc., but now technically restricted to the lizards or lacertilians. **2.** lizard-like. *–n.* **3.** a saurian animal, as a dinosaur or lizard. [NL *sauria* an order of reptiles (from Gk *saûros* lizard) + -AN]

**sauro-,** a word element meaning 'lizard'. [combining form of Gk *saûros*]

**sauropod** /ˈsɔrəpɒd/, *n.* **1.** any of the Sauropoda, a group of herbivorous dinosaurs with small head, long neck and tail, and five-toed limbs, the largest known land animals. *–adj.* **2.** belonging or pertaining to the Sauropoda. – **sauropodous** /sɔˈrɒpədəs/, *adj.*

**-saurus,** Latinised variant of **-saur.**

**saury** /ˈsɔri/, *n., pl.* **-ries. 1.** a sharp-snouted fish, *Scomberesox saurus,* of the Atlantic. **2.** any of various related fishes, esp. the **Pacific saury,** *Cololabis saira.* [apparently from Gk *saûros* sea fish (Aristotle)]

**sausage** /ˈsɒsɪdʒ/, *n.* **1.** minced pork, beef, or other meats (often combined), with various added ingredients and seasonings, and packed into a special skin, formerly prepared from the entrails of pigs or oxen, but now often made from a synthetic product. **2.** *Aeron.* a sausage-shaped observation balloon, formerly used in warfare. **3. not a sausage,** absolutely nothing. [ME *sausige,* from ONF *saussiche,* from LL *salsīcia,* from L *salsus* salted]

**sausage dog** /ˈ– dɒg/, *n. Colloq.* →**dachshund.**

**sausage meat** /ˈ– mit/, *n.* meat prepared for making sausages.

**sausage roll** /– ˈroʊl/, *n.* a roll of baked pastry filled with sausage meat.

**sauté** /ˈsoʊteɪ/, *adj., v.,* **-téed, -téeing,** *n.* *–adj.* **1.** cooked or browned in a pan containing a little fat. *–v.t.* **2.** to cook in a small amount of fat; pan fry. *–n.* **3.** a dish of sauté food. [F: tossed, pp. of *sauter* leap (used in causative sense), from L *saltāre*]

**sauterne** /soʊˈtɜn, sə-/, *n.* a rich sweet white table wine, esp. one produced near Bordeaux, France. Also, **sauternes.** [named after the district *Sauternes,* near Bordeaux, where it is made]

**sautoir** /soʊˈtwa/, *n.* a long ribbon, chain, beaded band, or the like, worn about the neck. [F]

**Sauvignon Blanc** /ˌsoʊvɪnjõ ˈblõk/, *n.* a highly regarded grape variety grown for the production of white wine. [F]

**sav** /sæv/, *n. Colloq.* a saveloy.

**savage** /ˈsævɪdʒ/, *adj., n., v.,* **savaged, savaging.** *–adj.* **1.** wild or rugged, as country or scenery: *savage wilderness.* **2.** uncivilised; barbarous: *savage tribes.* **3.** rude, boorish: *savage manners.* **4.** fierce, ferocious, or cruel; untamed: *savage beasts.* **5.** enraged, or furiously angry, as a person. *–n.* **6.** an uncivilised human being. **7.** a fierce, brutal, or cruel person. **8.** a rude, boorish person. *–v.t.* **9.** to assail violently; maul. [ME *sauvage,* from OF, from LL *salvāticus* of the woods, wild, replacing L *silvāticus*] – **savagely,** *adv.* – **savageness,** *n.*

**savagery** /ˈsævɪdʒri, -dʒəri/, *n., pl.* **-ries. 1.** uncivilised state or condition; a state of barbarism. **2.** savage nature, disposition, conduct, or act; barbarity.

**savanna** /səˈvænə/, *n.* **1.** a plain, characterised by coarse grasses and scattered tree growth, esp. on the margins of the tropics where the rainfall is seasonal, as in the Sudan of Africa. **2.** grassland region with scattered trees, grading into either open plain or woodland, usu. in subtropical or tropical regions. Also, **savannah.** [Sp. *zavana, savana,* from Carib]

**savant** /ˈsævənt/, *n.* a man of learning. [F, n. use of (former) ppr. of *savoir,* from L *sapere* be wise]

**savarin** /ˈsævərən/, *n.* a yeast-leavened dough, cooked in a special mould, soaked while still hot in one of various liqueur or fruit flavoured syrups.

**savate** /səˈvæt/, *n.* a French form of boxing in which the feet, as well as the hands, may be used to deliver blows. [F: lit., old shoe]

**save**[1] /seɪv/, *v.,* **saved, saving,** *n.* *–v.t.* **1.** to rescue from danger; preserve from harm, injury, or loss: *to save from drowning.* **2.** to keep safe, intact, or unhurt; safeguard: *God save the Queen.* **3.** to keep from being lost: *to save the game.* **4.** (in soccer, etc.) to prevent (a goal) being scored by stopping the ball from entering the net. **5.** to avoid the spending, consumption, or waste of: *to save fuel by keeping the fire low.* **6.** to set apart, reserve, or lay by: *to save money.* **7.** to treat carefully in order to reduce wear, fatigue, etc.: *to save one's eyes.* **8.** to prevent the occurrence, use, or necessity of; obviate: *a stitch in time saves nine.* **9.** *Theol.* to deliver from the power and consequences of sin. *–v.i.* **10.** to accumulate or put aside money, etc., as the result of economy (oft. fol. by *up*): *to save up for a new car.* **11.** to be economical in expenditure. **12.** to preserve something from harm, injury, loss, etc. **13.** (in soccer, etc.) to prevent a goal from being scored by stopping the ball from entering the net. **14.** *Colloq.* to admit of being kept without spoiling, as food. *–n.* **15.** the act or instance of saving, esp. in sports. [ME, from OF *sauver, salver,* from LL *salvāre*] – **savable,** *adj.* – **saver,** *n.*

**save**[2] /seɪv/, *prep.* **1.** except; but. *–conj.* **2.** except; but. **3.** *Archaic.* unless. [ME; var. of SAFE, adj., in obs. sense of reserving, making exception of]

**save-all** /ˈseɪv-ɔl/, *n.* a means, contrivance, or receptacle for preventing loss or waste.

**saved** /seɪvd/, *v.* **1.** past tense and past participle of **save**[1]. *–adj.* **2.** rescued. **3. saved by the bell, a.** (of a boxer) saved from being counted out by the bell marking the end of the round. **b.** rescued from a predicament at the last minute.

**saveloy** /ˈsævəlɔɪ/, *n.* **1.** →**frankfurt. 2.** a highly seasoned, smoked sausage, usu. of pork. [F, alteration of *cervelas* a kind of sausage orig. containing pigs' brains, from It. *cervellata,* from *cervello* brain, from L *cerebellum*]

**saver** /ˈseɪvə/, *n. Colloq.* a bet laid to offset another; a covering bet.

**savin** /ˈsævən/, *n.* **1.** a juniper, *Juniperus sabina,* whose dried tops are used as a drug. **2.** the drug itself. **3.** the red cedar. Also, **savine.** [ME and OE *savine,* from VL, from L (*herba*) *Sabīna,* lit., Sabine herb]

savin (def. 1)

**saving** /ˈseɪvɪŋ/, *adj.* **1.** that saves; rescuing; preserving. **2.** redeeming: *a saving sense of humour.* **3.** economical. **4.** making a reservation: *a saving clause.* *–n.* **5.** economy in expenditure, outlay, use, etc. **6.** a reduction or lessening of expenditure or outlay: *a saving of ten per cent.* **7.** that which is saved. **8.** (*pl.*) sums of money saved by economy and laid away. **9.** *Law.* a reservation or exception. *–prep.* **10.** except: *everyone came, saving Marcus.* **11.** with all due respect to or for: *saving your presence.* *–conj.* **12.** save. [SAVE[1] + -ING[2], -ING[1]] – **savingly,** *adv.*

**saving grace** /– ˈgreɪs/, *n.* a virtue or quality which compensates for faults.

**savings account** /ˈseɪvɪŋz əˌkaʊnt/, *n.* an account with a savings bank or permanent building society on which a rate of interest is paid and money can be withdrawn at short notice.

**savings bank** /ˈ– bæŋk/, *n.* a bank dealing in accounts operated by a bankbook and on which cheques may not be drawn. Cf. **trading bank.**

**saviour** /ˈseɪvjə/, *n.* **1.** one who saves, rescues, or delivers: *the saviour of the country.* **2.** (*cap.*) a title of God, esp. of Christ.

[ME *sauveour,* from OF, from LL *salvātor.* See SAVE[1]]

**savoiardi biscuit** /ˌsævɔɪˌadi ˈbɪskət/, *n.* a crisp, Italian-style sponge finger. [It. *savoiardo* of Savoy (a district in SE france)]

**savoir-faire** /ˌsævwa-ˈfɛə, ˌsʌv-/, *n.* knowledge of what to do in any situation; tact. [F: lit., to know how to act]

**savoir-vivre** /ˌsævwa-ˈvivrə, ˌsʌv-/, *n.* knowledge of the world and the usages of polite society. [F: lit., to know how to live]

**savor** /ˈseɪvə/, *n. U.S.* →**savour.**

**savorous** /ˈseɪvərəs/, *adj. Chiefly U.S.* having savour; savoury.

**savory**[1] /ˈseɪvəri/, *n., pl.* **-vories.** any of the aromatic plants constituting the genus *Satureja,* esp. *S. hortensis* (**summer savory**), a European herb used in cookery, or *S. montana* **(winter savory).** [ME *saverey,* OE *sætherie, saturēge,* from L *saturēia*]

**savory**[2] /ˈseɪvəri/, *adj., n. U.S.* →**savoury.**

**savour** /ˈseɪvə/, *n.* **1.** the quality in a substance which affects the sense of taste or of smell. **2.** a particular taste or smell. **3.** distinctive quality or property. **4.** power to excite or interest. *–v.i.* **5.** to have savour, taste, or smell. **6.** to exhibit the peculiar characteristics; smack (fol. by *of*). *–v.t.* **7.** to give a savour to; season; flavour. **8.** to perceive by taste or smell, esp. with relish. **9.** to give oneself to the enjoyment of. Also, *U.S.* **savor.** [ME *savour,* from OF, from L *sapor* taste, savour] – **savourer,** *n.* – **savourless,** *adj.*

**savoury** /ˈseɪvəri/, *adj., n., pl.* **-vouries.** *–adj.* **1.** having savour; agreeable in taste or smell: *a savoury smell.* **2.** piquant, pungent, or salty to the taste; not sweet. **3.** pleasing or morally respectable. *–n.* **4.** an unsweet, usu. salty, bite-sized morsel such as a smoked oyster, slice of egg topped with an anchovy, etc. on a small biscuit or crouton; canapé. **5.** *Brit.* an appetising, not sweet, dish served at the beginning, or at the end of a meal instead of a dessert. Also, *U.S.,* **savory.** [ME *savure,* from OF *savoure,* pp. See SAVOUR, *v.*] – **savouriness,** *n.*

**savoy** /səˈvɔɪ/, *n.* a variety of the common cabbage with a compact head and leaves reticulately wrinkled. [named after *Savoy,* a district in SE France]

**Savoyard** /səˈvɔɪad/, *n.* one enthusiastic about, or connected with, Gilbert and Sullivan operas. [so called from the *Savoy* Theatre, London, where the operas were first performed]

**savvy** /ˈsævi/, *v.,* **-vied, -vying,** *n., adj.,* **-vier, viest.** *Colloq.* *–v.t., v.i.* **1.** to know; understand. [Sp., alteration of *sabe* (*usted*) do you know] *–n.* **2.** understanding; intelligence; common sense. *–adj.* **3.** well-informed or experienced. [var. of d. Scot. *savie,* from F, alteration of *savoir* know, from L *sapere*]

**saw**[1] /sɔ/, *n., v.,* **sawed, sawn** or **sawed, sawing.** *–n.* **1.** a tool or device for cutting, typically a thin blade of metal with a series of sharp teeth. **2.** any similar tool or device, as a rotating disc in which a sharp continuous edge replaces the teeth. *–v.t.* **3.** to cut or divide with a saw. **4.** to form by cutting with a saw. **5.** to cut as if using a saw: *to saw the air with one's hands.* **6.** to work (something) from side to side like a saw. *–v.i.* **7.** to use a saw. **8.** to cut with, or as with, a saw. **9.** to cut as a saw does. [ME *sawe,* OE *saga, sagu,* c. D *zaag;* akin to G *Säge* saw, L *secāre* cut] – **sawer,** *n.*

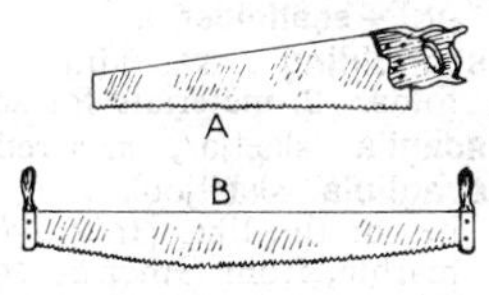

A, handsaw; B, two-handed crosscut saw

**saw**[2] /sɔ/, *v.* past tense of **see**[1].

**saw**[3] /sɔ/, *n.* a sententious saying; maxim; proverb: *he could muster an old saw for almost every occasion.* [ME; OE *sagu,* c. G *Sage,* Icel. *saga* SAGA; akin to SAY]

**sawbill** /ˈsɔbɪl/, *n.* any of the mergansers of the sub-family Merginae.

**sawbones** /ˈsɔbounz/, *n. Colloq.* a surgeon.

**sawdust** /ˈsɔdʌst/, *n.* small particles of wood produced in sawing.

**sawfish** /ˈsɔfɪʃ/, *n., pl.* **-fishes,** (*esp. collectively*) **-fish.** a large, elongate ray (genus *Pristis*) of tropical coasts and lowland rivers, with a bladelike snout bearing strong teeth on each side.

**sawfly** /ˈsɔflaɪ/, *n., pl.* **-flies.** any of the hymenopterous insects constituting the family Tenthredinidae, the females of which are characterised by a pair of saw-like organs for cutting slits in plants to hold their eggs.

sawfish

**sawgrass** /ˈsɔgras/, *n.* any of various plants of the family Cyperaceae, esp. of the genus *Cladium,* with the margins of the leaves toothed like a saw.

**sawhorse** /ˈsɔhɔs/, *n.* a movable frame for holding wood that is being sawn.

**sawlog** /ˈsɔlɒg/, *n.* a log large enough to saw into boards.

**sawmill** /ˈsɔmɪl/, *n.* an establishment in which timber is sawn into planks, boards, etc., by machinery.

**sawney** /ˈsɔni/, *adj.* **1.** sentimental. **2.** weak; effeminate. Also, **sorney.**

**sawn-off shotgun** /sɔn-ɒf ˈʃɒtgʌn/, *n.* a shotgun, the barrel of which has been sawn off.

**sawpit** /ˈsɔpɪt/, *n.* a pit in the ground over which trees are placed for sawing up.

**saw sedge** /ˈsɔ sɛdʒ/, *n.* any of various species of the genus *Gahnia,* esp. *G. aspera,* having long grass-like leaves with sharp, saw-edged margins; widespread in the sandy coastal areas of Australia.

**sawset** /ˈsɔsɛt/, *n.* an instrument used to bend the point of each alternate tooth of a saw out slightly so that the kerf made by the saw will be wider than its blade.

**saw shark** /ˈsɔ ʃak/, *n.* a shark, *Pristiophorus cirratus,* having an elongate snout with laterally projecting spines, differing from saw-fish in having two tentacles placed halfway along the saw and gills on the side of the head rather than under it.

**saw-toothed** /ˈsɔ-tuθt/, *adj.* having a shape or profile similar to the teeth of a saw.

**sawtooth roof** /ˈsɔtuθ ruf/, *n.* a roof which in section has a shape similar to the teeth of a saw. Also (in the Southern Hemisphere) **southlight roof,** and (in the Northern Hemisphere) **northlight roof.**

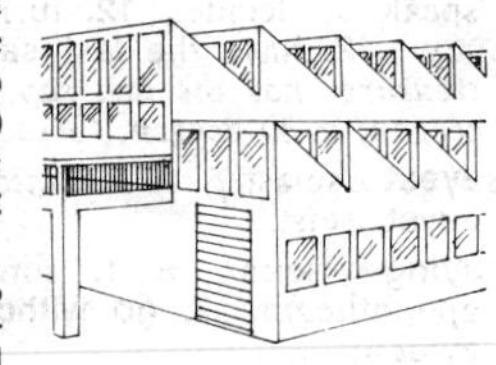
sawtooth roof

**saw-tooth tortoise** /sɔ-tuθ ˈtɔtəs/, *n.* a water tortoise, *Emydura latissternum,* of Australian inland rivers and lakes, distinguished by the serrated appearance of the posterior margin of the carapace.

**sawyer** /ˈsɔjə/, *n.* one who saws, esp. as an occupation. [ME *sawier,* from SAW[1] + -IER]

**sax**[1] /sæks/, *n.* an axelike tool for cutting roofing slate. [ME *sex,* OE *seax* knife]

**sax**[2] /sæks/, *n. Colloq.* a saxophone.

**saxatile** /ˈsæksətaɪl/, *adj.* living or growing on or among rocks. [L *saxātilis*]

**saxboard** /ˈsæksbɔd/, *n.* the part of each side of a rowing boat, stronger and thicker than the skin forming the hull, to which the riggers are attached.

**saxe blue** /sæks ˈblu/, *adj., n.* a shade of greenish light blue.

**saxhorn** /ˈsækshɔn/, *n.* any of a family of brass instruments close to the cornets and tubas. [named after Adolphe *Sax,* 1814-94, a Belgian, who invented the instrument]

saxhorn

**saxicolous** /sækˈsɪkələs/, *adj.* living or growing among rocks. Also, **saxicoline** /sækˈsɪkəlaɪn/. [L *saxi-* (combining form of *saxum* rock) + *-cola* dweller + -OUS]

**saxifragaceous** /sæksəfrəˈgeɪʃəs/, *adj.* belonging to the Saxifragaceae, or saxifrage family of plants.

**saxifrage** /ˈsæksəfrɪdʒ/, *n.* any of the plants, mostly perennial herbs, constituting the genus *Saxifraga,* many of which grow wild in the clefts of rocks, others being cultivated for their flowers. [ME, from L *saxifraga* (*herba*), lit., rock-breaking herb]

**Saxon** /ˈsæksən/, *n.* **1.** a person of the English race or of English descent. **2.** an Anglo-Saxon. **3.** Anglo-Saxon (language). **4.** the Old English dialects of the regions settled by the Saxons. **5.** the dialect of Old Low German spoken by the Saxons (def. 7). **6.** a native or inhabitant of Saxony in modern Germany. **7.** a member of a Germanic people anciently dwelling near the mouth of the Elbe, a portion of whom invaded and occupied parts of Britain in the 5th and 6th centuries. *–adj.* **8.** English. **9.** of or pertaining to the early Saxons (def. 7) or their language. **10.** of or pertaining to Saxony in modern Germany. [ME, from L *Saxo, Saxonēs* (pl.), from Gmc; replacing OE *Seaxan*, pl., from Gmc]

**saxony** /ˈsæksəni/, *n.* **1.** a fine woollen yarn for knitting, etc., originally made from the wool of sheep raised in Saxony, Germany. **2.** cloth made from this yarn.

**saxophone** /ˈsæksəfoun/, *n.* a musical wind instrument consisting of a conical metal tube (usu. brass) with keys or valves, and a clarinet mouthpiece. [*sax* (as in SAXHORN) + -O- + -PHONE] – **saxophonist** /sækˈsɒfənəst/, *n.*

saxophone

**saxtuba** /sæksˈtjubə/, *n.* a large (bass) form of saxhorn. [*sax* (as in SAXHORN) + TUBA]

**say** /seɪ/, *v.*, **said, saying,** *n.* *–v.t.* **1.** to utter or pronounce; speak. **2.** to express in words; state; declare. **3.** to state as an opinion, or with assurance. **4.** to recite or repeat: *to say one's prayers.* **5.** to assume as a hypothesis or an estimate: *to learn in, say, ten lessons.* **6.** to report or allege; maintain: *people say he will resign.* *–v.i.* **7.** to speak; declare; express an opinion. **8. that is to say,** in other words; otherwise. **9. I say,** an exclamation to attract attention or to express surprise, protest, joy, etc. *–n.* **10.** what a person says or has to say. **11.** *Colloq.* the right or opportunity to say, speak or decide. **12.** turn to say something: *it is now my say.* **13. have the last say,** to have the final authority: *the treasurer has the last say on a budget of this size.* [ME; OE *secgan*, c. D *zeggen*, G *sagen*, Icel. *segja*] – **sayer,** *n.*

**sayest** /ˈseɪəst/, *v. Archaic.* 2nd person singular of say. Also, **sayst** /seɪst/.

**saying** /ˈseɪɪŋ/, *n.* **1.** something said, esp. a proverb or apophthegm. **2. go without saying,** to be completely self-evident.

**say-so** /ˈseɪ-sou/, *n. Colloq.* **1.** one's personal statement or assertion. **2.** final authority. **3.** a command.

**sb,** stilb.

**sb.,** substantive.

**s.b.,** single-breasted.

**Sb,** antimony. [L *stibium*]

**S-bend** /ˈɛs-bɛnd/, *n.* **1.** an S-shaped bend in a pipe, as one forming an air-trap in a water closet. **2.** an S-shaped bend in a road, track, etc.

**SBR,** styrene-butadiene rubber.

**sc.,** **1.** scilicet. **2.** scene.

**s.c.,** **1.** self-contained. **2.** single column.

**Sc,** *Chem.* scandium.

**Sc.,** Science.

**S.C.,** **1.** Security Council. **2.** Signal Corps. **3.** Staff Corps. **4.** Supreme Court. **5.** Single Certificated.

**scab** /skæb/, *n., v.,* **scabbed, scabbing.** *–n.* **1.** the encrustation which forms over a sore during healing. **2.** *Vet. Sci.* a mangy disease in animals, esp. sheep; scabies. **3.** *Plant Pathol.* a hyperplasic plant disease with scablike lesions: *apple scab.* **4.** one who continues to work during a strike, takes a striker's place or refuses to join a union, etc.; blackleg. **5.** *Colloq.* a scoundrel. **6.** a fungus disease of potatoes. *–v.i.* **7.** to become covered with a scab. **8.** to act or work as a scab. **9.** *Civ. Eng.* (of a road surface) to loosen aggregate and form potholes. [ME, from Scand.; cf. Swed. *skabb*, c. d. E *shab*, OE *sceabb.* See SHABBY] – **scablike,** *adj.*

**scabbard** /ˈskæbəd/, *n.* **1.** a sheath or cover for the blade of a sword, dagger, or the like. *–v.t.* **2.** to put into a scabbard; sheathe. [ME *scauberd*, from AF *escauberz* (pl.); probably of Gmc orig.]

**scabbard fish** /ˈ– fɪʃ/, *n.* any salt-water fish of the family Trichiuridae, with dagger-like teeth and a thin, whip-shaped body; distributed throughout the world.

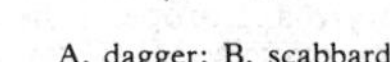


A, dagger; B, scabbard

**scabble** /ˈskæbəl/, *v.t.*, **-led, -ling.** to shape or dress (stone or concrete) roughly, as for providing a key for adhesion of a finish. Also, **scapple.** [F *escapeler* dress timber]

**scabby** /ˈskæbi/, *adj.*, **-bier, -biest.** **1.** covered with scabs; blotchy. **2.** consisting of scabs. **3.** affected with the scab. **4.** *Colloq.* mean or contemptible: *that was a scabby trick.*

**scabby mouth** /ˈ– mauθ/, *n.* a contagious disease of sheep and goats, caused by a virus and resulting in sores around the mouth.

**scabies** /ˈskeɪbiz, -biiz/, *n.* any of several infectious skin diseases occurring in sheep and cattle, and in man, caused by parasitic mites; itch. [L: roughness, the itch (from *scabere* scratch, scrape, c. SHAVE)] – **scabietic** /ˌskeɪbiˈɛtɪk/, *adj.*

**scabious**[1] /ˈskeɪbiəs/, *adj.* **1.** scabby. **2.** pertaining to or of the nature of scabies. [L *scabiōsus*]

**scabious**[2] /ˈskeɪbiəs/, *n.* any plant of the genus *Scabiosa*, comprising a large number of hairy herbs with flowers in dense heads, as *S. Caucasica*, a perennial plant, often cultivated. [ME *scabiose*, from ML *scabiōsa* (*herba*) scabies-curing (herb)]

**scabland** /ˈskæblænd/, *n.* rough, barren, badly eroded topography with thin soils and little vegetation.

**scabrous** /ˈskæbrəs, ˈskeɪ-/, *adj.* **1.** rough with minute points or projections. **2.** harsh; full of difficulties. **3.** bordering on the indecent; risqué. [LL *scabrōsus*, from L *scaber* rough] – **scabrously,** *adv.* – **scabrousness,** *n.*

**scad** /skæd/, *n.* (*usu. pl.*) *Colloq.* a large quantity: *he has scads of money.* [orig. uncert.]

**scaffold** /ˈskæfəld, -ould/, *n.* **1.** a temporary structure for holding workmen and materials during the erection, repair, cleaning, or decoration of a building. **2.** an elevated platform on which a criminal is executed. **3.** a raised platform or stage for exhibiting spectacles, seating spectators, etc. **4.** any raised framework. **5.** scaffolding. *–v.t.* **6.** to furnish with a scaffold or scaffolding. **7.** to support by or place on a scaffold. [ME, from OF *escafaud*, from *es-* E- + *cafaud*, from LL *catafalicum*, from *cata-* CATA- + *fala* tower, gallery + *-icum* -IC] – **scaffolder,** *n.*

**scaffolding** /ˈskæfəldɪŋ/, *n.* **1.** a scaffold or system of scaffolds. **2.** materials for scaffolds.

**scaglia** /ˈskæljə/, *n.* a reddish Italian limestone.

**scagliola** /skælˈjoulə/, *n.* plasterwork imitating marble, granite, or the like. [It. *scagliuola*, diminutive of *scaglia* chip of marble, from Gmc; cf. SCALE[1]]

**scalable** /ˈskeɪləbəl/, *adj.* that may be scaled: *the scalable slope of a mountain.*

**scalar** /ˈskeɪlə/, *Maths.* *–adj.* **1.** representable by position on a line; having only magnitude: *a scalar variable.* **2.** of or pertaining to a scalar, or something utilising scalars. *–n.* **3.** a quantity possessing only magnitude (contrasted with a *vector*). [L *scālāris*]

**scalare** /skəˈlari/, *n.* →**angelfish** (def. 3). [NL, from Pg., from L, neut. of *scālāris* ladder-like (from the markings)]

**scalariform** /skəˈlærəfɔm/, *adj. Biol.* ladder-like. [NL *scālāriformis*, from L *scālāris* SCALAR. See -FORM]

**scalawag** /ˈskæləwæg/, *n.* →**scallywag.**

**scald** /skɔld/, *v.t.* **1.** to burn or affect painfully with, or as with, hot liquid or steam. **2.** to subject to the action of boiling or hot liquid. **3.** to heat to a temperature just short of the boiling point: *to scald milk.* *–v.i.* **4.** to be or become scalded. *–n.* **5.** a burn caused by hot liquid or steam. **6.** any similar condition, esp. as the result of too much heat or sunlight. **7.** *Plant Pathol.* one of several non-parasitic diseases, esp. of the apple, which resemble the effects of too much heat or sunlight. [ME *skalde(n)*, from ONF *escalder* burn, scald, from LL *excaldāre* wash in hot water]

**scalding** /ˈskɔldɪŋ/, *adj.* **1.** hot enough to scald. **2.** bitter and crushing: *a scalding reply.*

**scale**[1] /skeɪl/, *n., v.,* **scaled, scaling.** *–n.* **1.** one of the thin, flat, horny or hard plates that form the covering of certain animals, as fishes. **2.** any thin platelike piece, lamina, or flake such as peels off from a surface. **3.** *Bot.* **a.** a small rudimentary body, usu. a specialised leaf, covering the leaf buds of deciduous trees in cold climates. **b.** a thin scarious or membranous part of a plant, as a bract of a catkin. **c.** the fleshy food storage structures of a bulb. **4.** a scale insect. **5.** the protective covering secreted by the scale insect. **6.** *Metall.* **a.** the crust of metallic oxide formed by cooling of hot metals in air. **b.** the encrustation caused in steam boilers by the evaporation of water containing mineral salts. **c.** a fault in glass or vitreous enamelware, in the form of an embedded particle of metal oxide or carbon. *–v.t.* **7.** to remove the scales or scale from: *to scale fish.* **8.** *Metall.* to remove the film of oxide formed on the surface of a metal. **9.** to remove in scales or thin layers. **10.** to cover with an encrustation or scale. **11.** to skip, as a stone over water. **12.** to change an amount according to a fixed proportion (oft. fol. by *down* for a reduction, *up* for an increase): *to scale the wage demands up or down.* *–v.i.* **13.** to come off in scales. **14.** to shed scales. **15.** to become coated with scale, as the inside of a boiler. [ME, from OF, aphetic modification of *escale;* of Gmc orig.] – **scalelike,** *adj.*

**scale**[2] /skeɪl/, *n., v.,* **scaled, scaling.** *–n.* **1.** the pan, or either of the pans or dishes, of a balance. **2.** (*usu. pl.*) a balance, or any of various other more or less complicated devices for weighing. **3. the Scales,** *Astron.* the zodiacal constellation or sign Libra; the Balance. **4. turn the scale(s),** to determine the outcome of something that has been in doubt. **5. tip the scale(s), a.** to weigh (fol. by *at*). **b.** to influence favourably. *–v.t.* **6.** to weigh in or as in scales. **7.** to have a weight of. [ME, from Scand.; cf. Icel. *skālar* (pl.), c. OE *scealu* scale (of a balance)]

**scale**[3] /skeɪl/, *n., v.,* **scaled, scaling.** *–n.* **1.** a succession or progression of steps or degrees; a graduated series. **2.** a point on such a scale. **3.** a series of marks laid down at determinate distances, as along a line, for purposes of measurement or computation: *the scale of a thermometer.* **4.** a graduated line, as on a map, representing proportionate size. **5.** a graduated table of prices, wages, etc. **6.** an instrument with graduated spaces, for measuring, etc. **7.** the proportion which the representation of an object bears to the object: *a model on a scale of one centimetre to a metre.* **8.** the ratio of distances (or, less commonly, of areas) on a map to the corresponding values on the earth. **9.** a certain relative or proportionate size or extent: *a residence on a yet more magnificent scale.* **10.** a standard of measurement or estimation. **11.** *Arith.* a system of numerical notation: *the decimal scale.* **12.** *Music.* a succession of notes ascending or descending according to fixed intervals, esp. such a series beginning on a particular note: *the major scale of C.* **13.** *Music.* the compass or range of a voice or an instrument. **14.** *Educ., Psychol.* a graded series of tests or tasks for measuring intelligence, achievement, adjustment, etc. **15.** *Obs.* anything by which one may ascend. **16.** *Obs.* a ladder; a flight of stairs. *–v.t.* **17.** to climb by, or as by, a ladder; climb up or over. **18.** *Colloq.* to ride on a public conveyance, esp. a tram, without paying a fare: *scale a rattler.* **19.** to make according to scale. **20.** to reduce in amount according to a fixed scale or proportion (oft. fol. by *down*): *to scale down wages.* **21.** to measure by, or as if by, a scale. *–v.i.* **22.** to climb; ascend; mount. **23.** to progress in a graduated series. [ME, from L *scāla* staircase, ladder]

scale[3] (def. 12): major diatonic scale

**scalebird** /ˈskeɪlbɜd/, *n.* →**pallid cuckoo.**

**scaleboard** /ˈskeɪlbɔd, ˈskæbəd/, *n.* **1.** a very thin board, as for the back of a picture. **2.** *Print.* a thin strip of wood used in justifying. **3.** a thin sheet of wood used as veneer, etc. [SCALE[1] + BOARD]

**scaled score** /ˈskeɪld skɔ/, *n.* the mark or result awarded to an examination candidate as a result of adjusting his raw score to be comparable to those of other candidates, classes, or schools.

**scale insect** /ˈskeɪl ˌɪnsɛkt/, *n.* any of various small plant-destroying insects of the homopterous family Coccidae, the females of which mostly have the body and eggs covered by a large scale or shield formed by secretions.

**scalene** /ˈskeɪlin/, *adj.* **1.** *Anat.* referring to one of a group of deep muscles in the front and sides of the neck. **2.** *Geom.* **a.** (of a cone, etc.) having the axis inclined to the base. **b.** (of a triangle) having three unequal sides. [LL *scalēnus,* from Gk *skalēnós* unequal]

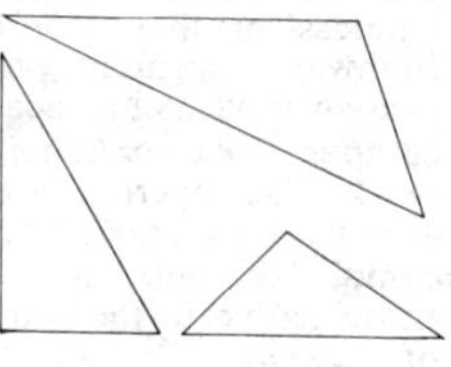

scalene triangles

**scaler** /ˈskeɪlə/, *n.* **1.** *Electronics.* any electronic device which produces an electrical pulse on an output line every time it receives a prescribed number of pulses on an input line. **2.** *Colloq.* one who evades paying a fare on a bus, train, etc.

**scallawag** /ˈskæləwæg/, *n.* →**scallywag.**

**scallion** /ˈskæljən/, *n. Chiefly U.S.* **1.** any onion which does not form a large bulb; spring onion. **2.** →**shallot. 3.** →**leek.** [ME *scalyon,* from AF *scal(o)un,* from L *(caepa) Ascalōnia* Ascalonian onion, from *Ascalon,* var. of *Ashkelon,* city in Palestine]

**scallop** /ˈskɒləp/, *n.* **1.** any of various bivalve molluscs of the genus *Pecten* and allied genera, having fluted shell valves that they clap together to accomplish swimming. **2.** the adductor muscle of certain species of such molluscs, esteemed as an article of food. **3.** one of the shells of such a mollusc, usu. having radial ribs and a wavy outer edge. **4.** a scallop shell or a dish in which flaked fish or the like is baked and served. **5.** one of a series of rounded projections along the edge of pastry, a garment, cloth, etc. **6.** →**potato scallop.** *–v.t.* **7.** to finish (an edge) with scallops. **8.** to bake (food, usu. cut in pieces) in a scallop shell or small container, usu. combined with a creamy sauce and topped with breadcrumbs; escallop. Also, **scollop.** [ME *scalop,* from OF, aphetic modification of *escalope* shell; of Gmc orig. Cf. D *schelp* shell] – **scalloper,** *n.*

**scallywag** /ˈskæliwæg/, *n.* (*oft. used indulgently of children*) a scamp; rascal. Also, **scalawag, scallawag.** [orig. uncert.]

**scaloppine** /skæləˈpini/, *n.* a small, thin slice of veal or other meat, esp. when cooked in a tomato or wine sauce. [It.]

**scalp** /skælp/, *n.* **1.** the integument of the upper part of the head, usu. including the associated subcutaneous structures. **2.** a part of this integument with the accompanying hair, taken by certain North American Indians as a trophy of victory. **3.** any token of victory. **4.** the integument on the top of an animal's head, esp. a canine's. **5.** a bed of oysters or mussels. **6.** *Colloq.* a small profit made in quick buying and selling. *–v.t.* **7.** to cut or tear the scalp from. **8.** *Colloq.* to buy and sell so as to make small, quick profits, as stocks. **9.** *Colloq.* to buy (tickets) cheap and sell at other than official rates. *–v.i.* **10.** *Colloq.* to scalp tickets, stocks, etc. [ME (northern d.), from Scand.; cf. Icel. *skālpr* leather sheath, d. Dan. *skalp* shell] – **scalper,** *n.*

**scalpel** /ˈskælpəl/, *n.* a small, light, usu. straight knife used in surgical and anatomical operations and dissections. [L *scalpellum,* diminutive of *scalprum* knife]

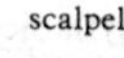

scalpel

**scalper** /ˈskælpə/, *n.* a person who sells at an exorbitant price tickets which he has obtained to a sporting event, pop concert, etc., which is sold out.

**scalp-lock** /ˈskælp-lɒk/, *n.* a long lock or tuft of hair left on the scalp by certain North American Indians as an implied challenge to their enemies.

**scaly** /ˈskeɪli/, *adj.,* **-lier, -liest. 1.** covered with or abounding in scales or scale. **2.** characterised by or consisting of scales; scalelike. **3.** peeling or flaking off in scales. **4.** *Colloq.* shabby; despicable. [SCALE[1] + -Y[1]] – **scaliness,** *n.*

**scaly anteater** /– ˈæntitə/, *n.* →**pangolin.**

**scaly foot** /ˈ– fʊt/, *n.* an elongated, pygopod lizard, *Pygopus lepidopodus,* with vestigial hind limbs resembling scaly flaps.

**scam** /skæm/, *n. Colloq.* an illegal business operation.

**scammony** /'skæməni/, *n.* **1.** a twining Asiatic species of convolvulus, *Convolvulus scammonia.* **2.** the cathartic gum resin obtained from its root. [ME and OE *scamonie,* from L *scammōnia,* from Gk *skammōnía*]

**scamp** /skæmp/, *n.* **1.** a worthless person; rascal. **2.** a mischievous child. *–v.t.* **3.** to perform (work, etc.) in a hasty or careless manner. [special uses of obs. *scamp,* v., go (on highways), apparently from D (obs.) *schampen* flee, from OF *escamper* DECAMP] – **scampish,** *adj.*

**scamper** /'skæmpə/, *v.i.* **1.** to run or go hastily or quickly. *–n.* **2.** a scampering; a quick run. **3.** one who or that which scamps. [obs. *scamp,* v., go + -ER[6]. See SCAMP, *n.*]

**scampi** /'skæmpi/, *n.pl.* very large prawns, esp. and originally those native to the Adriatic, used in Italian cookery. [It., pl. of *scampo*]

**scan** /skæn/, *v.,* **scanned, scanning,** *n. –v.t.* **1.** to examine minutely; scrutinise. **2.** to glance at or run through hastily: *to scan a page.* **3.** to analyse (verse) as to its prosodic or metrical structure; read or recite so as to indicate or test the metrical form. **4.** *Television.* to traverse (a surface) with a beam of light or electrons in order to reproduce or transmit a picture. **5.** *Radar.* to sweep a region with a beam from a radar transmitter. **6.** *Computers.* to examine every item in (a record or file). *–v.i.* **7.** to examine the metre of verse. **8.** (of verse) to conform to the rules of metre. **9.** *Television.* to scan a surface. *–n.* **10.** the act of scanning; close examination or scrutiny. [ME *scanne,* from LL *scandere* scan verse, from L: climb] – **scannable,** *adj.* – **scanner,** *n.*

**Scand.,** **1.** Scandinavia. **2.** Scandinavian.

**scandal** /'skændl/, *n., v.,* **-dalled, -dalling** or (*U.S.*) **-daled, -daling.** *–n.* **1.** a disgraceful or discreditable action, circumstance, etc. **2.** offence caused by faults or misdeeds. **3.** damage to reputation; disgrace. **4.** defamatory talk; malicious gossip. **5.** *Colloq.* gossip in general. **6.** a person whose conduct brings disgrace or offence. *–v.t.* **7.** *Archaic.* to spread scandal concerning. [LL *scandalum* cause of offence, from Gk *skándalon* trap; replacing ME *scandle,* from ONF]

**scandalise** /'skændəlaɪz/, *v.t.,* **-lised, -lising.** to shock or horrify by something considered immoral or improper. Also, **scandalize.** – **scandaliser,** *n.*

**scandalmonger** /'skændlmʌŋgə/, *n.* one who spreads scandal.

**scandalous** /'skændələs/, *adj.* **1.** disgraceful to reputation; shameful or shocking. **2.** defamatory or libellous, as a speech or writing. – **scandalously,** *adv.*

**scandent** /'skændənt/, *adj.* climbing, as a plant. [L *scandens,* ppr.]

**scandia** /'skændiə/, *n.* oxide of scandium, $Sc_2O_3$, a white infusible powder. [special use of L *Scandia* Scandinavia]

**scandic** /'skændɪk/, *adj.* of or pertaining to scandium: *scandic oxide.*

**Scandinavia** /skændə'neɪviə/, *n.* **1.** the collective name of Norway, Sweden, Denmark, and sometimes also Finland and Iceland. **2.** the peninsula consisting of Norway and Sweden. [L (Pliny), of Gmc orig.; cf. OE *Scedenig*]

**Scandinavian** /skændə'neɪviən/, *adj.* **1.** of or pertaining to Scandinavia, its inhabitants, or their languages. *–n.* **2.** a native or inhabitant of Scandinavia. **3.** the subgroup of Germanic languages that includes the languages of Scandinavia and Iceland in their historical and modern forms; North Germanic.

**scandium** /'skændiəm/, *n.* a silvery white, trivalent metal present in euxenite and wolframite, quite common but difficult to separate. *Symbol:* Sc; *at. wt.:* 44.956; *at. no.:* 21; *sp.gr.:* 2.99 at 20°C. [NL. See SCANDIA, -IUM]

**scanner** /'skænə/, *n.* **1.** one who or that which scans. **2.** *Television.* →**flying spot scanner.** **3.** *Computers.* →**optical scanner.**

**scansion** /'skænʃən/, *n.* the metrical analysis of verse. The usual marks for scansion are ˘ or × for a short or unaccented syllable, ¯ or ´ for a long or accented syllable, ˆ for a rest,| for a foot division, and ‖ for a caesura or pause. [L *scansio,* lit., a climbing]

**scansorial** /skæn'sɔriəl/, *adj.* **1.** capable of or adapted for climbing, as the feet of certain birds, lizards, etc. **2.** habitually climbing, as a woodpecker. [L *scansōrius* used for climbing + -AL[1]]

**scant** /skænt/, *adj.* **1.** barely sufficient in amount or quantity; not abundant; inadequate: *to do scant justice.* **2.** limited; not large: *a scant amount.* **3.** barely amounting to as much as indicated: *a scant two hours.* **4.** having an inadequate or limited supply (fol. by *of*): *scant of breath.* *–v.t.* **5.** to make scant; cut down; diminish. **6.** to stint the supply of; withhold. **7.** to treat slightly or inadequately. *–adv.* **8.** *Archaic.* scarcely; barely; hardly. [ME, from Scand.; cf. Icel. *skamt,* neut. of *skammr* short] – **scantly,** *adv.* – **scantness,** *n.*

**scanties** /'skæntiz/, *n.pl. Colloq.* very short close-fitting panties, of fine, soft material, for women.

**scantling** /'skæntlɪŋ/, *n.* **1.** a timber of comparatively small cross-section, as a rafter or a purlin. **2.** such timbers collectively. **3.** the size of a timber in width and thickness, or the dimensions of a stone or other building material. **4.** a small quantity or amount. **5.** (*pl.*) *Naut.* the sizes of the component parts of a ship. [late ME *scantillon,* from OF, aphetic modification of *escantillon,* from ML *scandalium,* from L *scandere* climb]

**scanty** /'skænti/, *adj.,* **scantier, scantiest.** **1.** scant in amount, quantity, etc.; barely sufficient. **2.** meagre; not adequate. **3.** lacking amplitude in extent or compass. – **scantily,** *adv.* – **scantiness,** *n.*

**scape**[1] /skeɪp/, *n.* **1.** *Bot.* a leafless peduncle rising from the ground. **2.** *Zool.* a stemlike part, as the shaft of a feather. **3.** *Archit.* the shaft of a column. [L *scāpus,* from Gk (Doric) *skâpos* staff, sceptre]

**scape**[2] /skeɪp/, *n., v.t., v.i.,* **scaped, scaping.** *Archaic.* →**escape.** Also, **'scape.** [ME, aphetic var. of ESCAPE]

**-scape,** a suffix indicating a view or expanse of the particular location indicated: *streetscape, desertscape, sandscape, cityscape.* [from (LAND)SCAPE]

S, scape[1]

**scapegoat** /'skeɪpgoʊt/, *n.* one who is made to bear the blame for others or to suffer in their place. [SCAPE[2], *v.* + GOAT; orig. with ref. to the goat, in ancient Jewish ritual, sent into the wilderness after the chief priest on the Day of Atonement had symbolically laid the sins of the people upon it (see Lev. 16)]

**scapegrace** /'skeɪpgreɪs/, *n.* a reckless, good-for-nothing person; a ne'er-do-well; a scamp. [short for phrase, '(one who) *escapes* (divine) *grace*']

**scapewheel** /'skeɪpwil/, *n.* →**escape wheel.** [SCAPE[2] + WHEEL]

**scaphoid** /'skæfɔɪd/, *adj.* **1.** boat-shaped. **2.** *Anat.* denoting esp. a bone of the radial side of the carpus, or a bone on the inner side of the tarsus. *–n.* **3.** *Anat.* a scaphoid bone. [NL *scaphoīdēs,* from Gk *skaphoeidḗs*]

**scaphopod** /'skæfəpɒd/, *n.* a member of the Scaphopoda, a class of molluscs with a tubular shell open at both ends. – **scaphopodous** /skæ'fɒpədəs/, *adj.*

**scapolite** /'skæpəlaɪt/, *n.* any of a group of minerals of variable composition, essentially silicates of aluminium, calcium, and sodium, occurring in crystals and also massive, and usually white or greyish white; wernerite. [G *Skapolith.* See SCAPE[1], -LITE]

**scapose** /'skeɪpoʊs/, *adj.* **1.** (of a plant) having scapes. **2.** (of a plant part) consisting of a scape; resembling a scape. [SCAPE[1] + -OSE[1]]

**scapple** /'skæpəl/, *v.t.,* **-led, -ling.** →**scabble.**

**s. caps,** small capitals.

**scapula** /'skæpjələ/, *n., pl.* **-lae** /-li/. **1.** *Anat.* either of two flat, triangular bones, each forming the back part of a shoulder; a shoulder-blade. **2.** *Zool.* a dorsal bone of the pectoral arch. [NL: shoulder blade (in L only in pl.)]

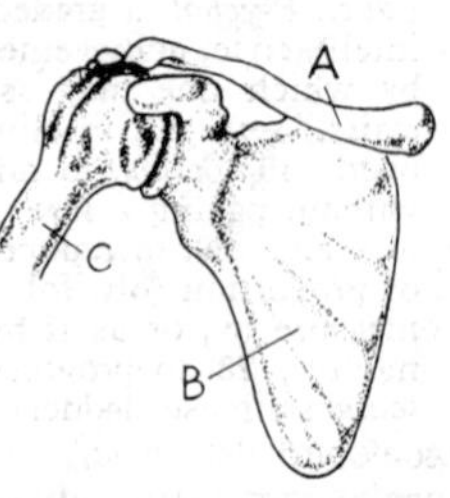

A, clavicle; B, scapula; C, humerus

**scapular** /'skæpjələ/, *adj.* **1.** of or pertaining to the shoulders or the scapula or scapulae. [NL *scapularis*] *–n.* **2.** *Eccles.* a loose, sleeveless monastic garment, hanging from the shoulders. **3.** two small pieces of woollen cloth, joined by strings passing over the shoulders, worn under the ordinary clothing as a badge of affiliation with a religious order, a token of devotion, etc. **4.** *Surg.* a shoulder dressing which keeps the shoulder or another bandage in place. **5.** *Ornith.* a scapular feather. [ME *scapulare,* from LL, from L *scapulae* shoulders]

**scapulary** /ˈskæpjələri/, *adj., n., pl.* **-laries.** →**scapular.**

**scar**[1] /ska/, *n., v.,* **scarred, scarring.** *–n.* **1.** the mark left by a healed wound, sore, or burn. **2.** any blemish remaining as a trace or result: *scars upon one's good name.* **3.** *Bot.* a mark indicating a former point of attachment, as where a leaf has fallen from a stem. *–v.t.* **4.** to mark with a scar. *–v.i.* **5.** to heal with a resulting scar. [ME, from OF, aphetic modification of *escare,* from LL *eschara* scab, from Gk: lit., hearth]

**scar**[2] /ska/, *n.* **1.** a precipitous rocky place; a cliff. **2.** a low or submerged rock in the sea. [ME *skerre,* from Scand.]

**scarab** /ˈskærəb/, *n.* **1.** any scarabaeid beetle, esp. *Scarabaeus sacer,* regarded as sacred by the ancient Egyptians. **2.** a representation or image of a beetle, much used among the ancient Egyptians as a symbol, seal, amulet, or the like. **3.** a gem (as of emerald, green felspar, etc.) cut in the form of a beetle. [L *scarabaeus;* cf. Gk *kárabos* a kind of beetle]

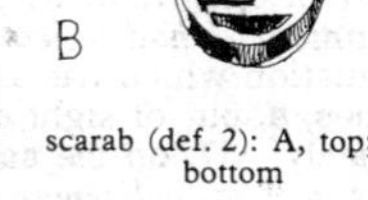

scarab (def. 2): A, top; B, bottom

**scarabaeid** /skærəˈbiəd/, *adj.* **1.** belonging or pertaining to the Scarabaeidae, a family of lamellicorn beetles, including the scarabs, June bugs, dung beetles, cockchafers, etc. *–n.* **2.** any scarabaeid beetle. [NL *scarabaeidae,* from L *scarabaeus.* See SCARAB, -ID[2]]

**scarabaeoid** /skærəˈbiɔɪd/, *adj.* Also, **scaraboid** /ˈskærəbɔɪd/. **1.** resembling a scarab. **2.** of the nature of, or resembling, a scarabaeid. *–n.* **3.** an imitation or counterfeit scarab (def. 3).

**scarabaeus** /skærəˈbiəs/, *n., pl.* **-baeuses, -baei** /-ˈbiaɪ/. →**scarab** (defs 2 and 3).

**Scaramouch** /ˈskærəmuʃ, -mutʃ, -maʊtʃ/, *n.* **1.** a stock character in Italian comedy and farce, a cowardly braggart who is constantly beaten by Harlequin. **2.** (*l.c.*) a rascal or scamp. Also, **Scaramouche.** [F *Scaramouche,* from It. *Scaramuccia,* lit., SKIRMISH]

**scarce** /skɛəs/, *adj.,* **scarcer, scarcest,** *adv. –adj.* **1.** insufficient for the need or demand; not abundant: *commodities scarce in wartime.* **2.** seldom met with; rare: *a scarce book.* **3. make oneself scarce,** *Colloq.* to make off; keep out of the way. *–adv.* **4.** *Obs.* scarcely. [ME *scars,* from ONF: scanty, stingy, from LL *excarpere,* replacing L *excerpere* excerpt, pluck] – **scarceness,** *n.*

**scarcely** /ˈskɛəsli/, *adv.* **1.** barely; hardly; not quite. **2.** definitely not. **3.** probably not.

**scarcement** /ˈskɛəsmənt/, *n.* a footing or ledge formed by an offset in a wall.

**scarcity** /ˈskɛəsəti/, *n., pl.* **-ties.** **1.** insufficiency or shortness of supply; dearth. **2.** rarity; infrequency.

**scare** /skɛə/, *v.,* **scared, scaring,** *n. –v.t.* **1.** to strike with sudden fear or terror. **2.** to drive off; frighten away. *–v.i.* **3.** to become frightened: *that horse scares easily. –n.* **4.** a sudden fright or alarm, esp. with little or no ground. **5.** a time or state of widespread fear, worry, etc. **6.** *Golf.* the part of a club where the head joins the shaft. [unexplained var. of ME *skerre,* from Scand.; cf. Icel. *skirra,* from *skjarr* shy, timid, startled] – **scarer,** *n.* – **scaringly,** *adv.*

**scarecrow** /ˈskɛəkroʊ/, *n.* **1.** an object, usu. a figure of a man in old clothes, set up to frighten crows, etc., away from crops. **2.** a person having a ragged, untidy appearance. **3.** a very thin person. **4.** anything frightening but not really dangerous.

**scared** /skɛəd/, *adj.* **1.** frightened; alarmed. **2. scared stiff,** *Colloq.* very frightened. *–adv.* **3. run scared,** *Colloq.* to panic; retreat in disarray.

**scaredy-cat** /ˈskɛədi-kæt/, *n. Colloq.* a coward.

**scaremonger** /ˈskɛəmʌŋgə/, *n.* one who creates or spreads rumours of a terrifying nature.

**scarf**[1] /skaf/, *n., pl.* **scarfs, scarves** /skavz/, *v. –n.* **1.** a long, broad strip of silk, wool, lace, etc., worn about the neck, shoulders, or head for ornament or protection. **2.** →**headscarf.** *–v.t.* **3.** to cover or wrap with, or as with, a scarf. **4.** to use in the manner of a scarf. [? ONF *escarpe* sash, sling for arm, probably var. of OF *escharpe* a pilgrim's scrip hung round the neck. Cf. Icel. *skreppa* SCRIP[2]]

**scarf**[2] /skaf/, *n., pl.* **scarfs,** *v. –n.* **1.** either of the tapered or specially cut ends of the pieces forming a scarf-joint. **2.** a notch; groove. **3.** *Whaling.* a strip of skin along the body of the whale. *–v.t.* **4.** to join by a scarf or over-lapping joint. **5.** to form a scarf, chamfer, or the like on, for a scarf-joint. **6.** to cut a vee notch in a tree to direct its falling. **7.** *Whaling.* to make a groove in (a whale) and remove the blubber and skin. [Scand.; cf. Swed. *skarf* in like senses] – **scarfer,** *n.*

**scarf-joint** /ˈskaf-dʒɔɪnt/, *n.* a joint by which the ends of two timbers or the like are fitted with long tapers or laps and glued, nailed, or bolted into a continuous piece.

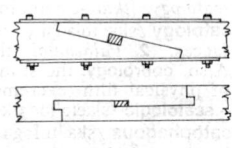

scarf-joints

**scarfskin** /ˈskafskɪn/, *n.* the outermost layer of the skin; the epidermis.

**scarification** /skærəfəˈkeɪʃən, skɛər-/, *n.* **1.** the act of scarifying. **2.** the result of scarifying; a scratch or scratches.

**scarificator** /ˈskærəfəkeɪtə, ˈskɛər-/, *n.* **1.** one who scarifies. **2.** a surgical instrument for scarifying. [NL, from LL *scarīficāre* SCARIFY]

**scarify** /ˈskærəfaɪ, ˈskɛər-/, *v.t.,* **-fied, -fying.** **1.** to make scratches or superficial incisions in (the skin, a wound, etc.), as in surgery. **2.** to lacerate by severe criticism. **3.** to loosen (the soil) with a type of cultivator. **4.** to hasten the sprouting of (hard-covered seeds) by making incisions in the seedcoats. [late ME, from LL *scarīficāre,* from Gk *skariphasthai* scratch an outline] – **scarifier,** *n.*

**scarious** /ˈskɛəriəs/, *adj.* (of a plant part) thin, dry, and membranous, as certain bracts. [NL *scariōsus,* from L *scaria* thorny shrub]

**scarlatina** /skaləˈtinə/, *n.* **1.** →**scarlet fever.** **2.** a mild form of scarlet fever. [NL, from It. *scarlattina* (fem.), diminutive of *scarlatto* scarlet]

**scarlatinoid** /skaləˈtinɔɪd, skəˈlætənɔɪd/, *adj.* resembling scarlatina or its eruption.

**scarlet** /ˈskalət/, *n.* **1.** bright red colour inclining towards orange. **2.** cloth or garments of this colour. *–adj.* **3.** of the colour scarlet. [ME, from OF, aphetic modification of *escarlate,* ? from Pers. *saqalāt* a rich cloth]

**scarlet fever** /– ˈfivə/, *n.* a contagious febrile disease, now chiefly of children, caused by streptococci and characterised by a scarlet eruption.

**scarlet letter** /– ˈlɛtə/, *n.* a scarlet letter 'A', formerly worn esp. in Puritan communities by one convicted of adultery.

**scarlet pimpernel** /– ˈpɪmpənɛl/, *n.* →**pimpernel.**

**scarlet runner** /– ˈrʌnə/, *n.* a climbing bean, *Phaseolus coccinea,* native to South America, and widely cultivated for its edible pods.

**scarlet woman** /– ˈwʊmən/, *n.* a prostitute or immoral woman. [from the woman described in Rev. 17, variously explained as symbolising pagan Rome or (opprobriously) the Church of Rome]

**scarmorze** /skaˈmɔtsi/, *n.* a small, soft, moist, sweet cheese, originally made in Italy from buffalo's milk, but now from cow's milk; commonly used in pizza. [It.]

**scarp** /skap/, *n.* **1.** a steep face on the side of a hill. **2.** *Fort.* the side of a ditch next to a rampart; an escarp. *–v.t.* **3.** to form or cut into a scarp. [It. *scarpa.* See ESCARP]

**scarper** /ˈskapə/, *v.i. Colloq.* to run away; depart suddenly, esp. leaving behind debts or other commitments. [orig. unknown]

**scarves** /skavz/, *n.* plural of **scarf**[1].

**scary** /ˈskɛəri/, *adj.,* **scarier, scariest.** *Colloq.* **1.** causing fright or alarm. **2.** easily frightened; timid.

**scat**[1] /skæt/, *v.t.*, **scatted, scatting.** *Colloq.* to go off hastily (usu. in the imperative).

**scat**[2] /skæt/, *n.*, *v.*, **scatted, scatting.** *–n.* **1.** (in jazz) an improvised form of singing where the vocalist sings nonsense syllables to the tune. **2.** an instrumental equivalent or imitation of this. **3.** an act or instance of doing this. *–v.i.* **4.** to sing scat. [? imitative]

**scathe** /skeɪð/, *v.*, **scathed, scathing,** *n.* *–v.t.* **1.** to attack with severe criticism. **2.** *Archaic.* to hurt, harm, or injure; sear. *–n.* **3.** *Archaic.* hurt, harm, or injury. [ME, from Scand.; cf. Icel. *skathi* harm, damage, c. OE *sc(e)atha* malefactor, injury, G *Schade*] – **scatheless,** *adj.*

**scathing** /ˈskeɪðɪŋ/, *adj.* **1.** intended to hurt the feelings; scornful; contemptuous, as a remark. **2.** that scathes or sears. – **scathingly,** *adv.*

**scato-,** a word element indicating faeces or excrement, as in *scatology.* [*skato-,* combining form of Gk *skôr* dung]

**scatology** /skæˈtɒlədʒi/, *n.* **1.** *Med.* diagnosis by means of the faeces. **2.** *Palaeoniol.* the science of fossil excrement. **3.** Also, **coprology.** the study of, or preoccupation with, images of physical filth (excrement) in literature. [SCATO- + -LOGY] – **scatologic** /skætəˈlɒdʒɪk/, **scatological** /skætəˈlɒdʒɪkəl/, *adj.*

**scatophagous** /skæˈtɒfəgəs/, *adj.* feeding on excrement, as a beetle or fly. [SCATO- + -PHAGOUS]

**scatter** /ˈskætə/, *v.t.* **1.** to throw loosely about; distribute at irregular intervals. **2.** to separate and drive off in various directions; disperse. **3.** *Physics.* as in an interaction with matter, to deflect (any beam of radiation), electromagnetic or particle, into random directions. *–v.i.* **4.** to separate and disperse; go in different directions. *–n.* **5.** the act of scattering. **6.** that which is scattered. **7.** *Colloq.* a drinking spree; bender. [ME *scatere;* orig. uncert.] – **scatterer,** *n.* – **scatteringly,** *adv.*

**scatterbrain** /ˈskætəbreɪn/, *n.* one incapable of serious, connected thought. – **scatterbrained,** *adj.*

**scatter cushion** /ˈskætə kʊʃən/, *n.* a small cushion, often brightly coloured, placed at random on a couch, armchairs, etc.

**scattergood** /ˈskætəgʊd/, *n.* →**spendthrift.**

**scattergram** /ˈskætəgræm/, *n.* a graph displaying (often by a series of dots) the dispersion of a variable, as the examination results of a group of students.

**scattering** /ˈskætərɪŋ/, *adj.* **1.** distributed or occurring here and there at irregular intervals. **2.** straggling, as an assemblage of parts. **3.** *U.S.* (of votes) cast in small numbers for various candidates. **4.** that scatters. *–n.* **5.** a scattered number or quantity. **6.** *Physics.* the process by which any beam of radiation, electromagnetic or particle, is deflected into random directions as a result of its interaction with matter.

**scatter pin** /ˈskætə pɪn/, *n.* a woman's small ornamental pin usu. worn in groups of two or more on a dress, suit, etc.

**scatter rug** /ˈ– rʌg/, *n.* a rug small enough that several can be scattered about a room as partial floor-covering.

**scatty** /ˈskæti/, *adj.* scatterbrained; thoughtless; unreliable.

**scaup duck** /ˈskɒp dʌk/, *n.* any of certain diving ducks of the genus *Aythya,* esp. the **greater scaup,** *A. marila,* of Europe and America. [? phonetic var. of *scalp duck*]

**scavenge** /ˈskævəndʒ/, *v.*, **-enged, -enging.** *–v.t.* **1.** to search for, and take (anything useable) from discarded material. **2.** to expel or sweep out burnt gases from (the cylinder of an internal-combustion engine). **3.** *Metall.* to clean (molten metal) by the introduction of another substance which will combine chemically with the impurities in it. **4.** to cleanse from filth, as a street. *–v.i.* **5.** to act as a scavenger. **6.** to search amongst refuse or any discarded material for anything useable, as food, clothing, etc. **7.** to become scavenged of burnt gases. [backformation from SCAVENGER]

**scavenger** /ˈskævəndʒə/, *n.* **1.** one who, or that which scavenges, as any of various animals feeding on dead organic matter. **2.** a street cleaner. [alteration of ME *scavager* (cf. *passenger, messenger*), from AF *scawager,* from OF *escauver* inspect]

**scavenger hunt** /ˈ– hʌnt/, *n.* a game in which competitors are sent out to accumulate, without purchasing, a number of chosen objects, the winners being those who return first with all the objects on the target list.

**scena** /ˈʃeɪnə/, *n.* an operatic scene; a dramatic recitative, usu. followed by an aria.

**scenario** /səˈnarioʊ/, *n.*, *pl.* **-narios.** **1.** an outline of the plot of a dramatic work, giving particulars as to the scenes, characters, situations, etc. **2.** the outline or manuscript of a film, giving the action in the order in which it takes place, the description of scenes and characters, the printed matter to be shown on the screen, etc. **3.** the outline of a general situation; a plan to be followed or observed. [It., from LL *scēnārius* pertaining to stage scenes, from L *scēna* scene]

**scend** /sɛnd/, *Naut.* *–v.i.* **1.** to be heaved upwards by a swell. *–n.* **2.** this motion. [var. of SEND (def. 17)]

**scene** /sin/, *n.* **1.** the place where any action occurs. **2.** any view or picture. **3.** an incident or situation in real life. **4.** an exhibition or outbreak of excited or violent feeling before others. **5.** a division of a play or of an act of a play, now commonly representing what passes between certain of the actors in one place. **6.** a unit of dramatic action within a play, in which a single point or effect is made. **7.** the place in which the action of a play or part of a play is supposed to occur. **8.** →**scenery** (def. 2). **9.** an episode, situation, or the like, as described in writing. **10.** the setting of a story or the like. **11.** the stage, esp. of an ancient Greek or Roman theatre. **12.** any sphere or domain, esp. that of contemporary culture: *the pop scene.* **13.** *Colloq.* an area or sphere of interest or involvement: *politics is his scene.* **14.** a social environment: *I had to leave that scene.* **15. a good (bad) scene,** a situation which has a good (bad) ambience. **16. behind the scenes, a.** out of sight of the audience; offstage. **b.** secretly; privately. **17. on the scene, a.** present: *the first person on the scene was a policeman.* **b.** in fashion. **18. the scene,** the contemporary fashionable world. [L *scēna,* from Gk *skēnḗ* tent, stage]

**scene dock** /ˈ– dɒk/, *n.* a place for storing theatrical scenery, near or beneath the stage. Also, **dock.**

**scenery** /ˈsinəri/, *n.*, *pl.* **-neries.** **1.** the general appearance of a place; the aggregate of features that give character to a landscape. **2.** hangings, draperies, structures, etc., on the stage to represent some place or furnish decorative background.

**scene-shifter** /ˈsin-ʃɪftə/, *n.* one employed to change scenery between scenes of a play or the like.

**scenic** /ˈsinɪk/, *adj.* **1.** of or pertaining to natural scenery; having fine scenery. **2.** of or pertaining to the stage or to stage scenery; dramatic; theatrical. **3.** representing a scene, action, or the like, as painting or sculpture. Also, **scenical.** – **scenically,** *adv.*

**scenic railway** /– ˈreɪlweɪ/, *n.* **1.** a miniature or private railway which carries passengers on a tour of a natural landscape, zoo, etc. **2.** →**big dipper.**

**scenography** /siˈnɒgrəfi/, *n.* **1.** *Obs.* the representing of objects, as buildings, according to the rules of perspective. **2.** scene painting (used esp. with reference to ancient Greece). [L *scēnographia,* from Gk *skēnographía*] – **scenographic** /sinəˈgræfɪk/, **scenographical** /sinəˈgræfɪkəl/, *adj.*

**scent** /sɛnt/, *n.* **1.** distinctive smell, esp. when agreeable. **2.** a smell left in passing, by means of which an animal or person may be traced. **3.** a track or trail as indicated by such a smell. **4.** the small pieces of paper dropped by the hare in the game of hare and hounds. **5.** →**perfume.** **6.** the sense of smell. *–v.t.* **7.** to perceive or recognise by the sense of smell. **8.** to perceive or detect in any way: *to scent trouble.* **9.** to impregnate or sprinkle with perfume. *–v.i.* **10.** to hunt by the sense of smell, as a hound. [ME *sent,* from F *sentir* perceive, from L *sentīre*] – **scentless,** *adj.*

**sceptic** /ˈskɛptɪk/, *n.* **1.** one who questions the validity or authenticity of something purporting to be knowledge. **2.** one who mistrusts and who maintains a doubting pessimistic attitude towards people, plans, ideas, etc. **3.** one who doubts the truth of the Christian religion or of important elements of it. **4.** (*cap.*) *Philos.* a member of a philosophical school of ancient Greece, or any later thinker, who maintained that real knowledge of things is impossible. *–adj.* **5.** pertaining to sceptics or scepticism; sceptical. **6.** (*cap.*) pertaining to the Sceptics. Also, *U.S.*, **skeptic.** [L *scepticus* inquiring, reflective, from Gk *skeptikós*]

**sceptical** /ˈskɛptɪkəl/, *adj.* **1.** inclined to scepticism; having doubt. **2.** showing doubt: *a sceptical smile.* **3.** denying or questioning the tenets of religion. **4.** of or pertaining to Sceptics or scepticism. – **sceptically,** *adv.* – **scepticalness,** *n.*

**scepticism** /ˈskɛptəsɪzəm/, *n.* **1.** sceptical attitude or temper; doubt. **2.** doubt or unbelief with regard to the Christian religion. **3.** the doctrines or opinions of philosophical Sceptics; universal doubt.

**sceptre** /ˈsɛptə/, *n.* **1.** a rod or wand borne in the hand as an emblem of regal or imperial power. **2.** royal or imperial power or authority; sovereignty. *–v.t.* **3.** to give a sceptre to; invest with authority. Also, *U.S.,* **scepter.** [ME *sceptre,* from OF, from L *scēptrum,* from Gk *skêptron*] – **sceptred,** *adj.*

sceptre

**sch.,** school.

**Schadenfreude** /ˈʃadənfrɔɪdə/, *n.* pleasure in others' misfortunes. [G: malicious pleasure, from *Schade(n)* injury + *Freude* joy]

**schappe** /ˈʃæpə, ˈʃapə/, *v.,* **schapped** /ˈʃæpəd, ˈʃapəd/, **schapping,** *n.* *–v.t.* **1.** to remove gum from (silk) by fermentation. *–n.* **2.** Also, **schappe silk.** a silk waste used for embroidery and sewing silks, or for combining with other fibres. [G (Swiss d.): lit., leavings, from F *échappement* leakage]

**schedule** /ˈʃɛdʒul/; *Chiefly U.S.* /ˈskɛdʒul/, *n., v.,* **-uled, -uling.** *–n.* **1.** a plan of procedure for a specified project with reference to sequence of operations, time allotted for each part, etc.: *the proposed schedule allows four weeks for the completion of the book.* **2.** a list of items to be dealt with during a specified time: *he has a full schedule tomorrow.* **3.** a timetable. **4.** a written or printed statement of details, often in classified or tabular form, esp. one forming an appendix or explanatory addition to another document. **5.** *Obs.* a written paper. *–v.t.* **6.** to make a schedule of; enter in a schedule. **7.** to plan for a certain date: *to schedule publication for June.* [LL *scedula,* diminutive of L *sceda* leaf of paper, probably from L *scindere* split; replacing ME *cedule,* from OF] – **schedular,** *adj.*

**Scheele's green** /ʃilz ˈgrin/, *n.* cupric arsenite, $Cu_3(AsO_3)_2 \cdot 2H_2O$, used as a pigment and insecticide. [named after K. W. *Scheele,* 1742-86, Swedish chemist]

**scheelite** /ˈʃilaɪt/, *n.* calcium tungstate, $CaWO_4$, an important ore of tungsten usu. occurring in crystals. [*Scheele* + -ITE[1]. See SCHEELE'S GREEN]

**schema** /ˈskimə/, *n., pl.* **-mata** /-mətə/. **1.** a diagram, plan, or scheme. **2.** *Philos.* (in Kantianism) a transcendental product of imagination in accordance with a rule whereby a category of the understanding is made applicable to the manifold of sense. It mediates between the universality of the pure concept (which is opaque to sense) and the particularity of sense (which is opaque to the understanding). [Gk: form]

**schematic** /skiˈmætɪk/, *adj.* **1.** pertaining to or of the nature of a schema, diagram, or scheme; diagrammatic. *–n.* **2.** a schematic drawing or diagram. – **schematically,** *adv.*

**schematise** /ˈskimətaɪz/, *v.t.,* **-tised, -tising.** to reduce to or arrange according to a scheme. Also, **schematize.** [Gk *schēmatízein*] – **schematisation** /skimətaɪˈzeɪʃən/, *n.* – **schematiser,** *n.*

**schematism** /ˈskimətɪzəm/, *n.* **1.** the particular form or disposition of a thing. **2.** a schematic arrangement. [NL *schēmatismus,* from Gk *schēmatismós* formalisation]

**scheme** /skim/, *n., v.,* **schemed, scheming.** *–n.* **1.** a plan or design to be followed, as for building operations, etc.; a program of action; a project. **2.** a policy or plan officially adopted by a company, business, etc., as for pensions, loans, etc. **3.** an underhand plot; intrigue. **4.** a visionary or impractical project. **5.** a body or system of related doctrines, theories, etc.: *a scheme of philosophy.* **6.** any system of correlated things, parts, etc., or the manner of its arrangement. **7.** an analytical or tabular statement. **8.** a diagram, map, or the like. **9.** an astrological diagram of the heavens. *–v.t.* **10.** to devise as a scheme; plan; plot; contrive. *–v.i.* **11.** to lay schemes; devise plans; plot. [ML *schēma,* from Gk] – **schemer,** *n.*

**scheming** /ˈskimɪŋ/, *adj.* given to forming plans, esp. underhand ones; crafty.

**scherzando** /skɜtˈsændoʊ, ˈskɛət-/, *adv., adj., n., pl.* **-dos.** *–adv.* **1.** (a musical direction) playfully; sportively. *–adj.* **2.** playful; sportive. *–n.* **3.** a musical passage or movement played in this way.

**scherzo** /ˈskɜtsoʊ, ˈskɛət-/, *n., pl.* **-zos, -zi** /-si/. (in music) a movement or passage of lively, playful character, esp. as the second or third division of a sonata or a symphony. [It.: sport, jest, from G *Scherz*]

**Schick test** /ˈʃɪk tɛst/, *n.* a diphtheria-immunity test in which diphtheria toxoid is injected cutaneously, non-immunity being characterised by an inflammation at the injection site. [named after Dr Bela *Schick,* 1877-1967, U.S. paediatrician]

**Schiff base** /ˈʃɪf beɪs/, *n.* a class of compounds derived by chemical reaction (condensation) of aldehydes and ketones with primary amines and having the general formula RR′C=NR″; used in perfumes, as liquid crystals, and in dyes.

**schiller** /ˈʃɪlə/, *n.* a peculiar, almost metallic lustre, sometimes with iridescence, occurring on certain minerals. [G: play of colours]

**schillerise** /ˈʃɪləraɪz/, *v.t.,* **-rised, -rising.** to give a schiller to (a crystal) by developing microscopic inclusions along certain planes. Also, **schillerize.** – **schillerisation** /ˌʃɪləraɪˈzeɪʃən/, *n.*

**schipperke** /ˈʃɪpəki/, *n.* one of a breed of small black dogs, originally used as watchdogs on boats in the Netherlands and Belgium. [D: little boatman]

**schism** /ˈskɪzəm, ˈsɪzəm/, *n.* **1.** division or disunion, esp. into mutually opposed parties. **2.** the parties so formed. **3.** *Eccles.* **a.** a formal division within, or separation from, a church or religious body over some doctrinal difference. **b.** a sect or body formed by such a division. **c.** the offence of causing or seeking to cause such a division. [L *schisma,* from Gk; replacing ME *cisme,* from OF]

**schismatic** /skɪzˈmætɪk, sɪzˈmætɪk/, *adj.* **1.** Also, **schismatical.** of, pertaining to, or of the nature of schism; guilty of schism. *–n.* **2.** one who promotes schism; an adherent of a schismatic body.

**schist** /ʃɪst/, *n.* any of a class of crystalline rocks whose constituent minerals have a more or less parallel or foliated arrangement, due mostly to metamorphic action. [F *schiste,* from L *schistos* fissile, readily splitting, from Gk *schistós*]

**schistose** /ˈʃɪstoʊs/, *adj.* of, resembling, or in the form of schist. – **schistosity** /ʃɪsˈtɒsəti/, *n.*

**schistosome** /ˈʃɪstəsoʊm/, *n.* a fluke of long, slender form that inhabits the blood vessels of birds and mammals and is one of the most important and detrimental human parasites in tropical countries; bilharzia.

**schistosomiasis** /ʃɪstəsəˈmaɪəsəs/, *n.* a chronic disease of man and animals caused by the presence of schistosomes in the blood, common in tropical and sub-tropical climates; bilharziasis.

**schizanthus** /skɪtˈsænθəs/, *n.* a plant native to Chile, *Schizanthus pinnatus,* often grown in greenhouses for its graceful appearance and multitude of flowers in a variety of colours; poor-man's orchid.

**schizo** /ˈskɪtsoʊ/, *Colloq.* *–n.* **1.** →**schizophrenic.** *–adj.* **2.** →**schizophrenic.**

**schizo-,** a word element referring to cleavage. Also, before vowels, **schiz-.** [Gk: parted (cf. *schízein* split), as in *schizópous* with parted toes]

**schizocarp** /ˈskɪtsoʊkap/, *n.* a dry fruit which at maturity splits into two or more one-seeded indehiscent carpels. – **schizocarpous** /ˌskɪtsoʊˈkapəs/, *adj.*

**schizogenesis** /skɪtsoʊˈdʒɛnəsəs/, *n.* reproduction by fission. Also, **schizogomy** /skɪtˈsɒgəmi/. – **schizogenetic** /ˌskɪtsoʊdʒəˈnɛtɪk/, *adj.*

**schizoid** /ˈskɪtsɔɪd/, *adj.* **1.** related to, predisposed to, or afflicted with schizophrenia. *–n.* **2.** one who is afflicted with schizophrenia.

**schizomycete** /ˌskɪtsoʊmaɪˈsit/, *n.* any of the Schizomycetes, a class or group of plant organisms comprising the bacteria.

**schizomycosis** /ˌskɪtsoʊmaɪˈkoʊsəs/, *n.* any disease due to schizomycetes.

**schizophrenia** /skɪtsəˈfriniə/, *n.* a psychosis characterised by breakdown of integrated personality functioning, withdrawal from reality, emotional blunting and distortion, and disturbances in thought and behaviour.

**schizophrenic** /skɪtsə'frɛnɪk, -'frinɪk/, *n.* **1.** Also, **schizophrene.** a person who is suffering from schizophrenia. *–adj.* **2.** of or pertaining to schizophrenia.

**schizophyceous** /skɪtsoʊ'fɪʃəs/, *adj.* belonging to the Schizophyceae, a class or group of unicellular and multicellular green or bluish green algae, occurring in both salt and fresh water, and often causing pollution of drinking water.

**schizophyte** /'skɪtsoʊfaɪt/, *n.* any of the Schizophyta, a group of plants comprising the schizomycetes and the schizophyceous algae, characterised by a simple structure and by reproduction by simple fission or by spores. [NL *Schizophyta* (pl.). See SCHIZO-, -PHYTE] – **schizophytic** /ˌskɪtsoʊ'fɪtɪk/, *adj.*

**schizopod** /'skɪtsoʊpɒd/, *n.* **1.** any of the shrimplike crustacean orders Mysidacea or Euphausiacea, as the opossum shrimps. *–adj.* **2.** Also, **schizopodous** /skɪt'sɒpədəs/. belonging or pertaining to the schizopods.

**schizothymia** /skɪtsoʊ'θaɪmiə/, *n.* an emotional state or temperament out of keeping with the rational mind. [SCHIZO- + Gk *-thymia,* from *thymós* mind] – **schizothymic,** *adj.*

**schlanter** /'slæntə/, *n. Colloq.* →**slanter.**

**schlemiel** /ʃlə'mil/, *n. U.S. Colloq.* an awkward and unlucky person for whom things never turn out right. Also, **schlemihl.** [from *Schlemihl* surname of title character of a novel (1814) by Adelbert von Chamisso, 1781-1838; ? surname from Yiddish, from Heb. proper name *Shélūmīēl* God is my welfare]

**schlieren** /'ʃlɪərən/, *n.pl.* **1.** *Geol.* streaks or irregularly shaped masses in an igneous rock, which differ in texture or composition from the main mass. **2.** *Physics.* areas in a turbulent, transparent fluid which become visible in schlieren photographs because of their different density and refractive index to the bulk of the fluid. [G, pl. of *Schliere* streak] – **schlieric,** *adj.*

**schlieren photography** /– fə'tɒgrəfi/, *n.* a method of photographing flow patterns in a turbulent, transparent fluid which depends on differences in density and refractive index within the fluid. – **schlieren photograph,** *n.*

**schmalz** /ʃmɔlts, ʃmælts/, *n. Colloq.* excessive sentimentality, esp. in the arts. Also, **schmaltz.** [G: lit., dripping fat] – **schmalzy,** *adj.*

**Schmidt optics** /ʃmɪt 'ɒptɪks/, *n.* optical system (used in wide-field cameras and reflecting telescopes) by means of which spherical aberration and coma are reduced to a minimum by specially designed objectives. [named after Bernard *Schmidt,* 1879-1935, German inventor]

**Schmitt trigger** /ʃmɪt 'trɪgə/, *n.* a circuit which converts a sinusoidal or similar signal into a train of square pulses.

**schmo** /ʃmoʊ/, *n.* →**shmo.** [Yiddish *shmok* fool, from Slovenian *šmok*]

**schmuck** /ʃmʌk/, *n. Colloq.* a stupid person; idiot; fool. [Yiddish: penis, from G *Schmuck* ornament, from MHG *smucken* to press into]

**schnapper** /'snæpə/, *n.* →**snapper** (def. 1).

**schnapps** /ʃnæps/, *n.* a type of gin (def. 1) often flavoured with carroway or cumin. [G: dram, nip; akin to *schnappen* snap]

**schnauzer** /'ʃnaʊzə/, *n.* one of a German breed of terrier with a wiry grey coat. [G]

**Schneider python** /ʃnaɪdə 'paɪθən/, *n.* →**amethystine python.**

**schnorkle** /'ʃnɔkəl/, *n.* →**snorkel.**

**schnozzle** /'ʃnɒzəl/, *n. Colloq.* the nose. Also, **schnoz.** [? Yiddish *shnoitsl,* diminutive of *shnoits* snout, from G *Schouze*]

**schola cantorum** /ˌskoʊlə kæn'tɔrəm/, *n.* **1.** a choir school. **2.** the building in which a choir school is held, sometimes integral with the structure of the church or cathedral. [L]

**scholar** /'skɒlə/, *n.* **1.** a learned or erudite person. **2.** a student; pupil. **3.** a student who, because of merit, etc., is granted money or other aid to pursue his studies. [LL *scholāris;* replacing ME and OE *scolere,* from LL (as above)]

**scholarch** /'skɒlak/, *n.* **1.** the head of a school. **2.** the head of an ancient Athenian school of philosophy. [Gk *scholárchēs,* from *schol(ḗ)* school + *-archēs* ruler]

**scholarly** /'skɒləli/, *adj.* **1.** of, like, or befitting a scholar: *scholarly habits.* **2.** having the qualities of a scholar: *a scholarly person.* *–adv.* **3.** like a scholar. – **scholarliness,** *n.*

**scholarship** /'skɒləʃɪp/, *n.* **1.** learning; knowledge acquired by study; the academic attainments of a scholar. **2.** the position of a student who, because of merit, etc., is granted money or other aid to pursue his studies. **3.** the sum of money or other aid granted to a scholar. **4.** a foundation to provide financial assistance to students.

**scholastic** /skə'læstɪk/, *adj.* Also, **scholastical.** **1.** of or pertaining to schools, scholars, or education: *scholastic attainments.* **2.** of or pertaining to the medieval schoolmen. **3.** academic. **4.** pedantic. **5.** of or pertaining to scholasticism. *–n.* **6.** (*sometimes cap.*) a schoolman, a disciple of the schoolmen, or an adherent of scholasticism. **7.** a Jesuit student under primary vows, prior to the commencement of training. **8.** the position held by such a student. **9.** a pedantic person. [L *scholasticus,* from Gk *scholastikós* studious, learned] – **scholastically,** *adv.*

**scholasticism** /skə'læstəsɪzəm/, *n.* **1.** the doctrine of the schoolmen; the system of theological and philosophical teaching predominant in the Middle Ages, based chiefly upon the authority of the Church fathers and of Aristotle and his commentators, and characterised by marked formality in methods. **2.** narrow adherence to traditional teachings, doctrines, or methods.

**scholiast** /'skoʊliæst/, *n.* **1.** an ancient commentator upon the classics. **2.** one who writes scholia. [LL *scholiasta,* from LGk *scholiastḗs*] – **scholiastic** /skoʊli'æstɪk/, *adj.*

**scholium** /'skoʊliəm/, *n., pl.* **-lia** /-liə/. **1.** (*oft. pl.*) **a.** an explanatory note or comment. **b.** an ancient annotation upon a passage in a Greek or Latin author. **2.** a note added to illustrate or amplify, as in a mathematical work. [ML, from Gk *schólion* commentary]

**school**[1] /skul/, *n.* **1.** a place or establishment where instruction is given, esp. one for children. **2.** the body of students or pupils attending a school. **3.** a regular course of meetings of a teacher or teachers and students for instruction: *a school held during the summer months.* **4.** a session of such a course: *no school today.* **5.** a building, room, etc., in a university, set apart for the use of one of the faculties or for some particular purpose. **6.** a department or faculty in a university or similar educational institution. **7.** a group of departments or faculties in a university or similar institution associated through a common disciplinary or interdisciplinary interest, or through a common purpose. **8.** an instructive place, situation, etc. **9.** a body of scholars, artists, writers, etc., who have been taught by the same master, or who are united by a similarity of method, style, principles, etc.: *the Platonic school of philosophy.* **10.** any body of persons who agree. **11.** *Colloq.* a group of people settled (either on one occasion or habitually) into a session of drinking or gambling. **12. of the old school,** old-fashioned; high-principled. **13. school of thought, a.** a group of people all holding the same opinion or point of view. **b.** a point of view held by such a group. *–adj.* **14.** of or connected with a school or schools. *–v.t.* **15.** to educate in or as in a school; teach; train. **16.** *Archaic.* to reprimand. [ME *scole,* OE *scōl,* from L *schola,* from Gk *scholḗ,* orig., leisure, hence employment of leisure, study]

**school**[2] /skul/, *n.* **1.** a large number of fish, porpoises, whales, or the like, feeding or migrating together. *–v.i.* **2.** to form into, or go in, a school, as fish. [ME *schol(e),* from D *school* troop, multitude, c. OE *scolu* SHOAL[2]]

**school age** /'– eɪdʒ/, *n.* the age set by law for children to start school attendance.

**school-age** /'skul-eɪdʒ/, *adj.* of or pertaining to children who are of an age to be at school.

**schoolbook** /'skulbʊk/, *n.* a book for study in schools.

**schoolboy** /'skulbɔɪ/, *n.* a boy attending a school.

**school captain** /skul 'kæptən/, *n.* a senior boy or girl in a school, appointed or elected to lead and represent the other pupils, help maintain discipline, etc.; head boy; head girl.

**schoolfellow** /'skulfɛloʊ/, *n.* →**schoolmate.**

**schoolgirl** /'skulgɜl/, *n.* a girl attending school.

**schoolhouse** /'skulhaʊs/, *n.* **1.** a building in which a school is conducted, esp. a small school in a rural area. **2.** a house attached to a school for the use of the schoolteacher.

**schoolie**[1] /'skuli/, *n. Colloq.* a schoolteacher. [SCHOOL[1] + -IE]

**schoolie**[2] /'skuli/, *n. Colloq.* a school prawn. [SCHOOL (PRAWN) + -IE]

**schooling** /'skulɪŋ/, *n.* **1.** the process of being taught in a school. **2.** education received in a school. **3.** the act of teaching. **4.** *Archaic.* a reprimand.

**schoolkid** /ˈskulkɪd/, *n.* a child still of an age to go to school.

**school mackerel** /skul ˈmækərəl/, *n.* →**spotted mackerel.**

**schoolman** /ˈskulmən/, *n., pl.* **-men. 1.** one versed in scholastic learning or engaged in scholastic pursuits. **2.** (*sometimes cap.*) a master in one of the schools or universities of the Middle Ages; one of the medieval writers who dealt with theology and philosophy after the methods of scholasticism.

**schoolmarm** /ˈskulmam/, *n. Colloq.* **1.** a schoolmistress, esp. of the old-fashioned type. **2.** any prim woman.

**schoolmaster** /ˈskulmastə/, *n.* a man who presides over or teaches in a school.

**schoolmate** /ˈskulmeɪt/, *n.* a companion or associate at school.

**schoolmistress** /ˈskulmɪstrəs/, *n.* a woman who presides over or teaches in a school.

**school of arts,** *n.* a hall in a country town or a suburb with facilities for working people to study and attend educational lectures; mechanics' institute.

**school of the air,** *n.* a system of education using two-way wireless equipment to supplement correspondence lessons for children in outback areas.

**school prawn** /skul ˈprɒn/, *n.* a common commercial penaeid prawn, *Metapenaeus macleayi,* pale olive green in colour with an upward tilted rostrum.

**schoolroom** /ˈskulrum/, *n.* a room in which a school is conducted or pupils are taught.

**school shark** /skul ˈʃak/, *n.* a tope-like shark, *Notogaleus australis,* of eastern and southern Australian coasts.

**school ship** /ˈ– ʃɪp/, *n.* →**training ship.**

**school sores** /ˈ– sɔz/, *n. pl. Colloq.* →**impetigo.**

**schoolteacher** /ˈskultitʃə/, *n.* one who teaches in a school.

**schoolyard** /ˈskuljad/, *n.* the playground of a school.

**school year** /skul ˈjɪə/, *n.* the months during a year when a school is open and attendance is required.

**schooner** /ˈskunə/, *n.* **1.** a sailing vessel with two or more masts and fore-and-aft rig. **2.** a large glass, usu. a beer glass. [orig. uncert.; said to be from New England (U.S.) d. verb *scoon* skim along (as on water)]

schooner

**schooner-rigged** /ˈskunə-rɪgd/, *adj.* fore-and-aft rigged.

**schorl** /ʃɔl/, *n.* black tourmaline. [G *Schörl;* orig. unknown] – **schorlaceous** /ʃɔˈleɪʃəs/, *adj.*

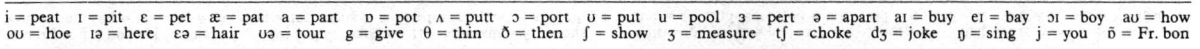

**schottische** /ʃɒˈtiʃ, -ˈtiz/, *n.* **1.** a round dance resembling the polka. **2.** its music. [G: Scottish (dance)]

**Schrödinger equation** /ˈʃrɜdɪŋər əkweɪʒən/, *n.* an equation that arises in the quantum mechanics of particles; of historical importance in the development of theories of quantum mechanics. [named after E. *Schrödinger,* 1887-1961, Austrian physicist]

**schuss** /ʃʊs/, *n.* **1.** a straight fast run in skiing. *–v.i.* **2.** to execute a schuss. [G: shot]

**schwa** /ʃwa/, *n.* **1.** the indeterminate vowel sound, or sounds, of most unstressed syllables of English, however represented, as the sound, or sounds, of *a* in *alone* and *sofa, e* in *system, i* in *terrible, o* in *gallop, u* in *circus.* **2.** the phonetic symbol ə. [G, from Heb. *sh'wa*]

**sci.,** **1.** science. **2.** scientific.

**sciaenoid** /saɪˈinɔɪd/, *adj.* **1.** belonging or pertaining to the Sciaenidae, a family of carnivorous acanthopterygian fishes including the drumfishes, certain kingfishes, etc. *–n.* **2.** a sciaenoid fish. Also, **sciaenid.** [NL *Sciaen(idae)* (from L *sciaena,* from Gk *skíaina* fish name) + -OID]

**sciamachy** /saɪˈæməki/, *n., pl.* **-chies.** an act or instance of fighting with a shadow or an imaginary enemy. Also, **sciomachy.** [Gk *skiamachía* shadow fighting]

**sciatic** /saɪˈætɪk/, *adj.* **1.** of the ischium or back of the hip: *sciatic nerve.* **2.** affecting the hip or the sciatic nerves. [ML *sciaticus,* alteration of L *ischiadicus* ISCHIADIC]

**sciatica** /saɪˈætɪkə/, *n.* **1.** pain and tenderness at some points of the sciatic nerve; sciatic neuralgia. **2.** any painful disorder extending from the hip down the back of the thigh and surrounding area. [late ME, from ML, properly fem. of adj. *sciaticus* SCIATIC]

**science** /ˈsaɪəns/, *n.* **1. a.** the systematic study of man and his environment based on the deductions and inferences which can be made, and the general laws which can be formulated, from reproducible observations and measurements of events and parameters within the universe. **b.** the knowledge so obtained. **2.** systematised knowledge in general. **3.** a particular branch of knowledge. **4.** skill; proficiency. [ME, from OF, from L *scientia* knowledge]

**science fiction** /– ˈfɪkʃən/, *n.* a form of fiction which draws imaginatively on scientific knowledge and speculation in its plot, setting, theme, etc.

**sciential** /saɪˈɛnʃəl/, *adj.* **1.** having knowledge. **2.** of or pertaining to science or knowledge.

**scientific** /saɪənˈtɪfɪk/, *adj.* **1.** of or pertaining to science or the sciences: *scientific studies.* **2.** occupied or concerned with science: *scientific men.* **3.** regulated by or conforming to the principles of exact science: *a scientific method.* **4.** systematic or accurate. [LL *scientificus.* See SCIENCE, -FIC] – **scientifically,** *adv.*

**scientist** /ˈsaɪəntəst/, *n.* one versed in or devoted to science, esp. physical or natural science.

**scientology** /saɪənˈtɒlədʒi/, *n.* an applied philosophy founded in 1950, deriving its allegedly scientific theory of knowledge from an empirical study of life. Its adherents believe that the application of the techniques derived therefrom can bring about desirable changes in the conditions of life. – **scientologist,** *n.*

**sci-fi** /saɪ-ˈfaɪ/, *n.;* /ˈsaɪ-faɪ/, *adj. Colloq.* *–n.* **1.** science fiction. *–adj.* **2.** science-fiction.

**scilicet** /ˈsɪləsət, ˈsaɪl-/, *adv.* to wit; that is to say; namely. [L, from *scīre licet* it is permitted to know]

**scilla** /ˈsɪlə/, *n.* any herb of the genus *Scilla,* family Liliaceae, of Eurasia and northern Africa, having bell-shaped flowers. Also, **squill.** [L, from Gk *skílla*]

**scimitar** /ˈsɪmətə/, *n.* a curved, single-edged sword of Oriental origin. Also, **scimiter, simitar.** [It. *scimitarra*]

scimitar

**scimitar pod** /ˈ– pɒd/, *n.* the seed of the Queensland bean.

**scincoid** /ˈsɪŋkɔɪd/, *adj.* **1.** resembling the skinks, as certain lizards. *–n.* **2.** a scincoid lizard. [NL *scincoīdēs,* from L *scincus* skink. See -OID]

**scintilla** /sɪnˈtɪlə/, *n.* a spark; a minute particle; a trace: *not a scintilla of recognition.* [L: spark]

**scintillant** /ˈsɪntələnt/, *adj.* scintillating; sparkling. [L *scintillans,* ppr.]

**scintillate** /ˈsɪntəleɪt/, *v.,* **-lated, -lating.** *–v.i.* **1.** to emit sparks. **2.** *Astron.* to sparkle; flash. **3.** to twinkle, as the stars. **4.** to be witty, brilliant in conversation. *–v.t.* **5.** to emit as sparks; flash forth. **6.** *Physics.* to produce a flash of light in a scintillator. [L *scintillātus,* pp.]

**scintillating** /ˈsɪntəleɪtɪŋ/, *adj.* **1.** sparkling; flashing; twinkling. **2.** witty; amusing: *a scintillating conversation.* **3.** stimulating interest or pleasure: *a scintillating evening.*

**scintillation** /sɪntəˈleɪʃən/, *n.* **1.** the act of scintillating. **2.** a spark or flash. **3.** *Astron.* the twinkling or tremulous motion of the light of the stars. **4.** *Physics.* a flash of light produced by a scintillator.

**scintillation counter** /ˈ– kaʊntə/, *n.* a device for detecting and measuring ionising radiation by counting the number of flashes it causes in a scintillator.

**scintillation spectrometer** /– spɛkˈtrɒmətə/, *n.* a device for determining the energy distribution of a radiation, which consists of a scintillation counter incorporating a suitable electronic circuit.

**scintillator** /ˈsɪntəleɪtə/, *n.* a phosphor in which the light energy is released only a short time after excitation.

**scintillometer** /sɪntəˈlɒmətə/, *n.* an instrument designed to make ionising radiation observable, esp. from radioactive materials.

**sciolism** /ˈsaɪəlɪzəm/, *n.* superficial knowledge. [LL *sciolus* one having little knowledge + -ISM] – **sciolist,** *n.* – **sciolistic** /saɪəˈlɪstɪk/, *adj.*

**sciomachy** /saɪˈɒməki/, *n., pl.* **-chies.** →**sciamachy.**

**sciomancy** /ˈsaɪəˌmænsi/, *n.* divination gained through the aid of supernatural agencies.

**scion** /ˈsaɪən/, *n.* **1.** a descendant. **2.** a shoot or twig, esp. one cut for grafting or planting; a cutting. [ME, from OF *cion,* from L *sectio* a cutting, b. with *scier* saw, from L *secāre* cut]

**sciosophy** /saɪˈɒsəfi/, *n.* a system of knowledge usu. based on tradition or the like, and not on scientific fact, as astrology.

**scire facias** /ˌsaɪəri ˈfeɪʃiˌæs/, *n. Law.* **1.** (formerly) a writ requiring the party against whom it is brought to show cause why a judgment, letters patent, etc., should not be executed, vacated, or annulled. **2.** such a proceeding. [L: lit., make (him) to know, after the words in the writ]

**scirrhus** /ˈsɪrəs/, *n., pl.* **scirrhi** /ˈsɪri/, **scirrhuses.** a hard, indolent tumour; a hard cancer. [NL, from Gk *skírrhos,* var. of *skíros* hard covering] – **scirrhous** /ˈsɪrəs/, **scirrhoid** /ˈsɪrɔɪd/, *adj.*

**scissile** /ˈsɪsaɪl/, *adj.* capable of being cut or divided; splitting easily. [L *scissilis*]

**scission** /ˈsɪʒən/, *n.* a cutting, dividing, or splitting; division; separation. [late ME, from LL *scissio*]

**scissor** /ˈsɪzə/, *v.t.* to cut or clip out with scissors.

**scissor link** /ˈ– lɪŋk/, *n.* a scissors-like device on an aeroplane, etc., linking fixed and movable parts of an undercarriage leg in order to maintain wheel alignment.

**scissors** /ˈsɪzəz/, *n.pl. or sing.* **1.** a cutting instrument consisting of two blades (with handles) so pivoted together that their edges work against each other (often called *a pair of scissors*). **2.** *Gymnastics.* exercises in which the legs execute a scissor-like motion. **3.** *Wrestling.* a hold in which a wrestler encircles the head or body of his opponent with his legs. **4. a.** *Athletics.* a high jumping style, in which the competitor straddles the bar with fully extended legs which cross the bar in succession. **b.** *Tennis.* a manoeuvre in which the server and his partner change sides immediately after the serve. **c.** *Rugby Football, etc.* an attack manoeuvre in which a supporting player runs diagonally across the path of the player with the ball, either to receive the pass and change the direction of play or to confuse the defending player. [ME *sisours, cysoures,* from OF *cisoires* (fem. pl.), from LL *cīsōria* (found only in sing., *cīsōrium* cutting instrument), from L *caesus,* pp., cut, slain; spelling due to confusion with L *scissor* one who cuts]

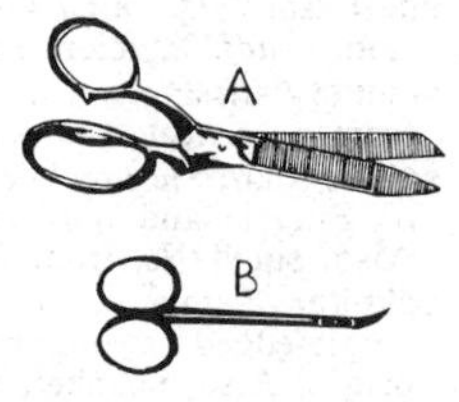

A, cloth-cutting scissors; B, manicure scissors

**scissors grinder** /ˈ– graɪndə/, *n.* →**restless flycatcher.**

**scissors jump** /ˈ– dʒʌmp/, *n.* →**scissors** (def. 4a).

**scissors kick** /ˈ– kɪk/, *n.* **1.** *Swimming.* a propelling motion of the legs in which they move somewhat like the blades of a pair of scissors, used in sidestroke and trudgeon. **2.** *Soccer.* a kick made by jumping, raising one leg, then kicking the ball with the other.

**sciurine** /ˈsaɪjəraɪn, -rən/, *adj.* of or pertaining to the squirrels and allied rodents of the family Sciuridae. [L *sciūrus* (from Gk *skíouros* squirrel) + -INE[1]]

**sciuroid** /ˈsaɪjərɔɪd, saɪˈjurɔɪd/, *adj.* **1.** →**sciurine. 2.** *Bot.* resembling a squirrel tail, as the spikes of certain grasses. [L *sciūrus* (see SCIURINE) + -OID]

**sclaff** /sklæf/, *Golf.* –*v.t., v.i.* **1.** to scrape (the ground) with the club before hitting the ball. –*n.* **2.** a sclaffing stroke. [special use of Scot. *sclaf* shuffle] – **sclaffer,** *n.*

**sclera** /ˈsklɪərə/, *n.* a dense, white, fibrous membrane forming with the cornea the external covering of the eyeball. [NL, from Gk *sklērá* (fem.) hard]

**sclerenchyma** /sklɪəˈreŋkɪmə/, *n.* (of plants) supporting or protective tissue composed of thickened and hardened cells from which the protoplasm has usu. disappeared. [SCLER(O)- + Gk *énchyma* infusion] – **sclerenchymatous** /sklɪəreŋˈkɪmətəs/, *adj.*

**sclerite** /ˈsklɛraɪt/, *n.* any chitinous, calcareous, or similar hard part, plate, spicule, or the like. [SCLER(O)- + -ITE[1]] – **scleritic** /skləˈrɪtɪk/, *adj.*

**scleritis** /skləˈraɪtəs/, *n.* inflammation of the sclera. Also, **sclerotitis.**

**sclero-,** a word element meaning 'hard'. Also, before vowels, **scler-.** [NL, from Gk *sklēro-,* combining form of *sklērós*]

**scleroderma** /sklɛroʊˈdɜmə/, *n.* a serious disease in which all the layers of the skin become hardened and rigid. Also, **sclerodermia** /sklɛroʊˈdɜmiə/. [NL. See SCLERO-, -DERM]

**sclerodermatous** /sklɛroʊˈdɜmətəs/, *adj.* covered with a hardened tissue, as scales.

**scleroid** /ˈsklɛrɔɪd/, *adj. Biol.* hard or indurated.

**scleroma** /skləˈroʊmə/, *n., pl.* **-mata** /-mətə/. a tumour-like induration of tissue. [NL, from Gk *sklḗrōma*]

**sclerometer** /skləˈrɒmətə/, *n.* an instrument for determining with precision the degree of hardness of a substance, esp. a mineral.

**sclerophyll** /ˈsklɛrəfɪl, ˈsklɪə-/, *n.* **1.** any of various plants, typically found in low rainfall areas, having tough leaves which help to reduce water loss. –*adj.* **2.** composed of or pertaining to such plants.

**sclerophylly** /ˈsklɛrəfɪli, ˈsklɪə-/, *n.* the normal formation of much sclerenchyma in the leaves of a plant, esp. certain plants of low rainfall areas, resulting in thick, tough leaves. – **sclerophyllous** /skləˈrɒfələs/, *adj.*

**scleroprotein** /sklɛroʊˈproʊtin, sklɪə-/, *n.* any of a group of simple proteins characterised by their insolubility.

**sclerosed** /ˈsklɪəroʊst/, *adj.* hardened or indurated, as by sclerosis.

**sclerosis** /skləˈroʊsəs/, *n., pl.* **-ses** /-siz/. **1.** *Pathol.* a hardening or induration of a tissue or part; increase of connective tissue or the like at the expense of more active tissue. **2.** *Bot.* a hardening of a tissue or cell wall by thickening or lignification. [ML, from Gk *sklḗrōsis* hardening] – **sclerosal,** *adj.*

**sclerotic** /skləˈrɒtɪk/, *adj.* **1.** *Anat.* designating or pertaining to sclera. **2.** *Pathol., Bot.* pertaining to or affected with sclerosis. [ML *sclērōtica,* from LGk *sklērōtikḗ,* fem. adj., pertaining to hardening]

**sclerotitis** /sklɛroʊˈtaɪtəs/, *n.* →**scleritis.** – **sclerotitic** /sklɛroʊˈtɪtɪk/, *adj.*

**sclerotium** /skləˈroʊʃiəm/, *n., pl.* **-tia** /-ʃə/. a vegetative, resting, food-storage body in certain higher fungi, composed of a compact mass of indurated mycelia. [NL, from *sclerot-* (from Gk *sklērṓtēs* hardness) + *-ium* -IUM] – **sclerotial,** *adj.*

**sclerotomy** /skləˈrɒtəmi/, *n., pl.* **-mies.** incision into the sclera, as to extract foreign bodies.

**sclerous** /ˈsklɛrəs/, *adj.* hard; firm; bony. [Gk *sklērós* hard]

**scoff**[1] /skɒf/, *n.* **1.** an expression of mockery, derision, or derisive scorn; a jeer. **2.** an object of mockery or derision. –*v.i.* **3.** to speak derisively; mock; jeer (oft. fol. by *at*). –*v.t.* **4.** *Obs.* to deride. [ME *scof,* from Scand.; cf. obs. Dan. *skof* mockery] – **scoffer,** *n.* – **scoffingly,** *adv.*

**scoff**[2] /skɒf/, *Colloq.* –*v.t., v.i.* **1.** to eat greedily and quickly. –*n.* **2.** food. [Afrikaans *schoft* meal, from D: quarter (of the day)]

**scold** /skoʊld/, *v.t.* **1.** to find fault with; chide. –*v.i.* **2.** to find fault; reprove. **3.** to use abusive language. –*n.* **4.** a person, esp. a woman, addicted to abusive speech. [ME, var. of *scald,* from Scand.; cf. Icel. *skāld* poet] – **scolder,** *n.* – **scolding,** *adj., n.* – **scoldingly,** *adv.*

**scolecite** /ˈskɒləsaɪt, ˈskoʊl-/, *n.* a zeolite mineral, a hydrous calcium aluminium silicate, $CaAl_2Si_3O_{10}\cdot 3H_2O$, occurring in masses and (usu.) needle-shaped crystals, commonly white. [Gk *skṓlēx* worm + -ITE[1]]

**scolex** /ˈskoʊlɛks/, *n., pl.* **scoleces** /skoʊˈlisiz/. the anterior segment or head of a tapeworm, provided with organs of attachment. It develops singly or in multiples in the larval stage; when it reaches the final host it gives rise to the chain of segments by growth from its posterior end or neck. [NL, from Gk *skṓlēx* worm]

**scoliosis** /skɒliˈoʊsəs/, *n.* lateral curvature of the spine. [NL, from Gk *skolíōsis* a bending]

**scollop** /ˈskɒləp/, *n., v.t.* →**scallop.**

**scolopendrid** /skɒləˈpɛndrəd/, *n.* any of the Scolopendrida, an order of myriapods including many large and poisonous centipedes. [NL *Scolopendridae* (pl.), from *scolopendra,* from Gk *skolópendra* kind of multiped. See -ID[2]] – **scolopendrine** /skɒləˈpɛndraɪn, -drən/, *adj.*

**scombroid** /ˈskɒmbrɔɪd/, *adj.* **1.** resembling the mackerel. **2.** belonging or pertaining to the mackerel family (Scombridae) or the superfamily (Scombroidea) containing the mackerel family. –*n.* **3.** a mackerel or related scombroid fish. Also, **scombrid.** [Gk *skómbros* mackerel + -OID]

**sconce**[1] /skɒns/, *n.* a wall bracket for holding one or more candles or other lights. [ME, from monastic L *sconsa,* from *absconsa,* fem. pp., hidden]

**sconce**[2] /skɒns/, *n., v.,* **sconced, sconcing.** –*n.* **1.** *Fort.* a small detached fort or earthwork, as for defence of a pass or ford. **2.** *Obs.* a shelter, screen, or protection. –*v.t.* **3.** *Fort.* to protect with a sconce. **4.** *Obs.* to fortify; shelter. [D *schans*]

**sconce**[3] /skɒns/, *n. Colloq.* **1.** the head or skull. **2.** sense or wit. [? special use of SCONCE[1] or SCONCE[2]]

**scone** /skɒn/, *n.* **1.** a light plain cake, quickly made, containing very little fat, either baked in a very hot oven or cooked on a hot plate or griddle (drop scone), usu. eaten split open and spread with butter, etc. **2.** *Colloq.* the head. **3. do one's scone,** *Colloq.* to lose one's temper. **4. off one's scone,** *Colloq.* mad; insane. –*v.t.* **5.** to strike a person, esp. on the head. [MD *schoon* (*brōt*) fine bread. See SHEEN, BREAD]

**scoob** /skub/, *n. Colloq.* a marijuana cigarette.

**scoop** /skup/, *n.* **1.** a ladle or ladle-like utensil, esp. a small, deep shovel with a short handle, for taking up flour, sugar, etc. **2.** the bucket of a dredge, steam-shovel, etc. **3.** *Surg.* a spoonlike apparatus used to remove substances or foreign objects. **4.** a place scooped out; a hollow. **5.** act of scooping; a movement as of scooping. **6.** the quantity taken up. **7.** *Colloq.* a big haul, as of money. **8.** an item of news, etc., published or broadcast in advance of, or to the exclusion of, rival newspapers, broadcasting organisations, etc. –*v.t.* **9.** to take up or out with, or as with a scoop. **10.** to gather together or appropriate with the arms or hands (oft. fol. by *up*): *he scooped up the jewels and put them into his pocket.* **11.** to empty with a scoop. **12.** to form a hollow or hollows in. **13.** to form with or as with a scoop. **14.** *Journalism Colloq.* to get the better of (a rival newspaper, broadcasting organisation, etc.) by publishing or broadcasting an item of news, etc., first. **15.** *Hockey.* to hit under the ball so that it rises into the air. –*v.i.* **16.** to remove or gather something with, or as with, a scoop. [ME *scope,* from MLG or MD: vessel used for drawing or bailing water] – **scooper,** *n.*

scoop (def. 1)

**scoop neck** /ˈ– nɛk/, *n.* a low rounded neckline on a woman's dress, blouse, etc. Also, **scoop neckline, scooped neckline.**

**scoop net** /ˈ– nɛt/, *n.* a small net used for fishing, prawning, etc.

**scoot** /skut/, *Colloq.* –*v.i.* **1.** to dart; go swiftly or hastily. –*v.t.* **2.** to send or impel at high speed. –*n.* **3.** a swift, darting movement or course. [of Scand. orig.; akin to SHOOT]

**scooter** /ˈskutə/, *n.* **1.** a child's vehicle with two wheels, one in front of the other, and a tread between them, and sometimes with an additional back wheel ensuring stability, steered by a handlebar and propelled by pushing against the ground with one foot. **2.** →**motor scooter.** –*v.i.* **3.** to go, or travel in or on a scooter.

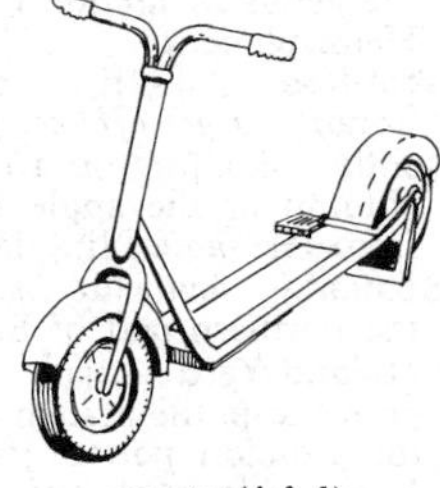

scooter (def. 1)

**scop** /ʃoʊp/, *n.* an Old English bard or poet. [OE, c. Icel. *skop* mockery. See SCOFF[1], SCOLD]

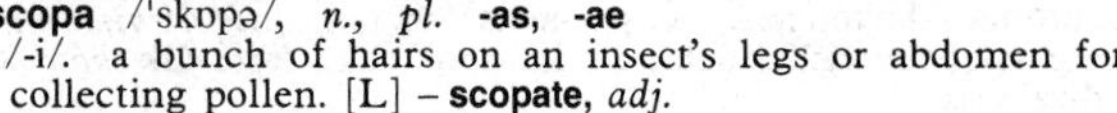

**scopa** /ˈskɒpə/, *n., pl.* **-as, -ae** /-i/. a bunch of hairs on an insect's legs or abdomen for collecting pollen. [L] – **scopate,** *adj.*

**scope** /skoʊp/, *n.* **1.** extent or range of view, outlook, application, operation, effectiveness, etc.: *an investigation of wide scope.* **2.** space for movement or activity; opportunity for operation: *to give one's fancy full scope.* **3.** extent in space; a tract or area. **4.** length, or a length. **5.** *Naut.* the length of cable at which a vessel rides when at anchor. **6.** short form of *microscope, periscope, radarscope, telescope,* etc. [It. *scopo,* from Gk *skopós* mark, aim]

**-scope,** a word element referring to instruments for viewing, as in *telescope.* [NL *-scopium,* from Gk *-skópion* or *-skopeîon,* from *skopeîn* look at]

**scopolamine** /skoʊˈpɒləmin, skoʊpəˈlæmin, -ən/, *n.* a crystalline alkaloid, $C_{17}H_{21}NO_4$, obtained from the rhizome of certain solanaceous plants, used as a depressant and mydriatic, and in producing the so-called twilight sleep. [NL *Scopola* (genus of plants named after G.A. *Scopoli,* 1723-88, Italian botanist) + AMINE]

**scopoline** /ˈskoʊpəlin, -lən/, *n.* a crystalline glucoside, $C_8H_{13}NO_2$, a derivative of scopolamine, used as a narcotic.

**scopophilia** /skoʊpəˈfɪliə/, *n.* the derivation of sexual pleasure from looking at sexual organs or erotic scenes, esp. as a substitute for actual sexual participation. Also, **scoptophilia** /skɒptəˈfɪliə/. [NL, from Gk *skopeîn* to view + *philía* fondness]

**scopula** /ˈskɒpjələ/, *n., pl.* **-las, -lae** /-li/. a small tuft of hairs, as on the feet of some spiders. [LL, from L *scōp*(*a*) broom + *-ula* -ULE]

**scopulate** /ˈskɒpjəleɪt, -lət/, *adj.* broom-shaped; brushlike.

**-scopy,** a word element for forming abstract action nouns related to *-scope,* as in *telescopy.* [Gk *-skopía,* lit., watching. See -SCOPE]

**scorbutic** /skɔˈbjutɪk/, *adj.* pertaining to, of the nature of, or affected with scurvy. Also, **scorbutical.** [NL *scorbūticus,* from ML *scorbūtus* scurvy, apparently from D *scheurbot* (now *scheurbuik*)]

**scorch** /skɔtʃ/, *v.t.* **1.** to affect in colour, taste, etc., by burning slightly. **2.** to parch or shrivel with heat. **3.** to criticise severely. –*v.i.* **4.** to be or become scorched. **5.** *Colloq.* to ride at high speed. –*n.* **6.** a superficial burn. [b. unrecorded *scorp* shrivel (from Scand.; cf. Icel. *skorpinn* shrivelled) and PARCH]

**scorched earth** /skɔtʃt ˈɜθ/, *n.* a condition or policy in which all things useful to an invading army are destroyed, as by fire.

**scorcher** /ˈskɔtʃə/, *n.* **1.** one who or that which scorches. **2.** *Colloq.* a very hot day. **3.** anything caustic or severe. **4.** *Obs. Colloq.* an excessively fast driver.

**scorching** /ˈskɔtʃɪŋ/, *adj.* **1.** burning; very hot. **2.** caustic or scathing. – **scorchingly,** *adv.*

**scordatura** /skɔdəˈturə/, *n.* the tuning of a stringed musical instrument to notes other than the normal in order to produce special effects. [It., from *scordato,* pp., played out of tune]

**score** /skɔ/, *n., v.,* **scored, scoring.** –*n.* **1.** the record of points made by the competitors in a game or match. **2.** the aggregate of points made by a side or individual. **3.** the scoring of a point or points. **4.** *Educ.* the performance of an individual, or sometimes of a group, in an examination or test, expressed by a letter, number, or other symbol. **5.** a notch or scratch; a stroke or line. **6.** a notch or mark for keeping an account or record. **7.** a reckoning or account so kept. **8.** any account showing indebtedness. **9.** an amount recorded as due. **10.** a line drawn as a boundary, the beginning of a race, etc. **11.** a group or set of twenty: *three score years and ten.* **12.** (*pl.*) a great many. **13.** account, reason, or ground: *to complain on the score of low pay.* **14.** a successful move, remark, etc. **15.** *Music.* **a.** a written or printed piece of music with all the vocal and instrumental parts arranged on staves, one under the other. **b.** the background music to a film, play, etc. **16.** *Colloq.* latest news or state of progress: *what's the score on the new space rocket?* **17. know the score,** to be aware of what is required. **18. pay off** or **settle a score, a.** to avenge a wrong. **b.** to fulfil an obligation. –*v.t.* **19.** to gain for addition to one's score in a game. **20.** to make a score of. **21.** to be worth (as points): *four aces score one hundred.* **22.** *Educ.* to evaluate the responses a person has made on (a test or an examination). **23.** *Music.* **a.** to orchestrate. **b.** to write out in score. **c.** to compose the music for (a film, play, etc.). **24.** *Cookery.* to cut with shallow slashes, as meat. **25.** to make notches, cuts, or lines in or on. **26.** to record by notches, marks, etc.; to reckon (oft. fol. by *up*). **27.** to write down as a debt. **28.** to record as a debtor. **29.** to gain or win: *a comedy scoring a great success.* **30.** *U.S.* to censure severely: *newspapers scored him severely for the announcement.* **31.** to be successful in obtaining (a commodity, esp. drugs): *he scored a deal of dope.* **32.** **score off,** gain an advantage over. *–v.i.* **33.** to make a point or points in a game or contest. **34.** to keep score, as of a game. **35.** to achieve an advantage or a success. **36.** to be successful in having sexual intercourse with. **37.** to make notches, cuts, lines, etc. **38.** to be successful in obtaining a commodity, esp. drugs. [ME; late OE *scoru,* from Scand.; cf. Icel. *skor* notch] – **scorer,** *n.*

**scoreboard** /'skɔbɔd/, *n.* a board on which the score of a game, match, etc., is exhibited, as at a cricket ground.

**scorebook** /'skɔbʊk/, *n.* a book in which scores, as of cricket matches, are kept.

**scorecard** /'skɔkad/, *n.* a card on which a score is kept.

**scoresheet** /'skɔʃit/, *n.* a sheet of paper on which a score is kept.

**scoria** /'skɔriə/, *n., pl.* **scoriae** /'skɔrii/. **1.** the refuse, dross, or slag left after smelting or melting metals. **2.** a clinker-like cellular lava. [L, from Gk *skōría* slag] – **scoriaceous** /skɔri'eɪʃəs/, *adj.*

**scorification** /skɔrəfə'keɪʃən/, *n.* the separation of gold or silver by heating it to a high temperature with a large amount of granulated lead and a little borax. The gold or silver dissolves in the molten lead which sinks, while the impurities form a slag with lead oxide.

**scorifier** /'skɔrəfaɪə/, *n.* a refractory crucible used in the process of scorification and other assaying techniques.

**scorify** /'skɔrəfaɪ/, *v.t.,* **-fied, -fying.** to reduce to scoria. [SCORI(A) + -FY]

**scorn** /skɔn/, *n.* **1.** open or unqualified contempt; disdain. **2.** mockery or derision. **3.** an object of derision or contempt. **4.** *Archaic.* a derisive or contemptuous action or speech. *–v.t.* **5.** to treat or regard with scorn. **6.** to reject or refuse with scorn. *–v.i.* **7.** to mock; jeer. [ME; var. of *skarn,* from OF *escarn* mockery, derision; of Gmc orig.] – **scorner,** *n.*

**scornful** /'skɔnfəl/, *adj.* full of scorn; derisive; contemptuous: *he smiled in a scornful way.* – **scornfully,** *adv.* – **scornfulness,** *n.*

**scorpaenid** /skɔ'pinɪd/, *adj.* **1.** of or pertaining to the Scorpaenidae, a large family of marine spiny-finned fishes found in all waters but particularly abundant in the Pacific. *–n.* **2.** a fish of the family Scorpaenidae, as the red rock cod or butterfly cod.

**scorpaenoid** /skɔ'pinɔɪd/, *adj.* **1.** of the scorpaenids. *–n.* **2.** →**scorpaenid.** [L *scorpaena* (from Gk *skórpaina* prickly fish) + -OID]

**Scorpio** /'skɔpioʊ/, *n.* **1.** a constellation and sign of the zodiac, represented by a scorpion. **2.** a person born under the sign of Scorpio, and (according to tradition) exhibiting the typical Scorpion personality traits in some degree. *–adj.* **3.** of or pertaining to Scorpio. **4.** of or pertaining to such a person or such a personality trait. [ME, from L. See SCORPION]

**scorpioid** /'skɔpiɔɪd/, *adj.* **1.** resembling a scorpion. **2.** belonging to the Scorpionida, the order of arachnids comprising the scorpions. **3.** curved (at the end) like the tail of a scorpion. **4.** *Bot.* of or pertaining to a type of cymose inflorescence in which the axis is coiled like the tail of a scorpion. [Gk *skorpioeidḗs*]

scorpion

**scorpion** /'skɔpiən/, *n.* **1.** any of numerous arachnids belonging to the order Scorpiones (Scorpionida) from the warmer parts of the world, having a long narrow tail terminating in a venomous sting. **2.** an insect which stings or which superficially resembles a true scorpion. **3.** a (supposed) whip or scourge armed with spikes. **4.** (*cap.*) the zodiacal constellation or sign Scorpio. [ME, from L *scorpio* (from *scorpius,* from Gk *skorpíos*)]

**scorpion-fish** /'skɔpiən-fɪʃ/, *n.* a rockfish, esp. of the genus *Scorpaena,* which has poisonous dorsal spines.

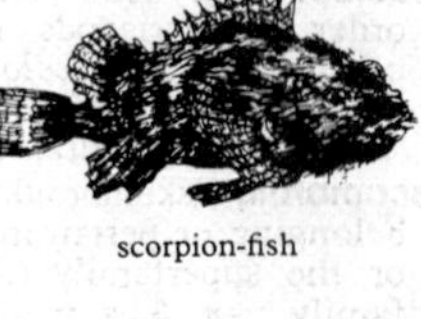
scorpion-fish

**scorpion-fly** /'skɔpiən-flaɪ/, *n.* any of the harmless insects of the order Mecoptera, in which the male has an abdominal structure resembling a scorpion sting.

**Scorpius** /'skɔpiəs/, *n.* →**Scorpio.**

**scot** /skɒt/, *n.* *Archaic.* **1.** a payment or charge; one's share of a payment. **2.** an assessment or tax. [ME, from Scand.; cf. Icel. *skot,* c. OE *gescot* payment]

**Scot** /skɒt/, *n.* a native or inhabitant of Scotland; a Scotsman. [ME; OE *Scottas* (pl.), from LL *Scottī* the Irish; of unknown origin]

**Scot.,** **1.** Scotland. **2.** Scottish. **3.** Scotch.

**scotch** /skɒtʃ/, *v.t.* **1.** to injure so as to make harmless. **2.** to cut, gash, or score. **3.** to put an end to; stamp out; suppress: *the spokesman soon scotched the rumours about a strike.* **4.** to block or prop with a scotch. *–n.* **5.** a cut, gash, or score. **6.** a block or wedge put under a wheel, barrel, etc., to prevent slipping. [b. SCORE and NOTCH]

**Scotch** /skɒtʃ/, *adj.* **1.** →**Scottish.** *–n.* **2.** →**Scotch whisky.** **3.** →**Scottish.** [var. of SCOTS]

**Scotch blackface** /– 'blækfeɪs/, *n.* one of a variety of black-faced domestic sheep popular in Scotland.

**Scotch bluebell** /– 'blubɛl/, *n.* →**harebell.**

**Scotch broth** /– 'brɒθ/, *n.* a thick soup made from beef stock and pearl barley.

**Scotch collops** /– 'kɒləps/, *n.* a savoury dish made of minced meat.

**Scotch egg** /– 'ɛg/, *n.* a hard-boiled egg enclosed in sausage meat, coated with egg and breadcrumbs and deep fried.

**Scotch fillet** /– 'fɪlət/, *n.* →**ribeye.**

**Scotch fir** /– 'fɜ/, *n.* →**Scots pine.**

**Scotch heather** /– 'hɛðə/, *n.* See **heather.**

**Scotchman** /'skɒtʃmən/, *n., pl.* **-men.** **1.** →**Scotsman.** **2.** *Naut.* a length of timber or metal fitted on half the circumference of a shroud or backstay to prevent chafing.

**Scotch pancake** /skɒtʃ 'pænkeɪk/, *n.* →**pikelet.**

**Scotch tape** /– 'teɪp/, *n.* →**sticky tape.** [Trademark]

**Scotch terrier** /– 'tɛriə/, *n.* →**Scottish terrier.**

**Scotch thistle** /– 'θɪsəl/, *n.* **1.** a large biennial thistle, *Onopordum acanthium,* widespread in Europe and western Asia, and introduced into Scotland where it became the national emblem. **2.** →**spear thistle.**

Scotch thistle

**Scotch whisky** /– 'wɪski/, *n.* any whisky distilled in Scotland, usu. a blended whisky.

**Scotch woodcock** /– 'wʊdkɒk/, *n.* scrambled eggs and anchovies on toast.

**scoter** /'skoʊtə/, *n.* any of the large diving ducks constituting the genus *Melanitta,* found in northern parts of the Northern Hemisphere.

**scot-free** /skɒt-'fri/, *adj.* **1.** free from penalty or payment; unhurt: *to get off scot-free.* **2.** free from payment of scot.

**scotia** /'skoʊʃə/, *n.* a concave moulding, as at the base of a column or the angle between the wall and the ceiling. [L, from Gk *skotía,* lit., darkness]

**Scotland** /'skɒtlənd/, *n.* a division of the United Kingdom in the northern part of Britain.

**Scotland Yard** /– 'jad/, *n.* **1.** the headquarters of the London police, esp. the branch engaged in criminal investigations. **2.** the London police. [from *Scotland Yard,* a short street in London, formerly the site of the London police headquarters]

**scotoma** /skɒ'toʊmə/, *n., pl.* **-mata** /-mətə/. loss of vision in a part of the visual field; a blind spot. [LL, from Gk *skótōma* dizziness]

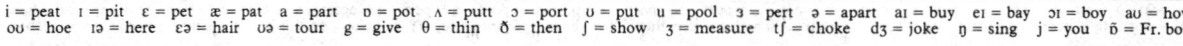

**scotopia** /skɒ'toʊpiə, skə-/, *n.* the ability of the eyes to adjust to darkness.

**Scots** /skɒts/, *n.* **1.** the Scottish dialect of English. *–adj.* **2.** Scottish or Scotch. [ME *Scottis,* northern var. of SCOTTISH]

**Scotsman** /'skɒtsmən/, *n., pl.* **-men.** a native of Scotland. Also, **Scotchman.**

**Scots pine** /skɒts 'paɪn/, *n.* a tall coniferous tree of Europe and temperate Asia, *Pinus sylvestris,* grown for its valuable timber. Also, **Scotch fir.**

**Scottie** /'skɒti/, *n. Colloq.* **1.** a Scotsman. **2.** →**Scottish terrier.** Also, **Scotty.**

**Scottish** /'skɒtɪʃ/, *adj.* **1.** of or pertaining to the Scots, their country, the dialect of English spoken there, or their literature. *–n.* **2.** the people of Scotland collectively. **3.** the dialects of English spoken in Scotland; Scottish English; Scots; Scotch.

**Scottish terrier** /– 'tɛriə/, *n.* one of a breed of terrier with short legs and wiry hair, originally from Scotland. Also, **Scotch terrier.**

Scottish terrier

**scotty** /'skɒti/, *Colloq. –n.* **1.** a Scotsman. **2.** →**Scottish terrier.** *–adj.* **3.** bad-tempered.

**scoundrel** /'skaʊndrəl/, *n.* **1.** an unprincipled, dishonourable man; a villain. *–adj.* **2.** *Rare.* scoundrelly. [orig. uncert.]

**scoundrelly** /'skaʊndrəli/, *adj.* **1.** having the character of a scoundrel. **2.** of or like a scoundrel.

**scour**[1] /'skaʊə/, *v.t.* **1.** to cleanse or polish by hard rubbing: *to scour pots and pans.* **2.** to remove (dirt, grease, etc.) from something by hard rubbing. **3.** to clear out (a channel, drain, etc.). **4.** to purge thoroughly, as an animal. **5.** to clear or rid of what is undesirable. **6.** to remove by, or as by, cleansing; get rid of. *–v.i.* **7.** to rub a surface in order to cleanse or polish it. **8.** to remove dirt, grease, etc. **9.** to become clean and shining by rubbing. **10.** to be capable of being cleaned by rubbing. **11.** (of animals, esp. cattle) to have diarrhoea. *–n.* **12.** act of scouring. **13.** the place scoured. **14.** an apparatus or a material used in scouring. **15.** (*pl.*) persistent diarrhoea in animals, esp. cattle. [ME, probably from MD or MLG *schūren,* probably from OF *escurer,* from L *ex-* EX-[1] and *cūrāre* care for, clean]

**scour**[2] /'skaʊə/, *v.i.* **1.** to move rapidly or energetically. **2.** to range about, as in search of something. *–v.t.* **3.** to run or pass quickly over or along. **4.** to range over, as in search. [ME *scoure.* Cf. Norw. *skura* rush]

**scoured wool** /skaʊəd 'wʊl/, *n.* wool that has been washed to remove impurities such as grease and dirt.

**scourer**[1] /'skaʊrə/, *n.* one who or that which scours or cleanses. [SCOUR[1] + -ER[1]]

**scourer**[2] /'skaʊrə/, *n.* **1.** one who scours or ranges about. **2.** *Brit.* (in the 17th and 18th centuries) a prankster who roamed the streets at night. [SCOUR[2] + -ER[1]]

**scourge** /skɜdʒ/, *n., v.,* **scourged, scourging.** *–n.* **1.** a whip or lash, esp. for the infliction of punishment or torture. **2.** any means of punishment. **3.** a cause of affliction or calamity. *–v.t.* **4.** to whip with a scourge; lash. **5.** to punish or chastise severely; afflict; torment. [ME, from AF *escorge,* from LL *excoriāre* strip off the hide] – **scourger,** *n.*

**scouring** /'skaʊrɪŋ/, *n.* **1.** diarrhoea in animals, esp. cattle. **2.** the act of one who or that which scours. **3.** (*pl.*) that which is removed by scouring.

**scouring rush** /'– rʌʃ/, *n.* **1.** Also, **Dutch rush.** a widespread plant, *Equisetum hyemale,* family Equisetaceae, having long, scarcely branched stems which were formerly used for scouring and polishing pots and pans. **2.** any of several other plants of the genus *Equisetum.*

**scouse** /skaʊs/, *n.* **1.** a baked food served to sailors, as **bread scouse** which contains no meat. See **lobscouse. 2.** (*cap.*) a person who lives in Liverpool, England. **3.** (*cap.*) the dialect of English spoken in Liverpool, England. [shortened form of LOBSCOUSE]

**scout**[1] /skaʊt/, *n.* **1.** a soldier, warship, aeroplane, or the like, employed in reconnoitring. **2.** a person sent out to obtain information. **3.** *Sport.* **a.** a person detailed to observe and report on the techniques, players, etc., of opposing teams. **b.** a person detailed to seek and recommend new players for recruitment to a club. **4.** a talent scout. **5.** the act of scouting. **6.** →**boy scout. 7.** *Colloq.* a fellow: *a good scout.* *–v.i.* **8.** to act as a scout; reconnoitre. *–v.t.* **9.** to examine, inspect, or observe for the purpose of obtaining information; reconnoitre: *to scout the enemy's defences.* **10.** *Colloq.* to seek; search for (usu. fol. by *out* or *up*): *try and scout out an entertainer for Saturday night.* **11.** to evaluate; seek opinions on: *we'll scout the idea of having a party.* [ME *scowte,* from OF *escoute* (fem.) action of listening, from *escouter* listen, from L *auscultāre*]

**scout**[2] /skaʊt/, *v.t., v.i.* to reject with scorn; flout. [Scand.; cf. Icel. *skūta* scold]

**scouter** /'skaʊtə/, *n.* **1.** one who or that which scouts. **2.** an officer in a company of boy scouts.

**scouting** /'skaʊtɪŋ/, *n.* **1.** the act or an instance of reconnoitring, gaining information, etc. **2.** the activities of a scout or scouts.

**scoutmaster** /'skaʊtmastə/, *n.* **1.** the leader or officer in charge of a band of scouts. **2.** the adult leader of a troop of boy scouts.

**scow** /skaʊ/, *n.* **1.** a large, flat-bottomed, unpowered vessel used chiefly for freight, as mud or coal; a low-grade lighter or barge. **2.** a coastal vessel, usu. fore-and-aft rigged, which carries cargo only on deck. [D *schouw* ferryboat]

**scowl** /skaʊl/, *v.i.* **1.** to draw down or contract the brows in a sullen or angry manner. **2.** to have a gloomy or threatening look. *–v.t.* **3.** to affect or express with a scowl. *–n.* **4.** a scowling expression, look, or aspect. [ME *skoul,* from Scand.; cf. Dan. *skule*] – **scowler,** *n.* – **scowlingly,** *adv.*

**SCR,** silicon-controlled rectifier.

**scrabble** /'skræbəl/, *v.,* **-bled, -bling,** *n.* *–v.i.* **1.** to scratch or scrape, as with the claws or hands. **2.** to scrawl; scribble. **3.** to struggle to gain possession of something. **4.** to scratch or grope about clumsily or blindly. *–v.t.* **5.** to scratch at. **6.** to write hurriedly; scribble. *–n.* **7.** a scrabbling or scramble. **8.** a scrawled character, writing, etc. **9.** a game similar to anagrams and crossword puzzles in which 2 to 4 players use counters of varying point values to form words on a playing board. [D *schrabbelen,* frequentative of *schrabben* scratch]

**scrag** /skræg/, *n., v.,* **scragged, scragging.** *–n.* **1.** a lean person or animal. **2.** the lean end of a neck of mutton, etc. **3.** *Colloq.* the neck of a human being. *–v.t.* **4.** *Colloq.* to wring the neck of; hang; garrotte. **5.** *Colloq.* to seize roughly by the neck. [probably akin to CRAG]

**scrag end** /– 'ɛnd/, *n. Colloq.* the remains of a meal; leftovers.

**scraggly** /'skrægli/, *adj.,* **-glier, -gliest.** irregular; ragged; straggling.

**scraggy** /'skrægi/, *adj.,* **-gier, -giest. 1.** lean or thin. **2.** meagre: *a scraggy meal.* **3.** irregular; jagged. – **scraggily,** *adv.* – **scragginess,** *n.*

**scram** /skræm/, *v.i.,* **scrammed, scramming.** *Colloq.* to get out quickly; go away. [alteration of SCRAMBLE]

**scramble** /'skræmbəl/, *v.,* **-bled, -bling,** *n.* *–v.i.* **1.** to make one's way hurriedly by use of the hands and feet, as over rough ground. **2.** to struggle with others for possession; strive rudely with others. **3.** to ride in a scramble. **4.** *Mil., Navy, etc.* (of the crew of an aircraft, submarine, etc., or the craft itself) to prepare for immediate action, as in intercepting the enemy. *–v.t.* **5.** to collect in a hurried or disorderly manner (fol. by *up,* etc.). **6.** to mix together confusedly. **7.** to cook (eggs) in a pan, mixing whites and yolks with butter, milk, etc. **8.** *Electronics.* to transmit (a radio signal) in a garbled form, so that it can be decoded only by a special receiver, and not by a normal instrument. *–n.* **9.** a climb or progression over rough, irregular ground, or the like. **10.** a form of motorcycle race in which competitors must race over very rough, uneven ground. **11.** a struggle for possession, as of the ball in soccer. **12.** any disorderly struggle or proceeding. **13.** *Mil., Navy, etc.* an emergency preparation for action. [nasalised var. of SCRABBLE] – **scrambler,** *n.*

**scramble crossing** /'– krɒsɪŋ/, *n.* a pedestrian crossing at which all traffic is halted by a system of phased traffic lights to allow pedestrians to cross in any direction.

**scran** /skræn/, *n. Colloq.* food. [orig. uncert.]

**scrannel** /ˈskrænəl/, *adj. Archaic.* **1.** thin or slight. **2.** squeaky or unmelodious. [cf. Norw. *skran* lean]

**scrap**[1] /skræp/, *n., adj., v.,* **scrapped, scrapping.** *–n.* **1.** a small piece or portion; a fragment: *scraps of paper.* **2.** (*pl.*) fragments of food, as those left over after a meal. **3.** a detached piece of something written or printed: *scraps of poetry.* **4.** (*pl.*) the remains of animal fat after the oil has been extracted. **5.** →**scrap metal.** **6.** anything discarded as useless, unwanted or worn-out. *–adj.* **7.** consisting of scraps or fragments: *scrap heap.* **8.** in the form of fragments or remnants of use only for reworking, as metal. **9.** discarded or left over. *–v.t.* **10.** to make into scraps or scrap; break up. **11.** to discard as useless or worthless. [ME *scrappe,* from Scand.; cf. Icel. *skrap* scraps, trifles, lit., scrapings]

**scrap**[2] /skræp/, *n., v.i.,* **scrapped, scrapping.** *Colloq.* fight or quarrel. [var. of SCRAPE (cf. defs 5, 6, 11)]

**scrapbook** /ˈskræpbʊk/, *n.* a blank book in which photographs, newspaper cuttings, etc., are pasted.

**scrape** /skreɪp/, *v.,* **scraped, scraping,** *n.* *–v.t.* **1.** to deprive of or free from an outer layer, adhering matter, etc., by drawing or rubbing something, esp. a sharp or rough instrument, over the surface. **2.** to remove (an outer layer, adhering matter, etc.) in this way. **3.** to scratch; produce as by scratching. **4.** to collect by or as by scraping, or laboriously, or with difficulty (fol. by *up* or *together*). **5.** to rub harshly on or across (something). **6.** to draw or rub (a thing) roughly across something. **7.** to level (an unpaved road) with a grader. **8.** (of a man) to have intercourse with (a woman). **9.** **scrape an acquaintance with somebody,** force one's attentions upon somebody in order to get acquainted with him. *–v.i.* **10.** to scrape something. **11.** to rub against something gratingly. **12.** to produce a grating and unmusical tone from a string instrument. **13.** to draw back the foot in making a bow. **14.** to practise laborious economy or saving. **15. bow and scrape,** to behave with exaggerated respect; be servile. **16. scrape through,** to manage to get by with difficulty; succeed by a narrow margin: *it was difficult having no money, but somehow we managed to scrape through.* *–n.* **17.** the act of scraping. **18.** a drawing back of the foot in making a bow. **19.** a scraping sound. **20.** a scraped place. **21.** *Med. Colloq.* curettage of the uterus. **22.** an embarrassing situation. **23.** a fight; struggle; scrap. [ME, from Scand.; cf. Icel. *skrapa*]

**scraper** /ˈskreɪpə/, *n.* **1.** one who or that which scrapes. **2.** any of various implements for scraping.

**scraperboard** /ˈskreɪpəbɔd/, *n.* a china clay coated cardboard covered with Indian ink, which is scratched to form a design in white against a black background.

**scrap heap** /ˈskræp hip/, *n.* **1.** a pile of scrap. **2. on the scrap heap,** useless; no longer employable: *there he was, on the scrap heap at forty-nine.*

**scraping** /ˈskreɪpɪŋ/, *n.* **1.** the act of one who or that which scrapes. **2.** the sound. **3.** (*usu. pl.*) that which is scraped off, up, or together.

**scrap iron** /ˈskræp aɪən/, *n.* old iron used for remelting or reworking.

**scrap merchant** /ˈ– mɜtʃənt/, *n.* **1.** a dealer in scrap metal. **2.** →**rag-and-bone man.**

**scrap metal** /ˈ– mɛtl/, *n.* pieces of old metal that can be reworked, esp. scrap iron.

**scrappy** /ˈskræpi/, *adj.,* **-pier, -piest.** **1.** made up of scraps or of odds and ends; fragmentary; disconnected. **2.** *Colloq.* given to fighting. – **scrappily,** *adv.* – **scrappiness,** *n.*

**scratch** /skrætʃ/, *v.t.* **1.** to break or mark slightly by rubbing, scraping, or tearing with something sharp or rough. **2.** to dig, scrape, or to tear (*out, off,* etc.) with the claws, the nails, etc. **3.** to rub or scrape lightly with the fingernails, etc., as to relieve itching. **4.** to rub gratingly, as a match, on something. **5.** to erase or strike out (writing, a name, etc.). **6.** to withdraw (a horse, etc.) from the list of entries in a race or competition. **7.** to write or draw by scraping or cutting into a surface. **8.** (formerly) to flog with a cat-o'-nine-tails. *–v.i.* **9.** to use the nails, claws, etc., for tearing, digging, etc. **10.** to relieve itching by rubbing with the nails, etc. **11.** to make a slight grating noise, as a pen. **12.** to manage with difficulty: *scratch along on very little money.* **13.** to withdraw from a contest. **14.** *Billiards.* to commit a scratch. *–n.* **15.** a mark produced by scratching, such as one on the skin. **16.** a rough mark of a pen, etc.; a scrawl. **17.** an act of scratching. **18.** the sound produced by scratching. **19.** the starting place, starting time, or status of a competitor in a handicap who has no allowance and no penalty. **20.** *Boxing.* (formerly) the mark in the centre of the ring at which bareknuckle fights were started. **21.** *Billiards.* **a.** a shot resulting in a penalty. **b.** a fluke. **22. from scratch,** from the beginning or from nothing. **23. up to scratch, a.** conforming to a certain standard; satisfactory. **b.** *Boxing.* (of a boxer) arriving at the fight by an agreed time (see def. 19). *–adj.* **24.** starting from scratch, or without allowance or penalty, as a competitor. **25.** *Colloq.* done by or dependent on chance: *a scratch shot.* **26.** *Colloq.* gathered hastily and indiscriminately: *a scratch crew, a scratch meal.* **27.** *Golf.* able to play the course in par figures: *a scratch player.* [b. obs. *scrat* and *cratch,* both meaning scratch] – **scratcher,** *n.*

**scratches** /ˈskrætʃəz/, *n.pl.* (*construed as sing.*) *Vet. Sci.* a disease of horses, in which dry rifts or chaps appear on the skin near the fetlock, behind the knee or in front of the hock.

**scratchy** /ˈskrætʃi/, *adj.,* **-ier, -iest.** **1.** that scratches: *a scratchy pen.* **2.** consisting of mere scratches. **3.** uneven; haphazard. **4.** suffering from scratches. **5.** irritable; out of sorts. – **scratchily,** *adv.* – **scratchiness,** *n.*

**scrawl** /skrɔl/, *v.t., v.i.* **1.** to write or draw in a sprawling awkward manner. *–n.* **2.** something scrawled, as a letter or a note. **3.** awkward or careless handwriting: *his scrawl is difficult to read.* [special use of obs. *scrawl* sprawl, influenced by SCRIBBLE[1], etc.] – **scrawler,** *n.* – **scrawly,** *adj.*

**scrawny** /ˈskrɔni/, *adj.,* **-nier, -niest.** lean; thin; scraggy: *a long scrawny neck.* [var. of *scranny,* var. of SCRANNEL] – **scrawniness,** *n.*

**scream** /skrim/, *v.i.* **1.** to utter a loud, sharp, piercing cry. **2.** to emit a shrill, piercing sound, as a whistle, etc. **3.** to laugh immoderately. **4.** to make something known by violent, startling words. **5.** to be startlingly conspicuous, used esp. of colours. **6.** to protest volubly, esp. to those in authority. **7. scream for,** to want desperately, be in great need of. **8. scream blue murder,** to complain vociferously. *–v.t.* **9.** to utter with a scream or screams. **10.** to make by screaming: *to scream oneself hoarse.* *–n.* **11.** a loud, sharp, piercing cry. **12.** a shrill, piercing sound. **13.** *Colloq.* someone or something that is very funny. [ME *screme;* orig. uncert.]

**screamer** /ˈskrimə/, *n.* **1.** one who or that which screams. **2.** *Colloq.* someone or something causing screams of astonishment, mirth, etc. **3.** *Print. Colloq.* an exclamation mark. **4.** *Aus. Rules Colloq.* a very high mark: *to pull down a screamer.* **5.** a newspaper poster incorporating blatant but not necessarily accurate headlines. **6.** any of the long-toed South and Central American birds which constitute the family Anhimidae, including *Anhima cornuta* **(horned screamer)** and *Chauna chavaria* and *C. torquata* (both known as **crested screamer**).

**screaming** /ˈskrimɪŋ/, *adj.* **1.** that screams. **2.** startling in effect: *screaming colours.* **3.** causing screams of mirth: *a screaming farce.* *–n.* **4.** the act or sound of one who or that which screams. – **screamingly,** *adv.*

**scree** /skri/, *n.* a steep mass of detritus on the side of a mountain. [Scand.; cf. Icel. *skridha* landslip and OE *scrīthan* go, glide]

**screech** /skritʃ/, *v.i.* **1.** to utter a harsh, shrill cry. *–v.t.* **2.** to utter with a screech. *–n.* **3.** a harsh, shrill cry. [var. of archaic *scritch;* probably imitative] – **screecher,** *n.* – **screechy,** *adj.*

**screech owl** /ˈ– aʊl/, *n.* any owl with a harsh cry, esp. the barn owl, *Tyto alba.*

**screed** /skrid/, *n.* **1.** a long speech or piece of writing; harangue. **2.** *Plastering.* **a.** a strip of plaster or wood of the proper thickness, applied to a wall as a guide or gauge for the rest of the work. **b.** the plaster, etc., laid to level off. *–v.i.* **3.** to apply screed to the required level. [ME *screde,* doublet of *shrede,* OE *scrēade* SHRED]

**screen** /skrin/, *n.* **1.** a covered frame or the like, movable or fixed, serving as a shelter, partition, etc.: *a firescreen.* **2.** an ornamental partition of wood, stone, etc., as in a church. **3.**

something affording a surface for displaying films, slides, etc. **4.** films collectively. **5.** (in a television set) the end of a cathode-ray tube on which the visible image is formed. **6.** →**sightscreen.** **7.** anything that shelters, protects, or conceals: *a screen of secrecy.* **8.** wire mesh serving as protection: *window screens.* **9.** a sieve or riddle, as for grain, sand, etc. **10.** *Mil.* a body of men sent out to cover the movement of an army. **11.** *Navy.* a protective formation of small vessels, as destroyers. **12.** *Physics.* a shield designed to prevent interference between various effects: *electric screens.* **13.** *Photoengraving.* **a.** a transparent plate containing two sets of the fine parallel lines, one crossing the other, used in the halftone process. **b.** a plastic sheet containing a special optical pattern for converting a continuous tone original into a series of dots of differing size. *–v.t.* **14.** to shelter, protect, or conceal with, or as with, a screen. **15.** to sift by passing through a screen. **16.** to project (pictures, etc.) on a screen. **17.** to photograph with a film camera. **18.** to provide with a screen or screens. **19.** to adapt (a story, play, etc.) for presentation, as a film. **20.** to check the loyalty, character, ability, etc., of applicants, employees, or the like. **21. screen off,** to conceal, shut off, behind a screen. *–v.i.* **22.** to be projected, or suitable for projection, on a screen. [ME *scren(e),* from OF *escren,* var. of *escrime,* from OHG *skirm* (G *Schirm*)] – **screenable,** *adj.* – **screener,** *n.*

**screen door** /– ˈdɔ/, *n.* a door consisting principally of a frame to which is attached fine wire or other mesh which allows ventilation but keeps out insects. Also, **stop door.**

**screening** /ˈskrinɪŋ/, *n.* **1.** the act or work of one who screens. **2.** →**fluoroscopy.** **3.** (*pl.*) matter separated out with a screen. **4.** *Mining.* a method of noodling in which a wire screen, bed frame, perforated drum, or anything else providing a mesh, is used to shake out dirt, leaving concentrates to be searched for opal.

**screenplay** /ˈskrinpleɪ/, *n.* the script of a film, including details of camera positions and movement, action, dialogue, lighting, etc.

**screen-print** /skrin-ˈprɪnt/, *n., v.t.* →**silk-screen.**

**screen test** /ˈskrin tɛst/, *n.* a test given to a person aspiring to act in a film, television show, etc., to judge their suitability on screen.

**screenwriter** /ˈskrinraɪtə/, *n.* one who writes the script of a film or television play.

**screw** /skru/, *n.* **1.** a metal device having a slotted head and a tapering body with a helical ridge usu. driven into wood with the aid of a screwdriver to assemble and secure parts of a building construction, furniture, etc. **2.** a mechanical device consisting of a cylinder having a helical ridge winding round it **(external** or **male screw). 3.** a corresponding part into which such a device fits when turned, consisting of a cylindrical socket in whose wall is cut a helical groove **(internal** or **female screw). 4.** something having a spiral form. **5.** →**propeller.** **6.** (*pl.*) *Colloq.* pressure; force: *to put the screws on a debtor.* **7.** a little tobacco, salt, etc., in a twisted paper. **8.** a twisting movement; a turn of a screw. **9.** *Colloq.* a hard bargainer; a miser. **10.** *Colloq.* a brokendown horse. **11.** *Colloq.* wages. **12.** *Colloq.* a prison warder. **13.** *Colloq.* sexual intercourse. **14.** a look; glance: *to have a screw (at).* **15. have a screw loose,** *Colloq.* to be slightly eccentric; have crazy ideas. **16. put the screws on,** *Colloq.* to apply pressure; intimidate. *–v.t.* **17.** to force, press, hold fast, stretch tight, etc., by or as by means of a screw. **18.** to operate or adjust by a screw, as a press. **19.** to attach with a screw or screws: *to screw a bracket to a wall.* **20.** to work (a screw, etc.) by turning. **21.** to twist; contort; distort. **22.** to force: *screw up one's courage.* **23.** to put compulsion on; force (a seller) to lower a price (oft. fol. by *down.*). **24.** *Colloq.* to extract or extort. **25.** *Colloq.* to make a mess of; impair; frustrate (oft. fol. by *up*). **26.** *Rugby Football.* of the loose head prop, to drop only one knee putting the scrum off balance and causing it to wheel around. **27.** *Colloq.* (of a man) to have sexual intercourse with. **28.** *Colloq.* to cause (someone) to become mentally and emotionally disturbed (fol. by *up*). *–v.i.* **29.** to turn as or like a screw. **30.** to be adapted for being connected or taken apart by means of a screw or screws (fol. by *on, together, off,* etc.). **31.** to turn with a twisting motion. **32.** *Colloq.* to practise extortion. **33.** to have sexual intercourse. [ME; cf. OF *escro(ue)* nut, MD *schrūve* screw]

screw (def. 1): flat-head woodscrew

**screw axis** /ˈ– æksəs/, *n.* an axis of symmetry about which the atoms in a crystal lattice are arranged.

**screwball** /ˈskrubɔl/, *Colloq.* *–n.* **1.** an erratic, eccentric, or unconventional person. *–adj.* **2.** erratic, eccentric, or unconventional.

**screwdriver** /ˈskrudraɪvə/, *n.* a tool fitting into the slotted head of a screw for driving in or withdrawing it by turning.

**screwed** /skrud/, *adj.* **1.** fastened with a screw or screws. **2.** having grooves like a screw. **3.** twisted; awry. **4.** *Colloq.* drunk; intoxicated. **5. screwed up, a.** mentally and emotionally disturbed. **b.** broken; impaired.

**screw-eye** /ˈskru-aɪ/, *n.* a screw having a ring-shaped head.

**screw-jack** /ˈskru-dʒæk/, *n.* a jack which obtains its lifting power by means of a screw. Also, **jackscrew.**

**screw pile** /ˈskru paɪl/, *n.* a bearing pile with a screw tip, turned into the ground with a capstan, used in soft mud or the like, for the foundation of bridges and other constructions.

**screw-pine** /ˈskru-paɪn/, *n.* a pandanus (plant), so called from its leaves, which have a spiral arrangement.

**screw-propeller** /skru-prəˈpɛlə/, *n.* a device consisting of a number of specially shaped blades radiating from a central hub, used to propel a vehicle, as a ship.

**screw thread** /ˈskru θrɛd/, *n.* **1.** the helical ridge of a screw. **2.** a full turn of the spiral ridge of a screw.

**screw-top** /ˈskru-tɒp/, *n.* **1.** a type of lid of a jar, bottle, or the like, designed to fit on by screwing. *–adj.* **2.** having a screw-top.

**screw-worm** /ˈskru-wɜm/, *n.* the larva of a dipteran insect, *Callitroga macellaria,* widespread in America, which feeds upon the skin of living domestic animals, occasionally man.

**screwy** /ˈskrui/, *adj.,* **-ier, -iest.** *Colloq.* **1.** eccentric; crazy. **2.** strange; peculiar.

**scribal** /ˈskraɪbəl/, *adj.* of, pertaining to, or denoting a scribe.

**scribble**[1] /ˈskrɪbəl/, *v.,* **-bled, -bling,** *n.* *–v.t.* **1.** to write hastily or carelessly: *to scribble a letter.* **2.** to cover with meaningless writing or marks (oft. fol. by *over*). *–v.i.* **3.** to write literary matter in a hasty, careless way. **4.** to make meaningless marks. *–n.* **5.** a hasty or careless piece of writing or drawing. [ME *scribyl, scrible,* from ML *scrībillāre.* Cf. L *conscrībillāre* scribble]

**scribble**[2] /ˈskrɪbəl/, *v.t.,* **-bled, -bling.** (of wool, cotton, etc.) to card; pass through a scribbler. [Flem. *schribbelen,* akin to SCRUB[1]]

**scribbler**[1] /ˈskrɪblə/, *n.* **1.** an unimportant writer or author. **2.** one who scribbles. **3.** Also, **scribble pad, scribbling block.** a writing pad for casual notes, memoranda, etc.

**scribbler**[2] /ˈskrɪblə/, *n.* **1.** a carding machine, as for wool. **2.** one who runs or looks after such a machine.

**scribbly gum** /ˈskrɪbli gʌm/, *n.* any species of the genus *Eucalyptus* with smooth bark marked by insects to resemble scribbling, esp. *E. haemastoma* of the Port Jackson district of New South Wales.

**scribe**[1] /skraɪb/, *n., v.,* **scribed, scribing.** *–n.* **1.** a penman or copyist, as one who, formerly, made copies of manuscripts, etc. **2.** any of various officials of ancient or former times who performed clerical duties. **3.** *Jewish Hist.* one of a class of teachers who interpreted the Jewish law to the people. **4.** a writer or author. *–v.t.* **5.** *Rare.* to write or write down. [ME, from L *scrība* writer]

**scribe**[2] /skraɪb/, *v.,* **scribed, scribing,** *n.* *–v.t.* **1.** to mark or score (wood, etc.) with a pointed instrument. *–n.* **2.** a pointed instrument for so marking (wood, etc.); scriber. [? aphetic var. of DESCRIBE]

**scriber** /ˈskraɪbə/, *n.* a tool for scribing wood, etc.

**scrim** /skrɪm/, *n.* **1.** a cotton or linen fabric of open weave, used for curtains, etc. **2.** such a fabric, used for cleaning, polishing, etc. **3.** a piece of such fabric, used as a drop to give the effect of opacity, hazy translucency, etc., in theatrical use, or in camouflage. [orig. uncert.]

**scrimmage** /ˈskrɪmɪdʒ/, *n., v.,* **-maged, -maging.** *–n.* **1.** a rough or vigorous struggle. **2. a.** *Aus. Rules, Rugby Football,*

*Soccer.* the action of a number of players struggling for the ball in no set pattern of play. **3.** *American Football.* the action between contesting lines of players when the ball is put into play. **4.** *Rugby Football.* →**scrum.** *–v.i.* **5.** to engage in a scrimmage. **6.** to search rapidly and in a disorderly fashion as through a drawer. Also, **scrummage.** [var. of *scrimish,* var. of SKIRMISH] – **scrimmager,** *n.*

**scrimp** /skrɪmp/, *v.t.* **1.** to be sparing of or in; stint. **2.** to keep on short allowance, as of food. *–v.i.* **3.** to use severe economy: *they scrimped on butter as best they could.* *–adj.* **4.** scant. [? akin to SHRIMP]

**scrimpy** /'skrɪmpi/, *adj.,* **-pier, -piest.** scanty; meagre. – **scrimpily,** *adv.* – **scrimpiness,** *n.*

**scrimshaw** /'skrɪmʃɔ/, *n.* **1.** carved or scratched work or articles of bone, ivory, steel, wood, etc., made by sailors in leisure times. *–v.t.* **2.** to make (scrimshaw). *–v.i.* **3.** to make scrimshaw. [orig. uncert.]

**scrip**[1] /skrɪp/, *n.* **1.** a writing, esp. a receipt or certificate. **2.** a scrap of paper. **3.** *Finance.* shares or stock issued to existing shareholders in a scrip issue. **4.** *Finance.* a certificate that part of the issue price of a debenture, bond, or share has been paid, and setting out the amounts and dates when further sums are due. **5.** →**prescription** (def. 1a). [var. of SCRIPT]

**scrip**[2] /skrɪp/, *n. Archaic.* a bag or wallet carried by wayfarers. [ME *scrippe,* from Scand.; cf. Icel. *skreppa*]

**Scrip.,** **1.** Scripture. **2.** Scriptural.

**scrip issue** /'skrɪp ˌɪʃu/, *n.* an issue of stock, etc., where the purchase price is payable by instalments according to the terms of the prospectus.

**scripsit** /'skrɪpsɪt/, *v.* he (she) wrote (it, this). [L]

**script** /skrɪpt/, *n.* **1.** handwriting; handwritten letters or lettering; the characters used in handwriting. **2.** the working text, manuscript, or the like, of a play, film, television program, etc., or the contents of such a document. **3.** a manuscript or document. **4.** the written work submitted by an examination candidate. **5.** *Law.* **a.** an original document. **b.** a draft of a will or codicil, or written instructions for it. **6.** *Print.* a typeface imitating handwriting. [L *scriptum,* neut. pp., (something) written, replacing ME *scrit,* from OF; *escrit*]

**Script.,** **1.** Scriptural. **2.** Scripture.

**scriptorium** /skrɪp'tɔriəm/, *n., pl.* **-toriums, -toria** /-'tɔriə/. a room in a monastery set apart for the writing or copying of manuscripts. [ML, properly neut. of L *scriptōrius* of writing]

**scriptural** /'skrɪptʃərəl/, *adj.* of, pertaining to, or in accordance with the Scriptures. Also, **Scriptural.** – **scripturally,** *adv.*

**Scripture** /'skrɪptʃə/, *n.* **1.** the sacred writings of the Old and the New Testaments or of either of them (often called **Holy Scripture** or **the Scriptures**); Holy Writ; the Bible. **2.** (*l.c.*) any writing or book, esp. of a sacred nature. [ME *scriptur,* from L *scriptūra* writing]

**scrivener** /'skrɪvnə/, *n. Archaic.* **1.** a professional or public writer; a clerk. **2.** →**notary.** [ME, from obs. *scriveyn* (from OF) + -ER[1]]

**scrobiculate** /skrə'bɪkjələt, -leɪt/, *adj.* (of plant and animal organs) furrowed or pitted. [LL *scrobiculus* (diminutive of *scrobis* ditch, trench) + -ATE[1]]

**scrod** /skrɒd/, *n. U.S.* a young codfish, esp. one that is split for cooking. [? akin to SHRED]

**scrofula** /'skrɒfjələ/, *n.* a constitutional disorder of a tuberculous nature, characterised chiefly by swelling and degeneration of the lymphatic glands, esp. of the neck, and by inflammation of the joints, etc.; king's evil. [ML, sing. of L *scrōfulae* glandular swelling]

**scrofulous** /'skrɒfjələs/, *adj.* **1.** pertaining to, of the nature of, or affected with scrofula. **2.** morally corrupt. – **scrofulously,** *adv.* – **scrofulousness,** *n.*

**scroggin** /'skrɒgən/, *n.* a mixture of dried fruits, nuts, etc., used as a light but sustaining food by bushwalkers. [? Scot. d.]

**scroll** /skroʊl/, *n.* **1.** a roll of parchment or paper, esp. one with writing on it. **2.** something, esp. an ornament, resembling a partly unrolled sheet of paper or having a spiral or coiled form. **3.** the ornamental carving, resembling this, at the head of a violin or similar instrument. **4.** a piece of writing; a list or schedule. *–v.t.* **5.** to cut into scrolls, as wooden ornamentation. **6.** to write, as in a scroll. *–v.i.* **7.** formed into, as, or like a scroll. [ME *scrowle,* var. of *scrowe,* from AF *escrowe;* of Gmc orig. and akin to SHRED]

**scroll-saw** /'skroʊl-sɔ/, *n.* **1.** a narrow saw mounted vertically in a frame and operated with an up-and-down motion, used for cutting curved ornamental designs. **2.** such a saw mounted in a power-driven machine.

**scrollwork** /'skroʊlwɜk/, *n.* **1.** decorative work in which scroll forms are important. **2.** ornamental work cut out with a scroll-saw.

**scrooge** /skrudʒ/, *n.* a miserly, ill-tempered person. [after Ebenezer *Scrooge,* a character in Dickens's story *A Christmas Carol* (1843)]

**scroop** /skrup/, *v.i.* **1.** to emit a harsh, grating sound. *–n.* **2.** a scrooping sound. **3.** the crisp rustle of silk or similar cloth that has been treated with dilute acids. [imitative]

**scrophulariaceous** /ˌskrɒfjəˌlɛəri'eɪʃəs/, *adj.* belonging to the Scrophulariaceae, family of plants, including the snapdragon, foxglove, toadflax, mullein, eyebright, etc. [NL *Scrophulāria,* the typical genus (reputed remedy for scrofula) + -ACEOUS]

**scrotum** /'skroʊtəm/, *n., pl.* **-ta** /-tə/. the pouch of skin that contains the testicles and their coverings. [L] – **scrotal,** *adj.*

**scrounge** /skraʊndʒ/, *v.,* **scrounged, scrounging.** *Colloq.* *–v.i.* **1.** to borrow, sponge, or pilfer. **2.** to gather, as by foraging; search out (oft. fol. by *around*). *–v.t.* **3.** to obtain by borrowing, scrounging, or pilfering. [var. of d. *scringe* to glean; ? akin to SCRIMP] – **scrounger,** *n.*

**scrub**[1] /skrʌb/, *v.,* **scrubbed, scrubbing,** *n.* *–v.t.* **1.** to rub hard with a brush, cloth, etc., or against a rough surface, in washing. **2.** to cleanse (a gas). **3.** *Colloq.* to cancel; get rid of. *–v.i.* **4.** to cleanse things by hard rubbing. **5.** *Horse-racing Colloq.* (of a jockey) to move the whip or arms rhythmically to and fro, to encourage the horse during the final stretch of the race. *–n.* **6.** the act of scrubbing. [ME *scrobbe,* apparently from MD *schrubben, schrobben* scratch, rub, scrub]

**scrub**[2] /skrʌb/, *n.* **1.** low trees or shrubs, collectively. **2.** a large area covered with scrub, as the Australian bush, or American sagebrush. **3.** tall, thick rainforest in eastern Australia. **4.** an animal of common or inferior breeding. **5.** a mean, insignificant person. **6.** anything undersized or inferior. **7. the scrub,** *Colloq.* country areas in general, as opposed to the city. *–v.i.* **8.** to remove the scrub from (a paddock, etc.). [var. of SHRUB[1]]

**scrub beefwood** /– 'bifwʊd/, *n.* a medium-sized tree, *Stenocarpus salignus,* family Proteaceae, found in coastal forests of eastern Australia.

**scrubber**[1] /'skrʌbə/, *n.* **1.** one who or that which scrubs. **2.** an apparatus for purifying gases. **3.** *Brit. Colloq.* a promiscuous or mercenary girl; a girl of loose morals (used as a term of abuse). **4.** a scruffy, untidy woman or girl. [SCRUB[1] + -ER[1]]

**scrubber**[2] /'skrʌbə/, *n.* a farm animal, as a horse, cow, etc., which has taken to the bush and run wild, thus losing condition. [SCRUB[2] + -ER[2]]

**scrubbing-board** /'skrʌbɪŋ-bɔd/, *n.* a board having a corrugated surface on which to scrub clothes. Also, **scrub-board.**

**scrubbing-brush** /'skrʌbɪŋ-brʌʃ/, *n.* **1.** a brush used for scrubbing, esp. floors, clothes, or very dirty hands. **2.** *Obs. Colloq.* bread with more chaff and bran in it than flour.

**scrub-bird** /'skrʌb-bɜd/, *n.* either of two species of elusive, ground-dwelling, Australian birds of the genus *Atrichornis* having fine, resonant voices as the rare **noisy scrub-bird,** *A. clamosus,* of south-western Australia and the **rufous scrub-bird,** *A. rufescens,* of coastal rainforest areas of southern Queensland and northern New South Wales.

**scrubby** /'skrʌbi/, *adj.,* **-bier, -biest.** **1.** low or stunted, as trees. **2.** consisting of or covered with stunted trees, etc., or scrub. **3.** undersized or inferior, as animals. **4.** wretched; shabby. – **scrubbiness,** *n.*

**scrub-cutter** /'skrʌb-kʌtə/, *n.* a man employed to clear land of scrub. – **scrub-cutting,** *n.*

**scrub fowl** /'skrʌb faʊl/, *n.* a chestnut-brown mound-building bird, with a prominent crest, *Megapodius freycinet,* of coastal forested areas of northern Australia, many parts of Asia and the Pacific islands. Also, **scrub hen, jungle fowl.**

**scrub land** /'– lænd/, *n.* land covered by scrub only.

**scrub muster** /'– mʌstə/, *n.* the mustering of a number of beasts (usu. cattle) which have been running wild in scrub.

**scrub robin** /– 'rɒbən/, *n.* either of two thrushes of the genus *Drymodes,* one of which is found in northern Australia and New Guinea, while the other is found in southern Australia.

**scrub turkey** /– 'tɜki/, *n.* →**brush turkey.**

**scrub wallaby** /– 'wɒləbi/, *n.* →**red wallaby.**

**scruff**[1] /skrʌf/, *n.* the nape or back of the neck. [var. of d. *scuft,* from D *schoft* horse's withers]

**scruff**[2] /skrʌf/, *n.* **1.** *Metall.* dross formed during tinplating. **2.** *Colloq.* a scruffy person. [metathetic var. of SCURF]

**scruffy** /'skrʌfi/, *adj. Colloq.* unkempt or dirty; shabby.

**scrum** /skrʌm/, *n., v.,* **scrummed, scrumming.** *Rugby Football.* *–n.* **1.** a method of restarting play after a rule infringement, in which the opposing forwards pack together and push in formation, heads down, in an attempt to gain ground, while the ball is thrown in and the hookers attempt to kick it back to their team-mates. It may be called for by the referee (**set scrum**), or it may form spontaneously (**loose scrum**). **2.** the formation. *–v.i.* **3.** to form a scrum (usu. fol. by *down*). **4.** to play as a member of a scrum. [short for SCRUMMAGE]

**scrum-half** /skrʌm-'haf/, *n. Chiefly Brit.* →**half-back** (def. 1a). Also, **scrum half.**

**scrummage** /'skrʌmɪdʒ/, *n., v.t., v.i.,* **-maged, -maging. 1.** →**scrum. 2.** →**scrimmage.** – **scrummager,** *n.*

**scrumptious** /'skrʌmpʃəs/, *adj. Colloq.* deliciously tasty; superlatively fine or nice; splendid: *to have a scrumptious time.* [orig. d., meaning 'stingy', from SCRIMP]

**scrunch** /skrʌntʃ/, *v.t., v.i.* **1.** to crunch; crush. *–n.* **2.** the act or sound of scrunching. [var. of CRUNCH]

**scruple** /'skrupəl/, *n., v.,* **-pled, -pling.** *–n.* **1.** hesitation or reluctance from conscientious or other restraining reasons. **2.** a very small portion or amount. **3.** a unit of weight in the imperial system, equal to 20 grams or $\frac{1}{3}$ of a drachm, apothecaries' weight, or approx. $1.3 \times 10^{-3}$ kg. *–v.i.* **4.** to have scruples. *–v.t.* **5.** *Obs.* to have scruples about; hesitate at. [L *scrūpulus,* lit., small stone, fig., anxiety, doubt, scruple (diminutive of *scrūpus* sharp stone)]

**scrupulous** /'skrupjələs/, *adj.* **1.** having scruples; having or showing a strict regard for what is right. **2.** punctiliously or minutely careful, precise, or exact. – **scrupulosity** /skrupjə'lɒsəti/, **scrupulousness,** *n.* – **scrupulously,** *adv.*

**scrutable** /'skrutəbəl/, *adj.* that may be penetrated or understood by investigation.

**scrutator** /skru'teɪtə/, *n.* one who investigates.

**scrutineer** /skrutə'nɪə/, *n.* **1.** one who is authorised, esp. by a candidate at an election, to inspect the counting of votes by electoral officers. **2.** one who checks cars, motor bikes, etc., for safety and to see that they comply with race regulations. **3.** an official in a race, contest, etc., who checks that the rules are observed. *–v.i.* **4.** to act as a scrutineer.

**scrutinise** /'skrutənaɪz/, *v.t.,* **-nised, -nising.** to examine closely or critically. Also, **scrutinize.** – **scrutiniser,** *n.* – **scrutinisingly,** *adv.*

**scrutiny** /'skrutəni/, *n., pl.* **-nies. 1.** searching examination or investigation; minute inquiry. **2.** a searching look. [LL *scrūtinium*]

**scry** /skraɪ/, *v.,* **scried, scrying.** *Archaic.* *–v.t.* **1.** to perceive, esp. by crystal-gazing. *–v.i.* **2.** to practise crystal-gazing. [var. of DESCRY]

**scuba** /'skubə/, *n.* a portable breathing device for free-swimming divers, consisting of a mouthpiece joined by hoses to one or two tanks of compressed air which are strapped on the back. [*s(elf-) c(ontained) u(nderwater) b(reathing) a(pparatus)*]

**scuba diving** /'– ˌdaɪvɪŋ/, *n.* underwater diving with the aid of scuba apparatus. – **scuba diver,** *n.*

**scud** /skʌd/, *v.,* **scudded, scudding,** *n.* *–v.i.* **1.** to run or move quickly or hurriedly. **2.** *Naut.* to run before a gale with little or no sail set. *–n.* **3.** the act of scudding. **4.** clouds, spray, or the like, driven by the wind; a driving shower; a gust of wind. **5.** low drifting clouds appearing beneath a cloud from which precipitation is falling. [Scand.; cf. Norw. *skudda* push]

**scuff** /skʌf/, *v.t.* **1.** to scrape with the feet. **2.** to mar by scraping or hard use, as shoes, furniture, etc. *–v.i.* **3.** to walk without raising the feet; shuffle. *–n.* **4.** the act or sound of scuffing. **5.** a type of slipper or sandal without a back. [? short for SCUFFLE]

**scuffle** /'skʌfəl/, *v.,* **-fled, -fling,** *n.* *–v.i.* **1.** to struggle or fight in a scrambling, confused manner. **2.** to go or move in hurried confusion. **3.** to move at a shuffle; scuff. *–n.* **4.** a confused struggle or fight. **5.** a shuffling: *a scuffle of feet.* **6.** *U.S.* a spadelike hoe which is pushed instead of pulled. [? of Scand. orig.; cf. Swed. *skuffa* push]

**scuffler** /'skʌflə/, *n.* **1.** one who or that which scuffles. **2.** a type of cultivator, drawn by hand or horse, and used principally as a weeder.

**scull** /skʌl/, *n.* **1. a.** an oar worked from side to side over the stern of a boat as a means of propulsion. **b.** one of a pair of oars operated, one on each side, by one person. **2.** a boat propelled by a scull or sculls, esp. a light racing boat propelled by one rower with a pair of oars. **3.** (*pl.*) a sculling race. **4.** an act of sculling. *–v.t.* **5.** to propel or convey by means of a scull or sculls. *–v.i.* **6.** to propel a boat with a scull or sculls. **7.** to swim while floating on the front or the back, with the arms close to the body, using only a wrist movement. [ME; orig. unknown] – **sculler,** *n.*

**scullery** /'skʌləri/, *n., pl.* **-leries. 1.** a small room where the rough, dirty work of a kitchen is done. **2.** the place in which kitchen utensils are cleaned and kept. [ME *squillerye,* from OF *escuelerie,* from *escuele* dish, from L *scutella* salver]

**scullion** /'skʌljən/, *n. Archaic.* **1.** a kitchen servant who does menial work. **2.** a low or contemptible person. [ME *sculyon,* ? from OF *escouillon* dishcloth]

**sculp** /skʌlp/, *v.t., v.i.* →**sculpt.** [L *sculpere* carve]

**sculpin** /'skʌlpən/, *n.* **1.** a small freshwater fish of the genus *Cottus* (family Cottidae), with a large head armed on each side with one or more spines; bullhead. **2.** any marine fish of the same family. [? NL *scorpæna.* See SCORPAENOID]

sculpin (def. 1)

**sculpsit** /'skʌlpsɪt/, *v.* (he or she) engraved, carved, or sculptured (it). [L]

**sculpt** /skʌlpt/, *v.t.* **1.** to make (a sculpture). **2.** to make a sculpture of (some person or thing). *–v.i.* **3.** to make a sculpture. **4.** to practise sculpture. [F *sculpter,* from L *sculptus* (pp. of *sculpere*). See SCULP]

**sculptor** /'skʌlptə/, *n.* one who practises the art of sculpture. [L] – **sculptress** /'skʌlptrəs/, *n. fem.*

**sculpture** /'skʌlptʃə/, *n., v.,* **-tured, -turing.** *–n.* **1.** the fine art of forming figures or designs in relief, in intaglio, or in the round by cutting marble, wood, granite, etc., by fashioning plastic materials, by modelling in clay, or by making moulds for casting in bronze or other metal. **2.** such work collectively. **3.** a piece of such work. *–v.t.* **4.** to carve, make, or execute by sculpture, as a figure, design, etc.; represent in sculpture. **5.** *Phys. Geog.* to change the form of (the land surface) by erosion. [ME, from L *sculptūra*] – **sculptural,** *adj.* – **sculpturally,** *adv.*

**sculpturesque** /skʌlptʃə'rɛsk/, *adj.* in the manner of, or suggesting, sculpture: *sculpturesque beauty.* – **sculpturesquely,** *adv.* – **sculpturesqueness,** *n.*

**scum** /skʌm/, *n., v.,* **scummed, scumming.** *–n.* **1.** a film of foul or extraneous matter on a liquid. **2.** refuse or offscourings: *scum of the earth.* **3.** low, worthless persons. **4.** the scoria of molten metals. *–v.t.* **5.** to remove the scum from. **6.** to remove as scum. *–v.i.* **7.** to form scum; become covered with scum. [ME, from MD *schūme,* c. G *Schaum* foam]

**scumble** /'skʌmbəl/, *v.,* **-bled, -bling,** *n.* *–v.t., v.i.* **1.** to modify the effect of (a painting) by overlaying parts of it with a thin application of opaque or semi-opaque colour. *–n.* **2.** application of such colour. **3.** the colour used. **4.** the effect produced by this technique. [from SCUM]

**scummy** /'skʌmi/, *adj.,* **-mier, -miest. 1.** consisting of or having scum. **2.** *Brit. Colloq.* worthless; despicable.

**scunge** /skʌndʒ/, *n. Colloq.* **1.** an unkempt, slovenly person. **2.** dirt, mess, slime, etc. **3.** messy, untidy objects: *I'll clear the scunge off this desk.*

**scungy** /'skʌndʒi/, *adj. Colloq.* mean, dirty, miserable, unpleasant. Also, **skungy.** [Brit. d.]

**scupper** /'skʌpə/, *n.* **1.** *Naut.* an opening in the side of a ship at or just below the level of the deck, to allow water to run off. *–v.t.* **2.** to sink (a ship) deliberately. **3.** *Brit. Colloq.* to deprive of any chance of success. [orig. uncert.]

**scur** /skɜ/, *n.* a rudimentary horn, or horn tissue attached to the skin of a horn pit of a polled animal.

**scurf** /skɜf/, *n.* **1.** the scales or small shreds of epidermis that are continually exfoliated from the skin; dandruff. **2.** any scaly matter or incrustation on a surface. [ME and OE, from Scand.; cf. Dan. *skurv,* c. OE *sceorf*] – **scurfy,** *adj.*

**scurf-pea** /'skɜf-pi/, *n.* any of many shrubs or herbs of the widespread genus *Psoralea,* family Papilionaceae.

**scurrile** /'skʌraɪl/, *adj.* →**scurrilous.** Also, **scurril** /'skʌrəl/. [L *scurrīlis*]

**scurrility** /skə'rɪləti/, *n., pl.* **-ties.** **1.** scurrilous quality. **2.** a scurrilous remark or attack.

**scurrilous** /'skʌrələs/, *adj.* **1.** grossly or indecently abusive: *a scurrilous attack.* **2.** characterised by or using low buffoonery; coarsely jocular or derisive: *a scurrilous jest.* [see SCURRILE, -OUS] – **scurrilously,** *adv.* – **scurrilousness,** *n.*

**scurry** /'skʌri/, *v.,* **-ried, -rying,** *n., pl.* **-ries.** *–v.i.* **1.** to go or move quickly or in haste. *–v.t.* **2.** to send hurrying along. *–n.* **3.** a scurrying rush: *we heard the scurry of little feet down the stairs.* **4.** a flurry or flittering passage, as of snow, leaves, birds, etc. **5.** a fairly short run or race. [abstracted from HURRY-SCURRY]

**scurvy** /'skɜvi/, *n., adj.,* **-vier, -viest.** *–n.* **1.** *Pathol.* a disease marked by swollen and bleeding gums, livid spots on the skin, prostration, etc., due to a diet lacking in vitamin C. *–adj.* **2.** low, mean, or contemptible: *a scurvy trick.* [orig. adj., from SCURF + -Y[1]] – **scurvily,** *adv.* – **scurviness,** *n.*

**scut** /skʌt/, *n.* a short tail, esp. that of a hare, rabbit, or deer. [Scand.; cf. Icel. *skott* tail]

**scutate** /'skuteɪt/, *adj.* **1.** *Bot.* formed like a round buckler. **2.** *Zool.* having scutes, shields, or large scales. [L *scūtātus* having a shield] – **scutation** /sku'teɪʃən/, *n.*

**scutch**[1] /skʌtʃ/, *v.t.* **1.** to dress (flax) by beating. **2.** →**thresh** (def. 1). *–n.* Also, **scutcher** (for defs 3, 4, 5). **3.** a device for scutching flax fibre. **4.** one who scutches flax fibres. **5.** →**thresher** (def. 2). **6.** a flat double-edged cutting head with a handle set perpendicularly to the cutting edges, used in trimming brick. [cf. OF *escousser* shake]

**scutch**[2] /skʌtʃ/, *n.* →**couch**[2].

**scutcheon** /'skʌtʃən/, *n.* **1.** →**escutcheon.** **2.** →**scute.**

**scute** /skut/, *n.* **1.** a dermal plate, as on an armadillo, turtle, etc. **2.** a large scale. [L *scūtum* shield]

**scutellate** /'skutəleɪt, -lət/, *adj.* **1.** having scutes. **2.** formed into a scutellum. Also, **scutellated.** [NL *scūtellātus.* See SCUTELLUM, -ATE[1]]

**scutellation** /skutə'leɪʃən/, *n. Zool.* **1.** scutellate state or formation; a scaly covering, as on a bird's leg. **2.** arrangement of scutella or scales.

**scutellum** /sku'tɛləm/, *n., pl.* **-tella** /-'tɛlə/. a small plate, scutum, or other shieldlike part. [NL, irregular diminutive of L *scūtum* shield]

**scutiform** /'skutəfɔm/, *adj.* shield-shaped. [NL *scūtiformis,* from L *scūti-* shield + *-formis* -FORM]

**scutter** /'skʌtə/, *v.i., n.* →**scurry.** [var. of SCUTTLE[2]]

**scuttle**[1] /'skʌtl/, *n.* **1.** a coalscuttle; a coal hod. **2.** a large basket. [ME and OE *scutel,* orig., a dish or platter, from L *scutella*]

**scuttle**[2] /'skʌtl/, *v.,* **-tled, -tling,** *n.* *–v.i.* **1.** to run with quick, hasty steps; hurry (oft. fol. by *off, away,* etc.). *–n.* **2.** a quick pace; a short, hurried run. [? var. of *scuddle,* frequentative of SCUD]

**scuttle**[3] /'skʌtl/, *n., v.,* **-tled, -tling.** *–n.* **1.** a small rectangular opening in a ship's deck, with a movable lid or cover. **2.** a similar opening in a ship's side. **3.** the part of a motor vehicle between the bonnet and the body. *–v.t.* **4.** to cut a hole or holes through the bottom, sides, or deck of (a ship or boat) for any purpose, esp. through the bottom or sides for the purpose of sinking it. **5.** to sink (a vessel) by cutting a hole below the waterline or opening the seacocks. [late ME *skottell* hatchway lid, apparently from D *schutten* to shut. Cf. F. *écoutille,* Sp. *escotilla* hatchway]

**scuttlebutt** /'skʌtlbʌt/, *n.* **1.** *Naut.* a cask having a hole cut in it for the introduction of a cup or dipper, and used to hold drinking water. **2.** *Colloq.* rumour; gossip.

**scutum** /'skjutəm/, *n., pl.* **-ta** /-tə/. **1.** *Zool.* →**scute** (def. 1). **2.** *Rom. Hist.* a large, oblong shield, as of heavy-armed legionaries. [L: shield]

**Scylla** /'sɪlə/, *n. in the phrase* **between Scylla and Charybdis** /kə'rɪbdɪs/, between two equal evils or dangers, where avoidance of one must bring exposure to the other. [from *Scylla* a dangerous rock on the Italian side of the Strait of Messina, facing *Charybdis* a whirlpool on the Sicilian side, both personified in classical mythology as female monsters]

**scyphiform** /'saɪfəfɔm/, *adj.* (of plants) shaped like a cup or goblet.

**scyphistoma** /sə'fɪstəmə/, *n.* the polyp stage of a jellyfish.

**scyphozoan** /saɪfə'zoʊən/, *n.* one of the Scyphozoa, a class of coelenterates comprising the larger medusae or jellyfishes. [NL *Scyphozo(a)* (from Gk *skypho-,* combining form of *skýphos* cup, can + *-zoa* -ZOA) + -AN]

**scyphus** /'saɪfəs/, *n., pl.* **-phi** /-faɪ/. a large ancient Greek drinking cup. [NL, special use of L *scyphus* goblet, from Gk *skýphos* can, cup]

**scythe** /saɪð/, *n., v.,* **scythed, scything.** *–n.* **1.** an agricultural implement consisting of a long, curved blade fastened at an angle to a handle, for mowing grass, etc., by hand. *–v.t., v.i.* **2.** to cut or mow with a scythe. [ME *sith,* OE *sīthe,* c. Icel. *sigdh;* spelling *sc* by pseudo-etymological association with L *scindere* cut]

**SD,** standard deviation.

**S.D.A.** /ɛs di 'eɪ/, Seventh-Day Adventist.

**se-,** a prefix applied mainly to stems not used as words, having a general meaning of setting apart or taking away, as in *seclude, seduce.* [L]

**Se,** *Chem.* selenium.

**SE,** **1.** south-east. **2.** south-eastern. Also, **S.E.**

**sea** /si/, *n.* **1.** the salt waters that cover the greater part of the earth's surface. **2.** a division of these waters, of considerable extent, more or less definitely marked off by land boundaries: *the Tasman Sea.* **3.** one of the seven seas. **4.** a large lake or landlocked body of water. **5.** the turbulence of the ocean or other body of water as caused by the wind; the waves. **6.** a large, heavy wave or swell: *heavy seas rocked the boat.* **7.** one of various more or less clearly defined areas on the surface of the moon, formerly thought to be areas of water. **8.** a widely extended, copious, or overwhelming quantity: *a sea of faces, a sea of troubles.* **9.** Some special noun phrases are:

**at sea,** **1.** out on the ocean. **2.** in a state of perplexity.

**by sea,** on a ship.

**follow the sea,** to follow a nautical career.

**go to sea,** **1.** to set out upon a voyage. **2.** to take up a nautical career.

**half seas over,** drunk.

**put to sea,** to set out from port.

**the high seas,** the sea away from land, esp. outside territorial waters.

*–adj.* **10.** of, pertaining to, or adapted for the sea. [ME *see,* OE *sǣ,* c. D *zee,* G *See,* Icel. *sǣr,* Goth. *saiws*]

**sea air** /– 'ɛə/, *n.* the air or atmosphere of the sea or seacoast, considered to be beneficial to the health.

**sea-anchor** /'si-æŋkə/, *n.* a floating anchor used at sea to prevent a ship from drifting or to keep its head to the wind, commonly consisting of a framed cone of canvas dragged along with its large open base towards the ship.

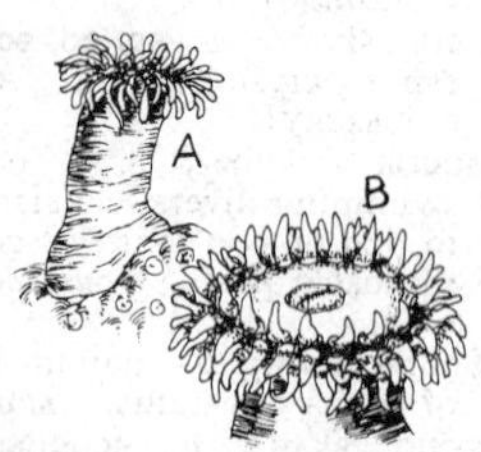

sea-anemone: A, columnar body; B, disc-shaped top bearing tentacles

**sea-anemone** /'si-əˌnɛməni/, *n.* any of the common marine animals of the phylum Coelenterata, class Anthozoa, of sedentary habits, having a columnar body topped by a disc bearing one or more circles of tentacles.

**seabag** /'sibæg/, *n.* a bag, usu. of canvas, closed at the top by a string, used by sailors and others for stowing kit; a nautical kitbag.

**sea-bank** /ˈsi-bæŋk/, *n.* **1.** an embankment to keep back the sea. **2.** the seashore.

**sea-bass** /ˈsi-bæs/, *n.* any of a number of marine serranoid fishes, as *Morone labrax* of the north Atlantic and Mediterranean.

**seabed** /ˈsibɛd/, *n.* the ground under the sea or an area of sea.

**seabird** /ˈsibɜd/, *n.* a bird frequenting the sea or coast.

**sea-biscuit** /ˈsi-bɪskət/, *n.* ship's biscuit; hardtack. Also, **sea-bread.**

**seablite** /ˈsiblaɪt/, *n.* any of several plants belonging to the genus *Suaeda,* as *S. maritima,* an annual herb widespread in salt marshes.

**seaboard** /ˈsibɔd/, *n.* **1.** the line where land and sea meet; the seashore. *–adj.* **2.** bordering on or adjoining the sea.

**seaborn** /ˈsibɔn/, *adj.* born in or of the sea; produced in or by the sea.

**seaborne** /ˈsibɔn/, *adj.* conveyed by sea; carried on the sea.

**sea-bream** /ˈsi-brɪm/, *n.* any marine sparoid foodfish.

**sea-breeze** /ˈsi-briz/, *n.* a thermally produced wind blowing during the day from the cool ocean surface on to the adjoining warm land.

**sea-butterfly** /si-ˈbʌtəflaɪ/, *n.* a pteropod mollusc, having feet with flat lateral lobes resembling the wings of a butterfly.

**sea-campion** /ˈsi-kæmpiən/, *n.* a perennial herb with white flowers, *Silene maritima,* which occurs on the coast and inland on mountains of western Europe.

**sea-canary** /ˈsi-kənɛəri/, *n.* the white whale, *Delphinapterus leucas,* which has a trilling voice.

**sea-captain** /ˈsi-kæptn/, *n.* the master of a ship, esp. a merchantman.

**sea change** /ˈsi tʃeɪndʒ/, *n.* **1.** a complete or radical transformation. **2.** a change brought about by the sea.

**sea-chest** /ˈsi-tʃɛst/, *n.* a chest used, esp. formerly, by sailors to store kit.

**seacoast** /ˈsikoʊst/, *n.* the land immediately adjacent to the sea.

**sea-cock** /ˈsi-kɒk/, *n.* **1.** a valve in the hull of a ship for admitting water, as to a ballast tank. **2.** →**gurnard.**

**sea-cow** /ˈsi-kaʊ/, *n.* **1.** any sirenian, as the manatee, dugong, etc. **2.** *Obs.* the hippopotamus.

**sea crayfish** /si ˈkreɪfɪʃ/, *n.* →**lobster** (def. 1).

**sea-cucumber** /si-ˈkjukʌmbə/, *n.* →**holothurian.**

**sea-dog** /ˈsi-dɒg/, *n.* **1.** a sailor, esp. one of long experience. **2.** →**harbour seal.**

**sea-dragon** /ˈsi-drægən/, *n.* **1.** →**dragonet** (def. 2). **2.** any of various pipefish, esp. the *Phycidurus eques* of Australian shores.

**sea-duck** /ˈsi-dʌk/, *n.* any diving duck of the subfamily Aythyinae, including the scaups, goldeneyes, scoters, eiders, etc., found principally on salt water.

**sea-eagle** /ˈsi-igəl/, *n.* any of various eagles of the genus *Haliaetus* which feed on fish, as the **white-breasted sea-eagle** of Australia and certain areas of Asia.

**sea-ear** /ˈsi-ɪə/, *n.* →**abalone.**

**sea elephant** /ˈsi ɛləfənt/, *n.* →**elephant seal.**

**sea-fan** /ˈsi-fæn/, *n.* any of certain anthozoans of the order Gorgonacea in which the colony assumes a fanlike form.

**seafarer** /ˈsifɛərə/, *n.* **1.** a sailor. **2.** a traveller on the sea.

**seafaring** /ˈsifɛərɪŋ/, *adj.* **1.** that travels by sea. **2.** following the sea as a calling. *–n.* **3.** the business or calling of a sailor. **4.** travelling by sea.

**sea-feather** /ˈsi-fɛðə/, *n.* any of various alcyonarians having a plume-like branched skeleton.

**sea-fight** /ˈsi-faɪt/, *n.* a fight between ships at sea.

**sea-floor** /ˈsi-flɔ/, *n.* →**seabed.**

**sea floor spreading,** *n.* a geological process affecting mid-ocean ridges by which molten lava is extruded and spreads to both sides of the ridge as it solidifies.

**sea-foam** /ˈsi-foʊm/, *n.* **1.** the foam of the sea. **2.** →**meerschaum** (def. 1).

**sea-fog** /ˈsi-fɒg/, *n.* a thick fog common along coastlines, caused by a difference between land and sea temperatures.

**seafood** /ˈsifud/, *n.* any saltwater fish or shellfish which is used for food.

**seafood cocktail** /– ˈkɒkteɪl/, *n.* a mixed dish of oysters, prawns, crabmeat, etc., usu. served with a sauce, often as an entree.

**seafowl** /ˈsifaʊl/, *n.* →**seabird.**

**sea-fox** /ˈsi-fɒks/, *n.* →**thresher** (def. 3).

**seafront** /ˈsifrʌnt/, *n.* **1.** the side or edge of land and buildings bordering on the sea. **2.** a road or promenade at a seaside town, running along the edge of the sea.

**seagirt** /ˈsigɜt/, *adj.* surrounded by the sea.

**seagoing** /ˈsigoʊɪŋ/, *adj.* **1.** designed or fit for going to sea, as a vessel. **2.** going to sea; seafaring.

**sea-gooseberry** /ˈsi-gʊzbəri, -bri/, *n.* a rounded pelagic ctenophore, esp. of the genera *Pleurobrachia* and *Hormiphora.*

**seagrass** /ˈsigras/, *n.* any of various marine plants of the genus *Zostera,* family Najadaceae, of temperate seas, having long strap-like leaves. Also, **eelgrass.**

**seagrass matting** /– ˈmætɪŋ/, *n.* matting made using certain grass fibres. Also, **Vietnamese matting.**

**sea green** /si ˈgrin/, *n.* a clear, light bluish-green (the colour of the sea on a clear day). – **sea-green,** *adj.*

**seagull** /ˈsigʌl/, *n.* **1.** a gull, esp. any of the marine species. **2.** *Colloq.* a man who does the interior painting in a ship. **3.** *N.Z. Colloq.* a casual wharf labourer who is not a member of a trade union.

**sea hare** /ˈsi hɛə/, *n.* any of the marine, slug-like, opisthobranch molluscs of the genera *Aplysia, Dolabella,* etc., having tentacles on the head which somewhat resemble the shape of a rabbit's ear.

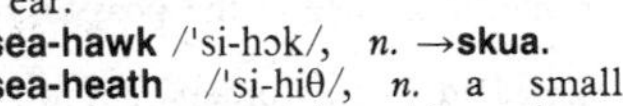

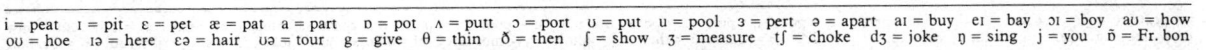

seagull (def. 1): silver gull of Australian and New Zealand waters

**sea-hawk** /ˈsi-hɔk/, *n.* →**skua.**

**sea-heath** /ˈsi-hiθ/, *n.* a small tough perennial with minute leaves and pink flowers, *Frankenia laevis,* occurring on salt marshes in Europe and western Asia.

**sea-hedgehog** /si-ˈhɛdʒhɒg/, *n.* **1.** →**sea-urchin. 2.** →**puffer** (def. 2).

**sea-holly** /ˈsi-hɒli/, *n.* →**eryngo.**

**seahorse** /ˈsihɔs/, *n.* **1.** any of a number of small fishes of the pipefish family, chiefly of the genus *Hippocampus,* with a prehensile tail and a beaked head that is turned at right angles to the body. **2.** a fabled marine animal with the foreparts of a horse and the hinder parts of a fish. **3.** →**walrus.**

**sea-kale** /ˈsi-keɪl/, *n.* a broad-leaved, maritime plant, *Crambe maritima,* of Europe, used as a pot herb.

**seal**[1] /sil/, *n.* **1.** a device impressed on a piece of wax or the like, or an impression, wafer, etc., affixed to a document as evidence of authenticity or attestation. **2.** a stamp engraved with such a device. **3.** an impression made with such a stamp. **4.** *Law.* a mark or symbol attached to a legal document and imparting a formal quality to it, originally defined as wax with an impression. **5.** a piece of wax or similar substance, affixed to a document, an envelope, a door, etc., which cannot be opened without breaking this. **6.** anything that effectively closes a thing. **7.** something for keeping a thing close or secret. **8.** a decorative stamp: *a Christmas seal.* **9.** a mark or the like serving as visible evidence of something. **10.** *Plumbing.* **a.** a small amount of water left standing in a trap to prevent the escape of foul air from below. **b.** the depth of the water between the dip and the overflow of a trap. **11.** a road surface of hard material, as tar, bitumen, etc.: *the tar seal.* **12. set one's seal on** or **to,** to approve or endorse. **13. the seals,** the tokens or signs of public office. *–v.t.* **14.** to affix a seal to an authorisation, confirmation, etc. **15.** to approve, authorise, or confirm: *to seal an agreement.* **16.** to impress a seal upon as an evidence of legal or standard exactness, measure, quality, etc. **17.** to fasten with a seal. **18.** to close by any form of fastening that must be broken before access can be had. **19.** to fasten or close as if by a seal. **20.** to decide irrevocably: *to seal someone's fate.* **21.** to grant under one's seal or authority, as a pardon. **22.** to surface a road with tar, bitumen, etc. **23.**

*Mormon Ch.* to make for ever binding, to give in marriage, or to join in family ties, according to the principle of marriage for eternity. **24.** *Elect.* to bring (a plug and jack or socket, etc.) into locked or fully aligned position. [ME *seel,* from OF, from LL *sigellum,* replacing L *sigillum*] – **sealable,** *adv.*

**seal**[2] /sil/, *n., pl.* **seals,** (*esp. collectively for def. 1*) **seal,** *v.* –*n.* **1.** any of the marine carnivores of the suborder Piniipedia, including the eared or fur seals, as the sea-lion and fur seal of commerce, and the earless or hair seals, of which the **harbour seal,** *Phoca vitulina,* is best known. **2.** the skin of the seal. **3.** leather made from it. **4.** the fur of the fur seal; sealskin. **5.** a fur used as a substitute for sealskin. –*v.i.* **6.** to hunt or take seals. [ME *sele,* OE *seolh,* c. Icel. *selr*]

seal[2]: fur seal

**sealant** /'silənt/, *n.* **1.** a substance used for sealing documents, etc., as sealing wax. **2.** →**sealer**[1] (def. 2).

**sea-lark** /'si-lak/, *n.* the name given to any of various shore birds, as the sandpiper, sanderling, etc.

**sea-lavender** /'si-lævəndə/, *n.* any plant of the genus *Limonium,* as *L. vulgare,* a perennial herb with bluish purple flowers which occurs on coastal salt marshes in northern temperate regions.

**seal brown** /sil 'braun/, *n., adj.* rich, dark brown suggestive of dressed and dyed sealskin.

**sea-leather** /'si-lɛðə/, *n.* the skin of sharks, porpoises, dogfishes, etc., prepared for the same purposes as ordinary leather.

**sealed book** /sild 'bʊk/, *n.* something beyond the possibility of understanding.

**sealed orders** /– 'ɔdəz/, *n. pl.* sealed written orders, not to be opened until after leaving port, given to the commander of a vessel to instruct him where to proceed on a voyage.

**sealed road** /– 'roud/, *n.* a bitumenised road.

**sea-legs** /'si-lɛgz/, *n.pl. Colloq.* **1.** the ability to walk with steadiness or ease on a rolling ship. **2.** the ability to resist seasickness.

**sea-lemon** /'si-lɛmən/, *n.* a large yellowish nudibranch mollusc, *Archidoris britannica,* common on coasts of Europe, including Britain.

**sea leopard** /'si lɛpəd/, *n.* **1.** Also, **leopard seal.** a large black-spotted, solitary, Southern Hemisphere seal that feeds preferentially on penguins and other sea birds. **2.** →**wolf-fish.**

**sealer**[1] /'silə/, *n.* **1.** one who or a device which affixes or impresses seals. **2.** Also, **sealant.** any of various fluids, chemical preparations, etc., used to give a tough, watertight coating to a surface, as on timber, concrete, or the like. **3.** *Obs. except U.S.* an officer appointed to examine and test weights and measures, and to set a stamp upon such as are true to the standard. [SEAL[1] + -ER[1]]

**sealer**[2] /'silə/, *n.* a person or vessel engaged in hunting seals. [SEAL[2] + -ER[1]]

**sealery** /'siləri/, *n., pl.* **-ries.** *Archaic.* **1.** the occupation of hunting or taking seals. **2.** a place where seals are caught.

**sea-letter** /'si-lɛtə/, *n.* a ship's passport carried in wartime by a neutral vessel describing its cargo, crew, destination, etc.

**sea lettuce** /'si lɛtəs/, *n.* an intertidal algae, *Ulva lactuca,* said to resemble lettuce leaves, and used as bait.

**sea-level** /'si-lɛvəl/, *n.* the horizontal plane or level corresponding to the surface of the sea when halfway between mean high and low water.

**sea-lily** /'si-lɪli/, *n.* →**crinoid.**

**sealing wax** /'silɪŋ wæks/, *n.* a resinous preparation, soft when heated, used for sealing letters, etc.

**sea lion** /'si laɪən/, *n.* **1.** the Australian white-naped hair seal, *Neophoca cinerea.* **2.** any of various eared seals of large size, as *Eumetopias jubata* of the northern Pacific, and *Zalophus californianus* of the Pacific coast of North America.

**sea loch** /'– lɒk/, *n.* →**loch** (def. 2).

**seal ring** /'sil rɪŋ/, *n.* a finger ring bearing a seal; a signet ring.

**sealskin** /'silskɪn/, *n.* **1.** the skin of the seal. **2.** the skin or fur of the fur seal, dressed for use. **3.** a garment or article made of this fur. –*adj.* **4.** made of or resembling sealskin.

**Sealyham** /'siliəm/, *n.* a terrier of Welsh origin having short legs, square jaws, and a shaggy white coat with markings on the head and ears. [named after *Sealyham,* village in Wales, where it was first bred]

Sealyham

**seam** /sim/, *n.* **1.** the line formed by sewing together pieces of cloth, leather, or the like. **2.** any line between abutting edges; a crack or fissure; a groove. **3.** any linear indentation or mark, as a wrinkle or a scar. **4.** *Knitting.* a line of stitches formed by purling. **5.** *Geol.* a comparatively thin stratum; a bed, as of coal. –*v.t.* **6.** to join with a seam; sew the seams of. **7.** to furrow; mark with wrinkles, scars, etc. **8.** →**cut** (def. 25b). –*v.i.* **9.** to become cracked, fissured, or furrowed. [ME *seme,* OE *sēam,* c. G *Saum;* akin to SEW] – **seamer,** *n.* – **seamless,** *adj.*

**seamaid** /'simeɪd/, *n. Poetic.* **1.** →**mermaid. 2.** a goddess or nymph of the sea.

**seaman** /'simən/, *n., pl.* **-men. 1.** one whose occupation it is to assist in the navigation of a ship; a sailor, specifically one below the rank of officer. **2.** *Navy.* a rating, esp. one who works on deck.

**seamanlike** /'simənlaɪk/, *adj.* like or befitting a seaman; showing good seamanship.

**seamanship** /'simənʃɪp/, *n.* the knowledge of and skill in all things pertaining to the operation, management, safety, and maintenance of ships and vessels other than in the engineering department.

**seamark** /'simak/, *n.* a conspicuous object on land, visible from the sea, serving as a guide, warning of danger, etc., to ships.

**seam bowling** /sim 'boulɪŋ/, *n.* bowling in which the seam of the ball is used to make it swing in flight and deviate on pitching. – **seam bowler,** *n.*

**sea-mew** /'si-mju/, *n.* a seagull, esp. a common European species, *Larus canus.*

**sea mile** /'si maɪl/, *n. Obs.* →**nautical mile.**

**sea-monster** /'si-mɒnstə/, *n.* a monster inhabiting or thought to inhabit the sea.

**sea-moss** /'si-mɒs/, *n.* →**bryozoan** (def. 1).

**sea-mouse** /'si-maus/, *n.* any of various large marine annelids of the genus *Aphrodite* and allied genera, of a somewhat mouselike appearance, due to a covering of long, fine, hair-like setae.

**seam-set** /'sim-sɛt/, *n.* a metalworker's tool for flattening seams.

**seamstress** /'simstrəs/, *n.* a woman whose occupation is sewing. Also, **sempstress.**

**sea mullet** /'si mʌlət/, *n.* →**bully mullet.**

**seam-welding** /sim-'wɛldɪŋ/, *n.* a process for joining sheets of thermoplastic material by softening, using direct or dielectric heating, and pressing the parts together along a prescribed line.

**seamy** /'simi/, *adj.,* **-mier, -miest. 1.** not pleasing or favourable; bad; sordid: *the seamy side of life.* **2.** having or showing seams; of the nature of a seam. – **seaminess,** *n.*

**seance** /'seɪɒns/, *n.* a meeting of people seeking to receive communications from spirits. Also, **séance.** [F: a sitting, from OF *seoir* (from L *sedēre*) sit]

**sea-onion** /'si-ʌnjən/, *n.* a herb, *Urginea maritima,* family Liliaceae, of the Mediterranean area, yielding the squill of medicine; sea-squill; squill.

**sea-otter** /'si-ɒtə/, *n.* a marine

sea-otter

otter, *Enhydra lutris,* of the shores of the northern Pacific, with a very valuable fur.

**sea-pen** /'si-pɛn/, *n.* a coelenterate consisting of a central fleshy axis bearing fleshy lateral leaves provided with small polyps, as of the genus *Pennatula* and related forms.

**sea perch** /'si pɜtʃ/, *n.* **1.** any of a number of Australian marine, usu. tropical fishes, mostly of the genus *Lutjanus* as the **scarlet sea perch,** *L. malabaricus,* of northern reef waters. **2.** elsewhere, any fish of the viviparous, almost exclusively marine family Embiotocidae.

**sea pie** /– 'paɪ/, *n.* a meat or fish stew with a scone dough or suet pastry topping, cooked by steaming.

**sea pike** /'– paɪk/, *n.* →**barracuda** (def. 1). Also, **pike.**

**sea-pink** /si-'pɪŋk/, *n.* an Old World, maritime, perennial herb, *Armeria maritima,* which has narrow tufted leaves and dense heads of pink or white flowers; thrift.

**seaplane** /'siplеɪn/, *n.* **1.** an aeroplane that can land on water, provided with floats instead of landing wheels. **2.** *U.S.* →**hydroplane.**

**seaport** /'sipɔt/, *n.* **1.** a port or harbour providing accommodation for seagoing vessels. **2.** a town or city at such a place.

**sea-power** /'si-paʊə/, *n.* **1.** a nation having an important navy or great influence on the sea. **2.** naval strength.

**sea-purse** /'si-pɜs/, *n.* the horny egg case of certain rays and sharks.

**seaquake** /'sikweɪk/, *n.* an agitation of the sea due to a submarine eruption or earthquake.

**sear**[1] /sɪə/, *v.t.* **1.** to burn or char the surface of. **2.** to mark with a branding iron. **3.** to burn or scorch injuriously or painfully. **4.** to harden, or make callous or unfeeling. **5.** to dry up or wither. **6.** to brown the surface of (meat) by a brief application of high heat. *–v.i.* **7.** to become dry or withered, as vegetation. *–n.* **8.** a mark or the like made by searing. *–adj.* **9.** *Chiefly Poetic.* →**sere**[1]. [ME *sere* (adj.), OE *sēar,* c. D *zoor*]

**sear**[2] /sɪə/, *n.* a pivoted piece in the firing mechanism of small arms which holds the hammer at full cock or half-cock. [OF *serre* lock, grasp, from *serrer* to grasp, hold, from LL *serāre* to bar, bolt (from L *sera* bar), b. with *serrāre* to saw (from L *serra* saw)]

**sea-raven** /'si-reɪvən/, *n.* a large marine fish of the genus *Hemitripterus,* as *H. americanus,* common on the northern Atlantic coast of America.

**search** /sɜtʃ/, *v.t.* **1.** to go or look through carefully in seeking to find something. **2.** to examine (a person) for concealed objects by going through his pockets or the like. **3.** to scrutinise or question: *to search one's feelings, search someone's face.* **4.** to probe (a wound, etc.). **5.** (of wind, cold, gunfire, etc.) to pierce or penetrate. **6.** *Mil.* to fire artillery over (an area) with successive changes in elevation. **7.** to bring or find (*out*) by a search: *to search out all the facts.* **8. search me,** *Colloq.* I don't know. *–v.i.* **9.** to seek; make examination or investigation. *–n.* **10.** the act of searching; careful examination or investigation. **11.** the search of a neutral vessel, or the examining of its papers, cargo, etc., as at sea, by officers of a belligerent state, in order to verify its nationality and ascertain whether it carries contraband, etc. **12.** *Law.* examination by a purchaser of records and registers at the Land Titles Office to find encumbrances affecting title to property. [ME *serch(en),* from OF *cerchier,* from LL *circāre,* from L *circus* circle] – **searchable,** *adj.* – **searcher,** *n.*

**searching** /'sɜtʃɪŋ/, *adj.* **1.** examining carefully or thoroughly. **2.** penetrating, as the eyes, gaze, etc. **3.** piercing or sharp, as the wind, etc. – **searchingly,** *adv.*

**searchlight** /'sɜtʃlaɪt/, *n.* **1.** a device, usu. consisting of a light and reflector, for throwing a beam of light in any direction. **2.** a beam of light so thrown.

**search-party** /'sɜtʃ-pati/, *n.* a group of people organised to search for someone or something missing.

**search-warrant** /'sɜtʃ-wɒrənt/, *n.* a court order authorising the searching of a house, etc., as for stolen goods.

**sea-robber** /'si-rɒbə/, *n.* →**pirate.**

**sea-rocket** /'si-rɒkət/, *n.* any succulent plant of the genus *Cakile* which occurs on coastal sand, esp. *C. maritima.*

**sea room** /'si rum/, *n.* space at sea free from obstruction in which a ship can be easily manoeuvred or navigated.

**sea-rover** /'si-roʊvə/, *n.* **1.** →**pirate. 2.** a pirate ship.

**seascape** /'siskeɪp/, *n.* a view or picture of the sea.

**sea-scorpion** /'si-skɔpiən/, *n.* a small, shore-living fish, *Cottus bubalis,* of Atlantic coasts.

**sea-scout** /'si-skaʊt/, *n.* a boy scout receiving training in seamanship, etc.

**sea-serpent** /'si-sɜpənt/, *n.* an enormous imaginary snake-like or dragon-like marine animal.

**sea-shell** /'si-ʃɛl/, *n.* the shell of any marine mollusc.

**seashore** /'siʃɔ/, *n.* **1.** land along the sea or ocean. **2.** *Law.* the ground between the ordinary high-water and low-water marks.

**seasick** /'sisɪk/, *adj.* affected with seasickness.

**seasickness** /'sisɪknəs/, *n.* nausea or other physical derangement caused by the motion of a vessel at sea.

**seaside** /'sisaɪd/, *n.* **1.** the seashore; the seacoast. *–adj.* **2.** situated at, or pertaining to, the seaside.

**sea-slug** /'si-slʌg/, *n.* any of various nudibranch, slug-like, marine, opisthobranch molluscs.

**sea-snail** /'si-sneɪl/, *n.* any of various molluscs found on the seashore, which resemble a snail.

**sea-snake** /'si-sneɪk/, *n.* any of the venomous marine snakes with a fin-like tail, constituting the family Hydrophiidae of tropical seas.

**sea-snipe** /'si-snaɪp/, *n.* the name given to any of various shore birds, as the sandpiper.

**season** /'sizən/, *n.* **1.** one of the four periods of the year (spring, summer, autumn, and winter), astronomically beginning each at an equinox or solstice, but geographically at different dates in different climates. **2.** a period of the year characterised by particular conditions of weather, temperature, etc. **3.** the period of the year when something is best or available: *the avocado season.* **4.** a period of the year marked by certain conditions, festivities, activities, etc.: *the cricket season, a dull season in trade.* **5.** any period or time. **6.** a suitable, proper, fitting, or right time. **7.** *Agric.* oestrus period in female stock; time for mating. **8.** →**season ticket. 9. in good season,** sufficiently early. **10. in season, a.** in the time or state for use, eating, hunting, etc. **b.** at the right time; opportunely. **c.** (of female animals) in a state of sexual excitement. **11. out of season, a.** not in the time or state for use, eating, hunting, etc. **b.** not at the right time. *–v.t.* **12.** to heighten or improve the flavour of (food) by adding condiments, spices, herbs, or the like. **13.** to give relish or a certain character to: *conversation seasoned with wit.* **14.** to mature, ripen, or condition by exposure to suitable conditions or treatment. **15.** to dry and harden (timber) by due process. **16.** to accustom or harden: *troops seasoned by battle.* **17.** to moderate, alleviate, or temper: *to season one's admiration.* *–v.i.* **18.** to become seasoned, matured, hardened, or the like. [ME *seson(e),* from OF *seson,* from L *satio* (time of) sowing] – **seasoner,** *n.*

**seasonable** /'sizənəbəl/, *adj.* **1.** suitable to the season: *seasonable weather.* **2.** timely; opportune. **3.** early. – **seasonableness,** *n.* – **seasonably,** *adv.*

**seasonal** /'sizənəl/, *adj.* pertaining to or dependent on the seasons of the year or some particular season; periodical: *seasonal work.* – **seasonally,** *adv.*

**seasonally-adjusted** /sizənəli-ə'dʒʌstəd/, *adj.* of or pertaining to sets of figures, as unemployment figures, which are altered to allow for seasonal fluctuations which would distort them.

**seasoning** /'sizənɪŋ/, *n.* **1.** something that seasons, esp. salt, spices, herbs, or other condiments. **2.** →**stuffing** (def. 3).

**season ticket** /sizən 'tɪkət/, *n.* a ticket valid any number of times for a specified period, usu. at a reduced rate.

**sea-spider** /'si-spaɪdə/, *n.* a slender, carnivorous, marine, eight-legged arthropod, as *Pycnogonum littorale* of northern African coasts.

**sea-squill** /'si-skwɪl/, *n.* →**sea-onion.**

**sea-squirt** /'si-skwɜt/, *n.* **1.** an ascidian; tunicate. **2.** →**cunjevoi** (def. 2).

**sea-state code** /si-steɪt 'koʊd/, *n.* a numerical code for indicating the state of the sea, from 0 for calm (glassy) to 9 for phenomenal. See **international sea and swell scale.**

**sea-swallow** /'si-swɒloʊ/, *n.* **1.** →**tern**[1]. **2.** →**storm-petrel.**

**seat** /sit/, *n.* **1.** something for sitting on, as a chair or bench; the place on or in which one sits. **2.** the part of a chair or the like on which one sits. **3.** the part of the body on which one sits; the buttocks. **4.** the part of the garment covering it. **5.** manner of sitting, as on horseback. **6.** that on which the base of anything rests. **7.** the base itself. **8.** *Carp.* any surface of intended contact, as the prepared bearing of a beam. **9.** a place in which something prevails or is established: *a seat of learning.* **10.** an established place or centre, as of government. **11.** a part of the body considered as the place in which a function or emotion is situated: *the head is the seat of the intellect.* **12.** site, location, or locality. **13.** abode or residence, esp. a country mansion with parkland. **14.** the throne or authority of a king, bishop, etc. **15.** a place for a spectator in a theatre or the like. **16.** right of admittance to such a place, esp. as indicated by ticket. **17.** a right to sit as a member in a legislative or similar body as the House of Representatives. **18.** a right to the privileges of membership in a stock exchange or the like. **19.** a parliamentary constituency. **20.** a directorship of a limited company. **21. take a seat,** to sit down. *–v.t.* **22.** to place on a seat or seats; cause to sit down. **23.** to find seats for; accommodate with seats: *a hall that seats a thousand persons.* **24.** to put a seat on or into (a chair, a garment, etc.). **25.** to fix firmly or accurately in a particular place. **26.** to put in a position of authority or in a legislative body. **27.** to commit pederasty on. [ME *sete,* from Scand.; cf. Icel. *sæti,* c. OE *sǣt* position for ambush, G *Gesäss*] – **seater,** *n.*

**seat belt** /'– bɛlt/, *n.* **1.** Also, **safety belt.** a belt attached to the frame of a motor vehicle for securing a driver or passenger against sudden turns, stops, collision, etc. Cf. **child restraint.** **2.** →**safety belt** (def. 1).

**seating** /'sitɪŋ/, *n.* **1.** the act of furnishing with seats. **2.** the arrangement of the seats in a building, etc. **3.** material for seats, esp. upholstery. **4.** manner of sitting, as on horseback. **5.** *Civ. Eng.* a supporting surface, as for a heavy load.

**SEATO** /'sitoʊ/, South-East Asia Treaty Organisation.

**sea-trout** /'si-traʊt/, *n.* **1.** any of various species of trout found in salt water, as the salmon trout, *Salmo trutta.* **2.** any of several fishes of the genus *Cynoscion.*

**seat-stick** /'sit-stɪk/, *n.* →**shooting stick.**

**sea-unicorn** /si-'junəkɔn/, *n.* →**narwhal.**

**sea-urchin** /'si-ɜtʃən/, *n.* any echinoderm of the class Echinoidea, comprising marine animals having a more or less globular or discoid form, and a spine-bearing shell composed of many calcareous plates.

sea-urchin

**seawall** /'siwɔl/, *n.* a strong wall or embankment to prevent the advance of the sea, act as a breakwater, etc.

**sea waratah** /'si wɒrə,ta/, *n.* →**waratah anemone.**

**seaward** /'siwəd/, *adj.* **1.** facing or tending towards the sea: *their seaward course.* **2.** coming from the sea, as a wind. *–n.* **3.** the direction towards the sea or away from the land. *–adv.* **4.** seawards.

**seawards** /'siwədz/, *adv.* towards the sea. Also, **seaward.**

**seaware** /'siwɛə/, *n.* seaweed, esp. coarse, large seaweed, used for manure, etc.

**sea wasp** /'si wɒsp/, *n.* any of certain box jellyfishes that have a highly venomous sting, as *Chironex fleckeri* of tropical Australian waters.

**sea water** /'– wɔtə/, *n.* the water which comprises the seas of the earth, consisting of about 96.4 per cent water, 2.8 per cent common salt, 0.4 per cent magnesium chloride, 0.2 per cent magnesium sulphate, 0.1 per cent each of calcium sulphate and potassium chloride (average composition excluding inland seas).

**seawater** /'siwɔtə/, *adj.* of, pertaining to, denoting, or existing in sea water.

**seaway** /'siweɪ/, *n.* **1.** a way over the sea. **2.** the open sea. **3.** the progress of a ship through the waves. **4.** a rough sea. **5.** an inland channel, canal, or waterway, navigable by ocean-going ships.

**seaweed** /'siwid/, *n.* **1.** any plant or plants growing in the ocean, esp. marine algae. **2.** *Colloq.* a surfie.

**sea-whip** /'si-wɪp/, *n.* a gorgonian coral with a flexible axis.

**sea-wife** /'si-waɪf/, *n.* →**wrasse.**

**sea-wolf** /'si-wʊlf/, *n.* any of several marine fishes, as the wolf-fish.

**seaworthy** /'siwɜði/, *adj.* (of a ship) adequately and safely constructed and equipped to sail at sea. – **seaworthiness,** *n.*

**sea-wrack** /'si-ræk/, *n.* seaweed, esp. of the larger kinds cast up on the shore.

**sebaceous** /sə'beɪʃəs/, *adj.* **1.** pertaining to, of the nature of, or resembling tallow or fat; fatty; greasy. **2.** secreting a fatty substance. [NL *sēbāceus,* from L *sēbum* tallow]

**sebaceous gland** /– 'glænd/, *n.* any of the cutaneous glands which secrete oily matter for lubricating hair and skin.

**sebacic acid** /sə,bæsɪk 'æsəd/, *n.* a white crystalline dibasic acid, $(CH_2)_8(COOH)_2$. [alteration of earlier SEBACEOUS *(acid),* replacing *-eous* with *-ic*]

**sebiferous** /sə'bɪfərəs/, *adj.* (of certain plants) producing vegetable wax or tallow. [*sebi-* (combining form representing L *sēbum* tallow, grease) + -FEROUS]

**seborrhoea** /sɛbə'riə/, *n.* an excessive and morbid discharge from the sebaceous glands. Also, *Chiefly U.S.,* **seborrhea.** [NL, from *sēbo-* (combining form representing L *sēbum* grease) + -(R)RHOEA]

**sebum** /'sibəm/, *n.* the fatty secretion of the sebaceous glands. [L: tallow, grease]

**sec,** secant.

**sec**[1] /sɛk/, *adj.* (of champagne) dry. [F]

**sec**[2] /sɛk/, *n. Colloq.* a second: *wait just a sec, please.*

**sec.,** **1.** second. **2.** secondary. **3.** secretary. **4.** section.

**Sec.,** Secretary.

**secant** /'sikənt/, *Maths. –n.* **1.** a straight line which cuts a circle or other curve. **2.** the ratio of the hypotenuse to the base in a right-angled triangle; the reciprocal of the cosine of an angle. *–adj.* **3.** cutting or intersecting, as one line or surface in relation to another. [L *secans,* ppr., cutting]

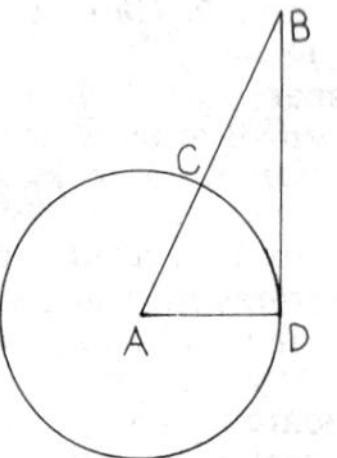


secant: AB is secant (def. 1) of arc CD; ratio of AB to AD, secant (def. 2) of angle A

**secateurs** /'sɛkətəz, sɛkə'tɜz/, *n.pl.* a scissor-like cutting instrument for pruning shrubs, etc., typically having a pair of crossed, short, curved blades, and a spring for returning them to the open position; pruning shears. [F, from L *secāre* cut]

**secco**[1] /'sɛkoʊ/, *adj.* **1.** *Music.* unaccompanied: *recitativo secco.* **2.** *Painting.* executed on dry plaster: *fresco secco.* [It.: dry]

**secco**[2] /'sɛkoʊ/, *n. Colloq.* a sex pervert.

**secede** /sə'sid/, *v.i.,* **-ceded, -ceding.** to withdraw formally from an alliance or association, as from a political or religious organisation. [L *sēcēdere* go back, withdraw] – **seceder,** *n.*

**secern** /sə'sɜn/, *v.t.* to distinguish; discriminate.

**secernent** /sə'sɜnənt/, *adj.* secreting. [L *sēcernens,* ppr., separating]

**secession** /sə'sɛʃən/, *n.* the act of seceding. [L *sēcessio*] – **secessional,** *adj.*

**secessionist** /sə'sɛʃənəst/, *n.* one who secedes or who favours secession. – **secessionism,** *n.*

**sech** /sɛʃ/, *n.* hyperbolic secant. See **hyperbolic functions.**

**seclude** /sə'klud/, *v.t.,* **-cluded, -cluding.** to shut off or keep apart; place in or withdraw into solitude. [L *sēclūdere*]

**secluded** /sə'kludəd/, *adj.* shut off or separated from others: *a secluded place.* – **secludedly,** *adv.* – **secludedness,** *n.*

**seclusion** /sə'kluʒən/, *n.* **1.** the act of secluding. **2.** the state of being secluded; retirement; solitude: *he sought seclusion in the country so that he could study undisturbed.* **3.** a secluded place.

**seclusionist** /sə'kluʒənəst/, *n.* one who favours seclusion or lives a secluded life.

**seclusive** /sə'klusɪv/, *adj.* **1.** tending to seclude. **2.** causing or providing seclusion. – **seclusively,** *adv.* – **seclusiveness,** *n.*

**second**[1] /ˈsɛkənd/, *adj.* **1.** next after the first in order, place, time, rank, value, quality, etc.; the ordinal of two. **2.** alternate: *every second Monday.* **3.** *Music.* the lower of two parts for the same instrument or voice: *second alto, second trombone.* **4.** additional; further: *to get a second chance.* **5.** closely resembling, imitating, or reaching the exceptional standard created by a historical person or event: *she's a second Nellie Melba.* *–n.* **6.** one who or that which comes next to or after the first, in order, quality, rank, etc.: *King Charles the Second.* **7.** the next to highest class of honours in a university degree examination. **8.** (*pl.*) *Colloq.* (at a meal) **a.** a second helping. **b.** a second course. **9.** *Motor Vehicles.* second gear. **10.** *Music.* **a.** a note on the next degree up from a given note. **b.** the interval between such notes. **c.** the harmonic combination of such notes. **d.** the lower of two parts in a piece of concerted music. **e.** a voice or instrument rendering such a part. **f.** →**alto.** **11.** *Boxing, Wrestling, etc.* one who assists a contestant in his corner between rounds. **12.** one who acts as representative of and an aid to a principal in a duel. **13.** one who aids or supports another; an assistant; a backer. **14.** (*sometimes pl.*) *Comm.* a product or material that is below the normal or required standard, though not unuseable, and is sold at a reduced price. **15. take seconds,** to reconsider. *–v.t.* **16.** to support, back up, or assist. **17.** to further or advance, as aims. **18.** to express support of (a motion, etc.) as a necessary preliminary to further discussion of the motion or to a vote on it. **19.** to act as second to (a duellist, etc.). *–adv.* **20.** in the second place, group, etc. [ME *seconde,* from F, from L *secundus*] – **seconder,** *n.* – **secondly,** *adv.*

**second**[2] /ˈsɛkənd/, *n.* **1.** a sixtieth part of a minute of time; the basic SI unit of time, now defined as the duration of 9 192 631 770 periods of the radiation corresponding to the transition between the two hyperfine levels of the ground state of the caesium-133 atom. **2.** *Geom., etc.* the sixtieth part of a minute of a degree equivalent to $4.848\ 136\ 8 \times 10^{-6}$ radians (often represented by the sign ″; thus, 12° 10′30″ means 12 degrees, 10 minutes, and 30 seconds). **3.** a moment or instant. [ME *seconde,* from F, from ML *secunda* (*minūta*), i.e., the result of the second sexagesimal division of the hour]

**second**[3] /səˈkɒnd/, *v.t.* to transfer (a military officer or other) temporarily to another post, organisation, or responsibility. [cf. F *en second* in the second rank] – **secondment,** *n.*

**Second Advent** /sɛkənd ˈædvɛnt/, *n.* →**Second Coming.**

**secondary** /ˈsɛkəndri/, *adj., n., pl.* **-aries.** *–adj.* **1.** next after the first in order, place, time, importance, etc. **2.** belonging or pertaining to a second order, division, stage, period, rank, or the like. **3.** derived or derivative; not primary or original. **4.** of or pertaining to the processing of primary products: *a secondary industry.* **5.** of minor importance; subordinate; auxiliary. **6.** *Educ.* denoting or pertaining to secondary education. **7.** *Chem.* **a.** involving, or obtained from replacement of, two atoms or radicals. **b.** denoting or containing a carbon atom united to two other carbon atoms in a chain or ring molecule. **8.** *Elect.* denoting or pertaining to the induced circuit, coil, or current in an induction coil or the like. **9.** *Geol.* **a.** denoting or pertaining to a clastic rock derived from older rocks. **b.** denoting or pertaining to a mineral produced from another mineral by decay, alteration, or the like. **c.** denoting or pertaining to a soil-formed rock material which has been transported. **10.** *Gram.* **a.** (of derivation) with an underlying element which is itself further analysable, as *likeably* composed of *likeable* + *ly,* but the first element *likeable* is further analysable into *like* + *able.* **b.** (of Latin, Greek, Sanskrit tenses) having reference to past time only. **11.** *Ornith.* pertaining to any of a set of flight feathers on the second segment (that corresponding to the forearm in higher vertebrates) of a bird's wing. *–n.* **12.** one who or that which is secondary. **13.** a subordinate; a delegate or deputy. **14.** *Elect.* a secondary circuit or coil. **15.** *Ornith.* a secondary feather. [ME, from L *secundārius*] – **secondarily,** *adv.*

**secondary accent** /– ˈæksɛnt/, *n.* →**secondary stress.**

**secondary boycott** /– ˈbɔɪkɒt/, *n.* a boycott placed by employees on dealings of their employer with another person, or an attempt by an employer to place a ban on or undermine free competition with another employer.

**secondary cell** /– ˈsɛl/, *n.* a voltaic cell which can be charged by passing a current through it in the opposite direction to the electromotive force, and which can therefore be used as a convenient device for storing electrical energy.

**secondary colour** /– ˈkʌlə/, *n.* a colour produced by mixing two or more primary colours, as orange, green, or violet.

**secondary education** /– ɛdʒəˈkeɪʃən/, *n.* education immediately following primary education, sometimes leading to further education.

**secondary emission** /– əˈmɪʃən/, *n.* the emission of electrons (**secondary electrons**) from a metal which is struck by a beam of fast-moving electrons (**primary electrons**) or ions from another source.

**secondary flow** /– ˈfloʊ/, *n.* the continuation of the input of irrigation water, probably at a slower rate, after the primary flow has reached the bottom end of the furrow.

**secondary group** /– ˈgrup/, *n.* a group of people with whom one's contacts are detached and impersonal.

**secondary industry** /– ˈɪndəstri/, *n.* an industry involved in the production of manufactured goods.

**secondary modern school,** *n. Brit.* a school providing secondary education, esp. in subjects which are intended to be primarily practical rather than academic, for children who fail the eleven-plus examination, or who are otherwise selected for this type of education.

**secondary school** /ˈsɛkəndri skul/, *n.* a school providing post-primary education; a high school.

**secondary stress** /– ˈstrɛs/, *n.* a stress accent weaker than primary stress, but stronger than lack of stress. Also, **secondary accent.**

**secondary wage** /– ˈweɪdʒ/, *n.* →**margin** (def. 9).

**second ballot** /sɛkənd ˈbælət/, *n.* a ballot held at certain kinds of election to ensure an absolute majority for the victor, when no candidate has secured one in a first ballot; the least successful candidate or candidates in the first ballot are excluded from the second, and all electors are entitled to vote again.

**second-best** /ˈsɛkənd-bɛst/, *adj.* **1.** next after the best in quality, performance, etc. **2. come off second best,** to be defeated in a contest. Also (*esp. in predicative use*), **second best** /sɛkənd ˈbɛst/.

**second childhood** /sɛkənd ˈtʃaɪldhʊd/, *n.* senility; dotage.

**second class** /– ˈklas/, *n.* **1.** a class of accommodation on a train, boat, etc., less luxurious and less expensive than first class. **2.** the standard of comfort of such accommodation. **3.** the next to highest class in a university honours degree examination.

**second-class** /ˈsɛkənd-klas/, *adj.* **1.** of or belonging to the second class. **2.** second-rate; inferior. **3.** treated as if inferior: *women were second-class citizens.*

**Second Coming** /sɛkənd ˈkʌmɪŋ/, *n.* the second coming of Christ to establish a personal reign upon the earth as its king. Also, **Second Advent.**

**second cousin** /ˈsɛkənd kʌzən/, *n.* See **cousin.**

**second cross** /– ˈkrɒs/, *n.* **1.** any progeny resulting from the mating of a true half-breed and a distinct breed. *–adj.* **2.** of or pertaining to such progeny.

**second cut** /– ˈkʌt/, *n.* **1.** (in shearing) another stroke with the shears, necessary because the fleece was not removed cleanly the first time. **2.** wool showing evidence of the first as well as the second cut.

**second-degree** /ˈsɛkənd-dəgri/, *adj.* of a degree which is next in seriousness to the first-degree, either more serious, as *second-degree burns* or less serious, as *second-degree murder.*

**second-degree murder** /– ˈmɜdə/, *n. U.S.* →**manslaughter.**

**seconde** /səˈkɒnd/, *n.* (in fencing) the second of eight defensive positions. [F, fem. of *second* SECOND[1]]

**second fiddle** /sɛkənd ˈfɪdl/, *n.* **1.** (in a musical score) the part written to be played by the second violin, or by the second group of violinists. **2.** one who plays such a part. **3. play second fiddle,** to take a minor or secondary part.

**second five-eighth** /ˈ– faɪv-eɪtθ/, *n. N.Z.* →**inside centre.** Also, **second five.**

**second floor** /– ˈflɔ/, *n.* **1.** the third storey of a building, counting upwards from ground level; the floor two above the ground floor. **2.** (sometimes) the second storey.

**second growth** /– 'grouθ/, *n.* the growth that follows the destruction of virgin forest.

**second-hand** /'sɛkənd-hænd, sɛkənd-'hænd/, *adj.;* /sɛkənd-'hænd/, *adv.* *–adj.* **1.** obtained from another; not original: *second-hand knowledge.* **2.** previously used or owned: *second-hand clothes.* **3.** dealing in previously used goods: *a second-hand bookseller.* *–adv.* **4.** after having been owned by another person: *to buy goods second-hand.*

**second-hand Sue** /– 'su/, *n. Colloq.* **1.** a prostitute of faded charms. **2.** a passive homosexual who is either old or unattractive.

**second lieutenant** /sɛkənd lɛf'tɛnənt/, *n.* the lowest commissioned rank in the army.

**second mortgage** /– 'mɔgɪdʒ/, *n.* a mortgage taken out in addition to an existing mortgage.

**second nature** /– 'neɪtʃə/, *n.* habit, tendency, etc., so long practised that it is inalterably fixed in one's character: *correcting the English of others is second nature to him.*

**secondo** /sə'kɒndou/, *n., pl.* **-di** /-di/. *Music.* **1.** the second or lower part in a duet, esp. in piano duets. **2.** its performer. [It., from L *secundus*]

**second person** /sɛkənd 'pɜsən/, *n.* →**person** (def. 11a).

**second-rate** /'sɛkənd-reɪt/, *adj.* **1.** of the second rate or class, as to size, quality, etc. **2.** inferior; mediocre: *a second-rate person.* – **second-rater** /sɛkənd-'reɪtə/, *n.*

**second rower** /sɛkənd 'rouə/, *n.* either of the two forwards who pack down in the second row of a rugby scrum. Also, **second row forward.**

**seconds** /'sɛkəndz/, *n.pl.* **1.** →**second**[1] (def. 7). **2.** goods with some slight manufacturing imperfections. **3.** second helpings of food.

**second sight** /sɛkənd 'saɪt/, *n.* a supposed faculty of seeing distant objects and future events; clairvoyance.

**second string** /– 'strɪŋ/, *n.* an alternative resort or recourse, intended to achieve one's aims upon the failure of an initial course of action. [shortened form of *second string to one's bow*]

**second-string** /'sɛkənd-strɪŋ/, *adj.* of or pertaining to an alternative plan, course of action, etc.

**second thigh** /sɛkənd 'θaɪ/, *n.* (of a horse) →**gaskin.**

**second thoughts** /– 'θɔts/, *n. pl.* a revised opinion; reconsideration.

**second wind** /– 'wɪnd/, *n.* **1.** the restoration of more comfortable breathing and the reduction of muscular strain in an ongoing energetic activity, after one has got over the initial stresses. **2. get one's second wind,** to experience a revival of interest, enthusiasm, etc., in a task in hand.

**secrecy** /'sikrəsi/, *n., pl.* **-cies. 1.** the state of being secret or concealed: *a meeting in strict secrecy.* **2.** privacy; retirement; seclusion. **3.** ability to keep a secret. **4.** secretive habits; lack of openness. [obs. *secre(e)* SECRET + -CY; replacing ME *secretee,* from *secre* secret + *-tee* -TY[2]]

**secret** /'sikrət/, *adj.* **1.** done, made, or conducted without the knowledge of others: *secret negotiations.* **2.** kept from the knowledge of any but the initiated: *a secret sign.* **3.** faithful or cautious in keeping secrets; close-mouthed; reticent. **4.** designed to escape observation or knowledge: *a secret drawer.* **5.** retired or secluded, as a place. **6.** beyond ordinary human understanding. *–n.* **7.** something secret, hidden, or concealed. **8.** a mystery: *the secrets of nature.* **9.** the reason or explanation, not immediately or generally apparent: *the secret of his success.* **10.** a method or art known only to the initiated or the few: *the secret of happiness.* **11.** (*cap.*) *Liturgy.* a variable prayer in the Roman and other Western liturgies, said inaudibly by the celebrant after the offertory, etc., and immediately before the preface. **12. in secret,** secretly. [ME *secrete,* from F, from L *sēcrētus* (adj.), orig. pp., divided off] – **secretly,** *adv.*

**secret agent** /– 'eɪdʒənt/, *n.* a spy.

**secretaire** /sɛkrə'tɛə/, *n.* a writing desk with drawers, etc., for papers, books, or the like. [F *secrétaire* SECRETARY]

**secretariat** /sɛkrə'tɛəriət/, *n.* **1.** the officials or office entrusted with maintaining records and performing secretarial duties, esp. for an international organisation. **2.** a group or department of secretaries. **3.** the place where a secretary transacts business, preserves records, etc. [F, from ML *sēcrētāriātus* the office of a secretary. See SECRETARY]

**secretary** /'sɛkrətri, 'sɛkrətəri/, *n., pl.* **-taries. 1.** a person who conducts correspondence, keeps records, etc., for an individual or an organisation. **2.** →**private secretary. 3.** a secretary of state. **4.** a writing desk; secretaire. **5.** a former style of handwriting. [ML *sēcrētārius* confidential officer, from L *sēcrētum* (something) secret. See SECRET] – **secretarial** /sɛkrə'tɛəriəl/, *adj.* – **secretaryship,** *n.*

**secretary bird** /'– bɜd/, *n.* a large, long-legged raptorial bird, *Sagittarius serpentarius,* of Africa, which feeds on reptiles (so called from its crest, which suggests pens stuck over the ear).

secretary bird

**secretary-general** /sɛkrətri-'dʒɛnrəl/, *n., pl.* **secretaries-general.** the head of a secretariat.

**secret ballot** /sikrət 'bælət/, *n.* a method of secret voting by means of printed or written ballots, or by means of voting machines.

**secrete** /sə'krit/, *v.t.,* **-creted, -creting. 1.** *Biol.* to separate off, prepare, or elaborate from the blood, as in the physiological process of secretion. **2.** to hide or conceal; keep secret. [L *sēcrētus,* pp., put apart] – **secretor,** *n.*

**secretin** /sə'kritn/, *n.* a hormone produced in the small intestine which activates the pancreas to secrete pancreatic juice.

**secretion** /sə'kriʃən/, *n.* **1.** the process or function of an animal body, executed in the glands, by which various substances, as bile, milk, etc., are separated and elaborated from the blood. **2.** the product secreted. [L *sēcrētio*] – **secretionary** /sə'kriʃənəri/, *adj.*

**secretive** /'sikrətɪv/, *adj.* **1.** having or showing a disposition to secrecy; reticent: *he seemed secretive about his new job.* **2.** secretory. – **secretively,** *adv.* – **secretiveness,** *n.*

**secretory** /sə'kritəri/, *adj., n., pl.* **-ries.** *–adj.* **1.** pertaining to secretion. **2.** performing the office of secretion. *–n.* **3.** a secretory organ, vessel, or the like.

**secret police** /sikrət pə'lis/, *n.* a police force, the activities of which are not available to public scrutiny, and which is usu. maintained to check political subversion.

**secret service** /– 'sɜvəs/, *n.* **1.** a department of government concerned with national security, particularly with espionage and counterespionage. **2.** official service of a secret nature; espionage.

**secret society** /– sə'saɪəti/, *n.* a society whose members use secret oaths, passwords, rites, etc., and conceal their activities from outsiders.

**secs,** seconds.

**sect** /sɛkt/, *n.* **1.** a body of persons adhering to a particular religious faith; a religious denomination. **2.** a group regarded as deviating from the general religious tradition or as heretical. **3.** (in the sociology of religion) a Christian denomination characterised by insistence on strict qualifications for membership, as distinguished from the more inclusive groups called churches. [ME *secte,* from L *secta* following]

**-sect,** a word element meaning 'cut', as in *intersect.* [L *sectus,* pp.]

**sect.,** section.

**sectarian** /sɛk'tɛəriən/, *adj.* **1.** of or pertaining to sectaries or sects. **2.** confined or devoted to a particular sect, esp. narrowly or excessively. *–n.* **3.** a member of a sect. **4.** a bigoted adherent of a sect. [SECTARY + -AN]

**sectarianise** /sɛk'tɛəriənaɪz/, *v.t.,* **-nised, -nising.** to make sectarian. Also, **sectarianize.**

**sectarianism** /sɛk'tɛəriənɪzəm/, *n.* the spirit or tendencies of sectarians; adherence or excessive devotion to a particular sect, esp. in religion.

**sectary** /'sɛktəri/, *n., pl.* **-ries.** a member of, or one zealously devoted to, a particular sect. [ML *sectārius,* from L *secta* sect]

**sectile** /'sɛktaɪl/, *adj.* capable of being cut smoothly by a knife. [L *sectilis*] – **sectility** /sɛk'tɪləti/, *n.*

**section** /'sɛkʃən/, *n.* **1.** a part cut off or separated. **2.** a distinct portion of a book, writing, newspaper, or the like; a subdivision, as of a chapter; a division of a legal code. **3.**

one of a number of parts that can be fitted together to make a whole: *sections of a fishing rod.* **4.** a distinct part of a country, community, class, or the like. **5.** the act of cutting; separation by cutting. **6.** a thin slice of a tissue, mineral, or the like, as for microscopic examination. **7.** a representation of an object as it would appear if cut by a plane, showing the internal structure; cross-section. **8.** *Mil.* **a.** a small unit, which may consist of two or more squads. **b. staff section,** one of the subdivisions of any staff. **9.** one of the administrative parts into which a subdivision of a police force is organised. **10.** *Surg.* any of various operations involving an incision, esp. a caesarian section. **11.** *Railways.* a length of track between two signal boxes, into which no train may enter or leave without authority. **12.** one of the divisions of a bus route, etc., for which a fare is fixed. **13.** a subdivision of a chapter in a book, etc. **14.** Also, **section mark.** a mark (§) used to denote a section of a book, chapter, or the like, or as a mark of reference to a footnote or the like. **15.** a division of an orchestra or band composed of all the instruments of one class: *the brass section.* **16.** *N.Z.* the part of a trainee teacher's course spent in school classrooms: *to be on section.* **17.** →**block** (def. 19). **18.** →**horde** (def. 5). **19. last section,** *Colloq.* the end, as of a marriage, friendship, etc. *–v.t.* **20.** to cut or divide into sections. **21.** to cut through so as to present a section. *–v.i.* **22.** (of a wave) to break unevenly. [L *sectio* a cutting]

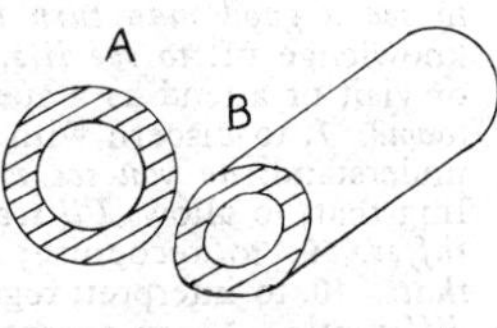

sections (def. 7) of a pipe: A, cross or transverse section; B, oblique section

**sectional** /ˈsɛkʃənəl/, *adj.* **1.** pertaining to a particular section; local; partial or partisan: *full of sectional pride.* **2.** composed of several independent sections. – **sectionally,** *adv.*

**sectionalise** /ˈsɛkʃənəlaɪz/, *v.t.,* **-lised, -lising. 1.** to render sectional. **2.** to divide into sections, esp. geographical sections. Also, **sectionalize.** – **sectionalisation** /sɛkʃənəlaɪˈzeɪʃən/, *n.*

**sectionalism** /ˈsɛkʃənəlɪzəm/, *n.* excessive regard for sectional or local interests; sectional spirit, prejudice, etc.

**section car** /ˈsɛkʃən ka/, *n.* a four wheeled vehicle, usu. motorised, used to carry fettlers along a railway line; quadracycle.

**section gang** /ˈ– gæŋ/, *n.* a group of workmen who maintain a section of railway track.

**sector** /ˈsɛktə/, *n.* **1.** *Geom.* a plane figure bounded by two radii and the included arc of a circle, ellipse, or the like. **2.** a mathematical instrument consisting of two flat rulers hinged together at one end and bearing various scales. **3.** *Mil.* one of the sections of a forward fighting area as divided for military operations, etc. **4.** any field or division of a field of activity. *–v.t.* **5.** to divide into sectors. [LL, special use of L *sector* cutter] – **sectoral,** *adj.*

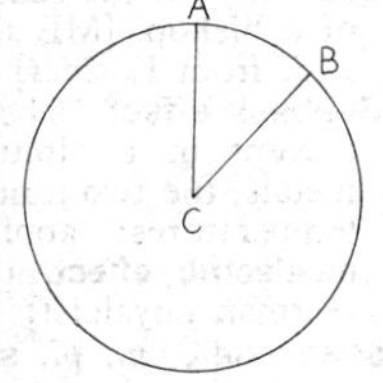

ACB, sector (def. 1) of a circle

**sectorial** /sɛkˈtɔriəl/, *adj.* **1.** sectoral. **2.** *Zool.* adapted for cutting, as teeth.

**secular** /ˈsɛkjələ/, *adj.* **1.** of or pertaining to the world, or to things not religious, sacred, or spiritual; temporal; worldly. **2.** not pertaining to or connected with religion, as literature, music, etc. **3.** dealing with non-religious subjects, or, esp., excluding religious instruction, as education, etc. **4.** (of members of the clergy) not belonging to a religious order (opposed to *regular*). **5.** occurring or celebrated once in an age or century: *the secular games of Rome.* **6.** going on from age to age; continuing through long ages. *–n.* **7.** →**layman. 8.** one of the secular clergy. [LL *saeculāris* worldly, from L: belonging to an age; replacing ME *seculer,* from OF] – **secularly,** *adv.*

**secularise** /ˈsɛkjələraɪz/, *v.t.,* **-rised, -rising. 1.** to make secular; separate from religious or spiritual connection or influences; make worldly or unspiritual; imbue with secularism. **2.** to change (clergy) from regular to secular. **3.** to transfer (property) from ecclesiastical to civil possession or use. Also, **secularize.** – **secularisation** /sɛkjələraɪˈzeɪʃən/, *n.* – **seculariser,** *n.*

**secularism** /ˈsɛkjələrɪzəm/, *n.* **1.** secular spirit or tendencies, esp. a system of political or social philosophy which rejects all forms of religious faith and worship. **2.** the view that public education and other matters of civil policy should be conducted without the introduction of a religious element. – **secularist,** *n.* – **secularistic** /sɛkjələˈrɪstɪk/, *adj.*

**secularity** /sɛkjəˈlærəti/, *n., pl.* **-ties. 1.** secularism. **2.** worldliness. **3.** a secular matter.

**secund** /səˈkʌnd/, *adj.* **1.** *Bot., Zool.* arranged on one side only. **2.** *Bot.* unilateral. [L *secundus* following]

**secundum** /səˈkʌndəm/, *prep.* according to. [L]

**secure** /səˈkjuə/, *adj., v.,* **-cured, -curing.** *–adj.* **1.** free from or not exposed to danger; safe. **2.** not liable to fall, yield, become displaced, etc., as a support or a fastening. **3.** affording safety, as a place. **4.** in safe custody or keeping. **5.** free from care; without anxiety. **6.** sure; certain: *to be secure of victory.* **7.** that can be counted on: *victory is secure.* *–v.t.* **8.** to get hold or possession of; obtain. **9.** to make secure from danger or harm; make safe. **10.** to make secure or certain; ensure. **11.** to make firm or fast. **12.** to confine or pinion. **13.** to make impregnable, or nearly so, as a military position. **14.** to assure a creditor of payment by the pledge or mortgaging of property. *–v.i.* **15.** to be safe; get security: *to secure against danger.* [L *sēcūrus* free from care] – **securely,** *adv.* – **secureness,** *n.* – **securer,** *n.*

**secured** /səˈkjuəd/, *adj.* (of a gaol or similar institution) guarded by manned watchtowers.

**security** /səˈkjurəti/, *n., pl.* **-ties. 1.** freedom from danger, risk, etc.; safety. **2.** freedom from care, apprehension, or doubt; confidence. **3.** something that secures or makes safe; a protection; a defence. **4.** protection from or measures taken against espionage, theft, infiltration, sabotage, or the like. **5.** an assurance; guarantee. **6.** *Law.* **a.** something given or deposited as surety for the fulfilment of a promise or an obligation, the payment of a debt, etc. **b.** one who becomes surety for another. **c.** an evidence of debt or of property, as a bond or a certificate of stock. **7.** (*usu. pl.*) stocks and shares, etc. [ME, from L *sēcūritas*]

**security blanket** /ˈ– blæŋkət/, *n.* something which affords a sense of security, well-being or comfort to the possessor. [from the comic strip *Peanuts* by U.S. cartoonist Charles Schulz, b. 1922, in which a character, Linus, carries round a blanket for security]

**security guard** /ˈ– gad/, *n.* one whose occupation is to guard money or valuables, esp. while in transit.

**security officer** /ˈ– ɒfəsə/, *n.* one whose occupation is to guard a business, factory, or the like against damage, industrial espionage, etc.

**security police** /ˈ– pəlis/, *n.* **1.** a force of security guards. **2.** a section of a police force having mainly secret duties, as the detection of espionage, protection of political leaders, etc.

**security risk** /ˈ– rɪsk/, *n.* one who is considered a threat to the security of the state or some other organisation.

**sedan** /səˈdæn/, *n.* **1.** Also, **saloon car.** a four-door passenger car seating four to six people. **2.** a sedan chair. [orig. uncert.; ? from It., from L *sēdes* seat]

**sedan chair** /ˈ– tʃɛə/, *n.* a portable wheelless vehicle for one person, borne on poles by two men, one before and one behind, much used during the 17th and 18th centuries.

sedan chair

**sedate** /səˈdeɪt/, *adj., v.,* **-dated, -dating.** *–adj.* **1.** calm, quiet, or composed; sober; undisturbed by passion or excitement. *–v.t.* **2.** to calm or put to sleep by means of sedatives. [L *sēdātus,* pp., calmed] – **sedately,** *adv.* – **sedateness,** *n.*

**sedation** /səˈdeɪʃən/, *n.* **1.** the state of being tranquillised or in an induced condition of reduced pain. **2.** the act or fact of soothing or allaying irritability or pain.

**sedative** /ˈsɛdətɪv/, *adj.* **1.** tending to calm or soothe. **2.** *Med.* allaying irritability or excitement; assuaging pain;

lowering functional activity. *–n.* **3.** a sedative agent or remedy.

**sedentary** /ˈsɛdəntri/, *adj.* **1.** characterised by or requiring a sitting posture: *a sedentary occupation.* **2.** accustomed to sit much or take little exercise. **3.** *Chiefly Zool.* **a.** abiding in one place; not migratory. **b.** referring to animals that seldom move about or are permanently attached to a stationary object. **4.** *Geol.* denoting or pertaining to a soil formed directly from the solid rocks under it. [L *sedentārius*] – **sedentarily,** *adv.* – **sedentariness,** *n.*

**Seder** /ˈseɪdə/, *n.* a Jewish ceremonial dinner which is held on the first night (or first two nights) of the Passover. [Heb. *sēdher* order]

**sedge** /sɛdʒ/, *n.* any of the rush or grass-like plants of the family Cyperaceae, often growing in wet places, esp. plants of the genus *Carex.* [ME *segge,* OE *secg;* akin to SAW[1]; apparently so named because of its sawlike edges]

**sedged** /sɛdʒd/, *adj.* **1.** made of sedge. **2.** abounding or bordered with sedge.

**sedge warbler** /ˈsɛdʒ wɔblə/, *n.* a small warbler, *Acrocephalus schoenobaenus,* inhabiting marshy places in Europe and western Asia.

**sedgy** /ˈsɛdʒi/, *adj.* **1.** abounding, covered, or bordered with sedge. **2.** of or like sedge.

**sedile** /səˈdaɪli/, *n., pl.* **sedilia** /səˈdaɪliə/. one of the seats (usu. three) on the south side of the chancel in Gothic-style churches, often recessed, for the use of the officiating clergy. [L: seat]

sedilia

**sediment** /ˈsɛdəmənt/, *n.* **1.** matter which settles to the bottom of a liquid; lees; dregs. **2.** *Geol.* mineral or organic matter deposited by water, air, or ice. [F, from L *sedimentum* a setting]

**sedimentary** /sɛdəˈmɛntəri/, *adj.* **1.** of, pertaining to, or of the nature of sediment. **2.** *Geol.* formed by deposition of sediment, as rocks. Also, **sedimental.** – **sedimentarily,** *adv.*

**sedimentation** /sɛdəmɛnˈteɪʃən/, *n.* the deposition or accumulation of sediment.

**sedition** /səˈdɪʃən/, *n.* **1.** incitement of discontent or rebellion against the government; action or language promoting such discontent or rebellion. **2.** *Archaic.* rebellious disorder. [ME *sedicion,* from L *sēditio,* lit., a going apart]

**seditionary** /səˈdɪʃənəri/, *adj., n., pl.* **-aries.** *–adj.* **1.** seditious. *–n.* **2.** one guilty of sedition.

**seditious** /səˈdɪʃəs/, *adj.* **1.** of, pertaining to, or of the nature of sedition. **2.** given to or guilty of sedition. – **seditiously,** *adv.* – **seditiousness,** *n.*

**seduce** /səˈdjus/, *v.t.,* **-duced, -ducing.** **1.** to induce to have sexual intercourse. **2.** to lead astray; entice away from duty or rectitude; corrupt. **3.** to lead or draw away, as from principles, faith, or allegiance. **4.** to win over; entice. [late ME, from L *sēdūcere* lead aside] – **seducer,** *n.* – **seducible,** *adj.*

**seduction** /səˈdʌkʃən/, *n.* **1.** the act or an instance of seducing. **2.** condition of being seduced. **3.** a means of seducing; an enticement. Also, **seducement.**

**seductive** /səˈdʌktɪv/, *adj.* tending to seduce; enticing; captivating: *a seductive smile, a seductive dress.* – **seductively,** *adv.* – **seductiveness,** *n.*

**seductress** /səˈdʌktrəs/, *n.* a woman who seduces, entices, or leads astray; a female seducer. [L *sēductrix*]

**sedulity** /səˈdjuləti/, *n.* sedulous quality.

**sedulous** /ˈsɛdʒələs/, *adj.* **1.** diligent in application or attention; persevering. **2.** persistently or carefully maintained: *sedulous flattery.* [L *sēdulus* busy, careful] – **sedulously,** *adv.* – **sedulousness,** *n.*

**sedum** /ˈsidəm/, *n.* any plant of the genus *Sedum,* which comprises fleshy, chiefly perennial, herbs with yellow, white, or pink flowers. Cf. **stonecrop.** [NL, special use of L *sedum* houseleek]

**see**[1] /si/, *v.,* **saw, seen, seeing.** *–v.t.* **1.** to observe, be aware of, or perceive, with the eyes. **2.** to look at; make an effort to observe in this way. **3.** to imagine, remember, or retain a mental picture of: *I see the house as it used to be.* **4.** to perceive or be aware of with any or all of the senses: *I hate to see a good man turn to crime.* **5.** to have experience or knowledge of: *to see life, to see a bit of variety.* **6.** to view, or visit or attend as a spectator: *have you seen the old part of town?* **7.** to discern with the intelligence; perceive mentally; understand: *do you see where you went wrong?* **8.** to be willing that; to allow: *I'll see you dead first, I can't see an animal suffer.* **9.** to recognise; appreciate: *I don't see the use of that.* **10.** to interpret; regard; consider: *I see the problem quite differently.* **11.** to accept as reasonable or likely; be able to conceive or believe without difficulty: *I just don't see him as Prime Minister.* **12.** to predict; foresee. **13.** to ascertain, find out, or learn, as by enquiry: *see who is knocking.* **14.** to meet socially; visit. **15.** to visit formally; consult: *to see a doctor.* **16.** to receive as a visitor or the like: *the Minister will see you now.* **17.** to spend time in the company of, esp. romantically. **18.** to accompany or escort: *may I see you home?* **19.** to ensure: *see that the work is done.* **20.** *Poker, etc.* to match (a bet) or match the bet of (another better) by making an equal bet. Cf. **raise.** *–v.i.* **21.** to have or use the power of sight. **22.** to understand; discern. **23.** to enquire or find out. **24.** to give attention or care: *go and see to it now.* **25.** to deliberate; consider; think. **26.** *Obs.* to look. *–n.* **27.** Some special verb phrases are:

**see about,** to deal with or attend to.

**see (someone) about his business,** to send away, esp. forcibly.

**see here,** (an expression used to attract attention, for emphasis or the like).

**see in,** to greet; celebrate: *see in the new year.*

**see into,** to investigate: *the manager must see into the circumstances of the dismissal of these workers.*

**see off, 1.** to attend the departure of, esp. as a courtesy; send off. **2.** to turn away, esp. forcibly; cause to leave.

**see out, 1.** to see off. **2.** to continue in (an undertaking) until it is finished. **3.** to live until the end of (a period) or outlive (a person).

**see over,** to inspect.

**see things,** to hallucinate.

**see through, 1.** to penetrate or detect: *to see through a disguise, see through an imposture.* **2.** to remain until the completion of; work to ensure the successful outcome of: *to see a project through.* **3.** to help or support in the achievement or completion of: *his family saw him through university.* [ME; OE *sēon,* c. D *zien,* G *sehen,* Icel. *sjā,* Goth. *saihwan*]

**see**[2] /si/, *n.* the seat, centre of authority, office, or jurisdiction of a bishop. [ME *se,* from OF, var. (influenced by L) of *sie, sied,* from L *sēdes*]

**Seebeck effect** /ˈsibɛk əfɛkt/, *n.* the production of an electric current in a circuit consisting of two wires of different metals, the two junctions of which are maintained at different temperatures; applied in the thermocouple. Also, **thermoelectric effect.** [named after T. J. *Seebeck,* 1770-1831, German physicist]

**seed** /sid/, *n., pl.* **seeds, seed,** *v.* *–n.* **1.** the propagative part of a plant, esp. as preserved for growing a new crop, including ovules, tubers, bulbs, etc. **2.** such parts collectively. **3.** *Bot.* a structure containing an embryo plant and food reserves, formed from an ovule after it has been fertilised. **4.** any small, seedlike part or fruit, as a grain of wheat. **5.** (*usu. pl.*) the germ or beginning of anything: *the seeds of discord.* **6.** offspring; progeny. **7.** semen or sperm. **8.** the ovum or ova of certain animals, as the lobster and the silkworm moth. **9.** →**seed oyster.** **10.** a small bubble in glass. **11.** a player who has been seeded: *Jones is number three seed this year.* **12. go** or **run to seed, a.** to pass to the stage of yielding seed. **b.** to approach the end of vigour, usefulness, prosperity, etc. *–v.t.* **13.** to sow (land) with seed. **14.** to sow or scatter (seed). **15.** *Chem.* to add a small crystal to (a super-saturated solution, or a supercooled liquid),

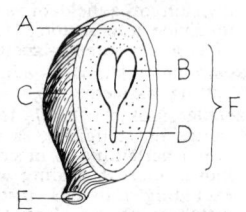

seed (def. 3) cross-section: A, endosperm; B, cotyledon; C, testa; D, radicle; E, hilum; F, embryo

in order to initiate crystallisation. **16.** to sow or scatter (clouds) with crystals or particles of silver iodide, solid carbon dioxide, etc., to induce precipitation. **17.** to place people with certain abilities or beliefs in positions of influence within an organisation. **18.** to remove the seeds from (fruit). **19.** to modify (the ordinary drawing of lots for position in a tournament, as at tennis) by distributing certain outstanding players so that they will not meet in the early rounds of play. **20.** to distribute (outstanding players) in this manner: *Jones was seeded fifth last year.* *–v.i.* **21.** to sow seed. **22.** to produce or shed seed. [ME; OE *sēd* (Anglian), *sǣd,* c. G *Saat*] – **seedless,** *adj.* – **seedlike,** *adj.*

**seedbed** /ˈsidbɛd/, *n.* an area of soil specially prepared for the germination of seeds, and usu. for raising the resulting seedlings prior to transplanting.

**seedcake** /ˈsidkeɪk/, *n.* a sweet cake containing aromatic seeds, esp. caraway.

**seed capsule** /ˈsid kæpʃul/, *n.* →**pericarp** (def. 1).

**seedcoat** /ˈsidkoʊt/, *n.* the outer integument of a seed.

**seed corn** /ˈsid kɔn/, *n.* ears or kernels of maize set apart as seed.

**seed crystal** /ˈ– krɪstl/, *n.* **1.** *Chem.* a small crystal added to a solution to initiate crystallisation. **2.** one of a large number of crystals scattered into clouds to induce precipitation.

**seed drill** /ˈ– drɪl/, *n.* a machine for sowing in rows and for covering the seeds when sown. Also, **drill.**

**seed-eater** /ˈsid-itə/, *n.* any of various tropical American and African finches, many of which resemble canaries.

**seeder** /ˈsidə/, *n.* **1.** one who or that which seeds. **2.** an apparatus for sowing seeds in the ground.

**seed leaf** /ˈsid lif/, *n.* →**cotyledon** (def. 1).

**seedling** /ˈsidlɪŋ/, *n.* a young plant developed from the embryo after germination of a seed.

**seed oyster** /ˈsid ɔɪstə/, *n.* one of a spat of oysters; a very young oyster.

**seed pearl** /ˈ– pɜl/, *n.* a very small pearl.

**seed plant** /ˈ– plænt/, *n.* a seed-bearing plant; a spermatophyte.

**seed potato** /– pəˈteɪtoʊ/, *n.* a potato tuber kept for planting for the next crop.

**seedsman** /ˈsidzmən/, *n., pl.* **-men. 1.** a dealer in seed. **2.** a sower of seed.

**seedtime** /ˈsidtaɪm/, *n.* the season for sowing seed.

**seed vessel** /ˈsid vɛsəl/, *n.* →**pericarp** (def. 1).

**seedy** /ˈsidi/, *adj.,* **-dier, -diest. 1.** abounding in seed. **2.** gone to seed. **3.** rather disreputable or shabby. **4.** wearing shabby clothes. **5.** *Colloq.* out of sorts physically. – **seedily,** *adv.* – **seediness,** *n.*

**seeing** /ˈsiɪŋ/, *conj.* in view of the fact (that); considering; inasmuch as.

**seek** /sik/, *v.,* **sought, seeking.** *–v.t.* **1.** to go in search or quest of: *to seek a new home.* **2.** to try to find by searching or endeavour: *to seek a solution.* **3.** to try to obtain: *to seek fame.* **4.** to try or attempt (fol. by an infinitive): *to seek to convince a person.* **5.** to ask for; request: *to seek advice.* **6. be sought after,** to be desired or in demand: *he is much sought after as an entertainer.* *–v.i.* **7.** to make search or inquiry. [ME *seke,* OE *sēcan,* c. G *suchen*] – **seeker,** *n.*

**seel** /sil/, *v.t.* **1.** *Falconry.* to close (the eyes of a hawk), esp. by sewing up the lids, in order to make it responsive to training. **2.** *Archaic.* to blind. **3.** *Archaic.* to deceive. [ME *sille(n),* from MF *siller,* from *cil* eyelash]

**seem** /sim/, *v.i.* **1.** to appear to be; appear (to be, feel, do, etc.). **2.** to appear to oneself (to be, do, etc.): *I seem to hear someone calling.* **3.** to appear to exist: *there seems no need to go now.* **4.** to appear to be true or the case: *it seems likely to rain.* [ME *seme,* from Scand.; cf. Icel. *sæma* (impers.) beseem, befit] – **seemer,** *n.*

**seeming** /ˈsimɪŋ/, *adj.* **1.** apparent; appearing to be such (whether truly or falsely): *a seeming advantage.* *–n.* **2.** appearance, esp. outward or deceptive appearance. – **seemingly,** *adv.*

**seemly** /ˈsimli/, *adj.,* **-lier, -liest,** *adv.* *–adj.* **1.** fitting or becoming with respect to propriety or good taste; decent; decorous. **2.** of pleasing appearance; handsome. **3.** *Archaic.* suitable. *–adv.* **4.** in a seemly manner; fittingly; becomingly. [ME *semeli,* from Scand.; cf. Icel. *sǣmilegr* becoming] – **seemliness,** *n.*

**seen** /sin/, *v.* past participle of **see**[1].

**seep** /sip/, *v.i.* **1.** to pass gradually, as liquid, through a porous substance; ooze. **2.** to enter or infiltrate gradually, as ideas. *–n.* **3.** moisture that seeps out. **4.** *U.S.* a small spring, or soakage of ground water at the surface. [? var. of d. *sipe,* OE *sīpian,* c. MLG *sīpen*]

**seepage** /ˈsipɪdʒ/, *n.* **1.** that which seeps or leaks out. **2.** the act or process of seeping; leakage.

**seer** /sɪə/, *n.* **1.** one who foretells future events; a prophet. **2.** a magician, clairvoyant, or other person claiming to have occult powers; a palmist, crystal-gazer, or the like. **3.** *Rare.* one who sees; an observer. [SEE[1] + -ER[1]]

**seersucker** /ˈsɪəsʌkə/, *n.* a fabric, usu. striped cotton with alternate stripes crinkled in the weaving. [Hind., from Pers., alteration of *shīr o shakkar,* lit., milk and sugar]

**seesaw** /ˈsiˌsɔ/, *n.* **1.** a plank or beam balanced at the middle so that its ends may rise and fall alternately. **2.** a children's game in which participants ride up and down on the ends of such a plank. **3.** moving up and down or back and forth. **4.** an up-and-down or a back-and-forth movement or procedure. **5.** *Whist.* →**crossruff.** *–v.i.* **6.** to move in the manner of a seesaw. *–v.t.* **7.** to cause to move in the manner of a seesaw. *–adj.* **8.** moving alternately in opposite directions. [varied reduplication suggested by SAW[1]]

**seethe** /sið/, *v.,* **seethed, seething,** *n.* *–v.i.* **1.** to surge or foam, as a boiling liquid. **2.** to be in a state of physical or mental agitation; to be excited, discontented, or agitated. **3.** to boil or stew, as meat. *–v.t.* **4.** *Obs.* to boil; prepare, cook, or extract the essence of by boiling, stewing, etc. **5.** *Obs.* to soak or steep. *–n.* **6.** an instance, state or act of seething; commotion or turmoil. [ME; OE *sēothan,* c. G *sieden*] – **seethingly,** *adv.*

**see-through** /ˈsi-θru/, *adj.* of or pertaining to garments which are either of an open weave or sheer, so that it is possible to see through them.

**seg.,** segment.

**seggar** /ˈsɛgə/, *n.* →**saggar.**

**segment** /ˈsɛgmənt/, *n.;* /sɛgˈmɛnt/, *v.* *–n.* **1.** one of the parts into which anything naturally separates or is naturally divided; a division or section. **2.** *Geom.* **a.** a part cut off from a figure (esp. a circular or a spherical one) by a line or a plane, as a part of a circular area contained by an arc and its chord, or by two parallel lines or planes. **b.** a finite section of a straight line or curve. **3.** *Zool.* any one of the rings that compose the body of an arthropod, or any other animal with a comparable structure, or one of the sections of a limb between the joints. **4.** *Elect.* one of the insulated elements which form a commutator. *–v.t., v.i.* **5.** to separate or divide into segments. [L *segmentum*] – **segmentary** /ˈsɛgməntəri, -tri/, *adj.*

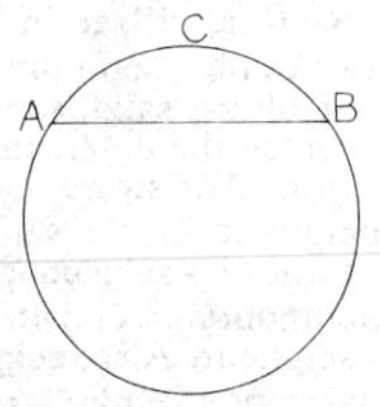

ACB, segment (def. 2a) of a circle

**segmental** /sɛgˈmɛntl/, *adj.* **1.** of or pertaining to segments. **2.** divided into segments. **3.** *Phonetics.* of or pertaining to those features of a sound which serve to identify it phonemically. Cf. **suprasegmental.** – **segmentally,** *adv.*

**segmentation** /sɛgmənˈteɪʃən/, *n.* **1.** division into segments. **2.** *Biol.* **a.** the subdivision of an organism or of an organ into more or less equivalent parts. **b.** cell-division.

**segmentation cavity** /ˈ– kævəti/, *n.* a blastocoel; the hollow of a blastula.

**segno** /ˈsɛnjoʊ/, *n., pl.* **-gni** /-nji/. *Music.* **1.** a sign. **2.** a sign or mark at the beginning or end of a repetition. [It., from L *signum*]

**segregate** /ˈsɛgrəgeɪt/, *v.,* **-gated, -gating;** /ˈsɛgrəgət/, *adj.* *–v.t.* **1.** to separate or set apart from the others or from the main body; isolate. **2.** to impose a policy of segregation on (a specific racial, religious or other group). **3.** to impose a policy of segregation on (a place, community, or state). *–v.i.* **4.** to separate or go apart; separate from the main body and collect in one place; become segregated. **5.** to practise, enforce, or adopt a policy of segregation. **6.** *Biol.* (of allelomorphic characters) to separate according to Mendel's laws. *–adj.* **7.** segregated; set apart. [ME, from L *sēgregātus,* pp., separated from the flock] – **segregative,** *adj.* – **segregator,** *n.*

**segregated** /ˈsɛgrəgeɪtəd/, *adj.* **1.** subject to a policy of, practising, or characterised by segregation. **2.** restricted to a single racial or other group. **3.** providing separate facilities for members of different racial or other groups. **4.** discriminating against a particular racial or other group.

**segregation** /sɛgrəˈgeɪʃən/, *n.* **1.** the act of segregating. **2.** the state of being segregated. **3.** something segregated. **4.** the policy or practice of providing separate facilities for racial groups living in the same area, and as far as possible preventing contact between them. **5.** a set of laws implementing this, as by restricting members of such races to certain residential areas, institutions, or facilities. **6.** *Biol.* the separation of genes in paternal chromosomes from those in maternal chromosomes at the reduction division, and the consequent separation of their hereditary characters as observed in the progeny of hybrids.

**segregationist** /sɛgrəˈgeɪʃənəst/, *n.* an advocate, adherent, or practitioner of racial segregation.

**segue** /ˈsɛgweɪ/, *adv.* **1.** (a musical direction) follow straight on without break. *–v.i.* **2.** to link without interruption, as of one segment of music to another (fol. by *with*). [It.]

**seguidilla** /sɛgəˈdiljə/, *n.* **1.** *Pros.* a stanza of four to seven lines with a distinctive rhythm. **2.** a Spanish dance in triple rhythm for two persons. **3.** the music for it. [Sp., from *seguida* following, sequence]

**seicento** /seɪˈtʃɛntoʊ/, *n.* the 17th century, with reference to the Italian art or literature of that period. [It., short for *mille seicento* one thousand six hundred]

**seiche** /seɪʃ/, *n.* an occasional rhythmical movement from side to side of the water of a lake, with fluctuation of the water-level. [Swiss F]

**Seidlitz powder** /ˈsɛdlɪts paʊdə/, *n.* an aperient consisting of two powders, one tartaric acid and the other a mixture of sodium bicarbonate and Rochelle salt, which are dissolved separately, mixed, and drunk while effervescing. [named after *Seidlitz,* village in Bohemia]

**seif-dune** /ˈseɪf-djun/, *n.* (in deserts, esp. the Sahara) a ridge of blown sand, sometimes several kilometres long, stretching across the desert in the direction of the prevailing wind. [*seif* from Ar.: sword]

**seigneur** /sɛnˈjɜ, seɪ-/, *n.* a feudal lord. [F, from L *senior.* See SENIOR] – **seigneurial,** *adj.*

**seigneury** /ˈseɪnjəri/, *n.* the domain, house, or status of a seigneur. Also, **seigneurie.**

**seignior** /seɪˈnjɔ/, *n. Archaic.* **1.** a lord; a ruler. **2.** the lord of a manor; a gentleman (also formerly used as a title of respect). [ME *segnour,* from AF, from L *senior.* See SENIOR]

**seigniorage** /ˈseɪnjərɪdʒ/, *n.* **1.** something claimed by a sovereign or superior as a prerogative, as a charge on bullion brought to the mint to be coined. **2.** the difference between the cost of the bullion plus minting expenses and the face value as money of the pieces coined.

**seigniory** /ˈseɪnjəri/, *n., pl.* **-ries. 1.** the rights, power, and authority of a seignior. **2.** *Hist.* a lord's domain. Also, **signory.**

**seignorial** /seɪnˈjɔriəl/, *adj.* of or pertaining to a seignior. Also, **seignioral** /ˈseɪnjərəl/.

**seine** /seɪn/, *n., v.,* **seined, seining.** *–n.* **1.** a fishing net which hangs vertically in the water, having floats at the upper edge and sinkers at the lower. **2.** *Colloq.* **a.** (formerly) the sum of £1. **b.** the sum of $1. *–v.t.* **3.** to fish for or catch with a seine. **4.** to use a seine in (water). *–v.i.* **5.** to fish with a seine. [ME *seyn(e),* OE *segne,* from L *sagēna,* from Gk *sagḗnē* fishing net] – **seiner,** *n.*

**seise** /siz/, *v.t.,* **seised, seising.** to put in seisin or legal possession of. Also, **seize.**

**seisin** /ˈsizən/, *n. Law.* **1.** (originally) possession of either land or chattel. **2.** the kind of possession, or right to possession, characteristic of estates of freehold. Also, **seizin.** [ME *saisine,* from OF, from *saisir* SEIZE]

**seism** /ˈsaɪzəm/, *n.* an earthquake. [Gk *seismós*]

**seismic** /ˈsaɪzmɪk/, *adj.* pertaining to, of the nature of, or caused by an earthquake. Also, **seismal, seismical.** [Gk *seismós* earthquake + -IC]

**seismic focus** /– ˈfoʊkəs/, *n.* a point within the earth's crust at which an earthquake originates.

**seismic prospecting** /– ˈprɒspɛktɪŋ/, *n.* a method of exploring the underlying strata of the earth, in which small explosive charges are fired, the resulting vibrations providing geological information.

**seismic survey** /– ˈsɜveɪ/, *n.* a determination of the composition of the earth's crust by means of seismic prospecting.

**seismo-** a word element meaning 'seismic', as in *seismology.* [Gk, combining form of *seismós* earthquake]

**seismogram** /ˈsaɪzməgræm/, *n.* a record made by a seismograph.

**seismograph** /ˈsaɪzməgræf, -graf/, *n.* an instrument for measuring and recording vibrations within the earth as earthquakes. – **seismographic** /saɪzməˈgræfɪk/, *adj.*

**seismography** /saɪzˈmɒgrəfi/, *n.* **1.** the scientific description of earthquake phenomena. **2.** the science of the use of the seismograph.

**seismology** /saɪzˈmɒlədʒi/, *n.* the science or study of earthquakes and their phenomena. – **seismologic** /saɪzməˈlɒdʒɪk/, **seismological** /saɪzməˈlɒdʒɪkəl/, *adj.* – **seismologically,** /saɪzməˈlɒdʒɪkli/, *adv.* – **seismologist,** *n.*

**seismometer** /saɪzˈmɒmətə/, *n.* an instrument for measuring the direction, intensity, and duration of earthquakes. – **seismometric** /saɪzməˈmɛtrɪk/, **seismometrical** /saɪzməˈmɛtrɪkəl/, *adj.*

**sei whale** /ˈseɪ weɪl/, *n.* a cetacean, *Balaenoptera borealis,* of the rorqual family, up to 18 metres long, with a worldwide distribution. [partial translation of Norw. *seihval,* lit., coalfish-whale]

**seize** /siz/, *v.,* **seized, seizing.** *–v.t.* **1.** to lay hold of suddenly or forcibly; grasp: *to seize a weapon.* **2.** to grasp with the mind: *to seize an idea.* **3.** to take possession of by force or at will: *to seize enemy ships.* **4.** to take possession or control of as if by suddenly laying hold: *panic seized the crowd.* **5.** to take possession of by legal authority; confiscate: *to seize smuggled goods.* **6.** →**seise. 7.** to capture; take into custody. **8.** to take advantage of promptly: *to seize an opportunity.* **9.** *Naut.* to bind, lash, or fasten together with several turns of light rope, cord, or the like. *–v.i.* **10.** to lay hold suddenly or forcibly: *to seize on a rope.* **11.** to become jammed or stuck solid, as an engine through excessive heat (fol. by *up*). [ME *sayse,* from OF *saisir,* from VL *sacīre* set, put (in possession), from Gmc; cf. Goth. *satjan* SET] – **seizer;** *Law,* **seizor** /ˈsizə,-zɔ/, *n.*

**seizin** /ˈsizən/, *n.* →**seisin.**

**seizing** /ˈsizɪŋ/, *n.* **1.** the act of seizing. **2.** *Naut.* a binding or lashing, consisting of several turns of light line, marline, wire, or the like, holding two ropes, etc., together.

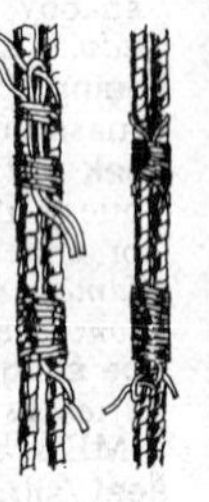
seizings (def. 2)

**seizure** /ˈsiʒə/, *n.* **1.** the act of seizing. **2.** a taking possession, legally or by force. **3.** a sudden attack, as of disease.

**sejant** /ˈsidʒənt/, *adj.* (in heraldry) in a sitting posture. [also *seiant,* from OF *seant,* ppr. of *seoir* sit, from L *sedēre*]

**selachian** /səˈleɪkiən/, *adj.* **1.** belonging to the Selachii, a large group of fishes comprising the sharks, skates, and rays. *–n.* **2.** a selachian fish, as a shark. [NL *Selachiī,* pl. (replacing *selachē,* from Gk: sharks) + -AN]

**selaginella** /sɛlədʒəˈnɛlə/, *n.* any of a genus of heterosporous vascular cryptogams, typical of the family Selaginellaceae, including species cultivated in conservatories. [NL, diminutive of L *selago* a genus of plant]

**selah** /ˈsilə/, *n.* a word occurring frequently in the Psalms, supposed to be a liturgical or musical direction, probably a direction by the leader to raise the voice, or perhaps indicating a pause. [Heb.]

**selamlik** /səˈlamlɪk/, *n.* the portion of a Turkish palace or house reserved for men. [Turk.]

**seldom** /ˈsɛldəm/, *adv.* **1.** rarely; infrequently; not often. *–adj.* **2.** *Obs.* rare; infrequent. [ME; OE *seldum,* var. of *seldan,* c. G *selten*]

**select** /səˈlɛkt/, *v.t.* **1.** to choose in preference to another or others; pick out. *–adj.* **2.** selected; chosen in preference to others. **3.** choice; of special value or excellence. **4.** carefully or fastidiously chosen; exclusive: *a select party.* [L *sēlectus,* pp., chosen] – **selectness,** *n.* – **selector,** *n.*

**select committee** /– kə'mɪti/, *n.* a committee selected from either the Senate or the House of Representatives to enquire into and report back on a specific matter.

**selectee** /səlɛk'ti/, *n. U.S.* one selected by draft for military or naval service.

**selection** /sə'lɛkʃən/, *n.* **1.** the act of selecting or the fact of being selected; choice. **2.** a thing or a number of things selected. **3.** a range of things from which selection may be made: *a shop with a wide selection of hats.* **4.** *Sport.* a contestant selected by someone, as a sports writer, to win a game or event. **5.** a block of land acquired under the system of free selection. **6.** a farm (usu. small). **7.** *Biol.* the singling out of certain forms of animal and vegetable life for reproduction and perpetuation, either by the operation of natural causes (cf. **natural selection**) which result in the survival of the fittest, or by man's agency (**artificial selection**) as in breeding animals and in cultivating fruits, vegetables, etc. **8.** *Linguistics.* **a.** the choice of one form instead of another in a position where both can occur, as the choice of *ask* instead of *tell* or *with* in the phrase *ask John.* **b.** the choice of one form class in a construction, to the exclusion of others which do not occur there, as the choice of a noun like *John* as direct object of *ask,* to the exclusion of adjectives and adverbs. **c.** the feature of a construction resulting from such a choice. The phrases *ask John* and *with John* differ in selection; no adjective or adverb occurs as direct object of a verb in English.

**selective** /sə'lɛktɪv/, *adj.* **1.** having the function or power of selecting; making selection. **2.** fastidious; discriminating. **3.** characterised by selection. **4.** *Radio.* having good selectivity.

**selective high school,** *n.* a secondary school which provided academic education for children chosen because of their high intellectual ability.

**selective service** /səlɛktɪv 'sɜvəs/, *n.* compulsory military service on a selective basis.

**selective transmission** /– trænz'mɪʃən/, *n.* a motor vehicle gearbox in which the available forward and reverse speeds may be engaged in any order, without passing progressively through the different changes of gear.

**selectivity** /səlɛk'tɪvəti/, *n.* **1.** the state or quality of being selective. **2.** *Elect.* the property of a circuit, instrument, or the like, by virtue of which it responds to electric oscillations of a particular frequency. **3.** *Radio.* (of a receiving set) the ability to receive any one of a band of frequencies or waves to the exclusion of others.

**selector** /sə'lɛktə/, *n.* **1.** one who or a device which selects. **2.** one who chooses the members of a team or the like. **3.** *Elect.* a mechanism which can be set to one of several positions, thus closing one of several circuits. **4.** →**free selector.**

**selenate** /'sɛləneɪt/, *n.* a salt of selenic acid.

**selenic** /sə'linɪk, -'lɛnɪk/, *adj.* of or containing selenium, esp. in the hexavalent state.

**selenic acid** /– 'æsəd/, *n.* a strong, corrosive, dibasic acid, $H_2SeO_4$, resembling sulphuric acid.

**selenious** /sə'liniəs/, *adj.* of or containing tetravalent or divalent selenium.

**selenite** /'sɛlənaɪt/, *n.* **1.** a variety of gypsum, found in transparent crystals and foliated masses. **2.** *Chem.* a salt of selenious acid. [L *selēnītēs,* from Gk: lit., (stone) of the moon]

**selenium** /sə'liniəm/, *n.* a non-metallic element chemically resembling sulphur and tellurium, occuring in several allotropic forms (crystalline, amorphous, etc.), and having an electrical resistance which varies under the influence of light. *Symbol:* Se; *at. wt:* 78.96; *at. no.:* 34; *sp. gr.:* (grey) 4.80 at 25°C, (red) 4.50 at 25°C. [NL, from Gk *selḗnē* moon + *-ium* -IUM]

**selenium cell** /'– sɛl/, *n.* a photoelectric cell which depends upon the influence of light on the conductivity of a strip of selenium supported between two metal electrodes.

**selenium rectifier** /– 'rɛktəfaɪə/, *n.* a rectifier which consists of alternate layers of iron and selenium in contact.

**seleno-,** **1.** a word element meaning 'moon', as in *selenology.* **2.** *Chem.* a combining form of *selenium.* [combining form of Gk *selḗnē* moon]

**selenodesy** /silə'nɒdəsi/, *n.* that branch of applied mathematics which determines, by observation and measurement, the exact positions of points and the figures and areas of large portions of the moon's surface, or the shape and size of the moon. – **selenodetik** /silənə'dɛtɪk/, *adj.*

**selenography** /silə'nɒgrəfi/, *n.* the science dealing with the moon, esp. with reference to its physical features. [See SELENO-, -GRAPHY] – **selenographer,** *n.* – **selenographic** /səlinoʊ'græfɪk/, *adj.*

**selenology** /silə'nɒlədʒi/, *n.* that branch of astronomy dealing with the moon. – **selenologist,** *n.*

**selenotropism** /silə'nɒtrəpɪzəm/, *adj.* the movement of parts of plants caused by moonlight. – **selenotropic** /səlinə'trɒpɪk/, *adj.*

**selenous acid** /səlinəs 'æsəd/, *n.* a weak, dibasic acid, $H_2SeO_3$.

**self** /sɛlf/, *n., pl.* **selves,** *adj., pron., pl.* **selves.** *–n.* **1.** a person or thing referred to with respect to individuality; one's own person: *one's own self.* **2.** one's nature, character, etc.: *one's better self.* **3.** personal interest; selfishness. **4.** *Philos.* the ego as opposed to the non-ego; the unifying condition of all one's knowing, feeling, and willing, as opposed to what one knows, feels, and wills. *–adj.* **5.** being the same throughout, as a colour; uniform. **6.** being of one piece or material with the rest. **7.** *Archaic.* same. *–pron.* **8.** myself, himself, etc.: *to make a cheque payable to self.* [ME and OE, c. D *zelf,* G *Selb*]

**self-,** prefixal use of *self,* appearing in various parts of speech, expressing principally reflexive action, e.g., subject identical with direct object, as in *self-control, self-government, self-help;* with indirect-object or adverbial-type relations, as in *self-conscious, self-centred, self-evident.*

**self-abasement** /sɛlf-ə'beɪsmənt/, *n.* abasement or humiliation of oneself, esp. as a penance or punishment administered from guilt or shame.

**self-abnegation** /ˌsɛlf-æbnə'geɪʃən/, *n.* self-denial.

**self-absorbed** /sɛlf-əb'sɔbd, -zɔbd/, *adj.* particularly preoccupied with one's own thoughts, interests, etc., esp. to the exclusion of others.

**self-absorption** /sɛlf-əb'sɔpʃən, -zɔp-/, *n.* preoccupation with oneself, esp. to the exclusion of other interests.

**self-abuse** /sɛlf-ə'bjus/, *n.* **1.** masturbation. **2.** criticism, deprecation, or disparagement of oneself.

**self-accusing** /sɛlf-ə'kjuzɪŋ/, *adj.* penitent; accepting or assuming blame.

**self-acting** /sɛlf-'æktɪŋ/, *adj.* automatic.

**self-actualisation** /ˌsɛlf-æktʃuəlaɪ'zeɪʃən/, *n.* the realisation of man's potential to develop as a mature, autonomous, creative being.

**self-addressed** /'sɛlf-ədrɛst/, *adj.* addressed to oneself.

**self-adjusting** /sɛlf-ə'dʒʌstɪŋ/, *adj.* capable of adjusting itself, or automatically returning to an original position, as a machine.

**self-aggrandisement** /sɛlf-ə'grændəzmənt/, *n.* increase of one's own power, wealth, etc., usu. aggressively. Also, **self-aggrandizement.**

**self-annealing** /sɛlf-ə'nilɪŋ/, *adj.* denoting or pertaining to certain metals, as lead, tin and zinc, which recrystallise at air temperatures so that they may be cold-worked without strain-hardening.

**self-appointed** /'sɛlf-əpɔɪntəd/, *adj.* acting or speaking as if having authority, without being authorised or requested to do so.

**self-assertion** /sɛlf-ə'sɜʃən/, *n.* insistence on or expression of one's own importance, claims, wishes, opinions, etc. – **self-assertive,** *adj.*

**self-assurance** /sɛlf-ə'ʃɔrəns/, *n.* self-confidence.

**self-assured** /sɛlf-ə'ʃɔd/, *adj.* self-confident.

**self-aware** /sɛlf-ə'wɛə/, *adj.* **1.** conscious of or knowing one's character, abilities, and weaknesses, etc. **2.** excessively aware of or obsessed with oneself. – **self-awareness,** *n.*

**self-binder** /sɛlf-'baɪndə/, *n.* a combine harvester which binds (corn, etc.) automatically.

**self-centred** /sɛlf-'sɛntəd/, *adj.* **1.** engrossed in self; selfish.

2. centred in oneself or itself. **3.** being itself fixed as a centre.

**self-centring** /sɛlf-ˈsɛntərɪŋ/, *adj.* **1.** automatically returning to a central position after displacement. **2.** (of a lathe chuck) containing a mechanism which ensures that the jaws are always concentric.

**self-cleaning** /ˈsɛlf-klinɪŋ/, *adj.* (of an oven, iron, etc.) designed so that it incorporates a cleaning mechanism or process.

**self-coloured** /ˈsɛlf-kʌləd/, *adj.* **1.** of one uniform colour. **2.** of the natural colour.

**self-command** /sɛlf-kəˈmænd, -ˈmand/, *n.* self-control.

**self-complacent** /sɛlf-kəmˈpleɪsənt/, *adj.* pleased with oneself; self-satisfied. – **self-complacently,** *adv.*

**self-composed** /sɛlf-kəmˈpoʊzd/, *adj.* calm within oneself; composed. – **self-composedly** /-ˈpoʊzədli/, *adv.*

**self-conceit** /sɛlf-kənˈsit/, *n.* an excessively good opinion of oneself, one's abilities, etc. – **self-conceited,** *adj.*

**self-confessed** /ˈsɛlf-kənfɛst/, *adj.* known to be such on one's own testimony: *a self-confessed murderer.*

**self-confidence** /sɛlf-ˈkɒnfədəns/, *n.* confidence in one's own judgment, ability, power, etc., sometimes to an excessive degree. – **self-confident,** *adj.* – **self-confidently,** *adj.*

**self-congratulation** /sɛlf-kənˌgrætʃəˈleɪʃən/, *n.* approval, esp. uncritical, of one's achievements, qualities, abilities, etc. – **self-congratulatory** /sɛlf-kənˈgrætʃələtri/, *adj.*

**self-conscious** /sɛlf-ˈkɒnʃəs/, *adj.* **1.** excessively conscious of oneself as an object of observation to others. **2.** conscious of oneself or one's own thoughts, etc. – **self-consciously,** *adv.* – **self-consciousness,** *n.*

**self-consistent** /sɛlf-kənˈsɪstənt/, *adj.* **1.** consistent with oneself or itself. **2.** consistent with one's stated principles.

**self-contained** /ˈsɛlf-kənteɪnd/, *adj.* **1.** containing in oneself or itself all that is necessary; independent. **2.** (of a flat or house) having its own kitchen, bathroom, and lavatory; not necessitating sharing. **3.** reserved or uncommunicative. **4.** self-possessed; calm. **5.** (of a machine) complete in itself.

**self-content** /sɛlf-kənˈtɛnt/, *n.* satisfaction with oneself; self-complacency. Also, **self-contentment.**

**self-contradiction** /ˌsɛlf-kɒntrəˈdɪkʃən/, *n.* **1.** the act or fact of contradicting oneself or itself. **2.** a statement containing contradictory elements. – **self-contradictory,** *adj.*

**self-control** /sɛlf-kənˈtroʊl/, *n.* control of oneself or one's actions, feelings, etc.

**self-cover** /ˈsɛlf-kʌvə/, *n.* a cover for a book, etc., which consists of the same material as the article itself.

**self-critical** /sɛlf-ˈkrɪtɪkəl/, *adj.* **1.** finding fault, esp. to an excessive degree, with one's own actions or motives. **2.** assessing one's actions, motives, or achievements impartially. – **self-critically,** *adv.* – **self-criticism,** *n.*

**self-deception** /sɛlf-dəˈsɛpʃən/, *n.* the act or fact of deceiving oneself. Also, **self-deceit** /sɛlf-dəˈsit/. – **self-deceptive,** *adj.*

**self-defeating** /sɛlf-dəˈfitɪŋ/, *adj.* (of an action, plan, argument, or the like) having inherent defects or contradictions which serve to frustrate or nullify the original purpose.

**self-defence** /sɛlf-dəˈfɛns/, *n.* **1.** the act of defending one's own person, reputation, etc. **2.** *Law.* the use of reasonable force against an attacker, constituting a defence in criminal law and tort. – **self-defensive,** *adj.*

**self-denial** /sɛlf-dəˈnaɪəl/, *n.* the sacrifice of one's own desires; unselfishness. – **self-denying,** *adj.* – **self-denyingly,** *adv.*

**self-deprecating** /sɛlf-ˈdɛprəkeɪtɪŋ/, *adj.* modest; understating one's worth. – **self-deprecatingly,** *adv.* – **self-deprecation** /ˌsɛlf-dɛprəˈkeɪʃən/, *n.*

**selfdestruct** /sɛlfdəˈstrʌkt/, *v.;* /ˈsɛlfdəstrʌkt/, *n., adj.* –*v.i.* **1.** to explode as a result of interference or according to some pre-set internal mechanism. –*n.* **2.** an autodestructing device. –*adj.* **3.** of or pertaining to, an aeroplane, missile, etc., equipped with a selfdestruct. Also, **autodestruct.**

**self-destruction** /sɛlf-dəˈstrʌkʃən/, *n.* the destruction of oneself or itself; suicide.

**self-determination** /sɛlf-dəˌtɜməˈneɪʃən/, *n.* **1.** determination by oneself or itself, without outside influence. **2.** the determining by a people or nationality of the form of government it shall have, without reference to the wishes of any other nation. – **self-determined** /sɛlf-dəˈtɜmənd/, *adj.* – **self-determining** /sɛlf-dəˈtɜmənɪŋ/, *adj., n.*

**self-devotion** /sɛlf-dəˈvoʊʃən/, *n.* devotion of oneself; self-sacrifice. – **self-devotional,** *adj.*

---

**self-accusation,** *n.*
**self-accusatory,** *adj.*
**self-accused,** *adj.*
**self-adhesive,** *adj.*
**self-administered,** *adj.*
**self-administering,** *adj.*
**self-admiration,** *n.*
**self-admiring,** *adj.*
**self-admiringly,** *adv.*
**self-adornment,** *n.*
**self-adulation,** *n.*
**self-advancement,** *n.*
**self-advertisement,** *n.*
**self-advertising,** *adj.*
**self-aligning,** *adj.*
**self-alignment,** *n.*
**self-amusement,** *n.*
**self-analysis,** *n.*
**self-applauding,** *adj.*
**self-applause,** *n.*
**self-appreciating,** *adj.*
**self-appreciation,** *n.*
**self-approval,** *n.*
**self-authorising,** *adj.*
**self-banishment,** *n.*
**self-benefiting,** *adj.*
**self-betrayal,** *n.*
**self-cancelled,** *adj.*
**self-cancelling,** *adj.*
**self-castigating,** *adj.*
**self-castigation,** *n.*
**self-chastisement,** *n.*
**self-closing,** *adj.*
**self-cocking,** *adj.*
**self-cognition,** *n.*
**self-commendation,** *n.*
**self-comprehending,** *adj.*
**self-comprehension,** *n.*
**self-condemnation,** *n.*
**self-condemnatory,** *adj.*
**self-condemned,** *adj.*
**self-confinement,** *n.*
**self-confining,** *adj.*
**self-consoling,** *adj.*
**self-consuming,** *adj.*
**self-contempt,** *n.*
**self-correcting,** *adj.*
**self-created,** *adj.*
**self-damnation,** *n.*
**self-debasement,** *n.*
**self-deceived,** *adj.*
**self-defining,** *adj.*
**self-definition,** *n.*
**self-degradation,** *n.*
**self-delusion,** *n.*
**self-depreciation,** *n.*
**self-deprivation,** *n.*
**self-destroyed,** *adj.*
**self-destructive,** *adj.*
**self-development,** *n.*
**self-directed,** *adj.*
**self-directing,** *adj.*
**self-disapproval,** *n.*
**self-discovery,** *n.*
**self-disengagement,** *n.*
**self-disgust,** *n.*
**self-disparagement,** *n.*
**self-disparaging,** *adj.*
**self-display,** *n.*
**self-dissatisfaction,** *n.*
**self-dissatisfied,** *adj.*
**self-dissolution,** *n.*
**self-doubt,** *n.*
**self-dramatisation,** *n.*
**self-driven,** *adj.*
**self-elected,** *adj.*
**self-election,** *n.*
**self-emptying,** *adj.*
**self-enamoured,** *adj.*
**self-engrossed,** *adj.*
**self-enrichment,** *n.*
**self-evaluation,** *n.*
**self-exultation,** *n.*
**self-exculpation,** *n.*
**self-excusing,** *adj.*
**self-exile,** *n.*
**self-exiled,** *adj.*
**self-exposure,** *n.*
**self-extermination,** *n.*
**self-filling,** *adj.*
**self-flagellation,** *n.*
**self-flattery,** *n.*
**self-focusing,** *adj.*
**self-fulfilment,** *n.*
**self-generated,** *adj.*
**self-giving,** *adj.*

**self-discipline** /sɛlf-ˈdɪsəplən/, *n.* discipline and training of oneself, usu. for improvement.

**self-distrust** /sɛlf-dɪsˈtrʌst/, *n.* lack of confidence in oneself, one's abilities, etc.

**self-educated** /sɛlf-ˈɛdʒəkeɪtəd/, *adj.* educated by one's own efforts, without formal instruction, or without financial assistance. – **self-education** /ˌsɛlf-ɛdʒəˈkeɪʃən/, *n.*

**self-effacement** /sɛlf-əˈfeɪsmənt/, *n.* the act or fact of keeping oneself in the background, as in humility. – **self-effacing,** *adj.*

**self-employed** /ˈsɛlf-əmplɔɪd/, *adj.* deriving one's income directly from one's own work, profession, or business, and not as a salary from an employer. – **self-employment,** *n.*

**self-esteem** /sɛlf-əsˈtim/, *n.* favourable opinion of oneself; conceit.

**self-evident** /sɛlf-ˈɛvədənt/, *adj.* evident in itself without proof; axiomatic. – **self-evidence,** *n.* – **self-evidently,** *adv.*

**self-examination** /ˌsɛlf-əgzæməˈneɪʃən/, *n.* examination of one's own state, conduct, motives, etc.

**self-excited** /sɛlf-əkˈsaɪtəd/, *adj.* denoting or pertaining to an electrical machine in which the magnetic field system is supplied by current from the machine itself, or an auxiliary machine attached to it.

**self-executing** /sɛlf-ˈɛksəkjutɪŋ/, *adj.* providing for its own execution, and needing no legislation to enforce it: *a self-executing treaty.*

**self-existent** /sɛlf-əgˈzɪstənt/, *adj.* **1.** existing independently of any cause, as God. **2.** having an independent existence. – **self-existence,** *n.*

**self-explanatory** /sɛlf-əksˈplænətri/, *adj.* needing no explanation; obvious. Also, **self-explaining.**

**self-expression** /sɛlf-əksˈprɛʃən/, *n.* the expression or assertion of one's personality by poetry, music, etc., or by one's behaviour, esp. unhampered by limitations imposed by an outside authority.

**self-feeder** /sɛlf-ˈfidə/, *n.* **1.** a machine that fuels itself, or feeds itself with raw materials or the like. **2.** a device attached to a machine that supplies it with fuel or raw materials or the like. **3.** *Agric.* an automatic machine for feeding livestock.

**self-fertilisation** /ˌsɛlf-fɜtəlaɪˈzeɪʃən/, *n.* the fertilisation of a flower by its own pollen (opposed to *cross-fertilisation*). Also, **self-fertilization.**

**self-forgetful** /sɛlf-fəˈgɛtfəl/, *adj.* forgetful, or not thinking, of one's own advantage, interest, etc.

**self-fulfilling prophecy** /ˌsɛlf-fʊlfɪlɪŋ ˈprɒfəsi/, *n.* a prediction which by its very pronouncement inclines a person towards bringing about its fulfillment.

**self-governed** /ˈsɛlf-gʌvənd/, *adj.* governed by itself, or having self-government, as a state or community; independent. – **self-governing,** *adj.*

**self-government** /sɛlf-ˈgʌvənmənt/, *n.* **1.** government of a state, community, or other body or persons by its members jointly; democratic government. **2.** political independence of a country, people, region, etc. **3.** the condition of being self-governed. **4.** self-control.

**self-hardening** /sɛlf-ˈhadnɪŋ/, *adj.* denoting or pertaining to any of certain steels which harden without the usual quenching, etc., necessary for ordinary steel. – **self-hardened,** *adj.*

**selfheal** /ˈsɛlfhil/, *n.* **1.** a small, perennial herb, *Prunella vulgaris,* once accredited with great remedial virtues. **2.** any of various other plants similarly credited.

**self-help** /sɛlf-ˈhɛlp/, *n.* the state or an act of achieving one's ends unaided by others.

**selfhood** /ˈsɛlfhʊd/, *n.* **1.** the state of being an individual person. **2.** one's personality. **3.** selfishness.

selfheal

**self-identity** /sɛlf-aɪˈdɛntəti/, *n.* the identity, or consciousness of identity, of a thing with itself.

**self-image** /sɛlf-ˈɪmɪdʒ/, *n.* the mental picture one has of oneself.

**self-immolate** /sɛlf-ˈɪməleɪt/, *v.i.,* **-lated, -lating.** to commit suicide by dowsing oneself with petrol and then setting oneself on fire, esp. as a political protest.

---

**self-glorifying,** *adj.*
**self-gratification,** *n.*
**self-hatred,** *n.*
**self-healing,** *adj.*
**self-humbling,** *adj.*
**self-humiliation,** *n.*
**self-hypnosis,** *n.*
**self-ignorant,** *adj.*
**self-immolation,** *n.*
**self-incriminating,** *adj.*
**self-incrimination,** *n.*
**self-incurred,** *adj.*
**self-inflating,** *adj.*
**self-inflation,** *n.*
**self-interrogation,** *n.*
**self-introduction,** *n.*
**self-invited,** *adj.*
**self-judgment,** *n.*
**self-laceration,** *n.*
**self-laudatory,** *adj.*
**self-levelling,** *adj.*
**self-locating,** *adj.*
**self-lubricating,** *adj.*
**self-maintained,** *adj.*
**self-maintaining,** *adj.*
**self-maintenance,** *n.*
**self-mortification,** *n.*
**self-multiplying,** *adj.*
**self-mutilation,** *n.*
**self-neglect,** *n.*
**self-obsessed,** *adj.*
**self-perception,** *n.*
**self-perfecting,** *adj.*
**self-perpetuating,** *adj.*
**self-perpetuation,** *n.*
**self-persuasion,** *n.*
**self-policing,** *adj.*
**self-powered,** *adj.*
**self-praise,** *n.*
**self-preoccupation,** *n.*
**self-preoccupied,** *adj.*
**self-preparation,** *n.*
**self-presentation,** *n.*
**self-proclaimed,** *adj.*
**self-propagating,** *adj.*
**self-propulsion,** *n.*
**self-proving,** *adj.*
**self-punishing,** *adj.*
**self-punishment,** *n.*
**self-purifying,** *adj.*
**self-quotation,** *n.*
**self-reconstruction,** *n.*
**self-reformation,** *n.*
**self-refuting,** *adj.*
**self-regulating,** *adj.*
**self-regulation,** *n.*
**self-representation,** *n.*
**self-repression,** *n.*
**self-reproof,** *n.*
**self-revealed,** *adj.*
**self-revealing,** *adj.*
**self-revelation,** *n.*
**self-reverence,** *n.*
**self-satisfying,** *adj.*
**self-schooled,** *adj.*
**self-scrutiny,** *n.*
**self-searching,** *adj.*
**self-serving,** *adj.*
**self-sinking,** *adj.*
**self-slain,** *adj.*
**self-sold,** *adj.*
**self-stabilising,** *adj.*
**self-stimulated,** *adj.*
**self-stimulating,** *adj.*
**self-stimulation,** *n.*
**self-suppression,** *n.*
**self-tapping,** *adj.*
**self-teaching,** *adj.*
**self-terminating,** *adj.*
**self-testing,** *adj.*
**self-threading,** *adj.*
**self-tightening,** *adj.*
**self-tipping,** *adj.*
**self-torment,** *n.*
**self-torture,** *n.*
**self-torturing,** *adj.*
**self-trained,** *adj.*
**self-transformation,** *n.*
**self-tuition,** *n.*
**self-unloading,** *adj.*
**self-valuation,** *n.*
**self-valuing,** *adj.*
**self-varying,** *adj.*
**self-vindicating,** *adj.*
**self-worship,** *n.*

---

i = peat ɪ = pit ɛ = pet æ = pat a = part ɒ = pot ʌ = putt ɔ = port ʊ = put u = pool ɜ = pert ə = apart aɪ = buy eɪ = bay ɔɪ = boy aʊ = how
oʊ = hoe ɪə = here ɛə = hair ʊə = tour g = give θ = thin ð = then ʃ = show ʒ = measure tʃ = choke dʒ = joke ŋ = sing j = you õ = Fr. bon

**self-important** /sɛlf-ɪm'pɔtnt/, *adj.* having or showing an exaggerated opinion of one's own importance; conceited or pompous. – **self-importance,** *n.* – **self-importantly,** *adv.*

**self-imposed** /'sɛlf-ɪmpoʊzd/, *adj.* imposed on one by oneself: *a self-imposed task.*

**self-improvement** /sɛlf-ɪm'pruvmənt/, *n.* improvement of one's mind, education, status, etc., by one's own efforts.

**self-induced** /'sɛlf-ɪndjust/, *adj.* **1.** induced by oneself or itself. **2.** produced by self-induction.

**self-inductance** /sɛlf-ɪn'dʌktəns/, *n.* **1.** the property of an electrical circuit in which self-induction occurs. **2.** a measure of this property coefficient of self-induction. See **inductance.**

**self-induction** /sɛlf-ɪn'dʌkʃən/, *n.* the production of an induced electromotive force in a circuit by a varying current in that circuit.

**self-indulgent** /sɛlf-ɪn'dʌldʒənt/, *adj.* **1.** indulging one's own desires, passions, etc., esp. at the expense of other considerations. **2.** characterised by such indulgence. – **self-indulgence,** *n.* – **self-indulgently,** *adv.*

**self-inflicted** /'sɛlf-ɪnflɪktəd/, *adj.* inflicted on one by oneself: *a self-inflicted wound.*

**self-insurance** /sɛlf-ɪn'ʃɔrəns/, *n.* **1.** the insuring of one's property, etc., through oneself, as by setting aside a fund for the purpose. **2.** the amount by which the actual value of one's property exceeds the cover provided by an insurance policy.

**self-interest** /sɛlf-'ɪntrəst/, *n.* **1.** regard for one's own interest or advantage, esp. with disregard of others. **2.** personal interest or advantage. – **self-interested,** *adj.*

**selfish** /'sɛlfɪʃ/, *adj.* **1.** devoted to or caring only for oneself, one's welfare, interests, etc. **2.** characterised by caring only for oneself: *selfish motives.* – **selfishly,** *adv.* – **selfishness,** *n.*

**self-justification** /ˌsɛlf-dʒʌstəfə'keɪʃən/, *n.* **1.** the act or fact of explaining or explaining away one's actions, motives, etc. **2.** a justification or raison d'être which is inherent in a thing. **3.** *Print.* the automatic adjustment of lines being typeset.

**self-justifying** /sɛlf-'dʒʌstəfaɪɪŋ/, *adj.* **1.** excusing or explaining one's actions, etc., as to avoid blame, esp. excessively. **2.** containing in itself its justification or raison d'être. **3.** *Print.* automatically adjusting the length of lines being typeset.

**self-knowledge** /sɛlf-'nɒlɪdʒ/, *n.* knowledge of oneself, one's character, abilities, etc.

**selfless** /'sɛlfləs/, *adj.* unselfish.

**self-liquidating** /sɛlf-'lɪkwədeɪtɪŋ/, *adj.* assured of being sold and converted into cash within a short period of time or before the date on which the supplier, etc., must be paid: *a self-liquidating loan.*

**self-loading** /sɛlf-'loʊdɪŋ/, *adj.* reloading automatically, as a firearm.

**self-locking** /sɛlf-'lɒkɪŋ/, *adj.* **1.** locking automatically when closed, as a door or lid. **2.** having a self-locking lid, door, or device.

**self-love** /sɛlf-'lʌv/, *n.* **1.** egotism; selfishness, narcissism, **2.** the instinct by which man's actions are directed to the promotion of his own welfare. **3.** *Philos.* the self-respect that constitutes a man's proper relation with himself. – **self-loving,** *adj.*

**self-made** /'sɛlf-meɪd/, *adj.* **1.** having succeeded in life, unaided by inheritance, class background, or other people: *a self-made man.* **2.** made by oneself.

**self-mastery** /sɛlf-'mastəri/, *n.* self-control.

**self-mate** /sɛlf-'meɪt/, *n.* *Chess.* **1.** a move or series of moves which lead inevitably to the mating of a player's own king. **2.** a problem in which this is the object. Also, **suimate.**

**self-moving** /sɛlf-'muvɪŋ/, *adj.* moving of itself, without external agency.

**self-murder** /sɛlf-'mɜdə/, *n.* suicide.

**self-opinion** /sɛlf-ə'pɪnjən/, *n.* **1.** opinion, esp. exaggerated opinion, of oneself. **2.** obstinacy in one's views.

**self-opinionated** /sɛlf-ə'pɪnjəneɪtəd/, *adj.* **1.** conceited. **2.** obstinate in one's own opinion.

**self-perpetuating** /sɛlf-pə'pɛtʃueɪtɪŋ/, *adj.* of or pertaining to a process or situation which, once brought into being, will continue to maintain itself.

**self-pity** /sɛlf-'pɪti/, *n.* exaggerated or self-indulgent pity for oneself, or exaggeration of one's misfortunes. – **self-pitying,** *adj.*

**self-pollinated** /sɛlf-'pɒləneɪtəd/, *adj.* having the pollen transferred from the anthers to the stigmas of the same flower, or another flower on the same individual plant. – **self-pollination** /ˌsɛlf-pɒlə'neɪʃən/, *n.*

**self-portrait** /sɛlf-'pɔtrət/, *n.* a portrait of an artist, photographer, or the like, by himself.

**self-possessed** /sɛlf-pə'zɛst/, *adj.* having or showing control of one's feelings, behaviour, etc. – **self-possession,** *n.*

**self-preservation** /ˌsɛlf-prɛzə'veɪʃən/, *n.* preservation of oneself from harm or destruction.

**self-pronouncing** /'sɛlf-prənaʊnsɪŋ/, *adj.* of or pertaining to a dictionary, tourist guide, etc., which indicates the pronunciation of a word by respelling it using the ordinary alphabet rather than transliterating it into a special phonetic alphabet.

**self-propelled** /sɛlf-prə'pɛld/, *adj.* **1.** propelled by itself. **2.** (of a vehicle, etc.) propelled by its own engine, motor, or the like, rather than drawn or pushed by a horse, locomotive, etc. – **self-propelling,** *adj.*

**self-protection** /sɛlf-prə'tɛkʃən/, *n.* protection of oneself or itself.

**self-raising flour** /sɛlf-'reɪzɪŋ flaʊə/, *n.* wheat flour with baking powder already added.

**self-realisation** /ˌsɛlf-riəlaɪ'zeɪʃən/, *n.* the fulfilment of one's potential capacities. Also, **self-realization.**

**self-recording** /sɛlf-rə'kɔdɪŋ/, *adj.* recording automatically, as an instrument.

**self-regard** /sɛlf-rə'gad/, *n.* **1.** consideration for oneself or one's own interests. **2.** self-respect. – **self-regarding,** *adj.*

**self-registering** /sɛlf-'rɛdʒəstrɪŋ, -tərɪŋ/, *adj.* registering automatically, as an instrument; self-recording.

**self-reliance** /sɛlf-rə'laɪəns/, *n.* reliance on oneself or one's own powers; confidence; independence. – **self-reliant,** *adj.*

**self-renunciation** /sɛlf-rəˌnʌnsi'eɪʃən/, *n.* renunciation of one's own will, interests, etc.; self-sacrifice. – **self-renunciatory,** *adj.*

**self-reproach** /sɛlf-rə'proʊtʃ/, *n.* **1.** blame or censure by one's own conscience. **2.** public self-criticism.

**self-respect** /sɛlf-rə'spɛkt/, *n.* proper esteem or regard for the dignity of one's character.

**self-respecting** /'sɛlf-rəspɛktɪŋ/, *adj.* having or showing self-respect.

**self-restraint** /sɛlf-rə'streɪnt/, *n.* restraint imposed on one by oneself; self-control.

**self-righteous** /sɛlf-'raɪtʃəs/, *adj.* righteous in one's own esteem; pharisaic. – **self-righteously,** *adv.* – **self-righteousness,** *n.*

**self-righting** /sɛlf-'raɪtɪŋ/, *adj.* denoting something, as a boat, which is built in such a way that it automatically rights itself after being upset.

**self-rule** /sɛlf-'rul/, *n.* achievement of independence by a former colony or dependent territory. – **self-ruling,** *adj.*

**self-sacrifice** /sɛlf-'sækrəfaɪs/, *n.* sacrifice of one's interests, desires, etc., as for duty or the good of another. – **self-sacrificing,** *adj.*

**selfsame** /'sɛlfseɪm/, *adj.* (the) very same; identical. – **self-sameness** /'sɛlf'seɪmnəs/, *n.*

**self-satisfaction** /ˌsɛlf-sætəs'fækʃən/, *n.* satisfaction with oneself, one's achievements, etc.; smugness.

**self-satisfied** /sɛlf-'sætəsfaɪd/, *adj.* feeling or showing satisfaction with oneself; complacent.

**self-sealing** /'sɛlf-silɪŋ/, *adj.* denoting or pertaining to a device, container, etc., which seals itself: *a self-sealing envelope.*

**self-seeker** /sɛlf-'sikə/, *n.* one who seeks his own interest or selfish ends.

**self-seeking** /sɛlf-'sikɪŋ/, *n.* **1.** the seeking of one's own interest or selfish ends. *–adj.* **2.** given to or characterised by self-seeking; selfish.

**self-service** /sɛlf-'sɜvəs/, *adj.* **1.** Also, **self-serve.** (of a restaurant, lift or other service) operating on the principle that the customers, passengers, etc., perform part or all of the service themselves. *–n.* **2.** a restaurant or section of a restaurant operating on this principle. **3.** the act of serving oneself.

**self-sharpening** /ˈsɛlf-ʃapənɪŋ/, *adj.* (of a knife) sharpened by insertion in and removal from a special holder fitted with a sharpening device.

**self-sown** /sɛlf-ˈsoʊn/, *adj.* **1.** sown by itself, or without human or animal agency. **2.** sown by any agency other than man, as by birds, the wind, etc. *–n.* **3.** a plant grown from a self-sown seed.

**self-starter** /sɛlf-ˈstatə/, *n.* **1. a.** a device which starts an internal combustion engine, other than a crank or an auxiliary turning engine. **b.** a machine or vehicle equipped with such a device. **2.** a person who acts on his own initiative and does not require external motivation to encourage him to work.

**self-styled** /ˈsɛlf-staɪld/, *adj.* (of a title or characterisation) applied to himself by the person so called, esp. undeservedly: *a self-styled genius.*

**self-sufficient** /sɛlf-səˈfɪʃənt/, *adj.* **1.** able to supply one's own needs. **2.** having undue confidence in one's own resources, powers, etc. Also, **self-sufficing** /sɛlf-səˈfaɪsɪŋ/. – **self-sufficiency,** *n.*

**self-support** /sɛlf-səˈpɔt/, *n.* the act or fact of supporting or maintaining oneself unaided. – **self-supported,** *adj.*

**self-supporting** /ˈsɛlf-səpɔtɪŋ/, *adj.* **1.** having an income great enough to cover all outgoings. **2.** requiring no props or other supports; independent: *a self-supporting wall.*

**self-sustaining** /sɛlf-səˈsteɪnɪŋ/, *adj.* self-supporting.

**self-tapping screw** /ˌsɛlf-tæpɪŋ ˈskru/, *n.* a screw which is capable of cutting a female thread in the hole into which it is screwed.

**self-taught** /ˈsɛlf-tɔt/, *adj.* taught by oneself without aid from others.

**self-will** /sɛlf-ˈwɪl/, *n.* **1.** wilfulness. **2.** obstinacy.

**self-willed** /sɛlf-ˈwɪld/, *adj.* obstinately or perversely insistent on one's own desires or opinions.

**self-winding** /sɛlf-ˈwaɪndɪŋ/, *adj.* (of a clock or watch) winding itself automatically by a motor, by its wearer's movements, or the like.

**sell** /sɛl/, *v.,* **sold, selling,** *n.* *–v.t.* **1.** to give up or make over for a consideration; dispose of to a purchaser for a price. **2.** to deal in; keep for sale. **3.** to act as a dealer in or seller of: *he sells insurance.* **4.** to facilitate or induce the sale of: *the package sells the product.* **5.** to induce or attempt to induce purchasers for: *he used to be a good actor, but now he is selling soap on television.* **6.** to cause to be accepted: *to sell an idea to the public.* **7.** *Colloq.* to cheat or hoax. *–v.i.* **8.** to sell something; engage in selling. **9.** to be on sale; find purchasers. **10.** to win acceptance, approval, or adoption. *–v.* **11.** Some special verb phrases are:

**be sold on,** *Colloq.* to be very enthusiastic about.

**sell dearly,** to part with after great and protracted resistance: *to sell one's life dearly.*

**sell down the river,** *Colloq.* to betray.

**sell off,** to sell at reduced prices, or with some other inducement for quick sale.

**sell out, 1.** to dispose of (goods or a particular product) entirely by selling; have none left (of). **2.** *Colloq.* to betray.

**sell up, 1.** to liquidate by selling the assets (of). **2.** to sell a business.

*–n.* **12.** *Colloq.* an act of selling or salesmanship. Cf. **hard sell, soft sell. 13.** *Colloq.* a hoax or deception. **14.** *Colloq.* a disappointment. [ME *selle(n),* OE *sellan,* c. LG *sellen*]

**seller** /ˈsɛlə/, *n.* **1.** one who sells; a vendor. **2.** an article, as a book, considered with reference to its sale: *one of the worst sellers in its price range.*

**seller's market** /sɛləz ˈmakət/, *n.* a market in which the seller is at an advantage because of scarcity of supply.

**Sellotape** /ˈsɛləteɪp/, *n.* →**sticky tape.** [Trademark]

**sell-out** /ˈsɛl-aʊt/, *n. Colloq.* **1.** a betrayal. **2.** a play, show, etc., for which all seats are sold.

**Seltzer** /ˈsɛltsə/, *n.* **1.** a natural effervescent mineral water containing common salt and small quantities of sodium, calcium, and magnesium carbonates. **2.** (*also l.c.*) an artificial water of similar composition. Also, **Seltzer water.** [G *Selterser,* from *Selters,* village near Wiesbaden, Germany]

**selvedge** /ˈsɛlvɪdʒ/, *n.* **1.** the edge of woven fabric finished to prevent fraying, often in a narrow tape effect, different from the body of the fabric. **2.** any similar strip or part of surplus material, as at the side of wallpaper. **3.** *Meat Industry.* the fatty edge on a cut of meat. Also, **selvage.** [late ME, from SELF + EDGE. Cf. D *zelfegge*]

**selves** /sɛlvz/, *n.* plural of **self.**

**Sem., 1.** Seminary. **2.** Semitic.

**semantic** /səˈmæntɪk/, *adj.* **1.** pertaining to signification or meaning. **2.** *Linguistics.* concerning the meaning of words and other linguistic forms. [Gk *sēmantikós* significant]

**semantic painting** /– ˈpeɪntɪŋ/, *n.* a style of art of the post-1950s in which differing elements, as circles, spirals, loops, etc., are systematically and rationally arranged to form the whole pictorial composition.

**semantics** /səˈmæntɪks/, *n.* **1.** *Linguistics.* the systematic study of the meanings of words and changes thereof. **2.** *Logic.* that branch of modern logic which studies the relations between signs and what they denote or signify.

**semaphore** /ˈsɛməfɔ/, *n., v.,* **-phored, -phoring.** *–n.* **1.** an apparatus for conveying information by means of signals. **2.** a system of signalling by hand, in which a flag is held in each hand at arm's length in various positions. *–v.t., v.i.* **3.** to signal by semaphore. [Gk *sêma* sign + -PHORE] – **semaphoric** /sɛməˈfɒrɪk/, *adj.*

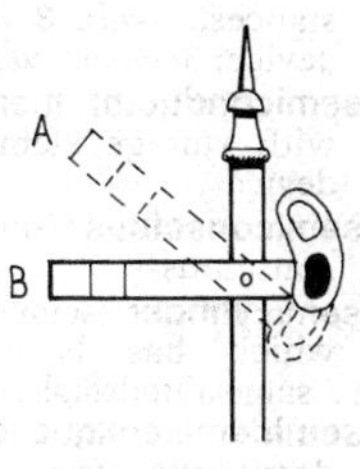

semaphore signal device: A, clear; B, stop

**semasiology** /səmeɪziˈɒlədʒi/, *n.* semantics, esp. the study of semantic change. [Gk *sēmasía* signification + -o- + -LOGY] – **semasiological** /səˌmeɪziəˈlɒdʒɪkəl/, *adj.* – **semasiologist,** *n.*

**sematic** /səˈmætɪk/, *adj.* serving as a sign or warning of danger, as the conspicuous colours or markings of certain poisonous animals. [Gk *sêma* sign + -IC]

**semblable** /ˈsɛmbləbəl/, *Archaic.* *–adj.* **1.** like or similar. **2.** seeming or apparent. *–n.* **3.** likeness; resemblance. [ME, from OF, from *sembler* appear. See SEMBLANCE] – **semblably,** *adv.*

**semblance** /ˈsɛmbləns/, *n.* **1.** an outward aspect or appearance. **2.** an assumed or unreal appearance; a mere show. **3.** a likeness, image, or copy. [ME, from OF, from *sembler* be like, seem, from L *similāre,* for *simulāre*]

**semé** /ˈsɛmeɪ/, *adj.* (in heraldry) strewn or covered with small figures of the same kind, as stars or flowers. Also, **semée.** [F, pp. of *semer* sow, strew, from L *sēmināre*]

**semeiology** /sɛmiˈɒlədʒi/, *n.* →**semiology.**

**semeiotic** /sɛmiˈɒtɪk, -meɪ-/, *adj.* →**semiotic.** Also, **semeiotical.**

**semeiotics** /sɛmiˈɒtɪks, -meɪ-/, *n.* →**semiotics.**

**semen** /ˈsimən/, *n.* the impregnating fluid produced by male reproductive organs; seed; sperm. [L: seed]

**semester** /səˈmɛstə/, *n.* (in educational institutions) one of two (or sometimes in the U.S., three) divisions of the academic year. See **term.** [G, from L *sēme(n)stris,* from *sē-* (combining form of *sex* six) + *menstris* monthly] – **semestral,** *adj.*

**semi** /ˈsɛmi/, *n. Colloq.* **1.** a semidetached house. **2.** semitrailer. **3.** *Sport.* a semifinal.

**semi-,** a prefix modifying the latter element of the word, meaning 'half' in its precise and less precise meanings, as in *semicircle, semiannual, semidetached, semiaquatic.* [L, c. Gk *hēmi-,* OE *sām-, sōm-* half]

**semi-acoustic** /ˈsɛmi-əkustɪk/, *adj.* (of an instrument) designed to be played either as an acoustic or an electric instrument: *semi-acoustic guitar.*

**semiaquatic** /sɛmiəˈkwɒtɪk/, *adj.* partly aquatic; growing or living close to water, and sometimes found in or entering water.

**semiarid** /sɛmiˈærəd/, *adj.* (of regions of the earth) being appreciably dry but not as dry as arid regions. – **semiaridity** /sɛmiəˈrɪdəti/, *n.*

**semiautomatic** /sɛmiɔtəˈmætɪk/, *adj.* **1.** of or pertaining to a machine with a partly automatic function, as certain washing machines. **2.** of or pertaining to a firearm which loads automatically after each shot but fires only one round for each pull of the trigger. *–n.* **3.** such a firearm. – **semiautomatically,** *adv.*

**semibreve** /'sɛmibriv/, *n.* a note having half the length of a breve, being the longest note in common use.

**semicircle** /'sɛmisɜkəl/, *n.* **1.** the half of a circle. **2.** anything having, or arranged in, the form of a half of a circle. – **semicircular** /sɛmi'sɜkjələ/, *adj.*

**semicircular canal** /sɛmi,sɜkjələ kə'næl/, *n.* any of three curved tubular canals in the labyrinth of the ear, concerned with equilibrium.

**semicolon** /sɛmi'koʊlən, 'sɛmikoʊlən/, *n.* a mark of punctuation (;) used to indicate a more distinct separation between parts of a sentence than that indicated by a comma.

**semiconductor** /,sɛmikən'dʌktə/, *n.* **1.** a substance whose electrical conductivity at normal temperatures is intermediate between that of a metal and an insulator, and whose conductivity increases with a rise in temperature over a certain range, as germanium and silicon. **2.** a device, as a transistor, which is based on the electronic properties of such substances. *–adj.* **3.** of or pertaining to such a substance or device: *semiconductor diode.*

**semiconductor memory** /– 'mɛmri/, *n.* a computer memory with storage elements formed by integrated semiconductor devices.

**semiconscious** /sɛmi'kɒnʃəs/, *adj.* half-conscious; not fully conscious.

**semicylinder** /sɛmi'sɪləndə/, *n.* one of the halves of a cylinder which has been dissected lengthways. – **semicylindrical** /,sɛmisə'lɪndrɪkəl/, *adj.*

**semidemisemiquaver** /,sɛmidɛmi'sɛmikweɪvə/, *n.* →**hemidemisemiquaver.**

**semidetached** /,sɛmidə'tætʃt/, *adj.* partly detached (used esp. of a pair of houses joined by a common wall but detached from other buildings).

**semidiameter** /,sɛmidaɪ'æmətə/, *n.* **1.** the half of a diameter; a radius. **2.** half the angular diameter of a celestial body.

**semidiurnal** /,sɛmidaɪ'ɜnəl/, *adj.* **1.** pertaining to, consisting of, or accomplished in half a day. **2.** occurring every twelve hours.

**semidocumentary** /,sɛmidɒkjə'mɛntəri/, *adj.* **1.** (of a film) having both documentary and imaginary elements, as a fictional story with an actual background. *–n.* **2.** a semidocumentary film.

**semidome** /'sɛmidoʊm/, *n.* half a dome, esp. as formed by a vertical section, as over a semicircular apse.

**semielliptical** /,sɛmiə'lɪptɪkəl/, *adj.* shaped like the half of an ellipse, esp. one whose base is the major axis of the ellipse.

**semifinal** /sɛmi'faɪnəl/, *Sport.* *–adj.* **1.** designating a round, contest, match, etc., between any two of the last four contestants in a competition. **2.** pertaining to such a round, contest, etc. *–n.* **3.** a semifinal round, contest, etc.

**semifinalist** /sɛmi'faɪnələst/, *n.* a player or team contesting a semifinal.

**semifluid** /sɛmi'fluəd/, *adj.* **1.** imperfectly fluid, having both fluid and solid characteristics. *–n.* **2.** a semifluid substance. Also, **semiliquid** /sɛmi'lɪkwəd/.

**semi-government authority** /sɛmi-,gʌvənmənt ɔ'θɒrəti/, *n.* a government instrumentality responsible to parliament through a minister.

**Semillon** /'sɛmijɔ̃/, *n.* a widely grown white grape variety used in the making of white wines. [F]

**semilunar** /sɛmi'lunə/, *adj.* shaped like a half-moon; crescent.

**semilunar bone** /– 'boʊn/, *n.* the second bone from the thumb side of the proximal row of the carpus.

**semilunar cartilage** /– 'katəlɪdʒ/, *n.* one of two cartilages inside the knee joint.

**semilunar valve** /– 'vælv/, *n.* **1.** a crescent-shaped valve consisting of three flaps, in the orifice of the aorta, which prevents blood from flowing back into the left ventricle. **2.** a similar valve in the pulmonary artery, which prevents blood from flowing back into the right ventricle.

**semi-monocoque** /sɛmi-'mɒnəkɒk/, *adj.* a form of fuselage construction in which the stresses are shared by the frame and skin.

**semimonthly** /sɛmi'mʌnθli/, *adj., n., pl.* **-lies,** *adv.* *–adj.* **1.** occurring every half month. *–n.* **2.** a thing occurring every

---

**semiabsorbent,** *adj.*
**semiabstract,** *adj.*
**semiacademic,** *adj.*
**semiactive,** *adj.*
**semiactively,** *adv.*
**semiactiveness,** *n.*
**semiadhesive,** *adj.*
**semiadhesively,** *adv.*
**semiadhesiveness,** *n.*
**semiagricultural,** *adj.*
**semianarchistic,** *adj.*
**semianimate,** *adj.*
**semiarch,** *n.*
**semiarid,** *adj.*
**semiaridity,** *n.*
**semiarticulate,** *adj.*
**semiautonomous,** *adj.*
**semibiographical,** *adj.*
**semibiographically,** *adv.*
**semicapitalist,** *adj.*
**semicartilaginous,** *adj.*
**semichaotic,** *adj.*
**semiclassical,** *adj.*
**semiclassically,** *adv.*
**semiclerical,** *adj.*
**semicolloquial,** *adj.*
**semicolonial,** *adj.*
**semicontinuous,** *adj.*
**semicrystalline,** *adj.*
**semicultivated,** *adj.*
**semicultured,** *adj.*
**semidesert,** *n.*
**semidiaphanous,** *adj.*
**semidivine,** *adj.*
**semidomesticated,** *adj.*
**semidormant,** *adj.*
**semiductile,** *adj.*
**semidurable,** *adj., n.*
**semierect,** *adj.*
**semiexperimental,** *adj.*
**semiexperimentally,** *adv.*
**semifictional,** *adj.*
**semifigurative,** *adj.*
**semifiguratively,** *adv.*
**semifinished,** *adj.*
**semifitted,** *adj.*
**semiformal,** *adj.*
**semiheretical,** *adj.*
**semihysterical,** *adj.*
**semi-industrialised,** *adj.*
**semi-instinctive,** *adj.*
**semi-instinctive,** *adj.*
**semi-instinctively,** *adv.*
**semi-intellectual,** *adj., n.*
**semi-intoxicated,** *adj.*
**semi-ironic,** *adj.*
**semi-ironical,** *adj.*
**semi-ironically,** *adv.*
**semi-isolated,** *adj.*
**semiliquid,** *adj., n.*
**semiliterate,** *adj.*
**semimat,** *adj.*
**semimobile,** *adj.*
**semimonarchical,** *adj.*
**semimonopolistic,** *adj.*
**seminarrative,** *adj.*
**seminationalistic,** *adj.*
**seminocturnal,** *adj.*
**seminomadic,** *adj.*
**seminude,** *adj.*
**seminudity,** *n.*
**semiobjective,** *adj.*
**semiparalysed,** *adj.*
**semipervious,** *adj.*
**semipolitical,** *adj.*
**semireactionary,** *adj., n.*
**semirealistic,** *adj.*
**semirealistically,** *adv.*
**semirefined,** *adj.*
**semirespectability,** *n.*
**semirespectable,** *adj., n.*
**semiretired,** *adj.*
**semiretirement,** *n.*
**semirhythmic,** *adj.*
**semiround,** *adj.*
**semirural,** *adj.*
**semisocialist,** *adj., n.*
**semisoft,** *adj.*
**semisubterranean,** *adj.*
**semisweet,** *adj.*
**semisynthetic,** *adj.*
**semitraditional,** *adj.*
**semiurban,** *adj.*
**semiwild,** *adj.*

half month. **3.** a semimonthly publication. *–adv.* **4.** every half month.

**seminal** /ˈsɛmənəl/, *adj.* **1.** of, pertaining to, or of the nature of semen. **2.** *Bot.* of or pertaining to seed. **3.** highly original and influential. **4.** having possibilities of development. **5.** rudimentary; embryonic. [ME, from L *sēmen* seed + -AL[1]] – **seminally,** *adv.*

**seminar** /ˈsɛməna/, *n.* **1.** a small group of students, as in a university, engaged in advanced study and original research under a professor or the like. **2.** the gathering place of such a group. **3.** a course or subject of study for advanced graduate students. **4.** a meeting of students, usu. at an advanced level, for discussion of and instruction in a specified topic, usu. chaired by a teacher. **5.** a meeting organised to discuss a specific topic: *a public seminar on uranium mining.* [G, from L *sēminārium* (neut.) of or for seed]

**seminarian** /sɛməˈnɛəriən/, *n.* **1.** one who attends a seminary, as in training for the priesthood. **2.** one who teaches in a seminary. – **seminarist** /ˈsɛmənərəst/, *n.*

**seminary** /ˈsɛmənri/, *n., pl.* **-naries. 1.** *Rom. Cath. Ch.* a college for the education of men for the priesthood or ministry. **2.** a school, esp. one of higher level. **3.** (formerly) a school for young ladies. **4.** a place of origin and development. [late ME, from L *sēminārium* nursery]

**semination** /sɛməˈneɪʃən/, *n.* →**dissemination.**

**seminiferous** /sɛməˈnɪfərəs/, *adj.* **1.** *Anat.* conveying or containing semen. **2.** *Bot.* bearing or producing seed. [*semini-* (from NL, combining form representing L *sēmen* seed) + -FEROUS]

**semiofficial** /sɛmiəˈfɪʃəl/, *adj.* having some degree of official authority. – **semiofficially,** *adv.*

**semiology** /sɛmiˈɒlədʒi/, *n. Obs.* the branch of medical science dealing with symptoms. Also, **semeiology.** [Gk *sēmeîo(n)* sign + -LOGY]

**semiotic** /sɛmiˈɒtɪk/, *adj.* **1.** pertaining to semiotics. **2.** pertaining to medical symptoms; symptomatic. Also, **semeiotic, semiotical.** [Gk *sēmeîon* sign + -OTIC]

**semiotics** /sɛmiˈɒtɪks/, *n.pl. (construed as sing.)* **1.** the study of systems of signs or symbols. **2.** *Med.* →**semiology.**

**semipalmate** /sɛmiˈpælmeɪt/, *adj.* partially or imperfectly palmate as the feet of some wading birds; half-webbed. Also, **semipalmated.**

semipalmate foot

**semiparasitic** /ˌsɛmipærəˈsɪtɪk/, *adj.* **1.** *Biol.* commonly parasitic but capable of living on dead or decaying animal matter. **2.** *Bot.* partly parasitic and partly photosynthetic.

**semipermanent** /sɛmiˈpɜmənənt/, *adj.* intended to last for some time but not for ever, as a position subject to review, or a dye that will wash out after frequent washing or special treatment.

**semipermeable** /sɛmiˈpɜmiəbəl/, *adj.* permeable to some substances more than to others: *a semipermeable membrane.*

**semiplastic** /sɛmiˈplæstɪk/, *adj.* imperfectly plastic.

**semipolar bond** /ˌsɛmipoʊlə ˈbɒnd/, *n. Chem.* a valency bond in which two electrons are donated by one atom to another atom which requires both of them to complete its octet. Also, **coordinate covalent bond; donor bond.**

**semiporcelain** /sɛmiˈpɔsələn/, *n.* a partly vitrified, somewhat porous and non-translucent pottery ware, inferior to porcelain.

**semiprecious** /sɛmiˈprɛʃəs/, *adj.* (of a gem) having value, but not classified as precious, as the amethyst, garnet, etc.

**semipublic** /sɛmiˈpʌblɪk/, *adj.* partly or to some degree public.

**semiquaver** /ˈsɛmikweɪvə/, *n.* a note equivalent to one-sixteenth of a semibreve; half a quaver.

**semirigid** /sɛmiˈrɪdʒəd/, *adj.* designating a type of airship whose shape is maintained by means of a rigid keel-like structure and by internal gas pressure.

**semiskilled** /sɛmiˈskɪld/, *adj.* partly skilled or trained.

**semisolid** /sɛmiˈsɒləd/, *adj.* **1.** not completely solid; very viscous. *–n.* **2.** a semisolid substance.

**Semite** /ˈsimaɪt/, *n.* **1.** a member of a speech family comprising the Hebrews, Arabs, Assyrians, etc., supposedly descended from Shem, eldest son of Noah. **2.** a Jew. [NL *Sēmīta,* from L *Sēm* Shem, from Gk. See -ITE[1]]

**Semitic** /səˈmɪtɪk/, *n.* **1.** an important family of languages, including Akkadian, Hebrew, Aramaic, Arabic, and Amharic. *–adj.* **2.** of or pertaining to the Semites or their languages. **3.** Jewish.

**Semitics** /səˈmɪtɪks/, *n.* the study of the Semitic languages, literature, etc.

**Semitism** /ˈsɛmətɪzəm/, *n.* **1.** Semitic characteristics, esp. the ways, ideas, influence, etc., of the Jewish people. **2.** a Semitic word or idiom.

**Semitist** /ˈsɛmətəst/, *n.* an authority on Semitics.

**semitone** /ˈsɛmitoʊn/, *n.* the smallest interval in the chromatic scale of Western music. Also, *U.S.,* **half-tone.**

**semitone-bird** /ˈsɛmitoʊn-ˌbɜd/, *n.* →**pallid cuckoo.**

**semitrailer** /sɛmiˈtreɪlə/, *n.* an articulated goods vehicle consisting of a prime mover and a detachable trailer, supported at the front by the prime mover and at the back by its own wheels; rig.

**semitranslucent** /ˌsɛmitrænzˈlusənt/, *adj.* imperfectly translucent.

**semitransparent** /ˌsɛmitrænsˈpɛərənt/, *adj.* imperfectly transparent.

**semitropical** /sɛmiˈtrɒpɪkəl/, *adj.* subtropical.

**semivitreous** /sɛmiˈvɪtriəs/, *adj.* partially vitreous, as mineral constituents of volcanic rocks.

**semivowel** /ˈsɛmivaʊəl/, *n.* a speech sound of vowel quality used as a consonant, such as *w* in *wet* or *y* in *yet.*

**semiweekly** /sɛmiˈwikli/, *adj., n., pl.* **-lies,** *adv. –adj.* **1.** occurring or appearing every half week. *–n.* **2.** a semiweekly publication. *–adv.* **3.** every half week.

**semiyearly** /sɛmiˈjɪəli/, *adj., n., pl.* **-lies,** *adv. –adj.* **1.** semiannual. *–n.* **2.** a semiannual thing, as a publication. *–adv.* **3.** semiannually.

**semolina** /sɛməˈlinə/, *n.* the large, hard parts of wheat grains retained in the bolting machine after the fine flour has passed through it, which are used for making puddings, etc. [It. *semolino,* diminutive of *semola* bran, from L *simila* fine flour]

**sempiternal** /sɛmpəˈtɜnəl/, *adj. Archaic.* everlasting; eternal. [ME, from LL *sempiternālis,* from L *sempiternus* everlasting] – **sempiternity** /sɛmpəˈtɜnəti/, *n.*

**semplice** /sɛmˈplitʃeɪ/, *adv.* (a musical direction) in a plain and simple manner. [It.]

**sempre** /ˈsɛmpreɪ/, *adv.* (a musical direction) throughout. [It.]

**sempstress** /ˈsɛmpstrəs, ˈsɛmstrəs/, *n.* →**seamstress.**

**sen** /sɛn/, *n.* a monetary unit of Japan, Indonesia and Malaysia equivalent to a hundredth of a yen, rupiah or ringgit. [Chinese *ch'ien* coin]

**Sen., 1.** Senate. **2.** Senator. **3.** Senior.

**senary** /ˈsinəri/, *adj.* of or pertaining to the number six. [L *sēnārius*]

**senate** /ˈsɛnət/, *n.* **1.** an assembly or council of citizens having the highest deliberative functions in the government; a legislative assembly of a state or nation. **2.** *(cap.)* the upper and smaller house of the Australian Parliament consisting of 64 senators, ten from each of the six States, two from the Northern Territory and two from the Australian Capital Territory. **3.** a similar body in certain other countries. **4.** the supreme council of state in ancient Rome, whose membership and functions varied at different periods. **5.** a governing, advisory, or disciplinary body, as in certain universities. [ME *senat,* from L *senātus*]

**senator**[1] /ˈsɛnətə/, *n.* a member of a senate. [ME *senatour,* from L *senātor*] – **senatorship,** *n.*

**senator**[2] /ˈsɛnətə/, *n. Colloq.* a schooner of beer. [rhyming slang, *Senator Spooner* schooner]

**senatorial** /sɛnəˈtɔriəl/, *adj.* **1.** of or pertaining to a senator or senators; characteristic of or befitting a senator. **2.** consisting of senators. **3.** *U.S.* entitled to elect a senator: *a senatorial district.*

**send** /sɛnd/, *v.,* **sent, sending,** *n. –v.t.* **1.** to cause to go; direct or order to go: *to send a messenger.* **2.** to cause to be conveyed or transmitted to a destination: *to send a letter.* **3.** to compel, order, or force to go: *to send someone away.* **4.** to impel, or throw: *he sent down a fast ball.* **5.** to cause to become: *to send somebody mad.* **6.** to give (fol. by *forth, out,* etc.), as light, smell, or sound. **7.** *Elect.* **a.** to transmit. **b.** to transmit (an electromagnetic wave, etc.) in the form of pulses. **8.** *Colloq.* to excite or inspire (as a jazz musician, listener, or other person). **9. send back,** *Cricket.* to dismiss a batsman (sending him back to the pavilion). **10. send down, a.** to expel from a university. **b.** to imprison; sentence to a term of imprisonment. **11. send in,** to submit, as an application, request, competition entry, etc. **12. send off,** *Colloq.* to cause to depart. **b.** to be present at a departure, as of a friend. **13. send on,** to dispatch in advance as luggage. **14. send packing,** *Colloq.* to dismiss; send away. **15. send up,** *Colloq.* **a.** to mock or ridicule; satirise. **b.** to imprison. *–v.i.* **16.** to dispatch a message, messenger, etc. **17.** *Naut.* **a.** to lurch forward from the force of a wave. **b.** →**scend. 18. send for,** to summon: *send for a doctor.* *–n.* **19.** *Naut.* **a.** the driving impulse of a wave or waves upon a ship. **b.** the act of sending; a sudden plunge of a vessel. [ME *sende(n),* OE *sendan,* c. G *senden*]

**sendal** /ˈsɛndl/, *n.* a silk fabric in use during the Middle Ages, or a piece or garment of it. [ME, from OF *cendal,* probably from Gk *sindōn* fine linen]

**sender** /ˈsɛndə/, *n.* **1.** one who or that which sends. **2.** a transmitter of electrical pulses, as in telegraphy.

**send-off** /ˈsɛnd-ɒf/, *n. Colloq.* **1.** a party or other social arrangement in honour of a person who is setting out on a journey, career, etc. **2.** a start given to a person or thing.

**send-up** /ˈsɛnd-ʌp/, *n. Colloq.* a satire or parody.

**senega** /ˈsɛnɪgə/, *n.* **1.** the root of a milkwort, *Polygala senega,* of the eastern U.S., dried and used as an expectorant. **2.** the plant. [var. of *Seneca,* American Indian tribe, from its use by this people]

**Senegal** /ˈsɛnəgal/, *n.* a republic in western Africa.

**Senegalese** /sɛnəgəˈliz/, *adj., n., pl.* **-lese.** *–adj.* **1.** of or pertaining to Senegal. *–n.* **2.** a native or inhabitant of Senegal.

**senescent** /səˈnɛsənt/, *adj.* growing old; ageing. [L *senescens,* ppr., growing old] – **senescence,** *n.*

**seneschal** /ˈsɛnəʃəl/, *n.* an officer in the household of a medieval prince or dignitary, who had full charge of domestic arrangements, ceremonies, the administration of justice, etc.; a steward. [ME, from OF, from ML *seniscalcus,* from Gmc; cf. OHG *siniscalh,* lit., old servant]

**senile** /ˈsenaɪl, ˈsinaɪl/, *adj.* **1.** of, pertaining to, or characteristic of old age. **2.** mentally or physically infirm due to old age. **3.** *Phys. Geog.* (of topographical features) having advanced in reduction by erosion, etc., to a featureless plain that stands everywhere at base level. [L, neut. of *senīlis*]

**senility** /səˈnɪləti/, *n.* senile state; old age; the weakness or mental infirmity of old age.

**senior** /ˈsinjə/, *adj.* **1.** older or elder (often used after the name of the older of two persons bearing the same name). *Abbrev.:* Sr *or* Sen. **2.** of higher rank or standing, esp. by virtue of longer service. *–n.* **3.** a person who is older than another. **4.** one of higher rank or standing, esp. by virtue of longer service. **5.** a senior barrister, esp. Queen's Counsel. **6.** a member of the senior class in a university, college, or school. **7.** *Rowing.* an oarsman who has won a top-class event. **8.** an amateur wrestler over 48 kg in weight. [ME, from L, compar. of *senex* old]

**senior citizen** /– ˈsɪtəzən/, *n.* an old person.

**seniority** /siniˈɒrəti/, *n., pl.* **-ties. 1.** the state or fact of being senior; priority of birth; superior age. **2.** priority or precedence in age or service.

**senior resident medical officer,** *n.* a medical graduate, appointed to and resident in a hospital in the second and subsequent years after graduation.

**senior school** /ˈsinjə skul/, *n.* the senior classes in a school, grouped together.

**senior service** /– ˈsɜvəs/, *n.* (*sometimes cap.*) *Colloq.* the Navy (contrasted with the Army and Air Force).

**senna** /ˈsɛnə/, *n.* **1.** a cathartic drug consisting of the dried leaflets of various plants of the genus *Cassia,* as **Alexandrian senna** from *C. acutifolia,* or **Arabian senna** from *C. angustifolia.* **2.** any plant yielding this drug. **3.** any of various similar plants as *C. odorata,* **Australian senna** and *Sutherlandia frutescens,* **bladder senna.** [NL, from Ar. *sanā*]

**sennet** /ˈsɛnət/, *n.* a call on a trumpet or the like to announce the entrance or exit of actors in Elizabethan drama. [var. of SIGNET]

**sennight** /ˈsɛnaɪt/, *n. Archaic.* a week. Also, **se'nnight.** [ME *sennyght, sevenyght,* OE *seofan nihta* seven nights. See SEVEN, NIGHT. Cf. FORTNIGHT]

**sennit** /ˈsɛnət/, *n.* a kind of flat braided cordage used on shipboard, formed by plaiting strands of rope yarn or other fibre. Also, **sinnet.** [earlier *sinnet;* ? from SEVEN + KNIT]

**señor** /sɛˈnjɔ/, *n., pl.* **-ñores** /–ˈnjɔrəz/. **1.** the conventional Spanish title of respect and form of address for a man (equivalent to *Mr* and *sir*). **2.** a gentleman. [Sp., from L *senior.* See SENIOR]

**señora** /sɛˈnjɔrə/, *n.* **1.** the conventional Spanish title of respect and form of address for a married woman (equivalent to *Mrs* and *madam*). **2.** lady; gentlewoman. [Sp.]

**señorita** /sɛnjəˈritə/, *n.* **1.** the conventional Spanish title of respect and form of address for an unmarried woman (equivalent to *Miss*). **2.** young lady. [Sp.]

**sensate** /ˈsɛnseɪt/, *adj.* **1.** perceived by the senses. **2.** endowed with the faculty of sensation. [LL *sensātus,* pp. See SENSE, -ATE[1]]

**sensation** /sɛnˈseɪʃən/, *n.* **1.** the operation or function of the senses; perception through the senses. **2.** a mental condition produced through an organ of sense or resulting from a particular condition of some part of the body; a physical feeling, as of cold, dizziness, etc. **3.** *Physiol.* the faculty of perception of stimuli. **4.** *Psychol.* an experience arising directly from stimulation of sense organs. **5.** a mental feeling, esp. a state of excited feeling. **6.** a mental impression or feeling of seeming to perceive: *he had the sensation that he was being watched.* **7. a.** a state of excited feeling or interest caused among a number of persons or throughout a community by some occurrence, etc. **b.** an expression of such a feeling, as sound or movement of a crowd. **8.** a cause of such feeling or interest. [ML *sensātio,* from LL *sensātus* having sense]

**sensational** /sɛnˈseɪʃənəl/, *adj.* **1.** such as to produce a startling impression, esp. of an erotic, sadistic, or horrific kind: *a sensational novel.* **2.** aiming at such impressions, as a writer, etc. **3.** of or pertaining to sensation or the senses. **4.** *Colloq.* extremely pleasing or exciting; especially or extraordinarily good or excellent. **5.** causing a sensation (def. 7). – **sensationally,** *adv.*

**sensationalise** /sɛnˈseɪʃənəlaɪz/, *v.t.,* **-ised, -ising.** to present in a sensational manner.

**sensationalism** /sɛnˈseɪʃənəlɪzəm/, *n.* **1.** matter, language, or style producing or designed to produce startling or thrilling impressions, or to excite and please vulgar taste. **2.** the exploitation of cheap emotional excitement by popular newspapers, novels, etc. **3.** the tendency of a writer, artist, etc, to be obsessed with a desire to thrill. **4.** *Ethics.* the doctrine that the good is to be judged only by the gratification of the senses; sensualism. **5.** *Philos.* the doctrine that sensation is the sole origin of knowledge; sensuism. – **sensationalist,** *n.*

**sensationism** /sɛnˈseɪʃənɪzəm/, *n.* a school of psychology which holds that mental life is constituted solely of sensations. – **sensationist,** *n.*

**sensation-monger** /sɛnˈseɪʃən-ˌmʌŋgə/, *n.* one who busies himself with or purveys sensationalism, esp. for financial gain.

**sense** /sɛns/, *n., v.,* **sensed, sensing.** *–n.* **1.** each of the special faculties connected with bodily organs by which man and other animals perceive external objects and their own bodily changes (commonly reckoned as sight, hearing, smell, taste, and touch). **2.** these faculties collectively. **3.** their operation or function; sensation. **4.** a feeling or perception produced through the organs of touch, taste, etc., or resulting from a particular condition of some part of the body: *to have a sense of cold.* **5.** a faculty or function of the mind analogous to sensation: *the moral sense.* **6.** any special capacity for perception, estimation, appreciation, etc.: *a sense of humour.* **7.** (*usu. pl.*) clear or sound mental faculties; sanity. **8.** any more or less vague perception or impression: *a sense of security.* **9.** a mental discernment, realisation, or recognition: *a just sense of the worth of a thing.* **10.** the recognition of something as incumbent or fitting: *a sense of duty.* **11.** sound practical intelligence; commonsense: *he has no sense.* **12.** what is sensible or reasonable: *to talk sense.* **13.** the meaning, or one of the meanings, of a word, statement, or a passage. **14.** interpretation; understanding. **15.** the approximate, or the general overall meaning of a speech, book, essay, etc. **16.** an opinion or judgment formed or held, now esp. by an assemblage or body of persons: *the sense of a meeting.* **17.** *Maths.* one of two opposite directions in which a vector may point. **18. in a sense,** according to one interpretation; in a way; in one but not every way. **19. make sense, a.** to be intelligible or acceptable. **b.** to understand. *–v.t.* **20.** to perceive by or as by the senses; become aware of. **21.** to perceive without certainty; be aware of dimly, vaguely or without positive sensory confirmation. **22.** to comprehend or understand, esp. instinctively rather than by rational means. [ME, from L *sensus*]

**sense datum** /'– deɪtəm/, *n., pl.* **-data.** *Psychol.* any experiential factor that results from the action of a stimulus on a sense organ.

**senseless** /'sɛnsləs/, *adj.* **1.** unconscious. **2.** destitute or deprived of sensation; insentient. **3.** destitute of mental perception or appreciation. **4.** stupid or foolish, as persons or actions. **5.** nonsensical or meaningless, as words: *this letter is either ingenious code or senseless.* – **senselessly,** *adv.* – **senselessness,** *n.*

**sense organ** /'sɛns ɔgən/, *n.* a specialised structure which receives impressions, such as one of the tastebuds or tactile corpuscles.

**sensibility** /sɛnsə'bɪləti/, *n., pl.* **-ties.** **1.** capacity for sensation or feeling; responsiveness to sensory stimuli. **2.** mental susceptibility or responsiveness; quickness and acuteness of apprehension or feeling. **3.** keen consciousness or appreciation. **4.** (*pl.*) emotional capacities. **5.** (*sing. or pl.*) liability to feel hurt or offended; sensitive feelings. **6.** capacity for the higher or more refined feelings; delicate sensitiveness of taste. **7.** the property, as in plants or instruments, of being readily affected by external influences.

**sensible** /'sɛnsəbəl/, *adj.* **1.** having, using, or showing good sense or sound judgment. **2.** cognisant; keenly aware (usu. fol. by *of*): *sensible of his fault.* **3.** appreciable; considerable: *a sensible reduction.* **4.** capable of being perceived by the senses: *the sensible universe.* **5.** capable of feeling or perceiving, as organs or parts of the body. **6.** perceptible to the mind. **7.** conscious: *speechless but still sensible.* **8.** *Obs.* sensitive. [ME, from LL *sensibilis*] – **sensibleness,** *n.* – **sensibly,** *adv.*

**sensillum** /sɛn'sɪləm/, *n.* a very small, simple sense organ.

**sensitise** /'sɛnsətaɪz/, *v.t.,* **-tised, -tising.** **1.** to render sensitive. **2.** *Photog.* to render (a plate, film, etc.) sensitive to light or other forms of radiant energy. Also, **sensitize.** – **sensitisation** /sɛnsətaɪ'zeɪʃən/, *n.* – **sensitiser,** *n.*

**sensitive** /'sɛnsətɪv/, *adj.* **1.** endowed with sensation. **2.** readily affected by external agencies or influences. **3.** having acute mental or emotional sensibility; easily affected, pained, annoyed, etc. **4.** highly susceptible to adverse criticism: *he was sensitive about his short stature.* **5.** (of an issue, topic, etc.) arousing strong feelings or reaction. **6.** pertaining to or connected with the senses or sensation. **7.** *Physiol.* having a low threshold of sensation or feeling. **8.** responding to stimulation, as leaves which move when touched. **9.** highly susceptible to certain agents, as photographic plates, films, or paper to light. **10.** constructed to indicate, measure, or be affected by small amounts or changes, as a balance or thermometer. **11.** *Radio.* easily affected by external influences, esp. by radio waves. [ME, from ML *sensitīvus,* from L *sensus* sense] – **sensitively,** *adv.* – **sensitiveness,** *n.*

**sensitive plant** /'– plænt/, *n.* **1.** a tropical American plant, *Mimosa pudica,* with bipinnate leaves whose leaflets fold together when touched. **2.** any of various other plants sensitive to touch, as *Neptunia gracilis.*

**sensitivity** /sɛnsə'tɪvəti/, *n., pl.* **-ties.** **1.** the state or quality of being sensitive. **2.** *Physiol.* **a.** the ability of an organism or part of an organism to react to stimuli; irritability. **b.** degree of susceptibility to stimulation. **3.** *Radio.* the ability to react to incoming radio waves. **4.** *Elect.* the change in deflection of an electrical instrument per unit of applied torque.

**sensitometer** /sɛnsə'tɒmətə/, *n.* an instrument for making a series of accurately known exposures on photographic surfaces, used to determine sensitivity and other properties.

**sensor** /'sɛnsə/, *n.* **1.** an electronic device in a spacesuit or the like which detects a change in some function of the wearer, esp. a physiological change, and converts it into a signal for measuring, recording, or for the taking of some action. **2.** any similar device which detects a variable quantity and converts it into a signal.

**sensorimotor** /sɛnsəri'moʊtə/, *adj.* **1.** *Physiol.* of or pertaining to sensation and motor activity. **2.** *Psychol.* of or pertaining to motor activity triggered by sensory stimuli.

**sensorium** /sɛn'sɔriəm/, *n., pl.* **-soria** /-'sɔriə/, **-soriums.** the supposed seat of sensation in the brain, usu. taken as the cortex or grey matter. [LL, from L *sensus,* pp., felt]

**sensory** /'sɛnsəri/, *adj.* **1.** pertaining to sensation. **2.** *Physiol.* denoting a structure that conveys an impulse which results or tends to result in sensation, as a nerve. Also, **sensorial** /sɛn'sɔriəl/.

**sensory deprivation** /– dɛprə'veɪʃən/, *n.* the blocking of normal input to all the human senses, used in psychological experimentation and in the torture of political prisoners.

**sensual** /'sɛnʃuəl/, *adj.* **1.** excessively inclined to the gratification of the senses; voluptuous. **2.** lewd or unchaste. **3.** pertaining to or given to the gratification of the senses or the indulgence of appetite. **4.** of or pertaining to the senses or physical sensation. **5.** pertaining to the doctrine of sensationalism. [late ME, from LL *sensuālis.* See SENSE, -AL[1]] – **sensually,** *adv.*

**sensualise** /'sɛnʃuəlaɪz/, *v.t.,* **-lised, -lising.** to render sensual. Also, **sensualize.** – **sensualisation** /,sɛnʃuəlaɪ'zeɪʃən/, *n.*

**sensualism** /'sɛnʃuəlɪzəm/, *n.* **1.** subjection to sensual appetites; sensuality. **2.** *Ethics.* the theory that the highest good consists in sensual gratification. **3.** *Philos.* the doctrine of sensationalism. **4.** *Aesthetics.* emphasis on objective sensuality, or on the quality of the sensual as the most important in the beautiful.

**sensualist** /'sɛnʃuələst/, *n.* **1.** one given to the indulgence of the senses or appetites. **2.** one who holds the doctrine of sensationalism. – **sensualistic** /sɛnʃuə'lɪstɪk/, *adj.*

**sensuality** /sɛnʃu'æləti/, *n., pl.* **-ties.** **1.** sensual nature. **2.** excessive indulgence in sensual pleasures. **3.** lewdness; unchastity. Also, **sensualness.**

**sensuism** /'sɛnʃuɪzəm/, *n.* →**sensationalism.**

**sensuous** /'sɛnʃuəs/, *adj.* **1.** of or pertaining to the senses. **2.** perceived by or affecting the senses: *the sensuous qualities of music.* **3.** readily affected through the senses: *a sensuous temperament.* – **sensuously,** *adv.* – **sensuousness,** *n.*

**sent** /sɛnt/, *v.* past tense and past participle of **send.**

**sentence** /'sɛntəns/, *n., v.,* **-tenced, -tencing.** *–n.* **1.** a linguistic form (a word or a sequence of words arranged in a grammatical construction) which is not part of any larger construction, typically expressing an independent statement, inquiry, command, or the like, as, *Fire!* or *Summer is here* or *Who's there?* **2.** *Law.* **a.** an authoritative decision; a judicial judgment or decree, esp. the judicial determination of the punishment to be inflicted on a convicted criminal. **b.** the punishment itself. **3.** *Obs.* a saying, apophthegm, or maxim. **4.** *Obs.* an opinion pronounced on some particular question. *–v.t.* **5.** to pronounce sentence upon; condemn to punishment. [ME, from F, from L *sententia* opinion] – **sentencer,** *n.*

**sentential** /sɛn'tɛnʃəl/, *adj.* pertaining to or of the nature of a sentence.

**sentential calculus** /– 'kælkjələs/, *n.* any symbolic systematic set of rules for joining or dividing sentences to form other sentences.

**sentential connective** /– kə'nɛktɪv/, *n.* a symbol, such as 'not', 'or', 'implies', used to combine two or more sentences to form a new sentence.

**sententious** /sɛn'tɛnʃəs/, *adj.* **1.** abounding in pithy sayings or maxims: *sententious style.* **2.** affectedly judicial in utterance; moralising; self-righteous. **3.** given to or using pithy sayings or maxims. **4.** of the nature of a maxim; pithy. [late ME, from L *sententiōsus*] – **sententiously,** *adv.* – **sententiousness,** *n.*

**sentience** /ˈsɛntiənsˌ ˈ-ʃəns/, *n.* sentient condition or character; capacity for sensation or feeling. Also, **sentiency.**

**sentient** /ˈsɛntiənt, ˈsɛnʃənt/, *adj.* **1.** that feels; having the power of perception by the senses. **2.** characterised by sensation. *–n.* **3.** one who or that which is sentient. **4.** the mind. [L *sentiens,* ppr., feeling] – **sentiently,** *adv.*

**sentiment** /ˈsɛntəmənt/, *n.* **1.** mental attitude with regard to something; opinion. **2.** a mental feeling; emotion: *a sentiment of pity.* **3.** refined or tender emotion; manifestation of the higher or more refined feelings. **4.** exhibition or manifestation of feeling or sensibility, or appeal to the tender emotions, in literature, art, or music. **5.** a thought influenced by or proceeding from feeling or emotion. **6.** the thought or feeling intended to be conveyed by words as distinguished from the words themselves. [LL *sentīmentum,* from L *sentīre* feel; replacing ME *sentement,* from OF]

**sentimental** /sɛntəˈmɛntl/, *adj.* **1.** expressive of or appealing to sentiment or the tender emotions: *a sentimental song.* **2.** pertaining to or dependent on sentiment: *sentimental reasons.* **3.** weakly emotional; mawkishly susceptible or tender: *a sentimental schoolgirl.* **4.** characterised by or showing sentiment or refined feeling. – **sentimentally,** *adv.*

**sentimentalise** /sɛntəˈmɛntəlaɪz/, *v.,* **-lised, -lising.** *–v.i.* **1.** to indulge in sentiment. *–v.t.* **2.** to render sentimental, as a person, etc. **3.** to be sentimental over; turn into an object of sentiment. Also, **sentimentalize.**

**sentimentalism** /sɛntəˈmɛntəlɪzəm/, *n.* **1.** sentimental tendency or character; predominance of sentiment over reason. **2.** weak emotionalism; excessive indulgence in sentiment. **3.** a display of sentimentality.

**sentimentalist** /sɛntəˈmɛntələst/, *n.* one given to sentiment or sentimentality.

**sentimentality** /sɛntəmɛnˈtæləti/, *n., pl.* **-ties.** sentimental quality, disposition, behaviour, etc.

**sentimental value** /sɛntəˈmɛntl ˈvælju/, *n.* the value which something often of little or no monetary value has because of its ability to arouse sentiments.

**sentinel** /ˈsɛntənəl/, *n., v.,* **-nelled, -nelling** or (*U.S.*) **-neled, -neling.** *–n.* **1.** one who or that which watches, or stands as if watching. **2.** a soldier stationed as a guard to challenge all comers and prevent a surprise attack: *to stand sentinel.* *–v.t.* **3.** to watch over or guard as a sentinel. [F *sentinelle,* from It. *sentinella,* from LL **sentīnāre* avoid danger, from L *sentīre* perceive]

**sentry** /ˈsɛntri/, *n., pl.* **-tries. 1.** a soldier stationed at a place to keep guard and prevent the passage of unauthorised persons, watch for fires, etc.; a sentinel. **2.** a member of a guard or watch. [? short for obs. *centrinel,* var. of SENTINEL]

**sentry-box** /ˈsɛntri-bɒks/, *n.* a small structure for sheltering a sentry from bad weather.

**sentry-go** /ˈsɛntri-goʊ/, *n.* the duty performed by a sentry pacing his beat while on guard duty, etc.

**senza** /ˈsɛnzə/, *adv.* (a musical direction) without. [It.]

**sep** /sɛp/, *n.* →**septic tank.**

**sep.,** separate. Also, **separ.**

**Sep.,** September.

**sepal** /ˈsipəl/, *n.* any of the individual leaves or parts of the calyx of a flower. [NL *sepalum,* b. *sep-* (irregularly from Gk *sképē* covering) and L (*pet*)*alum* petal]

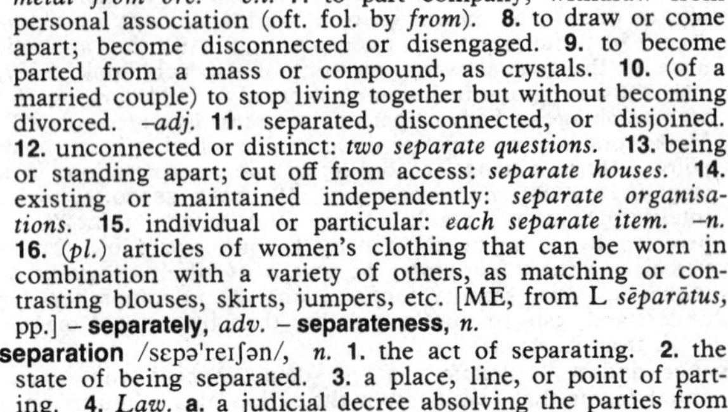

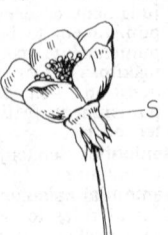

S, sepal

**-sepalous,** a word element meaning 'having sepals', as in *polysepalous.* [SEPAL + -OUS]

**separable** /ˈsɛprəbəl, ˈsɛpərəbəl/, *adj.* capable of being separated. – **separability** /sɛprəˈbɪləti, sɛpərə-/, **separableness,** *n.* – **separably,** *adv.*

**separate** /ˈsɛpəreɪt/, *v.,* **-rated, -rating;** /ˈsɛprət/, *adj., n.* *–v.t.* **1.** to keep apart or divide, as by an intervening barrier, space, etc. **2.** to put apart; part: *to separate persons fighting.* **3.** to disconnect; disunite: *to separate Church and state.* **4.** to remove from personal association, as a married person. **5.** to part or divide (an assemblage, mass, compound, etc.) into individuals, components, or elements. **6.** to take (fol. by *from* or *out*) by such parting or dividing: *separate metal from ore.* *–v.i.* **7.** to part company; withdraw from personal association (oft. fol. by *from*). **8.** to draw or come apart; become disconnected or disengaged. **9.** to become parted from a mass or compound, as crystals. **10.** (of a married couple) to stop living together but without becoming divorced. *–adj.* **11.** separated, disconnected, or disjoined. **12.** unconnected or distinct: *two separate questions.* **13.** being or standing apart; cut off from access: *separate houses.* **14.** existing or maintained independently: *separate organisations.* **15.** individual or particular: *each separate item.* *–n.* **16.** (*pl.*) articles of women's clothing that can be worn in combination with a variety of others, as matching or contrasting blouses, skirts, jumpers, etc. [ME, from L *sēparātus,* pp.] – **separately,** *adv.* – **separateness,** *n.*

**separation** /sɛpəˈreɪʃən/, *n.* **1.** the act of separating. **2.** the state of being separated. **3.** a place, line, or point of parting. **4.** *Law.* **a.** a judicial decree absolving the parties from the duty of cohabitation. **b.** cessation of conjugal cohabitation, as by mutual consent.

**separation allowance** /ˈ– əlaʊəns/, *n.* an allowance made by a soldier to his wife and augmented by the state.

**separatist** /ˈsɛprətəst, ˈsɛpərə-/, *n.* **1.** one who separates, withdraws, or secedes, as from an established Church. **2.** an advocate of separation, esp. ecclesiastical or political separation. **3.** formerly, one who advocated the separation from England of the administrative and judicial functions of the colonies in Australia, and their independence of each other. – **separatism,** *n.*

**separative** /ˈsɛprətɪv, ˈsɛpərətɪv/, *adj.* tending to separate; causing separation.

**separator** /ˈsɛpəreɪtə/, *n.* **1.** one who or that which separates. **2.** an apparatus for separating one thing from another, as cream from milk, steam from water, wheat from chaff, valuable minerals from one another, etc. **3.** *Elect.* a thin, perforated insulator used to separate the plates in a secondary cell. – **separatory,** *adj.*

**Sephardim** /səˈfadɪm/, *n.pl.* Spanish-Portuguese Jews and their descendants. Cf. **Ashkenazim.** [Heb., from *s'phārādh,* country mentioned in Obad. 20] – **Sephardic,** *adj.*

**sepia** /ˈsipiə/, *n.* **1.** a brown pigment obtained from the ink-like secretion of various cuttlefish, and used with brush or pen in drawing. **2.** a drawing made with sepia. **3.** a dark brown. **4.** *Photog.* a brown-coloured image, supposed to duplicate sepia ink. **5.** a cuttlefish of the genus *Sepia* or some allied genus. *–adj.* **6.** of a brown similar to that from sepia ink. [L, from Gk]

**sepiolite** /ˈsipiəlaɪt/, *n.* →**meerschaum.** [G *Sepiolith,* from Gk *sēpio(n)* cuttlebone + *-lith* -LITE]

**sepoy** /ˈsipɔɪ/, *n.* (formerly) an Indian soldier in the military service of Europeans, esp. of the British. [Pg. *sipae,* from Hind. and Pers. *sipāhī* horseman, from *sipāh* army]

**sepsis** /ˈsɛpsəs/, *n.* local or generalised bacterial invasion of the body, esp. by pyogenic organisms: *dental sepsis, wound sepsis.* [NL, from Gk]

**sept** /sɛpt/, *n.* **1.** a clan (originally with reference to tribes or families in Ireland). **2.** *Anthrop.* a group believing itself derived from a common ancestor. [special use of *sept* enclosure, fold (from L *sēptum*), by association with obs. *sect* clan (Irish)]

**sept-,** a prefix meaning 'seven', as in *septet.* Also, **septem-, septe-, septi-**[1]. [L, combining form of *septem*]

**Sept.,** September.

**septa** /ˈsɛptə/, *n.* plural of **septum.**

**septal** /ˈsɛptl/, *adj.* of or pertaining to a septum.

**septarium** /sɛpˈtɛəriəm/, *n., pl.* **-taria** /-ˈtɛəriə/. a concretionary nodule or mass, usu. of calcium carbonate or of argillaceous carbonate of iron, traversed within by a network of cracks filled with calcite and other minerals. [NL, from L *sēptum* enclosure] – **septarian,** *adj.*

**septate** /ˈsɛpteɪt/, *adj.* divided by a septum or septa. [NL *sēptātus.* See SEPTUM, -ATE[1]]

**septavalent** /sɛptəˈveɪlənt/, *adj.* →**heptavalent.**

**September** /sɛpˈtɛmbə/, *n.* the ninth month of the year, containing 30 days. [OE, from L, the seventh month in the early Roman calendar]

**septempartite** /sɛptɛm'pataɪt/, *adj.* separated into seven sections.

**septenary** /sɛp'tinəri/, *adj., n., pl.* **-naries.** *–adj.* **1.** of or pertaining to the number seven; forming a group of seven. **2.** →**septennial.** *–n.* **3.** a group or set of seven. **4.** a period of seven years. **5.** the number seven. **6.** *Pros.* a line with seven feet. [L *septēnārius*]

**septennial** /sɛp'tɛniəl/, *adj.* **1.** occurring every seven years. **2.** of or for seven years. [L *septennium* seven years + -AL[1]] – **septennially,** *adv.*

**septet** /sɛp'tɛt/, *n.* **1.** any group of seven persons or things. **2.** a company of seven singers or players. **3.** a musical composition for seven voices or instruments. Also, **septette.** [G. See SEPT-, -ET]

**septi-**[1], variant of **sept-,** before most consonants.

**septi-**[2], a word element representing **septum,** as in *septicidal.*

**septic**[1] /'sɛptɪk/, *adj.* **1.** infective, usu. with a pus-forming microbe. **2.** pertaining to or of the nature of sepsis; infected. *–n.* **3.** an agent which causes sepsis. **4.** →**septic tank.** [L *sēpticus,* from Gk *sēptikós*] – **septicity** /sɛp'tɪsəti/, *n.*

**septic**[2] /'sɛptɪk/, *n. Colloq.* a Yank. [rhyming slang, *septic tank* Yank]

**septicaemia** /sɛptə'simiə/, *n.* the invasion and persistence of pathogenic bacteria in the bloodstream. Also, **septicemia.** [NL, from Gk. See SEPTIC[1] -AEMIA] – **septicaemic,** *adj.*

**septicidal** /sɛptə'saɪdl/, *adj.* (of a seed capsule) characterised by splitting through the septa or dissepiments, as a mode of dehiscence. [SEPTI-[2] + L *-cīdere* cut + -AL[1]]

septicidal dehiscence: A, valves; B, dissepiments; C, axis

**septic system** /'sɛptɪk ˌsɪstəm/, *n.* a sewerage system using a septic tank.

**septic tank** /– 'tæŋk/, *n.* a tank in which solid organic sewage is decomposed and purified by anaerobic bacteria.

**septic throat** /– 'θroʊt/, *n.* an acute, toxic, streptococcus infection of the throat producing fever, tonsillitis, and other serious effects.

**septifragal** /sɛp'tɪfrəgəl/, *adj.* (of a fruit) characterised by the breaking away of the valves from the septa or dissepiments, in dehiscence. [SEPTI-[2] + L *frag-* break + -AL[1]]

**septillion** /sɛp'tɪljən/, *n.* **1.** (usu. with *one* or *a*) a cardinal number represented by one followed by 42 zeros, and (in the U.S. and France) by one followed by 24 zeros. *–adj.* **2.** (usu. with *one* or *a*) amounting to one septillion in number. [F, from L *sept(em)* + *(m)illion* MILLION] – **septillionth,** *n., adj.*

**septime** /'sɛptim/, *n.* (in fencing) the seventh of eight defensive positions. [L *septimus*]

**septivalent** /sɛptə'veɪlənt/, *adj.* →**heptavalent.** Also, **septavalent.**

**septuagenarian** /ˌsɛptʃuədʒə'nɛəriən/, *adj.* **1.** of the age of 70 years, or between 70 and 80 years old. *–n.* **2.** a septuagenarian person.

**septuagenary** /ˌsɛptʃuə'dʒinəri/, *adj., n., pl.* **-naries.** →**septuagenarian.** [L *septuāgēnārius*]

**Septuagesima** /ˌsɛptʃuə'dʒɛsəmə/, *n.* the third Sunday before Lent (more fully, **Septuagesima Sunday**). [L *septuāgēsima (dies)* seventieth day]

**Septuagint** /'sɛptʃuəˌdʒɪnt/, *n.* the Greek version of the Old Testament traditionally said to have been made at the request of Ptolemy II, king of Egypt (309-247? B.C.), by 72 Jewish scholars, in 72 days. [L *septuāginta* seventy]

S, septum: transverse section of the ovary of flax

**septum** /'sɛptəm/, *n., pl.* **septa** /'sɛptə/. **1.** *Biol.* a dividing wall, membrane, or the like in a plant or animal structure; a dissepiment. **2.** an osmotic membrane. [L: enclosure]

**septuple** /sɛp'tjupəl/, *adj., v.,* **-pled, -pling.** *–adj.* **1.** sevenfold; seven times as great. *–v.t., v.i.* **2.** to make or become seven times as great. [LL *septuplus*]

**septuplet** /sɛp'tʌplət, -'tju-/, *n.* **1.** any group or combination of seven related items. **2.** one of seven offspring born at one birth. **3.** *Music.* a group of seven notes to be played in the time of four or six.

**sepulchral** /sə'pʌlkrəl/, *adj.* **1.** of, pertaining to, or serving as a tomb. **2.** of or pertaining to burial. **3.** proper to or suggestive of a tomb; funereal or dismal. **4.** hollow and deep: *sepulchral tone.* – **sepulchrally,** *adv.*

**sepulchre** /'sɛpəlkə/, *n., v.,* **-chred, -chring.** *–n.* **1.** a tomb, grave, or burial place. **2.** *Eccles.* a structure or a recess in some churches of the Middle Ages in which the sacred elements, the cross, etc., were deposited with due ceremonies on Good Friday to be taken out at Easter, in commemoration of Christ's entombment and resurrection (often called **Easter sepulchre**). *–v.t.* **3.** to place in a sepulchre; bury. Also, *U.S.,* **sepulcher.** [ME *sepulcre,* from OF, from L *sepulcrum*]

**sepulture** /'sɛpəltʃə/, *n.* **1.** the act of placing in a sepulchre or tomb; burial. **2.** *Archaic.* sepulchre; tomb. [ME *sepulture,* from OF, from L *sepultūra*]

**sequacious** /sə'kweɪʃəs/, *adj.* **1.** *Archaic.* following another person, esp. unreasoningly. **2.** following with smooth regularity, as musical notes, thoughts, etc. [SEQUACI(TY) (from L *sequācitas* facility in following) + -OUS] – **sequaciously,** *adv.* – **sequacity** /sə'kwæsəti/, *n.*

**sequel** /'sikwəl/, *n.* **1.** a literary work, film, etc., complete in itself, but continuing a preceding work. **2.** an event or circumstance following something; subsequent course of affairs. **3.** a result, consequence, or inference. [ME *sequele,* from L *sequēla*]

**sequela** /sə'kwilə/, *n., pl.* **-lae** /-li/. a morbid condition resulting from a previous disease. [L]

**sequence** /'sikwəns/, *n.* **1.** the following of one thing after another; succession. **2.** order of succession: *a list of books in alphabetical sequence.* **3.** a continuous or connected series: *a sonnet sequence.* **4.** something that follows; a subsequent event; result; consequence. **5.** *Music.* a melodic or harmonic pattern repeated at different pitches, with or without modulation. **6.** a medieval chant or hymn with a non-biblical text, sometimes sung after the gradual and before the gospel. **7.** *Rom. Cath. Ch.* a hymn sometimes sung after the gradual and before the gospel; a prose. **8.** *Films.* a portion of a film story set in the same place and time, and without interruptions or breaks of any kind. **9.** *Cards.* a set of three or more cards following one another in order of value. **10.** *Maths.* a finite or countable set of numbers, arranged in order. [ME, from LL *sequentia,* from L *sequens,* ppr., following]

**sequencer** /'sikwənsə/, *n. Aerospace, Electronics.* an electronic device which arranges for a number of actions to take place in a predetermined order.

**sequent** /'sikwənt/, *adj.* **1.** following; successive. **2.** following logically or naturally; consequent. **3.** characterised by continuous succession; consecutive. *–n.* **4.** that which follows in order or as a result. [L *sequens,* ppr., following]

**sequential** /sə'kwɛnʃəl, si-/, *adj.* **1.** characterised by regular sequence of parts. **2.** following; subsequent; consequent. – **sequentially,** *adv.*

**sequential pill** /– 'pɪl/, *n.* a form of oral contraceptive medication where an oestrogen is consumed for 15 days commencing on the 5th day after the start of menstruation and followed by combined oestrogen and progestogen for a further 5 days.

**sequester** /sə'kwɛstə, si-/, *v.t.* **1.** to remove or withdraw into solitude or retirement; seclude. **2.** to remove or separate. **3.** *Law.* to remove (property) temporarily from the possession of the owner; seize and hold, as the property and income of a debtor, until legal claims are satisfied. **4.** *Internat. Law.* to requisition, hold, and control (enemy property). [ME *sequestre,* from LL *sequestrāre* separate, from L *sequester* depositary, trustee]

**sequestered** /sə'kwɛstəd, si-/, *adj.* secluded or out-of-the-way: *a sequestered village.*

**sequestrate** /sə'kwɛstreɪt, si-/, *v.t.,* **-trated, -trating. 1.** *Law.* **a.** to sequester (property). **b.** to confiscate. **c.** to make bankrupt. **2.** *Archaic.* to separate; seclude. – **sequestrator** /'sɛkwəstreɪtə, 'si-/, *n.*

**sequestrating agent** /ˌsɛkwəstreɪtɪŋ 'eɪdʒənt/, *n.* any chemical, as a chelating agent, which induces sequestration. Also, **sequestering agent.**

**sequestration** /sɛkwəs'treɪʃən/, *n.* **1.** removal or separation; banishment or exile. **2.** withdrawal, retirement or seclusion. **3.** *Law.* **a.** the sequestering of property. **b.** confiscation or seizure. **4.** *Chem.* the formation of a coordination complex by adding material so that the metallic ions in solution are prevented from exhibiting their usual properties, as in the addition of certain softeners to hard water which prevents the formation of calcium soap precipitates.

**sequestrectomy** /sikwəs'trɛktəmi/, *n., pl.* **-mies.** the removal of dead spicules or portions, esp. of bone.

**sequestrum** /sə'kwɛstrəm/, *n., pl.* **-tra** /-trə/. a dead portion of bone separated from the living bone. [NL, special use of L *sequestrum* something detached, properly neut. of *sequester* mediating]

**sequin** /'sikwən/, *n.* **1.** a small shining disc or spangle used to ornament a dress, etc. [F, from It. *zecchino,* a Venetian coin, from *zecca* mint, from Ar. *sikka* a die for coins] – **sequined,** *adj.*

**sequoia** /sə'kwɔɪə/, *n.* either of two related, extremely large coniferous trees of the south-western U.S., the big tree, genus *Sequoiadendron,* and the redwood, genus *Sequoia,* both formerly included in the genus *Sequoia.* [NL, named after *Sikwâyi,* d. 1843, a Cherokee Indian, inventor of a syllabary for writing Cherokee]

**sequoiadendron** /səkwɔɪə'dɛndrən/, *n.* the sequoia, *Sequoiadendron giganteum.*

**ser.,** series.

**serac** /'sɛræk/, *n.* a large block or pinnacle-like mass of ice on a glacier, formed by melting or movement of the ice. [Swiss F, orig. the name of a white cheese]

**seraglio** /sə'raliou/, *n., pl.* **-raglios.** **1.** the part of a Muslim house or palace in which the wives and concubines are secluded; a harem. **2.** a Turkish palace, esp. of the Sultan. [It. *serraglio* (rendering Turk. *seraī* SERAI), from L *serāre* lock up]

**serai** /sɛ'raɪ/, *n., pl.* **-rais.** →**caravanserai.** [Turk., from Pers.: lodging, palace]

**serape** /sə'rapi/, *n.* a kind of shawl or blanket, often of gay colours, worn by Spanish-Americans. [Mex. Sp.]

**seraph** /'sɛrəf/, *n., pl.* **-aphs, -aphim** /-əfɪm/. **1.** one of the celestial beings hovering above God's throne in Isaiah's vision. Isa. 6. **2.** a member of the highest order of angels, often represented as a child's head with wings above, below, and on each side. [backformation from *seraphim* (pl.), ME *serafin,* from LL *seraphīm,* from Heb.]

**seraphic** /sə'ræfɪk/, *adj.* of, like, or befitting a seraph. Also, **seraphical.** – **seraphically,** *adv.*

**seraphim** /'sɛrəfɪm/, *n.* a plural of **seraph.**

**Serapis** /'sɛrəpɪs/, *n.* a deity of Egyptian origin who was worshipped as the dead Apis under the attributes of Osiris. His cult was started under the Ptolemies and introduced into Greece and Rome.

**Serbian** /'sɜbiən/, *adj.* **1.** of Serbia, its inhabitants, or their language. *–n.* **2.** a native or inhabitant of Serbia, esp. one of the Slavic race inhabiting it. **3.** Serbo-Croat, esp. as spoken in Serbia.

**Serbo-Croat** /sɜbou-'krouæt/, *n.* the principal Slavic language of Yugoslavia, usu. written with Cyrillic letters in Serbia but with Roman letters in Croatia. Also, **Serbo-Croatian** /ˌsɜbou-krou'eɪʃən/.

**Sercial** /'sɜʃəl/, *n.* **1.** a grape variety used in the making of white wines. **2.** (*l.c.*) a type of madeira.

**sere**[1] /sɪə/, *adj.* dry; withered. [var. of SEAR[1]]

**sere**[2] /sɪə/, *n.* the series of stages in an ecological succession. [backformation from SERIES]

**serein** /sə'reɪn/, *n.* a very fine rain falling from a clear sky after sunset. [F: evening damp, OF *serain* nightfall, from L *sērum* evening, *sērus* late]

**serenade** /sɛrə'neɪd/, *n., v.,* **-naded, -nading.** *–n.* **1.** a complimentary performance of vocal or instrumental music in the open air at night, as by a lover under the window of his lady. **2.** a piece of music suitable for such performance. *–v.t.* **3.** to entertain with a serenade. *–v.i.* **4.** to perform a serenade. [F, from It. *serenata.* See SERENATA] – **serenader,** *n.*

**serenata** /sɛrə'natə/, *n., pl.* **-tas, -te** /-ti/. *Music.* **1.** a form of pastoral cantata, often of a dramatic or imaginative character. **2.** an instrumental composition in several movements, intermediate between the suite and the symphony. [It.: an evening song, from *sereno* the open air, n. use of adj. *sereno* serene (from L *serēnus*), influenced by L *sērum* evening]

**serendipity** /sɛrən'dɪpəti/, *n.* the faculty of making desirable but unsought-for discoveries. [*Serendip* (former name of Sri Lanka (Ceylon) + -ITY; coined by Horace Walpole, 1717-97, English author, from the Persian fairytale *The Three Princes of Serendip,* in which the heroes have this faculty]

**serene** /sə'rin/, *adj.* **1.** calm; peaceful; tranquil: *serene sea, a serene old age.* **2.** clear; fair: *serene weather.* **3.** (*oft. cap.*) an epithet used in titles of princes, etc.: *his Serene Highness.* **4.** **all serene,** *Colloq.* all right. *–n.* **5.** *Archaic.* a clear or tranquil expanse of sky, sea, etc. [L *serēnus*] – **serenely,** *adv.* – **sereneness,** *n.*

**serenity** /sə'rɛnəti/, *n., pl.* **-ties.** **1.** the state or quality of being serene; calmness; tranquillity. **2.** clearness, as of the sky, air, etc. **3.** (*usu. cap.,* with **his, your,** etc.) a title of honour given to certain reigning princes, etc.

**serf** /sɜf/, *n.* **1.** a person in a condition of servitude, required to render services to his lord, and commonly attached to the lord's land and transferred with it from one owner to another. **2.** *Obs.* a slave. [late ME, from F, from L *servus* slave] – **serfdom** /'sɜfdəm/, **serfhood,** *n.*

**serge** /sɜdʒ/, *n.* **1.** a twilled worsted or woollen fabric used esp. for clothing. **2.** cotton, rayon, or silk in a twill weave. [F; replacing ME *sarge,* from OF, from var. of L *sērica* silken]

**sergeant** /'sadʒənt/, *n.* **1.** a non-commissioned army officer of rank above that of corporal. **2.** a police officer ranking between constable and inspector. [ME *sergeaunte,* from OF *sergent,* from L *serviens,* ppr., serving] – **sergeancy** /'sadʒənsi/, **sergeantship,** *n.*

**sergeant baker** /– 'beɪkə/, *n.* a deep-reddish to purple fish of the genus *Latropiscis,* found in reef areas of Australasian temperate waters. [named after *Sergeant* William *Baker,* an early colonist of Norfolk Island]

**sergeant fish** /'– fɪʃ/, *n.* →**cobia.**

**sergeant major** /– 'meɪdʒə/, *n.* a non-commissioned officer of the highest rank; a warrant officer.

**Sergt,** Sergeant.

**serial** /'sɪəriəl/, *n.* **1.** anything published, broadcast, etc., in instalments at regular intervals, as a novel appearing in successive issues of a magazine. *–adj.* **2.** published in instalments or successive parts: *a serial story.* **3.** pertaining to such publication. **4.** of, pertaining to, or arranged in a series. **5.** *Telecom., Computers.* of or pertaining to a system in which information is transmitted along a path digit by digit. [NL *seriālis,* from L *series* series] – **serially,** *adv.*

**serialise** /'sɪəriəlaɪz/, *v.t.,* **-lised, -lising.** to publish, broadcast, televise, etc., in serial form. Also, **serialize.** – **serialisation** /ˌsɪəriəlaɪ'zeɪʃən/, *n.*

**serial music** /'sɪəriəl mjuzɪk/, *n.* music composed by using serial technique.

**serial number** /'– nʌmbə/, *n.* an individual number given to a particular person, article, etc., for identification.

**serial technique** /'– tɛkˌnik/, *n.* a method of composition in which not only the notes may be ordered in a strictly defined manner, as in twelve-tone music, but also their durations, timbres, etc.

**seriate** /'sɪəriət/, *adj.* arranged or occurring in one or more series. – **seriately,** *adv.*

**seriatim** /sɛri'atəm, sɪə-, -'eɪtəm/, *adv.* in a series; one after another. [ML, from L *series* series; modelled on *literatim, verbatim,* etc.]

**sericeous** /sə'rɪʃəs/, *adj.* **1.** silky. **2.** covered with silky down, as a leaf. [L *sēriceus*]

**sericin** /'sɛrəsən/, *n.* a gelatinous organic compound obtained from silk.

**sericite** /'sɛrəsaɪt/, *n.* a mineral, similar in composition to muscovite, occurring in small scales, often as a decomposition product of orthoclase. [G *Sericit,* from *seric-* (representing L *sēricum* silk) + *-it* -ITE[1]]

**sericulture** /'sɛrəkʌltʃə/, *n.* the rearing and keeping of silkworms, for the production of raw silk. Also, **sericiculture.** [F *sériciculture,* from *sérici-* (representing L *sēricum* silk) + *culture* CULTURE] – **sericultural** /sɛrə'kʌltʃərəl/, *adj.* – **sericulturist** /sɛrə'kʌltʃərəst/, *n.*

**seriema** /sɛri'imə/, *n.* **1.** a large bird, *Cariama cristata,* with long legs and a crested head, native to southern Brazil and surrounding regions. **2.** a smaller allied bird, *Chunga burmeisteri,* native to Argentina. [NL, from Tupi *siriema* crested]

**series** /'sɪəriz/, *n., pl.* **-ries,** *adj.* –*n.* **1.** a number of things, events, etc., ranged or occurring in spatial, temporal, or other succession; a sequence. **2.** a set, as of coins, stamps, etc. **3.** a set of volumes, as of a periodical, or as issued in like form with similarity of subject or purpose. **4.** *Maths.* the formal summation of the elements of a sequence. **5.** *Rhet.* a succession of coordinate sentence elements. **6.** *Music.* an arrangement of twelve notes in a particular order taken as the basis of a composition. **7.** *Geol.* a division of a system of rocks, marked by sedimentary deposits formed during a geological epoch. **8.** *Elect.* an arrangement of conductors or cells such that the same current flows through each. The components are said to be **in series** (opposed to *in parallel*). –*adj.* **9.** *Elect.* consisting of, or having, components in series. [L]

**series-wound** /'sɪəriz-waʊnd/, *adj.* of or pertaining to an electrical commutator in which the main magnetic field is provided by a winding connected in series with the armature.

**serif** /'sɛrəf/, *n.* a smaller line used to finish off a main stroke of a letter, as at the top and bottom of M. Also, **seriph.** [probably from D *schreef* stroke, line, from *schrijwen* write]

**serigraphy** /sə'rɪgrəfi/, *n.* the creation of original prints by the silk-screen method, the artist designing, making and printing his own stencils, and using paint as the printing medium. [*seri-* (representing L *sēricum* silk) + -GRAPHY]

**serin** /'sɛrən/, *n.* a small finch, *Serinus serinus,* of Europe, north-western Africa, etc., from which the common canary has been developed. [F; orig. uncert.]

**serine** /'sɪərin/, *n.* an amino acid, $CH_2OH \cdot CH(NH_3^+)COO^-$, occurring in all proteins. [SER(UM) + -INE[2]]

**seringa** /sə'rɪŋgə/, *n.* **1.** any of several South American trees of the genus *Hevea,* yielding rubber. **2.** a graceful deciduous tree, *Kirkia acuminata,* of southern Africa. [Pg.]

**seriocomic** /ˌsɪərioʊ'kɒmɪk/, *adj.* partly serious and partly comic. Also, **seriocomical.**

**serious** /'sɪəriəs/, *adj.* **1.** of grave or solemn disposition or character; thoughtful. **2.** of grave aspect. **3.** being in earnest; not trifling. **4.** demanding earnest thought or application: *serious reading, serious music.* **5.** weighty or important: *a serious matter.* **6.** giving cause for apprehension; critical: *a serious illness.* [ME, from LL *sēriōsus,* from L *sērius*] – **seriously,** *adv.* – **seriousness,** *n.*

**serjeant-at-arms** /sadʒənt-ət-'amz/, *n.* an executive officer of a legislative or other body, whose duty it is to enforce the commands of the body, preserve order, and arrest individuals of distinction, as the officer who attends on the lower house in parliament.

**sermon** /'sɜmən/, *n.* **1.** a discourse for the purpose of religious instruction or exhortation, esp. one based on a text of Scripture and delivered from a pulpit. **2.** any similar serious discourse or exhortation. **3.** a long, tedious speech. [ME, from OF, from L *sermo* discourse]

**sermonic** /sɜ'mɒnɪk/, *adj.* pertaining to, of the nature of, or resembling a sermon. Also, **sermonical.**

**sermonise** /'sɜmənaɪz/, *v.,* **-nised, -nising.** –*v.i.* **1.** to deliver or compose a sermon; preach. –*v.t.* **2.** to give serious exhortation to; lecture. Also, **sermonize.** – **sermoniser,** *n.*

**sero-,** a word element representing **serum,** as in *serology.*

**serology** /sɪə'rɒlədʒi/, *n.* the scientific study of the properties and action of the serum of the blood.

**seromucous** /sɪəroʊ'mjukəs/, *adj. Med.* both serous and mucous.

**serosa** /sə'roʊsə/, *n.* a serous membrane.

**serotine**[1] /'sɛrətaɪn/, *adj. Rare.* late. Also, **serotinous** /sə'rɒtənəs/. [F, from L *sērōtinus* late]

**serotine**[2] /'sɛrətaɪn/, *n.* a small European bat, *Vespertilio (Vesperugo) serotinus.* [F, from L *sērōtina* (fem.) late, i.e. flying late in the evening]

**serotonin** /sɛrə'toʊnən/, *n.* a hormone which induces muscular contraction, found in the brain, intestines, and platelets. [SERO- + TON(E) + -IN[2]]

**serous** /'sɪərəs/, *adj.* **1.** of a watery nature, or resembling serum. **2.** containing or secreting serum. **3.** pertaining to or characterised by serum. [L *sērōsus*] – **serosity** /sə'rɒsəti/, *n.*

**serous fluid** /– 'fluəd/, *n.* any of various animal liquids resembling blood serum, as the fluids of the serous membranes.

**serous membrane** /– 'mɛmbreɪn/, *n.* any of various thin membranes, as the peritoneum, which line certain cavities of the body and exude a serous fluid.

**serow** /'sɛroʊ/, *n.* a goat antelope, genus *Capricornis,* of eastern Asia, related to the goral. [Lepcha *saro*]

**serpent** /'sɜpənt/, *n.* **1.** a snake. **2.** a wily, treacherous, or malicious person. **3.** Satan. **4.** a kind of firework which burns with serpentine motion or flame. **5.** an old wooden musical wind instrument of serpentine form and deep tone. [ME, from L *serpens* creeping thing, properly ppr. of *serpere* creep, c. Gk *hérpein*]

serpent (def. 5)

**serpentine**[1] /'sɜpəntaɪn/, *adj.* **1.** of or pertaining to a serpent. **2.** moving in a winding course or having a winding form; tortuous; winding. **3.** having the qualities of a serpent; subtle, artful, or cunning. [ME, from L *serpentīnus*]

**serpentine**[2] /'sɜpəntaɪn/, *n.* a common mineral, hydrous magnesium silicate, $H_4Mg_3Si_2O_9$, usu. oily green and sometimes spotted, occurring in many varieties, and used for architectural and decorative purposes. [ME, from ML *serpentīnum,* properly neut. of L *serpentīnus*]

**serpentinite** /sə'pɛntənaɪt/, *n.* a rock composed almost entirely of serpentine minerals.

**serpigo** /sɜ'paɪgoʊ/, *n.* a creeping or spreading skin disease, as ringworm. [ME, from ML, from L *serpere* creep] – **serpiginous** /sɜ'pɪdʒənəs/, *adj.*

**serradella** /sɛrə'dɛlə/, *n.* any of several herbs of the genus *Ornithopus,* family Papilionaceae, grown as pasture legumes in temperate areas.

**serranoid** /'sɛrənɔɪd/, *adj.* **1.** belonging to the Serranidae, a numerous family of fishes including the sea-basses, groupers, jewfishes, etc. –*n.* **2.** a serranoid fish. [NL *Serrānus,* genus of fishes (from L *serra* saw, sawfish) + -OID]

**serrate** /'sɛreɪt, -rət/, *adj.;* /sə'reɪt/, *v.,* **-rated, -rating.** –*adj.* **1.** having notches or teeth along the edge like a saw: *a serrate leaf, a serrate blade.* **2.** having a grooved edge, as certain coins. **3.** having notches or teeth along the edge. –*v.t.* **4.** to make serrate or serrated. [L *serrātus* saw-shaped]

**serrated** /sə'reɪtəd/, *adj.* serrate; having a notched or grooved edge.

**serrated tussock** /– 'tʌsək/, *n.* a tussock-forming grass, *Nassella trichotoma,* native to South America but a troublesome weed in New Zealand and the tablelands of eastern Australia. Also, **nassella tussock, Yass river tussock.**

serrate leaf

**serration** /sə'reɪʃən/, *n.* **1.** serrated condition or form. **2.** a serrated edge or formation. **3.** one of the notches or teeth of such an edge or formation. Also, **serrature** /'sɛrətʃə/.

**serriform** /'sɛrəfɔm/, *adj.* resembling the notched edge of a saw; serrate. [*serri-* (from NL, combining form representing L *serra* saw) + -FORM]

**serrulate** /'sɛrəleɪt, -lət/, *adj.* finely or minutely serrate, as a leaf. Also, **serrulated.** [NL *serrulātus,* from L *serrula,* diminutive of *serra* saw]

**serrulation** /sɛrə'leɪʃən/, *n.* **1.** serrulate condition or form. **2.** a fine or minute serration.

**serry** /'sɛri/, *v.i., v.t.,* **-ried, -rying.** to crowd closely together. [apparently from F *serré,* pp. of *serrer* press close, from L *serāre* bar, bolt, from *sera* bar] – **serried,** *adj.*

**sertularian** /sɜtʃə'lɛəriən/, *n.* a type of hydroid that forms stiff feathery colonies in which the cups holding the zooids are sessile. [NL *Sertulāria,* genus name (from L *sertula,*

i = peat ɪ = pit ɛ = pet æ = pat a = part ɒ = pot ʌ = putt ɔ = port ʊ = put u = pool ɜ = pert ə = apart aɪ = buy eɪ = bay ɔɪ = boy aʊ = how
oʊ = hoe ɪə = here ɛə = hair ʊə = tour g = give θ = thin ð = then ʃ = show ʒ = measure tʃ = choke dʒ = joke ŋ = sing j = you õ = Fr. bon

diminutive of *serta* garland) + -AN]

**serum** /ˈsɪərəm/, *n., pl.* **sera** /ˈsɪərə/, **serums.** **1.** the clear, pale yellow liquid which separates from the clot in the coagulation of blood; blood serum. **2.** a fluid of this kind obtained from the blood of an animal which has been rendered immune to some disease by inoculation, used as an antitoxic or therapeutic agent. **3.** any watery animal fluid. **4.** (of milk) **a.** that portion left after butterfat, casein, and albumin have been removed. **b.** that portion left after the manufacture of cheese. [L: whey]

**serum hepatitis** /ˈ- hɛpəˌtaɪtəs/, *n.* a form of hepatitis transmitted by means of an infected hypodermic needle or by the transfusion of infected blood.

**serval** /ˈsɜvəl/, *n.* a long-limbed African cat, *Felis serval,* having a tawny coat spotted with black. [NL, from Pg. (*lobo*) *cerval* lynx, from L (*lupus*) *cervus* (wolf) deer]

serval

**servant** /ˈsɜvənt/, *n.* **1.** a person employed in domestic duties. **2.** a person in the service of another. **3.** a person employed by the government: *a public servant.* [ME, from OF, properly ppr. of *servir* SERVE]

**serve** /sɜv/, *v.,* **served, serving,** *n.* *–v.i.* **1.** to act as a servant. **2.** to wait at table; hand food to guests. **3.** to render assistance; help. **4.** to go through a term of service; do duty as a soldier, sailor, councillor, juror, etc. **5.** to have definite use; be of use. **6.** to answer the purpose: *that will serve to explain my actions.* **7.** to be favourable, suitable, or convenient, as weather, time, etc. **8.** *Tennis, etc.* to put the ball in play. **9.** *Eccles.* to act as server. *–v.t.* **10.** to be in the service of; work for. **11.** to render service to; help. **12.** to go through (a term of service, imprisonment, etc.). **13.** to render active service to (a king, commander, etc.). **14.** to render obedience or homage to (God, a sovereign, etc.). **15.** to perform the duties of (an office, etc.): *to serve his mayoralty.* **16.** to be useful or of service to. **17.** to answer the requirements of; suffice. **18.** to contribute to; promote. **19.** to wait upon; set food before. **20.** to set (food) on a table. **21.** to act as a host or hostess in presenting (someone) with food or drink: *may I serve you with some savouries?* **22.** to act as a host or hostess in offering (food or drink) to someone: *she served cocktails to her guests.* **23.** to provide with a regular or continuous supply of something. **24.** to treat in a specified manner: *his car served him well.* **25.** to gratify (desire, etc.). **26.** (of a male animal) to mate with. **27.** *Tennis, etc.* to put (the ball) in play. **28.** *Law.* **a.** to make legal delivery of (a process or writ). **b.** to present (a person) with a writ. **29.** to operate or work (a gun, etc.). **30.** *Naut., etc.* to bind or wind (a rope, etc.) with small cord or the like, as to strengthen or protect it. **31. serve out,** to distribute. *–n.* **32.** the act, manner, or right of serving, as in tennis. **33.** *Colloq.* a strong rebuke; a tongue lashing: *she gave him a real serve when he came home drunk.* [ME *serven,* from OF *servir,* from L *servīre*]

**server** /ˈsɜvə/, *n.* **1.** one who serves. **2.** that which serves or is used in serving, as a salver, serving spoon or fork. **3.** *Eccles.* an attendant on the priest at mass, who arranges the altar, makes the responses, etc. **4.** *Tennis, etc.* the player who puts the ball in play.

**servery** /ˈsɜvəri/, *n.* a room or an area near the kitchen in which food is set out on plates.

**service** /ˈsɜvəs/, *n., adj., v.,* **-viced, -vicing.** *–n.* **1.** an act of helpful activity. **2.** the supplying or supplier of any articles, commodities, activities, etc., required or demanded. **3.** the providing or a provider of some accommodation required by the public, as messengers, telegraphs, telephones, or conveyance. **4.** the organised system of apparatus, appliances, employees, etc., for supplying some accommodation required by the public. **5.** the supplying or a supplier of water, gas, or the like to the public. **6.** the performance of duties as a servant; occupation or employment as a servant. **7.** employment in any duties or work for another, a government, etc. **8.** a department of public employment, or the body of public servants in it: *the diplomatic service.* **9.** the duty or work of public servants. **10.** the serving of a sovereign, state, or government in some official capacity. **11.** *Mil.* **a.** (*pl.*) the armed forces: *in the services.* **b.** period or duration of active service. **c.** a branch of the armed forces, as the army or navy. **12.** (*oft. pl.*) the performance of any duties or work for another; helpful activity: *medical services.* **13.** the act of servicing a piece of machinery, esp. a motor vehicle. **14.** public religious worship according to prescribed form and order: *divine service.* **15.** a ritual or form prescribed for public worship or for some particular occasion: *the marriage service.* **16.** the serving of God by obedience, piety, etc. **17.** a musical setting of the sung portions of a liturgy. **18.** a set of dishes, utensils, etc., for a particular use: *a dinner service.* **19.** *Law.* the serving of a process or writ upon a person. **20.** *Naut., etc.* a small cord or the like wound about a rope, etc., as for strengthening or protection. **21.** *Tennis, etc.* **a.** the act or manner of putting the ball in play. **b.** the ball as put in play. **22.** the insemination of a female animal by the male. **23. at someone's service,** ready to help; at one's disposal: *my chauffeur will be at your service during your stay here.* **24. be of service,** to be helpful or useful: *if I can be of service to you please call me.* *–adj.* **25.** of service; useful. **26.** of, pertaining to, or used by, servants, tradesmen, etc.: *service stairs.* **27.** of or pertaining to the armed forces. *–v.t.* **28.** to make fit for service; restore to condition for service: *to service a car.* **29.** (of a male animal) to inseminate (a female animal). **30.** to meet interest and other payments on, as a government debt: *to service a debt.* **31.** to seek to vary an industrial award or conditions in it: *to service an award.* [ME; OE *serfise,* from OF *servise,* from L *servitium*]

**serviceable** /ˈsɜvəsəbəl/, *adj.* **1.** being of service; useful. **2.** capable of doing good service. **3.** wearing well; durable: *serviceable cloth.* **4.** *Archaic.* diligent or attentive in serving. – **serviceability** /sɜvəsəˈbɪləti/, **serviceableness,** *n.* – **serviceably,** *adv.*

**serviceberry** /ˈsɜvəsbɛri/, *n., pl.* **-ries.** **1.** a North American shrub or small tree, *Amelanchier canadensis,* with a berry-like fruit. **2.** any of various other plants of the genus *Amelanchier.*

**service book** /ˈsɜvəs bʊk/, *n.* a book containing the order of a religious service.

**service break** /ˈ- breɪk/, *n.* (in tennis) a game won by the receiver.

**service car** /ˈ- ka/, *n.* **1.** Also, **service bus.** a car, sometimes large and having several rows of seats, which provides passenger transport, usu. in country areas, and may carry mail and small quantities of supplies. **2.** *N.Z.* →**coach** (def. 3).

**service charge** /ˈ- tʃadʒ/, *n.* a proportion of a bill, as at a restaurant, hotel, etc., added on to the total to pay for service.

**service court** /ˈ- kɔt/, *n.* (in tennis) etc., that area of a court into which a served ball must fall.

**serviced flat** /sɜvəst ˈflæt/, *n.* a flat in which certain services, as cleaning, meals, etc., are provided.

**service dress** /ˈsɜvəs drɛs/, *n.* the ordinary dress for members of the armed forces, as opposed to full dress, battledress, etc.

**service hatch** /ˈ- hætʃ/, *n.* an opening in a wall through which food can be passed from the kitchen to the dining room. Also, **serving hatch.**

**service industry** /ˈ- ɪndəstri/, *n.* an industry providing services such as transport or entertainment (opposed to *manufacturing industry*).

**service lift** /ˈ- lɪft/, *n.* a goods lift.

**service line** /ˈ- laɪn/, *n.* a line drawn between the sidelines of a tennis court, parallel to and 6.4 metres from the net, which marks the rear of a service court.

**service man** /ˈ- mæn/, *n.* a man who comes to the house, office, etc., to repair appliances, as television sets, telephones, etc., or attend to faulty service installation, as electric power supply, etc.

**serviceman** /ˈsɜvəsmən/, *n., pl.* **-men.** a member of the armed forces. – **servicewoman,** *n. fem.*

**service pipe** /ˈsɜvəs paɪp/, *n.* a pipe connecting a building with a gas or water main.

**service road** /ˈ- roʊd/, *n.* a minor road running parallel to a main road and serving local traffic.

**service station** /ˈ- steɪʃən/, *n.* commercial premises selling petrol, oil, etc., for motor vehicles, and sometimes offering mechanical repairs. Also, **gas station, petrol station.**

**service tree** /'– tri/, *n.* either of two European trees, *Sorbus domestica,* bearing a small, acid fruit that is edible when overripe, or *S. torminalis* **(wild service tree),** with similar fruit.

**servient tenement** /sɜviənt 'tɛnəmənt/, *n.* See **dominant tenement.**

**serviette** /sɜvi'ɛt/, *n.* a rectangular piece of linen, cotton, cloth or paper, used at table to wipe the lips and hands and to protect the clothes. Also, **dinner napkin, table napkin, napkin.** [F, from *servir* serve]

**serviette ring** /'– rɪŋ/, *n.* a ring of metal, wood, etc., used to contain a folded serviette.

**servile** /'sɜvaɪl/, *adj.* **1.** obsequious: *servile flatterers.* **2.** of or pertaining to slaves; proper to or customary for slaves; characteristic of a slave; abject: *servile obedience.* **3.** yielding slavishly, or truckling (fol. by *to*). **4.** slavishly exact; without originality. **5.** being in slavery; oppressed. *–n.* **6.** a servile person. [ME, from L *servīlis*] **– servilely,** *adv.* **– servility** /sɜ'vɪləti/, **servileness,** *n.*

**serving** /'sɜvɪŋ/, *n.* **1.** the act of one who, or that which serves. **2.** a portion of food or drink; a helping. *–adj.* **3.** used for dishing out and distributing food at the table: *serving spoon.* **4.** of or pertaining to one still in office: *a serving vice-president.*

**serving hatch** /'– hætʃ/, *n.* →**service hatch.**

**serving spoon** /'– spun/, *n.* a large spoon designed for serving food.

**servitor** /'sɜvətə/, *n.* one who is in or at the service of another; an attendant. [ME, from OF, from LL]

**servitude** /'sɜvətjud/, *n.* **1.** slavery; bondage: *political or intellectual servitude.* **2.** compulsory service or labour as a punishment for criminals: *penal servitude.* **3.** *Law.* a right possessed by one person with respect to some other person's property, and consisting either of a right to use such property, or of power to prevent certain uses of the other property. [late ME, from L *servitūdo*]

**servo** /'sɜvoʊ/, *n.* →**servomechanism.**

**servo-assisted** /ˌsɜvoʊ-ə'sɪstəd/, *adj.* of or pertaining to a mechanism the operation of which is controlled by a servomechanism.

**servocontrol** /ˌsɜvoʊkən'troʊl/, *n., v.,* **-trolled, -trolling.** *–n.* **1.** a servomechanism used as a control. **2.** *Aeron.* **a.** a servo tab. **b.** a control system operated by the pilot of an aircraft which is powered, or power-assisted. *–v.t.* **3.** to control by means of a servomechanism.

**servomechanism** /'sɜvoʊˌmɛkənɪzəm/, *n.* a mechanism which is used to convert a low-powered mechanical motion into one which requires considerably greater power. The output power is usu. proportional to the input power and the device is often electronically controlled. Also, **servosystem** /'sɜvoʊˌsɪstəm/. [SERV(E) + -O- + MECHANISM] **– servomechanical** /ˌsɜvoʊmə'kænɪkəl/, *adj.*

**servomotor** /'sɜvoʊmoʊtə/, *n.* any motor which provides the power for a servomechanism.

**servo tab** /'sɜvoʊ tæb/, *n.* (in aeronautics) a control surface tab which is operated by the control stick, the movement from which operates the control surface to which it is attached.

**sesame** /'sɛsəmi/, *n.* **1.** a tropical herbaceous plant, *Sesamum indicum,* whose small oval seeds are edible and yield an oil. **2.** the seeds themselves. **3.** See **open sesame.** [Gk; replacing late ME *sysane,* from Gk *sēsámē*]

**sesamoid** /'sɛsəmɔɪd/, *adj.* shaped like a sesame seed, as certain small nodular bones and cartilages. [L *sēsamoīdēs,* from Gk *sēsamoeidḗs*]

**sesqui-,** **1.** a word element meaning 'one and a half', as in *sesquicentennial.* **2.** a prefix applied to compounds where the ratio of radicals is 2 : 3, as in *iron sesquichloride* ($Fe_2Cl_3$). [L, contraction of *sēmis* a half + *-que* besides]

**sesquicentenary** /ˌsɛskwisən'tinəri/, *adj., n., pl.* **-ries.** *–adj.* **1.** of or pertaining to a 150th anniversary. *–n.* **2.** a 150th anniversary. **3.** its celebration.

**sesquicentennial** /ˌsɛskwisən'tɛniəl/, *adj.* **1.** consisting of or marking the completion of a period of a century and a half, or 150 years. **2.** consisting of or recurring every 150 years. *–n.* **3.** a sesquicentenary.

**sesquioxide** /sɛskwi'ɒksaɪd/, *n.* an oxide containing three atoms or equivalents of oxygen to two of the other element or of some radical.

**sesquipedalian** /ˌsɛskwipə'deɪliən/, *adj.* **1.** measuring a foot and a half. **2.** given to using long words. **3.** (of words or expressions) very long. *–n.* **4.** a sesquipedalian word. [*sesquipedal* (from L *sesquipedālis*) + -IAN]

**sessile** /'sɛsaɪl/, *adj. Biol.* **1.** attached by the base, or without any distinct projecting support, as a leaf issuing directly from the stem. **2.** permanently attached. [L, neut. of *sessilis* sitting down]

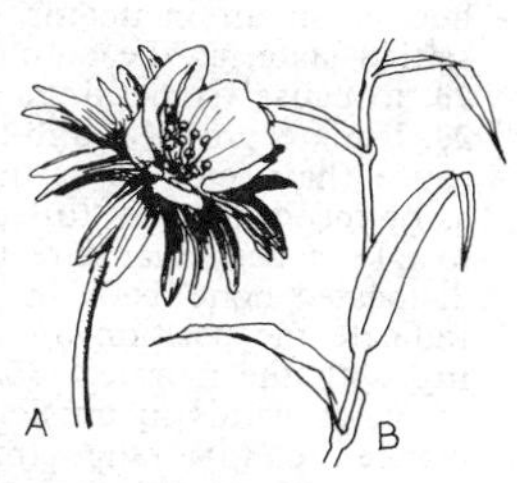

sessile (def. 1): A, sessile flower; B, sessile leaves

**session** /'sɛʃən/, *n.* **1.** the sitting together of a court, council, legislature, or the like, for conference or the transaction of business: *Parliament is now in session.* **2.** a single continuous sitting, or period of sitting, of persons so assembled. **3.** a continuous series of sittings or meetings of a court, legislature, or the like. **4.** the period or term during which such a series is held. **5.** (*pl.*) the sittings or a sitting of justices in court, to execute the powers confided to them by commission, charter, or statute. **6.** a single continuous course or period of lessons, study, etc., in the work of a day at school: *two afternoon sessions a week.* **7.** a portion of the year into which instruction is organised at a college or other educational institution. **8.** a period of time during which a person or group of persons performs an activity: *a dancing session, a cards session.* **9.** *Qld, W.A.* the hours on Sunday during which a particular hotel may open. [ME, from L *sessio*]

**sessional** /'sɛʃənəl/, *adj.* **1.** of or pertaining to a session. **2.** of a pre-school, etc., organised so that two (or more) groups of children attend in one day, in successive sessions, and follow the same program.

**sessional committee** /– kə'mɪti/, *n.* a parliamentary committee appointed for the duration of one session of parliament.

**sessional order** /– 'ɔdə/, *n.* an order of a parliamentary chamber operative for the full duration of the parliamentary session.

**sessionman** /'sɛʃənmæn/, *n. Colloq.* →**studio musician.**

**session work** /'sɛʃən wɜk/, *n.* employment for musicians in which they are paid for performing as required in recording sessions.

**sesterce** /'sɛstɜs/, *n.* an ancient Roman coin equal to a quarter of a denarius. [L *sestertius,* properly adj., two and a half]

**sestet** /sɛs'tɛt/, *n.* **1.** the last six lines of a sonnet. **2.** →**sextet** (def. 2). [It. *sestetto,* diminutive of *sesto* sixth, from L *sextus*]

**sestina** /sɛs'tinə/, *n.* a poem of six six-line stanzas and a three-line envoy, originally without rhyme, in which each stanza repeats the end words of the lines of the first stanza, but in different order, the envoy using the six words again, three in the middle of the lines and three at the end. Also, **sextain.** [It., from *sesto* sixth. See SESTET]

**set** /sɛt/, *v.,* **set, setting,** *n., adj.* *–v.t.* **1.** to put in a particular place or position: *to set a vase on a table.* **2.** to put into some condition or relation: *to set a house on fire.* **3.** to apply: *to set fire to a house.* **4.** to cause to begin: *to set someone thinking.* **5.** to put (a price or value) upon something. **6.** to fix the value of at a certain amount or rate. **7.** to put (much, little store, etc.) as a measure of esteem. **8.** to post, station, or appoint for the purpose of performing some duty: *to set a watch over a camp.* **9.** to incite or urge to attack: *to set the dogs on an intruder.* **10.** to fix, appoint, or ordain: *to set a limit.* **11.** to place or prescribe in an estimation: *to set an early date.* **12.** to present or fix for others to follow: *to set an example.* **13.** to prescribe or assign, as a task. **14.** to prescribe for study for examination: *the examiners have set 'King Lear' this year.* **15.** to compile and prescribe (an examination, etc.). **16.** to put in the proper position, order, or condition for use; adjust or arrange. **17.** to cover with a cloth or cloths and arrange cutlery, crockery, etc., on; lay: *to set the table.* **18.** to adjust according to a standard: *to set a clock.* **19.** to fix or mount (a gem, etc.) in gold or the like;

place in a frame or setting. **20.** to adorn with, or as with, precious stones. **21.** to fix at a given point or calibration: *to set a micrometer.* **22.** to sharpen as by honing: *to set a razor.* **23.** to bend out the points of alternate teeth of (a saw) in opposite directions. **24.** to cause to sit; seat. **25.** to put (a hen) on eggs to hatch them. **26.** to place (eggs) under a hen or in an incubator. **27.** to put into a fixed, rigid, or settled state, as the countenance, the muscles, or the mind. **28.** to cause (something, as mortar) to become firm or hard. **29.** *U.S.* to prove (dough). **30.** to change into a curd. **31.** to cause (hair, etc.) to assume a desired shape, style, or form, as by inserting clips, rollers, etc., when it is wet. **32.** to cause to take a particular direction. **33.** *Surg.* to put (a broken or dislocated bone) back in position. **34.** (of a hunting dog) to indicate the position of (game) by standing stiffly and pointing with the muzzle. **35.** to pitch, as a tune. **36.** *Music.* **a.** to fit, as words to music. **b.** to arrange for musical performance. **c.** to arrange (music) for certain voices or instruments. **37.** to put on (stage) the scenery and properties for an act or scene. **38.** to spread (a sail) so as to catch the wind. **39.** *Print.* **a.** to arrange (type) in the order required for printing. **b.** to put together types corresponding to (copy): *to set an article.* **40.** to begin to form (fruit, etc.). **41.** to sink (a nail head) with a nail set. *–v.i.* **42.** to pass below the horizon; sink: *the sun sets every evening.* **43.** to decline; wane. **44.** to assume a fixed or rigid state, as the countenance, the muscles, etc. **45.** to become firm (as jelly) or solid (as mortar). **46.** to become a curd, as junket. **47.** (of hair) to assume a desired shape, style, form, etc., by the insertion of clips, rollers, etc., when it is wet. **48.** to sit on eggs, as a hen. **49.** to hang or fit, as clothes. **50.** (of the ovary of a flower) to develop into fruit. **51.** (of a hunting dog) to indicate the position of game. **52.** to have a certain direction or course, as a wind, current, etc. **53.** (of a sail) to fill and take shape. **54.** *Dancing.* to face in a certain direction while moving backwards and forwards or in opposite directions, esp. in country-dancing and square-dancing: *set to your partners.* **55.** *Print.* to occupy a certain width: *this copy should be set to fifty ems.* *–v.* **56.** Some special verb phrases are:

**set about, 1.** to begin; start. **2.** to attack. **3.** to begin to fight: *he set about him with a club.*

**set against,** to cause to be hostile or antagonistic to.

**set aside, 1.** to put to one side. **2.** to discard from use. **3.** to dismiss from the mind. **4.** to annul or quash: *to set aside a verdict.*

**set back, 1.** to hinder: stop; delay. **2.** *Colloq.* to cost someone: *it set him back $10.*

**set down, 1.** to put down in writing or print. **2.** to consider: *to set someone down as a fool.* **3.** to rebuke or snub. **4.** to ascribe or attribute. **5.** to allow (passengers) to alight from a bus, etc.

**set eyes on,** to see.

**set forth, 1.** to give an account of; expound. **2.** to start.

**set in, 1.** to begin: *darkness set in.* **2.** (of wind, tide, or the like) to blow or flow towards the shore.

**set off, 1.** to explode. **2.** to cause to explode. **3.** to begin; start, as on a journey. **4.** to intensify or improve by contrast. **5.** *Banking.* to hold a credit balance on (one account) against a debit balance on another account held by the same person, company, etc.

**set on, 1.** to attack: *three men suddenly set on him.* **2.** to urge or persuade.

**set the world on fire,** to achieve fame or notable success.

**set out, 1.** to arrange. **2.** to state or explain methodically. **3.** to start, as on a journey. **4.** to have an intention or goal: *to set out to become prime minister.*

**set to, 1.** to apply oneself; start, as to work. **2.** to start to fight.

**set sail,** to start a voyage.

**set (someone) up,** *Colloq.* to arrange a situation in which (a person) appears in a bad light or is incriminated falsely.

**set up, 1.** to erect. **2.** to start (a business, etc.). **3.** to provide (with): *his parents set him up with books for university.* **4.** to claim to be: *to set up as an expert.* **5.** to raise (a cry, etc.).

**set upon,** to attack, esp. suddenly.

*–n.* **57.** the act or state of setting. **58.** a number of things customarily used together or forming a complete assortment, outfit, or collection: *a set of dishes.* **59.** a series of volumes by one author, about one subject, or the like. **60.** a number or group of persons associating or classed together: *the smart set.* **61.** the fit or hang of an article of clothing: *the set of his coat.* **62.** fixed direction or bent, as of the mind, etc. **63.** a grudge, a feeling of ill-will (fol. by *against* or *on*): *to have a set on (someone).* **64.** bearing or carriage: *the set of one's shoulder.* **65.** the indication by a hunting dog of the position of game. **66.** a permanent deformation or change in shape, as to a piece of machinery. **67.** the assumption of a fixed, rigid or hard state, as by mortar, etc. **68.** a radio or television receiving apparatus. **69.** *Tennis.* a group of games, considered as a unit in a match. **70.** *Surfing.* **a.** the succession of waves, progressing from small ones to large ones to form one group, usu. of about seven. **b.** a large wave, suitable for surfing. **71.** a construction representing a place in which action takes place in a film, television production, or the like. **72.** a number of pieces of stage scenery arranged together. **73.** *Mach.* the bending out of the points of alternate teeth of a saw in opposite directions. **74.** *Hort.* a young plant, or a slip, tuber, or the like, suitable for setting out or planting. **75.** *Dancing, etc.* **a.** the number of couples required to execute a quadrille or the like. **b.** a series of movements or figures that make up a quadrille or the like. **76.** the direction of a wind, current, etc. **77.** *Naut.* the fit and shape of sails. **78.** *Psychol.* readiness to respond in a specific way. **79.** *Maths.* any collection of numbers or objects which have some common property. **80.** a nail set. **81.** →**sett. 82. a (dead) set,** *Colloq.* an unfavourable or hostile attitude; a grudge (fol. by *against* or *on*). *–adj.* **83.** fixed beforehand: *a set time.* **84.** prescribed beforehand: *set rules.* **85.** deliberately composed; customary: *set phrases.* **86.** fixed; rigid: *a set smile.* **87.** resolved or determined; habitually or stubbornly fixed: *to be set in one's opinions.* **88.** ready; prepared; organised: *all set to go.* **89.** formed, built, or made (as specified): *stockily set.* **90.** *Colloq.* **a.** determined (fol. by on): *she was set on going to England.* **b.** hostile to (fol. by *against*): *she was dead set against housework.* **91.** *Colloq.* marked for dislike, attack, or destruction: *she had him set.* **92. dead set,** *Colloq.* true; certain. [ME *sette(n)* to set, place, from OE *settan;* for some n. defs, ME *sette* sect, set, from OF, from L *secta* SECT (by confusion with *set* a group placed or set together)]

**seta** /ˈsitə/, *n., pl.* **-tae** /-ti/. (in plants and animals) a stiff hair; a bristle-like part. [L: bristle]

**setaceous** /səˈteɪʃəs/, *adj.* **1.** bristlelike. **2.** furnished with bristles. [NL *sētāceus*]

**setback** /ˈsɛtbæk/, *n.* **1.** a check to progress; reverse. **2.** *Archit.* **a.** a flat, plain offset in a wall. **b.** such a setting back at a particular height in a tall building, or one of a number of such recessions at different heights, for allowing better light and ventilation in the street. **3.** *Bldg Trades.* the minimum distance from any boundary to which a structure may be built.

**set chisel** /ˈsɛt tʃɪzəl/, *n.* →**cold chisel.**

**set-down** /ˈsɛt-daʊn/, *n.* **1.** stop at which to alight from a bus, tram, etc.: *first set-down Market Street.* **2.** a brief landing made by an aeroplane at an airport en route to its destination.

**se-tenant** /si-ˈtɛnənt/, *adj.* not separated, as of postage stamps joined together in the original sheet. [F: holding together]

**seteriasis** /sɛtəˈraɪəsəs/, *n. Vet. Sci.* an infection of the abdomen of cattle most commonly caused by a worm, *Seteria ceryi,* carried by bloodsucking flies and mosquitos.

**seti-,** a word element meaning 'bristle'. [combining form representing L *sēta*]

**setiform** /ˈsitəfɔm/, *adj.* bristle-shaped; setaceous.

**setigerous** /səˈtɪdʒərəs/, *adj.* having setae or bristles. Also, **setiferous** /səˈtɪfərəs/. [L *sētiger* having bristles + -OUS]

**set-in** /ˈsɛt-ɪn/, *adj.* (of a sleeve) joined to the body of a garment by a seam at the shoulder. Cf. **raglan.**

**set-off** /ˈsɛt-ɒf/, *n.* **1.** anything that counterbalances or makes up for something else. **2.** a counterbalancing debt or claim. **3.** *Archit.* →**offset. 4.** *Print.* a faulty transfer of superabundant or undried ink on a printed sheet to any opposed surface, as the opposite page.

**set of ribs** /sɛt əv ˈrɪbz/, *n.* the standard cut of beef containing those ribs posterior to the fourth rib and excluding the brisket.

**seton** /ˈsitn/, *n. Surg.* **1.** a thread or the like inserted beneath the skin in order to maintain an artificial passage or issue. **2.** the issue itself. [F, from It. *setone,* from *seta* silk]

**setose** /ˈsitous/, *adj.* covered with setae or bristles; bristly. [L *sētōsus*]

**set piece** /ˈsɛt pis/ *for def. 1,* /sɛt ˈpis/ *for defs 2 and 3,* *n.* **1.** a piece of theatrical scenery used as part of a stage set. **2.** an arrangement of fireworks on a scaffolding forming a design or picture when lighted. **3.** a work of art, literature, music, or the like, conforming to a conventional structure, style, etc.

**set point** /– ˈpɔɪnt/, *n.* (in tennis) the point needed to win a set.

**setscrew** /ˈsɛtskru/, *n.* a screw holding firmly together two machine parts, one being otherwise subject to movement along the other. Also, **grubscrew.**

**set square** /ˈ– skwɛə/, *n.* a flat piece of wood, plastic, or the like, in the shape of a right-angled triangle, used in mechanical drawing.

**set stocking** /ˈ– stɒkɪŋ/, *n.* the practice of grazing stock in a paddock at a fixed ratio of stock to hectares, or hectares to stock.

**sett** /sɛt/, *n.* **1.** a small rectangular paving block of stone or wood. **2.** any of various tools for shaping, as a hammer-shaped chisel for paring or cutting metal. **3.** the adjustment of a weaver's reed, determining the pattern. **4.** a square or pattern of a tartan. **5.** the home or burrow of a badger. Also, **set.** [var. of SET]

**settecento** /sɛtəˈtʃɛntou/, *n.* the 18th century, used commonly with reference to Italian art and literature of that period. [It.: seven hundred, short for *mille settecento* one thousand seven hundred]

**settee** /sɛˈti, səˈti/, *n.* a seat for two or more persons with a back, sometimes with arms, and usu. upholstered. [? diminutive of SEAT]

**setter** /ˈsɛtə/, *n.* **1.** one who or that which sets. **2.** one of a breed of long-haired hunting dogs which originally had the habit of crouching when game was scented, but which are now trained to stand stiffly and point the muzzle towards the scented game, the breed being made up of three distinct groups: Irish setters, English setters, and Gordon setters.

**set theory** /ˈsɛt θɪəri/, *n.* the branch of mathematics that deals with the properties of sets (def. 79).

**setting** /ˈsɛtɪŋ/, *n.* **1.** the act of one who or that which sets. **2.** the surroundings or environment of anything. **3.** that in which something, as a jewel, is set or mounted. **4.** a group of all the combined articles, as of cutlery, china, etc., required for setting a table, or a single place at a table. **5.** the period or locale in which the action of a play, film, etc., takes place. **6.** the scenery, costumes, etc., of a play. **7.** *Music.* **a.** a piece of music composed for certain words. **b.** a piece of music composed for a particular medium, or arranged for a medium other than the original.

**setting coat** /ˈ– kout/, *n.* the finishing coat in plastering; skimming coat.

**setting lotion** /ˈ– louʃən/, *n.* a liquid applied to hair preparatory to setting it.

**settle**[1] /ˈsɛtl/, *v.,* **-tled, -tling.** *–v.t.* **1.** to appoint or fix definitely; agree upon (a time, price, conditions, etc.). **2.** to place in a desired position or in order. **3.** to pay (a bill, account due, or the like). **4.** to close (an account) by payment. **5.** to take up residence in (a country, place, house, etc.). **6.** to cause to take up residence. **7.** to furnish (a place) with inhabitants or settlers. **8.** to establish in a way of life, a business, etc. **9.** to bring to rest; quiet (the nerves, stomach, etc.). **10.** *Colloq.* to cause to cease from opposition or annoyance. **11.** to make stable; place on a permanent basis. **12.** to cause (a liquid) to deposit dregs. **13.** to cause (dregs, etc.) to sink. **14.** to cause to sink down gradually; make firm or compact. **15.** to close up; dispose of finally: *to settle an estate.* **16.** *Law.* **a.** to secure (property, title, etc.) on or to a person by formal or legal process. **b.** to terminate (legal proceedings) by mutual consent of the parties. *–v.i.* **17.** to decide; arrange (oft. fol. by *on* or *upon*): *to settle on a plan of action.* **18.** to make a financial arrangement; pay (oft. fol. by *up*). **19.** to take up residence in a new country or place. **20.** to come to rest, as from flight: *a bird settled on a bough.* **21.** to come to rest in a particular place: *a cold settles in one's head.* **22.** to sink down gradually; subside. **23.** to become clear, by the sinking of particles, as a liquid. **24.** to sink to the bottom, as sediment. **25.** to become firm or compact, as the ground. **26. settle down, a.** to come to a rest; become calm or composed. **b.** to apply oneself to serious work. **c.** to set oneself to a regular way of life, esp. upon marrying. **27. settle in,** to move into a new home and adapt oneself to new surroundings. **28. settle with, a.** to pay one's debts to. **b.** to come to an agreement with. [ME; OE *setlan* (c. D *zetelen* place, settle), from *setl* SETTLE[2]]

**settle**[2] /ˈsɛtl/, *n.* a long seat or bench, usu. wooden and with arms and high back. [ME; OE *setl,* c. G *Sessel.* See SIT, *v.*]

**settlement** /ˈsɛtlmənt/, *n.* **1.** the act of settling. **2.** the state of being settled. **3.** the act of making stable or putting on a permanent basis. **4.** the resulting state. **5.** arrangement; adjustment. **6.** the establishment of a person in an employment, office, or charge. **7.** the settling of persons in a new country or place. **8.** a colony, esp. in its early stages. **9.** a small village or collection of houses, esp. in a sparsely populated area. **10.** the satisfying of a claim or demand; a coming to terms. **11.** *Law.* **a.** final disposition of an estate or the like. **b.** the settling of property, title, etc., upon a person. **c.** the property so settled. **12.** legal residence in a particular place, or the right to maintenance, if a pauper. **13.** *Sociol.* a welfare establishment in an underprivileged area providing social, cultural, and educational facilities for the people in the area, including personnel to assist them. **14.** a subsidence or sinking of a structure or part of one.

**settlement of minutes,** *n.* a procedure in industrial relations, in which parties to proceedings agree upon and produce a written statement of the decision of a tribunal contained in an order or award.

**settlement worker** /ˈsɛtlmənt wɜkə/, *n.* one who devotes time to a settlement (def. 13).

**settler** /ˈsɛtlə/, *n.* **1.** one who or that which settles. **2.** one who settles in a new country, esp. one who is freeborn and who takes up portions of the land for agriculture. **3.** *Law.* one who disposes of property by creating a succession of interests in it.

**settler's clock** /sɛtləz ˈklɒk/, *n.* →**kookaburra** (def. 1).

**settler's flax** /– ˈflæks/, *n.* →**settler's twine.**

**settler's matches** /– ˈmætʃəz/, *n.pl.* the long pieces of dead bark which trail loosely from certain gum trees.

**settler's twine** /– ˈtwaɪn/, *n.* →**caterpillar-flower.** Also, **settler's flax.**

**settling** /ˈsɛtlɪŋ/, *n.* **1.** the act of one who or that which settles. **2.** (*usu. pl.*) →**sediment.**

**settling day** /ˈ– deɪ/, *n.* a day fixed for the settling of accounts and completion of transactions, esp. with respect to book-makers.

**set-to** /ˈsɛt-tu/, *n., pl.* **-tos.** a fight; argument. [SET + TO]

**setula** /ˈsɛtʃələ/, *n., pl.* **setulae** /ˈsɛtʃəli/. (of plants and animals) a short blunt seta or bristle-like part. Also, **setule.** [NL, diminutive of *seta* SETA]

**setulose** /ˈsɛtʃəlous/, *adj.* (of plant and animal parts) having or covered with setulae. Also, **setulous** /ˈsɛtʃələs/.

**set-up** /ˈsɛt-ʌp/, *n.* **1.** organisation; arrangement; general state of affairs. **2.** *Survey.* a station or point at which a surveying instrument is set up for taking a number of readings. **3.** *Colloq.* contest or undertaking which presents no real challenge or problems, as a fixed boxing match. **4.** *Colloq.* a racket; swindle. **5.** *Colloq.* a trap; ambush. **6.** of or pertaining to a set-up.

**set width** /sɛt ˈwɪdθ/, *n.* the width of the lower-case alphabet of a given face and size of type, used to assess the amount of type matter that can be set in a given area.

**seven** /ˈsɛvən/, *n.* **1.** a cardinal number, six plus one. **2.** a symbol for this number, as 7 or VII. **3.** a set of seven persons or things. **4.** a playing card with seven pips. **5.** (*pl.*) *Cards.* a game in which the players lay down their cards to form sequences in the same suits, the winner being the player who gets rid of his cards first. **6. throw a seven,** *Colloq.* to fall unconscious; to die. *–adj.* **7.** amounting to seven in number. [ME; OE *seofon,* c. G *sieben*]

**sevenfold** /ˈsɛvənfould/, *adj.* **1.** comprising seven parts or members; seven times as great or as much. *–adv.* **2.** in sevenfold measure.

**seven-gill shark** /ˌsɛvən-gɪl ˈʃak/, *n.* a primitive shark, *Notorhynchus cepedianus,* having only one dorsal fin and seven gill slits, found in southern Australian and New Zealand waters.

**seven seas** /sɛvən ˈsiz/, *n.pl.* the navigable waters of the world.

**seventeen** /sɛvənˈtin/, *n.* **1.** a cardinal number, ten plus seven. **2.** a symbol for this number, as 17 or XVII. **3.** a set of this many persons or things. *–adj.* **4.** amounting to seventeen in number. [ME *seventene,* OE *seofontene,* c. D *zeventien*]

**seventeen door sedan,** *n. Colloq.* →**sanitary cart.**

**seventeenth** /sɛvənˈtinθ/, *adj.* **1.** next after the sixteenth. **2.** being one of seventeen equal parts. *–n.* **3.** a seventeenth part, esp. of one ($\frac{1}{17}$). **4.** the seventeenth member of a series.

**seventh** /ˈsɛvənθ/, *adj.* **1.** next after the sixth. **2.** being one of seven equal parts. *–n.* **3.** a seventh part, esp. of one ($\frac{1}{7}$). **4.** the seventh member of a series. **5.** *Music.* **a.** a note on the seventh degree from a given note (counted as the first). **b.** the interval between such notes. **c.** the harmonic combination of such notes.

**seventh chord** /– ˈkɔd/, *n.* →**dominant seventh chord.**

**seventh-day** /ˈsɛvənθ-deɪ/, *adj.* (*oft. cap.*) designating certain Christian sects who make Saturday their chief day of rest and religious observance: *Seventh-Day Adventists.*

**seventh heaven** /sɛvənθ ˈhɛvən/, *n.* a state of extreme happiness: *she was in (the) seventh heaven at the news of her husband's release from gaol.* [orig. with ref. to the highest heaven in Talmudic literature, where God and the most exalted angels dwell]

**seventy** /ˈsɛvənti/, *n., pl.* **-ties,** *adj.* *–n.* **1.** a cardinal number, ten times seven. **2.** a symbol for this number, as 70 or LXX. **3. the Seventy,** the body of (seventy-two) scholars who, according to tradition, made the Septuagint. **4.** (*pl.*) the numbers from 70 to 79 of a series, esp. with reference to the years of a person's age, or the years of a century, esp. the twentieth. *–adj.* **5.** amounting to seventy in number. [ME; OE *seofontig,* c. G *siebzig*] – **seventieth** /ˈsɛvəntiəθ/, *adj., n.*

**seventy-eight** /sɛvənti-ˈeɪt/, *n.* a gramophone record which revolves seventy-eight times a minute when being played.

**seven-up** /sɛvən-ˈʌp/, *n. Cards.* all fours.

**seven-year itch** /ˌsɛvən-jɪər ˈɪtʃ/, *n. Colloq.* marital boredom or discontent considered to develop after about seven years of marriage.

**sever** /ˈsɛvə/, *v.t.* **1.** to put apart; separate. **2.** to divide into parts, esp. forcibly; cut; cleave. **3.** to break off or dissolve (ties, relations, etc.). *–v.i.* **4.** to separate or part, from each other or one from another; to become divided into parts. **5.** to make a separation or division, as between things. [ME *severe(n),* from AF *severer,* from LL *sēperāre,* replacing L *sēparāre*]

**severable** /ˈsɛvrəbəl, ˈsɛvərəbəl/, *adj.* **1.** capable of being severed. **2.** *Law.* separable or capable of being treated as separate from a whole legal right or obligation: *a severable contract obligation.*

**several** /ˈsɛvrəl/, *adj.* **1.** being more than two or three, but not many. **2.** respective; individual: *they went their several ways.* **3.** separate; different: *three several occasions.* **4.** single; particular. **5.** divers; various: *the several steps in a process.* **6.** *Law.* binding two or more persons who may be sued separately on a common obligation. *–n.* **7.** several persons or things; a few; some. [ME, from AF, from L *sēpar* distinct + *-ālis* -AL[1]]

**severally** /ˈsɛvrəli/, *adv.* **1.** separately; singly. **2.** respectively.

**severalty** /ˈsɛvrəlti, ˈsɛvərəlti/, *n., pl.* **-ties.** **1.** the state of being separate. **2.** the condition, as of land, of being held or owned by separate or individual right.

**severance** /ˈsɛvərəns, ˈsɛvrəns/, *n.* **1.** the act of severing. **2.** the state of being severed. **3.** *Law.* a dividing into parts, as in a contract. **4.** a breaking off, as of relations. [ME, from AF. See SEVER, -ANCE]

**severance pay** /ˈ– peɪ/, *n.* money paid by a firm to employees or directors in compensation for loss of employment.

**severe** /səˈvɪə/, *adj.,* **-verer, -verest.** **1.** harsh; harshly extreme: *severe criticism or laws.* **2.** serious; stern: *a severe face.* **3.** grave: *a severe illness.* **4.** rigidly restrained in style or taste; simple; plain. **5.** causing discomfort or distress by extreme character or conditions, as weather, cold, heat, etc.; unpleasantly violent, as rain or wind, a blow or shock, etc. **6.** hard to endure, perform, fulfil, etc.: *a severe test.* **7.** rigidly exact, accurate, or methodical: *severe conformity to standards.* [L *sevērus*] – **severely,** *adv.* – **severeness,** *n.*

**severity** /səˈvɛrəti/, *n., pl.* **-ties.** **1.** harshness, sternness, or rigour. **2.** austere simplicity, as of style or taste. **3.** violence or sharpness, as of cold, pain, etc. **4.** grievousness; hard or trying character or effect. **5.** gravity; austerity. **6.** rigid exactness or accuracy.

**Seville orange** /ˌsɛvəl ˈɒrɪndʒ/, *n.* See **orange** (def. 2).

**Sevres** /ˈsɛvrə/, *n.* a kind of porcelain, noted for the clarity of its colours and the elaborateness of its decorations. [first manufactured in the 16th cent. in *Sèvres,* a suburb of Paris]

**sew** /soʊ/, *v.,* **sewed, sewn** or **sewed, sewing.** *–v.t.* **1.** to join or attach by a thread or the like, as with a needle. **2.** to make, repair, etc., (a garment) by such means. **3.** to fasten or secure with stitches: *to sew flour in bags.* **4.** to close (a hole, wound, etc.) by means of stitches (usu. fol. by *up*). **5. sew up,** *Colloq.* to complete or conclude (arrangements, discussions, etc.) successfully or satisfactorily. *–v.i.* **6.** to work with a needle and thread, or with a sewing machine. [ME *sewe(n),* OE *siw(i)an;* akin to L *suere*]

**sewage** /ˈsuɪdʒ/, *n.* the waste matter which passes through sewers.

**sewage ejector** /ˈ– ədʒɛktə/, *n.* a device for lifting sewage from one level to another.

**sewage farm** /ˈ– fam/, *n.* a place where sewage is rendered harmless, by turning it in rotation over a large area of land.

**sewer**[1] /ˈsuə/, *n.* an artificial conduit, usu. underground, for carrying off waste water and refuse, as from a town or city. [ME, from OF *sewiere* channel from a fishpond, from Rom. **exaquāria,* from L *ex* out of + *aqua* water]

**sewer**[2] /ˈsoʊə/, *n.* one who or that which sews. [SEW + -ER[1]]

**sewer**[3] /ˈsuə/, *n.* (formerly) a household officer or head servant in charge of the service of the table. [ME, from AF *asseour* seater, from L *assidēre* sit at]

**sewerage** /ˈsuərɪdʒ/, *n.* **1.** the removal of waste water and refuse by means of sewers. **2.** a system of sewers. **3.** the pipes and fittings conveying sewage.

**sewer gas** /ˈsuə gæs/, *n.* the contaminated air of sewers, containing methane and carbon dioxide. Also, **sewage gas.**

**sewermat** /ˈsuəmæt/, *n.* →**electric eel**[2].

**sewer rat** /ˈsuə ræt/, *n.* any rat inhabiting sewers, as the brown rat, *Rattus norvegicus.*

**sewing** /ˈsoʊɪŋ/, *n.* **1.** the act or work of one who sews. **2.** something sewn or to be sewn.

**sewing circle** /ˈ– sɜkəl/, *n.* a group of women who meet regularly to sew for the benefit of charity or the like.

**sewing machine** /ˈ– məʃin/, *n.* any of various hand-operated, foot-operated or electric machines used for sewing, embroidery, etc.

**sewn** /soʊn/, *v.* a past participle of **sew.**

**sex** /sɛks/, *n.* **1.** the character of being either male or female: *persons of different sexes.* **2.** the sum of the anatomical and physiological differences with reference to which the male and the female are distinguished, or the phenomena depending on these differences. **3.** the instinct or attraction drawing one sex towards another, or its manifestation in life and conduct. **4.** men collectively or women collectively: *the fair sex.* **5.** *Colloq.* sexual intercourse. **6. to have sex,** *Colloq.* to have sexual intercourse. *–v.t.* **7.** to ascertain the sex of. [ME, from L *sexus* sex, ? orig., division]

**sex-,** a word element meaning 'six', as in *sexcentenary.* [L, combining form of *sex*]

**sexagenarian** /sɛksədʒəˈnɛəriən/, *adj.* **1.** of the age of 60 years, or between 60 and 70 years old. *–n.* **2.** a sexagenarian person.

**sexagenary** /sɛksəˈdʒinəri/, *adj., n., pl.* **-ries.** *–adj.* **1.** of or pertaining to the number 60. **2.** composed of or proceeding by sixties. **3.** →**sexagenarian.** *–n.* **4.** →**sexagenarian.** [L *sexāgēnārius*]

**Sexagesima** /sɛksəˈdʒɛsəmə/, *n.* the second Sunday before Lent (more fully, **Sexagesima Sunday**). [L *sexāgēsima* (*dies*) sixtieth day]

**sexagesimal** /sɛksəˈdʒɛsəməl/, *adj.* **1.** pertaining to or based upon the number 60. *–n.* **2.** a fraction whose denominator is 60 or a power of 60. [ML *sexāgēsimālis,* from L *sexāgēsimus* sixtieth]

**sex aid** /ˈsɛks eɪd/, *n.* an item of clothing, a pornographic book, or a device as a vibrator, dildo, etc., to stimulate erotic response.

**sex appeal** /ˈ– əpil/, *n.* the quality of attracting the opposite sex.

**sexcentenary** /ˌsɛkssɛnˈtinəri/, *adj., n., pl.* **-ries.** *–adj.* **1.** pertaining to six hundred or a period of six hundred years; marking the completion of six hundred years. *–n.* **2.** a six-hundredth anniversary, or its celebration.

**sex chromosome** /ˈsɛks ˌkroʊməsoʊm/, *n.* any chromosome carrying sex-determining factors, esp. such chromosomes that differ morphologically from the ordinary autosomes, called X and Y, W and Z chromosomes.

**sexed** /sɛkst/, *adj.* having sexuality to a specified degree: *she was highly sexed.*

**sexennial** /sɛksˈɛniəl/, *adj.* **1.** of or for six years. **2.** occurring every six years. *–n.* **3.** *U.S.* a sexcentenary. [L *sexennium* + -AL[1]] – **sexennially,** *adv.*

**sex hormone** /ˈsɛks hɔmoʊn/, *n.* a hormone which plays a part in the development of sexual organs, characteristics and inclinations.

**sex hygiene** /ˈ– ˌhaɪdʒin/, *n.* a branch of hygiene which concerns itself with sex and sexual behaviour as it relates to the well-being of the individual and the community.

**sexism** /ˈsɛksɪzəm/, *n.* the upholding or propagation of sexist attitudes.

**sexist** /ˈsɛksəst/, *adj.* **1.** of an attitude which stereotypes a person according to gender, or sexual preference, rather than judging on individual merits. **2.** of or pertaining to sexual exploitation or discrimination, esp. in advertising, language, job opportunities, etc. *–n.* **3.** a person who displays sexist attitudes.

**sexivalent** /sɛksəˈveɪlənt/, *adj.* →**hexavalent.** Also, **sexavalent.**

**sex kitten** /ˈsɛks kɪtn/, *n. Colloq.* a sexually attractive and provocative young woman.

**sexless** /ˈsɛksləs/, *adj.* **1.** having or seeming to have no sex. **2.** having or seeming to have no sexual desires. **3.** having no sex appeal. – **sexlessly,** *adv.* – **sexlessness,** *n.*

**sex-linkage** /ˈsɛks-ˌlɪŋkɪdʒ/, *n.* inheritance in which both parents do not contribute equally to their progeny because the genes involved are borne on the sex chromosomes in which the parents differ.

**sexology** /sɛksˈɒlədʒi/, *n.* the study of the sexual behaviour of human beings.

**sexpartite** /sɛksˈpataɪt/, *adj.* divided into or consisting of six parts, as a vault, etc. [SEX- + PARTITE]

**sexploitation** /sɛksplɔɪˈteɪʃən/, *n. Colloq.* **1.** the use of sex to help sell a product, film, etc. **2.** the exploitation of sex in books, films, magazines, etc.

**sexpot** /ˈsɛkspɒt/, *n.* a blatantly sexually attractive female.

**sex-sell** /ˈsɛks-sɛl/, *n.* the use of sexually stimulating copy and illustrations in advertising.

**sex shop** /ˈsɛks ʃɒp/, *n.* a shop in which articles associated with sexual behaviour are sold.

**sex symbol** /ˈ– sɪmbəl/, *n.* a woman or man publicised as embodying sexual attractiveness.

**sext** /sɛkst/, *n.* the third of the seven canonical hours, or the service for it, originally fixed for the sixth hour of the day (or noon). [ME, from L *sexta (hōra)* sixth (hour)]

**sextain** /ˈsɛksteɪn/, *n.* →**sestina.**

**sextan** /ˈsɛkstən/, *adj.* **1.** (of a fever, etc.) characterised by paroxysms which recur every sixth day. *–n.* **2.** a sextan fever or ague. [NL *sextāna* (from L *sextus* sixth), short for *sextāna febris*]

**sextant** /ˈsɛkstənt/, *n.* an astronomical instrument used in measuring angular distances, esp. the altitudes of sun, moon, and stars at sea in determining latitude and longitude. [L *sextans* sixth part]

**sextet** /sɛksˈtɛt/, *n.* **1.** any group or set of six. **2.** Also, **sestet. a.** a company of six singers or players. **b.** a musical composition for six voices or instruments. Also, **sextette.** [alteration of SESTET, from L *sex* six]

**sextile** /ˈsɛkstaɪl/, *Astron. –adj.* **1.** denoting or pertaining to the aspect or position of two heavenly bodies when 60° distant from each other. *–n.* **2.** a sextile position or aspect. [L *sextīlis* sixth]

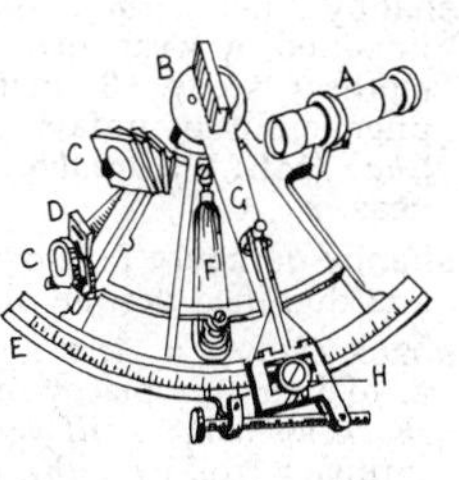


sextant: A, telescope; B, mirror; C, coloured glass; D, half-mirror, half-glass; E, graduated arc; F, handle; G, movable index arm; H, magnifying glass

**sextillion** /sɛksˈtɪljən/, *n.* **1.** (usu. with *one* or *a*) a cardinal number represented by one followed by 36 zeros, or (in the U.S. and France) by one followed by 21 zeros. *–adj.* **2.** (usu. with *one* or *a*) amounting to one sextillion in number. [F, from L *sextus* sixth (power of) + *(m)illion* MILLION] – **sextillionth,** *adj., n.*

**sexto** /ˈsɛkstoʊ/, *n.* a page with an area which is one sixth of the whole printing sheet. [L, abl. sing. of *sextus* sixth]

**sextodecimo** /sɛkstoʊˈdɛsəmoʊ/, *n., pl.* **-mos,** *adj. –n.* **1.** a volume printed from sheets folded to form 16 leaves or 32 pages. *Abbrev.:* 16mo or 16°. *–adj.* **2.** in sextodecimo. Also, **sixteenmo.** [L, abl. sing. of *sextusdecimus* sixteenth]

**sexton** /ˈsɛkstən/, *n.* a church officer and guardian who is charged with taking care of the church, its contents, and the graveyard, ringing the bell, gravedigging, etc. [ME *segerstone,* from AF *segrestaine,* from ML *sacristānus* sacristan]

**sextuple** /ˈsɛkstəpəl/, *adj., v.,* **-pled, -pling.** *–adj.* **1.** sixfold; consisting of six parts; six times as great. *–v.t., v.i.* **2.** to make or become six times as great. [L *sextus* sixth + *-uple,* as in QUINTUPLE]

**sextuplet** /sɛksˈtʌplət, -ˈtju-/, *n.* **1.** one of the six children born at one birth. **2.** a group or combination of six things.

**sexual** /ˈsɛkʃuəl/, *adj.* **1.** of or pertaining to sex. **2.** occurring between or involving the two sexes. **3.** having sex or sexual organs, or reproducing by processes involving both sexes, as animals or plants. **4.** having a strong sex drive or having the ability to arouse strong sexual interest. [LL *sexuālis*] – **sexually,** *adv.*

**sexual intercourse** /– ˈɪntəkɔs/, *n.* the insertion of the penis into the vagina followed by ejaculation; coitus; copulation.

**sexuality** /sɛkʃuˈæləti/, *n.* **1.** sexual character; possession of sex. **2.** the recognition or emphasising of sexual matters.

**sexual selection** /ˌsɛkʃuəl səˈlɛkʃən/, *n.* the theory, first propounded by Darwin, that the selection by some animals of attractive mates has resulted in the evolution of features which are in other respects disadvantageous.

**sexy** /ˈsɛksi/, *adj.* **-ier, -iest.** **1.** having or involving a predominant or excessive concern with sex: *a sexy novel.* **2.** sexually interesting or exciting; having sex appeal. – **sexily,** *adv.* – **sexiness,** *n.*

**Seychelles** /seɪˈʃɛlz/, **The,** *n.pl.* a country consisting of a group of ninety-two islands in the Indian Ocean, north-east of Madagascar.

**sf.,** sforzando. Also, **sfz.**

**SF,** science fiction.

**s.f.a.** /ɛs ɛf ˈeɪ/, *n. Colloq.* very little; next to nothing. [abbrev. for *s(weet) f(uck)-a(ll)* or *s(weet) F(anny) A(dams)*]

**sforzando** /sfɔtˈsændoʊ/, *adv.* **1.** with force (used as a musical direction, to indicate that a note or chord is to be rendered with special emphasis). *Abbrev.:* sf., sfz. *–adj.* **2.** forceful; emphatic. Also, **sforzato.** [It., ger. of *sforzare* force]

**sfumato** /sfuˈmatoʊ/, *n.* the transition in a work of art of tone or colour from light to dark by imperceptible stages. [It., pp. of *sfumare* smoke out, fade; c. FUME]

**s.g.,** specific gravity.

**sgd,** signed.

**sgl.,** single.

**sgraffito** /sgræˈfitoʊ, skræ-/, *n., pl.* **-ti** /-ti/. **1.** a technique of decoration in which a top layer of paint, etc., is incised with a pattern partially to reveal a second layer usu. of another colour. **2.** an object decorated by this technique. [It.]

**Sgt,** Sergeant.

**sh** /ʃ/, *interj.* (an exclamation requesting or demanding silence.)

**sh.**, shilling.

**shabby** /'ʃæbi/, *adj.*, **-bier, -biest.** **1.** having the appearance impaired by wear, use, etc.: *shabby clothes.* **2.** wearing worn clothes; seedy. **3.** making a poor appearance. **4.** meanly ungenerous or unfair; contemptible, as persons, actions, etc. [*shab* (ME; OE *sceabb* scab) + -Y[1]] – **shabbily,** *adv.* – **shabbiness,** *n.*

**shabby-genteel** /ʃæbi-dʒɛn'til/, *adj.* trying to appear genteel and dignified despite shabbiness.

**shack** /ʃæk/, *n.* **1.** a rough cabin; shanty. *–v.i.* **2. shack up, a.** to live at a place; reside (fol. by *with*): *you can come and shack up with us till your house is ready.* **b.** to live in sexual intimacy (fol. by *with*). [short for *shackle* in same sense, itself short for RAMSHACKLE]

**shackle** /'ʃækəl/, *n., v.,* **-led, -ling.** *–n.* **1.** a ring or fastening of iron or the like for securing the wrist, ankle, etc.; a fetter. **2.** a hobble or fetter for a horse or other animal. **3.** any of various fastening or coupling devices, as the curved bar of a padlock which passes through the staple. **4.** anything that serves to prevent freedom of procedure, thought, etc. *–v.t.* **5.** to put a shackle or shackles on; confine or restrain. **6.** to fasten or couple with a shackle. **7.** to restrain in action, thought, etc. [ME *shackle,* OE *sceacel* fetter, c. LG *schakel* hobble (for a horse)] – **shackler,** *n.*

**shad** /ʃæd/, *n., pl.* **shad,** (*for different species*) **shads. 1.** a deep-bodied herring of North America, *Alosa sapidissima,* that runs up streams to spawn, and is valued as a food fish. **2.** any other species of *Alosa* or of related genera. **3.** any of several unrelated fishes. [OE *sceadd;* cf. LG *schade*]

**shaddock** /'ʃædək/, *n.* **1.** the large roundish or pear-shaped, usu. pale yellow, orange-like edible fruit of the tree, *Citrus grandis,* grown extensively in the Orient; pomelo. **2.** the tree itself. [named after Captain *Shaddock,* 17th-cent. English sea-captain, who brought the seed from the East Indies to Jamaica]

**shade** /ʃeɪd/, *n., v.,* **shaded, shading.** *–n.* **1.** the comparative darkness caused by the interception of rays of light. **2.** an area of comparative darkness; a shady place. **3.** (*pl.*) darkness gathering at the close of day. **4.** (*chiefly pl.*) a retired or obscure place. **5.** comparative obscurity. **6.** a spectre or ghost. **7.** a lampshade. **8.** anything used for protection against excessive light, heat, etc. **9.** (*pl.*) *Colloq.* →**sunglasses. 10.** *Class. Myth.* **a.** an inhabitant of Hades. **b.** (*pl.*) the spirits of the dead collectively. **c.** the world or abode of the dead; Hades. **11.** a shadow. **12.** degree of darkening of a colour by adding black or by decreasing the illumination. **13.** comparative darkness as represented pictorially; the dark part, or a dark part, of a picture. **14.** a slight variation, amount, or degree: *there is not a shade of difference between them.* **15. cast** or **put in the shade,** to surpass; render insignificant by comparison. *–v.t.* **16.** to produce shade in or on. **17.** to obscure, dim, or darken. **18.** to screen or hide from view. **19.** to protect (something) from light, heat, etc., as by a screen; to cover or screen (a light, candle, etc.). **20.** to introduce degrees of darkness into (a drawing or painting) for effects of light and shade or different colours. **21.** to render the values of light and dark in (a painting or drawing). **22.** to change by imperceptible degrees into something else. *–v.i.* **23.** to pass or change by slight graduations, as one colour or one thing into another. [ME; OE *sceadu.* See SHADOW] – **shadeless,** *adj.*

**shade tree** /'– tri/, *n.* a tree planted, retained or valued for the shade it gives.

**shading** /'ʃeɪdɪŋ/, *n.* **1.** a slight variation or difference of colour, character, etc. **2.** the act of one who or that which shades. **3.** the representation of the different values in a painting or drawing.

**shadoof** /ʃə'duf/, *n.* a contrivance used in Egypt and other Middle Eastern countries for raising water, esp. for irrigation, consisting of a long suspended rod with a bucket at one end and a weight at the other. Also, **shaduf.** [Egypt. Ar. *shādūf*]

shadoofs

**shadow** /'ʃædoʊ/, *n.* **1.** a dark figure or image cast on the ground or some surface by a body intercepting light. **2.** shade or comparative darkness; an instance or area of comparative darkness. **3.** (*pl.*) darkness coming after sunset. **4.** shelter; protection. **5.** a slight suggestion; a trace: *not a shadow of a doubt.* **6.** a spectre or ghost: *pursued by shadows.* **7.** a shadowy or faint image: *shadows of things to come.* **8.** a mere semblance: *the shadow of power.* **9.** a reflected image. **10.** the dark part, or shade, or a dark part, of a picture. **11.** a cloud, as on friendship or reputation. **12.** a constant or dominant threat, influence, etc.: *under the shadow of the atomic bomb.* **13.** an inseparable companion. **14.** one who follows a person in order to keep watch upon him, as a spy or detective. *–v.t.* **15.** to overspread with shadow; shade. **16.** to cast a gloom over; cloud. **17.** to screen or protect from light, heat, etc. **18.** to follow (a person) about secretly, in order to keep watch over his movements. **19.** to represent faintly, prophetically, etc. (oft. fol. by *forth*). **20.** *Obs.* to shade in painting, drawing, etc. [ME; OE *scead(u)we,* oblique case of *sceadu* SHADE, c. D *schaduw;* akin to G *Schatten*] – **shadower,** *n.* – **shadowless,** *adj.*

**shadow bands** /'– bændz/, *n.pl.* parallel bands of light and shade which can sometimes be seen to sweep across the ground just before totality in a solar eclipse, caused by irregular refraction of light from the thin crescent formed by the earth's atmosphere.

**shadow-boxing** /'ʃædoʊ-ˌbɒksɪŋ/, *n.* boxing carried on with an imaginary opponent, as for exercise.

**shadow cabinet** /ʃædoʊ 'kæbənət/, *n.* the group of members of the chief opposition party who act as party spokesmen on major issues.

**shadowgraph** /'ʃædoʊgræf, -graf/, *n.* **1.** a picture produced by throwing a shadow, as of the hands, on a lighted screen. **2.** →**radiograph. 3.** *Aerospace.* an image which shows the density gradients in the flow about a body which is itself presented in silhouette.

**shadow-mask** /'ʃædoʊ-mask/, *adj.* of or pertaining to a type of picture tube commonly used in colour television receivers.

**shadow minister** /ʃædoʊ 'mɪnəstə/, *n.* a member of a shadow cabinet.

**shadow ministry** /– 'mɪnəstri/, *n.* the members of the opposition party who have a special responsibility for the ministerial portfolios held by their counterparts in the party in government.

**shadow play** /'– pleɪ/, *n.* a theatrical entertainment consisting of the shadows of puppets, live actors, etc., projected on to a screen illuminated from behind.

**shadowy** /'ʃædoʊi/, *adj.* **1.** resembling a shadow in faintness, slightness, etc.: *shadowy outlines.* **2.** unsubstantial, unreal, or illusory. **3.** abounding in shadow; shady: *a shadowy path.* **4.** enveloped in shadow. **5.** casting a shadow.

**shaduf** /ʃə'duf/, *n.* →**shadoof.**

**shady** /'ʃeɪdi/, *adj.,* **-dier, -diest. 1.** abounding in shade; shaded: *shady paths.* **2.** giving shade. **3.** shadowy; indistinct; spectral. **4.** *Colloq.* uncertain; questionable; of dubious character or reputation. **5. on the shady side of,** *Colloq.* beyond in age: *on the shady side of forty.* – **shadily,** *adv.* – **shadiness,** *n.*

**shaft** /ʃaft/, *n.* **1.** a long pole or rod forming the body of various weapons, as a spear, lance, or arrow. **2.** something directed as in sharp attack: *shafts of sarcasm.* **3.** a ray or beam: *shaft of sunlight.* **4.** the handle of a hammer, axe, golf club, or other long implement. **5.** a revolving bar serving to transmit motion, as from an engine to various machines. **6.** →**flagpole. 7.** the body of a column or pillar between the base and the capital; a column. **8.** a monument in the form of a column, obelisk, or the like. **9.** either of the parallel bars of wood between which the animal drawing a vehicle is placed. **10.** any well-like passage or vertical enclosed space, as in a building: *a lift shaft.* **11.** an inclined (sloping) or vertical passageway into a mine. **12.** *Bot.* the trunk of a tree. **13.** *Zool.* the main stem of a feather distal to the superior umbilicus. **14.** that part of a candlestick which supports its branches. [ME; OE *sceaft,* c. G *Schaft*]

**shafting** /'ʃaftɪŋ/, *n.* **1.** shafts for communicating motion. **2.** a system of such shafts. **3.** material for such shafts.

**shag**[1] /ʃæg/, *n.*, *v.*, **shagged, shagging.** *–n.* **1.** rough, matted hair, wool, or the like. **2.** a mass of this. **3.** a cloth with a nap, at times one of silk but commonly a heavy or rough woollen fabric. **4.** a coarse tobacco cut into fine shreds. *–v.t.* **5.** to make rough or sharp. [OE *sceacga* wool, etc., c. Icel. *skegg* beard, from *skaga* stick out]

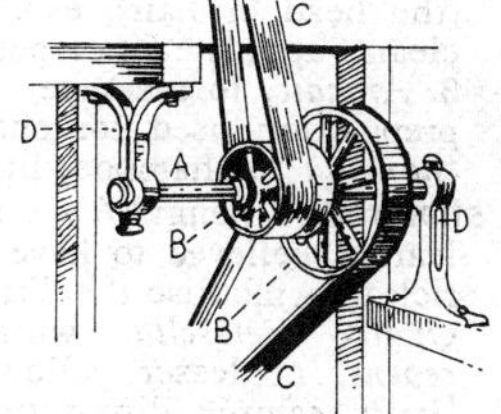

shafting: A, shaft; B, pulley; C, belt; D, support

**shag**[2] /ʃæg/, *n.* **1.** →**cormorant** (def. 1). **2.** →**darter** (def. 2). **3. like a shag on a rock,** *Colloq.* alone; deserted; forlorn. [? from the shaggy crest]

**shag**[3] /ʃæg/, *v.*, **shagged, shagging,** *n. Colloq. –v.t.* **1.** to have sexual intercourse with. **2.** to tire; exhaust (oft. fol. by *out*). **3.** to chase; run after. **4. get shagged** (an expression of contempt or rejection). *–v.i.* **5.** to masturbate. *–n.* **6.** an act or instance of sexual intercourse, esp. group sexual activity. [orig. unknown] – **shagger,** *n.*

**shagbark** /ˈʃægbak/, *n. U.S.* **1.** a species of hickory, *Carya ovata,* with rough bark, yielding light-coloured, ellipsoidal, slightly angular nuts, but most valued for its wood. **2.** the wood. **3.** the nut of this tree. Also, **shagbark hickory** (for defs 1 and 2).

**shagged** /ʃægd/, *adj. Colloq.* tired out; exhausted. Also, **shagged-out.**

**shagger's back** /ˈʃægəz bæk/, *n. Colloq.* any pain in a man's back, jocularly attributed to sexual intercourse.

**shaggin' wagon** /ˈʃægən wægən/, *n. Colloq.* a panel van or a station wagon, often luxuriously appointed with carpet, curtains, etc., as a suitable place for sexual intercourse.

**shaggy** /ˈʃægi/, *adj.*, **-gier, -giest. 1.** covered with or having long, rough hair. **2.** unkempt. **3.** rough and matted; forming a bushy mass, as the hair, mane, etc. **4.** having a rough nap, as cloth. – **shaggily,** *adv.* – **shagginess,** *n.*

**shaggy dog story,** *n.* a generally long and involved funny story whose humour lies in the pointlessness or irrelevance of its conclusion.

**shaggy pea** /ʃægi ˈpi/, *n.* any shrub of the endemic Australian genus *Oxylobium,* family Papilionaceae, with red to yellow pea-shaped flowers.

**shagpile** /ˈʃægpaɪl/, *n.* carpet pile which is long and thick.

**shagreen** /ʃəˈgrin/, *n.* **1.** a kind of untanned leather with a granular surface, prepared from the skin of the horse, shark, seal, etc. **2.** the rough skin of certain sharks, used as an abrasive. *–adj.* **3.** Also, **shagreened.** consisting of or covered with shagreen. [formerly *chagrin,* from F, from Turk. *çāghrī,* lit., the rump of a horse]

**shah** /ʃa/, *n.* king, esp. used (*usu. cap.*) as a title of the former rulers of Iran. Cf. **Padishah.** [Pers.]

**shake** /ʃeɪk/, *v.*, **shook, shaken, shaking,** *n. –v.i.* **1.** to move or sway with short, quick, irregular vibratory movements. **2.** to tremble with emotion, cold, etc. **3.** to fall (fol. by *down, off,* etc.) by such motion: *sand shakes off readily.* **4.** to totter; become unsteady. **5.** to clasp a person's hand in greeting, agreement, etc. **6.** *Music.* to execute a trill. **7. shake down, a.** to settle in or retire to a bed, esp. a makeshift or temporary one. **b.** to settle comfortably in or adapt oneself to new surroundings, etc. *–v.t.* **8.** to move to and fro with short, quick, forcible movements. **9.** to brandish or flourish. **10.** to bring, throw, force, rouse, etc., by or as by some vigorous movement to and fro; cause to quiver or tremble: *leaves shaken by the breeze.* **11.** to cause to totter or waver: *to shake the very foundations of society.* **12.** to agitate or disturb profoundly in feeling. **13.** to unsettle; weaken: *to shake one's faith.* **14.** →**trill** (defs 1 and 2). **15.** to mix (dice) before they are cast. **16.** *Colloq.* to get rid of; escape from; elude. (fol. by *off*). **17.** *Colloq.* to steal. **18. shake down, a.** to bring down. **b.** to cause to settle. **c.** to condition: *to shake down a vessel by a first voyage.* **d.** *Colloq.* to extort money from. **e.** *Colloq.* to search (someone); frisk. **19. shake hands,** to clasp hands in greeting, congratulation, agreement, etc. **20. shake off, a.** to get rid of; free oneself from. **b.** to get away from; elude. **21. shake one's head,** to turn the head from side to side to indicate reluctance, disapproval, disbelief, etc. **22. shake the dust from one's feet,** to make one's departure, esp. with a determination not to return. **23. shake up, a.** to shake in order to mix, loosen, etc. **b.** to upset. **c.** to disturb or agitate mentally or physically. *–n.* **24.** the act of shaking. **25.** tremulous motion. **26.** a tremor. **27.** a disturbing blow; shock. **28.** something resulting from shaking. **29.** *Colloq.* an earthquake. **30.** a fissure in the earth. **31.** a crack or fissure in timber, produced during growth by wind, sudden change of temperature, or the like. **32.** a shingle, about a metre long, split from a piece of log. **33.** →**trill** (def. 9). **34.** a drink made by shaking ingredients together: *a milk shake.* **35.** (*pl.*) *Colloq.* a state of trembling, esp. that induced by alcoholism, drugs or nervous disorder. **36.** a dance in which the body is shaken violently in time to music. **37.** *Colloq.* a moment, a short time: *just a shake.* **38. a brace of shakes,** a very short time; an instant. **39. in two shakes of a dog's tail,** *Colloq.* in a very short time. **40. no great shakes,** *Colloq.* of no particular importance; unimpressive. [ME; OE *sceacan,* c. LG *schacken*]

**shakedown** /ˈʃeɪkdaʊn/, *n.* **1.** a bed of straw, blankets, or other bedding spread on the floor. **2.** any makeshift bed. **3.** the process of shaking down. **4.** *Colloq.* extortion, esp. by blackmail or threatened violence. **5.** *U.S. Colloq.* a thorough search. *–adj.* **6.** (of a course, flight, etc.) intended to test a new ship, aircraft, etc., under normal operating conditions.

**shake-out** /ˈʃeɪk-aʊt/, *n.* **1.** *Stock Exchange.* a sharp drop in certain share values. **2.** *Comm.* the elimination of companies, products, etc., owing to increased competition in a declining market or rising standards of quality.

**shaker** /ˈʃeɪkə/, *n.* **1.** one who or that which shakes. **2.** that with which or from which something is shaken: *a cocktail shaker, flour shaker.* **3.** (*cap.*) *U.S.* a member of a communistic celibate religious sect, so called, popularly, from the movements of the body which form part of their ceremonial. – **Shakerism,** *n.*

**Shakespearian** /ʃeɪkˈspɪəriən/, *adj.* **1.** of, pertaining to, or suggestive of William Shakespeare, 1564-1616, poet and dramatist, or of his works. *–n.* **2.** a Shakespearian scholar; a specialist in the study of the works of Shakespeare. Also, **Shakespearean, Shaksperian.** – **Shakespearianism,** *n.*

**shake-up** /ˈʃeɪk-ʌp/, *n.* a thorough change in a business, department, or the like, as by dismissals, demotions, etc.

**shaking** /ˈʃeɪkɪŋ/, *n.* **1.** the act of one who or that which shakes. **2.** ague, with or without chill and fever.

**shaking palsy** /– ˈpɔlzi/, *n.* a disease of the brain, characterised by tremors, esp. of fingers and hands, rigidity of muscles, slowness of movements and speech, and a masklike, expressionless face; Parkinson's disease.

**shakings** /ˈʃeɪkɪŋz/, *n. Naut.* a collection or tangle, as of ropes, canvas, etc.

**shako** /ˈʃækoʊ/, *n.*, *pl.* **-os.** a military cap in the form of a cylinder or truncated cone, with a peak and a plume or pompom. [Magyar *csákó* peaked (cap)]

shako

**shakuhachi** /ʃækuˈhatʃi/, *n.* a Japanese end-blown bamboo flute, traditionally played by samurai, the only known musical instrument to serve also as a weapon. [Jap.]

**shaky** /ˈʃeɪki/, *adj.*, **-kier, -kiest. 1.** shaking. **2.** trembling; tremulous. **3.** liable to break down or give way; insecure; not to be depended upon: *a shaky ladder.* **4.** wavering, as in allegiance. **5. the Shaky Isles,** *Colloq.* New Zealand. – **shakily,** *adv.* – **shakiness,** *n.*

**shale** /ʃeɪl/, *n.* a rock of fissile or laminated structure formed by the consolidation of clay or argillaceous material. [special use of obs. *shale* scale (of a fish, etc.), OE *scealu* shell, husk. See SCALE[1]]

**shale oil** /ˈ– ɔɪl/, *n.* oil obtained by the distillation of various forms of shale.

**shall** /ʃæl/; *weak form* /ʃəl/, *aux. v., pres. sing.* 1 **shall;** 2 **shall** or (*Archaic*) **shalt;** 3 **shall;** *pl.* **shall;** *pt.* 1 **should;** 2 **should** or (*Archaic*) **shouldst** or **shouldest;** 3 **should;** *pl.* **should;** imperative, infinitive, and participles lacking. **1.** (used, generally, in the first person to indicate simple future time): *I shall go* *today.* **2.** (used, generally in the second and third persons, to indicate promise or determination): *you shall do it.* **3.** (used interrogatively, in questions that admit of *shall* in the answer): *Shall he be told? He shall.* **4.** (used conditionally in all persons to indicate future time): *if he shall come.* [ME *shal,* OE *sceal,* c. Icel. *skal;* akin to G *soll*]

**shalloon** /ʃə'lun/, *n.* a light, twilled woollen fabric used chiefly for linings. [ME *chalon* coverlet, apparently from F *chalon,* from *Châlons*-sur-Marne, town in NE France]

**shallop** /'ʃæləp/, *n.* (formerly) a small, light boat. [F *chaloupe,* from D *sloep*]

**shallot** /ʃə'lɒt/, *n.* **1.** a plant of the lily family, *Allium ascalonicum,* whose bulb forms bulblets which are used for flavouring in cookery and as a vegetable. **2.** the bulb or bulblet. Also, **eschalot.** [aphetic var. of *eschalot,* from F *eschalotte,* alteration of OF *eschaloigne.* See SCALLION]

**shallow** /'ʃæloʊ/, *adj.* **1.** of little depth; not deep: *shallow water, a shallow dish.* **2.** lacking depth; superficial: *a shallow mind.* *–n.* **3.** (*usu. pl.*) a shallow part of a body of water; a shoal. *–v.t.* **4.** to make shallow. *–v.i.* **5.** to become shallow. [ME *schalowe.* Cf. OE *sceald* shallow] – **shallowly,** *adv.* – **shallowness,** *n.*

**shallow-fry** /ʃæloʊ-'fraɪ/, *v.t.,* **-fried, -frying.** *v.t.* to fry in a small amount of fat or oil.

**shallow sinking** /ʃæloʊ 'sɪŋkɪŋ/, *n.* the obtaining of ore by shallow excavations.

**shalt** /ʃælt/, *v. Archaic.* 2nd person singular of **shall.**

**shaly** /'ʃeɪli/, *adj.* of, like, or containing shale.

**sham** /ʃæm/, *n., adj., v.,* **shammed, shamming.** *–n.* **1.** something that is not what it purports to be; a spurious imitation. **2.** *Obs.* a hoax. *–adj.* **3.** pretended; counterfeit: *sham attacks.* **4.** designed or used as a sham. *–v.t.* **5.** to produce an imitation of; pretend to be. **6.** to assume the appearance of: *to sham illness.* *–v.i.* **7.** to make a false pretence; pretend. [special use of Brit. d. *sham,* northern var. of SHAME]

**shaman** /'ʃamən, 'ʃeɪ-/, *n.* a medicine man and priest who works with the supernatural. [G *Schamane,* from Russ. *shaman,* from Tungusic *samân*] – **shamanic** /ʃə'mænɪk/, *adj.*

**shamanism** /'ʃamənɪzəm, 'ʃeɪ-/, *n.* **1.** the primitive religion of northern Asia embracing a belief in controlling spirits who can be influenced only by shamans. **2.** any similar religion. – **shamanist,** *n., adj.* – **shamanistic** /ʃamə'nɪstɪk, ʃeɪ-/, *adj.*

**shamble**[1] /'ʃæmbəl/, *n.* **1.** (*pl. oft. construed as sing.*) **a.** →**slaughterhouse. b.** any place of carnage. **c.** any place or thing in confusion or disorder. [ME *shamel,* OE *sc(e)amel* stool, table, from L *scamellum,* diminutive of *scamnum* bench]

**shamble**[2] /'ʃæmbəl/, *v.,* **-bled, -bling,** *n.* *–v.i.* **1.** to walk or go awkwardly; shuffle. *–n.* **2.** a shambling gait. [v. use of *shamble,* adj., awkward, itself attributive use of SHAMBLE[1]]

**shame** /ʃeɪm/, *n., v.,* **shamed, shaming.** *–n.* **1.** the painful feeling arising from the consciousness of something dishonourable, improper, ridiculous, etc., done by oneself or another. **2.** susceptibility to this feeling: *to be without shame.* **3.** disgrace; ignominy. **4.** a fact or circumstances bringing disgrace or regret. **5. for shame!** *Archaic.* you should feel shame! **6. put to shame, a.** to disgrace. **b.** to outdo or surpass. *–v.t.* **7.** to cause to feel shame; make ashamed. **8.** to drive, force, etc., through shame. **9.** to cover with ignominy or reproach; disgrace. [ME; OE *sc(e)amu,* c. G *Scham*]

**shamefaced** /'ʃeɪmfeɪst/, *adj.* **1.** modest or bashful. **2.** showing shame: *shamefaced apologies.* [SHAME, *n.* + FACE, *n.* + -ED[3]; replacing *shamefast,* OE *sceamfæst* (see FAST[1], *adj.*)] – **shamefacedly** /'ʃeɪmfeɪsədli, 'ʃeɪmfeɪstli/, *adv.* – **shamefacedness,** *n.*

**shameful** /'ʃeɪmfəl/, *adj.* **1.** that causes or ought to cause shame. **2.** disgraceful or scandalous: *shameful treatment.* – **shamefully,** *adv.* – **shamefulness,** *n.*

**shameless** /'ʃeɪmləs/, *adj.* **1.** completely lacking in shame; immodest; audacious. **2.** insensible to disgrace. **3.** showing no shame: *shameless conduct.* – **shamelessly,** *adv.* – **shamelessness,** *n.*

**shammer** /'ʃæmə/, *n.* one who shams.

**shammy** /'ʃæmi/, *n., pl.* **-mies.** →**chamois** (def. 2). [respelling of CHAMOIS to indicate pronunciation]

**shampoo** /ʃæm'pu/, *v.,* **-pooed, -pooing,** *n.* *–v.t.* **1.** to wash (the head or hair), esp. with a cleaning preparation. **2.** to clean (upholstery, carpets, etc.), with a special preparation. **3.** *Archaic.* to massage. *–n.* **4.** the act of shampooing. **5.** a preparation used for shampooing. [Hind. *chāmpo,* impv. of *chāmpnā* to shampoo, lit., to press, squeeze] – **shampooer,** *n.*

**shamrock** /'ʃæmrɒk/, *n.* a plant with trifoliate leaflets believed to have been used by St Patrick to symbolise the Trinity, esp. wood sorrel, *Oxalis acetosella,* white clover, *Trifolium repens,* or lesser yellow trefoil, *T. dubium.* [Irish *seamróg,* diminutive of *seamar* clover]

shamrock

**shamus** /'ʃeɪməs/, *n.* →**private investigator.** [possibly var. of *shammes* a sexton in a synagogue, from Yiddish *shames,* from Heb. *shammāsh,* from Aram. *shĕmāsh* to serve; jocular comparison of the duties of a house detective with those of a sexton]

**Shan** /ʃan/, *n.* a northern Thai language, spoken in the Shan States.

**shandigaff** /'ʃændigæf/, *n.* →**shandygaff.**

**shandrydan** /'ʃændrədæn/, *n.* a rickety, old-fashioned vehicle.

**shandy** /'ʃændi/, *n.* a mixed drink of beer with ginger beer or lemonade. [shortened form of SHANDYGAFF]

**shandygaff** /'ʃændigæf/, *n.* **1.** *Obs.* →**shandy. 2.** *Colloq.* any mixture, as of wet and dry sheep for shearing. Also, **shandigaff.** [orig. uncert.]

**shandy system** /'ʃændi sɪstəm/, *n. Colloq.* →**composite rating.**

**shanghai**[1] /'ʃæŋhaɪ, ʃæŋ'haɪ/, *v.,* **-haied, -haiing;** /'ʃæŋhaɪ/, *n.* *–v.t.* **1.** *Naut.* to obtain (a man) for the crew of a ship by unscrupulous means, as by force, drugs, or fraud. **2.** *Colloq.* to involve someone in an activity, usu. without their knowledge or against their wishes. **3.** *Colloq.* to steal. **4.** *Prison Colloq.* to transfer without warning to another gaol. *–n.* **5.** *Prison Colloq.* an unexpected transfer to another gaol. [apparently short for 'to ship to *Shanghai*', seaport in E China]

**shanghai**[2] /'ʃæŋhaɪ/, *n., v.,* **-haied, -haiing.** *–n.* **1.** a child's catapult; sling. *–v.t.* **2.** to shoot with a catapult. [Brit. d. *shangan* a cleft stick for putting on a dog's tail]

**Shangri-la** /ʃæŋgri-'la/, *n.* a paradise on earth. Also, **Shangrila.** [from *Shangri-la,* a hidden paradise in *Lost Horizon* (1933) by James Hilton, 1900-54, English novelist]

**shank** /ʃæŋk/, *n.* **1.** that part of the leg in man between the knee and the ankle. **2.** a part in certain animals corresponding or analogous to the human shank. **3.** the whole leg. **4.** a cut of meat from the top part of the front **(fore shank)** or back **(hind shank)** leg. **5.** that portion of an instrument, tool, etc., connecting the acting part with the handle or any like part. **6.** the long, straight, middle part of an anchor. **7.** →**crook**[1] (def. 6). **8.** the latter end or part of anything. **9.** the narrow part of a shoe connecting the broad part of the sole with the heel. **10.** the piece of metal or fibre used to give it form. **11.** *Print.* the body of a type, between the shoulder and the foot. *–v.i.* **12.** (of a leaf, flower, fruit, etc.) to decay as a result of disease. **13.** *Chiefly Scot.* to travel on foot. [ME; OE *sc(e)anca,* c. LG *schanke* leg, thigh]

**shanks** /ʃæŋks/, *n.* →**shank** (def. 4).

**shanks's pony** /ʃæŋksəz 'poʊni/, *n. Colloq.* one's own legs, esp. as a means of travelling, as opposed to riding on horseback or in a conveyance. Also, **shanks's mare.**

**shan't** /ʃant/, *v. Colloq.* contraction of *shall not.*

**shantung** /ʃæn'tʌŋ/, *n.* **1.** a silk fabric, a heavy variety of pongee made of rough, spun wild silk. **2.** a fabric imitating this made of rayon or cotton. [from *Shantung,* maritime province in NE China]

**shanty**[1] /'ʃænti/, *n., pl.* **-ties.** a roughly built hut, cabin, or house. [probably from Canadian F *chantier* log hut, from F: shed, from L *canthērius* framework]

**shanty**[2] /'ʃænti/, *n., pl.* **-ties.** a sailors' song, esp. one sung in rhythm to work. Also, **chanty, chantey.** [alteration of F *chanter* sing. See CHANT]

**shanty**[3] /'ʃænti/, *n., pl.* **-ties.** a small, rough bush hotel, often unlicensed. [? Irish *sean-tig* old, miserable hut; or Canadian F *chantier* log hut]

**shanty-keeper** /'ʃænti-kipə/, *n.* the proprietor of a shanty; lamber-down.

**shantytown** /'ʃæntitaʊn/, *n.* a town or section of a town consisting of roughly built, dilapidated huts, shacks, etc.

**shape** /ʃeɪp/, *n., v.,* **shaped, shaping.** *–n.* **1.** the quality of a thing depending on its outline or external surface. **2.** the form of a particular thing, person, or being. **3.** something seen indistinctly, as in outline or silhouette. **4.** an imaginary form; phantom. **5.** an assumed appearance; guise. **6.** a particular or definite form or nature: *things taking shape.* **7.** proper form; orderly arrangement. **8.** condition: *affairs in bad shape.* **9.** something used to give form, as a mould or a pattern. **10. take shape,** to assume a definite or concrete form. [ME, n. use of SHAPE, *v.;* replacing ME *shap,* OE *(ge)sceap* form, creature, c. Icel. *skap* state, mood] *–v.t.* **11.** to give definite form, shape, or character to; fashion or form. **12.** to couch or express in words: *to shape a statement.* **13.** to adjust; adapt. **14.** to direct (one's course). *–v.i.* **15.** to develop; take place in a specified manner; assume a definite form or character (oft. fol. by *up*). **16.** to stand ready to fight (fol. by *up*). **17. shape up or ship out,** to perform as required or leave. [ME; replacing ME *schippe,* OE *scieppan* create, shape (pp. *scapen,* whence current present form), c. Goth. *gaskapjan* create] – **shaper,** *n.*

**shapeless** /ˈʃeɪpləs/, *adj.* **1.** having no definite or regular shape or form. **2.** lacking beauty or elegance of form. – **shapelessly,** *adv.* – **shapelessness,** *n.*

**shapely** /ˈʃeɪpli/, *adj.,* **-lier, -liest.** having a pleasing shape; well-formed. – **shapeliness,** *n.*

**shard** /ʃad/, *n.* **1.** a fragment, esp. of broken earthenware. **2.** *Zool.* **a.** a scale. **b.** a shell, as of an egg or snail. **3.** *Entomol.* the elytron of a beetle. Also, **sherd.** [ME; OE *sceard,* c. LG *schaard*]

**share**[1] /ʃɛə/, *n., v.,* **shared, sharing.** *–n.* **1.** the portion or part allotted or belonging to, or contributed or owed by, an individual or group. **2.** one of the equal fractional parts into which the capital stock of a limited company is divided. *–v.t.* **3.** to divide and distribute in shares; apportion. **4.** to use, participate in, enjoy, etc., jointly. *–v.i.* **5.** to have a share or part; take part (oft. fol. by *in*). [ME; OE *scearu* cutting, division, c. G *Schar* troop. See SHEAR, *v.*] – **sharer,** *n.*

**share**[2] /ʃɛə/, *n.* →**ploughshare.** [ME; OE *scear,* c. G *Schar;* akin to SHARE[1], SHEAR]

**sharebroker** /ˈʃɛəbroʊkə/, *n.* →**stockbroker.**

**share certificate** /ˈʃɛə səˌtɪfəkət/, *n.* a document showing the entitlement of its owner to a number of shares in a company.

**sharecropper** /ˈʃɛəkrɒpə/, *n. Chiefly U.S.* a tenant farmer who pays as rent a share of the crop.

**sharefarmer** /ˈʃɛəfamə/, *n.* a farmer who lives on and works the land of another, with whom he shares the proceeds from his farming.

**shareholder** /ˈʃɛəhoʊldə/, *n.* one who holds or owns a share or shares, as in a company.

**shareholders' funds** /ˈʃɛəhoʊldəz ˌfʌndz/, *n. pl.* in a company, the net amount owned by the shareholders.

**sharemilker** /ˈʃɛəmɪlkə/, *n. N.Z.* a tenant farmer who pays as rent a share from the profits of the dairy produce. – **share-milking,** *n.*

**share-out** /ˈʃɛər-aʊt/, *n.* a distribution, as of profits, etc.

**share-pusher** /ˈʃɛə-pʊʃə/, *n.* a dealer in stocks and shares who uses means, often fraudulent, to induce the public to buy them.

**share register** /ˈʃɛə rɛdʒəstə/, *n.* a register of all shareholders in a company, showing their names and addresses and the number of shares held by each shareholder.

**shark**[1] /ʃak/, *n.* any of a group of elongate elasmobranch (mostly marine) fishes, certain species of which are large and ferocious, and destructive to other fishes and sometimes dangerous to man. [orig. obscure] – **sharklike,** *adj.*

**shark**[2] /ʃak/, *n.* **1.** a person who preys greedily on others, as by swindling, usury, etc. *–v.t.* **2.** to obtain by trickery or fraud; steal. **3.** *Ball Games.* to take (the ball) from a team-mate or an opponent. *–v.i. Ball Games* **4.** to take more than one's share of play from team-mates. [G *Schork,* var. of *Schurke* rascal]

**shark bait** /ˈ– beɪt/, *n. Colloq.* one who swims where there is danger of a shark attack.

**shark bell** /ˈ– bɛl/, *n.* a bell or siren rung or sounded at a beach when a shark is sighted offshore, to order surfers from the water.

**shark fence** /ˈ– fɛns/, *n.* fencing or netting surrounding a swimming area or pool, as at a harbour beach, specifically to protect swimmers from shark attack. Also, **shark net.**

**shark-fenced** /ˈʃak-fɛnst/, *adj.* of or pertaining to a swimming area or pool with a shark fence.

**shark meshing** /ˈʃak mɛʃɪŋ/, *n.* the practice of netting sharks near heavily used surfing beaches in an attempt to reduce risk of shark attack.

**shark net** /ˈ– nɛt/, *n.* a net stretched across a bathing area to prevent sharks entering it.

**shark patrol** /ˈ– pətroʊl/, *n.* a patrol of surfing beaches, usu. conducted from an aeroplane or a motor boat, in order to give warning of sharks.

**shark-proof** /ˈʃak-pruf/, *adj.* of or pertaining to a swimming area, pool, etc., protected by a shark fence. Also, **shark-proofed.**

**shark siren** /ˈʃak saɪrən/, *n.* →**shark bell.**

**sharkskin** /ˈʃakskɪn/, *n.* a heavy rayon suiting with a dull or chalklike appearance.

**sharp** /ʃap/, *adj.* **1.** having a thin cutting edge or a fine point; well adapted for cutting or piercing. **2.** terminating in an edge or point; not blunt or rounded. **3.** having sudden change of direction, as a turn. **4.** abrupt, as an ascent. **5.** composed of hard, angular lines, as a person's features. **6.** clearly outlined; distinct. **7.** marked, as a contrast: *a sharp distinction.* **8.** pungent or biting in taste. **9.** piercing or shrill in sound. **10.** keenly cold, as weather, etc. **11.** of sand, containing very little or no clay. **12.** intensely painful; distressing: *sharp pain.* **13.** harsh; merciless: *sharp words.* **14.** fierce or violent: *a sharp struggle.* **15.** keen or eager: *sharp desire.* **16.** quick or brisk. **17.** vigilant: *a sharp watch.* **18.** mentally acute: *a sharp mind.* **19.** shrewd or astute: *sharp at making a bargain.* **20.** shrewd to the point of dishonesty: *sharp practice.* **21.** *Music.* **a.** above an intended pitch, as a note; too high. **b.** (of a note) raised a semitone in pitch: *F sharp.* **22.** *Phonet.* fortis; voiceless. **23.** stylish or elegant, esp. in an ostentatious manner. *–v.t.* **24.** *Music.* to raise in pitch, esp. one semitone. *–v.i.* **25.** *Music.* to sound above the true pitch. *–adv.* **26.** keenly or acutely. **27.** abruptly or suddenly: *to pull a horse up sharp.* **28.** punctually: *at one o'clock sharp.* **29.** vigilantly: *look sharp!* **30.** briskly; quickly. **31.** *Music.* above the true pitch. *–n.* **32.** something sharp. **33.** a needle with a very sharp point. **34.** →**sharper.** **35.** (formerly) a criminal. **36.** *Music.* **a.** a note one semitone above a given note. **b.** (in musical notation) the symbol (#) indicating this. [ME; OE *scearp,* c. G *scharf*] – **sharply,** *adv.* – **sharpness,** *n.*

**sharp-cut** /ˈʃap-kʌt/, *adj.* clearly defined; having distinct outlines.

**sharp-edged** /ˈʃap-ɛdʒd/, *adj.* having a sharp edge or edges.

**sharpen** /ˈʃapən/, *v.t.* **1.** to make sharp or sharper. *–v.i.* **2.** to become sharp or sharper. – **sharpener,** *n.*

**sharper** /ˈʃapə/, *n.* **1.** a shrewd swindler. **2.** →**cardsharper.**

**sharp-eyed** /ˈʃap-aɪd/, *adj.* having keen sight.

**sharpie** /ˈʃapi/, *n.* **1.** a kind of long, flat-bottomed boat with one or (commonly) two masts, each rigged with a triangular sail, formerly in use along the North Atlantic coast of the U.S. **2. a.** →**sharper. b.** an alert, quick-witted person. **3.** a young man belonging to a gang distinguished by efforts to dress stylishly and aggressive, anti-social behaviour.

sharpie

**sharp-set** /ˈʃap-sɛt/, *adj.* **1.** very hungry. **2.** keen or eager. **3.** set to present a sharply angled edge.

**sharpshooter** /ˈʃapʃutə/, *n.* one skilled in shooting, esp. with a rifle; marksman; sniper. – **sharpshooting,** *n.*

**sharp-sighted** /ˈʃap-saɪtəd/, *adj.* **1.** having keen sight. **2.** having or showing mental acuteness. – **sharp-sightedness,** *n.*

**sharp-tongued** /ˈʃap-tʌŋd/, *adj.* characterised by harshness or bitterness in speech.

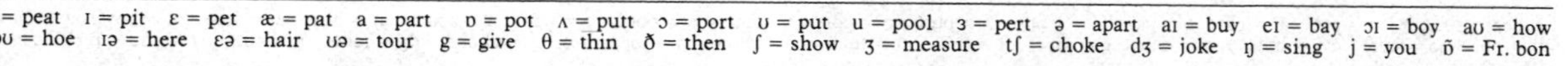

**sharp-witted** /ˈʃap-wɪtəd/, *adj.* having or showing a keen intelligence; acute. – **sharp-wittedness,** *n.*

**shashlik** /ˈʃæʃlɪk/, *n.* →**shish kebab.** Also, **shashlick, shaslick.** [Russ. *shashlyk,* of Turkic orig.]

**shasta daisy** /ʃæstə ˈdeɪzi/, *n.* a perennial herb, *Chrysanthemum maximum,* with large white flowers often 10 cm in diameter usu. borne singly on long leafless peduncles.

**shat** /ʃæt/, *v.* **1.** *Colloq.* past tense and past participle of **shit. 2. be shat off,** to have had enough of, be upset with (usu. fol. by *with*).

**shatter** /ˈʃætə/, *v.t.* **1.** to break in pieces, as by a blow. **2.** to damage, as by breaking or crushing: *ships shattered by storms.* **3.** to impair; weaken; destroy (health, nerves, etc.). *–v.i.* **4.** to break suddenly into fragments. [ME *schater(en).* Cf. SCATTER]

**shatterproof glass** /ˌʃætəpruf ˈglas/, *n.* **1.** →**laminated glass. 2.** glass strengthened by tempering so that it breaks into relatively harmless granules rather than large jagged pieces.

**shave** /ʃeɪv/, *v.,* **shaved, shaved** or **shaven, shaving,** *n.* *–v.i.* **1.** to remove a growth of beard with a razor. *–v.t.* **2.** to remove hair from (the face, legs, etc.) by cutting it close to the skin. **3.** to cut off (hair, esp. the beard) close to the skin (oft. fol. by *off* or *away*). **4.** to cut or scrape away the surface of with a sharp-edged tool: *to shave hides in preparing leather.* **5.** to reduce to shavings or thin slices: *to shave wood.* **6.** to cut or trim closely: *to shave a lawn.* **7.** to scrape or graze; come very near to: *to shave a corner.* *–n.* **8.** the act or process of shaving. **9.** a thin slice; a shaving. **10.** a narrow miss or escape: *a close shave.* **11.** any of various tools for shaving, scraping, removing thin slices, etc. [ME; OE *sceafan,* c. D, LG *schaven,* G *schaben*]

**shave coat** /ˈ– koʊt/, *n.* →**shaving jacket.**

**shaveling** /ˈʃeɪvlɪŋ/, *n. Archaic.* **1.** a shaven-headed clergyman. **2.** young fellow; youngster.

**shaver** /ˈʃeɪvə/, *n.* **1.** one who shaves. **2.** that which shaves: *electric shaver.* **3.** *Colloq.* a youngster; fellow. **4.** one who makes close bargains or is extortionate.

**Shavian** /ˈʃeɪviən/, *adj.* **1.** of, pertaining to, or characteristic of George Bernard Shaw, 1856-1950, dramatist, critic and novelist: *Shavian wit.* *–n.* **2.** an admirer of George Bernard Shaw or of his works.

**shaving** /ˈʃeɪvɪŋ/, *n.* **1.** (*oft. pl.*) a very thin piece or slice, esp. of wood. **2.** the act of one who or that which shaves.

**shaving jacket** /ˈ– dʒækət/, *n.* a man's short-length dressing gown.

**shaving rash** /ˈ– ræʃ/, *n.* a minor irritation of the skin caused by shaving.

**shawl** /ʃɔl/, *n.* a piece of material, worn as a covering for the shoulders, head, etc., chiefly by women, in place of coat or hat, sometimes as a decoration. [Pers. *shāl*]

**shawm** /ʃɔm/, *n.* an early woodwind instrument with a double reed, forerunner of the modern oboe. [ME *schallemelle,* from OF *chalemel,* from LL *calamellus* little pipe, from L *calamus* reed]

**shay** /ʃeɪ/, *n. Colloq.* →**chaise.** [backformation from CHAISE, taken as pl.]

**shd,** should.

**she** /ʃi/, *pron., poss.* **her,** *obj.* **her,** *pl.* **they;** *n., pl.* **shes;** *adj.* *–pron.* **1.** the female in question or last mentioned. **2.** used (instead of *it*) of things to which female sex is attributed, as a ship. **3.** used (instead of *it*) in phrases: *she'll be right, she's apples.* *–n.* **4.** any woman or any female person or animal (correlative to *he*). *–adj.* **5.** female or feminine, esp. of animals. [ME, sandhi var. of ME *ghe,* OE *hēo.* See HE]

**shea** /ʃɪə/, *n.* an African tree, *Butyrospermum parkii,* the seeds of which yield a butter-like fat (**shea butter**), used as food, in making soap, etc. [Mandingo *sye*]

**sheaf** /ʃif/, *n., pl.* **sheaves,** *v.* *–n.* **1.** one of the bundles in which cereal plants, as wheat, rye, etc., are bound after reaping. **2.** any bundle, cluster, or collection: *a sheaf of papers.* *–v.t.* **3.** to bind into a sheaf or sheaves. [ME *shefe,* OE *scēaf,* c. D *schoof,* G *Schaub* wisp of straw]

**shear** /ʃɪə/, *v.,* **sheared** or (*Archaic*) **shore; sheared** or **shorn; shearing;** *n.* *–v.t.* **1.** to remove by or as by cutting with a sharp instrument: *to shear wool from sheep.* **2.** to cut the hair, fleece, wool, etc., from. **3.** to strip or deprive (fol. by *of*): *shorn of its legislative powers.* **4.** to reap with a sickle. **5.** *Archaic.* to cut with a sharp instrument (usu. fol. by *through*). *–v.i.* **6.** *Physics.* to become fractured by a shear or shears. **7.** to reap grain, etc., with a sickle. *–n.* **8.** (*pl.*) scissors of large size. **9.** (*pl.*) any of various other cutting implements or machines resembling or suggesting scissors. **10.** one blade of a pair of shears. **11.** the act or process of shearing. **12.** a shearing of sheep (used in stating the age of sheep): *a sheep of one shear (one year old).* **13.** a quantity of wool, grass, etc., cut off at one shearing. **14.** any machine using an adaption of the shearing principle, esp. to cut metal sheets. **15.** *Physics.* the tendency produced by loads to deform or fracture a member by sliding one section against another. **16.** (*pl.*) shearlegs. [ME *shere(n),* OE *sceran,* c. D and G *scheren,* Icel. *skera*] – **shearer,** *n.*

**shearer** /ˈʃɪərə/, *n.* **1.** one who shears sheep. **2.** one who uses shears on metal, textiles, leather or other materials. **3.** a sheep that is fit and ready for shearing, or that yields a good fleece: *that sheep is a good shearer.*

shearer (def. 1)

**shear-hog** /ˈʃɪə-hɒg/, *n.* a sheep after its first shearing. Also, **shearling.**

**shearing** /ˈʃɪərɪŋ/, *n.* **1.** the act of shearing sheep. **2.** the time or season of shearing sheep.

**shearing board** /ˈ– bɔd/, *n.* the wooden floor of a shed, about two metres wide, on which sheep are shorn.

**shearing paddock** /ˈ– pædək/, *n.* →**holding paddock.**

**shearing shed** /ˈ– ʃɛd/, *n.* a building on a sheep station in which the shearing is done.

**shearlegs** /ˈʃɪəlɛgz/, *n.* an apparatus for hoisting heavy weights, consisting of two or more spars fastened together near the top with their lower ends separated and a tackle suspended from the top and steadying guys. Also, **shears, sheerlegs.**

**shear modulus** /ˈʃɪə mɒdʒələs/, *n.* →**modulus of rigidity.**

**shear pin** /ˈ– pɪn/, *n.* a replaceable pin inserted at a critical point in a machine and designed to break off when subjected to excess stress. Also, **break pin.**

**shear strain** /ˈ– streɪn/, *n.* the lateral deformation produced in a body by a shearing force, usu. expressed as the ratio of the lateral displacement between two points lying in parallel planes to the vertical distance between them.

**shear stress** /ˈ– strɛs/, *n.* the magnitude of a shearing force per unit area of cross-section.

**shearwater** /ˈʃɪəwɔtə/, *n.* any of various long-winged seabirds, esp. of the genus *Puffinus,* allied to the petrels, appearing, when flying low, to cleave the water with their wings. [SHEAR, *v.* + WATER, *n.*]

**shear zone** /ˈʃɪə zoʊn/, *n.* a geological zone in which shearing has occurred on a large scale, so that the rock is crushed and brecciated.

**sheatfish** /ˈʃitfɪʃ/, *n., pl.* **-fishes,** (*esp. collectively*) **-fish.** a large freshwater fish, *Silurus glanis,* the great catfish of central and eastern Europe, sometimes reaching 180 kilograms. [alteration of *sheathfish,* perhaps influenced by G *Schaid* sheatfish; see SHEATH, FISH[1]]

**sheath** /ʃiθ/, *n., pl.* **sheaths** /ʃiðz, ʃiθs/, *v.* *–n.* **1.** a case or covering for the blade of a sword, dagger, or the like. **2.** any similar covering. **3.** *Biol.* a closely enveloping part or structure, as in an animal or plant organism. **4.** *Bot.* the leaf base when it forms a vertical coating surrounding the stem. **5.** *Elect.* the metal covering of a cable. **6.** →**contraceptive sheath. 7.** a close-fitting dress which follows the contours of the body, usu. having no belt. *–v.t.* **8.** to sheathe. [ME *sheth(e),* OE *scēath,* c. G *Scheide*]

**sheathbill** /ˈʃiθbɪl/, *n.* either of two seabirds with white plumage, *Chionis alba* and *C. minor,* of the colder parts of the Southern Hemisphere, so called from the horny case which partly sheathes the bill.

**sheathe** /ʃið/, *v.t.,* **sheathed, sheathing. 1.** to put (a sword, etc.) into a sheath. **2.** to plunge (a sword, etc.) in something as if in a sheath. **3.** to enclose in or as in a casing or covering. **4.** to cover or provide with a protective layer or sheathing: *to sheathe a roof with copper.* [ME *shethe,* from SHEATH] – **sheather,** *n.*

**sheathing** /ˈʃiðɪŋ/, *n.* **1.** the act of one who sheathes. **2.** that which sheathes; a covering or outer layer of metal, wood, or other material, as one of the metal plates on a ship's bottom, the first covering of boards on a house, etc. **3.** material for forming any such covering.

**sheath-knife** /ˈʃiθ-naɪf/, *n.* a knife carried in a sheath.

**sheath rot** /ˈʃiθ rɒt/, *n.* →**pizzle rot.**

**sheave**[1] /ʃiv/, *v.t.,* **sheaved, sheaving.** to gather, collect, or bind into a sheaf or sheaves. [from SHEAF]

**sheave**[2] /ʃiv/, *n.* **1.** a grooved wheel forming a pulley. **2.** any of various other wheels or discs with a grooved rim. [ME *sheeve;* akin to G *Scheibe* disc]

**sheave-block** /ˈʃiv-blɒk/, *n.* an iron or wooden shell on a ship, etc., containing a revolving sheave or sheaves through which a rope runs.

**sheaves** /ʃivz/, *n.* **1.** plural of **sheaf. 2.** plural of **sheave.**

**shebang** /ʃəˈbæŋ/, *n. Colloq.* **1.** thing; affair; business. **2.** a hut; shanty; shack. **3.** *N.Z.* a disturbance; brawl.

**shebeen** /ʃəˈbin/, *n.* **1.** *Irish and Scot.* a place where alcoholic drinks are sold illegally. **2.** *S. African.* such an illegal tavern for Africans. **3.** any cheap or sordid tavern. [Irish *sībīn* small mug, small beer]

**sheckles** /ˈʃɛkəlz/, *n. pl.* →**shekel** (def. 3).

**shed**[1] /ʃɛd/, *n.* **1.** a slight or rough structure built for shelter, storage, etc. **2.** a large, strongly built structure, often open at the sides or end. **3.** →**outhouse. 4.** *N.Z.* →**freezing works. 5.** a shearing shed; woolshed. *–v.t.* **6.** to herd (sheep) into a shed. **7.** to place or keep (animals) under cover. [ME *shadde,* OE *scead, sced* shelter, SHADE]

**shed**[2] /ʃɛd/, *v.,* **shed, shedding,** *n. –v.t.* **1.** to pour forth (water, etc.) as a fountain. **2.** to emit and let fall (tears). **3.** to cast; give or send forth (light, sound, fragrance, etc.). **4.** to throw off readily: *cloth that sheds water.* **5.** to cast off or let fall by natural process (leaves, hair, feathers, skin, shell, etc.). **6. shed blood, a.** to cause blood to flow. **b.** to kill by violence. *–v.i.* **7.** to fall off, as leaves, etc.; drop out, as seed, grain, etc. **8.** to cast off hair, feathers, skin, or other covering or parts by natural process. *–n.* **9.** →**watershed. 10.** *Textiles.* an opening in the warp threads made by the heddles through which the shuttle passes. [ME; OE *scēadan,* earlier *sc(e)ādan,* c. D and G *scheiden*]

**she'd** /ʃid/, contraction of: **1.** she had. **2.** she would.

**shed-boss** /ˈʃɛd-bɒs/, *n.* the boss of a shearing shed.

**shedder** /ˈʃɛdə/, *n.* **1.** one who or that which sheds. **2.** a lobster, crab, etc., just before it sheds its shell.

**shedhand** /ˈʃɛdhænd/, *n.* (in a shearing shed) an unskilled worker who moves the wool from the shearers to the classers.

**sheen** /ʃin/, *n.* **1.** lustre; brightness; radiance. **2.** *Poetic.* gleaming attire. *–adj. Archaic.* **3.** shining. **4.** beautiful. [ME *sheene,* d. OE *scēne* beautiful, bright, c. G *schön*]

**sheeny**[1] /ˈʃini/, *adj.* shining; lustrous.

**sheeny**[2] /ˈʃini/, *n. Brit. (derog.)* a Jew.

**sheep** /ʃip/, *n., pl.* **sheep. 1.** any of the ruminant mammals constituting the genus *Ovis* (family Bovidae), closely allied to the goats, esp. *O. aries,* which has many domesticated varieties or breeds, valuable for their flesh, fleece, etc. **2.** leather made from the skin of these animals. **3.** a meek, timid, or stupid person. **4. separate the sheep from the goats,** to distinguish the good, worthy, or superior people or things from the rest. [ME; OE *scēp* (Anglian), *scēap,* c. G *Schaf*] – **sheeplike,** *adj.*

sheep (def. 1): a merino

**sheepcote** /ˈʃipkoʊt/, *n. Chiefly Brit.* a pen or covered structure for sheltering sheep.

**sheep dip** /ˈʃip dɪp/, *n.* **1.** a lotion or wash applied to the fleece or skin of sheep to kill vermin. **2.** a deep trough containing such a liquid through which sheep are driven.

**sheepdog** /ˈʃipdɒg/, *n.* a dog trained to watch and muster sheep.

**sheepdog trial** /ˈ– traɪəl/, *n.* a competition for sheepdogs in which their ability to round up and manoeuvre sheep is tested.

**sheepfold** /ˈʃipfoʊld/, *n.* an enclosure for sheep.

**sheepish** /ˈʃipɪʃ/, *adj.* **1.** awkwardly bashful or embarrassed. **2.** like sheep, as in meekness, timidity, etc. – **sheepishly,** *adv.* – **sheepishness,** *n.*

**sheepman** /ˈʃipmæn/, *n.* a farmer who raises sheep.

**sheep measles** /ˈʃip mizəlz/, *n.* infestation of the muscles of a sheep with cysticerci of a tapeworm, *Taenia ovis.*

**sheep nuts** /ˈ– nʌts/, *n.pl.* a food concentrate in pellet form for feeding to sheep.

**sheepo** /ˈʃipoʊ/, *n.* a shearing-shed hand employed to keep shearers' pens full of sheep.

**sheep-run** /ˈʃip-rʌn/, *n.* a property on which sheep are grazed for wool or mutton production. Also, **sheep station.**

**sheep's bit** /ˈʃips bɪt/, *n.* a biennial herb with dense heads of small blue flowers, *Jasione montana,* occurring in grasslands in Europe.

**sheep's eyes** /ˈ– aɪz/, *n. pl.* amorous or love-sick glances.

**sheep's fescue** /– ˈfɛskju/, *n.* a variable perennial grass, *Festuca ovina.*

**sheepshank** /ˈʃipʃæŋk/, *n.* a kind of knot, hitch, or bend made on a rope to shorten it temporarily.

**sheepshearing** /ˈʃipʃɪərɪŋ/, *n.* **1.** the act of shearing sheep. **2.** the time or season of shearing sheep, or a feast held then. – **sheepshearer,** *n.*

**sheep-sick** /ˈʃip-sɪk/, *adj.* (of land) depleted or exhausted through overstocking with sheep.

**sheepskin** /ˈʃipskɪn/, *n.* **1.** the skin of a sheep, esp. such a skin dressed with the wool on, as for a garment. **2.** leather, parchment, or the like made from the skin of sheep. *–adj.* **3.** made from the skin of a sheep.

**sheep's sorrel** /ʃips ˈsɒrəl/, *n.* a widespread herb, *Acetosella vulgaris,* with hastate leaves of an acid taste, abounding in poor, dry soils of temperate regions.

**sheep station** /ˈʃip steɪʃən/, *n.* a property on which sheep are raised. Also, **sheep run.**

**sheep strike** /ˈ– straɪk/, *n.* an infestation of the flesh of a living sheep by the maggots of a blowfly, esp. the blue blowfly. Also, **blowfly strike.**

**sheep tick** /ˈ– tɪk/, *n.* a parasitic, wingless fly, *Melophagus ovinus,* of the dipterous family Hippoboscidae which afflicts sheep.

**sheep vanner** /ˈ– vænə/, *n. Colloq.* a very young calf, small enough to be transported in a sheep van.

**sheepwalk** /ˈʃipwɔk/, *n.* **1.** *Brit.* a tract of land on which sheep are pastured. **2.** the track made by sheep walking through a paddock.

**sheer**[1] /ʃɪə/, *adj.* **1.** transparently thin; diaphanous, as fabrics, etc. **2.** unmixed with anything else. **3.** unqualified; utter: *a sheer waste of time.* **4.** extending down or up very steeply: *a sheer descent of rock.* **5.** *Obs.* bright; shining. *–adv.* **6.** clear; completely; quite. **7.** down or up very steeply. *–n.* **8.** thin, diaphanous material, as chiffon or voile. [ME *schere,* c. Icel. *skǣrr* clear, bright, pure; akin to OE *scīr*] – **sheerly,** *adv.* – **sheerness,** *n.*

**sheer**[2] /ʃɪə/, *v.i.* **1.** to deviate from a course, as a ship; swerve. *–v.t.* **2.** to cause to sheer. *–n.* **3.** a deviation or divergence, as of a ship from her course; a swerve. **4.** the upward longitudinal curve of a ship's deck or bulwarks. **5.** the position in which a ship at anchor is placed to keep her clear of the anchor. [special use of SHEAR, *v.* Cf. D and G *scheren* depart]

**sheerlegs** /ˈʃɪəlɛgz/, *n. pl.* →**shearlegs.**

**sheet**[1] /ʃit/, *n.* **1.** a large rectangular piece of linen, cotton, or other material, used as an article of bedding, commonly one of a pair spread immediately above and below the sleeper. **2.** a broad, thin mass, layer, or covering. **3.** a broad, relatively thin, piece of iron, glass, etc. **4.** an oblong or square piece of paper or parchment, esp. one on which to write or print. **5.** a newspaper. **6.** *Print., Bookbinding.* a piece of paper printed and folded so as to form pages of the required size. **7.** *Philately.* the impression from a plate, etc., on a single piece of paper, before the individual stamps have been separated. **8.** an extent, stretch, or expanse, as of lightning, water, etc.: *sheets of flame.* **9.** *Geol.* a more or less horizontal mass of rock, esp. eruptive rock, intruded between strata or spread over a surface. *–v.t.* **10.** to furnish with sheets. **11.** to wrap in a sheet. **12.** to cover with a sheet or layer of something: *sheeted with ice.* [ME *shete,* OE *scēte* (Anglian), *scīete,* from *scēat* lap, c. G *Schoss,* Icel. *skaut* skirt]

**sheet**² /ʃit/, *n.* **1.** *Naut.* a rope or chain fastened: **a.** to a lower aftercorner of a sail, or to the boom of a fore-and-aft sail, to control its trim. **b.** to both lower corners of a square sail to extend them to the yardarms below. **2.** (*pl.*) the spaces beyond the thwarts in the forward or the after end of an open boat. **3. three sheets in** (or **to**) **the wind,** *Colloq.* intoxicated. *–v.t.* **4.** *Naut.* to trim, extend, or secure by means of a sheet or sheets. **5. sheet home, a.** to extend (sails) to the utmost by hauling on the sheets. **b.** to attach (blame, responsibility, etc.). [ME *schete,* OE *scēata* rope tied to lower corner of a sail, c. LG *schote;* in some senses akin to SHOOT]

**sheet anchor** /'– æŋkə/, *n.* **1.** a large anchor used only in cases of emergency. **2.** a final reliance or resource. [late ME *shute anker;* orig. uncert.]

**sheet bend** /'– bɛnd/, *n. Naut.* a knot used to bend the end of a line on to a bight or eye of another line, used esp. with large lines.

sheet bend

**sheethand** /'ʃithænd/, *n.* a member of a sailing crew who handles the sheets, esp. mainsheet.

**sheeting** /'ʃitɪŋ/, *n.* **1.** the act of covering with or forming into sheets. **2.** material used for making sheets, as cotton, linen, etc.

**sheet iron** /'ʃit aɪən/, *n.* iron in sheets or thin plates.

**sheet lightning** /'– laɪtnɪŋ/, *n.* lightning appearing merely as a general illumination over a broad surface, usu. due to the reflection of the lightning of a distant thunderstorm.

**sheet metal** /'– mɛtl/, *n.* metal in sheets or thin plates.

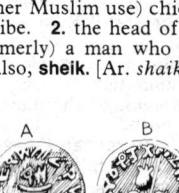

**sheet music** /'– mjuzɪk/, *n.* musical compositions printed on unbound sheets.

**sheikh** /ʃik, ʃeɪk/, *n.* **1.** (in Arab and other Muslim use) chief or head; the headman of a village or tribe. **2.** the head of a Muslim religious body. **3.** *Colloq.* (formerly) a man who is boldly amorous towards many women. Also, **sheik.** [Ar. *shaikh* old man]

**sheikhdom** /'ʃikdəm, 'ʃeɪk-/, *n.* the land or territory under the control of a sheikh. Also, **sheikdom.**

Hebrew shekel (def. 2): A, obverse; B, reverse

**sheila** /'ʃilə/, *n. Colloq.* **1.** a girl or woman: *a beaut sheila.* **2.** a girlfriend. [probably from *Sheila,* Irish girl's name]

**shekel** /'ʃɛkəl/, *n.* **1.** an ancient, originally Babylonian, unit of weight. **2.** a coin of this weight, esp. the chief silver coin of the Hebrews. **3.** (*pl.*) Also, **sheckles.** *Colloq.* money. [Heb. *sheqel,* akin to *shāqal* weigh]

**sheldrake** /'ʃɛldreɪk/, *n., pl.* **-drakes,** (*esp. collectively*) **-drake.** a male shelduck. [ME *shelded-rake,* from *sheld* particoloured (now obs.) + DRAKE]

sheldrake

**shelduck** /'ʃɛldʌk/, *n., pl.* **-ducks,** (*esp. collectively*) **-duck. 1.** any of the Old World ducks constituting the genera *Tadorna* and *Casarca,* certain of which are highly variegated in colour. **2.** any of various other ducks, esp. the goosander or merganser. [SHEL(DRAKE) + DUCK¹]

**shelf** /ʃɛlf/, *n., pl.* **shelves,** *v.* *–n.* **1.** a thin slab of wood or other material fixed horizontally to a wall, or in a frame, for supporting objects. **2.** the contents of such a shelf. **3.** a shelf-like surface or projection; a ledge. **4.** a sandbank or submerged extent of rock in the sea or a river. **5.** *Mining, etc.* bedrock, as under alluvial deposits. **6.** *Archery.* the upper portion of the hand, as it grasps the bow, on which the arrow rests. **7.** *Colloq.* →**informer. 8. on the shelf,** (of a woman) unattached or unmarried, and without prospects of marriage. *–v.t.* **9.** *Colloq.* to inform on (someone). [ME. Cf. LG *schelf;* akin to OE *scylfe*] – **shelf-like,** *adj.*

**shelf life** /'– laɪf/, *n.* the period in which a product may remain on the shelf before being purchased, and still be marketable.

**shelf mark** /'– mak/, *n.* a symbol on the spine of a book indicating the place where it belongs in a library.

**shell** /ʃɛl/, *n., pl.* **shells** or (*for defs 7-10*) **shell. 1.** a hard outer covering of an animal, as the hard case of a mollusc, or either half of the case of a bivalve mollusc. **2.** any of various objects resembling a shell, as in shape, or in being more or less concave or hollow. **3.** the material constituting any of various kinds of shells. **4.** the hard exterior of an egg. **5.** a more or less hard outer covering of a seed, fruit, or the like, as the hard outside portion of a nut, the pod of peas, etc. **6.** an enclosing case or cover suggesting a shell. **7.** a hollow projectile for a cannon, etc., filled with an explosive charge arranged to explode during flight or upon impact or after penetration. **8.** a metallic cartridge used in small arms and small artillery pieces. **9.** a cartridge. **10.** a cartridge-like pyrotechnic device which explodes in the air. **11.** *Cookery.* a flan-case; pastry-case. **12.** *Physics.* a class of electron orbits in an atom, all of which have the same energy. **13.** *Rowing.* a light racing boat having a very thin, carvel-built hull; best boat; fine boat. **14.** →**tortoiseshell. 15.** →**mollusc. 16.** the walls, external structure, etc., of an unfinished building, ship, etc., or of one whose interior has been destroyed: *after the fire only the shell of the factory remained.* **17.** *Bldg Trades.* a roof whose surface is used as a structural membrane. **18. come out of one's shell,** to emerge from a state of shyness or reserve. *–v.t.* **19.** to take out of the shell, pod, etc. **20.** to remove the shell of. **21.** to separate (maize, etc.) from the ear or cob. **22.** to throw shells or explosive projectiles into, upon, or among; bombard. **23. shell out,** *Colloq.* to hand over; pay up. *–v.i.* **24.** to fall or come out of the shell, husk, etc. **25.** to come away or fall off, as a shell or outer coat. [ME; OE *scell* (Anglian), *sciell,* c. D *schel.* See SCALE¹] – **shell-like,** *adj.*

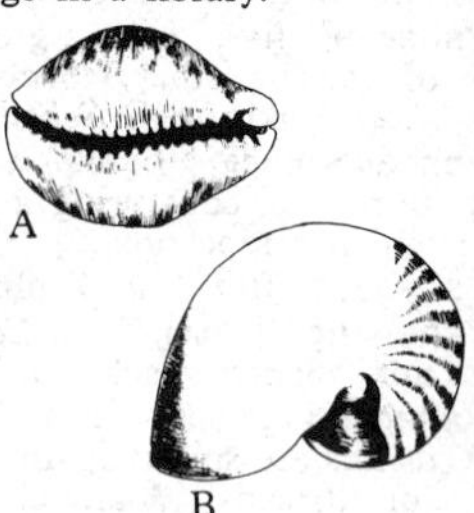


shells (def. 1): A, cowry; B, nautilis

**she'll** /ʃil/; *weak form* /ʃəl/, contraction of: **1.** she will. **2.** she shall.

**shellac** /ʃə'læk/, *n., v.,* **-lacked, -lacking.** *–n.* **1.** lac which has been purified and formed into thin plates, used for making varnish, polish, and sealing wax, and in electrical insulation. **2.** a varnish (**shellac varnish**) made by dissolving this material in alcohol or a similar solvent. *–v.t.* **3.** to coat or treat with shellac. [SHELL + LAC, translation of F *laque en écailles* lac in thin plates] – **shellacker,** *n.*

**shellacking** /'ʃɛlækɪŋ/, *n. Colloq.* a beating; thrashing.

**shellback** /'ʃɛlbæk/, *n.* an experienced sailor, esp. an old one.

**shellbark** /'ʃɛlbak/, *n.* →**shagbark.**

**shell bean** /'ʃɛl bin/, *n. U.S.* **1.** any of the various kinds of bean (plant) which are cultivated for their edible seeds. **2.** the seed itself.

**shellfire** /'ʃɛlfaɪə/, *n.* the firing of explosive shells or projectiles.

**shellfish** /'ʃɛlfɪʃ/, *n., pl.* **-fishes,** (*esp. collectively*) **-fish.** an aquatic animal (not a fish in the ordinary sense) having a shell, as the oyster and other molluscs and the lobster and other crustaceans. [ME *shelfish,* OE *scilfisc,* c. Icel. *skelfiskr.* See SHELL, FISH¹]

**shell-like** /'ʃɛl-laɪk/, *n. Colloq.* (*joc.*) an ear: *a word in your shell-like, please.*

**shellproof** /'ʃɛlpruf/, *adj.* protected against the explosive

i = peat ɪ = pit ɛ = pet æ = pat a = part ɒ = pot ʌ = putt ɔ = port ʊ = put u = pool ɜ = pert ə = apart aɪ = buy eɪ = bay ɔɪ = boy aʊ = how oʊ = hoe ɪə = here ɛə = hair ʊə = tour g = give θ = thin ð = then ʃ = show ʒ = measure tʃ = choke dʒ = joke ŋ = sing j = you õ = Fr. bon

effect of shells or bombs.

**shell shock** /'ʃɛl ʃɒk/, *n.* nervous or mental disorder in various forms, characterised by loss of self-command, memory, speech, sight, etc., at first supposed to be brought on by the explosion of shells in battle, but now explained as the result of the cumulative strain of modern warfare. – **shell-shocked,** *adj.*

**shelly** /'ʃɛli/, *adj.,* **-lier, -liest. 1.** abounding in shells. **2.** consisting of a shell or shells. **3.** like a shell or shells.

**Shelta** /'ʃɛltə/, *n.* a tinkers' jargon of Ireland and parts of Britain, based on deliberately altered Gaelic. [orig. obscure]

**shelter** /'ʃɛltə/, *n.* **1.** something which affords protection or refuge, as from bad weather, bombing, etc.; a place of refuge or safety. **2.** protection afforded; refuge. **3.** an institution for the care of destitute or delinquent children. *–v.t.* **4.** to be a shelter for; afford shelter to. **5.** to provide with a shelter; placed under cover. **6.** to protect as by shelter; take under one's protection. *–v.i.* **7.** to take shelter; find a refuge. [orig. uncert.] – **shelterer,** *n.* – **shelterless,** *adj.*

**sheltered housing** /ʃɛltəd 'haʊzɪŋ/, *n.* housing for elderly or disabled people in which each person lives in a separate unit, the whole complex being under the care of a resident supervisor.

**sheltered workshop** /ʃɛltəd 'wɜkʃɒp/, *n.* a factory or workshop set up to provide work for handicapped people.

**shelter-shed** /'ʃɛltə-ʃɛd/, *n.* **1.** a shed in a school playground to house children when eating their lunch, or when it rains. **2.** any of various rustic sheds set up by councils, park authorities, etc., to protect picnickers, bushwalkers, and others, from the weather.

**sheltie** /'ʃɛlti/, *n.* →**Shetland pony.**

**shelve**[1] /ʃɛlv/, *v.t.,* **shelved, shelving. 1.** to place on a shelf or shelves. **2.** to lay or put aside from consideration: *to shelve the question.* **3.** to remove from active service; cease to employ; dismiss. **4.** to furnish with shelves. **5.** to betray (a person who has committed a misdemeanour) to the authorities. [backformation from *shelves,* pl. of SHELF]

**shelve**[2] /ʃɛlv/, *v.i.,* **shelved, shelving.** to slope gradually. [orig. disputed; cf. OE *sceolh* squinting, awry, Icel. *skelgja* make squint]

**shelving** /'ʃɛlvɪŋ/, *n.* **1.** material for shelves. **2.** shelves collectively.

**shemozzle** /ʃə'mɒzl/, *n. Colloq.* **1.** a confused state of affairs; muddle. **2.** an uproar; row. [Yiddish *schlemozzel,* from Heb. *shellōmazzāl* bad luck]

**shenanigan** /ʃə'nænəgən/, *n.* (*oft. pl.*) *Colloq.* nonsense; deceit; trickery. [orig. uncert.]

**she-oak** /'ʃi-oʊk/, *n.* **1.** any casuarina which has slender, grooved, green branches bearing whorls of scale leaves, and hard durable wood. **2.** *Obs. Colloq.* beer.

**Sheol** /'ʃioʊl, 'ʃiɒl/, *n.* **1.** the abode of the dead or of departed spirits. **2.** (*l.c.*) hell. [Heb.]

**shepherd** /'ʃɛpəd/, *n.* **1.** a man who minds sheep in the pasture or while they are being driven from one place to another. **2.** one who watches over or protects a group of people. **3.** a clergyman. **4. the Shepherd,** Jesus Christ. **5.** a miner who retains a claim without working it. *–v.t.* **6.** to tend or guard as a shepherd. **7.** to watch over carefully. **8.** to move (people) along. **9.** (of a miner) to retain (a claim) without working it. **10.** *Aus. Rules.* to protect (a team-mate) by blocking or shouldering a member of the opposing side who comes within a short distance of the ball, so as to give the team-mate a clear area of play. **11.** *Rugby Football.* illegally to protect (a team-mate) from attack by opponents. [ME *shepherde,* OE *scēphyrde.* See SHEEP, HERD[2]] – **shepherdess** /'ʃɛpədɛs/, *n. fem.*

**shepherd dog** /'– dɒg/, *n.* →**sheepdog.**

**shepherd's check** /ʃɛpədz 'tʃɛk/, *n.* →**shepherd's plaid.**

**shepherd's cress** /– 'krɛs/, *n.* a small, annual herb, *Teesdalia nudicaulis,* of sandy places in Europe and northern Africa.

**shepherd's needle** /– 'nidl/, *n.* an annual umbelliferous herb with long narrow fruits, *Scandix pecten-veneris,* a widespread weed of cultivated land in temperate regions.

**shepherd's pie** /– 'paɪ/, *n.* a cooked dish of seasoned mince, topped with a crust of browned mashed potato; cottage pie.

**shepherd's plaid** /– 'plæd/, *n.* a woollen shawl-like material, made in a checked pattern. Also, **shepherd's check.**

**shepherd's-purse** /ʃɛpədz-'pɜs/, *n.* a herb of the family Cruciferae, *Capsella bursa-pastoris,* with white flowers and purselike pods.

**sherardise** /'ʃɛrədaɪz/, *v.t.,* **-dised, -dising.** to plate iron or steel with zinc by heating the metal in contact with zinc powder to a temperature slightly below the melting point of zinc. Also, **sherardize.** [named after *Sherard* Cowper-Coles, d. 1936, English inventor]

**Sheraton** /'ʃɛrətən/, *adj.* a style of furniture characterised by straight lines, graceful proportions, wood inlay, and sparing use of carving. [named after Thomas *Sheraton,* 1751-1806, English cabinet-maker and furniture designer]

**sherbet** /'ʃɜbət/, *n.* **1.** a powdered confection eaten dry or used to make effervescent drinks. **2.** Also, **sorbet.** a frozen fruit-flavoured mixture, made with egg whites, gelatine, etc. **3.** *Colloq.* beer. [Turk. and Pers., from Ar. *sharbah,* lit., a drink]

**sherd** /ʃɜd/, *n.* →**shard.**

**sherif** /ʃə'rif/, *n.* **1.** the governor of Mecca, traditionally a descendant of the Prophet Mohammed. **2.** an Arab prince or ruler. **3.** →**emir** (def. 2). Also, **shereef.** [Ar. *sharīf* noble, glorious, from *sharafa* be exalted]

**sheriff** /'ʃɛrəf/, *n.* **1.** *Law.* an officer of the Supreme Court with duties relating to service and execution of processes, summoning of juries, etc. **2.** *Brit.* the chief officer of the Crown in a county, appointed annually. **3.** *U.S.* the law enforcement officer of a county or other civil subdivision of a state. [ME *sher(r)ef,* OE *scīrgerēfa.* See SHIRE, REEVE[1]]

**sheriff's officer** /ʃɛrəfs 'ɒfəsə/, *n.* →**bailiff.**

**sherry** /'ʃɛri/, *n., pl.* **-ries.** a fortified and blended wine of southern Spain, or a similar wine made elsewhere. [earlier *sherris,* taken as pl., from Sp. (*vino de*) *Xeres* (wine of) Xeres, now Jerez in S Spain]

**Shetland pony** /ʃɛtlənd 'poʊni/, *n.* a pony of a small, sturdy, rough-coated breed. Also, **sheltie.** [from the *Shetland* Islands, a Scottish island group NE of the mainland, where the ponies were orig. bred]

Shetland pony

**Shetland wool** /– 'wʊl/, *n.* **1.** the wool of Shetland sheep. **2.** thin, loosely twisted, wool yarn for knitting or weaving.

**shew** /ʃoʊ/, *v.t., v.i.,* **shewed, shewn, shewing,** *n. Chiefly Archaic.* →**show.**

**shewbread** /'ʃoʊbrɛd/, *n.* (among the ancient Jews) the bread placed every Sabbath before Jehovah, on the table beside the altar of incense, and eaten at the end of the week by the priests alone. Also, **showbread.** [translation of G *Schaubrot,* L (Vulgate) *pānes prōpositionis,* Gk (Septuagint) *ártoi enṓpioi,* rendering Heb. *lechem pānīm*]

**SHF,** *Radio.* super high frequency.

**shibboleth** /'ʃɪbəlɛθ/, *n.* **1.** a peculiarity of pronunciation, or a habit, mode of dress, etc., which distinguishes a particular class or set of persons. **2.** a test word or pet phrase of a party, sect, etc. [Heb.: stream in flood; a word used by Jephthah as a test word by which to distinguish the fleeing Ephraimites (who could not pronounce the *sh*) from his own men, the Gileadites (Judges 12:4-6.)]

**shicer** /'ʃaɪsə/, *n. Colloq.* **1.** an unproductive gold mine. **2.** a swindler.

**shicker** /'ʃɪkə/, *Colloq.* *–n.* **1.** alcoholic drink. **2.** a drunkard. **3. on the shicker,** intoxicated; drunk. *–adj.* **4.** →**shickered.** [Yiddish *shiker,* from Heb. *shikkōr,* from *shikhar* to be drunk]

**shickered** /'ʃɪkəd/, *adj. Colloq.* drunk; intoxicated. Also, **shicker.** [SHICKER + -ED[3]]

**shied** /ʃaɪd/, *v.* past tense and past participle of **shy.**

**shield** /ʃild/, *n.* **1.** a piece of defensive armour of various shapes, carried on the left arm or in the hand to protect the body in battle. **2.** something shaped like a shield, as a trophy, etc. **3.** anything used or serving to protect. **4.** *Ordn.* a steel screen attached to a gun to protect its gunners, mechanism, etc. **5.** *Mining.* a movable framework for protecting a miner at the place at which he is working. **6.** *Physics.* a mass of material used to prevent the passage of radiation from one place to another, esp. to prevent the escape of radiation from a reactor. **7.** *Zool.* a protective plate or the like on the body of an animal, as a scute, enlarged scale, etc. **8.** *Geol.* a large, exposed mass of pre-Cambrian rocks forming a stable part of the earth's crust. **9.** *Her.* a shield-shaped escutcheon on which armorial bearings are displayed. *–v.t.* **10.** to protect with or as with a shield. **11.** to serve as a protection for. **12.** *Obs.* to avert; forbid. *–v.i.* **13.** to act or serve as a shield. [ME *shelde,* OE *sceld,* c. D *schild,* G *Schild*] – **shielder,** *n.* – **shieldlike,** *adj.*

ancient Roman shield

**shield-fern** /ˈʃild-fɜn/, *n.* any fern of the genus *Polystichum* which has peltate indusia, as **mother shield-fern,** *P. proliferum.*

**shift** /ʃɪft/, *v.i.* **1.** to move from one place, position, etc., to another. **2.** to manage to get along or succeed. **3.** to get along by indirect methods; employ shifts or evasions. **4.** to change gear in driving a motor vehicle. **5.** *Linguistics.* to undergo a systematic phonetic change. **6.** to travel at great speed: *the car was really shifting.* **7.** *Archaic.* to change one's clothes. *–v.t.* **8.** to put by and replace by another or others; change. **9.** to transfer from one place, position, person, etc., to another: *to shift the blame on someone else.* **10. shift house,** to move to a new place of residence. *–n.* **11.** a shifting from one place, position, person, etc., to another; a transfer. **12.** the portion of the day scheduled as a day's work when a factory, etc., operates continuously during the 24 hours, or works both day and night: *night shift.* **13.** a group of workers so employed. **14.** *Mining.* a fault, or the dislocation of a seam or stratum. **15.** *Music.* (in playing the violin or a similar instrument) any change in position of the left hand on the fingerboard. **16.** *Linguistics.* a change, or system of parallel changes, which seriously affects the phonetic or phonemic structure of the language, as the change in English vowels from Middle English to Modern English. **17.** an expedient; ingenious device. **18.** an evasion, artifice, or trick. **19.** change or substitution. **20. a.** a woman's loose-fitting dress. **b.** *Archaic.* a woman's chemise or undergarment. **21.** *Motor Vehicles.* →**gearstick. 22. make shift, a.** to manage to get along or succeed. **b.** to manage with effort or difficulty. **c.** to do one's best (fol. by *with*). [ME; OE *sciftan,* c. G *schichten* arrange] – **shifter,** *n.*

**shift allowance** /ˈ– əlaʊəns/, *n.* an allowance paid to employees on shift work as compensation for their having to work outside the usual span of hours fixed for day workers. Also, **shift loading, shift premium.**

**shifter** /ˈʃɪftə/, *n.* →**shifting spanner.**

**shifting spanner** /ˈʃɪftɪŋ spænə/, *n.* an adjustable spanner used for nuts and bolts.

**shift key** /ˈʃɪft ki/, *n.* a device on a typewriter for adjusting the position of the keys or carriage to type capital letters.

**shiftless** /ˈʃɪftləs/, *adj.* lacking in resource or ambition; inefficient; lazy. – **shiftlessly,** *adv.* – **shiftlessness,** *n.*

**shift register** /ˈʃɪft rɛdʒəstə/, *n.* a computer register in which binary bits are moved as a contiguous group a specified number of positions right or left.

**shifty** /ˈʃɪfti/, *adj.,* **-tier, -tiest. 1.** given to or full of evasions; deceitful; furtive. **2.** resourceful; fertile in expedients. – **shiftily,** *adv.* – **shiftiness,** *n.*

**Shih tzu** /ʃi ˈtsu/, *n.* a small breed of dog, related to the Pekingese and Lhasa apso, with a long, thick, black and white coat, a broad head, and drooping ears heavily fringed with hair.

**shikari** /ʃəˈkæri/, *n., pl.* **-ris.** (in India) a hunter or guide. Also, **shikaree.** [Urdu, from *shikār* shikar, from Pers.]

**shikkered** /ˈʃɪkəd/, *adj.* →**shickered.** Also, **shikker.**

**shillelagh** /ʃəˈleɪli/, *n.* (in Ireland) a cudgel of blackthorn or oak. Also, **shillalah, shillala, shillelah.** [from the name of a barony and village in County Wicklow, in Ireland]

**shilling** /ˈʃɪlɪŋ/, *n.* **1.** (formerly) a cupronickel or silver coin equal to $\frac{1}{20}$ of a pound. **2.** any similar coin or banknote of certain other countries. **3. cut (someone) off with (without) a shilling,** to cut (an heir) out of one's will. *–adj.* **4.** of the price or value of a shilling. *Abbrev.:* s., sh. [ME; OE *scilling,* c. D *schelling,* G *Schilling,* Icel. *skillingr*]

**shillyshally** /ˈʃɪliˌʃæli/, *v.,* **-lied, -lying,** *n., pl.* **-lies,** *adj., adv.* *–v.i.* **1.** to be irresolute; vacillate. *–n.* **2.** irresolution; indecision; vacillation. *–adj.* **3.** irresolute; undecided; vacillating. *–adv.* **4.** irresolutely. [dissimilated var. of repeated question *Shall I? Shall I?* Cf. DILLYDALLY]

**shim** /ʃɪm/, *n., v.,* **shimmed, shimming.** *–n.* **1.** a thin strip of metal, wood, or the like, for filling in, as for bringing one part in line with another. *–v.t.* **2.** to fill out or bring to a level by inserting a shim or shims. [orig. uncert.]

**shimmer** /ˈʃɪmə/, *v.i.* **1.** to shine with a subdued, tremulous light; gleam faintly. *–n.* **2.** a subdued, tremulous light or gleam. [ME *schimere,* late OE *scimerian,* apparently frequentative of *scīmian* shine. Cf. G *schimmern*]

**shimmery** /ˈʃɪməri/, *adj.* shimmering; shining softly.

**shimmy** /ˈʃɪmi/, *n., pl.* **-mies,** *v.,* **-mied, -mying.** *–n.* **1.** a U.S. ragtime dance, marked by shaking of the hips or shoulders. **2.** excessive wobbling in the front wheels of a motor vehicle. **3.** *Colloq.* →**chemise.** *–v.i.* **4.** to dance the shimmy. **5.** to vibrate; shake. [alteration of CHEMISE]

**shin** /ʃɪn/, *n., v.,* **shinned, shinning.** *–n.* **1.** the front part of the leg from the knee to the ankle. **2.** the lower part of the foreleg in cattle; the metacarpal bone. **3.** the shinbone or tibia, esp. its sharp edge or front portion. **4.** a cut of beef, usu. used for stewing. *–v.t., v.i.* **5.** to climb by holding fast with the hands or arms and legs and drawing oneself up. [ME *s(c)hine,* OE *scinu,* c. D *scheen,* G *Schienbein*]

**shinbone** /ˈʃɪnboʊn/, *n.* →**tibia.**

**shindig** /ˈʃɪndɪg/, *n. Colloq.* **1.** a dance, party, or other festivity, esp. a noisy one. **2.** a disturbance; quarrel; row. [var. of SHINDY]

**shindy** /ˈʃɪndi/, *n., pl.* **-dies. 1.** a row; rumpus. **2.** a merrymaking; party. [? for SHINTY]

**shine** /ʃaɪn/, *v.,* **shone** or (*esp. for def. 8*) **shined, shining,** *n.* *–v.i.* **1.** to give forth, or glow with, light; shed or cast light. **2.** to be bright with reflected light; glisten; sparkle. **3.** to be unusually bright, as the eyes or face. **4.** to appear with brightness or clearness, as feelings. **5.** to excel; be conspicuous: *to shine at sports.* *–v.t.* **6.** to cause to shine. **7.** to direct the light of (a lamp, etc.): *shine the torch over here.* **8.** to put a gloss or polish on (shoes, etc.). *–n.* **9.** radiance; light. **10.** lustre; polish. **11.** sunshine; fair weather: *come rain or shine.* **12.** a polish given to shoes. **13.** a giving of such a polish. **14.** *Colloq.* a caper; prank. **15.** *Colloq.* a liking; fancy: *to take a shine to.* **16. take the shine out of, a.** to remove or spoil the lustre or brilliance of. **b.** to surpass; excel; get the better of; humiliate. [ME; OE *scīnan,* c. G *scheinen*]

**shiner** /ˈʃaɪnə/, *n.* **1.** one who or that which shines. **2.** *Colloq.* a black eye. **3.** any of various small American freshwater fishes, mostly minnows, with glistening scales, as the **golden shiner,** *Notemigonus crysoleucas,* and the numerous species of the genus *Notropis.*

**shingle**[1] /ˈʃɪŋgəl/, *n., v.,* **-gled, -gling.** *–n.* **1.** a thin piece of wood, slate, etc., usu. oblong and with one end thicker than the other, used in overlapping rows to cover the roofs and sides of houses. **2.** a woman's close-cropped haircut. **3.** *Colloq.* a small signboard, esp. that of a professional man. **4. be a shingle short,** to be eccentric; mentally disturbed. *–v.t.* **5.** to cover (a roof, etc.) with shingles. **6.** to cut (hair) close to the head. [ME; var. of *shindle,* from L *scindula*] – **shingler,** *n.*

**shingle**[2] /ˈʃɪŋgəl/, *n.* **1.** small, water-worn stones or pebbles such as lie in loose banks or layers on the seashore. **2.** an extent of small, loose stones or pebbles. [earlier *chingle;* ? of imitative orig.]

**shingleback** /ˈʃɪŋgəlbæk/, *n.* →**stump-tailed skink.**

**shingles** /ˈʃɪŋgəlz/, *n. sing. or pl.* a cutaneous disease characterised by vesicles which sometimes form a girdle about the body; herpes zoster. [ME *schingles,* from ML *cingulus* (var. of *cingulum* girdle) used to translate Gk *zṓnē* or *zōstḗr,* name of the disease]

**shingly** /ˈʃɪŋgli/, *adj.* consisting of or covered with shingle, or small, loose stones or pebbles.

**shining** /ˈʃaɪnɪŋ/, *adj.* **1.** radiant; gleaming; bright. **2.** resplendent; brilliant: *shining talents.* **3.** conspicuously fine: *a shining example.* – **shiningly,** *adv.*

**shining starling** /ˈ– stalɪŋ/, *n.* →**metallic starling.**

**shinny**[1] /ˈʃɪni/, *n., pl.* **-nies,** *v.i.,* **-nied, -nying.** →**shinty.**

**shinny**[2] /ˈʃɪni/, *v.t.,* **-nied, -nying.** *Colloq.* to climb using the shins. [from SHIN, *n.*]

**shin plaster** /ˈʃɪn plastə/, *n. Obs.* **1.** *U.S.* a square piece of paper saturated with vinegar, etc., used as a plaster for sore legs. **2.** *U.S.* similar paper on which promissory notes were written, used as currency. **3.** a promissory note issued by outback storekeepers and used as currency.

**Shinto** /ˈʃɪntoʊ/, *n.* the native religion of Japan, primarily a system of nature and ancestor worship. Also, **Shintoism.** [Jap., from Chinese *shin tao* way of the gods] – **Shintoist,** *n., adj.*

**shinty** /ˈʃɪnti/, *n., pl.* **-ties,** *v.,* **-tied, -tying. 1.** a simple variety of hockey, played with a ball or the like and clubs curved at one end. **2.** the club used. *–v.i.* **3.** to play shinty. **4.** to drive the ball at shinty. Also, **shinny.** [? var. of *shin ye,* cry used in the game]

**shiny** /ˈʃaɪni/, *adj.,* **-nier, -niest. 1.** bright; glossy. **2.** worn to a glossy smoothness, as clothes. – **shininess,** *n.*

**shiny-arse** /ˈʃaɪni-as/, *n. Colloq.* **1.** a soldier in a base unit, as opposed to one in the fighting line. **2.** a male office worker.

**ship** /ʃɪp/, *n., v.,* **shipped, shipping.** *–n.* **1.** any vessel intended or used for navigating the water, esp. one of large size and not propelled by oars, paddles, or the like. **2.** *Naut.* a vessel with a bowsprit and three or more masts (foremast, mainmast, and mizzenmast), each consisting of a lower mast, a topmast, and topgallant mast. **3.** the crew of a vessel. **4.** an airship or aeroplane. **5. take ship,** to embark. **6. when one's ship comes in** or **home,** when one has become prosperous or acquired a fortune. *–v.t.* **7.** to put or take on board a ship or the like, for transportation; to send or transport by ship, rail, etc. **8.** *Naut.* to take in (water) over the side, as a vessel does when waves break over it. **9.** to bring (an object) into a ship or boat. **10.** to engage for service on a ship. **11.** to fix (oars, etc.) in a ship or boat in the proper place for use. **12.** *Colloq.* to send away or get rid of. *–v.i.* **13.** to go on board a ship; embark. **14.** to engage to serve on a ship. [ME; OE *scip,* c. D *schip,* G *Schiff*]

**-ship,** a suffix of nouns denoting condition, character, office, skill, etc., as in *kingship, friendship, statesmanship.* [ME; OE *-scipe,* c. West Fris. and West Flemish *-schip;* akin to G *-schaft*]

**shipboard** /ˈʃɪpbɔd/, *n.* **1.** a ship, or its deck or interior. **2. on shipboard,** on or in a ship. *–adj.* **3.** occurring while on a ship: *a shipboard romance.*

**ship-breaker** /ˈʃɪp-breɪkə/, *n.* a contractor who buys and breaks up old ships.

**ship-broker** /ˈʃɪp-broʊkə/, *n.* an agent who transacts business for shipowners, as procuring cargoes and arranging insurance, etc.

**shipbuilder** /ˈʃɪpbɪldə/, *n.* one whose occupation is the construction of ships. – **shipbuilding,** *n., adj.*

**ship canal** /ˈʃɪp kənæl/, *n.* a canal navigable by ships.

**ship chandler** /ˈ– tʃændlə/, *n.* one who deals in cordage, canvas, and other supplies for ships.

**shipload** /ˈʃɪploʊd/, *n.* **1.** a full load for a ship. **2.** the amount of cargo or passengers carried by a ship.

**ship-loader** /ˈʃɪp-loʊdə/, *n.* a conveyor system for transferring grain, earth, etc., onto a bulk cargo ship.

**shipman** /ˈʃɪpmən/, *n., pl.* **-men.** *Archaic or Poetic.* **1.** a sailor. **2.** the master of a ship.

**shipmaster** /ˈʃɪpmastə/, *n.* the master, commander, or captain of a ship.

**shipmate** /ˈʃɪpmeɪt/, *n.* one who serves with another on the same vessel.

**shipment** /ˈʃɪpmənt/, *n.* **1.** the act of shipping goods, etc.; the delivery of goods, etc., for transporting. **2.** the quantity of goods shipped. **3.** that which is shipped.

**ship money** /ˈʃɪp mʌni/, *n. Brit.* (formerly) a tax levied in time of war on ports, maritime towns, etc., to provide ships.

**ship of the line,** *n.* (formerly) a ship with heavy enough armour and gunpowder to be in the line of battle; a battleship.

**shipowner** /ˈʃɪpoʊnə/, *n.* an owner of a ship or ships.

**shipper** /ˈʃɪpə/, *n.* one who ships goods, or makes shipments.

**shipping** /ˈʃɪpɪŋ/, *n.* **1.** the act of one who ships goods, etc. **2.** the action or business of sending or transporting goods, etc., by ship, rail, etc. **3.** ships collectively, or their aggregate tonnage.

**shipping agent** /ˈ– eɪdʒənt/, *n.* the representative of a shipowner, who transacts business on his behalf.

**shipping clerk** /ˈ– klak/, *n.* a clerk who attends to shipments.

**shipping fever** /ˈ– fivə/, *n.* →**haemorrhagic septicaemia.**

**shipping master** /ˈ– mastə/, *n.* an official who supervises the engagement and discharge of seamen.

**shipping office** /ˈ– ɒfəs/, *n.* **1.** the office of a shipping agent. **2.** an office where seamen are engaged.

**shipping room** /ˈ– rum/, *n.* a place in a business concern where goods are packed and shipped.

**ship-rigged** /ˈʃɪp-rɪgd/, *adj.* rigged with three or more masts, with square sails on all masts.

**ship's articles** /ʃɪps ˈatɪkəlz/, *n. pl.* the terms on which seamen serve on a ship.

**ship's biscuit** /– ˈbɪskət/, *n.* a kind of coarse, hard biscuit.

**shipshape** /ˈʃɪpʃeɪp/, *adj.* **1.** in good order; well arranged; neat; tidy. *–adv.* **2.** in a shipshape manner.

**ship's husband** /ʃɪps ˈhʌzbənd/, *n.* a person appointed as an agent or manager of a ship by the owner.

**ship's papers** /– ˈpeɪpəz/, *n. pl.* →**paper** (def. 8).

**shipway** /ˈʃɪpweɪ/, *n.* **1.** the structure which supports a ship being built. **2.** →**ship canal.**

**shipworm** /ˈʃɪpwɜm/, *n.* any of various marine bivalve molluscs which burrow into the timbers of ships, etc.

**shipwreck** /ˈʃɪprɛk/, *n.* **1.** the destruction or loss of a ship, as by sinking. **2.** the remains of a ship. **3.** destruction or ruin: *the shipwreck of one's hopes.* *–v.t.* **4.** to cause to suffer shipwreck. **5.** to destroy; ruin. *–v.i.* **6.** to suffer shipwreck.

**shipwright** /ˈʃɪpraɪt/, *n.* one employed in the construction or repair of ships.

**shipyard** /ˈʃɪpjad/, *n.* a yard or enclosure near the water, in which ships are built or repaired.

**shiralee** /ʃɪrəˈli, ˈʃɪrəˌli/, *n.* **1.** a burden, or bundle. **2.** →**swag** (def. 1). [orig. unknown]

**Shiraz** /ʃəˈræz/, *n.* a popular red grape variety grown in Australia for the making of dry red table wines as well as sweet red wines. [from *Shiraz,* city in Iran]

**shire** /ˈʃaɪə/, *n.* **1.** an area of land delineated for the purposes of local government, usu. larger than that designated as a town, municipality or borough and, at least originally, more sparsely populated. **2.** *Brit.* one of the counties of Britain. [ME; OE *scīr,* c. OHG *scīra* care, official charge]

**shire horse** /– ˈhɔs/, *n.* one of a breed of large, strong draught horses.

**shirk** /ʃɜk/, *v.t.* **1.** to evade (work, duty, etc.). *–v.i.* **2.** to evade work, duty, etc. *–n.* **3.** Also, **shirker.** one who seeks to avoid work, duty, etc. [? G *Schurke* parasite, sharper. Cf. SHARK[2]]

**shirr** /ʃɜ/, *v.t.* **1.** to draw up or gather (cloth) on parallel threads. **2.** to bake (food, usu. eggs) in a small shallow container or ramekin dish. *–n.* **3.** Also, **shirring.** a shirred arrangement of cloth, etc. [orig. uncert.]

**shirt** /ʃɜt/, *n.* **1.** a garment for the upper part of a man's body, usu. with buttons down the front, a collar and short sleeves, or long sleeves with cuffs. **2.** *U.S.* an undershirt; vest; singlet. **3.** →**nightshirt. 4. in one's shirt sleeves,** not wearing a jacket. **5. keep one's shirt on,** to refrain from losing one's temper or becoming impatient. **6. put one's shirt on,** to bet heavily or all one has on (a horse, etc.). **7. lose one's shirt,** to lose everything. [ME *schirte,* OE *scyrte;* akin to G *Schürze* apron. Cf. SKIRT]

**shirt-band** /ˈʃɜt-bænd/, *n.* the neckband of a shirt.

**shirt-front** /ˈʃɜt-frʌnt/, *n.* **1.** the starched front of a white dress shirt. **2.** *Aus. Rules.* Also, **shirt-fronter.** a head-on charge aimed at bumping an opponent to the ground. *–v.t.* **3.** *Aus. Rules.* to bump (an opponent) thus.

**shirting** /ˈʃɜtɪŋ/, *n.* a fabric for men's shirts.

**shirtmaker** /ˈʃɜtmeɪkə/, *n.* a woman's dress with a collar, sleeves and buttoned front like a shirt.

**shirt-tail** /ˈʃɜt-teɪl/, *n.* that part of a shirt below the waist.

**shirty** /ˈʃɜti/, *adj. Colloq.* bad-tempered; annoyed.

**shish kebab** /ˈʃɪʃ kəbæb/, *n.* a dish consisting of cubes of meat, marinated, and grilled on a skewer, often with onion, tomato, green pepper, etc. Also, **kebab.** [Turk *şiş kebabi,* from *şiş* skewer + *kebap* roast meat]

**shit** /ʃɪt/, *v.,* **shitted, shat** or **shit; shitted** or (*Obs.*) **shitten; shitting;** *n., interj. Colloq.* *–v.i.* **1.** to defecate. **2.** win or succeed easily (fol. by *in*). *–v.t.* **3.** to anger or disgust. **4. shit it in,** to win easily. *–n.* **5.** faeces; dung; excrement. **6.** the act of defecating. **7.** a contemptible or despicable person. **8.** nonsense; rubbish; lies. **9.** marijuana or hashish. **10. get the shits,** to become exasperated or angry (oft. fol. by *with*). **11. give (someone) the shits,** to arouse dislike, resentment, annoyance in (someone). **12. have the shits, a.** to have diarrhoea. **b.** to feel fed up or weary. **c.** to feel fed up or angry with (someone) (fol. by *with*). **13. have shit for brains,** to be extremely stupid. **14. in the shit,** in trouble. **15. not worth a pinch of shit,** completely worthless. **16. put shit on, a.** to denigrate; criticise. **b.** to hoodwink; deceive. **17. the shit hits the fan,** (the trouble begins). **18. up shit creek (without a paddle),** in trouble; in difficulties. **19. up to shit,** worthless; useless. *–interj.* **20.** (an exclamation expressing anger, disgust, disappointment, disbelief, etc.). [ME *shiten,* OE *scitan* (n. *scite* dung); c. MLG *schiten,* D *schijten,* G *scheissen*]

**shitcan** /ˈʃɪtkæn/, *v.t.,* **-canned, -canning.** *Colloq.* to denigrate unmercifully: *one by one the lawyers shitcanned him.*

**shithead** /ˈʃɪthɛd/, *n. Colloq.* **1.** a mean contemptible person. **2.** a no-hoper; dullard. **3.** a person who smokes marijuana regularly.

**shithouse** /ˈʃɪthaʊs/, *Colloq.* *–n.* **1.** a toilet. *–adj.* **2.** foul; wretchedly bad. Also, **shouse.**

**shitkicker** /ˈʃɪtkɪkə/, *n. Colloq.* **1.** an assistant, esp. one doing menial or repetitive jobs. **2.** a person of little consequence. **3.** *Prison.* a prisoner serving a short sentence.

**shit-scared** /ˈʃɪt-skɛəd/, *adj. Colloq.* very frightened.

**shit-stirrer** /ˈʃɪt-stɜrə/, *n. Colloq.* **1.** an activist, esp. in a political context. **2.** a trouble-maker.

**shittim wood** /ˈʃɪtɪm wʊd/, *n.* the wood of which the ark of the covenant and various parts of the Jewish tabernacle were made. Also, **shittim.**

**shitty** /ˈʃɪti/, *Colloq.* *–adj.* **1.** annoyed; bad tempered. **2.** unpleasant; disagreeable; of low quality. *–n.* **3. pack a shitty,** *Colloq.* to sulk.

**shitty-livered** /ˈʃɪti-lɪvəd/, *adj. Colloq.* ill-tempered; angry.

**shiv** /ʃɪv/, *n. Brit. Colloq.* a knife. [alteration of *chiv* blade, from Gipsy]

**Shiva** /ˈʃivə/, *n.* one of the three chief divinities, the third member of the Hindu trinity, known also as 'the Destroyer'. Also, **Siva.** [Hind., from Skt *çiva* propitious] – **Shivaism,** *n.* – **Shivaist,** *n.* – **Shivaistic** /ʃiveɪˈɪstɪk, ʃɪv-/, *adj.*

**shivaree** /ʃɪvəˈri/, *n., v.,* **-reed, -reeing.** *U.S.* *–n.* **1.** a mock serenade with kettles, pans, horns, etc. **2.** a noisy celebration. *–v.t.* **3.** to serenade with kettles, etc. [alteration of CHARIVARI]

**shive**[1] /ʃaɪv/, *n.* **1.** a thin wooden, cork or plastic bung for casks. **2.** a thin flat cork for stopping a wide-mouthed bottle. **3.** *Archaic.* a slice. [ME: slice, probably from MD or MLG *schīve*]

**shive**[2] /ʃaɪv/, *n.* a small fragment of plant matter, as a splinter of the woody part of flax, or a grass seed caught in a fleece. [ME *schyff,* probably from LG, akin to MLG *schīve* slice]

**shiver**[1] /ˈʃɪvə/, *v.i.* **1.** to shake or tremble with cold, fear, excitement, etc. *–v.i.* **2.** (of a sail) to shake when too close to the wind. *–n.* **3.** a tremulous motion; a tremble or quiver. **4. cold shivers,** a sensation of fear, anxiety, distaste. **5. the shivers,** a fit or attack of shivering. [ME *chivere;* orig. uncert.]

**shiver**[2] /ˈʃɪvə/, *v.t., v.i.* **1.** to break or split into fragments. *–n.* **2.** a fragment; a splinter. [ME *schivere,* n., splinter; akin to G *Schiefer* slate]

**shivery**[1] /ˈʃɪvəri/, *adj.* **1.** shivering; quivering; tremulous. **2.** inclined to shiver or shake. **3.** causing shivering. [SHIVER[1] + -Y[1]]

**shivery**[2] /ˈʃɪvəri/, *adj.* readily breaking into shivers or fragments; brittle. [SHIVER[2] + -Y[1]]

**shivery grass** /ˈ– gras/, *n.* a small, soft, annual grass, *Briza minor,* with small heart-shaped spikelets on slender pedicels in open panicles; native to Europe and Asia.

**shivoo** /ʃəˈvu/, *n. Colloq.* a party; celebration; spree. Also, **chavoo, shavoo.** [Brit. d. *shebo* or *shivoo;* ? from F *chez vous* at your place]

**shlemiel** /ʃləˈmil/, *n.* an innocent fool. Also, **schlemiel.** [Yiddish]

**S.H.M.,** simple harmonic motion.

**shmo** /ʃmoʊ/, *n. Colloq.* a foolish, boring or stupid person. Also, **schmo.** [Yiddish]

**sho** /ʃoʊ/, *n.* a Japanese chord-producing mouth organ used notably in gagaku. [Jap.]

**shoad** /ʃoʊd/, *n.* **1.** a loose, waterworn fragment of mineral ore on the surface, away from the outcrop of the lode. *–v.i.* **2.** to locate a lode by following occurrences of shoad. [? Cornish d.]

**shoal**[1] /ʃoʊl/, *n.* **1.** a place where a body of water is shallow. **2.** a sandbank or sandbar in the bed of a body of water, esp. one which shows at low water. *–adj.* **3.** of little depth, as water; shallow. *–v.i.* **4.** to become shallow or more shallow. *–v.t.* **5.** to cause to become shallow. **6.** *Naut.* to proceed from a greater to a lesser depth of (water). [ME *schold, schald,* OE *sceald* shallow]

**shoal**[2] /ʃoʊl/, *n.* **1.** any large number of persons or things. **2.** a group of fish crowded fairly close together. *–v.i.* **3.** to collect in a shoal; throng. [OE *scolu* shoal (of fishes), multitude, troop, c. D *school.* See SCHOOL[2]]

**shoaly** /ˈʃoʊli/, *adj.* full of shoals or shallows.

**shoat** /ʃoʊt/, *n.* a young weaned pig. Also, **shote.** [ME. Cf. Flemish *schote* young pig]

**shock**[1] /ʃɒk/, *n.* **1.** a sudden and violent blow, or impact, collision, or encounter. **2.** a sudden disturbance or commotion. **3.** something that shocks mentally, emotionally, etc. **4.** *Pathol.* a sudden collapse of the nervous mechanism caused by violent physical or psychic factors, such as severe injuries or a strong emotional disturbance. **5.** the physiological effect produced by the passage of an electric current through the body. *–v.t.* **6.** to strike with intense surprise, horror, disgust, etc. **7.** to strike against violently. **8.** to give an electric shock to. *–v.i.* **9.** to come into violent contact; collide. [apparently from F *choc,* from *choquer* strike against, shock, from MD *schokken*] – **shockable,** *adj.* – **shock,** *adj.*

**shock**[2] /ʃɒk/, *n.* →**stook.** [ME; c. LG *schok* stook of grain, group of sixty, from G *Schock* sixty]

**shock**[3] /ʃɒk/, *n.* **1.** a thick, bushy mass, as of hair. *–adj.* **2.** shaggy, as hair. [? var. of SHAG[1]]

**shock absorber** /ˈ– əbsɔbə/, *n.* **1.** *Mach.* a device for deadening shock or concussion, esp. one on a motor vehicle for checking sudden or excessive movements of the suspension. **2.** *Aeron.* the part of an aircraft undercarriage which absorbs the impact on landing.

**shocker** /ˈʃɒkə/, *n.* **1.** one who or that which shocks. **2.** *Colloq.* a sensational work of fiction. **3.** *Colloq.* an unpleasant or disagreeable person.

**shockheaded** /ˈʃɒkhɛdəd/, *adj.* having a shock or thick mass of hair on the head.

**shocking** /ˈʃɒkɪŋ/, *adj.* **1.** causing intense surprise, disgust, horror, etc. **2.** *Colloq.* very bad: *shocking manners.* – **shockingly,** *adv.*

**shocking pink** /– ˈpɪŋk/, *n.* a very bright pink colour.

**shockproof** /ˈʃɒkpruf/, *adj.* protected against damage likely to result from shocks.

**shock tactics** /ˈʃɒk tæktɪks/, *n. pl.* a method of attack by mobile units in which the suddenness, violence, and massed weight of the first impact produce the main effect.

**shock treatment** /ˈ– tritmənt/, *n.* **1.** Also, **shock therapy.** a method of treating certain mental disorders, as schizophrenia, by shocks induced either by drugs or by electroconvulsive therapy. **2.** *Colloq.* any sudden or violent action as a brutal verbal confrontation calculated to achieve its aim by shock.

**shock troops** /ˈ– trups/, *n. pl.* troops especially selected, trained, and equipped for engaging in assault. Also, **storm troops.**

**shock wave** /ˈ– weɪv/, *n.* a region of abrupt change of pressure and density moving in a gas or liquid at or above the velocity of sound.

**shod** /ʃɒd/, *v.* past tense and past participle of **shoe.**

**shoddy** /ˈʃɒdi/, *n., pl.* **-dies,** *adj.,* **-dier, -diest.** *–n.* **1.** a fibrous material obtained by shredding woollen rags or waste. **2.** anything inferior made to resemble what is of superior quality; anything inferior but pretentious. **3.** pretence, as in art, manufacture, etc. *–adj.* **4.** pretending to a superiority not possessed; sham. **5.** of poor quality or badly made: *shoddy workmanship, shoddy goods.* **6.** made of or containing shoddy. [orig. uncert.] – **shoddily,** *adv.* – **shoddiness,** *n.*

**shoe** /ʃu/, *n., pl.* **shoes,** (*Archaic*) **shoon;** *v.,* **shod, shoeing.** *–n.* **1.** an external covering, usu. of leather, for the human foot, consisting of a more or less stiff or heavy sole and a lighter upper part. **2.** *U.S.* →**boot**[1] (def. 1). **3.** some thing or part resembling a shoe in form, position, or use. **4.** a horseshoe, or a similar plate for the hoof of some other animal. **5.** a ferrule or the like, as of iron, for protecting the end of a staff, pole, etc. **6.** the part of a brake mechanism fitting into the drum and expanded outwardly to apply the friction lining to the drum rim for stopping or slowing a car, etc. **7.** the outer casing of a pneumatic tyre. **8.** a drag or skid for a wheel of a vehicle. **9.** a part having a larger area than the end of an object on which it fits, serving to disperse or apply its thrust. **10.** the sliding contact by which an electric locomotive takes its current from the conductor rail. **11.** *Bldg Trades.* the bearing surface or area of contact of a roof truss, girder, etc. **12.** a band of iron on the bottom of the runner of a sledge. **13. in someone's shoes,** in the position or situation of another: *I shouldn't like to be in his shoes.* **14. know where the shoe pinches,** to know the cause or real meaning of trouble, misfortune, sorrow, etc., esp. from personal experience. *–v.t.* **15.** to provide or fit with a shoe or shoes. **16.** to protect or arm at the point, edge, or face with a ferrule, metal plate, or the like. [ME *shoo,* OE *scōh,* c. G *Schuh*]

**shoebill** /ˈʃubɪl/, *n.* a large African wading bird, *Balaeniceps rex,* with a broad bill shaped somewhat like a shoe, found esp. on the White Nile.

**shoeblack** /ˈʃublæk/, *n.* →**bootblack.**

**shoehorn** /ˈʃuhɔn/, *n.* a shaped piece of horn, metal, or the like, inserted in a shoe at the heel to make it slip on more easily.

**shoelace** /ˈʃuleɪs/, *n.* a string or lace for fastening a shoe.

**shoemaker** /ˈʃumeɪkə/, *n.* one who makes or mends shoes.

**shoemaker's children** /ˈʃumeɪkəz ˌtʃɪldrən/, *n.pl. Colloq.* children of technically skilled parents who get no benefit from their parents' expertise in a particular field.

**shoer** /ˈʃuə/, *n.* one who shoes horses, etc.

**shoeshine** /ˈʃuʃaɪn/, *n.* **1.** the polished surface of a shoe. **2.** the act or instance of cleaning or polishing a shoe or shoes.

**shoestring** /ˈʃustrɪŋ/, *n.* **1.** →**shoelace. 2. on a shoestring,** with a very small amount of money.

**shoestring potatoes** /– pəˈteɪtoʊz/, *n. pl.* thin strips of potato, deep fried.

**shoetree** /ˈʃuˌtri/, *n.* a device, usu. of metal or wood, placed in shoes when they are not being worn, to maintain the shape.

**shofar** /ˈʃoʊfa/, *n.* →**shophar.**

**shogun** /ˈʃoʊgʌn/, *n.* (in Japan) **1.** a title originating in the 8th century, in the wars against the Ainus, equivalent to commander-in-chief. **2.** (in later history) a member of a quasi-dynasty, holding real power while the imperial dynasty remained theoretically and ceremonially supreme. [Jap., from Chinese *chiang chün* lead army (i.e., general)]

**shogunate** /ˈʃoʊgənеɪt/, *n.* the office or rule of a shogun.

**shone** /ʃɒn/, *v.* past tense and past participle of **shine.**

**shonkie** /ˈʃɒŋki/, *adj. Colloq.* **1.** of dubious integrity or honesty. **2.** mechanically unreliable.

**shoo** /ʃu/, *interj., v.,* **shooed, shooing.** *–interj.* **1.** (an exclamation used to scare or drive away poultry, birds, etc.) *–v.t.* **2.** to drive away by calling 'shoo'. **3.** to ask or compel (a person) to leave. *–v.i.* **4.** to call out 'shoo'. [cf. G *schu*]

**shooftee** /ˈʃʊfti/, *n. Colloq.* a look.

**shook**[1] /ʃʊk/, *n.* **1.** a set of staves and headings sufficient for one hogshead, barrel, or the like. **2.** a set of the parts of a box, piece of furniture, or the like, ready to be put together. **3.** *U.S.* a shock of sheaves or the like. [? var. of SHOCK[2], *n.*]

**shook**[2] /ʃʊk/, *v.* **1.** past tense of **shake.** *–adj.* **2. shook on, a.** in love with or infatuated by (a person). **b.** disposed favourably towards (a thing or course of action).

**shoon** /ʃun/, *n. Archaic.* plural of **shoe.**

**shoot** /ʃut/, *v.,* **shot** /ʃɒt/, **shooting,** *n.* *–v.t.* **1.** to hit, wound, or kill with a missile discharged from a weapon. **2.** to execute or put to death with a bullet. **3.** to send forth (arrows, bullets, etc.) from a bow, firearm, or the like. **4.** to discharge (a weapon): *to shoot a gun.* **5.** to send forth like an arrow or bullet: *to shoot questions at someone.* **6.** to fling; throw; propel; direct. **7.** to send swiftly along. **8.** to go over (country) in shooting game. **9.** to pass rapidly along with: *to shoot a rapid, a wave.* **10.** to emit (rays, etc.) swiftly. **11.** to variegate by threads, streaks, etc., of another colour. **12.** to cause to extend or project. **13.** to discharge or empty; send down a chute. **14.** *Football, Hockey, etc.* to kick or drive (the ball, etc.) as at the goal. **15.** to accomplish by kicking or driving the ball, etc.: *to shoot a goal.* **16.** to propel (a marble or the like) from the thumb and forefinger. **17.** *Dice.* to toss (the dice). **18.** *Photog.* to photograph or film. **19.** to put forth (buds, branches, etc.), as a plant. **20.** to slide (a bolt, etc.) into or out of its fastening. **21.** to take the altitude of (a heavenly body): *to shoot the sun.* **22.** *Mining.* to detonate. **23.** to inject intravenously any form of drug (oft. fol. by *up*). **24. shoot a line,** *Colloq.* to boast. **25. shoot down, a.** to kill or cause to fall by hitting with a shot. **b.** to bring down (an aircraft) by gunfire. **c.** to defeat decisively (an argument or person putting forward an argument). **26. shoot off one's mouth,** *Colloq.* **a.** to talk indiscreetly, esp. to reveal secrets, etc.; talk wildly or tactlessly. **b.** to exaggerate; boast. **27. shoot one's bolt,** *Colloq.* **a.** to do one's utmost. **b.** to ejaculate prematurely. **28. shoot up,** *Colloq.* to cause damage, confusion, etc., by reckless or haphazard shooting. *–v.i.* **29.** to send forth missiles, from a bow, firearm, or the like. **30.** to send forth missiles, or be discharged, as a firearm. **31.** to move, start to move, or pass suddenly or swiftly; dart; be propelled (fol. by *ahead, away, into, off,* etc.). **32.** to come forth from the ground, as a stem, etc. **33.** to put forth buds or shoots, as a plant; germinate. **34.** to grow, esp. rapidly (oft. fol. by *up*). **35.** *Photog.* to photograph or film. **36.** *Films.* to begin to film a scene. **37.** to extend; jut: *a cape shooting out into the sea.* **38.** to propel a ball, etc., in a particular direction or way, as in games. **39.** to cause sharp, darting pains in a part of the body: *pain shot through his arm.* **40.** to kill game with a gun for sport. **41.** *Colloq.* to begin, esp. to begin to talk. **42. shoot off,** *Colloq.* to go away quickly. **43. shoot through,** *Colloq.* **a.** to go away, usu. absenting oneself improperly: *instead of going to the exam, he shot through.* **b.** to move away rapidly: *to shoot through like a Bondi tram.* **44. shoot the moon,** *Colloq.* to abscond. **45. shoot up,** *Colloq.* to take drugs intravenously. *–n.* **46.** an act of shooting with a bow, firearm, etc. **47.** an expedition for shooting game. **48.** a match or contest at shooting. **49.** a growing or sprouting, as of a plant. **50.** a new or young growth which shoots off from some portion of a plant. **51.** the amount of such growth. **52.** a young branch, stem, twig, or the like. **53.** a sprout which is not one metre high. **54.** *Rowing.* the interval between strokes. **55.** →**chute**[1] (def. 1). [ME *shote,* var. of *shete,* OE *scēotan,* c. G *schiessen,* Icel. *skjōta*]

**shooter** /ˈʃutə/, *n.* **1.** one who shoots. **2.** *Colloq.* something that shoots; a gun, pistol, or the like. **3.** *Cricket.* a ball which, upon pitching, fails to rise, or rises only a little. **4.** *Colloq.* a fast surfboard. **5.** *Colloq.* a photograph.

**shooting brake** /ˈʃutɪŋ breɪk/, *n. Brit.* **1.** →**station wagon. 2.** (formerly) a horsedrawn open carriage used on shooting expeditions, to carry equipment, etc.

**shooting gallery** /ˈ– gæləri/, *n.* a place, usu. indoors, equipped with targets, used to practise shooting.

**shooting iron** /ˈ– aɪən/, *n. Colloq.* a firearm, esp. a pistol or revolver.

**shooting lodge** /ˈ– lɒdʒ/, *n. Chiefly Brit.* a small house or lodge for the accommodation of a sportsman or sportsmen during the shooting season. Also, **shooting box.**

**shooting match** /ˈ– mætʃ/, *n.* **1.** a contest between marksmen. **2. the whole shooting match,** *Colloq.* everything under consideration.

**shooting script** /ˈ– skrɪpt/, *n.* a script for a film, etc., in which the order of the shooting of the scenes is listed together with details of proposed camera work, visual effects, etc., to be attempted in each scene.

**shooting star** /– ˈsta/, *n.* **1.** a falling star; a meteor. **2.** the American cowslip, *Dodecatheon meadia,* having bright nodding flowers and reflexed lobes of the corolla.

**shooting stick** /ˈ– stɪk/, *n.* a walking stick with a spike at one end and a small, folding seat at the other, used by spectators at sporting events, etc.; seat-stick.

**shooting war** /ˈ– wɔ/, *n.* open war between countries involving actual conflict between armies, etc. Cf. **cold war.**

**shoot-out** /ˈʃut-aʊt/, *n. U.S.* a gunfight between two or more people.

**shop** /ʃɒp/, *n., v.,* **shopped, shopping.** *–n.* **1.** a building where goods are sold retail. **2.** a place for doing certain work; a workshop. **3. all over the shop,** *Colloq.* all over the place; in confusion. **4. set up shop,** to set oneself up in business. **5. shut up shop,** to close a business either temporarily or permanently. **6. talk shop,** to discuss one's trade, profession, or business. **7. the shop,** *Colloq.* the University of Melbourne, Victoria. *–v.i.* **8.** to visit shops for purchasing or examining goods. **9. shop around, a.** to visit a number of shops comparing quality and price before making a purchase. **b.** to make general and wide-ranging inquiries. *–v.t.* **10.** to inform against, betray, to the police. [ME *shoppe,* OE *sceoppa* booth, c. G *Schopf* lean-to]

**shop assistant** /ˈ– əsɪstənt/, *n.* one who sells goods in a retail shop.

**shop awning** /ˈ– ɔnɪŋ/, *n.* a rooflike structure over the pavement in front of a shop, etc., as a protection for pedestrians against sun and rain.

**shop committee** /ˈ– kəmɪti/, *n.* a committee made up of members of all unions represented in an establishment, set up principally to coordinate union policy and to facilitate negotiations with the employer.

**shopfitter** /ˈʃɒpfɪtə/, *n.* a person employed to decorate and build and sometimes design the interiors and facades of shops, showrooms and the like.

**shop floor** /ʃɒp ˈflɔ/, *n.* **1.** that part of a factory where the machines, etc., are situated. **2.** workers collectively, esp. factory workers. – **shopfloor,** *adj.*

**shopfront** /ˈʃɒpfrʌnt/, *n.* **1.** that part of a shop which fronts the street. **2.** that part of an organisation which deals directly with the public. *–adj.* **3.** of or pertaining to the place or the people functioning as a shopfront.

**shopfront lawyer** /– ˈlɔjə/, *n.* a lawyer who sets up his practice in a main shopping area with the aim of making legal services readily accessible to people.

**shopgirl** /ˈʃɒpgɜl/, *n.* a girl employed as a shop assistant.

**shophar** /ˈʃoʊfa/, *n.* an ancient Jewish musical instrument of the trumpet kind, usu. made of the curved horn of a ram, still used in Jewish religious services. Also, **shofar.** [Heb.]

shophar

**shopkeeper** /ˈʃɒpkipə/, *n.* one who owns or runs a shop.

**shoplift** /ˈʃɒplɪft/, *v.t.* **1.** to steal (goods) from a shop while appearing to be a legitimate shopper. *–v.i.* **2.** to be engaged in this activity. [backformation from SHOPLIFTER]

**shoplifter** /ˈʃɒplɪftə/, *n.* a person who shoplifts. [obs. *shoplift* shoplifter (from SHOP + LIFT) + -ER[1]]

**shopman** /ˈʃɒpmən/, *n., pl.* **-men. 1.** one employed to sell goods in a shop. **2.** *Rare.* a shopkeeper.

**shopper** /ˈʃɒpə/, *n.* one who shops.

**shopping** /ˈʃɒpɪŋ/, *n.* **1.** the act of one who shops. **2.** the articles bought.

**shopping basket** /ˈ– baskət/, *n.* a basket, bag, etc., used for carrying goods purchased.

**shopping buggy** /ˈ– bʌgi/, *n.* →**shopping stroller.**

**shopping centre** /ˈ– sɛntə/, *n.* that part of a town or suburb where shops are most densely concentrated.

**shopping complex** /ˈ– ˌkɒmplɛks/, *n.* a group of many shops and associated facilities within a single architectural plan. plan. Also, **shopping mall.**

**shopping precinct** /ˈ– prisɪŋkt/, *n. Brit.* →**shopping complex.**

**shopping stroller** /ˈ– stroʊlə/, *n.* a deep cloth or plastic bag mounted on a metal frame with wheels. Also, **shopping buggy.**

**shoppingtown** /ˈʃɒpɪŋtaʊn/, *n.* →**shopping complex.**

**shopping trolley** /ˈʃɒpɪŋ trɒli/, *n.* a basket-shaped metal trolley used by customers for carrying purchases in supermarkets.

**shopsoiled** /ˈʃɒpsɔɪld/, *adj.* **1.** worn, dirtied, faded, etc., as goods handled and displayed in a shop or store. **2.** (of people) affected by sordid experience. Also, **shopworn.**

**shop steward** /ˈʃɒp stjuəd/, *n.* a trade-union official representing workers in a factory, workshop, etc.

**shoptalk** /ˈʃɒptɔk/, *n.* talk about the business in which people are engaged, esp. on social occasions when it would be more polite to join in the general conversation.

**shopwalker** /ˈʃɒpwɔkə/, *n.* a person employed in a large shop or store to direct customers, supervise assistants, etc.

**shopwindow** /ʃɒpˈwɪndoʊ/, *n.* a window used for display of merchandise.

**shore**[1] /ʃɔ/, *n.* **1.** land along the edge of a sea, lake, large river, etc. **2.** some particular country: *my native shore.* **3.** land: *marines serving on shore.* **4.** *Law.* the space between the ordinary high-water mark and low-water mark. *–adj.* **5.** of, pertaining to, or situated on land. [ME *schore,* probably from MLG, c. D *schoor* sea marsh]

**shore**[2] /ʃɔ/, *n., v.,* **shored, shoring.** *–n.* **1.** a supporting post or beam and auxiliary members, esp. one placed obliquely against the side of a building, a ship in dock, or the like; a prop; a strut. *–v.t.* **2.** to support by a shore or shores; prop (usu. fol. by *up*). [ME, probably from MLG *schore,* c. D *schoor* prop]

**shore**[3] /ʃɔ/, *v. Archaic.* past tense and past participle of **shear.**

**shorebird** /ˈʃɔbɜd/, *n.* a limicoline bird, as one which frequents the seashore, estuaries, etc., esp. the snipes, sandpipers, plovers, turnstones, etc., constituting the families Charadriidae and Scolopacidae.

**shore break** /ˈʃɔ breɪk/, *n.* a wave which breaks right at the water's edge.

**shore leave** /ˈ– liv/, *n. Navy.* **1.** permission to spend time ashore. **2.** the time spent ashore.

**shoreless** /ˈʃɔləs/, *adj.* **1.** boundless. **2.** without a shore for landing on: *a shoreless island.*

**shoreline** /ˈʃɔlaɪn/, *n.* the line where shore and water meet.

**shore patrol** /ˈʃɔ pətroʊl/, *n. U.S.* a naval detachment acting as military police.

**shoreward** /ˈʃɔwəd/, *adj.* **1.** situated near, directed towards, or facing the shore. *–adv.* **2.** shorewards.

**shorewards** /ˈʃɔwədz/, *adv.* towards the shore or land. Also, **shoreward.**

**shore whaling** /ˈʃɔ weɪlɪŋ/, *n.* (formerly) whaling from a whaling-station rather than from a ship.

**shoring** /ˈʃɔrɪŋ/, *n.* **1.** shores or props for supporting a building, a ship, etc. **2.** the act of setting up shores.

**shorn** /ʃɔn/, *v.* past participle of **shear.**

**shornie** /ˈʃɔni/, *n. Colloq.* a newly-shorn sheep.

**short** /ʃɔt/, *adj.* **1.** having little length; not long. **2.** having little height; not tall; low. **3.** extending or reaching only a little way. **4.** brief; not extensive: *a short speech.* **5.** concise, as writing. **6.** rudely brief; curt; hurting: *short temper; he was short with her.* **7.** low in amount; scanty: *short rations; short commons.* **8.** not reaching a mark or the like, as a throw or a missile. **9.** below the standard in extent, quantity, duration, etc.: *short measure.* **10.** less than; inferior to (fol. by *of*): *little short of the best.* **11.** having a scanty or insufficient amount of (money, food, etc.): *we are short of bread.* **12.** deficient in (fol. by *on*): *short on sense.* **13.** breaking or crumbling readily, as pastry that contains a large proportion of butter or other shortening. **14.** (of metals) deficient in tenacity; friable; brittle. **15.** (of the head or skull) of less than ordinary length from front to back. **16.** *Comm.* **a.** not possessing at the time of sale commodities or stocks that one sells. **b.** denoting or pertaining to sales of commodities or stocks which the seller does not possess; depending for profit on a decline in prices. **17.** *Phonet.* **a.** lasting a relatively short time: *bit* has a shorter vowel than *bid* or *bead.* **b.** belonging to a class of sounds considered as usu. shorter in duration than another class, such as the vowel of *hot* as compared to *bought;* conventionally, the vowels of *bat, bet, bit, hot, good,* and *but.* **18.** (of an alcoholic drink) small, usu. with a comparatively high alcoholic content. **19.** *Cricket.* of a ball which pitches well down the wicket from the batsman. **20. make short work of,** to finish or dispose of quickly. **21. nothing short of,** nothing less than. **22. short for,** being a shorter form of: *'phone' is short for 'telephone'.* *–adv.* **23.** abruptly or suddenly: *to stop short.* **24.** briefly; curtly. **25.** on the nearer side of an intended or particular point: *to fall short.* **26.** without going to the length (fol. by *of*): *to stop short of actual crime.* **27.** *Comm.* without possessing at the time the stocks, etc., sold: *to sell short.* **28.** *Cricket.* pitching well down the wicket from the batsman. **29. be caught short,** *Colloq.* **a.** to discover an inconvenient lack of something, as money. **b.** to have a sudden and urgent need to urinate or defecate. **30. cut short,** to end abruptly; curtail; interrupt. **31. sell oneself short,** *Colloq.* **a.** to underestimate one's abilities or achievements. **b.** to behave in a fashion considered to be unworthy of one. *–n.* **32.** something that is short. **33.** what is deficient or lacking. **34.** *Mil.* a shot which strikes or bursts short of the target. **35.** *Elect.* a short circuit. **36.** *Comm.* one who has sold short. **37.** *Pros.* a short sound or syllable. **38.** *Films.* **a.** (*usu. pl.*) a short film made up of excerpts from a feature film soon to be released; trailer. **b.** any short film. **39. for short,** by way of abbreviation. **40. in short,** in a few words; in brief; briefly. *–v.i.* **41.** *Colloq.* to short-circuit. **42.** *Colloq.* to sell short. *–v.t.* **43.** *Colloq.* to short-circuit. [ME; OE *sc(e)ort*] – **shortness,** *n.*

**short account** /'– əkaʊnt/, *n. Banking.* **1.** a short seller's account. **2.** the total short sales in a market, or the total short sales of a particular commodity.

**shortage** /'ʃɔtɪdʒ/, *n.* **1.** deficiency in quantity. **2.** an amount deficient.

**short and curlies,** *n. pl. Colloq.* →**short hairs.**

**short arm** /ʃɔt 'am/, *n., Colloq.* →**penis.**

**short-arm parade** /ˌʃɔt-am pə'reɪd/, *n. Colloq.* in an establishment of the armed forces, a parade called for the medical inspection of the men's genitalia. Also, **short-arm inspection.**

**short arse** /'ʃɔt as/, *n. Colloq.* a person of below average height.

**short black** /– 'blæk/, *n.* a small cup of strong black coffee.

**shortbread** /'ʃɔtbrɛd/, *n.* a thick, crisp biscuit, rich in butter, often baked in one piece and cut into pieces when cool.

**shortcake** /'ʃɔtkeɪk/, *n.* a rich biscuit dough, baked as a cake, and when cool, split, and filled with fruit, esp. strawberries, and topped with cream.

**short-change** /ʃɔt-'tʃeɪndʒ/, *v.t.,* **-changed, -changing.** *Colloq.* **1.** to give less than proper change to. **2.** to cheat. – **short-changer,** *n.*

**short circuit** /ʃɔt 'sɜkət/, *n.* an abnormal connection of relatively low resistance, whether made accidentally or intentionally, between two points of different potential in an electrical circuit.

**short-circuit** /ʃɔt-'sɜkət/, *v.t.* **1.** to establish a short circuit in. **2.** to carry (a current) as a short circuit. **3.** to cut off by a short circuit. *–v.i.* **4.** to form a short circuit.

**short circuiting** /ʃɔt 'sɜkətɪŋ/, *n. Colloq.* an operation to remove portions of the small intestine, so as to allow the body less opportunity to digest food, thereby causing weight loss.

**shortcoming** /'ʃɔtkʌmɪŋ/, *n.* a failure or defect in conduct, condition, etc.

**short covering** /'ʃɔt kʌvərɪŋ/, *n.* purchases made to provide for sales already made without possessing the commodities or stocks sold.

**shortcrust** /'ʃɔtkrʌst/, *adj.* →**short** (def. 13).

**short cut** /'ʃɔt kʌt/, *n.* a shorter or quicker way.

**short-dated** /'ʃɔt-deɪtəd/, *adj.* having little time to run.

**short division** /ʃɔt də'vɪʒən/, *n.* division in which all working out is done mentally and not written down.

**short-eared bandicoot** /ˌʃɔt-ɪəd 'bændikut/, *n.* any of several bandicoots of the genus *Perameles* **(long-nosed bandicoot)** or *Isoodon* **(short-nosed bandicoot).**

**shorten** /'ʃɔtn/, *v.t.* **1.** to make shorter; curtail. **2.** to take in; reduce: *to shorten sail.* **3.** to make (pastry, etc.) short, as with butter or other fat. *–v.i.* **4.** to become shorter. **5.** (of odds) to decrease. – **shortener,** *n.*

**short engine** /'ʃɔt ɛndʒən/, *n.* a reconditioned engine without a cylinder head and other removable parts such as the distributor, carburettor, etc. Also, **short motor.**

**shortening** /'ʃɔtnɪŋ/, *n.* butter, lard, or other fat, used to make pastry, etc., short.

**shortfall** /'ʃɔtfɔl/, *n.* the extent to which production or output falls short of expectation.

**short game** /'ʃɔt geɪm/, *n.* (in golf) the part of the game involving the approach to the green and putting.

**short-grain** /'ʃɔt-greɪn/, *adj.* (of paper) cut so that the grain of the paper runs parallel to the shorter side.

**short hairs** /ʃɔt 'hɛəz/, *n. pl. Colloq.* **1.** pubic hair. **2. have by the short hairs,** to have at one's mercy. Also, **short and curlies.**

**shorthand** /'ʃɔthænd/, *n.* **1.** a method of rapid handwriting using extremely simple strokes in place of letters, often with other abbreviating devices. *–adj.* **2.** using shorthand. **3.** written in shorthand.

**shorthanded** /ʃɔt'hændəd/, *adj.* not having the necessary number of workers, helpers, etc.

**shorthand typist** /'ʃɔthænd taɪpəst/, *n.* a person trained both to use shorthand and to type.

**shorthead** /'ʃɔthɛd/, *n.* **1.** a brachycephalic person. **2.** a head with a cephalic index of 81 and over. – **shortheaded,** *adj.*

**Shorthorn** /'ʃɔthɔn/, *n.* one of a breed of dairy or beef cattle, with white, red, or roan markings, having short horns.

**shortie** /'ʃɔti/, *n.* **1.** *Colloq.* a short person or thing. *–adj.* **2.** of or denoting a garment designed to be of short length, as a nightdress.

**shortish** /'ʃɔtɪʃ/, *adj.* rather short.

**short leg** /ʃɔt 'lɛg/, *n. Cricket.* **1.** the on-side fielding position close to and more or less square of the batsman. **2.** a fielder in this position.

**short life** /'– laɪf/, *n.* a short period of consummability, esp. as of perishable foods.

**short-life** /'ʃɔt-laɪf/, *adj.* having a short shelf life; perishable.

**short list** /'– lɪst/, *n.* a list of especially favoured candidates for a position, promotion, etc., who have been selected from a larger group of applicants.

**short-list** /'ʃɔt-lɪst/, *v.t.* to put (someone) on a short list.

**short-lived** /'ʃɔt-lɪvd/, *adj.* living or lasting only a little while.

**short loin chop,** *n.* a lamb chop from the top end of the loin, below the ribs.

**shortly** /'ʃɔtli/, *adv.* **1.** in a short time; soon. **2.** briefly; concisely. **3.** curtly; abruptly.

**short motor** /'ʃɔt moʊtə/, *n.* →**short engine.**

**short-nosed bandicoot** /ˌʃɔt-noʊzd 'bændikut/, *n.* See **short-eared bandicoot.**

**short octave** /'ʃɔt ɒktəv/, *n.* (formerly) the incomplete bottom octave in a harpsichord, organ, etc., in which some seldom-used notes are retuned to more frequently needed pitches below the original compass of the instrument.

**short order** /'– ɔdə/, *n. U.S.* a meal which can be quickly and easily prepared, as in a diner or cafe.

**short-order cook** /ˌʃɔt-ɔdə 'kʊk/, *n. U.S.* a cook employed to prepare short orders.

**short-range** /'ʃɔt-reɪndʒ/, *adj.* having a limited extent in distance or time.

**shorts** /ʃɔts/, *n.pl.* short trousers, not extending beyond the knee.

**short score** /'ʃɔt skɔ/, *n.* a condensation of a full score for piano rehearsals with the instrumentation indicated.

**shortsheet** /ʃɔt'ʃit/, *v.t.* **1.** to make (a bed) using only one sheet folded in half from the bottom up. **2.** to play a joke on (a person) by making his bed in this way.

**shortship** /ʃɔt'ʃɪp/, *v.t.,* **-shipped, -shipping.** to omit from shipment (a consignment or part thereof).

**short-sighted** /'ʃɔt-saɪtəd/, *adj.* **1.** unable to see far; near-sighted; myopic. **2.** lacking in foresight. – **short-sightedly,**

*adv.* – **short-sightedness,** *n.*

**short soup** /'ʃɔt sup/, *n.* a Chinese soup consisting largely of chicken stock and small pieces of noodle pastry enclosing forcemeat.

**short-spoken** /ʃɔt-'spoʊkən/, *adj.* speaking in a short, brief, or curt manner.

**short-staffed** /ʃɔt-'staft/, *adj.* not having the usual number of personnel present, esp. as a result of sickness, understaffing, etc.

**shortstop** /'ʃɔtstɒp/, *n. Baseball.* **1.** the position of the player who covers the infield between second and third base. **2.** the fielder in this position.

**short story** /ʃɔt 'stɔri/, *n.* a piece of prose fiction, usu. confined to a small group of characters and a single main event, and much shorter than a novel.

**short-story writer** /ʃɔt-'stɔri ˌraɪtə/, *n.* **1.** an author who writes short stories. **2.** *Prison Colloq.* a forger (esp. of cheques).

**short-tailed shearwater** /ˌʃɔt-teɪld 'ʃɪəwɔtə/, *n.* a large, dark seabird, *Puffinus tenuirostris,* breeding on islands in Bass Strait and in coastal areas of Tasmania and south-eastern Australia, and migrating to the Northern Hemisphere in winter; mutton-bird.

**short-tempered** /ʃɔt-'tɛmpəd/, *adj.* having a hasty temper; inclined to become angry on little provocation.

**short-term** /'ʃɔt-tɜm/, *adj.* **1.** covering a comparatively short period of time. **2.** having a maturity within a comparatively short time: *a short-term loan.*

**short-term memory** /– 'mɛmri/, *n.* the part of the memory that can store small amounts of information for a short period, as used in dialling telephone numbers, etc. Cf. **long-term memory.**

**short-term money market,** *n.* a market in which large loans (usu. of more than $50 000 at a time) are made for short periods of time, as short as a few days.

**short-time** /'ʃɔt-taɪm/, *n.* a compulsory reduction in working hours in order to cut costs but avoid standing workers down.

**short-timer** /ʃɔt-'taɪmə/, *n. Prison Colloq.* a prisoner serving a short sentence (usu. less than two years).

**short ton** /'ʃɔt tʌn/, *n.* See **ton**[1] (def. 1).

**short-waisted** /ʃɔt-'weɪstəd/, *adj.* of less than average length from the shoulders to the waist.

**short wave** /'ʃɔt weɪv/, *n.* an electromagnetic wave 60 metres or less in length. – **short-wave** /'ʃɔt-weɪv/, *adj.*

**short-winded** /ʃɔt-'wɪndəd/, *adj.* **1.** short of breath; liable to difficulty in breathing. **2.** brief; succinct. **3.** choppy; disconnected.

**Short Wool breed,** *n.* one of several British breeds of sheep which are short and symmetrical in body and which excel in mutton production. Their wool is short and deficient in quality and texture.

**Shoshonean** /ʃoʊ'ʃoʊniən, ʃoʊʃə'niən/, *adj.* **1.** belonging to or constituting a linguistic group of North American Indians of the western U.S., including the Shoshone, Comanche, Ute, Paiute, Hopi, etc.; a subdivision of the great Uto-Aztecan speech family. *–n.* **2.** the Shoshonean languages collectively.

**shot**[1] /ʃɒt/, *n., pl.* **shots** or *(for defs 5 and 7)* **shot;** *v.,* **shotted, shotting.** *–n.* **1.** the discharge or a discharge of a firearm, bow, etc. **2.** the range of the discharge, or the distance covered by the missile in its flight. **3.** an attempt to hit with a projectile discharged from a gun or the like. **4.** the act of shooting. **5.** a small ball or pellet of lead, of which a number are used for one charge of a sportsman's gun. **6.** such pellets collectively: *a charge of shot.* **7.** a projectile for discharge from a firearm or cannon. **8.** such projectiles collectively. **9.** a person who shoots: *he was a good shot.* **10.** anything like a shot. **11.** a heavy metal ball which competitors cast as far as possible in shot-putting contests. **12.** an aimed stroke, throw, or the like, as in games, etc. **13.** an attempt or try. **14.** a remark aimed at some person or thing. **15.** a guess at something. **16.** *Colloq.* an injection of a drug, vaccine, etc. **17.** *U.S.* a small quantity of something, esp. of liquor. **18.** *Photog., Films.* **a.** the making of a photograph. **b.** a photograph. **c.** a length of cinefilm taken without stopping or cutting. **19.** *Mining, etc.* an explosive charge in place for detonation. **20. big shot,** *Colloq.* an important person. **21.** (*pl.*) **call the shots,** *Colloq.* to be in command. **22. have a shot at (someone),** *Colloq.* to criticise; ridicule. **23. like a shot,** *Colloq.* instantly; very quickly. **24. shot in the arm,** *Colloq.* something that gives renewed confidence, vigour, etc. **25. shot in the dark,** a wild or random guess. **26. that's the shot!** (an exclamation of approval). *–v.t.* **27.** to load or supply with shot. **28.** to weight with shot. **29. to be** or **get shot of,** *Colloq.* to be rid of. [ME; OE *sc(e)ot, gesceot,* c. G *Schoss, Geschoss;* akin to SHOOT]

**shot**[2] /ʃɒt/, *v.* **1.** past tense and past participle of **shoot.** *–adj.* **2.** woven so as to present a play of colours, as silk. **3.** spread or streaked with colour.

**shote** /ʃoʊt/, *n.* →**shoat.**

**shot grass** /'ʃɒt gras/, *n.* a hardy native perennial, *Paspalidium globoideum,* common in north-western New South Wales, the seeds of which are spherical and resemble gun shot; used as a stock feed.

**shotgun** /'ʃɒtgʌn/, *n.* **1.** a smoothbore gun for firing small shot to kill small game, though often used with buckshot to kill larger animals. *–adj.* **2.** of, pertaining to, or used in a shotgun.

**shotgun wedding** /– 'wɛdɪŋ/, *n.* a wedding hastened or forced by the pregnancy of the bride.

**shot noise** /'ʃɒt nɔɪz/, *n.* fluctuation in a circuit due to the random motion of electrons.

**shot point** /'– pɔɪnt/, *n.* (in geophysical exploration) a point at which an explosion is set off to create seismic waves.

**shot-put** /'ʃɒt-pʊt/, *n.* **1.** the athletic exercise of putting the shot. See **shot**[1] (def. 11). **2.** one throw of the shot in this exercise.

**shot-putter** /'ʃɒt-pʊtə/, *n.* one who takes part in the shot-put.

**shott** /ʃɒt/, *n.* **1.** a shallow, temporary salt lake or salt marsh in the deserts of North Africa. **2.** a hollow or depression containing such a salt lake or marshy area. [Ar.]

**shotten** /'ʃɒtn/, *adj.* **1.** (of fish, esp. herring) that has recently spawned. **2.** *Pathol.* dislocated. [old pp. of SHOOT]

**shot tower** /'ʃɒt taʊə/, *n.* a tower in which shot is made by pouring molten lead through a sieve and then letting it drop into a tank of water.

**should** /ʃʊd/, *v.* **1.** past tense of **shall.** **2.** (specially used) **a.** to denote duty, propriety, or expediency: *you should not do that.* **b.** to make a statement less direct or blunt: *I should hardly say that.* **c.** to emphasise the uncertainty in conditional and hypothetical clauses: *if it should be true.* [ME *sholde,* OE *sc(e)olde.* See SHALL]

**shoulder** /'ʃoʊldə/, *n.* **1.** either of two corresponding parts of the human body, situated at the top of the trunk and extending respectively from the right side and left side of the neck to the upper joint of the corresponding arm. **2.** (*pl.*) these two parts together with the portion of the back joining them, forming a place where burdens are sometimes carried. **3.** a corresponding part in animals. **4.** the upper foreleg and adjoining parts of a sheep, etc. **5.** the joint connecting the arm or the foreleg with the trunk. **6.** a shoulder-like part or projection. **7.** a cut of meat including the upper joint of the foreleg. **8.** *Fort.* the angle of a bastion between the face and the flank. **9.** *Print.* the flat surface on a type body extending beyond the base of the letter or character. **10.** that part of a garment which covers, or fits over the shoulder. **11.** *Leather Mfg.* that part of the hide anterior to the butt. **12.** either of two strips of land bordering a road, esp. that part on which vehicles can be parked in an emergency. **13.** the unbroken, tapering part of the wave, away from the curl. **14. give the cold shoulder to,** *Colloq.* to treat coldly; ignore; snub. **15. have broad shoulders,** to be able to accept responsibility. **16. put one's shoulder to the wheel,** to work hard. **17. rub shoulders with,** to associate with; come into contact with. **18. shoulder to shoulder,** with united action and support. **19. straight from the shoulder,** without evasion. *–v.t.* **20.** to push, as with the shoulder, esp. roughly. **21.** to take upon or support with the shoulder. **22.** to assume as a burden, or responsibility: *to shoulder the expense.* *–v.i.*

shoulder (def. 1): A, clavicle; B, acromion; C, scapula; D, humerus

**23.** to push with the shoulder. **24. shoulder arms,** to execute a movement in arms drill, in which the rifle is brought into a vertical position, muzzle pointing upwards, on the right side of the body, and held by the right hand at the trigger guard. [ME *sholder,* OE *sculdor,* c. G *Schulter*]

**shoulder-bag** /ˈʃoʊldə-bæg/, *n.* a small travelling bag or handbag with a long strap, to be slung over the shoulder.

**shoulder-blade** /ˈʃoʊldə-bleɪd/, *n.* →**scapula.**

**shoulder-flash** /ˈʃoʊldə-flæʃ/, *n.* a cloth emblem worn on the shoulder to signify regiment or special duties.

**shoulder knot** /ˈʃoʊldə nɒt/, *n.* a knot of ribbon or lace worn on the shoulder, as by men of fashion in the 17th and 18th centuries, by servants in livery, or by women or children.

**shoulder-strap** /ˈʃoʊldə-stræp/, *n.* a strap worn over the shoulder as to support a garment.

**shouldn't** /ˈʃʊdnt/, *v.* contraction of *should not.*

**shouldst** /ʃʊdst/, *v. Archaic.* 2nd person singular of **should.** Also, **shouldest** /ˈʃʊdəst/.

**shouse** /ʃaʊs/, *n., adj. Colloq.* →**shithouse.** [contraction of SHITHOUSE]

**shout** /ʃaʊt/, *v.i.* **1.** to call or cry out loudly and vigorously. **2.** to speak or laugh noisily or unrestrainedly. *–v.t.* **3.** to express by a shout or shouts. **4.** *Colloq.* **a.** to stand (the company) a round of drinks. **b.** to pay for something for another person; treat: *I'll shout you to the pictures; I'll shout you a new dress.* **5. shout down,** to drown (another's words) by shouting or talking loudly. *–n.* **6.** a loud call or cry. **7.** a loud burst, as of laughter. **8.** the act of shouting, as by providing drinks. **9.** one's turn to shout. **10.** →**shout song.** [ME; c. Icel. *skūta* scold, chide] – **shouter,** *n.* – **shouting,** *n.*

**shout song** /ˈ– sɒŋ/, *n.* a traditional American Negro religious song, characterised by strong rhythm and responsive utterances between leader and congregation, now incorporated into gospel music, etc.

**shove** /ʃʌv/, *v.,* **shoved, shoving,** *n.* *–v.t.* **1.** to move along by force from behind. **2.** to push roughly or rudely; jostle. *–v.i.* **3.** to push. **4. shove off, a.** to push a boat off. **b.** *Colloq.* to leave; start. *–n.* **5.** an act of shoving. *–interj.* **6. shove it!** *Colloq.* (an expression of dismissal, contempt, etc.). [ME *showve,* OE *scūfan,* c. G *schauben* (obs.)] – **shover,** *n.*

**shovel**[1] /ˈʃʌvəl/, *n., v.,* **-elled, -elling,** or (*U.S.*) **-eled, -eling.** *–n.* **1.** an implement consisting of a broad blade or scoop attached to a handle, used for taking up and removing loose matter, as earth, snow, coal, etc. **2.** a contrivance or machine for shovelling, removing matter, etc. **3.** →**shovelful. 4.** *Colloq.* a shovel hat. *–v.t.* **5.** to take up and cast or remove with a shovel. **6.** to gather or put in quantities or carelessly: *to shovel food into one's mouth.* **7.** to dig or clear with a shovel: *to shovel a path.* *–v.i.* **8.** to work with a shovel. [ME *schovel,* OE *scofl;* akin to G *Schaufel*]

**shovel**[2] /ˈʃʌvəl/, *n. Colloq.* a room; living quarters. [rhyming slang, *shovel and broom* room]

**shovelboard** /ˈʃʌvəlbɔd/, *n.* →**shuffleboard.**

**shoveler** /ˈʃʌvələ/, *n.* **1.** Also, **blue-winged shoveler.** an Australian duck, *Anas rhynchotis,* with a broad, flat, olive-brown bill. **2.** Also, **shovel-bill.** a similar Northern Hemisphere bird, *Anas clypeata;* spoonbill. **3.** *U.S.* →**shoveller** (def. 1). Also, **shoveller.**

**shovelful** /ˈʃʌvəlfʊl/, *n.* as much as a shovel will hold.

**shovel hat** /ˈʃʌvəl hæt/, *n.* a hat with a broad brim turned up at the sides and projecting with a shovel-like curve in front and behind; worn by some ecclesiastics.

**shoveller** /ˈʃʌvələ/, *n.* **1.** Also, *U.S.,* **shoveler.** one who or that which shovels. **2.** →**shoveler.**

**shovel-nosed lobster** /ˌʃʌvəl-noʊzd ˈlɒbstə/, *n.* an edible crustacean, *Thenus orientalis,* found in Moreton Bay, Queensland, similar in appearance and related to the Balmain bug.

**shovel-nose ray** /ˌʃʌvəl-noʊz ˈreɪ/, *n.* any of a number of species of flattened, triangular-shaped rays of the family Rhinobatidae, having long, powerful, shark-like tails and often growing to a considerable size.

**show** /ʃoʊ/, *v.,* **showed, shown** or **showed, showing,** *n.* *–v.t.* **1.** to cause or allow to be seen; exhibit; display; present. **2.** to point out: *to show the way.* **3.** to guide; escort: *he showed me to my room.* **4.** to make clear; make known; explain. **5.** to prove; demonstrate. **6.** to indicate; register: *the thermometer showed ten degrees below zero.* **7.** to allege, as in a legal document; plead, as a reason or cause. **8.** to produce, as facts in an affidavit or at a hearing. **9.** to make evident by appearance, behaviour, etc.: *to show one's feelings.* **10.** to accord or grant (favour, etc.). **11. show off,** to exhibit for approval or admiration, or ostentatiously: *she was showing off her new dress.* **12. show up, a.** to expose (faults, etc.); reveal. **b.** to appear superior to (another); outdo. *–v.i.* **13.** to be seen; be or become visible. **14.** to look or appear: *to show to advantage.* **15.** *Colloq.* to give an exhibition, display, or performance. **16.** *U.S.* to finish in third place in a horse race, etc. **17. show off,** to display one's abilities, cleverness, etc., with the object of gaining attention. **18. show up, a.** to stand out in a certain way; appear: *blue shows up well against that background.* **b.** to turn up; appear at a certain place. *–n.* **19.** a display: *a show of freedom.* **20.** ostentatious display. **21.** any kind of public exhibition. **22.** the act of showing. **23.** appearance: *to make a sorry show.* **24.** an unreal or deceptive appearance. **25.** an indication; trace. **26.** a non-commercial quantity of oil or gas encountered in drilling. **27.** *Pathol.* (in pregnancy) a discharge of blood and mucosal tissue, indicating the onset of labour. **28.** *Colloq.* a theatrical performance or company. **29.** *Chiefly U.S.* a chance: *to get a fair show.* **30.** a sight or spectacle. **31.** any undertaking, organisation, etc.; affair. **32.** a public collection of things on display; a competitive exhibition of farm produce, livestock, etc. **33. a show of hands,** a voting procedure in which hands are raised to show assent for or dissent from a proposition. **34. give the show away,** to reveal all the details of a plan, scheme, etc. **35. run the show,** to control or manage a business, etc. **36. steal the show,** to attract most attention; be the most popular person or item, in a theatrical performance, etc. **37. stop the show,** (in a theatrical performance, etc.) to be applauded so enthusiastically as to cause the performance to be temporarily interrupted. *–adj.* **38.** of or pertaining to an animal bred or trained to be entered into a show (def. 32). [ME *showen,* var. of *shewan* look at, show, OE *scēawian* look at, c. D *schowen,* G *schauen* look at] – **shower,** *n.*

**showbill** /ˈʃoʊbɪl/, *n.* a poster advertising a show.

**showboat** /ˈʃoʊboʊt/, *n.* **1.** *U.S.* a boat, esp. a paddlewheel steamer, used as a travelling theatre. **2.** a boat which takes people on a short cruise in sheltered waters and on which food and entertainment are provided.

**showbread** /ˈʃoʊbrɛd/, *n.* →**shewbread.**

**show business** /ˈʃoʊ bɪznəs/, *n.* the entertainment industry, esp. that part concerned with variety. Also, **show biz.**

**showcase** /ˈʃoʊkeɪs/, *n.* **1.** a glass case for the display and protection of articles in shops, museums, etc. **2.** a setting or display for exhibiting something at its best, or on a trial basis.

**showdown** /ˈʃoʊdaʊn/, *n.* **1.** the laying down of one's cards, face upwards, in a card game, esp. poker. **2.** a confrontation of parties for the final settlement of a contested issue.

**shower** /ˈʃaʊə/, *n.* **1.** a brief fall of rain, hail, sleet or snow. **2.** a similar fall, as of sparks or bullets. **3.** a large supply or quantity: *a shower of questions.* **4.** →**shower tea. 5. a.** an apparatus for spraying water for bathing, usu. set overhead above a bath or in a shower recess. **b.** a washing of the body in the water sprayed from such an apparatus. **6.** a dust storm: *Wilcannia shower.* **7.** *Physics.* a group of high-energy particles which originate from one fast particle, from cosmic radiation, or from an accelerator. **8.** →**throwover. 9.** *Brit. Colloq.* an unpleasant group or person. **10. (someone) didn't come down in the last shower,** *Colloq.* (someone) is not naive or gullible. *–v.t.* **11.** to wet with a shower. **12.** to pour (something) down in a shower. **13.** to bestow liberally or lavishly. *–v.i.* **14.** to rain in a shower. **15.** (of a person) to take a shower (def. 5). [ME *shour,* OE *scūr,* c. G *Schauer*] – **showery,** *adj.*

**shower-bath** /ˈʃaʊə-baθ/, *n.* →**shower** (def. 5).

**showerproof** /ˈʃaʊəpruf/, *adj.* **1.** (of clothing) treated so as to repel water, yet retain air permeability. *–v.t.* **2.** to treat clothing in this fashion.

**shower recess** /ˈʃaʊə rəsɛs/, *n.* a small closed-off area, esp. in a bathroom, in which a shower is fitted.

**shower tea** /– ˈti/, *n.* a party for a bride-to-be to which the guests, usu. other women, bring a present for her future home.

**show floor** /ˈʃoʊ flɔ/, *n.* **1.** a covered space, esp. at ground level, in which large goods such as cars are displayed for sale. **2.** a showroom in a wool store where baled wool may be inspected by buyers.

**showgirl** /ˈʃoʊgɜl/, *n.* a girl who sings, dances, etc., usu. in a chorus, in a variety show, nightclub, or the like.

**showing** /ˈʃoʊɪŋ/, *n.* **1.** an exhibition; show. **2.** a setting forth or presentation, as of facts or conditions.

**showjumping** /ˈʃoʊdʒʌmpɪŋ/, *n.* the riding of horses in competitions in order to display skill in riding over and between obstacles. – **showjumper,** *n.*

**showman** /ˈʃoʊmən/, *n., pl.* **-men. 1.** one who exhibits a show. **2.** one who presents things well. – **showmanship,** *n.*

**shown** /ʃoʊn/, *v.* past participle of **show.**

**show-off** /ˈʃoʊ-ɒf/, *n.* one given to pretentious display or exhibitionism.

**showpiece** /ˈʃoʊpis/, *n.* **1.** an article to be displayed in an exhibition, show, etc. **2.** an article worthy of exhibition as an excellent example of its kind. **3.** a brilliant piece of music, dance, acrobatic routine, etc., which shows to advantage the skill of the performer.

**showplace** /ˈʃoʊpleɪs/, *n.* **1.** a building or estate renowned for its beauty or historical interest, and open to the public. **2.** any building renowned for its beauty or design: *the Opera House is a real showplace.*

**showroom** /ˈʃoʊrum/, *n.* a room used for the display of goods or merchandise.

**show stopper** /ˈʃoʊ stɒpə/, *n.* **1.** a song, act, performance, etc., that temporarily interrupts a show because of the enthusiastic applause of the audience. **2.** any utterance that interrupts a conversation due to its surprising, controversial or hilarious nature.

**show trial** /ˈ– traɪəl/, *n.* a trial which is held less for its own sake than for some impression it is calculated to create, as a demonstration of power of the state or a demonstration of the fairness of the judicial system.

**show window** /ˈ– wɪndoʊ/, *n.* a display window in a store.

**showy** /ˈʃoʊi/, *adj.,* **showier, showiest. 1.** making an imposing display: *showy flowers.* **2.** ostentatious; gaudy. – **showily,** *adv.* – **showiness,** *n.*

**shrank** /ʃræŋk/, *v.* past tense of **shrink.**

**shrapnel** /ˈʃræpnəl/, *n.* **1. a.** a hollow projectile containing bullets or the like and a bursting charge, designed to explode before reaching its target, and to set free a shower of missiles. **b.** such projectiles collectively. **2.** shell fragments. **3.** *Colloq.* small change, esp. silver. [named after the inventor, H. *Shrapnel,* 1761-1842, officer in the British army]

**shred** /ʃrɛd/, *n., v.,* **shredded** or **shred, shredding.** *–n.* **1.** a piece cut or torn off, esp. in a narrow strip. **2.** a bit; scrap. *–v.t.* **3.** to cut or tear into small pieces, esp. small strips; reduce to shreds. *–v.i.* **4.** to tear; be reduced to shreds. [ME *schrede,* OE *scrēade,* c. G *Schrot* chips]

**shredder** /ˈʃrɛdə/, *n.* **1.** one who or that which shreds. **2.** office equipment designed to shred paper and used principally to destroy unwanted confidential documents.

**shrew** /ʃru/, *n.* **1.** any of various small, insectivorous mammals of the genus *Sorex* and allied genera, having a long, sharp snout and a mouselike form, as the **watershrew,** *Neomys fodiens,* of Europe and the British Isles. **2.** a woman of violent temper and speech; a termagant. [OE *scrēawa;* of unknown orig.]

shrew (def. 1)

**shrewd** /ʃrud/, *adj.* **1.** astute or sharp in practical matters: *a shrewd politician.* **2.** *Archaic.* keen; piercing. **3.** *Archaic.* malicious. [ME *shrewed,* pp. of *shrew* curse (now obs.), v. use of SHREW, *n.*] – **shrewdly,** *adv.* – **shrewdness,** *n.*

**shrewdie** /ˈʃrudi/, *n. Colloq.* **1.** Also, **shrewd head.** a shrewd person. **2.** a shrewd trick.

**shrewish** /ˈʃruɪʃ/, *adj.* having the disposition of a shrew. – **shrewishly,** *adv.* – **shrewishness,** *n.*

**shrewmouse** /ˈʃrumaʊs/, *n., pl.* **-mice.** a shrew, esp. *Sorex araneus,* the common shrew of Europe.

**shriek** /ʃrik/, *n.* **1.** a loud, sharp, shrill cry. **2.** a loud, high sound of laughter. **3.** any loud, shrill sound, as of a whistle. *–v.i.* **4.** to utter a loud, sharp, shrill cry, as birds. **5.** to cry out sharply in a high voice: *to shriek with pain.* **6.** to utter loud, high-pitched sounds in laughing. **7.** (of a musical instrument, a whistle, the wind, etc.) to give forth a loud, shrill sound. *–v.t.* **8.** to cry in a shriek: *to shriek defiance.* [earlier *shrick,* northern Brit. var. of *shritch* (now d.), ME *schriche;* akin to Scand. *skrækja*] – **shrieker,** *n.*

**shrieve** /ʃriv/, *v.t., v.i.,* **shrieved, shrieving.** *Archaic.* →**shrive.**

**shrift** /ʃrɪft/, *n. Archaic.* **1.** the imposition of penance by a priest on a penitent after confession. **2.** absolution or remission of sins granted after confession and penance. **3.** confession to a priest. **4.** the act of shriving. **5. short shrift, a.** little consideration in dealing with someone or something; summary treatment. **b.** *Obs.* a brief space of time for confession allowed to a condemned criminal before his execution. [ME; OE *scrift* (c. D *schrift* and G *Schrift* writing), from SHRIVE]

**shrike** /ʃraɪk/, *n.* **1.** any of numerous predacious oscine birds of the European family Laniidae, with a strong hooked and toothed bill, which feed on insects and sometimes on small birds and other animals. **2.** any of various other birds resembling shrikes but belonging to different families, as the Australian butcherbird of the genus *Cracticus.* [OE *scrīc*]

**shrike-thrush** /ˈʃraɪk-θrʌʃ/, *n.* **1.** any of several Australian singing birds of the genus *Colluricincla* as the **grey shrike-thrush,** *C. harmonica.* **2.** an Indian bird of the genus *Gampsorhynchus.*

**shrike-tit** /ˈʃraɪk-tɪt/, *n.* any of several small, insectivorous birds of genus *Falcunculus* with powerful hooked bills and prominent crests.

**shrill** /ʃrɪl/, *adj.* **1.** high-pitched and piercing: *a shrill cry.* **2.** producing such sound. **3.** full of such sound. **4.** *Poetic.* keen; piercing. *–v.t., v.i.* **5.** to cry shrilly. *–n.* **6.** a shrill sound. *–adv.* **7.** shrilly. [ME *shrille,* c. G *schrill* (of LG orig.); akin to OE *scrallettan* sound loudly] – **shrillness,** *n.* – **shrilly,** *adv.*

**shrimp** /ʃrɪmp/, *n.* **1.** any of various small, long-tailed, chiefly marine, decapod crustaceans of the genus *Crangon* and allied genera (suborder Macrura), as the European *C. vulgaris,* esteemed as a table delicacy. **2.** *Colloq.* a diminutive or insignificant person. *–v.i.* **3.** to catch or attempt to catch shrimps. [ME *shrimpe.* Cf. G *shrumpfen* shrink up, and OE *scrimman* shrink] – **shrimper,** *n.*

shrimp

**shrine** /ʃraɪn/, *n., v.,* **shrined, shrining.** *–n.* **1.** a receptacle for sacred relics; a reliquary. **2.** a structure, often of a stately or sumptuous character, enclosing the remains or relics of a saint or other holy objects and forming an object of religious veneration and pilgrimage. **3.** any structure or place consecrated or devoted to some saint or deity, as an altar, chapel, church, or temple. **4.** any place or object hallowed by its history or associations. *–v.t.* **5.** to enshrine. [ME *schrine,* OE *scrīn* (c. G *Schrein*), from L *scrīnium* case for books and papers]

**shrink** /ʃrɪŋk/, *v.,* **shrank** or **shrunk, shrunk** or **shrunken, shrinking,** *n.* *–v.i.* **1.** to draw back, as in retreat or avoidance. **2.** to contract with heat, cold, moisture, etc. **3.** to become reduced in extent or compass. *–v.t.* **4.** to cause to shrink or contract. **5.** *Textiles.* to cause to shrink in order to prevent future shrinkage. *–n.* **6.** a shrinking. **7.** a shrinking movement. **8.** *Colloq.* Also, **headshrinker.** →**psychiatrist.** [ME *schrinke(n),* OE *scrincan,* c. MD *schrinken;* akin to Swed. *skrynka* wrinkle] – **shrinkable,** *adj.* – **shrinker,** *n.* – **shrinkingly,** *adv.*

**shrinkage** /ˈʃrɪŋkɪdʒ/, *n.* **1.** the act or fact of shrinking. **2.** the amount or degree of shrinking. **3.** reduction or depreciation in quantity, value, etc. **4.** contraction of a fabric in finishing or washing. **5.** the difference between the original weight of livestock and its weight after it has been prepared, shipped, etc., for marketing.

**shrive** /ʃraɪv/, *v.*, **shrove** or **shrived, shriven** or **shrived, shriving.** *–v.t.* **1.** to impose penance on for sin. **2.** to grant absolution to (a penitent). **3.** to confess to a priest, for the purpose of obtaining absolution. **4.** to hear the confession of. *–v.i.* **5.** to hear confessions. **6.** to go to or make confession. Also, *Archaic,* **shrieve.** [ME; OE *scrifan* (c. G *schreiben* write), from L *scrībere* write]

**shrivel** /ˈʃrɪvəl/, *v.t., v.i.,* **-elled, -elling** or (*U.S.*) **-eled, -eling. 1.** to contract and wrinkle, as from great heat or cold. **2.** to wither; make or become impotent. [orig. unknown]

**Shropshire** /ˈʃrɒpʃɪə, -ʃə/, *n.* a hornless breed of mutton sheep having dark brown or black face and legs, and fleece of a white wool. [from *Shropshire,* county in W England]

**shroud** /ʃraʊd/, *n.* **1.** a white cloth or sheet in which a corpse is wrapped for burial. **2.** something which covers or conceals like a garment: *a shroud of rain.* **3.** (*usu. pl.*) *Naut.* one of a set of strong ropes extended from the mastheads to the sides of a ship to help support the masts. **4.** *Mech.* **a.** circular webs used to stiffen the sides of gear teeth, esp. non-metallic gears. **b.** a strip used to strengthen turbine blades. **c.** a deflecting wall close to the inlet part of an internal-combustion engine used to promote turbulence of the incoming air. **5.** *Aeron.* the rearward extension of the skin of a fixed aerofoil surface to cover all or part of the leading edge of a control surface. *–v.t.* **6.** to wrap or clothe for burial. **7.** to cover; hide from view. **8.** to veil, as in obscurity or mystery. **9.** *Obs.* to shelter. *–v.i.* **10.** *Archaic.* to take shelter. [ME; OE *scrūd,* c. Icel. *skrūdh;* akin to SHRED] – **shroudless,** *adj.*

**shroud-laid** /ˈʃraʊd-leɪd/, *adj.* (of a rope) made with four strands and (usu.) a central core or heart.

**shrove** /ʃroʊv/, *v.* past tense of **shrive.**

**Shrove Sunday** /ʃroʊv ˈsʌndeɪ/, *n.* the Sunday before Ash Wednesday.

**Shrovetide** /ˈʃroʊvtaɪd/, *n.* the three days before Ash Wednesday, once a time of confession and absolution.

**Shrove Tuesday** /ʃroʊv ˈtjuzdeɪ/, *n.* the last day of Shrovetide, long observed as a season of merrymaking before Lent; Pancake Day.

**shrub**[1] /ʃrʌb/, *n.* a woody perennial plant smaller than a tree, usu. having permanent stems branching from or near the ground. [ME *shrubbe,* OE *scrybb* brushwood, c. d. Dan. *skrub*] – **shrublike,** *adj.*

**shrub**[2] /ʃrʌb/, *n.* a cordial made of different fruits, spirits, and sugar, formerly popular. [Ar., metathetic var. of *shurb* drink]

**shrubbery** /ˈʃrʌbəri/, *n., pl.* **-beries. 1.** shrubs collectively. **2.** a plantation or plot of shrubs.

**shrubby** /ˈʃrʌbi/, *adj.,* **-bier, -biest. 1.** shrublike. **2.** abounding in shrubs. **3.** consisting of shrubs. – **shrubbiness,** *n.*

**shrug** /ʃrʌg/, *v.,* **shrugged, shrugging,** *n.* *–v.t.* **1.** to raise and lower (the shoulders), expressing indifference, disdain, etc. **2. shrug off,** to disregard; take no notice of: *to shrug off an insult.* *–v.i.* **3.** to raise and lower the shoulders, expressing indifference, disdain, etc. *–n.* **4.** this movement. [ME]

**shrunk** /ʃrʌŋk/, *v.* past participle and a past tense of **shrink.**

**shrunken** /ˈʃrʌŋkən/, *v.* a past participle of **shrink.**

**sh tn,** short ton.

**shuck** /ʃʌk/, *U.S.* *–n.* **1.** a husk, shell, or pod, as the outer covering of maize, hickory nuts, chestnuts, etc. **2.** (*pl.*) *Colloq.* something useless: *not worth shucks.* **3.** the shell of an oyster or clam. *–v.t.* **4.** to remove the shucks from: *she sat there placidly shucking the peas.* **5.** to remove as or like shucks. [orig. unknown] – **shucker,** *n.*

**shucks** /ʃʌks/, *interj. U.S. Colloq.* (an exclamation of disgust or regret.)

**shudder** /ˈʃʌdə/, *v.i.* **1.** to tremble with a sudden convulsive movement, as from horror, fear, or cold. *–n.* **2.** a convulsive movement of the body, as from horror, fear, or cold. [ME *shodder, shuder* (c. G *schaudern*), frequentative of OE *scūdan* move, shake] – **shudderingly,** *adv.*

**shuffle** /ˈʃʌfəl/, *v.,* **-fled, -fling,** *n.* *–v.i.* **1.** to walk without lifting the feet or with clumsy steps and a shambling gait. **2.** to scrape the feet over the floor in dancing. **3.** to get (*into,* etc.) in a clumsy manner: *to shuffle into one's clothes.* **4.** to get (*in, out of,* etc.) in an underhand or evasive manner: *to shuffle out of responsibilities.* **5.** to act in a shifty or evasive manner; employ deceitful pretences; equivocate. **6.** to mix cards in a pack so as to change their relative position. *–v.t.* **7.** to move (the feet, etc.) along the ground or floor without lifting them. **8.** to perform (a dance, etc.) with such movements. **9.** to move this way and that. **10.** to put, thrust, or bring (*in, out,* etc.) trickily, evasively, or haphazardly. **11.** to mix (cards in a pack) so as to change their relative position. **12.** to jumble together; mix in a disorderly heap. **13. shuffle off, a.** to thrust aside or get rid of. **b.** to go off with a shuffling gait. *–n.* **14.** a scraping movement; a dragging gait. **15.** an evasive trick; evasion. **16.** the act of shuffling. **17.** a shuffling of cards in a pack. **18.** right or turn to shuffle in card-playing. **19.** a dance in which the feet are shuffled along the floor. [LG *schuffeln* walk clumsily or with dragging feet. See SHOVE] – **shuffler,** *n.*

**shuffleboard** /ˈʃʌfəlbɔd/, *n.* **1.** a game in which coins or discs are driven along a smooth board, table, or other surface, towards certain lines, etc., on it. **2.** the board, table, or the like. **3.** a similar game played as on board a ship's deck with large discs pushed with a cue. Also, **shovelboard.**

**shun** /ʃʌn/, *v.t.,* **shunned, shunning.** to keep away from (a place, person, etc.), from dislike, caution, etc.; take pains to avoid. [ME *shunen,* OE *scunian;* orig. obscure] – **shunner,** *n.*

**shunt** /ʃʌnt/, *v.t.* **1.** to move or turn aside or out of the way. **2.** to sidetrack; get rid of. **3.** *Elect.* to divert (a part of a current) by connecting a circuit element in parallel with another; to place on or furnish with a shunt. **4.** to move (a train, or part of it) from one line of rails to another or from the main track to a siding. *–v.i.* **5.** to move or turn aside or out of the way. **6.** (of a train) to move from one railway track to another, or from one point to another; to move railway trucks about as in a goods yard. *–n.* **7.** the act of shunting; a move. **8.** *Med.* a bypass or anastomosis, either occurring naturally or established by surgical means. **9.** *Elect.* a conducting element bridged across a circuit or a portion of a circuit, establishing a current path auxiliary to the main circuit. **10.** a railway siding. **11. get the shunt,** *Colloq.* to be dismissed from a job. [ME; orig. obscure, ? from SHUN] – **shunter,** *n.*

**shunt-wound** /ˈʃʌnt-waʊnd/, *adj.* of or pertaining to an electrical commutator in which the main magnetic field is provided by a field winding connected in shunt (i.e. in parallel) with the armature.

**shush** /ʃʊʃ/, *interj.* **1.** hush (a command to be quiet or silent). *–v.t.* **2.** to make silent. *–v.i.* **3.** to become silent.

**shut** /ʃʌt/, *v.,* **shut, shutting,** *adj., n.* *–v.t.* **1.** to put (a door, cover, etc.) in position to close or obstruct. **2.** to close the doors of (oft. fol. by *up*): *shut up the shop.* **3.** to close by bringing together or folding: *to shut one's eyes.* **4.** to confine; enclose: *to shut a bird into a cage.* **5.** to bar; exclude: *to shut a person from one's house.* **6.** to close down; cease normal operations: *they decided to shut the office during redecoration.* *–v.i.* **7.** to become shut or closed; close. *–v.* **8.** Some special verb phrases are:

**keep one's mouth shut, 1.** to remain silent. **2.** to keep a secret.

**shut away,** to hide or confine.

**shut down, 1.** to close by lowering, as a lid. **2.** to cover or envelop, as fog. **3.** to close down, esp. for a time, as a factory. **4.** *Colloq.* to put a stop or check to (fol. by *on* or *upon*). **5.** to stop (a machine, engine, etc.).

**shut in,** to imprison; confine; enclose.

**shut off, 1.** to stop the flow of (water, electricity, etc.). **2.** to keep separate; isolate.

**shut one's eyes to,** to refuse to notice; ignore.

**shut out,** to exclude; keep out.

**shut up, 1.** to imprison; confine; hide from view. **2.** *Colloq.* to stop talking; become silent. **3.** *Colloq.* to stop (someone) from talking; silence.

*–adj.* **9.** closed; fastened up. *–n.* **10.** the act or time of shutting or closing. **11.** the line where two pieces of welded metal are united. [ME *schutte,* OE *scyttan* bolt (a door); akin to SHOOT]

**shutdown** /ˈʃʌtdaʊn/, *n.* a shutting down; a closing of a factory or the like.

**shut-eye** /ˈʃʌt-aɪ/, *n. Colloq.* sleep.

**shut-out** /ˈʃʌt-aʊt/, *n.* **1.** the act of shutting out. **2.** the state of being shut out.

**shutter** /ˈʃʌtə/, *n.* **1.** a hinged or otherwise movable cover for a window. **2.** a movable cover, slide, etc., for an opening. **3.** one who or that which shuts. **4.** *Photog.* a mechanical device for opening and closing the aperture of a camera lens to expose a plate or film. *–v.t.* **5.** to close or provide with shutters.

**shutterbug** /ˈʃʌtəbʌg/, *n. Colloq.* a keen photographer.

**shuttle** /ˈʃʌtl/, *n., v.,* **-tled, -tling.** *–n.* **1.** a device in a loom for passing or shooting the weft thread through the shed from one side of the web to the other, usu. consisting of a boat-shaped piece of wood containing a bobbin on which the weft thread is wound. **2.** the sliding container that carries the lower thread in a sewing machine. **3.** →**shuttle service.** *–v.t., v.i.* **4.** to move quickly to and fro like a shuttle. [ME *schutylle, shittle,* OE *scytel* dart, arrow, c. Icel. *skutill* harpoon; akin to SHUT, SHOOT]

**shuttle car** /ˈ– ka/, *n.* a vehicle on rubber tyres or caterpillar treads and usu. propelled by electric motors, diesel or cable, designed to transfer raw materials such as coal and ore from loading machines in a trackless area of a mine to the main transportation system.

**shuttlecock** /ˈʃʌtlkɒk/, *n.* **1.** a piece of cork, or similar light material, with feathers stuck in one end, intended to be struck to and fro, as with a racquet in the game of badminton or with a battledore in the game of battledore. **2.** the game of battledore. *–v.t.* **3.** to send, or bandy to and fro, like a shuttlecock. *–v.i.* **4.** to move to and fro like a shuttlecock.

shuttlecock

**shuttle diplomacy** /ʃʌtl dəˈploʊməsi/, *n.* a form of diplomacy in which a mediator travels between the parties or countries in an international dispute, in order to effect a reconciliation or settlement.

**shuttle service** /ˈ– sɜvəs/, *n.* a transport service, usu. running at frequent intervals directly between two points.

**shy**[1] /ʃaɪ/, *adj.,* **shyer, shyest** or **shier, shiest,** *v.,* **shied, shying,** *n., pl.* **shies.** *–adj.* **1.** bashful; retiring. **2.** easily frightened away; timid. **3.** suspicious; distrustful. **4.** reluctant; wary. **5.** short: *shy of funds.* **6.** *Colloq.* failing to pay something due, as one's ante in poker. **7.** not bearing or breeding freely, as plants or animals. **8. fight shy of,** to avoid; keep away from. *–v.i.* **9.** to start back or aside, as in fear, esp. a horse. **10.** to draw back; recoil. *–n.* **11.** a sudden start aside, as in fear. [ME *schey,* OE *scēoh,* c. MHG *schiech;* akin to G *scheu*] – **shyer,** *n.* – **shyly,** *adv.* – **shyness,** *n.*

**shy**[2] /ʃaɪ/, *v.,* **shied, shying,** *n., pl.* **shies.** *–v.t.* **1.** to throw with a sudden swift movement: *to shy a stone.* *–n.* **2.** a sudden swift throw. **3.** →**cockshy.** [orig. uncert.]

**Shylock** /ˈʃaɪlɒk/, *n.* **1.** an extortionate usurer. **2.** any mean person. Also, **shylock.** [after *Shylock,* character in *The Merchant of Venice,* a play by William Shakespeare, 1564-1616]

**shypoo** /ʃaɪˈpu/, *n. Colloq.* inferior quality liquor.

**shyster** /ˈʃaɪstə/, *n. Colloq.* **1.** one who gets along by petty, sharp practices. **2.** a lawyer who uses unprofessional or questionable methods. [apparently alteration of *Scheuster,* an unscrupulous 19th C New York lawyer; perhaps influenced by G *Scheisser,* from *scheissen* SHIT]

**si** /si/, *n.* (in solfège) the syllable used for the seventh note of the scale. See **solfège.** [see GAMUT]

**Si,** *Chem.* silicon.

**SI** /ɛs ˈaɪ/, →**International System of Units.** [F *S(ystème) I(nternational) (d' Unités)*]

**sial** /ˈsaɪəl/, *n.* the lighter granitic layer of the lithosphere which forms the continents, overlying the sima, and composed largely of silica and alumina. [b. SI(LICA) + AL(UMINA)]

**sialagogic** /saɪələˈgɒdʒɪk/, *Med. –adj.* **1.** encouraging salivary flow. *–n.* **2.** →**sialagogue.**

**sialagogue** /ˈsaɪələgɒg, saɪˈæləgɒg/, *Med. –adj.* **1.** promoting the flow or secretion of saliva. *–n.* **2.** a sialagogue agent or medicine. [NL *sialagōgus,* from Gk *síalon* saliva + *agōgós* leading, drawing forth]

**sialoid** /ˈsaɪəlɔɪd/, *adj.* resembling saliva. [Gk *síalon* saliva + -OID]

**Siam** /saɪˈæm/, *n.* former name of **Thailand.**

**siamang** /ˈsaɪəmæŋ/, *n.* a large black gibbon, *Hylobates syndactylus,* of Sumatra and the Malay Peninsula, with very long arms and having the second and third digits united. [Malay, from *āmang* black]

**Siamese** /saɪəˈmiz/, *adj., n., pl.* **-mese.** *–adj.* **1.** of or pertaining to Siam, its people, or their language. **2.** (in allusion to Siamese twins) inseparable; closely connected; similar. *–n.* **3.** a native of Siam. **4.** the official language of Thailand, and the most important Thai language.

**Siamese cat** /– ˈkæt/, *n.* one of a breed of slender, short-haired cats, originating in Siam, having blue eyes, a small head, and a fawn or grey colour with extremities of a darker shading.

Siamese cat

**Siamese fighting fish,** *n.* a bony fish, *Betta splendens,* originating in Thailand, which has become highly coloured as a result of selective breeding, and the males of which are very pugnacious.

**Siamese twins** /ˌsaɪəmiz ˈtwɪnz/, *n.pl.* any twins who are born joined together in any manner. [from two Chinese men, Chang and Eng (1811-74), who were born in *Siam* joined to each other by a short, tubular, cartilaginous band]

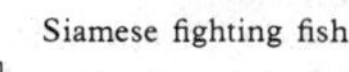

Siamese fighting fish

**sib**[1] /sɪb/, *adj.* **1.** related by blood; akin. *–n.* **2.** a kinsman; relative. **3.** one's kin or kindred. [ME *(i)sib,* OE *(ge)sibb* related (as n., a relation); cf. Icel. *sifi* kinsman]

**sib**[2] /sɪb/, *n. Colloq.* →**sibling.**

**Siberia** /saɪˈbɪəriə/, *n.* a part of the Soviet Union, in northern Asia, extending from the Ural mountains to the Pacific Ocean. – **Siberian,** *adj.*

**Siberian wallflower** /saɪˌbɪəriən ˈwɔlflaʊə/, *n.* a cultivated perennial of obscure origin with orange flowers, called *Cheiranthus allionii* by gardeners but probably a hybrid of *Erysimum.*

**sibilant** /ˈsɪbələnt/, *adj.* **1.** hissing. **2.** *Phonet.* characterised by a hissing sound; denoting sounds like those spelt with *s* in *this, rose, pressure, pleasure.* *–n.* **3.** *Phonet.* a sibilant sound. [L *sibilans,* ppr.] – **sibilance, sibilancy,** *n.* – **sibilantly,** *adv.*

**sibilate** /ˈsɪbəleɪt/, *v.,* **-lated, -lating.** *–v.i.* **1.** to hiss. *–v.t.* **2.** to utter or pronounce with a hissing sound. – **sibilation** /sɪbəˈleɪʃən/, *n.*

**sibling** /ˈsɪblɪŋ/, *n.* a brother or sister. [OE]

**sibyl** /ˈsɪbəl/, *n.* **1.** any of certain women of antiquity reputed to possess powers of prophecy or divination. **2.** a prophetess or witch. [ME *sibil,* from ML *Sibilla,* L *Sibylla,* from Gk] – **sibylic** /səˈbɪlɪk/, **sibylline** /ˈsɪbəlaɪn, səˈbɪlaɪn/, *adj.*

**sic**[1] /sɪk/, *adv.* so; thus (often used parenthetically to show that something has been copied exactly from the original). [L]

**sic**[2] /sɪk/, *v.t.,* **sicked, sicking. 1.** to attack (esp. of a dog). **2.** to incite to attack. [var. of SEEK]

**siccative** /ˈsɪkətɪv/, *adj.* **1.** causing or promoting absorption of moisture; drying. *–n.* **2.** a siccative substance, esp. in paint. [LL *siccātīvus,* from *siccāre* to dry]

**sicilienne** /səsɪliˈɛn/, *n.* a moderately slow dance of Sicilian peasant origin in 6/8 or 12/8 time, often in a minor key. Also, **siciliana.**

**sick** /sɪk/, *adj.* **1.** affected with nausea; inclined to vomit, or vomiting. **2.** affected with any disorder of health; ill, unwell, or ailing. **3.** of or attended with sickness. **4.** of or appropriate to sick persons: *on sick leave.* **5.** deeply affected with some feeling comparable to physical disorder, as sorrow, longing, repugnance, weariness, etc.: *sick at heart.* **6.** morbid; macabre: *sick humour, a sick joke.* **7.** *Colloq.* disgusted; chagrined. **8.** pale; wan. **9.** not in proper condition;

impaired. **10.** *Agric.* **a.** failing to sustain adequate harvests of some crop, usu. specified: *a lucerne-sick soil.* **b.** containing harmful micro-organisms: *a sick field.* **11. be sick of,** to feel fed up with; have had enough of: *he was sick of his employer's complaints about his work.* **12. sick as a dog,** *Colloq.* very sick. *–n.* **13. the sick,** sick people. **14.** vomit. *–v.t., v.i.* **15. sick up,** to vomit. [ME *sik, sek,* OE *sēoc,* c. G *siech*]

**sick bay** /'– beɪ/, *n.* a hospital or infirmary, as on board a ship.

**sickbed** /'sɪkbɛd/, *n.* a bed used by a sick person.

**sicken** /'sɪkən/, *v.i.* **1.** to become sick. *–v.t.* **2.** to make sick.

**sickening** /'sɪkənɪŋ/, *adj.* making sick; causing nausea, disgust, or loathing: *a sickening display of bad temper.* – **sickeningly,** *adv.*

**sick headache** /ˌsɪk 'hɛdeɪk/, *n.* headache accompanied by nausea; migraine.

**sickie** /'sɪki/, *n. Colloq.* a day taken off work with pay, because of genuine or feigned illness.

**sickish** /'sɪkɪʃ/, *adj.* **1.** somewhat sickening or nauseating. **2.** somewhat sick or ill. – **sickishly,** *adv.* – **sickishness,** *n.*

**sickle** /'sɪkəl/, *n.* an implement for cutting grain, grass, etc., consisting of a curved, hooklike blade mounted in a short handle. [ME *sikel,* OE *sicol* (c. G *Sichel*), from L *secula*]

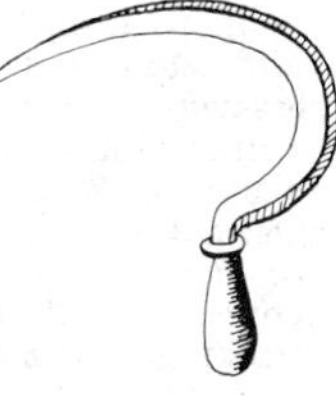
sickle

**sick leave** /'sɪk liv/, *n.* leave of absence granted because of illness.

**sicklebill** /'sɪkəlbɪl/, *n.* **1.** any of various birds with a curved bill, esp. the white ibis, *Threskiornis molucca,* of Australia. *–adj.* **2.** of or pertaining to any such bird.

**sickle cell** /'sɪkəl sɛl/, *n.* a cell containing a mutant gene which affects the blood of humans, usu. Negroes, and which is thought to offer resistance to malaria. – **sickle-cell,** *adj.*

**sickle-cell anaemia** /ˌsɪkəl-sɛl ə'nimiə/, *n.* a hereditary disease characterised by the crystallisation of sickle cells within erythrocytes, distorting them and clogging blood vessels.

**sickle feather** /'sɪkəl fɛðə/, *n.* one of the paired, elongated, sickleshaped, middle feathers of the tail of the cock.

**sickle fern** /'– fɜn/, *n.* any one of the numerous species of the fern genus *Pellaea,* often found in rainforests.

**sick list** /'sɪk lɪst/, *n.* **1.** a list of persons who are ill. **2. on the sick list,** *Colloq.* not well; ill: *he has been on the sick list for a week now.*

**sickly** /'sɪkli/, *adj.,* **-lier, -liest,** *adv., v.,* **-lied, -lying.** *–adj.* **1.** not strong; unhealthy; ailing. **2.** of, connected with, or arising from ill health: *a sickly complexion.* **3.** marked by the prevalence of ill health, as a region. **4.** causing sickness. **5.** (of food) rich; too sweet. **6.** nauseating. **7.** weak; mawkish: *sickly sentimentality.* **8.** faint or feeble, as light, colour, etc. *–adv.* **9.** *Obs.* in a sick or sickly manner. *–v.t.* **10.** *Obs.* to cover with a sickly hue. – **sickliness,** *n.*

**sickness** /'sɪknəs/, *n.* **1.** a particular disease or malady. **2.** state of being sick; illness. **3.** nausea.

**sickness benefit** /'– bɛnəfət/, *n.* money paid by the state to somebody who is out of work because of illness.

**sick parade** /'sɪk pəreɪd/, *n. Mil., etc.* a special parade held for those personnel who require medical attention.

**sick pay** /'– peɪ/, *n.* a wage or salary or a proportion of one paid to an employee absent from work owing to illness.

**sick room** /'– rum/, *n.* a room in which a sick person is confined.

**sida weed** /'saɪdə wid/, *n.* →**Paddy's lucerne.**

**siddur** /'sɪdʊə, 'sɪdə/, *n., pl.* **-durim, -durs.** *Judaism.* the book containing daily, Sabbath and festival prayers. [Heb.: order]

**side** /saɪd/, *n., adj., v.,* **sided, siding.** *–n.* **1.** one of the surfaces or lines bounding a thing. **2.** either of the two surfaces of paper, cloth, etc. **3.** one of the two surfaces of an object other than the front, back, top, and bottom. **4.** either of the two lateral (right and left) parts of a thing. **5.** either lateral half of the body of a person or an animal, esp. of the trunk. **6.** the space immediately beside someone or something: *the girl stood at his side.* **7.** an aspect; phase: *all sides of a question.* **8.** region, direction, or position with reference to a central line, space, or point: *the east side of a city.* **9.** a department or division, as of teaching in a school: *the science side, the arts side.* **10.** a slope, as of a hill. **11.** one of two or more parties concerned in a case, contest, etc. **12.** line of descent through either the father or the mother: *his maternal side.* **13.** *Colloq.* an affectedly superior manner; pretentious airs: *to put on side, to bung on side.* **14.** either of two lateral parts of the framework of a ship. **15.** *Billiards.* a spinning motion imparted to a ball by a quick stroke on one side of its centre. **16. on the side, a.** separate from the main subject. **b.** *Colloq.* as a sideline; secretly. **17. on the ... side,** tending towards the quality or condition specified: *this coffee is a little on the weak side.* **18. put on one side,** to leave for later consideration; shelve. **19. side by side,** next to one another; together; in close proximity. **20. take sides,** to support or show favour for one person or party in a dispute, contest, or the like. *–adj.* **21.** being at or on one side: *the side aisles of a theatre.* **22.** coming from one side: *side glance.* **23.** directed towards one side: *side blow.* **24.** subordinate: *a side issue.* *–v.i.* **25. side with** or **against,** to place oneself with or against a side or party to support or oppose an issue. [ME and OE; c. G *Seite*]

**side-arms** /'saɪd-amz/, *n.pl.* weapons (as pistols, swords, etc.) carried at the side or in the belt.

**side band** /'saɪd bænd/, *n.* the band of frequencies lying on either side of a modulated carrier wave.

**side bet** /'– bɛt/, *n.* **1.** a bet secondary to the main bet. **2.** (in two-up) a bet made between two people outside the ring on the outcome of the toss. – **side-better,** *n.*

**sideboard** /'saɪdbɔd/, *n.* **1.** a piece of furniture, as in a dining room, often with shelves, drawers, etc., for holding articles of table service. **2.** (*pl.*) →**sidelevers.**

**sideburns** /'saɪdbɜnz/, *n.pl. Orig. U.S.* →**sidelevers.** [alteration of BURNSIDES]

**side by side,** *n. Colloq.* a shotgun or rifle with two barrels arranged side by side.

**sidecar** /'saɪdka/, *n.* **1.** a small car attached on one side to a motorcycle and supported on the other by a wheel of its own: used for a passenger, parcels, etc. *–adv.* **2.** in a sidecar: *he rode sidecar.*

**side card** /'saɪd kad/, *n.* **1.** *Poker.* the highest card in a hand that is not part of a scoring combination, determining the ranking of two otherwise equal hands by its denomination. **2.** any card other than a trump.

**side chain** /'– tʃeɪn/, *n.* a group of atoms which is attached to an atom, forming part of a larger chain or a cyclic compound, esp. such a group of atoms which has replaced an atom of hydrogen.

**sided** /'saɪdəd/, *adj.* denoting the width of a frame in ship construction.

**side delivery rake,** *n.* a mechanical hay rake which pushes the mown hay to one side to form windrows.

**side-dish** /'saɪd-dɪʃ/, *n.* a dish served in addition to the principal dish of a course.

**side-dress** /saɪd-'drɛs/, *v.t.* to give (plants etc.) fertiliser by working it into the soil along the side of a row.

**side-drum** /'saɪd-drʌm/, *n.* a small double-headed drum, traditionally carried at the side, having snares across the lower head to produce a rattling or reverberating effect.

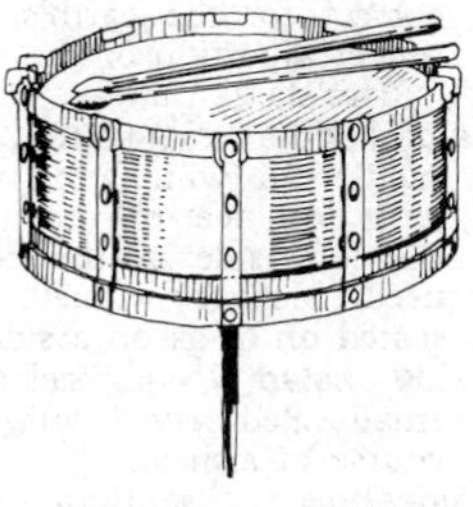
side-drum

**side effect** /'saɪd əfɛkt/, *n.* any effect produced, as of a drug, other than those originally intended, esp. an unpleasant or harmful effect.

**side heading** /'– hɛdɪŋ/, *n.* a heading or subheading which appears in the margin of printed matter.

**side issue** /'– ɪʃu/, *n.* a matter of secondary importance.

**sidekick** /'saɪdkɪk/, *n. Colloq.* **1.** an assistant. **2.** a close friend.

**sidelevers** /'saɪdlivəz/, *n. pl.* short whiskers extending from the hairline to below the ears and worn with an unbearded chin. Also, **sideboards, sideburns.**

**sidelight** /ˈsaɪdlaɪt/, *n.* **1.** light coming from the side. **2.** incidental information. **3.** either of the two small lights at the front of a vehicle used at night for indicating the width of the vehicle to other road-users, and for parking. **4.** either of two lights carried by a vessel under way at night, a red one on the port side and a green on the starboard. **5.** a window or other aperture for light, in the side of a building, ship, etc. **6.** a window at the side of a door or another window.

**sideline** /ˈsaɪdlaɪn/, *n., v.,* **-lined, -lining.** *–n.* **1.** a line at the side of something. **2.** an additional or auxiliary line of goods or of business. **3.** *Sport.* **a.** a line or mark defining the limit of play on the side of the field in football, etc. **b.** (*pl.*) the area immediately beyond any of the sidelines. **c.** the place occupied by those not playing in the contest. **d.** the place occupied by those not wishing to be involved in the main action. *–v.t.* **4.** to cause (a player) to become a non-participant, an observer from the sidelines: *the accident sidelined him for eight months.*

**sideling** /ˈsaɪdlɪŋ/, *n. N.Z.* a steep but negotiable ridge or spur. Also, **siding.**

**sidelong** /ˈsaɪdlɒŋ/, *adj.* **1.** directed to one side. *–adv.* **2.** towards the side; obliquely.

**sideman** /ˈsaɪdmən/, *n., pl.* **-men.** a member of a jazz band other than the leader.

**side-necked** /ˈsaɪd-nɛkt/, *adj.* (of a tortoise) able to withdraw the neck sideways to a horizontal position beneath the carapace but not able to retract it in a straight line.

**sidenote** /ˈsaɪdnoʊt/, *n.* a note made in the margin of a page.

**sidepiece** /ˈsaɪdpis/, *n.* a piece forming a side or a part of a side, or fixed by the side, of something.

**sidereal** /saɪˈdɪəriəl/, *adj.* **1.** determined by the stars: *sidereal time.* **2.** of or pertaining to the stars. [L *sīdereus* pertaining to the stars + -AL[1]]

**sidereal day** /– ˈdeɪ/, *n.* See **day** (def. 3e).

**sidereal hour** /– ˈaʊə/, *n.* one 24th part of a sidereal day.

**sidereal period** /– ˈpɪəriəd/, *n.* (of a planet) the time taken to complete one revolution of the sun with reference to the fixed stars.

**sidereal year** /– ˈjɪə/, *n.* See **year** (def. 6).

**siderite** /ˈsaɪdəraɪt/, *n.* **1.** a common mineral, iron carbonate, $FeCO_3$, usu. occurring in yellowish to deep brown cleavable masses; chalybite. **2.** a meteorite consisting almost entirely of metallic minerals. [L *sidērītes* lodestone, from Gk; in later use from SIDER(O)- + -ITE[1]] – **sideritic** /saɪdəˈrɪtɪk/, *adj.*

**sidero-**, a word element meaning 'iron', 'steel', as in *siderolite.* Also, before vowels, **sider-.** [Gk, combining form of *sídēros* iron]

**side road** /ˈsaɪd roʊd/, *n.* a minor road, turning off a main road; a byroad.

**siderolite** /ˈsaɪdərəlaɪt/, *n.* a meteorite of roughly equal proportions of metallic iron and stony matter.

**siderosis** /saɪdəˈroʊsəs/, *n.* a disease of the lungs due to inhaling iron or other metallic particles. – **siderotic** /sɪdəˈrɒtɪk/, *adj.*

**siderostat** /ˈsɪdərəstæt/, *n.* a device attached to an astronomical telescope which, by rotating the reflecting surface to correct for the earth's rotation, enables the instrument to reflect a portion of the sky in a fixed direction. – **siderostatic** /sɪdərəˈstætɪk/, *adj.*

**side-saddle** /ˈsaɪd-sædl/, *n.* **1.** a saddle on which the rider sits with both feet on the same (usu. the left) side of the horse, and used chiefly by women. *–adv.* **2.** seated on or as on a side-saddle.

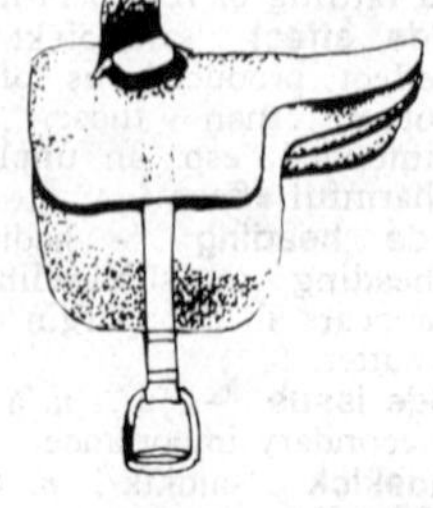
side-saddle

**side salad** /ˈsaɪd sæləd/, *n.* a small salad served with the main course of a meal.

**sideshow** /ˈsaɪdʃoʊ/, *n.* **1.** a minor show or exhibition in connection with a principal one as at a fair, circus, or the like. **2.** any subordinate event or matter.

**sideslip** /ˈsaɪdslɪp/, *v.,* **-slipped, -slipping,** *n.* *–v.i.* **1.** to slip to one side. **2.** (of an aeroplane when banked excessively) to slide sideways in a downward direction, towards the centre of the curve executed in turning. *–n.* **3.** the act of sideslipping.

**sidesman** /ˈsaɪdzmən/, *n., pl.* **-men.** a person who assists the churchwardens of a parish, esp. in distributing books and taking up the collection in church.

**side-splitting** /ˈsaɪd-splɪtɪŋ/, *adj.* convulsively uproarious: *side-splitting farce.* – **side-splittingly,** *adv.*

**sidestep** /ˈsaɪdstɛp/, *v.,* **-stepped, -stepping,** *n.* *–v.i.* **1.** to step to one side, as in avoidance. **2.** to be evasive in reaching a decision, solving a problem, etc. **3.** *Skiing.* to climb a short hill by edging the skis into the slope and climbing sideways, at right angles to the slope. *–v.t.* **4.** to avoid by stepping to one side. **5.** to evade (a decision, problem, etc.). *–n.* **6.** an act or instance of sidestepping. – **sidestepper,** *n.*

**sidestick** /ˈsaɪdstɪk/, *n.* a strip of wood on metal which is placed beside type either in galley or in a printing forme in order to hold the type in position.

**side-stitch** /ˈsaɪd-stɪtʃ/, *v.t.* to secure sections of (a book) by passing thread or wire through from the first sheet to the last.

**side street** /ˈsaɪd strit/, *n.* a separate, private, or obscure street; a bystreet.

**sidestroke** /ˈsaɪdstroʊk/, *n.* a swimming stroke in which the body is turned sideways in the water, the hands pulling alternately, and the legs performing a scissors kick.

**sideswipe** /ˈsaɪdswaɪp/, *v.,* **-swiped, -swiping,** *n.* *–v.t.* **1.** to strike with a sweeping stroke or blow with or along the side. *–n.* **2.** such a stroke or blow.

**sidetrack** /ˈsaɪdtræk/, *v.t.* **1.** to distract from the main subject or course. *–v.i.* **2.** to move from the main subject or course. *–n.* **3.** *U.S.* →**siding** (def. 1). **4.** an act of sidetracking; a diversion; distraction. **5.** a temporary road constructed as a detour for the use of traffic while work is being done on the main road.

**side-valve engine** /ˈsaɪd-vælv ˌɛndʒən/, *n.* a type of internal-combustion engine in which the valves are housed in the cylinder block and are operated from below.

**sidewalk** /ˈsaɪdwɔk/, *n. U.S.* →**pavement.**

**sidewall** /ˈsaɪdwɔl/, *n.* the part of a pneumatic tyre between the edge of the tread and the rim of the wheel.

**sideward** /ˈsaɪdwəd/, *adj.* **1.** directed or moving towards one side. *–adv.* **2.** sidewards.

**sidewards** /ˈsaɪdwədz/, *adv.* towards one side.

**sideway** /ˈsaɪdweɪ/, *n.* **1.** →**byway. 2.** a passage, as at the side of a house. *–adj., adv.* **3.** *U.S.* →**sideways.**

**sideways** /ˈsaɪdweɪz/, *adv.* **1.** with the side foremost. **2.** facing or inclining to the side. **3.** towards or from one side. *–adj.* **4.** moving from or towards one side. **5.** towards or from one side. Also, **sidewise** /ˈsaɪdwaɪz/.

**side-wheel** /ˈsaɪd-wil/, *adj.* having a paddle-wheel on each side, as a steamer. – **side-wheeler,** *n.*

**side-whiskers** /ˈsaɪd-wɪskəz/, *n.pl.* →**sidelevers.** – **side-whiskered,** *adj.*

**sidewinder** /ˈsaɪdwaɪndə/, *n.* **1.** *U.S. Colloq.* a disabling swinging blow from the side. **2.** the small species of rattlesnake, *Crotalus cerastes,* that moves in loose sand by throwing loops of the body forward.

**siding** /ˈsaɪdɪŋ/, *n.* **1.** a short branch off a railway track, often connected at both ends to the main-line track, and used for shunting or for loading, unloading, and storing goods trucks. **2.** the timber, metal or composite material forming the cladding of a framed building. **3.** *N.Z.* →**sideling.**

**sidle** /ˈsaɪdl/, *v.,* **-dled, -dling,** *n.* *–v.i.* **1.** to move sideways or obliquely. **2.** *N.Z.* to negotiate a steep slope or sideling. **3.** to edge along furtively. *–n.* **4.** a sidling movement. [back-formation from *sideling* SIDELONG]

**siècle** /siˈɛəklə/, *n.* an age; a century; a generation. [F (in OF *secle*), from L *saeculum* generation]

**siege** /sidʒ/, *n., v.,* **sieged, sieging.** *–n.* **1.** the operation of reducing and capturing a fortified place by surrounding it, cutting off supplies, undermining, bringing guns to bear, bombing, and other offensive operations. **2.** any prolonged or persistent endeavour to overcome resistance. **3.** *Obs.* a seat. **4.** *Obs.* rank. **5.** *Obs.* a throne. **6. lay siege to,** to besiege. *–v.t.* **7.** to lay siege to; besiege. [ME, from OF *sege, siege,* from L *sedēre* sit]

**siemens** /ˈsimənz/, *n., pl.* **siemens.** the SI unit of electrical conductance, formerly called the mho; the conductance of a conductor that has an electrical resistance of one ohm. *Symbol:* S [named after E.W. von *Siemens,* 1816-92, German electrical engineer and inventor]

**sienna** /si'ɛnə/, *n.* **1.** a ferruginous earth used as a yellowish brown pigment (**raw sienna**) or, after roasting in a furnace, as a reddish brown pigment (**burnt sienna**). **2.** the colour of such a pigment. [short for It. *terra di Sien(n)a* earth of Siena, town in central Italy]

**sierra** /si'ɛrə/, *n.* a chain of hills or mountains the peaks of which suggest the teeth of a saw. [Sp.: lit., saw, from L *serra*]

**Sierra Leone** /si,ɛrə li'oʊn/, *n.* a republic in western Africa.

**siesta** /si'ɛstə/, *n.* a midday or afternoon rest or nap, esp. as taken in Spain and other hot countries. [Sp., from L *sexta* sixth (hour), midday]

**sieve** /sɪv/, *n., v.,* **sieved, sieving.** *–n.* **1.** an instrument, with a meshed or perforated bottom, used for separating coarse from fine parts of loose matter, for straining liquids, etc., esp. one with a circular frame and fine meshes or perforations. **2.** *Colloq.* one who cannot keep a secret. **3. have a head like a sieve,** *Colloq.* to be very forgetful. *–v.t.* **4.** to put or force through a sieve; sift. [ME *sive,* OE *sife,* c. G *Sieb*]

**sieve cell** /'– sɛl/, *n.* an elongated, nucleated, food-conducting cell of the phloem of pteridophytes and gymnosperms with perforations in the walls **(sieve pores)** arranged in circumscribed areas **(sieve areas)** which afford cytoplasmic communication with similar adjacent cells.

**sieve tube** /'– tjub/, *n.* a longitudinal, food-conducting, tube-like structure present in the phloem of angiosperms composed of **sieve tube elements** (cells containing cytoplasm but not nuclei) placed end to end with perforations **(sieve pores)** confined mostly to their ends **(sieve plates)** where they are in contact with each other.

**sift** /sɪft/, *v.t.* **1.** to separate the coarse parts of (flour, ashes, etc.) with a sieve. **2.** to scatter by means of a sieve: *to sift sugar on to cake.* **3.** to separate by or as by a sieve. **4.** to examine closely. **5.** to question closely. *–v.i.* **6.** to use a sieve; sift something. **7.** to pass through, or as through a sieve. [ME *siften,* OE *siftan* (from *sife* SIEVE), c. G *sichten*] **– sifter,** *n.*

**sig.,** **1.** signature. **2.** signification. **3.** signifies. **4.** signor.

**sigatoka** /sɪgə'toʊkə/, *n.* a leaf spot disease of bananas caused by a sooty mould. [named after *Sigatoka,* district and river in Fiji]

**sigh** /saɪ/, *v.i.* **1.** to let out one's breath audibly, as from sorrow, weariness, relief, etc. **2.** to yearn or long. **3.** to make a sound suggesting a sigh: *sighing wind.* *–v.t.* **4.** to express with a sigh. **5.** to lament with sighing. *–n.* **6.** the act or sound of sighing. [ME *sighe(n),* backformation from *sihte* sighed, past tense of ME *siken, sichen,* OE *sīcan,* of unknown orig.] **– sigher,** *n.*

**sight** /saɪt/, *n.* **1.** the power or faculty of seeing; vision. **2.** the act or fact of seeing. **3.** range of vision: *in sight of land.* **4.** a view; glimpse. **5.** mental view or regard. **6.** something seen or to be seen; spectacle: *the sights of the town.* **7.** *Colloq.* something that looks odd or unsightly: *she looks a sight in her new hat.* **8.** *Colloq.* a great deal: *it's a sight better here than at the last hotel.* **9.** an observation taken with a surveying or other instrument. **10.** a device on or used with a surveying instrument, a firearm, etc., serving to guide the eye. **11.** *Obs.* insight. **12. a. raise one's sights,** to adopt a more lofty ambition. **b. lower one's sights,** to adopt a less lofty ambition. **13. at sight,** on presentation: *a bill of exchange payable at sight.* **14. catch sight of,** to glimpse; see, esp. briefly or momentarily. **15. know by sight,** to recognise (somebody or something) seen previously. **16. not by a long sight,** on no account; definitely not. **17. on sight,** as soon as one sees a thing. **18. sight unseen, a.** without an examination of the goods before purchase. **b.** without an interview previous to employment. *–v.t.* **19.** to get sight of: *to sight a ship.* **20.** to take a sight or observation of, esp. with an instrument. **21.** to direct by a sight or sights, as a firearm. **22.** to provide with sights, or adjust the sights of, as a gun. *–v.i.* **23.** to take a sight, as in shooting. [ME; OE *gesiht* (c. G *Gesicht*), *sihth,* from *sēon* SEE[1]]

**sight bill** /'– bɪl/, *n.* a bill of exchange payable on presentation, without any days of grace. Also, *Chiefly U.S.,* **sight draft.**

**sightless** /'saɪtləs/, *adj.* **1.** blind. **2.** invisible.

**sightly** /'saɪtli/, *adj.,* **-lier, -liest.** pleasing to the sight. **– sightliness,** *n.*

**sight-read** /'saɪt-rid/, *v.t.,* **-read, -reading.** to play, read, or sing (music) from a written or printed score without previous rehearsal or study. **– sight-reader,** *n.*

**sightscreen** /'saɪtskrin/, *n.* (in cricket) a white screen set on the boundary behind the wicket, as an aid to the batsman in sighting the ball. Also, **sightboard.**

**sightseeing** /'saɪtsiɪŋ/, *n.* the act of seeing objects or places of interest. **– sightseer,** *n.*

**sigil** /'sɪdʒəl/, *n.* a seal; signet. [LL *sigillum,* diminutive of *signum* mark] **– sigillary** /'sɪdʒələri/, *adj.*

**sigma** /'sɪgmə/, *n.* **1.** the eighteenth letter (Σ, σ, ς = English S, s) of the Greek alphabet. **2.** *Maths.* capital sigma, Σ, is the summation sign. $\Sigma_n$ means the sum of all the values n may take under the given conditions.

**sigmate** /'sɪgmət, -meɪt/, *adj.* having the form of the Greek sigma or the letter S.

**sigmoid** /'sɪgmɔɪd/, *adj.* **1.** curved in one direction like the letter C. **2.** curved in two directions like the letter S. **3.** pertaining to the sigmoid flexure: *the sigmoid artery* (which supplies this flexure). Also, **sigmoidal** /sɪg'mɔɪdl/. [Gk *sigmoeidḗs.* See -OID]

**sigmoid flexure** /– 'flɛkʃə/, *n.* **1.** *Zool.* an S-shaped curve consisting of several parts. **2.** *Anat.* the last curve of the large intestine before terminating in the rectum.

**sigmoidoscope** /sɪg'mɔɪdəskoʊp/, *n.* a medical instrument for the inspection of the sigmoid flexure.

**sign** /saɪn/, *n.* **1.** a token; indication. **2.** a conventional mark, figure, or symbol used technically instead of the word or words which it represents, as an abbreviation. **3.** *Music.* a signature. **4.** *Maths.* the plus or minus sign. **5.** a motion or gesture intended to express or convey an idea. **6.** an inscribed board, space, etc., serving for information, advertisement, warning, etc., on a building, along a street, or the like. **7.** *Med.* the objective indications of a disease. **8.** a trace; vestige. **9.** an omen; portent. **10.** *Astron.* any of the twelve divisions of the zodiac, each denoted by the name of a constellation or its symbol, and each (because of the precession of the equinoxes) now containing the constellation west of the one from which it took its name. *–v.t.* **11.** to affix a signature to. **12.** to write as a signature: *to sign one's name.* **13.** to engage by written agreement: *to sign a new player.* **14.** to indicate; betoken. **15.** to communicate by a sign. **16.** to mark with a sign, esp. the sign of the cross. **17.** *Obs.* to direct or appoint by a sign. *–v.i.* **18.** to write one's signature, as a token of agreement, obligation, receipt, etc. **19.** to make a sign or signal. *–v.* **20.** Some special verb phrases are:

**sign away,** to dispose of by affixing one's signature to a document.

**sign off, 1.** to cease broadcasting a radio or television program, as at the end of the day. **2.** to withdraw from some responsibility, project, etc.

**sign on, 1.** to employ; hire. **2.** to commit oneself to employment, as by signing a contract.

**sign up, 1.** to enlist, as for the armed services. **2.** to commit a person to a contract by having him sign it. [ME, from OF *signe,* from L *signum* mark, signal]

**signal** /'sɪgnəl/, *n., adj., v.,* **-nalled, -nalling** or (*U.S.*) **-naled, -naling.** *–n.* **1.** a gesture, act, light, etc., serving to warn, direct, command, or the like. **2.** anything agreed upon or understood as the occasion for concerted action. **3.** an act, event, or the like, which precipitates an action: *the signal for revolt.* **4.** a token; indication. **5.** *Radio, etc.* **a.** the impulses, waves, sounds, etc., transmitted or received. **b.** the wave which modulates the carrier wave. **6.** *Cards.* a play which reveals to one's partner a wish that he continue or discontinue the suit led. *–adj.* **7.** serving as a sign: *a signal flag.* **8.** conspicuous or notable: *a signal exploit.* *–v.t.* **9.** to make a signal to. **10.** to make known by a signal. *–v.i.* **11.** to make communication by a signal or signals. [ME, from ML *signāle,* properly neut. adj., from L *signum* SIGN] **– signaller,** *n.*

**signal box** /'– bɒks/, *n.* a raised cabin above a railway line, from which railway signals, points, etc., are worked.

**signal generator** /'– dʒɛnəreɪtə/, *n.* a device which generates artificial signals to test electronic equipment.

**signalise** /'sɪgnəlaɪz/, *v.t.*, **-lised, -lising. 1.** to make notable. **2.** to point out particularly. Also, **signalize.**

**signally** /'sɪgnəli/, *adv.* conspicuously; notably.

**signalman** /'sɪgnəlmən/, *n., pl.* **-men. 1.** a man employed to operate railway signals and points. **2.** Also, **signaller. a.** a private soldier of the Royal Australian Corps of Signals. **b.** a soldier trained to send and receive messages. **c.** a soldier concerned with communications.

**signatory** /'sɪgnətri/, *adj., n., pl.* **-ries.** *–adj.* **1.** that has signed, or has joined in signing, a document: *the signatory powers to a treaty.* *–n.* **2.** a signer, or one of the signers, of a document, as a treaty.

**signature** /'sɪgnətʃə/, *n., v.,* **-tured, -turing.** *–n.* **1.** a person's name, or a mark representing it, as signed or written by himself or by deputy, as in subscribing a letter or other document. **2.** the act of signing a document. **3.** *Music.* a sign or set of signs at the beginning of a stave to indicate the key or the time of a piece. **4.** a signature tune. **5.** *Pharm.* that part of a prescription which gives the directions to be marked on the container of the medicine. **6.** *Print.* **a.** a letter or other symbol generally placed by the printer at the foot of the first page of every section to guide the binder in arranging the sections in sequence. **b.** a sheet thus marked. **c.** a printed sheet folded to form a section of a book. *–v.t.* **7.** to identify (a radio or television program) with a signature tune. [ML *signātūra*]

**signature tune** /'– tjun/, *n.* **1.** a short tune or jingle played as an identification signal by a radio, television station, etc., to introduce a particular program, etc. **2.** a tune adopted by or associated with the name of a person, esp. a radio or television entertainer.

**signboard** /'saɪnbɔd/, *n.* a board bearing an inscription, advertisement, or the like.

**sign digit** /'saɪn dɪdʒət/, *n.* a zero or figure one preceding a number stored in a computer to show whether the number is positive or negative.

**signer** /'saɪnə/, *n.* **1.** one who signs. **2.** one who writes his name, as in token of agreement, etc.

**signet** /'sɪgnət/, *n.* **1.** a small seal, as in a finger ring. **2.** a small official seal. **3.** an impression made by or as if by a signet. *–v.t.* **4.** to stamp or mark with a signet. [ME, from ML *signētum,* from L *signum* SIGN]

**signet ring** /'– rɪŋ/, *n.* a finger ring containing a small seal, one's initials, or the like.

**significance** /sɪg'nɪfəkəns/, *n.* **1.** importance; consequence. **2.** meaning; import. **3.** the quality of being significant or having a meaning. Also, **significancy.**

**significant** /sɪg'nɪfəkənt/, *adj.* **1.** important; of consequence. **2.** expressing a meaning; indicative. **3.** having a special or covert meaning; suggestive. *–n.* **4.** *Archaic.* something significant; a sign. [L *significans,* ppr., signifying] – **significantly,** *adv.*

**significant figures** /– 'fɪgəz/, *n.pl.* the digits in a number excluding the zeros after an integral number or before a decimal fraction (except those added to signify accuracy). In 0.0352 and in 35 200 the significant figures are 352.

**signification** /sɪgnəfə'keɪʃən/, *n.* **1.** meaning; import; sense. **2.** the act or fact of signifying; indication.

**significative** /sɪg'nɪfəkətɪv/, *adj.* **1.** serving to signify. **2.** significant; suggestive.

**signify** /'sɪgnəfaɪ/, *v.,* **-fied, -fying.** *–v.t.* **1.** to make known by signs, speech, or action. **2.** to be a sign of; mean; portend. *–v.i.* **3.** to be of importance or consequence. [ME *signefie(n),* from L *significāre* show by signs] – **signifier,** *n.*

**sign language** /'saɪn ˌlæŋgwɪdʒ/, *n.* a substitute for speech using gestures, as the methods used by deaf-mutes, between speakers of different languages, etc.

**sign of the cross,** *n.* the movement of the other hand from the forehead to the breast and then from one shoulder to the other so as to trace out the form of a cross; made with religious purpose by Christians.

**sign of the zodiac,** *n.* **1.** See **zodiac. 2.** the depictions of animals, figures, etc., which conventionally represent the signs of the zodiac.

**signor** /si'njɔ/, *n., pl.* **-nori** /-'njɔri/. the conventional Italian title of respect and form of address for a man (equivalent to *Mr*). [It.]

**signora** /si'njɔrə/, *n., pl.* **-re** /-'njɔreɪ/. the conventional Italian title of respect and form of address for a married woman (equivalent to *Mrs* and *madam*). [It., fem., from *signore.* See SIGNORE]

**signore** /si'njɔri/, *n., pl.* **-ri** /-ri/. the conventional Italian form of address for a man (when used alone equivalent to *sir*).

**signorina** /sinjɔ'rinə/, *n., pl.* **-ne** /-neɪ/. the conventional Italian title of respect and term of address for an unmarried woman (corresponding to *miss*). [It., diminutive of *signora* SIGNORA]

**signory** /'sinjəri/, *n.* →**seigniory.**

**signpost** /'saɪnpoʊst/, *n.* a post by the roadside or at an intersection bearing a sign for the guidance of travellers.

**sign-writer** /'saɪn-raɪtə/, *n.* one who designs and produces signs, as for shops, hotels, etc. – **sign-writing,** *n.*

**Sikh** /sik/, *n.* **1.** a member of a religious sect founded in the early 16th century near Lahore in north-western India by a Hindu reformer. *–adj.* **2.** of or pertaining to the Sikhs or Sikhism. [Hind.: lit., disciple]

**Sikhism** /'sikɪzəm/, *n.* the religious system and practices of the Sikhs. Starting in the 16th century as an attempt to effect a peaceful harmony of Hinduism and Islam in India, Sikhism has branched off into a new independent religion.

**silactic prosthesis** /saɪˌlæktɪk prɒs'θisəs/, *n.* a surgical operation to enlarge the breasts.

**silage** /'saɪlɪdʒ/, *n.* green fodder preserved in a silo, silage pit, or mound. [alteration (influenced by SILO) of ENSILAGE]

**silage pit** /'– pɪt/, *n.* a pit dug for the storage of green fodder.

**silane** /'sɪleɪn/, *n.* any one of a group of silicon hydrides with the general formula, $Si_nH_{2n+2}$.

**sild** /sɪld/, *n.* a young herring. [Norw.]

**silence** /'saɪləns/, *n., v.,* **-lenced, -lencing,** *interj.* *–n.* **1.** absence of any sound or noise; stillness. **2.** the state or fact of being silent; muteness. **3.** omission of mention: *to pass over a matter in silence.* **4.** oblivion. **5.** secrecy. *–v.t.* **6.** to put or bring to silence; still. **7.** to put to rest (doubts, etc.); quiet. **8.** *Mil.* to still (enemy guns, etc.), as by more effective fire. *–interj.* **9.** be silent! [ME, from OF, from L *silentium*]

**silencer** /'saɪlənsə/, *n.* **1.** one who or that which silences. **2.** an expansion chamber fitted to the exhaust pipe of an internal-combustion engine to reduce the noise made by the exhaust gases; muffler. **3.** a device for deadening the report of a firearm.

**silent** /'saɪlənt/, *adj.* **1.** making no sound; quiet; still. **2.** refraining from speech. **3.** speechless; mute. **4.** taciturn; reticent. **5.** characterised by absence of speech or sound: *a silent prayer, a silent film.* **6.** tacit: *a silent assent.* **7.** omitting mention of something, as in a narrative. **8.** inactive or quiescent, as a volcano. **9.** not sounded or pronounced: *a silent letter,* such as 'b' in 'doubt'. [L *silens,* ppr., being silent] – **silently,** *adv.* – **silentness,** *n.*

**silent cop** /– 'kɒp/, *n. Colloq.* →**traffic dome.**

**silent number** /– 'nʌmbə/, *n.* a telephone number omitted from a directory and not disclosed to enquirers.

**silent partner** /– 'patnə/, *n.* a partner taking no active or public part in the conduct of a business.

**silhouette** /sɪlu'ɛt, sɪlə'wɛt/, *n., v.,* **-etted, -etting.** *–n.* **1.** an outline drawing, uniformly filled in with black, like a shadow. **2.** a dark image outlined against a lighter background. *–v.t.* **3.** to show in, or as in, a silhouette. [named after Etienne de *Silhouette,* 1709-67, French author and politician]

silhouette

**silic-,** a word element meaning 'flint', 'silica', 'silicon', as in *silicide.* Also, **silici-, silico-.** [combining form representing L *silex* flint]

**silica** /'sɪlɪkə/, *n.* silicon dioxide, $SiO_2$, appearing as quartz, sand, flint, and agate. [NL, from L *silex* flint]

**silica gel** /– 'dʒɛl/, *n.* a highly absorbent gelatinous form of silica, used as a drying agent and catalyst support.

**silica glass** /'– glas/, *n.* a vitreous material consisting almost entirely of silica. Also, **quartz glass, vitreous silica, fused silica.**

**silicane** /'sɪləkeɪn/, *n. Obs.* →**monosilane.**

**silicate** /'sɪləkət, -keɪt/, *n.* any salt derived from the silicic acids or from silica.

**siliceous** /sə'lɪʃəs/, *adj.* **1.** containing, consisting of, or resembling silica. **2.** growing in soil rich in silica. Also, **silicious.** [L *siliceus* of flint or limestone]

**silicic** /sə'lɪsɪk/, *adj.* **1.** containing silicon. **2.** of or pertaining to silica or acids derived from it.

**silicic acid** /– 'æsəd/, *n.* any of certain acids formed when alkaline silicates are treated with acids to form amorphous gelatinous masses, which dissociate readily into silica and water.

**silicide** /'sɪləsaɪd/, *n.* a compound, usu. of two elements only, one of which is silicon.

**silicified wood** /səˌlɪsəfaɪd 'wʊd/, *n.* wood which has been changed into quartz by a replacement of the cellular structure of the wood by siliceous waters.

**silicify** /sə'lɪsəfaɪ/, *v.t., v.i.,* **-fied, -fying.** to convert or be converted into silica. – **silicification** /səlɪsəfə'keɪʃən/, *n.*

**silicium** /sə'lɪsiəm/, *n. Obs.* →**silicon.** [NL, from *silic-* SILIC- + *-ium* -IUM]

**silicle** /'sɪləkəl/, *n.* →**silicule.**

**silico-,** variant of *silic-*, before consonants.

**silico-methane** /ˌsɪləkoʊ-'miθeɪn/, *n. Obs.* →**monosilane.**

**silicon** /'sɪləkən/, *n.* a non-metallic element, having amorphous and crystalline forms, occurring in the combined state in minerals and rocks and constituting more than one fourth of the earth's crust; used in steel-making, etc. *Symbol:* Si; *at. wt:* 28.086; *at. no.:* 14; *sp. gr.:* 2.33 at 20°C. [SILIC- + *-on,* modelled on BORON, CARBON]

**silicon carbide** /– 'kabaɪd/, *n.* a very hard crystalline compound, SiC, made by fusing carbon and sand, used as an abrasive, refractory, and an electrical resistance; carbon silicide.

**silicon-controlled rectifier** /ˌsɪləkən-kəntroʊld 'rɛktəfaɪə/, *n.* a type of semiconductor switch often used in control circuits; thyristor. *Abbrev.:* SCR

**silicone** /'sɪləkoʊn/, *n.* any of a large group of polymers based on a structure consisting of alternate silicon and oxygen atoms with various organic radicals attached to the silicon; characterised by greater stability and resistance to extremes of temperature than the corresponding carbon compounds; among the silicones are oils, greases, resins, and a group of synthetic rubbers. [SILIC- + -ONE]

**silicosis** /sɪlə'koʊsəs/, *n.* a disease of the lungs due to inhaling siliceous particles, as by stonecutters. [SILIC- + -OSIS]

**silicule** /'sɪləkjul/, *n.* a short siliqua. Also, **silicle.** [L *silicula,* diminutive of *siliqua* pod]

**siliculose** /sɪ'lɪkjəloʊs/, *adj.* **1.** (of a plant) bearing silicules. **2.** (of a plant part) having the form or appearance of a silicule.

**siliqua** /sɪ'likwə, 'sɪlɪkwə/, *n., pl.* **-quae** /-kwi/, **-quas.** the elongated, dry dehiscent fruit, characteristic of plants of the family Cruciferae, in which the loculus is divided by a false septum or replum. Also, **silique** /sɪ'lik, 'sɪlik/. [L: pod]

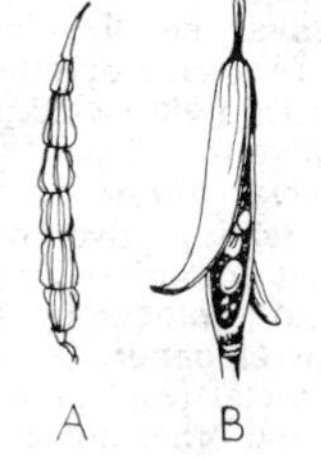

siliquae: A, charlock; B, black mustard

**siliquose** /'sɪləkwoʊs/, *adj.* **1.** (of a plant) bearing siliquae. **2.** resembling a siliqua or silicule.

**silk** /sɪlk/, *n.* **1.** the fine, soft, lustrous fibre obtained from the cocoon of the silkworm. **2.** thread made of this fibre. **3.** cloth made of this fibre. **4.** a garment of this cloth. **5.** the gown of such material, worn distinctively by a Queen's or King's Counsel at the bar. **6.** any fibre or filamentous matter resembling silk. **7.** the hair-like styles on an ear of maize. **8.** *Colloq.* a Queen's or King's Counsel. **9. to take silk,** to become a Queen's or King's Counsel. *–adj.* **10.** made of silk. **11.** resembling silk; silky. **12.** of or pertaining to silk. *–v.i.* **13.** *U.S.* (of corn) to be in the course of forming silk. *–v.t.* **14.** to clothe or cover with silk. [ME; OE *sioloc, seoloc* (c. Icel. *silki*), from Baltic or Slavic. Cf. German d. (Prussian) *silkas,* Russ. *sheolk*]

**silk cotton** /– 'kɒtn/, *n.* the silky covering of the seeds of certain tropical trees of the family Bombacaceae, used for stuffing cushions, etc. See **kapok.**

**silk-cotton tree** /sɪlk-'kɒtn ˌtri/, *n.* any of several trees of the family Bombacaceae, having seeds surrounded by silk cotton, esp. *Ceiba pentandra,* from which kapok is obtained.

**silk department** /'sɪlk dəpatmənt/, *Colloq. –adj.* **1.** top quality: *that girl is silk department. –n.* **2.** an easy, pleasant job that is often well-paid. Also, **the silk.**

**silken** /'sɪlkən/, *adj.* **1.** made of silk. **2.** like silk. **3.** smooth; soft. **4.** clad in silk. **5.** elegant; luxurious.

**silks** /sɪlks/, *n.pl.* the shirt and cap of a jockey worn in a race.

**silk-screen** /'sɪlk-skrin/, *n.* **1.** a process of printing from stencils, which may be photographically made or cut by hand, through a fine mesh of silk, metal or other material. *–v.t.* **2.** to print using this process.

**silkweed** /'sɪlkwid/, *n.* any milkweed of the family Asclepiadaceae, so called from the silky down in the pod.

**silkworm** /'sɪlkwɜm/, *n.* the caterpillar of any moth of the families Bombycidae, and Saturniidae, which spins a fine, soft filament (silk) to form a cocoon, in which it is enclosed while in the pupal stage, esp. the **Chinese silk-worm,** *Bombyx mori.* [ME *sylkewyrme,* OE *seolcwyrm.* See SILK, WORM]

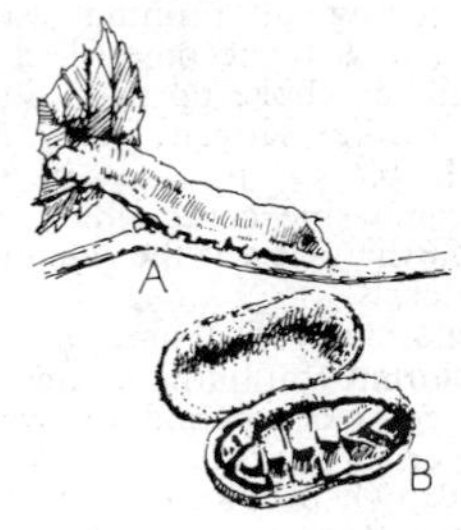

A, silkworm; B, section of cocoon showing pupa

**silky** /sɪlki/, *adj.* **-kier, -kiest. 1.** of or like silk; lustrous; smooth. **2.** *Bot.* covered with fine, soft, closely set hairs, as a leaf; sericeous. – **silkily,** *adv.* – **silkiness,** *n.*

**silky anteater** /– 'æntitə/, *n.* an arboreal, prehensile-tailed anteater, *Cyclopes didactylus,* of tropical South America, about the size of a squirrel and having silky, golden fur. Also, **two-toed anteater.**

**silky browntop** /– 'braʊntɒp/, *n.* a drought-resistant perennial grass, *Eulalia fulva,* with long slender stems, having at their base short bract-like sheaths and producing a seedhead consisting of three branches with spikelets clothed in dense, silky brown hairs; its leaves are palatable to stock, esp. horses. Also, **sugar grass.**

**silky oak** /– 'oʊk/, *n.* any of several Australian trees of the family Proteaceae with satiny timbers and oak-like grain, esp. *Grevillea robusta* which is also widely cultivated as an ornamental.

silky oak: flower and leaf

**sill** /sɪl/, *n.* **1.** a horizontal timber, block, or the like, serving as a foundation of a wall, house, etc. **2.** the horizontal piece or member beneath a window, door, or other opening. **3.** *Geol.* a tabular body of intrusive igneous rock, ordinarily between beds of sedimentary rocks or layers of volcanic ejecta. [ME *sille,* OE *syl, syll(e),* c. LG *süll;* akin to G *Schwelle*]

**sillabub** /'sɪləbʌb/, *n.* a dish made of milk or cream poured over wine, cider, or ale, sweetened and flavoured with spices, lemon rind, etc. Also, **syllabub.**

**sillimanite** /'sɪləmənaɪt/, *n.* a mineral, aluminium silicate, $Al_2SiO_5$, occurring as aggregates of thin fibrous crystals in metamorphic rocks such as shales and mudstones; fibrolite. [named after Benjamin *Silliman,* 1779-1864, U.S. geologist. See -ITE[1]]

**silly** /'sɪli/, *adj.,* **-lier, -liest,** *n., pl.* **-lies.** *–adj.* **1.** lacking good sense; foolish; stupid. **2.** absurd or ridiculous. **3.** *Colloq.* stunned. **4.** *Cricket.* (of a fielding position) close in to the batsman's wicket: *silly mid-off.* **5.** *Archaic.* simple-minded. **6.** *Obs.* simple; homely. **7.** *Obs.* weak; helpless. **8. silly as a wet hen,** stupid; idiotic; erratic. *–n.* **9.** *Colloq.* a silly person. [var. of earlier *seely* happy, helpless, silly, ME *seli*, OE *sēlig* (Anglian), *sælig* (c. G *selig*), from *sēl, sæl* happiness + *-ig* -Y[1]] – **sillily,** *adv.* – **silliness,** *n.*

**silly-billy** /'sɪli-bɪli/, *n.* (*usu. in an affectionate remonstrance, esp. to children*) a foolish person.

**silly season** /'sɪli sizən/, *n.* **1.** the time of the year, esp. the end-of-year break, when regular and serious activities have ceased and newspapers, broadcasts, etc., contain more frivolous material than usual. **2.** a time of year, when one's normal routines are complicated by the social demands of the season, as at the end of a school year.

**silo** /'saɪloʊ/, *n., pl.* **-los,** *v.,* **-loed, -loing.** *–n.* **1.** a tower-like structure, proofed against weather and vermin, for storing grain. **2.** a similar structure in which fermenting green fodder is preserved for future use as silage. **3.** Also, **pit silo.** *Chiefly U.S.* a pit or underground watertight space for storing grain, green feeds, etc. **4.** an underground launching site for a ballistic missile. *–v.t.* **5.** to put into or preserve in a silo. [Sp., from L *sīrus,* from Gk *sīrós* pit to keep grain in]

**siloxane** /sə'lɒksein/, *n.* any of a group of compounds with the general formula $(R_3Si)_2O$.

**silt** /sɪlt/, *n.* **1.** earthy matter, fine sand, or the like, carried by moving or running water and deposited as a sediment. *–v.i.* **2.** to become filled or choked up with silt. *–v.t.* **3.** to fill or choke up with silt. [ME *silte.* Cf. OE *unsylt* unsalted, G *Sülze* saltpan] – **silty,** *adj.*

**silt pit** /'– pɪt/, *n.* in stormwater drainage, a pit with a removable cover which traps silt and prevents it from going farther down the channel and facilitates the removal of debris.

**siltstone** /'sɪltstoʊn/, *n.* a consolidated silt; a fine sandstone.

**Silurian** /saɪ'ljuriən/, *adj.* **1.** pertaining to an early Palaeozoic geological period or system of rocks. *–n.* **2.** the Silurian period or system of rocks. [named after the *Silures,* an ancient British people who lived chiefly in SE Wales at the time of the Roman conquest of Britain]

**silurid** /saɪ'lurəd/, *n.* **1.** any of the Siluridae, or catfish family, comprising chiefly freshwater fishes with long barbels and without true scales, and including many species used for food. *–adj.* **2.** belonging to or pertaining to the Siluridae. Also, **siluroid.** [NL *Silūridae,* from L *silūrus* a river-fish, from Gk *sílouros*]

**silvan** /'sɪlvən/, *adj., n.* →**sylvan.** [L *silvānus,* from *silva* wood. See -AN]

**silver** /'sɪlvə/, *n.* **1.** *Chem.* a white ductile metallic element, used for making mirrors, coins, ornaments, table utensils, etc. *Symbol:* Ag (for argentum); *at.wt:* 107.87; *at.no.:* 47; *sp.gr.:* 10.5 at 20°C. **2.** coin made of silver or of a metal resembling silver; money. **3.** silverware; table articles made of or plated with silver. **4.** something resembling this metal in colour, lustre, etc. **5.** a lustrous greyish-white or whitish-grey; colour of metallic silver. *–adj.* **6.** consisting or made of silver; plated with silver. **7.** of or pertaining to silver. **8.** (of coins) made of a metal or alloy resembling silver, as cupronickel. **9.** producing or yielding silver. **10.** resembling silver: *the silver waves.* **11.** having the colour silver, or tinted with silver: *a silver dress, silver blue.* **12.** clear and soft: *silver sounds.* **13.** eloquent; persuasive: *a silver tongue.* **14.** indicating the 25th event of a series, as a wedding anniversary. *–v.t.* **15.** to coat with silver or some silver-like substance. **16.** to give a silvery colour to. *–v.i.* **17.** to become a silver colour. [ME; OE *siolfor,* c. G *Silber*] – **silverer,** *n.* – **silver-like,** *adj.*

**silver age** /'sɪlvər eɪdʒ/, *n.* (in Greek and Roman mythology) the second of the ages of mankind, inferior to the first or golden age, and a period of luxury and impiety.

**silver beech** /sɪlvə 'bitʃ/, *n.* a New Zealand forest tree, *Nothofagus menziesii,* with a silvery bark.

**silver beet** /– 'bit/, *n.* a form of beet, *Beta vulgaris cicla,* with large, firm, strongly veined, green leaves and a long fleshy stalk, and used as a vegetable; chard.

**silverbell** /'sɪlvəbɛl/, *n.* any of the handsome North American shrubs or small trees, with white bell-shaped flowers, constituting the genus *Halesia.* Also, **silverbell tree.**

**silver belly** /'sɪlvə ˌbɛli/, *n.* **1.** any of various small, silvery fish of the family Gerridae, found in tropical Australian coastal waters. **2.** *N.Z.* a freshwater eel.

**silver birch** /– 'bɜtʃ/, *n.* **1.** a widely-distributed Old World tree, *Betula pendula,* having a whitish papery bark. **2.** any other member of the genus *Betula* with a similar bark. **3.** *N.Z. Colloq.* →**silver beech.**

**silver bromide** /– 'broʊmaɪd/, *n.* a light-sensitive compound, AgBr, which is of basic importance in photography. It is obtained from the reaction of a bromide with a silver salt.

**silver chloride** /– 'klɔraɪd/, *n.* a light-sensitive compound, AgCl, used in sensitising photographic paper.

**silver-eye** /'sɪlvər-aɪ/, *n.* any of various white-eyes predominantly of yellow or olive colouring, as the **grey-breasted silver-eye,** *Zosterops lateralis,* of eastern and south-eastern Australia and Tasmania, the **western silver-eye,** *Z. gouldi,* of south-western Australia, the **yellow silver-eye,** *Z. lutea,* of northern Australia, and the **pale silver-eye,** *Z. chloris,* of north-eastern Australia.

**silver fern** /'sɪlvə fɜn/, *n.* a handsome tree fern, *Cyathea dealbata,* of New Zealand characterised by the white undersurface of its fronds.

**silver fir** /– 'fɜ/, *n.* a coniferous tree with leaves that are whitish beneath, *Abies alba,* native to south and central Europe widely planted for ornament.

**silverfish** /'sɪlvəfɪʃ/, *n., pl.* **-fishes,** (*esp. collectively*) **-fish. 1.** a white or silvery goldfish, *Carassius auratus.* **2.** any of various other silvery fishes, as the tarpon, or shiner. **3.** a food fish of southern African coasts, *Polysteganus argyrozona,* of the bream family. **4.** any of certain small, wingless, thysanuran insects (genus *Lepisma*) damaging to books, wallpaper, etc.

silverfish (def. 4)

**silver fluoride** /sɪlvə 'fluraɪd/, *n.* a brownish water-soluble solid, AgF, used as a disinfectant.

**silver foil** /– 'fɔɪl/, *n.* →**silver paper.**

**silver fox** /– 'fɒks/, *n.* the common red fox of North America, *Vulpes fulva,* in a melanistic variation, with a black pelage overlaid with silvery grey ends of the longer hairs.

**silver frost** /'– frɒst/, *n.* →**glaze ice.**

**silver glance** /'– glans/, *n.* →**argentite.**

**silver gull** /– 'gʌl/, *n.* the common seagull of Australia, *Larus novaehollandiae,* having white plumage with a grey back, black-tipped flight feathers, red eye-ring, bill and legs.

**silvering** /'sɪlvərɪŋ/, *n.* **1.** the act or process of coating with silver or a substance resembling silver. **2.** the coating thus applied.

**silver iodide** /sɪlvər 'aɪədaɪd/, *n.* a light-sensitive compound, AgI, used in photography and medicine.

**silver lining** /– 'laɪnɪŋ/, *n. Colloq.* some pleasing or beneficial component of a generally adverse situation.

**silverly** /'sɪlvəli/, *adv.* with a silvery appearance or sound.

**silver maple** /sɪlvə 'meɪpəl/, *n.* a large North American tree, *Acer saccharinum,* frequently cultivated for its attractive foliage.

**silver medal** /– 'mɛdl/, *n.* the prize awarded for second place in a race or other competition, esp. in the Olympic Games. See **gold medal, bronze medal.**

**silvern** /'sɪlvən/, *adj. Archaic.* of or like silver.

**silver nitrate** /sɪlvə 'naɪtreɪt/, *n.* a salt, $AgNO_3$, obtained by treating silver with nitric acid, and appearing in commerce as colourless crystals or white fused or moulded masses, used in photography, medicine, etc.

**silver paper** /– 'peɪpə/, *n.* a thin sheet of silver, or silver-like metal (esp. aluminium), used for wrapping foods, tobaccos, and other domestic articles. Also, **silver foil.**

**silver pine** /– 'paɪn/, *n. N.Z.* a small tree, *Dacrydium colensoi,* having timber specially useful for poles and railway sleepers.

**silver plate** /– 'pleɪt/, *n.* **1.** a thin silver coating deposited on the surface of another metal, usu. by electrolysis. **2.** silver-plated tableware.

**silver-plate** /sɪlvə-'pleɪt/, *v.t.,* **-plated, -plating.** to deposit a layer of silver on another (baser) metal, usu. by electrolysis.

**silver screen** /sɪlvə 'skrin/, *n.* **1.** motion pictures collectively. **2.** a special type of screen for a picture theatre.

**silverside** /ˈsɪlvəsaɪd/, *n.* a cut of beef from the outside portion of a full butt, below the aitchbone and above the leg, usu. boiled or pickled.

**silversmith** /ˈsɪlvəsmɪθ/, *n.* one who makes and repairs articles of silver.

**silver standard** /ˈsɪlvə stændəd/, *n.* a monetary system with silver of specified weight and fineness as the unit of value.

**silvertail** /ˈsɪlvəteɪl/, *n. Colloq.* **1.** a member of a wealthy elite. **2.** a highly placed official. **3.** a social climber. **4.** a prisoner (def. 1) who helps warders, as by informing, and receives special privileges.

**silver-tongued** /ˈsɪlvə-tʌŋd/, *adj.* eloquent; persuasive.

**silver tree** /ˈsɪlvə tri/, *n.* a small tree, *Leucadendron argenteum,* having hairy leaves with a silvery sheen, indigenous to the Cape peninsula in southern Africa.

**silverware** /ˈsɪlvəwɛə/, *n.* articles, esp. for table use, made of silver.

**silver wattle** /sɪlvə ˈwɒtl/, *n.* a small tree, *Acacia dealbata,* with somewhat silvery foliage, native to south-eastern Australia but planted elsewhere, as an ornamental.

**silver wedding** /– ˈwɛdɪŋ/, *n.* the 25th anniversary of a wedding.

**silverweed** /ˈsɪlvəwid/, *n.* a plant, *Potentilla anserina,* with pinnate leaves having on the underside a silvery pubescence.

**silvery** /ˈsɪlvəri/, *adj.* **1.** resembling silver; of a lustrous greyish-white colour. **2.** having a clear, ringing sound like that of silver. **3.** containing or covered with silver. – **silveriness,** *n.*

**silviculture** /ˈsɪlvəkʌltʃə/, *n.* the cultivation of forest trees; forestry. [L *silvi-* (combining form of *silva* wood) + CULTURE] – **silvicultural** /sɪlvəˈkʌltʃərəl/, *adj.* – **silviculturist** /sɪlvəˈkʌltʃərəst/, *n.*

**sim.,** **1.** similar. **2.** similarly. **3.** simile.

**sima** /ˈsaɪmə/, *n.* the denser layer of the lithosphere underlying the sial, which forms the floor of much of the oceans and is composed largely of silica and magnesia. [b. SI(LICA) + MA(GNESIA)]

**simarouba** /sɪməˈrubə/, *n.* **1.** any of the trees of the genus *Simarouba,* of tropical America, with pinnate leaves, a drupaceous fruit, and a root whose bark contains a tonic principle. **2.** the bark. Also, **simaruba.** [Carib]

**simian** /ˈsɪmiən/, *adj.* **1.** of or pertaining to an ape or monkey. **2.** characteristic of apes or monkeys. *–n.* **3.** an ape or monkey. [L *sīmia* ape + -AN]

**similar** /ˈsɪmələ/, *adj.* **1.** having likeness or resemblance, esp. in a general way. **2.** *Geom.* (of figures) having the same shape; having corresponding sides proportional and corresponding angles equal. [L *similis* like + -AR[1]] – **similarly,** *adv.*

**similarity** /sɪməˈlærəti/, *n., pl.* **-ties. 1.** state of being similar; likeness. **2.** a point of resemblance.

**simile** /ˈsɪməli/, *n.* **1.** a figure of speech directly expressing a resemblance, in one or more points, of one thing to another, as *a man like an ox.* **2.** an instance of this figure, or a use of words exemplifying it. [ME, from L, neut. of *similis* like]

**similitude** /səˈmɪlətjud/, *n.* **1.** likeness; resemblance. **2.** a person or thing that is the like, match, or counterpart of another. **3.** semblance; image. **4.** a likening or comparison; a parable or allegory. [ME, from L *similitūdo*]

**simious** /ˈsɪmiəs/, *adj.* →**simian** (defs 1 and 2).

**simitar** /ˈsɪmətə/, *n.* →**scimitar.**

**Simmental** /ˈsɪməntal/, *n.* one of a breed of cattle of Swiss origin, pale yellow to dark red in colour, excellent for milk or meat production. [from *Simmental,* valley of the Simme river in central Switzerland]

**simmer** /ˈsɪmə/, *v.i.* **1.** (of food) to cook in a liquid just below the boiling point. **2.** to make a gentle murmuring sound, as liquids just below the boiling point. **3.** to be in a state of subdued activity, excitement, etc. **4. simmer down,** *Colloq.* to become calm or calmer. *–v.t.* **5.** to cook (food) in a liquid just below the boiling point. *–n.* **6.** state or process of simmering. [earlier *simber,* ME *simper;* orig. unknown]

**simnel cake** /ˈsɪmnəl keɪk/, *n.* a rich fruit cake traditionally eaten at mid-Lent. [ME *simnel,* from OF *simenel,* from L *simila.* See SEMOLINA]

**simoniac** /səˈmoʊniæk/, *n.* one who practises simony. – **simoniacal** /saɪməˈnaɪəkəl/, *adj.* – **simoniacally,** *adv.*

**Simon says** /saɪmən ˈsɛz/, *n.* a children's game in which the leader gives instructions which are to be obeyed only when preceded by 'Simon says'. Also, **O'Grady says.**

**simony** /ˈsaɪməni/, *n.* **1.** making profit out of sacred things. **2.** the sin of buying or selling ecclesiastical preferments, benefices, etc. Also, **simonism.** [ME *symonie,* from ML *simōnia,* from *Simon* Magus, a sorcerer of Samaria. See Acts 8:18-19] – **simonist,** *n.*

**simoom** /səˈmum/, *n.* a hot, suffocating sand-laden wind of the deserts of Arabia, Syria, Africa, etc. Also, **simoon.** [Ar. *semūm,* from *samm* poison]

**simpatico** /sɪmˈpætɪkoʊ/, *adj.* **1.** of like mind or temperament; compatible. **2.** having attractive qualities; pleasing. [It., from *simpatia* SYMPATHY]

**simper** /ˈsɪmpə/, *v.i.* **1.** to smile in a silly, self-conscious way. *–v.t.* **2.** to say with a simper. *–n.* **3.** a silly, self-conscious smile. [orig. uncert. Cf. G *zimper* affected] – **simperer,** *n.* – **simperingly,** *adv.*

**simple** /ˈsɪmpəl/, *adj.,* **-pler, -plest,** *n. –adj.* **1.** easy to understand, deal with, use, etc.: *a simple matter, simple tools.* **2.** not elaborate or artificial: *a simple style.* **3.** not ornate or luxurious. **4.** unaffected; unassuming. **5.** not complex or complicated: *a simple design.* **6.** occurring or considered alone; mere; bare: *the simple truth or fact.* **7.** sincere; innocent. **8.** common or ordinary: *a simple soldier.* **9.** plain; unpretentious. **10.** humble or lowly. **11.** unimportant or insignificant. **12.** unlearned; ignorant. **13.** lacking mental acuteness or sense. **14.** *Chem.* **a.** composed of one substance or element: *a simple substance.* **b.** not mixed. **15.** *Bot.* not divided into parts: *a simple leaf* (one having only a single blade), *a simple stem* (one that does not branch). **16.** *Zool.* not compound: *a simple ascidian.* **17.** *Music.* single; uncompounded or without overtones: *simple note.* *–n.* **18.** an ignorant or foolish person. **19.** something simple, unmixed, or uncompounded. **20.** *Archaic.* a herb or plant used for medicinal purposes. **21.** *Archaic.* a person of humble condition. [ME, from OF, from L *simplus* or *simplex*] – **simpleness,** *n.*

**simple fraction** /– ˈfrækʃən/, *n.* a ratio of two whole numbers.

**simple fruit** /– ˈfrut/, *n.* a fruit formed from one pistil.

**simple harmonic motion,** *n.* a form of vibratory motion which may be represented by projecting on to the diameter of a circle the uniform motion of a point round its circumference. *Abbrev.:* S.H.M.

**simple-hearted** /ˈsɪmpəl-hatəd/, *adj.* sincere; open; frank.

**simple interest** /sɪmpəl ˈɪntrəst/, *n.* interest which is not compounded, that is, payable only on the principal amount of a debt.

**simple machine** /– məˈʃin/, *n.* one of the six (sometimes more) elementary mechanisms: the lever, wheel and axle, pulley, screw, inclined plane, and wedge.

**simple majority** /– məˈdʒɒrəti/, *n.* →**majority** (def. 3).

**simple-minded** /ˈsɪmpəl-maɪndəd/, *adj.* **1.** artless; unsophisticated. **2.** lacking in mental acuteness or sense. **3.** mentally deficient. – **simple-mindedly,** *adv.* – **simple-mindedness,** *n.*

**simple sentence** /sɪmpəl ˈsɛntəns/, *n.* a sentence with only one clause.

**simple sound** /– ˈsaʊnd/, *n.* a sound caused by vibrations operating at only one frequency at any given moment.

**simple time** /ˈ– taɪm/, *n.* a musical rhythm characterised by a metrical unit divisible by two.

**simpleton** /ˈsɪmpəltən/, *n.* a foolish, ignorant, or half-witted person; fool. [SIMPLE + -TON]

**simple vow** /ˈsɪmpəl vaʊ/, *n.* See **vow** (def. 4).

**simplex** /ˈsɪmplɛks/, *adj.* simple; consisting of or characterised by a single element, action, or the like: *a simplex circuit* (in which one telephone call and one telegraph message are transmitted simultaneously over a single pair of wires). [L]

**simplicidentate** /ˌsɪmplɪsiˈdɛnteɪt/, *adj.* belonging or pertaining to the Simplicidentata, in which there is only one pair of upper incisor teeth, formerly regarded as a suborder or division of rodents (including all except the hares, rabbits, and pikas), but now regarded as a separate order, the Lesomorpha. [*simplici-* (combining form of L *simplex* simple) + DENTATE]

**simplicity** /sɪm'plɪsəti/, *n., pl.* **-ties. 1.** state or quality of being simple. **2.** freedom from complexity, intricacy, or division into parts. **3.** absence of luxury, pretentiousness, ornament, etc.; plainness. **4.** naturalness; sincerity; artlessness. **5.** lack of acuteness or shrewdness. [ME *symplicite,* from L *simplicitas*]

**simplify** /'sɪmpləfaɪ/, *v.t.,* **-fied, -fying.** to make less complex or complicated; make plainer or easier. [F *simplifier,* from ML *simplificāre.* See -FY] – **simplification** /sɪmpləfə'keɪʃən/, *n.* – **simplifier,** *n.*

**simplism** /'sɪmplɪzəm/, *n.* the tendency to over-simplify problems by ignoring some of the difficulties, etc. [F *simplisme,* from *simple* SIMPLE + *-isme* -ISM]

**simplistic** /sɪm'plɪstɪk/, *adj.* characterised by extreme simplification; oversimplified. – **simplistically,** *adv.*

**simply** /'sɪmpli/, *adv.* **1.** in a simple manner. **2.** plainly; unaffectedly. **3.** artlessly. **4.** merely; only. **5.** unwisely; foolishly. **6.** absolutely: *simply irresistible.* [ME *simpleliche,* from SIMPLE + *-liche* -LY]

**simulacrum** /sɪmjə'leɪkrəm/, *n., pl.* **-cra** /-krə/. **1.** a mere, faint, or unreal semblance. **2.** a representation. [L]

**simulant** /'sɪmjələnt/, *adj.* **1.** simulating; imitating. **2.** *Biol., Bot.* similar in form or position (usu. fol. by *of*). *–n.* **3.** one who or that which simulates.

**simular** /'sɪmjələ/, *n.* **1.** one who or that which simulates. *–adj.* **2.** simulated; false. **3.** simulative (fol. by *of*). [SIMUL(ATE) + -AR[3]]

**simulate** /'sɪmjəleɪt/, *v.,* **-lated, -lating;** /'sɪmjələt, -leɪt/, *adj. –v.t.* **1.** to make a pretence of. **2.** to assume or have the appearance of. **3.** *Maths.* to set up an analogue of (a system) in order to study its properties. *–adj.* **4.** *Archaic.* simulated. [L *simulātus,* pp., made like] – **simulative,** *adj.* – **simulatively,** *adv.*

**simulation** /sɪmjə'leɪʃən/, *n.* **1.** pretending; feigning. **2.** assumption of a particular appearance or form. **3.** *Maths.* the use of an analogue in order to study the properties of a system. **4.** *Psychiatry.* the conscious attempt to imitate some mental or physical disorder to escape punishment or to gain some desirable objective. **5.** *Computers.* **a.** the technique of establishing a routine for one computer to make it function as nearly as possible like another computer. **b.** the representation of physical systems, phenomena, etc., by computers. **6.** the practice of constructing a model of a machine in order to test behaviour.

**simulator** /'sɪmjəleɪtə/, *n.* **1.** one who or that which simulates. **2.** a training or experimental device that simulates movement, flight, or some other condition.

**simulcast** /'sɪməlkast, 'saɪ-/, *n.* simultaneous broadcast of the same radio program by two separate radio stations or by a radio and a television station.

**simultaneous** /sɪməl'teɪniəs/, *adj.* existing, occurring, or operating at the same time: *simultaneous movements, simultaneous announcements.* [ML *simultāneus* simulated; meaning altered by association with L *momentāneus* and L *simul* at the same time as] – **simultaneously,** *adv.* – **simultaneousness, simultaneity** /sɪməltə'nɪəti/, *n.*

**simultaneous equations** /– ə'kweɪʒənz/, *n. pl.* algebraic equations which must each be satisfied by the same values of the unknowns.

**sin**[1] /sɪn/, *n., v.,* **sinned, sinning.** *–n.* **1.** transgression of divine law. **2.** an act regarded as such transgression, or any violation, esp. a wilful or deliberate one of some religious or moral principle. **3.** any serious transgression or offence. *–v.i.* **4.** to do a sinful act. **5.** to offend against a principle, standard, etc. **6.** to take advantage of; abuse or offend (fol. by *against*). *–v.t.* **7.** to do or perform sinfully. **8.** to bring, drive, etc., by sinning. [ME; OE *syn(n)*; akin to D *zonde,* G *Sünde* sin, L *sons* guilty]

**sin**[2] /saɪn/, *n.* →**sine**[1].

**sin-bin** /'sɪn-bɪn/, *n. Colloq.* **1.** →**shaggin' wagon. 2.** →**penalty box.**

**since** /sɪns/, *adv.* **1.** from then till now (oft. prec. by *ever*). **2.** between a particular past time and the present; subsequently: *he at first refused, but has since consented.* **3.** ago; before now: *long since. –prep.* **4.** continuously from or counting from: *since noon.* **5.** between (a past time or event) and the present: *changes since the war. –conj.* **6.** in the period following the time when: *he has written once since he left.* **7.** continuously or counting from the time when: *busy since he came.* **8.** because; inasmuch as. [ME *syns, synnes,* from *syn, sine* (contracted var. of *sithen,* OE *siththan* then) + adv. suffix *-es*]

**sincere** /sɪn'sɪə, sən-/, *adj.,* **-cerer, -cerest. 1.** free from any element of deceit, dissimulation, duplicity or hypocrisy. **2.** *Archaic.* pure; unmixed. **3.** *Obs.* sound; unimpaired. [L *sincērus*] – **sincerely,** *adv.* – **sincereness,** *n.*

**sincerity** /sɪn'sɛrəti, sən-/, *n., pl.* **-ties.** freedom from deceit, dissimulation, or duplicity; honesty. [L *sincēritas*]

**sinciput** /'sɪnsəpʊt/, *n.* the forepart of the skull. Cf. **occiput.** [L: half a head] – **sincipital** /sɪn'sɪpətl, sən-/, *adj.*

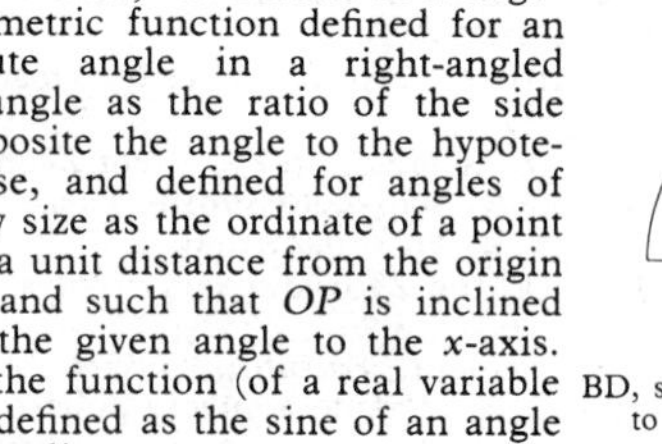

**sine**[1] /saɪn/, *n. Maths.* **a.** a trigonometric function defined for an acute angle in a right-angled triangle as the ratio of the side opposite the angle to the hypotenuse, and defined for angles of any size as the ordinate of a point *P,* a unit distance from the origin *O* and such that *OP* is inclined at the given angle to the *x*-axis. **b.** the function (of a real variable *x*) defined as the sine of an angle of radian measure *x;* any extension of this function. *Abbrev.:* sin. [L *sinus* curve, used to translate Ar. *jaib* chord of an arc]

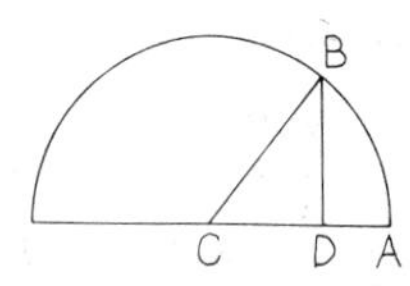


BD, sine of arc AB; ratio of BD to CB, sine of angle ACB

**sine**[2] /'saɪni, 'sineɪ/, *prep.* without. [L]

**sinecure** /'sɪnəkjʊə, 'saɪnəkjʊə/, *n.* **1.** an office requiring little or no work, esp. one yielding profitable returns. **2.** an ecclesiastical benefice without cure of souls. [short for L phrase (*beneficium*) *sine cūrā,* with E *cure* substituted for *cūrā*] – **sinecurist,** *n.*

**sine die** /saɪni 'daɪi, sineɪ 'dieɪ/, *adv.* without fixing a day for future action or meeting. [L]

**sine qua non** /ˌsaɪni kwa 'nɒn, ˌsineɪ kwa 'noʊn/, *n.* something essential; an indispensable condition. [L: lit., without which not]

**sinew** /'sɪnju/, *n.* **1.** a tendon. **2.** that which supplies strength. **3.** strength; vigour. *–v.i.* **4.** to furnish with sinews; strengthen as by sinews. [ME; OE *sinu* (nom.), *sinuwe* (gen.), c. G *Sehne,* Icel. *sin*] – **sinewless,** *adj.*

**sine wave** /'saɪn weɪv/, *n.* a periodic oscillation which can be represented geometrically by a curve having an equation of the form $y = a \sin x$.

**sinewy** /'sɪnjui/, *adj.* **1.** having strong sinews; strong. **2.** vigorous; forcible, as language, style, etc. **3.** like a sinew; tough; stringy. **4.** from or characteristic of strong sinews.

**sinfonia** /sɪn'foʊniə, sɪnfə'nɪə/, *n., pl.* **sinfonias, sinfonie** /sɪnfə'nieɪ/. →**symphony.** [It.]

**sinful** /'sɪnfəl/, *adj.* full of sin; wicked. – **sinfully,** *adv.* – **sinfulness,** *n.*

**sing** /sɪŋ/, *v.,* **sang** or **sung, sung, singing,** *n. –v.i.* **1.** to utter words or sounds in succession with musical modulations of the voice. **2.** to execute a song or voice composition, as a professional singer. **3.** to produce melodious sounds, as certain birds, insects, etc. **4.** to compose verse; tell of something in verse. **5.** to admit of being sung, as verses. **6.** to give out a continuous ringing, whistling, murmuring, or sound of musical quality, as a kettle coming to the boil, a brook, etc. **7.** to make a short ringing, whistling, or whizzing sound: *the bullet sang past his ear.* **8.** to have the sensation of a ringing or humming sound, as the ear. **9.** *Colloq.* to turn informer. **10.** (formerly), (of convicts) to scream while being flogged. **11. sing out, a.** *Colloq.* to call out in a loud voice; shout. **b.** to sing loudly: *ask the altos to sing out more. –v.t.* **12.** to utter with musical modulations of the voice, as a song. **13.** to escort or accompany with singing. **14.** to proclaim enthusiastically: *to sing a person's praises.* **15.** to bring, send, put, etc., with or by singing: *to sing a child to sleep.* **16.** to chant or intone. **17.** (in Aboriginal magic) to sing an incantation which is believed to have the power to kill the person against whom it is directed. *–n.* **18.** the act or performance of singing. **19.** a singing, ringing, or whistling sound, as of a bullet. [ME; OE *singan,* c. G *singen*] – **singable,** *adj.*

**sing.**, singular.

**Singapore** /'sɪŋəpɔ/, *n.* an island state in South-East Asia, at the southern end of the Malay Peninsula. – **Singaporean** /sɪŋə'pɔriən/, *n.*

**singe** /sɪndʒ/, *v.*, **singed, singeing,** *n.* *–v.t.* **1.** to burn superficially. **2.** to burn the ends or projections of (hair, etc.). **3.** to subject to flame in order to remove hair, etc. *–v.i.* **4.** to burn slightly; scorch. *–n.* **5.** a superficial burn. **6.** the act of singeing. [ME *senge,* OE *sencgan,* c. G *sengen;* akin to Icel. *sangr* singed, burnt]

**singer** /'sɪŋə/, *n.* **1.** one who sings, esp. a trained or professional vocalist. **2.** a poet. **3.** a singing bird.

**singer/songwriter** /ˌsɪŋə'sɒŋraɪtə/, *n.* a person who writes and sings his own songs.

**Singhalese** /sɪŋə'liz/, *adj., n., pl.* **-lese.** *–adj.* **1.** pertaining to Sri Lanka, formerly Ceylon, certain natives of that country, or their language. *–n.* **2.** a member of the Singhalese people or the Singhalese people collectively. **3.** the Indic language spoken by the Singhalese; the leading language of Sri Lanka. Also, **Sinhalese.** [Skt *Sinhala* Ceylon + -ESE]

**singing bushlark** /sɪŋɪŋ 'bʊʃlak/, *n.* a bird of the open grasslands of Australia, *Mirafra javanica,* whose song is not as loud or sustained as the introduced skylark, but is more varied and includes mimicry of other species. Also, **Horsfield's bushlark.**

**single** /'sɪŋgəl/, *adj., v.,* **-gled, -gling,** *n.* *–adj.* **1.** one only; separate; individual. **2.** of or pertaining to one person, family, etc.: *a single room.* **3.** alone; solitary. **4.** unmarried. **5.** pertaining to the unmarried state. **6.** of one against one, as combat or fight. **7.** consisting of one part, element, or member. **8.** sincere; honest: *single devotion.* **9.** having but one set of petals, as a flower. **10.** *Archaic.* of only moderate strength or body, as ale, etc. **11.** (of the eye) seeing rightly. *–v.t.* **12.** to pick or choose out from others (usu. fol. by *out*): *to single out a fact for special mention.* *–n.* **13.** something single or separate; a single one. **14.** a ticket for a train, bus, etc., valid for a one-way journey only. **15.** a gramophone record which contains only one short musical piece on each side. **16.** *Colloq.* an unmarried person. **17.** *Aus. Rules.* →**behind. 18.** (*pl.*) *Tennis, etc.* a game or match played with one person on each side. **19.** *Golf.* a contest between two golfers (as differentiated from a *foursome*). **20.** *Cricket.* a hit for which one run is scored. [ME *sengle,* from OF, from L *singulus*]

**single-acting** /'sɪŋgəl-æktɪŋ/, *adj.* (of any reciprocating machine or implement) acting effectively in only one direction (distinguished from *double-acting*).

**single-action** /'sɪŋgəl-ækʃən/, *adj.* (of a firearm) requiring cocking of the hammer before firing: *a single-action rifle.*

**single bond** /'sɪŋgəl bɒnd/, *n.* a single covalent bond linking two atoms of a molecule together.

**single-breasted** /'sɪŋgəl-brɛstəd/, *adj.* (of a coat, jacket, or the like) having a single row of buttons in the front for fastening. See **double-breasted.**

**single cream** /sɪŋgəl 'krim/, *n. Brit.* a thin cream containing a minimum of 18 per cent butterfat.

**single-cross** /sɪŋgəl-'krɒs/, *n.* (in genetics) the first-generation hybrid between two inbred lines.

**single-decker** /sɪŋgəl-'dɛkə/, *n.* a bus, tram, or the like without an upper deck. Cf. **double-decker.**

**single entry** /sɪŋgəl 'ɛntri/, *n.* a simple accounting system in which each transaction is noted by only one entry.

**single file** /– 'faɪl/, *n.* a line of persons or things arranged one behind the other; Indian file.

**single-foot** /'sɪŋgəl-fʊt/, *n.* **1.** a horse's showy gait in which the feet strike the ground as for a walk, but with faster, higher steps. *–v.i.* **2.** (of a horse) to move with such a gait.

**single-handed** /sɪŋgəl-'hændəd/, *adj.* **1.** acting or working alone or unaided. **2.** performed or accomplished by one person alone. **3.** having, using, or requiring the use of but one hand or one person. – **single-handedly,** *adv.*

**single-hearted** /sɪŋgəl-'hatəd/, *adj.* sincere in feeling or spirit; without duplicity. – **single-heartedly,** *adv.*

**single-minded** /sɪŋgəl-'maɪndəd/, *adj.* **1.** having or showing undivided purpose. **2.** having or showing a sincere mind; steadfast. – **single-mindedly,** *adv.* – **single-mindedness,** *n.*

**singleness** /'sɪŋgəlnəs/, *n.* the state or quality of being single.

**single-phase** /'sɪŋgəl-feɪz/, *adj.* denoting or pertaining to an electrical circuit having an alternating current of one phase.

**single room** /sɪŋgəl 'rum/, *n.* a bedroom for one person, esp. in a hotel or motel.

**singlestick** /'sɪŋgəlstɪk/, *n.* **1.** a stick requiring the use of one hand only, used in fencing, etc. **2.** fencing, etc., with such a stick. **3.** any short, heavy stick.

**singlet** /'sɪŋlət, 'sɪŋglət/, *n.* **1.** a short garment, with or without sleeves, usu. worn next to the skin under a shirt, jumper or dress. **2.** a similar garment worn to cover the torso by boxers, athletes, etc. **3.** *Chem.* a chemical bond consisting of one shared electron.

**singleton** /'sɪŋgəltn/, *n.* **1.** something occurring singly. **2.** *Cards.* a card which is the only one of a suit in a hand. [SINGLE + -TON]

**singly** /'sɪŋgli/, *adv.* **1.** apart from others; separately. **2.** one at a time; as single units. **3.** single-handed. [ME *senglely.* See SINGLE, -LY]

**sing-sing** /'sɪŋ-sɪŋ/, *n.* a concert of communal singing, usu. with dancing, among native, esp. Melanesian, peoples.

**singsong** /'sɪŋsɒŋ/, *n.* **1.** verse, or a piece of verse, of a jingling or monotonous character. **2.** monotonous rhythmical cadence, tone, or sound. **3.** an informal gathering at which the company sing; community singing. *–adj.* **4.** characterised by a regular rising and falling intonation. **5.** monotonous in rhythm.

**singspiel** /'sɪŋspil, 'zɪŋʃpil/, *n.* a form of music drama indigenous to Germany and Austria and akin to ballad opera. [G]

**singular** /'sɪŋgjələ/, *adj.* **1.** extraordinary; remarkable: *singular success.* **2.** unusual or strange; odd; eccentric. **3.** being the only one of the kind; unique. **4.** separate; individual. **5.** *Gram.* designating the number category that normally implies one person, thing, or collection, as English *man, thing, he, goes.* **6.** *Logic.* of or pertaining to a proposition that concerns one specified member of a class: *'Croesus was wealthy' is a singular proposition.* Cf. **particular** (def. 8); **universal** (def. 9). **7.** *Obs.* pertaining to an individual. **8.** *Obs.* private. *–n.* **9.** *Gram.* the singular number, or a form therein. [ME, from L *singulāris*] – **singularly,** *adv.* – **singularness,** *n.*

**singularise** /'sɪŋgjələraɪz/, *v.t.,* **-rised, -rising.** to make singular. Also, **singularize.**

**singularity** /sɪŋgjə'lærəti/, *n., pl.* **-ties. 1.** the state, fact, or quality of being singular. **2.** something singular; a peculiarity.

**sinh** /ʃaɪn, saɪn'eɪtʃ/, *n.* hyperbolic sine. See **hyperbolic functions.**

**Sinhalese** /sɪnhə'liz/, *adj., n., pl.* **-lese.** →**Singhalese.**

**sinhalite** /'sɪnəlaɪt, 'sɪnhə-/, *n.* a mineral, magnesium aluminium borate, used as a gem. [SINHAL(ESE) + -ITE[1]]

**Sinicism** /'saɪnəsɪzəm/, *n.* Chinese methods or customs; a Chinese usage. [*Sinic* Chinese (from ML *Sinicus,* from MGk *Sinikós*) + -ISM]

**sinister** /'sɪnəstə/, *adj.* **1.** threatening or portending evil; ominous. **2.** bad; evil; base. **3.** unfortunate; disastrous; unfavourable. **4.** of or on the left side; left. **5.** *Her.* on the shield at the left of the bearer. [ME, from L; orig. referring to omens observed on the left (the unlucky) side] – **sinisterly,** *adv.* – **sinisterness,** *n.* – **sinisterwise,** *adv.*

**sinistral** /'sɪnəstrəl/, *adj.* of or pertaining to the left side; left (opposed to *dextral*). – **sinistrally,** *adv.*

**sinistrorse** /'sɪnəstrɔs, sɪnəs'trɔs/, *adj.* rising spirally from right to left (from a point of view at the centre of the spiral), as a stem. [L *sinistrorsus* towards the left] – **sinistrorsal** /sɪnəs'trɔsəl/, *adj.*

**sinistrous** /'sɪnəstrəs/, *adj.* **1.** ill-omened; unlucky; disastrous. **2.** sinistral.

**sink** /sɪŋk/, *v.,* **sank** or **sunk, sunk** or **sunken, sinking,** *n.* *–v.i.* **1.** to descend gradually to a lower level, as water, flames, etc. **2.** to go down towards or below the horizon. **3.** to slope downwards, as ground. **4.** to go under or to the bottom; become submerged. **5.** to settle or fall gradually, as a heavy structure. **6.** to fall slowly from weakness, fatigue, etc. **7.** to pass gradually (into slumber, silence, oblivion, etc.). **8.** to pass or fall into some lower state, as of fortune, estimation, etc. **9.** to degenerate; decline. **10.** to fail in physical strength. **11.** to decrease in amount, extent, degree, etc., as value, prices, rates, etc. **12.** to become lower in tone or pitch, as sound. **13.** to enter or permeate the mind; become understood (fol. by *in, into,* etc.). **14.** to fall in; become hollow, as the cheeks. **15.** to be or become deeply absorbed in a mental state (usu. fol. by *in* or *into*): *he sank into a state of deep depression.* **16.** to drop or fall (on to a seat, bed, etc.) through weariness or fatigue: *she put down her books and sank thankfully into the nearest armchair.* **17.** to sit or lie down in a slow, luxurious manner: *he sank back into the soft cushions and dreamed.* **18. sink or swim,** to make a desperate attempt to succeed, esp. unaided, in the knowledge that the alternative is complete failure. *–v.t.* **19.** to cause to fall or descend. **20.** to cause to sink or become submerged. **21.** to depress (a part, area, etc.), as by excavating. **22.** to put down or lay (a pipe, post, etc.), as into the ground. **23.** *Golf, Billiards, etc.* to cause (the ball) to run into a hole. **24.** to bring to a worse state; lower. **25.** to bring to ruin or perdition. **26.** to reduce in amount, extent, etc., as value or prices. **27.** to lower (the voice, etc.). **28.** to suppress; ignore; omit. **29.** to invest (money), now esp. unprofitably. **30.** to lose (money) in an unfortunate investment, etc. **31.** to make (a hole, shaft, well, etc.) by excavating or boring downwards; hollow out (any cavity). **32.** *Colloq.* to drink: *let's sink a middy.* *–n.* **33.** a basin with a water supply and outlet, installed esp. in a kitchen, used for washing dishes, etc. **34.** a low-lying area where waters collect or where they disappear by sinking down into the ground or by evaporation. **35.** a place of vice or corruption. **36.** a drain or sewer. **37.** *Physics.* any device, place, or part of a system in which energy is consumed or drained from the system. **38.** *Rare.* →**cesspool.** [ME; OE *sincan,* c. G *sinken*] – **sinkable,** *adj.*

**sinkage** /ˈsɪŋkɪdʒ/, *n.* the act, process, or amount of sinking.

**sinker** /ˈsɪŋkə/, *n.* **1.** one who or that which sinks. **2.** one employed in sinking, as one who sinks shafts. **3.** a weight of lead, etc., for sinking a fishing line, fishing net, or the like in the water. **4.** *U.S. Colloq.* →**doughnut** (def. 1).

**sinkhole** /ˈsɪŋkhoʊl/, *n.* **1.** Also, **pothole, swallow-hole.** a hole formed in soluble rock by the action of water, serving to conduct surface water to an underground passage. **2.** →**sink** (def. 34). **3.** a cavern about a metre wide at ground level but widening as it increases in depth.

**sinking fund** /ˈsɪŋkɪŋ fʌnd/, *n.* a fund created to liquidate a debt by degrees.

**sinless** /ˈsɪnləs/, *adj.* free from or without sin. – **sinlessly,** *adv.* – **sinlessness,** *n.*

**sinner** /ˈsɪnə/, *n.* one who sins; a transgressor.

**sinnet** /ˈsɪnət/, *n.* →**sennit.**

**Sino-,** a word element meaning 'Chinese', as in *Sino-Tibetan, Sinology.* [NL, combining form representing L *Sinae* the Chinese (from Gk *Sínai*)]

**Sinologist** /saɪˈnɒlədʒəst, sə-/, *n.* one versed in Sinology. Also, **Sinologue** /ˈsaɪnəlɒg, ˈsɪnə-/.

**Sinology** /saɪˈnɒlədʒi, sə-/, *n.* the study of the language, literature, history, customs, etc., of China. – **Sinological** /saɪnəˈlɒdʒɪkəl, sɪnə-/, *adj.*

**sinopia** /sɪˈnoʊpiə/, *n.* **1.** a red-brown earth pigment. **2.** a preliminary drawing made on a wall as a guide for fresco painting. [named after *Sinope,* ancient seaport in Asia Minor, famous for the pigment; It., from L, from Gk]

**Sino-Tibetan** /ˌsaɪnoʊ-təˈbɛtn, ˌsɪnoʊ-/, *n.* **1.** a linguistic family, including languages spoken from Tibet to the coast, and from north China to Thailand (principally, Tibeto-Burman, Chinese, and Thai). *–adj.* **2.** denoting or pertaining to this linguistic group.

**sin-shifter** /ˈsɪn-ʃɪftə/, *n. Colloq.* a priest.

**sinter** /ˈsɪntə/, *n.* **1.** siliceous or calcareous matter deposited by springs, as that formed around the vent of a geyser. **2.** *Metall.* the product of a sintering operation. *–v.t.* **3.** *Metall.* to bring about the agglomeration of particles of a metal (or other substance as glass or carbides) by heating, usu. under pressure, to just below the melting point of the substance, or in the case of a mixture, to the melting point of the lowest melting constituent. [G: dross. See CINDER]

**sinuate** /ˈsɪnjuət, -eɪt/, *adj.* **1.** bent in and out; winding; sinuous. **2.** *Bot.* having the margin strongly or distinctly wavy, as a leaf. Also, **sinuated.** [L *sinuātus,* pp., bent, wound] – **sinuately,** *adv.*

sinuate leaf

**sinuation** /sɪnjuˈeɪʃən/, *n.* a winding; a sinuosity.

**sinuosity** /sɪnjuˈɒsəti/, *n., pl.* **-ties. 1.** (*oft. pl.*) a curve, bend, or turn. **2.** sinuous form or character.

**sinuous** /ˈsɪnjuəs/, *adj.* **1.** having many curves, bends, or turns; winding. **2.** indirect; devious. [L *sinuōsus*] – **sinuousness,** *n.* – **sinuously,** *adv.*

**sinus** /ˈsaɪnəs/, *n., pl.* **-nuses. 1.** a curve; bend. **2.** a curving part or recess. **3.** *Anat.* **a.** any of various cavities, recesses, or passages, as a hollow in a bone, or a reservoir or channel for venous blood. **b.** one of the hollow cavities in the skull connecting with the nasal cavities. **c.** an expanded area in a canal or tube. **4.** *Pathol.* a narrow, elongated abscess with a small orifice; a narrow passage leading to an abscess or the like. **5.** *Bot.* a small, rounded depression between two projecting lobes, as of a leaf. [L]

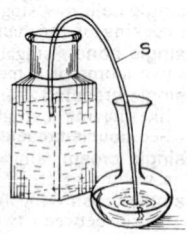

**sinusitis** /saɪnəˈsaɪtəs/, *n.* inflammation of a sinus or sinuses.

**sinus node** /ˈsaɪnəs noʊd/, *n.* a dense network of specialised conduction fibres at the junction of the superior vena cava and the right atrium; normally originates the cardiac rhythm and has been called the 'pacemaker' of the heart.

**sinusoid** /ˈsaɪnəsɔɪd/, *n.* **1.** *Maths.* a curve having an equation of the form $y = a \sin x$. **2.** *Zool.* a thin-walled, irregularly shaped space, usu. containing venous blood, found in some vertebrates.

**sinusoidal** /saɪnəˈsɔɪdl/, *adj.* **1.** of or pertaining to a sinusoid. **2.** *Physics.* having a characteristic which can be represented geometrically by a sine wave, as a *sinusoidal current.*

**-sion,** a suffix having the same function as **-tion,** as in *compulsion.* [L *-sio,* from *-s,* final surd in pp. stem + *-io,* noun suffix. Cf. -TION]

**Sion** /ˈsaɪən/, *n.* →**Zion.**

**Siouan** /ˈsuən/, *n.* **1.** a North American Indian linguistic family formerly widespread in the central and south-eastern parts of the continent. *–adj.* **2.** denoting or pertaining to this linguistic group.

**sip** /sɪp/, *v.,* **sipped, sipping,** *n.* *–v.t.* **1.** to drink a little at a time. **2.** to drink from by sips. **3.** to take in; absorb. *–v.i.* **4.** to drink by sips. *–n.* **5.** an act of sipping. **6.** a small quantity taken by sipping. [ME *sippe,* OE *sypian* drink in] – **sipper,** *n.*

**siphon** /ˈsaɪfən/, *n.* **1.** a tube or conduit in the form of an inverted U through which liquid flows over the wall of a tank or reservoir to a lower elevation by atmospheric pressure. **2.** →**soda siphon. 3.** a projecting tubular part of some animals, through which water enters or leaves the body. *–v.t., v.i.* **4.** to convey or pass through a siphon. Also, **syphon.** [L *sīpho,* from Gk *sīphōn* pipe, tube] – **siphonal, siphonic** /saɪˈfɒnɪk/, *adj.*

S

S, siphon

**siphonage** /ˈsaɪfənɪdʒ/, *n.* the action of a siphon.

**siphono-,** combining form meaning 'siphon', 'tube', as in *siphonostele.* [Gk, combining form of *sīphōn*]

**siphonophore** /səˈfɒnəfɔ, ˈsɪfənəfɔ/, *n.* any of the Siphonophora, an order of pelagic hydrozoans occurring in many diverse forms but consisting typically of a hollow stem or stock, budding into a number of polyps and bells. [NL *sīphōnophora* (pl.), from Gk *sīphōnophóros* tube-carrying. See SIPHONO-, -PHORE]

**siphonostele** /ˈsaɪfənəˌstili, -ˌstil/, *n.* (in a plant) a hollow tube of vascular tissue enclosing a pith and embedded in ground tissue.

**sippet** /ˈsɪpət/, *n.* a small piece of bread served with soup, etc.; crouton. [alteration of SOP + -ET]

**sipunculid** /saɪˈpʌŋkjəlɪd/, *n.* any of a group of annelid worms of the family Sipunculidae.

**sir** /sɜ/, *n.* **1.** a respectful or formal term of address used to a man. **2.** (*cap.*) the distinctive title of a knight or baronet: *Sir Walter Scott.* **3.** (*cap.*) a title of respect for some notable personage of ancient times: *Sir Pandarus of Troy.* **4.** a lord; gentleman. **5.** an ironic or humorous title of respect: *sir critic.* **6.** *Archaic.* a title of respect prefixed to a noun designating profession, rank, etc.: *sir priest.* [weak var. of SIRE]

**sire** /ˈsaɪə/, *n., v.,* **sired, siring.** *–n.* **1.** the male parent of an animal, esp. a domesticated quadruped, as a horse. **2.** a respectful term of address, now used only to a sovereign. **3.** *Poetic.* a father or forefather. **4.** *Obs.* a lord; person of importance. *–v.t.* **5.** to beget. [ME, from OF, from L *senior* SENIOR]

**siren** /ˈsaɪrən/, *n.* **1.** *Class Myth.* one of several sea nymphs, part woman and part bird, supposed to lure mariners to destruction by their seductive singing. **2.** any alluring or seductive woman. **3.** an acoustic instrument for producing sounds, consisting essentially of a disc pierced with holes arranged equidistantly in a circle, rotated over a jet or stream of compressed air, steam, or the like, so that the stream is alternately interrupted and allowed to pass. **4.** a device of this kind used as a whistle, fog signal, warning sound on an ambulance, fire-engine, or the like, etc. **5.** any of certain eel-like salamanders of the family Sirenidae with small forelimbs and no hind ones, and permanent external gills. *–adj.* **6.** of or like a siren. **7.** dangerously alluring. [ME, from L, from Gk *seirēn* sea nymph]

**sirenian** /saɪˈriniən/, *n.* any of the Sirenia, an order of aquatic herbivorous mammals that includes the manatee, dugong, etc. [NL *Sīrēnia* (from L *sīrēn* SIREN) + -AN]

**sirloin** /ˈsɜlɔɪn/, *n.* the portion of the loin of beef in front of the rump, used whole as a roast or cut into steaks. [earlier *surloyn.* Cf. OF *surlonge,* from *sur* over, above + *longe* loin]

**sirocco** /səˈrɒkoʊ/, *n., pl.* **-cos.** **1.** a hot, dry, dust-laden wind blowing from northern Africa and affecting parts of southern Europe; the chili. **2.** a warm, sultry south or south-east wind accompanied by rain, occurring in the same regions. **3.** any hot, oppressive wind, esp. one in the warm sector of a cyclone. [F *siroco,* from It. *scirocco,* from Ar. *shoruq,* from *sharq* east]

**Siromark** /ˈsaɪroʊmak/, *n.* a scourable branding fluid with a lanoline base for branding sheep. [(*C.*)*S.I.R.O.* + MARK[1]]

**sironise** /ˈsaɪrənaɪz/, *v.t.,* **-nised, -nising.** to treat (a wool textile) with a chemical process which prevents it from wrinkling or creasing after washing. [(*C.*)*S.I.R.O.* + *-n-* + -ISE[1]]

**siroset** /ˈsaɪroʊsɛt/, *adj.* **1.** of or pertaining to wool garments which have been treated with a chemical solution to render them permanent-press. **2.** of or pertaining to this process. [(*C.*)*S.I.R.O.* + SET]

**sirrah** /ˈsɪrə/, *n. Archaic.* a term of address used to inferiors in impatience, contempt, etc. [unexplained var. of SIR]

**sirup** /ˈsɪrəp/, *n. U.S.* →**syrup.**

**sisal** /ˈsaɪsəl/, *n.* **1.** Also, **sisal hemp.** a fibre yielded by *Agave sisalana* of southern Mexico, used for making ropes, etc. **2.** a plant yielding such fibre. [named after *Sisal,* port in Yucatan, a peninsula in S Mexico]

**siskin** /ˈsɪskɪn/, *n.* a small fringilline bird, esp. *Carduelis spinus* of Europe. [earlier *syskin,* from Flemish, var. of *sijsken* (now *sijsje*). Cf. MLG *sisek,* apparently from Pol. *czyzik*]

**sissy** /ˈsɪsi/, *n. Colloq.* **1.** an effeminate man or boy. **2.** a timid or cowardly person. Also, **cissy.** [from SISTER]

**sissy bar** /ˈ– ba/, *n.* a structure made from a U-shaped tubular bar behind the saddle of a bicycle and at right angles to the saddle bar. Also, **cissy bar.**

**sister** /ˈsɪstə/, *n.* **1.** a daughter of the same parents **(full sister** or **sister-german).** **2.** a daughter of only one of one's parents. **3.** member of the same kinship group, nationality, profession, etc.; a female associate; a female. **4.** a thing regarded as feminine and associated as if by kinship with something else. **5.** a female member of a religious community, which observes the simple vows of poverty, chastity, and obedience: *a Sister of Charity.* **6.** a senior nurse, esp. one in charge of a hospital ward. *–adj.* **7.** being a sister; related by, or as by, sisterhood: *sister ships.* [ME, from Scand.; cf. Icel. *systir,* c. OE *sweostor,* G *Schwester,* Goth. *swistar;* akin to Russ. *sestra,* L *soror*]

**sisterhood** /ˈsɪstəhʊd/, *n.* **1.** state of being a sister. **2.** a group of sisters, esp. of women bound by religious vows or similarly devoted. **3.** any organisation of women with a common aim or interest.

**sister-in-law** /ˈsɪstər-ɪn-lɔ/, *n., pl.* **sisters-in-law.** **1.** a husband's or wife's sister. **2.** a brother's wife. **3.** a husband's or wife's brother's wife.

**sisterly** /ˈsɪstəli/, *adj.* of, like, or befitting a sister.

**sistroid** /ˈsɪstrɔɪd/, *adj.* included between the convex sides of two intersecting curves (opposed to *cissoid*): *a sistroid angle.* [orig. unknown]

**sistrum** /ˈsɪstrəm/, *n., pl.* **-tra** /-trə/. an ancient Egyptian musical instrument, a form of metal rattle, used esp. in the worship of Isis. [L, from Gk *seîstron*]

sistrum

**Sisyphean** /sɪsəˈfiən/, *adj.* endless and unavailing, as labour or a task. [from *Sisyphus,* a king of Corinth, in Greek mythology condemned after death to roll a heavy stone up a steep hill, only to have it always roll down again when he neared the top]

**sit** /sɪt/, *v.,* **sat** or (*Archaic*) **sate, sitting.** *–v.i.* **1.** to rest on the lower part of the body; be seated. **2.** to be situated; dwell. **3.** to rest or lie. **4.** to place oneself in position for an artist, photographer, etc.: *to sit for a portrait.* **5.** to act as a model. **6.** to remain quiet or inactive. **7.** (of a bird) to perch or roost. **8.** to cover eggs to hatch them. **9.** to fit or be adjusted, as a garment. **10.** to occupy a seat in an official capacity, as a judge or bishop. **11.** to have a seat, be an elected representative, as in parliament. **12.** to be convened or in session, as an assembly. **13.** to act as a babysitter. **14.** to be a candidate for an examination; take an examination. *–v.t.* **15.** to cause to sit; seat (oft. with *down*). **16.** to sit upon (a horse, etc.). **17.** to provide seating room for; seat: *a table which sits eight people.* *–v.* **18.** Some special verb phrases are:

**be sitting pretty,** *Colloq.* to be comfortably established; be at an advantage.

**sit down,** to take a seat; be seated.

**sit in** (of a performer) to attach oneself temporarily to a band.

**sit in for,** to take the place of temporarily: *he'll be out for an hour so I'll sit in for him.*

**sit in on,** take part in as a spectator, observer, or visitor: *we were allowed to sit in on the debate.*

**sit on** or **upon, 1.** to have a place (on a committee, etc.): *he has sat on several committees during the past few years.* **2.** *Colloq.* to check; rebuke; repress. **3.** to prevent (a document) from becoming public knowledge so as to avoid the action demanded by it: *the government is sitting on the report.*

**sit out, 1.** to stay till the end of: *though the film was boring we sat it out.* **2.** to take no part in; keep one's seat during (a dance, etc.): *she sat out the last few dances because she was tired.*

**sit pat,** *Colloq.* to stick to one's decision, policy, etc.

**sit tight,** to take no action; bide one's time: *I'll sit tight till I know what the decision is.*

**sit up, 1.** to raise oneself from a lying to a sitting position. **2.** to stay up later than usual; not go to bed. **3.** to sit upright or erect. **4.** to be startled; become interested or alert: *the speaker's next announcement made us sit up.* [ME *sitte*(*n*), OE *sittan,* c. D *zitten,* G *sitzen,* Icel. *sitja;* akin to L *sedēre*]

**sit.,** **1.** sitting room. **2.** situation.

**sitar** /ˈsɪta, ˈsita/, *n.* a guitar-like instrument of India, having a long neck and usu. three strings. Also, **sittar.** [Hind.] – **sitarist,** *n.*

**sitcom** /ˈsɪtkɒm/, *n. Colloq.* →**situation comedy.**

**sit-down** /ˈsɪt-daʊn/, *n.* **1.** a sit-down strike. **2.** a period or instance of sitting for relaxation, talk, etc.: *they had a pleasant half-hour's sit-down together.* **3.** an organised passive protest in which demonstrators sit down in a public place in order to draw attention to their cause.

sitar

**sit-down money** /ˈ– ˌmʌni/, *n. Colloq.* unemployment benefits.

**sit-down strike** /ˌ– ˈstraɪk/, *n.* a strike during which workers refuse either to leave their place of employment or to work or to allow others to work until the strike is settled. Also, **sit-down.**

**site** /saɪt/, *n., v.,* **sited, siting.** *–n.* **1.** the position of a town, building, etc., esp. as to its environment. **2.** the area on which anything, as a building, is, has been or is to be situated. *–v.t.* **3.** to locate; place; provide with a site: *to site a gun.* [L *situs* position]

**site cover** /ˈ– kʌvə/, *n.* the percentage of a site which may be legally covered by a building.

**site index** /ˈ– ˌɪndɛks/, *n.* →**floor-space index.**

**sith** /sɪθ/, *adv., conj., prep. Archaic.* since.

**sit-in** /ˈsɪt-ɪn/, *n.* an organised passive protest in which the demonstrators occupy places normally prohibited to them and refuse to move.

**sito-,** a word element referring to food. [Gk, combining form of *sîtos* food made from grain]

**sitomania** /saɪtoʊˈmeɪniə/, *n.* morbid craving for food.

**sitophobia** /saɪtoʊˈfoʊbiə/, *n.* morbid aversion to food.

**sitosterol** /saɪˈtɒstərɒl/, *n.* a sterol, $C_{29}H_{49}OH$, derived from wheat, corn, Calabar beans, etc. [SITO- + (CHOLE)STEROL]

**sittar** /ˈsɪta, ˈsɪta/, *n.* →**sitar.**

**sittella** /səˈtɛlə/, *n.* any of various nuthatches found in dry forests throughout Australia.

**sitter** /ˈsɪtə/, *n.* **1.** one who sits, as for a portrait. **2.** a brooding bird. **3.** →**baby-sitter. 4.** *Colloq.* something easily accomplished, as a catch in cricket, a mark to be shot at, etc.

**sitting** /ˈsɪtɪŋ/, *n.* **1.** the act of one who or that which sits. **2.** a period of remaining seated, as for a portrait. **3.** an uninterrupted period of sitting, as to read a book. **4.** a brooding, as of a hen upon eggs, or the number of eggs on which a bird sits during one hatching. **5.** a session, as of a court or legislature. **6.** an occasion of serving a meal to a company, in a restaurant, etc.

**sitting duck** /– ˈdʌk/, *n.* **1.** any particularly easy mark to shoot at. **2.** *Colloq.* one who is easily duped or defeated.

**sitting room** /ˈ– rum/, *n.* a room for sitting in, as by a family communally; living room; drawing room.

**situate** /ˈsɪtʃueɪt/, *v.,* **-ated, -ating;** /ˈsɪtʃueɪt, -ət/, *adj.* *–v.i.* **1.** to give a site to; locate. *–adj.* **2.** *Archaic.* located; placed. [LL *situātus,* pp., from L *situs* site]

**situated** /ˈsɪtʃueɪtəd/, *adj.* **1.** located; placed. **2.** in certain circumstances: *well situated financially.*

**situation** /sɪtʃuˈeɪʃən/, *n.* **1.** manner of being situated; a location or position with reference to environment. **2.** a place or locality. **3.** condition; case; plight. **4.** the state of affairs; combination of circumstances: *to meet the demands of the situation.* **5.** a position or post of employment.

**situation comedy** /ˈ– kɒmədi/, *n.* comedy derived from the situations of ordinary life.

**situs** /ˈsaɪtəs/, *n.* **1.** position; situation. **2.** the proper or original position, as of a part or organ. [L]

**sit. vac.** /sɪt ˈvæk/, situation vacant.

**sitz bath** /ˈsɪts baθ/, *n.* **1.** a bathtub resembling a chair, in which the thighs and trunk of the body to the waistline are immersed in warm water. **2.** the bath so taken. [half adoption, half translation of G *Sitzbad,* from *Sitz* seat and *Bad* bath]

**SI unit** /ɛs ˈaɪ junət/, *n.* a unit of the International System of Units (Système International d'Unités).

**Siva** /ˈʃivə/, *n.* →**Shiva.** – **Sivaism,** *n.* – **Sivaist,** *n.* – **Sivaistic,** *adj.*

**six** /sɪks/, *n.* **1.** a cardinal number, five plus one. **2.** a symbol for this number, as 6 or VI. **3.** a set of this many persons or things. **4.** a playing card, die face, etc., with six pips. **5.** *Cricket.* a hit scoring six runs, the ball reaching the boundary without touching the ground. **6. at sixes and sevens,** in disorder or confusion. **7. go for six,** to suffer a major setback, as falling over heavily. **8. hit for six,** to despatch or destroy utterly. *–adj.* **9.** amounting to six in number. [ME and OE, c. D *zes,* LG *ses,* G *sechs,* Icel. *sex,* L *sex*]

**sixer** /ˈsɪksə/, *n. Colloq.* **1.** *Cricket.* →**six** (def. 5). **2.** a patrol leader of the cubs in the Boy Scouts. **3. go for a sixer,** →**six** (def. 7).

**sixfold** /ˈsɪksfoʊld/, *adj.* **1.** comprising six parts or members. **2.** six times as great or as much. *–adv.* **3.** in sixfold measure.

**six-footer** /sɪks-ˈfʊtə/, *n. Colloq.* **1.** one who is six feet tall or over. **2.** that which is six feet long.

**six o'clock swill,** *n. Colloq.* (formerly) the accelerated hectic consumption of alcohol in a hotel in the period just before six p.m. when the bars closed for the day.

**sixpence** /ˈsɪkspəns/, *n.* **1.** six pennies. **2.** (formerly) a silver coin of this value. **3.** any similar coin of other countries. **4.** *Colloq.* a five cent coin.

**sixpenny** /ˈsɪkspəni/, *adj.* **1.** of the amount or value of sixpence; costing sixpence. **2.** of trifling value; cheap; paltry.

**six-shooter** /ˈsɪks-ʃutə/, *n. Colloq.* a revolver with which six shots can be fired without reloading.

**six-stitcher** /sɪks-ˈstɪtʃə/, *n. Colloq.* a cricket ball with a leather covering sewn together with six rows of stitches around the seam.

**sixte** /sɪkst/, *n.* (in fencing) the sixth of eight defensive positions; part of the target. [F]

**sixteen** /sɪksˈtin/, *n.* **1.** a cardinal number, ten plus six. **2.** a symbol for this number, as 16 or XVI. *–adj.* **3.** amounting to sixteen in number. [ME *sixtene,* OE *sixtēne,* c. D *zestien,* G *sechzehn,* Icel. *sextān*]

**sixteenmo** /sɪksˈtinmoʊ/, *n., pl.* **-mos,** *adj. Bookbinding.* →**sextodecimo.**

**sixteenth** /sɪksˈtinθ/, *adj.* **1.** next after the fifteenth. **2.** being one of sixteen equal parts. *–n.* **3.** a sixteenth part, esp. of one ($\frac{1}{16}$). **4.** the sixteenth member of a series.

**sixteenth note** /ˈ– noʊt/, *n. U.S.* →**semiquaver.**

**sixth** /sɪksθ/, *adj.* **1.** next after the fifth. **2.** being one of six equal parts. *–n.* **3.** a sixth part, esp. of one ($\frac{1}{6}$). **4.** the sixth member of a series. **5.** sixth form. **6.** *Music.* **a.** a note on the sixth degree from a given note (counted as the first). **b.** the interval between such notes. **c.** the harmonic combination of such notes. – **sixthly,** *adv.*

**sixth chord** /ˈ– kɔd/, *n.* (in music) an inversion of a triad in which the second note (next above the root) is in the bass; the first inversion of a triad. Also, **chord of the sixth, six-three chord.**

**sixth sense** /– ˈsɛns/, *n.* a power of perception beyond the five senses; intuition.

**sixtieth** /ˈsɪkstiəθ/, *adj.* **1.** next after the fifty-ninth. **2.** being one of sixty equal parts. *–n.* **3.** a sixtieth part, esp. of one ($\frac{1}{60}$). **4.** the sixtieth member of a series.

**sixty** /ˈsɪksti/, *n., pl.* **-ties,** *adj.* *–n.* **1.** a cardinal number, ten times six. **2.** a symbol for this number, as 60 or LX. **3.** (*pl.*) the numbers from 60 to 69 of a series, esp. with reference to the years of a person's age, or the years of a century. *–adj.* **4.** amounting to sixty in number. [ME; OE *sixtig,* c. D *zestig,* G *sechzig,* Icel. *sextigir*]

**sixty-four dollar question,** *n.* the crucial, decisive, or fundamental issue of a matter. Also, **sixty-four thousand dollar question.** [named after the final prize of a popular U.S. television quiz program]

**sixty-fourth note** /ˌsɪksti-ˈfɔθ noʊt/, *n. U.S.* →**hemidemisemiquaver.**

**sixty-miler** /sɪksti-ˈmaɪlə/, *n.* a collier travelling short distances along the coast from Sydney, esp. between Sydney and Newcastle.

**sixty-nine** /sɪksti-ˈnaɪn/, *n. Colloq.* simultaneous fellatio and cunnilingus; soixante-neuf; furburger.

**sizable** /ˈsaɪzəbəl/, *adj.* →**sizeable.** – **sizableness,** *n.* – **sizably,** *adv.*

**size**[1] /saɪz/, *n., v.,* **sized, sizing.** *–n.* **1.** the dimensions, proportions, or magnitude of anything: *the size of a city, the size of a problem.* **2.** considerable or great magnitude: *to seek size rather than quality.* **3.** one of a series of graduated measures for articles of manufacture or trade: *children's sizes of shoes.* **4.** *Colloq.* actual condition, circumstances, etc. **5.** *Obs.* a fixed standard, as for food or drink. *–v.t.* **6.** to separate or sort according to size. **7.** to make of a certain size. **8. to size up,** to form an estimate of; to come up to a certain standard. **9.** *Obs.* to regulate according to a standard. [ME *syse,* from OF *sise,* aphetic var. of *assize* ASSIZE; later meanings arose from def. 9]

**size**[2] /saɪz/, *n., v.,* **sized, sizing.** *–n.* **1.** any of various gelatinous or glutinous preparations made from glue, starch, etc., used for glazing or coating paper, cloth, etc. *–v.t.* **2.** to coat or treat with size. [ME *syse;* ? special use of SIZE[1]]

**sizeable** /ˈsaɪzəbəl/, *adj.* **1.** of considerable size; fairly large: *he inherited a sizeable fortune.* **2.** *Obs.* of convenient size. Also, **sizable.** – **sizeableness,** *n.* – **sizeably,** *adv.*

**sized** /saɪzd/, *adj.* having size as specified: *middle-sized.*

**sizing** /ˈsaɪzɪŋ/, *n.* **1.** the act or process of applying size or preparing with size. **2.** size, as for glazing paper.

**sizzle** /ˈsɪzəl/, *v.,* **-zled, -zling,** *n.* *–v.i.* **1.** to make a hissing sound, as in frying or burning. **2.** *Colloq.* to be very hot. *–n.* **3.** a sizzling sound. [imitative] – **sizzler,** *n.*

**sizzle plate** /ˈ– pleɪt/, *n.* a heavy cast-iron plate for cooking steak, etc., over a direct flame, and, with the addition of a wooden base, suitable for serving at the table.

**ska** /ska/, *n.* an early form of reggae revived in Britain as a style of music suitable for dancing.

**skag** /skæg/, *n. Colloq.* **1.** a cigarette. **2.** heroin. [orig. unknown]

**skald** /skɔld/, *n.* an ancient Scandinavian poet. Also, **scald.** [Icel.: poet]

**skarn** /skan/, *n.* rock composed almost entirely of lime-bearing silicates derived by addition of silicon, aluminium, iron and magnesium to nearly pure limestones and dolomites.

**skat** /skæt/, *n.* a card game in which there are three active players, 32 cards being used. [G, from It. *scarto* a discard, from *scartare* to discard]

**skate**[1] /skeɪt/, *n., v.,* **skated, skating.** *–n.* **1.** a steel blade attached to the bottom of a shoe, enabling a person to glide on ice. **2.** a shoe with such a blade attached. **3.** →**roller-skate.** **4.** *Elect.* the sliding contact which collects current in an electric traction system. *–v.i.* **5.** to glide over ice, the ground, etc., on skates. **6.** to glide or slide smoothly along. **7.** to avoid, as in conversation (fol. by *round* or *over*). **8. skate on thin ice,** to place oneself in a delicate situation; touch on a contentious topic. [D *schaats,* MD *schaetse,* from ONF *escache* stilt]

**skate**[2] /skeɪt/, *n., pl.* **skates,** (*esp. collectively*) **skate.** any of certain rays (genus *Raja*), usu. having a pointed snout and spines down the back, but no serrated spine on the tail, as the common skate, *Raja australis* of Australian waters, or *Raja batis* of European coastal waters. [ME *scate,* from Scand.; cf. Icel. *skata*]

skate[2]

**skate**[3] /skeɪt/, *n. U.S. Colloq.* a person, a fellow. [see SKITE]

**skateboard** /ˈskeɪtbɔd/, *n.* a short plank on roller-skate wheels, ridden, usu. standing up, as a recreation.

**skater** /ˈskeɪtə/, *n.* **1.** one who skates. **2.** →**water-strider.**

**skean** /skin/, *n.* a kind of knife or dagger formerly used in Ireland and among the Scottish Highlanders. [Irish and Gaelic *sgian*]

**skedaddle** /skəˈdædl/, *v.,* **-dled, -dling,** *n. Orig. U.S. Colloq.* *–v.i.* **1.** to run away; disperse in flight. *–n.* **2.** a hasty flight. Also, **skidaddle,** *U.S.* **skiddo.** [orig. obscure]

**skeet** /skit/, *n.* a form of claypigeon shooting, in which clay targets are thrown from two traps about 40 metres apart and the shooter moves to different stations, thus firing from various angles as in real game shooting. [? special use of Brit. d. *skeet* scatter, var. of SCOOT]

**skeeter** /ˈskitə/, *n. Colloq.* **1.** a mosquito. **2.** (a nickname for a man of small build).

**skeg** /skɛg/, *n.* **1.** the afterpart of a ship's keel. **2.** a projection abaft a ship's keel for the support of a rudder. **3.** a small stabilising fin attached to the underside of a surfboard. [D *scheg,* from Scand.; cf. Icel. *skegg* beard]

**skein** /skeɪn/, *n.* **1.** a length of thread or yarn wound in a coil. **2.** anything resembling this, as coil of hair or the like. **3.** a flock of geese or similar birds in flight formation. [ME *skayne,* from OF *escaigne*]

**skeletal** /ˈskɛlətəl, skəˈlitl/, *adj.* **1.** of or pertaining to a skeleton. **2.** like a skeleton.

**skeleton** /ˈskɛlətn/, *n.* **1.** the bones of a human or other animal body considered together, or assembled or fitted together as a framework; the bony or cartilaginous framework of a vertebrate animal. **2.** *Colloq.* a very lean person or animal. **3.** a supporting framework, as of a leaf, building, or ship. **4.** mere lifeless, dry, or meagre remains. **5.** an outline, as of a literary work; basic essentials. **6. skeleton in the cupboard,** some fact in the history or lives of a family which is kept secret as a cause of shame. *–adj.* **7.** of or pertaining to a skeleton. **8.** like a skeleton or mere framework. **9.** reduced to the essential minimum: *skeleton staff.* [NL, from Gk, neut. of *skeletós* dried up]

**skeleton exercise** /– ˈɛksəsaɪz/, *n.* a military training exercise for the benefit of the commanders and staff, where only a skeleton number of troops are employed.

**skeletonise** /ˈskɛlətənaɪz/, *v.t.,* **-ised, -ising.** **1.** to reduce to a skeleton. **2.** to construct in outline. Also, **skeletonize.**

**skeleton key** /skɛlətn ˈki/, *n.* a key with nearly the whole substance of the bit filed away, so that it may open various locks. Also, **pass key.**

**skeleton weed** /ˈ– wid/, *n.* a leafless herb, *Chondrilla juncea,* from central Asia which has become a weed of crops in Australia.

**skep** /skɛp/, *n.* **1.** a basket or hamper, as of wicker. **2.** a specific quantity such as would be contained by such a basket. **3.** a beehive, esp. one made of wicker or straw. [ME *skeppe,* from Scand.; cf. Icel. *skeppa* half-bushel]

**skeptic** /ˈskɛptɪk/, *n., adj. U.S.* →**sceptic.** – **skeptical,** *adj.* – **skepticism,** *n.*

**skerrick** /ˈskɛrɪk/, *n.* a very small quantity; a scrap: *not a skerrick left.* [Brit. d.; orig. obscure]

**sketch** /skɛtʃ/, *n.* **1.** a simply or hastily executed drawing or painting, esp. a preliminary one, giving the essential features without the details. **2.** a rough design, plan, or draft, as of a literary work. **3.** a brief or hasty outline of facts, occurrences, etc. **4. a.** a brief and usu. light literary composition, as a story or essay. **b.** *Music.* a brief composition, esp. for the piano. **c.** a short play, usu. of a comic or musical nature, or slight dramatic performance, as one forming part of a revue. *–v.t.* **5.** to make a sketch of. **6.** to set forth in a brief or general account. *–v.i.* **7.** to make a sketch or sketches. [D *schets,* from It. *schizzo,* from L *schedium* extemporaneous poem, from Gk *schédios* extempore] – **sketcher,** *n.*

**sketchable** /ˈskɛtʃəbəl/, *adj.* suitable for being sketched.

**sketchbook** /ˈskɛtʃbʊk/, *n.* **1.** a book for making sketches in. **2.** a book of literary or other sketches. Also, **sketchblock, sketchpad.**

**sketchy** /ˈskɛtʃi/, *adj.,* **sketchier, sketchiest.** **1.** like a sketch; giving only outlines. **2.** slight; imperfect; incomplete; superficial. – **sketchily,** *adv.* – **sketchiness,** *n.*

**skete** /skit/, *n.* a settlement of monks or ascetics of the Greek Church. [L Gk *Skētís* desert in Egypt famous as a retreat for hermits]

skew arch

**skew** /skju/, *v.i.* **1.** to turn aside or swerve; take an oblique course. **2.** to look obliquely; squint. **3.** to drive a skewnail. *–v.t.* **4.** to give an oblique direction to; shape or form obliquely. **5.** *Carp.* to drive (a nail) obliquely; to drive a skewnail. **6.** to distort; depict unfairly. *–adj.* **7.** having an oblique direction or position; slanting. **8.** having a part which deviates from a straight line, right angle, etc.: *skew gearing.* **9.** *Geom.* not coplanar. *–n.* **10.** an oblique movement, direction, or position. [ME *skewe,* from ONF *eskiu(w)er* escape. See ESCHEW]

S, skewback

**skew arch** /ˈ– atʃ/, *n.* an arch whose axis is not perpendicular to the faces of its abutments, as where a railway crosses a road at an angle.

**skewback** /ˈskjubæk/, *n.* **1.** a sloping surface against which the end of an arch rests. **2.** a stone, course of masonry, or the like, presenting such a surface.

**skewbald** /ˈskjubəld/, *adj.* **1.** (of horses, etc.) having patches of different colours, esp. of white and brown. *–n.* **2.** a skewbald horse or pony. Cf. **piebald.** [cf. obs. E *skewed* skewbald (orig. uncert.)]

**skewer** /ˈskjuə/, *n.* **1.** a long pin of wood or metal for putting through meat to hold it together or in place while being cooked. **2.** any similar pin for some other purpose. *–v.t.* **3.** to fasten with, or as with, skewers. [earlier *skiver,* of unknown orig.]

**skewnail** /ˈskjuneɪl/, *n.* a nail driven obliquely.

**skew-whiff** /skju-ˈwɪf/, *adv. Colloq.* askew. Also, **skewiff.**

**ski** /ski/, *n., pl.* **skis, ski,** *v.,* **ski'd** or **skied, skiing.** *–n.* **1.** one of a pair of long, slender pieces of hard wood, metal, or plastic, one fastened to each shoe, used for travelling or gliding over snow, and often (esp. as a sport) down slopes. **2.** a water-ski. *–v.i.* **3.** to travel on or use skis. **4.** to water-ski. [Norw., var. of *skid,* c. Icel. *skīdh,* OE *scid* thin slip of wood, G *Scheit* thin board]

**skiascope** /ˈskaɪəskoup/, *n.* an apparatus which determines the refractive power of the eye by observing the lights and shadows on the pupil when a mirror illumines the retina; retinoscope. [Gk *skía* shadow + -SCOPE] **– skiascopy** /skaɪˈæskəpi/, *n.*

**skibob** /ˈskibɒb/, *n., v.,* **-bobbed, -bobbing.** *–n.* **1.** a vehicle used for gliding down snow slopes, consisting of a low seat and steering handle supported by two short skis; the rider wears small skis for balance. *–v.i.* **2.** to ride such a vehicle. [SKI + BOB(SLEIGH)]

**skid** /skɪd/, *n., v.,* **skidded, skidding.** *–n.* **1.** a plank, bar, log, or the like, esp. one of a pair, on which something heavy may be slid or rolled along. **2.** *U.S.* one of a number of such logs or planks forming a skidway. **3.** a plank or the like, esp. one of a number, on or by which something is supported. **4.** *Agric.* a low platform on metal runners, towed behind a tractor, used for transporting food, esp. hay, for stock. **5.** (*pl.*) *N.Z.* →**skidway** (def. 1.). **6.** *Naut.* **a.** (*pl.*) a skidboard. **b.** (*usu. pl.*) a framework above the main deck on which ships' boats are carried. **7.** a shoe or some other device for preventing the wheel of a vehicle from rotating, as when descending a hill. **8.** a runner on the underpart of some aeroplanes, enabling the machine to slide along the ground when alighting. **9.** an act of skidding: *the car went into a skid on the icy road.* **10. on the skids,** deteriorating fast. **11. put the skids under,** to place (someone) in a precarious position; to ensure the downfall (of someone). *–v.t.* **12.** to place on or slide along a skid or skids. **13.** to check with a skid, as a wheel. *–v.i.* **14.** to slide along without rotating, as a wheel to which a brake has been applied. **15.** to slip or slide sideways relative to direction of wheel rotation, as a car in turning a corner rapidly. **16.** to slide forward under its own momentum, as a car when the wheels have been braked. **17.** (of an aeroplane when not banked sufficiently) to slide sideways, away from the centre of the curve executed in turning. [orig. uncert.; ? irregularly from Scand.; cf. Icel. *skīdh,* akin to SKI]

**skidaddle** /skəˈdædl/, *v.i., n. Colloq.* →**skedaddle.**

**skidboard** /ˈskɪdbɔd/, *n.* **1.** a piece of light board, sometimes with the edge turned up, on which one can skid on the wet sand of a beach just as a wave is retreating. **2.** Also, **skids.** a large wooden framework on a quay used to slide cargo up and down when loading a ship.

**skiddoo** /skəˈdu/, *v.i., n. U.S. Colloq.* →**skedaddle.**

**skiddy** /ˈskɪdi/, *n.* one who works at a skidway.

**skid fin** /ˈskɪd fɪn/, *n.* an auxiliary aerofoil over the upper main wing in some early aeroplanes.

**skidlid** /ˈskɪdlɪd/, *n. Colloq.* a motorcyclist's crash-helmet.

**skidoo** /skəˈdu/, *n.* a small motorised over-snow vehicle, similar to a sled.

**skidpan** /ˈskɪdpæn/, *n.* a place where motorists or the like may learn and practise the control of skidding vehicles on a prepared slippery surface.

**skid row** /skɪd ˈrou/, *n.* **1.** a disreputable district inhabited by derelicts. **2. on skid row,** destitute.

**skidway** /ˈskɪdweɪ/, *n.* **1.** a platform, often sloping, on which logs are piled ready for sawing. **2.** a path or way made of logs along which objects are rolled.

**skier** /ˈskiə/, *n.* one who skis.

**skiey** /ˈskaɪi/, *adj.* →**skyey.**

**skiff** /skɪf/, *n.* any of various types of small boat, usu. propelled by oars or sails. [F *esquif,* from It. *schifo,* from OHG *scif* SHIP]

**skiffle** /ˈskɪfəl/, *n.* a style of music popular during the 1950s based on American folksongs and played on an arbitrary mixture of guitars and improvised instruments, esp. the washboard.

**skiing** /ˈskiɪŋ/, *n.* the use of skis, for travelling, or sport.

**skijoring** /skiˈdʒɔrɪŋ/, *n.* a sport in which a skier is pulled over snow or ice, generally by a horse. [Norw. *skikjøring* ski-driving] **– skijorer,** *n.*

**ski-jump** /ˈski-dʒʌmp/, *n.* **1.** a jump made by a skier. **2.** the runway designed for such a jump consisting of a ramp overhanging a slope. **– ski-jumper,** *n.*

**skilful** /ˈskɪlfəl/, *adj.* **1.** having or exercising skill. **2.** showing or involving skill: *a skilful display of fancy diving.* **3.** *Obs.* reasonable. Also, *U.S.,* **skillful. – skilfully,** *adv.* **– skilfulness,** *n.*

**ski-lift** /ˈski-lɪft/, *n.* a device for carrying skiers up a slope, typically consisting of chairs suspended from an endless cable; cable lift.

**skill** /skɪl/, *n.* **1.** the ability that comes from knowledge, practice, aptitude, etc., to do something well. **2.** competent excellence in performance; expertness; dexterity. **3.** *Obs.* understanding. **4.** *Obs.* a reason; cause. [ME, from Scand.; cf. Icel. *skil* distinction]

**skilled** /skɪld/, *adj.* **1.** having skill; trained or experienced. **2.** showing, involving, or requiring skill, as work. **3.** of or pertaining to workers performing a specific operation requiring apprenticeship or other special training or experience.

**skillet** /ˈskɪlət/, *n.* a frying pan. [orig. obscure]

**skillful** /ˈskɪlfəl/, *adj. U.S.* →**skilful.**

**skillion** /ˈskɪljən/, *n.* **1.** Also, **skilling.** a lean-to or outhouse. **2.** a hill or bluff sloping in one direction, with a sheer fall on the other side.

**skillion roof** /ˈ– ruf/, *n.* the roof of a lean-to in which the flat surface slopes in one direction, without a ridge or peak.

**skilly** /ˈskɪli/, *n. Brit.* a thin soup, broth, or gruel, formerly used in prisons and workhouses. [shortened form of obs. *skilligalee;* ult. orig. unknown]

**skim** /skɪm/, *v.,* **skimmed, skimming,** *n.* *–v.t.* **1.** to take up or remove (floating matter) from a liquid with a spoon, ladle, etc.: *to skim cream.* **2.** to clear (liquid) thus: *to skim milk.* **3.** to move or glide lightly over or along the surface of (the ground, water, etc.). **4.** to cause (a thing) to fly over or near a surface, or in a smooth course: *to skim stones.* **5.** to go over in reading, treatment, etc., in a superficial manner. **6.** to cover (liquid, etc.) with a thin layer. *–v.i.* **7.** to pass or glide lightly along over or near a surface. **8.** to go, pass, glance, etc., over something in a superficial way (usu. fol. by *over*). **9.** to become covered with a thin layer. *–n.* **10.** the act of skimming. **11.** that which is skimmed off as skimmed milk. **12.** *Obs.* scum. [d. var. of obs. *scum,* v., skim. See SCUM]

**skim board** /ˈ– bɔd/, *n.* a small board, usu. plywood, used by surfers to skim over the shallow water at the edge of the beach.

**skimmer** /ˈskɪmə/, *n.* **1.** one who or that which skims. **2.** a shallow utensil, usu. perforated, used in skimming liquids. **3.** any of various gull-like birds of the family Rynchopidae, which skim the water with the elongated lower mandible touching the water in obtaining food.

**skim milk** /skɪm ˈmɪlk/, *n.* milk from which the cream has been removed. Also, **skimmed milk.**

**skimming** /ˈskɪmɪŋ/, *n.* **1.** (*usu. pl.*) that which is removed by skimming. **2.** (*pl.*) *Metall.* dross.

**skimming coat** /ˈ– kout/, *n.* →**setting coat.**

**skimp** /skɪmp/, *v.t.* **1.** to do hastily or inattentively; scamp. **2.** to be sparing with; scrimp. *–v.i.* **3.** to be extremely thrifty (oft. fol. by *on*). *–adj.* **4.** skimpy. [orig. uncert.]

**skimpy** /ˈskɪmpi/, *adj.,* **skimpier, skimpiest. 1.** lacking in size, fullness, etc.; scanty. **2.** too thrifty; stingy: *a skimpy housewife.* **– skimpily,** *adv.* **– skimpiness,** *n.*

**skin** /skɪn/, *n., v.,* **skinned, skinning.** *–n.* **1.** the external covering or integument of an animal body, esp. when soft and flexible. **2.** such an integument stripped from the body of an animal; pelt. **3.** any integumentary covering, outer coating, or surface layer, as an investing membrane, the rind or peel of fruit, or a film on liquid. **4.** a single nacreous layer in a pearl, the outermost at any time. **5.** the planking or iron plating which covers the ribs of a ship. **6.** a sheathing or casing forming the outside surface of a structure, as an exterior wall of a building, etc. **7.** *Colloq.* a contraceptive sheath. **8.** a container made of animal skin, used for holding liquids. **9.** one's resistance or sensitivity to criticism, censure, etc.: *a thick skin, a thin skin.* **10. jump out of one's skin,** to be very frightened, surprised, or the like. **11. save one's skin,** to escape harm. **12. by the skin of one's teeth,** scarcely; just; barely. **13. get under one's skin, a.** to irritate one. **b.** to fascinate or attract one. *–v.t.* **14.** to strip or deprive of skin; flay; peel. **15.** to strip off, as or like skin. **16.** to cover with or as with skin. **17.** *Colloq.* to strip of money or belongings; fleece, as in gambling. *–v.i.* **18.** *U.S. Colloq.* to slip off hastily. [ME, from Scand.; cf. Icel. *skinn,* c. d. G *Schind, Schinde* skin of fruit]

**skin and bones,** *n.* **1.** an extremely emaciated physique. **2.** a person having such a physique.

**skinbound** /ˈskɪnbaʊnd/, *adj.* having the skin drawn tightly over the flesh, as in scleroderma.

**skin classing** /ˈskɪn klasɪŋ/, *n.* the grading of sheep skins according to type, fineness and length in preparation for sale.

**skin-deep** /skɪn-ˈdip/, *adj.* **1.** superficial; slight. *–adv.* **2.** slightly; superficially.

**skin depth** /ˈskɪn dɛpθ/, *n.* the effective depth to which an alternating current, esp. at radio frequencies, penetrates the conductor in the skin effect.

**skindiving** /ˈskɪndaɪvɪŋ/, *n.* underwater swimming for which the diver is equipped with a lightweight mask, an aqualung or snorkel, and foot fins. – **skindiver,** *n.*

**skin effect** /ˈskɪn əfɛkt/, *n.* the effect which causes an alternating current, esp. of radio frequencies, to concentrate near the surface of a conductor, so increasing its effective resistance.

**skin flic** /ˈ– flɪk/, *n. Colloq.* a pornographic movie. Also, **skin flick.**

**skinflint** /ˈskɪnflɪnt/, *n.* a mean, niggardly person.

**skin friction drag,** *n.* aerodynamic resistance due to the tangential forces of moving air on the surface of a body.

**skinful** /ˈskɪnfʊl/, *n. Colloq.* **1.** a large amount, esp. of alcoholic drink. **2. have a skinful, a.** to be drunk. **b.** to be fed up.

**skin game** /ˈskɪn geɪm/, *n. Colloq.* **1.** a dishonest activity, business, etc. **2.** a swindle. [SKIN (def. 17) + GAME[1]]

**skin grafting** /ˈ– graftɪŋ/, *n.* the transplanting of healthy skin from the patient's or another's body to a wound or burn, to form new skin.

**skinhead** /ˈskɪnhɛd/, *n. Colloq.* a member of any group of young men identified by close-cropped hair and sometimes indulging in aggressive activities.

**skink** /skɪŋk/, *n.* any of the harmless, generally smooth-scaled lizards constituting the family Scincidae, as the land mullet *Egernia major bungana* of eastern Australia, or as *Scincus scincus* of northern Africa, formerly much used for medicinal purposes. [L *scincus,* from Gk *skínkos*]

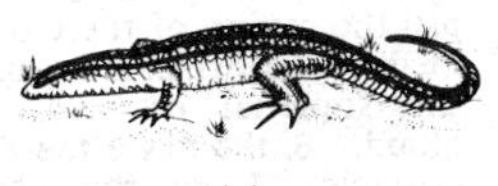
skink

**skinned** /skɪnd/, *adj.* **1.** having a skin, esp. as specified: *light-skinned.* **2. keep one's eyes skinned,** to be extremely vigilant.

**skinner** /ˈskɪnə/, *n.* **1.** one who skins. **2.** one who prepares, or deals in, skins. **3.** *Horseracing Colloq.* a horse which wins a race at very long odds. **4.** *Horseracing Colloq.* a betting coup. **5. a skinner,** *N.Z. Colloq.* **a.** empty; finished: *the beer's a skinner.* **b.** broke: *I'm a skinner.*

**Skinner box** /ˈskɪnə bɒks/, *n.* a box or cage, used in animal-conditioning experiments, in which the animal must learn to operate a mechanism correctly in order to gain a reward or escape a punishment. [from B.F. *Skinner,* b. 1904, U.S. psychologist]

**Skinnerian** /skɪˈnɪəriən/, *adj.* of or pertaining to the theories of operant conditioning and behaviour therapy associated with the work of the U.S. psychologist, B.F. Skinner.

**skinnery** /ˈskɪnəri/, *n., pl.* **-neries.** a place where skins are prepared, as for the market.

**skinny** /ˈskɪni/, *adj.,* **-nier, -niest. 1.** lean; emaciated. **2.** of or like skin. – **skinniness,** *n.*

**skinny-dip** /ˈskɪni-dɪp/, *Colloq. –v.i.* **1.** to bathe in the nude. *–n.* **2.** a nude swim. – **skinny-dipper,** *n.*

**skinny rib** /ˈskɪni rɪb/, *n.* a tight-fitting sweater in a rib knit.

**skinpop** /ˈskɪnpɒp/, *Colloq. –n.* **1.** an injection of a drug into the skin. *–v.i.* **2.** to inject drugs into the skin.

**skins** /skɪnz/, *n.pl. Colloq.* drums; bongos.

**skint** /skɪnt/, *adj. Colloq.* completely without money; broke. [from *skinned,* pp. of SKIN (def. 17)]

**skin-tight** /ˈskɪn-taɪt/, *adj.* fitting as tightly as skin.

**skin wool** /ˈskɪn wʊl/, *n.* scoured wool from a fellmongered sheep.

**skip**[1] /skɪp/, *v.,* **skipped, skipping,** *n. –v.i.* **1.** to spring, jump, or leap lightly; gambol. **2.** to pass from one point, thing, subject, etc., to another, disregarding or omitting what intervenes. **3.** *Colloq.* to go away hastily; abscond. **4.** *Educ.* to be advanced more than one class. **5.** to ricochet, as a missile passing with rebounds along a surface. **6.** to use a skipping-rope. *–v.t.* **7.** to jump lightly over. **8.** to miss out, as part of a continuum or one of a series. **9.** to pass over without reading, notice, mention, action, etc. **10.** to send (a missile) ricocheting along a surface. **11.** *Colloq.* to leave hastily, or flee from, as a place. *–n.* **12.** a skipping movement; a light jump. **13.** a gait marked by such jumps. **14.** a passing from one point or thing to another, with disregard of what intervenes. **15.** *U.S. Music.* a leap. [ME. Cf. MSwed. *skuppa* skip]

**skip**[2] /skɪp/, *n. Chiefly Sport Colloq.* →**skipper**[1] (def. 2). [short for SKIPPER[1]]

**skip**[3] /skɪp/, *n.* **1.** a container attached to a crane or cable for transporting materials or refuse in building operations. **2.** a truck used in an underground railway system for transporting coal, minerals, etc. **3.** →**skep.** [OE *skep* a basket]

**skip**[4] /skɪp/, *n. Colloq.* (*derog., used esp. by Australians of non-British background*) an Australian person of British background. Also, **skippy.** [from *Skippy,* the name of a kangaroo in a children's television series]

**skip distance** /ˈ– dɪstns/, *n.* the minimum distance from a radio transmitter at which waves reflected from the ionosphere can be detected.

**skipjack** /ˈskɪpdʒæk/, *n., pl.* **-jacks,** (*esp. collectively*) **-jack. 1.** any of various fishes that leap from the water. **2.** an important tuna, *Katsuwonus pelamis,* of tropical waters.

**ski-plane** /ˈski-pleɪn/, *n.* an aircraft fitted with skis, able to land on snow.

**ski-pole** /ˈski-poʊl/, *n.* **1.** Also, **pole.** one of two slender poles, metal-tipped and having a disc near the lower end to prevent it from sinking into the snow, used by a skier for balance and to increase speed; stock. **2.** one of a set of poles set at prescribed distances to mark out a snow-covered track for skiers.

**skipper**[1] /ˈskɪpə/, *n.* **1.** the master or captain of a ship, esp. of a small trading or fishing vessel. **2.** a captain or leader, as of a team. *–v.t.* **3.** to act as skipper of. [ME, from MD *schipper,* from *schip* SHIP]

**skipper**[2] /ˈskɪpə/, *n.* **1.** one who or that which skips. **2.** any of various insects that hop or fly with jerky motions. **3.** any of the quick-flying lepidopterous insects constituting the family Hesperiidae, closely related to the true butterflies. **4.** →**saury.** [SKIP[1] + -ER[1]]

**skippet** /ˈskɪpət/, *n.* a small round box for protecting a seal as attached by a ribbon or cord to a document. [orig. uncert.; ? from SKIP[3] + -ET]

**skipping-rope** /ˈskɪpɪŋ-roʊp/, *n.* a rope, usu. having handles at the ends, which is swung in a loop so that the holder or others jump over it.

**skipping stones** /ˈskɪpɪŋ stoʊnz/, *n.* the game of throwing flat stones at water so that they repeatedly hit and rebound from the surface; ducks and drakes.

**skirl** /skɜl/, *Chiefly Scot. –v.i.* **1.** to sound loudly and shrilly (used esp. of the bagpipes). **2.** to shriek. *–v.t.* **3.** to play (the bagpipes, etc.). *–n.* **4.** the sound of the bagpipes. **5.** a shrill sound. [metathetic var. of ME *scrille,* from Scand.; cf. Norw. *skrylla*]

**skirmish** /ˈskɜmɪʃ/, *n.* **1.** *Mil.* a fight between small bodies of troops, esp. advanced or outlying detachments of opposing armies. **2.** any brisk encounter. *–v.i.* **3.** to engage in a skirmish. [ME *skirmysshe,* from OF *eskirmiss-,* stem of *eskirmir,* from OHG *skirman* defend, from *skirm* shield. See SCREEN] – **skirmisher,** *n.*

**skirr** /skɜ/, *v.i.* **1.** to go rapidly; fly; scurry. **2.** to go rapidly over. *–n.* **3.** a grating or whirring sound. [imitative]

**skirret** /ˈskɪrət/, *n.* an umbelliferous plant, *Sium sisarum,* cultivated in Europe for its edible tuberous root. [ME *skirwhit(e),* from *skire* pure (from Scand.; cf. Icel. *skīrr*) + WHITE]

**skirt** /skɜt/, *n.* **1.** the lower part of a gown, coat, or the like, hanging from the waist. **2.** a separate garment (outer or under) worn by women and girls, extending from the waist downwards. **3.** some part resembling or suggesting the skirt of a garment. **4.** one of the flaps hanging from the sides of a saddle. **5.** a skirting board or bordering finish in building. **6.** (*usu. pl.*) the bordering, marginal, or outlying part of a place, group, etc. **7.** a cut of beef from the flank. **8.** *Colloq.* a woman or girl. *–v.t.* **9.** to lie on or along the border of. **10.** to border or edge with something. **11.** to pass along or around the border or edge of: *to skirt a town.* **12.** to remove skirtings from (fleeces). *–v.i.* **13.** to be, lie, live, etc., on or along the edge of something. **14.** to pass or go around the border of something. [ME, from Scand.; cf. Icel. *skyrta* SHIRT]

**skirter** /ˈskɜtə/, *n.* →**roller** (def. 11).

**skirting** /ˈskɜtɪŋ/, *n.* **1.** material for making skirts. **2.** a skirting board. **3.** (*pl.*) the trimmings or inferior parts of fleece.

**skirting board** /ˈ– bɔd/, *n.* **1.** Also, **skirting.** a line of boarding protecting an interior wall next to the floor. **2.** Also, **skirting table.** the table on which a fleece is skirted.

**skirting table** /ˈ– teɪbəl/, *n.* →**wool table.**

**skirty** /ˈskɜti/, *adj.* (of wool) inferior in quality because it contains or resembles skirtings.

**ski run** /ˈski rʌn/, *n.* a snow-covered slope regularly used for skiing.

**ski-stick** /ˈski-stɪk/, *n. Brit.* →**ski-pole** (def. 1).

**skit** /skɪt/, *n.* **1.** a slight parody, satire, or caricature, esp. dramatic or literary. **2.** a short satirical play. [ME: harlot; cf. d. *skite* move fast. See SKITTER]

**skite** /skaɪt/, *Colloq. v.i.* **1.** to boast; brag. *–n.* **2.** a boast; brag. **3.** Also, **skiter.** a boaster; braggart. [Scot. and northern d. *skate* (derog.)] – **skiting,** *n.*

**skitebook** /ˈskaɪtbʊk/, *n. Colloq.* a scrapbook in which actors, etc., keep notices of their performances, photographs, etc., esp. for purposes of promotion.

**skitter** /ˈskɪtə/, *v.i.* **1.** to go, run, or glide lightly or rapidly. **2.** to skim along a surface. **3.** *Angling.* to draw a spoon or a baited hook over the water with a skipping motion. *–v.t.* **4.** to cause to skitter. [frequentative of d. *skite* move fast, ? from Scand.; cf. Icel. *skeyti* dart]

**skittish** /ˈskɪtɪʃ/, *adj.* **1.** apt to start or shy. **2.** restlessly or excessively lively. **3.** fickle; uncertain. **4.** coy. [akin to SKITTER] – **skittishly,** *adv.* – **skittishness,** *n.*

**skittle** /ˈskɪtl/, *n.* **1.** (*pl.*) ninepins. **2.** one of the pins. *–v.t.* **3.** to knock over or send flying, in the manner of skittles. [Scand.; cf. Dan. *skyttel* kind of ball (child's plaything)]

**skive** /skaɪv/, *v.t.,* **skived, skiving.** to split or cut (leather, etc.) into layers or slices; shave (hides, etc.). [Scand.; cf. Icel. *skīfa,* v., n., slice, c. ME *schive* slice (of bread)]

**skiver** /ˈskaɪvə/, *n.* **1.** one who or that which skives. **2.** a thin sheepskin used for bookbinding, gloves, etc.

**skivvy** /ˈskɪvi/, *n.* **1.** a close-fitting garment with long sleeves and a turtle neck, similar to a jumper, but usu. made of machine-knitted cotton. **2.** Also, **skivv.** *Colloq.* (*usu. derog.*) a female servant, esp. one who does rough work.

**skol** /skɒl/, *interj., v.,* **skolled, skolling.** *–interj.* **1.** to your health. *–v.t. Colloq.* **2.** to consume (a drink) at one draught. Also, **skoal** /skoʊl/. [Scand.; cf. Dan. *skaal* bowl, toast]

**Skt,** Sanskrit.

**skua** /ˈskjuə/, *n.* any of several strong-flying, predatory, gull-like seabirds of the family Stercorariidae, which pursue weaker birds in order to make them disgorge their prey. [NL, from ON *skufr* skua, tassel, c. Icel. *skūfr;* orig. uncert.]

great skua

**skulduggery** /skʌlˈdʌgəri/, *n.* dishonourable proceedings; mean dishonesty or trickery. Also, **skullduggery.** [var. of d. *sculduddery;* orig. obscure]

**skulk** /skʌlk/, *v.i.* **1.** to lie or keep in hiding, as for some evil or cowardly reason. **2.** to shirk duty; malinger. **3.** to move or go in a mean, stealthy manner; sneak; slink. *–n.* **4.** one who skulks. **5.** an act of skulking. [ME, from Scand.; cf. Dan. *skulke*] – **skulker,** *n.*

**skull** /skʌl/, *n.* **1.** the bony framework of the head, enclosing the brain and supporting the face; the skeleton of the head. **2.** (*usu. derog.*) the head as the seat of intelligence or knowledge. **3.** a death's-head. [ME *scolle,* from Scand.; cf. d. Norw. *skol, skul* shell (of an egg or a nut)]

**skull and crossbones,** *n.* a representation of a front view of a human skull above two crossed bones, originally used on pirate's flags, and now used as a warning sign, as in designating poisons.

**skullcap** /ˈskʌlkæp/, *n.* **1.** a brimless cap of silk, velvet, or the like, fitting closely to the head. **2.** any member of the genus *Scutellaria,* herbaceous plants in which the calyx resembles a helmet.

skullcap

**skungy** /ˈskʌndʒi/, *adj.* →**scungy.**

**skunk** /skʌŋk/, *n.* **1.** a small, striped, fur-bearing, bushy-tailed, North American mammal, *Mephitis mephitis,* of the weasel family, Mustelidae, which ejects a fetid fluid when attacked. **2.** its fur, used in garments. **3.** any of various allied or similar animals, as a spotted variety (genus *Spilogale*) or the members of the genus *Conepatus.* **4.** *Colloq.* a thoroughly contemptible person. *–v.t.* **5.** *U.S. Colloq.* (in games) to beat so completely as to keep from scoring. [Amer. Ind. (Algonquian) *segankw* or *segongw*]

skunk

**skutterudite** /ˈskʌtərədaɪt/, *n.* a mineral arsenide of cobalt and nickel occurring in greyish-white cubic crystals; used as a source of cobalt and nickel. [named after *Skutterud* in Norway]

**sky** /skaɪ/, *n., pl.* **skies,** *v.,* **skied** or **skyed, skying.** *–n.* **1.** (*oft. pl.*) the region of the clouds or the upper air. **2.** (*oft. pl.*) the heavens or firmament, appearing as a great arch or vault. **3.** the supernal or celestial heaven. **4.** climate. **5.** *Obs.* a cloud. **6. the sky's the limit,** *Colloq.* there is no limitation or obstacle. **7. to the skies,** highly; extravagantly. *–v.t.* **8.** *Colloq.* to raise aloft; strike (a ball) high into the air. **9.** *Colloq.* to hang (a picture, etc.) high on the wall of a gallery. **10.** *Rowing.* to lift (the blade of an oar) too high above the water before a stroke. **11. sky the towel,** *Colloq.* give up, admit defeat. *–v.i.* **12.** *Rowing.* to sky a blade. [ME, from Scand.; cf. Icel. *skȳ* cloud, c. OE *scēo* cloud] – **skylike,** *adj.*

**sky blue** /– ˈblu/, *n.* the colour of the unclouded sky in daytime; azure. – **sky-blue,** *adj.*

**skydiving** /ˈskaɪdaɪvɪŋ/, *n.* the sport of free-falling from an aeroplane for a great distance, controlling one's course by changes in body position, before releasing one's parachute. – **skydiver,** *n.*

**Skye terrier** /skaɪ ˈtɛriə/, *n.* a small short-legged, very shaggy terrier, native to the Isle of Skye, an island off the north-western coast of Scotland.

**skyey** /ˈskaii/, *adj. Chiefly Poetic.* **1.** of or from the sky. **2.** in the sky; lofty. **3.** skylike; sky blue. Also, **skiey.**

**sky-high** /skaɪ-ˈhaɪ/, *adv., adj.* very high.

**skyjack** /ˈskaɪdʒæk/, *Colloq.* *–v.t.* **1.** to hijack (an aeroplane). *–n.* **2.** the act of hijacking an aeroplane. – **skyjacker,** *n.*

Skye terrier

**skylark**[1] /ˈskaɪlak/, *n.* **1.** a European lark, *Alauda arvensis,* noted for its singing in flight. **2.** any of several native Australian birds of similar habit, esp. the brown fieldlark, *Mirafra javanica.*

**skylark**[2] /ˈskaɪlak/, *v.i.* **1.** to frolic, sport or play about, esp. boisterously or in high spirits; play tricks. *–v.t.* **2.** to trick or play a trick on. [SKY + LARK[2], associated with LARK[1]]

skylark[1]

**skylight** /ˈskaɪlaɪt/, *n.* **1.** an opening in a roof or ceiling, fitted with glass, for admitting daylight. **2.** the frame set with glass fitted to such an opening.

**skyline** /ˈskaɪlaɪn/, *n.* **1.** the boundary line between earth and sky; the apparent horizon. **2.** the outline of something seen against the sky.

**skyman** /ˈskaɪmən/, *n., pl.* **-men.** *Colloq.* an aviator.

**sky pilot** /ˈskaɪ paɪlət/, *n.* **1.** *Colloq.* a clergyman. **2.** *U.S. Colloq.* an aviator.

**skyrocket** /ˈskaɪrɒkət/, *n.* **1.** a firework that ascends into the air and explodes at a height. *–v.i.* **2.** to move like a skyrocket. **3.** to rise suddenly or rapidly in amount, position, reputation, etc.

**skysail** /ˈskaɪseɪl, -səl/, *n.* (in a square-rigged vessel) a light square sail next above the royal.

**skyscraper** /ˈskaɪskreɪpə/, *n.* a tall building of many storeys, esp. one for office or commercial use.

**skyward** /ˈskaɪwəd/, *adj.* **1.** directed or tending towards the sky. *–adv.* **2.** skywards.

**skywards** /ˈskaɪwədz/, *adv.* towards the sky. Also, **skyward.**

**sky wave** /ˈskaɪ weɪv/, *n.* a radio wave reflected by the ionosphere (opposed to *ground wave*).

**skywonkie** /ˈskaɪwɒŋki/, *n. Colloq.* a person who can predict the weather.

**skywriting** /ˈskaɪraɪtɪŋ/, *n.* **1.** the act or practice of writing against the sky with chemically produced smoke released from an aeroplane. **2.** the words, etc., thus traced.

**sl,** (in knitting) slip.

**S.L.,** **1.** solicitor-at-law. **2.** south latitude.

**slab** /slæb/, *n., v.,* **slabbed, slabbing.** *–n.* **1.** a broad, flat, somewhat thick piece of stone, wood, or other solid material. **2.** a thick slice of anything: *a slab of bread.* **3.** a rough outside piece cut from a log, as in sawing it into boards. **4.** *Colloq.* a mortuary table. **5.** *Print.* ink table. **6.** *Colloq.* a tall, awkward fellow. *–v.t.* **7.** to make into a slab or slabs. **8.** to prop up the sides of (a mine shaft) with wooden slabs. **9.** to cover or lay with slabs. **10.** to cut the slabs or outside pieces from (a log, etc.). [ME *slabbe, sclabbe;* orig. uncert.]

**slabby** /ˈslæbi/, *n. N.Z. Colloq.* a timber worker who handles slabs.

**slab-heap** /ˈslæb-hip/, *n. N.Z.* **1.** *Timber Industry.* the place where slabs are piled. **2. be on the slab-heap,** *Colloq.* to be set aside as no longer useful or needed.

**slab hut** /slæb ˈhʌt/, *n.* a rough dwelling made from slabs of wood.

slab hut

**slack**[1] /slæk/, *adj.* **1.** not tense or taut; loose: *slack rope.* **2.** indolent; negligent; remiss. **3.** slow; sluggish. **4.** lacking in activity; dull; not brisk: *slack times for business.* **5.** sluggish, as the water, tide, or wind. **6.** promiscuous. *–adv.* **7.** in a slack manner; slackly. *–n.* **8.** a slack condition, interval, or part. **9.** part of a rope, sail, or the like, that hangs loose, without strain upon it. **10.** a decrease in activity, as in business, work, etc. **11.** a period of decreased activity. **12.** *Geog.* a cessation in a strong flow, as of a tide at its turn. **13.** an act or period of lazing or idling. **14.** a promiscuous woman. **15.** *Pros.* (in sprung rhythm) the unaccented syllable or syllables. *–v.t.* **16.** to be remiss in respect to (some matter, duty, right, etc.); shirk; leave undone. **17.** to make or allow to become less active, vigorous, intense, etc.; relax or abate (efforts, labour, speed, etc.). **18.** to moderate. **19.** to make loose, or less tense or taut, as a rope; loosen. **20.** to slake (lime). *–v.i.* **21.** to be remiss; shirk one's duty or part. **22.** to become less active, vigorous, rapid, etc. **23.** to moderate; slacken. **24.** to become less tense or taut, as a rope; to ease off. **25.** to become slaked, as lime. [ME *slac,* OE *sleac, slæc,* c. Icel. *slakr*] – **slackly,** *adv.* – **slackness,** *n.*

**slack**[2] /slæk/, *n.* the fine screenings of coal; small or refuse coal. [ME *slac,* from MLG or MD *schlacke* dross, splinterings. See SLAG[1]]

**slacken** /ˈslækən/, *v.t.* **1.** to make less active, vigorous, intense, etc. **2.** to make looser or less taut. *–v.i.* **3.** to slow down; abate activity. **4.** to loosen; become less taut.

**slacker** /ˈslækə/, *n. Colloq.* one who avoids work, effort, etc.

**slacks** /slæks/, *n.pl.* long trousers, worn by either men or women as informal wear.

**slacks suit** /ˈslæk sut/, *n.* an outfit designed for a woman and consisting of matching slacks and top. Also, **slacksuit.**

**slack water** /– ˈwɔtə/, *n.* the period of still water between tides.

**slackwire** /ˈslækwaɪə/, *n.* **1.** a wire stretched between two points but with some slack in it. **2. walk a slackwire, a.** to walk along a slackwire as an acrobatic performance. **b.** to be in a precarious situation. Cf. **tightrope.**

**slag**[1] /slæg/, *n., v.,* **slagged, slagging.** *–n.* **1.** the more or less completely fused and vitrified matter separated during the reduction of a metal from its ore. **2.** the scoria from a volcano. *–v.t.* **3.** to convert into slag. *–v.i.* **4.** to form slag; become a slaglike mass. [MLG *slagge,* c. G *Schlacke* dross, slag] – **slaggy,** *adj.*

**slag**[2] /slæg/, *Colloq.* *–n.* **1.** spittle. *–v.i.* **2.** to spit.

**slagheap** /ˈslæghip/, *n.* a pile or small hill, formed of waste matter from coal-mining, smelting, or some other process.

**slain** /sleɪn/, *v.* past participle of **slay.**

**slake** /sleɪk/, *v.,* **slaked, slaking.** *–v.t.* **1.** to allay (thirst, desire, wrath, etc.) by satisfying. **2.** to cool or refresh. **3.** to disintegrate or treat (lime) with water or moist air, causing it to change into calcium hydroxide (**slaked lime**). **4.** to make less active, vigorous, intense, etc.; refresh. **5.** *Obs.* to make loose or less tense. *–v.i.* **6.** (of lime) to become slaked. **7.** *Rare.* to become less active, vigorous, etc. [ME; OE *slacian,* from *slæc* slack]

**slalom** /ˈsleɪləm/, *n.* **1.** a downhill skiing race over a winding course defined by artificial obstacles. **2.** a similar race for canoes. [Norw.]

**slam**[1] /slæm/, *v.,* **slammed, slamming,** *n.* *–v.t.* **1.** to shut with force and noise. **2.** to dash, strike, etc., with violent and noisy impact. **3.** *Colloq.* to criticise severely. *–v.i.* **4.** to shut or swing into place so as to produce a loud noise. **5.** to hit or fall against something with force; crash. *–n.* **6.** a violent and noisy closing, dashing, or impact. **7.** the noise made. **8.** *Colloq.* a severe criticism. [orig. uncert.]

**slam**[2] /slæm/, *n. Cards.* **1.** the winning of all the tricks in one deal, as at whist (in bridge, called **grand slam**), or of all but one (in bridge, called **little slam**). **2.** an old type of card game associated with ruff. [orig. obscure]

**slam-bang** /slæm-ˈbæŋ/, *adv.* →**slap-bang.**

**slammer** /ˈslæmə/, *n. Colloq.* gaol.

**slander** /ˈslændə/, *n.* **1.** defamation; calumny. **2.** a malicious, false, and defamatory statement or report. **3.** *Law.* defamation in a transient form, as speech. *–v.t.* **4.** to utter slander concerning; defame. *–v.i.* **5.** to utter or circulate slander. [ME *sclandre,* from AF *esclaundre,* from L *scandalum.* See SCANDAL] – **slanderer,** *n.* – **slanderous,** *adj.* – **slanderously,** *adv.* – **slanderousness,** *n.*

**slang** /slæŋ/, *n.* **1.** language differing from standard or writ-

i = peat ɪ = pit ɛ = pet æ = pat a = part ɒ = pot ʌ = putt ɔ = port ʊ = put u = pool ɜ = pert ə = apart aɪ = buy eɪ = bay ɔɪ = boy aʊ = how
oʊ = hoe ɪə = here ɛə = hair ʊə = tour g = give θ = thin ð = then ʃ = show ʒ = measure tʃ = choke dʒ = joke ŋ = sing j = you õ = Fr. bon

ten speech in vocabulary and construction, involving extensive metaphor, ellipsis, humorous usage, etc., less conservative and more informal than standard speech, and sometimes regarded as being in some way inferior. **2.** vulgar or abusive language. **3.** the jargon of a particular class, profession, etc. **4.** →**back slang.** **5.** →**rhyming slang.** *–v.i.* **6.** to use slang or abusive language. *–v.t.* **7.** to assail with abusive language. [orig. uncert.]

**slanging match** /ˈslæŋɪŋ ˌmætʃ/, *n.* a quarrelsome exchange, esp. of abuse.

**slangy** /ˈslæŋi/, *adj.*, **slangier, slangiest.** **1.** pertaining to or of the nature of slang. **2.** using much slang. – **slangily,** *adv.* – **slanginess,** *n.*

**slant** /slænt, slant/, *v.i.* **1.** to slope; be directed or lie obliquely. *–v.t.* **2.** to slope; direct or turn so as to make (something) oblique. **3. a.** to distort or give partisan emphasis to (a newspaper story, article, etc.) in order to present a point of view, esp. a critical one. **b.** to present (a publication, piece of writing, etc.) so as to attract a specified class of people. *–n.* **4.** slanting or oblique direction; slope: *the slant of a roof.* **5.** a slanting line, surface, etc. **6.** a mental leaning or tendency, esp. unusual or unfair; bias. **7.** an attitude, approach, or way of treating subjects, as the mood of a piece of writing, a mental tendency, etc. [defs 1-3 var. of *slent* (from Scand.; cf. Norw. *slenta*), with vowel of ASLANT. Defs 4-7 aphetic var. of ASLANT] – **slanting,** *adj.* – **slantingly, slantly,** *adv.*

**slanter** /ˈslæntə/, *n.* **1.** *Colloq.* a trick. **2. work a slanter,** to trick or con someone. Also, **schlanter, slinter.** [S. African *schlenter,* from D *slenter*]

**slantwise** /ˈslæntwaɪz, ˈslant-/, *adv.* **1.** aslant; obliquely. *–adj.* **2.** slanting; oblique.

**slap** /slæp/, *n., v.,* **slapped, slapping,** *adv.* *–n.* **1.** a smart blow, esp. with the open hand or with something flat. **2.** the sound of such a blow. **3.** a sarcastic or censuring hit or rebuke. *–v.t.* **4.** to strike smartly, esp. with the open hand or with something flat. **5.** to bring (the hands, etc.) against with a smart blow. **6. a.** to put or apply vigorously, haphazardly or in large quantities. **b.** to dash or cast forcibly. **7. slap down, a.** to put down forcibly. **b.** to rebuke or suppress the enthusiasm of. *–adv.* **8.** smartly; suddenly. **9.** *Colloq.* directly; straight. [LG *slapp, slappe;* imitative]

**slap-and-tickle** /slæp-ən-ˈtɪkəl/, *n.* sexual play, usu. lighthearted.

**slap-bang** /slæp-ˈbæŋ/, *adv. Colloq.* **1.** Also, **slam-bang.** violently; suddenly. **2.** exactly; precisely; just: *slap-bang in the middle.*

**slapdash** /ˈslæpdæʃ/, *adv., adj.* **1.** in a hasty, haphazard manner. **2.** carelessly hasty or offhand. *–n.* **3.** roughcast.

**slaphappy** /ˈslæphæpi/, *adj. Colloq.* **1.** cheerful. **2.** irresponsible; lackadaisical.

**slapjack** /ˈslæpdʒæk/, *n.* **1.** a simple card game. **2.** *U.S.* a pancake.

**slaps** /slæps/, *n.pl. Colloq.* thick, rectangular thongs made from bamboo, material, etc.

**slapstick** /ˈslæpstɪk/, *n.* **1.** broad comedy in which rough play and knockabout methods prevail. **2.** a stick or lath used by harlequins, clowns, etc., as in pantomime, for striking other performers, often a combination of laths which make a loud, clapping noise without hurting a person struck. *–adj.* **3.** marked by the use of slapstick.

**slap-up** /ˈslæp-ʌp/, *adj. Colloq.* first-rate; excellent.

**slash** /slæʃ/, *v.t.* **1.** to cut with a violent sweep or by striking violently and at random. **2.** to lash. **3.** to cut, reduce, or alter, esp. drastically. **4.** to make slits in (a garment) to show an underlying fabric. *–v.i.* **5.** to lay about one with sharp strokes; make one's way by cutting. **6.** to make a sweeping, cutting stroke. *–n.* **7.** a sweeping stroke. **8.** a cut or wound made with such a stroke; a gash. **9.** an ornamental slit in a garment showing an underlying fabric. **10.** →**solidus.** **11.** *N.Z.* **a.** an open area strewn with debris of trees from felling or from wind or fire. **b.** the debris itself. **12.** *Colloq.* the act of urinating. [ME *slasch(en),* ? from OF *eslachier* break]

**slasher** /ˈslæʃə/, *n.* **1.** one that slashes, as one who uses a knife or other weapon on another. **2.** one that cuts down timber in a wasteful or destructive manner. **3.** a machine used in timber-getting for sawing logs, etc., into pieces suitable for disposal as firewood, pulpwood, etc. **4.** a machine with a rotary cutting action used to control excess growth of weeds, etc. **5.** *N.Z.* a form of billhook, usu. with curved blade.

**slashing** /ˈslæʃɪŋ/, *n.* **1.** slash. *–adj.* **2.** sweeping; cutting. **3.** violent; severe. **4.** severely critical or sarcastic. **5.** dashing; impetuous. **6.** *Colloq.* very large or fine: *a slashing fortune.* – **slashingly,** *adv.*

**slash pine** /slæʃ ˈpaɪn/, *n.* a valuable softwood timber tree, *Pinus elliottii.*

**slat** /slæt/, *n., v.,* **slatted, slatting.** *–n.* **1.** a long, thin, narrow strip of wood, metal, etc., used as a support for a bed, as one of the horizontal laths of a venetian blind, etc. **2.** *Aeron.* an auxiliary aerofoil constituting the forward part of a slotted aerofoil. **3.** *Colloq.* a rib. **4.** (*pl.*) *Colloq.* **a.** bottom; buttocks. **b.** ribs. *–v.t.* **5.** to furnish or make with slats. [ME *slatt,* var. of *sclat,* from OF *esclat* piece broken or split off, akin to *escalater* burst]

**slate**[1] /sleɪt/, *n., v.,* **slated, slating.** *–n.* **1.** a fine-grained rock formed by the compression of mudstone, that tends to split along parallel cleavage planes, usu. at an angle to the planes of stratification. **2.** a thin piece or plate of this rock or a similar material, used esp. for roofing, or (when framed) for writing on. **3.** a dull, dark bluish grey. **4.** a tentative list of candidates, officers, etc., for acceptance by a nominating convention or the like. **5. clean slate,** a good record. **6. put on the slate,** to record a debt, as on a slate; give credit for. *–v.i.* **7.** to cover with or as with slate. **8.** to write or set down for nomination or appointment; to appoint, schedule. [ME *sclate,* from OF *esclate* (fem.). See SLAT]

**slate**[2] /sleɪt/, *v.t.,* **slated, slating.** **1.** to censure or reprimand severely. **2.** *Colloq.* to criticise or review adversely. [special use of SLATE[1]]

**slater** /ˈsleɪtə/, *n.* any of various small, terrestrial isopods, chiefly of the genera *Oniscus* and *Porcellio,* having a flattened elliptical, segmented body often able to roll into a ball, commonly pale brown or greyish in colour and found under stones or logs; woodlouse.

**slather** /ˈslæðə/, *v.t.* **1.** to use in large quantities, to lavish. **2.** to spread thickly with or on. *–n.* **3.** a lot; a large quantity. **4. open slather,** complete freedom; free rein. [Brit. d. *slather* to slip, slide, related to *slidder* slippery, *sludder* mud] – **slathering,** *n.*

**slating** /ˈsleɪtɪŋ/, *n.* **1.** the operation of covering with slates. **2.** slates collectively. **3.** the material for slating.

**slattern** /ˈslætn/, *n.* a slovenly, untidy woman or girl; a slut.

**slatternly** /ˈslætnli/, *adj.* **1.** having the appearance or ways of a slattern. **2.** characteristic or suggestive of a slattern. *–adv.* **3.** in the manner of a slattern.

**slaty** /ˈsleɪti/, *adj.,* **slatier, slatiest.** **1.** consisting of, resembling, or pertaining to slate. **2.** slate-coloured.

**slaughter** /ˈslɔtə/, *n.* **1.** the killing or butchering of cattle, sheep, etc., esp. for food. **2.** the brutal or violent killing of a person. **3.** the killing by violence of great numbers of persons; carnage; massacre. *–v.t.* **4.** to kill or butcher (animals), esp. for food. **5.** to kill in a brutal or violent manner. **6.** to slay in great numbers; massacre. **7.** *Colloq.* to defeat thoroughly. [ME *slaghter,* from Scand.; cf. Icel. *slātr* butcher's meat, *slātra* kill; akin to SLAY] – **slaughterer,** *n.* – **slaughterman,** *n.*

**slaughterhouse** /ˈslɔtəhaʊs/, *n.* →**abattoirs.**

**slaughterman** /ˈslɔtəmən/, *n.* a person working at an abattoirs whose job is to kill animals and remove the hides and stomach contents.

**slaughterous** /ˈslɔtərəs/, *adj.* murderous; destructive.

**Slav** /slav/, *n.* **1.** one of a race of peoples widely spread over eastern, south-eastern, and central Europe, including the Russians and Ruthenians **(Eastern Slavs),** the Bulgars, Serbs, Croats, Slavonians, Slovenes, etc. **(Southern Slavs),** and the Poles, Czechs, Moravians, Slovaks, etc. **(Western Slavs).** **2.** Slavic. *–adj.* **3.** of, pertaining to, or characteristic of, the Slavs; Slavic. [ML *Slavus;* replacing ME *Sclave,* from ML *Sclavus*]

**slave** /sleɪv/, *n., v.,* **slaved, slaving.** *–n.* **1.** one who is the property of and wholly subject to, another; a bondservant. **2.** one who works for and is the prisoner of another; one who works under duress and without payment. **3.** one entirely under the domination of some influence: *a slave to cigarettes.* **4.** a drudge. *–v.i.* **5.** to work like a slave; drudge. *–v.t.* **6.** to enslave. [ME *sclave,* from OF *esclave,* from ML *sclavus* slave, SLAV; from the fact that many Slavs were reduced to slavery]

**slave-ant** /'sleɪv-ænt/, *n.* an ant, as *Formica fusca,* held in captivity by any other species, as *Formica sanguinea* (called **slave-making ants**).

**slavedriver** /'sleɪvdraɪvə/, *n.* **1.** an overseer of slaves. **2.** a hard taskmaster.

**slaveholder** /'sleɪvhouldə/, *n.* one who owns slaves.

**slave-labour** /sleɪv-'leɪbə/, *n.* **1.** work performed by slaves. **2.** persons working under duress considered collectively, as prisoners in concentration camps or labour camps. **3.** *Colloq.* work considered as very badly paid.

**slaver**[1] /'sleɪvə/, *n.* **1.** a dealer in or an owner of slaves. **2.** a vessel engaged in the traffic in slaves. [SLAVE + -ER[1]]

**slaver**[2] /'slævə/, *v.i.* **1.** to let saliva run from the mouth; slobber. **2.** to fawn. **3.** to express great desire by or as by slavering. *–v.t.* **4.** to wet or smear with saliva. *–n.* **5.** saliva coming from the mouth. [ME, apparently from Scand.; cf. Icel. *slafra*]

**slavery** /'sleɪvəri/, *n.* **1.** the condition of a slave; bondage. **2.** the keeping of slaves as a practice or institution. **3.** a state of subjection like that of a slave. **4.** severe toil; drudgery.

**slave state** /'sleɪv steɪt/, *n.* any of the states of the southern U.S. in which domestic slavery was practised and advocated up to the Civil War.

**slave trade** /'– treɪd/, *n.* **1.** (*also caps*) the transport of Negroes from Africa to America from the 17th to 19th centuries. **2.** any commercial trading in slaves. Also, **slave traffic.** – **slave-trader,** *n.* – **slave-trading,** *n.*

**slavey** /'sleɪvi/, *n., pl.* **-veys.** *Colloq.* a female domestic servant; maid of all work.

**Slavic** /'slævɪk, 'slavɪk/, *n.* **1.** one of the principal groups of Indo-European languages, usu. divided into **West Slavic** (Polish, Czech, Slovak, Serbian), **East Slavic** (Russian, Ukrainian, Ruthenian), and **South Slavia** (Old Church Slavonic, Bulgarian, Serbo-Croat, and Slovene). *–adj.* **2.** of or pertaining to the Slavs, or their languages.

**slavish** /'sleɪvɪʃ/, *adj.* **1.** of or befitting a slave: *slavish submission.* **2.** being or resembling a slave; abjectly submissive. **3.** base; mean; ignoble: *slavish fears.* **4.** painstakingly faithful, as a copy; lacking originality: *a slavish reproduction.* – **slavishly,** *adv.* – **slavishness,** *n.*

**Slavism** /'slavɪzəm/, *n.* the racial character, spirit, or tendencies of the Slavs.

**Slavo-,** form of **Slav** used in combination, as in *Slavo-Germanic.*

**slavocracy** /sleɪ'vɒkrəsi/, *n., pl.* **-cies.** **1.** the rule or domination of slaveholders. **2.** a dominating body of slaveholders. [SLAV(E) + -O- + -CRACY]

**Slavonian** /slə'vouniən/, *adj.* **1.** of or pertaining to Slavonia or its inhabitants. **2.** Slavic. *–n.* **3.** a native or inhabitant of Slavonia. **4.** →**Slav.**

**Slavonic** /slə'vɒnɪk/, *adj.* **1.** →**Slavonian.** **2.** →**Slavic.**

**slaw** /slɔ/, *n.* sliced or chopped cabbage served uncooked or cooked (cold or hot) with seasoning or dressing; coleslaw. [D *sla,* short for *salade* SALAD]

**slay** /sleɪ/, *v.t.,* **slew, slain, slaying.** **1.** *Archaic.* to kill by violence. **2.** *Archaic.* to destroy; extinguish. **3.** *Colloq.* to amuse (someone) greatly: *that comedian really slays me.* **4.** *Obs.* to strike; smite. [ME; OE *slēan,* c. G *schlagen*] – **slayer,** *n.*

**sleave** /sliv/, *v.,* **sleaved, sleaving,** *n.* *–v.t.* **1.** to divide or separate into filaments, as silk. *–n.* **2.** a filament of silk obtained by separating a thicker thread. **3.** a silk in the form of such filaments. **4.** *Poetic, Lit.* anything matted or ravelled. [OE *slǣfan,* akin to *slīfan* split]

**sleazy** /'slizi/, *adj.,* **-zier, -ziest.** **1.** shabby, shoddy, untidy, or grubby. **2.** thin or poor in texture, as a fabric; flimsy. [orig. uncert.] – **sleazily,** *adv.* – **sleaziness,** *n.*

**sled** /slɛd/, *n., v.,* **sledded, sledding.** *–n.* **1.** a vehicle mounted on runners for conveying loads over snow, ice, rough ground, etc. **2.** a sledge, esp. a small one. **3.** a small vehicle of this kind used in tobogganing, etc.; a toboggan. *–v.i.* **4.** to ride or be carried on a sled. *–v.t.* **5.** to convey on a sled. [ME *sledde,* from MFlemish or MLG; akin to G *Schlitten* sled]

sled

**sledder** /'slɛdə/, *n.* **1.** one who rides on a sled. **2.** a horse or other animal that draws a sled.

**sledding** /'slɛdɪŋ/, *n.* **1.** the state of the ground permitting use of a sled. **2.** the going, or kind of travel, for sleds, as determined by the ground, etc.: *rough sledding.* **3.** the act of conveying or riding on a sled.

**sledge**[1] /slɛdʒ/, *n., v.,* **sledged, sledging.** *–n.* **1.** any of various vehicles mounted on runners for travelling or conveying loads over snow, ice, rough ground, etc. **2.** a vehicle mounted on runners, and of various forms, used for travelling over snow and ice, as in northern countries; a sleigh. **3.** a sled, esp. a large one. **4.** →**toboggan.** *–v.t., v.i.* **5.** to convey or travel by sledge. [MD *sleedse*]

sledge[1]: traditional Russian

**sledge**[2] /slɛdʒ/, *n., v.,* **sledged, sledging.** *–n.* **1.** a sledge-hammer. *–v.t.* **2.** to strike, beat with or strike down with or as with a sledge-hammer. [ME *slegge,* OE *slecg,* c. D *slegge*]

**sledge-hammer** /'slɛdʒ-hæmə/, *n.* **1.** a large heavy hammer, often held with both hands, as used by blacksmiths, etc.; sledge. *–adj.* **2.** like a sledge-hammer; powerful or ruthless. **3.** crude; heavy-handed. *–v.t.* **4.** to strike or fell with, or as with, a sledge-hammer.

**sledging** /'slɛdʒɪŋ/, *n.* (in cricket) the practice among bowlers and fielders of heaping abuse and ridicule on the batsman.

**sleek**[1] /slik/, *adj.* **1.** smooth; glossy, as hair, an animal, etc. **2.** well-fed or well-groomed. **3.** smooth of manners, speech, etc. **4.** suave; insinuating. [var. of SLICK[1]] – **sleekly,** *adv.* – **sleekness,** *n.*

**sleek**[2] /slik/, *v.t.* to make sleek; smooth. [var. of SLICK[2]] – **sleeker,** *n.*

**sleeky** /'sliki/, *adj.* **1.** sleek; smooth. **2.** artful; sly. Also, *Scot.,* **sleekit** /'slikɪt/.

**sleep** /slip/, *v.,* **slept, sleeping,** *n.* *–v.i.* **1.** to take the repose or rest afforded by a suspension of the voluntary exercise of the bodily functions and the natural suspension, complete or partial, of consciousness. **2.** to be dormant, quiescent, or inactive, as faculties. **3.** to be unalert or inattentive. **4.** to lie in death. **5. sleep around,** to be sexually promiscuous. **6. sleep in,** to sleep later than usual. **7. sleep out, a.** to sleep away from the place of one's work. **b.** to sleep in the open air. **8. sleep on,** to postpone (a decision, etc.) overnight. **9. sleep under the house,** *Colloq.* to be in disgrace or disfavour. **10. sleep with,** to have sexual intercourse with. *–v.t.* **11.** to take rest in (sleep). **12.** to have beds or sleeping accommodation for: *a caravan that sleeps four.* **13.** to spend or pass (time, etc.) in sleep (fol. by *away* or *out*). **14.** to get rid of (a headache, etc.) by sleeping (fol. by *off* or *away*). *–n.* **15.** the state of a person, animal, or plant that sleeps. **16.** a period of sleeping: *a brief sleep.* **17.** dormancy or inactivity. **18.** the repose of death. **19.** the mucous congealed in the corner of the eyes which has been secreted while sleeping. **20.** *Prison Colloq.* a prison sentence longer than seven days but less than three months. [ME *slepe,* OE *slēpan, slāpan,* c. G *schlafen*]

**sleeper** /'slipə/, *n.* **1.** one who or that which sleeps. **2.** a timber, concrete, or steel beam forming part of a railway track, serving as a foundation or support for the rails. **3.** a bed, place, or compartment in a sleeping-car. **4.** →**sleeping car.** **5.** a small ring, bar, etc., worn in the ear lobe after piercing to prevent the hole from closing. **6.** *Colloq.* a sedative drug. **7.** *Colloq.* **a.** someone or something that unexpectedly achieves success or fame, such as an unadvertised television show. **b.** a book, item of manufacture, etc., which has slow but constant sales. **8.** a spy who is allowed to carry on a normal life, sometimes for years, before he is required to undertake any espionage.

**sleeper cutter** /'– kʌtə/, *n.* one who prepares wooden sleepers (def. 2).

**sleep-in** /'slip-ɪn/, *n.* an occasion on which one remains sleeping till well after one's usual hour of arising from bed.

**sleeping** /'slipɪŋ/, *n.* **1.** condition of being asleep. *–adj.* **2.** that sleeps. **3.** used for sleeping.

**sleeping-bag** /'slipɪŋ-bæg/, *n.* a large bag, usu. waterproof and warmly lined, for sleeping in, esp. for use out of doors.

**sleeping car** /'slipɪŋ ka/, *n.* a carriage on a passenger train, with provision for sleeping overnight.

**sleeping-draught** /'slipɪŋ-draft/, *n.* a drink containing a drug which induces sleep.

**sleeping partner** /slipɪŋ 'patnə/ *for def. 1;* /'slipɪŋ patnə/ *for def. 2, n.* **1.** →**silent partner. 2.** a person with whom one has regular sexual intercourse.

**sleeping-pill** /'slipɪŋ-pɪl/, *n.* a tablet, capsule, or pill, containing a soporific drug.

**sleeping sickness** /'slipɪŋ ˌsɪknəs/, *n.* **1.** →**African sleeping sickness. 2.** a form of inflammation of the brain marked by extreme weakness, drowsiness, or sleepiness, usu. associated with paralysis of some cerebral nerves.

**sleepless** /'slipləs/, *adj.* **1.** without sleep: *a sleepless night.* **2.** alert. **3.** always active: *the sleepless ocean.* – **sleeplessly,** *adv.* – **sleeplessness,** *n.*

**sleep-movement** /'slip-muvmənt/, *n.* one of the movements of leaves and flowers or their parts, when they close at night. See **nyctitropic.**

**sleep-out** /'slip-aʊt/, *n.* a partially enclosed porch or verandah, used as sleeping quarters.

**sleepwalking** /'slipwɔkɪŋ/, *n.* **1.** the state or act of walking or performing other activities while asleep. *–adj.* **2.** of or pertaining to the state of walking while asleep. – **sleepwalker,** *n.*

**sleepy** /'slipi/, *adj.,* **sleepier, sleepiest. 1.** ready or inclined to sleep; drowsy. **2.** of or showing drowsiness. **3.** languid; languorous. **4.** lethargic; sluggish. **5.** quiet: *a sleepy village.* **6.** inducing sleep. – **sleepily,** *adv.* – **sleepiness,** *n.*

**sleepy cod** /– 'kɒd/, *n.* an Australian freshwater gobiid fish, *Oxyeleotris lineolatus,* esteemed as a food fish.

**sleepyhead** /'slipihɛd/, *n. Colloq.* a sleepy or lazy person.

**sleepy lizard** /slipi 'lizəd/, *n.* **1.** →**stump-tailed skink. 2.** →**blue-tongue.**

**sleet** /slit/, *n.* **1.** snow or hail and rain falling together. **2.** *Chiefly U.S.* the frozen coating on trees, wires, and other bodies that sometimes forms when rain or sleet falls at a low temperature. **3.** *U.S.* frozen or partly frozen rain. *–v.i.* **4.** to send down sleet. **5.** to fall as or like sleet. [ME *slete,* akin to LG *slote,* G *Schlossen* hail] – **sleety,** *adj.*

**sleeve** /sliv/, *n., v.,* **sleeved, sleeving.** *–n.* **1.** the part of a garment that covers the arm, varying in form and length but commonly tubular. **2.** *Mach.* a tubular piece, as of metal, fitting over a rod or the like. **3.** *Bldg Trades.* metal inserts in walls and floors to allow pipes conducts and ducts fitted within the sleeve to move, independently of the structure. **4.** a cover or container for a gramophone record. **5. laugh up one's sleeve,** to be secretly or inwardly amused. **6. up one's sleeve,** secretly ready or at hand. **7. wear one's heart on one's sleeve,** to display one's emotions openly. *–v.t.* **8.** to furnish with sleeves. **9.** *Mech.* to fit with a sleeve; join or fasten by means of a sleeve. [ME *sleve,* OE *slēfe* (Anglian), c. D *sloof* apron] – **sleeveless,** *adj.*

**sleeve note** /'– noʊt/, *n.* the blurb on the sleeve of a record.

**sleeve valve** /'– vælv/, *n.* a thin metal sleeve with ports cut in it which is made to rotate and reciprocate between the cylinder and the piston of an internal-combustion engine so that it acts either as an inlet or exhaust valve.

**sleigh** /sleɪ/, *n.* **1.** a vehicle on runners, drawn by horses, dogs, etc., and used for transport on snow or ice. **2.** →**toboggan.** *–v.i.* **3.** to travel or ride in a sleigh. [D *slee,* short for *slede* SLED] – **sleigher,** *n.*

**sleighbell** /'sleɪbɛl/, *n.* a small bell attached to a sleigh or its harness.

**sleight** /slaɪt/, *n.* **1.** skill; dexterity. **2.** *Rare.* an artifice; stratagem. **3.** *Obs.* cunning; craft. [ME, var. of *slegthe,* from Scand.; cf. Icel. *slǣgdh,* from *slægr* SLY]

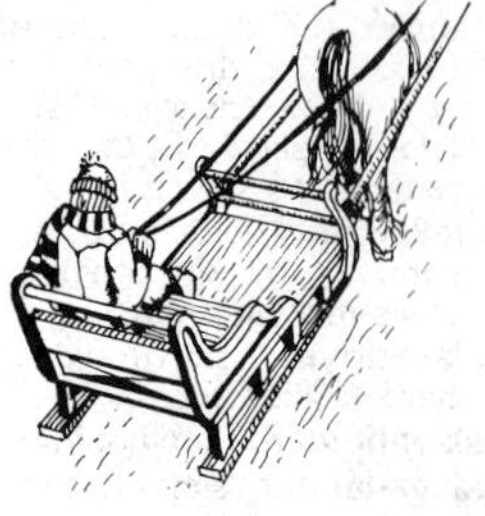
sleigh

**sleight of hand,** *n.* **1.** skill in feats of jugglery or legerdemain. **2.** the performance of such feats. **3.** a feat of jugglery or legerdemain.

**slender** /'slɛndə/, *adj.* **1.** small in circumference in proportion to height or length: *slender column.* **2.** small in size, amount, extent, etc.: *a slender income.* **3.** having little value, force or justification: *slender prospects.* **4.** thin or weak, as sound. [ME *slendre, sclendre;* orig. uncert.] – **slenderly,** *adv.* – **slenderness,** *n.*

**slenderise** /'slɛndəraɪz/, *v.t.,* **-rised, -rising. 1.** to make slender or more slender. **2.** *U.S.* to cause to appear slender: *dresses that slenderise the figure.* Also, **slenderize.**

**slept** /slɛpt/, *v.* past tense and past participle of **sleep.**

**sleuth** /sluθ/, *n.* **1.** *Colloq.* a detective. **2.** a sleuthhound or bloodhound. *–v.t., v.i.* **3.** to track or trail as a detective does. [ME *sloth,* from Scand.; cf. Icel. *slōdh* track, trail]

**sleuthhound** /'sluθhaʊnd/, *n.* **1.** →**bloodhound** (def. 1). **2.** a detective.

**slew**[1] /slu/, *v.* past tense of **slay.**

**slew**[2] /slu/, *v.t.* **1.** to turn or twist (something), esp. upon its own axis or without moving it from its place. **2.** to cause to swing round. *–v.i.* **3.** to swerve awkwardly; swing round; twist. **4.** *Colloq.* to relax vigilance. *–n.* **5.** such a movement. **6.** the position reached by slewing. [orig. uncert.]

**slewed** /slud/, *v.* **1.** past tense and past participle of slew. *–adj.* **2.** *Colloq.* lost; astray. **3.** *Colloq.* intoxicated; drunk.

**slice** /slaɪs/, *n., v.,* **sliced, slicing.** *–n.* **1.** a thin, broad, flat piece cut from something: *a slice of bread.* **2.** a part; portion. **3.** any of various implements with a thin, broad blade or part, as for turning food in a frying pan, for serving fish at table, for taking up printing ink, etc. **4.** *Sport.* a slicing stroke, kick, hit, etc. **5.** *Colloq.* **a.** (formerly) the sum of £5. **b.** the sum of $5. **6. a slice of the cake,** *Colloq.* a share in the profits. *–v.t.* **7.** to cut into slices; divide into parts. **8.** to cut through or cleave like a knife: *the ship sliced the sea.* **9.** to cut (*off, away, from,* etc.) as or like a slice. **10.** to remove by means of a slice (implement), slice bar, or the like. **11.** *Sport.* **a.** (in cricket, golf, soccer, etc.) to hit or kick the ball with the striking surface oblique, deliberately or accidentally, so that it does not travel along the line of force of the stroke. **b.** (in rowing) to put the blade slantwise into the water instead of square to the surface, so that it goes too deep. *–v.i.* **12.** *Sport.* to slice the ball. [ME, from OF *esclice, esclisse* splinter, sliver of wood, from Gmc; cf. OHG *slitz* slit] – **sliceable,** *adj.* – **slicer,** *n.*

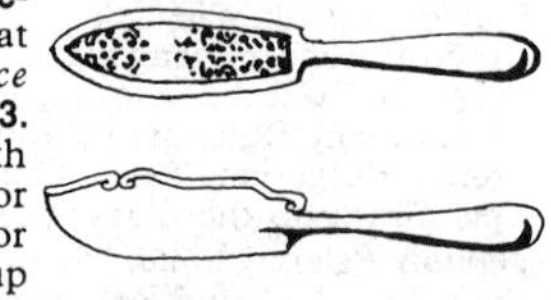
slices (def. 3)

**slice bar** /'– ba/, *n.* a long-handled instrument with a blade at the end, for clearing away or breaking up clinkers, etc., in a furnace.

**slick**[1] /slɪk/, *adj.* **1.** sleek; glossy. **2.** smooth of manners, speech, etc. **3.** sly; shrewdly adroit. **4.** ingenious; cleverly devised. **5.** slippery, as though covered with oil. *–n.* **6.** a smooth place or spot, as an oil-covered area on the sea. **7.** a patch or film of oil or the like, as on the sea. **8.** *U.S. Colloq.* a magazine in which the paper is finished to have a more or less glossy surface, implying a high-grade content, but sometimes regarded as intellectually shallow. **9.** *Colloq.* **a.** a tyre with a smooth tread used on racing cars. **b.** a very large tyre with a smooth tread used in underground mining operations. *–adv.* **10.** smoothly; cleverly. [ME *slike,* adj., c. Flemish *sleek* even, smooth] – **slickly,** *adv.* – **slickness,** *n.*

**slick**[2] /slɪk/, *v.t.* **1.** to make sleek or smooth. **2.** *U.S. Colloq.* to make smart or fine (fol. by *up*). [ME *slike(n),* v., OE *-slician;* akin to Icel. *slīkja* give a gloss to]

**slickensides** /'slɪkənsaɪdz/, *n.* a rock surface which has become more or less polished and striated from the sliding or grinding motion of an adjacent mass of rock. [*slicken* (d. var. of SLICK[1]) + SIDE]

**slicker** /'slɪkə/, *n.* **1.** a long, loose oilskin or waterproof outer coat. **2.** →**city slicker.** **3.** a swindler; con man. **4.** *Foundry.* a small trowel used for smoothing the surface of the mould. **5.** a tool used for burnishing leather. **6.** an account which balances correctly on the first calculation.

**slide** /slaɪd/, *v.,* **slid, slid** or **slidden, sliding,** *n.* *–v.i.* **1.** to move along in continuous contact with a smooth or slippery surface: *to slide down a snow-covered hill.* **2.** to slip, as one losing foothold or as a vehicle skidding. **3.** to glide or pass smoothly onwards. **4.** to slip easily, quietly, or unobtrusively (fol. by *in, out, away,* etc.). **5.** to go unregarded: *to let things slide.* **6.** to pass or fall gradually into a specified state, character, practice, etc. *–v.t.* **7.** to cause to slide, as over a surface or with a smooth, gliding motion. **8.** to slip (something) easily or quietly (fol. by *in, into,* etc.). *–n.* **9.** the act of sliding. **10.** a smooth surface for sliding on. **11.** *Geol.* **a.** a landslide or the like. **b.** the mass of matter sliding down. **12.** a single image for projection in a projector; transparency (def. 3b). **13.** a plate of glass or other material on which objects are placed for microscopic examination. **14.** Also, **hair slide.** a clip for holding a woman's hair in place. **15.** that which slides, as part of a machine. **16.** *Music.* **a.** an embellishment or grace-note consisting of an upward or downward series of three or more notes, the last of which is the principal note. **b.** →**portamento.** **c.** (in instruments of the trumpet class, esp. the trombone) a section of the tube, usu. U-shaped, which can be pushed in or out to alter the length of the air column and thus the pitch of the notes. **d.** any of various devices with a smooth surface as a bottle neck, a blunt knife, a copper or glass tube, etc., used for producing portamento effects from the strings of a guitar, rather than the regular pitches measured by the frets. **17.** *Rowing.* a sliding seat or its runners. [ME; OE *slīdan,* c. MLG *slīden*] – **slider,** *n.*

**slide-action** /'slaɪd-ækʃən/, *adj.* of or pertaining to a gun fired from the shoulder which is reloaded by the action of a sliding lever.

**slide bars** /'slaɪd baz/, *n. pl.* →**guide bars.**

**slide fastener** /'– fasənə/, *n.* →**zip** (def. 1).

**slide guitar** /– gə'ta/, *n.* **1.** a style of playing guitar in which glissando effects, etc., are produced by using a slide instead of stopping the strings with the fingers. **2.** a type of guitar with special adaptations for such a style of playing, such as a hawaiian guitar, pedal steel guitar, or resonator guitar. *–adj.* **3.** of or pertaining to such a style of music.

**slide rule** /'– rul/, *n.* a device for rapid calculation, consisting essentially of a rule having a sliding piece moving along it, both marked with graduated logarithmic scales.

**slide valve** /'– vælv/, *n.* **1.** *Mach.* a valve that slides (without lifting) to open or close an aperture, as the valves of the ports in the cylinders of certain steam-engines. **2.** *Music.* a perforated slide used to cut off the air supply to a rank of organ pipes when a key is depressed.

**sliding scale** /ˌslaɪdɪŋ 'skeɪl/, *n.* **1.** a variable scale, esp. of industrial costs, as wages, raw materials, etc., which may be adapted to demand. **2.** a wage scale varying with the selling price of goods produced, the cost of living, or profits.

**sliding seat** /'– sit/, *n.* a seat on runners which moves forward and back with the rower's movement to lengthen his stroke.

**sliding tackle** /– 'tækəl/, *n.* a tackle in which one player attempts to deprive another of the ball by sliding feet first at it.

**slight** /slaɪt/, *adj.* **1.** small in amount, degree, etc.: *a slight increase, a slight smell.* **2.** of little weight, or importance; trifling. **3.** slender; slim. **4.** frail; flimsy. **5.** lacking in solid or substantial qualities. *–v.t.* **6.** to treat as of slight importance. **7.** to treat with indifference; ignore. **8.** to snub; ignore pointedly. *–n.* **9.** slighting indifference or treatment. **10.** an instance of slighting treatment. **11.** a pointed and contemptuous ignoring; an affront. [ME; OE *sliht* smooth (in *eorthslihtes* close to earth), c. Icel. *slēttr* smooth, G *schlicht* smooth, *schlecht* bad, Goth. *slaihts* smooth] – **slightly,** *adv.* – **slightness,** *n.*

**slight breeze** /– 'briz/, *n.* a wind of Beaufort scale force 2, i.e. one with an average wind speed of 4 to 6 knots, or 6 to 11 km/h.

**slighting** /'slaɪtɪŋ/, *adj.* derogatory; disparaging. – **slightingly,** *adv.*

**slim** /slɪm/, *adj.,* **slimmer, slimmest,** *v.,* **slimmed, slimming.** *–adj.* **1.** slender, as in girth or form; slight in build or structure. **2.** poor; insufficient; meagre: *a slim chance, a slim excuse.* **3.** small, inconsiderable, or scanty: *a slim income.* **4.** *Obs.* crafty. *–v.t.* **5.** to make slim. *–v.i.* **6.** to make oneself slim, as by dieting, exercise, etc. **7.** to become slim. [D or LG; c. G *schlimm* bad] – **slimly,** *adv.* – **slimness,** *n.*

**slime** /slaɪm/, *n., v.,* **slimed, sliming.** *–n.* **1.** thin, glutinous mud. **2.** any ropy or viscous liquid matter, esp. of a foul or offensive kind. **3.** a viscous secretion of animal or vegetable origin. **4.** *Colloq.* servility; quality of being ingratiating. *–v.t.* **5.** to cover or smear with, or as with, slime. **6.** to remove slime from, as fish for canning. **7.** *Colloq.* to flatter. [ME *slyme,* OE *slīm,* c. G *Schleim*]

**slime mould** /'– moʊld/, *n.* a group of primitive organisms having a motile amoeboid stage and a non-motile spore-producing stage, thus showing characteristics of both the animal and plant kingdoms.

**slimey** /'slaɪmi/, *adj.,* **slimier, slimiest,** *n.* →**slimy.**

**slimmer** /'slɪmə/, *n.* one who makes himself, or tries to make himself, slimmer or lighter by dieting, etc.

**slimy** /'slaɪmi/, *adj.,* **slimier, slimiest,** *n.* *–adj.* **1.** of or like slime. **2.** abounding in or covered with slime. **3.** foul; vile. **4.** *Colloq.* servile; unpleasantly ingratiating. *–n.* **5.** a beachworm, *Australonuphis parateres,* found on the southern and eastern coast of Australia, growing up to 300 cm long and 1.5 cm wide, greenish in colour but without the brown bands of the kingworm, and giving off a greater amount of mucous when handled; it lives in the sand from the slopes downwards but prefers sandbanks and is commonly used for bait. Also, **slimey.** – **slimily,** *adv.* – **sliminess,** *n.*

**sling**[1] /slɪŋ/, *n., v.,* **slung, slinging.** *–n.* **1.** an instrument for hurling stones, etc., by hand, consisting of a strap or piece for holding the missile, with two strings attached, the ends of which are held in the hand (or attached to a staff), the whole being whirled rapidly before discharging the missile. **2.** →**catapult** (def. 1). **3.** a rope or chain used in hoisting cargo in and out of a ship. **4.** a bandage used to suspend an injured part of the body, as an arm or hand, by looping round the neck. **5.** a strap, band, or the like forming a loop by which something is suspended or carried, as a strap attached to a rifle and passed over the shoulder. **6.** the act of slinging. **7.** (*usu. pl.*). *Naut.* **a.** a rope or chain supporting a yard. **b.** a rope, wire, or chain forming a loop, used for hoisting cargo, etc. **8.** *Colloq.* money given as a bribe; protection money. *–v.t.* **9.** *Football.* to catch a player around the neck and throw him to the ground. **10.** to throw, cast or hurl; fling, as from the hand. **11.** to place in or secure with a sling to raise or lower. **12.** to raise, lower, etc., by such means. **13.** to hang in a sling or so as to swing loosely: *to sling a rifle over one's shoulder.* **14.** *Prison Colloq.* to bribe. **15.** to suspend. **16. sling it in,** to abandon an occupation, situation, etc. **17. sling the hook,** to pass on the responsibility for a task, etc. *–v.i.* **18.** to give money as a bribe. **19. sling off,** to speak disparagingly of someone (fol. by *at*): *he slings off at his teachers.* [ME *slynge(n),* from Scand.; cf. Icel. *slyngva*] – **slinger,** *n.*

**sling**[2] /slɪŋ/, *n.* an iced alcoholic drink, containing gin or the like, water, sugar, and lemon or lime juice. [cf. G *schlingen* swallow]

**slingshot** /'slɪŋʃɒt/, *n.* **1.** →**catapult** (def. 1). **2.** →**sling**[1] (def. 1).

**slink** /slɪŋk/, *v.,* **slunk** or (*Archaic*) **slank; slunk; slinking;** *n., adj.* *–v.i.* **1.** to go in a furtive, abject manner, as from fear, cowardice, or shame. **2.** to move stealthily, as to evade notice. *–v.t.* **3.** (of cows, etc.) to bring forth (young) prematurely. *–n.* **4.** a prematurely born calf or other animal. *–adj.* **5.** born prematurely: *a slink calf.* [ME *slynke,* OE *slincan* creep, crawl, c. LG *slinken,* G *schlinken*] – **slinkingly,** *adv.*

**slinky** /'slɪŋki/, *adj. Colloq.* **1.** sinuous; gliding; slender and flowing. **2.** stealthy; sinister, or menacing, esp. in movement. *–n.* **3.** the unborn foetus of the deer.

**slinter** /'slɪntə/, *n. Colloq.* →**slanter.**

**slip**[1] /slɪp/, *v.*, **slipped** or (*Archaic*) **slipt; slipped; slipping;** *n.* *–v.i.* **1.** to pass or go smoothly or easily; glide; slide (fol. by *along, away, down, off, over, through,* etc.): *water slips off a smooth surface.* **2.** to slide suddenly and involuntarily, as on a smooth surface; to lose one's foothold. **3.** to move, slide, or start from place, position, fastening, the hold, etc. **4.** to get away, escape, or be lost: *to let an opportunity slip.* **5.** to go, come, get, etc., easily or quickly: *to slip into a dress.* **6.** to pass insensibly, as from the mind or by, etc., as time. **7.** to go quietly; steal. **8.** to move quickly and lightly. **9.** to pass superficially, carelessly, or without attention, as over a matter. **10.** to make a slip, mistake, or error (oft. fol. by *up*). **11.** *Colloq.* to become somewhat reduced in quantity or quality: *the market slipped today.* **12. be slipping,** to be losing one's acuteness, abilities, or the like. **13.** *Motor Vehicles.* (of a clutch) to engage with difficulty as a result of wear. *–v.t.* **14.** to cause to slip, pass, put, draw, etc., with a smooth, easy, or sliding motion: *to slip one's hand into a drawer.* **15.** to put or draw quickly or stealthily: *to slip a letter into a person's hand.* **13.** to put (*on*) or take (*off*) easily or quickly, as a garment. **17.** to let slip from fastenings, the hold, etc. **18.** to release from a leash or the like, as a hound or a hawk. **19.** to untie or undo (a knot). **20.** *Naut.* to let go entirely, as an anchor cable or an anchor. **21.** to haul (a boat) out of the water onto a slipway. **22.** to let pass unheeded; neglect or miss. **23.** to pass over or omit, as in speaking or writing. **24.** to slip away from, escape from or elude, as a pursuer. **25.** to release oneself from (restraint, etc.). **26.** to escape (one's memory, notice, knowledge, etc.). **27.** (of animals) to bring forth (off-spring) prematurely. **28.** *Motor Vehicles.* to operate (the clutch) gradually so that the drive to the wheels increases speed smoothly. **29. let slip,** to say or reveal unintentionally. **30. slip it,** *Colloq.* (of a male) to have sexual intercourse (oft. fol. by *to*). *–n.* **31.** the act of slipping. **32.** a slipping of the feet, as on slippery ground. **33.** a mishap. **34.** a mistake, often inadvertent, as in speaking or writing: *a slip of the tongue.* **35.** an error in conduct; an indiscretion. **36.** the eluding of a pursuer, guard, or other person: *to give someone the slip.* **37.** something easily slipped on or off. **38.** a kind of dog's lead. **39.** a woman's sleeveless underdress. **40.** a pillowcase. **41.** →**slipway. 42.** *Naut.* the difference between the theoretical speed at which a screw propeller or paddlewheel would move if it were working against a solid and the actual speed at which it advances through the water. **43.** *U.S.* a space between two wharves or in a dock, for vessels to lie in. **44.** (in pumps) the difference between the actual volume of water or other liquid delivered by a pump during one complete stroke, and the theoretical volume as determined by calculation of the displacement. **45.** *Elect.* the fraction by which the rotor speed of an induction motor is less than the speed of rotation of the stator field. **46.** *Cricket.* **a.** the position of a fielder who stands behind and to the offside of the wicket-keeper. **b.** the fielder himself. **47.** *Geol.* **a.** →**fault** (def. 5). **b.** a smooth joint or crack where the strata have moved upon each other. **c.** the relative displacement of formerly adjacent points on opposite sides of a fault, measured in the fault plane. **d.** a form of landslide caused by the downhill movement of a mass of soil when saturated. **48.** *Metall.* the deformation of a metallic crystal caused by one part gliding over another part along a plane (**slip plane**). **49.** (*pl.*) *Theat.* **a.** the space on either side of the stage. **b.** similar parts of the auditorium. **50. give (someone) the slip,** to escape; [ME *slyppe,* probably from MLG *slippen,* c. d. G *schlippen,* akin to OE *slipor* slippery]

**slip**[2] /slɪp/, *n., v.,* **slipped, slipping.** *–n.* **1.** a piece suitable for propagation cut from a plant; a scion or cutting. **2.** any long, narrow piece or strip, as of wood, paper, land, etc. **3.** a young person, esp. one of slender form. **4.** a small paper form on which information is noted: *a withdrawal slip.* **5.** →**galley proof. 6.** a small whetstone with a wedge-shaped cross-section in which one or two sides are rounded. *–v.t.* **7.** to take slips or cuttings from (a plant); take (a part), as a slip from a plant. [late ME, from MD or MLG *slippe* cut, slit, strip, etc.]

**slip**[3] /slɪp/, *n.* potter's clay made semifluid with water, used for coating or decorating pottery. [ME and OE *slype;* orig. uncert. Cf. Norw. *slip* slime]

**slip cover** /'– kʌvə/, *n.* →**loose cover.**

**slipe** /slaɪp/, *n.* unscoured wool from a fellmongered sheep. Also, **slipe wool.** [Brit. d.]

**slipknot** /'slɪpnɒt/, *n.* a knot which slips easily along the cord or line round which it is made.

**slipnoose** /'slɪpnus/, *n.* a noose with a knot that slides along the rope, thus forming a noose that tightens as the rope is pulled.

**slip-on** /'slɪp-ɒn/, *adj.* **1.** designed to be slipped on easily, as a loose blouse. **2.** slipover. *–n.* **3.** a slip-on garment or article of dress.

**slipover** /'slɪpoʊvə/, *adj.* designed for slipping over the head, as a blouse or sweater; a pullover.

**slippage** /'slɪpɪdʒ/, *n.* **1.** the act of slipping. **2.** the amount or extent of slipping. **3.** *Mach.* the amount of work dissipated by slipping of parts, excess play, etc.

**slipped disc** /slɪpd 'dɪsk/, *n.* a protrusion of an intervertebral disc, often responsible for pain in the back radiating down the back of the leg.

**slipper** /'slɪpə/, *n.* **1.** a light shoe into which the foot may be easily slipped for indoor wear. **2.** any similar shoe, as a woman's shoe for dancing. *–v.t.* **3.** to beat with a slipper. [SLIP[1], *v.* + -ER[1]] – **slippered,** *adj.* – **slipper-like,** *adj.*

**slipper satin** /'– sætn/, *n.* fine satin with a dull finish.

**slippery** /'slɪpəri, 'slɪpri/, *adj.*, **-perier, -periest. 1.** tending to cause slipping or sliding, as ground, surfaces, things, etc. **2.** tending to slip from the hold or grasp or from position: *a slippery rope.* **3.** likely to slip away or escape. **4.** not to be depended on; fickle; shifty, tricky, or deceitful. **5.** unstable or insecure, as conditions, etc. [obs. *slipper* slippery (ME *sliper,* OE *slipor*) + -Y[1]] – **slipperiness,** *n.*

**slippery dip** /'– dɪp/, *n.* a construction bearing an inclined smooth slope for children to slide down for amusement; slide. Also, **slippery slide.**

**slippery elm** /'– ɛlm/, *n.* **1.** a species of elm, *Ulmus fulva,* of eastern North America, with a mucilaginous inner bark. **2.** the bark, used as a demulcent.

**slip plane** /'slɪp pleɪn/, *n.* See **slip**[1] (def. 47).

**slippy** /'slɪpi/, *adj. Colloq.* **1.** slippery. **2.** nimble, quick, or sharp. – **slippiness,** *n.*

**sliprail** /'slɪpreɪl/, *n.* one of a number of movable rails, forming a fence which can be taken out in order to make a gateway.

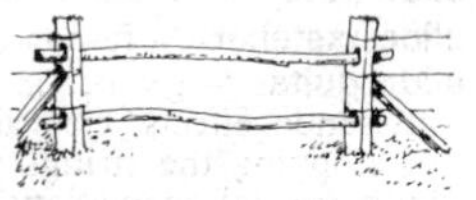

simple sliprail gate

**slipring** /'slɪprɪŋ/, *n. Elect.* a metal ring, usu. of copper or cast iron, mounted so that current may be conducted through stationary brushes into or out of a rotating member.

**slip-road** /'slɪp-roʊd/, *n. Brit.* a road for entering or leaving a motorway.

**slipshod** /'slɪpʃɒd/, *adj.* **1.** untidy, or slovenly; careless or negligent. **2.** wearing slippers or loose shoes, esp. ones down at the heel.

**slipslop** /'slɪpslɒp/, *n. Colloq.* **1.** a sloppy food or drink. **2.** meaningless, loose, or trifling talk or writing. [varied reduplication of SLOP[1]]

**slip-stitch** /'slɪp-stɪtʃ/, *n.* **1.** one of a series of stitches used for dress hems, etc., in which only a few threads of material are caught up from the outer material, and the stitches which hold it are invisible from the outside. **2.** a stitch slipped, or not worked, in knitting, crocheting, etc.

**slipstream** /'slɪpstrim/, *n.* **1.** *Aeron.* the air current forced back by an aircraft propeller or jet at speeds greater than the surrounding air. **2.** any similar air current behind any moving object.

**slipt** /slɪpt/, *v. Archaic.* past tense of **slip**[1].

**slip-up** /'slɪp-ʌp/, *n. Colloq.* a mistake or blunder: *several minor slip-ups in spelling.*

**slipway** /'slɪpweɪ/, *n.* an inclined plane or ramp, esp. one sloping to the water, serving as a landing place or a site on which vessels are built or repaired.

**slit** /slɪt/, *v.*, **slit, slitting,** *n.* *–v.t.* **1.** to cut apart or open along a line; make a long cut, fissure, or opening in. **2.** to cut or rend into strips; split. *–n.* **3.** a straight, narrow cut, opening, or aperture. **4.** *Colloq.* vagina. [ME *slitte,* OE *-slittan* (N d.), c. OHG *slizzan* (G *schlitzen*) split, slit. See

SLICE] – **slitter,** *n.*

**slither** /ˈslɪðə/, *v.i.* **1.** to slide down or along a surface, esp. unsteadily or with more or less friction or noise. **2.** to go or walk with a sliding motion. *–v.t.* **3.** to cause to slither or slide. *–n.* **4.** a slithering movement; a slide. [ME; var. of d. *slidder* (c. LG *slidderan*), OE *slidrian,* frequentative of *slīdan* SLIDE]

**slit trench** /ˈslɪt trɛntʃ/, *n.* **1.** *Mil.* Also, **slitty.** a narrow trench for one or more persons for protection against enemy fire and shrapnel. **2.** →**foxhole.** **3.** any narrow trench.

**sliver** /ˈslɪvə/, *n.* **1.** a slender piece, as of wood, split, broken, or cut off, usu. lengthwise or with the grain; splinter. **2.** a continuous strand or band of loose, untwisted wool, cotton, etc., ready for roving or slubbing. *–v.t.* **3.** to split or cut off, as a sliver; split or cut into slivers. **4.** to form (wool, cotton, etc.) into slivers. *–v.i.* **5.** to split. [ME *slivere,* from *slyve,* OE *slīfan* split]

**slivovitz** /ˈslɪvəvɪts/, *n.* a colourless plum brandy, common in south-eastern Europe. [Serbo-Croat *sljivovica*]

**slob** /slɒb/, *n.* **1.** *Irish.* mud or ooze, or a stretch of mud, esp. along a shore. **2.** *Colloq.* a stupid, clumsy, uncouth, or slovenly person. [Irish *slab* mud, from obs. E *slab* thick in consistency. Cf. Dan. *slab* mire, Icel. *slabb* slush]

**slobber** /ˈslɒbə/, *v.i.* **1.** to let saliva, etc., run from the mouth; slaver; dribble. **2.** to indulge in mawkish sentimentality. *–v.t.* **3.** to wet or make foul by slobbering. **4.** to utter with slobbering. *–n.* **5.** saliva or liquid dribbling from the mouth; slaver. **6.** mawkishly sentimental speech or actions. [var. of *slabber.* See SLOB] – **slobberer,** *n.*

**slobbery** /ˈslɒbəri/, *adj.* **1.** characterised by slobbering. **2.** disagreeably wet; sloppy.

**sloe** /sloʊ/, *n.* **1.** the small, sour, blackish fruit (drupe) of *Prunus spinosa.* **2.** the shrub itself. [ME *slo,* OE *slā(h),* c. G *Schlehe*]

**sloe-eyed** /ˈsloʊ-aɪd/, *adj.* having eyes like sloes; dark-eyed or having attractively narrow eyes.

**sloe gin** /sloʊ ˈdʒɪn/, *n.* a cordial or liqueur flavoured with sloe.

**slog** /slɒg/, *v.,* **slogged, slogging,** *n. Colloq. –v.t.* **1.** to hit hard, as in boxing, cricket, etc. **2.** to drive with blows. *–v.i.* **3.** to deal heavy blows. **4.** to walk steadily and firmly; plod heavily. **5.** to toil. *–n.* **6.** a strong blow with little finesse. **7.** a spell of hard work or walking. [var. of SLUG², *v.*] – **slogger,** *n.*

**slogan** /ˈsloʊgən/, *n.* **1.** a distinctive cry or phrase of any party, class, body, or person; a catchword. **2.** a war cry or gathering cry, as formerly used among the Scottish clans. [Gaelic *sluagh-ghairm* army cry]

**slommock** /ˈslʌmək/, *n., v.i.* →**slummock.**

**sloop** /slup/, *n.* a single-masted sailing vessel carrying fore-and-aft sails consisting of jibs, foresail, and mainsail and gaff-topsail. [D *sloep,* c. G *Schlup;* akin to OE *slūpan* glide]

sloop

**slop**¹ /slɒp/, *v.,* **slopped, slopping,** *n. –v.t.* **1.** to spill or splash (liquid). **2.** to spill liquid upon. *–v.i.* **3.** to spill or splash liquid (sometimes fol. by *about*). **4.** (of liquid) to run (over) in spilling. **5.** *Colloq.* (of persons, etc.) to be unduly effusive; gush (fol. by *over*). **6.** to walk or go through mud, slush, or water. *–n.* **7.** a quantity of liquid carelessly spilled or splashed about. **8.** (*oft. pl.*) weak or unappetising liquid or semiliquid food. **9.** (*oft. pl.*) the dirty water, liquid refuse, etc., of a household or the like. **10.** swill, or the refuse of the kitchen, etc., often used as food for pigs or the like. **11.** liquid mud. **12.** (*pl.*) *Distilling.* the mash remaining after distilling. **13.** (*pl.*) *Colloq.* beer. **14.** *Colloq.* a choppy sea. [ME *sloppe* mudhole, OE *-sloppe* (in *cusloppe* cowslip, lit., cow slime); akin to SLIP³]

**slop**² /slɒp/, *n.* (*oft. pl.*) **1.** clothing, bedding, tobacco, etc., supplied or sold to seamen from the ship's stores. **2.** a loose outer garment, as a jacket, tunic, or smock. **3.** cheap ready-made clothing in general. **4.** *Archaic.* wide knickerbockers. [ME *sloppe,* OE *-slop* (in *oferslop* overgarment), c. Icel. *sloppr* gown]

**slop-basin** /ˈslɒp-beɪsən/, *n.* a small bowl for the reception of teacup dregs at table. Also, **slop-bowl.**

**slop-bucket** /ˈslɒp-bʌkət/, *n.* bucket for removing slops. Also, **slop-pail.**

**slope**¹ /sloʊp/, *v.,* **sloped, sloping,** *n. –v.i.* **1.** to take or have an inclined or slanting direction, esp. downwards or upwards from the horizontal. **2.** to descend or ascend at a slant. *–v.t.* **3.** to direct at a slope or inclination; incline from the horizontal. **4.** to form with a slope or slant. *–n.* **5.** inclination or slant, esp. downwards or upwards. **6.** deviation from the horizontal. **7.** an inclined surface. **8.** (*oft. pl.*) an area of sloping ground. **9.** *Mil.* the position of standing with the rifle resting at a slope on the shoulder. **10. slope arms,** to bring one's rifle to the slope position. [aphetically from *aslope,* adv., on a slant] – **sloper,** *n.* – **sloping,** *adj.* – **slopingly,** *adv.* – **slopingness,** *n.*

**slope**² /sloʊp/, *v.i.,* **sloped, sloping.** *Colloq.* **1.** to move or go. **2. slope off,** to go away, esp. furtively.

**sloppy** /ˈslɒpi/, *adj.,* **-pier, -piest.** **1.** muddy, slushy, or very wet, as ground, walking, weather, etc. **2.** splashed or soiled with liquid. **3.** of the nature of slops, as food; watery and unappetising. **4.** *Colloq.* weak, silly, or maudlin: *sloppy sentiment.* **5.** *Colloq.* loose, careless, or slovenly: *to use sloppy English.* **6.** *Colloq.* untidy, as dress. – **sloppily,** *adv.* – **sloppiness,** *n.*

**sloppy joe** /– ˈdʒoʊ/, *n.* a loose, thick sweater.

**slopshop** /ˈslɒpʃɒp/, *n.* a cheap clothing shop.

**slopwork** /ˈslɒpwɜk/, *n.* **1.** the manufacture of cheap clothing. **2.** clothing of this kind. **3.** any work done cheaply or poorly. – **slopworker,** *n.*

**slosh** /slɒʃ/, *n.* **1.** →**slush.** **2.** *Brit. Colloq.* watery or weak drink. **3.** *Colloq.* a heavy blow. *–v.i.* **4.** to splash in slush, mud, or water. *–v.t.* **5.** to stir in some fluid: *to slosh the mop in the pail.* **6.** to pour, stir, spread, etc., a liquid or similar (oft. fol. by *in, on round,* etc.). **7. sloshing wine,** wine (esp. in large containers) for quaffing. [b. SLOP¹ and SLUSH] – **sloshy,** *adj.*

**sloshed** /slɒʃt/, *adj. Colloq.* drunk.

two-toed sloth

**slot**¹ /slɒt/, *n., v.,* **slotted, slotting.** *–n.* **1.** a narrow, elongated depression or aperture, esp. one to receive or admit something. **2. a.** a position within a system. **b.** *Linguistics.* a position within a given grammatical construction, such as that in which a subject or modifier may occur, and which therefore defines the function of any words which fill it. **3.** *Aeron.* an air passage in an aerofoil directing the air from the lower to the upper surface. **4.** →**timeslot.** **5.** *Prison Colloq.* a cell. **6. work one's slot out,** *Colloq.* to work very hard. *–v.t.* **7.** to provide with a slot or slots; make a slot in. **8.** to insert into a slot (usu. fol. by *in*). **9.** *Prison Colloq.* to lock up in a cell. *–v.i.* **10.** to allocate a timeslot. [ME, from OF *esclot* hollow between breasts] – **slotter,** *n.*

sloth-bear

**slot**² /slɒt/, *n.* **1.** the track or trail of a deer or other animal, as shown by the marks of the feet. **2.** the track, trace, or trail of anything. [AF and OF *esclot* hoofprint of a horse; probably akin to SLEUTH]

**sloth** /sloʊθ/, *n.* **1.** habitual disinclination to exertion; indolence; laziness. **2.** *Zool.* either of two genera of sluggish arboreal edentates of the family Bradypodidae of tropical America: the **two-toed sloth,** *Chloepus,* having two toes on the front foot, and the **three-toed sloth,** *Bradypus,* having three toes on the front foot. [ME *slowth* (SLOW + -TH¹), replacing OE *slǣwth* (from *slǣw,* var. of *slaw* SLOW)]

**sloth-bear** /ˈsloʊθ-bɛə/, *n.* a coarse-haired, long-snouted bear,

*Melursus ursinus,* of South-East Asia.

**slothful** /ˈslouθfəl/, *adj.* sluggardly; indolent; lazy. – **slothfully,** *adv.* – **slothfulness,** *n.*

**slot machine** /ˈslɒt məʃin/, *n.* **1.** a machine for vending small articles, weighing, etc., operated by dropping a coin in a slot. **2.** *U.S.* →**poker machine.**

**slouch** /slautʃ/, *v.i.* **1.** to sit or stand in an awkward, drooping posture. **2.** to move or walk with loosely drooping body and careless gait. **3.** to have a droop or downward bend, as a hat. –*v.t.* **4.** to cause to droop or bend down, as the shoulders or a hat. –*n.* **5.** a drooping or bending forward of the head and shoulders; an awkward, drooping carriage of a person. **6.** a drooping or hanging down of the brim of a hat, etc. **7.** an awkward, ungainly, or slovenly person. **8. no slouch,** *Colloq.* efficient; quick; expert: (oft. fol. by *at*): *he's no slouch at bricklaying.* [orig. uncert.; first occurs as n.] – **slouchy,** *adj.* – **slouchily,** *adv.* – **slouchiness,** *n.*

**slouch hat** /– ˈhæt/, *n.* **1. a.** an army hat of soft felt, having a brim capable of being attached to the crown on one side to facilitate the carrying of rifles at the slope. **b.** such a hat regarded in Australia as a symbol of courage, past greatness, virtue or national feeling. **2.** any soft hat, esp. one with a broad, flexible brim.

slouch hat: Australian World War I soldier

**slough**[1] /slau/, *n.* **1.** a piece of soft, muddy ground; a hole full of mire, as in a road; marsh; swamp. **2.** a condition of degradation, embarrassment, or helplessness. **3.** *Prison Colloq.* a cell. –*v.t.* **4.** *Prison Colloq.* to lock someone in a cell (fol. by *up*). [ME; OE *slōh,* c. MLG *slōch,* MHG *sluoche* ditch] – **sloughy,** *adj.*

**slough**[2] /slʌf/, *n.* **1.** the skin of a snake, esp. the outer skin which is shed periodically. **2.** *Pathol.* a mass or layer of dead tissue which separates from the surrounding or underlying tissue. **3.** *Bridge.* a discard. –*v.i.* **4.** to be shed or cast off, as the slough of a snake. **5.** to cast off a slough. **6.** *Pathol.* to separate from the sound flesh, as a slough. –*v.t.* **7.** to cast (fol. by *off*). **8.** to shed as or like a slough. **9.** *Bridge.* to dispose of (a losing card). [ME *slugh(e), slouh,* c. G *Schlauch* skin, bag] – **sloughy,** *adj.*

**sloven** /ˈslʌvən/, *n.* **1.** one who is habitually negligent of neatness or cleanliness in dress, appearance, etc. **2.** one who works, or does anything, in a negligent, slipshod manner. [ME *sloveyn.* Cf. D *slof* careless, negligent]

**slovenly** /ˈslʌvənli/, *adj.,* **-lier, -liest,** *adv.* –*adj.* **1.** having the habits of a sloven; untidy. **2.** characteristic of a sloven; slipshod. –*adv.* **3.** in a slovenly manner. – **slovenliness,** *n.*

**slow** /slou/, *adj.* **1.** taking or requiring a comparatively long time for moving, going, acting, occurring, etc.; not fast, rapid or swift. **2.** leisurely; gradual, as change, growth, etc. **3.** sluggish in nature, disposition, or function. **4.** dull of perception or understanding, as a person, the mind, etc. **5.** not prompt, readily disposed, or in haste (fol. by *to* or an infinitive): *slow to take offence.* **6.** burning or heating with little speed or intensity, as a fire or an oven. **7.** slack, as trade. **8.** showing a time earlier than the correct time, as a clock. **9.** passing heavily, or dragging, as time. **10.** not progressive; behind the times. **11.** dull, humdrum, uninteresting or tedious. **12.** *Photog.* (of film) requiring a long exposure. **13.** *Sport.* (of a pitch, track, court, etc., or its surface) tending to slow down movement, as of a ball. –*adv.* **14.** in a slow manner; slowly. –*v.t.* **15.** to make slow or slower. **16.** to retard; reduce the speed of (oft. fol. by *up, down,* etc.). –*v.i.* **17.** to become slow or slower; slacken in speed (oft. fol. by *up, down,* etc.). [ME; OE *slāw* sluggish, dull, c. D *sleeuw.* Cf. SLOTH] – **slowly,** *adv.* – **slowness,** *n.*

**slow bullet** /– ˈbulət/, *n.* →**rubber bullet.**

**slowcoach** /ˈsloukoutʃ/, *n. Colloq.* a slow or dull person.

**slowdown** /ˈsloudaun/, *n.* a slowing down.

**slow handclap** /slou ˈhændklæp/, *n.* clapping by an audience, slow, and often in unison, usu. to express displeasure, impatience at delay, or the like.

**slow-learner** /slou-ˈlɜnə/, *n.* a child whose response to educational stimuli indicates a mild degree of intellectual handicap and for whom special classes are provided at both primary and secondary levels of education.

**slow march** /slou ˈmatʃ/, *n.* a march in slow time.

**slow match** /– ˈmætʃ/, *n.* a slow-burning match or fuse, often consisting of a rope or cord soaked in a solution of saltpetre.

**slow-motion** /ˈslou-mouʃən/, *adj.* denoting or pertaining to films in which the images move more slowly than their originals, due to having been photographed at a greater number of frames per second than normal, or being projected more slowly than normal.

**slow neutron** /slou ˈnjutrɒn/, *n.* a neutron whose kinetic energy is less than ten electron volts.

**slowpoke** /ˈsloupouk/, *n.* a slow or dull person.

**slowup** /ˈsloʊʌp/, *n.* →**slowdown.**

**slow-witted** /slou-ˈwɪtəd/, *adj.* slow of wit or intelligence; dull of understanding.

**slow worker** /slou ˈwɜkə/, *n.* a worker who is certified as slow because of a particular disability, and may therefore earn less than the normal minimum rate prescribed for his classification, without creating a breach of the appropriate award.

**slow-worm** /ˈslou-wɜm/, *n.* **1.** →**blind snake. 2.** a European species of limbless lizard, *Anguis fragilis;* blindworm.

**slub** /slʌb/, *v.,* **slubbed, slubbing,** *n.* –*v.t.* **1.** to draw out and twist slightly after carding or slivering, as wool or cotton. –*n.* **2.** the partially twisted wool or the like produced by slubbing. **3.** yarn made with bunches of untwisted fibres at intervals. [orig. uncert.] – **slubby,** *adj.*

**sludge** /slʌdʒ/, *n.* **1.** mud, mire, or ooze; slush. **2.** a deposit of ooze at the bottom of bodies of water. **3.** any of various more or less mudlike deposits or mixtures. **4.** the sediment in a steam boiler or water tank. **5.** a later stage of sea freezing than frazil, in which the ice particles coagulate to form a thick, soupy surface layer having a matt appearance. **6.** a mixture of some finely powdered substance and water. **7.** sediment deposited during the treatment of sewage. **8.** a fine, mudlike powder produced by a mining drill. [ME *slich* slime; ? imitative] – **sludgy,** *adj.*

**slug**[1] /slʌg/, *n.* **1.** any of various slimy, elongated terrestrial gastropods related to the terrestrial snails, but having no shell or only a rudimentary one. **2.** a slow-moving animal, vehicle, or the like. **3.** any heavy piece of crude metal. **4.** a piece of lead or other metal for firing from a gun. **5.** a metal disc used as a coin, generally counterfeit. **6.** *Print.* **a.** a thick strip of type metal less than type-high. **b.** such a strip containing a type-high number, etc., for temporary use. **c.** a line of type in one piece, as produced by a linotype machine. **7.** *Mech.* a unit of mass in the imperial system, equal to about 32.2 pounds, or about 14.59 kg, which, if acted upon by a force of one pound, will have an acceleration of one foot per second squared. [ME *slugge,* from Scand.; cf. d. Norw. *sluggje* heavy, slow person]

common garden slug

**slug**[2] /slʌg/, *v.,* **slugged, slugging,** *n.* –*v.t.* **1.** to strike heavily; hit hard, esp. with the fist; to slog. **2.** to exact heavy payment, either by price or tax: *he slugged you for this motor car.* –*n.* **3.** a heavy blow, esp. with the fist. **4.** a high price, tax: *the income tax these days is a real slug.* **5.** *Colloq.* a disadvantage: *take the slug out of rail travel.* **6.** →**shot**[1] (def. 17). [? orig., hit with a slug (piece of lead)]

**sluggard** /ˈslʌgəd/, *n.* **1.** one who is habitually inactive or slothful. –*adj.* **2.** sluggardly. [ME *slogard(e),* from obs. *sluggy* sluggish + -ARD]

**sluggardly** /ˈslʌgədli/, *adj.* like or befitting a sluggard; slothful; lazy.

**slugger** /ˈslʌgə/, *n. Colloq.* **1.** one who strikes hard, esp. with the fists or a baseball bat. **2.** →**prize-fighter.**

**sluggish** /ˈslʌgɪʃ/, *adj.* **1.** indisposed to action or exertion, esp. by nature; inactive, slow, or of little energy or vigour. **2.** not acting or working with full vigour, as bodily organs. **3.** moving slowly, or having little motion, as a stream. **4.** slow, as motion. – **sluggishly,** *adv.* – **sluggishness,** *n.*

**sluice** /slus/, *n., v.,* **sluiced, sluicing.** *–n.* **1.** an artificial channel for conducting water, fitted with a sluicegate. **2.** the body of water held back or controlled by a sluicegate. **3.** any contrivance for regulating a flow from or into a receptacle. **4.** a channel, esp. one carrying off surplus water; a drain. **5.** a stream of surplus water. **6.** an artificial channel of water for moving solid matter on or in, as in timber-getting. **7.** *Mining.* **a.** a long, sloping trough or the like, with grooves in its bottom, into which water is directed to separate gold from gravel or sand. **b.** a long inclined trough to wash ores in. **8.** *Colloq.* a brief wash, esp. in running water. *–v.t.* **9.** to let out (water, etc.) or draw off the contents of (a pond, etc.) by, or as by, the opening of a sluice. **10.** to open a sluice upon. **11.** to flush or cleanse with a rush of water. **12.** *Mining.* to wash in a sluice. **13.** to send (logs, etc.) down a sluiceway. *–v.i.* **14.** to flow or pour through or as through a sluice. **15.** *Colloq.* to wash briefly, esp. in running water. [ME *scluse,* from OF *escluse,* from LL *exclūsa,* fem. pp., shut out]

**sluicegate** /ˈslusgeɪt/, *n.* a gate at the upper end of a sluice for regulating the flow.

**sluiceway** /ˈslusweɪ/, *n.* **1.** a channel controlled by a sluicegate. **2.** any artificial channel for water.

**slum** /slʌm/, *n., v.,* **slummed, slumming.** *–n.* **1.** (*oft. pl.*) an overpopulated, squalid part of a city, inhabited by the poorest people. **2.** a squalid street, place, dwelling, or the like. *–v.i.* **3.** to visit slums, esp. from curiosity. *–v.t.* **4.** to go about (a job, etc.) in a way that will result in work of inferior quality, as by using cheap materials, etc. **5. slum it,** *Colloq.* to be living in circumstances below one's usual or expected standard of living. [first occurs as slang word for room; orig. obscure] – **slummer,** *n.* – **slummy,** *adj.*

**slumber** /ˈslʌmbə/, *v.i.* **1.** to sleep, esp. deeply. **2.** to sleep lightly; doze; drowse. **3.** to be in a state of inactivity, negligence, quiescence, or calm. *–v.t.* **4.** to spend (time) in slumbering (fol. by *away,* etc.). **5.** to drive (away) by slumbering. *–n.* **6.** (*oft. pl.*) sleep, esp. deep sleep. **7.** light sleep. **8.** a period of sleep. **9.** a state of inactivity, quiescence, etc. [ME *slumeren,* frequentative of *slumen* slumber, doze, from OE *slūma,* n. Cf. G *schlummern*] – **slumberer,** *n.*

**slumberous** /ˈslʌmbərəs, -brəs/, *adj.* **1.** inclined to slumber; sleepy; heavy with drowsiness, as the eyelids. **2.** causing or inducing sleep. **3.** pertaining to, characterised by, or suggestive of slumber. **4.** inactive or sluggish; calm or quiet. Also, **slumbery, slumbrous.**

**slumber party** /ˈslʌmbə pati/, *n.* →**pyjama party.**

**slummock** /ˈslʌmək/, *n. Colloq.* **1.** a careless, untidy person. *–v.i.* **2.** to act in a slovenly way. [Brit. d. *slammock*] – **slummoky,** *adj.*

**slump** /slʌmp/, *v.i.* **1.** to drop heavily and limply. **2.** to sink into a bog, muddy place, etc., or through ice or snow. **3.** to fall suddenly and markedly, as prices, the market, etc. **4.** to have a decided falling off in progress, as an enterprise, a competitor, etc. **5.** to sink heavily, as the spirits, the posture, etc. *–n.* **6.** the act of slumping. **7.** a considerable decline in the economy, a market, etc. **8.** a decline in prices or sales. **9.** a decided falling off in progress, as in an undertaking. [v. use of Brit. d. *slump* bog, c. LG *schlump*]

**slung** /slʌŋ/, *v.* past tense and past participle of **sling.**

**slunk** /slʌŋk/, *v.* past tense and past participle of **slink.**

**slur** /slɜ/, *v.,* **slurred, slurring,** *n.* *–v.t.* **1.** to pass over lightly, or without due mention or consideration (oft. fol. by *over*). **2.** to pronounce (a syllable, word, etc.) indistinctly, as in hurried or careless utterance. **3.** *Music.* **a.** to sing in a single breath, or play without a break (two or more notes of different pitch). **b.** to mark with a slur. **4.** to calumniate, disparage, or deprecate. **5.** *Obs.* to smirch or sully. *–v.i.* **6.** to go through anything hurriedly and carelessly. *–n.* **7.** a slurred utterance or sound. **8.** *Music.* **a.** the combination of two or more notes of different pitch, sung to a single syllable or played without a break. **b.** a curved mark indicating this. **9.** a disparaging remark; a slight. **10.** a blot or stain, as upon reputation; discredit. **11.** *Print.* a spot which is blurred or unclear. [Brit. d. *slur* fluid mud, ? akin to Icel. *slor* offal (of fish)]

slur (def. 8)

**slurp** /slɜp/, *v.t.* **1.** to eat or drink (something) with a lot of noise. *–v.i.* **2.** to eat or drink noisily. *–n.* **3.** the noise produced by eating in such a manner. [MD *slorpen* to sip]

**slurry** /ˈslʌri/, *n.* **1.** a suspension of a solid in a liquid, esp. a thin paste containing cement. **2.** a semifluid mixture of clay or the like and water.

**slush** /slʌʃ/, *n.* **1.** snow in a partly melted state. **2.** liquid mud; watery mire. **3.** fat, grease, etc. discarded from the galley of a ship. **4.** *Colloq.* silly, sentimental, or weakly emotional writing, talk, etc. *–v.t.* **5.** to splash with slush. [apparently c. Norw. *slusk* slops]

**slush box** /ˈ– bɒks/, *n. Colloq.* →**automatic transmission.**

**slush fund** /ˈ– fʌnd/, *n.* **1.** a fund for use in campaign propaganda or the like, esp. secretly or illicitly, as in bribery. **2.** a fund from the sale of slush, refuse fat, etc., aboard ship, spent for any small luxuries.

**slush lamp** /ˈ– læmp/, *n.* a makeshift lamp, esp. one made from a stick wrapped in cloth, serving as a wick, in a tin of fat.

**slush money** /ˈ– mʌni/, *n.* money from a slush fund.

**slushy** /ˈslʌʃi/, *adj.,* **-shier, -shiest.** **1.** of or pertaining to slush. *–n.* **2.** Also, **slusher.** *Colloq.* a cook's assistant.

**slut** /slʌt/, *n.* **1.** a dirty, slovenly woman. **2.** an immoral woman. **3.** a female dog. [ME; cf. d. E *slut* mud, d. Norw. *slutr* sleet, impure liquid] – **sluttish,** *adj.*

**sly** /slaɪ/, *adj.,* **slyer, slyest** or **slier, sliest.** **1.** cunning or wily, as persons or animals, or their actions, ways, etc. **2.** stealthy, insidious, or secret. **3.** playfully artful, mischievous, or roguish: *sly humour.* **4. on the sly,** secretly. [ME *sly, sley,* from Scand.; cf. Icel. *slægr* sly, cunning, Swed. *slög* dexterous] – **slyly,** *adv.* – **slyness,** *n.*

**sly boots** /ˈ– buts/, *n. Colloq.* a deceitful person.

**sly grog** /– ˈgrɒg/, *n. Colloq.* illegally sold liquor.

**sly grogger** /– ˈgrɒgə/, *n. Colloq.* a person selling alcoholic drink illegally.

**slype** /slaɪp/, *n. Archit.* a covered passage, esp. one from the transept of a cathedral to the chapterhouse. [cf. West Flemish *slijpe* secret path]

**sm.,** small.

**s.m.,** stipendiary magistrate.

**Sm,** *Chem.* samarium.

**smack**[1] /smæk/, *n.* **1.** a taste or flavour, esp. a slight flavour distinctive or suggestive of something. **2.** a trace, touch, or suggestion of something. **3.** a taste, mouthful, or small quantity. *–v.i.* **4.** to have a taste, flavour, trace, or suggestion (oft. fol. by *of*). [ME *smacke,* OE *smæc,* c. MLG *smak,* G *(Ge)schmack* taste]

**smack**[2] /smæk/, *v.t.* **1.** to strike smartly, esp. with the open hand or anything flat. **2.** to bring, put, throw, send, etc., with a sharp, resounding blow or a smart stroke. **3.** to separate (the lips) smartly so as to produce a sharp sound, often as a sign of relish, as in eating. *–v.i.* **4.** to smack together, as the lips. **5.** to come or strike smartly or forcibly, as against something. **6.** to make a sharp sound as of striking against something. *–n.* **7.** a smart, resounding blow, esp. with something flat. **8.** a resounding or loud kiss. **9.** a smacking of the lips, as in relish. **10.** *Colloq.* heroin. **11. have a smack at,** to attempt. **12. smack in the eye,** *Colloq.* **a.** a snub. **b.** a setback or disappointment. *–adv.* **13.** *Colloq.* with a smack; suddenly and sharply. **14.** *Colloq.* directly; straight. [cf. D and LG *smakken,* d. G *schmacken;* of imitative orig.]

**smack**[3] /smæk/, *n.* **1.** a sailing vessel, usu. sloop-rigged, used esp. in coasting and fishing. **2.** a fishing vessel with a well to keep fish alive. [D *smak*]

**smacked-out** /smækt-ˈaʊt/, *adj.* heavily under the influence of heroin. Also (*esp. in predicative positions*), **smacked out.**

**smacker**[1] /ˈsmækə/, *n.* **1.** one who or that which smacks. **2.** →**smack**[2] (def. 7). **3.** →**smack**[2] (def. 8). **4.** *Colloq.* a dollar (formerly a pound).

**smacker**[2] /ˈsmækə/, *n. Colloq.* **1.** a young boy. **2.** (*in familiar address*) any young male.

**smackhead** /ˈsmækhɛd/, *n. Colloq.* a person who takes or is

i = peat ɪ = pit ɛ = pet æ = pat a = part ɒ = pot ʌ = putt ɔ = port ʊ = put u = pool ɜ = pert ə = apart aɪ = buy eɪ = bay ɔɪ = boy aʊ = how
oʊ = hoe ɪə = here ɛə = hair ʊə = tour g = give θ = thin ð = then ʃ = show ʒ = measure tʃ = choke dʒ = joke ŋ = sing j = you õ = Fr. bon

addicted to taking heroin.

**smacking** /ˈsmækɪŋ/, *adj.* **1.** smart, brisk, or strong, as a breeze. **2.** unusually big or large.

**small** /smɔl/, *adj.* **1.** of limited size; of comparatively restricted dimensions; not big; little. **2.** slender, thin, or narrow. **3.** not large, as compared with other things of the same kind. **4.** not great in amount, degree, extent, duration, value, etc. **5.** not great numerically. **6.** of low numerical value; denoted by a low number. **7.** having only little land, capital, etc., or carrying on business on a limited scale: *a small businessman.* **8.** of minor importance, moment, weight, or consequence. **9.** (of a letter) lower-case. **10.** humble, modest, or unpretentious. **11.** characterised by or indicative of littleness of mind or character; mean-spirited; ungenerous. **12.** ashamed or mortified: *to feel small.* **13.** of little strength or force. **14.** (of sound or the voice) gentle, soft, or low. **15.** (of a child) young. **16.** weak; diluted. *–adv.* **17.** in a small manner. **18.** into small pieces: *to slice small.* **19.** in low tones; softly. *–n.* **20.** that which is small. **21.** persons or things which are small considered collectively. **22.** the lower central part of the back. **23.** (*pl.*) *Chiefly Brit. Colloq.* small items of personal laundry; underclothes. [ME *smal(e),* OE *smæl,* c. D *smal,* G *schmal*] – **smallness,** *n.*

**smallage** /ˈsmɔlɪdʒ/, *n. Obs.* celery, *Apium graveolens,* esp. in its wild state. [ME *smalege, smalache,* from *smal* small + *ache* parsley (from OF, from L *apium*)]

**small arms** /ˈsmɔl amz/, *n. pl.* firearms collectively which are small enough to be carried by a man, as rifles, revolvers, etc. – **small-arms,** *adj.*

**small beer** /– ˈbɪə/, *n.* **1.** weak beer. **2.** *Colloq.* matters or persons of little or no importance.

**small burr grass,** *n.* a fast-growing annual grass with small burrs, *Tragus australianus,* found in inland areas of Australia and used as a stock feed.

**small calorie** /ˈsmɔl kæləri/, *n.* See **calorie** (def. 1).

**small capitals** /– ˈkæpətəlz/, *n.pl.* small capital letters; letters having the form of regular upper-case letters of a particular printing type, but being about the same height as the lower-case letters. Also, **small caps.** *Abbrev.:* s.c.

**small change** /– ˈtʃeɪndʒ/, *n.* **1.** metallic money of small denomination. **2.** that which is trifling, ordinary, or common.

**small circle** /– ˈsɜkəl/, *n.* a circle on a sphere, whose plane does not pass through the centre of the sphere.

**small crofton weed,** *n.* →**mist flower.** Also, **creeping crofton weed.**

**small end** /ˈsmɔl ɛnd/, *n.* the end of a connecting rod in an engine which is connected to the piston or the piston rod.

**smallest room** /smɔləst ˈrum/, *n. Colloq.* a toilet. Also, **smallest room in the house.**

**small farmer** /smɔl ˈfamə/, *n.* a farmer who engages in usu. mixed farming on a small scale.

**small fry** /ˈ– fraɪ/, *n.* **1.** small or young fish. **2.** young or unimportant persons or objects.

**smallgoods** /ˈsmɔlgʊdz/, *n. pl.* **1.** processed meats, as salami, frankfurts. **2.** goods sold in a delicatessen.

**smallholding** /ˈsmɔlhoʊldɪŋ/, *n.* a holding of agricultural land smaller than an ordinary farm.

**small hours** /ˈsmɔl aʊəz/, *n.pl.* the early hours of the morning; the hours following midnight.

**small intestine** /ˈ– ɪntɛstən/, *n.* See **intestine.**

**smallish** /ˈsmɔlɪʃ/, *adj.* rather small.

**small letter** /smɔl ˈlɛtə/, *n.* a lower-case letter.

**small-minded** /smɔl-ˈmaɪndəd/, *adj.* selfish or narrow in attitude. – **small-mindedness,** *n.*

**small potatoes** /smɔl pəˈteɪtoʊz/, *n.pl. Colloq.* matters or persons of little or no importance; small beer.

**smallpox** /ˈsmɔlpɒks/, *n.* an acute, highly contagious, febrile disease characterised by a pustular eruption which often leaves permanent pits or scars.

**small print** /smɔl ˈprɪnt/, *n.* →**fine print.**

**small-scale** /ˈsmɔl-skeɪl/, *adj.* **1.** relatively small and showing little detail, as a map, model, etc. **2.** unambitious, or of small extent, as an enterprise.

**small screen** /ˈsmɔl skrin/, *n. Colloq.* television.

**smallsword** /ˈsmɔlsɔd/, *n.* a light, tapering sword for thrusting, used esp. in fencing from the 16th to 18th centuries.

**small talk** /ˈsmɔl tɔk/, *n.* light, unimportant talk; chitchat.

**small-time** /ˈsmɔl-taɪm/, *adj. Colloq.* of insignificant or petty style, or importance.

**smalt** /smɔlt/, *n.* **1.** a deep blue pigment prepared by powdering a glass coloured with cobalt. **2.** a glass made by fusing cobalt oxide and silica. [F, from It. *smalto,* from G *Schmalte;* akin to SMELT[1]]

**smaltite** /ˈsmɔltaɪt/, *n.* a mineral diarsenide of cobalt which often also contains a diarsenide of nickel.

**smarm** /smam/, *v.t., v.i. Colloq.* **1.** to fawn ingratiatingly; flatter; be servile. *–n.* **2.** flattery; unctuousness; fulsomeness. [Brit. d. *smarm,* var. of *smalm;* orig. uncert.]

**smarmy** /ˈsmami/, *adj.,* **-mier, -miest.** ingratiating, falsely charming, or flattering.

**smart** /smat/, *v.i.* **1.** to be a source of sharp local and usu. superficial pain, as a wound. **2.** to cause a sharp pain, as an irritating application, a blow, etc. **3.** to wound the feelings, as with words. **4.** to feel a sharp pain, as in a wounded surface. **5.** to suffer keenly from wounded feelings. **6.** to suffer in punishment or in return for something. *–v.t.* **7.** to cause a sharp pain to or in. *–adj.* **8.** sharp or keen, as pain. **9.** sharply severe, as blows, strokes, etc. **10.** sharply brisk, vigorous, or active. **11.** quick or prompt in action, as persons. **12.** having or showing quick intelligence or ready capability; clever. **13.** shrewd or sharp, as a person in dealing with others, or as dealings, bargains, etc. **14.** cleverly ready or effective, as a speaker or a speech, rejoinder, etc. **15.** dashingly or effectively neat or trim in appearance, as persons, dress, etc. **16.** socially elegant, or fashionable. **17.** of or pertaining to a machine with some intelligence (def. 8). *–adv.* **18.** in a smart manner; smartly. *–n.* **19.** sharp local pain, usu. superficial, as from a wound or sting. **20.** keen mental suffering, as from wounded feelings, affliction, grievous loss, etc. [ME *smerten,* OE *smeortan,* c. G *schmerzen* smart; probably akin to L *mordēre* bite] – **smartly,** *adv.* – **smartness,** *n.*

**smart alec** /ˈ– ælɪk/, *n. Colloq.* one who is ostentatious in the display of knowledge or skill, often despite basic ignorance or lack of ability. Also, **smart aleck.**

**smart arse** /ˈ– as/, *n. Colloq.* →**smart alec.** – **smart-arse, smart-arsed,** *adj.*

**smarten** /ˈsmatn/, *v.t.* (sometimes fol. by *up*) **1.** to make more trim or spruce; improve in appearance. **2.** to make more brisk, as a pace.

**smartie** /ˈsmati/, *n. Colloq.* a smug know-all.

**smart set** /ˈsmat sɛt/, *n.* collectively, sophisticated, fashionable people.

**smartweed** /ˈsmatwid/, *n.* a summer annual, *Polygonum hydropiper,* native to Europe and Asia, which grows in low-lying areas, and whose reddish green stems and leaves contain an acrid juice; waterpepper.

**smartypants** /ˈsmatipænts/, *n. Colloq.* (*derog.*) a foolishly conceited person.

**smash** /smæʃ/, *v.t.* **1.** to break to pieces with violence and often with a crashing sound, as by striking, letting fall, or dashing against something; shatter; crush. **2.** to defeat utterly, as a person; overthrow or destroy, as a thing. **3.** to ruin financially. **4.** *Tennis.* to strike (the ball) hard and fast with an overhand stroke. *–v.i.* **5.** to break to pieces from a violent blow or collision. **6.** to dash with a shattering or crushing force or with great violence; crash (fol. by *against, into, through,* etc.). **7.** to become financially ruined or bankrupt (oft. fol. by *up*). *–n.* **8.** a smashing or shattering, or the sound of it. **9.** a destructive collision. **10.** smashed or shattered condition. **11.** a process or state of collapse, ruin, or destruction. **12.** financial failure or ruin. **13.** →**smash-hit.** **14.** *Tennis.* a forceful overhead stroke. [? b. SMACK[2] and MASH] – **smasher,** *n.*

**smash-and-grab** /smæʃ-ən-ˈgræb/, *n.* a robbery performed swiftly by breaking a shopwindow, as of a jeweller's, snatching the goods, and running away.

**smashed** /smæʃt/, *adj. Colloq.* incapacitated as a result of taking drugs, alcohol, etc.

**smasher** /ˈsmæʃə/, *n.* **1.** *Colloq.* an extremely attractive person. **2.** one who or that which smashes. **3.** a smash.

**smash-hit** /smæʃ-ˈhɪt/, *n. Colloq.* an immediately and extremely successful play, film, record, or the like.

**smashing** /ˈsmæʃɪŋ/, *adj. Colloq.* extremely fine; first-rate.

**smash-up** /ˈsmæʃ-ʌp/, *n.* a complete smash; a violent collision.

**smatter** /ˈsmætə/, *v.t.* **1.** *Obs.* to speak (a language, words, etc.) with superficial knowledge or understanding. **2.** to dabble in. *–n.* **3.** slight or superficial knowledge; a smattering. [ME, from Scand.; cf. Swed. *smattra* patter, rattle] – **smatterer,** *n.*

**smattering** /ˈsmætərɪŋ/, *n.* a slight or superficial knowledge of something. – **smatteringly,** *adv.*

**smear** /smɪə/, *v.t.* **1.** to rub or spread with oil, grease, paint, dirt, etc.; daub with anything. **2.** to spread or daub (oil, grease, etc.) on or over something. **3.** to rub or draw (something) over a thing so as to produce a smear. **4.** to rub something over (a thing) so as to cause a smear, sully, or blur. **5.** to soil or sully, as one's reputation. *–n.* **6.** a mark or stain made by, or as by, smearing. **7.** something smeared, or to be smeared, on a thing, as a glaze for pottery. **8.** a small quantity of something smeared on a slide for microscopic examination. **9.** an act of defamation; slur. [ME *smere,* OE *smeoru,* c. G *Schmer* grease]

**smear campaign** /ˈ– kæmpeɪn/, *n.* an organised effort to ruin a person by vilification, as by means of newspaper articles.

**smear test** /ˈ– tɛst/, *n.* →**Papanicolaou smear.**

**smear-word** /ˈsmɪə-wɜd/, *n.* a slanderous or defaming term or epithet.

**smeary** /ˈsmɪəri/, *adj.,* **smearier, smeariest. 1.** showing smears; smeared; bedaubed. **2.** tending to smear or soil. – **smeariness,** *adj.*

**smectic** /ˈsmɛktɪk/, *adj. Physics.* denoting or pertaining to one of the forms of liquid crystals.

**smegma** /ˈsmɛgmə/, *n.* a secretion or sebum, esp. from the penis. [L, from Gk *smêgma* soap, unguent]

**smell** /smɛl/, *v.,* **smelled** or **smelt, smelling,** *n. –v.t.* **1.** to perceive through the nose, by means of the olfactory nerves; inhale the odour of. **2.** to test by the sense of smell. **3.** to perceive, detect, or discover by shrewdness or sagacity. **4.** to search or find as if by smell (fol. by *out*). *–v.i.* **5.** to have the sense of smell. **6.** to search or investigate (usu. fol. by *around*). **7.** to give out an odour, esp. as specified: *to smell sweet.* **8.** to give out an offensive odour. **9.** to have the odour (fol. by *of*). **10.** to have a trace or suggestion (fol. by *of*). **11.** to seem or be unpleasant or bad. *–n.* **12.** the faculty or sense of smelling. **13.** that quality of a thing which is or may be smelled; odour. **14.** a trace or suggestion. **15.** the act of smelling. [ME *smellen, smullen;* orig. uncert.]

**smeller** /ˈsmɛlə/, *n.* **1.** one who smells. **2.** one who tests by smelling. **3.** *Colloq.* the nose.

**smelling bottle** /ˈsmɛlɪŋ bɒtl/, *n.* a small bottle or the like to hold smelling salts or some similar preparation.

**smelling salts** /ˈ– sɒlts/, *n.pl.* a preparation for sniffing, consisting essentially of ammonium carbonate with some agreeable scent, used as a restorative in cases of faintness, headache, etc.

**smelly** /ˈsmɛli/, *adj.,* **smellier, smelliest,** *n. –adj.* **1.** emitting a strong or offensive smell. *–n.* **2.** *Colloq.* a fart.

**smelt**[1] /smɛlt/, *v.t.* **1.** to fuse or melt (ore) in order to separate the metal contained. **2.** to obtain or refine (metal) in this way. [probably from MD or MLG *smelten,* c. G *schmelzen* melt, smelt. See MELT]

**smelt**[2] /smɛlt/, *n., pl.* **smelts,** (*esp. collectively*) **smelt.** a small silvery food fish, *Osmerus eperlanus,* of Europe. [ME and OE. Cf. Norw. *smelta* whiting]

**smelt**[3] /smɛlt/, *v.* past tense and past participle of **smell.**

**smelter** /ˈsmɛltə/, *n.* **1.** one who or that which smelts. **2.** the owner of, or a workman in, a smeltery. **3.** a place or establishment where ores are smelted.

**smeltery** /ˈsmɛltəri/, *n., pl.* **-ries.** →**smelter** (def. 3).

**smew** /smju/, *n.* a small saw-billed duck or merganser, *Mergus albellus,* of northerly parts of the eastern hemisphere, the adult male of which is white, marked with black and grey, and, on the crested head, with green. [orig. uncert.; ? var. of MEW[2]]

**smidgin** /ˈsmɪdʒən/, *n.* a very small quantity; a bit. Also, **smidgen, smidgeon.** [probably from Brit. d.]

**smilax** /ˈsmaɪlæks/, *n.* **1.** any plant of the genus *Smilax,* of the tropical and temperate zones, consisting mostly of vines with woody stems. **2.** a delicate, twining plant, *Asparagus asparagoides,* with glossy, bright green leaves, often used in floral decoration. [L, from Gk]

**smile** /smaɪl/, *v.,* **smiled, smiling,** *n. –v.i.* **1.** to assume a facial expression, characterised esp. by a widening of the mouth, indicative of pleasure, favour, kindliness, amusement, derision, scorn, etc. **2.** to look with such an expression, esp. (fol. by *at, on,* or *upon*) in a pleasant or kindly way, or (fol. by *at*) in amusement. **3.** to have a pleasant or agreeable aspect, as natural scenes, objects, etc. *–v.t.* **4.** to assume or give (a smile). **5.** to express by a smile: *to smile approval.* **6.** to bring, put, drive, etc., by smiling: *to smile one's tears away.* **7.** to look with favour, or support (fol. by *on* or *upon*). *–n.* **8.** the act of smiling; a smiling expression of the face. **9.** favouring look or regard: *fortune's smile.* **10.** pleasant or agreeable look or aspect. [ME, c. OHG *smīlan,* Dan. *smile*] – **smiler,** *n.* – **smilingly,** *adv.*

**smirch** /smɜtʃ/, *v.t.* **1.** to discolour or soil with some substance, as soot, dust, dirt, etc., or as the substance does. **2.** to sully or tarnish, as with disgrace. *–n.* **3.** a dirty mark or smear. **4.** a stain or blot, as on reputation. [ME *smorch;* b. SMEAR and SMUTCH]

**smirk** /smɜk/, *v.i.* **1.** to smile in an affected, would-be agreeable, or offensively familiar way. *–v.t.* **2.** to utter with a smirk. *–n.* **3.** the smile or the facial expression of one who smirks. [ME; OE *sme(a)rcian*] – **smirker,** *n.* – **smirkingly,** *adv.*

**smite** /smaɪt/, *v.,* **smote** or (*Obs.*) **smit; smitten** or **smit; smiting.** *–v.t.* **1.** to strike or hit hard, as with the hand, a stick or weapon, etc., or as the hand or a weapon does. **2.** to deal (a blow, etc.) by striking hard. **3.** to render by, or as by, a blow: *to smite a person dead.* **4.** to strike down or slay. **5.** to afflict, chasten, or punish in a grievous manner. **6.** to fall upon or attack with deadly or disastrous effect, as lightning, blight, pestilence, etc., do. **7.** to affect mentally with a sudden pang: *his conscience smote him.* **8.** to affect suddenly and strongly with a specified feeling: *smitten with terror.* **9.** to impress favourably; charm; enamour. *–v.i.* **10.** to strike; deal a blow or blows. **11.** to come, fall, etc., with or as with the force of a blow. [ME; OE *smītan,* c. G *schmeissen* strike] – **smiter,** *n.*

**smith** /smɪθ/, *n.* **1.** a worker in metal. **2.** →**blacksmith.** *–v.t.* **3.** to make by forging. [ME and OE, c. G *Schmied*]

**smithereens** /smɪðəˈrinz/, *n.pl. Colloq.* small fragments. [*smithers* (orig. unknown), with Irish diminutive suffix *-een*]

**smithery** /ˈsmɪθəri/, *n., pl.* **-eries. 1.** the work or craft of a smith. **2.** →**smithy.**

**smithing** /ˈsmɪθɪŋ, -ðɪŋ/, *n.* the art or process of forging iron or steel.

**smithsonite** /ˈsmɪθsənaɪt/, *n.* a native carbonate of zinc, $ZnCO_3$; an important ore of zinc. [named after James *Smithson,* 1765-1829, English chemist]

**smithy** /ˈsmɪθi, ˈsmiði/, *n., pl.* **smithies. 1.** the workshop of a smith, esp. a blacksmith. **2.** a forge.

**smitten** /ˈsmɪtn/, *adj.* **1.** struck, as with a hard blow. **2.** stricken with affliction, etc. **3.** *Colloq.* very much in love. *–v.* **4.** past participle of **smite.**

**smock** /smɒk/, *n.* **1.** any loose overgarment, esp. one worn to protect the clothing while at work: *an artist's smock.* *–v.t.* **2.** to clothe in a smock. **3.** to draw (a fabric) by needlework into a honeycomb pattern with diamond-shaped recesses. [ME; OE *smocc,* c. OHG *smoccho;* orig. name of garment with a hole for the head. Cf. Icel. *smjūga* to put on (a garment) over the head]

smocking

**smocking** /ˈsmɒkɪŋ/, *n.* **1.** smocked needlework, esp. as ornament. **2.** embroidery stitches used to hold gathered cloth in a pattern of even folds.

**smog** /smɒg/, *n.* a mixture of smoke and fog. – **smoggy,** *adj.*

**smoke** /smoʊk/, *n., v.,* **smoked, smoking.** *–n.* **1.** the visible exhalation given off by a burning or smouldering substance, esp. the grey, brown, or blackish mixture of gases and suspended carbon particles resulting from the combustion of wood, peat, coal, or other organic matter. **2.** something resembling this, as vapour or mist, flying particles, etc. **3.** something unsubstantial, evanescent, or without result. **4.** obscuring conditions. **5.** an act or spell of smoking tobacco, or the like. **6.** that which is smoked, as a cigar or cigarette. **7.** *Phys. Chem.* a dispersed system of solid particles in a gaseous medium. **8. go** or **end up in smoke, a.** to be burnt up completely. **b.** to have no solid result; end or disappear without coming to anything. **9. go into smoke,** *Colloq.* to disappear. *–v.i.* **10.** to give off or emit smoke. **11.** to give out smoke offensively or improperly, as a stove. **12.** to send forth steam or vapour, dust, or the like. **13.** to draw into the mouth and puff out the smoke of tobacco or the like, as from a pipe, cigar, or cigarette. *–v.t.* **14.** to draw into the mouth and puff out (the smoke of tobacco, etc.). **15.** to use (a pipe, cigarette, etc.) in this process. **16.** to expose to smoke. **17.** →**fumigate. 18.** to colour or darken by smoke. **19.** to cure (meat, fish, etc.) by exposure to smoke. **20.** to drive by means of smoke, as an animal from its hole or a person from a hiding place (fol. by *out,* etc). **21.** to force into public view or knowledge (fol. by *out*). [ME; OE *smoca;* akin to Scot. *smeek* (OE *smeocan*) emit smoke]

**smokebomb** /ˈsmoʊkbɒm/, *n.* a bomb which, when set off, emits a large quantity of smoke, as used for military purposes, in theatricals, demonstrations, etc.

**smoke-bush** /ˈsmoʊk-bʊʃ/, *n.* any of the mostly western Australian species of the genus *Conospermum,* with diffuse greyish inflorescences.

**smoked cheese** /smoʊkt ˈtʃiz/, *n.* a processed cheese to which the delicate tangy flavour of smoked wood is added.

**smokehouse** /ˈsmoʊkhaʊs/, *n.* a building or place in which meat, fish, etc., are treated with smoke.

**smokejack** /ˈsmoʊkdʒæk/, *n.* (formerly) an apparatus for turning a roasting spit, set in motion by the current of ascending gases in a chimney.

**smokeless** /ˈsmoʊkləs/, *adj.* emitting, producing, or having no (or little) smoke.

**smokeless powder** /– ˈpaʊdə/, *n.* any of various substitutes for ordinary gunpowder which give off little or no smoke, esp. one composed wholly or mostly of guncotton.

**smoker** /ˈsmoʊkə/, *n.* **1.** one who or that which smokes. **2.** a railway carriage or compartment in which passengers are permitted to smoke.

**smoker concert** /ˈ– kɒnsət/, *n.* (formerly) an informal gathering of men, usu. at a club or the like, for light entertainment.

**smokeroom** /ˈsmoʊkrum/, *n.* a room set apart for smoking, as in a hotel, ship, clubhouse, etc.

**smokescreen** /ˈsmoʊkskrin/, *n.* **1.** a mass of dense smoke produced to conceal an area, vessel, or aeroplane from the enemy. **2.** any device or artifice used for concealment of the truth, as a mass of verbiage.

**smokestack** /ˈsmoʊkstæk/, *n.* a pipe for the escape of the smoke or gases of combustion, as on a steamship, locomotive, or building.

**smoke tree** /ˈsmoʊk tri/, *n.* **1.** a treelike shrub, *Cotinus coggygria,* native to southern Europe and Asia Minor, bearing small flowers in large panicles, that develop a light, feathery appearance suggestive of smoke. **2.** a related American species, *Cotinus americanus.*

**smoking-jacket** /ˈsmoʊkɪŋ-ˌdʒækət/, *n.* a loose, comfortable jacket, usu. of a soft decorative fabric as velvet, worn by men for informal use at home.

**smoking room** /ˈsmoʊkɪŋ ˌrum/, *n.* →**smokeroom.**

**smoko** /ˈsmoʊkoʊ/, *n. Colloq.* a rest from work; tea-break. Also, **smoke-o, smoke-oh.**

**smoky** /ˈsmoʊki/, *adj.,* **smokier, smokiest. 1.** emitting smoke, or much smoke, as a fire, a torch, etc. **2.** hazy; darkened or begrimed with smoke. **3.** having the character or appearance of smoke. **4.** pertaining to or suggestive of smoke. **5.** of a dull or brownish grey; cloudy. – **smokily,** *adv.* – **smokiness,** *n.*

**smolder** /ˈsmoʊldə/, *v.i., n. U.S.* →**smoulder.**

**smolt** /smoʊlt/, *n.* a young, silvery salmon going down to the sea. [akin to SMELT[2]]

**smooch** /smutʃ/, *Colloq. –v.i.* **1.** to kiss; cuddle; behave amorously. *–n.* **2.** the act of smooching. [orig. unknown]

**smoodge** /smudʒ/, *v.i. Colloq.* **1.** to kiss; caress. **2.** to flatter; curry favour. Also, **smooge.** [probably from Brit. d.] – **smoodger,** *n.* – **smoodging,** *n.*

**smooth** /smuð/, *adj.* **1.** free from projections or irregularities of surface such as would be perceived in touching or stroking. **2.** free from hairs or a hairy growth. **3.** free from inequalities of surface, ridges or hollows, obstructions, etc. **4.** generally flat or unruffled, as a calm sea. **5.** of uniform consistency; free from lumps, as a batter, a sauce, etc. **6.** free from or proceeding without breaks, abrupt bends, etc. **7.** free from unevenness or roughness: *smooth driving.* **8.** easy and uniform, as an outline, motion, the working of a machine, etc. **9.** having projections worn away: *a tyre worn smooth.* **10.** free from hindrances or difficulties. **11.** undisturbed, tranquil, or equable, as the feelings, temper, etc. **12.** easy, flowing, elegant, or polished, as speech, a speaker, etc. **13.** pleasant, agreeable, or ingratiatingly polite, as manner, persons, etc.; bland or suave. **14.** free from harshness or sharpness of taste, as wine. **15.** not harsh to the ear, as sound. **16.** *Phonet.* without aspiration. **17.** *Tennis.* of or pertaining to the back of a racquet (from the texture of the strings on that side). *–adv.* **18.** in a smooth manner; smoothly. *–v.t.* **19.** to make smooth of surface, as by scraping, planing, pressing, stroking, etc. (sometimes fol. by *down*). **20.** to remove (projections, etc.) in making something smooth (oft. fol. by *away* or *out*). **21.** to tranquillise, calm, or soothe, as the feelings. **22.** to gloss over or palliate, as something unpleasant or wrong (usu. fol. by *over*). **23.** *Obs.* to make more polished, elegant, agreeable, or plausible, as wording, verse, manners, the person, etc. *–n.* **24.** the act of smoothing. **25.** that which is smooth; a smooth part or place. **26.** the smooth side of a racquet. [ME *smothe,* OE *smōth.* Cf. OE *smēthe* smooth, c. OS *smōthi*] – **smoother,** *n.* – **smoothly,** *adv.* – **smoothness,** *n.*

**smoothbore** /ˈsmuðbɔ/, *adj.* **1.** (of firearms) having a smooth bore; not rifled. *–n.* **2.** such a firearm.

**smooth breathing** /smuð ˈbriðɪŋ/, *n. Gk Gram.* a symbol (ʼ) indicating non-aspiration of the initial vowel. Cf. **rough breathing.** Also, **soft breathing.** [translation of L *spiritus lēnis*]

**smoothen** /ˈsmuðən/, *v.t.* **1.** to make smooth. *–v.i.* **2.** to become smooth.

**smooth-faced** /ˈsmuð-feɪst/, *adj.* **1.** beardless or clean-shaven. **2.** having a smooth surface, as cloth. **3.** deceitfully ingratiating.

**smoothing-iron** /ˈsmuðɪŋ-aɪən/, *n.* **1.** →**iron** (def. 4). **2.** a tool resembling this, used in the process of smoothing hot asphalt.

**smoothing plane** /ˈsmuðɪŋ pleɪn/, *n.* a small plane used for finishing wooden surfaces.

**smooth-spoken** /ˈsmuð-spoʊkən/, *adj.* **1.** speaking easily and well. **2.** polished in speech and manner. **3.** →**smooth-tongued.**

**smooth-tongued** /ˈsmuð-tʌŋd/, *adj.* **1.** Also, **smooth-spoken.** plausible. **2.** flattering; glib.

**smorgasbord** /ˈsmɔgəzbɔd/, *n.* **1.** a buffet meal of various hot and cold hors d'oeuvres, salads, meat dishes, etc. **2.** a wide choice or variety. [Swed. *smorgasbord,* equivalent to *smörgås* sandwich + *bord* table]

**smote** /smoʊt/, *v.* past tense of **smite.**

**smother** /ˈsmʌðə/, *v.t.* **1.** to stifle or suffocate, esp. by smoke or by depriving of the air necessary for life. **2.** to extinguish or deaden (fire, etc.) by covering so as to exclude air. **3.** to cover closely or thickly (oft. fol. by *up*); envelop (in). **4.** to surround with (love, kindness, etc.) to an extent that it inhibits personal development. **5.** to suppress: *to smother a scandal.* **6.** to repress, as feelings impulses, etc. *–v.i.* **7.** to become stifled or suffocated; be prevented from breathing freely by smoke or otherwise. **8.** to be stifled; be suppressed or concealed. *–n.* **9.** dense, stifling smoke. **10.** a smoking or smouldering state, as of burning matter; a smouldering fire. **11.** dust, fog, spray, etc., in a dense or enveloping cloud. **12.** an overspreading profusion of anything. [ME *smorther,* from OE *smorian* suffocate] – **smothery,** *adj.*

**smother tackle** /ˈ– tækəl/, *n.* a tackle in which the player holding the ball is enveloped by his opponent so that he cannot pass the ball.

**smoulder** /ˈsmoʊldə/, *v.i.* **1.** to burn or smoke without flame. **2.** to exist or continue in a suppressed state or without outward demonstration. **3.** to display repressed feelings, esp. of indignation: *his eyes smouldered.* –*n.* **4.** dense smoke resulting from slow or suppressed combustion. **5.** a smouldering fire. Also, *U.S.*, **smolder.** [ME *smoulder(en)*, from *smoulder* smoky vapour, dissimilated var. of earlier *smorther* SMOTHER, *n.*]

**smudge** /smʌdʒ/, *n.*, *v.*, **smudged, smudging.** –*n.* **1.** a dirty mark or smear. **2.** a smeary state. **3.** a blurred mass: *the house was a smudge on the horizon.* **4.** a stifling smoke. –*v.t.* **5.** to mark with dirty streaks or smears. –*v.i.* **6.** to form a smudge on something. **7.** to be or become smudged. [ME *smoge;* orig. uncert.]

**smudgy** /ˈsmʌdʒi/, *adj.*, **smudgier, smudgiest.** **1.** marked with smudges; smeared; smeary. **2.** emitting a stifling smoke; smoky. – **smudgily,** *adv.* – **smudginess,** *n.*

**smug** /smʌg/, *adj.*, **smugger, smuggest.** **1.** complacently proper, righteous, clever, etc.; self-satisfied. **2.** trim; spruce; smooth; sleek. [? D *smuk* neat] – **smugly,** *adv.* – **smugness,** *n.*

**smuggle** /ˈsmʌgəl/, *v.*, **-gled, -gling.** –*v.t.* **1.** to import or export (goods) secretly, without payment of legal duty or in violation of law. **2.** to bring, take, put, etc., surreptitiously: *she smuggled the gun into prison inside a cake.* –*v.i.* **3.** to smuggle goods. [LG *smuggeln,* c. G *schmuggeln*] – **smuggler,** *n.*

**smut** /smʌt/, *n.*, *v.*, **smutted, smutting.** –*n.* **1.** a particle of soot; sooty matter. **2.** a black or dirty mark; a smudge. **3.** indecent talk or writing; obscenity. **4.** a fungous disease of plants, esp. cereals, in which the affected parts are converted into a black powdery mass of spores, caused by fungi of the order Ustilaginales. **5.** the fungus itself. –*v.t.* **6.** to soil or smudge. –*v.i.* **7.** to become affected with smut, as a plant. [alteration of earlier *smit* (OE *smitte*) by association with SMUDGE, SMUTCH]

**smutch** /smʌtʃ/, *v.t.* **1.** to smudge or soil. –*n.* **2.** a smudge or stain. **3.** dirt, grime, or smut. [? MHG *smutzen* smear] – **smutchy,** *adj.*

**smutty** /ˈsmʌti/, *adj.*, **-tier, -tiest.** **1.** soiled with smut, soot, or the like; grimy; dirty. **2.** vulgar, but without strong connotations of indecency: *a smutty novel.* **3.** given to such talk, etc., as a person. **4.** (of plants) affected with the smut disease. – **smuttily,** *adv.* – **smuttiness,** *n.*

**Sn,** *Chem.* tin. [L *stannum*]

**S/N,** Shipping Note.

**snack** /snæk/, *n.* **1.** a small portion of food or drink; a light meal. **2.** *Colloq.* anything easily done. [n. use of *snack,* v., snap. Cf. MD *snacken* snap]

**snack bar** /ˈ– ba/, *n.* a bar, on the roadside or in a hotel or cafe, where snacks are served.

**snaffle**[1] /ˈsnæfəl/, *n.*, *v.*, **-fled, -fling.** –*n.* **1.** a slender, jointed bit used on a bridle. –*v.t.* **2.** to put a snaffle on (a horse, etc.); control by or as by a snaffle. [cf. D *snavel,* G *Schnabel* beak, mouth]

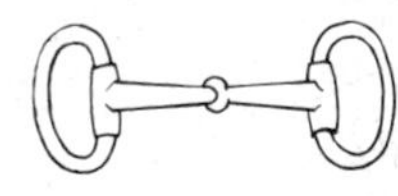

snaffle[1]

**snaffle**[2] /ˈsnæfəl/, *v.t.*, **-fled, -fling.** *Colloq.* **1.** to steal. **2.** to take away quickly before anyone else: *early shoppers snaffled up the sales bargains.* Also, **snavel.**

**snafu** /ˈsnæfu/, *n.*, *adj.*, *v.*, **-fued, -fuing.** *U.S. Orig. Mil. Colloq.* –*n.* **1.** chaos; a muddled situation. –*adj.* **2.** in disorder; out of control; chaotic. –*v.t.* **3.** to throw into disorder; muddle. [from the initial letters of *s(ituation) n(ormal): a(ll) f(ouled) u(p)*]

**snag** /snæg/, *n.*, *v.*, **snagged, snagging.** –*n.* **1.** a short, projecting stump, as of a branch broken or cut off. **2.** any sharp or rough projection. **3.** a tree or part of a tree held fast in the bottom of a river or other water and forming an impediment or danger to navigation. **4.** a stump of a tooth; a projecting tooth. **5.** any obstacle or impediment: *to strike a snag in carrying out plans.* **6.** a small hole or ladder caused by catching a stocking, or the like, on a sharp object. **7.** *Colloq.* a sausage. –*v.t.* **8.** to ladder; catch upon, or damage by, a snag. **9.** to obstruct or impede, as a snag does. [cf. d. Norw. *snag* stump, etc., Icel. *snagi* clothes peg] – **snaglike,** *adj.*

**snagger** /ˈsnægə/, *n. Colloq.* **1.** a shearer who does his job roughly or inexpertly. **2.** a person employed to remove snags from the river. **3.** a boat which removes snags from the river. [SNAG + -ER[1]]

**snaggle-tooth** /ˈsnægəl-tuθ/, *n.* a tooth which is broken or not properly in line with its fellows. [Brit. d. *snaggle* irregularly-shaped tooth] – **snaggle-toothed,** *adj.*

**snaggy** /ˈsnægi/, *adj.*, **-gier, -giest.** **1.** having snags or sharp projections, as a tree. **2.** abounding in snags or obstructions, as a river. **3.** snaglike; projecting sharply or roughly.

**snail** /sneɪl/, *n.* **1.** a mollusc of the class Gastropoda having a single, usu. spirally coiled shell. **2.** a slow or lazy person; a sluggard. [ME; OE *snegel,* c. G *Schnägel*] – **snail-like,** *adj.*

common garden snail

**snail-paced** /ˈsneɪl-peɪst/, *adj.* slow of pace or motion, like a snail; sluggish.

**snaily** /ˈsneɪli/, *n.* a bullock with a curled horn.

**snaily-horn** /ˈsneɪli-ˌhɔn/, *Colloq.* –*adj.* **1.** of cattle, having slightly twisted horns. –*n.* **2.** such a beast.

**snake** /sneɪk/, *n.*, *v.*, **snaked, snaking.** –*n.* **1.** a scaly, limbless, usu. slender reptile, occurring in venomous and nonvenomous forms, widely distributed in numerous genera and species and constituting the order (or suborder) Serpentes. **2.** a treacherous person; an insidious enemy. **3.** something resembling a snake in form or manner. **4.** any of various flexible coil springs used for clearing drains, threading wires, etc., through tubes, or the like. **5. like a cut snake,** *Colloq.* in a frenzy of activity. **6. snake in the grass,** a very deceitful or treacherous person; a hidden enemy. –*v.i.* **7.** to move, twist, or wind in the manner of a snake: *the path snakes through the field.* –*v.t.* **8.** to follow (a course) in the shape of a snake: *he snaked his way through the jungle.* [ME; OE *snaca,* c. MLG *snake.* Cf. Icel. *snākr*] – **snakelike,** *adj.*

**snakebird** /ˈsneɪkbɜd/, *n.* →**darter** (def. 2).

**snakebite** /ˈsneɪkbaɪt/, *n.* a bite from a snake, esp. a poisonous one.

**snake-charmer** /ˈsneɪk-tʃamə/, *n.* **1.** (esp. in Eastern countries) one who provides entertainment by presenting apparently dangerous snakes which dance to the music of his flute. **2.** anyone who displays snakes as an entertainment. **3.** *Colloq.* →**fettler.**

**snake-eater** /ˈsneɪk-itə/, *n.* →**black-headed python.**

**snake fence** /ˈsneɪk fɛns/, *n. Chiefly U.S.* →**worm fence.**

**snake juice** /ˈ– dʒus/, *n. Colloq.* any alcoholic beverage.

**snake-lizard** /ˈsneɪk-lɪzəd/, *n.* **1.** a smooth-scaled, elongated skink, *Lygosoma verreauxii,* resembling pygopod legless lizards in that its limbs are very small; glass snake. **2.** →**legless lizard.**

**snake-necked tortoise** /ˌsneɪk-nɛkt ˈtɔtəs/, *n.* →**long-necked tortoise.**

**snakeroot** /ˈsneɪkrut/, *n.* **1.** any of various plants whose roots have been regarded as a remedy for snakebites, as *Aristolochia serpentaria* (**Virginia snakeroot**), a herb with medicinal rhizome and rootlets. **2.** the root or rhizome of such a plant.

**snakes and ladders,** *n.* a game of chance played on a board with pictures of snakes and ladders, which, if landed on, advance or retard one's progress to the top.

**snakeskin** /ˈsneɪkskɪn/, *n.* the skin of a snake, esp. as used for leather.

**snakeweed** /ˈsneɪkwid/, *n.* any of a number of plants of the genus *Stachytarpheta,* a common weed of tropical and subtropical areas.

**snaky** /ˈsneɪki/, *adj.*, **snakier, snakiest.** **1.** of or pertaining to a snake or snakes. **2.** abounding in snakes, as a place. **3.** snakelike; twisting, winding, or sinuous. **4.** venomous; treacherous or insidious. **5.** consisting of, entwined with, or bearing snakes or serpents. **6.** *Colloq.* annoyed; angry or spiteful.

**snap** /snæp/, *v.*, **snapped, snapping,** *n.*, *adj.*, *adv.* –*v.i.* **1.** to make a sudden, sharp sound; crackle. **2.** to click, as a mechanism. **3.** to move, strike, shut, catch, etc. with a sharp sound, as a lid. **4.** to break suddenly, esp. with a sharp, cracking sound, as something slender and brittle. **5.** to flash, as the eyes. **6.** to act or move with quick, neat motions of the body: *to snap to attention.* **7.** *Photog.* to take snapshots. **8.** to make a quick or sudden bite or snatch. **9.** to utter a quick, sharp speech, reproof, retort, etc. **10. snap out of it,** to recover quickly from a mood, as anger, unhappiness, etc. **11.** *Football.* to make a hurried shot at goal. *–v.t.* **12.** to seize with, or as with, a quick bite or snatch (usu. fol. by *up* or *off*). **13.** to secure hastily, as a decision not subjected to due deliberation. **14.** to cause to make a sudden, sharp sound: *to snap one's fingers.* **15.** to bring, strike, shut, open, operate, etc., with a sharp sound or movement: *to snap a lid down.* **16.** to utter or say in a quick, sharp manner (sometimes fol. by *out*). **17.** to break suddenly, esp. with a crackling sound. **18.** *Photog.* to take a snapshot of. **19.** to fire (a pistol, or the like) quickly and spontaneously. **20.** *Football.* to kick (a goal or behind) under pressure. **21. snap one's fingers at,** to disregard; scorn. **22. snap (someone's) head off,** to speak angrily and sharply to. *–n.* **23.** a sharp, crackling or clicking sound, or a movement or action causing such a sound: *a snap of the fingers.* **24.** a catch or the like operating with such a sound. **25.** a sudden breaking, as of something brittle or tense, or a sharp crackling sound caused by it. **26.** a small, thin, brittle or crisp biscuit. **27.** *Colloq.* briskness, vigour, or energy, as of persons or actions. **28.** a quick, sharp speech, or manner of speaking. **29.** a quick or sudden bite or snatch, as at something. **30.** something obtained by or as by biting or snatching. **31.** a short spell, as of cold weather. **32.** →**snapshot.** **33.** a simple card game in which cards are thrown in turn on to a pile. When a card of equal value to the preceding card is put down, the first player to call 'snap' wins the pile. **34.** *Colloq.* an easy and profitable or agreeable position, piece of work, or the like. **35.** *Football.* a hurried shot at goal. *–adj.* **36.** denoting devices closing by pressure on a spring catch, or articles using such devices. **37.** made, done, taken, etc., suddenly or offhand: *a snap judgment.* *–adv.* **38.** in a brisk, sudden manner. *–interj.* **39.** (used in the game of snap to take cards from an opponent.) [D or LG *snappen*]

**snapbean** /ˈsnæpbin/, *n. U.S.* **1.** any of various kinds of beans (plant) whose unripe pods are used as foods. **2.** the pod itself.

**snap-brim** /ˈsnæp-brɪm/, *n.* a hat with a flexible brim usu. worn with the brim down in the front and up at the back.

**snapdragon** /ˈsnæpdrægən/, *n.* **1.** a plant of the genus *Antirrhinum*, esp. *A. majus*, a plant long cultivated for its spikes of showy flowers, of various colours, with a corolla that is supposed to look like the mouth of a dragon. **2.** the game of flapdragon.

snapdragon

**snap fastener** /ˈsnæp fasnə/, *n.* →**press-stud.**

**snap-freeze** /snæp-ˈfriz/, *v.t.*, **-froze, -frozen, -freezing.** to freeze (fresh food) rapidly.

**snapper** /ˈsnæpə/, *n.* **1.** Also, **schnapper.** a marine food fish of the family Sparidae, *Chrysophrys auratus*, widely distributed in Australian and New Zealand coastal waters, and known as cockney bream when very young, then with increasing age as red bream, squire and 'old man'; wollomai. **2.** elsewhere, **a.** any of various large marine fishes of the family Lutjanidae of warm seas, as the **red snapper,** *Lutjanus blackfordii*, a food fish of the Gulf of Mexico. **b.** any of various other fishes, as the bluefish, *Pomatomus saltratix.* **3.** →**snapping turtle.** **4.** *Colloq.* →**ticket snapper.** **5.** *Colloq.* (a form of address to a thin person).

**snapping beetle** /ˈsnæpɪŋ bitl/, *n.* →**click beetle.**

**snapping turtle** /– ˈtɜtl/, *n.* a large and savage turtle, *Chelydra serpentina*, of American rivers, having powerful jaws with which it lunges and snaps at an enemy.

**snappish** /ˈsnæpɪʃ/, *adj.* **1.** apt to snap or bite, as a dog. **2.** disposed to speak or reply quickly and sharply, as a person. **3.** impatiently or irritably sharp; curt. – **snappishly,** *adv.* – **snappishness,** *n.*

**snappy** /ˈsnæpi/, *adj.*, **-pier, -piest.** **1.** snappish, as a dog, a person, the speech, etc. **2.** snapping or crackling in sound, as a fire. **3.** quick or sudden in action or performance. **4.** *Colloq.* crisp, smart, lively, brisk, etc. **5. make it snappy,** *Colloq.* to hurry up. – **snappily,** *adv.* – **snappiness,** *n.*

snapping turtle

**snap-roll** /ˈsnæp-roʊl/, *n.* (in aeronautics) a rapidly executed roll. Also, **flick-roll.**

**snapshot** /ˈsnæpʃɒt/, *n.* **1.** a photograph taken quickly without any formal arrangement of the subject, mechanical adjustment of the camera, etc. **2.** a quick shot from a gun, taken without deliberate aim.

**snare**[1] /snɛə/, *n.*, *v.*, **snared, snaring.** *–n.* **1.** a device, usu. consisting of a noose, for capturing birds or small animals. **2.** anything serving to entrap, entangle, or catch unawares; a trap. **3.** *Surg.* a noose which removes tumours, etc., by the roots or the base. *–v.t.* **4.** to catch with a snare; entrap; entangle. **5.** to catch or involve by trickery or wile. [ME, from Scand. (cf. Icel. *snara*); replacing OE *snearh*, c. OHG *snarahha*] – **snarer,** *n.*

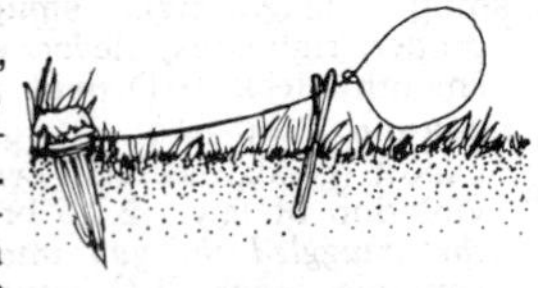
snare: rabbit snare

**snare**[2] /snɛə/, *n.* one of the strings of gut stretched across the skin of a side-drum. [LG: string]

**snare-drum** /ˈsnɛə-drʌm/, *n.* →**side-drum.**

**snark** /snak/, *n.* a mysterious, imaginary animal. [b. SNAKE and SHARK[1]; coined by Lewis Carroll, 1832-98, English writer and mathematician]

**snarl**[1] /snal/, *v.i.* **1.** to growl angrily or viciously, as a dog. **2.** to speak in a savagely sharp, angry, or quarrelsome manner. *–v.t.* **3.** to utter or say with a snarl. *–n.* **4.** the act of snarling. **5.** a snarling sound or utterance. [frequentative of obs. *snar* snarl, c. D and LG *snarren*, G *schnarren*] – **snarler,** *n.* – **snarlingly,** *adv.* – **snarly,** *adj.*

**snarl**[2] /snal/, *n.* **1.** a tangle, as of thread or hair. **2.** a complicated or confused condition or matter, as a traffic snarl. **3.** a knot in wood. *–v.t.* **4.** to bring into a tangled condition, as thread, hair, etc; tangle. **5.** to render complicated or confused. **6.** to raise or emboss, as parts of a thin metal vessel, by hammering on a tool **(snarling iron)** held against the inner surface of the vessel. *–v.i.* **7.** to become tangled; get into a tangle. [ME *snarle* snare, from Scand.; cf. OSwed. *snarel* noose, from *snara* SNARE[1]]

**snarler** /ˈsnalə/, *n. N.Z. Colloq.* a sausage.

**snarl-up** /ˈsnal-ʌp/, *n. Colloq.* any upset to the accustomed or expected progression of events, as a traffic jam.

**snarly** /ˈsnali/, *adj.* irritable; cantankerous.

**snatch** /snætʃ/, *v.i.* **1.** to make a sudden effort to seize something, as with the hand (usu. fol. by *at*). **2.** *Rowing.* to make a hurried, jerky movement at the beginning of a stroke. *–v.t.* **3.** to seize by a sudden or hasty grasp (oft. fol. by *up, from, out of, away,* etc.). **4.** to take, get, secure, etc., suddenly or hastily. **5.** to rescue or save by prompt action. **6.** *Bldg Trades Colloq.* to leave a task or contract uncompleted. *–n.* **7.** the act of snatching. **8.** a sudden motion to seize something. **9.** *Colloq.* a robbery by a quick seizing of goods. **10.** a bit, scrap, or fragment of something: *snatches of conversation.* **11.** a brief spell of effort, activity, or any experience: *to work in snatches.* **12.** a brief period of time. **13.** *Colloq.* **a.** the female pudenda. **b.** a woman as a sexual object. **14.** *Weightlifting.* a lift where the barbell is lifted from the floor to a position above the head with arms locked, in one swift, smooth movement. [ME *snacchen*, var. of earlier *snecchen*; orig. uncert.] – **snatcher,** *n.*

**snatch block** /ˈ– blɒk/, *n.* a block with a hinged piece that is lifted to admit the rope and then secured.

**snatchy** /ˈsnætʃi/, *adj.* consisting of, occurring in, or characterised by snatches; spasmodic; irregular.

**snath** /snæθ/, *n.* the shaft or handle of a scythe. Also, **snathe** /sneɪð/. [unexplained var. of *snead*, ME *snede*, OE *snǣd*;

orig. uncert.]

**snavel** /'snævəl/, *v.t.*, **-elled, -elling.** →**snaffle.**

**snazzy** /'snæzi/, *adj.*, **-zier, -ziest.** *Colloq.* **1.** very smart; strikingly fashionable; stylish. **2.** (of a person) very well-dressed. **3.** brightly patterned; having gay designs.

**sneak** /snik/, *v.*, **sneaked** or *Colloq.* **snuck, sneaking.** *–v.i.* **1.** to go in a stealthy or furtive manner; slink; skulk (fol. by *about, along, in, off, out,* etc.). **2.** to act in a furtive, underhand, or mean way. **3.** to let out secrets, esp. deceitfully; tell tales. **4.** *Colloq.* to leave quickly and quietly (fol. by *out, off, away,* etc.). *–v.t.* **5.** to move, put, pass, etc., in a stealthy or furtive manner. **6.** *Colloq.* to take surreptitiously, or steal. *–n.* **7.** one who sneaks; a sneaking, underhand, or contemptible person. **8.** a telltale. **9.** *Colloq.* an act of sneaking; a quiet departure. [akin to OE *snīcan* sneak along]

**sneaker** /'snikə/, *n.* **1.** *Colloq.* a shoe with a rubber or other soft sole used esp. in gymnasiums. **2.** one who sneaks; a sneak.

**sneaking** /'snikɪŋ/, *adj.* **1.** acting in a furtive or underhand way. **2.** deceitfully underhand, as actions, etc.; contemptible. **3.** secret; not generally avowed, as a feeling, notion, suspicion, etc. – **sneakingly,** *adv.*

**sneak preview** /snik 'privju/, *n.* the showing of an unreleased film more or less unannounced to try to estimate future audience reaction.

**sneakthief** /'snikθif/, *n.* a burglar who steals by sneaking into houses through open doors, etc.

**sneaky** /'sniki/, *adj.*, **sneakier, sneakiest.** like or suggestive of a sneak; sneaking. – **sneakily,** *adv.* – **sneakiness,** *n.*

**sneer** /snɪə/, *v.i.* **1.** to smile or curl the lip in a manner that shows scorn, contempt, etc. **2.** to speak or write in a manner expressive of derision, scorn, or contempt. *–v.t.* **3.** to utter or say in a sneering manner. **4.** to bring, put, force, etc., by sneering. *–n.* **5.** a look or expression suggestive of derision, scorn, or contempt. **6.** a derisive or scornful utterance or remark, esp. one more or less covert or insinuative. **7.** an act of sneering. [ME *snere,* c. N Fris. *sneere* scorn, of unknown orig.] – **sneerer,** *n.* – **sneering,** *adj.* – **sneeringly,** *adv.*

**sneeze** /sniz/, *v.*, **sneezed, sneezing,** *n.* *–v.i.* **1.** to emit air or breath suddenly, forcibly, and audibly through the nose and mouth by involuntary, spasmodic action. **2.** *Colloq.* to show contempt for, or treat with contempt (fol. by *at*). **3. not to be sneezed at,** worth consideration. *–n.* **4.** an act or sound of sneezing. [late ME *snese,* earlier *fnese,* OE *fnēosan,* c. MHG *fnūsen*] – **sneezer,** *n.* – **sneezy,** *adj.*

**sneeze weed** /'– wid/, *n.* **1.** any species of *Centipeda,* of Asia, Australia and New Zealand, herbs with a pungent aroma irritating to the mucous membranes. **2.** any species of *Helenium,* esp. *H. autumnale* of North America.

**sneezewood** /'snizwʊd/, *n.* a small tree, *Ptaeroxylon obliquum,* producing durable timber; native to southern and tropical Africa.

**sneezewort** /'snizwɜt/, *n.* a plant, *Achillea ptarmica,* native to Europe, the powdered leaves of which cause sneezing.

**snell** /snɛl/, *n.* a short piece of gut or the like by which a fishhook is attached to a longer line. [orig. unknown]

**Snell's law** /'snɛlz lɔ/, *n.* the law that for a ray of light refracted at a surface separating two media, the ratio of the sine of the angle of incidence to the sine of the angle of refraction is a constant. [named after Willebrod *Snell* van Royen, d. 1626, Dutch mathematician]

**snib** /snɪb/, *n.*, *v.*, **snibbed, snibbing.** *–n.* **1.** a mechanism which is usu. part of a lock and which can be operated from only one side of a door, holding the lock in position independently of the key. **2.** →**latch** (def. 1). *–v.t.* **3.** to hold (a lock) by means of a snib.

**snick** /snɪk/, *v.t.* **1.** to cut, snip, or nick. **2.** to strike sharply. **3.** to snap (a gun, etc.). **4.** *Cricket.* to hit (the ball), esp. accidentally, with the edge of the bat. *–v.i.* **5.** to click. *–n.* **6.** a small cut; a nick. **7.** a click. **8.** *Cricket.* **a.** a glancing blow given to the ball. **b.** the ball so hit. [orig. uncert. Cf. Scot. *sneck* cut (off), Icel. *snikka* whittle]

**snicker** /'snɪkə/, *v.i.* **1.** (of a horse) to make a low snorting neigh. **2.** →**snigger.** *–v.t.* **3.** →**snigger.** [orig. unknown] *–n.* **4.** →**snigger.**

**snide** /snaɪd/, *adj.* derogatory in a nasty, insinuating manner: *snide remarks about the Mayor.*

**sniff** /snɪf/, *v.i.* **1.** to draw air through the nose in short, audible inhalation. **2.** to clear the nose by so doing; sniffle, as with emotion. **3.** to smell by short inhalations. **4.** to show disdain, contempt, etc., by a sniff (oft. fol. by *at*). *–v.t.* **5.** to draw in or up through the nose by sniffing, as air, smells, liquid, powder, etc.; inhale. **6.** to perceive by, or as if by, smelling. *–n.* **7.** an act of sniffing; a single short, audible inhalation. **8.** the sound made. **9.** a scent or smell perceived. [ME; backformation from SNIVEL] – **sniffer,** *n.*

**sniffle** /'snɪfəl/, *v.*, **-fled, -fling,** *n.* *–v.i.* **1.** to sniff repeatedly, as from a cold in the head or in repressing tearful emotion. *–n.* **2.** an act or sound of sniffling. **3. the sniffles,** a cold, or other condition marked by sniffling. [frequentative of SNIFF]

**sniffy** /'snɪfi/, *adj.*, **sniffier, sniffiest.** *Colloq.* inclined to sniff, as in disdain; disdainful; supercilious.

**snifter** /'snɪftə/, *n.* **1.** *Colloq.* a small drink of an alcoholic beverage. **2.** →**balloon glass.** *–adj.* **3.** *Colloq.* excellent; very fine. [Brit. d., from ME *sniftеren,* probably akin to ME *snivelen* to snivel]

**snig** /snɪg/, *v.t.*, **snigged, snigging.** **1.** to drag (a long object) along the ground after first raising one end clear (used of logs, etc.) **2.** to trim (fallen timber); remove small branches, leaves, etc. [Brit. d.]

**snigger** /'snɪgə/, *v.i.* **1.** to laugh in a half-suppressed, often indecorous or disrespectful, manner. *–v.t.* **2.** to utter with a snigger. *–n.* **3.** a sniggering laugh. [imitative]

**snigging track** /'snɪgɪŋ træk/, *n.* a rough trail through forest country used by timber-getters; to draw or snig out fallen timber. Also, **snigging trail.**

**snip** /snɪp/, *v.*, **snipped, snipping,** *n.* *–v.t.* **1.** to cut with a small, quick stroke, or a succession of such strokes, with scissors or the like. **2.** to take off by, or as by, cutting thus. **3.** *Colloq.* to borrow or get money from: *can I snip you for $2?* *–v.i.* **4.** to cut with small, quick strokes. *–n.* **5.** the act of snipping, as with scissors. **6.** a small cut, notch, slit, etc., made by snipping. **7.** the sound made by snipping. **8.** a small piece snipped off. **9.** a small piece, bit, or amount of anything. **10.** a bargain; a certainty of success. **11.** a light mark, patch, or the like on the nose or lip of a horse. **12.** (*pl.*) small, stout hand shears for the use of sheet metal workers. [cf. D and LG *snippen* snip, snatch, clip]

**snipe** /snaɪp/, *n.*, *v.*, **sniped, sniping.** *–n.* **1.** any of several small shorebirds of the genus *Gallinago* having plump bodies, striped heads and long, straight bills, frequenting swamps and wet grasslands in many parts of the world and some of which, as the **Japanese snipe,** *G. hardwickii,* are seen in Australia as non-breeding migrants. **2.** a bird of genus *Rostratula,* rather similar in appearance but having a down curved tip to its bill, as the **painted snipe,** *Rostratula benghalensis* of Australia, Africa and southern Asia. **3.** a shot, usu. from a hidden position. **4.** a long, thin poster displayed during election campaigns and usu. bearing just the name of the candidate and his party. *–v.i.* **5.** to shoot or hunt snipe. **6.** to shoot at individual soldiers, etc., as opportunity offers from a concealed or long-range position. **7.** to make critical or damaging comments about (someone) without entering into open conflict (fol. by *at*). [ME *snype,* from Scand.; cf. Icel. *snípa*] – **snipelike,** *adj.*

snipe (def. 1)

**sniper** /'snaɪpə/, *n.* **1.** one who or that which snipes. **2.** a non-union labourer, usu. on the waterfront.

**snippet** /'snɪpət/, *n.* **1.** a small piece snipped off; a small bit, scrap, or fragment. **2.** *Colloq.* a small or insignificant person.

**snitch**[1] /snɪtʃ/, *v.t.* *Colloq.* to snatch or steal. [? var. of SNATCH]

**snitch**[2] /snɪtʃ/, *Colloq.* *–v.i.* **1.** to turn informer. *–n.* **2.** Also, **snitcher.** an informer. **3.** a feeling of ill-will: *she has a snitch against you.* [orig. uncert.]

**snitchy** /'snɪtʃi/, *adj.* *Colloq.* bad-tempered.

**snivel** /'snɪvəl/, *v.*, **-elled, -elling** or (*U.S.*) **-eled, -eling,** *n.*

–*v.i.* **1.** to weep or cry with sniffing. **2.** to affect a tearful state; whine. **3.** to run at the nose. **4.** to draw up mucus audibly through the nose. –*v.t.* **5.** to utter with snivelling or sniffing. –*n.* **6.** weak or pretended weeping. **7.** a light sniff, as in weeping. **8.** a hypocritical show of feeling. **9.** mucus running from the nose. [ME *snyvele.* Cf. OE *snyflung,* from *snofl* mucus] – **sniveller,** *n.* – **snivelly,** *adj.*

**S.N.L.R.,** services no longer required.

**snob** /snɒb/, *n.* **1.** one who admires, imitates, or seeks association with those with social rank, wealth, etc., and is condescending or overbearing to others. **2.** one who affects social importance and exclusiveness. **3.** one who has, or assumes, knowledge of a subject or subjects, and scorns anyone without this. **4.** →**cobbler**[2]. [nickname for cobbler or cobbler's apprentice; orig. uncert.]

**snobbery** /ˈsnɒbəri/, *n., pl.* **-beries.** snobbish character, conduct, trait, or act.

**snobbish** /ˈsnɒbɪʃ/, *adj.* **1.** of, pertaining to, or characteristic of a snob. **2.** having the character of a snob. Also, *Colloq.,* **snobby.** – **snobbishly,** *adv.* – **snobbishness, snobbism,** *n.*

**snodger** /ˈsnɒdʒə/, *adj. Obs. Colloq.* excellent; first-rate.

**snoek** /snuk/, *n.* **1.** (in Australia) usu. the barracouta. **2.** (elsewhere) variously the barracouta or the barracuda. [Afrikaans]

**snood** /snud/, *n.* **1.** the distinctive headband formerly worn by young unmarried women in Scotland and northern England. **2.** a band or fillet for the hair. **3.** a netlike hat or part of a hat, or material worn to confine a woman's hair. **4.** the fleshy protuberance at the base of the beak of a turkey. **5.** →**snell.** –*v.t.* **6.** to bind or confine (the hair) with a snood. [OE *snōd;* orig. uncert.]

**snook**[1] /snuk/, *n.* a gesture of defiance or cheekiness, made by putting the thumb to the nose. [orig. unknown]

**snook**[2] /snuk/, *n.* **1.** the Spanish mackerel, *Scomberomorus commerson.* **2.** the school mackerel, *S. queenslandicus.* **3.** a barracuda, esp. the **short-finned barracuda,** *Australuzza novaehollandiae.*

**snooker** /ˈsnukə/, *n.* **1.** a game played on a billiard table with fifteen red balls and six balls of other colours, the object being to pocket them. **2.** *Colloq.* a hiding place. –*v.t.* **3.** *Colloq.* to obstruct or hinder (someone), esp. from reaching some object, aim, etc. –*v.i.* **4.** *Colloq.* to hide. [orig. unknown]

**snookums** /ˈsnʊkəmz/, *n. Colloq.* (a term of endearment, used esp. of a baby or child). Also, **snooks** /snʊks/.

**snoop** /snup/, *Colloq.* –*v.i.* **1.** to prowl or pry; go about in a sneaking, prying way; pry in a mean, sly manner. –*n.* **2.** an act or instance of snooping. **3.** one who snoops. [D *snoepen* take and eat (food or drink) on the sly] – **snooper,** *n.* – **snoopy,** *adj.*

**snoot** /snut/, *n. Colloq.* **1.** the nose. **2.** a snob.

**snooty** /ˈsnuti/, *adj.,* **snootier, snootiest.** *Colloq.* **1.** snobbish. **2.** haughty; supercilious.

**snooze** /snuz/, *v.,* **snoozed, snoozing,** *n. Colloq.* –*v.i.* **1.** to sleep; slumber; doze; nap. –*n.* **2.** a rest; nap. **3.** *Prison.* a period of imprisonment of three months. [orig. uncert.]

**snoozer** /ˈsnuzə/, *n. Obs. Colloq.* a person; bloke.

**snore** /snɔ/, *v.,* **snored, snoring,** *n.* –*v.i.* **1.** to breathe during sleep with hoarse or harsh sounds. –*v.t.* **2.** to spend or pass (time) in snoring (fol. by *away* or *out*). –*n.* **3.** an act of snoring, or the sound made. [ME; ? b. SNIFF and ROAR] – **snorer,** *n.*

**snorkel** /ˈsnɔkəl/, *n.* **1.** a device on a submarine consisting of two vertical tubes for the intake and exhaust of air for diesel engines and general ventilation, thus permitting cruising at periscope depth for very long periods. **2.** a tube enabling a person swimming face downwards in the water to breathe, consisting of a tube, one end of which is put in the mouth while the other projects above the surface. –*v.i.* **3.** to swim using such a device, usu. in order to look at the seabed, fish, etc. Also, **schnorkle.** [G *Schnorchel*]

**snorker** /ˈsnɔkə/, *n. Colloq.* a sausage.

**snort** /snɔt/, *v.i.* **1.** to force the breath violently through the nostrils with a loud, harsh sound, as a horse, etc. **2.** to express contempt, indignation, etc., by such a sound. **3.** *Colloq.* to laugh outright or boisterously. **4.** *Colloq.* to sniff (a powdered drug, as cocaine). –*v.t.* **5.** to utter with a snort. **6.** to expel by or as by snorting. –*n.* **7.** the act or sound of snorting. **8. a.** a shot (def. 17) of spirits. **b.** *Colloq.* an alcoholic drink. [ME; ? b. SNORE and ME *route* snore (OE *hrūtan*)]

**snorter** /ˈsnɔtə/, *n.* **1.** one who or that which snorts. **2.** *Colloq.* anything unusually strong, large, difficult, dangerous, as a fast ball in cricket, a gale, etc. **3.** *Colloq.* an alcoholic drink.

**snot** /snɒt/, *n. Colloq.* **1.** mucus from the nose. **2.** →**snotnose.** [OE *gesnot*]

**snotnose** /ˈsnɒtnoʊz/, *n. Colloq.* a snobbish or affected person. – **snotnosed,** *adj.*

**snotty** /ˈsnɒti/, *adj. Colloq.* **1.** of or pertaining to snot. **2.** (esp. of a child) dirty. **3.** snobbish; arrogant. **4.** ill-tempered; cranky.

**snotty nose** /ˈ– noʊz/, *n. Colloq.* →**snotnose.** – **snotty-nosed,** *adj.*

**snout** /snaʊt/, *n.* **1.** the part of an animal's head projecting forward and containing the nose and jaws; the muzzle. **2.** *Entomol.* a prolongation of the head bearing the feeding organs, as in scorpion-flies and snout-beetles. **3.** anything that resembles or suggests an animal's snout in shape, function, etc. **4.** a nozzle or spout. **5.** *Colloq.* a person's nose, esp. when large or prominent. **6. have a snout on,** *Colloq.* to bear a grudge, ill-will, against. [ME, c. D *snuit,* G *Schnauze*]

**snout-beetle** /ˈsnaʊt-bitl/, *n.* a weevil (def. 1) having a protruding snout or rostrum.

**snow** /snoʊ/, *n.* **1.** the aqueous vapour of the atmosphere precipitated in partially frozen crystalline form and falling to the earth in white flakes. **2.** these flakes as forming a layer on the ground, etc. **3.** the fall of these flakes. **4.** something resembling snow. **5.** the white hair of age. **6.** *Poetic.* white blossoms. **7.** *Poetic.* the white colour of snow. **8.** *Chem.* carbon dioxide snow. **9.** *Colloq.* cocaine or heroin. **10.** white spots on a television screen caused by a weak signal. **11.** an opaque liquid used in correcting typescript. **12.** →**snow pudding.** –*v.i.* **13.** to send down snow; fall as snow. **14.** to descend like snow. **15. be snowed under,** to be overcome by something, as work. **16. it's snowing down south,** *Colloq.* (*euph.*) pointing out that someone's underwear is showing. –*v.t.* **17.** to let fall as or like snow. **18.** to cover, obstruct, isolate, etc., with snow (fol. by *in, over, under, up,* etc.). **19.** to overwhelm (someone) with facts and information in an attempt to distract attention from some aspect of the situation. [ME; OE *snaw,* c. D *sneeuw,* G *Schnee*] – **snowlike,** *adj.*

**snowball** /ˈsnoʊbɔl/, *n.* **1.** a ball of snow pressed or rolled together. **2.** Also, **snowball tree.** any of certain shrubs, varieties of the genus *Viburnum,* esp. the sterile cultivated variety of the guelder rose, *V. opulus,* with white flowers borne in large snowball-like clusters. **3.** a ball of marshmallow coated in cocoa or chocolate and rolled in desiccated coconut. **4.** any of various similar confections. **5.** a dance begun by one couple who, after a few minutes, take different partners who in turn do likewise until all the members of the company are dancing. –*v.t.* **6.** to throw snowballs at. –*v.i.* **7.** to accumulate or grow larger at an accelerating rate.

**snowberry** /ˈsnoʊbɛri/, *n., pl.* **-ries. 1.** a shrub, *Symphoricarpos albus,* native to North America, cultivated for its ornamental white berries. **2.** Also, **waxberry.** any of several species of the genus *Gaultheria* of Tasmania and New Zealand which have white, red or purple berries.

**snowbird** /ˈsnoʊbɜd/, *n. U.S. Colloq.* a cocaine or heroin addict.

**snow blindness** /ˈsnoʊ blaɪndnəs/, *n.* conjunctivitis and deteriorated vision caused by reflection of strong light on snow or ice. – **snow-blind,** *adj.*

**snowblink** /ˈsnoʊblɪŋk/, *n.* the peculiar reflection that arises from fields of snow or ice.

**snowbound** /ˈsnoʊbaʊnd/, *adj.* shut in and prevented from travelling by heavy snowfalls.

**snow bunny** /ˈsnoʊ bʌni/, *n. Colloq.* a young woman in whose mind the social events at a ski resort figure rather more than skiing.

**snow-bunting** /ˈsnoʊ-bʌntɪŋ/, *n.* a fringilline bird, *Plectro-*

*phenax nivalis,* inhabiting cold parts of the Northern Hemisphere, including Britain, where it is a winter migrant.

**snow cap** /ˈsnoʊ kæp/, *n.* a cap of snow on the top of a mountain, over a polar region, etc. – **snow-capped,** *adj.*

**snowcat** /ˈsnoʊkæt/, *n.* →**snowmobile.** Also, **sno-cat.** [Trademark]

**snow chains** /ˈsnoʊ tʃeɪnz/, *n. pl.* chains placed around the driving wheels of a motor vehicle to give added traction in icy conditions, etc.

**snow-clad** /ˈsnoʊ-klæd/, *adj.* covered with snow.

**snow comb** /ˈsnoʊ koʊm/, *n.* a thick shearing comb used in cold climates or for shearing stud sheep, which leaves a protective length of wool on the sheep's skin.

**snow country** /ˈ– kʌntri/, *n.* an area in which some snow usu. falls in winter.

**snow daisy** /ˈ– deɪzi/, *n.* any of a number of herbs of the Australasian, esp. New Zealand, genus *Celmisia,* as *C. longifolia* found at high altitudes in Australia.

**snowdrift** /ˈsnoʊdrɪft/, *n.* **1.** a mass or bank of snow driven together by wind. **2.** snow driven before wind.

**snowdrop**[1] /ˈsnoʊdrɒp/, *n.* **1.** a low spring-blooming herb, *Galanthus nivalis,* bearing drooping white flowers. **2.** its bulbous root or flower. **3.** the snowflake, a plant of the genus *Leucojum.*

**snowdrop**[2] /ˈsnoʊdrɒp/, *v.i.* **-dropped, -dropping.** *Colloq.* to steal laundry from clothes lines. – **snowdropper,** *n.*

**snowdrop tree** /ˈ– tri/, *n.* any tree or shrub of the genus *Halesia,* as *H. carolina,* with attractive, white, bell-shaped flowers; silverbell.

**snowfall** /ˈsnoʊfɔl/, *n.* **1.** a fall of snow. **2.** the amount of snow at a particular place or in a given time.

**snowfield** /ˈsnoʊfild/, *n.* **1.** an area of permanent snow found at high altitude or latitude. **2.** (*pl.*) snow country, esp. that developed for winter sports.

**snowflake** /ˈsnoʊfleɪk/, *n.* **1.** one of the small feathery masses or flakes in which snow falls. **2.** any of certain European plants resembling the snowdrop, as plants of the genus *Leucojum.*

**snow gauge** /ˈsnoʊ geɪdʒ/, *n.* an instrument for measuring the depth of a snowfall.

**snow goose** /ˈ– gus/, *n.* a large white bird of the family Anatidae, *Anser caerulescens* widespread in the Northern Hemisphere.

**snowgrass** /ˈsnoʊgras/, *n.* **1.** any of many species of the tussock grass *Poa.* **2.** *N.Z.* any of certain mountain grasses of the genus *Danthonia* which often form large tussocks at high altitudes.

**snowguard** /ˈsnoʊgad/, *n.* →**roofguard.**

**snow gum** /ˈsnoʊ gʌm/, *n.* any of several trees of the genus *Eucalyptus* found growing at high altitudes in Australia, esp. *E. pauciflora* ssp. *niphophila.*

**snow-in-summer** /snoʊ-ɪn-ˈsʌmə/, *n.* **1.** →**dusty miller.** **2.** any of various other white-flowered or white-leaved plants.

**snow job** /ˈsnoʊ dʒɒb/, *n.* an attempt to distract attention away from certain aspects of a situation by supplying an overwhelming amount of often extraneous information; a cover-up.

**snow leopard** /ˈ– lɛpəd/, *n.* →**ounce**[2]

**snowline** /ˈsnoʊlaɪn/, *n.* **1.** the general level on mountains, etc., above which snow never completely disappears, or the lower limit of perpetual snow. **2.** the lower limit of snow at a particular season.

**snowman** /ˈsnoʊmæn/, *n., pl.* **-men** /-mən/. a figure, resembling that of a man, made out of packed snow.

**snowmobile** /ˈsnoʊməbil/, *n.* an automotive vehicle for use in snow.

**snowplough** /ˈsnoʊplaʊ/, *n.* **1.** a contrivance for clearing away snow from roads, railways, etc. **2.** *Skiing.* a technique in which a skier moves slowly down hill or to a stop, by edging the skis inward, the tips touching, with the skis in a V position. Also, *Chiefly U.S.,* **snowplow.**

**snow pole** /ˈsnoʊ poʊl/, *n.* one of a set of poles put at the edges of a road, etc., to delineate it when snow-covered.

**snow pudding** /– ˈpʊdɪŋ/, *n.* a light pudding, prepared by folding whipped eggwhites into a gelatine mixture, flavoured with lemon or other fruit.

**snowshed** /ˈsnoʊʃɛd/, *n.* a structure, as over an extent of railway on a mountainside, for protection against snow.

**snowshoe** /ˈsnoʊʃu/, *n., v.,* **-shoed, -shoeing.** *–n.* **1.** a contrivance attached to the foot to enable the wearer to walk on deep snow without sinking in, as a ski, or esp., a light racquet-shaped frame across which is stretched a network of rawhide. *–v.i.* **2.** to walk or travel on snowshoes. – **snowshoer,** *n.*

snowshoes

**snowslip** /ˈsnoʊslɪp/, *n.* the sliding down of a mass of snow on a slope. Also, **snowslide.**

**snowstorm** /ˈsnoʊstɔm/, *n.* a storm accompanied by a heavy fall of snow.

**snow-white** /ˈsnoʊ-waɪt/, *adj.* white as snow.

**snowy** /ˈsnoʊi/, *adj.,* **snowier, snowiest. 1.** abounding in or covered with snow. **2.** characterised by snow, as weather, etc. **3.** consisting of snow; pertaining to or resembling snow. **4.** snow-white. **5.** immaculate; unsullied; stainless. – **snowily,** *adv.* – **snowiness,** *n.*

**snowy owl** /– ˈaʊl/, *n.* a large owl, *Nyctea scandiaca,* of northern Europe, Asia, and North America.

**snoz** /snɒz/, *n. Colloq.* the nose.

**snr,** senior.

**snub** /snʌb/, *v.,* **snubbed, snubbing,** *n., adj. –v.t.* **1.** to treat with disdain or contempt. **2.** to put, force, etc., by doing this: *to snub one into silence.* **3.** to check or rebuke sharply. **4.** to check or stop suddenly (a rope or cable running out). **5.** *Naut.* to stop or bring up (a boat, or the like) by means of a rope or line made fast to a buoy, anchor, etc. **6.** *U.S.* to check (an animal, or the like) in a similar way. **7.** to pull up thus. *–n.* **8.** an act of snubbing; a sharp rebuke. **9.** a disdainful affront or slight. **10.** a sudden check given to a rope or cable running out of a moving boat, or the like. **11.** a snub nose. *–adj.* **12.** (of the nose) short, and turned up at the tip. [ME, from Scand.; cf. Icel. *snubba* rebuke] – **snubber,** *n.*

**snubby** /ˈsnʌbi/, *adj.,* **-bier, -biest. 1.** somewhat snub, as the nose. **2.** tending to snub people.

**snuck** /snʌk/, *v. Colloq.* past tense and past participle of **sneak.**

**snuff**[1] /snʌf/, *v.t.* **1.** to draw in through the nose by inhaling. **2.** to perceive by or as by smelling. **3.** to examine by smelling, as an animal does. *–v.i.* **4.** to draw air, etc., into the nostrils by inhaling, as in order to smell something. **5.** to inhale powdered tobacco; take snuff. **6.** *Obs.* to express disdain, contempt, displeasure, etc., by sniffing (oft. fol. by *at*). *–n.* **7.** an act of snuffing; an inhalation; a sniff. **8.** smell or scent. **9.** a preparation of powdered tobacco, usu. taken into the nostrils by inhalation. **10.** a pinch of such tobacco. [MD *snuffen* snuffle]

**snuff**[2] /snʌf/, *n.* **1.** the charred or partly consumed portion of a candlewick or the like. **2.** a thing of little or no value, esp. if left over. *–v.t.* **3.** to cut off or remove the snuff of (a candle, etc.). **4.** to extinguish (fol. by *out*). *–v.i.* **5. snuff it,** *Colloq.* to die. [ME *snoffe;* orig. uncert.]

**snuffbox** /ˈsnʌfbɒks/, *n.* a box for holding snuff, esp. one small enough to be carried in the pocket.

**snuffer**[1] /ˈsnʌfə/, *n.* **1.** one who snuffs or sniffs. **2.** one who takes snuff. [SNUFF[1] + -ER[1]]

**snuffer**[2] /ˈsnʌfə/, *n.* **1.** (*usu. pl.*) an instrument for snuffing out candles, etc. **2.** one who snuffs candles. [SNUFF[2] + -ER[1]]

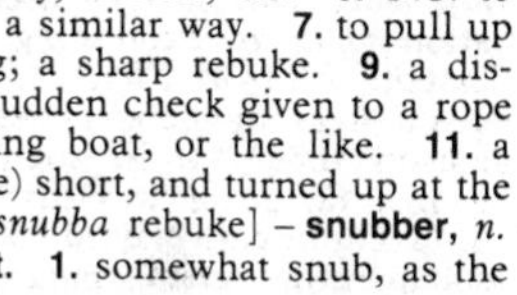

snuffer[2]

**snuffle** /ˈsnʌfəl/, *v.,* **-fled, -fling,** *n. –v.i.* **1.** to draw air into the nose for the purpose of smelling something. **2.** to draw the breath or mucus through the nostrils in an audible or noisy manner. **3.** to speak through the nose or with a nasal twang (often implying canting or hypocritical speech). **4.** to sniff; snivel. *–v.t.* **5.** to utter in a snuffling or nasal tone. *–n.* **6.** an act of snuffling. **7.** a nasal tone of voice. **8. the snuffles,** *Colloq.* a condition of the nose, as from a cold, causing snuffling. [D or Flem. *snuffelen,* frequentative of *snuffen.* See SNUFF[1], *v.*] – **snuffler,** *n.*

**snufflebuster** /ˈsnʌfəlbʌstə/, *n. Colloq.* →**wowser.**

**snuffy** /ˈsnʌfi/, *adj.,* **snuffier, snuffiest. 1.** resembling snuff. **2.** soiled with snuff. **3.** given to the use of snuff. **4.** easily displeased; huffy. – **snuffiness,** *n.*

**snug** /snʌg/, *adj.,* **snugger, snuggest,** *v.,* **snugged, snugging,** *adv.* –*adj.* **1.** comfortable or cosy, as a place, living quarters, etc. **2.** trim, neat, or compactly arranged, as a ship or its parts. **3.** fitting closely, but comfortably, as a garment. **4.** more or less compact or limited in size, and sheltered or warm. **5.** comfortably situated, as persons, etc. **6.** pleasant or agreeable, esp. in a small, exclusive way. **7.** enabling one to live in comfort: *a snug fortune.* **8.** *Obs.* secret. –*v.i.* **9.** to lie closely or comfortably; nestle. –*v.t.* **10.** to make snug or secure. **11.** *Naut.* to prepare (a ship) for a storm by taking in sail, lashing deck gear, etc. (usu. fol. by *down*). –*adv.* **12.** in a snug manner. [MD *snuggher* smart, ship-shape] – **snugly,** *adv.* – **snugness,** *n.*

**snuggery** /ˈsnʌgəri/, *n., pl.* **-geries. 1.** a snug place or position. **2.** a comfortable or cosy room.

**snuggle** /ˈsnʌgəl/, *v.,* **-gled, -gling.** –*v.i.* **1.** to lie or press closely, as for comfort or from affection; nestle; cuddle (oft. fol. by *up, in,* etc). –*v.t.* **2.** to draw or press closely, as for comfort or from affection. –*n.* **3.** a cuddle; embrace. [frequentative of SNUG, *v.*]

**sny** /snaɪ/, *n.* the upward curving of a plank, esp. a boat's outer planking. [orig. unknown]

**so**[1] /soʊ/, *adv.* **1.** in the way or manner indicated, described, or implied: *do it so.* **2.** as stated or reported: *is that so?* **3.** in the aforesaid state or condition: *it is broken, and has long been so.* **4.** to that extent; in that degree: *do not walk so fast.* **5.** very or extremely: *you are so kind.* **6.** very greatly: *my head aches so!* **7.** (used as the antecedent in the correlation *so ... as,* expressing comparison) to such a degree or extent: *so far as I know.* **8.** having the purpose of. **9.** for a given reason; hence; therefore. **10.** because of; for the reason that. **11.** in such manner as to follow or result from. **12.** in the way that follows; in this way. **13. and so, a.** (a continuative used to confirm or emphasise a previous statement): *I said I would come, and so I will.* **b.** likewise or correspondingly: *he is going, and so am I.* **c.** consequently or accordingly: *she is ill, and so cannot come.* **d.** thereupon or thereafter: *and so they were married.* **14. and so forth, a.** continuing in the same way. **b.** etcetera. **15. and so on,** et cetera. **16. just so,** in perfect order; carefully arranged: *her room was just so.* **17. or so,** about thus, or about that amount or number: *a day or so ago.* **18. quite so,** exactly as you have just stated. **19. so as, a.** with the result or purpose (fol. by an infinitive). **b.** provided that. **20. so called, a.** called or designated thus. **b.** incorrectly called or styled thus. **21. so much,** an unspecified amount. **22. so much for,** there is no more to be said or done about: *so much for your childhood ideals.* **23. so that, a.** with the effect or result that. **b.** in order that: *he wrote so that they might expect him.* **c.** *Obs.* provided that. **24. so to speak** (or **say**), to use such manner of speaking. **25. so what!** *Colloq.* what does that matter. –*conj.* **26.** *Colloq.* consequently; with the result that. **27.** under the condition that (oft. fol. by *that*). –*pron.* **28.** such as has been stated: *to be good and stay so.* –*interj.* **29.** how can that be! **30.** that will do! stop! [ME; OE *swā,* c. D *zoo,* G *so*]

**so**[2] /soʊ/, *n.* →**soh.** [See GAMUT]

**soak** /soʊk/, *v.i.* **1.** to lie in and become saturated or permeated with water or some other liquid. **2.** to pass, as a liquid, through pores or interstices (usu. fol. by *in, through, out,* etc.). **3.** to be thoroughly wet. **4.** to become known slowly to: *the facts soaked into his mind.* –*v.t.* **5.** to place and keep in liquid in order to saturate thoroughly; steep. **6.** to wet thoroughly, or drench. **7.** to permeate thoroughly, as liquid or moisture. **8.** to take in or up by absorption (oft. fol. by *up*): *blotting paper soaks up ink.* **9.** *Colloq.* to drink (alcohol) esp. to excess (fol. by *up*). **10.** to draw (*out*) by or as by soaking. –*n.* **11.** the act of soaking. **12.** the state of being soaked. **13.** the liquid in which anything is soaked. **14.** Also, **soak hole.** a shallow depression holding rainwater. **15.** *Colloq.* a heavy drinker. **16.** *Colloq.* a prolonged drinking bout. [ME *soke,* OE *socian;* akin to SUCK, *v.*] – **soaker,** *n.*

**soakage** /ˈsoʊkɪdʒ/, *n.* **1.** the act of soaking. **2.** liquid which has oozed out or been absorbed.

**soakage pit** /ˈ– pɪt/, *n.* a pit filled with rubble, etc., into which rainwater, or waste water, is sometimes drained. Also, **soakaway.**

**so-and-so** /ˈsoʊ-ən-soʊ/, *n., pl.* **-sos. 1.** someone or something not definitely named: *Mr So-and-so.* **2.** *Colloq.* a very unpleasant or unkind person: *he really is a so-and-so.*

**soap** /soʊp/, *n.* **1.** a substance used for washing and cleansing purposes, usu. made by treating a fat with an alkali (as sodium or potassium hydroxide), and consisting chiefly of the sodium or potassium salts of the acids contained in the fat. **2.** any metallic salt of an acid derived from a fat. **3.** →**soap opera.** –*v.t.* **4.** to rub, cover or treat with soap. **5.** to flatter (oft. fol. by *up*). [ME *sope,* OE *sāpe,* c. G *Seife*]

**soapbark** /ˈsoʊpbak/, *n.* **1.** a Chilean tree, *Quillaja saponaria,* bearing undivided evergreen leaves and small white flowers. **2.** the inner bark of this tree, used as a substitute for soap; quillai bark.

**soapberry** /ˈsoʊpbɛri/, *n., pl.* **-ries. 1.** any of certain tropical and subtropical trees of the genus *Sapindus,* esp. *S. saponaria,* used as a substitute for soap. **2.** a tree bearing such fruit, as *S. drummondii,* of the south-western U.S., which yields a useful wood.

**soapbox** /ˈsoʊpbɒks/, *n.* **1.** a box, usu. wooden, in which soap has been packed, esp. one used as a temporary platform by speakers addressing a street audience. **2.** any place, means, or the like, used by a person to make a speech, voice opinions, etc. **3.** →**billycart.**

**soapbox derby** /– ˈdabi/, *n.* a race for billycarts.

**soap flakes** /ˈsoʊp fleɪks/, *n. pl.* soap manufactured into flakes and sold esp. for washing clothes, etc.

**soapie** /ˈsoʊpi/, *n. Colloq.* a soap opera.

**soap opera** /ˈsoʊp ɒprə/, *n. Colloq.* a radio or television play presented serially in short regular programs, dealing usu. with domestic problems, esp. in a highly emotional manner. [so called because orig. sponsored on U.S. radio networks by soap manufacturers]

**soap powder** /ˈ– paʊdə/, *n.* **1.** soap in a powdered form, esp. as sold for washing clothes. **2.** detergent in powder form.

**soapstone** /ˈsoʊpstoʊn/, *n.* a massive variety of talc with a soapy or greasy feel, used to make hearths, tabletops, carved ornaments, etc.; steatite.

**soapsuds** /ˈsoʊpsʌdz/, *n.pl.* suds made with water and soap.

**soapwort** /ˈsoʊpwɜt/, *n.* a herb, *Saponaria officinalis,* whose leaves were formerly used for cleansing.

**soapy** /ˈsoʊpi/, *adj.,* **soapier, soapiest. 1.** containing, or impregnated with, soap: *soapy water.* **2.** covered with soap or lather. **3.** of the nature of soap; resembling soap; of the texture of soap. **4.** pertaining to or characteristic of soap. **5.** *Colloq.* flattering; given to using smooth words. –*n.* **6.** *Colloq.* →**soap opera.** – **soapily,** *adv.* – **soapiness,** *n.*

**soar** /sɔ/, *v.i.* **1.** to fly upwards, as a bird. **2.** to fly at a great height, without visible movements of the pinions, as a bird. **3.** *Aeron.* to fly without engine power, esp. in a sailplane, using ascending air currents. **4.** to rise or ascend to a height, as a mountain. **5.** to rise or aspire to a higher or more exalted level. –*n.* **6.** the act of soaring. **7.** the height attained in soaring. [ME *sore,* from OF *essorer* fly up, soar, from LL *exaurāre,* from *ex-* out of + *aura* air] – **soarer,** *n.*

**sob** /sɒb/, *v.,* **sobbed, sobbing,** *n.* –*v.i.* **1.** to weep with a sound caused by a convulsive catching of the breath **2.** to make a sound resembling this. –*v.t.* **3.** to utter with sobs. **4.** to put, send, etc., by sobbing or with sobs: *to sob oneself to sleep.* –*n.* **5.** the act of sobbing; a convulsive catching of the breath in weeping. **6.** any sound suggesting this. [ME *sobbe(n);* apparently imitative] – **sobbingly,** *adv.*

**S.O.B.** /ɛs oʊ ˈbi/, *n. U.S. Colloq.* (*derog.*) a despicable or contemptible person. [*s(on) o(f) (a) b(itch)*]

**sobeit** /soʊˈbiɪt/, *conj. Archaic.* if it be so that; provided.

**sober** /ˈsoʊbə/, *adj.* **1.** not intoxicated or drunk. **2.** habitually temperate, esp. with alcoholic drink. **3.** quiet or sedate in demeanour, as persons. **4.** marked by seriousness, gravity, solemnity, etc., as demeanour, speech, etc. **5.** subdued in tone, as colour; not gay or showy, as clothes. **6.** free from excess, extravagance, or exaggeration: *sober facts.* **7.** showing self-control. **8.** sane or rational. *–v.i., v.t.* **9.** to make or become sober. [ME, from OF *sobre,* from L *sōbrius*] **– soberly,** *adv.* **– soberness,** *n.*

**soberminded** /soubə'maɪndəd/, *adj.* self-controlled; sensible. **– sober-mindedness,** *n.*

**sobersides** /'soubəsaɪdz/, *n. Colloq.* a serious person.

**sobriety** /sə'braɪəti/, *n.* **1.** the state or quality of being sober. **2.** temperance or moderation, esp. in the use of strong drink. **3.** seriousness, gravity, or solemnity. [ME *sobrietie,* from L *sōbrietas*]

**sobriquet** /'soubrəkeɪ/, *n.* a nickname. Also, **soubriquet.** [F; orig. uncert.]

**sob-sister** /'sɒb-sɪstə/, *n.* **1.** a woman journalist who writes a newspaper or magazine feature in a sentimental style. **2.** a person who plays on one's emotions.

**sob-story** /'sɒb-stɔri/, *n. Colloq.* **1.** a story full of sentiment and pathos. **2.** an excuse: *he arrived very late and gave them a sob-story about a broken clock.*

**sob-stuff** /'sɒb-stʌf/, *n. Colloq.* sentimental matter as in literature, in the cinema, a story of bad luck, etc., designed to arouse the emotions.

**Soc.,** **1.** socialist. **2.** society. **3.** social.

**so-called** /'sou-kɔld/, *adj.* **1.** called or designated thus. **2.** incorrectly called or styled thus.

**soccer** /'sɒkə/, *n.* a form of football in which there are eleven players in a team, the ball is spherical, and the use of the hands and arms is prohibited except to the goalkeeper; association football. [(AS)SOC(IATION) + -ER[2]]

**Socceroos** /sɒkə'ruz/, *n. pl.* the Australian Soccer international touring team.

**sociability** /souʃə'bɪləti/, *n., pl.* **-ties.** sociable disposition; inclination for the society of others.

**sociable** /'souʃəbəl/, *adj.* **1.** inclined to associate with or be in the company of others. **2.** friendly or agreeable in company; companionable. **3.** characterised by or pertaining to companionship with others. [L *sociābilis*] **– sociableness,** *n.* **– sociably,** *adv.*

**social** /'souʃəl/, *adj.* **1.** pertaining to, devoted to, or characterised by friendly companionship or relations: *a social club.* **2.** friendly or sociable, as persons or the disposition, spirit, etc. **3.** pertaining to, connected with, or suited to polite or fashionable society: *a social function.* **4.** living, or disposed to live, in companionship with others or in a community, rather than in isolation. **5.** of or pertaining to human society, esp. as a body divided into classes according to worldly status: *social rank.* **6.** of or pertaining to the life and relation of human beings in a community: *social problems.* **7.** denoting or pertaining to activities designed to remedy or alleviate certain unfavourable conditions of life in a community, esp. among the poor: *social work.* **8.** pertaining to or advocating socialism. **9.** (of animals) living together in communities, as bees, ants, etc. (opposed to *solitary*). **10.** *Bot.* growing in patches or clumps. *–n.* **11.** a social gathering or party. [L *sociālis*] **– socially,** *adv.* **– socialness,** *n.*

**social bandaid** /– 'bændeɪd/, *n.* a superficial attempt, usu. by a government, to solve a social problem.

**social class** /– 'klas/, *n.* **1.** a group which is part of the hierarchical structure of a society, usu. classified by occupation, and having common economic, cultural or political status. **2.** the phenomenon of horizontal stratification in society in terms of economic, cultural, or political status.

**social climber** /– 'klaɪmə/, *n.* one who tries to move up into a higher social class, esp. by associating with people from that class. **– social climbing,** *n.*

**social contract** /– 'kɒntrækt/, *n.* an agreement between a government and the unions limiting wage demands in return for legislation designed to improve living standards generally.

**social control** /– kən'troul/, *n.* **1.** the enforcement of conformity by society upon its members, either by law or by attitudes. **2.** the influence of any element in social life working to maintain the pattern of such life.

**social credit** /– 'krɛdət/, *n.* the doctrine that the state should control retail prices, and profits should be distributed among consumers.

**social development** /– də'vɛləpmənt/, *n.* the formation and transformation of social life, customs, institutions, etc. Also, **social evolution.**

**social differentiation** /– ˌdɪfərɛnʃi'eɪʃən/, *n.* the state or process by which elements in society possess or develop distinct characteristics, as in the specialisation resulting from division of labour.

**social disease** /'– dəziz/, *n.* **1.** *Colloq.* any venereal disease. **2.** a disease which is prevalent amongst members of a particular social group, because factors relating to environment, conditions of work, etc., predispose them to it.

**social disorganisation** /– dɪsˌɔgənaɪ'zeɪʃən/, *n. Sociol.* **1.** the breaking-up of the structure of a social organisation. **2.** the non-existence of a social organisation.

**social distance** /– 'dɪstns/, *n.* the extent to which individuals or groups are removed from or excluded from participating in each other's life.

**social environment** /– ən'vaɪrənmənt/, *n.* →**culture factor.**

**social evolution** /– ɛvə'luʃən/, *n.* →**social development.**

**social heritage** /– 'hɛrətɪdʒ/, *n.* the entire inherited pattern of cultural activity present in a society.

**social interaction** /– ɪntər'ækʃən/, *n.* the reciprocal stimulation and response taking place between individuals and between groups, with particular reference to cultural activity.

**socialisation** /ˌsouʃəlaɪ'zeɪʃən/, *n.* **1.** the modifying of behaviour, esp. that of a growing infant, to what is acceptable in a particular society. **2.** the process of such modification.

**socialise** /'souʃəlaɪz/, *v.,* **-lised, -lising.** *–v.t.* **1.** to make social; educate to conform to society. **2.** to make socialistic; establish or regulate according to the theories of socialism. **3.** *Educ.* to turn from an individual activity into one involving all or a group of pupils. *–v.i.* **4.** to go into society; frequent social functions. **5.** to be sociable and mix freely, as at a social gathering. Also, **socialize.** **– socialisation** /souʃəlaɪ'zeɪʃən/, *n.*

**socialism** /'souʃəlɪzəm/, *n.* **1.** a theory or system of social organisation which advocates the vesting of the ownership and control of the means of production, capital, land, etc., in the community as a whole. **2.** procedure or practice in accordance with this theory.

**social isolation** /souʃəl ˌaɪsə'leɪʃən/, *n.* a state or process in which persons, groups, or cultures lose or do not have communication or cooperation with one another.

**socialist** /'souʃələst/, *n.* **1.** an advocate of socialism. *–adj.* **2.** pertaining to socialists or socialism.

**socialistic** /souʃə'lɪstɪk/, *adj.* **1.** socialist. **2.** tending towards or sympathising with socialism.

**socialistically** /souʃə'lɪstɪkli/, *adv.* in a socialist or socialistic manner or direction.

**socialite** /'souʃəlaɪt/, *n.* a member of the social elite, or one who aspires to be such.

**sociality** /souʃi'æləti/, *n., pl.* **-ties.** **1.** social nature or tendencies as shown in the assembling of individuals in communities. **2.** the action on the part of individuals of associating together in communities. **3.** the state or quality of being social.

**social mix** /souʃəl 'mɪks/, *n.* the sociological groupings combined in a given area, institution, etc.

**social organisation** /ˌsouʃəl ɔgənaɪ'zeɪʃən/, *n.* the structure of relations inside a group, usu. the relations of subgroups and of institutions.

**social process** /– 'prousɛs/, *n.* the means by which culture and social organisation change or are preserved.

**social realism** /– 'riəlɪzəm/, *n.* a movement in American painting, originating in the depression of the 1930s, and involving the artistic representation of contemporary social and political life, usu. from a left wing standpoint.

**social science** /– 'saɪəns/, *n.* →**social studies.**

**social security** /– sə'kjurəti/, *n.* the provision by the state for the economic and social welfare of the public by means of old-age pensions, sickness and unemployment benefits.

**social service** /– 'sɜvəs/, *n.* organised welfare efforts carried on under professional rules by trained personnel.

**social settlement** /– 'sɛtlmənt/, *n.* →**settlement** (def. 13).

**social studies** /– 'stʌdiz/, *n. pl.* a broad group of subjects, as economics, social history, esp. as taught in schools, sociology, etc., relating to man's function as a social being. Also, **social science.**

**social sub-set** /– 'sʌb-sɛt/, *n.* those who belong to one small group of society, as members of a street gang, workers in a particular trade, etc.

**social welfare** /– 'wɛlfɛə/, *n.* a system of services set up by a state for the benefit of the community.

**social work** /'– wɜk/, *n.* **1.** organised work directed towards the betterment of social conditions in the community, as by seeking to improve the condition of the poor, to promote the welfare of children, etc. **2.** the study of the methods by which this can be effected. – **social worker,** *n.*

**societal** /sə'saɪətl/, *adj.* →**social** (def. 6).

**society** /sə'saɪəti/, *n., pl.* **-ties.** **1.** a body of individuals living as members of a community: *a society of human beings.* **2.** the body of human beings generally, associated or viewed as members of a community: *the evolution of human society.* **3.** human beings collectively regarded as a body divided into classes according to worldly status: *the lower classes of society.* **4.** an organisation of persons associated together for religious, benevolent, literary, scientific, political, patriotic, or other purposes. **5.** a body of persons associated by their calling, interests, etc.: *diplomatic society.* **6.** those with whom one has companionship. **7.** companionship or company: *to enjoy one's society.* **8.** the social relations, activities, or life of the polite or fashionable world. **9.** the body of those associated in the polite or fashionable world; the rich upper class. **10.** the condition of those living in companionship with others, or in a community, rather than in isolation. **11.** any community. **12.** *Ecol.* a closely integrated grouping of organisms of the same species held together by mutual dependence and showing division of labour. *–adj.* **13.** of or pertaining to polite society: *a society party.* [L *societas*]

**Society of Friends,** *n.* a Christian sect, founded by George Fox, 1624-91, which rejects formal creed or ordained ministers, and which advocates peace and plain living.

**socio-,** a word element representing 'social', 'sociological', as in *sociometry.* [combining form representing L *socius* companion]

**socioeconomic** /ˌsoʊsioʊˌɛkə'nɒmɪk, ˌsoʊʃioʊ-, -ˌik-/, *adj.* of or pertaining to both social and economic considerations. – **socioeconomically,** *adv.*

**sociol.,** **1.** sociological. **2.** sociologist. **3.** sociology.

**sociolinguistics** /ˌsoʊsioʊlɪŋ'gwɪstɪks/, *n.* the study of language as it relates to social structures and attitudes. – **sociolinguistic,** *adj.* – **sociolinguist** /ˌsoʊsioʊ'lɪŋgwəst/, *n.*

**sociology** /soʊsi'ɒlədʒi/, *n.* the science or study of the origin, development, organisation, and functioning of human society; the science of the fundamental laws of social relations, institutions, etc. – **sociological** /soʊsiə'lɒdʒɪkəl/, *adj.* – **sociologist,** *n.*

**sociometry** /soʊsi'ɒmətri/, *n.* the measurement of attitudes of social acceptance or rejection through expressed preferences among members of a social grouping.

**sociopolitical** /ˌsoʊsioʊpə'lɪtɪkəl, ˌsoʊʃioʊ-/, *adj.* of or pertaining to both social and political considerations. – **sociopolitically,** *adv.*

**sock**[1] /sɒk/, *n.* **1.** a short stocking reaching about halfway to the knee, or only above the ankle. **2.** a light shoe worn by ancient Greek and Roman comic actors, sometimes taken as a symbol of comedy. **3. pull one's socks up,** *Colloq.* to make more effort. **4. put a sock in it,** *Colloq.* to be quiet. *–v.t.* **5. sock away,** *Colloq.* **a.** to accumulate a store of something, esp. in secret (from the habit of storing money in an old sock). **b.** to consume large quantities of (something, esp. alcohol). See **buskin.** [ME *sokke,* OE *socc,* from L *soccus* (def. 2)]

**sock**[2] /sɒk/, *Colloq.* *–v.t.* **1.** to strike or hit hard. *–n.* **2.** a hard blow. [orig. uncert.]

**socket** /'sɒkət/, *n.* **1.** a hollow part or piece for receiving and holding some part or thing. **2.** one of a set of different-sized circular heads with flanges on the inner circumference, for use with a ratchet spanner. **3.** *Elect.* a connecting device to which the wires of a circuit may be attached and which is arranged for the insertion of a plug. **4.** *Anat.* **a.** a hollow in one part, which receives another part: *the socket of the eye.* **b.** the concavity of a joint: *the socket of the hip.* **5.** the shank of a golf club. *–v.t.* **6.** to place in or fit with a socket. **7.** *Golf.* to hit (the ball) with the shank of the club. [ME *socket,* from AF, diminutive of *soc* ploughshare; of Celtic orig.]

**socket outlet** /'– aʊtlɛt/, *n.* →**socket** (def. 3).

**socketwood** /'sɒkətwʊd/, *n.* a large tree, *Daphnandra micrantha,* of rainforests of eastern Australia, characterised by swellings at the base of the branches.

**sockeye** /'sɒkaɪ/, *n.* the red salmon, *Oncorhynchus nerka,* most highly valued of the Pacific salmons. [Salishan (an Amer. Ind. language); alteration of *sukkegh*]

**socle** /'soʊkəl/, *n.* (in architecture) a low, plain member supporting a wall, pedestal, or the like. [F, from It. *zoccolo,* from L *socculus,* diminutive of *soccus* SOCK[1]]

**Socratic** /sə'krætɪk/, *adj.* **1.** of or pertaining to Socrates (469?-399 B.C.), philosopher, or his philosophy, followers, etc. *–n.* **2.** a follower of Socrates. **3.** one of the Greek philosophers stimulated by Socrates. – **Socratically,** *adv.*

**Socratic irony** /– 'aɪrəni/, *n.* See **irony**[1] (def. 3).

**Socratic method** /– 'mɛθəd/, *n.* the use of questions as employed by Socrates to develop a latent idea, as in the mind of a pupil, or to elicit admissions, as from an opponent, tending to establish or to confute some proposition.

**sod**[1] /sɒd/, *n., v.,* **sodded, sodding.** *–n.* **1.** a piece (usu. square or oblong) cut or torn from the surface of grassland, containing the roots of grass, etc. **2.** the surface of the ground, esp. when covered with grass; turf; sward. **3.** *Colloq.* a damper which is doughy from being badly cooked. *–v.t.* **4.** to cover with sods. [ME, from MD or MLG *sode* turf]

**sod**[2] /sɒd/, *n. Colloq.* **1.** sodomite. **2.** a disagreeable person. *–v.t.* **3. sod it,** *Colloq.* (a strong exclamation of annoyance, disgust, etc.).

**soda** /'soʊdə/, *n.* **1.** sodium hydroxide, NaOH; caustic soda. **2.** the oxide of sodium, $Na_2O$. **3.** sodium (in phrases): *carbonate of soda.* **4.** soda-water. **5.** a drink made with soda-water, served with fruit or other syrups, ice-cream, etc. **6.** (in faro) the turned-up card in the dealing box before one begins to play. **7.** *Colloq.* something which can be done easily and successfully: *the exam was a soda.* **8. on a soda,** *Colloq.* secure in an easy, comfortable way of life. [ML, from It., ? backformation from ML *sodānum* glasswort, from Ar. *suwwād* or *sudā* headache (for which the plant was used as a remedy)]

**soda ash** /'soʊdər æʃ/, *n.* See **sodium carbonate.**

**soda biscuit** /'soʊdə bɪskət/, *n.* a biscuit using soda and sour milk or buttermilk as leavening agents.

**soda bread** /'– brɛd/, *n.* a yeastless bread, risen by the addition of bicarbonate of soda and cream of tartar.

**soda fountain** /'– faʊntn/, *n.* **1.** *U.S.* a counter at which sodas, ice-cream, snacks, etc., are served. **2.** *U.S.* a milk bar. **3.** a container from which soda-water is drawn by taps.

**soda lime** /'– laɪm/, *n.* a mixture of sodium hydroxide and calcium hydroxide.

**sodalite** /'soʊdəlaɪt/, *n.* a mineral, sodium aluminium silicate with sodium chloride, $3NaAlSiO_4 \cdot NaCl$, occurring in crystals and in massive form, white, grey, or blue in colour; found in certain alkali-rich igneous rocks.

**sodality** /soʊ'dæləti/, *n., pl.* **-ties.** **1.** fellowship. **2.** an association or society. **3.** *Rom. Cath. Ch.* a society with religious or charitable objects. [L *sodālitas*]

**soda nitre** /'soʊdə naɪtə/, *n.* impure naturally occurring sodium nitrate; caliche; Chile saltpetre.

**soda siphon** /'– saɪfən/, *n.* a bottle filled with carbonated water, fitted with a bent tube through the neck, the soda-water being forced out, when a valve is opened, by the pressure on its surface from the gas accumulating within the bottle.

**soda-water** /'soʊdə-wɔtə/, *n.* **1.** an effervescent beverage consisting of water charged with carbon dioxide. **2.** (originally) a beverage made with sodium bicarbonate.

**sodden** /'sɒdn/, *adj.* **1.** soaked with liquid or moisture. **2.** heavy, doughy, or soggy, as food. **3.** having the appearance of having been soaked. **4.** bloated, as the face. **5.** expressionless, dull, or stupid. *–v.i.* **6.** to become sodden. *–v.t.* **7.** to make sodden. [ME *sothen,* pp. of SEETHE] – **soddenly,** *adv.* – **soddenness,** *n.*

**sodium** /'soʊdiəm/, *n.* a soft, silver-white metallic element which oxidises rapidly in moist air, occurring in nature only in the combined state. The metal is used in the synthesis of sodium peroxide, sodium cyanide, and lead tetraethyl. *Symbol:* Na (for *natrium*); *at. wt:* 22.9898; *at. no.:* 11; *sp. gr.:* 0.97 at 20°C. [SOD(A) + -IUM]

**sodium bicarbonate** /– baɪ'kabənət/, *n.* a white, crystalline compound, $NaHCO_3$, used in cooking, medicine, etc. Also, **sodium hydrogen carbonate.**

**sodium carbonate** /– 'kabənət/, *n.* a compound of sodium, $Na_2CO_3$, occurring in an anhydrous form as a white powder, called **soda ash,** and as a hydrate, $Na_2CO_3 \cdot 10H_2O$, known as **washing soda.**

**sodium chlorate** /– 'klɔreɪt/, *n.* a sodium salt, $NaClO_3$, used in explosives, as an antiseptic in toothpastes, etc.

**sodium chloride** /– 'klɔraɪd/, *n. Chem.* common salt, NaCl.

**sodium dichromate** /– daɪ'kroʊmeɪt/, *n. Chem.* a red, water-soluble, crystalline salt, $Na_2Cr_2O_7 \cdot 2H_2O$, used as an oxidising agent, in electroplating, and in the manufacture of inks and dyes. Also, **sodium bichromate.**

**sodium glycocholate** /– glaɪkə'koʊleɪt/, *n.* sodium salt of glycocholic acid, found in bile.

**sodium hydroxide** /– haɪ'drɒksaɪd/, *n.* a white caustic solid, NaOH, used in making soap, etc.; caustic soda.

**sodium metabisulphite** /– mɛtəbaɪ'sʌlfaɪt/, *n.* a white crystalline solid, $Na_2S_2O_5$, which is the chief constituent of commercial dry sodium bisulphite, used as a laboratory reagent and as a food preservative. Also, **sodium pyrosulphite.**

**sodium nitrate** /– 'naɪtreɪt/, *n.* a crystalline water-soluble compound, $NaNO_3$, which occurs naturally as Chile saltpetre, used in fertilisers, explosives, and glass.

**sodium pentothal** /– 'pɛntəθæl/, *n.* a barbiturate, $C_{11}H_{17}O_2N_2SNa$, injected intravenously as a general anaesthetic. Also, **pentothal sodium, thiopentone sodium.**

**sodium peroxide** /– pə'rɒksaɪd/, *n.* a yellow, water-soluble compound, $Na_2O_2$, formed when sodium burns in air; used as an oxidising agent and in bleaching.

**sodium pyrosulphite** /– paɪroʊ'sʌlfaɪt/, *n.* →**sodium metabisulphite.**

**sodium silicate** /– 'sɪləkeɪt/, *n.* a white, water-soluble compound, $Na_2SiO_3$, used in dyeing, printing, fireproofing, and preserving; waterglass.

**sodium sulphate** /– 'sʌlfeɪt/, *n.* a white, water-soluble compound, $Na_2SO_4 \cdot 10H_2O$, used in the manufacture of dyes, soaps, detergents, etc.; Glauber salt.

**sodium sulphite** /– 'sʌlfaɪt/, *n.* a white crystalline water-soluble powder, $Na_2SO_3$ (when hydrated $Na_2SO_3 \cdot 7H_2O$), which decomposes on heating to give $SO_2$ and which is used in the paper industry, in the treatment of water, in bleaching and photography, and as a food preservative and an anti-oxidant.

**sodium taurocholate** /– tɔrə'koʊleɪt/, *n.* sodium salt of taurocholic acid, found in bile.

**sodium thiosulphate** /– θaɪoʊ'sʌlfeɪt/, *n.* a water-soluble crystalline salt, $Na_2S_2O_3 \cdot 5H_2O$, sometimes called **sodium hyposulphite** (the 'hypo' of photographers, used as a fixing bath).

**sodium-vapour lamp** /soʊdiəm-'veɪpə læmp/, *n.* an electric lamp in which sodium vapour is activated by current passing between two electrodes, producing a yellow, glareless light which is widely used for street lighting.

**Sodom** /'sɒdəm/, *n.* any very wicked place. [from *Sodom,* an ancient city near the Dead Sea which was destroyed by fire from heaven because of the wickedness of its inhabitants]

**sodomite** /'sɒdəmaɪt/, *n.* one who practises sodomy. [from *Sodomite* an inhabitant of Sodom. See SODOM]

**sodomy** /'sɒdəmi/, *n.* **1.** sexual intercourse using the anal orifice, esp. of one man with another. **2.** →**bestiality** (def. 3). **3.** any sexual practice regarded as unnatural or perverted. [ME, from OF *sodomie.* See SODOM, -Y[3]]

**sod-seed** /'sɒd-sid/, *v.t.* to sow (established sod or pasture) which has not been ploughed, by using a pasture drill with a narrow, sharp-edged sowing shoe. – **sod-seeder,** *n.*

**soever** /soʊ'ɛvə/, *adv.* at all; in any case; of any kind; in any way (used with generalising force after *who, what, when, where, how, any, all,* etc., sometimes separated by intervening words, often in composition): *choose what person soever you please.*

**sofa** /'soʊfə/, *n.* a long upholstered seat, or couch, with a back, and two arms or raised ends. [Ar. *soffeh* part of floor made higher for use as a seat]

**soffit** /'sɒfət/, *n.* the under surface of a beam, arch, stair, architrave, or the like. [earlier *soffita, -o,* from It., from *so-* (from L *sub*) under + *-fita, -fito,* pp. of *figgere* (from L *figere*) fix]

**soft** /sɒft/, *adj.* **1.** yielding readily to touch or pressure; easily penetrated, divided, or altered in shape; not hard or stiff. **2.** relatively deficient in hardness, as metal. **3.** smooth and agreeable to the touch; not rough or coarse. **4.** producing agreeable sensations; pleasant, easeful, or comfortable: *soft slumber.* **5.** low or subdued in sound; gentle and melodious. **6.** not harsh or unpleasant to the eye; not glaring, as light or colour. **7.** not hard or sharp, as outlines. **8.** gentle or mild, as wind, rain, etc.; genial or balmy, as climate, air, etc. **9.** gentle, mild, lenient, or compassionate. **10.** smooth, soothing, or ingratiating, as words. **11.** not harsh or severe, as terms. **12.** yielding readily to the tender emotions, as persons; impressionable. **13.** sentimental, as language. **14.** not strong or robust; delicate; incapable of great endurance or exertion. **15.** *Colloq.* not hard, trying, or severe; involving little effort: *a soft job.* **16.** (of water) relatively free from mineral salts that interfere with the action of soap. **17.** *Photog.* having delicate gradations of tone (opposed to *contrasty*). **18.** *Physics.* (of radiation) having a relatively long wavelength and low penetrating power. **19.** *Metall.* **a.** (of solder) having a relatively low melting point, usu. below 370°C. **b.** (of iron) containing little carbon; incapable of retaining magnetic properties when the magnetising field is removed. **20.** *Astronautics.* (of a landing of a space vehicle) gentle, not harmful to the vehicle or its contents, usu. implying an impact velocity of less than 30 km/h. **21.** *Phonet.* **a.** (of consonants) lenis, esp. lenis and voiced. **b.** (of *c* and *g*) pronounced as in *cent* and *gem.* **c.** (of consonants in languages) palatalised. **22.** (of drugs) non-addictive, as marijuana and LSD. **23.** *Colloq.* easily influenced or swayed, as a person, the mind, etc.; easily imposed upon. **24.** *Colloq.* foolish; feeble; weak. **25. be soft on someone,** *Colloq.* **a.** to be sentimentally inclined towards someone. **b.** to act towards someone in a less harsh manner than expected. **26. have a soft spot for someone** or **something,** to be fond of someone or something. **27. a soft touch,** *Colloq.* one who yields too easily to requests for money, etc. **28. soft in the head,** *Colloq.* stupid; insane. *–n.* **29.** that which is soft or yielding; the soft part; softness. *–adv.* **30.** in a soft manner. *–interj. Archaic.* **31.** be quiet! hush! **32.** not so fast! stop! [ME *softe,* OE *softe,* c. G *sanft*] – **softly,** *adv.* – **softness,** *n.*

**softball** /'sɒftbɔl/, *n.* **1.** a form of baseball played with a larger and softer ball, in which the pitcher delivers the ball underarm. **2.** the ball itself.

**soft-boiled** /'sɒft-bɔɪld/, *adj.* (of an egg) lightly boiled so that the yoke remains unset.

**soft breathing** /sɒft 'briðɪŋ/, *n.* →**smooth breathing.**

**soft coal** /'– koʊl/, *n.* →**bituminous coal.**

**soft-core pornography** /ˌsɒft-kɔ pɔ'nɒgrəfi/, *n.* pornography in which erotic activity is not explicitly presented (opposed to *hard-core pornography*).

**softcover** /'sɒftkʌvə/, *n., adj.* →**paperback.**

**soft drink** /'sɒft drɪŋk/, *n.* a drink which is not alcoholic or intoxicating, as ginger beer, lemonade, etc.

**soften** /'sɒfən/, *v.t.* **1.** to make soft or softer. *–v.i.* **2.** to become soft or softer. – **softener,** *n.*

**softening of the brain,** *n.* **1.** a softening of the cerebral tissues, which are transformed into a mushy, fatlike substance. **2.** *Obs.* dementia associated with general paresis. **3.** any observed or alleged diminution of intellectual power.

**soft-finned** /'sɒft-fɪnd/, *adj.* (of fish) having fins supported by articulated rays rather than by spines, as a malacopterygian (contrasted with *spiny-finned*).

**soft furnishings** /sɒft 'fɜnəʃɪŋz/, *n.pl.* materials used for interior decoration, as for curtains and chair covers.

**soft goods** /'– gʊdz/, *n.pl.* merchandise as textiles, furnishings, etc.

**softgrass** /'sɒftgras/, *n.* →**Yorkshire fog.**

**soft hail** /sɒft 'heɪl/, *n.* hail comprising easily compressible, crisp, opaque pellets of ice; graupel.

**soft-headed** /ˈsɒft-hɛdəd/, *adj.* foolish; stupid. – **soft-headedness,** *n.*

**soft-hearted** /ˈsɒft-hatəd/, *adj.* very generous or sympathetic. – **soft-heartedness,** *n.*

**softie** /ˈsɒfti/, *n. Colloq.* **1.** a generous or soft-hearted person. **2.** one who is easily duped. **3.** one (esp. a man) who is not as brave or hardy as others consider proper. Also, **softy.**

**soft landing** /ˈsɒft lændɪŋ/, *n.* a landing by a spacecraft on the moon or some other celestial body which is so gentle that no injury is caused to equipment or crew. Cf. **hard landing.**

**soft palate** /– ˈpælət/, *n.* →**palate.**

**soft pedal** /ˈ– pɛdl/, *n.* a pedal, as on a piano, for lessening the volume.

**soft-pedal** /sɒft-ˈpɛdl/, *v.,* **-alled, -alling** or (*U.S.*) **-aled, -aling.** *–v.i.* **1.** to use the soft pedal. **2.** *Colloq.* to make concessions or be conciliatory, as in an argument. *–v.t.* **3.** to soften the sound of by means of the soft pedal. **4.** *Colloq.* to tone down; make less strong, uncompromising, noticeable, or the like.

**soft rock** /sɒft ˈrɒk/, *n.* a form of rock music which is related to folk music in its use of the style of playing associated with the acoustic guitar and of lyrical melody.

**soft rot** /– ˈrɒt/, *n.* any plant disease caused by bacteria or fungi resulting in a marked softening of the tissue, esp. that due to the bacterium *Erwinia carotovora.*

**soft sell** /ˈ– sɛl/, *n.* a method of advertising or selling which is quietly persuasive, subtle, and indirect. See **hard sell.**

**soft-shelled crab** /ˌsɒft-ʃɛld ˈkræb/, *n.* the common edible crab, *Cancer pagurus,* recently moulted and therefore in a suitable state to be cooked and eaten in its entirety.

**soft-shelled turtle** /– ˈtɜtl/, *n.* any of various turtles of the family Trionychiadae, having a leathery shell overlying the bony carapace and plastron, instead of the usual one of horny plates. See **leatherback.**

**soft-shoe** /ˈsɒft-ʃu/, *adj.* of or pertaining to tap-dancing done in shoes with soft soles without metal taps: *soft-shoe shuffle.*

**soft shower** /sɒft ˈʃauə/, *n.* →**cascade shower.**

**soft soap** /– ˈsoup/, *n.* **1.** the semifluid soap produced when potassium hydroxide is used in the saponification of a fat or an oil. **2.** *Colloq.* smooth words; flattery.

**soft-soap** /ˈsɒft-soup/, *v.t.* **1.** to apply soft soap to. **2.** *Colloq.* to ply with smooth words; cajole; flatter. *–v.i.* **3.** to use soft soap in washing. – **soft-soaper,** *n.*

**soft-spoken** /ˈsɒft-spoukən/, *adj.* **1.** (of persons) speaking with a soft or gentle voice; mild. **2.** (of words) softly or mildly spoken; persuasive.

**software** /ˈsɒftwɛə/, *n.* a collection of computer programs which is normally provided along with a computer, enabling it to be used efficiently.

**softwood** /ˈsɒftwud/, *n.* **1.** any wood which is relatively soft or easily cut. **2.** a tree yielding such a wood. **3.** *Forestry.* a coniferous tree or its wood.

**softy** /ˈsɒfti/, *n. Colloq.* →**softie.**

**soggy** /ˈsɒgi/, *adj.,* **-gier, -giest.** **1.** soaked; thoroughly wet. **2.** damp and heavy, as ill-baked bread. **3.** spiritless, dull, or stupid. [Brit. d. *sog* bog Cf. d. Norw. *soggjast* get soaked] – **soggily,** *adv.* – **sogginess,** *n.*

**soh** /sou/, *n.* (in solfa) the syllable used for the fifth note of the scale. See **solfa.**

**soi-disant** /swa-diˈzɒ̃/, *adj.* **1.** calling oneself thus; self-styled: *a soi-disant marquess.* **2.** so-called or pretended: *a soi-disant science.* [F]

**soignée** /ˈswanjeɪ/, *adj.* **1.** carefully done. **2.** well groomed. [F *soignée* (fem.), *soigné* (mase.) *adj.*]

**soil¹** /sɔɪl/, *n.* **1.** that portion of the earth's surface in which plants grow; a well-developed system of inorganic and organic material and of living organisms. **2.** a particular kind of earth: *sandy soil.* **3.** the ground as producing vegetation or cultivated for its crops: *fertile soil.* **4.** a country, land, or region: *on foreign soil.* **5.** the ground or earth. [ME *soyle,* from AF *soyl,* from L *solium* seat, confused with *solum* ground]

**soil²** /sɔɪl/, *v.t.* **1.** to make dirty or foul, esp. on the surface: *to soil one's clothes.* **2.** to smirch, smudge, or stain. **3.** to sully or tarnish, as with disgrace; defile morally, as with sin. *–v.i.* **4.** to become soiled. *–n.* **5.** the act of soiling. **6.** the fact or state of being soiled. **7.** a spot, mark or stain due to soiling. **8.** dirty or foul matter; filth; sewage. **9.** ordure; manure or compost. [ME *soilen,* from OF *suill(i)er, soill(i)er,* from *souille* pigsty, from L *sus* pig]

**soil³** /sɔɪl/, *v.t.* **1.** to feed (cattle, etc.) on freshly cut green fodder, for fattening. **2.** to feed (horses, cattle, etc.) on green food, for purging. [orig. uncert.]

**soilage** /ˈsɔɪlɪdʒ/, *n.* freshly cut green fodder for animals kept in a confined area.

**soil creep** /ˈsɔɪl krip/, *n.* slow, almost imperceptible, downslope movement of soil under the influence of gravity.

**soil mechanics** /ˈ– məkænɪks/, *n.* the science of the study of soils and their behaviour.

**soil pipe** /ˈ– paɪp/, *n.* a pipe carrying liquid wastes from all fixtures, including water closets. Cf. **wastepipe.**

**soiree** /swaˈreɪ, ˈswareɪ/, *n.* an evening party or social gathering, often for a particular purpose: *a musical soiree.* Also, **soirée.** [F, from *soir* evening, from L *sērō* late, adv., from *sērus* late]

**soixante-neuf** /ˌswʌzɒnt-ˈnɜf/, *n.* simultaneous fellatio and cunnilinctus. [F: sixty-nine, from the position of two people engaged in this practice, resembling the figures 69. The French term is *six-à-neuf*]

**sojourn** /ˈsoudʒɜn, ˈsɒdʒɜn, ˈsʌdʒ-, -ən/, *v.i.* **1.** to dwell for a time in a place; make a temporary stay. *–n.* **2.** a temporary stay. [ME *sojurne,* from OF *sojorner,* from *so-* (from L *sub-* SUB-) + *jorn* day (from L *diurnum* daily)] – **sojourner,** *n.*

**sol¹** /sɒl/, *n.* (in solfège) the syllable used for the fifth note of a scale. See **solfège.** [ME, from L. See GAMUT]

**sol²** /sɒl/, *n.* a colloidal suspension of a solid in a liquid. [abstracted from (HYDRO)SOL]

**sol.,** **1.** soluble. **2.** solution.

**sola¹** /ˈsoulə/, *adj.* feminine of **solus.**

**sola²** /ˈsoulə/, *n.* **1.** an Indian pithy-stemmed plant, *Aeschynomene aspera.* **2.** its pith, used for making topees.

**solace** /ˈsɒləs/, *n., v.,* **-aced, -acing.** *–n.* **1.** comfort in sorrow or trouble; alleviation of distress or discomfort. **2.** something that gives comfort, consolation, or relief. *–v.t.* **3.** to comfort, console, or cheer (a person, oneself, the heart, etc.). **4.** to alleviate or relieve (sorrow, distress, etc.). [ME *solas,* from OF, from L *solācium*] – **solacement,** *n.* – **solacer,** *n.*

**solan** /ˈsoulən/, *n.* the gannet. Also, **solan goose.** [ME *soland,* from Scand.; cf. Icel. *sūla* gannet, Dan. *and* duck]

**solander** /səˈlændə/, *n.* a box, esp. one for botanical specimens, made in the form of a book, the front cover being the lid. [named after its inventor, D. C. *Solander,* 1736-82, Swedish botanist]

**solanine** /ˈsɒlənin/, *n.* the poisonous alkaloid present in immature fruit of the *Solanum* genus.

**solanum** /souˈleɪnəm/, *n.* any plant of the genus *Solanum,* which comprises gamopetalous herbs, shrubs, and small trees, including the nightshades, aubergine, common potato, etc. [L: nightshade]

**solar** /ˈsoulə/, *adj.* **1.** of or pertaining to the sun: *solar phenomena.* **2.** determined by the sun: *solar hour.* **3.** proceeding from the sun, as light or heat. **4.** operating by the light or heat of the sun, as a mechanism. **5.** indicating time by means of or with reference to the sun: *a solar chronometer.* **6.** *Astrol.* subject to the influence of the sun. *–n.* **7.** any room, esp. a large room or one on an upper storey, for family use in a large house or castle. [L *sōlāris*] – **solarian,** *adj.*

**solar apex** /soulər ˈeɪpɛks/, *n.* the point on the celestial sphere towards which the solar system is moving, relative to the stars.

**solar battery** /soulə ˈbætri/, *n.* a battery containing solar cells, usu. mounted in panels. Also, **solar paddle.**

**solar cell** /– ˈsɛl/, *n.* a photovoltaic cell that converts sunlight directly into electrical energy.

**solar constant** /– ˈkɒnstənt/, *n.* the average rate at which energy from the sun would be received by one sq. cm of the earth's surface in the absence of the atmosphere, assuming that the incident radiation is normal to the surface and that the earth is at its mean distance from the sun; equal to approximately 14 000 joule per second per square metre.

**solar day** /– ˈdeɪ/, *n.* See **day** (def. 3c).

**solar energy** /soulər 'ɛnədʒi/, *n.* energy derived from the sun, as for home heating, industrial use, etc.

**solar flare** /– 'flɛə/, *n.* a short-lived, high-temperature outburst, seen as a bright area in the sun's atmosphere.

**solar furnace** /– 'fɜnəs/, *n.* a furnace using sunlight as the direct source of heat.

**solarimeter** /soulə'rɪmətə/, *n.* a device for measuring solar radiation.

**solarise** /'souləraɪz/, *v.,* **-rised, -rising.** *–v.t.* **1.** *Photog.* to produce partial reversal in, as from a negative to a positive image, by exposure to light during development. **2.** to affect by sunlight. *–v.i.* **3.** *Photog.* to become injured by over-exposure. Also, **solarize.** – **solarisation** /ˌsouləraɪ'zeɪʃən/, *n.*

**solarism** /'soulərɪzəm/, *n.* the interpretation of myths by reference to the sun, esp. such interpretation carried to an extreme. – **solarist,** *n.*

**solarium** /sə'lɛəriəm/, *n., pl.* **-laria** /-'lɛəriə/. **1.** a room, gallery, or the like, exposed to the sun's rays, as at a seaside hotel or, for convalescents, in a hospital. **2.** a room in which one takes treatment under a sunlamp. [L]

**solar keratosis** /ˌsoulə kɛrə'tousəs/, *n.* keratosis caused by prolonged exposure of skin to the rays of the sun.

**solar month** /soulə 'mʌnθ/, *n.* See **month** (def. 1).

**solar paddle** /– 'pædl/, *n.* →**solar battery.**

**solar parallax** /– 'pærəlæks/, *n.* the angle subtended by the mean equatorial radius of the earth at a distance of one astronomical unit.

**solar plexus** /– 'plɛksəs/, *n.* **1.** *Anat.* a network of nerves situated at the upper part of the abdomen, behind the stomach and in front of the aorta. **2.** *Colloq.* a point on the stomach wall, just below the sternum, where a blow will affect this nerve centre.

**solar salt** /– 'sɒlt/, *n.* salt obtained by evaporation of seawater or other brine in the sun.

**solar system** /'– sɪstəm/, *n.* the sun together with all the planets, satellites, asteroids, etc., revolving around it.

**solar wind** /– 'wɪnd/, *n.* the streams of ionised atoms (esp. hydrogen) or electrons constantly emanating from the sun.

**solar year** /– 'jɪə/, *n.* See **year** (def. 5).

**sold** /sould/, *v.* past tense and past participle of **sell.**

**solder** /'sɒldə/, *n.* **1.** any of various fusible alloys, some (**soft solders**) fusing readily, and others (**hard solders**) fusing only at red heat, applied in a melted state to metal surfaces, joints, etc., to unite them. **2.** anything that joins or unites. *–v.t.* **3.** to unite with solder or some other substance or device. **4.** to join closely and intimately. **5.** to mend; repair; patch up. *–v.i.* **6.** to unite things with solder. **7.** to become soldered or become united; grow together. [ME *soudur,* from OF *soldure,* from *solder* to solder, from L *solidāre* make firm] – **solderer,** *n.*

**soldering-iron** /'sɒldərɪŋ-aɪən/, *n.* a tool used for soldering.

**soldier** /'souldʒə/, *n.* **1.** one who serves in an army for pay; one engaged in military service. **2.** one of the rank and file in such service, sometimes including non-commissioned officers. **3.** a man of military skill or experience. **4.** one who contends or serves in any cause. **5.** *Zool.* (in certain ants and termites) an individual with powerful jaws or other device for protecting the colony. *–v.i.* **6.** to act or serve as a soldier. **7. soldier on,** to continue, persist. [ME *souldeour,* from OF, from *soulde* pay, from L *solidus.* See SOL[2]] – **soldiership,** *n.*

**soldier ant** /'souldʒər ænt/, *n.* one of the ants in a colony whose function is to defend the nest.

**soldier beetle** /'souldʒə bitl/, *n.* any of various elongated, soft-bodied, brightly-coloured beetles of the family Cantharidae, as *Cantharis lugubris,* whose larvae prey upon the larvae of codling moths.

**soldier bird** /'– bɜd/, *n.* →**noisy miner.**

**soldier crab** /'– kræb/, *n.* a small pale blue Australian estuarine crab of genus *Mictyris,* which assembles in large numbers and gives the impression of soldiers drilling and manoeuvring in formation.

**soldierlike** /'souldʒəlaɪk/, *adj.* **1.** having the character, appearance, etc., of a soldier. **2.** soldierly.

**soldierly** /'souldʒəli/, *adj.* of, like, or befitting a soldier.

**soldier of fortune,** *n.* **1.** a man whose life is principally shaped by an opportunist response to chance encounters and events. **2.** a mercenary.

**soldier settlement** /souldʒə 'sɛtlmənt/, *n.* a scheme whereby soldiers were allotted blocks of land, esp. previously unsettled land, on their return from war. – **soldier settler,** *n.*

**soldiery** /'souldʒəri/, *n., pl.* **-ries. 1.** soldiers collectively. **2.** a body of soldiers. **3.** military training.

**sole**[1] /soul/, *adj.* **1.** being the only one or ones; only. **2.** being the only one of the kind; unique. **3.** belonging or pertaining to one individual or group to the exclusion of all others; exclusive: *the sole right to a thing.* **4.** functioning automatically or with independent power. [L *sōlus* alone; replacing ME *soul(e),* from OF]

**sole**[2] /soul/, *n., v.,* **soled, soling.** *–n.* **1.** the bottom or under surface of the foot. **2.** the corresponding under part of a shoe, boot, or the like, or this part exclusive of the heel. **3.** a separate, shaped piece of material fitted into a shoe at the bottom. **4.** the bottom, under surface, or lower part of anything. [ME and OE, from L *solea* sandal, shoe] – **soled,** *adj.*

**sole**[3] /soul/, *n., pl.* **soles,** (*esp. collectively*) **sole. 1.** any flatfish of the families Soleidae and Cynoglossidae, with a hooklike snout. **2.** any of several other flatfishes used as food, especially when filleted. [ME, from F, from L *solea.* See SOLE[2]]

**solecism** /'sɒləsɪzəm/, *n.* **1.** a substandard intrusion into standard speech, as 'they was'. **2.** a breach of good manners or etiquette. **3.** any error, impropriety, or inconsistency. [L *soloecismus,* from Gk *soloikismós* incorrectness of speech] – **solecistic** /sɒlə'sɪstɪk/, *adj.*

**solely** /'souli, 'soulli/, *adv.* **1.** as the only one or ones: *solely responsible.* **2.** exclusively or only: *plants found solely in the tropics.* **3.** wholly; merely.

**solemn** /'sɒləm/, *adj.* **1.** grave, sober, or mirthless, as a person, the face, speech, tone, mood, etc. **2.** gravely or sombrely impressive; such as to cause serious thoughts or a grave mood: *solemn music.* **3.** serious or earnest: *solemn assurances.* **4.** characterised by dignified or serious formality, as proceedings; of a formal or ceremonious character. **5.** made in due legal or other express form, as a declaration, agreement, etc. **6.** marked or observed with religious rites; having a religious character. **7.** made according to religious forms. [ME *solempne,* from L *sōlempnis*] – **solemnly,** *adv.* – **solemness,** *n.*

**solemnify** /sə'lɛmnəfaɪ/, *v.t.,* **-fied, -fying.** to make solemn or serious, esp. a ceremony. – **solemnification** /səlɛmnəfə'keɪʃən/, *n.*

**solemnise** /'sɒləmnaɪz/, *v.t.,* **-nised, -nising. 1.** to observe or commemorate with rites or ceremonies. **2.** to hold or perform (ceremonies, etc.) in due manner. **3.** to perform the ceremony of (marriage). **4.** to go through with ceremony or formality. **5.** to render solemn, serious or grave. Also, **solemnize.** – **solemnisation** /ˌsɒləmnaɪ'zeɪʃən/, *n.* – **solemniser,** *n.*

**solemnity** /sə'lɛmnəti/, *n., pl.* **-ties. 1.** the state or character of being solemn; earnestness; gravity; impressiveness. **2.** (*oft. pl.*) a solemn observance, ceremonial proceeding, or special formality. **3.** observance of rites or ceremonies, esp. a formal, solemn, ecclesiastical observance, as of a feast day. [ME *solempnete,* from L *sōlempnitas*]

**solenodon** /sə'lɛnədən/, *n.* a rare insectivore, *Atopogale cubana,* about the size of a rat, now confined to Cuba and Haiti. [NL, from Gk *sōlḗn* pipe + *odṓn* (Ionic) tooth]

**solenoid** /'sɒlənɔɪd/, *n.* an electrical conductor wound as a helix with a small pitch, or as two or more coaxial helices, a current passing through which establishes a magnetic field usu. so as to activate a metal bar within the helix and so perform some mechanical task. [Gk *sōlḗn* channel, pipe, shellfish + -OID] – **solenoidal** /soulə'nɔɪdəl/, *adj.* – **solenoidally** /soulə'nɔɪdəli/, *adv.*

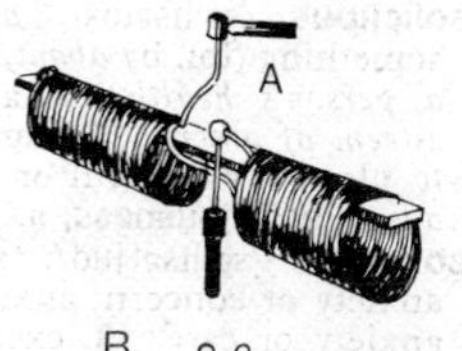

A, solenoid with both ends returned to the middle; B, diagram of A

**solero sherry** /səˌlɛərou 'ʃɛri/, *n.* sherry blended by the solero system.

**solero system** /ˈ– sɪstəm/, *n.* a method of blending sherry in which casks are banked in tiers. Young wine enters the top tier and progresses down, blending with the more mature wine in the lower tiers. [Sp. *solera* mother liquor, from *suelo* dregs, from L *solum* ground, base]

**solfa** /sɒlˈfa/, *n., v.,* **-faed, -faing.** *–n.* **1.** *Music.* the set of syllables *doh, ray, me, fah, soh, lah* and *te,* used to represent the notes of the scale. **2.** the system of singing notes to these syllables. *–v.i.* **3.** to use the solfa syllables in singing, or to sing these syllables. *–v.t.* **4.** to sing to the solfa syllables, as a tune. Cf. →**solfège.** [SOL[1] + FA. See GAMUT] – **solfaist,** *n.*

**solfatara** /sɒlfəˈtarə/, *n.* a volcanic vent or area which gives off only sulphurous gases, steam, and the like. [It. (Neapolitan), from *solfo,* from L *sulfur* SULPHUR] – **solfataric,** *adj.*

**solfège** /sɒlˈfeɪʒ, -ˈfɛʒ/, *n. Music* **1.** the set of syllables *do, re, mi, fa, sol, la and si,* used to represent the notes of the scale. **2.** the system of singing notes to these syllables. Cf. **solfa.**

**solfeggio** /sɒlˈfɛdʒioʊ/, *n., pl.* **-feggi** /-ˈfɛdʒi/, **-feggios.** →**solfège.** [It., from *sol, fa.* See SOLFA]

**solferino** /sɒlfəˈrinoʊ/, *n.* **1.** a dye obtained from rosaniline. **2.** vivid purplish pink. [named after *Solferino,* village in Italy where a battle was fought in 1859, the year of the dye's introduction]

**soli-**[1], a word element meaning 'alone', 'solitary', as in *solifidian.* [L, combining form of *solus*]

**soli-**[2], a word element meaning 'sun'. [L, combining form of *sōl*]

**solicit** /səˈlɪsət/, *v.t.* **1.** to seek for by entreaty, earnest or respectful request, formal application, etc.: *to solicit contributions.* **2.** to entreat or petition (a person, etc.) for something or to do something; urge; importune. **3.** to seek to influence or incite to action, esp. unlawful or wrong action. **4.** to accost (another) with immoral intention, as a prostitute. *–v.i.* **5.** to make petition or request, as for something desired. **6.** to accost another with immoral intention. **7.** to endeavour to obtain orders or trade, as for a business house. [ME, from L *sōlicitāre* disturb, incite]

**solicitation** /səlɪsəˈteɪʃən/, *n.* **1.** the act of soliciting. **2.** entreaty, urging, or importunity; a petition or request. **3.** enticement or allurement. **4.** *Law.* **a.** the crime of asking another to commit or to aid in a crime. **b.** loitering and importuning passers-by for the purpose of prostitution.

**solicitor** /səˈlɪsətə/, *n.* **1.** one who solicits. **2.** a member of that branch of the legal profession whose services consist of advising clients, representing them before the lower courts, and preparing cases for barristers to try in the higher courts. **3.** *U.S.* an officer having charge of the legal business of a city, town, etc.

**solicitor-general** /səlɪsətə-ˈdʒɛnrəl/, *n., pl.* **solicitors-general, solicitor-generals.** usu. the second legal officer of the government whose principal functions are to appear on behalf of the government in litigation to which the government is a party and to offer such legal advice to the government as is requested by the attorney-general.

**solicitous** /səˈlɪsətəs/, *adj.* **1.** anxious or concerned over something (fol. by *about, for,* etc., or a clause): *solicitous about a person's health.* **2.** anxiously desirous: *solicitous of the esteem of others.* **3.** eager (fol. by infinitive): *to be solicitous to please.* **4.** careful or particular. [L *sōlicitus*] – **solicitously,** *adv.* – **solicitousness,** *n.*

**solicitude** /səˈlɪsətjud/, *n.* **1.** the state of being solicitous; anxiety or concern; anxious desire or care. **2.** (*pl.*) causes of anxiety or care. **3.** excessive anxiety or assistance. [L *sōlicitūdo*]

**solid** /ˈsɒləd/, *adj.* **1.** having three dimensions (length, breadth, and thickness), as a geometrical body or figure. **2.** of or pertaining to bodies or figures of three dimensions: *solid geometry.* **3.** having the interior completely filled up, free from cavities, or not hollow: *a solid ball of matter.* **4.** without openings or breaks: *a solid wall.* **5.** firm, hard, or compact in substance: *solid ground.* **6.** having relative firmness, coherence of particles, or persistence of form, as matter that is not liquid or gaseous: *solid particles floating in a liquid.* **7.** pertaining to such matter: *ice is water in a solid state.* **8.** dense, thick, or heavy in nature or appearance: *solid masses of cloud.* **9.** substantial, or not flimsy, slight, or light, as buildings, furniture, fabrics, food, etc. **10.** of a substantial character; not superficial, trifling, or frivolous: *solid learning.* **11.** undivided or continuous: *a solid row of buildings.* **12.** whole or entire: *one solid hour.* **13.** forming the whole; being the only substance or material: *solid gold.* **14.** uniform in tone or shade, as a colour. **15.** real or genuine: *solid comfort.* **16.** sound or good, as reasons, arguments, etc. **17.** sober-minded or sensible. **18.** financially sound or strong. **19.** *Obs.* cubic: *a solid foot contains 1728 solid inches.* **20.** having the lines not separated by leads, or having few open spaces, as type or printing. **21.** thorough, vigorous, great, big, etc. (with emphatic force, often after *good*): *a good solid blow.* **22.** firmly united or consolidated: *a solid combination.* **23.** united in opinion, policy, etc., or unanimous. **24.** *Colloq.* on a friendly, favourable, or advantageous footing. **25. a bit solid,** *Colloq.* unreasonable; harsh; severe. *–n.* **26.** a body or magnitude having three dimensions (length, breadth, and thickness). **27.** a solid substance or body; a substance exhibiting rigidity. **28.** (*pl.*) food that is not in liquid form. **29.** an opal which has been cut and polished but not modified in any other way (opposed to *doublet, triplet*). [ME, from L *solidus*] – **solidly,** *adv.* – **solidness,** *n.*

**solidago** /sɒləˈdeɪgoʊ/, *n., pl.* **-gos.** any plant of the genus *Solidago,* mostly native to North America; a goldenrod. [NL, special use of ML *solidago* comfrey, from L *solidus* SOLID]

**solid angle** /ˈsɒləd æŋgəl/, *n.* an angle formed by three or more planes intersecting in a common point or at the vertex of a cone; the supplementary SI unit of solid angle is the steradian.

**solidarity** /sɒləˈdærəti/, *n., pl.* **-ties.** **1.** solidary character or relation. **2.** union or fellowship arising from common responsibilities and interests, as between members of a group or between classes, peoples, etc. **3.** community of interests, feelings, purposes, etc. [F *solidarité,* from *solidaire,* from L *solidus* solid]

**solidary** /ˈsɒlədri/, *adj.* characterised by or involving responsibilities and interests in common.

**solid geology** /ˌsɒləd dʒiˈɒlədʒi/, *n.* the geological features of a district without the regolith.

**solid geometry** /– dʒiˈɒmətri/, *n.* the geometry of solid figures; geometry of three dimensions.

**solidify** /səˈlɪdəfaɪ/, *v.,* **-fied, -fying.** *–v.t.* **1.** to make solid; make into a hard or compact mass; change from a liquid or gaseous to a solid form. **2.** to unite firmly or consolidate. **3.** to form into crystals. *–v.i.* **4.** to become solid. **5.** to form into crystals. [see SOLID, -(I)FY] – **solidification** /səlɪdəfəˈkeɪʃən/, *n.*

**solidity** /səˈlɪdəti/, *n., pl.* **-ties.** **1.** the state, property, or quality of being solid. **2.** substantialness. **3.** strength of mind, character, finances, etc.

**solid of revolution,** *n.* a solid generated by revolving a plane area about a line.

**solid propellant** /sɒləd prəˈpɛlənt/, *n.* a rocket propellant in solid form, usu. a mixture of fuel and oxidant.

**solid solution** /– səˈluʃən/, *n.* **1.** a solid homogeneous mixture of two or more substances, as some alloys, glasses, etc. **2.** *Chem.* a mixed crystal of two or more isomorphous substances.

**solid-state** /ˈsɒləd-steɪt/, *adj.* **1.** *Physics.* of or pertaining to the structure and properties of solids. **2.** *Electronics.* of or pertaining to electronic devices which are composed of components in the solid state as transistors, semiconductor diodes, integrated circuits, etc.

**solid-state lamp** /ˌsɒləd-steɪt ˈlæmp/, *n.* →**light-emitting diode.**

**solidus** /ˈsɒlədəs/, *n., pl.* **-di** /-daɪ/. **1.** a Roman gold coin introduced by Constantine, which continued under the Byzantine Empire and received in western Europe the name bezant. Cf. **bezant** (def. 1). **2.** (in medieval Europe) a money of account valued at 12 denarii. **3.** the shilling mark, a sloping line [/] representing the old long form of the letter s (abbreviation of solidus) generally used as a dividing line, as in dates, fractions, etc.; diagonal. [LL. See SOL[2]]

**solifidian** /sɒləˈfɪdiən/, *n.* one who maintains that religious faith alone, without works, is all that is necessary for justification. [SOLI-[1] + L *fid(es)* faith + -IAN]

**solifluction** /ˈsɒləflʌkʃən/, *n.* **1.** slow, downward, movement of rock debris or soil saturated with melt-water over permanently frozen subsoil in tundra regions. **2.** →**soil creep.** **3.** down-slope movement of soil, faster than soil creep. Also, **solifluxion.**

**soliloquise** /səˈlɪləkwaɪz/, *v.*, **-quised, -quising.** *–v.t.* **1.** to utter a soliloquy; talk to oneself. *–v.t.* **2.** to utter in a soliloquy; say to oneself. Also, **soliloquize.** – **soliloquist, soliloquiser,** *n.* – **soliloquisingly,** *adv.*

**soliloquy** /səˈlɪləkwi/, *n., pl.* **-quies.** the act of talking when alone or as if alone; an utterance or discourse by one who is talking to himself or is regardless of any hearers present. [LL *sōliloquium*]

**solipsism** /ˈsɒləpsɪzəm/, *n.* the theory that the self is the only object of verifiable knowledge, or that nothing but the self exists. [SOL(I)-[1] + L *ips(e)* self + -ISM] – **solipsist,** *n.*

**solitaire**[1] /ˈsɒlətɛə/, *n.* **1.** a game played by one person alone, as a game played with marbles or pegs on a board having hollows or holes. **2.** *U.S.* →**patience** (def. 4). **3.** a precious stone, esp. a diamond, set by itself, as in a ring. [F, from L *sōlitārius* alone]

**solitaire**[2] /ˈsɒlətɛə/, *n.* an extinct flightless bird, *Pezohaps solitaria,* related to and resembling the dodo, and formerly found on the island of Rodriguez in the Indian Ocean.

**solitary** /ˈsɒlətri/, *adj., n., pl.* **-ries.** *–adj.* **1.** quite alone; without companions; unattended. **2.** living alone; avoiding the society of others. **3.** alone by itself. **4.** characterised by the absence of companions: *solitary confinement.* **5.** done without assistance or accompaniment; done in solitude. **6.** being the only one or ones: *a solitary exception.* **7.** characterised by solitude, as a place; unfrequented, secluded, or lonely. **8.** *Zool.* not social, as certain wasps. *–n.* **9.** one who lives alone or in solitude, or avoids the society of others. **10.** one who lives in solitude from religious motives. **11.** *Colloq.* solitary confinement. [ME, from L *sōlitārius*] – **solitarily,** *adv.* – **solitariness,** *n.*

**solitude** /ˈsɒlətjud/, *n.* **1.** the state of being or living alone; seclusion. **2.** remoteness from habitations, as of a place; absence of human life or activity. **3.** a lonely, unfrequented place. [ME, from L *sōlitūdo*]

**solleret** /sɒləˈrɛt/, *n.* flexible armour for the foot, made of overlapping plates. [OF *soleret,* diminutive of *soler* shoe, from LL *subtel* arch of foot]

solleret

**sollicker** /ˈsɒlɪkə/, *adj. Colloq.* anything or anyone remarkably big, good, great, etc. [orig. uncert.] – **sollicking,** *adj.*

**solmisation** /sɒlməˈzeɪʃən/, *n.* the act, process, or system of using certain syllables, esp. the solfa syllables, to represent the notes of the scale. Also, **solmization.** [F *solmisation,* from *solmiser,* from *sol* SOL[1] + *mi* MI]

**solo** /ˈsoʊloʊ/, *n., pl.* **-los, -li** /-li/ *adj., adv.* *–n.* **1.** a musical composition performed by or intended for one singer or player, with or without accompaniment. **2.** any performance, as a dance, by one person. **3.** a flight in an aeroplane during which the aviator is unaccompanied by an instructor or other person. **4.** *Cards.* any of certain games in which one person plays alone against others. **5.** a motorcycle without a sidecar. *–adj.* **6.** *Music.* performing alone, as an instrument or its player. **7.** performed alone; not combined with other parts of equal importance; not concerted. **8.** alone; without a companion or partner: *a solo flight in an aeroplane.* *–adv.* **9.** alone: *he made his first flight solo.* **10. go solo,** of a musician, to leave a group and embark upon a solo career. [It., from L *sōlus* alone]

**soloist** /ˈsoʊloʊəst/, *n.* one who performs a solo or solos.

**Solomon's-seal** /sɒləmənz-ˈsil/, *n.* any of various plants of the genus *Polygonatum,* with a thick rootstock bearing seal-like scars.

**Solon** /ˈsoʊlɒn/, *n.* a wise lawgiver. [from *Solon, c.* 638 - *c.* 558 B.C., a statesman noted for his political reforms and his wisdom]

**so long** /soʊ ˈlɒŋ/, *interj. Colloq.* goodbye.

**solstice** /ˈsɒlstəs/, *n.* **1.** *Astron.* either of the two times in the year when the sun is at its greatest distance from the celestial equator and apparently does not move either north or south about June 21st when it enters the sign of Cancer, and about December 22nd, when it enters the sign of Capricorn (called respectively, in the Southern Hemisphere, *winter solstice* and *summer solstice*). **2.** either of the two points in the ecliptic farthest from the equator. **3.** a farthest or culminating point; a turning point. [ME, from OF, from L *sōlstitium*]

**solstitial** /sɒlˈstɪʃəl/, *adj.* **1.** of or pertaining to a solstice or the solstices: *a solstitial point.* **2.** occurring at or about the time of a solstice. **3.** characteristic of the summer solstice. [L *sōlstitiālis*]

**solubility** /sɒljəˈbɪləti/, *n., pl.* **-ties.** **1.** the quality or property of being capable of being dissolved; relative capability of being dissolved. **2.** the extent to which a solute will dissolve in a solvent, usu. expressed in grams of solute per 100 grams of solvent, at a specified temperature.

**soluble** /ˈsɒljəbəl/, *adj.* **1.** capable of being dissolved or liquefied. **2.** capable of being solved or explained. [ME, from L *solūbilis*] – **solubleness,** *n.* – **solubly,** *adv.*

**soluble glass** /– ˈglas/, *n.* →**sodium silicate.**

**solus** /ˈsoʊləs/, *adj. masc.* alone; by oneself; used formerly in stage directions. [L] – **sola** /ˈsoʊlə/, *adj. fem.*

**solute** /ˈsɒljut/, *n.* **1.** the substance dissolved in a given solution. *–adj.* **2.** dissolved; in solution. **3.** *Bot.* not adhering; free. [L *solūtus* pp.]

**solution** /səˈluʃən/, *n.* **1.** the act of solving a problem, etc., or state of being solved. **2.** a particular instance or method of solving; an explanation or answer. **3.** *Maths.* **a.** the act of determining the answer to a problem. **b.** the answer. **4.** the act by which a gas, liquid, or solid is dispersed homogeneously in a gas, liquid, or solid without chemical change. **5.** the fact of being dissolved; dissolved state: *salt in solution.* **6.** a homogeneous molecular mixture of two or more substances. [ME *solucion,* from L *solūtio*]

**solvable** /ˈsɒlvəbəl/, *adj.* **1.** capable of being solved, as a problem. **2.** capable of being dissolved. – **solvability** /sɒlvəˈbɪləti/, **solvableness,** *n.*

**solvate** /ˈsɒlveɪt/, *n., v.,* **-vated, -vating.** *Chem. –n.* **1.** a substance formed by solvation. *–v.t.* **2.** to convert into a solvate.

**solvation** /sɒlˈveɪʃən/, *n.* the process of association or combination between solvent molecules and molecules or ions of the solute being dissolved.

**Solvay process** /ˈsɒlveɪ ˌproʊsɛs/, *n.* a process for manufacturing soda from sodium chloride (common salt). It consists essentially of saturating a concentrated solution of sodium chloride with ammonia, and passing carbon dioxide through it; the product of this reaction (sodium bicarbonate) is then calcined, and yields soda. [named after Ernest *Solvay,* 1838-1922, Belgian chemist]

**solve** /sɒlv/, *v.t.,* **solved, solving.** **1.** to clear up or explain; find the answer to. **2.** to work out the answer or solution to (a mathematical problem). [ME, from L *solvere* loosen, dissolve] – **solver,** *n.*

**solvency** /ˈsɒlvənsi/, *n., pl.* **-cies.** solvent condition; ability to pay all just debts.

**solvent** /ˈsɒlvənt/, *adj.* **1.** able to pay all just debts. **2.** having the power of dissolving; causing solution. *–n.* **3.** the component of a solution which dissolves the other component: *water is a solvent for sugar.* **4.** something that solves or explains. [L *solvens,* ppr., dissolving]

**soma** /ˈsoʊmə/, *n., pl.* **-mata** /-mətə/. the body of an organism as contrasted with its germ cells. [NL, from Gk: body]

**Somali** /səˈmali/, *n., pl.* **-li, lis.** **1.** a member of a Hamitic race dwelling in Somaliland and adjacent regions. **2.** a modern Cushitic language.

**Somalia** /səˈmaliə/, *n.* a republic on the east coast of Africa. Official name: **Somali Democratic Republic.**

**Somaliland** /səˈmalilænd/, *n.* a coastal region in eastern Africa, including French Somaliland, an overseas territory of France, Somalia, and part of Ethiopia.

**somatic** /soʊˈmætɪk/, *adj.* **1.** *Anat., Zool.* pertaining to the cavity of the body of an animal, or, more esp. to its walls. **2.** *Biol.* pertaining to the soma. **3.** of the body; bodily; physical.

[Gk *sōmatikós* of the body]

**somatic cell** /– 'sɛl/, *n.* one of the cells which take part in the formation of the body, becoming differentiated into the various tissues, organs, etc.

**somatology** /soumə'tɒlədʒi/, *n.* that branch of anthropology which deals with man's physical characteristics. [from *somato-* (combining form representing Gk *sôma* body) + -LOGY] – **somatological** /soumətə'lɒdʒɪkəl/, *adj.* – **somatologist** /soumə'tɒlədʒəst/, *n.*

**somatopleure** /'soumətəpluə, -plɜ/, *n.* the outer of the two layers into which the mesoderm of vertebrates splits, and which forms the body wall.

**sombre** /'sɒmbə/, *adj.* **1.** gloomily dark, shadowy, or dimly lit. **2.** dark and dull, as colour, or as things in respect to colour. **3.** gloomy, depressing, or dismal. Also, *U.S.,* **somber;** *Archaic,* **sombrous.** [Fr, from VL *subombrāre* to shade, from L *sub* under + *umbra* shade] – **sombrely,** *adv.* – **sombreness,** *n.*

**sombrero** /sɒm'brɛərou/, *n., pl.* **-ros.** a broad-brimmed hat, usu. of felt, worn in Spain, Mexico, the south-western U.S., etc. [Sp, from *sombra* shade, ? from L *umbra*]

sombrero

**some** /sʌm/; *weak form* /səm/, *adj.* **1.** being an undetermined or unspecified one: *some poor fellow.* **2.** certain (with plural nouns): *some friends of mine.* **3.** of a certain unspecified number, amount, degree, etc.: *some variation.* **4.** unspecified but considerable in number, amount, degree, etc.: *he was here some weeks.* **5.** (used with numerals and with words expressing extent, etc., to indicate an approximate amount): *some four or five of us.* **6.** *Colloq.* of considerable account or consequence; notable of the kind: *that was some storm.* –*pron.* **7.** certain persons, instances, etc., not specified: *some think he is dead.* **8.** an unspecified number, amount, etc., as distinguished from the rest. –*adv.* **9.** *Colloq.* to some degree or extent; somewhat. **10.** *U.S. Colloq.* to a great degree or extent; considerably: *that's going some!* [ME; OE *sum,* c. MLG and MHG *sum,* Icel. *sumr,* Goth. *sums*]

**-some**[1], suffix found in some adjectives showing esp. a tendency, as in *quarrelsome, burdensome.* [ME; OE *-sum,* akin to G *-sam*]

**-some**[2], collective suffix used with numerals, as in *twosome, threesome, foursome.* [special use of SOME]

**-some**[3], a word element meaning 'body', as in *chromosome.* [see SOMA]

**somebody** /'sʌmbɒdi, 'sʌmbədi/, *pron., n., pl.* **-bodies.** –*pron.* **1.** some person. –*n.* **2.** a person of some note or importance.

**some day** /'sʌm deɪ/, *adv.* at an indefinite future time.

**somehow** /'sʌmhau/, *adv.* **1.** in some way not specified, apparent, or known. **2. somehow or other,** in a way not as yet determined.

**someone** /'sʌmwʌn/, *pron., n.* somebody.

**somersault** /'sʌməsɔlt, -sɒlt/, *n.* **1.** an acrobatic movement of the body in which it describes a complete revolution, heels over head. **2.** a complete overturn or reversal, as of opinion. –*v.i.* **3.** to perform a somersault. **4.** *Prison Colloq.* to alter one's plea from guilty to not guilty. [OF *sombresaut,* from Pr. *sobresaut,* from *sobre* (from L *suprā*) above + *saut* (from L *saltus*) leap]

**something** /'sʌmθɪŋ/, *pron.* **1.** some thing; a certain undetermined or unspecified thing. –*n.* **2.** a thing or person of some value or consequence. –*adv.* **3.** in some degree; to some extent; somewhat.

**sometime** /'sʌmtaɪm/, *adv.* **1.** at some indefinite or indeterminate point of time: *he will arrive sometime next week.* **2.** at an indefinite future time: *come over sometime.* **3.** *Rare.* sometimes; on some occasions. **4.** at one time; formerly. **5.** *Obs.* on a certain occasion in the past. –*adj.* **6.** having been formerly; former: *sometime professor of history at Sydney.*

**sometimes** /'sʌmtaɪmz/, *adv.* **1.** on some occasions; at times; now and then. **2.** *Obs.* once; formerly.

**someway** /'sʌmweɪ/, *adv.* in some way; somehow.

**somewhat** /'sʌmwɒt/, *adv.* **1.** in some measure or degree; to some extent. –*n.* **2.** some part, portion, amount, etc.

**somewhere** /'sʌmwɛə/, *adv.* **1.** in or at some place not specified, determined, or known. **2.** to some place not specified or known. **3.** at or to some point in amount, degree, etc. (fol. by *about,* etc.): *he is somewhere about 60.* **4.** at some point of time (fol. by *about, between, in,* etc.): *this happened somewhere between 3 o'clock and 5 o'clock.* –*n.* **5.** an unspecified or uncertain place.

**somite** /'soumaɪt/, *n.* any of the longitudinal series of segments or parts into which the body of certain animals is divided; a metamere. [SOM(A) + -ITE[1]] – **somital** /'soumətl/, **somitic** /sou'mɪtɪk/, *adj.*

**somnambulate** /sɒm'næmbjəleɪt/, *v.,* **-lated, -lating.** –*v.i.* **1.** to walk during sleep, as a somnambulist does. –*v.t.* **2.** to traverse during sleep. [L *somnus* sleep + *ambulate* (from L *ambulātus,* pp., walked)] – **somnambulant** /sɒm'næmbjələnt/, *adj., n.* – **somnambulation** /sɒmˌnæmbjə'leɪʃən/, *n.* – **somnambulator** /sɒm'næmbjəleɪtə/, *n.*

**somnambulism** /sɒm'næmbjəlɪzəm/, *n.* the fact or habit of walking about, and often of performing various other acts, while asleep; sleepwalking. – **somnambulist** /sɒm'næmbjələst/, *n.* – **somnambulistic** /sɒmˌnæmbjə'lɪstɪk/, *adj.*

**somniferous** /sɒm'nɪfərəs/, *adj.* inducing sleep, as drugs, etc. [L *somnifer* sleep-bearing + -OUS]

**somnific** /sɒm'nɪfɪk/, *adj.* causing sleep; soporific; somniferous. [L *somnificus*]

**somniloquy** /sɒm'nɪləkwi/, *n.* the act or habit of talking while asleep. – **somniloquist,** *n.*

**somnolent** /'sɒmnələnt/, *adj.* **1.** sleepy; drowsy. **2.** tending to cause sleep. [late ME, from L *somnolentus*] – **somnolence, somnolency,** *n.* – **somnolently,** *adv.*

**son** /sʌn/, *n.* **1.** a male child or person in relation to his parents. **2.** one adopted as a son; one in the legal position of a son. **3.** any male descendant. **4.** a son-in-law. **5.** one related as if by ties of sonship. **6.** a male person looked upon as the product or result of particular agencies, forces, influences, etc.: *sons of liberty.* **7.** (a familiar term of address to a man or boy from an older person, an ecclesiastic, etc.) **8. the Son,** the second person of the Trinity; Jesus Christ. [ME *sone,* OE *sunu,* c. D *zoon,* G *Sohn,* Icel. *sunr, sonr,* Goth. *sunus*]

**sonagram** /'sɒnəgræm/, *n.* →**spectrogram.**

**sonagraph** /'sɒnəgræf, -graf/, *n.* an apparatus for making a sonagram. [Trademark]

**sonance** /'sounəns/, *n.* **1.** the condition or quality of being sonant. **2.** *Obs.* a sound; a tune.

**sonant** /'sounənt/, *adj.* **1.** sounding; having sound. **2.** *Phonet.* voiced. –*n.* **3.** *Phonet.* **a.** a speech sound which by itself makes a syllable or subordinates to itself the other sounds in the syllable; a syllabic sound (opposed to *consonant*). **b.** a voiced sound. **c.** (in Indo-European) a sonorant. [L *sonans,* ppr., sounding] – **sonantal** /sou'næntl/, *adj.*

**sonar** /'souna/, *n.* **1.** any device or method of echo ranging or echolocation involving underwater sonics. **2.** an echo sounder. Also, **SONAR.** [*so(und) n(avigation) a(nd) r(anging)*]

**sonata** /sə'natə/, *n.* an extended instrumental composition usu. in several (commonly three or four) movements in contrasted moods and keys, each movement being developed with a balanced form in mind. [It., fem. pp. of *sonare* sound; orig. a sounded (i.e. instrumental) composition as opposed to one sung]

**sonata form** /'– fɔm/, *n.* the formal exposition and development of contrasting themes in the first movement and sometimes later movements of a sonata or symphony.

**sonatina** /sɒnə'tinə/, *n., pl.* **-nas, -ne** /-neɪ/. a short or simplified sonata. [It., diminutive of *sonata* SONATA]

**sondage** /'sɒndɪdʒ/, *n.* a deep, narrow trench, showing the stratigraphy of a site.

**sonde** /sɒnd/, *n.* a rocket, balloon, or the like carrying equipment to a high altitude or in space. [F: plumbline, from Gmc; cf. SOUND[3]]

**son et lumière** /ˌsɒn eɪ lumi'ɛə/, *n.* a dramatic presentation staged at night in a building of historical interest, as a palace, castle, etc., and portraying by means of actors, music, and lighting effects, episodes in the history of the building and important events associated with it. [F: sound and light]

**song** /sɒŋ/, *n.* **1.** a short metrical composition combining words and music; a ballad; a lyric. **2.** a piece adapted for singing or simulating a piece to be sung: *Mendelssohn's 'Songs without Words'.* **3.** poetical composition; poetry. **4.** the act or art of singing; vocal music. **5.** that which is sung. **6.** the musical or tuneful sounds produced by certain birds, insects, etc. **7. for a song,** at a very low price. **8. make a song (and dance) about,** *Colloq.* to make a fuss about. [ME and OE, c. G *Sang,* Icel. *söngr*]

**song and dance,** *n. Colloq.* a fuss or commotion: *Bill kicked up a great song and dance about that.*

**songbird** /'sɒŋbɜd/, *n.* **1.** a bird that sings. **2.** any of the passerine birds of the suborder Oscines, which contains those with the most highly developed vocal organs. **3.** a woman who sings.

**song cycle** /'sɒŋ saɪkəl/, *n.* a series of songs unified by their subject or musical content.

**songful** /'sɒŋfəl/, *adj.* abounding in song; melodious.

**song lark** /'sɒŋ lak/, *n.* either of two warblers of the genus *Cinclorhamphus,* found generally throughout Australia and noted for their song.

**songless** /'sɒŋləs/, *adj.* devoid of song; lacking the power of song, as a bird.

**songster** /'sɒŋstə/, *n.* **1.** one who sings; a singer. **2.** a writer of songs or poems; a poet. **3.** a songbird. [ME; OE *sangestre,* c. D *zangster.* See SONG, -STER] – **songstress** /'sɒŋstrəs/, *n.fem.*

**songsticks** /'sɒŋstɪks/, *n.* →**music sticks.**

**song thrush** /'sɒŋ θrʌʃ/, *n.* a common European songbird, *Turdus philomelos.*

**songwriter** /'sɒŋraɪtə/, *n.* one who writes the words or music, or both, for popular songs.

**sonhood** /'sʌnhʊd/, *n.* →**sonship.**

**sonic** /'sɒnɪk/, *adj.* **1.** of or pertaining to sound. **2.** denoting a speed approximating that of the propagation of sound.

**sonic barrier** /'– bæriə/, *n.* →**sound barrier.**

**sonic boom** /– 'bum/, *n.* a sudden loud sound caused by the shock waves generated by an aircraft, or other object, travelling at or above the speed of sound.

**soniferous** /sɒ'nɪfərəs/, *adj.* conveying or producing sound. [*soni-* (from L, combining form of *sonus* sound) + -FEROUS]

**son-in-law** /'sʌn-ɪn-lɔ, -ən-/, *n., pl.* **sons-in-law.** the husband of one's daughter.

**sonky** /'sɒŋki/, *adj. Colloq.* foolish; silly.

**sonnet** /'sɒnət/, *n.* **1.** *Pros.* a poem, properly expressive of a single complete thought, idea, or sentiment, of 14 lines (usu. in 5-foot iambic metre) with rhymes arranged according to one of certain definite schemes, being in the strict or Italian form divided into a major group of 8 lines (the octave) followed by a minor group of 6 lines (the sestet), and in a common English form into 3 quatrains followed by a couplet. **2.** *Obs.* a short, usu. amatory poem. *–v.i.* **3.** to compose sonnets. *–v.t.* **4.** to celebrate in a sonnet or sonnets. [F, from It. *sonetto,* from OPr. *sonet,* from *son* sound, from L *sonus*]

**sonneteer** /sɒnə'tɪə/, *n.* **1.** a composer of sonnets. *–v.i.* **2.** to compose sonnets.

**sonny** /'sʌni/, *n., pl.* **-nies.** little boy; young man (often used as a familiar term of address).

**sonobuoy** /'soʊnəbɔɪ/, *n.* a sonar device used to detect submerged submarines.

**son of a bitch,** *n. Colloq.* (*derog.*) **1.** a mean and contemptible man. **2.** an object as a car, etc., which has incurred one's wrath.

**son of a gun,** *n. Chiefly U.S. Colloq.* **1.** an approving term for a man, esp. one who has demonstrated his masculinity in some way. **2. I'll be a son of a gun!,** (an exclamation of surprise, admiration, etc.).

**sonorant** /'sɒnərənt/, *n.* a voiced sound less sonorous than a vowel but more sonorous than a stop or fricative, as /l, r, m, n, j, w/.

**sonority** /sə'nɒrəti/, *n., pl.* **-ties.** the condition or quality of being resonant or sonorous.

**sonorous** /'sɒnərəs/, *adj.* **1.** giving out, or capable of giving out, a sound, esp. a deep resonant sound, as a thing or a place. **2.** loud, deep, or resonant, as a sound. **3.** rich and full in sound, as language, verse, etc. **4.** highflown; grandiloquent: *a sonorous address.* [L *sonōrus*] – **sonorously,** *adv.* – **sonorousness,** *n.*

**-sonous,** a word element used in adjectives to refer to sounds, as in *unisonous.* [L *-sonus*]

**sonship** /'sʌnʃɪp/, *n.* the state, fact, or relation of being a son.

**sonsy** /'sɒnsi/, *adj.,* **-sier, -siest.** *Scot., Irish.* buxom or comely. [Brit. d. *sonse* prosperity (from Gaelic *sonas*) + -Y[1]]

**sook** /sʊk/, *n.* **1.** Also, **sookie.** a poddy calf. **2.** (usu. of children) a timid, shy, cowardly person; a cry-baby. [? OE *sūcan* to suck, influenced by Welsh *swci swead* tame] – **sooky,** *adj.*

**sool** /sul/, *v.t.* to incite (a dog, etc.) to attack or chase an animal or person.

**soon** /sun/, *adv.* **1.** within a short period after this (or that) time, event, etc.: *we shall soon know.* **2.** before long; in the near future; at an early date. **3.** promptly or quickly. **4.** readily or willingly: *I would as soon walk as ride.* **5.** *Obs.* immediately, or at once. [ME; OE *sōna* at once, c. OHG *sān,* akin to Goth. *suns*]

**sooner** /'sunə/, *n. Colloq.* **1.** a lazy person. **2.** a horse which pulls back. [one who would *sooner* loaf than work, *sooner* go backwards than forwards, etc.]

**soot** /sʊt/, *n.* **1.** a black carbonaceous substance produced during the imperfect combustion of coal, wood, oil, etc., rising in fine particles and adhering to the sides of the chimney or pipe conveying the smoke. *–v.t.* **2.** to mark, cover, or treat with soot. [ME; OE *sōt,* c. d. D *zoet*]

**sooth** /suθ/, *n.* **1.** *Archaic.* truth, reality, or fact. *–adj.* **2.** *Poetic.* soothing, soft, or delicious. **3.** *Archaic.* true or real. [ME; OE *sōth,* c. OS *sōth,* Icel. *sannr,* akin to Goth. *sunjis* true] – **soothly,** *adv.*

**soothe** /suð/, *v.,* **soothed, soothing.** *–v.t.* **1.** to tranquillise or calm, as a person, the feelings, etc.; relieve, comfort, or refresh. **2.** to mitigate, assuage, or allay, as pain, sorrow, doubt, etc. *–v.i.* **3.** to exert a soothing influence; bring tranquillity, calm, ease, or comfort. [ME *sothe,* OE *sōthian,* from *sōth* SOOTH, *adj.*] – **soother,** *n.* – **soothing,** *adj.* – **soothingly,** *adv.*

**soothsay** /'suθseɪ/, *v.i.,* **-said, -saying.** to foretell events; prophesy.

**soothsayer** /'suθseɪə/, *n.* one who professes to foretell events. [ME *sothseyere;* from SOOTH, *adj.* or *n.,* + SAY, *v.,* + -ER[1]]

**soothsaying** /'suθseɪ-ɪŋ/, *n.* **1.** the practice or art of foretelling events. **2.** a prediction or prophecy.

**sooty** /'sʊti/, *adj.,* **-ier, -iest. 1.** covered, blackened, or smirched with soot. **2.** consisting of or resembling soot. **3.** of a black, blackish, or dusky colour. – **sootily,** *adv.* – **sootiness,** *n.*

**sooty blotch** /– 'blɒtʃ/, *n.* →**sooty mould.**

**sooty kangaroo** /– kæŋgə'ru/, *n.* →**western grey kangaroo.**

**sooty mould** /– 'moʊld/, *n.* fungus growth, black in colour, which damages many plants. Also, **sooty blotch.**

**sooty oystercatcher** /– 'ɔɪstəkætʃə/, *n.* a sooty-black coloured bird, *Haematopus fuliginosus,* with red eyes and bill, having a loud carrying call and found on rocky beaches and estuaries around the Australian seashore.

**sooty shearwater** /– 'ʃɪəwɔtə/, *n.* a brown bird with pale wing linings, *Puffinus griseus,* breeding in south-eastern Australia, New Zealand and some Southern Hemisphere islands; king mutton-bird.

**sop** /sɒp/, *n., v.,* **sopped, sopping.** *–n.* **1.** a piece of bread or the like dipped, or for dipping, in liquid food. **2.** anything thoroughly soaked. **3.** something given to pacify or quiet, or as a bribe. **4.** *Colloq.* a weak or cowardly person. *–v.t.* **5.** to dip or soak (bread, etc.) in some liquid. **6.** to drench. **7.** to take up (water, etc.) by absorption (usu. fol. by *up*). *–v.i.* **8.** to become or be soaking wet. **9.** (of a liquid) to soak (*in,* etc.). [ME; OE *sopp*]

**sop.,** soprano.

**sophism** /'sɒfɪzəm/, *n.* **1.** a specious but fallacious argument, used to display ingenuity in reasoning or to deceive someone. **2.** any false argument; a fallacy. [L *sophisma,* from Gk: clever device, argument; replacing ME *sophime,* from OF]

**sophist** /'sɒfəst/, *n.* **1.** (*oft. cap.*) **a.** any of a class of professional teachers in ancient Greece who gave instruction in various fields, as in general culture, rhetoric, politics, or disputation. **b.** any member of a portion of this class at a later period who, while professing to teach skill in reasoning, concerned himself with ingenuity and specious effectiveness rather than soundness of argument. **2.** one who reasons adroitly and speciously rather than soundly. **3.** a man of learning. [L *sophista,* from Gk *sophistḗs*]

**sophistic** /sə'fɪstɪk/, *adj.* **1.** of the nature of sophistry; fallacious. **2.** characteristic or suggestive of sophistry. **3.** given to the use of sophistry. **4.** of or pertaining to sophists or sophistry. Also, **sophistical.** – **sophistically,** *adv.* – **sophisticalness,** *n.*

**sophisticate** /sə'fɪstəkeɪt/, *v.,* **-cated, -cating;** /sə'fɪstəkət/, *n.* *–v.t.* **1.** to make less natural, simple, or ingenuous; to make worldly-wise. **2.** to mislead or pervert. *–v.i.* **3.** to use sophistry; quibble. *–n.* **4.** a sophisticated person. [ML *sophisticātus,* pp., from L *sophisticus* sophistic. See SOPHIST]

**sophisticated** /sə'fɪstəkeɪtəd/, *adj.* **1.** (of a person, the ideas, tastes, manners, etc.) altered by education, experience, etc., to be worldly-wise; changed from the natural character or simplicity; refined; artificial. **2.** of intellectual complexity; reflecting a high degree of skill, intelligence, etc.; subtle: *sophisticated music.* **3.** deceptive; misleading. **4.** (of machinery, etc.) complex; intricate.

**sophistication** /səfɪstə'keɪʃən/, *n.* **1.** sophisticated character, ideas, tastes, or ways as the result of education, worldly experience, etc. **2.** change from the natural character or simplicity, or the resulting condition. **3.** impairment or debasement, as of purity or genuineness. **4.** the use of sophistry; a sophism or quibble. **5.** advanced refinement or complexity: *solid-state technology has advanced electronics to a new level of sophistication.*

**sophistry** /'sɒfəstri/, *n., pl.* **-ries.** **1.** a subtle, tricky, specious, but generally fallacious method of reasoning. **2.** a false argument; sophism.

**sophomore** /'sɒfəmɔ/, *n. Chiefly U.S.* a student in the second year of the course at a university, college, or school. [*sophom* (var. of SOPHISM, def. 1, with reference to the fact that such arguments were used as school exercises) + -OR[2]] – **sophomoric** /sɒfə'mɔrɪk/, **sophomorical** /sɒfə'mɔrɪkəl/, *adj.*

**-sophy,** a word element referring to systems of thought, as in *theosophy.* [Gk *-sophia,* combining form of *sophía* skill, wisdom]

**sopor** /'soʊpə/, *n.* a deep, unnatural sleep; lethargy. [L]

**soporiferous** /sɒpə'rɪfərəs/, *adj.* bringing sleep; soporific. [L *sopōrifer* sleep-bringing + -OUS] – **soporiferously,** *adv.* – **soporiferousness,** *n.*

**soporific** /sɒpə'rɪfɪk/, *adj.* **1.** causing or tending to cause sleep. **2.** pertaining to or characterised by sleep or sleepiness; sleepy; drowsy. *–n.* **3.** something causing sleep, as a drug or medicine. [SOPOR + -I- + -FIC]

**sopping** /'sɒpɪŋ/, *adj.* soaked; drenched: *sopping wet.*

**soppy** /'sɒpi/, *adj.,* **-pier, -piest.** **1.** soaked, drenched, or very wet, as ground. **2.** rainy, as weather. **3.** *Colloq.* excessively sentimental; mawkish; silly. – **soppily,** *adv.* – **soppiness,** *n.*

**soprano** /sə'pranoʊ/, *n., pl.* **-pranos, -prani** /-'prani/, *adj. Music.* *–n.* **1.** the uppermost part or voice. **2.** the highest singing voice in women and boys. **3.** a part for such a voice. **4.** a singer with such a voice. *–adj.* **5.** of or pertaining to soprano; having the compass of a soprano. [It., from *sopra* above, from L *suprā*]

**soprano clef** /'– klɛf/, *n.* a sign locating middle C on the bottom line of the stave.

**sorb** /sɔb/, *n.* **1.** a European service tree, *Sorbus domestica.* **2.** its fruit (**sorb apple**). [L *sorbum* serviceberry, or *sorbus* service tree]

**sorbet** /'sɔbət/, *n.* **1.** an iced dessert made with fruit and liqueurs or heavy wines; served between meals to clear the palate. **2.** a water-ice. **3.** →**sherbet** (def. 2). [F: water-ice, from Turk. and Pers. See SHERBET]

**sorbic acid** /sɔbɪk 'æsəd/, *n.* a white crystalline solid, $CH_3CH$: CHCH: CHCOOH, used as a fungicide and food preservative.

**sorbite** /'sɔbaɪt/, *n.* **1.** a steel microstructure consisting of ferrite and finely divided cementite, which is produced when martensite is tempered above 450°C. **2.** a constituent of steel produced by the decomposition of austenite when the rate of cooling is too slow to yield a troostitic structure, and too rapid to produce a pearlitic structure. [named after H.C. *Sorby,* 1829-1908, English metallurgist. See -ITE[1]] – **sorbitic** /sɔ'bɪtɪk/, *adj.*

**sorbitol** /'sɔbətɒl/, *n.* a white crystalline powder, $CH_2OH(CHOH)_4CH_2OH$, which occurs in certain fruits and which is isomeric with mannitol; used in the manufacture of resins and varnishes and as a substitute for sugar. Also, **sorbit, sorbol.**

**sorbose** /'sɔboʊz, -boʊs/, *n.* a ketohexose, $C_6H_{12}O_6$, derived from trees of the genus *Sorbus* (the European and American mountain ash), and industrially by bacterial oxidation, and used in the synthesis of vitamin C. [SORB(ITOL) + -OSE[2]]

**sorcerer** /'sɔsərə/, *n.* one supposed to exercise supernatural powers through evil spirits; a magician or enchanter. [SORCER(Y) + -ER[2]; replacing ME *sorser,* from OF *sorcier,* from VL **sortiārius*] – **sorceress** /'sɔsərəs/, *n. fem.*

**sorcerous** /'sɔsərəs/, *adj.* **1.** of the nature of or involving sorcery. **2.** using sorcery.

**sorcery** /'sɔsəri/, *n., pl.* **-ceries.** the art, practices, or spells of a sorcerer; magic, esp. black magic in which supernatural powers are exercised through the aid of evil spirits; witchcraft. [ME, from ML *sorceria,* from L *sors* lot]

**sordid** /'sɔdəd/, *adj.* **1.** dirty or filthy; squalid. **2.** morally mean or ignoble: *sordid gains.* **3.** meanly selfish, selfseeking, or mercenary. [L *sordidus,* dirty, base] – **sordidly,** *adv.* – **sordidness,** *n.*

**sordino** /sɔ'dinoʊ/, *n., pl.* **-ni** /-ni/. →**mute**[1] (def. 11). Also, **sourdine.** [It., from L *surdus* deaf, mute]

**sore** /sɔ/, *adj.,* **sorer, sorest,** *n., adv.* *–adj.* **1.** physically painful or sensitive, as a wound, hurt, diseased part, etc. **2.** suffering bodily pain from wounds, bruises, etc., as a person. **3.** suffering mental pain; grieved, distressed, or sorrowful: *to be sore at heart.* **4.** causing great mental pain, distress, or sorrow: *a sore bereavement.* **5.** causing very great suffering, misery, hardship, etc.: *sore need.* **6.** *Colloq.* irritated, offended, or feeling aggrieved: *What are you sore about?* **7.** being an occasion of annoyance or irritation: *a sore subject.* **8. done up like a sore finger** (**toe**), *Colloq.* dressed up in one's best clothes. **9. stand** (**stick**) **out like a sore finger,** *Colloq.* to catch the eye by virtue of a contrast with surrounding people or objects. *–***10.** a sore spot or place on the body. **11.** a source or cause of grief, distress, irritation, etc. *–adv.* **12.** *Archaic or Poetic.* sorely. [ME; OE *sār,* c. D *zeer,* G *sehr* very] – **sorely,** *adv.* – **soreness,** *n.*

**sorehead** /'sɔhɛd/, *n. Colloq.* a disgruntled or vindictive person, esp. an unsportsmanlike loser.

**sore mouth** /'sɔ maʊθ/, *n.* ecthyma of sheep.

**sorghum** /'sɔgəm/, *n.* **1.** a cereal grass, *Sorghum bicolor,* of many varieties, which may be divided into four groups, the **sweet sorghums** (used esp. for making molasses or syrup and for forage), the **grain sorghums** (used for forage and as a food for man), the **grass sorghums** (used principally for producing hay), and the **broomcorns** (used for making brooms and brushes). **2.** the syrup made from the sweet or saccharine sorghums. **3.** any grass of the genus *Sorghum,* as wild sorghum. [NL, from It. *sorgo,* from L *syricum* Syrian]

sorghum

**sorgo** /'sɔgoʊ/, *n., pl.* **-gos.** any of the sweet sorghums. Also, **sorgho.** [It. See SORGHUM]

**sori** /'sɔraɪ/, *n.* plural of **sorus.**

**soricine** /'sɒrəsin/, *adj.* of or resembling the shrews. See **shrew** (def. 1). [L *sōricīnus*]

**sorites** /sə'raɪtiz/, *n.* a form of argument having several premises and one conclusion, and resolvable into a number of syllogisms, the conclusion of each of which is a premise of the next. [L, from Gk *sōreítēs,* lit., heaped] – **soritical** /sə'rɪtɪkəl/, *adj.*

**sorney** /'sɔni/, *adj.* →**sawney.**

**soroptimist** /sə'rɒptəməst/, *n. Chiefly U.S.* a member of an association of professional and business women, devoted mainly to charity work. [L *sor(ōr)* sister + OPTIMIST]

**sororate** /'sɒrəreɪt/, *n.* marriage with a wife's sister.

**sororicide** /sə'rɒrəsaɪd, -'rɔ-/, *n.* **1.** one who kills his or her sister. **2.** the act of killing one's sister. [L *sorōricīda* (def. 1), *sorōricīdium* (def. 2). See -CIDE] – **sororicidal,** *adj.*

**sorority** /sə'rɒrəti, -'rɔ-/, *n., pl.* **-ties.** *U.S.* a society or club of women or girls, as in a college. [ML *sorōritas*]

**sorosis** /sə'roʊsəs/, *n., pl.* **-ses** /-siz/. a fleshy multiple fruit composed of many flowers, seed capsules, and receptacles consolidated, as in the pineapple and mulberry. [NL, from Gk *sōrós* heap + *-ōsis* -OSIS]

**sorption** /'sɔpʃən/, *n.* the binding of one substance by another by any mechanism, such as absorption, adsorption, or persorption. [abstracted from ABSORPTION, etc.]

**sorrel**[1] /'sɒrəl/, *n.* **1.** light reddish brown. **2.** a horse of this colour. *–adj.* **3.** having the colour sorrel. [ME *sorel,* from OF, from *sore* yellowish brown, from Gmc; cf. MLG *sōr* sere]

**sorrel**[2] /'sɒrəl/, *n.* **1.** any of various plants of the genus *Rumex* and related genera, having succulent acid leaves often used in salads, sauces, etc. **2.** any of various sour-juiced plants of the genus *Oxalis;* wood sorrel. **3.** any of various similar plants. [ME *sorell,* from OF *surele,* from *sur,* adj., from Gmc: SOUR]

**sorrel tree** /'– tri/, *n.* a North American tree, *Oxydendrum arboreum,* having leaves with an acid flavour and racemes of white flowers.

**sorrow** /'sɒroʊ/, *n.* **1.** distress caused by loss, affliction, disappointment, etc.; grief, sadness, or regret. **2.** a cause or occasion of grief or regret. **3.** an affliction, misfortune, or trouble. *–v.i.* **4.** to feel sorrow; grieve. [ME; OE *sorg,* c. G *Sorge*] – **sorrower,** *n.*

**sorrowful** /'sɒrəfəl/, *adj.* **1.** full of or feeling sorrow; grieved; sad. **2.** indicative or expressive of sorrow; mournful; plaintive. **3.** involving or causing sorrow; distressing. – **sorrowfully,** *adv.* – **sorrowfulness,** *n.*

**sorry** /'sɒri/, *adj.,* **-rier, -riest. 1.** feeling regret, compunction, sympathy, pity, etc.: *to be sorry for a remark.* **2.** of a deplorable, pitiable, or miserable kind: *to come to a sorry end.* **3.** sorrowful, grieved, or sad. **4.** associated with sorrow; suggestive of grief or suffering; melancholy; dismal. **5.** wretched, poor, mean, or pitiful: *a sorry horse.* [ME; OE *sārig* (c. LG *sērig,* OHG *sērag*), from *sār* SORE] – **sorrily,** *adv.* – **sorriness,** *n.*

**sort** /sɔt/, *n.* **1.** a particular kind, species, variety, class, group, or description, as distinguished by the character or nature: *to discover a new sort of mineral.* **2.** character, quality, or nature. **3.** a more or less adequate or inadequate type or example of something: *he's some sort of friend.* **4.** manner, fashion, or way. **5.** (*usu. pl.*). *Print.* one of the kinds of characters of a fount of type. **6.** *Colloq.* a woman or girl: *a good sort, a drack sort.* **7. a good sort,** *Colloq.* **a.** one who is likeable, trustworthy, reliable. **b.** a sexually attractive woman or man. **8. of sorts, a.** of a mediocre or poor kind. **b.** of one sort or another; of an indefinite kind. **9. out of sorts, a.** not in a normal condition of good health, spirits, or temper. **b.** *Print.* short of certain characters of a fount of type. **10. sort of,** to a certain extent; in some way; as it were. *–v.t.* **11.** to arrange according to sort, kind, or class; separate into sorts; classify. **12.** to separate or take (*out*) from other sorts, or from others. **13.** to assign to a particular class, group, or place (fol. by *with, together,* etc.). **14.** *Agric.* (of wool) to prepare for manufacture by breaking up fleeces into bales of matching types, according to quality, number, length and colour. [ME, from OF *sorte,* from L *sors* lot, condition, LL class, order] – **sortable,** *adj.*

**sorter** /'sɔtə/, *n.* **1.** one who or that which sorts. **2.** a post-office employee who sorts letters.

**sortie** /'sɔti/, *n., v.,* **-tied, -tieing.** *–n.* **1.** a sally of troops from a besieged place to attack the besiegers. **2.** a body of troops making such a sally. **3.** the flying of a military aircraft on a mission, as a bombing raid. *–v.i.* **4.** to go out on a sortie. [F: a going out, from *sortir* go out]

**sortilege** /'sɔtəlɪdʒ/, *n.* **1.** the drawing of lots for divination; divination by lot. **2.** sorcery; magic. [ME, from ML *sortilegium,* from L *sortilegus* diviner]

**sorus** /'sɔrəs/, *n., pl.* **sori** /'sɔri/. **1.** one of the clusters of sporangia on the back of the fronds of ferns. **2.** a similar cluster on some fungi and other low plants. [NL, from Gk *sōrós* heap]

**SOS** /ɛs oʊ 'ɛs/, *n.* **1.** the letters represented by the radio telegraphic signal used, as by ships in distress, to call for help. **2.** any call for help. [said to stand for *Save Our Souls*]

**so-so** /'soʊ-soʊ, soʊ-'soʊ/, *adj.* **1.** indifferent; neither very good nor very bad. *–adv.* **2.** in an indifferent or passable manner; indifferently; tolerably.

sorus: fern sori

**sost.,** *Music.* sustained. [L *sostenuto*]

**sostenuto** /sɒstə'njutoʊ/, *adj., n., pl.* **-tos, -ti** /-ti/. *–adj. Music.* **1.** sustained or prolonged in the time value of the notes. *–n.* **2.** a movement or passage played in this manner. [It., pp. of *sostenere* sustain]

**sot** /sɒt/, *n.* **1.** a confirmed drunkard. **2.** one befuddled by drink. [ME *sotte,* OE *sott,* from VL *sottus;* orig. uncert.]

**soteriology** /sɒˌtɪəri'ɒlədʒi/, *n.* the doctrine of salvation through the Saviour, Jesus Christ. [Gk *sōtērio(s)* saving + -LOGY] – **soteriologic** /sɒˌtɪəriə'lɒdʒɪk/, **soteriological** /sɒˌtɪəriə'lɒdʒɪkəl/, *adj.*

**Sothic** /'soʊθɪk, 'sɒθɪk/, *adj.* of Sirius, the Dog Star, the brightest star in the heavens. [Gk *Sôthis,* Egyptian name for Sirius, the Dog Star, + -IC]

**Sothic cycle** /– 'saɪkəl/, *n.* (in the ancient Egyptian calendar) a period of 1460 Sothic years. Also, **Sothic period.**

**Sothic year** /– 'jɪə/, *n.* the fixed year of the ancient Egyptians, determined by the heliacal rising of Sirius, and equivalent to 365¼ days.

**sottish** /'sɒtɪʃ/, *adj.* **1.** stupefied, as with drink. **2.** given to excessive drinking. **3.** pertaining to or befitting a sot. – **sottishly,** *adv.* – **sottishness,** *n.*

**sotto voce** /sɒtoʊ 'voʊtʃeɪ/, *adv.* in a low tone intended not to be overheard. [It.: under (normal) voice (level)]

**sou** /su/, *n.* (formerly) a French bronze coin equal to either 5 or 10 centimes. [F, in OF *sol,* from L *solidus* (*nummus*) solid (coin)]

**sou'** /saʊ/, *n., adj., adv. Chiefly Naut.* south.

**souari nut** /su'ari ˌnʌt/, *n.* the large, edible, oily nut of a tall tree, *Caryocar nuciferum,* of tropical South America; butternut. [Carib (Galibi) *saouari*]

**soubise** /su'biz/, *n.* a strained white onion sauce for meats, etc. [named after Charles de Rohan, Prince de *Soubise,* 1715-87, marshal of France]

**soubrette** /su'brɛt/, *n.* **1.** a maidservant or lady's maid in a play or opera, esp. one displaying coquetry, pertness, and intrigue. **2.** an actress playing such a role. **3.** any lively or pert young woman character. [F, from Pr. *soubreto,* fem. of *soubret* coy, reserved, from *soubra* to set aside, (earlier) be left over, from L *superāre* be above] – **soubrettish,** *adj.*

**soubriquet** /'subrɪkeɪ/, *n.* →**sobriquet.**

**souchong** /su'ʃɒŋ, -'tʃɒŋ/, *n.* a variety of black tea grown in India, Ceylon and China. [Chinese Cantonese *siu-chung* small sort]

**souffle** /'sufəl/, *n. Physiol.* a murmuring or blowing sound. [F, from *souffler* blow. See SOUFFLÉ]

**soufflé** /'sufleɪ/, *n.* **1.** a light baked dish made fluffy with beaten eggwhites combined with egg yolks, white sauce, and fish, cheese, or other ingredients. **2.** a similar sweet or savoury cold dish like a mousse. *–adj.* **3.** puffed-up; made light, as by beating and cooking. [F, pp. of *souffler* blow, puff, from L *sufflāre* blow up]

**sough** /saʊ/, *v.i.* **1.** to make a rushing, rustling, or murmuring sound. *–n.* **2.** such a sound. [ME *swoghe,* OE *swōgan* make a noise, c. OS *swōgan* and akin to OE *swēgan* make a noise (c. Goth. *-swōgjan*)]

**sought** /sɔt/, *v.* past tense and past participle of **seek.**

**soul** /soʊl/, *n.* **1.** the principle of life, feeling, thought, and action in man, regarded as a distinct entity separate from the body, and commonly held to be separable in existence from the body; the spiritual part of man as distinct from the physical. **2.** the spiritual part of man regarded in its moral aspect, or as believed to survive death and be subject to happiness or misery in a life to come. **3.** the emotional part of man's nature, or the seat of the feelings or sentiments. **4.** high-mindedness; noble warmth of feeling, spirit or courage, etc. **5.** the animating principle or essential element or part of something. **6.** the inspirer or moving spirit of some action, movement, etc. **7.** the embodiment of some quality. **8.** a disembodied spirit of a deceased person. **9.** a human being; person. **10.** →**soul music.** **11.** the sincere and heartfelt expression of Negro emotion. *–adj.* **12.** *Chiefly U.S.* of or pertaining to American Negros. [ME; OE *sāwl,* c. Goth. *saiwala,* akin to D *ziel,* G *Seele,* Icel. *sāl*]

**soul-destroying** /ˈsoʊl-dəstrɔɪɪŋ/, *adj.* (of a job, way of life, etc.) demoralising, dispiriting, usu. because of the drudgery or monotony involved: *the soul-destroying tasks of a production-line worker.*

**soulful** /ˈsoʊlfəl/, *adj.* of, or expressive of, deep feeling or emotion: *soulful eyes.* – **soulfully,** *adv.* – **soulfulness,** *n.*

**soulless** /ˈsoʊlləs/, *adj.* **1.** without a soul. **2.** lacking in nobility of soul, as persons; without spirit or courage. **3.** harsh; unsympathetic. – **soullessly,** *adv.* – **soullessness,** *n.*

**soul mate** /ˈsoʊl meɪt/, *n.* one of two or more persons who share common interests, temperaments, and aspirations.

**soul music** /ˈ– mjuzɪk/, *n.* commercial American Negro blues music which combines gospel music with a blues style.

**soul-searching** /ˈsoʊl-sɜtʃɪŋ/, *n.* the act or process of close and penetrating analysis of oneself, to determine one's true motives and sentiments.

**sound**[1] /saʊnd/, *n.* **1.** the sensation produced in the organs of hearing when certain vibrations (**soundwaves**) are caused in the surrounding air or other elastic medium, as by a vibrating body. **2.** the vibrations in the air, or vibrational energy, producing this sensation; longitudinal vibrations are propagated at about 335 metres per second. **3.** the particular auditory effect produced by a given cause: *the sound of music.* **4.** any auditory effect, or vibrational disturbance such as to be heard. **5.** a noise, vocal utterance, musical note, or the like. **6.** *Phonet.* a segment of speech corresponding to a single articulation or to a combination of articulations constantly associated in the language; a phone. **7.** the quality of an event, letter, etc., as it affects a person: *this report has a bad sound.* **8.** the distance within which the noise of something may be heard. **9.** mere noise, without meaning. **10.** *Obs.* a report; news; tidings. *–v.i.* **11.** to make or emit a sound. **12.** to give forth a sound as a call or summons. **13.** to be heard, as a sound. **14.** to convey a certain impression when heard or read: *to sound strange.* **15.** to give a specific sound: *to sound loud.* **16.** to give the appearance of being: *to sound true.* **17.** *Law.* to have as its basis or the import of (usu. fol. by *in*): *his action sounds in contract.* **18. sound off,** *Colloq.* **a.** to speak or complain frankly. **b.** to speak angrily; lose one's temper. **c.** to boast; exaggerate. **d.** *U.S.* to call one's name, sequence, number, etc. *–v.t.* **19.** to cause (an instrument, etc.) to make or emit a sound. **20.** to give forth (a sound). **21.** to announce, order, or direct by a sound as of a trumpet: *to sound a retreat.* **22.** to utter audibly, pronounce, or express: *to sound each letter.* **23.** to examine by percussion or auscultation. *–adj.* **24.** of, pertaining to, or by the medium of radio broadcasting (as opposed to television broadcasting). [ME *soune(n),* from OF *soner,* from L *sonāre*]

**sound**[2] /saʊnd/, *adj.* **1.** free from injury, damage, decay, defect, disease, etc.; in good condition; healthy; robust: *a sound heart.* **2.** financially strong, secure, or reliable: *a sound business.* **3.** reliable: *sound judgment.* **4.** without defect as to truth, justice, or reason: *sound advice.* **5.** of substantial or enduring character: *sound value.* **6.** without logical defect, as reasoning. **7.** without legal defect, as a title. **8.** theologically correct or orthodox, as doctrines or a theologian. **9.** free from moral defect or weakness; upright, honest, or good; honourable; loyal. **10.** unbroken and deep, as sleep. **11.** vigorous, hearty, or thorough, as a beating. **12. sound as a bell,** in perfect health or condition. *–adv.* **13.** in a sound manner. [ME *sund,* OE *gesund,* c. D *gezond,* G *gesund*] – **soundly,** *adv.* – **soundness,** *n.*

**sound**[3] /saʊnd/, *v.t.* **1.** to measure or try the depth of (water, a deep hole, etc.) by letting down a lead or plummet at the end of a line or by some equivalent means. **2.** to measure (depth) in such a manner, as at sea. **3.** to examine or test (the bottom of water, etc.) with a lead that brings up adhering bits of matter. **4.** to examine or investigate; seek to fathom or ascertain: *to sound a person's views.* **5.** to seek to elicit the views or sentiments of (a person) by indirect inquiries, suggestive allusions, etc. (oft. fol. by *out*). **6.** *Surg.* to examine, as the urinary bladder, with a sound (def. 10). *–v.i.* **7.** to use the lead and line, (or some other device) for measuring depth, etc., as at sea. **8.** to go down or touch bottom, as a lead. **9.** to plunge downwards or dive, as a whale. *–n.* **10.** *Surg.* a long, solid, slender instrument for sounding or exploring body cavities or canals. [ME; OE *sund* channel (in *sundgyrd* sounding pole, lit., channel pole), from Scand.; cf. Icel. *sund* channel, c. OE *sund* sea; akin to SWIM]

**sound**[4] /saʊnd/, *n.* **1.** a relatively narrow passage of water, not a stream, between larger bodies or between the mainland and an island: *Marlborough Sounds.* **2.** an inlet, arm, or recessed portion of the sea: *Milford Sound.* **3.** the air-bladder of a fish. [ME; OE *sund* swimming, channel, sea. See SOUND[3]]

**sound barrier** /ˈ– bæriə/, *n.* a point near the speed of sound at which an aircraft or projectile meets a sudden increase in air resistance and creates a shock wave; a sonic barrier. This point is viewed as a barrier separating subsonic from supersonic speed.

**soundboard** /ˈsaʊndbɔd/, *n.* →**sounding-board.**

**soundbox** /ˈsaʊndbɒks/, *n.* **1.** a chamber in a musical instrument, as the body of a violin, for increasing the sonority of its tone. **2.** the part of an acoustic gramophone pick-up in which the mechanical movements of the needle are converted into acoustic impulses, usu. based upon a diaphragm vibrated by the needle.

**sound change** /ˈsaʊnd tʃeɪndʒ/, *n.* an alteration which, as the language develops over the centuries, affects all members of certain groups of speech sounds in the same way.

**sound effect** /ˈ– əfɛkt/, *n.* (*usu. pl.*) any sound other than speech or music forming part of a radio or television program or a film and used to create an effect, as the noise of a train, storm, gunfire, etc.

**sound engineer** /ˈ– ɛndʒəˌnɪə/, *n.* one who controls the audio equipment in a recording studio.

**sounder**[1] /ˈsaʊndə/, *n.* one who or that which makes a sound or noise, or sounds something.

**sounder**[2] /ˈsaʊndə/, *n.* one who or that which sounds the depth of water, etc. [SOUND[3] + -ER[1]]

**sound hole** /ˈsaʊnd hoʊl/, *n.* a hole, usu. in the shape of an *f,* cut in the sounding-board of a violin or similar stringed instrument, with the object of increasing vibration.

**sounding**[1] /ˈsaʊndɪŋ/, *adj.* **1.** emitting or producing a sound or sounds. **2.** resounding or sonorous. **3.** having an imposing sound; high-sounding; pompous. [SOUND[1] + -ING[2]] – **soundingly,** *adv.*

**sounding**[2] /ˈsaʊndɪŋ/, *n.* **1.** (*oft. pl.*) the act or process of measuring depth, examining the bottom of water, etc., with or as with a lead and line. **2.** the act or process of making measurements of remote atmospheric characteristics, by such means as a balloon or rocket, esp. for meteorological purposes. **3.** (*pl.*) depths of water ascertained by means of a lead and line, or sonar apparatus, as at sea. **4.** (*pl.*) parts of the water in which the ordinary sounding lead will reach bottom. [SOUND[3] + -ING[1]]

**sounding balloon** /ˈ– bəlun/, *n.* a small free balloon used to obtain meteorological information from the upper atmosphere.

**sounding-board** /ˈsaʊndɪŋ-bɔd/, *n.* **1.** a thin, resonant plate of wood forming part of a musical stringed instrument, and so placed as to enhance the power and quality of the tone. **2.** a structure over, or behind and above, a speaker, orchestra, etc., to reflect the sound towards the audience. **3.** a board used in the deadening of floors, partitions, etc. **4.** one whose reactions to new methods, ideas, etc., serve as a test of their general acceptability or effectiveness. **5.** one who propagates opinions or ideas. Also, **soundboard.**

**sounding line** /ˈsaʊndɪŋ laɪn/, *n.* a line weighted with a lead or plummet (**sounding lead**) and bearing marks to show the length paid out, used for sounding, as at sea.

**sounding rocket** /ˈ– rɒkət/, *n.* **1.** *Meteorol.* a research rocket used to obtain meteorological information from the upper atmosphere. **2.** *Aerospace.* a rocket used to explore regions up to 6500 km above the surface of the earth.

**soundless**[1] /ˈsaʊndləs/, *adj.* without sound. [SOUND[1] + -LESS] – **soundlessly,** *adv.*

**soundless**[2] /ˈsaʊndləs/, *adj.* unfathomable. [SOUND[3] + -LESS]

**sound library** /ˈsaʊnd laɪbri/, *n.* a library of recorded music for specific theatrical or media use.
**sound mixer** /ˈ– mɪksə/, *n.* **1.** a piece of electronic equipment which unites sound signals from various sources, as several microphones, tape recorders, etc., in proportions which are controllable. **2.** *Films, T.V., etc.,* one who employs such a device, as when making records, films, etc.
**sound-mouth** /ˈsaʊnd-maʊθ/, *n.* a sheep, usu. aged, but whose teeth are still firm and retain their natural position.
**sound on sound,** *n.* **1.** the process of recording additional sounds on to a sound track which already has sound on it. *–adj.* **2.** of or pertaining to this process.
**sound piece** /ˈsaʊnd pis/, *n.* music without melody or harmony, comprised of different sounds either contrived or taken from nature, and arranged according to some principle related to timbre or colour.
**soundpost** /ˈsaʊndpoʊst/, *n.* a small wooden post separating the belly and back of stringed instruments, and used both to support the structure and to act as a focus for the vibrations.
**soundproof** /ˈsaʊndpruf/, *adj.* **1.** impervious to sound. *–v.t.* **2.** to cause to be soundproof.
**sound ranging** /ˈsaʊnd reɪndʒɪŋ/, *n.* the location of a sound source by microphonic detection of the sound signals.
**soundshell** /ˈsaʊndʃɛl/, *n.* a building having a roof in the form of a shell (def. 17), for accommodating performers, bands at outdoor entertainments, etc.
**sound shift** /ˈsaʊnd ʃɪft/, *n.* a sound change, esp. one affecting vowels, as the Great Vowel Shift.
**sound spectrograph** /– ˈspɛktrəgræf/, *n.* →**spectrograph.**
**sound system** /ˈsaʊnd sɪstəm/, *n.* →**audio system.**
**soundtrack** /ˈsaʊndtræk/, *n.* **1.** a strip at the side of a cinema film which carries the sound recording. **2.** such a recording, esp. when transferred on to a gramophone record.
**soundwave** /ˈsaʊndweɪv/, *n.* a longitudinal vibration in an elastic medium by which sound is propagated.
**soup** /sup/, *n.* **1.** a liquid food made from meat, fish, or vegetables, with various added ingredients, by boiling or simmering. **2.** *Surfing. Colloq.* foaming water, caused by the breaking of a wave. **3. in the soup,** *Colloq.* in trouble. *–v.t.* **4. soup up,** *Colloq.* to modify (an engine, esp. of a motor car) in order to increase its power. [F, *soupe,* sop, broth, of Gmc orig.; cf. OE *sūpan* sip, *sopp* SOP]
**soupçon** /ˈsupsɒn/, *n.* **1.** a suspicion; a slight trace or flavour. **2.** a very small amount. [F, from LL *suspectio,* replacing L *suspicio* suspicion]
**soupe du jour** /sup də ˈʒuə/, *n.* the variety of soup being served in a restaurant on a particular day. [F: soup of the day]
**souped-up** /ˈsupt-ʌp/, *adj.* (of an engine, esp. a motor-car engine) increased in power as a result of some modification.
**soup kitchen** /ˈsup kɪtʃən/, *n.* **1.** a place where food, usu. soup, is served free or at little charge to the poor. **2.** *Mil.* a mobile kitchen.
**soup plate** /ˈ– pleɪt/, *n.* a deep plate used for serving soup.
**soup-spoon** /ˈsup-spun/, *n.* a large spoon, usu. with a rounded bowl, used for eating soup.
**soupy** /ˈsupi/, *adj.* **1.** reminiscent of the consistency of a thick soup: *a soupy fog.* **2.** excessively sentimental: *wallowing in soupy music.*
**sour** /ˈsaʊə/, *adj.* **1.** having an acid taste, such as that of vinegar, lemon juice, etc.; tart. **2.** rendered acid or affected by fermentation; fermented. **3.** characteristic of what is so affected: *a sour smell.* **4.** distasteful or disagreeable; unpleasant. **5.** harsh in spirit or temper; austere; morose; embittered; peevish. **6.** *Agric.* (of soil) having excessive acidity. **7.** (of substances such as petrol) contaminated by sulphur compounds. *–n.* **8.** that which is sour; something sour. **9.** a drink, as whisky or gin with lemon juice, sugar, etc. *–v.i., v.t.* **10.** to become or make sour. [ME; OE *sūr,* c. G *sauer*] – **sourish,** *adj.* – **sourly,** *adv.* – **sourness,** *n.*
**source** /sɔs/, *n.* **1.** any thing or place from which something comes, arises, or is obtained; origin. **2.** a spring of water from the earth, etc., or the place of issue; a fountain; the beginning or place of origin of a stream or river. **3.** a book, statement, person, etc., supplying information. **4.** *Elect.* one of the three electrodes of a field effect transistor. *–v.t.* **5.** to establish the source of or the authority for (a statement, document, etc.). [ME, from OF, n. use of pp. of *sourdre* rise, spring up, from L *surgere* rise]
**source book** /ˈ– bʊk/, *n.* a book, collection of documents, etc., serving as an authoritative basis for the historical study of a subject.
**source material** /ˈ– mətɪəriəl/, *n.* original authoritative materials used in research, as diaries, manuscripts, records, etc.
**sour cream** /saʊə ˈkrim/, *n.* **1.** cream naturally soured by the action of lactic acid bacteria, used in baking some breads and cakes. **2.** a smooth cream artificially soured by the addition of certain bacteria, and used as a garnish in soups, sauces, etc.
**sourdine** /sʊəˈdin/, *n.* **1.** →**sordino. 2.** →**kit**[2]. **3.** *Hist.* an obsolete member of the oboe family. [F, from *sourd* deaf, from L *surdus*]
**sourdough** /ˈsaʊədoʊ/, *n.* **1.** leaven, esp. fermented dough kept from one baking to start the next instead of beginning each time with fresh yeast. **2.** *U.S.* a prospector or pioneer, esp. in Alaska or Canada.
**sour fig** /saʊə ˈfɪg/, *n.* →**Hottentot fig.**
**sour gourd** /– ˈgʊəd/, *n.* **1.** the acid fruit of the baobab. **2.** the tree itself.
**sour grapes** /– ˈgreɪps/, *n.* the pretence of despising something, only because one cannot have it. [after the fox (in a fable by Aesop) who pretended that the grapes he could not reach were sour]
**sour gum** /– ˈgʌm/, *n.* the tupelo, *Nyssa sylvatica.*
**sourpuss** /ˈsaʊəpʊs/, *n. Colloq.* one having a sour or gloomy disposition; an embittered person.
**soursob** /ˈsaʊəsɒb/, *n.* any plant of the genus *Oxalis,* as *O. pes-caprae,* a yellow-flowered herb. [probably alteration of SOURSOP]
**soursop** /ˈsaʊəsɒp/, *n.* **1.** a small tree, *Annona muricata,* originally from the West Indies, grown in Queensland. **2.** the large fruit of this tree, having short spines, and a slightly acid, fibrous pulp; guanabana.

soursop

**sousaphone** /ˈsuzəfoʊn/, *n.* a form of bass tuba, similar to the helicon, used in brass bands. [named after John Philip *Sousa,* 1854-1932, U.S. composer of marches]
**souse**[1] /saʊs/, *v.,* **soused, sousing,** *n.* *–v.t.* **1.** to plunge into water or other liquid. **2.** to drench with water, etc. **3.** to dash or pour as water. **4.** to steep in pickling liquid; pickle. **5.** *Colloq.* to intoxicate. *–v.i.* **6.** to plunge into water, etc.; fall with a splash. **7.** to be soaked or drenched. **8.** to be steeping or soaking in something. **9.** *Colloq.* to drink to intoxication. *–n.* **10.** an act of sousing. **11.** something kept or steeped in pickle, esp. the head, ears, and feet of a pig. **12.** a liquid used as a pickle. **13.** *Colloq.* a drunkard. [ME *sows,* from OF *souce,* from OHG *sulza* brine; akin to SALT]

sousaphone

**souse**[2] /saʊs/, *v.,* **soused, sousing,** *n.* *Archaic.* *–v.i.* **1.** to swoop. *–v.t.* **2.** to swoop or pounce on. *–n.* **3.** *Falconry.* **a.** a rising while in flight. **b.** a swooping or pouncing. [var. of SOURCE in (now obs.) sense 'rise']
**soutache** /suˈtæʃ/, *n.* a narrow braid, commonly of mohair, silk, or rayon, used for trimming. [F, from Hung. *sujtas* trimming]
**soutane** /suˈtan, -ˈtæn/, *n.* →**cassock.** [F, from It. *sottana,* from *sotto* under, from L *subtus*]
**south** /saʊθ/, *n.* **1.** a cardinal point of the compass directly opposite to the north. **2.** the direction in which this point lies. **3.** (*l.c. or cap.*) a quarter or territory situated in this direction. **4.** *Chiefly Poetic.* the south wind. **5. the South,** *Qld.* the southern States of Australia, esp. Victoria and New South Wales. *–adj.* **6.** lying towards or situated in the south. **7.** directed or proceeding towards the south. **8.** coming from the south, as a wind. **9.** (*cap.*) designating the southern part of a region, nation, country, etc.: *South Pacific.* *–adv.* **10.** towards or in the south. **11.** from the south. Also, *esp. Naut.,* **sou'** /saʊ/. [ME; OE *sūth,* c. OHG *sund-;*

akin to G *Süd*]

**South Africa** /saʊθ ˈæfrəkə/, *n.* a republic in southern Africa. Official name: **Republic of South Africa.** – **South African,** *adj.*

**South African Dutch,** *n.* **1.** →**Afrikaans.** **2.** →**Boer.**

**South America** /saʊθ əˈmɛrɪkə/, *n.* a continent in the southern part of the Western Hemisphere. – **South American,** *n.*

**South Australia** /– əsˈtreɪljə/, *n.* a State in central southern Australia, one of the six States of Australia. *Abbrev.:* SA, S.A.

South Australia: coat of arms

**South Australian** /– əsˈtreɪljən/, *n.* **1.** one who was born in South Australia or who has come to regard it as his home State. *–adj.* **2.** of or pertaining to the State of South Australia.

**southbound** /ˈsaʊθbaʊnd/, *adj.* travelling towards the south.

**south by east,** *n.* 11° 15′ (one point) east of south. *Abbrev.:* S by E. Also, *esp. Naut.,* **sou' by east.**

**south by west,** *n.* 11° 15′ (one point) west of south. *Abbrev.:* S by W. Also, *esp. Naut.,* **sou'by west.**

**South Caucasian** /ˌsaʊθ kɔˈkeɪʒən/, *n.* **1.** a family of languages of southern Caucasia. *–adj.* **2.** of or pertaining to South Caucasian.

**South China Sea,** *n.* a part of the Pacific Ocean, partially enclosed by south-east China, Vietnam, the Malay Peninsula, Borneo and the Philippines.

**Southdown** /ˈsaʊθdaʊn/, *n.* one of the purest strains of the British short wool breeds, particularly suited for the production of export fat lambs. [from the *South Downs* of England, where the sheep were orig. reared]

**south-east** /saʊθ-ˈist/, *n.* **1.** the point or direction midway between south and east. **2.** a region in this direction. *–adj.* **3.** lying towards or situated in the south-east. **4.** directed or proceeding towards the south-east. **5.** coming from the south-east, as a wind. *–adv.* **6.** towards or in the south-east. **7.** from the south-east. Also, *esp. Naut.,* **sou'-east.** – **south-easterner,** *n.*

**South-East Asia** /saʊθ-ist ˈeɪʒə/, *n.* the area which includes Brunei, Burma, Indonesia, Cambodia, Laos, Malaysia, the Philippines, Thailand and Vietnam; the south-eastern corner of Asia. – **South-East Asian,** *adj.*

**south-east by east,** *n.* 11° 15′ (one point) east of south-east; 123° 45′ from due north. *Abbrev.:* SE by E. Also, *esp. Naut.,* **sou'-east by east.**

**south-east by south,** *n.* 11° 15′ (one point) south of south-east; 146° 15′ from due north. *Abbrev.:* SE by S. Also, *esp. Naut.,* **sou'-east by sou'.**

**south-easter** /saʊθ-ˈistə/, *n.* a wind, gale, or storm from the south-east. Also, *esp. Naut.,* **sou'-easter** /saʊ-ˈistə/.

**south-easterly** /saʊθ-ˈistəli/, *adj.* **1.** of or situated in the south-east. **2.** towards or from the south-east. *–adv.* **3.** towards or from the south-east. Also, *esp. Naut.,* **sou'-easterly** /saʊ-ˈistəli/.

**south-eastern** /saʊθ-ˈistən/, *adj.* situated in, proceeding towards, or coming from the south-east. Also, *esp. Naut.,* **sou'-eastern** /saʊ-ˈistən/.

**south-eastward** /saʊθ-ˈistwəd/, *adj., adv.* **1.** Also, **south-eastwardly;** *esp. Naut.,* **sou'-eastwardly.** towards the south-east. *–n.* **2.** the south-east. Also, *esp. Naut.,* **sou'-eastward** /saʊ-ˈistwəd/.

**south-eastwards** /saʊθ-ˈistwədz/, *adv.* south-eastward. Also, *esp. Naut.,* **sou'-eastwards** /saʊ-ˈistwədz/.

**southerly** /ˈsʌðəli/, *adj.* **1.** moving, directed, or situated towards the south. **2.** coming from the south, as a wind. *–adv.* **3.** towards the south. **4.** from the south. *–n.* **5.** a wind from the south. – **southerliness,** *n.*

**southerly buster** /– ˈbʌstə/, *n.* a violent, cold southerly wind blowing on the south-eastern coast of Australia, causing a sudden drop in temperature and often accompanied by dust squalls.

**southern** /ˈsʌðən/, *adj.* **1.** lying towards, or situated in the south. **2.** directed or proceeding southwards. **3.** (*cap.*) coming from the south, as wind. **4.** of or pertaining to the south. [ME; OE *sūtherne.* See SOUTH, -ERN]

**Southern Cross** /sʌðən ˈkrɒs/, *n.* **1.** the southern constellation Crux, whose four chief stars are in the form of a cross. **2.** (*l.c.*) a western Australian plant, *Xanthosia rotundifolia,* with an attractive, somewhat cross-shaped inflorescence.

Southern Cross (def. 1)

**southern figbird** /sʌðən ˈfɪgbɜd/, *n.* a medium-sized, greenish fruit-eating bird, *Sphecotheres vieilloti,* of eastern Australia; mulberry bird; banana-bird.

**Southern Hemisphere** /sʌðən ˈhɛməsfɪə/, *n.* the half of the earth between the South Pole and the equator.

**southernmost** /ˈsʌðənmoʊst/, *adj.* farthest south.

**Southern Rhodesia** /sʌðən roʊˈdiʒə/, *n.* former name of **Rhodesia.**

**southern sassafras** /sʌðən ˈsæsəfræs/, *n.* a rainforest tree, *Atherosperma moschatum,* widely distributed on the Australian east coast and in Tasmania, with aromatic, rigid leaves, grey or white on the undersurface, and a smooth grey bark which was used by early settlers as a tea substitute.

**southern stone curlew,** *n.* a nocturnal bird, *Burhinus magnirostris,* of dark grey colour streaked with black, with cream patches showing in flight, and having an eerie, mournful cry; found throughout Australia and southern New Guinea.

**southernwood** /ˈsʌðənwʊd/, *n.* a woody-stemmed wormwood, *Artemisia abrotanum,* of southern Europe, having aromatic, finely dissected leaves.

**southing** /ˈsaʊðɪŋ/, *n.* **1.** *Astron.* **a.** the transit of a heavenly body across the celestial meridian. **b.** south declination. **2.** movement or deviation towards the south. **3.** distance due south made by a ship.

**South Korea** /saʊθ kəˈriə/, *n.* a republic in eastern Asia; formed in 1948 after the division of Korea at 38°N. Official name: **Republic of Korea.** – **South Korean,** *adj., n.*

**southland** /ˈsaʊθlænd/, *n.* **1.** a land lying in or towards the south. **2.** the southern part of a country.

**southlight roof** /ˌsaʊθlaɪt ˈruf/, *n.* (in the Southern Hemisphere) a sawtooth roof in which the spandrels are glazed and faced south, giving light without glare.

**southmost** /ˈsaʊθmoʊst/, *adj.* southernmost.

**southpaw** /ˈsaʊθpɔ/, *Colloq.* *–n.* **1.** a person who is left-handed. **2.** *Boxing.* a boxer who stands with his right arm and right leg forward. *–adj.* **3.** left-handed.

**South Pole** /saʊθ ˈpoʊl/, *n.* **1.** that end of the earth's axis of rotation marking the southernmost point of the earth. **2.** *Astron.* the zenith of the earth's south pole; the point at which the earth's axis produced cuts the southern half of the celestial sphere.

**south-south-east** /ˌsaʊθ-ˌsaʊθ-ˈist/, *n.* **1.** the point of the compass midway between south and south-east; 157° 30′ from north. *–adj.* **2.** lying or situated in this direction. *–adv.* **3.** to, in, or from this direction. *Abbrev.:* SSE. Also, *esp. Naut.,* **sou'-sou'-east** /ˌsaʊ-ˌsaʊ-ˈist/.

**south-south-west** /ˌsaʊθ-ˌsaʊθ-ˈwɛst/, *n.* **1.** the point of the compass midway between south and south-west; 202° 30′ from north. *–adj.* **2.** lying or situated in this direction. *–adv.* **3.** to, in, or from this direction. *Abbrev.:* SSW. Also, *esp. Naut.,* **sou'-sou'-west** /ˌsaʊ,-saʊ-ˈwɛst/.

**southward** /ˈsaʊθwəd/; *Naut.* /ˈsʌðəd/, *adj.* **1.** moving, bearing, facing, or situated towards the south. *–n.* **2.** the southward part, direction, or point. *–adv.* **3.** southwards. – **southwardly,** *adj., adv.*

**southwards** /ˈsaʊθwədz/, *adv.* towards the south. Also, **southward.**

**south-west** /saʊθ-ˈwɛst/, *n.* **1.** the point or direction midway between south and west. **2.** a region in this direction. *–adj.* **3.** lying towards or situated in the south-west. **4.** directed or proceeding towards the south-west. **5.** coming from the south-west, as a wind. *–adv.* **6.** in the direction of a point midway between south and west. **7.** from this direction. Also, *esp. Naut.,* **sou'-west** /saʊ'-ˈwɛst/.

**south-west by south,** *n.* 11° 15′ (one point) south of

south-west; 213° 45′ from due north. *Abbrev.:* SW by S. Also, *esp. Naut.,* **sou'-west by sou'.**

**south-west by west,** *n.* 11° 15′ (one point) west of south-west; 236° 15′ from due north. *Abbrev.:* SW by W. Also, *esp. Naut.,* **sou'-west by west.**

**south-wester** /saʊθ-'wɛstə/, *n.* a wind, gale, or storm from the south-west. Also, *esp. Naut.,* **sou'-wester** /saʊ-'wɛstə/.

**south-westerly** /saʊθ-'wɛstəli/, *adj., adv.* towards or from the south-west. Also, *esp. Naut.,* **sou'-westerly** /saʊ-'wɛstəli/.

**south-western** /saʊθ-'wɛstn/, *adj.* situated in, proceeding towards, or coming from the south-west. Also, *esp. Naut.,* **sou'-western** /saʊ-'wɛstn/.

**south-westward** /saʊθ-'wɛstwəd/, *adv., adj.* **1.** Also, **south-westwardly;** *esp. Naut.,* **sou'-westwardly.** towards the south-west. *–n.* **2.** the south-west. Also, *esp. Naut.,* **sou'-westward** /saʊ-'wɛstwəd/.

**south-westwards** /saʊθ-'wɛstwədz/, *adv.* south-westward. Also, *esp. Naut.,* **sou'-westwards** /saʊ-'wɛstwədz/.

**South Yemen** /saʊθ 'jɛmən/, *n.* an independent state in South Arabia. Official name: **Democratic People's Republic of Yemen.**

**souvenir** /suvə'nɪə/, *n.* **1.** something given or kept for remembrance; a memento. **2.** a memory. *–v.t.* **3.** *Colloq.* to pilfer. [F, n. use of *souvenir* (reflex.) to remember, from L *subvenīre* come to mind]

**sou'wester** /saʊ'wɛstə/, *n.* **1.** a waterproof hat, usu. of oil-skin, having the brim very broad behind, worn esp. by seamen. **2.** south-wester.

**sovereign** /'sɒvrən/, *n.* **1.** a monarch; a king or queen. **2.** one who has sovereign power or authority. **3.** a group or body of persons or a state possessing sovereign authority. **4.** a former British gold coin. *–adj.* **5.** belonging to or characteristic of a sovereign or sovereignty. **6.** having supreme rank, power, or authority. **7.** supreme, as power, authority, etc. **8.** greatest in degree; utmost or extreme. **9.** being above all others in character, importance, excellence, etc. **10.** efficacious or potent, as a remedy. [ME, from OF *soverain,* from L *super* above] – **sovereignly,** *adv.*

**sovereignty** /'sɒvrənti/, *n., pl.* **-ties.** **1.** the quality or state of being sovereign. **2.** the status, dominion, power, or authority of a sovereign. **3.** supreme and independent power or authority in government as possessed or claimed by a state or community. **4.** a sovereign state, community, or political unit.

**soviet** /'soʊviət, 'sɒ-/, *n.* **1.** (in the Soviet Union) **a.** (before the revolution) a council of any kind, presumably elected by all. **b.** (after the revolution) a local council, orig. elected only by manual workers, with certain powers of local administration. **c.** (after the revolution) a higher local council elected by a local council, part of a pyramid of soviets, culminating in the **Supreme Soviet.** **2.** any similar assembly connected with a socialist governmental system elsewhere. *–adj.* **3.** of a soviet. **4.** (*cap.*) of the Soviet Union: *a Soviet statesman.* [Russ. *souyet* council]

**sovietise** /'soʊviətaɪz/, *v.t.,* **-tised, -tising.** to bring under the influence or domination of the Soviet Union. Also, **sovietize.** – **sovietisation** /ˌsoʊviətaɪ'zeɪʃən/, *n.*

**sovietism** /'soʊviətɪzəm/, *n.* the soviet system of government. – **sovietist,** *n., adj.*

**Soviet Union** /ˌsoʊviət 'junjən/, *n.* a federal union of fifteen constituent republics, in eastern Europe and western and northern Asia. Official name: **Union of Soviet Socialist Republics.**

**sovran** /'sɒvrən/, *n., adj. Poetic.* →**sovereign.**

**sow**[1] /soʊ/, *v.,* **sowed, sown** or **sowed, sowing.** *–v.t.* **1.** to scatter (seed) over land, earth, etc., for growth; plant (seed, and hence a crop). **2.** to scatter seed over (land, earth, etc.) for the purpose of growth. **3.** to introduce for development; seek to propagate or extend; disseminate: *to sow distrust or dissension.* **4.** to strew or sprinkle with anything. *–v.i.* **5.** to sow seed, as for the production of a crop. [ME *sowen,* OE *sāwan,* c. G *säen;* akin to L *serere*] – **sower,** *n.*

**sow**[2] /saʊ/, *n.* **1.** an adult female pig. **2.** the adult female of various other animals. **3.** *Metall.* a mould of larger size than a pig. **4. a.** *Metall.* a channel which conducts the molten metal to the rows of moulds in the pig bed. **b.** a mass of metal solidified in such a channel or mould. **5.** *Metall.* an accretion that frequently forms in the hearth or crucible of a furnace and which consists mainly of iron. [ME *sow(e),* from OE *sugu*]

**sowbane** /'saʊbeɪn/, *n.* a herb, *Chenopodium hybridum,* of Europe, commonly found on waste ground, and considered fatal to swine.

**sowbread** /'saʊbrɛd/, *n.* **1.** a common wild cyclamen, of central Europe, *Cyclamen europaeum,* with dark green leaves spotted with white. **2.** a related herb, *Cyclamen neapolitanum,* widely cultivated for its showy pink or white flowers. [SOW[2] (from the fact that its rootstocks are eaten by swine) + BREAD]

**sowbug** /'saʊbʌg/, *n. U.S.* →**slater.**

**sown** /soʊn/, *v.* past participle of **sow**[1].

**sow-thistle** /'saʊ-θɪsəl/, *n.* any plant of the genus *Sonchus,* esp. *S. oleraceus,* a common, noxious weed having thistle-like leaves, yellow flowers, and a milky juice.

sow-thistle

**Soxhlet apparatus** /'sɒkslət æpəˌratəs/, *n.* a laboratory apparatus for extracting the soluble portion of any substance by continuously circulating a boiling solvent through it. [named after Franz von *Soxhlet,* 1848-1926, German agricultural chemist]

**soya bean** /'sɔɪjə bin/, *n.* **1.** a bushy, leguminous plant, *Glycine max,* of south-east Asia. **2.** the seed of this plant which is used as food, livestock feed, etc., and which yields an oil used as a food and in the manufacture of soap, candles, etc. Also **soy, soybean.**

**soya sauce** /'– sɔs/, *n.* a salty dark brown sauce, made by fermenting soya beans in brine. Also, **soy sauce.** [Jap., var. of *shoy,* short for *shō-yu,* from Chinese *shī-yu* (from *shī* kind of bean + *yu* oil)]

**sozzled** /'sɒzəld/, *adj. Colloq.* drunk. [obs. *sozzle* drunken stupor (akin to SOUSE[1]) + -ED[3]]

**sp.,** **1.** special. **2.** species. **3.** specific. **4.** specimen. **5.** spelling. **6.** spirit.

**s.p.,** without issue. [L *sine prole*]

**Sp.,** **1.** Spain. **2.** Spaniard. **3.** Spanish.

**S.P.,** starting price.

**spa** /spa/, *n.* **1.** a mineral spring, or a locality in which such springs exist. **2.** an enclosed section of a swimming pool through which heated, aerated water is pumped at some pressure. [from *Spa,* town in E Belgium, famous for its mineral springs]

**SPA,** Socialist Party of Australia.

**space** /speɪs/, *n., v.,* **spaced, spacing.** *–n.* **1.** the unlimited or indefinitely great general receptacle of things, commonly conceived as an expanse extending in all directions (or having three dimensions), in which, or occupying portions of which, all material objects are located. **2.** the portion or extent of this in a given instance; extent or room in three dimensions: *the space occupied by a body.* **3.** that part of the universe which lies outside the earth's atmosphere in which the density of matter is very low; outer space. **4.** extent or area; a particular extent of surface: *to fill in blank spaces in a document.* **5. a.** the area or position for a person to stand, sit, etc.: *save me a space in the queue.* **b.** a seat, berth, or room on an aeroplane, train, etc. **6.** linear distance; a particular distance: *trees set at equal spaces apart.* **7.** extent, or a particular extent, of time: *a space of two hours.* **8.** an interval of time; a while: *after a space he continued his story.* **9.** *Music.* one of the degrees or intervals between the lines of the stave. **10.** *Print.* one of the blank pieces of metal used to separate words, etc. **11.** *Teleg.* a period of time having a fixed relation to dots and dashes, during which no signal is transmitted in morse or similar systems. *–v.t.* **12.** to fix the space or spaces of; divide into spaces. **13.** to set some distance apart. **14.** *Print., etc.* **a.** to separate (words, letters, or lines) by spaces. **b.** to extend by inserting more space or spaces (usu. fol. by *out*). [ME, from OF *espace,* from L *spatium*]

**space age** /'– eɪdʒ/, *n.* the period in the history of man when exploration of and travel in space is possible.

**space-age** /'speɪs-eɪdʒ/, *adj.* **1.** of or pertaining to the space age, esp. to its advanced technology. **2.** ultra-modern; highly sophisticated: *a car with space-age styling.*

**space-bar** /ˈspeɪs-ba/, *n.* a horizontal bar on a typewriter which is depressed in order to move the carriage one space to the left.

**space capsule** /ˈspeɪs ˌkæpʃul/, *n.* a container for instruments or astronauts which is capable of being sent into space and which can be recovered on its return.

**spacecraft** /ˈspeɪskraft/, *n.* a vehicle capable of travelling in space.

**spaced** /speɪst/, *adj.* →**spaced-out.**

**spaced-out** /speɪst-ˈaʊt/, *adj.* in a euphoric or dreamy state, as if under the influence of a hallucinogen. Also, *esp. in predicative use,* **spaced out.**

**space heater** /ˈspeɪs hitə/, *n.* a domestic or industrial heater used for heating an enclosed area, as a room or workshop.

**space lattice** /ˈ– lætəs/, *n.* →**lattice** (def. 3).

**spaceless** /ˈspeɪsləs/, *adj.* **1.** independent of space; infinite. **2.** occupying no space.

**spaceman** /ˈspeɪsmæn/, *n.* a traveller in outer space. – **spacewoman,** *n. fem.*

**spaceport** /ˈspeɪspɔt/, *n.* a place where rockets are launched, esp. rockets carrying manned spacecraft.

**space probe** /ˈspeɪs proʊb/, *n.* **1.** a rocket-propelled missile capable of travelling in space and of radioing back to earth information concerning its environment.

**spacer** /ˈspeɪsə/, *n.* **1.** one who or that which spaces. **2.** *Bldg Trades.* a member (def. 4) which separates one material or element in building construction from another.

**spaceship** /ˈspeɪsʃɪp/, *n.* a manned spacecraft.

**space shuttle** /ˈspeɪs ʃʌtl/, *n.* a re-useable rocket-propelled spacecraft designed to transport equipment and personnel between earth and a satellite.

**space station** /ˈ– steɪʃən/, *n.* a manned artificial satellite in orbit around the earth.

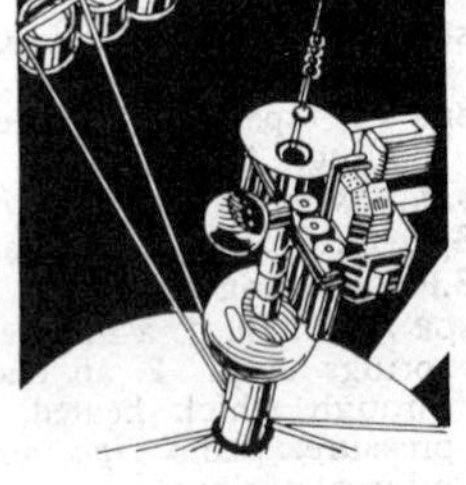

space station

**spacesuit** /ˈspeɪssut/, *n.* →**pressure suit.**

**space-time** /speɪs-ˈtaɪm/, *n.* **1.** a four-dimensional continuum in which the coordinates are the three spatial coordinates and time. The events and objects of any spatial and temporal region may be conceived as part of this continuum. *–adj.* **2.** of or pertaining to any system with three spatial and one temporal coordinates. **3.** of or pertaining to both space and time.

**space travel** /ˈspeɪs trævəl/, *n.* flight in space in a manned spacecraft.

**spacewalk** /ˈspeɪswɔk/, *v.i.* an excursion from a spacecraft during which one floats weightlessly in space, while held to the craft by a lifeline.

**spacey** /ˈspeɪsi/, *adj. Colloq.* dreamy; hallucinatory.

**spacing** /ˈspeɪsɪŋ/, *n.* **1.** the act of one who or that which spaces. **2.** the fixing or arranging of spaces.

**spacious** /ˈspeɪʃəs/, *adj.* **1.** containing much space, as a house, room, court, street, etc.; amply large. **2.** occupying much space; vast. **3.** of a great extent or area; broad; large; great. **4.** broad in scope, range, inclusiveness, etc. [ME, from L *spatiōsus*] – **spaciously,** *adv.* – **spaciousness,** *n.*

**spade**[1] /speɪd/, *n., v.,* **spaded, spading.** *–n.* **1.** a tool for digging, having an iron blade adapted for pressing into the ground with the foot, and a long handle commonly with a grip or crosspiece at the top. **2.** some implement, piece, or part resembling this. **3.** a sharp projection on a guncarriage embedded in the ground to restrict backward movement of the carriage during recoil. **4.** a cutting tool used to strip the blubber or skin, as from a whale. **5. call a spade a spade,** to call a thing by its real name; speak plainly or bluntly. *–v.t.* **6.** to dig, cut, or remove with a spade. [ME; OE *spadu,* c. G *Spaten*] – **spadeful** /ˈspeɪdfʊl/, *n.*

**spade**[2] /speɪd/, *n.* **1.** a black figure shaped like an inverted heart with a short stem at the cusp opposite the point, used on playing cards. **2.** a card of the suit bearing such figures. **3.** (*pl.*) the suit of cards bearing this figure. **4.** *Colloq.* (*derog.*) someone of very dark skin, as a Negro, Aborigine, etc. [It., pl. of *spada,* orig., sword, later mark on cards, from L *spatha,* from Gk *spáthē* wooden blade]

**spadefoot** /ˈspeɪdfʊt/, *n.* any of several toads of the family Pelobatidae, widely distributed in Europe and Asia, usu. in sandy areas, where they burrow into the earth for concealment.

**spadework** /ˈspeɪdwɜk/, *n.* preliminary or initial work, esp. of a laborious or tedious nature.

**spadger** /ˈspædʒə/, *n. Colloq.* a sparrow. Also, **spag.** [fanciful alteration of SPARROW]

**spadiceous** /speɪˈdɪʃəs/, *adj.* **1.** *Bot.* **a.** of the nature of a spadix. **b.** bearing a spadix. **2.** of a bright brown colour. [NL *spādiceus,* from L *spādix* SPADIX]

**spadix** /ˈspeɪdɪks/, *n., pl.* **spadices** /speɪˈdaɪsiz/. an inflorescence consisting of a spike with a fleshy or thickened axis, usu. enclosed in a spathe, as in the arum lily. [L, from Gk: torn-off palm bough, as adj., brown, palm-coloured]

**spado** /ˈspeɪdoʊ/, *n., pl.* **spadones** /spəˈdoʊniz/. an impotent or castrated man. [L, from Gk *spádōn* eunuch]

**spag**[1] /spæg/, *n. Colloq.* **1.** spaghetti. **2.** (*derog.*) an Italian. **3.** (*derog.*) the Italian language.

**spag**[2] /spæg/, *n. Colloq.* a sparrow. [var. of SPADGER]

**spaghetti** /spəˈgɛti/, *n.* **1.** a kind of pasta of Italian origin, made from wheat flour, in long, thin, solid strips or tubes, and cooked by boiling. **2.** *Elect. Colloq.* plastic sleeving for wires. [It., pl. of *spaghetto,* diminutive of *spago* cord]

**spaghetti bol** /– ˈbɒl/, *n. Colloq.* →**spaghetti bolognaise.**

**spaghetti bolognaise** /– bɒləˈneɪz/, *n.* a dish of spaghetti with bolognaise sauce.

**spaghetti western** /– ˈwɛstn/, *n.* a film made in Italy in the genre of a western, usu. technically excellent but with a simple story-line.

**spagyric** /spəˈdʒɪrɪk/, *Rare. –adj.* **1.** pertaining to alchemy. *–n.* **2.** an alchemist. [NL *spagiricus,* probably coined by Paracelsus] – **spagyrist** /ˈspædʒərəst/, *n.*

**Spain** /speɪn/, *n.* a country in south-western Europe.

**spake** /speɪk/, *v. Archaic.* past tense of **speak.**

**spall** /spɔl/, *n.* **1.** a chip or splinter, as of stone or ore. *–v.t.* **2.** to break into smaller pieces, as ore; split or chip. *–v.i.* **3.** to break or split off in chips or bits. [ME *spalle* chip. Cf. E d. *spale* chip and *spald,* v., split, c. G *spalten*]

**spallation** /spəˈleɪʃən/, *n.* a nuclear reaction in which a high-energy incident particle, or photon, causes the struck nucleus to emit several particles or fragments.

**spam** /spæm/, *n. Chiefly Brit.* a type of ready-cooked tinned meat. [Trademark: *sp(iced) (h)am*]

**span**[1] /spæn/, *n., v.,* **spanned, spanning.** *–n.* **1.** the distance between the tip of the thumb and the tip of the little finger when the hand is fully extended. **2.** a unit of length corresponding to this distance, commonly taken as 9 inches or 23 cm. **3.** a distance, amount, piece, etc., of this length or of some small extent. **4.** the distance or space between two supports of a bridge, beam, or similar structure. **5.** the full extent, stretch, or reach of anything: *the span of memory.* **6.** *Aeron.* the distance between the wingtips of an aeroplane. **7.** a short space of time, as the term or period of living. *–v.t.* **8.** to measure by, or as by, the hand with the thumb and little finger extended. **9.** to encircle with the hand or hands, as the waist. **10.** to extend over or across (a space, a river, etc.). **11.** to provide with something that extends over: *to span a river with a bridge.* **12.** to extend, reach, or pass over (space or time). [ME and OE, c. G *Spanne*]

**span**[2] /spæn/, *n.* a pair of horses or other animals harnessed and driven together. [Flem., D, or LG, from *spannen* fasten, unite]

**span**[3] /spæn/, *v. Archaic.* past tense of **spin.**

**Span.,** Spanish.

**spandrel** /ˈspændrəl/, *n. Archit.* **1.** the triangular space between either half of the extrados of an arch and a rectangular moulding or part enclosing the

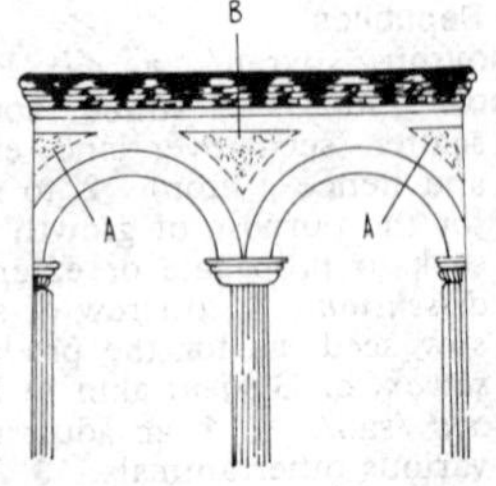


A, spandrel (def. 1); B, spandrel (def. 2)

i = peat ɪ = pit ɛ = pet æ = pat a = part ɒ = pot ʌ = putt ɔ = port ʊ = put u = pool ɜ = pert ə = apart aɪ = buy eɪ = bay ɔɪ = boy aʊ = how oʊ = hoe ɪə = here ɛə = hair ʊə = tour g = give θ = thin ð = then ʃ = show ʒ = measure tʃ = choke dʒ = joke ŋ = sing j = you ɒ̃ = Fr. bon

arch. **2.** the space included between the extradoses of two adjacent arches and a horizontal moulding or part above. [ME *spaundrell,* apparently diminutive of AF *spaundre;* orig. uncert.]

**spangle** /'spæŋgəl/, *n., v.,* **-gled, -gling.** *–n.* **1.** a small, thin, often circular piece of glittering material, as metal, for decorating garments, etc. **2.** any small, bright drop, object, spot, or the like. *–v.t.* **3.** to decorate with spangles. **4.** to sprinkle or stud with small, bright pieces, objects, spots, etc. *–v.i.* **5.** to glitter with, or like spangles. [ME *spangele,* from *spange* spangle (from MD) + *-le,* diminutive suffix]

**spangled drongo** /spæŋgəld 'drɒŋgoʊ/, *n.* a glossy black, green-spotted, migratory bird, *Chibea bracheata,* the sole Australian representative of the widespread family Dicruridae.

spangled drongo

**Spaniard** /'spænjəd/, *n.* **1.** a native or inhabitant of Spain. **2.** (*l.c.*) Also, **spaniard plant.** *N.Z.* →**spear grass.**

**spaniel** /'spænjəl/, *n.* **1.** a dog of any of various breeds of small or medium size, usu. with a long, silky coat and drooping ears, used in hunting and as pets. **2.** a submissive, fawning, or cringing person. [ME *spaynel,* from OF *espaigneul* Spanish (dog), from L *Hispāniolus*]

**Spanish** /'spænɪʃ/, *adj.* **1.** of or pertaining to Spain, its people, or their language. *–n.* **2.** the Spanish people collectively. **3.** a Romance language, the language of Spain, standard also in Latin America (except Brazil).

**Spanish bayonet** /– 'beɪənət/, *n.* any of certain plants of the genus *Yucca,* with narrow, spine-tipped leaves.

**Spanish broom** /– 'brum/, *n.* a papilionaceous shrub with long rush-like stems and yellow flowers, *Spartium junceum,* a frequently cultivated native of southern Europe.

**Spanish chestnut** /– 'tʃɛsnʌt/, *n.* **1.** a large, deciduous tree, *Castanea sativa,* a native of southern Europe and Asia Minor but frequently cultivated elsewhere for its edible nut and valuable timber. **2.** the nut itself.

**Spanish cream** /– 'krim/, *n.* a stirred egg custard with gelatine, flavourings and whipped egg whites folded in before allowing to set. Also, **spanish delight.**

**Spanish dancer** /– 'dænsə/, *n. Colloq.* cancer. [rhyming slang]

**Spanish fly** /– 'flaɪ/, *n.* **1.** a blister beetle, *Lytta vesicatoria.* **2.** a preparation, esp. used as an aphrodisiac, made from this beetle dried and powdered; cantharides.

**Spanish mackerel** /– 'mækərəl/, *n.* **1.** Also, **Queensland kingfish.** a valuable commercial fish, *Scomberomorus commerson,* of Queensland waters. **2.** any of several related marine food fishes, as the school mackerel, *S. queenslandicus.* **3.** any of various scombroid marine food fishes found elsewhere, as the European *Pneumatophorus colias,* or *Scomberomorus maculatus,* of the American Atlantic coast.

**Spanish moss** /– 'mɒs/, *n.* an epiphytic plant, *Tillandsia usneoides,* that hangs from the branches of trees in long greyish-green tufts; found in the southern U.S. and the West Indies. Also, **Florida moss.**

**Spanish omelette** /– 'ɒmlət/, *n.* **1.** an omelette made with strips of pimento, garlic, and tomatoes and cooked like a pancake. **2.** an omelette made with sauté potatoes.

**Spanish onion** /– 'ʌnjən/, *n.* a large-sized, mild, succulent onion.

**Spanish rice** /– 'raɪs/, *n.* rice cooked with onions, herbs, and spices; served as a side-dish.

**spank**[1] /spæŋk/, *v.t.* **1.** to strike (a person, usu. a child) with the open hand, a slipper, etc., esp. on the buttocks, as in punishment. *–n.* **2.** a blow given in spanking; a smart or resounding slap. [imitative]

**spank**[2] /spæŋk/, *v.i.* to move quickly, vigorously, or smartly. [backformation from SPANKING[1]]

**spanker** /'spæŋkə/, *n. Naut.* **1.** the lower fore-and-aft sail on the aftermost mast of a ship or barque. **2.** (on a schooner-rigged vessel having more than three masts) the fourth mast and sail counting aft from the bow. [SPANK[2] + -ER[1]]

**spanking**[1] /'spæŋkɪŋ/, *adj.* **1.** moving rapidly and smartly. **2.** quick and vigorous, as the pace. **3.** blowing briskly, as a breeze. **4.** *Colloq.* unusually fine, great, large, etc. [cf. Dan. *spanke* strut]

**spanking**[2] /'spæŋkɪŋ/, *n.* **1.** the act of one who spanks. **2.** this act administered as a punishment.

**span-loading** /'spæn-loʊdɪŋ/, *n.* See **loading** (def. 5).

**spanner** /'spænə/, *n.* **1.** one who or that which spans. **2.** a tool for catching upon or gripping and turning or twisting the head of a bolt, a nut, a pipe, or the like, commonly consisting of a bar of metal with fixed or adjustable jaws. **3. spanner in the works,** *Colloq.* any cause of confusion or impediment. [G]

**spanner crab** /'– kræb/, *n.* →**frog crab.**

**span of hours,** *n.* a formula prescribing a period in each day during which an employee's hours of work are to be performed, and outside which no work is to be performed except at overtime rates. Also, **spread of hours.**

**span roof** /spæn 'ruf/, *n.* a roof having two equally inclined sloping sides.

**spar**[1] /spa/, *n., v.,* **sparred, sparring.** *–n.* **1.** *Naut.* a stout pole such as those used for masts, etc.; a mast, yard, boom, gaff, or the like. **2.** *Aeron.* a principal lateral member of the framework of a wing of an aeroplane. *–v.t.* **3.** to provide or make with spars. [ME *sparre.* Cf. G *sparren,* Icel. *sperra* rafter]

**spar**[2] /spa/, *v.,* **sparred, sparring,** *n.* *–v.i.* **1.** *Boxing.* **a.** to make the motions of attack and defence with the arms and fists; practise boxing. **b.** to box with light blows, esp. while seeking an opening in an opponent's defence. **2.** to strike or fight with the feet or spurs, as cocks, etc. **3.** to bandy words; engage in a verbal dispute of a not particularly serious or acrimonious kind. *–n.* **4.** a motion of sparring. **5.** a boxing match. **6.** a dispute. [ME; orig. meaning thrust (n. and v.); orig. uncert.]

**spar**[3] /spa/, *n.* any of various more or less lustrous, transparent or translucent, easily cleavable crystalline minerals, as fluorspar. [backformation from *spar-stone* spar, OE *spærstan* gypsum. Cf. MLG *spar*]

**sparable** /'spærəbəl/, *n.* a small, headless nail used by shoemakers. [var. of *sparrow bill*]

**sparaxis** /spə'ræksəs/, *n.* any small plant of the genus *Sparaxis,* family Iridaceae, of southern Africa, several species of which are grown for their brightly coloured flowers.

**spar buoy** /'spa bɔɪ/, *n.* a buoy shaped like a log or spar, anchored vertically.

**spar deck** /'– dɛk/, *n.* the upper deck of a vessel, extending from stem to stern.

**spare** /spɛə/, *v.,* **spared, sparing,** *adj.,* **sparer, sparest,** *n.* *–v.t.* **1.** to refrain from harming or destroying; leave uninjured; forbear to punish: *to spare a fallen adversary.* **2.** to deal gently or leniently with; show consideration for: *to spare a person's feelings.* **3.** to save from strain, discomfort, annoyance, or the like, or from a particular cause of it: *to spare oneself trouble.* **4.** to refrain from, forbear, omit, or withhold, as action or speech. **5.** to refrain from employing, as some instrument, means, aid, etc.: *to spare the rod.* **6.** to set aside for a particular purpose: *to spare land for a garden.* **7.** to part with or let go, as from a supply, esp. without inconvenience or loss: *to spare a few cents.* **8.** to dispense with or do without. **9.** to use economically or frugally; refrain from using up or wasting. **10.** to have left over or unused: *we have room to spare.* *–v.i.* **11.** to use economy; be frugal. **12.** to refrain from action; forbear. **13.** to refrain from inflicting injury or punishment; exercise lenience or mercy. *–adj.* **14.** kept in reserve, as for possible use: *a spare tyre.* **15.** being in excess of present need; free for other use: *spare time.* **16.** frugally restricted; meagre, as living, diet, etc. **17.** lean or thin, as a person. **18.** scanty or scant, as in amount, fullness, etc. **19.** sparing, economical, or temperate, as persons. *–n.* **20.** a spare thing, part, etc., as an extra tyre for emergency use. **21.** *Tenpin Bowling.* **a.** the knocking down of all the pins in two consecutive bowls. **b.** the score made by bowling a spare. **22.** *Colloq.* →**spare part.** [ME; OE *sparian,* c. D and G *sparen*] – **sparely,** *adv.* – **spareness,** *n.* – **sparer,** *n.*

**spare boy** /– 'bɔɪ/, *n.* an assistant to the driver of a bullock team.

i = peat ɪ = pit ɛ = pet æ = pat a = part ɒ = pot ʌ = putt ɔ = port ʊ = put u = pool ɜ = pert ə = apart aɪ = buy eɪ = bay ɔɪ = boy aʊ = how
oʊ = hoe ɪə = here ɛə = hair ʊə = tour g = give θ = thin ð = then ʃ = show ʒ = measure tʃ = choke dʒ = joke ŋ = sing j = you õ = Fr. bon

**spare part** /– 'pat/, *n.* a part which replaces a faulty, worn, or broken part of a machine, esp. a motor vehicle. Also, **spare.**

**spare ribs** /'– rɪbz/, *n.pl.* a cut of meat, esp. pork, containing ribs from the upper or fore end of the row, where there is little meat adhering. [transposed var. of *ribspare,* from MHG *ribbespēr* rib cut. Cf. E *spare,* n., cut, slit]

**spare tyre** /– 'taɪə/, *n.* **1.** an extra tyre carried on a car, etc., in case a replacement is needed. **2.** *Colloq.* a roll of fat around a person's midriff.

**sparge** /spadʒ/, *v.t., v.i.,* **sparged, sparging.** *Rare.* to scatter or sprinkle. [L *spargere* sprinkle] – **sparger,** *n.*

**sparge arms** /'– amz/, *n.pl.* perforated tubes that spray hot water on to the malt mash in the manufacture of beer.

**sparid** /'spærəd/, *adj.* of or belonging to the Sparidae, a family of deep-bodied, marine fishes, as the Australian snapper and bream.

**sparing** /'spɛərɪŋ/, *adj.* **1.** that spares. **2.** economical (*in*); chary (*of*). **3.** lenient or merciful. **4.** frugally restricted. **5.** scanty; limited. – **sparingly,** *adv.* – **sparingness,** *n.*

**spark**[1] /spak/, *n.* **1.** an ignited or fiery particle such as is thrown off by burning wood, etc., or produced by one hard body striking against another. **2.** *Elect.* **a.** the light produced by a sudden discontinuous discharge of electricity through air or another dielectric. **b.** the discharge itself. **c.** any electric arc of relatively small energy content. **d.** such a spark in the spark plug of an internal-combustion engine. **e.** the arrangement of devices producing and governing this spark. **3.** a small amount or trace of something. **4.** a trace of life or vitality. *–v.i.* **5.** to emit or produce sparks. **6.** to issue as or like sparks. **7.** to send forth gleams or flashes. **8.** (of the ignition in an internal-combustion engine) to function correctly in forming the sparks. *–v.t.* **9.** *Colloq.* to kindle or stimulate (interest, activity, etc.). **10. spark off,** to bring about; cause; precipitate. [ME; OE *spearca,* c. MD and MLG *sparke*]

**spark**[2] /spak/, *n.* **1.** a gay, elegant, or showily dressed young man. **2.** a beau, lover, or suitor. *–v.t.* **3.** *U.S. Colloq.* to pay attentions to (a woman); court. *–v.i.* **4.** *U.S. Colloq.* to engage in courtship; be the beau or suitor. [either fig. use of SPARK[1]; or metathetic var. of *sprack* lively, from Scand.; cf. Icel. *sprækr* sprightly] – **sparkish,** *adj.*

**spark coil** /'– kɔɪl/, *n.* an induction coil for producing the spark in an internal combustion engine.

**sparker** /'spakə/, *n.* **1.** something that produces sparks. **2.** an apparatus used to test insulation on wires.

**spark gap** /'spak gæp/, *n.* a space between two electrodes across which a discharge of electricity may take place.

**spark generator** /'– dʒɛnəreɪtə/, *n.* an alternating current power source with a capacitor discharging across a spark gap.

**sparking potential** /'spakɪŋ pətɛnʃəl/, *n.* the difference in potential required to make an electrical spark pass across a given gap. Also, **sparking voltage.**

**sparkle** /'spakəl/, *v.,* **-kled, -kling,** *n. –v.i.* **1.** to issue in or as in little sparks, as fire, light, etc. **2.** to emit little sparks, as burning matter. **3.** to shine with little gleams of light, as a brilliant gem; glisten brightly; glitter. **4.** to effervesce, as wine. **5.** to be brilliant, lively, or vivacious. *–v.t.* **6.** to cause to sparkle. *–n.* **7.** a little spark or fiery particle. **8.** a sparkling appearance, lustre, or play of light: *the sparkle of a diamond.* **9.** brilliance; liveliness or vivacity. [frequentative of SPARK[1]]

**sparkler** /'spaklə/, *n.* **1.** one who or that which sparkles. **2.** a handheld firework that burns slowly, with a bright white glow, and gives off a shower of sparks. **3.** *Colloq.* a diamond.

**sparkling wine** /spaklɪŋ 'waɪn/, *n.* a wine that is naturally carbonated by a secondary fermentation.

**spark photography** /spak fə'tɒgrəfi/, *n.* photography using a spark as a source of illumination when a very brief exposure is required, as for photographing fast-moving objects, etc.

**spark plug** /'– plʌg/, *n.* a device inserted in the cylinder of an internal-combustion engine, containing two terminals between which passes the electric spark for igniting the explosive gases. Also, **sparking plug.**

**sparks** /spaks/, *n. Colloq.* a radio operator or electrician.

**spark transmitter** /'spak trænzmɪtə/, *n.* a radio transmitting set which generates electromagnetic waves because of the characteristic of a spark gap and a tuned circuit through which energy can surge.

**sparling** /'spalɪŋ/, *n.* the European smelt, *Osmerus eperlanus.* [ME *sperlyng(e),* from OF *esperlinge,* of Gmc orig.]

**sparoid** /'spærɔɪd/, *adj.* resembling or related to the Sparidae, a family of deep-bodied marine fishes, as the Australian snapper and bream. [NL *sparoīdēs,* from L *sparus,* from Gk *spáros* kind of fish. See -OID]

**sparring partner** /'sparɪŋ patnə/, *n.* **1.** one who spars with a boxer in training. **2.** *Colloq.* one with whom one has happily shared experiences but with whom it has seldom been possible to agree.

**sparrow** /'spæroʊ/, *n.* **1.** a small, hardy, pugnacious weaverbird, *Passer domesticus,* of Europe, introduced into Australia, America, etc., as a destroyer of insects, but now commonly regarded as a pest; house sparrow. **2.** any of various weaverbirds (family Ploceidae) of the Old World. **3.** any of numerous American finches (family Fringillidae), as the **chipping sparrow** (*Spizella passerina*). [ME *sparowe,* OE *spearwa,* c. Goth. *sparwa,* Icel. *spörr*]

**sparrow fart** /'– fat/, *n. Colloq.* dawn; very early morning.

**sparrowgrass** /'spæroʊgras/, *n. Colloq.* asparagus.

**sparrowhawk** /'spæroʊhɔk/, *n.* **1.** a small, brownish, square-tailed hawk which preys on smaller birds, the **collared sparrowhawk,** *Accipiter cirrocephalus,* of Australia, Tasmania and New Guinea. **2.** →**nankeen kestrel. 3.** a small European hawk, *Accipiter nisus,* which preys extensively on birds. **4.** an American falcon, *Falco sparverius,* which preys esp. on grasshoppers and small mammals.

**sparrowpeck** /'spæroʊpɛk/, *v.t.* to treat a building surface by chipping to provide a key for subsequent finishes. – **sparrowpecking,** *n.* Also, **sparrowpick.**

**sparry** /'spari/, *adj.* of or pertaining to mineral spar.

**sparry coal** /– 'koʊl/, *n.* coal filled with calcite.

**sparse** /spas/, *adj.,* **sparser, sparsest. 1.** thinly scattered or distributed: *a sparse population.* **2.** thin; not thick or dense: *sparse hair.* **3.** scanty; meagre. [L *sparsus,* pp., scattered] – **sparsely,** *adv.* – **sparseness, sparsity** /'spasəti/, *n.*

**Spartan** /'spatn/, *adj.* **1.** rigorously simple, frugal, or austere; sternly disciplined; brave. *–n.* **2.** a person of Spartan characteristics. [orig. with ref. to *Sparta,* an ancient city in S Greece, famous for strict discipline and training of soldiers] – **Spartanism,** *n.*

**sparteine** /'spatin, -iən/, *n.* a bitter, poisonous, liquid alkaloid, $C_{15}H_{26}N_2$, obtained from the common broom, *Cytisus scoparius,* used in medicine. [NL *spartium* genus of broom (from Gk *spártos* broom) + -INE[2]]

**spasm** /'spæzəm/, *n.* **1.** *Pathol.* a sudden, abnormal, involuntary muscular contraction; an affection consisting of a continued muscular contraction (**tonic spasm**), or of a series of alternating muscular contractions and relaxations (**clonic spasm**). **2.** any sudden, brief spell of great energy, activity, feeling, etc. [ME *spasme,* from L *spasmus* or *spasma,* from Gk *spasmós* or *spásma*]

**spasmodic** /spæz'mɒdɪk/, *adj.* **1.** pertaining to or of the nature of a spasm; characterised by spasms. **2.** resembling a spasm or spasms; sudden and violent, but brief; intermittent: *spasmodic efforts.* **3.** given to or characterised by bursts of excitement. Also, **spasmodical.** [ML *spasmodicus,* from Gk *spasmṓdēs*] – **spasmodically,** *adv.*

**spastic** /'spæstɪk/, *adj.* **1.** pertaining to, of the nature of, or characterised by spasm, esp. tonic spasm. **2.** idiotic; clumsy. *–n.* **3.** a person exhibiting such spasms, esp. one who has cerebral palsy. **4.** *Colloq.* **a.** a fool. **b.** a clumsy person. [L *spasticus,* from Gk *spastikós*] – **spastically,** *adv.*

**spastic centre** /'– sɛntə/, *n.* a centre for the treatment, diagnosis and training of children suffering from cerebral palsy.

**spat**[1] /spæt/, *n., v.,* **spatted, spatting.** *–n.* **1.** a light blow; a slap; a smack. **2.** a petty quarrel. *–v.i.* **3.** to slap. **4.** to engage in a petty quarrel or dispute. **5.** to splash; spatter. *–v.t.* **6.** to strike lightly; slap. [probably imitative]

**spat**[2] /spæt/, *v.* past tense and past participle of **spit.**

**spat**[3] /spæt/, *n.* (*usu. pl.*) a short gaiter worn over the instep, usu. fastened under the foot with a strap. [short for SPATTERDASH]

**spat**[4] /spæt/, *n.* **1.** the spawn of an oyster or similar shellfish. **2.** young oysters collectively. **3.** a young oyster. [orig. uncert.; ? akin to SPIT[1], *v.*]

**spatchcock** /'spætʃkɒk/, *n.* **1.** a chicken, esp. a small one, split in half, and usu. served grilled. *–v.t.* **2.** to prepare a chicken for serving in this manner. [probably alteration of SPITCHCOCK]

**spate** /speɪt/, *n.* **1.** a sudden, almost overwhelming, outpouring: *a spate of words.* **2.** a flood or inundation; a state of flood. **3.** a sudden heavy downpour of rain. [ME; orig. obscure]

**spathaceous** /spə'θeɪʃəs/, *adj. Bot.* **1.** of the nature of or resembling a spathe. **2.** having a spathe.

**spathe** /speɪð/, *n.* (in a plant) a bract or pair of bracts, often large and coloured, subtending or enclosing a spadix or flower cluster. See **spadix.** [Gk: sword blade] – **spathed,** *adj.* – **spathose** /'speɪθoʊs, 'spæ-/, *adj.*

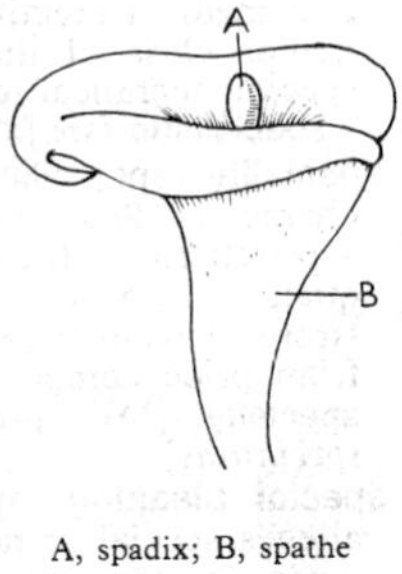

**spathic** /'spæθɪk/, *adj. Mineral.* like spar. Also, **spathose** /'spæθoʊs/. [G *Spath* spar + -IC]

**spathulate** /'spæθjələt/, *adj. Bot.* →**spatulate.**

**spatial** /'speɪʃəl/, *adj.* **1.** of or pertaining to space. **2.** existing or occurring in space; having extension in space. [L *spatium* SPACE + -AL[1]] – **spatiality** /speɪʃi'æləti/, *n.* – **spatially,** *adv.*

A, spadix; B, spathe

**spatio-,** a word element meaning space. [L *spatium* SPACE + -O-]

**spätlese** /'spætleɪz, ʃpɛt'leɪzə/, *adj.* (of wine) made from berries picked late in the season, and therefore naturally sweet. Also, **spatlese.** [G *spät* late + *(aus)lesen* to select]

**spatter** /'spætə/, *v.t.* **1.** to scatter or dash in small particles or drops: *to spatter mud.* **2.** to splash with something in small particles: *to spatter the ground with water.* **3.** to sprinkle or spot with something that soils or stains. *–v.i.* **4.** to send out small particles or drops, as boiling matter. **5.** to strike as in a shower, as bullets. *–n.* **6.** the act or the sound of spattering: *the spatter of rain on a roof.* **7.** a splash or spot of something spattered. [apparently a frequentative of D and LG *spatten* burst, spout] – **spatteringly,** *adv.*

**spatterdash** /'spætədæʃ/, *n.* **1.** *(usu. pl.)* a kind of long gaiter worn to protect the trousers or stockings from mud, etc., as in riding. **2.** *Bldg Trades.* a cement and sand mixture thrown on to a wall as a primer for a first coat of plaster. [SPATTER + DASH[1]]

**spatterdock** /'spætədɒk/, *n.* **1.** a coarse yellow-flowered pond lily, *Nuphar advena,* common in stagnant waters. **2.** any pond lily of genera *Nymphaea* and *Nuphar,* esp. one with yellow flowers.

**spatula** /'spætʃələ/, *n.* an implement with a broad, flat, flexible blade, used for blending foods, mixing drugs, spreading plasters and paints, etc. [L, var. of *spathula,* diminutive of *spatha.* See SPADE[2]] – **spatular,** *adj.*

**spatulate** /'spætʃələt/, *adj.* **1.** shaped like a spatula; rounded more or less like a spoon. **2.** Also, **spathulate.** *Bot.* having a broad, rounded end and a narrow, attenuate base, as a leaf.

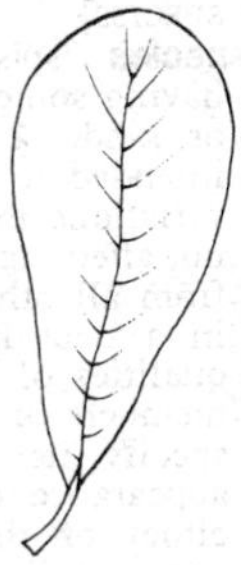

**spavin** /'spævən/, *n. Vet. Sci.* **1.** any disease of the hock joint of horses in which enlargements occur, after causing lameness. The enlargement may be due to collection of fluids (**bog spavin**) or to bony growth (**bone spavin**). **2.** an excrescence or enlargement so formed. [ME *spaveyne,* from OF *espavain;* orig. obscure] – **spavined,** *adj.*

**spa water** /'spa wɔtə/, *n.* →**mineral water** (def. 1).

spatulate leaf

**spawn** /spɒn/, *n.* **1.** *Zool.* the mass of sex cells of fishes, amphibians, molluscs, crustaceans, etc., after being emitted. **2.** *Bot.* the mycelium of mushrooms, esp. of the species grown for the market. **3.** *(usu. offensive)* **a.** a swarming brood or numerous progeny. **b.** any person or thing regarded as the offspring of some stock, idea, etc. *–v.i.* **4.** to shed the sex cells, esp. as applied to animals that shed eggs and sperm directly into water. *–v.t.* **5.** to produce (spawn). **6.** to give birth to; give rise to. **7.** *(usu. derog.)* to produce in large numbers, or with excessive fecundity. **8.** to plant with mycelium. [ME, from AF *espaundre* spill, from L *expandere* expand] – **spawner,** *n.*

**spay** /speɪ/, *v.t.* to remove the ovaries of (a female animal). [ME, from AF *espeier* cut with a sword, from *espee* sword. See ÉPÉE]

**SP bookmaker** /ˌɛs pi 'bʊkmeɪkə/, *n.* an unlicensed bookmaker operating off racetracks paying the starting price odds.

**speak** /spik/, *v.,* **spoke** or *(Archaic)* **spake; spoken** or *(Archaic)* **spoke; speaking.** *–v.i.* **1.** to utter words or articulate sounds with the ordinary (talking) voice. **2.** to make oral communication or mention: *to speak to a person of various matters.* **3.** to converse. **4.** to deliver an address, discourse, etc. **5.** to make a statement in written or printed words. **6.** to make communication or disclosure by any means; convey significance. **7.** to emit a sound, as a musical instrument; make a noise or report. **8.** (of hunting dogs) to give tongue; bay. *–v.t.* **9.** to utter orally and articulately: *to speak words of praise.* **10.** to express or make known with the voice: *to speak the truth.* **11.** to declare in writing or printing, or by any means of communication. **12.** to make known, indicate, or reveal. **13.** to use, or be able to use, in oral utterance, as a language: *to speak French.* **14.** *Naut.* to communicate with (a passing vessel, etc.) at sea, as by voice or signal. **15.** *Archaic.* to speak to or with. *–v.* **16.** Some special verb phrases are:

**so to speak,** to use a certain way of speaking; as one might say.

**speak for, 1.** to recommend; intercede for; to act as spokesman for. **2.** to reserve; bespeak: *this dress is already spoken for.*

**speak for oneself,** to express only one's own views.

**speak for yourself,** (an expression of disagreement.)

**speak of,** worth mentioning: *he has no money to speak of.*

**speak out,** to express one's views openly and without reserve.

**speak up,** to speak loudly and clearly.

**speak well for,** to be favourable evidence for. [ME *spek(en),* OE *specan,* unexplained var. of *sprecan,* c. G *sprechen*] – **speakable,** *adj.*

**-speak,** a suffix used to indicate a particular variety of spoken language as in *newspeak, doublespeak.*

**speak-easy** /'spik-izi/, *n., pl.* **-easies.** *U.S.* a place where alcoholic drinks are illegally sold, esp. between 1919 and 1933 when prohibition was in force.

**speaker** /'spikə/, *n.* **1.** one who speaks. **2.** one who speaks formally before an audience; an orator. **3.** *(usu. cap.)* the presiding officer of the lower house of a parliament, as in the House of Representatives. **4.** a loudspeaker. – **speakership,** *n.*

**speaking** /'spikɪŋ/, *n.* **1.** the act, utterance, or discourse of one who speaks. *–adj.* **2.** highly expressive. **3.** lifelike: *a speaking likeness.* **4.** used in, suited to, or involving speaking or talking: *the speaking voice.* **5.** permitting of speaking, as in greeting or conversation: *they are no longer on speaking terms.* **6.** of or pertaining to declamation.

**speaking trumpet** /'– trʌmpət/, *n.* **1.** a trumpet-shaped device for amplifying sounds, held to the ear by a deaf person to enable him to hear better. **2.** a megaphone.

**speaking tube** /'– tjub/, *n.* a tube for conveying the voice to a distance, as from one part of a building to another.

**spear**[1] /spɪə/, *n.* **1.** a weapon for thrusting or throwing, being a long staff with a sharp head, as of iron or steel. **2.** a similar weapon for spearing fish. **3.** a man armed with a spear. **4.** *Colloq.* dismissal, the sack. **5.** *Colloq.* a surfboard. *–v.t.* **6.** to pierce with or as with a spear. *–v.i.* **7.** *Colloq.* to move rapidly, esp. in a restricted passage: *a racehorse spearing down the rails.* **8. spear on,** *Colloq.* to proceed rapidly. [ME and OE *spere,* c. D *speer,* G *Speer*] – **spearer,** *n.*

**spear**[2] /spɪə/, *n.* **1.** a sprout or shoot of a plant; an acrospire of grain; a blade of grass, grain, etc. *–v.i.* **2.** to sprout; shoot; send up or rise in a spear or spears. [var. of SPIRE[1], ? influenced by SPEAR[1]]

**spearfish** /'spɪəfɪʃ/, *n., pl.* **-fishes,** *(esp. collectively)* **-fish.** →**marlin.**

**spearfisherman** /ˈspɪəfɪʃəmən/, *n.* a skindiver armed with a spear gun.

**spear grass** /ˈspɪə gras/, *n.* **1.** a native, dry-weather resistant grass of the genus *Stipa* with narrow leaves, twisted awns, and seeds which are spear-shaped and can cause damage to stock, as plains grass. **2.** either of two native, perennial grasses of the genus *Heteropogon,* found in northern Australia, which can cause damage to livestock with their sharp-pointed seeds. **3.** →**wire grass. 4.** a New Zealand perennial, umbelliferous plant, *Aciphylla squarrosa,* having a large basal rosette of stiff, narrow leaves about 60cm long and inflorescences up to 3 metres high.

**spear gun** /ˈ– gʌn/, *n.* a gun, propelling a spear, powered by compressed air, a powerful spring, etc., used in underwater fishing.

**spearhead** /ˈspɪəhɛd/, *n.* **1.** the sharp-pointed head which forms the piercing end of a spear. **2.** any person or thing that leads an attack, undertaking, etc. **3.** *Aus. Rules.* →**full-forward.** *–v.t.* **4.** to act as a spearhead for.

**spear lily** /ˈspɪə lɪli/, *n.* a robust herb, *Doryanthes palmeri,* with a tall flowering stem bearing a large head of flowers, native to northern New South Wales and Queensland.

**spearman** /ˈspɪəmən/, *n., pl.* **-men.** one who is armed with or uses a spear.

**spearmint** /ˈspɪəmɪnt/, *n.* the common garden mint, *Mentha spicata,* an aromatic herb much used for flavouring. [SPEAR[1] + MINT[1]]

**spear side** /ˈspɪə saɪd/, *n.* the male side, or line of descent, of a family (opposed to *distaff side*).

**spear tackle** /ˈ– tækəl/, *n. Rugby League.* an illegal tackle in which the player with the ball is lifted into the air, turned upside down, then thrust violently head first into the ground, and exposed to the possibility of serious injury.

**spear thistle** /ˈ– θɪsəl/, *n.* a biennial weed, *Cirsium vulgare,* having purple flowers and prickly leaves, and found in temperate regions; black thistle.

**spec** /spɛk/, *Colloq. –n.* **1.** speculation. **2. on spec,** as a guess, risk, or gamble: *to buy shares on spec. –adj.* **3.** speculative.

**spec.,** **1.** special. **2.** specially. **3.** specification. **4.** speculation.

**spec builder** /spɛk ˈbɪldə/, *n.* one who builds houses, etc., as a speculative enterprise, rather than under contract.

**spec-built** /ˈspɛk-bɪlt/, *adj.* (of a house) built on spec without an order from a purchaser.

**special** /ˈspɛʃəl/, *adj., n., v.,* **specialled, specialling.** *–adj.* **1.** of a distinct or particular character. **2.** being a particular one; particular, individual, or certain. **3.** pertaining or peculiar to a particular person, thing, instance, etc.: *the special features of a plan.* **4.** having a particular function, purpose, application, etc.: *a special messenger.* **5.** dealing with particulars, or specific, as a statement. **6.** distinguished or different from what is ordinary or usual: *a special occasion.* **7.** extraordinary; exceptional; exceptional in amount or degree; especial: *special importance.* **8.** great; being such in an exceptional degree: *a special friend. –n.* **9.** a special person or thing. **10.** a special train. **11.** an item sold at a special, usu. bargain price. **12. on special,** *Colloq.* available at a bargain price. **13.** (formerly) a convict receiving special indulgence because of his birth or ability. **14.** a special edition of a newspaper. **15.** a special constable. *–v.t.* **16.** (of a nurse) to care for (a patient) as a special responsibility, esp. in a private home. *–v.i.* **17.** (of a nurse) to special a patient. [ME, from L *specialis*] – **specially,** *adv.*

**special constable** /– ˈkʌnstəbəl/, *n.* a man temporarily or periodically serving as a policeman, in time of emergency, for extra duties, etc.

**special delivery** /– dəˈlɪvəri/, *n.* a delivery of mail outside normal hours, on payment of an extra fee.

**special drawing rights,** *n.* credits which central banks in the western world extend to each other.

**special education** /spɛʃəl ɛdʒəˈkeɪʃən/, *n.* education for children who are physically or mentally handicapped.

**special effects** /– əˈfɛkts/, *n.pl.* (*Films, T.V., etc.*) effects, esp. visual, of a startling or fantastic nature, produced by sophisticated techniques, as computer animation, etc.

**specialise** /ˈspɛʃəlaɪz/, *v.,* **-lised, -lising.** *–v.i.* **1.** to pursue some special line of study, work, etc.; make a speciality. **2.** *Biol.* to become specialised. *–v.t.* **3.** to render special or specific; invest with a special character, function, etc. **4.** to adapt to special conditions; restrict to specific limits. **5.** to restrict payment of (a negotiable instrument) by endorsing over to a specific payee. **6.** *Biol.* to modify or differentiate (an organism or one of its organs) to adapt it to a special function or environment. **7.** to specify; particularise. Also, **specialize.** – **specialisation** /spɛʃəlaɪˈzeɪʃən/, *n.*

**specialism** /ˈspɛʃəlɪzəm/, *n.* devotion or restriction to a special branch of study, etc.

**specialist** /ˈspɛʃələst/, *n.* **1.** one who devotes himself to one subject, or to one particular branch of a subject or pursuit. **2.** a medical practitioner who devotes his attention to a particular class of diseases, etc. **3.** *U.S. Mil.* a soldier with special technical qualifications ranking below a corporal. – **specialistic** /spɛʃəˈlɪstɪk/, *adj.*

**speciality** /spɛʃiˈæləti/, *n., pl.* **-ties. 1.** special or particular character. **2.** a special or distinctive quality or characteristic; a peculiarity. **3.** an article of unusual or superior design or quality. **4.** a novelty; a new article. **5.** an article with such strong consumer demand that it is at least partially removed from price competition. **6.** →**specialty** (defs 1, 2, 3). Also, **specialty.** [ME *specialite,* from OF *(e)specialite,* from LL *speciālitas*]

**special pleading** /spɛʃəl ˈplidɪŋ/, *n.* **1.** *Law.* pleading that alleges special or new matter in avoidance of the allegations made by the opposite side. **2.** pleading or arguing that ignores unfavourable features of a case.

**special school** /– ˈskul/, *n.* **1.** a school providing education for children suffering from some physical or mental disability. **2.** a school providing for children with unusual needs or talents, as musically gifted children.

**special sort** /– ˈsɔt/, *n.* a printing character not normally found in a type fount, as an accented letter, etc.; a peculiar; an arbitrary.

**special theory of relativity,** *n.* that part of the theory of relativity which applies to observers in uniform motion.

**specialty** /ˈspɛʃəlti/, *n., pl.* **-ties. 1.** a special point or item; a particular detail. **2.** a special study line of work, or the like. **3.** an article particularly dealt in, manufactured, etc., or one to which the dealer or manufacturer professes to devote special care. **4.** *Law.* **a.** a special agreement, contract, etc., expressed in an instrument under seal. **b.** a negotiable instrument not under seal. **5.** →**speciality. 6. specialty of the house,** a dish by which a restaurant claims to be distinguished from others. [ME *specialte,* from OF *(e)specialte,* var. of *(e)specialte* SPECIALITY]

**specialty cut** /ˈ– kʌt/, *n.* a quality meat cut, often not for general sale.

**speciation** /spiʃiˈeɪʃən/, *n.* (in biology) the development of a new species by evolutionary processes.

**specie** /ˈspiʃi/, *n.* **1.** coin; coined money. **2. in specie, a.** in kind. **b.** (of money) in actual coin. [L, abl. sing. of *species* SPECIES]

**species** /ˈspisiz, -ʃiz/, *n., pl.* **-cies. 1.** a group of individuals having some common characteristics or qualities; distinct sort or kind. **2.** the basic category of biological classification, intended to designate a single kind of animal or plant, any variations existing among the individuals being regarded as not affecting the essential sameness which distinguishes them from all other organisms. **3.** *Logic.* **a.** any group contained in a next larger group (the genus). **b.** the sum of those qualities of such a contained group that are common to all members of the group and are sufficient to identify it, i.e. to specify its members. **4.** *Eccles.* **a.** the external form or appearance of the bread or the wine in the Eucharist. **b.** either of the Eucharistic elements. **5.** *Obs.* →**specie.** [L: appearance, sort]

**specif.,** **1.** specific. **2.** specifically.

**specifiable** /ˈspɛsəfaɪəbəl/, *adj.* that may be specified.

**specific** /spəˈsɪfɪk/, *adj.* **1.** having a special application, bearing, or reference; specifying, explicit, or definite: *specific mention.* **2.** specified, precise, or particular: *a specific sum of money.* **3.** peculiar or proper to something, as qualities, characteristics, effects, etc. **4.** of a special or particular kind. **5.** *Zool., Bot.* of or pertaining to a species: *specific characters.* **6.** *Med.* **a.** (of a disease) produced by a special cause or infection. **b.** (of a remedy) having special effect in the prevention or cure of a certain disease. **7.** *Comm.* denoting customs or duties levied in fixed amounts per unit (number, volume, weight, etc.). **8.** *Physics.* denoting a physical quantity which has been divided by man, as specific activity, specific charge, specific heat, etc. **9.** something specific, as a statement, quality, etc. **10.** *Med.* a specific remedy. [ML *specificus,* from L *species*] – **specifically,** *adv.* – **specificity** /spɛsə'fɪsəti/, *n.*

**specific activity** /– æk'tɪvəti/, *n.* **1.** *Physics.* the activity per unit mass of a pure radioactive isotope. **2.** *Physics.* the activity of a radioactive isotope in a material per unit mass of that material. **3.** *Biochem.* the activity of an enzyme in units per milligram of protein.

**specification** /spɛsəfə'keɪʃən/, *n.* **1.** the act of specifying. **2.** a statement of particulars; a detailed description setting forth the dimensions, materials, etc., for a proposed building, engineering work, or the like. **3.** something specified, as in a bill of particulars; a specified particular, item, or article. **4.** the act of making specific. **5.** the state of having a specific character.

**specific charge** /spə,sɪfɪk 'tʃadʒ/, *n.* the charge to mass ratio of an elementary particle.

**specific gravity** /– 'grævəti/, *n.* the ratio of the mass of a given volume of any substance to that of the same volume of some other substance taken as a standard, water being the standard for solids and liquids, and hydrogen or air for gases; relative density. *Abbrev:* s.g.

**specific heat** /– 'hit/, *n.* **1.** the heat required to raise unit mass of a substance through one degree of temperature, expressed in joules per kilogram per kelvin, calories per gram per degree C, or B.T.U.s per pound per degree F. **2.** (orig.) the ratio of the heat capacity of a substance to that of some standard material.

**specific impulse** /– 'ɪmpʌls/, *n. Aeron.* a measure of the efficiency of a rocket propellant in terms of the ratio of the thrust produced to the rate of consumption.

**specific learning difficulty,** *n.* a specific or particular deficiency of perception or cognition, as dyslexia.

**specific performance** /spə,sɪfɪk pə'fɔməns/, *n.* remedy available in equity compelling a party to certain forms of contract to perform what he has undertaken.

**specific volume** /– 'vɒljum/, *n.* the volume occupied by one gram of a substance at a specified temperature and pressure; the reciprocal of density.

**specify** /'spɛsəfaɪ/, *v.,* **-fied, -fying.** *–v.t.* **1.** to mention or name specifically or definitely; state in detail. **2.** to give a specific character to. **3.** to name or state as a condition. *–v.i.* **4.** to make a specific mention or statement. [ME, from ML *specificāre,* from *specificus* specific, from L *species* sort, kind]

**specimen** /'spɛsəmən/, *n.* **1.** a part or an individual taken as exemplifying a whole mass or number; a typical animal, plant, mineral, part, etc. **2.** *Med.* a sample of a substance to be examined or tested for a specific purpose. **3.** *Colloq.* a person as a specified kind, or in some respect a peculiar kind, of human being. [L]

**speciosity** /spiʃi'ɒsəti/, *n., pl.* **-ties. 1.** the state of being specious or plausible. **2.** something pleasing to the eye but deceptive. **3.** *Obs.* the state of being beautiful.

**specious** /'spiʃəs/, *adj.* **1.** apparently good or right but without real merit; superficially pleasing: *specious arguments.* **2.** pleasing to the eye, but deceptive. **3.** *Obs.* pleasing to the eye; fair. [ME, from L *speciōsus* fair, fair-seeming, from *species* sort, kind] – **speciously,** *adv.* – **speciousness,** *n.*

**speck** /spɛk/, *n.* **1.** a small spot differing in colour or substance from that of the surface or material upon which it appears. **2.** a very little bit or particle. **3.** something appearing small by comparison or by distance. **4.** a damaged piece of fruit. **5.** a small piece of gold, opal, etc., on a surface heap near a mine. *–v.t.* **6.** to mark with, or as with, a speck or specks. [ME *specke,* OE *specca*]

**specking** /'spɛkɪŋ/, *n.* fossicking for small pieces of gold, opal, etc., left exposed on a surface heap near a mine, and which glint, esp. after wind or rain.

**speckle** /'spɛkəl/, *n., v.,* **-led, -ling.** *–n.* **1.** a small speck, spot, or mark, as on skin. **2.** speckled colouring or marking. *–v.t.* **3.** to mark with, or as with, speckles. [SPECK + *-le,* diminutive and frequentative suffix]

**speckled hen** /spɛkəld 'hɛn/, *n. Colloq.* a sandstone or conglomerate band; mottled sandstone; cuckoo sandstone.

**specs** /spɛks/, *n. pl. Colloq.* spectacles; glasses.

**spectacle** /'spɛktəkəl/, *n.* **1.** anything presented to the sight or view, esp. something of a striking kind. **2.** a public show or display, esp. on a large scale. **3.** (*pl.*) a device to aid defective vision or to protect the eyes from light, dust, etc., consisting usu. of two glass lenses set in a frame which rests on the nose and is held in place by pieces passing over or around the ears (often called **a pair of spectacles**). **4.** (*oft. pl.*) something resembling spectacles in shape or function. **5.** (*oft. pl.*) any of various devices suggesting spectacles, as one attached to a semaphore to display lights of different colours by coloured glass. **6. make a spectacle of oneself,** to draw attention to oneself by unseemly behaviour. [ME, from L *spectāculum*]

**spectacled** /'spɛktəkəld/, *adj.* **1.** provided with or wearing spectacles. **2.** *Zool.* having a marking resembling a pair of spectacles.

**spectacular** /spɛk'tækjələ/, *adj.* **1.** pertaining to or of the nature of a spectacle; marked by or given to great display. **2.** dramatic; thrilling. *–n.* **3.** a lavishly produced film, television show, etc. – **spectacularly,** *adv.*

**spectator** /spɛk'teɪtə, 'spɛkteɪtə/, *n.* **1.** one who looks on; an onlooker. **2.** one who is present at and views a spectacle or the like. [L]

**spectator sport** /'– spɔt/, *n.* **1.** a sport, as football, cricket, car-racing, etc., which attracts an exceptionally large audience. **2.** (*joc.*) any activity in which one plays no active part, being present merely as an onlooker.

**spectra** /'spɛktrə/, *n.* plural of **spectrum.**

**spectral** /'spɛktrəl/, *adj.* **1.** pertaining to or characteristic of a spectre; of the nature of a spectre. **2.** resembling or suggesting a spectre. **3.** of, pertaining to, or produced by a spectrum or spectra. – **spectrality** /spɛk'træləti/, *n.* – **spectrally,** *adv.*

**spectral classification** /– klæsəfə'keɪʃən/, *n.* a method of classifying stars, according to their emission spectra, into ten major classes.

**spectral series** /– 'sɪəriz/, *n.* a series of lines in the emission spectrum of a substance, each line representing a particular energy level of an atom of an element.

**spectre** /'spɛktə/, *n.* **1.** a visible incorporeal spirit, esp. one of a terrifying nature; ghost; phantom; apparition. **2.** some object or source of terror or dread. Also, *U.S.,* **specter.** [L *spectrum* apparition]

**spectro-,** a word element representing **spectrum.**

**spectrobolometer** /,spɛktroʊbə'lɒmətə/, *n.* a combined spectroscope and bolometer, for determining the distribution of radiant heat or energy in a spectrum.

**spectrogram** /'spɛktrəgræm/, *n.* a representation or photograph of a spectrum as a speech spectrogram or sonagram, a mass spectrogram, etc.

**spectrograph** /'spɛktrəgræf, -graf/, *n.* **1.** an apparatus for making a spectrogram, as a speech spectrograph, a mass spectrograph, etc. **2.** →**spectrogram.** – **spectrographic** /spɛktrə'græfɪk/, *adj.*

**spectroheliogram** /spɛktroʊ'hiliə,græm/, *n.* a photograph of the sun made with a spectroheliograph.

**spectroheliograph** /spɛktroʊ'hiliə,græf, -graf/, *n.* an apparatus for making photographs of the sun with monochromatic light, to show the details of the sun's surface and surroundings as they would appear if only that one kind of light were emitted.

**spectrometer** /spɛk'trɒmətə/, *n.* any of certain optical instruments for observing a spectrum and measuring the deviation of refracted rays, used for determining wavelengths, angles between faces of a prism, etc.

**spectrophotometer** /,spɛktroʊfə'tɒmətə/, *n.* an instrument for making photometric comparisons between parts of spectra. – **spectrophotometry,** *n.*

**spectroscope** /'spɛktrəskoʊp/, *n.* an optical instrument for producing and examining the spectrum of the light or radiation from any source. – **spectroscopic** /spɛktrə'skɒpɪk/,

**spectroscopical** /spɛktrəˈskɒpɪkəl/, *adj.* – **spectroscopically** /spɛktrəˈskɒpɪkli/, *adv.*

**spectroscopy** /spɛkˈtrɒskəpi/, *n.* the science dealing with the use of the spectroscope and with spectrum analysis. – **spectroscopist** /spɛkˈtrɒskəpəst/, *n.*

**spectrum** /ˈspɛktrəm/, *n. Physics.* **1.** the band of colours (red, orange, yellow, green, blue, indigo, violet) obscured when white light passes through a prism. **2.** a continuous range of frequencies within which waves have some specified common characteristic (as in audio-frequency spectrum, radio-frequency spectrum, visible spectrum, etc.). **3.** a visual display, a photographic record or a graph of the intensity of radiation as a function of wavelength, energy or frequency, etc. **4.** a display, etc. of the abundances (def. 5) of isotopes as a function of mass. **5.** a range of interrelated values, objects, opinions, etc.: *the spectrum of Australian English speech varieties.* [L: appearance, form]

**spectrum analysis** /– əˈnæləsəs/, *n.* the determination of the constitution or condition of bodies and substances by means of the spectra they produce. Also, **spectrographic analysis.**

**spectrum of Australian English,** *n.* a continuum along which the variant pronunciations of Australian English are ranged. The position of a person's pronunciation on the spectrum is determined by the habitual choices he makes; four areas are commonly delineated: broad, general, cultivated and modified Australian.

**specular** /ˈspɛkjələ/, *adj.* **1.** pertaining to, or having the properties of, a mirror. **2.** pertaining to a speculum. [L *speculāris* of or like a mirror]

**speculate** /ˈspɛkjəleɪt/, *v.i.*, **-lated, -lating. 1.** to engage in thought or reflection, or meditate (oft. fol. by *on, upon,* or a clause). **2.** to indulge in conjectural thought. **3.** *Comm.* to buy and sell commodities, shares, etc., in the expectation of profit through a change in their market value; engage in any business transaction involving considerable risk, or the chance of large gains. [L *speculātus*, pp., observed, examined]

**speculation** /spɛkjəˈleɪʃən/, *n.* **1.** the contemplation or consideration of some subject. **2.** a single instance or process of consideration. **3.** a conclusion or opinion reached thereby. **4.** conjectural consideration of a matter; conjecture or surmise. **5.** trading in commodities, shares, etc., in the hope of profit from changes in the market price; engagement in business transactions involving considerable risk but offering the chance of large gains. **6.** a speculative commercial venture or undertaking.

**speculative** /ˈspɛkjələtɪv/, *adj.* **1.** pertaining to, of the nature of, or characterised by speculation, contemplation, conjecture, or abstract reasoning. **2.** theoretical, rather than practical. **3.** given to speculation, as persons, the mind, etc. **4.** of the nature of or involving commercial or financial speculation. **5.** engaging in or given to such speculation. – **speculatively,** *adv.* – **speculativeness,** *n.*

**speculative philosophy** /– fəˈlɒsəfi/, *n.* any philosophy in which the thinker's own intuition provides a part of the data that is subjected to rational criticism.

**speculator** /ˈspɛkjəleɪtə/, *n.* **1.** one engaged in commercial or financial speculation. **2.** one devoted to mental speculation. [L: scout, explorer]

**speculum** /ˈspɛkjələm/, *n., pl.* **-la** /-lə/, **-lums. 1.** a mirror or reflector, esp. one of polished metal, as on a reflecting telescope. **2.** *Surg.* an instrument for rendering a part accessible to observation, as by enlarging an orifice. **3.** *Zool.* a lustrous or specially coloured area on the wing of certain birds. [L]

**speculum metal** /– ˈmɛtl/, *n.* any of several copper and tin alloys used for mirrors and reflectors.

**sped** /spɛd/, *v.* past tense and past participle of **speed.**

**speech** /spitʃ/, *n.* **1.** the faculty or power of speaking; oral communication; expression of human thought and emotions by speech sounds and gesture. **2.** that which is spoken; an utterance, remark, or declaration: *an eloquent speech.* **3.** a form of communication in spoken language, made by a speaker before an audience for a given purpose. **4.** any single utterance of an actor in the course of a play, etc. **5.** the form of utterance characteristic of a particular people or region; a language or dialect. **6.** manner of speaking, as of a person. **7.** a field of study devoted to the theory and practice of oral communication. **8.** *Archaic.* rumour. [ME *speche,* OE *spǣc,* unexplained var. of *sprǣc,* c. G *Sprache*]

**speech community** /– kəˈmjunəti/, *n.* **1.** the aggregate of all the people who use a given language or dialect. **2.** a group of people geographically distributed so that there is no break in intelligibility from place to place.

**speech day** /ˈ– deɪ/, *n.* an annual ceremony at a school, attended by parents, when speeches are made and prizes distributed.

**speechify** /ˈspitʃəfaɪ/, *v.i.*, **-fied, -fying.** to make a speech or speeches.

**speechless** /ˈspitʃləs/, *adj.* **1.** temporarily deprived of speech by strong emotion, physical weakness, exhaustion, etc.: *speechless with horror.* **2.** characterised by absence or loss of speech: *speechless astonishment.* **3.** lacking the faculty of speech; dumb. **4.** not expressed in speech or words. **5.** refraining from speech. – **speechlessly,** *adv.* – **speechlessness,** *n.*

**speech night** /ˈspitʃ naɪt/, *n.* See **speech day.**

**speech sound** /ˈ– saʊnd/, *n.* any vocal or articulated sound used in human oral communication.

**speech spectrogram** /– ˈspɛktrəgræm/, *n.* →**spectrogram.**

**speech spectrograph** /– ˈspɛktrəgræf, -graf/, *n.* a spectrograph designed for use within the frequency range of the human voice.

**speech synthesiser** /– ˈsɪnθəsaɪzə/, *n.* →**synthesiser** (def. 2).

**speech therapy** /– ˈθɛrəpi/, *n.* the correction of defects of articulation resulting from psychological or physical disorders.

**speed** /spid/, *n., v.,* **sped** or **speeded, speeding.** –*n.* **1.** rapidity in moving, going, travelling, or any proceeding or performance; swiftness; celerity. **2.** the ratio of the distance covered by a moving body to the time taken. **3.** *Motor Vehicles.* a transmission gear-ratio. **4.** *Photog.* a measure of the exposure required by an emulsion. **5.** *Archaic.* success or prosperity. **6.** *Colloq.* amphetamines; pep pills. **7. at full speed,** as fast as possible. –*v.t.* **8.** to promote the success of (an affair, undertaking, etc.); further, forward, or expedite. **9.** to direct (the steps, course, way, etc.) with speed. **10.** to increase the rate of speed of (usu. fol. by *up*): *to speed up industrial production.* **11.** to bring to a particular speed, as a machine. **12.** to cause to move, go, or proceed, with speed. **13.** to expedite the going of: *to speed the parting guest.* **14.** *Archaic.* to cause (a person, etc.) to succeed or prosper. –*v.i.* **15.** to move, go, pass, or proceed with speed or rapidity. **16.** to drive a vehicle at a rate exceeding the maximum permitted by law. **17.** to increase the rate of speed or progress (fol. by *up*). **18.** to get on or fare in a specified or particular manner. **19.** *Archaic.* to succeed or prosper. [ME *spede,* OE *spēd* (c. D *spoed*). Cf. OE *spōwan* prosper, succeed] – **speeder,** *n.* – **speedster,** *n.*

**speedball nib** /spidbɔl ˈnɪb/, *n.* a nib with an overlaying piece ending in a rounded point. [Trademark]

**speedboat** /ˈspidboʊt/, *n.* a small motor boat designed for speed.

**speed brake** /ˈspid breɪk/, *n.* →**air-brake.**

**speed bumps** /ˈspid bʌmps/, *n. pl.* transverse ridges spaced at intervals in a road to deter a motorist from speeding; humps.

**speed-cop** /ˈspid-kɒp/, *n. Colloq.* a policeman, often a motorcyclist, who enforces the observation of speed-limits.

**speed-limit** /ˈspid-lɪmət/, *n.* **1.** the maximum speed at which a vehicle is legally permitted to travel, as on a particular road in certain conditions. **2.** the regulation prescribing this.

**speed-merchant** /ˈspid-mɜtʃənt/, *n. Colloq.* one who drives a motor vehicle extremely fast.

**speedo** /ˈspidoʊ/, *n.* →**speedometer.**

**speedometer** /spiˈdɒmətə/, *n.* a device attached to a motor vehicle or the like to record the distance covered and the rate of travel. Also, **speedo.**

**speedster** /ˈspidstə/, *n. Colloq.* one who or that which speeds.

**speed-trap** /ˈspid-træp/, *n.* **1.** any of various devices used by the police, as radar, etc., to verify the speed of motor vehicles. **2.** a place on a road where such a device is set up. **3.** →**speed bumps.**

**speed-up** /ˈspid-ʌp/, *n.* an increasing of speed.

**speedway** /ˈspidweɪ/, *n.* **1.** a racing track for motor vehicles, esp. motorcycles. **2.** a road or course for fast driving, motoring, or the like, or on which more than ordinary speed is allowed.

**speedwell** /'spidwɛl/, *n.* any of various herbs and softwooded shrubs of the genus *Veronica* and allied genera, often with blue flowers, as the water speedwell, *V. anagallis-aquatica.* [so called because its period of flowering is speedily over]

**speedy** /'spidi/, *adj.,* **-dier, -diest. 1.** characterised by speed; rapid; swift; fast. **2.** coming, given, or arrived at, quickly or soon; prompt; not delayed: *a speedy recovery.* – **speedily,** *adv.* – **speediness,** *n.*

**speeler** /'spilə/, *n.* a fast horse. [Brit. d. *speel* to run fast; orig. uncert.]

**speiss** /spaɪs/, *n.* a product consisting chiefly of one or more metallic arsenides (as of iron, nickel, etc.), obtained in smelting certain ores. [G *Speise,* lit., food]

**spelaean** /spə'liən/, *adj.* of, pertaining to, or inhabiting caves. Also, **spelean.** [NL *spēlaeus* (from L *spēlaeum* cave, from Gk *spēlaion*) + -AN]

**speleology** /spili'ɒlədʒi/, *n.* the exploration and study of caves. Also, **spelaeology.** – **speleological** /spiliə'lɒdʒɪkəl/, *adj.* – **speleologist** /spili'ɒlədʒəst/, *n.*

**spell**[1] /spɛl/, *v.,* **spelt** or **spelled, spelling.** *–v.t.* **1.** to name, write, or otherwise give (as by signals), in order, the letters of (a word, syllable, etc.). **2.** (of letters) to form (a word, syllable, etc.). **3.** to read letter by letter or with difficulty (oft. fol. by *out*). **4.** to discern or find, as if by reading or study (oft. fol. by *out*). **5.** to make absolutely clear and understandable (fol. by *out*). **6.** to signify; amount to: *this delay spells disaster for us.* *–v.i.* **7.** to name, write, or give the letters of words, etc. **8.** to express words by letters, esp. correctly. [ME, from OF *espeller,* of Gmc orig.; akin to SPELL[2]]

**spell**[2] /spɛl/, *n.* **1.** a form of words supposed to possess magic power; a charm, incantation, or enchantment. **2.** any dominating or irresistible influence; fascination. [ME and OE *spell* discourse. Cf. SPIEL]

**spell**[3] /spɛl/, *n.* **1.** a continuous course or period of work or other activity: *to take a spell at the wheel.* **2.** a turn of work so taken. **3.** a turn, bout, fit, or period of anything experienced or occurring: *a spell of coughing.* **4.** *Colloq.* an interval or space of time, usu. indefinite or short. **5.** a period of weather of a specified kind: *a hot spell.* **6.** an interval or period of rest. **7.** *Rare.* a person or set of persons taking a turn of work to relieve another. *–v.t.* **8.** to take the place of or relieve (a person, etc.) for a time. **9.** to give an interval of rest to. *–v.i.* **10.** to take an interval of rest. [var. of Brit. d. *spele,* OE *spelian* represent]

**spellbind** /'spɛlbaɪnd/, *v.t.,* **-bound, -binding.** to render spellbound; bind or hold as by a spell.

**spellbinder** /'spɛlbaɪndə/, *n. Colloq.* a speaker, esp. a politician, who holds his audience spellbound.

**spellbound** /'spɛlbaʊnd/, *adj.* bound by, or as by, a spell; enchanted, entranced, or fascinated: *a spellbound audience.* [SPELL[2] + BOUND[1]]

**speller** /'spɛlə/, *n.* **1.** one who spells words, etc. **2.** a spelling book.

**spelling** /'spɛlɪŋ/, *n.* **1.** the manner in which words are spelt; orthography. **2.** a group of letters representing a word. **3.** the act of a speller. **4.** the ability to spell or degree of proficiency in spelling.

**spelling bee** /'– bi/, *n.* a competition to see who can spell the most words in accordance with traditional orthography.

**spelling book** /'– bʊk/, *n.* a textbook to teach spelling.

**spelling pronunciation** /'– prəˌnʌnsieɪʃən/, *n.* a pronunciation based on the spelling, usu. a variant of the traditional pronunciation.

**spelt**[1] /spɛlt/, *v.* past tense and past participle of **spell**[1].

**spelt**[2] /spɛlt/, *n.* a kind of wheat, *Triticum spelta* (or a variety of *T. sativum*), anciently much cultivated, used in developing improved varieties of wheat. [OE (c. G *Spelz, Spelt*), from LL *spelta*]

**spelter** /'spɛltə/, *n.* zinc, esp. in the form of ingots. [orig. obscure; akin to MD *speauter* and PEWTER]

**spelunker** /spə'lʌŋkə/, *n.* one who explores caves. [L *spēlunca* + -ER[1]]

**spencer**[1] /'spɛnsə/, *n.* **1.** a short coat or jacket, formerly worn by men. **2.** a jacket or bodice, formerly worn by women. **3.** a kind of woman's vest, worn for extra warmth. [named after George John *Spencer,* 1758-1834, 2nd Earl Spencer]

**spencer**[2] /'spɛnsə/, *n.* a kind of wig worn in the 18th century. [named after Charles *Spencer,* 1674-1722, 3rd Earl of Sunderland]

**spencer**[3] /'spɛnsə/, *n.* a type of spanker sail, set on a gaff from the after mast of a square-rigged ship.

**spencer roll** /– 'roʊl/, *n.* a boneless cut of beef from the ribs.

**spend** /spɛnd/, *v.,* **spent, spending.** *–v.t.* **1.** to pay out, disburse, or expend; dispose of (money, wealth, resources, etc.). **2.** to employ (labour, thought, words, time, etc.) on some object, in some proceeding, etc. **3.** to pass (time) in a particular manner, place, etc. **4.** to use up, consume, or exhaust: *the storm had spent its fury.* **5.** to give (one's blood, life, etc.) for some cause. *–v.i.* **6.** to spend money, etc. **7.** *Obs.* to be used up. [ME *spende,* OE *spendan* (c. G *spenden*), from L *expendere* EXPEND] – **spendable,** *adj.* – **spender,** *n.*

**spending money** /'spɛndɪŋ ˌmʌni/, *n.* money for small personal expenses; pocket-money.

**spendthrift** /'spɛndθrɪft/, *n.* **1.** one who spends his possessions or money extravagantly or wastefully; a prodigal. *–adj.* **2.** wastefully extravagant; prodigal.

**Spenserian** /spɛn'sɪəriən/, *adj.* **1.** of or characteristic of Edmund Spenser, c. 1552-99, poet, or of his work. *–n.* **2.** an imitator of Spenser. **3.** a Spenserian stanza. **4.** verse in Spenserian stanzas.

**Spenserian stanza** /– 'stænzə/, *n.* the stanza used by Spenser in his *Faerie Queene* and employed since by other poets, consisting of eight iambic pentameter lines and a final Alexandrine, with a rhyme scheme of ababbcbcc.

**spent** /spɛnt/, *v.* **1.** past tense and past participle of **spend.** *–adj.* **2.** used up, consumed, or exhausted.

**spent grains** /– 'greɪnz/, *n.pl.* the refuse malt and other insoluble residue left after the wort has been run off.

**sperm**[1] /spɜm/, *n.* **1.** →**spermatic fluid. 2.** a male reproductive cell; a spermatozoon. [ME *sperme,* from L *sperma,* from Gk]

**sperm**[2] /spɜm/, *n.* **1.** →**spermaceti. 2.** →**sperm whale. 3.** →**sperm oil.** [abbrev. of defs above]

**sperm-,** a word element representing **sperm**[1]. Also, **spermo-.**

**-sperm,** a terminal combining form of **sperm**[1], as in *angiosperm.*

**spermaceti** /spɜmə'sɛti, -'siti/, *n.* a whitish, waxy substance obtained from the oil in the head of the sperm whale, used in making ointments, cosmetics, etc. [ML, orig. phrase *sperma cēti* sperm of whale]

**-spermal,** a word element used to form adjectives related to **sperm**[1]. [-SPERM + -AL[1]]

**spermary** /'spɜməri/, *n., pl.* **-ries.** a sperm gland; an organ in which spermatozoa are generated; testis.

**spermatic** /spɜ'mætɪk/, *adj.* **1.** of, pertaining to, or of the nature of sperm; seminal; generative. **2.** pertaining to a spermary.

**spermatic cord** /– 'kɔd/, *n.* the solid neck of the spermatic sac by which the testicle is suspended within the scrotum; it contains the vas deferens, the blood vessels and nerves of the testicles, etc.

**spermatic fluid** /– 'fluəd/, *n.* the male generative fluid; semen.

**spermatic sac** /– 'sæk/, *n.* the hollow portion of the inguinal bursa which contains the testis and is lined by the peritoneum.

**spermatium** /spɜ'meɪtiəm/, *n., pl.* **-tia** /-tiə/. **1.** the non-motile male gamete of the red algae. **2.** a minute, colourless cell (conjectured to be a male reproductive body) developed within spermogonia. [NL, from Gk *spermátion,* diminutive of *spérma* SPERM[1]]

**spermato-,** variant of **sperm-.** Also, **spermat-.** [Gk, combining form of *spérma* SPERM[1]]

**spermatocyte** /'spɜmətoʊˌsaɪt/, *n.* a male germ cell at the maturation stage, giving rise to spermatozoids and spermatozoa.

**spermatogenesis** /ˌspɜmətoʊ'dʒɛnəsəs/, *n.* the genesis or origin and development of spermatozoa. Also, **spermatogeny** /spɜmə'tɒdʒəni/. – **spermatogenetic** /ˌspɜmətoʊdʒə'nɛtɪk/, *adj.*

**spermatogonium** /ˌspɜmətoʊˈgoʊniəm/, *n., pl.* **-nia** /-niə/. one of the primitive germ cells giving rise to spermatocytes. [NL. See SPERMATO-, -GONIUM] – **spermatogonial,** *adj.*

**spermatoid** /ˈspɜmətɔɪd/, *adj.* resembling sperm.

**spermatophore** /ˈspɜmətoʊˌfɔ/, *n.* a special case or capsule containing a number of spermatozoa, produced by the male of certain insects, molluscs, annelids, etc., and some vertebrates. – **spermatophoral** /spɜməˈtɒfərəl/, *adj.*

**spermatophyte** /ˈspɜmətoʊˌfaɪt/, *n.* any of the Spermatophyta, a primary division or group of plants embracing those that bear seeds. – **spermatophytic** /ˌspɜmətoʊˈfɪtɪk/, *adj.*

**spermatorrhoea** /ˌspɜmətəˈriə/, *n.* abnormally frequent involuntary emission of semen. Also, *U.S.,* **spermatorrhea.**

**spermatozoid** /ˌspɜmətoʊˈzoʊɪd/, *n.* (of some plants) a motile male gamete produced in an antheridium; antherozoid. [SPERMATOZO(ON) + -ID[2]]

**spermatozoon** /ˌspɜmətoʊˈzoʊɒn/, *n., pl.* **-zoa** /-ˈzoʊə/. one of the minute, usu. actively motile, gametes in semen, which serve to fertilise the ovum; a mature male reproductive cell. – **spermatozoal, spermatozoan, spermatozoic,** *adj.*

**spermic** /ˈspɜmɪk/, *adj.* →**spermatic.**

**spermo-,** variant of **sperm-,** before consonants.

**spermogonium** /spɜməˈgoʊniəm/, *n., pl.* **-nia** /-niə/. one of the cup-shaped or flask-shaped receptacles in which spermatia of certain fungi are produced. [NL. See SPERMO-, -GONIUM]

**sperm oil** /ˈspɜm ɔɪl/, *n.* an oil from the sperm whale.

**spermophile** /ˈspɜməfaɪl/, *n.* any of various American terrestrial rodents of the squirrel family, esp. of the genus *Citellus* (or *Spermophilus*), sometimes sufficiently numerous to do much damage to crops, as the ground squirrels, susliks, etc.

**spermophyte** /ˈspɜməfaɪt/, *n.* →**spermatophyte.**

**spermous** /ˈspɜməs/, *adj.* of the nature of or pertaining to sperm.

**sperm whale** /ˈspɜm weɪl/, *n.* a large, square-headed whale, *Physeter macrocephalus,* valuable for oil and spermaceti; cachalot.

sperm whale

**sperrylite** /ˈsperəlaɪt/, *n.* a mineral, platinum arsenide, $PtAs_2$, occurring in minute tin-white crystals, usu. cubes, a minor ore of platinum. [named after F.L. *Sperry,* 19th-cent. Canadian mineralogist. See -LITE]

**spew** /spju/, *v.i.* **1.** to discharge the contents of the stomach through the mouth; vomit. *–v.t.* **2.** to eject from the stomach through the mouth; vomit. **3.** to thrust forth or discharge violently. *–n.* **4.** that which is spewed; vomit. Also, **spue** (for defs 1, 2). [ME; OE *spīwan,* c. G *speien.* Cf. L *spuere*] – **spewer,** *n.*

**sp. gr.,** specific gravity.

**sphacelate** /ˈsfæsəleɪt/, *v.t., v.i.,* **-lated, -lating.** to affect or be affected with sphacelus; mortify. – **sphacelation** /sfæsəˈleɪʃən/, *n.*

**sphacelus** /ˈsfæsələs/, *n.* a gangrenous or mortified mass of tissue; necrosis. [L, from Gk *sphákelos*]

**sphagnous** /ˈsfægnəs/, *adj.* pertaining to, abounding in, or consisting of sphagnum.

**sphagnum** /ˈsfægnəm/, *n.* any of the bog mosses constituting the genus *Sphagnum,* found chiefly in temperate regions of high rainfall and low insolation, where they may build up deep layers of peat; used by gardeners in potting and packing plants, and (formerly) in surgery for dressing wounds, etc. [NL, from Gk *sphágnos* a moss]

**sphalerite** /ˈsfælərait, ˈsfeɪlə-/, *n.* a very common mineral, zinc sulphide, ZnS, usu. containing some iron and a little cadmium, occurring in yellow, brown, or black crystals or cleavable masses with resinous lustre, the principal ore of zinc and cadmium; blende; blackjack. [Gk *sphalerós* deceptive, uncertain + -ITE[1]]

**sphene** /sfin/, *n.* a mineral, calcium titanium silicate, $CaTiSiO_5$, occurring in many rocks, usu. in wedge-shaped crystals; titanite. [Gk *sphḗn* wedge (with reference to the shape of its crystals)]

**sphenic** /ˈsfinɪk/, *adj.* wedge-shaped. [Gk *sphḗn* wedge + -IC]

**sphenogram** /ˈsfinəgræm/, *n.* a cuneiform character. [*spheno-* (from Gk, combining form of *sphḗn* wedge) + -GRAM[2]]

**sphenoid** /ˈsfinɔɪd/, *adj.* Also, **sphenoidal** /sfiˈnɔɪdl/. **1.** wedge-shaped. **2.** *Anat.* denoting or pertaining to the compound bone of the base of the skull, at the roof of the pharynx. *–n.* **3.** *Anat.* the sphenoid bone. [NL *sphēnoīdes,* from Gk *sphēnoeidḗs* wedgelike]

**spheral** /ˈsfɪərəl/, *adj.* **1.** of or pertaining to a sphere. **2.** spherical. **3.** symmetrical; perfect in form.

**sphere** /sfɪə/, *n., v.,* **sphered, sphering.** *–n.* **1.** a solid geometrical figure generated by the revolution of a semi-circle about its diameter; a round body whose surface is at all points equidistant from the centre. **2.** any rounded body approximately of this form; a globular mass, shell, etc. **3.** a heavenly body; a planet or star. **4.** →**celestial sphere. 5.** *Ancient Astron.* any of the transparent, concentric, spherical shells, or 'heavens', in which the planets, fixed stars, etc., were supposed to be set. **6.** the place or environment within which a person or thing exists; a field of activity or operation: *to be out of one's sphere.* **7.** a particular social world, stratum of society, or walk of life. **8.** a field of something specified: *a sphere of influence.* *–v.t.* **9.** to enclose in, or as in, a sphere. **10.** to form into a sphere. **11.** *Poetic.* to place among the heavenly spheres. [ME, from LL *sphēra,* L *sphaera,* from Gk *sphaîra*] – **spherelike,** *adj.*

**-sphere,** a word element representing **sphere,** as in *planisphere;* having a special use in the names of the layers of gases, etc., surrounding the earth and other celestial bodies, as in *ionosphere.*

**spherical** /ˈsfɛrəkəl/, *adj.* **1.** having the form of a sphere; globular. **2.** formed in or on a sphere, as a figure. **3.** of or pertaining to a sphere or spheres: *spherical trigonometry.* **4.** pertaining to the heavenly bodies, or to their supposed revolving spheres or shells. **5.** pertaining to the heavenly bodies regarded astrologically as exerting influence on mankind and events. Also, **spheric.** – **sphericality** /sfɛrəˈkæləti/, *n.* – **spherically,** *adv.*

**spherical aberration** /– æbəˈreɪʃən/, *n.* variation in focal length of a lens from centre to edge due to its spherical shape.

**spherical angle** /– ˈæŋgəl/, *n.* an angle formed by arcs of great circles of a sphere.

**spherical triangle** /– ˈtraɪæŋgəl/, *n.* a triangle formed by arcs of great circles of a sphere.

**sphericity** /sfəˈrɪsəti/, *n., pl.* **-ties.** spherical state or form.

**spherics**[1] /ˈsfɛrɪks/, *n.* the geometry and trigonometry of figures formed on the surface of a sphere. [pl. of SPHERIC(AL). See -ICS]

**spherics**[2] /ˈsfɛrɪks/, *n.* a branch of meteorology in which weather forecasting and atmospheric conditions are studied by means of electronic devices. [(ATMO)SPHERIC + *-s.* See -ICS]

**spheroid** /ˈsfɪərɔɪd/, *n.* **1.** a solid of revolution obtained by rotating an ellipse about one of its two axes. *–adj.* **2.** →**spheroidal.**

**spheroidal** /sfɪəˈrɔɪdl/, *adj.* **1.** pertaining to a spheroid or spheroids. **2.** shaped like a spheroid; approximately spherical. Also, **spheroidic.** – **spheroidally,** *adv.*

**spheroidicity** /sfɪərɔɪˈdɪsəti/, *n.* spheroidal state or form. Also, **spheroidity** /sfɪəˈrɔɪdəti/.

**spherometer** /sfəˈrɒmətə/, *n.* an instrument for measuring the curvature of spheres and curved surfaces.

**spherule** /ˈsfɛrul/, *n.* a small sphere or spherical body. [L *sphaerula,* diminutive of *sphaera* SPHERE] – **spherular,** *adj.*

**spherulite** /ˈsfɛrəlaɪt/, *n.* a rounded aggregate of radiating crystals formed in certain igneous rocks. – **spherulitic** /sfɛrəˈlɪtɪk/, *adj.*

**sphery** /ˈsfɪəri/, *adj.* **1.** having the form of a sphere; sphere-like. **2.** pertaining to the heavenly bodies, or to their supposed revolving spheres or shells. **3.** resembling a heavenly body; star-like.

**sphincter** /ˈsfɪŋktə/, *n.* a circular band of voluntary or involuntary muscle which encircles an orifice of the body or one of its hollow organs. [L, from Gk *sphinktḗr* band] – **sphincteral,** *adj.*

**sphingomyelin** /sfɪŋgəˈmaɪlən/, *n.* any of a group of closely related phospholipids occurring in the brain and other tissues.

**Sphinx** /sfɪŋks/, *n., pl.* **sphinxes, sphinges** /ˈsfɪndʒəz/. **1.** a figure of an imaginary creature having the head of a man, woman or animal and the body of a lion. **2.** some similar monster. **3.** a sphinx-like person or thing, as one given to enigmatic or inscrutable behaviour. [from the *Sphinx,* a similar monster of Greek mythology, which proposed a riddle to passers-by, killing those unable to guess it; Oedipus solved it and the Sphinx killed itself]

**sphinx-moth** /ˈsfɪŋks-mɒθ/, *n.* →**hawkmoth.**

**sphragistic** /sfrəˈdʒɪstɪk/, *adj.* of or pertaining to signet rings and seals. [Gk *sphrāgistikós*]

**sphragistics** /sfrəˈdʒɪstɪks/, *n.* the study of signet rings and seals.

**sp. ht,** specific heat.

**sphygmic** /ˈsfɪgmɪk/, *adj.* of or pertaining to the pulse. [Gk *sphygmikós*]

**sphygmo-,** a word element meaning 'pulse'. Also, before vowels, **sphygm-.** [Gk, combining form of *sphygmós*]

**sphygmogram** /ˈsfɪgməgræm/, *n.* a tracing or diagram produced by a sphygmograph.

**sphygmograph** /ˈsfɪgməgræf, -graf/, *n.* an instrument for recording the rapidity, strength, and uniformity of the arterial pulse. – **sphygmographic** /sfɪgməˈgræfɪk/, *adj.* – **sphygmography** /sfɪgˈmɒgrəfi/, *n.*

**sphygmoid** /ˈsfɪgmɔɪd/, *adj.* resembling the pulse; pulse-like.

**sphygmomanometer** /ˌsfɪgmoʊməˈnɒmətə/, *n.* an instrument for measuring the pressure of the blood in an artery. [SPHYGMO- + MANOMETER]

**sphygmometer** /sfɪgˈmɒmətə/, *n.* an instrument for measuring the strength of the pulse.

**sphygmus** /ˈsfɪgməs/, *n.* the pulse. [NL, from Gk *sphygmós* pulsation]

**spic** /spɪk/, *n.* (*derog.*) **1.** any person of European descent. **2.** *U.S.* a person from a Spanish-speaking community. Also, **spick, spik.** [? Sp. mispronunciation of *speak*]

**spica** /ˈspaɪkə/, *n., pl.* **-cae** /-si/. **1.** *Archaeol.* an ear of grain. **2.** a type of bandage extending from an extremity to the trunk by means of successive turns and crosses. **3.** a spike, as of a flower.

**spicate** /ˈspaɪkeɪt/, *adj.* **1.** (of a plant) having spikes. **2.** (of flowers) arranged in spikes. **3.** (of an inflorescence) in the form of a spike. [L *spīcātus,* pp., furnished with spikes]

**spiccato** /spəˈkatoʊ/, *adv.* **1.** (a musical direction) in a detached manner, esp. in violin playing denoting distinct notes produced by short, abrupt, rebounding motions of the bow. *–adj.* **2.** detached. [It., pp. of *spiccare* detach, separate]

**spice** /spaɪs/, *n., v.,* **spiced, spicing.** *–n.* **1.** any of a class of pungent or aromatic substances of vegetable origin, as pepper, cinnamon, cloves, and the like, used as seasoning, preservatives. **2.** such substances as material or collectively. **3.** *Poetic.* a spicy or aromatic smell or fragrance. **4.** something that gives interest; a piquant element or quality. **5.** piquancy, or interest. **6.** a trace, flavour, or suggestion: *a spice of humour in conversation.* **7.** *Colloq.* (formerly) plausible patter used by showmen to draw the public. *–v.t.* **8.** to prepare or season with a spice or spices. **9.** to give flavour, piquancy, or interest to by something added. [ME, from OF *espice,* from L *species* SPECIES]

**spicebush** /ˈspaɪsbʊʃ/, *n.* a yellow-flowered shrub, *Lindera benzoin,* of North America, whose bark and leaves have a spicy smell.

**spicery** /ˈspaɪsəri/, *n., pl.* **-eries. 1.** spices. **2.** spicy flavour or fragrance. **3.** *Obs.* a storeroom or place for spices. [ME, from OF *espicerie,* from *espice* SPICE]

**spick-and-span** /spɪk-ən-ˈspæn/, *adj.* **1.** neat and clean. **2.** perfectly new; fresh. Also, **spick and span.** [short for *spick-and-span-new,* var. of *span-new,* from Scand.; cf. Icel. *spānnȳr,* lit., chip-new]

**spicula** /ˈspɪkjələ/, *n., pl.* **-lae** /-li/. →**spicule.** [NL, diminutive of L *spīca* SPIKE[2]. Cf. SPICULUM]

**spiculate** /ˈspɪkjəleɪt, -lət/, *adj.* **1.** having the form of a spicule. **2.** covered with or having spicules; consisting of spicules. Also, **spicular.** [L *spīculātus,* pp., pointed]

**spicule** /ˈspɪkjul, ˈspaɪkjul/, *n.* **1.** a small or minute, slender, sharp-pointed body or part; a small, needle-like crystal, process, or the like. **2.** *Zool.* one of the small, hard, calcareous or siliceous bodies which serve as the skeletal elements of various animals. **3.** *Bot.* →**spikelet.** Also, **spicula.** [L. See SPICULA]

**spiculum** /ˈspɪkjələm/, *n., pl.* **-la** /-lə/. *Zool.* a small, needle-like body, part, process, or the like. [L, diminutive of *spīca* SPIKE[2]]

**spicy** /ˈspaɪsi/, *adj.,* **spicier, spiciest. 1.** seasoned with or containing spice. **2.** characteristic or suggestive of spice. **3.** of the nature of or resembling spice. **4.** abounding in or yielding spices. **5.** aromatic or fragrant. **6.** piquant or pungent: *spicy criticism.* **7.** of a somewhat improper, scandalous, or sensational nature. – **spicily,** *adv.* – **spiciness,** *n.*

**spider** /ˈspaɪdə/, *n.* **1.** *Zool.* any of the eight-legged wingless, predatory, insectlike arachnids which constitute the order Arachnida, most of which spin webs that serve as nests and as traps for prey. **2.** any of various other arachnids resembling or suggesting these. **3.** any of various things resembling or suggesting a spider. **4.** a device consisting of several elastic cables held together at a central point, used to strap down a load; octopus. **5.** a trivet or tripod, as for supporting a pot or pan on a hearth. **6.** a lightly built cart, phaeton, or wagon with a high body and large slender wheels; a trotting sulky. **7.** a person who entraps others, or lures them by his wiles. **8.** *Agric.* a pulverising instrument used with a cultivator. **9.** a type of harness with radiating straps for a horse, bullock, etc. **10.** a small iron instrument with a ring or spike to hold a candle, often used in mines. **11.** an aerated soft drink to which ice-cream is added. **12.** *Colloq.* (formerly) a drink of lemonade or ginger beer with brandy. **13.** a bowling contest held to raise money for charity, in which all the contestants simultaneously bowl towards the jack, the winner being the one whose bowl actually hits it. [ME *spithre,* OE *spīthra,* c. Dan. *spinder,* lit., spinner]

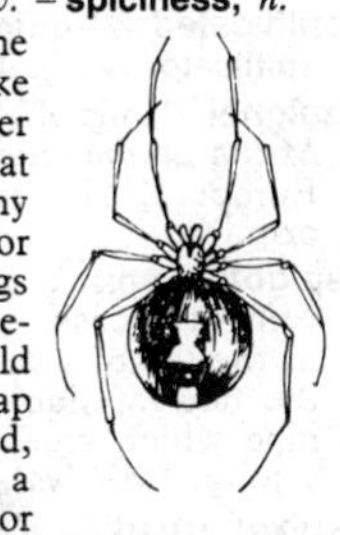

Red-back spider

**spider crab** /ˈ– kræb/, *n.* any of various crabs with long, slender legs and comparatively small triangular body.

**spider flower** /ˈ– flaʊə/, *n.* **1.** any of several species of the Australian genus *Grevillea* with inflorescences resembling spiders, as the **grey spider flower,** *G. buxifolia.* **2.** any of certain species of the genus *Cleome,* as *C. spinosa* which has pinkish flowers with long protruding stamens. **3.** any of certain species of the genus *Strophanthus.*

**spider lily** /ˈ– lɪli/, *n.* any of the bulbs of the genera *Lycoris* and *Nerine* grown for their umbels of coloured flowers.

**spiderling** /ˈspaɪdəlɪŋ/, *n.* a very young, small spider.

**spiderman** /ˈspaɪdəmæn/, *Brit. n.* **1.** one who works on high buildings, esp. as an erector of the steel framework. **2.** →**steeplejack.**

**spider monkey** /ˈspaɪdə mʌŋki/, *n.* any of various acrobatic monkeys of tropical America, genera *Ateles,* with a slender body, long slender limbs, and a long prehensile tail.

**spider-orchid** /ˈspaɪdər-ɔkəd/, *n.* **1.** any of many species of the widespread mostly Australian genus *Caladenia.* **2.** any of several other orchids with flowers thought to resemble a spider.

**spiderwort** /ˈspaɪdəwɜt/, *n.* **1.** any plant of the genus *Tradescantia,* comprising perennial herbs with blue-, purple-, or rose-coloured flowers. **2.** any plant of the same family.

**spidery** /ˈspaɪdəri/, *adj.* **1.** like a spider or a spider's web; very thin and attenuated. **2.** full of spiders.

**spiegeleisen** /ˈspigəlaɪzən/, *n. Metall.* a lustrous, crystalline pig-iron containing a large amount of manganese, sometimes 15 per cent or more, used as a deoxidising agent in steel-making. Also, **spiegel.** [G: lit., mirror-iron]

**spiel** /spil, ʃpil/, *Colloq. –n.* **1.** glib or plausible talk, esp. for the purpose of persuasion, swindling, seduction, etc. **2.** a salesman's, conjurer's, or swindler's patter. **3.** any talk or speech. *–v.i.* **4.** to talk plausibly; deliver a patter or sales talk. *–v.t.* **5.** to attempt to lure, persuade, or deceive (someone) by glib talk. [G: play]

**spieler** /ˈspilə, ˈʃpilə/, *n. Colloq.* **1.** one who delivers or is proficient at, delivering a spiel, a glib talker. **2.** a salesman, barker, etc. **3.** a swindler; cardsharper. [SPIEL + -ER[1]]

**spier** /ˈspaɪə/, *n.* one who spies, watches, or discovers. Also, **spyer.**

**spiff** /spɪf/, *n.* a form of incentive given to sales people, usu. in the form of money or goods to an appropriate value.

**spiffing** /'spɪfɪŋ/, *adj. Brit. Colloq.* first-rate; excellent. [orig. uncert.; ? akin to SPIFFY]

**spiffy** /'spɪfi/, *adj.*, **spiffier, spiffiest.** *Brit. Colloq.* spruce; smart; fine. [Brit. d. *spiff* smartness + -Y[1]]

**spiflicate** /'spɪfləkeɪt/, *v.t.*, **-cated, -cating.** *Colloq.* (*oft. joc.*) to destroy utterly; hurt, punish, or damage; destroy or kill. Also, **spifflicate.** [orig. uncert.]

**spiflicated** /'spɪfləkeɪtəd/, *Colloq.* *–v.* **1.** past participle of **spiflicate.** *–adj.* **2.** drunk. Also, **spifflicated.**

**spignel** /'spɪgnəl/, *n.* a small, umbelliferous, perennial herb, *Meum athamanticum,* occurring among grass in mountains in Europe. [ME *spigurnel,* from ML *spigurnella,* of obscure orig.]

**spigot** /'spɪgət/, *n.* **1.** a small peg or plug for stopping the vent of a cask, etc. **2.** a small peg which stops the passage in the tap of a cask, etc. **3.** *U.S.* a tap or cock for controlling the flow of liquid from a pipe or the like. **4.** the end of a pipe which enters the enlarged end of another pipe to form a joint. [ME, var. of *spicket,* from SPIKE[1]]

**spike**[1] /spaɪk/, *n., v.,* **spiked, spiking.** *–n.* **1.** a large, strong nail or pin, esp. of iron. **2.** such a nail used for fastening rails to sleepers. **3.** a stiff, sharp-pointed piece or part. **4.** a sharp-pointed piece of metal, etc., fastened in something, with a point outwards, as for defence. **5.** a needle or syringe used for injecting drugs. **6.** a sharp metal projection on the sole of a shoe, as that of a golf player, to prevent slipping. **7.** (*pl.*) running shoes having such projections; track shoes. **8.** the antler of a young deer, when straight and without branches. **9.** *Elect.* a very short pulse of large amplitude. **10.** *Colloq.* a High Churchman. *–v.t.* **11.** to fasten or secure with a spike or spikes. **12.** to provide or set with a spike or spikes. **13.** to pierce with or impale on a spike. **14.** to set or stud with something suggesting spikes. **15.** to render (a muzzle-loading gun) useless by driving a spike into the touch-hole. **16.** to make ineffective, or frustrate the action or purpose of: *to spike a rumour.* **17.** *Colloq.* (of a newspaper editor) to reject (a story). **18.** *Colloq.* **a.** to add alcoholic liquor to a usu. non-alcoholic drink. **b.** to add a hard drug to a soft drug. **c.** to add anything to any drink or food. **19.** to increase the impact, interest or attractiveness of a speech, conversation, etc. **20. spike someone's guns,** to frustrate (someone's) plans. [ME, from Scand.; cf. Norw. *spik* nail, c. OE *spic-* in spicing nail] – **spikelike,** *adj.*

**spike**[2] /spaɪk/, *n.* **1.** an ear, as of wheat or other grain. **2.** *Bot.* an inflorescence in which the flowers are sessile (or apparently so) along an elongated, unbranched axis. [ME *spik,* from L *spica* ear of grain]

spikes[2]: A, barley; B, plantain

**spike lavender** /– 'lævəndə/, *n.* a species of lavender, *Lavandula latifolia,* having spikes of pale purple flowers, and yielding an oil (**oil of spike**) used in painting, etc.

**spikelet** /'spaɪklət/, *n.* **1.** *Bot.* a small or secondary spike in grasses; one of the flower clusters; the unit of inflorescence (consisting of two or more flowers and subtended by one or more glumes disposed around one axis). **2.** a small spike in which each flower is subtended by a glume as in plants of the family Cyperaceae as in sedges. Also, **spicule.**

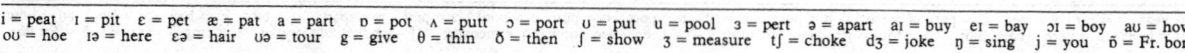

**spikenard** /'spaɪknad/, *n.* **1.** an aromatic East Indian plant, *Nardostachys jatamansi,* supposedly the same as the ancient nard. **2.** an aromatic substance used by the ancients, supposed to be obtained from this plant. **3.** any of various similar or related plants. [ME, from ML *spica nardi* spike of nard]

**spiker** /'spaɪkə/, *n.* a stag with his first set of antlers.

**spike-rush** /'spaɪk-rʌʃ/, *n.* any plant of the genus *Eleocharis,* family Cyperaceae, as the **tall spike-rush,** *E. sphacelata.*

**spiky** /'spaɪki/, *adj.* **1.** having a spike or spikes. **2.** having the form of a spike; spikelike. **3.** (of a person or one's temperament) short-tempered; easily irritated; difficult to deal with, or unyielding. **4.** *Colloq.* high-church Anglican.

**spile** /spaɪl/, *n., v.,* **spiled, spiling.** *–n.* **1.** a peg or plug of wood, esp. one used as a spigot. **2.** *U.S.* a spout for conducting sap from the sugar maple. **3.** a heavy stake or beam driven into the ground, etc., as a support; a pile. *–v.t.* **4.** to stop up (a hole) with a spile or peg. **5.** to furnish with a spigot or spout, as for drawing off a liquid. **6.** to tap by means of a spile. **7.** to furnish, strengthen, or support with spiles or piles. [MD or MLG, c. G *Speil*]

**spiling** /'spaɪlɪŋ/, *n.* **1.** piles; spiles. **2.** the dimensions of the curve of a ship's timbers.

**spill**[1] /spɪl/, *v.,* **spilt** or **spilled, spilling,** *n.* *–v.t.* **1.** to cause or allow (liquid, or any matter in grains or loose pieces) to run or fall from a container, esp. accidentally or wastefully. **2.** to shed (blood), as in killing or wounding. **3.** to scatter. **4.** *Naut.* to let the wind out of (a sail). **5.** to cause to fall from a horse, vehicle, or the like. **6.** *Colloq.* to divulge, disclose, or tell. *–v.i.* **7.** (of a liquid, loose particles, etc.) to run or escape from a container, esp. by accident or in careless handling. *–n.* **8.** a spilling, as of liquid. **9.** a quantity spilt. **10.** the mark made. **11.** a throw or fall from a horse, vehicle, or the like. **12.** the vacating of positions of political leadership preliminary to new ballots, appointments, etc. **13.** type which is transferred by a compositor to another page because of a lack of space. [ME; OE *spillan,* c. MLG *spillen*]

**spill**[2] /spɪl/, *n.* **1.** a splinter. **2.** a slender piece of wood or twisted paper, for lighting candles, lamps, etc. **3.** a peg made of metal. **4.** a small pin for stopping a cask; spile. [ME *spille;* akin to SPILE]

**spillage** /'spɪlɪdʒ/, *n.* **1.** an act of spilling. **2.** that which has been spilled: *a great spillage of oil.*

**spillway** /'spɪlweɪ/, *n.* a passageway through which surplus water escapes from a reservoir.

**spilt** /spɪlt/, *v.* past tense and past participle of **spill**[1].

**spin** /spɪn/, *v.,* **spun** or (*Archaic*) **span; spun; spinning;** *n.* *–v.t.* **1.** to make (yarn) by drawing out, twisting, and winding fibres. **2.** to form (any material) into thread. **3.** (of spiders, silkworms, etc.) to produce (a thread, cobweb, gossamer, silk, etc.) by extruding from the body a long, slender filament of a natural viscous matter that hardens in the air. **4.** to cause to turn round rapidly, as on an axis; twirl; whirl: *to spin a coin on a table.* **5.** (in sheet metalwork) to shape into hollow, rounded form, during rotation on a lathe or wheel, by pressure with a suitable tool. **6.** to produce, fabricate, or evolve in a manner suggestive of spinning thread, as a story. **7. a.** *Cricket.* of a bowler, to cause (the ball) to revolve on its axis so that on bouncing it changes direction or speed. **b.** *Tennis, etc.* to hit (the ball) so that it behaves thus. **8.** *Two-up.* to toss the coins. **9. spin a yarn, a.** to tell a tale. **b.** to tell a false or improbable story or version of an event. **10. spin out, a.** to draw out, protract, or prolong: *to spin out a story tediously.* **b.** to spend (time, one's life, etc.). **c.** to make last, as money; eke out. *–v.i.* **11.** to turn round rapidly, as on an axis, as the earth, a top, etc. **12.** to produce a thread from the body, as spiders, silkworms, etc. **13.** to move, go, run, ride, or travel rapidly. **14.** to be affected with a sensation of whirling, as the head. **15.** to fish with a spinning or revolving bait. *–n.* **16.** the act of causing a spinning or whirling motion. **17.** a spinning motion given to a ball or the like when thrown or struck. **18.** *Aeron.* a condition of stalled flight in which the aircraft is rotating about all its axes simultaneously. **19.** a moving or going rapidly along. **20.** a rapid run, ride, drive, or the like, as for exercise or enjoyment. **21.** *Colloq.* a state of confusion or excitement. **22.** *Colloq.* experience or chance generally: *a rough spin, a fair spin.* **23.** *Colloq.* **a.** (formerly) the sum of £5. **b.** the sum of $5. **24.** *Prison Colloq.* a prison sentence of five years' duration. **25.** *Physics.* the angular momentum of a molecule, atom, or particle, when it has no velocity of translation. [ME *spinne(n),* OE *spinnan,* c. D and G *spinnen*]

**spina bifida** /spaɪnə 'bɪfədə/, *n.* a congenital defect in the development of the vertebral column giving rise to a hernial protrusion of the meninges.

**spinach** /'spɪnɪtʃ/, *n.* **1.** an annual herb, *Spinacia oleracea,* cultivated for its succulent leaves, which are eaten boiled. **2.** the leaves. **3.** any related plant as species of the genus *Tetragonia,* whose leaves can be eaten boiled. [OF *(e)spinache, espinage,* from ML *spinachia,* from Sp. *espinaca,* from Ar. *isfinā̄j,* b. with L *spina* thorn]

**spinal** /ˈspaɪnəl/, *adj.* of, pertaining, or belonging to any spine or thornlike structure, esp. to the backbone. [LL *spīnālis*]

**spinal canal** /– kəˈnæl/, *n.* the tube formed by the vertebrae in which the spinal cord and its membranes are located.

**spinal column** /ˈ– kɒləm/, *n.* (in a vertebrate animal) the bones of vertebrae forming the axis of the skeleton and protecting the spinal cord; the spine; the backbone.

human spinal column: A, seven cervical vertebrae; B, twelve dorsal vertebrae; C, five lumbar vertebrae; D, five sacral vertebrae; E, four caudal or coccygeal vertebrae, forming a coccyx

**spinal cord** /ˈ– kɔd/, *n.* the cord of nervous tissue extending through the spinal column.

**spin bowler** /ˈspɪn boʊlə/, *n.* (in cricket) a bowler who has a special skill in spinning the ball.

**spindle** /ˈspɪndl/, *n., adj., v.,* **-dled, -dling.** *–n.* **1.** a rounded rod, usu. of wood, tapering towards each end, used in spinning by hand to twist into thread the fibres drawn from the mass on the distaff, and to wind the thread on as it is spun. **2.** the rod on a spinning wheel by which the thread is twisted and on which it is wound. **3.** one of the rods of a spinning machine which bear the bobbins on which the thread is wound as it is spun. **4.** any rod or pin suggestive of a spindle used in spinning, as one which turns round or on which something turns; an axle, axis, or shaft. **5.** either of the two shaft-like parts in a lathe which support the work to be turned, one (**live spindle**) rotating and imparting motion to the work, and the other (**dead spindle**) not rotating. **6.** a small axis, arbor, or mandrel. **7.** a measure of length of yarn, varying according to the material. **8.** →**hydrometer.** **9.** *Biol.* the fine threads of achromatic material arranged within the cell, during mitosis, in a fusiform manner. **10.** a short turned or circular ornament, as in a baluster or stair rail. *–adj.* **11.** of or resembling spindles. **12.** *U.S.* denoting the maternal line of descent; distaff: *the spindle side of the house.* *–v.t.* **13.** to fit with a spindle or spindles. **14.** to give the form of a spindle to. *–v.i. Obs. or U.S.* **15.** to shoot up, or grow, into a long, slender stalk or stem, as a plant. **16.** to grow tall and slender, often disproportionately so. [ME *spindel,* OE *spinel* (c. D *spindel,* G *Spindel*), from *spinnan* SPIN]

**spindlelegs** /ˈspɪndlˌlɛgz/, *n.pl.* →**spindleshanks.** – **spindle-legged** /ˈspɪndl-ˌlɛgd, -ˌlɛgəd/, *adj.*

**spindleshanks** /ˈspɪndlʃæŋks/, *n.pl. Colloq.* **1.** long, thin legs. **2.** (*construed as sing.*) a tall, thin person with such legs. – **spindle-shanked** /ˈspɪndl-ʃæŋkt/, *adj.*

**spindle tree** /ˈspɪndl tri/, *n.* **1.** a shrub or small tree of Europe and western Asia, *Euonymus europaeus* (family Celastraceae), with a hard wood formerly much used for making spindles. **2.** any of various allied plants.

**spindling** /ˈspɪndlɪŋ/, *adj.* **1.** long or tall and slender, often disproportionately so. **2.** growing into a long, slender stalk or stem, often a too slender or weakly one. *–n.* **3.** *Rare.* a spindling person or thing.

**spindly** /ˈspɪndli/, *adj.,* **-dlier, -dliest.** long or tall and slender; attenuated; slender and fragile.

**spin-drier** /spɪn-ˈdraɪə/, *n.* a machine for spin-drying laundry, often forming part of an automatic washing machine. Also, **spin-dryer.**

**spindrift** /ˈspɪndrɪft/, *n.* spray swept by a violent wind along the surface of the sea. Also, **spoondrift.**

**spin-dry** /spɪn-ˈdraɪ/, *v.t.,* **-dried, -drying.** to dry (laundry) by spinning it in a tub so that the moisture is extracted by centrifugal force.

**spine** /spaɪn/, *n.* **1.** the vertebral or spinal column; the backbone. **2.** any backbone-like part. **3.** a pointed process or projection, as of a bone. **4.** a stiff, pointed process or appendage on an animal, as a quill of a porcupine, or a sharp, bony ray in a fish's fin. **5.** a ridge, as of ground, rock, etc. **6.** a sharp-pointed, hard or woody outgrowth on a plant; a thorn. **7.** *Bookbinding.* the part of a book's cover that holds the front and back together, and which usu. indicates the title and author. [ME, from L *spīna*] – **spined,** *adj.* – **spinelike,** *adj.*

**spinebash** /ˈspaɪnbæʃ/, *v.i. Colloq.* **1.** to rest; loaf. *–n.* **2.** a rest. – **spinebasher,** *n.* – **spinebashing,** *n.*

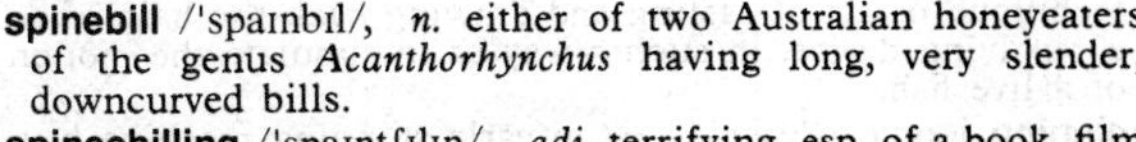

**spinebill** /ˈspaɪnbɪl/, *n.* either of two Australian honeyeaters of the genus *Acanthorhynchus* having long, very slender, downcurved bills.

**spinechilling** /ˈspaɪntʃɪlɪŋ/, *adj.* terrifying, esp. of a book, film etc. – **spinechiller,** *n.*

**spinefoot** /ˈspaɪnfʊt/, *n.* any of several rabbit-fish of the genus *Siganus,* of Indo-Pacific tropical waters, having venomous fin spines.

**spinel** /spəˈnɛl/, *n.* **1.** any of a group of minerals composed principally of oxides of magnesium, aluminium, iron, manganese, chromium, etc., characterised by their hardness and octahedral crystals. **2.** a mineral of this group, essentially magnesium aluminate, $MgAl_2O_4$, and having varieties used as ornamental stones in jewellery. [F *(e)spinelle,* from It. *spinella,* diminutive of *spina* thorn, from L]

**spineless** /ˈspaɪnləs/, *adj.* **1.** without spines. **2.** having no spine. **3.** having a weak spine; limp. **4.** without moral force, resolution, or courage; feeble. – **spinelessly,** *adv.* – **spinelessness,** *n.*

**spinescent** /spaɪnˈɛsənt/, *adj.* **1.** *Bot.* **a.** becoming spine-like. **b.** ending in a spine. **c.** bearing spines. **2.** *Zool.* somewhat spinelike; coarse, as hair. [LL *spīnescens,* ppr., growing thorny]

**spinet** /ˈspɪnət/, *n.* **1.** a small keyboard instrument resembling the harpsichord, the main difference being that the strings run across the instrument more or less in the direction of the keyboard, not at right angles to it. **2.** an early small square piano. **3.** *U.S.* a commercial name for a modern small upright piano. [F *espinette,* ? named after Giovanni *Spinetti,* fl. 1500, Venetian inventor]

**spine-tailed chowchilla** /ˌspaɪn-teɪld tʃaʊˈtʃɪlə/, *n.* →**chowchilla** (def. 2).

**spiniferous** /spaɪˈnɪfərəs/, *adj.* →**spiny.**

**spinifex** /ˈspɪnəfɛks/, *n.* **1.** any of the spiny grasses of the genus *Spinifex,* chiefly of Australia, often useful for binding sand on the seashore. **2.** any species of the genus *Triodia,* spiny-leaved tussock-forming grasses of inland Australia. [NL *spina* spine + *-fex* maker]

spinifex (def. 1)

**spinifex bird** /ˈ– bɜd/, *n.* a wren-like bird, *Eremiornis carteri,* inhabiting the spinifex and low scrubs of Australian arid zones.

**spinifex hopping-mouse** /– ˈhɒpɪŋ-maʊs/, *n.* →**dargawarra.**

**spinnaker** /ˈspɪnəkə/, *n.* a large triangular sail with a light boom (**spinnaker boom**), carried by yachts on the side opposite the mainsail when running before the wind, or with the wind abaft the beam. [supposedly from *Sphinx* (mispronounced *spinks*), name of yacht on which this sail was first regularly used]

spinnaker

**spinner** /ˈspɪnə/, *n.* **1.** one who or that which spins. **2.** a revolving bait used in trolling or casting for fish. **3.** a spider. **4.** **a.** a delivery in which the bowler imparts lateral spin to the ball, making it deviate upon pitching. **b.** a bowler specialising in such deliveries. **5.** *Two-up.* the person who tosses the coins. **6.** **come in spinner!** (an expression indicating to the spinner that play has reached the point where he should now toss the coins). **7.** *Aeron.* a streamlined housing enclosing a propeller hub.

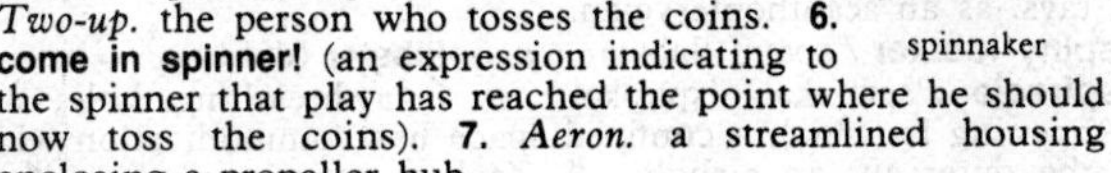

**spinneret** /ˈspɪnərɛt/, *n.* **1.** an organ or part by means of which a spider, insect larva, or the like spins a silky thread for its web or cocoon. **2.** a finely perforated tube or plate through which a viscous liquid passes into the solidifying medium during the course of manufacture of man-made fibres. [diminutive of SPINNER]

**spinner's type** /ˈspɪnəz taɪp/, *n.* a superior combing wool which is sound, regular, of good colour and free from vegetable fault and dust.

**spinney** /ˈspɪni/, *n., pl.* **-neys.** *Brit.* **1.** a thicket or copse. **2.** a small plantation or group of trees. [ME *spenne,* from OF *espinei* thorny place, from *espine* SPINE]

**spinning** /ˈspɪnɪŋ/, *n.* **1.** the technique or act of changing fibrous substances into yarn or thread. **2.** *Angling.* the technique or act of casting and drawing back the bait, often a revolving device, in such a way as to simulate the motion of a live fish.

**spinning jenny** /–ˈdʒɛni/, *n.* an early spinning machine having more than one spindle, whereby one person could spin a number of yarns simultaneously.

**spinning wheel** /ˈ– wil/, *n.* a device for spinning wool, flax, etc., into yarn or thread consisting essentially of a single spindle driven by a large wheel operated by hand or foot.

spinnning wheel

**spinode** /ˈspɪnoʊd/, *n.* →**cusp** (def. 3). [L *spī(na)* spine + NODE]

**spin-off** /ˈspɪn-ɒf/, *n.* **1.** an object, product or enterprise derived as an incidental or secondary development of a larger enterprise: *the non-stick frying pan is a commercially valuable spin-off of space research.* **2.** *Econ.* the formation of a new company by an already existing company, with shareholders in the existing company entitled to subscribe for shares in the new company.

**spinose** /ˈspaɪnoʊs/, *adj. Chiefly Biol.* full of spines; spiniferous; spinous. [L *spīnōsus*] – **spinosely,** *adv.* – **spinosity** /spaɪnˈɒsəti/, *n.*

**spinous** /ˈspaɪnəs/, *adj.* **1.** covered with or having spines; thorny, as a plant. **2.** armed with or bearing sharp-pointed processes, as an animal; spiniferous. **3.** spinelike.

**spin rod** /ˈspɪn rɒd/, *n.* (in angling) a rod used in spinning with a high speed reel.

**spin stabilisation** /– steɪbəlaɪˈzeɪʃən/, *n.* stabilisation of a spacecraft, etc., by spinning, so that the craft remains pointing in a given direction. – **spin-stabilised,** *adj.*

**spinster** /ˈspɪnstə/, *n.* **1.** a woman still unmarried beyond the usual age of marrying; an old maid. **2.** *Chiefly Law.* a woman who has never married. **3.** *Obs.* a woman (sometimes, any person) who spins, esp. as a regular occupation. [ME, from SPIN + -STER] – **spinsterhood,** *n.* – **spinsterish,** *adj.*

**spinthariscope** /spɪnˈθærəskoʊp/, *n.* an apparatus for observing the scintillations produced in a prepared screen, as of zinc sulphide, by the action of radioactive rays. [Gk *spintharí(s)* spark + -SCOPE]

**spinule** /ˈspaɪnjul/, *n.* a small spine or thorn. [L *spīnula,* diminutive of *spina* SPINE] – **spinulose** /ˈspaɪnjəloʊs/, *adj.*

**spiny** /ˈspaɪni/, *adj.,* **spinier, spiniest.** **1.** abounding in or having spines; thorny, as a plant. **2.** covered with or having sharp-pointed processes, as an animal. **3.** in the form of a spine; resembling a spine; spinelike. **4.** perplexing or troublesome, as a problem; thorny. – **spininess,** *n.*

**spiny anteater** /– ˈæntitə/, *n.* →**echidna.**

**spiny burr grass,** *n.* a summer growing annual, *Cenchrus panciflorus,* a native of America, having sharp, spined burrs which damage animals' feet and skins and infest fleeces.

**spiny emex** /spaɪni ˈimɛks/, *n.* →**cat's head.**

**spiny-finned** /ˈspaɪni-fɪnd/, *adj.* having fins with sharp bony rays, as an acanthopterygian.

**spiny lobster** /ˌspaɪni ˈlɒbstə/, *n.* →**lobster** (def. 1).

**spiracle** /ˈspaɪrəkəl, ˈspɪrəkəl/, *n.* **1.** a breathing hole; an opening by which a confined space has communication with the outer air; an airhole. **2.** *Zool.* **a.** an aperture or orifice through which air or water passes in the act of respiration, as the blowhole of a cetacean. **b.** an opening in the head of sharks and rays through which water is drawn and passed over gills. **c.** one of the external orifices of a tracheal respiratory system, usu. on the sides of the body. [ME, from L *spīrāculum*] – **spiracular** /spəˈrækjələ/, *adj.* – **spiraculate** /spəˈrækjələt/, *adj.*

**spiraea** /spaɪˈriə/, *n.* any of the herbs or shrubs constituting the genus *Spiraea,* with racemes, cymes, panicles, or corymbs of small white or pink flowers, certain species of which are much cultivated for ornament, esp. the **Japanese spiraea,** *S. japonica.* Also, **spirea.** [L, from Gk *speiraía* meadowsweet]

**spiral**[1] /ˈspaɪrəl/, *n., adj., v.,* **-ralled, -ralling** or (*U.S.*) **-raled, -raling.** *–n.* **1.** a plane curve traced by a point which runs continuously round and round a fixed point or centre while constantly receding from or approaching it. **2.** a single circle or ring of a spiral or helical curve or object. **3.** a spiral or helical object, formation, or form. **4.** →**helix.** **5.** *Aeron.* a manoeuvre in which an aeroplane descends in a helix of small pitch and large radius, with the angle of incidence within that of the normal flight range. **6.** *Econ.* a reciprocal interaction of price and cost changes forming an overall economic change upwards (**inflationary spiral**) or downwards (**deflationary spiral**). *–adj.* **7.** resembling or arranged in a spiral or spirals. **8.** (of a curve) like a spiral. **9.** →**helical.** *–v.i.* **10.** to take a spiral form or course. **11.** *Aeron.* to move an aeroplane through a spiral course. *–v.t.* **12.** to cause to take a spiral form or course. [ML *spīrālis*] – **spirally,** *adv.*

**spiral**[2] /ˈspaɪrəl/, *adj.* pertaining to or of the nature of a spire; spirelike; tall and tapering. [SPIR(E)[1] + -AL[1]]

**spiral galaxy** /– ˈgæləksi/, *n.* one of the extragalactic stellar systems which shows spiral structure. Also, **spiral nebula.**

**spiral punt** /ˈ– pʌnt/, *n.* →**torpedo punt.**

**spiral staircase** /– ˈstɛəkeɪs/, *n.* a staircase whose steps rise to form a spiral around a central axis. Also, **spiral stairway.**

**spirant** /ˈspaɪrənt/, *n., adj. Phonet. Obsolesc.* →**fricative.** [L *spīrans,* ppr., breathing]

**spire**[1] /ˈspaɪə/, *n., v.,* **spired, spiring.** *–n.* **1.** a tall, tapering structure, generally an elongated, upright cone or pyramid, erected on a tower, roof, etc. **2.** such a structure forming the upper part of the steeple, or the whole steeple. **3.** a tapering, pointed part of something; a tall, sharp-pointed summit, peak, or the like. **4.** the highest point or summit of something. **5.** a sprout or shoot of a plant; an acrospire of grain; a blade or spear of grass, etc. *–v.i.* **6.** to shoot or rise into spirelike form; rise or extend to a height in the manner of a spire. [ME; OE *spīr,* c. D *spier,* G *Spier*] – **spirelike,** *adj.*

**spire**[2] /ˈspaɪə/, *n.* **1.** a coil or spiral. **2.** one of the series of convolutions of a coil or spiral. **3.** *Zool.* the upper, convoluted part of a spiral shell, above the aperture. [L *spīra,* from Gk *speîra* coil, winding] – **spirelike,** *adj.*

**spirea** /spaɪˈriə/, *n.* →**spiraea.**

**spired** /ˈspaɪəd/, *adj.* having a spire.

**spireme** /ˈspaɪrim/, *n.* (of a plant or animal) the chromatin of a cell nucleus, when appearing in a continuous or segmented threadlike form, during mitosis. [Gk *speírēma* coil]

**spiriferous** /spaɪˈrɪfərəs/, *adj.* **1.** having a spire, or spiral upper part, as a univalve shell. **2.** having spiral appendages, as a brachiopod.

**spirillum** /spaɪˈrɪləm/, *n., pl.* **-rilla** /-ˈrɪlə/. **1.** any of the bacteria constituting the genus *Spirillum,* characterised by spirally twisted, rigid forms and having a bundle of 5 to 20 flagella. **2.** any of various similar micro-organisms. [NL, diminutive of L *spīra* SPIRE[2]]

**spirit** /ˈspɪrət/, *n.* **1.** the principle of conscious life, originally identified with the breath; the vital principle in man, animating the body or mediating between body and soul. **2.** the incorporeal part of man: *present in spirit though absent in body.* **3.** the soul as separable from the body at death. **4.** conscious, incorporeal being, as opposed to matter: *the world of spirit.* **5.** a supernatural, incorporeal being, esp. one inhabiting a place or thing or having a particular character: *evil spirits.* **6.** a fairy, sprite, or elf. **7.** an angel or demon. **8.** an inspiring or animating principle such as pervades and tempers thought, feeling, or action: *a spirit of reform.* **9.** (*cap.*) the divine influence as an agency working in the heart of man. **10.** (in biblical use) a divine inspiring or animating being or influence. **11.** the third person of the Trinity; Holy Spirit. **12. the Spirit,** God. **13.** the soul or heart as the seat of feelings or sentiments, or as prompting to action: *to break a person's spirit.* **14.** (*pl.*) feelings with respect to exaltation or depression: *in low spirits.* **15.** fine or brave vigour or liveliness; mettle. **16.** temper or disposition: *meek in spirit.* **17.** a person characterised according to character, disposition, action, etc. **18.** mental or moral attitude; mood: *take something in the right spirit.* **19.** the dominant tendency or character of anything: *the spirit of the age.* **20.** vigorous sense of membership in a group: *team spirit.* **21.** the true or general meaning or intent of a statement, etc. (opposed to *letter*). **22.** *Chem.* **a.** an aqueous solution of ethyl alcohol, esp. one obtained by distillation. **b.**

the essence or active principle of a substance as extracted in liquid form, esp. by distillation. **23.** (*oft. pl.*) a strong distilled alcoholic liquor. **24.** *Pharm.* a solution in alcohol of an essential or volatile principle. **25.** any of certain subtle fluids formerly supposed to permeate the body. *–adj.* **26.** pertaining to something which works by burning alcoholic spirits. **27.** of or pertaining to spiritualist bodies or activities. *–v.t.* **28.** to animate with fresh ardour or courage; inspirit. **29.** to encourage; urge (*on*) or stir (*up*), as to action. **30.** to carry (*away, off,* etc.) mysteriously or secretly. [ME, from L *spīritus* breathing]

**spirited** /ˈspɪrətəd/, *adj.* **1.** having a spirit, or having spirits, as specified: *low-spirited.* **2.** having or showing mettle, courage, vigour, liveliness, etc. – **spiritedly,** *adv.* – **spiritedness,** *n.*

**spirit gum** /ˈspɪrət gʌm/, *n.* a spirit-soluble, fast-drying preparation, as used for attaching false hair to an actor's skin.

**spiritism** /ˈspɪrətɪzəm/, *n.* the doctrine or practices of spiritualism. – **spiritist** /ˈspɪrətəst/, *n.* – **spiritistic** /spɪrəˈtɪstɪk/, *adj.*

**spiritless** /ˈspɪrətləs/, *adj.* **1.** without spirit. **2.** without ardour, vigour, animation, etc. – **spiritlessly,** *adv.* – **spiritlessness,** *n.*

**spirit level** /ˈspɪrət lɛvəl/, *n.* a device for testing horizontality, consisting of a glass tube containing an oil or spirit, as alcohol, with a movable bubble which is only in the centre of the tube if the device is horizontal.

**spiritoso** /spɪrəˈtoʊsoʊ/, *adv.* **1.** (a musical direction) in a lively and spirited manner. *–adj.* **2.** lively; spirited. [It.]

**spiritous** /ˈspɪrətəs/, *adj. Obs.* **1.** of the nature of spirit; immaterial, ethereal, or refined. **2.** high-spirited. **3.** spirituous.

**spirit-rapping** /ˈspɪrət-ˌræpɪŋ/, *n.* supposed communication between the living and the dead by rapping out messages on a table or the like. – **spirit-rapper,** *n.*

**spirits of hartshorn,** *n.* an aqueous solution of ammonia.

**spirits of salt,** *n.* a solution of hydrochloric acid in water.

**spirits of turpentine,** *n.* oil of turpentine.

**spirits of wine,** *n.* alcohol.

**spirit stove** /ˈspɪrət stoʊv/, *n.* →**primus.**

**spiritual** /ˈspɪrətʃuəl, -tʃəl/, *adj.* **1.** of, pertaining to, or consisting of spirit or incorporeal being. **2.** of or pertaining to the spirit or soul as distinguished from the physical nature. **3.** standing in a relationship of the spirit; non-material: *a spiritual attitude, a spiritual father.* **4.** characterised by or suggesting predominance of the spirit; ethereal or delicately refined. **5.** of or pertaining to the spirit as the seat of the moral or religious nature. **6.** of or pertaining to sacred things; pertaining or belonging to the church; ecclesiastical; religious; devotional; sacred. **7.** of or relating to the conscious thoughts and emotions. *–n.* **8.** a traditional religious song, esp. of American Negroes. **9.** (*pl.*) affairs of the church. **10.** a spiritual thing or matter. [L *spīrituālis*] – **spiritually,** *adv.* – **spiritualness,** *n.*

**spiritualise** /ˈspɪrətʃəlaɪz/, *v.t.,* **-lised, -lising. 1.** to make spiritual. **2.** to invest with a spiritual meaning. Also, **spiritualise.** – **spiritualisation** /spɪrətʃəlaɪˈzeɪʃən/, *n.*

**spiritualism** /ˈspɪrətʃəlɪzəm/, *n.* **1.** the belief or doctrine that the spirits of the dead, surviving after the mortal life, can and do communicate with the living, esp. through a person (a medium) particularly susceptible to their influence. **2.** the practices or the phenomena associated with this belief. **3.** the belief that all or some reality is immaterial and therefore spiritual. **4.** *Metaphys.* any doctrine that asserts the separate but related existence of God, human (or other rational) beings, and physical nature. **5.** spiritual quality or tendency. **6.** insistence on the spiritual side of things, as in philosophy or religion.

**spiritualist** /ˈspɪrətʃələst/, *n.* **1.** an adherent of spiritualism. **2.** one who concerns himself with or insists on the spiritual side of things. *–adj.* **3.** Also, **spiritualistic** /ˌspɪrətʃəˈlɪstɪk/. of or pertaining to spiritualists or spiritualism.

**spirituality** /spɪrətʃuˈæləti/, *n., pl.* **-ties. 1.** the quality or fact of being spiritual. **2.** incorporeal or immaterial nature. **3.** predominantly spiritual character, as shown in thought, life, etc.; spiritual tendency or tone. **4.** (*oft. pl.*) property or revenue of the church or of an ecclesiastic in his official capacity.

**spiritualty** /ˈspɪrətʃʊəlti/, *n., pl.* **-ties.** *Obs. or Hist.* **1.** (*oft. pl.*) ecclesiastical property or revenue. **2.** the body of ecclesiastics; the clergy.

**spirituel** /ˈspɪrɪtʃuˌɛl/, *adj.* **1.** showing a refined and graceful mind or wit. **2.** light and airy in movement; ethereal. [F. See SPIRITUAL] – **spirituelle,** *adj., fem.*

**spirituous** /ˈspɪrətʃuəs/, *adj.* **1.** containing, of the nature of, or pertaining to alcohol; alcoholic. **2.** (of liquors) distilled, as opposed to fermented. – **spirituousness,** *n.*

**spiritus asper** /spɪrətəs ˈæspə/, *n.* →**rough breathing.** [L]

**spiritus lenis** /– ˈleɪnəs/, *n.* →**smooth breathing.** [L]

**spirit varnish** /ˈspɪrət ˌvanɪʃ/, *n.* a varnish consisting of a solution of resin, or resins, in industrial methylated spirits.

**spirket** /ˈspɜkət/, *n.* (in shipbuilding) a space between the floor timbers of a wooden ship. [orig. uncert.; ? akin to OE *spircing* scattering]

**spirketting** /ˈspɜkətɪŋ/, *n. Naut.* the planks of the deck nearest the sides of a wooden ship. Also, *U.S.,* **spirketing.**

**spirketting plate** /ˈ– pleɪt/, *n.* the spirketting in a steel ship.

**spiro-**[1], a word element referring to 'respiration', as in *spirograph.* [combining form representing L *spīrāre* breathe]

**spiro-**[2], a word element meaning 'coil', 'spiral', as in *spirochaete.* [Gk *speiro-*, combining form of *speîra*]

**spirochaete** /ˈspaɪrəkit/, *n.* slender, corkscrew-like bacterial micro-organisms constituting the genus *Spirochaeta,* and found on man, animals, and plants, and in soil and water. Some cause disease, as the *Spirochaeta pallida* or *Treponema pallidum* (the causative agent of syphilis); most, however, are saprophytic. Also, *Chiefly U.S.,* **spirochete.** [NL *Spirochaeta,* from Gk *speiro-* SPIRO-[2] + *chaítē* hair]

**spirochaetosis** /ˌspaɪroʊkəˈtoʊsəs/, *n. Vet. Sci.* **a.** a specific, infectious, usu. fatal, blood disease of chickens caused by a spirochaete, *Borrelia anserina.* **b.** an infection of pigs caused by an organism, *B. suilla,* entering the animal through a wound, often occurring after castration if animals are in unsanitary conditions. Also, **spirochetosis.**

**spirograph** /ˈspaɪrəgræf, -graf/, *n.* an instrument for recording respiratory movements.

**spirogyra** /spaɪrəˈdʒaɪrə/, *n.* a widely distributed freshwater green alga (genus *Spirogyra*) having peripheral, spiral chromatophores. [NL, from Gk *speiro-* SPIRO-[2] + *gŷros* circle, ring]

**spiroid** /ˈspaɪrɔɪd/, *adj.* more or less spiral; resembling a spiral. [NL *spīroīdes.* See SPIRO-[2], -OID]

**spirometer** /spaɪˈrɒmətə/, *n.* an instrument for determining the capacity of the lungs. [SPIRO-[1] + -METER[1]] – **spirometric** /spaɪrəˈmɛtrɪk/, *adj.* – **spirometry,** *n.*

**spirt** /spɜt/, *v.i., v.t., n.* →**spurt.**

**spirula** /ˈspaɪrələ/, *n., pl.* **-lae** /-li/. any of the small decapod dibranchiate cephalopods of the genus *Spirula,* having in the hinder part of the body, but not completely internal, a shell in the form of a flat spiral with separated whorls, which is divided by partitions into a series of chambers. [NL, diminutive of L *spīra* SPIRE[2]]

spirula

**spiry**[1] /ˈspaɪri/, *adj.* **1.** having the form of a spire, slender shoot, or tapering pointed body; tapering up to a point like a spire. **2.** abounding in spires or steeples. [SPIRE[1] + -Y[1]]

**spiry**[2] /ˈspaɪri/, *adj.* spiral; coiled; curling. [SPIRE[2] + -Y[1]]

**spit**[1] /spɪt/, *v.,* **spat** or **spit, spitting,** *n.* *–v.i.* **1.** to eject saliva from the mouth; expectorate. **2.** to do this at or on a person, etc., to express hatred, contempt, etc. **3.** to sputter. **4.** to fall in scattered drops or flakes, as rain or snow. **5.** to make a noise as of spitting. *–v.t.* **6.** to eject (saliva, etc.) from the mouth. **7.** to throw out or emit, esp. violently. **8.** to utter vehemently. **9. spit chips,** *Colloq.* to be very annoyed. **10. spit it out,** *Colloq.* speak up. *–n.* **11.** saliva, esp. when ejected. **12.** the act of spitting. **13.** a frothy or spitlike secretion exuded by various insects; spittle. **14.** a light fall of rain or snow. **15.** Also, **dead spit.** *Colloq.* the image, likeness, or counterpart of a person, etc. **16. the big spit,** *Colloq.* vomit. [ME; OE *spittan* c. d. G *spitzen,* akin to OE *spǣtan* spit] – **spitlike,** *adj.* – **spitter,** *n.*

**spit**[2] /spɪt/, *n., v.,* **spitted, spitting.** *–n.* **1.** a sharply pointed, slender rod or bar for thrusting into or through and holding meat to be roasted at a fire or grilled. **2.** any of various rods, pins, or the like used for particular purposes. **3.** a device for roasting meat, etc., comprising such a rod, together with a mechanism for revolving it, and a source of heat; a rotisserie. **4.** a narrow point of land projecting into the water. **5.** a long, narrow shoal extending from the shore. *–v.t.* **6.** to pierce, stab, or transfix, as with a spit; impale on something sharp. **7.** to thrust a spit into or through. [ME; OE *spitu,* c. D and LG *spit*]

**spital** /ˈspɪtl/, *n. Obs.* **1.** a hospital, esp. one for the poor. **2.** a shelter on a highway. [short for HOSPITAL; replacing earlier *spittle,* ME *spitel,* c. G *Spital.* Cf. d. It. *spitale*]

**spit and polish,** *n.* assiduous attention to smartness, esp. of soldiers; excessive concern with discipline.

**spitchcock** /ˈspɪtʃkɒk/, *n.* **1.** an eel, split, cut into pieces, and broiled or fried. *–v.t.* **2.** to split, cut up, and broil or fry (an eel, chicken, etc.). **3.** *Rare.* to treat severely. [orig. uncert.]

**spite** /spaɪt/, *n., v.,* **spited, spiting.** *–n.* **1.** a keen, ill-natured desire to humiliate, annoy, or injure another; venomous ill will. **2.** a particular instance of such ill will; a grudge. **3.** *Archaic.* vexation or chagrin. **4. in spite of,** in disregard or defiance of; notwithstanding. *–v.t.* **5.** to wreak one's spite or malice on. **6.** to annoy or thwart, out of spite. **7.** *Archaic.* to fill with spite; vex; offend. [ME; aphetic var. of DESPITE, *n.*]

**spiteful** /ˈspaɪtfəl/, *adj.* full of spite or malice; showing spite; malicious; malevolent; venomous: *she was a spiteful and jealous old woman.* – **spitefully,** *adv.* – **spitefulness,** *n.*

**spitfire** /ˈspɪtfaɪə/, *n.* **1.** a person of fiery temper, easily provoked to outbursts, esp. a girl or woman. **2.** (*cap.*) a British single-engined fighter aircraft much used in World War II. **3.** the slug-like larva of a cup moth, most of which are brightly coloured and possess clusters of retractable nettle-like spines that can inflict a most painful sting.

**spitter** /ˈspɪtə/, *n.* **1.** one who, or that which spits. **2.** *Bldg Trades.* a short outlet pipe from a gutter, balcony, etc., directing water out of a building.

**spitting distance** /ˈspɪtɪŋ dɪstns/, *n. Colloq.* a very short distance: *they lived within spitting distance of each other.*

**spitting image** /ˌspɪtɪŋ ˈɪmɪdʒ/, *n.* →**spit**[1] (def. 15).

**spitting snake** /ˈ– sneɪk/, *n.* →**ringhals.**

**spittle** /ˈspɪtl/, *n.* **1.** saliva; spit. **2.** the frothy protective secretion exuded by spittle insects. [alteration (conformed to SPIT[1]) of obs. or d. *spattle,* ME *spatel,* OE *spātl,* akin to *spǣtan* spit]

**spittle insect** /ˈ– ˌɪnsɛkt/, *n.* →**froghopper.**

**spittoon** /spɪˈtun/, *n.* a bowl, etc., for spitting into.

**spitz** /spɪts/, *n.* any of a number of small or medium-sized breeds of dog having dense hair, pointed muzzle, and erect ears, as the elkhound. [G: pointed, with ref. to the muzzle]

spitz

**spiv** /spɪv/, *n. Orig. Brit. Colloq.* one who lives by his wits, without working or by dubious business activity, and usu. affecting ostentatious dress and tastes. [back-formation from Brit. d. *spiving* smart. See SPIFFY] – **spivvy,** *adj.*

**S.P.J.,** Senior Puisne Judge.

**splade** /spleɪd/, *n.* a spoon-shaped fork with a cutting edge. [Trademark]

**splanchnic** /ˈsplæŋknɪk/, *adj.* of or pertaining to the viscera or entrails; visceral. [NL *splanchnicus,* from Gk *splanchnikós*]

**splash** /splæʃ/, *v.t.* **1.** to wet or soil by dashing masses or particles of water, mud, or the like; spatter. **2.** to fall upon (something) in scattered masses or particles, as a liquid does. **3.** to cause to appear spattered. **4.** to dash (water, etc.) about in scattered masses or particles. **5.** to make (one's way) with splashing. **6.** *Colloq.* to display or print very noticeably, as in a newspaper. **7.** *Colloq.* to spend (money) freely. *–v.i.* **8.** to dash a liquid or semiliquid substance about. **9.** to fall, move, or go with a splash or splashes. **10.** (of liquid) to dash or fall in scattered masses or particles. **11.** (of a bullet) to disintegrate on impact. **12.** *Colloq.* to spend money freely (oft. fol. by *out*). *–n.* **13.** the act of splashing. **14.** the sound of splashing. **15.** a quantity of some liquid or semiliquid substance splashed upon or in a thing. **16.** a spot caused by something splashed. **17.** a patch, as of colour or light. **18.** a striking show, or an ostentatious display; sensation or excitement. **19. make a splash,** to be noticed; make an impression on people. [alteration of PLASH[1]]

**splashback** /ˈsplæʃbæk/, *n.* a vertical waterproof surface on a wall backing a horizontal surface such as a bench top, basin, etc.

**splashboard** /ˈsplæʃbɔd/, *n.* **1.** a board, guard, or screen to protect from splashing, as a dashboard of a vehicle or a guard placed over a wheel to intercept water, dirt, etc. **2.** a screen to prevent water or spray from coming on the deck of a boat.

**splash coat** /ˈsplæʃ koʊt/, *n.* an initial coat of paint, render, plaster, etc., which is splashed roughly on a surface to form a key for a final surface.

**splash cymbal** /ˈ– sɪmbəl/, *n.* a cymbal whose resonance is limited to the extent that when struck the sound produced is immediately stifled.

**splashdown** /ˈsplæʃdaʊn/, *n.* the landing of a space vehicle on a body of water.

**splasher** /ˈsplæʃə/, *n.* **1.** one who or that which splashes. **2.** something that protects from splashes.

**splashy** /ˈsplæʃi/, *adj.,* **splashier, splashiest.** **1.** making a splash or splashes. **2.** making the sound of splashing. **3.** full or marked by splashes, or irregular spots, spotty. **4.** wet, soft, or muddy. **5.** *Colloq.* making a show or display.

**splat** /splæt/, *n.* **1.** a broad, flat piece of wood, as the central upright part of the back of a chair. **2.** a slapping sound as made with something wet. [cf. OE *splātan* split]

**S-plate** /ˈɛs-pleɪt/, *n.* an S-shaped piece of metal securing a bolt which braces a weak brick wall.

**splatter** /ˈsplætə/, *v.i., v.t.* to splash.

**splay** /spleɪ/, *v.t.* **1.** to spread out, expand, or extend. **2.** to form with an oblique angle; make slanting; bevel. **3.** to make with a splay or splays. **4.** to disjoin; dislocate. *–v.i.* **5.** to have an oblique or slanting direction. **6.** to spread or flare. *–n.* **7.** *Archit.* Also, **reveal.** a surface which makes an oblique angle with another, as where the opening through a wall for a window or door widens from the window or door proper towards the face of the wall. *–adj.* **8.** spread out; wide and flat; turned outwards. **9.** oblique or awry. [aphetic var. of DISPLAY]

S, splay (def. 7)

**splayfoot** /ˈspleɪfʊt/, *n.* a broad, flat foot, esp. one outwards. – **splayfooted,** *adj.*

**spleen** /splin/, *n.* **1.** a highly vascular, glandlike but ductless organ, situated in man near the cardiac end of the stomach, in which the blood undergoes certain corpuscular changes. **2.** *Obs.* this organ as supposed (variously) to be the seat of mirth, spirit or courage, ill humour, melancholy, etc. **3.** ill humour, peevish temper, or spite: *venting his spleen on his unfortunate wife.* **4.** *Archaic.* melancholy. [ME, from L *splēn,* Gk] – **spleenish, spleeny,** *adj.*

**spleenful** /ˈsplinfəl/, *adj.* **1.** full of or displaying spleen. **2.** ill-humoured; irritable or peevish; spiteful.

**spleenwort** /ˈsplinwɜt/, *n.* any of various ferns of the genus *Asplenium,* having linear or oblong sori on the undersurface of the leaf along the acropetal side of an oblique veinlet, as *A. flaccidum.*

**splendent** /ˈsplɛndənt/, *adj.* **1.** shining or radiant, as the sun; gleaming or lustrous, as metal, marble, etc. **2.** brilliant in appearance, colour, etc.; gorgeous; magnificent; splendid. **3.** very conspicuous; illustrious. [late ME, from L *splendens,* ppr., shining]

**splendid** /ˈsplɛndəd/, *adj.* **1.** gorgeous; magnificent; sumptuous. **2.** grand; superb, as beauty. **3.** glorious, as a name, reputation, victory, etc. **4.** strikingly admirable or fine: *splendid talents.* **5.** excellent, fine, or very good: *to have a splendid time.* **6.** *Rare.* brilliant in appearance, colour, etc. [L *splendidus*] – **splendidly,** *adv.* – **splendidness,** *n.*

**splendiferous** /splɛnˈdɪfərəs/, *adj. Colloq.* splendid; magnificent; fine. [ML *splendifer* (replacing LL *splendōrifer*) splendour-bearing + -OUS]

**splendour** /ˈsplɛndə/, *n.* **1.** brilliant or gorgeous appearance, colouring, etc.; magnificence, grandeur, or pomp, or display of it: *the splendour and pomp of his coronation.* **2.** brilliant distinction; glory: *the splendour of ancient Roman architecture.* **3.** great brightness; brilliant light or lustre. **4. sun in splendour,** *Her.* the sun depicted with its rays, and a human face. Also, *U.S.*, **splendor.** [late ME, from L] – **splendorous,** *adj.*

**splenectomy** /spləˈnɛktəmi/, *n., pl.* **-mies.** excision or removal of the spleen.

**splenetic** /spləˈnɛtɪk/, *adj.* Also, **splenetical. 1.** of the spleen; splenic. **2.** irritable, peevish; spiteful. **3.** *Obs.* melancholy. *–n.* **4.** a splenetic person. [LL *splēnēticus*] – **splenetically,** *adv.*

**splenic** /ˈsplɛnɪk, ˈsplinɪk/, *adj.* of or pertaining to, connected with, or affecting the spleen: *splenic nerves.* [L *splēnicus* from Gk *splēnikós*]

**splenitis** /spləˈnaɪtəs/, *n.* inflammation of the spleen.

**splenius** /ˈspliniəs/, *n., pl.* **-nii** /-niaɪ/. one of a pair of bandage-shaped muscles which run obliquely upwards on the back and sides of the neck. [NL, from Gk *splēnion* bandage] – **splenial,** *adj.*

**splenomegaly** /ˌsplinoʊˈmɛgəli/, *n.* an enlargement of the spleen. [Gk *splēn* SPLEEN + *megálē,* fem. of *mégas* great]

**splice** /splaɪs/, *v.,* **spliced, splicing,** *n. –v.t.* **1.** to join together or unite, as two ropes or parts of a rope, by the interweaving of strands. **2.** to unite, as two pieces of timber, etc., by overlapping. **3.** to join or unite. **4.** *Colloq.* to join in marriage. **5. splice the mainbrace,** *Naut.* to issue an extra allowance of drink, esp. rum. *–n.* **6.** a joining of two ropes or parts of a rope by splicing. **7.** the union so effected. **8.** a joining or junction of two pieces of timber, etc., by overlapping and fastening the ends. **9.** the wedge-shaped extension of the handle of a cricket bat or the like that fits into the blade. [MD *splissen;* ? akin to SPLIT] – **splicer,** *n.*

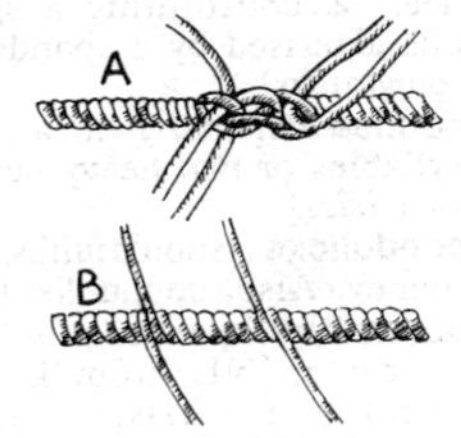

rope splices: A, short splice; B, long splice

**spliced** /splaɪst/, *adj. Colloq.* drunk.

**splice graft** /ˈsplaɪs graft/, *n.* a type of horticultural graft in which a V-shaped cut is made in the stock, into which the scion is fitted.

**spline** /splaɪn/, *n., v.,* **splined, splining.** *–n.* **1.** a long, narrow, relatively thin strip of wood, metal, etc.; a slat. **2.** a long, flexible strip of wood or the like used in drawing curves. **3.** *Mach.* one of a number of uniformly spaced keys cut into a shaft parallel to its axis. *–v.t. Mach.* **4.** to fit with a spline or key. **5.** to provide with a groove for a spline or key. [orig. E Anglian d.; ? akin to SPLINTER]

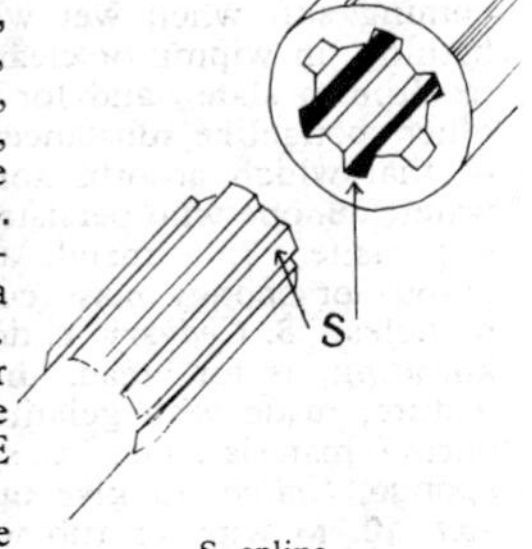

S, spline

**splint** /splɪnt/, *n.* **1.** a thin piece of wood or other rigid material used to immobilise a fractured or dislocated bone, or to maintain any part of the body in a fixed position. **2.** one of a number of thin strips of wood woven together to make a chair seat, basket, etc. **3.** *Vet. Sci.* an exostosis or bony enlargement of a splint-bone of a horse or a related animal. **4.** one of a number of overlapping bands or strips of metal in armour for protecting the body and limbs. *–v.t.* **5.** to secure, hold in position, or support by means of a splint or splints, as a fractured bone. **6.** to support as if with splints. [ME *splente,* from MLG metal plate or pin; akin to SPLINTER] – **splintlike,** *adj.*

**splint-bone** /ˈsplɪnt-boʊn/, *n.* one of the rudimentary, splint-like metacarpal or metatarsal bones of the horse or some allied animal, closely applied one on each side of the back of each cannon bone.

**splinter** /ˈsplɪntə/, *n.* **1.** a rough piece of wood, bone, etc., usu. comparatively long, thin, and sharp, split or broken off from a main body. **2.** a fragment of metal resulting from the explosion of a bomb or shell. *–v.t.* **3.** to split or break into splinters. **4.** to break off in splinters. *–v.i.* **5.** to be split or broken into splinters. **6.** to break off in splinters. [ME, from MD or MLG. See SPLINT] – **splintery,** *adj.*

**splinter-bone** /ˈsplɪntə-boʊn/, *n. Colloq.* →**fibula** (defs 1 and 2).

**splinter group** /ˈsplɪntə grup/, *n.* a group of members of an organisation, party, or the like, who set up independently, as after disagreement with the parent body on some matter of principle.

**split** /splɪt/, *v.,* **split, splitting,** *n., adj. –v.t.* **1.** to rend or cleave lengthwise; separate or part from end to end or between layers, often forcibly or by cutting. **2.** to separate off by rending or cleaving lengthwise: *to split a piece from a block.* **3.** to tear or break asunder; rend or burst. **4.** to divide into distinct parts or portions. **5.** to separate (a part) by such division. **6.** to divide (persons) into different groups, factions, parties, etc., as by discord. **7.** *Stock Exchange.* to divide (a company's shares) into smaller units. **8.** to separate off (a group, etc.) by such division. **9.** to share between two or more persons, etc.: *to split a bottle of wine.* **10.** to separate into parts by interposing something: *to split an infinitive.* **11.** *Chem.* to divide (molecules or atoms) by cleavage into smaller parts. **12.** to make (a vote) less effective by offering more than one candidate with a similar policy: *Liberal intervention in the Country Party seat split the anti-Labor vote and won Labor the seat.* **13. split one's sides,** to laugh heartily. **14. split the difference,** to reach a compromise by which each side concedes an equal amount. *–v.i.* **15.** to break or part lengthways, or suffer longitudinal division. **16.** to part, divide, or separate in any way. **17.** to break as under; part by striking on a rock, by the violence of a storm, etc., as a ship. **18.** to become separated off by such a division as a piece or part from a whole. **19.** to break up or separate through disagreement, etc. **20.** *Colloq.* to divide something with another or others. **21.** *Colloq.* to commit a betrayal by divulging information. **22.** *Colloq.* to leave hurriedly. **23. split on,** *Colloq.* to betray, denounce, or divulge secrets concerning. **24. split up,** *Colloq.* to part; leave each other; become separated. *–n.* **25.** the act of splitting. **26.** a crack, rent, or fissure caused by splitting. **27.** a piece or part separated by or as by splitting. **28.** a strip split from an osier, used in basket-making. **29.** a breach or rupture in a party, etc., or between persons. **30.** a faction, party, etc., formed by a rupture or schism. **31.** *Colloq.* something combining different elements, as a drink composed of half spirits, half soda-water. **32.** *Colloq.* a dish made from sliced fruit (usu. banana) and ice-cream, and covered with syrup and nuts. **33.** *Colloq.* a drink containing only half the usual quantity. **34.** a small bottle usu. with a crown seal and containing aerated drink, as tonic water, soda water etc., for mixing with alcoholic drinks. **35.** (*usu. pl.*) the feat of separating the legs while sinking to the floor, until they extend at right angles to the body, as in stage performances. **36.** *Tenpin Bowling.* the arrangement of the remaining pins after the first bowl so that a spare is practically impossible. **37.** one of the thicknesses of leather into which a skin is cut. **38.** *Colloq.* an act or arrangement of splitting, as of a sum of money. *–adj.* **39.** that has undergone splitting; parted lengthwise; cleft. **40.** divided. [MD *splitten,* akin to G *spleissen*] – **splitter,** *n.*

**split ends** /– ˈɛndz/, *n.pl.* a condition of damaged hair where the ends are split.

**split infinitive** /– ɪnˈfɪnətɪv/, *n.* a simple infinitive with a word between the *to* and the verb, as *to readily understand.*

**split-level** /ˈsplɪt-lɛvəl/, *adj.* **1.** denoting or pertaining to a building having certain floors at other than main storey level, or a room with a floor at more than one level. *–n.* **2.** a house, etc., built like this.

**split pea** /splɪt ˈpi/, *n.* a pea dried and split, used in soups and as a vegetable.

**split personality** /– pɜsəˈnæləti/, *n.* **1.** *Colloq.* →**schizophrenia. 2.** *Psychiatry.* a neurotic state characterised by dissociation of mental processes, as the adoption of multiple personalities.

**split-phase** /ˈsplɪt-feɪz/, *adj.* pertaining to an electric current from a single-phase source which has been split into two separate phases in two branches of a circuit.

**split pin** /ˈsplɪt pɪn/, *n.* →**cotter pin.**

**split ring** /– ˈrɪŋ/, *n.* a ring, as a key ring, having a split by means of which things may be attached and removed.

**split-screen** /ˈsplɪt-skrin/, *adj.* pertaining to a film technique whereby two separate images are projected simultaneously on different parts of a screen.

**split second** /– ˈsɛkənd/, *n.* a very short period of time.

**split-second** /ˈsplɪt-sɛkənd/, *adj.* **1.** performed with great precision. **2.** achieved or arrived at immediately.

**splitter** /ˈsplɪtə/, *n.* **1.** one who or that which splits. **2.** one who splits tree trunks into posts, rails, railway sleepers, etc.

**splitting** /ˈsplɪtɪŋ/, *adj.* **1.** that splits. **2.** overpoweringly noisy, as if to split the ears. **3.** violent or severe, as a headache.

**splosh** /splɒʃ/, *n.* **1.** *Colloq.* money. **2.** splash.

**splotch** /splɒtʃ/, *n.* **1.** a large, irregular spot; blot; stain. *–v.t.* **2.** to mark with splotches. Also, **splodge** /splɒdʒ/. [? b. OE *splott* spot and PATCH] – **splotchy,** *adj.*

**splurge** /splɜdʒ/, *n., v.,* **splurged, splurging.** *Colloq.* *–n.* **1.** an ostentatious display, esp. of wealth. *–v.t.* **to spend (money) extravagantly.** *–v.i.* **2.** to be extravagant: *we splurged and bought champagne.* [? b. SPLASH and SURGE]

**splutter** /ˈsplʌtə/, *v.i.* **1.** to talk hastily and confusedly or incoherently, as in excitement or embarrassment. **2.** to make a spluttering sound, or emit particles of something explosively, as something frying or a pen scattering ink. **3.** to fly or fall in particles or drops; spatter, as a liquid. *–v.t.* **4.** to utter hastily and confusedly or incoherently; sputter. **5.** to spatter (a liquid, etc.). **6.** to bespatter (a person, etc.). *–n.* **7.** spluttering utterance or talk; a dispute; a noise or fuss. **8.** a sputtering or spattering of liquid, etc. [b. SPLASH and SPUTTER] – **splutterer,** *n.*

**spodumene** /ˈspɒdʒəmin/, *n.* a mineral, lithium aluminium silicate, $LiALSi_2O_6$, occurring in prismatic crystals, transparent varieties being used as gems; an ore of lithium. [Gk *spodoúmenos,* ppr., burning to ashes]

**spoil** /spɔɪl/, *v.,* **spoiled** or **spoilt, spoiling,** *n.* *–v.t.* **1.** to damage or impair (a thing) irreparably as to excellence, value, usefulness, etc.: *to spoil a sheet of paper.* **2.** to impair in character or disposition by unwise treatment, benefits, etc., esp. by excessive indulgence. **3.** *Aus. Rules.* to prevent (an opponent) from marking by punching the ball away. **4.** *Archaic.* to strip (persons, places, etc.) of goods, valuables, etc.; plunder, pillage, or rob. **5.** *Archaic.* to take by force, or carry off as booty. *–v.i.* **6.** to become spoiled, bad, or unfit for use, as food or other perishable substances; become tainted or putrid. **7.** to plunder, pillage, or rob. **8. be spoiling for,** eager for (a fight, action, etc.) *–n.* **9.** (*oft. pl.*) booty, loot, or plunder taken in war or robbery. **10.** (*usu. pl.*) emoluments and advantages associated with a powerful or prestigious position: *the spoils of office.* **11.** treasures won or accumulated. **12.** waste materials, as those cast up in mining, excavating, quarrying, etc. [ME, from OF *espoillier,* from L *spoliāre;* ? also an aphetic var. of DESPOIL]

**spoilage** /ˈspɔɪlɪdʒ/, *n.* **1.** an act or instance of spoiling. **2.** that which is spoiled: *spoilage of fruit on the way to market.*

**spoiler** /ˈspɔɪlə/, *n.* **1.** one who or that which spoils. **2.** *Aeron.* a device fitted to an aircraft wing, designed to reduce lift as required.

**spoil ground** /ˈspɔɪl graʊnd/, *n. Naut.* a charted area designated for the deposit of dredgings.

**spoil heap** /ˈ– hip/, *n.* the pile of earth, stones, etc., produced by an archaeological excavation.

**spoilsport** /ˈspɔɪlspɔt/, *n.* one who interferes with the pleasure of others.

**spoilt** /spɔɪlt/, *v.* **1.** a past tense and past participle of **spoil.** *–adj.* **2.** selfish; used to getting one's own way.

**spoke**[1] /spoʊk/, *v.* past tense and archaic past participle of **speak.**

**spoke**[2] /spoʊk/, *n., v.,* **spoked, spoking.** *–n.* **1.** one of the bars, rods, or rungs radiating from the hub or nave of a wheel and supporting the rim or felloe. **2.** one of a number of pins or handles projecting from a cylinder or wheel, or joining hub and rim, esp. on a steering wheel. **3.** a rung of a ladder. **4. put a spoke in one's wheel,** to interfere with one's plans. *–v.t.* **5.** to fit or furnish with or as with spokes. [ME; OE *spāca,* c. D *speek,* G *Speiche*]

**spoken** /ˈspoʊkən/, *v.* **1.** past participle of **speak.** *–adj.* **2.** uttered or expressed by speaking; oral (opposed to *written*). **3.** (in compounds) speaking, or using speech, as specified: *fair-spoken, plain-spoken.*

**spokeshave** /ˈspoʊkʃeɪv/, *n.* a cutting tool having a blade set between two handles, originally for shaping spokes, but now in general use for dressing curved edges of wood and in forming round bars and shapes.

**spokesperson** /ˈspoʊkspɜsən/, *n.* **1.** one who speaks for another or others. **2.** the principal advocate or practitioner (of a movement, organisation, etc.), considered as speaking on its behalf. **3.** a public speaker. – **spokeswoman,** *n. fem.* – **spokesman,** *n. masc.*

**spoliate** /ˈspoʊlieɪt/, *v.t., v.i.,* **-ated, -ating.** to despoil; plunder.

**spoliation** /spoʊliˈeɪʃən/, *n.* the act of spoiling, plundering, or despoiling. [ME *spoliacio(u)n,* from L *spoliātio*] – **spoliative** /ˈspoʊliətɪv/, *adj.* – **spoliator** /ˈspoʊlieɪtə/, *n.*

**spon** /spɒn/, *n. Colloq.* money. Also, **spons.** [short for SPONDULICKS]

**spondaic** /spɒnˈdeɪɪk/, *adj.* **1.** of or pertaining to a spondee. **2.** constituting a spondee. **3.** consisting of spondees; characterised by a spondee or spondees. Also, **spondaical.** [L *spondaicus*]

**spondee** /ˈspɒndi/, *n.* a metrical foot consisting of two long syllables or two heavy beats. [ME, from L *spondēus,* from Gk *spondeîos*]

**spondulicks** /spɒnˈdjulɪks/, *n. pl., construed as sing. Colloq.* money. Also, **spondulix.** [orig. unknown]

**spondylitis** /spɒndəˈlaɪtəs/, *n.* inflammation of one or more vertebrae. [NL, from L *spondylus* (from Gk *sphóndylos* vertebra) + *-itis* -ITIS]

**spondylolisthesis** /ˌspɒndəloʊləsˈθisəs/, *n.* forward displacement of a vertebra over a lower segment.

**sponge** /spʌndʒ/, *n., v.,* **sponged, sponging.** *–n.* **1.** any of a group of aquatic (mostly marine) animals (phylum Porifera) which are characterised by a porous structure and (usu.) a horny, siliceous, or calcareous skeleton or framework, and which, except in the larval state, are fixed, occurring in large, complex, often plant-like colonies. **2.** the light, yielding, porous, fibrous skeleton or framework of certain animals, or colonies of this group, from which the living matter has been removed, characterised by readily absorbing water, and becoming soft when wet while retaining toughness, used in bathing, in wiping or cleansing surfaces, in removing marks (as from a slate), and for other purposes. **3.** any of various other spongelike substances. **4.** a sponge-down. **5.** one who or that which absorbs something freely, as a sponge does water. **6.** one who persistently lives at the expense of others; a parasite. **7.** a metal, as platinum, when obtained as a porous or spongy mass consisting of fine, loosely cohering particles. **8.** *Cookery.* **a.** dough raised with yeast, esp. before kneading, as for bread. **b.** a light sweet pudding of spongy texture, made with gelatine, eggs, fruit juice or other flavouring material, etc. **c.** sponge cake. **9. throw in (up) the sponge,** *Colloq.* to give up; abandon hope or one's efforts. *–v.t.* **10.** to wipe or rub with a wet sponge, as in order to clean or moisten. **11.** to remove with a wet sponge (fol. by *off, away,* etc.). **12.** to wipe out or efface with or as with a sponge (oft. fol. by *out*). **13.** to take up or absorb with a sponge or the like (oft. fol. by *up*): *to sponge up water.* **14.** to get from another or at another's expense by indirect exactions, trading on generosity, etc.: *to sponge a dinner.* *–v.i.* **15.** to take in liquid by absorption. **16.** to gather sponges. **17.** *Colloq.* to live at the expense of others. **18. sponge on,** to live as a parasite of. [ME and OE, from L *spongia,* from Gk] – **spongelike,** *adj.*

**sponge bag** /ˈ– bæg/, *n.* a waterproof bag for holding toilet articles, as used when travelling.

**sponge bath** /ˈ– baθ/, *n.* (the washing of the body) with a wet sponge or cloth, rather than by immersing in water; pommy wash.

**sponge cake** /ˈ– keɪk/, *n.* a very light kind of sweet cake, made with a comparatively large proportion of eggs and very little shortening.

**sponge-down** /ˈspʌndʒ-daʊn/, *n.* a wash in a small amount of water, esp. with a sponge or washer, rather than by immersion.

**sponge finger** /ˈspʌndʒ fɪŋgə/, *n.* a small sponge cake, approximately finger-shaped, and often coated with a hard layer of crystallised sugar.

**sponger** /ˈspʌndʒə/, *n.* **1.** one who or that which sponges. **2.** a person who sponges on others. **3.** a person or a vessel engaged in gathering sponges.

**sponge rubber** /spʌndʒ ˈrʌbə/, *n.* →**foam rubber.**

**sponge sandwich** /ˈ– sænwɪtʃ/, *n.* a sponge cake split horizontally and filled with jam, cream, etc.

**spongy** /ˈspʌndʒi/, *adj.*, **-gier, -giest.** **1.** of the nature of or resembling a sponge; light, yielding, and porous; without firmness and readily compressible, as pith, flesh, etc. **2.** absorbing or holding water or the like, as a sponge does, or yielding it as when pressed. **3.** pertaining to a sponge. **4.** porous but hard, as bone. – **sponginess,** *n.*

**sponsion** /ˈspɒnʃən/, *n.* **1.** an engagement or promise, esp. one made on behalf of another. **2.** the act of becoming surety for another. [L *sponsio*]

**sponson** /ˈspɒnsən/, *n.* **1.** a structure projecting from the side of a ship, as a gun platform, or a platform for handling gear. **2.** a buoyant appendage at the gunwale of a canoe to resist capsizing. **3.** the projection which covers and protects the paddlewheels of a paddle-steamer. **4.** a protuberance at the side of a flying-boat hull designed to increase lateral stability in the water. [var. of EXPANSION]

**sponsor** /ˈspɒnsə/, *n.* **1.** one who vouches or is responsible for a person or thing. **2.** one who makes an engagement or promise on behalf of another; a surety. **3.** one who answers for an infant at baptism, making the required professions and promises; a godfather or godmother. **4.** a person, firm, or other organisation that finances a radio or television program in return for advertisement of a commercial product, a service, etc. **5.** *Parl. Proc.* a member of a legislative assembly responsible for the introduction of a particular bill (usu. with reference only to private bills). *–v.t.* **6.** to act as sponsor for; promise, vouch, or answer for. [L] – **sponsorial** /spɒnˈsɔriəl/, *adj.* – **sponsorship,** *n.*

**spontaneity** /spɒntəˈniəti, -ˈneɪəti/, *n., pl.* **-ties.** **1.** the state, quality, or fact of being spontaneous. **2.** spontaneous activity. **3.** (*pl.*) spontaneous impulses, movements, or actions.

**spontaneous** /spɒnˈteɪniəs/, *adj.* **1.** proceeding from a natural personal impulse, without effort or premeditation; natural and unconstrained: *a spontaneous action or remark.* **2.** (of impulses, motion, activity, natural processes, etc.) arising from internal forces or causes, or independent of external agencies. **3.** growing naturally or without cultivation, as plants, fruits, etc. **4.** produced by natural process. [L *spontāneus*] – **spontaneously,** *adv.* – **spontaneousness,** *n.*

**spontaneous combustion** /– kəmˈbʌstʃən/, *n.* the ignition of a substance or body from the rapid oxidation of its own constituents, without heat from any external source.

**spontaneous cure** /– ˈkjuə/, *n.* the cure of a disease not due to medical treatment.

**spontaneous generation** /– dʒɛnəˈreɪʃən/, *n.* →**abiogenesis.**

**spontoon** /spɒnˈtun/, *n.* a shafted weapon with broad blade and basal crossbar used in the 18th and 19th centuries. [F *sponton,* from It. *spuntone,* from *puntone* point, from *punto,* from L *punctum*]

**spoof**[1] /spuf/, *n., v.t., v.i., adj. Colloq.* parody; hoax. [coined by Arthur Roberts, 1852-1933, British comedian] – **spoofer,** *n.*

**spoof**[2] /spʊf/, *n. Colloq.* →**semen.**

**spook** /spuk/, *n. Colloq.* **1.** a ghost; a spectre. **2.** an agent of an intelligence organisation; a spy. [D, c. G *Spuk*]

**spooked** /spukt/, *adj.* frightened; on edge; nervous.

**spooky** /ˈspuki/, *adj.*, **spookier, spookiest.** *Colloq.* **1.** like or befitting a spook or ghost; suggestive of spooks; eerie. **2.** (of a surf) difficult; unpredictable. Also, **spookish.**

**spool** /spul/, *n.* **1.** any cylindrical piece or appliance on which something is wound. **2.** such a device for holding film, magnetic tape, or the like, which is stopped from slipping off by a disc on each side. **3.** a small cylindrical piece of wood or other material on which yarn is wound in spinning, for use in weaving; a bobbin. **4.** →**reel**[1] (def. 3). *–v.t.* **5.** to wind on a spool. [ME *spole,* from MD or MLG; c. G *Spule*]

**spoon** /spun/, *n.* **1.** a utensil consisting of a bowl or concave part and a handle, for taking up or stirring liquid or other food, or other matter. **2.** any of various implements, objects, or parts resembling or suggesting this. **3.** Also, **spoonbait.** *Angling.* a lure used in casting or trolling for fish, consisting of a bright spoon-shaped piece of metal or the like, swivelled above one or more fishhooks and revolved as it is drawn through the water. **4.** *Golf.* a club (No. 3 wood) with a wooden head whose face is more lofted than that of the brassy, and with a shorter shaft. **5.** a curved piece projecting from the top of a torpedo tube to guide the torpedo in a horizontal direction and prevent it from striking the side of the ship. **6. be born with a silver spoon in one's mouth,** to inherit social or financial advantages and privileges. *–v.t.* **7.** to take up or transfer in or as in a spoon. **8.** to hollow out or shape like a spoon. **9.** *Sport.* **a.** to push or shove (the ball) with a lifting motion instead of striking it soundly, as in croquet or golf. **b.** to hit (the ball) up in the air as in cricket. **10.** *Colloq.* to show affection towards, esp. in an openly sentimental manner. *–v.i.* **11.** *Sport.* to spoon the ball. **12.** to fish with a spoon. **13.** *Colloq.* to show affection, esp. in an openly sentimental manner. **14.** *Angling.* to rise a spoon. [ME and OE *spōn,* c. LG *spon,* Icel. *spōnn;* akin to G *Span*]

**spoonbill** /ˈspunbɪl/, *n.* **1.** any of several wading birds closely related to the ibis and having a long, flat bill with a spoon-like tip, as the **royal spoonbill,** *Platalea regia,* of Australasia and certain islands to the north. **2.** any of various birds having a similar bill, as the shoveler, of the Northern Hemisphere. **3.** →**paddlefish.**

spoonbill (def. 1)

**spoon drain** /ˈspun dreɪn/, *n.* an open drain for storm water, in the form of a shallow trough.

**spoondrift** /ˈspundrɪft/, *n.* →**spindrift.** [from *spoon* scud, run before the wind (orig. uncert.) + DRIFT]

**spoonerism** /ˈspunərɪzəm/, *n.* a slip of the tongue whereby initial or other sounds of words are transposed, as in 'our queer old dean' for 'our dear old queen'. [named after Rev. W. A. *Spooner,* 1844-1930, of New College, Oxford, noted for such slips]

**spooney** /ˈspuni/, *adj.*, **spoonier, spooniest,** *n., pl.* **spoonies.** *Colloq.* →**spoony.**

**spoon-feed** /ˈspun-fid/, *v.t.*, **-fed, -feeding.** **1.** to give food by means of a spoon. **2.** to treat with excessive solicitude. **3.** to deprive of a chance to act or think for oneself.

**spoonful** /ˈspunfʊl/, *n., pl.* **-fuls.** **1.** as much as a spoon can hold. **2.** a small quantity.

**spoony** /ˈspuni/, *adj.*, **spoonier, spooniest,** *n., pl.* **spoonies.** *Colloq. –adj.* **1.** foolishly or sentimentally amorous. **2.** foolish; silly. *–n.* **3.** one who is foolishly or sentimentally amorous. **4.** a simple or foolish person.

**spoor** /spɔ/, *n.* **1.** a track or trail, esp. that of a wild animal pursued as game. *–v.t.* **2.** to track by a spoor. *–v.i.* **3.** to follow a spoor. [Afrikaans, from D; c. OE and Icel. *spor,* akin to G *Spur*] – **spoorer,** *n.*

**spor-,** variant of **sporo-,** before vowels, as in *sporangium.*

**sporadic** /spəˈrædɪk/, *adj.* **1.** appearing or happening at intervals in time; occasional: *sporadic outbreaks.* **2.** appearing in scattered or isolated instances, as a disease. **3.** occurring singly, or widely apart, in locality: *sporadic genera of plants.* Also, **sporadical.** [ML *sporadicus,* from Gk *sporadikós*] – **sporadically,** *adv.* – **sporadicalness,** *n.*

**sporadic cholera** /– ˈkɒlərə/, *n.* See **cholera.**

**sporangium** /spəˈrændʒiəm/, *n., pl.* **-gia** /-dʒiə/. (in ferns, mosses and fungi) the case or sac within which spores (asexual reproductive cells) are produced. Also, **spore case.** [NL, from *spor-* SPOR- + Gk *angeîon* vessel] – **sporangial,** *adj.*

**spore** /spɔ/, *n., v.,* **spored, sporing.** *–n.* **1.** *Biol.* a walled body that contains or produces one or more uninucleate organisms that develop into an adult individual, esp.: **a.** a reproductive body **(asexual spore)** produced asexually and capable of growth into a new individual, such individuals often, as in ferns, etc., being one (a gametophyte) unlike that which produced the spore. **b.** a walled reproductive body **(sexual spore)** produced sexually (by the union of two gametes). **2.** a germ, germ cell, seed, or the like. *–v.i.* **3.** to bear or produce spores. [NL *spora,* from Gk: seed]

**spore case** /ˈ– keɪs/, *n.* →**sporangium.**

**sporiferous** /spəˈrɪfərəs/, *adj.* bearing spores.

**sporo-,** a word element meaning 'seed'. Also, **spor-.** [combining form representing Gk *sporá* seed]

**sporocarp** /ˈspɔroʊkap, ˈspɒ-/, *n.* (in higher fungi, lichens, and red algae) a multicellular body developed for the formation of spores.

**sporocyst** /ˈspɔrəsɪst, ˈspɒ-/, *n.* **1.** a walled body resulting from the multiple division of a sporozoan, which produces one or more sporozoites. **2.** a stage in development of trematodes which gives rise, non-sexually, to daughter cercaria.

**sporogenesis** /ˌspɔroʊˈdʒɛnəsəs, ˌspɒ-/, *n.* **1.** the production of spores; sporogony. **2.** reproduction by means of spores. – **sporogenous** /spəˈrɒdʒənəs/, *adj.*

**sporogony** /spəˈrɒgəni/, *n.* the process of multiplication in the sexual phase of parasitic protozoans of the class Sporozoa, giving rise to sporozoites.

**sporophore** /ˈspɔroʊfɔ, ˈspɒ-/, *n.* **1.** a simple or branched fungal hypha specialised to bear spores. **2.** the whole spore-producing structure of a gill-bearing fungus; a toadstool. **3.** a spore-bearing organ in some other plants.

**sporophyll** /ˈspɔroʊfɪl, ˈspɒ-/, *n.* a more or less modified leaf which bears sporangia. Also, **sporophyl.**

**sporophyte** /ˈspɔrəfaɪt, ˈspɒ-/, *n.* the asexual form of a plant in the alternation of generations (opposed to *gametophyte*).

**sporotrichosis** /ˌspɔroʊtrəˈkoʊsəs, ˈspɒ-/, *n.* an infectious fungus disease of horses and man, marked by ulceration of superficial lymphatic vessels of the skin.

**sporozoan** /spɔrəˈzoʊən, spɒ-/, *n.* **1.** one of the Sporozoa, a class of the phylum Protozoa, consisting of parasites that multiply by sporogenesis, i.e. by dividing into reproductive bodies. *–adj.* **2.** belonging or pertaining to the Sporozoa.

**sporozoite** /spɔrəˈzoʊaɪt, spɒ-/, *n.* one of the minute active bodies into which the spore of certain sporozoans divides, each developing into an adult individual.

**sporran** /ˈspɒrən/, *n.* (in Scottish Highland costume) a large pouch, commonly of fur, worn hanging from the belt over the front of the kilt. [Gaelic *sporan,* c. Irish *sparān*]

S, sporran

**sport** /spɔt/, *n.* **1.** an activity pursued for exercise or pleasure, usu. requiring some degree of physical prowess, as hunting, fishing, racing, baseball, tennis, golf, bowling, wrestling, boxing, etc. **2.** a particular form of pastime. **3.** (*pl.*) a meeting for athletic competition. **4.** the pastime of hunting, shooting, or fishing with reference to the pleasure achieved: *we had good sport today.* **5.** diversion; recreation; pleasant pastime. **6.** playful trifling, jesting, or mirth: *to do or say a thing in sport.* **7.** derisive jesting; ridicule. **8.** an object of derision; a laughing-stock. **9.** something sported with or tossed about like a plaything: *to be the sport of circumstances.* **10.** *Colloq.* (used as a term of address, usu. between males) any person approached as a friend: *Goodday, sport.* **11.** *Colloq.* one who is interested in pursuits involving betting or gambling. **12.** *Biol.* an animal or a plant, or a part of a plant, that shows an unusual or singular deviation from the normal or parent type; a mutation. **13.** *Obs.* amorous dalliance. **14. a good sport,** *Colloq.* **a.** a person of sportsmanlike or admirable qualities; one who exhibits boldness or good humour in the face of risk or ridicule. **b.** a person who is easygoing, good-natured and agreeable. **15. be a sport,** *Colloq.* **a.** to play fair. **b.** to accede to a request; be agreeable. *–v.i.* **16.** to amuse oneself with some pleasant pastime or recreation. **17.** to play, frolic, or gambol, as a child or an animal. **18.** to engage in some open-air or athletic pastime or sport. **19.** to deal lightly; trifle. **20.** to ridicule. **21.** *Bot.* to mutate. **22.** *Archaic.* to trifle playfully. *–v.t.* **23.** to have or wear, esp. ostentatiously, proudly, etc. **24.** *Colloq.* to display freely or with ostentation: *to sport a roll of money.* **25.** to pass (time) in amusement or sport. **26.** to spend or squander recklessly or lightly (oft. fol. by *away*). **27.** *Obs.* to amuse (esp. oneself). [ME *sporte;* aphetic var. of DISPORT] – **sporter,** *n.* – **sportful,** *adj.* – **sportfully,** *adv.* – **sportfulness,** *n.*

**sportfish** /ˈspɔtfɪʃ/, *n.* →**game fish.**

**sporting** /ˈspɔtɪŋ/, *adj.* **1.** engaging in, given to, or interested in open-air or athletic sport. **2.** concerned with or suitable for such sport. **3.** sportsmanlike. **4.** interested in or connected with sport or pursuits involving betting or gambling. **5.** willing to take a chance. **6.** even or fair; involving reasonable odds, as a gamble: *a sporting chance.* – **sportingly,** *adv.*

**sportive** /ˈspɔtɪv/, *adj.* **1.** playful or frolicsome; jesting, jocose, or merry. **2.** done in sport, rather than in earnest. **3.** pertaining to or of the nature of sport or sports. **4.** *Biol.* mutative. **5.** *Obs.* amorous. – **sportively,** *adv.* – **sportiveness,** *n.*

**sports** /spɔts/, *adj.* **1.** of, pertaining to, or devoted to a sport or sports: *the sports department of a store.* **2.** concerned with sport: *the sports editor of a newspaper.* **3.** (of garments, etc.) suitable for use in open-air sports, or for outdoor or informal use.

**sports car** /ˈ– ka/, *n.* a high-powered car with rakish lines, usu. a two-seater.

**sports complex** /ˈ– kɒmplɛks/, *n.* a group of interconnected buildings and other facilities designed for the playing of various sports.

**sports day** /ˈ– deɪ/, *n.* a day when a school or the like holds athletic contests.

**sportsground** /ˈspɔtsgraʊnd/, *n.* an area set aside for sports, usu. with one or more playing fields, grandstands for spectators and facilities for players.

**sports jacket** /ˈ– dʒækət/, *n.* a man's jacket for informal wear, typically made of tweed or checked cloth. Also, **sports coat.**

**sportsman** /ˈspɔtsmən/, *n., pl.* **-men. 1.** a man who engages in sport, esp. in some open-air sport such as hunting, fishing, racing, etc. **2.** one who exhibits qualities especially esteemed in those who engage in sports, such as fairness, good humour when losing, willingness to take risks, etc. – **sportsmanlike, sportsmanly,** *adj.* – **sportswoman,** *n. fem.*

**sportsmanship** /ˈspɔtsmənʃɪp/, *n.* **1.** sportsmanlike conduct. **2.** the character, practice, or skill of a sportsman.

**sports shirt** /ˈspɔts ʃɜt/, *n.* a casual shirt, usu. brightly coloured, with long or short sleeves, and worn without a tie.

**sports uniform** /ˈ– junəfɔm/, *n.* a loose-fitting garment, often in a school's distinguishing colours, worn by school students for sport, gymnastics, etc.

**sportswear** /ˈspɔtswɛə/, *n.* **1.** clothing for wear while engaged in some sport. **2.** clothing for outdoor or other leisure use.

**sporty** /ˈspɔti/, *adj.,* **sportier, sportiest.** *Colloq.* **1.** flashy; vulgarly showy. **2.** stylish. **3.** like or befitting a sportsman. – **sportiness,** *n.*

**sporulate** /ˈspɒrəleɪt/, *v.,* **-lated, -lating.** *–v.i.* **1.** to undergo multiple division resulting in the production of spores. *–v.t.* **2.** to cause such division. – **sporulation** /spɒrəˈleɪʃən/, *n.*

**sporule** /ˈspɒrul/, *n.* a small spore. [NL *sporula,* diminutive of *spora* SPORE]

**spot** /spɒt/, *n., v.,* **spotted, spotting,** *adj.* *–n.* **1.** a mark made by foreign matter, as mud, blood, paint, ink, etc.; a stain, blot, or speck, as on a surface. **2.** a blemish of the skin, as a pimple. **3.** a relatively small, usu. roundish, part of a surface differing from the rest in appearance or character. **4.** a moral blemish, as on character or reputation; stain or flaw. **5.** a place or locality: *a monument marks the spot.* **6.** a position or period of time in a program of entertainment assigned to a particular performer. **7.** a short period of advertising time on radio or television: *they booked ten twenty-second spots per week.* **8.** a spotlight. **9.** *Billiards.* **a.** any of several marked points on a billiard table. **b.** the spot-ball. **10.** *Soccer.* **a.** the centre spot. **b.** a penalty spot. **11.** *Colloq.* a small quantity of something: *a spot of tea.* **12.** *Colloq.* an alcoholic drink:

*he stopped at the pub for a spot.* **13.** *Colloq.* a predicament: *he was in a bit of a spot when the crash came.* **14.** *Colloq.* **a.** (formerly) the sum of £100. **b.** the sum of $100. **15.** *U.S.* an object bearing a specified device or numeral: *he gave the waiter a five-spot.* **16. change one's spots,** to alter one's fundamental character. **17. knock spots off,** *Colloq.* to outdo without difficulty or by a large margin. **18. on the spot, a.** instantly. **b.** at the place in question. **c.** obliged to deal with a situation. **d.** in trouble, embarrassment, or danger. **e.** without change of location. **19. soft spot,** a special sympathy or affection: *she has a soft spot for small animals.* **20. tight spot,** a serious predicament. **21. weak spot,** an aspect of a person's character which is liable to criticism or opposition. *–v.t.* **22.** to stain with spots. **23.** to sully; blemish. **24.** to mark or diversify with spots, as of colour. **25.** →**spot-clean. 26.** to pick the best portions out of; peacock. **27.** to see or perceive, esp. suddenly, by chance, or when it is difficult to do so. **28.** *Colloq.* to detect or recognise. **29.** to scatter in various spots. **30.** *Billiards.* to place (a ball) on a particular spot. *–v.i.* **31.** to make a spot; cause a stain. **32.** to become or tend to become spotted, as some fabrics when spattered with water. *–adj.* **33.** *Comm.* made, paid, delivered, etc., at once: *a spot sale.* [ME *spotte,* c. MD and LG *spot* speck, Icel. *spotti* bit, small piece]

**spot-ball** /ˈspɒt-bɔl/, *n.* (in billiards) one of the white balls, distinguished from the other by being marked with a small black spot. Also, **spot.**

**spot cash** /spɒt ˈkæʃ/, *n.* payment for goods immediately on their delivery.

**spot check** /– ˈtʃɛk/, *n.* **1.** an inspection made without warning, as of motor vehicles, etc. **2.** a check made on a random sample, as of manufactured articles.

**spot-clean** /ˈspɒt-klin/, *v.t.* to clean the soiled part of a garment, usu. before dry-cleaning it. Also, **spot.**

**spot kick** /ˈspɒt kɪk/, *n. Soccer Colloq.* →**penalty kick.**

**spotless** /ˈspɒtləs/, *adj.* **1.** free from spot, stain, blemish, marks, etc. **2.** immaculate; well-dressed. – **spotlessly,** *adv.* – **spotlessness,** *n.*

**spotlight** /ˈspɒtlaɪt/, *n.* **1.** (in theatrical use) a strong light with a narrow beam thrown upon a particular spot on the stage in order to render some object, person, or group especially conspicuous. **2.** the lamp producing such light. **3.** a similar lamp attached to a car, usu. not able to be swivelled. **4.** conspicuous public attention. *–v.t.* **5.** to direct a spotlight at.

**spot month** /ˈspɒt mʌnθ/, *n.* (in futures trading) the month when all contracts dated for that month mature.

**spot-on** /spɒt-ˈɒn/, *Colloq.* *–adj.* **1.** absolutely right or accurate; excellent. *–interj.* **2.** (an exclamation of approbation, etc.).

**spot price** /ˈspɒt praɪs/, *n.* (in commodities trading) the price agreed on for immediate delivery of the commodity.

**spotted** /ˈspɒtəd/, *adj.* **1.** marked with or characterised by a spot or spots. **2.** sullied; blemished.

**spotted black snake,** *n.* →**blue-bellied black snake.**

**spotted crake** /spɒtəd ˈkreɪk/, *n.* **1.** a small rail, *Porzana fluminea,* of Australia and Tasmania. **2.** a similar bird, *Porzana porzana,* of Europe and western Asia. Also, **water crake.**

**spotted dick** /– ˈdɪk/, *n.* a steamed or boiled suet pudding containing currants, etc. Also, **spotted dog.**

**spotted dog** /– ˈdɒg/, *n.* **1.** *Colloq.* →**Dalmatian** (def. 4). **2.** →**spotted dick.**

**spotted fever** /– ˈfivə/, *n.* **1.** any of several fevers characterised by spots on the skin, esp. as in cerebrospinal meningitis or typhus. **2.** →**tick fever** (def. 1).

**spotted gum** /ˈ– gʌm/, *n.* a tall tree with a spotted smooth bark, *Eucalyptus maculata,* which forms forests in coastal districts of eastern Australia.

**spotted hyena** /– haɪˈinə/, *n.* See **hyena.**

**spotted laurel** /– ˈlɒrəl/, *n.* →**laurel** (def. 5).

**spotted mackerel** /– ˈmækərəl/, *n.* a small mackerel, *Scomberomorus queenslandicus,* of northern Australian waters; doggie. Also, **school mackerel.**

**spotted native cat,** *n.* →**tiger cat** (def. 1).

**spotted pardalote** /spɒtəd ˈpadəlout/, *n.* a small bird, *Pardalotus punctatus,* of southern Australia, with buff underparts and a grey-brown back spotted with buff.

**spotted-sided finch** /ˌspɒtəd-saɪdəd ˈfɪntʃ/, *n.* →**diamond firetail.**

**spotted turtledove** /spɒtəd ˈtɜtldʌv/, *n.* See **turtledove** (def. 2).

**spotter** /ˈspɒtə/, *n.* **1.** *Mil.* the person who determines for the gunner the fall of shots in relation to the target. **2.** Also, **spotter plane.** a light aircraft that determines targets for artillery. **3.** one who watches for enemy aircraft, as in civil defence. **4.** one whose pastime is to spot and note the numbers or types of buses, trains, etc. **5.** →**talent scout. 6.** a person employed at a laundry or dry cleaning works to remove dirt spots from garments.

**spotty** /ˈspɒti/, *adj.,* **-tier, -tiest. 1.** full of or having spots; occurring in spots: *a spotty face.* **2.** irregular or uneven in quality or character. – **spottily,** *adv.* – **spottiness,** *n.*

**spot-weld** /ˈspɒt-wɛld/, *v.t.* **1.** to weld (two pieces of metal) together by compressing them between two electrodes through which a heavy current passes for a short time. **2.** to join (thermoplastic materials) together at a number of spots by using dielectric heating. *–n.* **3.** the welded joint so formed.

**spousal** /ˈspauzəl/, *n.* **1.** (*oft. pl.*) the ceremony of marriage; nuptials. *–adj.* **2.** nuptial; matrimonial.

**spouse** /spaus, spauz/, *n., v.,* **spoused, spousing.** *–n.* **1.** either member of a married pair in relation to the other; one's husband or wife. *–v.t.* **2.** *Obs.* to join, give, or take in marriage. [ME, from OF *spus* (masc.), *spuse* (fem.), from L *sponsus,* pp., betrothed]

**spout** /spaut/, *v.t.* **1.** to discharge or emit (a liquid, etc.) in a stream with some force. **2.** *Colloq.* to utter or declaim in an oratorical manner. *–v.i.* **3.** to discharge a liquid, etc., in a jet or continuous stream. **4.** to issue with force, as liquid through a narrow orifice. **5.** *Colloq.* to talk or speak at some length or in an oratorical manner. *–n.* **6.** a pipe or tube, or a tubular or liplike projection, by which a liquid is discharged or poured. **7.** a trough or chute for discharging or conveying grain, flour, etc. **8.** Also, **spouting.** →**downpipe. 9.** a continuous stream of liquid, etc., discharged from, or as if from, a spout, upwards under pressure or falling from a higher to a lower level. **10.** a chute or shaft formerly common in pawnbrokers' shops, up which pawned articles were sent to a storage room. **11. up the spout,** *Colloq.* **a.** ruined; lost. **b.** pawned. [ME *spoute(n),* c. D *spuiten;* akin to Icel. *spýta* SPIT[1]] – **spouter,** *n.* – **spoutless,** *adj.*

**spp.,** species (*pl.*).

**S.P.Q.R.,** the Senate and the People of Rome. [L *S(enatus) P(opulus)q(ue) R(omanus)*]

**spraddle** /ˈsprædl/, *v.t.* **1.** to straddle. *–v.i.* **2.** to sprawl.

**spraddle legs** /ˈ– lɛgz/, *n.* →**perosis.**

**sprag** /spræg/, *n.* **1.** a chock or pointed steel bar hinged to the rear axle of a vehicle and let down to arrest backward movement on gradients; dogstick. **2.** *Mining.* a short, round piece of hard wood, sharpened at both ends, inserted between the spokes of the wheels of a mine car to prevent motion. **3.** a spoke of a wheel. **4.** a post or support used in mining. **5.** *Mining.* a short wooden prop set in a slanting position for keeping up coal during the operation of extracting the coal. **6.** a worker in a railway marshalling yard; a shunter. [special use of Brit. d. *sprag* twig, OE *spræc* shoot]

**sprain** /spreɪn/, *v.t.* **1.** to overstrain or wrench (the ankle, wrist, or other part of the body at a joint) so as to injure without fracture or dislocation. *–n.* **2.** a violent straining or wrenching of the parts around a joint, without dislocation. **3.** the condition of being sprained. [orig. uncert.]

**sprang** /spræŋ/, *v.* past tense of **spring.**

**sprat** /spræt/, *n.* **1.** a small, herring-like marine fish, *Clupea sprattus,* of European waters; brisling. **2. a sprat to catch a mackerel,** something given in expectation of a larger return. [var. of earlier *sprot,* ME and OE *sprott,* c. G *Sprote*]

**sprawl** /sprɔl/, *v.i.* **1.** to be stretched out in irregular or ungraceful movements, as the limbs. **2.** to lie or sit with the limbs stretched out in a careless or ungraceful posture. **3.** to fall in such a manner. **4.** to work one's way awkwardly along with the aid of all the limbs; scramble. **5.** to spread out in a straggling or irregular manner, as vines, buildings, handwriting, etc. *–v.t.* **6.** to stretch out (the limbs) as in sprawling. **7.** to spread out or distribute in a straggling manner. *–n.* **8.** the act of sprawling; a sprawling posture. **9.** a straggling array of something. [ME *spraule(n)*, OE *sprēawlian.* c. N Fris. *spraweli*] – **sprawler,** *n.*

**sprawly** /ˈsprɔli/, *adj.* tending to sprawl; straggly.

**spray**[1] /spreɪ/, *n.* **1.** water or other liquid broken up into small particles and blown or falling through the air. **2.** a jet of fine particles of liquid discharged from an atomiser or other appliance, as for medicinal treatment, etc. **3.** a liquid to be discharged in such a jet. **4.** an appliance for discharging it. **5.** a quantity of small objects, flying or discharged through the air: *a spray of bullets.* *–v.t.* **6.** to scatter in the form of fine particles. **7.** to apply as a spray: *to spray insecticide upon plants.* **8.** to sprinkle or treat with a spray: *to spray plants with insecticide.* **9.** to direct a spray of particles, missiles, etc., upon. *–v.i.* **10.** to scatter spray; discharge a spray. **11.** to issue as spray. [cf. MD *sprayen* sprinkle] – **sprayer,** *n.*

**spray**[2] /spreɪ/, *n.* **1.** a single slender shoot, twig, or branch with its leaves, flowers, or berries, growing or detached. **2.** an ornament, decorative figure, etc., with a similar form. **3.** a single flower or small bouquet of flowers designed to be pinned to one's clothes as an adornment. [ME; orig. uncert.]

**spray dip** /ˈ– dɪp/, *n.* a method of showering sheep with a sheep dip to control or destroy external parasites.

**spray-gun** /ˈspreɪ-gʌn/, *n.* a device for forcing paint, etc., through a small nozzle so that it issues in a fine, even spray.

**spray irrigation** /ˌspreɪ ɪrəˈgeɪʃən/, *n.* a controlled method of irrigating crops, pastures or orchards by fixed or portable sprays.

**spray-on** /ˈspreɪ-ɒn/, *adj.* (of a hair spray, deodorant, sun-tan lotion, etc.) sprayed on from a pressure pack.

**spray painter** /ˈspreɪ peɪntə/, *n.* a painter who uses a spray gun to apply paint.

**spread** /sprɛd/, *v.,* **spread, spreading,** *n.* *–v.t.* **1.** to draw or stretch out to the full width, as a cloth, a rolled or folded map, folded wings, etc. (oft. fol. by *out*). **2.** to extend over a greater or a relatively great area, space, or period (oft. fol. by *out*): *to spread out handwriting.* **3.** to force apart, as walls, rails, etc., under pressure. **4.** to flatten out: *to spread the end of a rivet by hammering.* **5.** to display the full extent of; set forth in full. **6.** to dispose or distribute in a sheet or layer: *to spread hay to dry.* **7.** to apply in a thin layer or coating. **8.** to extend or distribute over a region, place, etc. **9.** to overlay, cover, or coat with something. **10.** to set or prepare (a table, etc.), as for a meal. **11.** to send out in various directions, as light, sound, mist, etc. **12.** to shed or scatter abroad; diffuse or disseminate, as knowledge, news, disease, etc. **13.** *Phonet.* to spread (the lips), as for the vowel ē of *me.* **14.** *Colloq.* to exert (oneself) to an unusual extent to produce a good effect or fine impression. *–v.i.* **15.** to become stretched out or extended, as a flag in the wind; expand, as in growth. **16.** to extend over a greater or a considerable area or period. **17.** to be or lie outspread or fully extended or displayed, as a landscape or scene. **18.** to admit of being spread or applied in a thin layer, as a soft substance. **19.** to become extended or distributed over a region, as population, animals, plants, etc. **20.** to become diffused abroad, or disseminated, as light, influences, rumours, ideas, infection, etc. **21.** to be forced apart, as rails; go out of gauge. *–n.* **22.** expansion; extension; diffusion. **23.** the extent of spreading: *to measure the spread of branches.* **24.** the distribution of cards in a hand. **25.** capacity for spreading: *the spread of an elastic material.* **26.** widening of girth: *middle-age spread.* **27.** a stretch, expanse, or extent of something. **28.** *Chiefly U.S.* a property; station; ranch. **29.** a cloth covering for a bed, table, or the like, esp. a bedspread. **30.** *Colloq.* a meal set out, esp. a feast. **31.** *Colloq.* a pretentious display made. **32.** any food preparation for spreading on bread, etc., as fruit, jam, or peanut butter. **33.** *Aeron.* the wingspan. **34.** *Stock Exchange.* **a.** the difference between the highest and the lowest prices at which business has been done during one day. **b.** the difference between the prices quoted by a stockjobber for buying and selling. **35.** a pair of facing pages of a book, magazine, or the like, or any part of them. **36.** *Journalism* a balance in the coverage of a newspaper, in relation to news, entertainment, sports, picture, etc. **37. a good spread,** *Colloq.* a lot of publicity, esp. in the various channels of the media. *–adj.* **38.** extended, esp. fully. **39.** *Jewellery.* (of a gem) flat and shallow. **40.** *Phonet.* (of the lips) forming a long, narrow opening, as for the vowel [i] in *me.* [ME *sprede(n)*, OE *sprǣdan*, c. G *spreiten*]

**spread eagle** /– ˈigəl/, *n.* **1.** a representation of an eagle with outspread wings (used as an emblem of the U.S.). **2.** an ice-skating movement, in which the skater describes a circular figure.

spread eagle

**spread-eagle** /sprɛd-ˈigəl/, *adj., v.,* **-gled, -gling.** *–adj.* **1.** having or suggesting the form of a spread eagle. **2.** *U.S. Colloq.* boastful or bombastic, esp. in the display of patriotism or national vanity. *–v.t.* **3.** to stretch out in the manner of a spread eagle. **4.** *Colloq.* to knock (a person) out. *–v.i.* **5.** to perform the spread eagle in skating. **6.** *Colloq.* to form a shape or take a position resembling a spread eagle. Also, **spreadeagle.**

**spreader** /ˈsprɛdə/, *n.* **1.** one who, or that which spreads. **2.** *Bldg Trades.* a piece of piping at the bottom of a downpipe from a higher roof which spreads rain water over a lower roof.

**spread of hours,** *n.* →**span of hours.**

**Sprechgesang** /ˈʃprɛkgəzʌŋ/, *n.* (in music) a type of vocalising between speech and song, originated by Schönberg. [G: lit., speech song]

**Sprechstimme** /ˈʃprɛkʃtɪmə/, *n.* (in music) a vocal part employing Sprechgesang. [G: lit., speech voice]

**spree** /spri/, *n.* **1.** a lively frolic. **2.** a bout or spell of drinking to intoxication. **3.** a session or period of indulgence: *a spending spree.* [orig. uncert.]

**sprig** /sprɪg/, *n., v.,* **sprigged, sprigging.** *–n.* **1.** a small spray of some plant with its leaves, flowers, etc. **2.** a shoot, twig, or small branch. **3.** an ornament or a decorative figure having the form of such a spray. **4.** (*joc.*) a person as a scion or offshoot of a family or class. **5.** a youth or young fellow. **6.** a small wedge-shaped piece of tin for holding glass in a sash. **7.** a headless brad. **8.** a stud on the sole of a boot, running shoe, etc., which gives the wearer greater purchase on the ground. **9.** (*pl.*) sports shoes with sprigged soles. *–v.t.* **10.** to decorate (fabrics, pottery, etc.) with a design of sprigs. **11.** to fasten with brads. **12.** to remove a sprig or sprigs from (plants or trees). **13.** to fit (the sole of a shoe) with sprigs. **14.** to injure with the sprigs of one's shoe. [ME *sprigge,* orig. uncert.] – **spriggy,** *adj.*

**sprightly** /ˈspraɪtli/, *adj.,* **-lier, -liest,** *adv.* *–adj.* **1.** animated, vivacious, or gay; lively. *–adv.* **2.** in a sprightly manner. [from *spright,* var. of SPRITE + -LY] – **sprightliness,** *n.*

**spring** /sprɪŋ/, *v.,* **sprang** or **sprung, sprung, springing,** *n., adj.* *–v.i.* **1.** to rise or move suddenly and lightly as by some inherent power: *to spring into the air, a tiger about to spring.* **2.** to go or come suddenly as if with a leap: *blood springs to the face.* **3.** to fly back or away in escaping from a forced position, as by resilient or elastic force or from the action of a spring: *a trap springs.* **4.** to start or work out of place, as parts of a mechanism, structure etc. **5.** to issue suddenly, as water, blood, sparks, fire, etc. (oft. fol. by *forth, out,* or *up*). **6.** to come into being; rise or arise (oft. fol. by *up*): *industries spring up.* **7.** to arise by growth, as from a seed or germ, bulb, root, etc.; grow, as plants. **8.** to proceed or originate, as from a source or cause. **9.** to have one's birth, or be descended, as from a family, person, stock, etc. **10.** to rise or extend upwards, as a spire. **11.** to take an upward course or curve from a point of support, as an arch. **12.** to start or rise from cover, as partridges, pheasants, etc. **13.** to become bent or warped, as boards. **14.** to explode, as a mine. **15.** (of a cricket bat or the like) to lose its resilience, as by perishing of the rubber springs. **16.** *Archaic.* to begin to appear, as day, light, etc. *–v.t.* **17.** to cause to spring. **18.** to cause to fly back, move, or act by elastic force, a spring, etc.: *to spring*

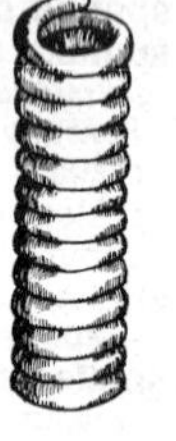
spiral spring (def. 43)

i = peat ɪ = pit ɛ = pet æ = pat a = part ɒ = pot ʌ = putt ɔ = port ʊ = put u = pool ɜ = pert ə = apart aɪ = buy eɪ = bay ɔɪ = boy aʊ = how oʊ = hoe ɪə = here ɛə = hair ʊə = tour g = give θ = thin ð = then ʃ = show ʒ = measure tʃ = choke dʒ = joke ŋ = sing j = you õ = Fr. bon

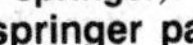

*a lock.* **19.** to cause to start out of place or work loose. **20. a.** to undergo the splitting or cracking of: *the ship sprang a mast.* **b.** to cause or bring about the splitting or cracking of: *the last blow sprang the axe-handle.* **21.** to come to have by cracking, etc.: *to spring a leak.* **22.** to bend by force, or force (*in*) by bending, as a slat or bar. **23.** to explode (a mine). **24.** to bring out, disclose, produce, make, etc., suddenly: *to spring a surprise.* **25.** to equip or fit with springs. **26.** to cause (a cricket bat or the like) to lose its resilience. **27.** to leap over. **28.** to make a surprise attack on (someone). **29.** *Colloq.* to catch out; to come upon unexpectedly. **30.** *Colloq.* to cause or enable (someone) to escape from prison. **31.** to obtain the release of a prisoner on bail. *–n.* **32.** a leap, jump, or bound. **33.** a springing or starting from place. **34.** a flying back from a forced position. **35.** an elastic or springy movement. **36.** elasticity or springiness. **37.** a split or crack, as in a mast; a bend or warp, as in a board. **38.** an issue of water from the earth, flowing away as a small stream or standing as a pool or small lake, or the place of such an issue: *mineral springs.* **39.** a source of something; a beginning or cause of origin. **40.** the rise of an arch, or the point or line at which an arch springs from its support. **41.** the first season of the year, between winter and summer. **42.** the first and freshest period: *the spring of life.* **43.** an elastic contrivance or body, as a strip or wire of steel coiled spirally, which recovers its shape after being compressed, bent, etc. **44.** any device or contrivance designed to impart resilience or elasticity, as one of a set of rubber strips running down the inside of the handle of a cricket bat. **45.** *Naut.* a mooring rope passing astern from the bow or ahead from the stern. **46.** (of pork) the belly. **47.** *Archaic.* the dawn, as of day; light, etc. *–adj.* **48.** of, pertaining to, characteristic of, or suitable for the season of spring: *spring flowers.* **49.** sown in the spring, as a cereal forming a second crop. **50.** young: *spring chicken.* **51.** resting on or containing springs: *a spring bed; spring mattress.* [ME; OE *springan.* c. D and G *springen,* Icel. *springa*] – **springless,** *adj.*

**spring balance** /'– bæləns/, *n.* a balance in which weight is determined by the extent to which a coiled spring is extended.

**springboard** /'sprɪŋbɔd/, *n.* **1.** a projecting semiflexible board from which persons dive. **2.** a flexible board used as a take-off in vaulting, tumbling, etc., to increase the height of leaps. **3.** anything serving to assist departure, initiation of a project, or the like. **4.** the short plank on which an axeman stands when chopping a tree at a point above shoulder height; jiggerboard.

**springbok** /'sprɪŋbɒk/, *n., pl.* **-boks,** (*esp. collectively*) **-bok. 1.** Also, **springbuck** /'sprɪŋbʌk/. a gazelle, *Antidorcas marsupialis,* of southern Africa which has a habit of springing upwards in play or when alarmed. **2.** (*pl. cap.*) the South African representative Rugby Union team. [Afrikaans, from *spring(en)* SPRING + *bok* goat, antelope]

springbok (def. 1)

**spring chicken** /sprɪŋ 'tʃɪkən/, *n. Colloq.* (*usu. with a negative*) a very young person: *I'm no spring chicken.*

**spring-clean** /sprɪŋ-'klin/, *v.t.* **1.** to clean (a house, etc.) thoroughly and completely, as traditionally done to homes in the spring of each year. *–n.* **2.** such a cleaning. – **spring-cleaner,** *n.* – **spring-cleaning,** *n.*

**spring dead spot,** *n.* a disease of lawn grasses, appearing as circular bleached patches, and caused by a soil-inhabiting fungus which attacks the root system of the grass.

**springe** /sprɪndʒ/, *n., v.,* **springed, springing.** *–n.* **1.** a snare for catching small game. *–v.t.* **2.** to catch in a springe. *–v.i.* **3.** to set springes. [ME *sprengen,* akin to obs. *sprenge,* v., cause to spring, OE *sprengean*]

**springer** /'sprɪŋə/, *n.* **1.** one who or that which springs. **2.** a springer spaniel. **3.** *Archit.* the impost of an arch, or the bottom stone of an arch resting upon the impost. **4.** a sea fish, *Mugil cephalus;* harder. **5.** a heifer or cow about to calve, either early (**backward springer**) or late (**forward springer**).

**springer paddock** /'– pædək/, *n.* a paddock reserved for cows about to calve.

**springer spaniel** /– 'spænjəl/, *n.* either of two breeds of short-haired spaniel, used to flush game.

springer spaniel

**spring fever** /sprɪŋ 'fivə/, *n.* a listless or restless feeling felt by some people at the beginning of spring weather.

**springform tin** /ˌsprɪŋfɔm 'tɪn/, *n.* a circular mould or pan with an upright rim that may be detached from the bottom to facilitate the removal of baked or moulded food.

**spring gun** /'sprɪŋ gʌn/, *n.* a gun fired as a result of a person coming into contact with a string or wire attached to it, used to deter trespassers.

**springhalt** /'sprɪŋhɔlt/, *n.* →**stringhalt.**

**springhead** /'sprɪŋhɛd/, *n.* **1.** the spring or fountain-head from which a stream flows. **2.** the source of something.

**springhouse** /'sprɪŋhaʊs/, *n. Chiefly U.S.* a shed or outhouse built over a spring, for cool or moist storage.

**spring lamb** /sprɪŋ 'læm/, *n.* a lamb of the late winter or spring drop which is raised on lush spring pastures.

**springlet** /'sprɪŋlət/, *n.* a little spring (of water).

**spring-loaded** /'sprɪŋ-loʊdəd/, *adj.* (of a machine part) held in or returned to position by means of a spring. – **spring-loading,** *n., adj.*

**springlock** /'sprɪŋlɒk/, *n.* a lock which fastens automatically by a spring.

**spring of pork,** *n.* a cut of meat from the belly of a pig along the rib line, usu. pickled or boned for smallgoods.

**spring onion** /sprɪŋ 'ʌnjən/, *n.* a type of onion having a small bulb, chiefly used raw as a salad vegetable.

**spring roll** /– 'roʊl/, *n.* a Chinese delicacy consisting of a savoury filling wrapped in a thin dough and deep fried.

**springtail** /'sprɪŋteɪl/, *n.* any of various wingless insects of the order Collembola, having a pair of elastic tail-like appendages which are ordinarily folded under the abdomen, but when suddenly extended enable the insect to spring into the air.

**spring tide** /sprɪŋ 'taɪd/, *n.* **1.** the large rise and fall of the tide at or soon after the new or the full moon. **2.** any great flood or swelling rush. Also, **king tide.**

**springtime** /'sprɪŋtaɪm/, *n.* **1.** the season of spring. **2.** the first or earliest period. Also, **springtide.**

**springwood** /'sprɪŋwʊd/, *n.* that part of an annual growth ring which, esp. in trees of the northern hemisphere, grows in the spring and early summer, and is characterised by larger thin-walled cells (distinguished from *summerwood*). Also, **earlywood.**

**springy** /'sprɪŋi/, *adj.,* **springier, springiest. 1.** characterised by spring or elasticity; elastic; resilient: *a springy step.* **2.** abounding in or having springs (of water), as land. – **springily,** *adv.* – **springiness,** *n.*

**sprinkle** /'sprɪŋkəl/, *v.,* **-kled, -kling,** *n. –v.t.* **1.** to scatter, as a liquid or a powder, in drops or particles. **2.** to disperse or distribute here and there. **3.** to overspread with drops or particles of water, powder, or the like. **4.** to diversify or intersperse with objects scattered here and there. *–v.i.* **5.** to scatter or disperse a liquid, powder, or the like in drops or particles. **6.** to be sprinkled. **7.** to rain slightly. *–n.* **8.** the act of sprinkling. **9.** that which is sprinkled. **10.** a light rain. **11.** a small quantity or number. [ME *sprenkle,* c. G *sprenkeln*]

**sprinkler** /'sprɪŋklə/, *n.* **1.** any device which sprinkles, esp. a small stand or the like with a rose or perforated hose for watering with a fine, even spray. **2.** one who sprinkles.

**sprinkler system** /'– sɪstəm/, *n.* **1.** a system of ceiling pipes in a building with valves which open automatically at certain temperatures, used for extinguishing fires. **2.** a system of pipes, etc. for watering gardens, lawns.

**sprinkling** /'sprɪŋklɪŋ/, *n.* **1.** a small quantity or number scattered here and there. **2.** a small quantity sprinkled.

**sprint** /sprɪnt/, *v.i.* **1.** to race at full speed, esp. for a short distance, as in running, rowing, etc. *–v.t.* **2.** to cover by sprinting: *to sprint a hundred metres.* *–n.* **3.** a short race at full speed. **4.** a spell of running at full speed, as to the finish of a long race. **5.** a brief spell of great activity. [Scand.; cf. Icel. *spretta* (where *tt* is for early *nt*)] – **sprinter,** *n.*

**sprit** /sprɪt/, *n.* a small pole or spar crossing a fore-and-aft sail diagonally from the mast to the upper aftermost corner of a sailing vessel, thus serving to extend the sail. [ME *spret,* OE *sprēot,* c. D *spriet,* G *Spriet*]

S, sprit

**sprite** /spraɪt/, *n.* an elf, fairy, or goblin. [ME, from OF *esprit,* or similarly reduced from *esperit(e),* AF *spirit(e)* SPIRIT]

**spritsail** /ˈsprɪtseɪl/; *Naut.* /-səl/, *n.* a sail extended by a sprit.

**spritzig** /ˈsprɪtsɪg/, *adj.* (of wine) showing a slight degree of gassiness or prickle caused by secondary fermentation in the bottle. [G]

**sprocket** /ˈsprɒkət/, *n.* **1.** *Mach.* one of a set of projections on the rim of a wheel which engage the links of a chain. **2.** *Mach.* a sprocket wheel. **3.** *Carp.* a wedge-shaped piece fitted to the bottom of a rafter to flatten the slope at the eaves. [from *sprock* (of obscure orig.; ? akin to SPUR + -ET]

**sprocket wheel** /ˈ– wil/, *n.* a wheel having sprockets.

**sprog** /sprɒg/, *n. Colloq.* **1.** a child or youngster. **2.** a new recruit, as in an airforce. [orig. obscure]

**sprout** /spraʊt/, *v.i.* **1.** to begin to grow; shoot forth, as a bud from a seed or stock. **2.** (of a seed, plant, the earth, etc.) to put forth buds or shoots. **3.** to develop or grow quickly. *–v.t.* **4.** to cause to sprout. **5.** to remove sprouts from. *–n.* **6.** a shoot of a plant. **7.** a new growth from a germinating seed, or from a rootstock, tuber, bud, or the like. **8.** something resembling or suggesting a sprout, as in growth. **9.** a scion or descendant. **10.** →**brussels sprout.** [ME *spruten,* OE *sprūtan,* c. G *spriessen*]

**spruce**[1] /sprus/, *n.* **1.** any member of the coniferous genus *Picea,* consisting of evergreen trees with short angular needle-shaped leaves attached singly around twigs, as *P. abies* **(Norway spruce),** *P. glauca* **(white spruce** or **Canadian spruce),** and *P. mariana* **(black spruce). 2.** any of various allied trees, as the Douglas fir and the hemlock spruce. **3.** the wood of any such tree. *–adj.* **4.** made of or containing such trees or such wood. [ME, sandhi var. of *Pruce* Prussia, from OF, from ML *Prussia*]

**spruce**[2] /sprus/, *adj.,* **sprucer, sprucest,** *v.,* **spruced, sprucing.** *–adj.* **1.** smart in dress or appearance; trim; neat; dapper. *–v.t.* **2.** to make spruce or smart (oft. fol. by *up*). *–v.i.* **3.** to make oneself spruce (usu. fol. by *up*). [? special use of SPRUCE[1] through (obs.) *Spruce leather,* a leather from Prussia used in jerkins, etc.] – **sprucely,** *adv.* – **spruceness,** *n.*

**sprue**[1] /spru/, *n.* **1.** an opening through which molten metal is poured into a mould. **2.** the waste piece of metal cast in this opening. [orig. uncert.]

**sprue**[2] /spru/, *n.* a chronic disease, occurring chiefly in the tropics, characterised by diarrhoea, ulceration of the mucous membrane of the digestive tract, and a smooth, shining tongue; psilosis. [D *spruw*]

**spruik** /spruk/, *v.i. Colloq.* **1.** to harangue or address a meeting. **2.** (of a showman) to harangue prospective customers to entice them into his tent, stripjoint, etc. [orig. uncert.; ? from D *spreken* speak] – **spruiker,** *n.*

**sprung** /sprʌŋ/, *v.* past tense and past participle of **spring.**

**sprung rhythm** /– ˈrɪðəm/, *n.* a system of prosody with the accent always on the first syllable of every foot followed by a varying number of unaccented syllables, all feet being given equal time length.

**spry** /spraɪ/, *adj.,* **spryer, spryest** or **sprier, spriest.** active; nimble; brisk. [orig. obscure] – **spryly,** *adv.* – **spryness,** *n.*

**spud** /spʌd/, *n., v.,* **spudded, spudding.** *–n.* **1.** a spade-like instrument, esp. one with a narrow blade, as for digging up or cutting the roots of weeds. **2.** a chisel-like tool for removing bark. **3.** *Surg.* a blunt-ended instrument used to remove wax from ears, and foreign bodies from eyes. **4.** *Colloq.* a potato. **5.** *Colloq.* an Irishman. *–v.t.* **6.** to remove with a spud. **7.** to begin to drill (an oil well) by using a broad, dull drilling tool (oft. fol. by *in*). *–v.i.* **8.** to dig with a spud. [ME *spudde* kind of knife]

**spud-bashing** /ˈspʌd-bæʃɪŋ/, *n. Colloq.* the act of peeling potatoes.

**spudder** /ˈspʌdə/, *n. Colloq.* **1.** an employee at an oil well. **2.** a rig or oil rig, esp. one used to begin a well.

**spue** /spju/, *v.i., v.t.,* **spued, spuing.** →**spew.**

**spume** /spjum/, *n., v.,* **spumed, spuming.** *–n.* **1.** foam; froth; scum. *–v.i.* **2.** to foam; froth. *–v.t.* **3.** to send forth as or like foam or froth. [ME, from L *spūma*] – **spumous, spumy,** *adj.*

**spumescent** /spjuˈmɛsənt/, *adj.* foamy; foamlike; frothy. – **spumescence,** *n.*

**spumone** /spəˈmoʊni/, *n.* Italian ice-cream of a very fine and smooth texture, usu. containing chopped fruit or nuts. Also, **spumoni.** [It.]

**spun** /spʌn/, *v.* **1.** past tense and past participle of **spin.** *–adj.* **2.** formed by or as by spinning: *spun rayon, spun silk.*

**spun glass** /– ˈglas/, *n.* →**fibreglass.**

**spunk** /spʌŋk/, *n.* **1.** *Colloq.* pluck; spirit; mettle. **2.** *Colloq.* semen. **3.** a good-looking person. [b. SPARK[1] and obs. *funk* spark, touchwood (c. D *vonk,* G *Funke* spark]

**spunky** /ˈspʌŋki/, *adj.* **spunkier, spunkiest.** *Colloq.* **1.** plucky; spirited. **2.** good-looking; attractive. – **spunkily,** *adv.* – **spunkiness,** *n.*

**spun protein** /spʌn ˈproʊtin/, *n.* vegetable protein which is forced through spinnerets, hardened into fibres, and bound together into bundles which can then be given flavour and colour to resemble the textured protein of meat or fish. See **extruded protein.**

**spun sugar** /– ˈʃʊgə/, *n.* →**fairy floss.**

**spun yarn** /– ˈjan/, *n.* cord formed of rope yarns loosely twisted together, for serving ropes, bending sails, etc.

**spur** /spɜ/, *n., v.,* **spurred, spurring.** *–n.* **1.** a pointed device attached to a horseman's boot heel, for goading a horse onwards, etc. **2.** anything that goads, impels, or urges to action or speed. **3.** something projecting, and resembling or suggesting a spur. **4.** a sharp piercing or cutting instrument fastened on the leg of a gamecock, for use in fighting. **5.** a stiff, usu. sharp, horny process on the leg of various birds, esp. the domestic cock. **6.** a short or stunted branch or shoot, as of a tree. **7.** one of the principal lateral roots of a tree. **8.** a slender, usu. hollow, projection from some part of a flower, as from the calyx of the larkspur or the corolla of the violet. **9.** *Phys. Geog.* a ridge or line of elevation projecting from or subordinate to the main body of a mountain or mountain range. **10.** a structure built to protect a river bank from a fast current; a river groyne. **11.** griff. **12.** *Archit.* **a.** a short wooden brace, usu. temporary, for strengthening a post or some other part. **b.** any offset from a wall, etc., as a buttress. **13.** *Railways.* a siding. **14. on the spur of the moment,** suddenly; without premeditation. **15. win one's spurs,** to achieve one's first distinction or success. *–v.t.* **16.** to prick with, or as with, spurs or a spur, as in order to urge on. **17.** to strike or wound with the spur, as a gamecock. **18.** to furnish with spurs or a spur. *–v.i.* **19.** to prick one's horse with the spur; ride quickly. **20.** to proceed hurriedly; press forward. [ME; OE *spura,* c. G *Sporn*] – **spurlike,** *adj.* – **spurer,** *n.*

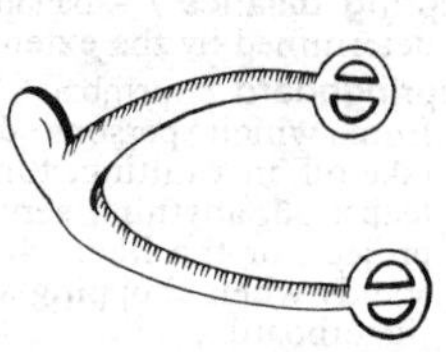
spur (def. 1)

**spurge** /spɜdʒ/, *n.* any plant of the genus *Euphorbia,* some species of which have purgative properties. [ME, from OF *espurge,* from *espurgier* purge, from L *expurgāre*]

**spur gear** /ˈspɜ gɪə/, *n. Mach.* a gear in which spur wheels are employed. Also, **spur gearing.**

**spurge laurel** /spɜdʒ ˈlɒrəl/, *n.* an evergreen shrub, *Daphne laureola,* of southern and western Europe and western Asia, with fragrant green axillary flowers.

**spurious** /ˈspjuriəs/, *adj.* **1.** not genuine or true; counterfeit; not from the reputed, pretended, or right source; not authentic. **2.** of illegitimate birth; bastard. **3.** *Bot.* bearing superficial resemblances but having morphological differences. [L *spurius* false] – **spuriously,** *adv.* – **spuriousness,** *n.*

**spurling pipe** /'spɜlɪŋ paɪp/, *n.* the pipe which leads the chain cable of a ship from the windlass down to the chain locker; navel pipe.

**spurn** /spɜn/, *v.t.* **1.** to reject with disdain; treat with contempt; scorn; despise. **2.** *Obs.* to kick. *–v.i.* **3.** to show disdain or contempt. **4.** *Obs.* to kick (oft. fol. by *against*). *–n.* **5.** disdainful rejection; contemptuous treatment. **6.** a kick. [ME; OE *spurnan,* akin to OHG *spurnan*] – **spurner,** *n.*

**spurred** /spɜd/, *adj.* **1.** having spurs or a spur. **2.** bearing spurs or spurlike spines. **3.** having the form of a spur. **4.** urged or encouraged.

**spurrey** /'spʌri/, *n., pl.* **-ries.** →**spurry.**

**spurrier** /'spʌriə/, *n.* a maker of spurs.

**spurry** /'spʌri/, *n.* **1.** →**corn spurry.** **2.** →**sand spurry.** [MD *spurie.* Cf. ML *spergula*]

**spurt** /spɜt/, *v.i.* **1.** to gush or issue suddenly in a stream or jet, as a liquid. **2.** to show marked activity or energy for a short period. *–v.t.* **3.** to throw or force out suddenly in a stream or jet, as a liquid. *–n.* **4.** a forcible gush of water, etc., as from a confined place. **5.** a sudden outburst, as of feeling. **6.** a marked increase of effort for a short period or distance, as in running, rowing, etc. Also, **spirt.** [var. of *spirt,* metathetic var. of *sprit,* ME *sprutten,* OE *spryttan* come forth; akin to SPROUT]

**spur wheel** /'spɜ wil/, *n. Mach.* a wheel with projecting teeth on the periphery, which are placed radially about and parallel to the axis; cogwheel.

spur wheel

**spur-winged plover** /ˌspɜ-wɪŋd 'plʌvə/, *n.* a large brown-winged, black-marked Australian plover, *Vanellus miles novaehollandiae,* frequenting well-watered paddocks and the margins of swamps; alarm bird.

**sputnik** /'spʌtnɪk, 'spʊtnɪk/, *n.* an artificial satellite, esp. an early Soviet one. [Russ.: companion]

**sputter** /'spʌtə/, *v.i.* **1.** to emit particles of anything in an explosive manner, as a candle does in burning. **2.** to eject particles of saliva, food, etc., from the mouth in a similar manner. **3.** to utter words or sounds in an explosive, incoherent manner. *–v.t.* **4.** to emit (anything) in small particles, as if by spitting. **5.** to eject (saliva, food, etc.) in small particles explosively and involuntarily, as in excitement. **6.** to utter explosively and incoherently. **7.** to deposit (a thin film of a metal) on a surface by making a disc of the metal the cathode of a low-pressure discharge system and introducing the surface between this cathode and a high-voltage anode. *–n.* **8.** the act, process, or sound of sputtering. **9.** explosive, incoherent utterance. **10.** matter ejected in sputtering. [frequentative of SPOUT, c. D *sputteren*] – **sputterer,** *n.*

**sputum** /'spjutəm/, *n., pl.* **-ta** /-tə/. **1.** spittle mixed with mucus, purulent matter, or the like. **2.** that which is expectorated; spittle. [L]

**spy** /spaɪ/, *n., pl.* **spies,** *v.,* **spied, spying.** *–n.* **1.** one who keeps secret watch on the actions of others. **2.** one employed by a government to obtain secret information or intelligence, esp. with reference to military or naval affairs of other countries. **3.** the act of spying; a careful view. *–v.i.* **4.** to make secret observations. **5.** to be on the lookout; keep watch. **6.** to examine or search closely or carefully. *–v.t.* **7.** to make secret observations in (a place) with hostile intent (now usu. fol. by *out*). **8.** to inspect or examine closely or carefully. **9.** to find (*out*) by observation or scrutiny. **10.** to catch sight of; descry; see. [ME *spien,* from OF *espier* ESPY]

**spyer** /'spaɪə/, *n.* →**spier.**

**spyglass** /'spaɪglas/, *n.* a small telescope.

**spy-hole** /'spaɪ-hoʊl/, *n.* a peephole, esp. one in a front door, as of a flat, through which those inside may examine callers before opening the door.

**sq.,** **1.** the following one. [L *sequens*] **2.** square.

**Sq.,** Square (in place-names).

**sqdn,** squadron.

**Sqn Ldr,** squadron leader.

**sqq.,** *pl.* the following ones. [L *sequentia*]

**squab** /skwɒb/, *n.* **1.** a nestling pigeon, marketed when fully grown but still unfledged. **2.** a short, stout person. **3.** a thickly stuffed, soft cushion. **4.** the back part, often detachable, of the seat of certain motor cars. *–adj.* **5.** short and thick or broad. **6.** (of birds) unfledged or lately hatched. [Scand.; cf. d. Swed. *sqvabb* loose fat flesh, d. Norw. *skvabb* soft wet mass]

**squabble** /'skwɒbəl/, *v.,* **-bled, -bling,** *n.* *–v.i.* **1.** to engage in a petty quarrel. *–n.* **2.** a petty quarrel. [? imitative.; cf. d. Swed. *sqvabbel*] – **squabbler,** *n.*

**squabby** /'skwɒbi/, *adj.,* **-bier, -biest.** short and stout; squat. – **squabbily,** *adv.*

**squad** /skwɒd/, *n., v.,* **squadded, squadding.** *–n.* **1.** any small group of soldiers operating as a unit. **2.** any small group or party of persons engaged in a common enterprise, etc. **3.** a group of sportsmen, often selected for a tour, from whom teams for specific occasions are drawn. [F *escouade,* var. of *esquadre* squadron, from It. *squadra* SQUARE]

**squad car** /'– ka/, *n.* →**patrol-car.**

**squadron** /'skwɒdrən/, *n.* **1.** a portion of a naval fleet, or a detachment of warships employed on a particular service; a subdivision of a fleet. **2.** an armoured cavalry or cavalry unit consisting of two or more troops (companies), a headquarters, and certain supporting units. **3.** the basic administrative and tactical unit of an airforce, smaller than a group and composed of two or more flights. **4.** a number of persons grouped or united together for some purpose; a group or body in general. *–v.t.* **5.** to form into a squadron or squadrons; marshal or array in or as in squadrons. [It. *squadrone,* from *squadra* SQUARE]

**squadron leader** /'– lidə/, *n.* **1.** a commissioned officer in the Royal Australian Air Force ranking above a flight lieutenant and below a wing-commander. **2.** an officer of equivalent rank in any of various other airforces.

**squalene** /'skweɪlin/, *n.* a terpene, $C_{30}H_{50}$, an intermediate in cholesterol biosynthesis, found in large quantities in shark liver.

**squalid** /'skwɒləd/, *adj.* **1.** foul and repulsive, as from the want of care or cleanliness; dirty; filthy. **2.** wretched; miserable; degraded. [L *squālidus*] – **squalidly,** *adv.* – **squalidity** /skwɒ'lɪdəti/, **squalidness,** *n.*

**squall**[1] /skwɔl/, *n.* **1.** *Meteorol.* a sudden strong wind which dies away rapidly after lasting only a few minutes, often associated with a temporary change of wind direction. **2.** *Colloq.* a disturbance or commotion. *–v.i.* **3.** to blow in a squall. [? akin to SQUALL[2]]

**squall**[2] /skwɔl/, *v.i.* **1.** to cry out loudly; scream violently. *–v.t.* **2.** to utter in a screaming tone. *–n.* **3.** the act or sound of squalling. [imitative] – **squaller,** *n.*

**squally** /'skwɔli/, *adj.,* **squallier, squalliest.** **1.** characterised by squalls. **2.** *Colloq.* threatening.

**squalor** /'skwɒlə/, *n.* filth and misery. [L]

**squama** /'skweɪmə/, *n., pl.* **-mae** /-mi/. a scale or scale-like part, as of epidermis or bone. [L]

**squamate** /'skweɪmeɪt/, *adj.* provided or covered with squamae or scales; scaly. [L *squāmātus*]

**squamation** /skwə'meɪʃən/, *n.* **1.** the state of being squamate. **2.** the arrangement of the squamae or scales of an animal.

**squamosal** /skwə'moʊsəl/, *adj.* **1.** *Anat.* pertaining to the thin scale-like bone (an element of the temporal bone) in the side of the skull above and behind the ear. **2.** *Zool.* pertaining to a corresponding bone in other vertebrates. **3.** squamous. *–n.* **4.** a squamosal bone.

**squamose** /'skweɪmoʊs/, *adj.* →**squamous.** – **squamosely,** *adv.* – **squamoseness,** *n.*

**squamous** /'skweɪməs/, *adj.* covered with or formed of squamae or scales; scale-like. [L *squāmōsus*] – **squamously,** *adv.* – **squamousness,** *n.*

**squamulose** /'skwæmjəloʊs, 'skweɪmjə-/, *adj.* furnished or covered with small scales.

**squander** /'skwɒndə/, *v.t.* **1.** to spend (money, etc.) extravagantly or wastefully (oft. fol. by *away*). *–n.* **2.** extravagant or wasteful expenditure. [orig. obscure] – **squanderer,** *n.*

**square** /skwɛə/, *n.*, *v.*, **squared, squaring,** *adj.*, **squarer, squarest,** *adv.* *–n.* **1.** a four-sided plane having all its sides equal and all its angles right angles. **2.** anything having this form or a form approximating it. **3.** one of the rectangular or otherwise shaped divisions of a game board, as a chess or draughts board. **4.** an open area in a city or town, as at the intersection of streets, often planted with grass, trees, etc. **5.** a block of buildings in a town marked off by neighbouring and intersecting streets along each side. **6.** an L-shaped or T-shaped instrument for determining or testing right angles, and for other purposes. **7.** *Maths.* the second power of a number or quantity: *the square of 4 is 4 × 4, or 16.* **8.** *Bldg Trades.* a former unit of surface measurement equalling 100 square feet. **9.** *Mil.* (formerly) a body of troops drawn up in quadrilateral form. **10.** *Colloq.* one who is ignorant of or uninterested in the latest fads. **11.** *Rowing.* the position of the blade of an oar at right angles to the water before it is dropped in to begin a stroke. **12.** *Obs.* a true standard. **13. on the square, a.** fair; fairly. **b.** abstaining from alcohol; teetotal. **14. out of square,** not at right angles. *–v.t.* **15.** to reduce to square, rectangular, or cubic form. **16.** to mark out in squares or rectangles. **17.** to test for deviation from a right angle, straight line, or plane surface. **18.** *Maths.* **a.** to multiply (a number or quantity) by itself. **b.** to describe or find a square which is equivalent to: *to square a circle.* **19.** to bring to the form of a right angle or right angles; set at right angles to something else. **20.** to make the score of (a contest, etc.) even. **21.** to set (the shoulders, arms, etc.) so as to present an approximately rectangular outline. **22.** to make straight, level, or even. **23.** to regulate, as by a standard. **24.** to adjust harmoniously or satisfactorily; balance; settle: *to square a debt.* **25.** *Rowing.* to turn (the blade of an oar) from the feather to a right angle to the surface before dropping it to begin a stroke. **26.** *Colloq.* to bribe. *–v.i.* **27.** to accord or agree (oft. fol. by *with*): *his theory does not square with the facts.* **28. square away, a.** *Naut.* to arrange the yards so that they are at right angles to the fore-and-aft line of the ship. **b.** to complete; fix up. **29. square off, a.** to assume a posture of offence or defence, as in boxing. **b.** to apologise; make recompense (fol. by *with*). **c.** to get revenge; pay back (fol. by *with*). **30. square the circle,** to attempt the impossible. **31. square up,** to pay or settle a bill, debt, etc. **32. square up to,** to face, esp. courageously; prepare to contest or resist. *–adj.* **33.** of the form of a right angle; having some part or parts rectangular: *a square corner.* **34.** having four sides and four right angles, but not equilateral; cubical or approximately so; rectangular and of three dimensions: *a square box.* **35.** at right angles, or perpendicular: *one line square to another.* **36.** *Naut.* at right angles to the mast and the keel, as a yard. **37.** designating a unit representing an area in the form of a square: *a square metre.* **38.** pertaining to such units, or to surface measurement: *square measure.* **39.** *Maths.* **a.** See **square number. b.** See **square root.** **40.** of a specified length on each side of a square: *an area 2 metres square.* **41.** having a square section, or one that is merely rectangular: *a square file.* **42.** having a solid, sturdy form with rectilinear and angular outlines. **43.** straight, level, or even, as a surface or surfaces. **44.** leaving no balance of debt on either side; having all accounts settled: *to make accounts square.* **45.** just, fair, or honest. **46.** straightforward, direct, or unequivocal. **47.** *Colloq.* substantial or satisfying: *a square meal.* **48.** conservative in manners, dress, or behaviour, esp. regarding sex or drug-taking. *–adv.* **49.** so as to be square; in square or rectangular form. **50.** at right angles. **51.** *Colloq.* solidly or directly: *to hit a nail square on the head.* **52.** *Colloq.* fairly, honestly or uprightly. **53. break square,** to have one's credits or profits equal one's debits or losses. [ME, from OF *esquarrer,* from L *ex-* EX[1] + *quadrāre* to square, QUADRATE] **– squarely,** *adv.* **– squareness,** *n.* **– squarer,** *n.*

**square bracket** /– 'brækət/, *n.* either of the two parenthetical marks: [ ].

**square-cut** /'skwɛə-kʌt/, *Cricket.* *–n.* **1.** a cut (def. 37) in the direction of square leg. *–v.t.* **2.** to cut (def. 25) in the direction of square leg.

**square dance** /'skwɛə dæns/, *n.* a dance, as a quadrille, by couples arranged in a square or in some set form.

**square-dance** /'skwɛə-dæns/, *v.i.*, **-danced, -dancing.** to perform or take part in a square dance. **– square-dancer,** *n.*

**square deal** /skwɛə 'dil/, *n. Colloq.* **1.** a mutually fair and honest arrangement or attitude. **2.** a distribution of cards according to the rules of a game, without cheating.

**squared ring** /skwɛəd 'rɪŋ/, *n. Colloq.* the boxing ring. Also, **squared circle.**

**square-drive** /'skwɛə-draɪv/, *Cricket.* *–n.* **1.** a drive (def. 23) in the direction of square leg. *–v.t.* **2.** to drive (a ball) in this direction.

**squarehead** /'skwɛəhɛd/, *n.* **1.** *Colloq.* a conservative in manners, dress and behaviour. **2.** *Prison Colloq.* a law-abiding person.

**square knot** /'skwɛə nɒt/, *n. U.S.* →**reef knot.**

**square-law detector** /skwɛə-'lɔ də,tɛktə/, *n.* an electronic circuit which produces an output proportional to the square of its input voltage.

**square leg** /skwɛə 'lɛg/, *n.* (in cricket) a fielding position on the leg side at right angles to the pitch opposite the batsman's wicket.

**square measure** /'– mɛʒə/, *n.* a system of units for the measurement of surfaces or areas.

**square number** /– 'nʌmbə/, *n.* a number which is the square of some integer number, as 1, 4, 9, 16, 25, etc., with respect to 1, 2, 3, 4, 5, etc.

**square-off** /'skwɛər-ɒf/, *n.* something offered in order to mollify someone having suffered a hurt, slight or injustice.

**square one** /skwɛə 'wʌn/, *n. Colloq.* the beginning; the point of departure: *we're back to square one.*

**square piano** /– pi'ænoʊ/, *n.* See **piano**[1] (def. 4).

**square-rigged** /'skwɛə-rɪgd/, *adj. Naut.* having square sails as the principal sails.

**square root** /skwɛə 'rut/, *n. Maths.* the quantity of which a given quantity is the square: *4 is the square root of 16.*

**square sail** /'– seɪl/, *n. Naut.* See **sail** (def. 1).

**square-shooter** /'skwɛə-ʃutə/, *n. Colloq.* an honest, fair person.

**square-shouldered** /skwɛə-'ʃoʊldəd/, *adj.* having shoulders set so as to present an approximately rectangular outline.

**square thread** /skwɛə 'θrɛd/, *n.* a screw thread with a deep pitch in which the thread profile is U-shaped instead of V-shaped, used for transmitting thrust.

**square-toed** /skwɛə-'toʊd/, *adj.* having a broad, square toe, as a shoe.

**square wave** /'skwɛə weɪv/, *n. Physics.* a wave form which alternates between two fixed values for equal lengths of time, the time of transition between the two values being very short.

**squarish** /'skwɛərɪʃ/, *adj.* approximately square.

**squarrose** /'skwæroʊs, 'skwɒroʊs/, *adj.* denoting any rough or ragged surface. [L *squarrōsus*]

**squash**[1] /skwɒʃ/, *v.t.* **1.** to press into a flat mass or pulp; crush. **2.** to suppress or put down; quash. **3.** *Colloq.* to silence, as with a crushing retort. *–v.i.* **4.** to be pressed into a flat mass or pulp. **5.** (of a soft, heavy body) to fall heavily. **6.** to make a splashing sound; splash. *–n.* **7.** the act or sound of squashing. **8.** the fact of being squashed. **9.** something squashed or crushed. **10.** something soft and easily crushed. **11.** a great number of people in a comparatively small space. **12.** Also, **squash racquets.** a game for two players, played in a small walled court with light raquets and a small rubber ball. **13.** Also, **squash tennis.** *U.S.* a game resembling squash racquets, played with a larger ball and racquet. **14.** a small indiarubber ball used in squash racquets. **15.** a beverage based upon a fruit juice, often diluted. **16.** →**social** (def. 11). [OF *esquasser.* See QUASH[1]; ? partly imitative] **– squasher,** *n.*

**squash**[2] /skwɒʃ/, *n.* **1.** any of various varieties of *Cucurbita pepo,* usu. round in shape and having paler flesh and softer skin than the pumpkin, *Cucurbita maxima.* **2.** *North America.* many of various edible pumpkins. [Algonquian abbrev. of *askutasquash,* lit., vegetables eaten green]

**squashy** /'skwɒʃi/, *adj.*, **squashier, squashiest. 1.** easily squashed; pulpy. **2.** soft and wet, as ground, etc. **3.** having a squashed appearance. **– squashily,** *adv.* **– squashiness,** *n.*

**squat** /skwɒt/, *v.*, **squatted** or **squat, squatting,** *adj.*, *n.*

–*v.i.* **1.** to assume a posture close to the ground with the knees bent and the back more or less straight resting either on the balls of the feet, or with feet flat. **2.** to crouch or cower down, as an animal. **3.** to adopt a low position, as a heavily laden ship. **4.** (formerly) to settle on land, often large tracts, without government permission, security of tenure not being granted until the mid 19th century. **5.** to occupy a building without title or right. –*v.t.* **6.** to cause (a person, oneself, etc.) to squat. –*adj.* **7.** short and thickset or thick, as persons, animals, the body, etc. **8.** low and thick or broad. **9.** seated or being in a squatting position; crouching. –*n.* **10.** the act or fact of squatting. **11.** a squatting position or posture. [ME, from OF *esquatir,* from *es-* (from L *ex-* EX-[1]) out + *quatir* press down (from L *coactus,* pp., driven together)] – **squatly,** *adv.* – **squatness,** *n.*

**squatter** /ˈskwɒtə/, *n.* **1.** one who or that which squats. **2.** (formerly) one who settled on Crown land to run stock, esp. sheep, initially without government permission, but later with a lease or licence. **3.** one of a group of rich and influential rural landowners. **4.** one who occupies a building without right or title.

squatter (def. 2)

**squatterdom** /ˈskwɒtədəm/, *n.* **1.** squatters and their families as a social class. **2.** the milieu of this class.

**squattocracy** /skwɒˈtɒkrəsi/, *n.* the long-established and wealthy landowners who regard themselves as an aristocracy. [SQUAT(TER) + (ARIS)TOCRACY] – **squattocratic** /skwɒtəˈkrætɪk/, *adj.*

**squatty** /ˈskwɒti/, *adj.,* **-tier, -tiest.** short and thick; low and broad.

**squaw** /skwɔ/, *n.* a North American Indian woman or wife. [Algonquian *eskaw* woman]

**squawk** /skwɔk/, *v.i.* **1.** to utter a loud, harsh cry, as a duck or other fowl when frightened. **2.** *Colloq.* to complain loudly and vehemently. –*v.t.* **3.** to give forth with a squawk. –*n.* **4.** a loud, harsh cry or sound. **5.** *Colloq.* a loud, vehement complaint. [b. SQUALL[2] and CROAK] – **squawker,** *n.*

**squaw man** /ˈskwɔ mæn/, *n.* a white or other non-Indian man married to a North American Indian woman.

**squeak** /skwik/, *n.* **1.** a short, sharp, shrill cry; a sharp, high-pitched sound. **2.** *Colloq.* a narrow escape. –*v.i.* **3.** to utter or emit a squeak or squeaky sound. **4.** *Colloq.* to confess or turn informer. –*v.t.* **5.** to utter or produce with a squeak or squeaks. [ME *squeke,* apparently from Scand.; cf. Swed. *sqväka* croak]

**squeaker** /ˈskwikə/, *n.* **1.** one who or that which squeaks. **2.** any of various birds as the grey currawong, the noisy miner, or the whiteface, which make a squeaking noise. **3.** the short-nosed rat kangaroo. **4.** any of various cicadas which make a squeaking noise. **5.** *Shooting.* a shot which narrowly misses or just touches a scoring ring.

**squeaky** /ˈskwiki/, *adj.,* **squeakier, squeakiest.** squeaking; tending to squeak: *his squeaky shoes could be heard along the corridor.* – **squeakily,** *adv.* – **squeakiness,** *n.*

**squeaky-clean** /ˈskwiki-klin/, *adj. Colloq.* **1.** very clean. **2.** morally irreproachable.

**squeal** /skwil/, *n.* **1.** a more or less prolonged, sharp, shrill cry, as of pain, fear, etc. **2.** *Colloq.* a protest or complaint. –*v.i.* **3.** to utter or emit a squeal or squealing sound. **4.** *Colloq.* to turn informer. **5.** *Colloq.* to protest or complain. –*v.t.* **6.** to utter or produce with a squeal. **7.** *Colloq.* to disclose or reveal, as something secret. [imitative] – **squealer,** *n.*

**squeamish** /ˈskwimɪʃ/, *adj.* **1.** easily nauseated or sickened; qualmish. **2.** easily shocked by anything slightly immodest; prudish. **3.** excessively particular or scrupulous as to the moral aspect of things. **4.** fastidious or dainty. [late ME *squaymysch,* replacing ME *squaymous,* earlier *scoymous,* from AF *escoymous;* orig. unknown] – **squeamishly,** *adv.* – **squeamishness,** *n.*

**squeegee** /ˈskwiˌdʒi/, *n., v.,* **-geed, -geeing.** –*n.* **1.** an implement edged with rubber or the like, for removing water from windows after washing, sweeping water from wet decks, etc. **2.** *Photog.* a device for removing surplus water from negatives or prints. –*v.t.* **3.** to sweep, scrape, or press with a squeegee. Also, **squilgee.** [? from *squeege,* var. of SQUEEZE]

**squeeze** /skwiz/, *v.,* **squeezed, squeezing,** *n.* –*v.t.* **1.** to press forcibly together; compress. **2.** to apply pressure to in order to extract something: *to squeeze a lemon.* **3.** to thrust forcibly; force by pressure; cram: *to squeeze three suits into a small suitcase.* **4.** to force out, extract, or procure by pressure (usu. fol. by *out* or *from*): *to squeeze juice from an orange.* **5.** to embrace; hug. **6.** to press (someone's hand, arm, etc.) as an expression of affection, sympathy, etc. **7.** to harass or oppress (a person, etc.) by exactions. **8.** *Colloq.* to put pressure upon (a person or persons) to act in a given way, esp. by blackmail. **9.** to obtain a facsimile impression of. –*v.i.* **10.** to exert a compressing force. **11.** to force a way through some narrow or crowded place (fol. by *through, in, out,* etc.). –*n.* **12.** the act of squeezing. **13.** the fact of being squeezed. **14.** a tight pressure of another's hand within one's own, as in friendliness. **15.** a hug or close embrace. **16.** *Colloq.* a situation from which extrication is difficult: *in a tight squeeze.* **17.** a crowded gathering or assembly. **18.** a restriction, demand, or pressure, as imposed by a government: *a credit squeeze.* **19.** a small quantity or amount of anything obtained by squeezing. **20.** a facsimile impression of an inscription or the like, obtained by pressing some plastic substance over or around it. **21.** *Colloq.* the act of blackmailing. [var. of obs. *squize* squeeze, OE *cwȳsan* (with *s-* by false division of words in sandhi)] – **squeezer,** *n.*

**squeezebox** /ˈskwizbɒks/, *n. Colloq.* →**accordion.**

**squelch** /skwɛltʃ/, *v.t.* **1.** to strike or press with crushing force; crush down; squash. **2.** *Colloq.* to put down or suppress completely; silence, as with a crushing retort. –*v.i.* **3.** to make a splashing sound. **4.** to tread heavily in water, mud, wet shoes, etc., with such a sound. –*n.* **5.** a squelched or crushed mass of anything. **6.** a squelching sound. **7.** *Electronics.* a circuit which cuts off the output of a radio receiver until a signal begins. **8.** *Colloq.* a crushing argument or retort. [var. of *quelch* (b. QUELL and CRUSH), with *s-* by false division of words in sandhi] – **squelcher,** *n.*

**squeteague** /skwəˈtig/, *n.* any of several fishes of the genus *Cynoscion,* of the North American Atlantic coast, esp. *C. regalis,* an important food fish. [Algonquian *pesukwiteag,* lit., they give glue]

**squib** /skwɪb/, *n., v.,* **squibbed, squibbing.** –*n.* **1.** a short witty or sarcastic saying or writing. **2.** a firework consisting of a tube or ball filled with powder, which burns with a hissing noise terminated usu. by a slight explosion. **3.** any firework. **4.** a pyrotechnic device used to fire the igniter in a rocket. **5.** Also, **damp squib.** any plan, project, etc., which does not eventuate. **6.** a mean or paltry fellow. **7.** *Racing.* a horse, dog, etc., which lacks stamina. –*v.i.* **8.** to write squibs. **9.** to shoot a squib. **10.** to go off with a small, sharp sound. **11.** to move swiftly and irregularly. **12.** *Colloq.* to behave in a fearful or cowardly manner. **13.** to desert (someone) to save one's own skin (fol. by *on*). –*v.t.* **14.** to assail in squibs or lampoons. **15.** to toss, shoot, or utilise as a squib. **16.** to withdraw from, usu. through fear. [orig. uncert.]

**squid** /skwɪd/, *n., pl.* **squids,** (*esp. collectively*) **squid.** any of various decapod dibranchiate cephalopods, esp. any of certain small species (as of the genera *Loligo* and *Ommastrephes*) having slender bodies and caudal fins and much used for bait. [orig. uncert.]

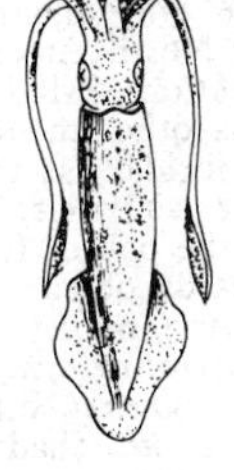

squid

**squiffy** /ˈskwɪfi/, *adj. Colloq.* **1.** slightly intoxicated; tipsy. **2.** crooked; askew. [orig. uncert.]

**squiggle** /ˈskwɪgəl/, *n., v.,* **-gled, -gling.** –*n.* **1.** a short twist or curve, as in drawing or writing. –*v.i.* **2.** to twist or curve; appear as squiggles. –*v.t.* **3.** to form squiggles; scribble. [b. SQUIRM and WRIGGLE] – **squiggly,** *adj.*

**squill** /skwɪl/, *n.* **1.** the bulb of the sea-onion, *Urginea maritima,* of the genus *Scilla,* cut into thin slices and dried, and used in medicine chiefly as an expectorant. **2.** the plant itself. **3.** →**scilla.** [ME, from L *squilla,* var. of *scilla,* from Gk *skilla*]

**squilla** /ˈskwɪlə/, *n., pl.* **squillas, squillae** /ˈskwɪli/. →**mantis crab.** [L. See SQUILL]

**squinch** /skwɪntʃ/, *n.* a small arch, corbelling, or the like, built across the interior angle between two walls, as in a square tower for supporting the side of a superimposed octagonal spire. [var. of Brit. obs. or d. *scunch* for *scuncheon,* ME *sconchon,* from OF *escoinson,* apparently from *es-* (from L *ex-* EX-[1]) out + *coin* angle (from L *cuneus* wedge)]

squinch

**squint** /skwɪnt/, *v.i.* **1.** to look with the eyes partly closed. **2.** to be affected with strabismus; be cross-eyed. **3.** to look or glance obliquely or sideways; look askance. **4.** to make or have an indirect reference; tend or incline (fol. by *towards,* etc.). *–v.t.* **5.** to close (the eyes) partly in looking. **6.** to cause to squint; cause to look obliquely. *–n.* **7.** *Pathol.* an affection of the eye consisting in non-coincidence of the optic axes; strabismus. **8.** *Colloq.* a furtive glance. **9.** a looking obliquely or askance. **10.** an indirect reference; inclination. **11.** an oblique or perverse tendency. **12.** Also, **hagioscope.** a small opening in a church wall giving a view of the altar. **13.** *Bldg Trades.* (in brickwork) a special component consisting of a brick with splayed ends. *–adj.* **14.** looking obliquely; looking with a side glance; looking askance. **15.** affected with strabismus, as the eyes. [aphetic var. of ASQUINT, *adv.* (used as adj.)] – **squinter,** *n.*

**squint-eyed** /ˈskwɪnt-aɪd/, *adj.* **1.** affected with or characterised by strabismus. **2.** looking obliquely or askance.

**squire** /ˈskwaɪə/, *n., v.,* **squired, squiring.** *–n.* **1.** (in England) a country gentleman, esp. the chief landed proprietor in a district. **2.** *U.S.* a justice of the peace, local judge, or other local dignitary (chiefly used as a title) in country districts and small towns. **3.** a young man of gentle birth who, as an aspirant to knighthood, attended upon a knight; an esquire. **4.** a personal attendant, as of a person of rank. **5.** a man who attends or escorts a lady in public. **6.** *Colloq.* (*joc.*) (a form of address to a man). **7.** See **snapper** (def. 1). *–v.t.* **8.** to attend as or in the manner of a squire. [ME *squier,* from OF *esquier.* See ESQUIRE]

**squirearchy** /ˈskwaɪəraki/, *n., pl.* **-archies.** **1.** the class of squires collectively. **2.** rule or government by a squire or squires. Also, **squirarchy.** [SQUIRE + -ARCHY]

**squireling** /ˈskwaɪəlɪŋ/, *n.* a petty squire.

**squirm** /skwɜm/, *v.i.* **1.** to wriggle or writhe. **2.** to feel or display discomfort or disgust as from reproof, embarrassment, or repulsion. *–n.* **3.** a squirming or wriggling movement. [b. SKEW and WORM *v.*] – **squirmy,** *adj.*

**squirrel** /ˈskwɪrəl/, *n.* **1.** any of the arboreal, bushy-tailed rodents constituting the genus *Sciurus* (family Sciuridae), as the **red squirrel** of Europe (including Britain) and Asia, *S. vulgaris,* and the **grey squirrel,** *S. carolinensis,* of North America and (by introduction) Britain. **2.** any of various other members of the family Sciuridae, as the chipmunks, flying squirrels, woodchucks, etc. **3.** the pelt or fur of such an animal. **4.** *Colloq.* a person who hoards objects of little value. *–v.t.* **5.** to hoard or save, as saving money in times of economic depression: *people are squirreling away funds in the savings banks.* [ME *squirel,* from AF *esquirel,* diminutive from LL *sciūrus,* from Gk *skiouros,* from *skiá* shadow + *ourá* tail] – **squirrel-like,** *adj.*

squirrel

**squirrel cage** /ˈ– keɪdʒ/, *n.* a cage containing a cylindrical framework that is rotated by a squirrel or the like running around inside it.

**squirrel-cage motor** /ˈskwɪrəl-keɪdʒ ˌmoʊtə/, *n.* a type of induction motor in which the rotor consists of a number of copper bags parallel to the axis of the motor, resembling a squirrel cage.

**squirrelfish** /ˈskwɪrəlfɪʃ/, *n.* any fish of the tropical marine family Holocentridae, or of the related family Melamplaidae, having large eyes and a usu. reddish body.

**squirrel glider** /ˈskwɪrəl glaɪdə/, *n.* a medium-sized gliding possum of eastern Australia and Norfolk Island, *Petaurus norfolcensis.*

**squirt** /skwɜt/, *v.i.* **1.** to eject liquid in a jet from a narrow orifice. **2.** to issue in a jetlike stream. *–v.t.* **3.** to cause (liquid) to issue in a jet from a narrow orifice. **4.** to wet or bespatter with a liquid so ejected. *–n.* **5.** the act of squirting. **6.** a jet, as of water. **7.** an instrument for squirting, as a syringe. **8.** a small quantity of liquid squirted. **9.** *Colloq.* **a.** an insignificant, self-assertive fellow. **b.** a short person. **10.** *Colloq.* →**expert** (def. 2). [orig. obscure] – **squirter,** *n.*

**squirting cucumber** /ˌskwɜtɪŋ ˈkjukʌmbə/, *n.* a plant, *Ecballium elaterium,* native to the Mediterranean region, whose ripened fruit forcibly ejects the seeds and juice.

**squish** /skwɪʃ/, *Colloq.* *–v.t.* **1.** to squeeze or squash. *–v.i.* **2.** (of water, soft mud, etc.) to make a gushing sound. *–n.* **3.** a noise made by squishing. – **squishy,** *adj.*

**squiz** /skwɪz/, *Colloq.* *–v.t.* **1.** to look at quickly but closely. *–n.* **2.** a quick but close look.

**sr,** steradian.

**Sr,** **1.** Senior. **2.** Senor. **3.** Sir. **4.** *Chem.* strontium.

**S.R.,** self-raising.

**S.R.C.,** Student's Representative Council.

**Sri Lanka** /ʃri ˈlæŋkə/, *n.* an island nation in the Indian Ocean, south of India. – **Sri Lankan,** *adj., n.*

**ss.,** sections.

**SS,** **1.** Saints. [L *Sancti*] **2.** storm-trooper.

**S.S.,** **1.** Social Security. **2.** Steamship. **3.** Sunday School.

**SSB,** *Radio.* single side-band.

**SS.D.,** Most Holy Lord (a title of the pope). [L *Sanctissimus Dominus*]

**SSE,** south-south-east. Also, **S.S.E.**

**S-shaped bend** /ˌɛs-ʃeɪpt ˈbɛnd/, *n.* →**swan neck.**

**ssp.,** subspecies.

**SSR,** Soviet Socialist Republic. Also, **S.S.R.**

**SSW,** south-south-west. Also, **S.S.W.**

**st,** **1.** stet. **2.** strait. **3.** street. **4.** stitch. **5.** stumped. **6.** stone (weight).

**s.t.,** short ton.

**St,** **1.** Saint. **2.** Strait. **3.** Street. **4.** Stokes.

**stab** /stæb/, *v.,* **stabbed, stabbing,** *n.* *–v.t.* **1.** to pierce or wound with, or as with, a pointed weapon. **2.** to thrust or plunge (a knife, etc.) into something. **3.** to penetrate sharply, like a knife. **4.** to make a thrusting or plunging motion at or in. **5.** to roughen the surface of (brickwork) so that it will hold plaster. **6. stab (someone) in the back,** *Colloq.* to do harm to (somebody), esp. somebody defenceless or unsuspecting, as by making a treacherous attack upon his reputation. *–v.i.* **7.** to thrust with or as with a knife or other pointed weapon: *to stab at an adversary.* **8.** to deliver a wound, as with a pointed weapon. *–n.* **9.** the act of stabbing. **10.** a thrust or blow with, or as with, a pointed weapon. **11.** a wound made by stabbing. **12.** a sudden, usu. painful sensation. **13.** *Colloq.* an attempt; try. **14.** *Rugby, Aus. Rules.* →**stab kick.** [ME, var. of Brit. d. *stob* in same sense, ? v. use of ME *stob* stick] – **stabber,** *n.*

**stabile** /ˈsteɪbaɪl/, *adj.* **1.** fixed in position; stable. **2.** *Med.* **a.** resistant to moderate degrees of heat. **b.** denoting or pertaining to a mode of application of electricity in which the active electrode is kept stationary over the part to be acted upon (opposed to *labile*). *–n.* **3.** a sculpture or construction of sheet metal, wood, etc., similar in concept and design to a mobile, but motionless. [L *stabilis* STABLE[2]]

**stabilise** /ˈsteɪbəlaɪz/, *v.,* **-lised, -lising.** *–v.t.* **1.** to make stable. **2.** to maintain at a given or unfluctuating level or quantity. **3.** *Aeron.* to put or keep (an aircraft) in stable equilibrium, as by some special device. *–v.i.* **4.** to become stable. Also, **stabilize.** – **stabilisation** /ˌsteɪbəlaɪˈzeɪʃən/, *n.*

**stabiliser** /ˈsteɪbəlaɪzə/, *n.* **1.** one who or that which stabilises. **2.** one of a pair of retractable horizontal planes fitted to a ship below the waterline to stabilise it. **3.** *Chem.* any substance which is added to explosives, plastics, paints, foods, chemicals, etc., in order to retard any undesirable spontaneous chemical or physical changes; an inhibitor. **4.** *U.S. Aeron.* tailplane. Also, **stabilizer.**

**stability** /stəˈbɪləti/, *n., pl.* **-ties. 1.** firmness in position. **2.** continuance without change; permanence. **3.** steadfastness, as of character or purpose. **4.** resistance to change, esp. adverse change. **5.** the ability of a ship or aircraft to return to its original upright position when laterally displaced. **6.** *Rom. Cath. Ch.* a vow taken by a Benedictine monk, binding him to remain a member of the same community and house.

**stab kick** /ˈstæb kɪk/, *n.* (in Rugby and Australian Rules) a short low drop kick, to send the ball to a team-mate or to gain distance quickly. Also, **stab.**

**stable**[1] /ˈsteɪbəl/, *n., v.,* **-bled, -bling.** *–n.* **1.** a building for the lodging and feeding of horses, cattle, etc. **2.** such a building with stalls. **3.** a collection of animals belonging in such a building. **4.** *Racing.* **a.** an establishment where racehorses are kept and trained. **b.** the horses belonging to, or the persons connected with, such an establishment. **5.** any centre of production or connected group of such centres as a group of newspapers, car factories, etc: *Jaguar and Morris are from the same stable.* **6.** *Music.* the performers who record for a particular recording company. **7.** the artists, potters, etc., who have a close association with a particular gallery. **8.** the writers, editors, etc., associated with a particular publishing house. *–v.t.* **9.** to put or lodge in or as in a stable. *–v.i.* **10.** to live in or as in a stable. [ME, from OF *estable,* from L *stabulum*]

**stable**[2] /ˈsteɪbəl/, *adj.* **1.** not likely to fall or give way, as a structure, support, foundation, etc.; firm; steady. **2.** able or likely to continue or last; enduring or permanent: *a stable government.* **3.** steadfast; not wavering or changeable, as a person, the mind, etc. **4.** *Physics.* having or showing an ability or tendency to maintain or re-establish position, form, etc.: *stable equilibrium.* **5.** *Chem.* not readily decomposing, as a compound; resisting molecular or chemical change. [ME, from F, from L *stabilis*] – **stableness,** *n.* – **stably,** *adv.*

**stableboy** /ˈsteɪbəlbɔɪ/, *n.* one who works in a stable. Also, **stableman** /ˈsteɪbəlmæn, -mən/.

**stable door** /ˈsteɪbəl dɔ/, *n.* a door cut through horizontally at half its height, with each half separately hung. Also, **Dutch door.**

**stable equilibrium** /– ikwəˈlɪbriəm/, *n.* a state of a body such that after any displacement the body will return to its original position.

**stabling** /ˈsteɪblɪŋ/, *n.* **1.** the act of putting into a stable. **2.** accommodation for horses, etc., in a stable or stables. **3.** stables collectively.

**stablish** /ˈstæblɪʃ/, *v.t. Archaic.* →**establish.**

**stab pass** /ˈstæb pas/, *n.* (in Australian Rules) a stab kick aimed at delivering the ball to a team-mate.

**stacc.,** *Music.* staccato.

**staccato** /stəˈkatoʊ/, *Music. –adj.* **1.** detached, disconnected, or abrupt. **2.** with breaks between the successive notes. *–adv.* **3.** in a staccato manner. Cf. **legato.** [It., pp. of *staccare,* short for *distaccare* DETACH]

**stack** /stæk/, *n.* **1.** a large, usu. circular or rectangular pile of hay, straw, or the like. **2.** any more or less orderly pile or heap. **3.** a number of chimneys or flues grouped together. **4.** a single chimney or funnel for smoke, or a vertical pipe inside or outside a building for passing waste products down, circulating heat, or expelling exhaust gases. **5.** *Geol.* a column or pillar of rock, isolated from the shore by the erosive action of waves. **6.** *Colloq.* a great quantity or number. **7.** a number of muskets or rifles hooked together to stand on the ground in a conical group. **8.** *Colloq.* a combination of amplifiers and speaker boxes. **9.** a measure for coal and wood, equal to 108 cubic feet or 3.06 cubic metres. **10.** *Aeron.* a number of aircraft circling at different altitudes above an aerodrome awaiting their signal to land. **11.** a motor vehicle accident, esp. one involving a number of vehicles. **12.** *Bldg Trades.* a pipe which conveys sewage and sullage waste to drainage in the ground. **13.** that part of a library to which the general user is denied access and in which the main holdings of a library are kept. **14.** (*pl.*) *Colloq.* a great amount. *–v.t.* **15.** to pile or arrange in a stack: *to stack hay.* **16.** to place (rifles, etc.) in a stack. **17.** to cover or load with something in stacks or piles. **18.** to arrange (playing cards in the pack) in an unfair manner. **19.** to bring a large number of one's own supporters to (a meeting) in order to outvote those of opposing views. **20.** *Aeron.* to control the aircraft waiting to land at an airport, so that they form a stack. **21.** to crash (a motor vehicle). **22. stack it on,** *Colloq.* to exaggerate one's concern, grief, anger, etc. **23. stack on a blue,** *Colloq.* to start; instigate. *–v.i.* **24.** to accumulate; add up (fol. by *up*). [ME *stak,* from Scand.; cf. Icel. *stakkr* haystack; akin to Russ. *stog* haystack] – **stacker,** *n.*

**stacked** /stækt/, *v.* **1.** past participle of **stack.** *–adj.* **2.** Also, **well stacked.** *Colloq.* (of a woman) having big breasts; buxom.

**stacks on the mill,** *n.* a children's game in which the participants form a stack, each newcomer lying on top of the others. [from the children's rhyme '*stacks on the mill,* more on still']

**stack-up** /ˈstæk-ʌp/, *n.* **1.** *Colloq.* an accident involving a number of vehicles, railway carriages, etc. *–adj.* **2.** of or pertaining to furniture, esp. chairs, designed so that one unit fits into another to form a stack for storage.

**stacte** /ˈstækti/, *n.* one of the sweet spices which composed the holy incense of the ancient Jews. Ex. 30:34. [L, from Gk *staktḗ,* fem. of *staktós* distilling in drops; replacing ME *stacten,* from L, acc. of *stactē*]

**staddle** /ˈstædl/, *n.* **1.** the lower part of a stack of corn, hay, etc. **2.** a supporting frame for a stack; a platform upon which a stack or rick is placed. **3.** any supporting base or framework. [ME *stathel,* OE *stathol,* Icel. *stödhull* milking place]

**stadholder** /ˈstædhoʊldə/, *n.* →**stadtholder.**

**stadia**[1] /ˈsteɪdiə/, *n.* **1.** a method of surveying in which distances are read by noting the interval on a graduated rod (**stadia rod**) intercepted by two parallel crosshairs (**stadia hairs** or **wires**) mounted in the telescope of a surveyor's level, the rod being placed at one end of the distance to be measured and the theodolite at the other. *–adj.* **2.** pertaining to stadia surveying. [orig. uncert.; probably special use of STADIA[2]]

**stadia**[2] /ˈsteɪdiə/, *n.* plural of **stadium.**

**stadiometer** /steɪdiˈɒmətə/, *n.* an instrument for measuring the lengths of curves, dashed lines, etc., by running a toothed wheel over them. [*stadio-* (combining form of STADIUM) + -METER[1]]

**stadium** /ˈsteɪdiəm/, *n., pl.* **-dia** /-diə/, **-diums. 1.** a sporting facility, often, though not necessarily, enclosed, comprising an arena, tiers or seats for spectators, parking, etc. **2.** an ancient Greek course for races, typically semicircular. **3.** a stage of development in a process, disease, etc. [L, from Gk *stádion,* an ancient Greek unit of length]

**stadtholder** /ˈstædhoʊldə/, *n.* **1.** the chief magistrate of the former republic of the United Provinces of the Netherlands. **2.** (formerly, in the Netherlands) the viceroy or governor of a province. Also, **stadholder.** [D *stadhouder,* from *stad* place, city + *houder* holder]

**staff**[1] /staf/, *n., pl.* **staffs, staves** /steɪvz/, *adj., v. –n.* **1.** a stick, pole, rod, or wand for aid in walking or climbing, for use as a weapon, etc. **2.** a rod or wand serving as an ensign of office or authority, as a crosier, baton, truncheon, or mace. **3.** a pole on which a flag is hung or displayed. **4.** something which serves to support or sustain: *bread is the staff of life.* **5.** a body of assistants to a manager, superintendent, or executive head. **6.** a body of persons charged with carrying out the work of an establishment or executing some undertaking. **7.** the teaching personnel of a school, college, or the like. **8.** *Mil., Navy.* **a.** a body of officers without command authority, appointed to assist a commanding officer. **b.** the parts of any army concerned with administrative matters, planning, etc., instead of with actual participation in combat. **9.** *Railways.* a bar without which the driver of a locomotive about to enter a section of the permanent way with only a single track may not proceed, and the receipt of which constitutes his signal to proceed. **10.** *Music.* →**stave** (def. 5). **11.** *Archaic.* a stick or pole forming part of something, as the shaft of a spear, a rung of a ladder, etc. *–adj.* **12.** of, or being a member of, a military or naval staff or unit: *staff officer. –v.t.* **13.** to provide with a staff.

[ME; OE *stæf*, c. D *staf*, G *Stab*, Icel. *stafr*]

**staff**[2] /staf/, *n.* a kind of plaster combined with fibrous material, used for temporary ornamental buildings, etc. [orig. unknown]

**staff hand** /'– hænd/, *n.* an employee who is principally engaged in the direction and control of other employees.

**staff notation** /– noʊ'teɪʃən/, *n.* musical notation in which a stave is used.

**staff officer** /'– ɒfəsə/, *n.* a commissioned officer appointed to a staff position at a senior military headquarters.

**Staffordshire terrier** /stæfədʃə 'tɛriə/, *n.* one of a breed of stocky dogs having a short, glossy coat of various colours.

**staffroom** /'stafrum/, *n.* a common room for the staff of a school, college, etc.

**staff sergeant** /'staf sadʒənt/, *n.* a non-commissioned officer with the rank of sergeant, acting in a specialised capacity, usu. in an administrative position.

**stag** /stæg/, *n., v.,* **stagged, stagging,** *adj.* –*n.* **1.** an adult male deer. **2.** the male of various other animals. **3.** *Colloq.* a man, esp. one at a social gathering exclusively for men. **4.** an animal castrated after maturation of the sex organs. **5.** *Stock Exchange.* one who applies for shares of a new issue in the hope of a quick sale at a profit. –*v.i.* **6.** *Colloq.* to go to a social function without a woman partner. –*adj.* **7.** *Colloq.* for or of men only: *a stag party.* [ME *stagge,* OE (unrecorded) *stagga,* akin to Icel. *steggr* male fox, tomcat]

stag

**stag-beetle** /'stæg-bitl/, *n.* any of the lamellicorn beetles constituting the family Lucanidae. The males have mandibles resembling a stag's antlers.

**stage** /steɪdʒ/, *n., v.,* **staged, staging.** –*n.* **1.** a single step or degree in a process; a particular period in a process of development. **2.** a raised platform or floor, as for speakers, performers, etc. **3.** *Theat.* **a.** the platform in a theatre on which the actors perform. **b.** this platform with all the parts of the theatre, and all the apparatus behind the proscenium. **4.** the theatre, the drama, or the dramatic profession. **5.** the scene of any action. **6.** a stagecoach. **7.** (formerly) a place of rest on a journey; a regular stopping place of a stagecoach or the like, for the change of horses, etc. **8.** →**section** (def. 12). **9.** the distance between two places of rest on a journey; each of the portions of a journey. **10.** a portion or period of a course of action, of life, etc. **11.** *N.Z.* each year in the study of a university subject. **12.** *Zool.* **a.** any one of the major time periods in the development of an insect, as the embryonic, larval, pupal, and imaginal stages. **b.** any one of the periods of larval growth between moults. **13.** *Econ., Sociol.* a major phase of the economic or sociological life of man or society: *the matriarchal stage.* **14.** *Geol.* a division of stratified rocks next in rank to series, representing deposits formed during the fraction of an epoch that is called an age. **15.** the small platform of a microscope on which the object is examined. **16.** *Radio.* a part of a complex circuit, as a transistor and its associated passive elements in an amplifier having several transistors. **17.** a powered section of a rocket which can be jettisoned after firing. **18. by easy stages,** without rushing; working or travelling with many stops. **19. go on the stage,** to take up acting as a career. **20. hold the stage,** to be the centre of attention. –*v.t.* **21.** to put, represent, or exhibit on or as on a stage. **22.** to furnish with a stage or staging. **23.** to write, direct, or produce (a play) as if the action were taking place in a specific place or period of time. **24.** to plan, organise, or carry out (an action) in which each participant has a specific task to perform. **25.** to arrange; set up, as for a particular event: *he staged a comeback.* –*v.i.* **26.** to be suitable for presentation on the stage. **27.** to travel by stages, or by stagecoach. [ME, from OF *estage,* from L *stāre* stand]

**stagecoach** /'steɪdʒkoʊtʃ/, *n.* a coach that runs regularly over a fixed route with passengers, parcels, etc.

**stagecraft** /'steɪdʒkraft/, *n.* skill in or the art of writing, adapting, or staging plays.

**stage direction** /'steɪdʒ dəˌrɛkʃən/, *n.* an instruction written into the script of a play, indicating actions or movements of the performers, or requirements for the settings, costumes, etc.

stagecoach

**stage door** /– 'dɔ/, *n.* a door at the back or side of a theatre, used by performers and other authorised theatre personnel.

**stage-door johnny** /ˌsteɪdʒ-dɔ 'dʒɒni/, *n.* a man who loiters near a stage door in the hope of escorting one of the female performers after the show.

**stage effect** /'steɪdʒ əfɛkt/, *n.* an effect, as of noise, music, lighting, used in producing a play, etc.

**stage fright** /'– fraɪt/, *n.* nervousness experienced on facing an audience, esp. for the first time.

**stagehand** /'steɪdʒhænd/, *n.* a person employed to move properties, regulate lighting, etc., in a dramatic production.

**stage left** /steɪdʒ 'lɛft/, *n.* the part of a theatre stage that is left of the centre as an actor faces the audience.

**stage-manage** /'steɪdʒ-mænɪdʒ/, *v.t.,* **-aged, -aging. 1.** to superintend the performance, as of a play and to regulate the stage arrangements. **2.** to contrive unobtrusively to produce a particular response in a group, as at a political meeting.

**stage-manager** /'steɪdʒ-mænədʒə/, *n.* one who superintends the performance of a play and regulates the stage arrangements. – **stage-management,** *n.*

**stage-name** /'steɪdʒ-neɪm/, *n.* a name, other than the real one, assumed by an actor or actress.

**stager** /'steɪdʒə/, *n.* **1.** Also, **old stager.** a person of experience in some profession, way of life, etc.; an old hand. **2.** *Archaic.* an actor.

**stage race** /'steɪdʒ reɪs/, *n.* (in cycling, etc.) a road race held over a number of days, won by the rider, driver, etc. who covers the distance in the shortest time.

**stage right** /– 'raɪt/, *n.* the part of a theatre stage which is right of the centre as an actor faces the audience.

**stagestruck** /'steɪdʒstrʌk/, *adj.* obsessed with the desire to go on the stage.

**stage whisper** /'steɪdʒ wɪspə/, *n.* **1.** a loud whisper on a stage, meant to be heard by the audience. **2.** a whisper meant to be heard by others than the person addressed.

**stagflation** /stæg'fleɪʃən/, *n.* a situation in the economy in which stagnant economic growth is accompanied by inflation.

**stagger** /'stægə/, *v.i.* **1.** to walk, move, or stand unsteadily; sway. **2.** to begin to doubt or waver, as in opinion; hesitate. –*v.t.* **3.** to cause to reel, totter, or become unsteady. **4.** to shock; render helpless with amazement or the like. **5.** to cause to waver or falter. **6.** to arrange in a zigzag order or manner, as spokes in the hub of a wheel. **7.** *Aeron.* to arrange the upper wing of a biplane **a.** ahead of the lower wing (**positive stagger**) or **b.** behind the lower wing (**negative stagger**). **8.** to arrange in some other order or manner than the regular, uniform, or usual one, esp. at such intervals that there is a continuous overlapping: *to stagger lunch hours so that the cafeteria is not overcrowded.* –*n.* **9.** the act of staggering; a reeling or tottering movement or motion. **10.** a staggered order or arrangement. **11.** *Aeron.* **a.** a staggered arrangement of planes. **b.** the amount of staggering. [var. of obs. or d. *stacker,* ME *staker(en),* from Scand.; cf. Icel. *stakra*] – **staggerer,** *n.* – **staggeringly,** *adv.*

**stagger-bush** /'stægə-bʊʃ/, *n.* an American shrub, *Lyonia mariana,* with a foliage poisonous to animals.

**staggered start** /stægəd 'stat/, *n.* a method of starting a race in which competitors running in the outer lanes of a circular track are deployed progressively further ahead of the starting judge so that they run the same distance as the runner on the inner lane.

**staggering bob** /stægərɪŋ 'bɒb/, *n.* **1.** a very young calf. **2.** meat from such a calf.

**stagger-weed** /'stægə-wid/, *n.* a cosmopolitan annual herb, *Stachys arvensis,* a common weed of cultivated ground.

**staghorn fern** /'stæghɔn fɜn/, *n.* any of various ferns of the tropical and subtropical genus *Platycerium,* family Polypodiaceae, having large fertile leaves resembling the horns of a stag, as *P. grande* of Queensland. Also, **elkhorn fern.**

**staghound** /'stæghaʊnd/, *n.* a hound resembling the foxhound, but larger, used for hunting stags, etc.

**staging** /'steɪdʒɪŋ/, *n.* **1.** the act or process of putting a play on the stage. **2.** a temporary platform or structure of posts and boards for support, as in buildings; scaffolding. **3.** the business of running stagecoaches. **4.** the act of travelling by stages or by stagecoach.

**staging area** /'– ɛəriə/, *n.* a predetermined place of assembly for troops to form up prior to an action, embarkation, etc. Also, **staging camp.**

**stagnant** /'stægnənt/, *adj.* **1.** not running or flowing, as water, air, etc. **2.** foul from standing, as a pool of water. **3.** inactive, sluggish, or dull. **4.** making no progress; not developing. [L *stagnans,* ppr.] – **stagnancy,** *n.* – **stagnantly,** *adv.*

**stagnate** /'stægneɪt, stæg'neɪt/, *v.i.,* **-nated, -nating. 1.** to cease to run or flow, as water, air, etc. **2.** to become foul from standing, as a pool of water. **3.** to become inactive, sluggish, or dull. **4.** to make no progress; stop developing. [L *stagnātus,* pp.] – **stagnation** /stæg'neɪʃən/, *n.*

**stag party** /'stæg pati/, *n.* **1.** a party exclusively for men. **2.** →**bucks party.**

**stag's-horn moss** /ˌstægz-hɔn 'mɒs/, *n.* a small club moss, *Lycopodium clavatum,* a homosporous pteridophyte of hills and mountains.

**stagy** /'steɪdʒi/, *adj.,* **stagier, stagiest.** of, pertaining to or suggestive of the stage; theatrical. – **stagily,** *adv.*

**staid** /steɪd/, *adj.* **1.** of settled or sedate character; not flighty or capricious. **2.** *Rare.* fixed, settled, or permanent. *–v.* **3.** a past tense and past participle of **stay**[1]. [var. of *stayed,* pp. of STAY[1]] – **staidly,** *adv.* – **staidness,** *n.*

**stain** /steɪn/, *n.* **1.** a discolouration produced by foreign matter; a spot. **2.** a natural spot or patch of different colour, as on the body of an animal. **3.** a cause of reproach; blemish: *a stain on one's reputation.* **4.** a solution or suspension of colouring matter in water, spirit, or oil, designed to colour a surface (esp. wooden) by penetration without hiding it. **5.** a dye made into a solution and used to colour textiles, etc. **6.** a reagent or dye used in staining microscopic specimens. *–v.t.* **7.** to discolour with spots or streaks of foreign matter. **8.** to bring reproach upon; blemish. **9.** to sully with guilt or infamy; corrupt. **10.** to colour in a particular way. **11.** to colour with something which penetrates the substance. **12.** to treat (a microscopic specimen) with some reagent or dye in order to colour the whole or parts and so give distinctness, contrast of tissues, etc. *–v.i.* **13.** to produce a stain. **14.** to become stained; take a stain. [ME *steyne,* from Scand. (cf. Icel. *steina* to paint); in some senses, aphetic var. of DISTAIN] – **stainable,** *adj.* – **stainer,** *n.* – **stainless,** *adj.* – **stainlessly,** *adv.*

**stained glass** /steɪnd 'glas/, *n.* coloured, enamelled, or painted glass, as used in church windows. – **stained-glass,** *adj.*

**stainer** /'steɪnə/, *n.* **1.** one who or that which stains. **2.** a coloured pigment which is added in small quantity to a prepared paint in order to modify its colour.

**stainless steel** /steɪnləs 'stil/, *n.* a hard steel alloyed with a high percentage of chromium, from 8 to approximately 25 per cent, proof against rust and many corrosive agents.

**stair** /stɛə/, *n.* **1.** one of a series or flight of steps forming a means of passage from one storey or level to another, as in a building. **2.** (*pl.*) such steps collectively, esp. as forming a flight or a series of flights. **3.** a series or flight of steps; a stairway: *a winding stair.* **4. below stairs,** in the servants quarters. [ME *steire,* OE *stǣger,* c. D and LG *steiger* landing stage]

**stair-carpet** /'stɛə-kapət/, *n.* a long, narrow carpet used for covering stairs.

**staircase** /'stɛəkeɪs/, *n.* a flight of stairs with its framework, bannisters, etc., or a series of such flights.

**stairfoot** /'stɛəfʊt/, *n.* the bottom of a staircase.

**stairhead** /'stɛəhɛd/, *n.* the top of a staircase.

**stair-rod** /'stɛə-rɒd/, *n.* one of a series of rods fixed into the angles of a flight of stairs for holding the stair-carpet in place.

**stairway** /'stɛəweɪ/, *n.* a way up and down by a series of stairs; a staircase.

**stairwell** /'stɛəwɛl/, *n.* the vertical shaft or opening containing a stairway.

**staithe** /steɪð/, *n.* a riverside berth or pier at which ships can load coal by gravity into their holds. [ME, from Scand.; cf. Icel. *stöth,* c. OE *stæth* shore]

**stake**[1] /steɪk/, *n., v.,* **staked, staking.** *–n.* **1.** a stick or post pointed at one end for driving into the ground as a boundary mark, a part of a fence, a support for a plant, etc. **2.** a post, esp. one to which a person is bound for execution, usu. by burning. **3.** one of a number of vertical posts fitting into sockets or staples on the edge of the platform of a vehicle, as to retain the load. **4. pull up stakes,** *Colloq.* to leave one's job, home, etc., and move away. **5. the stake,** the punishment of death by burning. *–v.t.* **6.** to mark with stakes (oft. fol. by *off* or *out*). **7.** to possess, lay claim to or reserve a share of (land, profit, etc.) (sometimes fol. by *out* or *off*): *to stake a claim.* **8.** to protect, separate, or close off by a barrier of stakes. **9.** to support with a stake or stakes, as a plant. **10.** to tether or secure to a stake, as an animal. **11.** to fasten with a stake or stakes. **12.** to surround (a building, etc.) for the purposes of a raid, a siege or keeping watch (fol. by *out*). [ME; OE *staca,* c. D *staak,* G *Stake;* akin to STICK[1]]

**stake**[2] /steɪk/, *n., v.,* **staked, staking.** *–n.* **1.** that which is wagered in a game, race, or contest. **2.** an interest held in something. **3.** *Colloq.* personal concern, interest, involvement, etc. **4.** the funds with which a gambler operates. **5.** (*oft. pl.*) a prize in a race or contest. **6.** (*pl. construed as sing.*) a race in which equal amounts are contributed by all the owners of the competing horses for prize money. **7.** (*pl. construed as sing.*) (*joc.*) a fictitious race or contest: *beauty stakes.* **8.** *U.S. Colloq.* →**grubstake. 9. at stake,** involved; in a state of being staked or at hazard. *–v.t.* **10.** to put at hazard upon the result of a game, the event of a contingency, etc.; wager; venture or hazard. **11.** to furnish with necessaries or resources, often by way of a business venture with a view to a possible return. **12.** to place under surveillance (fol. by *out*). [cf. D *staken* fix, place]

**stakeboat** /'steɪkboʊt/, *n.* a moored boat from which the stern of a competing boat is held before starting a race.

**stakeholder** /'steɪkhoʊldə/, *n.* the holder of the stakes of a wager, etc.

**stake-out** /'steɪk-aʊt/, *n.* the act of secretly surrounding a building, etc., usu. by police, in order to keep watch on it, make a raid, or place it under siege.

**Stakhanovism** /stæ'kænəˌvɪzəm/, *n.* a method developed (1935) in the Soviet Union to increase production by rewarding individual initiative. [named after A. G. *Stakhanov,* b. 1905, Russian coal-miner. See -ISM] – **Stakhanovite,** *adj., n.*

**stalactite** /'stæləktaɪt/, *n.* a deposit, usu. of calcium carbonate, shaped like an icicle, hanging from the roof of a cave or the like, and formed by the dripping of percolating calcareous water. [NL *stalactītēs,* from *stalact-* (from Gk *stalaktós* dripping) + *-ītēs* -ITE[1]] – **stalactitic** /stælək'tɪtɪk/, **stalactitical** /stælək'tɪtɪkəl/, *adj.*

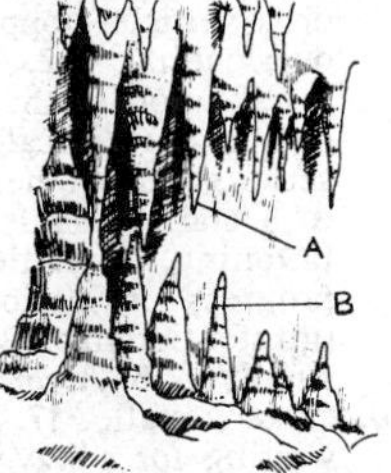

A, stalactite; B, stalagmite

**stalag** /'stælæg/, *n.* a German camp for prisoners of war. [G *Sta(mm)lag(er)* group camp]

**stalagmite** /'stæləgmaɪt/, *n.* a deposit, usu. of calcium carbonate, more or less resembling an inverted stalactite, formed on the floor of a cave or the like by the dripping of percolating calcareous water. [NL *stalagmītēs,* from *stalagm-* (from Gk *stalagmós* dropping) + *-ītēs* -ITE[1]] – **stalagmitic** /stæləg'mɪtɪk/, **stalagmitical** /stæləg'mɪtɪkəl/, *adj.*

**stalagmometry** /stæləg'mɒmətri/, *n.* the measurement of surface tension by determining the weight or volume of liquid drops.

**stale**[1] /steɪl/, *adj.,* **staler, stalest,** *v.,* **staled, staling.** *–adj.* **1.** not fresh; vapid or flat, as beverages; dry or hardened, as bread. **2.** having lost novelty or interest; hackneyed; trite: *a stale joke.* **3.** having lost fresh vigour, quick intelligence, initiative, or the like, as from overstrain, boredom, etc. **4.** *Law.* having lost force or effectiveness through absence of action, as a claim. *–v.t.* **5.** to make stale. *–v.i.* **6.** to become

i = peat ɪ = pit ɛ = pet æ = pat a = part ɒ = pot ʌ = putt ɔ = port ʊ = put u = pool ɜ = pert ə = apart aɪ = buy eɪ = bay ɔɪ = boy aʊ = how
oʊ = hoe ɪə = here ɛə = hair ʊə = tour g = give θ = thin ð = then ʃ = show ʒ = measure tʃ = choke dʒ = joke ŋ = sing j = you õ = Fr. bon

stale. [ME, ? from AF **estale* (F *étale* still (water), from *estaler* stop] – **stalely,** *adv.* – **staleness,** *n.*

**stale**[2] /steɪl/, *n., v.,* **staled, staling.** *–n.* **1.** urine, esp. of horses and cattle. *–v.i.* **2.** (of livestock, esp. horses and cattle) to urinate. [ME; special use of STALE[1]]

**stalemate** /ˈsteɪlmeɪt/, *n., v.,* **-mated, -mating.** *–n.* **1.** *Chess.* a position of the pieces when no move can be made by a player without putting his own king in check, the result being a draw. **2.** any position in which no action can be taken; a deadlock. *–v.t.* **3.** to subject to a stalemate. **4.** to bring to a standstill. [*stale* a standstill (special use of STALE[1]) + MATE[2]]

**stalk**[1] /stɔk/, *n.* **1.** the stem or main axis of a plant. **2.** any slender supporting or connecting part of a plant, as the petiole of a leaf, the peduncle of a flower, or the funicle of an ovule. **3.** a similar structural part of an animal. **4.** a stem, shaft, or slender supporting part of anything. [ME *stalke,* from OE *stæla* stalk + *-k* suffix] – **stalkless,** *adj.* – **stalklike,** *adj.*

**stalk**[2] /stɔk/, *v.i.* **1.** to pursue or approach game, etc., stealthily. **2.** to walk with slow, stiff, or haughty strides. **3.** to proceed with slow, implacable and often sinister movement: *famine stalked through the land.* **4.** *Obs.* to walk or go stealthily along. *–v.t.* **5.** to pursue (game, a person, etc.) stealthily. **6.** to stalk over or through. *–n.* **7.** an act or course of stalking game or the like. **8.** a slow, stiff stride or gait. [ME *stalke,* OE *-stealcian* move stealthily, apparently from (with *-k* suffix) OE *stalian* go stealthily. See STEAL] – **stalker,** *n.*

**stalking-horse** /ˈstɔkɪŋ-hɔs/, *n.* **1.** a horse, or a figure of a horse, behind which a hunter conceals himself in stalking game. **2.** anything put forward to mask plans or efforts; a pretext. **3.** *Chiefly U.S. Politics.* a candidate used to screen a more important candidate or to draw votes from a rival and hence cause his defeat.

**stalky** /ˈstɔki/, *adj.* **1.** abounding in stalks. **2.** stalk-like; long and slender. **3.** (of wine) denoting the presence of the bitter flavour of stalks in a wine. – **stalkily,** *adv.* – **stalkiness,** *n.*

**stall**[1] /stɔl/, *n.* **1.** a compartment in a stable or shed, for the accommodation of one animal. **2.** a stable or shed for horses or cattle. **3.** a booth, bench, table, or stand on which merchandise is displayed or exposed for sale. **4.** →**carrel. 5.** one of a number of fixed enclosed seats in the choir or chancel of a church for the use of the clergy. **6.** a chair-like seat in a theatre, separated from others by armrests. **7.** (*pl.*) the front part of the auditorium on the ground floor of a theatre. **8.** a small compartment or chamber for any of various purposes. **9.** a working area in a mine. **10.** a sheath or cover for a finger or toe. **11.** the fact or an instance of an engine or a vehicle stopping, as through inadequate fuel supply or overloading. **12.** *Aeron.* a condition of an aeroplane in which a reduction in the lift of the wings caused by their being at or above a critical angle or by too low an airspeed results in serious loss of height and control. *–v.t.* **13.** to put or keep in a stall or stalls, as animals. **14.** to confine in a stall for fattening, as cattle. **15.** to bring to a standstill; check the progress or motion of, esp. of a vehicle or an engine by unintentionally overloading it or giving an inadequate fuel supply. **16.** *Aeron.* to fly (an aeroplane) in such a way as to cause a stall. **17.** *Surfing.* to slow down (the board), as while waiting for a wave to build up height. **18.** to cause to stick fast, as in mire or snow. *–v.i.* **19.** to come to a standstill; be brought to a stop, esp. unintentionally. **20.** to stick fast, as in mire. **21.** *Aeron.* **a.** (of an aeroplane) to become stalled. **b.** (of an aviator) to stall an aeroplane. **22.** to occupy a stall, as an animal. [ME; OE *steall,* c. G *Stall*]

**stall**[2] /stɔl/, *Colloq.* *–n.* **1.** anything used as a pretext, pretence, or trick. *–v.i.* **2.** to act evasively or deceptively. **3.** *Sport.* to play below one's best in order to deceive for any reason. **4. stall for time,** to engage in a delaying tactic. *–v.t.* **5.** to put off, evade, or deceive (oft. fol. by *off*). [var. of late ME *stale* decoy bird, from AF *estale,* from OE *stæl* (in *stælhrān* decoy reindeer), akin to G *Stell* (in *Stellvogel* decoy bird)]

**stallage** /ˈstɔlɪdʒ/, *n.* rent for the right to erect a stall in a marketplace, on a fairground, or elsewhere.

**stall-feed** /ˈstɔl-fid/, *v.t.,* **-fed, -feeding. 1.** to keep and feed (an animal) in a stall. **2.** to fatten by this process, as an animal for killing.

**stalling angle** /ˈstɔlɪŋ ˌæŋgəl/, *n.* the angle of attack providing maximum lift for an aircraft; below this angle the airflow becomes turbulent, leading to an abrupt loss of lift. Also, **stall angle.**

**stallion** /ˈstæljən/, *n.* a male horse not castrated, esp. one kept for breeding. [ME *stalun,* from OF *estalon;* of Gmc orig.]

**stall speed** /ˈstɔl spid/, *n.* the slowest speed at which an aircraft can maintain level flight and below which it stalls.

**stalwart** /ˈstɔlwət/, *adj.* **1.** strongly and stoutly built; well-developed and robust. **2.** strong and brave; valiant. **3.** firm, steadfast, or uncompromising. *–n.* **4.** a physically stalwart person. **5.** a steadfast or uncompromising partisan. [ME; Scot. var. of *stalward,* earlier *stalwurthe,* OE *stælwierthe* serviceable, from *stǣl* (contraction of *stathol* foundation) + *wierthe* WORTH[1]] – **stalwartly,** *adv.* – **stalwartness,** *n.*

**stamen** /ˈsteɪmən/, *n., pl.* **stamens, stamina** /ˈstæmənə/. the pollen-bearing organ of a flower, consisting of the filament and the anther. [L: thread, warp in the upright loom]

S

S, stamens of a lily

**stamin** /ˈstæmən/, *n.* a coarse woollen fabric. [ME, from MF *(e)stamine,* from L *staminea,* adj., consisting of threads; akin to STAMEN]

**stamina**[1] /ˈstæmənə/, *n.* **1.** strength of physical constitution; power to endure disease, fatigue, privation, etc. [L, pl. of *stāmen* thread (specifically, those spun by the Fates determining length of life)]

**stamina**[2] /ˈstæmənə/, *n.* a plural of **stamen.**

**staminal** /ˈstæmənəl/, *adj.* **1.** of or pertaining to stamina. **2.** *Bot.* of or pertaining to stamens.

**staminate** /ˈstæmənət, -neɪt/, *adj.* **1.** having a stamen or stamens. **2.** having stamens but no pistils.

**staminiferous** /stæməˈnɪfərəs/, *adj.* bearing or having a stamen or stamens.

**staminodium** /stæməˈnoudiəm/, *n., pl.* **-dia** /-diə/. **1.** a sterile or abortive stamen. **2.** a part resembling such a stamen. Also, **staminode** /ˈstæmənoud/. [NL. See STAMEN, -ODE[1], -IUM]

**staminody** /ˈstæməˌnoudi/, *n.* the metamorphosis of any of various flower organs (as a sepal or a petal) into a stamen.

**stammel** /ˈstæməl/, *Obs.* *–n.* **1.** a coarse woollen cloth, usu. dyed red. **2.** the colour red. *–adj.* **3.** red. [ME, from MF *(e)stamel;* akin to STAMEN]

**stammer** /ˈstæmə/, *v.i.* **1.** to speak with involuntary breaks and pauses or with spasmodic repetitions of syllables or sounds. *–v.t.* **2.** to say with a stammer (oft. fol. by *out*). *–n.* **3.** a stammering mode of utterance. **4.** a stammered utterance. [ME; OE *stamerian,* akin to G *stammeln*] – **stammerer,** *n.* – **stammeringly,** *adv.*

**stamp** /stæmp/, *v.t.* **1.** to strike or beat with a forcible downward thrust of the foot. **2.** to bring (the foot) down forcibly or smartly on the ground, floor, etc. **3.** to trample, force, drive, etc., by or as by beating down with the foot (usu. fol. by *out* or *on*): *to stamp out a fire or a rebellion.* **4.** to crush or pound with or as with a pestle. **5.** to impress with a particular mark or device, as to indicate genuineness, approval, ownership, etc. **6.** to impress with an official mark. **7.** to mark or impress with any characters, words, designs, etc. **8.** to impress (a design, figure, words, etc.) on something; imprint deeply or permanently on anything. **9.** to affix an adhesive paper stamp to (a letter, etc.). **10.** to characterise, distinguish, or reveal. *–v.i.* **11.** to bring the foot down forcibly or smartly, as in crushing something, expressing rage, etc. **12.** to walk with forcible or heavy, resounding steps: *to stamp out of a room in anger.* *–n.* **13.** the act or an instance of stamping. **14.** a die, engraved block, or the like, for impressing a design, characters, words, or marks. **15.** an impression, design, characters, words, etc., made with or as with a stamp. **16.** an official mark indicating genuineness, validity, etc., or payment of a duty or charge. **17.** the impression of a public seal required for revenue purposes, to be obtained from a government office, for a fee, on the paper or parchment on which deeds, bills, receipts, etc., are written. **18.** a peculiar or distinctive impress or mark: *a story which bears the stamp of truth.* **19.** character, kind, or type. **20.** a small adhesive piece of paper printed with a distinctive design, issued by a government for a fixed sum, for attaching to documents, goods subject to duty, letters, etc., to show that a charge has been paid: *an excise stamp, a postage stamp.* **21.** a similar piece of paper issued by a private organisation to show that the charges for postage have been paid: *a local stamp.* **22.** a similar piece of paper issued privately for various purposes: *a trading stamp.* **23.** an instrument for stamping, crushing, or pounding. **24.** a heavy piece of iron or the like, as in a stamp mill, for dropping on and crushing ore or other material. [early ME *stampen,* c. G *stampfen*]

**stamp-collector** /ˈstæmp-kəlɛktə/, *n.* a philatelist. – **stamp-collecting,** *n.*

**stamp duty** /ˈstæmp djuti/, *n.* a tax imposed on certain legal documents, as cheques, receipts, conveyances, etc., on which a stamp is impressed or affixed.

**stampede** /stæmˈpid/, *n., v.,* **-peded, -peding.** *–n.* **1.** a sudden scattering or headlong flight of a body of cattle or horses in fright. **2.** any headlong general flight or rush. *–v.i.* **3.** to scatter or flee in a stampede. **4.** to make an unconcerted general rush. *–v.t.* **5.** to cause to stampede. [Mex. Sp. *estampida,* from *estampar* press, of Gmc orig. See STAMP] – **stampeder,** *n.*

**stamper** /ˈstæmpə/, *n.* **1.** one who or that which stamps. **2.** one who applies postmarks and cancels postage stamps in a post office. **3.** an instrument for stamping. **4.** a pestle, esp. one in a stamp mill. **5.** the final negative metal mould used in manufacturing gramophone records.

**stamp-head** /ˈstæmp-hɛd/, *n.* a cast iron weight, fixed on the end of a shank and used as a pestle in a stamp mill.

**stamping ground** /ˈstæmpɪŋ graʊnd/, *n. Colloq.* the habitual place of resort of an animal or person.

**stamp mill** /ˈstæmp mɪl/, *n.* a mill or machine in which ore is crushed to powder by means of heavy stamps or pestles.

**stamp office** /ˈ– ɒfəs/, *n.* an office at which stamp duties are received and stamps issued.

**stance** /stæns/, *n.* **1.** the position or bearing of the body while standing: *a boxer's stance.* **2.** emotional or intellectual attitude to something: *a hostile stance towards modern poetry.* **3.** *Cricket, Golf, etc.* the relative position of a player's feet when making a stroke. **4.** *Mountaineering.* **a.** the position of a climber when belaying another. **b.** a ledge where a belay can be made. [F, from It. *stanza* station, stopping place, room, from L *stans,* ppr., standing]

**stanch**[1] /stæntʃ, stantʃ/, *v.t., v.i., n.* →**staunch**[1]. [ME, from OF *estanchier*] – **stancher,** *n.*

**stanch**[2] /stantʃ, stɒntʃ/, *adj.* →**staunch**[2]. – **stanchly,** *adv.* – **stanchness,** *n.*

**stanchion** /ˈstæntʃən, -ʃən/, *n.* **1.** an upright bar, beam, post, or support, as in a window, stall, ship, etc. *–v.t.* **2.** to furnish with stanchions. **3.** to secure by or to a stanchion or stanchions. [ME *stanchon,* from OF *estanchon,* from *estance* STANCE]

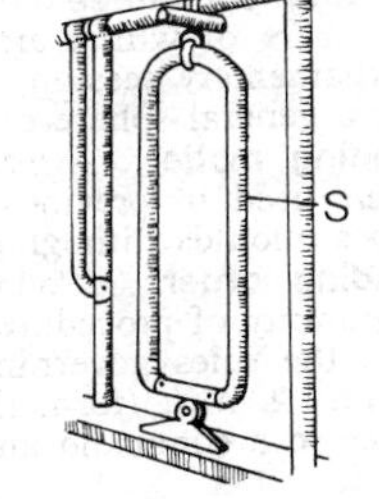

S, stanchion of a cattle stall

**stand** /stænd/, *v.,* **stood, standing,** *n. –v.i.* **1.** to take or keep an upright position on the feet (opposed to *sit, lie,* etc.). **2.** to have a specified height when in this position: *he stands two metres in his socks.* **3.** to remain motionless or steady on the feet. **4.** to cease moving; halt; stop: *stand and deliver!, to stand and fight.* **5.** to take a position or stand as indicated: *to stand aside.* **6.** to remain firm or steadfast, as in a cause. **7.** to take up or maintain a position or attitude with respect to a person, question, or the like: *to stand sponsor for a person.* **8.** to adopt a certain course or attitude, as of adherence, support, opposition, or resistance. **9.** (of things) to be in an upright position (opposed to *lie*); be set on end; rest on or as on a support; be set, placed, or fixed. **10.** to be located or situated. **11.** to be at a certain degree: *the temperature stands at 25° C.* **12.** (of an account, score, etc.) to show a specified position of the parties concerned: *the account stands in my favour.* **13.** to remain erect and entire; resist change, decay, or destruction. **14.** to continue in force or remain valid. **15.** to become or remain still or stationary. **16.** to be or become stagnant, as water. **17.** (of persons or things) to be or remain in a specified state, condition, relation, etc.: *he stood alone in his opinion.* **18.** to be likely or in a position as specified: *to stand to lose.* **19.** to become or be a candidate, as for parliament. **20.** *Naut.* **a.** to take or hold a particular course at sea. **b.** to move in a certain direction: *to stand offshore.* **21.** (of a stallion) to be at stud. *–v.t.* **22.** to cause to stand; set upright; set. **23.** to face or encounter: *to stand an assault.* **24.** to endure, undergo, or submit to: *to stand trial.* **25.** to endure or undergo without hurt or damage, or without giving way: *he cannot stand the sun.* **26.** to tolerate. **27.** *Colloq.* to bear the expense of; pay for. *–v.* **28.** Some special verb phrases are:

**stand a chance,** to have a chance or possibility, esp. of winning, surviving, or the like.

**stand back,** to get out of the way, as by moving backwards.

**stand by, 1.** to wait in a state of readiness: *stand by for further instructions.* **2.** to aid, uphold, or sustain. **3.** to adhere to (an agreement, promise, etc.); abide by.

**stand down, 1.** to go off duty. **2.** to withdraw, as from a contest. **3.** *Law.* to leave the witness box. **4.** to dismiss (employees) who are not involved in direct strike action but who are not able to carry out their normal duties as a result.

**stand for, 1.** to endure or tolerate: *I won't stand for any nonsense.* **2.** to represent: *the symbol x stands for an unknown quantity.* **3.** to be an advocate of: *he stands for racial equality.* **4.** to be a candidate for: *to stand for parliament.*

**stand in, 1.** to act as a substitute or representative. **2.** to join in; take a part in.

**stand in good stead,** to be of use or advantage to: *his knowledge of Indonesian stood him in good stead in Jakarta.*

**stand off, 1.** to keep at a distance. **2.** to suspend from employment, esp. temporarily: *owing to the drop in sales, the factory is standing men off.* **3.** *Rugby Football.* to stand outside the centre of play waiting for the ball to come free and an opportunity to attack.

**stand on, 1.** to rest or depend on. **2.** to be punctilious about (ceremony, etc.); claim respect for (one's rights, dignity, etc.) **3.** *Naut.* to continue on the same course or tack.

**stand on one's dig,** to claim respect.

**stand one's ground,** to be unyielding; remain steadfast in the face of opposition or attack.

**stand out, 1.** to project or protrude. **2.** to be prominent or conspicuous. **3.** to hold aloof. **4.** to persist in opposition or resistance.

**stand over,** to intimidate.

**stand to,** *Naval.* to assemble or take up assigned posts in readiness, as for inspection or awaiting orders.

**stand to reason,** to be in accordance with reason.

**stand up, 1.** to assume a standing position, esp. from sitting. **2.** *Colloq.* to fail to keep an appointment with, esp. with a member of the opposite sex.

**stand up for,** to defend the cause of; support.

**stand up to, 1.** to remain in good condition despite: *to stand up well to wear.* **2.** to resist or oppose, esp. bravely.

**stand with,** to ally oneself with.

*–n.* **29.** the act of standing; an assuming of or a remaining in upright position. **30.** a coming to a position of rest; a halt or stop. **31.** a halt to give battle or repel an attack. **32.** a determined opposition to or support for some cause, circumstance, or the like. **33.** *Cricket.* a period of batting and scoring, usu. of some length, during which neither batsman is out: *a ninth wicket stand of 44.* **34.** the place where a person or thing stands; station. **35.** a shearer's place in a shed. **36.** a witness box. **37.** a raised platform or other structure, as for spectators at a racecourse or a sports field, or along the route of a ceremonial parade, or for a band or the like. **38.** a place, usu. under cover, from which a hunter or sportsman shoots game. **39.** a framework on or in which articles are placed for support, exhibition, etc. **40.** a piece of furniture of various forms, on or in which to put articles. **41.** a stall where articles are displayed for sale or for some other purpose, esp. at a show or exhibition. **42.** a place or station occupied by vehicles available for hire. **43.** the growing trees, or those of a particular species, on a given area. **44.** a standing growth, as of grass, wheat, etc. **45.** a halt of a theatrical company on tour, to give a performance

or performances. **46.** the town at which a theatrical company gives a performance. [ME; OE *standan,* c. MD *standen,* OHG *stantan,* Icel. *standa,* Goth. *standan*]

**stand-alone** /'stænd-əloʊn/, *adj.* **1.** of or pertaining to any computerised device which does not need to be linked up to a larger computer system. *–n.* **2.** such a device.

**standard** /'stændəd/, *n.* **1.** anything taken by general consent as a basis of comparison; an approved model. **2.** the authorised exemplar of a unit of weight or measure. **3.** a certain commodity in which the basic monetary unit is stated, historically usu. either gold or silver **(gold standard, silver standard,** or **single standard),** or both gold and silver in a fixed proportion to each other **(bimetallic standard).** **4.** the legal rate of intrinsic value for coins. **5.** the prescribed degree of fineness for gold or silver. **6.** a grade or level of excellence, achievement, or advancement: *a high standard of living.* **7.** a level of quality which is regarded as normal, adequate, or acceptable. **8.** a fitting or size, as for clothes, which is regarded as normal or average. **9.** (*usu. pl.*) behaviour, beliefs, etc., regarded as socially desirable or acceptable. **10.** a class in certain schools. **11.** a flag, emblematic figure, or other object raised on a pole to indicate the rallying point of an army, fleet, etc. **12.** a flag indicating the presence of a sovereign. **13.** *Mil.* **a.** any of various military or naval flags. **b.** the colours of a mounted unit. **14.** *Her.* a long tapering flag or ensign, as of a king or a nation. **15.** something which stands or is placed upright. **16.** an upright support or supporting part. **17.** an upright timber, bar, or rod. **18.** *Hort.* a tree, shrub, or other plant having a tall, erect stem, and not grown in bush form or trained upon a trellis or other support. **19.** *Bot.* →**vexillum.** **20.** a piece of music or the like of lasting popularity, esp. one often revived with new arrangements. **21.** standard petrol. *–adj.* **22.** serving as a basis of weight, measure, value, comparison, or judgment. **23.** of recognised excellence or established authority: *a standard author.* **24.** normal, adequate, acceptable, or average: *standard goods, a standard fitting.* **25.** (of a variety of a given language, or of usage in the language) characterised by preferred pronunciations, expressions, grammatical constructions, etc., the use of which is considered essential to social or other prestige, failure to conform to them tending to bring the speaker into disfavour. [ME, from OF: aphetic modification of *estandard,* from Gmc (cf. G *Standort* standing-place), conformed to suffix *-ard* -ARD]

**standard atmosphere** /– 'ætməsfɪə/, *n.* **1.** *Meteorol.* any hypothetical atmosphere the physical properties of which are given arbitrary values, approximating to mean conditions, for such puposes as comparing the performance of aircraft, ballistic calculations, etc. **2.** *Physics.* a standard unit of atmospheric pressure equal to 101.325 kilopascals. *Symbol:* atm

**standard-bearer** /'stændəd-bɛərə/, *n.* **1.** an officer or soldier of an army or military unit who bears a standard. **2.** a conspicuous leader of a movement, political party, etc.

**standard cell** /stændəd 'sɛl/, *n.* a specially prepared primary cell, providing an electromotive force which is constant over long periods of time.

**standard deviation** /– divi'eɪʃən/, *n.* the square root of the average of the squares of a set of deviations about an arithmetic mean; the root mean square of the deviations of a set of values.

**Standard English** /'stændəd ɪŋglɪʃ/, *n.* **1.** that form of written English characterised by the spelling, syntax and morphology which educated writers of all English dialects adopt with only minor variation. **2.** (loosely) **a.** the pronunciation of educated speakers of the south-eastern English dialect. **b.** the pronunciation of the educated speakers of other dialects of English which resemble it. **3.** those words and phrases which in a dictionary do not have limiting labels as *Colloq., Obs.,* etc.

**standard error** /stændəd 'ɛrə/, *n.* **1.** →**standard deviation.** **2.** standard deviation divided by the square root of the number of items in the sample; the standard deviation of the sample mean.

**standard gauge** /– 'geɪdʒ/, *n.* See **gauge** (def. 13).

**standard hours** /– 'aʊəz/, *n. pl.* the number of hours worked by an employee at ordinary rates of pay, determined either by a legally constituted authority or by general acceptance.

**standardise** /'stændədaɪz/, *v.t.,* **-dised, -dising.** **1.** to bring to or make of an established standard size, weight, quality, strength, or the like: *to standardise manufactured parts.* **2.** to compare with or test by a standard. Also, **standardize.** – **standardisation** /ˌstændədaɪ'zeɪʃən/, *n.* – **standardiser,** *n.*

**standard lamp** /'stændəd læmp/, *n.* a lamp having a tall support, standing on the floor of a room.

**standard of living,** *n.* a grade or level of subsistence and comforts in everyday life enjoyed by a community, a class in a community, or an individual: *widespread unemployment will depress the nation's standard of living.*

**standard solution** /stændəd sə'luʃən/, *n.* a solution of known concentration, as a normal solution.

**standard time** /– 'taɪm/, *n.* the civil time officially adopted for a country or region, usu. the civil time of some specific meridian lying within the region.

**stand-by** /'stænd-baɪ/, *n., pl.* **-bys.** **1.** a staunch supporter or adherent; one who can be relied upon. **2.** something upon which one can rely; a chief support. **3.** something kept in a state of readiness for use, as for an emergency. **4.** a recipe, piece of music, theme of discourse, etc., often simple and well-known, which one falls back on when disinclined to be adventurous. **5.** a person who is on standby. **6. on stand-by, a.** (of doctors, etc.) available for duty at short notice. **b.** in readiness, as of a person wishing to travel on an aeroplane, to take up a cancelled booking.

**stand-down** /'stænd-daʊn/, *n.* the standing down of employees.

**stand-in** /'stænd-ɪn/, *n.* **1.** a substitute for a film actor or actress during the preparation of lighting, cameras, etc., or in dangerous scenes. **2.** any substitute.

**standing** /'stændɪŋ/, *n.* **1.** position or status, as to rank, credit, reputation, etc.: *men of good standing.* **2.** good position, financial viability, or credit. **3.** length of existence, continuance, residence, membership, experience, etc. **4.** the act of one who or that which stands. **5.** the period during which a person or thing stands. **6.** a place where a person or thing stands. *–adj.* **7.** that stands erect or upright. **8.** performed in or from a stationary or an erect position: *a standing start; a standing jump.* **9.** still; not flowing or stagnant, as water; stationary. **10.** continuing without cessation or change; lasting or permanent. **11.** continuing in operation, force, use, etc.: *a standing rule.* **12.** out of use; idle: *a standing engine.*

**standing army** /– 'ami/, *n.* a permanently organised military force kept up by a nation.

**standing-by time** /ˌstændɪŋ-'baɪ taɪm/, *n.* time outside of normal working hours during which some employees are required to keep themselves ready for work.

**standing committee** /stændɪŋ kə'mɪti/, *n.* a committee, the members of which are appointed at the beginning of each parliamentary session, which has a continuing responsibility for a general sphere of government activity.

**standing matter** /'– mætə/, *n.* printing material which has been used in previous publications, as type, blocks, stereotypes, moulds, lithographic negatives or plates.

**standing order** /– 'ɔdə/, *n.* **1.** any of the rules ensuring continuity of procedure during the meetings of an assembly, esp. the rules governing the conduct of business in parliament. **2.** *Mil.* (formerly) a general order that is always in force in a command and that establishes uniform procedures for it.

**standing rigging** /– 'rɪgɪŋ/, *n. Naut.* the stays, shrouds, etc., which secure the masts.

**standing room** /'– rum/, *n.* **1.** room or space in which to stand. **2.** accommodation for standing only, as in a theatre where all the seats have been taken.

**standing start** /– 'stat/, *n.* a start to a race from a stationary position (opposed to *flying start*).

**standing stone** /'– stoʊn/, *n. Archaeol.* →**menhir.**

**standing wave** /– 'weɪv/, *n.* **1.** Also, **stationary wave.** *Physics.* a distribution of wave displacements, such that the distribution in space is periodic, with fixed maximum and minimum points, with the maxima occurring everywhere at the same time, as in vibrations of strings, electric potentials, acoustic pressures, etc. **2.** *Meteorol.* an ascending or descending current of air associated in certain circumstances with wind flow over mountains or hills.

**stand-off** /ˈstænd-ɒf/, *n.* **1.** →**stand-off half.** *–adj.* **2.** standing off or apart; aloof; reserved.

**stand-off half** /– ˈhaf/, *n. Brit.* →**five-eighth.**

**stand-offish** /stænd-ˈɒfɪʃ/, *adj.* aloof; reserved; unfriendly. – **stand-offishly,** *adv.* – **stand-offishness,** *n.*

**stand oil** /ˈstænd ɔɪl/, *n.* a thick oil used in paints, etc., made by heating linseed oil to temperatures of 315° C, and higher.

**standover man** /ˈstændouvə ˌmæn/, *n.* one who practices standover tactics; a hoodlum. Also, **standover merchant.**

**standover tactics** /ˈ– ˌtæktɪks/, *n.pl.* intimidation; threats of violence to gain a desired result.

**standpipe** /ˈstændpaɪp/, *n.* **1.** a vertical pipe or tower into which water is pumped to obtain a required head. **2.** any vertical pipe with a tap, as one in a garden for a hose fitting.

**standpoint** /ˈstændpɔɪnt/, *n.* **1.** the point at which one stands to view something. **2.** the mental position from which one views and judges things.

**St Andrew's Cross spider,** *n.* a large reddish-coloured spider, *Argyope aetherea,* with white and yellow transverse bands on the abdomen, which constructs a white silken cross in the centre of its snare, along the arms of which it arranges its legs in pairs.

St Andrew's Cross spider

**standstill** /ˈstændstɪl/, *n.* a standing still; a state of cessation of movement or action; a halt; a pause; a stop.

**stand-to** /stænd-ˈtu/, *n.* an assembly or taking up of posts, as for inspection or to await orders.

**stand-up** /ˈstænd-ʌp/, *adj.* **1.** standing erect; upright, as a collar. **2.** performed, taken, etc., while one stands: *a stand-up meal.* **3.** (of a fight) characterised by hard and frequent blows rather than defensive skill or evasiveness.

**stang** /stæŋ/, *v. Obs.* past tense of **sting.**

**stanhope** /ˈstænəp/, *n.* a kind of light, two-wheeled, open, one-seat carriage hung on four springs. [named after Fitzroy *Stanhope,* 1787-1864]

stanhope

**stank**[1] /stæŋk/, *v.* a past tense of **stink.**

**stank**[2] /stæŋk/, *Brit. –n.* **1.** *Civ. Eng.* a small timber cofferdam made watertight with clay. *–v.t.* **2.** to make watertight, esp. with clay, as the banks of a stream. [ME, from OF *estanc* STAUNCH[2]]

**stannary** /ˈstænəri/, *n., pl.* **-ries. 1.** a tin-mining region or district. **2.** a place where tin is mined or smelted. [ML *stannāria,* from LL *stannum* tin]

**stannate** /ˈstæneɪt/, *n.* a salt of stannic acid.

**stannic** /ˈstænɪk/, *n.* of or containing tin, esp. in the tetravalent state. [LL *stannum* tin + -IC]

**stannic acid** /–ˈæsəd/, *n.* any of a series of amorphous powders with the general formula $SnO_2 \cdot XH_2O$; **alpha-stannic acid** is formed by the action of alkalis on stannic chloride and **beta-stannic acid** by the action of nitric acid on metallic tin.

**stannic oxide** /– ˈɒksaɪd/, *n.* a white, amorphous, insoluble powder, $SnO_2$, used in polishing powders, etc.

**stannic sulphide** /– ˈsʌlfaɪd/, *n.* a yellowish compound, $SnS_2$, used in making gilding preparations; mosaic gold.

**stanniferous** /stænˈɪfərəs/, *adj.* bearing tin.

**stannite** /ˈstænaɪt/, *n.* **1.** a mineral, copper iron tin sulphide, $Cu_2FeSnS_4$, an ore of tin, iron-black to steel-grey in colour, with a metallic lustre; tin pyrites. **2.** *Chem.* a salt of stannous acid.

**stannous** /ˈstænəs/, *adj.* containing divalent tin.

**stannum** /ˈstænəm/, *n.* →**tin.** *Symbol:* Sn [LL: tin, in L, alloy of silver and lead]

**stanza** /ˈstænzə/, *n.* a group of lines of verse, commonly four or more in number, arranged and repeated according to a fixed plan as regards the number of lines, the metre, and the rhyme, and forming a regularly repeated metrical division of a poem. [It., from L *stans,* ppr., standing] – **stanzaic** /stænˈzeɪɪk/, *adj.*

**stapelia** /stəˈpiljə/, *n.* any of the plants constituting the genus *Stapelia,* native to southern Africa, with short, fleshy, leafless stems, and flowers which are often oddly coloured or mottled and in most species emit a fetid, carrion-like smell. [named after J.B. *Stapel,* d. 1636, Dutch botanist]

**stapes** /ˈsteɪpiz/, *n.* the innermost of three small bones in the middle ear of man and other mammals, having a stirrup-like shape. [NL, special use of ML *stapes* stirrup] – **stapedial** /stəˈpidiəl/, *adj.*

**staphylo-,** **1.** a word element referring to **staphylococcus. 2.** a word element referring to the uvula. [combining form representing Gk *staphylḗ* bunch of grapes]

**staphylococcus** /stæfələˈkɒkəs/, *n., pl.* **-cocci** /-ˈkɒksaɪ/. any of certain species of micrococcus in which the individual organisms form irregular clusters, as *Micrococcus* (or *Staphylococcus*) *pyogenes,* which causes pus formation. [STAPHYLO- + COCCUS] – **staphylococcal** /stæfələˈkɒkəl/, **staphylococcic** /stæfələˈkɒksɪk/, *adj.*

**staphyloma** /stæfəˈloumə/, *n., pl.* **-mata** /-mətə/. any of various local bulgings of the eyeball.

**staphyloplasty** /ˈstæfələˌplæsti/, *n.* the remedying of defects of the soft palate by plastic surgery.

**staphylorrhaphy** /stæfəˈlɔrəfi/, *n.* the uniting of a cleft palate by plastic surgery. [STAPHYLO- + *-rrhaphy* (from Gk *-rhaphia,* from *rhaphḗ* suture)]

**staple**[1] /ˈsteɪpəl/, *n., v.,* **-pled, -pling.** *–n.* **1.** a bent piece of wire used to bind papers, sections of a book, etc., together. **2.** a U-shaped or other piece of metal with pointed ends for driving into a surface to hold a hasp, hook, pin, bolt, or the like. **3.** a similar device used in medical operations. *–v.t.* **4.** to secure or fasten by a staple or staples: *to staple three sheets together.* [ME; OE *stapol* support, c. G *Stapel*]

**staple**[2] /ˈsteɪpəl/, *n., adj., v.,* **-pled, -pling.** *–n.* **1.** a principal commodity grown or manufactured in a locality. **2.** a principal commodity in a mercantile field; goods in steady demand; goods of known or recognised quality. **3.** a principal item, thing, feature, element, or part. **4.** the fibre of wool, cotton, flax, rayon, etc., considered with reference to length and fineness. **5.** a particular length and degree of fineness of the fibre of wool, cotton, etc. *–adj.* **6.** chief or prominent among the products exported or produced by a country or district; chiefly or largely dealt in or consumed. **7.** chief or principal, as industries. **8.** principally used: *staple subjects of conversation.* *–v.t.* **9.** sort or classify according to the staple or fibre, as wool. [late ME *stapull, staple* (def. 6), from MD (directly or through AF) *stapel* mart, orig. support. See STAPLE[1]]

**staple diet** /– ˈdaɪət/, *n.* those foods which are the major constituents of the diet of a community.

**stapler**[1] /ˈsteɪplə/, *n.* **1.** a stapling machine. **2.** one who operates a stapling machine or who staples by hand. [STAPLE[1] + -ER[1]]

**stapler**[2] /ˈsteɪplə/, *n.* one who sorts according to the staple or fibre. [STAPLE[2] + -ER[2]]

**stapling machine** /ˈsteɪplɪŋ məˌʃin/, *n.* a wire-stitching machine, esp. one used in bookbinding.

**star** /sta/, *n., adj., v.,* **starred, starring.** *–n.* **1.** any of the heavenly bodies appearing as apparently fixed luminous points in the sky at night. **2.** *Astron.* any of the self-luminous bodies outside the solar system, as distinguished from planets, comets, and meteors. The sun is classed with the stars and appears to be a typical member of the galaxy. **3.** any heavenly body. **4.** *Astrol.* **a.** a heavenly body, esp. a planet that is considered as influencing mankind and events. **b.** (*pl.*) a horoscope, esp. one in a magazine, etc. **5.** one's destiny, fortune, or luck, esp. as regarded as influenced by the heavenly bodies. **6.** a conventional figure having rays (commonly five or six) proceeding from, or angular points disposed in a regular outline about, a central point, and considered as representing a star of the sky. **7.** *Jewellery.* a brilliant having six, not eight, triangular facets just below the table. **8.** a white mark on the forehead of an animal, esp. a horse; a blaze. **9.** *Print., etc.* an asterisk. **10.** a person who is pre-eminent or distinguished in some art, profession, or other field. **11.** a prominent actor, singer, or the like, esp. one who plays the leading role in a performance. **12.** a starfish. **13. see stars,** to seem to see bright flashes of light, as after a heavy blow on the head. **14. under the stars,**

exposed to the night sky: *we slept under the stars.* –*adj.* **15.** brilliant, prominent, or distinguished; chief. –*v.t.* **16.** to set with, or as with, stars; spangle. **17.** to present or feature (an actor, etc.) as a star. **18.** to mark with a star or asterisk, as for special notice. –*v.i.* **19.** to shine as a star; be brilliant or prominent. **20.** (of an actor, etc.) to appear as a star. [ME *sterre,* OE *steorra,* c. D *ster,* MHG *sterre,* akin to L *stella,* Gk *astēr*]

**star-anise** /star-ˈænəs/, *n.* an aromatic, evergreen shrub or small tree, *Illicium anisatum,* native to Japan.

**star-apple** /star-ˈæpəl/, *n.* **1.** the edible fruit of a West Indian tree, *Chrysophyllum cainito,* of the size of an apple, and when cut across presenting a star-shaped figure within. **2.** the tree.

**starboard** /ˈstabəd/, *Naut.* –*n.* **1.** the side of a ship to the right of a person looking towards the bow (opposed to *larboard* and *port*). –*adj.* **2.** pertaining to the starboard; on the right side. –*adv.* **3.** towards the right side. –*v.t.* **4.** to turn (the helm) to starboard. [ME *sterbord,* OE *stēorbord,* from *stēor* steering + *bord* side (of a ship). See STEER[1], V., BOARD, n.]

**starch** /statʃ/, *n.* **1.** a white, tasteless solid, chemically a carbohydrate, $(C_6H_{10}O_5)_n$, occurring in the form of minute grains in the seeds, tubers, and other parts of plants, and forming an important constituent of rice, corn, wheat, beans, potatoes, and many other vegetable foods; amylum. Starch is separable into amylose and amylopectin fractions. **2.** a commercial preparation of this substance used (dissolved in water) to stiffen linen, etc., in laundering, and employed also for many industrial purposes. **3.** (*pl.*) foods rich in starch. **4.** stiffness or formality, as of manner. –*v.t.* **5.** to stiffen or treat with starch. **6.** to make stiff or rigidly formal (sometimes fol. by *up*). [ME *sterce,* v., OE *stercean* make stiff or resolute (in *stercedferhth* made resolute in mind), from *stearc* STARK] – **starcher,** *n.* – **starchless,** *adj.*

**Star Chamber** /ˈsta tʃeɪmbə/, *n.* any tribunal, committee, or the like, which proceeds by arbitrary or unfair methods. [from the *Star Chamber,* a former court of inquisitorial and criminal jurisdiction in England, which sat in secret without a jury, and was noted for its arbitrary methods and severe punishments (abolished 1641)]

**starch-gum** /ˈstatʃ-gʌm/, *n.* →**dextrin.**

**starch-reduced** /ˈstatʃ-rədjust/, *adj.* (of foodstuffs, esp. bread) prepared so as to contain less starch than normal, in order to aid slimming.

**starchy** /ˈstatʃi/, *adj.,* **starchier, starchiest. 1.** pertaining to, or of the nature of, starch. **2.** containing starch. **3.** stiffened with starch. **4.** stiff and formal, as in manner. – **starchily,** *adv.* – **starchiness,** *n.*

**star connection** /sta kəˈnɛkʃən/, *n.* a form of three-phase circuit arrangement in which three line conductors are connected to terminals of three circuit elements, as represented by the three arms of a Y, the centre connection becoming the so-called 'neutral'.

**star-crossed** /ˈsta-krɒst/, *adj.* characterised by consistent ill fortune; having much bad luck, as if brought about by the influence of the stars: *Romeo and Juliet were star-crossed lovers.*

**stardom** /ˈstadəm/, *n.* **1.** the world or class of professional stars, as in films. **2.** the status of a star.

**star drift** /ˈsta drɪft/, *n.* a very slow motion common to a number of fixed stars in the same part of the heavens.

**stardust** /ˈstadʌst/, *n.* **1.** a mass of distant stars seen as dust. **2.** a dreamy romantic quality.

**stare** /stɛə/, *v.,* **stared, staring,** *n.* –*v.i.* **1.** to gaze fixedly, esp. with the eyes wide open. **2.** to stand out boldly or obtrusively to view. **3.** (of hair, feathers, etc.) to stand on end; bristle. –*v.t.* **4.** to stare at. **5.** to put, bring, etc., by staring: *to stare one out of countenance.* **6. stare out,** to gaze fixedly at (someone) until he looks away. **7. stare one in the face, a.** to be inescapably obvious. **b.** to be impending and require immediate action. –*n.* **8.** a staring gaze; a fixed look with the eyes wide open: *the banker greeted him with a glassy stare.* [ME; OE *starian,* c. D *staren,* Icel. *stara*] – **starer,** *n.*

**star finch** /ˈsta fɪntʃ/, *n.* an Australian finch, *Bathilda ruficauda,* marked with numerous small white dots.

**starfish** /ˈstafɪʃ/, *n., pl.* **-fishes,** (*esp. collectively*) **-fish.** any echinoderm of the class Asteroidea, comprising marine animals having the body radially arranged, usu. in the form of a star, with five or more rays or arms radiating from a central disc; an asteroid.

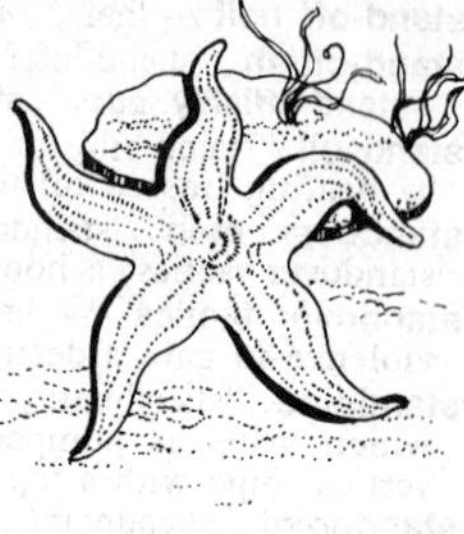
starfish

**star fruit** /ˈsta frut/, *n.* an erect aquatic plant, *Damasonium minus,* family Alismataceae, found on pond margins.

**stargaze** /ˈstageɪz/, *v.i.,* **-gazed, -gazing. 1.** to gaze at or observe the stars. **2.** to daydream. – **stargazing,** *n.*

**stargazer** /ˈstageɪzə/, *n.* **1.** one who gazes at the stars; an astrologer or an astronomer. **2.** a dreamy, vacant, abstracted person. **3.** any of the fishes constituting the family Uranoscopidae, having eyes directed upwards. **4.** *Horseracing.* a horse which looks around the track instead of directly ahead, and is therefore prone to stumbling.

stargazer (def. 3)

**stark** /stak/, *adj.* **1.** sheer, utter, downright, or arrant: *stark madness.* **2.** absolutely naked. **3.** stiff or rigid in substance, muscles, etc. **4.** rigid in death. **5.** harsh, grim, or desolate to the view, as places, etc. **6.** *Archaic.* hard, stern, or severe. –*adv.* **7.** utterly, absolutely, or quite: *stark mad.* [ME; OE *stearc* stiff, c. G *stark* strong] – **starkly,** *adv.*

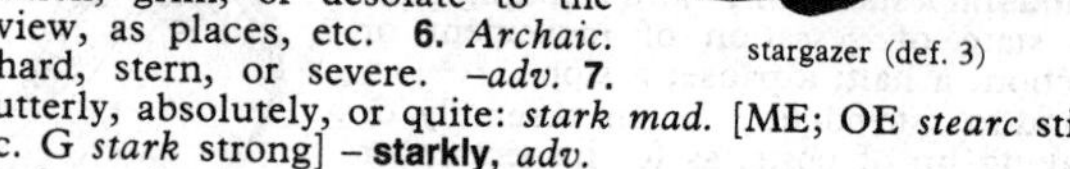

**starkers** /ˈstakəz/, *adj. Colloq.* **1.** stark-naked. **2.** absolutely mad; insane.

**stark-naked** /stak-ˈneɪkəd/, *adj.* completely naked. [STARK + NAKED; replacing ME *start-naked (start* from OE *steort* tail)]

**starless** /ˈstaləs/, *adj.* having no stars visible: *a starless night.*

**starlet** /ˈstalət/, *n.* **1.** a small star. **2.** a young actress who plays small and usu. sexy parts, esp. in films, and who receives publicity as a potential star.

**starlight** /ˈstalaɪt/, *n.* **1.** the light proceeding from the stars. –*adj.* **2.** of or pertaining to starlight. **3.** starlit.

**starlike** /ˈstalaɪk/, *adj.* **1.** star-shaped. **2.** shining like a star.

**starling**[1] /ˈstalɪŋ/, *n.* **1.** any of numerous passerine birds constituting the family Sturnidae, esp. the common European species, *Sturnus vulgaris,* introduced and now widespread in eastern Australia. **2.** →**metallic starling.** [ME; OE *stærling,* from *stær* starling, c. G *Star.* See -LING[1]]

**starling**[2] /ˈstalɪŋ/, *n.* a set of piles driven into a riverbed upstream of a bridge pier to protect it from floating debris, the force of the current, etc. [? alteration of obs. *staddling,* akin to STADDLE]

starling[1]

**starlit** /ˈstalɪt/, *adj.* illuminated by the stars.

**star-nosed** /ˈsta-noʊzd/, *adj.* having a starlike ring of small, fleshy radiating processes about the end of the snout, as an American mole, *Condylura cristata.*

**star-of-Bethlehem** /star-əv-ˈbɛθləhɛm/, *n.* a plant of Europe and Asia, *Ornithogalum umbellatum,* with star-shaped flowers.

**Star of David,** *n.* a figure resembling a six-pointed star, formed of two equilateral triangles interlaced, one being inverted, used as a symbol of Judaism.

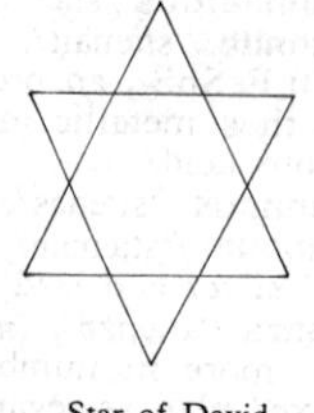
Star of David

**Starr-Bowkett** /sta-ˈboʊkət/, *adj.* **1.** of or pertaining to a building society to which members contribute a regular fixed amount and from which an interest-free loan is made when sufficient funds become available to a member selected by ballot. **2.** of or pertaining to such a loan. [from R. B. *Starr* and Dr. T. E. *Bowkett* who in the 1840s set up such a cooperative society]

**starred** /stad/, *adj.* **1.** set or studded with, or as with stars. **2.** presented as a star, as an actor. **3.** decorated with a star, as

i = peat ɪ = pit ɛ = pet æ = pat a = part ɒ = pot ʌ = putt ɔ = port ʊ = put u = pool ɜ = pert ə = apart aɪ = buy eɪ = bay ɔɪ = boy aʊ = how oʊ = hoe ɪə = here ɛə = hair ʊə = tour g = give θ = thin ð = then ʃ = show ʒ = measure tʃ = choke dʒ = joke ŋ = sing j = you õ = Fr. bon

of an order. **4.** marked with a starlike figure or spot. **5.** having luck or fortune as specified, thought to be due to the influence of the stars. **6.** having ill fortune.

**starred first** /– 'fɜst/, *n. Brit.* (at Cambridge and some other universities) a first-class honours degree with a distinction.

**starry** /'stari/, *adj.*, **-rier, -riest. 1.** abounding with or lit by stars: *a starry sky.* **2.** of, pertaining to, or proceeding from the stars. **3.** of the nature of or consisting of stars: *starry worlds.* **4.** resembling a star; star-shaped or stellate. **5.** shining like stars: *starry eyes.* **6.** studded with starlike figures or markings. – **starrily,** *adv.* – **starriness,** *n.*

**starry-eyed** /stari-'aɪd/, *adj.* **1.** having brightly shining eyes, as with emotion. **2.** excessively optimistic or romantic.

**Stars and Bars,** *n.* the flag adopted by the Confederate States of America, consisting of two broad horizontal bars of red separated by one of white, with a blue union marked with as many white stars, arranged in a circle, as the number of Confederate States.

**Stars and Stripes,** *n.* the national flag of the United States, consisting of thirteen horizontal stripes, alternately red and white, equal to the number of the original states, with a blue union marked with white stars equal in number to the whole number of states.

**star sapphire** /sta 'sæfaɪə/, *n.* a sapphire which exhibits by reflected light a star composed of three bright rays, resulting from the crystalline structure of the gem.

star sapphire

**star shell** /'– ʃɛl/, *n.* a shell which bursts in the air and produces a bright light, used to illuminate enemy positions.

**star-spangled** /'sta-spæŋgəld/, *adj.* spangled with stars.

**Star-Spangled Banner, The,** *n.* **1.** the national flag of the United States. **2.** the national anthem of the United States, composed in 1814 by Francis Scott Key.

**star stone** /'sta stoʊn/, *n.* any precious stone exhibiting asterism.

**star-studded** /'sta-stʌdəd/, *adj.* **1.** having many stars visible: *a clear, star-studded night.* **2.** marked by the presence of many notable or famous persons, esp. actors.

**start** /stat/, *v.i.* **1.** to begin to move, go, or act; set out, as on a journey. **2.** to begin any course of action or procedure, as one's career, life, etc. **3.** (of a process or performance) to begin. **4.** to come suddenly into activity, life, view, etc.; come, rise, or issue suddenly. **5.** to spring or move suddenly from a position or place: *to start from one's seat.* **6.** to move with a sudden, involuntary jerk or twitch, as from a shock of surprise, alarm, or pain. **7.** to protrude: *eyes starting from their sockets.* **8.** to spring, slip, or work loose from place or fastenings, as timbers or other structural parts. **9.** to be among the starters in a race, contest, or the like. *–v.t.* **10.** to set moving, going, or acting: *to start an engine, a fire, etc.* **11.** to set in operation; establish: *to start a newspaper.* **12.** to enter upon or begin: *to start a letter.* **13.** to cause or enable (a person, etc.) to set out on a journey, a course of action, a career, or the like: *to start one's son in business.* **14.** to cause (timbers, structural parts, etc.) to start from place or fastenings. **15.** to rouse (game) from its lair or resting place; flush. **16.** to draw or discharge (liquid or other contents) from a vessel or container, or empty (a container). **17.** to force (a screw, nail, or the like) into a surface a little way to give it a hold before driving. *–n.* **18.** a beginning to move, go, or act; the beginning or outset of anything; a setting in motion. **19.** an impulse to move or proceed; a signal to start, as on a course or in a race. **20.** the place or point from which competitors in a race, travellers, or the like set out: *Hobart was the start to our tour of Tasmania.* **21.** the first part of anything: *the start of his article was good, but later it became unreadable.* **22.** a sudden, springing movement from a position. **23.** a sudden, involuntary jerking movement of the body: *to awake with a start.* **24.** a lead or advance of specified amount, as over competitors or pursuers. **25.** the position or advantage of one who starts first; the lead: *she has got the start on the rest of us.* **26.** a chance or opportunity given to one of starting on a course or career. **27.** a spurt of activity: *to work by fits and starts.* **28.** a starting of parts from their place or fastenings in a structure. **29.** the resulting condition. **30.** *Archaic.* a burst, outburst, or sally, as of emotion, wit, or fancy. [ME; akin to STARTLE and OE *styrtan* start, c. G *sturzen* fall, rush, make fall]

**starter** /'statə/, *n.* **1.** one who or that which starts. **2.** a person who gives the signal for starting, as in a race. **3.** a self-starter. **4.** any competitor who begins a race, contest, or the like. **5.** a bacterial culture used to start fermentation, as in the manufacture of cheese or the like. **6.** the first course of a meal. **7.** a likely prospect.

**star thistle** /sta 'θɪsəl/, *n.* a biennial herb with reddish purple flower-heads, *Centaurea calcitrapa,* native to Europe and western Asia.

star thistle

**starting block** /'statɪŋ blɒk/, *n.* one of a pair of angled supports for the feet, nailed to the track, to increase the power of a sprinter from a crouching start.

**starting box** /'– bɒks/, *n.* **1.** *Horseracing.* a stall in a starting gate. **2.** *Greyhound-racing.* a box from which the dogs are released to start the race.

**starting gate** /'– geɪt/, *n.* a device to start a race of horses, greyhounds, or the like, typically a set of stalls having barriers which are lifted simultaneously at the moment of starting.

**starting grid** /'– grɪd/, *n.* the starting area, usu. marked with bays on which the cars in a race are positioned according to speeds in practice.

**starting handle** /'– hændl/, *n.* a handle used to crank an internal-combustion engine to start it.

**starting price** /'– praɪs/, *n.* the betting odds on a horse, greyhound, etc., at the time when a race begins.

**startle** /'statl/, *v.*, **-tled, -tling,** *n. –v.t.* **1.** to disturb or agitate suddenly by a surprise, alarm, or the like. **2.** to cause to start involuntarily, as under a sudden shock. *–v.i.* **3.** to start involuntarily, as from a surprise or alarm. *–n.* **4.** a sudden surprise, alarm, or the like. **5.** something that startles. [ME *stertle* rush, caper, OE *steartlian* kick, struggle. See START, *v.*] – **startler,** *n.* – **startling,** *adj.* – **startlingly,** *adv.*

**starvation** /sta'veɪʃən/, *n.* **1.** the condition of being starved. **2.** the process of starving.

**starvation diet** /'– daɪət/, *n.* a diet containing so little nutriment as to cause or be likely to cause slow starvation. Also, **starvation rations.**

**starvation wages** /'– weɪdʒəz/, *n. pl.* wages insufficient to support the earner and his dependants, if any, above subsistence level.

**starve** /stav/, *v.*, **starved, starving.** *–v.i.* **1.** to die or perish from hunger. **2.** to be in process of perishing, or to suffer severely, from hunger. **3.** *Colloq.* to be hungry. **4.** to suffer from extreme poverty and need. **5.** to pine or suffer for lack of something specified (fol. by *for*). **6.** *Obs.* to die. *–v.t.* **7.** to cause to starve; weaken or reduce by lack of food. **8.** to subdue, or force to some condition or action, by hunger: *to starve a besieged garrison into surrender.* **9.** to cause to suffer for lack of something needed or craved. [ME *sterve(n),* OE *steorfan* die, c. G *sterben*]

**starveling** /'stavlɪŋ/, *adj.* **1.** starving; suffering from lack of nourishment; pining with want; poverty-stricken. **2.** poor in condition or quality. **3.** such as to entail or suggest starvation. *–n.* **4.** a person, animal, or plant that is starving.

**starwort** /'stawɜt/, *n.* **1.** any plant belonging to the genus *Callitriche,* small aquatics with star-shaped rosettes of floating leaves. **2.** any of several species of *Stellaria,* low herbs with white flowers. **3.** any of several species of aster.

**stash** /stæʃ/, *v.t.* **1.** to put away, as for safekeeping or in a prepared place. *–n.* **2.** a hoard. [b. STOW and CACHE]

**stasis** /'steɪsəs/, *n.* stagnation in the flow of any of the fluids of the body, as of the blood in an inflamed area, the intestinal contents proximal to an obstruction, etc. [NL, from Gk]

**stat-,** a prefix attached to the name of electrical units to indicate the corresponding electrostatic unit, as *statconlomb.*

**-stat,** a word element meaning 'standing', 'stationary', as in *thermostat.* [Gk *-statēs* that stands]

**stat.,** **1.** statuary. **2.** statute.

**state** /steɪt/, *n., adj., v.,* **stated, stating.** *–n.* **1.** the condition of a person or thing, as with respect to circumstances or attributes: *a state of disrepair.* **2.** condition with respect to constitution, structure, form, phase, or the like: *a liquid state, the larval state.* **3.** a mode or form of existence: *the future state.* **4.** a person's condition or position in life, or estate, station, or rank. **5.** the style of living befitting a person of high rank and great wealth; sumptuous, imposing, or ceremonious display of dignity; pomp: *a hall used on occasions of state.* **6.** a particular condition of mind or feeling: *to be in an excited state.* **7.** a particularly tense, nervous, or excited condition: *to be in quite a state over a matter.* **8.** a body of people occupying a definite territory and organised under one government, esp. a sovereign government. **9.** (*sometimes cap.*) any of the territories, each more or less independent as regards internal affairs, which together make up a federal union, as in the Commonwealth of Australia or the United States of America. **10.** the domain or the authority of a state. **11.** (*oft. cap.*) the body politic as organised for civil rule and government (often contrasted with the Church). **12.** the operations or activities of supreme civil government, or the sphere of supreme civil authority and administration: *affairs of state.* **13.** *Mil.* a statement or report, esp. one giving details of numbers, casualties, etc. **14. lie in state,** (of a body) to be publicly displayed in honour before burial. **15. the state of play,** the current situation. **16. the States.** →**United States.** *–adj.* **17.** of or pertaining to the supreme civil government or authority. **18.** (*oft. cap.*) of or pertaining to one of the territories which make up a federal union, as any of the States of Australia. **19.** characterised by, attended with, or involving ceremony: *a state dinner.* **20.** used on or reserved for occasions of ceremony. *–v.t.* **21.** to declare definitely or specifically: *to state one's views.* **22.** to set forth formally in speech or writing: *to state a case.* **23.** to set forth in proper or definite form: *to state a problem.* **24.** to say. **25.** to fix or settle, as by authority. [ME; partly var. of ESTATE; partly from L *status* in defs 8-12 a development from L *status rērum* state of things, or *status reī publicae* state of the republic] – **statable, stateable,** *adj.*

**state aid** /– 'eɪd/, *n.* financial support from the state, esp. to non-government schools.

**state-aided** /'steɪt-eɪdəd/, *adj.* receiving financial support from the state, as a school.

**statecraft** /'steɪtkraft/, *n.* **1.** the art of government and diplomacy. **2.** *Archaic.* crafty statesmanship.

**stated** /'steɪtəd/, *adj.* **1.** fixed or settled: *for a stated fee.* **2.** explicitly set forth; declared as fact. **3.** recognised or official. – **statedly,** *adv.*

**statehood** /'steɪthʊd/, *n.* the condition or status of a state.

**state house** /'steɪt haʊs/, *n. N.Z.* a private dwelling built and owned by the State.

**statehouse** /'steɪthaʊs/, *n. U.S.* the building in which the legislature of a state sits.

**stateless** /'steɪtləs/, *adj.* without nationality. – **statelessness,** *n.*

**stately** /'steɪtli/, *adj.,* **-lier, -liest,** *adv. –adj.* **1.** dignified or majestic; imposing in magnificence, elegance, etc.: *a stately palace.* *–adv.* **2.** in a stately manner. – **stateliness,** *n.*

**statement** /'steɪtmənt/, *n.* **1.** something stated. **2.** a communication or declaration in speech or writing setting forth facts, particulars, etc. **3.** *Comm.* an abstract of an account, as one rendered to show the balance due. **4.** the occurrence of a theme, subject, or motif in a piece of music. **5.** the act or manner of stating something.

**state-of-the-art** /steɪt-əv-ðɪ-'at/, *adj.* embodying the latest techniques or developments.

**state paper** /'steɪt peɪpə/, *n.* an official document relating to affairs of state.

**state prison** /– 'prɪzən/, *n. Chiefly U.S.* a prison maintained by a state for the confinement of felons.

**state prisoner** /– 'prɪzənə/, *n. Chiefly U.S.* **1.** a prisoner held by a state for offences against the body politic or views thought to be inimical to the state, rather than for crimes against the law. **2.** an inmate of a state prison.

**stater** /'steɪtə/, *n.* any of various gold or silver or electrum coin units or coins of the ancient Greek states or cities. [L, from Gk: standard of weight or money]

**state religion** /steɪt rə'lɪdʒən/, *n.* the official religion of a country, as established by law.

**state-righter** /steɪt-'raɪtə/, *n.* one who supports state government powers against encroachments by a federal government. Also, **states'-righter.**

**state rights** /steɪt 'raɪts/, *n.pl.* (in a federation) the rights belonging to the states. Also, **states' rights.**

**stateroom** /'steɪtrum/, *n.* **1.** a private room or cabin on a ship. **2.** *U.S.* a private sleeping compartment on a train. **3.** any magnificent room for use on state occasions.

**state's attorney** /steɪts ə'tɜni/, *n. U.S.* (in judicial proceedings) the legal representative of the state; a public prosecuter.

**state school** /'steɪt skul/, *n.* a school maintained at public expense for the education of the children and youth of a community or district, as part of a system of public, free education, commonly forming one of a series of graded schools including primary and secondary schools.

**state's evidence** /steɪts 'ɛvədəns/, *n. Chiefly U.S.* →**queen's evidence.**

**stateside** /'steɪtsaɪd/, *U.S. –adj.* **1.** of, in, or towards the United States. *–adv.* **2.** in or towards the United States.

**statesman** /'steɪtsmən/, *n., pl.* **-men.** **1.** a man who is versed in the management of affairs of state. **2.** one who exhibits ability of the highest kind in directing the affairs of a government or in dealing with important public issues. [from *state's,* gen. of STATE + MAN, after F *homme d'état*] – **statesmanlike, statesmanly,** *adj.* – **stateswoman** /'steɪtswʊmən/, *n.fem.*

**statesmanship** /'steɪtsmənʃɪp/, *n.* the character or procedure of a statesman; skill in the management of public affairs.

**states'-righter** /steɪts-'raɪtə/, *n.* →**state-righter.**

**states' rights** /steɪts 'raɪts/, *n.pl.* →**state rights.**

**state trial** /steɪt 'traɪəl/, *n.* a trial for offences against the state.

**state trooper** /– 'trupə/, *n. U.S.* a member of a paramilitary force having jurisdiction only within the boundaries of a state.

**state university** /– junə'vɜsəti/, *n. U.S.* a university maintained by the government of a state as the highest public educational institution.

**static** /'stætɪk/, *adj.* Also, **statical.** **1.** pertaining to or characterised by a fixed or stationary condition. **2.** *Elect.* denoting or pertaining to electricity at rest, as that produced by friction, or the production of such electricity. **3.** denoting or pertaining to atmospheric electricity interfering with the sending and receiving of radio messages, etc. **4.** *Physics.* acting by mere weight without producing motion: *static pressure.* **5.** *Sociol.* denoting or pertaining to a condition of social life in which no changes are taking place. **6.** *Econ.* pertaining to fixed relations, or different combinations of fixed quantities: *static population.* *–n. Elect.* **7.** static or atmospheric electricity. **8.** Also, **atmospherics.** *Radio.* extraneous noises, crackling, etc., caused by electrical currents from storms or other atmospheric disturbances picked up by the receiver. [NL *staticus,* from Gk *statikós*] – **statically,** *adv.*

**statice** /'stætəs/, *n.* any of several plants of the genus *Limonium,* as *L. latifolium* of eastern Europe, frequently cultivated for their inflorescences which are dried and used for indoor decoration. [NL, from Gk *statikḗ,* fem., astringent, STATIC]

**static firing** /ˌstætɪk 'faɪərɪŋ/, *n.* the firing of a rocket, held down on a special test stand, to measure thrust, etc.

**static machine** /– mə'ʃin/, *n. Physics.* →**Wimshurst machine.**

**static-pressure tube** /stætɪk-'prɛʃə tjub/, *n.* an open-ended tube used to measure the static pressure of a fluid by positioning it so that the pressure recorded is unaffected by movements of the fluid itself or of a body (as an aircraft) passing through it.

**statics** /'stætɪks/, *n.* (*pl. construed as sing.*) that branch of mechanics which deals with bodies at rest or forces in equilibrium. [see STATIC, -ICS]

**station** /ˈsteɪʃən/, *n.* **1.** a position assigned for standing or remaining in; the place in which anything stands. **2.** the place at which something stops; a regular stopping place, as on a railway. **3.** the building or buildings at a railway stopping place or terminal. **4.** a terminal for buses or coaches. **5.** police station. **6.** a fire station. **7.** a place equipped for some particular kind of work, service, or the like: *a power station.* **8. a.** (formerly) a government-run agricultural or pastoral establishment employing convicts. **b.** a privately-owned rural establishment for raising sheep or cattle; a sheep-run or cattle-run. **9.** standing, as of persons or things, in a scale of estimation, rank, or dignity. **10.** *Mil.* **a.** a military place of duty. **b.** a semipermanent army post. **11.** *Navy.* **a.** a place or region to which a warship or fleet is assigned for duty. **b.** a position assigned to a member of the crew of a warship during action. **12.** (in India) formerly, a place where the British officials of a district or the officers of a garrison reside. **13.** a radio station. **14.** the wave-length on which a radio or television program is broadcast; a frequency or channel: *tune in to another station.* **15.** *Biol.* a particular place or the kind of place where a given animal or plant is found. **16.** *Survey.* a point where an observation is taken. **17.** a position, office, rank, calling, or the like. **18.** *Eccles.* one of the stations of the cross. *–adj.* **19.** of or pertaining to a station: *station buildings.* **20.** in charge of a station: *a station sergeant in the police force.* *–v.t.* **21.** to assign a station to; place or post in a station or position. [ME, from L *statio*]

**station agent** /ˈ– eɪdʒənt/, *n. U.S.* →**stationmaster.**

**stationary** /ˈsteɪʃənri, ˈsteɪʃənəri/, *adj., n., pl.* **-aries.** *–adj.* **1.** standing still; not moving. **2.** having a fixed position; not movable. **3.** established in one place; not itinerant or migratory. **4.** remaining in the same condition or state; not changing. *–n.* **5.** one who or that which is stationary. [ME, from L *statiōnārius*] – **stationarily,** *adv.* – **stationariness,** *n.*

**stationary engine** /– ˈɛndʒən/, *n.* a steam engine or other heat engine which remains in a fixed place.

**stationary orbit** /– ˈɔbət/, *n.* →**synchronous equatorial orbit.**

**stationary state** /– ˈsteɪt/, *n.* an energy state of a system, as an atom or molecule, when it is not emitting electromagnetic radiation.

**stationary wave** /– ˈweɪv/, *n.* →**standing wave** (def. 1).

**station break** /ˈsteɪʃən breɪk/, *n.* one of the interruptions to a program on commercial radio or television during which advertisements, station identification, etc., are presented.

**stationer** /ˈsteɪʃənə/, *n.* **1.** one who sells the materials used in writing, as paper, pens, pencils, ink, etc. **2.** *Obs.* a bookseller. **3.** *Obs.* a publisher. [ME, from L *statiōnārius* stationary, in ML applied to a tradesman who had a shop, as contrasted with a vendor]

**stationery** /ˈsteɪʃənri, ˈsteɪʃənəri/, *n.* **1.** writing paper. **2.** writing materials, as pens, pencils, paper, etc.

**station hand** /ˈsteɪʃən hænd/, *n.* an employee involved in routine work on a rural property or station.

**station house** /ˈ– haʊs/, *n.* **1.** a house or building at or serving as a station, esp. a police station or railway station. **2.** the homestead on a rural property.

**station identification** /– aɪˌdɛntəfəˈkeɪʃən/, *n.* a short jingle or other advertisement used periodically on radio or television to identify the station to its audience.

**station manager** /ˈ– mænədʒə/, *n.* one who manages a rural property.

**stationmaster** /ˈsteɪʃənmastə/, *n.* a person in charge of a railway station.

**station-owner** /ˈsteɪʃən-oʊnə/, *n.* a person who owns a sheep or cattle station.

**stations of the cross,** *n.pl. Eccles.* a series of fourteen representations of successive incidents from the Passion of Christ, each with a wooden cross, or a series of wooden crosses alone, set up in a church (or sometimes in the open air) and visited in order, for prayer and meditation.

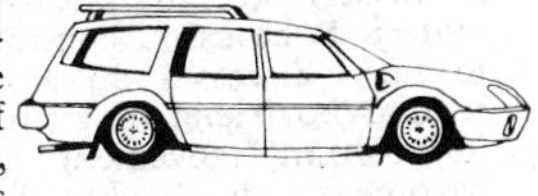

station wagon

**station wagon** /ˈsteɪʃən wægən/, *n.* a car with an extended interior, allowing extra space behind the rear seat, and a door or tailgate at the back.

**statism** /ˈsteɪtɪzəm/, *n.* **1.** the principle or policy of concentrating extensive economic, political, and related controls in the state at the cost of individual liberty. **2.** support of or belief in the sovereignty of a state, usu. a republic. **3.** *Obs.* statecraft; politics.

**statist** /ˈsteɪtəst/, *n.* **1.** a supporter of statism. **2.** *Obs.* a statesman. *–adj.* **3.** of or pertaining to statism or statists. [STAT(E) + -IST]

**statistical** /stəˈtɪstɪkəl/, *adj.* of or pertaining to statistics; consisting of or based on statistics. Also, **statistic.** – **statistically,** *adv.*

**statistical independence** /– ɪndəˈpɛndəns/, *n. Statistics.* a condition on the two-way probability distribution of two variables such that the conditional probability distribution of one variable for a given value of a second variable is identical with that for any other given value of the second variable.

**statistical mechanics** /– məˈkænɪks/, *n.* the application of statistics to the dynamics of large numbers of particles, as in the kinetic theory of gases which deals with large numbers of gas molecules.

**statistician** /stætəsˈtɪʃən/, *n.* an expert in, or compiler of, statistics.

**statistics** /stəˈtɪstɪks/, *n.* **1.** (*construed as sing.*) the science which deals with the collection, classification, and use of numerical facts or data, bearing on a subject or matter. **2.** (*construed as pl.*) the numerical facts or data themselves. [pl. of *statistic,* from G *Statistik,* from NL *statisticus,* orig., pertaining to a statist]

**stative** /ˈsteɪtɪv/, *adj. Linguistics.* (of verbs) expressing a state or condition.

**statocyst** /ˈstætəsəst/, *n.* a type of sense organ consisting of a sac enclosing sensory hairs and particles of sand, lime, etc., that has an equilibrating function serving to indicate position in space. [Gk *statό(s)* standing + -CYST]

**stator** /ˈsteɪtə/, *n.* **1.** *Elect.* the fixed part of an electrical machine (motor or generator) which contains the stationary magnetic circuits. **2.** *Aeron.* the system of fixed radial aerofoils in an axial compressor or turbine.

**statoscope** /ˈstætəskoʊp/, *n.* **1.** *Physics.* a form of aneroid barometer for registering minute variations of atmospheric pressure. **2.** *Aeron.* an instrument for detecting a small rate of rise or fall of an aircraft. [Gk *statό(s)* standing + -SCOPE]

**statuary** /ˈstætʃuəri/, *n., pl.* **-aries,** *adj.* *–n.* **1.** statues collectively. *–adj.* **2.** of, pertaining to, or suitable for statues. [L *statuārius* of statues]

**statue** /ˈstætʃu/, *n.* a representation of a person or an animal carved in stone or wood, moulded in a plastic material, or cast in bronze or the like, esp. one of some size, in the round. [ME, from F, from L *statua*]

**statuesque** /stætʃuˈɛsk/, *adj.* like or suggesting a statue, as in formal dignity, grace, immobility, proportions, or beauty. – **statuesquely,** *adv.* – **statuesqueness,** *n.*

**statuette** /stætʃuˈɛt/, *n.* a small statue. [F, diminutive of *statue* STATUE]

**stature** /ˈstætʃə/, *n.* **1.** the height of an animal body, esp. of man. **2.** the height of any object. **3.** degree of development or achievement attained. **4.** impressive achievement; moral greatness. [ME, from OF, from L *statūra*]

**status** /ˈsteɪtəs/, *n.* **1.** condition, position, or standing socially, professionally, or otherwise. **2.** the relative rank or social position of an individual or group. **3.** the relative standing, position, or condition of anything. **4.** the state or condition of affairs. **5.** *Law.* the standing of a person before the law. [L]

**status quo** /– ˈkwoʊ/, *n.* the existing or previously existing state or condition. Also, **status in quo.** [L: state in which]

**status symbol** /ˈ– sɪmbəl/, *n.* a possession which is considered to be proof of the owner's prestige, wealth, social position, etc.

**statutable** /ˈstætʃətəbəl/, *adj.* **1.** (of an offence) recognised by statute; legally punishable. **2.** prescribed, authorised, or permitted by statute.

**statute** /ˈstætʃut/, *n.* **1.** *Law.* **a.** an enactment made by a legislature and expressed in a formal document. **b.** the document in which such an enactment is expressed. **2.**

*Internat. Law.* an instrument annexed or subsidiary to an international agreement, as a treaty. **3.** a permanent rule established by an institution, corporation, etc., for the conduct of its internal affairs. [ME, from F *statut,* from LL *statūtum,* properly neut. of L *statūtus,* pp., decreed, set up]

**statute book** /'– bʊk/, *n.* a register of statutes enacted by a legislature.

**statute law** /'– lɔ/, *n.* law established by legislative enactments.

**statute of limitations,** *n. Law.* a statute defining the period within which a claim may be prosecuted.

**statutory** /'stætʃətri, 'stætʃətəri/, *adj.* **1.** of, pertaining to, or of the nature of a statute. **2.** prescribed or authorised by statute. **3.** conforming to statute. **4.** (of an offence) recognised by statute; legally punishable.

**statutory authority** /– ɔ'θɒrəti/, *n.* a government instrumentality independent of ministerial control and responsible directly to parliament.

**statutory declaration** /– dɛklə'reɪʃən/, *n.* a written statement on oath, sworn to before an authorised official, as a justice of the peace, public notary, etc.

**statutory instrument** /– 'ɪnstrəmənt/, *n.* a statutory rule or order, often required to be laid before parliament.

**statutory rape** /– 'reɪp/, *n. U.S.* sexual intercourse with a girl younger than the age of consent.

**statutory reserve deposit,** *n.* the minimum deposit which each trading bank is required to maintain with the Reserve Bank.

**staunch**[1] /stɔntʃ/, *v.t.* **1.** to stop the flow of (a liquid, esp. blood). **2.** to stop the flow of blood from (a wound). **3.** *Archaic.* to check, appease, allay, or assuage. *–v.i.* **4.** to stop flowing, as blood; be stanched. *–n.* **5.** *Civ. Eng.* a device on primitive river navigation systems in which changes of level are overcome by sending boats down in a rush of water. Also, **stanch.** – **stauncher,** *n.*

**staunch**[2] /stɔntʃ/, *adj.* **1.** firm or steadfast in principle, adherence, loyalty, etc., as a person. **2.** characterised by firmness or steadfastness. **3.** strong; substantial. **4.** impervious to water or other liquids; watertight. Also, **stanch.** [late ME *sta(u)nch,* from OF *estanche,* fem. of *estanc;* akin to STANCH[1]] – **staunchly,** *adv.* – **staunchness,** *n.*

**staurolite** /'stɔrəlaɪt/, *n.* a mineral, basic iron aluminium silicate, $HFeAl_5Si_2O_{13}$, occurring in brown to black prismatic crystals, which are often twinned in the form of a cross. [F, from Gk *stauró(s)* cross + *-lite* -LITE] – **staurolitic** /stɔrə'lɪtɪk/, *adj.*

**stauroscope** /'stɔrəskoʊp/, *n.* an optical instrument for determining the position of the planes of light vibration in sections of crystals.

**stave** /steɪv/, *n., v.,* **staved** or **stove, staving.** *–n.* **1.** one of the thin, narrow, shaped pieces of wood which form the sides of a cask, tub, or similar vessel. **2.** a stick, rod, pole, or the like. **3.** a rung of a ladder, chair, etc. **4.** *Pros.* **a.** a verse or stanza of a poem or song. **b.** the alliterating sound in a line of verse, thus, *w* is the stave in *the way of the wind.* **5.** Also, **staff.** *Music.* a set of horizontal lines, now five in number, with the corresponding four spaces between them, music being written on both the lines and spaces. *–v.t.* **6.** to break in a stave or staves of. **7.** to break a hole in; crush inwards (oft. fol. by *in*). **8.** to break (a hole) in a boat, etc. **9.** to break to pieces, splinters, etc. **10.** to furnish with a stave or staves. **11.** to beat with a stave or staff. **12. stave off,** to put, ward, or keep off, as by force or evasion. *–v.i.* **13.** to become staved in, as a boat; break in or up. [ME; backformation from STAVES, pl. of STAFF[1]]

**staves** /steɪvz/, *n.* **1.** a plural of **staff**[1]. **2.** plural of **stave.**

**stavesacre** /'steɪvzeɪkə/, *n.* **1.** a larkspur, *Delphinium staphisagria,* native to Europe and Asia Minor, having violently emetic and cathartic poisonous seeds. **2.** the seeds. [ME *staphisagrie,* from L *staphisagria* wild raisin, from Gk]

**stay**[1] /steɪ/, *v.,* **stayed** or **staid, staying,** *n.* *–v.i.* **1.** to remain in a place, situation, company, etc.; dwell or reside: *we cannot stay at home.* **2.** to continue to be (as specified), as to condition, etc.: *to stay clean.* **3.** to hold out or endure, as in a contest. **4.** to keep up, as with a competitor in a race (usu. fol. by *with*). **5.** *Poker.* to continue in a hand by meeting a bet, ante, or raise. **6.** to stop or halt. **7.** to pause or wait, as for a moment, before proceeding or continuing; linger or tarry. **8.** *Archaic.* to cease or desist. **9.** *Archaic.* to stand firm. **10. stay put,** to remain where placed; not to move from a position. *–v.t.* **11.** to stop or halt. **12.** to hold back, detain, or restrain, as from going further. **13.** to suspend or delay (proceedings, etc.). **14.** to suppress or quell (violence, strife, etc.). **15.** to appease or satisfy temporarily the cravings of (the stomach, appetite, etc.). **16.** to remain through or during (a period of time, etc.). **17.** to remain to the end of; last out; endure. **18.** *Archaic.* to await. *–n.* **19.** an act of stopping. **20.** a stop, halt, or pause; a standstill. **21.** a sojourn or temporary residence. **22.** *Law.* a stoppage or arrest of action; a suspension of a judicial proceeding. **23.** *Colloq. U.S.* staying power; endurance. **24.** *Obs.* a cause of stoppage or restraint. [late ME, probably OF from *estai-,* stem of *ester* stand, from L *stāre*]

**stay**[2] /steɪ/, *n., v.,* **stayed, staying.** *–n.* **1.** something used or serving to support or steady a thing; a prop; a brace. **2.** a flat strip of steel, plastic, etc., for stiffening corsets, etc. **3.** (*pl.*) a corset. *–v.t.* **4.** to support, prop, or hold up (sometimes fol. by *up*). **5.** to rest for support. **6.** to sustain or strengthen mentally or spiritually. **7.** to fix or rest in dependence or reliance. [apparently same as STAY[3]. Cf. F *étayer,* of Gmc orig.]

**stay**[3] /steɪ/, *n., v.,* **stayed, staying.** *Chiefly Naut.* *–n.* **1.** a strong rope, now commonly of wire, used to support a mast. **2.** any rope similarly used; a guy. **3. in stays,** heading into the wind while going about from one tack to the other. *–v.t.* **4.** to support or secure with a stay or stays: *to stay a mast.* **5.** to put (a ship) on the other tack. *–v.i.* **6.** (of a ship) to change to the other tack. [ME *stey(e),* OE *stæg,* c. D *stag,* G *Stag*]

**stay-at-home** /'steɪ-ət-hoʊm/, *adj.* **1.** unadventurous; not inclined to travel. *–n.* **2.** a stay-at-home person.

**stayer** /'steɪə/, *n.* a horse, dog, athlete, etc., who performs best in races over long distances.

**staying power** /'steɪɪŋ paʊə/, *n.* ability or strength to last or endure; stamina.

**staysail** /'steɪseɪl/; *Naut.* /-səl/ *n.* any sail hoisted on a stay, as a triangular sail between two masts.

**St Bernard** /sənt 'bɜnəd/, *n.* →**Saint Bernard.**

**STD** /ɛs ti 'di/, Subscriber Trunk Dialling. Also, **S.T.D.**

**STD code** /ɛs ti 'di koʊd/, *n.* →**area code.**

**stead** /stɛd/, *n.* **1.** the place of a person or thing as occupied by a successor or substitute: *since he could not come, his brother came in his stead.* **2.** *Archaic.* a place or locality. **3. stand in good stead,** to be useful or advantageous to. *–v.t.* **4.** *Archaic.* to be of service, advantage, or avail to. [ME and OE *stede,* c. G *statt*]

**steadfast** /'stɛdfast, -fəst/, *adj.* **1.** fixed in direction; steadily directed: *a steadfast gaze.* **2.** firm in purpose, resolution, faith, attachment, etc., as a person. **3.** unwavering, as resolution, faith, adherence, etc. **4.** firmly established, as an institution or a state of affairs. **5.** firmly fixed in place or position. Also, **stedfast.** [ME *stedefast,* OE *stedefæst,* from *stede* STEAD + *fæst* FAST[1]] – **steadfastly,** *adv.* – **steadfastness,** *n.*

**steady** /'stɛdi/, *adj.,* **steadier, steadiest,** *interj., n., pl.* **steadies,** *v.,* **steadied, steadying,** *adv.* *–adj.* **1.** firmly placed or fixed; stable in position or equilibrium; even or regular in movement: *a steady ladder.* **2.** free from change, variation, or interruption; uniform; continuous: *a steady wind.* **3.** constant, regular, or habitual: *steady drinkers.* **4.** free from excitement or agitation: *steady nerves.* **5.** firm, unwavering, or steadfast, as persons or their principles, policy, etc. **6.** settled, staid, or sober, as a person, habits, etc. **7.** *Naut.* (of a vessel) keeping nearly upright, as in a heavy sea. *–interj.* **8.** be calm! control yourself! **9.** *Naut.* (a helm order to keep a vessel on a certain course.) *–n.* **10.** *Colloq.* a regular boyfriend or girlfriend. *–v.t.* **11.** to make steady, as in position, movement, action, character, etc. *–v.i.* **12.** to become steady. *–adv.* **13.** in a firm or steady manner. **14. go steady,** *Colloq.* to go about regularly with the same boyfriend or girlfriend. [STEAD + -Y[1]] – **steadier,** *n.* – **steadily,** *adv.* – **steadiness,** *n.*

**steady state theory,** *n.* the cosmological theory that the universe has always existed in a steady state and that the expansion of the universe is compensated by the continuous creation of matter as a property of space itself. Cf. **big bang theory.**

**steak** /steɪk/, *n.* **1.** Also, **cutlet. a.** a slice of meat, beef unless indicated otherwise, as ham steak, usu. cut thick and across the grain of the muscle. **b.** a thick slice of a large fish cut across the body and including part of the backbone. **2.** chopped or minced meat formed to resemble steak and cooked in the manner of steak. [ME *steike* from ON *steik*]

**steak diane** /– daɪ'æn/, *n.* grilled steak served with a highly flavoured sauce, usu. including cream, pepper and garlic.

**steakhouse** /'steɪkhaʊs/, *n.* an eating house making a speciality of chops, steaks, grills, and the like.

**steak tartare** /steɪk ta'tɛə/, *n.* raw minced steak, served with a spicy sauce. Also, **steak tartar, tartar steak.**

**steal** /stil/, *v.*, **stole, stolen, stealing,** *n.* *–v.t.* **1.** to take or take away dishonestly or wrongfully, esp. secretly. **2.** to appropriate (ideas, credit, words, etc.) without right or acknowledgment. **3.** to take, get, or win by insidious, surreptitious, or subtle means: *to steal a nap during a sermon.* **4.** to move, bring, convey, or put secretly or quietly (fol. by *away, from, in, into, etc.*). **5.** (in various games) to gain (a point, etc.) by strategy, by chance, or by luck. **6.** to obtain more than one's share; appropriate entirely to oneself: *the new baby stole everybody's attention.* **7. steal a march on,** to obtain an advantage over, esp. by surreptitious means. **8. steal someone's thunder,** to appropriate or use another's idea, plan, etc. **9. steal the show,** to achieve great success, as an actor in a play, etc. *–v.i.* **10.** to commit or practise theft. **11.** to move, go, or come secretly, quietly, or unobserved. **12.** to pass, come, spread, etc., imperceptibly, gently or gradually: *the years steal by.* *–n.* **13.** *Colloq.* something acquired at very little cost or at a cost well below its true value. [ME *stele(n),* OE *stelan, G stehlen,* Icel. *stela*] – **stealer,** *n.*

**stealing** /'stilɪŋ/, *n.* **1.** the act of one who steals. *–adj.* **2.** that steals.

**stealth** /stɛlθ/, *n.* secret, clandestine, or surreptitious procedure. [ME *stelthe.* See STEAL, *v.*, -TH[1]]

**stealthy** /'stɛlθi/, *adj.*, **stealthier, stealthiest.** done, characterised, or acting by stealth; furtive: *stealthy footsteps.* – **stealthily,** *adv.* – **stealthiness,** *n.*

**steam** /stim/, *n.* **1.** water in the form of an invisible gas or vapour. **2.** water changed to this form by boiling, and extensively used for the generation of mechanical power, for heating purposes, etc. **3.** the mist formed when the gas or vapour from boiling water condenses in the air. **4.** an exhalation. **5.** *Colloq.* power or energy. **6. let off steam,** *Colloq.* to release repressed emotions, by behaving in an unrestrained manner. **7.** *Colloq.* cheap wine. *–v.i.* **8.** to emit or give off steam or vapour. **9.** to rise or pass off in the form of steam, as vapour. **10.** to become covered with condensed steam, as a surface. **11.** to generate or produce steam, as in a boiler. **12.** to move or travel by the agency of steam. *–v.t.* **13.** to expose to or treat with steam, as in order to heat, cook, soften, renovate, or the like. **14.** to emit or exhale (steam or vapour); send out in the form of steam. **15.** to convey by the agency of steam, as in a steamship. *–adj.* **16.** heated by or heating with steam: *steam radiator.* **17.** propelled by or propelling with a steam-engine: *a steam train.* **18.** operated by steam. **19.** conducting steam: *a steampipe.* **20.** bathed with, or affected by, steam. **21.** *Colloq. (joc.)* antiquated; old-fashioned; belonging to the age of steam: *steam radio.* [ME *steme,* OE *stēam,* c. D *stoom*]

**steam bath** /'– baθ/, *n.* **1.** →**Turkish bath. 2.** *Chem.* such a bath used particularly in organic chemistry as a source of steady, uniform heat. **3.** a vessel used for such a bath.

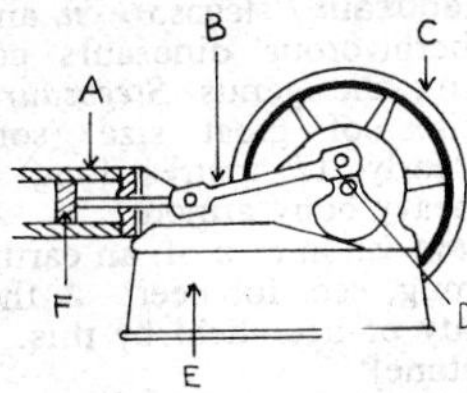

steam-engine: A, cylinder; B, connecting rod; C, flywheel; D, crankshaft; E, frame; F, piston

**steamboat** /'stimboʊt/, *n.* a steamship, esp. a small one.

**steam-boiler** /'stim-bɔɪlə/, *n.* a receptacle in which water is boiled to generate steam.

**steam-chest** /'stim-tʃɛst/, *n.* (in a steam-engine) the chamber from which the steam enters the cylinder. Also, **steam box.**

**steamed-up** /stimd-'ʌp/, *adj. Colloq.* excited or angry.

**steam-engine** /'stim-ɛndʒən/, *n.* an engine worked by steam, typically one in which a sliding piston in a cylinder is moved by the expansive action of the steam generated in a boiler.

**steamer** /'stimə/, *n.* **1.** something propelled or operated by steam, as a steamship or steamcar. **2.** one who or that which steams. **3.** a device or container in which something is steamed. **4.** (formerly) a stew: *kangaroo steamer.*

**steam hammer** /'stim hæmə/, *n.* a heavy, steam-operated, mechanical hammer, used in forges.

**steam heat** /– 'hit/, *n.* heat obtained by the condensation of steam in pipes, radiators, etc.

**steaming coal** /'stimɪŋ koʊl/, *n.* black coal used in the production of steam.

**steam iron** /'stim aɪən/, *n.* an iron which releases steam during use, facilitating ironing.

**steam jacket** /'– dʒækət/, *n.* an outer casing enclosing a hollow space through which steam is circulated to heat the contents of an inner container.

**steampipe** /'stimpaɪp/, *n.* a pipe for conveying steam from a boiler.

**steam point** /'stim pɔɪnt/, *n.* the equilibrium temperature of the liquid and vapour phases of water at a pressure of 101 325 pascals, approx. equal to 373.15k (100°C).

**steam radio** /– 'reɪdioʊ/, *n.* radio seen as being technologically old fashioned, esp. in comparison with television.

**steamroll** /'stimroʊl/, *v.t.* to persuade to agree to a point of view or a proposal, by overruling any objections in an overbearing manner.

**steamroller** /'stimroʊlə/, *n.* **1.** a heavy locomotive, originally steam-powered, having a roller or rollers, for crushing or levelling materials in road-making. **2.** an overpowering force, esp. one that crushes opposition with ruthless disregard of rights. *–v.t.* **3.** to go over or crush as with a steamroller or an overpowering force. **4.** *Politics.* to put pressure on a recalcitrant party member to make him vote for or support party policy. *–adj.* **5.** suggestive of a steamroller: *steamroller tactics.*

**steam room** /'stim rum/, *n.* a room filled with steam in which one takes a Turkish bath.

**steamship** /'stimʃɪp/, *n.* a ship propelled by a steam-driven engine.

**steam-shovel** /'stim-ʃʌvəl/, *n.* a machine for digging or excavating, operated by its own engine and boiler.

**steam turbine** /stim 'tɜbaɪn/, *n.* See **turbine** (def.2).

**steamy** /'stimi/, *adj.*, **steamier, steamiest. 1.** consisting of or resembling steam. **2.** full of or abounding in steam; emitting steam. **3.** covered with or as if with condensed steam. – **steamily,** *adv.* – **steaminess,** *n.*

**steapsin** /sti'æpsən/, *n.* the lipase of the pancreatic juice. [b. STEA(RIN) and (PE)PSIN]

**stearate** /'stɪəreɪt/, *n.* a salt or ester of stearic acid.

**stearic** /sti'ærɪk/, *adj.* **1.** of or pertaining to suet or fat. **2.** *Chem.* of or derived from stearic acid.

**stearic acid** /– 'æsəd/, *n.* a monobasic organic acid, $C_{17}H_{35}$-COOH, the glycerides of which are the principal components of animal fats.

**stearin** /'stɪərən/, *n.* **1.** *Chem.* any of the three glyceryl esters of stearic acid, esp. $C_3H_5(C_{18}H_{35}O_2)_3$, a soft, white, odourless solid found in many natural fats; tristearin. **2.** a crude mixture of stearic and palmitic acids used for making candles. Also, **stearine** /'stɪərin/. [F *stéarine,* from Gk *stéar* fat + *-ine* -IN[2]]

**stearoptene** /stɪə'rɒptin/, *n.* the oxygenated solid part of an essential oil (opposed to *eleoptene,* the liquid part). [from *stearo-* (representing Gk *stéar* tallow, fat, suet) + *-ptene* (from Gk *ptēnós* winged, volatile)]

**steatite** /'stiətaɪt/, *n.* →**soapstone.** [L *steatītis,* from Gk: doughlike (stone)] – **steatitic** /stiə'tɪtɪk/, *adj.*

**steatopygia** /ˌstiətoʊ'pɪdʒiə, -'pidʒiə/, *n.* abnormal accumulation of fat on and about the buttocks, as among the Hottentots, Bushmen, and other South African peoples, esp. the women. Also, **steatopyga** /ˌstiətoʊ'paɪgə/. [NL, from *steato-* (representing Gk *stéar* fat) + *-pȳgia* (from Gk *pȳgḗ* rump)] – **steatopygic, steatopygous** /stiə'tɒpəgəs/, *adj.*

**steatorrhoea** /stiətə'riə/, *n.* a condition in which an excess of fat is excreted causing frothy, foul-smelling faeces.

**stedfast** /ˈstɛdfast, -fəst/, *adj.* steadfast.

**steed** /stid/, *n.* **1.** a horse, esp. one for riding. **2.** a high-spirited horse. [ME *stēde,* OE *stēda* stallion, from *stōd* STUD[2]; cf. Icel. *stedda* mare]

**steel** /stil/, *n.* **1.** iron in a modified form, artificially produced, containing a certain amount of carbon (more than in wrought iron and less than in cast iron) and other constituents, and possessing a hardness, elasticity, strength, etc., which vary with the composition and the heat treatment. It is commonly made by removing a certain amount of the carbon from pig-iron, and used in making tools, girders, etc. **2. high** or **hard steel,** steel with a comparatively high percentage of carbon. **3. low, mild,** or **soft steel,** steel with a comparatively low percentage of carbon. **4. medium steel,** a tough-tempering steel having a medium carbon content. **5.** something made of steel, as a knife-sharpener, for striking sparks from flints, etc. **6.** a sword; instrument or tool of this metal. **7.** a flat strip of steel for stiffening corsets, etc. **8.** *Stock Exchange.* **a.** the market quotation of a steel concern. **b.** stocks, shares, etc., of steel companies. *–adj.* **9.** pertaining to or made of steel. **10.** like steel in colour, hardness, or strength. *–v.t.* **11.** to fit with steel, as by pointing, edging, or overlaying. **12.** to cause to resemble steel in some way. **13.** to render insensible, inflexible, unyielding, determined, etc. [ME and d. OE *stēle,* c. D *staal,* G *Stahl,* Icel. *stāl*]

**steel band**[1] /– ˈbænd/, *n.* a style of band originating in the Caribbean islands and using instruments made from petrol drums, usu. tuned to a specific pitch. [STEEL + BAND[1]]

**steel band**[2] /– ˈbænd/, *n.* a thin band or layer of pyrite in a coal seam. [STEEL + BAND[2]]

**steel blue** /– ˈblu/, *n.* a dark bluish-grey colour.

**steel engraving** /– ənˈgreɪvɪŋ/, *n. Print.* **1.** a method of incising (letters, designs, etc.) on steel. **2.** the imprint, as on paper, from a plate of engraved steel.

**steel grey** /– ˈgreɪ/, *n.* a dark metallic grey with a bluish tinge.

**steel guitar** /– gəˈta/, *n.* **1.** →**pedal steel guitar. 2.** →**Hawaiian guitar. 3.** an acoustic guitar with steel strings.

**steel wool** /– ˈwʊl/, *n.* fine threads or shavings of steel, tangled into a small pad, and used for scouring, etc.

**steelwork** /ˈstilwɜk/, *n.* steel parts or articles.

**steelworker** /ˈstilwɜkə/, *n.* one employed in the manufacturing of steel.

**steelworks** /ˈstilwɜks/, *n.pl. or sing.* an establishment where steel is made and often manufactured into girders, rails, etc.

**steely** /ˈstili/, *adj.,* **steelier, steeliest. 1.** consisting or made of steel. **2.** resembling or suggesting steel; hard or strong like steel. **3.** unfeeling or merciless. **4.** (of wool) lacking character, or possessing a steely or glassy sheen, as a result of sheep grazing on pastures deficient in certain trace elements. **– steeliness,** *n.*

**steelyard** /ˈstiljad/, *n.* a portable balance with two unequal arms, the longer one having a movable counterpoise, and the shorter one bearing a hook or the like for holding the object to be weighed. [G: mistaken translation of *Stahlhof* sample (court) yard]

**steenbok** /ˈstinbɒk/, *n.* a small antelope, *Raphicerus campestris,* southern African, frequenting rocky places, and lacking dewclaws. Also, **steinbok.** [Afrikaans: lit., stonebuck]

**steep**[1] /stip/, *adj.* **1.** having an almost perpendicular slope or pitch, or a relatively high gradient, as a hill, an ascent, stairs, etc. **2.** *Colloq.* unduly high, or exorbitant, as a price or amount. **3.** *Colloq.* extreme or extravagant, as a statement. *–n.* **4.** a steep place; a declivity, as of a hill. [ME *stepe,* OE *stēap;* akin to STOOP] **– steeply,** *adv.* **– steepness,** *n.*

**steep**[2] /stip/, *v.t.* **1.** to soak in water or other liquid, as for the purpose of softening, cleansing, or the like, or of extracting some constituent. **2.** to wet thoroughly in or with any liquid, or as a liquid does; drench, saturate, or imbue. **3.** to immerse in some pervading, absorbing, or stupefying influence or agency: *a mind steeped in romance.* *–v.i.* **4.** to lie soaking in a liquid. *–n.* **5.** the act or process of steeping. **6.** the state of being steeped. **7.** a liquid in which something is steeped. [ME *stepe,* c. Swed. *stöpa*] **– steeper,** *n.*

**steepen** /ˈstipən/, *v.t.* **1.** to make steeper. *–v.i.* **2.** to become steeper.

**steeple** /ˈstipəl/, *n.* **1.** a lofty tower attached to a church, temple, or the like, and often containing bells. **2.** such a tower with a spire or other superstructure surmounting it. **3.** a spire on the top of the tower or roof of a church or the like. [ME *stepyl,* OE *stēpel,* from *stēap* high, steep]

A, steeple; B, spire

**steeplechase** /ˈstipəltʃeɪs/, *n.* **1.** a horserace over a course furnished with artificial ditches, hedges, and other obstacles. **2.** a horserace across country; point-to-point. **3.** a race run on foot by persons across country or over a course having obstacles, as ditches, hurdles, etc. *–v.i.* **4.** to ride or run in a steeplechase. **– steeplechaser,** *n.*

**steeple grass** /ˈstipəl gras/, *n.* a race course suitable for steeplechasers.

**steeplejack** /ˈstipəldʒæk/, *n.* a man who climbs steeples, tall chimneys, etc., to make repairs. Also, **spiderman.**

**steer**[1] /stɪə/, *v.t.* **1.** to guide the course of (anything in motion) by a rudder, helm, wheel, etc.: *to steer a ship.* **2.** to follow or pursue (a particular course). **3.** *Colloq.* to direct the course of. *–v.i.* **4.** to direct the course of a vessel, vehicle, aeroplane, or the like by the use of a rudder or other means. **5.** to direct the course, or pursue a course (as specified). **6.** (of a vessel, etc.) to admit of being steered; be steered or guided in a particular direction. **7. steer clear of,** to avoid. *–n.* **8. bum steer,** a misleading idea or suggested course of action. [ME *stere,* OE *stēoran,* c. D *sturen,* G *steuern,* Icel. *stȳra*] **– steerable,** *adj.* **– steerer,** *n.*

**steer**[2] /stɪə/, *n.* a castrated male bovine, esp. one raised for beef; ox; bullock. [ME; OE *steor,* c. D *stier,* G *Stier*]

**steerage** /ˈstɪərɪdʒ/, *n.* **1.** a part or division of a ship, originally that containing the steering apparatus, later varying in use. **2.** (in a passenger ship) the part allotted to the passengers who travel at the cheapest rate.

**steerageway** /ˈstɪərɪdʒweɪ/, *n.* sufficient forward movement to permit a ship to be manoeuvred.

**steering committee** /ˈstɪərɪŋ kəˌmɪti/, *n.* a committee, esp. one of a legislative body, entrusted with the preparation of the agenda of a conference, session, etc.

**steering gear** /ˈ– gɪə/, *n.* the apparatus or mechanism for steering a ship, motor vehicle, bicycle, aeroplane, etc.

**steering lock** /ˈ– lɒk/, *n.* **1.** a locking device on a steering wheel. **2.** →**lock** (def. 7).

**steering wheel** /ˈ– wil/, *n.* a wheel turned by the driver, pilot, etc., in steering a motor vehicle, ship, etc.

**steersman** /ˈstɪəzmən/, *n., pl.* **-men. 1.** one who steers a ship; helmsman. **2.** one who drives a machine.

**steeve**[1] /stiv/, *v.,* **steeved, steeving,** *n.* *–v.t.* **1.** to pack tightly, as cotton or other cargo in a ship's hold. *–n.* **2.** a long derrick or spar, with a block at one end, used in stowing cargo. [late ME, from F *estiver,* or from Pr. *estibar,* from L *stīpāre* pack]

**steeve**[2] /stiv/, *v.,* **steeved, steeving,** *n. Naut.* *–v.i.* **1.** (of a bowsprit, etc.) to incline upwards at an angle instead of extending horizontally. *–v.t.* **2.** to set (a bowsprit, etc.) at an upward inclination. *–n.* **3.** the angle that a bowsprit or the like makes with the horizontal. [cf. OE *stifig* steep]

**stego-,** a word element meaning 'cover', as in *stegosaur.* [combining form representing Gk *stégos,* var. of *stégē* roof]

**stegosaur** /ˈstɛgəsɔ/, *n.* any of the herbivorous dinosaurs constituting the genus *Stegosaurus,* reptiles of great size (sometimes nearly 12 metres long) with a heavy bony armour.

stegosaur

**stein** /staɪn/, *n.* **1.** an earthenware mug, esp. for beer. **2.** the quantity of beer held by this. [G: lit., stone]

**steinbok** /ˈstaɪnbɒk/, *n.* **1.** the steenbok. **2.** ibex.

**stela** /ˈstilə/, *n., pl.* **stelae** /ˈstili/. →**stele** (defs 1-3).

**stele** /ˈstili/, *n., pl.* **-lae** /-li/, **-les** /-liz/. **1.** *Archaeol.* an upright slab or pillar of stone bearing an inscription, sculptural design, or the like. **2.** *Archit.* a prepared surface on the face of a building, a rock, etc., bearing an inscription or the like. **3.** (in ancient Greece and Rome) a burial stone. **4.** *Bot.* the central cylinder of vascular tissue, etc., in the stem or root of a plant. Also, **stela** (for defs 1-3). [Gk: standing block (of stone)]

**stellar** /ˈstɛlə/, *adj.* **1.** of or pertaining to the stars; consisting of stars. **2.** starlike. **3.** pertaining to a leading actor, etc. [LL *stellāris,* from L *stella* star]

**stellarator** /ˈstɛləreɪtə/, *n.* an experimental apparatus for research in thermonuclear reactions, consisting of a toroid containing magnetically controlled plasma.

**stellar evolution** /ˌstɛlər ˌɛvəˈluʃən/, *n.* the process by which stars evolve during the course of their histories.

**stellate** /ˈstɛlət, -eɪt/, *adj.* being or arranged in the form of a conventional star; star-shaped. Also, **stellated.** [L *stellātus*] – **stellately,** *adv.*

**stelliferous** /stəˈlɪfərəs/, *adj. Obs.* having or abounding with stars. [L *stellifer* star-bearing + -OUS]

**stelliform** /ˈstɛləfɔm/, *adj.* star-shaped. [NL *stelliformis*]

**stellular** /ˈstɛljələ/, *adj.* **1.** having the form of a small star or small stars. **2.** spotted with star-shaped specks of colour. [LL *stellula* small star + -AR[1]]

**St Elmo's fire,** *n.* →**corposant.**

**stem**[1] /stɛm/, *n., v.,* **stemmed, stemming.** –*n.* **1.** the ascending axis of a plant, whether above or below ground, which ordinarily grows in an opposite direction to the root or descending axis. **2.** the stalk which supports a leaf, flower, or fruit. **3.** the main body of that portion of a tree, shrub, or other plant which is above ground; a trunk; a stalk. **4.** a petiole; a peduncle; a pedicel. **5.** a stalk of bananas. **6.** something resembling or suggesting the stem of a plant, flower, etc. **7.** a long, slender part: *the stem of a tobacco pipe.* **8.** the slender, upright part of a goblet, wineglass, etc. **9.** the cylindrical projection on a watch, having a knob at the end for winding. **10.** the circular rod of some locks about which the key fits and rotates. **11.** the stock, or line of descent, of a family; ancestry or pedigree. **12.** *Gram.* the element common to all the forms of an inflectional paradigm, or to some subset thereof, usu. more than a root. Thus *ten-* or *tan-* would be the root of Latin *tendere* and *tend-* would be the stem. **13.** *Music.* the vertical line forming part of a note. **14.** the main or relatively thick stroke of a letter in printing, etc. –*v.t.* **15.** to remove the stem from (a fruit, etc.). –*v.i.* **16.** to originate (usu. fol. by *from*). [ME; OE *stemn,* akin to G *Stamm*] – **stemless,** *adj.*

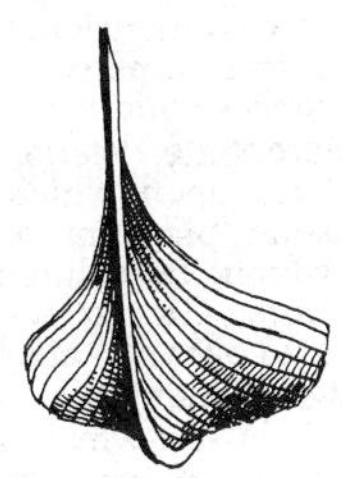

stem[4] of viking ship

**stem**[2] /stɛm/, *v.t.,* **stemmed, stemming. 1.** to stop or check. **2.** to dam up (a stream, etc.). **3.** to tamp, plug, or make tight, as a hole or a joint. **4.** *Scot.* to stanch (bleeding, etc.). –*v.i.* **5.** *Skiing.* to perform a stem turn. [ME, from Scand.; cf. Icel. *stemma,* c. G *stemmen*] – **stemless,** *adj.*

**stem**[3] /stɛm/, *v.t.,* **stemmed, stemming. 1.** to make headway against (a tide, current, gale, etc.). **2.** to make progress against (any opposition). [v. use of STEM[4]]

**stem**[4] /stɛm/, *n. Naut.* **1.** an upright at the bow of a ship into which the side timbers or plates are jointed. **2.** the forward part of a ship: *from stem to stern.* [OE *stefn, stemn* prow, stern (special use of STEM[1])]

**stem christiania** /– krɪstiˈaniə/, *n.* (in skiing) a turn executed by stemming one ski and bringing the skis parallel into a christiania during the turn. Also, **stem christie.**

**stemmer**[1] /ˈstɛmə/, *n.* **1.** one who stems (tobacco, etc.). **2.** a device for stemming (grapes, etc.).

**stemmer**[2] /ˈstɛmə/, *n.* an implement for stemming or tamping.

**stemson** /ˈstɛmsən/, *n. Naut.* a curved timber in the bow, having its lower end scarfed into the keelson. [from STEM[4], modelled after KEELSON]

**stem turn** /ˈstɛm tɜn/, *n.* (in skiing) a turn in which the ski heel is pushed outwards so that the ski slides over the snow at an angle to the direction of movement.

**stemware** /ˈstɛmwɛə/, *n.* glassware with stems.

**stem-winder** /ˈstɛm-waɪndə/, *n.* a watch wound by turning a knob at the stem.

**stem-winding** /ˈstɛm-waɪndɪŋ/, *adj.* wound, as a watch, by turning a knob at the stem.

**stench** /stɛntʃ/, *n.* **1.** an offensive smell; stink. **2.** ill-smelling quality. [ME; OE *stenc,* c. D *stank,* G *Stank*]

**stench trap** /ˈ– træp/, *n.* →**trap**[1] (def. 5).

**stencil** /ˈstɛnsəl/, *n., v.,* **-cilled, -cilling,** or (*U.S.*) **-ciled, -ciling.** –*n.* **1.** a thin sheet of paper, cardboard or metal cut through so as to reproduce a design, letters, etc., when colour is rubbed through it. **2.** the letters, designs, etc., produced. –*v.t.* **3.** to mark or paint (a surface) or produce (letters, etc.) by means of a stencil. [earlier *stanesile,* apparently from ME *stansel(en)* adorn with a variety of colours, from OF *estanceler,* from *estencele,* from L *scintilla* spark]

**sten gun** /ˈstɛn gʌn/, *n.* a light submachine gun. [*sten* formed from *S(hephard and) T(urpin)* + *En(field)* the inventors and the place of manufacture in England]

**steno-,** a word element meaning 'little', 'narrow', referring especially to shorthand, as in *stenography.* [combining form representing Gk *stenós* narrow, close]

**stenograph** /ˈstɛnəgræf/, *n.* **1.** a character written in shorthand. **2.** any of various keyboard instruments, somewhat resembling a typewriter, used for writing in shorthand, as by means of phonetic or arbitrary symbols. –*v.t.* **3.** to write in shorthand.

**stenographer** /stəˈnɒgrəfə/, *n.* a person who specialises in taking dictation in shorthand. Also, **stenographist.**

**stenography** /stəˈnɒgrəfi/, *n.* the art of writing in shorthand. – **stenographic** /stɛnəˈgræfɪk/, **stenographical** /stɛnəˈgræfɪkəl/, *adj.* – **stenographically** /stɛnəˈgræfɪkli/, *adv.*

**stenosis** /stəˈnoʊsəs/, *n., pl.* **-ses** /-siz/. *Pathol.* a narrowing or constriction of a passage or vessel of the body. [NL, from Gk]

**stenotype** /ˈstɛnətaɪp/, *n.* **1.** a keyboard instrument resembling a typewriter, used in a system of phonetic shorthand. **2.** the symbols typed in one stroke on a stenotype machine. [Trademark]

**stenotypy** /ˈstɛnəˌtaɪpi/, *n.* shorthand in which alphabetic letters or types are used to produced shortened forms of words or groups of words.

**stentor** /ˈstɛntɔ/, *n.* a person having a very loud or powerful voice. [from *Stentor,* a Greek herald in 'The Iliad' with a loud voice]

**stentorian** /stɛnˈtɔriən/, *adj.* very loud or powerful in sound: *a stentorian voice.*

**step** /stɛp/, *n., v.,* **stepped, stepping.** –*n.* **1.** a movement made by lifting the foot and setting it down again in a new position, as in walking, running, marching, or dancing. **2.** the space passed over or measured by one movement of the foot in stepping: *to move a step nearer.* **3.** the sound made by the foot in stepping. **4.** a mark or impression made by the foot on the ground; footprint. **5.** the manner of walking; gait. **6.** pace uniform with that of another or others, or in time with music: *to that step.* **7.** (*pl.*) movements or course in stepping or walking: *to retrace one's steps.* **8.** a move or proceeding, as towards some end or in the general course of action: *the first step towards peace.* **9.** a degree on a scale. **10.** a support for the foot in ascending or descending: *a step of a ladder, stair, etc.* **11.** a very short distance; a distance easily walked. **12.** a repeated pattern or unit of movement in a dance formed by a combination of foot and body motions. **13.** *Music.* **a.** a degree of the scale. **b.** the interval between two adjacent scale degrees; a second. **14.** (*pl.*) a stepladder. **15.** *Mech., etc.* a part or offset resembling a step of a stair. **16.** *Naut.* a socket, frame, or platform for supporting the lower end of a mast. **17.** *Quarrying.* a flat-topped ledge on the face of a quarry. **18. break step,** to stop marching or walking in step. **19. in step, a.** moving at the same pace as others. **b.** in harmony or conformity. **20. out of step, a.** not moving at the same pace as others. **b.** not in harmony or conformity. **21. step by step,** by degrees; gradually. **22. take steps,** to initiate a course of action. **23. watch one's step,** to go, behave, etc., with caution. –*v.i.* **24.** to move, go, etc., by lifting the foot and setting it down again in a new position, or by using the feet alternately in this manner: *to step forward.* **25.** to walk, or go on foot, esp. for a few steps or a short distance: *please step this way.* **26.** to move with measured steps, as in a dance. **27.** to go briskly or fast, as a horse. **28.** to come easily as if by a step of the foot: *to step into a fortune.* **29.** to put the foot down, as on the ground, a support, etc.; tread (*on* or *upon*), by intention or accident: *to step on a worm.* **30.** to press with the foot, as on a lever, spring, or the like, in order to operate some mechanism. *–v.t.* **31.** to take (a step, pace, stride, etc.). **32.** to go through or perform the steps of (a dance). **33.** to move or set (the foot) in taking a step. **34.** to measure (a distance, ground, etc.) by steps (sometimes fol. by *off* or *out*). **35.** to make or arrange in the manner of a series of steps. **36.** *Naut.* to fix (a mast) in its step. *–v.* **37.** Some special verb phrases are:

**step down, 1.** to decrease. **2.** to resign; relinquish a position, etc.

**step in,** to intervene; become involved.

**step on it,** *Colloq.* to hasten; hurry.

**step out, 1.** to leave a place, esp. for a short time. **2.** to walk briskly. **3.** *U.S.* to go out to a social gathering, etc.; walk out.

**step up,** to increase. [ME; d. OE *steppe,* var. of OE *stepe, stæpe,* c. D and LG *stap*] – **steplike,** *adj.* – **stepper,** *n.*

**step-,** a prefix indicating connection between members of a family by the remarriage of a parent, and not by blood. [ME; OE *stēop-,* c. G *Stief-,* Icel. *stjūp* bereaved, orphaned]

**stepbrother** /ˈstɛpbrʌðə/, *n.* one's stepfather's or stepmother's son by a former marriage.

**step-by-step** /ˌstɛp-baɪ-ˈstɛp/, *n.* a type of telephone exchange in which a series of rotating selectors operating sequentially route a call through to its destination.

**stepchild** /ˈstɛptʃaɪld/, *n., pl.* **-children.** a child of a husband or wife by a former marriage.

**step-cut** /ˈstɛp-kʌt/, *adj. Jewellery.* (of the facets) cut in sloping steps; trap-cut.

**stepdame** /ˈstɛpdeɪm/, *n. Archaic.* →**stepmother.**

**stepdaughter** /ˈstɛpdɔtə/, *n.* a daughter of one's husband or wife by a former marriage.

**step-down** /ˈstɛp-daʊn/, *adj.* converting from a higher to a lower voltage: *a step-down transformer.*

**stepfather** /ˈstɛpfaðə/, *n.* a man who occupies one's father's place by marriage to one's mother.

**step function** /ˈstɛp fʌŋkʃən/, *n. Maths.* a function whose graph resembles a step.

**stephanotis** /stɛfəˈnoʊtəs/, *n.* a climbing shrub of the genus *Stephanotis,* widespread in the tropics and subtropics, having large white flowers.

**step-in** /ˈstɛp-ɪn/, *adj.* (of garments, shoes, etc.) put on by being stepped into.

**step-ins** /ˈstɛp-ɪnz/, *n. pl.* a woman's elasticised foundation garment, without fastenings; roll-ons.

**stepladder** /ˈstɛplædə/, *n.* a ladder having flat steps or treads in place of rungs and a hinged support to keep it upright.

**stepmother** /ˈstɛpmʌðə/, *n.* a woman who occupies one's mother's place by marriage to one's father.

**step-out** /ˈstɛp-aʊt/, *n.* **1.** (in geophysical exploration) the effect which the horizontal distance between the shot point and the seismometer has on the time taken for the reflection of seismic waves. **2.** Also, **step-out well.** an oil well drilled some distance from a successful well to discover the extent of the field.

**step-parent** /ˈstɛp-pɛərənt/, *n.* a stepfather or stepmother.

**steppe** /stɛp/, *n.* an extensive plain, esp. one without trees. [Russ. *step*]

**stepped floor** /ˈstɛpt flɔ/, *n.* (of auditoriums) a floor, usu. with fixed seating, sloping down in steps towards the stage, each row of the seating being on a separate step. See **raked floor, flat floor.**

**stepping stone** /ˈstɛpɪŋ stoʊn/, *n.* **1.** a stone, or one of a line of stones, in shallow water, a marshy place, or the like, used for stepping on in crossing. **2.** a stone for use in mounting or ascending. **3.** any means of advancing or rising.

**stepping switch** /ˈ– swɪtʃ/, *n.* a rotating device which closes each of a set of electric circuits in turn.

**step rocket** /ˈstɛp rɒkət/, *n.* a multistage rocket.

**stepsister** /ˈstɛpsɪstə/, *n.* one's stepfather's or stepmother's daughter by a former marriage.

**stepson** /ˈstɛpsʌn/, *n.* a son of one's husband or wife by a former marriage.

**step-up** /ˈstɛp-ʌp/, *adj.* converting from a lower to a higher voltage: *a step-up transformer.*

**stepwise** /ˈstɛpwaɪz/, *adv.* in a step-like arrangement.

**-ster,** a suffix of personal nouns, often derogatory, referring esp. to occupation or habit, as in *songster, gamester, trickster,* also having less apparent connotations, as in *youngster, roadster.* [ME; OE *-estre, -istre,* c. D *-ster,* MLG *-(e)ster*]

**steradian** /stəˈreɪdiən/, *n.* a unit of measurement of solid angle, being the solid angle which, having its vertex in the centre of a sphere, cuts off an area of the surface of the sphere equal to that of a square with sides equal to the radius of the sphere. *Symbol:* sr

**stercoraceous** /stɜkəˈreɪʃəs/, *adj.* consisting of, resembling, or pertaining to dung or faeces. Also, **stercorous** /ˈstɜkərəs/. [L *stercorāceus*]

**stereo** /ˈstɛrioʊ, ˈstɪərioʊ/, *n., pl.* **stereos,** *adj.* *–n.* **1.** stereophonic sound reproduction. **2.** any system, equipment, etc., for reproducing stereophonic sound. **3.** a stereoscopic photograph. **4.** stereoscopic photography. **5.** *Print.* →**stereotype.** *–adj.* **6.** pertaining to stereoscopic sound, stereoscopic photography, etc.

**stereo-,** a word element referring to hardness, solidity, three-dimensionality, as in *stereogram, stereoscope.* Also, before some vowels, **stere-.** [combining form representing Gk *stereós* solid]

**stereobate** /ˈstɛriəˌbeɪt, ˈstɪə-/, *n. Archit.* **1.** the foundation or base upon which a building or the like is erected. **2.** the solid platform or structure (including the stylobate) upon which the columns of a classical building rest. [L *stereobata,* from Gk *stereo-* STEREO- + *-bátēs* stepping, going. Cf. STYLOBATE] – **stereobatic** /ˌstɛriəˈbætɪk, ˌstɪə-/, *adj.*

**stereochemistry** /ˌstɛrioʊˈkɛməstri, ˌstɪə-/, *n.* that branch of chemistry which deals with the relative arrangement in space of the atoms or groups of atoms constituting a molecule.

**stereochrome** /ˈstɛriəkroʊm, ˈstɪə-/, *n., v.* **-chromed, -chroming.** *–n.* **1.** a picture produced by a process in which waterglass is used as a vehicle or as a preservative coating. *–v.t.* **2.** to produce (a picture) by stereochromy. – **stereochromic** /stɛriəˈkroʊmɪk, stɪə-/, *adj.* – **stereochromically** /stɛriəˈkroʊmɪkli, stɪə-/, *adv.*

**stereochromy** /ˈstɛriəˌkroʊmi, ˈstɪə-/, *n.* the stereochrome process. [G *Stereochromie.* See STEREOCHROME, -Y[3]]

**stereogram** /ˈstɛriəgræm, ˈstɪə-/, *n.* **1.** a diagram or picture representing objects in a way to give the impression of solidity. **2.** a stereograph. **3.** a stereo gramophone.

**stereograph** /ˈstɛriəgræf, ˈstɪə-/, *n.* a single or double picture for a stereoscope.

**stereographic** /stɛriəˈgræfɪk, stɪə-/, *adj.* of or pertaining to stereography. – **stereographical,** *adj.* – **stereographically,** *adv.*

**stereography** /ˌstɛriˈɒgrəfi, ˌstɪə-/, *n.* the art of delineating the forms of solid bodies on a plane; a branch of solid geometry dealing with the construction of regularly defined solids.

**stereo-isomer** /ˌstɛrioʊ-ˈaɪsəmə, ˌstɪə-/, *n.* a compound which is stereo-isomeric with one or more other compounds.

**stereo-isomerism** /ˌstɛrioʊ-aɪˈsɒməˌrɪzəm, ˌstɪə-/, *n.* the isomerism ascribed to different relative positions of the atoms or groups of atoms in the molecules of optically active compounds. – **stereo-isomeric** /ˌstɛrioʊ-ˌaɪsəˈmɛrɪk, ˌstɪə-/, *adj.*

**stereometry** /ˌstɛriˈɒmətri, ˌstɪə-/, *n.* the measurement of volumes. – **stereometric** /ˌstɛrioʊˈmɛtrɪk, ˌstɪə-/, **stereometrical** /ˌstɛrioʊˈmɛtrɪkəl, ˌstɪə-/, *adj.*

**stereophonic** /stɛriəˈfɒnɪk, stɪə-/, *adj.* **1.** of or pertaining to a three-dimensional auditory perspective. **2.** of or pertaining to the multi-channel reproduction or broadcasting of sound which simulates three-dimensional auditory perspective. Most commonly two channels are used and reproduction is from two speakers or speaker systems placed apart in front of the listener. **3.** of or pertaining to the discs, tapes, equipment, etc., used in creating stereophonic effects. Cf. **monophonic, quadraphonic.** [STEREO- + PHONIC] – **stereophonically,** *adv.*

**stereophony** /stɛriˈɒfəni, stɪə-/, *n.* **1.** stereophonic perception. **2.** stereophonic reproduction. Also, **stereophonics.**

**stereophotography** /ˌstɛrioʊfəˈtɒgrəfi, ˌstɪə-/, *n.* photography which produces stereoscopic images. – **stereophotograph** /ˌsteriouˈfoutəˌgræf, ˌstɪə-/, *n.* – **stereophotographic** /ˌsteriouˌfoutəˈgræfɪk, ˌstɪə-/, *adj.*

**stereopsis** /ˌsteriˈɒpsəs, ˌstɪə-/, *n.* stereoscopic vision. [NL. See STEREO-, -OPSIS]

**stereopticon** /ˌsteriˈɒptəkən, ˌstɪə-/, *n.* an improved form of projector usu. consisting of two complete lanterns arranged so that one picture appears to dissolve while another is forming. [NL, from Gk *stere-* STERE(O)- + *optikón* OPTIC]

**stereo-regular rubber** /ˌsteriou-regjələ ˈrʌbə, ˌstɪə-/, *n.* any of a group of synthetic elastomers manufactured by the process of solution polymerisation using specific catalysts capable of controlling the stereo-isomerism of the products, thus enabling the structure and properties of natural rubber to be substantially copied.

**stereoscope** /ˈsteriəskoup, ˈstɪə-/, *n.* an optical instrument through which two pictures of the same object, taken from slightly different points of view, are viewed, one by each eye, producing the effect of a single picture of the object, with the appearance of depth or relief.

**stereoscopic** /steriəˈskɒpɪk, stɪə-/, *adj.* of or pertaining to stereoscopy. – **stereoscopical,** *adj.* – **stereoscopically,** *adv.*

**stereoscopy** /ˌsteriˈɒskəpi, ˌstɪə-/, *n.* **1.** the study of the stereoscope and its techniques. **2.** three-dimensional vision. – **stereoscopist,** *n.*

**stereospecific polymer** /ˌsteriouspəˌsɪfɪk ˈpɒləmə, ˌstɪə-/, *n.* a polymer whose molecular structure has a definite, regular spatial arrangement in contrast to an atactic polymer. See **isotactic, syndiotactic.**

**stereotaxis** /ˌsteriəˈtæksəs, ˌstɪə-/, *n.* a movement of an organism in response to contact with a solid.

**stereotropism** /ˌsteriˈɒtrəpɪzəm, ˌstɪə-/, *n.* a tropism determined by contact with a solid.

**stereotype** /ˈsteriətaɪp, ˈstɪə-/, *n., v.,* **-typed, -typing.** *–n.* **1.** a process of making metal plates to use in printing by taking a mould of composed type or the like in papier-mâché or other material and then taking from this mould a cast (plate) in type metal. **2.** a plate made by this process. **3.** a set form; convention; standardised idea or concept. *–v.t.* **4.** to make a stereotype of. **5.** to give a fixed form to. – **stereotyper,** *n.* – **stereotypic** /ˌsteriəˈtɪpɪk, ˌstɪə-/, **stereotypical** /ˌsteriəˈtɪpɪkəl, ˌstɪə-/, *adj.*

**stereotyped** /ˈsteriəˌtaɪpt, ˈstɪə-/, *adj.* **1.** reproduced in stereotype plates. **2.** fixed or settled in form; hackneyed; conventional.

**stereotypy** /ˈsteriəˌtaɪpi, ˈstɪə-/, *n.* the sterotype process.

**stereovision** /ˈstɪəriouˌvɪʒən/, *n.* →**stereoscopy** (def. 2).

**steric** /ˈsterɪk, ˈstɪərɪk/, *adj.* pertaining to the spatial relationship of atoms in the molecule. Also, **sterical.** [STER(EO)- + -IC]

**sterile** /ˈsteraɪl/, *adj.* **1.** free from living germs or microorganisms: *sterile bandage.* **2.** incapable of producing, or not producing, offspring. **3.** barren; unproductive of vegetation, as soil. **4.** *Bot.* **a.** denoting a plant in which reproductive structures fail to develop. **b.** bearing no stamens or pistils. **5.** unproductive of results; fruitless. [L *sterilis* barren] – **sterilely,** *adv.* – **sterility** /stəˈrɪləti/, *n.*

**sterilisation** /ˌsterəlaɪˈzeɪʃən/, *n.* **1.** the act of sterilising. **2.** the condition of being sterilised. **3.** the destruction of all living micro-organisms, as pathogenic or saprophytic bacteria, vegetative forms, and spores. Also, **sterilization.**

**sterilise** /ˈsterəlaɪz/, *v.t.,* **-lised, -lising.** **1.** to destroy micro-organisms in, usu. by bringing to a high temperature with steam, dry heat, or boiling liquid. **2.** to destroy (one's) ability to reproduce by removing sex organs or inhibiting their functions. Also, **sterilize.** – **steriliser,** *n.*

**sterling** /ˈstɜlɪŋ/, *adj.* **1.** consisting of or pertaining to British money. **2.** (of silver) being of standard quality, 92½ per cent pure silver. **3.** made of sterling silver: *sterling cutlery.* **4.** thoroughly excellent: *a man of sterling worth.* **5.** (formerly) born in Britain or Ireland (opposed to *currency*). *–n.* **6.** the standard of fineness of legal coin in Britain: **a.** for silver (sterling silver), before 1920, 0.925; now, 0.500. **b.** for gold at one time, 0.995 but now, 0.916 66. **7.** silver having the sterling fineness of 0.925, used esp. in manufacture. **8.** manufactured goods of sterling silver. **9.** (formerly) one born in Britain or Ireland (opposed to *currency*). [ME, name of a silver coin, ? from *ster* STAR + -LING[1] (with ref. to the little star on some of the coins)]

**stern**[1] /stɜn/, *adj.* **1.** firm, strict, or uncompromising: *stern discipline.* **2.** hard, harsh, or severe: *a stern warning.* **3.** rigorous or austere; of an unpleasantly serious character: *stern times.* **4.** grim or forbidding in aspect: *a stern face.* [ME; OE *styrne;* akin to G *starr* stiff, Gk *stereós* hard, solid] – **sternly,** *adv.* – **sternness,** *n.*

**stern**[2] /stɜn/, *n.* **1.** the hinder part of a ship or boat (often opposed to *stem*). **2.** the hinder part of anything. [ME, ? from Scand.; cf. Icel. *stjōrn* steering (see STERNPOST)]

**sternal** /ˈstɜnəl/, *adj.* of or pertaining to the sternum.

**stern chase** /ˈstɜn tʃeɪs/, *n.* a chase in which the pursuing vessel follows in the wake of the other or astern of it.

**stern-chaser** /ˈstɜn-tʃeɪsə/, *n.* a cannon mounted in the stern of a sailing ship.

**stern door** /ˈstɜn dɔ/, *n.* the large, strong, mechanically-operated water-tight door at the stern of a vehicle-deck ship giving vehicular access by a ramp from the shore.

**sternmost** /ˈstɜnmoust/, *adj.* **1.** farthest astern or in the rear. **2.** nearest the stern.

**sternpost** /ˈstɜnpoust/, *n.* the principal piece of timber or iron in the stern of a vessel, having its lower end fastened to the keel, and usu. serving as a support for the rudder.

**stern sheets** /ˈstɜn ʃits/, *n.pl.* the afterpart of an open boat, occupied by the person in command and by passengers.

**sternum** /ˈstɜnəm/, *n., pl.* **-na** /-nə/, **-nums.** a bone or series of bones extending along the middle line of the ventral portion of the body of most vertebrates, consisting in man of a flat, narrow bone connected with the clavicles and the true ribs; the breastbone. [NL, from Gk *stérnon* chest, breast]

**sternutation** /stɜnjəˈteɪʃən/, *n.* the act of sneezing. [L *sternūtātio*]

**sternutator** /ˈstɜnjəteɪtə/, *n.* a chemical agent causing nose irritation, coughing, etc., used in chemical warfare, etc.

**sternutatory** /stəˈnjutətri, -təri/, *adj., n., pl.* **-ries.** *–adj.* **1.** Also, **sternutative.** causing or tending to cause sneezing. *–n.* **2.** a sternutatory substance.

**sternwards** /ˈstɜnwədz/, *adv.* towards the stern; astern.

**sternway** /ˈstɜnweɪ/, *n.* the movement of a ship backwards, or stern foremost.

**stern-wheel** /ˈstɜn-wil/, *adj.* propelled by a paddle-wheel at the stern. – **stern-wheeler,** *n.*

**steroid** /ˈsterɔɪd, ˈstɪə-/, *n.* any of a large group of lipids most of which have specific physiological action, as the sterols, bile acids, and many hormones.

**steroid enema** /– ˈenəmə/, *n.* an enema containing a cortisone derivative, used in the treatment of some diseases of the colon.

**sterol** /ˈsterɒl/, *n.* any of a group of steroid alcohols derived from plants or animals, as cholesterol and ergosterol. [abstracted from (CHOLE)STEROL, (ERGO)STEROL]

**stertor** /ˈstɜtə/, *n.* a heavy snoring sound accompanying respiration in certain diseases. [NL, from L *stertere* snore]

**stertorous** /ˈstɜtərəs/, *adj.* **1.** characterised by stertor or heavy snoring. **2.** breathing in this manner. – **stertorously,** *adv.* – **stertorousness,** *n.*

**stet** /stet/, *v.,* **stetted, stetting.** *–v.i.* **1.** let it stand (a direction on a printer's proof, a manuscript, or the like to retain cancelled matter, usu. accompanied by a row of dots under or beside the matter). *–v.t.* **2.** to mark with the word 'stet' or with dots. [L: let it stand]

**stetho-,** a word element meaning 'chest'. Also, before vowels, **steth-.** [combining form representing Gk *stêthos*]

**stethometer** /stəˈθɒmətə/, *n.* an instrument for measuring the respiratory movements of the walls of the chest and abdomen.

**stethoscope** /ˈsteθəskoup/, *n.* an instrument used in auscultation to convey sounds in the chest or other parts of the body to the ear of the examiner. – **stethoscopy** /stəˈθɒskəpi/, *n.*

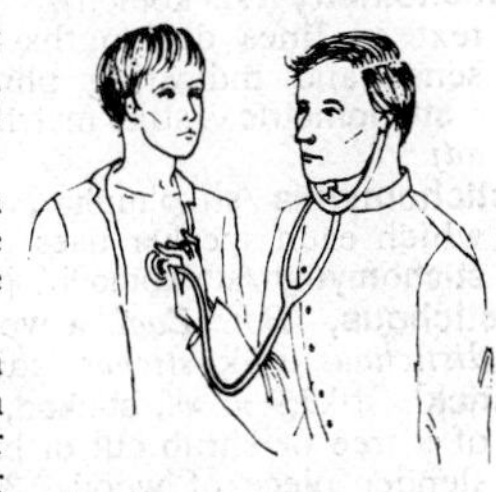

stethoscope

**stethoscopic** /stεθə'skɒpɪk/, *adj.* **1.** pertaining to the stethoscope or to stethoscopy. **2.** made or obtained by the stethoscope. Also, **stethoscopical.** – **stethoscopically,** *adv.*

**stetson** /'stεtsən/, *n.* a man's hat having a broad brim and a wide crown, formerly common in the western U.S. [named after the designer, John *Stetson,* 1830-1906, American hatmaker]

**stevedore** /'stivədɔ/, *n., v.,* **-dored, -doring.** *–n.* **1.** a firm or individual engaged in the loading or unloading of a vessel. *–v.t.* **2.** to load or unload the cargo of (a ship). *–v.i.* **3.** to load or unload a vessel. [Sp. *estivador,* from *estivar* pack, stow, from L *stīpāre* press]

**stevedore's knot** /'stivədɔz ˌnɒt/, *n.* a knot which forms a lump in a line to prevent it from passing through a hole, etc.

**stew** /stju/, *v.t.* **1.** to cook (food) by simmering or slow boiling. *–v.i.* **2.** to undergo cooking by simmering or slow boiling. **3.** *Colloq.* to fret, worry, or fuss. **4. stew in one's own juice,** to suffer one's own misfortunes or the consequences of one's own actions without help. *–n.* **5.** a preparation of meat, fish or other food cooked by stewing. **6.** *Colloq.* a state of uneasiness, agitation, or worry. **7.** (*usu. pl.*) *Archaic.* a brothel. **8.** a sporting event, esp. racing or trotting, the outcome of which has been fixed beforehand. **9.** any underhand trick. [ME, from OF *estuver,* from VL *extūfāre* perspire, from *tūfus* vapour, from Gk *tŷphos*]

**steward** /'stjuəd/, *n.* **1.** one who manages another's property or financial affairs; one who administers anything as the agent of another or others. **2.** one who has charge of the household of another, providing for the table, directing the servants, etc. **3.** an employee who has charge of the table, the servants, etc., in a club or other establishment. **4.** any attendant on a ship or aircraft who waits on passengers. **5.** one responsible for arranging the details and conduct of a public meeting, race meeting, public entertainment, etc. **6.** *U.S. Navy.* a petty officer in charge of officers' quarters and mess. *–v.t.* **7.** to act as steward of; manage. *–v.i.* **8.** to act or serve as steward. [ME; OE *stīweard, stigweard,* from *stig* hall + *weard* keeper, WARD] – **stewardship,** *n.*

**stewardess** /'stjuədəs, stjuəd'εs/, *n.* a woman attendant on board an aircraft or ship who waits on passengers.

**stewed** /stjud/, *adj.* **1.** cooked by simmering or slow boiling, as food. **2.** (of tea) made disagreeably strong by being infused too long. **3.** *Colloq.* intoxicated or drunk.

**sthenia** /sθə'niə, 'sθiniə/, *n. Pathol.* strength; excessive vital force. [NL, abstracted from *asthenia* ASTHENIA]

**sthenic** /'sθεnɪk/, *adj.* sturdy; heavily and strongly built. [abstracted from ASTHENIC]

**Sthn,** Southern.

**stibine** /'stɪbaɪn/, *n.* antimonous hydride, $SbH_3$, a colourless poisonous gas. [STIB(IUM) + -INE[2]]

**stibium** /'stɪbiəm/, *n.* →**antimony.** [L] – **stibial,** *adj.*

**stibnite** /'stɪbnaɪt/, *n.* a mineral, antimony sulphide, $Sb_2S_3$, lead grey in colour with a metallic lustre, occurring in crystals, often acicular, or in bladed masses, the most important ore of antimony. [STIB(I)N(E) + -ITE[1]]

**stich** /stɪk/, *n.* a verse or line of poetry. [Gk *stíchos* row, line, verse]

**stichic** /'stɪkɪk/, *adj.* **1.** pertaining to or consisting of stichs. **2.** composed of lines of the same metrical form throughout. [Gk *stichikós*]

**stichometry** /stə'kɒmətri/, *n.* the practice of writing a prose text in lines of lengths corresponding to divisions in the sense and indicating phrasal rhythms. [LGk *stichometría*] – **stichometric** /stɪkə'mεtrɪk/, **stichometrical** /stɪkə'mεtrɪkəl/, *adj.*

**stichomythia** /stɪkə'mɪθiə/, *n.* dramatic practice of dialogue in which each speaker uses exactly one line of the verse. Also, **stichomythy** /stə'kɒməθi/. [Gk] – **stichomythic,** *adj.*

**-stichous,** *Bot., Zool.* a word element referring to rows, as in *distichous.* [Gk *-stichos* (adj. suffix) having stichs]

**stick**[1] /stɪk/, *n., v.,* **sticked, sticking.** *–n.* **1.** a branch or shoot of a tree or shrub cut or broken off. **2.** a relatively long and slender piece of wood. **3.** an elongated piece of wood for burning, for carpentry, or for any special purpose. **4.** a rod or wand; a baton. **5.** a walking stick or cane. **6.** a club or cudgel. **7.** an elongated, stick-like piece of some material: *a stick of rock.* **8.** *Sport.* the stick or racquet used to hit the ball in hockey or lacrosse. **9.** (*pl.*) the goal posts. **10.** *Aeron.* a lever, usu. with a handle, by which the longitudinal and lateral motions of an aeroplane are controlled; joystick. **11.** *Naut.* a mast, or a part of a mast. **12.** *Print.* →**composing stick.** **13.** *Mil.* **a.** a group of bombs so arranged as to be released in a row across a target. **b.** the bombload. **c.** a group of parachutists jumping in sequence. **14. the sticks,** *Colloq.* **a.** an area or district regarded as lacking in the amenities of urban life. **b.** →**back country.** **15.** a piece of furniture. **16.** *Colloq.* a person: *a decent stick.* **17.** *Colloq.* a surfboard. **18.** *U.S. Colloq.* a marijuana cigarette. **19. in a cleft stick,** in a dilemma, awkward position, etc. **20. more than one can poke (shake) a stick at,** *Colloq.* a lot of; many; much. **21. wrong end of the stick,** a complete misunderstanding of facts, a situation, etc. *–v.t.* **22.** to furnish with a stick or sticks in order to support or prop, as a plant. **23.** *Print.* to set (type) in a composing stick. [ME *stiffe,* OE *sticca,* akin to G *stecken*]

**stick**[2] /stɪk/, *v.,* **stuck, sticking,** *n.* *–v.t.* **1.** to pierce or puncture with a pointed instrument, as a dagger, spear, or pin; stab. **2.** to kill by this means: *to stick a pig.* **3.** to thrust (something pointed) in, into, through etc.: *to stick a pin into a balloon.* **4.** to fasten in position by thrusting the point or end into something: *to stick a nail in a wall.* **5.** to fasten in position by, or as by, something thrust through: *to stick a badge on one's coat.* **6.** to fix or impale upon something pointed: *to stick a potato on a fork.* **7.** to set with things piercing the surface: *to stick a cushion full of pins.* **8.** to furnish or adorn with things attached or set here and there. **9.** to place upon a stick or pin for exhibit: *to stick butterflies.* **10.** to thrust or poke into a place or position indicated: *to stick one's head out of the window.* **11.** to place in a specified position: *stick your books on the table.* **12.** to fasten or attach by causing to adhere: *to stick a stamp on a letter.* **13.** to bring to a standstill; render unable to proceed or go back: *to be stuck in the mud.* **14.** to endure; tolerate. **15.** to confuse; perplex; puzzle. **16.** to impose an unpleasant task upon. *–v.i.* **17.** to have the point piercing, or embedded in something. **18.** to remain attached by adhesion: *the mud sticks to one's shoes.* **19.** to hold, cleave, or cling: *to stick to a horse's back.* **20.** to remain persistently or permanently: *a fact that sticks in the mind.* **21.** to remain firm in resolution, opinion, statement, attachment, etc.; hold faithfully, as to a promise or bargain. **22.** to keep steadily or unremittingly at a task, undertaking, or the like (fol. by *at* or *to*): *to stick at a job.* **23.** to become fastened, hindered, checked, or stationary by some obstruction. **24.** to be at a standstill, as from difficulties. **25.** to hesitate or scruple (usu. fol. by *at*). **26.** to be thrust, or extend, project, or protrude (fol. by *through, from, out, up,* etc.). **27.** to remain or stay, usu. for a considerable time: *I can't bear to stick indoors all day.* *–v.* **28.** Some special verb phrases are:

**stick around,** *Colloq.* to stay nearby; linger.

**stick by or to,** to remain loyal or faithful to.

**stick in one's throat,** to be hard to accept.

**stick it!** *Colloq.* (an expression of contempt, dismissal, disgust, etc.).

**stick on,** to remain; stay behind.

**stick one's neck out,** to expose oneself to blame, criticism, etc.; to take a risk.

**stick one's nose in,** to pry; interfere.

**stick out, 1.** to protrude; thrust out. **2.** to be obvious, conspicuous, etc.: *to stick out a mile.* **3.** to endure; stand one's ground.

**stick out for,** to continue to ask for; be persistent in demanding.

**stick (something) out,** to endure; put up with until the very end: *they were bored by the film but stuck it out for two hours.*

**stick together,** to remain friendly, loyal, etc., to one another.

**stick up, 1.** to project or protrude upwards. **2.** *Colloq.* to rob, esp. at gunpoint.

**stick up for,** to speak or act in favour of; defend; support.

**stick up to,** to confront boldly; resist strongly.

**stick with,** to remain loyal to.

**(you can) stick that for a joke (lark),** *Colloq.* (an expression indicating complete and often derisive rejection of a proposal,

plan, etc.).
–*n.* **29.** a thrust with a pointed instrument; a stab. **30.** the quality of adhering or of causing things to adhere. **31.** something causing adhesion. **32.** *Obs.* a stoppage or standstill. **33.** *Obs.* something causing delay or difficulty. **34.** *Mil.* a number of missiles or bombs fired or released in rapid succession from a single aircraft. **35.** *Mil.* a number of parachutists who jump from one aperture or door of an aircraft during one run over a dropping zone. [ME *stike* (*n*), OE *stician,* akin to (M) LG *stikken*]

**stick commander** /'– kəmændə, -man-/, *n.* →**jumpmaster.**

**sticker** /'stɪkə/, *n.* **1.** one who or that which sticks. **2.** an adhesive label, usu. with an advertisement, publicity slogan, or other message printed on it. **3.** a persistent, diligent person. **4.** *Colloq.* something that nonplusses or puzzles one. **5.** a burr, thorn, or the like. **6.** a weapon used for piercing or stabbing. **7.** *N.Z. Colloq.* a traffic-offence notice, usu. stuck to the offending vehicle.

**stickful** /'stɪkfʊl/, *n., pl.* **-fuls.** (in printing) as much set type as a composing stick will hold.

**sticking** /'stɪkɪŋ/, *n.* the neck of a beef carcass.

**sticking place** /'– pleɪs/, *n.* the place in an animal's neck where the knife is thrust in slaughtering. Also, **sticking point.**

**sticking plaster** /'– plastə/, *n.* an adhesive cloth or other material for covering and closing superficial wounds, etc.

**sticking point** /'– pɔɪnt/, *n.* **1.** a point at which further progress is impeded or becomes impossible. **2.** →**sticking place.**

**stick insect** /'stɪk ˌɪnsɛkt/, *n.* any of certain orthopterous insects of the family Phasmidae, with long, slender, twig-like bodies.

stick insect

**stick-in-the-mud** /'stɪk-ən-ðə-mʌd/, *n.* one who is unadventurous, lacking initiative, or opposed to new ideas, progress, novelty, etc.

**stickjaw** /'stɪkdʒɔ/, *n. Colloq.* any glutinous toffee, chewing gum, pudding, etc.

**stickle** /'stɪkəl/, *v.i.,* **-led, -ling. 1.** to argue or haggle insistently, esp. on trivial matters. **2.** to raise objections; scruple; demur. [ME *stightle* set in order, frequentative of obs. *stight,* OE *stihtan,* c. G *stiften*]

**stickleback** /'stɪkəlbæk/, *n.* any of the small, pugnacious, spiny-backed fishes of the family Gasterosteidae, of fresh waters and sea inlets, esp. *Gasterosteus aculeatus,* **the three-spined stickleback,** and *G. spinachia,* **the fifteen-spined stickleback,** a saltwater species. [ME *stykylbak,* from OE *sticol* scaly + *bæc* back]

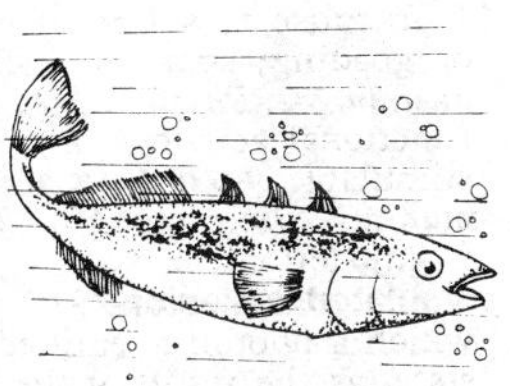
three-spined stickleback

**stickler** /'stɪklə/, *n.* **1.** a person who insists on something unyieldingly (fol. by *for*): *a stickler for ceremony.* **2.** any puzzling or difficult problem.

**stick-nest rat** /ˌstɪk-nɛst 'ræt/, *n.* a primitive, gregarious Australian rodent of the genus *Leporillus,* which builds nests or houses of sticks and twigs.

**stick-picker** /'stɪk-pɪkə/, *n. Colloq.* →**emu-bobber.**

**stickpin** /'stɪkpɪn/, *n. U.S.* →**tiepin.**

**sticktight** /'stɪktaɪt/, *n.* any of several species of *Bidens,* as *B. pilosa,* having flat, barbed achenes which adhere to clothing, etc.

**stick-up** /'stɪk-ʌp/, *n. Colloq.* a hold-up or robbery.

**sticky**[1] /'stɪki/, *adj.,* **stickier, stickiest. 1.** having the property of adhering, as glue; adhesive. **2.** covered with adhesive matter: *sticky hands.* **3.** *Cricket.* (of a wicket) affected by rain causing the ball to veer off in an unpredictable direction on the bounce. **4.** (of the weather, etc.) humid: *an unbearably sticky day.* **5.** *Colloq.* difficult to deal with; awkward; troublesome. **6.** *Colloq.* disagreeable; painful. –*n.* **7.** *Cricket Colloq.* →**sticky wicket** (def. 1). – **stickily,** *adv.* – **stickiness,** *n.*

**sticky**[2] /'stɪki/, *n. Colloq.* **1.** a look. **2. have a sticky,** *Colloq.* to take a look. [short for STICKYBEAK]

**stickybeak** /'stɪkibik/, *v.i.* **1.** to pry; meddle. –*n.* **2.** one who pries.

**sticky end** /stɪki 'ɛnd/, *n.* **1.** an unhappy final situation: *that girl will come to a sticky end.* **2.** a wretched or violent death: *he met a sticky end in Mexico.*

**sticky-nose** /'stɪki-noʊz/, *v.i.,* **-nosed, -nosing,** *n.* →**stickybeak.**

**sticky tape** /'stɪki ˌteɪp/, *n. Colloq.* an adhesive tape, made of cellulose and usu. transparent; durex. Also, **Scotch tape.**

**sticky wicket** /– 'wɪkət/, *n.* **1.** *Cricket.* a wicket, affected by rain, which gives an unpredictable bounce. **2.** *Colloq.* a delicate, difficult or disadvantageous situation: *he's on a sticky wicket now that his father has disinherited him.*

**stiff** /stɪf/, *adj.* **1.** rigid or firm in substance; not flexible, pliant, or easily bent: *a stiff collar.* **2.** not moving or working easily: *a stiff hinge.* **3.** (of a person, etc.) moving only with difficulty, as from cold, age, exhaustion, etc. **4.** unfortunate; unlucky: *that's stiff, mate.* **5.** blowing violently, strongly, or with steady force: *stiff winds.* **6.** strong, as alcoholic beverages. **7.** firm in purpose or resolution; unyielding; stubborn. **8.** stubbornly maintained, as a struggle, etc. **9.** firm against any lowering action, as prices, etc. **10.** rigidly formal, as persons, manners, proceedings, etc. **11.** lacking ease and grace; awkward: *a stiff style of writing.* **12.** excessively regular, as a design; not graceful in form or arrangement. **13.** laborious or difficult, as a task. **14.** severe, as a penalty. **15.** excessive; unusually high or great, as a price, demand, etc. **16.** firm from tension; taut: *to keep a stiff rein.* **17.** relatively firm in consistency, as semisolid matter: *a stiff jelly.* **18.** dense, compact, or tenacious: *stiff soil.* **19.** *Naut.* (of a ship) resistant to heeling; stable. **20.** *Colloq.* drunk. **21. stiff cheese (cheddar) (luck),** *Colloq.* **a.** bad luck. **b.** (an off-hand expression of sympathy). **c.** (a rebuff to an appeal for sympathy). **22. stiff with,** *Colloq.* bristling with: *the area was stiff with cops.* **23.** *Prison Colloq.* a letter sent illegally out of gaol. –*n. Colloq.* **24.** a dead body; corpse. **25.** a drunk. **26.** a racehorse that is certain to lose. **27.** Also, **stiffy, stiffie.** an erect penis. –*adv.* **28.** in a rigid state: *the clothes were frozen stiff.* **29.** completely; extremely: *we were all scared stiff.* [ME; OE *stīf,* c. G *steif;* akin to L *stīpāre* crowd, pack] – **stiffish,** *adj.* – **stiffly,** *adv.* – **stiffness,** *n.*

**stiff-arm** /'stɪf-am/, *Rugby Football.* –*n.* **1.** →**stiff-arm tackle.** –*v.t.* **2.** to give (someone) a stiff-arm tackle.

**stiff-arm tackle** /– 'tækəl/, *n.* (in football) the illegal felling of an opponent by combining a punch with the action of a tackle.

**stiffen** /'stɪfən/, *v.t.* **1.** to make stiff. –*v.i.* **2.** to become stiff or tense. – **stiffener,** *n.*

**stiff-necked** /'stɪf-nɛkt/, *adj.* **1.** having a stiff neck. **2.** stubborn; perversely obstinate; refractory.

**stiffy** /'stɪfi/, *n. pl.* **-fies.** *Colloq.* an erect penis. Also, **stiffie.**

**stifle**[1] /'staɪfəl/, *v.,* **-fled, -fling.** –*v.t.* **1.** to kill by impeding respiration; smother. **2.** to keep back or repress: *to stifle a yawn.* **3.** to suppress, crush, or stop: *to stifle a revolt.* –*v.i.* **4.** to become stifled or suffocated. **5.** to suffer from difficulty in breathing, as in a close atmosphere. [Scand.; cf. Icel. *stifla* stop up] – **stifler,** *n.*

**stifle**[2] /'staɪfəl/, *n.* the joint of the hind leg of a horse, dog, etc., between the femur and the tibia. Also, **stifle joint.** [ME; orig. uncert.]

**stifling** /'staɪflɪŋ/, *adj.* suffocating; oppressively close: *a stifling atmosphere.* – **stiflingly,** *adv.*

**stigma** /'stɪgmə/, *n., pl.* **stigmata** /'stɪgmətə/, **stigmas** (*esp. defs 4 and 5*). **1.** a mark of disgrace; a stain, as on one's reputation. **2.** a characteristic mark or sign of defect, degeneration, disease, etc. **3.** *Pathol.* a spot or mark on the skin, esp. a place or point on the skin which bleeds during certain mental states, as in hysteria. **4.** *Zool.* a small mark, spot, pore, or the like, on an animal or organ, as: **a.** the eyespot, usu. red, of a protozoan. **b.** (in insects) an entrance into the respiratory system. **5.** *Bot.* that part of a pistil which receives the pollen. **6.** *Rom. Cath. Ch.* marks said to have been supernaturally impressed upon certain persons in the semblance of the wounds on the crucified body of Christ. **7.** *Archaic.* a mark made by a branding iron on the skin of a criminal or slave. [L, from Gk]

**stigmatic** /stɪgˈmætɪk/, *adj.* **1.** pertaining to a stigma, mark, spot, or the like. **2.** *Bot.* pertaining to or having the character of a stigma (part of the pistil). **3.** *Optics.* converging to a point; anastigmatic. *–n.* **4.** *Rom. Cath. Ch.* one marked with stigmata.

**stigmatise** /ˈstɪgmətaɪz/, *v.t.*, **-tised, -tising.** **1.** to mark with a stigma or brand. **2.** to set some mark of disgrace or infamy upon. **3.** to produce stigmata, marks, spots, or the like on. Also, **stigmatize.** – **stigmatisation** /ˌstɪgmətaɪˈzeɪʃən/, *n.* – **stigmatiser** /ˈstɪgmətaɪzə/, *n.*

**stigmatism** /ˈstɪgmətɪzəm/, *n.* **1.** *Optics.* a condition in which there is no astigmatism. **2.** *Pathol.* the condition in which stigmata are present.

**stilb** /stɪlb/, *n.* a unit of luminance equal to 10 000 candela per square metre.

**stilbene** /ˈstɪlbin/, *n.* a colourless, crystalline insoluble substance, $C_6H_5 \cdot CH{:}CH \cdot C_6H_5$, used in the dyestuffs industry.

**stilbite** /ˈstɪlbaɪt/, *n.* a white to brown or red zeolite mineral, a hydrous silicate of calcium, sodium and aluminium, occurring in sheaf-like aggregates of crystals and in radiating masses. [Gk *stilbein* glitter + -ITE[2]]

**stilboestrol** /stɪlˈbistrɒl/, *n.* a synthetic hormone, $C_{18}H_{20}O_2$, the parent substance of a group of oestrogenic agents, some of which are more active than those of the human body. Also, *U.S.*, **stilbestrol.**

**stile**[1] /staɪl/, *n.* **1.** a series of steps or the like for ascending and descending in getting over a fence, etc., which remains closed to cattle. **2.** →**turnstile.** [ME; OE *stigel*, from *stīgan*, c. G *steigen* ascend, go]

stile[1]

**stile**[2] /staɪl/, *n.* a vertical member in a wainscot, panelled door, or other piece of framing. [probably from D *stijl* pillar, doorpost, prop]

**stiletto** /stəˈlɛtoʊ/, *n.*, *pl.* **-tos,** *v.*, **-toed, -toing.** *–n.* **1.** a dagger having a narrow blade, thick in proportion to its width. **2.** a small sharp-pointed instrument for making eyelet holes in needlework. **3.** →**stiletto heel.** *–v.t.* **4.** to stab or kill with a stiletto. [It., diminutive of *stilo* dagger, from L *stilus* pointed instrument]

**stiletto heel** /– ˈhil/, *n.* a high heel on a woman's shoe that tapers to an extremely small base. Also, **stiletto.**

**still**[1] /stɪl/, *adj.* **1.** remaining in place or at rest; motionless; stationary: *to stand still.* **2.** free from sound or noise, as a place, time, etc.; silent. **3.** subdued or low in sound; hushed: *a still small voice.* **4.** free from commotion of any kind; quiet; tranquil; calm. **5.** without waves or perceptible current, as water. **6.** not effervescent or sparkling, as wine. **7.** *Photog.* denoting or pertaining to a still (photograph). *–n.* **8.** *Poetic.* stillness or silence. **9.** a single photographic picture, esp. a print of one of the frames of a film. *–adv.* **10.** at this or that time; as previously: *is she still here?* **11.** up to this or that time: *points still unsettled.* **12.** in the future as in the past: *objections will still be made.* **13.** even or yet (with comparatives or the like): *still more complaints.* **14.** even then; yet; nevertheless: *to be rich and still crave for more.* **15.** without sound or movement. **16.** *Poetic.* steadily; constantly; always. *–conj.* **17.** and yet; but yet; nevertheless: *it was futile, still they fought.* *–v.t.* **18.** to silence or hush (sounds, etc.). **19.** to calm, appease, or allay. **20.** to quiet (waves, winds, commotion, tumult, passion, pain, etc.). *–v.i.* **21.** to become still or quiet. [ME and OE *stille*, c. G *Still*]

**still**[2] /stɪl/, *n.* **1.** a distilling apparatus, consisting of a vessel, in which the substance is heated and vaporised, and a cooling device or coil for condensing the vapour. **2.** →**distillery.** *–v.t., v.i.* **3.** *Obs.* to distil. [aphetic var. of DISTIL]

**stillbirth** /ˈstɪlbɜθ/, *n.* **1.** the birth of a dead child or organism. **2.** a foetus dead at birth.

**stillborn** /ˈstɪlbɔn/, *adj.* **1.** dead when born. **2.** (of a project) not proceeding beyond the planning stage.

**stiller** /ˈstɪlə/, *n. Obs.* →**distiller.**

**still hunt** /stɪl ˈhʌnt/, *n. U.S.* **1.** a hunt for game carried on stealthily, as by stalking or under cover. **2.** *Colloq.* a quiet or secret pursuit of any object.

**still-hunt** /ˈstɪl-hʌnt/, *U.S.* *–v.t.* **1.** to pursue by a still hunt. *–v.i.* **2.** to carry on a still hunt.

**stilliform** /ˈstɪləfɔm/, *adj.* drop-shaped. [*stilli-* (combining form of L *stilla* drop) + -FORM]

**still life** /stɪl ˈlaɪf/, *n.*, *pl.* **still lifes** /stɪl ˈlaɪfs/. a picture representing inanimate objects, such as fruit, flowers, etc. – **still-life,** *adj.*

Stillson wrench

**stillness** /ˈstɪlnəs/, *n.* **1.** absence of motion. **2.** quiet; silence; hush.

**Stillson wrench** /ˈstɪlsən rɛntʃ/, *n.* **1.** a monkey-wrench with a pivoted adjustable jaw that grips pipes, etc., more tightly when pressure is exerted on the handle. **2.** a trademark for such a wrench.

**stilly** /ˈstɪlli/, *adv.*; /ˈstɪli/, *adj.* *–adv.* **1.** quietly; silently. *–adj.* **2.** *Poetic.* still; quiet.

**stilt** /stɪlt/, *n.* **1.** one of two poles, each with a support for the foot at some distance above the ground. **2.** one of several high posts underneath any structure built above land or over water. **3.** any of various limicoline birds, esp. of the genus *Himantopus*, with very long legs, long neck, and slender bill, and living esp. in marshes. *–v.t.* **4.** to raise on or as on stilts. [ME *stilte*, c. LG *stilte*, Norw. *stilta* pole]

stilted arch

**stilted** /ˈstɪltəd/, *adj.* **1.** stiffly dignified or formal, as speech, literary style, etc.; pompous. **2.** *Archit.* raised on or as on stilts: *a stilted arch.* – **stiltedly,** *adv.* – **stiltedness,** *n.*

**stilton** /ˈstɪltən/, *n.* a rich, waxy, white cheese, veined with mould. [after *Stilton* in Huntingdonshire, England]

**stimulant** /ˈstɪmjələnt/, *n.* **1.** *Physiol., Med.* something that temporarily quickens some vital process or the functional activity of some organ or part. **2.** any beverage or food that stimulates. **3.** *Rare.* a stimulus or incentive. *–adj.* **4.** *Physiol., Med.* temporarily quickening some vital process or functional activity. **5.** stimulating. [L *stimulans*, ppr., stimulating, inciting]

stilts

**stimulate** /ˈstɪmjəleɪt/, *v.*, **-lated, -lating.** *–v.t.* **1.** to rouse to action or effort, as by pricking or goading; spur on; incite: *to stimulate production.* **2.** *Physiol., Med., etc.* to excite (an organ, etc.) to its functional activity. **3.** to invigorate by an alcoholic or other stimulant. *–v.i.* **4.** to act as a stimulus or stimulant. [L *stimulātus*, pp., goaded on] – **stimulator,** *n.* – **stimulation** /stɪmjəˈleɪʃən/, *n.*

**stimulated emission** /ˌstɪmjəleɪtəd əˈmɪʃən/, *n.* the process by which a photon is emitted by an atom in an excited quantum state, as the result of the impact from outside of a photon of exactly equal energy. It is on this principle that masers and lasers work.

**stimulative** /ˈstɪmjələtɪv/, *adj.* **1.** serving to stimulate. *–n.* **2.** a stimulating agency.

**stimulus** /ˈstɪmjələs/, *n.*, *pl.* **-li** /-li, -laɪ/, **-luses.** **1.** something that incites to action or exertion, or quickens action, feeling, thought, etc.; an incentive. **2.** *Physiol., etc.* something that excites an organism or part to functionable activity. [NL, special use of L *stimulus* goad, sting]

**sting** /stɪŋ/, *v.*, **stung, stinging,** *n.* *–v.t.* **1.** to prick or wound with some sharp-pointed, often venom-bearing, organ, with which certain animals are furnished: *to be stung by a bee.* **2.** to affect painfully or irritatingly, esp. as a result of contact with certain plants: *to be stung by nettles.* **3.** to cause mental or moral suffering: *to be stung with remorse.* **4.** to goad or drive as by sharp irritation. **5.** *Colloq.* to get money from, esp. by begging, overcharging, or swindling. **6.** to use or have a sting, as bees. **7.** to cause a sharp, smarting pain, as some plants, an acrid liquid or gas, etc. **8.** to cause acute mental pain or irritation, as annoying thoughts, etc. **9.** to feel acute mental pain or irritation. **10.** to feel a smarting pain, as from the sting of an insect or from a blow. *–n.* **11.**

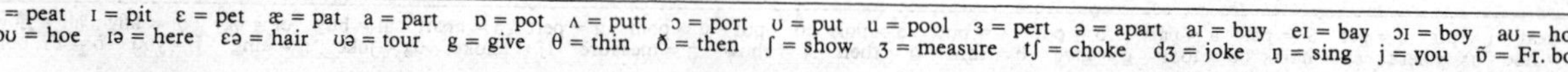

the act of stinging. **12.** a wound, pain, or smart caused by stinging. **13.** any sharp or smarting wound, hurt, or pain (physical or mental). **14.** anything, or an element in anything, that wounds, pains, or irritates: *to feel the sting of defeat.* **15.** capacity to wound or pain. **16.** a sharp stimulus or incitement: *driven by the sting of jealousy.* **17.** *Bot.* a glandular hair on certain plants, as nettles, which emits an irritating fluid. **18.** *Zool.* any of various sharp-pointed, often venom-bearing, organs of insects and other animals, capable of inflicting painful or dangerous wounds. **19.** *Colloq.* a drug, esp. in a hypodermic injection, given to a racehorse. **20.** an alcoholic drink, esp. spirits. **21.** *U.S. Colloq.* a confidence trick. [ME; OE *stingan,* c. Icel. *stinga*]

**stingaree** /ˈstɪŋəri, stɪŋəˈri/, *n.* →**stingray.** [alteration of STINGRAY]

**stinger** /ˈstɪŋə/, *n.* **1.** one who or that which stings. **2.** an animal or plant that stings. **3.** the sting of an insect or the like. **4.** *Colloq.* a stinging blow, remark, or the like. **5.** *U.S.* a cocktail of brandy and a liqueur.

**stinging hair** /ˈstɪŋɪŋ hɛə/, *n.* →**sting** (def. 17).

**stinging nettle** /ˈ– nɛtl/, *n.* →**nettle.**

**stinging tree** /ˈ– tri/, *n.* any species of the genus *Laportea* bearing rigid stinging hairs.

**sting moth** /ˈstɪŋ mɒθ/, *n.* a mottled cup-moth, *Doratifera vulnerans,* the larvae of which can be found on eucalypts, guava and apricot trees.

**stingray** /ˈstɪŋreɪ/, *n.* any of the rays, esp. of the family Dasyatidae, having a long, flexible tail armed near the base with a strong, serrated bony spine with which they can inflict severe and very painful wounds.

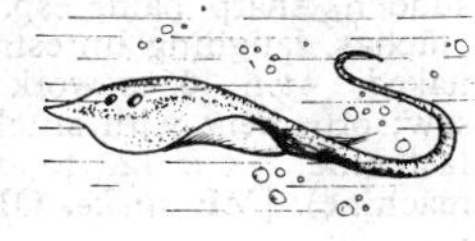
stingray

**stingy**[1] /ˈstɪndʒi/, *adj.,* **-gier, -giest.** **1.** reluctant to give or spend; niggardly; penurious. **2.** scanty or meagre. [orig. meaning 'having a sting', 'bad-tempered', from d. *stinge* sting, OE *steng*] – **stingily,** *adv.* – **stinginess,** *n.*

**stingy**[2] /ˈstɪŋi/, *adj.* having a sting. [STING + -Y[1]]

**stink** /stɪŋk/, *v.,* **stank** or **stunk, stunk, stinking,** *n.* –*v.i.* **1.** to emit a strong offensive smell. **2.** to be in extremely bad repute or disfavour. **3.** *Colloq.* to be very inferior in quality. **4.** *Colloq.* to have a large quantity of something, esp. money (usu. fol. by *of* or *with*). –*v.t.* **5. stink out, a.** to cause to stink. **b.** to repel, drive out, etc., by an offensive smell. –*n.* **6.** a strong offensive smell; stench. **7.** *Colloq.* a commotion; fuss; scandal: *kick up a stink.* **8. play stink finger,** to engage in erotic play of the fingers with the female genitals. [ME; OE *stincan,* c. D and LG *stiken.* Cf. STENCH] – **stinking,** *adj.* – **stinkingly,** *adv.*

**stink bomb** /ˈ– bɒm/, *n.* a small bomb which emits a foul smell when it explodes.

**stinker** /ˈstɪŋkə/, *n.* **1.** one who or that which stinks. **2.** *Colloq.* a dishonourable, disgusting, or objectionable person. **3.** any device emitting a stink, as a bomb, pot, etc. **4.** any of several large petrels. **5.** *Colloq.* something difficult, as a task, problem, etc. **6.** something unpleasant, as a very hot day.

**stinkfish** /ˈstɪŋkfɪʃ/, *n. S.A.* →**dragonet.**

**stink grass** /ˈstɪŋk gras/, *n.* a common weed of cultivation, *Eragrostis cilianensis,* having black seedheads, and a pungent smell, native to Mediterranean regions.

**stinkhorn** /ˈstɪŋkhɔn/, *n.* any of various ill-smelling fungi, as *Phallus impudicus.*

stinkhorn

**stinking** /ˈstɪŋkɪŋ/, *adj.* **1.** foul-smelling. **2.** *Colloq.* disgusting; disgraceful. **3.** *Colloq.* drunk. **4.** *Colloq.* very rich. **5.** *Colloq.* (an intensifier): *stinking hot, stinking bastard.*

**stinking gum** /ˈ– gʌm/, *n.* a gum tree, *Eucalyptus tereticornis,* the leaves of which emit a pungent smell.

**stinking roger** /ˈ– ˈrɒdʒə/, *n.* a very tall annual plant, *Tagetes minuta,* native to North America but a weed elsewhere, characterised by strongly-scented vegetative parts.

**stinking smut** /ˈ– ˈsmʌt/, *n.* a type of smut on wheat; bunt.

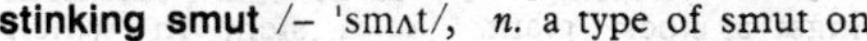

**stinking wattle** /ˈ– ˈwɒtl/, *n.* →**gidgee** (def. 1).

**stinko** /ˈstɪŋkoʊ/, *adj. Colloq.* **1.** stinking. **2.** drunk.

**stinkpipe** /ˈstɪŋkpaɪp/, *n.* a pipe which provides an outlet for escaping gases from drains, sewers, etc.

**stinkpot** /ˈstɪŋkpɒt/, *n.* **1.** a jar containing combustibles, etc., which generate offensive and suffocating vapours, formerly used in warfare. **2.** *Colloq.* one who or that which stinks.

**stinkstone** /ˈstɪŋkstoʊn/, *n.* any of various stones which emit a fetid smell on being struck or rubbed, as from embedded decomposed organic matter.

**stinkweed** /ˈstɪŋkwid/, *n.* any of various ill-smelling plants, as the jimson weed.

**stinkwood** /ˈstɪŋkwʊd/, *n.* **1.** one of several trees or shrubs with fetid wood, as the dogwood. **2.** the wood of any of these trees or shrubs.

**stinkwort** /ˈstɪŋkwɜt/, *n.* an erect, hairy annual, *Inula graveolens,* from the Mediterranean, with yellow flowers and an unpleasant odour.

stinkwort

**stint**[1] /stɪnt/, *v.t.* **1.** to limit to a certain amount, number, share, or allowance, often unduly; set limits to; restrict. **2.** *Archaic.* to discontinue, cease, or bring to an end. –*v.i.* **3.** to be sparing or frugal; get along on a scanty allowance. **4.** *Archaic.* to cease action; desist. –*n.* **5.** limitation or restriction, esp. as to amount: *to give without stint.* **6.** a limited or prescribed quantity, share, rate, etc.: *to exceed one's stint.* **7.** an allotted amount or piece of work: *to do one's daily stint.* **8.** a period of time, usu. short, allotted to a particular activity. **9.** *Obs.* a stop; halt. [ME; OE *styntan* make blunt, dull, c. Icel. *stytta* shorten. Cf. STUNT[1], *v.*] – **stinter,** *n.* – **stintingly,** *adv.*

**stint**[2] /stɪnt/, *n.* any of various small shorebirds, as the red-necked stint.

**stipe**[1] /staɪp/, *n.* **1.** Also, **stipes.** *Bot.* a stalk or slender support, as the petiole of a fern frond, the stem supporting the pileus of a mushroom, or a stalk-like elongation of the receptacle of a flower. **2.** *Zool.* a stem-like part, as a footstalk; a stalk. [F, from L *stīpes* log, post]

**stipe**[2] /staɪp/, *n. Colloq.* a stipendary steward at a racecourse.

**stipel** /ˈstaɪpəl/, *n.* a secondary stipule situated at the base of a leaflet of a compound leaf. [NL *stipella,* diminutive of L *stipula.* See STIPULE] – **stipellate** /staɪˈpɛlət, -eɪt/, *adj.*

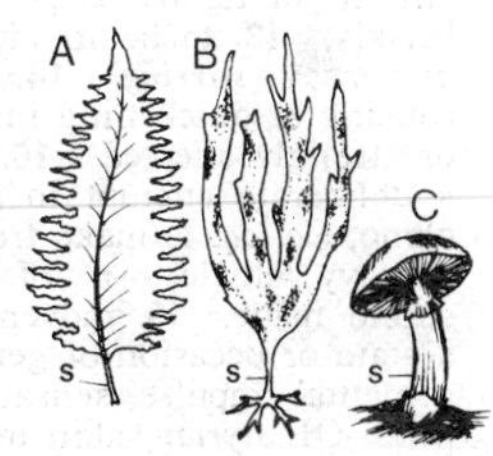

S, stipe: A, fern; B, kelp; C, mushroom

**stipend** /ˈstaɪpɛnd/, *n.* fixed or regular pay; periodic payment; salary. [ME *stipendy,* from L *stīpendium*]

**stipendiary** /staɪˈpɛndəri/, *adj., n., pl.* **-ries.** –*adj.* **1.** receiving a stipend; performing services for regular pay. **2.** paid for by a stipend, as services. **3.** pertaining to or of the nature of a stipend. –*n.* **4.** one who receives a stipend.

**stipendiary magistrate** /– ˈmædʒəstreɪt/, *n.* a legally qualified paid magistrate who may do alone all acts authorised to be done by two justices of the peace.

**stipes** /ˈstaɪpiz/, *n., pl.* **stipites** /ˈstaɪpətiz/. **1.** *Zool.* (of crustaceans and insects) the second joint of a maxilla. **2.** *Bot.* →**stipe** (def. 1). [L: log, post]

**stipitate** /ˈstɪpəteɪt/, *adj.* (of a plant part) having, or supported by, a stipe. [NL *stipitātus,* from *stīpes* STIPE[1] + *-ātus* -ATE[1]]

**stipitiform** /ˈstɪpətəfɔm/, *adj.* having the form of a stipe.

**stipple** /ˈstɪpəl/, *v.,* **-pled, -pling,** *n.* –*v.t.* **1.** to paint, engrave, or draw by means of dots or small touches. –*n.* Also, **stippling. 2.** the method of painting, engraving, etc., by stippling. **3.** stippled work; a painting, engraving, or the like, executed by means of dots or small spots. [D *stippelen,* frequentative of *stippen* dot, speckle] – **stippler,** *n.*

**stipulate**[1] /ˈstɪpjəleɪt/, *v.*, **-lated, -lating.** *–v.i.* **1.** to make an express demand or arrangement (*for*), as a condition of agreement. *–v.t.* **2.** to arrange expressly or specify in terms of agreement: *to stipulate a price.* **3.** to require as an essential condition in making an agreement. **4.** to promise, in making an agreement. [L *stipulātus,* pp.] – **stipulator,** *n.* – **stipulatory,** *adj.*

**stipulate**[2] /ˈstɪpjələt, -leɪt/, *adj.* having stipules. [STIPULE + -ATE[1]]

**stipulation** /stɪpjəˈleɪʃən/, *n.* **1.** the act of stipulating. **2.** something stipulated; a condition in an agreement or contract.

**stipule** /ˈstɪpjul/, *n.* (of some plants) one of a pair of lateral appendages, often leaf-like, sometimes thorns, at the base of a leaf petiole. [L *stīpula,* diminutive of *stīpes.* See STIPE[1]] – **stipular,** *adj.*

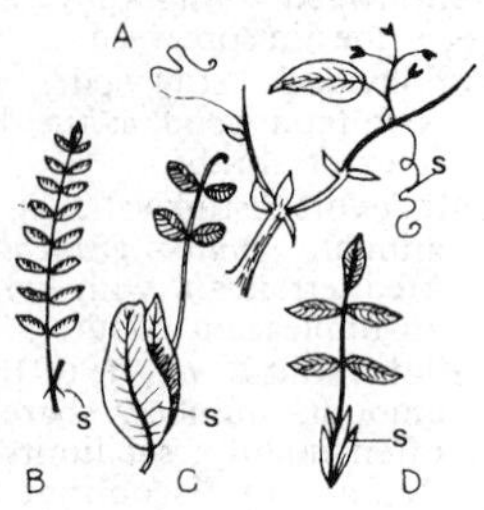

S, stiple: A, smilax; B, false acacia; C, pea; D, dog rose

**stir**[1] /stɜ/, *v.*, **stirred, stirring,** *n.* *–v.t.* **1.** to move or agitate (a liquid, or any matter in separate particles or pieces) so as to change the relative position of component parts, as by passing an implement continuously or repeatedly through: *to stir one's coffee with a spoon.* **2.** to move, esp. in some slight way: *the leaves stirred in the breeze.* **3.** to set in tremulous, fluttering, or irregular motion; shake: *leaves stirred by the wind.* **4.** to move briskly; bestir: *to stir oneself.* **5.** to rouse from inactivity, quiet, contentment, indifference, etc. (oft. fol. by *up*). **6.** to incite, instigate, or prompt (oft. fol. by *up*): *to stir up a people to rebellion.* **7. stir the possum,** to instigate a debate on a controversial topic, esp. in the public arena. **8.** to take an active part in proceedings so as to upset the equanimity of others involved in them. **9.** to affect strongly; excite: *to stir pity, the heart, etc.* **10.** *Rare.* to bring up for notice or discussion. *–v.i.* **11.** to move, esp. slightly or lightly: *not a leaf stirred.* **12.** to move about, esp. briskly. **13.** to be in circulation, current, or afoot: *is there any news stirring?* **14.** to become active, as from some rousing or quickening impulse. **15.** to be emotionally moved or strongly affected. **16.** to touch on controversial topics in a deliberate attempt to incite a heated discussion. **17. stir along,** *Colloq.* to make frequent use of the gears when driving a heavy vehicle. *–n.* **18.** the act of stirring or moving, or the sound made. **19.** movement; brisk or busy movement. **20.** a state or occasion of general excitement; a commotion. **21.** a mental impulse, sensation, or feeling. **22.** a jog or thrust. [ME; OE *styrian,* akin to G *storen* disturb. Cf. STORM]

**stir**[2] /stɜ/, *n. Colloq.* a prison. [orig. unknown]

**stir-crazy** /ˈstɜ-kreɪzi/, *adj. Colloq.* crazy as a result of being institutionalised in gaol.

**stir-fry** /ˈstɜ-fraɪ/, *v.t.*, **-fried, -frying.** to fry lightly in a little hot fat or oil, while stirring continually.

**stirk veal** /stɜk ˈvil/, *n.* veal from a carcass over 32 kg in weight. Also, **bobby veal.**

**stirpiculture** /ˈstɜpəkʌltʃə/, *n.* the production of special stocks or strains by careful breeding. [*stirpi-* (combining form of STIRPS) + CULTURE] – **stirpicultural** /stɜpəˈkʌltʃərəl/, *adj.* – **stirpiculturist** /stɜpəˈkʌltʃərɪst/, *n.*

**stirps** /stɜps/, *n., pl.* **stirpes** /ˈstɜpiz/. **1.** a stock; a family, or a branch of a family; a line of descent. **2.** *Law.* one from whom a family is descended. [L: stem, root, stock]

**stirrer** /ˈstɜrə/, *n.* **1.** one who or that which stirs. **2.** an implement or device for stirring something. **3.** an agitator, troublemaker.

**stirring** /ˈstɜrɪŋ/, *adj.* **1.** that stirs; moving, active, bustling, or lively. **2.** rousing, exciting, or thrilling: *a stirring speech.* – **stirringly,** *adv.*

**stirrup** /ˈstɪrəp/, *n.* **1.** a loop, ring, or other contrivance of metal, wood, leather, etc., suspended from the saddle of a horse to support the rider's foot. **2.** any of various similar supports, or any of various clamps, etc., used for special purposes. **3.** *Naut.* a short rope with an eye at the end, hung from a yard to support a footrope, the footrope being rove through the eye. **4.** one of a series of vertical steel loops used in a reinforced concrete beam to resist shear. [ME; OE *stigrāp* (from *stige* ascent + *rāp* ROPE), c. G *Stegreif*]

**stirrup bone** /ˈ– boʊn/, *n.* →**stapes.**

**stirrup cup** /ˈ– kʌp/, *n.* a farewell drink, esp. one offered to a rider already mounted for departure.

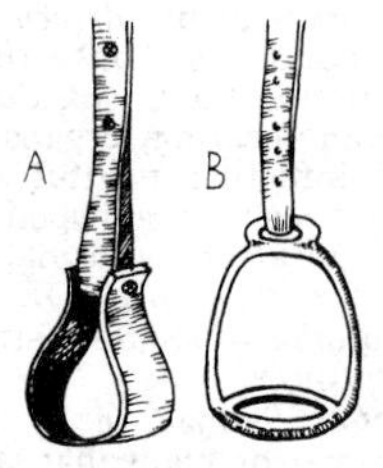

stirrups (def. 1): A, leather; B, metal

**stirrup leather** /ˈ– lɛðə/, *n.* the strap which holds the stirrup of a saddle.

**stirrup pump** /ˈ– pʌmp/, *n.* a small hand pump held steady by a foot bracket and used in fire fighting.

**stitch** /stɪtʃ/, *n.* **1.** one complete movement of a threaded needle through a fabric or material such as to leave behind it a single loop or portion of thread, as in sewing, embroidery, surgical closing of wounds, etc. **2.** a loop or portion of thread disposed in place by one movement in sewing: *to rip out stitches.* **3.** a particular mode of disposing the thread in sewing, or the style of work produced. **4.** one complete movement of the needle or other implement used in knitting crocheting, netting, tatting, etc. **5.** the portion of work produced. **6.** a thread or bit of any fabric or of clothing, etc.: *every stitch of clothing.* **7.** a sudden, sharp pain, esp. in the intercostal muscles. **8. in stitches,** laughing unrestrainedly. **9. not a stitch on,** *Colloq.* naked. *–v.t.* **10.** to work upon, join, or fasten with stitches; sew; ornament with stitches. **11.** to put staples through for fastening. *–v.i.* **12.** to make stitches; sew (by hand or machine). [ME *stiche,* OE *stice,* c. G *Stich* prick] – **stitcher,** *n.*

**stitchwort** /ˈstɪtʃwɜt/, *n.* any of certain herbs of the genus *Stellaria* (or *Alsine*), as *S. holostea,* an Old World white-flowered species. [STITCH + WORT[2]]

**stithy** /ˈstɪði/, *n., pl.* **stithies,** *v.*, **stithied, stithying.** *–n.* **1.** →**anvil** (def. 1). **2.** a forge or smithy. *–v.t.* **3.** *Archaic.* to forge. [ME *stithie,* var. of *stethie,* from Scand.; cf. Icel. *stedhja* (acc.)]

**stiver** /ˈstaɪvə/, *n.* **1.** a former coin of the Netherlands of low value. **2.** a small amount of anything. [D *stuiver*]

**St John's bread,** *n.* →**carob** (def. 1).

**St John's wort,** *n.* any of various herbs or shrubs of the genus *Hypericum,* having yellow flowers and pellucid-dotted leaves, esp. *H. perforatum,* a troublesome weed.

**stn,** station.

**stoa** /ˈstoʊə/, *n., pl.* **stoae** /ˈstoʊi/, **stoas.** a portico, usu. a detached portico of considerable length, that is used as a promenade or meeting place. [Gk]

**stoat** /stoʊt/, *n.* the ermine, *Mustela erminea,* of Europe, Asia and North America, esp. when in brown summer pelage. [ME *stote;* orig. unknown]

stoat

**Stobie pole** /ˈstoʊbi poʊl/, *n.* a pole of steel and concrete used to carry electricity wires, etc. [from J.C. *Stobie,* design engineer with the Adelaide Electric Supply Company]

**stochastic** /stəˈkæstɪk/, *adj.* based on one item in the probability distribution of an ordered set of observations; conjectural. [Gk *stochastikós,* from *stóchos* mark, aim]

stocks (def. 23)

**stock** /stɒk/, *n.* **1.** an aggregate of goods kept on hand by a merchant, business firm, manufacturer, etc., for the supply of customers. **2.** a quantity of something accumulated, as for future use: a *stock of provisions.* **3.** →**livestock.** **4.** →**dead stock.** **5.** *Hort.* **a.** a tree, stem, or plant that furnishes slips or cuttings; a stock plant. **b.** a stem in which a graft is inserted and which is its support. **6.** the trunk or main stem of a tree or other plant, as distinguished from roots and branches. **7.** →**rootstock.** **8.** the type from which a group of animals or plants has been derived. **9.** a race or other related group of animals or plants. **10.** the person from whom a given line of descent is derived; the original progenitor. **11.** a line of descent; a tribe, race, or ethnic group. **12.** *Ethnol.* a major division of mankind, as Caucasoid, Mongoloid, Negroid. **13.** a group of languages having certain features in common and considered to be ultimately related. **14.** *Zool.* a compound organism. **15.** the handle of a whip, etc. **16.** *Firearms.* **a.** the wooden or metal piece to which the barrel and mechanism of a rifle or like firearm are attached. **b.** a part of an automatic weapon, as a machine-gun, similar in position or function. **17.** the stump of a tree left standing. **18.** a log or block of wood. **19.** a dull or stupid person. **20.** something lifeless or senseless. **21.** the main upright part of anything, esp. a supporting structure. **22.** →**ski-pole.** **23.** (*pl.*) an instrument of punishment (no longer in use), consisting of a framework with holes for the ankles and (sometimes) the wrists of an offender exposed to public derision. **24.** (*pl.*) a frame in which a horse or other animal is secured in a standing position for shoeing or for a veterinary operation. **25.** (*pl.*) the frame on which a boat rests while under construction. **26.** a tool for holding dies used in cutting screwthreads on a rod. **27.** the piece of metal or wood which constitutes the body of a carpenter's plane. **28.** *Bldg Trades.* the base plate of the timber mould on which bricks are formed. **29.** the raw material from which anything is made: *paper stock.* **30.** *Cookery.* the liquor or broth prepared by boiling meat, fish, vegetables, etc., used esp. as a foundation for soups and sauces. **31.** any of various widely cultivated plants of the genus *Matthiola,* esp. *M. incana* and the **nightscented stock,** *M. bicornis.* **32.** a collar or a neckcloth fitting like a band about the neck. **33.** *Cards.* that portion of a pack of cards which, in certain games, is not dealt out to the players, but is left on the table, to be drawn from as occasion requires. **34.** *Theat.* the repertoire of pieces produced by a stock company. **35.** *Finance.* **a.** the capital of a company converted from fully paid shares. **b.** the shares of a particular company. **c.** →**capital stock.** **36.** a stocking. **37.** repute; standing. **38.** the part of a plough to which the irons, handles, etc., are attached. **39. in stock,** available for use or sale. **40. on the stocks,** under construction; in preparation. **41. out of stock,** not available for use or sale. **42. take stock, a.** to make an inventory of stock on hand. **b.** to make an appraisal of resources, prospects, etc. **43. take** or **put stock in,** *Chiefly U.S.* to put confidence in; trust; believe. *–adj.* **44.** kept regularly on hand, as for use or sale; staple; standard: stock articles. **45.** having as one's job the care of a concern's goods: *a stock clerk.* **46.** of the common or ordinary type; in common use: *a stock argument.* **47.** commonplace: *a stock remark.* **48.** designating or pertaining to livestock raising; stock farming. **49.** *Comm.* of or pertaining to the stock of a company. **50.** *Theat.* **a.** pertaining to repertory plays or pieces, or to a stock company. **b.** appearing together in a repertoire, as a company. **c.** forming part of a repertoire, as a play. *–v.t.* **51.** to furnish with a stock or supply. **52.** to furnish with stock, as a farm with horses, cattle, etc. **53.** to lay up in store, as for future use. **54.** to fasten to or provide with a stock, as a rifle, plough, bell, anchor, etc. **55.** *Obs.* to put in the stocks as a punishment. *–v.i.* **56.** to lay in a stock of something (oft. fol. by *up*). [ME; OE *stoc(c),* c. G *Stock*]

**stockade** /stɒˈkeɪd/, *n., v.,* **-aded, -ading.** *–n.* **1.** *Fort.* a defensive barrier consisting of strong posts or timbers fixed upright in the ground. **2.** an enclosure or pen made with posts and stakes. **3.** (formerly) an enclosure in which convict labourers employed in road gangs, etc., were held at night. **4.** *U.S.* a prison for military personnel. *–v.t.* **5.** to protect, fortify, or encompass with a stockade. [F (obs.) *estocade,* from OPr. *estaca* stake, of Gmc orig. See STAKE[1]]

**stock and station agent,** *n.* **1.** one engaged in the business of buying and selling rural properties and stock. **2.** a firm which supplies provisions to rural properties. Also, **stock agent.**

**stock book** /ˈstɒk bʊk/, *n.* a ledger for recording amounts of goods bought and sold.

**stockbreeder** /ˈstɒkbridə/, *n.* one who breeds and raises livestock.

**stockbroker** /ˈstɒkbroʊkə/, *n.* a broker who buys and sells stocks and shares for customers for a commission. **– stockbrokerage, stockbroking,** *n.*

**stock-camp** /ˈstɒk-kæmp/, *n.* a temporary shelter established by stockmen when mustering.

**stock car** /ˈstɒk ka/, *n.* **1.** a car, esp. an old one, adapted for stock-car racing. **2.** *U.S.* →**cattle truck.** **– stock-car,** *adj.*

**stock-car racing** /ˈstɒk-ka ˌreɪsɪŋ/, *n.* a type of motor racing using stock cars, characterised by frequent collisions.

**stock certificate** /ˈstɒk səˌtɪfəkət/, *n.* a certificate evidencing ownership of one or more shares of a company's stock.

**stock company** /ˈ– kʌmpəni/, *n.* **1.** *U.S.* →**joint-stock company.** **2.** *U.S.* →**repertory** (def. 2).

**stock dove** /ˈ– dʌv/, *n.* a wild pigeon of Europe, *Columba oenas.*

**stock-driver** /ˈstɒk-draɪvə/, *n. N.Z.* →**drover.**

**stock exchange** /ˈstɒk əkstʃeɪndʒ/, *n.* **1.** (*oft. caps.*) a building or place where stocks and shares are bought and sold. **2.** an association of brokers, jobbers, and dealers in stocks and bonds, who meet to transact business according to fixed rules.

**stock farm** /ˈ– fam/, *n.* a farm devoted to breeding livestock. **– stock farmer,** *n.* **– stock farming,** *n.*

**stockfeed** /ˈstɒkfid/, *n.* food for livestock.

**stockfish** /ˈstɒkfɪʃ/, *n., pl.* **-fishes,** (*esp. collectively*) **-fish.** fish, as the cod or haddock, cured by splitting and drying in the air without salt.

**stockholder** /ˈstɒkhoʊldə/, *n.* **1.** →**shareholder.** **2.** an owner of livestock.

**stockhorse** /ˈstɒkhɔs/, *n.* a horse trained in the handling of stock.

**stockinet** /stɒkəˈnɛt/, *n.* an elastic machine-knitted fabric used in making undergarments, etc. [alteration of *stockinget,* from STOCKING + -ET]

**stocking** /ˈstɒkɪŋ/, *n.* **1.** a close-fitting covering, usu. knitted (by hand or machine) and of wool, cotton, nylon, silk, etc., for the foot and leg. **2.** something resembling such a covering. [STOCK, (def. 36) + -ING[1]] **– stockingless,** *adj.*

**stockinged** /ˈstɒkɪŋd/, *adj.* **1.** wearing socks or stockings. **2. in one's stockinged feet,** wearing socks or stockings but without shoes.

**stocking rate** /ˈ– reɪt/, *n.* the number of stock to the hectare or, in the marginal pastoral areas of Australia, hectares to stock.

**stock-in-trade** /stɒk-ɪn-ˈtreɪd/, *n.* **1.** goods, assets, etc., necessary for carrying on a business. **2.** the abilities, resources, etc., characteristic of or belonging to a particular group: *eloquence is part of a salesman's stock in trade.*

**stockist** /ˈstɒkəst/, *n.* a vendor, as a retailer or distributor, who keeps goods in stock.

**stockjobber** /ˈstɒkdʒɒbə/, *n.* **1.** a stock exchange dealer who acts as an intermediary between brokers and buyers but does not deal directly with the public. **2.** *U.S.* a seller of stock, esp. of worthless securities. **– stockjobbery, stockjobbing,** *n.*

**stockkeep** /ˈstɒkkip/, *v.t.* to manoeuvre moving livestock, esp. at speed: *my dog could stockkeep a fly into a bottle.*

**stockkeeper** /ˈstɒkkipə/, *n.* **1.** one who tends livestock. **2.** one who keeps records of goods on hand, received or dispatched, as in a warehouse.

**stockman** /ˈstɒkmən/, *n., pl.* **-men.** **1.** a man employed to tend livestock, esp. cattle. **2.** *Chiefly U.S.* a man who raises livestock. **3.** *U.S.* a man in charge of a stock of goods.

**stock market** /ˈstɒk makət/, *n.* a market where stocks and shares are bought and sold; a stock exchange.

**stock mortgage** /ˈ– ˌmɔgɪdʒ/, *n. Law.* mortgage of cattle, sheep and horses as security for a loan.

**stockpile** /ˈstɒkpaɪl/, *n., v.* **-piled, -piling.** *–n.* **1.** a supply of material, as a pile of gravel in road maintenance. **2.** a large supply of essential materials, held in reserve for use during a period of shortage, etc. **3.** a supply of munitions, weapons, etc., accumulated for possible future use. *–v.t.* **4.** to accumulate for future use. *–v.i.* **5.** to accumulate in a stockpile. **– stockpiler,** *n.*

**stockpot** /ˈstɒkpɒt/, *n.* a pot in which stock for soup, etc., is made and kept.

**stock raising** /ˈstɒk reɪzɪŋ/, *n.* the breeding and rearing of different kinds of livestock. – **stock raiser,** *n.*

**stockrider** /ˈstɒkraɪdə/, *n.* a man employed on a sheep or cattle station in such work as mustering, branding, droving, etc.

**stockroom** /ˈstɒkrum/, *n.* a room in which a stock of materials or goods is kept for use or sale.

**stock-route** /ˈstɒk-rut/, *n.* a right of way for travelling cattle, sheep, etc.

**stock run** /ˈstɒk rʌn/, *n.* a tract of grazing land.

**stock-still** /stɒk-ˈstɪl/, *adj.* motionless.

**stocktaking** /ˈstɒkteɪkɪŋ/, *n.* **1.** the examination and listing of goods, assets, etc., in a shop, business, etc. **2.** a reappraisal or reassessment of one's position, progress, prospects, etc.

**stock unit** /ˈstɒk junət/, *n.* →**share**[1] (def. 2).

**stockwhip** /ˈstɒkwɪp/, *n.*, *v.*, **-whipped, -whipping.** *–n.* **1.** a long, bullock-hide whip used in handling stock. *–v.t.* **2.** to control (cattle, etc.) with a stockwhip.

stockwhip

**stocky** /ˈstɒki/, *adj.*, **-ier, -iest. 1.** of solid and sturdy form or build; thickset, often short. **2.** having a strong, stout stem, as a plant. – **stockily,** *adv.* – **stockiness,** *n.*

**stockyard** /ˈstɒkjad/, *n.* **1.** an enclosure with pens, sheds, etc., connected with a slaughterhouse, railway, market, etc., for the temporary keeping of cattle, sheep, swine, or horses. **2.** a yard for livestock.

**stodge** /stɒdʒ/, *n.*, *v.*, **stodged, stodging.** *Colloq. –n.* **1.** heavy, indigestible, and unappetising food. **2.** uninteresting or difficult reading matter. *–v.t.* **3.** to stuff full with food, etc. *–v.i.* **4.** to stuff oneself full of food. [b. STUFF and GORGE]

**stodgy** /ˈstɒdʒi/, *adj.*, **-ier, -iest. 1.** heavy, dull, or uninteresting; tediously commonplace. **2.** of a thick, semisolid consistency; heavy, as food. **3.** stocky; thickset. – **stodgily,** *adv.* – **stodginess,** *n.*

**stoechiology** /ˌstikiˈɒlədʒi/, *n.* →**stoichiology.** – **stoechiological** /ˌstikiəˈlɒdʒɪkəl/, *adj.*

**stoechiometry** /ˌstikiˈɒmətri/, *n.* →**stoichiometry.**

**Stoic** /ˈstoʊɪk/, *adj.* **1.** of or pertaining to the school of philosophy founded by Zeno, fl. *c.* 475 B.C., who taught that men should be free from passion, unmoved by joy or grief, and submit without complaint to unavoidable necessity. **2.** (*l.c.*) stoical. *–n.* **3.** a member or adherent of the Stoic school of philosophy. **4.** (*l.c.*) one who maintains or affects a mental attitude of austere fortitude. [ME, from L *stōicus,* from Gk *stōikós,* from *stoá* a porch, specifically the porch in Athens where Zeno lectured]

**stoical** /ˈstoʊɪkəl/, *adj.* impassive; characterised by calm or austere fortitude, as in repression of emotion: *a stoical sufferer.* – **stoically,** *adv.* – **stoicalness,** *n.*

**stoichiology** /ˌstɔɪkiˈɒlədʒi/, *n.* a physiological study of the cellular components of tissues. Also, **stoechiology, stoicheiology.** – **stoichiological** /ˌstɔɪkiəˈlɒdʒɪkəl/, *adj.*

**stoichiometric** /ˌstɔɪkiəˈmɛtrɪk/, *adj. Chem.* **1.** of or pertaining to stoichiometry. **2.** (of a compound) containing its component elements in the exact proportions represented by its formula. **3.** (of a mixture) yielding on complete reaction a stoichiometric compound. Also, **stoichiometrical.**

**stoichiometry** /ˌstɔɪkiˈɒmətri/, *n. Chem.* **1.** the calculation of the quantities of chemical elements or compounds involved in chemical reactions. **2.** the branch of chemistry dealing with relationships of combining elements, esp. quantitatively. Also, **stoechiometry, stoicheiometry.** [Gk *stoicheio-* (combining form of *stoicheîon* component) + -METRY]

**stoicism** /ˈstoʊəsɪzəm/, *n.* **1.** the stoic philosophy. **2.** conduct conforming to stoic precepts; repression of emotion; indifference to pleasure or pain.

**stoke**[1] /stoʊk/, *v.*, **stoked, stoking.** *–v.t.* **1.** to poke, stir up, and feed (a fire). **2.** to tend the fire of (a furnace, esp. one used with a boiler to generate steam for an engine); supply with fuel. *–v.i.* **3.** to shake up the coals of a fire. **4.** to tend a fire or furnace; act as a stoker: *to make a living by stoking.* **5.** *Colloq.* to eat (fol. by *up*). [backformation from STOKER]

**stoke**[2] /stoʊk/, *n.* a unit of viscosity equal to the viscosity of a fluid in poises divided by its density in grams per cubic centimetre. [named after Sir George *Stokes,* 1819-1903, British physicist]

**stoked** /stoʊkt/, *adj. Colloq.* **1.** under the influence or as if under the influence of drugs or alcohol. **2.** thrilled; delighted.

**stokehold** /ˈstoʊkhoʊld/, *n.* the space or compartment containing the furnaces, boilers, etc., of a ship.

**stokehole** /ˈstoʊkhoʊl/, *n.* **1.** a compartment where furnace fires are worked, as in a steamship. **2.** a hole through which a furnace is stoked.

**stoker** /ˈstoʊkə/, *n.* **1.** one who or that which stokes. **2.** one employed to tend a furnace used in generating steam, as on a steamship. **3.** a mechanical device for supplying solid fuel to a furnace. [D, from *stoken* feed a fire]

**stokes** /stoʊks/, *n.* a non-SI unit of kinematic viscosity, equal to 0.1 x $10^{-3}$ square metres per second. *Symbol:* St

**Stokes' law** /ˈstoʊks lɔ/, *n.* the law of physics which states that a small sphere falling under the action of gravity through a viscous medium reaches a constant velocity which is proportional to the square of the diameter of the sphere, and the difference between the density of the sphere and the medium through which it is falling, as well as inversely proportional to the viscosity of the viscous medium. [see STOKE[2]]

**STOL** /stɒl/, *n.* an aircraft capable of taking of and landing on a relatively short runway. Also, **S.T.O.L.** [*S(hort) T(ake)-O(ff and) L(anding)*]

**stole**[1] /stoʊl/, *v.* past tense of **steal.**

**stole**[2] /stoʊl/, *n.* **1.** an ecclesiastical vestment, a narrow strip of silk or other material worn over the shoulders and hanging down in front to the knee or below. **2.** a woman's scarf or similar garment of fur or cloth, usu. worn with the ends hanging down in front. **3.** *Archaic.* a long robe, esp. one worn by Roman matrons. [ME and OE, from L *stola,* from Gk *stolḗ* clothing, robe]

**stolen** /ˈstoʊlən/, *v.* past participle of **steal.**

**stolid** /ˈstɒləd/, *adj.* not easily moved or stirred mentally; impassive; unemotional; dull; unenterprising or unimaginative. [L *stolidus*] – **stolidity** /stɒˈlɪdəti/, **stolidness,** *n.* – **stolidly,** *adv.*

**stolon** /ˈstoʊlɒn/, *n.* **1.** *Bot.* **a.** a slender branch or shoot, usu. a runner or prostrate stem, which takes root at the tip and eventually develops into a new plant. **b.** a rhizome, as of some grasses, used for vegetative reproduction. **2.** *Zool.* a root-like extension in a compound organism, usu. giving rise to new zooids by budding. [L *stolo*]

S, stolon (def. 1a)

**stoloniferous** /stoʊləˈnɪfərəs/, *adj.* producing stolons.

**stoma** /ˈstoʊmə/, *n.*, *pl.* **stomata** /ˈstoʊmətə, ˈstɒm-/. **1.** *Bot.* any of various small apertures, esp. one of the minute orifices or slits in the epidermis of leaves, etc. **2.** *Zool.* a mouth or ingestive opening, esp. when in the form of a small or simple aperture. [NL, from Gk: mouth]

**stomach** /ˈstʌmək/, *n.* **1.** (in man and other vertebrates) **a.** a sac-like enlargement of the alimentary canal, forming an organ of storage, dilution, and digestion. **b.** such an organ, or an analogous portion of the alimentary canal, when divided into two or more sections or parts, or any one of these sections. **2.** any analogous digestive cavity or tract in invertebrates. **3.** the part of the body

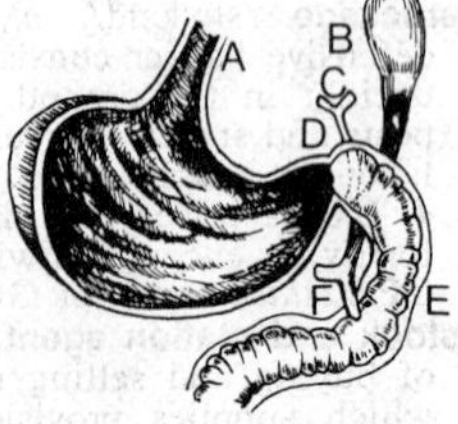


human stomach (def. 1a): A, oesophagus; B, gall bladder; C, biliary duct; D, pylorus; E, duodenum; F, pancreatic duct

i = peat ɪ = pit ɛ = pet æ = pat a = part ɒ = pot ʌ = putt ɔ = port ʊ = put u = pool ɜ = pert ə = apart aɪ = buy eɪ = bay ɔɪ = boy aʊ = how oʊ = hoe ɪə = here ɛə = hair ʊə = tour g = give θ = thin ð = then ʃ = show ʒ = measure tʃ = choke dʒ = joke ŋ = sing j = you õ = Fr. bon

containing the stomach; the belly or abdomen. **4.** appetite for food. **5.** desire, inclination, or liking. **6.** *Obs.* spirit or courage. **7.** *Obs.* pride. *–v.t.* **8.** to take into or retain in the stomach. **9.** to endure or tolerate. **10.** *Obs.* to be offended at or resent. [ME *stomak,* from OF *estomac,* from L *stomachus,* from Gk *stómachos* throat, gullet, stomach]

**stomach-ache** /ˈstʌmək-eɪk/, *n.* a pain in the stomach or abdomen; gastralgia; colic.

**stomacher** /ˈstʌməkə/, *n.* an ornamented article of dress for covering the stomach and chest, formerly worn by both men and women, esp. one worn by women under a bodice.

stomacher

**stomachic** /stəˈmækɪk/, *adj.* **1.** of or pertaining to the stomach; gastric. **2.** beneficial to the stomach; stimulating gastric digestion; sharpening the appetite. *–n.* **3.** a stomachic agent or drug. Also, **stomachical.**

**stomach pump** /ˈstʌmək pʌmp/, *n.* **1.** a small pump or syringe used for withdrawing the contents of the stomach, or for injecting into the stomach. **2.** withdrawal of the contents of the stomach by means of such an instrument.

**stomach stapling** /ˈ– steɪplɪŋ/, *n.* an operation to reduce the size of the stomach by stapling together a section of it, thereby reducing food intake.

**stomach worm** /ˈ– wɜm/, *n.* a nematode worm of the family Trichostrongylidae, *Haemonchus contortus,* parasitic in sheep and related animals; wireworm.

**stomata** /ˈstoʊmətə, ˈstɒm-/, *n.* plural of **stoma.**

**stomatal** /ˈstoʊmətl, ˈstɒm-/, *adj.* **1.** of, pertaining to, or of the nature of a stoma. **2.** having stomata.

**stomatic** /stoʊˈmætɪk/, *adj.* **1.** pertaining to the mouth. **2.** acting as a remedy for diseases of the mouth, as a drug. **3.** stomatal.

**stomatitis** /stoʊməˈtaɪtəs, stɒm-/, *n.* inflammation of the mouth. [NL, from Gk *stóma* mouth + *-ītis* -ITIS]

**stomato-,** a word element referring to the mouth, as in *stomatoplasty.* Also, before vowels, **stomat-.** [Gk, combining form of *stóma* mouth]

**stomatology** /stoʊməˈtɒlədʒi, stɒm-/, *n.* the science dealing with the mouth and its diseases.

**stomatoplasty** /ˈstoʊmətəplæsti, ˈstɒm-/, *n.* plastic surgery of the mouth.

**stomatopod** /ˈstoʊmətəpɒd, ˈstɒm-/, *n.* any of the Stomatopoda, an order of crustaceans having some of the legs close to the mouth and having the gills borne on the abdominal segments.

**stomatous** /ˈstoʊmətəs, ˈstɒm-/, *adj.* →**stomatal.**

**-stome,** a word element referring to the mouth, as in *cyclostome.* [combining form representing (1) Gk *stóma* mouth, (2) Gk *stómion* little mouth]

**stomodaeum** /stoʊməˈdiəm, stɒm-/, *n., pl.* **-daea** /-ˈdiə/. the part of the primary oral cavity which begins as an invagination of the ectoderm. Also, **stomodeum.** [NL *stom-* (see -STOME) + *odaeum* (from Gk *hodaîon,* neut., on the way)] – **stomodaeal,** *adj.*

**-stomous,** an adjectival suffix corresponding to **-stome,** as in *monostomous.*

**stomp** /stɒmp/, *n.* **1.** a form of jazz music. **2.** a dance, usu. characterised by stamping of the feet, done to such music. *–v.i.* **3.** *Colloq.* to stamp. **4.** to perform the stomp. *–v.t.* **5.** *Colloq.* to stamp.

**-stomy,** a combining form used in names of surgical operations for making an artificial opening, as *colostomy.* [Gk *-stomia,* from *stóma* mouth]

**stone** /stoʊn/, *n., pl.* **stones** (*except* **stone** *for def. 8*), *adj., v.,* **stoned, stoning,** *adv.* *–n.* **1.** the hard substance of which rocks consist. **2.** a particular kind of rock. **3.** *Mining.* opal-bearing material. **4.** a piece of rock of definite size, shape, etc., for a particular purpose. **5.** a piece of rock of small or moderate size. **6.** precious stone. **7.** *Mining Colloq.* opal. **8.** a unit of mass in the imperial system, equal to 14 lb avoirdupois, or approx. 6.35 kg. **9.** something resembling a small stone or pebble. **10.** any hard, stone-like seed. **11.** *Bot.* the hard endocarp of a drupe. **12.** *Med.* a calculous concretion in the body, as in the kidney, gall bladder, or urinary bladder. **13.** a gravestone or tombstone. **14.** a grindstone. **15.** a millstone. **16.** a hailstone. **17.** a polished granite stone used in curling. **18.** a light grey or beige colour. **19.** *Print.* a table with a smooth surface used for composing page formes, formerly made of stone. **20.** a piece in the game of dominoes, backgammon, etc. **21.** (*pl.*) *Obs.* testicles. *–adj.* **22.** made of or pertaining to stone. **23.** made of stoneware: *a stone jug or bottle.* *–v.t.* **24.** to throw stones at; drive by pelting with stones. **25.** to put to death by pelting with stones. **26.** to provide or fit with stones, as by paving, lining, facing, etc. **27.** to rub with or on a stone, as to sharpen, polish, smooth, etc. **28.** to free from stones, as fruit. **29.** *Obs.* to turn into stone; petrify. [ME; OE *stān,* c. G *Stein*] – **stoneless,** *adj.* – **stoner,** *n.*

**Stone Age** /ˈstoʊn eɪdʒ/, *n.* the time during which early man lived and made implements of stone, chiefly of flint; it corresponds to the Pleistocene and Holocene epochs up to the beginning of the Bronze Age.

**stone-bass** /ˈstoʊn-bæs/, *n.* a deep-water sea-perch, *Polyprion cernium* up to 1.3 metres long, found chiefly in the Mediterranean Sea and southern Atlantic Ocean.

**stone-blind** /stoʊn-ˈblaɪnd/, *adj.* completely blind.

**stone-broke** /stoʊn-ˈbroʊk/, *adj. Colloq.* →**stony-broke.**

**stone-cold** /stoʊn-ˈkoʊld/, *adj.* **1.** as cold as stone; very cold; lifeless. **2. stone-cold sober,** *Colloq.* completely sober.

**stonecrop** /ˈstoʊnkrɒp/, *n.* **1.** any plant of the genus *Sedum,* esp. a mosslike herb, *Sedum acre,* with small, fleshy leaves and yellow flowers, frequently growing on rocks and walls. **2.** any of various plants of related genera. [ME *stooncroppe,* OE *stāncrop.* See STONE, CROP]

**stone-curlew** /stoʊn-ˈkɜlju/, *n.* any of various large, nocturnal birds of the family Burhinidae, as the beach stone curlew and the bush stone curlew.

**stonecutter** /ˈstoʊnkʌtə/, *n.* **1.** Also, **stone-dresser.** one who cuts or carves stone in preparation for building. **2.** a machine for cutting or dressing stone.

**stoned** /stoʊnd/, *adj. Colloq.* completely drunk or under the influence of drugs.

**stone-dead** /stoʊn-ˈdɛd/, *adj.* completely lifeless; utterly dead.

**stone-deaf** /stoʊn-ˈdɛf/, *adj.* completely deaf.

**stonefish** /ˈstoʊnfɪʃ/, *n.* any of several species of highly venomous, tropical fishes of *Synanceja* or a related genus, remarkably camouflaged to resemble weathered coral or rock, having erectile dorsal spines capable of inflicting an extremely painful and sometimes fatal sting.

stonefish

**stonefly** /ˈstoʊnflaɪ/, *n.* any of the insects constituting the order Plecoptera, whose larvae abound under stones in streams.

**stone fruit** /ˈstoʊn frut/, *n.* a fruit with a stone or hard endocarp, as a peach or a plum; drupe.

**stone ground** /ˈ– graʊnd/, *adj.* ground with a grindstone.

**stonehand** /ˈstoʊnhænd/, *n.* the printing craftsman responsible for imposing type prior to printing.

**stone-lily** /ˈstoʊn-lɪli/, *n.* a fossil crinoid.

**stone-marten** /ˈstoʊn-matn/, *n.* a marten, *Mustela foina,* of Europe, Asia, and northern Africa, having a white mark on the throat and breast.

**stonemason** /ˈstoʊnmeɪsən/, *n.* a dresser of or builder in stone. – **stonemasonry,** *n.*

**stone shield** /ˈstoʊn ʃild/, *n.* a shield which can be fitted to the windscreen of a motor vehicle to protect it from damage by flying stones.

**stone's-throw** /ˈstoʊnz-θroʊ/, *n.* the distance a stone may be thrown; a short distance.

**stonewall** /stoʊnˈwɔl, ˈstoʊnwɔl/, *v.i.* **1.** *Cricket.* (of a batsman) to play a defensive game only. *–v.t.* **2.** to obstruct, hinder, as the passage of a parliamentary bill. – **stonewaller,** *n.*

**stoneware** /ˈstoʊnwɛə/, *n.* a more or less vitrified pottery ware, usu. made from a single clay.

**stonework** /ˈstoʊnwɜk/, *n.* **1.** work in stone; stone masonry. **2.** (*usu. pl.*) an establishment where stone is prepared for building, etc. – **stoneworker,** *n.*

**stonewort** /ˈstoʊnwɜt/, *n.* a green alga of the class *Charophyceae,* having a jointed plant body frequently encrusted with lime and usu. growing in fresh water.

**stonk** /stɒŋk/, *n. Colloq.* heavy shelling; a severe bombardment.

**stonkered** /ˈstɒŋkəd/, *adj. Colloq.* **1.** defeated; destroyed; overthrown. **2.** exhausted. **3.** confounded; discomfited. **4.** drunk. **5.** extremely lethargic or incapacitated, as after a large meal.

**stony** /ˈstoʊni/, *adj.,* **stonier, stoniest.** **1.** full of or abounding in stones or rock. **2.** pertaining to or characteristic of stone. **3.** resembling or suggesting stone, esp. hard like stone. **4.** unfeeling; merciless; obdurate. **5.** motionless or rigid; without expression, as the eyes or look. **6.** petrifying: *stony fear.* **7.** having a stone or stones, as a fruit. **8.** *Colloq.* →**stony-broke.** – **stonily,** *adv.* – **stoniness,** *n.*

**stony-broke** /stoʊni-ˈbroʊk/, *adj. Colloq.* having no money whatever.

**stony coral** /stoʊni ˈkɒrəl/, *n.* a true coral or madrepore consisting of numerous anthozoan polyps embedded in the calcareous material that they secrete.

**stony-hearted** /ˈstoʊni-hatəd/, *adj.* hard-hearted.

**stood** /stʊd/, *v.* past tense and past participle of **stand.**

**stooge** /studʒ/, *n., v.,* **stooged, stooging.** *Colloq.* *–n.* **1.** an entertainer who feeds lines to a comedian and is often the object of his ridicule. **2.** one who acts on behalf of another, esp. in obsequious, corrupt, or secretive fashion. *–v.i.* **3.** to act as a stooge. [orig. uncert.]

**stook** /stuk, stʊk/, *n.* **1.** a group of sheaves of grain placed on end supporting one another in the field. *–v.t.* **2.** to make into stooks. [ME *stouk;* c. MLG *stūke,* G *Stauche* muff]

**stool** /stul/, *n.* **1.** a seat, either low or high, without arms or a back, usu. for a single person. **2.** a short, low support for resting the feet on, kneeling on, sitting on, etc. **3.** *Archaic.* a chair, seat, or position of authority. **4.** the stump, base, or root of a tree or other plant which has been cut down, from which new shoots or stems appear annually. **5.** the base of plants which annually produce new stems, etc. **6.** a cluster of shoots or stems springing up from a stool or from any root, or a single shoot or layer. **7.** *U.S.* a bird fastened as a decoy. **8.** *U.S.* a decoy duck or similar decoy. **9.** a privy. **10.** the mass of matter evacuated at each movement of the bowels; faeces. **11.** *U.S.* the sill of a window. **12. fall between two stools,** to fail to select either of two alternatives, as through indecision or hesitation. *–v.i.* **13.** to throw up shoots from the base or root, as a plant; form a stool. [ME; OE *stōl,* c. G *Stuhl*]

**stool pigeon** /ˈ– pɪdʒən/, *n.* **1.** a pigeon used as a decoy. **2.** *Chiefly U.S.* →**nark** (def. 1). **3.** *Colloq.* a person employed as a decoy or secret confederate, as by gamblers.

**stoop** /stup/, *v.i.* **1.** to bend the head and shoulders, or the body generally, forwards and downwards from an erect position: *to stoop over a desk.* **2.** to carry the head and shoulders habitually bowed forwards: *to stoop from age.* **3.** to bend, bow, or lean (said of trees, precipices, etc.). **4.** to descend from one's level of dignity; condescend; deign. **5.** to lower oneself by undignified or unworthy behaviour. **6.** to swoop down, as a hawk at prey. **7.** *Rare.* to submit; yield. **8.** *Obs.* to come down from a height. *–v.t.* **9.** to bend (oneself, one's head, etc.) forwards and downwards. **10.** *Archaic.* to abase, humble, or subdue. *–n.* **11.** the act of stooping; a stooping movement. **12.** a stooping position or carriage of body. **13.** a descent from dignity or superiority; a condescension. **14.** a downward swoop, as of a hawk. [ME *stoupe,* OE *stūpian;* akin to STEEP[1]]

**stop** /stɒp/, *v.,* **stopped** or (*Poetic*) **stopt, stopping,** *n.* *–v.t.* **1.** to cease from, leave off, or discontinue: *to stop running.* **2.** to cause to cease; put an end to: *to stop noise in the street.* **3.** to interrupt, arrest, or check (a course, proceeding, process, etc.). **4.** to cut off, intercept, or withhold: *to stop supplies.* **5.** to restrain, hinder, or prevent (fol. by *from*): *to stop a person from doing something.* **6.** to prevent from proceeding, acting, operating, continuing, etc.: *to stop a speaker, a car, etc.* **7.** to block, obstruct, or close (a passageway, channel, opening, duct, etc.) (oft. fol. by *up*). **8.** to fill the hole or holes in (a wall, a decayed tooth, etc.). **9.** to close (a container, tube, etc.) with a cork, plug, bung, or the like. **10.** to close the external orifice of (the ears, nose, mouth, etc.). **11.** *Fencing, Boxing, etc.* **a.** to check (a stroke, blow, etc.); parry; ward off. **b.** to defeat by a knockout or the like: *the local boy stopped his opponent in the fourth round.* **12.** *Banking.* to notify a banker not to honour (a cheque) on presentation. **13.** *Bridge.* to have an honour card and a sufficient number of protecting cards to keep an opponent from continuing to win in (a suit). **14.** *Music.* **a.** to close (a fingerhole, etc.) in order to produce a particular note from a wind instrument. **b.** to press down (a string of a violin, etc.) in order to alter the pitch of the note produced from it. **c.** to insert the hand in (the bell of a horn) in order to alter the pitch and quality of the note. **d.** to produce (a particular note) by so doing. **15.** to stay: *I stopped there for dinner.* *–v.i.* **16.** to come to a stand, as in a course or journey; halt. **17.** to cease moving, proceeding, speaking, acting, operating, etc.; to pause; desist. **18.** to cease; come to an end. *–v.* **19.** Some special verb phrases are:

**stop by,** to call somewhere briefly on the way to another destination.

**stop down,** *Photog.* to reduce the aperture size of (a camera).

**stop off at,** to halt for a brief stay in (a place) before leaving for another destination.

**stop over,** to make a stopover.

*–n.* **20.** the act of stopping. **21.** a cessation or arrest of movement, action, operation, etc.; end. **22.** a stay or sojourn made at a place, as in the course of a journey. **23.** a place where buses or other vehicles halt. **24.** a closing or filling up, as of a hole. **25.** a blocking or obstructing, as of a passage or way. **26.** *Fencing.* the action of a fencer who stands still instead of parrying a blow and then thrusting, allowing his opponent to run on his sword. **27.** a plug or other stopper for an opening. **28.** an obstacle, impediment, or hindrance. **29.** any piece or device that serves to check or control movement or action in a mechanism. **30.** *Banking.* stop order. **31.** *Music.* **a.** the act of closing a finger hole, etc., or of pressing down a string, of an instrument, in order to produce a particular note. **b.** a device or contrivance, as on an instrument, for accomplishing this. **c.** (in an organ) a graduated set of pipes of the same kind and giving tones of the same quality. **d.** a knob or handle which is drawn out or pushed back to permit or prevent the sounding of such a set of pipes or to control some other part of the organ. **e.** a similar group of reeds on a reed organ. **32.** *Zool.* the angle between the forehead and the nose or the face of a mammal, esp. that of a dog. **33.** *Naut.* a piece of small line used to lash or fasten something, as a furled sail. **34.** *Phonet.* **a.** an articulation which interrupts the flow of air from the lungs. **b.** a consonant sound resulting from stop articulation: *p, b, t, d, k,* and *g* are the English stops. **35.** *Photog.* the aperture size of a lens, esp. as indicated by an f number. **36.** →**full stop.** **37.** the word 'stop' spelt out, and used instead of a full stop in telegraphic and cable messages. **38.** (*pl.*) a family of games in which a player continues to play cards in a certain sequence until he is stopped, and can no longer play. **39.** *Cards.* **a.** a card which interrupts the run of a sequence. **b.** *Bridge.* an honour card covered by a sufficient number of lesser cards to prevent an opponent from continuing to win a suit. **40. pull out all (the) stops,** *Colloq.* **a.** to speak with extreme emotion. **b.** to push oneself or a machine to the utmost. [ME *stoppe,* OE *stoppian,* c. D and LG *stoppen,* G *stopfen,* all from VL. Cf. It. *stoppare* plug (with tow), from *stoppa,* from L *stuppa* tow, from Gk *stýppē*]

**stop-action camera** /ˌstɒp-ækʃən ˈkæmrə/, *n.* an automatically-operated camera for exposing successive frames of a film at regular but lengthy intervals, as in shooting the growth of a flower in accelerated motion.

**stopbank** /ˈstɒpbæŋk/, *n.* a dyke preventing a river from flooding the surrounding land; levee.

**stop bath** /ˈstɒp baθ/, *n.* (in photography) a bath of weakly acidic solution into which films, etc., being developed are immersed to stop the action of the developer.

**stopcock** /ˈstɒpkɒk/, *n.* a valve, with a tapered plug operated by a handle, used to control the flow of a liquid or gas from a receptacle or through a pipe.

**stopcylinder press** /ˈstɒpsɪləndə ˌprɛs/, *n.* a press in which the cylinder revolves only during the printing of the sheet and is stationary whilst the forme returns to print the next sheet.

**stop door** /ˈstɒp dɔ/, *n.* →**screen door.**

**stope** /stoʊp/, *n., v.,* **stoped, stoping.** *–n.* **1.** any excavation made in a mine to remove the ore which has been rendered accessible by the shafts and drifts. *–v.t., v.i.* **2.** to mine or work by stopes. [apparently akin to STEP, *n.*]

**stoper** /ˈstoʊpə/, *n.* a rock drill, originally one used for making stopes.

**stopgap** /ˈstɒpgæp/, *n.* **1.** something that fills the place of something lacking; a temporary substitute; a makeshift. *–adj.* **2.** makeshift.

**stop-go** /stɒp-ˈgoʊ/, *Colloq. –n.* **1.** a period of successive inflation and deflation. *–adj.* **2.** of or pertaining to such a period: *stop-go policies.*

**stoping** /ˈstoʊpɪŋ/, *n.* **1.** *Mining.* the act of creating a mine stope. **2.** *Geol.* the breaking off and assimilation of blocks of rock by an intruding magma, a process by which magmas move upwards through the earth's crust. Also, **magmatic stoping.** [pres. part. of STOPE]

**stoplight** /ˈstɒplaɪt/, *n.* **1.** a light placed at intersections, pedestrian crossings, etc., to indicate that traffic should stop. **2.** →**brakelight.**

**stoploss** /ˈstɒplɒs/, *adj.* (of a share trading system) designed to prevent or minimise financial loss to the trader.

**stoploss order** /– ˈɔdə/, *n.* an order given by a share trader to a stockbroker to buy or sell shares at a particular price.

**stop order** /ˈstɒp ɔdə/, *n.* (in banking) an order, as by the drawer of a cheque, etc., not to make payment.

**stopout** /ˈstɒpaʊt/, *n. Colloq.* one who habitually stays out till late at night at parties, etc.

**stopover** /ˈstɒpoʊvə/, *n.* any brief stop in the course of a journey, esp. one with the privilege of proceeding later on the ticket originally issued.

**stoppage** /ˈstɒpɪdʒ/, *n.* **1.** the act of stopping; cessation of activity, etc. **2.** the state of being stopped. **3.** the amount of anything stopped.

**stop payment** /ˈstɒp peɪmənt/, *n.* an order by the drawer of a cheque to his bank not to pay a specified cheque.

**stopped** /stɒpt/, *adj.* **1.** halted or checked. **2.** closed, filled up, or obstructed. **3.** *Music.* **a.** having the upper end plugged or closed, as an organ pipe. **b.** acted upon by stopping, as a string. **c.** produced by the stopping of a string, etc. **d.** having the bell stopped by the inserted hand, as in a French horn, to lower the pitch or to muffle the sound. **4.** *Phonet.* involving stop articulation.

**stopper** /ˈstɒpə/, *n.* **1.** one who or that which stops. **2.** a plug or piece for closing a bottle, tube, or the like. **3.** *Naut.* a short length of small or medium-sized Manila rope or light chain secured to a ringbolt or the like, used to hold a larger rope while it is being made fast permanently. **4.** *Colloq.* any kind of sleeping pill. *–v.t.* **5.** to close, secure, or fit with a stopper.

**stopping** /ˈstɒpɪŋ/, *n.* **1.** the action of one who or that which stops. **2.** *Mining.* a barrier erected to stop the passage of air, gas, fire, or an explosion. **3.** *Bldg Trades.* the material used to fill holes in timber, etc., before finishing with paint, etc.

**stopple** /ˈstɒpəl/, *n., v.,* **-pled, -pling.** *Archaic. –n.* **1.** a stopper for a bottle or the like. *–v.t.* **2.** to close or fit with a stopple.

**stop press** /ˈstɒp prɛs/, *n.* **1.** news inserted in a newspaper after printing has begun. **2.** the space for this.

**stop-ridge** /ˈstɒp-rɪdʒ/, *n.* the raised part of the blade of an axe, sword, etc., which stops it from penetrating too deeply.

**stop sign** /ˈstɒp saɪn/, *n.* a sign at a road junction, indicating that the driver must stop completely and give way to all traffic on his left and right.

**stop volley** /ˈ– vɒli/, *n.* (in tennis) a gentle volley played close to the net, so that the ball falls into the opponent's court with little bounce.

**stopwatch** /ˈstɒpwɒtʃ/, *n.* a watch with a hand or hands that can be stopped or started at any instant, and which is adapted for indicating fractions of a second (used for timing races, etc.).

**stop-work meeting** /ˈstɒp-wɜk ˌmitɪŋ/, *n.* a meeting of employees held during working time to consult with unions or management over conditions of work, etc.

**storage** /ˈstɔrɪdʒ/, *n.* **1.** the act of storing. **2.** the state or fact of being stored. **3.** capacity or space for storing. **4.** *Computers.* the capacity of a device to hold information. **5.** a place where something is stored. **6.** the price charged for storing goods.

**storage battery** /ˈ– bætəri/, *n.* a battery of secondary cells used for storing electricity; an accumulator.

**storage cell** /ˈ– sɛl/, *n.* a cell in a storage battery.

**storage device** /ˈ– dəvaɪs/, *n.* the memory of a computer.

**storage heater** /ˈ– hitə/, *n.* an appliance in which heat is stored when cheap or easily obtainable, and given out when expensive or unobtainable; heat reservoir.

**storage ring** /ˈ– rɪŋ/, *n.* a toroidal vacuum chamber for storing high-energy particles from a particle accelerator.

**storax** /ˈstɔræks/, *n.* **1.** any shrub or tree of the genus *Styrax,* having attractive white flowers. **2.** a solid resin with a vanilla-like scent obtained from a small styracaceous tree, *Styrax officinalis,* formerly much used in medicine and perfumery. **3.** a liquid balsam (**liquid storax**) obtained from species of liquidambar, esp. from the wood and inner bark of *Liquidambar orientalis* (**Levant storax**), a tree of Asia Minor, etc., and used in medicine, perfumery, etc. [L, from Gk *stýrax*]

**store** /stɔ/, *n., v.,* **stored, storing.** *–n.* **1.** a large shop with many departments or branches. **2.** a supply or stock (of something), esp. one for future use. **3.** (*pl.*) supplies of food, clothing, or other requisites, as for a household or other establishment, a ship, naval or military forces, or the like. **4.** (*pl.*) **the stores,** (formerly) government rations. **5.** a beast in store condition. **6.** a shop. **7.** a storehouse or warehouse. **8.** measure of esteem or regard: *to set little store by a thing.* **9.** quantity, esp. great quantity; abundance, or plenty. **10.** a computer memory. **11. in store, a.** kept in readiness for future use. **b.** coming in the future: *she did not know what was in store for her.* **c.** deposited in a warehouse until needed. *–adj.* **12.** of or pertaining to sheep, cattle, etc., bought to be fattened for market. *–v.t.* **13.** to supply or stock with something, as for future use. **14.** to lay up or put away, as a supply for future use (oft. with *up* or *away*). **15.** to deposit in a storehouse, warehouse, or other place, for keeping. [ME, aphetic var. of *astore,* from OF *estorer* build, furnish, stock, from L *instaurare* renew, restore, make] – **storable,** *adj.*

**store condition** /ˈ– kəndɪʃən/, *n.* the condition of an animal, esp. of sheep or cattle, which is in good condition, but not fat.

**storehouse** /ˈstɔhaʊs/, *n.* **1.** a house or building in which things are stored. **2.** any repository or source of abundant supplies, as of facts or knowledge.

**storekeeper** /ˈstɔkipə/, *n.* **1.** one who has charge of a store or stores. **2.** a shopkeeper.

**storeroom** /ˈstɔrum/, *n.* **1.** a room in which stores are kept. **2.** room or space for storage.

**storey** /ˈstɔri/, *n., pl.* **-reys. 1.** a complete horizontal section of a building, having one continuous or approximately continuous floor. **2.** the set of rooms on the same floor or level of a building. **3.** each of the stages separated by floors, one above another, of which a building consists. Also, *Chiefly U.S.,* **story.** [ME, from OF *estorer* build. See STORE]

**storeyed** /ˈstɔrid/, *adj.* having storeys or floors: *a two-storeyed house.* Also, *Chiefly U.S.,* **storied.** [STOREY + -ED[3]]

**storied**[1] /ˈstɔrid/, *adj.* **1.** recorded or celebrated in history or story. **2.** ornamented with designs representing historical, legendary or similar subjects. [STORY[1] + -ED[3]]

**storied**[2] /ˈstɔrid/, *adj. Chiefly U.S.* →**storeyed.**

**stork** /stɔk/, *n.* one of the long-legged, long-necked, long-billed wading birds, allied to the ibises and herons, which constitute the family Ciconiidae, esp. *Ciconia ciconia* (white stork) of Europe, or, in Australia, the jabiru. [ME; OE *storc,* c. G *Storch*]

**stork's-bill** /ˈstɔks-bɪl/, *n.* any herbaceous plant of the genus

i = peat ɪ = pit ɛ = pet æ = pat a = part ɒ = pot ʌ = putt ɔ = port ʊ = put u = pool ɜ = pert ə = apart aɪ = buy eɪ = bay ɔɪ = boy aʊ = how
oʊ = hoe ɪə = here ɛə = hair ʊə = tour g = give θ = thin ð = then ʃ = show ʒ = measure tʃ = choke dʒ = joke ŋ = sing j = you õ = Fr. bon

*Erodium,* as *E. cicutarium,* the **common stork's bill,** so called from the long-beaked fruit.

**storm** /stɔm/, *n.* **1.** a disturbance of the normal condition of the atmosphere, manifesting itself by winds of unusual force or direction, often accompanied by rain, snow, hail, thunder and lightning, or flying sand or dust. **2.** a heavy fall of rain, snow, or hail, or a violent outbreak of thunder, and lightning, unaccompanied by strong wind. **3.** *Meteorol.* a wind of Beaufort scale force 10, i.e., one with average wind speed of 48 to 55 knots, or 89 to 102 km/h. **4.** a violent assault on a fortified place, strong position, or the like. **5.** a heavy descent or discharge of missiles, blows, or the like. **6.** a violent disturbance of affairs, as a civil, political, social, or domestic commotion. **7.** a violent outburst or outbreak: *a storm of applause.* **8. cook up a storm,** to engage in activities which will lead to a confrontation or quarrel. **9. storm in a teacup,** a great deal of fuss arising out of a very unimportant matter. **10. take by storm, a.** to take by military assault. **b.** to captivate and overwhelm completely. *–v.i.* **11.** *Chiefly U.S.* to blow with unusual force, or to rain, snow, hail, etc., esp. with violence (used impersonally): *it stormed all day.* **12.** to rage or complain with violence or fury. **13.** to deliver a violent attack or fire, as with artillery. **14.** to rush to an assault or attack. **15.** to rush with angry violence: *to storm out of a room.* *–v.t.* **16.** to subject to or as to a storm. **17.** to utter or say with angry vehemence. **18.** to assault (a fortified place). [ME and OE, c. D *storm,* G *Sturm*]

storm centre (as seen in satellite photograph)

**stormbound** /ˈstɔmbaund/, *adj.* confined or detained by storms.

**storm cellar** /ˈstɔm sɛlə/, *n. U.S.* a cellar or underground chamber for refuge during violent storms.

**storm centre** /ˈ– sɛntə/, *n.* **1.** the centre of a cyclonic storm, the area of lowest pressure and of comparative calm. **2.** a centre of disturbance, tumult, trouble, or the like.

**storm-cloud** /ˈstɔm-klaud/, *n.* a large black cloud, usu. signifying that a storm is imminent.

**storm-cock** /ˈstɔm-kɒk/, *n.* →**missel thrush.**

**storm door** /ˈstɔm dɔ/, *n. U.S.* an outer or additional door for protection against inclement weather, as during the winter.

**storm jib** /ˈ– dʒɪb/, *n.* a small jib made of very strong material, used in stormy weather.

**storm-lantern** /ˈstɔm-læntən/, *n. Brit.* →**hurricane lamp.**

**stormless** /ˈstɔmləs/, *adj.* without storms.

**storm mould** /ˈstɔm mould/, *n.* a member fixed over the gap between a window and the masonry into which it is built to conceal and protect the flashing.

**storm-petrel** /ˈstɔm-pɛtrəl/, *n.* any of various small, dark, swallow-like seabirds of the family Hydrobatidae.

storm-petrel

**stormproof** /ˈstɔmpruf/, *adj.* proof against storms or storming.

**storm sail** /ˈstɔm seɪl/, *n.* a sail of very strong and heavy material of smaller dimensions than usual, set in gales and storms.

**storm signals** /ˈ– sɪgnəlz/, *n.pl.* signals in the form of flags, shapes, or lights exhibited at points round the coast to warn vessels of the approach of bad weather.

**storm-trooper** /ˈstɔm-trupə/, *n.* a member of a body of storm troops or shock troops.

**storm troops** /ˈstɔm trups/, *n.* →**shock troops.**

**stormwater** /ˈstɔmwɔtə/, *n.* a sudden, excessive run-off of water following a storm.

**stormwater channel** /ˈ– tʃænəl/, *n.* an artificial passage for stormwater and floodwater; floodway. Also, **stormwater canal, stormwater drain.**

**storm window** /ˈstɔm wɪndou/, *n.* a glass covering over a window, providing extra insulation and protection from cold and wind.

**stormy** /ˈstɔmi/, *adj.,* **stormier, stormiest. 1.** affected or characterised by, or subject to, storms; tempestuous: *a stormy sea.* **2.** characterised by violent commotion, actions, speech, passions, etc.: *a stormy debate.* – **stormily,** *adv.* – **storminess,** *n.*

**stormy petrel** /– ˈpɛtrəl/, *n.* **1.** →**storm-petrel. 2.** a person whose coming is supposed to portend trouble.

**story**[1] /ˈstɔri/, *n., pl.* **-ries,** *v.,* **-ried, -rying.** *–n.* **1.** narrative, either true or fictitious, in prose or verse, designed to interest or amuse the hearer or reader; a tale. **2.** a fictitious tale, shorter and less elaborate than a novel. **3.** such narratives or tales as a branch of literature. **4.** the plot, or succession of incidents of a novel, poem, drama, etc. **5.** a narration of a series of events, or a series of events that are or may be narrated. **6.** a narration of the events in the life of a person or the existence of a thing, or such events as a subject for narration. **7.** a report or account of a matter; a statement. **8.** *Journalism.* an account of some event, situation, etc., in a newspaper. **9.** *Media.* a news item; an account of an event or situation, as in a newspaper, on television, etc.: *we are having trouble with that film and will go on to the next story.* **10.** *Colloq.* a lie; a fib. **11.** *Obs.* history. *–v.t.* **12.** to ornament with pictured scenes, as from history or legend. **13.** *Rare.* to tell the history or story of; tell as a story. [ME, from AF *estorie,* from L *historia*]

**story**[2] /ˈstɔri/, *n., pl.* **-ries.** *Chiefly U.S.* →**storey.**

**storybook** /ˈstɔribʊk/, *n.* **1.** a book containing a story or stories, fiction or non-fiction, esp. for children. *–adj.* **2.** of or pertaining to childish fiction: *he lives in a storybook world.*

**story-line** /ˈstɔri-laɪn/, *n.* →**plot.**

**storyteller** /ˈstɔritɛlə/, *n.* **1.** one who tells stories. **2.** *Colloq.* one who tells untrue or fantastic stories, as if they were true.

**stoss** /stɒs, ʃtɒs/, *adj.* denoting the end or side, as of a hill, drumlin, etc., that receives, or has received, the thrust of a glacier. [G: thrust, push]

**stoup** /stup/, *n.* **1.** a basin for holy water, as at the entrance of a church. **2.** *Scot.* a pail or bucket. **3.** *Archaic and Scot.* **a.** a drinking vessel of various sizes, as a cup or tankard. **b.** the amount it holds. [ME *stowpe,* from Scand.; cf. Icel. *staup,* c. OE *stēap*]

stoup (def. 1)

**stoush** /stauʃ/, *Colloq.* *–n.* **1.** a fight. **2.** an artillery bombardment. **3. the big stoush,** World War I. *–v.t.* **4.** to fight (someone or something). [var. Scot. *stash, stashie* uproar]

**stout** /staut/, *adj.* **1.** bulky in figure, solidly built, or thickset; corpulent or fat. **2.** bold, hardy, or dauntless: *a stout heart.* **3.** a firm; stubborn: *stout resistance.* **4.** strong of body, stalwart, or sturdy: *stout fellows.* **5.** having endurance or staying power, as a horse. **6.** strong in substance or construction. **7.** strong and thick or heavy. *n.* **8.** any of various beers brewed by the top-fermentation method but darker and heavier than ales, deriving colour and flavour from the roasted malt used in the brewing process. [ME, from OF *estout* brave, proud, from Gmc; cf. MLG *stolt*] – **stoutly,** *adv.* – **stoutness,** *n.*

**stout-hearted** /ˈstaut-hatəd/, *adj.* brave and resolute; dauntless. – **stout-heartedly,** *adv.*

**stove**[1] /stouv/, *n., v.,* **stoved, stoving.** *–n.* **1.** an apparatus, portable or fixed, and in many forms, for furnishing heat, as for comfort, cooking, or mechanical purposes, commonly using coal, oil, gas, or electricity. **2.** a heated chamber or box for some special purpose, as a drying room, or a kiln for firing pottery. *–v.t.* **3.** to apply heat to (metalware, etc.) in a kiln to fuse paint to its surface. [ME; OE *stofa* hot air bathroom, c. G *Stube* sitting room]

**stove**[2] /stouv/, *v.* a past tense and past participle of **stave.**

**stovepipe** /ˈstouvpaɪp/, *n.* **1.** a pipe, as of sheet metal, serving as a stove chimney or to connect a stove with a chimney flue. **2.** *Colloq.* →**stovepipe hat.**

**stovepipe hat** /– ˈhæt/, *n. Colloq.* a tall silk hat.

**stover** /ˈstouvə/, *n.* **1.** coarse roughage used as feed for livestock. **2.** *Chiefly U.S.* stalks and leaves, not including grain, of such forages as corn and sorghum. [ME, from OF *estover* necessaries, ESTOVERS]

**stovette** /stoʊvˈɛt/, *n.* a small stove.

**stow** /stoʊ/, *v.t.* **1.** *Naut.* to place (cargo, etc.) in the hold or some other part of a ship. **2.** to put in a place or receptacle as for storage or reserve; pack. **3.** to fill (a place or receptacle) by packing. **4.** (of a place or receptacle) to afford room for; hold. **5.** to put away, as in a safe convenient place (fol. by *away*). **6.** to desist from. **7. stow it,** *Colloq.* be quiet. *–v.i.* **8. stow away,** to conceal oneself aboard a ship or other conveyance in order to get a free trip. [ME, from *stowe* place, OE *stow,* c. Icel. *-stō* (in *eldstō* fireplace)]

**stowage** /ˈstoʊɪdʒ/, *n.* **1.** the act or operation of stowing. **2.** the state or manner of being stowed. **3.** room or accommodation for stowing something. **4.** a place in which something is or may be stowed. **5.** that which is stowed or to be stowed. **6.** a charge for stowing something.

**stowaway** /ˈstoʊəweɪ/, *n.* one who conceals himself aboard a ship or other conveyance, as to get a free trip.

**S.T.P.** /ɛs ti ˈpi/, *n.* standard temperature and pressure; a temperature of 0°C and a pressure of 101 325 pascals. Also, **N.T.P.**

**St Peters wort,** *n.* a stoloniferous perennial herb, *Hypericum tetrapterum,* native to Mediterranean regions but naturalised elsewhere.

**strabismus** /strəˈbɪzməs/, *n.* a disorder of vision due to the turning of one eye or both eyes from the normal position so that both cannot be directed at the same point or object at the same time; squint; cross-eye. [NL, from Gk *strabismós*] – **strabismal, strabismic, strabismical,** *adj.*

**strabotomy** /strəˈbɒtəmi/, *n., pl.* **-mies.** the operation of dividing one or more of the muscles of the eye for the cure of strabismus.

**strachino** /strəˈtʃinoʊ/, *n.* one of several whole-milk cheeses, soft and white, with a mild, delicate flavour, used in cakes and pastries.

**straddle** /ˈstrædl/, *v.,* **-dled, -dling,** *n.* *–v.i.* **1.** to walk, stand, or sit with the legs wide apart; stand or sit astride. **2.** to stand wide apart, as the legs. *–v.t.* **3.** to walk, stand, or sit with one leg on each side of; stand or sit astride of. **4.** to spread (the legs) wide apart. **5.** *Mil.* to cover (an area) with bombs. **6.** *Gunnery.* to fire (shots) beyond and short of (a target) in order to fix range. *–n.* **7.** the act of straddling. **8.** the distance straddled over. **9.** *Athletics.* a style of high jumping in which the athlete crosses the bar horizontally and face down, rolling forward to land on his back. [apparently northern var. of *stroddle,* akin to *striddle,* frequentative of STRIDE] – **straddler,** *n.* – **straddlingly,** *adv.*

**strafe** /straf, streɪf/, *v.t.,* **strafed, strafing.** **1.** to attack (ground troops or installations) by aircraft with machine-gun fire. **2.** to bombard heavily. **3.** *Colloq.* to punish. *–n.* **4.** an attack or assault. [G; from the phrase *Gott strafe England* God punish England] – **strafer,** *n.*

**straggle** /ˈstrægəl/, *v.i.,* **-gled, -gling.** **1.** to stray from the road, course, or line of march. **2.** to wander about in a scattered fashion; ramble. **3.** to go, come, or spread in a scattered, irregular fashion. **4.** to fail to keep up with one's companions in a journey, walk, etc.; drop behind. [ME; b. STRAY and DRAGGLE]

**straggler** /ˈstræglə/, *n.* **1.** one who, or that which straggles. **2.** *Agric.* **a.** an animal missed in a muster. **b.** one that is not the property of the holding on which it is found. **3.** one who falls behind, as in a journey.

**straggly** /ˈstrægli/, *adj.* straggling; rambling.

**straight** /streɪt/, *adj.* **1.** without a bend, crook, or curve; not curved; direct: *a straight path.* **2.** flat; horizontal. **3.** *Cricket.* **a.** (of a bat) held perpendicular to the ground. **b.** (of a stroke) playing the ball down the wicket past the bowler: *a straight drive.* **4.** (of a line) lying evenly between its points; generated by a point moving constantly in the same direction. **5.** evenly formed or set: *straight shoulders.* **6.** delivered with arm extended straight from the shoulder, as a blow: *straight left.* **7.** without circumlocution; candid: *a straight answer.* **8.** honest, honourable, or upright, as conduct, dealings, methods, persons, etc. **9.** *Colloq.* conforming to orthodox, conservative forms of behaviour, as heterosexuality, avoidance of illegal drugs, etc. **10.** *Colloq.* reliable, as reports, information, etc. **11.** right or correct, as reasoning, thinking, a thinker, etc. **12.** continuous or unbroken: *in straight succession.* **13.** thoroughgoing or unreserved: *a straight comedy.* **14.** undiluted, as an alcoholic beverage; neat. **15.** *Theat.* (of a play, acting style, etc.) serious; without music or dancing and not primarily comic in intent. **16.** *Cards.* made up of cards in consecutive denominations, as the two, three, four, five, and six. **17. play a straight bat,** *Colloq.* to act in a straightforward and honest fashion. *–adv.* **18.** in a straight line: *to walk straight.* **19.** in an even form or position: *pictures hung straight.* **20.** directly: *to go straight to a place.* **21.** without circumlocution (oft. fol. by *out*). **22.** honestly, honourably, or virtuously: *to live straight.* **23.** in a continuous course: *to keep straight on.* **24.** at once; immediately; without delay: *I'll come straight over.* **25.** in the proper order or condition, as a room: *he set the room straight after the meeting.* **26. set (put) someone straight,** to point out an error to someone. **27.** *U.S.* without discount regardless of the quantity bought: *candy bars are ten cents straight.* **28. go straight,** to lead an honest life, esp. after a prison sentence. *–n.* **29.** the condition of being straight. **30. the straight and narrow,** a way of life governed by strict moral principles. **31.** a straight form or position. **32.** a straight line. **33.** a straight part, as of a racecourse or a railway. **34.** a person who is straight (def. 9). **35.** *Poker.* a sequence of five cards of various suits. Cf. **sequence.** [ME, orig. pp. of STRETCH] – **straightly,** *adv.* – **straightness,** *n.*

**straight angle** /ˈ– æŋgəl/, *n.* an angle of 180°.

**straight-arm** /ˈstreɪt-am/, *v.t.* *Football.* to ward off an opponent by holding the arm straight and pushing with the palm of the hand; fend (off).

**straightaway** /streɪtəˈweɪ/, *adv.* **1.** immediately; at once; right away. *–adj.* **2.** *U.S.* straight onwards, without turn or curve, as a racecourse. *–n.* **3.** *U.S.* a straightaway course or part.

**straight bat** /streɪt ˈbæt/, *n.* **1.** *Cricket.* a bat held in a defensive position vertical to the ground. **2.** *Cricket.* a bat moving in a curve vertical to the ground as for a drive. **3. play with a straight bat,** *Colloq.* to act honestly, straightforwardly.

**straightedge** /ˈstreɪtɛdʒ/, *n.* a bar or strip of wood or metal, of various sizes, having at least one edge of sufficiently reliable straightness, for use in obtaining or testing straight lines, plane surfaces, etc.

**straighten** /ˈstreɪtn/, *v.t.* **1.** to make straight in direction, form, position, character, conduct, condition, etc. *–v.i.* **2.** to become straight. – **straightener,** *n.*

**straight face** /streɪt ˈfeɪs/, *n.* a deliberately serious expression, esp. in an attempt to suppress laughter: *she managed to keep a straight face despite their antics.* – **straight-faced,** *adj.*

**straight fight** /– ˈfaɪt/, *n.* a contest, as at an election, between two candidates only.

**straight flush** /– ˈflʌʃ/, *n.* (in poker) a sequence of five cards of the same suit.

**straightforward** /streɪtˈfɔwəd/, *adj.* **1.** going or directed straight forward: *a straightforward glance.* **2.** proceeding without circuity; direct. **3.** free from crookedness or deceit; honest: *straightforward in one's dealings.* **4.** without difficulty; uncomplicated: *the subject set was very straightforward.* *–adv.* **5.** Also, **straightforwards.** *Chiefly U.S.* straight ahead; directly or continuously forward. – **straightforwardly,** *adv.* – **straightforwardness,** *n.*

**straightjacket** /ˈstreɪtdʒækət/, *n.* →**straitjacket.**

**straight joint** /ˈstreɪt dʒɔɪnt/, *n.* a fault in brick or stone masonry, by which one vertical joint is situated immediately above another.

**straight line** /– ˈlaɪn/, *n.* a line of stock developed by breeding through one family, excluding close relations.

**straight-line** /ˈstreɪt-laɪn/, *adj.* *Mach.* **1.** indicating a linear arrangement of the working parts of a machine, as in some compressors. **2.** denoting an apparatus copying or initiating motion along a straight line.

**straight-line motion** /ˈ– ˌmoʊʃən/, *n.* (in machines) a device, as a linkage, initiating motion in a straight line, or transferring motion from a curved line to a straight.

**straight man** /ˈstreɪt mæn/, *n.* an entertainer who plays his part straight, usu. as a foil for a comedian.

**straight-out** /ˈstreɪt-aʊt/, *adj.* *Colloq.* **1.** thorough-going: *a* *straight-out Democrat.* **2.** frank; aboveboard. **3.** (of a bet) for a win only.

**straightshooter** /streɪtˈʃutə/, *n. Colloq.* a person who is honest and open in his dealings.

**straight-up** /ˈstreɪt-ʌp/, *adj.* **1.** honest; fair. **2.** of or pertaining to sexual intercourse in the more usual positions: *she likes only straight-up sex.*

**straightway** /streɪtˈweɪ/, *adv. Archaic.* immediately; at once.

**strain**[1] /streɪn/, *v.t.* **1.** to draw tight or taut; stretch, esp. to the utmost tension: *to strain a rope.* **2.** to exert to the utmost: *to strain one's ears to catch a sound.* **3.** to impair, injure, or weaken by stretching or overexertion, as a muscle. **4.** to cause mechanical deformation in (a body or structure) as the result of stress. **5.** to stretch beyond the proper point or limit: *to strain the meaning of a word.* **6.** to make excessive demands upon: *to strain one's resources, credit, etc.* **7.** to pass (liquid matter) through a filter, sieve, or the like, in order to hold back the denser or solid constituents. **8.** to draw off (clear liquid) or hold back (solid particles, etc.) from liquid matter by using a filter, sieve, or the like. **9.** to clasp tightly in the arms, the hand, etc. **10.** *Obs.* to constrain, as to a course of action. *–v.i.* **11.** to pull forcibly: *a dog straining at a leash.* **12.** to stretch one's muscles, nerves, etc., to the utmost. **13.** to make violent physical efforts; strive hard. **14.** to be subjected to tension or stress; suffer strain. **15.** to filter, percolate, or ooze. **16.** to trickle or flow. *–n.* **17.** any force or pressure tending to alter shape, cause fracture, etc. **18.** strong muscular or physical effort; great or excessive effort of any kind. **19.** an injury to a muscle, tendon, etc., due to excessive tension or use; a sprain. **20.** *Colloq.* →**urethritis** (def. 1). **21. a.** an injury to or deformation of any body or structure resulting from stress. **b.** *Physics.* the extent of such deformation expressed as the ratio of the dimensional change to the original unstrained dimension (length, area, or volume). **22.** the condition of being strained or stretched. **23.** extreme or excessive striving after some object or effect. **24.** severe, trying, or wearing pressure or effect: *the strain of hard work.* **25.** a severe demand on resources, feelings, a person, etc.: *a strain on one's hospitality.* **26.** *Obs.* a flow or burst of language, eloquence, etc. **27.** (*sing. or pl., oft. collective pl.*) a passage of music or song as rendered or heard: *the strains of a violin.* **28.** *Music.* a section of a piece of music more or less complete in itself. **29.** a passage or piece of poetry. **30.** tone, style, or spirit in expression: *a humorous strain.* **31.** *Rare.* a particular degree, height, or pitch attained. [ME *streyne,* from OF *estrein-, estreindre* bind tightly, clasp, squeeze, from L *stringere* draw tight]

**strain**[2] /streɪn/, *n.* **1.** the body of descendants of a common ancestor, as a family or stock. **2.** any of the different lines of ancestry united in a family or an individual. **3.** a group of plants distinguished from other plants of the variety to which it belongs by some intrinsic quality, such as a tendency to yield heavily. **4.** an artificial variety of a species of domestic animal or cultivated plant. **5.** a variety, esp. of micro-organisms. **6.** ancestry or descent. **7.** hereditary or natural character, tendency, or trait: *a strain of insanity in a family.* **8.** a streak or trace. **9.** *Rare.* a kind or sort. [ME *straine,* unexplained var. of *strene,* OE *gestrēon* acquisition, c. OHG *gistriuni*]

**strained** /streɪnd/, *adj.* affected or produced by effort; forced; not natural or spontaneous.

**strainer** /ˈstreɪnə/, *n.* **1.** one who or that which strains. **2.** a filter, sieve, or the like for straining liquids. **3.** a stretcher or tightener, as on a wire fence. **4.** Also, **strainer post.** a solid post against which the wires in a post and wire fence are tightened or strained.

**strain gauge** /ˈstreɪn geɪdʒ/, *n.* a grid of fine wires attached to a surface under stress so that any change in the dimensions of the surface is imparted to the wires causing a change in their electrical resistance. This change in resistance is proportional to the strain produced by the stress.

**strain-hardening** /streɪn-ˈhadnɪŋ/, *n.* an increase in the hardness of a metal resulting from the permanent change to its crystalline structure caused by cold working. Also, **work-hardening.** – **strain-hardened,** *adj.*

**straining beam** /ˈstreɪnɪŋ bim/, *n.* (in a queen-post roof) a horizontal beam uniting the tops of the two queen posts, and resisting the thrust of the roof. Also, **straining piece.**

**strait** /streɪt/, *n.* **1.** (*oft. pl. with sing. sense*) a narrow passage of water connecting two large bodies of water. **2.** (*oft. pl.*) a position of difficulty, distress, or need. **3.** *Archaic.* a narrow passage, space, or area. **4.** *Rare.* →**isthmus.** *–adj.* **5.** *Archaic.* narrow. **6.** *Archaic or Lit.* affording little room, as a place, bounds, etc. **7.** *Archaic.* strict in requirements, principles, etc. [ME, from OF *estreit* tight, narrow, from L *strictus,* pp., bound] – **straitly,** *adv.*

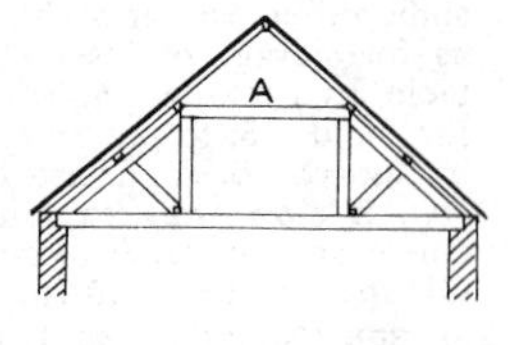

A, straining beam

**straiten** /ˈstreɪtn/, *v.t.* **1.** to put into difficulties, esp. financial ones: *in straitened circumstances.* **2.** to restrict in range, extent, amount, pecuniary means, etc. **3.** *Archaic or Lit.* to make narrow. **4.** *Archaic.* to confine within narrow limits.

**straitjacket** /ˈstreɪtdʒækət/, *n.* a kind of coat for confining the arms of violently insane persons, etc. Also, **straightjacket.**

**straitlaced** /ˈstreɪtleɪst/, *adj.* **1.** excessively strict in conduct or morality; puritanical; prudish. **2.** *Archaic.* tightly laced, or wearing tightly laced garments.

**Straitsman** /ˈstreɪtsmən/, *n.* a person living on an island in Bass Strait.

**strake** /streɪk/, *n.* **1.** *Naut.* one continuous longitudinal line or breadth of planking or plate on the side or bottom of a vessel. **2.** *Mech.* any one section of the metal tyre on a wooden wheel. **3.** *Mech.* a metal plate let into a rubber tyre. **4.** *Mining.* a relatively wide trough set at an angle and covered with a blanket or corduroy for catching comparatively coarse gold and valuable mineral. **5.** *Mining.* a trough in which ore, gravel etc., are washed; a launder. **6.** *Mining.* the place where ore is sorted on the floor of a mine; a dressing floor. [ME; apparently akin to STRETCH]

**stramineous** /strəˈmɪniəs/, *adj.* **1.** of straw; straw-like. **2.** straw-coloured; yellowish. [L *strāmineus*]

**stramonium** /strəˈmoʊniəm/, *n.* **1.** →**jimson weed. 2.** the dried leaves of this plant, used in medicine as an analgesic, antispasmodic, etc. [NL; orig. uncert.]

**strand**[1] /strænd/, *v.t.* **1.** to drive aground on a shore, esp. of the sea, as a ship, a fish, etc. **2.** (*usu. in the passive*) to bring into a helpless position. **3.** to leave without means of transport. *–v.i.* **4.** to be driven or run ashore, as a ship, etc.; run aground. *–n.* **5.** *Poetic.* the land bordering the sea or ocean, or, formerly, a river; the shore. [ME and OE, c. D and G *Strand*]

**strand**[2] /strænd/, *n.* **1.** each of a number of strings or yarns which are twisted together to form a rope, cord, or the like. **2.** a similar part of a wire rope. **3.** a fibre or filament, as in animal or plant tissue. **4.** a thread of the texture of anything, as cloth. **5.** a tress of hair. **6.** a string of pearls, beads, etc. *–v.t.* **7.** to form (a rope, etc.) by twisting strands. **8.** to break one or more strands of (a rope). [ME *strond;* orig. uncert.]

**strandline** /ˈstrændlaɪn/, *n.* a shoreline, esp. one from which the sea or a lake has receded.

**strange** /streɪndʒ/, *adj.,* **stranger, strangest,** *adv. –adj.* **1.** unusual, extraordinary, or curious; odd; queer: *a strange remark to make.* **2.** out of one's natural environment: *to feel strange in a place.* **3.** situated, belonging, or coming from outside one's own or a particular locality: *to move to a strange place.* **4.** outside one's previous experience; hitherto unknown; unfamiliar: *the writing is strange to me.* **5.** unacquainted; unaccustomed (to) or inexperienced (at). **6.** distant or reserved. **7.** *Archaic.* foreign. *–adv.* **8.** *Colloq.* slightly unbalanced mentally; *she is a little strange.* **9.** *Colloq.* in a strange manner. [ME, from OF *estrange,* from L *extrāneus* external, foreign] – **strangely,** *adv.* – **strangeness,** *n.*

**strangeness** /ˈstreɪndʒnəs/, *n.* **1.** the fact or quality of being strange. **2.** *Physics.* a quantum number used to account for the slowness with which certain transformations between elementary particles happen.

**strange particle** /ˈstreɪndʒ ˌpatɪkəl/, *n.* an elementary particle the strangeness (def. 2) of which is not zero.

**stranger** /ˈstreɪndʒə/, *n.* **1.** a person with whom one has, or has hitherto had, no personal acquaintance. **2.** an outsider.

3. a visitor or guest. 4. a newcomer in a place or locality. 5. **a (the) little stranger,** *Colloq.* an unborn or new-born infant. 6. a person or thing that is unaccustomed or new (fol. by *to*): *he is no stranger to poverty.* 7. *Law.* one not privy or party to an act, proceeding, etc. 8. *Archaic.* a foreigner or alien. 9. a floating tea leaf in a cup of tea. 10. →**herring cale.**

**strangle** /ˈstræŋgəl/, *v.*, **-gled, -gling,** *n.* –*v.t.* 1. to kill by compression of the windpipe, as by a cord around the neck. 2. to kill by stopping the breath in any manner; choke; stifle; suffocate. 3. to prevent the continuance, growth, rise, or action of; suppress. –*v.i.* 4. to be choked, stifled, or suffocated. –*n.* 5. (*pl. construed as sing.*) an infectious febrile disease of equine animals, characterised by catarrh of the upper air passages and suppuration of the submaxillary and other lymphatic glands; distemper. [ME, from OF *estrangler,* from L *strangulāre,* from Gk *strangalân*] – **strangler,** *n.*

**stranglehold** /ˈstræŋgəlhoʊld/, *n.* 1. *Wrestling.* a hold by which the adversary's breathing is stopped. 2. anything which prevents motion or development of a person or group.

**strangulate** /ˈstræŋgjəleɪt/, *v.t.*, **-lated, -lating.** 1. *Pathol., Surg.* to compress or constrict (a duct, intestine, vessel, etc.) so as to prevent circulation or suppress function. 2. to strangle. [L *strangulātus,* pp., strangled] – **strangulation** /stræŋgjəˈleɪʃən/, *n.*

**strangury** /ˈstræŋgjəri/, *n.* a condition of the urinary organs in which the urine is painfully emitted, drop by drop. [ME, from L *strangūria,* from Gk *strangouría*]

**S trap** /ˈɛs træp/, *n.* →**trap** (def. 5).

**strap** /stræp/, *n., v.,* **strapped, strapping.** –*n.* 1. a narrow strip of flexible material, esp. leather, for fastening or holding things together, etc. 2. a looped band of leather, strong material, etc., for lifting, holding, pulling, or attaching. 3. a strop for a razor. 4. a long, narrow piece or object; strip; band. 5. a straplike ornament, as a watch-strap. 6. See **shoulder-strap.** 7. *Elect.* a short thick conductor connecting two points in a circuit. –*v.t.* 8. to fasten or secure with a strap or straps. 9. *Obs.* to sharpen on a strap or strop. 10. to beat or flog with a strap. [var. of STROP] – **straplike,** *adj.*

**straphanger** /ˈstræphæŋə/, *n.* 1. *Colloq.* a passenger in an overfull bus, train, or the like who has to stand holding on to a strap suspended from above. 2. *Colloq.* a commuter. – **straphanging,** *n.*

**strapless** /ˈstræpləs/, *adj.* 1. having no straps. 2. designed to have no shoulder-straps, leaving the shoulders bare, as a woman's evening gown.

**strappado** /strəˈpeɪdoʊ, -ˈpadoʊ/, *n., pl.* **-does.** 1. a form of punishment or torture in which the victim, tied to a rope, was raised to a height and suddenly let fall almost to the ground. 2. the instrument used for this purpose. [It. *strappata,* from *strappare* drag, pull]

**strapper** /ˈstræpə/, *n.* 1. one who or that which straps. 2. *Colloq.* a tall, robust person. 3. one employed to attend and groom racehorses in the stables.

**strapping** /ˈstræpɪŋ/, *adj. Colloq.* 1. tall, robust, and strongly built. 2. very large of its kind; whopping. 3. a thrashing. –*n.* 4. straps collectively.

**strasbourg** /ˈstræzbɜg/, *n.* 1. a spiced sausage of pork, veal, etc. [from *Strasbourg,* a city in NE France, near the river Rhine] 2. →**Devon** (def. 3). Also, **stras** /stræz/.

**strass**[1] /stræs/, *n.* →**paste** (def. 7). [G, from F *stras,* probably named after Josef *Strasser,* 18th-cent. German jeweller, the inventor]

**strass**[2] /stræs/, *n.* silk waste resulting from the making of skeins. [F *strasse,* from It. *straccio*]

**strata** /ˈstratə/, *n.* a plural of **stratum.**

**stratagem** /ˈstrætədʒəm/, *n.* 1. a plan, scheme, or trick for deceiving the enemy. 2. any artifice, ruse, or trick. [F *stratagème,* from L *stratēgēma,* from Gk]

**stratal** /ˈstratl/, *adj.* of a stratum or strata.

**strata title** /stratə ˈtaɪtl/, *n.* a system of registration of strata of air space in multistorey buildings, similar to the registration of titles under the Torrens System, to create a type of interest similar to the interest a person has in the land with a single storey building.

**strategic** /strəˈtidʒɪk/, *adj.* 1. pertaining to, characterised by, or of the nature of strategy: *strategic movements.* 2. important in strategy: *a strategic point.* 3. important; highly crucial to one's position. Also, **strategical.** – **strategically,** *adv.*

**strategic grazing** /– ˈgreɪzɪŋ/, *n.* the technique of concentrating stock on a limited pasture area for a period of time, thus allowing pasture establishment or recovery elsewhere.

**strategic plan** /– ˈplæn/, *n.* a formulation of policy about land use and development in an area: *the City of Sydney strategic plan.*

**strategist** /ˈstrætədʒəst/, *n.* one versed in strategy: *a great military strategist.*

**strategy** /ˈstrætədʒi/, *n., pl.* **-gies.** 1. Also, *Chiefly U.S.* **strategics** /strəˈtidʒɪks/. generalship; the science or art of combining and employing the means of war in planning and directing large military movements and operations. 2. the use, or a particular use, of this science or art. 3. skilful management in getting the better of an adversary or attaining an end. 4. the method of conducting operations, esp. by the aid of manoeuvring or stratagem. [Gk *stratēgía* generalship]

**strath** /stræθ/, *n.* a wide valley. [Gaelic *srath*]

**strathspey** /stræθˈspeɪ/, *n.* 1. a Scottish dance, similar to a reel, but slower. 2. the music for this. [named after *Strath Spey,* a district and valley in Inverness-shire, Scotland]

**strati-,** a word element representing **stratum,** as in *stratify.*

**stratification** /strætəfəˈkeɪʃən/, *n.* 1. the act of stratifying. 2. stratified state or appearance: *the stratification of medieval society.* 3. *Geol.* **a.** formation of strata; deposition or occurrence in strata. **b.** →**stratum** (def. 3).

**stratiform** /ˈstrætəfɔm/, *adj.* 1. *Geol.* occurring as a bed or beds; arranged in strata. 2. *Anat.* noting a cartilage occurring in thin layers in bones. 3. *Meteorol.* having the appearance or character of a stratus.

**stratify** /ˈstrætəfaɪ/, *v.,* **-fied, -fying.** –*v.t.* 1. to form in strata or layers. 2. to preserve or germinate (seeds) by placing them between layers of earth. –*v.i.* 3. to form strata. 4. *Geol.* to lie in beds or layers. 5. *Sociol.* to develop horizontal status groups in society. [NL *strātificāre.* See STRATI-, -FY]

**stratig.,** stratigraphy.

**stratigraphic column** /strætəˌgræfɪk ˈkɒləm/, *n. Geol.* a description of the sequence and stratigraphic relations of rock units in a region.

**stratigraphy** /strəˈtɪgrəfi/, *n.* a branch of geology dealing with the classification, nomenclature, correlation, and interpretation of stratified rocks. – **stratigrapher** /strəˈtɪgrəfə/, **stratigraphist** /strəˈtɪgrəfəst/, *n.* – **stratigraphic** /strætəˈgræfɪk/, **stratigraphical** /strætəˈgræfɪkəl/, *adj.*

**strato-,** a word element meaning 'low and horizontal', as in *stratosphere.* [NL, combining form representing L *strātus,* a spreading out]

**stratocracy** /stræˈtɒkrəsi/, *n.* government by the army. – **stratocrat** /ˈstrætəkræt/, *n.* – **stratocratic** /strætəˈkrætɪk/, *adj.*

**stratocruiser** /ˈstrætoʊˌkruzə/, *n.* a passenger or transport aeroplane designed to fly at stratospheric altitudes.

**stratocumulus** /strætoʊˈkjumjələs/, *n., pl.* **-li** /-laɪ/. a low cloud or cloud layer consisting of large, dark, rounded masses, in groups, lines, or waves, the individual elements being larger than in an altocumulus.

stratocumulus

**stratosphere** /ˈstrætəsfɪə/, *n.* 1. the region of the atmosphere outside the troposphere but within the ionosphere, characterised by relatively uniform temperature over considerable differences in altitude or by a markedly different lapse rate from that of the troposphere below. 2. *Obs.* all of the earth's atmosphere lying outside the troposphere. – **stratospheric** /ˌstrætəsˈfɛrɪk/, *adj.*

**stratum** /ˈstratəm/, *n., pl.* **strata** /ˈstratə/, **stratums.** 1. a layer of material, formed either naturally or artificially, often one of a number of parallel layers placed one upon another. 2. one of a number of portions likened to layers or levels. 3. *Geol.* a single bed of sedimentary rock, generally consisting of one kind of matter representing continuous deposition. 4. *Biol.* a layer of tissue; a lamella. 5. a layer of the ocean or the atmosphere distinguished by natural or arbitrary limits. 6. *Sociol.* a level or grade of a people or population with reference to social position or education: *the lowest stratum of society.* [NL; in L something spread out]

**stratus** /ˈstreɪtəs/, *n., pl.* **-ti** /-taɪ/. a continuous horizontal sheet of cloud, resembling fog but not resting on the ground, usu. of uniform thickness and comparatively low altitude.

**stratus fractus** /- ˈfræktəs/, *n.* a stratus cloud broken up into irregular, ragged fragments.

**straw** /strɔ/, *n.* **1.** a single stalk or stem, esp. of certain species of grain, chiefly wheat, rye, oats, and barley. **2.** a mass of such stalks, esp. after drying and threshing, used as fodder, as material for hats, etc. **3.** a hollow paper tube, plant stem, etc., used in drinking some beverages, etc. **4.** anything of trifling value or consequence: *not to care a straw.* **5.** a desperate and insubstantial expedient: *to clutch at a straw.* **6. a straw in the wind,** an indication of how things will turn out. **7. man of straw, a.** a person having little or no position, financial or moral resources, or the like. **b.** an imaginary person, as one set up to represent a point of view. **8. the last straw,** the final fact, circumstance, etc., which makes a situation unbearable. *–adj.* **9.** of, pertaining to, or made of straw. [ME; OE *strēaw*]

**straw bail** /- ˈbeɪl/, *n.* bail papers signed by a corrupt policeman on worthless surety.

**strawberry** /ˈstrɔbəri, -bri/, *n., pl.* **-ries.** **1.** the fruit of any of the stemless herbs constituting the genus *Fragaria,* consisting of an enlarged fleshy receptacle bearing achenes on its exterior. **2.** the plant bearing it. *–adj.* **3.** of the colour of a strawberry; reddish; strawberry blonde.

**strawberry blonde** /- ˈblɒnd/, *n.* **1.** a redhead, usu. female. **2.** a drink consisting usu. of cherry brandy and lemonade.

**strawberry mark** /ˈ- ˌmak/, *n.* a reddish birthmark.

**strawberry tomato** /- təˈmatoʊ/, *n.* **1.** the small, edible, tomato-like fruit of the plant *Physalis pruinosa.* **2.** the plant bearing it.

**strawberry tree** /ˈ- ˌtri/, *n.* an evergreen shrub or tree, *Arbutus unedo,* native to southern Europe, bearing a scarlet, strawberry-like fruit.

**strawboard** /ˈstrɔbɔd/, *n.* coarse, yellow paper board made of straw pulp, used in packing, and for making boxes, etc.

**straw boss** /ˈstrɔ bɒs/, *n. Chiefly U.S.* a subordinate boss.

**straw colour** /ˈ- kʌlə/, *n.* a pale yellow similar to the colour of straw. – **straw-coloured,** *adj.*

**straw company** /ˈ- kʌmpəni/, *n.* a company set up not to produce anything but simply on a legal device to obtain some benefit, exp. tax benefits.

**straw vote** /ˈ- voʊt/, *n.* an unofficial vote taken, as at a casual gathering or in a particular district, to obtain some indication of the general drift of opinion. Also, **straw poll.**

**strawy** /ˈstrɔi, ˈstrɔri/, *adj.* **1.** of, containing, or resembling straw. **2.** strewed or thatched with straw.

**stray** /streɪ/, *v.i.* **1.** to go from the proper course or place or beyond the proper limits, esp. without settled course or purpose; ramble; roam. **2.** to wander (fol. by *away, off, from, into, to,* etc.). **3.** to deviate, as from the set or right course; go astray; get lost. **4.** to digress. *–n.* **5.** a domestic animal found wandering at large or without an owner. **6.** any homeless or friendless creature or person; a thing that has strayed. *–adj.* **7.** straying, or having strayed, as a domestic animal. **8.** found or occurring apart from others, or as an isolated or casual instance. [aphetic var. of ME *astray,* from OF *estraier,* from L *extrā vagārī* wander outside] – **strayer,** *n.*

**strayline** /ˈstreɪlaɪn/, *n.* a section of the logline, between the logchip and the mark on the line which indicates the precise point at which the computation of the speed of the vessel shall begin. The strayline is not counted in this computation.

**streak** /strik/, *n.* **1.** a long, narrow mark, smear, band of colour, or the like: *streaks of mud, a streak of lightning.* **2.** a portion or layer of something, distinguished by colour or nature from the rest; a vein or stratum: *streaks of fat in meat.* **3.** a vein, strain, or admixture of anything: *a streak of humour.* **4.** *Colloq.* a run (of luck): *to have a streak of bad luck.* **5.** *Colloq.* a tall, thin person. **6.** *Mining.* rock which shows good colour opal. **7.** *Mineral.* the line of powder obtained by scratching a mineral or rubbing it upon a hard, rough white surface, often differing in colour from the mineral in the mass, and forming an important distinguishing character. **8.** *Bacteriol.* the inoculation of a medium with a loop which contains the material to be inoculated, by passing the loop in a direct or zigzag line over the medium, without scratching the surface. **9. be on a streak,** *Mining.* to come across rock showing good colour opal. **10. streak of misery,** *Colloq.* a very tall, thin, unhappy person. *–v.t.* **11.** to mark with a streak or streaks. **12.** to dispose in the form of a streak or streaks. *–v.i.* **13.** to become streaked. **14.** to flash or go rapidly, like a streak of lightning. **15.** to run stark naked through a crowd of people in a street, at a cricket match, etc., for dramatic effect. [ME *streke,* OE *strica;* akin to STRIKE]

**streaker** /ˈstrikə/, *n. Colloq.* one who streaks (def. 15).

**streaky** /ˈstriki/, *adj.,* **streakier, streakiest. 1.** occurring in streaks or a streak. **2.** marked with or characterised by streaks. **3.** *Colloq.* varying or uneven in quality, etc. – **streakily,** *adv.* – **streakiness,** *n.*

**stream** /strim/, *n.* **1.** a body of water flowing in a channel or bed, as a river, rivulet, or brook. **2.** a steady current in water, as in a river or the ocean: *to row against the stream.* **3.** any flow of water or other liquid or fluid: *streams of blood.* **4.** a current of air, gas, or the like; a beam or trail of light. **5.** a continuous flow or succession of anything: *a stream of words.* **6.** prevailing direction; drift: *the stream of opinion, a stream of cars.* **7.** *Educ.* a division of children in a school to bring together those of similar age and ability in one class. **8. on stream,** (of a factory etc.) productive, operating. *–v.i.* **9.** to flow, pass, or issue in a stream, as water, tears, blood, etc. **10.** to send forth or throw off a stream; run or flow (fol. by *with*): *eyes streaming with tears.* **11.** to extend in a beam or trail, as light. **12.** to move or proceed continuously like a flowing stream, as a procession. **13.** to wave or float outwards, as a flag in the wind. **14.** to hang in a loose, flowing manner, as long hair. *–v.t.* **15.** to send forth or discharge in a stream. **16.** to cause to stream or float outwards, as a flag. **17.** to overspread or suffuse with a stream or streams. **18.** *Educ.* to divide into streams. [ME; OE *strēam,* c. G *Strom*]

**streamer** /ˈstrimə/, *n.* **1.** something that streams. **2.** a long, narrow flag or pennant. **3.** a long, flowing ribbon, feather, or the like, used for ornament, as in dress. **4.** a long, narrow strip of paper, usu. brightly coloured, thrown in festivities, or used for decorating rooms or the like. **5.** any long, narrow piece or thing, as a spray of a plant or a strip of cloud. **6.** a stream of light, esp. one appearing in some forms of the aurora borealis. **7.** the headline which extends across the width of the newspaper, usu. at the top of the first page, and often sensational.

**streamlet** /ˈstrimlət/, *n.* a small stream; a rivulet.

**streamline** /ˈstrimlaɪn/, *n., v.,* **-lined, -lining.** *–n.* **1.** a teardrop line of contour, as of a motor car. **2.** *Physics.* a line of motion in a fluid; the actual path of a particle in a flowing fluid mass whose motion is steady. *–v.t.* **3.** to make streamlined.

**streamlined** /ˈstrimlaɪnd/, *adj.* **1.** denoting, pertaining to, or having a shape designed to offer the least possible resistance in passing through the air, etc., allowing an uninterrupted flow of the fluid about it: *a streamlined motor car.* **2.** designed to make more efficient, often by simplifying methods, organisation, etc.

**streamline flow** /ˌstrimlaɪn ˈfloʊ/, *n.* a type of fluid flow in which the motion of the fluid is such that continuous streamlines can be drawn through the whole length of its course at any instant.

**stream of consciousness,** *n.* thought regarded as a succession of states constantly moving onwards in time.

**stream-of-consciousness novel** /ˌstrim-əv-kɒnʃəsnəs ˈnɒvəl/, *n.* a novel in which the action is reported through, or together with, the thoughts of one or several characters.

**streamy** /ˈstrimi/, *adj.* **1.** abounding in streams or watercourses. **2.** flowing in a stream; streaming.

**street** /strit/, *n.* **1.** a public way or road, paved or unpaved, in a town, or city, sometimes including a pavement or pavements, and having houses, shops, or the like, on one side or both sides. **2.** such a way or road together with the adjacent buildings. **3.** a main way or thoroughfare, as distinct from a lane, alley, or the like. **4.** the inhabitants of or the people in a street. **5. on the streets, a.** earning one's living as a prostitute. **b.** destitute; homeless. **6. the man in the street,** the average person; a typical citizen. **7. streets ahead,** a long way ahead. **8. up one's street,** in the sphere that one knows or likes best. [ME; d. OE *strēt,* OE *strǣt,* c. D *straat,* G *Strasse,* all from L (*via*) *strāta* paved (road)]

**street Arab** /'– ærəb/, *n.* a child having no home and making his way by begging, stealing, etc. Also, **street urchin.**

**streetcar** /'stritka/, *n. U.S.* →**tram**[1] (def. 1).

**street furniture** /'strit fɜnɪtʃə/, *n.* the conventional equipment of urban streets, as bus-shelters, streetlights, litter bins, etc.

**streetlight** /'stritlaɪt/, *n.* an electric light for illuminating streets, roads, etc., often supported by a wooden or metal pole.

**streetwalker** /'stritwɔkə/, *n.* one who walks the streets, esp. a soliciting prostitute. – **streetwalking,** *n.*

**street-wise** /'strit-waɪz/, *adj.* skilled in living in an urban environment; knowing how to survive on the streets.

**strelitzia** /strə'lɪtsiə/, *n.* any of the large perennial herbs of the genus *Strelitzia,* family Musaceae, esp. *S. reginae* with large ornamental orange and purple flowers.

**strength** /streŋθ/, *n.* **1.** the quality or state of being strong; bodily or muscular power; vigour, as in robust health. **2.** mental power, force, or vigour. **3.** moral power, firmness, or courage. **4.** power by reason of influence, authority, resources, numbers, etc. **5.** number, as of men or ships in a force or body: *a regiment of a strength of three thousand.* **6.** effective force, potency, or cogency, as of inducements or arguments. **7.** power of resisting force, strain, wear, etc. **8.** vigour of action, language, feeling, etc. **9.** large proportion of the effective or essential properties of a beverage, chemical, or the like. **10.** a particular proportion of these properties; intensity, as of light, colour, sound, flavour, or smell. **11.** something that makes strong; a support or stay. **12.** *Finance.* a commodity or price which is either firm or rising. **13. get with the strength,** to side with the most powerful, influential person or group. **14. on the strength of,** relying on; on the basis of. **15. the strength of (something),** the reliable information concerning (something). [ME; OE *strength(u),* from STRONG]

**strengthen** /'streŋθən/, *v.t.* **1.** to make stronger; give strength to. *–v.i.* **2.** to gain strength; grow stronger. – **strengthener,** /'streŋθənə/, *n.*

**strenuous** /'strenjuəs/, *adj.* **1.** vigorous, energetic, or zealously active, as a person, etc. **2.** characterised by vigorous exertion, as action, efforts, life, etc.: *a strenuous opposition.* [L *strēnuus;* akin to Gk *strēnḗs* strong] – **strenously,** *adv.* – **strenuousness, strenuosity** /strenju'ɒsəti/.

**strephosymbolia** /ˌstrefousɪm'bouliə/, *n.* difficulty in learning to read because of inability to distinguish similar letters, due to mixed dominance of right and left cerebral hemispheres.

**strepitous** /'strepətəs/, *adj.* noisy. [L *strepitus* noise + -OUS]

**strepsipterous** /strep'sɪptərəs/, *adj.* belonging or pertaining to the Strepsiptera, an order of minute insects with reduced fore wings and large hind wings, the females of which are usu. degenerate worm-like parasites.

**strep throat** /strep 'θrout/, *n. Colloq.* a streptococcal infection of the throat.

**strepto-,** a word element meaning 'curved', as in *streptococcus.* [Gk, combining form of *streptós*]

**streptococcus** /streptə'kɒkəs/, *n., pl.* **-cocci** /-'kɒksaɪ/. one of a group of organisms of the genus *Streptococcus,* which divide in one plane only and remain attached to one another, forming long, short, or conglomerated chains. Some cause very important diseases such as scarlet fever, erysipelas, puerperal sepsis, sepsis, etc. – **streptococcic** /streptə'kɒksɪk/, – **streptococcal** /streptə'kɒkəl/, *adj.*

**streptomycin** /streptə'maɪsən/, *n.* an antibiotic effective against diseases caused by bacteria, including several against which penicillin is ineffective, as tuberculosis.

**streptothricin** /streptə'θraɪsən/, *n.* an antibacterial substance derived from the soil fungus, *Actinomyces lavendulae.* Also, **streptothrysin.**

**stress** /stres/, *v.t.* **1.** to lay stress or emphasis on; emphasise. **2.** *Phonet.* to pronounce strongly or with a stress accent. **3.** to subject to stress or strain. **4.** *Mech.* to subject to mechanical stress. *–n.* **5.** importance or significance attached to a thing; emphasis: *to lay stress upon successive incidents.* **6.** *Phonet.* relative loudness resulting from special effort or emphasis in utterance. **7.** accent or emphasis on a syllable or syllables in speech, esp. so as to form a metrical pattern. **8.** the syllable accented. **9.** emphasis in music, rhythm, etc. **10.** the physical pressure, pull, or other force exerted on one thing by another. **11.** *Physics.* **a.** the forces on a body which produce a deformation or strain. **b.** a measure of the amount of stress, expressed as a force per unit area. **c.** a load, force, or system of forces producing a strain. **d.** the internal resistance or reaction of an elastic body to the external forces applied to it. **12.** a disturbing physiological or psychological influence which produces a state of severe tension in an individual. **13.** *Rare.* strong or straining exertion. [aphetic var. of DISTRESS]

**-stress,** a feminine equivalent of **-ster,** as in *seamstress, songstress.* [*-str* (syncopated var. of -STER) + -ESS]

**stressed skin** /strest 'skɪn/, *n.* →**monocoque.**

**stretch** /stretʃ/, *v.t.* **1.** to draw out or extend (oneself, the body, limbs, wings, etc.) to the full length or extent (oft. fol. by *out*): *to stretch oneself out on the ground.* **2.** to hold out, reach forth, or extend (the hand or something held, the head etc.). **3.** to extend, spread, or place so as to reach from one point or place to another: *to stretch a rope across a road.* **4.** to draw tight or taut: *to stretch the strings of a violin.* **5.** to lengthen, widen, distend, or enlarge by tension: *to stretch a rubber band.* **6.** to draw out, extend, or enlarge unduly: *a sweater stretched at the elbows.* **7.** to extend or force beyond the natural or proper limits; strain: *to stretch the facts.* **8.** to extend the fuselage of a plane, the body of a car, etc. **9. stretch a point,** to go beyond the usual limits; make concessions. **10. stretch one's legs,** to take a walk. *–v.i.* **11.** to recline at full length (usu. fol. by *out*): *to stretch out on a couch.* **12.** to extend the hand, or reach, as for something. **13.** to extend over a distance, area, period of time, or in a particular direction: *the forest stretches for as far as the eye can see.* **14.** to stretch oneself by extending the limbs, straining the muscles, etc. **15.** to become stretched, or admit of being stretched, to greater length, width, etc., as any elastic material. *–n.* **16.** the act of stretching. **17.** the state of being stretched. **18.** capacity for being stretched. **19.** a continuous length, distance, tract, or expanse: *a stretch of bush.* **20.** one of the two straight sides of a racecourse, as distinguished from the bend or curve at each end, esp. that part of the course (**home stretch**) between the last turn and the winning post. **21.** an extent in time or duration: *a stretch of ten years.* **22.** *Colloq.* a term of imprisonment. **23.** *Colloq.* (a form of address to a tall person). *–adj.* **24.** made to stretch in order to fit different shapes and sizes, as clothing: *stretch stockings.* [ME; OE *streccan,* c. G *strecken*] – **stretchable,** *adj.*

**stretched** /stretʃt/, *adj.* exhausted; nervously debilitated.

**stretcher** /'stretʃə/, *n.* **1.** a light, folding bed; camp stretcher. **2.** one who or that which stretches. **3.** any of various instruments for extending, widening, distending, etc. **4.** a bar, beam, or fabricated material, serving as a tie or brace. **5.** a narrow crosspiece in a boat, for a rower to push his feet against. **6.** a brick or stone laid horizontally with its length in the direction of the face of a wall, usu. planned to give added strength to the structure. **7.** a simple wooden framework on which the canvas of an oil painting is stretched.

**stretcher-bearer** /'stretʃə-beərə/, *n.* a man, esp. a serviceman, who helps to carry a stretcher, as in removing the wounded from a battlefield.

**stretcher bond** /stretʃə 'bɒnd/, *n.* a common arrangement of brickwork, in which each brick is laid as a stretcher, the bricks in each alternate course laid so that the perpend of the brick is in the centre of the one above and below. Cf. **English bond.**

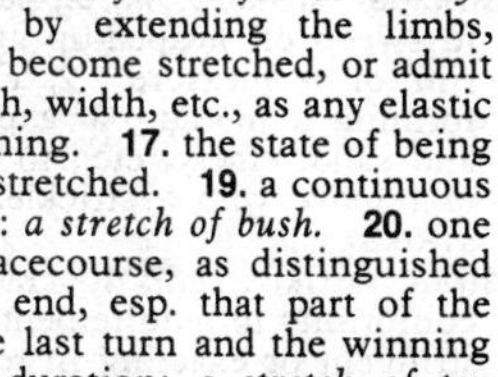

stretcher bond

**stretchy** /'stretʃi/, *adj.* **1.** capable of being stretched; elastic. **2.** liable to stretch unduly.

**stretta** /'stretə/, *n., pl.* **-te** /-teɪ/, **-tas.** **1.** the concluding passage of a piece of music, taken at an accelerated speed. **2.** →**stretto.**

i = peat ɪ = pit ɛ = pet æ = pat a = part ɒ = pot ʌ = putt ɔ = port ʊ = put u = pool ɜ = pert ə = apart aɪ = buy eɪ = bay ɔɪ = boy aʊ = how
oʊ = hoe ɪə = here ɛə = hair ʊə = tour g = give θ = thin ð = then ʃ = show ʒ = measure tʃ = choke dʒ = joke ŋ = sing j = you õ = Fr. bon

**stretto** /ˈstrɛtoʊ/, *n., pl.* **-ti** /-ti/, **-tos.** (in a musical fugue) the close overlapping of voices so that each succeeding one enters before the preceding one has completed its statement of the subject, often in the final section. [It.: narrow, from L *strictus,* pp., drawn tight]

**strew** /stru/, *v.t.,* **strewed, strewed** or **strewn, strewing. 1.** to let fall in separate pieces or particles over a surface; scatter or sprinkle: *to strew seed in a garden bed.* **2.** to cover or overspread (a surface, place, etc.) with something scattered or sprinkled: *to strew a floor with rushes.* **3.** to be scattered or sprinkled over (a surface, etc.). [ME *strewe,* OE *strēowian,* c. G *streuen*]

**strewth** /struθ/, *interj.* →**struth.**

**stria** /ˈstraɪə/, *n., pl.* **striae** /ˈstraɪi/. **1.** a slight furrow or ridge; a narrow stripe or streak, esp. one of a number in parallel arrangement. **2.** (*pl.*) *Geol.* scratches or tiny grooves on the surface of a rock, resulting from the action of moving ice, as of a glacier. **3.** (*pl.*) *Mineral.* parallel lines or tiny grooves on the surface of a crystal, or on a cleavage face of a crystal, due to its molecular organisation. **4.** *Pathol.* a linear mark on the abdomen which may appear in pregnancy or obesity or in some endocrine abnormalities. **5.** Also, **strix.** *Archit.* a fillet between the flutes of a column. [L: furrow, channel]

**striate** /ˈstraɪeɪt/, *v.,* **-ated, -ating;** /ˈstraɪət/, *adj.* *–v.t.* **1.** to mark with striae; furrow; stripe; streak. *–adj.* **2.** Also, **striated.** marked with striae; furrowed; striped.

**striation** /straɪˈeɪʃən/, *n.* **1.** striated condition or appearance. **2.** a stria; one of many parallel striae.

**stricken** /ˈstrɪkən/, *adj.* **1.** struck; hit or wounded by a weapon, missile, or the like. **2.** smitten or afflicted, as with disease, trouble, or sorrow. **3.** deeply affected, as with horror, fear, or other emotions. **4.** characterised by or showing the effects of affliction, trouble, misfortune, a mental blow, etc.

**strickle** /ˈstrɪkəl/, *n., v.,* **-led, -ling.** *–n.* **1.** a straightedge used to sweep off heaped-up grain or the like to a level with the rim of a measure. **2.** *Foundry.* a shaped board used for forming a mould. **3.** a piece of wood covered with grease and sand, emery, etc., to sharpen scythes. *–v.t.* **4.** to sweep or remove with a strickle. [ME *strikylle,* OE *stricel;* akin to STRIKE]

**strict** /strɪkt/, *adj.* **1.** characterised by or acting in close conformity to requirements or principles: *strict observance.* **2.** stringent or exacting in requirements, obligations, etc.: *strict laws, a strict judge.* **3.** closely or rigorously enforced or maintained. **4.** exact or precise: *a strict statement of facts.* **5.** narrowly or carefully limited: *a strict construction of the constitution.* **6.** close, careful, or minute: *a strict search.* **7.** absolute, perfect, or complete: *told in strict confidence.* [L *strictus,* pp., drawn together, tight, severe] – **strictly,** *adv.* – **strictness,** *n.*

**striction** /ˈstrɪkʃən/, *n.* the act of drawing tight, constricting, or straining. [L *strictio*]

**stricture** /ˈstrɪktʃə/, *n.* **1.** a remark or comment, esp. an adverse criticism. **2.** a morbid contraction of any passage or duct of the body. [ME, from L *strictūra*]

**stride** /straɪd/, *v.,* **strode, stridden, striding,** *n.* *–v.i.* **1.** to walk with long steps, as with vigour, haste, impatience, or arrogance. **2.** to take a long step. **3.** to straddle. *–v.t.* **4.** to walk with long steps along, on, through, over, etc.: *to stride the deck.* **5.** to pass over or across by one stride: *to stride a ditch.* **6.** to straddle. *–n.* **7.** a striding or a striding gait. **8.** a long step in walking. **9.** (in animal locomotion) act of progressive movement, completed when all the feet are returned to the same relative position as at the beginning. **10.** the distance covered by such a movement. **11.** a regular or steady course, pace, etc.: *to take it in one's stride.* **12.** a step forward in development or progress: *John made rapid strides in mastering algebra.* **13.** (*pl.*) *Colloq.* trousers. [ME; OE *strīdan,* c. LG *strīden.* Cf. also G *streiten* quarrel] – **strider,** *n.*

**strident** /ˈstraɪdnt/, *adj.* making or having a harsh sound; grating; creaking. [L *strīdens,* ppr., creaking] – **stridence, stridency,** *n.* – **stridently,** *adv.*

**stride piano** /ˈstraɪd piˌænoʊ/, *n.* a left-hand playing style characterised by an alternation between low single tones and medium register chords.

**stridor** /ˈstraɪdɔ/, *n.* **1.** a harsh, grating, or creaking sound. **2.** *Pathol.* a harsh respiratory sound due to any of various forms of obstruction. [L]

**stridulate** /ˈstrɪdʒəleɪt/, *v.i.,* **-lated, -lating.** to produce a shrill grating sound, as a cricket, by rubbing together certain parts of the body; shrill. – **stridulation** /strɪdʒəˈleɪʃən/, *n.* – **stridulator,** *n.* – **stridulatory** /ˈstrɪdʒəleɪtəri/, *adj.*

**stridulous** /ˈstrɪdʒələs/, *adj.* **1.** making or having a harsh, or grated sound. **2.** *Pathol.* pertaining to or characterised by stridor. [L *strīdulus*] – **stridulously,** *adv.* – **stridulousness,** *n.*

**strife** /straɪf/, *n.* **1.** conflict, discord, or variance: *to be at strife.* **2.** a quarrel, struggle, or clash. **3. in strife,** *Colloq.* in trouble. [ME, from OF, aphetic modification of *estrif.* See STRIVE] – **strifeful, strifeless,** *adj.*

**striges** /ˈstraɪdʒiz/, *n.* plural of **strix.**

**strigiform** /ˈstrɪdʒəfɔm/, *adj.* belonging or pertaining to the Strigiformes, the order of birds which includes the owls.

**strigil** /ˈstrɪdʒəl/, *n.* **1.** an instrument with a curved blade, used by the ancient Greeks and Romans for scraping the skin at the bath and in the gymnasium. **2.** *Archit.* one of a series of decorative S-shaped flutings, esp. in Roman architecture. [L *strigilis*]

**strigose** /ˈstraɪgoʊs/, *adj.* **1.** *Bot.* set with stiff bristles or hairs; hispid. **2.** *Zool.* marked with fine ridges or grooves. [NL *strigōsus,* from L *striga* row of bristles]

**strike** /straɪk/, *v.,* **struck, struck** or (*esp. for defs 30-33*) **stricken, striking,** *n.* *–v.t.* **1.** to deliver a blow, stroke, or thrust with (the hand, a weapon, etc.). **2.** to deal a blow or stroke to (a person or thing), as with the fist, a weapon, or a hammer; hit. **3.** to deal or inflict (a blow, stroke, etc.). **4.** to drive or thrust forcibly: *to strike the hands together.* **5.** to produce (fire, sparks, light, etc.) by percussion, friction, etc.; cause (a match) to ignite by friction. **6.** to smite or blast with some natural or supernatural agency: *struck by lightning.* **7.** to come into forcible contact or collision with: *the ship struck a rock.* **8.** to fall upon (something), as light or sound. **9.** to enter the mind of; occur to: *a happy thought struck him.* **10.** to catch or arrest (the eyes, etc.): *the first object that strikes one's sight.* **11.** to impress strongly: *a picture which strikes one's fancy.* **12.** to impress in a particular manner: *how does it strike you?* **13.** to come across, meet with, or encounter suddenly or unexpectedly: *to strike the name of a friend in a newspaper.* **14.** to come upon or find (ore, oil, etc.) in prospecting, boring, or the like. **15.** to send down or put forth (a root, etc.), as a plant, cutting, etc. **16.** to balance (a ledger, etc.). **17.** to remove from the stage (the scenery and properties of an act or scene). **18.** *Bldg Trades.* to remove formwork from (concrete, etc.) after it has gained its initial set. **19.** *Naut.* **a.** to lower or take down (a sail, mast, etc.). **b.** to lower (a sail, flag, etc.) as a salute or as a sign of surrender. **c.** to lower (something) into the hold of a vessel by means of a rope and tackle. **20.** to hook (a fish) by a jerk or sudden movement of the tackle. **21.** to harpoon, spear, as in hunting. **22.** (in various technical uses) to make level or smooth. **23.** to make level or even, as a measure of grain, salt, etc., by drawing a strickle across the top, or as potatoes, by making the projections equal to the depressions. **24.** to efface or cancel with, or as with, the stroke of a pen (fol. by *off, out,* etc.). **25.** to forbid (someone) to continue practising his profession because of unprofessional conduct, or the like (fol. by *off*): *the doctor was struck off for advertising.* **26.** to stamp (a coin, medal, etc.) or impress (a device), by a stroke. **27.** to remove or separate with a cut (usu. fol. by *off*). **28.** *Rowing.* to make (a specified number of strokes) in a given time: *Grammar struck forty in the first minute.* **29.** to indicate (the hour of day) by a stroke or strokes, as a clock: *to strike twelve.* **30.** to afflict suddenly, as with disease, suffering, or death. **31.** to affect deeply or overwhelm, as with terror, fear, etc. **32.** to render (blind, dumb, etc.) suddenly, as if by a blow. **33.** to cause (a feeling) to enter suddenly: *to strike terror into a person.* **34.** to induce a favourable reaction in: *he was struck by her beauty.* **35.** to start suddenly into (vigorous movement): *the horse struck a gallop.* **36.** to assume (an attitude or posture). **37.** to cause (chill, warmth, etc.) to pass or penetrate quickly. **38.** to come upon or reach in travelling or in a course of procedure. **39.** to make, conclude, or ratify (an agreement, treaty, etc.). **40.** to reach by agreement, as a compromise: *to strike a rate of payment.* **41.** to enter upon or form (an acquaintance, etc.) (usu. fol. by *up*). **42.** to estimate or determine (a mean or average). **43.** to break (camp). **44. strike me lucky!,** (an exclamation of surprise, etc.). **45. strike me pink!,** (an exclamation of surprise, indignation, etc.). *–v.i.* **46.** to deal or aim a blow or stroke, as with the fist, a weapon, or a hammer; *make an attack.* **47.** to knock, rap, or tap. **48.** to hit or dash on or against something, as a moving body; come into forcible contact. **49.** to run upon a bank, rock, or other obstacle, as a ship. **50.** to fall, as light or sound (fol. by *on* or *upon*). **51.** to make an impression on the mind, senses, etc., as something seen or heard. **52.** to come suddenly or unexpectedly (fol. by *on* or *upon*): *to strike on a new way of doing a thing.* **53.** to sound by percussion: *the clock strikes.* **54.** to be indicated by such sounding: *the hour has struck.* **55.** to be ignited by friction, as a match. **56.** to make a stroke, as with the arms or legs in swimming or with an oar in rowing. **57.** to produce a sound, music, etc., by touching a string or playing upon an instrument. **58.** (of an orchestra or band) to begin to play: *strike up a tune.* **59.** to take root, as a slip of a plant. **60.** to go, proceed, or advance, esp. in a new direction. **61.** (of an employee or employees) to engage in a strike. **62.** *Naut.* **a.** to lower the flag or colours, esp. as a salute or as a sign of surrender. **b.** to run up the white flag of surrender. **63.** *Angling.* to swallow or grasp the bait (applied to fish). **64. strike out, a.** to direct one's course boldly. **b.** *Baseball.* (of a batter) to make three strikes and to be declared 'out'. *–n.* **65.** an act of striking. **66.** a concerted stopping of work or withdrawal of workers' services in order to compel an employer to accede to demands or in protest against terms or conditions imposed by employer. **67.** *Baseball.* an unsuccessful attempt on the part of the batter to hit a pitched ball, or anything ruled to be equivalent to this. **68.** *Cricket.* the obligation to face the bowling. **69.** *Tenpin Bowling.* **a.** the knocking down of all the pins with the first bowl. **b.** the score made by bowling a strike. **70.** *Brewing.* the critical temperature of the water during mashing. **71.** *Angling.* the process of grabbing at the bait. **72.** *Geol.* **a.** the direction of the line formed by the intersection of the bedding plane of a bed or stratum of sedimentary rock with a horizontal plane. **b.** the direction or trend of a structural feature, as an anticlinal axis or the lineation resulting from metamorphism. **73.** the discovery of a rich vein of ore in mining, of oil in drilling, etc. **74. in** or **on strike,** *Cricket.* at the striker's end of the pitch. [ME; OE *strīcan*, c. G *streichen.* Cf. STREAK, STROKE[1]]

**strike-a-light** /straɪk-ə-ˈlaɪt/, *interj.* (an exclamation of surprise, etc.).

**strikebound** /ˈstraɪkbaʊnd/, *adj.* unable to function because of a strike.

**strikebreaker** /ˈstraɪkbreɪkə/, *n.* one who takes part in breaking up a strike of workers, either by working or by furnishing workers for the employer.

**strikebreaking** /ˈstraɪkbreɪkɪŋ/, *n.* action directed at breaking up a strike of workers.

**strike fault** /ˈstraɪk fɔlt/, *n.* a fault the trend of which is parallel to the strike of the affected rocks.

**strike-on composition** /ˌstraɪk-ɒn kɒmpəˈzɪʃən/, *n.* a process in which the image to be used as a photographic copy for printing is first produced as on a typewriter.

**strike pay** /ˈstraɪk peɪ/, *n.* an allowance paid by a trade union to members on strike. Also, **strike benefit.**

**striker** /ˈstraɪkə/, *n.* **1.** one who or that which strikes. **2.** a worker who is on strike. **3.** the clapper in a clock that strikes the hours or rings an alarm. **4.** *Cricket.* the batsman who is facing the bowling. **5.** *Tennis.* Also, **striker out.** →**receiver. 6.** one who strikes fish, etc., with a spear or harpoon. **7.** *Whaling.* →**harpoon.**

**striker's end** /ˈstraɪkəz ɛnd/, *n.* (in cricket) the end of the wicket towards which the ball is being bowled.

**strike-through** /ˈstraɪk-θru/, *n.* a printing imperfection where an image is evident on the reverse of the paper on which it is printed.

**striking** /ˈstraɪkɪŋ/, *adj.* **1.** that strikes. **2.** attractive; impressive. **3.** being on strike, as workmen. – **strikingly,** *adv.*

**striking circle** /ˈ– sɜkəl/, *n.* →**circle** (def. 10).

**strine** /straɪn/, *n. Colloq.* **1.** Australian English, humorously and affectionately regarded. **2.** the form of it which appeared in the books of Alastair Morrison, pen-name 'Afferbeck Lauder', where it was written in scrambled form to suggest excessive assimilation, metanalysis, ellipsis etc. as in *Gloria Soame* for *glorious home, muncer go* for *months ago,* etc.

**string** /strɪŋ/, *n., v.,* **strung; strung** or (*Rare*) **stringed; stringing.** *–n.* **1.** a line, cord, or thread, used for tying parcels, etc. **2.** a narrow strip of cloth, leather, etc., for tying parts together: *strings of a bonnet.* **3.** something resembling a string or thread. **4.** a number of objects, as beads or pearls, threaded or arranged on a cord. **5.** any series of things arranged or connected in a line or following closely one after another: *a string of islands or of vehicles; to ask a string of questions.* **6.** a set or number, as of animals: *a string of racehorses.* **7.** (in musical instruments) a tightly stretched cord or wire which produces a note when caused to vibrate, as by plucking, striking, or friction of a bow. **8.** (*pl*) **a.** stringed musical instruments, esp. such as are played with a bow. **b.** players on such instruments in an orchestra or band. **9. two strings to one's bow.** See **second string. 10.** a cord or fibre in a plant. **11.** the tough piece uniting the two parts of a pod: *the strings of beans.* **12.** *Archit.* **a.** a string-course. **b.** →**stringer** (def. 3). **13.** *Billiards.* a stroke made by each player from the head of the table to the opposite cushion and back, to determine, by means of the resultant positions of the balls, who shall open the game. **14.** *Colloq.* limitations on any proposal: *a proposal with no strings attached.* **15.** *Obs.* a ligament, tendon, nerve, or the like, in an animal body. **16. keep on a string,** to have someone under one's control, esp. emotionally: *she kept him on a string and then agreed to marry him.* **17. pull strings,** *Colloq.* to seek one's own advancement by using social contacts and other means not directly connected with one's ability or suitability. *–v.t.* **18.** to furnish with or as with a string or strings. **19.** to extend or stretch (a cord, etc.) from one point to another. **20.** to thread on, or as on, a string: *to string beads.* **21.** to connect in, or as in, a line; arrange in a series or succession. **22.** to provide or adorn with something suspended or slung: *a room strung with festoons.* **23.** to deprive of a string or strings; strip the strings from: *to string beans.* **24.** to make tense, as the sinews, nerves, mind, etc. **25.** to kill by hanging (usu. fol. by *up*). *–v.i.* **26.** to form into or move in a string or series. **27.** to form into a string or strings, as glutinous substances do when pulled. *–v.* **28.** Some special verb phrases are:

**string along** or **on,** *Colloq.* to deceive (someone) in a progressive series of falsehoods; con.

**string along with,** *Colloq.* to go along with; accompany; cooperate with; agree with.

**string out, 1.** to extend or spread out at intervals. **2.** to extend over a period of time; prolong. [ME; OE *streng,* c. D *streng;* akin to G *strang,* L *stringere* bind, Gk *strangálē* halter]

**string bag** /– ˈbæg/, *n.* a loosely woven bag, originally made of string, now often made of plastic, or the like.

**string band** /– ˈbænd/, *n.* a band of stringed instruments.

**string bass** /– ˈbeɪs/, *n.* →**double bass** (def. 1).

**string bean** /– ˈbin/, *n.* **1.** any of various kinds of bean (plant) the unripe pods of which are used as food, usu. after stripping off the fibrous thread along the side. **2.** the pod itself.

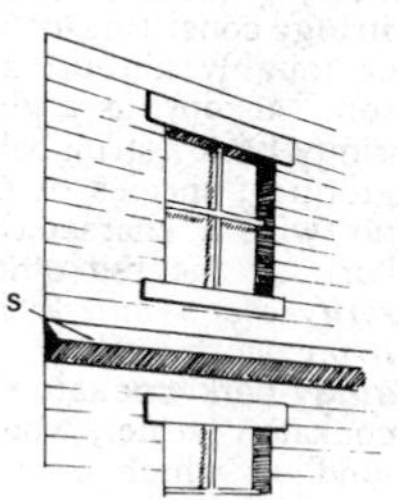

S, string-course

**string bikini** /ˈ– bəkini/, *n.* a very small bikini made from patches of material tied together with cord or similar fastenings.

**stringboard** /ˈstrɪŋbɔd/, *n.* a board or the like covering the ends of the steps in a staircase.

**string-course** /ˈstrɪŋ-kɔs/, *n.* a horizontal band or course of stone, etc., projecting beyond or flush with the face of a building, often moulded and sometimes richly carved.

**stringed** /strɪŋd/, *adj.* **1.** (of a musical instrument) having a string or strings. **2.** pertaining to such instruments: *stringed music.*

**stringency** /ˈstrɪndʒənsi/, *n., pl.* **-cies.** **1.** stringent character or condition. **2.** strictness; closeness; rigour. **3.** tightness; straitness: *stringency in the money market.*

**stringendo** /strɪnˈdʒɛndoʊ/, *adv.* **1.** (a musical direction) indicating a progressively quickening of the tempo. *–adj.* **2.** progressively quickening the tempo. [It., ppr. of *stringere* compress, draw tight, from L]

**stringent** /ˈstrɪndʒənt/, *adj.* **1.** narrowly binding; rigorously exacting; strict; severe: *stringent laws.* **2.** compelling, constraining, or urgent: *stringent necessity.* **3.** convincing or forcible, as arguments, etc. **4.** (of the money market) tight; characterised by a shortage of loan money. [L *stringens,* ppr., drawing tight] – **stringently,** *adv.*

**stringer** /ˈstrɪŋə/, *n.* **1.** one who or that which strings. *–n.* **2.** a longitudinal timber, metal rod, etc., which is fitted to frames or ribs in the construction of a boat, the fusilage or wing of an aeroplane, etc. **3.** *Bldg Trades.* **a.** a long horizontal timber connecting upright posts, supporting a floor, or the like. **b.** a cross-member keeping horizontal timbers in position. **4.** Also, **string.** *Archit.* one of the sloping sides of a stair, supporting the treads and risers. **5.** *Chiefly U.S.* a longitudinal timber spanning a bent of a railway trestle or bridge; girder. **6.** *Naut.* a narrow, flat steel plate, extending the whole length of a ship, and forming part of the skeleton construction which strengthens and supports the hull of the ship. **7.** *Journalism.* one who corresponds on an irregular or part-time basis for one newspaper, news publication, periodical or news service, usu. while working full-time for another.

**string game** /ˈstrɪŋ geɪm/, *n.* a game, esp. played by children, in which a piece of string is twined around the fingers to form various patterns.

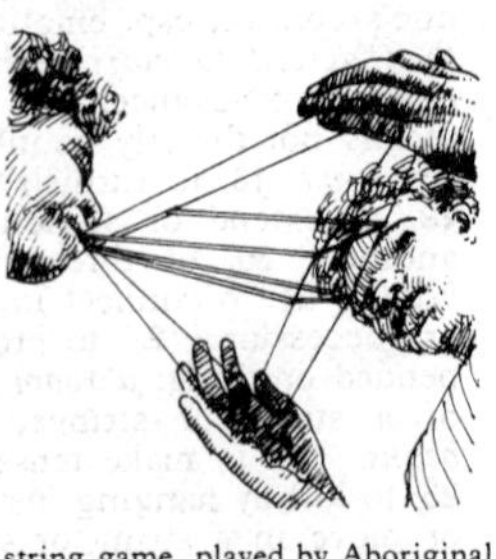

string game, played by Aboriginal children of northern Australia

**stringhalt** /ˈstrɪŋhɔlt/, *n.* a nervous disorder in horses, causing exaggerated flexing movements of the hind legs in walking. Also, **springhalt.**

**string line** /ˈstrɪŋ laɪn/, *n.* →**baulk line.**

**stringline** /ˈstrɪŋlaɪn/, *n.* a length of string or cord stretched between two points to indicate a level, as in bricklaying.

**string orchestra** /strɪŋ ˈɔkəstrə/, *n.* an orchestra which normally consists of violins, violas, cellos, and double basses.

**stringpiece** /ˈstrɪŋpis/, *n.* a long piece of timber or the like (esp. a horizontal one) in a framework or structure, as for strengthening the structure or connecting or supporting parts.

**string-pulling** /ˈstrɪŋ-pʊlɪŋ/, *n. Colloq.* the act or fact of seeking one's own advancement by using social contacts and other means not directly connected with one's ability or suitability. – **string-puller,** *n.*

**string quartet** /strɪŋ kwɔˈtɛt/, *n.* a quartet, usu. consisting of two violins, a viola, and a cello.

**stringy** /ˈstrɪŋi/, *adj.,* **stringier, stringiest.** **1.** resembling a string; consisting of strings or stringlike pieces. **2.** coarsely or toughly fibrous, as meat. **3.** sinewy or wiry, as a person. **4.** ropy, as a glutinous liquid. – **stringiness,** *n.*

**stringy-bark** /ˈstrɪŋi-bak/, *n.* **1.** any of a group of species of the genus *Eucalyptus* with a characteristic tough fibrous bark as the **red stringy-bark,** *E. Macrorhyncha.* *–adj.* **2.** rustic, uncultured: *stringy-bark settler.*

**stringy-bark cockatoo** /– kɒkəˈtu/, *n.* a cockatoo farmer, who farms the poorest land, or which only stringy-bark gums would grow.

stringy-bark

**strip**[1] /strɪp/, *v.,* **stripped** or (*Rare*) **stript, stripping.** *–v.t.* **1.** to deprive of covering: *to strip a fruit of its rind.* **2.** to deprive of clothing; make bare or naked. **3.** to take away or remove: *to strip pictures from a wall.* **4.** to deprive or divest: *to strip a tree of its fruit.* **5.** to clear out or empty: *to strip a house of its contents.* **6.** to deprive of equipment; dismantle: *to strip a ship of rigging.* **7.** to rob, plunder, or dispossess: *to strip a man of his possessions.* **8.** to separate the leaves from the stalks of (tobacco). **9.** to remove the midrib, etc., from (tobacco leaves). **10.** *Mach.* to tear off the thread of (a screw, bolt, etc.) or the teeth of (a gear, etc.), as by applying too much force. **11.** *Agric.* to harvest part of a plant, using a specially constructed machine, as grains of wheat. **12.** to remove old paint, distemper, etc., from a surface prior to redecorating. **13.** *Chem.* to remove the most volatile components from a mixture by distillation or evaporation. **14.** to draw the last milk from (a cow), esp. by a stroking and compressing movement. **15.** to draw out (milk) thus. **16.** (in filmsetting) to make up a composite sheet of film using individual pieces (oft. fol. by *in*). *–v.i.* **17.** to strip something; esp., to strip oneself of clothes. **18.** to perform a striptease. **19.** to become stripped. [ME *stripe,* OE *-strȳpan,* c. D *stroopen*]

**strip**[2] /strɪp/, *n., v.,* **stripped, stripping.** *–n.* **1.** a narrow piece, comparatively long and usu. of uniform width: *a strip of cloth, metal, land, etc.* **2.** *Colloq.* a sporting uniform. **3.** a continuous series of pictures, as in a newspaper, illustrating incidents, conversation, etc. See **comic strip.** **4.** *Philately.* three or more stamps joined either in a horizontal or vertical row. **5.** →**airstrip.** *–v.t.* **6.** to cut into strips. [late ME, ? from MLG *strippe* strap; akin to STRIPE[1]]

**strip cartoon** /– kaˈtun/, *n.* See **comic strip.**

**strip club** /ˈ– klʌb/, *n.* →**strip joint.**

**strip cropping** /– ˈkrɒpɪŋ/, *n.* the planting of cover crops between rows of trees in an orchard.

**stripe**[1] /straɪp/, *n., v.,* **striped, striping,** *adj.* *–n.* **1.** a relatively long, narrow band of a different colour, appearance, weave, material, or nature from the rest of a surface or thing: *the stripes of a zebra.* **2.** a striped fabric or material. **3.** a strip of braid or the like. **4.** (*pl.*) a number or combination of such strips, worn on a military, naval, or other uniform as a badge of rank, service, good conduct, wounds, etc. **5.** a strip, or long, narrow piece of anything. **6.** a streak or layer of a different nature within a substance. **7.** *Chiefly U.S.* style, variety, sort, or kind: *a man of quite a different stripe.* *–v.t.* **8.** to mark or furnish with a stripe or stripes. *–adj.* **9.** furnished with racing stripes: *stripe swimwear.* [MD]

**stripe**[2] /straɪp/, *n.* a stroke with a whip, rod, etc., as in punishment. [late ME; ? special use of STRIPE[1]]

**striped** /straɪpt/, *adj.* having stripes or bands. Also, **stripy.**

**striped hyena** /– haɪˈinə/, *n.* a scavenging carnivorous mammal, *Hyaena hyaena,* of south-western Asia and Africa.

**striped possum** /– ˈpɒsəm/, *n.* a tropical, non-gliding possum, with stripes from crown to rump, and an extended fourth finger with a hooked nail for digging grubs out of timber.

**stripe smut** /ˈstraɪp smʌt/, *n.* any of several diseases of grasses caused by fungi of the order Ustilaginales, as *Urocystis agropyri* on wheat. Also, **flag smut.**

**strip footing** /strɪp ˈfʊtɪŋ/, *n.* →**footing** (def. 6).

**strip grazing** /– ˈgreɪzɪŋ/, *n.* controlled grazing of crops or pasture fenced off by electric or temporary fencing.

**strip heater** /– ˈhitə/, *n.* a long strip radiator (def. 2) frequently designed to be attached to a wall.

**strip joint** /ˈ– dʒɔɪnt/, *n.* a place of entertainment where striptease is performed.

**strip lighting** /– ˈlaɪtɪŋ/, *n.* lighting by long cylindrical glass strips which are either fluorescent tubes or which contain long filaments.

**stripling** /ˈstrɪplɪŋ/, *n.* a youth just passing from boyhood to manhood. [STRIP[2] + -LING[1]]

**strip mill** /ˈstrɪp mɪl/, *n.* part of a steel-making complex in which steel ingots are rolled into strips.

**strip mining** /ˈ– maɪnɪŋ/, *n.* →**open cut.**

**stripper** /ˈstrɪpə/, *n.* **1.** one who strips. **2.** a striptease dancer. **3.** that which strips, as an appliance, machine or solvent for stripping.

**strip poker** /strɪp ˈpoʊkə/, *n.* a form of poker in which the stakes are items of apparel worn by the players.

**striptease** /ˈstrɪptiz/, *n.* **1.** an act in which a person, usu. a woman, disrobes garment by garment, usu. to the accompaniment of music before an audience. *–adj.* **2.** of or pertaining to such an act.

**strive** /straɪv/, *v.i.*, **strove, striven, striving.** **1.** to exert oneself vigorously; try hard. **2.** to make strenuous efforts towards any end: *to strive for success.* **3.** to contend in opposition, battle, or any conflict. **4.** to struggle vigorously, as in opposition or resistance: *to strive against fate.* **5.** *Archaic.* to contend in rivalry; vie. [ME, from OF *estriver* quarrel, contend; of Gmc orig.] – **striver,** *n.*

**strix** /strɪks/, *n., pl.* **striges.** a channel or groove in a fluted column. Also, **stria.**

**strobe** /stroʊb/, *n.* a high-intensity flash device used in stroboscopic photography or an analogous electronic system. [short for STROBOSCOPE]

**strobe lighting** /– ˈlaɪtɪŋ/, *n.* **1.** flashing light of great intensity, as at a theatre, dance, etc., obtained by using a strobe. **2.** lighting designed to be similar in effect to that of a strobe.

**strobila** /strəˈbaɪlə/, *n.* a segmented structure produced by transverse fission, such as the entire body of a tapeworm, or in jellyfish a body in the process of division so as to produce other jellyfish. [NL, from Gk *strobílē* plug of lint twisted into the shape of a fir cone]

**strobilus** /ˈstroʊbələs/, *n., pl.* **-luses, -li** /-laɪ/. (in plants) a compact reproductive structure consisting of a central axis bearing either simple sporophylls, as in club-mosses and male cones of conifers, or compound scales bearing ovules as in female cones of conifers. Also, **strobile** /ˈstroʊbaɪl/.

**stroboscope** /ˈstroʊbəskoʊp/, *n.* an instrument used in studying the motion of a body (esp. one in rapid revolution or vibration) by rendering it visible at frequent intervals, as by illuminating it with an electric spark or the like, or by viewing it through openings in a revolving disc. [*strobo-* (combining form representing Gk *stróbos* a twisting) + -SCOPE] – **stroboscopic** /stroʊbəˈskɒpɪk/, *adj.*

**strode** /stroʊd/, *v.* past tense of **stride.**

**stroganoff** /ˈstrɒgənɒf/, *n.* a dish of meat cooked in a sauce of sour cream, mushrooms, etc. [named after Count Paul *Stroganoff,* 19th cent. Russian diplomat]

**stroke**[1] /stroʊk/, *n., v.,* **stroked, stroking.** *–n.* **1.** an act of striking, as with the fist, a weapon, a hammer, etc.; a blow. **2.** a hitting of or upon anything. **3.** a striking of a clapper or hammer, as on a bell, or the sound produced by this. **4.** a throb or pulsation, as of the heart. **5.** something likened to a blow in its effect, as in causing pain, injury, or death, as an attack of apoplexy or paralysis. **6.** a destructive discharge of electricity. **7.** a piece of luck, fortune, etc., befalling one: *a stroke of good luck.* **8.** a vigorous movement, as if in dealing a blow. **9.** a single complete movement, esp. one continuously repeated in some process. **10.** *Mech.* **a.** one of a series of alternating continuous movements of something back and forth over or through the same line. **b.** the complete movement of a moving part (esp. a reciprocating part) in one direction. **c.** the distance traversed. **d.** a halfway revolution of an engine during which the piston travels from one extreme of its range to the other. **11.** each of the succession of movements of the arms and legs in swimming. **12.** a type or method of swimming: *the crawl is a rapid stroke.* **13.** a vigorous attempt to attain some object: *a bold stroke for liberty.* **14.** a measure adopted for a particular purpose. **15.** a feat or achievement: *a stroke of genius.* **16.** an act, piece, or amount of work, etc.: *not to do a stroke of work.* **17.** a distinctive or effective touch in a literary composition. **18.** a movement of a pen, pencil, brush, graver, or the like. **19.** a mark traced by or as if by a pen, pencil, brush, or the like. **20.** (in some games) a hitting of the ball in a certain manner: *an overhand stroke.* **21.** *Rowing.* **a.** a single pull of the oar. **b.** manner or style of moving the oars. **c.** the oarsman nearest to the stern of the boat, to whose strokes those of the other oarsmen must conform. **d.** the position in the boat occupied by this oarsman. **22.** *Squash.* the time during which the ball is in play after a service. *–v.t.* **23.** to mark with a stroke or strokes, as of a pen; cancel, as by a stroke of a pen. **24.** to row as stroke oarsman of (a boat or crew); row as stroke in (a race). [ME, c. G *Streich;* akin to STRIKE]

**stroke**[2] /stroʊk/, *v.,* **stroked, stroking,** *n.* *–v.t.* **1.** to pass the hand or an instrument over (something) lightly or with little pressure; rub gently, as in soothing or caressing. *–n.* **2.** the act or an instance of stroking; a stroking movement. [ME; OE *strācian,* c. G *streichen;* akin to STRIKE]

**stroke play** /ˈ– pleɪ/, *n.* →**medal play.**

**stroll** /stroʊl/, *v.i.* **1.** to walk leisurely as inclination directs; ramble; saunter; take a walk. **2.** to wander or rove from place to place; roam: *strolling minstrels.* *–n.* **3.** a leisurely walk; a ramble; a saunter: *a short stroll before supper.* [orig. uncert.]

**stroller** /ˈstroʊlə/, *n.* **1.** a person taking a walk or a stroll. **2.** an itinerant performer. **3.** Also, **pushchair, pusher.** a light collapsible chair on wheels, used for carrying small children.

**stroma** /ˈstroʊmə/, *n., pl.* **-mata** /-mətə/. **1.** the colourless, sponge-like, framework of a red blood corpuscle or other cell. **2.** the connective tissue forming the framework of an organ (contrasted with *parenchyma*). **3.** *Bot.* a dense mass of hyphae in which a fungus may develop. [NL; in LL bed covering, from Gk: a spread] – **stromatic** /stroʊˈmætɪk/, **stromatous,** *adj.*

**strong** /strɒŋ/, *adj.* **1.** having, showing, or involving great bodily or muscular power; physically vigorous or robust. **2.** mentally powerful or vigorous: *a strong mind.* **3.** esp. powerful, able, or competent in a specified field or respect (oft. fol. by *on* or *in*): *strong in maths.* **4.** of great moral power, firmness, or courage: *strong under temptation.* **5.** powerful in influence, authority, resources, or means of prevailing or succeeding: *a strong nation.* **6.** clear and firm; loud: *a strong voice.* **7.** well-supplied or rich in something specified: *a strong hand at cards.* **8.** of great force, effectiveness, potency, or cogency: *strong arguments.* **9.** able to resist force or stand strain, wear, etc.: *strong walls, cloth, etc.* **10.** firm or unfaltering under trial: *strong faith.* **11.** moving or acting with force or vigour: *strong wind.* **12.** containing alcohol, or much alcohol: *strong drink.* **13.** intense, as light or colour. **14.** distinct, as marks or impressions; marked, as a resemblance or contrast. **15.** strenuous or energetic; forceful or vigorous: *strong efforts.* **16.** (of language, speech, etc.) **a.** forceful; forthright. **b.** indecent; vulgar. **17.** hearty, fervent, or thoroughgoing: *strong prejudice.* **18.** having a large proportion of the effective or essential properties or ingredients: *strong tea.* **19.** having a high degree of flavour or smell: *strong perfume.* **20.** of an unpleasant or offensive flavour or smell: *strong butter.* **21.** *Comm.* characterised by steady or advancing prices. **22.** *Gram.* **a.** (of Germanic verbs) indicating differentiation in tense by internal vowel change rather than by the addition of a common inflectional ending, as *sing, sang, sung; ride, rode, ridden.* **b.** (of Germanic nouns and adjectives) inflected with endings generally distinctive of case, number, and gender, as German *alter Mann* 'old man'. *–adv.* **23.** in a strong manner; powerfully; forcibly; vigorously. **24.** in number: *the army was twenty thousand strong.* **25. going strong,** continuing vigorously, in good health: *he is very old but still going strong.* *–n.* **26. the strong of,** *Colloq.* the meaning of; the truth about. [ME and OE, c. MD *stranc;* akin to D and G *streng* severe, strict] – **strongly,** *adv.*

**strongarm** /ˈstrɒŋam/, *Colloq.* *–adj.* **1.** having, using, or involving the use of muscular or physical force: *strongarm methods.* *–v.t.* *U.S.* **2.** to employ violent methods upon. **3.** to steal from by force.

**strongbox** /ˈstrɒŋbɒks/, *n.* a strongly made chest for preserving money, jewels, etc.

**strong breeze** /strɒŋ ˈbriz/, *n.* a wind of Beaufort scale force 6, i.e. one with average wind speed of 22 to 27 knots, or 39 to 49 km/h.

**strong gale** /– ˈgeɪl/, *n.* a wind of Beaufort scale force 9, i.e. with average wind speed of 41 to 47 knots, or 75 to 88 km/h.

**stronghold** /ˈstrɒŋhoʊld/, *n.* **1.** a strong or well-fortified place; a fortress. **2.** a place where anything, as an ideology, opinion, etc., is strong.

**strong man** /ˈstrɒŋ mæn/, *n.* **1.** a man who performs feats of strength for entertainment, as in a circus. **2.** the most powerful person in an organisation, state, or the like.

**strong-minded** /strɒŋ-ˈmaɪndəd/, *adj.* having or showing a strong mind or vigorous mental powers. – **strong-mindedly,** *adv.* – **strong-mindedness,** *n.*

**strong nuclear interaction,** *n.* the interaction which binds protons and neutrons together in the nucleus of an atom; the strongest interaction known in nature. Also, **strong interaction.**

**strong point** /ˈstrɒŋ pɔɪnt/, *n.* a person's special quality or talent.

**strongroom** /ˈstrɒŋrum/, *n.* a room for valuables in a bank or the like, built so as to resist fire and theft.

**strong-willed** /ˈstrɒŋ-wɪld/, *adj.* **1.** having a powerful will; resolute. **2.** stubborn.

**strongyle** /ˈstrɒndʒəl/, *n.* any of the nematode worms constituting the family Strongylidae, parasitic as adults in the intestine principally of horses; in the larval stage they burrow into the mucosa, and some enter the circulatory system, giving rise to serious pathological conditions. [NL *Strongylus* (name of typical genus), from Gk *strongýlos* round]

**strontia** /ˈstrɒntiə/, *n.* **1.** strontium oxide, SrO, a white amorphous powder resembling lime in its general character. **2.** strontium hydroxide, $Sr(OH)_2$. [NL, from *Strontian,* parish in Argyllshire, Scotland, where discovered]

**strontian** /ˈstrɒntiən/, *n.* **1.** strontianite. **2.** strontia. **3.** strontium.

**strontianite** /ˈstrɒntiənaɪt/, *n.* a mineral, strontium carbonate, $SrCO_3$, a minor ore of strontium, occurring in radiating, fibrous, or granular aggregates and crystals, varying from white to yellow and pale green. [*Strontian* (see STRONTIA) + -ITE[1]]

**strontium** /ˈstrɒntiəm/, *n.* a bivalent metallic element whose compounds resemble those of calcium, found in nature only in the combined state, as in strontianite. The radioactive isotope **strontium-90,** produced in certain nuclear reactions and sometimes present in fall-out, is extremely dangerous to mammals as it tends to be assimilated in bones in place of calcium which it resembles chemically. *Symbol:* Sr; *at. wt:* 87.62; *at. no.:* 38; *sp. gr.:* 2.6. – **strontic** /ˈstrɒntɪk/, *adj.*

**strontium unit** /ˈ– junət/, *n.* a measure of the concentration of **strontium-90** in an organic medium, as milk, bone, soil, etc., relative to the concentration of calcium in the same medium. One strontium unit is equivalent to $10^{-12}$ curies of strontium-90 per gram of calcium. *Abbrev.:* S.U.

**strop** /strɒp/, *n., v.,* **stropped, stropping.** *–n.* **1.** a strip of leather or other flexible material, or a long, narrow piece of wood having its faces covered with leather or an abrasive, or some similar device, used for sharpening razors. **2.** *Naut.* **a.** a ring of rope fitted round a block or spar, with an eye used for connecting. **b.** a large ring of rope used as a sling. *–v.t.* **3.** to sharpen on, or as on, a strop. [ME *stroppe,* OE *strop,* c. D and LG *strop,* probably from L *stroppus* strap]

**strophanthin** /stroʊˈfænθən/, *n.* a bitter, poisonous glycoside obtained from the ripe seeds of various species of *Strophanthus,* esp. *S. Kombe,* used in medicine as a cardiac stimulant. [STROPHANTH(US) + -IN[2]]

**strophanthus** /stroʊˈfænθəs/, *n.* **1.** any of the shrubs or small trees of the genus *Strophanthus,* mostly native to tropical Africa. **2.** the seed. [NL, from Gk *stróphos* twisted band + *ánthos* flower]

**strophe** /ˈstroʊfi/, *n.* **1.** the part of an ancient Greek choral ode sung by the chorus when moving from right to left. **2.** the first of two metrically corresponding series of lines forming divisions of a lyric poem (the second being the antistrophe), or in a longer poem, the first section of such a metrical pattern whenever it is repeated. **3.** (in modern poetry) any separate or extended section in a poem, opposed to the stanza, a group of lines which necessarily repeats a metrical pattern. [Gk: a turning] – **strophic** /ˈstrɒfɪk/, *adj.*

**strophulus** /ˈstrɒfjələs/, *n.* a papular eruption of the skin in infants, occurring in several forms and usu. harmless. [NL, alteration of ML *scrophulus* red gum, itself alteration of L *scrōfulae* SCROFULA]

**stroppy** /ˈstrɒpi/, *adj. Colloq.* rebellious and difficult to control; awkward; complaining. [alteration of OBSTREPEROUS]

**strove** /stroʊv/, *v.* past tense of **strive.**

**strow** /stroʊ/, *v.,* **strowed, strown** or **strowed, strowing.** *Archaic.* →**strew.**

**struck** /strʌk/, *v.* **1.** past tense and a past participle of **strike.** **2. struck on,** *Colloq.* in love or infatuated with.

**struck measure** /– ˈmɛʒə/, *n.* a measure, esp. of grain, level with the top of a receptacle.

**structural** /ˈstrʌktʃərəl/, *adj.* **1.** of or pertaining to structure; pertaining or essential to a structure. **2.** *Biol.* pertaining to organic structure; morphological. **3.** *Geol.* pertaining to the structure of rock, etc. **4.** *Chem.* pertaining to or showing the arrangement or mode of attachment of the atoms which constitute the molecule of a substance. **5.** resulting from, or pertaining to, political or economic structure. – **structurally,** *adv.*

**structural formula** /– ˈfɔmjələ/, *n.* See **formula** (def. 4).

**structuralism** /ˈstrʌktʃərəlɪzəm/, *n.* **1.** *Linguistics.* the view of a language as a coherent entity in which each part acquires its value by virtue of its relationships with the other parts in the entity. **2.** *Archit.* a style which emphasises the structural components of a building, esp. load-bearing structures such as beams, columns, etc.

**structure** /ˈstrʌktʃə/, *n., v.,* **-tured, -turing.** *–n.* **1.** mode of building, construction, or organisation; arrangement of parts, elements or constituents. **2.** something built or constructed; a building, bridge, dam, framework, etc. **3.** a complex system considered from the point of view of the whole rather than of any single part: *the structure of modern science.* **4.** anything composed of parts arranged together in some way; an organisation. **5.** *Biol.* mode of organisation; construction and arrangement of tissues, parts, or organs. **6.** *Geol.* **a.** the attitude of a bed or stratum, or of beds or strata, of sedimentary rocks, as indicated by the dip and strike. **b.** coarser features of rocks as contrasted with their texture. **7.** the manner by which atoms in a molecule are joined to each other, esp. in organic chemistry where it is represented by a diagram of the molecular arrangement. *–v.t.* **8.** to give form or organisation to. [L *structūra*]

**strudel** /ˈstrudəl/, *n.* a very thin sheet of pastry, spread with a filling, such as apples, sour cherries, cottage cheese, etc., rolled up, brushed with butter and baked slowly. [G]

**struggle** /ˈstrʌgəl/, *v.,* **-gled, -gling,** *n.* *–v.i.* **1.** to contend with an adversary or opposing force. **2.** to contend resolutely with a task, problem, etc.; strive: *to struggle for existence.* **3.** advance with violent effort: *to struggle through the snow.* *–v.t.* **4.** to make (one's way) with violent effort. *–n.* **5.** the act or process of struggling. **6.** a strong effort, or series of efforts, against any adverse agencies or conditions. **7.** a fight, usu. on a small scale involving only a few people. [ME; ? from *strug-* (b. STRIVE and TUG) + *-le* frequentative suffix] – **struggler,** *n.*

**struggle for existence,** *n.* **1.** *Biol.* the ability of an organism to adapt to changes in environment, pressure of populations, means of subsistence, esp. as a factor in evolution. **2.** *Colloq.* everyday living.

**strum** /strʌm/, *v.,* **strummed, strumming,** *n.* *–v.t.* **1.** to play on (a stringed musical instrument) unskilfully or carelessly. **2.** to produce (notes, etc.) by such playing: *to strum a tune.* **3.** to play (chords, etc., esp. on a guitar) by sweeping across the strings with the fingers or with a plectrum. *–v.i.* **4.** to play chords on a stringed instrument unskilfully or as a simple accompaniment. *–n.* **5.** the act of strumming. [b. STRING and THUMB] – **strummer,** *n.*

**struma** /ˈstrumə/, *n., pl.* **-mae** /-mi/. **1.** *Pathol.* **a.** →**scrofula.** **b.** →**goitre.** **2.** *Bot.* a cushion-like swelling on an organ, as that at one side of the base of the capsule in many mosses. [NL special use of L: scrofulous tumour]

**strumose** /ˈstrumoʊs/, *adj.* having a struma or strumae.

**strumous** /ˈstruməs/, *adj. Pathol.* **1.** affected with struma. **2.** characteristic of or of the nature of struma.

**strumpet** /ˈstrʌmpət/, *n.* a prostitute; a harlot. [*strump-* (cf. G *strumpf* stump) + -ET]

**strung** /strʌŋ/, *v.* past tense and past participle of **string.**

**strut**[1] /strʌt/, *v.,* **strutted, strutting,** *n.* *–v.i.* **1.** to walk with a vain, pompous bearing, as with head erect and chest thrown out, as if expecting to impress observers. *–n.* **2.** the act of strutting; a strutting walk or gait. [ME *stroute,* OE *strūtian* stand stiffly; akin to STRUT[2]] – **strutter,** *n.*

**strut**[2] /strʌt/, *n., v.,* **strutted, strutting.** *–n.* **1.** a piece of wood or iron, or some other member of a structure, designed for the reception of pressure or weight in the direction of its length. *–v.t.* **2.** to brace or support by a strut or struts. [cf. LG *strutt* stiff; akin to STRUT[1]]

**struth** /struθ/, *interj.* (an exclamation expressing surprise or verification: *Did he say that? Struth!; Struth he did!*) Also,

**strewth, 'struth.** [from *God's truth*]

**struthious** /ˈstruθiəs/, *adj.* related to or resembling the ostrich. [LL *strūthi(o)* ostrich (from Gk *strouthíon*) + -OUS]

**strut suspension** /strʌt səˈspɛnʃən/, *n.* a method of suspension in a motor vehicle involving an integral shock absorber and strut encased in a spring. Also, **McPherson strut suspension.**

**strutting** /ˈstrʌtɪŋ/, *adj.* that struts; walking pompously; pompous. – **struttingly,** *adv.*

**strychnic** /ˈstrɪknɪk/, *adj.* of or obtained from strychnine.

**strychnine** /ˈstrɪknin, -nən/, *n.* a colourless crystalline poison, $C_{21}H_{22}N_2O_2$, derived from the nux vomica. It has a powerful stimulating effect on the central nervous system and can be used in small quantities to stimulate the appetite. Also, *Archaic.* **strychnia** /ˈstrɪkniə/. [F, from L *strychnos* (from Gk: kind of nightshade) + *-ine* -INE[2]]

**strychninism** /ˈstrɪkniˌnɪzəm/, *n. Obs.* a morbid condition induced by an overdose, or by excessive use, of strychnine.

**stub** /stʌb/, *n., v.,* **stubbed, stubbing.** *–n.* **1.** a short projecting part. **2.** the end of a fallen tree, shrub, or plant left fixed in the ground; a stump. **3.** a short remaining piece, as of a pencil, a candle, a cigar, etc. **4.** something unusually short, as a short, thick nail or a short-pointed, blunt pen. **5.** a worn horseshoe nail. **6.** the counterfoil of a chequebook, etc. *–v.t.* **7.** to strike, as one's toe, against something projecting from a surface. **8.** to clear of stubs, as land. **9.** to dig up by the roots; grub up (roots). **10. stub out,** to extinguish (a cigarette) by pressing the lighted end against a hard surface. [ME and OE, c. MLG and MD *stubbe*]

**stub axle** /ˈ– æksəl/, *n.* a short axle which carries a wheel used for steering a vehicle, and which is capable of restricted angular movement about a kingpin.

**stubbed** /stʌbd/, *adj.* **1.** reduced to or resembling a stub; short and thick; stumpy. **2.** abounding in or rough with stubs. – **stubbedness,** *n.*

**stubble** /ˈstʌbəl/, *n.* **1.** (*usu. pl.*) the stump of a grain stalk or the like, left in the ground when the crop is cut. **2.** such stumps collectively. **3.** any short, rough growth, as of beard. [ME, from OF *stuble,* from LL *stupula.* See STIPULE] – **stubbled, stubbly,** *adj.*

**stubborn** /ˈstʌbən/, *adj.* **1.** unreasonably obstinate; obstinately perverse. **2.** fixed or set in purpose or opinion; resolute. **3.** obstinately maintained, as a course of action: *a stubborn resistance.* **4.** hard to deal with or manage. **5.** hard, tough, or stiff, as stone or wood. [ME *stiborn(e),* apparently from OE *stybb* STUB] – **stubbornly,** *adv.* – **stubornness,** *n.*

**stubby** /ˈstʌbi/, *adj.,* **-bier, -biest,** *n., pl.* **-bies.** *–adj.* **1.** of the nature of or resembling a stub. **2.** short and thick or broad; thickset. **3.** consisting of or abounding in stubs. **4.** bristly, as the hair or beard. *–n.* Also, **stubbie. 5.** a short surfboard. **6.** a small squat beer bottle. **7.** the contents of such a bottle. – **stubbiness,** *n.*

stubby (def. 6)

**stubby cooler** /ˈ– kulə/, *n.* a polystyrene casing designed as insulation for a stubby (def. 6).

**stub floor** /stʌb ˈflɔ/, *n.* a floor made by sinking transverse sections of a tree flat into the earth floor of a hut, etc.

**stub nail** /ˈ– neɪl/, *n.* **1.** a short, thick nail. **2.** an old or worn horseshoe nail.

**stucco** /ˈstʌkoʊ/, *n., pl.* **-coes, -cos,** *v.,* **-coed, -coing.** *–n.* **1.** a plaster (as of slaked lime, chalk, and pulverised white marble, or of plaster of Paris and glue) used for cornices and mouldings of rooms and for other decorations. **2.** a cement or concrete imitating stone, for coating exterior walls of houses, etc. **3.** any of various plasters, cements, etc. **4.** work made of such materials. *–v.t.* **5.** to cover or ornament with stucco. [It., from Gmc; cf. OHG *stukki* crust] – **stuccoer,** *n.*

**stuccowork** /ˈstʌkoʊwɜk/, *n.* work made of stucco.

**stuck** /stʌk/, *v.* **1.** past tense and past participle of **stick**[2]. **2. stuck on,** *Colloq.* infatuated with. **3. get stuck into,** *Colloq.* **a.** to set about a task vigorously. **b.** to attack (someone) vigorously either physically or verbally. **c.** to eat hungrily.

**stuck fermentation** /– fɜmɛnˈteɪʃən/, *n.* a fermentation which has stopped prematurely.

**stuck-up** /ˈstʌk-ʌp/, *adj. Colloq.* conceited; haughty.

**stud**[1] /stʌd/, *n., v.,* **studded, studding.** *–n.* **1.** a boss, knob, nailhead, or other protuberance projecting from a surface or part, esp. as an ornament. **2.** a post or upright prop, as in the wall of a building. **3.** any of various projecting pins, lugs, or the like on machines, etc. **4.** a short rod, threaded on both ends, screwed in and projecting from something, used to fasten parts together or used as a short journal as in the change gears on a screw-cutting lathe. **5.** a kind of small button or fastener, commonly of metal, bone, or the like, in the form of a small knob and a disc connected by a stem, used (when passed through small buttonholes or the like) for holding together parts of clothing (as detachable collars to shirts) or for ornament. **6.** →**stud poker.** *–v.t.* **7.** to set with or as with studs, bosses, or the like. **8.** to scatter over with things set at intervals. **9.** (of things) to be scattered over the surface of. **10.** to set or scatter (objects) at intervals over a surface. **11.** to furnish with or support by studs or upright props. [ME *stude,* OE *studu,* c. MHG *stud;* akin to G *Stütze*]

**stud**[2] /stʌd/, *n.* **1.** a number of horses, as for racing or hunting, belonging to one owner. **2.** an establishment in which horses cattle, etc., are kept for breeding. **3.** *U.S.* a studhorse or stallion. **4.** a young man of obvious sexual power. *–adj.* **5.** of, associated with, or pertaining to a studhorse. **6.** retained for breeding purposes. [ME and OE *stōd,* c. Icel. *stōdh*]

**studbook** /ˈstʌdbʊk/, *n.* **1.** a genealogical register of a stud; a book giving the pedigree of horses. **2.** *Colloq.* a list of seniority in a public service department.

**studding** /ˈstʌdɪŋ/, *n.* **1.** studs of a wall, partition, or the like, collectively. **2.** material for such studs.

**studdingsail** /ˈstʌdɪŋseɪl/; *Naut.* /-səl/ *n.* a light sail sometimes set outboard of either of the leeches of a square sail, and extended by booms.

**student** /ˈstjudnt/, *n.* **1.** one who is engaged in a course of study and instruction, as at a college, university, or professional or technical school. **2.** one who studies a subject systematically or in detail. [ME, from L *studens,* ppr., being eager, studying; replacing ME *studiant,* from OF]

**studentship** /ˈstjudntˌʃɪp/, *n.* **1.** the state or condition of being a student. **2.** a grant of money for a student; scholarship.

**stud-farm** /ˈstʌd-fam/, *n.* a place where horses, cattle, etc. are bred.

**stud game** /ˈstʌd geɪm/, *n.* →**stud poker.**

**studhorse** /ˈstʌdhɔs/, *n.* a stallion kept for breeding.

**studied** /ˈstʌdid/, *adj.* **1.** marked by or suggestive of effort, rather than spontaneous or natural: *studied simplicity.* **2.** carefully considered. **3.** *Rare.* learned. – **studiedly,** *adv.* – **studiedness,** *n.*

**studio** /ˈstjudioʊ/, *n., pl.* **-dios. 1.** the workroom or atelier of an artist, as a painter or sculptor. **2.** a room or place in which some form of art is pursued: *a music studio.* **3.** a room or set of rooms specially equipped for broadcasting radio or television programs or making recordings. **4.** (*oft. pl.*) all the buildings occupied by a company engaged in making films. [It., from L *studium* zeal, study, LL a place for study]

**studio couch** /ˈ– kaʊtʃ/, *n.* a kind of divan used as both a couch and a bed.

**studio musician** /ˈ– mjuzɪʃən/, *n.* a musician often of great versatility, who makes his living by playing in recording sessions.

**studious** /ˈstjudiəs/, *adj.* **1.** disposed or given to study: *a studious boy.* **2.** concerned with, characterised by, or pertaining to study: *studious tastes.* **3.** zealous, assiduous, or painstaking: *studious care.* **4.** studied or carefully maintained. **5.** *Poetic.* (of places) used or frequented for purposes of study. [ME, from L *studiōsus*] – **studiously,** *adv.* – **studiousness,** *n.*

**stud poker** /stʌd ˈpoʊkə/, *n.* a variety of poker in which some rounds of cards are dealt face up.

**studwork** /ˈstʌdwɜk/, *n.* **1.** construction with studs or upright scantlings. **2.** work containing or supported by studs.

**study** /ˈstʌdi/, *n., pl.* **studies,** *v.,* **studied, studying.** *–n.* **1.** application of the mind to the acquisition of knowledge, as by reading, investigation, or reflection. **2.** the cultivation of a particular branch of learning, science, or art: *the study of* *law.* **3.** a particular course of effort to acquire knowledge: *to pursue special medical studies.* **4.** something studied or to be studied. **5.** a thorough examination and analysis of a particular subject. **6.** a written account of this. **7.** zealous endeavour or assiduous effort. **8.** the object of the endeavour or effort. **9.** deep thought, reverie, or a state of abstraction: *to be in a brown study.* **10.** a room, in a house or other building, set apart for private study, reading, writing, or the like. **11.** *Music.* a composition, usu. instrumental, combining the instructive purpose of an exercise with a certain amount of artistic value; an étude. **12.** *Lit.* **a.** a composition, executed for exercise or as an experiment in a particular method of treatment. **b.** such a composition dealing in detail with a particular subject. **13.** *Art.* something produced as an educational exercise, or as a memorandum or record of observations or effects, or as a guide for a finished production. *–v.i.* **14.** to apply oneself to the acquisition of knowledge, as by reading, investigation, practice, etc. **15.** to apply oneself, or endeavour. **16.** to think deeply, reflect, or consider. *–v.t.* **17.** to apply oneself to acquiring a knowledge of (a branch of learning, science, or art, or a subject), esp. systematically. **18.** to examine or investigate carefully and in detail: *to study the political situation.* **19.** to observe attentively; scrutinise: *to study a person's face.* **20.** to read (a book, document, etc.) with careful effort. **21.** to seek to learn or memorise, as a part in a play. **22.** to give careful consideration to. **23.** to aim at; seek to acquire. [ME *studie,* from L *studium* zeal, application, study, LL a place for study]

**study leave** /'– liv/, *n.* →**sabbatical** (def. 4).

**stuff** /stʌf/, *n.* **1.** the material of which anything is made. **2.** material to be worked upon, or to be used in making something. **3.** matter or material indefinitely: *cushions filled with some soft stuff.* **4.** woven material or fabric. **5.** *Colloq.* property, as personal belongings, equipment, etc. **6.** something to be swallowed, as food, drink, or medicine. **7.** inward character, qualities, or capabilities. **8.** *Colloq.* actions, performances, talk, etc.: *to cut out the rough stuff.* **9.** worthless matter or things. **10.** worthless or foolish ideas, talk, or writing. **11.** *Colloq.* literary, artistic, or musical material, productions, compositions, etc. **12.** *Colloq.* one's own trade, profession, occupation, etc.: *to know one's stuff.* **13.** *Colloq.* money. **14. do one's stuff,** *Colloq.* to do what is expected of one; show what one can do. **15. not to give a stuff,** *Colloq.* to be unconcerned. **16. that's the stuff,** *Colloq.* that is what is needed, right, proper, etc. *–v.t.* **17.** to fill (a receptacle), esp. by packing the contents closely together; cram full. **18.** to fill (an aperture, cavity, etc.) by forcing something into it. **19.** to fill or line with some kind of material as a padding or packing. **20.** to fill or cram (oneself, one's stomach, etc.) with food. **21.** to fill (a chicken, turkey, piece of meat, etc.) with seasoned breadcrumbs or other savoury matter. **22.** to fill the skin of (a dead animal) with material, preserving the natural form and appearance. **23.** to thrust or cram (something) tightly into a receptacle, cavity, or the like. **24.** to pack tightly in a confined place; crowd together. **25.** to crowd (a vehicle, room, etc.) with persons. **26.** to fill (the mind) with details, facts, etc. **27.** *Leather Mfg.* to treat (a skin, etc.) with a composition of tallow and other ingredients. **28.** to stop up or plug; block or choke (usu. fol. by *up*). **29.** *Colloq.* (of males) to have sexual intercourse with. **30.** *Colloq.* to cause to fail; render useless. **31. stuff it!,** *Colloq.* (an exclamation indicating anger, frustration, etc.). *–v.i.* **32.** to cram oneself with food; feed gluttonously. [ME, from OF *estoffe* material, provision, from *estoffer* provide, from Gmc (cf. MHG *stopfen*), from LL *stuppāre,* from *stuppa* tow. Cf. STOP]

**stuffed** /stʌft/, *v.* **1.** past tense and past participle of **stuff.** *–adj. Colloq.* **2. stuffed up,** having the nasal passages blocked with mucus, usu. as a result of a cold. **3. get stuffed,** (*offensive*) to go away; leave (one) alone.

**stuffed shirt** /'– ʃɜt/, *n. Colloq.* a pompous, pretentious person.

**stuffing** /'stʌfɪŋ/, *n.* **1.** the act of one who or that which stuffs. **2.** that with which anything is or may be stuffed. **3.** seasoned breadcrumbs or other filling used to stuff a chicken, turkey, etc., before cooking. **4. knock** or **beat the stuffing out of,** *Colloq.* to destroy the self-confidence of or defeat utterly.

**stuffing box** /'– bɒks/, *n.* a contrivance for securing a steamtight, airtight, or watertight joint at the place or hole where a movable rod (as a piston rod) enters a vessel, consisting typically of a cylindrical box or chamber through the middle of which the rod passes, the rest of the space being filled with packing held in by a cover or adjustable member at one end of the box.

**stuffing nut** /'– nʌt/, *n.* the nut on a stuffing box that serves to condense the packing and so to tighten the seal.

**stuff-up** /'stʌf-ʌp/, *n. Colloq.* a failure which has arisen from a foolish or thoughtless error.

**stuffy** /'stʌfi/, *adj.,* **stuffier, stuffiest. 1.** close or ill-ventilated, as a room; oppressive from lack of freshness, as the air, etc. **2.** lacking in interest, as writing or discourse. **3.** affected with a sensation of obstruction in the respiratory passages, as a person. **4.** boring; tedious. **5.** conceited; self-important. **6.** straitlaced; prim; easily shocked. **7.** old-fashioned; immune to new ideas. – **stuffily,** *adv.* – **stuffiness,** *n.*

**stull** /stʌl/, *n.* **1.** *Mining.* a timber prop. **2.** one piece of timber set for a mine support, usu. the top piece. **3.** a platform in an underground workings. [cf. G *Stollen* prop]

**stultify** /'stʌltəfaɪ/, *v.t.,* **-fied, -fying. 1.** to make, or cause to appear, foolish or ridiculous. **2.** to render absurdly or wholly futile or ineffectual, as efforts. **3.** *Law.* to allege or prove to be of unsound mind; allege (oneself) to be insane. [LL *stultificāre,* from L *stultus* foolish. See -FY] – **stultification** /stʌltəfə'keɪʃən/, *n.* – **stultifier,** *n.*

**stumble** /'stʌmbəl/, *v.,* **-bled, -bling,** *n. –v.i.* **1.** to strike the foot against something in walking, running, etc., so as to stagger or fall; trip. **2.** to walk or go unsteadily. **3.** to make a slip, mistake, or blunder, esp. a verbal one. **4.** to proceed in a hesitating or blundering manner, as in action or speech. **5.** to come accidentally or unexpectedly (fol. by *on, upon, across,* etc.). **6.** to falter or hesitate, as at an obstacle to progress or belief. *–v.t.* **7.** to cause to stumble; trip. **8.** to give pause to; puzzle or perplex. *–n.* **9.** the act of stumbling. **10.** a moral lapse or error. **11.** a slip or blunder. [ME, c. Norw. *stumla;* akin to STAMMER] – **stumbler,** *n.* – **stumblingly,** *adv.*

**stumbling block** /'stʌmblɪŋ blɒk/, *n.* an obstacle or hindrance to progress, belief, etc.

**stumer** /'stjumə/, *n. Colloq.* **1.** a worthless cheque. **2. come a stumer,** to suffer a reversal of fortune, esp. financial.

**stumered** /'stjuməd/, *adj. Colloq.* bankrupt; without any money.

**stump** /stʌmp/, *n.* **1.** the lower end of a tree or plant left after the main part falls or is cut off; a standing tree trunk from which the upper part and the branches have been removed. **2.** the part of a limb of the body remaining after the rest has been amputated or cut off. **3.** a part of a broken or decayed tooth left in the gum. **4.** a short remnant of a pencil, candle, cigar, etc. **5.** any basal part remaining after the main or more important part has been removed. **6.** *Qld.* one of the piles on which a house is raised above the ground. **7.** a wooden or artificial leg. **8.** (*usu. pl.*) *Colloq.* a leg: *to stir one's stumps.* **9.** a short, stumpy person. **10.** a heavy step or gait, as of a wooden-legged or lame person. **11.** *Chiefly U.S.* the platform or place of political speech-making: *to go on the stump.* **12.** an instrument consisting of a short, thick, roll of paper or soft leather, or a bar of indiarubber or other soft material, usu. cut to a blunt point at each end, used for rubbing the lights and shades in crayon drawing or charcoal drawing, or for otherwise altering the effect. **13.** *Cricket.* each of the three upright sticks which, with the two bails laid on the top of them, form a wicket. **14.** (*pl.*) *Cricket.* the end of a day's play. **15.** *Colloq.* union dues. **16. beyond** (**back of**) **the black stump,** *Colloq.* in the far outback; in country areas beyond the reach of civilised comforts and facilities. **17. draw stumps,** *Cricket.* to cease play. **18. get up on the stump,** to address a public meeting. *–v.t.* **19.** to reduce to a stump; truncate; lop. **20.** to clear of stumps, as land. **21.** *U.S. Colloq.* to stub, as one's toe. **22.** to nonplus, embarrass, or render completely at a loss. **23.** *Chiefly U.S. Colloq.* to make political speeches in or to. **24.** *Cricket.* (of the wicket-keeper) to put (a batsman) out by knocking down a stump or by dislodging a bail with the ball held in the hand, at a moment when the batsman is out of his ground. **25.** to tone or modify (crayon drawings, etc.) by means of a stump. *–v.i.* **26.** to walk heavily or clumsily, as if with a wooden leg: *the sailor stumped across the deck.* **27.** *Chiefly U.S. Colloq.* to make speeches in an election campaign. **28. stump up,** *Colloq.* to pay up or hand over money required. [ME *stomp,* c. G *Stumpf*]

**stumpage** /ˈstʌmpɪdʒ/, *n. U.S.* **1.** standing timber with reference to its value. **2.** the right to cut such timber on the owner's land. **3.** the value of such timber.

**stumper** /ˈstʌmpə/, *n.* **1.** one who or that which stumps. **2.** *Cricket Colloq.* a wicket-keeper. **3.** a puzzling question; poser; problem.

**stump-jump plough** /stʌmp-dʒʌmp ˈplaʊ/, *n.* a plough designed to rise and fall over roots and stumps in newly cleared ground.

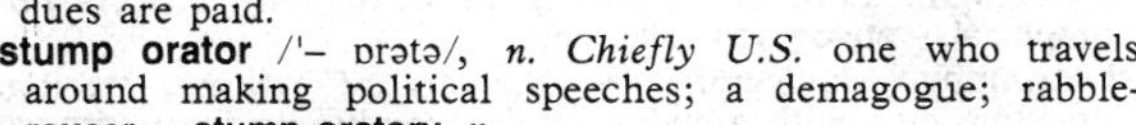

**stump office** /ˈstʌmp ɒfəs/, *n. Colloq.* an office into which union dues are paid.

stump-jump plough

**stump orator** /ˈ– ɒrətə/, *n. Chiefly U.S.* one who travels around making political speeches; a demagogue; rabble-rouser. – **stump oratory,** *n.*

**stump-tailed skink** /stʌmp-teɪld ˈskɪŋk/, *n.* a common Australian lizard, *Trachydosaurus rugosus,* having a stout body, wedge-shaped head, stumpy tail and distinctive large, rough scales on the upper surface; shingleback; sleepy lizard; pine-cone lizard. Also, **stump-tail lizard.**

stump-tailed skink

**stumpy**[1] /ˈstʌmpi/, *adj.,* **stumpier, stumpiest. 1.** of the nature of or resembling a stump. **2.** short and thick; stubby; stocky. **3.** abounding in stumps. – **stumpily,** *adv.* – **stumpiness,** *n.*

**stumpy**[2] /ˈstʌmpi/, *n.* the juvenile kingworm, up to 50 cm long and 1 cm wide, found on the slopes of the beach.

**stun** /stʌn/, *v.,* **stunned, stunning,** *n.* *–v.t.* **1.** to deprive of consciousness or strength by or as by a blow, fall, etc. **2.** to strike with astonishment; astound; amaze. **3.** to daze or bewilder by distracting noise. *–n.* **4.** the act of stunning. **5.** the condition of being stunned. [ME; OE *stunian* resound, crash. Cf. OF *estoner* resound, stun]

**stung** /stʌŋ/, *v.* **1.** past tense and past participle of **sting.** *–adj.* **2.** *Colloq.* drunk. **3.** *Colloq.* tricked; cheated.

**stunned** /stʌnd/, *v.* **1.** past tense and past participle of **stun. 2. like a stunned mullet,** *Colloq.* **a.** in complete bewilderment or astonishment. **b.** in a state of inertia.

**stunner** /ˈstʌnə/, *n.* **1.** one who or that which stuns. **2.** *Colloq.* a person or thing of striking excellence, beauty, attractiveness, etc.

**stunning** /ˈstʌnɪŋ/, *adj.* **1.** that stuns. **2.** *Colloq.* of striking excellence, beauty, etc. – **stunningly,** *adv.*

**stunsail** /ˈstʌnsəl/, *n.* →**studdingsail.**

**stunt**[1] /stʌnt/, *v.t.* **1.** to check the growth or development of; dwarf; hinder the increase or progress of. *–n.* **2.** a check in growth or development. **3.** arrested development. **4.** a creature hindered from attaining its proper growth. [v. use of *stunt,* adj. (now d.), dwarfed, stubborn (in ME and OE foolish), c. MHG *stunz,* Icel. *stuttr* short]

**stunt**[2] /stʌnt/, *n.* **1.** a performance serving as a display of strength, activity, skill, or the like, as in athletics, etc.; a feat. **2.** anything done to attract publicity. *–v.i.* **3.** to do a stunt or stunts. [orig. uncert.]

**stunted** /ˈstʌntəd/, *adj.* having failed to reach full growth; dwarfish; underdeveloped.

**stuntman** /ˈstʌntmæn/, *n.* one who is paid to perform hazardous or acrobatic feats, esp. one who replaces a film actor in scenes requiring such feats.

**stupa** /ˈstupə/, *n.* a monumental pile of earth or other material, either dome-shaped or pyramidal, in memory of Buddha or a Buddhist saint, and commemorating some event or marking a sacred spot. [Skt]

**stupe** /stjup/, *n.* two or more layers of flannel or other cloth soaked in hot water, applied to the skin as a counter-irritant. [ME, from L *stūpa* tow]

**stupefacient** /stjupəˈfeɪʃənt/, *adj.* **1.** stupefying; producing stupor. *–n.* **2.** a drug or agent that produces stupor. [L *stupefaciens,* ppr., stupefying]

**stupefaction** /stjupəˈfækʃən/, *n.* **1.** the act of stupefying. **2.** the state of being stupefied; stupor; numbness of the faculties. **3.** overwhelming amazement.

**stupefactive** /stjupəˈfæktɪv/, *adj.* serving to stupefy.

**stupefy** /ˈstjupəfaɪ/, *v.t.,* **-fied, -fying. 1.** to put into a state of stupor; dull the faculties of. **2.** to stun as with a narcotic, a shock, strong emotion, etc. **3.** to overwhelm with amazement; astound. [L *stupefacere*] – **stupefier,** *n.*

**stupendous** /stjuˈpɛndəs/, *adj.* **1.** such as to cause amazement; astounding; marvellous. **2.** amazingly large or great; immense: *a stupendous mass of information.* [L *stupendus,* ger., to be wondered at] – **stupendously,** *adv.* – **stupendousness,** *n.*

**stupid** /ˈstjupəd/, *adj.* **1.** lacking ordinary activity and keenness of mind; dull. **2.** characterised by, indicative of, or proceeding from mental dullness: *a stupid act.* **3.** tediously dull or uninteresting: *a stupid book.* **4.** in a state of stupor; stupefied. *–n.* **5.** *Colloq.* a stupid person. [L *stupidus*] – **stupidly,** *adv.* – **stupidness,** *n.*

**stupidity** /stjuˈpɪdəti/, *n., pl.* **-ties. 1.** the state, quality, or fact of being stupid. **2.** a stupid act, notion, speech, etc.

**stupor** /ˈstjupə/, *n.* **1.** suspension or great diminution of sensibility, as in disease or as caused by narcotics, intoxicants, etc. **2.** a state of suspended or deadened sensibility. **3.** mental torpor, or apathy; stupefaction. [ME, from L] – **stuporous,** *adj.*

**sturdy**[1] /ˈstɜdi/, *adj.,* **-dier, -diest. 1.** strongly built, stalwart, or robust. **2.** strong, as in substance, construction, texture, etc.: *sturdy walls.* **3.** firm, stout, or indomitable: *sturdy defenders.* **4.** of strong or hardy growth, as a plant. [ME, from OF *estourdi* dazed, reckless, pp. of *estourdir* stun, LL *exturdīre* deafen (with chatter), from *turdus* turtledove] – **sturdily,** *adv.* – **sturdiness,** *n.*

**sturdy**[2] /ˈstɜdi/, *n. Vet. Sci.* →**gid.** [ME adj. meaning 'giddy', from OF. See STURDY[1]] – **sturdied,** *adj.*

**sturgeon** /ˈstɜdʒən/, *n.* any of various large ganoid fishes of the family Acipenseridae, found in fresh and salt waters of the northern temperate zone, and valued for their flesh and as a source of caviar and isinglass. [ME, from AF, var. of OF *sturg(i)un,* from VL *sturio,* from Gmc; cf. OHG *sturio*]

sturgeon

**sturt** /stɜt/, *n.* a rich return earned by a party of miners working on a tribute system. [Cornish d.]

**Sturt's desert pea,** *n.* an Australian plant, *Clianthus formosus,* with brilliant scarlet and black flowers, found in inland desert country; the floral emblem of South Australia. [named after Charles *Sturt,* 1795-1869, explorer]

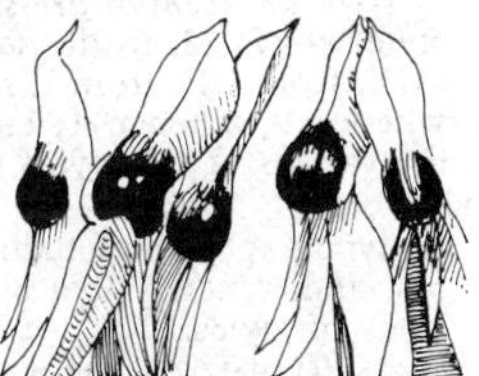

Sturt's desert pea

**Sturt's desert rose,** *n.* a shrub of inland Australia, *Gossypium sturtianum,* with attractive mauve flowers; the floral emblem of the Northern Territory. [named after Charles *Sturt,* 1795-1869, explorer]

**stutter** /ˈstʌtə/, *v.t., v.i.* **1.** to utter (sounds) in which the rhythm is interrupted by blocks or spasms, repetitions, or prolongation of sounds or syllables, sometimes accompanied by facial contortions. *–n.* **2.** unrhythmical and distorted speech characterised principally by blocks or spasms interrupting the rhythm. [frequentative of Brit. d. *stut,* ME *stutte(n),* akin to D *stotteren*] – **stutterer,** *n.* – **stutteringly,** *adv.*

**St Vitus dance** /sənt ˈvaɪtəs dæns/, *n.* →**chorea** (def. 2). Also, **St Vitus's dance.** [from *St Vitus* legendary martyr, venerated for his gift of healing, effected esp. on those who danced before his image at his festival]

**sty**[1] /staɪ/, *n., pl.* **sties,** *v.,* **stied, stying.** *–n.* **1.** a pen or enclosure for pigs. **2.** any filthy abode. **3.** a place of bestial debauchery. *–v.t.* **4.** to keep or lodge in or as in a sty. *–v.i.* **5.** to live in or as in a sty. [ME; OE *stig,* c. Icel. *stī;* akin to D *stijg*]

**sty**[2] /staɪ/, *n., pl.* **sties.** a circumscribed inflammatory swelling, like a small boil, on the edge of the eyelid. Also, **stye.** [backformation from ME *styanye,* from *styan* (OE *stīgend* sty, lit., rising) + *ye* EYE, but taken to mean sty on eye]

**stygian** /ˈstɪdʒiən/, *adj.* **1.** *Class. Myth.* of or pertaining to the lower world river Styx, over which the souls of the dead were ferried. **2.** dark; gloomy. **3.** infernal; hellish. [L *Stygius* (from Gk *Stýgios*) + -AN]

**styl-,** var. of **stylo-,** before vowels, as in *stylar.*

**stylar** /ˈstaɪlə/, *adj.* having the shape of a stylus resembling a pen, pin, or peg.

**style** /staɪl/, *n., v.,* **styled, styling.** *–n.* **1.** a particular kind, sort, or type, as with reference to form, appearance, or character. **2.** a particular, distinctive, or characteristic mode of action. **3.** a mode of living, as with respect to expense or display. **4.** an elegant or fashionable mode of living: *they live in style.* **5.** a mode of fashion, as in dress, esp. good or approved fashion; elegance; smartness. **6.** characteristic mode of writing or speaking, as determined by period, literary form, personality, etc.: *the style of Henry Lawson.* **7.** the features of a literary composition belonging to the form of expression other than the content. **8.** a manner or tone adopted in speaking to others. **9.** a particular, distinctive, or characteristic mode or form of construction or execution in any art or work. **10.** a descriptive or distinguishing appellation, esp., a legal, official, or recognised title: *a firm trading under the style of Smith, Jones & Co.* **11.** Also, **stylus.** an instrument of metal, bone, or the like, used by the ancients for writing on a waxed tablet, having one end pointed for incising the letters, and the other end blunt for rubbing out writing and smoothing the tablet. **12.** something resembling or suggesting such an instrument. **13.** a pointed instrument for drawing, etching, or writing. **14.** the gnomon of a sundial. **15.** a mode of reckoning time. **16.** *Bot.* a narrow, usu. cylindrical and more or less filiform extension of the ovary, which, when present, bears the stigma at its apex. **17.** *Zool.* a small, slender, pointed process or part. **18.** the rules of spelling, punctuation, capitalisation, etc., observed by a publishing house, newspaper, etc. *–v.t.* **19.** to call by a particular style or appellation (as specified); to denominate; name; call. **20.** to design in accordance with a given or new style: *to style an evening dress.* **21.** to make conform to a specific style. *–v.i.* **22.** to do decorative work with a style or stylus. [ME, from OF, from L *stilus* (incorrectly *stylus*); orig. def. 11, whence 9, whence 1, etc. In defs 14 and 16, confused with derivatives of Gk *stŷlos* pillar] – **styler,** *n.*

S, style (def. 16)

**stylebook** /ˈstaɪlbʊk/, *n.* **1.** a book containing rules of usage in typography, punctuation, etc., employed by printers, editors, and writers. **2.** a book featuring styles, fashions, or the rules of styles.

**stylet** /ˈstaɪlət/, *n.* **1.** a stiletto or dagger. **2.** some similar sharp-pointed instrument. **3.** *Med.* **a.** a probe. **b.** a wire run through the length of a catheter, cannula, or needle to make it rigid or to clear it. **4.** *Zool.* →**style** (def. 17). [F, from It. *stiletto* STILETTO]

**styliform** /ˈstaɪləfɔm/, *adj.* having the shape of a style (def. 11); stylar.

**stylise** /ˈstaɪlaɪz/, *v.t.,* **-lised, -lising.** to bring into conformity with a particular style, as of representation or treatment in art; conventionalise. Also, **stylize.** – **stylisation** /staɪlaɪˈzeɪʃən/, *n.* – **styliser,** *n.*

**stylish** /ˈstaɪlɪʃ/, *adj.* characterised by style, or by conforming to the fashionable standard; modishly elegant; smart. – **stylishly,** *adv.* – **stylishness,** *n.*

**stylist** /ˈstaɪləst/, *n.* **1.** a writer or speaker who is skilled in or who cultivates a literary style. **2.** one who designs clothing, interior decorations, etc. **3.** one who cultivates any particular style.

**stylistic** /staɪˈlɪstɪk/, *adj.* of or pertaining to style. – **stylistically,** *adv.*

**stylistics** /staɪˈlɪstɪks/, *n.* **1.** the study of style in literary or other writing. **2.** the stylistic features of a written work.

**stylite** /ˈstaɪlaɪt/, *n.* one of a class of solitary ascetics who lived on the top of high pillars or columns, chiefly in Syria. [Eccel. Gk *stȳlítēs,* from Gk *stŷlos* pillar]

**stylo** /ˈstaɪloʊ/, *n.* a variable species, *Stylosanthes guyanensis,* which is grown in tropical areas as a pasture legume.

**stylo-,** a combining form, frequent in scientific terminology, representing (1) **style,** (2) **styloid.**

**stylobate** /ˈstaɪləbeɪt/, *n.* a continuous base supporting a row of columns; that part of a stereobate immediately beneath the columns. [L *stylobata,* from Gk *stȳlobátēs*]

**stylograph** /ˈstaɪləgræf, -graf/, *n.* a fountain pen in which the writing point is a hollow tube instead of a nib, inside of which is a plunger which releases ink under pressure.

**stylographic** /staɪləˈgræfɪk/, *adj.* **1.** of or pertaining to a stylograph. **2.** of or pertaining to stylography. Also, **stylographical.** – **stylographically,** *adv.*

**stylography** /staɪˈlɒgrəfi/, *n.* the art of writing, tracing, drawing, etc., with a stylus. [*stylo-* (combining form STYLUS) + -GRAPHY]

**styloid** /ˈstaɪlɔɪd/, *adj. Anat.* **1.** resembling a style; slender and pointed. **2.** denoting several bony processes on the temporal bone, radius, ulna, etc. [NL *stȳloīdēs,* from Gk *stȳloeidḗs*]

**stylolite** /ˈstaɪləlaɪt/, *adj.* **1.** of or pertaining to a column-like structure found in certain limestones, the columns having grooved sides and being composed of limestone and generally at right angles or highly inclined to the bedding planes. *–n.* **2.** a stylolite structure. [Gk *stŷlo(s)* pillar + -LITE]

**stylo pen** /staɪloʊ ˈpɛn/, *n.* a dry pen which perforates the waxed fibre of a stencil, allowing ink to print from it.

**stylopodium** /staɪləˈpoʊdiəm/, *n., pl.* **-dia** /-diə/. a glandular disc or expansion surmounting the ovary in umbelliferous plants and supporting the styles.

**stylus** /ˈstaɪləs/, *n.* **1. a.** a pointed instrument for writing on wax or other suitable surfaces. **b.** →**style** (def. 11). **2.** a cutting tool, often needle-shaped, used to cut grooves in making gramophone records. **3.** a needle tipped with diamond, sapphire, etc., for reproducing the sound of a gramophone record. **4.** any of various pointed instruments used in drawing, tracing, stencilling, etc. [L, var. of *stilus*]

**stymie** /ˈstaɪmi/, *n., v.,* **-mied, -mieing.** *–n.* **1.** *Golf.* a position in which an opponent's ball is lying directly between the player's ball and the hole for which he is playing. **2.** any problem which is difficult to resolve. *–v.t.* **3.** to hinder or block, as with a stymie; thwart; frustrate.

**stymy** /ˈstaɪmi/, *n., pl.* **-mies,** *v.t.,* **-mied, -mying.** →**stymie.**

**styphelia** /staɪˈfiliə/, *n.* any shrub of the genus *Styphelia,* family Epacridaceae, with long tubular flowers and drupaceous fruits with a 5-cornered stone; five-corners.

**stypsis** /ˈstɪpsəs/, *n.* the employment or application of styptics. [LL, from Gk]

**styptic** /ˈstɪptɪk/, *adj.* Also, **styptical. 1.** contracting organic tissue; astringent; binding. **2.** checking haemorrhage or bleeding, as a drug; haemostatic. *–n.* **3.** a styptic agent or substance. [ME; from L *stypticus,* from Gk *styptikós*] – **stypticity** /stɪpˈtɪsəti/, *n.*

**styrene** /ˈstaɪrin/, *n.* a colourless liquid hydrocarbon, $C_6H_5CH:CH_2$, with a fragrant, aromatic smell, used in making synthetic rubber. [L *styr(ax)* STORAX + -ENE]

**styrene-butadiene rubber** /ˌstaɪrin-bjutəˌdaɪin ˈrʌbə/, *n.* a widely used, general-purpose, synthetic rubber consisting of a copolymer of butadiene and about 35 per cent styrene. *Abbrev.:* SBR

**styrene resin** /staɪrin ˈrɛzən/, *n.* the transparent plastic formed by the polymerisation of styrene and characterised by its thermo-plastic properties.

**styrienne** /stɪriˈɛn/, *n.* a slow air in 2/4 time and in a minor key, originally with a yodel between each verse. [from *Styria,* province in SE Austria]

**styrofoam** /ˈstaɪrəfoʊm/, *n.* a polystyrene foam. [Trademark]

**su-**, variant of **sub-** before *sp*.

**Su.**, Sunday.

**S.U.**, *Physics.* strontium unit.

**suable** /ˈsuəbəl/, *adj.* capable of being sued; liable to be sued. – **suability** /suəˈbɪləti/, *n.*

**suasion** /ˈsweɪʒən/, *n.* **1.** the act of advising or urging, or attempting to persuade. **2.** an instance of this; a persuasive effort. [ME, from L *suāsio*] – **suasive** /ˈsweɪsɪv/, **suasory** /ˈsweɪsəri/, *adj.*

**suave** /swav/, *adj.* (of persons or their manner, speech, etc.) smoothly agreeable or polite; agreeably or blandly urbane. [L *suāvis* gentle; replacing *suaif,* from F] – **suavely,** *adv.*

**suavity** /ˈswavəti/, *n., pl.* **-ties.** **1.** suave or smoothly agreeable quality (of persons, manner, etc.). **2.** (*pl.*) suave or courteous actions or manners; amenities. Also, **suaveness.**

**sub** /sʌb/, *n., adj., v.,* **subbed, subbing.** *Colloq.* –*n.* **1.** subaltern. **2.** subeditor. **3.** submarine. **4.** subordinate. **5.** subscription. **6.** substitute. **7.** *Brit.* an advance against wages, etc. –*adj.* **8.** substandard. –*v.i.* **9.** to act as a substitute for another. **10.** *Brit.* to pay or receive an advance against wages, etc. –*v.t.* **11.** *Brit.* to pay or receive (an advance against wages, etc.). **12.** to subedit.

**sub-**, **1.** a prefix meaning 'under', 'not quite', or 'somewhat', freely used as a formative (*subarctic, subcortex, substandard, subacid*), also attached to stems not used independently, with various extensions of meaning (*subject, subtract, subvert*). **2.** *Chem.* **a.** a prefix indicating a basic compound, as in *subacetate, subcarbonate, subnitrate.* **b.** a prefix indicating that the element is present in a relatively small proportion, i.e. in a low oxidation state, as in *subchloride, suboxide.* Also, **su-, suc-, suf-, sug-, sum-, sup-.** [L, representing *sub,* prep., under, close to; akin to HYPO-]

**sub.**, **1.** subeditor. **2.** subject. **3.** subjunctive. **4.** submarine. **5.** subscription. **6.** substitute. **7.** suburb.

**subacid** /sʌbˈæsəd/, *adj.* **1.** slightly or moderately acid or sour: *a subacid fruit.* **2.** (of speech, temper, etc., or a person) somewhat tart or sharp. – **subacidity** /sʌbəˈsɪdəti/, **subacidness,** *n.*

**subacute** /sʌbəˈkjut/, *adj.* somewhat or moderately acute.

**subagent** /sʌbˈeɪdʒənt/, *n.* **1.** one to whom agency duties are assigned by an agent. **2.** one who works for or under the supervision of an agent.

**subalpine** /sʌbˈælpaɪn/, *adj.* **1.** pertaining to the regions at the foot of an alpine mountain system. **2.** *Bot.* growing on mountains below the limit of tree growth, and above the foothill, or montane, zone.

**subaltern** /ˈsʌbəltən/, *adj.* **1.** having an inferior or subordinate position or rank; subordinate. **2.** *Mil.* of or pertaining to a commissioned officer below the rank of captain. **3.** *Logic.* denoting the relation of one proposition to another when the first is implied by the second but not conversely. In Aristotelian logic, a particular proposition stands in this relation to the universal proposition having the same subject, predicate, and quality as the particular. –*n.* **4.** one who has a subordinate position. **5.** *Mil.* a commissioned officer below the rank of captain. **6.** *Logic.* a subaltern proposition. [LL *subalternus,* from L *sub* under + *alternus* one after the other, alternate]

**subalternate** /sʌbɔlˈtɜnət/, *adj. Bot.* placed singly along an axis, but tending to become grouped oppositely. – **subalternation** /ˌsʌbɔltəˈneɪʃən/, *n.*

**subantarctic** /sʌbænˈtaktɪk/, *adj.* of, or pertaining to, or similar to the region lying immediately to the north of the Antarctic Circle.

**subapostolic** /ˌsʌbæpəsˈtɒlɪk/, *adj.* of or pertaining to the period of time immediately after the apostles.

**subaquatic** /sʌbəˈkwɒtɪk/, *adj.* living or growing partly on land, partly in water.

**subaqueous** /sʌbˈækwiəs, -ˈeɪk-/, *adj.* **1.** existing or situated under water. **2.** occurring or performed under water. **3.** used under water.

**subarctic** /sʌbˈaktɪk/, *adj.* of, pertaining to, or similar to the region immediately south of the Arctic Circle.

**subarid** /sʌbˈærəd/, *adj.* moderately arid.

**sub-artesian bore** /ˌsʌb-atiʒən ˈbɔ/, *n.* an artesian bore in which the water level rises but not to the surface.

**sub-artesian water** /– ˈwɔtə/, *n.* underground water which, when tapped by a bore hole, does not rise sufficiently high to flow naturally above the surface of the ground.

**subassembly** /ˈsʌbəsɛmbli/, *n.* an assembly, as of machine parts, forming part of a larger assembly but capable of being treated as a separate unit for certain purposes.

**subastringent** /sʌbəˈstrɪndʒənt/, *adj.* slightly astringent.

**subatomic** /sʌbəˈtɒmɪk/, *adj. Physics.* **1.** denoting or pertaining to a particle which is smaller than an atom. **2.** denoting or pertaining to any process which occurs within an atom.

**subaudition** /sʌbɔˈdɪʃən/, *n.* **1.** the act of understanding or mentally supplying something not expressed. **2.** something mentally supplied; understood or implied meaning. [L *subaudītio*]

**subauricular** /sʌbɔˈrɪkjələ/, *adj.* situated below the ear.

**subaxillary** /sʌbˈæksɪləri/, *adj.* situated or placed beneath an axil.

**sub-base** /ˈsʌb-beɪs/, *n.* (in architecture) the lowest part of a base (as of a column) which consists of two or more horizontal members. – **sub-basal** /sʌb-ˈbeɪsəl/, *adj.*

**sub-basement** /ˈsʌb-beɪsmənt/, *n.* a basement, or one of a series of basements, below the main basement of a building.

**sub-bass** /sʌb-ˈbeɪs/, *n.* a pedal stop producing the lowest notes of an organ.

**subcalibre** /sʌbˈkæləbə/, *adj. Mil.* **1.** (of a projectile) having a diameter less than the calibre of the gun from which it is fired, the projectile being fitted with a disc large enough to fill the bore, or being fired from a tube attached to the inside or the outside of the gun. **2.** used in firing such a projectile: *a subcalibre gun.*

**subcartilaginous** /ˌsʌbkatəˈlædʒənəs/, *adj. Anat., Zool.* **1.** partially or incompletely cartilaginous. **2.** situated below or beneath cartilage.

**subcategory** /sʌbˈkætəgri/, *n.* a subordinate category.

**subcelestial** /sʌbsəˈlɛstiəl/, *adj.* **1.** being beneath, the heavens; mundane. –*n.* **2.** a subcelestial being.

**subcellar** /ˈsʌbsɛlə/, *n.* a cellar beneath another cellar.

**subclass** /ˈsʌbklas/, *n.* **1.** a primary division of a class. **2.** a category of related orders within a class. –*v.t.* **3.** to place in a subclass.

**subclavian** /sʌbˈkleɪviən/, *Anat.* –*adj.* **1.** situated or extending beneath the clavicle, as certain arteries, veins, etc. **2.** pertaining to such an artery, vein, or the like. –*n.* **3.** a subclavian artery, vein, or the like. [NL *subclāvius* (from L *sub-* SUB- + *clāvis* key) + -AN]

**subclavian groove** /–ˈgruv/, *n.* either of two shallow depressions on the first rib, one for the subclavian artery and the other for the subclavian vein.

**subclimax** /sʌbˈklaɪmæks/, *n. Ecol.* the imperfect development of a climax community because of some factor (such as repeated fires in a forest) which arrests the normal succession.

**subclinical** /sʌbˈklɪnɪkəl/, *adj.* of or pertaining to a disease whose symptoms are so mild that they remain undetected in usual clinical examinations.

**subcommittee** /ˈsʌbkəˌmɪti/, *n.* a secondary committee appointed out of a main committee.

**subconscious** /sʌbˈkɒnʃəs/, *adj.* **1.** existing or operating beneath or beyond consciousness: *the subconscious self.* **2.** imperfectly or not wholly conscious. –*n.* **3.** the totality of mental processes of which the individual is not aware; unreportable mental activities. – **subconsciously,** *adv.* – **subconsciousness,** *n.*

**subcontinent** /sʌbˈkɒntənənt/, *n.* a large land mass, smaller than a continent: *the Indian subcontinent.*

**subcontract** /sʌbˈkɒntrækt/, *n.;* /sʌbkənˈtrækt/, *v. Law.* –*n.* **1.** a contract by which one agrees to render services or to provide materials necessary for the performance of another contract. –*v.t.* **2.** to make a subcontract for. –*v.i.* **3.** to make a subcontract.

**subcontractor** /sʌbˈkɒntræktə, sʌbkənˈtræktə/, *n.* one who contracts to render some performance for another which the latter requires for the performance of his own contract.

**subcontrary** /sʌbˈkɒntrəri/, *Logic.* –*adj.* **1.** pertaining to the relation between any two propositions, both of which may be true, but only one of which can be false. –*n.* **2.** any such proposition.

**subcortex** /sʌb'kɔtɛks/, *n., pl.* **-tices** /-təsiz/. the portions of the brain situated beneath the cerebral cortex.

**subcortical** /sʌb'kɔtɪkəl/, *adj.* situated beneath the cerebral cortex.

**subcritical** /sʌb'krɪtɪkəl/, *adj.* denoting or pertaining to a nuclear reaction or a nuclear reactor in which the chain-reaction is not self-sustaining. Cf. **supercritical.**

**subculture** /'sʌbkʌltʃə/, *v.,* **-tured, -turing,** *n.* *–v.t.* **1.** *Bacteriol.* to cultivate (a bacterial strain) again on a new medium. *–n.* **2.** *Bacteriol.* a culture derived in this way. **3.** *Sociol.* a distinct network of behaviour, beliefs and attitudes existing within a larger culture.

**subcutaneous** /sʌbkju'teɪniəs/, *adj.* **1.** situated or lying under the skin, as tissue. **2.** performed or introduced under the skin, as an injection by a syringe. **3.** living below the several layers of the skin, as certain parasites. – **subcutaneously,** *adv.*

**subdeacon** /sʌb'dikən/, *n.* a member of the clerical order next below that of deacon. – **subdeaconate,** *n.*

**subdean** /sʌb'din/, *n.* an assistant dean. – **subdeanery** /sʌb'dinəri/, *n.*

**subdelirium** /sʌbdə'lɪəriəm/, *n., pl.* **-liriums, -liria** /-'lɪəriə/. a mild or intermittent delirium.

**subdiaconal** /sʌbdaɪ'ækənəl/, *adj.* of or pertaining to a subdeacon.

**subdiaconate** /sʌbdaɪ'ækənət/, *n.* **1.** the office or dignity of a subdeacon. **2.** a body of subdeacons.

**subdistrict** /'sʌb,dɪstrɪkt/, *n.* a division of a district.

**subdivide** /'sʌbdəvaɪd, sʌbdə'vaɪd/, *v.,* **-vided, -viding.** *–v.t.* **1.** to divide (a part, or an already divided whole) into smaller parts; divide anew after a first division. **2.** to divide into parts. *–v.i.* **3.** to become separated into subdivisions. – **subdivider,** *n.*

**subdivision** /'sʌbdəvɪʒən/, *n.* **1.** the act or process of subdividing, or the fact of being subdivided. **2.** an instance of this. **3.** one of the parts into which something is subdivided. **4.** (of land) an area of land divided into lots for specified development: *urban subdivision; rural subdivision.* **5.** *Agric.* a fence on a property other than a boundary fence. **6.** *Naut.* the separation of the hull of a ship into compartments by water-tight bulkheads to ensure that flooding of one compartment resulting from damage does not enter adjacent spaces.

**subdominant** /sʌb'dɒmənənt/, *n.* the fourth note of a scale, next below the dominant.

**subdual** /səb'djuəl/, *n.* **1.** the act of subduing. **2.** the state of being subdued.

**subduct** /səb'dʌkt/, *v.t. Rare.* to take away or withdraw; deduct. – **subduction** /səb'dʌkʃən/, *n.*

**subdue** /səb'dju/, *v.t.,* **-dued, -duing.** **1.** to conquer and bring into subjection. **2.** to overpower by superior force; overcome. **3.** to bring into mental subjection, as by persuasion or by inspiring awe or fear; render submissive. **4.** to repress (feelings, impulses, etc.). **5.** to bring (land) under cultivation. **6.** to reduce the intensity, force, or vividness of (sound, light, colour, etc.); tone down; soften. **7.** to allay (inflammation, etc.). [ME, through AF, from OF *so(u)duire* seduce, from L *subdūcere* remove by stealth; sense development in AF affected by L *subdere* (subdue)] – **subduable,** *adj.* – **subduedly,** *adv.* – **subduedness, subduer,** *n.*

**subdued** /səb'djud/, *adj.* **1.** quiet; gentle; cowed; inhibited. **2.** (of colours, etc.) not harsh; reduced in intensity; muted.

**subedit** /sʌb'ɛdət/, *v.t.* (in journalism) to edit and correct (material written by others). *–v.i.* **1.** to act as a subeditor.

**subeditor** /sʌb'ɛdətə/, *n.* **1.** *Journalism.* one who edits and corrects material written by others. **2.** an assistant or subordinate editor. – **subeditorial** /,sʌbɛdə'tɔriəl/, *adj.* – **subeditorship,** *n.*

**subereous** /su'bɪəriəs/, *adj.* of the nature of or resembling cork; suberose. [L *sūbereus*]

**suberic** /su'bɛrɪk/, *adj.* of or pertaining to cork. [F *suberique,* from L *sūber* cork + *-ique* -IC]

**suberic acid** /– 'æsəd/, *n.* a crystalline dibasic acid, $(CH_2)_6(COOH)_2$, derived from cork.

**suberin** /'subərən/, *n.* a substance contained in and characteristic of cork tissue.

**suberisation** /subəraɪ'zeɪʃən/, *n.* the impregnation of cell walls with suberin, causing the formation of cork. Also, **suberization.**

**suberise** /'subəraɪz/, *v.t.,* **-rised, -rising.** to change into cork tissue. Also, **suberize.** [L *sūber* cork + -ISE]

**suberose** /'subərous/, *adj.* of the nature of cork; cork-like; corky. Also, **suberous** /'subərəs/.

**subfamily** /'sʌbfæmli/, *n., pl.* **-lies.** **1.** *Biol.* a category of related genera within a family. **2.** *Linguistics.* (in the classification of languages) a category of a lower order than a family.

**subfebrile** /sʌb'fɛbraɪl, -'fi-/, *adj.* of or denoting a condition in which the temperature is slightly above normal.

**subfusc** /'sʌbfʌsk/, *adj.* **1.** of sombre hue; dusky; somewhat dark. *–n.* **2.** clothes of a dark or drab colour. [L *subfuscus,* equivalent to *sub-* SUB- + *fuscus* dark]

**subgenus** /'sʌb,dʒinəs/, *n., pl.* **-genera** /-,dʒɛnərə/, **-genuses.** a subordinate genus; a subdivision of a genus. – **subgeneric** /sʌbdʒə'nɛrɪk/, *adj.*

**subglacial** /sʌb'gleɪʃəl, -'gleɪsiəl/, *adj.* **1.** beneath a glacier: *a subglacial stream.* **2.** formerly beneath a glacier: *a subglacial deposit.* – **subglacially,** *adv.*

**subglottal** /sʌb'glɒtl/, *adj.* below the glottis; tracheal.

**subgroup** /'sʌbgrup/, *n.* **1.** a subordinate group; a division of a group. **2.** *Chem.* a vertical division of a group in the periodic table; family.

**subheading** /'sʌbhɛdɪŋ/, *n.* **1.** a title or heading of a subdivision or subsection in a chapter, treatise, essay, newspaper article, etc. **2.** a subordinate division of a heading or title. Also, **subhead.**

**subhuman** /sʌb'hjumən/, *adj.* **1.** below the human race or type; less than or not quite human. **2.** almost human.

**subhumid** /sʌb'hjuməd/, *adj.* (of regions of the earth) having appreciable amounts of water, esp. as water vapour in the air, but less than in humid regions.

**subincision** /sʌbɪn'sɪʒən/, *n.* the making of an incision of the urethra through the underside of the penis, a custom traditionally performed by the Aboriginals and in some other pre-literate societies.

**subindex** /sʌb'ɪndɛks/, *n., pl.* **-dices** /-dəsiz/, **-dexes.** →**subscript** (def. 4).

**subirrigate** /sʌb'ɪrəgeɪt/, *v.t.,* **-gated, -gating.** to irrigate beneath the surface of the ground, as with water passing through a system of underground pipes or transmitted through the subsoil from ditches, etc. – **subirrigation** /sʌbɪrə'geɪʃən/, *n.*

**subito** /'subitou/, *adv.* (in music) suddenly; abruptly: *f. subito, p. subito.* [It., from L, abl. of *subitus* sudden]

**subj.,** **1.** subject. **2.** subjective. **3.** subjunctive.

**subjacent** /sʌb'dʒeɪsənt/, *adj.* **1.** situated or occurring underneath or below; underlying. **2.** forming a basis. **3.** being in a lower situation, though not directly beneath. [L *subjacens,* ppr., lying under] – **subjacency,** *n.*

**subject** /'sʌbdʒɛkt/, *n., adj.;* /səb'dʒɛkt/, *v.* *–n.* **1.** something that forms a matter of thought, discourse, investigation, etc.: *a subject of conversation.* **2.** a branch of knowledge organised into a system so as to form a suitable course of study. **3.** a ground, motive, or cause: *a subject for complaint.* **4.** the theme of a sermon, book, story, etc. **5.** a theme or melodic phrase on which a musical work or movement is based. **6.** an object, scene, incident, or the like, chosen by an artist for representation, or as represented in art. **7.** one who is under the dominion or rule of a sovereign. **8.** one who owes allegiance to a government and lives under its protection: *a Swedish subject.* **9.** such people collectively. **10.** *Gram.* (in English and many other languages) the word or words of a sentence which represent the person or object performing the action expressed in the predicate, as, *he* in *he raised his hat.* **11.** one who or that which undergoes, or may undergo, some action. **12.** one who or that which is under the control or influence of another. **13.** a person as an object of medical, surgical, or psychological treatment or experiment. **14.** a dead body as used for dissection. **15.** *Logic.* that part of a proposition of which the predicate is asserted or denied. **16.** *Philos.* **a.** the substance in which attributes inhere. **b.** substance; external reality as distinguished from its appearance;

that which is the object of reference in predication. **c.** the self or ego to which all experiences or mental operations are attributed. *–adj.* **17.** being under domination, control, or influence (oft. fol. by *to*). **18.** being under dominion, rule, or authority, as of a sovereign or a state, or some governing power; owing allegiance or obedience (*to*). **19.** open or exposed (fol. by *to*): *subject to ridicule.* **20.** being dependent or conditional upon something (fol. by *to*): *his consent is subject to your approval.* **21.** being under the necessity of undergoing something (fol. by *to*): *all men are subject to death.* **22.** liable, as to something (esp. something undesirable) that may or often does befall (fol. by *to*): *subject to headaches.* *–v.t.* **23.** to bring under domination, control, or influence (usu. fol. by *to*). **24.** to bring under dominion, rule, or authority, as of a conqueror or a governing power (usu. fol. by *to*). **25.** to cause to undergo or experience something (fol. by *to*): *to subject metal to a white heat.* **26.** to make liable, lay open, or expose (fol. by *to*): *to subject oneself to ridicule.* [L *subjectus,* pp., placed under; replacing ME *suget,* from OF]

**subject catalogue** /'– ˌkætəlɒg/, *n.* (in libraries) a catalogue with entries listed by subject only.

**subjectify** /səb'dʒɛktəfaɪ/, *v.t.,* **-fied, -fying.** **1.** to make subjective. **2.** to identify with (a subject); interpret in a subjective manner. – **subjectification** /səbdʒɛktəfə'keɪʃən/, *n.*

**subjection** /səb'dʒɛkʃən/, *n.* **1.** the act of subjecting. **2.** the state or fact of being subjected.

**subjective** /səb'dʒɛktɪv/, *adj.* **1.** existing in the mind; belonging to the thinking subject rather than to the object of thought (opposed to *objective*). **2.** pertaining to or characteristic of an individual thinking subject; personal; individual: *subjective poetry.* **3.** belonging to the thinking subject rather than to the object of thought. **4.** introspective. **5.** relating to or of the nature of a subject as it is known in the mind as distinct from a thing in itself. **6.** relating to properties or specific conditions of the mind as distinct from general or universal experience. **7.** pertaining to the subject or substance in which attributes inhere; essential. **8.** *Gram.* **a.** pertaining to or constituting the subject of a sentence. **b.** (in English and some other languages) denoting a case specialised for that use: in *he hit the ball, he* is in the subjective case. **c.** similar to such a case in meaning. **9.** *Philos.* **a.** of or pertaining to thought, as opposed to an object of thought. **b.** descriptive of a philosophy that regards thought as real and substantial. **10.** *Obs.* pertaining to or befitting one who is subject to dominion, rule, or control. – **subjectively,** *adv.* – **subjectivity** /sʌbdʒɛk'tɪvəti/, **subjectiveness,** *n.*

**subjectivism** /səb'dʒɛktəvɪzəm/, *n.* **1.** the philosophical theory that one mind can know nothing but itself and its characteristics. (See **idealism**, def. 5a). **2.** any epistemological theory that attaches preponderating importance to the subjective factor of knowledge. **3.** the ethical theory that the rightness or wrongness of an action depends upon the mental state of a particular person. **4.** any theological theory that attaches preponderating importance to religious experience as opposed to revelation or historical evidence. **5.** subjectivity. – **subjectivist,** *n.* – **subjectivistic** /səbdʒɛktə'vɪstɪk/, *adj.*

**subject matter** /'sʌbdʒɛkt mætə/, *n.* **1.** the substance of a discourse, book, writing, or the like, as distinguished from its form or style. **2.** the matter which is subject to some action or operation. **3.** the matter out of which a thing is formed.

**subjoin** /sʌb'dʒɔɪn, səb-/, *v.t.* **1.** to add at the end, as of something said or written; append. **2.** to place in sequence or juxtaposition to something else.

**sub judice** /sʌb 'dʒudəsi/, *adv.* before a judge or court of law; under judicial consideration. [L]

**subjugate** /'sʌbdʒəgeɪt/, *v.t.,* **-gated, -gating.** **1.** to bring under complete control or into subjection; subdue; conquer. **2.** to make submissive or subservient. [L *subjugātus,* pp., brought under the yoke] – **subjugation** /sʌbdʒə'geɪʃən/, *n.* – **subjugator,** *n.*

**subjunction** /səb'dʒʌŋkʃən/, *n.* **1.** the act of subjoining. **2.** the state of being subjoined. **3.** something subjoined.

**subjunctive** /səb'dʒʌŋktɪv/, *Gram. –adj.* **1.** (in many languages) designating or pertaining to a verb mood having among its functions the expression of contingent or hypothetical action. For example, in the sentence *Were I but king, things would alter,* the verb *were* is in the subjunctive mood. Cf. **indicative.** *–n.* **2.** the subjunctive mood. **3.** a verb in the subjunctive mood, as *be* in *if it be true.* [LL *subjunctīvus,* from L *subjunctus,* pp., subjoined]

**subkingdom** /sʌb'kɪŋdəm/, *n.* →**phylum.**

**sublapsarianism** /sʌblæp'sɛəriənɪzəm/, *n.* →**infralapsarianism.** [NL *sublapsārius* (from L *sub-* SUB- + *lapsus* fall + *-ārius,* adj. suffix) + -AN + -ISM]

**sublate** /sʌb'leɪt/, *v.t.,* **-lated, -lating.** (in Hegelian philosophy) to set aside but not wholly to dispense with; supersede while retaining something of the nature of what is superseded. [L *sub-* SUB- + *latus,* pp., borne; translation of G *aufheben* as used by Hegel]

**sublease** /'sʌblis/, *n.;* /sʌb'lis/, *v.,* **-leased, -leasing.** *–n.* **1.** a lease granted by one who is himself a lessee of the property. *–v.t.* **2.** →**sublet.** – **sublessee** /sʌblɛ'si/, *n.* – **sublessor** /sʌblɛ'sɔ/, *n.*

**sublet** /sʌb'lɛt/, *v.t.,* **-let, -letting.** **1.** to let to another person, the party letting being himself a lessee. **2.** to let (work, etc.) under a subcontract.

**sublethal** /sʌb'liθəl/, *adj.* almost lethal or fatal.

**sublieutenant** /sʌblɛf'tɛnənt/, *n.* a naval officer ranking below a lieutenant. – **sublieutenancy,** *n.*

**sublimate** /'sʌbləmeɪt/, *v.,* **-mated, -mating;** /'sʌbləmət/, *n., adj.* *–v.t.* **1.** *Psychol.* to deflect (sexual or other biological energies) into socially constructive or creative channels. **2.** *Chem., etc.* **a.** to sublime (a solid substance); extract by this process. **b.** to refine or purify (a substance). **3.** to make nobler or purer. *–v.i.* **4.** to become sublimated; undergo sublimation. *–n.* **5.** *Chem.* the crystals, deposit, or material obtained when a substance is sublimated; esp. corrosive sublimate. *–adj.* **6.** sublimated. [L *sublīmātus,* pp., elevated] – **sublimation** /sʌblə'meɪʃən/, *n.*

**sublime** /sə'blaɪm/, *adj., n., v.,* **-limed, -liming.** *–adj.* **1.** elevated or lofty in thought, language, etc.: *sublime poetry.* **2.** impressing the mind with a sense of grandeur or power; inspiring awe, veneration, etc.: *sublime scenery.* **3.** supreme or perfect: *a sublime moment.* **4.** *Poetic.* of lofty bearing. **5.** *Poetic.* haughty or proud. **6.** *Archaic.* raised aloft. *–n.* **7.** that which is sublime: *the sublime in art.* **8.** the highest degree or example (fol. by *of*). *–v.t.* **9.** to make higher, nobler, or purer. **10.** *Chem., etc.* to convert (a solid substance) by heat into a vapour, which on cooling condenses again to solid form, without apparent liquefaction. **11.** *Chem., etc.* to cause to be given off by this or some analogous process. *–v.i.* **12.** *Chem., etc.* to volatilise from the solid state to a gas, and then condense again as a solid without passing through the liquid state. [ME, from L *sublīmāre* elevate, from *sublīmis,* adj., lofty] – **sublimely,** *adv.* – **sublimeness,** *n.*

**subliminal** /sə'blɪmənəl/, *adj.* (of stimuli, etc.) being or operating below the threshold of consciousness or perception; subconscious: *subliminal advertising.* – **subliminally,** *adv.*

**sublimity** /sə'blɪməti/, *n., pl.* **-ties.** **1.** the state or quality of being sublime. **2.** a sublime person or thing.

**sublingual** /sʌb'lɪŋgwəl/, *Anat. –adj.* **1.** situated under the tongue, or on the underside of the tongue. *–n.* **2.** a sublingual gland, artery, or the like.

**sublunary** /sʌb'lunəri/, *adj.* **1.** situated beneath the moon. **2.** of, on, or being the earth; terrestrial. **3.** mundane or worldly. Also, **sublunar** /sʌb'lunə/.

**subluxate** /sʌb'lʌkseɪt/, *v.t.,* **-ated, -ating.** to dislocate partially. [backformation from SUBLUXATION]

**subluxation** /sʌblʌk'seɪʃən/, *n.* a partial dislocation; sprain. [NL *subluxatio,* from L *sub-* under, away + *luxāre* dislocate]

**submachine gun** /sʌbmə'ʃin gʌn/, *n.* a lightweight automatic or semiautomatic gun, fired from the shoulder or hip.

**subman** /'sʌbmæn/, *n., pl.* **-men.** a man of very low mental or physical capacity.

**submarginal** /sʌb'madʒənəl/, *adj.* **1.** *Biol.* near the margin. **2.** below the margin. **3.** not worth cultivating, as land; unproductive. – **submarginally,** *adv.*

**submarine** /'sʌbmərin, sʌbmə'rin/, *n.* **1.** a type of vessel that can be submerged and navigated under water, esp. one used in warfare for the discharge of torpedoes, guided missiles, etc. **2.** something submarine, as a plant,

submarine

animal, etc. **3.** a long, thin bread roll with elaborate salad-type fillings. *–adj.* **4.** situated, occurring, operating, or living under the surface of the sea. **5.** of, pertaining to, or carried on by submarine ships: *submarine warfare.* – **submariner** /sʌbˈmærənə/, *n.*

**submaxilla** /sʌbmækˈsɪlə/, *n., pl.* **-maxillae** /-mækˈsɪli/. *Anat., Zool.* the lower jaw or lower jawbone.

**submaxillary** /sʌbmækˈsɪləri/, *adj.* of or pertaining to the lower jaw or lower jawbone.

**submaxillary gland** /– ˈglænd/, *n.* either of two saliva-producing glands beneath the lower jaw, one on each side.

**submediant** /sʌbˈmidiənt/, *n.* the sixth note of a musical scale, being midway between the subdominant and the upper tonic.

**submerge** /səbˈmɜdʒ/, *v.,* **-merged, -merging.** *–v.t.* **1.** to put under water; plunge below the surface of water or any enveloping medium. **2.** to cover with or as water; immerse. *–v.i.* **3.** to sink or plunge under water, or beneath the surface of any enveloping medium. [L *submergere*] – **submergence,** *n.*

**submerged** /səbˈmɜdʒd/, *adj.* **1.** under the surface of water or any other enveloping medium. **2.** hidden or obscured. **3.** overwhelmed by circumstances, etc.

**submergible** /səbˈmɜdʒəbəl/, *adj., n.,* →**submersible.** – **submergibility** /səbmɜdʒəˈbɪləti/, *n.*

**submerse** /səbˈmɜs/, *v.t.,* **-mersed, -mersing.** →**submerge.** [L *submersus,* pp., submerged] – **submersion** /səbˈmɜʒən/, *n.*

**submersed** /səbˈmɜst/, *adj.* **1.** submerged. **2.** (of a plant) growing under water.

**submersible** /səbˈmɜsəbəl/, *adj.* **1.** that may be submersed. *–n.* **2.** (formerly) a submarine.

**submicroscopic** /ˌsʌbmaɪkrəˈskɒpɪk/, *adj.* smaller than can be seen through a microscope.

**submission** /səbˈmɪʃən/, *n.* **1.** the act of submitting. **2.** the condition of having submitted. **3.** submissive conduct or attitude. **4.** that which is submitted. **5.** *Law.* an agreement to abide by a decision or obey an authority in some matter referred to arbitration. **6.** *Wrestling.* inability to stand an opponent's hold. In professional wrestling, the first contestant to win the best of three pinfalls or submissions is declared the winner. [ME, from L *submissio*]

**submissive** /səbˈmɪsɪv/, *adj.* **1.** inclined or ready to submit; unresistingly or humbly obedient. **2.** marked by or indicating submission: *a submissive reply.* – **submissively,** *adv.* – **submissiveness,** *n.*

**submit** /səbˈmɪt/, *v.,* **-mitted, -mitting.** *–v.t.* **1.** to yield in surrender, compliance, or obedience. **2.** to subject (esp. oneself) to conditions imposed, treatment, etc. **3.** to refer to the decision or judgment of another or others. **4.** to state or urge with deference (usu. fol. by a clause): *I submit that full proof should be required.* *–v.i.* **5.** to yield in surrender, compliance, or obedience: *to submit to a conqueror.* **6.** to allow oneself to be subjected to something imposed or to be undergone: *to submit to punishment.* **7.** to defer to the opinion, judgment, etc., of another. [ME *submitte,* from L *submittere* lower, put under] – **submittable, submissible** /səbˈmɪsəbəl/, *adj.* – **submittal,** *n.* – **submitter,** *n.*

**submontane** /sʌbˈmɒnteɪn/, *adj.* **1.** under or beneath a mountain or mountains. **2.** at or near the foot of mountains. **3.** pertaining to the lower slopes of mountains. – **submontanely,** *adv.*

**submultiple** /sʌbˈmʌltəpəl/, *n.* **1.** a number which is contained within another an exact number of times without a remainder. *–adj.* **2.** pertaining to or denoting a number that is a submultiple.

**subnormal** /sʌbˈnɔməl/, *adj.* **1.** below the normal; less than or inferior to the normal. **2.** lacking in one or more important psychological traits, as intelligence, personality, etc. *–n.* **3.** a subnormal person. – **subnormality** /ˌsʌbnɔˈmæləti/, *n.*

**suboceanic** /ˌsʌboʊʃiˈænɪk/, *adj.* beneath the ocean.

**suborbital** /sʌbˈɔbətl/, *adj.* **1.** *Anat.* lying below the orbit of the eye. **2.** (of a spacecraft, etc.) not in orbit.

**suborder** /sʌbˈɔdə/, *n.* a group of related plants or animals ranking above a family and below an order.

**subordinal** /sʌbˈɔdənəl/, *adj.* of, pertaining to, or ranked as a suborder.

**subordinate** /səˈbɔdənət/, *adj., n.;* /səˈbɔdəneɪt/, *v.,* **-nated, -nating.** *–adj.* **1.** placed in or belonging to a lower order or rank. **2.** of lesser importance; secondary. **3.** subject to or under the authority of a superior. **4.** subservient. **5.** dependent. **6.** *Gram.* **a.** denoting or pertaining to a subordinate clause or other dependent phrase. **b.** denoting or pertaining to a subordinating conjunction. **7.** *Obs.* submissive. *–n.* **8.** a subordinate person or thing. *–v.t.* **9.** to place in a lower order or rank. **10.** to make secondary (fol. by *to*). **11.** to make subject, subservient, or dependent (fol. by *to*). [late ME, from ML *subordinātus,* pp., subordinated] – **subordination** /səbɔdəˈneɪʃən/, *n.* – **subordinately,** *adv.* – **subordinative,** *adj.*

**subordinate clause** /– ˈklɔz/, *n.* (in grammar) a clause that modifies and is dependent upon a main clause, as *'when I came'* in the sentence *'They were glad when I came'.*

**subordinate set** /ˈ– sɛt/, *n.* →**subset.**

**subordinating conjunction** /səˌbɔdəneɪtɪŋ kənˈdʒʌŋkʃən/, *n.* a conjunction introducing a subordinate clause, as *'when'* in *'They were glad when I came'.*

**subordinationism** /səbɔdəˈneɪʃənɪzəm/, *n.* the doctrine that the first person of the Holy Trinity is superior to the second and the third. – **subordinationist,** *adj.*

**suborn** /səˈbɔn/, *v.t.* to bribe or procure (a person) to commit some unlawful or wrongful act, usu. perjury. [L *subornāre* equip secretly] – **subornation** /ˌsʌbɔˈneɪʃən/, *n.* – **subornative,** *adj.* – **suborner,** *n.*

**suboxide** /sʌbˈɒksaɪd/, *n.* the oxide of an element containing the smallest proportion of oxygen.

**subphylum** /sʌbˈfaɪləm/, *n., pl.* **-la** /-lə/. a category in biological classification ranking below a phylum.

**subplot** /ˈsʌbplɒt/, *n.* a secondary plot in a play, novel, etc., as distinct from the main plot.

**subpoena** /səˈpinə/, *n., v.,* **-naed, -naing.** *Law.* *–n.* **1.** the usual writ process for the summoning of witnesses. *–v.t.* **2.** to serve with a subpoena. [ME, from L *sub poenā* under penalty, the first words of the writ]

**subpolar** /sʌbˈpoʊlə/, *adj.* **1.** →**subantarctic. 2.** →**subarctic.**

**subprincipal** /sʌbˈprɪnsəpəl/, *n.* **1.** an assistant or deputy principal. **2.** *Carp.* an auxiliary rafter or additional supporting member. **3.** *Music.* (in an organ) a sub-bass of the open diapason class.

**subregion** /ˈsʌbridʒən/, *n.* a division or subdivision of a region, esp. a division of a zoogeographical region. – **subregional,** *adj.*

**subreption** /səbˈrɛpʃən/, *n.* **1.** the act of obtaining something, as an ecclesiastical dispensation, by suppression or fraudulent concealment of facts. **2.** a fallacious representation, or an inference from it. [L *subreptio* theft] – **subreptitious** /sʌbrɛpˈtɪʃəs/, *adj.*

**subrogate** /ˈsʌbrəgeɪt/, *v.t.,* **-gated, -gating.** **1.** to put into the place of another; substitute for another. **2.** *Civil. Law.* to substitute a claim against one person for a claim against another person, or transfer a lien originally imposed on one piece of property to another piece of property. [L *subrogātus,* pp., put in another's place] – **subrogation** /sʌbrəˈgeɪʃən/, *n.*

**sub rosa** /sʌb ˈroʊzə/, *adv.* confidentially; privately. [L: under the rose; the rose being the symbol of the Egyptian god Horus, identified by the Greeks with Harpocrates, god of silence]

**subroutine** /ˈsʌbrutin/, *n.* (in computers) a routine used by a computer program to perform some function necessary to carry out the program.

**subscapular** /sʌbˈskæpjələ/, *adj.* **1.** beneath, or on the deep surface of, the scapula, as a muscle, artery, etc. *–n.* **2.** a subscapular muscle, artery, etc.

**subscribe** /səbˈskraɪb/, *v.,* **-scribed, -scribing.** *–v.t.* **1.** to promise, as by signing an agreement, to give or pay (a sum of money) as a contribution, payment, share, etc. **2.** to give or pay in fulfilment of such a promise. **3.** to express assent or adhesion to (a contract, etc.) by signing one's name; attest by signing, as a statement or a will. **4.** to write or inscribe (something) beneath or at the end of a thing; sign (one's name) to a document, etc. *–v.i.* **5.** to undertake, as by signing an agreement, to give or pay money for some special purpose. **6.** to obtain a subscription to a magazine, newspaper, etc. **7.** to give or pay money as a contribution, payment, etc. **8.** to sign one's name to something. **9.** to assent by, or as by, signing one's name. **10.** to give consent or sanction. [ME, from L *subscrībere*]

**subscriber** /səb'skraɪbə/, *n.* **1.** one who subscribes, esp. to a magazine. **2.** one who rents telephone equipment for use through an exchange.

**subscriber trunk dialling,** *n.* a system for making trunk calls in which the subscriber dials the required number himself. *Abbrev.:* STD

**subscript** /'sʌbskrɪpt/, *adj.* **1.** written below (distinguished from *adscript*). **2.** placed low on the line, as the '2' in '$H_2O$'. *–n.* **3.** something written below. **4.** a specifying or distinguishing figure or letter following and slightly below a figure, letter or symbol, as 'x' in '$B_x$'. [L *subscriptus,* pp.]

**subscription** /səb'skrɪpʃən/, *n.* **1.** a monetary contribution towards some object or a payment for shares, a book, a periodical, etc. **2.** the right to receive a periodical for a sum subscribed. **3.** the dues paid by a member of a club, society, etc. **4.** a fund raised through sums of money subscribed. **5.** a sum subscribed. **6.** the act of subscribing; the signing of one's name, as to a document. **7.** something written beneath or at the end of a thing. **8.** a signature attached to a paper. **9.** assent, agreement, or approval expressed by, or as by, signing one's name. **10.** *Eccles.* assent to or acceptance of a body of principles or doctrines, the purpose of which is to establish uniformity. [late ME, from L *subscriptio*] – **subscriptive** /səb'skrɪptɪv/, *adj.* – **subscriptively,** *adv.*

**subscription concert** /'– kɒnsət/, *n.* one of a series of concerts for which a single ticket or subscription per person is issued for the entire series.

**subscription library** /'– ˌlaɪbri/, *n.* a commercially owned library which charges a fee for each book borrowed; circulating library.

**subsection** /'sʌbsɛkʃən/, *n.* **1.** a part or division of a section. **2.** a division within a section of an Aboriginal tribe with its own particular totem, as a hunting group.

**subsequence** /'sʌbsəkwəns/, *n.* **1.** the state or fact of being subsequent. **2.** that which is subsequent; sequel. **3.** *Maths.* a sequence whose elements belong to a given sequence.

**subsequent** /'sʌbsəkwənt/, *adj.* **1.** occurring or coming later or after: *subsequent events.* **2.** following in order or succession: *a subsequent section in a treaty.* [late ME, from L *subsequens,* ppr.] – **subsequently,** *adv.*

**subserve** /səb'sɜv/, *v.t.,* **-served, -serving.** to be useful or instrumental in promoting (a purpose, action, etc.). [L *subservīre*]

**subservient** /səb'sɜviənt/, *adj.* **1.** serving or acting in a subordinate capacity; subordinate. **2.** (of persons, their conduct, etc.) servile; excessively submissive; obsequious. **3.** of use as a means to promote a purpose or end. [L *subserviens,* ppr.] – **subservience, subserviency,** *n.* – **subserviently,** *adv.*

**subset** /'sʌbsɛt/, *n.* a set whose elements belong to a given set; a subordinate set.

**subside** /səb'saɪd/, *v.i.,* **-sided, -siding.** **1.** to sink to a low or lower level. **2.** to become quiet, less violent, or less active; abate: *the laughter subsided.* **3.** to sink or fall to the bottom; settle, as lees; precipitate. [L *subsīdere* settle down] – **subsidence** /səb'saɪdns, 'sʌbsədəns/, *n.* – **subsider,** *n.*

**subsidiary** /səb'sɪdʒəri/, *adj., n., pl.* **-ries.** *–adj.* **1.** serving to assist or supplement; auxiliary; supplementary; tributary, as a stream. **2.** subordinate or secondary. *–n.* **3.** a subsidiary thing or person. **4.** *Music.* a subordinate theme or subject. [L *subsidiārius* belonging to a reserve] – **subsidiarily,** *adv.*

**subsidiary company** /'– ˌkʌmpəni/, *n.* a company the controlling interest in which is owned by another company.

**subsidise** /'sʌbsədaɪz/, *v.t.,* **-dised, -dising.** **1.** to furnish or aid with a subsidy. **2.** to purchase the assistance of by the payment of a subsidy. **3.** to secure the cooperation of by bribery; buy over. Also, **subsidize.** [SUBSID(Y) + -ISE] – **subsidisation** /sʌbsədaɪ'zeɪʃən/, *n.* – **subsidiser,** *n.*

**subsidy** /'sʌbsədi/, *n., pl.* **-dies.** **1.** a direct pecuniary aid furnished by a government to a private industrial undertaking, a cultural organisation, or the like. **2.** a sum paid, often in accordance with a treaty, by one government to another, to secure some service in return. **3.** a grant or contribution of money.

**subsist** /səb'sɪst/, *v.i.* **1.** to exist, or continue in existence. **2.** to continue alive; live, as on food, resources, etc., esp. when these are limited. **3.** to have existence in, or by reason of, something. **4.** to reside, lie, or consist (fol. by *in*). **5.** *Philos.* **a.** to have existence of some kind or other. **b.** to possess the quality of truth and of amenability to thought and to logical construction. *–v.t.* **6.** to provide sustenance or support for; maintain. [L *subsistere* stand firm, be adequate to]

**subsistence** /səb'sɪstəns/, *n.* **1.** the state or fact of subsisting; continuance. **2.** the state or fact of existing. **3.** the providing of sustenance or support. **4.** means of supporting life; a living or livelihood. **5.** *Philos.* **a.** the process of substance assuming individualisation; a single autonomous human being with certain rights. **b.** the rank of something possessing the quality of truth and the ability of being construed logically.

**subsistence allowance** /'– əlaʊəns/, *n.* **1.** money paid in advance to an employee to enable him to supply his immediate needs, until his regular payday. **2.** money paid to an employee in addition to his salary to cover incidental expenses. **3.** money paid to members of the armed forces in lieu of meals; an allowance for food. Also, **subsistence money.**

**subsistence farming** /'– 'famɪŋ/, *n.* farming in which the produce is consumed by the farmer and his family leaving little or no surplus for marketing. Also, **subsistence agriculture.**

**subsistence level** /'– lɛvəl/, *n.* a standard of living just sufficient to maintain life.

**subsoil** /'sʌbsɔɪl/, *n.* **1.** the bed or stratum of earth or earthy material immediately under the surface soil. *–v.t., v.i.* **2.** to plough so as to break up part of the subsoil.

**subsolar** /sʌb'soʊlə/, *adj.* **1.** directly beneath the sun. **2.** between the tropics.

**subsonic** /sʌb'sɒnɪk/, *adj.* **1.** (of sound frequencies) below the audible limit. **2.** (of velocities) below the velocity of sound in the medium.

**subsp.,** subspecies.

**subspecies** /'sʌbspisiz/, *n., pl.* **-cies.** a subdivision of a species, esp. a geographical or ecological subdivision. – **subspecific** /sʌbspə'sɪfɪk/, *adj.*

**subst.,** substantive.

**subs' table** /'sʌbz ˌteɪbəl/, *n.* (in journalism) the desk at which news stories, etc., are edited and prepared for printing.

**substance** /'sʌbstəns/, *n.* **1.** that of which a thing consists; matter or material. **2.** a species of matter of definite chemical composition. **3.** the matter with which thought, discourse, study, or the like, is occupied; subject matter. **4.** the actual matter of a thing, as opposed to the appearance or shadow; reality. **5.** substantial or solid character or quality: *claims lacking in substance.* **6.** body: *soup without much substance.* **7.** the meaning or gist, as of speech or writing. **8.** something that has separate or independent existence. **9.** *Philos.* **a.** that which exists by itself, and in which accidents or attributes inhere; that which receives modifications, and is not itself a mode; that which is causally active; that which is more than an event. **b.** the essential part, or essence, of a thing. **c.** the thing as a continuing whole. **10.** possessions, means, or wealth: *to squander one's substance.* **11. in substance, a.** substantially. **b.** actually; really. [ME, from OF, from L *substantia*]

**substandard** /sʌb'stændəd/, *adj.* **1.** below standard; inadequate; inferior. **2.** denoting or pertaining to a dialect or a feature of usage differing from the standard language in such a way that the use is often considered uneducated or socially inferior.

**substantial** /səb'stænʃəl/, *adj.* **1.** of a corporeal or material nature; real or actual. **2.** of ample or considerable amount, quantity, size, etc.: *a substantial sum of money.* **3.** of solid character or quality; firm, stout, or strong. **4.** being such with respect to essentials: *two stories in substantial agreement.* **5.** wealthy or influential: *one of the substantial men of the town.* **6.** of real worth or value: *substantial reasons.* **7.** pertaining to the substance, matter, or material of a thing. **8.** of or pertaining to the essence of a thing; essential, material, or important. **9.** being a substance; having independent existence. **10.** *Philos.* pertaining to or of the nature of substance rather than accidents. *–n.* **11.** something substantial. [ME *substancial,* from LL *substantiālis*] – **substantiality** /səbstænʃi'æləti/, **substantialness,** *n.* – **substantially,** *adv.*

**substantialism** /səb'stænʃəlɪzəm/, *n.* the doctrine that there are substantial realities behind phenomena. – **substantialist,** *n.*

**substantiate** /səb'stænʃieɪt/, *v.t.,* **-ated, -ating. 1.** to establish by proof or competent evidence: *to substantiate a charge.* **2.** to give substantial existence to. **3.** to present as having substance. – **substantiation** /səbstænʃi'eɪʃən/, *n.* – **substantiative** /səb'stænʃiətɪv/, *adj.*

**substantive** /sʌb'stæntɪv, 'sʌbstəntɪv/, *n.* **1.** *Gram.* **a.** a noun. **b.** a noun, pronoun, or other word or phrase having nominal function in sentences or inflected like a noun. **c.** (in Latin and other languages where adjectives are inflected like nouns) a noun or adjective, as Latin *puella* 'girl' and *bona* 'good' in *puella bona est* 'the girl is good'. *–adj.* **2.** *Gram.* **a.** pertaining to substantives. **b.** used in a sentence like a noun: *a substantive adjective.* **c.** expressing existence: *'to be' is a substantive verb.* **3.** having independent existence; independent. **4.** belonging to the real nature or essential part of a thing; essential. **5.** real or actual. **6.** of considerable amount or quantity. **7.** *Law.* pertaining to the rules of right which courts are called on to apply, as distinguished from rules of procedure (opposed to *adjective*). **8.** *Dyeing.* (of colours) attaching directly to the material without the aid of a mordant or the like (opposed to *adjective*). [ME, from LL *substantīvus* standing by itself, from L *substantia* substance] – **substantival** /sʌbstən'taɪvəl/, *adj.* – **substantively** /sʌb'stæntɪvli/, *adv.* – **substantiveness** /sʌb'stæntɪvnəs/, *n.*

**substantive rank** /'– ræŋk/, *n.* a permanent rank in the forces, attained after a suitable length of service and usu. after successfully taking certain qualifying examinations.

**substation** /'sʌbsteɪʃən/, *n.* **1.** a subsidiary station. **2.** *Elect.* an installation in an electrical distribution system, between the generating station and the low-tension network, in which transformation, conversion, or switching takes place.

**substituent** /sʌb'stɪtʃuənt/, *n.* an atom or atomic group which takes the place of another atom or group present in the molecule of the original compound. [L *substituens,* ppr., substituting]

**substitute** /'sʌbstətjut/, *n., v.,* **-tuted, -tuting.** *–n.* **1.** a person or thing acting or serving in place of another. **2.** (formerly) one who, for a consideration, served in an army or navy in the place of a conscript. **3.** *Gram.* a word which under given conditions replaces any of a class of other words or constructions, as English *do* replacing verbs (I *know* but he *doesn't*). *–v.t.* **4.** to put (one person or thing) in the place of another. **5.** to take the place of; replace. *–v.i.* **6.** to act as substitute. **7.** *Chem.* to replace one or more elements or radicals in a compound by other elements or radicals. [ME, from L *substitūtus,* pp.] – **substitution** /sʌbstə'tjuʃən/, *n.* – **substitutional** /sʌbstə'tjuʃənəl/, **substitutionary** /sʌbstə'tjuʃənəri/, *adj.* – **substitutionally** /sʌbstə'tjuʃənli/, *adv.*

**substitutive** /'sʌbstətjutɪv/, *adj.* **1.** serving as, or capable of serving as, a substitute. **2.** pertaining to or involving substitution.

**substrate** /'sʌbstreɪt/, *n.* **1.** →**substratum.** (def. 2). **2.** *Biochem.* the substance acted upon by an enzyme.

**substratum** /sʌb'stratəm/, *n., pl.* **-strata** /-'stratə/. **1.** that which is spread or laid under something else; a stratum or layer lying under another. **2.** Also, **substrate.** something which underlies, or serves as a basis or foundation. **3.** *Agric.* →**subsoil. 4.** *Biol.* the base or material on which an organism lives. **5.** *Metaphys.* that which is regarded as supporting accidents or attributes; substance, as that in which qualities inhere. [NL: (neut. pp.) spread underneath] – **substrative,** *adj.*

**substruction** /sʌb'strʌkʃən/, *n.* a foundation or substructure. [L *substructio*] – **substructional,** *adj.*

**substructure** /'sʌbstrʌktʃə/, *n.* **1.** a structure forming the foundation of a building or the like. **2.** the foundations, piers, abutments, and other parts of a bridge upon which the superstructure rests. – **substructural,** *adj.*

**subsume** /səb'sjum/, *v.t.,* **-sumed, -suming. 1.** to consider (an idea, term, proposition, etc.) as part of a more comprehensive one. **2.** bring (a case, instance, etc.) under a rule. **3.** to take up into or include in a larger or higher class or a more inclusive classification. [NL *subsūmere,* from L *sub-* SUB- + *sūmere* take]

**subsumption** /səb'sʌmpʃən/, *n.* **1.** the act of subsuming. **2.** the state of being subsumed. **3.** that which is subsumed. **4.** a proposition subsumed under another. – **subsumptive** /səb'sʌmptɪv/, *adj.*

**subteen** /sʌb'tin/, *n. Colloq.* a young person approaching adolescence.

**subtemperate** /sʌb'tɛmpərət, -prət/, *adj.* pertaining to or occurring in the colder parts of the Temperate Zone.

**subtenant** /sʌb'tɛnənt/, *n.* one who rents land, a house, or the like from a tenant. – **subtenancy,** *n.*

**subtend** /səb'tɛnd/, *v.t.* **1.** *Geom., etc.* to extend under; be opposite to: *a chord subtending an arc.* **2.** *Bot.* (of a leaf, bract, etc.) to enclose or embrace in its axil. [L *subtendre* stretch under]

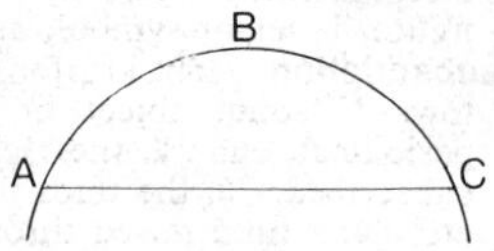

B

A C

chord AC subtends arc ABC

**subter-,** a prefix meaning 'position underneath', with figurative applications, as in *subterfuge.* [L, combining form of *subter,* prep. and adv.]

**subterfuge** /'sʌbtəfjudʒ/, *n.* an artifice or expedient employed to escape the force of an argument, to evade unfavourable consequences, hide something etc. [LL *subterfugium,* from L *subterfugere* flee secretly]

**subternatural** /sʌbtə'nætʃərəl, -'nætʃrəl/, *adj.* below what is natural; less than natural.

**subterranean** /sʌbtə'reɪniən/, *adj.* **1.** existing, situated, or operating below the surface of the earth; underground. **2.** existing or operating out of sight or secretly; hidden or secret. Also, **subterraneous.** [L *subterrāneus* below the earth + -AN]

**subterranean clover** /– 'kloʊvə/, *n.* a herbaceous pasture species, *Trifolium subterraneum,* with cream-coloured flowers and pods which ripen in the soil.

**subtilise** /'sʌtəlaɪz/, *v.,* **-lised, -lising.** *–v.t.* **1.** to elevate in character; sublimate. **2.** to render (the mind, senses, etc.) acute or keen. **3.** to make thin, rare, or more fluid or volatile; refine. *–v.i.* **4.** to make subtle distinctions; argue subtly. Also, **subtilize.** – **subtilisation** /ˌsʌtəlaɪ'zeɪʃən/, *n.*

**subtitle** /'sʌbtaɪtl/, *n.* **1.** a secondary or subordinate title of a literary work, usu. of explanatory character. **2.** a repetition of the leading words in the full title of a book at the head of the first page of text. **3.** *Films.* **a.** one of a series of captions projected on to the lower part of the screen which translate and summarise the dialogue of foreign language films. **b.** (in silent films) a title or caption usu. giving an explanation to a following scene. *–v.t.* **4.** to give a subtitle to.

**subtle** /'sʌtl/, *adj.* **1.** thin, tenuous, or rarefied, as a fluid, scent, etc. **2.** fine or delicate, often when likely to elude perception or understanding: *subtle irony.* **3.** delicate or faint and mysterious: *a subtle smile.* **4.** requiring mental acuteness, penetration, or discernment: *a subtle point.* **5.** characterised by mental acuteness or penetration: *a subtle understanding.* **6.** cunning, wily, or crafty. **7.** insidious in operation, as poison, etc. **8.** skilful, clever, or ingenious. [ME *sutell,* from OF *soutil,* from L *subtīlis* fine, delicate] – **subtleness,** *n.* – **subtly** /'sʌtli/, *adv.*

**subtlety** /'sʌtlti/, *n., pl.* **-ties. 1.** the state or quality of being subtle. **2.** delicacy or nicety of character or meaning; acuteness or penetration of mind; delicacy of discrimination. **3.** a fine-drawn distinction. **4.** something subtle.

**subtonic** /sʌb'tɒnɪk/, *n.* the seventh note of a musical scale, being the next below the upper tonic.

**subtopia** /sʌb'toʊpiə/, *n. Brit.* a partially built-up country area in which the use of standardised materials in building, street furniture, etc., has created the impression of a suburb and blurred the distinction between town and country. [SUB(URBAN) + (U)TOPIA]

**subtract** /səb'trækt/, *v.t.* **1.** to withdraw or take away, as a part from a whole. **2.** *Maths.* to take (one number or quantity) from another; deduct. *–v.i.* **3.** to take away something or a part, as from a whole. [L *subtractus,* pp., carried away] – **subtracter,** *n.*

**subtraction** /səb'trækʃən/, *n.* **1.** the act of subtracting. **2.** *Maths.* the operation of finding the difference between two numbers or quantities (denoted by the symbol −).

**subtractive** /səbˈtræktɪv/, *adj.* **1.** tending to subtract; having power to subtract. **2.** *Maths.* (of a quantity) that is to be subtracted; having the minus sign (−). **3. a.** (of a colour) reflecting light of a particular wavelength and absorbing (subtracting) other wavelengths. **b.** designating a process of colour photography which is based on the three colours magenta, blue-green, and yellow, which, when mixed, selectively absorb light.

**subtractive process** /ˈ– ˌprousɛs/, *n.* a process of colour photography in which the colours are formed by combinations of the subtractive colours.

**subtrahend** /ˈsʌbtrəhɛnd/, *n.* (in mathematics) the number or quantity to be taken from another (the minuend) in subtraction. [L *subtrahendus,* ger., to be subtracted]

**subtropical** /sʌbˈtrɒpɪkəl/, *adj.* **1.** bordering on the tropics; nearly tropical. **2.** pertaining to or occurring in a region intermediate between tropical and temperate.

**subtropics** /sʌbˈtrɒpɪks/, *n.pl.* subtropical regions.

**subtype** /ˈsʌbtaɪp/, *n.* **1.** a subordinate type. **2.** a special type included in a more general type.

**subulate** /ˈsʌbjələt, -leɪt/, *adj.* **1.** awl-shaped. **2.** *Bot., Zool., etc.* slender, more or less cylindrical, and tapering to a point. [NL *sūbulātus,* from L *sūbula* awl]

**sub-underwrite** /sʌb-ˈʌndəraɪt/, *v.t.,* **-wrote, -written, -writing.** *Econ.* to subcontract the obligation of an underwriter.

**sub-unit** /ˈsʌb-junət/, *n.* a military organisational unit smaller than the parent unit: *a platoon is a sub-unit of a company, a company is a sub-unit of a battalion.*

**suburb** /ˈsʌbɜb/, *n.* **1.** a district, usu. residential and to some degree remote from the business or administrative centre of a city or large town and enjoying its own facilities, as schools, shopping centres, railway stations. **2.** an outlying part. [ME *suburbe,* from L *suburbium*]

**suburban** /səˈbɜbən/, *adj.* **1.** pertaining to, inhabiting, or being in a suburb or the suburbs of a city or town. **2.** characteristic of a suburb or suburbs. **3.** narrow-minded; conventional in outlook. *–n.* **4.** →**suburbanite.**

**suburbanise** /səˈbɜbənaɪz/, *v.t.,* **-nised, -nising.** to make into a suburb; give suburban characteristics to. Also, **suburbanize.** – **suburbanisation** /səbɜbənaɪˈzeɪʃən/, *n.*

**suburbanite** /səˈbɜbənaɪt/, *n.* one who lives in the suburbs of a city or town.

**suburbia** /səˈbɜbiə/, *n.* **1.** the suburbs collectively esp. as they embody the middle range of community standards and values. **2.** suburban inhabitants collectively. **3.** the characteristic life of people in suburbs.

**suburbicarian** /səbɜbəˈkɛəriən/, *adj.* **1.** being near the city (of Rome). **2.** denoting or pertaining to any of the dioceses surrounding Rome, each of which is under the jurisdiction of a cardinal bishop. [LL *suburbicārius* suburban + -AN]

**subvention** /səbˈvɛnʃən/, *n.* **1.** a grant of pecuniary aid, esp. by a government or some other authority, in aid or support of some object, institution, or undertaking. **2.** the furnishing of aid or relief. [L *subventio,* from *subvenīre* come to the aid of] – **subventionary** /səbˈvɛnʃənəri/, *adj.*

**subversion** /səbˈvɜʒən/, *n.* **1.** the act of subverting; overthrow. **2.** the state of being subverted; destruction. **3.** that which subverts or overthrows. Also, **subversal** /səbˈvɜsəl/. [ME, from, LL *subversio*]

**subversive** /səbˈvɜsɪv/, *adj.* **1.** tending to subvert; such as to cause subversion. *–n.* **2.** one who adopts subversive principles or policies.

**subvert** /səbˈvɜt/, *v.t.* **1.** to overthrow (something established or existing). **2.** to cause the downfall, ruin, or destruction of. **3.** to undermine the principles of; corrupt. [ME, from L *subvertere*] – **subverter,** *n.*

**subway** /ˈsʌbweɪ/, *n.* **1.** an underground passage or tunnel enabling pedestrians to cross beneath a street, railway line, etc. **2.** *U.S.* an underground railway.

**suc-,** variant of **sub-** (by assimilation) before *c.*

**succeed** /səkˈsid/, *v.i.* **1.** to turn out or terminate according to desire; turn out successfully; have the desired result. **2.** to have (good or ill) success: *I have succeeded very badly.* **3.** to accomplish what is attempted or intended. **4.** to achieve success in a particular field; prosper. **5.** to follow or replace another by descent, election, appointment, etc. (oft. fol. by *to*). **6.** to come next after something else in an order or series. *–v.t.* **7.** to come after and take the place of, as in an office or estate. **8.** to come next after in an order or series, or in the course of events; follow. [ME *succede,* from L *succēdere* go up, be successful] – **succeeder,** *n.*

**succentor** /səkˈsɛntə/, *n.* a precentor's deputy. [LL, from L *succinere* accompany, sing to]

**success** /səkˈsɛs/, *n.* **1.** the favourable or prosperous termination of attempts or endeavours. **2.** the gaining of wealth, position, or the like. **3.** a successful performance or achievement. **4.** a thing or a person that is successful. [L *successus*]

**successful** /səkˈsɛsfəl/, *adj.* **1.** achieving or having achieved success. **2.** having succeeded in obtaining wealth, position, or the like. **3.** resulting in or attended with success. – **successfully,** *adv.*

**succession** /səkˈsɛʃən/, *n.* **1.** the coming of one after another in order, sequence, or the course of events; sequence. **2.** a number of persons or things following one another in order or sequence. **3.** the right, act or process, by which one person succeeds to the office, rank, estate or the like, of another. **4.** the order or line of those entitled to succeed. **5.** the descent or transmission, or the principle or mode of transmission, of a throne, dignity, estate, or the like. **6.** *Ecol.* the progressive replacement of one community by another in development towards climax vegetation. [ME, from L *successio*] – **successional,** *adj.* – **successionally,** *adv.*

**successive** /səkˈsɛsɪv/, *adj.* **1.** following in order or in uninterrupted course: *three successive days.* **2.** following another in a regular sequence: *the second successive day.* **3.** characterised by or involving succession. – **successively,** *adv.* – **successiveness,** *n.*

**successor** /səkˈsɛsə/, *n.* **1.** one who or that which succeeds or follows. **2.** one who succeeds another in an office, position, or the like. [L; replacing ME *successour,* from AF]

**succinate dehydrogenase** /ˌsʌkəneɪt dihaɪˈdrɒdʒəneɪz/, *n.* a key enzyme in the citric acid cycle catalysing the oxidation of succinic acid to fumaric acid.

**succinct** /səkˈsɪŋkt/, *adj.* **1.** expressed in few words; concise; terse. **2.** characterised by conciseness or verbal brevity. **3.** compressed into a small area or compass. **4.** *Archaic.* encircled, as by a girdle. [ME, from L *succinctus,* pp., girded up] – **succinctly,** *adv.* – **succinctness,** *n.*

**succinic** /sʌkˈsɪnɪk/, *adj.* **1.** pertaining to or obtained from amber. **2.** *Chem.* of or derived from succinic acid. [F *succinique,* from L *succinum* amber + *-ique* -IC]

**succinic acid** /– ˈæsəd/, *n.* a white crystalline soluble acid, $(CH_2)_2(COOH)_2$, which is found in nearly all cells as an intermediate in the citric acid cycle. It occurs naturally in amber and is manufactured synthetically and used in dyes, perfumes and lacquers.

**succory** /ˈsʌkəri/, *n., pl.* **-ries.** →**chicory.**

**succotash** /ˈsʌkətæʃ/, *n.* a dish of North American Indian origin, consisting of green maize and beans. [Algonquian *msiquatash*]

**succour** /ˈsʌkə/, *n.* **1.** help; relief; aid; assistance. **2.** one who or that which gives help, relief, aid, etc. *–v.t.* **3.** to help or relieve in difficulty, need, or distress; aid; assist. Also, *U.S.,* **succor.** [ME *sucurs,* from AF, OF, from *secourir* to help, from L *succurrere*] – **succourer,** *n.*

**succuba** /ˈsʌkjəbə/, *n., pl.* **-bae** /-bi/. →**succubus.**

**succubus** /ˈsʌkjəbəs/, *n., pl.* **-bi** /-baɪ/. **1.** a demon in female form fabled to have sexual intercourse with men in their sleep. **2.** any demon or evil spirit. [ME, from ML: masc. form of *succuba* strumpet]

**succulent** /ˈsʌkjələnt/, *adj.* **1.** full of juice; juicy. **2.** rich in desirable qualities. **3.** affording mental nourishment; not dry. **4.** (of plants, etc.) having fleshy and juicy tissues. *–n.* **5.** a fleshy or juicy plant, as a cactus. [L *succulentus*] – **succulence, succulency,** *n.* – **succulently,** *adv.*

**succumb** /səˈkʌm/, *v.i.* **1.** to give way to superior force; yield. **2.** to yield to disease, wounds, old age, etc.; die. [late ME, from L *succumbere*]

**succursal** /səˈkɜsəl/, *adj.* subsidiary; esp. denoting a religious establishment which is dependent upon a principal one. [F, from L *succursus* SUCCOUR]

**succuss** /sə'kʌs/, *v.t.* **1.** to shake up; shake. **2.** *Med.* to shake (a patient) in order to determine if a fluid is present in the thorax or elsewhere. [L *succussus*, pp., tossed up]

**succussion** /sə'kʌʃən/, *n.* the act or an instance of succussing. [L *succussio*] – **successive** /sə'kʌsɪv/, *adj.*

**such** /sʌtʃ/, *adj.* **1.** of the kind, character, degree, extent, etc., of that or those indicated or implied: *such a man is dangerous.* **2.** of that particular kind or character: *the food, such as it was, was plentiful.* **3.** like or similar: *tea, coffee, and such commodities.* **4.** (preceding an adjective used attributively) so, or in such a manner or degree: *such terrible deeds.* **5.** (with omission of an indication of comparison) of so extreme a kind; so great, good, bad, etc.: *he is such a liar.* **6.** being as stated or indicated: *such is the case.* **7.** being the person or thing, or the persons or things, indicated: *if any member be behind in his payments, such member shall be suspended.* **8.** Also, **such and such.** being definite or particular, but not named or specified: *it happened at such a time in such a town.* *–pron.* **9.** such a person or thing, or such persons or things. **10.** the person or thing, or the persons or things, indicated: *he claims to be a friend but is not such.* **11. as such, a.** as being what is indicated; in that capacity: *the leader, as such, is entitled to respect.* **b.** in itself or themselves: *wealth, as such, does not appeal to him.* **12. such as, a.** of the kind specified: *people such as these are not to be trusted.* **b.** for example: *he likes outdoor sports such as tennis and football.* [ME; OE *swulc*, var. of *swylc*, c. G *solch*]

**suchlike** /'sʌtʃlaɪk/, *adj.* **1.** of any such kind; similar. *–pron.* **2.** persons or things of such a kind.

**suck** /sʌk/, *v.t.* **1.** to draw into the mouth by action of the lips and tongue which produces a partial vacuum: *to suck lemonade through a straw.* **2.** to draw (water, moisture, air, etc.) by any process resembling this: *plants suck up moisture from the earth.* **3.** to apply the lips or mouth to, and draw upon by producing a partial vacuum, esp. for extracting fluid contents: *to suck an orange.* **4.** to apply the mouth to, or take into the mouth, and draw upon similarly, for some other purpose: *to suck one's thumb.* **5.** to take into the mouth and absorb by action of the tongue, etc.: *to suck a piece of toffee.* **6.** to render or bring (as specified) by or as by sucking. **7.** *Colloq.* to cause orgasm by oral stimulation of the genitalia (fol. by *off*). *–v.i.* **8.** to draw something in by producing a partial vacuum in the mouth, esp. to draw milk from the breast. **9.** to draw or be drawn by, or as by, suction. **10.** (of a pump) to draw air instead of water, as when the water is low or a valve is defective. **11. suck in,** to cheat; swindle; deceive; defraud. **12. suck up to,** to flatter; toady; fawn upon. *–n.* **13.** the act or instance of sucking with the mouth or otherwise. **14.** a sucking force. **15.** the sound produced by sucking. **16.** that which is sucked; nourishment drawn from the breast. **17.** *Colloq.* a small draught of liquid. [ME *soke, souke(n)*, OE *sūcan*, c. L *sūgere;* akin to OE *sūgan*, G *saugen*]

**sucker** /'sʌkə/, *n.* **1.** one who or that which sucks. **2.** an infant or a young animal that is suckled, esp. a suckling pig. **3.** a part or organ of an animal adapted for sucking nourishment, or for adhering to an object as by suction. **4.** any member of the cyprinoid family Catostomidae, comprising freshwater fishes which are mostly North American and often used as food. **5.** the piston of a pump which works by suction, or the valve of such a piston. **6.** a pipe or tube through which anything is drawn. **7.** *Colloq.* a person easily deceived or imposed upon; dupe. **8.** *Bot.* a shoot rising from a subterranean stem or a root. **9.** *Colloq.* a lollipop, esp. an all-day sucker. *–v.t.* **10.** to strip off suckers or shoots from (a plant); remove superfluous shoots from (tobacco, etc.). *–v.i.* **11.** to send out suckers or shoots, as a plant.

**suckerfish** /'sʌkəfɪʃ/, *n., pl.* **-fishes,** (*esp. collectively*) **-fish.** →**remora** (def. 1).

**sucker lamb** /'sʌkə læm/, *n.* a lamb still suckling its mother but which is sufficiently developed to be slaughtered.

**sucker punch** /'– pʌntʃ/, *n. Boxing Colloq.* an unorthodox punch or move which succeeds only because of its element of surprise.

**sucking-pig** /'sʌkɪŋ-pɪg/, *n.* a newborn or very young pig, esp. one suitable for roasting.

**suckle** /'sʌkəl/, *v.,* **-led, -ling.** *–v.t.* **1.** to nurse at the breast. **2.** to nourish or bring up. **3.** to put to suck. *–v.i.* **4.** to suck at the breast. [frequentative of SUCK]

**suckling** /'sʌklɪŋ/, *n.* an infant or a young animal that is not yet weaned.

**sucrase** /'sukreɪz, -eɪs/, *n.* →**invertase.**

**sucroclastic** /sukroʊ'klæstɪk/, *adj.* (of enzymes) capable of hydrolysing complex carbohydrates.

**sucrose** /'sukroʊz, -oʊs/, *n.* a crystalline disaccharide, $C_{12}H_{22}O_{11}$, the sugar obtained from the sugar cane, the sugar beet, and sorghum, and forming the greater part of maple sugar. Also, **saccharose.** [F *sucr(e)* SUGAR + -OSE²]

**suction** /'sʌkʃən/, *n.* **1.** the act, process, or condition of sucking. **2.** the tendency to suck a substance into an interior space when the atmospheric pressure is reduced in the space. **3.** the reduction of pressure in order to cause such a sucking. **4.** the act or process of sucking a gas or liquid by such means. [L *suctio*]

**suction pump** /'– pʌmp/, *n.* a pump for raising water or the like by suction, consisting essentially of a vertical cylinder in which a piston works up and down, both with valves.

**suction stop** /'– stɒp/, *n.* →**click** (def. 3).

**suctorial** /sʌk'tɔriəl/, *adj.* **1.** adapted for sucking or suction, as an organ; functioning as a sucker, whether for imbibing or for adhering. **2.** having sucking organs; imbibing or adhering by suckers. **3.** pertaining to or characterised by suction.

**Sudan** /su'dæn/, *n.* a republic in north-eastern Africa, south of Egypt and bordering the Red Sea.

**Sudanese** /sudə'niz/, *n., pl.* **-nese,** *adj.* *–n.* **1.** a native of Sudan. *–adj.* **2.** of or pertaining to Sudan or its people.

**sudarium** /sju'dɛəriəm/, *n., pl.* **-daria** /-'dɛəriə/. **1.** a cloth for wiping the face; a handkerchief. **2.** →**veronica**¹ (def. 3). [L]

**sudatorium** /sjudə'tɔriəm/, *n., pl.* **-toria** /-'tɔriə/. a hot-air bath for inducing sweating. [L, prop. neut. of *sūdātōrius* sweat-producing]

**sudatory** /'sjudətəri, -tri/, *adj.* **1.** pertaining to or causing sweating. **2.** pertaining to a sudatorium. *–n.* **3.** →**sudatorium.** [see SUDATORIUM]

**sudd** /sʌd/, *n.* (in the White Nile) floating vegetable matter which often obstructs navigation. [Ar.]

**sudden** /'sʌdn/, *adj.* **1.** happening, coming, made, or done quickly, without warning or unexpectedly: *a sudden attack.* **2.** sharp; abrupt: *a sudden turn.* **3.** *Archaic.* unpremeditated, as actions. **4.** *Archaic.* quickly made, prepared, provided, etc. *–adv.* **5.** *Poetic.* suddenly. *–n.* **6.** an unexpected occasion or occurrence. **7. all of a sudden,** suddenly; without warning; quite unexpectedly. [ME *soden*, from AF *sodein*, from L *subitāneus*] – **suddenly,** *adv.* – **suddenness,** *n.*

**sudden-death** /'sʌdn-dɛθ/, *adj.* of or pertaining to a method of resolving a contest which has resulted in a tie by a simpler win-or-lose form of the game, as one extra hole in golf, or one spin in two-up: *sudden-death play-off.*

**sudden-death syndrome** /– 'sɪndroʊm/, *n.* →**cot death.** Also, **sudden infant-death syndrome.**

**sudor** /'sjudɔ/, *n.* sweat; perspiration. [L] – **sudoral** /'sjudərəl/, *adj.*

**sudoriferous** /sjudə'rɪfərəs/, *adj.* bearing or secreting sweat. [LL *sūdōrifer* sweat-bringing + -OUS]

**sudorific** /sjudə'rɪfɪk/, *adj.* **1.** causing sweat; diaphoretic. **2.** →**sudoriparous.** *–n.* **3.** a sudorific agent. [NL *sūdōrificus*, from L *sūdor* sweat]

**sudoriparous** /sjudə'rɪpərəs/, *adj.* producing or secreting sweat. [NL *sūdōriparus*]

**suds** /sʌdz/, *n.pl.* **1.** soapy water; foam; lather. **2.** *Colloq.* **a.** the head on a glass of beer, etc. **b.** beer. [MD *sudse* marsh] – **sudsy,** *adj.*

**sue** /su/, *v.,* **sued, suing.** *–v.t.* **1.** to institute process in law against, or bring a civil action against. **2.** to make petition or appeal to. **3.** *Archaic.* to woo or court. *–v.i.* **4.** to institute legal proceedings, or bring suit. **5.** to make petition or appeal. **6.** *Archaic.* to be suitor to a woman. [ME, from AF *suer*, var. of OF *sivre*, from VL *sequere*, replacing L *sequī* follow] – **suer** /'suə/, *n.*

**suede** /sweɪd/, *n.* **1.** kid or other leather finished on the flesh side with a soft, napped surface, or on the outer side after removal of a thin outer layer. **2.** a napped fabric suggesting this. Also, **suède.** [F: lit., Sweden] – **sueded,** *adj.*

**suet** /ˈsuət/, *n.* the hard fatty tissue about the loins and kidneys of cattle, sheep, etc., used in cookery, etc., and prepared as tallow. [ME, from AF *su(e)* (from L *sēbum* tallow, suet) + -ET] – **suety,** *adj.*

**suet pudding** /– ˈpʊdɪŋ/, *n.* a pudding mixture with suet added in place of butter, boiled and served with a sweet sauce.

**suf-,** variant of **sub-** (by assimilation) before *f.*

**suf.,** suffix. Also, **suff.**

**suffer** /ˈsʌfə/, *v.i.* **1.** to undergo or feel pain or distress. **2.** to sustain injury, disadvantage or loss. **3.** to undergo a penalty, esp. of death. **4.** to be the object of some action. **5.** to endure patiently or bravely. *–v.t.* **6.** to undergo, experience, or be subjected to (pain, distress, injury, loss, or anything unpleasant). **7.** to undergo (any action, process, etc.): *to suffer change.* **8.** to tolerate or allow. **9.** to allow or permit (to do or be as stated). [L *sufferre;* replacing ME *suffre(n),* from AF *suffrir,* from LL *sufferīre*] – **sufferable,** *adj.* – **sufferableness,** *n.* – **sufferably,** *adv.* – **sufferer,** *n.*

**sufferance** /ˈsʌfərəns, ˈsʌfrəns/, *n.* **1.** tolerance, as of a person or thing; tacit permission. **2.** capacity to endure pain, hardship, etc. **3.** *Archaic.* the suffering of pain, distress, injury, etc. **4.** *Archaic.* patient endurance. **5. on sufferance,** reluctantly tolerated.

**suffering** /ˈsʌfərɪŋ, ˈsʌfrɪŋ/, *n.* **1.** the act of one who suffers. **2.** a particular instance of this.

**suffice** /səˈfaɪs/, *v.,* **-ficed, -ficing.** *–v.i.* **1.** to be enough or adequate, as for needs, purposes, etc. *–v.t.* **2.** to be enough or adequate for; satisfy. [L *sufficere;* replacing ME *suffyse,* from OF] – **sufficer,** *n.*

**sufficiency** /səˈfɪʃənsi/, *n., pl.* **-cies.** **1.** the state or fact of being sufficient; adequacy. **2.** a sufficient number or amount; enough. **3.** adequate provision or supply, esp. of wealth.

**sufficient** /səˈfɪʃənt/, *adj.* **1.** that suffices; enough or adequate: *sufficient proof or protection.* **2.** *Archaic.* competent or capable, as a person. [ME, from L *sufficiens,* ppr., sufficing] – **sufficiently,** *adv.*

**suffix** /ˈsʌfɪks/, *n.* **1.** *Gram.* an affix which follows the element to which it is added, as *-ly* in *kindly.* **2.** something suffixed. *–v.t.* **3.** *Gram.* to add as a suffix. **4.** to affix at the end of something: *to suffix a syllable to a word.* **5.** to fix or put under. *–v.i.* **6.** *Gram.* (of a linguistic form) to admit a suffix. [NL *suffixum,* prop. neut. pp., fastened on] – **suffixal** /ˈsʌfɪksəl/, *adj.* – **suffixion** /sʌˈfɪkʃən/, *n.*

**suffocate** /ˈsʌfəkeɪt/, *v.,* **-cated, -cating.** *–v.t.* **1.** to kill by preventing the access of air to the blood through the lungs or analogous organs, as gills. **2.** to impede the respiration of. **3.** to cause discomfort to through lack of cool or fresh air. **4.** to overcome or extinguish; suppress. *–v.i.* **5.** to become suffocated; stifle; smother. **6.** to feel discomfort through lack of cool or fresh air. [L *suffōcātus,* pp., choked] – **suffocatingly,** *adv.* – **suffocation** /sʌfəˈkeɪʃən/, *n.* – **suffocative,** *adj.*

**suffragan** /ˈsʌfrəgən/, *adj.* **1.** assistant or subsidiary, applied: **a.** to a bishop appointed to help a diocesan bishop in the administration of a diocese. **b.** to any bishop in relation to the archbishop or metropolitan who is his superior. **2.** (of a see or diocese) subordinate to an archiepiscopal or metropolitan see. *–n.* **3.** a suffragan bishop. [ME *suffragane,* from ML *suffrāgāneus* assistant, from L *suffrāgor* I support (vote for). See SUFFRAGE]

**suffrage** /ˈsʌfrɪdʒ/, *n.* **1.** the right of voting, esp. in political elections. **2.** a vote given in favour of a proposed measure, a candidate, or the like. **3.** *Eccles.* a prayer, esp. a short intercessory prayer or petition. [ME, from L *suffrāgium*]

**suffragette** /sʌfrəˈdʒɛt/, *n.* a woman who advocates female suffrage. – **suffragettism,** *n.*

**suffragist** /ˈsʌfrədʒəst/, *n.* an advocate of the grant or extension of political suffrage, esp. to women.

**suffumigate** /səˈfjuməgeɪt/, *v.t.,* **-gated, -gating.** to fumigate from below; apply fumes or smoke to. [L *suffūmigātus,* pp.] – **suffumigation** /səfjuməˈgeɪʃən/, *n.*

**suffuse** /səˈfjuz/, *v.t.,* **-fused, -fusing.** to overspread with or as with a liquid, colour, etc. [L *suffūsus,* pp., overspread] – **suffusion** /səˈfjuʒən/, *n.* – **suffusive** /səˈfjusɪv/, *adj.*

**Sufi** /ˈsufi/, *n., pl.* **-fis.** a member of an ascetic and mystical Muslim sect. [Ar. *çūfī* man of wool, probably with ref. to the woollen garments worn]

**Sufism** /ˈsufɪzəm/, *n.* the ascetic and mystical system of the Sufis. Also, **Sufiism** /ˈsufiɪzəm/. – **Sufistic** /suˈfɪstɪk/, *adj.*

**sug-,** variant of **sub-** (by assimilation) before *g.*

**sugar** /ˈʃʊgə/, *n.* **1.** a sweet crystalline substance, sucrose, cane sugar, or beet sugar, $C_{12}H_{22}O_{11}$, obtained chiefly from the juice of the sugar cane or sugar beet, but present in sorghum, maple sap, etc., and extensively used for food purposes. **2.** a member of the same class of carbohydrates. **3.** *Colloq.* (a term of endearment). *–v.t.* **4.** to cover, sprinkle, mix, or sweeten with sugar. **5.** to make agreeable. *–v.i.* **6.** to form sugar. [ME *sugure, zugure,* from ML *zugurum,* from Ar. *sukkar;* replacing ME *sucure, zucure,* from OF *sukere, suchre,* from Ar.]

**sugarbag** /ˈʃʊgəbæg/, *n.* **1.** any bag containing sugar, esp. one made of hessian. **2.** →**honeybag.**

**sugar basin** /ˈʃʊgə beɪsən/, *n.* a small basin for serving sugar at the table. Also, **sugar bowl.**

**sugar beet** /ˈ– bit/, *n.* a variety of beet, *Beta vulgaris,* with a white root, cultivated for the sugar it yields.

**sugarbird** /ˈʃʊgəbɜd/, *n.* →**sunbird.**

**sugar bush** /ˈʃʊgə bʊʃ/, *n.* a large shrub native to southern Africa, *Protea repens,* with large heads of whitish flowers which is grown in some parts of Australia. [translation of *suikerbos, suikerbosch* from Afrikaans, from *suiker* sugar (from MD *suker,* from MF *sucre*) + *bos, bosch* bush, from MD *bosch*]

**sugar candy** /– ˈkændi/, *n.* a confection made by suspending strings in a strong sugar solution, which is left standing in a cool place until the candy is deposited on the string.

**sugarcane** /ˈʃʊgəkeɪn/, *n.* a tall grass, *Saccharum officinarum,* of tropical and warm regions, having a stout, jointed stalk, and constituting the chief source of sugar.

**sugar-coated** /ˈʃʊgə-koʊtəd/, *adj.* **1.** covered with sugar. **2.** (of something unpleasant) disguised so as to appear agreeable, pleasant, or acceptable.

**sugar daddy** /ˈʃʊgə ˌdædi/, *n. Colloq.* a rich middle-aged or old man who lavishes money and gifts on a young woman or boy in return for sexual favours or companionship.

**sugared** /ˈʃʊgəd/, *adj.* **1.** covered, mixed, or sweetened with sugar. **2.** sweetened as if with sugar; made agreeable; honeyed, as words, speech, etc.

**sugar farmer** /ˈʃʊgə famə/, *n.* →**canegrower.**

**sugar glider** /ˈ– glaɪdə/, *n.* a honey-eating possum, *Petaurus breviceps,* capable of short gliding flight.

**sugar grass** /ˈ– gras/, *n.* →**silky browntop.**

**sugar gum** /ˈ– gʌm/, *n.* a species of *Eucalyptus, E. cladocalyx,* of southern Australia, widely planted esp. for windbreaks and occasionally poisonous to stock.

**sugar loaf** /ˈ– loʊf/, *n.* **1.** a large approximately conical loaf or mass of hard refined sugar. **2.** anything resembling this in shape. – **sugar-loaf,** *adj.*

sugar glider

**sugar maple** /ˈ– meɪpəl/, *n.* any of several maples having a sweet sap, esp. *Acer saccharum,* of eastern North America, which yields a timber used in making furniture and is the chief source of maple sugar.

**sugar of lead,** *n.* →**lead acetate.**

**sugar of milk,** *n.* →**lactose.**

**sugar orchid** /ˈʃʊgər ɔkəd/, *n.* a terrestrial orchid, *Caladenia saccharata,* widespread in south-western Australia.

**sugarplum** /ˈʃʊgəplʌm/, *n.* a small sweetmeat made of sugar with various flavouring and colouring ingredients; a bonbon.

**sugar soap** /ˈʃʊgə soʊp/, *n.* a substance with the appearance of brown sugar, which when dissolved in water gives an alkaline solution; used for cleaning surfaces to be painted.

**sugar titty** /ˈ– tɪti/, *n. Colloq.* (formerly) a tiny bag made of muslin, or other material, filled with sugar, given to a baby to suck.

**sugar tongs** /ˈ– tɒŋz/, *n.pl.* small tongs used for serving cubes of sugar at table.

**sugary** /ˈʃʊgəri/, *adj.* **1.** of, containing, or resembling sugar. **2.** sweet; excessively sweet. **3.** dulcet: honeyed; cloying; deceitfully agreeable: *her sugary words of greetings sounded insincere.* – **sugariness,** *n.*

**suggest** /səˈdʒɛst/, *v.t.* **1.** to place or bring (an idea, proposition, plan, etc.) before a person's mind for consideration or possible action. **2.** to propose (a person or thing) as suitable or possible. **3.** (of things) to prompt the consideration, making, doing, etc., of. **4.** to bring before a person's mind indirectly or without plain expression. **5.** (of a thing) to call up in the mind (another thing) through association or natural connection of ideas. [L *suggestus,* pp., placed under, added, furnished] – **suggester,** *n.*

**suggestible** /səˈdʒɛstəbəl/, *adj.* **1.** capable of being influenced by suggestion. **2.** that may be suggested. – **suggestibility** /sədʒɛstəˈbɪləti/, *n.*

**suggestion** /səˈdʒɛstʃən/, *n.* **1.** the act of suggesting. **2.** the state of being suggested. **3.** something suggested, as a proposal, plan, etc. **4.** a slight trace: *he speaks English with just a suggestion of a foreign accent.* **5.** the calling up in the mind of one idea by another by virtue of some association or of some natural connection between the ideas. **6.** the idea thus called up. **7.** *Psychol.* **a.** the process of accepting a proposition for belief or action in the absence of the intervening and critical thought that would normally occur. **b.** a proposition for belief or action accepted in this way. **c.** the offering of a stimulus in such a way as to produce an uncritical response. [ME, from L *suggestio*]

**suggestive** /səˈdʒɛstɪv/, *adj.* **1.** that suggests; tending to suggest thoughts, ideas, etc. **2.** pertaining to hypnotic suggestion. **3.** such as to suggest something improper or indecent. – **suggestively,** *adv.* – **suggestiveness,** *n.*

**sui** /ˈsjui/, *n. Chess Colloq.* →**self-mate.** [short for SUIMATE]

**suicidal** /ˈsuəsaɪdl, suəˈsaɪdl/, *adj.* **1.** pertaining to, involving, or suggesting suicide; tending or leading to suicide. **2.** dangerously rash or foolish. – **suicidally** /suəˈsaɪdəli/, *adv.*

**suicide** /ˈsuəsaɪd/, *n. v.,* **-cided, -ciding. 1.** one who intentionally takes his own life. **2.** the intentional taking of one's own life. **3.** deliberate destruction of one's own interests or prospects. **4. commit suicide,** to kill oneself intentionally. *–v.i.* **5.** to commit suicide. **6.** to embark on a course which is disasterous to oneself, esp. financially. [NL *suīcīdium.* See -CIDE]

**sui generis** /suaɪ ˈdʒɛnərɪs/, *adj.* of his, her, its, or their own kind; unique. [L]

**sui juris** /– ˈdʒurɪs/, *n.* one capable of managing his affairs and assuming legal responsibility for his acts, as distinguished from others, as lunatics and infants, whose legal capacity is limited. [L: of one's own right]

**suimate** /ˈsjuimeɪt/, *n. Chess.* →**self-mate.** Also, **sui.** [L *suī-* of oneself + MATE²]

**suint** /ˈsuɪnt, swɪnt/, *n.* the natural grease of the wool of sheep, consisting of a mixture of fatty matter and potassium salts, used as a source of potash and in the preparation of ointments. [F, from *suer* sweat]

**suit** /sut/, *n.* **1.** a set of garments, vestments, or armour, intended to be worn together. **2.** a set of outer garments of the same material, worn by men, normally consisting of trousers, jacket, and sometimes a waistcoat. **3.** a set of outer garments worn by women, usu. consisting of skirt and jacket, and sometimes a blouse. **4.** the act or process of suing in a court of law; legal prosecution. **5.** *Cards.* **a.** one of the sets or classes (usu. four: spades, clubs, hearts, and diamonds) into which playing cards are divided. **b.** the aggregate of cards belonging to one of these sets held in a player's hand at one time. **6.** a number of things of this kind or purpose forming a series or set. **7.** the wooing or courting of a woman. **8.** the act of making petition or appeal. **9.** a petition, as to a person of exalted station. **10. follow suit, a.** to play a card of the suit led. **b.** to follow another's example. **11. strong suit,** something one is very good at; one's forte. *–v.t.* **12.** to provide with a suit of clothes; clothe; array. **13.** to make appropriate, adapt, or accommodate, as one thing to another. **14.** to be appropriate or becoming to. **15.** to be or prove satisfactory, agreeable, or acceptable to; satisfy or please. **16. suit oneself,** to do what one chooses, regardless of the interests or advice of others. *–v.i.* **17.** to be appropriate or suitable; accord. **18.** to be satisfactory, agreeable, or acceptable. [ME, from AF *suite,* var. of OF *sieute,* from *s(u)ivre* follow. See SUE]

**suitable** /ˈsutəbəl/, *adj.* such as to suit; appropriate; fitting; becoming. – **suitability** /sutəˈbɪləti/, **suitableness,** *n.* – **suitably,** *adv.*

**suitcase** /ˈsutkeɪs/, *n.* a portable rectangular travelling bag, usu. with stiffened frame, for carrying clothes, etc.

**suite** /swit/, *n.* **1.** a company of followers or attendants; a train or retinue. **2.** a number of things forming a series or set. **3.** a connected series of rooms to be used together by one person or a number of persons. **4.** a set of furniture of similar design and complementary in function: *a three-piece suite consists of a settee and two armchairs.* **5.** *Music.* **a.** an ordered series of instrumental dances, in the same or related keys, commonly preceded by a prelude. **b.** an ordered series of instrumental movements of any character. [F, from *suivre.* See SUIT]

**suiting** /ˈsutɪŋ/, *n.* a fabric for making suits.

**suitor** /ˈsutə/, *n.* **1.** one who courts or woos a woman. **2.** *Law.* a petitioner or plaintiff. **3.** one who sues or petitions for anything.

**sukiyaki** /sʊkiˈjaki/, *n.* a Japanese dish containing fried meat, vegetables, onions, etc., usu. cooked with soya sauce, often at the table. [Jap.]

**Sukkoth** /ˈsʊkoʊt, -oʊθ/, *n.pl.* the Jewish holiday of the Feast of Tabernacles (Lev. 23:34-43), beginning on the eve of the 15th of Tishri and lasting originally eight days, and in later Judaism nine days. [Heb.]

**sulcate** /ˈsʌlkeɪt/, *adj.* **1.** having long, narrow grooves or channels, as a leaf; furrowed. **2.** cleft, as a hoof. Also, **sulcated.** [L *sulcātus,* pp., furrowed] – **sulcation** /sʌlˈkeɪʃən/, *n.*

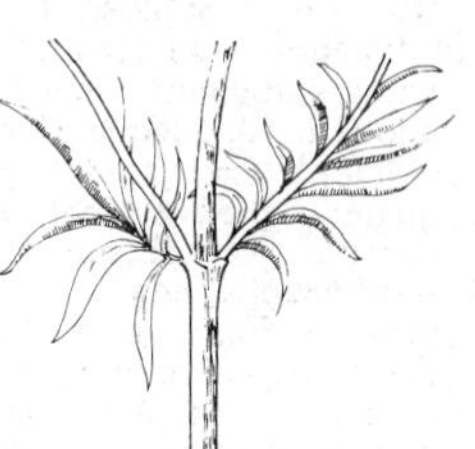

sulcate stalk

**sulcus** /ˈsʌlkəs/, *n., pl.* **-ci** /-saɪ/. **1.** a furrow or groove. **2.** *Anat.* a fissure between two convolutions of the brain. [L]

**sulf-,** *U.S.* variant of **sulph-.**

**sulfadiazine** /sʌlfəˈdaɪəzin/, *n. U.S.* →**sulphadiazine.**

**sulfamic acid** /sʌlˌfæmɪk ˈæsəd/, *n. U.S.* →**sulphamic acid.**

**sulfur** /ˈsʌlfə/, *n. U.S.* →**sulphur.**

**sulfuret** /ˈsʌlfjərət/, *n.;* /ˈsʌlfjərɛt/, *v.t.,* **-reted, -reting.** *U.S.* →**sulphuret.**

**sulk** /sʌlk/, *v.i.* **1.** to hold aloof in a sullen, morose, ill-humoured, or offended mood. *–n.* **2.** a state or fit of sulking. **3.** (*pl.*) ill humour shown by sulking: *to have the sulks.* **4.** Also, **sulker.** one who sulks. [backformation from SULKY]

**sulky** /ˈsʌlki/, *adj.,* **sulkier, sulkiest,** *n., pl.* **sulkies.** *–adj.* **1.** sullenly ill-humoured or resentful; marked by ill-humoured aloofness. **2.** (of weather, etc.) gloomy. *–n.* **3.** a light two-wheeled one-horse carriage. [? from OE *-solcen* slothful, remiss; cf. N Fris. *sulkig* sulky; in def. 3, so called as holding only one person] – **sulkily,** *adv.* – **sulkiness,** *n.*

**sullage** /ˈsʌlɪdʒ/, *n.* **1.** refuse, scum, or filth. **2.** *Bldg Trades.* dirty water, as from bathrooms, laundries, kitchens, etc., excluding sewage. **3.** scoria. **4.** silt. [cf. OE *sol* mire]

**sullage pit** /ˈ– pɪt/, *n.* a pit in which waste, esp. sewage, is held.

**sullage tanker** /ˈ– tæŋkə/, *n.* a road tanker into which the contents of domestic and other cess pits are pumped for ultimate disposal elsewhere.

**sullen** /ˈsʌlən/, *adj.* **1.** showing ill humour by a gloomy silence or reserve. **2.** silently and persistently ill-humoured; morose. **3.** indicative of gloomy ill humour: *sullen silence.* **4.** gloomy or dismal, as weather, sounds, etc.: *a sullen sky.* **5.** sluggish, as a stream. **6.** *Obs.* malignant, as planets, influences, etc. [ME *solein,* from AF, from *sol* SOLE¹] – **sullenly,** *adv.* – **sullenness,** *n.*

**sullivan** /ˈsʌləvən/, *n. Colloq.* (*derog., used esp. by Australians of non-British background*) an Australian of British background. [from the *Sullivans,* a television show which began in Nov. 1976, in which the hero is a stereotype of the average Australian male]

**sully** /'sʌli/, *v.*, **-lied, -lying,** *n., pl.* **-lies.** *–v.t.* **1.** to soil, stain, or tarnish. **2.** to mar the purity or lustre of; defile. *–v.i.* **3.** to become sullied, soiled, or tarnished. *–n. Obs.* **4.** the act of sullying. **5.** a stain. [ME *solien,* OE *(ā)solian* become dirty, from *sol* dirty]

**sulph-,** *Chem.* a prefix indicating a compound in which sulphur has been substituted for oxygen, as *sodium sulphantimonate* ($Na_3SbS_4$) compared with sodium antimonate ($Na_3SbO_4$). Thus, formulas such as *sulphantimonite, sulpharsenate,* etc., can be deduced from the formulas of the corresponding antimonite, arsenate, etc. Also, before consonants, **sulpho-;** *U.S.,* **sulf-, sulfo-.** [combining form representing SULPHUR]

**sulphadiazine** /sʌlfə'daɪəzin/, *n.* a sulphanilamide derivative, $C_{10}H_{10}N_4O_2S$, particularly effective against staphylococcal and gonococcal infections. Also, *U.S.,* **sulfadiazine.**

**sulpha drugs** /'sʌlfə drʌgz/, *n.pl.* a group of compounds containing the radical-$SO_2NH_2$, used as antibacterials in treatment of various diseases, wounds, burns, etc. Also, **sulphas** /'sʌlfəz/; *U.S.,* **sulfa drugs, sulfas.**

**sulphafurazole** /sʌlfə'fjurəzoʊl/, *n.* a sulpha drug used to cure urinary infections. Also, *U.S.,* **sulfafurazole.**

**sulphaguanidine** /sʌlfə'gwanədin/, *n.* a sulphanilamide derivative, $C_7H_{10}N_4O_2S$, effective against bacterial dysentery. Also, *U.S.* **sulfaguanidine.**

**sulphamic acid** /sʌl,fæmɪk 'æsəd/, *n.* a white crystalline solid, $HSO_3NH_2$, which gives weakly acid water solutions; used as a metal and ceramic cleaner and as a stabilising agent for chlorine and hypochlorite in swimming pools, etc. Also, *U.S.,* **sulfamic acid.**

**sulphanilamide** /sʌlfə'nɪləmaɪd/, *n.* a white crystalline amide of sulphanilic acid, $NH_2C_6H_4SO_2NH_2$, effective against infections caused by haemolytic streptococci, the gonococci, etc. Also, *U.S.,* **sulfanilamide.**

**sulphapyridine** /sʌlfə'pɪrədaɪn, -din/, *n.* a sulphanilamide derivative, $C_{11}H_{11}N_3O_3S$, more toxic than sulphanilamide but somewhat more effective against infections caused by pneumococci. Also, *U.S.,* **sulfapyridine.**

**sulpharsphenamine** /sʌlfas'fɛnəmin, -fə'næmən/, *n.* a compound having the same characteristics as arsphenamine but less efficient and not so irritating to the body. Also, *U.S.,* **sulfarsphenamine.**

**sulphate** /'sʌlfeɪt/, *n., v.,* **-phated, -phating.** *–n.* **1.** *Chem.* a salt of sulphuric acid. *–v.t.* **2.** to combine, treat, or impregnate with sulphuric acid, or with a sulphate or sulphates. **3.** to convert into a sulphate. **4.** *Elect.* to deposit lead sulphate on during sulphation. *–v.i.* **5.** to become sulphated. Also, *U.S.,* **sulfate.** [NL *sulphātum,* from L *sulph(ur)* SULPHUR + *-ātum* -ATE[2]] – **sulphatic** /sʌl'fætɪk/, *adj.*

**sulphathiazole** /sʌlfə'θaɪəzɒl/, *n.* a sulphanilamide derivative, $C_9H_9N_3O_2S_2$, effective in the treatment of pneumonia and staphylococcus infections. Also, *U.S.,* **sulfathiazole.**

**sulphation** /sʌl'feɪʃən/, *n.* the process of forming a deposit of lead sulphate on the lead plates of an accumulator. Also, *U.S.,* **sulfation.**

**sulphatise** /'sʌlfətaɪz/, *v.t.,* **-tised, -tising.** to convert into a sulphate as by the roasting of ores. Also, **sulphatize;** *U.S.,* **sulfatize.**

**sulphide** /'sʌlfaɪd/, *n.* a compound of sulphur with a more electropositive element or, less often, a radical. Also, **sulphid** /'sʌlfəd/; *U.S.,* **sulfide, sulfid.**

**sulphite** /'sʌlfaɪt/, *n.* a salt of sulphurous acid. Also, *U.S.,* **sulfite.**

**sulpho-,** variant of **sulph-** before a consonant. Also, *U.S.,* **sulfo-.**

**sulphonamide** /sʌl'fɒnəmaɪd/, *n.* **1.** *Chem.* an amide of a sulphonic acid, containing the radical –$SO_2NH_2$. **2.** *Pharm.* any of a group of sulphonamide compounds possessing antibacterial activity, as sulphanilamide. Also, *U.S.,* **sulfonamide.**

**sulphonate** /'sʌlfəneɪt/, *n., v.,* **-nated, -nating.** *–n.* **1.** an ester or salt derived from a sulphonic acid. *–v.t.* **2.** to make into a sulphonic acid, as by treating an aromatic hydrocarbon with concentrated sulphuric acid. Also, *U.S.,* **sulfonate.**

**sulphonation** /sʌlfə'neɪʃən/, *n.* the process of attaching the sulphonic acid radical, –$SO_3H$, directly to carbon in an organic compound. Also, *U.S.,* **sulfonation.**

**sulphone** /'sʌlfoʊn/, *n.* any of a class of organic compounds containing the bivalent $SO_2$ group united with two hydrocarbon radicals. Also, *U.S.,* **sulfone.**

**sulphonic** /sʌl'fɒnɪk/, *adj.* **1.** denoting or pertaining to the group $SO_2OH$. **2.** denoting or pertaining to any of the acids, mostly organic, containing the $SO_3H$ group. Also, *U.S.,* **sulfonic.**

**sulphonic acid** /– 'æsəd/, *n.* any of a large group of organic compounds containing the sulphonic radical. They are strong acids, giving neutral sodium salts and used in the synthesis of phenols, dyes, and other substances. Also, *U.S.,* **sulfonic acid.**

**sulphonium** /sʌl'foʊniəm/, *n.* the ion obtained by adding a proton to hydrogen sulphide, as $(H_3S)^+$. Also, *U.S.,* **sulfonium.**

**sulphonyl** /'sʌlfənɪl/, *n.* →**sulphuryl.** Also, *U.S.,* **sulfonyl.**

**sulphonyl chloride** /– 'klɔraɪd/, *n.* denoting the radical –$SO_2Cl$. Also, *U.S.,* **sulfonyl chloride.**

**sulphur** /'sʌlfə/, *n.* **1.** *Chem.* a non-metallic element which exists in several forms, the ordinary one being a yellow rhombic crystalline solid, and which burns with a blue flame and a suffocating smell; used esp. in making gunpowder and matches, in vulcanising rubber, in medicine, etc. *Symbol:* S; *at. wt:* 32.064; *at. no.:* 16; *sp. gr.:* 2.07 at 20°C. **2.** a pale yellow with a greenish tinge. **3.** any of various yellow or orange butterflies of the family Pieridae. *–v.t.* **4.** to treat or fumigate with sulphur. Also, *U.S.,* **sulfur.** [ME, from L] – **sulphury,** *adj.*

**sulphurate** /'sʌlfjəreɪt/, *v.t.,* **-rated, -rating.** to combine, treat, or impregnate with sulphur, the fumes of burning sulphur, or the like. Also, *U.S.,* **sulfurate.** – **sulphuration** /sʌlfjə'reɪʃən/, *n.* – **sulphurator,** *n.*

**sulphur-bottom** /'sʌlfə-bɒtəm/, *n.* →**blue whale.**

**sulphur-crested cockatoo** /,sʌlfə-krɛstəd kɒkə'tu/, *n.* a large common Australian parrot, *Cacatua galerita,* predominantly white, with yellow on the undersides of wings and tail and a forward curving yellow crest. Also, **white cockatoo.**

sulphur-crested cockatoo

**sulphur dioxide** /sʌlfə daɪ'ɒksaɪd/, *n.* a colourless gas or liquid with a strong pungent odour which is non-combustible and is soluble in water, ether and alcohol; it is used as an oxidising and reducing agent, a preservative for beer and wine, a disinfectant, a bleaching agent of oils and fuels and for various other industrial uses; when dissolved in water it gives sulphurous acid.

**sulphureous** /sʌl'fjuriəs/, *adj.* consisting of, containing, pertaining to, or resembling sulphur; sulphur-coloured. Also, *U.S.,* **sulfureous.** – **sulphureously,** *adv.* – **sulphureousness,** *n.*

**sulphuret** /'sʌlfjərət/, *n.;* /'sʌlfjərɛt/, *v.,* **-retted, -retting.** *–n.* **1.** →**sulphide.** *–v.t.* **2.** to treat or combine with sulphur. Also, *U.S.,* **sulfuret.** [NL *sulphurētum.* See SULPHUR, -URET]

**sulphuretted hydrogen** /sʌlfjə,rɛtəd 'haɪdrədʒən/, *n.* →**hydrogen sulphide.**

**sulphuric** /sʌl'fjurɪk, -'fjʊə-/, *adj.* of, pertaining to, or containing sulphur, esp. in the hexavalent stage. Also, *U.S.,* **sulfuric.**

**sulphuric acid** /– 'æsəd/, *n.* the dibasic acid of sulphur. $H_2SO_4$, a colourless oily liquid, made from sulphur trioxide and used in many industrial processes; oil of vitriol. Also, *U.S.,* **sulfuric acid.**

**sulphuric ether** /– 'iθə/, *n.* →**ether** (def. 1a). Also, *U.S.,* **sulfuric ether.**

**sulphurise** /'sʌlfjəraɪz/, *v.t.,* **-rised, -rising.** **1.** to combine, treat, or impregnate with sulphur. **2.** to fumigate with sulphur dioxide. Also, **sulphurize;** *U.S.,* **sulfurize.** – **sulphurisation** /sʌlfjəraɪ'zeɪʃən/, *n.*

**sulphurous** /'sʌlfərəs/, *adj.* **1.** *Chem.* relating to sulphur. **2.** of the yellow colour of sulphur. **3.** *Chem.* containing tetravalent sulphur. **4.** pertaining to the fires of hell; hellish. **5.** fiery or heated. **6.** thundery. Also, *U.S.,* **sulfurous.**

**sulphurous acid** /– 'æsəd/, *n.* an acid, $H_2SO_3$, formed by dissolving sulphur dioxide in water, known mainly by its salts (sulphites). Also, *U.S.,* **sulfurous acid.**

**sulphur point** /'sʌlfə pɔɪnt/, *n.* the temperature at which liquid sulphur is in equilibrium with its vapour at one standard atmosphere; equal to 444.6°C. Also, *U.S.,* **sulfur point.**

**sulphur trioxide** /– traɪ'ɒksaɪd/, *n.* an irritant, corrosive, low-melting solid, $SO_3$, prepared by oxidation of sulphur dioxide; an intermediate in the manufacture of sulphuric acid. Also, *U.S.,* **sulfur trioxide.**

**sulphuryl** /'sʌlfjərəl, -fərəl/, *n.* the bivalent radical of sulphuric acid, $-SO_2-$. Also, *U.S.,* **sulfuryl.**

**sulphuryl chloride** /– 'klɔraɪd/, *n.* a colourless fluid, $SO_2Cl_2$, with a very pungent smell, used as a chlorinating agent, etc. Also, *U.S.,* **sulfuryl chloride.**

**sul ponticello** /,sʊl pɒntɪ'tʃɛloʊ/, *adv.* (a musical direction to a string player) on or near the bridge. [It.]

**sultan** /'sʌltən/, *n.* **1.** the sovereign of a Muslim country. **2.** (*cap.*) any of the former sovereigns of Turkey. [ML *sultānus,* from Ar. *sultān* king, ruler, power] – **sultanic** /sʌl'tænɪk/, *adj.* – **sultanship,** *n.*

**sultana** /sʌl'tanə, səl-/, *n.* **1.** a wife or concubine of a sultan. **2.** any close female relative of a sultan. **3.** a small, green, seedless grape. **4.** a raisin made from such a grape. [It., fem of *sultano* SULTAN]

**sultana bird** /'– bɜd/, *n.* →**swamphen.**

**sultanate** /'sʌltənət/, *n.* **1.** the office or rule of a sultan. **2.** the territory ruled over by a sultan.

**sultry** /'sʌltri/, *adj.,* **-trier, -triest. 1.** oppressively hot and close or moist; sweltering. **2.** oppressively hot, as the weather, etc. **3.** characterised by or associated with sweltering heat. **4.** characterised by or arousing temper or passion. [*sulter* (var. of SWELTER) + -Y[1]] – **sultrily,** *adv.* – **sultriness,** *n.*

**sum** /sʌm/, *n., v.,* **summed, summing.** *–n.* **1.** the aggregate of two or more numbers, magnitudes, quantities, or particulars as determined by mathematical process: *the sum of 5 and 7 is 12.* **2.** a particular aggregate or total, esp. with reference to money: *the expenses came to an enormous sum.* **3.** a quantity or amount, esp. of money: *to lend small sums.* **4.** a series of numbers or quantities to be added up. **5.** an arithmetical problem to be solved, or such a problem worked out and having the various steps shown. **6.** the total amount, or the whole. **7.** the substance or gist of a matter, comprehensively viewed or expressed: *the letter contains the sum and substance of his opinions.* **8.** concise or brief form: *in sum.* **9.** a summary. *–v.t.* **10.** to combine into an aggregate or total (oft. fol. by *up*). **11.** to ascertain the sum of, as by addition. **12.** to bring into or contain in a small compass (oft. fol. by *up*). **13. sum up, a.** to reckon: *to sum up advantages and disadvantages.* **b.** to bring into or contain in a brief and comprehensive statement: *the article sums up the work of the year.* **c.** to form a quick estimate of: *to sum someone up.* **d.** to give a brief and comprehensive statement or summary. *–adj.* **14.** denoting or pertaining to a sum: *sum total.* [L *summa,* prop. fem. of *summus* highest; replacing ME *somme,* from OF]

**sum-,** occasional variant of **sub-** (by assimilation) before *m.*

**sumach** /'sumæk, 'ʃumæk/, *n.* **1.** any of the plants of the genus *Rhus* as *R. coriaria* of southern Europe. **2.** a preparation of dried and powdered leaves of certain species of *Rhus,* used in dyeing, tanning, etc. **3.** the wood of any of these plants. Also, (esp. def. 2) **sumac.** [ME, from OF, from Ar. *summāq*]

**Sumerian** /su'mɪəriən/, *adj.* **1.** of or pertaining to Sumer, its inhabitants, their civilisation, or language. *–n.* **2.** one of the Sumerian people. **3.** the language of the Sumerians, of unknown relationship, preserved in very ancient cuneiform inscriptions.

**summa** /'sʊmə/, *n., pl.* **summae** /'sʊmi/. a treatise giving a summary or synthesis of a whole subject, esp. a detailed exposition of religious doctrine. [L]

**summa cum laude** /,sʊmə kʊm 'laʊdeɪ/, with the highest honour or praise (used chiefly in American universities to grant the highest of three special honours for above-average academic performance). [L]

**summand** /'sʌmænd, sʌ'mænd/, *n.* a part or item of a sum.

**summarise** /'sʌməraɪz/, *v.t.,* **-rised, -rising. 1.** to make a summary of; state or express in a concise form. **2.** to constitute a summary of. Also, **summarize.** – **summarisation** /sʌmərаɪ'zeɪʃən/, *n.* – **summariser, summarist,** *n.*

**summary** /'sʌməri/, *n., pl.* **-ries,** *adj.* *–n.* **1.** a brief and comprehensive presentation of facts or statements; an abstract, compendium, or epitome. *–adj.* **2.** brief and comprehensive; concise. **3.** direct and prompt; unceremoniously fast. **4.** (of legal proceedings, jurisdiction, etc.) conducted without or exempt from the various steps and delays of full proceedings. [ME, from ML *summārius,* from L *summa* sum] – **summarily** /'sʌmərəli/, *adv.* – **summariness,** *n.*

**summat** /'sʌmət/, *adv., pron., n. Colloq.* somewhat or something. [spelling var. of SOMEWHAT]

**summation** /sʌ'meɪʃən/, *n.* **1.** the process of summing. **2.** the result of this; an aggregate or total. **3.** *U.S. Law.* the final arguments of opposing counsel before a case goes to the jury.

**summer**[1] /'sʌmə/, *n.* **1.** the second and the warmest season of the year, between spring and autumn. **2.** a period of warm, sunny weather associated with this season. **3.** a whole year as represented by this season: *a child of eight summers.* **4.** the period of finest development, perfection, or beauty previous to any decline: *the summer of life.* *–adj.* **5.** of, pertaining to, or characteristic of summer; *summer resorts.* **6.** suitable for use or wear in summer. **7.** having the weather or warmth of summer. *–v.i.* **8.** to spend or pass the summer. [ME *sumer,* OE *sumor,* c. G *Sommer*] – **summer-like,** *adj.*

**summer**[2] /'sʌmə/, *n.* **1.** a principal timber or beam, as in a floor or any spanning structure. **2.** a stone at the top of a pier, column, or the like, as to support an arch. **3.** →**lintel.** [ME, from AF *sumer* beam, packhorse, from LL *sagma* packsaddle, from Gk]

**summer grass** /'– gras/, *n.* any grasses, as grasses of the genus *Digitaria,* which are summer garden weeds.

**summerhouse** /'sʌməhaʊs/, *n.* a simple, often rustic structure in a park or garden, intended to provide a shady, cool place in the summer.

**summer lightning** /'sʌmə ,laɪtnɪŋ/, *n.* lightning which can be seen but is too far away for the resulting thunder to be heard.

**summer pudding** /– 'pʊdɪŋ/, *n.* a cold sweet sponge cake, the centre of which is filled with stewed fruit, as berries or currents.

**summersault** /'sʌməsɒlt, -sɔlt/, *n., v.i.* →**somersault.**

**summer school** /'sʌmə skul/, *n.* a course of teaching which takes place during summer for groups usu. other than regular students.

**summer solstice** /– 'sɒlstəs/, *n.* See **solstice** (def. 1).

**summertime** /'sʌmətaɪm/, *n.* **1.** the season of summer. **2.** any daylight-saving time.

**summerwood** /'sʌməwʊd/, *n.* that part of an annual ring of a tree which, esp. in trees of the northern hemisphere, grows in summer and the later part of the main growth season, and is characterised by thick-walled cells (distinguished from *springwood*). Also, **latewood.**

**summery** /'sʌməri/, *adj.* of, like, or befitting summer.

**summing-up** /sʌmɪŋ-'ʌp/, *n.* **1.** a recapitulation or review of the leading points of an argument or the like. **2.** the survey of the evidence given by a judge to a jury before it withdraws to consider its verdict.

**summit** /'sʌmət/, *n.* **1.** the highest point or part, as of a hill, a line of travel, or any object; the top; the apex. **2.** the highest point of attainment or aspiration. **3.** the highest state or degree. **4.** a meeting or conference between heads of state or the heads of any other organisation. **5.** diplomacy at the highest level. *–adj.* **6.** (in diplomacy) between heads of state: *summit conference.* [late ME *sommet,* from F, from L *summum,* prop. neut. of *summus* highest]

**summitry** /'sʌmətri/, *n.* the interplay and bargaining between figures of supreme political power, each attempting to maintain a particular position without regard to repercussions upon weaker individuals or states.

**summon** /'sʌmən/, *v.t.* **1.** to call as with authority to some duty, task, or performance; call upon (to do something). **2.** to call for the presence of, as by command, message, or signal; call (fol. by *to, away, from,* etc.). **3.** to call or notify to appear at a specified place, esp. before a court: *to summon a defendant.* **4.** to call together (an assembly, council, or other body) by authority, as for deliberation or action: *to summon a parliament.* **5.** to call into action; rouse; call forth (oft. fol. by *up*): *to summon up all one's courage.* **6.** to call upon to surrender. [L *summonēre* suggest, ML summon; replacing ME *somonen,* from OF] – **summonable,** *adj.* – **summoner,** *n.*

**summons** /ˈsʌmənz/, *n., pl.* **-monses,** *v.* –*n.* **1.** an authoritative command, message, or signal by which one is summoned. **2.** a call to do something: *a summons to surrender.* **3.** *Law.* a call or citation by authority to appear before a court, or the writ by which the call is made. **4.** an authoritative call or notice to appear at a specified place, as for a particular purpose or duty. **5.** a call issued for the meeting of an assembly or parliament. –*v.t.* **6.** to serve with a summons; summon. [ME *somonse,* from AF, OF, from *somondre* SUMMON]

**summum bonum** /sʊmʊm ˈbɒnʊm/, *n.* the highest or chief good. [L]

**sumo** /ˈsumoʊ/, *n.* a style of wrestling in Japan, in which the object is to force the opponent out of the ring or to make any part of his body other than the feet touch the ground. [Jap.]

**sump** /sʌmp/, *n.* **1.** a pit, well, or the like in which water or other liquid is collected. **2.** *Mach.* a container situated at the lowest point in a circulating system, esp. the crankcase of an internal-combustion engine, which acts as an oil reservoir. **3.** *Mining.* **a.** a space at the bottom of a shaft or below a passageway where water is allowed to collect. **b.** a pilot shaft or tunnel pushed out in front of a main bore. [ME *sompe,* muddy pool, bog, from MLG or MD *sump,* c. G *Sumpf*]

**sumpbuster** /ˈsʌmpbʌstə/, *n. Colloq.* a road having a particularly rough surface.

**sumptuary** /ˈsʌmptʃəri/, *adj.* pertaining to, dealing with, or regulating expense or expenditure. [L *sumptuārius*]

**sumptuary law** /ˈ– ˌlɔ/, *n.* a law regulating personal habits which offend the moral or religious conscience of the community.

**sumptuous** /ˈsʌmptʃuəs/, *adj.* **1.** entailing great expense, as from fine workmanship, choice materials, etc.; costly: *a sumptuous residence.* **2.** luxuriously fine; splendid or superb. [late ME, from L *sumptuōsus* expensive] – **sumptuously,** *adv.* – **sumptuousness,** *n.*

**sun** /sʌn/, *n., v.,* **sunned, sunning.** –*n.* **1.** the star which is the central body of the solar system and around which the planets revolve, and from which they receive light and heat. Its mean distance from the earth is about $1.5 \times 10^8$ kilometres, its diameter about $1.4 \times 10^6$ kilometres, and its mass about 332 958 times that of the earth. Its period of surface rotation is about 26 days at its equator but longer in greater latitudes. **2.** the sun considered with reference to its position in the sky, its visibility, the season of the year, the time at which or the place where it is seen, etc. **3.** a self-luminous heavenly body. **4.** sunshine: *to be exposed to the sun.* **5.** a figure or representation of the sun, as a heraldic bearing usu. surrounded with rays and charged with the features of a human face. **6.** something likened to the sun in brightness, splendour, etc. **7. a place in the sun,** a pleasant or advantageous situation. **8. under the sun,** anywhere on earth: *the most beautiful girl under the sun.* –*v.t.* **9.** to expose to the sun's rays. **10.** to warm, dry, etc., in the sunshine. **11.** to put, bring, make, etc. (as specified), by exposure to the sun's rays. –*v.i.* **12.** to expose oneself to the sun's rays. [ME and OE *sunne,* c. G *Sonne*]

**Sun.,** Sunday.

**sun-and-planet** /sʌn-ən-ˈplænət/, *adj.* denoting a system of toothed gearing in which a small wheel moves round a larger wheel.

**sun animalcule** /ˌsʌn ænəˈmælkjul/, *n.* →**heliozoan.**

**sunbake** /ˈsʌnbeɪk/, *v.i.,* **-baked, -baking.** to expose one's body to the sun in order to acquire a suntan or as a relaxation. – **sunbaker,** *n.*

**sunbaked** /ˈsʌnbeɪkt/, *adj.* baked or dried and hardened by the heat of the sun.

**sunbath** /ˈsʌnbaθ/, *n.* an exposure of the body directly to the rays of the sun.

**sunbathe** /ˈsʌnbeɪð/, *v.i.,* **-bathed, -bathing.** →**sunbake.**

**sunbeam** /ˈsʌnbim/, *n.* **1.** a beam or ray of sunlight. **2.** *Colloq.* a plate, utensil, etc. which is not used at a meal, and does not need to be washed.

**sunbird** /ˈsʌnbɜd/, *n.* any of various small, brilliantly coloured birds of the family Nectariniidae.

**sun-bittern** /ˈsʌn-bɪtn/, *n.* a South American bird, *Eurypyga helias,* with variegated plumage, allied to the rails.

**sunblind** /ˈsʌnblaɪnd/, *n.* a shade, as a venetian blind or an awning, on a window to afford protection from the sun.

**sunbonnet** /ˈsʌnbɒnət/, *n.* a large bonnet of cotton or other light material shading the face and projecting down over the neck, formerly worn by women and small girls.

**sunbow** /ˈsʌnboʊ/, *n.* a bow or arc of prismatic colours like a rainbow, appearing in the spray of cataracts, etc.

**sunbreak** /ˈsʌnbreɪk/, *n.* →**brise-soleil.** [translation of F BRISE-SOLEIL, modelled on WINDBREAK]

**sunburn** /ˈsʌnbɜn/, *n., v.,* **-burnt** or **-burned, -burning.** –*n.* **1.** superficial inflammation of the skin, caused by excessive or too sudden exposure to the sun's rays. –*v.t., v.i.* **2.** to affect or be affected with sunburn.

**sunburst** /ˈsʌnbɜst/, *n.* **1.** a burst of sunlight; a sudden shining of the sun through rifted clouds. **2.** a firework, a piece of jewellery, an ornament, or the like, resembling the sun with rays issuing in all directions. **3.** a tool used for making a sun ray pattern on leather.

**sun-cured** /ˈsʌn-kjuəd/, *adj.* cured or preserved by exposure to the sun.

**sundae** /ˈsʌndeɪ/, *n.* a portion of ice-cream with fruit or other syrup poured over it, and often whipped cream, chopped nuts, or other additions. [orig. uncert.]

**sun-dance** /ˈsʌn-dæns, -dans/, *n.* a religious ceremony associated with the sun, practised by North American Indians of the Plains, consisting of dancing attended with various symbolic rites, commonly including self-torture.

**Sunday** /ˈsʌndeɪ, -di/, *n.* **1.** the first day of the week, the Sabbath of most Christian sects, observed in commemoration of the resurrection of Christ. **2. a month of Sundays,** an extremely long time. –*adj.* **3.** of, pertaining to, occurring on, or suitable for Sunday. [ME; OE *sunnandæg,* c. G *Sonntag;* translation of L *dies sōlis,* Gk *hēméra hēlíou*]

**Sunday best** /– ˈbɛst/, *n.* one's best clothes.

**Sunday driver** /– ˈdraɪvə/, *n. Colloq.* (*derog.*) an unusually slow and cautious driver.

**Sunday-go-to-meeting** /ˌsʌndeɪ-goʊ-tə-ˈmitɪŋ/, *adj. U.S. Colloq.* most dressed-up; most presentable; best: *Sunday-go-to-meeting shoes.*

**Sunday school** /ˈsʌndeɪ skul/, *n.* **1.** a school, now usu. in connection with a church, for religious (and formerly also secular) instruction on Sunday. **2.** the members of such a school. Also, **Sabbath school.**

**sundeck** /ˈsʌndɛk/, *n.* **1.** a flat roof or platform adjoining a house, hotel, etc. used for sunbathing. **2.** a deck of a passenger ship exposed to the sun.

**sunder** /ˈsʌndə/, *v.t.* **1.** to separate; part; divide; sever. –*v.i.* **2.** to become separated; part. [ME; late OE *sundrian,* c. G *sondern*] – **sunderer,** *n.*

**sunderance** /ˈsʌndərəns, -drəns/, *n.* separation.

**sundew** /ˈsʌndju/, *n.* any of a group of small bog plants, species of the genus *Drosera,* with sticky hairs that capture insects.

**sundial** /ˈsʌndaɪəl/, *n.* an instrument for indicating the time of day by the position of a shadow (as of a gnomon) cast by the sun on a graduated plate or surface.

sundial

**sun-disc** /ˈsʌn-dɪsk/, *n.* **1.** the disc of the sun. **2.** a figure or representation of this, esp. in religious symbolism.

**sundog** /ˈsʌndɒg/, *n.* **1.** →**parhelion. 2.** a small or incomplete rainbow.

**sundown** /ˈsʌndaʊn/, *n.* sunset; the time of sunset.

**sundowner** /ˈsʌndaʊnə/, *n.* **1.** a swagman who arrives at a homestead at nightfall, too late for work, but obtains shelter for the night. **2.** an alcoholic drink taken in the evening, traditionally at sundown.

sundowner (def. 1)

**sun-drenched** /ˈsʌn-drɛntʃt/, *adj.* exposed to intense light and heat from the sun: *the sun-drenched beaches of the Gold Coast.*

**sundress** /ˈsʌndrɛs/, *n.* a low-cut, sleeveless, light summer dress.

**sun-dried** /ˈsʌn-draɪd/, *adj.* **1.** dried in the sun, as bricks, raisins, etc. **2.** dried up or withered by the sun.

**sundries** /ˈsʌndriz/, *n.pl.* sundry things or items.

**sundry** /ˈsʌndri/, *adj.* **1.** various or divers: *sundry persons.* *–n.* **2.** *Cricket.* (*usu. pl.*) a score or run not made by hitting the ball with the bat, as a bye or a wide; an extra. *–pron.* **3. all and sundry,** everyone collectively and individually. [ME; OE *syndrig* private, separate, from *sundor* apart. See -Y[1]]

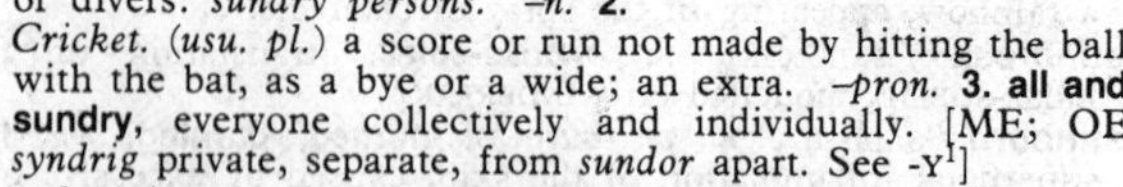

**sunfast** /ˈsʌnfast/, *adj.* not subject to fading in sunlight.

**sunfish** /ˈsʌnfɪʃ/, *n., pl.* **-fishes,** (*esp. collectively*) **-fish. 1.** a huge fish, the **ocean sunfish,** *Mola mola,* found in Australian waters and elsewhere, having a deep body abbreviated behind, seeming to consist of little more than the head. **2.** any fish of the same family, Molidae. **3.** any of the small freshwater fishes of the family Centrarchidae, of North America, closely related to the perch.

**sunflower** /ˈsʌnflaʊə/, *n.* any plant of the genus *Helianthus,* characterised by yellow-rayed flowers, as *H. annuus,* the common species of North America, a tall plant grown for its showy flowers, and for its seeds which are valued as food for poultry and as the source of an oil.

sunflower

**sung** /sʌŋ/, *v.* past tense and past participle of **sing.**

**sunglass** /ˈsʌnglas/, *n.* →**burning-glass.**

**sunglasses** /ˈsʌnglasəz/, *n.pl.* spectacles having tinted, darkened, or polaroid lenses to protect the eyes from the glare of the sun.

**sunglow** /ˈsʌngloʊ/, *n.* a diffused hazy light seen round the sun, due to particles of foreign matter in the atmosphere.

**sun-god** /ˈsʌn-gɒd/, *n.* **1.** the sun considered or personified as a deity. **2.** a god identified or associated with the sun.

**sunhat** /ˈsʌnhæt/, *n.* **1.** a soft, usu. light-coloured hat with a shady brim. **2.** →**sunbonnet.**

**sun-helmet** /ˈsʌn-hɛlmət/, *n.* →**topee.**

**sunhood** /ˈsʌnhʊd/, *n. Archit.* a part of a building designed to keep glare from the windows without excluding light.

**sunk** /sʌŋk/, *v.* a past tense and past participle of **sink.**

**sunken** /ˈsʌŋkən/, *v.* **1.** a past participle of **sink.** *–adj.* **2.** having sunk or having been sunk beneath the surface; submerged. **3.** having settled down to a lower level, as walls. **4.** depressed or lying below the general level, as a garden. **5.** hollow: *sunken cheeks.*

**sunken garden** /– ˈgadn/, *n.* a garden or part of a garden lying below the level of the surrounding ground.

**sunk fence** /sʌŋk ˈfɛns/, *n.* See **ha-ha**[2].

**sunlamp** /ˈsʌnlæmp/, *n.* **1.** a lamp which generates ultraviolet rays, used as a therapeutic device, to induce artificial suntan, etc. **2.** a source of light used in cinema photography, consisting essentially of a bright lamp whose light is intensified and directed by an arrangement of parabolic mirrors.

**sunless** /ˈsʌnləs/, *adj.* **1.** characterised by lack of sunlight; dark: *a sunless room.* **2.** overcast: *a sunless day.* **3.** gloomy; dismal; depressing: *a sunless attitude to life.* – **sunlessly,** *adv.* – **sunlessness,** *n.*

**sunlight** /ˈsʌnlaɪt/, *n.* the light of the sun.

**sunlit** /ˈsʌnlɪt/, *adj.* lit by the sun.

**sun lizard** /ˈsʌn lɪzəd/, *n.* →**garden lizard.**

**sunlounge** /ˈsʌnlaʊndʒ/, *n.* →**sunroom.**

**sunn** /sʌn/, *n.* **1.** a tall East Indian shrub, *Crotalaria juncea,* with slender branches and yellow flowers, and an inner bark which yields a hemp-like fibre used for making ropes, sacking, etc. **2.** the fibre. Also, **sunn hemp.** [Hind. *san*]

**sunnies** /ˈsʌniz/, *n. pl. Colloq.* →**sunglasses.**

**sunny** /ˈsʌni/, *adj.,* **-nier, -niest. 1.** abounding in sunshine: *a sunny day.* **2.** exposed to, lit or warmed by the direct rays of the sun: *a sunny room.* **3.** pertaining to or proceeding from the sun; solar. **4.** resembling the sun. **5.** cheery, cheerful, or joyous: *a sunny disposition.* – **sunnily,** *adv.* – **sunniness,** *n.*

**sunny side** /ˈ– saɪd/, *n.* **1.** the side exposed to most sunlight, as the north-facing side of a house. **2.** a comparatively cheerful or optimistic point of view. **3. sunny side up,** *Colloq.* (of eggs) fried on one side only.

**sun orchid** /ˈsʌn ɔkəd/, *n.* any species of the terrestrial orchid genus *Thelymitra,* some species of which expand their flowers only in bright sunshine.

**sun-porch** /ˈsʌn-pɔtʃ/, *n.* a porch or veranda, sometimes partially enclosed with glass, positioned so as to catch much sunlight.

**sun-power** /ˈsʌn-paʊə/, *n.* power obtained from concentrated heat of the sun's rays.

**sunproof** /ˈsʌnpruf/, *adj.* impervious to damage by the rays of the sun.

**sunray** /ˈsʌnreɪ/, *n.* **1.** a ray of the sun. **2.** (*pl.*) ultraviolet rays, as from a sunlamp. *–adj.* **3.** sending forth ultraviolet rays: *a sunray lamp.*

**sunrise** /ˈsʌnraɪz/, *n.* **1.** the rise or ascent of the sun above the horizon in the morning. **2.** the atmospheric phenomena accompanying this. **3.** the time when the sun rises.

**sunroof** /ˈsʌnruf/, *n.* **1.** →**sundeck** (def. 1). **2.** →**sunshine roof.**

**sunroom** /ˈsʌnrum/, *n.* a room having extensive windows positioned so as to admit much sunlight.

**sunset** /ˈsʌnsɛt/, *n.* **1.** the setting or descent of the sun below the horizon in the evening. **2.** the atmospheric phenomena accompanying this. **3.** the time when the sun sets. **4.** the close or final stage of any period.

**sunshade** /ˈsʌnʃeɪd/, *n.* **1.** something used as a protection from the rays of the sun. **2.** →**parasol. 3.** *Chiefly U.S.* a sunblind, esp. one over a shopwindow.

**sun shield** /ˈsʌn ʃild/, *n.* a strip usu. of metal affixed outside the upper part of a car's windscreen, so as to provide protection for the interior from sun.

**sunshine** /ˈsʌnʃaɪn/, *n.* **1.** the shining of the sun; the direct light of the sun. **2.** brightness or radiance; cheerfulness, happiness, or prosperity. **3.** a source of cheer or happiness. **4.** the effect of the sun in lighting and heating a place. **5.** a place where the direct rays of the sun fall. *–adj.* **6.** bright, cheerful, or prosperous. – **sun-shiny,** *adj.*

**sunshine roof** /ˈ– ruf/, *n.* a part of a car roof which can be slid open to admit sunlight. Also, **sun roof.**

**sunshine wattle** /– ˈwɒtl/, *n.* a shrub, *Acacia botrycephala,* found in south-eastern Australia where it flowers profusely in springtime.

**sunspot** /ˈsʌnspɒt/, *n.* **1.** one of the relatively dark patches which appear periodically on the surface of the sun, and which have a certain effect on terrestrial magnetism and other terrestrial phenomena. Their appearance is spasmodic but their number reaches a maximum approximately every eleven years (the **sunspot cycle**). **2.** →**hyperkeratosis.**

**sun spurge** /ˈsʌn spɜdʒ/, *n.* a small annual herb, *Euphorbia helioscopia,* with a flat inflorescence which is turned towards the sun, a common weed of Europe.

**sunstone** /ˈsʌnstoʊn/, *n.* aventurine felspar.

**sunstroke** /ˈsʌnstroʊk/, *n.* a condition caused by excessive exposure to the sun, marked by prostration, which may lead to convulsions, coma, and death.

**sunstruck** /ˈsʌnstrʌk/, *adj.* affected with sunstroke.

**sunsuit** /ˈsʌnsut/, *n.* a playsuit, as worn for sunbathing, on the beach, etc.

**suntan** /ˈsʌntæn/, *n.* brownness of the skin induced by exposure to the sun, cultivated by some as a mark of health or beauty. Also, **tan.** – **sun-tanned,** *adj.*

**suntrap** /ˈsʌntræp/, *n.* any place which is built or situated so that it receives a large amount of sun.

**sun-up** /ˈsʌn-ʌp/, *n.* →**sunrise.**

**sun visor** /ˈsʌn vaɪzə/, *n.* **1.** →**visor** (def. 4). **2.** a fixed shield mounted outside the car above the windscreen as a protection against glare.

**sunward** /ˈsʌnwəd/, *adj.* **1.** directed towards the sun. *–adv.* **2.** sunwards.

**sunwards** /ˈsʌnwədz/, *adv.* towards the sun. Also, **sunward.**

**sunwise** /ˈsʌnwaɪz/, *adv.* **1.** in the direction of the sun's apparent daily motion. **2.** clockwise.

**sun-worship** /ˈsʌn-wɜʃəp/, *n.* the practice of giving reverence to the sun as a deity. – **sunworshipper,** *n.*

**suo jure** /suoʊ ˈdʒʊəri/, *adv.* in his (her, its, one's) own right. [L]

**suo loco** /suoʊ ˈlɒkoʊ/, *adv.* in one's own or rightful place. [L]

**sup**[1] /sʌp/, *v.,* **supped, supping.** *–v.i.* **1.** to eat the evening meal; take supper. *–v.t.* **2.** to provide with or entertain at supper. [ME *sope,* from OF *soper*]

**sup**[2] /sʌp/, *v.,* **supped, supping,** *n.* *–v.t.* **1.** to take (liquid food, or any liquid) into the mouth in small quantities, as from a spoon or a cup. *–v.i.* **2.** to take liquid into the mouth in small quantities, as by spoonfuls or sips. *–n.* **3.** a mouthful or small portion of liquid food or of drink. [ME *suppe,* OE *suppa,* akin to OE *sūpan,* c. G *saufen* drink. Cf. SIP, SOP, SUP[1], SOUP]

**sup-,** variant of **sub-** (by assimilation) before *p.*

**sup.,** superior.

**super** /ˈsupə/, *n. Colloq.* **1.** →**superannuation.** **2.** high-octane petrol. **3.** →**superintendent.** **4.** →**supernumerary.** **5.** →**superphosphate.** **6.** →**supervisor.** *–adj.* **7.** of a superior quality, grade, size, etc. **8.** extremely fine, pleasing, etc. *–v.t.* **9.** to treat (land) with superphosphate.

**super-,** **1.** a prefix meaning 'superior to' or 'over-', applied variously, as of quality (*superman*), size (*superdreadnought*), degree (*superheat, supersensitive*), space (*superstructure*), and other meanings (*supersede, supernatural*). **2.** *Chem.* a prefix having the same sense as 'per-'. [L, combining form of *super,* adv. and prep., above, beyond, in addition]

**Super.,** Superintendent.

**superable** /ˈsupərəbəl/, *adj.* capable of being overcome; surmountable. [L *superābilis*] – **superably,** *adv.*

**superabound** /supərəˈbaʊnd/, *v.i.* **1.** to abound beyond something else. **2.** to be very abundant or too abundant (fol. by *in* or *with*).

**superabundant** /supərəˈbʌndənt/, *adj.* exceedingly or excessively abundant; being more than sufficient. – **superabundance,** *n.* – **superabundantly,** *adv.*

**superacute** /supərəˈkjut/, *adj.* extremely acute.

**superadd** /supərˈæd/, *v.t.* to add over and above; join as a further addition; add besides. [L *superaddere*] – **superaddition** /supərəˈdɪʃən/, *n.*

**superalloy** /supərˈælɔɪ/, *n. Metall.* an alloy developed for very high temperature service where relatively high stresses (tensile, vibratory and shock) are encountered and where oxidation resistance is frequently required.

**superannuate** /supərˈænjueɪt/, *v.t.,* **-ated, -ating.** **1.** to allow to retire from service or office on a pension, on account of age or infirmity. **2.** to set aside as out of date; remove as too old. [ML *superannātus* over a year old (said of cattle); for *-u-* see ANNUAL]

**superannuated** /supərˈænjueɪtəd/, *adj.* **1.** retired on account of age or infirmity. **2.** too old for use, work, service, or a position. **3.** antiquated or obsolete.

**superannuation** /ˌsupərænjuˈeɪʃən/, *n.* **1.** the act of superannuating. **2.** the state of being superannuated. **3.** a pension or allowance to a superannuated person. **4.** a sum paid periodically as contribution to a superannuation fund.

superb blue wren

**superannuation fund** /ˈ– fʌnd/, *n.* a retirement fund to which an employee (and usu. also his employer) contribute during the period of his employment, and which provides benefits to him during illness and after retirement. Also, **provident fund.**

**superb** /səˈpɜb, su-/, *adj.* **1.** stately, majestic, or grand: *superb jewels.* **2.** admirably fine or excellent: *a superb performance.* **3.** of a proudly imposing appearance or kind: *superb beauty.* [L *superbus* proud, distinguished] – **superbly,** *adv.* – **superbness,** *n.*

**superb blue wren,** *n.* a small bird, *Malurus cyaneus,* the adult male in breeding plumage having bright blue feathers on the crown and upper back, while the female is brown; widely distributed throughout south-eastern coastal areas of Australia.

**superb lyrebird** /səpɜb ˈlaɪəbɜd/, *n.* the larger of the two lyrebird species, *Menura novaehollandiae,* the male being noted for its fine tail and for building mounds upon which to display; native pheasant.

**supercalender** /supəˈkæləndə/, *v.t.* **1.** to give a highgloss finish to (paper) by pressing in a calender. *–n.* **2.** a calender for doing this.

**supercalendered paper** /supəˌkæləndəd ˈpeɪpə/, *n.* paper with a surface glazed by repeated runs through highly polished copper or zinc rollers.

**supercargo** /ˈsupəˌkagoʊ/, *n., pl.* **-goes.** an officer on merchant ship who is in charge of the cargo and the commercial concerns of the voyage. [earlier *supracargo,* from Sp. *sobrecargo*]

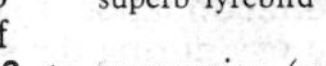

superb lyrebird

**supercharge** /ˈsupətʃadʒ/, *v.t.,* **-charged, -charging.** **1.** to supply air to (an internal-combustion engine) at greater than atmospheric pressure; boost. **2.** to charge with an excessive amount of emotion, tension, energy, or the like. **3.** to pressurise (a gas or liquid).

**supercharger** /ˈsupətʃadʒə/, *n.* a mechanism attached to an internal-combustion engine to deliver to the cylinders a volume of air greater than that from the suction of the pistons alone, used to increase power; booster.

**superciliary** /supəˈsɪljəri/, *adj.* **1.** situated over the eye. **2.** *Anat., Zool.* **a.** of or pertaining to the eyebrow. **b.** having a conspicuous line or marking over the eye, as certain birds. **3.** on the frontal bone at the level of the eyebrow. *–n.* **4.** a superciliary ridge or mark. [NL *superciliāris,* from L *supercilium* eyebrow]

**supercilious** /supəˈsɪliəs/, *adj.* haughtily disdainful or contemptuous, as persons, their expression, bearing, etc. [L *superciliōsus*] – **superciliously,** *adv.* – **superciliousness,** *n.*

**superclass** /ˈsupəklas/, *n.* a group or category of related classes in biological classification within a phylum or subphylum.

**superconductivity** /ˌsupəˌkɒndʌkˈtɪvəti/, *n.* the phenomenon of greatly increased electrical conductivity shown by certain substances at temperatures approaching absolute zero. – **superconductor** /supəkənˈdʌktə/, *n.* – **superconducting** /supəkənˈdʌktɪŋ/, *adj.*

**supercool** /ˈsupəkul/, *v.t.* **1.** to cool (a liquid) below its freezing point without producing solidification. *–v.i.* **2.** to become supercooled. *–adj* **3.** *Colloq.* extremely sophisticated, fashionable, smart, etc.

**supercritical** /supəˈkrɪtɪkəl/, *adj.* denoting or pertaining to a nuclear reaction or a nuclear reactor in which a chain-reaction is self-sustaining. Cf. **subcritical.**

**superdense** /supəˈdɛns/, *adj.* extremely dense or compressed. – **superdensity,** *n.*

**superdense theory** /ˈ– ˌθɪəri/, *n.* the cosmological theory that the universe has evolved from one superdense agglomeration

---

**supercelestial,** *adj.*
**superexaltation,** *n.*
**superexcellence,** *n.*
**superexcellent,** *adj.*
**superordinary,** *adj.*
**superrational,** *adj.*
**superrationally,** *adv.*
**supersalesman,** *n.*
**supersalesmanship,** *n.*
**supersubstantial,** *adj.*
**supersuperlative,** *n.*
**supertemporal,** *adj.*

of matter which suffered an explosion; the observed expansion of the universe is regarded as a result of this explosion, the galaxies flying apart like fragments from an exploding bomb.

**superdreadnought** /supə'drɛdnɔt/, *n.* a battleship of the general type of the dreadnought, but much larger and with superior armament.

**super-duper** /'supə-dupə/, *adj. Colloq.* extremely fine, great, pleasing, etc. [dissimilated reduplication of SUPER (def. 8)]

**superego** /supər'igoʊ/, *n.* a personification of the development of the ego in the direction of social ideals, etc., so that distress is felt when the ego is unduly influenced by primitive impulses; similar to 'conscience', but is largely unconscious.

**superelevated** /supər'ɛləveɪtəd/, *adj.* (of a curve in a road or railway track) having superelevation; banked.

**superelevation** /ˌsupərɛlə'veɪʃən/, *n.* **1.** an elevation at a curve of the outer rail of a railway track or outer side of a road above the inner, to counteract centrifugal force of vehicles; cant. **2.** the vertical difference between the inner and outer rails of a track, or sides of road, at a curve.

**supereminent** /supər'ɛmənənt/, *adj.* of superior eminence, rank, or dignity; distinguished, conspicuous, or noteworthy above others. [L *supereminens*] – **supereminence,** *n.* – **supereminently,** *adv.*

**supererogate** /supər'ɛrəgeɪt/, *v.i.*, **-gated, -gating.** to do more than duty requires. [LL *superērogātus,* pp., from L *super* above + *ērogātus,* pp., paid out] – **supererogation** /ˌsupərɛrə'geɪʃən/, *n.*

**supererogatory** /ˌsupərə'rɒgətri/, *adj.* **1.** going beyond the requirements of duty. **2.** →**superfluous.**

**superette** /supə'rɜt/, *n. N.Z.* a grocery store or small supermarket, which is open after normal trading hours.

**superfamily** /'supəˌfæməli/, *n., pl.* **-lies.** a group or category ranking above a family.

**superfecundation** /ˌsupəfikən'deɪʃən/, *n.* the fertilisation of two ova during the same menstrual cycle by two different acts of coition.

**superfetate** /supə'fiteɪt/, *v.i.*, **-tated, -tating.** to fertilise an ovum after a prior conception but before the first one has run its course. [LL *superfētātus,* pp.] – **superfetation** /supəfə'teɪʃən/, *n.*

**superficial** /supə'fɪʃəl/, *adj.* **1.** of or pertaining to the surface: *superficial measurement.* **2.** being at, on, or near the surface: *a superficial wound.* **3.** external or outward: *a superficial resemblance.* **4.** concerned with or comprehending only what is on the surface or obvious: *a superficial observer.* **5.** shallow; not profound or thorough: *a superficial writer.* **6.** apparent, rather than real: *superficial piety.* [ME, from LL *superficiālis,* from L *superficies* SUPERFICIES] – **superficiality** /ˌsupəfɪʃi'æləti/, **superficialness,** *n.* – **superficially,** *adv.*

**superficial foot** /– 'fʊt/, *n.* a unit of volume of timber in the imperial system, equal to 1 $ft^2$ × 1 in. (144 cu. in.) or 2.359 737 216 × $10^{-3}$ $m^3$. Also, **board foot, super foot.**

**superficies** /supə'fɪʃiz/, *n., pl.* **-cies.** **1.** the surface, outer face, or outside of a thing. **2.** the outward appearance, esp. as distinguished from the inner nature. [L]

**superfine** /'supəfaɪn/, *adj.* **1.** extra fine; unusually fine. **2.** excessively fine, refined, or nice.

**superfix** /'supəfɪks/, *n.* (in linguistics) a suprasegmental feature such as lexical stress. Cf. **prefix, suffix.**

**superfluid** /'supəfluəd/, *n.* **1.** liquid helium at temperatures below about 2K with special reference to its negligible internal friction and very high thermal conductivity. *–adj.* **2.** denoting a superfluid. – **superfluidity** /supəflu'ɪdəti/, *n.*

**superfluity** /supə'fluəti/, *n., pl.* **-ties.** **1.** the state of being superfluous. **2.** superabundant or excessive amount. **3.** something superfluous, as a luxury.

**superfluous** /su'pɜfluəs/, *adj.* **1.** being over and above what is sufficient or required. **2.** unnecessary or needless. **3.** *Obs.* lavish or extravagant. [ME, from L *superfluus* overflowing] – **superfluously,** *adv.* – **superfluousness,** *n.*

**superflux** /'supəflʌks/, *n.* →**superfluity.**

**super foot** /'supə fʊt/, *n.* →**superficial foot.**

**super ft,** superficial foot.

**supergene** /'supədʒin/, *adj.* **1.** deposited or enriched by solutions which generally move downwards, used esp. of an ore deposit (opposed to *hypogene*). **2.** of, or pertaining to a process of deposition by these solutions. [SUPER- + *-gene* (var. of -GEN)]

**supergiant** /'supədʒaɪənt/, *n.* any of a number of very large, highly luminous, low-density stars, as Betelgeuse or Antares.

**superglacial** /supə'gleɪʃəl, -siəl/, *adj.* **1.** on the surface of a glacier. **2.** believed to have been formerly on the surface of a glacier: *superglacial debris.*

**super group** /'supə grup/, *n.* a band which is totally comprised of recognised virtuoso performers.

**superheat** /'supəhit/, *n.* **1.** the state of being superheated. **2.** the amount of superheating. *–v.t.* **3.** to heat to an extreme degree or to a very high temperature. **4.** to heat (a liquid) above its boiling point without the formation of bubbles of vapour. **5.** to heat (a gas, as steam not in contact with water) to such a degree that its temperature may be lowered or its pressure increased without the conversion of any of the gas into liquid. – **superheater** /supə'hitə/, *n.*

**superheavy** /'supəhɛvi/, *adj.* (of a nucleus) having mass numbers above those of the actinides.

**superhero** /'supəhɪəroʊ/, *n.* a comic book or fantasy character, distinctively dressed, endowed with superhuman or magical powers, and involved in a struggle with the forces of evil.

**superheterodyne** /supə'hɛtərədaɪn/, *adj.* **1.** denoting or pertaining to a method of receiving radio signals by which the incoming modulated wave is changed by the heterodyne process to a lower frequency (the intermediate frequency, which is inaudible) to facilitate amplification and the rejection of unwanted signals. *–n.* **2.** a superheterodyne receiver.

**super high frequency,** *n.* a radio frequency of between 3000 and 30 000 megacycles per second. *Abbrev.:* SHF

**superhuman** /'supəhjumən/, *adj.* **1.** above or beyond what is human; having a higher nature or greater powers than man. **2.** exceeding ordinary human power, achievement, experience, etc.: *a superhuman effort.* – **superhumanity** /supəhju'mænəti/, *n.* – **superhumanly,** *adv.*

**superimpose** /supərɪm'poʊz/, *v.t.*, **-posed, -posing.** **1.** to impose, place, or set on something else. **2.** to put or join as an addition (fol. by *on* or *upon*). – **superimposition** /ˌsupərɪmpə'zɪʃən/, *n.*

**superincumbent** /supərɪn'kʌmbənt/, *adj.* **1.** lying or resting on something else. **2.** situated above; overhanging. **3.** exerted from above, as pressure. – **superincumbence, superincumbency,** *n.*

**superinduce** /supərɪn'djus/, *v.t.*, **-duced, -ducing.** to bring in or induce as an added feature, circumstance, etc.; superimpose. [LL *superindūcere*] – **superinducement,** *n.* – **superinduction** /supərɪn'dʌkʃən/, *n.*

**superintend** /supərɪn'tɛnd, suprɪn-/, *v.t., v.i.* to oversee and direct (work, processes, affairs, etc.); exercise supervision over (an institution, place, etc.). [LL *superintendere*] – **superintendence,** *n.*

**superintendency** /supərɪn'tɛndənsi, suprɪn-/, *n., pl.* **-cies.** **1.** a district under a superintendent. **2.** the position or work of a superintendent.

**superintendent** /supərɪn'tɛndənt, suprɪn-/, *n.* **1.** one who has the oversight or direction of some work, enterprise, (esp. farming, grazing, etc.), establishment, institution, house, etc. **2.** a police officer ranking above chief inspector and below chief superintendent. **3.** the rank. **4.** (formerly) one who has charge of a gang of convicts. *–adj.* **5.** superintending. – **superintendentship,** *n.*

**superior** /sə'pɪəriə, su-/, *adj.* **1.** higher in station, rank, degree, or grade: *a superior officer.* **2.** above the average in excellence, merit, intelligence, etc. **3.** of higher grade or quality. **4.** greater in quantity or amount: *superior numbers.* **5.** showing a consciousness or feeling of being above others in such respects: *superior airs.* **6.** not yielding or susceptible (fol. by *to*): *to be superior to temptation.* **7.** *Bot.* **a.** situated above some other organ. **b.** (of a calyx) seeming to originate from the top of the ovary. **c.** (of an ovary) free from the calyx. **8.** *Print.* higher than the main line of type, as algebraic exponents, reference figures, etc.; superscript. **9.** *Astron.* **a.** (of a planet) having an orbit outside that of the earth. **b.** (of a conjunction of an inferior planet) denoting a conjunction in which the sun is between the earth and the planet. *–n.* **10.** one superior to another or others. **11.** *Print.*

a superior letter or figure. **12.** *Eccles.* the head of a monastery, convent, or the like. [ME, from L, compar. of *superus* above] – **superiorly,** *adv.*

**superior court** /'– ˌkɔt/, *n.* (in law) any court above the summary or equivalent inferior courts, as the State Supreme Courts, the Courts of Criminal Appeal, etc.

**superiority** /səpɪəri'ɒrəti, su-/, *n.* the quality or fact of being superior.

**superiority complex** /'– kɒmpleks/, *n. Colloq.* an exaggerated estimation of one's own worth. [modelled on INFERIORITY COMPLEX]

**superjacent** /supə'dʒeɪsənt/, *adj.* lying above or upon something else. [LL *superjacens,* ppr.]

**superl.,** superlative.

**superlative** /su'pɜlətɪv/, *adj.* **1.** of the highest kind or order; surpassing all other or others; supreme; extreme: *superlative wisdom.* **2.** being more than is proper or normal; exaggerated in language or style. **3.** *Gram.* **a.** denoting the highest degree of the comparison of adjectives and adverbs, as English *smoothest* in contrast to *smooth* and *smoother.* **b.** having or pertaining to the function or meaning of this degree of comparison. *–n.* **4.** something superlative; a superlative example. **5.** the utmost degree. **6.** *Gram.* the superlative degree, or a form therein. [ME, from LL *superlātīvus,* from L *superlātus,* pp., carried beyond] – **superlatively,** *adv.* – **superlativeness,** *n.*

**superlunary** /supə'lunəri/, *adj.* **1.** situated above or beyond the moon. **2.** celestial, rather than earthly. Also, **superlunar.**

**superman** /'supəmæn/, *n., pl.* **-men.** **1.** a man of more than human powers. **2.** an ideal superior being conceived by Nietzsche as the product of human evolution, being in effect a ruthless egoist of superior strength, cunning, and force of will. **3.** a man who prevails by virtue of such characteristics. [translation of G *Übermensch*]

**supermarket** /'supəmakət/, *n.* a large, usu. self-service, retail store or market selling food and other domestic goods.

**supermedial** /supə'midiəl/, *adj.* above the middle or centre.

**supermundane** /supə'mʌndeɪn/, *adj.* above earthly or worldly things.

**supernal** /su'pɜnəl/, *adj.* **1.** being in or belonging to the heaven of divine beings; heavenly, celestial, or divine. **2.** lofty; of more than earthly or human excellence, powers, etc. **3.** being on high or in the sky or visible heavens. [late ME, from L *supernus* being above, on high + -AL[1]] – **supernally,** *adv.*

**supernatant** /supə'neɪtnt/, *adj.* floating above, or on the surface. [L *supernatans,* ppr.]

**supernational** /supə'næʃnəl/, *adj.* **1.** supranational. **2.** extremely or fanatically patriotic. – **supernationally,** *adv.* – **supernationalism,** *n.* – **supernationalist,** *n.*

**supernatural** /supə'nætʃrəl, -'nætʃərəl/, *adj.* **1.** being above or beyond what is natural; not explicable in terms of natural laws or phenomena. **2.** of or pertaining to supernatural beings, as ghosts, spirits, etc. **3.** abnormal; extraordinary; unprecedented: *a man of supernatural intelligence.* *–n.* **4.** supernatural forces, effects, and beings collectively. **5.** the action of the supernatural as it intervenes in the natural order. **6.** a supernatural being. – **supernaturally,** *adv.*

**supernaturalise** /supə'nætʃrəlaɪz, -'nætʃərə-/, *v.t.,* **-lised, -lising.** to make supernatural or attribute supernatural qualities. Also, **supernaturalize.**

**supernaturalism** /supə'nætʃrəlɪzəm, -'nætʃərə-/, *n.* **1.** supernatural character or agency. **2.** belief in the doctrine of supernatural (divine) agency as manifested in the world, in human events, religious revelation, etc. – **supernaturalist,** *n., adj.* – **supernaturalistic** /ˌsupənætʃrə'lɪstɪk/, *adj.*

**supernormal** /supə'nɔməl/, *adj.* **1.** beyond that which is normal. **2.** in greater number, amount, concentration, or the like than normal. – **supernormality** /supənɔ'mæləti/, *n.* – **supernormally,** *adv.*

**supernova** /supə'noʊvə/, *n.* an extremely bright nova which can become up to $10^8$ times brighter than the sun during the explosive process; only two have been observed in the Milky Way.

**supernumerary** /supə'njumərəri/, *adj., n., pl.* **-aries.** *–adj.* **1.** being in excess of the usual, proper, or prescribed number; additional; extra. **2.** associated with a regular body or staff as an assistant or substitute in case of necessity. *–n.* **3.** a supernumerary or extra person or thing. **4.** a supernumerary official or employee. **5.** *Theat.* one not belonging to the regular company, who appears on the stage but has no lines to speak. [LL *supernumerārius* in excess, from L phrase *super numerum* beyond the number]

**superorder** /'supərɔdə/, *n.* a group or category of related orders within a class or subclass.

**superordinate** /supər'ɔdənət/, *adj., n.;* /supər'ɔdəneɪt/, *v.,* **-nated, -nating.** *–adj.* **1.** higher in rank, degree, etc. **2.** *Logic.* of superior order or generality, as genus to species or as universal to particular. *–n.* **3.** one who or something which is superordinate. **4.** *Logic.* a proposition or a class of higher generality than another. *–v.t.* **5.** to place in a superordinate position or relation.

**superordination** /ˌsupərɔdə'neɪʃən/, *n. Logic.* the act of making a proposition or a class superordinate to another.

**superorganic** /supərɔ'gænɪk/, *adj.* **1.** above or beyond what is organic. **2.** *Sociol.* of or pertaining to elements of a society or culture conceived as independent of the individual members of the society.

**superoxide** /supər'ɒksaɪd/, *n.* a higher oxide of a metal which yields hydrogen peroxide on treatment with a dilute acid.

**superphosphate** /supə'fɒsfeɪt/, *n.* **1.** an artificial fertiliser consisting of a mixture of calcium sulphate and calcium dihydrogen phosphate, $Ca(H_2PO_4)_2$, made by treating phosphate rock with sulphuric acid. **2.** any fertiliser containing this mixture.

**superphysical** /supə'fɪzɪkəl/, *adj.* above or beyond what is physical; hyperphysical.

**superporker** /'supəpɔkə/, *n.* a prime bacon pig.

**superpose** /supə'poʊz/, *v.t.,* **-posed, -posing.** **1.** to place above or upon something else, or one upon another. **2.** *Geom.* to place (one figure) ideally in the space occupied by another, so that the two figures coincide throughout their whole extent. [F *superposer,* from *super-* SUPER- + *poser* POSE[1], after L *superpōnere*] – **superposable,** *adj.*

**superposition** /supəpə'zɪʃən/, *n.* **1.** the act or fact of superposing. **2.** *Geol.* the principle that in sedimentary rocks an upper stratum is younger than a lower one, unless earth movements have reversed the order of strata.

**superpower** /'supəpaʊə/, *n.* **1.** power, esp. mechanical or electric power, on an extraordinary scale secured by the linking together of a number of separate power systems, with a view to more efficient and economical generation and distribution. **2.** an extremely powerful and influential nation.

**super-regenerative** /supə-rə'dʒenərətɪv/, *adj. Radio.* denoting a type of receiver using regeneration.

**supersaturate** /supə'sætʃəreɪt/, *v.t.,* **-rated, -rating.** to increase the concentration of (a solution) beyond saturation; saturate abnormally. – **supersaturation** /ˌsupəsætʃə'reɪʃən/, *n.*

**superscribe** /'supəskraɪb/, *v.t.,* **-scribed, -scribing.** **1.** to write (words, letters, one's name, etc.) above or on something. **2.** to inscribe or mark (something) with writing at the top or on the outside or surface; put an inscription above or on. [LL *superscrībere*]

**superscript** /'supəskrɪpt/, *adj.* **1.** written above, as a diacritical mark or a correction of a word. **2.** higher than the main line of type; superior. *–n.* **3.** a superscript or superior letter, figure, etc. **4.** a specifying or distinguishing letter or symbol following and slightly above a figure, letter or symbol: *i, j, are superscripts in* $b^{i,j}$. **5.** *Obs.* a superscription, as of a letter.

**superscription** /supə'skrɪpʃən/, *n.* **1.** the act of superscribing. **2.** that which is superscribed. **3.** an address on a letter or the like. **4.** *Pharm.* the Latin word *recipe* (take), or the symbol ℞ in a prescription.

**supersede** /supə'sid/, *v.t.,* **-seded, -seding.** **1.** to replace in power, authority, effectiveness, acceptance, use, etc., as by another person or thing. **2.** to set aside, as void, useless, or obsolete, now usu. in favour of something mentioned. **3.** to displace in office or promotion by another. **4.** to succeed to the position, function, office, etc., of; supplant. [L *supersedēre* sit above] – **superseder,** *n.*

**supersedeas** /supə'sidiæs/, *n. Law.* (formerly) a writ showing good cause to stay proceedings.

**supersedure** /supə'sidʒə/, *n.* **1.** the act of superseding. **2.** the state of being superseded. Also, **supersession** /supə'sɛʃən/.

**supersensible** /supə'sɛnsəbəl/, *adj.* beyond the reach of the senses. – **supersensibly,** *adv.*

**supersensitise** /supə'sɛnsətaɪz/, *v.t.,* **-tised, -tising.** to make supersensitive. Also, **supersensitize.** – **supersensitisation** /ˌsupəsɛnsətaɪ'zeɪʃən/, *n.* – **supersensitiser,** *n.*

**supersensitive** /supə'sɛnsətɪv/, *adj.* →**hypersensitive.** – **supersensitiveness,** *n.*

**supersensory** /supə'sɛnsəri/, *adj.* beyond, or independent of, the organs of sense.

**supersensual** /supə'sɛnʃuəl/, *adj.* **1.** beyond the range of the senses. **2.** spiritual. **3.** very sensual.

**supersession** /supə'sɛʃən/, *n.* **1.** the state of being superseded. **2.** →**supersedure.**

**supersonic** /supə'sɒnɪk/, *adj.* **1.** (of sound frequencies) above the audible limit; ultrasonic. **2.** (of velocities) above the velocity of sound in the medium.

**supersonics** /supə'sɒnɪks/, *n.* →**ultrasonics.**

**superstar** /'supəsta/, *n.* a singer, actor, or showbusiness personality who is very famous.

**superstate** /'supəsteɪt/, *n.* a state or a governing power presiding over states subordinated to it.

**superstition** /supə'stɪʃən/, *n.* **1.** a belief or notion entertained, regardless of reason or knowledge, of the ominous significance of a particular thing, circumstance, occurrence, proceeding, or the like. **2.** any blindly accepted belief or notion. **3.** a system or collection of superstitious beliefs and customs. **4.** irrational fear of what is unknown or mysterious, esp. in connection with religion. **5.** (*pejor.*) belief in a religion or sect other than one's own. [ME, from L *superstitio,* lit., a standing over, as in wonder or awe]

**superstitious** /supə'stɪʃəs/, *adj.* **1.** of the nature of, characterised by, or proceeding from superstition: *superstitious fears.* **2.** pertaining to or connected with superstition: *superstitious legends.* **3.** full of or addicted to superstition. – **superstitiously,** *adv.* – **superstitiousness,** *n.*

**superstratum** /supə'stratəm/, *n., pl.* **-ta** /-tə/, **-tums.** an overlying stratum or layer.

**superstructure** /'supəstrʌktʃə/, *n.* **1.** all of an edifice above the basement or foundation. **2.** any structure built on something else. **3.** *Naut.* the parts of a vessel, as a warship, built above the main deck. **4.** that part of a bridge which rests on the piers and abutments. **5.** anything erected on a foundation or basis.

**supersubtle** /supə'sʌtl/, *adj.* extremely or excessively subtle; oversubtle. – **supersubtlety,** *n.*

**supertanker** /'supətæŋkə/, *n.* a very large tanker (ship).

**supertax** /'supətæks/, *n.* **1.** a tax in addition to a normal tax, as one upon income above a certain amount. **2.** →**surtax.**

**superterrestrial** /supətə'rɛstriəl/, *adj.* above the earth or earthly things; celestial.

**supertonic** /supə'tɒnɪk/, *n.* the second note of a musical scale, being the next above the tonic.

**supervene** /supə'vin/, *v.i.,* **-vened, -vening.** **1.** to come as something additional or extraneous (sometimes fol. by *on* or *upon*). **2.** to ensue. [L *supervenīre* follow] – **supervenience, supervention** /supə'vɛnʃən/, *n.* – **supervenient,** *adj.*

**supervise** /'supəvaɪz/, *v.t.,* **-vised, -vising.** to oversee (a process, work, workers, etc.) during execution or performance; superintend; have the oversight and direction of. [ML *supervīsus,* pp.]

**supervision** /supə'vɪʒən/, *n.* the act or function of supervising; oversight; superintendence.

**supervisor** /'supəvaɪzə/, *n.* **1.** one who supervises; a superintendent. **2.** (at some universities) a teacher who supervises the work of a student, esp. a research student or one studying for a higher degree. – **supervisorship,** *n.*

**supervisory** /'supəvaɪzəri/, *adj.* pertaining to or having supervision.

**supinate** /'sjupəneɪt/, *v.,* **-nated, -nating.** *–v.t.* **1.** to render supine; rotate or place (the hand or forelimb) so that the palmar surface is upwards when the limb is stretched forwards horizontally. *–v.i.* **2.** to become supinated. [L *supīnātus,* pp., bent backwards, laid on the back]

**supination** /sjupə'neɪʃən/, *n.* **1.** a turning of the hand so that the palm is facing upwards and the bones of the forearm are parallel (opposed to *pronation*). **2.** a comparable motion of the foot, consisting of adduction followed by inversion. **3.** the result of this rotation; the position so assumed.

**supinator** /'sjupəneɪtə/, *n.* a muscle which causes supination. [NL. See SUPINATE, -OR[2]]

**supine** /'sjupaɪn/, *adj.* **1.** lying on the back, or with the face or front upwards. **2.** having the palm upwards, as the hand. **3.** inactive; passive; inert; esp., inactive or passive from indolence or indifference. *–n.* **4.** (in Latin) a noun form derived from verbs, appearing only in the accusative and the dative-ablative, as *dictū* in *mirābile dictū* 'wonderful to say'. **5.** an analogous form in some other language. [L *supīnus*] – **supinely,** *adv.* – **supineness,** *n.*

**supp.,** **1.** supplement. **2.** supplementary. Also, **suppl.**

**supper** /'sʌpə/, *n.* **1.** a very light meal, as of a biscuit and a cup of tea taken at night, which is the last meal of the day. **2.** *Chiefly Brit. and U.S.* the evening meal; the last major meal of the day, taken in the evening. **3.** any evening meal often one forming part of a social entertainment. [ME, from OF *so(u)per,* n. use of *souper* SUP[1]]

**suppertime** /'sʌpətaɪm/, *n.* **1.** the time in the evening when supper is eaten. *–adj.* **2.** denoting, pertaining to, or taking place at this time.

**suppl.,** **1.** supplement. **2.** supplementary.

**supplant** /sə'plænt/, *v.t.* **1.** to displace or supersede, as one thing does another. **2.** to take the place of (another), as in office or favour, through scheming, strategy, or the like. **3.** to replace (one thing) by something else. [ME *supplante(n),* from L *supplantāre* trip up, overthrow] – **supplantation** /sʌplæn'teɪʃən/, *n.* – **supplanter,** *n.*

**supple** /'sʌpəl/, *adj.,* **-pler, -plest,** *v.,* **-pled, -pling.** *–adj.* **1.** bending readily without breaking or deformation; pliant; flexible: *a supple rod.* **2.** characterised by ease in bending; limber; lithe: *supple movements.* **3.** characterised by ease and adaptability in mental action. **4.** compliant or yielding. **5.** obsequious; servile. *–v.t., v.i.* **6.** to make or become supple. [ME *souple,* from OF, from L *supplex* bending under] – **suppleness,** *n.*

**supplejack** /'sʌpəldʒæk/, *n.* **1.** a strong, pliant cane or walking stick. **2.** any of various climbing shrubs with strong stems suitable for making walking sticks. **3.** a tree of inland Australia, *Ventilago viminalis.*

**supplely** /'sʌpəli/, *adv.* →**supply**[2].

**supplement** /'sʌpləmənt/, *n.;* /'sʌpləmɛnt/, *v.* *–n.* **1.** something added to complete a thing, supply a deficiency, or reinforce or extend a whole. **2.** a part added to a book, document, or the like to supply deficiencies or correct errors. **3.** a part, usu. of special character, issued as an additional feature of a newspaper or other periodical. **4.** *Maths.* the quantity by which an angle or an arc falls short of 180° or a semicircle. *–v.t.* **5.** to complete, add to, or extend by a supplement; form a supplement or addition to. **6.** to supply (a deficiency). [ME, from L *supplēmentum*] – **supplementation** /sʌpləmɛn'teɪʃən/, *n.* – **supplementer,** *n.*

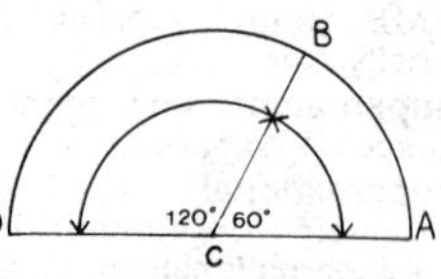

supplement (def. 4): angle BCD, supplement of angle BCA

**supplemental** /sʌplə'mɛntl/, *adj.* **1.** supplementary. **2.** *Law.* additional. – **supplementally,** *adv.*

**supplementary** /sʌplə'mɛntri/, *adj.* **1.** of the nature of or forming a supplement; additional. *–n.* **2.** one who or that which is supplementary. – **supplementarily,** *adv.*

**supplementary angle** /– 'æŋgəl/, *n.* either of two angles whose sum is 180°.

**suppletion** /sə'pliʃən/, *n.* **1.** the presence of one or more suppletive forms in a paradigm. **2.** the use of suppletive forms, or an instance of such use.

**suppletive** /sə'plitɪv, 'sʌplətɪv/, *adj.* **1.** (of a linguistic form) serving as an inflected form of a word with a totally different stem, e.g., *went* as the preterite of *go.* **2.** (of a paradigm) including one or more suppletive forms. **3.** (of inflection) characterised by the use of suppletive forms.

**suppletory** /'sʌplətəri, -tri/, *adj.* supplying a deficiency. [LL *supplētorius,* from L *supplētus,* pp., filled up]

**suppliance**[1] /sə'plaɪəns/, *n.* the act of supplying. Also, **supplial** /sə'plaɪəl/.

**suppliance**[2] /'sʌpliəns/, *n.* the act of supplicating; entreaty; supplication.

**suppliant** /'sʌpliənt/, *n.* **1.** one who supplicates; a humble petitioner. *–adj.* **2.** supplicating. **3.** expressive of supplication, as words, actions, etc. [ME, from F, ppr. of *supplier,* OF *souplier,* from L *supplicāre* supplicate] – **suppliantly,** *adv.* – **suppliantness, suppliance,** *n.*

**supplicant** /'sʌpləkənt/, *adj.* **1.** supplicating. *–n.* **2.** a suppliant. [L *supplicans,* ppr.]

**supplicate** /'sʌpləkeɪt/, *v.,* **-cated, -cating.** *–v.i.* **1.** to pray humbly; make humble and earnest entreaty or petition. *–v.t.* **2.** to pray humbly to; entreat or petition humbly. **3.** to seek by humble entreaty. [late ME, from L *supplicātus,* pp., begged]

**supplication** /sʌplə'keɪʃən/, *n.* the act of supplicating; humble prayer, entreaty, or petition.

**supplicatory** /'sʌpləkətri, sʌplə'keɪtəri/, *adj.* making or expressing supplication.

**supply**[1] /sə'plaɪ/, *v.,* **-plied, -plying,** *n., pl.* **-plies.** *–v.t.* **1.** to furnish (a person, establishment, place, etc.) with what is lacking or requisite. **2.** to furnish or provide (something wanting or requisite): *to supply electricity to a community.* **3.** to make up (a deficiency); make up for (a loss, lack, absence, etc.); satisfy (a need, demand, etc.). **4.** to fill (a place, vacancy, etc.); occupy as a substitute. *–v.i.* **5.** to fill the place of another, temporarily, or as a substitute. *–n.* **6.** the act of supplying, furnishing, providing, satisfying, etc. **7.** that which is supplied. **8.** a quantity of something provided or on hand, as for use; a stock or store. **9.** (*usu. pl.*) a provision, stock, or store of food or other things necessary for maintenance. **10.** a parliamentary grant or provision of money for the expenses of government. **11.** *Econ.* the quantity of a commodity, etc., that is in the market and available for purchase, or that is available for purchase at a particular price. **12.** *Elect.* a source of electrical energy. **13.** (*pl.*) *Mil.* **a.** articles and materials used by an army or navy of types rapidly used up, such as food, clothing, soap, and fuel. **b.** the furnishing of supplies, and the management of supply units and installations. **14.** *Obs.* reinforcements. **15.** *Obs.* aid. *–adj.* **16.** *Elect.* denoting or pertaining to a source of electrical energy or its characteristics. [ME *supplye,* from OF *so(u)pl(e)ier,* from L *supplēre* fill up] – **supplier,** *n.*

**supply**[2] /'sʌpli/, *adv.* in a supple manner. Also, **supplely.** [SUPP(LE) + -LY]

**support** /sə'pɔt/, *v.t.* **1.** to bear or hold up (a load, mass, structure, part, etc.). **2.** to sustain or withstand (weight, etc.) without giving way. **3.** to undergo or endure, esp. with patience or submission; tolerate. **4.** to sustain (a person, the mind, spirits, courage, etc.) under trial or affliction. **5.** to maintain (a person, family, establishment, institution, etc.) by supplying with things necessary to existence; provide for. **6.** to uphold (a person, cause, policy, etc.) by aid or countenance; back; second (efforts, aims, etc.) **7.** to maintain or advocate (a theory, etc.) **8.** to corroborate (a statement, etc.). **9.** to sustain or act (a part, role, or character). **10.** to act with or second (a leading actor), as on a stage; assist in any performance. **11.** to form a secondary part of a program with: *the main film will be supported by two short documentaries.* *–n.* **12.** the act of supporting. **13.** the state of being supported. **14.** maintenance, as of a person, family, etc., with necessities, means, or funds. **15.** a thing or a person that supports. **16.** a prop or stay for carrying part of the weight of a structure. **17.** a device, usu. of elastic cotton webbing, for holding up some part of the body, as a jockstrap. **18.** a thing or a person that gives aid or assistance. **19.** an actor, actress, or company playing secondary or subordinate roles. **20.** the material, as canvas or wood, on which a picture is painted. **21.** *Gymnastics.* any of several positions of the body in which its weight is supported on the arms, usu. on a beam. [ME, from OF *supporter* bear, from L *supportāre* convey]

**supportable** /sə'pɔtəbəl/, *adj.* capable of being supported; endurable; maintainable. – **supportability** /səpɔtə'bɪləti/, **supportableness,** *n.* – **supportably,** *adv.*

**supporter** /sə'pɔtə/, *n.* **1.** one who or that which supports. **2.** →**support** (def. 17). **3.** one who supports a sporting team, esp. by attending matches to shout encouragement. **4.** an upholder, backer, or advocate. **5.** *Her.* a figure as of an animal or a man, holding up an escutcheon or standing beside it.

**supposal** /sə'poʊzəl/, *n.* →**supposition.**

**suppose** /sə'poʊz/, *v.,* **-posed, -posing.** *–v.t.* **1.** to assume (something), without reference to its being true or false, for the sake of argument or for the purpose of tracing the consequences: *suppose the distance to be one kilometre.* **2.** to consider as a possibility suggested or an idea or plan proposed (used in the imperative): *suppose we wait till tomorrow.* **3.** to assume as true, or believe, in the absence of positive knowledge or of evidence to the contrary: *it is supposed that the occurrence was an accident.* **4.** to take for granted, assume, or presume, without especial thought of possible error: *I supposed that you had gone.* **5.** to think, with reference to mere opinion: *what do you suppose he will do?* **6.** (of a proposition, theory, etc.) to make or involve the assumption of: *this theory supposes the existence of life on Mars.* **7.** (of facts, circumstances, etc.) to require logically; imply; presuppose. **8.** *Obs.* to expect. *–v.i.* **9.** to assume something; presume; think. [ME, from OF *sup(p)oser,* from *sup-* SUB- + *poser* POSE[1], after L *suppōnere*] – **supposable,** *adj.* – **supposably,** *adv.* – **supposer,** *n.*

**supposed** /sə'poʊzd/, *adj.* **1.** assumed as true, regardless of fact; hypothetical: *a supposed case.* **2.** accepted or received as true, without positive knowledge and perhaps erroneously: *the supposed site of an ancient temple.* **3.** merely thought to be such: *to sacrifice real for supposed gains.* – **supposedly** /sə'poʊzədli/, *adv.*

**supposing** /sə'poʊzɪŋ/, *conj.* on the supposition or premise that.

**supposition** /sʌpə'zɪʃən/, *n.* **1.** the act of supposing. **2.** that which is supposed; an assumption; a hypothesis. [late ME, from ML *suppositio* (in L: a putting under) used as translation of Gk *hypóthesis* HYPOTHESIS] – **suppositional,** *adj.* – **suppositionally,** *adv.*

**suppositious** /sʌpə'zɪʃəs/, *adj.* **1.** supposititious. **2.** suppositional.

**supposititious** /səpɒzə'tɪʃəs/, *adj.* **1.** fraudulently substituted or pretended; spurious; not genuine. **2.** hypothetical. [L *supposititius*] – **supposititiously,** *adv.* – **supposititiousness,** *n.*

**suppositive** /sə'pɒzətɪv/, *adj.* **1.** of the nature of or involving supposition; suppositional. **2.** supposititious or false. **3.** *Gram.* expressing supposition, as the words *if, granting,* or *provided.* *–n.* **4.** *Gram.* a suppositive word. – **suppositively,** *adv.*

**suppository** /sə'pɒzətri/, *n., pl.* **-ries.** a solid or encapsulated medicinal substance inserted into the rectum or vagina to be dissolved therein. [LL *suppositōrium* (thing) placed under, from L *suppositus,* pp., placed under]

**suppress** /sə'prɛs/, *v.t.* **1.** to put an end to the activities of (a person, body of persons, etc.). **2.** to do away with by or as by authority; abolish; stop (a practice, etc.). **3.** to keep in or repress (a feeling, smile, groan, etc.). **4.** to withhold from disclosure or publication (truth, evidence, a book, names, etc.). **5.** to arrest (a flow, haemorrhage, etc.). **6.** to quell; crush; vanquish or subdue (a revolt, rebel, etc.). **7.** *Elect.* **a.** to reduce or eliminate any unwanted oscillations in a circuit. **b.** to reduce current surges in the high-tension circuit of a motor-car engine to eliminate interference with the car radio. [ME, from L *suppressus,* pp., put down] – **suppressible,** *adj.* – **suppressive,** *adj.*

**suppression** /sə'prɛʃən/, *n.* **1.** the act of suppressing or state of being suppressed. **2.** *Psychol.* conscious inhibition of an impulse. **3.** *Elect.* the reduction or elimination of unwanted oscillations in a circuit. **4.** *Radio, etc.* the elimination of a frequency or group of frequencies from a signal. **5.** *Bot.* the elimination of parts of a plant by the action of frost, disease, insects, etc.

**suppressor** /sə'prɛsə/, *n.* **1.** Also, **suppresser.** one who or that which suppresses. **2.** *Elect.* **a.** a circuit which reduces or eliminates unwanted oscillations in an electrical system. **b.** a device which reduces current surges in the high-tension circuit of a motor-car engine. **c.** one of the grids in a multigrid vacuum tube.

**suppurate** /'sʌpjəreɪt/, *v.i.,* **-rated, -rating.** to produce or discharge pus, as a wound; maturate. [L *suppūrātus*, pp., caused to secrete pus]

**suppuration** /sʌpjəˈreɪʃən/, *n.* **1.** the process of suppurating. **2.** the matter produced by suppuration.

**suppurative** /ˈsʌpjərətɪv/, *adj.* **1.** suppurating, or characterised by suppuration. **2.** promoting suppuration. *–n.* **3.** a medicine that promotes suppuration.

**supra** /ˈsuprə/, *adv.* (esp. used in making reference to parts of a text) above. [L: above, beyond]

**supra-**, a prefix meaning 'above', equivalent to **super-**, but emphasising situation or position, as in *supraorbital, suprarenal.* [L, representing *suprā*, adv. and prep.]

**supraglottal** /ˈsuprəglɒtl/, *adj.* above the glottis.

**supralapsarianism** /ˌsupræləpˈsɛəriənɪzəm/, *n.* a Calvinistic doctrine that God, to demonstrate divine grace and justice, predetermined those of mankind who would be amongst the elect, and those who would be damned, before decreeing the creation and fall of man, as a means to achieve the end (opposed to *infralapsarianism* and *sublapsarianism*).

**supraliminal** /suprəˈlɪmənəl/, *adj.* above the limen or threshold of consciousness; of or in consciousness.

**supramolecular** /suprəməˈlɛkjələ/, *adj.* **1.** above the molecule; of greater complexity than a molecule. **2.** composed of an aggregation of molecules.

**supranational** /suprəˈnæʃnəl/, *adj.* overriding national sovereignty; outside the authority of a single national government. – **supranationalism**, *n.* – **supranationally**, *adv.*

**supraorbital** /suprəˈɔbətl/, *adj.* situated above the eye socket.

**supra protest** /ˌsuprə ˈproutɛst/, *adv.* upon or after protest (a phrase used with reference to an acceptance or a payment of a bill by a third person for the honour of the drawer after protest for non-acceptance or non-payment by the drawee). [It. *sopra protesto* upon protest]

**suprarenal** /suprəˈrinəl/, *adj.* **1.** situated above or on the kidney. **2.** pertaining to or connected with a suprarenal. *–n.* **3.** a suprarenal body, capsule, or gland.

**suprarenal gland** /ˈ– ˌglænd/, *n.* either of a pair of ductless glands, located in man at the upper end, and in most vertebrates at the anterior end, of the kidneys, which secrete adrenaline and a number of steroid hormones; adrenal gland.

**suprasegmental** /suprəsɛgˈmɛntl/, *adj.* of or pertaining to those features of a sound segment, or group of sound segments, which do not serve to identify the segments phonemically; they include expressive duration, loudness, etc., in the case of one segment, and also rhythm, intonation, etc., in the case of numbers of segments bound into words, phrases and larger structures.

**supremacist** /səˈprɛməsəst, su-/, *n.* **1.** a believer in the supremacy of one particular group, esp. a racial group: *white supremacist.* *–adj.* **2.** advocating or believing in such supremacy. – **suprematism**, *n.*

**supremacy** /səˈprɛməsi, su-/, *n.* **1.** the state of being supreme. **2.** supreme authority or power. Also, **supremity**.

**suprematism** /səˈprɛməˌtɪzəm, su-/, *n.* a type of abstract art originating in Russia in 1913, which used the rectangle, triangle, circle and cross as symbols to express feelings in a visual form.

**supreme** /suˈprim, sə-/, *adj.* **1.** highest in rank or authority; paramount; sovereign; chief. **2.** of the highest quality, character, importance, etc.: *supreme courage.* **3.** greatest, utmost, or extreme: *supreme disgust.* **4.** last (with reference to the end of life): *the supreme moment.* [L *suprēmus*, superl. of *superus* that is above] – **supremely**, *adv.* – **supremeness**, *n.*

**suprême** /suˈprim/, *n.* **1.** the breast and wings of poultry and game, esp. when served with a rich cream sauce. **2.** the best cut of any meat. [F]

**Supreme Being** /suprim ˈbiɪŋ/, *n.* the sovereign of the universe; God.

**supreme commander** /suprim kəˈmændə/, *n. U.S.* the military, naval, or air officer commanding all allied forces in a theatre of war.

**Supreme Court** /suˈprim kɔt/, *n.* the highest State court with inherent common law jurisdiction; a court of record presided over by a Justice.

**supreme sacrifice** /suprim ˈsækrəfaɪs/, *n.* the sacrifice of one's own life.

**supremo** /suˈprimoʊ/, *n.* a supreme ruler; dictator, esp. a military dictator. [Sp., short for *generalissimo supremo* supreme general]

**Supt**, superintendent. Also, **supt.**

**sur-**[1], a prefix corresponding to **super-** but mainly attached to stems not used as words and having figurative applications (*survive, surname*), used esp. in legal terms (*surrebuttal*). [late ME, from F, from L *super-* SUPER-]

**sur-**[2], occasional variant of **sub-** (by assimilation) before *r.*

**surah** /ˈsjurə/, *n.* a soft twilled silk or rayon fabric. [apparently named after *Surat*, a seaport in W India]

**sural** /ˈsjurəl/, *adj.* of or pertaining to the calf of the leg. [NL *sūrālis*, from L *sūra* calf of the leg]

**surbase** /ˈsɜbeɪs/, *n.* a moulding above a base, as that immediately above a skirting board, the crowning moulding of a pedestal, etc. – **surbasement** /sɜˈbeɪsmənt/, *n.*

**surbased** /ˈsɜbeɪst/, *adj.* **1.** having a surbase. **2.** depressed; flattened. **3.** (of an arch) having a rise of less than half the span. [Anglicisation of F *surbaissé*, from *sur-* (intensive) + *baissé* lowered. See BASE[2]]

**surcease** /sɜˈsis/, *v.*, **-ceased, -ceasing**, *n. Archaic.* *–v.i.* **1.** to cease from some action; desist. **2.** to come to an end. *–v.t.* **3.** to cease from; leave off. *–n.* **4.** cessation; end. [ME *sursese*, from OF *sursis*, pp. of *surseoir* refrain, suspend, from L *supersedēre* desist, conformed to CEASE]

**surcharge** /ˈsɜtʃadʒ/, *n.*; /ˈsɜtʃadʒ, sɜˈtʃadʒ/, *v.*, **-charged, -charging.** *–n.* **1.** an additional or excessive charge for payment, tax, etc. **2.** an excessive sum or price charged. **3.** *Philately.* an overprint which alters or restates the face value or denomination of a stamp to which it has been applied. **4.** *Law.* the act of surcharging. **5.** an additional or excessive load or burden. **6.** an additional sum added to the usual cost, in restaurants, etc., as *holiday surcharge, weekend surcharge.* *–v.t.* **7.** to subject to an additional or extra charge (for payment). **8.** to over-charge. **9.** to show an omission in (an account) of something that operates as a charge against the accounting party. **10.** *Philately.* to print a surcharge on. **11.** to put an additional or excessive burden upon; overload. [ME, from OF. See SUR-[1], CHARGE, *v.*] – **surcharger**, *n.*

**surcingle** /ˈsɜsɪŋgəl/, *n.* **1.** a girth for a horse or other animal, esp. a large girth passing over and keeping in place a blanket, pack, or the like. **2.** a girdle with which a garment, esp. a cassock, is fastened. [ME *sursengle*, from OF *surcengle*, from *sur-* SUR-[1] + *cengle* (from L *cingula* girdle)]

**surcoat** /ˈsɜkoʊt/, *n.* **1.** a garment worn over medieval armour, often embroidered with heraldic arms. **2.** an outer coat or garment. [ME *surcote*, from OF. See SUR-[1], COAT]

surcoat

**surculose** /ˈsɜkjəloʊs/, *adj.* (of a plant) producing suckers. [L *surculōsus*]

**surd** /sɜd/, *adj.* **1.** *Maths.* (of a quantity) not capable of being expressed in rational numbers; irrational. **2.** *Phonet.* voiceless. *–n.* **3.** *Maths.* a surd quantity; a root the value of which is a non-terminating decimal as $\sqrt{3}$ or $\sqrt{(1\text{-}5\sqrt[3]{2})}$. **4.** *Phonet.* a voiceless consonant. [L *surdus* deaf, indistinct]

**sure** /ʃɔ/, *adj.*, **surer, surest**, *adv.* *–adj.* **1.** free from apprehension or doubt as to the reliability, character, action, etc., of something (oft. fol. by *of*): *to be sure of one's data.* **2.** confident, as of something expected: *sure of ultimate success.* **3.** convinced, fully persuaded, or positive, as of something firmly believed: *sure of a person's guilt.* **4.** assured or certain beyond question: *man*

**supra-axillary**, *adj.*
**supraciliary**, *adj.*
**supraclavicular**, *adj.*
**supracostal**, *adj.*
**supralunar**, *adj.*
**supramaxillary**, *adj.*
**supramundane**, *adj.*
**supranormal**, *adj.*
**suprarational**, *adj.*
**suprasensible**, *adj.*
**suprasensory**, *adj.*
**supratemporal**, *adj.*

*is sure of death.* **5.** worthy of confidence; reliable: *a sure messenger.* **6.** firm or stable: *to stand on sure ground.* **7.** unfailing; never disappointing expectations: *a sure cure.* **8.** unerring; never missing, slipping, etc.: *a sure aim.* **9.** admitting of no doubt or question: *sure proof.* **10.** inevitable: *death is sure.* **11.** destined; bound inevitably; certain: *he is sure to come.* **12.** *Archaic.* secure or safe. **13. a sure thing,** *Colloq.* a certainty; something assured beyond any doubt. **14. be sure,** be certain or careful (to do or be as specified): *be sure to close the windows.* **15. for sure,** as a certainty; surely. **16. make sure, a.** to be certain (that something is done). **b.** to be confident in the support or possession (*of*). **17. sure thing,** *Chiefly U.S. Colloq.* assuredly; certainly. **18. to be sure,** surely; certainly; without doubt. *–adv.* **19.** *Colloq.* surely, undoubtedly, or certainly. **20.** *U.S. Colloq.* inevitably or without fail. [ME, from OF, from L *sēcūrus* secure] **– sureness,** *n.*

**sure enough** /ʃɔr əˈnʌf/, *adv. Colloq.* as expected; in actual fact: *he was expected to win, and sure enough he did.*

**sure-fire** /ˈʃɔ-faɪə/, *adj. Colloq.* certain to succeed; assured: *a sure-fire winner for tomorrow's race.*

**sure-footed** /ˈʃɔ-fʊtəd/, *adj.* **1.** not liable to stumble, slip, or fall. **2.** proceeding surely; unerring. **– sure-footedly,** *adv.* **– surefootedness,** *n.*

**surely** /ˈʃɔli/, *adv.* **1.** firmly; unerringly; without missing, slipping, etc. **2.** undoubtedly, assuredly, or certainly: *the results are surely encouraging.* **3.** (in emphatic utterances that are not necessarily sustained by fact) assuredly: *surely you are mistaken.* **4.** inevitably or without fail: *slowly but surely the end approached.*

**surety** /ˈʃɔrəti, ˈʃurəti/, *n., pl.* **-ties. 1.** security against loss or damage; security for the fulfilment of an obligation, the payment of a debt, etc.; a pledge, guaranty, or bond. **2.** one who has made himself responsible for another. **3.** the state or quality of being sure. **4.** certainty. **5.** that which makes sure; ground of confidence or safety. **6.** one who is legally answerable for the debt, default, or miscarriage of another. **7.** the quality of being sure; assurance or sureness. [ME *seurte,* from OF, from L *sēcūritas*]

**suretyship** /ˈʃɔrəti͵ʃɪp, ˈʃurə-/, *n.* the relationship between the surety, the principal debtor, and the creditor.

**surf** /sɜf/, *n.* **1.** the swell of the sea which breaks upon a shore or upon shoals. **2.** the mass or line of foamy water caused by the breaking of the sea upon a shore, etc. *–v.i.* **3.** to engage in surfing. [earlier *suff,* ? var. of SOUGH]

**surface** /ˈsɜfəs/, *n., adj., v.,* **-faced, -facing.** *–n.* **1.** the outer face, or outside, of a thing. **2.** any face of a body or thing: *the six surfaces of a cube.* **3.** extent or area of outer face; superficial area. **4.** the outward appearance, esp. as distinguished from the inner nature: *to look below the surface of a matter.* **5.** *Geom.* any figure having only two dimensions; part or all of the boundary of a solid. **6.** *Aeron.* an aerofoil. *–adj.* **7.** of, on, or pertaining to the surface. **8.** superficial; external; apparent, rather than real. **9.** of, on, or pertaining to land and/or sea: *surface travel.* *–v.t.* **10.** to finish as to surface; give a particular kind of surface to; make even or smooth. *–v.i.* **11.** to rise to the surface. **12.** *Colloq.* **a.** to wake up. **b.** to emerge at the end of a period of activity elsewhere. **c.** to appear in public, as arriving at one's job. **13.** *Mining.* **a.** to wash surface deposits of ore. **b.** to mine at or near the surface. **14.** to work on or at the surface. [F, from *sur-* SUR-[1] + *face* FACE. Cf. SUPERFICIES] **– surfacer,** *n.*

**surface-active agent** /ˈsɜfəs-͵æktɪv ͵eɪdʒənt/, *n.* any substance which when added to a liquid reduces its surface tension and thus increases its spreading or wetting properties. Also, **surfactant.**

**surface chemistry** /ˈsɜfəs ͵kɛməstri/, *n.* the study of forces acting at the surfaces of gases, liquids, and solids, or at the interfaces between them.

**surface dressing** /– ˈdrɛsɪŋ/, *n.* **1.** a method of repairing roads by spreading chippings or gravel over a coat of hot tar. **2.** the dressing applied.

**surface indication** /– ɪndəˈkeɪʃən/, *n.* a particular feature of the earth's surface which suggests a possible hidden deposit below, as of opal, iron-ore, etc.

**surface mail** /ˈ– meɪl/, *n.* mail carried in a surface vehicle (opposed to *airmail*).

**surface plate** /ˈ– pleɪt/, *n.* a flat plate used by mechanics for testing surfaces which are to be made perfectly flat.

**surface reef** /ˈ– rif/, *n.* (in mining) a reef outcropping on the surface, or a reef covered only by shallow soil.

**surface structure** /ˈ– strʌktʃə/, *n.* **1.** *Linguistics.* the relationship between the elements of an actually produced sentence (opposed to *deep structure*). **2.** the appearance of a situation, as opposed to the hidden reality.

**surface tension** /ˈ– tɛnʃən/, *n.* a property of liquid or solid matter due to unbalanced molecular forces near a surface, and the measure thereof; an apparent tension in an actually non-existent surface film associated with capillary phenomena, cohesion, and adhesion.

**surface-to-air missile** /sɜfəs-tu-ˈɛə mɪsaɪl/, *n.* a missile which is designed to be launched from the ground against airborne targets.

**surface-to-surface missile** /sɜfəs-tə-ˈsɜfəs mɪsaɪl/, *n.* a missile which is designed to be launched from the ground against a surface target.

**surface zero** /sɜfəs ˈzɪəroʊ/, *n.* →**ground zero.**

**surfacing** /ˈsɜfəsɪŋ/, *n.* **1.** the act or process of giving a surface to anything. **2.** the material for a surface layer: *surfacing for a road.* **3.** the act of rising to the surface. **4.** *Mining.* the act or process of washing surface deposits.

**surfactant** /sɜˈfæktənt/, *n.* →**surface-active agent.** [SURF(ACE)-ACT(IVE) A(GE)NT]

**surf beach** /ˈsɜf bitʃ/, *n.* a beach where there is surf, as opposed to a beach on a lake, harbour, river, etc. Also, **ocean beach.**

**surfboard** /ˈsɜfbɔd/, *n.* a long, narrow board, slightly rounded and usu. longer than body-length, used by surfers in riding waves towards the shore.

**surfboard riding** /ˈ– raɪdɪŋ/, *n.* →**surfing.**

**surfboat** /ˈsɜfboʊt/, *n.* a strong buoyant six-oared rowing boat with sweep, designed for use in surf and employed in beach rescue and patrol work.

surfboard

**surf carnival** /ˈsɜf kanəvəl/, *n.* a sporting event held on a beach and including swimming, running and rowing contests.

**surf club** /ˈ– klʌb/, *n.* **1.** a group of surf lifesavers who patrol one particular beach, together with their organisation and equipment. **2.** the clubhouse of such a group of lifesavers, usu. on the beach they patrol, housing their equipment and usu. offering changing and other facilities to the public.

**surfeit** /ˈsɜfət/, *n.* **1.** excess; an excessive amount. **2.** excess in eating or drinking. **3.** oppression or disorder of the system due to excessive eating or drinking. **4.** general disgust caused by excess or satiety. *–v.t.* **5.** to bring to a state of surfeit by excess of food or drink. **6.** to supply with anything to excess or satiety; satiate. *–v.i.* **7.** *Archaic.* to overindulge, esp. in eating or drinking. [ME *sorfait,* from OF: excess, properly pp. of *sorfaire* overdo, from *sor-* SUR-[1] + *faire* do (from L *facere*)] **– surfeiter,** *n.*

**surfer** /ˈsɜfə/, *n.* one engaged in surfing.

**surf flag** /ˈsɜf flæg/, *n.* one of a pair of flags on a beach marking the area where it is safe to enter the water.

**surfie** /ˈsɜfi/, *n. Colloq.* **1.** a devotee of surfing, esp. of surfboard riding. **2.** a person with tanned skin and sun-bleached hair, as from surfboard riding.

**surfing** /ˈsɜfɪŋ/, *n.* **1.** the sport in which one paddles a surfboard out over the surf, and then, usu. standing on the board, attempts to ride on or with a wave towards the shore; surfboard riding. **2.** Also, **body-surfing.** the sport of swimming in the surf, and esp. of riding waves, by holding the body stiff, usu. with the arms outstretched, as if it were a board, and allowing oneself to be carried along by the force of the water.

**surf-lifesaver** /sɜf-ˈlaɪfseɪvə/, *n.* →**lifesaver.**

**surf-lifesaving** /sɜf-ˈlaɪfseɪvɪŋ/, *n.* →**lifesaving.**

**surf-line** /'sɜf-laɪn/, *n.* a rope which is attached, at one end, to the beltman and at the other end to the surf-reel, with which the beltman and the person rescued are pulled to safety, by rewinding the surf-reel.

**surf mat** /'sɜf mæt/, *n.* →**surfoplane.** [Trademark]

**surfoplane** /'sɜfəpleɪn/, *n.* a small, inflatable rubber float used esp. for shooting waves. [Trademark]

**surf-reel** /'sɜf-ril/, *n.* a large reel on which a surf-line is wound.

**surf rescue boat,** *n.* a motor boat with a high bow designed for passing through surf and used in beach rescue and patrol work.

**surf-ride** /'sɜf-raɪd/, *v.i.* **-rode, -ridden, -riding.** to ride a surfboard. – **surf-riding,** *n.*

**surf ski** /'sɜf ski/, *n.* a small narrow craft propelled usu. by one rider using a double ended paddle.

**surfy** /'sɜfi/, *adj.,* **surfier, surfiest.** abounding with surf; forming or resembling surf.

**surg.,** **1.** surgeon. **2.** surgery. **3.** surgical.

**surge** /sɜdʒ/, *n., v.,* **surged, surging.** *–n.* **1.** a strong forward or upward movement, rush, or sweep, like that of swelling or rolling waves: *the onward surge of an angry mob.* **2.** a strong, wave-like volume or body of something: *a surge of smoke.* **3.** the rolling swell of the sea. **4.** the swelling and rolling sea; *the surge was seething free.* **5.** a swelling wave; billow. **6.** a large swelling or abrupt wave, the change in depth or pressure generally being maintained after passage. **7.** *Elect.* a sudden rush of current, a violent oscillatory disturbance, or the like. **8.** *Mach.* an unevenness or irregularity in motion or action in an engine. **9.** *Naut.* a surging, or slipping back, as of a rope. *–v.i.* **10.** to rise and fall, or move along, on the waves, as a ship: *to surge at anchor.* **11.** to rise or roll in waves, or like waves: *a crowd surges about a spot.* **12.** to rise as if by a heaving or swelling force: *blood surges to the face.* **13.** *Elect.* to increase suddenly, as a current; oscillate violently. **14.** *Naut.* **a.** to slack off or loosen a rope or cable around a capstan or windlass. **b.** to slip back, as a rope. *–v.t.* **15.** to cause to surge or roll in or as in waves. **16.** to heave or sway with a waving motion. **17.** *Naut.* to slacken (a rope). [orig. uncert. Cf. F *surgeon* spring]

**surge area** /'– ɛəriə/, *n.* an area of land which is inundated by high seas, as in a cyclone.

**surge line** /'– laɪn/, *n.* a line along the shore beyond which a surge does not reach.

**surgeon** /'sɜdʒən/, *n.* **1.** one who treats injuries, deformities, and diseases by manual operation or instrumental appliances. **2.** a medical practitioner or physician qualified to practise surgery. **3.** an army or naval medical officer. **4.** a surgeonfish. [ME *surgien,* from AF, contraction of OF *serurgien.* See CHIRURGEON]

**surgeoncy** /'sɜdʒənsi/, *n., pl.* **-cies.** the office or position of a surgeon, as in the army or navy. Also, **surgeonship.**

**surgeonfish** /'sɜdʒənfɪʃ/, *n., pl.* **-fishes,** (*esp. collectively*) **-fish.** any tropical coral-reef fish of the family Acanthuridae, with one or more spines near the base of the tail fin.

**surgeon general** /sɜdʒən 'dʒɛnrəl/, *n., pl.* **surgeons general.** the chief of medical service in the navy.

**surgeon's knot** /ˌsɜdʒənz 'nɒt/, *n.* a knot resembling a reef knot but with a double turn in the first part, used by surgeons for tying ligatures, etc.

**surgery** /'sɜdʒəri/, *n., pl.* **-geries.** **1.** the art, practice, or work of treating diseases, injuries, or deformities by manual operation or instrumental appliances. **2.** the branch of medicine concerned with such treatment. **3.** treatment, operations, etc., performed by a surgeon. **4.** a room or place for surgical operations. **5.** the consulting room of a medical practitioner, dentist, or the like. [ME, from OF *surgerie*]

**surgical** /'sɜdʒɪkəl/, *adj.* **1.** pertaining to or involving surgery. **2.** used in surgery. – **surgically,** *adv.*

**surgical appliance** /– ə'plaɪəns/, *n.* any device designed to be worn to support a damaged or deformed part of the body.

**surgical boot** /– 'but/, *n.* a specially constructed boot or shoe designed to support or correct a deformed foot or leg.

**surgical spirit** /– 'spɪrət/, *n.* ethyl alcohol, usu. containing oil of wintergreen and castor oil, used for cleansing the skin of a patient before an operation, etc.

**surgy** /'sɜdʒi/, *adj.,* **surgier, surgiest.** billowy; surging or swelling.

**suricate** /'sjurəkeɪt/, *n.* the meerkat, *Suricata suricatta.* [earlier *surikate,* from F, from D *surikat* macaque]

**Surinam** /surə'næm/, *n.* a country on the north-eastern coast of South America.

**Surinam toad** /– 'toud/, *n.* →**pipa.** [named after *Surinam,* a region in N South America]

**surloin** /'sɜlɔɪn/, *n.* →**sirloin.**

**surly** /'sɜli/, *adj.,* **-lier, -liest.** **1.** churlishly rude or ill-humoured, as a person or the manner, tone, expression, etc. **2.** (of an animal) ill-tempered and unfriendly. **3.** *Obs.* lordly; arrogant. [var. of obs. *sirly* (from SIR + -LY) lordly] – **surlily,** *adv.* – **surliness,** *n.*

**surmise** /sɜ'maɪz/, *v.,* **-mised, -mising;** /sɜ'maɪz, 'sɜmaɪz/, *n.* *–v.t.* **1.** to think or infer without certain or strong evidence; conjecture; guess. *–v.i.* **2.** to conjecture or guess. *–n.* Also, **surmisal.** **3.** a matter of conjecture. **4.** an idea or thought of something as being possible or likely, although without any certain or strong evidence. **5.** conjecture or surmising. [ME from OF, pp. of *surmettre* accuse] – **surmisable,** *adj.* – **surmiser,** *n.*

**surmount** /sɜ'maunt/, *v.t.* **1.** to mount upon; get on the top of; mount upon and cross over: *to surmount a hill.* **2.** to get over or across (barriers, obstacles, etc.). **3.** to prevail over. **4.** to be on top of or above: *a statue surmounting a pillar.* **5.** to furnish with something placed on top or above: *to surmount a tower with a spire.* **6.** *Obs.* to surpass or excel; exceed in amount. [ME *surmounte(n),* from OF *surmonter.* See SUR-[1], MOUNT[1]] – **surmountable,** *adj.* – **surmounter,** *n.*

**surmullet** /sɜ'mʌlət/, *n.* →**goatfish.**

**surname** /'sɜneɪm/, *n., v.,* **-named, -naming.** *–n.* **1.** the name which a person has in common with the other members of his family, as distinguished from his Christian or first name; a family name. **2.** a name added to a person's name or names, as from birth or abode or from some characteristic or achievement. *–v.t.* **3.** to give a surname to; call by a surname. [ME; half adoption, half translation of F *surnom*]

**surpass** /sɜ'pas/, *v.t.* **1.** to go beyond in amount, extent, or degree; be greater than; exceed. **2.** to go beyond in excellence or achievement; be superior to; excel. **3.** to be beyond the range or capacity of; transcend: *misery that surpasses description.* [F *surpasser,* from *sur-* (intensive) + *passer* PASS] – **surpassable,** *adj.*

**surpassing** /sɜ'pasɪŋ/, *adj.* **1.** that surpasses, exceeds, or excels; extraordinary: *structures of surpassing magnificence.* *–adv.* **2.** *Obs.* surpassingly. – **surpassingly,** *adv.* – **surpassingness,** *n.*

**surplice** /'sɜpləs/, *n.* **1.** a loose-fitting, broad-sleeved white vestment properly of linen, worn over the cassock by certain clergymen and choristers. **2.** a garment in which the fronts cross each other diagonally. [ME, from AF *surpliz,* syncopated var. of OF *sourpeliz* over-fur (garment)] – **surpliced,** *adj.*

surplice

**surplus** /'sɜpləs/, *n.* **1.** that which remains above what is used or needed. **2.** an amount of assets in excess of what is requisite to meet liabilites. **3.** *Accounting.* the excess of assets over liabilities accumulated throughout the existence of a business, excepting assets against which stock certificates have been issued. *–adj.* **4.** being a surplus; being in excess of what is required: *the surplus wheat of Australia.* [ME, from OF. Cf. ML *superplus.* See PLUS]

**surplusage** /'sɜpləsɪdʒ/, *n.* **1.** surplus; excess. **2.** an excess of words.

**surprint** /'sɜprɪnt/, *v.t.* **1.** to print over with additional marks or matter; overprint. **2.** to print (additional marks, etc.) over something already printed. *–n.* **3.** something surprinted.

**surprisal** /sə'praɪzəl/, *n.* **1.** the act of surprising. **2.** the state of being surprised. **3.** a surprise.

**surprise** /sə'praɪz/, *v.,* **-prised, -prising,** *n.* *–v.t.* **1.** to come upon suddenly and unexpectedly; catch (a person, etc.) in the act of doing something; discover (a thing) suddenly. **2.** to assail, attack, or capture suddenly or without warning, as an army, fort, or person that is unprepared. **3.** to strike with a sudden feeling of wonder that arrests the thoughts, as at something unexpected or extraordinary. **4.** to bring out, esp. by a surprise: *to surprise the facts from the witness.* **5.** to lead or bring (a person, etc.) unawares, as into doing something not intended. *–n.* **6.** an act of surprising. **7.** a sudden assault, attack, or capture. **8.** a sudden and unexpected event, action, or the like. **9.** the state or feeling of being surprised as by something unexpected. **10.** something that excites this feeling, as an unexpected or extraordinary occurrence. **11.** **take by surprise, a.** to come upon unawares or without visible preparation. **b.** to catch unprepared. **c.** to amaze; astonish. *–adj.* **12.** sudden and unexpected: *a surprise attack.* [late ME, from F, pp. of *surprendre* surprise, from *sur-* SUR-[1] + *prendre* take] – **surpriser,** *n.*

**surprising** /sə'praɪzɪŋ/, *adj.* that surprises. – **surprisingly,** *adv.* – **surprisingness,** *n.*

**surreal** /sə'ril/, *adj.* **1.** of or pertaining to the dreamlike experiences, etc., dealt with by surrealism. *–n.* **2. the surreal,** the world of these experiences.

**surrealism** /sə'riəlɪzəm/, *n.* a movement in literature and art from about 1919, based on the expression of imagination uncontrolled by reason, and seeking to suggest the activities of the subconscious mind. [F *surréalisme.* See SUR-[1], REALISM] – **surrealist,** *n., adj.* – **surrealistic** /sə,riə'lɪstɪk/, *adj.* – **surrealistically** /sə,riə'lɪstɪkli/, *adv.*

**surrender** /sə'rɛndə/, *v.t.* **1.** to yield (something) to the possession or power of another; deliver up possession of (something) upon demand or compulsion: *to surrender a fort.* **2.** to give (oneself) up, esp. as a prisoner or to some emotion, course of action, or the like. **3.** to give up, abandon, or relinquish (comfort, hope, etc.). **4.** to yield or resign (an office, privilege, etc.) in favour of another. **5.** *Obs.* to return: *to surrender thanks.* *–v.i.* **6.** to give oneself up, as into the power of another or of an emotion, course of action, etc.; submit or yield. *–n.* **7.** the act of surrendering. **8.** *Insurance.* the abandonment of a policy by the party insured, for a consideration, the amount receivable (**surrender value**) depending on the number of years elapsed from the commencement of the risk. **9.** the deed by which a legal surrendering is made. [late ME, from AF, from *sur-* SUR-[1] + *rendre* RENDER]

**surreptitious** /sʌrəp'tɪʃəs/, *adj.* **1.** obtained, done, made, etc., by stealth; secret and unauthorised; clandestine: *a surreptitious glance.* **2.** acting in a stealthy way. **3.** obtained by subreption; subreptitious. [late ME, from L *surreptītius,* from *subreptus,* pp., snatched away secretly] – **surreptitiously,** *adv.* – **surreptitiousness,** *n.*

**surrey** /'sʌri/, *n., pl.* **-reys.** *U.S.* a light, four-wheeled, two-seat horse-drawn carriage, with or without a top, for four persons.

surrey

**surrogate** /'sʌrəgət/, *n.;* /'sʌrəgeɪt/, *v.,* **-gated, -gating.** *–n.* **1.** one appointed to act for another; a deputy. **2.** the deputy of an ecclesiastical judge, esp. of a bishop or his chancellor. **3.** a substitute. *–v.t.* **4.** to put into the place of another as a successor, substitute, or deputy; substitute for another. **5.** to subrogate. [L *surrogātus,* pp., put in another's place] – **surrogateship,** *n.* – **surrogation** /sʌrə'geɪʃən/, *n.*

**surround** /sə'raʊnd/, *v.t.* **1.** to enclose on all sides, or encompass. **2.** to form an enclosure round; encircle. **3.** to enclose (a body of troops, fortification, or the like) so as to cut off communication or retreat. *–n.* **4.** a border which surrounds, as of uncovered floor around a carpet. **5.** (*pl.*) surroundings. [late ME *suround,* from AF *surounder,* from LL *superundāre* overflow; conformed to SUR-[1] + ROUND]

**surrounding** /sə'raʊndɪŋ/, *n.* **1.** that which surrounds. **2.** (*pl.*) environing circumstances, conditions, etc.; environment. **3.** the act of encircling or enclosing. *–adj.* **4.** that encloses or encircles. **5.** neighbouring; nearby; in the environment of.

**surtax** /'sɜtæks/, *n.* **1.** one of a graded series of additional taxes levied on incomes exceeding a certain amount. **2.** an additional or extra tax on something already taxed. *–v.t.* **3.** to put an additional or extra tax on; charge with a surtax.

**surveillance** /sɜ'veɪləns/, *n.* **1.** watch kept over a person, etc., esp. over a suspect, a prisoner, or the like. **2.** supervision or superintendence. [F, from *surveiller.* See SURVEILLANT]

**surveillant** /sɜ'veɪlənt/, *adj.* **1.** exercising surveillance. *–n.* **2.** one who exercises surveillance. [F, properly ppr. of *surveiller,* from *sur-* SUR-[1] + *veiller* (from L *vigilāre*) watch over]

**survey** /sɜ'veɪ, 'sɜveɪ/, *v.;* /'sɜveɪ/, *n., pl.* **-veys.** *–v.t.* **1.** to take a general or comprehensive view of. **2.** to view in detail, esp. to inspect or examine formally or officially in order to ascertain condition, value, etc. **3.** to determine the form, boundaries, position, extent, etc., of, as a part of the earth's surface, by linear and angular measurements and the application of the principles of geometry and trigonometry. **4.** to collect sample opinions, facts, figures or the like in order to estimate the total overall situation. *–v.i.* **5.** to survey land, etc.; practise surveying. *–n.* **6.** the act of surveying; a comprehensive view. **7.** a formal or official examination of the particulars of something made in order to ascertain condition, character, etc. **8.** a statement or description embodying the result of this. **9.** a determining of form, boundaries, position, extent, etc., as of a part of the earth's surface, by linear and angular measurements, etc. **10.** an organisation or body of persons engaged in such an operation. **11.** the plan or description resulting from such an operation. **12.** a partial poll or gathering of sample opinions, facts or figures in order to estimate the total or overall situation. [ME *surveie(n),* from OF *surveier,* from L *super-* SUPER- + *vidēre* see] – **surveyable,** *adj.*

**survey.,** **1.** surveying. **2.** surveyor. Also, **surv.**

**surveying** /sɜ'veɪɪŋ/, *n.* **1.** the process, occupation, or art of making surveys of land, etc. **2.** the act of one who surveys.

**surveyor** /sɜ'veɪə/, *n.* **1.** one whose business it is to survey land, etc. **2.** an overseer or supervisor. **3.** one who inspects something officially for the purpose of ascertaining condition, value, etc. – **surveyorship,** *n.*

**Surveyor General** /sɜ,veɪə 'dʒɛnrəl/, *n.* an officer employed by the Lands Department to supervise all survey work and mapping within a state.

**surveyor's chain** /sɜ,veɪəz 'tʃeɪn/, *n.* See **chain** (def. 9).

**surveyor's level** /– 'lɛvəl/, *n.* See **level** (defs 8 and 9).

**surveyor's measure** /– 'mɛʒə/, *n.* (formerly) a system of units of length used in surveying land, based on the surveyor's chain of 66 feet.

**survival** /sə'vaɪvəl/, *n.* **1.** the act or fact of surviving. **2.** one who or that which survives, esp. a surviving custom, observance, belief, or the like. – **survivalist,** *n.*

**survival level feeding,** *n.* →**drought-feed** (def. 1).

**survival of the fittest,** *n.* the fact or the principle of the survival of the forms of animal and vegetable life best fitted for existing conditions, while related but less fit forms become extinct. See **natural selection.**

**survive** /sə'vaɪv/, *v.,* **-vived, -viving.** *–v.i.* **1.** to remain alive after the death of someone or after the cessation of something or the occurrence of some event; continue to live. **2.** to remain in existence after some person, thing, or event; continue to exist. **3.** *Colloq.* to remain unaffected or nearly so: *she doesn't love me, but I'll survive.* *–v.t.* **4.** to continue to live or exist after the death, cessation, or occurrence of; outlive. **5.** *Colloq.* to remain unaffected or nearly unaffected by. [late ME, from AF *survivre,* from *sur-* SUR-[1] + *vivre* live, from L *vīvere*] – **surviving,** *adj.*

**survivor** /sə'vaɪvə/, *n.* **1.** one who or that which survives. **2.** one who copes successfully with the difficulties and disappointments of life. **3.** *Law.* that one of two or more designated persons, as joint tenants or others having a joint interest, who outlives the other or others. – **survivorship,** *n.*

**susceptance** /sə'sɛptəns/, *n.* the ratio of the reactance to the square of the impedance in an alternating-current circuit.

**susceptibility** /səsɛptə'bɪləti/, *n., pl.* **-ties.** **1.** the state or character of being susceptible: *susceptibility to disease.* **2.** capability of being affected, esp. easily; capacity for receiving mental or moral impressions; tendency to be emotionally affected. **3.** (*pl.*) capacities for emotion; sensitive feelings. **4.** *Elect.* (of a material) **a.** a constant relating the electric polarisation to the applied electric field. **b.** a constant relating the magnetisation to the applied magnetic field.

**susceptible** /sə'sɛptəbəl/, *adj.* **1.** capable of receiving, admitting, undergoing, or being affected by, something (fol. by *of* or *to*): *susceptible of a high polish, of various interpretations, etc.* **2.** accessible or esp. liable: *susceptible to a disease, flattery.* **3.** capable of being affected, esp. easily; readily impressed; impressionable. [ML *susceptibilis,* from L *susceptus,* pp., taken up] – **susceptibleness,** *n.* – **susceptibly,** *adv.*

**susceptive** /sə'sɛptɪv/, *adj.* **1.** →**receptive. 2.** →**susceptible.** – **susceptivity** /ˌsʌsɛp'tɪvəti/, **susceptiveness,** *n.*

**suslik** /'sʌslɪk/, *n.* **1.** a common ground squirrel or spermophile, *Citellus* (or *Spermophilus*) *citellus,* of Europe and Asia. **2.** the fur of this animal. [Russ.]

**susp.,** suspended.

**suspect** /sə'spɛkt/, *v.;* /'sʌspɛkt/, *n., adj.* –*v.t.* **1.** to imagine to be guilty, false, counterfeit, undesirable, defective, bad, etc., with insufficient proof or with no proof. **2.** to imagine or believe to be rightly chargeable with something stated, usu. something wrong or something considered as undesirable, on little or no evidence: *to suspect a person of murder.* **3.** to imagine to be the case or to be likely; surmise: *I suspect his knowledge did not amount to much.* –*v.i.* **4.** to imagine something, esp. something evil, wrong, or undesirable, to be the case; have suspicion. –*n.* **5.** one suspected; a person suspected of a crime, offence, or the like. –*adj.* **6.** suspected; open to suspicion. [ME, from L *suspectus,* pp.] – **suspecter** /sə'spɛktə/, *n.*

**suspend** /sə'spɛnd/, *v.t.* **1.** to hang by attachment to something above. **2.** to attach so as to allow free movement, as on a hinge. **3.** to keep from falling or sinking, as if by hanging: *solid particles suspended in a liquid.* **4.** to hold or keep undetermined; refrain from forming or concluding definitely: *to suspend one's judgment.* **5.** to defer or postpone, as sentence on a convicted person. **6.** to cause to cease, or bring to a stop or stay, usu. for a time: *to suspend payment.* **7.** to cause to cease for a time from operation or effect, as a law, rule, privilege, or the like. **8.** to debar, usu. for a time, from the exercise of an office or function or the enjoyment of a privilege: *a student may be suspended for a breach of discipline.* **9.** to put or hold in a state of suspense. –*v.i.* **10.** to come to a stop, usu. temporarily; cease from operation for a time. **11.** to stop payment; be unable to meet financial obligations. [ME *suspende(n),* from L *suspendere*]

**suspended animation** /səˌspɛndəd ænə'meɪʃən/, *n.* temporary cessation of the vital functions, as due to asphyxia.

**suspender** /sə'spɛndə/, *n.* **1.** a strap with fastenings to support women's stockings, attached to a corset, step-ins or belt. **2.** a similar device attached to a garter below the knee to support men's socks. **3.** (*pl.*) *U.S.* →**braces** (def. 11). **4.** (in a suspension bridge) one of the cables or chains which support the deck from the main suspension cables. **5.** one who or that which suspends.

**suspender belt** /'– bɛlt/, *n.* a narrow belt or wide band of fabric or elastic, having suspenders attached to support women's stockings. Also, *U.S.,* **garter belt.**

**suspense** /sə'spɛns/, *n.* **1.** a state of mental uncertainty, as in awaiting a decision or outcome, usu. with more or less apprehension or anxiety. **2.** a state of mental indecision. **3.** undecided or doubtful condition, as of affairs: *for a few days matters hung in suspense.* **4.** the state or condition of being suspended; suspension. [ME, from AF *suspens,* in phrase *en suspens* in suspense, from L *suspensus,* pp., suspended] – **suspenseful,** *adj.*

**suspense account** /'– əkaʊnt/, *n.* an account in which items are entered which, for some reason, cannot at once be placed in the account to which they are intended to go.

**suspensible** /sə'spɛnsəbəl/, *adj.* capable of being suspended. – **suspensibility** /səspɛnsə'bɪləti/, *n.*

**suspension** /sə'spɛnʃən/, *n.* **1.** the act of suspending. **2.** the state of being suspended. **3.** temporary abrogation, as of a law or privilege. **4.** stoppage of payment of debts, etc., through financial inability, or insolvency. **5.** *Phys. Chem.* the state in which particles of a solid are mixed with a fluid but are undissolved. **6.** *Phys. Chem.* a substance in such a state. **7.** *Phys. Chem.* a system consisting of small particles kept dispersed by agitation (in **mechanical suspension**), or by the molecular motion in the surrounding medium (in **colloidal suspension**). **8.** something on or by which something else is hung. **9.** the arrangement of springs, shock absorbers, hangers, etc., in a motor vehicle, railway carriage, etc., connecting the wheel-suspension units or axles to the chassis frame. **10.** *Elect.* a wire or filament by which the moving part of an instrument or device is suspended. **11.** *Music.* **a.** the prolongation of a note in one chord into the following chord, usu. producing a temporary dissonance. **b.** the note so prolonged. **c.** the dissonance produced. [LL *suspensio*]

S, suspension (def. 11a)

**suspension bridge** /'– brɪdʒ/, *n.* a bridge in which the roadway or deck is suspended from cables, usu. hung between towers of masonry or steel, and fastened at the extremities.

**suspension point** /'– pɔɪnt/, *n. Chiefly U.S.* one of a group of dots or full stops which indicates ellipsis.

**suspensive** /sə'spɛnsɪv/, *adj.* **1.** pertaining to or characterised by suspension. **2.** undecided in mind. **3.** pertaining to or characterised by suspense. **4.** (of words, phrases, etc.) keeping one in suspense. **5.** having the effect of suspending the operation of something. – **suspensively,** *adv.* – **suspensiveness,** *n.*

**suspensoid** /sə'spɛnsɔɪd/, *n. Chem.* a sol in which the disperse phase is solid. [b. SUSPENS(ION) + (COLL)OID]

**suspensor** /sə'spɛnsə/, *n.* **1.** a suspensory ligament, bandage, etc. **2.** *Bot.* a row of cells formed by divisions of the zygote which push the embryo into the endosperm during the early development of a seed. [ML, from L *suspensus,* pp., suspended]

**suspensory** /sə'spɛnsəri/, *adj., n., pl.* **-ries.** –*adj.* **1.** serving or fitted to suspend or hold up, as a ligament, muscle, bandage, etc. **2.** suspending the operation of something. –*n.* **3.** a suspensory bandage, ligament, muscle, or the like.

**sus. per coll.,** *Law.* the note formerly made by a judge against the name of one convicted of a capital crime. [L *suspendātur per collum* let him be hanged by the neck]

**supercollate** /sʌspə'kɒleɪt/, *v.t.,* **-ated, -ating.** *Law* →**hang** (def. 3). [from SUS. PER COLL.]

**suspicion** /sə'spɪʃən/, *n.* **1.** the act of suspecting; imagination of the existence of guilt, fault, falsity, defect, or the like, on slight evidence or without evidence. **2.** the state of mind or feeling of one who suspects. **3.** the state of being suspected. **4.** an instance of suspecting something. **5.** imagination of anything to be the case or to be likely; a vague notion of something. **6.** a slight trace: *a suspicion of a smile.* [late ME, from L *suspicio;* replacing ME *suspecioun,* from AF, from L *suspectio*]

**suspicional** /sə'spɪʃənəl/, *adj.* of or pertaining to suspicion, esp. morbid or insane suspicions.

**suspicious** /sə'spɪʃəs/, *adj.* **1.** liable to cause or excite suspicion; questionable. **2.** inclined to suspect; esp., inclined to suspect evil; distrustful. **3.** full of or feeling suspicion. **4.** expressing or indicating suspicion. – **suspiciously,** *adv.* – **suspiciousness,** *n.*

**suspiration** /sʌspə'reɪʃən/, *n.* a long, deep sigh.

**suspire** /sə'spaɪə/, *v.i.,* **-spired, -spiring.** *Archaic.* **1.** to sigh. **2.** to breathe. [L *suspīrāre* sigh]

**suss**[1] /sʌs/, *v.t. Colloq.* to attempt to determine the possibilities of a situation, esp. one involving a particular challenge or presenting probable difficulties (fol. by *out*): *before the minister proposed his bill, he sussed out the likely reaction of the opposition.* [orig. uncert.; ? shortened form of SUSPECT]

**suss**[2] /sʌs/, *n. Obs. Colloq.* **1.** a form of payment given by the government to an unemployed person; dole. **2. on the suss,** unemployed and in receipt of such payment. Also, **susso.** [short for *Sustenance Payment*]

**Sussex** /'sʌsəks/, *n.* **1.** one of an English breed of chickens having white plumage with black markings. **2.** one of a breed of English red beef cattle.

**Sussex spaniel** /– 'spænjəl/, *n.* one of a breed of spaniels having short legs and a golden-liver coat.

**susso** /'sʌsoʊ/, *n. Obs. Colloq.* **1.** the dole: *on the susso.* **2.** an unemployed person. [sustenance]

**sustain** /sə'steɪn/, *v.t.* **1.** to hold or bear up from below; bear the weight of; be the support of, as in a structure. **2.** to bear (a burden, charge, etc.). **3.** to undergo, experience, or suffer (injury, loss, etc.); endure without giving way or yielding. **4.** to keep (a person, the mind, the spirits, etc.) from giving way, as under trial or affliction. **5.** to keep up or keep going, as an action or process: *to sustain a conversation.* **6.** to supply with food and drink, or the necessities of life, as persons. **7.** to provide for by furnishing means or funds, as an institution. **8.** to support by aid or countenance, as a person or cause. **9.** to uphold as valid, just, or correct, as a claim or the person making it. **10.** to confirm or corroborate, as a statement. [ME *susteine,* from OF *sustenir,* from L *sustinēre*] – **sustainable,** *adj.* – **sustainment,** *n.*

**sustainer** /səˈsteɪnə/, *n.* an engine that maintains the velocity of a rocket vehicle, once it has achieved its programmed velocity through the use of a booster engine.

**sustaining pedal** /səˈsteɪnɪŋ ˌpɛdl/, *n.* a pedal on a piano operated by the right foot, which holds the dampers off the strings and thus prolongs the note. Also, **loud pedal.**

**sustenance** /ˈsʌstənəns/, *n.* **1.** means of sustaining life; nourishment. **2.** means of livelihood. **3.** the process of sustaining. **4.** the state of being sustained.

**sustentacular** /ˌsʌstɛnˈtækjələ/, *adj.* supporting. [L *sustentāculum* a support + -AR[1]]

**sustentation** /ˌsʌstɛnˈteɪʃən/, *n.* **1.** maintenance in being or activity; the sustaining of life through vital processes. **2.** provision with means or funds for upkeep. **3.** means of sustaining life; sustenance. [ME, from L *sustentātio*] – **sustentative** /ˈsʌstɛnˌteɪtɪv, səˈstɛntətɪv/, *adj.*

**sustention** /səˈstɛnʃən/, *n.* **1.** the act of sustaining. **2.** the state or quality of being sustained. [coinage on model of DETENTION] – **sustentive** /səˈstɛntɪv/, *adj.*

**susurrant** /sjuˈsʌrənt/, *adj.* softly murmuring; whispering. [L *susurrans,* ppr.]

**susurration** /sjusəˈreɪʃən/, *n.* a soft murmur; whisper.

**susurrus** /sjuˈsʌrəs/, *n.* a soft murmuring sound; whisper. [L]

**sutler** /ˈsʌtlə/, *n.* (formerly) a person who followed an army and sold provisions, etc., to the soldiers. [early mod. D *soeteler,* from *soetelen* have a humble occupation]

**sutra** /ˈsutrə/, *n.* **1.** (*also cap.*) *Sanskrit Lit.* one of a body of aphoristic rules forming a link between the Vedic and the later Sanskrit literature. **2.** concise rules or teachings, chiefly in Hindu or Buddhist literature. Also, **sutta** /ˈsʊtə/. [Skt: thread, rule]

**suttee** /sʌˈti, ˈsʌti/, *n.* **1.** a former Hindu practice in which a widow immolated herself on the funeral pyre of her husband. **2.** a Hindu widow who immolated herself in this manner. [Skt *satī* faithful wife] – **sutteeism** /sʌˈtiɪzəm/, *n.*

**suture** /ˈsutʃə/, *n., v.,* **-tured, -turing.** *–n.* **1.** *Surg.* **a.** a joining of the lips or edges of a wound or the like by stitching or some similar process. **b.** a particular method of doing this. **c.** one of the stitches or fastenings employed. **2.** *Anat.* **a.** the line of junction of two bones, esp. of the skull, in an immovable articulation. **b.** the articulation itself. **3.** *Zool., Bot.* the line of junction, or the junction, of contiguous parts, as the line of closure between the valves of a bivalve shell, a seam where carpels of a pericarp join, etc. **4.** a seam as formed in sewing; a line of junction between two parts. **5.** a sewing together, or a joining as by sewing. *–v.t.* **6.** to unite by or as by a suture. [L *sūtūra*] – **sutural,** *adj.* – **suturally,** *adv.*

**suzerain** /ˈsuzəreɪn/, *n.* **1.** a sovereign or a state exercising political control over a dependent state. **2.** *Hist.* a feudal overlord. *–adj.* **3.** characteristic of, or being, a suzerain. [F, from *sus* above (from L *su(r)sum* upwards), modelled on *souverain* sovereign]

**suzerainty** /ˈsuzərənti/, *n., pl.* **-ties.** the position or authority of a suzerain.

**s.v.,** sailing vessel.

**S.V.,** **1.** Holy Virgin. [L *Sancta Virgo*] **2.** Your Holiness. [L *Sanctitas Vestra*]

**svelte** /svɛlt, sfɛlt/, *adj.* slender, esp. gracefully slender in figure; lithe. [F, from It. *svelto,* lit., plucked]

**SW,** **1.** south-west. **2.** south-western. **3.** short wave. Also, **S.W.**

**swab** /swɒb/, *n., v.,* **swabbed, swabbing.** *–n.* **1.** a large mop used on shipboard for cleaning decks, etc. **2.** *Med., Vet. Sci.* a piece of sponge, cloth, cottonwool, or the like, often mounted on a stick, for cleansing the mouth of a sick person, or for applying medicaments, taking specimens of discharges and secretions, etc. **3.** the material collected with a swab. **4.** a cleaner for the bore of a firearm. **5.** *Colloq.* a contemptible or useless person. *–v.t.* **6.** to clean with or as with a swab. **7.** to take up, or apply, as moisture, with or as with a swab. **8.** to pass (a swab, etc.) over a surface. **9.** to test (a racehorse) for possible drugging by taking a saliva sample with a swab. Also, **swob.** [backformation from SWABBER]

**swabbing stall** /ˈswɒbɪŋ stɔl/, *n.* a stall at a racecourse in which a horse is placed while undergoing swab tests.

**swaddle** /ˈswɒdl/, *v.,* **-dled, -dling,** *n.* *–v.t.* **1.** to bind (an infant, esp. a newborn infant) with long, narrow strips of cloth to prevent free movement; wrap tightly with clothes. **2.** to wrap (anything) round with bandages. *–n.* **3.** a long, narrow strip of cloth used for swaddling or bandaging. [ME *swathel,* OE *swæthel* swaddling band, akin to SWATHE[1], *v.*]

**swaddling clothes** /ˈswɒdlɪŋ ˌkloʊðz/, *n.pl.* **1.** clothes consisting of long, narrow strips of cloth for swaddling an infant. **2.** long clothes for an infant. **3.** the earliest period of existence of a person or thing; a period of infancy, immaturity, etc. **4.** a constricting influence; rigid supervision of actions, movement, etc.

**swag** /swæg/, *n., v.,* **swagged, swagging.** *–n.* **1.** a bundle or roll carried across the shoulders or otherwise, and containing the personal belongings of a traveller through the bush, a miner, etc.; shiralee; bluey. **2.** *Colloq.* plundered property; booty. **3.** *Colloq.* an unspecified but large number or quantity: *a swag of people.* *–v.i.* **4.** to travel about carrying one's bundle of personal belongings. [Brit. d.]

**swage** /sweɪdʒ/, *n., v.,* **swaged, swaging.** *–n.* **1.** a tool for bending cold metal to a required shape. **2.** a tool, die, or stamp for giving a particular shape to metal on an anvil, in a stamping press, etc. **3.** →**swage block.** *–v.t.* **4.** to bend or shape by means of a swage. [ME, from OF *souage*]

**swage block** /ˈ– blɒk/, *n.* an iron block containing holes and grooves of various sizes, used for heading bolts and shaping objects not easily worked on an anvil.

**swagger** /ˈswægə/, *v.i.* **1.** to walk or strut with a defiant or insolent air. **2.** to boast or brag noisily. *–v.t.* **3.** to bring, drive, force, etc., by blustering. *–n.* **4.** swaggering gait, bearing, or air; arrogant show of affected superiority. **5.** *N.Z.* →**swagman.** [frequentative of SWAG[1]] – **swaggerer,** *n.* – **swaggeringly,** *adv.*

**swagger stick** /ˈ– stɪk/, *n.* a short stick or cane sometimes carried by military personnel.

**swaggie** /ˈswægi/, *n. Colloq.* →**swagman.**

**swagman** /ˈswægmən/, *n.* **1.** a man who travels about the country on foot, living on his earnings from occasional jobs, or gifts of money or food. **2.** one who carries a swag.

swagman

**Swahili** /swaˈhili/, *n., pl.* **-lis,** (*esp. collectively*) **-li.** **1.** a member of a Bantu people with a large amount of Arab blood, who inhabit Zanzibar and the neighbouring coast of Africa. **2.** their language, a lingua franca in East and central Africa. [Ar.: coastal] – **Swahilian,** *adj.*

**swain** /sweɪn/, *n. Chiefly Poetic.* **1.** a country lad. **2.** a country gallant. **3.** a lover. [early ME *swein* servant, from Scand.; cf. Icel. *sveinn* boy] – **swainish,** *adj.* – **swainishness,** *n.*

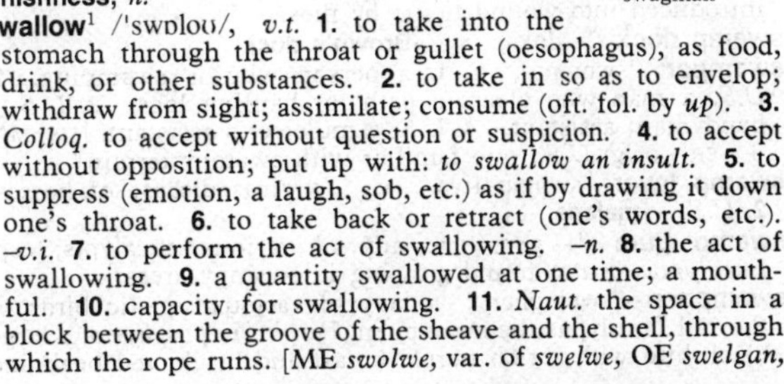

**swallow**[1] /ˈswɒloʊ/, *v.t.* **1.** to take into the stomach through the throat or gullet (oesophagus), as food, drink, or other substances. **2.** to take in so as to envelop; withdraw from sight; assimilate; consume (oft. fol. by *up*). **3.** *Colloq.* to accept without question or suspicion. **4.** to accept without opposition; put up with: *to swallow an insult.* **5.** to suppress (emotion, a laugh, sob, etc.) as if by drawing it down one's throat. **6.** to take back or retract (one's words, etc.). *–v.i.* **7.** to perform the act of swallowing. *–n.* **8.** the act of swallowing. **9.** a quantity swallowed at one time; a mouthful. **10.** capacity for swallowing. **11.** *Naut.* the space in a block between the groove of the sheave and the shell, through which the rope runs. [ME *swolwe,* var. of *swelwe,* OE *swelgan,*

c. G *schwelgen*] – **swallowable,** *adj.* – **swallower,** *n.*

**swallow**² /ˈswɒloʊ/, *n.* **1.** any of numerous small, long-winged passerine birds constituting the family Hirundinidae, notable for their swift, graceful flight and for the extent and regularity of their migrations, as the barn swallow, *Hirundo rustica,* of both Old and New Worlds and the welcome swallow. **2.** a swallow-like bird not of this family, as, in America, the chimney swallow, *Chaetura pelagica.* [ME *swalwe,* OE *swealwe,* akin to G *Schwalbe*] – **swallow-like,** *adj.*

swallow²

**swallow dive** /ˈ– daɪv/, *n.* a dive in which the diver while in the air assumes a position with arms outstretched to the side, legs straight and together.

**swallow-hole** /ˈswɒloʊ-hoʊl/, *n.* →**sinkhole** (def. 1).

**swallowtail** /ˈswɒloʊˌteɪl/, *n.* **1.** a swallow's tail, or a deeply forked tail like that of a swallow. **2.** any of various butterflies of the family Papilionidae, having the hind wings prolonged so as to suggest the tail of a swallow, as the Northern Hemisphere *Papilio machaon* or *Papilio aegeus* of eastern Australia, New Guinea and adjacent islands.

swallowtail butterfly

**swallow-tailed** /ˈswɒloʊ-teɪld/, *adj.* **1.** having a deeply forked tail like that of a swallow, as various birds. **2.** having an end or part suggesting a swallow's tail.

**swallow-tailed coat** /– ˈkoʊt/, *n.* a man's dress coat having the lower part cut away over the hips and descending in a pair of tapering skirts behind.

**swallow-wort** /ˈswɒloʊ-wɜt/, *n.* **1.** →**celandine** (def. 1). **2.** any of various plants of the family Asclepiadaceae, esp. a herb, *Cynanchum vincetoxicum,* of Europe, with an emetic root formerly esteemed as a counterpoison.

**swam** /swæm/, *v.* past tense of **swim.**

**swami** /ˈswami/, *n., pl.* **-mis.** a title for a Hindu religious teacher. [Hind.: master, from Skt *svāmin*]

**swamp**¹ /swɒmp/, *n.* **1.** a piece or tract of wet, spongy land; marshy ground; an area of still, often stagnant water. **2.** a tract of soft, wet ground having a growth of certain kinds of trees, but unfit for cultivation. *–v.t.* **3.** to flood or drench with water or the like. **4.** *Naut.* to sink or fill (a boat) with water. **5.** to plunge or sink in or as in a swamp. **6.** to overwhelm. **7.** to render helpless. *–v.i.* **8.** to fill with water and sink, as a boat. **9.** to sink or stick in or as in a swamp. **10.** to be plunged into or overwhelmed with difficulties, etc. [alteration of ME *sompe* swamp, probably influenced by LG *swampen* to quake and MHG *swamp* sponge, fungus. See SUMP]

**swamp**² /ˈswɒmp/, *v.i.* **1.** to act as an assistant to a bullock-driver. **2.** to travel on foot beside a bullock team, carrier's wagon, etc., on which one's swag, gear, etc., is being carried, giving assistance if needed to the driver. [backformation from SWAMPER]

**swamp cancer** /ˈ– kænsə/, *n.* an ulcerated condition of the skin of horses due to infestation with *Habronema* larvae, introduced into wound tissue by flies.

**swamp dock** /ˈ– dɒk/, *n.* →**Brown's dock.**

**swamper** /ˈswɒmpə/, *n.* **1.** a person who is swamping. **2.** *U.S.* a man who clears a path for hauling logs. **3.** *U.S.* a handyman; assistant. **4.** *U.S.* a muleteer's assistant. [SWAMP¹ + -ER¹; orig. *U.S.,* one familiar with swampy terrain]

**swamp fever** /ˈswɒmp fivə/, *n.* **1.** a virus disease of horses. **2.** *U.S.* →**malaria.**

**swamp gum** /ˈ– gʌm/, *n.* any of various eucalypts, esp. *Eucalyptus ovata,* found growing in swampy areas.

**swamphen** /ˈswɒmphɛn/, *n.* any of various aquatic birds of the rail family, as the swamphen, *Porphyrio porphyrio,* a large black bird with a rich purple breast and bright red beak and shield, which inhabits the margins of lakes, swamps and rivers throughout Australia, southern Eurasia and Africa.

**swampland** /ˈswɒmplænd/, *n.* land covered with swamps.

**swamp oak** /ˈswɒmp oʊk/, *n.* a tree, *Casuarina glauca,* found on the east coast of Australia esp. along tidal rivers and on brackish soil.

swamphen

**swamp pheasant** /– ˈfɛzənt/, *n.* →**coucal.** Also, **swamp cuckoo.**

**swamp wallaby** /ˈ– ˌwɒləbi/, *n.* a large, distinctive wallaby, *Wallabia bicolor,* inhabiting regions of dense, moist undergrowth in eastern Australia. Also, **black wallaby, black-tailed wallaby.**

**swampy** /ˈswɒmpi/, *adj.,* **-pier, -piest. 1.** of the nature of, resembling, or abounding in swamps. **2.** found in swamps.

**swan** /swɒn/, *n.* **1.** any large, stately swimming bird of the subfamily Cygninae, having a long, slender neck, such as the **mute swan** (*Cygnus olor*) of Europe and Asia introduced to parks and gardens throughout the world, and the black swan. **2.** a person or thing of unusual beauty, excellence, purity, or the like. **3.** a sweet singer or poet. [ME and OE, c. G *Schwan*] – **swanlike,** *adj.*

**swanee whistle** /ˌswɒni ˈwɪsəl/, *n.* a simple woodwind musical instrument, usu. of metal, worked by a plunger.

**swanherd** /ˈswɒnhɜd/, *n.* one who tends swans.

**swank** /swæŋk/, *n.* **1.** *Colloq.* dashing smartness, as in bearing, appearance, etc.; style. **2.** swagger. *–adj.* **3.** *Colloq.* pretentiously stylish. *–v.i.* **4.** to swagger in behaviour; show off. [? akin to MLG *swank* supple, MHG *swanken* sway]

**swanky** /ˈswæŋki/, *adj.,* **-kier, -kiest.** *Colloq.* **1.** conceited; boastful. **2.** expensive; smart; luxurious. – **swankily,** *adv.* – **swankiness,** *n.*

**swan neck** /swɒn ˈnɛk/, *n.* a curve in a tube, pipe, handrail, etc., shaped like the neck of a swan; S-shaped bend.

**swannery** /ˈswɒnəri/, *n., pl.* **-ries.** a place where swans are kept and reared.

**Swan River daisy,** *n.* a herbaceous plant, *Brachycome iberidifolia,* of western Australia, often cultivated for its attractive flowers.

**swan's-down** /ˈswɒnz-daʊn/, *n.* **1.** the down or under plumage of a swan, used for trimming, powder puffs, etc. **2.** a fine, soft, thick woollen cloth. Also, **swandown, swansdown.**

**swanskin** /ˈswɒnskɪn/, *n.* **1.** the skin of a swan, with the feathers on. **2.** a kind of fine twilled flannel.

**swan song** /ˈswɒn sɒŋ/, *n.* **1.** the fabled song of the dying swan. **2.** the last work, utterance, or achievement of a poet, a composer, or other person, before his death or retirement.

**swan-upping** /ˈswɒn-ʌpɪŋ/, *n. Brit.* the taking up of young swans to mark them with nicks on the beak as a sign of being owned by the Crown or some corporation. [SWAN + *upping,* from UP, *v.*]

**swap** /swɒp/, *v.,* **swapped, swapping,** *n.* *–v.t.* **1.** to exchange, barter, or trade, as one thing for another. *–v.i.* **2.** to make an exchange. *–n.* **3.** an exchange. Also, **swop.** [ME *swappe* strike, strike hands (in bargaining), c. d. G *schwappen* box (the ear)] – **swapper,** *n.*

**sward** /swɔd/, *n.* **1.** the grassy surface of land; turf. **2.** a stretch of turf; a growth of grass. *–v.t.* **3.** to cover with sward or turf. *–v.i.* **4.** to become covered with sward. [ME; OE *sweard* skin, c. G *Schwarte* rind]

**sware** /swɛə/, *v. Archaic.* past tense of **swear.**

**swarf** /swɔf, swaf/, *n.* chips of metal, plastic, etc., removed by a cutting tool during machining or grinding. [ME, OE *(ge)swearf;* c. Icel. *svarf*]

**swarm**¹ /swɔm/, *n.* **1.** a body of honeybees which emigrate from a hive and fly off together under the direction of a queen, to start a new colony. **2.** a body of bees settled together, as in a hive. **3.** a great number of things or persons, esp. in motion. **4.** *Biol.* a group of aggregation of free-floating or free-swimming cells or organisms. *–v.i.* **5.** to fly off together in a body from a hive to start a new colony, as bees. **6.** to move about, along, forth, etc., in great numbers, as things or persons. **7.** to congregate or occur in swarms or multitudes; be exceedingly numerous, as in a place or area. **8.** (of a place) to be thronged or overrun; abound or teem (fol. by *with*). **9.** *Biol.* to move or swim about in a swarm. *–v.t.* **10.** to swarm about, over, or in; throng; overrun. **11.** to produce a swarm of. [ME; OE *swearm*, c. G *Schwarm*, Icel. *svarmr* tumult]

**swarm**[2] /swɔm/, *v.i., v.t.* to climb (a tree, pole, or the like) by clasping it with the hands or arms and legs and drawing oneself up; shin (usu. fol. by *up*). [special use of SWARM[1]]

**swarmer** /'swɔmə/, *n.* **1.** one of a number that swarm; one of a swarm. **2.** *Biol.* →**swarm spore.**

**swarm spore** /swɔm 'spɔ/, *n.* any minute, motile, naked reproductive body produced in great numbers or occurring in groups or aggregations.

**swart** /swɔt/, *adj. Archaic.* swarthy. Also, **swarth.** [ME; OE *sweart*, c. G *schwarz*] – **swartness,** *n.*

**swarthy** /'swɔði/, *adj.,* **-thier, -thiest.** dark-coloured, now esp. as the skin, complexion, etc., of a person. [var. of *swarty*, from SWART + -Y[1]] – **swarthily,** *adv.* – **swarthiness,** *n.*

**swash** /swɒʃ/, *v.i.* **1.** to splash as things in water, or as water does. **2.** to dash about, as things in violent motion. **3.** to swagger. *–v.t.* **4.** to dash or cast violently, esp. to dash (water, etc.) about, down, etc. *–n.* **5.** a swashing blow, stroke, or movement, or the sound of it. **6.** the dashing of water, waves, etc. **7.** the sound made by such a dashing. **8.** the ground over which water washes. **9.** a channel of water through or behind a sandbank. [probably imitative] – **swashingly,** *adv.*

**swashbuckler** /'swɒʃbʌklə/, *n.* a swaggering swordsman or bully. Also, **swasher.** [SWASH (i.e., strike swords against shields) + BUCKLER] – **swashbuckling,** *adj., n.*

**swash letter** /'swɒʃ lɛtə/, *n.* (in printing) a decorative letter available in addition to normal ones, in certain founts of type.

**swastika** /'swɒstɪkə/, *n.* **1.** a figure used as a symbol or an ornament in the Old World and in America since prehistoric times, consisting of a cross with arms of equal length, each arm having a continuation at right angles, and all four continuations turning the same way. **2.** this figure with clockwise arms as the official emblem of the Nazi Party and the Third Reich. [Skt *svastika*, from *svastī* well-being]

Nazi swastika

**swat**[1] /swɒt/, *v.,* **swatted, swatting,** *n. Colloq. –v.t.* **1.** to hit with a smart or violent blow. *–n.* **2.** a smart or violent blow. Also, *U.S.,* **swot.** [orig. var. of SQUAT] – **swatter,** *n.*

**swat**[2] /swɒt/, *v.,* **swatted, swatting,** *n.* →**swot**[2].

**swatch** /swɒtʃ/, *n.* a sample of cloth or other material.

**swath** /swɔθ/, *n.* **1.** the space covered by the stroke of a scythe or the cut of a mowing machine. **2.** the piece or strip so cut. **3.** a line or ridge of grass, grain, or the like, cut and thrown together by a scythe or mowing machine. **4.** a strip, belt, or long and relatively narrow extent of anything. Also, **swathe.** [ME; OE *swæth*, c. G *Schwade*]

**swathe**[1] /sweɪð/, *v.,* **swathed, swathing,** *n.* *–v.t.* **1.** to wrap, bind, or swaddle with bands of some material; wrap up closely or fully. **2.** to enfold or envelop, as wrappings do. **3.** to wrap (cloth, a bandage, etc.) round something. *–n.* **4.** a band of linen or the like in which something is wrapped; a wrapping; a bandage. [ME; late OE *swathian*, from *swath-* (in *swathum* bandages)] – **swather,** *n.*

**swathe**[2] /sweɪð/, *n.* →**swath.**

**swatter** /'swɒtə/, *n.* one who or that which swats.

**sway** /sweɪ/, *v.i.* **1.** to move to and fro, as something fixed at one end or resting on a support; swing to and fro. **2.** to move or incline to one side or in a particular direction. **3.** to incline in opinion, sympathy, tendency, etc. **4.** to fluctuate or vacillate, as in opinion. **5.** to wield power; exercise rule. *–v.t.* **6.** to cause to move to and fro; cause to incline from side to side. **7.** to cause to move to one side or in a particular direction. **8.** *Naut.* to hoist or raise, as a yard or topmast (usu. fol. by *up*). **9.** to cause to fluctuate or vacillate. **10.** to cause (the mind, etc., or the person) to incline or turn in a specified way. **11.** to cause to swerve, as from a purpose or a course of action. **12.** to dominate; direct. **13. a.** *Archaic or Poetic.* to wield (a weapon or instrument, esp. the sceptre). **b.** to exercise rule or sovereignty over. *–n.* **14.** the act of swaying; swaying movement. **15.** rule; dominion. **16.** dominating power or influence. [ME, from Scand.; cf. Icel. *sveigja* sway] – **swayer,** *n.* – **swayingly,** *adv.*

**sway-back** /'sweɪ-bæk/, *n.* an excessive downward curvature of the spinal column in the dorsal region, esp. of horses.

**sway-backed** /'sweɪ-bækt/, *adj.* having the back sagged to an unusual degree; having a sway-back.

**Swaziland** /'swazilænd/, *n.* a country in southern Africa between southern Mozambique and south-eastern Transvaal in the Republic of South Africa; an independent member of the British Commonwealth.

**sweal** /swil/, *v.t., v.i.* **1.** to burn. **2.** to melt, as a candle; waste away. [ME *swelen*, OE *swǣlan* to burn; c. G *schwälen*, Icel. *svæla* burn out]

**swear** /swɛə/, *v.,* **swore** or (*Archaic*) **sware; sworn; swearing.** *–v.i.* **1.** to make a solemn declaration with an appeal to God or some superhuman being in confirmation of what is declared; make affirmation in a solemn manner by some sacred being or object, as the deity or the Bible. **2.** to engage or promise on oath or in a solemn manner; vow; bind oneself by oath (usu. fol. by *to*). **3.** to give evidence or make any statement on oath or by solemn declaration (usu. fol. by *to*). **4.** to use profane or taboo oaths or language, as in imprecation or anger or for mere emphasis. *–v.t.* **5.** to declare or affirm by swearing by a deity, some sacred object, etc. **6.** to affirm or say with solemn earnestness or great emphasis. **7.** to promise or undertake on oath or in a solemn manner; vow. **8.** to testify or state on oath or by solemn declaration; make oath to (something stated or alleged). **9.** to take (an oath), as in order to give solemnity or force to a declaration, promise, etc. **10.** to administer an oath to; bind by an oath (usu. fol. by *to*): *to swear someone to secrecy.* *–v.* **11.** Some special verb phrases are:

**swear at,** to speak to with curses or blasphemies; abuse.

**swear by, 1.** to name (some sacred being or thing, etc.) as one's witness or guarantee in swearing. **2.** to rely on; have confidence in.

**swear in,** to admit to office or service by administering an oath.

**swear off,** *Colloq.* to promise to give up something, esp. intoxicating drink.

**swear out,** to secure (a warrant for arrest) by making an accusation under oath.

*–n.* **12.** *Colloq.* the act of swearing or cursing. [ME *swere(n)*, OE *swerian*, c. G *schwören*] – **swearer,** *n.*

**swearword** /'swɛəwɜd/, *n.* a word used in swearing or cursing; an obscene or blasphemous word.

**sweat** /swɛt/, *v.,* **sweat** or **sweated, sweating,** *n.* *–v.i.* **1.** to excrete watery fluid through the pores of the skin, as from heat, exertion, etc.; perspire, esp. freely or profusely. **2.** to exude moisture, as green plants piled in a heap. **3.** to gather moisture from the surrounding air by condensation. **4.** (of tobacco) to ferment. **5.** *Colloq.* to exert oneself strenuously; work hard. **6.** *Colloq.* to feel distress, as from anxiety, impatience, vexation, etc. *–v.t.* **7.** to emit (watery fluid, etc.) through the pores of the skin. **8.** to exude (moisture, etc.) in drops or small particles. **9.** to send forth or get rid of with or like perspiration (oft. fol. by *out* or *off*). **10.** to wet or stain with perspiration. **11.** to cause (a person, a horse, etc.) to sweat. **12.** to cause (substances, etc.) to exude moisture, esp. as a step in some industrial process of treating or preparing. **13.** to cause (persons, etc.) to work hard. **14.** to employ (workers) at low wages, for long hours or under other unfavourable conditions. **15.** *Colloq.* to deprive (a person) of money, etc. as by exaction. **16.** *Colloq.* to subject a person to severe questioning in order to extract information. **17.** *Metall.* **a.** to heat (metal) to partial fusion in order to remove an easily fusible constituent. **b.** to heat (solder or the like) until it melts; join (metal parts) by heating, esp. after applying solder. **18.** to remove part of the metal from (coins, esp. gold) by friction, as by shaking them in a bag. **19.** to cause (tobacco) to ferment. **20. sweat blood,** *Colloq.* to be under a strain; be anxious; worry. **21. sweat it out,** *Colloq.* to hold out; endure until the end. **22. sweat on,** to await anxiously. **23. sweat out,** to get rid of by sweating. *–n.* **24.** the process of sweating or perspiring, as from heat, exertion, perturbation, disease, etc. **25.** the secretions of sweat glands; the product of sweating. **26.** a state or period of sweating. **27.** process of inducing sweat as medical or other treatment. **28.** moisture or liquid matter exuded from something or gathered on a surface in drops or small particles. **29.** an exuding of moisture by a substance, etc., or an inducing of such exudation, as in some industrial process. **30.** a run given to a horse for exercise, as before a race. **31.** *Colloq.* a state of perturbation, anxiety, or impatience. **32.** *Colloq.* hard work. **33. no sweat!,** *Colloq.* it's no problem! [ME *swete(n)*, OE *swǣtan*, c. D *zweeten*, G *schweissen*] – **sweatless,** *adj.*

**sweatband** /ˈswɛtbænd/, *n.* **1.** a band in a hat or cap to protect it against sweat from the head. **2.** a headband worn by athletes, tennis players, etc., to absorb perspiration.

**sweat bee** /ˈswɛt bi/, *n.* any of various small short-tongued bees, esp. a bee of the genus *Halictus.*

**sweatbox** /ˈswɛtbɒks/, *n.* **1.** a device for sweating various vegetable products, as figs and tobacco leaves. **2.** any confined space in which a person is made to sweat, esp. a prison cell.

**sweated** /ˈswɛtəd/, *adj.* **1.** made by underpaid workers. **2.** underpaid and overworked. **3.** having poor working conditions.

**sweater** /ˈswɛtə/, *n.* **1.** a knitted jumper, usu. of wool. **2.** one who or that which sweats. **3.** an employer who underpays and overworks employees.

**sweat gland** /ˈswɛt glænd/, *n.* one of the minute, coiled, tubular glands of the skin that secrete sweat; a sudoriferous gland.

**sweating sickness** /ˈswɛtɪŋ ˌsɪknəs/, *n.* a febrile epidemic disease which appeared in the 15th and 16th centuries, characterised by profuse sweating, and frequently fatal in a few hours.

**sweating system** /ˈ– ˌsɪstəm/, *n.* the practice of employing workers in sweatshops.

**sweat-rag** /ˈswɛt-ræg/, *n.* a scarf or handkerchief tied around the neck to catch perspiration.

**sweatshirt** /ˈswɛtˌʃɜt/, *n.* a loose pullover worn esp. by athletes to prevent chill or to induce sweating.

**sweatshop** /ˈswɛtˌʃɒp/, *n.* a workshop, or the like, employing workers at low wages during overlong hours, under insanitary or otherwise unfavourable conditions.

**sweatsuit** /ˈswɛtsut/, *n.* a one-piece suit, opening at the front, usu. of cotton and fitting tightly at the wrists and ankles; used by athletes in training.

**sweaty** /ˈswɛti/, *adj.*, **-ier, -iest.** **1.** covered, moist, or stained with sweat. **2.** causing sweat. **3.** laborious. – **sweatily,** *adv.* – **sweatiness,** *n.*

**Swede** /swid/, *n.* **1.** a native or inhabitant of Sweden. **2.** (*l.c.*) a cultivated variety of a plant, *Brassica napus,* frequently grown for its edible, swollen taproot. **3.** the root itself. [MLG or MD]

**Sweden** /ˈswidən/, *n.* a kingdom in northern Europe, in the eastern part of the Scandinavian peninsula.

**Swedish** /ˈswidɪʃ/, *adj.* **1.** of or pertaining to Sweden, its inhabitants, or their language. *–n.* **2.** a Germanic language, the language of Sweden and parts of Finland, closely related to Danish and Norwegian. **3.** the people of Sweden collectively.

**sweeny** /ˈswini/, *n.* atrophy of the shoulder muscles in horses. [cf. d. G *Schweine* atrophy]

**sweep**[1] /swip/, *v.,* **swept, sweeping,** *n. –v.t.* **1.** to move, drive, or bring, by passing a broom, brush, or the like over the surface occupied, or as the broom or other object does: *to sweep dust away.* **2.** to move, bring, take, etc., by or as by a steady, driving stroke or with continuous, forcible actions: *the wind sweeps the snow into drifts.* **3.** *Cricket.* to strike (the ball) with a cross bat close to the ground, on the leg side, usu. backward of square leg. **4.** to pass or draw (something) over a surface, or about, along, etc., with a steady, continuous stroke or movement: *to sweep a brush over a table.* **5.** to clear or clean (a floor, room, chimney, etc.) of dirt, litter, etc., by means of a broom or the like. **6.** to make (a path, etc.) by clearing a space with a broom or the like. **7.** to clear (a surface, place, etc.) of something on or in it: *to sweep the sea of enemy ships.* **8.** to pass over (a surface, region, etc.) with a steady, driving movement or unimpeded course, as winds, floods or fire. **9.** to direct the gaze over (a region, etc.) with the unaided eye or with a telescope or the like; survey with a continuous view over the whole extent. **10.** to win an overwhelming victory, as in an election: *the Labor Party swept the polls in the 1972 election.* **11.** *Music.* **a.** to pass the fingers or bow over (a musical) instrument, its strings or keys, etc.) as in playing. **b.** to bring forth (music) thus. **12.** *Electronics.* to scan (a band of frequency) when receiving a signal, or to generate a signal which moves across (a band of frequency). **13. sweep under the carpet,** to remove inconvenient issues from consideration. *–v.i.* **14.** to sweep a floor, room etc., as with a broom, or as a broom does: *a new broom sweeps clean.* **15.** to move steadily and strongly or swiftly (fol. by *along, by, down over,* etc.). **16.** to pass in a swift but stately manner, as a person, a procession, etc. **17.** to walk in long, trailing garments. **18.** to trail, as garments, etc. **19.** to move or pass in a continuous course, esp. a wide curve or circuit: *his glance swept about the room.* **20.** to extend in a continuous or curving stretch, as a road, a shore, fields, etc. **21.** to conduct an underwater search by towing a drag under the surface of the water, as for mines, a lost anchor, or the like. **22.** *Cricket.* to execute a sweep. *–n.* **23.** the act of sweeping, esp. a moving, removing, clearing, etc., by or as by the use of a broom: *to abolish all class distinctions at one sweep.* **24.** the steady, driving motion or swift onward course of something moving with force or unimpeded: *the sweep of the wind or waves.* **25.** a trailing movement, as of garments. **26.** *Cricket.* the action of a batsman who sweeps (def. 3). **27.** a swinging or curving movement or stroke, as of the arm or a weapon, oar, etc. **28.** *Canoeing.* a paddle stroke used to turn a canoe to the left or right in a large arc. **29.** reach, range or compass, as of something about: *the sweep of a road about a marsh.* **30.** a continuous extent or stretch: *a broad sweep of sand.* **31.** *Navy.* a wire or rope dragged beneath the surface of the water by two mine-sweeping ships to cut mines loose. **32.** a curving, esp. widely or gently curving, line, form, part, or mass. **33.** matter removed or gathered by sweeping. **34.** a lever-like device for raising or lowering a bucket in a well, consisting essentially of a long pole pivoted on an upright post. **35.** a large oar used in small vessels, sometimes to assist the rudder in turning the vessel but usu. to propel the craft. **36.** (in a life-saving boat) the man who steers by means of a sweep (def. 35) at the stern. **37.** one who sweeps, esp. a chimneysweep. **38.** *Cards.* **a.** (in whist) the winning of all the tricks in a hand. Cf. **slam**[2] (def. 1). **b.** (in a casino) a pairing or combining, and hence taking, of all the cards on the board. **39.** *Physics.* **a.** an irreversible process tending towards thermal equilibrium. **b.** the motion of the spot across the screen of a cathode-ray tube. **40.** →**sweepstake.** **41.** *Colloq.* a disreputable person; scoundrel. **42.** *Cricket.* a stroke played with a cross bat close to the ground, aimed at despatching the ball square or fine on the leg side. **43. make a clean sweep,** to get rid of completely. [ME *swepe;* cf. OE *geswēpa* sweepings, akin to *swāpan* sweep, c. G *schweifen*]

**sweep**[2] /swip/, *n.* an Australian marine fish of prized edible quality, of the family Scorpidae.

**sweepback** /ˈswipbæk/, *n.* the shape of, or the angle formed by, an aeroplane wing whose leading or trailing edges slope backwards.

**sweeper** /ˈswipə/, *n.* **1.** one who or that which sweeps. **2.** a train which stops at all stations; picker-up.

**sweeping** /ˈswipɪŋ/, *adj.* **1.** of wide range or scope; far-reaching. **2.** moving or passing about over a wide area: *a sweeping glance.* **3.** moving, driving, or passing steadily or forcibly on. **4.** without limitations; indiscriminate; disregarding details: *a sweeping statement.* **5.** decisive; overwhelming: *a sweeping victory.* *–n.* **6.** the act of one that sweeps. **7.** (*pl.*) matter swept out or up, as dust, refuse, etc.: *put the sweepings in this box.* – **sweepingly,** *adv.* – **sweepingness,** *n.*

**sweepstake** /ˈswipsteɪk/, *n.* **1.** a race or other contest in which the prize consists of the stakes contributed by the various competitors. **2.** the prize itself. **3.** a method of gambling, as on the outcome of a horserace, in which each participant contributes a stake, usu. by buying a numbered ticket entitling him to draw the name of a competitor, the winnings being provided from the stake money. Also, **sweepstakes.** [SWEEP[1] + STAKE[2]]

**sweet** /swit/, *adj.* **1.** pleasing to the taste, esp. having the pleasant taste or flavour characteristic of sugar, honey, etc. **2.** not rancid, or stale; fresh. **3.** fresh as opposed to salt, as water. **4.** pleasing to the ear; making a pleasant or agreeable sound; musical. **5.** pleasing to the smell; fragrant; perfumed. **6.** pleasing or agreeable; yielding pleasure or enjoyment; delightful. **7.** pleasant in disposition or manners; amiable; kind or gracious as a person, action, etc. **8.** dear; beloved; precious. **9.** easily managed; done or effected without effort. **10.** (of wine) sweet-tasting (opposed to *dry*). **11.** free from sourness or acidity, as soil. **12.** *Chem.* **a.** devoid of corrosive or acidic substances. **b.** (of substances such as petrol) containing no sulphur compounds. **13.** *Jazz.* performed with a regular beat, moderate tempo, and with melodic harmony. **14.** *Colloq.* satisfactory as arranged; *she's sweet.* **15. sweet on,** *Colloq.* in love with; fond of. *–adv.* **16.** in a sweet manner; sweetly. *–n.* **17.** sweet taste or flavour; sweet smell; sweetness. **18.** that which is sweet. **19.** Also, **sweetie.** any of various small confections made wholly or partly from sugar. **20.** (*oft. pl.*) any sweet dish, as a pudding, tart, etc., served at the end of a meal. **21.** something pleasant to the mind or feelings. **22.** a beloved person; darling; sweetheart. [ME and OE *swēte,* c. D *zoet* G *süss,* Icel. *sætr,* akin to Goth. *suts,* L *suāvis*] – **sweetly,** *adv.* – **sweetness,** *n.*

**sweet alyssum** /– 'æləsəm/, *n.* a garden plant, *Lobularia maritima,* with small white, pink or violet flowers.

**sweet-and-sour** /swit-n-'sauə/, *adj.* (of a sauce) flavoured with sugar and vinegar and used with meat, esp. pork, fish, etc., as in oriental cookery.

**sweet basil** /swit 'bæzəl/, *n.* →**basil**[1].

**sweet bay** /– 'beɪ/, *n.* **1.** →**laurel** (def. 1). **2.** →**bay**[4] (def. 1).

**sweetbread** /'switbrɛd/, *n.* **1.** the pancreas (**stomach sweetbread**) of an animal, esp. a calf or a lamb, used for food. **2.** the thymus gland (**neck sweetbread** or **throat sweetbread**), likewise so used.

**sweetbriar** /swit'braɪə/, *n.* a rosaceous shrub, *Rosa rubiginosa,* of Eurasia, now widely naturalised in temperate regions, having hooked prickles often mixed with bristles, and single pink flowers; eglantine. Also, **sweetbrier, briar.**

**sweet cherry** /swit 'tʃɛri/, *n.* any of several cultivated forms of the tree, *Prunus avium,* having sweet fruit.

**sweet cicely** /– 'sɪsəli/, *n.* any of several umbelliferous plants nearly allied to chervil, as an English species, *Myrrhis odorata,* sometimes used as a potherb, or some species of the North American genus *Osmorhiza.*

**sweet cider** /– 'saɪdə/, *n.* cider which has not fermented.

**sweet clover** /– 'klouvə/, *n.* →**Bokhara clover.**

**sweet corn** /'– kɔn/, *n.* **1.** any maize of a sweetish flavour and suitable for eating, esp. a particularly sweet variety, *Zea mays* var. *saccharata.* **2.** the unripe and tender ears of maize, esp. when used as a table vegetable and when the kernels have been removed from the cob; green corn.

**sweeten** /'switn/, *v.t.* **1.** to make sweet. **2.** to make mild or kind; soften. **3.** to make (the breath, air, etc.) sweet or fresh, as with a mouthwash, spray, etc. **4.** to alleviate; make less disagreeable. **5.** *Colloq.* to bribe. **6.** *Colloq.* (in poker) to increase (a pot) by adding stakes before opening. *–v.i.* **7.** to become sweet.

**sweetener** /'switənə/, *n.* **1.** one who or that which sweetens. **2.** *Colloq.* a bribe.

**sweetening** /'switənɪŋ/, *n.* **1.** something that sweetens food, etc. **2.** the process of causing something to be sweet.

**sweet F.A.** /swit ɛf 'eɪ/, *n.* very little; next to nothing. [abbrev. of *sweet Fanny Adams,* euph. for *sweet fuck-all;* Fanny Adams was a young British girl who was murdered and cut up into small pieces]

**sweet flag** /– 'flæg/, *n.* a plant, *Acorus calamus,* with long, sword-shaped leaves and a pungent, aromatic rootstock; calamus.

**sweet gale** /– 'geɪl/, *n.* →**bog myrtle.**

**sweet gum** /'– gʌm/, *n.* →**liquidambar** (def. 1).

**sweetheart** /'swithat/, *n.* **1.** one of a pair of lovers with relation to the other, sometimes esp. the girl or woman. **2.** a beloved person (often used in affectionate address).

**sweetheart deal** /'– dil/, *n.* an agreement between employers and employees, which contains benefits well over those of the normal award. Also, **sweetheart agreement.**

**sweetie** /'switi/, *n. Colloq.* **1.** a sweetheart (often used as a term of endearment). **2.** a sweet; confection.

**sweeting** /'switɪŋ/, *n.* **1.** *Chiefly Brit.* a sweet variety of apple. **2.** *Archaic.* a beloved person; darling; sweetheart.

**sweetish** /'switɪʃ/, *adj.* somewhat sweet. – **sweetishly,** *adv.* – **sweetishness,** *n.*

**sweetlips** /'switlɪps/, *n.* **1.** a fat-lipped fish of the family Plectorhynchidae. **2.** a name used erroneously for some of the emperor fish.

**sweet lupin** /swit 'lupən/, *n.* any variety of lupin which, unlike the majority of lupins which are high in alkaloids and bitter to taste, is relatively sweet and palatable to stock, as the western Australian blue lupin.

**sweetmeat** /'switmit/, *n.* **1.** a sweet delicacy, prepared with sugar, honey, or the like, as preserves, sweets or (formerly) cakes or pastry. **2.** (*usu. pl.*) any sweet delicacy of the confectionery kind, as crystallised fruit, sugar-covered nuts, sweets, bonbons, etc.

**sweet oil** /swit 'ɔɪl/, *n. Chiefly U.S.* an edible oil, esp. olive oil.

**sweet pea** /– 'pi/, *n.* an annual climbing plant, *Lathyrus odoratus,* bearing sweet-scented flowers.

**sweet pepper** /– 'pɛpə/, *n.* any of the mild-flavoured peppers, *Capsicum frutescens* var. *grossum,* used for stuffing, pickling, or as a vegetable; bell pepper.

**sweet potato** /– pə'teɪtou/, *n.* **1.** a plant of central America, *Ipomaea batatas,* widely cultivated in the tropics for its edible root. **2.** the root.

**sweet-scented** /'swit-sɛntəd/, *adj.* having a pleasantly sweet smell; fragrant.

**sweetshop** /'swit,ʃɒp/, *n.* a shop that sells sweets.

**sweetsop** /'switsɒp/, *n.* **1.** a tropical American tree, *Annona squamosa.* **2.** the sweet pulpy fruit of this tree, with a green scaly rind, and shining black seeds.

**sweet spirit of nitre,** *n.* an alcoholic solution of ethyl nitrite, $C_2H_5NO_2$, employed medicinally as a diaphoretic, diuretic, and antispasmodic.

**sweet-talk** /'swit-tɔk/, *v.t. Colloq.* **1.** to flatter excessively. **2.** to win over (someone) by ingratiating talk; con (fol. by *into*). – **sweet-talker,** *n.*

**sweet-tempered** /'swit-tɛmpəd/, *adj.* having a kind and gentle disposition.

**sweet tooth** /swit 'tuθ/, *n. Colloq.* a strong liking for sweets, sweet dishes, etc.

**sweet vernal grass,** *n.* a perennial grass with a strong smell of new-mown hay, *Anthoxanthum odoratum,* widespread in temperate regions.

**sweet william** /swit 'wɪljəm/, *n.* a kind of pink, *Dianthus barbatus,* bearing small flowers of various colours in dense clusters.

**swell** /swɛl/, *v.,* **swelled, swollen** or **swelled, swelling,** *n., adj.* *–v.i.* **1.** to grow in bulk, as by absorption of moisture, by inflation or distention, by addition of material in the process of growth, or the like. **2.** to rise in waves, as the sea. **3.** to well up, as a spring or as tears. **4.** to bulge out or be protuberant, as a sail, a cask in the middle. **5.** to grow in amount, degree, force, or the like. **6.** to increase gradually in volume or intensity, as sound. **7.** to arise and grow within one, as a feeling or emotion. **8.** to become puffed up with pride; behave or talk arrogantly or pretentiously. *–v.t.* **9.** to cause to grow in bulk. **10.** to increase gradually in loudness, as a musical note. **11.** to cause (a thing) to bulge out or be protuberant. **12.** to increase in amount, degree, force, etc. **13.** to affect with swelling emotion. **14.** to puff up with pride. *–n.* **15.** the act of swelling. **16.** condition of being swollen. **17.** increase in bulk; inflation or distention. **18.** a part that bulges out, or a protuberant part. **19.** a wave, esp. when long and unbroken, or such waves collectively. **20.** a gradually rising elevation of the land. **21.** increase in amount, degree, force, etc. **22.** gradual increase in loudness of sound. **23.** *Music.* **a.** a gradual increase (crescendo) followed by a gradual decrease (diminuendo) in loudness or force of musical sound. **b.** the sign (< >) for indicating this. **c.** a contrivance, as in an organ, by which the loudness of notes may be varied. **24.** a swelling of emotion within one. **25.** *Colloq.* **a.** a fashionably dressed person. **b.** a person of high social standing. *–adj. Colloq.* **26.** (of things) stylish; elegant; grand: *a swell hotel.* **27.** (of persons) fashionably dressed; of high standing, esp. socially. **28.** first-rate; excellent. [ME; OE *swellan,* c. G *schwellen*]

**swell box** /'– bɒks/, *n.* a box or chamber containing a set of pipes in a pipe organ or of reeds in a reed organ, and having movable slats or shutters which can be opened or closed to increase or diminish the loudness of the notes.

**swelled head** /swɛld 'hɛd/, *n. Colloq.* an excessively high opinion of oneself; conceit. – **swelled-headed,** *adj.*

**swellfish** /'swɛlfɪʃ/, *n., pl.* **-fishes,** (*esp. collectively*) **-fish.** →**puffer** (def. 2).

**swelling** /'swɛlɪŋ/, *n.* **1.** the act of one that swells. **2.** the condition of being swollen. **3.** a swollen part; a protuberance or prominence. **4.** *Pathol.* an abnormal enlargement or protuberance.

**swell organ** /'swɛl ɔgən/, *n.* **1.** the section of an organ which is fitted with a swell box. **2.** the stops which control it.

**swelter** /'swɛltə/, *v.i.* **1.** to suffer or languish with oppressive heat; perspire profusely from heat. *–v.t.* **2.** to oppress, or cause to languish, with heat. **3.** *Archaic.* to exude like sweat, as venom. *–n.* **4.** a sweltering condition. [ME *sweltre,* frequentative of *swelt* die, swoon, OE *sweltan,* c. Icel. *svelta*]

**sweltering** /'swɛltərɪŋ/, *adj.* **1.** suffering or languishing with oppressive heat. **2.** characterised by oppressive heat, as a place, the weather, etc.; sultry. – **swelteringly,** *adv.*

**swept** /swɛpt/, *v.* past tense and past participle of **sweep**[1].

**sweptback** /'swɛptbæk/, *adj.* (of the wing of an aircraft) having its leading and trailing edges slanted backwards relative to its longitudinal axis.

**swept frequency oscillator,** *n.* a device which has a swept frequency output which allows it to be set to a centre frequency about which the signal deviates.

**sweptwing** /'swɛptwɪŋ/, *adj.* (of an aircraft, etc.) having sweptback wings.

**swerve** /swɜv/, *v.,* **swerved, swerving,** *n. –v.i.* **1.** to turn aside abruptly in movement or direction; deviate suddenly or sharply from the straight or direct course. *–v.t.* **2.** to cause to turn aside. *–n.* **3.** the act of swerving; a turning aside; a deviation. **4.** that which swerves. **5.** *Cricket.* deviation of a ball in mid-air, usu. as a result of spin rather than swing. [ME; OE *sweorfan* rub, file, c. D *zwerven* rove] – **swerver,** *n.*

**swidden** /'swɪdn/, *n.* a field cleared from the forest, used to grow crops until the soil is exhausted, and then abandoned. [Scand.]

**swift** /swɪft/, *adj.* **1.** moving with great speed or velocity; fleet; rapid: *a swift ship.* **2.** coming, happening, or performed quickly or without delay. **3.** quick or prompt to act, etc.: *swift to act. –adv.* **4.** swiftly. *–n.* **5.** any of the rapidly flying birds of the families Apodidae and Hemiprocnidae, as *Hirundapus caudacutus,* which migrates to Australia and Tasmania. **6.** any of various small lizards, esp. of the genus *Sceloporus,* which run with great swiftness. **7.** an adjustable device upon which a hank of yarn is placed in order to wind off skeins or balls. [ME and OE; akin to SWEEP[1]] – **swiftly,** *adv.* – **swiftness,** *n.*

swift (def. 5)

**swifter** /'swɪftə/, *n. Naut.* **1.** a small line joining the outer ends of the bars of a capstan to confine them to their sockets while the capstan is being turned. **2.** the forward shroud of the lower rigging on either side of a mast. [Brit. d. *swift,* v., tie fast; cf. Icel. *svipta* to reef (sails)]

**swift-footed** /'swɪft-fʊtəd/, *adj.* swift in running.

**swiftie** /'swɪfti/, *n. Colloq.* **1.** an unfair act; a deceitful practice. **2. pull (put over) a swiftie,** to hoodwink; to deceive.

**swift moth** /'swɪft mɒθ/, *n.* any of various moths of the family Hepialidae, having reduced mouth parts, short antennae and larvae which tunnel in trees or soil and are agricultural and forestry pests. Also, **ghost moth.**

**swift-talk** /'swɪft-tɔk/, *v.t.* to attempt to advantage (oneself) by talking rapidly, usu. with specious arguments.

**swig** /swɪg/, *n., v.,* **swigged, swigging.** *Colloq. –n.* **1.** a large or deep drink, esp. of alcoholic liquor, taken in one swallow; draught. *–v.t., v.i.* **2.** to drink heartily or greedily. – **swigger,** *n.*

**swill** /swɪl/, *n.* **1.** liquid or partly liquid food for animals, esp. kitchen refuse given to pigs; pig-swill. **2.** kitchen refuse in general; rubbish. **3.** any liquid matter; slops. **4.** a session of heavy drinking, often hurried: *the six o'clock swill.* **5.** *Colloq.* the public bar of a hotel: *in the swill. –v.i.* **6.** to drink greedily or excessively. *–v.t.* **7.** to drink (something) greedily or to excess; guzzle. **8.** to wash or cleanse by flooding with water. [ME *swile(n),* OE *swilian,* var. of *swillan;* orig. unknown] – **swiller,** *n.*

**swim** /swɪm/, *v.,* **swam, swum, swimming,** *n. –v.i.* **1.** to move along or in water by movements of the limbs, fins, tail, etc.; move on or in water or other liquid in any way, esp. on the surface. **2.** to float on the surface of water or other liquid. **3.** to move, rest, or be suspended in air or the like, as if swimming in water. **4.** to move, glide, or go smoothly over a surface. **5.** to be immersed or steeped in, or overflowed or flooded with, a liquid. **6.** to be dizzy or giddy; have a whirling sensation; seem to whirl. *–v.t.* **7.** to move along on or in by swimming; float on or in; cross by swimming, as a stream. **8.** to cause to swim; cause to float, as on a stream. **9.** to furnish with sufficient water to swim or float. **10.** to perform (a particular stroke) in swimming. *–n.* **11.** an act, instance, or period of swimming. **12.** a motion as of swimming; a smooth gliding movement. **13. in the swim,** actively engaged in current affairs, social activities, etc. [ME *swimme(n),* OE *swimman,* c. G *schwimmen*] – **swimmer,** *n.*

**swim bladder** /'– ˌblædə/, *n.* →**air-bladder** (def. 2).

**swimmeret** /'swɪmərɛt/, *n.* (in many crustaceans) one of a number of abdominal limbs or appendages, usu. adapted for swimming, and for carrying eggs, and thus distinguished from other limbs adapted for walking or seizing.

**swimmers** /'swɪməz/, *n.* →**swimsuit.**

**swimming** /'swɪmɪŋ/, *n.* **1.** the act or technique of swimming. **2.** vertigo; dizziness. *–adj.* **3.** capable of, adapted for, or used in swimming. **4.** immersed in or overflowing with, or as with, water. **5.** having a sensation of dizziness, vertigo, etc.

**swimming costume** /'– ˌkɒstjum/, *n.* →**swimsuit.**

**swimmingly** /'swɪmɪŋli/, *adv.* without difficulty; with great success.

**swimming pool** /'swɪmɪŋ pul/, *n.* an artificial pool, esp. one in the open air, for swimming in.

**swimming trunks** /'– trʌŋks/, *n.pl.* a man's swimsuit.

**swimsuit** /'swɪmsut/, *n.* a garment or garments worn for swimming.

**swimwear** /'swɪmwɛə/, *n.* clothing designed to be worn for swimming or on the beach, as a swimsuit, bathing cap, beach robe or cover-up, etc.

**swindle** /'swɪndl/, *v.,* **-dled, -dling,** *n. –v.t.* **1.** to cheat (a person) out of money, etc. **2.** to obtain by fraud or deceit. *–v.i.* **3.** to put forward plausible schemes or use unscrupulous artifice to defraud others; cheat; defraud. *–n.* **4.** the act of swindling; a fraudulent transaction or scheme. **5.** anything deceptive; a fraud. [backformation from *swindler,* from G *Schwindler,* from *schwindeln* be giddy, swindle] – **swindler,** *n.*

**swine** /swaɪn/, *n., pl.* **swine. 1.** the domestic pig. **2.** any animal of the same family, Suidae, of the artiodactyl suborder Suina, as the European wildboar, *Sus scrofa,* or of the closely related peccary family of the New World, Tayassuidae. **3.** a coarse, gross, or brutishly sensual person. **4.** a contemptible person. [ME; OE *swīn,* c. G *Schwein;* akin to SOW[2]]

**swinecress** /'swaɪnkrɛs/, *n.* any of the small herbs constituting the genus *Coronopus,* family Cruciferae, of Europe, northern Africa and America, as an ill-smelling bittercress, *C. didymus,* of temperate South America, now widespread in temperate regions as a weed and tainter of dairy products. Also, **wartcress.**

**swine fever** /swaɪn 'fivə/, *n.* a specific, acute, usu. fatal, contagious disease of pigs caused by a filterable virus; hog cholera.

**swine flu** /– 'flu/, *n.* *U.S.* an influenza affecting swine and also people in contact with this virus.

**swineherd** /'swaɪnhɜd/, *n.* one who herds or tends swine.

**swine pox** /'swaɪn pɒks/, *n.* **1.** a variety of chickenpox. **2.** *Vet. Sci.* a mild pox disease of pigs, caused by a virus related to that of cowpox and characterised by the appearance of pustules in the skin, esp. of the abdomen.

**swing**[1] /swɪŋ/, *v.*, **swung** or (*Archaic*) **swang; swung; swinging,** *n.* *–v.t.* **1.** to cause to move to and fro, sway, or oscillate, as something suspended from above: *ladies swinging their parasols.* **2.** to cause to move in alternate directions, or in either direction, about a fixed point or line of support, as a door on its hinges. **3.** *Cricket.* (of a bowler) to cause the ball to deviate to the left or right in its flight towards the wicket, as a result of the action of air on the seam of a shiny ball. **4.** to move (something held or grasped) with an oscillating or rotary movement: *swing a club about one's head.* **5.** to cause to move in a curve as if about a central point. **6.** to suspend so as to hang freely, as a hammock or a door. **7.** to sway, influence, or manage as desired: *to swing the voting in an election.* *–v.i.* **8.** to move to and fro, as something suspended from above, as a pendulum. **9.** to move to and fro on a swing, as for amusement. **10.** to move in alternate directions, or in either direction, about a point or line of support, as a gate on its hinges. **11. a.** to move in a curve as if about a central point, as around a corner. **b.** *Cricket.* (of a ball) to deviate to the left or right in its flight toward the wicket, through atmospheric action on the seam. **12.** to move with a free, swaying motion, as soldiers on the march. **13.** to be suspended so as to hang freely, as a bell, etc. **14.** *Colloq.* to suffer death by hanging. **15.** to change or shift one's attention, opinion, interest, etc.; fluctuate. **16.** to aim at or hit something with a sweeping movement of the arm. **17.** *Colloq.* (of two people) to be in mental or spiritual harmony; be in accord in outlook or feeling. **18.** *Colloq.* (of the members of a group) to agree to exchange sexual partners on a casual basis. *–n.* **19.** the act or the manner of swinging; movement in alternate directions, or in a particular direction. **20.** the amount of such movement. **21.** a curving movement or course. **22.** a moving of the body with a free, swaying motion, as in walking. **23.** a steady, marked rhythm or movement, as of verse or music. **24.** *U.S.* freedom of action: *have free swing.* **25.** active operation: *to get into the swing of things.* **26.** something that is swung or that swings. **27.** a seat suspended from above as in a loop of rope or between ropes or rods, in which one may sit and swing to and fro for amusement. **28.** a steady rhythm or movement, as in a piece of poetry, music, etc. **29.** *Cricket.* deviation of a ball in mid-air, as a result of atmospheric action on the seam. **30. in full swing,** *Colloq.* fully active; operating at maximum speed or with maximum efficiency. [ME; OE *swingan,* c. G *Schwingen* cf. OE *swinge* blow]

**swing**[2] /swɪŋ/, *n., adj., v.,* **swung, swinging.** *–n.* **1.** Also, **swing music.** a smooth, orchestral type of jazz popular in the 1930s, often arranged for big bands. **2.** the rhythmic element that excites dancers and listeners to move in time to jazz music. *–adj.* **3.** of, pertaining to, or characteristic of, swing music. *–v.t.* **4.** to play (a piece of music) in the style of swing. *–v.i.* **5.** *Colloq.* to be characterised by a lively, modern, or knowledgeable attitude to life. **6.** *Colloq.* (of a place) to have a lively atmosphere. [special use of SWING[1]]

**swing boat** /'– boʊt/, *n.* a boat-shaped carriage suspended from a frame for swinging in at a fairground.

**swing bridge** /'– brɪdʒ/, *n.* **1.** a bridge which is pivoted at its centre and opens horizontally to allow ships to pass; pivot bridge. **2.** *N.Z.* a pedestrian suspension bridge.

**swing door** /– 'dɔ/, *n.* a door that opens on being pushed or pulled from either side and swings shut by itself.

**swinge** /swɪndʒ/, *v.t.,* **swinged, swinging.** *Archaic.* to whip; punish. [ME *swenge* shake, smite, OE *swengan,* causative of *swingan* SWING[1]] **– swinger** /'swɪndʒə/, *n.*

**swingeing** /'swɪndʒɪŋ/, *adj. Colloq.* **1.** forcible; strong. **2.** great; large.

**swinger** /'swɪŋə/, *n.* **1.** one who or that which swings. **2.** *Colloq.* an active, lively, or modern person. **3.** *Colloq.* **a.** a person who exchanges sexual partners frequently. **b.** a member of a group of people who agree to exchange sexual partners on a casual basis. **4.** *Colloq.* a motor cycle side-car rider.

**swing gate** /swɪŋ 'geɪt/, *n.* a gate designed to close one entrance to a yard while another is opened, for drafting livestock; a drafting gate.

**swinging** /'swɪŋɪŋ/, *adj.* **1.** characterised by or capable of swinging or being swung. **2.** *Colloq.* fine; excellent. **3.** *Colloq.* lively, active, vigorous, and modern. **4.** of or pertaining to a swinger (def. 3). **– swingingly,** *adv.*

**swinging post** /'– ˌpoʊst/, *n.* the post from which a door or gate hangs.

**swinging seat** /– 'sit/, *n.* a constituency which elects representatives of different political parties at different elections.

**swinging voter** /– 'voʊtə/, *n.* a person who changes his political allegiance at different elections.

**swingle** /'swɪŋgəl/, *n., v.,* **-gled, -gling.** *–n.* **1.** a wooden instrument shaped like a large knife, for beating flax or hemp and scraping from it the woody or coarse portions. *–v.t.* **2.** to clean (flax or hemp) by beating and scraping with a swingle. [ME *swyngel,* from MD *swinghel,* c OE *swingell* rod]

**swingletree** /'swɪŋgəltri/, *n.* →**whippletree.**

**swing music** /'swɪŋ ˌmjuzɪk/, *n.* →**swing**[2]**.**

**swing-wing** /'swɪŋ-wɪŋ/, *adj.* **1.** denoting or pertaining to an aircraft wing which can be swung from one position to another in flight in order to provide the best characteristics both for take-off and low speeds as well as for supersonic flight. *–n.* **2.** an aircraft fitted with such wings.

**swinish** /'swaɪnɪʃ/, *adj.* like or befitting swine; brutishly gross or sensual. **– swinishly,** *adv.* **– swinishness,** *n.*

**swink** /swɪŋk/, *v.i.,* **swank** or **swonk, swonken, swinking,** *n.* *Archaic.* labour; toil. [ME; OE *swincan,* akin to SWING[1]] **– swinker,** *n.*

**swipe** /swaɪp/, *n., v.,* **swiped, swiping.** *–n.* **1.** *Colloq.* a sweeping stroke; a stroke with full swing of the arms, as in cricket or golf. **2.** a lever-like device for raising or lowering a weight, esp. a bucket in a well; a sweep. *–v.t.* **3.** *Colloq.* to strike with a sweeping blow. **4.** *Colloq.* to steal. **5.** *Colloq.* to borrow without the owner's knowledge. *–v.i.* **6.** *Colloq.* to make a sweeping stroke. [akin to SWEEP[1]]

**swipes** /swaɪps/, *n.pl. Brit.* **1.** poor, washy beer; small beer. **2.** malt liquor in general. [? from *swipe,* v., drink at a gulp, special use of SWIPE]

**swipple** /'swɪpəl/, *n.* the freely swinging part of a flail, which falls upon the grain in threshing; a swingle. Also, **swiple.** [ME *swepelles* broom, OE *swæples(e)* robe; akin to sweep]

**swirl** /swɜl/, *v.i.* **1.** to move about or along with a whirling motion; whirl; eddy. **2.** to be dizzy or giddy, or swim, as the head. *–v.t.* **3.** to cause to swirl or whirl; twist. *–n.* **4.** a swirling movement; a whirl; an eddy. **5.** a twist, as of hair about the head or of trimming on a hat. [? imitative. ? akin to d. Norw. *svirla,* D *zwirrelen* whirl, d. G *schwirrlen* totter]

**swirly** /'swɜli/, *adj.* swirling, whirling, or twisted.

**swish** /swɪʃ/, *v.i.* **1.** to move with or make a sibilant sound, as a slender rod cutting sharply through the air, or as small waves washing on the shore. **2.** to rustle, as silk. *–v.t.* **3.** to flourish, whisk, etc., with a swishing movement or sound: *to swish a cane.* **4.** to bring, take, etc., with or as with such a movement or sound: *to swish off the tops of plants with a cane.* **5.** to flog or whip. *–n.* **6.** a swishing movement or sound. **7.** a stock or rod for flogging, or a stroke with this. **8.** *U.S. Colloq.* a male homosexual. **9. put (a bit of) swish into,** *Colloq.* to cause to pay attention or take heed. **10.** *Colloq.* Also, **swishy.** smart; stylish; glamorous. [imitative]

**Swiss** /swɪs/, *adj.* **1.** of, pertaining to, associated with or characteristic of Switzerland. **2.** Also, **Swiss muslin.** a thin crisp fabric, often with woven or printed dots or figures. [F *Suisse,* from MHG *Swiz*]

**Swiss chard** /– 'tʃad/, *n.* →**chard** (def. 3).

**Swiss cheese** /– 'tʃiz/, *n.* a firm whitish cheese with a smooth, mellow flavour and a nutty, sweetish tang. It has characteristic holes or eyes in it made by the expansion of gas within the curd; emmenthaler.

**Swiss roll** /– 'roʊl/, *n.* a thin, rolled sponge cake filled with jam or cream.

**Swiss steak** /– 'steɪk/, *n.* a slice of round steak coated on both sides with flour, fried in fat, with onions, tomatoes and other vegetables.

**switch** /swɪtʃ/, *n.* **1.** a slender, flexible shoot, rod, etc., used esp. in whipping, beating, etc. **2.** the act of switching; a stroke, lash, or whisking movement. **3.** a slender growing shoot, as of a plant. **4.** a separate bunch or tress of long hair (or some substitute) fastened together at one end, worn by women to supplement their hair. **5.** *Elect.* a device for turning on or off or directing an electric current, or making or breaking a circuit. **6.** *Chiefly U.S.* →**point** (def. 45). **7.** a turning, shifting, or changing: *a switch of votes to another candidate.* **8.** *Bridge.* a change to a suit other than the one played or bid previously. **9.** a tuft of hair at the end of the tail of some animals. **10.** *Colloq.* →**switchboard** (def. 2). *–v.t.* **11.** to whip or beat with a switch or the like; lash: *he switched the lad with a cane.* **12.** to move, swing, or whisk (a cane, a fishing line, etc.) like a switch or with a swift, lashing stroke. **13.** to exchange; shift. **14.** to turn, shift, or divert: *to switch conversation from a painful subject.* **15.** **switch on, a.** to cause an electric current to flow or an electric appliance to operate. **b.** *Colloq.* to cause (a person) to be interested and enthused: *Bach switched him on.* **16.** *Chiefly U.S.* →**shunt** (def. 4). *–v.i.* **17.** to strike with or as with a switch. **18.** to change direction or course; turn, shift, or change. **19.** to be shifted, turned, etc., by means of a switch. **20.** **switch off, a.** to cause an electric current or appliance to stop. **b.** *Colloq.* to become oblivious of (or *to*). **21.** **switch on, a.** (of electric lights, appliances, etc.) to begin to operate. **b.** *Colloq.* (of a person) to become interested and enthused. [cf. LG *swutsche*] – **switcher,** *n.* – **switchlike,** *adj.*

**switchback** /'swɪtʃbæk/, *n.* **1.** a mountain road having many hairpin bends. **2.** *Railways.* a zigzag track arrangement for climbing a steep gradient. **3.** →**big dipper.**

**switchblade** /'swɪtʃbleɪd/, *n.* →**flick-knife.**

**switchboard** /'swɪtʃbɔd/, *n. Elect.* **1.** a structural unit mounting switches, instruments, and/or meters necessary for the control of electrical energy. **2.** an arrangement of switches, plugs, and jacks mounted on a board or frame enabling an operator to make temporary connections between telephone users.

**switchbox** /'swɪtʃbɒks/, *n.* a box housing one or more electrical switches.

**switched-on** /'swɪtʃt-ɒn/, *adj.* with heightened awareness.

**switcheroo** /swɪtʃə'ru/, *n. Colloq.* a change; a turnabout.

**switchgear** /'swɪtʃgɪə/, *n.* any form of electrical switch, esp. for high voltages.

**switchgirl** /'swɪtʃgɜl/, *n.* a girl who operates a telephone switchboard.

**switch hitter** /'swɪtʃ hɪtə/, *n. Colloq.* a bisexual person.

**switchman** /'swɪtʃmən/, *n., pl.* **-men.** *U.S.* →**signalman** (def. 1).

**switch-over** /'swɪtʃ-oʊvə/, *n.* →**changeover.**

**Switzerland** /'swɪtsələnd/, *n.* a republic in central Europe.

**swive** /swaɪv/, *v.t., v.i.,* **swived, swiving.** *Archaic.* to copulate (with). [ME *swyve(n)*, OE *swīfan* revolve. Cf. SWIVEL]

**swivel** /'swɪvəl/, *n., v.,* **-elled, -elling** or (*U.S.*) **-eled, -eling.** *–n.* **1.** a fastening device which allows the thing fastened to turn round freely upon it. **2.** such a device consisting of two parts, each of which turns round independently, as a compound link of a chain one part of which turns freely in the other by means of a headed pin or the like. **3.** a pivoted support for allowing a gun to turn round in a horizontal plane. **4.** →**swivel gun.** *–v.t.* **5.** to turn on or as on a swivel. **6.** to fasten by a swivel; furnish with a swivel. *–v.i.* **7.** to turn on a swivel, pivot, or the like. [ME *swyvel,* from Scand.; cf. Icel. *sweifla* swing, akin to OE *swīfan* revolve] – **swivel-like,** *adj.*

**swivel chair** /'– tʃɛə/, *n.* a chair whose seat revolves on a swivel.

**swivel gun** /'– gʌn/, *n.* a gun mounted on a pedestal so that it can be turned from side to side or up and down.

**swivel pin** /'– pɪn/, *n.* →**kingpin** (def. 1).

**swiz** /swɪz/, *n. Colloq.* **1.** a disappointment. **2.** a fraud; swindle.

**swizzle** /'swɪzəl/, *n. v.,* **-zled, -zling.** *n.* **1.** a drink composed of rum, crushed ice, lemon or lime juice, bitters and sugar. **2.** *Colloq.* a swindle. *–v.t. Colloq.* **3.** to swindle. [orig. unknown] – **swizzler,** *n.*

**swizzle stick** /'– stɪk/, *n. Colloq.* a small rod for stirring drinks.

**swob** /swɒb/, *n., v.t.,* **swobbed, swobbing.** →**swab.**

**swollen** /'swoʊlən/, *v.* **1.** past participle of **swell.** *–adj.* **2.** Also, *Archaic,* **swoln** /swoʊln/. swelled; enlarged by or as by swelling; puffed up; tumid. **3.** turgid or bombastic. – **swollenly,** *adv.* – **swollenness,** *n.*

**swollen-headed** /swoʊlən-'hɛdəd/, *adj.* inordinately proud of oneself; conceited; vain.

**swoon** /swun/, *v.i.* **1.** to faint; lose consciousness. **2.** to become enraptured; enter a state of ecstasy. *–n.* **3.** a faint or fainting fit; syncope. [ME *swo(w)ne,* OE *geswōgen* in a swoon] – **swooningly,** *adv.*

**swoop** /swup/, *v.i.* **1.** to sweep through the air, as a bird or a bat, esp. down upon prey. **2.** to come down in a sudden swift attack (oft. fol. by *down* or *on* or *upon*): *the enemy troops swooped down on the town.* *–v.t.* **3.** to take, lift, or remove, with, or as with, a sweeping motion (oft. fol. by *up*). *–n.* **4.** the act of swooping; a sudden, swift descent. **5.** **at one fell swoop,** all at once. [var. of ME *swope,* OE *swāpan* sweep]

**swop** /swɒp/, *v.t., v.i.,* **swopped, swopping,** *n.* →**swap.**

**sword** /sɔd/, *n.* **1.** a weapon having various forms but consisting typically of a long, straight or slightly curved blade, sharp-edged on one side or both sides, with one end pointed and the other fixed in a hilt or handle. **2.** this weapon as the symbol of military power, punitive justice, authority, etc. **3.** a cause of death or destruction. **4.** war, combat, or slaughter; military force or power. **5.** (*pl.*) *Shearing Colloq.* hand shears. **6.** **cross swords, a.** to join in combat. **b.** to argue; disagree violently. **c.** *Colloq.* (of men) to urinate at the same time, in the same toilet or urinal. **7.** **put to the sword,** to massacre; slaughter. **8.** **have had the sword,** *Colloq.* to be finished or ruined. **9.** **give (something) the sword,** *Colloq.* to discard (something) as broken or no longer useful. [ME; OE *sweord,* c. G *Schwert*] – **swordless,** *adj.* – **swordlike,** *adj.*

**sword bayonet** /– 'beɪənət/, *n.* a kind of short sword for attaching to the muzzle of a gun, to be used as a bayonet.

**sword bean** /'– bin/, *n.* a trailing leguminous plant, *Canavalia gladiata,* grown as a vegetable in the tropics and subtropics.

**sword-bearer** /'sɔd-bɛərə/, *n.* an official who carries a sword on certain ceremonial occasions.

**sword-belt** /'sɔd-bɛlt/, *n.* a belt from which a sword is hung.

**swordbill** /'sɔdbɪl/, *n.* a hummingbird, *Ensifera ensifera,* of South America, whose slender bill is longer than its body.

**sword cane** /'sɔd keɪn/, *n.* →**swordstick.**

**swordcraft** /'sɔdkraft/, *n.* **1.** knowledge of, or skill with, the sword. **2.** military skill or power.

**sword dance** /'sɔd dæns/, *n.* any of various dances performed with a sword in the hand or in which swords are laid on the ground and danced around.

**swordfish** /'sɔdfɪʃ/, *n.* a large marine sport fish of the genus *Xiphias,* with the upper jaw elongated into a swordlike weapon; broadbill.

swordfish

**sword grass** /'sɔd gras/, *n.* any of various grasses or plants with swordlike or sharp leaves, as the sword lily.

**sword knot** /'– nɒt/, *n.* a looped strap, ribbon, etc., attached to the hilt of a sword, as a support or ornament.

**sword lily** /'– lɪli/, *n.* →**gladiolus.**

**sword of Damocles,** *n.* an immediate threat or danger, esp. in otherwise favourable circumstances. [from the Greek legend in which *Damocles,* a flatterer, attended a banquet of Dionysius, the tyrant of Syracuse, and found that he was sitting with a sword suspended over his head by a single hair]

**swordplay** /'sɔdpleɪ/, *n.* the action, practice, or art of wielding a sword; fencing.

**swordsman** /'sɔdzmən/, *n., pl.* **-men.** **1.** one who uses, or is skilled in the use of, a sword. **2.** a fencer. **3.** a soldier. Also, **swordman.** – **swordsmanship,** *n.*

**swordstick** /'sɔdstɪk/, *n.* a cane walking stick or the like, having a hollow shaft which serves as a sheath for a sword. Also, **sword cane.**

**swordtail** /'sɔdteɪl/, *n.* any of several small, viviparous, Mexican cyprinodont fishes of the genus *Xiphophorus,* commonly cultivated in home aquariums.

**swore** /swɔ/, *v.* past tense of **swear.**

**sworn** /swɔn/, *v.* **1.** past participle of **swear.** *–adj.* **2.** having taken an oath; bound by or as by an oath. **3.** confirmed; inveterate; avowed.

**swot**[1] /swɒt/, *v.t.,* **swotted, swotting,** *n. U.S.* →**swat**[1].

**swot**[2] /swɒt/, *v.,* **swotted, swotting,** *n. Colloq. –v.i.* **1.** to study hard. *–v.t.* **2.** to study (a subject) hard (fol. by *up*). *–n.* **3.** one who studies hard. [d. var. of SWEAT]

**swound** /swaʊnd, swund/, *n., v.i. Archaic* →**swoon.**

**swounds** /zwaʊndz, zaʊndz, zwundz, zundz/, *interj. Obs.* →**zounds.**

**swum** /swʌm/, *v.* past participle of **swim.**

**swung** /swʌŋ/, *v.* past tense and past participle of **swing.**

**swy** /swaɪ/, *n. Colloq.* **1.** Also, **swy-game.** →**two-up.** **2.** *Prison Colloq.* a prison sentence of two year's duration. **3.** (formerly) a two-shilling coin. [G *zwei* two]

**sy-,** variant of **syn-,** before *s* followed by a consonant, and before *z,* as in *systaltic.*

**S.Y.,** steam yacht.

**sybarite** /'sɪbəraɪt/, *n.* one devoted to luxury and pleasure; an effeminate voluptuary. [from *Sybaris,* an ancient Greek city in S Italy, destroyed 510 B.C., famed for its wealth and luxury] – **sybaritic** /sɪbə'rɪtɪk/, *adj.* – **sybaritically** /sɪbə'rɪtɪkli/, *adv.*

**sycamine** /'sɪkəmaɪn/, *n.* a mulberry (tree), probably the black mulberry. [L *sȳcamīnus,* from Gk *sȳkáminos,* from Aram. *shiqmīn* pl.). See Luke 17.6]

**sycamore** /'sɪkəmɔ/, *n.* **1.** (in Europe) a maple, *Acer pseudoplatanus,* grown as a shady ornamental tree and for its wood. **2.** (in the U.S.) the plane tree or buttonwood, *Platanus occidentalis.* **3.** a tree, *Ficus sycomorus,* of the Near East, allied to the common fig and bearing an edible fruit. **4.** any of various trees resembling the sycamore, as the sandalwood. [ME *sycomore,* from LL *sȳcomorus,* from Gk *sȳkómoros*]

**sycee** /saɪ'si/, *n.* fine uncoined silver in lumps of various sizes usu. bearing a banker's or assayer's stamp or mark, used in China as a medium of exchange. Also, **sycee silver.** [Chinese *sai sz',* Cantonese var. of Mandarin *si sz'* fine silk, so called because when pure it may be drawn out into fine threads]

**sycomancy** /'saɪkəmænsi/, *n.* divination by means of writing messages on the leaves of trees and waiting for them to dry.

**syconium** /saɪ'koʊniəm/, *n., pl.* **-nia** /-niə/. a multiple fruit developed from a hollow fleshy receptacle containing numerous flowers, as in the fig. [NL, from Gk *sŷkon* fig + *-ium* -IUM]

**sycophancy** /'sɪkəfənsi, 'saɪ-, -fænsi/, *n., pl.* **-cies.** **1.** self-seeking or servile flattery. **2.** the character or conduct of a sycophant.

**sycophant** /'sɪkəfənt, 'saɪ-, -fænt/, *n.* a self-seeking flatterer; a fawning, servile parasite. [L *sȳcophanta,* from Gk *sȳkophántēs* slanderer, false accuser] – **sycophantic** /sɪkə'fæntɪk/, **sycophantical** /sɪkə'fæntɪkəl/, *adj.* – **sycophantically** /sɪkə'fæntɪkli/, *adv.*

**sycosis** /saɪ'koʊsəs/, *n.* an inflammatory disease of the hair follicles, marked by a pustular eruption. [NL, from Gk *sȳkōsis*]

**Sydharb** /'sɪdab/, *n.* an unofficial unit of measurement of the volume of water in a lake, dam, etc., equivalent to the volume of water in Sydney Harbour. [*Syd(ney) Harb(our)*]

**Sydney** /'sɪdni/, *n. in the phrase* **Sydney or the bush!** *Colloq.* all or nothing!

**Sydney blue gum,** *n.* a tall forest tree, *Eucalyptus saligna,* found in coastal areas of New South Wales, with an attractive pale, smooth, straight trunk and useful timber.

**Sydney golden wattle,** *n.* a yellow-flowered shrub, *Acacia longifolia,* found on sandy soil in eastern Australia and flowering profusely in springtime.

**Sydney Harbour** /sɪdni 'habə/, *n. Colloq.* a barber. [rhyming slang]

**Sydneyite** /'sɪdniaɪt/, *n.* →**Sydneysider.**

**Sydney red gum,** *n.* the smooth-barked angophora, *Angophora costata,* with reddish wood.

**Sydney rock oyster,** *n.* a type of oyster, *Crassostrei commercialis,* cultivated in Sydney waters, and valued for its unique flavour.

**Sydney rose** /sɪdni 'roʊz/, *n.* →**native rose.**

**Sydneysider** /'sɪdnisaɪdə/, *n.* **1.** one who was born in Sydney, the capital city of New South Wales, or who has come to regard it as his home town. *–adj.* **2.** of or pertaining to the city of Sydney. Also, **Sydneyite.**

**Sydney silky** /sɪdni 'sɪlki/, *n.* →**Australian silky terrier.**

**syenite** /'saɪənaɪt/, *n.* a granular igneous rock consisting typically of felspar (orthoclase) and hornblende. [L *Syēnītēs (lapis)* (stone) of *Syene,* the ancient name of Aswan, a town in SE Egypt] – **syenitic** /saɪə'nɪtɪk/, *adj.*

**syl-,** variant of **syn-** (by assimilation) before *l,* as in *syllepsis.*

**syll.,** syllable.

**syllabary** /'sɪləbəri/, *n., pl.* **-baries.** **1.** a list or catalogue of syllables. **2.** a set of written symbols, each of which represents a syllable of the language to be written.

**syllabi** /'sɪləbaɪ/, *n.* a plural of **syllabus.**

**syllabic** /sə'læbɪk/, *adj.* **1.** of, pertaining to, or consisting of a syllable or syllables. **2.** pronounced with careful distinction of syllables. **3.** of or pertaining to poetry based on the number of syllables as distinct from poetry depending on stresses or quantities. **4.** (of chanting, etc.) having each syllable sung to one note only. **5.** *Phonet.* syllable-forming or syllable-dominating; sonantal. *–n.* **6.** *Phonet.* a syllabic sound. See **sonant** (def. 3a). – **syllabically,** *adv.*

**syllabicate** /sə'læbəkeɪt/, *v.t.,* **-cated, -cating.** →**syllabify.** – **syllabication** /səlæbə'keɪʃən/, *n.*

**syllabify** /sə'læbəfaɪ/, *v.t.,* **-fied, -fying.** to form or divide into syllables. – **syllabification** /səlæbəfə'keɪʃən/, *n.*

**syllabise** /'sɪləbaɪz/, *v.t.,* **-bised, -bising.** →**syllabify.** Also, **syllabize.**

**syllabism** /'sɪləbɪzəm/, *n.* **1.** the use of syllabic characters, as in writing. **2.** division into syllables.

**syllable** /'sɪləbəl/, *n., v.,* **-bled, -bling.** *–n.* **1.** *Phonet.* a segment of speech uttered with a single impulse of air-pressure from the lungs, and consisting of one sound of relatively great sonority (see **sonant,** def. 3a), with or without one or more subordinated sounds of relatively small sonority (see **consonant,** def. 1). **2.** (in writing systems) a character or a set of characters representing (more or less exactly) such an element of speech. **3.** the least portion or amount of speech or writing; the least mention: *do not breathe a syllable of all this.* *–v.t.* **4.** to utter in syllables; articulate. **5.** to represent by syllables. *–v.i.* **6.** to utter syllables; speak. [ME *sillable,* from AF, var. of OF *sillabre,* from L *syllaba,* from Gk *syllabḗ*]

**syllabub** /'sɪləbʌb/, *n.* →**sillabub.**

**syllabus** /'sɪləbəs/, *n., pl.* **-buses, -bi** /-baɪ/. **1.** an outline or summary of a course of studies, lectures, etc. **2.** subjects to be studied on a particular course, as at a school, university, etc. **3.** a list: *the syllabus of errors.* [NL, mistake for L *sittyba* title-slip on a book, from Gk]

**syllepsis** /sə'lɛpsəs/, *n., pl.* **-ses** /-siz/. in grammar and rhetoric, the use of one word for two syntactical functions, as *are* in *neither he nor we are willing,* or in two senses, as *fought* in *he fought with desperation and his trusty sword.* [LL, from Gk: a taking together] – **sylleptic** /sə'lɛptɪk/, *adj.* – **sylleptically** /sə'lɛptɪkli/, *adv.*

**syllogise** /'sɪlədʒaɪz/, *v.i., v.t.,* **-gised, -gising.** to argue or reason by syllogisms. Also, **syllogize.** – **syllogisation** /ˌsɪlədʒaɪ'zeɪʃən/, *n.* – **syllogiser,** *n.*

**syllogism** /'sɪlədʒɪzəm/, *n.* **1.** *Logic.* an argument with two premises and a conclusion. Both the premises of a **categorical syllogism** are categorical propositions, containing just three distinct terms between them, e.g. *all men are mortal* (major premise), *Socrates is a man* (minor premise), therefore *Socrates is mortal* (conclusion); at least one premise in a **hypothetical syllogism** is a hypothetical proposition, e.g. *if*

*Smith is eligible to vote he is a citizen* (major premise), *Smith is eligible to vote* (minor premise), *therefore Smith is a citizen* (conclusion); at least one premise in a **disjunctive syllogism** is a disjunctive proposition, e.g. *either Smith is out of town or he is ill* (major premise). *Smith is not ill* (minor premise), *therefore he is out of town* (conclusion). **2.** deductive reasoning. [L *syllogismus,* from Gk *syllogismós;* replacing ME *silogime,* from F]

**syllogistic** /sɪlə'dʒɪstɪk/, *adj.* Also, **syllogistical. 1.** of or pertaining to a syllogism. **2.** like or consisting of syllogisms. *–n.* **3.** that part of logic which deals with syllogisms. **4.** syllogistic reasoning. – **syllogistically,** *adv.*

**sylph** /sɪlf/, *n.* **1.** a slender, graceful, lightly moving woman or girl. **2.** one of a race of imaginary beings, supposed (originally by P.A. Paracelsus, 1493?-1541, Swiss physician and alchemist) to inhabit the air. [NL *sylphes* (pl.), coined by Paracelsus]

**sylphid** /'sɪlfəd/, *n.* **1.** a little or young sylph. **2.** a female sylph. [F *sylphide,* from *sylphe* SYLPH]

**sylvan** /'sɪlvən/, *adj.* **1.** of, pertaining to, or inhabiting the woods. **2.** consisting of or abounding in woods or trees; wooded; woody. *–n.* **3.** a person dwelling in a woodland region. **4.** a fabled deity or spirit of the woods. Also, **silvan.** [L *silvānus, sylvānus,* from *silva* forest]

**Sylvaner** /sɪl'vanə/, *n.* a grape variety used for producing white wines. [G]

**sylvanite** /'sɪlvənaɪt/, *n.* a mineral, gold silver telluride, $(AuAg)Te_2$, silver-white with metallic lustre, often occurring in crystals so arranged as to resemble written characters, and an ore of gold. [(*Tran*)*sylvan*(*ia*), where it was first found, + -ITE[1]]

**sylvic acid** /sɪlvɪk 'æsəd/, *n.* →**abietic acid.**

**sylviculture** /'sɪlvəkʌltʃə/, *n.* →**silviculture.**

**sylvinite** /'sɪlvənaɪt/, *n.* a mineral consisting of a mixture of sylvite and halite.

**sylvite** /'sɪlvaɪt/, *n.* a common mineral, potassium chloride, KCl, colourless to milky white or red, bitter in taste, occurring in crystals, usu. cubes, and masses with cubic clearage; the most important source of potassium. Also, **sylvin, sylvine** /'sɪlvin/. [from *Sylv-* (in NL *sal digestivus Sylvii* digestive salt of Sylvius, probably after Franz de la Boë *Sylvius,* 1614-1672, Dutch physician) + -ITE[1]]

**sym-,** variant of **syn-**, before *b, p,* and *m,* as in *sympathy.*

**sym.,** **1.** symbol. **2.** *Chem.* symmetrical. **3.** symphony. **4.** symptom.

**symbiont** /'sɪmbiɒnt, -baɪ-/, *n.* an organism living in a state of symbiosis. [Gk *symbiôn,* ppr., living together] – **symbiontic** /sɪmbi'ɒntɪk/, *adj.* – **symbiontically** /sɪmbi'ɒntɪkli/, *adv.*

**symbiosis** /sɪmbi'oʊsəs, -baɪ-/, *n.* the living together of two species of organisms, a term usu. restricted to cases in which the union of the two animals or plants is advantageous or necessary to both, as the case of the fungus and alga which together make up the lichen; mutualism. [NL, from Gk] – **symbiotic** /sɪmbi'ɒtɪk/, **symbiotical** /sɪmbi'ɒtɪkəl/, *adj.* – **symbiotically** /sɪmbi'ɒtɪkli/, *adv.*

**symbol** /'sɪmbəl/, *n., v.,* **-bolled, -bolling** or (*U.S.*) **-boled, -boling.** *–n.* **1.** something used or regarded as standing for or representing something else; a material object representing something immaterial; an emblem, token, or sign. **2.** a letter, figure, or other character or mark, or a combination of letters or the like, used to represent something: *the algebraic symbol, x; the chemical symbol, Au.* **3.** something which expresses, through suggestion, an idea or mood which would otherwise remain inexpressible or incomprehensible; the meeting-point of many analogies. *–v.t.* **4.** to symbolise. [LL *symbolum,* from Gk *sýmbolon* mark, token, ticket]

**symbolic** /sɪm'bɒlɪk/, *adj.* **1.** serving as a symbol of something (oft. fol. by *of*). **2.** of, pertaining to, or expressed by a symbol. **3.** characterised by or involving the use of symbols: *symbolic language.* Also, **symbolical.** – **symbolically,** *adv.* – **symbolicalness,** *n.*

**symbolic logic** /– 'lɒdʒɪk/, *n.* a system of logic that has been reduced to a set of precise rules, used in mathematical proofs and also in constructing digital computers.

**symbolics** /sɪm'bɒlɪks/, *n.* the study and comparison of the expression of the creed of different churches and sects.

**symbolise** /'sɪmbəlaɪz/, *v.,* **-lised, -lising.** *–v.t.* **1.** to be a symbol of; stand for, or represent, as a symbol does. **2.** to represent by a symbol or symbols. **3.** to regard or treat as symbolic. *–v.i.* **4.** to use symbols. Also, **symbolize.** – **symbolisation** /ˌsɪmbəlaɪ'zeɪʃən/, *n.*

**symbolism** /'sɪmbəlɪzəm/, *n.* **1.** the practice of representing things by symbols, or of investing things with a symbolic meaning or character. **2.** a set or system of symbols. **3.** symbolic meaning or character. **4.** the principles and practice of symbolists in art or literature. **5.** (*usu. cap.*) a movement of the late 19th century in French literature. See **symbolist** (def. 3b). **6.** the belief that in the Eucharist the bread and wine undergo no change of any kind, but represent the body and blood of Christ in a purely figurative way.

**symbolist** /'sɪmbələst/, *n.* **1.** one who uses symbols or symbolism. **2.** one versed in the study or interpretation of symbols. **3.** *Lit.* **a.** a writer who seeks to express or suggest ideas, emotions, etc., by emphasising the symbolic value of language as a means of communicating otherwise inexpressible experiences of reality, as by the use of words or even word-sounds (as vowels) to convey a meaning, often with a mystical or vague effect. **b.** (*oft. cap.*) a member of a group of French and Belgian poets characterised by such procedure (including Verlaine, Mallarmé, and Maeterlinck), which arose during the latter part of the 19th century. **4.** *Art.* an artist who seeks to symbolise or suggest particular ideas by the objects represented, the colours used, etc. **5.** (*oft. cap.*) *Eccles.* a person who rejects the doctrine of transubstantiation and views the Eucharist symbolically. **6.** a person who favours the use of symbols in religious services. *–adj.* **7.** Also, **symbolistic** /sɪmbə'lɪstɪk/. of or pertaining to symbolists or symbolism.

**symbology** /sɪm'bɒlədʒi/, *n.* **1.** the study of symbols. **2.** the use of symbols; symbolism. [NL *symbologia,* from (by haplology) *symbolo-* (see SYMBOL) + *-logia* -LOGY]

**symmetallism** /sɪ'mɛtəlɪzəm/, *n.* the use of two (or more) metals, as gold and silver, combined in assigned proportions as a monetary standard.

**symmetric** /sə'mɛtrɪk/, *adj.* **1.** →**symmetrical. 2.** *Logic., Maths.* denoting a relation, such that if it is valid between *a* and *b* it is valid between *b* and *a:* as, $a = b$ implies $b = a$.

**symmetrical** /sə'mɛtrɪkəl/, *adj.* **1.** characterised by or exhibiting symmetry; well proportioned, as a body or whole; regular in form or arrangement of corresponding parts. **2.** →**symmetric** (def. 2). **3.** *Bot.* **a.** →**actinomorphic. b.** (of a flower) having the same number of parts in each whorl. **4.** *Chem.* **a.** having a structure which exhibits a regular repeated pattern of the component parts. **b.** denoting a benzene derivative in which three substitutions have occurred at alternate carbon atoms. **5.** *Pathol.* affecting corresponding parts simultaneously, as certain diseases. Also, **symmetric.** – **symmetrically,** *adv.* – **symmetricalness,** *n.*

**symmetrise** /'sɪmətraɪz/, *v.t.,* **-trised, -trising.** to reduce to symmetry; make symmetrical. Also, **symmetrize.** – **symmetrisation** /ˌsɪmətraɪ'zeɪʃən/, *n.*

**symmetry** /'sɪmətri/, *n., pl.* **-tries. 1.** the correspondence, in size, form, and arrangement, of parts on opposite sides of a plane, line, or point; regularity of form or arrangement with reference to corresponding parts. **2.** the proper or due proportion of the parts of a body or whole to one another with regard to size and form; excellence of proportion. [LL *symmetria,* from Gk]

**sympathectomy** /sɪmpə'θɛktəmi/, *n.* surgical excision of a portion of the sympathetic nervous system.

**sympathetic** /sɪmpə'θɛtɪk/, *adj.* **1.** characterised by, proceeding from, exhibiting, or feeling sympathy; sympathising; compassionate. **2.** acting or affected by, of the nature of, or pertaining to a special natural sympathy or affinity; congenial. **3.** looking with favour or liking upon (oft. fol. by *to* or *towards*): *he is sympathetic to the project.* **4.** *Anat., Physiol.* **a.** pertaining to that portion of the autonomic nervous system which is made up of a system of nerves and ganglia which arise from the thoracic and lumbar regions of the spinal cord, and which supply the walls of the vascular system and the various viscera and glands where they function in opposition to the parasympathetic system, as in dilating the pupil of the eye, etc. **b.** *Obs.* designating the autonomic nervous system in its entirety. **5.** *Physics.* (of vibrations, sounds, etc.) produced by vibrations conveyed through the air (or other medium) from a body already in vibration. Cf. **resonance** (def. 4). – **sympathetically,** *adv.*

**sympathetic ink** /– 'ɪŋk/, *n.* →**invisible ink.**

**sympathetic magic** /– 'mædʒɪk/, *n.* magic depending upon the belief that an object or event can affect another at a distance because of a supposed sympathetic connection between them.

**sympathetic string** /– 'strɪŋ/, *n.* a thin wire string used in various musical instruments, and not played upon, but set into vibration by the plucked or bowed strings, to reinforce the sound.

**sympathise** /'sɪmpəθaɪz/, *v.i.*, **-thised, -thising. 1.** to be in sympathy, or agreement of feeling; share in a feeling or feelings (oft. fol. by *with*). **2.** to feel a compassionate sympathy, as for suffering or trouble (oft. fol. by *with*). **3.** to express sympathy or condole (oft. fol. by *with*). **4.** to be in approving accord, as with a person, cause, etc.: *sympathise with a person's aims.* **5.** to agree, correspond, or accord. Also, **sympathize.** [F *sympathiser,* from *sympathie* SYMPATHY. See -ISE[1]] – **sympathiser,** *n.* – **sympathisingly,** *adv.*

**sympathy** /'sɪmpəθi/, *n., pl.* **-thies. 1.** community of or agreement in feeling, as between persons or on the part of one person with respect to another. **2.** the community of feeling naturally existing between persons of like tastes or opinion or of congenial dispositions. **3.** the fact or the power of entering into the feelings of another, esp. in sorrow or trouble; fellow feeling, compassion, or commiseration. **4.** (*pl.*) feelings or impulses of compassion. **5.** favourable or approving accord; favour or approval. **6.** agreement, consonance, or accord. **7.** *Psychol.* a relation between persons whereby the condition of one induces a responsive condition in another. **8.** *Physiol., Pathol.* the relation between parts or organs whereby a condition, affection, or disorder of one part induces some effect in another. [L *sympathīa,* from Gk *sympátheia,* lit., feeling with another]

**sympathy strike** /'– straɪk/, *n.* a strike by a body of workers, not because of grievances against their own employer, but by way of endorsing and aiding another body of workers who are on strike or have been locked out.

**sympetalous** /sɪm'pɛtələs/, *adj.* →**gamopetalous.**

**symphonic** /sɪm'fɒnɪk/, *adj.* **1.** *Music.* of, pertaining to, or having the character of a symphony. **2.** of or pertaining to symphony, or harmony of sounds. **3.** characterised by similarity of sound, as words.

**symphonic poem** /– 'poʊəm/, *n.* a form of tone poem scored for a symphony orchestra, originated by Liszt in the mid 19th century and developed esp. by Richard Strauss, in which a literary or pictorial 'plot' is treated with considerable program detail.

**symphonious** /sɪm'foʊniəs/, *adj.* harmonious; in harmonious agreement or accord. – **symphoniously,** *adv.*

**symphonist** /'sɪmfənəst/, *n.* one who performs or composes symphonies.

**symphony** /'sɪmfəni/, *n., pl.* **-nies. 1.** *Music.* **a.** an elaborate instrumental composition, usu. in several (traditionally three or four) movements, similar in form to a sonata but written for an orchestra, and usu. of far grander proportions and more varied elements. **b.** an instrumental passage occurring in a vocal composition, or between vocal movements in a composition. **c.** an instrumental piece, often in several movements, forming the overture to an opera or the like. **2.** anything characterised by a harmonious combination of elements and esp. an effective combination of colours. **3.** *Archaic or Poetic.* harmony of sounds. **4.** *Archaic or Poetic.* harmony in general. [ME *symphonie,* from L *symphōnia,* from Gk: lit., a sounding together]

**symphony orchestra** /– 'ɔkəstrə/, *n.* a large orchestra composed of wind, string, and percussion instruments, and designed to perform symphonic compositions.

**symphysial** /sɪm'fɪziəl/, *adj.* referring to a symphyis. Also, **symphyseal.**

**symphysiotomy** /ˌsɪmfɪzi'ɒtəmi/, *n.* the operation of dividing the pubic symphysis in order to facilitate the delivery of a baby. Also, **symphyseotomy.**

**symphysis** /'sɪmfəsəs/, *n., pl.* **-ses** /-siz/. **1.** *Anat., Zool.* **a.** the growing together, or the fixed or nearly fixed union, of bones, as that of the two halves of the lower jaw in man, or of the pubic bones in the anterior part of the pelvic girdle. **b.** a line of junction or articulation so formed. **2.** *Bot.* a coalescence or growing together of parts. [NL, from Gk] – **symphystic** /sɪm'fɪstɪk/, *adj.*

**sympodium** /sɪm'poʊdiəm/, *n., pl.* **-dia** /-diə/. (in plants) an axis or stem which simulates a simple stem but is made up of the bases of a number of axes which arise successively as branches one from another, as in the grapevine. Cf. **monopodium.** [NL. See SYM-, PODIUM]

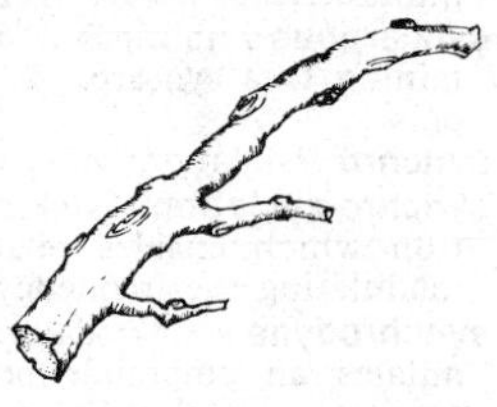
sympodium

**symposiac** /sɪm'poʊziˌæk/, *adj.* **1.** of, pertaining to, or suitable for a symposium. –*n.* **2.** a symposium.

**symposiarch** /sɪm'poʊziˌak/, *n.* **1.** the president, director, or master of a symposium. **2.** the toastmaster. [Gk *symposíarchos*]

**symposium** /sɪm'poʊziəm/, *n., pl.* **-siums, -sia** /-ziə/. **1.** a meeting or conference for discussion of some subject. **2.** a collection of opinions expressed, or articles contributed, by several persons on a given subject or topic. **3.** an account of such a meeting or of the conversation at it. **4.** (among the ancient Greeks) a convivial meeting, usu. following a dinner, for drinking, conversation, and intellectual discussion. [L, from Gk *sympósion* (def. 4)]

**symptom** /'sɪmptəm/, *n.* **1.** any phenomenon or circumstance accompanying something and serving as evidence for it. **2.** a sign or indication of something. **3.** *Pathol.* a phenomenon which arises from and accompanies a particular disease or disorder and serves as an indication of it. [LL *symptōma,* from Gk] – **symptomless,** *adj.*

**symptomatic** /sɪmptə'mætɪk/, *adj.* **1.** pertaining to a symptom or symptoms. **2.** of the nature of or constituting a symptom; indicative (oft. fol. by *of*). **3.** according to symptoms: *a symptomatic classification of disease.* Also, **symptomatical.** – **symptomatically,** *adv.*

**symptomatology** /sɪmptəmə'tɒlədʒi/, *n.* that branch of medical science which deals with symptoms. [NL *symptōmatologia.* See SYMPTOM, -LOGY]

**syn-,** a prefix in learned words having the same function as **co-** (def. 1), as in *synthesis, synoptic.* Also, **sy-, syl-, sym-, sys-.** [Gk, combining form of *sýn,* prep., with, and adv., together]

**syn.,** **1.** synonym. **2.** synonymous. **3.** synonymy.

**synaeresis** /sɪ'nɪərəsəs/, *n.* **1.** the contraction of two syllables or two vowels into one; esp. the contraction of two vowels so as to form a diphthong (opposed to *diaeresis*). **2.** synizesis. Also, *U.S.* **syneresis.** [LL, from Gk *synaíresis,* lit., a taking together]

**synaesthesia** /sɪnəs'θiʒə/, *n.* a sensation produced in one physical sense when a stimulus is applied to another sense, as when the hearing of a certain sound induces the visualisation of a certain colour. Also, *U.S.,* **synesthesia.**

**synagogue** /'sɪnəgɒg/, *n.* **1.** a Jewish house of worship, usu. also providing religious instruction. **2.** an assembly or congregation of the Jews for the purposes of worship. [ME *sinagoge,* from LL *synagōga,* from Gk *synagōgḗ* meeting, assembly] – **synagogical** /sɪnə'gɒdʒɪkəl/, **synagogal** /'sɪnəgɒgəl/, *adj.*

**synaloepha** /sɪnə'lifə/, *n.* the blending of two successive vowels into one. Also, **synalepha, synalephe** /sɪnə'lifi/. [L, from Gk *synaloiphḗ*]

**synapse** /'saɪnæps/, *n.* the region of contact between processes of two or more nerve cells, across which an impulse passes. [Gk *sýnapsis* connection]

**synapsis** /sə'næpsəs/, *n., pl.* **-ses** /-siz/. **1.** *Biol.* the conjugation of homologous chromosomes, one from each parent, during early meiosis. **2.** *Physiol.* →**synapse.** [NL, from Gk] – **synaptic** /sə'næptɪk/, *adj.*

**synarthrodia** /sɪna'θroʊdiə/, *n., pl.* **-diae** /-dii/. →**synarthrosis.** [NL] – **synarthrodial,** *adj.*

**synarthrosis** /sɪna'θroʊsəs/, *n., pl.* **-ses** /-siz/. (in anatomy) immovable articulation; a fixed or immovable joint; a suture. [NL, from Gk]

**sync** /sɪŋk/, *Films, Computers, etc. Colloq.* –*n.* **1.** synchronisation. *–v.i., v.t.* **2.** to synchronise.

**syncarp** /ˈsɪnkap/, *n. Bot.* **1.** an aggregate fruit. **2.** a collective fruit. [NL *syncarpium,* from Gk *syn-* SYN- + *karpíon,* diminutive of *karpós* fruit]

**syncarpous** /sɪnˈkapəs/, *adj. Bot.* **1.** of the nature of or pertaining to a syncarp. **2.** composed of or having united carpels.

**synchro** /ˈsɪŋkroʊ/, *adj., n. Colloq.* →**synchromesh.**

**synchro-cyclotron** /ˌsɪŋkroʊ-ˈsaɪklətrɒn/, *n.* a type of cyclotron which enables relativistic energies to be achieved by modulating the frequency of the accelerating electric field.

**synchrodyne** /ˈsɪŋkrədaɪn/, *n.* a radio receiver which demodulates an amplitude-modulated signal by mixing a local oscillator signal at the carrier frequency with the side bands.

**synchroflash** /ˈsɪŋkroʊflæʃ/, *adj.* of or pertaining to photography which synchronises the operation of the flashgun with the opening of the shutter.

**synchromesh** /ˈsɪŋkroʊmɛʃ/, *Motor Vehicles. –adj.* **1.** of, pertaining to or fitted with a system consisting of small friction clutches, by means of which the speeds of the driven and driving gears in a gearbox are automatically synchronised before they engage, to assist gear changing and reduce wear. *–n.* **2.** such a system. [SYNCHRO(NOUS) + MESH]

**synchromism** /ˈsɪŋkrəmɪzəm/, *n.* an abstract art movement, originating among American artists in Paris in 1912 which concentrated on the effects of pure colours applied alone or in juxtaposition.

**synchronic** /sɪŋˈkrɒnɪk/, *adj.* **1.** synchronous. **2.** studying phenomena at a given time or stage without reference to historical data. **3.** descriptive or classificatory: *synchronic linguistics.* Cf. **diachronic.**

**synchronise** /ˈsɪŋkrənaɪz/, *v.,* **-nised, -nising.** *–v.i.* **1.** to occur at the same time, or coincide or agree in time. **2.** to go on at the same rate and exactly together; recur together. *–v.t.* **3.** to cause to indicate the same time, as one clock with another. **4.** to cause to go on at the same rate and exactly together. **5.** to cause to agree in time of occurrence; assign to the same time or period, as in a history. Also, **synchronize.** [Gk *synchronízein* be contemporary with] – **synchronisation** /ˌsɪŋkrənaɪˈzeɪʃən/, *n.* – **synchroniser,** *n.*

**synchronised swimming** /ˌsɪŋkrənaɪzd ˈswɪmɪŋ/, *n.* a sport in which teams of swimmers perform movements to music.

**synchronism** /ˈsɪŋkrənɪzəm/, *n.* **1.** coincidence in time; contemporaneousness; simultaneousness. **2.** the arrangement or treatment of synchronous things or events in conjunction, as in a history. **3.** a tabular arrangement of historical events or personages, grouped together according to their dates. **4.** *Physics, Elect., etc.* the state of being synchronous. – **synchronistic** /sɪŋkrəˈnɪstɪk/, **synchronistical** /sɪŋkrəˈnɪstɪkəl/, *adj.* – **synchronistically** /sɪŋkrəˈnɪstɪkli/, *adv.*

**synchronoscope** /sɪŋˈkrɒnəˌskoʊp/, *n.* →**synchroscope.**

**synchronous** /ˈsɪŋkrənəs/, *adj.* **1.** occurring at the same time; coinciding in time; contemporaneous; simultaneous. **2.** going on at the same rate and exactly together; recurring together. **3.** *Physics, Elect., etc.* having the same frequency and no phase difference. **4.** →**synchronic.** [LL *synchronus,* from Gk *sýnchronos*] – **synchronously,** *adv.* – **synchronousness,** *n.*

**synchronous computer** /– kəmˈpjutə/, *n.* a computer whose operation is controlled by an electronic clock.

**synchronous converter** /– kənˈvɜtə/, *n.* →**rotary converter.**

**synchronous equatorial orbit,** *n.* a circular orbit in which a satellite moves around the earth once while the earth rotates once on its axis and thus remains fixed above a particular point above the equator; geostationary orbit; stationary orbit.

**synchronous motor** /sɪŋkrənəs ˈmoʊtə/, *n.* an alternating-current motor in which the average speed of normal operation is exactly proportional to the frequency of the system to which it is connected.

**synchronous speed** /– ˈspid/, *n.* the speed at which an alternating-current machine must operate to generate electromotive force at a given frequency.

**synchroscope** /ˈsɪŋkrəskoʊp/, *n.* an instrument for indicating synchronism between two related motions, as two aircraft engines or two electrical machines. Also, **synchronoscope.**

**synchrotron** /ˈsɪŋkrətrɒn/, *n.* an accelerator of the cyclotron type in which the magnetic field is modulated but the electric field is maintained at a constant frequency.

**synchrotron radiation** /– reɪdiˈeɪʃən/, *n.* the emission of radio-frequency electromagnetic radiation by interstellar gas clouds in radio galaxies, believed to be analogous to the light emitted by high-energy electrons in a synchrotron.

**synchro unit** /ˈsɪŋkroʊ junət/, *n.* a type of alternating-current motor designed to maintain continuously, at some remote place, the same rotational angle that may be imposed by force upon the electrically connected rotating element of a similar motor.

**synclastic** /sɪŋˈklæstɪk/, *adj.* denoting or pertaining to a point of a surface (such as a sphere) at which the two principal curvatures have the same sign (opposed to *anticlastic).* [SYN- + Gk *klastós* broken + -IC]

**synclinal** /sɪŋˈklaɪnəl/, *adj.* **1.** sloping downwards in opposite directions so as to meet in a common point or line. **2.** *Geol.* **a.** inclining upwards on both sides from a median line or axis, as a downward fold of rock strata. **b.** pertaining to such a fold. [Gk *synklī́nein* lean together + -AL[1]]

Axis

synclinal folds

**syncline** /ˈsɪŋklaɪn/, *n.* a synclinal fold.

**syncopate** /ˈsɪŋkəpeɪt/, *v.t.,* **-pated, -pating.** **1.** *Music.* **a.** to place (the accents) on beats which are normally unaccented. **b.** to employ notes so affected in (a passage, piece, etc.). **2.** *Gram.* to contract (a word) by omitting one or more sounds from the middle, as in reducing *Gloucester* to *Gloster.* [LL *syncopātus,* pp., cut short, from *syncopē* SYNCOPE] – **syncopator,** *n.*

**syncopation** /sɪŋkəˈpeɪʃən/, *n.* **1.** *Music.* a shifting of the normal accent, usu. by stressing normally unaccented beats. **2.** *Gram.* a syncope.

**syncope** /ˈsɪŋkəpi/, *n.* **1.** *Gram.* the contraction of a word by omitting one or more sounds from the middle, as in the reduction of *never* to *ne'er.* **2.** *Pathol.* brief loss of consciousness associated with transient cerebral anaemia, as in heart block, sudden lowering of the blood pressure, etc.; fainting. [ME, from L, from Gk *synkopḗ* a cutting up] – **syncopic** /sɪŋˈkɒpɪk/, *adj.*

**syncretise** /ˈsɪŋkrətaɪz/, *v.t., v.i.,* **-tised, -tising.** to attempt to combine or unite, as different or opposing principles, parties, etc. Also, **syncretize.** [NL *syncrētizāre,* from Gk *synkrētizein* from *Krḗtē* Crete, an island in the E Mediterranean, whose inhabitants were notorious for their factious quarrels]

**syncretism** /ˈsɪŋkrətɪzəm/, *n.* **1.** the attempted reconciliation or union of different or opposing principles, practices, or parties, as in philosophy or religion. **2.** (in linguistic change) the merging into one of two or more former categories, as the substandard English usage of *was* in *'we was, you was, they was'* as well as in *'I was, he was'.* [NL *syncrētismus,* from Gk *synkrētismós*] – **syncretic** /sɪŋˈkrɛtɪk/, **syncretistic** /sɪŋkrəˈtɪstɪk/, **syncretistical** /sɪŋkrəˈtɪstɪkəl/, *adj.*

**syncytium** /sɪnˈsɪtiəm/, *n., pl.* **-cytia** /-ˈsɪtiə/. animal tissue with many nuclei but without cell walls. [NL. See SYN-, CYTO-, -IUM]

**syndactyl** /sɪnˈdæktəl/, *adj.* **1.** having certain digits growing joined together. *–n.* **2.** an animal characterised by being syndactyl. Also, **syndactyle.** [SYN- + Gk *-dáktylos* fingered, toed] – **syndactylism** /sɪnˈdæktəˌlɪzəm/, *n.*

**syndesmosis** /ˌsɪndɛsˈmoʊsəs/, *n., pl.* **-ses** /-siz/. a connection of bones by ligaments, fasciae, or membranes other than in a joint. [NL, from Gk *sýndesmos* ligament + *-ōsis* -OSIS] – **syndesmotic** /ˌsɪndɛsˈmɒtɪk/, *adj.*

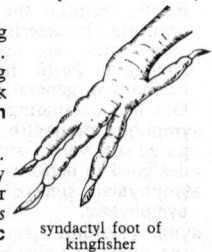

syndactyl foot of kingfisher

**syndetic** /sɪnˈdɛtɪk/, *adj.* **1.** serving to unite or connect; connective; copulative. **2.** →**conjunctive** (def. 3b). Also, **syndetical.** [Gk *syndetikós*] – **syndetically,** *adv.*

**syndic** /ˈsɪndɪk/, *n.* **1.** a person chosen to represent and

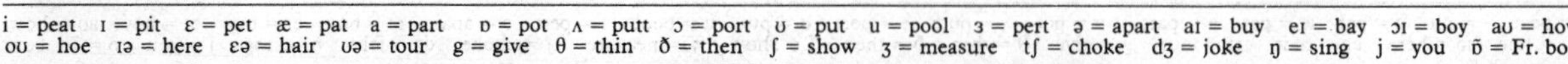

transact business for a society, corporation or the like. **2.** a magistrate having different powers in different countries. [LL *syndicus* advocate, delegate, from Gk *sýndikos* defendant's advocate]

**syndical** /'sɪndɪkəl/, *adj.* **1.** denoting or pertaining to a union of persons engaged in a particular trade. **2.** of or pertaining to syndicalism.

**syndicalism** /'sɪndɪkə,lɪzəm/, *n.* a form or development of trade unionism, originating in France, which aims at the possession of the means of production and distribution, and ultimately at the control of society, by the federated bodies of industrial workers, and which seeks to realise its purposes through general strikes, terrorism, sabotage, or other means. – **syndicalist,** *adj., n.* – **syndicalistic** /,sɪndɪkə'lɪstɪk/, *adj.*

**syndicate** /'sɪndəkət/, *n.;* /'sɪndəkeɪt/, *v.,* **-cated, -cating.** *–n.* **1.** a combination of persons, as business associates, commercial firms, etc., formed for the purpose of carrying out some project, esp. one requiring large resources of capital. **2.** any agency which buys and supplies articles, stories, etc., for simultaneous publication in a number of newspapers or other periodicals in different places. **3.** a council or body of syndics. **4.** (formerly) a local organisation of employers or employees in Italy under the fascist regime. *–v.t.* **5.** to combine into a syndicate. **6.** to publish simultaneously, or supply for simultaneous publication, in a number of newspapers or other periodicals in different places. [F *syndicat,* from *syndic* SYNDIC] – **syndication** /sɪndə'keɪʃən/, *n.*

**syndiotactic** /,sɪndioʊ'tæktɪk/, *adj.* (of a polymer) having substituent groups or atoms located symmetrically in a recurring fashion, along the backbone of a polymer chain.

**syndrome** /'sɪndroʊm/, *n.* the pattern of symptoms in a disease or the like; a number of characteristic symptoms occurring together. [NL, from Gk: a running together] – **syndromic** /sɪn'drɒmɪk/, *adj.*

**synecdoche** /sɪ'nɛkdəki/, *n.* a figure of speech by which a part is put for the whole or the whole for a part, the special for the general or the general for the special, as in 'a fleet of ten *sail*' (for *ships*), or 'a *Croesus*' (for a *rich man*). [LL, from Gk *synekdochē*; replacing ME *synodoche,* from ML] – **synecdochic** /,sɪnɛk'dɒkɪk/, **synecdochical** /,sɪnɛk'dɒkɪkəl/, *adj.*

**synecious** /sə'niʃəs/, *adj.* →**synoicous.**

**synecology** /sɪnə'kɒlədʒi/, *n.* that branch of autecology which deals with the relation between the species or group and its environment. Cf. **autecology.**

**syneresis** /sə'nɪərəsəs/, *n.* **1.** →**synaeresis. 2.** *Chem.* the separation of liquid from a gel.

**synergetic** /sɪnə'dʒɛtɪk/, *adj.* working together; cooperative.

**synergic curve** /sə,nɜdʒɪk 'kɜv/, *n.* the optimum path that a rocket should follow to put a satellite in orbit with the least expenditure of energy.

**synergism** /'sɪnədʒɪzəm, sə'nɜ-/, *n.* **1.** *Theol.* the doctrine that the human will cooperates with the Holy Ghost in the work of regeneration. **2.** the joint action of two substances, as drugs, which increase each other's effectiveness when taken together.

**synergist** /'sɪnədʒəst, sə'nɜdʒəst/, *n.* **1.** *Physiol., Med.* a bodily organ, a medicine, etc., that cooperates with another or others; an adjuvant. **2.** *Theol.* one who holds the doctrine of synergism. **3.** *Chem.* any substance which increases the effect of some other substance.

**synergistic** /sɪnə'dʒɪstɪk/, *adj.* working together; synergetic.

**synergy** /'sɪnədʒi/, *n., pl.* **-gies. 1.** combined action. **2.** the cooperative action of two or more bodily organs or the like. **3.** the cooperative action of two or more stimuli or drugs. [NL *synergia,* from Gk] – **synergic** /sə'nɜdʒɪk/, *adj.* – **synergise,** *v.*

**synesis** /'sɪnəsəs/, *n.* a grammatical construction having a feature which is syntactically extraordinary, as the replacement of an expected singular verb by a plural verb to agree with the sense rather than the syntax of a subject, e.g. *a number of men are going.* [NL, from Gk: comprehension]

**synesthesia** /sɪnəs'θiʒə/, *n.* →**synaesthesia.**

**syngamy** /'sɪŋgəmi/, *n.* (of plants and animals) union of gametes, as in fertilisation or conjugation; sexual reproduction. – **syngamic** /sɪn'gæmɪk/, *adj.* – **syngamous,** *adj.*

**syngenesis** /sɪn'dʒɛnəsəs/, *n.* **1.** *Biol.* sexual reproduction. **2.** *Geol.* the formation of ores at the same time as the enclosing rock. Cf. **epigenesis.**

**syngenetic** /sɪndʒə'nɛtɪk/, *adj.* **1.** *Biol.* of or pertaining to sexual reproduction. **2.** *Geol.* of or pertaining to ores which were formed at the same time as the enclosing rock.

**synizesis** /sɪnə'zisəs/, *n.* the combination into one syllable of two vowels (or of a vowel and a diphthong) that do not form a diphthong. Also, **synaeresis.** [LL, from Gk]

**synod** /'sɪnəd/, *n.* **1.** an assembly of ecclesiastics or other church delegates duly convoked, pursuant to the law of the church, for the discussion and decision of ecclesiastical affairs; an ecclesiastical council. **2.** any council. [ME, from LL *synodus,* from Gk *sýnodos* assembly] – **synodal,** *adj.*

**synodic** /sə'nɒdɪk/, *adj.* pertaining to a conjunction, or to two successive conjunctions of the same bodies. Also, **synodical.** – **synodically,** *adv.*

**synodic month** /– 'mʌnθ/, *n.* →**month** (def. 5).

**synoicous** /sə'nɔɪkəs/, *adj.* (of a plant) having male and female flowers on one flower head, as in many plants of the family Compositae. Also, **synecious, synoecious.** [Gk *synoíkia* a living together + -OUS]

**synonym** /'sɪnənɪm/, *n.* **1.** a word having the same, or nearly the same, meaning as another in the language, as *joyful, elated, glad.* **2.** a word or expression accepted as another name for something, as *Arcadia* for *pastoral simplicity.* **3.** *Bot., Zool.* a rejected scientific name, other than a homonym. [ME, from LL *synōnymum,* from Gk *synṓnymon,* prop. neut. of *synṓnymos* synonymous] – **synonymic** /sɪnə'nɪmɪk/, **synonymical** /sɪnə'nɪməkəl/, *adj.* – **synonymity** /sɪnə'nɪməti/, *n.*

**synonymise** /sə'nɒnəmaɪz/, *v.t.,* **-mised, -mising.** to give synonyms for (a word, name, etc.); furnish with synonyms. Also, **synonymize.**

**synonymous** /sə'nɒnəməs/, *adj.* having the character of synonyms or a synonym; equivalent in meaning; expressing or implying the same idea. [ML *synōnymus,* from Gk *synṓnymos*] – **synonomously,** *adv.* – **synonymousness,** *n.*

**synonymy** /sə'nɒnəmi/, *n., pl.* **-mies. 1.** the character of being synonymous; equivalence in meaning. **2.** the study of synonyms. **3.** a set, list, or system of synonyms. **4.** *Bot., Zool.* **a.** a list of the scientific names for a particular species or other group, or for various species, etc., with discriminations or explanatory matter. **b.** these names collectively, whether listed or not. [LL *synōnymia,* from Gk]

**synop.,** synopsis.

**synopsis** /sə'nɒpsəs/, *n., pl.* **-ses** /-siz/. **1.** a brief or condensed statement giving a general view of some subject. **2.** a compendium of headings or short paragraphs giving a view of the whole. **3.** the outline of the plot of a novel, play, film, etc. [LL, from Gk: general view]

**synoptic** /sə'nɒptɪk/, *adj.* **1.** pertaining to or constituting a synopsis; affording or taking a general view of the whole or of the principal parts of a subject. **2.** (*oft. cap.*) taking a common view (applied to the first three Gospels, Matthew, Mark, and Luke, from their similarity in contents, order, and statement). **3.** (*oft. cap.*) pertaining to the synoptic Gospels. *–n.* **4.** one of the synoptic Gospels. **5.** one of their authors. [NL *synopticus,* from Gk *synoptikós*] – **synoptically,** *adv.*

**synoptic chart** /– 'tʃat/, *n.* a chart showing distribution of meteorological conditions over a region at a given moment.

**synoptic meteorology** /– mitiə'rɒlədʒi/, *n.* a branch of meteorology analysing data taken simultaneously over a large area, for the purpose of weather forecasting.

**synovia** /saɪ'noʊviə, sə-/, *n.* a lubricating liquid resembling the white of an egg, secreted by certain membranes, as those of the joints. [NL coined by Paracelsus 1493?-1541, Swiss-German physician and alchemist]

**synovitis** /,saɪnoʊ'vaɪtəs, ,sɪnoʊ-/, *n.* inflammation of a synovial membrane. [SYNOV(IA) + -ITIS]

**synsepalous** /sɪn'sɛpələs/, *adj.* →**gamosepalous.**

**syntactical** /sɪn'tæktɪkəl/, *adj.* of or pertaining to syntax. Also, **syntactic.** – **syntactically,** *adv.*

**syntactic construction** /sɪn,tæktɪk kən'strʌkʃən/, *n.* a construction composed wholly of independent words, without bound forms.

**syntax** /'sɪntæks/, *n.* **1.** *Gram.* **a.** the patterns of formation of sentences and phrases from words in a particular language. **b.** the study and description thereof. **2.** the rules governing the order or structure (as opposed to the meaning) of symbols or expressions used in a computer language. **3.** *Logic.* **a.** that branch of modern logic which studies the various kinds of signs that occur in a system and the possible arrangements of those signs, complete abstraction being made of the meaning of the signs. **b.** the outcome of such a study when directed upon a specified language. **4.** *Obs.* a system. [LL *syntaxis,* from Gk: arrangement]

**synthesis** /ˈsɪnθəsəs/, *n., pl.* **-ses** /-siz/. **1.** the combination of parts or elements, as material substances or objects of thought, into a complex whole (opposed to *analysis*). **2.** a complex whole made up of parts or elements combined. **3.** *Chem.* the forming or building up of a more complex substance or compound by the union of elements or the combination of simpler compounds or radicals. **4. a.** reasoning from the universal or general to the particular, or from a principle to its exemplification. **b.** (in Kant) the unification, by the understanding, of one concept with another not contained in it. **c.** (in Fichte) the union of thesis and antithesis. **d.** a forerunner of the Hegelian dialectic, which claims to unite contradictory judgments in a higher truth. [L, from Gk: lit., a taking together] – **synthesist,** *n.*

**synthesise** /ˈsɪnθəsaɪz/, *v.t.,* **-sised, -sising. 1.** to make up by combining parts or elements. **2.** to combine into a complex whole. **3.** to treat synthetically. **4.** *Chem.* to manufacture (a complex product, esp. a product resembling one of natural origin) by combining simple substances. Also, **synthesize.** – **synthesisation** /ˌsɪnθəsaɪˈzeɪʃən/, *n.*

**synthesiser** /ˈsɪnθəsaɪzə/, *n.* **1.** one who or that which synthesises. **2.** Also, **music synthesiser.** a machine which creates speech or music by combining the controlled outputs of a number of electronic circuits. Also, **synthesizer.**

**synthetase** /sɪnθəˈteɪz/, *n.* a non-specific name for any enzyme which will catalyse the synthesis of a named product, as glutamine synthetase.

**synthetic** /sɪnˈθɛtɪk/, *adj.* Also, **synthetical. 1.** of, pertaining to, proceeding by, or involving synthesis (opposed to *analytic*). **2.** denoting or pertaining to chemical compounds, resins, rubbers, etc., formed by chemical reaction in a laboratory or chemical plant, as opposed to those of natural origin. **3.** (of languages) characterised by the use of affixes (bound forms) to express relationships between words, as in Latin; as opposed to *analytic,* as in English. *–n.* **4.** something made by a synthetic (chemical) process. [NL *syntheticus,* from Gk *synthetikós*] – **synthetically,** *adv.*

**synthetic geometry** /– dʒiˈɒmətri/, *n.* elementary geometry as distinct from analytic geometry.

**synthetise** /ˈsɪnθətaɪz/, *v.t.,* **-tised, -tising.** →**synthesise.** Also, **synthetize.** – **synthetisation** /ˌsɪnθətaɪˈzeɪʃən/, *n.* – **synthetiser,** *n.*

**syntonic** /sɪnˈtɒnɪk/, *adj.* adjusted to oscillations of the same or a particular frequency. Also, **syntonical.** – **syntonically,** *adv.*

**syntonise** /ˈsɪntənaɪz/, *v.t.,* **-nised, -nising.** to render syntonic; to tune to the same frequency. Also, **syntonize.** [SYNTON(Y) + -ISE] – **syntonisation** /ˌsɪntənaɪˈzeɪʃən/, *n.*

**syntony** /ˈsɪntəni/, *n.* the state or condition of being syntonic. [Gk *syntonía* tension]

**syphilis** /ˈsɪfələs/, *n.* a chronic, infectious venereal disease, caused by the micro-organism *Spirochaeta pallida,* or *Treponema pallidum* (see **spirochaete**), and communicated by contact or heredity, usu. having three stages, the first (**primary syphilis**), in which a hard chancre forms at the point of inoculation, the second (**secondary syphilis**), characterised by skin affections and constitutional disturbances, and the third (**tertiary syphilis**), characterised by affections of the bones, muscles, viscera, nervous system, etc. [NL, from *Syphilus,* name of shepherd suffering from the disease in L poem of 16th cent. by G. Fracastoro]

**syphilitic** /sɪfəˈlɪtɪk/, *adj.* **1.** pertaining to or affected with syphilis. *–n.* **2.** one affected with syphilis.

**syphiloid** /ˈsɪfəlɔɪd/, *adj.* resembling syphilis.

**syphilology** /sɪfəˈlɒlədʒi/, *n.* the study or science of syphilis. – **syphilologist,** *n.*

**syphon** /ˈsaɪfən/, *n., v.t., v.i.* →**siphon.**

**syr.,** *Pharm.* syrup.

**syrette** /sɪˈrɛt/, *n.* a collapsible tube with an attached hypodermic needle for the subcutaneous administration of medication. [Trademark SYR(INGE) + -ETTE]

**Syria** /ˈsɪriə/, *n.* a republic in south-western Asia at the eastern end of the Mediterranean. – **Syrian,** *adj., n.*

**Syriac** /ˈsɪriæk/, *n.* an Aramaic language. [L *Syriacus,* from Gk *Syriakós*]

**Syrian Arab Republic,** *n.* official name of **Syria.**

**syringa** /sɪˈrɪŋgə/, *n.* **1.** →**mock orange. 2.** a lilac of the genus *Syringa.* [NL, from Gk *syrinx* pipe]

**syringe** /səˈrɪndʒ, ˈsɪrɪndʒ/, *n., v.,* **-ringed, -ringing.** *–n.* **1.** *Med.* a small device consisting of a glass, metal, rubber, or plastic tube, narrowed at its outlet, and fitted with either a piston or a rubber bulb for drawing in a quantity of fluid and ejecting it in a stream, used for cleaning wounds, injecting fluids into the body, etc. **2.** any similar device for pumping and spraying liquids through a small aperture. *–v.t.* **3.** to cleanse, wash, inject, etc., by means of a syringe. [backformation from *syringes,* from Gk, pl. of *sŷrinx* pipe; replacing late ME *siryng,* from ML]

syringe

**syringeal** /səˈrɪndʒiəl/, *adj.* of, pertaining to, or connected with the syrinx.

**syringomyelia** /sɪˌrɪŋgoʊmaɪˈiliə/, *n.* a disease of the spinal cord in which the nerve tissue is replaced by a cavity filled with fluid. [NL, from *syringo-* (combining form of Gk *sŷrinx* pipe) + Gk *myelós* marrow (of the spinal cord) + *-ia* -IA]

**syrinx** /ˈsɪrɪŋks/, *n., pl.* **syringes** /səˈrɪndʒiz/, **syrinxes. 1.** →**Eustachian tube. 2.** *Ornith.* the vocal organ of birds, situated at or near the bifurcation of the trachea into the bronchi. [from a nymph of Greek mythology who was pursued by Pan, God of forests, and, to escape him, was turned into a reed, of which he made the panpipe; L, from Gk]

syrinx of bird: A, modified tracheal and bronchial rings forming syrinx; B, trachea; C, bronchi

**syrphid** /ˈsɜfɪd/, *n.* any of the Syrphidae, or hoverflies, a family of dipterous insects or flies, some of which are beneficial, their larvae feeding on plant lice. Also, **syrphian.** [Gk *sýrphos* gnat + -ID[2]]

**syrup** /ˈsɪrəp/, *n.* **1.** any of various sweet, more or less viscid liquids, consisting of fruit, juices, water, etc., boiled with sugar. **2.** →**molasses. 3.** any of various solutions of sugar used in pharmacy. **4.** any of various thick sweet liquids for use in cooking, prepared from molasses, glucose, etc., water, and often with a flavouring agent. **5.** *Colloq.* excessive or cloying sweetness or sentimentality. *–v.t.* **6.** to bring to the form or consistency of syrup. **7.** to cover, fill or sweeten with syrup. Also, U.S., **sirup.** [ME *syrope,* from OF *sirop,* from Ar *sharāb* beverage] – **syruplike,** *adj.*

**syrupy** /ˈsɪrəpi/, *adj.* **1.** resembling syrup in appearance or quality. **2.** *Colloq.* excessively sentimental; cloying: *syrupy music.*

**sys-,** variant of **syn-,** before *s,* as in *syssarcosis.*

**syssarcosis** /sɪsaˈkoʊsəs/, *n.* the union of bones by muscle. [NL, from Gk]

**systaltic** /sɪsˈtæltɪk/, *adj.* **1.** rhythmically contracting. **2.** of the nature of contraction. **3.** characterised by alternate contraction (systole) and dilatation (diastole), as the action of the heart. [LL *systalticus,* from Gk *systaltikós* contractile]

**system** /ˈsɪstəm/, *n.* **1.** an assemblage or combination of things or parts forming a complex or unitary whole: *a mountain system, a railway system.* **2.** any assemblage or set of correlated members: *a system of currency, a system of shorthand characters.* **3.** an ordered and comprehensive assemblage of facts, principles, doctrines, or the like in a particular field of knowledge or thought: *a system of philosophy.* **4.** a coordinated body of methods, or a complex scheme or plan of procedure: *a system of marking, numbering, or measuring.* **5.** due method, or orderly manner of arrangement or procedure: *have system in one's work.* **6.** a number of heavenly bodies associated and acting together according to certain natural laws: *the solar system.* **7.** the world or universe. **8.** *Astron.* a hypothesis or theory of the disposition and arrangements of the heavenly bodies by which their phenomena, motions, changes, etc., are explained: *the Ptolemaic system, the Copernican system.* **9.** *Biol.* **a.** an assemblage of parts of organs of the same or similar tissues, or concerned with the same function: *the nervous system, the digestive system.* **b.** the entire human or animal body: *to expel poison from the system.* **10.** a method or scheme of classification: *the Linnean system of plants.* **11.** (*also pl.*) *Computers.* (in data-processing) the interrelation of personnel, procedure, hardware, and software, which combine to accomplish a set of specific functions. **12.** *Geol.* a major division of rocks comprising sedimentary deposits and igneous masses formed during a geological period. **13.** *Phys. Chem.* **a.** any substance or group of substances considered apart from the surroundings. **b.** a sample of matter consisting of one or more components in equilibrium in one or more phases; a system is called binary if containing two components, ternary, if containing three, etc. **14.** *Colloq.* society at large or an organisation within it: *to buck the system.* [LL *systēma,* from Gk: organised whole] – **systemless,** *adj.*

**systematic** /sɪstə'mætɪk/, *adj.* **1.** having, showing, or involving a system, method, or plan: *a systematic course of reading, systematic efforts.* **2.** characterised by system or method; methodical: *a systematic person, systematic habits.* **3.** arranged in or comprising an ordered system: *systematic theology.* **4.** concerned with classification: *systematic botany.* **5.** pertaining to, based on, or in accordance with a system of classification: *the systematic names of plants.* Also, **systematical.** – **systematically,** *adv.*

**systematics** /sɪstə'mætɪks/, *n.* the study of systems, or of classification.

**systematise** /'sɪstəmətaɪz/, *v.t.,* **-tised, -tising.** to arrange in or according to a system; reduce to a system; make systematic. Also, **systematize.** – **systematisation** /ˌsɪstəmətaɪ'zeɪʃən/, *n.* – **systematiser,** *n.*

**systematism** /'sɪstəmətɪzəm/, *n.* **1.** the practice of systematising. **2.** adherence to system.

**systematist** /'sɪstəmətəst/, *n.* **1.** one who constructs a system. **2.** a naturalist engaged in classification. **3.** one who adheres to system.

**systematology** /ˌsɪstəmə'tɒlədʒi/, *n.* the science of systems or their formation.

**system city** /sɪstəm 'sɪti/, *n.* a city planned in accordance with a systems analysis of its total operation.

**systemic** /sɪs'tɛmɪk, sɪs'timɪk/, *adj.* **1.** of or pertaining to a system. **2.** *Physiol., Pathol.* **a.** pertaining to or affecting the entire bodily system, or the body as a whole. **b.** pertaining to a particular system of parts or organs of the body. – **systemically,** *adv.*

**systemise** /'sɪstəmaɪz/, *v.t.,* **-mised, -mising.** →**systematise.** Also, **systemize.** – **systemisation** /sɪstəmaɪ'zeɪʃən/, *n.* – **systemiser,** *n.*

**systems analysis** /'sɪstəmz ənæləsəs/, *n.* the analysis of an activity or project, usu. with the aid of a computer, to determine its aims, methods and effectiveness. – **systems analyst,** *n.*

**systems engineer** /'– ɛndʒənɪə/, *n.* an engineer who is concerned with the design of systems in the light of systems analysis and information theory. – **systems engineering,** *n.*

**systole** /'sɪstəli, 'sɪstoʊl/, *n.* **1.** *Physiol.* the normal rhythmical contraction of the heart, esp. that of the ventricles, which drives the blood into the aorta and the pulmonary artery. Cf. **diastole. 2.** *Class. Pros.* the shortening of a syllable regularly long. [NL, from Gk: contraction] – **systolic** /sɪs'tɒlɪk/, *adj.*

**syzygy** /'sɪzədʒi/, *n., pl.* **-gies. 1.** *Astron.* the conjunction or opposition of two heavenly bodies; a point in the orbit of a body, as the moon, at which it is in conjunction with or in opposition to the sun. **2.** *Class. Pros.* a group or combination of two feet (by some restricted to a combination of two feet of different kinds). [LL *sȳzygia,* from Gk: conjunction] – **syzygial** /sɪ'zɪdʒiəl/, **syzygetic** /sɪzə'dʒɛtɪk/, *adj.* – **syzygetically** /sɪzə'dʒɛtɪkli/, *adv.*

**sz.,** size.

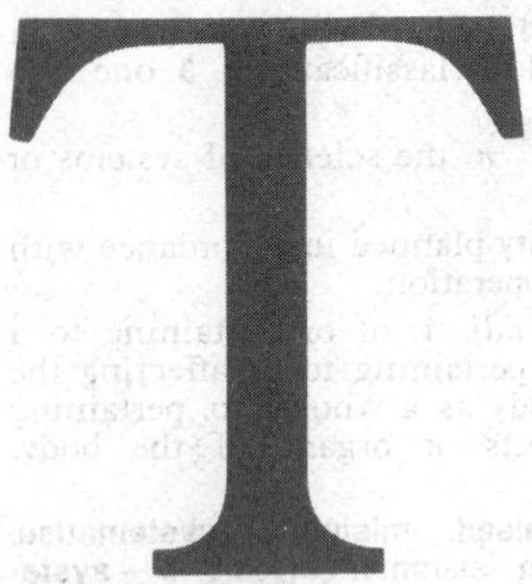

Tt Roman KORINNA

Tt Sans Serif GERMANIC

Script FORMAL

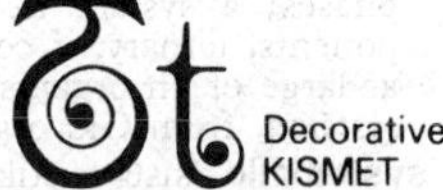

Decorative KISMET

*Although there are numerous typefaces in the world they can be divided into four main classifications. These are:*

*ROMAN or SERIF. This typeface came into being from the technique of the Roman masons who, working in stone, finished off each letter with a serif or small stroke projecting from the top or bottom. This was done to correct any feeling of unevenness or imbalance they may have created in cutting the characters in stone.*

*SANS SERIF (without serif). This typeface is geometric in design and has straight-edged characters and lines of a regular thickness.*

*SCRIPT. Based on the movement of the hand, this typeface is often italicised or slanted, as if drawn by a brush or quill pen.*

*DECORATIVE. Any typeface that exaggerates the characteristics of any of the other three classifications to a degree that places it outside of them.*

*The dictionary entries in this book use a SANS SERIF typeface called Helvetica (set in a bold face for the head words) and a SERIF typeface Plantin (used throughout the body of the entries).*

**T, t** /ti/, *n., pl.* **T's** or **Ts, t's** or **ts. 1.** a consonant, the 20th letter of the English alphabet. **2.** something shaped like the letter T. **3. to a T,** exactly: *to suit or fit to a T.*

**t, 1.** *Statistics.* distribution. **2.** tonne.

**t-,** *Chem.* **1.** tertiary (def. 3a). **2.** trans- (def. 2).

**-t,** a suffix forming the past tense or past participle of certain verbs; an equivalent of **-ed.** [(1) pp., ME and OE *-t, -(e)d,* OE *-od;* (2) past tense, ME and OE *-te, -(e)de,* OE *-ode*]

**'t,** a shortened form of *it,* before or after a verb, as in *'twas, 'tis, do't, see't.*

**t., 1.** taken from. **2.** tare. **3.** teaspoon. **4.** temperature. **5.** in the time of. [L *tempore*] **6.** tenor. **7.** *Gram.* tense. **8.** territory. **9.** time. **10.** tome. **11.** ton. **12.** transitive.

**T, 1.** absolute temperature. **2.** (surface) tension. **3.** *Physics.* tesla.

**T., 1.** Territory. **2.** Tuesday. **3.** Tenor.

**ta** /ta/, *interj. Colloq.* thankyou. [shortened and altered form of *thankyou*]

**Ta,** *Chem.* tantalum.

**Taal** /tal/, *n.* →**Afrikaans** (usu. prec. by *the*). [D: speech]

**tab**[1] /tæb/, *n., v.,* **tabbed, tabbing.** *–n.* **1.** a small flap, strap, loop, or similar appendage, as on a garment, etc. **2.** a tag or label. **3.** *Aeron.* a hinged portion at the trailing edge of an aileron or other control surface on an aircraft. **4.** a stiffened projecting piece from file, paper, or the like, for ready identification; tag. **5.** *Archery.* a flat piece of leather used to protect the fingers when drawing the bow. **6. keep tabs on,** *Colloq.* to keep account of or a check on: *keep tabs on your expenses.* **7. pick up the tab,** *Colloq.* to pay the bill. *–v.t.* **8.** to furnish or ornament with a tab or tabs. [orig. uncert.]

**tab**[2] /tæb/, *n. Colloq.* →**tabulator.**

**tab**[3] /tæb/, *n. Colloq.* a tablet.

**tab.,** tablet.

**TAB** /tæb, ti eɪ 'bi/, *n.* **1.** a government-run betting shop. **2.** a bet placed on a TAB betting shop. Also, **T.A.B.** [*T(otalisator) A(gency) B(oard)*]

**T.A.B.,** Typhoid A and B (bacilli); a vaccine made from dead typhoid-paratyphoid A and B bacilli.

**tabanid** /'tæbənɪd/, *n.* **1.** a large bloodsucking dipterous fly of the family Tabanidae, esp. a horsefly. *–adj.* **2.** belonging or pertaining to the Tabanidae.

**tabard** /'tæbəd/, *n.* **1.** a loose outer garment with short sleeves or without sleeves, worn by knights over their armour and usu. emblazoned with the arms of the wearer. **2.** an official garment of a herald, emblazoned with the arms of his sovereign or ruler. **3.** a coarse, heavy, short coat with or without sleeves, formerly used as an outdoor garment. [ME, from OF]

T, tabard

**tabaret** /'tæbərət/, *n.* a durable upholstery fabric made of satin and watered silk stripes. [? from TABBY (def. 7)]

**tabasco** /tə'bæskoʊ/, *n.* **1.** a pungent sauce used as a condiment, prepared from the fruit of a variety of capsicum. **2.** (*cap.*) a trademark for this. [named after *Tabasco,* State of Mexico]

**tabbed** /tæbd/, *v.* **1.** past participle of **tab.** *–adj.* **2. have someone tabbed,** *Colloq.* to identify: *I had him tabbed as a footballer.*

**tabbinet** /'tæbənɛt/, *n.* a fabric resembling poplin, made of silk and wool. Also, **tabinet.** [obs. *tabine* (? from TABB(Y) + -INE[2]) + -ET]

**tabby** /'tæbi/, *n., pl.* **-bies,** *adj., v.,* **-bied, -bying.** *–n.* **1.** a cat with a striped or brindled coat. **2.** a female cat. **3.** an old maid; a spinster. **4.** *Colloq.* a girl. **5.** any spiteful female gossip or tattler. **6.** plain weave. **7.** a watered silk fabric, or any other watered material, as moreen. *–adj.* **8.** striped or brindled. **9.** made of or resembling tabby. *–v.t.* **10.** to give a wavy or watered appearance to (silk, etc.). [aphetic var. of ME *attaby,* from OF *atabis,* from Ar. *'attābī* rich watered silk, from *'Attābīya* quarter of Baghdad where first made]

**tabby weave** /'– wiv/, *n. Textiles.* a plain simple weave, used often in such fabrics as calico, muslin, hopsack, tweeds and some Scottish tartans.

**tabernacle** /'tæbənækəl/, *n., v.,* **-nacled, -nacling. 1.** the tent used by the Jews as a portable sanctuary before their final settlement in Palestine. **2.** any place of worship, esp. one designed for a large congregation. **3.** a canopied niche or recess, as for an image. **4.** *Eccles.* an ornamental receptacle for the reserved Eucharist, now generally found on the altar. **5.** the human body as the temporary abode of the soul. **6.** *Archaic.* a temporary habitation, as a tent or hut. **7.** *Archaic.* a dwelling place. **8.** *Naut.* an upright support to house the foot of a mast which can be raised and lowered. *–v.i., v.t.* **9.** to dwell or place in or as in a tabernacle. [ME, from L *tabernāculum* tent, booth, from L *taberna* hut, booth] **– tabernacular** /tæbə'nækjələ/, *adj.*

**tabes** /'teɪbiz/, *n.* **1.** syphilis of the spinal cord and its appendages, characterised by shooting pains and other sensory disturbances, and in the later stages by locomotor ataxia and paralysis. **2.** a gradually progressive emaciation; consumption. [L: a decay]

**tabescent** /tə'bɛsənt/, *adj.* wasting away. [L *tābescens,* ppr.] – **tabescence,** *n.*

**tabes dorsalis** /teɪbiz dɔ'saləs/, *n.* →**locomotor ataxia.** [NL: tabes of the back]

**tabetic** /tə'bɛtɪk/, *adj.* **1.** Also, **tabid** /'tæbəd/. pertaining to or affected with tabes. *–n.* **2.** one affected with tabes.

**tabinet** /'tæbənɛt/, *n.* →**tabbinet.**

**tabi song** /'tabi sɒŋ/, *n.* an Aboriginal solo narrative song performed at a corroboree.

**tabla** /'tæblə/, *n.* **1.** a set of two hand drums used in North Indian Music. **2.** the cylindrical wooden member of this set, played with the right hand. Cf. **baya.**

**tablature** /'tæblətʃə/, *n.* **1.** a tabular space, surface, or structure. **2.** *Music.* any of various former systems of notation using symbols, as letters or numbers, indicating the strings or frets to be played. [F, from It. *tavolatura,* from *tavola,* from L *tabula* table]

**table** /'teɪbəl/, *n., v.,* **-bled, -bling.** *–n.* **1.** an article of furniture consisting of a flat top resting on legs or on a pillar. **2.** such an article of furniture designed for the play of any various games: *a billiard table.* **3.** the board at or round which persons sit at meals. **4.** the food placed on a table to be eaten. **5.** a company of persons at a table, as for a meal, game, or business transaction. **6.** a flat or plane surface; a level area. **7.** a tableland or plateau. **8.** *Cricket.* the surface of the pitch. **9.** a flat and relatively thin piece of wood, stone, metal, or other hard substance, esp. one artificially shaped for a particular purpose. **10.** anything resembling a table, as a horizontal gravestone supported on pillars. **11.** *Print.* →**ink table. 12.** *Archit.* a flat, vertical, usu. rectangular surface forming a distinct feature in a wall, and often ornamental. **13.** a smooth, flat board or slab on which inscriptions, etc., may be put. **14.** (*pl.*) **a.** the tablets on which certain collections of laws were anciently inscribed, used most often of the Twelve Tables. **b.** the laws themselves. **15.** an arrangement of words, numbers, or signs, or combinations of them, as the multiplication tables, to exhibit a set of facts or relations in a definite, compact, and comprehensive form; a synopsis or scheme. **16.** *Anat.* the inner or outer hard layer or any of the flat bones of the skull. **17.** *Music.* the sounding-board of a violin or similar stringed instrument. **18.** *Jewellery.* **a.** the upper horizontal surface of a faceted gem. **b.** a gem with such a surface. **19. keep a good table,** to provide plentiful, high-quality food. **20. on the table,** *Parl. Proc.* under discussion; put forward for discussion. **21. turn the tables,** to cause a complete reversal of circumstances. **22. under the table, a.** drunk to the extent of being incapable. **b.** given as a bribe. *–v.t.* **23.** to enter in or form into a table or list. **24.** to place or lay on a table. **25.** *Parl. Proc.* to place (a proposal, resolution, etc.) on the table of an assembly for discussion. [ME; OE *tablu,* var. of *tabule,* from L *tabula* board] – **tableless,** *adj.*

**tableau** /'tæbloʊ/, *n., pl.* **-leaux, -leaus. 1.** a picture, as of a scene. **2.** a picturesque grouping of persons or objects; a striking scene. **3.** →**tableau vivant.** [F: a table, picture, from *table* TABLE]

**tableau vivant** /– vi'võ/, *n., pl.* **tableaux vivants** /tæbloʊ vi'võ/. a representation of a picture, statue, scene, etc., by one or more persons suitably costumed and posed. [F]

**table-book** /'teɪbəl-bʊk/, *n.* a notebook or notepad.

**tablecloth** /'teɪbəlklɒθ/, *n.* a cloth for covering the top of a table, esp. during a meal.

**table-cut** /'teɪbəl-kʌt/, *adj.* (of jewels) cut with a very large table joined to the girdle with a bevel.

**table d'hôte** /tablə 'doʊt/, *n., pl.* **tables d'hôte** /tabləz 'doʊt/. a meal of prearranged courses served at a fixed time and price, for guests at a hotel or restaurant. [F: the host's table]

**table hand** /'teɪbəl hænd/, *n.* a shearing shed hand who works on a fleece preparation table.

**table-hop** /'teɪbəl-hɒp/, *v.i.,* **-hopped, -hopping.** to move from table to table in a restaurant, etc. to greet friends. – **table-hopper,** *n.*

**tableland** /'teɪbəllænd/, *n.* an elevated and generally level region of considerable extent; a plateau.

**table-lifting** /'teɪbəl-lɪftɪŋ/, *n.* **1.** the supposed lifting of tables by supernatural rather than physical forces. **2.** →**spiritualism.**

**table linen** /'teɪbəl lɪnən/, *n.* tablecloths, serviettes, etc., for use at meals.

**tablemat** /'teɪbəlmæt/, *n.* a mat, usu. bearing an ornamental design, made of some heat-absorbing material, placed under hot dishes on a table.

**table napkin** /'teɪbəl næpkən/, *n.* →**serviette.**

**table skittles** /'– skɪtlz/, *n.pl.* (*construed as sing.*) a game in which a ball suspended on a string is swung to knock down pins standing on a board.

**tablespoon** /'teɪbəlspun/, *n.* **1.** a spoon larger than a teaspoon and a dessertspoon, used in the service of the table and as a standard measuring unit in recipes. **2.** a unit of capacity, equal to 3 household teaspoons. **3.** →**tablespoonful.**

**tablespoonful** /'teɪbəlspun,fʊl/, *n., pl.* **-fuls.** the quantity a tablespoon holds, equal to about three teaspoonfuls.

**tablet** /'tæblət/, *n.* **1.** a number of sheets of writing paper or the like fastened together at the edge; a pad. **2.** a small, flat slab or surface, esp. one bearing or intended to bear an inscription, carving, or the like. **3.** a leaf or sheet of some inflexible material for writing or marking on, esp. one of a pair or set hinged or otherwise fastened together. **4.** (*pl.*) the set as a whole. **5.** a small, flat or flattish, cake or piece of some solid or solidified substance, as a drug, chemical or the like. **6.** a cake, as of soap. [ME *tablette,* from F, from *table* TABLE]

**table talk** /'teɪbəl tɔk/, *n.* informal conversation at meals.

**table tennis** /'– tɛnəs/, *n.* a miniature tennis game usu. played indoors, on a table with small bats and a hollow celluloid or plastic ball; ping-pong.

**table-top** /'teɪbəl-tɒp/, *adj.* **1.** of or pertaining to a truck, wagon, etc., with a flat open tray. **2.** with a top flattened like a table, as a mountain. *–n.* **3.** a table-top vehicle.

**tabletop** /'teɪbəltɒp/, *n.* **1.** the top of a table. **2.** a flat surface resembling this.

**table-turning** /'teɪbəl-tɜnɪŋ/, *n.* **1.** the movement of a table supposedly due to supernatural forces. **2.** →**spiritualism.**

**tableware** /'teɪbəlwɛə/, *n.* dishes, utensils, etc., used at table or meals.

**table wine** /'teɪbəl waɪn/, *n.* unfortified wine usu. taken with meals.

**tabloid** /'tæblɔɪd/, *n.* **1.** a newspaper, about one half the ordinary page size, emphasising pictures and concise writing. **2.** a compressed portion of various drugs, chemicals, etc. **3.** anything short or condensed, as a play. *–adj.* **4.** compressed in or as in a tabloid: *a tabloid newspaper.* [TABL(ET) + -OID]

**tabo** /'tæboʊ/, *n. Colloq.* a girl. [TABBY (def. 4) + -O]

**taboo** /tə'bu, tæ-/, *adj., n., pl.* **-boos,** *v.,* **-booed, -booing.** *–adj.* **1.** forbidden to general use; placed under a prohibition or ban. **2.** (among the Polynesians and other peoples of the southern Pacific) separated or set apart as sacred or unclean. *–n.* **3.** a prohibition or interdiction of anything; exclusion from use or practice. **4.** (among the Polynesians, etc.) **a.** the system or practice, or an act, whereby things are set apart as sacred, forbidden to general use, or placed under a prohibition or interdiction. **b.** the fact of being so set apart, forbidden, or placed. **5.** exclusion from social relations; ostracism. *–v.t.* **6.** to put under a taboo; prohibit or forbid. **7.** to ostracise, as a person. Also, **tabu.** [Tongan *tabu*]

**tabor** /'teɪbə/, *n.* **1.** a kind of small drum formerly in use, esp. as an accompaniment to a pipe or fife. *–v.i.* **2.** to play upon, or as upon, a tabor; drum. *–v.t.* **3.** to strike or beat, as a tabor. Also, **tabour.** [ME *tabour,* from OF; of Oriental orig.; cf. Pers. *tabūrāk* drum] – **taborer,** *n.*

**taboret** /'tæbərət/, *n.* **1.** a low seat without back or arms, for one person; a stool. **2.** a frame for embroidery. **3.** a small tabor. Also, **tabouret.** [ME *taberett,* from *taber* TABOR + *-ett* -ET]

**taborin** /'tæbərən/, *n.* a small tabor. Also, **tabourin.**

**tabret** /'tæbrət/, *n.* a small tabor.

**tabu** /tə'bu, tæ'bu/, *adj., n., v.t.* →**taboo.**

**tabular** /'tæbjələ/, *adj.* **1.** pertaining to or of the nature of a table or tabulated arrangement. **2.** ascertained from or computed by the use of tables. **3.** having the form of a table, tablet, or tablature. **4.** flat and expansive. [L *tabulāris* relating to a board or plate] – **tabularly,** *adv.*

**tabula rasa** /tæbjələ 'razə, 'rasə/, *n.* a mind as yet free from impressions. [L: scraped tablet]

**tabularise** /'tæbjələraɪz/, *v.t.*, **-rised, -rising.** →**tabulate.** Also, **tabularize.** – **tabularisation** /tæbjələraɪ'zeɪʃən/, *n.*

**tabulate** /'tæbjəleɪt/, *v.*, **-lated, -lating;** /'tæbjələt, -leɪt/, *adj.* –*v.t.* **1.** to put or form into a table, scheme, or synopsis; formulate tabularly. –*v.i.* **2.** to operate or set the tabulator on a typewriter. –*adj.* **3.** shaped like a table or tablet; tabular. **4.** having transverse dissepiments, as certain corals. [L *tabulātus,* pp., boarded, planked] – **tabulation** /tæbjə'leɪʃən/, *n.*

**tabulator** /'tæbjəleɪtə/, *n.* **1.** one who or that which tabulates. **2.** an attachment to a typewriter for moving the carriage a set number of spaces along each time it is pressed and used for setting out matter in tabular form, as accounts. **3.** a machine which reads punched cards, performs certain simple calculations and prints the results.

**tacamahac** /'tækəməhæk/, *n.* **1.** any of certain resinous substances used in incenses, ointments, etc. **2.** any tree yielding such a product. **3.** (in North America) the balsam poplar, *Populus balsamifera.* Also, **tacamahaca.** [Sp. *tacama(ha)ca,* from Nahuatl *tecomah(a)ca* scented copal]

**tacet** /'teɪsɛt/, (in a music score) an indication that an instrument or voice is to be silent for a time. [L: (it) is silent]

**tache** /tæʃ, taʃ/, *n. Archaic.* a buckle; clasp. Also, **tach.** [late ME, from F. See TACK[1]]

**tacheometer** /tæki'ɒmətə/, *n.* **1.** an instrument for determining the speed of blood in the vessels. **2.** an instrument used in surveying to measure the distance from the point of observation to another point at which a staff is held. The length of the staff seen between two reference hairs in the telescope of the instrument is multiplied by a factor to give the distance. **3.** any of various other instruments for measuring speed. Also, **tachometer, tachymeter.** [F *tachéomètre,* from *taché-* (Gk *tácheos,* gen. sing. of *táchos* speed) + *-mètre* -METER[1]] – **tacheometric** /ˌtækiə'mɛtrɪk/, **tacheometrical** /ˌtækiə'mɛtrɪkəl/, *adj.* – **tacheometrically** /ˌtækiə'mɛtrɪkli/, *adv.* – **tacheometry,** *n.*

**tachina fly** /'tækənə flaɪ/, *n.* any of the dipterous insects of the family Tachinidae, the larvae of which are parasitic on other insects such as caterpillars, beetles, etc. [NL *tachina* (from Gk, fem. of *tachinós* swift) + FLY[2]]

**tachisme** /'taʃɪzəm/, *n.* a style of action painting of the post 1950s, originating in France, whose adherents painted in a wholly spontaneous manner regarding each irregular dab of colour as an emotional projection and the whole as an act of dynamic creation. – **tachist,** *adj., n.*

**tachistoscope** /tə'kɪstəskoup/, *n.* an apparatus used in experimental psychology which exposes to view an object, group of objects, letters, words, etc., for a selected brief period of time. [Gk *táchisto(s)* swiftest + -SCOPE] – **tachistoscopic** /təkɪstə'skɒpɪk/, *adj.*

**tacho** /'tækou/, *n. Colloq.* →**tachometer.**

**tacho-,** a word element meaning 'swift'. [Gk, combining form of *táchos* speed, akin to *tachýs.* See TACHY-]

**tachogram** /'tækəgræm/, *n.* the record produced by the action of a tachometer.

**tachograph** /'tækəgræf, -graf/, *n.* **1.** a recording tachometer. **2.** a record made by such an instrument. [TACHO- + -GRAPH]

**tachometer** /tæ'kɒmətə/, *n.* **1.** an instrument for measuring the number of revolutions per minute made by a revolving shaft. **2.** →**tacheometer.** [TACHO- + -METER[1]] – **tachometric** /tækə'mɛtrɪk/, **tachometrical** /tækə'mɛtrɪkəl/, *adj.* – **tachometrically** /tækə'mɛtrɪkli/, *adv.* – **tachometry,** *n.*

**tachy-,** a word element meaning swift, as in *tachygraphy.* [Gk, combining form of *tachýs*]

**tachycardia** /tæki'kadiə/, *n.* an abnormally fast heartbeat. – **tachycardiac** /tæki'kadiæk/, *adj.*

**tachygraph** /'tækigræf, -graf/, *n.* **1.** tachygraphic writing. **2.** a tachygraphic writer.

**tachygraphy** /tæ'kɪgrəfi/, *n.* the Greek and Roman handwriting used for rapid stenography and writing. – **tachygrapher, tachygraphist,** *n.* – **tachygraphic** /tæki'græfɪk/, **tachigraphical** /tæki'græfɪkəl/, *adj.*

**tachylyte** /'tækəlaɪt/, *n.* a black, glassy form of basalt, readily fusible and of a high lustre. Also, **tachylite.** [G *Tachylit,* from Gk *tachy-* TACHY- + *lytós* soluble] – **tachylytic** /tækə'lɪtɪk/, *adj.*

**tachymeter** /tæ'kɪmətə/, *n.* →**tacheometer.** [TACHY- + -METER[1]] – **tachymetric** /tækə'mɛtrɪk/, **tachymetrical** /tækə'mɛtrɪkəl/, *adj.* – **tachymetrically** /tækə'mɛtrɪkli/, *adv.* – **tachymetry,** *n.*

**tachyon** /'tækiɒn/, *n.* a hypothetical elementary particle which travels faster than the velocity of light.

**tachyphemia** /tæki'fimiə/, *n.* rapidity and volubility of speech, esp. as the result of a nervous disorder. [NL, from TACHY- + Gk *-phēmia,* from *phḗmē* speech]

**tachypnoea** /tækɪp'niə/, *n.* abnormally rapid breathing. Also, *U.S.,* **tachypnea.** [TACHY- + *-pnoea* (from Gk *-pnoia,* Doric d. for *pnoḗ* breath)]

**tacit** /'tæsət/, *adj.* **1.** silent; saying nothing. **2.** not openly expressed, but implied; understood or inferred. **3.** unspoken: *tacit consent.* [L *tacitus,* pp.] – **tacitly,** *adv.* – **tacitness,** *n.*

**taciturn** /'tæsətɜn/, *adj.* inclined to silence, or reserved in speech; not inclined to conversation. [L *taciturnus*] – **taciturnity** /tæsə'tɜnəti/, *n.* – **taciturnly,** *adv.*

**tack**[1] /tæk/, *n.* **1.** a short, sharp-pointed nail or pin, usu. with a flat and comparatively large head. **2.** a stitch, esp. a long stitch used in fastening seams, etc., preparatory to a more thorough sewing. **3.** a fastening, esp. in a temporary manner. **4.** the quality of being tacky; stickiness. **5.** *Naut.* **a.** a rope which confines the foremost lower corner of a course on a square-rigged ship. **b.** the part of a sail to which such a rope is fastened. **c.** the lower forward corner of a fore-and-aft sail. **d.** a line secured to the lower outboard corner of a studding-sail to haul it to the end of the boom. **6.** *Naut.* **a.** the direction or course of a ship in relation to the position of her sails: *the starboard tack* (when close-hauled with the wind on the starboard side); *the port tack* (when close-hauled with the wind on the port side). **b.** a course obliquely against the wind. **c.** one of the series of straight runs which make up the zigzag course of a ship proceeding to windward. **7.** a course of action or conduct, esp. one differing from some preceding or other course. **8.** one of the movements of a zigzag course on land. **9.** the equipment collectively which pertains to the saddling and harnessing of horses; saddlery. **10. on the wrong tack,** following a false line of reasoning; under a wrong impression. –*v.t.* **11.** to fasten by a tack or tacks: *to tack a rug.* **12.** to secure by some slight or temporary fastening. **13.** to join together; unite or combine. **14.** to attach as something supplementary; append or annex (usu. fol. by *on* or *on to*). **15.** *Naut.* **a.** to change the course of (a ship) to the opposite tack. **b.** navigate (a ship) by a series of tacks. –*v.i.* **16.** *Naut.* **a.** to change the course of a ship by bringing her head into the wind and then causing it to fall off on the other side: *he ordered us to tack at once.* **b.** to change its course in this way, as a ship. **c.** to proceed to windward by a series of courses as close to the wind as the vessel will sail, the wind being alternately on one bow and then on the other. **17.** to follow a zigzag course or route. **18.** to change one's course of action or conduct. [ME, from AF *taque* a fastening, clasp, nail, from Gmc; cf. G *Zacken* prong, D *tak* twig] – **tacker,** *n.* – **tackless,** *adj.*

**tack**[2] /tæk/, *n.* food; fare: *hard tack.* [orig. obscure]

**tackle** /'tækəl/, *n., v.,* **-led, -ling.** –*n.* **1.** equipment, apparatus, or gear, esp. for fishing. **2.** a mechanism or apparatus, as a rope and block or a combination of ropes and blocks, for hoisting, lowering, and shifting objects or materials. **3.** any system of leverage using several pulleys. **4.** *Naut.* **a.** the gear and rigging used in handling a ship, esp. that used in working the sails, etc. **b.** a purchase consisting of a rope running over two or more sheaves or pulleys. **c.** an arrangement of rope and blocks or sheaves for multiplying power. **5.** an act of tackling, as in football. –*v.t.* **6.** to undertake to deal with, master, solve, etc. **7.** *Colloq.* to lay hold upon, attack, or encounter. **8.** *Soccer, Hockey, etc.* to get or attempt to get the ball from (an opponent). **9.** *Rugby Football, etc.* to seize and pull down (an opponent having the ball). **10.** to harness (a horse). –*v.i.* **11.** *Football, Hockey, etc.* to tackle an opponent. [ME *takel* gear, from MLG, from *taken* seize, c. TAKE, *v.*] – **tackler,** *n.*

**tackling** /ˈtæklɪŋ/, *n.* gear; tackle.

**tack room** /ˈtæk rum/, *n.* a room in which riding gear is stored.

**tacky**[1] /ˈtæki/, *adj.*, **-ier, -iest.** adhesive; sticky, as a paint, varnish, or the like, when partly dry. [TACK[1] + -Y[1]]

**tacky**[2] /ˈtæki/, *adj.*, **-ier, -iest.** *Colloq.* **1.** shabby; dowdy. **2.** superficially attractive but lacking quality or craftsmanship. [orig. obscure]

**taco** /ˈtakoʊ, ˈtækoʊ/, *n.* a tortilla folded around a savoury filling and usu. fried. [Mex. Sp.]

**Taconic** /təˈkɒnɪk/, *adj.* of or pertaining to the major mountain-building episode which occurred at the end of the Ordovician period in North America. [name of mountain range forming part of the Appalachian Mountains on the E coast of N America]

**taconite** /ˈtækənaɪt/, *n. U.S.* a low-grade iron ore found in the region of Lake Superior as a hard rock formation, containing about 51 per cent silica and 27 per cent iron.

**tact** /tækt/, *n.* **1.** a keen sense of what to say or do to avoid giving offence; skill in dealing with difficult or delicate situations. **2.** touch; the sense of touch. [L *tactus* sense of touch]

**tactful** /ˈtæktfʊl/, *adj.* discreet; diplomatic; considerate.

**tactic** /ˈtæktɪk/, *n.* **1.** (*pl.*) →**tactics. 2.** a system or a detail of tactics. **3.** a plan or procedure for achieving a desired end. *–adj.* **4.** of or pertaining to arrangement or order; tactical. [NL *tactica,* from Gk *taktikḗ,* fem. of *taktikós,* from *taktós* ordered]

**tactical** /ˈtæktɪkəl/, *adj.* **1.** of or pertaining to tactics, esp. military or naval tactics. **2.** characterised by skilful tactics or adroit manoeuvring or procedure: *tactical movements.* – **tactically,** *adv.*

**tactical unit** /– ˈjunət/, *n.* a group organised to operate independently in action and sharing a specific objective.

**tactician** /tækˈtɪʃən/, *n.* one versed in tactics.

**tacticity** /tækˈtɪsəti/, *n. Chem.* regularity or symmetry in the molecular arrangement or structure of a polymer molecule.

**tactics** /ˈtæktɪks/, *n.pl.* **1.** (*construed as sing.*) the art or science of disposing military or naval forces for battle and manoeuvring them in battle. **2.** the manoeuvres themselves. **3.** mode of procedure for gaining advantage or success. [pl. of TACTIC. See -ICS]

**tactile** /ˈtæktaɪl/, *adj.* **1.** of or pertaining to the organs or sense of touch; endowed with the sense of touch. **2.** perceptible to the touch; tangible. [L *tactilis* tangible] – **tactility** /tækˈtɪləti/, *n.*

**taction** /ˈtækʃən/, *n. Obs.* touch; contact.

**tactless** /ˈtæktləs/, *adj.* without tact; showing no tact: *a tactless person.* – **tactlessly,** *adv.* – **tactlessness,** *n.*

**tactual** /ˈtæktʃuəl/, *adj.* **1.** of or pertaining to touch. **2.** communicating or imparting the sensation of contact; arising from or due to touch. [L *tactu(s)* touch + -AL[1]] – **tactually,** *adv.*

**taddie** /ˈtædi/, *n. Colloq.* a tadpole.

**tadpole** /ˈtædpoʊl/, *n.* the aquatic larva or immature form of frogs, toads, etc., esp. after the enclosure of the gills and before the appearance of the forelimbs and the resorption of the tail. [ME *taddepol,* from *tadde* TOAD + *pol* POLL[1] (head)]

tadpole: A, early stage; B, after appearance of forelimbs

**taedium vitae** /tidiəm ˈvitaɪ/, *n.* a feeling that life is unbearably wearisome. Also, **tedium vitae.** [L: wearisome of life]

**tael** /teɪl/, *n.* **1.** any of various units of weight in the Far East. **2.** a former Chinese monetary unit based on this weight of standard silver. [Pg., from Malay *tahil* weight]

**ta'en** /teɪn/, *v. Poetic.* taken.

**taenia** /ˈtiniə/, *n., pl.* **-niae** /-nii/. **1.** *Archit.* the fillet or band on the Doric architrave, which separates it from the frieze. **2.** *Anat.* a ribbon-like structure, as certain bands of white nerve fibres in the brain. **3.** *Zool.* →**tapeworm.** Also, *U.S.,* **tenia.** [L, from Gk *tainía*]

**taeniacide** /ˈtiniəsaɪd/, *n.* an agent that destroys tapeworms. Also, *U.S.,* **teniacide.** – **taeniacidal** /tiniəˈsaɪdl/, *adj.*

**taeniafuge** /ˈtiniəfjudʒ, -fjuʒ/, *adj.* **1.** expelling tapeworms, as a medicine. *–n.* **2.** an agent or medicine to expel tapeworms from the body.

**taeniasis** /təˈnaɪəsəs/, *n.* a diseased condition due to the presence of taeniae or tapeworms.

**T.A.F.E.** /teɪf/, Technical and Further Education. Also, **TAFE.**

**taffel** /ˈtæfəl/, *n.* a smooth, delicately flavoured cheese with a close texture, and resilient body with a few, very small, shiny holes through it, originally made in Denmark. [G *tafel,* table]

**taffeta** /ˈtæfətə/, *n.* **1.** a lustrous silk or rayon fabric of plain weave. **2.** any of various other fabrics of silk, linen, wool, etc., in use at different periods. *–adj.* **3.** of or resembling taffeta. [ME *taffata,* from ML, from Pers. *tāftah* silken or linen cloth]

**taffrail** /ˈtæfreɪl/, *n.* **1.** the upper part of the stern of a vessel. **2.** the rail across the stern. [earlier *tafferel,* from D *tafereel* panel (diminutive of *tafel* TABLE)]

**taffy** /ˈtæfi/, *n. U.S.* toffee. [var. of TOFFEE]

**Taffy** /ˈtæfi/, *n. Colloq.* a Welshman. [Welsh form of *Davy,* shortened form of *David,* proper name and name of patron saint of Wales]

**tafia** /ˈtæfiə/, *n.* a kind of rum made from the lower grades of molasses, refuse sugar, etc., in Haiti. [orig. uncert.]

**tag**[1] /tæg/, *n., adj., v.,* **tagged, tagging.** *–n.* **1.** a piece or strip of strong paper, leather, or the like, for attaching by one end to something as a mark or label. **2.** any small hanging or loosely attached part or piece; tatter. **3.** a loop of material sewn on a garment so that it can be hung up. **4.** a point or binding of metal, plastic, or other hard substance at the end of a cord, lace, or the like. **5.** *Angling.* a small piece made of tinsel or the like, tied to the shank of a hook at the body of an artificial fly. **6.** a tag end. **7.** the refrain of a song or poem. **8.** the last words of a speech in a play, etc., as a curtain line or cue. **9.** (in popular music) a coda. **10.** an addition to a speech or writing, as the moral of a fable. **11.** a trite quotation or cliché, esp. one in Latin. **12.** a word or phrase applied as characteristic of a person or group. **13.** a curlicue in writing. **14.** a lock of hair. **15.** a matted lock of wool on a sheep. **16.** the tip of the tail of a fox. **17.** *Obs.* the rabble. *–v.t.* **18.** to furnish with a tag or tags; to attach a tag to. **19.** to append as a tag to something else. **20.** to apply as characteristic a word or phrase to (a person or group). **21.** *Colloq.* to follow closely. **22.** to attach a price tag to; to price. *–v.i.* **23.** to follow closely; go along or about as a follower (usu. fol. by *along*). [ME; orig. obscure, ? related to TACK[1]. Cf. Swed. *tagg* prickle, point]

**tag**[2] /tæg/, *n., v.,* **tagged, tagging.** *–n.* **1.** Also, **tig.** →**chasings. 2.** *Baseball.* an act of tagging. **3.** *Wrestling.* an act of touching hands over the top rope by two team-mates in tag wrestling. *–adj.* **4.** denoting or pertaining to a form of professional wrestling in which two teams of two compete one at a time but with partners interchanging. *–v.t.* **5.** Also, **tig.** to touch in or as in the game of tag. **6.** *Baseball.* to touch (a runner) with the ball or the hand holding the ball, thereby putting him out of the game. [? special use of TAG[1]]

**Tagalog** /təˈgalɒg/, *n.* **1.** a member of a Malayan people native in the Philippines. **2.** the principal Indonesian language of the Philippines.

**tagasaste** /tægəˈsæsti/, *n.* a small soft-wooded tree or tall shrub, *Chamaecytisus prolifer,* with white, pea-shaped flowers, native to the Canary Islands, and occasionally planted as a hedge; tree lucerne.

**tag end** /ˈtæg ɛnd/, *n.* the tail end or concluding part, as of a proceeding; fag-end.

**tagger** /ˈtægə/, *n.* **1.** one who or that which tags. **2.** (*pl.*) iron in very thin sheets, either uncoated or coated with tin.

**tagliatelle** /tæljəˈtɛli/, *n.* a kind of pasta made with egg and shaped into long, flat pieces. [It., from *tagliato* (pp. of *tagliare* to cut) + *-elle* fem. pl. diminutive suffix]

**tagmeme** /ˈtægmim/, *n.* (in tagmemics) the basic unit of analysis conceived as a slot and the class of items that can occur in that slot, e.g., the word *I* denoting 'actor' as subject in *I came early.* [Gk *tágma* order + (PHON)EME] – **tagmemic** /tægˈmimɪk/, *adj.*

**tagmemics** /tægˈmimɪks/, *n.* a school of linguistic analysis in which the basic unit is the tagmeme.

**tagrope** /ˈtægroup/, *n.* a short rope attached to a corner of the ring, which a tag wrestler outside the ring must be holding when he touches hands to change places with his team-mate in the ring.

**taguan** /ˈtægwən/, *n.* the largest of the flying squirrels, *Petaurista philippensis,* of India and South-East Asia.

**tahina** /təˈhinə/, *n.* a paste used in Middle Eastern dishes, made by thickening sesame oil with vinegar, water and lemon juice, and sometimes seasoned with pepper, onion, garlic, etc. [Ar.]

**tahr** /ta/, *n.* any of various wild goats of the genus *Hemitragus,* of southern Asia, as the **Himalayan tahr,** *H. jemlahicus;* mountain ibex. Also, **thar.** [Nepalese]

**Tai** /taɪ/, *n., adj.* →**Thai.**

**taiaha** /ˈtaɪəha/, *n.* a long-handled Maori weapon made of wood with a carved and decorated head and used by chiefs. [Maori]

**taiga** /ˈtaɪgə/, *n.* the coniferous, evergreen forests of sub-arctic lands, covering vast areas of northern North America and Eurasia. [Russ.]

**taihoa** /ˈtaɪhouə/, *interj.* by and by; wait a bit. [Maori]

**tail**[1] /teɪl/, *n.* **1.** the hindmost part of an animal esp. when forming a distinct flexible appendage to the trunk. **2.** something resembling or suggesting this in shape or position: *the tail of a kite.* **3.** the hinder, bottom, or concluding part of anything; the rear. **4.** *Elect.* the small piece of wiring from a meter or mains to which wiring from a house is attached. **5.** the final or concluding part of anything, as in cricket, the last batsmen to bat. **6.** the inferior or refuse part of anything. **7.** a long braid or tress of hair. **8.** *Astron.* the luminous train extending from the head of a comet. **9.** *Colloq.* (*pl.*) the reverse of a coin. **10.** an arrangement of objects or persons which extends like a tail. **11.** a downward stroke, as of a printed or written letter, the stem of a musical note, etc. **12.** →**retinue.** **13.** *Aeron.* the stabilising and control surfaces at the after end of an aircraft. **14.** (*pl.*) **a.** the skirts of certain coats, as a swallow-tailed coat. **b.** →**swallow-tailed coat.** **c.** full-dress attire. **15.** the lower part of a pool or section of a stream. **16.** *Colloq.* the buttocks. **17.** *Colloq.* a person who follows another, esp. one who is employed to do so in order to observe or hinder escape. **18.** *Colloq.* **a.** the vagina. **b.** a woman considered as a sex object: *a nice bit of tail.* **19. turn tail, a.** to turn the back, as in aversion or fright. **b.** to run away; flee. **20. with one's tail between one's legs,** in a state of utter defeat or humiliation; abjectly. *–adj.* **21.** coming from behind: *a tail wind.* **22.** being at the back or rear: *a tail-light.* *–v.t.* **23.** to form or furnish with a tail. **24.** to form or constitute the tail or end of (a procession, etc.). **25.** to terminate; follow like a tail. **26.** to join or attach (one thing) at the tail or end of another. **27.** *Bldg Trades.* to fasten (a beam, etc.) by one of its ends (fol. by *in, into,* etc.). **28.** to tend or herd (sheep or cattle). **29.** to dock the tail of: *tailed lambs.* **30.** to remove the stalk of. **31.** to seize by the tail: *to tail an otter.* **32.** *Colloq.* to follow in order to hinder escape or to observe: *to tail a suspect.* *–v.i.* **33.** to form or move in a line or continuation suggestive of a tail: *hikers tailing up a narrow path.* **34. tail out,** to guide timber as it comes off the saw. **35.** (of a boat, etc.) to have or take a position with the stern in a particular direction. **36.** *Colloq.* to follow close behind. **37.** *Bldg Trades.* (of a beam, etc.) to be fastened by the end (fol. by *in, into,* etc.). **38. tail away** or **off,** to decrease gradually; decline. [ME; OE *tægel,* c. Icel. *tagl*] **–tailless,** *adj.* **–tail-like,** *adj.*

**tail**[2] /teɪl/, *n.* **1.** *Law.* the limitation of an estate to a person and the heirs of his body, or some particular class of such heirs. **2.** *Print., Bookbinding.* the bottom of a page or book. *–adj.* **3.** *Law.* limited to a specified line of heirs; being in tail. [ME, from OF *taille* cutting, tax, from *taillier,* v., cut] **–tailless,** *adj.*

**tail-block** /ˈteɪl-blɒk/, *n.* a sheave-block with a small length of rope spliced round it for making fast in any position.

**tailboard** /ˈteɪlbɔd/, *n.* →**tailgate** (def. 1).

**tail coat** /ˈteɪl kout/, *n.* a man's evening coat with a pair of divided tapering skirts behind; a swallow-tailed coat.

**tail end** /ˈ– ɛnd/, *n.* **1.** the rear part of anything. **2.** the tag end; the final part.

**tail ender** /– ˈɛndə/, *n.* one who is last, esp. one who is running last in a competition. Also, **tailender.**

**tailer**[1] /ˈteɪlə/, *n.* a man employed to tend cattle, or other stock, and track down strays, esp. on foot.

**tailer**[2] /ˈteɪlə/, *n.* →**tailor** (def. 2).

**tailer-out** /ˈteɪlər-aʊt/, *n.* one who guides timber as it comes off the saw.

**tailer-up** /teɪlər-ˈʌp/, *n.* the drover at the rear of a mob.

**tailgate** /ˈteɪlgeɪt/, *n.* **1.** Also, **tailboard.** the board at the back of a truck, wagon, etc., which can be removed or let down for convenience in loading and unloading. **2.** *Jazz.* the flamboyant style of trombone-playing characteristic of traditional New Orleans jazz, so called because in processions the trombonist sat at the rear of a lorry. *–adj.* **3.** *Jazz.* denoting, pertaining to, or of this style of trombone-playing. *–v.i.* **4.** to drive in a motor vehicle close behind the vehicle in front. *–v.t.* **5.** to drive close behind (another vehicle).

**tailgater** /ˈteɪlgeɪtə/, *n.* **1.** a tailgate trombone-player. **2.** a driver who persistently drives too close to the vehicle in front.

**tailing** /ˈteɪlɪŋ/, *n.* **1.** the part of a projecting stone or brick tailed or inserted in a wall. **2.** (*pl.*) the residue of any product, as in mining; leavings.

**tail-light** /ˈteɪl-laɪt/, *n.* a light, usu. red, at the rear of a motor vehicle, train, etc. Also, **tail-lamp** /ˈteɪl-læmp/.

**tailor** /ˈteɪlə/, *n.* **1.** one whose business it is to make or mend outer garments, esp. for men. **2.** Also, **tailer, taylor.** an Australian sport fish (named because of the scissor-like meshing of its teeth) of the genus *Pomatomus.* *–v.i.* **3.** to do the work of a tailor. *–v.t.* **4.** to make by tailor's work. **5.** to fit or furnish with clothing. **6.** to design for a particular need or taste: *to tailor prices for the market.* [ME, from OF *tailleor* cutter, from *taillier* cut] **–tailorless,** *adj.*

**tailorbird** /ˈteɪləbɜd/, *n.* **1.** →**golden-headed cisticola.** **2.** any of various small Asiatic passerine birds of the genus *Orthotomus* which build similar nests.

**tailoring** /ˈteɪlərɪŋ/, *n.* **1.** the business or work of a tailor. **2.** the skill or craft of a tailor.

**tailor-made** /ˈteɪlə-meɪd/, *adj.* **1.** made by or as by a tailor (applied esp. to women's garments made of more substantial fabrics or with plainness of cut and finish). **2.** made by a tailor to a particular order for an individual customer. **3.** designed for a particular need or taste. **4.** *Colloq.* of or pertaining to a cigarette made by machine, i.e., not hand rolled. *–n.* **5.** a cigarette made by machine.

**tailor's chalk** /teɪləz ˈtʃɔk/, *n.* →**pipeclay.**

**tailpiece** /ˈteɪlpis/, *n.* **1.** a piece added at the end; an end piece or appendage. **2.** *Print.* a small decorative design at the end of a chapter or at the bottom of a page. **3.** (in musical instruments of the violin family) a triangular piece of wood, usu. of ebony, to which the lower ends of the strings are fastened.

**tailpipe** /ˈteɪlpaɪp/, *n.* the exhaust pipe of a motor vehicle.

**tailplane** /ˈteɪlpleɪn/, *n.* a horizontal surface at the rear end of an aircraft providing longitudinal stability; horizontal stabiliser.

**tailrace** /ˈteɪlreɪs/, *n.* **1.** the race, flume, or channel leading away from a waterwheel or the like. **2.** *Mining.* the channel for conducting tailings or refuse away in water.

**tail rotor** /ˈteɪl routə/, *n.* the small propeller at the rear of a helicopter.

**tail shaft** /ˈteɪl ʃaft/, *n.* the shaft which transmits power from the engine of a motor vehicle from the gearbox to the differential.

**tail skid** /ˈteɪl skɪd/, *n.* a runner under the tail of an aeroplane.

**tail spin** /ˈ– spɪn/, *n.* **1.** →**spin** (def. 18). **2.** *Colloq.* a sudden collapse into a state of utter confusion; flat spin.

**tailstock** /ˈteɪlstɒk/, *n.* (on a lathe or grinder) the movable or sliding frame supporting the dead spindle.

**tail wind** /ˈteɪl wɪnd/, *n.* a favourable wind blowing from behind an aircraft or vessel, etc., thus increasing its speed.

**Taino** /ˈtaɪnou/, *n., pl.* **-nos.** **1.** a member of an extinct Arawakan Indian tribe of the West Indies. **2.** their language.

**taint** /teɪnt/, *n.* **1.** a touch of something offensive or deleterious; a latent or incipient defect or corruption. **2.** a trace of infection, contamination, or the like. **3.** a trace of dishonour or discredit. **4.** *Obs.* colour or tinge. *–v.t.* **5.** to modify as by a touch of something offensive or deleterious. **6.** to infect, contaminate, or corrupt. **7.** to sully or tarnish. **8.** *Obs.* to colour or tinge. *–v.i.* **9.** to become tainted. [ME *taynte,* b. OF *teint* (pp. of *teindre* colour, from L *tingere*) and aphetic var. of ATTAINT] – **taintless,** *adj.*

**tainture** /ˈteɪntʃə/, *n. Obs.* →**taint.**

**taipan** /ˈtaɪpæn/, *n.* a long-fanged, highly venomous snake, *Oxyuranus scutellatus,* of northern Australia and New Guinea, brownish in colour, with a long head and slender body, averaging 2 to 2.5 metres in length. [Aboriginal]

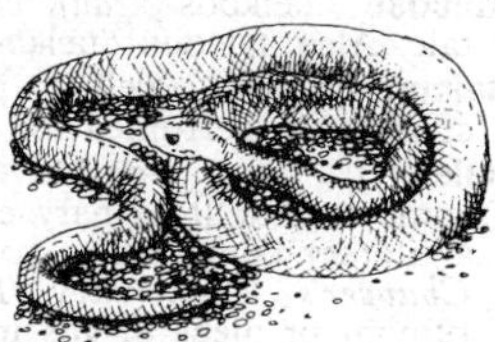
taipan

**taipo** /ˈtaɪpoʊ/, *n. N.Z.* **1.** a ghost; fearsome person or thing. **2.** →**weta.** [Maori]

**tait** /teɪt/, *n.* →**honey possum.**

**Taiwan** /taɪˈwan/, *n.* a Chinese island separated from south-eastern China by Taiwan Strait, homeland of Nationalist Chinese since 1949. See **Nationalist China.** – **Taiwanese** /taɪwənˈiz/, *adj., n.*

**taj** /tadʒ/, *n., pl.* **tajes** /ˈtadʒəz/. a tall, conical cap worn in Muslim countries. [Ar.]

**takable** /ˈteɪkəbəl/, *adj.* →**takeable.**

**takahe** /ˈtakahi/, *n. N.Z.* →**notornis.** [Maori]

**takapu** /ˈtakapu/, *n. N.Z.* the gannet, *Morus serrator.* [Maori]

**take** /teɪk/, *v.,* **took, taken, taking,** *n.* *–v.t.* **1.** to get into one's hands or possession by force or artifice. **2.** to seize, catch, or capture. **3.** to grasp, grip or hold. **4.** to get into one's hold, possession, control, etc., by one's own action but without force or artifice. **5.** to select; pick out from a number: *take a chocolate from a box.* **6.** to receive or accept willingly. **7.** to receive by way of payment or charge. **8.** to obtain by making payment: *to take a house in Paddington.* **9.** to get or obtain from a source; derive. **10.** to receive into the body or system, as by swallowing or inhaling: *to take food.* **11.** to eat or use habitually, as a foodstuff, flavouring, etc.: *to take sugar in tea.* **12.** to quote, esp. without acknowledgment: *this writer has taken whole pages from Eliot.* **13.** to carry off or remove (fol. by *away,* etc.). **14.** to remove by death. **15.** to subtract or deduct: *to take 2 from 5.* **16.** to carry or convey: *take your lunch with you.* **17.** to convey or transport: *we took the children to the seaside by car.* **18.** to have recourse to (a vehicle, etc.) as a means of progression or travel: *to take a bus to the top of the hill.* **19.** to effect a change in the position or condition of: *his ability took him to the top.* **20.** to conduct or lead: *where will this road take me?* **21.** to attempt to get over, through, round, etc. (something that presents itself), or succeed in doing this: *the horse took the hedge with an easy jump.* **22.** (of a disease, illness, or the like) to attack or affect: *to be taken with a fit.* **23.** to become affected by: *a stone which will take a high polish.* **24.** to absorb or become impregnated with (a colour, etc.). **25.** to surprise; detect; come upon: *to take a thief in the act of stealing.* **26.** to receive or adopt (a person) into some specified or implied relation: *to take a woman in marriage.* **27.** to have sexual intercourse with: *to take a woman by force.* **28.** to secure regularly by payment: *to take a magazine.* **29.** to adopt and enter upon (a way, course, etc.); proceed to deal with in some manner: *to take a matter under consideration.* **30.** to proceed to occupy: *to take a seat.* **31.** to receive in a specified manner: *to take a thing kindly.* **32.** to avail oneself of (an opportunity, etc.). **33.** to obtain or exact (satisfaction or reparation). **34.** to receive, or be the recipient of (something bestowed, administered, etc.): *to take first prize.* **35.** to have, undergo, enjoy, etc., as for one's benefit: *to take a bath, take a rest.* **36.** to occupy, use up, or consume (space, material, time, etc.). **37.** to attract and hold: *a well-dressed shop window takes one's eye.* **38.** to captivate or charm: *a pretty ring takes one's fancy.* **39.** to assume or adopt (a symbol, badge, or the like): *to take the veil.* **40.** to make, put forth, etc.: *to take exception.* **41.** to write down (notes, a copy, etc.: *to take a record of (a speech, etc.).* **42.** to go into or enter: *to take the field.* **43.** to make (a reproduction, picture, or photograph of something). **44.** to make a figure or picture, esp. a photograph, of (a person or thing). **45.** to make or perform (a measurement, observation, etc.). **46.** to ascertain by enquiry, examination, measurement, scientific observation, etc. **47.** to begin to have (a certain feeling or state of mind); experience or feel (delight, pride, etc.). **48.** to form and hold in the mind: *to take a gloomy view.* **49.** to understand in a specified way: *how do you take this?* **50.** to regard or consider: *he was taken to be wealthy.* **51.** to assume or undertake (a function, duty, responsibility, etc.). **52.** to assume the obligation of (a vow, pledge, etc.); perform or discharge (a part, service, etc.). **53.** to assume or adopt as one's own (a part or side in a contest, etc.); assume or appropriate as if by right: *to take the credit for something, to take a liberty.* **54.** to grasp or apprehend, understand, or comprehend. **55.** to do, perform, execute, etc.: *to take a walk.* **56.** to accept and comply with (advice, etc.). **57.** to suffer or undergo: *to take insults.* **58.** to enter into the enjoyment of (recreation, a holiday, etc.). **59.** to employ for some specified or implied purpose: *to take measures to check an evil.* **60.** to require: *it takes courage to do that.* **61.** *Cards, Chess, etc.* to capture or win (a trick, piece, etc.). **62.** *Gram.* to have by usage, either as part of itself or with it in construction (a particular form, accent, etc., or a case, mode, etc.), as a word or the like. *–v.i.* **63.** to catch or engage, as a mechanical device. **64.** to strike root, or begin to grow, as a plant. **65.** to adhere, as ink, etc. **66.** to win favour or acceptance, as a play. **67.** to have the intended result or affect as a medicine, inoculation, etc. **68.** to enter into possession, as of an estate. **69.** to apply or devote oneself. **70.** to make one's way; proceed; go. **71.** to become (sick or ill). **72.** to admit of being photographed (well, badly, etc.). **73.** to admit of being taken (out, apart, etc.). **74.** *Angling.* (of a fish) to bite. *–v.* **75.** Some special verb phrases are:

**take aback,** to surprise; disconcert; startle.

**take after, 1.** to resemble (a parent, etc.). **2.** *U.S.* to pursue.

**take back, 1.** to retrieve; regain possession of. **2.** to retract or withdraw. **3.** to allow to return: *to take back one's erring husband.* **4.** to return for exchange, etc.: *to take a faulty radio back to the shop.*

**take care,** to act or think cautiously.

**take care of,** to look after; protect.

**take down, 1.** to pull down. **2.** to remove by pulling apart or taking apart. **3.** to write down. **4.** to take advantage of (someone); cheat; swindle. **5.** to lessen in power, strength, pride, arrogance, etc.: *I'll take him down a peg or two.*

**take for,** to believe or assume to be, esp. mistakenly: *I took him for the postman.*

**take for a ride,** *Colloq.* **1.** to deceive; con. **2.** to murder.

**take for granted, 1.** to accept or assume without question. **2.** to fail to ascribe credit, merit, worth, or the like to: *it is very upsetting to have one's work taken for granted.*

**take from,** to detract from or reduce: *he may behave foolishly, but that does not take from the value of his work.*

**take in, 1.** to receive and accommodate; provide lodging for. **2.** to alter (a garment or garments) in order to make smaller; reduce the size or measurement of. **3.** to include; encompass. **4.** to comprehend; understand; grasp the meaning of. **5.** to deceive, trick, or cheat.

**take it, 1.** *Colloq.* to endure pain, misfortune or the like with fortitude. **2.** to react in a manner specified: *when I broke the news, he took it very badly.* **3.** to assume: *I take it from your silence that this is true.*

**take it out of,** to exhaust; sap one's strength or energy.

**take it out on,** to vent wrath, anger, or the like, on.

**take off, 1.** to remove, as of clothing; to undress. **2.** to lead off or away. **3.** to set off; take one's departure; go away. **4.** to leave the ground, as an aeroplane. **5.** to withdraw, as from service. **6.** to become popular: *surfboard riding took off as a national sport.* **7.** to escalate: *prices took off.* **8.** to become excited. **9.** *Colloq.* to imitate or mimic. **10.** to reach a level of excellence, success, flair, etc.: *the play took off in the last act.*

**take on, 1.** to hire. **2.** to undertake to handle. **3.** to acquire: *to take on a new aspect.* **4.** *Colloq.* to start a quarrel or fight with: *take on someone your own size.* **5.** *Colloq.* to show great excitement, grief, or other emotion. **6.** *Colloq.* to win popularity: *yoyos took on rapidly with children.* **7.** to stand

up to in a situation of conflict, esp. political.
**take out,** **1.** to extract: *to take out a tooth.* **2.** to escort or accompany (a woman). **3.** to treat (someone) to dinner at a restaurant, an entertainment, etc. **4.** to obtain; apply for and get; *to take out an insurance policy.* **5.** to vent: *to take out one's rage on the dog.* **6.** to destroy; eliminate; render harmless: *to take out a military installation by bombing.*
**take over,** to assume or acquire control of.
**take place,** to happen; occur.
**take the bull by the horns,** *Colloq.* to act directly and promptly, particularly in a difficult situation.
**take to,** **1.** to apply, devote, or addict oneself to: *to take to drink.* **2.** to respond kindly or favourably to. **3.** to go to: *to take to one's bed.* **4.** to resort to; have recourse to: *to take to one's heels.*
**take up,** **1.** to lift; pick up. **2** to occupy oneself with; adopt the practice or study of: *to take up Greek.* **3.** to occupy (time, space, or the like). **4.** to resume or continue: *to take up where one left off.* **5.** *Mining Colloq.* to reopen and mine an abandoned mine.
**take upon oneself,** to assume the responsibility for.
**take up with,** to associate with.
*–n.* **76.** an act or instance of taking. **77.** that which is taken. **78.** the quantity of fish, etc. taken at one time. **79.** money taken; gross profit; takings. **80.** *Journalism.* a portion of copy assigned to a keyboard operator or compositor, usu. part of a story or article. **81.** *Parl. Proc.* a ten-minute interval of reporting done by a parliamentary reporter working on roster. **82.** *Films, etc.* **a.** a scene or a portion of a scene photographed at one time without any interruption or break. **b.** an instance of such continuous operation of the camera. **83.** *Recording.* a single uninterrupted sequence of recorded sound. **84.** *Colloq.* a cheat; swindle. **85.** *Med.* a successful inoculation, vaccination, or the like. **86.** *Mining.* a two-month period for which tributers would work on a pitch of ore at a set percentage. **87.** *Mining.* a mineral-bearing area which a miner is permitted to work; a holding. [ME; late OE *tacan,* from Scand.; cf. Icel. *taka,* c. MD *taken* grasp, seize; akin to Goth. *tēkan* touch] – **taker,** *n.*

**takeable** /ˈteɪkəbəl/, *adj.* of or pertaining to something one is permitted to take, as a fish above a legally specified minimum size. Also, **takable.** [TAKE + -ABLE]

**take-all** /ˈteɪk-ɔl/, *n.* a disease of wheat caused by the fungus, *Ophiobolus graminis,* which attacks the base of the plant.

**takeaway** /ˈteɪkəweɪ/, *n.* **1.** a hot or cold meal purchased for consumption elsewhere. *–adj.* **2.** of or pertaining to such a meal or the place where it is sold.

**take-down** /ˈteɪk-daʊn/, *n. Colloq.* **1.** the state of being humbled, disadvantaged. **2.** a fraudulent transaction.

**take-home pay** /ˈteɪk-hoʊm ˌpeɪ/, *n.* salary remaining after all deductions, esp. tax deductions, have been made.

**take-off** /ˈteɪk-ɒf/, *n.* **1.** the leaving of the ground, as in leaping or jumping. **2.** the place or point at which one leaves the ground, as in jumping. **3.** the initial phase of an aeroplane flight in which the aeroplane leaves the ground. **4.** *Showjumping.* the initial phase of the leap made by a horse attempting to jump an obstacle. **5.** *Colloq.* an imitating or mimicking; caricature.

**takeover** /ˈteɪkoʊvə/, *n.* **1.** acquisition of control, esp. of a business company, by the purchase of the majority of its shares. **2.** the acquisition of control over another country, usu. by means of force. *–adj.* **3.** denoting or pertaining to such acquisition: *a takeover bid.*

**take-up** /ˈteɪk-ʌp/, *n.* **1.** the act of taking up. **2.** a stop where a bus, tram, etc., will take up passengers. **3.** *Mach.* any device for taking up slack, speed or lost motion.

**take-up spool** /ˈ– spul/, *n.* (in a tape-recorder, cine-projector, etc.) a spool which receives the tape or film after it has been played or projected.

**taking** /ˈteɪkɪŋ/, *n.* **1.** the act of one who or that which takes. **2.** the state of being taken. **3.** that which is taken. **4.** (*pl.*) receipts. *–adj.* **5.** captivating, winning or pleasing. – **takingly,** *adv.* – **takingness,** *n.*

**tala** /ˈtalə/, *n.* a rhythmic pattern in Indian music. [Hindi]

**talapoin** /ˈtæləpɔɪn/, *n.* a small, yellowish monkey, *Cercopithecus talapoin,* of West Africa, the smallest of the guenons. [F: Buddhist monk, talapoin (from fancied resemblance), from Pg., from Mon (Talaing) *tala pôi* my lord]

**talc** /tælk/, *n., v.,* **talcked** or **talced** /tælkt/, **talcking** or **talcing** /ˈtælkɪŋ/. *–n.* **1.** Also, **talcum** /ˈtælkəm/. a soft greenish grey mineral, hydrous magnesium silicate, $Mg_3Si_4O_{10}(OH)_2$ or $3MgO \cdot 4SiO_2 \cdot H_2O$, unctuous to the touch, and occurring usu. in foliated, granular or fibrous masses, used in making lubricants, talcum powder, electrical insulation, etc. *–v.t.* **2.** to treat or rub with talc. [ML *talcum,* from Ar *ṭalq*]

**talcose** /ˈtælkoʊs/, *adj.* containing, or composed largely of, talc. Also, **talcous** /ˈtælkəs/.

**talcum powder** /ˈtælkəm paʊdə/, *n.* powdered talc or soapstone, usu. perfumed for toilet use.

**tale** /teɪl/, *n.* **1.** a narrative purporting to relate the facts about some real or imaginary event, incident, or case; a story. **2.** a literary composition having the form of such a narrative: *Chaucer's 'Canterbury Tales'.* **3.** a falsehood; lie. **4.** a rumour or piece of gossip, esp. when malicious. **5.** *Archaic.* the full number or amount. **6.** *Archaic.* enumeration, numbering, or counting. **7.** *Obs.* talk or discourse. [ME; OE *talu* reckoning, speech, c. D *taal* speech, language, G *Zahl* number]

**tale-bearer** /ˈteɪl-bɛərə/, *n.* one who carries tales or gossip likely to breed mischief. – **tale-bearing,** *adj., n.*

**talent** /ˈtælənt/, *n.* **1.** a special natural ability or aptitude: *a talent for drawing.* **2.** a capacity for achievement or success; natural ability: *young men of talent.* **3.** persons of ability. **4.** a power of mind or body considered as committed to one for use and improvement (from the parable in Matt. 25: 14-30). **5.** an ancient unit of weight, varying with time and place, the later Attic talent being estimated at about 26 kg and the Hebrew talent about double this. **6.** this weight of gold, silver, or the like as a monetary unit. **7.** *Obs.* inclination or disposition. **8.** *Colloq.* at a party, dance, etc., women or men viewed as possible sexual partners. **9.** (in television and radio) anyone who is either invited as a guest or employed as a performer on a particular program. [ME and OE *talente,* from L *talenta,* pl. of *talentum,* from Gk *tálanton* (defs 5 and 6); def. 7 from OF *talent*]

**talented** /ˈtæləntəd/, *adj.* having talent; gifted.

**talent scout** /ˈtælənt skaʊt/, *n.* a person whose business is to discern and engage people with potential talent, esp. in the entertainment business.

**taler** /ˈtalə/, *n., pl.* **-ler.** →**thaler.**

**tales** /ˈteɪliz/, *n.* **1.** (*orig. as pl.*) persons chosen from among the bystanders or those present in court to serve on the jury when the original panel has become deficient in number. **2.** the order or writ summoning them. [ML *tālēs* (*dē circumstantibus*) such (of the bystanders)]

**talesman** /ˈteɪlizmən, ˈteɪlzmən/, *n., pl.* **-men.** a person summoned as one of the tales.

**taleteller** /ˈteɪltɛlə/, *n.* a tale-bearer. – **taletelling,** *adj., n.*

**tali-,** a word element meaning 'ankle', as in *taligrade.* [combining form representing L *tālus*]

**taligrade** /ˈtæləgreɪd/, *adj. Zool.* walking on the outer side of the foot.

**talion** /ˈtæljən/, *n.* retaliation as authorised by law, esp. when the punishment inflicted corresponds in kind and degree to the injury, as 'eye for eye' (Lev. 24:20). [ME, from L *tāliō*]

**taliped** /ˈtæləpɛd/, *adj.* **1.** (of a foot) twisted or distorted out of shape or position. **2.** (of a person) club-footed. *–n.* **3.** a taliped person or animal.

**talipes** /ˈtæləpiz/, *n.* **1.** →**club foot.** **2.** the condition of being club-footed. [TALI- + L *pēs* foot]

**talipot** /ˈtæləpɒt/, *n.* a tall palm, *Corypha umbraculifera* of southern India and Ceylon, whose large leaves are much used for making fans and umbrellas, for covering houses, and in place of writing paper. [Malayalam *tālipat,* from Hind. *tālpat,* from Skt *tālapattra* leaf of the fan palm]

**talisman** /ˈtæləzmən/, *n., pl.* **-mans.** **1.** a stone, ring, or other object, engraved with figures or characters under certain superstitious observances of the heavens, which is supposed to possess occult powers, and is worn as an amulet or charm. **2.** any amulet or charm. **3.** anything of almost magic power. [Ar. *tilsaman,* pl. of *tilsam* from LGk *têlesma* talisman, (earlier) religious rite, performance, completion] – **talismanic** /tæləzˈmænɪk/, **talismanical** /tæləzˈmænɪkəl/, *adj.*

**talk** /tɔk/, *v.i.* **1.** to speak or converse; perform the act of speaking. **2.** to make known or interchange ideas, information, etc., by means of spoken words. **3.** to consult or confer. **4.** to gossip. **5.** to chatter or prate. **6.** to reveal information: *to make a spy talk.* **7.** to communicate ideas by other means than speech, as by writing, signs, or signals. **8.** to make sounds imitative or suggestive of human speech. *–v.t.* **9.** to express in words; utter: *to talk sense.* **10.** to use as a spoken language; speak: *he can talk three languages.* **11.** to discuss: *to talk politics.* **12.** to persuade, bring, put, influence, etc., by talk: *to talk a person into buying something.* *–v.* **13.** Some special verb phrases are:
**talk back,** to reply sharply, rudely: to argue with. (fol. by *to* or *at*).
**talk big,** *Colloq.* to speak boastfully.
**talk (someone** or **something) down, 1.** to override in argument by speaking in a loud, persistent manner. **2.** *Aeron.* to radio landing instructions to (an aircraft or pilot) when landing is difficult.
**talk down to,** to speak condescendingly to.
**talk into,** to persuade someone to take some course, esp. against his original intention.
**talk out, 1.** to resolve (differences) by discussion: *unions and management usually attempt to talk out their differences before resorting to industrial action.* **2.** *Parl. Proc.* to thwart (the passage of a piece of legislation) by prolonging discussion until the adjournment.
**talk over,** to discuss.
**talk round, 1.** to discuss generally and discursively, without coming to the essential point. **2.** to persuade; bring around to one's own way of thinking.
*–n.* **14.** the act of talking; speech; conversation, esp. of a familiar or informal kind. **15.** a lecture or informal speech. **16.** a conference. **17.** report or rumour; gossip. **18.** a subject or occasion of talking, esp. of gossip. **19.** mere empty speech. **20.** a way of talking: *baby talk.* **21.** language, dialect, or lingo. **22.** sound imitative or suggestive of human speech: *the talk of monkeys.* **23. talk off the top of one's head, a.** to speak without prior preparation. **b.** to speak nonsense. **24. talk through the back of one's neck,** to talk nonsense. [ME, c. East Fris. *talken;* akin to TALE, *n.,* TELL, *v.*] **– talkable,** *adj.* **– talker,** *n.* **– talkatively,** *adv.* **– talkativeness,** *n.*

**talkative** /ˈtɔkətɪv/, *adj.* inclined to talk a great deal. **– talkatively,** *adv.* **– talkativeness,** *n.*

**talkback** /ˈtɔkbæk/, *n.* **1.** *Television, Radio, etc.* a communications system enabling spoken directions from the control room to be conveyed to cameramen, directors, comperes, actors, etc., in the studio. **2.** a radio program in which members of the public participate by telephone. *–adj.* **3.** of or pertaining to such a radio program.

**talkdown** /ˈtɔkdaʊn/, *n.* the radioing of instructions to an aircraft to enable it to land in fog or other difficult circumstances.

**talkie** /ˈtɔki/, *n. Colloq.* a film (def. 4) having a soundtrack.

**talking book** /tɔkɪŋ ˈbʊk/, *n.* a tape recording of a book, for the use of the blind.

**talking head** /– ˈhɛd/, *n.* a person interviewed or speaking at length on television.

**talking picture** /– ˈpɪktʃə/, *n. Obs.* a film (def. 4) with a soundtrack.

**talking point** /ˈ– pɔɪnt/, *n.* a subject for discussion or dispute.

**talking shop** /ˈ– ʃɒp/, *n. Colloq.* parliament.

**talking-to** /ˈtɔkɪŋ-tu/, *n. Colloq.* a scolding.

**talk show** /ˈtɔk ʃoʊ/, *n. Colloq.* an informal interview program on television or radio. Also, **chat show.**

**tall** /tɔl/, *adj.* **1.** having a relatively great stature; of more than average height: *tall grass.* **2.** having stature or height as specified: *a man 1·9 metres tall.* **3.** *Colloq.* high, great, or large in amount: *a tall price.* **4.** *Colloq.* extravagant; difficult to believe: *a tall story.* **5.** *Colloq.* difficult to accomplish: *a tall order.* **6.** *Colloq.* high-flown or grandiloquent. [ME *tal,* OE *getæl* prompt; c. OHG *gizal* swift, OS *gital* quick] **– tallish,** *adj.* **– tallness,** *n.*

**tallage** /ˈtælɪdʒ/, *n.* **1.** a tax imposed upon the tenants of a manor by the lord. **2.** a compulsory tax levied by the Norman and early Angevin kings of England upon the demesne lands of the Crown and upon all royal towns. [ME, from OF *taillage,* from *taillier* cut, limit, tax]

**tallboy** /ˈtɔlbɔɪ/, *n.* **1.** a tall chest of drawers supported on a low stand. **2.** a tall chimneypot. **3.** a tall-stemmed glass for wine, etc.

**tall hat** /ˈtɔl hæt/, *n.* →**top hat.**

**tallith** /ˈtælɪθ/, *n.* a mantle or a scarf-like garment with fringes at the four corners, worn over the shoulders by male Jews at prayer. [Heb., from *tālal* cover]

**tall oil** /ˈtal ɔɪl/, *n.* a resinous secondary product resulting from the manufacture of chemical wood pulp, used in making soaps, etc. [Swed. *tallöl* pine beer]

**tallow** /ˈtæloʊ/, *n.* **1.** the fatty tissue or suet of animals. **2.** the harder fat of sheep, cattle, etc., separated by melting from the fibrous and membranous matter naturally mixed with it, and used to make candles, soap, etc. **3.** any of various similar fatty substances: *vegetable tallow.* *–v.t.* **4.** to smear with tallow. *–v.i.* **5.** to produce tallow. [ME *talgh,* c. G *Talg*] **– tallow-like,** *adj.* **– tallowy,** *adj.*

**tallowwood** /ˈtæloʊwʊd/, *n.* **1.** a large tree, *Eucalyptus microcorys,* family Myrtaceae, of New South Wales and Queensland, growing in coastal forests and yielding a strong timber and nectar much prized by apiarists. **2.** →**banyalla.**

**tall poppy** /tɔl ˈpɒpi/, *n. Colloq.* a person who is outstanding in any way.

**tall posture** /ˈ– pɒstʃə/, *n.* a position of strength, as in argument or negotiation.

**tall story** /– ˈstɔri/, *n.* a far-fetched or incredible tale. Also, **tall tale.**

**tally** /ˈtæli/, *n., pl.* **-lies,** *v.,* **-lied, lying.** *–n.* **1.** (formerly) a stick of wood with notches cut to indicate the amount of a debt or payment, often split lengthwise across the notches, the debtor retaining one piece and the creditor the other. **2.** anything on which a score or account is kept. **3.** a notch or mark made on or in a tally. **4.** an account or reckoning; a record of debit and credit, of the score of a game, or the like. **5.** a number or group of objects recorded. **6. a.** a mark made to register a certain number of objects, in keeping account, as, for instance, a group of five. **b.** the number of sheep shorn in a given period. **7.** a number of objects serving as a unit of computation. **8.** a ticket, label, or mark used as a means of identification, etc. **9.** anything corresponding to another thing as a counterpart. *–v.t.* **10.** to mark or enter on a tally; register; record. **11.** to count or reckon up. **12.** to furnish with a tally or identifying label. **13.** to cause to correspond or agree. *–v.i.* **14.** to correspond, as one part of a tally with the other; accord or agree: *Does his story tally with John's?* [ME *taly,* from AF *tallie,* from L *tālea* rod. See TAIL[2]] **– tallier,** *n.*

**tallyclerk** /ˈtæliklak/, *n.* a clerk employed to check cargoes and other goods against a list or manifest.

**tally-hi** /tæli-ˈhaɪ/, *n.* a modern Australian method of shearing which results in higher tallies and cleaner shearing.

**tally-ho** /tæli-ˈhoʊ/, *n., pl.* **-hos,** *interj., v.,* **-hoed** or **-ho'd, -hoing.** *–n.* **1.** a mail coach or a four-in-hand pleasure coach. **2.** a cry of 'tally-ho'. *–interj.* **3.** (a huntsman's cry on catching sight of the fox). *–v.t.* **4.** to arouse (hounds in hunting, etc.) by crying 'tally-ho'. *–v.i.* **5.** to utter a cry of 'tally-ho'. [F *taiaut*]

**tallyman** /ˈtælimæn/, *n., pl.* **-men. 1.** →**tallyclerk. 2.** one who sells goods, esp. cheap and shoddy goods, and collects payment by instalments. **3.** a man who lives with a woman outside marriage. **– tallywoman,** *n.fem.*

**tally-room** /ˈtæli-rum/, *n.* a room in which voting figures for an election are collated and from which progress reports are disseminated.

**tallyshop** /ˈtæliʃɒp/, *n.* a shop where goods are sold to be paid for by instalments.

**Talmud** /ˈtælmʊd/, *n.* **1.** the two commentaries on the Mishnah, one produced in Palestine (in about A.D. 375) and the other in Babylonia (in about A.D. 500). **2.** the Mishnah and the commentary on it. [Heb.: study, instruction] **– Talmudic** /tælˈmʊdɪk/, **Talmudical** /tælˈmʊdɪkəl/, *adj.*

**Talmudist** /ˈtælmʊdəst/, *n.* **1.** one of the writers or compilers of the Talmud. **2.** one who accepts the doctrines of the Talmud. **3.** one versed in the Talmud.

**talon** /ˈtælən/, *n.* **1.** a claw, esp. of a bird of prey. **2.** *Colloq.* a finger or fingernail, esp. when regarded as grasping or attacking. **3.** (in a lock) the shoulder on the bolt against which the key presses in shooting the bolt. **4.** *Cards.* the cards left over after the deal; the stock. [ME, from OF: heel, from LL *tālo* talon, replacing L *tālus* ankle, heel] – **taloned,** *adj.*

**talus**[1] /ˈteɪləs/, *n., pl.* **-li** /-laɪ/. →**astragalus.** [L]

**talus**[2] /ˈteɪləs/, *n.* **1.** a slope. **2.** *Geol.* a sloping mass of rocky fragments at the base of a cliff. **3.** *Fort.* the sloping side or face of a wall. [F, from L: ankle]

**talweg** /ˈtalvɛg, -wɛg/, *n.* →**thalweg.**

**tam** /tæm/, *n.* →**tam-o'-shanter.**

**tamable** /ˈteɪməbəl/, *adj.* →**tameable.**

**tamale** /təˈmali/, *n.* a Mexican dish made of crushed maize and minced meat, seasoned with red peppers, etc., wrapped in maize husks, and steamed. Also, **tamal.** [backformation from *tamales,* from Mex. Sp., pl. of *tamal,* from Aztec *tamalli*]

**tamandua** /tæmənˈduə/, *n.* the four-toed anteater, *Tamandua tetradactyla,* a prehensile-tailed, arboreal edentate of the forests of tropical America. Also, **tamandu** /tæmənˈdu/. [Pg., from Tupi, from *taa* ant + *munden* trap]

tamandua

**tamara** /təˈmarə/, *n.* a mixture of spices, esp. cinnamon and cloves, used in Italian cooking.

**tamarack** /ˈtæməræk/, *n.* **1.** an American larch, *Larix laricina,* yielding a useful timber. **2.** any of several very similar related trees. **3.** the wood of these trees. [N Amer. Ind. (Algonquian)]

**tamarau** /ˈtæməraʊ/, *n.* a small, sturdy wild buffalo, *Babalus mindorensis,* of Mindoro, in the Philippines, having thick brown hair and short, massive horns. [Tagalog]

**tamarillo** /tæməˈrɪloʊ/, *n.* →**tree tomato.**

**tamarin** /ˈtæmərən/, *n.* any of various South American primates of the genus *Callithrix,* allied to the marmosets, lacking ear tufts and tail rings. [F, from Carib d.]

**tamarind** /ˈtæmərənd/, *n.* **1.** the fruit of a large tropical tree, *Tamarindus indica,* a pod containing seeds enclosed in a juicy acid pulp that is used in beverages and food. **2.** the tree, cultivated throughout the tropics for its fruit, fragrant flowers, shade and timber. [ML *tamarindus,* from Ar. *tamrhindī* date of India]

tamarind

**tamarisk** /ˈtæmərəsk/, *n.* a plant of the Old World genus *Tamarix,* esp. *T. gallica,* native to the Mediterranean region, an ornamental shrub or small tree with slender, feathery branches. [ME *tamariscus,* from LL. Cf. L *tamarix*]

**tamasha** /təˈmaʃə/, *n.* (in the East Indies) a spectacle; entertainment. [Urdu, from Ar.: a short walk]

**Tambaroora muster** /tæmbəˌrurə ˈmʌstə/, *n.* a bar game where men put an agreed amount of money in a hat and gamble for it, the winner shouting a round of drinks with his winnings. [from the *Tambaroora* N.S.W., a goldrush town of the 1860s]

**tambour** /ˈtæmbʊə/, *n.* **1.** a drum. **2.** a drummer. **3.** a circular frame consisting of two hoops, one fitting within the other, in which cloth is stretched for embroidering. **4.** embroidery done on this. **5.** a vestibule in a church porch. **6.** *Royal Tennis.* a sloping buttress in the court. *–adj.* **7.** shaped like a drum, as the rolling mechanism of a roll-top desk. *–v.t., v.i.* **8.** to embroider on a tambour. [late ME, from F. See TABOR]

**tamboura** /tæmˈburə/, *n.* an Indian musical instrument, with four strings and a long neck without frets, used to provide a drone accompaniment to the sitar or sarod. Also, **tambura.** [Pers. *tanbūr*]

**tambourin** /ˈtæmbərɪn/, *n.* **1.** a Provençal dance in 2/4 time, with a drone bass. **2.** the tune or rhythm for this dance.

**tambourine** /tæmbəˈrin/, *n.* a small drum consisting of a circular wooden frame with a skin stretched over it and several pairs of jingles (metal discs) inserted into the frame, played by striking with the knuckles, shaking, etc. [F *tambourin,* diminutive of *tambour* TAMBOUR] – **tambourinist,** *n.*

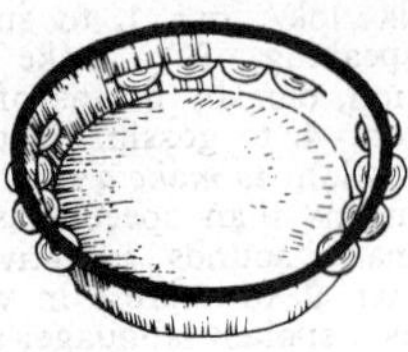
tambourine

**tambura** /tæmˈburə/, *n.* →**tamboura.**

**tame** /teɪm/, *adj.,* **tamer, tamest,** *v.,* **tamed, taming.** *–adj.* **1.** changed from the wild or savage state; domesticated: *a tame bear.* **2.** gentle, fearless, or without shyness, as if domesticated, as an animal. **3.** tractable, docile, or submissive, as a person, the disposition, etc. **4.** lacking in animation; dull; insipid: *a tame existence.* **5.** spiritless or pusillanimous. **6.** cultivated, or improved by cultivation, as a plant, its fruit, etc. **7.** local: *a tame genius.* **8.** rendered manageable for human or domestic use: *a tame water supply.* *–v.t.* **9.** to make tame; domesticate; make tractable; subdue. **10.** to deprive of courage, ardour, or interest. **11.** to soften; tone down. **12.** to bring under control or render manageable, as for domestic or human use: *to tame the natural resources of a country.* [ME; OE *tam,* c. G *zahm;* akin to Goth. *tamjan,* v., L *domāre*] – **tameability, tamability** /teɪməˈbɪləti/, **tameableness, tamableness,** *n.* – **tameable, tamable,** *adj.* – **tamely,** *adv.* – **tameness,** *n.* – **tamer,** *n.*

**tameable** /ˈteɪməbəl/, *adj.* that may be tamed. Also, **tamable.**

**tameless** /ˈteɪmləs/, *adj.* untamed or untameable. – **tamelessness,** *n.*

**Tamil** /ˈtæməl/, *n.* **1.** a member of a people of Dravidian stock of southern India and Sri Lanka. **2.** their language, spoken chiefly to the south of Madras. *–adj.* **3.** of or pertaining to the Tamils or their language.

**tamis** /ˈtæmi, -əs/, *n., pl.* **tamises** /ˈtæmiz, ˈtæməsiz/. a cloth sieve or strainer. Also, **tammy.** [F: sieve; replacing OE *temes*]

**Tammany-Hall** /ˌtæməni-ˈhɔl/, *adj.* employing methods of exerting political influence which are unscrupulous or corrupt. [orig. ref. to a fraternal benevolent society (*Tammany Society*), a political organisation in New York, founded 1789. From Amer. Ind. *taminy,* a form of name of an Indian Chief]

**tammar** /ˈtæmə/, *n.* a small scrub wallaby, *Macropus eugenii,* of south and south-western Australia and offshore islands. Also, **dama.** [Aboriginal]

**tammy**[1] /ˈtæmi/, *n.* a fabric of glazed woollen or mixed fibres, used for linings, underwear, etc. [orig. unknown]

**tammy**[2] /ˈtæmi/, *n., pl.* **-mies,** *v.,* **-mied, mying.** *–n.* **1.** →**tamis.** *–v.t.* **2.** *Cookery.* to strain a sauce through a tamis to give the sauce an especially smooth texture and glossy appearance.

**tam-o'-shanter** /tæm-ə-ˈʃæntə/, *n.* a cap, of Scottish origin, with a flat crown larger in diameter than the headband. Also, **tam, tammy.** [named after *Tam O'Shanter,* the hero of a poem by Robert Burns, 1759-96, Scottish poet]

tam-o'-shanter

**tamp** /tæmp/, *v.t.* **1.** to force in or down by repeated, somewhat light strokes. **2.** (in blasting) to fill (the hole made by the drill) with earth, etc., after the powder or explosive has been introduced. [apparently akin to TAMPION]

**tamper**[1] /ˈtæmpə/, *v.i.* **1.** to meddle, esp. for the purpose of altering, damaging, misusing, etc. (fol. by *with*): *to tamper with a lock.* **2.** to engage secretly or improperly in something. **3.** to undertake underhand or corrupt dealings, as in order to influence improperly (fol. by *with*): *to tamper with a witness.* [var. of TEMPER, *v.*] – **tamperer,** *n.*

**tamper**[2] /ˈtæmpə/, *n.* one who or that which tamps. [TAMP + -ER[1]]

**tampion** /ˈtæmpiən/, *n.* a wooden plug or stopper placed in the muzzle of a piece of ordnance when not in use, to keep out dampness and dust. Also, **tompion.** [F *tampon,* variant of *tapon,* from *tape* plug]

**tampon** /ˈtæmpɒn/, *n.* **1.** a plug of cotton or the like inserted into an orifice, wound, etc., as to stop haemorrhage. **2.** a

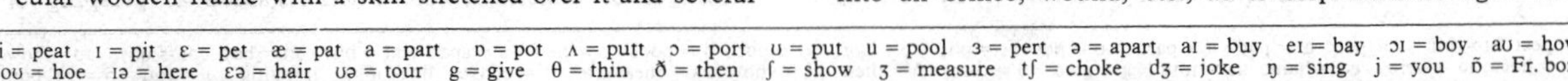
i = peat ɪ = pit ɛ = pet æ = pat a = part ɒ = pot ʌ = putt ɔ = port ʊ = put u = pool ɜ = pert ə = apart aɪ = buy eɪ = bay ɔɪ = boy aʊ = how
oʊ = hoe ɪə = here ɛə = hair ʊə = tour g = give θ = thin ð = then ʃ = show ʒ = measure tʃ = choke dʒ = joke ŋ = sing j = you õ = Fr. bon

similar device used internally to absorb menstrual flow. *–v.t.* **3.** to fill or plug with a tampon. [F. See TAMPION]

**tamponade** /tæmpə'neɪd/, *n.* **1.** *Surg.* the use of a tampon, as to stop haemorrhage. **2.** *Pathol.* a condition in which the action of the heart is impaired because of pressure created by fluid collecting in the pericardium.

**tam-tam** /'tæm-tæm/, *n.* **1.** a gong with indefinite pitch. **2.** →**tom-tom.** [var. of TOM-TOM]

**tan**[1] /tæn/, *v.*, **tanned, tanning,** *n., adj.* *–v.t.* **1.** to convert (a hide) into a leather, esp. by soaking or steeping in a bath prepared from bark, as wattle, etc., or synthetically. **2.** to make brown by exposure to ultraviolet rays, as of the sun. **3.** *Colloq.* to beat or thrash: *to tan one's hide.* *–v.i.* **4.** to become tanned. *–n.* **5.** the brown colour imparted to the skin by exposure to the sun or open air; suntan. **6.** yellowish or tawny brown. **7.** the bark of the wattle, oak, etc., bruised and broken by a mill, and used for tanning hides. *–adj.* **8.** of the colour of tan; tawny or yellowish brown. **9.** used in or relating to tanning processes, materials, etc. [ME *tanne,* late OE *tannian,* from ML *tannāre,* from *tannum,* n.] – **tannable,** *adj.* **able,** *adj.*

**tan**[2] /tæn/, *n.* →**tangent.** (def. 5).

**tana** /'tanə/, *n.* a large tree shrew of the family Tupaiidae, *Tupaia tana,* of Sumatra and Borneo. [Malay (*tupai*) *tanah* ground (shrew)]

**tanager** /'tænədʒə/, *n.* any of numerous small, usu. brightly coloured oscinine birds constituting the New World family Thraupidae, most of which inhabit the warmer parts of South America. [NL *tanagra,* from Tupi *tangara*]

**tanagrine** /'tænəgrin/, *adj.* of or pertaining to the tanagers; belonging to the tanager family.

**tanbark** /'tænbak/, *n.* **1.** bark used in tanning; tan. **2.** such bark, after the tanning process is completed, broken up in chips and used as a ground-cover, as in playgrounds, landscape gardening, etc.,

**tandan** /'tændən/, *n.* any of various Australian eel-tailed catfishes, particularly freshwater forms of the genera *Tandanus* and *Neosilurus;* dewfish; dhufish. [Aboriginal]

**tandem** /'tændəm/, *adv.* **1.** one behind another; in single file: *to drive horses tandem.* *–adj.* **2.** having animals, seats, parts, etc., arranged tandem, or one behind another: *a tandem bicycle.* *–n.* **3.** a bicycle for two riders, having twin seats, pedals, etc. **4.** a team of horses harnessed in tandem. **5.** *Rowing.* a method of rigging the boat to allow successive oarsmen on the same side of the boat to neutralise uneven thrust. **6.** a two-wheeled carriage, with a high driver's seat, drawn by two or more horses. **7.** any mechanism having a tandem arrangement. **8. in tandem,** one behind the other. [L: at length (in time), probably at first humorously used]

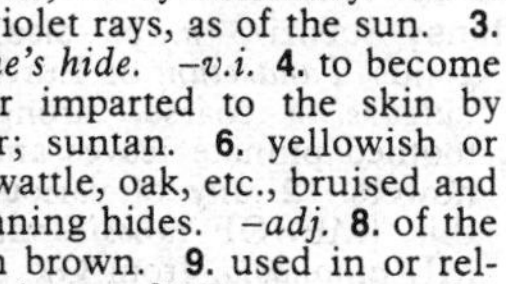

tandem (def. 6)

**tandem generator** /– 'dʒɛnəreɪtə/, *n.* an accelerator consisting of two electrostatic generators in tandem.

**tandem trailer** /– 'treɪlə/, *n.* a large trailer on four wheels.

**tanekaha** /tanə'kaha/, *n. N.Z.* →**celery-top pine.** [Maori]

**tang** /tæŋ/, *n.* **1.** a strong taste or flavour. **2.** the distinctive flavour or quality of a thing. **3.** a pungent or distinctive smell. **4.** a smack, touch, or suggestion of something. **5.** a long and slender projecting strip, tongue, or prong forming part of an object, as a chisel, file, knife, etc., and serving as a means of attachment for another part, as a handle or stock. **6.** →**surgeonfish.** **7.** the white-fronted chat. *–v.t.* **8.** to furnish with a tang. [ME *tange,* from Scand.; cf. Icel. *tangi* pointed object, akin to TONG[1]]

**tangelo** /'tændʒəloʊ/, *n., pl.* **-los.** **1.** a hybrid between the tangerine and the pomelo (grapefruit) tree. **2.** its fruit. [b. TANG(ERINE) and (POM)ELO]

**tangency** /'tændʒənsi/, *n.* the state of being tangent.

**tangent** /'tændʒənt/, *adj.* **1.** touching. **2.** *Geom.* touching, as a straight line in relation to a curve or surface; passing through two (or more) consecutive points of a curve or surface. **3.** in contact along a single line or element, as a plane with a cylinder. *–n.* **4.** *Geom.* a tangent line or plane. **5.** *Maths.* a trigonometric function, defined for an acute angle in a right angled triangle as the ratio of the opposite side to the adjacent side, and defined for angles of any sine as the ratio of the sine of the angle to the cosine of the angle. *Abbrev:* tan. **6.** *Survey.* the straight portion of a survey line between curves, as on railway or road alignment. **7.** the metal pin that strikes the strings on a clavichord, causing it to sound. **8.** a sudden divergence from one course, thought, etc., to another: *to fly off at a tangent.* [L *tangens,* ppr., touching]

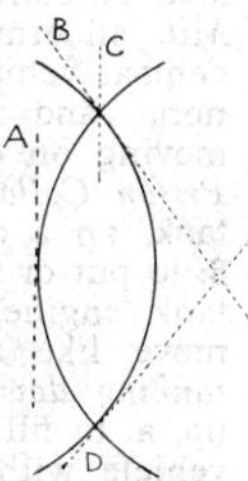

tangents: A, ordinary; B, inflectional; C, cuspidal; D, nodal

**tangent galvanometer** /– gælvə'nɒmətə/, *n.* a galvanometer consisting of a coil of wire held in a vertical plane parallel to the earth's magnetic field with a small magnetic needle pivoted at the centre of the coil; the current passing through the coil is proportional to the tangent of the angle of deflection of the needle.

**tangential** /tæn'dʒɛnʃəl/, *adj.* **1.** pertaining to or of the nature of a tangent; being or moving in the direction of a tangent. **2.** merely touching; slightly connected. **3.** divergent or digressive. Also, **tangental** /tæn'dʒɛntl/. – **tangentially,** *adv.*

**tangerine** /tændʒə'rin/, *n.* **1.** a small, loose-skinned variety of mandarin. See **mandarin** (def. 5). **2.** deep orange; reddish orange. *–adj.* **3.** of a deep orange colour. [*Tangier,* a seaport in N Morocco, + -INE[1]]

**tangi** /'tʌŋi/, *n. N.Z.* **1.** a Maori mourning for the dead; a wake. *–v.i.* **2.** to mourn; to take part in a tangi. [Maori]

**tangible** /'tændʒəbəl/, *adj.* **1.** capable of being touched; discernible by the touch; material or substantial. **2.** real or actual, rather than imaginary or visionary. **3.** definite; not vague or elusive: *no tangible grounds for suspicion.* **4.** (of an asset) capable of being possessed or realised; having the form of real property or chattels. *–n.* **5.** (*usu. pl.*) something capable of being possessed or realised. [L *tangibilis*] – **tangibility** /tændʒə'bɪləti/, **tangibleness,** *n.* – **tangibly,** *adv.*

**tangle** /'tæŋgəl/, *v.*, **-gled, -gling,** *n.* *–v.t.* **1.** to bring together into a mass of confusedly interlaced or intertwisted threads, strands, or other like parts; snarl. **2.** to involve in something that hampers, obstructs, or overgrows: *bushes tangled with vines.* **3.** to catch and hold in, or as in, a net or snare. *–v.i.* **4.** to be or become tangled. **5.** *Colloq.* to conflict, quarrel, or argue (usu. fol. by *with*). *–n.* **6.** a tangled condition. **7.** a tangled or confused mass or assemblage of something. **8.** a confused jumble: *a tangle of contradictory statements.* **9.** *Colloq.* a conflict, quarrel, or disagreement. [ME *tangil,* nasalised var. of *tagil* entangle, from Scand.; cf. d. Swed. *taggla* disarrange] – **tangler,** *n.* – **tangly,** *adj.*

**tangle orchid** /– ɔkəd/, *n.* an epiphytic orchid, *Plectorrhiza tridentata,* common in dense forests of eastern Australia.

**tango** /'tæŋgoʊ/, *n., pl.* **-gos,** *v.*, **-goed, -going.** *–n.* **1.** a dance of Spanish-American origin, danced by couples, and having many varied steps, figures, and poses. **2.** music for this dance. *–v.i.* **3.** to dance the tango. [Amer. Sp.] – **tangoist,** *n.*

**tangram** /'tæŋgræm/, *n.* a Chinese puzzle consisting of a square cut into five triangles, a square, and a rhomboid, which can be combined so as to form a great variety of other figures.

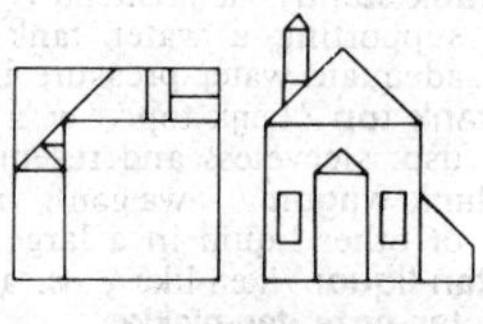

tangram: A, the square card; B, an assembly of its pieces representing a house

**tangy** /'tæŋi/, *adj.*, **tangier, tangiest.** having a tang.

**tanh** /θæn, tæn'eɪtʃ/, *n.* See **hyperbolic functions.**

**tanist** /'tænəst/, *n.* the successor apparent to a Celtic chief, usu. the oldest or worthiest of his kin, chosen by election among the tribe during the chief's lifetime. [Irish, Gaelic *tānaiste* immediate heir to estate]

**tanistry** /'tænəstri/, *n.* the system among various Celtic tribes of choosing a tanist.

**taniwha** /'tʌnifa, 'tænəwa/, *n. N.Z.* a mythical water monster. [Maori]

**tank** /tæŋk/, *n.* **1.** a large receptacle or structure for holding water or other liquid or a gas: *tanks for storing oil.* **2.** an artificial pond made by building walls of earth either excavated or conveyed to the site. **3.** *Mil.* an armoured, self-propelled combat vehicle, armed with cannon, and machine-guns and moving on caterpillar tracks. **4.** *Prison Colloq.* a safe. **5. on the tank,** on a drinking spree. *–v.t.* **6.** to put or store in a tank. **7.** a tank engine. *–v.i.* **8.** *Colloq.* to move like a tank: *a footballer tanking down the wing.* **9. tank up, a.** to fill the tank of a motor vehicle with fuel. **b.** *Colloq.* to drink heavily. [Gujarati *tānkh* pool; replacing ME *stank,* from OF *estanc* pool. See STANCH[1]] **–tankless,** *adj.* **–tanklike,** *adj.*

tank (def. 3)

**tanka**[1] /'tæŋkə/, *n.* a Japanese poem or verse form of 31 syllables arranged in 5 lines, of which the first and third have 5 syllables and the other lines 7 each. [Japanese *tanka* short verse]

**tanka**[2] /'tæŋkə/, *n.* a Tibetan religious scroll painting, usu. displayed as a banner. [Tibetan *thaṅka*]

**tankage** /'tæŋkɪdʒ/, *n.* **1.** the capacity of a tank or tanks. **2.** the act or process of storing liquid in a tank. **3.** the price charged for this. **4.** *Brit.* the residue from tanks in which carcases and other offal have been steamed and the fat has been rendered, used as a fertiliser.

**tankard** /'tæŋkəd/, *n.* a large drinking cup, now usu. with a handle and (sometimes) a hinged cover. [ME; cf. MD *tanckaert*]

tankard

**tanked** /tæŋkt/, *adj. Colloq.* intoxicated, esp. with beer.

**tank engine** /'tæŋk ɛndʒən/, *n.* a steam locomotive that carries its own water and coal, and does not have a tender.

**tanker** /'tæŋkə/, *n.* a ship, aircraft, road or rail vehicle designed to carry oil or other liquid in bulk.

**tanker service** /'– sɜvəs/, *n.* **1.** a service for the provision of water, petrol, etc., by tanker. **2.** the pumping out of cesspits, usu. domestic, in unsewered areas.

**tank farming** /'tæŋk famɪŋ/, *n.* →**hydroponics.**

**tank furnace** /'– fɜnəs/, *n.* a furnace in which glass is melted in a bath constructed from refractory blocks.

**tank glass** /'– glas/, *n.* glass melted in a tank furnace rather than in a pot.

**tank loaf** /'– loʊf/, *n.* a loaf of bread, usu. white, baked in a cylindrical tin with corrugated sides resembling a water tank.

**tankman** /'tæŋkmən/, *n. Prison Colloq.* a person who specialises in stealing from safes.

**tank sinker** /'tæŋk sɪŋkə/, *n.* a man employed to excavate dams.

**tank-stand** /'tæŋk-stænd/, *n.* a structure of steel, stone, etc., supporting a water tank at a height sufficient to generate adequate water pressure in the pipes running from it.

**tank top** /'tæŋk tɒp/, *n.* a tight fitting garment worn as a top, usu. sleeveless and resembling a singlet.

**tank wagon** /'– wægən/, *n.* a railway wagon for carrying oil or other liquid in a large tank. Also, **tank car.**

**tan-liquor** /'tæn-lɪkə/, *n.* an aqueous extract of tanbark. Also, **tan-ooze, tan-pickle.**

**tannage** /'tænɪdʒ/, *n.* **1.** →**tanning. 2.** that which has been tanned; the product of tanning.

**tannate** /'tæneɪt/, *n.* a salt of tannic acid.

**tanner**[1] /'tænə/, *n.* one whose occupation it is to tan hides. [ME and OE *tannere.* See TAN[1]]

**tanner**[2] /'tænə/, *n. Colloq.* (formerly) sixpence.

**tannery** /'tænəri/, *n., pl.* **-neries.** a place where tanning is carried on.

**tannic** /'tænɪk/, *adj.* pertaining to, derived from, or related to tan or its tanning principle.

**tannin** /'tænən/, *n.* any of a group of astringent vegetable principles or compounds as that which gives the tanning properties to wattle bark, or that which in grape skins, stalks and seeds gives a distinctive tannin taste to some wines. [ML *tannum* TAN[1], *n.,* + -IN[2], on model of F *tanin*]

**tanning** /'tænɪŋ/, *n.* **1.** the process or art of converting hides or skins into leather. **2.** a making brown, as by exposure to the sun. **3.** *Colloq.* a thrashing.

**Tanoan** /'tanoʊən/, *n.* **1.** an American Indian linguistic stock, which includes three surviving languages spoken in pueblos in northern New Mexico, including Taos. *–adj.* **2.** of or pertaining to this stock.

**tanrec** /'tænrɛk/, *n.* →**tenrec.**

**tansy** /'tænzi/, *n., pl.* **-sies. 1.** any plant of the genus *Tanacetum* of Europe and Asia, esp. *T. vulgare,* a coarse, strong-scented herb with toothed pinnate leaves and corymbs of yellow flowers. **2.** any of various plants resembling this. [ME, OF *tanesie,* var. of *athanasie,* from ML *athanasia,* from Gk: immortality]

tansy

**tantalate** /'tæntəleɪt/, *n.* a salt of any tantalic acid.

**tantalic** /tæn'tælɪk/, *adj.* of or pertaining to tantalum, esp. in the pentavalent state.

**tantalic acid** /– 'æsəd/, *n.* an acid which forms complex salts (tantalates); tantalum pentoxide-hydrate, $Ta_2O_5 \cdot xH_2O$.

**tantalise** /'tæntəlaɪz/, *v.t.,* **-lised, -lising.** to torment with, or as with, the sight of something desired but out of reach; tease by arousing expectations that are repeatedly disappointed. Also, **tantalize.** [*Tantal(us)* + -ISE[1]. See TANTALUS] **–tantalisation** /tæntəlaɪ'zeɪʃən/, *n.* **–tantaliser,** *n.* **–tantalisingly,** *adv.*

**tantalite** /'tæntəlaɪt/, *n.* a mineral, iron tantalate, $FeTa_2O_6$, usu. containing manganese and columbium, occurring in heavy (sp. gr. 6.0-7.4) black crystals; the principal ore of tantalum.

**tantalous** /'tæntələs/, *adj.* containing trivalent tantalum.

**tantalum** /'tæntələm/, *n.* a rare element usu. associated with columbium. On account of its resistance to strong acids, it is used for handling such reactive acids as hydrochloric. *Symbol:* Ta; *at. wt:* 180.948; *at. no.:* 73; *sp. gr.:*16.6. [NL; from *Tantalus,* from its incapacity to absorb acid. See TANTALUS]

**tantalus** /'tæntələs/, *n.* a stand containing visible decanters, secured by a lock. [from *Tantalus,* in Greek mythology a son of Zeus and the nymph Pluto, who, for revealing secrets of the gods, was condemned to stand, hungry and thirsty, in water up to his chin, under a tree laden with fruit]

**tantamount** /'tæntəmaʊnt/, *adj.* equivalent, as in value, force, effect, or signification. [apparently from F *tant* (from L, *tantum* so much) + AMOUNT]

**tantara** /'tæntərə, tæn'tarə, tæntə'ra/, *n.* **1.** a blast of a trumpet or horn. **2.** any similar sound. [imitative]

**tantivy** /tæn'tɪvi/, *adv., adj., n., pl.* **-tivies,** *interj. –adv.* **1.** at full gallop or speed: *to ride tantivy. –adj.* **2.** swift; rapid. *–n.* **3.** a gallop; a rush. **4.** a hunting cry; a cry of 'tantivy'. *–interj.* **5.** (a hunting cry when the chase is at full speed). [? imitative]

**tanto** /'tæntoʊ/, *adv.* (in music) too much; so much. [It., from L *tantum* so much]

**Tantra** /'tæntrə, 'tʌn-/, *n.* **1.** *Hinduism.* one of several books in dialogue form setting out the requirements of ritual, discipline, etc. **2.** one of a similar series of Buddhist devotional books. **3.** →**Tantrism.** [Skt: lit., loom]

**Tantrism** /'tæntrɪzəm, 'tʌn-/, *n. Hinduism.* the doctrine of the books of Tantra, teaching that the visible world presents an unending dance of the believers with the Divine, in which unity of the worshipper with the worshipped is ultimately achieved.

**tantrum** /'tæntrəm/, *n.* a sudden burst of ill humour; a fit of ill temper or passion. [orig. uncert.]

**Tanzania** /tænzə'niə/, *n.* a republic in eastern Africa.

**Tao** /'teɪoʊ, taʊ, daʊ/, *n.* **1.** the concept or the Taoist philosophy, that all existence has been only in relation to an external absolute. **2.** the ideal striven for by Taoists. **3.** (in Taoist belief) the course of life and its foundation in relation to eternal truth. [Chinese: path or way (i.e. way of belief)]

**Taoism** /ˈteɪoʊˌɪzəm, ˈtaʊɪzəm, ˈdaʊɪzəm/, *n.* **1.** a philosophical system developed by Lao-tse advocating a discipline of nonintervention with the course of nature and of absolute sincerity and honesty, whereby the disciple can attain a state of harmony with Tao. **2.** a system of religious belief founded upon the teachings of Lao-tse but incorporating in its present form elements drawn from several more primitive and animistic sources, including sorcery and pantheism. It is one of the principal religions of China. – **Taoist,** *n., adj.* – **Taoistic** /teɪoʊˈɪstɪk, taʊˈɪstɪk, daʊˈɪstɪk/, *adj.*

**tap**[1] /tæp/, *v.,* **tapped, tapping,** *n.* *–v.t.* **1.** to strike lightly but audibly; strike with slight blows. **2.** to make, put, etc., by tapping. **3.** to strike (the hand, foot, etc.) lightly upon or against something. **4.** to add a thickness of leather to the sole or heel of (a boot or shoe), as in repairing. *–v.i.* **5.** to strike lightly but audibly, as to attract attention. **6.** to strike light blows. *–n.* **7.** a light but audible blow. **8.** the sound made by this. **9.** (*pl.*) *U.S. Mil.* →**last post.** **10.** a thickness of leather added to the sole or heel of a boot or shoe, as in repairing. **11.** a piece of metal attached to the toe or heel of a shoe to make the tapping of a dancer more audible. **12.** a minimum amount; skerrick: *one had done a tap of work.* **13. off tap,** *Prison Colloq.* convicted. [ME *tappen,* from F *taper* strike, slap; of Gmc orig.] – **tappable,** *adj.*

**tap**[2] /tæp/, *n., v.,* **tapped, tapping.** *–n.* **1.** any device for controlling the flow of liquid from a pipe or the like by opening or closing an orifice; a cock. **2.** a cylindrical stick, long plug, or stopper for closing an opening through which liquid is drawn, as in a cask; a spigot. **3.** the liquid, esp. beer, drawn through a particular tap. **4.** *Surg.* withdrawal of gas or fluid. **5.** a taphouse or taproom. **6.** an instrument for cutting the thread of a female screw. **7.** a hole made in tapping, as one in a pipe to furnish connection for a branch pipe. **8.** *Elect.* a connection brought out of a winding at some point between its extremities. **9.** *Archaic.* a particular kind or quality of drink. **10. on tap, a.** ready to be drawn off and served, as drink, esp. beer, in a cask. **b.** furnished with a tap or cock, as a barrel containing drink, esp. beer. **c.** ready for immediate use. *–v.t.* **11.** to draw off (liquid) by drawing out or opening a tap, or by piercing the container; draw liquid from (any vessel or reservoir). **12.** to draw the tap or plug from, or pierce (a cask, etc.). **13.** to penetrate, reach, etc., for the purpose of drawing something off: *to tap one's resources.* **14.** *Surg.* to penetrate for the purpose of drawing off fluid or gas: *tap the abdomen.* **15.** *Colloq.* to extract money from, esp. in a crafty manner. **16.** to gain or effect secret access to: *to tap telephone wires to hear conversations.* **17.** to furnish (a cask, etc.) with a tap. **18.** to cut a female screw thread in (a hole, etc.). **19.** to open outlets from (power lines, roads, pipes, etc.). [ME; OE *tæppa,* c. G *zapfen*] – **tappable,** *adj.*

**tapa** /ˈtapə/, *n.* **1.** an unwoven cloth of the Pacific islands, made by steeping and beating the inner bark of the paper-mulberry tree, *Broussonetia papyrifera.* **2.** the bark. **3.** the tree. Also, **tappa.** [Polynesian]

**tap-bolt** /ˈtæp-boʊlt/, *n.* →**stud**[1] (def. 4).

**tap-cinder** /ˈtæp-sɪndə/, *n.* slag produced in iron-founding.

**tap dance** /ˈtæp dæns, dans/, *n.* a dance in which the rhythm or rhythmical variation is audibly tapped out by the toe or heel.

**tap-dance** /ˈtæp-dæns, -dans/, *v.i.,* **-danced, -dancing.** to perform a tap dance. – **tap-dancer,** *n.*

**tape** /teɪp/, *n., v.,* **taped, taping.** *–n.* **1.** a long narrow strip of linen, cotton, or the like, used for tying garments, etc. **2.** a long narrow strip of paper, metal, etc. **3.** a tape measure. **4.** →**magnetic tape.** **5.** a string or the like stretched across the finishing line in a race and broken by the winning contestant. **6.** *Horseracing.* the starting line of a race when no barrier stalls are used, as in trotting, picnic races, etc. **7.** the ribbon of white paper on which a ticker prints quotations or news. *–v.t.* **8.** to furnish with a tape or tapes. **9.** to tie up or bind with tape. **10.** to measure with, or as if with a tape measure. **11.** to tape-record. **12. have (someone) taped,** *Colloq.* to understand thoroughly, esp. a person's weakness or guile. **13. have (something) taped,** *Colloq.* to be in complete control of or be easily able to do (something). [ME, unexplained var. of ME *tappe,* OE *tæppe* strip (of cloth)] – **taper,** *n.* – **tapeless,** *adj.* – **tapelike,** *adj.*

**tape deck** /ˈ– dɛk/, *n.* **1.** a tape-recorder without built-in amplifiers or speakers, used as a component in a high fidelity sound system. **2.** *Computers.* →**tape unit.**

**tape-grass** /ˈteɪp-gras/, *n.* a submerged aquatic plant with narrow leaves, *Vallisneria spiralis,* family Hydrocharitaceae, of warm temperate regions and frequently grown in aquaria.

**tape loop** /ˈteɪp lup/, *n.* a length of magnetic recording tape which has one end joined to the other so that it will play continuously once started.

**tape machine** /ˈ– məʃin/, *n.* a telegraphic instrument which automatically prints share prices, market reports, etc., on a tape **(ticker tape).**

**tape measure** /ˈ– mɛʒə/, *n.* a long strip or ribbon, as of linen or steel, marked with subdivisions of the foot or metre for measuring. Also, *Chiefly U.S.,* **tapeline** /ˈteɪplaɪn/.

**tape punch** /ˈ– pʌntʃ/, *n.* *Computers.* a machine which punches information on to paper tape.

**taper** /ˈteɪpə/, *v.i.* **1.** to become gradually slenderer towards one end. **2.** to grow gradually lean. *–v.t.* **3.** to make gradually smaller towards one end. **4.** to reduce gradually. *–n.* **5.** gradual diminution of width or thickness in an elongated object. **6.** gradual decrease of force, capacity, etc. **7.** a spire or slender pyramid; anything having a tapering form. **8.** a candle, esp. a very slender one. **9.** a long wick coated with wax, tallow, or the like, as for use in lighting candles or gas. **10.** a feeble light. [ME *tapere* candle, OE *tapor;* orig. uncert.] – **taperer,** *n.* – **taperingly,** *adv.*

**tape-reader** /ˈteɪp-ridə/, *n.* *Computers.* a machine that converts information on punched paper tape into electrical impulses as the tape is drawn through the machine.

**tape-record** /ˈteɪp-rəkɔd/, *v.t.* to transcribe on to magnetic tape.

**tape-recorder** /ˈteɪp-rəkɔdə/, *n.* a device for recording an electrical signal, esp. one produced by sound, in which a magnetic tape moves past an inductance coil which magnetises the tape in relation to the input signal. The signal is recovered from the magnetised tape by a playback circuit and can be erased by demagnetising the tape.

**tape-recording** /ˈteɪp-rəkɔdɪŋ/, *n.* **1.** a magnetic tape on which speech, music, etc. has been recorded. **2.** the act of recording on magnetic tape.

**tapestry** /ˈtæpəstri/, *n., pl.* **-tries,** *v.,* **-tried, -trying.** *–n.* **1.** a fabric consisting of a warp upon which coloured threads are woven by hand to produce a design, often pictorial, and used for wall hangings, furniture coverings, etc. **2.** a machine-woven reproduction of true tapestry. *–v.t.* **3.** to furnish, cover, or adorn with tapestry. [ME *tapestrye,* from F *tapisserie,* from *tapissier* maker of tapestry, from *tapis* TAPIS] – **tapestry-like,** *adj.*

**tapetum** /təˈpitəm/, *n., pl.* **-ta** /-tə/. **1.** *Bot.* a layer of cells often investing the archespore in a developing sporangium and absorbed as the spores mature. **2.** *Anat., Zool.* any of certain membranous layers or the like, as in the choroid or retina. [LL, replacing L *tapēte* carpet] – **tapetal,** *adj.*

**tape unit** /ˈteɪp junət/, *n.* a machine that handles magnetic tape in a computer system.

**tapeworm** /ˈteɪpwɜm/, *n.* any of various flat or tapelike worms of the class Cestoda, lacking any alimentary canal, and parasitic when adult in the alimentary canal of man and other vertebrates, usu. characterised by having the larval and adult stages in different hosts.

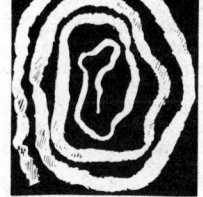

tapeworm

**taphole** /ˈtæphoʊl/, *n.* a hole in a blast furnace or the like through which molten metal or slag is drawn off.

**taphouse** /ˈtæphaʊs/, *n., pl.* **-houses.** a house where alcoholic drink is kept on tap for sale; a tavern.

**tapioca** /tæpiˈoʊkə/, *n.* a granular farinaceous food substance prepared from cassava starch by drying while moist on heated plates, used for making puddings, thickening soups, etc. [Pg., from Brazilian (Tupi-Guarani) *tipioca,* from *tipi* residue +

*og, ók* squeeze out]

**tapir** /'teɪpə/, *n.* any of various slate-coloured stout-bodied perissodactyl ungulates (family Tapiridae) of the genus *Tapirus* of tropical America and South-East Asia, somewhat resembling swine and having a flexible snout. [Brazilian (Tupi) *tapira*]

**tapis** /'tæpi/, *n., pl.* **tapis. 1.** a carpet, tapestry, or other covering. **2. on the tapis,** under consideration or discussion. [F, from LL *tapētium,* from Gk *tapḗtion,* diminutive of *tápēs* cloth wrought with figures]

South American tapir

**tap-kick** /'tæp-kɪk/, *n.* (in rugby football) a form of penalty kick in which a player kicks the ball only a short distance and then picks it up himself.

**tappa** /'tæpə/, *n.* →**tapa.**

**tapper**[1] /'tæpə/, *n.* one who or that which taps or strikes lightly. [TAP[1] + -ER[1]]

**tapper**[2] /'tæpə/, *n.* **1.** one who or that which taps, as trees for the sap or juice. **2.** one who cuts screw threads in a hole. [TAP[2] + -ER[1]]

**tappet** /'tæpət/, *n.* (in a machine or engine) a projecting part, arm, or the like which intermittently comes in contact with another part to which it communicates or from which it receives an intermittent motion. [TAP[1] + -ET]

**tapping**[1] /'tæpɪŋ/, *n.* **1.** the act of one who or that which taps or strikes lightly. **2.** the sound so made. [TAP[1] + -ING[1]]

**tapping**[2] /'tæpɪŋ/, *n.* **1.** the act of one who or that which taps casks, etc. **2.** that which is drawn by tapping. **3.** the operation of cutting a screw thread in a hole. [TAP[2] + -ING[1]]

**taproom** /'tæprum/, *n. Brit.* a room, as in a tavern, in which alcoholic drink is sold; bar.

**taproot** /'tæprut/, *n.* a main root descending downwards from the radicle and giving off small lateral roots.

**tapster** /'tæpstə/, *n. Archaic.* a bartender or barmaid. [ME; OE *tæppestre.* See TAP[2], *n.*, -STER] – **tapstress,** *n. fem.*

**tapu** /'tapu/, *adj. N.Z.* sacred; taboo. [Maori]

**tap-water** /'tæp-wɔtə/, *n.* water from a household tap; domestic water.

**tar**[1] /ta/, *n., v.,* **tarred, tarring.** *–n.* **1.** any of various dark-coloured viscid products obtained by the destructive distillation of certain organic substances, such as coal, wood, etc. **2.** coal-tar pitch. *–adj.* **3.** made of or covered with tar. *–v.t.* **4.** to smear or cover with, or as with, tar. **5. tar and feather,** to punish or have revenge on (someone) by covering with tar and feathers. **6. tarred with the same brush,** having similar faults. [ME *terre,* OE *terw-* (stem *teru*), c. D *teer,* G *Teer;* akin to TREE]

**tar**[2] /ta/, *n. Colloq.* a sailor. [said to be short for TARPAULIN]

**taradiddle** /'tærədɪdl/, *n.* →**tarradiddle.**

**taraire** /tə'raɪri/, *n.* a large New Zealand forest tree, *Beilschmiedia taraire.* [Maori]

**tarakihi** /'tærəkihi/, *n. N.Z.* →**terakihi.**

**taranaki gate** /ˌtærənæki 'geɪt/, *n. N.Z.* a makeshift wire and batten gate. [first used on dairy farms in *Taranaki,* province of N.Z.]

**taranaki topdressing** /– 'tɒpdresɪŋ/, *n. N.Z.* cow manure.

**tarantella** /tærən'telə/, *n.* **1.** a rapid, whirling southern Italian dance in very quick sextuple (originally quadruple) time, usu. performed by a single couple, and formerly supposed to be a remedy for tarantism. **2.** a popular dance derived from it. **3.** a piece of music for either dance or in its rhythm. [It., diminutive of *Taranto,* where tarantism was common. See TARANTULA]

**tarantism** /'tærəntɪzəm/, *n.* a nervous disorder characterised by an uncontrollable impulse to dance, esp. as prevalent in southern Italy from the 15th to the 17th century and popularly attributed to the bite of the tarantula (def. 2). [It. *Tarant(o)* + -ISM. See TARANTULA]

**tarantula** /tə'ræntʃələ/, *n., pl.* **-las, -lae** /-li/. **1.** in Australia, a huntsman spider of the genus *Isopoda,* esp. the large, swift *Isopoda immanis,* which often seeks shelter in houses during rain; a triantelope. **2.** a large spider of southern Europe, *Lycosa tarantula,* whose bite was formerly supposed to cause tarantism. **3.** any large spider, esp. one of the family Theraphosidae of America. **4.** a name given to several animals which are thought to be venomous, as certain snakes and lizards. [ML, from It. *tarantola,* from *Taranto* (from L *Tarentum*), sea-port in SE Italy, where def. 2 is common]

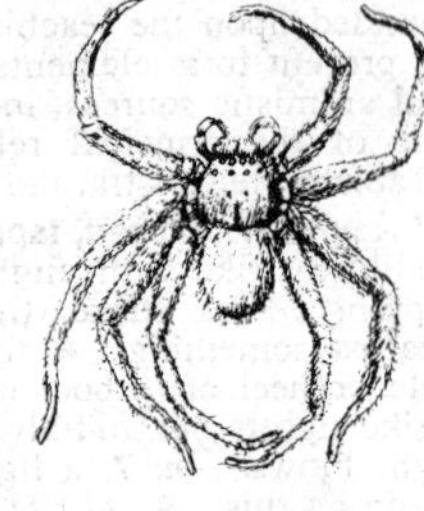
tarantula (def. 1)

**tarata** /tə'ratə/, *n. N.Z.* →**lemonwood.** [Maori]

**taraxacum** /tə'ræksəkəm/, *n.* **1.** any of the plants, mostly stemless herbs, constituting the genus *Taraxacum,* as the dandelion. **2.** the root of the dandelion, used in medicine as a tonic, diuretic, and aperient. [ML, from Ar. *tarakhshaqōq,* from Pers. *talkh chakōk* bitter herb]

**tarboosh** /ta'buʃ/, *n.* a cap of cloth or felt (nearly always red) with a tassel, worn by Muslim men either by itself or as the inner part of the turban. Also, **tarbush, tarbouche.** [Ar. *tarbūsh*]

tarboosh

**tarboy** /'tabɔɪ/, *n.* one who, during the shearing of sheep, smears cuts, etc., with tar or antiseptics.

**tarbrush** /'tabrʌʃ/, *n.* **1.** a brush for applying tar. **2. a touch of the tarbrush,** (*derog.*) Negro or other coloured ancestry or appearance.

**tarbuttite** /'tabətaɪt/, *n.* a mineral basic zinc phosphate which occurs in sheaf-like aggregates. [named after Percy *Tarbutt,* 20th C Australian mining engineer]

**Tardenoisian** /tadə'nɔɪziən, -'nwa-/, *adj.* belonging to the Mesolithic stage of culture transitional between Palaeolithic and Neolithic recognised from Iberia to Central Europe and esp. in southwest France. [named after *Tardenois,* village in France, site of finds]

**tardigrade** /'tadəgreɪd/, *adj.* **1.** slow in pace or movement. **2.** of or pertaining to the Tardigrada, a class or subclass of minute herbivorous arthropods, lacking well-developed circulatory or respiratory systems. *–n.* **3.** a tardigrade animal. [L *tardigradus*]

**tardo** /'tadoʊ/, *adv.* **1.** (a musical direction) slowly. *–adj.* **2.** slow. [It., from L *tardus*]

**tardy** /'tadi/, *adj.,* **-dier, -diest. 1.** moving or acting slowly; slow; sluggish. **2.** late or behindhand. **3.** delaying through reluctance. [ME *tardive,* from F, from LL *tardivus,* L *tardus* slow] – **tardily,** *adv.* – **tardiness,** *n.*

**tare**[1] /tɛə/, *n.* **1.** any of various vetches, esp. *Vicia sativa.* **2.** the seed of a vetch. **3.** (in biblical use) some injurious weed, possibly the darnel. [ME; cf. MD *tarwe* wheat]

**tare**[2] /tɛə/, *n., v.,* **tared, taring.** *–n.* **1.** the weight of the wrapping, receptacle, or conveyance containing goods. **2.** a deduction from the gross weight to allow for this. **3.** the weight of a vehicle without cargo, passengers, etc. **4.** *Chem.* a counterweight used to balance the weight of a container. *–v.t.* **5.** to ascertain, note, or allow for, the tare of. [late ME, from ML *tara,* from Ar. *tarha* deduction]

**targe** /tadʒ/, *n. Archaic.* a round shield. [ME, from OF; replacing OE *targa,* from Scand.; cf. Icel. *targa* shield, c. OHG *zarga* frame]

**target** /'tagət/, *n.* **1.** a device, usu. marked with concentric circles, to be aimed at in shooting practice or contests. **2.** any object used for this purpose. **3.** anything fired at or aimed at. **4.** a goal to be reached. **5.** *Boxing, Fencing.* the portion of the opponent's body which may be punched or touched for the scoring of points. **6.** an object of abuse, scorn, derision, etc.; a butt. **7.** *Survey.* **a.** the sliding sight on a levelling rod. **b.** any marker on which sights are taken. **8.** *Hist.* a small round shield or buckler. [late ME, from F *targuete.* See TARGE] – **targetless,** *adj.*

**target language** /'– læŋgwɪdʒ/, *n.* **1.** the language into which a text is translated, or a loan word borrowed. **2.** (in language teaching) the foreign language being taught.

**target-practice** /'tagət-præktəs/, *n.* the act of shooting at targets for practice in accuracy in aiming.

**target response** /tagət rə'spɒns/, *n.* the effect on men, material, and equipment of blast, heat, light, and nuclear radiation resulting from the explosion of a nuclear weapon.

**tar guard** /'ta gad/, *n.* a cigarette holder with built-in filter.

**tariff** /'tærəf/, *n.* **1.** an official list or table showing the duties or customs imposed by a government on exports or, esp., imports. **2.** the system of duties so imposed. **3.** any duty in such a list or system. **4.** any table of charges, as of a transport undertaking. **5.** a bill of fare. *–v.t.* **6.** to subject to a tariff. **7.** to put a valuation on according to a tariff. [It. *tariffa,* from Ar. *tarif* notification, information] – **tariffless,** *adj.*

**tarlatan** /'talətən/, *n.* a thin, open, stiff cotton fabric, not washable. [F *tarlatane;* orig. uncert.]

**tarmac** /'tamæk/, *n., adj., v.,* **-macked, -macking.** *–n.* **1.** →**tarmacadam.** **2.** a road or airport runway made of tarmacadam. *–adj.* **3.** made of or surfaced with tarmacadam. *–v.t.* **4.** to surface (a road, runway or the like) with tarmacadam.

**tarmacadam** /tamə'kædəm/, *n.* **1.** a road-surfacing mixture consisting of small stones or gravel bound together with tar or a mixture of tar and bitumen. *–adj.* **2.** made of or having a surface of such a mixture. [TAR[1] + MACADAM]

**tarn** /tan/, *n.* a small mountain lake or pool. [ME *terne,* from Scand.; cf. Icel. *tjörn*]

**tarnation** /ta'neɪʃən/, *Colloq.* *–interj.* **1.** damnation. *–n.* **2.** an act or instance of saying 'tarnation'. **3.** eternal damnation. *–adj.* **4.** damned: *I can't get the tarnation car to start.* ['*tarn(al)* d. var. of ETERNAL + (DAMN)ATION]

**tarnish** /'tanɪʃ/, *v.i.* **1.** to dull or alter the lustre of (esp. a metallic surface by oxidation, etc.); discolour. **2.** to diminish or destroy the purity of; stain; sully. *–v.i.* **3.** to grow dull or discoloured; lose lustre. **4.** to become sullied. *–n.* **5.** a tarnished coating. **6.** tarnished condition; discolouration; alteration of the lustre. **7.** stain or blemish. [F *terniss-,* stem of *ternir,* from *terne* dull, dark, probably of Gmc orig.; cf. MHG *ternen* darken, OE *derne* obscure] – **tarnishable,** *adj.* – **tarnisher,** *n.*

**taro** /'taroʊ/, *n., pl.* **-ros.** **1.** a tuberous herb, *Colocasia esculenta,* cultivated in the tropics for the root which, though poisonous, is made edible by boiling. **2.** the root. [Polynesian]

**tarogato** /tærə'gatoʊ/, *n.* a Hungarian clarinet-like musical instrument.

**tarot** /'tæroʊ/, *n.* **1.** one of a pack of 78 cards, made up of four suits of 14 cards each, with 22 trump cards. **2.** a trump card in such a pack, bearing a symbolic or mythological character, now chiefly used in cartomancy. **3.** (*pl.*) *Obs.* a game played with these cards. *–adj.* **4.** of or pertaining to the tarots, esp. the trump cards. [F, from It. *tarocco*]

tarot: 15th century Italian playing card

**tarp** /tap/, *n. Colloq.* a tarpaulin.

**tarpan** /'tapæn/, *n.* a variety of wild horse, *Equus caballus gomelini,* widespread in Europe in prehistoric times, but now extinct. [Russ., from Kirghiz, a Turkic language of W central Asia]

**tarpaulin** /ta'pɔlən/, *n.* **1.** a protective covering of canvas or other material waterproofed with tar, paint, or wax. **2.** a hat, esp. a sailor's made of or covered with such material. **3.** *Rare.* a sailor. [earlier *tarpauling,* from TAR[1] + PALL[1] + -ING[1]]

**tarpaulin muster** /'– mʌstə/, *n.* a collection of donations for a specific purpose, as a charity, sometimes involving the use of a tarpaulin to collect coins.

**tarpon** /'tapɒn/, *n.* **1.** in Australia, the ox-eye herring. **2.** a large fish, *Tarpon atlanticus,* of the warmer waters of the Atlantic, with compressed body and huge silvery scales. [orig. uncert.; cf. D *tarpoen*]

tarpon (def. 2)

**tarpot** /'tapɒt/, *n.* →**black-headed python.**

**tarradiddle** /'tærədɪdl/, *n.* **1.** a lie about a small matter; fib. **2.** nonsense; rubbish. Also, **taradiddle.**

**tarragon** /'tærəgən/, *n.* **1.** an Old World plant, *Artemisia dracunculus,* whose aromatic leaves are used for flavouring. **2.** the leaves themselves. Also, **estragon.** [Sp. *taragona,* from Ar. *tarkhūm,* probably from Gk *drakōn* dragon, or *drakōntion* type of arum]

**tarriance** /'tæriəns/, *n. Archaic.* **1.** delay; tarrying; waiting. **2.** →**sojourn.**

**tarry**[1] /'tæri/, *v.,* **-ried, -rying,** *n., pl.* **-ries.** *–v.i.* **1.** to remain or stay, as in a place; sojourn. **2.** to delay or be tardy in acting, starting, coming, etc.; linger or loiter. **3.** to wait. *–v.t.* **4.** *Archaic.* to wait for. *–n.* **5.** *Archaic.* a stay; sojourn. [ME; orig. uncert.] – **tarrier,** *n.*

**tarry**[2] /'tari/, *adj.* of or like tar; smeared with tar. [TAR[1] + -Y[1]] – **tarriness,** *n.*

**tarsal** /'tasəl/, *adj.* **1.** of or pertaining to the tarsus of the foot or leg. **2.** pertaining to the tarsi of the eyelids. *–n.* **3.** a tarsal bone, joint, or the like.

**tarseal** /'tasil/, *v.t.* **1.** to finish (a road) with a bitumen surface. *–n. N.Z.* **2.** the surface of such a road.

**tarsia** /'tasiə/, *n.* inlay or marquetry in wood; intarsia. [It.]

**tarsier** /'tasiə/, *n.* a small arboreal primate, genus *Tarsius,* with enormous eyes, sole representative of a suborder, Tarsiodea, and found in Indonesia and parts of the Philippines. [F, from *tarse* TARSUS]

tarsier

**tarsometatarsus** /,tasoʊmɛtə'tasəs/, *n., pl.* **-si** /-saɪ/. the large bone in the lower leg of a bird with which the toe bones articulate; the third segment from the body in the leg of a bird. [*tarso-* (combining form of TARSUS) + METATARSUS] – **tarsometatarsal,** *adj.*

**tarsus** /'tasəs/, *n., pl.* **-si** /-saɪ/. **1.** the proximal segment of the foot; the collection of bones between the tibia and the metatarsus, entering into the construction of the ankle joint and into the instep of man. **2.** the small plate of connective tissue along the border of an eyelid. **3.** →**tarsometatarsus.** **4.** the fifth segment of an insect's leg. [NL, from Gk *tarsós* flat of the foot]

**tart**[1] /tat/, *adj.* **1.** sharp to the taste; sour or acid: *tart apples.* **2.** sharp in character, spirit, or expression; cutting; caustic: *a tart remark.* [ME; OE *teart* sharp, rough. Cf. G *trotz*] – **tartish,** *adj.* – **tartishly,** *adv.* – **tartly,** *adv.* – **tartness,** *n.*

**tart**[2] /tat/, *n.* **1.** a small and saucer-shaped shell of pastry, filled with cooked fruit or other sweetened preparation, and having no top crust. **2.** a similar but larger pastry concoction. **3.** *Colloq.* a girl or woman, now esp. of low character. **4.** *Colloq.* a prostitute. *–v.t.* **5. tart up,** *Colloq.* to adorn; make attractive, esp. with cheap ornaments and cosmetics. [ME *tarte,* from OF *tart(r)e,* from L *tortula* (from *torta,* pp., twisted) or ? b. L *tortula* and *tartarun* baked crust] – **tarty,** *adj.*

**tartan**[1] /'tatn/, *n.* **1.** a woollen or worsted cloth woven with stripes of different colours and widths crossing at right angles, worn chiefly by the Scottish Highlanders, each clan having its distinctive pattern. **2.** a design of such a plaid known by name of the clan wearing it. **3.** any plaid. *–adj.* **4.** of, pertaining to, or resembling tartan. **5.** made of tartan. [apparently from F *tiretaine* linsey-woolsey]

tartan[1]

**tartan**[2] /'tatn/, *n.* a single-masted vessel with a lateen sail and a jib, used in the Mediterranean. [F *tartane,* from It. *tartana,* from Ar. *tartaneh*]

**tartar** /'tatə/, *n.* **1.** a hard substance deposited on the teeth by the saliva, consisting of calcium phosphate, mucus, etc. **2.** the deposit from wines, potassium bitartrate. **3.** the partially purified product midway between the crude form (argol) and the further purified form (cream of tartar). [ML *tartarum,* from Gk *tártaron* (of Ar. orig.); replacing ME *tartre,* from F]

**Tartar** /'tatə/, *n.* **1.** a member of any of a mingled host of Mongolian, Turkish, and other tribes who, under the leadership of Genghis Khan, overran Asia and eastern Europe during the Middle Ages. **2.** a member of the descendants of this people variously intermingled with other races and tribes, now inhabiting parts of the European and western and central Asiatic Soviet Union. **3.** any of several Turkic languages of western central Asia, particularly Uzbek. **4.** (*also l.c.*) a savage, intractable person. **5.** (*l.c.*) a shrew or vixen. **6. catch a Tartar,** to catch or have dealings with something that or someone who proves unexpectedly troublesome or powerful. *–adj.* **7.** pertaining to a Tartar or Tartars, or to their language. Also, **Tatar.** [ME, from ML *Tartarus,* from Pers. *Tatar,* by association with *Tartarus,* which, in classical mythology was a sunless abyss below Hades, in which Zeus imprisoned the Titans; Tartarus was also known as Hades]

**tartar emetic** /tatər ə'mɛtɪk/, *n.* potassium antimonyl tartrate, $K(SbO)C_4H_4O_6 \cdot \frac{1}{2}H_2O$, a poisonous salt with a sweetish metallic taste, occurring in white crystals or as a white granular powder, used in medicine, dyeing, etc.

**tartare sauce** /ˌtatɛə 'sɔs, ˌtata/, *n.* a mayonnaise dressing usu. with chopped pickles, onions, olives, capers, and green herbs, etc. added, often served with fish. Also, **tartar sauce.** [F *sauce tartare*]

**tartaric** /ta'tærɪk/, *adj.* pertaining to or derived from tartar.

**tartaric acid** /– 'æsəd/, *n.* an organic acid, $(CHOHCOOH)_2$ existing in four isomeric modifications, the common or dextrorotatory form being a colourless crystalline compound found in grapes and as one of the principal acids of wine.

**tartarise** /'tatəraɪz/, *v.t.,* **-rised, -rising.** to impregnate, combine, or treat with tartar, or potassium bitartrate. Also, **tartarize.** – **tartarisation** /tatəraɪ'zeɪʃən/, *n.*

**tartarous** /'tatərəs/, *adj.* of or containing tartar.

**tartar steak** /tatə 'steɪk/, *n.* →**steak tartare.**

**tartlet** /'tatlət/, *n.* a small tart.

**tartrate** /'tatreɪt/, *n.* a salt or ester of tartaric acid. [F, from *tartre* TARTAR]

**tartrated** /'tatreɪtəd/, *adj.* formed into a tartrate; combined with tartaric acid.

**tartrazine** /'tatrəzin/, *n.* a type of yellow dye used in food materials. [*tartro-* (combining form representing TARTAR) + AZ(O)- + -INE[2]]

**Tartuffe** /ta'tuf/, *n.* a hypocritical pretender to piety. [name of the hero of a comedy (1667) by Molière, 1622-73, French writer] – **Tartuffian,** *adj.*

**tar-vine** /'ta-vaɪn/, *n.* any species of the genus *Boerhavia,* of inland Australia, esp. *B. diffusa,* a widespread weed.

**tarwhine** /'tawaɪn/, *n.* an eastern Australian bream, *Rhabdosargus sarba,* distinguished by golden streaks on a generally silver background. [Aboriginal]

**tarwine** /ta'wɪni/, *n. N.Z.* →**tawine.**

**Tarzan** /'tazən, ta'zæn/, *n. Colloq.* a person of superior strength and agility. [name of the hero of a series of jungle stories by Edgar Rice Burroughs, 1875-1950, U.S. writer]

**Tas** /tæz/, *n. Colloq.* Tasmania. Also, **Tassie.**

**Tas.,** Tasmania.

**task** /task/, *n.* **1.** a definite piece of work assigned or falling to a person; a duty. **2.** any piece of work. **3.** a matter of considerable labour or difficulty. **4. take to task,** to call to account, as for fault; blame or censure. **5.** *Obs.* a tax or impost. *–v.t.* **6.** to subject to severe or excessive labour or exertion; put a strain upon (powers, resources, etc.). **7.** to impose a task on. **8.** *Obs.* to tax. [ME, from ML *tasca,* metathetic var. of *taxa* TAX] – **tasker,** *n.* – **taskless,** *adj.*

**task force** /'– fɔs/, *n.* a temporary grouping of units under one commander, formed for the purpose of carrying out a specific operation or mission.

**taskmaster** /'taskmastə/, *n.* one whose function it is to assign tasks to others, esp. burdensome tasks. – **taskmistress,** *n. fem.*

**taskwork** /'taskwɜk/, *n.* **1.** work imposed or done as a task, esp. unpleasant work. **2.** work done or paid for by the job, rather than by the time it takes. **3.** →**bonus work.**

**Tasmania** /tæz'meɪniə/, *n.* an island State off the south-eastern mainland of Australia, one of the six States of Australia. *Abbrev.:* Tas., TAS.

Tasmania: coat of arms

**Tasmanian** /tæz'meɪniən/, *n.* **1.** one who was born in Tasmania or who has come to regard it as his home State. *–adj.* **2.** of or pertaining to the State of Tasmania. Also, **Taswegian.**

**Tasmanian barred bandicoot,** *n.* →**Gunn's bandicoot.**

**Tasmanian blue gum,** *n.* a tall smooth-barked species of *Eucalyptus, E. globulus,* native to Tasmania and Victoria but widely cultivated; the floral emblem of Tasmania.

**Tasmanian bluey** /tæzˌmeɪniən 'blui/, *n.* a blue woollen cloth, formerly manufactured in Tasmania. See **Wonga bluey.**

**Tasmanian devil** /– 'dɛvəl/, *n.* a ferocious carnivorous marsupial, *Sarcophilus harrisii,* of Tasmania having a black coat with white markings; ursine dasyure.

Tasmanian devil

**Tasmanian kingfish** /– 'kɪŋfɪʃ/, *n.* →**king barracouta.**

**Tasmanian mutton-bird** /– 'mʌtn-bɜd/, *n.* →**short-tailed shearwater.**

**Tasmanian myrtle** /– 'mɜtl/, *n.* the tree *Nothofagus cunninghamii,* and its timber.

**Tasmanian scallop** /– 'skɒləp/, *n.* a scallop, esp. *Notovola meridionalis,* found in Tasmania and marketed commercially.

**Tasmanian tiger** /– 'taɪgə/, *n.* →**Tasmanian wolf.**

**Tasmanian wolf** /– 'wʊlf/, *n.* a rare carnivorous, wolf-like marsupial, *Thylacinus cynocephalus,* of Tasmania, tan-coloured, with black stripes across the back. Also, **Tasmanian tiger.** [NL *Thȳlacīnus,* from Gk *thȳlakos* pouch + *-īnus* -INE[1]]

Tasmanian wolf

**tasmanite** /'tæzmənaɪt/, *n.* an impure coal transitional between cannel coal and oil shale. [from *Tasmania,* where it was first discovered]

**tasse** /tæs/, *n.* →**tasset.**

**tassel** /'tæsəl/, *n., v.,* **-selled, -selling** or (*U.S.*) **-seled, -seling.** *–n.* **1.** a pendent ornament, originally a clasp consisting commonly of a bunch of threads, small cords, or strand hanging from a roundish knob or head. **2.** something resembling this, as the inflorescence of certain plants, esp. that at the summit of a stalk of sugarcane, maize, etc. **3.** *Colloq.* the penis. *–v.t.* **4.** to furnish or adorn with tassels. **5.** to form into a tassel or tassels. **6.** to remove the tassel from (growing maize), as in order to improve the crop. *–v.i.* **7.** (of maize, sugarcane, etc.) to put forth tassels. [ME, from OF: fastening for a cloak] – **tasselly,** *adj.*

tassel: 19th century Italian

**tassel-fish** /'tæsəl-fɪʃ/, *n.* →**threadfin.**

**tasseography** /tæsi'ɒgrəfi/, *n.* the art of reading tea-leaves.

**tasset** /'tæsət/, *n.* one of a pair of defences for the upper thighs suspended from the waist plates by straps. Also, **tasse.**

**Tassie** /'tæzi/, *n., adj. Colloq.* →**Tasmanian.**

**taste** /teɪst/, *v.,* **tasted, tasting,** *n.* *–v.t.* **1.** to try the flavour or quality of (something) by taking some into the mouth: *to taste food.* **2.** to eat or drink a little of: *he hadn't tasted food for three days.* **3.** to perceive or distinguish the flavour of: *to taste the wine in a sauce.* **4.** to have or get experience, esp. a slight experience. **5.** *Archaic.* to perceive in any way, esp. by smell. **6.** *Archaic.* to enjoy or appreciate. **7.** *Obs.* to touch, feel, or handle; test or try. *–v.i.* **8.** to try the flavour or quality of something. **9.** to eat or drink a little (usu. fol.

by *of*): *Harry tasted slyly of the cake.* **10.** to perceive or distinguish the flavour of anything. **11.** to have experience, or make trial in experience, of something. **12.** to have a particular flavour: *the milk tastes sour.* **13.** to smack or savour (usu. fol. by *of*). *–n.* **14.** the act of tasting food, drink, or the like. **15.** the sense by which the flavour or savour of things is perceived when they are brought into contact with special organs of the tongue. **16.** sensation, flavour, or quality as perceived by these organs. **17.** a small quantity tasted; a morsel, bit, or sip. **18.** a relish, liking, or predilection for something: *a taste for music.* **19.** the sense of what is fitting, harmonious, or beautiful; the perception and enjoyment of what constitutes excellence in the fine arts, literature, etc. **20.** manner, style, or general character as showing perception, or lack of perception, of what is fitting or beautiful; characteristic or prevailing style. **21.** a slight experience or a sample of something. **22. to one's taste,** agreeable or pleasing to one: *he couldn't find a tie to his taste.* [ME, from OF *taster* try by touching, from b. L *tangere* touch and *gustāre* taste] – **tastable,** *adj.*

**tastebud** /ˈteɪstbʌd/, *n.* any of a number of small, flask-shaped bodies in the epithelium of the tongue, etc., the special organs of taste.

**tasteful** /ˈteɪstfəl/, *adj.* having, displaying, or in accordance with, good taste. – **tastefully,** *adv.* – **tastefulness,** *n.*

**tasteless** /ˈteɪstləs/, *adj.* **1.** having no taste or flavour; insipid. **2.** dull; uninteresting. **3.** lacking in good taste; showing lack of good taste. **4.** *Rare.* lacking the sense of taste. – **tastelessly,** *adv.* – **tastelessness,** *n.*

**taste powder** /ˈteɪst paʊdə/, *n.* →**monosodium glutamate.**

**taster** /ˈteɪstə/, *n.* **1.** one who tastes, esp. one skilled in distinguishing the qualities of wine, tea, etc., by the taste. **2.** *Colloq.* one who samples and reports on manuscripts for a publisher. **3.** a container for taking samples or tasting. **4.** a wide shallow vessel, usu. metal, in which wine is tested. **5.** →**pipette.**

**tasto** /ˈtastoʊ/, *n. Music.* **1.** →**fingerboard.** **2. sul tasto,** (a direction to string players) bowed on or near the fingerboard. **3. tasto solo,** (a direction, esp. in baroque music) with only the single notes of the figured bass or continuo part played, without the chords or harmonies founded on them. [It. touch]

**tasty** /ˈteɪsti/, *adj.,* **tastier, tastiest.** **1.** pleasing to the taste; savoury; appetising. **2.** *Colloq.* having or showing good taste. – **tastily,** *adv.* – **tastiness,** *n.*

**tasty cheese** /ˈ– tʃiz/, *n.* matured cheese.

**Tasway** /ˈtæzweɪ/, *n. Colloq.* Tasmania. [backformation from TASWEGIAN, by analogy with NORWEGIAN, *adj.,* from NORWAY]

**Taswegian** /tæzˈwidʒən/, *n.* →**Tasmanian.** [TAS(MANIAN) + *-wegian* (by analogy with *Norwegian, Glaswegian,* etc.)]

**tat**[1] /tæt/, *v.i., v.t.,* **tatted, tatting.** to do, or make by, tatting. [orig. unknown]

**tat**[2] /tæt/, *n.* See **tit for tat.**

**ta-ta** /tæ-ˈta/, *interj. Colloq.* good-bye.

**Tatar** /ˈtatə/, *n., adj.* →**Tartar.** – **Tatarian** /taˈtɛəriən, -ˈtari-/, **Tataric** /taˈtærɪk/, *adj.*

**tater** /ˈteɪtə/, *n. Colloq.* a potato. Also, **tatie** /ˈteɪti/.

**tatouay** /ˈtætueɪ, tatuˈaɪ/, *n.* an armadillo, *Tatoua unicintus,* of tropical South America. [Pg. (Brazilian) *tatuay,* from Guarani, from *tatu* armadillo + *ay* valueless (i.e. inedible as food)]

**tats** /tæts/, *n.pl. Colloq.* tatters.

**tatter**[1] /ˈtætə/, *n.* **1.** a torn piece hanging loose from the main part, as of a garment, etc. **2.** a separate torn piece. **3.** (*pl.*) torn or ragged clothing. *–v.t.* **4.** to tear or wear to tatters. *–v.i.* **5.** to become ragged. [backformation from TATTERED]

**tatter**[2] /ˈtætə/, *n.* one who makes tatting. [TAT[1] + -ER[1]]

**tatterdemalion** /tætədəˈmeɪliən/, *n.* a person in tattered clothing; a ragged fellow. [TATTER[1]; + second element of uncert. orig.]

**tattered** /ˈtætəd/, *adj.* **1.** torn to tatters; ragged. **2.** wearing ragged clothing. [TATTER[1], *n.* + -ED[3]]

**tatters** /ˈtætəz/, *n.pl. Colloq.* a denture; set of false teeth.

**tattersall** /ˈtætəsɔl/, *n.* **1.** a fabric with brightly coloured crossbars in a plaid pattern. *–adj.* **2.** made of this fabric: *a tattersall vest.* [from *Tattersall's,* London horse market, where brightly coloured blankets were used]

**tatting** /ˈtætɪŋ/, *n.* **1.** the process or work of making a kind of knotted lace of cotton or linen thread with a shuttle. **2.** such lace. [orig. unknown]

**tattle** /ˈtætl/, *v.,* **-tled, -tling,** *n.* *–v.i.* **1.** to let out secrets. **2.** to chatter, prate, or gossip. *–v.t.* **3.** to utter idly; disclose by gossiping. *–n.* **4.** the act of tattling. **5.** idle talk; chatter; gossip. [ME *tatle,* apparently from M Flemish *tatelen,* c. LG *tateln* gabble] – **tattingly,** *adv.*

**tattler** /ˈtætlə/, *n.* **1.** one who tattles; a telltale. **2.** any of various sandpipers with a vociferous cry which spend the northern winter in Australia and South-East Asia.

**tattletale** /ˈtætlteɪl/, *n.* **1.** →**tale-bearer.** *–adj.* **2.** telltale; revealing.

**tattoo**[1] /tæˈtu/, *n., pl.* **-toos.** **1.** a signal on a drum, bugle, or trumpet at night, for soldiers or sailors to retire to their quarters. **2.** any similar beating or pulsation. **3.** an outdoor military pageant or display. [D *taptoe,* lit., the tap (is) to, i.e. the taproom is shut]

**tattoo**[2] /tæˈtu/, *n., pl.* **-toos,** *v.,* **-tooed, -tooing.** *–n.* **1.** the act or practice of marking the skin with indelible patterns, pictures, legends, etc., by making punctures in it and inserting pigments. **2.** a pattern, picture, legend, etc., so made. *–v.t.* **3.** to mark with tattoos. **4.** to put pictures, legends, etc., on the skin. [earlier *tattow,* from Polynesian *tatau*] – **tattooer,** *n.*

tattoo[2]

**tatts** /tæts/, *n. pl. Colloq.* false teeth.

**tatty** /ˈtæti/, *adj.* untidy; shabby; tawdry.

**tau** /taʊ, tɔ/, *n.* the nineteenth letter (Τ,τ) of the Greek alphabet.

**tau cross** /– ˈkrɒs/, *n.* a T-shaped cross.

**taught** /tɔt/, *v.* past tense and past participle of **teach.**

**tauhinu** /taʊˈhinu/, *n. N.Z.* →**cottonwood** (def. 2).

**taunt** /tɔnt/, *v.t.* **1.** to reproach in a sarcastic or insulting manner. **2.** to provoke by taunts; mock. *–n.* **3.** an insulting gibe or sarcasm; scornful reproach or challenge. **4.** *Obs.* an object of insulting gibes or scornful reproaches. [orig. uncert.] – **taunter,** *n.* – **tauntingly,** *adv.*

**taupata** /ˈtaʊpətə/, *n.* a New Zealand shrub of the genus *Coprosma,* esp. *C. repens* with dark shiny leaves and orange-red berries. [Maori]

**taupe** /tɔp, toʊp/, *n.* dark grey usu. slightly tinged with brown, purple, yellow, or green. [F, from L *talpa* mole]

**Taurean** /ˈtɔriən/, *n.* **1.** a person born under the sign of Taurus, and (according to tradition) exhibiting the typical Taurean personality traits in some degree. *–adj.* **2.** of or pertaining to Taurus. **3.** of or pertaining to such a person or such a personality trait.

**taurine**[1] /ˈtɔraɪn/, *adj.* **1.** of, pertaining to, or resembling a bull. **2.** pertaining to the zodiacal sign Taurus. [L *taurīnus* pertaining to a bull]

**taurine**[2] /ˈtɔrin/, *n.* a neutral crystalline substance, $H_2NCH_2CH_2SO_3H$, obtained from the bile of oxen and other animals, from muscles, lung tissue, etc., and as a decomposition product of taurocholic acid. [TAURO(CHOLIC ACID) + -INE[2]]

**taurobolium** /tɔrəˈboʊliəm/, *n., pl.* **-lia** /-liə/. a ceremony forming part of certain ancient Mediterranean cults in which the worshippers were baptised with the blood of a sacrificed bull. Also, **tauroboly** /tɔˈrɒbəli/.

**taurocholic acid** /tɔrə,kɒlɪk ˈæsəd/, *n.* an acid, $C_{26}H_{45}NO_7S$, occurring as a sodium salt in the bile of oxen, etc., which on hydrolysis yields taurine and cholic acid. [*tauro-* (combining form of Gk *taûros* bull, ox) + CHOLIC ACID]

**tauromachy** /tɔˈrɒməki/, *n.* the art or practice of bullfighting.

**Taurus** /ˈtɔrəs/, *n.* **1.** a constellation and sign of the zodiac, represented by a bull. **2.** →**Taurean.** [L: bull]

**taut** /tɔt/, *adj.* **1.** tightly drawn; tense; not slack. **2.** in good order or condition; tidy; neat. [ME *toght,* apparently b. *towen* (OE *togen* drawn) and TIGHT] – **tautly,** *adv.* – **tautness,** *n.*

**tauten** /ˈtɔtn/, *v.t., v.i.* to make or become taut.

**tauto-,** a word element meaning same, as in *tautonym.* [Gk, combining form of *tautó,* contraction of *tò autó* the same]

**tautog** /ˈtɔtɒg/, *n.* a black labroid fish, *Tautoga onitis,* of the North Atlantic coast of the U.S. [Algonquian *tautauog* (sheepsheads, pl. of *tau, tautau*)]

**tautologise** /tɔˈtɒlədʒaɪz/, *v.i.,* **-gised, -gising.** to use tautology. Also, **tautologize.**

**tautology** /tɔˈtɒlədʒi/, *n., pl.* **-gies. 1.** needless repetition of an idea, esp. in other words in the immediate context, without imparting additional force or clearness, as *to descend down.* **2.** an instance of this. **3.** *Logic.* a proposition that can be shown to be true because it includes every possibility: *either Smith owns a car or he doesn't own a car.* [LL *tautologia,* from Gk] – **tautological** /tɔtəˈlɒdʒɪkəl/, *adj.* – **tautologically** /tɔtəˈlɒdʒɪkli/, *adv.* – **tautologist,** *n.*

**tautomer** /ˈtɔtəmə/, *n.* a compound which is tautomeric with one or more other compounds. [backformation from TAUTOMERISM]

**tautomerisation** /tɔˌtɒmərаɪˈzeɪʃən/, *n.* conversion into a tautomeric structure. Also, **tautomerization.**

**tautomerism** /tɔˈtɒmərɪzəm/, *n.* the ability of certain organic compounds to react in isomeric structures which differ from each other in the position of a hydrogen atom and a double bond. The individual tautomers are in equilibrium and some pairs of tautomeric isomers have been isolated. [TAUTO- + Gk *méros* part + -ISM] – **tautomeric** /tɔtəˈmɛrɪk/, *adj.*

**tautonym** /ˈtɔtənɪm/, *n.* a scientific name in which the generic and the specific name are the same, as *Chloris chloris* (the greenfinch). [Gk *tautṓnymos* of same name] – **tautonymic** /tɔtəˈnɪmɪk/, *adj.*

**tavern** /ˈtævən/, *n.* **1.** premises where food and alcoholic drink are served, but where no accommodation is provided. **2.** *Chiefly Brit.* a hotel; inn.

**taverner** /ˈtævənə/, *n. Brit.* **1.** *Archaic.* the owner of a tavern. **2.** *Obs.* a frequenter of taverns. [ME, from OF *tavernier*]

**taw**[1] /tɔ/, *n.* **1.** a choice or fancy marble with which to shoot. **2.** (*pl.*) a game of marbles. **3.** the line from which the players shoot. **4.** a token such as a stone, piece of slate, etc., used by children in certain games, as hopscotch. **5.** *Colloq.* **go back to taws** or **start from taws,** to begin at the beginning. [? Scand.; cf. Icel. *taug* string, rope]

**taw**[2] /tɔ/, *v.t.* **1.** to prepare or dress (some raw material) for use or further manipulation. **2.** *Obs.* to beat; flog. [ME *tawe,* OE *tawian,* c. D *touwen*] – **tawer,** *n.*

**tawa** /ˈtawə/, *n.* a tall New Zealand timber tree, *Beilschmiedia tawa,* with edible purple berries. [Maori]

**tawdry** /ˈtɔdri/, *adj.,* **-drier, -driest.** (of finery, etc.) gaudy; showy and cheap. [short for *(Sain)t Audrey lace,* i.e. lace bought at her fair in the Isle of Ely] – **tawdrily,** *adv.* – **tawdriness,** *n.*

**tawhai** /ˈtafaɪ, ˈtawaɪ/, *n.* any of various New Zealand species of *Nothofagus,* beech. [Maori]

**tawine** /taˈwɪni/, *n. N.Z.* →**cottonwood** (def. 2). Also, **tarwine.**

**tawny** /ˈtɔni/, *adj.,* **-nier, -niest,** *n.* –*adj.* **1.** of a dark yellowish or yellowish brown colour. –*n.* **2.** a shade of brown tinged with yellow; dull yellowish brown. [ME, from OF *tane,* pp., TANNED] – **tawniness,** *n.* Also, **tawney.**

**tawny frogmouth** /– ˈfrɒgmaʊθ/, *n.* a medium-sized frogmouth, *Podargus strigoides,* with variously coloured, mottled plumage and a low but penetrating call, widely distributed throughout Australia.

tawny frogmouth

**tawny port** /– ˈpɔt/, *n.* **1.** a port wine, made from a blend of several vintages, and matured in wood, thus losing some of its colour and acquiring a brownish tinge. **2.** a wine of lighter colour and body than standard port.

**tawse** /tɔz/, *n. Chiefly Scot.* a leather strap divided at the end into narrow strips used for inflicting corporal punishment. Also, **taws.** [pl. of *taw* thong, n. use of TAW[2]]

**tax** /tæks/, *n.* **1.** a compulsory monetary contribution demanded by a government for its support and levied on incomes, property, goods purchased, etc. **2.** a burdensome charge, obligation, duty, or demand. –*v.t.* **3.** to impose tax on. **4.** to lay a burden on; make serious demands. **5.** to take to task; censure; reprove; accuse. **6.** to assess (a solicitor's fees) in order to establish that a reasonable amount has been charged. **7.** *U.S. Colloq.* to charge. [ME, from L *taxāre* reprove, appraise, ML impose a tax] – **taxability** /tæksəˈbɪləti/, **taxableness,** *n.* – **taxably,** *adv.* – **taxer,** *n.* – **taxless,** *adj.*

**taxable** /ˈtæksəbəl/, *adj.* **1.** capable of being taxed; subject to tax. –*n.* **2.** (*usu. pl.*) *U.S.* persons, property, etc., subject to tax.

**taxation** /tækˈseɪʃən/, *n.* **1.** the act of taxing. **2.** the fact of being taxed. **3.** a tax imposed. **4.** the revenue raised by taxes.

**tax avoidance** /tæks əˈvɔɪdns/, *n.* the taking of lawful measures to minimise one's tax liabilities. Cf. **tax evasion.**

**tax collector** /ˈ– kəlɛktə/, *n.* an official who collects taxes.

**tax-deductible** /ˈtæks-dədʌktəbəl/, *adj.* any expense, loss, etc., which can be legally claimed as a deduction from taxable income.

**taxeme** /ˈtæksim/, *n.* (in linguistics) a feature of the arrangement of elements in a construction, as selection, order, modification, or modulation. [TAX(IS), modelled after PHONEME]

**tax evasion** /ˈtæks əveɪʒən/, *n.* the taking of illegal steps to deprive the revenue of fiscal dues.

**tax-free** /ˈtæks-fri/, *adj.* free from taxation.

**tax haven** /ˈtæks heɪvən/, *n.* a country or territory in which resident individuals and resident companies pay little or no tax.

**taxi** /ˈtæksi/, *n., pl.* **taxis,** *v.,* **taxied, taxiing** or **taxying.** –*n.* **1.** Also, **taxicab.** a motor car for public hire, esp. one fitted with a taximeter. –*v.i.* **2.** to ride or travel in a taxi. **3.** (of an aeroplane) to move over the surface of the ground or water under its own power, except when preparing to take off or just after landing. –*v.t.* **4.** to cause (an aeroplane) to taxi. [short for TAXICAB]

**taxicab** /ˈtæksikæb/, *n.* →**taxi.** (def. 1). [short for *taximeter cab.* See TAXIMETER]

**taxi dancer** /ˈtæksi dænsə, dansə/, *n. U.S.* a girl or woman employed in a dance hall, etc., to dance with patrons, who pay a stipulated amount for each dance.

**taxidermy** /ˈtæksəˌdɜmi/, *n.* the art of preparing and preserving the skins of animals, and stuffing and mounting them in lifelike form. [*taxi-* (combining form of Gk *táxis* arrangement) + *-dermy* (Gk *-dermia,* from *dérma* skin)] – **taxidermal** /tæksəˈdɜməl/, **taxidermic** /tæksəˈdɜmɪk/, *adj.* – **taxidermist,** *n.*

**taximeter** /ˈtæksiˌmitə/, *n.* a device fitted to a taxi or other vehicle, for automatically computing and indicating the fare due. [F *taximètre,* from *taxe* charge. See -METER[1]]

**tax indexation** /ˌtæks ɪndɛkˈseɪʃən/, *n.* the indexing of tax scales in accordance with certain economic variables such as the consumer price index.

**taxi rank** /ˈtæksi ræŋk/, *n.* a place in the street reserved for taxicabs to stand awaiting passengers. Also, **cab rank.**

**taxis** /ˈtæksəs/, *n.* **1.** arrangement, order, as in one of the physical sciences. **2.** *Biol.* the movement of an organism in a particular direction in response to an external stimulus. **3.** *Surg.* the replacing of a displaced part, or the reducing of a hernial tumour or the like, by manipulation without cutting. [NL, from Gk: arrangement]

**-taxis,** a word element meaning 'arrangement', as in *chemotaxis.* [Gk]

**taxite** /ˈtæksaɪt/, *n.* a lava appearing to be formed from fragments, because of its parts having different colours, textures, etc. [(TAX(IS) + -ITE[1]] – **taxitic** /tækˈsɪtɪk/, *adj.*

**taxi truck** /ˈtæksi trʌk/, *n.* a truck for hire.

**taxiway** /ˈtæksiweɪ/, *n.* a paved or cleared strip leading from an air terminal apron to the runway.

**tax lurk** /ˈtæks lɜk/, *n.* a scheme or trick by which one avoids paying tax. Also, **tax dodge.**

**taxon** /ˈtæksɒn/, *n.* a term used to denote any taxonomic category, as species, genus, etc.

**taxonomy** /tækˈsɒnəmi/, *n.* **1.** classification, esp. in relation to its principles or laws. **2.** that department of science, or of a particular science, which deals with classification. [F *taxonomie,* from Gk *táxis* arrangement + *nomia* distribution]

–**taxonomic** /tæksəˈnɒmɪk/, **taxonomical** /tæksəˈnɒmɪkəl/, *adj.* –**taxonomically** /tæksəˈnɒmɪkli/, *adv.* –**taxonomist, taxonomer,** *n.*

**taxpayer** /ˈtækspeɪə/, *n.* one who pays a tax or is subject to taxation.

**tax rate** /ˈtæks reɪt/, *n.* the percentage of income assessed as payable as tax.

**tax return** /ˈ– rətɜn/, *n.* a statement of personal income required annually by tax authorities, used in assessing a person's tax liability.

**tax revolt** /ˈtæks rəvoʊlt/, *n.* a revolt by taxpayers against excessive taxation.

**tax shelter** /ˈ– ʃɛltə/, *n.* an investment, allowance, etc., used by a person or company to reduce or avoid tax liability.

**-taxy,** variant of **-taxis**, as in *heterotaxy.*

**taylor** /ˈteɪlə/, *n.* →**tailor** (def. 2).

**tayra** /ˈtaɪrə/, *n.* a mammal, *Eira barbara,* related to the martens, found in the forests of Central and South America.

**tazza** /ˈtætsə/, *n.* a shallow, saucer-like ornamental bowl, usu. on a high base or foot. [It.]

**t.b.,** **1.** trial balance. **2.** tuberculosis.

**Tb,** *Chem.* terbium.

**T.B.** /ti ˈbi/, *n.* tuberculosis.

**T-bar** /ˈti-ba/, *n.* a metal or wooden bar which is shaped like the letter T, as the gearstick of certain cars.

**T-bar lift** /ˈ– lɪft/, *n.* a ski-lift consisting of metal or wooden T-bars, suspended from the towing cable, which skiers straddle to be towed uphill.

T-bar lift

**T-bone steak** /ˌti-boʊn ˈsteɪk/, *n.* a cut of steak from the loin including sirloin and fillet on either side of a T-shaped bone.

**tbs.,** tablespoon; tablespoons. Also, **tbsp.**

**Tc,** *Chem.* technetium.

**TC,** Triple certificated.

**Tchad** /tʃæd/, *n.* →**Chad.**

**tcharibeena** /tʃærəˈbinə/, *n.* →**Bennett's tree-kangaroo.** [Aboriginal]

**tchurunga** /tʃəˈrʌŋgə/, *n.* →**churinga.**

**te**[1] /ti/, *n.* (in the solfa system) the seventh degree of the scale. Also, **ti.** See **solfa.** [See GAMUT]

**te**[2] /ti/, *n.* →**ti**[1].

**Te,** *Chem.* tellurium.

**tea** /ti/, *n.* **1.** the dried and prepared leaves of the shrub, *Thea sinensis,* from which a somewhat bitter, aromatic beverage is made by infusion in boiling water. **2.** the shrub itself, which is extensively cultivated in China, Japan, India, etc., and has fragrant white flowers. **3.** the beverage so prepared, served hot or iced. **4.** any kind of leaves, flowers, etc., so used, or any plant yielding them. **5.** any of various infusions prepared from the leaves, flowers, etc., of other plants, and used as beverages or medicines. **6.** →**beef tea. 7.** a light meal taken in the late afternoon. **8.** the main evening meal. **9.** *Colloq.* →**marijuana. 10. cup of tea,** *Colloq.* a task, topic, person, or object, etc., well suited to one's experience, taste, or liking: *that show wasn't my cup of tea.* [Chinese *t'e,* d. var. of Mandarin and Cantonese *ch'a*] –**tealess,** *adj.*

**tea-and-sugar bushranger** /ˌti-ən-ʃʊgə ˈbʊʃreɪndʒə/, *n.* a station owner who steals from his neighbours in order to set up his own herd.

**tea bag** /ˈti bæg/, *n.* a small container of paper or cloth filled with tea-leaves; infused in boiling water for making tea.

**tea ball** /ˈ– bɔl/, *n. U.S.* a perforated metal ball in which tea-leaves are to be immersed in boiling water to make tea.

**teaberry** /ˈtibəri, -bri/, *n., pl.* **-ries.** the spicy red fruit of the American wintergreen, *Gaultheria procumbens.*

**tea biscuit** /ˈti bɪskət/, *n.* a small, round, soft biscuit, usu. made with shortening and sugar.

**tea-break** /ˈti-breɪk/, *n.* a pause from work, usu. in the middle of the morning or afternoon, for tea, coffee, etc.

**tea caddy** /ˈti kædi/, *n.* a small box, tin, etc., for holding tea.

**teacake** /ˈtikeɪk/, *n.* **1.** a flat round cake made with a sweetened bread dough, often served toasted and buttered. **2.** a plain cake, often spiced and served buttered.

**teacart** /ˈtikat/, *n. U.S.* →**tea-trolley.**

**teach** /titʃ/, *v.,* **taught, teaching.** –*v.t.* **1.** to impart knowledge of or skill in; give instruction in: *he teaches mathematics.* **2.** to impart knowledge or skill to; give instruction to: *he teaches a large class.* –*v.i.* **3.** to impart knowledge or skill; give instruction. [ME *teche(n),* OE *tǣcan;* akin to TOKEN]

**teachable** /ˈtitʃəbəl/, *adj.* **1.** capable of being instructed, as a person; docile. **2.** capable of being taught, as a subject. –**teachability** /titʃəˈbɪləti/, **teachableness,** *n.* –**teachably,** *adv.*

**teacher** /ˈtitʃə/, *n.* one who teaches or instructs, esp. as a profession; instructor. –**teacherless,** *adj.*

**teacher aide** /ˈtitʃər eɪd/, *n.* a person employed in a non-professional capacity to assist a teacher. Also, **teacher's aide.**

**teachers' college** /ˈtitʃəz ˌkɒlɪdʒ/, *n.* a tertiary institution offering courses of training for teachers of all levels of primary and secondary education.

**tea-chest** /ˈti-tʃɛst/, *n.* a large wooden box or crate in which tea is packed.

**tea-chest bass** /– ˈbeɪs/, *n.* a bass musical instrument used in bush bands and consisting of a large hollow box, a pole, and a string for plucking stretched taut between the pole and the edge of the box.

**teach-in** /ˈtitʃ-ɪn/, *n., pl.* **teach-ins.** a prolonged public debate about a subject of topical interest conducted by persons having a special knowledge of the subject.

**teaching** /ˈtitʃɪŋ/, *n.* **1.** the act of one who or that which teaches; the work or profession of a teacher. **2.** that which is taught; a doctrine or precept.

**teaching aid** /ˈ– eɪd/, *n.* an item of prepared material, or a piece of equipment such as a tape recorder, film strip, etc., used by a teacher to assist in the presentation of a lesson.

**teaching fellow** /ˈ– fɛloʊ/, *n.* a university teacher below the rank of lecturer, appointed on a temporary basis while studying for a higher degree.

**teaching hospital** /ˈ– hɒspətl/, *n.* a hospital associated with a medical school and providing students, etc., with facilities in various branches of medical study.

**teaching machine** /ˈ– məʃin/, *n.* a mechanical or computerised teaching device, operated by the user, which presents him with items of information in a planned sequence, allowing him to pass to the next item only when he has answered correctly questions about the previous one.

**tea-cloth** /ˈti-klɒθ/, *n.* →**tea-towel.**

**tea-cosy** /ˈti-koʊzi/, *n.* a covering for a teapot to keep the tea hot.

**teacup** /ˈtikʌp/, *n.* **1.** a cup in which tea is served, usu. of small or moderate size. **2.** a teacupful. **3. a storm in a teacup,** *Colloq.* a great fuss about nothing very much.

**teacupful** /ˈtikʌpfʊl/, *n., pl.* **-fuls.** as much as a teacup will hold.

**tea-garden** /ˈti-gadn/, *n.* an open-air cafe, restaurant, etc., in which tea and other refreshments are served.

**tea-gown** /ˈti-gaʊn/, *n.* (formerly) a loose gown worn by women at afternoon tea.

**tea-house** /ˈti-haʊs/, *n.* a restaurant where tea is served, esp. in Japan and China.

**tea infuser** /ˈti ɪnfjuzə/, *n.* a device in the form of tongs with perforated spoonlike extremities to contain tealeaves, over which boiling water can be poured to make tea in a cup. Also, **tea maker.**

**teak** /tik/, *n.* **1.** a large East Indian tree, *Tectona grandis,* with a hard, durable, yellowish brown, resinous wood, used for shipbuilding, making furniture, etc. **2.** the wood. **3.** any of various similar trees or woods as *Flindersia australis.* [earlier *teke,* Pg. *teca,* from Malayalam *tēkka*]

**teakettle** /ˈtikɛtl/, *n.* →**kettle** (def. 1).

**teal** /til/, *n., pl.* **teals,** (*esp. collectively*) **teal.** any of various small freshwater ducks, as the grey teal, *Anas gibberifrons,* a wide-ranging bird of Australia, Indonesia, New Zealand and Pacific islands.

**tea lady** /ˈti ˌleɪdi/, *n.* one who makes and distributes tea, coffee, etc., in offices, factories, etc.

**tea-leaf**[1] /ˈti-lif/, *n., pl.* **-leaves** /-livz/. a fragment of the leaf of the tea plant, esp. when remaining in the teapot or cup after the tea has been infused.

**tea-leaf**[2] /ˈti-lif/, *Colloq.* *–n.* **1.** a thief. *–v.t.* **2.** to steal. [rhyming slang]

**team** /tim/, *n.* **1.** a number of persons associated in some joint action, esp. one of the sides in a match: *a team of football players.* **2.** two or more horses, oxen, or other animals harnessed together to draw a vehicle, plough or the like. **3.** two or more draught animals, or one such animal, together with the harness and the vehicle drawn. **4.** *Colloq.* a family or brood of young animals. **5.** *Obs.* offspring or progeny; race or lineage. *–v.t.* **6.** to join together in a team. **7.** *U.S.* to convey or transport by means of a team. *–v.i.* **8.** *U.S.* to drive a team. **9. team up with,** to work together with; collaborate with. [ME *teme,* OE *tēam,* c. G *Zaum,* Icel. *taumr* bridle, rein]

**tea maker** /ˈti meɪkə/, *n.* →**tea infuser.**

**team cream** /ˈ– krim/, *n.* *Colloq.* →**gang bang.**

**team-mate** /ˈtim-meɪt/, *n.* a member of the same team.

**tea money** /ˈti mʌni/, *n.* a meal allowance paid to employees required to work overtime during their normal evening meal period.

**teamster** /ˈtimstə/, *n.* **1.** one who drives a team, esp. as an occupation. **2.** *U.S.* one who drives a truck, esp. as an occupation; haulier.

**team-teach** /tim-ˈtitʃ/, *v.i.,* **-taught, -teaching.** to engage in team teaching.

**team teaching** /ˈtim titʃɪŋ/, *n.* a method of teaching in a school, whereby the members of a group of teachers have joint responsibility for a number of students often from different classes, and plan and conduct the teaching program as a team.

**teamwork** /ˈtimwɜk/, *n.* **1.** the work of a team with reference to coordination of effort and to collective efficiency. **2.** work done with a team.

**tea-party** /ˈti-pati/, *n.* an afternoon social gathering at which tea and other refreshments are served.

**tea-planter** /ˈti-plæntə, -plantə/, *n.* one who cultivates tea plants for a living.

**teapot** /ˈtipɒt/, *n.* a container with a lid, spout, and handle, in which tea is made and from which it is poured.

teapot

**teapoy** /ˈtipɔɪ/, *n.* **1.** a small three-legged table or stand. **2.** a small table for use in serving or storing tea. [from *ti* three (from Hind. *tīn*) + *poy* foot (from Pers. *pāi*) influenced by tea]

**tear**[1] /tɪə/, *n.* **1.** a drop of the limpid fluid secreted by the lachrymal gland, appearing in or flowing from the eye, chiefly as the result of emotion, esp. of grief. **2.** something resembling or suggesting a tear, as a drop of a liquid or a tear-like mass of a solid substance. **3.** (*pl.*) grief; sorrow. **4. in tears,** weeping. [ME *tere,* OE *tēar* (c. Icel. *tār*), Vernerian var. of *teagor,* c. Goth. *tagr;* akin to Gk *dákry,* Cornish *dagr*] – **tearless,** *adj.*

**tear**[2] /tɛə/, *v.,* **tore, torn, tearing,** *n.* *–v.t.* **1.** to pull apart or in pieces by force, esp. so as to leave ragged or irregular edges. **2.** to pull or pluck violently or with force. **3.** to distress greatly: *a heart torn with anguish.* **4.** to rend or divide: *a country torn by civil war.* **5.** to wound or injure by, or as by, rending; lacerate. **6.** to produce or effect by rending: *to tear a hole in one's coat.* **7.** to remove by force: *to be unable to tear oneself away from a place.* *–v.i.* **8.** to become torn. **9.** to make a tear or rent. **10.** *Colloq.* to move or go with violence or great haste. *–v.* **11.** Some special verb phrases are:

**tear at,** to pluck violently at; attempt to tear.

**tear down,** to pull down; destroy; demolish.

**tear into,** to attack violently, either physically or verbally.

**tear off, 1.** to pull or pluck violently. **2.** *Colloq.* to perform or do, esp. rapidly or casually. **3.** to leave hurriedly.

**tear strips off,** to reprove severely.

**tear up, 1.** to tear into small pieces. **2.** to cancel; annul.

*–n.* **12.** the act of tearing. **13.** a rent or fissure. **14.** a rage or passion; violent flurry or outburst. **15.** *Colloq.* a spree: *on the tear.* [ME *tere,* OE *teran,* c. D *teren,* G *zehren* destroy consume, Goth. *gatairan* destroy; akin to Gk *dérein* flav]

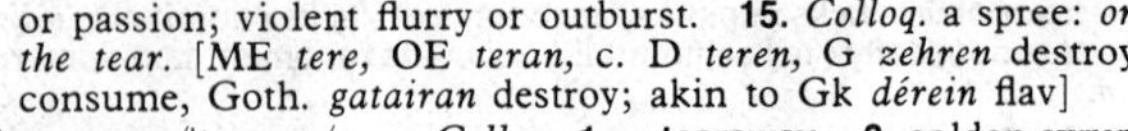

**tear-arse** /ˈtɛər-as/, *n.* *Colloq.* **1.** →**tearaway. 2.** golden syrup or treacle.

**tearaway** /ˈtɛərəweɪ/, *Colloq.* *–n.* **1.** an impetuous or unruly person. *–adj.* **2.** uncontrolled; impetuous.

**teardrop** /ˈtɪədrɒp/, *n.* a tear.

**tear duct** /ˈtɪə dʌkt/, *n.* a short tube in the inner corner of the lower eyelid which drains tears away into the nose.

**tearful** /ˈtɪəfəl/, *adj.* **1.** full of tears; weeping. **2.** causing tears. – **tearfully** /ˈtɪəfəli/, *adv.* – **tearfulness,** *n.*

**tear gas** /ˈtɪə gæs/, *n.* a gas used in warfare or in riots, which makes the eyes smart and water, thus producing a temporary blindness; lachrymator.

**tearing** /ˈtɛərɪŋ/, *adj.* extreme; violent: *he's in a tearing hurry.*

**tear-jerker** /ˈtɪə-dʒɜkə/, *n.* *Colloq.* an excessively sentimental novel, film, or the like.

**tearoom** /ˈtirum/, *n.* **1.** Also, **teashop.** a room or restaurant where tea and other refreshments are served to customers. **2.** a room in an office, etc., where staff take refreshments or meals.

**tea-rose** /ˈti-roʊz/, *n.* any of several varieties of cultivated roses having a scent supposed to resemble that of tea.

**tear sheet** /ˈtɛə ʃit/, *n.* a sheet or page in a magazine, journal, etc., perforated or cut so that it may be torn out easily if required.

**teary** /ˈtɪəri/, *adj.* **1.** of or like tears. **2.** tearful.

**tease** /tiz/, *v.,* **teased, teasing,** *n.* *–v.t.* **1.** to worry or irritate by persistent petty requests, trifling raillery, or other annoyances often in jest. **2.** to pull apart or separate the adhering fibres of, as in combing or carding wool; comb or card (wool, etc.); shred. **3.** to raise a nap on (cloth) with teasels; teasel. **4.** to give height and body to a hairdo by combing the hair from the end towards the scalp. **5.** to flirt. *–v.i.* **6.** to worry or disturb a person, etc., by importunity or persistent petty annoyance. *–n.* **7.** the act of teasing. **8.** the state of being teased. **9.** one who or that which teases or annoys. [ME *tese,* OE *tǣsan* tear up, c. D *teezen* pull] – **teasingly,** *adv.*

**teasel** /ˈtizəl/, *n., v.,* **-selled, -selling** or (*U.S.*) **-seled, -seling.** *–n.* **1.** any of the herbs with prickly leaves and flower heads constituting the dipsacaceous genus *Dipsacus.* **2.** the dried flower head or burr of *D. fullonum,* used for teasing or teaselling cloth. **3.** any mechanical contrivance used for teaselling. *–v.t.* **4.** to raise a nap on (cloth) with teasels; dress by means of teasels. Also, **teazel, teazle.** [ME *tesel,* OE *tǣsel;* akin to TEASE, *v.*] – **teaseller,** *n.*

**teaser** /ˈtizə/, *n.* **1.** one who or that which teases. **2.** a problem, puzzle. **3.** *Television.* an opening segment of a program designed to attract an audience. **4.** *Colloq.* →**prick-teaser.**

**teaser ad** /ˈtizər æd/, *n.* an advertisement designed primarily to attract customers to a shop by making a special offer on one item.

**teaser ram** /ˈ– ræm/, *n.* a vasectomised ram turned in among ewes to show which ewes are in season.

**tea-set** /ˈti-sɛt/, *n.* a number of cups, saucers, plates, etc., with a teapot, usu. of the same pattern, used in serving tea. Also, **tea-service** /ˈti-sɜvəs/.

**teasey** /ˈtizi/, *adj.* (of babies) fretful; suffering from an unidentified malaise. [Brit. colloq. (rare) TEASE + -Y[1]]

**teashop** /ˈtiʃɒp/, *n.* *Brit.* a small restaurant where tea and other light refreshments are served.

**teaspoon** /ˈtispun/, *n.* **1.** the small spoon commonly used to stir tea, coffee, etc. **2.** a teaspoonful.

**teaspoonful** /ˈtispunfʊl/, *n., pl.* **-spoonfuls, -spoonsful.** as much as a teaspoon can hold, about 5 millilitres.

**tea-strainer** /ˈti-streɪnə/, *n.* a device for holding back tea-leaves when pouring out tea.

**teat** /tit/, *n.* **1.** the protuberance on the breast or udder in female mammals (except the monotremes), where the milk ducts discharge; a nipple or mamilla. **2.** something resembling a teat, esp. for feeding a baby from a bottle. [ME *tete,* OF. See TIT[2]]

**tea-table** /ˈti-teɪbəl/, *n.* a table at which tea is served.

**tea-taster** /ˈti-teɪstə/, *n.* one whose occupation is to test and grade samples of tea by tasting them. – **tea-tasting,** *n.*

**teatime** /'titaɪm/, *n.* the time of day at which tea is served.

**tea-towel** /'ti-taʊl/, *n.* a cloth for drying crockery, etc., after it has been washed. Also, **tea-cloth.**

**tea-tray** /'ti-treɪ/, *n.* a tray on which articles used in serving tea are carried.

**tea-tree** /'ti-tri/, *n.* any species of *Leptospermum* or any of several species of the allied genus *Melaleuca,* as *L. scoparium,* of Australia and New Zealand, frequently developed as an ornamental with white, pink, or red flowers. Also, **ti-tree** (by confusion with **ti**[1]). [so called from its use as a tea substitute in the early days of the colony in Australia]

tea-tree

**tea-trolley** /'ti-trɒli/, *n.* a small table on wheels for carrying articles for use in serving tea.

**tea-urn** /'ti-ɜn/, *n.* an urn in which tea is made in large quantities.

**tea-wagon** /'ti-wægən/, *n.* →**tea-trolley.**

**teazel** /'tizəl/, *n., v.t.,* **-zelled, -zelling** or (*U.S.*) **-zeled, -zeling.** →**teasel.**

**teazle** /'tizəl/, *n., v.t.,* **-zled, -zling.** →**teasel.**

**tec** /tɛk/, *n. Colloq.* a detective. Also, **'tec.**

**tech** /tɛk/, *n. Colloq.* a technical college or school.

**tech.,** **1.** technical. **2.** technology.

**technetium** /tɛk'niʃəm/, *n.* an element of the manganese family, the first element to be made artificially, which does not occur in nature but is present in the fission products of uranium. *Symbol:* Tc; *at. no.:* 43. The most stable isotope has *at. wt.:* 99. Also, *Obs.,* **masurium.** [Gk *technētós* artificial + -IUM]

**technic** /'tɛknɪk/, *n.* **1.** technique. **2.** a technicality. **3.** →**technics** (def. 2). *–adj.* **4.** technical. [Gk *technikos* pertaining to art, skilful, technical]

**technical** /'tɛknɪkəl/, *adj.* **1.** belonging or pertaining to an art, science, or the like: *technical skill.* **2.** peculiar to or characteristic of a particular art, science, profession, trade, etc.; *technical details.* **3.** using terms or treating a subject in a manner peculiar to a particular field, as a writer or a book. **4.** skilled in, or familiar in a practical way with, a particular art, trade, etc., as a person. **5.** pertaining to or connected with the mechanical or industrial arts and the applied sciences: *a technical school.* **6.** so considered from a strictly legal point of view or a rigid interpretation of the rules: *a military engagement ending in a technical defeat.* **7. get technical,** *Colloq.* to propound or apply a strict interpretation of the rules. – **technically,** *adv.* – **technicalness,** *n.*

**technical atmosphere** /– 'ætməsfɪə/, *n.* a unit used on the European continent equal to one kilogram force per square centimetre, which equals 98 066.5 pascals. *Abbrev.:* at

**technical college** /'– kɒlɪdʒ/, *n.* a state institution providing technical education at the tertiary level.

**technical education** /– ɛdʒə'keɪʃən/, *n.* education for tradespeople, technicians and technologists specialising in courses in specific vocational skills, as wool classing, motor mechanics, industrial electronics, etc.

**technicality** /tɛknə'kæləti/, *n., pl.* **-ties.** **1.** technical character. **2.** the use of technical methods or terms. **3.** something that is technical; a technical point, detail, or expression. **4.** a literal, often narrow-minded interpretation of a rule, law, etc.; quibble: *he was ruled ineligible on a technicality.*

**technical knockout** /,tɛknɪkəl 'nɒkaʊt/, *n.* the decision of the referee of a boxing contest to award the victory to one contestant as though he had delivered a knockout, because the other contestant is in the estimation of the referee not in a fit state to continue.

**technical school** /'– skul/, *n.* a secondary school offering technical education.

**technical sergeant** /– 'sadʒənt/, *n. U.S.* (in the Air Force and Marine Corps) a non-commissioned officer ranking below a master sergeant and above a staff sergeant.

**technician** /tɛk'nɪʃən/, *n.* **1.** one versed in the technicalities of a subject. **2.** one skilled in the technique of an art, as music or painting. **3.** a person considered from the point of view of his or her technical skill: *a good technician; a bad technician.*

**technicolour** /'tɛknɪkʌlə, -nə-/, *n.* **1.** Also, **technicolor.** a process of making cinema films in colour by superimposing the three primary colours to produce a final coloured print. *–adj.* **2.** bright, vivid, esp. of colours: *a technicolour dream.* [Trademark *Technicolor*]

**technicolour yawn** /– 'jɔn/, *n. Colloq.* the act of vomiting.

**technics** /'tɛknɪks/, *n.* **1.** technique. **2.** the study or science of an art or of arts in general, esp. of the mechanical or industrial arts.

**technique** /tɛk'nik/, *n.* **1.** method or performance; way of accomplishing. **2.** technical skill, esp. in artistic work. [F. See TECHNIC]

**techno-,** a word element referring to 'technic', 'technology'. [Gk, combining form of *téchnē* art, skill]

**technocracy** /tɛk'nɒkrəsi/, *n.* **1.** a theory and movement (prominent about 1932) advocating control of industrial resources and reorganisation of the social system, based on the findings of technologists and engineers. **2.** a system of government which applies this theory. **3.** people who occupy senior positions in various technical fields, as engineering, science, economics, etc., considered as a class exercising a strong influence over society as a whole. – **technocrat** /'tɛknəkræt/, *n.* – **technocratic** /tɛknə'krætɪk/, *adj.*

**technography** /tɛk'nɒgrəfi/, *n.* description of the arts.

**technol.,** **1.** technology. **2.** technological.

**technological** /tɛknə'lɒdʒɪkəl/, *adj.* of or pertaining to technology; relating to science and industry. Also, **technologic.** – **technologically,** *adv.*

**technology** /tɛk'nɒlədʒi/, *n.* **1.** the branch of knowledge that deals with science and engineering, or its practice, as applied to industry; applied science. **2.** the terminology of an art, science, etc.; technical nomenclature. [Gk *technologīa* systematic treatment] – **technologist,** *n.*

**techy** /'tɛtʃi/, *adj.,* **-ier, -iest.** →**tetchy.** – **techily,** *adv.* – **techiness,** *n.*

**tectonic** /tɛk'tɒnɪk/, *adj.* **1.** of or pertaining to building or construction; constructive; architectural. **2.** *Geol.* **a.** pertaining to the structure of the earth's crust. **b.** referring to the forces or conditions within the earth that cause movements of the crust such as earthquakes, folds, faults and the like. **c.** designating the results of such movements: *tectonic valleys.* [LL *tectonicus,* from Gk *tektonikós* (def. 1)] – **tectonically,** *adv.*

**tectonics** /tɛk'tɒnɪks/, *n.* **1.** the science or art of assembling, shaping, or ornamenting materials in construction; the constructive arts in general. **2.** structural geology.

**ted**[1] /tɛd/, *v.t.,* **tedded, tedding.** to spread out for drying, as newly mown hay. [ME, c. d. G *zetten* scatter]

**ted**[2] /tɛd/, *n. Brit. Colloq.* a teddy boy.

**tedder** /'tɛdə/, *n.* **1.** one who teds. **2.** an implement that spreads and turns newly mown grass or hay from the swath for the purpose of drying.

**teddy bear** /'tɛdi bɛə/, *n.* a stuffed toy bear. [said to be named after *Theodore* Roosevelt, President of the U.S. 1901-09]

**Teddy Bear** /'tɛdi bɛə/, *n. Colloq.* a lair. [rhyming slang]

**teddy boy** /'tɛdi bɔɪ/, *n. Brit. Colloq.* (in the mid 1950s) a boy in his teens or early twenties who dressed in a fashion resembling that of the Edwardian era and identified himself with others affecting a similar style of dress.

**Te Deum** /teɪ 'deɪəm, ti 'diəm/, *n.* **1.** an ancient Latin hymn of praise, in the form of a psalm, sung regularly at matins. **2.** a musical setting of the hymn. **3.** a service of thanksgiving in which this hymn forms a prominent part. [L, first two words of the hymn]

**tedious** /'tidiəs/, *adj.* **1.** marked by tedium; long and tiresome: *tedious tasks, journeys, etc.* **2.** prolix so as to cause weariness, as a speaker. [ME, from LL *taediōsus*] – **tediously,** *adv.* – **tediousness,** *n.*

**tedium** /'tidiəm/, *n.* the state of being wearisome; irksomeness; tediousness. [L *taedium*]

**tee**[1] /ti/, *n.* **1.** the letter T, t. **2.** something shaped like a T, as a three-way joint used in fitting pipes together. **3.** the mark aimed at in various games, as curling. *–adj.* **4.** having a crosspiece at the top; shaped like a T.

**tee**[2] /ti/, *n., v.,* **teed, teeing.** *–n.* **1.** *Golf.* Also, **teeing ground.** the starting place, usu. a hard mound of earth, at the beginning of each fairway. **2.** *Golf.* a small heap of sand, or a rubber, plastic, or wooden object, on which the ball is placed and from which it is driven at the beginning of a hole. *–v.t.* **3.** *Golf.* to place (the ball) on a tee. *–v.i.* **4.** *Golf.* to strike the ball from a tee (fol. by *off*). **5.** to organise, plan (fol. by *up*). [orig. uncert.]

**teehee** /ti'hi/, *interj., n., v.,* **-heed, -heeing.** *–interj.* **1.** (the sound of a tittering laugh.) *–n.* **2.** a titter; a snigger. *–v.i.* **3.** to titter; snigger. [ME; imitative]

**teem**[1] /tim/, *v.i.* **1.** to abound or swarm; be prolific or fertile (fol. by *with*). **2.** *Obs.* to be or become pregnant; bring forth young. *–v.t.* **3.** *Obs.* to produce (offspring). [ME *teme(n)*, OE *tēman, tīeman* produce (offspring), from *tēam* child-bearing, offspring] – **teemer,** *n.*

**teem**[2] /tim/, *v.i.* **1.** to empty or pour out; discharge. **2.** to rain very hard. *–v.t.* **3.** to empty liquid from (a vessel). [ME *teme(n)*, from Scand.; cf. Icel. *tæma*, from *tōmr,* adj.]

**teeming** /'timɪŋ/, *adj.* **1.** abounding or swarming with something, as with people. **2.** prolific or fertile.

**teen** /tin/, *adj. Colloq.* teenage.

**-teen,** a termination forming the cardinal numerals from 13 to 19. [ME and OE *-tēne,* combining form of TEN, c. G *-zehn*]

**teenage** /'tineɪdʒ/, *adj.* of, pertaining to, or characteristic of a teenager.

**teenager** /'tineɪdʒə/, *n.* a person in his or her teens.

**teens** /tinz/, *n. pl.* the period of one's life between the ages of 12 and 20.

**teeny** /'tini/, *adj.,* **-nier, -niest.** tiny.

**teeny-bopper** /'tini-bɒpə/, *n.* a young teenager (12-15 years) who conforms to the style of dress, music, etc., of current pop groups. [TEEN(AGER) + BOP + -ER[1]]

**teeny-weeny** /'tini-wini/, *adj.* (*esp. in children's speech*) very small. Also, **teensy-weensy.**

**teepee** /'tipi/, *n.* →**tepee.**

**tee-shirt** /'ti-ʃɜt/, *n.* →**T-shirt.**

**teeter** /'titə/, *v.i.* **1.** to seesaw. **2.** to move unsteadily. *–v.t.* **3.** to move (anything) with a seesaw motion. *–n.* **4.** a seesaw. **5.** a seesaw motion. [var. of *titter,* from Scand.; cf. Icel. *titra,* c. G *zittern* tremble, quiver]

**teeth** /tiθ/, *n.* **1.** plural of **tooth. 2.** the punitive sections of a legislation, ruling, etc., meant to ensure its enforcement: *give a regulation teeth.* **3. be fed (up) to the (back) teeth,** *Colloq.* to be heartily sick of; have had more than enough of (fol. by *with*). **4. get one's teeth into,** to start to cope effectively with (a problem, etc.). **5. have the bit in (between) one's teeth,** to tackle a task, problem, etc., in a determined and energetic fashion. **6. in one's teeth, a.** in direct opposition or conflict. **b.** to one's face; openly. **7. in the teeth of, a.** so as to face or confront; straight against. **b.** in defiance of; in spite of. **c.** in the face or presence of. **8. scarce (rare) as hen's teeth,** *Colloq.* very rare. **9. to the teeth,** fully: *armed to the teeth.*

**teethe** /tið/, *v.i.,* **teethed, teething.** to grow teeth; cut one's teeth.

**teething** /'tiðɪŋ/, *n.* **1.** the first growth of teeth. **2.** the phenomena associated with this.

**teething ring** /'– rɪŋ/, *n.* a circular disc, usu. of plastic, ivory, bone, etc., on which a teething baby may bite.

**teething stage** /'– steɪdʒ/, *n.* that stage of a project, etc., usu. early, at which difficulties tend to occur.

**teething troubles** /'– trʌbəlz/, *n. pl.* difficulties, usu. temporary ones, which occur at the initial stages of an enterprise. Also, **teething difficulties, teething problems.**

**teethridge** /'tiθrɪdʒ/, *n.* →**alveolar ridge.**

**teetotal** /'titoʊtl, ti'toʊtl/, *adj.* **1.** of or pertaining to, advocating, or pledged to total abstinence from intoxicating drink. **2.** *U.S. Colloq.* absolute; complete. [from TOTAL, with reduplication of initial *t-* for emphasis] – **teetotally,** *adv.*

**teetotalism** /ti'toʊtəlɪzəm/, *n.* the principle or practice of total abstinence from intoxicating drink.

**teetotaller** /'titoʊtələ, ti'toʊtələ/, *n.* one who abstains totally from intoxicating drink. Also, *U.S.,* **teetotaler.**

**teetotum** /ti'toʊtəm/, *n.* **1.** any small top spun with the fingers. **2.** a kind of die having four sides, each marked with a different initial letter, spun with the fingers in an old game of chance. [earlier *T totum,* from *T.* (abbrev. for *tōtum,* used on toy) + *tōtum* (neut. of L *tōtus* all)]

**teflon** /'tɛflɒn/, *n.* **1.** a lining for saucepans, frying pans, etc., made from polytetrafluoroethylene, to which food does not adhere. *–adj.* **2.** of or pertaining to saucepans, frying pans, etc., which are coated with teflon. [Trademark]

**teg** /tɛg/, *n.* a sheep that is one or two years old. [orig. uncert.]

**tegmen** /'tɛgmən/, *n., pl.* **-mina** /-mənə/. **1.** a cover, covering, or integument. **2.** *Bot.* the delicate inner integument or coat of a seed. **3.** (in certain orthopterous insects) one of a pair of leathery forewings serving as a protective covering for the hind wings in certain insects. [L: covering] – **tegminal** /'tɛgmənəl/, *adj.*

**tegular** /'tɛgjələ/, *adj.* **1.** pertaining to or resembling a tile. **2.** consisting of or arranged like tiles. [L *tēgula* tile + -AR[1]] – **tegularly,** *adv.*

**tegument** /'tɛgjəmənt/, *n.* a covering or investment; an integument. [L *tegumentum*] – **tegumental** /tɛgjə'mɛntl/, **tegumentary** /tɛgjə'mɛntəri/, *adj.*

**tehee** /ti'hi/, *interj., n., v.i.,* **-heed, -heeing.** →**teehee.**

**tektite** /'tɛktaɪt/, *n.* a small glass-like body, whose chemical composition is unrelated to the geological formation in which it is found; believed to be of meteoric origin. **Carbonaceous tektites** contain traces of carbon compounds. [Gk *tēktós* molten + -ITE[1]]

tektite

**tel-**[1], variant of **tele-**[1], as in *telaesthesia.* Properly, this form should occur wherever the following word or word element begins with a vowel. However, **teleo-** is more frequently found.

**tel-**[2], variant of **tele-**[2], as in *telencephalon.* For form, see **tel-**[1].

**tel., 1.** telegram. **2.** telegraph. **3.** telephone.

**telaesthesia** /tɛləs'θiʒə, -'θiziə/, *n.* sensation or perception received at a distance without the normal operation of the recognised organs. Also, *U.S.,* **telesthesia.** [NL. See TEL-[1], AESTHESIA]

**telamon** /'tɛləmən/, *n., pl.* **telamones** /tɛlə'moʊniz/. a figure of a man used like a supporting column; an atlas (def. 5). [L, from Gk: name of mythological hero]

**telangiectasis** /təlændʒi'ɛktəsəs/, *n., pl.* **-ses** /-siz/. chronic dilatation of the capillaries and other small blood vessels, as seen in the faces of alcoholics, those exposed to raw, cold climates, and certain congenital sufferers. [NL, from Gk *télos* end + *angeîon* receptacle + *éktasis* extension] – **telangiectatic** /tə,lændʒiɛk'tætɪk/, *adj.*

**tele-**[1], **1.** a word element meaning 'distant', esp. 'transmission over a distance', as in *telegraph.* Also, **tel-**[1], **telo-**[1]. **2.** a word element referring to *television* or *telephone.* [combining form representing Gk *têle* far]

**tele-**[2], a word element referring to the end, as in *teleological.* Also, **tel-**[2], **teleo-, telo-**[2]. [combining form representing Gk *télos* end, *téleos* complete]

**telecast** /'tɛləkast, 'tɛli-/, *v.,* **-cast** or **-casted, -casting,** *n.* *–v.i., v.t.* **1.** to broadcast by television. *–n.* **2.** a television broadcast.

**teleceptor** /'tɛlisɛptə, 'tɛlə-/, *n.* a sense organ, as the nose, eyes, ears, or skin, responding to and conveying stimuli from the external environment. [TELE-[1] + -CEPTOR]

**telecine** /'tɛli,sɪni/, *n.* **1.** cinematography specifically for television use. *–adj.* **2.** of or pertaining to such cinematography.

**telecom.,** telecommunications.

**telecommunication** /,tɛləkəmjunə'keɪʃən, ,tɛli-/, *n.* **1.** (*pl.*) the science or technology of telegraphic or telephonic communications by line or radio transmission. **2.** a message so communicated.

**teledex** /'tɛlədɛks/, *n.* a device in which names with appropriate telephone numbers are listed alphabetically, which can be opened at the letter of the alphabet selected.

**teledu** /ˈtɛlədu/, *n.* a small badger-like mammal, *Mydaus javanensis,* of the mountains of Java, Sumatra, and Borneo, which (like the skunk) ejects a fetid secretion, and which is coloured like the skunk but has a short tail. [Malay]

teledu

**telefacsimile** /ˌtɛlifækˈsɪməli/, *n.* a system for transmitting and reproducing printed matter by telephone.

**teleferic** /tɛləˈfɛrɪk/, *n.* **1.** →**cableway.** *–adj.* **2.** of or denoting a cableway. [F *téléphérique*]

**telefilm** /ˈtɛlifɪlm/, *n.* a feature film made for television.

**teleg.**, **1.** telegram. **2.** telegraph. **3.** telegraphy.

**telega** /təˈleɪgə/, *n.* a crude Russian cart having four wheels and no springs. [Russ.]

**telegony** /təˈlɛgəni/, *n.* the supposed influence of a previous sire upon the progeny subsequently borne by the same mother to other sires. – **telegonic** /tɛləˈgɒnɪk/, *adj.*

**telegram** /ˈtɛləgræm/, *n.* a communication sent by telegraph; a telegraphic message. – **telegrammic** /tɛləˈgræmɪk/, **telegrammatic** /tɛləgrəˈmætɪk/, *adj.*

**telegraph** /ˈtɛləgræf, -graf/, *n.* **1.** an apparatus, system, or process for transmitting messages or signals to a distance, esp. by means of an electrical device consisting essentially of a transmitting or sending instrument and a distant receiving instrument connected by a conducting wire, or other communications channel, the making and breaking of the circuit at the sending end causing a corresponding effect, as on a sounder, at the receiving end. **2.** a telegraphic message. *–v.t.* **3.** to transmit or send (a message, etc.) by telegraph. **4.** to send a message to (a person) by telegraph. **5.** *Sport Colloq.* to give prior indication of (one's moves). **6. telegraph one's punches,** *Colloq.* to give prior indication of one's plans or intentions, esp. to an opponent. *–v.i.* **7.** to send a message by telegraph. – **telegrapher** /təˈlɛgrəfə/, **telegraphist** /təˈlɛgrəfəst/, *n.* – **telegraphic** /tɛləˈgræfɪk/, **telegraphical** /tɛləˈgræfɪkəl/, *adj.* – **telegraphically** /tɛləˈgræfɪkli/, *adv.*

**telegraphese** /tɛləgrəˈfiz/, *n.* a manner of writing or speaking characterised by the concise and elliptical style in which telegrams are worded.

**telegraphic transfer** /ˌtɛləgræfɪk ˈtrænsfɜ/, *n.* the transfer, by telegraph, radio, or telephone, of credit from one person or firm to another.

**telegraphoscope** /tɛləˈgræfəskoup/, *n.* a telegraphic device by means of which a picture may be reproduced at a distance.

**telegraph plant** /ˈtɛləgræf plænt/, *n.* an East Indian plant, *Desmodium gyrans,* remarkable for the spontaneous, jerking, signal-like motions of its leaflets.

**telegraph pole** /ˈ– poul/, *n.* a pole for supporting telegraph wires.

**telegraphy** /təˈlɛgrəfi/, *n.* the art or practice of constructing or operating telegraphs.

**telekinesis** /tɛləkaɪˈnisəs, -kə-/, *n.* the production of motion in a body, apparently without the application of material force, a power long claimed by spiritualist mediums; teleportation. [TELE-[1] + Gk *kinēsis* movement]

**telemark** /ˈtɛlimak/, *n.* **1.** *Skiing.* a turn made by placing one ski well in front of the other, and gradually turning the tip of the forward ski in the direction to be turned. **2.** *Canoeing.* a paddle stroke in which the paddle is held to one side and then leaned on to make the canoe turn sharply in the water. [from *Telemark,* county in Norway]

**telemeter** /təˈlɛmətə, ˈtɛləmitə/, *n.* **1.** any of certain devices or attachments for determining distances by measuring the angle subtending a known distance. **2.** the device in a telemetric system which automatically scans what is being measured and transmits its information to another place. **3.** *Photog.* a small rangefinder. *–v.t.* **4.** to transmit the results of measurements over a distance.

**telemetry** /təˈlɛmətri/, *n.* the automatic measurement of something distant or inaccessible and the transmission of the measurements to a device for recording or displaying them, as when radiation, etc., in space is measured by sensors on a spacecraft and the results are monitored on earth, or information about some bodily process is collected from a device implanted in the body. – **telemetric** /tɛləˈmɛtrɪk/, *adj.*

**telemotor** /ˈtɛləmoutə/, *n.* a mechanical, electrical or hydraulic system, by which power is applied at and controlled from a distant point, esp. such a system actuating a ship's rudder.

**telencephalon** /tɛlɛnˈsɛfəlɒn/, *n.* the anterior end of the embryonic nervous system which forms the cerebral hemisphere in the adult vertebrate. – **telencephalic** /ˌtɛlɛnsəˈfælɪk/, *adj.*

**teleo-**, variant of **tele-**[2], as in *teleology.*

**teleological argument** /ˌtiliəlɒdʒɪkəl ˈagjəmənt/, *n.* the argument for the existence of God based on the assumption that order in the universe implies an orderer and cannot be a natural feature of the universe.

**teleology** /tiliˈɒlədʒi, tɛl-/, *n.* **1.** the doctrine of final causes or purposes. **2.** the study of the evidences of design or purpose in nature. **3.** such design or purpose. **4.** the belief that purpose and design are a part of, or are apparent in, nature. **5.** the doctrine in vitalism that phenomena are guided not only by mechanical forces but also by the ends towards which they move. **6.** *Ethics.* the doctrine that right and wrong are to be determined solely by the efficacy of actions in attaining desirable ends. [NL *teleologia,* from Gk. See TELEO-, -LOGY] – **teleological** /tiliəˈlɒdʒɪkəl/, *adj.* – **teleologically** /tiliəˈlɒdʒɪkli/, *adv.* – **teleologist** /tiliˈɒlədʒəst/, *n.*

**teleost** /ˈtɛliɒst/, *adj.* **1.** belonging or pertaining to the Teleostei, the group of fishes that have a skeleton composed at least in part of bone rather than of cartilage, including the large majority of living species. *–n.* **2.** a teleost fish. [NL, backformation from *teleostei,* pl. (from Gk *tele-* TELE-[2] + *ostéon* bone), by false analysis of pl. form] – **teleostean** /tɛliˈɒstiən/, *adj., n.*

**telepathist** /təˈlɛpəθəst/, *n.* **1.** a student of or believer in telepathy. **2.** one having telepathic powers.

**telepathy** /təˈlɛpəθi/, *n.* communication of one mind with another by some means other than the normal use of the senses. – **telepathic** /tɛləˈpæθɪk/, *adj.* – **telepathically** /tɛləˈpæθɪkli/, *adv.*

**teleph.**, telephony.

**telephone** /ˈtɛləfoun/, *n., v.,* **-phoned, -phoning.** *–n.* **1.** an apparatus, system, or process for transmission of sound or speech to a distant point, esp. by an electrical device. **2. on (off) the telephone,** engaged (unengaged) in a telephone conversation. *–v.t.* **3.** to speak to or summon (a person) by telephone. **4.** to send (a message, etc.) by telephone. *–v.i.* **5.** to send a message by telephone. – **telephoner,** *n.* – **telephonic** /tɛləˈfɒnɪk/, *adj.* – **telephonically** /tɛləˈfɒnɪkli/, *adv.*

**telephone box** /ˈ– bɒks/, *n.* a small booth or enclosure containing a public telephone. Also, **phone box, telephone booth.**

**telephone directory** /ˈ– dəˌrɛktəri/, *n.* a book listing names, addresses and telephone numbers of the telephone subscribers of a particular city or region.

**telephonist** /təˈlɛfənəst/, *n.* one who operates a telephone or a telephone switchboard.

**telephony** /təˈlɛfəni/, *n.* the art or practice of constructing or operating telephones.

**telephoto** /ˈtɛlifoutou, ˈtɛlə-/, *adj.* **1.** denoting or pertaining to telephotography. **2.** denoting or pertaining to a form of photographic lens used in telephotography (def. 1) which produces magnified images.

**telephotograph** /tɛliˈfoutəgræf, -graf, tɛlə-/, *n.* **1.** a picture made with a telephoto lens. **2.** a picture transmitted by wire or radio.

**telephotography** /ˌtɛlifəˈtɒgrəfi, ˌtɛlə-/, *n.* **1.** the art of photographing objects too distant for the ordinary camera, by the use of telephoto lenses. **2.** the art of electrically reproducing photographs or facsimiles over a communications channel. – **telephotographic** /ˌtɛlifoutəˈgræfɪk, ˌtɛlə-/, *adj.*

**telephoto lens** /ˌtɛləfoutou ˈlɛnz/, *n.* a lens used in or attached to a camera for producing an enlarged image of a distant object.

**teleplay** /ˈtɛlipleɪ/, *n.* a play written or produced especially for television.

**teleplayer** /ˈtɛlipleɪə/, *n.* a device for playing pre-recorded television programs through a domestic television set.

**teleportation** /tɛlipɔˈteɪʃən/, *n.* →**telekinesis.**

**teleprinter** /ˈtɛliprɪntə, ˈtɛlə-/, *n.* an instrument having a typewriter keyboard which transmits and receives messages by telegraphic transmission, or to and from a computer. Also, **teletype.**

**teleprocessing** /'tɛliˌprousɛsɪŋ/, *n.* the processing of information held at another place, by means of an on-line computer.

**teleprompter** /'tɛləprɒmptə/, *n.* an electronic prompting device used esp. by television performers, speakers, etc., on which the magnified text of the script is unrolled at a pace suitable to the speaker's speed of delivery. [Trademark]

**teleran** /'tɛləræn/, *n.* a system of aircraft navigation using radar to map the sky above an airfield, which, together with the map of the airfield itself and other pertinent data, is transmitted by television to the aeroplane approaching the field. [short for *Tele(vision) R(adar) A(ir) N(avigation)*]

**telerecord** /tɛlirə'kɔd, tɛlə-/, *v.t.* to record (a program, etc.) for showing on television.

**telerecording** /ˌtɛlirə'kɔdɪŋ, ˌtɛlə-/, *n.* a recorded television program.

**telescope** /'tɛləskoup/, *n., adj., v.,* **-scoped, -scoping.** *–n.* **1.** an optical instrument for making distant objects appear nearer and larger. There are two principal forms, one (**refracting telescope**) consisting essentially of a lens or object glass for forming an image of the object and an eyepiece or combination of lenses for magnifying this image, and the other (**reflecting telescope**) having a similar arrangement but containing a concave mirror or speculum instead of an object glass. **Astronomical telescopes** are used for viewing objects outside the earth; **terrestrial telescopes** are used for viewing distant objects on the earth's surface. *–adj.* **2.** consisting of parts which fit and slide one within another. *–v.t.* **3.** to force together, one into another, or force into something else, in the manner of the sliding tubes of a jointed telescope. **4.** to condense; shorten. *–v.i.* **5.** to slide together, or into something else in the manner of the tubes of a jointed telescope. **6.** to be driven one into another, as railway carriages in a collision. [NL *telescopium,* from Gk *teleskópos* far-seeing + *-ium* -IUM]

**telescopic** /tɛlə'skɒpɪk/, *adj.* **1.** of, pertaining to, or of the nature of a telescope. **2.** obtained by means of a telescope: *a telescopic view of the moon.* **3.** seen by a telescope; visible only through a telescope. **4.** far-seeing: *a telescopic eye.* **5.** consisting of parts which slide one within another like the tubes of a jointed telescope, and thus capable of being extended or shortened. Also, **telescopical.** – **telescopically,** *adv.*

**telescopic sight** /– 'saɪt/, *n.* a telescope mounted on a gun and used for sighting.

**telescopy** /tə'lɛskəpi/, *n.* **1.** the use of the telescope. **2.** telescopic investigation. – **telescopist** /tə'lɛskəpəst/, *n.*

**telesis** /'tɛləsəs/, *n. Sociol.* deliberate, purposeful utilisation of the processes of nature and society to obtain particular goals. [Gk: completion]

**telespectroscope** /tɛli'spɛktrəskoup/, *n.* an instrument for analysing the spectra of astronomical bodies, consisting of a telescope attached to a spectroscope.

**telestereoscope** /tɛli'stɛriəskoup, -'stɪə-/, *n.* a binocular optical instrument used for stereoscopic viewing of distant objects; a small rangefinder.

**telesthesia** /tɛləs'θiʒə, -'θiziə/, *n. U.S.* →**telaesthesia.**

**teletext** /'tɛlitɛkst/, *n.* a data service provided via a conventional television system.

**telethermometer** /tɛliθə'mɒmətə/, *n.* any of various thermometers that indicate or record temperatures at a distance, as by means of an electric current. – **telethermometry,** *n.*

**telethon** /'tɛləθɒn/, *n.* a television program lasting for many hours, soliciting contributions from viewers in support of a charity or other community effort.

**teletype** /'tɛlitaɪp, 'tɛlə-/, *n.* →**teleprinter.** [Trademark]

**teletypewriter** /tɛli'taɪpraɪtə/, *n.* →**teleprinter.**

**teleview** /'tɛlivju/, *v.t., v.i.* to view with a television receiver; watch television. – **televiewer,** *n.*

**televise** /'tɛləvaɪz/, *v.t.,* **-vised, -vising.** to broadcast by television.

**television** /'tɛləvɪʒən/, *n.* **1.** the broadcasting of a still or moving image via radio waves to receivers which project it on a picture tube for viewing at a distance from the point of origin. **2.** the process employed. **3.** the field of broadcasting by television. **4.** a television receiver; television set. – **televisional** /tɛlə'vɪʒənəl/, **televisionary** /tɛlə'vɪʒənri/, *adj.*

**television station** /'– steɪʃən/, *n.* **1.** a combination of devices for television transmission and/or receiving. **2.** a complete installation for television broadcasting, including transmitting apparatus, television studios, etc. **3.** an organisation engaged in broadcasting, on a fixed channel, programs of news, entertainment, propaganda, etc.

**telex** /'tɛlɛks/, *n.* **1.** an international service provided by postal authorities in which teleprinters are loaned to subscribers. **2.** →**teleprinter.** **3.** a message received or sent by teleprinter. *–v.i.* **4.** to send a message by telex. *–v.t.* **5.** to send (someone) a message by telex. **6.** to send (a message) by telex.

**telfer** /'tɛlfə/, *n., adj., v.t.* →**telpher.** – **telferage,** *n.*

**telic** /'tɛlɪk/, *adj.* **1.** *Gram.* expressing end or purpose, as a clause. **2.** tending to a definite end. [Gk *telikós* final]

**teliospore** /'tiliəspɔ, 'tɛli-/, *n.* a spore of certain rust fungi which carries the fungus through the winter and which, on germination, produces the promycelium.

**telium** /'tiliəm, 'tɛli-/, *n.* the sorus of the rust fungi bearing teliospores.

**tell**[1] /tɛl/, *v.,* **told, telling.** *–v.t.* **1.** to give an account or narrative of; narrate; relate (a story, tale, etc.): *to tell one's life story.* **2.** to make known by speech or writing (a fact, news, information, etc.); communicate. **3.** to announce or proclaim. **4.** to utter (the truth, a lie, etc.). **5.** to express in words (thoughts, feelings, etc.). **6.** to reveal or divulge (something secret or private). **7.** to say plainly or positively: *he won't tell me if it's true or not.* **8.** to discern (a distant person or thing) so as to be able to identify or describe: *can you tell who that is over there?* **9.** to recognise or distinguish: *you could hardly tell the difference between them.* **10.** to inform or apprise (a person, etc.) of something. **11.** to assure emphatically: *I won't, I tell you!* **12.** to bid, order, or command: *tell him to stop.* **13.** to count or enumerate, as votes. **14. tell off, a.** to mention one after another, as in enumerating; count or set one by one or in exact amount: *to tell off five metres.* **b.** to separate from the whole, a group, etc., and assign to a particular task. **c.** *Colloq.* to scold; rebuke severely. **15. tell tales (out of school)** to report the misdemeanours, true or fictitious, of one's friends, peers, relatives, etc. *–v.i.* **16.** to give an account or report: *he told about his experience.* **17.** to give evidence or be an indication (fol. by *of*): *to tell of wonders!* **18.** to disclose something secret or private; play the informer (usu. fol. by *on*). **19.** to know; be certain: *how can we tell if there is a life after death?* **20.** to have force or effect; operate effectively: *a contest in which every stroke tells.* **21.** to produce a marked or severe effect: *the strain was telling on his health.* [ME *telle,* OE *tellan,* c. D *tellen* reckon, count, Icel. *telja* tell, count, akin to TALE] – **tellable,** *adj.*

**tell**[2] /tɛl/, *n.* a large mound of earth usu. covering the ruins of an ancient city. Also, **tel.** [Ar.]

**teller** /'tɛlə/, *n.* **1.** one who or that which tells, relates, or communicates; a narrator. **2.** one employed in a bank to receive or pay out money over the counter. **3.** one who tells, counts, or enumerates, as one appointed to count votes.

**tellie** /'tɛli/, *n. Colloq.* television. Also, **telly.**

**telling** /'tɛlɪŋ/, *adj.* **1.** having force or effect; effective; striking: *a telling blow.* **2.** indicative of one's feelings; revealing: *a telling blush.* – **tellingly,** *adv.*

**telltale** /'tɛlteɪl/, *n.* **1.** Also, **telltale-tit.** one who heedlessly or maliciously reveals private or confidential matters; a tattler; a tale-bearer. **2.** a thing serving to reveal or disclose something. **3.** any of various indicating or registering devices, as a time clock. **4.** *Music.* a gauge on an organ for indicating the air pressure. **5.** an indicator showing the position of a ship's rudder. **6.** *Naut.* a pennant, feather, or piece of wool, etc., flown at the masthead or on the shrouds to indicate wind direction; dogvane. *–adj.* **7.** that reveals or betrays what is not intended to be known: *a telltale blush.* **8.** giving notice or warning of something, as a mechanical device.

**telltale compass** /– 'kʌmpəs/, *n.* a ship's compass normally placed overhead in the captain's cabin to enable him to check the steering.

**tellur-**, a prefix indicating the presence of tellurium, as in *tellurite.*

**tellurate** /ˈtɛljəreɪt/, *n.* a salt of telluric acid.

**tellurian**[1] /tɛlˈjuriən, təˈlu-/, *adj.* **1.** of or characteristic of the earth or an inhabitant of the earth. *–n.* **2.** an inhabitant of the earth. [L *tellūs* earth + -IAN]

**tellurian**[2] /tɛlˈjuriən, təˈlu-/, *n.* →**tellurion.**

**telluric**[1] /tɛlˈjurɪk, təˈlu-/, *adj.* **1.** of or pertaining to the earth; terrestrial. **2.** of or proceeding from the earth or soil. [L *tellūs* earth + -IC]

**telluric**[2] /tɛlˈjurɪk, təˈlu-/, *adj. Chem.* **1.** of or containing tellurium, esp. in the hexavalent state. **2.** containing tellurium in a higher valency state than the corresponding tellurous compound. [TELLUR- + -IC]

**telluric acid** /– ˈæsəd/, *n.* a very weak dibasic acid, $H_6TeO_6$, which is a moderately strong oxidising agent.

**telluride** /ˈtɛljəraɪd/, *n.* a compound of tellurium with an electropositive element or, less often, a radical.

**tellurion** /tɛlˈjuriən, təˈlu-/, *n.* an apparatus for showing how the diurnal rotation and annual revolution of the earth and the obliquity of its axis produce the alternation of day and night and the changes of the seasons. Also, **tellurian**[2]. [var. of TELLURIUM]

**tellurise** /ˈtɛljəraɪz/, *v.t.*, **-rised, -rising.** to mix or cause to combine with tellurium. Also, **tellurize.**

**tellurite** /ˈtɛljəraɪt/, *n. Chem.* **1.** a salt of tellurous acid, of the type $H_2TeO_3$. **2.** a mineral, tellurium dioxide, $TeO_2$.

**tellurium** /tɛlˈjuriəm, təˈlu-/, *n.* a rare silver-white element resembling sulphur in its chemical properties, and usu. occurring in nature combined with gold, silver, or other metals of high atomic weight. Used in alloys and the electrolytic refining of zinc. *Symbol:* Te; *at. wt:* 127.60; *at. no.:* 52; sp. gr.: 6.25 at 20°C. [NL, from L *tellūs* earth + *-ium* -IUM]

**tellurous** /ˈtɛljərəs, tɛlˈjurəs, təˈlurəs/, *adj.* containing tetravalent tellurium.

**telly** /ˈtɛli/, *n. Colloq.* television. Also, **tellie.**

**telo-**[1], variant of **tele-**[1], as in *telodynamic.*

**telo-**[2], variant of **tele-**[2], as in *telophase.*

**telodynamic** /ˌtɛloudaɪˈnæmɪk/, *adj.* pertaining to the transmission of power over considerable distances, as by means of endless wire ropes on pulleys.

**telophase** /ˈtɛləfeɪz/, *n.* the final stage of mitotic cell division, in which new nuclei are formed.

**telpher** /ˈtɛlfə/, *n.* **1.** a travelling unit, car, or carrier in a telpherage. **2.** →**telpherage.** *–adj.* **3.** of or pertaining to a system of telpherage. *–v.t.* **4.** to transport by means of a telpherage. Also, **telfer.** [var. of *telephore,* from TELE-[1] + -PHORE]

**telpherage** /ˈtɛlfərɪdʒ/, *n.* a transport system in which cars or carriers are suspended from or run on wire cables or the like, esp. one in which the cars are individually operated by electricity. Also **telferage.**

**telson** /ˈtɛlsən/, *n.* the last segment, or an appendage of the last segment, of certain crustaceans and arachnids, as the middle flipper of a lobster's tail. [Gk: boundary, limit]

**Telugu** /ˈtɛləgu/, *n., pl.* **-gu, -gus,** *adj. –n.* **1.** a Dravidian language spoken in south-eastern India. **2.** one of the people speaking this language. *–adj.* **3.** of Telugu or the Telugu.

**temblor** /ˈtɛmblə, -blɔ/, *n., pl.* **-blors** /-blɔz/, **-blores** /-ˈblɔreɪz/. *n. Chiefly U.S.* a tremor; an earthquake. [Sp., from *temblar* tremble, from Rom. *tremulāre,* from L *tremulus* trembling]

**temerarious** /tɛməˈrɛəriəs/, *adj.* reckless; rash. [L *temerārius*] **– temerariously,** *adv.* **– temerariousness,** *n.*

**temerity** /təˈmɛrəti/, *n.* reckless boldness; rashness. [late ME *temeryte,* from L *temeritas*]

**temp**[1] /tɛmp/, *n. Colloq.* →**temporary** (def. 2).

**temp**[2] /tɛmp/, *n. Colloq.* →**temperature** (def. 2.)

**temp.,** **1.** temperate. **2.** temporary.

**temper** /ˈtɛmpə/, *n.* **1.** a particular state of mind or feelings. **2.** habit of mind, esp. with respect to irritability or impatience, outbursts of anger, or the like. **3.** heat of mind or passion, shown in outbursts of anger, resentment, etc. **4.** calm disposition or state of mind. **5.** a substance added to something to modify its properties or qualities. **6.** the particular degree of hardness and elasticity imparted to steel, etc., by tempering. **7.** *Archaic.* a middle course; compromise. **8.** *Obs.* the constitution or character of a substance. **9. keep one's temper,** to remain calm or patient, esp. despite provocation. **10. lose one's temper,** to become suddenly angry or enraged. *–v.t.* **11.** to moderate or mitigate. **12.** to soften or tone down. **13.** to bring to a proper, suitable, or desirable state by, or as by, blending or admixture. **14.** to moisten, mix, and work up into proper consistency, as clay or mortar. **15.** to heat and cool or quench (metal) to bring to the proper degree of hardness, elasticity, etc. **16.** to produce internal stresses in (glass) by sudden cooling from low red heat; toughen. **17.** to tune (a keyboard instrument, as a piano, organ, etc.) so as to make the notes available in different keys or tonalities. **18.** *Archaic.* to combine or blend in due proportions. **19.** *Obs.* to pacify. *–v.i.* **20.** to be or become tempered. [ME; OE *temprian,* from L *temperāre* divide or proportion duly, temper] **– temperable,** *adj.* **– temperability** /tɛmpərəˈbɪləti/, *n.* **– temperer,** *n.*

**tempera** /ˈtɛmpərə/, *n.* paint made from pigment ground in water and mixed with an emulsion of egg yolk or some similar substance. [It., in phrase *pingere a tempera* paint in distemper, from *temp(e)rare* temper, from L]

**temperament** /ˈtɛmprəmənt/, *n.* **1.** the individual peculiarity of physical organisation by which the manner of thinking, feeling, and acting of every person is permanently affected; natural disposition. **2.** unusual personal make-up manifested by peculiarities of feeling, temper, action, etc., with disinclination to submit to ordinary rules or restraints. **3.** the combination of the four cardinal humours, the relative proportions of which were supposed to determine physical and mental constitution. **4.** *Music.* **a.** the tuning of a keyboard instrument as the piano, organ, etc., so that it can be played in all keys. **b.** a particular system of doing this. **5.** *Obs.* the act of tempering or moderating. **6.** *Obs.* climate. **7.** *Obs.* temperature. [late ME, from L *temperāmentum* due mixture]

**temperamental** /tɛmprəˈmɛntl/, *adj.* **1.** having or exhibiting a strongly marked individual temperament. **2.** moody, irritable or sensitive. **3.** liable to behave erratically; unstable; unreliable. **4.** of or pertaining to temperament; constitutional. **– temperamentally,** *adv.*

**temperance** /ˈtɛmpərəns, ˈtɛmprəns/, *n.* **1.** moderation or self-restraint in action, statement, etc.; self-control. **2.** habitual moderation in the indulgence of a natural appetite or passion, esp. in the consumption of alcoholic drink. **3.** total abstinence from alcoholic drink. [ME, from AF *temperaunce,* from L *temperantia* moderation]

**temperate** /ˈtɛmpərət, ˈtɛmprət/, *adj.* **1.** moderate or self-restrained; not extreme in opinion, etc. **2.** moderate as regards indulgence of appetite or passion, esp. in the consumption of alcoholic drink. **3.** not excessive in degree, as things, qualities, etc. **4.** moderate in respect of temperature. [ME, from L *temperātus,* pp.] **– temperately,** *adv.* **– temperateness,** *n.*

**Temperate Zone** /ˈtɛmpərət zoun/, *n.* the parts of the earth's surface lying between each of the tropics and the polar circle nearest to it. Also, **Variable Zone.**

**temperature** /ˈtɛmprətʃə/, *n.* **1.** a measure of the degree of hotness or coldness of a body or substance which determines the rate at which heat will be transferred to or from it. As this is related to the kinetic energies of the constituent atoms, ions, or molecules of the substance, which cannot be directly ascertained, temperature has to be measured with respect to an arbitrary scale. See **thermometer.** **2.** *Physiol., Pathol.* **a.** the degree of heat of a living body, esp. the human body. **b.** the excess of this above the normal (which in the adult human being is about 37°C or about 98.4°F). [L *temperātūra*]

**temperature gradient** /ˈ– greɪdiənt/, *n.* the rate of change of temperature with altitude.

**temperature inversion** /ˈ– ɪnˌvɜʒən/, *n.* an anomalous increase of temperature with height in the troposphere.

**tempered** /ˈtɛmpəd/, *adj.* **1.** having a temper or disposition (as specified): *good-tempered.* **2.** *Music.* tuned in accordance with some other temperament than just or pure temperament; specifically, tuned in equal temperament. **3.** made less intense or violent, esp. by the influence of something added. **4.** (of metal, glass, etc.) having had internal stresses altered by heat treatment.

**tempest** /'tɛmpəst/, *n.* **1.** an extensive current of wind rushing with great velocity and violence, esp. one attended with rain, hail, or snow; a violent storm. **2.** a violent commotion, disturbance, or tumult. *–v.t.* **3.** *Obs.* to affect by or as by a tempest; disturb violently. [ME *tempeste,* from OF, from Rom. *tempesta* time, storm, from L *tempestas* season]

**tempestuous** /tɛm'pɛstʃuəs/, *adj.* **1.** characterised by or subject to tempests: *the tempestuous ocean.* **2.** of the nature of or resembling a tempest: *a tempestuous wind.* **3.** tumultuous; turbulent: *a tempestuous period.* [late ME, from LL *tempestuōsus*] – **tempestuously,** *adv.* – **tempestuousness,** *n.*

**template** /'tɛmplət, -leɪt/, *n.* **1.** a pattern, mould, or the like, usu. consisting of a thin plate of wood, metal or plastic, used as a guide in mechanical work or for transferring a design onto a work surface, etc. **2.** *Bldg Trades.* a horizontal piece of timber, stone, or the like, in a wall, to receive and distribute the pressure of a girder, beam, etc. **3.** *Shipbuilding.* either of two wedges in each of the temporary blocks forming the support for the keel of a ship while building. Also, **templet.** [orig. uncert.; ? from F *templet* stretcher, from L *templum* small timber, purlin]

**temple**[1] /'tɛmpəl/, *n.* **1.** an edifice or place dedicated to the service or worship of a deity or deities. **2.** a synagogue. **3.** an edifice erected as a place of worship; a church, esp. a large or imposing one. **4.** any place or object regarded as occupied by the Divine Presence, as the body of a Christian. **5.** (in France) a Protestant church. **6.** a Mormon church. **7.** a building, usu. large or pretentious, devoted to some public use: *a temple of music.* [ME *tempel,* OE *templ,* from L *templum*] – **temple-like,** *adj.*

**temple**[2] /'tɛmpəl/, *n.* **1.** the flattened region on either side of the human forehead. **2.** a corresponding region in lower animals. **3.** *U.S.* either sidepiece of a pair of spectacles, extending back above the ears. [ME, from OF, from Rom. *tempula,* replacing L *tempora,* pl., temples]

**temple**[3] /'tɛmpəl/, *n.* (in a loom) a device for keeping the cloth stretched to the proper width during the weaving. [late ME *tempylle,* from F *temple* TEMPLATE]

**templet** /'tɛmplət/, *n.* →**template.**

**tempo** /'tɛmpoʊ/, *n., pl.* **-pos, -pi** /-pi/. **1.** *Music.* relative rapidity or rate of movement (usu. indicated by such terms as adagio, allegro, etc., or by reference to the metronome). **2.** characteristic rate, rhythm, or pattern of work or activity: *the tempo of city life.* [It., from L *tempus* time]

**tempo giusto** /– 'dʒustoʊ/, *adv.* (a musical direction) at an appropriate speed. [It.]

**temporal**[1] /'tɛmpərəl, 'tɛmprəl/, *adj.* **1.** of or pertaining to time. **2.** pertaining to or concerned with the present life or this world; worldly. **3.** enduring for a time only; temporary; transitory. **4.** *Gram.* **a.** of, pertaining to, or expressing time: *a temporal adverb.* **b.** of or pertaining to the tenses of a verb. **5.** secular, lay, or civil (as opposed to *spiritual* or *ecclesiastical*). *–n.* **6.** (*chiefly pl.*) a temporal possession, estate, or the like; a temporality. **7.** (*chiefly pl.*) that which is temporal; a temporal matter or affair. [ME, from L *temporālis* pertaining to or enduring for a time] – **temporally,** *adv.*

**temporal**[2] /'tɛmpərəl, 'tɛmprəl/, *Anat. –adj.* **1.** of, pertaining to, or situated near the temple or a temporal bone. *–n.* **2.** any of several parts in the temporal region, esp. the temporal bone. [L *temporālis*]

**temporal bone** /'– boʊn/, *n.* either of a pair of complex bones forming part of the sides and base of the skull.

**temporality** /tɛmpə'rælәti/, *n., pl.* **-ties.** **1.** temporal character or nature; temporariness. **2.** something temporal. **3.** (*chiefly pl.*) a temporal possession, revenue, or the like, as of the church or clergy.

**temporal lobe** /'tɛmpərəl loʊb/, *n.* the lower lateral lobe of each cerebral hemisphere, the centre of sound perception.

**temporary** /'tɛmpri, -prəri/, *adj.* **1.** lasting, existing, serving, or effective for a time only; not permanent: *a temporary need.* **2.** (of an employee) not on the permanent staff and therefore not enjoying job security or fringe benefits, as superannuation. *–n.* Also, **temp.** **3.** *Colloq.* a temporary member of an office staff, esp. a secretary. **4.** a person who works for an agency which fills temporary staffing needs in offices. – **temporarily,** *adv.* – **temporariness,** *n.*

**temporary headquarters** /– 'hɛdkwɔtəz/, *n.pl. or sing.* a place of employment other than an employee's usual place of work, where he is required to work for at least two weeks continuously under supervision, and where there are amenities available.

**temporise** /'tɛmpəraɪz/, *v.i.,* **-rised, -rising.** **1.** to act indecisively or evasively to gain time or delay matters. **2.** to comply with the time or occasion; yield temporarily or ostensibly to the current of opinion or circumstances. **3.** to treat or parley so as to gain time (fol. by *with*). **4.** to come to terms (usu. fol. by *with*). **5.** to effect a compromise (usu. fol. by *between*). Also, **temporize.** [ML *temporizāre,* from *temporāre* delay] – **temporisation** /tɛmpəraɪ'zeɪʃən/, *n.* – **temporiser,** *n.* – **temporisingly,** *adv.*

**tempt** /tɛmpt/, *v.t.* **1.** to induce or persuade by enticement or allurement. **2.** to allure, appeal strongly to, or invite: *the offer tempts me.* **3.** to render strongly disposed (to do something). **4.** to try to dispose or incite; assail with enticements, esp. to evil. **5.** to put to the test in a venturesome way; risk provoking; provoke: *to tempt one's fate.* **6.** *Obs.* to try or test. [ME, from L *temptāre* handle, touch, try, test] – **temptable,** *adj.*

**temptation** /tɛm'teɪʃən/, *n.* **1.** the act of tempting; enticement or allurement. **2.** something that tempts, entices, or allures. **3.** the fact or state of being tempted, esp. to evil. **4.** an instance of it. [ME *temptacion,* from L *temptātio*]

**tempter** /'tɛmptə/, *n.* **1.** one who or that which tempts, esp. to evil. **2. the Tempter,** the devil. – **temptress** /'tɛmptrəs/, *n. fem.*

**tempting** /'tɛmptɪŋ/, *adj.* that tempts; enticing or inviting. – **temptingly,** *adv.* – **temptingness,** *n.*

**tempura** /tɛm'purə/, *n.* a Japanese dish in which seafood or vegetables are coated in a light batter and deep-fried in oil. [Jap: fried food]

**ten** /tɛn/, *n.* **1.** a cardinal number, nine plus one. **2.** a symbol for this number, as 10 or X. **3.** a set of this many persons or things. **4.** a playing card with ten pips. *–adj.* **5.** amounting to ten in number. [ME; OE *tēn,* c. G *zehn,* Goth. *taihun,* L *decem,* Gk *déka*]

**ten.,** tenuto.

**tenable** /'tɛnəbəl/, *adj.* capable of being held, maintained, or defended, as against attack or objection: *a tenable theory.* [F, from *tenir,* from L *tenēre* hold, keep] – **tenability** /tɛnə'bɪləti/, **tenableness,** *n.* – **tenably,** *adv.*

**tenace** /'tɛneɪs/, *n.* (in whist and bridge) a combination of the best and third best cards of a suit (**major tenace**), or of the second and fourth best cards (**minor tenace**). [Sp. *tenaza* pincers (referring to cards)]

**tenacious** /tə'neɪʃəs/, *adj.* **1.** holding fast; characterised by keeping a firm hold (oft. fol. by *of*). **2.** highly retentive: *a tenacious memory.* **3.** pertinacious, persistent, stubborn, or obstinate. **4.** adhesive or sticky; viscous or glutinous. **5.** holding together; cohesive; not easily pulled asunder; tough. [TENACI(TY) + -OUS] – **tenaciously,** *adv.* – **tenaciousness,** *n.*

**tenacity** /tə'næsəti/, *n.* **1.** the quality or property of being tenacious. **2.** →**tensile strength.** [L *tenācitas*]

**tenaculum** /tə'nækjələm/, *n., pl.* **-la** /-lə/. a small sharp-pointed hook set in a handle, used for seizing and picking up parts, etc., in operations and dissections. [LL: instrument for holding, from L *tenēre* hold]

**tenakoe** /tə'nakwɔɪ/, *interj. N.Z.* (a Maori greeting). [Maori]

**tenancy** /'tɛnənsi/, *n., pl.* **-cies.** **1.** a holding, as of lands, by any kind of title; tenure; occupancy of land, a house, or the like, under a lease or on payment of rent. **2.** the period of a tenant's occupancy. **3.** occupation of or residence in any place, position, etc. **4.** *Obs.* a holding, or piece of land held by a tenant.

**tenant** /'tɛnənt/, *n.* **1.** one who holds land, a house, or the like, of another (the landlord) for a period of time, as a lessee or occupant for rent. **2.** *Law.* **a.** a person or body of persons holding land under a landlord in leasehold tenure. **b.** any holder of land. **3.** an occupant or inhabitant of any place. *–v.t.* **4.** to hold or occupy as a tenant; dwell in; inhabit. *–v.i.* **5.** to dwell or live (fol. by *in*). [ME *tenaunt,* from F *tenant,* ppr. of *tenir* hold, from L *tenēre*] – **tenantable,** *adj.* – **tenantless,** *adj.*

**tenant farmer** /– 'famə/, *n.* one who farms land which he has rented from another.

**tenant in common,** *n.* one who holds property in common with another person or persons so that each has quantum of interest in the whole property; on death, this quantum of interest passes to an heir or devisee who then becomes a tenant in common with the surviving co-owner or co-owners.

**tenantry** /'tɛnəntri/, *n., pl.* **-tries. 1.** tenants collectively; the body of tenants on an estate. **2.** the state or condition of being a tenant.

**tench** /tɛntʃ/, *n.* a European freshwater cyprinoid fish, *Tinca tinca,* introduced into Australia in the 1870s.

**tend**[1] /tɛnd/, *v.i.* **1.** to be disposed or inclined in action, operation, or effect (to do something): *the particles tend to unite.* **2.** to be disposed towards a state of mind, emotion, quality, etc. **3.** to incline in operation or effect; lead or conduce, as to some result or resulting condition: *measures tending to improved working conditions; governments are tending towards democracy.* **4.** to be directed or lead, as a journey, course, road, etc. (usu. fol. by *to, towards,* etc.). [ME, from F *tendre,* from L *tendere* stretch, go, strive; akin to Gk *teínein,* Skt *tan* stretch]

**tend**[2] /tɛnd/, *v.t.* **1.** to attend to by work or services, care, etc.: *to tend a fire.* **2.** to look after; watch over and care for; minister to or wait on with service. **3.** *Naut.* to handle or watch (a line, etc.). *–v.i.* **4.** to attend by action, care, etc. (usu. fol. by *to*). **5.** *Obs.* to attend or wait upon; serve (usu. fol. by *on* or *upon*). [ME *tende;* aphetic var. of ATTEND]

**tendance** /'tɛndəns/, *n.* attention; care; ministration, as to the sick.

**tendencious** /tɛn'dɛnʃəs/, *adj.* →**tendentious.**

**tendency** /'tɛndənsi/, *n., pl.* **-cies. 1.** natural or prevailing disposition to move, proceed, or act in some direction or towards some point, end, or result: *the tendency of falling bodies towards the earth.* **2.** an inclination, bent, or predisposition to something. **3.** special and definite purpose in a novel or other literary work. [ML *tendentia,* from L *tendere* TEND[1]]

**tendendum** /tɛn'dɛndəm/, *n.* a clause in a conveyance which says that the land is to be held by the grantee.

**tendentious** /tɛn'dɛnʃəs/, *adj.* having or showing a definite tendency, bias, or purpose; described or written so as to influence in a desired direction or present a particular point of view: *a tendentious novel.* Also, **tendencious.** – **tendentiously,** *adv.* – **tendentiousness,** *n.*

**tender**[1] /'tɛndə/, *adj.* **1.** soft or delicate in substance; not hard or tough: *a tender steak.* **2.** weak or delicate in constitution; not strong or hardy. **3.** *Wool.* of wool fibres that have a weakness at a certain point of the staple such that if tension is applied the staple will break. **4.** young or immature: *children of tender age.* **5.** delicate or soft in quality: *tender blue.* **6.** delicate, soft, or gentle: *the tender touch of her hand.* **7.** soft-hearted; easily touched; sympathetic; compassionate. **8.** affectionate or loving; sentimental or amatory. **9.** considerate or careful; chary or reluctant (usu. fol. by *of*). **10.** acutely or painfully sensitive. **11.** readily made uneasy, as the conscience. **12.** yielding readily to force or pressure; easily broken; fragile. **13.** of a delicate or ticklish nature; requiring careful or tactful handling: *a tender subject.* **14.** (of a ship) apt to lean over easily; having a low measure of stability. *–v.t.* **15.** to make tender. [ME, from F *tendre,* from L *tener* soft, delicate, tender] – **tenderly,** *adv.* – **tenderness,** *n.*

**tender**[2] /'tɛndə/, *v.t.* **1.** to present formally for acceptance; make formal offer of: *to tender one's resignation.* **2.** to offer or proffer. **3.** *Law.* to offer, as money or goods, in payment of a debt or other obligation, esp. in exact accordance with the terms of the law and of the obligation. *–n.* **4.** the act of tendering; an offer of something for acceptance. **5.** that which is tendered or offered, esp. money in payment of something. **6.** *Comm.* an offer made in writing by one party to another to execute certain work, supply certain commodities, etc., at a given cost. **7.** *Law.* an offer, as of money or goods, in payment or satisfaction of a debt or other obligation. [AF, from L *tendere*] – **tenderer,** *n.*

**tender**[3] /'tɛndə/, *n.* **1.** one who tends; one who attends to or takes charge of something. **2.** an auxiliary vessel employed to attend one or more other vessels, as for supplying provisions. **3.** a small rowing boat or motor boat carried or towed by a yacht. **4.** a wagon attached to a steam locomotive, for carrying coal, water, etc. [late ME; aphetic var. of ATTENDER. See TEND[2]]

**tenderfoot** /'tɛndəfʊt/, *n., pl.* **-foots, -feet** /-fit/. **1.** *Colloq.* a raw, inexperienced person; a novice. **2. a.** (formerly) the initial membership award in the boy scout movement. **b.** a holder of this award.

**tender-hearted** /'tɛndə-hatəd/, *adj.* soft-hearted; sympathetic. – **tender-heartedness,** *n.*

**tenderise** /'tɛndəraɪz/, *v.t.,* **-rised, -rising.** to make (meat) tender by beating, marinating, etc. Also, **tenderize.** – **tenderiser,** *n.*

**tenderloin** /'tɛndəlɔɪn/, *n.* **1.** a strip of tender meat forming part of the loin of beef, pork, etc., lying under the short ribs and consisting of the psoas muscle. **2.** Also, **fillet** (def. 6). a cut of beef lying between the sirloin and ribs.

**tenderstretch** /'tɛndəstrɛtʃ/, *adj.* of or pertaining to beef or lamb carcasses hung from the pelvis or aitchbone before chilling with the aim of producing extremely tender cuts for roasting and grilling.

**tendinous** /'tɛndənəs/, *adj.* **1.** of the nature of or resembling a tendon. **2.** consisting of tendons. [ML *tendinōsus* full of tendons]

**tendon** /'tɛndən/, *n.* a cord or band of dense, tough, inelastic, white fibrous tissue, serving to connect a muscle with a bone or part; a sinew. [ML *tendō,* from Gk *ténōn* sinew (by association with L *tendere* stretch)]

**tendril** /'tɛndrəl/, *n.* a filiform leafless organ of climbing plants, often growing in spiral form, which attaches itself to or twines round some other body, so as to support the plant. [F *tendrillon* tender shoot, from *tendron* tender part, OF *tendrun,* from LL *tenerumen,* from *tener* tender] – **tendrillar, tendrilous,** *adj.*

T, tendrils

**tenebrific** /tɛnə'brɪfɪk/, *adj.* producing darkness. [L *tenebrae,* pl., darkness + -I- + -FIC]

**tenebrism** /'tɛnəbrɪzəm/, *n.* a style of painting of the late 16th and early 17th centuries, characterised by a general darkness of tone relieved and illuminated by dramatic lights. [L *tenebrae* darkness + -ISM]

**tenebrous** /'tɛnəbrəs/, *adj.* dark; gloomy; obscure. [late ME, from L *tenebrōsus* dark]

**tenement** /'tɛnəmənt/, *n.* **1.** any house or building; dwelling house. **2.** a portion of a house or building occupied by a tenant as a separate dwelling. **3.** →**tenement house. 4.** any habitation, abode, or dwelling place. **5.** any species of permanent property, as lands, houses, rents, an office, a franchise, etc., that may be held of another. **6.** (*pl.*) freehold interests in things immovable considered as subjects of property. [ME, from OF, from *tenir* hold, from L *tenēre*] – **tenemental** /tɛnə'mɛntl/, **tenementary** /tɛnə'mɛntəri/, *adj.*

**tenement house** /'– haʊs/, *n.* a house divided into flats, esp. one in the poorer, crowded parts of a large city.

**tenesmus** /tə'nɛzməs/, *n.* the urgent desire to urinate or defecate, without the ability to do so. [ML, from L *tenesmos,* from Gk: straining]

**tenet** /'tɛnət/, *n.* any opinion, principle, doctrine, dogma, or the like, held as true. [L: he holds]

**tenfold** /'tɛnfoʊld/, *adj.* **1.** comprising ten parts or members. **2.** ten times as great or as much. *–adv.* **3.** in tenfold measure.

**10-4** /tɛn-'fɔ/, *interj.* **1.** (an exclamation signifying agreement acceptance, etc., esp. used by C.B. radio operators). *–adj.* **2.** okay; all right: *that's 10-4 by me.* Also, **ten-four.**

**ten-gallon hat** /ˌtɛn-gælən 'hæt/, *n.* a cowboy's broad-brimmed hat with a high, soft crown.

**tenia** /'tiniə/, *n., pl.* **-niae** /-nii/. *U.S.* →**taenia.**

**teniacide** /'tiniəsaɪd/, *n. U.S.* →**taeniacide.**

**tennantite** /'tɛnəntaɪt/, *n.* a mineral, copper arsenic sulphide, $Cu_3AsS_3$, usu. containing some antimony and grading into tetrahedrite; an ore of copper. [named after Smithson *Tennant,* 1761-1815, English chemist. See -ITE[1]]

**tenner** /'tɛnə/, *n. Colloq.* **1.** a ten-dollar note. **2.** (formerly) a ten-pound note.

**tennis** /ˈtɛnəs/, *n.* **1.** a game, played on a tennis court, in which two players, or two pairs of players, hit a tennis ball backwards and forwards with racquets over a centrally placed net. When a player commits a fault, points are awarded to the other side. **2.** →**royal tennis.** [ME *tenetz, teneys,* from AF *tenetz,* impv., hold, take]

**tennis ball** /ˈ– bɔl/, *n.* a hollow rubber ball covered with felt, used in tennis.

**tennis court** /ˈ– kɔt/, *n.* See **court** (def. 5).

**tennis elbow** /– ˈɛlboʊ/, *n.* a painful condition of the elbow accompanied by inflammation, caused by undue exertion while playing tennis or other games.

**tennis racquet** /ˈ– rækət/, *n.* See **racquet.**

**tennis shoe** /ˈ– ʃu/, *n.* →**sandshoe.**

**teno-,** a word element meaning 'tendon', as in *tenotomy.* [combining form representing Gk *ténōn*]

**tenon** /ˈtɛnən/, *n.* **1.** a projection shaped on an end of a piece of wood, etc., for insertion in a corresponding cavity (mortise) in another piece, so as to form a joint. *–v.t.* **2.** to provide with a tenon. **3.** to shape so as to fit into a mortise. **4.** to join securely. [ME, from OF, from *tenir* hold, from L *tenēre*]

**tenonitis** /tɛnənˈaɪtəs/, *n.* inflammation of a tendon.

**tenon saw** /ˈtɛnən sɔ/, *n.* a saw consisting of a thin, parallel-sided blade, whose upper edge is reinforced, and whose lower (cutting) edge has some 4-6 teeth per centimetre.

**tenor** /ˈtɛnə/, *n.* **1.** the course of thought or meaning which runs through something written or spoken; purport; drift. **2.** continuous course, progress, or movement. **3.** *Music.* **a.** the highest natural male voice. **b.** a part sung by or written for such a voice, esp. the next to the lowest part in four-part harmony. **c.** a singer with such a voice. **d.** an instrument corresponding in compass to this voice, esp. the viola. **e.** the lowest-toned bell of a peal. *–adj.* **4.** *Music.* of, pertaining to, or having the compass of, a tenor. [ME, from (M)L: course, etc.] **– tenorless,** *adj.*

**tenor clef** /– ˈklɛf/, *n.* (in music) a sign placing middle C on the next to the top line of the stave.

**tenorite** /ˈtɛnəraɪt/, *n.* a mineral, copper oxide, which occurs as small black scales in volcanic regions or in copper veins. [named after G. *Tenore,* d. 1861, Italian botanist. See -ITE[1]]

**tenorrhaphy** /təˈnɒrəfi/, *n., pl.* **-phies.** suture of a tendon. [TENO- + Gk *-(r)rhaphia*]

**tenosynovitis** /ˌtɛnoʊˌsaɪnəˈvaɪtəs/, *n.* inflammation of the tendon sheath.

**tenotomy** /təˈnɒtəmi/, *n., pl.* **-mies.** the cutting or division of a tendon.

**ten-per-center** /tɛn-pə-ˈsɛntə/, *n. Colloq.* **1.** an actor's agent. **2.** a person who sponges off other people's abilities.

**tenpin** /ˈtɛnpɪn/, *n.* one of the pins used in tenpin bowling.

**tenpin bowling** /– ˈboʊlɪŋ/, *n.* a form of bowling played with ten wooden pins at which a ball is bowled to knock them down. Also, *U.S.,* **tenpins.**

**tenrec** /ˈtɛnrɛk/, *n.* any of several insectivorous mammals of Madagascar, which constitute the family Tenrecidae, esp. a common tailless species, *Tenrec ecaudatus.* Also, **tanrec.** [F, from Malagasy *tàndraka*]

tenrec

**tense**[1] /tɛns/, *adj.,* **tenser, tensest,** *v.,* **tensed, tensing.** *–adj.* **1.** stretched tight, as a cord, fibre, etc.; drawn taut; rigid. **2.** in a state of mental or nervous strain, as a person. **3.** characterised by a strain upon the nerves or feelings: *a tense moment.* **4.** *Phonet.* pronounced with relatively tense muscles. *–v.t., v.i.* **5.** to make or become tense. [L *tensus,* pp., stretched, taut] **– tensely,** *adv.* **– tenseness,** *n.*

**tense**[2] /tɛns/, *n.* **1.** a category of verb inflection found in some languages which specifies the time and length of occurrence of the action or state expressed by the verb. **2.** a set of such categories or constructions in a particular language. **3.** the meaning of, or typical of, such a category. **4.** such categories or constructions, or their meanings collectively. [ME *tens,* from OF, from L *tempus* time]

**tensible** /ˈtɛnsəbəl/, *adj.* capable of being stretched; tensile. **– tensibility** /tɛnsəˈbɪləti/, *n.* **– tensibly,** *adv.*

**tensile** /ˈtɛnsaɪl/, *adj.* **1.** of or pertaining to tension: *tensile stress.* **2.** capable of being stretched or drawn out; ductile. [NL *tensilis,* from L *tendere* stretch] **– tensility** /tɛnˈsɪləti/, *n.*

**tensile strength** /ˈ– strɛŋθ/, *n.* the resistance offered by a material to tensile stresses, as measured by the tensile force per unit cross-sectional area required to break it.

**tensimeter** /tɛnˈsɪmətə/, *n.* an instrument for determining vapour pressure or tension. [TENSI(ON) + -METER[1]]

**tensiometer** /tɛnsiˈɒmətə/, *n.* an apparatus for measuring tensile stress, as in aeroplane members.

**tension** /ˈtɛnʃən/, *n.* **1.** the act of stretching or straining. **2.** the state of being stretched or strained. **3.** mental or emotional strain; intense suppressed anxiety, suspense, or excitement. **4.** a strained relationship between individuals, groups, countries, etc. **5.** *Physics.* pressure: *vapour tension.* **6.** *Mech.* **a.** a state in which a body is stretched or increased in size in one direction with a decrease in size in a certain ratio in a perpendicular direction. **b.** a force tending to elongate a body. **7.** *Elect.* **a.** the condition of a dielectric body when its opposite surfaces are oppositely electrified. **b.** electromotive force; potential. **8.** *Mach.* a device for stretching or pulling something. **9.** a device to hold the proper tension on the material being woven in a loom. [LL *tensio* act of stretching] **– tensional,** *adj.* **– tensionless,** *adj.*

**tensity** /ˈtɛnsəti/, *n.* the state of being tense.

**tensive** /ˈtɛnsɪv/, *adj.* stretching or straining. [TENSE[1] + -IVE. Cf. F *tensif*]

**tensor** /ˈtɛnsə, -sɔ/, *n.* **1.** *Anat.* a muscle that stretches or tightens some part of the body. **2.** *Maths.* a set of functions which, when changing from one set of co-ordinates to another, are transformed in a precisely defined manner. [NL: stretcher]

**tent**[1] /tɛnt/, *n.* **1.** a portable shelter of skins, coarse cloth, esp. canvas, supported by one or more poles and usu. extended by ropes fastened to pegs in the ground. *–v.t.* **2.** to provide with or lodge in tents; cover as with a tent. *–v.i.* **3.** to live in a tent; encamp. [ME *tente,* from OF, from L *tenta,* from *tentus,* pp., stretched] **– tentless,** *adj.* **– tentlike,** *adj.*

**tent**[2] /tɛnt/, *Surg. –n.* **1.** a roll or pledget, usu. of soft, absorbent material, as a lint or gauze, for dilating an orifice, keeping a wound open, etc. *–v.t.* **2.** to keep (a wound) open with a tent. [ME *tente* a probe, from MF, from *tenter*]

**tentacle** /ˈtɛntəkəl/, *n.* **1.** *Zool.* any of various slender, flexible processes or appendages in animals, esp. invertebrates, which serve as organs of touch, prehension, etc.; a feeler. **2.** *Bot.* a sensitive filament or process, as one of the glandular hairs of the sundew. [NL *tentāculum,* from L *tentā(re)* feel, try + *-culum,* diminutive suffix] **– tentacle-like,** *adj.* **– tentacular** /tɛnˈtækjələ/, *adj.*

**tentacled** /ˈtɛntəkəld/, *adj.* having tentacles. Also, **tentaculate** /tɛnˈtækjələt/.

**tentage** /ˈtɛntɪdʒ/, *n.* tents collectively; equipment or supply of tents.

**tentation** /tɛnˈteɪʃən/, *n.* a method of making mechanical adjustments or the like by a succession of trials. [L *tentātio,* late var. of *temptātio* attempt]

**tentative** /ˈtɛntətɪv/, *adj.* **1.** of the nature of, or made or done as, a trial, experiment, or attempt; experimental. **2.** hesitant; cautious; diffident. [ML *tentātīvus,* from L *tentāre* (*temptāre*) try] **– tentatively,** *adv.* **– tentativeness,** *n.*

**tent caterpillar** /ˈtɛnt ˌkætəpɪlə/, *n.* any of several caterpillars or moths (family Lasiocampidae), which spin tentlike, silken webs in which they live gregariously.

**tenter** /ˈtɛntə/, *n.* **1.** (in the manufacture of cloth) a framework on which the cloth is stretched so that it may set or dry evenly. **2.** *Obs.* →**tenterhook.** *–v.t.* **3.** to stretch (cloth) on a tenter or tenters. *–v.i.* **4.** to be capable of being tentered. [ME *tentour,* from L *tentus,* pp., stretched + *-our* -OR[2]]

**tenterhook** /ˈtɛntəhʊk/, *n.* **1.** one of the hooks or bent nails which hold cloth stretched on a tenter. **2. on tenterhooks,** in a state of painful suspense or anxiety.

**tent-fly** /ˈtɛnt-flaɪ/, *n.* piece of fabric placed above a tent and extending beyond each side, designed to protect the tent from heat or bad weather.

**tenth** /tɛnθ/, *adj.* **1.** next after the ninth. **2.** being one of ten equal parts. *–n.* **3.** a tenth part, esp. of one ($\frac{1}{10}$). **4.** the tenth member of a series. **5.** *Music.* **a.** a note distant from another note by an interval of an octave and a third. **b.** the interval between such notes. **c.** the harmonic combination of such notes. – **tenthly**, *adv.*

**tent-pegging** /'tɛnt-pɛgɪŋ/, *n.* a sport, deriving from cavalry training in India, in which a team of horses and riders armed with lances ride in single file, each one removing with his lance a tent-peg stuck in the ground. – **tent-pegger**, *n.*

**tent stitch** /'tɛnt stɪtʃ/, *n.* a series of diagonal stitches thought to resemble the shape of a tent.

**tenuity** /tə'njuəti/, *n.* **1.** the state of being tenuous. **2.** slenderness. **3.** thinness of consistency; rarefied condition.

**tenuous** /'tɛnjuəs/, *adj.* **1.** thin or slender in form. **2.** thin in consistency; rare or rarefied. **3.** of slight importance or significance; unsubstantial. **4.** flimsy; lacking a firm or sound basis; weak; vague. [L *tenuis* slender + -OUS] – **tenuously**, *adv.* – **tenuousness**, *n.*

**tenure** /'tɛnjə/, *n.* **1.** the holding or possessing of anything: *the tenure of an office.* **2.** the holding of property, esp. real property, of a superior in return for services to be rendered. **3.** the period or terms of holding something. [ME, from OF, from *tenir,* from L *tenēre* hold] – **tenurial** /tɛn'juriəl/, *adj.* – **tenurially** /tɛn'juriəli/, *adv.*

**tenuto** /tə'njutoʊ/, *adj., n., pl.* **-tos, -ti** /-ti/. *Music. –adj.* **1.** held or sustained to its full time value, as a note or chord; not staccato. *–n.* **2.** the mark to indicate this. [It.: held]

**teosinte** /tioʊ'sɪnti/, *n.* a tall annual grass, *Euchlaena mexicana,* native to Mexico and Central America, closely related to maize, and occasionally cultivated as a fodder plant. [Sp., from Nahuatl *teocintli,* apparently from *teo(tl)* god + *cintli* dry ear of maize]

**tepee** /'tipi/, *n.* a tent or wigwam of the North American Indians. Also, **teepee, tipi.** [Dakota Siouan *tīpī,* from *ti* to dwell + *pi* used for]

tepee

**tepefy** /'tɛpəfaɪ/, *v.t.,* **-fied, -fying.** to make or become tepid or lukewarm. [L *tepefacere* make tepid] – **tepefaction** /tɛpə'fækʃən/, *n.*

**tephramancy** /'tɛfrə,mænsi/, *n.* divination by means of seeking messages in ashes.

**tephrite** /'tɛfraɪt/, *n.* a basaltic rock consisting essentially of pyroxene and plagioclase with nepheline or leucite. [Gk *tephrós* ash-coloured + -ITE[1]] – **tephritic** /tɛf'rɪtɪk/, *adj.*

**tepid** /'tɛpəd/, *adj.* moderately warm; lukewarm. [ME, from L *tepidus*] – **tepidity** /tə'pɪdəti/, **tepidness**, *n.* – **tepidly**, *adv.*

**tequila** /tə'kilə/, *n.* a Mexican drink produced by distillation of a fermented mash of agave. [named after *Tequila,* district of Mexico]

**Ter.**, **1.** Terrace. **2.** Territory.

**tera-** /'tɛrə-/, a prefix denoting $10^{12}$, of a given unit as in *terahertz. Symbol:* T [Gk *téras* monster. See TERATO-]

**teraglin** /tə'ræglən/, *n.* an eastern Australian offshore fish, *Zeluco atelodus,* of excellent eating quality. [Aboriginal]

**terakihi** /tɛrə'kihi/, *n. N.Z.* →**jackass fish.** Also, **teraki, tarakihi.** [Maori]

**terat.**, teratology.

**terato-**, a word element meaning 'monster', as in *teratogenic.* Also, (before vowels), **terat-**. [combining form representing Gk *téras* monster]

**teratogenic** /tɛrətə'dʒɛnɪk/, *adj.* leading to the production of foetal abnormalities.

**teratoid** /'tɛrətɔɪd/, *adj.* resembling a monster.

**teratology** /tɛrə'tɒlədʒi/, *n.* the science or study of monstrosities or abnormal formations in animals or plants. – **teratological** /tɛrətə'lɒdʒɪkəl/, *adj.* – **teratologist**, *n.*

**teratorn** /'tɛrətɔn/, *n.* a prehistoric bird as tall as a man, with a wingspan of 7.6 metres; believed to have been the world's largest flying bird. [TERATO- + Gk *órn(is)* bird]

**terbia** /'tɜbiə/, *n.* the oxide of terbium, $Tb_2O_3$, an amorphous white powder.

**terbium** /'tɜbiəm/, *n.* a rare-earth, metallic element present in certain minerals, and yielding colourless salts. *Symbol:* Tb; *at. no.:* 65; *at. wt:* 158.924; sp. gr.: 8.272 at 20°C. [(*Yt*)*terb*(*y*), name of Swedish town where found + -IUM. See YTTERBIUM] – **terbic,** *adj.*

**terbium metals** /– 'mɛtlz/, *n.pl.* See **rare-earth elements.**

**terce** /tɜs/, *n. Eccles.* →**tierce** (def. 3).

**tercel** /'tɜsəl/, *n.* a male hawk trained for falconry, esp. the male peregrine falcon. Also, **tiercel, tercelet** /'tɜslət/. [ME, from OF, from *tierz* third, from L *tertius*]

**tercentenary** /tɜsən'tinəri, -'tɛn-/, *adj., n., pl.* **-ries.** *–adj.* **1.** of or pertaining to a 300th anniversary. *–n.* **2.** a 300th anniversary. **3.** its celebration. **4.** a period of 300 years. Also, **tercentennial.** [L *ter* thrice + CENTENARY]

**tercentennial** /tɜsən'tɛniəl/, *adj.* **1.** consisting of or lasting 300 years. **2.** recurring every 300 years. *–n.* **3.** *U.S.* →**tercentenary.**

**tercet** /'tɜsət/, *n.* **1.** *Pros.* a group of three lines rhyming together, or connected by rhyme with the adjacent group or groups of three lines. **2.** →**triplet.** [F, from It. *terzetto,* diminutive of *terzo* third, from L *tertius*]

**terebene** /'tɛrəbin/, *n.* a paint and varnish drier consisting of linseed oil, natural resin, and salts of lead and manganese, thinned with turpentine. Also, **terebine.**

**terebic acid** /tərɛbɪk 'æsəd/, *n.* an acid, $C_7H_{10}O_4$, formed by the action of nitric acid on oil of turpentine. [TEREB(INTH) + -IC]

**terebinth** /'tɛrəbɪnθ/, *n.* a moderate sized tree, *Pistacia terebinthus,* of the Mediterranean regions, yielding turpentine. [L *terebinthus,* from Gk *terébinthos;* replacing ME *theribynte,* from OF]

**terebinthic** /tɛrə'bɪnθɪk/, *adj.* pertaining to or resembling turpentine.

**terebinthine** /tɛrə'bɪnθaɪn/, *adj.* **1.** of, pertaining to, consisting of, or resembling turpentine. **2.** of or pertaining to the terebinth.

**teredo** /tɛ'ridoʊ/, *n., pl.* **-dos, -dines** /-dəniz/. a shipworm (genus *Teredo*). [L, from Gk *terēdṓn* wood-boring worm]

**terephthalic acid** /tɛrəf,θælɪk 'æsəd/, *n.* white crystals or powder, $C_6H_4(COOH)_2$, insoluble in water, used in combination with glycols to form linear, crystalline fibres, as dacron and terylene.

**terete** /'tɛrit/, *adj.* **1.** slender and smooth, with a circular transverse section. **2.** cylindrical or slightly tapering. [L *teres* rounded]

**tergal** /'tɜgəl/, *adj.* of or pertaining to the tergum. [L *tergum* back + -AL[1]]

**tergite** /'tɜdʒaɪt/, *n.* **1.** a dorsal sclerite of an arthropod. **2.** the dorsal sclerite of an abdominal segment of an insect.

**tergiversate** /tɜ'dʒɪvə,seɪt, 'tɜdʒəvəseɪt/, *v.i.,* **-sated, -sating.** **1.** to change repeatedly one's attitude or opinions with respect to a cause, subject, etc. **2.** to turn renegade. [L *tergiversātus,* pp., having turned the back] – **tergiversation** /tɜdʒəvə'seɪʃən/, *n.* – **tergiversator** /tɜdʒəvə'seɪtə/, *n.*

**tergum** /'tɜgəm/, *n., pl.* **-ga** /-gə/. the dorsal surface of a body segment of an arthropod. [L: the back]

**teriyaki** /tɛri'jaki/, *n.* a Japanese dish consisting of meat, chicken or seafood, marinated in a mixture containing soy sauce, and grilled. [Jap. *teri* sunshine, thus flame, + *yaki* to grill]

**term** /tɜm/, *n.* **1.** any word or group of linguistic forms naming something, esp. as used in some particular field of knowledge, as *atom* in physics, *quietism* in theology, or *adze* in carpentry. **2.** any word or group of linguistic forms considered as a member of a construction or utterance. **3.** the time or period through which something lasts. **4.** a period of time to which limits have been set: *elected for a term of four years.* **5.** each of certain stated periods of the year into which instruction is regularly organised for students or pupils in universities, colleges, and schools. **6.** an appointed or set time or date, as for the payment of rent, interest, wages, etc. **7.** (*pl.*) conditions with regard to payment, price, charge, rates, wages, etc.: *reasonable terms.* **8.** (*pl.*) conditions or stipulations limiting what is proposed to be granted or done: *the terms of a treaty.* **9.** (*pl.*) footing or standing: *on good terms with a person.* **10.** *Alg., Arith., etc.* each of the members of which an expression, a series of quantities, or the like is composed, as one of two or more parts of an algebraic expression. **11.** *Logic.* **a.** the subject or predicate of a categorical proposition. **b.** the word or expression denoting the subject or predicate of a categorical preposition. **12.** *Law.* **a.** an estate or interest in land, etc., to be enjoyed for a fixed period: *a term of years.* **b.** the duration of an estate. **c.** each of the periods during which certain courts of law hold their sessions. **13.** the normal completion of the period of pregnancy. **14.** *Archaic.* end, conclusion, or termination. **15.** *Archaic.* a boundary or limit. **16.** *Aus. Rules.* →**quarter** (def. 8). **17.** →**terminus** (def. 7). **18. a contradiction in terms,** a statement which is self-contradictory. **19. bring to terms,** to compel to agree to stated conditions; force into submission. **20. come to terms, a.** to reach agreement. **b.** to become accustomed or resigned. *–v.t.* **21.** to apply a particular term or name to; name; call; designate. [ME, from OF *terme,* from L *terminus* boundary, limit, end]

**termagant** /'tɜməgənt/, *n.* **1.** a violent, turbulent, or brawling woman. *–adj.* **2.** violent; turbulent; brawling; shrewish. [ME *Termagaunt, Tervagant,* from OF *Tervagan* a supposed Muslim deity, represented in some medieval morality plays, etc., as a violent, overbearing person]

**term day** /'tɜm deɪ/, *n.* a fixed or appointed day, as for the payment of money due; a quarter-day.

**terminable** /'tɜmənəbəl/, *adj.* **1.** that may be terminated. **2.** (of an annuity) coming to an end after a certain term. **– terminability** /tɜmənə'bɪləti/, **terminableness,** *n.* **– terminably,** *adv.*

**terminal** /'tɜmənəl/, *adj.* **1.** situated at or forming the end or extremity of something. **2.** occurring at or forming the end of a series, succession, or the like; closing; concluding. **3.** pertaining to or lasting for a term or definite period; occurring at fixed terms or in every term. **4.** pertaining to, situated, at or forming the terminus of a railway. **5.** *Bot.* growing at the end of a branch or stem, as a bud, inflorescence, etc. **6.** pertaining to or placed at a boundary, as a landmark. **7.** occurring at or causing the end of life: *terminal cancer.* *–n.* **8.** a terminal part or structure; end or extremity. **9.** the end of a railway line, shipping route, air route, etc., at which large scale loading and unloading of passengers, goods, etc., takes place. **10.** *Elect.* **a.** the mechanical device by means of which an electrical connection to an apparatus is established. **b.** the point of current entry to, or point of current departure from, any conducting component in an electric circuit. **11.** →**computer terminal.** **12.** *Archit., etc.* a carving or the like at the end of something, as a finial. [L *terminālis* pertaining to an end or boundary] **– terminally,** *adv.*

**terminal bonus** /– 'boʊnəs/, *n.* free addition to the sum assured on a policy to reflect the excess of the market value of the life assurance company's assets over their book value; paid once only when the policy matures. See also, **reversionary bonus.**

**terminal velocity** /– və'lɒsəti/, *n.* **1.** *Physics.* the maximum velocity attained by a body which falls through a resisting medium. **2. a.** the velocity of a missile, rocket, shell, etc., on impact with its target. **b.** the maximum velocity attained by a missile, rocket, shell, etc., during the course of its flight.

**terminate** /'tɜməneɪt/, *v.,* **-nated, -nating.** *–v.t.* **1.** bring to an end; put an end to. **2.** to occur at or form the conclusion of. **3.** to bound or limit spatially; form or be situated at the extremity of. *–v.i.* **4.** to end, conclude, or cease. **5.** (of a train, bus, etc.) to complete a scheduled journey at a certain place. **6.** to come to an end (oft. fol. by *at, in,* or *with*). **7.** to issue or result (usu. fol. by *in*). [L *terminātus,* pp., ended, limited, determined] **– terminative** /'tɜmənətɪv/, *adj.* **– terminatively,** *adv.*

**terminating building society,** *n.* an association of individuals who make regular payments to a common fund, from which each obtains a housing loan, the order usu. being determined by ballot; the society is terminated when the last house is paid for.

**terminating loan** /'tɜməneɪtɪŋ loʊn/, *n.* a loan to a terminating building society.

**termination** /tɜmə'neɪʃən/, *n.* **1.** the act of terminating. **2.** the fact of being terminated. **3.** the place at which or the part in which anything terminates; bound or limit. **4.** an end or extremity; close or conclusion. **5.** an issue or result. **6.** *Gram.* a suffix or ending. **– terminational,** *adj.*

**terminator** /'tɜməneɪtə/, *n.* **1.** one who or that which terminates. **2.** *Astron.* the dividing line between the illuminated and the unilluminated part of a heavenly body, esp. the moon.

**terminology** /tɜmə'nɒlədʒi/, *n., pl.* **-gies. 1.** the system of terms belonging to a science, art, or subject; nomenclature: *the terminology of botany.* **2.** the science of terms, as in particular sciences or arts. [G *Terminologie,* from *termino-* (combining form representing ML *terminus* term) + *-logie* -LOGY] **– terminological** /tɜmənə'lɒdʒɪkəl/, *adj.* **– terminologically** /tɜmənə'lɒdʒɪkli/, *adv.* **– terminologist,** *n.*

**term insurance** /tɜm ɪn'ʃɔrəns/, *n.* an insurance policy taken out on an individual life, for a specified number of years, to cover a temporary need.

**terminus** /'tɜmənəs/, *n., pl.* **-ni** /-naɪ/, **-nuses. 1.** the end or extremity of anything. **2.** either end of a railway line, bus route, etc. **3.** the station or town at the end of a railway line, bus route, etc. **4.** the point to which anything tends; goal or end. **5.** a boundary or limit. **6.** a boundary post or stone. **7.** a figure of the Roman god, Terminus, representing the upper part of the body and terminating below in a rectangular pillar, which serves as a pedestal, often used as a boundary post. [L: boundary, limit, end]

**termitarium** /tɜmə'tɛəriəm/, *n., pl.* **-taria** /-'tɛəriə/. a termite colony's nest.

**termite** /'tɜmaɪt/, *n.* any of the pale-coloured, soft-bodied, mainly tropical, social insects constituting the order Isoptera, some of which are very destructive to buildings, furniture, household stores, etc.; white ant. [NL *termes* termite (LL woodworm)]

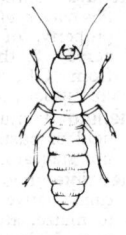

termite

**termless** /'tɜmləs/, *adj.* **1.** not limited; unconditional. **2.** boundless; endless.

**termor** /'tɜmə/, *n.* (in law) one who has an estate for a term of years or for life.

**terms of reference,** *n.pl.* See **reference** (def. 13).

**tern**[1] /tɜn/, *n.* any bird of the subfamily Sterninae (family Laridae), comprising numerous aquatic species which are allied to the gulls but usu. with a more slender body and bill, smaller feet, a long and deeply forked tail, and a more graceful flight, esp. any of those constituting the genus *Sterna,* as the crested tern, the little tern and the fairy tern. [Scand.; cf. Dan. *terne*]

tern[1]: common tern

**tern**[2] /tɜn/, *n.* **1.** a set of three. **2.** three winning numbers drawn together in a lottery. **3.** a prize won by drawing these. [ME, from F *terne,* from It. *terno,* from L *ternī* three each]

**ternary** /'tɜnəri/, *adj., n., pl.* **-ries.** *–adj.* **1.** consisting of or involving three; threefold; triple. **2.** third in order or rank. **3.** based on the number three. **4.** *Chem.* **a.** consisting of three different elements or radicals. **b.** *Obs.* consisting of three atoms. **5.** *Maths.* having three variables. **6.** *Metall.* (of an alloy) having three constituents. *–n.* **7.** a group of three. [ME, from LL *ternārius* made up of three]

**ternary form** /'– fɔm/, *n.* a form of musical composition consisting of two contrasting sections in sequence, the first of which is then repeated.

**ternate** /'tɜnət, -neɪt/, *adj.* **1.** consisting of three; arranged in threes. **2.** *Bot.* **a.** consisting of three leaflets, as a compound leaf. **b.** having leaves arranged in whorls of three, as a plant. **– ternately,** *adv.*

**terneplate** /'tɜnpleɪt/, *n.* an inferior tin plate in which sheet steel is covered with tin alloyed with a large proportion of lead. [*terne* (from F: dull. See TARNISH) + PLATE[1]]

**ternion** /'tɜniən/, *n.* a set or group of three; a triad. [L *ternio*]

**terpene** /'tɜpin/, *n.* **1.** any of certain monocyclic hydrocarbons with the formula $C_{10}H_{16}$, occurring in essential or volatile oils. **2.** any of various compounds which contain isoprene structural units for their carbon skeletons and have the general formula $(C_5H_8)_n$. [G *Terpen,* from *Terp(entin)* TURPENTINE + *-en* -ENE]

**terpinene** /ˈtɜpənin/, *n.* any of three isomeric liquid terpenes, $C_{10}H_{16}$, two of which occur naturally in various vegetable oils.

**terpineol** /tɜˈpɪnɪɒl/, *n.* any of several unsaturated tertiary alcohols, $C_{10}H_{17}OH$, occurring naturally in essential oils or prepared synthetically, used in perfumery. [*terpine* (from TERP(ENE) + -INE[2]) + -OL[1]]

**terpsichorean** /ˌtɜpsɪkəˈriən/, *adj.* **1.** pertaining to dancing. *–n.* **2.** *Colloq.* a dancer. [from *Terpsichore,* in Greek mythology, the muse of dancing and choral song]

**terr.**, **1.** terrace. **2.** territory. **3.** territorial.

**terra** /ˈtɛrə/, *n.* earth; land. [L and It.: earth]

**terra alba** /– ˈælbə/, *n.* any of various white, earthy or powdery substances as pipeclay, gypsum, kaolin, or magnesia. [L: white earth]

terrace (def. 4)

**terrace** /ˈtɛrəs/, *n., v.,* **-raced, -racing.** *–n.* **1.** a raised bank of earth with vertical or sloping sides, esp. one of a series of flat levels formed across a slope, mountain side, etc., usu. for the purposes of cultivation. **2.** a nearly level strip of land with a more or less abrupt descent along the margin of the sea, a lake, or a river. **3.** an open (usu. paved) area connected with a house and serving as an outdoor living area. **4.** a row of adjoining, identical houses, or a house in such a row, each house built to its side boundaries, and usu. of 19th century construction or design, often with two storeys and iron lace decoration. **5.** a city street. *–v.t.* **6.** to form into or supply with a terrace or terraces. [OF *terrasse* terrace, pile of earth, from F *terre* earth, from L *terra*]

**terrace house** /ˈ– haʊs/, *n.* one of a group of houses built in a terrace (def. 4).

**terracotta** /tɛrəˈkɒtə/, *n.* **1.** a hard, usu. unglazed earthenware of fine quality, used for architectural decorations, statuettes, vases, etc. **2.** something made of this, esp. a work of art. **3.** a brownish orange colour like that of much terracotta. *–adj.* **4.** made or having the colour of terracotta. [It.: baked earth, from L *terra cocta*]

**terra firma** /tɛrə ˈfɜmə/, *n.* firm or solid earth; dry land, as opposed to water or air. [L: solid earth]

**terrain** /təˈreɪn/, *n.* **1.** a tract of land, esp. as considered with reference to its natural features, military advantages, etc. **2.** *Geol.* →**terrane.** [F, from *terre* earth, from L *terra*]

**terra incognita** /ˌtɛrə ɪnkɒgˈnitə/, *n.* an unknown or unexplored land. [L: unknown land]

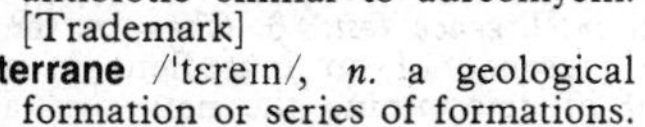
terrapin

**terramycin** /tɛrəˈmaɪsən/, *n.* an antibiotic similar to aureomycin. [Trademark]

**terrane** /ˈtɛreɪn/, *n.* a geological formation or series of formations. [see TERRAIN]

**terrapin** /ˈtɛrəpɪn/, *n.* **1.** any of various edible North American freshwater or tidewater turtles of the family Emydidae, esp. any of those constituting the genus *Malacylemmys* (**diamondback terrapins**). **2.** any of various similar turtles. [Algonquian, diminutive of *torope, torupe* tortoise]

**terraqueous** /tɛˈrækwiəs/, *adj.* consisting of land and water, as the earth. [L *terra* earth + AQUEOUS]

**terrar** /ˈtɛrə/, *n.* →**terrier**[2].

terrarium

**terrarium** /təˈrɛəriəm/, *n., pl.* **-rariums, -raria** /-ˈrɛəriə/. **1.** a closed glass container in which moisture-loving plants are grown. **2.** a container or small enclosure in which small animals, as lizards, turtles, etc., are kept. [NL, from *terra* earth; modelled on AQUARIUM]

**terra rossa** /tɛrə ˈrɒsə/, *n.* a reddish clay soil characteristic of limestone regions which have a Mediterranean climate. [It.: red earth]

**terrazzo** /təˈratsoʊ, -ˈraz-/, *n.* a floor material of chippings of broken stone and cement, polished when in place. [It.: terrace, balcony, from *terra* earth]

**terrene** /ˈtɛrin/, *adj.* **1.** earthly; worldly. **2.** earthy. *–n.* **3.** the earth. **4.** a land or region. [ME, from L *terrēnus* pertaining to earth]

**terreplein** /ˈtɛəpleɪn, ˈtɛrə-/, *n.* the top platform or horizontal surface of a rampart, used to support cannon. [F, from *terre* earth (from L *terra*) + *plein* full (from L *plēnus*)]

**terrestrial** /təˈrɛstriəl/, *adj.* **1.** pertaining to, consisting of, or representing the earth: *a terrestrial globe.* **2.** of or pertaining to the land as distinct from the water. **3.** *Bot.* **a.** growing on land; not aquatic. **b.** growing in the ground; not epiphytic or aerial. **4.** *Zool.* living on the ground; not aquatic, arboreal, or aerial. **5.** of or pertaining to the earth or this world; worldly; mundane. *–n.* **6.** an inhabitant of the earth, esp. a human being. [ME, from L *terrestri(s)* pertaining to earth + -AL[1]] **– terrestrially,** *adv.*

**terrestrial magnetism** /– ˈmægnətɪzəm/, *n.* the magnetic field associated with the earth, due to which a freely suspended magnetised needle anywhere on the surface of the earth will set itself so that it points in the direction of the earth's magnetic North Pole.

**terret** /ˈtɛrət/, *n.* **1.** one of the round loops or rings on a harness, through which the driving reins pass. **2.** a similar ring, as on a dog collar, etc., used for attaching a leash. [var. of ME *toret,* from OF, diminutive of *to(u)r* a round, circumference]

**terre-verte** /tɛə-ˈvɛət/, *n.* an olive-green pigment. [F: green earth]

**terrible** /ˈtɛrəbəl/, *adj.* **1.** exciting or fitted to excite terror or great fear; dreadful; awful. **2.** *Colloq.* very bad: *a terrible performance.* **3.** *Colloq.* very great: *a terrible liar.* [ME, from L *terribilis*] **– terribleness,** *n.* **– terribly,** *adv.*

**terricolous** /tɛˈrɪkələs/, *adj.* living on or in the ground. [L *terricola* earth-dweller + -OUS]

**terrier**[1] /ˈtɛriə/, *n.* one of a variety of dogs, typically small, with a propensity to pursue prey, as the fox, etc., into its burrow, occurring in many breeds including the fox-terrier, Irish terrier, Australian terrier. [ME *terrere,* from F *(chien) terrier* a hunting dog to start badgers, etc., from their earth or burrow, from *terre* earth, from L *terra*]

**terrier**[2] /ˈtɛriə/, *n.* (in law) a book or document in which are described the site, boundaries, area, etc., of lands privately owned by persons or corporations. Also, **terrar.** [ME *terrere,* from OF *terreoir,* from L *territōrium* territory]

**terrif** /təˈrɪf/, *adj. Colloq.* wonderful; terrific.

**terrific** /təˈrɪfɪk/, *adj.* **1.** causing terror; terrifying. **2.** *Colloq.* extraordinarily great, intense, etc.: *terrific speed.* **3.** *Colloq.* very good: *terrific food, fishing.* [L *terrificus* frightening] **– terrifically,** *adv.*

**terrify** /ˈtɛrəfaɪ/, *v.t.,* **-fied, -fying.** to fill with terror; make greatly afraid. [L *terrificāre*] **– terrifier,** *n.*

**terrigenous** /tɛˈrɪdʒənəs/, *adj.* **1.** produced by the earth. **2.** *Geol.* denoting or pertaining to sediments on the sea bottom derived directly from the neighbouring land, or to the rocks formed primarily by the consolidation of such sediments. [L *terrigenus* earthborn]

**terrine** /təˈrin/, *n.* **1.** an earthenware cooking dish. **2.** a pâté of meat or game served in such a dish. **3.** a tureen. [F. See TUREEN]

**territorial** /tɛrəˈtɔriəl/, *adj.* **1.** of or pertaining to territory or land. **2.** of, pertaining to, associated with, or restricted to a particular territory or district; local. **3.** pertaining or belonging to the territory of a state or ruler. **4.** of or pertaining to a territorial army. *–n.* **5.** *(sometimes cap.)* a soldier in a territorial army. **– territorially,** *adv.*

**territorial army** /– ˈami/, *n.* an army, often voluntary, organised for home or national defense.

**territorialise** /tɛrəˈtɔriəlaɪz/, *v.t.,* **-lised, -lising. 1.** to make a territory of. **2.** to extend by adding new territory. **3.** to organise or reorganise on a territorial basis. Also, **territorialize.** **– territorialisation** /tɛrəˌtɔriəlaɪˈzeɪʃən/, *n.*

**territorialism** /tɛrəˈtɔriəlɪzəm/, *n.* **1.** the principle of the predominance of the landed classes. **2.** organisation on a territorial basis. **3.** Also, **territorial system.** *Eccles.* the theory of Church policy according to which the supreme ecclesiastical authority is vested in the civil power. – **territorialist,** *n.*

**territoriality** /ˌtɛrətɔri'æləti/, *n.* **1.** territorial quality, condition, or status. **2.** the behaviour of an animal in claiming and defending its territory.

**territorial waters** /tɛrəˌtɔriəl 'wɔtəz/, *n.pl.* that part of the sea adjacent to the coast of a country regarded under international law as within the territorial sovereignty of that country.

**Territorian** /tɛrə'tɔriən/, *n.* **1.** one who was born in the Northern Territory, a self-governing territory of Australia, or who has come to regard it as his home. *–adj.* **2.** of or pertaining to the Northern Territory.

**territory** /'tɛrətri, -təri/, *n., pl.* **-ries. 1.** any tract of land; region or district. **2.** the land and waters belonging to or under the jurisdiction of a state, sovereign, etc. **3.** any separate tract of land belonging to a nation. **4.** (*oft. cap.*) a region administered by a government in which it is not fully represented. See **trust territory. 5. the Territory, a.** →**Northern Territory. b.** (formerly) →**Papua New Guinea. 6.** the field of action, thought, etc.; domain or province of something. **7.** the region or district assigned to a representative, agent, or the like, for making sales, etc. **8.** the area which an animal or pair of animals claim as their own and defend against intruders. [ME, from L *territōrium* land round a town, district]

**terror** /'tɛrə/, *n.* **1.** intense, sharp, overpowering fear: *to be frantic with terror.* **2.** a feeling, instance or cause of intense fear: *to be a terror to evildoers.* **3.** (*cap.*) a period when a political group uses violence to maintain or achieve supremacy. **4.** (*cap.*) any terrorist group, regime, etc. **5.** *Colloq.* a person or thing that is a particular nuisance: *that boy is a little terror.* [L; replacing ME *terrour,* from F or L] – **terrorless,** *adj.*

**terrorise** /'tɛrəraɪz/, *v.t.,* **-rised, -rising. 1.** to fill or overcome with terror. **2.** to dominate or coerce by intimidation. Also, **terrorize.** – **terrorisation** /tɛrəraɪ'zeɪʃən/, *n.* – **terroriser,** *n.*

**terrorism** /'tɛrərɪzəm/, *n.* **1.** the use of terrorising methods. **2.** the state of fear and submission so produced. **3.** a method of resisting a government or of governing by deliberate acts of armed violence.

**terrorist** /'tɛrərəst/, *n.* **1.** one who uses or favours terrorising methods of resisting a government or of governing. *–adj.* **2.** Also, **terroristic** /tɛrə'rɪstɪk/. denoting or pertaining to terrorists or their methods. [F *terroriste,* from L *terror* terror]

**terror-stricken** /'tɛrə-strɪkən/, *adj.* smitten with terror; terrified. Also, **terror-struck** /'tɛrə-strʌk/.

**terry** /'tɛri/, *n., pl.* **-ries,** *adj. –n.* **1.** the loop formed by the pile of a fabric when left uncut. *–adj.* **2.** having the pile loops uncut: *terry velvet.* [? var. of TERRET]

**terry towelling** /– 'taʊlɪŋ/, *n.* a cotton pile fabric with loops on both sides.

**Tersanctus** /tɜ'sæŋktəs/, *n.* →**Sanctus.** [NL, lit. thrice holy]

**terse** /tɜs/, *adj.,* **terser, tersest. 1.** neatly or effectively concise; brief and pithy, as language. **2.** abrupt or bad-tempered, esp. in one's speech. [L *tersus,* pp., polished] – **tersely,** *adv.* – **terseness,** *n.*

**tertial** /'tɜʃəl/, *adj.* **1.** pertaining to any of a set of flight feathers situated on the basal segment of a bird's wing. *–n.* **2.** a tertial feather. [L *tertius* third + -AL[1]]

**tertian** /'tɜʃən/, *adj.* **1.** recurring every other day, or, if considered inclusively, every third day. *–n.* **2.** a tertian fever or ague, esp. a form of malaria characterised by paroxysms associated with the 48 hour life-cycle of the invading parasite, *Plasmodium vivax.* [ME *tercian,* from L (*febris*) *tertiāna* tertian (fever), from *tertius* third]

**tertiary** /'tɜʃəri/, *adj., n., pl.* **-ries.** *–adj.* **1.** of the third order, rank, formation, etc.; third. **2.** *Educ.* denoting or pertaining to tertiary education. **3.** *Chem.* **a.** denoting or containing a carbon atom united to three other carbon atoms. **b.** formed by replacement of three atoms or radicals. **4.** (*cap.*) *Geol.* pertaining to a geological period or a system of rocks which precedes the Quaternary and constitutes the earlier principal division of the Cainozoic era. **5.** *Ornith.* tertial. **6.** *Eccles.* denoting or pertaining to a branch (third order) of certain religious orders which consists of lay members living in community (**regular tertiaries**) or living in the world (**secular tertiaries**). *–n.* **7.** (*cap.*) *Geol.* the period or system representing geological time from about 2 to 60 million years ago and comprising Palaeocene to Pliocene epochs or series. **8.** *Ornith.* a tertial feather. **9.** (*also cap.*) *Eccles.* a member of a tertiary branch of a religious order. [L *tertiārius* of third part or rank]

**tertiary colour** /– 'kʌlə/, *n.* a colour produced by mixing two or more secondary colours, as brown or grey.

**tertiary education** /– ɛdʒə'keɪʃən/, *n.* all forms of formal education beyond secondary education, including education at a university, college of advanced education, teacher's college, technical college, or other specialist college.

**tertium quid** /tɜtjəm 'kwɪd/, *n.* something related in some way to two things, but distinct from both; something intermediate between two things. [L, translation of Gk *tríton ti* some third thing]

**tervalent** /tɜ'veɪlənt/, *adj.* **1.** →**trivalent. 2.** possessing three different valencies, as cobalt with valencies 2, 3, and 4. [L *ter* thrice + -VALENT]

**terylene** /'tɛrəlin/, *n.* a synthetic polyester fibre, used in the manufacture of clothing, etc., made from ethylene glycol and terephthalic acid. [Trademark]

**terza rima** /tɛətsə 'rimə/, *n.* an Italian form of iambic verse consisting of eleven-syllable lines arranged in tercets, the middle line of each rhyming with the first and the third lines of the following tercet. [It.: third rhyme]

**tesla** /'tɛslə/, *n.* the SI derived unit of magnetic flux density, or magnetic intensity, defined as a magnetic flux of one weber per square metre ($Wb/m^2$). *Symbol:* T

**tesla coil** /'– kɔɪl/, *n.* a transformer for producing high voltages at high frequencies.

**tessellate** /'tɛsəleɪt/, *v.,* **-lated, -lating;** /'tɛsələt, -leɪt/, *adj. –v.t.* **1.** to form of small squares or blocks, as floors, pavements, etc.; form or arrange in a chequered or mosaic pattern. *–adj.* **2.** like a mosaic; tessellated. [LL *tessellātus,* pp., formed in mosaic]

**tessellation** /tɛsə'leɪʃən/, *n.* **1.** the act or art of tessellating. **2.** tessellated form or arrangement. **3.** tessellated work.

**tessera** /'tɛsərə/, *n., pl.* **tesserae** /'tɛsəri/. **1.** each of the small pieces used in mosaic work. **2.** a small square of bone, wood, or the like, anciently used as a token, tally, ticket, due, etc. [L, from d. Gk: lit., four] – **tesseral,** *adj.*

**tessitura** /tɛsə'turə, -'tjurə/, *n.* the range or compass of a voice or of a piece of music in relation to the normal range of a voice: *the song has a high tessitura.* [It.: lit., texture]

**test**[1] /tɛst/, *n.* **1.** that by which the presence, quality, or genuineness of anything is determined; a means of trial. **2.** the trial of the quality of something: *to put to the test.* **3.** a particular process or method of doing this. **4.** *Educ.* a form of examination for evaluating the performance and capabilities of a student or class. **5.** *Psychol.* a standardised procedure for eliciting responses upon which appraisal of the individual can be based: *an intelligence test.* **6.** *Chem.* **a.** the process of detecting the presence of an ingredient in a compound or the like, or of determining the nature of a substance, commonly by the addition of a reagent. **b.** the reagent used. **c.** an indication or evidence of the presence of an ingredient, or of the nature of a substance, obtained by such means. **7.** a cupel for assaying or refining metals. **8.** *Sport.* →**test match.** *–v.t.* **9.** to subject to a test of any kind; try. **10.** *Chem.* to subject to a chemical test. **11.** to assay or refine in a test or cupel. *–v.i.* **12.** to conduct a test or series of tests. [ME, from OF: cupel, from L *testu*(*m*), var. of *testa* tile, earthen vessel, pot] – **testable,** *adj.*

**test**[2] /tɛst/, *n.* **1.** *Zool.* the hard covering of certain invertebrates, as molluscs, arthropods, tunicates, etc.; shell; lorica. **2.** *Bot.* testa. [L *testa* (see TEST[1])]

**testa** /'tɛstə/, *n., pl.* **-tae** /-ti/. the outer, usu. hard, integument or coat of a plant seed. [L. See TEST[2]]

**testaceous** /tɛs'teɪʃəs/, *adj.* **1.** having a hard shell. **2.** of a brick red, brownish red, or brownish yellow colour. [L *testāceus* shell-covered]

**testacy** /'tɛstəsi/, *n.* the state of being testate.

**testament** /'tɛstəmənt/, *n.* **1.** *Law.* **a.** a formal declaration, usu. in writing, of a person's wishes as to the disposition of his property after his death. **b.** a disposition to take effect upon death and relating to personal property. **2.** a covenant, esp. between God and man. **3.** (*cap.*) either of the two main divisions of the Bible: **a.** the Mosaic or old covenant or dispensation. **b.** the Christian or new covenant or dispensation. **4.** (*cap.*) the New Testament, as distinct from the Old Testament. **5.** a copy of the New Testament. [ME, from L *testāmentum* will]

**testamentary** /tɛstəˈmɛntəri/, *adj.* **1.** of, pertaining to, or of the nature of a testament or will. **2.** given, bequeathed, done, or appointed by will. **3.** set forth or contained in a will.

**testamur** /tɛsˈteɪmə/, *n.* a certificate showing that the person named has been admitted to a particular degree or diploma by the academic institution which issues the certificate.

**testate** /ˈtɛsteɪt, ˈtɛstət/, *adj.* having made and left a valid will. [late ME, from L *testātus*, pp.]

**testation** /tɛsˈteɪʃən/, *n.* **1.** the disposal of property by will. **2.** *Obs.* attestation; witnessing.

**testator** /tɛsˈteɪtə/, *n.* **1.** one who makes a will. **2.** one who has died leaving a valid will. [L; replacing ME *testatour*, from AF]

**testatrix** /tɛsˈteɪtrɪks, ˈtɛstətrɪks/, *n., pl.* **-trices** /-trəsiz/. a female testator.

**testatum** /tɛsˈteɪtəm/, *n.* the witnessing part of a deed or agreement.

**test-ban** /ˈtɛst-bæn/, *adj.* denoting or pertaining to a treaty or agreement between nations not to test nuclear weapons, or to test them only under limited conditions, as not in the atmosphere.

**test bed** /ˈtɛst bɛd/, *n.* a framework and foundation on which an electrical machine or an engine is placed for the purpose of carrying out a test under load.

**test case** /ˈ– keɪs/, *n.* a legal or other case which establishes a precedent for reference in similar cases.

**tester**[1] /ˈtɛstə/, *n.* one who or that which tests. [TEST[1], *v.* + -ER[1]]

**tester**[2] /ˈtɛstə/, *n.* a canopy or support, or both, as over a bed, altar, etc. [late ME. Cf. OF *testre* headboard of bed, *testiere* head covering, from *teste* head, from L *testa* pot]

**tester**[3] /ˈtɛstə/, *n. Convict Obs. Colloq.* a flogging of twenty-five lashes. See **bob**[4], **bull**[2], **canary**[2]. [obs. Brit. *tester* thieves slang for sixpence]

**testes** /ˈtɛstiz/, *n.* plural of **testis.**

**test group** /ˈtɛst grup/, *n.* (in an experiment) that group which is exposed to the drug, condition, etc., to be tested (opposed to *control group*).

**testicle** /ˈtɛstɪkəl/, *n.* the male sex gland, either of two oval glands situated in the scrotal sac. [L *testiculus*, diminutive of *testis* TESTIS] – **testicular** /tɛsˈtɪkjələ/, *adj.*

**testiculate** /tɛsˈtɪkjələt/, *adj.* **1.** shaped like a testicle. **2.** having tubers shaped like testicles, as certain orchids.

**testification** /tɛstəfəˈkeɪʃən/, *n.* the act of testifying or bearing witness.

**testify** /ˈtɛstəfaɪ/, *v.*, **-fied, -fying.** *–v.i.* **1.** to bear witness; give or afford evidence. **2.** to make solemn declaration. **3.** *Law.* to give testimony under oath or solemn affirmation, usu. in court. *–v.t.* **4.** to bear witness to; affirm as fact or truth. **5.** to give or afford evidence of in any manner. **6.** to declare, profess, or acknowledge openly. **7.** *Law.* to state or declare under oath or affirmation, usu. in court. [ME, from L *testificārī* bear witness] – **testifier,** *n.*

**testimonial** /tɛstəˈmoʊniəl/, *n.* **1.** a writing certifying to a person's character, conduct, or qualifications, or to a thing's value, excellence, etc.; a letter or written statement of recommendation. **2.** something given or done as an expression of esteem, admiration, or gratitude. *–adj.* **3.** pertaining to or serving as testimony.

**testimonialise** /tɛstəˈmoʊniəlaɪz/, *v.t.*, **-lised, -lising.** to present with a testimonial. Also, **testimonialize.**

**testimony** /ˈtɛstəməni/, *n., pl.* **-nies. 1.** *Law.* the statement or declaration of a witness under oath or affirmation, usu. in court. **2.** evidence in support of a fact or statement; proof. **3.** open declaration or profession, as of faith. [late ME, from L *testimōnium* evidence, attestation]

**testis** /ˈtɛstəs/, *n., pl.* **-tes** /-tiz/. →**testicle.** [L]

**test match** /ˈtɛst mætʃ/, *n.* a match or one of a series of matches, esp. in cricket, between two nationally representative teams.

**testosterone** /tɛsˈtɒstəroʊn/, *n.* the hormone, $C_{19}H_{28}O_2$, secreted by the testes and obtained by extraction from animal testes and by synthesis. It stimulates the development of masculine characteristics. [*testo-* TESTIS + STER(OL) + -ONE]

**test paper** /ˈtɛst peɪpə/, *n.* **1.** a set of questions to be answered under examination conditions, as one used in practice for an examination. **2.** *Chem.* paper impregnated with a reagent, as litmus, which changes colour when acted upon by certain substances.

**test pilot** /ˈ– paɪlət/, *n.* a pilot employed to test new aircraft by flying them in such a way that they are subjected to maximum strains.

**test tube** /ˈ– tjub/, *n.* a hollow cylinder of thin glass with one end closed, used in chemical tests.

**test-tube baby** /ˈtɛst-tjub ˌbeɪbi/, *n.* **1.** a child born as a result of artificial insemination. **2.** a child conceived artificially outside a mother's body under simulated conditions suitable for its survival and then implanted in the womb.

**testudinate** /tɛsˈtjudənət, -neɪt/, *adj.* formed like the carapace of a tortoise; arched; vaulted.

**testudo** /tɛsˈtjudoʊ/, *n., pl.* **-dines** /-dəniz/. **1.** *Fort.* (among the ancient Romans) a movable shelter with a strong and usu. fireproof arched roof, used for protection of soldiers in siege operations. **2.** a shelter formed by soldiers overlapping their oblong shields above their heads. [ME, from L: tortoise]

testudo: detail from Trajan's Column in Rome

**testy** /ˈtɛsti/, *adj.*, **-tier, -tiest.** irritably impatient; touchy. [ME, from AF *testif* headstrong, from OF *teste* head, from L *testa* potsherd] – **testily,** *adv.* – **testiness,** *n.*

**tetanic** /təˈtænɪk/, *adj.* **1.** *Pathol.* pertaining to, of the nature of, or characterised by tetanus. **2.** *Med.* denoting a remedy which acts on the nerves and through them on the muscles, and which, if taken in overdoses, causes tetanic spasms of the muscles and death. Also, **tetanical.**

**tetanise** /ˈtɛtənaɪz/, *v.t.*, **-nised, -nising.** *Physiol.* to induce a condition of tetanus in (a muscle). Also, **tetanize.** – **tetanisation** /tɛtənaɪˈzeɪʃən/, *n.*

**tetanus** /ˈtɛtənəs/, *n.* **1.** *Pathol.* **a.** an infectious, often fatal disease, due to a specific micro-organism, the **tetanus bacillus,** which gains entrance to the body through wounds, characterised by more or less violent tonic spasms and rigidity of many or all the voluntary muscles, esp. those of the neck and lower jaw. Cf. **lockjaw. b.** the micro-organism, *Clostridium tetami,* which causes this disease. **2.** *Physiol.* tonic contractions of a skeletal muscle induced by rapid stimulation. [L, from Gk *tétanos* spasm (of muscles)] – **tetanoid,** *adj.*

**tetany** /ˈtɛtəni/, *n.* a state marked by severe intermittent tonic contractions and muscular pain, frequently due to a deficiency of calcium salts. [NL *tetania.* See TETANUS]

**tetartohedral** /təˌtatoʊˈhidrəl/, *adj.* (of a crystal) having one fourth the planes or faces required by the maximum symmetry of the system to which it belongs. [*tetarto-* (from Gk, combining form of *tétartos* fourth) + -HEDR(ON) + -AL[1]] – **tetartohedrally,** *adv.* – **tetartohedralism,** *n.*

**tetchy** /ˈtɛtʃi/, *adj.*, **tetchier, tetchiest.** irritable; touchy. Also, **techy.** [orig. uncert.] – **tetchily,** *adv.* – **tetchiness,** *n.*

**tete-a-tete** /teɪt-a-ˈteɪt/, *adj.* **1.** of, between, or for two persons together, without others. *–n.* **2.** a private conversation or interview, usu. between two people. **3.** a sofa shaped like an S so that two people are able to converse face to face. *–adv.* **4.** (of two persons) together in private: *to sit tete-a-tete.* Also, **tête-à-tête.** [F: head to head]

tete-a-tete

**tete-beche** /teɪt-ˈbɛʃ/, *adj.* (of an unsevered pair of stamps) reversed in relation to each other, either through error or intentionally. Also, **tête-bêche.** [from *tête* head + *bêche,* reduced from *bechenet* double-bed head]

**tether** /ˈtɛðə/, *n.* **1.** a rope, chain, or the like, by which an animal is fastened, as to a stake, so that its range of movement is limited. **2.** the utmost length to which one can go in action; the utmost extent or limit of ability or resources. **3. the end of one's tether,** the limit of one's possibilities, patience, or resources. *–v.t.* **4.** to fasten or confine with or as with a tether. [ME *tethir,* apparently from Scand.; cf. Icel. *tjōdhr*]

**tetra** /ˈtɛtrə/, *n.* any of several highly coloured tropical fish of the family Characinidae, often kept in home aquariums.

**tetra-,** a word element meaning 'four' as in *tetrabrach.* [Gk, combining form of *téttares*]

**tetrabasic** /tɛtrəˈbeɪsɪk/, *adj.* **1.** (of an acid) having four atoms of hydrogen replaceable by basic atoms or radicals. **2.** containing four basic atoms or radicals having a valency of one.

**tetrabrach** /ˈtɛtrəbræk/, *n.* a metrical foot or word of four short syllables. [Gk *tetrábrachys* having four short syllables]

**tetrabranchiate** /tɛtrəˈbræŋkiət, -eɪt/, *adj.* belonging or pertaining to the Tetrabranchiata, a subclass or order of cephalopods with four gills, including the pearly nautilus and numerous fossil forms. [NL *tetrabranchiātum,* from Gk *tetra-* TETRA- + Gk *bránchia* gills + *-ātum* -ATE[1]]

**tetrachloroethylene** /ˌtɛtrəˌklɔroʊˈɛθəlin/, *n.* a colourless liquid, $C_2Cl_4$, used as a solvent, esp. in dry cleaning; perchlorethylene.

**tetrachord** /ˈtɛtrəkɔd/, *n.* a diatonic series of four notes, the first and last separated by a perfect fourth. [Gk *tetráchordos* having four strings] – **tetrachordal** /tɛtrəˈkɔdl/, *adj.*

**tetracid** /tɛˈtræsəd/, *n.* a base or an alcohol containing four hydroxyl (OH) groups.

**tetracyanoplatinic acid** /ˌtɛtrəˌsaɪənoʊpləˌtɪnɪk ˈæsəd/, *n. Chem.* →**platinocyanic acid.**

**tetracycline** /tɛtrəˈsaɪklin/, *n.* **1.** *Chem.* a yellow crystalline powder, $C_{22}H_{24}N_2O_8$. **2.** *Biochem.* any of a group of broad-spectrum antibiotics, including aureomycin and terramycin, used to treat diseases of bacterial origin.

**tetrad** /ˈtɛtræd/, *n.* **1.** a group of four. **2.** the number four. **3.** *Chem.* a tetravalent or quadrivalent element, atom, or radical. [Gk *tetrás* group of four]

**tetradymite** /tɛˈtrædəmaɪt/, *n.* a mineral, bismuth telluride and sulphide, $Bi_2Te_2S$, occurring in soft grey to black foliated masses. [G *Tetradymit,* from Gk *tetrádymos* fourfold + *-it* -ITE[1]]

**tetradynamous** /tɛtrəˈdaɪnəməs, -ˈdɪnə-/, *adj.* having four long and two short stamens, as in many cruciferous flowers.

**tetraethyl lead** /ˌtɛtrəˌɛθəl ˈlɛd/, *n.* →**lead tetraethyl.**

**tetrafluoroethylene** /ˌtɛtrəˌfluroʊˈɛθəlin/, *n.* a colourless gas, $C_2F_4$, which polymerises into a thermoplastic material with good electrical-insulation properties.

**tetragon** /ˈtɛtrəgən, -gɒn/, *n.* a plane figure having four angles; a quadrangle; a quadrilateral. [Gk *tetrágōnon* quadrangle]

**tetragonal** /tɛˈtrægənəl/, *adj.* **1.** pertaining to a tetragon. **2.** *Crystall.* denoting or pertaining to the tetragonal system.

**tetragonal system** /ˈ– sɪstəm/, *n.* a system of crystallisation in which all three axes are at right angles to one another, and the two equal lateral axes differ in length from the vertical axis.

**tetragram** /ˈtɛtrəgræm/, *n.* **1.** a word of four letters. **2.** (*also cap.*) →**Tetragrammaton.** [Gk *tetrágrammon*]

**Tetragrammaton** /tɛtrəˈgræmətən/, *n.* the Hebrew word written JHVH (or JHWH, YHVH, YHWH), representing, without vowels, the 'ineffable name' of God, pronounced in Hebrew as 'Adonai' and commonly transliterated in English as 'Jehovah'. See **Yahweh.** [ME, from Gk: the four-letter (word)]

**tetrahedral** /tɛtrəˈhidrəl/, *adj.* **1.** pertaining to or having the form of a tetrahedron. **2.** having four lateral planes in addition to the top and bottom. – **tetrahedrally,** *adv.*

**tetrahedrite** /tɛtrəˈhidraɪt/, *n.* a steel-grey or blackish mineral with a brilliant metallic lustre, essentially copper and antimony sulphide (nearly $Cu_3SbS_3$), but often containing other elements, as silver, etc., occurring in tetrahedral crystals and massive, and forming an important ore of copper and sometimes of silver.

**tetrahedron** /tɛtrəˈhidrən/, *n., pl.* **-drons, -dra** /-drə/. a solid contained by four plane faces; a triangular pyramid. [LGk *tetráedron,* neut. of *tetráedros* four-sided. See -HEDRON]

**tetrahydrocannabinol** /ˌtɛtrəˌhaɪdroʊ- ˌkænəˈbinɒl/, *n.* a component of marijuana which causes a euphoric state.

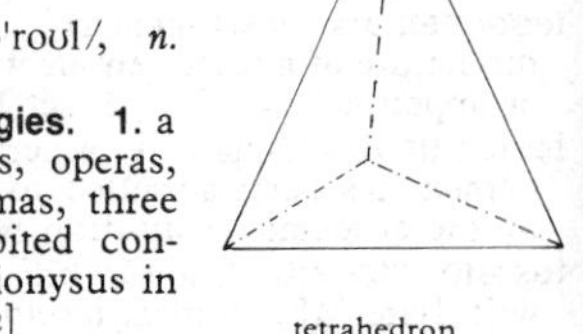

tetrahedron

**tetraiodofluorescein** /ˌtɛtrəaɪədoʊˈflurəsin/, *n.* →**iodeosin.**

**tetraiodopyrrole** /ˌtɛtrəaɪədoʊpəˈroʊl/, *n.* →**iodole.**

**tetralogy** /tɛˈtrælədʒi/, *n., pl.* **-gies. 1.** a series of four related dramas, operas, etc. **2.** a group of four dramas, three tragic and one satiric, exhibited consecutively at the festival of Dionysus in ancient Athens. [Gk *tetralogia*]

**tetramerous** /tɛˈtræmərəs/, *adj.* **1.** consisting of or divided into four parts. **2.** *Bot.* (of flowers) having four members in each whorl. [NL *tetramerus,* from Gk *tetramerés* four-parted]

**tetrameter** /tɛˈtræmətə/, *Pros.* *–adj.* **1.** having four measures. *–n.* **2.** a tetrameter line. In ancient poetry, it consisted of four dipodies (eight feet) in trochaic, iambic, or anapaestic metre. [L *tetrametrus,* from Gk *tetrámetros*]

**tetramorphism** /tɛtrəˈmɔfɪzəm/, *n.* the property of some substances of crystallising in four structurally distinct forms. – **tetramorphic, tetramorphous,** *adj.*

tetramerous flower

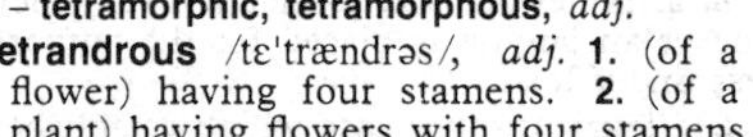

**tetrandrous** /tɛˈtrændrəs/, *adj.* **1.** (of a flower) having four stamens. **2.** (of a plant) having flowers with four stamens.

**tetrapetalous** /tɛtrəˈpɛtələs/, *adj.* having four petals.

**tetraplegia** /tɛtrəˈplidʒə/, *n.* →**quadriplegia.**

**tetrapod** /ˈtɛtrəpɒd/, *n.* any amphibian, reptile, bird, or mammal, the four classes of vertebrates, the members of which typically have four limbs.

**tetrapody** /tɛˈtræpədi/, *n.* a group of four metrical feet. – **tetrapodic** /tɛtrəˈpɒdɪk/, *adj.*

**tetrapterous** /tɛˈtræptərəs/, *adj.* **1.** *Zool.* having four wings or winglike appendages. **2.** *Bot.* having four winglike appendages. [Gk *tetrápteros*]

**tetrarch** /ˈtɛtrak/, *n.* **1.** any ruler of a fourth part, division, etc. **2.** a subordinate ruler generally. **3.** one of four joint rulers or chiefs. [ME, from LL *tetrarcha,* var. of L *tetrarchēs,* from Gk: ruler of one of four (parts)] – **tetrarchate** /tɛˈtrakeɪt, -kət/, **tetrarchy** /ˈtɛtraki/, *n.*

**tetrasporangium** /tɛtrəspɔˈrændʒiəm/, *n., pl.* **-gia** /-dʒiə/. a sporangium containing four asexual spores (tetraspores).

**tetraspore** /ˈtɛtrəspɔ/, *n.* one of the four asexual spores produced within a tetrasporangium. – **tetrasporic** /tɛtrəˈspɒrɪk/, **tetrasporous** /tɛtrəˈspɔrəs, tɛˈtræspərəs/, *adj.*

**tetrastich** /ˈtɛtrəstɪk/, *n.* a poem, stanza, or set of four lines. – **tetrastichic** /tɛtrəˈstɪkɪk/, **tetrastichal** /tɛˈtræstɪkəl/, *adj.*

**tetrastichous** /tɛˈtræstɪkəs/, *adj. Bot.* **1.** arranged in a spike of four vertical rows, as flowers. **2.** having four such rows of flowers, as a spike. [Gk *tetrástichos* having four rows]

**tetrasyllable** /ˈtɛtrəsɪləbəl/, *n.* a word of four syllables. – **tetrasyllabic** /tɛtrəsəˈlæbɪk/, **tetrasyllabical** /tɛtrəsəˈlæbɪkəl/, *adj.*

**tetratomic** /tɛtrəˈtɒmɪk/, *adj.* **1.** having four atoms in the molecule. **2.** having a valency of four. **3.** containing four replaceable atoms or groups.

**tetravalent** /tɛtrəˈveɪlənt/, *adj.* **1.** having a valency of four. **2.** →**quadrivalent.**

**tetrode** /ˈtɛtroʊd/, *n.* a radio valve containing four electrodes, usu. an anode, two grids, and a cathode.

**tetrose** /ˈtɛtroʊz, -oʊs/, *n.* a monosaccharide which contains four oxygen atoms in its molecule.

**tetroxide** /tɛˈtrɒksaɪd/, *n.* an oxide which contains in its molecule four atoms of oxygen. Also, **tetroxid** /tɛˈtrɒksəd/.

**tetryl** /ˈtɛtrəl/, *n.* a military explosive, $C_7H_5N_5O_8$, used as a detonator and as a bursting charge in small-calibre projectiles. [TETR(A)- + -YL]

**tetter** /ˈtɛtə/, *n.* any of various cutaneous diseases, as herpes, eczema, impetigo, etc. [ME; OE *teter,* c. Skt *dadru* kind of skin disease]

**Teut.,** **1.** Teuton. **2.** Teutonic.

**Teutonic** /tju'tɒnɪk/, *adj.* **1.** of or pertaining to the ancient Teutons. **2.** of or pertaining to the Teutons or Germans; German. **3.** denoting or pertaining to the northern European stock which includes the German, Dutch, Scandinavian, British, and related peoples. **4.** (of languages) Germanic. **5.** *Obs.* Nordic. *–n.* **6.** Germanic. – **Teutonically,** *adv.*

**tex** /tɛks/, *n.* a unit for expressing the linear density of fibres, equal to $10^{-6}$ kg/m.

**text** /tɛkst/, *n.* **1.** the main body of matter in a book or manuscript, as distinguished from notes, appendixes, etc. **2.** the original words of an author as distinct from a translation, paraphrase, commentary, or the like. **3.** the actual wording of anything written or printed. **4.** any of the various forms in which a writing exists. **5.** the wording adopted by an editor as representing the original words of an author. **6.** any theme or topic. **7.** the words of a song or the like. **8.** a textbook. **9.** a short passage of Scripture, esp. one chosen in proof of a doctrine, as the subject of a sermon, etc. **10.** *Eccles.* the letter of the Holy Scripture, or the Scriptures themselves. [ME, from ML *textus* wording (of the Gospel), L structure (of a discourse), orig. texture. See TEXTURE] – **textless,** *adj.*

**textbook** /'tɛkstbʊk/, *n.* a book used by students as a standard work for a particular branch of study.

**textile** /'tɛkstaɪl/, *n.* **1.** any material that is woven. **2.** a material suitable for weaving. *–adj.* **3.** woven or capable of being woven: *textile fabrics.* **4.** of or pertaining to weaving: *the textile industries.* [L *textilis* woven]

**textual** /'tɛkstʃuəl/, *adj.* **1.** of or pertaining to a text: *textual errors.* **2.** having the purpose of determining the true or best possible reading of a text: *textual criticism.* **3.** based on or conforming to the text, as of the Scriptures. [ME *textuel,* from ML *textu(s)* TEXT + *-el* -AL[1]] – **textually,** *adv.*

**textual criticism** /– 'krɪtəsɪzəm/, *n.* **1.** the scholarly study of manuscripts in order to establish the original text and elucidate questions of authorship. **2.** literary criticism working from close analysis of the text.

**textualism** /'tɛkstʃuəˌlɪzəm/, *n.* strict adherence to the text, esp. of the Scriptures.

**textualist** /'tɛkstʃuələst/, *n.* **1.** one who adheres closely to the text, esp. of the Scriptures. **2.** one who is well versed in the text of the Scriptures.

**textuary** /'tɛkstʃuəri/, *adj., n., pl.* **-aries.** *–adj.* **1.** of or pertaining to the text; textual. *–n.* **2.** →**textualist.**

**texture** /'tɛkstʃə/, *n., v.,* **-tured, -turing.** *–n.* **1.** the characteristic disposition of the interwoven or intertwined threads, strands, or the like, which make up a textile fabric. **2.** the characteristic disposition of the constituent parts of any body; general structure or constitution. **3.** the characteristic appearance or essential quality of something, esp. as conveyed to the touch. **4.** the structure of the surface of any work of art, or the simulation of the surface structure of the skin, garment, etc., of the object represented in paint, stone, or other medium. **5.** *Music.* **a.** a combination of timbres or tone colours. **b.** the pattern of relationships between the parts of a musical form: *contrapuntal texture, harmonic texture.* **6.** anything produced by weaving; woven fabric. *–v.t.* **7.** to give a specific or desired texture to, as clothes. [late ME, from L *textūra* weaving] – **textural,** *adj.* – **texturally,** *adv.*

**TG** /ti 'dʒi/, transformational grammar.

**T-group** /'ti-grup/, *n.* →**encounter group.** [abbrev. *Training group,* in some U.S. hospitals, a group of sociologists, psychologists, etc., training as a group]

**-th**[1], a noun suffix referring to condition, quality, or action, added to words (*warmth*) and to stems related to words (*depth, length*). [OE *-thu, -tho, -th,* c. Icel. *-th*]

**-th**[2], the suffix of ordinal numerals (*fourth, tenth, twentieth*), the form *-th* being added in one or two cases to altered stems of the cardinal (*fifth, twelfth*). [OE *-tha, -the;* c. L *-tus,* Gk *-tos*]

**Th,** *Chem.* thorium.

**Th.,** **1.** Theatre. **2.** Theology. **3.** Thursday.

**Thai** /taɪ/, *n.* **1.** a group of Sino-Tibetan languages spoken over a wide area of South-East Asia, including Siamese and Shan. **2.** the Siamese language. **3.** a native or inhabitant of Thailand. **4.** a Thai-speaking person. *–adj.* **5.** of, designating, or pertaining to the Thai languages or to the peoples that speak them. **6.** →**Siamese.** Also, **Tai.**

**Thailand** /'taɪlænd/, *n.* a kingdom in South-East Asia. Formerly, **Siam.**

**thalamencephalon** /θæləmɛn'sɛfəlɒn/, *n., pl.* **-la** /-lə/. →**diencephalon.** [NL. See THALAMUS, ENCEPHALON]

**thalamus** /'θæləməs/, *n., pl.* **-mi** /-maɪ/. **1.** *Anat.* the middle part of the diencephalon through which sensory impulses pass to reach the cerebral cortex; optic thalamus. **2.** *Bot.* a receptacle or torus. [L, from Gk *thálamos* inner room] – **thalamic** /θə'læmɪk/, *adj.*

**thalassic** /θə'læsɪk/, *adj.* **1.** of or pertaining to the seas and oceans (sometimes distinguishing smaller bodies of water from *oceanic* bodies). **2.** growing, living, or found in the sea; marine. [Gk *thálassa* sea + -IC]

**thalassography** /θælə'sɒgrəfi/, *n.* oceanography, esp. the branch dealing with coastal waters, seas, and gulfs. [Gk *thálassa* + -O- + -GRAPHY] – **thalassographer,** *n.* – **thalassographic** /θæləsə'græfɪk/, *adj.*

**thaler** /'talə/, *n., pl.* **-ler.** any of certain large silver coins of varying value formerly issued in Germany, esp. one of the value of 3 marks. Also, **taler.** [G: dollar]

**thalidomide** /θə'lɪdəmaɪd/, *n.* a crystalline solid, $C_{13}H_{10}N_2O_{41}$, formerly used as a sedative until it was discovered that it could affect the normal growth of the foetus if taken during pregnancy. [THAL(LIC) + (IM)IDO- + (*glutaril*)*mide* (from GLUT(EN) + (TART)AR(IC) + IMIDE)]

**thallic** /'θælɪk/, *adj.* of or containing thallium, esp. in the trivalent state.

**thallium** /'θæliəm, 'θeɪ-/, *n.* a soft, malleable, rare, metallic element, used in alloys; its salts are also used in rat poisons. *Symbol:* Tl; *at. wt:* 204.37; *at. no.:* 81; *sp.gr.:* 11.85 at 20°C. [NL, from Gk *thallós* green shoot + *-ium* -IUM]

**thalloid** /'θælɔɪd/, *adj.* resembling or consisting of a thallus.

**thallophyte** /'θæləfaɪt/, *n.* any member of the Thallophyta, a phylum of plants (including the algae, fungi, and lichens) in which the plant body of larger species is typically a thallus. [NL *thallophyta* (pl.). See THALLUS, -PHYTE] – **thallophytic** /θælə'fɪtɪk/, *adj.*

**thallous** /'θæləs/, *adj.* containing monovalent thallium. Also, **thallious** /'θæliəs/.

**thallus** /'θæləs/, *n., pl.* **thalli** /'θælaɪ/, **thalluses.** a simple vegetative plant body undifferentiated into true leaves, stem, and root, being the plant body of typical thallophytes. [NL, from Gk *thallós* young shoot, twig]

**thalofide cell** /'θæləfaɪd sɛl/, *n.* a photoconductive cell which uses thallium oxysulphide as the light sensitive agent. [*thalofide* from THAL(LIUM) + *o*(*xysul*)*fide* U.S. var. of OXYSULPHIDE]

**thalweg** /'talvɛg, -wɛg/, *n.* the line joining the deepest points of a stream channel. Also, **talweg.**

**than** /ðæn/; *weak form* /ðən/, *conj.* **1.** a particle used after comparative adjectives and adverbs and certain other words, such as *other, otherwise, else,* etc., to introduce the second member of a comparison: *he is taller than I am.* *–prep.* **2.** in comparison with: *he is taller than me.* [ME and OE; var. of ME and OE *thanne* than, then, c. G *denn.* See THEN]

**thanage** /'θeɪnɪdʒ/, *n.* **1.** the tenure by which lands were held by a thane. **2.** the lands so held. **3.** the office, rank, or jurisdiction of a thane.

**thanatophobia** /θænətə'foʊbiə/, *n.* morbid fear of death. [Gk *thánatos* death + -PHOBIA]

**thanatopsis** /θænə'tɒpsəs/, *n.* a view or contemplation of death. [Gk *thánatos* death + *ópsis sight, view*]

**thane** /θeɪn/, *n.* **1.** *Old Eng. Hist.* a member of any of several classes of men ranking between earls and ordinary freeman, and holding lands of the king or lord by military service. **2.** *Scot. Hist.* a person, ranking with an earl's son, holding lands of the king; the chief of a clan, who became one of the king's barons. Also, **thegn.** [late ME, var. of ME *thain,* OE *thegn,* c. G *Degen* servant, warrior; akin to Gk *téknon* child]

**thank** /θæŋk/, *v.t.* **1.** to give thanks to; express gratitude to. **2. have oneself to thank,** to be oneself responsible or at fault. **3. have someone to thank for,** to rightly place blame or responsibility for (something) on someone. *–n.* **4.** (*usu.*

*pl.*) the expression of grateful feeling, or grateful acknowledgment of a benefit or favour, by words or otherwise: *to return a borrowed book with thanks.* **5.** (*pl.*) a common elliptical expression used in acknowledging a favour, service, courtesy, or the like. **6. thanks to, a.** thanks be given to. **b.** as a result or consequence of. [ME; OE *thanc* gratitude, orig. thoughtfulness, thought. See THINK[1]] – **thanker,** *n.*

**thankful** /ˈθæŋkfəl/, *adj.* feeling or expressing thanks. – **thankfully,** *adv.* – **thankfulness,** *n.*

**thankless** /ˈθæŋkləs/, *adj.* **1.** not such as to be rewarded with thanks; not appreciated. **2.** ungrateful. – **thanklessly,** *adv.* – **thanklessness,** *n.*

**thank-offering** /ˈθæŋk-ˌɒfrɪŋ/, *n.* an offering, as to some deity, to express gratitude for the turn of events or the like.

**thanksgiver** /ˈθæŋksgɪvə/, *n.* one who gives thanks.

**thanksgiving** /θæŋksˈgɪvɪŋ, ˈθæŋksgɪvɪŋ/, *n.* **1.** the act of giving thanks; grateful acknowledgment of benefits or favours, esp. to God. **2.** an expression of thanks, esp. to God. **3.** a public celebration in acknowledgment of divine favour.

**thankworthy** /ˈθæŋkwɜði/, *adj.* deserving gratitude.

**thankyou** /ˈθæŋkju/, *interj.* **1.** (an expression of gratitude or thanks.) *–n.* **2.** the act of expressing thanks: *have you said your thankyous?* *–adj.* **3.** expressing thanks: *a thankyou letter.*

**thar** /ta/, *n.* →**tahr.**

**that** /ðæt/; *weak form* /ðət/, *pron. and adj., pl.* **those;** *adv., conj.* *–pron.* **1.** (a demonstrative pronoun used to indicate: **a.** a person, thing, idea, etc., as pointed out or present, before mentioned, about to be mentioned, supposed to be understood, or by way of emphasis. **b.** one of two or more persons, things, etc., already mentioned referring to the one more remote in place, time, or thought. **c.** one of two or more persons, things, etc., already mentioned, implying contradistinction (opposed to *this*).) **2.** (a relative pronoun used: **a.** as the subject or object of a relative clause, esp. one defining or restricting the antecedent (sometimes replaceable by *who, whom,* or *which*). **b.** as the object of a preposition, the preposition being at the end of the relative clause: *the man that I spoke of.* **c.** in various special or elliptical constructions: *fool that he is.*) **3. and all that,** together with all similar things (used dismissively). **4. at that,** additionally; besides: *it's an idea, and a good one at that.* **5. that is,** more precisely; in clarification or example. **6. that's that,** that is the end of the matter; the matter is closed or finished (used dismissively). **7. with that,** thereupon; immediately afterwards. *–adj.* **8.** (a demonstrative adjective used to indicate: **a.** a person, place, thing, idea, etc., as pointed out or present, before mentioned, supposed to be understood, or by way of emphasis. **b.** one of two or more persons, things, etc., already mentioned, referring to the one more remote in place, time, or thought. **c.** one of two or more persons, things, etc., already mentioned, implying contradistinction (opposed to *this*).) *–adv.* **9.** (an adverb used: **a.** with adjectives and adverbs of quality or extent to indicate precise degree or extent: *that much, that far.* **b.** *Colloq.* with other adjectives and adverbs to indicate extent or degree, or for emphasis: *poor lad, he was that weak!*). *–conj.* **10.** (a conjunction used: **a.** to introduce a clause as the subject or object of the principal verb or as the necessary complement to a statement made, or a clause expressing cause or reason, purpose or aim, result or consequence, etc.: *that he will come is certain.* **b.** elliptically, to introduce a sentence or clause expressing desire, surprise, or indignation.) [ME; OE *thæt* that, the, c. G *das*(*s*), Gk *tó*]

**thatch** /θætʃ/, *n.* **1.** a material, as straw, rushes, leaves, or the like, used to cover roofs, haystacks, etc. **2.** a covering of such a material. **3.** *Colloq.* the hair covering the head. *–v.t.* **4.** to cover with or as with thatch. *–v.i.* **5.** to thatch houses, haystacks, etc. [ME *thacche,* var. of *thack,* OE *thæc* roof, thatch, c. G *Dach,* L *toga* covering; akin to Gk *tégos* roof] – **thatcher,** *n.* – **thatchless,** *adj.* – **thatchy,** *adj.*

**thatching** /ˈθætʃɪŋ/, *n.* **1.** the act or skill of covering with thatch. **2.** the material used for thatching; thatch (def. 1).

**thaumatology** /θɔməˈtɒlədʒi/, *n.* the study or description of miracles. [*thaumato-* (Gk, combining form of *thaûma* wonder) + -LOGY]

**thaumatrope** /ˈθɔmətroup/, *n.* a card with different pictures on opposite sides (as a horse on one side and a rider on the other), which, when twirled rapidly, causes the pictures to appear as if combined, thus illustrating the persistence of visual impressions. [Gk *thaûma* wonder + -TROPE]

**thaumaturge** /ˈθɔmətɜdʒ/, *n.* a worker of wonders or miracles. Also, **thaumaturgist.**

**thaumaturgic** /θɔməˈtɜdʒɪk/, *adj.* **1.** pertaining to a thaumaturge or to thaumaturgy. **2.** having the powers of a thaumaturge. Also, **thaumaturgical.**

**thaumaturgy** /ˈθɔmətɜdʒi/, *n.* the working of wonders or miracles; magic. [Gk *thaumatourgía* wonder-working, conjuring]

**thaw** /θɔ/, *v.i.* **1.** to pass from a frozen to a liquid or semi-liquid state; melt. **2.** to be freed from the physical effect of frost or extreme cold (oft. fol. by *out*). **3.** (of the weather) to become warm enough to melt ice and snow: *it will probably thaw today.* **4.** to become less cold, formal, or reserved. **5.** to become less hostile, or aggressive: *relations between the Soviet Union and the U.S. have thawed.* *–v.t.* **6.** to cause to thaw. **7.** to make less cold, formal, reserved. *–n.* **8.** the act or process of thawing. **9.** a becoming less cold, formal, or reserved. **10.** a reduction in hostility or aggressiveness, esp. in international relations. **11.** a condition of the weather caused by the rise of the temperature above freezing point. [ME *thawe,* OE *thawian,* c. D *dooien,* Icel. *theyja*] – **thawer,** *n.* – **thawless,** *adj.*

**ThB,** Bachelor of Theology. [L *Theologiae Baccalaureus*]

**the**[1] /ði/ *before a vowel;* /ðə/ *before a consonant, def. art.* a word used esp. before nouns: **1.** with a specifying or particularising effect (opposed to *a* or *an*). **2.** to mark a noun as indicating something well known or unique: *the Alps, the earth.* **3.** with or as part of a title: *the Duke of Wellington, the Reverend John Smith.* **4.** to mark a noun as indicating the best-known, most approved, or most important of its kind: *the skiing centres of Europe.* **5.** to mark a noun as being used generically: *the dog is quadruped.* **6.** in place of a possessive pronoun, to denote a part of the body or a personal belonging: *to hang the head and weep.* **7.** before adjectives used substantively and denoting an individual, a class or number of individuals, or an abstract notion: *to visit the sick.* **8.** distributively, to denote any one separately, where *a* or *an* is more commonly employed: *at fifty cents the kilo.* **9.** to specify one of a class or type: *did you see the television last night?* **10.** to denote sufficiency or enough of something: *I don't have the money to buy a car.* [ME and OE, uninflected var. of demonstrative pronoun. See THAT]

**the**[2] /ði/ *before a vowel;* /ðə/ *before a consonant, adv.* a word used to modify an adjective or adverb in the comparative degree: **1.** signifying 'in or by that', 'on that account', 'in or by so much', or 'in some or any degree': *he is taking more care of himself, and looks the better.* **2.** used correlatively, in one instance with relative force and in the other with demonstrative force, and signifying 'by how much . . . by so much' or 'in what degree . . . in that degree': *the more the merrier.* [ME and OE; orig. a case form of demon. pronoun. See THAT]

**theandric** /θiˈændrɪk/, *adj.* →**theanthropic.** [MGk *theandrikós.* See THEO-, ANDRO-, -IC]

**theanthropic** /θiænˈθrɒpɪk/, *adj.* of or pertaining to both God and man; both divine and human.

**theanthropism** /θiˈænθrəˌpɪzəm/, *n.* **1.** the doctrine of the union of the divine and human natures, or of the manifestation of God as man in Christ. **2.** the attribution of human nature to the gods. [LGk *theánthrōpos* god-man + -ISM] – **theanthropist,** *n.*

**thearchy** /ˈθiaki/, *n., pl.* **-chies. 1.** the rule or government of God or of a god. **2.** an order or system of deities. [Eccl. Gk *thearchía.* See THEO-, -ARCHY] – **thearchic** /θiˈakɪk/, *adj.*

**theat.,** **1.** theatre. **2.** theatrical.

**theatre** /ˈθɪətə, ˈθiətə/, *n.* **1.** a building or room expressly designed to house dramatic presentations, stage entertainments, or the like. **2.** any site used for dramatic presentations, etc., as one in the open air. **3.** Also, **film theatre.** a cinema. **4.** the audience at a performance in a theatre. **5.** dramatic performances as a branch of art; the drama. **6.** dramatic works collectively, as of a literature, a nation, a period, or an author. **7.** acting, writing, or the like with reference to its suitability for dramatic performance: *it's fine writing, but it's just not theatre.* **8.** a room or hall, fitted with tiers of seats rising like steps, as used for lectures, anatomical demonstrations, etc. **9.** a room in a hospital or elsewhere in which surgical operations are performed: *an operating theatre.* **10.** a place of action; field of operations: *theatre of war, theatre of operations.* **11.** a natural formation of land rising by steps or gradations. Also, *U.S.*, **theater.** [ME, from L *theātrum,* from Gk *théātron* seeing place, theatre]

**theatregoer** /ˈθɪətəgoʊə/, *n.* one who regularly attends the theatre.

**theatre in the round,** *n.* a theatre with seats arranged round a central stage.

**theatre missile** /ˈθɪətə ˌmɪsaɪl/, *n.* a medium-range missile, esp. one deployed in Europe.

**theatre of the absurd,** *n.* a modern dramatic genre which expresses the belief that the condition of man is essentially absurd.

**theatrical** /θiˈætrəkəl/, *adj.* Also, **theatric. 1.** of or pertaining to the theatre, or dramatic or scenic representations: *theatrical performances.* **2.** suggestive of the theatre or of acting; artificial, pompous, spectacular, or extravagantly histrionic: *a theatrical display of grief.* *–n.* **3.** (*pl.*) dramatic performances, now esp. as given by amateurs. – **theatricalism,** *n.* – **theatricality** /θiˌætrəˈkæləti/, **theatricalness,** *n.* – **theatrically,** *adv.*

**theatricalise** /θiˈætrəkəlaɪz/, *v.,* **-lised, -lising.** *–v.t.* **1.** to represent, in dramatic form; dramatise. **2.** to express in a theatrical or extravagantly histrionic manner. *–v.i.* **3.** to behave in an extravagantly histrionic manner. Also, **theatricalize.**

**thebaine** /ˈθibəin, θəˈbeɪin, -aɪn/, *n.* a white crystalline poisonous alkaloid, $C_{19}H_{21}NO_3$, present in opium in small quantities. [NL *thēba(a)* thebaine (from Gk *Thêbai* Thebes, a city, + -INE[2]]

**theca** /ˈθikə/, *n., pl.* **-cae** /-si/. **1.** a case or receptacle. **2.** *Bot.* **a.** a sac, cell, or capsule. **b.** a spore case. **3.** *Anat., Zool.* a case or sheath enclosing an organ, etc., as the horny covering of an insect pupa. [L, from Gk *thḗkē* case, cover] – **thecal,** *adj.*

**thecate** /ˈθikət, -keɪt/, *adj.* having, or contained in, a theca.

**thee** /ði/, *pron.* **1.** *Archaic.* objective case of **thou.** [ME; OE *thē* (orig. dat., later dat. and acc.), c. LG *di,* G *dir*]

**theft** /θɛft/, *n.* **1.** the act of stealing; the wrongful taking and carrying away of the personal goods of another; larceny. **2.** an instance of this. [ME; OE *thēoft,* earlier *thēofth,* from *thēof* THIEF + -TH[1], c. Icel. *thýft,* obs. D *diefte*] – **theftless,** *adj.*

**thegn** /θeɪn/, *n.* →**thane.**

**theine** /ˈθiin, -ən/, *n.* caffeine found in tea. Also, **thein** /ˈθiən/. [NL *thea* TEA + -INE[2]]

**their** /ðɛə/, *adj.* **1.** the possessive form of *they* used before a noun. **2.** *Colloq.* (usu. considered to be bad usage) a possessive adjective with singular force used in place of 'his' or 'her' when the sex of the antecedent is not determined: *who has left their pen on my desk?* [ME, from Scand.; cf. Icel. *their(r)a* of those. See THEY]

**theirs** /ðɛəz/, *pron.* **1.** a form of the possessive *their* used predicatively or without a noun following. **2.** *Colloq.* (usu. considered to be bad usage) a possessive pronoun with singular force, used in place of 'his' or 'hers' when the sex of the antecedent is not determined: *does anybody recognise this pen as theirs?*

**theism** /ˈθiɪzəm/, *n.* **1.** the belief in one God as the creator and ruler of the universe, without rejection of revelation (distinguished from *deism*). **2.** belief in the existence of a God or gods (opposed to *atheism*). [Gk *theós* god + -ISM] – **theist,** *n., adj.* – **theistic** /θiˈɪstɪk/, **theistical** /θiˈɪstɪkəl/, *adj.* – **theistically** /θiˈɪstɪkli/, *adv.*

**thelitis** /θəˈlaɪtəs/, *n.* inflammation of the nipple. [NL, from Gk *thēlḗ* nipple + *-ītis* -ITIS]

**them** /ðɛm/; *weak form* /ðəm/, *pron.* **1.** the objective case of **they.** *–adj.* **2.** *Colloq.* (usu. considered to be bad usage) those: *take them things out of here.* [ME *theym,* from Scand.; cf. Icel. *theim* to those. See THEY]

**thematic** /θəˈmætɪk/, *adj.* **1.** of or pertaining to a theme. **2.** *Gram.* **a.** of, pertaining to, or producing a theme or themes (def. 4). **b.** pertaining to the theme or stem. The thematic vowel is the vowel that ends the stem and precedes the inflectional ending of a word form, as *i* in Latin *audio* I hear. – **thematically,** *adv.*

**theme** /θim/, *n.* **1.** a subject of discourse, discussion, meditation, or composition; a topic. **2.** a short, informal essay, esp. a school composition. **3.** *Music.* **a.** a principal subject in a musical composition. **b.** a short subject from which variations are developed. **4.** *Gram.* the element common to all or most of the forms of an inflectional paradigm, often consisting in turn of a root with certain formative elements or modifications. [ME, from L *thema,* from Gk] – **themeless,** *adj.*

**theme song** /ˈ– sɒŋ/, *n.* **1.** a melody in an operetta, film or musical comedy, so emphasised by repetition as to dominate the presentation. **2.** a melody associated with a particular character or the like in such a production. **3.** a signature tune. Also, **theme tune.**

**themselves** /ðəmˈsɛlvz/, *pron. pl.* **1.** a reflexive form of **them:** *they hurt themselves.* **2.** an emphatic form of **them** or **they** used: **a.** as object: *they used it for themselves.* **b.** in apposition to a subject or object: *they themselves did it.* **3.** their proper or normal selves; their usual state of mind (used after *be, become,* or *come to*): *they are themselves again.* **4.** Also, **themself.** *Colloq.* (usu. considered to be bad usage) a reflexive pronoun with singular force, used in place of 'himself' or 'herself' when the sex of the antecedent is not determined: *someone is deceiving themselves.*

**then** /ðɛn/, *adv.* **1.** at that time: *prices were lower then.* **2.** immediately or soon afterwards: *he stopped, and then began again.* **3.** next in order of time. **4.** at another time. **5.** next in order of place. **6.** in the next place; in addition; besides. **7.** in that case; in those circumstances. **8.** since that is so; therefore; consequently. **9. but then,** but at the same time; but on the other hand. *–adj.* **10.** being; being such; then existing: *the then prime minister.* *–n.* **11.** that time: *till then.* [ME, var. of ME *thenne,* OE *thænne;* orig. var. of THAN]

**thenar** /ˈθinə/, *n.* **1.** the fleshy mass of the outer side of the palm of the hand. **2.** the fleshy prominence or ball of muscle at the base of the thumb. *–adj.* **3.** of or pertaining to the thenar. [NL, from Gk: palm of hand or sole of foot]

**thenardite** /θəˈnadaɪt, tə-/, *n.* a mineral, sodium sulphate, $Na_2SO_4$, occurring in white crystals and masses, esp. in dried lakes. [named after L. J. *Thénard,* 1777-1857, French chemist. See-ITE[1]]

**Thenard's blue** /teɪnadz ˈblu/, *n.* a blue pigment consisting of a calcined mixture of cobalt oxide and alumina. [named after L. J. *Thénard.* See THENARDITE]

**thence** /ðɛns/, *adv.* **1.** from that place. **2.** from that time; thenceforth. **3.** from that source; for that reason; therefore. [ME *thennes,* from *thenne* (OE *thanone* thence; c. D *dan,* G *dannen*) + *-s,* adv. gen. suffix]

**thenceforth** /ðɛnsˈfɔθ/, *adv.* from that time or place onwards. Also, **thenceforward** /ðɛnsˈfɔwəd/, **thenceforwards.**

**thenceforward** /ðɛnsˈfɔwəd/, *adv.* from that time on; thence. Also, **thenceforwards.**

**theo-,** a word element meaning 'pertaining to the gods', 'divine'. Also, before vowels, **the-.** [Gk, combining form of *theós* god]

**theobromine** /θioʊˈbroʊmin/, *n.* a powder, $C_7H_8N_4O_2$, the lower homologue of caffeine, in the form of microscopic crystals, having alkaline properties, obtained from the seeds and leaves of species of the genus *Theobroma,* and used as a nerve stimulant and a diuretic. [NL *theobrom(a)* genus of trees typified by cacao (from Gk: lit., god-food) + -INE[2]]

**theocentric** /θiəˈsɛntrɪk/, *adj.* having God as a focal point of concern.

**theocracy** /θiˈɒkrəsi/, *n., pl.* **-cies. 1.** a form of government in which God or a deity is recognised as the supreme civil ruler, His laws being interpreted by the ecclesiastical authorities. **2.** a system of government by priests claiming a divine commission. **3.** a state or commonwealth under any such form or system of government. [Gk *theokratía.* See THEO-, -CRACY]

**theocrasy** /θiˈɒkrəsi/, *n.* **1.** a mixture of religious forms and deities worshipped. **2.** (in mysticism) the union of the soul and God. [Gk *theokrāsía* mingling with god]

**theocrat** /ˈθiəkræt/, *n.* **1.** the ruler, or a member of a governing body, in a theocracy. **2.** one who favours theocracy. – **theocratic** /θiəˈkrætɪk/, **theocratical** /θiəˈkrætɪkəl/, *adj.* – **theocratically** /θiəˈkrætɪkli/, *adv.*

**theodicy** /θiˈɒdəsi/, *n., pl.* **-cies.** a vindication of the divine attributes, particulary holiness and justice, in respect to the existence of physical and moral evil. [F *Théodicée,* title of work by Baron von Gottfried Wilhelm Leibniz, 1646-1716, German philosopher, from Gk: *theó(s)* god + *díkē* justice] – **theodicean** /θiˌɒdəˈsiən/, *adj., n.*

**theodolite** /θiˈɒdəlaɪt/, *n.* an instrument for measuring horizontal or vertical angles. [coined word; orig. unknown] – **theodolitic** /θiˌɒdəˈlɪtɪk/, *adj.*

theodolite: A, telescope; B, vertical scale; C, horizontal scale

**theogony** /θiˈɒgəni/, *n., pl.* **-nies. 1.** the origin of the gods. **2.** an account of this; a genealogical account of the gods. [Gk *theogonía*] – **theogonic** /θiəˈgɒnɪk/, *adj.* – **theogonist,** *n.*

**theol.,** **1.** theologian. **2.** theological. **3.** theology.

**theolog** /ˈθiəlɒg/, *n. Colloq.* a student of theology.

**theologian** /θiəˈloʊdʒən/, *n.* one versed in theology, esp. Christian theology.

**theological** /θiəˈlɒdʒɪkəl/, *adj.* **1.** of, pertaining to, or connected with theology. **2.** based upon the nature and will of God as revealed to man. Also, **theologic.** **theologically,** *adv.*

**theologise** /θiˈɒlədʒaɪz/, *v.,* **-gised, -gising.** *–v.i.* **1.** to theorise or speculate upon theological subjects. *–v.t.* **2.** to make theological; treat theologically. Also, **theologize.** – **theologisation** /θiˌɒlədʒaɪˈzeɪʃən/, *n.* – **theologiser,** *n.*

**theology** /θiˈɒlədʒi/, *n., pl.* **-gies. 1.** the science which treats of God, His attributes, and His relations to the universe; the science or study of divine things or religious truth; divinity. **2.** a particular form, system, or branch of this science or study. [ME *theologie,* from L *theologia,* from Gk]

**theomachy** /θiˈɒməki/, *n., pl.* **-chies.** a battle with or among the gods. [Gk *theomachía*]

**theomania** /θiəˈmeɪniə/, *n.* religious madness, esp. the belief that one is God. – **theomaniac** /θiəˈmeɪniæk/, *n.*

**theomorphic** /θiəˈmɔfɪk/, *adj.* having the form or likeness of God or a god. [Gk *theómorph(os)* of divine form + -IC] – **theomorphism,** *n.*

**theopathy** /θiˈɒpəθi/, *n.* religious emotion excited by the contemplation of God. [Gk *theopátheia* suffering of God] – **theopathetic** /θiəpəˈθɛtɪk/, **theopathic** /θiəˈpæθɪk/, *adj.*

**theophany** /θiˈɒfəni/, *n., pl.* **-nies.** a manifestation or appearance of God or a god to man. [LL *theophania,* from Gk] – **theophanic** /θiəˈfænɪk/, *adj.*

**theophylline** /θiəˈfɪlin, -aɪn/, *n.* a white crystalline alkaloid, $C_7H_8N_4O_2$, derived from tea; an isomer of theobromine. [*theo-* (irreg. combining form representing NL *thea* TEA) + PHYLL(O)- + -INE[2]]

**theor.,** theorem.

**theorbo** /θiˈɔboʊ/, *n., pl.* **-bos.** an obsolete musical instrument of the lute class, having two necks, one above the other; archlute. [It. *tiorba*] – **theorbist,** *n.*

**theorem** /ˈθɪərəm/, *n.* **1.** *Maths.* a theoretical proposition; a statement embodying something to be proved. **2.** a rule or law, esp. one expressed by an equation or formula. **3.** *Logic.* a proposition which can be deduced from the premises or assumptions of a system. [LL *theōrēma,* from Gk: spectacle, theory, thesis (to be proved)] – **theorematic** /θɪərəˈmætɪk/, *adj.*

**theoretical** /θiəˈrɛtɪkəl/, *adj.* **1.** of, pertaining to, or consisting in theory; not practical. **2.** existing only in theory; hypothetical. **3.** given to, forming, or dealing with theories; speculative. Also, **theoretic.** – **theoretically,** *adv.*

**theoretical arithmetic** /– əˈrɪθmətɪk/, *n.* →**arithmetic** (def. 2).

**theoretician** /θɪərəˈtɪʃən/, *n.* one who deals with or is expert in the theoretical side of a subject.

**theoretics** /θiəˈrɛtɪks/, *n.* the theoretical or speculative part of a science or subject.

**theorise** /ˈθɪəraɪz/, *v.i.,* **-rised, -rising. 1.** to form a theory or theories. **2.** to speculate or conjecture. Also, **theorize.** – **theorisation** /θɪəraɪˈzeɪʃən/, *n.* – **theoriser,** *n.*

**theorist** /ˈθɪərəst/, *n.* **1.** one who theorises. **2.** one who deals mainly with the theory of a subject: *a theorist in medical research.*

**theory** /ˈθɪəri/, *n., pl.* **-ries. 1.** a coherent group of general propositions used as principles of explanation for a class of phenomena: *Newton's theory of gravitation.* **2.** a proposed explanation whose status is still conjectural, in contrast to well-established propositions that are regarded as reporting matters of actual fact. **3.** *Maths.* a body of principles, theorems, or the like, belonging to one subject: *number theory.* **4.** that department of a science or art which deals with its principles or methods, as distinguished from the practice of it. **5.** a particular conception or view of something to be done or of the method of doing it; a system of rules or principles. **6.** conjecture or opinion. [LL *theōria,* from Gk: contemplation, theory]

**theos.,** **1.** theosophical. **2.** theosophy.

**theosophy** /θiˈɒsəfi/, *n.* **1.** any of various forms of philosophical or religious thought in which claim is made to a special insight into the divine nature or to a special divine revelation. **2.** the system of belief and doctrine, based largely on Brahmanic and Buddhistic ideas, of the **Theosophical Society** (founded in New York in 1875). [ML *theosophia,* from LGk. See THEO-, -SOPHY] – **theosophic** /θiəˈsɒfɪk/, **theosophical** /θiəˈsɒfɪkəl/, *adj.* – **theosophically** /θiəˈsɒfɪkli/, *adv.* – **theosophist,** *n.*

**theralite** /ˈθɛrəlaɪt/, *n.* a coarse-grained basic igneous rock comprised of plagioclase, nepheline, augite, and often biotite, analcite, or olivine. [Gk *thēra* prey + -LITE]

**therapeutic** /θɛrəˈpjutɪk/, *adj.* pertaining to the treating or curing of disease; curative. Also, **therapeutical.** [NL *therapeuticus,* from Gk *therapeutikós,* from *therapeutes* one who treats medically] – **therapeutically,** *adv.*

**therapeutics** /θɛrəˈpjutɪks/, *n.* the branch of medicine concerned with the remedial treatment of disease. [pl. of *therapeutic,* n., from NL *therapeutica,* properly fem. of *therapeuticus* THERAPEUTIC, *adj.* See -ICS]

**therapist** /ˈθɛrəpəst/, *n.* a person trained to give therapy by any of various physical or psychological methods. Also, **therapeutist** /θɛrəˈpjutəst/.

**therapy** /ˈθɛrəpi/, *n., pl.* **-pies. 1.** the treatment of disease, disorder, defect, etc., as by some remedial or curative process. **2.** a curative power or quality. [NL *therapīa,* from Gk *therapeía* healing]

**there** /ðɛə/, *adv.* **1.** in or at that place. **2.** at that point in an action, speech, etc. **3.** in that matter, particular, or respect. **4.** into or to that place; thither. **5.** (used less definitely and also unemphatically as by way of calling the attention to something): *there they go.* *–adj.* **6.** (used for emphasis with a demonstrative adjective, after the noun qualified): *that man there.* **7.** *Colloq.* used for emphasis between a demonstrative adjective and the noun qualified: *that there man.* **8. all there,** *Colloq.* **a.** of sound mind. **b.** shrewd; quick-witted. *–pron.* **9.** that place: *he comes from there too.* **10.** (used to introduce a sentence or clause in which the verb comes before its subject): *there is no hope.* **11.** used in interjectional phrases: *there's a good boy.* *–interj.* **12. a.** (an exclamation used to express satisfaction etc.): *there! it's done!* **b.** (an exclamation used to give consolation): *there, there, don't cry.* **c.** (an exclamation used to draw attention to something): *there! the jug's broken.* [ME; OE *thǣr,* c. D *daar,* G *da*]

**there-,** a word element meaning 'that (place)', 'that (time)', etc., used in combination with certain adverbs and prepositions. [special use of THERE, demonstrative adv.]

**thereabouts** /ðɛərəˈbaʊts, ˈðɛərəbaʊts/, *adv.* **1.** about or near that place or time. **2.** about that number, amount, etc. Also, **thereabout.**

**thereafter** /ðɛərˈaftə/, *adv.* **1.** after that in time or sequence; afterwards. **2.** *Obs.* accordingly.

**thereagainst** /ðɛərəˈgɛnst/, *adv. Archaic.* against, or in opposition to, that.

**thereat** /ðɛərˈæt/, *adv.* **1.** at that place, time, etc.; there. **2.** on that occasion; by reason of that.

**thereby** /ðɛəˈbaɪ, ˈðɛəbaɪ/, *adv.* **1.** by that; by means of that. **2.** in that connection or relation: *thereby hangs a tale.* **3.** by or near that place.

**therefor** /ðɛə'fɔ/, *adv.* for that or this; for it.
**therefore** /'ðɛəfɔ/, *adv.* in consequence of that; as a result; consequently. [ME *therefore*, from *ther* THERE + *fore*, var. of *for* FOR]
**therefrom** /ðɛə'frɒm/, *adv.* from that place, thing, etc.
**therein** /ðɛər'ɪn/, *adv.* **1.** in that place or thing. **2.** in that matter, circumstance, etc.
**thereinafter** /ðɛərɪn'aftə/, *adv.* afterwards in that document, statement, etc.
**thereinbefore** /ðɛərɪnbə'fɔ/, *adv.* before in that document, statement, etc.
**thereinto** /ðɛər'ɪntu/, *adv.* into that place, thing, matter, etc.
**theremin** /'θɛrəmən/, *n.* an electronic musical instrument whose pitch and tone volume are controlled by the distance between the player's hands and two metal rods serving as aerials. [named after Léon *Thérémin*, b. 1896, French inventor]
**thereof** /ðɛər'ɒv/, *adv.* **1.** of that or it. **2.** from or out of that as a source or origin.
**thereon** /ðɛər'ɒn/, *adv.* **1.** on or upon that or it. **2.** immediately after that; thereupon.
**thereout** /ðɛər'aʊt/, *adv. Archaic.* out of that.
**thereto** /ðɛə'tu/, *adv.* **1.** to that place, thing, matter, etc. **2.** *Archaic.* in addition to that. Also, **thereunto** /ðɛərʌn'tu, ðɛər'ʌntu/.
**theretofore** /ðɛətu'fɔ/, *adv.* before that time.
**thereunder** /ðɛər'ʌndə/, *adv.* **1.** under or beneath that. **2.** under the authority of, or in accordance with, that.
**thereupon** /ðɛərə'pɒn, 'ðɛərəpɒn/, *adv.* **1.** immediately following that. **2.** in consequence of that. **3.** upon that or it. **4.** with reference to that.
**therewith** /ðɛə'wɪθ, -'wɪð/, *adv.* **1.** with that. **2.** in addition to that. **3.** following upon that; thereupon.
**therewithal** /ðɛəwɪθ'ɔl, -wɪð-/, *adv.* **1.** together with that; in addition to that. **2.** following upon that.
**theriac** /'θɪəriæk/, *n.* an antidote to venomous bites, etc., esp. an electuary made with honey. – **theriacal** /θə'raɪəkəl/, *adj.*
**therianthropic** /ˌθɪəriæn'θrɒpɪk/, *adj.* **1.** being partly animal and partly human in form. **2.** of or pertaining to deities conceived or represented in such form. [Gk *thērion* wild beast + *ánthrōpos* man + -IC] – **therianthropism** /ˌθɪəri'ænθrəpɪzəm/, *n.*
**theriomorphic** /ˌθɪərioʊ'mɔfɪk/, *adj.* (of deities) conceived or represented as having the form of beasts. Also, **theriomorphous.** [Gk *thēriómorphos* having the shape of a wild beast + -IC]
**therm** /θɜm/, *n.* a unit of heat in the imperial system, used as a basis for the selling of gas; equal to 100 000 British thermal units, or about 105.5 × $10^6$ J. [Gk *thérmē* heat]
**therm-**, a word element representing **thermal.** Also, **thermo-.** [Gk, combining form of *thermós* hot, *thérmē* heat]
**thermae** /'θɜmi/, *n.pl.* **1.** hot springs; hot baths. **2.** a public bathing establishment of the ancient Greeks or Romans. [L, from Gk *thérmai*]
**thermaesthesia** /θɜməs'θiʒə, -'θiziə/, *n. Physiol.* ability to feel cold or heat; sensitiveness to heat. Also, *U.S.*, **thermesthesia.**
**thermal** /'θɜməl/, *adj.* **1.** Also, **thermic.** of or pertaining to heat or temperature: *thermal energy.* **2.** of, pertaining to, or of the nature of thermae. –*n.* **3.** *Aeron., Meteorol.* an ascending current of air caused by local heating, used by glider pilots to attain height. [Gk *thérmē* heat + -AL[1]] – **thermally,** *adv.*
**thermal barrier** /'– bæriə/, *n.* an obstacle to flight above very high speeds owing to heating of the aircraft by air friction. Also, **heat barrier.**
**thermal capacity** /– kə'pæsəti/, *n.* →**heat capacity.**
**thermal diffusion** /– də'fjuʒən/, *n.* a method of separating the constituents of fluid, as isotopes, due to diffusion along a temperature gradient within the fluid.
**thermal efficiency** /– ə'fɪʃənsi/, *n.* the ratio of the work done by a heat engine to the mechanical equivalent of the heat supplied by the fuel.
**thermal equator** /– ə'kweɪtə/, *n.* an imaginary line drawn round the earth for each month of the year, joining the point on each meridian where the highest average monthly temperature occurs.
**thermalise** /'θɜməlaɪz/, *v.t.*, **-lised, -lising.** to reduce the energy of neutrons with a moderator, in order to produce thermal neutrons. Also, **thermalize.**
**thermal neutrons** /θɜməl 'njutrɒnz/, *n.pl.* neutrons which have low speeds, their energy being of the same order as the thermal energy of the atoms or molecules of the substance through which they are passing.
**thermal radiation** /– reɪdi'eɪʃən/, *n.* **1.** the heat and light produced by a nuclear explosion. **2.** electromagnetic radiations emitted from a heat or light source as a consequence of its temperature; it consists essentially of ultraviolet, visible and infra-red radiation.
**thermal reactor** /– ri'æktə/, *n.* a nuclear reactor in which most of the fissions are caused by thermal neutrons.
**thermal springs** /– 'sprɪŋz/, *n.pl.* natural hot-water springs.
**thermal X-rays** /– 'ɛks-reɪz/, *n.pl.* the electromagnetic radiation, mainly in the soft low-energy, X-ray region, emitted by extremely hot weapon debris.
**thermanaesthesia** /ˌθɜmænəs'θiʒə, -'θiziə/, *n.* loss of ability to feel cold or heat; loss of temperature sense. Also, *U.S.*, **thermanesthesia.**
**thermesthesia** /θɜməs'θiʒə, -'θiziə/, *n. U.S.* →**thermaesthesia.**
**thermic** /'θɜmɪk/, *adj.* →**thermal** (def. 1).
**thermion** /'θɜmiən/, *n.* any of a class of electrically charged particles such as ions or electrons emitted by incandescent materials.
**thermionic** /θɜmi'ɒnɪk/, *adj.* pertaining to thermionics or thermions: *thermionic emission.*
**thermionic current** /– 'kʌrənt/, *n.* **1.** a flow of thermions. **2.** the electric current so produced.
**thermionics** /θɜmi'ɒnɪks/, *n.* the science of thermionic phenomena, esp. the design and study of thermionic valves.
**thermionic valve** /θɜmiˌɒnɪk 'vælv/, *n.* a radio valve which contains a heated cathode.
**thermistor** /θɜ'mɪstə/, *n.* an electronic semiconductor, the resistance of which decreases or increases rapidly with increase in temperature. [THERM- + (TRANS)ISTOR or THERM- + (RES)ISTOR]
**thermit** /'θɜmət/, *n.* Also, **thermite** /'θɜmaɪt/. a mixture of finely divided metallic aluminium and one or more oxides, as of iron, producing when ignited an extremely high temperature as the result of the union of the aluminium with the oxygen of the oxide; used in welding, etc. [Trademark G, from *therm-* THERM- + *-it* -ITE[1]]
**thermo-**, variant of **therm-**, before consonants, as in *thermochemistry.*
**thermobarograph** /θɜmoʊ'bærəgræf, -graf/, *n.* an apparatus combining a thermograph and a barograph.
**thermobarometer** /ˌθɜmoʊbə'rɒmətə/, *n.* **1.** an apparatus in which the change in boiling point indicates the pressure. **2.** a form of barometer so constructed that it may also be used as a thermometer.
**thermochemistry** /θɜmoʊ'kɛməstri/, *n.* the branch of chemistry that treats of the relations between chemical action and heat. – **thermochemical,** *adj.* – **thermochemist,** *n.*
**thermocouple** /'θɜmoʊkʌpəl/, *n.* two conductors of different metals joined at their ends and producing a thermoeletric current when there is a difference in temperature between the ends. Also, **thermoelectric couple.**
**thermoduric** /θɜmoʊ'djurɪk/, *adj.* resistant to relatively high temperatures.
**thermodynam.**, thermodynamics.
**thermodynamics** /ˌθɜmoʊdaɪ'næmɪks/, *n.* the science concerned with the relations between heat and mechanical energy or work, and the conversion of one into the other. – **thermodynamic, thermodynamical,** *adj.* – **thermodynamically,** *adv.*
**thermodynamic temperature scale,** *n.* a temperature scale of which the unit is the kelvin (K) which is 1/273.16 of the thermodynamic temperature of the triple point of water.
**thermoelectric** /ˌθɜmoʊə'lɛktrɪk/, *adj.* of or pertaining to thermoelectricity. Also, **thermoelectrical.** – **thermoelectrically,** *adv.*
**thermoelectric couple** /– 'kʌpəl/, *n.* →**thermocouple.**
**thermoelectric effect** /– ə'fɛkt/, *n.* →**Seebeck effect.**
**thermoelectricity** /ˌθɜmoʊəlɛk'trɪsəti/, *n.* electricity produced

directly from heat, as that generated (in the form of a current) when the ends of two dissimilar metallic conductors are joined to form a closed circuit and one of the junctions is heated.

**thermoelectric thermometer** /θɜmoʊəˌlɛktrɪk θəˈmɒmətə/, *n.* a thermometer based on thermoelectricity containing a thermocouple with an indicator.

**thermoelectromotive** /ˌθɜmoʊəlɛktrəˈmoʊtɪv/, *adj.* denoting or pertaining to electromotive force produced by heat, as with a thermocouple.

**thermogenesis** /θɜmoʊˈdʒɛnəsəs/, *n.* the production of heat, esp. in an animal body by physiological processes. – **thermogenetic** /ˌθɜmoʊdʒəˈnɛtɪk/, *adj.*

**thermograph** /ˈθɜməgræf, -graf/, *n.* a thermometer which records the temperature it indicates.

**thermography** /θɜˈmɒgrəfi/, *n.* a form of photography in which the brightness or colour of the photo corresponds to the temperature of the object. – **thermographer,** *n.*, **thermographic** /θɜməˈgræfɪk/, *adj.*

**thermolabile** /θɜmoʊˈleɪbəl, -ˈleɪbaɪl/, *adj.* subject to destruction or loss of characteristic properties through the action of moderate heat, as certain toxins and ferments (opposed to *thermostable*).

**thermoluminescence** /ˌθɜmoʊluməˈnɛsəns/, *n.* phosphorescence produced by heat. – **thermoluminescent,** *adj.*

**thermolysis** /θɜˈmɒləsəs/, *n.* **1.** *Physiol.* the dispersion of heat from the body. **2.** *Chem.* dissociation by heat. – **thermolytic** /θɜməˈlɪtɪk/, *adj.*

**thermometer** /θəˈmɒmətə/, *n.* an instrument for measuring temperature, as by means of the expansion and contraction of mercury or alcohol in a capillary tube and bulb. – **thermometric** /θɜməˈmɛtrɪk/, **thermometrical** /θɜməˈmɛtrɪkəl/, *adj.* – **thermometrically** /θɜməˈmɛtrɪkli/, *adv.*

thermometer (centigrade)

**thermometry** /θɜˈmɒmətri/, *n.* **1.** the measurement of temperature. **2.** the science of the construction and use of thermometers.

**thermomotive** /ˌθɜmoʊˈmoʊtɪv/, *adj.* **1.** pertaining to motion produced by heat. **2.** pertaining to a thermomotor.

**thermomotor** /ˈθɜmoʊmoʊtə/, *n.* an engine operated by heat, esp. one driven by the expansive force of heated air.

**thermonuclear** /ˌθɜmoʊˈnjukliə/, *adj.* designating, or capable of producing, extremely high temperatures resulting from, caused by, or associated with nuclear fusion.

**thermonuclear reaction** /– riˈækʃən/, *n.* a nuclear fusion reaction that takes place between atomic nuclei which form part of a substance which has been heated to a temperature of several million degrees centigrade.

**thermonuclear weapon** /– ˈwɛpən/, *n.* an atomic weapon which involves a fusion reaction, as a hydrogen bomb.

**thermophile** /ˈθɜməfaɪl/, *n.* an organism which flourishes at high temperatures. Cf. **mesophile, psychrophile.** – **thermophilic,** *adj.*

**thermophone** /ˈθɜməfoʊn/, *n.* a device for producing soundwaves in which an electrical conductor is heated and cooled according to the current passing through it; the soundwaves are produced by the expansion and contraction of the air around the conductor.

**thermopile** /ˈθɜməpaɪl/, *n.* a number of thermocouples joined so as to produce a combined effect, used for generating currents or measuring small differences in temperature. [THERMO- + PILE[1]]

**thermoplastic** /θɜmoʊˈplæstɪk/, *adj.* **1.** soft and pliable whenever heated, as some plastics, without any change of the inherent properties. –*n.* **2.** such a plastic.

**thermoplastic binding** /– ˈbaɪndɪŋ/, *n.* a type of binding in which the four edges of a book are trimmed and the spine is attached to the cover by means of a heat-set plastic. Also, **perfect binding.**

**thermos** /ˈθɜmɒs, -məs/, *n.* **1.** a double-walled container, usu. made of silvered glass and having a vacuum in the interior cavity; used to keep substances that are hotter or colder than their surroundings at a constant temperature; a commercially produced Dewar flask. Also, **thermos flask.** [Trademark; Gk: hot]

**thermoscope** /ˈθɜməskoʊp/, *n.* a device for indicating variations in temperature, usu. without measuring their amount. – **thermoscopic** /θɜməˈskɒpɪk/, **thermoscopical** /θɜməˈskɒpɪkəl/, *adj.* – **thermoscopically** /θɜməˈskɒpɪkli/, *adv.*

**thermosetting** /ˈθɜmoʊsɛtɪŋ/, *adj.* denoting or pertaining to a type of plastic which becomes hard and unmouldable when heated and, after setting, resistant to additional applications of heat, as the urea resins.

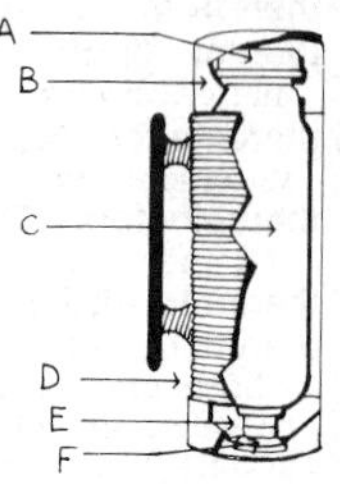

thermos flask: A, stopper; B, cup; C, vacuum insulated glass filler; D, plastic jacket; E, tip protector; F, filler support

**thermosiphon** /θɜmoʊˈsaɪfən/, *n.* an arrangement of siphon tubes serving to induce circulation of water in a heating apparatus.

**thermosphere** /ˈθɜməsfɪə/, *n.* the region of the earth's atmosphere in which the temperature increases with altitude.

**thermostable** /θɜmoʊˈsteɪbəl/, *adj.* capable of being subjected to a moderate degree of heat without loss of characteristic properties, as certain toxins and ferments (opposed to *thermolabile*). – **thermostability** /ˌθɜmoʊstəˈbɪləti/, *n.*

**thermostat** /ˈθɜməstæt/, *n.* a device, including a relay actuated by thermal conduction or convection, which establishes and maintains a desired temperature automatically, or signals a change in temperature for manual adjustment. – **thermostatic** /θɜməˈstætɪk/, *adj.* – **thermostatically** /θɜməˈstætɪkli/, *adv.*

**thermostatics** /θɜməˈstætɪks/, *n.* the science concerned with thermal equilibrium.

**thermotaxis** /θɜmoʊˈtæksəs/, *n.* **1.** *Biol.* the movement of an organism towards or away from a source of heat. **2.** *Physiol.* the regulation of the bodily temperature. – **thermotaxic,** *adj.*

**thermotensile** /θɜmoʊˈtɛnsaɪl/, *adj.* pertaining to tensile strength as affected by changes of temperature.

**thermotherapy** /θɜmoʊˈθɛrəpi/, *n.* treatment of disease by means of heat, either moist or dry.

**thermotropism** /θɜˈmɒtrəpɪzəm/, *n.* the property in plants or other organisms of turning or bending (towards or away), as in growth, under the influence of heat. – **thermotropic** /θɜməˈtrɒpɪk/, *adj.*

**-thermy,** a word element referring to heat. [combining form representing Gk *thérmē*]

**theroid** /ˈθɪərɔɪd/, *adj.* having animal propensities or characteristics. [Gk *thēroeidḗs*]

**thersitical** /θɜˈsɪtɪkəl/, *adj.* scurrilous; foul-mouthed. [from *Thersites* the most vindictive, impudent and foul-mouthed of the Greeks before Troy]

**thesaurus** /θəˈsɔrəs/, *n., pl.* **-sauri** /-ˈsɔraɪ/. **1.** a storehouse or repository, as of words or knowledge; a dictionary, encyclopaedia, or the like, esp. a dictionary of synonyms and antonyms. **2.** a treasury. [L, from Gk *thēsaurós* treasure, treasury]

**these** /ðiz/, *pron., adj.* plural of **this.** [ME; replacing OE *thās*]

**thesis** /ˈθisəs/; *also for defs 4 and 5* /ˈθɛsəs/, *n., pl.* **-ses** /-siz/. **1.** a proposition laid down or stated, esp. one to be discussed and proved or to be maintained against objections. **2.** a subject for a composition or essay. **3.** a dissertation, as one presented by a candidate for a diploma or degree, esp. a postgraduate degree. **4.** *Music.* (in conducting) the downward stroke in a measure (opposed to *arsis*). **5.** *Pros.* **a.** (originally) the accented syllable of a foot in verse (opposed to *arsis*). **b.** (later) the stressed part of a metrical unit. [ME, from Gk: setting down, something set down]

**Thespian** /ˈθɛspiən/, *adj.* **1.** pertaining to tragedy or to the dramatic art in general; tragic; dramatic. –*n.* **2.** a tragedian; an actor or actress. [from *Thespis*, a poet (fl. 6th cent. B.C.)]

**Thess.**, *Bible.* Thessalonians.

**theta** /ˈθitə/, *n.* the eighth letter (Θ, θ) of the Greek alphabet.

**thetic** /ˈθɛtɪk/, *adj.* positive; dogmatic. Also, **thetical.** [Gk *thetikós*, from *thetós* placed] – **thetically,** *adv.*

**theurgy** /ˈθiɜdʒi/, *n., pl.* **-gies. 1.** a system of magic practised by the Egyptian Platonists and others professing to have communication with and aid from beneficent deities. **2.** the working of some divine or supernatural agency in human affairs; the effects brought about among men by such agency. [L *theūrgia*, from Gk *theourgía* sorcery] – **theurgic** /θiˈɜdʒɪk/, **theurgical** /θiˈɜdʒɪkəl/, *adj.* – **theurgically** /θiˈɜdʒɪkli/, *adv.* – **theurgist**, *n.*

**thew** /θju/, *n.* **1.** (*usu. pl.*) muscle or sinew. **2.** (*pl.*) physical strength. [ME; OE *thēaw* custom, usage, c. OHG *dau* discipline] – **thewy**, *adj.*

**thewless** /ˈθjuləs/, *adj.* without vigour or energy.

**they** /ðeɪ/, *pron. pl., poss.* **theirs,** *obj.* **them. 1.** nominative plural of *he, she* and *it.* **2.** people in general: *they say he is rich.* **3.** *Colloq.* (generally regarded as bad usage) a person indefinitely (used in place of a singular pronoun where the sex of the antecedent is not determined): *if anybody moves they will get a bullet in their head.* [ME; from Scand.; cf. Icel. *their* those, c. OE *thā,* pl. of *thæt* THAT]

**they'd** /ðeɪd/, the contraction of: **1.** they had. **2.** they would.

**they'll** /ðeɪl/, the contraction of: **1.** they will. **2.** they shall.

**they're** /ðɛə, ˈðeɪə/, the contraction of: *they are.*

**they've** /ðeɪv/, the contraction of: *they have.*

**thi-**, variant of **thio-**, as in *thiazine.*

**thiamine** /ˈθaɪəmin/, *n.* a white crystalline solid forming part of the vitamin B complex, $C_{12}H_{17}ClN_4OS$; a vitamin ($B_1$) required by the nervous system, absence of which causes beri-beri and other disorders; aneurin. Also, **thiamin.** [THI(O)- + (VIT)AMIN]

**thiazine** /ˈθaɪəzin, -zaɪn/, *n.* any of a class of compounds containing a ring composed of one atom each of sulphur and nitrogen and four atoms of carbon. Also, **thiazin** /ˈθaɪəzən/. [THI- + AZ(O)- + -INE[2]]

**thiazole** /ˈθaɪəzoʊl/, *n.* **1.** a colourless liquid, $C_3H_3NS$, with a pungent smell, serving as the parent substance of important dyestuffs. **2.** any of various derivatives of this substance. Also, **thiazol** /ˈθaɪəzɒl/.

**Thibet** /təˈbɛt/, *n. Obs.* →**Tibet.**

**thick** /θɪk/, *adj.* **1.** having relatively great extent from one surface or side to its opposite; not thin: *a thick slice.* **2.** measuring as specified between opposite surfaces, or in depth, or in a direction perpendicular to that of the length and breadth: *a board one centimetre thick.* **3.** set close together; compact; dense: *a thick forest.* **4.** numerous, abundant, or plentiful. **5.** filled, covered, or abounding (fol. by *with*): *tables thick with dust.* **6.** having relatively great consistency; viscous: *a thick syrup.* **7.** (of darkness, etc.) dense, deep, or profound. **8.** husky, hoarse, muffled, or not clear in sound: *a thick voice.* **9.** (of an accent or dialect) very pronounced. **10.** containing much solid matter in suspension or solution. **11.** (of mist, smoke, etc.) having the component particles densely aggregated. **12.** (of the weather, etc.) foggy, misty, or hazy. **13.** sluggish; heavy-headed, as after dissipation. **14.** slow of mental apprehension; stupid; dull; slow-witted: *his mind is very thick.* **15.** *Colloq.* close in friendship; intimate. **16.** *Colloq.* disagreeably excessive: *his demands are a bit thick.* **17. a thick ear,** a swollen ear. *–adv.* **18.** in a thick manner. **19.** closely; near together: *flowers growing thick beside a wall.* **20. lay it on thick,** *Colloq.* to be extravagant in flattery, praise, or the like. *–n.* **21.** that which is thick. **22.** the thickest, densest, or most crowded part; the place, time, stage, etc., of greatest activity or intensity: *in the thick of the fight.* **23.** *Colloq.* a stupid, dull-witted person. **24. through thick and thin,** under all circumstances; unwaveringly. [ME; OE *thicce,* c. G *dick*] – **thickish,** *adj.* – **thickly,** *adv.*

**thicken** /ˈθɪkən/, *v.t., v.i.* **1.** to make or become thick or thicker. **2.** to make or grow more intense, profound, intricate, or complex. – **thickener,** *n.*

**thickening** /ˈθɪkənɪŋ/, *n.* **1.** a making or becoming thick. **2.** a thickened part or area. **3.** something used to thicken; thickener.

**thicket** /ˈθɪkət/, *n.* a thick or dense growth of shrubs, bushes, or small trees; a thick coppice. [OE *thiccet,* from *thicce* THICK + *-et,* n. suffix]

**thickhead** /ˈθɪkhɛd/, *n.* **1.** a stupid person; blockhead. **2.** any bird of the Australian family Pachycephalidae. – **thickheaded** /ˈθɪk-hɛdəd, θɪkˈhɛdəd/, *adj.* – **thickheadedness** /θɪkˈhɛdədnəs/, *n.*

**thick-knee** /ˈθɪk-ni/, *n.* a wading bird of the family Burhinidae, as *Burhinus oedicnemus,* of Europe, Africa, and Asia; stone curlew.

**thickness** /ˈθɪknəs/, *n.* **1.** the state or quality of being thick. **2.** the third dimension of a solid, as distinct from length and breadth. **3.** the thick part or body of something. **4.** a layer. *–v.t.* **5.** to cut or prepare to a required thickness.

**thickset** /ˈθɪksɛt/, *adj.* **1.** set thickly or in close arrangement; dense: *a thickset hedge.* **2.** set, studded, or furnished thickly: *a sky thickset with stars.* **3.** of thick form or build; heavily or solidly built. *–n.* **4.** →**thicket.**

**thick shake** /ˈθɪk ʃeɪk/, *n.* a milk shake with extra icecream or ice to thicken the consistency.

**thick-skinned** /ˈθɪk-skɪnd/, *adj.* **1.** having a thick skin. **2.** not sensitive to criticism, reproach, rebuff, etc.

**thick-skulled** /ˈθɪk-skʌld/, *adj.* **1.** having a thick skull. **2.** stupid; doltish.

**thick-witted** /ˈθɪk-wɪtəd/, *adj.* stupid; dull.

**thief** /θif/, *n., pl.* **thieves.** one who steals, esp. secretly or without open force; one guilty of theft or larceny. [ME; OE *thēof,* c. G *Dieb*]

**thief's cat** /θifs ˈkæt/, *n.* (formerly) a double cat-o-nine-tails.

**thieve** /θiv/, *v.,* **thieved, thieving.** *–v.t.* **1.** to take by theft; steal. *–v.i.* **2.** to act as a thief; commit theft; steal. [OE *thēofian,* from *thēof* THIEF]

**thievery** /ˈθivəri/, *n., pl.* **-eries. 1.** the act or practice of thieving; theft. **2.** something taken by theft.

**thievish** /ˈθivɪʃ/, *adj.* **1.** given to thieving. **2.** of, pertaining to, or characteristic of a thief; stealthy. – **thievishly,** *adv.* – **thievishness,** *n.*

**thigh** /θaɪ/, *n.* **1.** that part of the leg between the hip and the knee in man. **2.** a homologous or apparently corresponding part of the hind limb of other animals; the region of the femur. **3.** (in birds) **a.** the true femoral region, buried in the general integument of the body. **b.** the segment below, containing the fibula and tibia. **4.** →**femur.** [ME; OE *thēoh,* c. D *dij,* MHG *diech,* Icel. *thjō*]

**thighbone** /ˈθaɪboʊn/, *n.* →**femur.**

**thigmotaxis** /θɪgməˈtæksəs/, *n.* the movement of an organism towards or away from any object which provides a mechanical stimulus; stereotaxis. [NL, from Gk *thígma* touch + *-taxis* -TAXIS] – **thigmotactic** /θɪgməˈtæktɪk/, *adj.*

**thigmotropism** /θɪgˈmɒtrəpɪzəm/, *n.* the property in plants or other organisms of turning or bending (towards or away), as in growth, under the influence of mechanical contact. [Gk *thígma* touch + -O- + -TROPISM] – **thigmotropic** /θɪgməˈtrɒpɪk/, *adj.*

**thill** /θɪl/, *n.* either of the pair of shafts between which a single animal drawing a vehicle is placed. [ME *thylle.* Cf. OE *thille* plank, flooring]

**thimble** /ˈθɪmbəl/, *n.* **1.** a small cap, usu. of metal, worn on the finger to push the needle in sewing. **2.** *Mech.* any of various devices or attachments likened to this. **3.** a short length of pipe encasing one of smaller diameter, as where a stovepipe passes through a wooden roof. **4.** *Naut.* a metal ring with a concave groove on the outside, used to line the outside of a ring of rope forming an eye. [ME *thym(b)yl,* OE *thȳmel,* from *thūma* thumb] – **thimble-like,** *adj.*

**thimbleful** /ˈθɪmbəlfʊl/, *n., pl.* **-fuls.** as much as a thimble will hold; a small quantity.

**thimblerig** /ˈθɪmbəlrɪg/, *n., v.,* **-rigged, -rigging.** *–n.* **1.** a swindling game in which the operator apparently covers a small ball or pea with one of three thimble-like cups, and then, moving the cups about, offers to bet that no-one can tell under which cup the ball or pea lies. *–v.t.* **2.** to cheat by or as by the thimblerig. – **thimblerigger,** *n.*

**thin** /θɪn/, *adj.,* **thinner, thinnest,** *adv., v.,* **thinned, thinning.** *–adj.* **1.** having relatively little extent from one surface or side to its opposite; not thick: *thin ice.* **2.** of small cross-section in comparison with the length; slender: *a thin wire.* **3.** having little flesh; spare; lean. **4.** having the constituent or individual parts relatively few and not close together: *thin vegetation.* **5.** not dense; sparse; scanty. **6.** having relatively slight consistency, as a liquid; fluid; rare or rarefied, as air, etc. **7.** without solidity or substance; unsubstantial. **8.** easily seen through, transparent, or flimsy: *a thin excuse.* **9.**

lacking fullness or volume, as sound; weak and shrill. **10.** faint, slight, poor, or feeble. **11.** lacking body, richness, or growth. **12.** lacking in chroma; of light tint. **13.** *Photog.* (of a developed negative) lacking in opaqueness and yielding prints without strong contrasts of light and shade. *–adv.* **14.** in a thin manner. *–v.t.* **15.** to make thin or thinner (oft. fol. by *down, out,* etc.). *–v.i.* **16.** to become thin or thinner; become reduced or diminished; go, pass, etc. (fol. by *down, off, away,* etc.). [ME and OE *thynne,* c. G *dünn;* akin to L *tenuis*] **– thinly,** *adv.* **– thinness,** *n.*

**thine** /ðaɪn/, *pron., adj. Archaic.* the possessive form of *thou* used predicatively or without a noun following, or before a noun beginning with a vowel or *h.* Cf. **thy.** [ME; OE *thīn,* c. G *dein.* See THOU]

**thin-face** /ˈθɪn-feɪs/, *adj.* →**lean-face.**

**thin-film** /ˈθɪn-fɪlm/, *adj.* of or pertaining to the deposition of metals over insulating substrates, as for the making of magnetic films for certain computer memories.

**thing** /θɪŋ/, *n.* **1.** a material object without life or consciousness; an inanimate object. **2.** some entity, object, or creature which is not or cannot be specifically designated or precisely described: *the stick had a brass thing on it.* **3.** that which is or may become an object of thought, whether material or ideal, animate or inanimate, actual, possible, or imaginary. **4.** a matter or affair: *things are going well now.* **5.** a fact or circumstance: *it is a curious thing.* **6.** an action, deed, or performance: *to do great things.* **7.** a particular or respect: *perfect in all things.* **8.** what is desired or required: *just the thing.* **9.** (*pl.*) clothes or apparel, esp. articles of dress added to ordinary clothing when going outdoors. **10.** (*pl.*) *Colloq.* implements, utensils, or other articles for service: *to help with the breakfast things.* **11.** (*pl.*) *Colloq.* personal possessions or belongings, often such as one carries along on a journey. **12.** *Law.* anything that may be the subject of a property right. **13.** that which is signified or represented, as distinguished from a word, symbol, or idea representing it. **14.** a living being or creature. **15.** *Colloq.* an unaccountable attitude or feeling about something, as of fear or aversion: *I have a thing about minced meat.* **16. a good thing,** something warranting support. **17. do the right thing by** or **do the handsome thing by,** to treat generously. **18. like one thing,** *Colloq.* at great speed. **19. know a thing or two,** *Colloq.* to be shrewd. **20. make a good thing out of,** to obtain an advantage from. **21. make a thing of,** *Colloq.* to turn into a major issue: *OK, so I made a mistake, but there's no need to make a thing of it.* **22. not get a thing out of, a.** to fail to elicit something desired, as information, from. **b.** to fail to enjoy, appreciate, etc.: *I went to a performance of a play in Czech, but didn't get a thing out of it.* **23. old thing,** *Colloq.* (a familiar form of address). **24. one of those things,** an event which was unavoidable or which is no longer remediable. **25. do one's thing,** *Colloq.* to act in a characteristic manner, to do what is most satisfying to oneself. **26. on a good thing, a.** (in betting on horses, dogs etc.) backing a likely winner at favourable odds. **b.** engaged in a project which promises to be successful. **27. the thing, a.** that which is proper, correct, or fashionable. **b.** that which is important or necessary. **c.** the point or hub of a matter: *this is the thing.* [ME and OD, c. D and G *Ding* affair, matter, thing]

**thing-in-itself** /ˌθɪŋ-ɪn-ɪtˈsɛlf/, *n.* (in Kantian philosophy) reality as it is apart from experience; what remains to be postulated after space, time, and all the categories of the understanding are assigned to consciousness. See **noumenon.** [translation of G *Ding an sich*]

**thingummyjig** /ˈθɪŋəmidʒɪg/, *n. Colloq.* (an indefinite name for a thing or person which a speaker cannot or does not designate more precisely.) Also, **thingummybob** /ˈθɪŋəmibɒb/, **thingummy** /ˈθɪŋəmi/, **thingumabob** /ˈθɪŋəməbɒb/.

**think**[1] /θɪŋk/, *v.,* **thought, thinking,** *n. –v.t.* **1.** to form or conceive in the mind; have in the mind as an idea, conception, or the like. **2.** to turn over in the mind; meditate; ponder: *he was thinking what it could mean.* **3.** to have the mind full of (a particular subject or the like). **4.** to form or have an idea or conception of (a thing, fact, circumstance, etc.). **5.** to bear in mind, recollect, or remember. **6.** to have in mind, intent, or purpose. **7.** to hold as an opinion; believe; suppose: *they thought that the earth was flat.* **8.** to consider (something) to be (as specified): *he thought the lecture was very interesting.* **9.** to anticipate or expect: *I did not think to find you here.* **10.** to bring by thinking. *–v.i.* **11.** to use the mind, esp. the intellect, actively; cogitate or meditate. **12.** to form or have an idea or mental image (fol. by *of*). **13.** to reflect upon the matter in question: *think carefully before you begin.* **14.** to remember (usu. fol. by *of*): *I can't think of his name.* **15.** to have consideration or regard (usu. fol. by *of*): *to think of others first.* **16.** to make mental discovery; form or have a plan (usu. fol. by *of*): *he thought of it first.* **17.** to have a belief or opinion as indicated. **18.** to have a high, low, or other opinion of a person or thing (fol. by *of*): *to think well of a person.* **19.** to have an anticipation or expectation (fol. by *of*). **20.** to have an opinion as indicated: *he thought fit to act alone.* *–v.* **21.** Some special verb phrases are:
**think aloud,** to utter one's thoughts without considering all implications or putting them into a formal pattern.
**think better of,** to decide against an original intention.
**think little of,** to have a poor or low opinion of.
**think nothing of, a.** to have a very low opinion of. **b.** to disregard; take no account of.
**think out, a.** to finish or complete in thought. **b.** to understand or solve by process of thought. **c.** to devise or contrive by thinking.
**think over,** to consider carefully and at leisure.
**think through,** to think out.
**think twice,** to consider with great care (before taking action).
**think up,** to form as a concept; devise.
*–n.* **22.** *Colloq.* an act or process of thinking: *go away and have a good think.* [ME; OE *thencan* (c. D and G *denken*) from *thanc* thought. See THANK, *n.*] **– thinkable,** *adj.* **– thinker,** *n.*

**think**[2] /θɪŋk/, *v.t.,* **thought, thinking.** *Archaic.* to seem or appear (usu. impersonal, with indirect object; now only in *methinks* and *methought*). [ME; OE *thync(e)an,* c. G *dünken*]

**thinking** /ˈθɪŋkɪŋ/, *adj.* **1.** that thinks; reasoning. **2.** thoughtful; reflective. **3. put on one's thinking cap,** *Colloq.* to reflect upon or consider a matter; cogitate. *–n.* **4.** thought; reflection.

**think-tank** /ˈθɪŋk-tæŋk/, *n.* a group, usu. of highly qualified specialists, dedicated to the solving of particular problems and the generating of productive ideas.

**thinner** /ˈθɪnə/, *n.* **1.** one who or that which thins. **2.** a volatile liquid added to paints or varnishes to facilitate application and to aid penetration by lowering the viscosity.

**thin-skinned** /ˈθɪn-skɪnd/, *adj.* **1.** having a thin skin. **2.** sensitive to criticism, reproach, rebuff, or the like; easily offended; touchy.

**thio-,** a word element used in chemical nomenclature to indicate the replacement of part or all the oxygen atoms in a compound by sulphur, often used to designate sulphur analogues of oxygen compounds. Also, **thi-.** [combining form representing Gk *theîon* sulphur]

**thioalcohol** /θaɪoʊˈælkəhɒl/, *n.* an aliphatic mercaptan.

**thioaldehyde** /θaɪoʊˈældəhaɪd/, *n.* any of a class of compounds formed by the action of hydrogen sulphide on aldehydes, and regarded as aldehydes with the oxygen replaced by sulphur.

**thioamide** /θaɪoʊˈæmaɪd, -ˈæməd/, *n.* an amide group which contains a sulphur atom. See **polyamide.**

**thiocarbamide** /θaɪoʊˈkabəmaɪd/, *n.* →**thiourea.**

**thiocyanate** /θaɪoʊˈsaɪəneɪt/, *n.* a salt or ester of thiocyanic acid, characterised by the univalent NCS group, and used in hypertensions to relax and dilate smaller blood vessels.

**thiocyanic acid** /ˌθaɪoʊsaɪˌænɪk ˈæsəd/, *n.* an unstable acid, HNCS, known chiefly in the form of its salts.

**thiokol** /ˈθaɪəkɒl/, *n.* any of a group of rubber-like materials with the general formula $(RS_x)_n$, where R is a bivalent radical and *x* is a number usu. between 2 and 4, used when oil and petrol resistance are required. [Trademark]

**thiol** /ˈθaɪɒl/, *n.* any of a group of organic compounds containing the radical -SH; a thioalcohol.

**thionic** /θaɪˈɒnɪk/, *adj.* of or pertaining to sulphur. [*Gk theîon* sulphur + -IC]

**thionic acid** /– ˈæsəd/, *n.* any of four acids of sulphur of the type $H_2S_X O_6$, where *x* is a number from 2 to 5.

**thionine** /ˈθaɪənaɪn, -in/, *n.* **1.** a thiazine derivative occurring in dark crystalline plates, used as a violet dye, as in staining microscopic objects. **2.** any of various related dyes.

**thiopentone sodium** /ˌθaɪoʊˌpɛntoʊn ˈsoʊdiəm/, *n.* →**sodium pentothal.** Also, **thiopental sodium** /ˌθaɪoʊˌpɛntl ˈsoʊdiəm/.

**thiophen** /ˈθaɪoʊfɛn/, *n.* a colourless liquid, $C_4H_4S$, with physical properties resembling benzene, occurring in crude coal-tar benzene and prepared by high temperature interaction of butane and sulphur. Also, **thiophene** /ˈθaɪoʊfin/.

**thiosinamine** /θaɪoʊˈsɪnəmin, -səˈnæmən/, *n.* a colourless crystalline compound, $C_3H_5NHCSNH_2$, with bitter taste and faint garlic-like smell, obtained by the action of ammonia on a sulphur compound, present in mustard oil; allythiourea.

**thiosulphate** /θaɪoʊˈsʌlfeɪt/, *n.* a salt of thiosulphuric acid. Also, *U.S.*, **thiosulfate.**

**thiosulphuric acid** /ˌθaɪoʊsʌlˌfjurɪk ˈæsəd/, *n.* an acid, $H_2S_2O_3$, which may be regarded as sulphuric acid with one oxygen atom replaced by sulphur. Also, *U.S.*, **thiosulfuric acid.**

**thiourea** /ˌθaɪoʊjuˈriə, -ˈjuriə/, *n.* a colourless crystalline substance, $CS(NH_2)_2$, with a bitter taste, derived from urea by replacement of the oxygen with sulphur. Also, **thiocarbamide.**

**third** /θɜd/, *adj.* **1.** next after the second in order, place, time, rank, value, quality, etc. (the ordinal of three). **2.** one out of every three: *every third Monday.* **3.** *Music.* lowest of three parts for the same instrument or voice: *third cello.* **4.** uncommitted to either of two opposing extremes; following a middle course: *third force, Third World.* *–n.* **5.** one who or that which comes next after the second. **6.** a third part, esp. of one. **7.** the class of honours next below a second in a university degree examination. **8.** *Motor Vehicles.* →**third gear. 9.** (*usu. pl.*) *Law.* **a.** the third part of the personal property of a deceased husband, which in certain circumstances goes absolutely to the widow. **b.** a widow's dower. **10.** *Music.* **a.** a note on the third degree from a given note (counted as the first). **b.** the interval between such notes. **c.** the harmonic combination of such notes. [ME *thirde,* OE (North.) *thirda,* var. of *thridda,* c. D *derde,* G *dritte;* akin to L *tertius,* Gk *trítos*] – **thirdly,** *adv.*

**third class** /– ˈklas/, *n.* a class of accommodation, as on a train, esp. formerly in Britain, cheaper and less luxurious than second or first class.

**third-class** /ˈθɜd-klas/, *adj.* extremely shoddy and inferior.

**third degree** /θɜd dəˈgri/, *n.* the use of bullying or torture by the police (or others) in some countries in examining a person in order to extort information or a confession: *to give one the third degree.*

**third-degree** /ˈθɜd-dəgri/, *adj.* of a degree which is at the extreme end of a scale, either as the lowest (*third-degree murder*) or the highest (*third-degree burns*).

**third dimension** /θɜd dəˈmɛnʃən/, *n.* the dimension of thickness or depth in solid objects.

**third estate** /θɜd əˈsteɪt/, *n.* the commons. See **estate** (def. 6).

**third force** /– ˈfɔs/, *n.* a loosely defined term covering esp. certain humanist and existentialist psychologists opposed to the mechanism of behaviourism and psychoanalysis.

**third gear** /– ˈgɪə/, *n.* the third forward gear ratio, usu. the highest or next to highest.

**third half** /– ˈhaf/, *n. Sport Colloq.* a social gathering after a match.

**third-hand** /ˈθɜd-hænd/, *adj.* **1.** obtained after two previous possessors. **2.** old and shoddy. *–adv.* **3.** after having been owned by two previous persons.

**third man** /θɜd ˈmæn/, *n.* **1.** *Cricket.* **a.** a fielding position near the boundary on the off side behind the batsman's wicket. **b.** a fielder in this position. **2.** *Colloq.* the referee in a boxing or wrestling match.

**third party** /– ˈpati/, *n.* any person other than the principals to some transaction, proceeding, or agreement.

**third-party** /ˈθɜd-pati/, *adj.* denoting an insurance policy against liability caused by the insurer or his servants to the property or person of others.

**third person** /θɜd ˈpɜsən/, *n.* See **person** (def. 11).

**third rail** /– ˈreɪl/, *n.* a conductor in the form of a supplementary rail, laid beside or between the rails of the track of an electric railway to carry the current, which is collected by means of a sliding contact.

**third-rate** /ˈθɜd-reɪt/, *adj.* **1.** of the third rate or class. **2.** distinctly inferior.

**thirds** /θɜdz/, *n.pl.* →**third** (def. 7).

**third stream** /θɜd ˈstrim/, *n.* a style of musical composition in which classical techniques are applied to a jazz idiom.

**third world** /– ˈwɜld/, *n.* (*sometimes cap.*) developing countries collectively, esp. in Africa, South America and South-East Asia, which are not heavily industrialised, have a low standard of living and are usu. not politically aligned with either the Communist or the non-Communist blocs.

**thirst** /θɜst/, *n.* **1.** an uneasy or painful sensation of dryness in the mouth and throat caused by need of drink. **2.** the physical condition resulting from this need. **3.** strong or eager desire; craving: *a thirst for knowledge.* *–v.i.* **4.** to feel thirst; be thirsty. **5.** to have a strong desire. [ME *thirsten* (v.), OE *thyrstan,* from OE *thurst* (n.) c. D *dorst,* G *Durst*] – **thirster,** *n.* – **thirstless,** *adj.*

**thirsty** /ˈθɜsti/, *adj.,* **-tier, -tiest. 1.** having thirst; craving drink. **2.** needing moisture, as land; dry or arid. **3.** eagerly desirous; eager. **4.** *Colloq.* causing thirst. – **thirstily,** *adv.* – **thirstiness,** *n.*

**thirteen** /θɜˈtin/, *n.* **1.** a cardinal number, ten plus three. **2.** a symbol for this number, as 13 or XIII. *–adj.* **3.** amounting to thirteen in number. [ME *thrittene,* OE *thrēotēne,* c. G *dreizehn.* See THREE, -TEEN]

**thirteenth** /θɜˈtinθ/, *adj.* **1.** next after the twelfth. **2.** being one of thirteen equal parts. *–n.* **3.** a thirteenth part, esp. of one ($\frac{1}{13}$). **4.** the thirteenth member of a series.

**thirtieth** /ˈθɜtiəθ/, *adj.* **1.** next after the twenty-ninth. **2.** being one of thirty equal parts. *–n.* **3.** a thirtieth part, esp. of one ($\frac{1}{30}$). **4.** the thirtieth member of a series.

**thirty** /ˈθɜti/, *n., pl.* **-ties,** *adj.* *–n.* **1.** a cardinal number, ten times three. **2.** a symbol for this number, as 30 or XXX. **3.** (*pl.*) the numbers from 30 to 39 of a series, esp. with reference to the years of a person's age, or the years of a century, esp. the twentieth. *–adj.* **4.** amounting to thirty in number. [ME *thritty,* OE *thrītig,* from *thrī* THREE + *-tig* -TY[1], c. G *dreissig*]

**thirty-second note** /θɜti-ˌsɛkənd ˈnoʊt/, *n. U.S.* demisemiquaver.

**thirty-three** /θɜti-ˈθri/, *n.* a gramophone record which revolves thirty three and a third times a minute when being played.

**thirty-twomo** /θɜti-ˈtumoʊ/, *n., pl.* **-mos,** *adj.* →**trigesimo-secundo.**

**this** /ðɪs/, *pron. and adj., pl.* **these;** *adv.* *–pron.* **1.** a demonstrative pronoun used to indicate: **a.** a person, thing, idea, etc., as pointed out, present, or near, as before mentioned or supposed to be understood, as about to be mentioned, or by way of emphasis. **b.** one of two or more persons, things, etc., already mentioned, referring to the one nearer in place, time, or thought. **c.** one of two or more persons, things, etc., already mentioned, implying contradistinction (opposed to *that*). **2. with this,** here-upon; immediately after this. *–adj.* **3.** a demonstrative adjective used to indicate: **a.** a person, place, thing, idea, etc., as pointed out, present, or near, before mentioned, supposed to be understood, or by way of emphasis. **b.** one of two or more persons, things, etc., already mentioned, referring to one nearer in place, time, or thought. **c.** one of two or more persons, things, etc., already mentioned, implying contradistinction (opposed to *that*). *–adv.* **4.** an adverb used with adjectives and adverbs of quantity or extent: *this much.* [ME and OE, c. G *dies*]

**this place** /– ˈpleɪs/, *n.* a term used by a member of parliament to refer to the house which he is addressing. Cf. **another place.**

**thistle** /ˈθɪsəl/, *n.* **1.** any of various prickly plants of the genus *Cirsium,* as *C. vulgare,* the **spear thistle. 2.** any prickly plant of related genera, as *Carduus, Carlina,* and *Onopordum.* **3.** any of various other prickly plants. [ME and OE *thistel,* c. D *distel,* G *Distel*] – **thistlelike,** *adj.* – **thistly,** *adj.*

thistle

**thistledown** /ˈθɪsəldaʊn/, *n.* the tufted feathery parachutes of thistle seeds.

**thither** /ˈðɪðə/, *adv.* **1.** Also, **thitherwards** /ˈðɪðəwədz/,

**thitherward.** to or towards that place or point. *–adj.* **2.** on the side or in the direction away from the person speaking; farther; more remote. [ME; OE *thider,* earlier *thæder,* c. Icel. *thadhra* there; akin to THAT, THE]

**thitherto** /ðɪðəˈtu, ˈðɪðətu/, *adv. Rare.* up to that time; until then.

**thixotropy** /θɪkˈsɒtrəpi/, *n.* the property exhibited by certain gels of becoming liquid when stirred or shaken. [Gk *thíx(is)* a touch + -O- + -TROPY] – **thixotropic** /θɪksəˈtrɒpɪk/, *adj.*

**tho** /ðoʊ/, *conj., adv.* though. Also, **tho'**.

**thole** /θoʊl/, *n.* **1.** a pin inserted in a boat's gunwale or the like, to act as a fulcrum for the oar. **2.** either of two such pins between which the oar works. Also, **thole-pin** /ˈθoʊlpɪn/. [ME *tholle,* OE *tholl,* c. LG *dolle*]

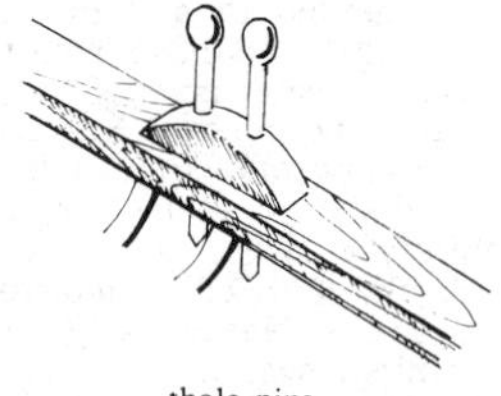
thole pins

**tholobate** /ˈθɒləbeɪt/, *n.* the substructure supporting a dome or cupola. [Gk *thólos* THOLUS + *-batēs* goer]

**tholus** /ˈθoʊləs/, *n., pl.* **tholi** /ˈθoʊlaɪ/. a circular building or part of one, as a dome, cupola, or lantern. Also, **tholos, thole.** [L, from Gk *thólos*]

**Thomism** /ˈtoʊmɪzəm/, *n.* a system of philosophy and theology as taught by St Thomas Aquinas. – **Thomist,** *n., adj.*

**Thompson machine gun,** *n.* a type of submachine gun. Also, **Tommy gun.** [named after J. T. *Thompson,* 1860-1940, U.S. army officer]

**Thomson effect** /ˈtɒmsən əfɛkt/, *n.* the production of a gradient of electrical potential along a conducting metal wire or strip which is subjected to a temperature gradient along its length. [named after Sir William *Thomson* Kelvin, 1st Baron 1824-1907, British physicist and mathematician]

**thong** /θɒŋ/, *n.* **1.** a narrow strip of hide or leather, used as a fastening, as the lash of a whip, etc. **2.** a similar strip of some other material. **3.** a sandal held loosely on the foot by two strips of leather, rubber, etc., passing between the first and second toes and over either side of the foot.

**thoracic** /θəˈræsɪk/, *adj.* of or pertaining to the thorax. Also, **thoracal** /ˈθɒrəkəl/.

**thoracic duct** /– ˈdʌkt/, *n.* the main trunk of the lymphatic system, passing along the spinal column in the thoracic cavity, and conveying a large amount of lymph and chyle into the venous circulation.

**thoracicolumbar** /θəˌræsikəˈlʌmbə/, *adj.* pertaining to the thoracic and lumbar areas of the body.

**thoracoplasty** /ˈθɔrəkoʊˌplæsti/, *n., pl.* **-ties.** the operation of removal of selected portions of the bony chest wall (ribs) to compress part of the underlying lung or an abnormal pleural space, usu. in the treatment of tuberculosis. [*thoraco-* (from Gk *thōrako-,* combining form of *thṓrāx* THORAX) + -PLASTY]

**thorax** /ˈθɔræks/, *n., pl.* **thoraces** /ˈθɔrəsiz, θɔˈreɪsiz/, **thoraxes.** **1.** (in man and the higher vertebrates) the part of the trunk between the neck and the abdomen, containing the cavity (enclosed by the ribs, etc.) in which the heart, lungs, etc., are situated; the chest. **2.** a corresponding part in other animals. **3.** (in insects) the portion of the body between the head and the abdomen. [ME, from L, from Gk: breastplate, chest]

**thoria** /ˈθɔriə/, *n.* an oxide of thorium, $ThO_2$, a white powder, used in making gas mantles. [THORI(UM) + *-a;* modelled on MAGNESIA]

**thorianite** /ˈθɔriəˌnaɪt/, *n.* a rare mineral, mainly thorium oxide, $ThO_2$, but containing also uranium, cerium, etc., occurring in small, black, cubic crystals, notable for its radioactivity.

**thoride** /ˈθɔraɪd/, *n.* any of several natural radioactive isotopes which occur in the radioactive series containing thorium.

**thorite** /ˈθɔraɪt/, *n.* a radioactive mineral, thorium silicate, $ThSiO_4$, occurring as black or yellow crystals.

**thorium** /ˈθɔriəm/, *n.* a radioactive metallic element present in thorite and monazite, and used in gas mantles, electrodes and nuclear fuel. *Symbol:* Th; *at. wt.:* 232.038; *at. no.:* 90; *sp. gr.:* 11.7. [NL, from *Thor,* the Scandinavian god of thunder, + *-ium* -IUM] – **thoric** /ˈθɔrɪk/, *adj.*

**thorn** /θɔn/, *n.* **1.** a sharp excrescence on a plant, esp. a sharp-pointed aborted branch; a spine; a prickle. **2.** any of various thorny shrubs or trees, esp. of the genus *Crataegus,* as *C. monogyna,* the common hawthorn, often planted for hedges. **3.** their wood. **4.** something that wounds, or causes discomfort or annoyance. **5.** the runic character þ for *th* (once in the English alphabet; still used in Iceland). **6. thorn in one's flesh** or **side,** a source of continual annoyance, discomfort, or the like. *–v.t.* **7.** to prick with a thorn; vex. [ME and OE, c. G *Dorn,* Icel. *thorn*] – **thornless,** *adj.* – **thornlike,** *adj.*

**thornapple** /ˈθɔnæpəl/, *n.* **1.** any of the poisonous plants constituting the genus *Datura,* the species of which bear capsules covered with prickly spines, as the jimson weed. **2.** a fruit of some species of thorn tree, genus *Crataegus;* haw. Also, **thorn-apple.**

**thornbill** /ˈθɔnbɪl/, *n.* any of various small, finch-like birds of the genus *Acanthiza,* with small but stout and sharp bills, as the **yellow-tailed thornbill,** *A. chrysorrhoa.*

**thornbush** /ˈθɔnbʊʃ/, *n.* any thorny plant or bush.

**thorn devil** /ˈθɔn dɛvəl/, *n.* →**moloch** (def. 2). Also, **thorny devil.**

**thorn lizard** /ˈ– lɪzəd/, *n.* →**moloch** (def. 2).

**thorny** /ˈθɔni/, *adj.,* **-nier, -niest.** **1.** abounding in or characterised by thorns; spiny; prickly. **2.** thornlike. **3.** overgrown with thorns or brambles. **4.** painful; vexatious. **5.** full of points of dispute; difficult: *a thorny question.* – **thorniness,** *n.*

**thoron** /ˈθɔrɒn/, *n.* a radioactive isotope of radon, produced by the disintegration of thorium. *Symbol:* Tn; *at. wt:* 220; *at. no.:* 86. [from *thoro-,* combining form of THORIUM, modelled on NEON]

**thorough** /ˈθʌrə/, *adj.* **1.** carried out through the whole of something; fully executed; complete or perfect: *a thorough search.* **2.** being fully or completely (such): *a thorough fool.* **3.** thoroughgoing in action or procedure; leaving nothing undone. Also, *Colloq.,* **thoro.** [ME; OE *thuruh,* var. of *thurh* THROUGH] – **thoroughly,** *adv.* – **thoroughness,** *n.*

**thoroughbass** /ˈθʌrəbeɪs/, *n.* **1.** a bass part written out in full throughout an entire piece of music and accompanied by figures which indicate the successive chords of the harmony. **2.** the science or method of indicating harmonies by such figures. **3.** harmonic composition in general.

**thorough brace** /ˈθʌrə breɪs/, *n. U.S.* either of two strong braces or bands of leather from the front to the back spring and supporting the body of a coach or other vehicle.

**thoroughbred** /ˈθʌrəbrɛd/, *adj.* **1.** of pure or unmixed breed, stock, or race, as a horse or other animal; bred from the purest and best blood. **2.** (*cap. or l.c.*) of or pertaining to the Thoroughbred breed of horses. **3.** (of human beings) having qualities characteristic of pure breeding; high-spirited; mettlesome; elegant or graceful. **4.** thoroughly educated or trained. *–n.* **5.** a thoroughbred animal. **6.** (*cap.*) a horse of the English breed of racehorses, developed by crossing domestic and Middle Eastern strains. **7.** a well-bred or thoroughly trained person.

**thoroughfare** /ˈθʌrəfɛə/, *n.* **1.** a road, street, or the like, open at both ends; esp. a main road. **2.** a passage or way through: *no thoroughfare.* **3.** a strait, river, or the like, affording passage.

**thoroughgoing** /ˈθʌrəgoʊɪŋ/, *adj.* **1.** doing things thoroughly. **2.** carried out to the full extent. **3.** complete; unqualified: *a thoroughgoing knave.*

**thoroughpaced** /ˈθʌrəpeɪst/, *adj.* **1.** trained to go through all the possible paces, as a horse. **2.** thoroughgoing, complete, or perfect.

**thoroughpin** /ˈθʌrəpɪn/, *n.* a morbid swelling just above the hock of a horse, usu. appearing on both sides of the leg and sometimes causing lameness.

**thorp** /θɔp/, *n. Archaic except in placenames.* a hamlet, village, or small town. Also, **thorpe.** [ME and OE, c. G *Dorf,* Icel. *thorp* village]

**those** /ðoʊz/, *pron., adj.* plural of **that.** [ME; OE *thās* these (change of meaning variously explained); replacing *thō* (d., obs.)]

**thou**[1] /ðaʊ/, *pron., sing., nom.* **thou** *poss.* **thy** or **thine;** *obj.* **thee;** *pl., nom.* **you** or **ye;** *poss.* **your** or **yours;** *obj.* **you** or **ye;** *v.*

*-pron.* **1.** the personal pronoun of the second person, in the singular number and nominative case, used to denote the person (or thing) spoken to: formerly in general use, often as indicating: **a.** equality, familiarity, or intimacy. **b.** superiority on the part of the speaker. **c.** contempt or scorn for the person addressed; but now little used (being regularly replaced by *you,* which is plural, and takes a plural verb) except provincially, archaically, in poetry or elevated prose, in addressing the Deity, and by the Friends or Quakers, who, however, usu. say not *thou* but *thee,* putting with it a verb in the third person singular (*thee is*). *-v.t.* **2.** to address as 'thou'. *-v.i.* **3.** to use 'thou' in discourse. [ME; OE *thū,* c. G and MD *du,* L *tū*]

**thou**[2] /θaʊ/, *n. Colloq.* **1.** a thousand (dollars, kilometres, etc.). **2.** one thousandth of (an inch, etc.).

**thou.**, thousandth.

**though** /ðoʊ/, *conj.* **1.** (introducing a subordinate clause, which is often marked by ellipsis) notwithstanding that; in spite of the fact that. **2.** even if; granting that. **3.** yet, still, or nevertheless (introducing an additional statement restricting or modifying a principal one): *I will go though I fear it will be useless.* **4.** if (usu. in *as though*). *-adv.* **5.** for all that; however. Also, **'tho, tho'**. [ME *thoh,* from Scand.; cf. Icel. *thō,* c. OE *thēah* however]

**thought**[1] /θɔt/, *n.* **1.** the product of mental activity; that which one thinks. **2.** a single act or product of thinking; an idea or notion: *to collect one's thoughts.* **3.** the act or process of thinking; mental activity. **4.** the capacity or faculty of thinking. **5.** a consideration or reflection. **6.** meditation: *lost in thought.* **7.** intention, design, or purpose, esp. a half-formed or imperfect intention: *we had some thought of going.* **8.** anticipation or expectation: *I had no thought of seeing you here.* **9.** consideration, attention, care, or regard: *taking no thought for her appearance.* **10.** a judgment, opinion, or belief. **11.** the intellectual activity or the ideas, opinions, etc., characteristic of a particular place, class, or time: *Greek thought.* **12.** a very small amount; a trifle. **13.** **second thoughts,** reconsideration. [ME *thoght,* OE *thoht* (akin to THINK[1]). Cf. D *gedachte*]

**thought**[2] /θɔt/, *v.* past tense and past participle of **think.**

**thoughtful** /ˈθɔtfəl/, *adj.* **1.** occupied with or given to thought; contemplative; meditative; reflective. **2.** characterised by or manifesting thought: *a thoughtful essay.* **3.** careful, heedful, or mindful: *to be thoughtful of one's safety.* **4.** showing consideration for others; considerate. **– thoughtfully,** *adv.* **– thoughtfulness,** *n.*

**thoughtless** /ˈθɔtləs/, *adj.* **1.** not taking thought; unthinking, careless, or heedless. **2.** characterised by or showing lack of thought. **3.** lacking in consideration for others; inconsiderate. **4.** devoid of or lacking capacity for thought. **– thoughtlessly,** *adv.* **– thoughtlessness,** *n.*

**thought-reading** /ˈθɔt-ridɪŋ/, *n.* →**mind-reading.** **– thought-reader,** *n.*

**thought transference** /ˈθɔt trænsfərəns/, *n.* →**telepathy.**

**thousand** /ˈθaʊzənd/, *n.* **1.** a cardinal number, ten times one hundred. **2.** a symbol for this number, as 1000 or M. **3.** a great number or amount. **4.** **one in a thousand,** exceedingly good; exceptional; outstanding. *-adj.* **5.** amounting to one thousand in number. [ME; OE *thūsend,* c. Dan. *tusind*]

**thousandfold** /ˈθaʊzənfoʊld/, *adj., adv.* a thousand times as great or as much.

**thousand island dressing,** *n.* a salad dressing consisting of mayonnaise with chilli sauce, green pepper, cream or milk, etc. [named after *Thousand Islands,* a group of about 1500 islands in southern Canada and northern U.S.]

**thousand-jacket** /ˈθaʊzənd-dʒækət/, *n.* →**houhere.**

**thousandth** /ˈθaʊzənθ/, *adj.* **1.** last in order of a series of a thousand. **2.** being one of a thousand equal parts. *-n.* **3.** a thousandth part, esp. of one (1/1000). **4.** the thousandth member of a series.

**thraldom** /ˈθrɔldəm/, *n.* the state of being a thrall; bondage; slavery; servitude. Also, *U.S.,* **thralldom.**

**thrall** /θrɔl/, *n.* **1.** one who is in bondage; a bondman or slave. **2.** one who is in bondage to some power, influence, or the like. **3.** thraldom. *-v.t.* **4.** *Archaic.* to put or hold in thraldom; enslave. *-adj.* **5.** *Archaic.* enslaved. [ME; OE *thrǣl,* from Scand.; cf. Icel. *thrǣll,* c. OHG *dregil* servant]

**thrash** /θræʃ/, *v.t.* **1.** to beat soundly by way of punishment; administer a beating to. **2.** to defeat thoroughly. **3.** *Naut.* to force (a ship) forward against the wind, etc. **4.** to thresh (wheat, grain, etc.). **5.** **thrash out,** to discuss (a matter) exhaustively; solve (a problem, etc.) by exhaustive discussion. *-v.i.* **6.** to beat, toss, or plunge wildly or violently about. **7.** *Naut.* to make way against the wind, tide, etc.; beat. **8.** →**thresh.** *-n.* **9.** the act of thrashing; a beating; a blow. **10.** *Swimming.* the upward and downward movement of the legs, as in the crawl. [var. of THRESH]

**thrasher** /ˈθræʃə/, *n.* **1.** one who or that which thrashes. **2.** any of various long-tailed thrushlike birds, esp. of the genus *Toxostoma,* allied to the mockingbird, as the **brown thrasher.** **3.** →**thresher** (def. 3).

**thrashing** /ˈθræʃɪŋ/, *n.* **1.** a beating. **2.** the act of one who or that which thrashes. **3.** a defeat.

**thrasonical** /θrəˈsɒnɪkəl/, *adj.* boastful; vainglorious. [L *Thraso* a boastful soldier in the play *'Eunuchus'* by the Roman dramatist Terence + -IC + -AL[1]] **– thrasonically,** *adv.*

**thread** /θrɛd/, *n.* **1.** a fine cord of flax, cotton, or other fibrous material spun out to considerable length; esp. such a cord composed of two or more filaments twisted together. **2.** twisted fibres of any kind used for sewing. **3.** one of the lengths of yarn forming the warp and woof of a woven fabric. **4.** a filament or fibre of glass or other ductile substance. **5.** something having the fineness or slenderness of a thread, as a thin continuous stream of liquid, a fine line of colour, or a thin seam of ore. **6.** the helical ridge of a screw. **7.** that which runs through the whole course of something, connecting successive parts, as the sequence of events in a narrative. **8.** something conceived as being spun or continuously drawn out, as the course of life supposed to be spun and cut by the Fates, the three goddesses of destiny in classical mythology. **9.** **hang by a thread,** to be in a dangerous or precarious position. *-v.t.* **10.** to pass the end of a thread through the eye of (a needle). **11.** to fix (beads, etc.) upon a thread that is passed through; string. **12.** to pass continuously through the whole course of (something); pervade. **13.** to make one's way through (a narrow passage, a forest, a crowd, etc.). **14.** to make (one's way, etc.) thus. **15.** to form a thread on or in (a bolt, hole, etc.). *-v.i.* **16.** to thread one's way, as through a passage or between obstacles. **17.** to move in a threadlike course; wind or twine. **18.** *Cookery.* (of boiling syrup) to form a fine thread when dropped from a spoon. [ME *threed,* OE *thrǣd,* c. G *Draht.* See THROW] **– threader,** *n.* **– threadless,** *adj.* **– threadlike,** *adj.*

**threadbare** /ˈθrɛdbɛə/, *adj.* **1.** having the nap worn off so as to lay bare the threads of the warp and woof, as a fabric, garment, etc. **2.** meagre, scanty, or poor. **3.** hackneyed or trite: *threadbare arguments.* **4.** wearing threadbare clothes; shabby: *a threadbare little old man.*

**threadfin** /ˈθrɛdfɪn/, *n.* any of the spiny-rayed fishes constituting the family Polynemidae, the lower part of whose pectoral fin is composed of numerous separate, slender, filamentous rays.

**thread mark** /ˈθrɛd mak/, *n.* a thin thread in paper currency used to prevent counterfeiting.

**threadworm** /ˈθrɛdwɜm/, *n.* any of various nematode worms, esp. a pinworm.

**thready** /ˈθrɛdi/, *adj.* **1.** consisting of or resembling a thread or threads; fibrous; filamentous. **2.** stringy or viscid, as a liquid. **3.** (of the pulse) thin and feeble. **4.** (of voice, etc.) lacking fullness; thin; weak. **– threadiness,** *n.*

**threat** /θrɛt/, *n.* **1.** a declaration of an intention or determination to inflict punishment, pain or loss on someone in retaliation for, or conditionally upon, some action or course; menace. **2.** an indication of probable evil to come; something that gives indication of causing evil or harm. [ME *threte,* OE *thrēat* throng, threat, distress. Cf. Icel. *thraut* labour, struggle] **– threatless,** *adj.*

**threaten** /ˈθrɛtn/, *v.t.* **1.** to utter a threat against; menace. **2.** to be a menace or source of danger to. **3.** to offer (a punishment, injury, etc.) by way of a threat. **4.** to give an ominous indication of: *the clouds threaten rain.* *-v.i.* **5.** to utter or use threats. **6.** to indicate impending evil or mischief. [ME *thretne,* OE *thrēatnian,* from *thrēat* THREAT] – **threatener,** *n.* – **threateningly,** *adv.*

**three** /θri/, *n.* **1.** a cardinal number, two plus one. **2.** a symbol for this number, as 3 or III. **3.** a set of this many persons or things. **4.** a playing card with three pips. *–adj.* **5.** amounting to three in number. [ME; OE *thrēo,* c. G *drei;* akin to Gk *treîs,* L *trēs*]

**three-awn grass** /ˈθri-ɔn gras/, *n.* any of various species of grass with a trifid awn, as wire grass or kerosene grass.

**three-colour** /ˈθri-kʌlə/, *adj.* **1.** having or characterised by the use of three colours. **2.** denoting or pertaining to a photomechanical process for making reproductions of paintings, etc., usu. carried out by making three plates or printing surfaces, each corresponding to a primary colour, by the halftone process, and taking superimposed impressions from these plates in three correspondingly coloured inks.

**three-cornered** /ˈθrɪ-kɔnəd/, *adj.* **1.** having three corners. **2.** pertaining to or involving three persons, parties, etc.

**3-D** /θri-ˈdi/, *adj.* **1.** three-dimensional: *3-D films.* *–n.* **2.** a three-dimensional form or appearance.

**three-day night** /θri-deɪ ˈnaɪt/, *n. Colloq.* a night full of excitement, danger, etc.

**three-decker** /θri-ˈdɛkə/, *n.* **1.** any vessel, etc., having three decks, tiers, etc. **2.** (formerly) one of a class of sailing warships which carried guns on three decks. **3.** a novel published in three volumes (esp. in 19th century). **4.** anything having three layers, levels, tiers, etc.

**three-dimensional** /θri-daɪˈmɛnʃənəl, -dəˈmɛn-/, *adj.* **1.** having or seeming to have, the dimension of depth as well as height and breadth. **2.** realistic; lifelike.

**threefold** /ˈθrifoʊld/, *adj.* **1.** having three elements or parts. **2.** three times as great or as much; treble. *–adv.* **3.** in threefold manner or measure; trebly.

**three-legged race** /θri-ˈlɛgəd reɪs, -ˈlɛgd/, *n.* a race run by a number of contestants in pairs, each pair having their inside legs tied together.

**three-master** /θri-ˈmastə/, *n.* a sailing ship with three masts.

**three-mile limit** /ˌθri-maɪl ˈlɪmət/, *n.* (in international law) the minimum extent of territorial waters; greater limits are now claimed by many states.

**three-on-the-tree** /ˌθri-ɒn-ðə-ˈtri/, *n. Colloq.* a column shift for a motor vehicle with three forward gears (opposed to *four-on-the-floor*).

**threepence** /ˈθrɪpəns/, *n.* **1.** a former silver coin valued at three pennies. **2.** a similar coin of other countries.

**threepenny** /ˈθrɪpəni/, *adj.* of the amount or value of threepence: *a threepenny bit.*

**threepenny bits** /– ˈbɪts/, *n.pl.* in the phrase **give (someone) the threepenny bits,** *Colloq.* to arouse dislike, anger, disgust, etc., in (someone). [rhyming slang, the shits]

**three-phase** /ˈθri-feɪz/, *adj. Elect.* **1.** denoting or pertaining to a circuit, system, or device which is energised by three electromotive forces which differ in phase by one third of a cycle, i.e., 120 degrees. **2.** having three phases.

**three-piece** /ˈθri-pis/, *adj.* **1.** consisting of three matching pieces, as a woman's coat, skirt and blouse, a man's jacket, trousers and waistcoat, or a lounge and two chairs. **2.** having three parts. *–n.* **3.** a three-piece outfit, suit, etc.

**three-ply** /ˈθri-plaɪ/, *adj.* **1.** consisting of three thicknesses, layers, strands, or the like. *–n.* **2.** wood which is three-ply.

**three-point landing** /θri-pɔɪnt ˈlændɪŋ/, *n.* a smooth aircraft landing in which the two main wheels of the landing gear and the tail or nose wheel all touch the ground simultaneously.

**three-point turn** /– ˈtɜn/, *n.* the complete reversal of the direction of motion of a vehicle by swinging it round in the road to the opposite kerb, reversing on the opposite lock, and driving off forwards in the new direction.

**three-quarter** /θri-ˈkwɔtə/, *adj.* **1.** consisting of or involving three quarters of a whole. **2.** *Rugby Football.* of or pertaining to a three-quarter. *–n.* **3.** *Rugby Football.* one of the four players in the three-quarter line.

**three-quarter binding** /– ˈbaɪndɪŋ/, *n.* a book binding in which the leather back extends farther towards the side covers than in half-binding.

**three-quarter line** /ˈ– laɪn/, *n.* (in Rugby football) the positions of right-wing, left-wing, inside centre and outside centre or the players occupying them.

**three-quarter time** /– ˈtaɪm/, *n.* the interval between the third and last quarters of a game, as basketball, Australian Rules, etc.

**three-ring circus** /θri-rɪŋ ˈsɜkəs/, *n.* **1.** a circus with performances taking place simultaneously in three separate rings. **2.** something spectacular, tumultuous, or confusing. **3.** an exhibitionistic performance, esp. considered highly pretentious or foolish.

**three R's** /θri ˈaz/, *n. pl.* reading, (w)riting, and (a)rithmetic, traditionally regarded as the fundamentals of education.

**threesome** /ˈθrisəm/, *adj.* **1.** consisting of three; threefold. **2.** performed or played by three persons. *–n.* **3.** three forming a group. **4.** something in which three persons participate. **5.** *Golf.* a match in which one player, playing his own ball, plays against two opponents with one ball, the two latter playing alternate strokes. [ME *thresum.* See THREE, -SOME[2]]

**three-square** /θri-ˈskwɛə/, *adj.* having an equilateral triangular cross-section, as certain files.

**three-toed skink** /ˌθri-toʊd ˈskɪŋk/, *n.* a small, smooth-scaled, shiny skink, *Siaphos equalis,* having greatly reduced limbs and somewhat resembling a snake.

**three-wheeler** /θri-ˈwilə/, *n.* a vehicle, esp. a motor car, or a child's tricycle, having three wheels.

**thremmatology** /θrɛməˈtɒlədʒi/, *n.* the science of breeding or propagating animals and plants under domestication. [Gk *thremmato-* (combining form of *thrémma* nursling) + -LOGY]

**threnode** /ˈθrinoʊd, ˈθrɛn-/, *n.* →**threnody.**

**threnody** /ˈθrɛnədi/, *n., pl.* **-dies.** a song of lamentation, esp. for the dead; a dirge or funeral song. [Gk *thrēnōidía*] – **threnodial** /θrəˈnoʊdiəl/, **threnodic** /θrəˈnɒdɪk/, *adj.* – **threnodist,** *n.*

**threonine** /ˈθrioʊnin/, *n.* an essential amino acid, $CH_3CHOHCH(NH_3^+)COO^-$, found in all proteins.

**thresh** /θrɛʃ/, *v.t.* **1.** to separate the grain or seeds from (a cereal plant, etc.) by some mechanical means, as by beating with a flail or by the action of a threshing machine. **2.** to beat as if with a flail. *–v.i.* **3.** to thresh wheat, grain, etc. **4.** to deliver blows as if with a flail. *–n.* **5.** the act of threshing. [ME *thresshe,* OE *threscan,* c. G *dreschen.* Cf. THRASH]

**thresher** /ˈθrɛʃə/, *n.* **1.** one who or that which threshes. **2.** one who separates grain or seeds from wheat, etc., by beating with a flail, using a threshing machine, etc. **3.** Also, **thrasher, thresher shark.** a large shark of the genus *Alopias,* esp. *A. vulpinus,* having a very long tail with which it threshes the water to drive together the small fish on which it feeds.

**threshing machine** /ˈθrɛʃɪŋ məʃin/, *n.* a machine for separating the grain and seeds from wheat, etc.

**threshold** /ˈθrɛʃhoʊld/, *n.* **1.** the sill of a doorway. **2.** the entrance to a house or building. **3.** any place or point of entering or beginning. **4.** *Aeron.* the beginning of the landing area on a runway or landing strip. **5.** *Psychol., Physiol.* the point at which a stimulus becomes perceptible or is of sufficient intensity to produce an effect; the limen. **6.** *Physics.* the lowest value of any signal, stimulus, or agency which will produce a specified effect, as a threshold frequency. [ME *threschold,* OE *threscold, -wold,* c. Icel. *threskjöldr;* apparently from THRESH, *v.*]

**threshold frequency** /ˈ– ˌfrikwənsi/, *n.* the lowest frequency of radiation which, when incident upon a photoelectric material, will produce a photoelectric effect.

**threw** /θru/, *v.* past tense of **throw.**

**thrice** /θraɪs/, *adv.* **1.** three times, as in succession; on three occasions. **2.** in threefold quantity or degree. **3.** very; greatly; extremely. [ME *thriefrom obs. thrie* thrice (OE *thrīga*) + *-s,* adv. gen. suffix]

**thrift** /θrɪft/, *n.* **1.** economical management; economy; frugality. **2.** vigorous growth, as of a plant. **3.** →**sea-pink.** [ME, from THRIVE. Cf. Icel. *thrift* prosperity] – **thriftless,** *adj.* – **thriftlessly,** *adv.* – **thriftlessness,** *n.*

**thrift shop** /ˈ– ʃɒp/, *n.* →**opportunity shop.**

**thrifty** /ˈθrɪfti/, *adj.,* **-tier, -tiest.** **1.** using or characterised by thrift or frugality; provident. – **thriftily,** *adv.* – **thriftiness,** *n.*

**thrill** /θrɪl/, *v.t.* **1.** to effect with a sudden wave of keen emotion, so as to produce a tremor or tingling sensation through the body. **2.** to cause to vibrate or quiver; utter or send forth tremulously, as a melody. *–v.i.* **3.** to affect one with a wave of emotion or excitement; produce a thrill. **4.** to be stirred by a thrill of emotion or excitement. **5.** to move tremulously; vibrate; quiver. *–n.* **6.** a tremor or tingling sensation passing through the body as the result of sudden keen emotion or excitement. **7.** thrilling property or quality, as of a story. **8.** a vibration or quivering. **9.** *Pathol.* an abnormal tremor or vibration, as in the respiratory system. **10. thrill to bits,** to delight: *she was thrilled to bits over her new job.* [ME; metathetic var. of ME *thirl* to pierce, from OE *thyrlian,* from *thyrel* hole]

**thriller** /ˈθrɪlə/, *n.* **1.** one who or that which thrills. **2.** a book, play, or film, dealing with crime, mystery, etc., in an exciting or sensational manner.

**thrilling** /ˈθrɪlɪŋ/, *adj.* **1.** exciting; pleasing. **2.** vibrant. **– thrillingly,** *adv.* **– thrillingness,** *n.*

**thrips** /θrɪps/, *n., pl.* **thrips.** any of numerous small insects of the order Thysanoptera, characterised by long, narrow wings fringed with hairs, many species of which are destructive to plants. [L, from Gk: woodworm]

**thrive** /θraɪv/, *v.i.,* **throve** or **thrived, thrived** or **thriven, thriving. 1.** to prosper; be fortunate or successful; increase in property or wealth; grow richer or rich. **2.** to grow or develop vigorously; flourish. [ME, from Scand.: cf. Icel. *thrīfask*] **– thriver,** *n.* **– thrivingly,** *adv.*

**thro** /θru/, *prep., adv., adj.* →**through.** Also, **thro'.**

**throat** /θroʊt/, *n.* **1.** the passage from the mouth to the stomach or to the lungs; the fauces, pharynx, and oesophagus; the larynx and trachea. **2.** some analogous or similar narrowed part or passage. **3.** the front of the neck below the chin and above the collarbones. **4.** *Naut.* →**nock** (def. 4). **5. cut one's (own) throat,** to pursue a course of action which is injurious or ruinous to oneself. **6. jump down someone's throat,** to deliver a strong verbal attack on; berate scold. **7. ram** or **thrust (something) down someone's throat,** to force something on someone's attention. **8. stick in one's throat, a.** to be difficult to express or utter. **b.** to be difficult to accept in one's mind. [ME and OE *throte.* Cf. THROTTLE] **– throatless,** *adj.*

**throatlatch** /ˈθroʊtlætʃ/, *n.* a strap which passes under a horse's throat and helps to hold a bridle or halter in place.

**throat microphone** /ˈθroʊt ˌmaɪkrəfoʊn/, *n.* a type of microphone designed to be held against the throat so as to pick up glottal pulses.

**throaty** /ˈθroʊti/, *adj.,* **-tier, -tiest.** produced or modified in the throat, as sounds; hoarse; guttural. **– throatily,** *adv.* **– throatiness,** *n.*

**throb** /θrɒb/, *v.,* **throbbed, throbbing,** *n. –v.i.* **1.** to beat with increased force or rapidity, as the heart under the influence of emotion or excitement; palpitate. **2.** to feel or exhibit emotion. **3.** to pulsate; vibrate. *–n.* **4.** the act of throbbing. **5.** a violent beat or pulsation, as of the heart. **6.** any pulsation or vibration. [ME (in ppr. *throbbant*); orig. unknown] **– throbber** *n.* **– throbbingly,** *adv.*

**throe** /θroʊ/, *n.* **1.** a violent spasm or pang; a paroxysm. **2.** a sharp attack of emotion. **3.** *(pl.)* the pains of childbirth. **4.** *(pl.)* the agony of death. **5.** *(pl.)* any violent convulsion or struggle. **6. in the throes of,** *Colloq.* engaged in; fully preoccupied with: *she was in the throes of writing her latest novel.* [ME *throwe,* var. of *thrawe;* akin to OE *thrēa, thrawu* threat, calamity]

**thrombin** /ˈθrɒmbən/, *n.* an enzyme catalysing the conversion of fibrinogen into fibrin in the clotting of blood. [THROMB(US) + -IN[2]]

**thrombosis** /θrɒmˈboʊsəs/, *n.* intravascular coagulation of the blood in any part of the circulatory system, as in the heart, arteries, veins, or capillaries. [NL, from Gk: curdling, clotting] **– thrombotic** /θrɒmˈbɒtɪk/, *adj.*

**thrombus** /ˈθrɒmbəs/, *n., pl.* **-bi** /-baɪ/. a fibrinous clot which forms in and obstructs a blood vessel, or which forms in one of the heart's chambers. [NL, from Gk *thrómbos* lump, clot]

**throne** /θroʊn/, *n., v.,* **throned, throning.** *–n.* **1.** the chair or seat occupied by a sovereign, bishop, or other exalted personage on ceremonial occasions, usu. raised on a dais and covered with a canopy. **2.** the office or dignity of a sovereign. **3.** the occupant of a throne; a sovereign. **4.** sovereign power or authority. **5.** episcopal office or authority. **6.** *(pl.)* an order of angels. **7. the throne,** *Colloq.* the toilet. *–v.t., v.i.* **8.** to set or sit on or as on a throne. [ME, from L *thronus,* from Gk *thrónos* high seat; replacing ME *trone,* from OF] **– throneless,** *adj.*

**throng** /θrɒŋ/, *n.* **1.** a multitude of people crowded or assembled together; a crowd. **2.** a great number of things crowded or considered together. *–v.i.* **3.** to assemble, collect, or go in large numbers; crowd. *–v.t.* **4.** to crowd or press upon; jostle. **5.** to fill or occupy with or as with a crowd. **6.** to bring or drive together into a crowd. **7.** to fill by crowding or pressing into. [ME; OE *gethrang;* akin to D *drang,* G *Drang*]

**throstle** /ˈθrɒsəl/, *n.* **1.** the Old World songthrush, *Turdus philomelus.* **2.** a machine for spinning wool, cotton, etc., in which the twisting and winding are simultaneous and continuous. [ME and OE, c. D *drossel,* G *Drossel,* akin to L *turdus* thrush]

**throttle** /ˈθrɒtl/, *n., v.,* **-tled, -tling.** *–n.* **1.** a lever, pedal, or other device to control the amount of fuel being fed to an engine. **2.** →**throttle valve.** *–v.t.* **3.** to stop the breath of by compressing the throat; strangle. **4.** to choke or suffocate in any way. **5.** to compress by fastening something tightly about. **6.** to silence or check as if by choking. **7.** *Mach.* to obstruct the flow of (steam, etc.) by means of a throttle valve or otherwise; check the supply of steam, etc. to (an engine) in this way. [late ME *throtel,* frequentative of earlier *throte, v.,* strangle (from *throte,* n., THROAT)] **– throttler,** *n.*

**throttle lever** /ˈ– livə/, *n.* a lever, handle, etc., for manipulating a throttle valve.

**throttle valve** /ˈ– vælv/, *n.* the valve which regulates the flow of vapour received by the cylinders of an engine.

**through** /θru/, *prep.* **1.** in at one end, side, or surface, and out at the other, of: *to pass through a tunnel.* **2.** past: *the car went through the traffic lights without stopping.* **3.** between or among the individual members or parts of: *to swing through the trees.* **4.** over the surface or within the limits of: *to travel through a country.* **5.** during the whole period of; throughout: *to work through the night.* **6.** having reached the end of: *to be through one's work.* **7.** having finished successfully: *to get through an examination.* **8.** by the means or instrumentality of: *it was through him they found out.* **9.** by reason of or in consequence of: *to run away through fear.* **10.** *U.S.* up to and including: *from Monday through Thursday.* *–adv.* **11.** in at one end, side, or surface and out at the other: *to push a needle through.* **12.** all the way; along the whole distance: *this train goes through to Flinders St.* **13.** throughout: *wet through.* **14.** from the beginning to the end: *to read a letter through.* **15.** to the end: *to carry a matter through.* **16.** to a favourable or successful conclusion: *to pull through.* **17.** having completed an action, process, etc.: *he is not yet through.* **18. go through,** to wear out: *he's gone through ten pairs of shoes.* **19. through and through, a.** through the whole extent or substance; from beginning to end. **b.** in all respects; thoroughly. **20. through with, a.** finished or done with. **b.** at an end of all relations or dealings with. *–adj.* **21.** passing or extending from one end, side, or surface to the other. **22.** that extends, goes, or conveys through the whole of a long distance with little or no interruption, obstruction, or hindrance: *a through train.* Also, **thro, thro', thru.** [ME; metathetic var. of *thourgh,* OE *thurh,* c. G *durch,* akin to Goth. *thairh*]

**through-composed** /ˌθru-kəmˈpoʊzd/, *adj.* of or pertaining to a type of musical setting of poems for which the music is different for every stanza, and not simply a repeated tune. [translation of G *durchcomponiert*]

**throughout** /θruˈaʊt/, *prep.* **1.** in or to every part of; everywhere in. **2.** from the beginning to the end of. *–adv.* **3.** in every part. **4.** at every moment or point.

**throughput** /ˈθrupʊt/, *n.* **1.** the quantity or amount of raw material processed within a given time. **2.** *Computers.* the work done by a computer in a given time.

**throve** /θroʊv/, *v.* a past tense of **thrive.**

**throw** /θroʊ/, *v.,* **threw, thrown, throwing,** *n. –v.t.* **1.** to project or propel forcibly through the air by a sudden jerk or straightening of the arm; propel or cast in any way. **2.** to hurl or project (a missile), as a gun does. **3.** to project or cast (light, a shadow, etc.). **4.** to project (the voice). **5.** to make (a voice) appear to be coming from a place other than its source, as a ventriloquist does. **6.** to direct (words, a glance, etc.). **7.** to cause to go or come into some place, position, condition, etc., as if by throwing: *to throw a man into prison, to throw a bridge across a river, to throw troops into action.* **8.** to put hastily: *to throw a shawl over one's shoulders.* **9.** *Mach.* **a.** to move (a lever, etc.) in order to connect or disconnect parts of an apparatus or mechanism. **b.** to connect, engage, disconnect, or disengage by such a procedure. **10.** to shape on a potter's wheel. **11.** to bring to bear or exert (influence, authority, power, etc.). **12.** to deliver (a blow or punch). **13.** *Cards.* **a.** to play (a card). **b.** to discard (a card). **14.** to cause to fall to the ground; bring to the ground, as an opponent in wrestling. **15.** *Colloq.* to permit an opponent to win (a race, contest, or the like) deliberately, as for a bribe. **16.** to cast (dice). **17.** to make (a cast) at dice. **18.** (of a horse, etc.) to cause to fall off. **19.** (of domestic animals) to bring forth (young). **20.** *Colloq.* to astonish; disconcert; confuse. **21.** *Textiles.* to wind or twist silk, etc., into threads. **22.** to arrange or host (a social event): *she threw a party last Saturday.* *–v.i.* **23.** to cast, fling, or hurl a missile, etc. *–v.* **24.** Some special verb phrases are:

**throw away, 1.** to discard; dispose of. **2.** to squander; waste. **3.** to fail to use; miss (an opportunity, chance, etc.).

**throw back,** to revert to a type found in one's ancestors; show atavism.

**throw in, 1.** to add as an extra, esp. in a bargain. **2.** to interpose; interpolate; contribute (a remark, etc.).

**throw in one's hand,** *Colloq.* to concede defeat; surrender.

**throw in the towel** or **sponge,** *Colloq.* to give in; accept defeat.

**throw it in,** *Colloq.* **1.** to accept defeat. **2.** to cease an activity.

**throw off, 1.** to free oneself from. **2.** to elude, escape from (a pursuer, etc.). **3.** to discard or remove hastily. **4.** to recover from (a cold, etc.). **5.** to utter, write, compose, etc., with ease. **6.** *Colloq.* to criticise or belittle (fol. by *at*).

**throw oneself at (someone),** to attempt to excite the interest of in order to win the love of.

**throw oneself into,** to work enthusiastically at.

**throw oneself on** or **upon,** to entrust oneself to the mercy of; commit oneself completely to.

**throw open, 1.** to open wide. **2.** to permit general access to.

**throw out, 1.** to discard; cast away. **2.** to emit; give forth. **3.** to utter casually or indirectly (a remark, hint, etc.). **4.** to expel; eject; remove forcibly. **5.** to reject; refuse to accept. **6.** to cause to make a mistake.

**throw over,** to abandon; forsake; desert.

**throw together, 1.** to assemble in a hasty or haphazard manner. **2.** to bring together; cause to associate.

**throw up, 1.** to give up; abandon. **2.** to build hastily. **3.** to vomit.

*–n.* **25.** an act of throwing or casting; a cast or fling. **26.** *Colloq.* a turn in a game involving throwing, as ball games, etc. **27.** the distance to which anything is or may be thrown: *a stone's throw.* **28.** a venture or chance: *it was his last throw.* **29.** *Mach.* **a.** the movement of a reciprocating part or the like from its central position to its extreme position in either direction, or the distance traversed (equivalent to one half of the travel or stroke). **b.** the arm or the radius of a crank or the like; the eccentric, or the radius of a crank to which an eccentric is equivalent, being equal to the distance between the centre of the disc and the centre of the shaft. **c.** the complete movement of a reciprocating part or the like in one direction, or the distance traversed (equivalent to the travel or stroke). **30.** *U.S.* a light blanket, as for use when reclining on a sofa; an afghan. **31.** a cast at dice. **32.** a number thrown. **33.** *Wrestling.* the act, instance, or method of throwing an opponent. **34.** *Geol., Mining.* the amount of vertical displacement produced by fault. [ME; OE *thrāwan* turn, twist, c. G *drehen* twist, twirl] – **thrower,** *n.*

**throwaway** /ˈθroʊəweɪ/, *n.* **1.** any advertisement, as a brochure or handbill, distributed in the streets, slipped under doors, etc. **2.** a manufactured object designed to be used once and then thrown away. *–adj.* **3.** (of a remark, witticism, etc.) uttered in a deliberately casual manner with apparent disregard for effect.

**throwaway society** /– səˈsaɪəti/, *n.* a society which is conditioned to regard all manufactured goods as instantly replaceable.

**throwback** /ˈθroʊbæk/, *n.* **1.** reversion to an ancestral type or character. **2.** a setback or check. **3.** an act of throwing back.

**throwdown** /ˈθroʊdaʊn/, *n.* a small firework designed to explode when thrown with force to the ground.

**throw-in** /ˈθroʊ-ɪn/, *n.* **1.** *Aus. Rules, Soccer.* the act of throwing the ball into play after it has crossed one of the boundary lines or touchlines. **2.** *Rugby Union.* the winger's act of throwing the ball from touch to the line-out.

**throwing stick** /ˈθroʊɪŋ stɪk/, *n.* an Aboriginal wooden implement with which a spear or dart is thrown.

**thrown** /θroʊn/, *v.t.* past participle of **throw.**

**thrown silk** /– ˈsɪlk/, *n.* raw silk that has been twisted into thread.

**throw-out** /ˈθroʊ-aʊt/, *n.* an item from a shop, warehouse, etc., which is being given away, being no longer needed.

**throwover** /ˈθroʊoʊvə/, *n.* a light, often embroidered, cloth used to cover food, etc. to protect from flies; shower.

**thru** /θru/, *prep., adv., adj.* →**through.**

**thrum**[1] /θrʌm/, *v.,* **thrummed, thrumming,** *n.* *–v.i.* **1.** to play on a stringed instrument, as a guitar, by plucking the strings, esp. in an idle, monotonous, or unskilful manner. **2.** to sound when thrummed on, as a guitar, etc. **3.** to drum or tap idly with the fingers. *–v.t.* **4.** to play (a stringed instrument, or a melody on it) by plucking the strings, esp. in an idle, monotonous, or unskilful manner. **5.** to drum or tap idly on. **6.** to recite or tell in a monotonous way. *–n.* **7.** the act or sound of thrumming; dull; monotonous sound. [imitative] – **thrummer,** *n.*

**thrum**[2] /θrʌm/, *n., v.,* **thrummed, thrumming.** *–n.* **1.** one of the ends of the warp threads in a loom, left unwoven and remaining attached to a loom when the web is cut off. **2.** (*pl.*) the row or fringe of such threads. **3.** any short piece of waste thread or yarn; a tuft, tassel, or fringe of threads, as at the edge of a piece of cloth. **4.** (*pl. or sing.*) *Naut.* short bits of rope yarn used for mops, etc. *–v.t.* **5.** *Naut.* to insert short pieces of rope yarn through (canvas) and thus give it a rough surface. [ME and OE, c. G *Trumm.* Cf. L *terminus* end]

**thruppence** /ˈθrʌpəns/, *n. Chiefly Brit.* →**threepence.**

**thrush**[1] /θrʌʃ/, *n.* **1.** any of numerous passerine birds belonging to the family Turdidae, most of which are moderate in size, migratory, gifted as songsters, and not brightly coloured, as the European **song thrush** (*Turdus philomelus*), which has been introduced into Australia, or the native **ground thrush** (*Zoothera dauma*) of eastern and southern Australia. **2.** any of various superficially similar birds of other families, as the quail-thrush or the shrike-thrush. [ME *thrusche,* OE *thrȳsce,* akin to OHG *drōsca*] – **thrushlike,** *adj.*

**thrush**[2] /θrʌʃ/, *n.* **1.** *Pathol.* a disease, esp. in children, characterised by whitish spots and ulcers on the membranes of the mouth, fauces, etc., due to a parasitic fungus, *Candida albicans;* monilia. **2.** *Vet. Sci.* (in horses) a diseased condition of the frog of the foot. [cf. Dan. *troske,* d. Swed. *torsk* (def. 1)]

**thrust** /θrʌst/, *v.,* **thrust, thrusting,** *n.* *–v.t.* **1.** to push forcibly; shove; put or drive with force: *he thrust a dagger into her back.* **2.** to put forcibly into some position, condition, etc.: *to thrust oneself into danger.* **3.** to stab or pierce, as with a sword. *–v.i.* **4.** to push against something. **5.** to push or force one's way, as against obstacles or through a crowd. **6.** to make a thrust, lunge, or stab at something. *–n.* **7.** the act of thrusting; a forcible push or drive; a lunge or stab. **8.** *Mach.* the linear force generated by an engine-driven propeller or by propulsive gases (as in jet propulsion). **9.** *Geol.* a compressive strain in the crust of the earth, which in its most characteristic development, produces reversed or thrust faults. **10.** *Mech., etc.* a pushing force or pressure exerted by a thing or a part against a contiguous one. **11.** *Archit.* the force exerted in a lateral direction by an arch, and tending to overturn the abutments. [ME *thruste(n),* from Scand.; cf. Icel. *thrȳsta*]

**thrust bearing** /ˈ– bɛərɪŋ/, *n.* a bearing designed to take an axial load.

**thruster** /ˈθrʌstə/, *n.* **1.** one who or that which thrusts. **2.** *Astronautics.* a small rocket used to control the attitude of a spacecraft; vernier rocket.

**thrust fault** /'θrʌst fɔlt/, *n.* a reversed fault (def. 5), the result of horizontal compression.

**thud** /θʌd/, *n., v.,* **thudded, thudding.** *–n.* **1.** a dull sound, as of a heavy blow or fall. **2.** a blow causing such a sound. **3. come a thud,** *Colloq.* to be disappointed in an expectation. *–v.i., v.t.* **4.** to beat or strike with a dull sound of heavy impact. [ME; OE *thyddan,* v.]

**thug** /θʌg/, *n.* a brutal, vicious, or murderous ruffian, robber, or gangster. [from *Thugs,* a former body of professional robbers and murderers in India who strangled their victims; Hind. *thag*] – **thuggery,** *n.* – **thuggish,** *adj.*

**thuggee** /θʌ'gi/, *n.* (*sometimes cap.*) the system or practices of the thugs in India. [Hind. *thagī*]

**thuja** /'θjudʒə/, *n.* any of the evergreen coniferous trees constituting the genus *Thuja,* esp. *T. occidentalis,* the common arborvitae, which yields an aromatic oil. [NL, from Gk *thyía* African tree]

**Thule** /θjul/, *n.* **1.** the ancient Greek and Latin name for an island or region (variously identified as one of the Shetland Islands, Iceland, Norway, etc.) supposed to be the most northerly region of the world. **2.** →**ultima Thule.** [L, from Gk *Thoúlē*; replacing ME and OE *Tyle,* from L *Thȳlē,* from Gk]

**thulium** /'θjuliəm/, *n.* a rare-earth metallic element found in the minerals euxenite, gadolinite, etc. *Symbol:* Tm; *at. wt:* 168.934; *at. no.:* 69. [NL, from L *Thūlē* THULE + *ium* -IUM]

**thumb** /θʌm/, *n.* **1.** the short, thick inner digit of the human hand, next to the forefinger. **2.** the corresponding digit in other animals; the pollex. **3.** that part of a glove, etc., which covers the thumb. **4.** *Archit.* →**ovolo. 5. all thumbs,** clumsy; awkward. **6. under the thumb of,** under the power or influence of. *–v.t.* **7.** to soil or wear with the thumbs in handling, as the pages of a book. **8.** to run through (the pages of a book, etc.) quickly (oft. fol. by *through*). **9.** (of a hitchhiker) to solicit or obtain (a ride) by pointing the thumb in the direction in which one wishes to travel. **10. thumb one's nose,** to put one's thumb to one's nose and extend the fingers in a gesture of defiance or contempt. [ME; OE *thūma,* c. G *Daumen*] – **thumbless,** *adj.* – **thumblike,** *adj.*

**thumb index** /'– ɪndɛks/, *n.* a series of notches or indentations on the outer edges of a book to indicate the various sections into which the book is divided.

**thumbnail** /'θʌmneɪl/, *n.* the nail of the thumb.

**thumbnail sketch** /'– skɛtʃ/, *n.* **1.** a rudimentary drawing. **2.** a brief description of a person or an account of an event.

**thumb position** /'θʌm pəzɪʃən/, *n.* the hand position for playing high notes on the cello, for which the thumb quits the neck of the instrument.

**thumbscrew** /'θʌmskru/, *n.* **1.** an ancient instrument of torture by which one or both thumbs were compressed. **2.** a screw whose head is so constructed that it may be turned easily with the thumb and a finger; used as a fastening device for window sashes.

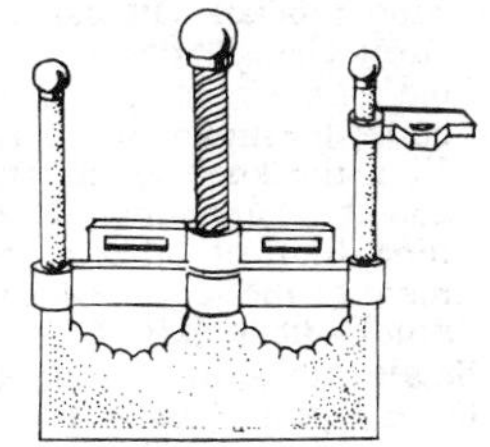

thumbscrew (def. 1)

**thumbs down** /θʌmz 'daʊn/, *n.* **1.** a gesture made by pointing the thumb of one hand downward, symbolising defeat or, in Roman times, death. **2.** rejection, disapproval, esp. of a proposal.

**thumbs up** /– 'ʌp/, *n.* **1.** a gesture made by clenching the fingers and holding the thumb vertical while the hand is moved slightly forward and down, symbolising success. **2.** (an exclamation indicating encouragement). **3.** a similar gesture but made with a vigorous upward thrust of the hand, symbolising contempt.

**thumbtack** /'θʌmtæk/, *n.* →**drawing-pin.**

**thump** /θʌmp/, *n.* **1.** a blow with something thick and heavy, producing a dull sound; a heavy knock. **2.** the sound made by such a blow. *–v.t.* **3.** to strike or beat with something thick and heavy, so as to produce a dull sound; pound. **4.** (of an object) to strike against (something) heavily and noisily. **5.** *Colloq.* to punch; thrash severely. *–v.i.* **6.** *Colloq.* to steal. **7.** to strike or beat heavily, with a dull sound; pound. **8.** to walk with heavy-sounding steps. **9.** to beat violently, as the heart. [imitative] – **thumper,** *n.*

**thumping** /'θʌmpɪŋ/, *adj. Colloq.* very great; remarkably or unusually large; exceptional. – **thumpingly,** *adv.*

**thunbergia** /θʌn'bɜdʒə, -dʒiə/, *n.* any plant of the tropical genus *Thunbergia,* evergreen climbers having blue, yellow, purple, or white flowers according to species. [named after Carl. P. *Thunberg,* Swedish botanist, died 1828]

**thunder** /'θʌndə/, *n.* **1.** the loud noise which accompanies a flash of lightning, due to violent disturbance of the air by a discharge of electricity. **2.** *Chiefly Poetic.* the destructive agent in a thunderstorm. **3.** any loud, resounding noise: *thunders of applause.* **4.** a threatening or startling utterance, denunciation, or the like. *–v.i.* **5.** to give forth thunder (oft. with impersonal *it* as subject): *it thundered last night.* **6.** to make a loud, resounding noise like thunder. **7.** to utter loud or vehement denunciations, threats, or the like. **8.** to speak in a very loud tone. **9.** to move or go with a loud noise. *–v.t.* **10.** to strike, drive, inflict, give forth, etc., with loud noise or violent action. [ME; OE *thunor,* c. G *Donner,* Icel. *Thōrr* Thor, akin to L *tonitrus* thunder] – **thunderless,** *adj.*

**thunderbird** /'θʌndəbɜd/, *n.* **1.** any of a number of Australian birds that will call in response to sudden loud noises as the **rufous whistler,** *Pachycephala rufiventris.* **2.** (in the folk belief of certain western American Indians) a huge bird capable of producing thunder, lightning and rain.

**thunderbolt** /'θʌndəboʊlt/, *n.* **1.** a flash of lightning with the accompanying thunder. **2.** an imaginary bolt or dart conceived as the material destructive agent cast to earth in a flash of lightning. **3.** →**thunder egg. 4.** something very destructive, terrible, severe, sudden, or startling. **5.** one who acts with fury or with sudden force.

**thunderbox** /'θʌndəbɒks/, *n. Colloq.* a toilet, esp. a sanitary can.

**thunderclap** /'θʌndəklæp/, *n.* a crash of thunder.

**thundercloud** /'θʌndəklaʊd/, *n.* an electrically charged cloud producing lightning and thunder.

**thunder egg** /'θʌndər ɛg/, *n.* any of various fossils, stones, or mineral concretions supposed to have been cast to earth by lightning.

**thundering** /'θʌndərɪŋ/, *adj.* **1.** that thunders. **2.** producing a noise or effect like thunder. **3.** *Colloq.* extraordinary; very great. – **thunderingly,** *adv.*

**thunder-mug** /'θʌndə-mʌg/, *n. Colloq.* →**chamber-pot.**

**thunderous** /'θʌndərəs/, *adj.* producing thunder or a loud noise like thunder. Also, **thundery.** – **thunderously,** *adv.*

**thunderpeal** /'θʌndəpil/, *n.* a crash of thunder.

**thundershower** /'θʌndəʃaʊə/, *n.* a shower accompanied by thunder and lightning, or a short heavy shower from a thundercloud.

**thunder stick** /'θʌndə stɪk/, *n.* →**bullroarer.**

**thunderstone** /'θʌndəstoʊn/, *n.* →**thunder egg.**

**thunderstorm** /'θʌndəstɔm/, *n.* a storm of thunder and lightning, and often rain.

**thunderstruck** /'θʌndəstrʌk/, *adj.* **1.** struck by a thunderbolt. **2.** overcome with consternation, confounded, or astounded: *he was thunderstruck by the news of his promotion.* Also, **thunderstricken** /'θʌndəstrɪkən/, *n.*

**thundery** /'θʌndəri/, *adj.* →**thunderous.**

**Thur.,** Thursday.

**Thurawal** /'ðʌrəwəl/, *n.* an Australian Aboriginal language still known by several speakers between Port Hacking and the Shoalhaven River, New South Wales.

**thurible** /'θjurəbəl/, *n.* →**censer.** [ME *turrible,* from L *t(h)ūribulum* censer, from *t(h)ūs* incense]

**thurifer** /'θjurəfə/, *n.* one who carries a thurible in religious ceremonies. [L: incense-bearing]

**Thurs.,** Thursday.

**Thursday** /'θɜzdeɪ, -di/, *n.* the fifth day of the week, following Wednesday. [ME, from Scand.; cf. Icel. *Thorsdagr,* c. OE *Thunresdæg,* G *Donnerstag,* day of *Thunor* or Thor (translation of LL *dies Jovis*)]

**thus** /ðʌs/, *adv.* **1.** in the way just indicated; in this way. **2.** in the following manner; in the manner now indicated. **3.** accordingly; consequently. **4.** to this extent or degree: *thus far.* [ME and OE, c. D *dus*]

**thwack** /θwæk/, *v.t.* **1.** to strike or beat vigorously with something flat; whack. *–n.* **2.** a sharp blow with something flat; whack. [apparently imitative] – **thwacker,** *n.*

**thwart** /θwɔt/, *v.t.* **1.** to oppose successfully; prevent from accomplishing a purpose; frustrate (a purpose, etc.); baffle. **2.** *Archaic.* to cross. **3.** *Archaic.* to extend across. *–n.* **4.** a seat across a boat, esp. one used by an oarsman. **5.** a transverse member spreading the gunwales of a canoe or the like. *–adj.* **6.** passing or lying crosswise or across; cross; transverse. **7.** *Archaic.* perverse; obstinate. **8.** adverse; unfavourable. *–prep., adv.* **9.** across; athwart. [ME *thwert,* adv., from Scand.; cf. Icel. *thvert* across, neut. of *thverr* transverse, c. OE *thweorh* crooked, cross] – **thwarter,** *n.*

**thy** /ðaɪ/, *pron., adj.* the possessive form corresponding to **thou** and **thee,** used before a noun. Cf. **thine.** [ME, var. of THINE]

**thylacine** /ˈθaɪləsin/, *n.* →**Tasmanian wolf.**

**thyme** /taɪm/, *n.* any of the plants of the mint family constituting the genus *Thymus,* as *T. vulgaris,* a low sub-shrub with aromatic leaves used for seasoning, or a wild creeping species, *T. serpyllum* **(wild thyme).** [ME, from L *thymum,* from Gk *thýmon*]

wild thyme

**thymic**[1] /ˈtaɪmɪk/, *adj.* pertaining to or derived from thyme. [THYME + -IC]

**thymic**[2] /ˈθaɪmɪk/, *adj.* of or pertaining to the thymus. [THYM(US) + -IC]

**thymidine** /ˈθaɪmədin/, *n.* a nucleoside of thymine and deoxyribose, present in all living cells, mainly in combined form, as in deoxyribonucleic acids.

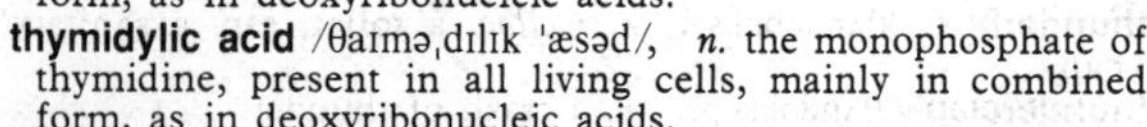

**thymidylic acid** /θaɪməˌdɪlɪk ˈæsəd/, *n.* the monophosphate of thymidine, present in all living cells, mainly in combined form, as in deoxyribonucleic acids.

**thymine** /ˈθaɪmin/, *n.* a white crystalline pyrimidine base, $C_5H_6N_2O_2$, which occurs in DNA and is one of the four units upon which the genetic code is based.

**thymol** /ˈθaɪmɒl/, *n.* a crystalline phenol, $C_{10}H_{13}OH$, present in an oil obtained from thyme, used as an antiseptic, etc. [THYM(E) + -OL[2]]

**thymol blue** /– ˈblu/, *n.* a brown-green powder or crystals, $C_{27}H_{30}O_5S$, used as an acid base indicator in pH range 8.0 (yellow) to 9.6 (blue).

**thymus** /ˈθaɪməs/, *n.* a glandular body or ductless gland of uncertain function found in vertebrate animals, in man lying in the thorax near the base of the neck and becoming vestigial in the adult. An animal thymus used as food is called **sweetbread.** Also, **thymus gland.** [NL, from Gk *thýmos*]

**thynnid** /ˈθɪnəd/, *adj.* **1.** of or pertaining to the Thynnidae, a family of wasplike insects largely confined to Australia, in which the females are wingless and smaller than the winged males. *–n.* **2.** an insect of the family Thynnidae.

**thyr-,** a combining form of **thyroid,** as in *thyroxine.* Also, before consonants, **thyro-.**

**thyratron** /ˈθaɪrətrɒn/, *n.* a gas-filled valve used as a high-speed switch.

**thyristor** /θaɪˈrɪstə/, *n.* →**silicon-controlled rectifier.**

**thyroid** /ˈθaɪrɔɪd/, *adj.* **1.** denoting or pertaining to the thyroid gland. **2.** denoting or pertaining to the principal cartilage of the larynx, forming the projection known in men as the Adam's apple. *–n.* **3.** →**thyroid gland. 4.** the thyroid cartilage. **5.** an artery, vein or the like, of the thyroid region. **6.** a preparation made from the thyroid glands of certain animals, used in treating hypothyroidism. [var. of *thyreoid,* from Gk *thyreoeidḗs* shield-shaped] – **thyroidless,** *adj.*

**thyroidectomy** /θaɪrɔɪdˈɛktəmi/, *n., pl.* **-mies.** excision of the whole or a part of the thyroid gland.

**thyroid gland** /ˈθaɪrɔɪd glænd/, *n.* a bilobate ductless gland lying on either side of the windpipe or trachea and connected below the larynx by a thin isthmus of tissue. Its internal secretion is important in regulating the rate of metabolism and, consequently, body growth.

**thyroiditis** /θaɪrɔɪdˈaɪtəs/, *n.* inflammation of the thyroid gland. [NL. See THYROID, -ITIS]

**thyrotoxicosis** /ˌθaɪroʊˌtɒksəˈkoʊsəs/, *n.* a disease caused by an overactive thyroid gland.

**thyroxine** /θaɪˈrɒksin/, *n.* the hormone of the thyroid gland (often produced synthetically), $C_{15}H_{11}O_4NI_4$, used in treating hypothyroidism. Also, **thyroxin** /θaɪˈrɒksən/. [THYR- + *-oxin(e),* modelled on TOXIN(E)]

**thyrsoid** /ˈθɜsɔɪd/, *adj.* having somewhat the form of a thyrsus. Also, **thyrsoidal** /θɜˈsɔɪdl/. [Gk *thyrsoeidḗs* thyrsus-like]

**thyrsus** /ˈθɜsəs/, *n., pl.* **-si** /-saɪ/. a form of mixed inflorescence, as in the lilac, in which the primary ramification is centripetal or indeterminate, and the secondary and successive ramifications are centrifugal or determinate. Also, **thyrse** /θɜs/. [L, from Gk *thýrsos* Bacchic staff, stem of plant; in Greek mythology a staff tipped with a pine cone and sometimes twined with ivy and vine branches, borne by Bacchus (Dionysus) and his votaries]

**thysanuran** /θɪsəˈnjurən/, *adj.* **1.** belonging or pertaining to the Thysanura, an order of wingless insects, with long filamentous caudal appendages, to which the bristletails belong. *–n.* **2.** a thysanuran insect. [NL *Thysanūra* (from Gk *thýsanos* tassel + *ourá* tail) + -AN] – **thysanurous,** *adj.*

**thyself** /ðaɪˈsɛlf/, *pron.* **1.** an emphatic appositive to **thou** or **thee. 2.** a substitute for reflexive **thee.**

**ti**[1] /ti/, *n., pl.* **tis.** a tropical palmlike plant, *Cordyline terminalis* and all New Zealand species of *Cordyline.* Also, **ti-palm, ti-tree.** [Polynesian]

**ti**[2] /ti/, *n.* →**te**[1].

**Ti,** *Chem.* titanium.

**T.I.** /ti ˈaɪ/, Thursday Island.

tiara (def. 2)

**tiara** /tiˈarə/, *n.* **1.** a jewelled ornamental coronet worn by women. **2.** a diadem worn by the pope, surmounted by the mound (or orb) and cross of sovereignty, and surrounded with three crowns. **3.** the papal position or dignity. **4.** a headdress or turban worn by the ancient Persians and others. [L, from Gk]

**tibby** /ˈtɪbi/, *n.* a section of a newspaper, either an insert or a lift-out, usu. in a different colour, as a racing guide or an advertisement. [the name given to the size of reel used in its printing]

**Tibet** /təˈbɛt/, *n.* an elevated country north of the Himalayas, a possession of China since 1950. Official name, **Tibetan Autonomous Region.** Also, *Obs.,* **Thibet.**

**Tibetan** /təˈbɛtn/, *adj.* **1.** of or pertaining to Tibet, its inhabitants, or their language. *–n.* **2.** a member of the native Mongoloid race of Tibet. **3.** the language of Tibet, a Sino-Tibetan language, esp. in its standard literary form. Also, *Obs.,* **Thibetan.**

**tibia** /ˈtɪbiə/, *n., pl.* **tibiae** /ˈtɪbii/, **tibias. 1.** *Anat.* the shinbone; the inner of the two bones of the lower leg, extending from the knee to the ankle, and articulating with the femur and the astragalus. **2.** *Zool.* **a.** a corresponding bone in the hind limb of other animals. **b.** (in insects) the fourth segment of the leg, between the femur and tarsus. [L: shinbone, flute] – **tibial,** *adj.*

**tibiale** /tɪbiˈali/, *n.* →**astragalus.**

**tic** /tɪk/, *n. Pathol.* **1.** a sudden, painless, purposeless muscular contraction in the face or extremities, which can be reproduced by the victim of this habit and can be stopped at will. **2.** →**tic douloureux.** [F, from It. *ticchis;* of Gmc origin]

**tic douloureux** /– duləˈrɜ/, *n.* trifacial or trigeminal neuralgia; paroxysmal darting pain and muscular twitching in the face which may be evoked by rubbing certain points of the face. [F: painful tic]

**tice** /taɪs/, *v.t.,* **ticed, ticing.** *Croquet.* to play (a ball) with the intention of enticing the opponent to play at it and miss. [shortened form of ENTICE]

**tick**[1] /tɪk/, *n.* **1.** a slight, sharp recurring click or beat, as of a clock. **2.** *Colloq.* a moment or instant: *hang on just a tick.* **3.** a small mark, as a dash (often formed by two small strokes at an acute angle) serving to draw attention to something, to indicate that an item on a list, etc., has been noted or checked, or to indicate the correctness of something, as a written work. **4. on the tick,** punctually. *–v.i.* **5.** to emit or produce a tick, like that of a clock. **6.** to pass as with ticks of a clock: *the hours ticked by.* –*v.t.* **7.** to sound or announce by a tick or ticks. **8.** to mark (an item, etc.) with a tick, as to indicate examination or correctness (oft. fol. by *off*). –*v.* **9.** Some special verb phrases are:

**tick off,** to rebuke; scold.

**tick over, 1.** (of an internal-combustion engine) to run slowly with the gears disengaged. **2.** to be inactive, often in preparation for action.

**what makes one tick,** what motivates one's behaviour. [late ME *tek* little touch, akin to D *tik,* LG *tikk* a touch]

**tick**[2] /tɪk/, *n.* **1.** any member of a group of blood-sucking mitelike animals (Acarina) of the families Ixodidae and Argasidae, provided with a barbed proboscis which it buries in the skin of vertebrate animals. **2.** any of the dipterous insects of the family Hippoboscidae, often wingless, which are parasitic on certain animals, as sheep, camels, bats, pigeons. [ME *teke, tyke,* OE *ticia* (? mistake for *ticca*). Cf. LG *tieke,* G *Zecke*]

**tick**[3] /tɪk/, *n.* **1.** the cloth case of a mattress, pillow, etc., containing hair, feathers, or the like. **2.** *Colloq.* ticking. [ME *tikke, teke, tyke* (c. D *tijk,* G *Zieche*). Cf. L *tēca, thēca,* from Gk *thḗkē* case]

**tick**[4] /tɪk/, *n. Colloq.* **1.** a score or account. **2.** credit or trust: *to buy on tick.* [short for TICKET]

**tick-bird** /ˈtɪk-bɜd/, *n.* either of two African species of birds of the genus *Buphagus,* of the family Sturnidae, which have the habit of perching upon large mammals and feeding upon ticks.

**tickbush** /ˈtɪkbʊʃ/, *n.* a bushy shrub, *Kunzea ambigua,* family Myrtaceae, with white flowers, often forming thickets in heath areas.

**ticker** /ˈtɪkə/, *n.* **1.** one who or that which ticks. **2.** *U.S.* →**tape machine. 3.** *Colloq.* a watch. **4.** *Colloq.* the heart.

**ticker tape** /ˈ– teɪp/, *n.* the paper tape on which the tape machine prints its information.

**ticket** /ˈtɪkət/, *n.* **1.** a slip, usu. of paper or cardboard, serving as evidence of the holder's title to some service, right, or the like: *a railway ticket, a theatre ticket.* **2.** a written or printed slip of paper, cardboard, etc., affixed to something to indicate its nature, price, or the like; a label or tag. **3.** a list of candidates nominated or put forward by a political party, faction, etc. **4.** *Colloq.* a certificate. **5.** *Colloq.* discharge from the armed forces: *to get one's ticket.* **6.** a preliminary recording of transactions prior to their entry in more permanent books of account. **7.** a summons issued for a traffic or parking offence. **8.** *Colloq.* blotting paper impregnated with LSD. **9.** *Colloq.* the correct, right, or proper thing: *that's the ticket!* **10.** *Rare.* a short note, notice, or memorandum. **11.** *Rare.* a placard. **12. have tickets on oneself,** *Colloq.* to be conceited. –*v.t.* **13.** to attach a ticket to; distinguish by means of a ticket; label. **14.** to furnish with a ticket. [F *etiquette* ticket, label. See ETIQUETTE]

**ticket collector** /ˈ– kəlɛktə/, *n.* one who checks or collects passengers' tickets, as at a railway station.

**ticket day** /ˈ– deɪ/, *n.* →**name-day.**

**ticket-of-leave** /tɪkət-əv-ˈliv/, *n.* a document which entitled a convict to freedom of occupation and lodging within a given district of a colony until the original sentence expired or he obtained a pardon. Also, **ticket of leave.**

**ticket-of-leaver** /tɪkət-əv-ˈlivə/, *n.* (formerly) a convict holding a ticket-of-leave. Also, **ticket-of-leave holder, ticket-of-leave man.**

**ticket snapper** /ˈtɪkət snæpə/, *n. Colloq.* a ticket inspector on the railways.

**tickety-boo** /tɪkəti-ˈbu/, *adj. Brit. Colloq.* fine; splendid: *everything is tickety-boo.*

**tick fever** /ˈtɪk fivə/, *n.* **1.** any fever transmitted by ticks. **2.** a cattle disease common in northern Australia caused mainly by *Babesia argenta* where the animal's urine is red coloured; redwater fever.

**ticking** /ˈtɪkɪŋ/, *n.* **1.** a strong cotton fabric, usu. twilled, used esp. for ticks. **2.** a similar cloth in satin weave or Jacquard, used esp. for mattress covers. [TICK[3] + -ING[1]]

**tickle** /ˈtɪkəl/, *v.,* **-led, -ling,** *n.* –*v.t.* **1.** to touch or stroke lightly with the fingers, a feather, etc., so as to excite a tingling or itching sensation in; titillate. **2.** to poke in some sensitive part of the body so as to excite spasmodic laughter. **3.** to excite agreeably; gratify: *to tickle someone's vanity.* **4.** to excite amusement in. **5.** to get, move, etc., by or as by tickling. **6. tickle the peter,** to rob the till. **7. tickled pink,** greatly pleased or amused. **8. tickled to bits,** delighted. –*v.i.* **9.** to be affected with a tingling or itching sensation, as from light touches or strokes. **10.** to produce such a sensation. –*n.* **11.** the act of tickling. **12.** a tickling sensation. [ME *tikel(en)*; ? frequentative of TICK[1] (in obs. sense) touch lightly]

**tickle box** /ˈ– bɒks/, *n.* a small box for filing cards.

**tickler** /ˈtɪklə/, *n.* **1.** one who or that which tickles. **2.** *U.S.* a memorandum book or the like kept to refresh the memory as to appointments, payments due, etc. **3.** *U.S. Accounting.* a single-entry account arranged according to the due dates of obligations. **4.** *Colloq.* a difficult or puzzling situation, problem, etc.

**tickler coil** /ˈ– kɔɪl/, *n.* the coil by which the anode circuit of a radio valve is inductively coupled with the grid circuit in the process of regeneration.

**ticklish** /ˈtɪklɪʃ/, *adj.* **1.** sensitive to tickling. **2.** requiring careful handling or action; risky; difficult: *a ticklish situation.* **3.** unstable or easily upset, as a boat; unsteady. –**ticklishly,** *adv.* –**ticklishness,** *n.*

**tick-tack** /ˈtɪk-tæk/, *n.* **1.** a system by which bookmakers make secret signals amongst themselves at a race meeting. –*v.i.* **2.** to signal by tick-tack. **3.** to have secret dealings or negotiations (fol. by *with*).

**tick-tack man** /ˈ– mæn/, *n.* an assistant to a bookmaker.

**tick-tack-toe** /ˌtɪk-tæk-ˈtoʊ/, *n.* **1.** a children's game consisting of trying, with the eyes shut, to bring a pencil down upon one of a set of numbers, as on a slate, the number hit being scored. **2.** *U.S.* →**noughts-and-crosses.** Also, **tick-tack-too** /ˌtɪk-tæk-ˈtu/, **tit-tat-toe.**

**tick-tock** /ˈtɪk-tɒk/, *n.* an alternating ticking sound, as that made by a clock. Also, **tic-toc.** [imitative. Cf. TICK[1]]

**tidal** /ˈtaɪdl/, *adj.* **1.** of, pertaining to, or characterised by tides. **2.** dependent on the state of the tide as to time of departure: *a tidal steamer.*

**tidal basin** /– ˈbeɪsən/, *n.* **1.** a dock affected by tidal movement. **2.** a basin with gates which is filled with water at high tide; the water is released at low tide, scouring the adjacent harbour.

**tidal current** /– ˈkʌrənt/, *n.* the flow of seawater into and out of an estuary or through a strait at the ebb and flow of the tide.

**tidal wave** /ˈ– weɪv/, *n.* **1.** a large destructive ocean wave produced by an earthquake or the like. **2.** either of the two great wavelike swellings of the ocean surface (due to the attraction of the moon and sun) which move round the earth on opposite sides and give rise to tide. **3.** any overwhelmingly widespread or powerful movement, opinion, or the like: *a tidal wave of popular indignation.*

**tidbit** /ˈtɪdbɪt/, *n. U.S.* →**titbit.** [Brit. d. *tyd* nice + BIT[2]]

**tiddler** /ˈtɪdlə/, *n.* **1.** a very small fish, esp. a stickleback or minnow. **2.** *Colloq.* a small child, esp. one who is undersized.

**tiddly** /ˈtɪdli/, *n.* **1.** *Colloq.* slightly drunk; tipsy. **2.** *Naut.* smart; trim. Also, **tiddley.** [d. var. of OE *tīdlic* timely; sense development obscure]

**tiddlywinks** /ˈtɪdliwɪŋks/, *n.* a game, the object of which is to flick small discs into a cup placed some distance away. Also, **tiddleywinks.**

tide: S, sun; E, earth; M[1], M[3], moon at neap tide; M[2], M[4], moon at spring tide

**tide** /taɪd/, *n., v.,* **tided, tiding.** –*n.* **1.** the periodic rise and fall of the waters of the ocean and its inlets, about every 12 hours and 26 minutes, due to the attraction of the moon and sun. **2.** the inflow, outflow, or current of water at any given place resulting from the tidal waves. **3.** →**flood tide. 4.** a stream or current. **5.** anything that alternately rises and falls, increases and decreases, etc. **6.** a tendency, trend, current, etc., as of events, ideas, public opinion, etc. **7.** a season or period in the course of the year, day, etc. (now chiefly in compounds): *wintertide.* **8.** *Eccles.*

a period of time which includes, and follows, an anniversary or festival, etc. **9.** *Archaic.* a suitable time or occasion. *–v.i.* **10.** to flow as the tide; flow to and fro. **11.** to float or drift with the tide. *–v.t.* **12.** to carry, as the tide does. **13.** **tide over,** to get (a person, etc.) over a period of difficulty, distress, etc.; enable (a person, etc.) to cope. [ME; OE *tīd,* c. G *Zeit* time; akin to TIME] – **tideless,** *adj.* – **tidelike,** *adj.*

**tide-gate** /'taɪd-geɪt/, *n.* a gate which admits water at flood tide and closes when the tide is at ebb.

**tide-gauge** /'taɪd-geɪdʒ/, *n.* a gauge for measuring tide level.

**tideland** /'taɪdlænd/, *n. U.S.* land in the intertidal zone.

**tide-lock** /'taɪd-lɒk/, *n.* a lock at the entrance to a tidal basin.

**tidemark** /'taɪdmak/, *n.* **1.** a mark left by the highest or lowest point of a tide. **2.** a mark made to indicate the highest or lowest point of a tide. **3.** any mark indicating the point which something has reached or below which it has fallen.

**tide-race** /'taɪd-reɪs/, *n.* a swift tidal current.

**tide-rip** /'taɪd-rɪp/, *n.* a rip associated with tidal movements in water. [TIDE + RIP[2]]

**tidewater** /'taɪdwɔtə/, *n.* **1.** water affected by the ebb and flow of the tide. **2.** the water covering land which is dry at low tide. **3.** *U.S.* seacoast.

**tideway** /'taɪdweɪ/, *n.* **1.** a channel in which a tidal current runs. **2.** a strong current running through such a channel.

**tidings** /'taɪdɪŋz/, *n.pl.* (*sometimes construed as sing.*) news, information, or intelligence: *sad tidings.* [ME; OE *tīdung* (c. G *Zeitung* news), from *tīdan* happen]

**tidivate** /'tɪdəveɪt/, *v.,* **-vated, -vating.** →**titivate.**

**tidy** /'taɪdi/, *adj.,* **-dier, -diest,** *v.,* **-died, -dying,** *n., pl.* **-dies.** *–adj.* **1.** neat; trim; orderly: *a tidy room.* **2.** *Colloq.* considerable: *a tidy sum.* *–v.t., v.i.* **3.** to make tidy or neat (oft. fol. by *up*). *–n.* **4.** any of various articles for keeping things tidy, as a receptacle or box; a rubbish tin or wastepaper basket. **5.** *Chiefly U.S.* an ornamental covering for protecting the back of a chair, etc.; an antimacassar. [ME, from *tīd* time, c. G *zeitig* timely] – **tidily,** *adv.* – **tidiness,** *n.*

**tie** /taɪ/, *v.,* **tied, tying,** *n.* *–v.t.* **1.** to bind or fasten with a cord, string, or the like, drawn together and knotted. **2.** to draw together the parts of with a knotted string or the like: *to tie a bundle.* **3.** to fasten by tightening and knotting the string or strings of: *to tie one's shoes.* **4.** to draw together into a knot, as a cord. **5.** to form by looping and interlacing, as a knot or bow. **6.** to fasten, join, or connect in any way. **7.** to bind or join closely or firmly. **8.** *Colloq.* to unite in marriage. **9.** to confine, restrict, or limit. **10.** to bind or oblige, as to do something. **11.** *Music.* to connect (notes) by a tie. **12.** **tie down, a.** to fasten down by tying. **b.** to hinder; confine; restrict; curtail. **13.** **tie up, a.** to fasten securely by tying. **b.** to bind or wrap up. **c.** to hinder. **d.** to bring to a stop or pause. **e.** to invest or place (money) in such a way as to make it unavailable for other purposes. **f.** to place (property) under such conditions or restrictions as to prevent sale or alienation. **g.** to occupy or engage completely. *–v.i.* **14.** to make a tie, bond, or connection. **15.** to make the same score; be equal in a contest. **16.** (of a ship) to moor. **17.** **tie in,** (of a fact, belief, etc.) to relate to; fit in; form a coherent whole with: *that ties in with his deprived childhood.* **18.** **tie up with,** to be closely connected or associated with. *–n.* **19.** that with which anything is tied. **20.** a cord, string, or the like, used for tying or fastening something. **21.** a narrow, decorative band, as of cotton or silk, worn round the neck, commonly under a collar, and tied in front. **22.** a low shoe fastened with a lace. **23.** a knot; an ornamental knot. **24.** anything that fastens, secures, or unites. **25.** a link, bond, or connection of kinship, affection, mutual interest, etc. **26.** something that restricts one's freedom of action. **27.** a state of equality in points, votes, etc., as among competitors: *the game ended in a tie.* **28.** a match or contest in which this occurs. **29.** anything, as a beam, rod, etc., connecting or holding together two or more things or parts. **30.** *Civ. Eng.* a member of a framework which is required to take only a tensile load. **31.** *Music.* a curved line connecting two notes on the same line or space to indicate that the sound is to be sustained for their joint value, not repeated. **32.** *U.S.* →**sleeper** (def. 2). [ME; OE *tīgan* bind, from *tēag* rope, c. Icel. *taug* rope, *teygja* draw]

**tie beam** /'– bim/, *n.* **1.** a timber or piece serving as a tie. **2.** a horizontal beam connecting the lower ends of two opposite principal rafters; collar tie.

**tie breaker** /'– breɪkə/, *n.* a game or a shortened version of a game, played to select a winner from among contestants with tied scores, as in tennis.

**tied cottage** /taɪd 'kɒtɪdʒ/, *n. Brit.* a cottage, usu. owned by a farmer, and rented to one of his employees as long as he is in the farmer's employment.

**tied house** /– 'haʊs/, *n.* a hotel tied to a brewery under an agreement to sell draught beer from that brewery only.

**tied island** /– 'aɪlənd/, *n.* an island linked to the mainland by a sand spit, etc.

tied island

**tie-dye** /taɪ-'daɪ/, *v.t.,* **-dyed, -dyeing.** to create a variegated pattern in the dyeing of fabric by tying off various sections.

**tie-in sale** /'taɪ-ɪn seɪl/, *n. U.S.* a sale in which the buyer is required to purchase, in addition, some undesired or undesirable item.

**tie line** /'taɪ laɪn/, *n.* a telephone line connecting two private branch exchanges or subscribers, which is not open to connection with the main telephone network, even though it may pass through a main exchange.

**tiepin** /'taɪpɪn/, *n.* an ornamental pin or clip for holding the halves of a tie together.

**tier**[1] /tɪə/, *n.* **1.** a row, range, or rank. **2.** one of a series of rows or ranks rising one behind or above another, as of seats in an amphitheatre, of boxes in a theatre, of guns in a man-of-war, or of oars in an ancient galley. **3.** a layer or level. **4.** (*pl.*) (esp. Tasmania) a range of mountains. *–v.t.* **5.** to arrange in tiers. *–v.i.* **6.** to rise in tiers. [F *tire* sequence]

**tier**[2] /'taɪə/, *n.* one who or that which ties. [TIE + -ER[1]]

**tierce** /tɪəs, tɜs/, *n.* **1.** an old measure of capacity equivalent to one third of a pipe, or 42 wine gallons or 159 litres. **2.** a cask or vessel holding this quantity. **3.** Also, **terce.** *Eccles.* the third of the seven canonical hours, or the service for it, originally fixed for the third hour of the day (or 9 a.m.). **4.** *Fencing.* the third of eight defensive positions. **5.** *Cards.* (esp. in piquet) a sequence of three cards. [ME *terce,* from OF, from L *tertius* third]

**tiercel** /'tɪəsəl/, *n.* →**tercel.**

**tie rod** /'taɪ rɒd/, *n.* a metal rod serving as a tie (def. 29).

**tie-up** /'taɪ-ʌp/, *n.* **1.** an association, link, or connection. **2.** a stoppage of business, transportation, etc., on account of a strike, storm, accident, etc.

**tiff** /tɪf/, *n.* **1.** a slight or petty quarrel. **2.** a slight fit of ill humour. *–v.i.* **3.** to have a petty quarrel. **4.** to be in a tiff. [orig. uncert.]

**tiffany** /'tɪfəni/, *n.* a gauze of silk-like texture. [? from MF *tiphanie* Epiphany, from LL *theophania.* See THEOPHANY]

**tiffin** /'tɪfən/, *n.* (in India) **1.** lunch. *–v.i.* **2.** to eat lunch. *–v.t.* **3.** to serve lunch to. [var. of *tiffing* drinking, from *tiff* an alcoholic drink]

**tiger**[1] /'taɪgə/, *n.* **1.** a large, carnivorous feline, *Panthera tigris,* of Asia, tawny-coloured, striped with black, ranging in several races from India and the Malay Peninsula to Siberia. **2.** the puma, jaguar, thylacine, or other animal resembling the tiger. **3.** one who resembles a tiger in fierceness, courage, etc. **4.** *U.S.* an additional cheer (often the word *tiger*) at the end of a round of cheering. **5.** a shearer. **6.** **a tiger for punishment** or **work,** someone who works hard, esp. beyond what is expected. *–v.i.* **7.** (formerly) to work hard. [ME *tigre,* OE *tīgras* (pl.), from L *tīgris, tigris,* from Gk] – **tigerlike,** *adj.*

tiger[1]

**tiger**[2] /'taɪgə/, *n. Colloq.* a swim. [rhyming slang, *tiger Tim* swim]

**tiger beetle** /'– bitl/, *n.* any beetle of the family Cicindelidae, of active, predatory habits.

**tiger cat** /'– kæt/, *n.* **1.** Also, **spotted native cat.** a common, carnivorous, cat-sized marsupial, *Dasyurus maculatus,* brownish in colour with white spots on body and tail, found in eastern and southern Australia and Tasmania. **2.** a small spotted felid carnivore, *Felis tigrina,* of Central and South America. **3.** → **margay. 4.** the golden cat, *Felis aurata,* of Africa.

tiger cat (def. 1)

**tiger country** /'– kʌntri/, *n.* **1.** rough, thickly wooded bush. **2.** remote, uncultivated country.

**tigereye** /'taɪgəraɪ/, *n.* →**tiger's-eye.**

**tigerfish** /'taɪgəfɪʃ/, *n.* any of various striped fish, esp. those of the family Theraponidae of marine and brackish waters of Asia and the Pacific, or freshwater fish of the genus *Hydrocyon* (family Cichlidae).

**tigerish** /'taɪgərɪʃ/, *adj.* **1.** tigerlike. **2.** fiercely cruel; bloodthirsty; relentless. Also, **tigrish.** – **tigerishly,** *adv.* – **tigerishness,** *n.*

**tiger lily** /'taɪgə lɪli/, *n.* **1.** a lily, *Lilium tigrinum,* with flowers of a dull orange colour spotted with black, and small bulbs or bulbils in the axils of the leaves. **2.** any lily, esp. *L. pardalinum,* of similar colouration.

**tiger moth** /'– mɒθ/, *n.* any of a group of moths (family Arctiidae), many of which have conspicuously spotted or striped wings.

**tiger pear** /'– pɛə/, *n.* a species of prickly pear, *Opuntia aurantiaca,* native to south-western South America.

**tiger prawn** /'– prɔn/, *n.* a large, edible prawn of Australian tropical and sub-tropical waters, *Penaeus esculentus,* with distinctive brown bands across the head and body; red when cooked.

**tiger's-eye** /'taɪgəz-aɪ/, *n.* **1.** a golden brown chatoyant stone used for ornament, formed by the alteration of crocidolite, and consisting essentially of quartz coloured by iron oxide. **2.** a glaze on pottery, etc., giving the appearance of this stone. Also, **tigereye.**

**tiger shark** /'taɪgə ʃak/, *n.* a large voracious striped shark, *Galeocerdo cuvieri* (family Carcharinidae), of tropical oceans.

**tiger snake** /'– sneɪk/, *n.* any of several highly venomous snakes (*Notechis* species) found in southern Australia, Tasmania and Bass Strait islands, of various shades of brown, tan, olive or grey, sometimes with creamy bands, and averaging about 1.5 metres in length.

tiger snake

**tiggy touchwood** /tɪgi 'tʌtʃwʊd/, *n.* chasings.

**tight** /taɪt/, *adj.* **1.** firmly or closely fixed in place; not easily moved; secure: *a tight knot.* **2.** drawn or stretched so as to be tense; taut. **3.** fitting closely, esp. too closely: *tight trousers.* **4.** difficult to deal with or manage: *to be in a tight corner.* **5.** of such close or compacted texture, or fitted together so closely, as to be impervious to water, air, steam, etc. **6.** strict; firm; rigid. **7.** closely packed; full. **8.** *Colloq.* close; nearly even: *a tight race.* **9.** *Colloq.* stingy; parsimonious. **10.** *Colloq.* drunk; tipsy. **11.** *Football.* of good play, in which the players, esp. forwards, move close together. **12.** *Rugby Football.* of the side of the scrum away from the loose side or loose head. **13.** *Comm.* (of a commodity) difficult to obtain. **14.** *Finance.* (of credit) not easily obtained. –*adv.* **15.** in a tight manner; closely; firmly; securely; tensely. [ME, sandhi var. of *thight* dense, solid, c. Icel. *thēttr* tight, D and G *dicht* tight, close, dense] – **tightly,** *adv.* – **tightness,** *n.*

**-tight,** a suffix meaning 'impervious to', as in *watertight.*

**tight-arsed** /'taɪt-asd/, *adj. Colloq.* **1.** mean; parsimonious. **2.** haughty.

**tighten** /'taɪtn/, *v.t., v.i.* to make or become tight or tighter. – **tightener,** *n.*

**tight-fisted** /'taɪt-fɪstəd/, *adj.* →**parsimonious.**

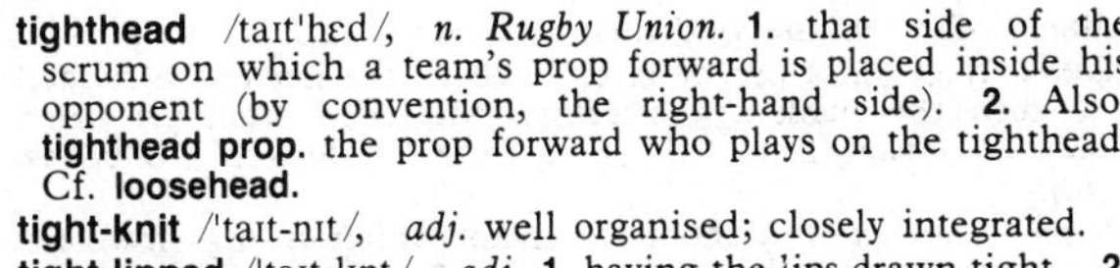

**tighthead** /taɪt'hɛd/, *n. Rugby Union.* **1.** that side of the scrum on which a team's prop forward is placed inside his opponent (by convention, the right-hand side). **2.** Also, **tighthead prop.** the prop forward who plays on the tighthead. Cf. **loosehead.**

**tight-knit** /'taɪt-nɪt/, *adj.* well organised; closely integrated.

**tight-lipped** /'taɪt-lɪpt/, *adj.* **1.** having the lips drawn tight. **2.** not saying much; taciturn.

**tightrope** /'taɪtroʊp/, *n.* **1.** a rope or wire stretched tight, on which acrobats perform feats of balancing. **2. walk a tightrope, a.** to walk along a tightrope as an acrobatic performance. **b.** to be in a precarious situation.

**tightrope-walker** /'taɪtroʊp-wɔkə/, *n.* an acrobat or stuntman who balances on a tightrope.

**tights** /taɪts/, *n.pl.* a close-fitting garment covering the body from the waist downwards, and the legs.

**tightwad** /'taɪtwɒd/, *n. Colloq.* a close-fisted or stingy person. [TIGHT + WAD[1]]

**tigon** /'taɪgən/, *n.* the offspring of a male tiger and a female lion. Cf. **liger.**

**tigress** /'taɪgrəs/, *n.* **1.** a female tiger. **2.** a fierce or cruel woman.

**tigrish** /'taɪgrɪʃ/, *adj.* →**tigerish.**

**tike** /taɪk/, *n.* →**tyke.**

**tiki** /'tiki/, *n.* a carved image representing an ancestor, worn as an amulet in some Polynesian cultures. [Maori]

**til** /tɪl, til/, *n.* the plant sesame. [Hind.: sesame]

**tilbury** /'tɪlbəri, -bri/, *n., pl.* **-ries.** a light two-wheeled carriage without a top. [named after the inventor]

**tilde** /'tɪldə/, *n.* a diacritical mark (˜) placed over a letter, as over the letter *n* in Spanish to indicate a palatal nasal sound, as in *señor.* [Sp., from ML *titulus* TITLE]

**tile** /taɪl/, *n., v.,* **tiled, tiling.** –*n.* **1.** a thin slab or shaped piece of baked clay, sometimes glazed and ornamented, used for covering roofs, lining walls, paving floors, draining land, in ornamental work, etc. **2.** any of various similar slabs or pieces, as of stone or metal. **3.** a pottery tube or pipe used for draining land. **4.** a hollow or cellular block used as a wall unit in masonry construction. **5. on the tiles,** *Colloq.* having a wild, riotous, or debauched night's entertainment. –*v.t.* **6.** to cover with or as with tiles. [ME; OE *tīgele,* c. G *Ziegel,* both from L *tēgula*] – **tiler,** *n.* – **tilelike,** *adj.*

**tilefish** /'taɪlfɪʃ/, *n., pl.* **-fishes,** (*esp. collectively*) **-fish. 1.** a colourful, deep water, marine fish, *Branchiostegus wardi,* of eastern Australian coastal waters. **2.** a large, brilliantly coloured food fish, *Lopholatilus chamaeleonticeps,* of the Atlantic Ocean.

tilefish

**tiling** /'taɪlɪŋ/, *n.* **1.** the operation of covering with tiles. **2.** tiles collectively. **3.** a tiled surface.

**till[1]** /tɪl/, *prep.* **1.** up to the time of; until: *to fight till death.* **2.** (with a negative) before: *he did not come till today.* –*conj.* **3.** to the time that or when; until. **4.** (with a negative) before [ME; OE (Northern) *til,* from Scand.; cf. Icel. *til* to]

**till[2]** /tɪl/, *v.t.* **1.** to labour, as by ploughing, harrowing, etc., upon (land) for the raising of crops; cultivate. **2.** to plough. –*v.i.* **3.** to cultivate the soil. [ME *tille,* OE *tilian* strive, get, c. D *telen* breed, cultivate, G *zielen* aim (at)] – **tillable,** *adj.*

**till[3]** /tɪl/, *n.* (in a shop, etc.) a container as a box, drawer, or the like, usu. having separate compartments for coins and notes of different denominations, in which cash for daily transactions is temporarily kept. [late ME *tylle,* n. use of *tylle,* v., draw (now obs.), OE *tyllan;* akin to L *dolus* trick]

**till[4]** /tɪl/, *n.* **1.** *Geol.* glacial drift consisting of an unassorted mixture of clay, sand, gravel, and boulders. **2.** a stiff clay. [orig. uncert.]

**tillage** /'tɪlɪdʒ/, *n.* **1.** the operation, practice, or art of tilling land. **2.** tilled land.

**tillandsia** /tɪ'lændziə/, *n.* any of the tropical and subtropical American plants constituting the genus *Tillandsia,* most of which are epiphytic on trees, as Spanish moss. [NL; named after E. *Tillands,* 17th C Swedish botanist]

**tiller**[1] /ˈtɪlə/, *n.* one who tills; a farmer. [TILL[2] + -ER[1]]

**tiller**[2] /ˈtɪlə/, *n.* a bar or lever fitted to the head of a rudder, to turn the rudder in steering. [ME *tiler,* from OF *telier* weaver's beam, from *teile* cloth, from L *tēla* web] – **tillerless,** *adj.*

**tiller**[3] /ˈtɪlə/, *n.* **1.** a shoot of a plant which springs from the root or bottom of the original stalk. **2.** a sapling. *–v.i.* **3.** (of a plant) to put forth new shoots from the root, or round the bottom of the original stalk. [OE *telgor* twig, shoot]

**Tilley lamp** /ˈtɪli læmp/, *n.* a portable form of light which ·operates by burning vaporised paraffin in a special type of mantle, used on building sites, yachts, etc. [Trademark]

**tillikin** /ˈtɪləkɪn/, *n.* the stick-nest rat, *Leporillus apicalis,* of central Australia, which has a white-tipped tail. [Aboriginal]

**tilly** /ˈtɪli/, *n. Qld. Colloq.* a utility truck. Also, **til.**

**tilsit** /ˈtɪlsət/, *n.* a firm, plastic-bodied cheese, made from whole or skim milk, with a mild to slightly sharp taste, a pungent aroma, and sometimes, small, round holes. Also, **ragnit.** [named after *Tilsit,* East Prussia, former name of the town Sovetsk, U.S.S.R.]

**tilt**[1] /tɪlt/, *v.t.* **1.** to cause to lean, incline, slope or slant. **2.** to rush at or charge, as in a joust. **3.** to hold poised for attack, as a lance. *–v.i.* **4.** to move into or assume a sloping position or direction. **5.** to strike, thrust, or charge with a lance or the like (fol. by *at*). **6.** to engage in a joust, tournament or similar contest. **7. tilt at windmills,** to fight imaginary enemies. *–n.* **8.** an act or instance of tilting. **9.** the state of being tilted; a sloping position. **10.** a slope. **11.** a joust or any other contest. **12.** a dispute. **13.** a thrust of a weapon, as at a tilt or joust. **14. full tilt,** with full force or speed. [ME *tylte,* from OE *tealt* unsteady] – **tilter,** *n.*

**tilt**[2] /tɪlt/, *n.* **1.** a cover of coarse cloth, canvas, etc., as for a wagon, boat, etc. **2.** an awning. *–v.t.* **3.** to furnish with a tilt. [ME, var. of *tild,* OE *teld,* c. G *Zelt* tent]

**tilth** /tɪlθ/, *n.* **1.** the act or operation of tilling; tillage. **2.** the state of being tilled. **3.** the physical condition of soil in relation to plant growth. **4.** tilled land. [ME and OE, from OE *tilian* TILL[2]]

**tilt hammer** /ˈtɪlt hæmə/, *n.* a drop hammer used in forging, etc., consisting of a heavy head at one end of a pivoted lever.

**tiltyard** /ˈtɪltjad/, *n.* a courtyard or other area for tilting or jousting.

**Tim.,** *Bible.* Timothy.

**timbal** /ˈtɪmbəl/, *n.* **1.** →**kettledrum.** **2.** *Entomol.* a vibrating membrane in certain insects, as the cicada. Also, **tymbal.** [F *timbale,* aphetic nasalised var. of *attabal,* from Sp. *atabal* Moorish drum, from Ar. *aṭṭabl*]

**timbale** /tæmˈbal/, *n.* **1.** a preparation of minced meat, fish, or vegetables, cooked in a cup-shaped mould. **2.** a small mould of paste, baked and filled with some cooked food. [F: kettledrum. See TIMBAL]

**timber** /ˈtɪmbə/, *n.* **1.** wood, esp. when suitable for building houses, ships, etc., or for use in carpentry, joinery, etc. **2.** the wood of growing trees suitable for structural uses. **3.** the trees themselves. **4.** *Chiefly U.S.* wooded land. **5.** a single beam or piece of wood forming, or capable of forming, part of a structure. **6.** *Naut.* (in a ship's frame) one of the curved pieces of wood which spring upwards and outwards from the keel; a rib. **7.** personal character or quality. *–v.t.* **8.** to furnish with timber. **9.** to support with timber. *–interj.* **10.** (a warning, as given by a lumberjack, that a tree is about to fall). [ME and OE; orig. building, material for building, c. G *Zimmer* room, Icel. *timbr* timber; akin to L *domus* house, Gk *dómos*] – **timberless,** *adj.*

**timbered** /ˈtɪmbəd/, *adj.* **1.** made of or furnished with timber. **2.** covered with growing trees; wooded: *timbered hills.*

**timber-framing** /ˈtɪmbə-freɪmɪŋ/, *n.* a method of building construction in which the frame of timber forming the structure is filled in with plaster or bricks.

**timber-getter** /ˈtɪmbə-gɛtə/, *n.* a person employed in timber-getting.

**timber-getting** /ˈtɪmbə-gɛtɪŋ/, *n.* the process of cutting and hauling forest trees for logs or firewood.

**timberhead** /ˈtɪmbəhɛd/, *n.* **1.** the top end of a timber, rising above the deck, and serving for belaying ropes, etc. **2.** a bollard resembling this in position and use.

**timber hitch** /ˈtɪmbə hɪtʃ/, *n.* a kind of hitch by which a rope is fastened to a spar.

**timbering** /ˈtɪmbərɪŋ/, *n.* **1.** building material of wood. **2.** →**timberwork.**

**timberland** /ˈtɪmbəlænd/, *n. U.S.* land covered with timber-producing forests.

**timber line** /ˈtɪmbə laɪn/, *n.* **1.** the altitude above sea-level at which timber ceases to grow. **2.** the arctic or antarctic limit of tree growth.

**timberman** /ˈtɪmbəmæn/, *n.* a person working in a timber yard.

**timber wolf** /ˈtɪmbə wʊlf/, *n.* the large brindled wolf, *Canis lupus lycaon,* of forested Canada and the northern U.S. Also, **grey wolf.**

timber wolf

**timberwork** /ˈtɪmbəwɜk/, *n.* work formed of timbers.

**timber yard** /ˈtɪmbə jad/, *n.* a place where timber is stored and sold.

**timbre** /ˈtɪmbə, ˈtæmbə/, *n.* **1.** *Acoustics, Phonet.* that characteristic quality of a sound, independent of pitch and loudness, from which its source or manner of production can be inferred. The saxophone and the clarinet have different timbres, and so do the vowels of *bait* and *boat.* Timbre depends on the relative strengths of the components of different frequencies, which are determined by resonance. **2.** *Music.* the characteristic quality of sound produced by a particular instrument or voice; tone colour. [F: quality of sound, orig., kind of tambourine, from L *tympanum,* from Gk *týmpanon* timbrel, kettledrum]

**timbrel** /ˈtɪmbrəl/, *n.* a tambourine or similar instrument. [diminutive of ME *timbre.* See TIMBRE]

**timbron** /ˈtɪmbrɒn/, *n.* an electronic musical instrument based on a synthesiser and having the capacity to alter timbre in response to varying pressure on a control board.

**Timbuktu** /tɪmbʌkˈtu/, *n.* any faraway place. [from *Timbuktu* town in central Mali, near the river Niger, Africa]

**time** /taɪm/, *n., adj., v.,* **timed, timing.** *–n.* **1.** the system of those relations which any event has to any other as past, present, or future; indefinite continuous duration regarded as that in which events succeed one another. **2.** duration regarded as belonging to the present life as distinct from the life to come, or from eternity. **3.** a system or method of measuring or reckoning the passage of time. **4.** a limited extent of time, as between two successive events: *a long time.* **5.** a particular period considered as distinct from other periods: *for the time being.* **6.** (*oft. pl.*) a period in the history of the world, or contemporary with the life or activities of a notable person: *ancient times.* **7.** (*oft. pl.*) the period or era now (or then) present. **8.** (*oft. pl.*) a period considered with reference to its events or prevailing conditions, tendencies, ideas, etc.: *hard times.* **9.** a prescribed or allotted period, as of one's life, for payment of a debt, etc. **10.** the normal or expected moment of death. **11.** the natural termination of the period of gestation. **12.** a period with reference to personal experience of a specified kind: *to have a good time.* **13.** a period of work of an employee, or the pay for it. **14.** *Colloq.* a term of imprisonment: *to do time.* **15.** the period necessary for or occupied by something: *to ask for time to consider.* **16.** leisure or spare time: *to have no time.* **17.** a particular or definite point in time: *what time is it?* **18.** a particular part of a year, day, etc.: *Christmas time.* **19.** an appointed, fit, due, or proper time: *there is a time for everything.* **20.** the particular moment at which something takes place: *opening time.* **21.** an indefinite period in the future: *time will tell.* **22.** the period in which an action is completed, esp. a performance in a race: *the winner's time was just under four minutes.* **23.** the right occasion or opportunity: *to watch one's time.* **24.** each occasion of a recurring action or event: *to do a thing five times.* **25.** (*pl.*) used as a multiplicative word in phrasal combinations expressing how many instances of a quantity or factor are taken together: *four times five.* **26.** *Drama.* one of the three unities. See **unity** (def. 10). **27.**

*Pros.* a unit or a group of units in the measurement of metre. **28.** *Music, etc.* **a.** tempo; relative rapidity of movement. **b.** the metrical duration of a note or rest. **c.** proper or characteristic tempo. **d.** the general movement of a particular kind of musical composition with reference to its rhythm, metrical structure, and tempo. **e.** the movement of a dance or the like to music so arranged: *waltz time.* **29.** *Mil.* the rate of marching, calculated on the number of paces taken per minute: *quick time.* **30. against time,** in an effort to finish something within a certain period. **31. ahead of one's time,** having ideas more advanced than those of the age in which one lives. **32. ahead of time,** before the time due; early. **33. at one time,** formerly. **34. at the same time,** nevertheless. **35. at times,** occasionally; at intervals. **36. behind the times,** old-fashioned. **37. do time,** to serve a prison sentence. **38. for the time being,** temporarily. **39. from time to time,** occasionally, at intervals. **40. in good time, a.** punctually; at the right time. **b.** early; with time to spare. **41. in no time,** very quickly. **42. in time, a.** soon or early enough. **b.** eventually; after a lapse of time. **c.** following the correct rhythm or tempo. **43. keep time, a.** to function accurately, as a clock. **b.** to observe the tempo or rhythm. **c.** to perform movements in unison in the same rhythm. **44. kill time,** to occupy oneself in some manner so as to make the time pass quickly. **45. many a time,** often; frequently. **46. no time,** a very short time. **47. on time,** punctually. **48. pass the time of day,** to have a brief conversation. **49. take one's time,** to be slow or leisurely. **50. take time out,** to spare the time, to make the effort (to do something). **51. time after time,** often; repeatedly. **52. time and (time) again,** often; repeatedly; again and again. **53. time of one's life,** *Colloq.* a very enjoyable experience. *–adj.* **54.** of, pertaining to, or showing the passage of time. **55.** (of an explosive device) containing a timing mechanism so that it will detonate at the desired moment: *a time bomb.* **56.** *Comm.* payable a stated period of time after presentment. **57.** of or pertaining to purchases with payment postponed. *–v.t.* **58.** to ascertain or record the time, duration, or rate of: *to time a race.* **59.** to fix the duration of. **60.** to fix or regulate the intervals between (actions, movements, etc.). **61.** to regulate as to time, as a train, a clock, etc. **62.** to appoint or choose the moment or occasion for. **63.** to mark the rhythm or measure of, as in music. **64.** *Music.* to classify (notes or syllables) according to metre, accent, rhythm, etc. *–v.i.* **65.** to keep time; sound or move in unison. [ME; OE *tīma,* c. Icel. *tīmi;* akin to TIDE]

**time allowance** /'– əlaʊəns/, *n.* an amount of time allowed off the normal working week without loss of pay, in consideration for working under certain unpleasant conditions.

**time and a half (quarter, third, etc.),** *n.* a rate of pay for overtime work equal to one and a half (quarter, third, etc.), times the regular hourly rate.

**time and motion study,** *n.* the systematic examination of methods of working, esp. in industrial organisations, in order to improve efficiency.

**time bomb** /'taɪm bɒm/, *n.* **1.** a bomb which contains a mechanism causing it to explode at a predetermined time. **2.** a situation, esp. political, which is expected to have a disastrous outcome.

**timebook** /'taɪmbʊk/, *n.* a book in which employees are required to sign their names and the times at which they arrive at work and depart.

**time capsule** /'taɪm kæpʃul/, *n.* a container in which are sealed objects and documents in the hope that they will display the current state of civilisation to whoever might eventually find it in later times.

**timecard** /'taɪmkad/, *n.* a card for recording the time at which an employee arrives and departs.

**time clock** /'taɪm klɒk/, *n.* a clock with an attachment by which a record may be made of the time of something, as of the arrival and departure of employees.

**time deposit** /'– dəpɒsət/, *n.* a deposit that can be withdrawn by the depositor only after he has given advance notice or after a period of time agreed upon has elapsed.

**time division multiplex,** *n.* a technique whereby two or more signals are formed into a single composite signal for transmitting over a link, and are recovered at the receiving end of the link.

**time-expired** /'taɪm-əkspaɪəd/, *adj.* (of a soldier, sailor, etc.) having completed a term of service.

**time exposure** /taɪm ɛk'spoʊʒə/, *n.* a long exposure in which the camera shutter is operated by hand, rather than by a built-in timing mechanism in the camera.

**time-honoured** /'taɪm-ɒnəd/, *adj.* revered or respected because of antiquity and long continuance: *a time-honoured custom.*

**time immemorial** /ˌtaɪm ɪmə'mɔriəl/, *n.* **1.** Also, **time out of mind.** a time extending back beyond memory or record. **2.** *Law.* time beyond legal memory, fixed by English statute as prior to the beginning of the reign of Richard I (1189).

**timekeeper** /'taɪmkipə/, *n.* **1.** one who or that which keeps time. **2.** (in a sports contest, etc.) one who observes and records the time taken by competitors in a race, the duration of an event, etc. **3.** →**timepiece. 4.** a person employed to keep account of the hours of work done by others and, sometimes, to pay them. **5.** one who beats time in music.

**time-lag** /'taɪm-læg/, *n.* the period of time between the occurrence of two closely connected events.

**time-lapse** /'taɪm-læps/, *adj.* of or pertaining to film, photography, etc., in which considerable time is allowed to elapse between successive exposures so that when the film is viewed at normal speed, the action photographed is enormously speeded up.

**time-lapse photography** /– fə'tɒgrəfi/, *n.* a method of recording a very slow process by making a large number of photographs on a film strip at regular intervals of time, these to be projected at normal speed, thus representing the process in a greatly condensed time span.

**timeless** /'taɪmləs/, *adj.* **1.** eternal; unending. **2.** referring to no particular time. **–timelessly,** *adv.* **–timelessness,** *n.*

**time limit** /'taɪm lɪmət/, *n.* a period of time within which something must be done.

**timely** /'taɪmli/, *adj.,* **-lier, -liest,** *adv.* *–adj.* **1.** occurring at a suitable time; seasonable; opportune; well-timed: *a timely warning.* **2.** *Rare.* early. *–adv.* **3.** seasonably; opportunely. **4.** *Archaic.* early or soon. **–timeliness,** *n.*

**time machine** /'taɪm məʃin/, *n.* an imagined machine in which people and objects may be taken into time past or time future.

**time-off** /taɪm-'ɒf/, *n.* →**time-out.**

**time-on** /taɪm-'ɒn/, *n.* **1.** resumption of play (in a football game, etc.) after time-out. **2.** extra time played at the completion of the normal period of the quarter to compensate for the stoppages of play.

**time-out** /taɪm-'aʊt/, *n.* **1.** a brief cessation of play at the request of a sports team for rest, consultation, or as a result of injury to a player. **2.** any short break from work or play.

**time out of mind,** *n.* →**time immemorial** (def. 1).

**time payment** /taɪm 'peɪmənt/, *n.* →**hire-purchase.**

**timepiece** /'taɪmpis/, *n.* **1.** an apparatus for measuring and recording the progress of time; a chronometer. **2.** a clock or a watch.

**timer** /'taɪmə/, *n.* **1.** one who or that which times. **2.** one who measures or records time. **3.** a device for indicating or measuring time, as a stopwatch.

**time-release capsule** /'taɪm-rəlis ˌkæpʃul/, *n.* a capsule (def. 2) in which the casing dissolves in sections, releasing dosages at intervals of time.

**timesaving** /'taɪmseɪvɪŋ/, *adj.* reducing time required: *timesaving devices or methods.*

**timeserver** /'taɪmsɜvə/, *n.* one who for selfish ends shapes his conduct to conform with the opinions of the time or of persons in power. **–timeserving,** *adj., n.*

**time-sharing** /'taɪm-ʃɛərɪŋ/, *n.* the handling by a computer of several programs at the same time.

**time sheet** /'taɪm ʃit/, *n.* a sheet or card recording the hours worked by an employee.

**time signal** /'– sɪgnəl/, *n.* a signal, esp. one sent by radio, indicating a precise moment of time and used as a means of regulating clocks, etc.

**time signature** /'– sɪgnətʃə/, *n.* a sign, usu. in the form of a fraction, indicating the rhythmical pattern of a piece or part of a piece of music, the numerator being the number of beats to the bar and the denominator the length of each beat as a fraction of a semibreve.

**timeslot** /'taɪmslɒt/, *n.* (in radio or television) the period of time, allocated for a program. Also, **slot.**

**time switch** /'taɪm swɪtʃ/, *n.* a switch operated by a clockwork or electric clock for activating a mechanism at a particular time.

**timetable** /'taɪmteɪbəl/, *n.* **1.** a schedule showing the times at which railway trains, buses, aeroplanes, etc., arrive and depart. **2.** a schedule of times of classes, lectures, etc., in a school, university, etc. **3.** any plan listing the times at which certain things are due to take place. *–v.t.* **4.** to incorporate into a timetable.

**time value** /'taɪm vælju/, *n.* the duration of a note in a musical score in relation to other notes in the musical system, and to the tempo of the composition.

**timeworn** /'taɪmwɔn/, *adj.* **1.** worn or impaired by time. **2.** showing the ravages or adverse effect of time.

**time zone** /'taɪm zoʊn/, *n.* one of the 24 regions or divisions of the globe approximately coinciding with meridians at successive hours from the observatory at Greenwich.

**timid** /'tɪməd/, *adj.* **1.** subject to fear; easily alarmed; timorous; shy. **2.** characterised by or indicating fear. [L *timidus* frightened] – **timidity** /tɪ'mɪdəti/, **timidness,** *n.* – **timidly,** *adv.*

**timing** /'taɪmɪŋ/, *n.* **1.** *Theat.* **a.** a synchronising of the various parts of a production for theatrical effect. **b.** the result or effect thus achieved. **c.** (in acting) the act of adjusting one's tempo of reading and movement for dramatic effect. **2.** *Sport.* the control of the speed of an action in order that it may reach its maximum at the proper moment. **3. a.** the mechanism which ensures that the valves in an internal-combustion engine open and close at the correct time. **b.** the process of adjusting this mechanism so that it operates correctly.

**timing chain** /'– tʃeɪn/, *n.* the chain which operates the timing in an internal-combustion engine by driving the camshaft from the crankshaft.

**timocracy** /taɪ'mɒkrəsi/, *n., pl.* **-cies. 1.** a form of government in which love of honour is the dominant motive of the rulers. **2.** a form of government in which a certain amount of property is requisite as a qualification for office. [earlier *timocratie,* from Gk *tīmokratía,* from *tīmḗ* price, (moral) worth] –**timocratic** /taɪmə'krætɪk/, **timocratical** /taɪmə'krætɪkəl/, *adj.*

**timorous** /'tɪmərəs/, *adj.* **1.** full of fear; fearful. **2.** subject to fear; timid. **3.** characterised by or indicating fear. [late ME, from ML *timōrōsus* fearful, frightened] – **timorously,** *adv.* – **timorousness,** *n.*

**timothy** /'tɪməθi/, *n.* a coarse grass, *Phleum pratense,* with cylindrical spikes, valuable as fodder. Also, **timothy grass.** [named after *Timothy* Hanson, U.S. farmer who first cultivated it in the early 18th C]

timothy

**timp.,** timpani.

**timpani** /'tɪmpəni/, *n.pl., sing.* **-no** /-noʊ/. a set of kettledrums. [It., from L *tympanum,* from Gk *týmpanon*]

**timpanist** /'tɪmpənəst/, *n.* →**tympanist.**

**tin** /tɪn/, *n., adj., v.,* **tinned, tinning.** *–n.* **1.** a low-melting, metallic element nearly approaching silver in colour and lustre, used in making alloys and in plating. *Symbol:* Sn (for *stannum*); *at. wt:* 118.69; *at. no.:* 50; *sp. gr.:* 7.31 at 20°C. **2.** tin plate. **3.** any shallow metal pan, esp. one used in baking. **4.** a hermetically sealed container for food, esp. one made of tin plate. **5.** any container made of tin plate. **6.** the contents of a tin. *–adj.* **7.** made or consisting of tin or tin plate. **8.** mean; worthless; counterfeit. **9.** indicating the tenth event of a series, as a wedding anniversary. *–v.t.* **10.** to cover or coat with a thin deposit of tin. **11.** to pack or preserve in tins, as foodstuffs. [ME and OE, c. G *Zinn*] – **tinlike,** *adj.*

**tinamou** /'tɪnəmu/, *n.* any of a group of birds (family Tinemidae), of South and Central America, superficially resembling the gallinaceous birds but more primitive, and hunted as game. [F, from Galibi *tinamu*]

**tin arse** /'tɪn as/, *n. Colloq.* a lucky person. Also, **tin bum.**

**tincal** /'tɪŋkəl/, *n.* crude native borax (the oriental name). [Malay *tingkal*]

**tin can** /tɪn 'kæn/, *n.* a sealed or covered metal can for foodstuffs, esp. one made of tin plate.

**tinct** /tɪŋkt/, *v.t.* **1.** *Obs.* to tinge or tint, as with colour. **2.** *Obs.* to imbue. *–adj.* **3.** *Poetic.* tinged; coloured; flavoured. *–n.* **4.** *Obs.* tint; tinge; colouring. [L *tinctus,* pp., coloured, tinged]

**tinctorial** /tɪŋk'tɔriəl/, *adj.* pertaining to colouring or dyeing.

**tincture** /'tɪŋktʃə/, *n., v.,* **-tured, -turing.** *–n.* **1.** *Pharm.* a solution of a medicinal substance in alcohol (or sometimes in a mixture of alcohol and ammonia or ether), prepared by maceration, digestion, or percolation. **2.** a slight infusion, as of some element or quality. **3.** a trace; a smack or smattering. **4.** *Her.* any of the metals, colours, or furs used in coats of arms, etc. **5.** *Obs.* a dye or pigment. *–v.t.* **6.** to impart a tincture or colour to; tinge. **7.** to imbue or impregnate with something. [ME, from L *tinctūra* dyeing, tingeing]

**tinder** /'tɪndə/, *n.* **1.** a material or preparation formerly used for catching the spark from a flint and steel struck together for fire or light. **2.** any dry substance that readily takes fire from a spark. [ME; OE *tynder,* c. G *Zunder*] – **tinder-like,** *adj.*

**tinderbox** /'tɪndəbɒks/, *n.* **1.** a box for holding tinder, usu. fitted with a flint and steel. **2.** one who or that which is highly excitable, inflammable, etc.

**tin disease** /'tɪn dəziz/, *n.* →**tin plague.**

**tine** /taɪn/, *n.* a sharp projecting point or prong, as of a fork or deer's antler. [ME *tyne,* var. of ME and OE *tind,* c. MHG *zint*]

**tinea** /'tɪniə/, *n.* any of several skin diseases caused by fungi. [NL, in L gnawing worm]

**tineid moth** /,tɪniɪd 'mɒθ/, *n.* any moth of the family Tineidae, as the clothes moth.

**tinfoil** /'tɪnfɔɪl/, *n.* **1.** tin, or an alloy of tin and lead, in the form of a thin sheet, formerly much used as a wrapping for drugs, confectionery, tobacco, etc. **2.** →**aluminium foil.**

**ting** /tɪŋ/, *v.t., v.i.* **1.** to cause to make, or to make, a high, clear, ringing sound. *–n.* **2.** a tinging sound. [imitative]

**ting-a-ling** /tɪŋ-ə-'lɪŋ/, *n.* a tingling sound, esp. one made by a small bell.

**tinge** /tɪnʒ/, *v.,* **tinged, tingeing** or **tinging,** *n.* *–v.t.* **1.** to impart a trace or slight degree of some colour to; tint. **2.** to impart a slight taste or smell to. *–n.* **3.** a slight degree of colouration. **4.** a slight admixture, as of some qualifying property or characteristic. [late ME, from L *tingere* dye, colour]

**tingle** /'tɪŋgəl/, *v.,* **-gled, -gling,** *n.* *–v.i.* **1.** to have a sensation of slight stings or prickly pains, from a sharp blow or from cold. **2.** to cause such a sensation. *–n.* **3.** a tingling sensation. **4.** the tingling action of cold, etc. **5.** *Colloq.* a telephone call. [ME; apparently var. of TINKLE] – **tingler,** *n.* – **tinglingly,** *adv.*

**tingle tingle** /'– tɪŋgəl/, *n.* either of two species of timber tree, *Eucalyptus jacksonii* and *E. guilfoylei,* found in south-western Australia.

**tin god** /tɪn 'gɒd/, *n.* **1.** a pompous, self-satisfied, dictatorial person, esp. one of minor importance who exercises some authority over others. **2.** an unworthy person who is mistakenly made the object of veneration or worship.

**tin hare** /– 'hɛə/, *n.* **1.** a single railway car, self-propelled by a diesel engine, commonly used on country lines. **2.** →**lure** (def. 4). **3.** *Colloq.* a delivery truck carrying beer. **4.** *Colloq.* the driver of such a truck.

**tin hat** /– 'hæt/, *n.* a steel helmet worn by soldiers.

**tinhorn** /'tɪnhɔn/, *U.S. Colloq.* *–n.* **1.** a pretentious or boastful person, esp. a gambler, who claims power, influence, resources, etc., which he does not possess. *–adj.* **2.** insignificant; petty; cheap.

**tinker** /'tɪŋkə/, *n.* **1.** a mender of pots, kettles, pans, etc., usu. an itinerant. **2.** an unskilful or clumsy worker; a bungler. **3.** one skilled in various minor kinds of mechanical work; a jack-of-all-trades. **4.** an act or instance of tinkering. **5.** a small species of mackerel, *Pneumatophorus grex,* of the Atlantic coast of the U.S. *–v.i.* **6.** to do the work of a tinker. **7.** to work unskilfully or clumsily at anything. **8.** to busy oneself with something, esp. a machine or an appliance, usu. without useful results. *v.t.* **9.** to mend as a tinker. **10.** to repair in an unskilful or makeshift way. [syncopated var.

of earlier *tinekere* worker in tin]

**tinker's cuss** /tɪŋkəz 'kʌs/, *n. Colloq.* something worthless or trivial: *his opinion is not worth a tinker's cuss.* Also, **tinker's damn.**

**tin-kettle** /tɪn-'kɛtl/, *v.t.*, **-tled, -tling.** *N.Z.* to welcome (a newly-wed couple) by noisy banging of tin-cans, etc.

**tinkle** /'tɪŋkəl/, *v.*, **-kled, -kling,** *n.* *–v.i.* **1.** to give forth or make a succession of short, light, ringing sounds. *–v.t.* **2.** to cause to tinkle or jingle. **3.** to make known, call attention to, attract, or summon by tinkling. *–n.* **4.** a tinkling sound. **5.** the act of tinkling. **6.** →**tingle** (def. 5). Also, **tingle.** [ME; frequentative of obs. *tink,* v., make a metallic sound; imitative] – **tinkling,** *n., adj.*

**tinktinkie** /'tɪŋktɪŋki/, *n.* a small, brown warbler-like bird with speckled breast, *Prinia maculosa,* family Muscicapidae, of southern Africa; Cape wren-warbler. [Afrikaans]

**tin lizzie** /tɪn 'lɪzi/, *n. Colloq.* any cheap, old, or decrepit motor vehicle.

**tinman** /'tɪnmən/, *n., pl.* **-men.** →**tinsmith.**

**tinman's solder** /tɪnmənz 'sɒldə/, *n.* a low-melting solder containing up to 65 per cent tin alloyed with lead, used for tinning.

**tinned** /tɪnd/, *adj.* **1.** covered or coated with tin or solder. **2.** preserved or packed in a can, as foodstuffs.

**tinned dog** /– 'dɒg/, *n. Colloq.* canned meat.

**tinner** /'tɪnə/, *n.* **1.** →**tinsmith.** **2.** →**canner** (def. 2).

**tinnie** /'tɪni/, *n. Colloq.* a can of beer. Also, **tinny.**

**tinnitus** /tə'naɪtəs, 'tɪnətəs/, *n.* a ringing or similar sensation of sound in the ears, due to disease of the auditory nerve, etc. [L: a ringing]

**tinny**[1] /'tɪni/, *adj.*, **-nier, -niest.** **1.** of or like tin. **2.** containing tin. **3.** characteristic of tin, as sounds; lacking resonance. **4.** not strong or durable. **5.** having the taste of tin. **6.** →**tinnie.** – **tinnily,** *adv.* – **tinniness,** *n.*

**tinny**[2] /'tɪni/, *adj. Colloq.* lucky.

**tin-opener** /'tɪn-oʊpnə/, *n.* a device for opening tins.

**tin-pan alley** /ˌtɪn-pæn 'æli/, *n.* **1.** the district of a city where most of the popular music is published. **2.** the realm of composers or publishers of popular music, or such persons as a group.

**tin plague** /'tɪn pleɪg/, *n.* an allotropic change which occurs to white tin, at low temperatures, causing it to change into the grey, powdery form. Also, **tin disease, tin pest.**

**tin plate** /– 'pleɪt/, *n.* thin sheet iron or sheet steel coated with tin.

**tin-plate** /'tɪn-pleɪt/, *v.t.*, **-plated, -plating.** to plate (sheet iron or steel) with tin.

**tin-pot** /'tɪn-pɒt/, *adj. Colloq.* inferior; petty; worthless.

**tin pyrites** /tɪn paɪ'raɪtiz/, *n.* →**stannite.**

**tinsel** /'tɪnsəl/, *n., adj., v.*, **-selled, -selling** or (*U.S.*) **-seled, -seling.** *–n.* **1.** an inexpensive glittering metallic substance, as copper, brass, etc., in thin sheets, used in pieces, strips, threads, etc., to produce a sparkling effect. **2.** a metallic yarn usu. wrapped around a core yarn of silk, rayon, or cotton, for weaving brocade or lamé. **3.** anything showy or attractive with little or no real worth; showy pretence. **4.** *Obs.* a fabric of silk or wool interwoven with threads of gold, silver, or (later) copper. *–adj.* **5.** consisting of or containing tinsel. **6.** showy; gaudy; tawdry. *–v.t.* **7.** to adorn with tinsel. **8.** to adorn with anything glittering. **9.** to make showy or gaudy. [F *étincelle* spark, flash, from L *scintilla*] – **tinsel-like,** *adj.*

**tinselly** /'tɪnsəli/, *adj.* cheap; gaudy; tawdry.

**tinsmith** /'tɪnsmɪθ/, *n.* one who works in or with tin; a maker of tinware. Also, **tinman, tinner, whitesmith.**

**tinsnips** /'tɪnsnɪps/, *n.* an implement designed to cut tin plate.

**tin soldier** /tɪn 'soʊldʒə/, *n.* **1.** a miniature toy soldier usu. made of lead. **2.** one who plays at being a soldier.

**tinstone** /'tɪnstoʊn/, *n.* →**cassiterite.**

**tint** /tɪnt/, *n.* **1.** a colour, or a variety of a colour; hue. **2.** a colour diluted with white; a colour of less than maximum chroma, purity, or saturation (as opposed to a *shade,* which is produced by adding black). **3.** a delicate or pale colour. **4.** *Engraving.* a uniform shading, as that produced by series of fine parallel lines. **5.** *Print.* a faintly or lightly coloured background upon which an illustration or the like is to be printed. **6.** any of various impermanent dyes for the hair. *–v.t.* **7.** to apply a tint or tints to; colour slightly or delicately; tinge. [var. of TINCT] – **tinter,** *n.*

**tintack** /'tɪntæk/, *n.* **1.** a short nail made of tin-plated iron. **2.** **get down to tintacks,** to deal with essentials.

**tintinnabular** /tɪntə'næbjələ/, *adj.* of or pertaining to bells or bellringing. Also, **tintinnabulary, tintinnabulous.** [L *tintinnābulum* bell + -AR[1]]

**tintinnabulation** /ˌtɪntənæbjə'leɪʃən/, *n.* the ringing or sound of bells.

**tintinnabulum** /ˌtɪntən'æbjələm/, *n.* a small bell. [L]

**tintometer** /tɪn'tɒmətə/, *n.* a colorimeter in which a colour is compared with a range of standard solutions or standard glass slides.

**tintype** /'tɪntaɪp/, *n.* a photograph (in the form of a positive) taken on a sensitised sheet of enamelled tin or iron; a ferrotype.

**tinware** /'tɪnwɛə/, *n.* articles made of tin plate.

**tinwork** /'tɪnwɜk/, *n.* **1.** something made of tin. **2.** (*pl., usu. construed as sing.*) an establishment for the mining or manufacture of tin or for the making of tinware.

**tiny** /'taɪni/, *adj.*, **-nier, -niest.** very small; minute; wee. [obs. *tine* very small (of unknown orig.) + -Y[1]]

**-tion,** a suffix used to form abstract nouns from verbs or stems not identical with verbs, whether as expressing action (*revolution, commendation*), or a state (*contrition, starvation*), or associated meanings (*relation, temptation*). Also, **-ation, -cion, -ion, -sion, -xion.** [L *-tio* (from *-t,* pp. stem ending, + *-io,* noun suffix); also representing F *-tion,* G *-tion,* etc., from L]

**tip**[1] /tɪp/, *n., v.*, **tipped, tipping.** *–n.* **1.** a slender or appointed exremity, esp. of anything long or tapered: *the tips of the fingers.* **2.** the top, summit, or apex. **3.** a small piece or part, as of metal or leather, forming the extremity of something. *–v.t.* **4.** to furnish with a tip. **5.** to serve as or form the tip of. **6.** to mark or adorn the tip of. [ME *typ,* c. D and LG *tip*] – **tipless,** *adj.*

**tip**[2] /tɪp/, *v.*, **tipped, tipping,** *n.* *–v.t.* **1.** to cause to assume a slanting or sloping position; incline; tilt. **2.** to overthrow, overturn, or upset (oft. fol. by *over* or *up*). **3.** to take off or lift (the hat) in salutation. **4.** to dispose of (rubbish, etc.) by dumping. **5.** *Print.* to print an illustration, map, etc. separately from the main work and paste it into the inner edge of the preceding or following page. (fol. by *in*). *–v.i.* **6.** to assume a slanting or sloping position; incline. **7.** to tilt up at one end and down at the other. **8.** to be overturned or upset. **9.** to tumble or topple (usu. fol. by *over* or *up*). *–n.* **10.** the act of tipping. **11.** the state of being tipped. **12.** a rubbish dump, esp. one near a mine, on which unwanted material is dumped. [ME *tipe;* orig. uncert.]

**tip**[3] /tɪp/, *n., v.*, **tipped, tipping.** *–n.* **1.** a small present of money given to someone, as a waiter, porter, etc., for performing a service; a gratuity. **2.** a piece of private or secret information, as for use in betting, speculation, etc. **3.** a useful hint or idea. *–v.t.* **4.** to give a small present of money to. **5. tip off** or **tip the wink,** *Colloq.* **a.** to give private or secret information about; inform. **b.** to warn of impending trouble, danger, etc. *–v.i.* **6.** to give a gratuity. [orig. unknown]

**tip**[4] /tɪp/, *n., v.*, **tipped, tipping.** *–n.* **1.** a light, smart blow; a tap. *–v.t.* **2.** to strike or hit with a light, smart blow; tap. **3.** *Cricket, etc.* to strike (the ball) with a glancing blow. [? akin to TAP[1]. Cf. G *tippen* tap]

**ti-palm** /'ti-pam/, *n.* →**ti-tree.**

**tip-and-run** /tɪp-ən-'rʌn/, *n.* a form of cricket in which the batsman must attempt to make a run each time he hits the ball.

**tip-cart** /'tɪp-kat/, *n.* →**tip-truck.**

**tipcat** /'tɪpkæt/, *n.* **1.** a game in which a short piece of wood, tapering at both ends, is struck lightly at one end with a stick so as to make it spring up, and while in the air is struck again for the purpose of driving it as far as possible. **2.** the piece of wood used in this game. Also, **cat, pussy.**

**tipi** /'tipi/, *n., pl.* **-pis.** →**tepee.**

**tip-off** /'tɪp-ɒf/, *n.* **1.** the act of tipping off. **2.** a hint or warning: *they got a tip-off about the raid.*

**tipper** /'tɪpə/, *n.* one who or that which tips.

**tippet** /'tɪpət/, *n.* **1.** a scarf, usu. of fur or wool, for covering the neck, or the neck and shoulders, and usu. having ends hanging down in front. **2.** *Eccles.* a band of silk or the like worn round the neck with the ends pendent in front. **3.** *Hist.* a long, narrow, pendent part of a hood, sleeve, etc. [ME: apparently from TIP[1]]

tippet (def. 3)

**tipple** /ˈtɪpəl/, *v.*, **-pled, -pling,** *n.* *–v.t.* **1.** to drink (wine, spirits, etc.), esp. repeatedly, in small quantities. *–v.i.* **2.** to drink alcoholic drink, esp. habitually or to some excess. *–n.* **3.** intoxicating liquor. [orig. uncert.; apparently akin to TIP[2]. Cf. Norw. *tipla* drink little and often] – **tippler,** *n.*

**tipstaff** /ˈtɪpstaf/, *n., pl.* **-staves** /-steɪvz/, **-staffs. 1.** an attendant or crier in a court of law. **2.** a staff tipped with metal, formerly carried as a badge of office, as by a constable. **3.** any official who carried such a staff.

**tipster** /ˈtɪpstə/, *n. Colloq.* one who makes a business of furnishing tips, as for use in betting, speculation, etc.

**tipsy** /ˈtɪpsi/, *adj.*, **-sier, -siest. 1.** slightly intoxicated. **2.** characterised by or due to intoxication: *a tipsy lurch.* **3.** tipping, unsteady, or tilted, as if from intoxication. [apparently from TIP[2] in obs. sense of intoxicate] – **tipsily,** *adv.* – **tipsiness,** *n.*

**tipsy cake** /ˈ– keɪk/, *n.* a kind of trifle decorated with almonds and soaked in wine. Also, **tipsy parson cake.**

**tiptoe** /ˈtɪptoʊ/, *n., v.*, **-toed, -toeing,** *adj., adv.* *–n.* **1.** the tip or end of a toe. **2. on tiptoe, a.** on the tips of the toes collectively: *to walk on tiptoe.* **b.** eagerly expectant. **c.** cautious; stealthy. *–v.i.* **3.** to move or go on tiptoe, as with caution or stealth. *–adj.* **4.** characterised by standing or walking on tiptoe. **5.** straining upwards. **6.** eagerly expectant. **7.** cautious; stealthy. *–adv.* **8.** on tiptoe.

**tiptop** /ˈtɪptɒp/, *n.* **1.** the extreme top or summit. **2.** *Colloq.* the highest point or degree, as of excellence. *–adj.* **3.** situated at the very top. **4.** *Colloq.* of the highest quality or excellence: *in tiptop condition.* [TIP[1] end + TOP[1] highest point; or varied reduplication of TOP[1]]

**tip-truck** /ˈtɪp-trʌk/, *n.* a truck whose body can be tilted to discharge the contents. Also, **dump-truck.**

**tirade** /taɪˈreɪd, təˈreɪd/, *n.* **1.** a prolonged outburst of denunciation. **2.** a long, vehement speech. **3.** a passage dealing with a single theme or idea, as in poetry. [F: draught, shot, from It. *tirata* volley, from *tirare* draw]

**tirage** /tɪˈraʒ/, *n.* **1.** the primary bottling of champagne-style wines. **2.** the act of drawing wine from a barrel. [Fr. *tirage,* drawing]

**tire**[1] /ˈtaɪə/, *v.*, **tired, tiring,** *n.* *–v.t.* **1.** to reduce or exhaust the strength of, as by exertion; make weary; fatigue (sometimes fol. by *out*). **2.** to exhaust the interest, patience, etc., of, as by long continuance or by dullness. *–v.i.* **3.** to have the strength reduced or exhausted, as by labour or exertion; become fatigued. **4.** to have one's appreciation, interest, patience, etc., exhausted; become or be weary (usu. fol. by *of*). [ME *tyre,* OE *tȳrian;* of unknown orig.]

**tire**[2] /ˈtaɪə/, *n., v.*, **tired, tiring.** *U.S.* →**tyre.**

**tire**[3] /ˈtaɪə/, *v.*, **tired, tiring,** *n.* *Archaic.* *–v.t.* **1.** to attire or array. **2.** to dress (the head or hair), esp. with a headdress. *–n.* **3.** attire or dress. **4.** a headdress. [ME; aphetic var. of ATTIRE]

**tired** /ˈtaɪəd/, *adj.* **1.** exhausted, as by exertion; fatigued. **2.** weary; bored (usu. fol. by *of*). **3.** *Colloq.* impatient or disgusted: *you make me tired!* **4.** trite; hackneyed; lacking originality. [TIRE[1] + -ED[2]] – **tiredly,** *adv.* – **tiredness,** *n.*

**tireless** /ˈtaɪələs/, *adj.* untiring; indefatigable: *a tireless worker.* – **tirelessly,** *adv.* – **tirelessness,** *n.*

**tiresome** /ˈtaɪəsəm/, *adj.* **1.** such as to tire one; wearisome. **2.** annoying or vexatious. – **tiresomely,** *adv.*

**tiring room** /ˈtaɪərɪŋ rum/, *n. Archaic.* a dressing-room, esp. in a theatre. [aphetic var. of *attiring room*]

**tiro** /ˈtaɪroʊ/, *n., pl.* **-ros.** →**tyro.**

**'tis** /tɪz/, contraction of *it is.*

**tisane** /təˈsan, -ˈzan/, *n.* **1.** a herbal tea. **2.** *Obs.* →**ptisan.** [F: barley water. See PTISAN]

**tissue** /ˈtɪʃu/, *n., v.*, **-sued, -suing.** *–n.* **1.** *Biol.* **a.** the substance of which an organism or part is composed. **b.** an aggregate of cells and cell products forming a definite kind of structural material in an animal or plant: *muscular tissue.* **2.** a woven fabric, esp. one of light or gauzy texture, originally woven with gold or silver. **3.** an interwoven or interconnected series or mass: *a tissue of falsehoods.* **4.** any of several kinds of soft gauzelike papers used for various purposes. **5.** a paper handkerchief. **6.** →**tissue paper. 7.** a cigarette paper. *–v.t. Rare.* **8.** to weave, esp. with threads of gold or silver. **9.** to clothe or adorn with tissue. [ME, from OF *tissu* rich kind of cloth, pp. of *tistre* weave, from L *texere*]

**tissue culture** /ˈ– kʌltʃə/, *n.* **1.** the science of cultivating animal tissue in a prepared medium. **2.** the process itself.

**tissue paper** /ˈ– peɪpə/, *n.* a very thin, almost transparent paper used for wrapping delicate articles, covering illustrations in books, copying letters, etc.

**tit**[1] /tɪt/, *n.* **1.** any of various small Australian birds, esp. a thornbill. **2.** any of various birds of the family Paridae, as the **blue tit,** *Parsus caeruleus.* **3.** any of various other small birds. [ME *tit-,* c. Icel. *tittr* titmouse, d. Norw. *titta* little girl]

**tit**[2] /tɪt/, *n.* **1.** a nipple. **2.** *Colloq.* a female breast. [ME and OE, c. G *Zitze,* MD, LG *titte*]

**Tit.,** *Bible.* Titus.

**titan** /ˈtaɪtn/, *n.* (*also cap.*) a person or thing of enormous size, strength, etc. [Gk *Titan,* one of a family of primordial deities, of gigantic size and strength]

**titanate** /ˈtaɪtəneɪt/, *n.* a salt of titanic acid (def. 2).

**titania** /taɪˈteɪniə/, *n.* →**titanium dioxide.**

**titanic**[1] /taɪˈtænɪk/, *adj.* of enormous size, strength, etc.; gigantic. [TITAN + -IC]

**titanic**[2] /taɪˈtænɪk/, *adj.* of or containing titanium, esp. in the tetravalent state. [TITAN(IUM) + -IC]

**titanic acid** /– ˈæsəd/, *n.* **1.** →**titanium dioxide. 2.** any of various acids derived from it.

**titanic oxide** /– ˈɒksaɪd/, *n.* →**titanium dioxide.**

**titaniferous** /taɪtənˈɪfərəs/, *adj.* containing or yielding titanium. [TITANI(UM) + -FEROUS]

**titanite** /ˈtaɪtənaɪt/, *n.* →**sphene.** [TITANIUM]

**titanium** /taɪˈteɪniəm/, *n.* a metallic element occurring combined in various minerals, and isolated as a dark grey powder with a metallic lustre and an ironlike appearance. It is used in metallurgy to remove oxygen and nitrogen from steel and to toughen it. *Symbol:* Ti; *at. wt.:* 47.90; *at. no.:* 22; *sp. gr.:* 4.5 at 20°C. [TITAN + -IUM]

**titanium dioxide** /– daɪˈɒksaɪd/, *n.* a white insoluble powder, $TiO_2$, used as a white pigment and in ceramics. Also, **titanium oxide, titanic oxide, titanic acid, titania.**

**titanosaurus** /taɪtənəˈsɔrəs/, *n.* a South American dinosaur (genus *Titanosaurus*) of the Cretaceous era. Also, **titanosaur.** [NL *Tītāno-* (from Gk, combining form of *Tītān* Titan) + *-saurus* -SAURUS]

**titanous** /taɪˈtænəs/, *adj.* containing trivalent titanium.

**titbit** /ˈtɪtbɪt/, *n.* **1.** a delicate bit of food. **2.** a choice or pleasing bit of anything. Also, *U.S.,* **tidbit.** [var. of TIDBIT]

**titer** /ˈtaɪtə, ˈti-/, *n. U.S.* →**titre.**

**titfer** /ˈtɪtfə/, *n. Colloq.* a hat. [rhyming slang, *tit for tat* hat]

**tit for tat,** *n.* blow for blow; an equivalent given in retaliation, repartee, etc. [? var. of earlier *tip for tap*]

**tithable** /ˈtaɪðəbəl/, *adj.* liable to be tithed; subject to the payment of tithes.

**tithe** /taɪð/, *n., v.*, **tithed, tithing.** *–n.* **1.** (*oft. pl.*) the tenth part of the annual produce of agriculture, etc., due or paid as a tax for the support of the priesthood, religious institutions, etc. **2.** any tax, levy, or the like, of one tenth. **3.** a tenth part, or any indefinitely small part, of anything. *–v.t.* **4.** to give or pay a tithe or tenth of (produce, earnings, etc.). **5.** to pay tithes on. **6.** to exact a tithe from (a person, etc.). **7.** to levy a tithe on (produce, goods, etc.). *–v.i.* **8.** *Obs.* to give or pay a tithe. [ME *tithen,* OE *te(o)g(o)thian,* v., from *teogotha* tenth part] – **titheless,** *adj.* – **tither,** *n.*

**tithing** /ˈtaɪðɪŋ/, *n.* **1.** a tithe. **2.** a giving or exacting of tithes. [ME; OE *tigething,* from *teogotha* TITHE]

**titi**[1] /ˈtiti/, *n., pl.* **-tis.** any of various small reddish or greyish monkeys of the genus *Callicebus* of South America. [native name; orig. uncert.]

**titi**[2] /'titi/, *n., pl.* **-tis.** any of the shrubs or small trees of the family Cyrillaceae of the southern U.S., esp. *Cliftonia monophylla* (**black titi**) and *Cyrilla racemiflora* (**white titi**), with glossy leaves and racemes of white flowers. [S Amer. Sp., from Aymara]

**titi**[3] /'titi/, *n. N.Z.* →**mutton-bird.** [Maori]

**titian** /'tɪʃən, 'ti-/, *n.* a reddish or reddish brown colour. [made famous by the Italian painter Tiziano Vecellio *Titian,* c. 1477-1576]

**titillate** /'tɪtəleɪt/, *v.t.,* **-lated, -lating. 1.** to tickle; excite a tingling or itching sensation in, as by touching or stroking lightly. **2.** to excite agreeably: *to titillate the fancy.* [L *titillātus* tickled] – **titillation** /tɪtə'leɪʃən/, *n.* – **titillative** /'tɪtəleɪtɪv/, *adj.*

**titivate** /'tɪtəveɪt/, *v.,* **-vated, -vating.** *Colloq. –v.t.* **1.** to make smart or spruce. *–v.i.* **2.** to make oneself smart or spruce. Also, **tittivate, tidivate.** [earlier *tiddivate,* ? from TIDY, modelled on CULTIVATE] – **titivation** /tɪtə'veɪʃən/, *n.* – **titivator,** *n.*

**titlark** /'tɪtlak/, *n.* any of the pipits, small lark-like birds, esp. of the genus *Anthus,* as *A. spinoletta,* a migratory bird of northern parts of both the New and Old Worlds. [TIT[1] + LARK[1]]

**title** /'taɪtl/, *n., v.,* **-tled, -tling.** *–n.* **1.** the distinguishing name of a book, poem, picture, piece of music, or the like. **2.** a descriptive heading or caption, as of a chapter, section, or other part of a book. **3.** a titlepage. **4.** a descriptive or distinctive appellation, esp. one belonging to a person by right of rank, office, attainment, etc. **5.** *Sport.* the championship: *he lost the title.* **6.** established or recognised right to something. **7.** a ground for a claim. **8.** anything affording ground for a claim. **9.** *Law.* **a.** legal right to the possession of property, esp. real property. **b.** the ground or evidence of such right. **c.** the instrument constituting evidence of such right. **d.** a unity combining all the requisites to complete legal ownership. **e.** a division of a statute, lawbook, etc., esp. one larger than an article or section. **f.** (in pleading) the designation of one's basis for judicial relief; the cause of action sued upon, as contract, tort, etc. **10.** *Eccles.* **a.** a fixed sphere of work and source of income, required as a condition of ordination. **b.** any of certain Catholic churches in Rome, the nominal incumbents of which are cardinals. *–v.t.* **11.** to furnish with a title; designate by an appellation; entitle. [ME, from OF, from L *titulus;* replacing OE *titul,* from L *titulus*]

**titled** /'taɪtld/, *adj.* having title, esp. of nobility.

**title deed** /'taɪtl did/, *n.* a deed or document containing or constituting evidence of ownership.

**titleholder** /'taɪtlhouldə/, *n.* **1.** one who holds a title. **2.** *Sport.* one who is the current holder of a championship.

**titlepage** /'taɪtlpeɪdʒ/, *n.* the page at the beginning of a volume which indicates the title, author's or editor's name, and publication information (usu. the publisher, and the place and date of publication).

**title role** /'taɪtl roul/, *n.* (in a play, opera, etc.) the role or character from which the title is derived. Also, **title part.**

**titmouse** /'tɪtmaus/, *n., pl.* **-mice** /-maɪs/. any of various small birds constituting the family Paridae, as *Parus atricapillus* of the New and Old Worlds. [ME *titmose,* from TIT[1] + *mose* (OE *māse*) titmouse, by association with MOUSE]

**titoki** /ti'touki/, *n.* a tough-timbered berry-bearing New Zealand forest tree, *Alectryon excelsum,* resembling the ash in foliage and wood. [Maori]

**titrate** /'taɪtreɪt/, *v.t., v.i.,* **-trated, -trating.** to ascertain the quantity of a given constituent present in a solution by accurately measuring the volume of a liquid reagent of known strength necessary to convert the constituent into another form. [F *titrer* titrate + -ATE[1]. See TITRE] – **titration** /taɪ'treɪʃən/, *n.*

**titre** /'taɪtə, 'ti-/, *n.* **1.** the amount of a substance by volume or weight which exactly fulfils certain given requirements of titration. **2.** the strength of a standard solution used in titration. Also, *U.S.,* **titer.** [F *titre* fineness, strength, from L *titulus* title]

**ti-tree** /'ti-tri/, *n.* **1.** →**ti**[1]. **2.** →**tea-tree.**

**tit-tat-toe** /tɪt-tæt-'tou/, *n.* →**tick-tack-toe.**

**titter** /'tɪtə/, *v.i.* **1.** to laugh in a low, half-restrained way, as from nervousness or in ill-suppressed amusement. *–n.* **2.** a tittering laugh. [cf. d. Swed. *tittra* giggle] – **titterer,** *n.* – **titteringly,** *adv.*

**tittivate** /'tɪtəveɪt/, *v.t., v.i.,* **-vated, -vating.** →**titivate.**

**tittle** /'tɪtl/, *n.* **1.** a dot or other small mark in writing or printing, used, for example, as a diacritic. **2.** a very small part or quantity; a particle, jot, or whit. [ME *titel,* from ML *titulus* mark over letter or word. See TITLE]

**tittle-tattle** /'tɪtl-tætl/, *n., v.,* **-tled, -tling.** *–n.* **1.** gossip; telltale. *–v.i.* **2.** to reveal private or confidential matters in idle gossip; act as a tale-bearer. [varied reduplication of TATTLE] – **tittle-tattler,** *n.*

**tittup** /'tɪtəp/, *n., v.,* **-tupped, -tupping.** *–n.* **1.** a prancing movement; a curvet. *–v.i.* **2.** to go with an up-and-down movement; prance; caper. [Brit. d. *tit* pull + UP]

**titty** /'tɪti/, *n.* **1.** a nipple. **2.** *Colloq.* a female breast. [OE *tittig*]

**titubation** /tɪtʃə'beɪʃən/, *n.* a disturbance of body equilibrium in standing or walking, resulting in an uncertain gait and trembling, the result of a disease of the cerebellum. [L *titubātio* staggering, stammering]

**titular** /'tɪtʃələ/, *adj.* **1.** of, pertaining to, or of the nature of a title. **2.** having a title, esp. of rank. **3.** existing or being such in title only: *a titular prince.* **4.** from whom or which a title or name is taken. **5.** designating any of the Roman Catholic churches in Rome whose nominal incumbents are cardinals. *–n.* **6.** one who bears a title. **7.** one from whom or that from which a title or name is taken. **8.** the benefice or cure conferring its name or style upon a dignitary who may delegate the obligations of this office; sinecure. [L *titulus* TITLE + -AR[1]] – **titularly,** *adv.*

**titulary** /'tɪtʃələri/, *adj., n., pl.* **-laries.** →**titular.**

**Tiwi** /'tiwi/, *n.* an Australian Aboriginal language, used by about one thousand speakers on Bathurst and Melville Islands, off the coast of the Northern Territory.

**tizz** /tɪz/, *n. Colloq.* a state of somewhat hysterical confusion and anxiety, often expressed in frantic but ineffectual activity: *don't get in a tizz.* Also, **tizzy.**

**tizzy** /'tɪzi/, *n., pl.* **-zies.** *Colloq.* **1.** →**tizz.** *–adj.* **2.** gaudy, vulgar; tinselly.

**T-junction** /'ti-dʒʌŋkʃən/, *n.* a junction where a road meets another going across it at right angles, as in the letter T. Also, **T-intersection.**

**tjuringa** /tjə'rɪŋgə/, *n.* →**churinga.**

**t.k.o.,** technical knockout.

**Tl,** *Chem.* thallium.

**TLC** /ti ɛl 'si/, *n. Colloq.* sympathetic attention. [*T(ender) L(oving) C(are)*]

**T.L.C.** /ti ɛl'si/, Trades and Labour Council. Also, **TLC.**

**Tm,** *Chem.* thulium.

**T.M.** /ti 'ɛm/, *n.* transcendental meditation.

**tmesis** /'tmisəs, 'misəs/, *n.* the separation of words that constitute a compound or construction by the insertion of other elements, as *a great man and good* instead of *a great and good man.* [Gk: a cutting]

**Tn,** *Chem.* thoron.

**TNB,** *Chem.* trinitrobenzene. Also, **T.N.B.**

**T note** /'ti nout/, *n. Colloq.* a Treasury note.

**TNT** /ti ɛn 'ti/, *Chem.* trinitrotoluene. Also, **T.N.T.**

**to** /tu/; *weak form* /tə/, *prep.* **1.** expressing motion or direction towards something: *from north to south.* **2.** indicating limit of movement or extension: *rotten to the core.* **3.** expressing contact or contiguity: *apply varnish to the surface.* **4.** expressing a point or limit in time: *to this day.* **5.** expressing time until and including: *Monday to Friday.* **6.** expressing aim, purpose, or intention: *going to the rescue.* **7.** expressing destination or appointed end: *sentenced to death.* **8.** indicating result or consequence: *to his dismay.* **9.** indicating state or condition: *he tore it to pieces.* **10.** indicating the object of inclination or desire: *they drank to his health.* **11.** expressing the object of a right or claim: *claimants to an estate.* **12.** expressing limit in degree or amount: *punctual to the minute; goods to the value of $100.* **13.** indicating addition or amount: *adding insult to injury; they danced to music.* **14.** expressing attachment or adherence: *the paper stuck to the wall; he held to his opinions.* **15.** expressing comparison or opposition: *the score was 9 to 5.* **16.** expressing agreement or accordance: *a position to one's liking.* **17.** expressing reference or relation: *what will he say to this?* **18.** expressing relative position: *one line parallel to another.* **19.** indicating proportion or ratio: *one teacher to every thirty students.* **20.** supplying the place or sense of the dative case in other languages, connecting transitive verbs with their indirect or distant objects, and adjectives, nouns, and intransitive or passive verbs with a following noun which limits their action or application. **21.** used as the ordinary sign or accompaniment of the infinitive (expressing originally motion, direction, purpose, etc., as in the ordinary uses with a substantive object, but now appearing in many cases as a mere meaningless sign). *–adv.* **22.** towards a person, thing, or point implied or understood. **23.** to a contact point or closed position: *pull the shutters to.* **24.** to a matter; to action or work: *we turned to with a will.* **25.** to consciousness; to one's senses: *after he came to.* **26. to and fro, a.** to and from some place or thing. **b.** in opposite or different directions alternately. [ME and OE *tō*, c. G *zu*]

**t/o,** turnover.

**T.O.** /ti 'oʊ/, Technical Officer.

**toad** /toʊd/, *n.* **1.** the terrestrial species of tailless (i.e., froglike) amphibians of the genus *Bufo* and allied genera. **2.** any of various tailless amphibians (order Salientia). **3.** any of various other animals, as certain lizards. See **horned toad. 4.** a person or thing as an object of disgust or aversion. [ME *tode,* OE *tādige;* orig. unknown] – **toadlike,** *adj.*

toad

**toadfish** /'toʊdfɪʃ/, *n.* **1.** in Australia, the toado. **2.** →**frogfish** (def. 1).

**toadflax** /'toʊdflæks/, *n.* **1.** a perennial herb, *Linaria vulgaris,* family Scrophulariaceae, of western Eurasia, now widely naturalised, having yellow and orange flowers; bacon-and-eggs. **2.** any of various herbs of the closely related genera *Linaria* and *Kickxia,* mainly of Mediterranean regions.

toadfish (def. 1)

**toad-in-the-hole** /toʊd-ɪn-ðə-'hoʊl/, *n.* meat, esp. sausages, baked in batter.

**toado** /'toʊdoʊ/, *n.* any of numerous species of poisonous, self-inflating fishes of the family Tetraodontidae, found in warm seas around Australia and elsewhere; a puffer. [TOAD + -O]

**toad-rush** /'toʊd-rʌʃ/, *n.* a small annual rush, *Juncus bufonius,* common in wet muddy places throughout temperate regions.

**toad spittle** /'toʊd spɪtl/, *n.* →**cuckoo-spit.**

**toadstone** /'toʊdstoʊn/, *n.* any of various stones or stone-like objects, formerly supposed to have been formed in the head or body of a toad, worn as jewels or amulets.

**toadstool** /'toʊdstul/, *n.* **1.** any of various fleshy fungi having a stalk with an umbrella-like cap, esp. the agarics. **2.** a poisonous agaric, as distinguished from an edible one. **3.** any of various other fleshy fungi, as the puffballs, coral fungi, etc.

**toady**[1] /'toʊdi/, *n., pl.* **toadies,** *v.,* **toadied, toadying.** *–n.* **1.** an obsequious sycophant; a fawning flatterer. *–v.t.* **2.** to be the toady to. *–v.i.* **3.** to be a toady. [shortened form of obs. *toadeater,* a mountebank's assistant who pretended to eat toads from which his master had supposedly removed the poison; hence a servile hanger-on] – **toadyish,** *adj.* – **toadyism,** *n.*

toadflax

**toady**[2] /'toʊdi/, *n. Colloq.* →**toado.**

**to-and-fro** /tu-ən-'froʊ/, *adv.* back and forth.

**to-and-from** /tu-ən-'frɒm/, *n. Colloq.* an Englishman. [rhyming slang, *to-and-from,* pom]

**toast**[1] /toʊst/, *n.* **1.** bread in slices browned on both surfaces by heat. *–v.t.* **2.** to brown, as bread or cheese, by exposure to heat. **3.** to heat or warm thoroughly at a fire. *–v.i.* **4.** to become toasted. [ME *tost(en),* from OF *toster,* from L *torrēre* dry, parch]

**toast**[2] /toʊst/, *n.* **1.** a person whose health is proposed and drunk; an event, sentiment, or the like, to which one drinks. **2.** a call on another or others to drink to some person or thing. **3.** the act of thus drinking. **4.** words of congratulation, appreciation, loyalty, etc., spoken before drinking. **5.** a person who is very popular, celebrated, suddenly famous: *she was the toast of the town. –v.t.* **6.** to propose as a toast. **7.** to drink to the health of, or in honour of. *–v.i.* **8.** to propose or drink a toast. [fig. use of TOAST[1], *n.,* with ref. to a piece of toast being put into a beverage to flavour it]

**toaster**[1] /'toʊstə/, *n.* **1.** one who toasts something. **2.** an instrument or apparatus for toasting bread, cheese, etc. [TOAST[1], *v.* + -ER[1]]

**toaster**[2] /'toʊstə/, *n.* one who proposes, or joins in, a toast or health. [TOAST[2], *v.* + -ER[1]]

**toastie pie** /toʊsti 'paɪ/, *n.* →**jaffle.**

**toasting fork** /'toʊstɪŋ fɔk/, *n.* a fork with a long handle on which bread, or the like, can be toasted over a fire.

**toastmaster** /'toʊstmastə/, *n.* **1.** one who presides at a dinner and introduces the after-dinner speakers. **2.** one who proposes or announces toasts. – **toastmistress,** *n. fem.*

**toast-rack** /'toʊst-ræk/, *n.* **1.** a stand in which slices of toast are placed to stand upright, separated by partitions. **2.** *Colloq.* (formerly) a type of tramcar used in Sydney.

**toatoa** /'toʊə,toʊə/, *n.* either of the small coniferous New Zealand trees, *Phyllocladus glaucus* and *P. alpinus.* [Maori]

**tobacco** /tə'bækoʊ/, *n., pl.* **-cos, -coes. 1.** any plant of the genus *Nicotiana,* esp. one of those species, as *N. tabacum,* whose leaves are prepared for smoking or chewing or as snuff. **2.** the leaves so prepared. **3.** any of various similar plants of other genera. [Sp. *tabaco,* from Arawak (from Guarani) pipe for smoking, or roll of leaves smoked, or plant] – **tobaccoless,** *adj.*

**tobacco heart** /'– hat/, *n.* a functional disorder of the heart, characterised by a rapid and often irregular pulse, due to excessive use of tobacco.

**tobacconist** /tə'bækənəst/, *n.* one who retails tobacco, cigarettes, and other items connected with smoking.

**to-be** /tə-'bi/, *adj.* future (esp. in combination): *mother-to-be.*

**toboggan** /tə'bɒgən/, *n.* **1.** a light sledge with low runners, used in the sport of tobogganing. **2.** a long, narrow, flat-bottomed sledge made of a thin board curved upwards and backwards at the front end, used originally for transport over snow. *–v.i.* **3.** to use, or coast on, a toboggan. **4.** *U.S.* to fall rapidly, as prices, one's fortune, etc. [Canadian F *tabagane,* etc., from Abnaki (Algonquian) *udaba'gan* (what is) used for dragging, from *uda'be* he drags; cf. *udabauask* sleigh] – **tobogganer, tobogganist,** *n.*

**toby** /'toʊbi/, *n.* a stick used to raddle sheep not shorn to the owner's satisfaction.

**toby jug** /'– dʒʌg/, *n.* **1.** Also, **toby.** a small jug or mug in the form of a stout old man wearing a three-cornered hat. **2.** *U.S. Colloq.* a long, slender, cheap cigar. [short for *Tobias*]

toby jug

**toccata** /tə'katə/, *n.* a composition in the style of an improvisation, for the piano, organ, or other keyboard instrument, intended to exhibit the player's technique. [It.: (pp. fem.) touched, from *toccare* TOUCH]

**tocology** /tə'kɒlədʒi/, *n.* →**obstetrics.** Also, **tokology.** [Gk *tóko(s)* child + -LOGY]

**tocopherol** /tə'kɒfərəl/, *n.* one of several alcohols which comprise the reproductive dietary factor known as vitamin E, occurring in wheat-germ oil, lettuce or spinach leaves, egg yolk, etc. The most active form is **alpha-tocopherol.** [Gk *tókos* child + Gk *phérein* + -OL[1]]

**tocsin** /'tɒksən/, *n.* **1.** a signal, esp. of alarm, sounded on a bell or bells. **2.** a bell used to sound an alarm. [F, from Pr. *tocasenh,* from *toca(r)* touch, strike + *senh* sign, bell (from L *signum* sign, ML bell)]

**tod** /tɒd/, *n.* **1.** an English unit of weight, chiefly for wool, commonly equal to 28 lbs but varying locally. **2.** a load. **3.**

a bushy mass, esp. of ivy. [ME *todde.* Cf. d. Swed. *todd* mass (of wool), Fris. *todde* small load]

**today** /tə'deɪ/, *n.* **1.** this present day. **2.** this present time or age. *–adv.* **3.** on this present day. **4.** at the present time; in these days. [ME; OE *to dæg.* See TO, prep., DAY]

**toddle** /'tɒdl/, *v.,* **-dled, -dling,** *n.* *–v.i.* **1.** to go with short, unsteady steps, as a child or an old person. *–n.* **2.** the act of toddling. **3.** an unsteady gait. [b. TOTTER and WADDLE]

**toddler** /'tɒdlə/, *n.* one who toddles, esp. a very young child.

**toddy** /'tɒdi/, *n., pl.* **-dies. 1.** a drink made of spirits and hot water, sweetened and sometimes spiced with cloves. **2.** the drawn sap, esp. when fermented, of various species of palm **(toddy palms),** used as a drink. [Hind. *tārī,* from *tār* palm tree]

**to-do** /tə-'du/, *n., pl.* **-dos.** *Colloq.* bustle; fuss.

**tody** /'toʊdi/, *n., pl.* **-dies.** any of the small insectivorous West Indian birds constituting the family Todidae, related to the motmots and kingfishers, and having a brightly coloured green and red plumage. [F *todier,* from L *todus,* name of small bird]

**toe** /toʊ/, *n., v.,* **toed, toeing.** *–n.* **1.** (in man) one of the terminal members or digits of the foot. **2.** an analogous part in other animals. **3.** the forepart of the foot or hoof of a horse or the like. **4.** a part, as of a stocking or shoe, to cover the toes. **5.** a part resembling a toe in shape or position. **6.** the outer end of the hitting surface of a golf club or hockey stick. **7.** *Railways.* the end of a frog in front of the point and in the direction of travel. **8.** *Mach.* **a.** a journal or part placed vertically in a bearing, as the lower end of a vertical shaft. **b.** an arm or projecting part on which a cam or the like strikes. **9. hit the toe,** *Prison Colloq.* to attempt to escape. **10. on one's toes,** prepared to act; wide-awake. **11. tread on someone's toes,** to offend, esp. by ignoring (another's) area of responsibility. **12. all done up like a sore toe,** *Colloq.* overdressed. **13. stick out like a sore toe,** *Colloq.* to be obvious. *–v.t.* **14.** to furnish with a toe or toes. **15.** to touch or reach with the toes. **16.** to kick with the toe. **17.** *Golf.* to strike (the ball) with the toe of the club. **18.** to adjust (the wheels of a motor car) so that each pair is at the angle of convergence or divergence required (fol. by *in, out*). **19. toe the line,** *Colloq.* to behave according to the rules; conform. [ME; OE *tā,* c. G *Zeh(e),* Icel. *tā*] **–toeless,** *adj.* **–toelike,** *adj.*

**toea** /'toʊiə/, *n.* the smaller of the two units of currency in Papua New Guinea; one hundredth of a kina. [Papuan]

**toecap** /'toʊkæp/, *n.* a cap to strengthen the toe of a shoe or boot.

**toe-crack** /'toʊ-kræk/, *n.* a sand-crack on the front of a horse's hoof.

**toed** /toʊd/, *adj.* having a toe or toes: *five-toed.*

**toehold** /'toʊhoʊld/, *n.* **1.** a small ledge or niche, just enough for the toe, in climbing. **2.** any means of support, entry, access, etc. **3.** *Wrestling.* a type of hold whereby the wrestler wrenches the foot of his opponent.

**toe-in** /'toʊ-ɪn/, *n.* a slight forward convergence of the wheels of a motor vehicle, used to improve steering stability.

**toe jam** /'toʊ dʒæm/, *n. Colloq.* the dirt which collects between the toes.

**toenail** /'toʊneɪl/, *n.* the nail growing on each of the toes of the human foot.

**toe-out** /'toʊ-aʊt/, *n.* the setting of the front wheels of a motor vehicle so that they point slightly outwards, common in front-wheel drive cars to improve steering stability.

**toe rag** /'toʊ ræg/, *n.* (formerly) a small piece of cloth wrapped around the toes to protect them from chafing, worn in place of socks.

**toe-ragger** /'toʊ-rægə/, *n. Colloq.* **1.** a swagman; a down-and-out. **2.** *Prison.* a prisoner serving a short sentence.

**toe sock** /'toʊ sɒk/, *n.* a sock with a separate place for each toe.

**toetoe** /'tɔɪtɔɪ, 'toʊitoʊi, toʊi'toʊi/, *n. N.Z.* →**cutting-grass.** [Maori]

**toey** /'toʊi/, *adj. Colloq.* **1.** anxious; apprehensive. **2.** →**randy** (def. 2). **3.** keen, ready to go. **4.** (of a horse) having an excitable temperament; fast.

**toff** /tɒf/, *n. Colloq.* a rich, upper-class, usu. well-dressed person; a gentleman. **–toffy,** *adj.*

**toffee** /'tɒfi/, *n.* a sweet made of sugar or treacle boiled down, often with butter, nuts, etc. Also, **toffy;** *U.S.,* **taffy.** [earlier *taffy, tuffy,* of unknown orig.; ? associated with TOUGH]

**toffee apple** /'– æpəl/, *n.* an apple coated with toffee, fixed onto a small stick.

**toffee-nosed** /'tɒfi-noʊzd/, *adj. Chiefly Brit. Colloq.* snobbish; pretentious; upper-class.

**tog** /tɒg/, *n., v.,* **togged, togging.** *Colloq.* *–n.* **1.** (*usu. pl.*) clothes: *football togs, swimming togs.* *–v.t.* **2.** to clothe; dress (oft. fol. by *out* or *up*). [apparently short for obs. cant term *togeman(s)* cloak, coat. Cf. D *tuig* trappings or L *toga* toga]

**tog.,** together.

**toga** /'toʊgə/, *n., pl.* **-gas. 1.** the loose outer garment of the citizens of ancient Rome when appearing in public in time of peace. **2.** a robe of office, a professional gown, or some other distinctive garment. [L] **–togaed** /'toʊgəd/, *adj.*

toga

**together** /tə'gɛðə/, *adv.* **1.** into or in one gathering, company, mass, place, or body: *to call the people together.* **2.** into or in union, proximity, contact, or collision, as two or more things: *to sew things together.* **3.** into or in relationship, association, business, or friendly relations, etc., as two or more persons: *to bring strangers together.* **4.** taken or considered collectively or conjointly: *this one cost more than all the others together.* **5.** (of a single thing) into or in a condition of unity, compactness, or coherence: *to squeeze a thing together; the argument does not hang together well.* **6.** at the same time; simultaneously: *you cannot have both together.* **7.** without intermission or interruption; continuously; uninterruptedly: *for days together.* **8.** in cooperation; with united action; conjointly: *to undertake a task together.* **9.** with mutual action; mutually; reciprocally: *to confer together.* *–adj.* **10.** capable and calm. [ME *togethir,* OE *tōgædere,* from TO, *prep.,* + *gædere,* adv., together, c. D *tegader.* Cf. GATHER]

**togetherness** /tə'gɛðənəs/, *n.* a feeling or quality of being united with other people.

**toggery** /'tɒgəri/, *n. Brit. Colloq.* garments; clothes; togs.

**toggle** /'tɒgəl/, *n., v.,* **-gled, -gling.** *–n.* **1.** a transverse pin, bolt, or rod placed through an eye of a rope, link of a chain, or the like, for various purposes. **2.** a toggle joint, or a device furnished with one. **3.** a small wooden bar around which a loop is passed, to fasten the front of a garment as a dufflecoat. *–v.t.* **4.** to furnish with a toggle or toggles. **5.** to secure or fasten with a toggle or toggles. [? akin to TACKLE]

**toggle joint** /'– dʒɔɪnt/, *n.* a device consisting of two arms pivoted together at their inner ends and pivoted to other parts at their outer ends, utilised in printing presses, etc., for pressure at the outer ends when the arms are put into a straight line by force applied at the bend between them.

**toggle switch** /'– swɪtʃ/, *n.* (in electronics) a switch in which a projecting knob or arm, moving through a small arc, causes the contacts to open or close the circuit suddenly.

**Togo** /'toʊgoʊ/, *n.* a country in western Africa. Official name: **Republic of Togo.**

**toheroa** /toʊə'roʊə/, *n.* **1.** a New Zealand shellfish, *Amphidesma ventricosum.* **2.** a soup made from this. [Maori]

**tohunga** /'tɒhʊŋə, toʊ'hʊŋə/, *n. N.Z.* a Maori wise man or priest. [Maori]

**toil**[1] /tɔɪl/, *n.* **1.** hard and continuous work; exhausting labour or effort. **2.** a laborious task. **3.** *Archaic.* battle; strife; struggle. *–v.i.* **4.** to engage in severe and continuous work; labour arduously. **5.** to move or travel with difficulty, weariness, or pain. *–v.t.* **6.** to bring or effect by toil. [ME *toile(n),* from AF *toiler* strive, dispute, wrangle, from L *tudiculāre* stir] **–toiler,** *n.*

**toil**[2] /tɔɪl/, *n.* **1.** (*usu. pl.*) a net or nets set about an area occupied by game, or into which game is driven. **2.** (*pl.*) power; clutches: *she was in the toils of her wicked uncle.* **3.** *Obs.* any snare or trap for wild beasts. [F *toile,* from L *tēla* web]

**toile** /twal/, *n.* **1.** a type of transparent linen. **2.** the made-up pattern in a cheap cloth of an exclusively designed gown before this is made in its intended material. [F. See TOIL[2]]

**toiler** /'tɔɪlə/, *n.* a conscientious worker.

**toilet** /'tɔɪlət/, *n.* **1.** a disposal apparatus of any type used for urination and defecation, esp. a water-closet. **2.** a room or booth fitted with a water-closet or urinal, often with means for washing face and hands. **3.** the act or process of dressing, including bathing, arranging the hair, etc. **4.** →**toilet set.** **5.** the dress or costume of a person; any particular costume: *toilet of white silk.* **6.** *Surg.* the cleansing of the part or wound after an operation, esp. in the peritoneal cavity. Also, **toilette** /twa'lɛt/ *for defs 3 and 5.* [F *toilette,* diminutive of *toile* cloth. See TOIL[2]]

**toilet block** /'– blɒk/, *n.* a building containing toilets, wash basins, etc., as in a school playground, barracks, public park, etc.

**toilet facilities** /'– fəsɪlətiz/, *n.pl.* handbasin and toilet, sometimes with a shower.

**toilet paper** /'– peɪpə/, *n.* soft, thin paper for sanitary use after defecation.

**toiletry** /'tɔɪlətri/, *n., pl.* **-tries.** an article or substance used in dressing or hygiene, as a soap, deodorant, shaving lotion, etc.

**toilet set** /'tɔɪlət sɛt/, *n.* the articles used in dressing, etc., as mirror, brush, comb, etc.

**toilet-train** /'tɔɪlət-treɪn/, *v.t.* to train (an infant) to control its natural excretory functions and void bodily wastes in socially acceptable ways. – **toilet-training,** *n.* – **toilet-trained,** *adj.*

**toilet water** /'tɔɪlət wɔtə/, *n.* a scented liquid used as a light perfume; cologne.

**toilful** /'tɔɪlfəl/, *adj.* characterised by or involving toil; laborious; toilsome. – **toilfully,** *adv.*

**toilinet** /tɔɪlə'nɛt/, *n.* a type of fine woollen cloth. Also, **toilinette, toilenette.** [? Trademark; from TOILE, modelled on SATINET]

**toilsome** /'tɔɪlsəm/, *adj.* characterised by or involving toil; laborious or fatiguing. – **toilsomely,** *adv.* – **toilsomeness,** *n.*

**toilworn** /'tɔɪlwɔn/, *adj.* **1.** worn by toil. **2.** showing the effects of toil.

**tokay**[1] /'toukeɪ/, *n.* a small lizard, *Gekko gecko* of the family Gekkonidae, of South-East Asia. [imitative of its cry]

**tokay**[2] /tou'keɪ/, *n.* **1.** a rich, sweet, aromatic wine made near Tokay, Hungary. **2.** (*cap.*) a variety of grape from which it is made. **3.** a similar wine made elsewhere.

**toke** /touk/, *n. Colloq.* a puff of a cigarette or joint.

**token** /'toukən/, *n.* **1.** something serving to represent or indicate some fact, event, feeling, etc.; sign: *to wear black as a token of mourning.* **2.** a characteristic mark or indication; symbol. **3.** a memento; a keepsake. **4.** something used to indicate authenticity, authority, etc. **5.** a ticket, metal disc, etc., certified as having a particular value, for payment or exchange, as for ferry fares, at a nominal value much greater than its commodity value. **6.** anything of only nominal value similarly used, as paper currency. **7.** a particular act or event, esp. as an instance of a class or type: *each subject in the experiment pronounced six tokens of the key word.* **8. by the same token,** in the same way; similarly. **9. in token of,** as a sign or evidence of. [ME; OE *tācen,* c. G *Zeichen;* akin to TEACH]

**token economy** /'– əˌkɒnəmi/, *n.* a system in behaviour therapy in which pleasing behaviour is rewarded with tokens which can be exchanged for goods, privileges, etc.

**tokenism** /'toukənɪzəm/, *n.* the policy of avoiding a real solution to a problem by a superficial gesture intended to impress and to distract attention from the real issues.

**token payment** /toukən 'peɪmənt/, *n.* a small payment binding an agreement or acknowledging a debt.

**tokology** /tɒ'kɒlədʒi/, *n.* →**tocology.**

**tokomak** /'tɒkəmæk/, *n.* an experimental apparatus for research in thermonuclear reactions, where the plasma is magnetically confined in a toroid. [Russ.]

**tolan** /'toulæn/, *n.* an unsaturated crystalline hydrocarbon, $C_6H_5C \equiv CCH_6H_5$. Also, **tolane** /'touleɪn/. [TOL(U) + -AN(E)]

**told** /tould/, *v.* **1.** past tense and past participle of **tell.** **2. all told,** in all.

**tole** /toul/, *n.* enamelled or lacquered metalware usu. with gilt decoration, often used (esp. in the 18th century) for trays, lampshades, etc. Also, **tôle.** [F]

**Toledo** /tə'leɪdou, tə'lidou/, *n.* (*sometimes l.c.*) a type of sword or sword blade. [from *Toledo,* Spain, a city formerly noted for the manufacture of fine sword blades]

**tolerable** /'tɒlərəbəl/, *adj.* **1.** that may be tolerated; endurable. **2.** fairly good; not bad. **3.** *Colloq.* in fair health. [ME, from L *tolerābilis* bearable] – **tolerableness,** *n.* – **tolerably,** *adv.*

**tolerance** /'tɒlərəns/, *n.* **1.** the disposition to be patient and fair towards those whose opinions or practices differ from one's own; freedom from bigotry. **2.** the disposition to be patient and fair to opinions which are not one's own. **3.** the ability to endure disagreeable circumstances. **4.** *Med.* **a.** the ability to endure the action of a drug, without adverse effects. **b.** physiological resistance to poison. **5. a.** *Mach.* an allowable variation in the dimensions of a machined article or part. **b.** an allowable variation in some other characteristic of an article as weight, quality, etc. **6.** *Coining.* a permissible deviation in the fineness and weight of coin, owing to the difficulty of securing exact conformity to the standard.

**tolerance limits** /'– lɪməts/, *n.pl.* (in statistics) a pair of numbers obtained from a sample such that it can be stated with a given degree of probability that the numbers will include between them at least a specified percentage of values of a variable in the population.

**tolerant** /'tɒlərənt/, *adj.* **1.** inclined or disposed to tolerate; showing tolerance; forbearing. **2.** favouring toleration. **3.** *Med.* able to endure the action of a drug, resist a poison, etc. **4.** able to survive in adverse conditions: *plants tolerant of the summer heat.* – **tolerantly,** *adv.*

**tolerate** /'tɒləreɪt/, *v.t.,* **-rated, -rating.** **1.** to allow to be, be practised, or be done without prohibition or hindrance; permit. **2.** to bear without repugnance; put up with. **3.** *Med.* to endure or resist the action of (a drug, poison, etc.). **4.** *Obs.* to endure or sustain, as pain or hardship. [L *tolerātus* endured] – **tolerative** /'tɒlərətɪv/, *adj.* – **tolerator,** *n.*

**toleration** /tɒlə'reɪʃən/, *n.* **1.** the tolerating, esp. of what is not actually approved; forbearance. **2.** allowance, by a government, of the exercise of religions other than the one which is officially established or recognised; recognition of the right of private judgment in matters of faith and worship. – **tolerationism,** *n.* – **tolerationist,** *n.*

**tolidine** /'tɒlədin, -dɪn/, *n.* any of three isomeric derivatives of toluene, $(C_6H_3(CH_3)NH_2)_2$, the orthoisomer of which is used in making dyes. [from TOL(U) + -ID(E) + -INE[2]]

**toll**[1] /toul/, *v.t.* **1.** to cause (a large bell) to sound with single strokes slowly and regularly repeated, as for summoning a congregation to church, or esp. for announcing a death. **2.** to sound (a knell, etc.) or strike (the hour), by such strokes. **3.** to announce (a death, etc.) by this means; ring a toll for (a dying or dead person). **4.** to summon or dismiss by tolling. **5.** *U.S.* to lure or decoy (game) by arousing curiosity. **6.** *Obs.* to attract, allure, or entice. *–v.i.* **7.** to sound with single strokes slowly and regularly repeated, as a bell. *–n.* **8.** the act of tolling a bell. **9.** a single stroke made in tolling a bell. **10.** the sound made. [ME; akin to OE *-tyllan* in *fortyllan* attract, allure]

**toll**[2] /toul/, *n.* **1.** Also, **tollage.** a payment exacted by the state, the local authorities, etc., for some right or privilege, as for passage along a road or over a bridge. **2.** *Obs.* the right to take such payment. **3.** a tax, duty, or tribute; a price. **4.** exaction, cost or the like, esp. in terms of death or loss: *the accident took a heavy toll of lives.* *–v.t.* **5.** to collect (something) as a toll. *–v.i.* **6.** to collect toll; levy toll. [ME and OE (c. G Zoll), var. of *toln,* from LL *tolōneum,* var. of L *telōnium,* from Gk *telōnion* tollhouse]

**tollah** /'tɒlə/, *n.* →**toolah.**

**tollbar** /'toulba/, *n.* a barrier, esp. a gate, across a road or bridge, where toll is taken.

**tollbooth** /'toulbuθ, -buð/, *n.* a booth or other small building at which toll is collected.

**toll bridge** /'toul brɪdʒ/, *n.* a bridge at which a toll is charged.

**tollgate** /'toulgeɪt/, *n.* a gate where toll is taken.

**tollhouse** /'toulhaus/, *n.* a house at a tollgate, occupied by a tollkeeper.

**tollkeeper** /'toulkipə/, *n.* the collector at a tollgate.

**tollway** /'toulweɪ/, *n.* a road on which drivers pay a toll.

**tolu** /tɒ'lu/, *n.* a fragrant yellowish brown balsam obtained from a South American tree, *Myroxylon balsamum,* used in medicine as a stomachic and expectorant, and in perfumery.

[named after *Tolu* (now Santiago de Tolu) in Columbia, where balsam is obtained]

**toluate** /ˈtɒljueɪt/, *n.* a salt or ester of toluic acid.

**toluene** /ˈtɒljuin/, *n.* a colourless liquid hydrocarbon, $C_6H_5CH_3$, obtained from tolu, coal tar, etc., used as a solvent and in the manufacture of coal-tar substances, as TNT. [TOLU + -ENE]

**toluic acid** /tɒlˌjuɪk ˈæsəd/, *n.* any of three isomeric acids, $CH_3C_6H_4COOH$, which are derivatives of toluene; methylbenzoic acid.

**toluide** /ˈtɒljuaɪd/, *n.* an amide which contains a tolyl group united to the nitrogen. Also, **toluid** /ˈtɒljuəd/.

**toluidine** /tɒlˈjuədin/, *n.* any of three isomeric amines, $CH_3C_6H_4NH_2$, derived from toluene, used in the dye and drug industries. Also, **toluidin** /tɒlˈjuədən/.

**toluol** /ˈtɒljuɒl/, *n.* **1.** →**toluene.** **2.** the commercial form of toluene. Also, **toluole** /ˈtɒljuoʊl/. [TOLU + -OL[2]]

**toluyl group** /ˈtɒljuəl ˌgrup/, *n.* a univalent radical, $CH_3C_6H_4CO$, present in toluic acids. Also, **toluyl radical.** [TOLU + -YL]

**tolyl group** /ˈtɒləl grup/, *n.* a univalent hydrocarbon radical, $CH_3C_6H_4$, from toluene. Also, **tolyl radical.** [TOL(U) + -YL]

**tom** /tɒm/, *n.* **1.** the male of various animals (often used in composition, as in *tomcat*). **2.** a tomcat. **3.** a name for a large bell. [short for *Thomas*]

**tomahawk** /ˈtɒməhɔk/, *n.* **1.** a small, short-handled axe for use with one hand; hatchet. **2.** a light axe used by the North American Indians as a weapon and tool, and serving as a token of war. *–v.t.* **3.** to strike, cut, or kill with or as with a tomahawk. **4.** to shear (a sheep) roughly, as if with a tomahawk. [Algonquian *tommahick,* etc., war club, ceremonial object]

tomahawk

**Tom and Jerry** /tɒm ən ˈdʒɛri/, *n. U.S.* a hot drink composed of rum and water (or milk) with beaten eggs, spiced and sweetened.

**tomato** /təˈmatoʊ/, *n., pl.* **-toes.** **1.** a widely cultivated plant, *Lycopersicon esculentum,* bearing a slightly acid, pulpy fruit, commonly red, sometimes yellow, used as a vegetable. **2.** the fruit itself. **3.** any plant of the same genus. **4.** its fruit. [Sp. *tomate,* from Nahuatl *tomatl*]

**tomato paste** /– ˈpeɪst/, *n.* a concentrated tomato purée, used in flavouring soups, stews, etc.

**tomato sauce** /– ˈsɔs/, *n.* a sauce made of cooked, puréed tomatoes with herbs or spices, esp. one commercially produced.

**tomb** /tum/, *n.* **1.** an excavation in earth or rock for the reception of a dead body. **2.** a grave or mausoleum. **3.** any sepulchral structure. **4.** the state of death. *–v.t.* **5.** to place in or as in a tomb; bury. [ME, from OF *tombe,* from LL *tumba,* from Gk *týmbos*] **–tombless,** *adj.* **–tomblike,** *adj.*

**tombola** /tɒmˈboʊlə/, *n.* →**housie-housie.** [Hindu]

**tombolo** /ˈtɒmbəloʊ/, *n.* a spit of sand or shingle thrown up by the tides, linking an island or rock with the mainland. [It.]

**tomboy** /ˈtɒmbɔɪ/, *n.* a boisterous, romping girl. **–tomboyish,** *adj.* **–tomboyishness,** *n.*

**tombstone** /ˈtumstoʊn/, *n.* a stone, usu. bearing an inscription, set to mark a tomb or grave.

**tomcat** /ˈtɒmkæt/, *n.* a male cat.

**Tom Collins** /tɒm ˈkɒlənz/, *n.* a long drink containing gin, lemon or lime juice, and soda-water, sweetened and served with ice.

**Tom, Dick, and Harry,** *n.* common people generally; anybody at all: *they invited every Tom, Dick, and Harry.*

**tome** /toʊm/, *n.* **1.** a volume forming a part of a larger work. **2.** any volume, esp. a ponderous one. [F, from L *tomus,* from Gk *tómos* volume, section of book]

**-tome,** a word element referring to cutting, used esp. in scientific terms, as *microtome, osteotome.* [combining form representing Gk *tomḗ* a cutting, section; *tómos* a cut, slice; *-tomos* cutting]

**tomentose** /təˈmɛntoʊs/, *adj.* **1.** *Anat.* fleecy; flocculent. **2.** *Bot., Entomol.* closely covered with down or matted hair. [NL *tōmentōsus,* from L *tōmentum* TOMENTUM]

**tomentum** /təˈmɛntəm/, *n., pl.* **-ta** /-tə/. (in botany) pubescence consisting of longish, soft, entangled hairs pressed close to the surface. [NL; special use of L *tōmentum* stuffing (of wool, hair, etc.) for cushions]

**tomfool** /ˈtɒmful/, *n.* **1.** a grossly foolish person; a silly fool. *–adj.* **2.** being, or characteristic of, a tomfool. *–v.i.* **3.** to play the fool.

**tomfoolery[1]** /tɒmˈfuləri/, *n., pl.* **-eries.** **1.** foolish or silly behaviour. **2.** a silly act, matter, or thing.

**tomfoolery[2]** /tɒmˈfuləri/, *n. Colloq.* jewellery. [rhyming slang]

**tommy** /ˈtɒmi/, *n., pl.* **-mies.** short for **Tommy Atkins.** Also, **Tommy.**

**Tommy Atkins** /tɒmi ˈætkənz/, *n.* **1.** any private of the British Army. **2.** the rank and file collectively. [a familiar name for typical British soldier, arising out of the use of the name *Thomas Atkins* in specimen forms given in official regulations from 1815]

**tommyaxe** /ˈtɒmiæks/, *n.* →**tomahawk** (def. 1).

**tommy bar** /ˈtɒmi ba/, *n.* a bar inserted into a capstan, box spanner, etc., to give leverage for turning.

**Tommy gun** /ˈtɒmi gʌn/, *n. Colloq.* →**Thompson machine gun.**

**tommyhawk** /ˈtɒmihɔk/, *n. Colloq.* a tomahawk.

**tommyrot** /ˈtɒmirɒt/, *n. Colloq.* nonsense.

**tommy ruff** /tɒmi ˈrʌf/, *n.* a small food and sport fish of the family Arripididae, related to the Australian salmon and found mainly in southern and western Australian waters; herring. Also, **roughie, ruff.**

**Tommy talker** /tɒmi ˈtɔkə/, *n.* →**kazoo.**

**tomo** /ˈtoʊmoʊ/, *n. N.Z.* a hole or pit; pothole. [Maori]

**tomogram** /ˈtɒməgræm/, *n.* an X-ray picture obtained by the process of tomography. Also, **tomograph** /ˈtɒməgræf, -graf/.

**tomography** /təˈmɒgrəfi/, *n.* the technique of obtaining an X-ray picture of a selected layer in an object. [Gk *tómos* slice + -GRAPHY]

**tomorrow** /təˈmɒroʊ/, *n.* **1.** the day after this day: *tomorrow will be fair.* **2.** a day immediately following or succeeding another day. **3.** some future day or time. *–adv.* **4.** on the morrow; on the day after this day: *come tomorrow.* Also, **to-morrow.** [ME *to morwe(n),* OE *tō morgen(ne)* on the morrow, in the morning]

tomtit

**tompion** /ˈtɒmpiən/, *n.* →**tampion.**

**Tom Thumb** /tɒm ˈθʌm/, *n.* **1.** a diminutive hero of folktales. **2.** a diminutive man; a dwarf. **3.** (*l.c.*) a very small cracker (def. 2).

**tomtit** /ˈtɒmtɪt/, *n.* the bluetit, *Parus caeruleus,* or less often any other of the titmice, family Paridae. [TOM + TIT[1]]

**tomtits** /tɒmˈtɪts/, *n. pl. Colloq.* the shits. [rhyming slang]

**tom-tom** /ˈtɒm-tɒm/, *n.* **1.** a native drum of indefinite pitch. **2.** a dully repetitious drumbeat or similar sound. Also, **tam-tam.** [Hind. or other East Ind. vernacular *tam-tam.* Cf. Malay *tong-tong;* both imitative]

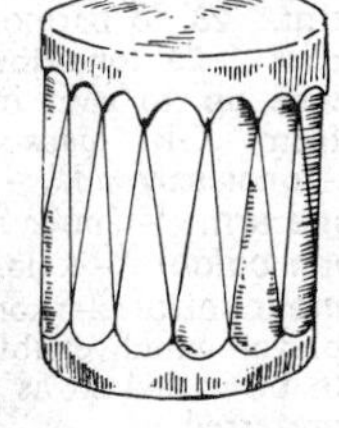

tom-tom

**-tomy,** a noun termination meaning a 'cutting', esp. relating to a surgical operation, as in *appendectomy, lithotomy, phlebotomy,* or sometimes a division, as in *dichotomy.* [Gk *-tomia*]

**ton[1]** /tʌn/, *n.* **1.** a unit of mass in the imperial system equal to 2240 lb (long ton), or approx. 1016 kg, and, in the U.S., 2000 lb (short ton), or approx. 907 kg. **2.** a unit of freight equal to 1000 kg or, formerly 40 cubic feet (freight ton). **3.** a unit of displacement of ships in the imperial system equal to 35 cubic feet of salt water (displacement ton or shipping ton), or approx. 0.99 cubic metres. **4.** a unit of internal capacity of ships in the imperial system, equal to 100 cubic feet, or approx. 2.83 cubic metres (gross ton). **5.** →**tonne.** **6.** *Colloq.* a heavy weight: *that book weighs a ton.* **7.** (*pl.*) *Colloq.* very many; a good deal: *tons of things to see.* [ME; var. of TUN]

**ton[2]** /tʌn/, *n.* **1.** a score of a hundred. **2.** *Obs. Colloq.* a speed of a hundred miles an hour, esp. on a motorcycle.

**-ton,** noun suffix, as in *simpleton, singleton.* [var. of Brit. d. *tone* ONE. Cf. TOTHER]

**tonal** /ˈtounəl/, *adj.* **1.** *Music.* pertaining to tonality (opposed to *modal*). **2.** pertaining to tone. – **tonally,** *adv.*

**tonal centre** /– ˈsɛntə/, *n.* the tone which most predominates in a musical passage; the tonic in traditional music.

**tonalist** /ˈtounələst/, *n.* one who adheres to tonality in music, painting, etc.

**tonality** /tounˈæləti/, *n., pl.* **-ties. 1.** *Music.* **a.** the sum of relations, melodic and harmonic, existing between the notes of a scale or musical system; key. **b.** particular scale or system of notes; a key. **2.** *Painting, etc.* the system of tones or tints, or the colour scheme, of a picture, etc.

**tone** /toun/, *n., v.,* **toned, toning.** *–n.* **1.** any sound considered with reference to its quality, pitch, strength, source, etc.: *shrill tones.* **2.** quality or character of sound. **3.** vocal sound; the sound made by vibrating muscular bands in the larynx. **4.** a particular quality, way of sounding, modulation, or intonation of the voice as expressive of some meaning, feeling, spirit, etc.: *a tone of command.* **5.** an accent peculiar to a person, people, locality, etc., or a characteristic mode of sounding words in speech. **6.** stress of voice on a syllable of a word. **7.** *Phonet.* a musical pitch or melody which may serve to distinguish between words composed of the same sounds, as in Chinese. **8.** *Music.* **a.** an interval equivalent to two semitones; a whole tone. **b.** any of the nine plainsong melodies or tunes, to which the psalms are sung (called **Gregorian tones**). **c.** *Chiefly U.S.* →**note. 9.** a variety of colour; a tint; a shade. **10.** hue; that distinctive quality by which colours differ from one another in addition to their differences indicated by chroma, tint, shade; a slight modification of a given colour: *green with a yellowish tone, light tone, dull tone, etc.* **11.** *Art.* the prevailing effect of harmony of colour and values. **12.** *Physiol.* **a.** the state of tension or firmness proper to the organs or tissues of the body. **b.** that state of the body or of an organ in which all its animal functions are performed with healthy vigour. **c.** healthy sensitivity to stimulation. **13.** normal healthy condition of the mind. **14.** a particular state or temper of the mind; spirit, character, or tenor. **15.** prevailing character or style, as of manners or morals. **16.** style, distinction, or elegance. *–v.t.* **17.** to sound with a particular tone. **18.** to give the proper tone to (a musical instrument). **19.** to modify the tone or general colouring of. **20.** to give the desired tone to (a painting, etc.). **21.** *Photog.* to change the colour of (a print), usu. by chemical means. **22.** to render (as specified) in tone or colouring. **23.** to modify the tone or character of. **24.** to give physical or mental tone to. **25. tone down, a.** *Painting.* to subdue; make (a colour) less intense in hue. **b.** to lower the tone, strength, intensity, etc., of; soften; moderate. **26. tone up, a.** to give a higher or stronger tone to. **b.** to make stronger or more vigorous: *walking tones up the muscles.* *–v.i.* **27.** to take on a particular tone; assume colour or tint. **28.** to harmonise in tone or colour (fol. by *with* or *in with*). **29. tone down,** to become softened or moderated. **30. tone up,** to gain in tone or strength. [ME, from ML *tonus,* from Gk *tónos* tension, pitch, key] – **toneless,** *adj.* – **tonelessly,** *adv.* – **tonelessness,** *n.* – **toner,** *n.*

**tone arm** /ˈ– am/, *n.* →**pick-up arm.**

**tone colour** /ˈ– kʌlə/, *n.* in music, quality of tone; timbre.

**tone control** /ˈ– kəntroul/, *n.* a device in a radio or record player which enables the intensities of range of frequencies to be varied so as to increase the bass or treble response as preferred.

**tone-deaf** /ˈtoun-dɛf/, *adj.* unable to distinguish differences in pitch in musical notes. – **tone-deafness,** *n.*

**tone language** /ˈtoun læŋgwɪdʒ/, *n.* a language in which systematic differences in vocal pitch level may make differences in lexical meaning, as in Mandarin Chinese.

**tone poem** /ˈ– pouəm/, *n.* an instrumental musical composition intended to suggest a train of poetic images or sentiments.

**tone row** /ˈ– rou/, *n.* a sequence of intervals which involves all the twelve tones of an octave without repetition, used in twelve-tone music.

**toney** /ˈtouni/, *adj. Colloq.* of high class or pretending to it. Also, **tony.** [TONE (def. 16) + -Y[1]]

**tong**[1] /tɒŋ/, *n.* **1.** (*pl., sometimes construed as sing.*) any of various implements consisting of two arms hinged, pivoted, or otherwise fastened together, for seizing, holding, or lifting something. [ME; OE *tang,* c. G *Zange*]

**tong**[2] /tɒŋ/, *n.* **1.** (in China) an association, society, or political party. **2.** in other countries, a Chinese society or association, usu. considered by its members to be a private, closed society, but often believed by others to indulge in criminal practices. [Chinese *t'ang* meeting place]

**Tonga** /ˈtɒŋə/, *n.* a Polynesian kingdom consisting of three groups of islands in the South Pacific. Also, **Tonga Islands** or **Friendly Islands.**

**Tongan** /ˈtɒŋən/, *n.* **1.** a native of Tonga. **2.** the language of the Tongans. *–adj.* **3.** of or pertaining to Tonga, the Tongans, or their language.

**tongue** /tʌŋ/, *n., v.,* **tongued, tonguing.** *–n.* **1.** an organ in man and most vertebrates occupying the floor of the mouth and often protrusible and freely movable, being the principal organ of taste, and, in man, of articulate speech. **2.** *Zool.* an organ in the mouth of invertebrates, frequently of a rasping nature. **3.** the tongue of an animal, as an ox, reindeer, or sheep, as used for food, often prepared by smoking or pickling. **4.** the human tongue as the organ of speech. **5.** the faculty or power of speech: *to find one's tongue, to lose one's tongue.* **6.** speech or talk, esp. mere glib or empty talk. **7.** manner or character of speech: *a flattering tongue.* **8.** the language of a particular people, country, or locality: *the Hebrew tongue.* **9.** a dialect. **10.** a people as distinguished by its language (a biblical use): *I will gather all nations and tongues.* **11.** something resembling or suggesting an animal's tongue in shape, position, or function. **12.** a strip of leather under the lacing or fastening of a shoe. **13.** a suspended piece inside a bell that produces a sound on striking against the side. **14.** a vibrating reed or the like in a musical instrument. **15.** the pole of a carriage or other vehicle, extending between the animals drawing it. **16.** *Carp.* a projecting strip along the centre of the edge of a board, for fitting into a groove in another board. **17.** a narrow strip of land extending into a body of water. **18.** *Mach.* a long, narrow projection on a machine. **19.** the pin of a buckle, brooch, etc. **20.** (*pl.*) →**gift of tongues. 21. give tongue, a.** to speak out, esp. loudly. **b.** (of a hunting dog) to bark or bay loudly when the scent has been picked up or the quarry sighted. **22. hold one's tongue,** to be quiet. **23. mind one's tongue,** to be careful what one says. **24. on the tip of one's tongue,** on the verge of being uttered. **25. slip of the tongue,** an inadvertent remark. **26. with one's tongue in one's cheek,** facetiously; mockingly; insincerely. *–v.t.* **27.** to articulate (the notes of a flute, cornet, etc.) by strokes of the tongue. **28.** *Carp.* **a.** to cut a tongue on (a board). **b.** to join or fit together by a tongue-and-groove joint. **29.** to touch with the tongue. **30.** to reproach or scold. **31.** to articulate or pronounce. **32.** *Archaic.* to speak or utter. *–v.i.* **33.** to tongue the notes of a flute, etc. **34.** to talk or prate. **35.** to project like a tongue or tongues. [ME and OE *tunge,* c. G *Zunge;* akin to L *lingua*] – **tongued,** *adj.* – **tongueless,** *adj.*

**tongue-and-groove joint** /ˌtʌŋ-ən-ˈgruv ˌdʒɔɪnt/, *n.* (in carpentry) a joint consisting of a tongue on the edge of one board and a matching groove on the edge of the next.

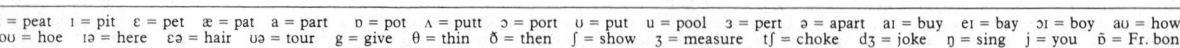

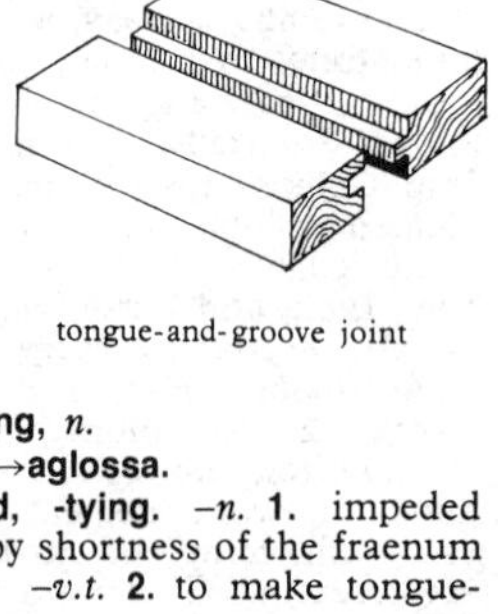

tongue-and-groove joint

**tongue graft** /ˈtʌŋ graft/, *n.* →**whip graft.**

**tongue-in-cheek** /tʌŋ-ɪn-ˈtʃik/, *adj.* facetious; mocking; insincere.

**tongue-lash** /ˈtʌŋ-læʃ/, *v.i., v.t.* to scold or reprimand. – **tongue-lashing,** *n.*

**tongueless frog** /tʌŋləs ˈfrɒg/, *n.* →**aglossa.**

**tongue-tie** /ˈtʌŋ-taɪ/, *n., v.,* **-tied, -tying.** *–n.* **1.** impeded motion of the tongue caused esp. by shortness of the fraenum which binds down its underside. *–v.t.* **2.** to make tongue-tied.

**tongue-tied** /ˈtʌŋ-taɪd/, *adj.* **1.** unable to speak, as from shyness. **2.** affected with tongue-tie.

**tongue twister** /ˈtʌŋ twɪstə/, *n.* **1.** a contrived sentence which is difficult to say because of the constant repetition of a certain letter, or certain similar sounds: *the Leith police dismisseth us.* **2.** any word or phrase that is difficult to say or pronounce without stumbling.

**tonguing** /'tʌŋɪŋ/, *n.* the manipulation of the tongue in playing a wind instrument to interrupt the note and produce a staccato effect.

**tonic** /'tɒnɪk/, *n.* **1.** a medicine that invigorates or strengthens. **2.** anything invigorating physically, mentally, or morally. **3.** *Music.* the first degree of the scale; the keynote. **4.** *Colloq.* tonic water: *gin and tonic.* *–adj.* **5.** pertaining to, maintaining, increasing, or restoring the tone or healthy condition of the system or organs, as a medicine. **6.** invigorating physically, mentally, or morally. **7.** *Physiol., Pathol.* **a.** pertaining to tension, as of the muscles. **b.** marked by continued muscular tension: *a tonic spasm.* **8.** characterised by distinctions of tone or accent: *a tonic language.* **9.** pertaining to tone or accent in speech. **10.** *Phonet.* accented, esp. with primary accent. **11.** *Music.* pertaining to or founded on the keynote, or first note, of a musical scale: *a tonic chord.* [Gk *tonikós* pertaining to tone]

**tonic accent** /– 'æksɛnt/, *n.* vocal accent, or syllabic stress, in pronunciation or speaking.

**tonicity** /toʊ'nɪsəti/, *n.* **1.** tonic quality or condition. **2.** the state of bodily tone. **3.** *Physiol.* the normal elastic tension of living muscles, arteries, etc., by which the tone of the system is maintained.

**tonic sol-fa** /tɒnɪk 'sɒl-fa/, *n.* a system of singing, in which tonality or key relationship is emphasised, the usual staff notation is discarded, and the notes are indicated by the initial letters of the syllables of the sol-fa system.

**tonic water** /'– wɔtə/, *n.* effervescent water with quinine, often added to spirits.

**tonight** /tə'naɪt/, *n.* **1.** this present or coming night; the night of this present day. **2.** *Obs.* last night. *–adv.* **3.** on this present night; on the night of this present day. [ME; OE *tō niht.* See TO, *prep.*, NIGHT]

**tonite** /'toʊnaɪt/, *n.* an explosive made of guncotton, a nitrate, and a nitro compound, used esp. for blasting. [L *tonāre* to thunder + -ITE[1]]

**tonk** /tɒŋk/, *n. Colloq.* **1.** a penis. **2.** (*derog.*) a passive homosexual.

**tonka bean** /'tɒŋkə bin/, *n.* **1.** the fragrant, black, almond-shaped seed of a tall leguminous tree, *Dipteryx odorata,* of tropical South America, used in perfumes and snuff. **2.** the tree itself. [? Carib (Galibi) *tonka* + BEAN]

**tonky** /'tɒŋki/, *adj. N.Z. Colloq.* →**toney.**

**tonn.,** tonnage.

**tonnage** /'tʌnɪdʒ/, *n.* **1.** the carrying capacity of a vessel expressed in gross tons. See **gross tonnage, register tonnage. 2.** ships collectively considered with reference to their carrying capacity or together with their cargoes. **3.** a duty on ships or boats at so much per ton of cargo or freight, or according to the capacity in tons. Also, **tunnage.**

**tonnage deck** /'– dɛk/, *n.* the upper deck in all ships which have less than three decks, the second deck from below in other ships.

**tonne** /tɒn/, *n.* a unit of mass equal to 1000 kilograms. *Symbol:* t

**tonneau** /'tɒnoʊ/, *n., pl.* **tonneaus, tonneaux** /'tɒnoʊz/. **1.** a rear body or compartment of a motor car with seats for passengers. **2.** a flexible material covering a convertible motor car, often with a part which folds back around the driver to protect him from the weather. [F: cask, diminutive of *tonne* TUN]

**tonometer** /tɒ'nɒmətə/, *n.* **1.** an instrument for measuring the frequencies of tones. **2.** a tuning fork. **3.** a graduated set of tuning forks, whose frequencies have been carefully determined. **4.** any of various physiological instruments, as for measuring the tension within the eyeball, or for determining blood pressure. [Gk *tóno(s)* tension, tone + -METER[1]] **– tonometric** /tɒnə'mɛtrɪk/, *adj.* **– tonometry,** *n.*

**tonsil** /'tɒnsəl/, *n.* either of two prominent oval masses of lymphoid tissue situated one on each side of the fauces. [L *tonsillae,* pl.] **– tonsillar,** *adj.*

**tonsillectomy** /tɒnsə'lɛktəmi/, *n., pl.* **-mies.** the operation of excising or removing one or both tonsils. [L *tonsillae* tonsils + -ECTOMY]

**tonsillitis** /tɒnsə'laɪtəs/, *n.* inflammation of a tonsil or the tonsils. [NL, from L *tonsillae* + *-ītis* -ITIS] **– tonsillitic** /tɒnsə'lɪtɪk/, *adj.*

**tonsorial** /tɒn'sɔriəl/, *adj.* (*oft. joc.*) of or pertaining to a barber or his work. [L *tonsōrius* pertaining to shaving + -AL[1]]

**tonsure** /'tɒnʃə/, *n., v.,* **-sured, -suring.** *–n.* **1.** the act of clipping the hair or shaving the head. **2.** the shaving of the head, or of some part of it, as a religious practice or rite, esp. in preparation for entering the priesthood or a monastic order. **3.** the part of a cleric's head left bare by shaving the hair. **4.** the state of being shorn. *–v.t.* **5.** to confer the ecclesiastical tonsure upon. **6.** to subject to tonsure. [ME, from L *tonsūra* shearing] **– tonsured,** *adj.*

tonsured monk

**tontine** /'tɒntin, tɒn'tin/, *n.* **1.** a scheme in which subscribers to a common fund share an annuity with the benefit of survivorship, the shares of the survivors being increased as the subscribers die, until the whole goes to the last survivor. **2.** the annuity shared. **3.** the share of each subscriber. **4.** the number who share. **5.** any of various forms of life assurance in which the chief benefits accrue to participants who are alive and whose policies are in force at the end of a specified period (**tontine period**). [F; named after Lorenzo *Tonti,* Neapolitan banker who started the scheme in France about 1653]

**ton-up** /tʌn-'ʌp/, *adj. Chiefly Brit. Colloq.* **1.** capable of travelling at a speed of a hundred miles an hour or more. **2.** of or pertaining to a person who derives pleasure or prestige from excessive speed.

**tonus** /'toʊnəs/, *n.* a normal state of slight continuous tension in muscle tissue which facilitates its response to stimulation. [NL: special use of L *tonus,* from Gk *tónos* tone]

**too** /tu/, *adv.* **1.** in addition; also; furthermore; moreover: *young, clever, and rich too.* **2.** to an excessive extent or degree; beyond what is desirable, fitting, or right: *too long.* **3.** more (as specified) than should be. **4.** very, extremely (esp. after *only* or a negative): *only too glad to help you, not too bad.* **5.** *Colloq.* indeed (used for emphasis): *I did so too!* **6.** **too right,** *Colloq.* (an emphatic expression of agreement). [var. of TO, *adv.*]

**too-hard basket** /tu-'had baskət/, *n.* (*joc.*) an imaginary basket (cf. **in-tray, out-tray**) in which papers coming into an office are placed if the recipient finds them difficult and wishes to delay making a decision.

**took** /tʊk/, *v.* past tense of **take.**

**tool** /tul/, *n.* **1.** an instrument, esp. one held in the hand, for performing or facilitating mechanical operations, as a hammer, saw, file, etc. **2.** any instrument of manual operation. **3.** that part of a lathe, planer, drill, or similar machine, which performs the cutting or machining operation. **4.** the machine itself; a machine tool. **5.** anything used like a tool to do work or effect some result. **6.** a person used by another for his own ends; a cat's paw. **7.** the design or ornament impressed upon a book cover. **8.** *Colloq.* the penis. *–v.t.* **9.** to work or shape with a tool. **10.** to work decoratively with a hand tool; to ornament with a bookbinder's tool, as on book covers. **11.** *Colloq.* to drive (a vehicle). *–v.i.* **12.** to work with a tool or tools. **13. tool up,** to equip, as a workshop for a particular job. **14.** *Colloq.* to drive or ride in a vehicle. [ME: OE *tol,* c. Icel. *tol,* pl.] **– tooler,** *n.*

**toolache** /tu'leɪtʃi/, *n.* a large, rare or possibly extinct wallaby, *Macropus greyi,* of the border country between South Australia and Victoria; Grey's brush wallaby. [Aboriginal]

**toolah** /'tulə/, *n.* →**green ringtail possum.** Also, **tollah** /'tɒlə/.

**tool allowance** /'tul əlaʊəns/, *n.* an allowance paid by an employer to tradesmen who equip themselves with the tools necessary for their work.

**tooling** /'tulɪŋ/, *n.* the provision of tools, as in a factory.

**tool-post** /'tul-poʊst/, *n.* a vertical post, which is usu. slotted and carries a clamping nut, for securing a lathe tool in its cutting position.

**toolshed** /'tulʃɛd/, *n.* a shed in the garden of, or attached to a house, in which tools are kept.

**tool steel** /'tul stil/, *n.* any of various steels, containing up to about 1.5 per cent carbon and various alloying metals, which are suitable for use in tools for cutting metal.

**toon** /tun/, *n.* **1.** any of several species of *Toona* (formerly *Cedrela toona*) yielding a red wood resembling mahogany, but softer, and extensively used for furniture, carving, etc. **2.** the wood. [Hind. *tūn*]

**toot**[1] /tut/, *v.i.* **1.** (of a horn) to give forth its characteristic sound. **2.** to make a sound resembling that of a horn or the like. **3.** to sound or blow a horn or other wind instrument. **4.** (of grouse) to give forth a characteristic cry or call. *–v.t.* **5.** to cause (a horn, etc.) to sound by blowing it. **6.** to sound (notes, etc.) on a horn or the like. *–n.* **7.** an act or sound of tooting. [late ME, cf. LG and G *tūten,* D *toeten* in same sense] **– tooter,** *n.*

**toot**[2] /tut/, *n. Colloq.* a toilet.

**toot**[3] /tut/, *n.* →**tutu**[2]. [Maori *tutu*]

**tooth** /tuθ/, *n., pl.* **teeth** /tiθ/, *v.* *–n.* **1.** (in most vertebrates) one of the hard bodies or processes usu. attached in a row to each jaw, serving for the prehension and mastication of food, as weapons of attack or defence, etc., and in mammals typically composed chiefly of dentine surrounding a sensitive pulp and covered on the crown with enamel. **2.** (in invertebrates) any of various similar or analogous processes occurring in the mouth or alimentary canal, or on a shell. **3.** any projection resembling or suggesting a tooth. **4.** one of the projections of a comb, rake, saw, etc. **5.** one of a series of projections (cogs) on the edge of a wheel, etc., which engage with corresponding parts of another wheel or body. **6.** *Bot.* one of the hard projections in the peristome of mosses. **7.** a sharp, distressing, or destructive attribute or agency. **8.** taste, relish, or liking. **9. a sweet tooth,** a liking for sweet things. **10. long in the tooth,** old. *–v.t.* **11.** to furnish with teeth. **12.** to cut teeth upon. *–v.i.* **13.** to interlock, as cogwheels. [ME; OE *tōth,* c. G *Zahn:* akin to L *dens,* Gk *odoús*] **– toothed** /tuθt/, *adj.* **– toothless,** *adj.*

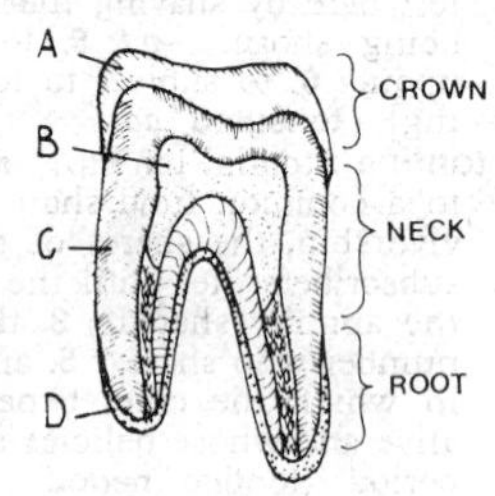


tooth (human): A, enamel; B, pulp; C, dentine; D, cementum

**toothache** /ˈtuθeɪk/, *n.* a pain in a tooth or teeth or in the jawbone.

**toothache tree** /ˈ– tri/, *n.* the eastern North American prickly ash, *Zanthoxylum americanum,* the bark of which is used as a remedy for toothache.

**tooth and nail,** *adv.* fiercely; with all one's might: *we fought tooth and nail but lost.*

**toothbrush** /ˈtuθbrʌʃ/, *n.* a small brush with a long handle, for cleaning the teeth.

**toothcomb** /ˈtuθkoʊm/, *n.* **1.** a comb with very fine teeth, usu. at each edge. **2. with a fine toothcomb,** in great detail; very painstakingly.

**toothing** /ˈtuθɪŋ/, *n.* a method of laying bricks so that stretchers project from a wall to bond with later work; indenting.

**toothpaste** /ˈtuθpeɪst/, *n.* a dentifrice in the form of paste.

**toothpick** /ˈtuθpɪk/, *n.* **1.** a small pointed piece of wood, etc., for removing food, etc., lodged between the teeth. **2.** *Colloq.* a sculling boat designed for racing.

**tooth shell** /ˈtuθ ʃɛl/, *n.* a member of the scaphopod mollusc genus *Dentalium,* having a long, tapering, tubular shell.

**toothsome** /ˈtuθsəm/, *adj.* pleasing to the taste; palatable: *a toothsome dish.* **– toothsomely,** *adv.* **– toothsomeness,** *n.*

**tooth-stick** /ˈtuθ-stɪk/, *n.* stick made of soft wood to clean the interdental spaces.

**toothy** /ˈtuθi/, *adj.* **1.** having prominent teeth. **2.** displaying the teeth: *a toothy grin.* **– toothily,** *adv.* **– toothiness,** *n.*

**tootle**[1] /ˈtutl/, *v.,* **-tled, -tling,** *n.* *–v.i.* **1.** to toot gently or repeatedly on a flute or the like. *–n.* **2.** the sound itself. [frequentative of TOOT[1]]

**tootle**[2] /ˈtutl/, *v.i.,* **-tled, -tling.** *Colloq.* **1.** to go or walk. **2.** to drive. **3. tootle off,** to depart.

**too-too** /tu-ˈtu/, *adj. Colloq.* excessive; absurd: *that dress is just too-too.*

**tootsy** /ˈtutsi/, *n., pl.* **-sies.** *Colloq.* **1.** a foot. **2.** Also, **toots.** a beloved one (often used in direct address). **3. play tootsy,** *Colloq.* **a.** (of two people) to touch feet secretly under a table as part of amorous play. **b.** (of a man) to have an affair. [Brit. d. *toot* foot (alteration of FOOT, or from OE *tōtian* to protrude) + *-sy* hypocoristic suffix]

**top**[1] /tɒp/, *n., adj., v.,* **topped, topping.** *–n.* **1.** the highest point or part of anything; the apex; the summit. **2.** the uppermost or upper part, surface, etc., of anything. **3.** the higher end of anything on a slope. **4.** a part considered as higher: *the top of a street.* **5.** the part of a plant above ground, as distinguished from the root. **6.** (*usu. pl.*) one of the tender tips of the branches or shoots of plants. **7.** that part of anything which is first or foremost; the beginning. **8.** the highest or leading place, position, rank, etc.: *at the top of the class.* **9.** the highest point, pitch, or degree: *to speak at the top of one's voice.* **10.** one who or that which occupies the highest or leading position. **11.** *Poetic.* the most perfect example, type, etc.: *the top of all honours.* **12.** the best or choicest part. **13.** a covering or lid, as of a box, motor car, carriage, etc. **14.** the head. **15.** the crown of the head. **16.** a blouse, skivvy, jumper, jacket or other outer garment, sometimes with sleeves, to cover the torso. **17.** *Motor Vehicles.* a transmission gear providing the highest forward speed ratio, usu. turning the drive shaft at the same rate as the engine crankshaft. **18.** *Naut.* a platform surrounding the head of a lower mast on a ship, and serving as a foothold, a means of extending the upper rigging, etc. **19.** *Chem.* that part of a mixture under distillation which volatilises first. **20.** *Golf, etc.* **a.** a stroke above the centre of the ball, usu. failing to give any height, distance, or accuracy. **b.** the forward spin given to the ball by such a stroke. **21.** (*pl.*) a continuous strand of untwisted fibres from which the shorter fibres, or noils, have been removed by combing. **22.** See **big top. 23. blow one's top,** *Colloq.* to lose one's temper. **24. off the top of one's head,** in an impromptu or improvised fashion. **25. from the top,** from the beginning. **26. on top,** successful; victorious; dominant. **27. on top of, a.** upon. **b.** close upon; following upon. **28. over the top,** *Mil.* over the top of the parapet before a trench, as in issuing to charge against the enemy. **29. the Top,** see **top end. 30. the tops, a.** the peaks or ridges of a high mountain range: *Barrington Tops.* **b.** Also, **tops.** *Colloq.* the very best: *that book really is the tops.* *–adj.* **31.** pertaining to, situated at, or forming the top; highest; uppermost; upper: *the top shelf.* **32.** highest in degree; greatest: *to pay top prices.* **33.** foremost, chief, or principal: *to win top honours in a competition.* **34.** *Colloq.* the best; excellent: *he's a top bloke.* **35.** denoting or pertaining to the highest forward gear on a vehicle. **36. top dog,** the person in the highest or most important position. *–v.t.* **37.** to furnish with a top; put a top on. **38.** to be at or constitute the top of. **39.** to reach the top of. **40.** to rise above: *the sun had topped the horizon.* **41.** to exceed in height, amount, number, etc. **42.** to surpass, excel, or outdo: *that tops everything!* **43.** to come up to or go beyond the requirements of (a part or character). **44.** to surmount with something specified. **45.** to complete by or as by putting the top on or constituting the top of. **46.** to remove the top of; crop; prune. **47.** to get or leap over the top of (a fence, etc.). **48.** *Chem.* to distil off only the most volatile part of a mixture. **49.** *Golf, etc.* **a.** to hit (the ball) above the centre. **b.** to make (a stroke, etc.) by hitting the ball in this way. **50.** to top-dress (land). **51.** *Colloq.* to inform on; tell on (fol. by *off*). **52. top off,** to complete with success (fol. by *with*). **53. top up,** to fill by adding liquid to (a partly filled container). *–v.i.* **54.** to rise aloft. **55.** *Golf, etc.* to hit the ball above the centre. [ME and OE, c. D *top(p),* G *Zopf* top, tuft of hair]

**top**[2] /tɒp/, *n.* **1.** a child's toy, often inversely conical, with a point on which it is made to spin. **2.** *Colloq.* →**amplifier** (def. 2). **3. sleep like a top,** to sleep very soundly. [ME and OE, c. Flem. *top.* Cf. G *Topf*]

**top-,** variant of **topo-,** before vowels, as in *toponym.*

**topaz** /ˈtoʊpæz/, *n.* **1.** a mineral, a fluosilicate of aluminium, usu. occurring in prismatic orthorhombic crystals of various colours, and used as a gem (**true topaz** or **precious topaz**). **2.** a yellow variety of sapphire (**oriental topaz**). **3.** a yellow variety of quartz (**false topaz** or **common topaz**). [L *topazus,* from Gk *tópazos;* replacing ME *topace,* from OF]

**top-boot** /'tɒp-but/, *n.* a high boot, esp. one having the upper part of a different material from the rest.

**topcoat** /'tɒpkoʊt/, *n.* **1.** a lightweight overcoat. **2.** an outer coat; an overcoat.

**top cross** /tɒp 'krɒs/, *n.* the progeny of the cross of a variety by one inbred line.

**top dog** /– 'dɒg/, *n.* **1.** *Colloq.* leader; boss. **2.** in a sawpit, the man who is above the log working the top end of the saw.

**top drawer** /– 'drɔ/, *n. Colloq.* the highest level, esp. of social class. – **topdrawer,** *adj.*

**top-dress** /'tɒp-drɛs/, *v.t.* to apply a top dressing to (land).

**top dressing** /'tɒp drɛsɪŋ/, *n.* **1.** a dressing of manure, soil, fertiliser, etc. on the surface of lawns, crops, etc. **2.** the action of one who top-dresses. **3.** a top layer of gravel, crushed rock, etc., on a roadway. **4.** any superficial treatment or surface covering.

**tope**[1] /toʊp/, *v.,* **toped, toping.** *–v.i.* **1.** to consume alcoholic drink habitually and to excess. *–v.t.* **2.** to drink (alcohol) habitually and to excess. [var. of obs. *top* drink, apparently special use of *top* tip, tilt, topple; ? akin to TOP[2]]

**tope**[2] /toʊp/, *n.* **1.** a small shark, *Galeorhinus galeus,* found along the European coast. **2.** any of various related sharks of small to medium size. [orig. uncert., ? from Cornish]

**tope**[3] /toʊp/, *n.* (in Buddhist countries) a dome-shaped monument, usu. for religious relics. [Hind. *tōp*]

tope[3]

**topee** /'toʊpi/, *n.* (in India) a helmet of sola pith. Also, **topi.** [Hind.: hat]

**top end** /'tɒp ɛnd/, *n.* (*sometimes caps.*) *Colloq.* the northern part of a geographical division, esp. the top end of the Northern Territory of Australia.

**top-ender** /tɒp-'ɛndə/, *n.* (*sometimes cap.*) *Colloq.* a person living in the northern part of the Northern Territory of Australia.

**toper** /'toʊpə/, *n.* a hard drinker; a chronic drunkard. [TOPE[1] + -ER[1]]

**top fermentation** /ˌtɒp fɜmɛn'teɪʃən/, *n.* a brewing method using a strain of yeast that rises to the top of the vessel at the completion of fermentation, producing old beer or ale. Cf. **bottom fermentation.**

**top-flight** /'tɒp-flaɪt/, *adj.* first-rate; superior.

**top forty** /tɒp 'fɔti/, *n.* a list of forty pop records, arranged according to assessed popularity.

**topgallant** /tɒp'gælənt/; *Naut.* /tə'gælənt/, *n.* **1.** the spars and rigging next above the topmast, in a square-rigged vessel. *–adj.* **2.** pertaining to the topgallant. [TOP[1] + GALLANT, *adj.*]

**tophamper** /'tɒphæmpə/, *n. Naut.* **1.** the light upper sails and their gear and spars, sometimes used to refer to all spars and gear above the deck. **2.** the fittings, furniture and tackle that are above the upper deck of a vessel, esp. those which are aloft.

**top hat** /'tɒp haet/, *n.* **1.** a man's tall silk hat. **2.** →**high hat** (def. 2).

**top-heavy** /'tɒp-hɛvi/, *adj.* **1.** having the top disproportionately heavy; liable to fall from too great weight above. **2.** *Finance.* **a.** having a financial structure overburdened with securities which have priority in the payment of dividends. **b.** overcapitalised. – **top-heaviness,** *n.*

**top-hole** /tɒp-'hoʊl/, *adj. Chiefly Brit. Colloq.* first-rate.

**tophus** /'toʊfəs/, *n., pl.* **-phi** /-faɪ/. a calcareous concretion formed in the soft tissue about a joint, in the pinna of the ear, etc., esp. in gout; a gouty deposit. [L, var. of *tōfus* sandstone]

**topi**[1] /'toʊpi/, *n., pl.* **-pis.** a medium-sized, short-horned East African antelope, *Damaliscus korrigum.*

**topi**[2] /'toʊpi/, *n., pl.* **-pis.** →**topee.**

**topiary** /'toʊpiəri/, *adj., n., pl.* **-aries.** *–adj.* **1.** (of hedges, trees, etc.) clipped or trimmed into (fantastic) shapes. **2.** of or pertaining to such trimming. *–n.* **3.** topiary work; the topiary art. **4.** a garden containing such work. [L *topiārius*] – **topiarian** /toʊpi'ɛəriən/, *adj.* – **topiarist,** *n.*

**topic** /'tɒpɪk/, *n.* **1.** a subject of conversation or discussion: *to provide a topic for discussion.* **2.** the subject or theme of a discourse or of one of its parts. **3.** *Rhet., Logic.* a general field of considerations from which arguments can be drawn. **4.** a general rule or maxim. [sing. of *topics,* from L, anglicisation of *topica,* pl., from Gk *tà topiká* name of work by Aristotle (lit., things pertaining to commonplaces)]

topiary

**topical** /'tɒpɪkəl/, *adj.* **1.** pertaining to or dealing with matters of current or local interest. **2.** pertaining to the subject of a discourse, composition, or the like. **3.** of a place; local. **4.** *Med.* pertaining or applied to a particular part of the body. – **topically,** *adv.*

**topknot** /'tɒpnɒt/, *n.* **1.** a tuft of hair growing on the top of the head. **2.** a knot of hair so worn in some styles of hairdressing. **3.** a knot or bow of ribbon worn on the top of the head. **4.** a tuft or crest of feathers on the head of a bird. **5.** any of the various flatfishes of the genus *Zeugopterus.* **6.** wool shorn from the top of a sheep's head.

**topknot pigeon** /– 'pɪdʒən/, *n.* a large, grey, nomadic pigeon, *Lopholaimus antarcticus,* with a black-banded tail and a round black and brown crest, usu. found in flocks in coastal forest areas of eastern Australia from Cape York to northern Victoria. Also, **flock pigeon.**

**topless** /'tɒpləs/, *adj.* **1.** without a top. **2.** having the breasts bare. **3.** allowing the breasts to be exposed, as a garment. *–n.* **4.** a topless garment, esp. a dress.

**top-line** /'tɒp-laɪn/, *adj.* of the highest importance; among the best. – **top-liner,** *n.*

**top lines** /tɒp 'laɪnz/, *n. pl.* the melodic line together with the chord chart of a musical composition, esp. jazz, rock or pop, as opposed to a fully notated arrangement.

**toplofty** /tɒp'lɒfti/, *adj. Colloq.* haughty; pompous; pretentious. – **toploftiness,** *n.*

**top maker's type,** *n.* a combing wool having faults which exclude it from the spinner's section.

**topman** /'tɒpmən/, *n., pl.* **-men.** a man stationed for duty in a ship's top.

**topmast** /'tɒpmast/; *Naut.* /-məst/, *n.* the second section of mast above the deck, being that just above the lower mast.

**top minnow** /tɒp 'mɪnoʊ/, *n.* any of several small surface-swimming cyprinodont fishes in North and South America, of the egg-laying family Cyprinodontidae and the live-bearing family Poeciliidae.

**topmost** /'tɒpmoʊst/, *adj.* highest; uppermost.

**topnotch** /'tɒpnɒtʃ/, *adj.* **1.** *Colloq.* first-rate: *a topnotch job.* *–n.* **2.** in a sawpit, the man who positions wedges in the log to prevent the saw from jamming.

**topnotcher** /tɒp'nɒtʃə/, *n.* a person or thing of unsurpassed excellence.

**topo-,** a word element meaning 'place', as in *topography.* Also, **top-.** [Gk, combining form of *tópos*]

**topochemistry** /tɒpoʊ'kɛməstri/, *n.* the study of chemical reactions which are confined to a specified part of a system.

**top-off** /'tɒp-ɒf/, *n. Colloq.* one who informs on another, usu. apparently in jest or by accident.

**topog.,** **1.** topographical. **2.** topography.

**topographer** /tə'pɒgrəfə/, *n.* **1.** a specialist in topography. **2.** one who describes the surface features of a place or region.

**topography** /tə'pɒgrəfi/, *n., pl.* **-phies.** **1.** the detailed description and analysis of the features of a relatively small area, district, or locality. **2.** the detailed description of particular localities, as cities, towns, estates, etc. **3.** the relief features or surface configuration of an area. [ME, from LL *topographia,* from Gk] – **topographic** /tɒpə'græfɪk/, **topographical** /tɒpə'græfɪkəl/, *adj.* – **topographically** /tɒpə'græfɪkli/, *adv.*

**topology** /tə'pɒlədʒi/, *n.* the study of those properties of geometric forms that remain invariant under certain transformations, as bending, stretching, etc. [TOPO- + -LOGY] – **topologic** /tɒpə'lɒdʒɪk/, **topological** /tɒpə'lɒdʒɪkəl/, *adj.*

– **topologically** /tɒpə'lɒdʒɪkli/, *adv.*

**toponym** /'tɒpənɪm/, *n.* **1.** a placename. **2.** a name derived from the name of a place. [TOP- + *-onym,* modelled on SYNONYM]

**toponymy** /tə'pɒnəmi/, *n., pl.* **-mies.** **1.** the study of the placenames of a region. **2.** *Anat.* the nomenclature of the regions of the body. – **toponymic** /tɒpə'nɪmɪk/, **toponymical** /tɒpə'nɪmɪkəl/, *adj.*

**topper** /'tɒpə/, *n.* **1.** one who or that which tops. **2.** *Colloq.* a top-hat. **3.** *Colloq.* anything excellent.

**topping** /'tɒpɪŋ/, *n.* **1.** the act of one who or that which tops. **2.** a distinct part forming a top to something. **3.** something put on a thing at the top to complete it. **4.** a sweet sauce for ice-cream, puddings, etc. *–adj.* **5.** *Chiefly Brit. Colloq.* excellent. **6.** *Obs.* rising above something else; overtopping.

**topping lift** /'– lɪft/, *n.* a rope or wire used for lifting the end of a derrick or boom.

**topping-out ceremony** /tɒpɪŋ-'aʊt ˌsɛrəməni/, *n.* a celebration held by construction workers, etc., when the highest point on the structure of a new building is completed.

**topple** /'tɒpəl/, *v.,* **-pled, -pling.** *–v.t.* **1.** to fall forwards as having too heavy a top; pitch or tumble down. **2.** to lean over or jut, as if threatening to fall. *–v.t.* **3.** to cause to topple. [frequentative of *top* topple. See TOPE[1]]

**topsail** /'tɒpseɪl/; *Naut.* /-səl/, *n.* **1.** a square sail (or either of two square sails) next above the lowest or chief square sail on a mast of a square-rigged vessel, or next above a chief fore-and-aft sail on topsail schooners, etc. **2.** in a fore-and-aft rig, a square or triangular sail set above the gaff.

**top-secret** /'tɒp-sikrət/, *adj.* extremely secret.

**topside** /'tɒpsaɪd/, *n.* **1.** the upper side. **2.** (*usu. pl.*) the upper part of a boat's or ship's side, above the main deck. **3.** the top section of a butt of beef, without bone, below the rump.

**topsoil** /'tɒpsɔɪl/, *n.* **1.** the surface or upper part of the soil. *–v.t.* **2.** to cover (land) with topsoil.

**top spin** /'tɒp spɪn/, *Cricket. –adj.* **1.** forward spin imparted to the ball by the bowler at the moment of delivery. *–n.* **2.** →**topspinner.**

**topspinner** /'tɒpspɪnə/, *n. Cricket.* **1.** a delivery in which forward spin is imparted to the ball, so that it does not deviate significantly on bouncing, but accelerates off the pitch, and often bounces unexpectedly high. **2.** a bowler specialising in such deliveries.

**topsy-turvy** /tɒpsi-'tɜvi/, *adv., adj., n., pl.* **-vies.** *–adv.* **1.** with the top where the bottom should be; upside down. **2.** in or into a reversed condition or order. **3.** in or into a state of confusion or disorder. *–adj.* **4.** turned upside down; inverted; reversed. **5.** confused or disorderly. *–n.* **6.** inversion of the natural order. **7.** a state of confusion or disorder. [akin to TOP[1] and ME *terve* overturn (cf. OE *tearflian* roll)] – **topsy-turvily,** *adv.* – **topsy-turviness,** *n.*

**topsy-turvydom** /tɒpsi-'tɜvidəm/, *n.* a state of affairs or a region in which everything is topsy-turvy.

**toque** /toʊk/, *n.* a hat with little or no brim and often with a soft or full crown, worn by women and (formerly) men. [F: a hat, bonnet, c. It. *tocca* cap, Sp. *toca* kerchief, Pg. *touca* coif]

**tor** /tɔ/, *n.* a rocky eminence; a hill. [ME; OE *torr,* from Celtic. Cf. Gael. *torr,* Welsh *twr* protuberance]

**Torah** /'tɔrə/, *n.* **1.** the teaching and judgments of the early Jewish priests. **2.** →**Pentateuch.** Also, **Tora.** [Heb: instruction, law]

**torbanite** /'tɔbənaɪt/, *n.* a dark brown oil shale which is rich in carbonaceous matter (70-80 per cent). [named after *Torbane* Hill in Scotland. See -ITE[1]]

**torbernite** /'tɔbənaɪt/, *n.* a mineral, hydrated copper uranium phosphate, $CuU_2P_2O_{12}\cdot 12H_2O$, a minor ore of uranium, occurring in square tabular crystals of a bright green colour; copper uranite. [named after *Torber* Bergmann, 1735-84, Swedish chemist. See -ITE[1]]

**torc** /tɔk/, *n.* →**torque** (def. 4).

**torch** /tɔtʃ/, *n.* **1.** a small portable electric lamp powered by dry batteries. **2.** a light to be carried in the hand, consisting of some combustible substance, as resinous wood, or of twisted flax or the like soaked with tallow or other inflammable substance. **3.** something considered as a source of illumination, enlightenment, guidance, etc.: *the torch of learning.* **4.** any of various lamplike devices which produce a hot flame and are used for soldering, burning off paint, etc; an oxyacetylene burner. **5.** a person who, for a fee, sets fire to someone's property so that the owner may collect the insurance money. **6. carry a torch for,** to suffer unrequited love for. [ME *torche,* from OF] – **torchless,** *adj.*

**torchbearer** /'tɔtʃbɛərə/, *n.* **1.** one who or that which carries a torch. **2.** one who brings knowledge or enlightenment, esp. in a new sphere of activity.

**torchlight** /'tɔtʃlaɪt/, *n.* the light of a torch or torches.

**torchon lace** /'tɔʃən leɪs/, *n.* **1.** bobbin-made linen or cotton lace with loosely twisted threads in simple, open patterns. **2.** a machine-made imitation of this, in linen or cotton. [*torchon,* from F: dishcloth]

**torch song** /'tɔtʃ sɒŋ/, *n.* a moody, romantic song, popular in the 1930s, sung by a woman singer, esp. in a nightclub. – **torch-singer,** *n.*

**torchwood** /'tɔtʃwʊd/, *n.* **1.** any of various resinous woods suitable for making torches, as the wood of the tree, *Amyris balsamifera,* of Florida, the West Indies, etc. **2.** any of the trees yielding these woods.

**tore**[1] /tɔ/, *v.* past tense of **tear**[2].

**tore**[2] /tɔ/, *n.* →**torus.** [F, from L *torus* TORUS]

**toreador** /'tɒriədɔ/, *n.* a Spanish bullfighter. [Sp., from *torear* fight bulls, from *toro* bull, from L *taurus*]

**torero** /tɒ'rɛəroʊ/, *n., pl.* **-ros** /-roʊz/. a bullfighter who fights on foot. [Sp.]

**toreutic** /tə'rutɪk/, *adj.* of or pertaining to toreutics or to objects decorated by this work. [Gk *toreutikós,* from *toreúein* to emboss]

**toreutics** /tə'rutɪks/, *n.* the art of decorating metal by embossing or engraving.

**toric** /'tɔrɪk/, *adj.* **1.** denoting or pertaining to a lens with a surface forming a portion of a torus, used for spectacles. **2.** *Geom.* of or pertaining to a torus. [TOR(US) + -IC]

**torii** /'tɔrii/, *n., pl.* **torii.** a form of decorative gateway or portal in Japan, consisting of two upright wooden posts connected at the top by two horizontal crosspieces, and commonly found at the entrance to Shinto temples. [Jap.]

**torment** /tɔ'mɛnt/, *v.;* /'tɔmɛnt/, *n.* *–v.t.* **1.** to afflict with great bodily or mental suffering; pain: *to be tormented with violent headaches.* **2.** to worry or annoy excessively: *to torment one with questions.* **3.** to throw into commotion; stir up; disturb. *–n.* **4.** a state of great bodily or mental suffering; agony; misery. **5.** something that causes great bodily or mental pain or suffering. **6.** a source of pain, anguish, trouble, worry, or annoyance. **7.** *Archaic.* **a.** an instrument of torture, as the rack or the thumbscrew. **b.** the infliction of torture by means of such an instrument. **c.** the torture inflicted. [ME, from OF *tormenter,* from *torment* torment, n., from L *tormentum* something operated by twisting] – **tormentingly,** *adv.*

**tormentil** /'tɔməntɪl/, *n.* a low herb, *Potentilla erecta,* of Europe and western Asia with small bright yellow flowers, and a strongly astringent root which is used in medicine and in tanning and dyeing. [ME *tormentille,* from ML *tormentilla,* diminutive of *tormentum* TORMENT]

**tormentor** /tɔ'mɛntə/, *n.* **1.** one who or that which torments. **2.** *Theat.* a curtain or framed structure behind the proscenium at each side of the stage to conceal stage lights, etc. Also, **tormenter.**

**torn** /tɔn/, *v.* **1.** past participle of **tear**[2]. **2. that's torn it,** everything is ruined. **3. torn between,** unable to choose between (conflicting desires, duties, etc.).

**tornado** /tɔ'neɪdoʊ/, *n., pl.* **-does, -dos.** **1.** *Meteorol.* **a.** a violent whirlwind of small radius, advancing over the land, in which winds of destructive force circulate round a centre. It is characterised by strong ascending currents and is generally made visible by a funnel-shaped cloud. **b.** a violent squall or whirlwind of small extent, as those occurring during the summer months on the west coast of Africa. **2.** a violent outburst, as of emotion or activity. [Sp., from *tornar* to turn, b. with *tronada* thunderstorm, from *tronar* to thunder, from L *tonāre*] – **tornadic** /tɔ'nædɪk/, *adj.* – **tornado-like,** *adj.*

**toroid** /'tɔrɔɪd/, *n.* **1.** a surface generated by the revolution of any closed plane curve or contour about an axis lying in its plane and outside it. **2.** the solid enclosed by such a surface. [TOR(US) + -OID]

**toroidal** /tɔ'rɔɪdl/, *adj.* denoting or pertaining to a torus.

**torose** /'tɔroʊs, tɔ'roʊs/, *adj.* **1.** *Bot.* cylindrical, with swellings or constrictions at intervals; knobbed. **2.** *Zool.* bulging. Also, **torous** /'tɔrəs/. [L *torōsus* bulging. See TORUS]

**torp** /tɔp/, *n. Colloq.* →**torpedo punt.**

**torpedo** /tɔ'pidoʊ/, *n., pl.* **-does,** *v.,* **-doed, -doing.** *–n.* **1.** a self-propelled cigar-shaped missile containing explosives which is launched from a tube in a submarine, torpedo-boat or the like, or from an aircraft, and explodes upon impact with the ship fired at. **2.** *Obs.* any of various submarine explosive devices for destroying hostile ships, as a mine. **3.** *U.S.* a cartridge of gunpowder, dynamite, or the like, exploded in an oilwell to start or increase the flow of oil, or elsewhere for other purposes. **4.** any of various other explosive devices. **5.** any of the fishes of the genus *Torpedo,* relatives of the rays and sharks, characterised by their ability to give electric shocks to aggressors. **6.** →**torpedo punt.** *–v.t.* **7.** to attack, hit, damage, or destroy with a torpedo or torpedoes. **8.** *U.S.* to explode a torpedo in (an oilwell) to start or increase the flow of oil. *–v.i.* **9.** to attack, damage, or sink a ship with torpedoes. [L: crampfish or electric ray, which disables its prey by electric discharge, from *torpēre* to be numb, inactive]

**torpedo-boat** /tɔ'pidoʊ-ˌboʊt/, *n.* a warship of small size and high speed used primarily for torpedo attacks.

**torpedo-boat destroyer** /– də'strɔɪə/, *n.* a vessel somewhat larger than the ordinary torpedo-boat, designed for the destruction of enemy torpedo-boats, or as a more powerful form of torpedo-boat.

**torpedo punt** /tɔ'pidoʊ pʌnt/, *n.* a punt kick executed to impart a torpedo-like, lateral spin to a football. Also, **spiral punt.**

**torpedo tube** /'– tjub/, *n.* **1.** a tube through which a self-propelled torpedo is launched, usu. by the detonation of a charge of explosive. **2.** a tube-shaped piece of polystyrene foam, about one metre long and covered with plastic, used in the water to support people in danger of drowning.

**torpid** /'tɔpəd/, *adj.* **1.** inactive or sluggish, as a bodily organ. **2.** slow; dull; apathetic; lethargic. **3.** dormant, as a hibernating or aestivating animal. [L *torpidus* numb] **– torpidity** /tɔ'pɪdəti/, **torpidness,** *n.* **– torpidly,** *adv.*

**torpor** /'tɔpə/, *n.* **1.** a state of suspended physical powers and activities. **2.** sluggish inactivity or inertia. **3.** dormancy, as of a hibernating animal. **4.** lethargic dullness or indifference; apathy. [L: numbness]

**torporific** /tɔpə'rɪfɪk/, *adj.* causing torpor.

**torquate** /'tɔkweɪt, -kweɪt/, *adj.* ringed about the neck, as with feathers or a colour; collared. [L *torquātus,* pp., adorned with a necklace]

**torque** /tɔk/, *n.* **1.** *Mech.* that which produces or tends to produce torsion or rotation; the moment of a system of forces which tends to cause rotation. **2.** *Mach.* the turning power of a shaft. **3.** the rotational effect on plane-polarised light passing through certain liquids or crystals. **4.** Also, **torc.** a collar, necklace, or similar ornament consisting of a twisted narrow band, usu. of precious metal, worn esp. by the ancient Gauls and Britons. [L *torques* twisted metal necklace]

**torque converter** /– kən'vɜtə/, *n.* See **fluid drive.**

**torquemeter** /'tɔkmitə/, *n.* a device for measuring the torque of a rotating shaft enabling the power transmitted, or the power of an engine to which it is attached, to be calculated.

**torques** /'tɔkwiz/, *n.* a ringlike band or formation about the neck of an animal, as of feathers, hair, or integument of distinctive colour or appearance; a collar. [L: twisted neck chain or collar]

**torr** /tɔ/, *n.* a non-SI unit of pressure, equal to 133.322 37 pascals, used in the field of high vacuum. [named after E. *Torricelli,* 1608-47, Italian physicist]

**torrefy** /'tɒrəfaɪ/, *v.t.,* **-fied, -fying. 1.** to dry or parch with heat, as drugs, etc. **2.** to roast, as metallic ores. Also, **torrify.** [L *torrefacere* make dry or hot] **– torrefaction** /tɒrə'fækʃən/, *n.*

**Torrens title** /tɒrənz 'taɪtl/, *n.* the name given to a system whereby title to land is evidenced by one document issued by a government department. [introduced by Sir Robert Richard Torrens in South Australia in 1858]

**torrent** /'tɒrənt/, *n.* **1.** a stream of water flowing with great rapidity and violence. **2.** a rushing, violent, or abundant and unceasing stream of anything: *a torrent of lava.* **3.** a violent downpour of rain. **4.** a violent, tumultuous, or overwhelming flow: *a torrent of abuse.* [L *torrens* torrent, lit., boiling; replacing ME *torrens,* from L]

**torrential** /tə'rɛnʃəl/, *adj.* **1.** pertaining to or having the nature of a torrent. **2.** resembling a torrent in rapidity or violence. **3.** falling in torrents. **4.** produced by the action of a torrent. **5.** violent, vehement, or impassioned. **6.** overwhelming; extraordinarily copious. **– torrentially,** *adv.*

**torrid** /'tɒrəd/, *adj.* **1.** subject to parching or burning heat, esp. of the sun, as regions, etc. **2.** oppressively hot, parching, or burning, as climate, weather, air, etc. **3.** ardent; passionate. [L *torridus*] **– torridity** /tə'rɪdəti/, **torridness,** *n.* **– torridly,** *adv.*

**Torrid Zone** /'tɒrəd zoʊn/, *n.* the part of the earth's surface between the tropics of Cancer and Capricorn.

**torrify** /'tɒrəfaɪ/, *v.t.,* **-fied, -fying.** →**torrefy.**

**torsade** /tɔ'seɪd/, *n.* **1.** a twisted cord. **2.** any ornamental twist, as of velvet. [F: twisted fringe, from *tordre,* from LL *torcēre,* replacing L *torquēre* twist]

**torsibility** /tɔsə'bɪləti/, *n.* **1.** capability of being twisted. **2.** resistance to being twisted. **3.** capacity to return to original shape after being twisted.

**torsion** /'tɔʃən/, *n.* **1.** the act of twisting. **2.** the resulting state. **3.** *Mech.* **a.** the twisting of a body by two equal and opposite torques. **b.** the internal torque so produced. [ME *torcion,* from LL *torsio,* from *torquēre* twist] **– torsional,** *adj.* **– torsionally,** *adv.*

**torsion balance** /'– bæləns/, *n.* an instrument for measuring small forces (as electrical attraction or repulsion) by determining the amount of torsion or twisting they cause in a slender wire or filament.

**torsion bar** /'– ba/, *n.* a metal bar with the function of a torsional spring, resembling a coiled spring that has been drawn out into a rod, and used in the suspension system of some motor vehicles.

**torsk** /tɔsk/, *n.* **1.** a deep-bodied fish with large scales, belonging to the family Ophidiidae, found in deep waters of the Great Australia Bight. **2.** an edible marine fish, *Brosmius brosme,* of both coasts of the North Atlantic.

**torso** /'tɔsoʊ/, *n., pl.* **-sos. 1.** the trunk of the human body. **2.** a sculptured form representing the trunk of a nude female or male figure. **3.** something mutilated or incomplete. Also, **torse.** [It.: trunk, stump, stalk, trunk of statue, from L *thyrsus* THYRSUS]

**tort** /tɔt/, *n. Law.* **1.** any wrong other than a criminal wrong, as negligence, defamation, etc. **2.** (*pl.*) the field of study of wrongs other than criminal wrongs. See **executor de son tort.** [F: a wrong]

**torte** /tɔt/, *n.* a large, highly decorated cake containing cream and other rich ingredients, usu. served on festive occasions. [G, from LL *torta.* See TORTILLA]

**tortellini** /tɔtə'lini/, *n.* a dish, originally from Bologna, Italy, which consists of small coils of pasta, filled with a rich stuffing, usu. of meat, eggs, and cheese, served with butter and grated cheese, or in a broth. [It.]

**tortfeasor** /tɔt'fizə/, *n. Law.* one who commits a tort.

**torticollis** /tɔtə'kɒləs/, *n.* a condition in which the neck is twisted and the head inclined to one side, by spasmodic contraction of the muscles of the neck. [NL crooked neck. See TORT, COLLAR]

**tortile** /'tɔtaɪl/, *adj.* twisted; coiled. [L *tortilis* twisted, winding]

**tortilla** /tɔ'tijə/, *n.* (in Mexico, etc.) a thin, round, unleavened cake prepared from cornmeal, baked on a flat plate of iron, earthenware, or the like. [Sp., diminutive of *torta* cake, from LL *torta* (*pānis*) twisted (bread)]

**tortious** /'tɔʃəs/, *adj. Law.* of the nature of or pertaining to a tort. [ME *torcious,* from AF, from ML *tortio* use of violence, in L torture] **– tortiously,** *adv.*

**tortoise** /'tɔtəs/, *n.* **1.** any terrestrial or freshwater reptile of the order Chelonia, having toed feet rather than flippers, as *Testudo chelodina.* **2.** *U.S.* →**turtle**[1] (defs 1 and 2). **3.** a very slow person or thing. **4.** →**testudo.** [ME *tortuce,* from ML *tortuca,* from L *tortus,* pp., twisted]

**tortoiseshell** /ˈtɔtəʃɛl/, *n.* **1.** the horny substance, with a mottled or clouded yellow-and-brown colouration, composing the plates or scales that cover the marine **tortoiseshell turtle,** of the genus *Eretmochelys,* formerly used for making combs and other articles, inlaying, etc. **2.** the shell of a tortoise. **3.** any synthetic substance made to appear like natural tortoiseshell. **4.** any of certain colourful butterflies (family Nymphalidae), as *Nymphalis polychloros,* with variegated undermarkings. **5.** Also, **tortoiseshell cat.** a domestic cat, usu. female, with yellow-and-black colouring. *–adj.* **6.** mottled or variegated like tortoiseshell, esp. with yellow and black and sometimes other colours. **7.** made of tortoiseshell.

long-necked tortoise

**tortuosity** /tɔtʃuˈɒsəti/, *n., pl.* **-ties. 1.** the state of being tortuous; twisted form or course; crookedness. **2.** a twist, bend, or crook. **3.** a twisting or crooked part, passage, or thing.

**tortuous** /ˈtɔtʃuəs/, *adj.* **1.** full of twists, turns, or bends; twisting, winding, or crooked. **2.** not direct or straightforward as in a course of procedure, thought, speech, or writing. **3.** deceitfully indirect or morally crooked, as proceedings, methods, policy, etc. **4.** *Geom.* not in one plane, as a curve, such as a helix, which does not lie in a plane. [ME, from L *tortuōsus* full of turns or twists] **– tortuously,** *adv.* **– tortuousness,** *n.*

**torture** /ˈtɔtʃə/, *n., v.,* **-tured, -turing.** *–n.* **1.** the act of inflicting excruciating pain, esp. from sheer cruelty or in hatred, revenge, or the like. **2.** a method of inflicting such pain. **3.** (*oft. pl.*) the pain or suffering caused or undergone. **4.** extreme anguish of body or mind; agony. **5.** a cause of severe pain or anguish. *–v.t.* **6.** to subject to torture. **7.** to afflict with severe pain of body or mind. **8.** to twist, force, or bring into some unnatural position or form: *trees tortured by storms.* **9.** to wrest, distort, or pervert (language, etc.). [L *tortūra* twisting, torment, torture] **– torturer,** *n.* **– torturous,** *adj.*

**torus** /ˈtɔrəs/, *n., pl.* **tori** /ˈtɔraɪ/. **1.** *Archit.* a large convex moulding, more or less semicircular in profile, commonly forming the lowest member of the base of a column, or that directly above the plinth (when present), and sometimes occurring as one of a pair separated by a scotia and fillets. **2.** *Geom.* **a.** a surface generated by the revolution of a circle about an axis lying in its plane and outside it. **b.** the solid enclosed by such a surface. **3.** *Bot.* the receptacle of a flower. **4.** *Anat., etc.* a rounded ridge; a protuberant part. [L: bulge, rounded moulding]

**torus palatinus** /– pæləˈtaɪnəs/, *n.* a rounded ridge on the hard palate. [NL]

**tory** /ˈtɔri/, *adj.* conservative; right-wing.

**tosh** /tɒʃ/, *n. Colloq.* nonsense.

**toss** /tɒs/, *v.,* **tossed** or (*Poetic*) **tost; tossing,** *n.* *–v.t.* **1.** to throw, pitch, or fling, esp. to throw lightly or carelessly: *to toss a piece of paper into the wastepaper basket.* **2.** to throw or send (a ball, etc.) from one to another, as in play. **3.** to throw or pitch with irregular or careless motions; fling or jerk about: *a ship tossed by the waves, a tree tosses its branches in the wind.* **4.** to agitate, disturb, or disquiet. **5.** to throw, raise, or jerk upwards suddenly: *she tossed her head disdainfully.* **6.** to throw (a coin, etc.) into the air in order to decide something by the side turned up when it falls (oft. fol. by *up*). **7.** to drink or eat very quickly (fol. by *off*): *he tossed off a few drinks and then left.* **8.** to produce quickly and easily: *he tossed off a few ideas.* **9.** (of an animal) to throw (someone or something) up into the air or to the ground. **10.** *Colloq.* to outwit; defeat. *–v.i.* **11.** to pitch, rock, sway, or move irregularly, as a ship on a rough sea, or a flag or plumes in the breeze. **12.** to fling or jerk oneself or move restlessly about, esp. on a bed or couch: *to toss in one's sleep.* **13.** to throw something. **14.** to throw a coin or other object into the air in order to decide something by the way it falls (oft. fol. by *up*). **15.** *Colloq.* to go with a fling of the body: *to toss out of a room.* **16. toss off,** *Colloq.* **a.** (of a male) to ejaculate sperm; have an orgasm. **b.** to masturbate. *–n.* **17.** the act of tossing. **18.** a pitching about or up and down. **19.** a throw or pitch. **20.** a tossing of a coin or the like to decide something; a toss-up. **21.** a sudden fling or jerk of the body, esp. a quick upward or backward movement of the head. **22. argue the toss,** to go on arguing after a dispute has been settled. **23. take a toss,** to fall from a horse. [apparently from Scand.; cf. d. Swed. *tossa* spread, strew] **– tosser,** *n.*

**tossed salad** /tɒst ˈsæləd/, *n.* a mixture of salad vegetables tossed in a dressing.

**tossil** /ˈtɒsəl/, *n. Colloq.* →**tassel** (def. 3). Also, **tossel, tassle.**

**tosspot** /ˈtɒspɒt/, *n. Colloq.* one who drinks to excess.

**toss-up** /ˈtɒs-ʌp/, *n.* **1.** the tossing up of a coin or the like to decide something by the side on which it falls. **2.** *Colloq.* an even chance.

**tost** /tɒst/, *v. Poetic.* past tense and past participle of **toss.**

**tot**[1] /tɒt/, *n.* **1.** a small child. **2.** a small portion of drink. **3.** a small quantity of anything. [? short for *totterer* child learning to walk]

**tot**[2] /tɒt/, *v.,* **totted, totting,** *n.* *Colloq.* *–v.t.* **1.** to add (oft. fol. by *up*). *–n.* **2.** a total. **3.** the act of adding. [L: so much, so many]

**tot.,** total.

**total** /ˈtoʊtl/, *adj., n., v.,* **-talled, -talling** or (*U.S.*) **-taled, -taling.** *–adj.* **1.** constituting or comprising the whole; entire; whole: *the total expenditure.* **2.** of or pertaining to the whole of something: *a total eclipse.* **3.** complete in extent or degree; absolute; unqualified; utter: *a total failure.* *–n.* **4.** the total amount; sum; aggregate: *to add the several items to find the total.* **5.** the whole; a whole or aggregate: *the costs reached a total of $200.* *–v.t.* **6.** to bring to a total; add up. **7.** to reach a total of; amount to. *–v.i.* **8.** to amount (oft. fol. by *to*). [ME, from ML *tōtālis,* from L *tōtus* entire]

**total abstainer** /– əbˈsteɪnə/, *n.* one who, for religious or other reasons, abstains from any form of alcoholic drink.

**total depravity** /– dəˈprævəti/, *n.* (in certain theological doctrines) the absolute unfitness of man, due to original sin, for the moral purposes of his being, until born again through the influence of the Spirit of God.

**total eclipse** /– əˈklɪps/, *n.* an eclipse in which the whole surface of the eclipsed body is obscured (opposed to *annular eclipse*).

**total heat** /– ˈhit/, *n.* →**enthalpy.**

**total internal reflection,** *n.* the total reflection of a light ray which occurs when light from one medium strikes another of refractive index or optical density, at an angle of incidence in excess of the critical angle.

**totalisator** /ˈtoʊtəlaɪˌzeɪtə/, *n.* **1.** an apparatus for registering and indicating the total of operations, measurements, etc. **2.** a form of betting, as on horseraces, in which those who bet on the winners divide the bets or stakes, less a percentage for the management, taxes, etc. **3.** the apparatus that records the bets. Also, **totalizator.**

**Totalisator Agency Board,** *n.* →**TAB.**

**totalise** /ˈtoʊtəlaɪz/, *v.t.,* **-lised, -lising.** to make total; combine into a total. Also, **totalize. – totalisation** /toʊtəlaɪˈzeɪʃən/, *n.*

**totaliser** /ˈtoʊtəlaɪzə/, *n.* **1.** →**totalisator. 2.** *Chiefly U.S.* →**adding machine.** Also, **totalizer.**

**totalitarian** /toʊˌtæləˈtɛəriən/, *adj.* **1.** of or pertaining to a centralised government in which those in control grant neither recognition nor tolerance to parties of differing opinion. *–n.* **2.** an adherent of totalitarian principles. **– totalitarianism,** *n.*

**totality** /toʊˈtæləti/, *n., pl.* **-ties. 1.** the state of being total; entirety. **2.** that which is total; the total; the total amount; a whole. **3.** *Astron.* total obscuration in an eclipse.

**totally** /ˈtoʊtəli/, *adv.* wholly; entirely; completely.

**total wage** /ˈtoʊtl weɪdʒ/, *n.* the normal wage paid to an employee considered as one total unit comprising both a basic wage and a margin for skill; gross wage.

**totara** /ˈtoʊtərə/, *n.* the conifer, *Podocarpus totara,* found in

New Zealand, the wood of which is widely used for building, furniture, etc. [Maori]

**tote**[1] /toʊt/, *v.*, **toted, toting,** *n. Colloq.* –*v.t.* **1.** to carry, as on the back or in the arms, as a burden or load. **2.** to carry or have on the person: *to tote a gun.* **3.** to transport or convey, as in a vehicle or boat. –*n.* **4.** the act or course of toting. **5.** that which is toted. [orig. uncert.]

**tote**[2] /toʊt/, *n.* →**totalisator.**

**tote bag** /'– bæg/, *n.* a bag with a large carrying capacity, used for shopping, etc.

**totem** /'toʊtəm/, *n.* **1.** an object or thing in nature, often an animal, assumed as the token or emblem of a clan, family, or related group. **2.** an object or natural phenomenon with which a primitive family or sib considers itself closely related, usu. by blood. **3.** a representation of such an object serving as the distinctive mark of the clan or group. [Algonquian *ototeman* his brother-sister kin, from *ote* parents, relations] – **totemic** /toʊ'tɛmɪk/, *adj.*

**totemism** /'toʊtəmɪzəm/, *n.* **1.** the practice of having totems. **2.** the system of tribal division according to totems.

**totemist** /'toʊtəməst/, *n.* a member of a clan or the like distinguished by a totem. – **totemistic** /toʊtəm'ɪstɪk/, *adj.*

**totem pole** /'toʊtəm poʊl/, *n.* a pole or post carved and painted with totemic figures, erected by Indians of the north-western coast of North America, esp. in front of their houses. Also, **totem post.**

**tother** /'tʌðə/, *adj., pron. Archaic.* the other. Also, **t'other.** [ME *the tother,* var. of *thet other* the other]

**t'othersider** /tʌðə'saɪdə/, *n. W.A. Colloq.* a person living on the other side of the Nullabor Plain.

**totipalmate** /toʊtə'pælmeɪt, -mət/, *adj.* having all toes fully webbed. [L *tōti-* (representing *tōtus* whole) + PALMATE]

**totipalmation** /toʊtəpæl'meɪʃən/, *n.* totipalmate condition or formation.

**totter** /'tɒtə/, *v.i.* **1.** to walk or go with faltering steps, as if from extreme weakness. **2.** to sway or rock on the base or ground, as if about to fall: *a tottering tower, a tottering government.* **3.** to shake or tremble: *a tottering load.* –*n.* **4.** the act of tottering; an unsteady movement or gait. **5.** *Colloq.* a rag-and-bone man; a scavenger. [ME *totre,* from Scand.; cf. d. Norw. *totra* quiver, shake] – **totterer,** *n.* – **totteringly,** *adv.*

**tottery** /'tɒtəri/, *adj.* tottering; shaky.

**toucan** /'tukæn/, *n.* any of various fruit-eating birds (family Ramphastidae) of tropical America, with an enormous beak and usu. a striking colouration. [Tupi *tucana*]

**touch** /tʌtʃ/, *v.t.* **1.** to put the hand, finger, etc., on or into contact with (something) to feel it. **2.** to come into contact with and perceive (something), as the hand or the like. **3.** to bring (the hand, finger, etc., or something held) into contact with something. **4.** to give a slight tap or pat to with the hand, finger, etc.; strike or hit gently or lightly. **5.** to hurt or injure. **6.** to come into or be in contact with. **7.** *Geom.* (of a line or surface) to be tangent to. **8.** to be adjacent to or border on. **9.** to come up to; reach; attain. **10.** to attain equality with; compare with (usu. with a negative). **11.** to mark by strokes of the brush, pencil, or the like. **12.** to modify or improve by adding a stroke of paint, etc., here and there (oft. fol. by *up*). **13.** to mark or relieve slightly, as with colour: *a grey dress touched with blue.* **14.** to strike the strings, keys, etc., of (a musical instrument) so as to cause it to sound. **15.** to play or perform, as a tune. **16.** to stop at (a place), as a ship. **17.** to treat or affect in some way by contact. **18.** to affect as if by contact; tinge; imbue. **19.** to affect with some feeling or emotion, esp. tenderness, pity, gratitude, etc.: *his heart was touched by their sufferings.* **20.** to handle, use, or have to do with (something) in any way: *he won't touch another drink.* **21.** to begin to eat; eat a little of: *he hardly touched his food.* **22.** to deal with or treat in speech or writing. **23.** to refer or allude to. **24.** to pertain or relate to: *a critic in all affairs touching the kitchen.* **25.** to be a matter of importance to; make a difference to. **26.** to stamp (tested metal) as being of standard purity, etc. **27.** *Colloq.* to apply to for money, or succeed in getting money from; to beg. **28. touch up, a.** to put finishing touches to. **b.** to repair, renovate, add points of detail to, as of photographs. –*v.i.* **29.** to place the hand, finger, etc., on or in contact with something. **30.** to come into or be in contact. **31.** to make a stop or a short call at a place, as a ship or those on board (usu. fol. by *at*). **32.** to speak or write briefly or casually (fol. by *on* or *upon*) in the course of a discourse, etc.: *he touched briefly on his own travels.* **33. touch down,** (of an aircraft) to land after a flight. –*n.* **34.** the act of touching. **35.** the state or fact of being touched. **36.** that sense by which anything material is perceived by means of the contact with it of some part of the body. **37.** the sensation or effect caused by touching something, regarded as a quality of the thing: *an object with a slimy touch.* **38.** a coming into or being in contact. **39.** a close relation of communication, agreement, sympathy, or the like: *to be in touch with public opinion.* **40.** a slight stroke or blow. **41.** a slight attack, as of illness or disease: *a touch of rheumatism.* **42.** a slight added action or effort in doing or completing any piece of work. **43.** manner of execution in artistic work. **44.** the act or manner of touching or fingering a musical instrument, esp. a keyboard instrument, so as to bring out the tone. **45.** the mode of action of the keys of an instrument. **46.** a partial series of changes on a peal of bells. **47.** a stroke or dash, as with a brush, pencil, or pen. **48.** a detail in any artistic work. **49.** a slight amount of some quality, attribute, etc.: *a touch of sarcasm in his voice.* **50.** a slight quantity or degree: *a touch of salt.* **51.** a distinguishing characteristic or trait: *the touch of the master.* **52.** quality or kind in general. **53.** the act of testing anything. **54.** something that serves as a test. **55.** *Colloq.* the act of applying to a person for money, as a gift or loan. **56.** *Colloq.* an obtaining of money thus. **57.** *Colloq.* the money obtained. **58.** *Colloq.* a person from whom such money can be obtained easily. **59.** an official mark or stamp put upon gold, silver, etc., after testing, to indicate standard fineness. **60.** a die, stamp, or the like for impressing such a mark. **61.** *Rugby Football, etc.* the area outside the field of play, including the touchlines. **62.** *Fencing.* a hit with the point of the weapon which scores a point. **63. keep (stay) in touch,** to maintain an association or friendship. [ME *touche(n),* from OF *tochier;* orig. uncert.] – **touchable,** *adj.*

**touch-and-go** /tʌtʃ-ən-'goʊ/, *adj.* **1.** hasty, sketchy, or desultory. **2.** precarious, risky: *a highly touch-and-go situation.* Also, (*esp. in predicative use*), **touch and go.**

**touchdown** /'tʌtʃdaʊn/, *n.* **1.** *Rugby Football.* the act of a player touching the ball down to the ground behind the opponent's goal line, so as to score a try. **2.** *American Football.* **a.** a similar act. **b.** the score made by this, counting 6 points. **3.** the landing of an aircraft.

**touché** /tu'ʃeɪ, 'tuʃeɪ/, *interj.* **1.** *Fencing.* (an expression indicating a touch by the point of a weapon.) **2.** good point! (said in acknowledging a telling remark or rejoinder). [F pp. of *toucher* to touch]

**touched** /tʌtʃt/, *adj.* **1.** moved; stirred. **2.** slightly crazy; unbalanced: *touched in the head.*

**toucher** /'tʌtʃə/, *n.* **1.** one who or that which touches. **2.** *Bowls.* a bowl which touches the jack after delivery and is then marked with chalk for final counting.

**touch football** /tʌtʃ 'fʊtbɔl/, *n.* a simplified form of the Rugby codes in which a player with the ball who is touched by an opponent is considered to have been tackled and must play the ball. Also, **tip football.**

**touch-hole** /'tʌtʃ-hoʊl/, *n.* (formerly) the vent in the breech of a firearm through which fire was communicated to the powder charge.

**touching** /'tʌtʃɪŋ/, *adj.* **1.** affecting; moving; pathetic. **2.** that touches. –*prep.* **3.** in reference or relation to; concerning; about. – **touchingly,** *adv.* – **touchingness,** *n.*

**touch-in-goal** /tʌtʃ-ɪn-'goʊl/, *n.* (in Rugby football) the extension of the touchline between the dead-ball line and the goal line.

**touch judge** /'tʌtʃ dʒʌdʒ/, *n.* (in Rugby football) one of two officials, one on each side of the field of play, who decide whether the ball has gone into touch and which side last played it.

**touchline** /'tʌtʃlaɪn/, *n.* (in Rugby football, etc.) any of the sidelines bordering the field of play.

**touchmark** /'tʌtʃmak/, *n.* an official mark or stamp indicating a standard of purity, used in marking pewter articles.

**touch-me-not** /'tʌtʃ-mi-ˌnɒt/, *n.* any of various plants of the genus *Impatiens,* whose ripe seeds burst open when touched.

**touchpaper** /ˈtʌtʃpeɪpə/, *n.* paper saturated with a substance, as potassium nitrate, which makes it smoulder slowly; used as a fuse in fireworks and explosives.

**touchstone** /ˈtʌtʃstoun/, *n.* **1.** a black siliceous stone used to test the purity of gold and silver by the colour of the streak produced on it by rubbing it with either metal. **2.** a test or criterion for the qualities of a thing.

**touch-type** /ˈtʌtʃ-taɪp/, *v.i.,* **-typed, -typing.** to type without looking at the keys of the typewriter.

**touchwood** /ˈtʌtʃwud/, *n.* **1.** wood converted into an easily ignitable substance by the action of certain fungi, and used as tinder. **2.** →**amadou.**

**touchy** /ˈtʌtʃi/, *adj.,* **touchier, touchiest. 1.** apt to take offence on slight provocation; irritable. **2.** precarious, risky, or ticklish, as a subject. **3.** sensitive to touch. **4.** easily ignited, as tinder. [var. of TETCHY, by association with TOUCH] – **touchily,** *adv.* – **touchiness,** *n.*

**tough** /tʌf/, *adj.* **1.** not easily broken or cut. **2.** not brittle or tender. **3.** difficult to masticate, as food. **4.** of viscous consistency, as liquid or semiliquid matter. **5.** capable of great endurance; sturdy; hardy. **6.** not easily influenced, as a person. **7.** hardened; incorrigible. **8.** difficult to perform, accomplish, or deal with; hard, trying, or troublesome. **9.** hard to bear or endure. **10.** vigorous; severe; violent: *a tough struggle.* **11.** rough, disorderly, or rowdyish. *–adv.* **12.** *Colloq.* aggressively; threateningly: *to act tough.* *–n.* **13.** a ruffian; a rowdy. [ME; OE *tōh.* Cf. D *taai,* G *zähe, zäh*] – **toughly,** *adv.* – **toughness,** *n.*

**toughen** /ˈtʌfən/, *v.i., v.t.* to make or become tough or tougher. – **toughener,** *n.*

**toughened glass** /tʌfənd ˈglas/, *n.* →**shatterproof glass** (def. 2).

**toupee** /ˈtupeɪ/, *n.* **1.** a wig or patch of false hair worn to cover a bald spot. **2.** (formerly) a curl or an artificial lock of hair on the top of the head, esp. as a crowning feature of a periwig. Also, **toupée.** [F *toupet,* from OF *to(u)p* tuft of hair. See TOP[1]]

**tour** /tuə, ˈtuə, tɔ/, *v.i.* **1.** to travel from place to place. **2.** to travel from place to place giving musical or theatrical performances. *–v.t.* **3.** to travel through (a place). **4.** (of a manager) to send or take (a theatrical company, its production, etc.) from place to place. *–n.* **5.** a travelling around from place to place. **6.** a long journey including the visiting of a number of places in sequence. **7.** *Chiefly Mil.* a period of duty at one place. **8.** *Cycling.* a road race extending over several days, starting and finishing at the same point. [ME, from F, from L *tornus,* tool for making a circle]

**touraco** /ˈturəkou/, *n., pl.* **-cos.** any of the large African birds constituting the family Musophagidae (genera *Turacus, Musophaga,* etc.), notable for their brilliant plumage and helmet-like crest. [some W African language. Cf. Twi *aturukuba* turtle-dove]

**tourbillion** /tuəˈbɪliən/, *n.* **1.** a whirlwind. **2.** a firework, as a rocket, which spirals in display. **3.** the whirl in the hair on the crown of the head. **4.** an astral force whch is said to be the base of the human spirit. [MF *tourbillon,* from L *turbō* whirlwind, top, whirl]

**tour de force** /tuə də ˈfɔs/, *n.* a feat requiring unusual strength, skill, or ingenuity. [F]

**tourer** /ˈtuərə, ˈtuə-, ˈtɔ-/, *n.* **1.** one who or that which tours. **2.** an open motor car; sports car.

**touring** /ˈtuərɪŋ, ˈtuə-, ˈtɔ-/, *adj.* **1.** of or pertaining to a sporting team, theatrical company, band, etc., which tours. **2.** of or pertaining to cross-country skiing.

**touring car** /ˈ– ka/, *n.* an open motor car designed for five or more passengers. Also, **tourer.**

**tourism** /ˈtuərɪzəm, ˈtuə-, ˈtɔ-/, *n.* **1.** the practice of touring, esp. for pleasure. **2.** the occupation of providing local services, as entertainment, lodging, food, etc., for tourists.

**tourist** /ˈtuərəst, ˈtuə-, ˈtɔ-/, *n.* **1.** one who tours, esp. for pleasure. **2.** a member of a touring international sporting team.

**tourist class** /ˈ– klas/, *n.* **1.** a type of lower-priced accommodation, as in a hotel, or as on a passenger ship or airliner. *adj.* **2.** of or pertaining to such accommodation or travel.

**touristy** /ˈtuərəsti/, *adj. Colloq.* **1.** abounding in, or attractive to, or designed for tourists. **2.** resembling a tourist in dress, behaviour, etc.

**tourmaline** /ˈtɔməlin/, *n.* a mineral, essentially a complex silicate containing boron, aluminium, sodium, lithium, magnesium and iron, occurring in various colours (black being common); the transparent varieties (red, pink, green and blue) are used in jewellery. [Singhalese *toramalli* cornelian]

**tournament** /ˈtɔnəmənt/, *n.* **1.** a meeting for contests in athletic or other sports. **2.** a trial of skill in some game, in which competitors play a series of contests: *a chess tournament.* **3.** *Hist.* **a.** a contest or martial sport in which two opposing parties of mounted and armoured combatants fought for a prize, with blunted weapons and in accordance with certain rules. **b.** a meeting at an appointed time and place for the performance of knightly exercises and sports. [ME *tornement,* from OF *torneiement,* from *torneier* TOURNEY, *v.*]

**tournedos** /ˈtuənədou/, *n., pl.* **-dos.** a small thick slice of fillet of beef fried in butter, often served on top of a fried crouton of similar size and shape, and wrapped in a rasher of bacon. [F from *tourne(r)* turn + *dos* the back]

**tourney** /ˈtuəni, ˈtɔ-/, *n., pl.* **-neys,** *v.,* **-neyed, -neying.** *Archaic.* *–n.* **1.** →**tournament** (def. 3). *–v.i.* **2.** to contend or engage in a tournament. [def. 1, ME from OF *tornei, tournay,* from *torneier* tourney, v. def. 2, ME, from OF *tourneier,* from *torn* turn, from L *tornus* lathe] – **tourneyer,** *n.*

**tourniquet** /ˈtɔnəkeɪ, ˈtuə-/, *n.* any device for arresting bleeding by forcibly compressing a blood vessel, as a pad pressed down by a screw, a bandage tightened by twisting, etc. [F, from *tourner* turn]

**tousle** /ˈtauzəl/, *v.,* **-sled, -sling,** *n.* *–v.t.* **1.** to disorder or dishevel: *his hair was tousled.* **2.** to handle roughly. *–n.* *Rare.* **3.** a tousled mass of hair. **4.** a tousled condition; a disordered mass. [ME *tousel;* frequentative of *touse* pull]

**tout** /taut/, *v.i.* **1.** to solicit business, employment, votes, etc., importunately. **2.** *Racing.* to sell betting information, take bets, etc., esp. in public places. **3.** to spy on a racehorse, etc., to obtain information for betting purposes. *–v.t.* **4.** to solicit support for importunately. **5.** to describe or proclaim, esp. favourably: *to tout a politician as a friend of the people.* **6.** to sell information on (a racehorse, etc.). **7.** to spy on (a racehorse, etc.) in order to gain information for betting purposes. **8.** to watch; spy on. *–n.* **9.** one who solicits custom, employment, support, etc., importunately. **10.** one who spies on racehorses, etc., to gain information for betting purposes, or who gives tips on racehorses, etc., as a business. [ME *tute(n);* akin to OE *tȳtan* peep out, become visible, shine (said of a star)]

**tout ensemble** /ˌtut õˈsõmblə/, *adv.* **1.** all together. *–n.* **2.** the assemblage of parts of details, as in a work of art, considered as forming a whole; the ensemble. [F]

**touter** /ˈtautə/, *n. Colloq.* one who touts; a tout.

**tow[1]** /tou/, *v.t.* **1.** to drag or pull (a boat, car, etc.) by means of a rope or chain. *–n.* **2.** the act of towing. **3.** the thing being towed. **4.** a rope, chain, etc., for towing. **5.** the state of being towed. **6. in tow, a.** in the condition of being towed. **b.** under guidance; in one's charge. **c.** in attendance; following or accompanying one around. **7. on** or **under tow,** in the condition of being towed. [ME *towe(n),* OE *togian* pull by force, drag, c. MHG *zogen* draw, tug, drag. Cf. TUG]

**tow[2]** /tou/, *n.* **1.** the fibre of flax, hemp, or jute prepared for spinning by scutching. **2.** the coarse and broken parts of flax or hemp separated from the finer parts in hackling. *–adj.* **3.** made of tow: *tow cloth.* **4.** resembling tow; pale yellow: *tow-coloured hair.* [ME; OE *tōw* (in *tōwlīc* pertaining to thread, *tōwhūs* spinning house). Cf. Icel. *tō* wool]

**towage** /ˈtouɪdʒ/, *n.* **1.** the act of towing. **2.** the state of being towed. **3.** a charge for towing.

**towai** /ˈtouwaɪ/, *n.* a New Zealand forest tree, *Weinmannia silvicola,* similar to the kamahi. [Maori]

**toward** /ˈtouəd/, *adj.;* /təˈwɔd, tɔd/, *prep.* *–adj.* **1.** going on; in progress: *when there is work toward.* **2.** *Obs.* promising, hopeful, or apt, as a young person. **3.** *Obs.* that is to come; imminent or impending. *–prep.* **4.** towards. [ME, OE *tōweard,* from *tō-* to + *-weard* -WARD]

**towardly** /ˈtouədli/, *adj. Archaic.* **1.** promising; apt; tractable or docile. **2.** favourable or propitious; seasonable or suitable. – **towardliness, towardness,** *n.*

**towards** /tə'wɔdz, tɔdz/, *prep.* **1.** in the direction of (with reference to either motion or position): *to walk towards the north.* **2.** with respect to; as regards: *one's attitude towards a proposition.* **3.** nearly as late as; shortly before: *towards two o'clock.* **4.** as a help or contribution to: *to give money towards a gift.* Also, **toward.** [See TOWARD]

**tow bar** /'toʊ ba/, *n.* a stout metal bar bolted or welded to a vehicle to facilitate the attachment of a caravan, trailer, etc., or the towing of another vehicle.

**towboat** /'toʊboʊt/, *n.* →**tugboat.**

**towel** /'taʊəl, taʊl/, *n., v.,* **-elled, -elling** or (*U.S.*) **-eled, -eling.** *–n.* **1.** a cloth or the like for wiping and drying something wet, esp. one for the hands, face, or body after washing or bathing. **2. throw in the towel,** to give up; admit defeat. *–v.t.* **3.** to wipe or dry with a towel. **4.** to give (someone) a hiding. [ME, from OF *toaille* cloth for washing or wiping, from Gmc; cf. MHG *twähele* towel, OE *thwēal* washbasin]

**towelling** /'taʊəlɪŋ/, *n.* **1.** any of various absorbent fabrics used for towels, and also for beachwear and the like. **2.** a rubbing with a towel. **3.** *Colloq.* a thrashing. Also, *U.S.,* **toweling.**

**tower** /'taʊə/, *n.* **1.** a building or structure high in proportion to its lateral dimensions, either isolated or forming part of any building. **2.** such a structure used as or intended for a stronghold, fortress, prison, etc. **3.** any of various tower-like structures, contrivances, or objects. **4.** a tall, movable structure used in ancient and medieval warfare in storming a fortified place. **5. tower of strength,** a source of mental and physical support, as a person; one who may be depended on. *–v.i.* **6.** to rise or extend far upwards like a tower; rise aloft. **7.** to surpass, as in ability, etc. (fol. by *over, above,* etc.). [ME *tour,* late OE *tūr,* from OF; replacing OE *torr,* from L *turris*] – **towered,** *adj.* – **towerless,** *adj.* – **tower-like,** *adj.*

**tower block** /'– blɒk/, *n.* a very tall building or part of a building, esp. one containing flats or offices.

**tower crane** /'– kreɪn/, *n.* a crane mounted on a tall, lattice tower, used in the erection of multistorey buildings.

**towering** /'taʊərɪŋ/, *adj.* **1.** that towers; very lofty or tall: *a towering oak.* **2.** very great. **3.** rising to an extreme degree of violence or intensity: *a towering rage.* – **toweringly,** *adv.*

**towershell** /'taʊəʃɛl/, *n.* a gastropod mollusc of the genus *Turritella,* with a long, spiral shell.

**towery** /'taʊəri/, *adj.* **1.** having towers. **2.** lofty.

**towhead** /'toʊhɛd/, *n.* **1.** a head of flaxen or light-coloured hair. **2.** a head of tousled hair. **3.** a person with such hair. – **towheaded,** *adj.*

**towie** /'toʊi/, *n. Colloq.* **1.** →**tow truck.** **2.** a tow truck driver.

**towline** /'toʊlaɪn/, *n.* a line, hawser, or the like, by which anything is or may be towed.

**town** /taʊn/, *n.* **1.** a distinct densely populated area of considerable size, having some degree of self-government. **2.** a group of buildings, larger than a village and administratively more independent, but smaller than a city. **3.** a city. **4.** *Brit.* →**borough** (defs 2 and 3). **5.** urban life, opposed to rural: *I prefer the town to the country.* **6.** the particular town in question, as that in which one is. **7.** the nearest large town. **8.** the main shopping, business, or entertainment centre of a large town, contrasted with the suburbs. **9.** an urban community; the people of a town. **10.** the inhabitants of a university town (opposed to *gown*). **11.** *U.S.* any of various administrative divisions, usu. urban, and smaller and less elaborately organised than a city; a township. **12. go to town, a.** to do something thoroughly. **b.** to do something enthusiastically; splash out. **c.** to overindulge or lose one's self-restraint. **d.** to celebrate. **e.** to be successful. **f.** to berate; tell off (usu. fol. by *on*). **13. man about town,** a sophisticated, pleasure-seeking and usu. sociable man of high social status. **14. on the town, a.** seeking amusement in a town. **b.** supported by the municipal authorities or public charity. **15. paint the town red,** *Colloq.* to indulge in riotous entertainment. **16. talk of the town,** the subject of general gossip or rumour. [ME; OE *tūn,* c. D *tuin,* G *Zaun* hedge. Cf. Irish *dūn* fortified place] – **townish,** *adj.* – **townless,** *adj.*

**town belt** /'– bɛlt/, *n. N.Z.* the land of a city set aside as a reserve.

**town bike** /– 'baɪk/, *n. Colloq.* a prostitute, usu. in a small town.

**town clerk** /– 'klak/, *n.* an appointed official of a council who is in charge of all responsibilities of local government.

**town council** /– 'kaʊnsəl/, *n.* the governing body of a town.

**town councillor** /– 'kaʊnsələ/, *n.* a member of a town council.

**town crier** /– 'kraɪə/, *n.* (formerly) a person employed by a town to make public proclamations.

**town gas** /'– gæs/, *n.* gas made for domestic or industrial use.

**town hall** /– 'hɔl/, *n.* a hall or building belonging to a town, used for the transaction of the town's business, etc., and often also as a place of public assembly.

**town house** /'– haʊs/, *n.* **1.** a house or mansion in a town, as distinguished from a country residence. **2.** a house designed as part of a small block of such, each being sold under strata title, and each with ground floor access.

**townie** /'taʊni/, *n.* **1.** one who lives in a town, esp. a country town. **2.** (*derog.*) an inhabitant of a university town. **3.** (*derog.*) one who comes from a town and is ignorant of country ways. Also, **townee.**

town hall: Sydney Town Hall

**town planning** /taʊn 'plænɪŋ/, *n.* the calculated control of urban physical conditions in the social interests of the community at large. – **town-planner** /taʊn-'plænə/, *n.*

**townscape** /'taʊnskeɪp/, *n.* a view or representation of an urban scene. Cf. **landscape.**

**townsfolk** /'taʊnzfoʊk/, *n.pl.* **1.** townspeople. **2.** people living or bred in towns or a town rather than the country.

**township** /'taʊnʃɪp/, *n.* **1.** a small town or settlement. **2.** *Hist.* a tract of surveyed land; town site. **3.** *Chiefly Brit. Hist.* **a.** one of the local divisions or districts of a large parish, each containing a village or small town, usu. with a church of its own. **b.** the manor, parish, etc., itself. **c.** its inhabitants. **4.** (in U.S. and Canada) an administrative division of a county with varying corporate powers. **5.** (in South Africa) an area set aside for black Africans, as in an urban locality; a location. [ME *tounshipe,* OE *tūnscipe,* from *tūn* TOWN + *-scipe* -SHIP]

**townsman** /'taʊnzmən/, *n., pl.* **-men. 1.** an inhabitant of a town. **2.** an inhabitant of one's own or the same town. – **townswoman,** *n.fem.*

**townspeople** /'taʊnzpipəl/, *n.pl.* the inhabitants collectively of a town. Also, **townsfolk.**

**towpath** /'toʊpaθ/, *n.* a path along the bank of a canal or river, for use in towing boats.

**towrope** /'toʊroʊp/, *n.* a rope, hawser, or the like, used in towing boats, cars, etc. Also, **tow rope.**

**tow truck** /'toʊ trʌk/, *n.* a truck for towing other vehicles, as from accidents, etc.

**towy** /'toʊi/, *adj.* of the nature of or resembling tow.

**tox-,** variant of **toxo-,** before vowels, as in *toxaemia.*

**toxaemia** /tɒk'simiə/, *n.* entry into, and persistence in, the bloodstream of bacterial toxins absorbed from a local lesion, by which stream these poisons are borne by the circulation to all parts of the body. Also, *Chiefly U.S.,* **toxemia.** [NL. See TOX-, -AEMIA]

**toxaemic** /tɒk'simɪk/, *adj.* **1.** pertaining to or of the nature of toxaemia. **2.** affected with toxaemia. Also, *Chiefly U.S.,* **toxemic.**

**toxaphene** /'tɒksəfin/, *n.* an organochlorine compound highly toxic to animal life and used as a systemic insecticide. [Trademark]

**toxic** /'tɒksɪk/, *adj.* **1.** of, pertaining to, affected with, or caused by a toxin or poison. **2.** poisonous. [ML *toxicus,* from L *toxicum* poison, from Gk *toxikón* (orig. short for *toxikòn* (*phármakon*), lit., (poison) pertaining to the bow, i.e. poison used on arrows)] – **toxically,** *adv.*

**toxicant** /ˈtɒksəkənt/, *adj.* **1.** poisonous; toxic. *–n.* **2.** a poison.

**toxication** /tɒksəˈkeɪʃən/, *n.* poisoning.

**toxicity** /tɒkˈsɪsəti/, *n., pl.* **-ties.** toxic quality; poisonousness.

**toxico-,** a combining form of **toxic.** Cf. **toxo-.** [combining form representing Gk *toxikón* poison. See TOXIC]

**toxicogenic** /ˌtɒksəkoʊˈdʒɛnɪk/, *adj.* **1.** generating or producing toxic products or poisons. **2.** formed by poisonous matter.

**toxicol.,** toxicology.

**toxicology** /tɒksəˈkɒlədʒi/, *n.* the science of poisons, their effects, antidotes, detection, etc. – **toxicological** /tɒksəkəˈlɒdʒɪkəl/, *adj.* – **toxicologically** /tɒksəkəˈlɒdʒɪkli/, *adv.* – **toxicologist,** *n.*

**toxicosis** /tɒksəˈkoʊsəs/, *n., pl.* **-ses** /-siz/. a morbid condition produced by the action of a poison. [NL. See TOXIC, -OSIS]

**toxic shock syndrome,** *n.* a particular kind of endotoxin shock syndrome caused by a bacterial infection in the vagina of women of menstruating age.

**toxin** /ˈtɒksən/, *n.* **1.** any of the specific poisonous products generated by pathogenic micro-organisms and constituting the causative agents in various diseases, as tetanus, diphtheria, etc. **2.** any of various organic poisons produced in living or dead organisms. **3.** their products, as a venom, etc. Also, **toxine** /ˈtɒksin, -sən/. [TOX(IC) + -IN(E)[2]]

**toxiphobia** /tɒksəˈfoʊbiə/, *n.* a morbid fear of being poisoned. [*toxi-* (var. of TOXO-) + -PHOBIA]

**toxo-,** a combining form representing **toxin,** or short for **toxico-,** as in *toxoplasmosis.*

**toxoid** /ˈtɒksɔɪd/, *n.* a toxin which has had its toxicity reduced by treatment with chemical agents or by physical means. [TOX(O)- + -OID]

**toxophilite** /tɒkˈsɒfəlaɪt/, *n.* a devotee of archery; archer. [*Toxophilus* (coined Gk proper name: bow-lover) + -ITE[1]] – **toxophilitic** /tɒkˌsɒfəˈlɪtɪk/, *adj.* – **toxophily,** *n.*

**toxoplasmosis** /ˌtɒksoʊplæzˈmoʊsəs/, *n.* an infection caused by bodies believed to be protozoa which are known as *Toxoplasma gondii,* and occurring in dogs, cats, sheep, and man, the nervous system usu. being the part involved.

**toy** /tɔɪ/, *n.* **1.** an object, often a small imitation of some familiar thing, for children or others to play with, or otherwise derive amusement; a plaything. **2.** a thing or matter of little or no value or importance; a trifle. **3.** a small article of little real value, but prized for some reason; a knick-knack; a trinket. **4.** something diminutive. **5.** any of various breeds of dog bred or selected for their smallness; toy dog. **6.** an object of amorous dalliance. *–adj.* **7.** of or like a toy, esp. in size. **8.** made as a toy: *a toy train.* *–v.i.* **9.** to handle affectionately; play. **10.** to act idly, absentmindedly, or without seriousness. **11.** to trifle; deal with as unimportant (usu. fol. by *with*). [ME *toye* dalliance; orig. uncert.] – **toyer,** *n.* – **toyless,** *adj.* – **toylike,** *adj.*

**toy dog** /ˈ– dɒg/, *n.* **1.** →**toy** (def. 5). **2.** any dog of unusually small size kept as a pet.

**toyshop** /ˈtɔɪʃɒp/, *n.* a shop in which toys are sold.

**TP** /ti ˈpi/, time payment.

**tpi,** **1.** teeth per inch. **2.** turns per inch.

**T.P.I.** /ti pi ˈaɪ/, *n.* **1.** a returned serviceman who is totally and permanently incapacitated by his injuries. *–adj.* **2.** of or pertaining to such a person: *T.P.I. pension.* [*T*(*otally and*) *P*(*ermanently*) *I*(*ncapacitated*)]

**TPN,** *Biochem.* triphosphopyridine nucleotide.

**tr.,** **1.** transitive. **2.** translated. **3.** translator. **4.** transitive. **5.** treble. **6.** *Music.* trill.

**Tr,** *Chem.* terbium.

**trabeated** /ˈtreɪbieɪtəd/, *adj. Archit.* **1.** constructed with horizontal beams, as a flat, unvaulted ceiling, or with a lintel or entablature, as an unarched doorway. **2.** pertaining to such construction, as distinct from the vaulted or arched kind. Also, **trabeate** /ˈtreɪbiət, -eɪt/. [*trabeat*(*ion*) beam structure, from L *trabe*(*m*) beam (acc. of *trabs*) + -ATION] – **trabeation** /treɪbiˈeɪʃən/, *n.*

**trabecula** /trəˈbɛkjələ/, *n., pl.* **-lae** /-li/. **1.** *Anat., Bot., etc.* a structural part resembling a small beam or crossbar. **2.** *Bot.* one of the projections from the cell wall which extend across the cell cavity of the ducts of certain plants, or the plate of cells across the cavity of the sporangium of a moss. [L, diminutive of *trabs* beam] – **trabecular,** *adj.*

**trac** /træk/, *n. Prison Colloq.* an intractable prisoner.

**trace[1]** /treɪs/, *n., v.,* **traced, tracing.** *–n.* **1.** a mark, token, or evidence of the former presence, existence, or action of something; a vestige. **2.** a mark, indication, or evidence. **3.** a scarcely discernible quantity of something; a very small amount. **4.** *Psychol.* the residual effect of an experience in memory; an engram. **5.** a record traced by a self-registering instrument. **6.** a tracing, drawing, or sketch of a thing. **7.** (*esp. in pl.*) the track made or left by the passage of a person, animal, or thing. **8.** a single such mark. *–v.t.* **9.** to follow the footprints, track, or traces of. **10.** to follow or make out the course or line of: *to trace a river to its source.* **11.** to follow (footprints, traces, the history of something, the course or line of something, a drawn line, etc.). **12.** to follow the course, development, or history of: *to trace a political movement.* **13.** to find by investigation; find out; discover. **14.** to copy (a drawing, plan, etc.) by following the lines of the original on a superimposed transparent sheet. **15.** to draw (a line, outline, figure, etc.). **16.** to make a plan, diagram, or map of. **17.** to mark or ornament with lines, figures, etc. **18.** to make an impression or imprinting of (a design, pattern, etc.). **19.** to print in a curved, broken, or wavy-lined manner. **20.** to put down in writing. [ME, from OF *tracer* delineate, trace, pursue, from L *tractus,* pp., drawn, trailed, or *tractus,* n., a dragging, trailing] – **traceable,** *adj.* – **traceability** /treɪsəˈbɪləti/, **traceableness,** *n.* – **traceably,** *adv.*

**trace[2]** /treɪs/, *n.* **1.** each of the two straps, ropes, or chains by which a carriage, wagon, or the like is drawn by a harness horse or other draught animal. **2.** *Mach.* a piece in a machine, as a bar, transferring the movement of one part to another part, being hinged to each. **3.** *Angling.* a short piece of gut or other strong material connecting the hook to a fishing line. **4. kick over the traces,** to reject discipline; to act in an independent manner. [ME *trays,* from OF *traiz,* pl. of *trait* strap for harness, act of drawing, from L *tractus,* pp., drawn, or *tractus,* n., draught]

**trace element** /ˈ– ɛləmənt/, *n.* a chemical element found in plants and animals in minute quantities which is a critical factor in physiological processes.

**tracer** /ˈtreɪsə/, *n.* **1.** one who or that which traces. **2.** any of various devices for tracing drawings, plans, etc. **3.** ammunition containing a chemical which by burning or smoking makes it visible, to show the path of the projectile and indicate the target to other firers. **4.** the composition contained in such ammunition. **5.** a radioactive substance used to study biological, chemical, and industrial processes by following its path on a photographic film, fluoroscope, or other detection device; radioactive tracer. **6.** one whose business is the tracing of missing property, parcels, etc. **7.** an enquiry form sent from point to point to trace a missing shipment, parcel, or the like.

**tracer bullet** /ˈ– bʊlət/, *n.* a bullet that leaves a trail of smoke or fire so that aim can be corrected.

**traceried** /ˈtreɪsərid/, *adj.* ornamented with tracery.

**tracery** /ˈtreɪsəri/, *n., pl.* **-ries.** **1.** ornamental work consisting of ramified ribs, bars, or the like, as in the upper part of a Gothic window, in panels, screens, etc. **2.** any delicate interlacing work of lines, threads, etc., as in carving, embroidery, etc.; network.

**trache-,** variant of **tracheo-** before vowels, as in *tracheid.*

**trachea** /trəˈkiə/, *n., pl.* **tracheae** /trəˈkii/. **1.** (in air-breathing vertebrates) the tube extending from the larynx to the bronchi, serving as the principal passage for conveying air to and from the lungs; the windpipe. **2.** (in insects and other arthropods) one of the air-conveying tubes of the respiratory system. **3.** *Bot.* a duct formed by a row of cells which have perforated end walls as in xylem vessels. [ML, var. of LL *trāchīa,* from Gk *trācheîa,* short for *artēría trācheîa* rough artery (i.e. windpipe)]

**tracheal** /trəˈkiəl/, *adj.* **1.** *Anat., Zool.* pertaining to or connected with the trachea or tracheae. **2.** *Bot.* of the nature of or composed of tracheae.

**tracheid** /ˈtreɪkiɪd/, *n.* an elongated, imperforate, dead xylem cell with a lignified wall. Also, **tracheide.**

**tracheitis** /træki'aɪtəs/, *n.* inflammation of the trachea. [NL. See TRACHE-, -ITIS]

**tracheo-,** a combining form representing **trachea**, as in *tracheoscopy.* Also, **trache-.**

**tracheoscopy** /træki'ɒskəpi/, *n.* examination of the interior of the trachea, as with a laryngoscope. – **tracheoscopic** /trækiə'skɒpɪk/, *adj.* – **tracheoscopist,** *n.*

**tracheostomy** /træki'ɒstəmi/, *n.* an opening into the trachea, in some cases permanent, made surgically.

**tracheotomy** /træki'ɒtəmi/, *n., pl.* **-mies.** the operation of cutting into the trachea. – **tracheotomist,** *n.*

**trachoma** /trə'koumə/, *n.* a contagious inflammation of the conjunctiva of the eyelids, characterised by the formation of granulations or papillary growths. [NL, from Gk: roughness] – **trachomatous** /trə'kɒmətəs, -'koumə-/, *adj.*

**trachyphonia** /træki'founiə/, *n.* roughness or hoarseness of the voice. [Gk *trāchýs* rough + ME *-phonie,* from L *-phonia,* from Gk *-phōnia,* from *-phōnos* sounding]

**trachyte** /'treɪkaɪt, 'træk-/, *n.* a volcanic rock, commonly of porphyritic texture, consisting essentially of alkali felspar and one or more subordinate minerals, as hornblende, mica, etc. [F, from Gk *trāchýtēs* roughness]

**trachytic** /trə'kɪtɪk/, *adj.* pertaining to the nearly parallel arrangement of felspar crystals in the ground-mass of volcanic rocks.

**tracing** /'treɪsɪŋ/, *n.* **1.** a copy of a drawing, etc., made by tracing. **2.** the act of one who or that which traces. **3.** that which is produced by tracing. **4.** the record traced by a self-registering instrument.

**tracing paper** /'– peɪpə/, *n.* a translucent paper used in tracing.

**track**[1] /træk/, *n.* **1.** a road, path, or trail. **2.** the structure of rails, sleepers, etc., on which a railway train or the like runs; a railway line. **3.** the mark, or series of marks, left by anything that has passed along. **4.** (*esp. pl.*) a footprint or other mark left by an animal, a person, or a vehicle. **5.** a rough roadway or path made or beaten by the feet of men or animals. **6.** a line of travel or motion: *the track of a bird.* **7.** a route, usu. only roughly defined: *the Birdsville Track.* **8.** an endless jointed metal band which is driven by the wheels of a track-laying vehicle to enable it to move, or pull loads, over rough ground. **9.** *Physics.* the path of an ionised particle which has been made visible in a cloud chamber or on a photographic emulsion. **10.** a course followed. **11.** a course of action or conduct; a method of proceeding: *to go on in the same track year after year.* **12.** a path or course made or laid out for some particular purpose. **13.** a course laid out for running or racing. **14. a.** the sports which are performed on a track, collectively; athletics. **b.** both track and field sports as a whole. **15.** *Motor Vehicles.* the measured distance at the ground line, between the centres of both front or rear tyres. **16.** *Aeron.* **a.** the distance between the port and starboard wheels of an undercarriage, or the distance between the centres of the port and starboard legs of multi-wheel landing gears. **b.** the projection of an aircraft's flight path on the surface of the earth. **17.** one of the distinct sections of a gramophone record containing a piece, or section of music, etc. **18.** one of the bands of material recorded lengthwise beside other such bands on magnetic tape, hence *2-track, 8-track, etc., tape-recorders,* referring to the number of tracks they can record and *half-track, quarter-track, etc., recordings,* referring roughly to the fraction of the width of the magnetic tape taken up by each track. **19.** *Prison Colloq.* a prison warder who will carry contraband messages or goods out of or into a prison for a prisoner. **20.** Some special noun phrases are:

**in one's tracks,** just where one is standing: *he was stopped in his tracks.*

**in the tracks of,** following; pursuing.

**keep track of,** to follow the course or progress of; keep sight or knowledge of.

**lose track of,** to fail to keep informed on or in view; fail to stay in touch with.

**make tracks,** *Colloq.* to leave or depart.

**make tracks for,** to head towards.

**off the beaten track,** secluded, unusual, or little known.

**off the track,** away from the subject in hand.

**on the track,** itinerant.

**on the track of,** pursuing; on the scent of.

**the right** or **wrong track,** *Colloq.* the right (or wrong) idea, plan, interpretation, etc.

**run off the track,** *Horseracing, etc.* to run wide at a turn.

**(on) the wrong side of the tracks,** *U.S.* (in) a low social position; (in) a low-class or poor neighbourhood.

*–v.t.* **21.** to follow up or pursue the tracks, traces, or footprints of. **22.** to hunt by following the tracks of. **23.** to follow the course of, as by radar. **24.** to catch or find, after pursuit or searching (fol. by *down*). **25.** to follow (a track, course, etc.). **26.** *Mil.* to keep a target-locating instrument or a weapon pointing continuously at a moving target. **27. a.** *U.S.* to make a track of footprints upon (a floor, etc.). **b.** to make a track with (earth, snow, etc., carried on the feet) in walking. **28.** *U.S. Railways.* **a.** to furnish with a track or tracks, as for trains. **b.** to have (a certain distance) between wheels, runners, rails, etc. *–v.i.* **29.** to follow up a track or trail. **30. a.** to run in the same track, as the wheels of a vehicle. **b.** to be in alignment, as one gearwheel with another. **31.** *Films, T.V., etc.* (of the camera) to move bodily in any direction while in operation. Cf. **pan**[3], **zoom. 32. track in (out),** *Films, T.V.* to move the camera towards (away) from the subject. **33.** make one's way. **34.** *Colloq.* to keep company; cohabit (fol. by *with*). *–adj.* **35.** *Athletics.* pertaining to those sports performed on a running track (contrasted with *field*). [late ME *trak,* from F *trac,* ? from Gmc; cf. D *trekken* draw, pull] – **tracker,** *n.* – **trackless,** *adj.*

**track**[2] /træk/, *v.t.* to tow (a boat), esp. from a river bank. [D *trekken* to pull]

**trackage** /'trækɪdʒ/, *n. U.S.* **1.** the tracks, collectively, of a railway. **2.** the provision of tracks. **3.** the right of one railway company to use the tracks of another. **4.** Also, **trackage charge.** the money paid for this right.

**tracked** /trækt/, *adj.* fitted with tracks, as a track-laying vehicle.

**tracker action** /'trækər ækʃən/, *n.* a completely mechanical action in a pipe organ.

**track event** /'træk əvɛnt/, *n.* an athletic event which takes place on a track, as running races, hurdling. Cf. **field event.**

**tracking shot** /'trækɪŋ ʃɒt/, *n. Films, T.V.* a shot taken with the camera moving on a truck or trolley.

**tracking station** /'– steɪʃən/, *n.* a station used for following an object, esp. a satellite, moving through the atmosphere or space, usu. by means of radio or radar.

**tracklayer** /'trækleɪə/, *n.* equipment used to lay prefabricated sections of railway track.

**tracklaying** /'trækleɪɪŋ/, *n.* the laying down of railway lines.

**tracklaying vehicle** /'– viːkəl/, *n.* a vehicle, as a tank or tractor, the wheels on each side of which move on a track (see **track**[1] def. 8); a caterpillar.

**trackless** /'trækləs/, *adj.* **1.** without paths, roads, etc. **2.** untrodden; unexplored. **3.** not running on rails, as a trolleybus. **4.** not leaving a track or trail. – **tracklessly,** *adv.* – **tracklessness,** *n.*

**trackman** /'trækmən/, *n., pl.* **-men.** *U.S.* **1.** a man who assists in inspecting, installing, or maintaining railway tracks. **2.** →**trackwalker.**

**track meet** /'træk mit/, *n.* an athletics meeting.

**track record** /'– rɛkɔd/, *n.* **1.** an account of a racehorse's successes and defeats on the racecourse. **2.** an account of a person's successes or failures in a specific field.

**track rod** /'– rɒd/, *n.* a rod which connects the two front wheels of a motor vehicle so that they can be steered together.

**track shoe** /'– ʃu/, *n.* See **spike**[1] (def. 7).

**tracksuit** /'træksut/, *n.* a loose, two-piece overgarment worn by athletes in training, between events, etc.

**trackwalker** /'trækwɔkə/, *n. U.S.* a man employed to walk over and inspect a certain section of railway track at intervals.

**tract**[1] /trækt/, *n.* **1.** a stretch or extent of land, water, etc.; region. **2.** *Anat.* **a.** a definite region or area of the body, esp. a group, series, or system of related parts or organs: *the digestive tract.* **b.** a bundle of nerve fibres having a common origin and destination. **3.** a space or extent of time; a period. **4.** *Rom. Cath. Ch.* an anthem consisting of verses of

Scripture. [late ME *tracte,* from L *tractus* drawing, stretch, extent, tract]

**tract²** /trækt/, *n.* a brief treatise or pamphlet suitable for general distribution, esp. one dealing with some topic of practical religion. [ME *tracte;* apparently short for L *tractātus* TRACTATE]

**tractable** /'træktəbəl/, *adj.* **1.** easily managed, or docile, as persons, their dispositions, etc. **2.** that may be easily handled or dealt with, as metals; malleable. [L *tractābilis*] – **tractability** /træktə'bɪləti/, **tractableness,** *n.* – **tractably,** *adv.*

**Tractarianism** /træk'tɛəriənɪzəm/, *n.* the principles or tenets held by a school of High Churchmen in the Church of England. [from *Tracts for the Times,* a series of pamphlets written by J.H. Newman and published at Oxford 1833-41]

**tractate** /'trækteɪt/, *n.* a treatise; a tract. [late ME, from L *tractātus* handling, discussion, treatise]

**tractile** /'træktaɪl/, *adj.* that may be drawn out in length; ductile. – **tractility** /træk'tɪləti/, *n.*

**traction** /'trækʃən/, *n.* **1.** the act of drawing or pulling. **2.** the state of being drawn. **3.** the drawing of a body, vehicle, train, or the like along a surface, road, track, railway, waterway, etc. **4.** the adhesive friction of a body, as of a wheel on a rail. **5.** the pulling or drawing of a muscle, organ, or the like. **6.** the form or type of propulsion of a vehicle; motive power. **7.** *Obs.* attracting power or influence. [ML *tractio* act of drawing, from L *trahere* draw] – **tractional,** *adj.*

**traction engine** /'– ɛndʒən/, *n.* a locomotive formerly used to drive farm machinery and to draw heavy loads along an ordinary road, over fields, etc., usu. driven by steam.

**traction motor** /'– moʊtə/, *n.* an electric motor, usu. mounted on the bogies of a diesel-electric or electric locomotive which turns the driving wheels.

**tractive** /'træktɪv/, *adj.* serving to draw; drawing.

**tractor** /'træktə/, *n.* **1.** a motor vehicle, usu. fitted with deeply treaded tyres, used to draw farm implements as the plough, seed-drill, etc., and loads and also as a source of power for agricultural machinery, etc. **2.** one who or that which draws or pulls. **3.** something used for drawing or pulling. **4.** Also, **tractor propeller.** a propeller mounted at the front of an aeroplane, thus exerting a pull. **5.** Also, **tractor aeroplane.** an aeroplane with a propeller so mounted. [obs. *tract,* v. draw (from L *tractus,* pp.) + -OR²]

tractor

**tractor shovel** /'– ʃʌvəl/, *n.* →**front-end loader.**

**trad** /træd/, *n. Colloq.* **1.** traditional jazz. *–adj.* **2.** traditional; old-fashioned; conventional.

**trad.,** traditional.

**trade** /treɪd/, *n., v.,* **traded, trading.** *–n.* **1.** the buying and selling, or exchanging, of commodities, either by wholesale or by retail, within a country or between countries: *domestic or foreign trade.* **2.** a purchase, sale, or exchange. **3.** a form of occupation pursued as a business or calling, as for a livelihood or profit. **4.** some line of skilled mechanical work: *the trade of a carpenter, plumber, or printer.* **5.** people engaged in a particular line of business: *a lecture of interest only to the trade.* **6.** traffic; amount of dealings: *a brisk trade in overcoats.* **7.** market: *the tourist trade.* **8.** commercial occupation (as against professional): *she could not marry him, for he was in trade.* **9.** (*pl.*) the trade winds. *–v.t.* **10.** to give in return; exchange; barter. **11.** to exchange: *to trade seats with a person.* **12. trade in,** to give in part exchange, as in a transaction. **13. trade on,** to exploit or take advantage of, esp. unfairly. *–v.i.* **14.** to carry on trade. **15.** to traffic (fol. by *in*): *to trade in wheat.* **16.** to make an exchange. *–adj.* **17.** of or pertaining to commerce, a particular trade or occupation, or trade as a whole. [ME, from MLG: a track] – **tradeless,** *adj.*

**trade cycle** /'– saɪkəl/, *n.* the recurrent alternation of boom-time and depression in a country's economy.

**trade discount** /– 'dɪskaʊnt/, *n.* a deduction from list prices made to members of the same or allied types of business, or by a wholesaler to a retailer.

**trade edition** /'– ədɪʃən/, *n.* an edition of a book intended for sale in bookshops, as distinct from mail-order or other special editions.

**trade gap** /'– gæp/, *n.* the difference between the value of a country's imports and of its exports when the former is a larger figure.

**trade-in** /'treɪd-ɪn/, *n.* **1.** goods given in whole or, usu. part payment of a purchase. *–adj.* **2.** of or pertaining to such goods, or to such a method of payment.

**trade journal** /'treɪd dʒɜnəl/, *n.* a periodical devoted to the activities and associations of a trade or profession and distributed among its members.

**trade magazine** /'treɪd ˌmægəzin/, *n.* a journal, usu. available by subscription only, to members of a particular profession or trade, and devoted to their occupational interests. Also, **trade journal.**

**trademark** /'treɪdmak/, *n.* the name, symbol, figure, letter, word, or mark adopted and used by a manufacturer or merchant in order to designate the goods he manufactures or sells, and to distinguish them from those manufactured or sold by others. Any mark entitled to registration under the provisions of a statute is a trademark. Also, **trade mark.**

**trade name** /'treɪd neɪm/, *n.* **1.** the name or style under which a firm does business. **2.** a word or phrase used in trade whereby a business or enterprise or a particular class of goods is designated, but which is not technically a trademark, either because it is not susceptible of exclusive appropriation as a trademark or because it is not affixed to goods sold in the market. **3.** the name by which an article or substance is known to the trade.

**trade-off** /'treɪd-ɒf/, *n.* a concession made in a negotiation in return for one given.

**trade price** /'– praɪs/, *n.* the price at which goods are sold to members of the same trade, or to retail dealers by wholesalers.

**trader** /'treɪdə/, *n.* **1.** one who trades; a merchant or businessman. **2.** a ship employed in trade, esp. in a limited sphere, as a chain of islands.

**trade rat** /'treɪd ræt/, *n.* →**pack rat.** Also, **trading rat.**

**trade reference** /'– rɛfrəns/, *n.* **1.** an individual or company in business to which one is referred for information concerning an applicant's credit standing. **2.** the reference itself.

**trade route** /'– rut/, *n.* a land or sea route habitually or commonly followed by caravans, trading ships, etc.

**tradescantia** /treɪdɛs'kænʃiə/, *n.* any plant of the genus *Tradescantia* (family Commelinaceae); a spiderwort (def. 1). [NL; named after John *Tradescant,* gardener to Charles I]

**trade school** /'treɪd skul/, *n.* a type of school for giving instruction in a trade or trades.

**tradesman** /'treɪdzmən/, *n., pl.* **-men. 1.** a man engaged in trade. **2.** a shopkeeper. **3.** a craftsman. **4.** one who calls on private houses to deliver goods. – **tradeswoman,** *n.fem.*

**tradespeople** /'treɪdzpipəl/, *n.pl.* **1.** people engaged in trade. **2.** shopkeepers collectively. Also, **tradesfolk** /'treɪdzfoʊk/.

**trade union** /treɪd 'junjən/, *n.* an organisation of employees for mutual aid and protection, and for dealing collectively with employers. Also, **trades union.**

**trade unionism** /– 'junjənɪzəm/, *n.* **1.** the system, methods, or practice of trade or labour unions. **2.** trade unions collectively. **3.** advocacy of the general adoption of trade unions.

**trade unionist** /– 'junjənəst/, *n.* **1.** a member of a trade union. **2.** one who favours trade unions.

**trade wind** /'– wɪnd/, *n.* **1.** one of the winds prevailing over the oceans from about 30° north latitude to about 30° south latitude, and blowing from north-east to south-west in the Northern Hemisphere, and from south-east to north-west in the Southern Hemisphere towards the equator. **2.** *Archaic.* a wind that blows in one regular course, or continually in the same direction.

**trading bank** /'treɪdɪŋ bæŋk/, *n.* a bank dealing in accounts on which cheques may be drawn. Cf. **savings bank.**

**trading certificate** /– sə'tɪfɪkət/, *n.* a licence without which a public company may not start to trade.

**trading estate** /'– əsteɪt/, *n. Brit.* an industrial area consisting of factories built or financed by the government or local authority.

**trading post** /'– poʊst/, *n.* a general store for carrying on trade in a sparsely settled region.

**trading stamp** /'– stæmp/, *n.* a stamp with a certain value given as a premium by a seller to a customer, specified quantities of these stamps being exchangeable for various articles when presented to the issuers of the stamps.

**trading stock** /'– stɒk/, *n.* stock not held for permanent investment.

**tradition** /trə'dɪʃən/, *n.* **1.** the handing down of statements, beliefs, legends, customs, etc., from generation to generation, esp. by word of mouth or by practice: *a story that has come down to us by popular tradition.* **2.** that which is so handed down: *the traditions of the Eskimos.* **3.** *Theol.* **a.** (among the Jews) an unwritten body of laws and doctrines, or any one of them, held to have been received from Moses and handed down orally from generation to generation. **b.** (among Christians) a body of teachings, or any one of them, held to have been delivered by Christ and His apostles but not committed to writing. **4.** *Law.* the act of handing over something to another, esp. in a formal legal manner; delivery; transfer. [ME, from L *trāditio* delivery, handing down]

**traditional** /trə'dɪʃənəl/, *adj.* **1.** pertaining to tradition. **2.** handed down by tradition. **3.** in accordance with tradition. **4.** *Jazz.* **a.** of the style of music played in New Orleans in the early 1900s, characterised by extensive improvisation within a set instrumental framework. **b.** of a modern imitation of this style. Also, **traditionary** /trə'dɪʃənəri/. – **traditionally**, *adv.*

**traditionalism** /trə'dɪʃənəlɪzəm/, *n.* **1.** adherence to tradition as authority, esp. in matters of religion. **2.** a system of philosophy according to which all knowledge of religious truth is derived from divine revelation and received by traditional instruction. – **traditionalist**, *n., adj.* – **traditionalistic** /trədɪʃənə'lɪstɪk/, *adj.*

**traditive** /'trædətɪv/, *adj.* traditional. [TRADIT(ION) + -IVE]

**traditor** /'trædətə/, *n.* an early Christian who betrayed his fellows at the time of the Roman persecutions. [ME, from L: traitor, betrayer]

**traduce** /trə'djus/, *v.t.*, **-duced, -ducing.** to speak evil or maliciously and falsely of; slander, calumniate, or malign: *to traduce someone's character.* [L *trādūcere* transport, disgrace] – **traducer**, *n.* – **traducingly**, *adv.*

**traducianism** /trə'djuʃənɪzəm/, *n. Theol.* **1.** the doctrine that a man's soul is born of his parents with his body, and hence inherits their characteristics. **2.** the teaching that original sin is transmitted at birth from parent to child. – **traducianist**, *n., adj.* – **traducianistic** /trəˌdjuʃə'nɪstɪk/, *adj.*

**traffic** /'træfɪk/, *n., v.*, **-ficked, -ficking.** *–n.* **1.** the coming and going of persons, vehicles, ships, etc., along a way of passage or travel: *heavy traffic in a street.* **2.** the persons, vehicles, etc., going along such a way. **3.** the transportation of goods for the purpose of trade, by sea or land: *ships of traffic.* **4.** trade; buying and selling; commercial dealings. **5.** trade between different countries or places; commerce. **6.** the business done by a railway or other carrier in the transportation of goods or passengers. **7.** the aggregate of goods, passengers, telephone or telegraph messages, etc., handled, esp. in a given period. **8.** trade or dealing in some commodity or thing, often trade of an illicit kind. **9.** dealings or exchanges of anything between parties, people, etc. *–v.i.* **10.** to carry on traffic, trade, or commercial dealings. **11.** to carry on dealings of an illicit or improper kind. [F *trafique,* from It. *traffico,* ult. orig. uncert.] – **trafficker**, *n.* – **trafficless**, *adj.* – **trafficable**, *adj.*

traffic dome

**trafficator** /'træfəkeɪtə/, *n.* (in a motor vehicle) a flashing light or an illuminated arm which indicates a driver's intention to turn left or right.

**traffic circle** /'træfɪk sɜkəl/, *n. U.S.* →**roundabout.**

**traffic dome** /'– doʊm/, *n.* a small raised circular device in a carriageway, used as a guide to control turning traffic; fried egg; silent cop; silent bobby.

**traffic jam** /'– dʒæm/, *n.* an acute congestion of motor vehicles, bringing traffic to a standstill.

**traffic light** /'– laɪt/, *n.* (*usu. pl.*) one of a set of coloured lights used to direct or control road traffic at crossings, junctions, etc.

**traffic warden** /'– wɔdn/, *n. Brit.* →**parking policeman.**

**tragacanth** /'trægəkænθ/, *n.* **1.** a mucilaginous substance derived from various low, spiny, Asiatic shrubs of the genus *Astragalus,* esp. *A. gummifer,* used to impart firmness to pills and lozenges, stiffen calicoes, etc. **2.** the plant itself. [L *tragacantha* goat's thorn, from Gk *tragákantha*]

**tragedian** /trə'dʒidiən/, *n.* **1.** a writer of tragedy. **2.** an actor of tragedy.

**tragedienne** /trədʒidi'ɛn/, *n.* an actress of tragedy.

**tragedy** /'trædʒədi/, *n., pl.* **-dies.** **1.** a dramatic composition of serious or sombre character, with an unhappy ending: *Shakespeare's tragedy of 'Hamlet'.* **2.** that branch of the drama which is concerned with this form of composition. **3.** the art and theory of writing and producing tragedies. **4.** any literary composition, as a novel, dealing with a sombre theme carried to a tragic conclusion. **5.** the tragic element of drama, of literature generally, or of life. **6.** a lamentable, dreadful, or fatal event or affair; a disaster or calamity. [ME *tragedie,* from ML *tragēdia,* L *tragoedia,* from Gk *tragōidía,* lit., goat song (reason for name variously explained)]

**tragic** /'trædʒɪk/, *adj.* **1.** characteristic or suggestive of tragedy: *tragic solemnity.* **2.** mournful, melancholy, or pathetic in the extreme: *a tragic expression.* **3.** dreadful, calamitous, or fatal: *a tragic death.* **4.** pertaining to or having the nature of tragedy: *the tragic drama.* **5.** acting in or composing tragedy. Also, **tragical.** [L *tragicus,* from Gk *tragikós* of tragedy] – **tragically**, *adv.* – **tragicalness**, *n.*

**tragicomedy** /trædʒi'kɒmədi/, *n., pl.* **-dies.** **1.** a dramatic or other literary composition combining elements of both tragedy and comedy. **2.** an incident or series of incidents of mixed tragic and comic character. [LL *tragicōmoedia,* replacing L *tragico-cōmoedia,* from *tragico-* TRAGIC + *cōmoedia* COMEDY] – **tragicomic, tragicomical**, *adj.* – **tragicomically**, *adv.*

**tragion** /'treɪgiən/, *n., pl.* **tragia** /'treɪgiə/. a point in the depth of the notch just over the tragus of the external ear.

**tragopan** /'trægəpæn/, *n.* any of the Asiatic pheasants constituting the genus *Tragopan,* characterised by two fleshy erectile horns on the head, and wattles on the throat. [NL, special use of L *tragopān* fabulous Ethiopian bird, from Gk]

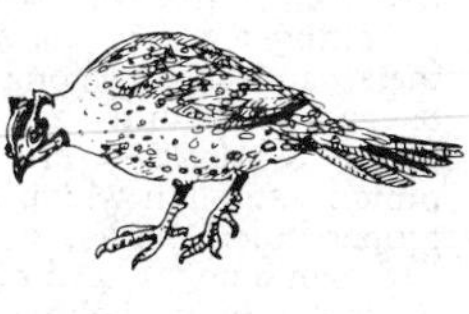

tragopan

**tragus** /'treɪgəs/, *n., pl.* **-gi** /-dʒaɪ/. a fleshy prominence at the front of the external opening of the ear. [LL, from Gk *trágos* hairy part of ear (lit., goat)] – **tragal**, *adj.*

**trail** /treɪl/, *v.t.* **1.** to drag or let drag along the ground or other surface; to draw or drag along behind. **2.** to bring or have floating after itself or oneself: *to trail clouds of dust.* **3.** to follow the track or trail of; track. **4.** to protract. **5.** to mark out, as a track. **6.** *U.S.* to beat down or make a path or way through (grass, etc.). **7.** *Colloq.* to follow along behind (another or others), as in a race. **8.** *Mil.* to carry (a rifle, etc.) in the right hand in a horizontal position, with the muzzle forwards and the butt near the ground. **9. trail a coat,** to provoke a heated reaction by persistent antagonistic remarks, in order to bring suspected latent hostility into the open. *–v.i.* **10.** to be drawn or dragged along the ground or some other surface, as when hanging from something moving: *her long gown trailed over the floor.* **11.** to hang down loosely from something. **12.** to stream or float from and after something moving, as dust, smoke, sparks, etc., do. **13.** to follow as if drawn along. **14.** to fish by trailing a line; to troll. **15.** to go slowly, lazily, or wearily along; straggle. **16.** to pass or extend in a straggling line. **17.** to move languidly. **18.** to pass by gradual change, as into silence; diminish (fol. by *off*): *her voice trailed off.* **19.** to fall behind the leaders, as a competitor in a race; be losing in a competition of any kind. **20.** to follow a track or scent, as of game. **21.** (of a plant) to extend itself in growth along the ground and over objects encountered, resting on these for support rather than taking root or clinging by tendrils, etc. *–n.* **22.** a path or track made across a wild region, over rough country, or the like, by the passage of men or animals: *to follow the trail.* **23.** the track, scent, or the like, left by an animal, person, or thing, esp. as followed by a hunter, hound, or other pursuer. **24.** something that is trailed or that trails behind, as the train of a skirt or robe. **25.** a stream of dust, smoke, light, people, vehicles, etc., behind something moving. **26.** *Greyhound Racing, Trotting, etc.* a position just behind the leader in a race. **27.** *Astron.* **a.** a long bright tail seen in the sky in the wake of certain meteors. **b.** the trace left on a stationary photographic plate by a star during a long exposure. **28.** *Ordn.* that part of a guncarriage which rests on the ground when the piece is unlimbered. **29.** the act of trailing. [ME *traile(n)*, from AF *trailler* trail, OF tow (a boat), from *traille* towrope, from L *trāgula* dragnet, from *trahere* draw, drag] **– trailless,** *adj.*

**trail bike** /'– baɪk/, *n.* a motorbike designed for cross-country conditions, built with a high engine and exhaust system, often of esp. light construction.

**trailblazer** /'treɪlbleɪzə/, *n.* **1.** a person who blazes a trail. **2.** a leader or innovator in a particular field.

**trailer** /'treɪlə/, *n.* **1.** one who or that which trails. **2.** a vehicle designed to be towed by a motor vehicle, and used in transporting loads. **3.** *Films.* an advertisement for a forthcoming film, usu. consisting of extracts from it. **4.** a trailing plant. **5.** *U.S.* a caravan.

**trail feeding** /'– fidɪŋ/, *n.* a method of feeding animals, esp. in times of drought whereby the feed, usu. grain, is laid out in a trail across the paddock.

**trail foot** /'– fʊt/, *n. Colloq.* a surfboard rider's back foot.

**trailing arbutus** /ˌtreɪlɪŋ a'bjutəs/, *n.* →**arbutus** (def. 2).

**trailing edge** /'– ɛdʒ/, *n.* the rear edge of a propeller blade or aerofoil.

**trailing tram** /'– træm/, *n.* a fully enclosed car of a cable tram designed to hook on to the dummy (def. 11).

**trail rope** /'treɪl roʊp/, *n.* a guide rope on a balloon.

**train** /treɪn/, *n.* **1.** *Railways.* **a.** a set of carriages or wagons, whether self-propelled or connected to a locomotive. **b.** such a series without any motive power. **c.** a railway locomotive. **2.** a line or procession of persons, vehicles, etc., travelling together. **3.** *Mil.* an aggregation of vehicles, animals, and men accompanying an army to carry supplies, baggage, ammunition, etc. **4.** a series or row of objects or parts. **5.** *Mach.* a series of connected parts, as wheels and pinions, through which motion is transmitted. **6.** order, esp. proper order: *matters were in good train.* **7.** something that is drawn along; a trailing part. **8.** an elongated part of a skirt or dress trailing behind on the ground. **9.** a trail or stream of something from a moving object. **10.** a line or succession of persons or things following after. **11.** a body of followers or attendants; a retinue. **12.** a succession or series of proceedings, events, circumstances, etc. **13.** a succession of connected ideas; a course of reasoning: *to lose one's train of thought.* **14.** the aftermath; the events proceeding from an event. **15.** proper sequence; order: *putting matters in train.* **16.** *Astron.* a trail (def. 27a) or the tail of a comet. **17.** a line of combustible material, as gunpowder, for leading fire to an explosive charge. **18.** *Physics.* a succession of wave cycles, pulses, or the like, esp. one caused by a periodic disturbance of short duration. *–v.t.* **19.** to subject to discipline and instruction; educate; drill. **20.** to make proficient by instruction and practice, as in some art, profession, or work: *to train soldiers.* **21.** to make (a person, etc.) fit by proper exercise, diet, etc., as for some athletic feat or contest. **22.** to discipline and instruct (an animal) to perform specified actions. **23.** to treat or manipulate so as to bring into some desired form, position, direction, etc. **24.** *Hort.* to bring (a plant, branch, etc.) into a particular shape or position, by bending, pruning, or the like. **25.** to bring to bear on some object or point, aim, or direct, as a firearm, a camera, a telescope, the glance, etc. *–v.i.* **26.** to give the discipline and instruction, drill, practice, etc., designed to impart proficiency or efficiency. **27.** to undergo discipline and instruction, drill, etc. **28.** to get oneself into condition by exercise, etc. **29.** to travel by train. [ME from OF *tra(h)iner,* v., from L *trahere* draw] **– trainer,** *n.* **– trainable,** *adj.* **– trainless,** *adj.*

**trainbearer** /'treɪnbɛərə/, *n.* one who holds up a train, as of a robe, cloak, or dress, in ceremonies, to prevent it from trailing on the ground.

**trainee** /treɪ'ni/, *n.* **1.** one receiving training. *–adj.* **2.** receiving training: *a trainee designer.*

**trainer** /'treɪnə/, *n.* **1.** a person who prepares racehorses for racing. **2.** a person who trains athletes in a sport. **3.** equipment used in training, esp. that which simulates the conditions of the sport.

**training** /'treɪnɪŋ/, *n.* **1.** the development in oneself or another of certain skills, habits, and attitudes. **2.** the resulting condition. **3. in training, a.** undergoing such discipline. **b.** physically fit, as a result of training. **4. out of training,** physically unfit.

**training college** /'– kɒlɪdʒ/, *n.* a college providing post-secondary education in specified skills, usu. associated with a professional qualification or vocation, as teaching.

**training school** /'– skul/, *n.* **1.** a school for giving training in some art, profession, or line of work. **2.** an institution for the reformation of juvenile delinquents.

**training ship** /'– ʃɪp/, *n.* a ship equipped for training boys in seamanship, as for naval service.

**train oil** /'treɪn ɔɪl/, *n.* oil obtained by boiling, from the blubber of whales, or from seals, fishes, etc. [*train* (now obs.), earlier *trane* train oil (from MLG or MD; apparently special use of MLG *trāne* tear, drop, c. G *Träne*) + OIL]

**trainsick** /'treɪnsɪk/, *adj.* made sick by the motion of riding in a train. **– trainsickness,** *n.*

**trainspotter** /'treɪnspɒtə/, *n.* See **spotter** (def. 4).

**traipse** /treɪps/, *v.i.,* **traipsed, traipsing.** *Colloq.* **1.** to walk so as to be, or having become, tired; trudge. **2.** to walk (about) aimlessly; gad about. Also, **trapes.** [orig. uncert; ? akin to TRAMP]

**trait** /treɪ, treɪt/, *n.* **1.** a distinguishing feature or quality; characteristic: *bad traits of character.* **2.** *Rare.* a stroke or touch. [late ME, from F: draught, from L *tractus*]

**traitor** /'treɪtə/, *n.* **1.** one who betrays a person, a cause, or any trust. **2.** one who betrays his country by violating his allegiance; one guilty of treason. [ME, from OF *traitre,* from L *trāditor* betrayer] **– traitress** /'treɪtrəs/, *n.fem.*

**traitorous** /'treɪtərəs/, *adj.* **1.** having the character of a traitor; treacherous; perfidious. **2.** characteristic of a traitor. **3.** having the nature of treason: *a traitorous action.* **– traitorously,** *adv.* **– traitorousness,** *n.*

**trajectory** /trə'dʒɛktəri/, *n., pl.* **-ries. 1.** the curve described by a projectile in its flight. **2.** the path described by a body moving under the action of given forces. **3.** *Geom.* a curve or surface which cuts all the curves or surfaces of a given system at a constant angle. [ML *trājectōrius,* adj., casting over]

**tram**[1] /træm/, *n., v.,* **trammed, tramming.** *–n.* **1.** a passenger vehicle running on a tramway, having flanged wheels and usu. powered by electricity taken by a current collector from an overhead conductor wire. **2.** →**tramway** (def. 5). **3.** the vehicle or cage of an overhead carrier. *–v.t.* **4.** to travel or convey by tram. **5.** to convey by truck (def. 6). *–v.i.* **6.** to travel by tram. [MLG or MD *trame* beam, rung, etc.] **– tramless,** *adj.*

**tram**[2] /træm/, *n., v.,* **trammed, tramming.** *–n.* **1.** →**trammel** (def. 2). **2.** *Mach.* correct position or adjustment: *the spindle is in tram.* *–v.t.* **3.** *Mach.* to adjust (something) correctly. [short for TRAMMEL]

**tram**[3] /træm/, *n.* silk yarn of two or more strands or weft. [F *trame,* from L *trāma* weft]

**tramcar** /'træmka/, *n.* →**tram**[1] (def. 1).

**Traminer** /'træmənə, trə'minə/, *n.* a grape variety used to produce a white wine with a perfumed bouquet and matching flavour. [G]

**tramline** /'træmlaɪn/, *n.* **1.** (*usu. pl.*) the track on which trams run. **2.** one of the rails of such track. **3.** the route of a tram. **4.** (*pl.*) *Tennis, etc.* the outer marking lines of a tennis court, etc.

**trammel** /'træməl/, *n., v.,* **-melled, -melling** or (*U.S.*) **-meled, -meling.** *–n.* **1.** (*usu. pl.*) anything that impedes or hinders free action; a restraint: *the trammels of custom.* **2.** an instrument for describing ellipses. **3.** a trammel net. **4.** a fowling net. **5.** a contrivance hung in a fireplace to support pots, kettles, etc., over the fire. **6.** a shackle, esp. one for teaching a horse to amble. *–v.t.* **7.** to involve or hold in trammels; hamper; restrain. **8.** to catch or entangle in or as in a net. [ME *tramail,* from OF: net with three layers of meshes, from LL *tremaculum,* from L *trē(s)* three + *macula* mesh] – **trammeller,** *n.*

**trammel net** /'– nɛt/, *n.* a three-layered net, the middle layer of which is fine-meshed, the others coarse-meshed, so that fish attempting to pass through the net will become entangled in one or more of the meshes.

**trammie** /'træmi/, *n. Colloq.* a tram driver or conductor.

**tramontana** /træmɒn'tanə/, *n.* a cool, dry wind which blows down from the mountains in the Mediterranean region. [It.]

**tramontane** /trə'mɒnteɪn/, *adj.* **1.** Also, **transmontane.** being or situated beyond the mountains, (originally, beyond the Alps as viewed from Italy). **2.** pertaining to the other side of the mountains. **3.** foreign; barbarous. *–n.* **4.** one who lives beyond the mountains (originally applied by the Italians to the peoples beyond the Alps, and by the latter to the Italians). **5.** a foreigner; a barbarian. [ME, from It. *tramontano,* from L *transmontānus,* from *trans* across + stem of *mons* mountain + *-ānus* -AN]

**tramp** /træmp/, *v.i.* **1.** to tread or walk with a firm, heavy, resounding step. **2.** to tread heavily or trample (fol. by *on* or *upon*): *to tramp on a person's toes.* **3.** to walk steadily; march; trudge. **4.** to go about as a vagabond or tramp. **5.** to make a voyage on a tramp (def. 19). **6.** to hike. *–v.t.* **7.** to tramp or walk heavily or steadily through or over. **8.** to traverse on foot: *tramp the streets.* **9.** to tread or trample underfoot. **10.** to travel over as a tramp. **11.** to run (a vessel) as a tramp (def. 19). *–n.* **12.** the act of tramping. **13.** a firm, heavy, resounding tread. **14.** the sound made. **15.** a long, steady walk; trudge. **16.** a walking excursion or expedition. **17.** a person who travels about on foot from place to place, esp. a vagabond living on occasional jobs or gifts of money or food. **18.** *Colloq.* a socially unacceptable woman, often promiscuous. **19.** a cargo boat which does not run regularly between ports, but goes wherever shippers desire. [ME *trampe(n),* c. LG *trampen* stamp] – **tramper,** *n.* – **tramping,** *n.*

**tram pinch** /'træm pɪntʃ/, *n.* See **pinch** (def. 26).

**trample** /'træmpəl/, *v.,* **-pled, -pling,** *n. –v.i.* **1.** to tread or step heavily and noisily; stamp. **2.** to tread heavily, roughly, or crushingly (fol. by *on, upon,* etc.), esp. repeatedly. **3.** to treat with contempt. **4.** to act in a harsh, domineering, or cruel way, as if treading roughly (fol. by *on, upon,* etc.): *to trample on an oppressed people. –v.t.* **5.** to tread heavily, roughly, or carelessly on or over; tread underfoot, etc. **6.** to treat with contempt. **7.** to domineer harshly over; crush: *to trample one's employees.* **8.** to put, force, reduce, etc., by trampling: *to trample out a fire. –n.* **9.** the act or sound of trampling. [ME, frequentative of TRAMP, c. G *trampeln*] – **trampler,** *n.*

**trampoline** /'træmpəlin, træmpə'lin/, *n., v.,* **-lined, -lining.** *–n.* **1.** a sheet of canvas attached by resilient cords to a horizontal frame a metre or so above the floor; used as a springboard when performing acrobatics. *–v.i.* **2.** to jump on a trampoline. [It.: springboard]

**tramp steamer** /'træmp stimə/, *n.* →**tramp** (def. 19).

**tramroad** /'træmroud/, *n.* a tracked road within a mine for ore trucks.

**tramway** /'træmweɪ/, *n.* **1.** usu. a system of grooved tracks laid in urban streets, forming routes for the conveyance of passengers in trams. **2.** such a system, together with the cars and other equipment. **3.** the company owning or operating it. **4.** an early type of railway, consisting of a crude track of wooden rails, or wooden rails capped with metal treads. **5.** *Mining.* **a.** a track (usu. elevated) or roadway for mine haulage. **b.** an overhead cable system for transporting ore and mine freight.

**trance** /træns, trans/, *n., v.,* **tranced, trancing.** *–n.* **1.** a half-conscious state, as between sleeping and waking. **2.** a dazed or bewildered condition. **3.** a fit of complete mental absorption or deep musing. **4.** an unconscious, cataleptic, or hypnotic condition. **5.** *Spiritualism.* a temporary state in which a medium, with suspension of personal consciousness, is controlled by an intelligence from without and used as a means of communication, as from the dead. *–v.t.* **6.** to put in a trance. [ME, from OF *transe* passage, esp. from life to death, deadly suspense or fear, from *transir* go across, pass over, from L *transīre*] – **trancelike,** *adj.*

**tranche** /træntʃ, trantʃ/, *n.* an additional block of stock, as bonds, etc., supplementary to an already existing issue. [F: slice]

**trannie**[1] /'træni/, *n. Colloq.* a transistor radio. [*tran(sistor)* + *-n-* + -IE]

**trannie**[2] /'træni/, *n. Colloq.* a transformer. [*tran(sformer)* + *-n-* + -IE]

**tranquil** /'træŋkwəl/, *adj.,* **-quiller, -quillest** or (*U.S.*) **-quiler, -quilest.** **1.** free from commotion or tumult; peaceful; quiet; calm: *a tranquil country place.* **2.** free from or unaffected by disturbing emotions; unruffled: *a tranquil life.* [earlier *tranquill,* from L *tranquillus*] – **tranquilly,** *adv.* – **tranquilness,** *n.*

**tranquillise** /'træŋkwəlaɪz/, *v.t., v.i.,* **-lised, -lising.** to make or become tranquil. Also, **tranquillise;** *U.S.,* **tranquilize.** – **tranquillisation** /ˌtræŋkwəlaɪ'zeɪʃən/, *n.*

**tranquilliser** /'træŋkwəlaɪzə/, *n.* **1.** a drug that has a sedative or calming effect without inducing sleep. **2.** one who or that which tranquillises. Also, **tranquillizer;** *U.S.,* **tranquilizer.**

**tranquillity** /træŋ'kwɪləti/, *n.* **1.** the state of being tranquil; calmness; peacefulness; quiet; serenity; composure. **2.** (*caps*) **Sea of,** a plain, *Mare Tranquillitatis,* in the first quadrant of the face of the moon, site of man's first landing on the moon, 20 July, 1969. Also, *U.S.,* **tranquility.**

**tranquillo** /træn'kwɪlou/, *adv.* **1.** (a musical direction) in a calm manner. *–adj.* **2.** calm. [It.]

**trans-,** **1.** a prefix meaning 'across', 'beyond', freely applied in geographical terms (*transcontinental, trans-Australian*), also found attached to stems not used as words, and in figurative meanings, as *transpire, transport, transcend.* **2.** *Chem.* See **cis-trans isomerism.** [L, combining form of *trans,* prep.]

**trans.,** **1.** transaction. **2.** transcript. **3.** transitive. **4.** translated. **5.** translation. **6.** translator. **7.** transport.

**transact** /trænz'ækt/, *v.t.* **1.** to carry through (affairs, business, negotiations, etc.) to a conclusion or settlement. **2.** to perform. *–v.i.* **3.** to carry through affairs or negotiations. [L *transactus,* pp., carried out, driven through, accomplished] – **transactor,** *n.*

**transaction** /trænz'ækʃən/, *n.* **1.** the act of transacting. **2.** the fact of being transacted. **3.** an instance or process of transacting something. **4.** that which is transacted; an affair; a piece of business. **5.** (*pl.*) **a.** records of the doings of a learned society or the like. **b.** reports of papers read, addresses delivered, discussions, etc., at the meetings. [late ME, from L *transactio* act of carrying out] – **transactional,** *adj.*

**transalpine** /trænz'ælpaɪn/, *adj.* **1.** across or beyond the Alps, a mountain system in southern Europe, esp. as viewed from Italy. **2.** passing through or over the Alps. **3.** pertaining to people or places beyond the Alps. *–n.* **4.** a native or inhabitant of a country beyond the Alps.

**transatlantic** /trænzət'læntɪk/, *adj.* **1.** passing or extending across the Atlantic: *a transatlantic liner.* **2.** beyond, or on the other side of, the Atlantic.

**transcalent** /træns'keɪlənt/, *adj.* pervious to heat; permitting the passage of heat. [TRANS- + L *calens,* ppr., being hot] – **transcalency,** *n.*

**transceiver** /træn'sivə/, *n.* a radio set capable of both transmitting and receiving.

**transcend** /træn'sɛnd/, *v.t.* **1.** to go or be above or beyond (a limit, something with limits, etc.); surpass or exceed. **2.** to go beyond in elevation, excellence, extent, degree, etc.; surpass, excel, or exceed. **3.** *Theol.* (of the Deity) to be above and independent of (the universe). *–v.i.* **4.** to be transcendent; excel. [ME, from L *transcendere* climb over or beyond]

**transcendence** /træn'sɛndəns/, *n.* **1.** the state, quality, or fact of being transcendent. **2.** transcendent character. Also, **transcendency.**

**transcendent** /træn'sɛndənt/, *adj.* **1.** transcending; going beyond ordinary limits; surpassing or extraordinary. **2.** superior or supreme. **3.** *Theol.* being beyond matter, and having a continuing existence therefore outside the created world. **4.** *Philos.* that which is beyond experience. – **transcendently,** *adv.* – **transcendentness,** *n.*

**transcendental** /trænsɛn'dɛntl/, *adj.* **1.** transcendent, surpassing, or superior. **2.** transcending ordinary or common experience, thought, or belief; extraordinary; supernatural; abstract or metaphysical. **3.** idealistic, lofty, or extravagant. **4.** speculative; obscure. **5.** *Philos.* **a.** belonging to every kind of thing, transcending all other distinctions. **b.** a form of argumentation that claims to establish the necessary presuppositions of our knowledge. **c.** a type of philosophy that rests primarily on such argumentation. **6.** *Maths.* (of a number) not algebraic; not producible by the algebraic operations of addition, subtraction, multiplication, division, and the extraction of roots, each repeated only a finite number of times. *–n.* **7.** *Maths.* a transcendental number, such as $\pi$ or *e.* **8.** (*pl.*) application as being, one, true, good. – **transcendentally,** *adv.*

**transcendentalism** /trænsɛn'dɛntəlɪzəm/, *n.* **1.** transcendental character, thought, or language. **2.** transcendental philosophy; any philosophy based upon the doctrine that the principles of reality are to be discovered by the study of the processes of thought, or emphasising the intuitive and spiritual above the empirical (associated with Kant and subsequent German idealism, esp. Schelling, and in the U.S., with Emerson). **3.** that which is vague and elusive in philosophy. – **transcendentalist,** *n., adj.*

**transcendental meditation** /trænsɛn,dɛntəl mɛdə'teɪʃən/, *n.* a state of rest deeper than sleep when the mind remains alert and stress is neutralised automatically. *Abbrev:* **T.M.**

**transcontinental** /,trænzkɒntə'nɛntl/, *adj.* **1.** passing or extending across a continent: *a transcontinental railway.* **2.** on the other side of a continent.

**transcribe** /træn'skraɪb/, *v.t.,* **-scribed, -scribing.** **1.** to make a copy of in writing: *to transcribe a document.* **2.** to reproduce in writing or print as from speech. **3.** to write out in other characters; transliterate: *to transcribe one's shorthand notes.* **4.** to make a transcription. **5.** *Music.* to arrange (a composition) for a medium other than that for which it was originally written. [L *transcrībere* copy off] – **transcriber,** *n.*

**transcript** /'trænskrɪpt/, *n.* **1.** something transcribed or made by transcribing; a written copy. **2.** a reproduction in writing or print. **3.** a form of something as rendered from one alphabet or language into another. **4.** *Law.* an official written copy of proceedings in a court. [ME, from L *transcriptum,* lit., thing copied, pp. (neut.) of *transcrībere* TRANSCRIBE; replacing ME *transcrit,* from OF]

**transcription** /træn'skrɪpʃən/, *n.* **1.** the act of transcribing. **2.** a transcript; a copy. **3.** *Music.* **a.** the arrangement of a composition for a medium other than that for which it was originally written. **b.** a composition so arranged. **4.** a recorded radio or television program. **5.** *Biochem.* the process whereby RNA is formed from DNA. – **transcriptive** /træn'skrɪptɪv/, *adj.*

**transcrystalline fracture** /trænz,krɪstəlaɪn 'frækʃə/, *n.* the fracture of a metal in which the line of failure passes through the crystals rather than round their boundaries. Cf. **intercrystalline fracture.**

**transducer** /trænz'djusə/, *n.* any device which receives energy from one medium or transmission system, and supplies related energy to another medium or transmission system. [var. of TRADUCER. See TRADUCE]

**transect** /træn'sɛkt/, *v.t.* to cut across; dissect transversely. – **transection,** *n.*

**transenna** /træn'sɛnə/, *n.* a lattice or openwork screen, generally of marble, enclosing a shrine in early Christian churches. [L: lit., latticework]

**transept** /'trænsɛpt/, *n.* **1.** the transverse portion (or, occasionally, portions) of a cruciform church. **2.** either of the two armlike divisions of this, one on each side of the crossing. [Anglo-L *transēptum,* from L *trans* across + *sēptum* enclosure] – **transeptal** /træn'sɛptl/, *adj.* – **transeptally** /træn'sɛptəli/, *adv.*

**transeunt** /'transiənt/, *adj. Philos.* passing outwards; producing an effect outside itself (usu. descriptive of activity, and then contrasted with *immanent*). Also, **transient.** [L *transiens,* ppr., going across]

**transfer** /træns'fɜ/, *v.,* **-ferred, -ferring;** /'trænsfɜ/, *n. –v.t.* **1.** to convey or remove from one place, person, etc., to another. **2.** *Law.* to make over or convey: *to transfer a title to land.* **3.** to convey (a drawing, design, pattern, etc.) from one surface to another. *–v.i.* **4.** to transfer oneself. **5.** to be transferred. **6.** to change from one bus, train, or the like, to another, as on a transfer (def. 12). **7.** (of a professional football player) to change from one club to another. *–n.* **8.** the means or system of transferring. **9.** the act of transferring. **10.** the fact of being transferred. **11.** a point or place for transferring. **12.** a ticket, issued with or without extra charge, entitling a passenger to continue his journey on another bus, train, or the like; a transfer-ticket. **13.** a drawing, pattern, etc., which may be transferred to a surface, esp. by direct contact. **14.** (of a football player) the fact or act of transferring or being transferred. **15.** *Law.* a conveyance, by sale, gift, or otherwise, of real or personal property, to another. **16.** *Finance.* the act of having the ownership of a stock or registered bond transferred upon the books of the issuing company or its agent. **17.** *Finance.* a deed completed when stocks and shares change hands, which is registered with the company issuing the shares. [ME *transferre(n),* from L *transferre* carry across] – **transferable** /træns'fɜrəbəl/, *adj.* – **transferability** /,trænsfɜrə'bɪləti/, *n.* – **transferal** /træns'fɜrəl/, *n.*

**transferable vote** /træns,fɜrəbəl 'voʊt/, *n.* a vote which can be transferred to a second choice if the candidate first voted for should be out of the running.

**transferase** /'trænsfəreɪz, -eɪs/, *n.* any enzyme that catalyses the transfer of a chemical group from one substrate to another.

**transferee** /trænsfə'ri/, *n.* **1.** one who is transferred or removed, as from one place to another. **2.** *Law.* one to whom a transfer is made, as of property.

**transference** /'trænsfərəns/, *n.* **1.** the act or process of transferring. **2.** the fact of being transferred. **3.** *Pyschoanal.* **a.** reproduction of emotions, originally experienced for the most part in childhood, towards a person other than the one towards whom they were initially experienced. **b.** →**displacement** (def. 8).

**transferential** /trænsfə'rɛnʃəl/, *adj.* pertaining to or involving transference.

**transfer fee** /'trænsfɜ fi/, *n.* **1.** a sum of money paid by one football club to another when a player is transferred between them. **2.** a sum of money paid to a bank to transfer funds.

**transfer list** /'– lɪst/, *n.* a list made by a football club of players to be transferred.

**transferor** /træns'fɜrə/, *n. Law.* one who makes a transfer, as of property.

**transfer-paper** /'trænsfɜ-,peɪpə/, *n.* a specially prepared paper formerly used to transfer images from letterpress or engraved surfaces to lithographic surfaces. Images could also be drawn direct on to transfer-paper and transferred to lithographic surfaces.

**transferrer** /træns'fɜrə/, *n.* one who or that which transfers.

**transfer-ticket** /'trænsfɜ-,tɪkət/, *n.* →**transfer** (def. 12).

**transfiguration** /,trænsfɪgə'reɪʃən/, *n.* **1.** the act of transfiguring. **2.** the state of being transfigured. **3.** (*cap.*) the change in the appearance of Christ when glorified in the presence of three chosen disciples. **4.** (*cap.*) the occasion when this happened. **5.** (*cap.*) the church festival commemorating this, observed on 6 August.

**transfigure** /træns'fɪgə/, *v.t.,* **-ured, -uring.** **1.** to change in outward form or appearance; transform, change, or alter. **2.** to change so as to glorify, exalt, or idealise. [ME, from L *transfigūrāre*] – **transfigurement,** *n.*

**transfinite** /træns'faɪnaɪt/, *adj.* (in mathematics) beyond any finite number or magnitude.

**transfix** /træns'fɪks/, *v.t.* **1.** to pierce through, as with a pointed weapon, or as the weapon does. **2.** to fix fast with or on something sharp; thrust through. **3.** to make motionless with amazement, terror, etc. [L *transfixus,* pp., pierced, transfixed] – **transfixion** /træns'fɪkʃən/, *n.*

**transform** /træns'fɔm/, *v.;* /'trænsfɔm/, *n. –v.t.* **1.** to change in form; change to something of a different form; metamorphose. **2.** to change in appearance, condition, nature, or character, esp. completely or extensively. **3.** to change (one substance, element, or nuclide) into another. **4.** *Elect.* to change the voltage and current characteristics of (a circuit) by the use of a transformer. **5.** *Maths.* to change the form of (a figure, expression, etc.) without in general changing the value. **6.** *Physics.* to change (one form of energy) into another. *–v.i.* **7.** to change in form, appearance, or character; become transformed. *–n.* **8.** *Maths.* a function obtained from a given function by a specified rule, as a Fourier transform. **9.** *Linguistics.* the result of applying a transformational rule to a group of words; *I am being hit* is the passive transform of *I am hitting.* [ME, from L *transformāre* change form] – **transformable,** *adj.* – **transformative** /træns'fɔmətɪv/, *adj.*

**transformation** /trænsfə'meɪʃən/, *n.* **1.** the act of transforming. **2.** the state of being transformed. **3.** change in form, appearance, nature, or character. **4.** *Physics.* the change of one nuclide or element into another. **5.** *Theat.* Also, **transformation scene.** a seemingly miraculous change in the appearance of scenery or actors in view of the audience. **6.** *Gram., Logic.* the substitution of symbols for other symbols in an expression according to strict rules, designed to bring out clearly the relations in which the parts of a complex expression stand to each other. **7.** *Linguistics.* **a.** the process of changing one linguistic structure into another according to certain rules; the sentence *He went home* is transformed into the interrogative *Did he go home?* **b.** the end result of a transformation. **8.** *Obs.* a wig for a woman. – **transformational,** *adj.*

**transformational grammar** /trænsfə,meɪʃənəl 'græmə/, *n.* a grammar which uses transformational rules in its description of a language.

**transformer** /træns'fɔmə/, *n.* **1.** one who or that which transforms. **2.** *Elect.* an electric device, without continuously moving parts, which by electromagnetic induction transforms electric energy from one or more circuits to one or more circuits at the same frequency, usu. with changed values of voltage and current; esp. one for transforming a comparatively small alternating current of higher voltage into a larger current of lower voltage (**step-down transformer**), or, conversely, a current of lower voltage into one of higher voltage (**step-up transformer**).

**transformism** /træns'fɔmɪzəm/, *n. Biol.* **1.** the doctrine of gradual transformation of one species into another by descent with modification through many generations. **2.** such transformation itself. **3.** any doctrine or instance of evolution. – **transformist,** *n.*

**transfuse** /træns'fjuz/, *v.t.*, **-fused, -fusing.** **1.** to pour from one container into another. **2.** to transfer or transmit as if by pouring; instil; impart. **3.** to diffuse through something; infuse. **4.** *Med.* **a.** to transfer (blood) from the veins or arteries of one person or animal into those of another. **b.** to inject, as a saline solution, into a blood vessel. [ME, from L *transfūsus,* pp., poured across] – **transfuser,** *n.* – **transfusible,** *adj.* – **transfusive** /træns'fjusɪv/, *adj.*

**transfusion** /træns'fjuʒən/, *n.* **1.** the act or process of transfusing. **2.** *Med.* **a.** the transferring of blood taken from one person or animal to another, as in order to renew a depleted blood supply. **b.** the injecting of some other liquid into the veins. **3.** an act of imparting, injecting, transmitting, or the like: *a transfusion of new capital into a business.* [L *transfūsio*]

**transgress** /trænz'grɛs/, *v.t.* **1.** to pass over or go beyond (a limit, etc.): *to transgress the bounds of prudence.* **2.** to go beyond the limits imposed by (a law, command, etc.); violate; infringe; break. *–v.i.* **3.** to violate a law, command, etc.; offend or sin (fol. by *against*). [L *transgressus,* pp., having stepped across] – **transgressive,** *adj.* – **transgressively,** *adv.* – **transgressor,** *n.*

**transgression** /trænz'grɛʃən/, *n.* the act of transgressing; violation of a law, command, etc.; sin.

**tranship** /trænz'ʃɪp/, *v.,* **-shipped, -shipping.** *–v.t.* **1.** to transfer from one ship or other conveyance to another. *–v.i.* **2.** to go or be taken from one ship or other conveyance to another. Also, **transship, trans-ship.** – **transhipment,** *n.*

**transhumance** /træns'hjuməns/, *n.* the seasonal migration of livestock, and the people who tend them, between lowlands and adjacent mountains. [F, from *transhumer,* from Sp. *trashumar* change ground. See TRANS-, HUMUS] – **transhumant,** *adj.*

**transience** /'trænziəns/, *n.* transient state or quality. Also, **transiency.**

**transient** /'trænziənt/, *adj.* **1.** passing with time; not lasting or enduring; transitory. **2.** lasting only for a time; temporary: *transient authority.* **3.** remaining for only a short time, as a guest at a hotel. **4.** *Philos.* →**transeunt.** *–n.* **5.** one who or that which is transient; a transient guest, boarder, etc. [TRANSEUNT (with *-ie-* from L nom.)] – **transiently,** *adv.* – **transientness,** *n.*

**transilient** /træn'sɪliənt/, *adj.* leaping or passing from one thing or state to another. [L *transiliens,* ppr., leaping across] – **transilience,** *n.*

**transilluminate** /trænzə'lumәneɪt/, *v.t.*, **-nated, -nating.** **1.** to cause light to pass through. **2.** *Med.* to throw a strong light through (an organ or part) as a means of diagnosis. – **transillumination** /,trænzəlumə'neɪʃən/, *n.* – **transilluminator,** *n.*

**transisthmian** /trænz'ɪsθmiən/, *adj.* passing or extending across an isthmus.

**transistor** /træn'zɪstə/, *n.* **1.** *Electronics.* a miniature solid-state device for amplifying or switching, using silicon or germanium semiconducting materials. **2.** a transistorised radio. *–adj.* **3.** equipped with transistors, as a radio or gramophone. [TRANS(FER) + (RES)ISTOR]

**transistorise** /træn'zɪstəraɪz/, *v.t.*, **-rised, -rising.** to equip with or convert to a circuit employing transistors. Also, **transistorize.**

**transit** /'trænzət/, *n., v.,* **-sited, -siting.** *–n.* **1.** the act or fact of passing across or through; passage from one place to another. **2.** conveyance from one place to another, as of persons or goods: *the problem of rapid transit in cities.* **3.** a transition or change. **4.** *Astron.* **a.** the passage of a heavenly body across the meridian of a place or through the field of a telescope. **b.** the passage of an inferior planet (Mercury or Venus) across the disc of the sun, or of a satellite or its shadow across the face of its primary. **5.** *Survey., U.S.* a theodolite. **6. in transit,** passing through a place; staying for only a short time. *–v.t.* **7.** to pass across or through. **8.** *Survey.* to turn (the telescope of a theodolite) about its horizontal transverse axis so as to make it point in the opposite direction; reverse, invert, or plunge (the instrument). *–v.i.* **9.** to pass across or through a place or thing. [late ME, from L *transitus* act of crossing]

**transit camp** /'– kæmp/, *n.* temporary accommodation, esp. army huts, tents, etc., provided for groups of people in transit between one country and another. Also, **transit site.**

**transition** /træn'zɪʃən/, *n.* **1.** passage from one position, state, stage, etc., to another. **2.** a passage or change of this kind. **3.** *Music.* **a.** a passing from one key to another; modulation. **b.** a brief or sudden modulation; a modulation used in passing. **c.** a passage serving as a connecting link between two more important passages. **4.** *Physics.* a change in the configuration of an atomic nucleus, either by changing to another nuclide with the emission of alpha or beta particles, or by changing its energy state with the emission of gamma rays. **5.** *Archit.* the period of change from one architectural style to another. **6.** →**transition handicap.** **7.** →**transition horse.** [L *transitio* act of going across] – **transitional, transitionary,** *adj.* – **transitionally,** *adv.*

**transition element** /'– ɛləmənt/, *n.* any of several elements which occur in the middle of the long periods of the periodic table, have incomplete inner electron shells, variable valencies, and properties which generally resemble those of their horizontal neighbours in the periodic table.

**transition handicap** /– 'hændikæp/, *n.* a restricted race for horses, which are specified as being the transition class in accordance with the rules operating in each State of Australia.

**transition horse** /– 'hɔs/, *n.* a horse eligible to run in a transition handicap. Also, **transition-class horse.**

**transition temperature** /'– tɛmprətʃə/, *n.* **1.** *Chem.* the temperature at which one form of a polymorphous substance changes into another; the temperature at which both forms can coexist (**transition point**). **2.** *Physics.* the temperature at which a superconducting material becomes superconducting.

**transitive** /'trænzətɪv/, *adj.* **1.** *Gram.* having the nature of a transitive verb. **2.** characterised by or involving transition; transitional; intermediate. **3.** passing over to or affecting something else; transeunt. *–n.* **4.** *Gram.* a transitive verb. [LL *transitīvus*] – **transitively,** *adv.* – **transitiveness,** *n.*

**transitive relation** /– rə'leɪʃən/, *n. Logic, Maths.* a relation which, if it is valid between *x* and *y* and between *y* and *z*, is also valid between *x* and *z*: *if x equals y and y equals z, then x equals z; if a is the ancestor of b, and b is the ancestor of c, then a is the ancestor of c.*

**transitive verb** /– 'vɜb/, *n.* a verb that is regularly accompanied by a direct object.

**transit lane** /'trænzət leɪn/, *n.* a traffic lane which is restricted during certain hours to particular categories of vehicles.

**transitory** /'trænzətri/, *adj.* **1.** passing away; not lasting, enduring, permanent or eternal. **2.** lasting for a short time; brief; transient. – **transitorily,** *adv.* – **transitoriness,** *n.*

**transit site** /'trænzət saɪt/, *n.* →**transit camp.**

**transit theodolite** /– θi'ɒdəlaɪt/, *n.* a theodolite in which the telescope can be rotated completely around its horizontal axis.

**transit van** /'– væn/, *n.* a small van with side and rear doors.

**Trans-Jordan** /trænz-'dʒɔdən/, *n.* former name of **Jordan.**

**translate** /trænz'leɪt/, *v.*, **-lated, -lating.** *–v.t.* **1.** to turn (something written or spoken) from one language into another: *to translate Arunta into English.* **2.** to change into another form; transform or covert. **3.** to bear, carry, or remove from one place, position, condition, etc., to another; transfer. **4.** to express in other terms; interpret; explain. **5.** *Physics.* to cause (a body) to move without rotation or angular displacement; subject to translation. **6.** *U.S. Teleg.* to retransmit or forward (a message), as by a relay. **7.** *Eccles.* **a.** to move (a bishop) from one see to another. **b.** to move (a see) from one place to another. **8.** to remove (the body of a saint) from one resting place to another, esp. a specially built shrine. **9.** to exalt in spiritual ecstasy or rapture. **10.** to convey or remove to heaven without death. *–v.i.* **11.** to practise translation. **12.** to admit of translation: *the book translates well.* [ME, from L *translātus,* pp., carried over] – **translatable,** *adj.* – **translatableness,** *n.*

**translation** /trænz'leɪʃən/, *n.* **1.** the rendering of something into another language. **2.** a version in a different language: *a French translation of 'Tree of Man'.* **3.** conversion to a different form. **4.** the act of translating. **5.** the state of being translated; removal to another place, etc. **6.** *Mech.* motion in which all particles of a body move in straight-line paths. **7.** *U.S. Teleg.* the process of forwarding a message, as by a relay. **8.** *Biochem.* protein synthesis. – **translational,** *adj.*

**translator** /trænz'leɪtə/, *n.* **1.** one who or that which translates. **2.** *Computers.* assembler; compiler.

**transliterate** /trænz'lɪtəreɪt/, *v.t.*, **-rated, -rating.** to change (letters, words, etc.) into corresponding characters of another alphabet or language: *to transliterate the Greek χ as ch.* [TRANS- + L *līterātus* lettered] – **transliteration** /ˌtrænzlɪtə'reɪʃən/, *n.* – **transliterator,** *n.*

**translocate** /trænzloʊ'keɪt/, *v.t.*, **-cated, -cating.** to remove from one place to another; cause to change place; displace; dislocate. – **translocation,** *n.*

**translucent** /trænz'lusənt/, *adj.* **1.** transmitting light diffusely or imperfectly, as frosted glass. **2.** *Rare.* clear. [L *translūcens,* ppr., shining through] – **translucence, translucency,** *n.* – **translucently,** *adv.*

**translucid** /trænz'lusəd/, *adj.* →**translucent.** – **translucidity** /trænzlu'sɪdəti/, *n.*

**translunary** /trænz'lunəri/, *adj.* **1.** situated beyond or above the moon; superlunary. **2.** celestial, rather than earthly. **3.** ideal; visionary.

**transmarine** /trænzmə'rin/, *adj.* overseas.

**transmeridional** /trænzmə'rɪdiənəl/, *adj.* crossing the meridians; running east and west.

**transmigrant** /'trænzmaɪgrənt/, *n.* **1.** a person passing through a country or place on his way from his own country to a country in which he intends to settle. *–adj.* **2.** transmigrating. [L *transmigrans,* ppr.]

**transmigrate** /trænzmaɪ'greɪt/, *v.*, **-grated, -grating.** *–v.i.* **1.** to remove or pass from one place to another. **2.** to migrate from one country to another in order to settle there. **3.** (of the soul) to be reborn with the same soul in another body, either immediately upon death or after a purgatorial or waiting period. *–v.t.* **4.** to cause to transmigrate, as a soul. [ME, from L *transmigrātus,* pp.] – **transmigrator,** *n.* – **transmigratory,** *adj.*

**transmigration** /trænzmaɪ'greɪʃən/, *n.* **1.** the act of transmigrating. **2.** the passage of a soul at death into another body; metempsychosis. [ME, from LL *transmigrātio*]

**transmissible** /trænz'mɪsəbəl/, *adj.* capable of being transmitted. – **transmissibility** /ˌtrænzmɪsə'bɪləti/, *n.*

**transmission** /trænz'mɪʃən/, *n.* **1.** the act of transmitting. **2.** the fact of being transmitted. **3.** that which is transmitted. **4.** *Mach.* **a.** the transmitting or transferring of motive force. **b.** a device for this purpose, esp. the mechanism or gearing for transmitting the power from the revolutions of the engine shaft in a motor vehicle to the driving wheels, at the varying rates of speed and direction of drive as selected in gear changes. **5.** *Radio, T.V., etc.* the broadcasting of electromagnetic waves from the transmitting station to the receiving station. **6. a.** an instance of broadcasting a television or radio program. **b.** such a program. [L *transmissio*] – **transmissive** /trænz'mɪsɪv/, *adj.*

**transmission line** /'– laɪn/, *n.* **1.** *Elect.* the system of conductors (often overhead wires) by which electric power at high voltages is transmitted from one place to another. **2.** *Radio.* the system of conductors (two parallel wires or a coaxial cable) by which radio frequency signals are transmitted from one place to another.

**transmission loss** /'– lɒs/, *n.* the electrical power lost in a transmission line.

**transmission tower** /'– taʊə/, *n.* a high metal tower which carries transmission lines.

**transmit** /trænz'mɪt/, *v.t.*, **-mitted, -mitting.** **1.** to send over or along, as to a recipient or destination; forward, dispatch, or convey. **2.** to communicate, as information, news, etc. **3.** to pass on or hand down, as to heirs, successors, or posterity. **4.** to broadcast (a radio or television program). **5.** *Physics.* **a.** to cause (light, heat, sound, etc.) to pass through a medium. **b.** to convey or pass along (an impulse, force, motion, etc.). **c.** to permit (light, heat, etc.) to pass through: *glass transmits light.* **6.** *Radio.* to emit (electromagnetic waves). [ME, from L *transmittere* send across] – **transmittable, transmittible,** *adj.*

**transmittal** /trænz'mɪtl/, *n.* the act of transmitting (defs 1-3). Also, **transmittance.**

**transmittance** /trænz'mɪtns/, *n.* →**transmittal.**

**transmitter** /trænz'mɪtə/, *n.* **1.** one who or that which transmits. **2.** Also, **transmitting set.** *Radio.* a device for sending electromagnetic waves; that part of the broadcasting apparatus which generates and modulates the radio frequency current and conveys it to the aerial. **3.** that part of a telephonic or telegraphic apparatus converting soundwaves or mechanical movements into corresponding electrical waves or impulses.

**transmogrify** /trænz'mɒgrəfaɪ/, *v.t.*, **-fied, -fying.** to change as by magic; transform. [humorous coinage] – **transmogrification** /trænzˌmɒgrəfə'keɪʃən/, *n.*

**transmontane** /trænz'mɒnteɪn/, *adj.* →**tramontane** (def. 1).

**transmundane** /trænz'mʌndeɪn/, *adj.* beyond the (or this) world.

**transmutation** /trænzmju'teɪʃən/, *n.* **1.** the act of transmuting. **2.** the fact or state of being transmuted. **3.** a change into another nature, substance, form, or condition. **4.** *Biol.* the transformation of one species into another. **5.** *Physics.* the change of one element into another. **6.** *Alchemy,* the (attempted) conversion of base metals into metals of greater value, esp. into gold or silver. – **transmutational, transmutative** /trænz'mjutətɪv/, *adj.*

**transmute** /trænz'mjut/, *v.t.*, **-muted, -muting.** to change from one nature, substance, or form into another; transform. [ME, from L *transmutāre*] – **transmutable,** *adj.* – **transmutability** /ˌtrænzmjutə'bɪləti/, **transmutableness,** *n.* – **transmutably,** *adv.* – **transmuter,** *n.*

**transnational** /trænz'næʃənəl/, *adj.* operating on a nationwide basis.

**transnormal** /trænz'nɔməl/, *adj.* beyond what is normal; supernormal.

**transoceanic** /ˌtrænzoʊʃi'ænɪk, -oʊsi-/, *adj.* across, crossing, or beyond the ocean.

**transom** /'trænsəm/, *n.* **1.** a crosspiece separating a door, window, etc., from a window or fanlight above it. **2.** *Chiefly U.S.* a window above such a crosspiece; a fanlight. **3.** a crossbar, as of wood or stone, dividing a window horizontally. **4.** a window so divided. **5.** a lintel. **6.** any of several transverse beams or timbers fixed across the sternpost of a ship, to strengthen and give shape to the afterpart. **7.** *Railways.* any of several transverse beams or timbers fixed across a bridge to strengthen it. [ME, from L *transtrum* (with loss of second *-tr-* by dissimilation)] – **transomed,** *adj.*

**transom stern** /'– stɜn/, *n.* a flat or slightly curved stern on a boat or ship.

**transonic** /træn'sɒnɪk/, *adj.* of or pertaining to the speed at which the airflow relative to the body is subsonic in some places and supersonic in others, moving at 1120-1250 km/h at sea-level.

**transpacific** /trænspə'sɪfɪk/, *adj.* **1.** passing or extending across the Pacific. **2.** beyond or on the other side of, the Pacific.

**transparency** /træns'pɛərənsi, -'pær-/, *n., pl.* **-cies. 1.** Also, **transparence.** the property or quality of being transparent. **2.** something which is transparent; a picture, design, etc., on glass or some translucent substance, made visible by light shining through from behind. **3.** *Photog.* **a.** the fraction of the incident light transmitted by a specific photographic density. **b.** a transparent positive photographic image used for projection.

**transparent** /træns'pɛərənt, -'pær-/, *adj.* **1.** having the property of transmitting rays of light through its substance so that bodies situated beyond or behind can be distinctly seen (opposed to *opaque,* and usu. distinguished from *translucent*). **2.** admitting the passage of light through interstices. **3.** diaphanous. **4.** open, frank, or candid: *the man's transparent honesty.* **5.** easily seen through or understood: *transparent excuses.* **6.** manifest or obvious. **7.** *Obs.* shining through, as light. [ME, from ML *transpārens,* from L *trans* across + *pārens,* ppr., appearing] – **transparently,** *adv.* – **transparentness,** *n.*

**transpire** /træns'paɪə/, *v.,* **-spired, -spiring.** *–v.i.* **1.** to occur, happen, or take place. **2.** to emit or give off waste matter, etc., through the surface, as of the body, of leaves, etc. **3.** to escape as through pores, as moisture, smell, etc. **4.** to escape from secrecy; leak out; become known. *–v.t.* **5.** to emit or give off (waste matter, watery vapour, a smell, etc.) through the surface, as of the body, of leaves, etc. [ML *transpīrāre,* from L *trans* across + *spīrāre* breathe] – **transpirable,** *adj.* – **transpiration** /trænspə'reɪʃən/, *n.* – **transpiratory** /træns'paɪrətri/, *adj.*

**transplant** /træns'plænt, -'plant/, *v.;* /'trænsplænt, -plant/, *n.* *–v.t.* **1.** to remove (a plant) from one place and plant it in another. **2.** *Surg.* to transfer, as an organ or a portion of tissue, from one part of the body to another or from one person or animal to another. **3.** to remove from one place to another. **4.** to bring (a colony, culture, etc.) from one country to another for settlement. *–v.i.* **5.** to be capable of being transplanted. *–n.* **6.** a transplanting. **7.** something transplanted. **8.** a seedling which has been transplanted once or several times. [late ME, from LL *transplantāre*] – **transplantable** /træns'plæntəbəl/, *adj.* – **transplantation** /trænsplæn'teɪʃən/, *n.* – **transplanter** /træns'plæntə/, *n.*

**transpolar** /trænz'poʊlə/, *adj.* across the (north or south) pole or polar region.

**transponder** /træns'pɒndə/, *n.* a transmitter controlled by a receiver so that it transmits information in response to interrogating signals.

**transponible** /træns'poʊnəbəl/, *adj.* capable of being transposed. [L *transpōnere* transpose + -IBLE] – **transponibility** /,trænspoʊnə'bɪləti/, *n.*

**transpontine** /trænz'pɒntaɪn/, *adj.* across or beyond a bridge. [TRANS- + L *pons* bridge + -INE[1]]

**transport** /træns'pɔt, 'trænspɔt/, *v.;* /'trænspɔt/, *n.* *–v.t.* **1.** to carry or convey from one place to another. **2.** to carry away by strong emotion. **3.** to carry into banishment, as a criminal to a penal colony. **4.** *Obs.* to kill. *–n.* **5.** the act or method of transporting or conveying; conveyance. **6.** a system of conveying passengers or freight: *public transport.* **7.** a means of transporting or conveying, as a ship employed for transporting soldiers or military stores, or convicts. **8.** a large truck. **9.** an aeroplane carrying goods or passengers as part of a transport system. **10.** strong emotion; ecstatic joy, bliss, etc. *–adj.* **11.** relating to means, systems, or the personnel or equipment of transport: *transport workers.* [ME *transporte(n),* from L *transportāre* carry across] – **transportable** /træns'pɔtəbəl/, *adj.* – **transportability** /,trænspɔtə'bɪləti/, *n.*

**transportation** /,trænspɔ'teɪʃən/, *n.* **1.** the act of transporting. **2.** the state of being transported. **3.** means of transport or conveyance. **4.** banishment, as of a criminal to a penal colony. **5.** *U.S.* cost of transport or travel by public conveyance. **6.** *U.S.* tickets or permits for transport or travel.

**transportee** /trænspɔ'ti/, *n.* (formerly) a person transported as a convict.

**transporter** /træns'pɔtə/, *n.* **1.** a truck designed to carry large or bulky loads. **2.** a transporter bridge, crane, etc.

**transporter bridge** /'– brɪdʒ/, *n.* a bridge having a tower on each bank connected by a span which supports a moving trolley from which a shore-level platform is suspended from cables; used for carrying vehicles, passengers, etc., over waterways.

**transporter crane** /'– kreɪn/, *n.* a crane having a high-level girder from which a grab or hoist is suspended; the structure can usu. move on wheels and can run astride ships, trains, etc., to unload at any point.

**transport number** /'trænspɔt nʌmbə/, *n.* (in an electrolytic process) the fraction of the total current passed which is carried by one specified species of ion.

**transpose** /træns'poʊz/, *v.t.,* **-posed, -posing. 1.** to alter the relative position or order of (a thing in a series, or a series of things). **2.** to cause (two or more things) to change places; interchange. **3.** to alter the order of (letters in a word, or words in a sentence). **4.** *Alg.* to bring (a term) from one side of an equation to the other, with change of the plus or minus sign. **5.** *Music.* to reproduce in a different key, by raising or lowering in pitch. **6.** *Rare.* to transfer or transport. **7.** *Obs.* to transform; transmute. [ME *transpose(n),* from F *transposer, trans-* across + *poser* place. See POSE[1]] – **transposable,** *adj.* – **transposer,** *n.*

**transposition** /trænspə'zɪʃən/, *n.* **1.** the act of transposing, or the state of being transposed. **2.** a transposed form of something. Also, **transposal** /træns'poʊzəl/. – **transpositional,** *adj.*

**transsexual** /træns'sɛkʃuəl/, *adj.* **1.** of or pertaining to one who has changed sex. **2.** of or pertaining to the medical procedures by which sex changes are effected. *–n.* **3.** one who has undergone a sex change operation. **4.** one who feels himself or herself, though physically of one sex, to be of the other sex in psychological disposition.

**transship** /trænzʃɪp/, *v.t., v.i.,* **-shipped, -shipping.** →**tranship.** Also, **trans-ship.**

**trans-Tasman** /trænz-'tæzmən/, *adj.* passing or extending across the Tasman Sea.

**transubstantiate** /trænsəb'stænʃieɪt/, *v.t.,* **-ated, -ating. 1.** to change from one substance into another; transmute. **2.** *Theol.* to change (the substance of bread and wine) into the substance or body and blood of Christ, the species (def. 4a) alone remaining of bread and wine. [ML *transubstantiātus,* pp.]

**transubstantiation** /,transəb,stænʃi'eɪʃən/, *n.* **1.** the changing of one substance into another. **2.** *Theol.* the conversion, in the Eucharist, of the whole substance of the bread into the body, and of the whole substance of the wine into the blood, of Christ, only the appearance of bread and wine remaining, following the philosophical concept that any object whatever could be separately conceived as to its tangible form and its true nature (a doctrine of the Roman Catholic Church). – **transubstantiationalist,** *n.*

**transudation** /trænsju'deɪʃən/, *n.* **1.** the act or process of transuding. **2.** a substance which has transuded. Also, **transudate** /'trænsjudeɪt/.

**transude** /træn'sjud/, *v.i.,* **-suded, -suding.** to pass or ooze through pores or interstices, as a fluid. [NL *transūdāre,* from L *trans* across + *sūdāre* sweat] – **transudatory** /træn'sjudətri/, *adj.*

**transumpt** /træn'sʌmpt, 'trænsʌmpt/, *n.* a copy of a legal document. [L *transumptus,* pp., transcribe]

**transuranic element** /trænzju,rænɪk 'ɛləmənt, -,reɪn-/, *n.* an element having a higher atomic number than uranium.

**transvalue** /trænz'vælju/, *v.t.,* **-ued, -uing.** to change the value of. – **transvaluation** /,trænzvælju'eɪʃən/, – **transvaluer,** *n.*

**transversal** /trænz'vɜsəl/, *adj.* **1.** transverse. *–n.* **2.** *Geom.* a line intersecting two or more lines. [late ME, from ML *transversālis.* See TRANSVERSE, -AL[1]] **– transversality** /trænzvɜ'sæləti/, *adj.* **– transversally,** *adv.*

**transverse** /'trænzvɜs, trænz'vɜs/, *adj.* **1.** lying or being across or in a crosswise direction; athwart. **2.** (of a flute) held across the body, and having a mouth hole in the side of the tube, near its end, across which the player's breath is directed. *–n.* **3.** something which is transverse. **4.** *Geom.* a transverse axis. [L *transversus,* pp., turned or directed across] **– transversely,** *adv.*

**transverse flute** /– 'flut/, *n.* a flute held transversely, as with the modern flute but not the fipple or block flute (recorder).

**transverse process** /– 'prouses/, *n.* a process which projects from the sides of a vertebra.

**transverse wave** /'– weɪv/, *n.* a wave in which the vibrations of particles of the medium (as in a wave motion in a stretched wire or string) or the directions of the oscillating electromagnetic fields (as in an electromagnetic wave) are perpendicular to the direction of propagation.

**transvestism** /trænz'vɛstɪzəm/, *n.* **1.** the abnormal desire to wear clothing appropriate to the opposite sex. **2.** the act or state of so dressing. **– transvestite** /trænz'vɛstaɪt/, *n., adj.*

**trap**[1] /træp/, *n., v.,* **trapped, trapping.** **1.** a contrivance used for taking game or other animals, as a mechanical device that springs shut suddenly, a pitfall, or a snare. **2.** any device, stratagem, or the like for catching one unawares. **3.** an ambush. **4.** any of various mechanical contrivances for preventing the passage of steam, water, etc. **5.** an arrangement in a pipe, as a double curve or a U-shaped section, in which liquid remains and forms a seal, for preventing the passage or escape of air or gases through the pipe from behind or below; P trap; S trap; gully trap. **6.** (*pl.*) percussion instruments, esp. a drum kit. **7.** a device for suddenly releasing or tossing into the air objects to be shot at, as pigeons or clay targets. **8.** a carriage, esp. a light two-wheeled one. **9.** a trapdoor. **10.** *Colloq.* the mouth. **11.** (*usu. pl.*) a policeman. **12. a trap for young players,** *Colloq.* a danger or risk to the inexperienced. **13. round the traps,** *Colloq.* in and about pubs, brothels, clubs, etc. *–v.t.* **14.** to catch in a trap: *to trap foxes.* **15.** to take by stratagem; lead by artifice or wiles. **16.** to furnish or set with traps. **17.** to provide (a drain, etc.) with a trap. **18.** to stop and hold by a trap, as air in a pipe. *–v.i.* **19.** to set traps for game: *he was busy trapping.* **20.** to engage in catching animals in traps for their furs. [ME *trappe,* OE *træppe,* c. MD *trappe.* Cf. ML *trappa*]

trap[1]: fish trap

**trap**[2] /træp/, *n., v.,* **trapped, trapping.** *–n.* **1.** (*pl.*) *Colloq.* personal belongings; luggage. **2.** *Obs.* a cloth or covering for a horse. *–v.t.* **3.** to furnish with trapping; caparison. [ME *trappe;* orig. uncert.]

**trap**[3] /træp/, *n.* any of various fine-grained dark-coloured igneous rocks having a more or less columnar structure, esp. some form of basalt. Also, **traprock.** [Swed. *trapp,* var. of *trappa* stair (so named from their appearance)]

**trap-cut** /'træp-kʌt/, *adj.* →**step-cut.**

**trapdoor** /'træpdɔ/, *n.* **1.** a door or the like, flush, or nearly so, with the surface of a floor, ceiling, roof, etc. **2.** the opening which it covers.

trapdoor spider

**trapdoor spider** /– 'spaɪdə/, *n.* any of various burrowing spiders of the family Ctenizidae that construct silk-lined tunnels in the ground, sometimes fitted with a lid, as the **brown trapdoor spider,** *Dyarcyops fuscipes,* of eastern Australia.

**trapes** /treɪps/, *v.i.,* **trapesed, trapesing.** *Colloq.* →**traipse.**

**trapeze** /trə'piz/, *n.* **1.** an apparatus for gymnastics consisting of a short horizontal bar attached to the ends of two suspended ropes. **2.** (on a small sailing boat) a device resembling this by which one may lean almost completely outboard. **3.** *Geom.* →**trapezium.** [F, from L *trapezium* small table, from Gk *trapézion*]

**trapeze artist** /'– atəst/, *n.* a performer in a circus, etc., who is skilled in the use of the trapeze.

**trapeziform** /trə'pizəfɔm/, *adj.* formed like a trapezium.

**trapezium** /trə'piziəm/, *n., pl.* **-ziums, -zia** /-ziə/. **1.** *Geom.* Also, **trapeze. a.** (as originally used by Euclid) any rectilinear quadrilateral plane figure not a parallelogram. **b.** a quadrilateral plane figure in which only one pair of opposite sides is parallel. **2.** *Anat.* a bone of the carpus articulating with the metacarpal bone of the thumb. [NL. See TRAPEZE] **– trapezial,** *adj.*

**trapezoid** /'træpəzɔɪd/, *n.* **1.** *Geom.* **a.** a quadrilateral plane figure of which no two sides are parallel. **b.** →**trapezium** (def. 1b). **2.** *Anat.* a bone of the carpus articulating with the metacarpal bone of the index finger. [NL *trapezoidēs* table-like, from LGk *trapezoeidḗs*] **– trapezoid, trapezoidal** /træpə'zɔɪdl/, *adj.*

**trapper** /'træpə/, *n.* **1.** one who traps. **2.** one who makes a business of trapping wild animals for their furs.

**trappings** /'træpɪŋz/, *n.pl.* **1.** articles of equipment or dress, esp. of an ornamental character. **2.** conventional or characteristic articles of dress or adornment. **3.** that which necessarily accompanies or adorns: *the trappings of power.* **4.** a covering for a horse, esp. when ornamental in character. [ME. See TRAP[2], -ING[1]]

**traprock** /'træprɒk/, *n.* →**trap**[3].

**trapshooting** /'træpʃutɪŋ/, *n.* the sport of shooting at live pigeons released from, or clay targets, etc., thrown into the air by, a trap (def. 7). **– trapshooter,** *n.*

**trapunto** /trə'puntou/, *n.* quilting made by outlining a design in running stitches through at least two layers of material and filling it out with cotton padding. [It. *trapungere* to embroider]

**trash** /træʃ/, *n.* **1.** anything worthless or useless; rubbish. **2.** foolish notions, talk, or writing; nonsense. **3.** worthless or disreputable persons. **4.** broken or torn bits, as twigs, splinters, rags, or the like. **5.** that which is broken or lopped off from anything in preparing it for use. **6.** the refuse of sugar cane after the juice has been expressed. **7. white trash, a.** *U.S.* the poor white inhabitants of the southern U.S. **b.** the poor white inhabitants of a region or district where some of the inhabitants are coloured people. *–v.t.* **8.** to free from trash or refuse, as outer leaves from growing sugar cane. **9.** to free from superfluous twigs or branches. [ME *trasche.* Cf. d. Norw. *trask,* Icel. *tros*] **– trasher,** *n.*

**trashy** /'træʃi/, *adj.,* **trashier, trashiest,** *n.* *–adj.* **1.** of the nature of trash; rubbishy or worthless: *trashy novels.* **2.** *U.S.* encumbered with trash, as a field. *–n.* **3.** *Colloq.* a garbage man. **– trashily,** *adv.* **– trashiness,** *n.*

**trasi** /'trasi/, *n.* a dry roasted form of blachan, darker in colour, used in Japanese cooking. [Bahasa Indonesia]

**trass** /træs/, *n.* a rock, common along the Rhine, composed chiefly of comminuted pumice or other volcanic material, used for making hydraulic cement. [D *tras,* earlier *tarasse,* var. of *terras,* probably from F. See TERRACE]

**trauma** /'trɔmə/, *n., pl.* **-mata** /-mətə/, **-mas.** **1.** *Pathol.* **a.** a bodily injury produced by violence, or any thermal, chemical, etc., extrinsic agent. **b.** the condition produced by this; traumatism. **c.** the injurious agent or mechanism itself. **2.** *Psychol.* a startling experience which has a lasting effect on mental life; a shock. [Gk: wound]

**traumatic** /trɔ'mætɪk/, *adj.* **1.** pertaining to or produced by a trauma or wound. **2.** adapted to the cure of wounds. [LL *traumaticus,* from Gk *traumatikós* pertaining to wound(s)]

**traumatise** /'trɔmətaɪz/, *v.t.,* **-tised, -tising.** **1.** *Pathol.* to injure (tissues) by force, or by thermal, chemical, electrical, etc., agents. **2.** to shock, agitate, upset. Also, **traumatize.**

**traumatism** /'trɔmətɪzəm/, *n.* **1.** any morbid condition produced by a trauma. **2.** the trauma or wound itself.

**travail** /'trævei1/, *n.* **1.** physical or mental toil or exertion, esp. when painful. **2.** the labour and pain of childbirth. *–v.i.* **3.** to suffer the pangs of childbirth; be in labour.

**trave** /treiv/, *n.* a device to inhibit a wild or untrained horse or one being shod. [ME *trave,* from OF, from L *trabs* beam]

**travel** /'trævəl/, *v.,* **-elled, -elling** or (*U.S.*) **-eled, -eling,** *n.* *–v.i.* **1.** to go from one place to another; make a journey: *to travel for pleasure.* **2.** to move or go from one place or point to another. **3.** to proceed or advance in any way. **4.** to go from place to place as a representative of a business firm. **5.** *Colloq.* to move with speed. **6.** to move in a fixed course, as a piece of mechanism. **7.** to pass, or be transmitted, as light, sound, etc. *–v.t.* **8.** to travel, journey, or pass through or over, as a country, district, road, etc. **9.** to journey (a specified distance). *–n.* **10.** the act of travelling; journeying, esp. in distant or foreign places. **11.** (*pl.*) journeys: *to start on one's travels.* **12.** (*pl.*) **a.** journeys as the subject of a written account or literary work. **b.** such an account or work. **13.** *Mach.* **a.** the complete movement of a moving part (esp. a reciprocating part) in one direction, or the distance traversed; stroke. **b.** length of stroke. **14.** movement or passage in general. [ME; var. of TRAVAIL]

**travelability** /trævələ'bıləti/, *n. Colloq.* the ability of wine to travel without detrimental effects.

**travel agency** /'trævəl eıdʒənsi/, *n.* a business that arranges journeys and accommodation for travellers, as by procuring tickets, reservations, etc. Also, **travel bureau.**

**travelled** /'trævəld/, *adj.* **1.** having travelled, esp. to distant places; experienced in travel. **2.** frequented by travellers, as a road. **3.** *Geol.* moved to a distance from the original site, as a boulder. Also, *U.S.,* **traveled.**

**traveller** /'trævlə, -vələ/, *n.* **1.** one who or that which travels. **2.** one who travels or has travelled in distant places or foreign lands. **3.** a travelling salesman; a commercial traveller. **4.** a piece of mechanism constructed to move in a fixed course. **5.** a swagman. **6.** *Naut.* **a.** a wooden or metal ring or hoop fitted to move freely round a mast or spar. **b.** the rope, spar, or rod itself. **c.** a ring attached to the sheet of a fore-and-aft sail and sliding from side to side on a metal rod fastened to the deck. Also, *U.S.,* **traveler.**

**traveller's cheque** /'trævləz tʃɛk/, *n.* a cheque issued by a bank, express company, etc., to a traveller, which may be cashed only by endorsement in sight of the payee. Also, *U.S.,* **traveler's check.**

**traveller's joy** /– 'dʒɔı/, *n.* any of a number of species of the genus *Clematis.*

**traveller's tree** /'– tri/, *n.* a Madagascan tree, *Ravenala madagascariensis,* having two rows of large leaves the bases of which accumulate water.

**travelling salesman** /,trævlıŋ 'seılzmən/, *n.* one who travels from place to place as the representative of a business firm, to solicit orders or sell goods; a representative; a traveller.

**travelogue** /'trævəlɒg/, *n.* **1.** a documentary film describing a country, travels, etc. **2.** a lecture describing travel, usu. illustrated, as with photographs, slides, etc. [TRAVEL + *-logue,* modelled on DIALOGUE]

**traverse** /trə'vɜs, 'trævɜs/, *v.,* **-ersed, -ersing,** *n., adj., adv.* *–v.t.* **1.** to pass across, over, or through. **2.** to go to and fro over or along, as a place. **3.** to extend across. **4.** to cause to move laterally. **5.** to pass in review; survey carefully. **6.** to go counter to; obstruct or thwart. **7.** *Law.* **a.** (in the law of pleading) to deny (an allegation of fact set forth in a previous pleading). **b.** to join issue upon. **c.** to deny formally, in pleading at law. **8.** to turn and point (a gun) in any direction. **9.** *Naut.* to brace (a yard) fore and aft. *–v.i.* **10.** to pass or go across; cross; cross over. **11.** to turn horizontally, as a gun. **12.** *Mach.* to move crosswise or sideways. **13.** *Fencing.* to glide the blade towards the hilt of the contestant's foil while applying pressure to the blade. **14.** *Mountaineering, Skiing, etc.* to move across a downhill slope, not directly down it. *–n.* **15.** the act of traversing, or passing across, over, or through. **16.** something that crosses, obstructs, or thwarts; obstacle. **17.** a transversal or similar line. **18.** a place where one may traverse or cross; a crossing. **19.** *Archit.* a transverse gallery or loft of communication in a church or other large building. **20.** a member placed or extending across; a crosspiece or crossbar. **21.** a railing, lattice, or screen serving as a barrier. **22.** *Naut.* **a.** the zigzag track of a vessel compelled by contrary winds or currents to sail on different courses. **b.** each of the runs in a single direction made in such sailing. **23.** *Fort.* **a.** a defensive barrier, parapet, etc., placed transversely. **b.** one thrown across the terreplein or the covered way of a fortification to protect it from enfilade fire. **24.** *Ordn.* the horizontal laying of a gun so as to make it point in any required direction. **25.** *Mach.* **a.** a crosswise or side movement or motion, as of a lathe carriage or tool. **b.** a part moving in this way. **26.** *Survey.* a movement across the country by a surveyor connected by continuous bearings and measurements. **27.** *Law.* a formal denial of some matter of fact alleged by the other side. *–adj.* **28.** lying, extending, or passing across; cross; transverse. *–adv.* **29.** *Obs.* across; crosswise; transversely. [defs 1-14, ME *traverse(n),* from F *traverser* cross, thwart, from *travers* TRAVERSE, *n.* or *adj.* Defs 15-29, ME; from OF *travers* lying athwart, from LL *trāversus,* L *transversus,* pp.] – **traversable,** *adj.* – **traverser,** *n.*

**traversing bridge** /trə'vɜsıŋ brıdʒ/, *n.* a bridge that may be withdrawn horizontally to permit the passage of ships, etc.

**travertine** /'trævətən/, *n.* **1.** a form of limestone deposited by springs, etc., used in Italy for building purposes. **2.** a crusty deposit of calcium carbonate around a hot spring. [It. *travertino,* b. *tivertino,* from L *Tīburtīnus* of Tibur (now Tivoli) and *tra-* across (from L *trans*)]

**travesty** /'trævəsti/, *n., pl.* **-ties,** *v.,* **-tied, -tying.** *–n.* **1.** any grotesque or debased likeness or imitation: *a travesty of justice.* **2.** a literary composition characterised by burlesque or ludicrous treatment of a serious work or subject. **3.** literary composition of this kind. *–v.t.* **4.** to make a travesty on; turn (a serious work or subject) to ridicule by burlesque imitation or treatment. **5.** to imitate grotesquely or absurdly. **6.** to be a travesty of. [F *travesti,* pp., disguised, from It. *travestire* disguise, from *tra-* across (from L *trans*) + *vestire* dress (from L)]

**trawl** /trɔl/, *n.* **1.** Also, **trawl net.** a strong fishing net dragged along the sea bottom in trawling. **2.** Also, *U.S.,* **trawl line.** a buoyed line used in sea fishing, having numerous short lines with baited hooks attached at intervals. *–v.i.* **3.** to fish with a net whose edge is dragged along the sea bottom to catch the fish living there. **4.** *U.S.* to fish with a trawl line. **5.** to troll. **6.** *Colloq.* to use a public address system attached to a moving vehicle to address people, as during a political election campaign. *–v.t.* **7.** to drag (a trawl net). **8.** to catch with a trawl net or a trawl line. **9.** to troll. [cf. MD *traghel* dragnet]

**trawler** /'trɔlə/, *n.* **1.** any of various types of vessels used in fishing with a trawl net. **2.** one who trawls.

**tray**[1] /treı/, *n.* **1.** any of various flat, shallow containers or receptacles of wood, metal, etc., with slightly raised edges used for carrying, holding, or exhibiting articles and for various other purposes. **2.** a removable receptacle of this shape in a cabinet, box, trunk, or the like, sometimes forming a drawer. **3.** (on a motor truck) a shallow open compartment behind the cab for holding and carrying goods. **4.** a tray and what is in it. [ME; OE *trēg.* c. OSw. *trö* corn measure; akin to TREE]

**tray**[2] /treı/, *n.* →**trey.**

**traymobile** /'treımәbil/, *n.* a small table on wheels, used for serving tea, etc.

**treacherous** /'trɛtʃərəs/, *adj.* **1.** violating faith or betraying trust; disloyal; traitorous. **2.** deceptive, untrustworthy, or unreliable. **3.** unstable or insecure. **4.** likely or ready to betray. – **treacherously,** *adv.* – **treacherousness,** *n.*

**treachery** /'trɛtʃəri/, *n., pl.* **-eries.** **1.** violation of faith; betrayal of trust; treason. **2.** an act of perfidy or faithlessness. **3.** readiness to betray. [ME *trecherie,* from OF, from *tricher* cheat; orig. uncert.]

**treacle** /'trikəl/, *n.* **1.** the dark, viscous, uncrystallised syrup obtained in refining sugar. **2.** →**golden syrup. 3.** *Colloq.* cloying sentimentality as of music or behaviour. **4.** *Obs.* any of various medicinal compounds formerly in repute as antidotes for poisonous bites or for poisons. **5.** *Obs.* a sovereign remedy. [ME, from OF *triacle* antidote, from L *thēriaca,* from Gk *thēriakḗ* (def. 4)] – **treacly** /'trikli/, *adj.* – **treacliness,** *n.*

**treacle mustard** /– 'mʌstəd/, *n.* an annual herb, *Erysimum* *cheiranthoides,* a common weed of cultivated land in temperate regions.

**tread** /trɛd/, *v.,* **trod** or (*Archaic*) **trode; trodden** or **trod; treading;** *n.* *–v.t.* **1.** to step or walk on, about, in, or along. **2.** to trample or crush underfoot. **3.** to put into some position or condition by trampling: *to tread grapes.* **4.** to domineer harshly over; crush. **5.** to execute by walking or dancing: *to tread a measure.* **6.** (of male birds) to copulate with. *–v.i.* **7.** to set down the foot or feet in walking; step; walk. **8.** to step, walk, or trample (fol. by *on* or *upon*). **9.** *Colloq.* to copulate esp. of male birds. **10. tread water,** *Swimming.* to move the arms and legs in such a way as to keep the body in an upright position with the head above water. *–n.* **11.** a treading, stepping, or walking, or the sound of this. **12.** manner of treading or walking. **13.** a single step as in walking. **14.** any of various things or parts on which a person or thing treads, stands, or moves. **15.** the sole of the foot or of a shoe that presses on the ground. **16.** the horizontal upper surface of a step in a stair, on which the foot is placed. **17.** the width of this from front to back. **18.** that part of a wheel, tyre, or runner which bears on the road, rail, etc. **19.** the part of a rail on which the wheels bear. [defs 1-10, ME *trede(n),* OE *tredan,* c. G *treten.* Defs 11-19, ME *trede, tredd*] – **treader,** *n.*

**treadle** /ˈtrɛdl/, *n., v.,* **-dled, -dling.** *–n.* **1.** a lever or the like worked by the foot to impart motion to a machine. **2.** *Colloq.* a bicycle. *–v.i.* **3.** to work a treadle. [ME and OE *tredel.* See TREAD, *v.*] – **treadler,** *n.*

**treadmill** /ˈtrɛdmɪl/, *n.* **1.** an apparatus for producing rotary motion by the weight of men or animals, treading on a succession of moving steps that form a kind of continuous path, as around the periphery of a horizontal cylinder. **2.** a monotonous or wearisome round, as of work or life.

treadmill

**Treas.,** **1.** Treasurer. **2.** Treasury.

**treason** /ˈtrizən/, *n.* **1.** violation by a subject of his allegiance to his sovereign or to the state; high treason. **2.** *Rare.* the betrayal of a trust or confidence; breach of faith; treachery. [ME, from AF *tre(y)soun,* from L *trāditio* act of betraying]

**treasonable** /ˈtrizənəbəl/, *adj.* **1.** of the nature of treason. **2.** involving treason; traitorous. – **treasonableness,** *n.* – **treasonably,** *adv.*

**treasonous** /ˈtrizənəs/, *adj.* treasonable. – **treasonously,** *adv.*

**treasure** /ˈtrɛʒə/, *n., v.,* **-ured, -uring.** *–n.* **1.** wealth or riches stored or accumulated, esp. in the form of precious metals or money. **2.** wealth, rich materials, or valuable things. **3.** any thing or person greatly valued or highly prized: *this book was his chief treasure.* *–v.t.* **4.** to put away for security or future use, as money; lay up in store. **5.** to retain carefully or keep in store, as in the mind. **6.** to regard as precious; prize; cherish. [ME *tresor,* from OF, from L *thēsaurus.* See THESAURUS] – **treasureless,** *adj.*

**treasure-house** /ˈtrɛʒə-haʊs/, *n.* **1.** a repository or storehouse for valuables or money. **2.** a source of valuable things, as ideas.

**treasurer** /ˈtrɛʒərə/, *n.* **1.** one who is in charge of treasure or a treasury. **2.** one who has charge of the funds of a company, private society, or the like. **3.** an officer of a state, city, etc., entrusted with the receipt, care, and disbursement of public money. **4.** (*cap.*) the government minister responsible for the Treasury. – **treasurership,** *n.*

**treasure-trove** /ˈtrɛʒə-troʊv/, *n.* **1.** *Law.* any money, bullion, or the like, of unknown ownership, found hidden in the earth or any other place. **2.** anything of similar nature which one finds. [AF *tresor trové* treasure found]

**treasury** /ˈtrɛʒəri/, *n., pl.* **-uries.** **1.** a place where public revenues, or the funds of a company, etc., are deposited, kept, and disbursed. **2.** the funds or revenue of a state or a public or private company, etc. **3.** (*cap.*) the department of government which has control over the collection, management, and disbursement of the public revenue. **4.** a building, room, chest, or other place for the preservation of treasure or valuable objects. **5.** a repository or a collection of treasures of any kind; a thesaurus.

**Treasury bench** /ˈtrɛʒəri bɛntʃ/, *n.* the first row of seats on the Speaker's right in the House of Representatives, occupied by members of the government.

**Treasury bill** /ˈ– bɪl/, *n. Brit.* a bill, not carrying interest, issued under the authority of the Treasury of the United Kingdom, payable at not more than twelve months from its date, which is tendered for at a discount and forms part of the unfunded debt of the United Kingdom.

**Treasury note** /ˈ– noʊt/, *n.* **1.** security issued with three and six month maturities by the Reserve Bank of Australia, to acknowledge a borrowing obligation. **2.** *U.S.* a note or bill issued by the United States Treasury, receivable as legal tender for all debts except as otherwise expressly provided.

**Treasury note rediscount rate,** *n.* the yield at which the Reserve Bank is prepared to buy back its Treasury notes before they are due to mature.

**treat** /trit/, *v.t.* **1.** to act or behave towards in some specified way: *to treat someone with respect.* **2.** to look upon, consider, or regard in a specified aspect, and deal with accordingly: *to treat a matter as unimportant.* **3.** to deal with (a disease, patient, etc.) in order to relieve or cure. **4.** to deal with in speech or writing; discuss. **5.** to deal with, develop, or represent artistically, esp. in some specified manner or style: *to treat a theme realistically.* **6.** to subject to some agent or action in order to bring about a particular result: *to treat a substance with an acid.* **7.** to entertain with food, drink, amusement, etc. **8.** to regale (another) at one's own expense. *–v.i.* **9.** to deal with a subject in speech or writing, or discourse. **10.** to give, or bear the expense of, a treat. **11.** to carry on negotiations with a view to a settlement, discuss terms of settlement, or negotiate. *–n.* **12.** an entertainment of food, drink, amusement, etc., given by way of compliment or as an expression of friendly regard. **13.** *Colloq.* anything that affords particular pleasure or enjoyment. **14.** the act of treating. **15.** one's turn to treat. **16. a (fair) treat,** *Colloq.* excessively. **17. stand treat,** to bear the expense of an entertainment. [ME *trete(n),* from OF *tretier, traitier,* from L *tractāre* drag, handle, treat] – **treatable,** *adj.* – **treater,** *n.*

**treatise** /ˈtritəs/, *n.* **1.** a book or writing treating of some particular subject. **2.** one containing a formal or methodical exposition of the principles of the subject. [ME *treatis,* from AF *tretiz,* from *traitier* TREAT]

**treatment** /ˈtritmənt/, *n.* **1.** the act or manner of treating. **2.** action or behaviour towards a person, etc. **3.** management in the application of medicines, surgery, etc. **4.** literary or artistic handling, esp. with reference to style. **5.** subjection to some agent or action. **6. the treatment,** *Colloq.* punishment; severe handling; thorough criticism: *the unions are getting the treatment from the media.*

**treaty** /ˈtriti/, *n., pl.* **-ties.** **1.** a formal agreement between two or more independent states in reference to peace, alliance, commerce, or other international relations. **2.** the formal document embodying such an international agreement. **3.** any agreement or compact. **4.** *Rare.* negotiation with a view to settlement. **5.** *Obs.* entreaty. [ME *tretee,* from AF *treté,* pp., handled, treated. See TREAT]

**Trebbiano** /trɛbiˈanoʊ/, *n.* a grape variety used in the making of white table wines.

**treble** /ˈtrɛbəl/, *adj., n., v.,* **-bled, -bling.** *–adj.* **1.** threefold; triple. **2.** *Music.* **a.** of or pertaining to the highest part in harmonised music; soprano. **b.** of the highest pitch or range, as a voice part, voice, singer, or instrument. **c.** high in pitch; shrill. *–n.* **3.** *Music.* **a.** the treble or soprano part. **b.** a treble voice, singer, or instrument. **c.** a piano part for the right hand. **4.** a high or shrill voice or sound. **5.** the highest-pitched peal of a bell. *–v.t.* **6.** to make three times as much or as many; triple. *–v.i.* **7.** to become three times as much. [ME, from OF, from L *triplus* triple] – **trebly** /ˈtrɛbli/, *adv.*

**treble clef** /– ˈklɛf/, *n.* a sign on a music score which indicates the G above middle C, placed on the second line of the stave, counting upwards.

**treble fleece** /ˈ– flis/, *n.* **1.** a fleece of wool consisting of three years' growth. **2.** Also, **treble fleecer.** a sheep carrying such a fleece.

**trebuchet** /ˈtrɛbjuʃɛt/, *n.* a medieval military engine for hurling stones and making a breach. [ME, from OF, from *trebucher* overturn, fall, from *tre(s)*, across, over (from L *trans*) + *buc* trunk of body, from Gmc; cf. OE *būc* belly]

**trecento** /treɪˈtʃɛntoʊ/, *n.* the 14th century, with reference to Italy, and esp. to its art or literature. [It., short for *mille trecento* thirteen hundred]

trebuchet

**tre corde** /treɪ ˈkɔdeɪ/, *adv.* (a direction in pianoforte music) with the soft pedal released, allowing the hammers to hit all three strings of each note. [It.: three strings.]

**tree** /tri/, *n., v.,* **treed, treeing.** *–n.* **1.** a perennial plant having a permanent, woody, self-supporting main stem or trunk, usu. growing to a considerable height, and usu. developing branches at some distance from the ground. **2.** any of various shrubs, bushes, and herbaceous plants, as the banana, resembling a tree in form or size. **3.** a family tree. **4.** something resembling a tree in shape, as a crosstree, etc. **5.** a pole, post, beam, bar, handle, or the like, as one forming part of some structure. **6.** a shoetree. **7.** a saddletree. **8.** a treelike group of crystals, as one forming in an electrolytic cell. **9.** *Maths.* a network with no loops. **10.** a gallows or gibbet. **11.** *Archaic or Poetic.* the cross on which Christ was crucified. *–v.t.* **12.** to drive into or up a tree, as a hunted animal, or a man pursued by an animal. **13.** *Colloq.* to put into a difficult position. **14.** to stretch or shape on a tree, as a shoe or boot. **15.** to furnish (a structure) with a tree. [ME; OE *trēo(w)*, c. Icel. *trē*, Goth. *triu;* akin to Gk *drŷs* tree, oak] **– treeless,** *adj.* **– treelessness,** *n.* **– treelike,** *adj.*

tree fern

**treecreeper** /ˈtrikripə/, *n.* **1.** any of a number of Australian birds of the genus *Climacteris,* which have slender downcurved bills and run up the trunks of trees searching for insects, as the **brown treecreeper,** *C. picumnus,* of the south-eastern part of Australia. **2.** any of various birds of similar habits, esp. the several species of the family Certhiidae of Europe and North America.

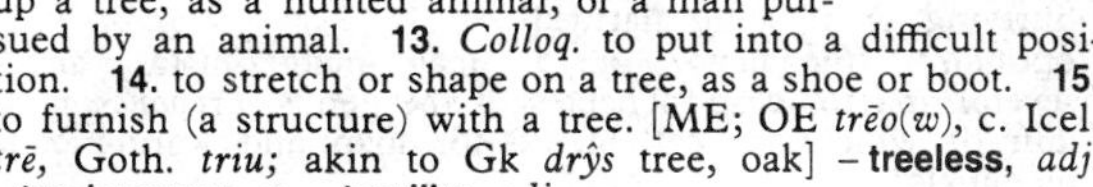

**tree diagram** /ˈtri ˌdaɪəgræm/, *n. Linguistics.* **1.** an illustration of the genealogical relationships between languages of one family. **2.** a diagrammed representation of the grammatical relationships between the words of a sentence.

**tree dragon** /ˈ– drægən/, *n.* →**jacky lizard.**

**tree-feller** /ˈtri-fɛlə/, *n.* one who is employed to fell trees.

**tree fern** /ˈtri fɜn/, *n.* any fern, as of the family Cyatheaceae, which attains the size of a tree, sending up a straight trunklike stem with foliage at the summit.

**tree frog** /ˈ– frɒg/, *n.* any of the arboreal frogs of various families, characterised usu. by toes with adhesive discs.

**tree goanna** /ˈ– goʊænə/, *n.* →**lace monitor.**

**tree heath** /ˈ– hiθ/, *n.* →**briar** (def. 1).

**tree-kangaroo** /ˈtri-kæŋgəˌru/, *n.* any of the medium-sized kangaroos of north-eastern Queensland and New Guinea, belonging to the genus *Dendrolagus,* highly adapted to arboreal life.

**tree lucerne** /ˈtri lusən/, *n.* →**tagasaste.**

**tree-mouse** /ˈtri-maʊs/, *n.* any of several arboreal rodents of Africa, belonging to the subfamily Dendromyinae.

tree frog

**treenail** /ˈtrineɪl, ˈtrɛnəl/, *n.* a cylindrical pin of hard wood for fastening together timbers in ships, etc. Also, **trenail, trunnel.** [ME *trenayl.* See TREE, NAIL]

**tree of heaven,** *n.* →**ailanthus.**

**tree-rat** /ˈtri-ræt/, *n.* any member of a distinctive group of native rodents of the genera *Mesembriomys* and *Conilurus,* occurring mostly in northern Australia, usu. living and nesting in trees.

**tree runner** /ˈtri rʌnə/, *n.* →**orange-winged sittella.**

**tree shrew** /ˈ– ʃru/, *n.* any mammal of the family Tupaiadae, of southern Asia and adjacent islands, squirrel-like in appearance and having a long snout.

**tree sparrow** /ˈ– spæroʊ/, *n.* **1.** a European weaverbird, *Passer montanus,* related to the house sparrow and introduced into Australia. **2.** a North American finch, *Spizella arborea,* common in winter in the northern U.S.

**tree-surgeon** /ˈtri-sɜdʒən/, *n.* one who practises tree-surgery.

tree-kangaroo

**tree-surgery** /ˈtri-sɜdʒəri/, *n.* the repair of damaged trees, as by the removal of diseased parts, filling of cavities, and prevention of further decay, and by strengthening branches with braces.

**tree tomato** /ˈtri təmatoʊ/, *n.* a tree-like shrub, *Cyphomandra betacea,* with large simple leaves and smooth, egg-shaped, somewhat acid red fruit, native to South America but widely cultivated; tamarillo.

**treetop** /ˈtritɒp/, *n.* the top part of a tree.

**trefoil** /ˈtrɛfɔɪl/, *n.* **1.** any of the herbs constituting the leguminous genus *Trifolium,* usu. having digitate leaves of three leaflets, and reddish, purple, yellow, or white flower heads, and including the common clovers. **2.** any of various similar plants, as the medic and the lotus (def. 6). **3.** an ornamental figure or structure resembling a trifoliolate leaf. [ME *treyfoyle,* from AF *trifoil,* from L *trifolium* triple leaf]

**trehala** /trəˈhalə/, *n.* an edible, sugar-like secretion of the larvae of certain beetles of the genus *Larinus,* found in Asia Minor and neighbouring countries, forming a cocoon. [Turk. *tīqālah*]

**trehalose** /ˈtrihəloʊz, -oʊs/, *n.* a white crystalline disaccharide, $C_{12}H_{22}O_{11}$, found in yeast, certain fungi, etc., and used to identify certain bacteria. [TREHAL(A) + -OSE[2]]

**treillage** /ˈtreɪlɪdʒ/, *n.* latticework; a lattice or trellis. [F, from *treille* arbour, trellis, from L *trichila* arbour]

**trek** /trɛk/, *v.,* **trekked, trekking,** *n.* *–v.i.* **1.** to travel or migrate, esp. with difficulty. *–n.* **2.** a journey, esp. a difficult one. [D *trekken* draw, travel] **– trekker,** *n.*

**trellis** /ˈtrɛləs/, *n.* **1.** a frame or structure of latticework; a lattice. **2.** a framework of this kind used for the support of growing vines, etc. *–v.t.* **3.** to furnish with a trellis. **4.** to enclose in a trellis. **5.** to train or support on a trellis: *trellised vines.* **6.** to form into or like a trellis. [ME *trelis,* from OF, orig. adj., from LL *trilīcius,* replacing L *trilix* woven with three threads] **– trellis-like,** *adj.*

**trelliswork** /ˈtrɛləswɜk/, *n.* →**latticework.**

**trematode** /ˈtrɛmətoʊd, ˈtrimə-/, *n.* any of the Trematoda, a class or group of platyhelminths or flatworms, having one or more suckers, and living as ectoparasites or endoparasites on or in various animals; fluke. [NL *Trēmatōda,* from Gk *trēmatṓdēs* having holes]

**tremble** /ˈtrɛmbəl/, *v.,* **-bled, -bling,** *n.* *–v.i.* **1.** (of persons, the body, etc.) to shake involuntarily with quick, short movements, as from fear, excitement, weakness, cold, etc.; quake; quiver; shiver. **2.** to be agitated with fear, apprehension, or the like. **3.** (of things) to be affected with vibratory motion. **4.** to be tremulous, as light, sound, etc.: *his voice trembled as he spoke.* *–n.* **5.** an act of trembling. **6.** a state or fit of trembling. **7.** (*pl.*) any condition or disease characterised by continued trembling or shaking, as ague. **8.** (*pl.*) *Vet. Sci.* a toxic condition of cattle and sheep contracted by eating white snakeroot (*Eupatorium rugosum*), and marked by muscular tremors. [ME, from F *trembler,* from LL *tremulāre,* from L *tremere*] **– trembler,** *n.* **– tremblingly,** *adv.*

**trembly** /ˈtrɛmbli/, *adj.* trembling; tremulous.

**tremendous** /trəˈmɛndəs/, *adj.* **1.** *Colloq.* extraordinarily great in size, amount, degree, etc. **2.** dreadful or awful, as in character or effect. **3.** *Colloq.* extraordinary; unusual; remarkable. [L *tremendus* dreadful] **– tremendously,** *adv.* **– tremendousness,** *n.*

**tremolant** /ˈtrɛmələnt/, *n.* →**tremulant.** [G, from It. *tremolante* tremulant]

**tremolite** /ˈtrɛməlaɪt/, *n.* a white or greyish variety of amphibole, $Ca_2Mg_5Si_8O_{22}(OH)_2$, occurring usu. in bladed crystals. [*Tremol(a)* valley in Switzerland + -ITE[1]]

**tremolo** /ˈtrɛməloʊ/, *n., pl.* **-los.** **1.** a tremulous or vibrating effect produced on certain instruments and in the human voice, as to express emotion. **2.** →**tremulant.** [It.: trembling, from L *tremulus*]

**tremolo unit** /ˈ– junət/, *n.* an electronic device which alters amplified sound to give a repetitive variation in intensity.

**tremor** /ˈtrɛmə/, *n.* **1.** involuntary shaking of the body or limbs, as from fear, weakness, etc.; a fit of trembling. **2.** any tremulous or vibratory movement; a vibration. **3.** a trembling or quivering effect, as of light, etc. **4.** a tremulous sound or note. [ME, from L: trembling, terror] – **tremorless,** *adj.*

**tremulant** /ˈtrɛmjələnt/, *adj.* **1.** trembling; tremulous. *–n.* **2.** Also, **tremolant, tremolo.** a mechanical device on an organ for producing a tremolo effect.

**tremulous** /ˈtrɛmjələs/, *adj.* **1.** (of persons, the body, etc.) characterised by trembling, as from fear, nervousness, weakness, excitement, etc. **2.** fearful; timorous. **3.** (of things) vibratory or quivering. **4.** (of writing, etc.) done with a trembling hand. [L *tremulus*] – **tremulously,** *adv.* – **tremulousness,** *n.*

**trench** /trɛntʃ/, *n.* **1.** *Fort.* a long, narrow excavation in the ground, the earth from which is thrown up in front to serve as a shelter from the enemy's fire, etc. **2.** (*pl.*) a system of such excavations, with their embankments, etc. **3.** (*pl.*) the front line of battle in Europe in World War I. **4.** a deep furrow, ditch, or cut. *–v.t.* **5.** to surround or fortify with a trench or trenches; entrench. **6.** to cut a trench or trenches in. **7.** to set or place in a trench. **8.** to form (a furrow, ditch, etc.) by cutting into or through something. **9.** to make a cut in; divide by cutting. **10.** *Obs.* to cut. *–v.i.* **11.** to dig a trench or trenches. **12.** to encroach or infringe (fol. by *on* or *upon*). **13.** to come close or verge (fol. by *on* or *upon*). **14.** *Obs.* to enter or penetrate so as to affect intimately (fol. by *into* or *unto*). [ME *trenche,* from OF: act of cutting, slice, from *trenchier,* v., from L *truncāre* cut off]

**trenchant** /ˈtrɛntʃənt/, *adj.* **1.** incisive or keen, as language or a person; cutting: *trenchant wit.* **2.** thorough-going, vigorous, or effective: *a trenchant policy.* **3.** clearly or sharply defined, as an outline. **4.** *Chiefly Poetic.* sharp; keen-edged: *a trenchant blade.* [ME, from OF, ppr. of *trenchier* cut] – **trenchancy,** *n.* – **trenchantly,** *adv.*

**trench coat** /ˈtrɛntʃ koʊt/, *n.* a belted, military-style raincoat.

**trencher** /ˈtrɛntʃə/, *n.* **1.** one who trenches; one who makes trenches. **2.** →**mortarboard** (def. 2). **3.** *Archaic* **a.** a rectangular or circular flat piece of wood on which meat, or other food, was formerly served or carved. **b.** such a piece of wood with that which it bears. **4.** *Archaic.* a supply of food. [ME, from AF *trenchour* a cutting place, trencher, from *trenchier* cut. See TRENCH]

**trencherman** /ˈtrɛntʃəmən/, *n., pl.* **-men.** **1.** one who has a hearty appetite. **2.** a parasite or hanger-on.

**trench fever** /trɛntʃ ˈfivə/, *n.* a recurrent fever, often suffered by soldiers in trenches in World War I, caused by a rickettsia transmitted by lice.

**trench foot** /– ˈfʊt/, *n.* a disease of the feet due to exposure to cold and wet, common among soldiers serving in trenches.

**trench mortar** /ˈ– mɔtə/, *n.* a mortar, usu. having a smooth bore, for firing projectiles short distances at high angles of elevation, used in trench warfare.

**trench mouth** /– ˈmaʊθ/, *n.* →**Vincent's angina.** [so called because of its prevalence among soldiers]

**trench warfare** /– ˈwɔfɛə/, *n.* warfare in which the opposing sides occupy a system of trenches facing each other.

**trend** /trɛnd/, *n.* **1.** the general course, drift, or tendency: *the trend of events.* **2.** the general direction which a road, river, coastline, or the like, tends to take. **3.** style; fashion. *–v.i.* **4.** to have a general tendency, as events, etc. **5.** to tend to take a particular direction; extend in some direction indicated. [ME *trende(n),* OE *trendan;* akin to OE *trinda* ball, D *trent* circumference, Swed. *trind* round. Cf. TRUNDLE]

**trendsetter** /ˈtrɛndsɛtə/, *n.* one who initiates a subsequently popular fashion or style.

**trendy** /ˈtrɛndi/, *Colloq.* *–adj.* **1.** forming part of or influenced by fashionable trends; ultrafashionable. *–n.* **2.** one who embraces an ultrafashionable life-style. **3.** one who adopts a set of avant-garde social or political viewpoints. – **trendiness, trendyism,** *n.*

**trente et quarante** /trɒnt eɪ kəˈrɒnt/, *n.* →**rouge et noir.** [F: thirty and forty]

**trepan**[1] /trəˈpæn/, *n., v.,* **-panned, -panning.** *–n.* **1.** a boring tool for sinking shafts or the like. **2.** →**trephine.** *–v.t.* **3.** *Mach.* **a.** to cut (circular discs) out of plate stock using a rotating cutter. **b.** to cut (a concentric groove) around a bored or drilled hole. **4.** to operate upon with a trepan; perforate by a trepan. [ME, from ML *trepanum* crown saw, from Gk *trýpanon* borer] – **trepanation** /trɛpəˈneɪʃən/, *n.*

**trepan**[2] /trəˈpæn/, *n., v.,* **-panned, -panning.** *Archaic.* *–n.* **1.** one who ensnares or entraps others. **2.** a stratagem; a trap. *–v.t.* **3.** to ensnare or entrap. **4.** to entice. **5.** to cheat or swindle. Also, **trapan.** [orig. *trapan,* from TRAP[1] and confused with TREPAN[1]] – **trepanner,** *n.*

**trepang** /ˈtripæŋ/, *n.* any of various wormlike holothurians or sea-cucumbers, as *Holothuria edulis,* used as food in China. [Malay *trīpang*]

**trephine** /trəˈfin/, *n., v.,* **-phined, -phining.** *–n.* **1.** *Surg.* a small circular saw with a centre pin mounted on a strong hollow metal shaft to which is attached a transverse handle, used in surgery to remove circular discs of bone from the skull. *–v.t.* **2.** to operate upon with a trephine. [orig. *trafine,* explained by inventor as L *trēs fīnēs* three ends]

**trepidation** /trɛpəˈdeɪʃən/, *n.* **1.** tremulous alarm or agitation; perturbation. **2.** vibratory movement; a vibration. **3.** *Pathol.* rapid, repeated, muscular flexion and extension of muscles of the extremities or lower jaw; clonus. [L *trepidātio* act of hurrying, or of being alarmed]

**treponema** /trɛpəˈnimə/, *n., pl.* **-mas, -mata** /-mətə/. any of several anaerobic spirochaetes of the genus *Treponema,* certain of which are pathogenic for man and warm-blooded mammals.

**Tresillian** /trəˈsɪljən/, *adj.* **1.** of or pertaining to a nurse trained in the care of mothers and newborn children according to the principles of the Tresillian organisation. **2.** of or pertaining to a nursing home or hospital run on those principles. [from *Tresillian* Bridge, village in Cornwall, England, whence the founders of the organisation came]

**trespass** /ˈtrɛspəs/, *n.* **1.** *Law.* **a.** an unlawful act causing injury to the person, property, or rights of another, committed with force or violence, actual or implied. **b.** a wrongful entry upon the lands of another. **c.** the action to recover damages for such an injury. **2.** an encroachment or intrusion. **3.** an offence, sin, or wrong. *–v.i.* **4.** *Law.* to commit a trespass. **5.** to make an improper inroad on a person's presence, time, etc.; encroach or infringe (usu. fol. by *on* or *upon*). **6.** to commit a transgression or offence; transgress; offend; sin. [ME *trespas(en),* from OF *trespasser,* v., from *tres* across (from L *trans*) + *passer* (from L *passāre* PASS)] – **trespasser,** *n.*

**tress** /trɛs/, *n.* **1.** (*usu. pl.*) any long lock or curl of hair, esp. of a woman, not plaited or braided. **2.** *Archaic.* a plait or braid of the hair of the head, esp. of a woman. [ME *tresse,* from F: plait or braid of hair; orig. uncert.] – **tressed** /trɛst/, *adj.*

**-tress,** a suffix forming some feminine agent-nouns, corresponding to masculine nouns in *-ter, -tor,* as *actor, actress,* etc. See **-ess.**

**tressure** /ˈtrɛʃə/, *n.* a diminutive of the orle, usu. decorated with fleur-de-lis round the edges, and often doubled. [ME, from OF *tressur* braid of hair, from *tresser* braid, plait. See TRESS]

**trestle** /ˈtrɛsəl/, *n.* **1.** a frame used as a support, consisting typically of a horizontal beam or bar fixed at each end to a pair of spreading legs. **2.** *Civ. Eng.* **a.** a supporting framework composed chiefly of vertical or inclined pieces with or without diagonal braces, etc., used for various purposes, as for carrying tracks across a gap. **b.** a bridge or the like of such structure. [ME, from OF *trestel* transom, beam, from diminutive of L *transtrum*]

**trestle bridge** /ˈ– brɪdʒ/, *n.* a bridge supported by trestles or trestlework.

**trestle table** /ˈ– teɪbəl/, *n.* a table made of a board or boards laid upon trestles.

**trestletree** /ˈtrɛsəlˌtri/, *n.* either of two horizontal fore-and-aft timbers or bars secured to a masthead, one on each side, to support the crosstrees.

**trestlework** /'trɛsəlwɜk/, *n.* structural work consisting of a trestle or trestles.

**tret** /trɛt/, *n.* (formerly) an allowance for waste, after a deduction for tare. [ME, from AF *trait* TRAIT]

**trevalla** /trə'vælə/, *n.* a large deep-sea fish, *Hyperoglyphe porosa,* of the colder Australian waters.

**trevally** /trə'væli/, *n.* any of numerous species of Australian sport and food fishes, esp. of the genus *Caranx,* typically fast-swimming with streamlined bodies tapering sharply towards a forked or lunate tail.

**trews** /truz/, *n.pl.* close-fitting tartan trousers, worn esp. by certain Scottish Lowland regiments. [var. of *trouse* TROUSERS]

**trey** /treɪ/, *n.* **1.** a playing card or a dice having three pips. **2.** *Colloq.* (formerly) a threepenny piece; threepence. [ME, from OF *trei(s),* from L *trēs* three]

**tri-,** a word element meaning 'three', as in *triacid.* [L, combining form of *trēs, tria* three; or from Gk, combining form of *treîs, tría* three and *trís* thrice]

**triable** /'traɪəbəl/, *adj.* **1.** that may be tried. **2.** subject or liable to judicial trial. [late ME, from AF. See TRY, -ABLE] – **triableness,** *n.*

**triacetate fibre** /traɪ,æsəteɪt 'faɪbə/, *n.* **1.** a fibre made from pure cellulose, similar in composition to acetate fibre. **2.** material made from the fibre, having greater elasticity and resilience than acetate.

**triacid** /traɪ'æsəd/, *adj.* **1.** capable of combining with three molecules of a monobasic acid: *a triacid base.* **2.** denoting acid salts containing three replaceable hydrogen atoms.

**triad** /'traɪæd/, *n.* **1.** a group of three, esp. of three closely related or associated persons or things. **2.** *Chem.* an element, atom, or radical having a valency of three. **3.** *Music.* a chord of three notes, esp. one consisting of a given note with its major or minor third and its perfect, augmented, or diminished fifth. [L *trias,* from Gk: group of three.] – **triadic,** *adj.*

**trial** /'traɪəl, traɪl/, *n.* **1.** *Law.* **a.** the examination before a judicial tribunal of the facts put in issue in a cause (often including issues of law as well as of fact). **b.** the determination of a person's guilt or innocence by due process of law. **2.** the act of trying or testing, or putting to the proof. **3.** a contest or competition: *car trial; a trial of arms.* **4.** test; proof. **5.** an attempt or effort to do something. **6.** tentative or experimental action in order to ascertain results; an experiment. **7.** the state or position of a person or thing being tried or tested; probation. **8.** subjection to suffering or grievous experiences; affliction: *comfort in the hour of trial.* **9.** an affliction or trouble. **10.** a trying, distressing, or annoying thing or person. **11.** *Ceramics.* a piece of ceramic material used to try the heat of the kiln and the progress of the firing of its contents. **12.** a competition, usu. over rough terrain and roads in which competitors are required to keep to an average speed; motor trial. **13.** →**trial handicap.** **14.** →**trial horse.** **15. on trial, a.** undergoing a trial before a court of law. **b.** undergoing a test; on approval. *–v.t.* **16.** to put a plan, etc. into operation, often on a small scale, to test its feasibility. *–adj.* **17.** pertaining to trial or a trial. **18.** done or used by way of trial, test, proof, or experiment. [from AF, *trier,* TRY]

**trial and error,** *n.* a process of experimentation to find the best way of achieving a desired result, in which various methods are tried and eliminated as unsuitable.

**trial balance** /traɪəl 'bæləns/, *n.* a statement of all the open debit and credit items, made preliminary to balancing a double-entry ledger.

**trial handicap** /– 'hændikæp/, *n.* a restricted race for horses which are specified as being in the trial class in accordance with the rules operating in each State in Australia.

**trial horse** /– 'hɔs/, *n.* a horse eligible to run in a trial handicap. Also, **trial-class horse.**

**trial marriage** /– 'mærɪdʒ/, *n.* cohabitation of a man and woman in order to discover if they are suitable marriage partners.

**trial run** /– 'rʌn/, *n.* **1.** a preliminary performance to test the efficiency of a motor vehicle, ship, etc. **2.** a preliminary testing period of anything.

**triandrous** /traɪ'ændrəs/, *adj.* **1.** (of a flower) having three stamens. **2.** (of a plant) having flowers with three stamens.

**triangle** /'traɪæŋgəl/, *n.* **1.** a geometrical plane figure formed by three (usu.) straight lines which meet two by two in three points, thus forming three angles. **2.** *Chiefly U.S.* →**set square.** **3.** any three-cornered or three-sided figure, object, or piece: *a triangle of land.* **4.** *Music.* an instrument of percussion, made of a steel rod bent into the form of a triangle open at one of the corners, and sounded by being struck with a small, straight steel rod. **5.** a group of three; triad. [ME, from L *triangulum,* lit. three-cornered object. See ANGLE[1]]

**triangular** /traɪ'æŋgjələ/, *adj.* **1.** pertaining to or having the form of a triangle; three-cornered. **2.** having a triangle as base or cross-section: *a triangular prism.* **3.** comprising three parts or elements; triple. **4.** pertaining to or involving a group of three, as three persons, parties, or things. – **triangularity** /traɪ,æŋgjə'lærəti/, *n.* – **triangularly,** *adv.*

**triangulate** /traɪ'æŋgjələt, -leɪt/, *adj.;* /traɪ'æŋgjəleɪt/, *v.,* **-lated, -lating.** *–adj.* **1.** triangular. **2.** composed of or marked with triangles. *–v.t.* **3.** to make triangular. **4.** to divide into triangles. **5.** *Survey.* **a.** to survey (a region, etc.) by dividing the area into triangles and measuring the angles of these triangles. **b.** to determine trigonometrically.

**triangulation** /traɪ,æŋgjə'leɪʃən/, *n.* **1.** the operation and immediate result of measuring, ordinarily with a theodolite, the angles of a network of triangles laid out on the earth's surface by marking their vertices. **2.** the triangles thus marked.

**triantelope** /traɪ'æntəloup/, *n.* →**tarantula** (def. 1). [b. TARANTULA + ANTELOPE]

**triarchy** /'traɪaki/, *n., pl.* **-chies.** **1.** government by three persons. **2.** a set of three joint rulers; a triumvirate. **3.** a country divided into three governments. **4.** a group of three countries or districts each under its own ruler. [Gk *triarchía* triumvirate. See TRI-, -ARCHY]

**Triassic** /traɪ'æsɪk/, *adj.* **1.** pertaining to the geological period or system that constitutes the earliest principal division of the Mesozoic era. *–n.* **2.** the period or system characterised by widespread land deposits following Permian and preceding Jurassic. [LL *trias* the number three (from Gk) + -IC; so called because deposits are divisible into three groups]

**triatic stay** /traɪ,ætɪk 'steɪ/, *n.* a wire rope fitted horizontally between the tops of the masts in schooners, or from the foremost to the funnel in power-driven ships. [orig. uncert.]

**triatomic** /traɪə'tɒmɪk/, *adj.* **1.** having three atoms in the molecule. **2.** containing three replaceable atoms or groups.

**triaxial** /traɪ'æksiəl/, *adj.* having three axes.

**triazine** /'traɪəzin, -zən, traɪ'æzin, -zən/, *n.* **1.** any of a group of three compounds, $C_3H_3N_3$, containing three nitrogen and three carbon atoms arranged in a six-membered ring. **2.** any of a number of their derivatives. Also, **triazin** /'traɪəzən, traɪ'æzən/. [TRI- + AZ(O)- + -INE[2]]

**triazoic** /traɪə'zouɪk/, *adj.* →**hydrazoic.**

**triazole** /'traɪəzɒl, traɪ'æzɒl/, *n.* any of a group of four compounds, $C_2H_3N_3$, containing three nitrogen and two carbon atoms arranged in a five-membered ring.

**tribade** /'trɪbəd/, *n.* a woman who practises tribadism, esp. a female homosexual who assumes the male role. [L *tribas* rubbing, from Gk]

**tribadism** /'trɪbədɪzəm/, *n.* →**lesbianism.**

**tribal** /'traɪbəl/, *adj.* of, pertaining to, or characteristic of, a tribe or tribes: *tribal customs.* – **tribally,** *adv.*

**tribalism** /'traɪbəlɪzəm/, *n.* **1.** the customs and belief of a tribe or tribes. **2.** loyalty to one's tribe, group, etc. – **tribalist,** *n., adj.* – **tribalistic** /traɪbə'lɪstɪk/, *adj.*

**tribasic** /traɪ'beɪsɪk/, *adj.* **1.** (of an acid) having three atoms of hydrogen replaceable by basic atoms or radicals. **2.** containing three basic atoms or radicals, each having a valency of one, as *tribasic sodium phosphate,* $Na_3PO_4$.

**tribe** /traɪb/, *n.* **1.** any aggregate of people united by ties of descent from a common ancestor, community of customs and traditions, adherence to the same leaders, etc. **2.** a local division of a primitive or aboriginal people. **3.** (in the culture of the Aborigines) a social group which claims hunting rights and religious sanction for its occupation of an area. **4.** a class, kind, or sort of animals, plants, articles, or other things. **5.** *Bot., Zool.* **a.** a classificatory group of animals or plants, ranking between a family and a genus. **b.** any group of plants or animals. **6.** a company, troop, or number of

T-V

persons or animals. **7.** (*joc.*) **a.** a class or set or persons. **b.** a family. [L *tribus;* replacing ME *tribu,* from OF] – **tribeless,** *adj.*

**tribesman** /ˈtraɪbzmən/, *n., pl.* **-men.** a man belonging to a tribe; a member of a tribe.

**tribo-,** a word element meaning 'friction', as in *triboelectricity.* [Gk, combining form of *tríbein* to rub]

**triboelectricity** /ˌtraɪbouəlɛkˈtrɪsəti/, *n.* electricity generated by friction.

**tribology** /traɪbˈɒlədʒi/, *n.* the study of the friction and wear between, and the lubrication of, interacting surfaces in relative motion.

**triboluminescence** /ˌtraɪbouˌluməˈnɛsəns/, *n.* the emission of light when certain crystals, as cane sugar, are crushed. – **triboluminescent,** *adj.*

**tribrach** /ˈtraɪbræk, ˈtrɪbræk/, *n.* a foot of three short syllables. [L *tribachys,* from Gk]

**tribromoethanol** /ˌtraɪbroumouˈɛθənɒl/, *n.* a colourless crystalline compound, $CBr_3CH_2OH$, used as an anaesthetic.

**tribulation** /trɪbjəˈleɪʃən/, *n.* **1.** grievous trouble; severe trial or experience. **2.** an instance of this, or an affliction, trouble, etc. [ME, from L *trībulātio,* from L *trībulāre* afflict, from *trībulum* threshing sledge]

**tribunal** /traɪˈbjunəl/, *n.* **1.** a court of justice. **2.** a place or seat of judgment. [L: judgment seat, from *tribūnus* tribune]

**tribunate** /ˈtrɪbjənət/, *n.* **1.** the office of tribune. **2.** a body of tribunes. [L *tribūnātus*]

**tribune**[1] /ˈtrɪbjun/, *n.* a person who upholds or defends popular rights. [ME, from L *tribūnus* an administrative officer in the ancient Roman republic] – **tribuneship,** *n.*

**tribune**[2] /ˈtrɪbjun/, *n.* **1.** a raised platform, or dais; a rostrum or pulpit. **2.** a raised part, or gallery, with seats, as in a church. **3.** (in a Christian basilica) the bishop's throne in a corresponding recess, or apse. **4.** the apse itself. [It. *tribuna* tribunal]

**tributary** /ˈtrɪbjətri/, *n., pl.* **-taries,** *adj.* –*n.* **1.** a stream contributing its flow to a larger stream or other body of water. **2.** one who pays tribute. –*adj.* **3.** (of a stream) flowing into a larger stream or other body of water. **4.** furnishing subsidiary aid; contributory; auxiliary. **5.** paying or required to pay tribute. **6.** paid as tribute. – **tributarily,** *adv.*

**tribute** /ˈtrɪbjut/, *n.* **1.** a personal offering, testimonial, compliment, or the like given as if due, or in acknowledgment of gratitude, esteem, or regard. **2.** a stated sum or other valuable consideration paid by one sovereign or state to acknowledgment of submission or as the price of peace, security, protection, or the like. **3.** a rent, tax, or the like, as that paid by a subject to a sovereign. **4.** anything paid as under exaction or by enforced contribution. **5.** *Chiefly S. Aust.* (in opal mining) one's share when working on a partnership basis. **6.** the state of being liable or the obligation to make such payment. –*v.t.* **7.** *Mining.* to work a mine for a share of the product. [ME *tribut,* from L *tribūtum*] – **tributer,** *n.*

**tributer** /ˈtrɪbjutə/, *n. Chiefly S. Aust.* (in opal mining) one who mines on a share basis or tribute. Also, **tributor.**

**tricarboxylic acid cycle,** *n.* →**citric acid cycle.**

**tricarpellary** /traɪˈkapələri/, *adj.* having three carpels.

**trice**[1] /traɪs/, *n.* a very short time; a moment; an instant: *to come back in a trice.* [ME *tryse,* special use of TRICE[2] (*at a trice* at one tug)]

**trice**[2] /traɪs/, *v.t.,* **triced, tricing.** *Naut.* **1.** to pull or haul with a rope. **2.** to haul up and fasten with a rope (usu. fol. by *up*). [ME, from MD *trīsen* hoist, apparently from *trīse* pulley]

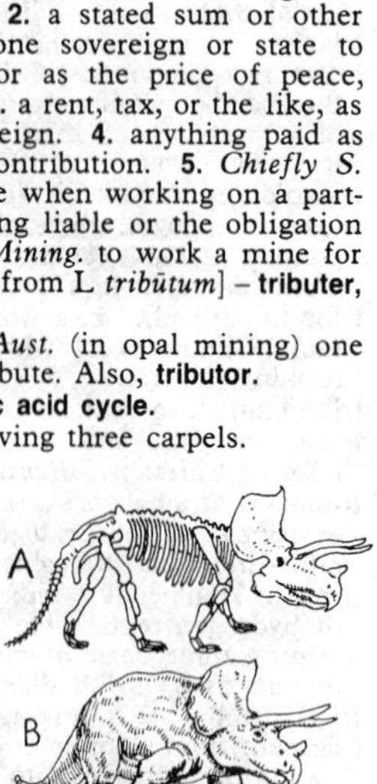

triceratops: A, skeleton; B, reconstruction

**tricentennial** /traɪsɛnˈtɛniəl/, *adj., n.* →**tercentenary.**

**triceps** /ˈtraɪsɛps/, *n.* a muscle having three heads, or points of origin, esp. the extensor muscle at the back of the upper arm. [L: three-headed]

**triceratops** /traɪˈsɛrətɒps/, *n.* any of the large, horned dinosaurs constituting the genus *Triceratops,* reptiles of great size with huge heads and heavily armoured necks.

**trich-,** variant of **tricho-,** before vowels, as in *trichite.*

**trichiasis** /trəˈkaɪəsəs/, *n. Pathol.* a state in which the eyelashes grow inwardly. [Gk, from *trichiân* be hairy]

**trichina** /trəˈkaɪnə/, *n., pl.* **-nae** /-ni/. the nematode worm, *Trichinella spiralis,* the adults of which live in the intestine and produce embryos which encyst in the muscle tissue, esp. in pigs, rats, and man. [NL, from Gk, n. use of fem. of *tríchinos* of hair]

**trichinise** /ˈtrɪkənaɪz/, *v.t.,* **-nised, -nising.** to infect with trichinae. Also, **trichinize.** – **trichinisation** /trɪkənaɪˈzeɪʃən/, *n.*

**trichinosis** /trɪkəˈnousəs/, *n.* a disease due to the presence of the trichina in the intestines and muscular tissues. [NL. See TRICHINA, -OSIS]

**trichinous** /ˈtrɪkənəs/, *adj.* **1.** pertaining to or of the nature of trichinosis. **2.** infected with trichinae.

**trichite** /ˈtrɪkaɪt/, *n.* any of various minute hairlike mineral bodies occurring in certain vitreous igneous rocks, esp. obsidian. [TRICH- + -ITE[1]] – **trichitic** /trəˈkɪtɪk/, *adj.*

**trichlorethylene** /traɪklɔrˈɛθəlin/, *n.* a colourless liquid, $CHCl{:}CCl_2$, used as a solvent, in dry-cleaning, and as an anaesthetic. Also, **trichloroethylene** /ˌtraɪklɔrouˈɛθəlin/, **trilene.**

**trichloride** /traɪˈklɔraɪd/, *n.* a chloride having three atoms of chlorine, as ferric chloride, $FeCl_3$. Also, **trichlorid** /traɪˈklɔrəd/.

**trichloroacetic acid** /traɪˌklɔrouəˌsitɪk ˈæsəd/, *n.* toxic, deliquescent colourless crystals, $CCl_3COOH$, having a sharp pungent odour; used in medicine and pharmacy, and as a herbicide.

**trichloronitromethane** /ˌtraɪklɔrouˌnaɪtrouˈmiθeɪn/, *n.* →**chloropicrin.**

**tricho-,** a word element referring to hair, as in *trichocyst.* [Gk, combining form of *thríx*]

**trichocyst** /ˈtrɪkəsɪst/, *n. Zool.* an organ of offence and defence embedded in the outer protoplasm of many infusorians, consisting of a small elongated sac containing a fine, hairlike filament capable of being ejected. – **trichocystic** /trɪkəˈsɪstɪk/, *adj.*

**trichogyne** /ˈtrɪkədʒaɪn, -dʒɪn/, *n.* a hairlike prolongation of a carpogonium, serving as a receptive organ for the spermatium. [TRICHO- + Gk *gynḗ* woman]

**trichoid** /ˈtrɪkɔɪd/, *adj.* hairlike.

**trichology** /trɪˈkɒlədʒi/, *n.* the science of the hair and its diseases. – **trichologist,** *n.*

**trichome** /ˈtraɪkoum, ˈtrɪkoum/, *n.* an outgrowth from the epidermis of plants, as a hair. [Gk *trichōma* growth of hair] – **trichomic** /trɪˈkɒmɪk/, *adj.*

**trichomonad** /trɪkouˈmɒnæd/, *n.* any flagellate protozoan of the genus *Trichomonas,* parasitic in man or animals.

**trichosis** /trɪˈkousəs/, *n.* any disease of the hair.

**trichotomy** /traɪˈkɒtəmi/, *n.* **1.** division into three parts. **2.** arrangement in three divisions. **3.** the three-part division of man into body, spirit, and soul. [*tricho-* (representing Gk *trícha* triply) + -TOMY] – **trichotomic** /trɪkəˈtɒmɪk/, **trichotomous,** *adj.*

**trichroic** /traɪˈkrouɪk/, *adj.* **1.** having or exhibiting three colours. **2.** →**pleochroic.** – **trichroism,** *n.*

**trichromatic** /traɪkrouˈmætɪk/, *adj.* **1.** pertaining to the use or combination of three different colours, as in printing, or in photography in natural colours. **2.** pertaining to, characterised by, or involving three colours.

**trichromatism** /traɪˈkroumətɪzəm/, *n.* **1.** trichromatic condition. **2.** the use or combination of three different colours.

**trichromatopsia** /traɪˌkrouməˈtɒpsiə/, *n.* normal vision, in which the three fundamental colours, red, blue, and green, can be distinguished.

**trick** /trɪk/, *n.* **1.** a crafty or fraudulent device, expedient, or proceeding; an artifice, stratagem, ruse, or wile. **2.** a deceptive or illusory appearance; mere semblance. **3.** a roguish or mischievous performance; prank: *to play a trick on someone.* **4.** a foolish, disgraceful, or mean performance or action. **5.** a clever device or expedient, dodge, or ingenious shift: *a rhetorical trick.* **6.** the art or knack of doing something. **7.** a clever or dexterous feat, as for exhibition or entertainment: *tricks in horsemanship.* **8.** a feat of jugglery, magic, or legerdemain. **9.** a particular habit or way of acting; characteristic quality, trait, or mannerism. **10.** *Cards.* the cards collectively which are played and won in one round. **11. do the trick,** to achieve the desired result. **12. not to be able to take a trick,** to have no success at all. *–adj.* **13.** pertaining to or having the nature of tricks. **14.** made for tricks. *–v.t.* **15.** to deceive by trickery. **16.** to cheat or swindle (fol. by *out of*). **17.** to beguile by trickery (fol. by *into*). **18.** to dress, array, or deck (oft. fol. by *out* or *up*). *–v.i.* **19.** to practise trickery or deception; cheat. **20.** become aware of, esp. of something previously concealed (fol. by *to*). [ME *trik,* from OF *trique* deceit, from *trichier* deceive; orig. uncert.] – **tricker,** *n.* – **trickless,** *adj.*

**trickery** /ˈtrɪkəri/, *n., pl.* **-eries. 1.** the use or practice of tricks; artifice. **2.** a trick.

**trickish** /ˈtrɪkɪʃ/, *adj.* tricky. – **trickishly,** *adv.* – **trickishness,** *n.*

**trickle** /ˈtrɪkəl/, *v.,* **-led, -ling,** *n. –v.i.* **1.** to flow or fall by drops, or in a small, broken, or gentle stream: *tears trickled down her cheeks.* **2.** to come, go, pass, or proceed bit by bit, slowly, irregularly, etc.: *subscriptions are trickling in. –v.t.* **3.** to cause to trickle. *–n.* **4.** a trickling flow or stream. **5.** a small, slow, or irregular quantity of anything coming, going, or proceeding: *a trickle of visitors.* [sandhi var. of obs. *strickle,* frequentative of STRIKE]

**trickle charger** /ˈ– tʃadʒə/, *n.* an apparatus which supplies a very small current to an accumulator.

**trickster** /ˈtrɪkstə/, *n.* **1.** a deceiver; a cheat. **2.** one who practises tricks.

**tricksy** /ˈtrɪksi/, *adj.* **1.** tricky, crafty, or wily. **2.** mischievous, frolicsome, or playful. **3.** deceptive; uncertain. **4.** *Obs.* trim, spruce, or fine. – **tricksily,** *adv.* – **tricksiness,** *n.*

**tricktrack** /ˈtrɪktræk/, *n.* a variety of backgammon. Also, **trictrac.**

**tricky** /ˈtrɪki/, *adj.,* **trickier, trickiest. 1.** given to or characterised by deceitful or clever tricks; clever; wily. **2.** deceptive, uncertain or ticklish to deal with or handle. – **trickily,** *adv.* – **trickiness,** *n.*

**triclinic** /traɪˈklɪnɪk/, *adj.* denoting or pertaining to a system of crystallisation in which the three axes are unequal and intersect at oblique angles. [TRI- + Gk *klī́ne* lean, slope + -IC]

**tricolour** /ˈtrɪkələ, ˈtraɪkʌlə/, *adj.* **1.** Also, **tricoloured** /ˈtraɪkʌləd/. having three colours. *–n.* **2.** a tricolour flag or the like. Also, *U.S.,* **tricolor.** [F *tricolore,* from LL *tricolor,* adj., from *tri-* TRI- + *-color* coloured]

**tricorn** /ˈtraɪkɔn/, *adj.* **1.** having three horns, or hornlike projections, as a hat with the brim turned up on three sides. *–n.* **2.** a tricorn hat. Also, **tricorne.**

**tricostate** /traɪˈkɒsteɪt/, *adj.* having three ribs, costae, or raised lines.

**tricot** /ˈtrikoʊ/, *n.* a warp-knit fabric, usu. of rayon, with the right and wrong sides different. [F, from *tricoter* knit, ult. of Gmc orig.]

**tricresol** /traɪˈkrisɒl/, *n.* a mixture of the three isomers of cresol.

**trictrac** /ˈtrɪktræk/, *n.* →**tricktrack.**

**tricuspid** /traɪˈkʌspəd/, *adj.* Also, **tricuspidal. 1.** having three cusps or points, as a tooth. **2.** *Anat.* denoting or pertaining to a valve of three segments, guarding the opening from the right auricle into the right ventricle of the heart. *–n.* **3.** *Anat.* a tricuspid valve. [L *tricuspis* having three points]

**tricuspidate** /traɪˈkʌspədeɪt/, *adj. Anat.* having three cusps or flaps.

**tricyanic acid** /traɪsaɪˌænɪk ˈæsəd/, *n.* →**cyanuric acid.**

tricycle

**tricycle** /ˈtraɪsɪkəl/, *n.* **1.** a cycle with three wheels (usu. one in front and one on each side behind) propelled by pedals or hand levers. **2.** →**three-wheeler.** [F, from *tri-* TRI- + *cycle* (see CYCLE)]

**tricyclic** /traɪˈsaɪklɪk/, *adj.* **1.** pertaining to or embodying three cycles. *–n.* **2.** →**tricyclic antidepressant.**

**tricyclic antidepressant** /– ˌæntidəˈprɛsənt/, *n.* an antidepressant which has three rings in its chemical structure.

**trident** /ˈtraɪdnt/, *n.* **1.** a three-pronged instrument or weapon. **2.** a fish spear having three prongs. *–adj.* **3.** having three prongs or tines. [L *tridens* having three teeth]

**tridimensional** /traɪdəˈmɛnʃənəl/, *adj.* having three dimensions. – **tridimensionality** /ˌtraɪdəmɛnʃəˈnæləti/, *n.*

**triecious** /traɪˈiʃəs/, *adj. U.S.* →**trioecious.**

**tried** /traɪd/, *v.* **1.** past tense and past participle of **try.** *–adj.* **2.** tested; proved; having sustained the tests of experience.

**triella** /traɪˈɛlə/, *n.* (in horseracing) three selected races on which off-course jackpot betting by totalisator is allowed.

**triennial** /traɪˈɛniəl/, *adj.* **1.** lasting three years. **2.** occurring every three years. *–n.* **3.** a period of three years. **4.** a third anniversary. [L *triennium* period of three years + -AL[1]] – **triennially,** *adv.*

**triennium** /traɪˈɛniəm/, *n., pl.* **-enniums, -ennia** /-ˈɛniə/. a period of three years.

**trier** /ˈtraɪə/, *n.* one who continually works hard despite failure.

**triethylamine** /traɪˈɛθələmin/, *n.* a colourless liquid, $N(C_2H_5)_3$, used as a solvent.

**trifacial** /traɪˈfeɪʃəl/, *adj.* →**trigeminal.**

**trifecta** /traɪˈfɛktə/, *n.* a form of betting in which the punter is required to select the first three placegetters in a nominated race in the correct order. [TRI- + *per(fecta)* a U.S. form of betting]

**trifid** /ˈtraɪfəd/, *adj.* cleft into three parts or lobes. [L *trifidus* split in three. See -FID]

**trifle** /ˈtraɪfəl/, *n., v.,* **-fled, -fling.** *–n.* **1.** an article or thing of small value. **2.** a matter of slight importance; a trivial or insignificant affair or circumstance. **3.** a small, inconsiderable, or trifling sum of money. **4.** a small quantity or amount of anything; a little: *he's still a trifle angry.* **5.** a kind of pewter of medium hardness. **6.** (*pl.*) articles made of this. **7.** a dish typically consisting of sponge cake soaked in wine or liqueur, with jam, fruit, jelly, or the like topped with custard and whipped cream and (sometimes) almonds. *–v.i.* **8.** to deal lightly or without due seriousness or respect (usu. fol. by *with*): *he was in no mood to be trifled with.* **9.** to amuse oneself or dally (usu. fol. by *with*). **10.** to play or toy by handling or fingering (usu. fol. by *with*): *he sat trifling with a pen.* **11.** to act or talk in an idle or frivolous way. **12.** to pass time idly or frivolously; waste time; idle. *–v.t.* **13.** to pass (time, etc.) idly or frivolously (usu. fol. by *away*). [ME *treoflen,* from OF *trufler* make sport of, deceive; orig. uncert.] – **trifler,** *n.*

**trifling** /ˈtraɪflɪŋ/, *adj.* **1.** of slight importance; trivial; insignificant: *a trifling matter.* **2.** of small value, cost, or amount: *a trifling sum.* **3.** frivolous, shallow, or light. – **triflingness,** *n.* – **triflingly,** *adv.*

**trifoliata** /traɪˌfoʊliˈatə/, *n.* →**trifoliate orange.**

**trifoliate** /traɪˈfoʊliət, -eɪt/, *adj.* **1.** having three leaves, leaflike parts or lobes, or three foils. **2.** →**trifoliolate.** Also, **trifoliated.** [TRI- + L *foliātus* leaved]

**trifoliate orange** /– ˈɒrɪndʒ/, *n.* a small, thorny tree, *Poncirus trifoliata,* native to China, widely cultivated as an ornamental and for hedges and used as a stock for other citrus fruits. Also, **trifoliata.**

**trifoliolate** /traɪˈfoʊliəleɪt/, *adj.* **1.** having three leaflets, as a compound leaf. **2.** having leaves with three leaflets, as a plant.

**trifolium** /traɪˈfoʊliəm/, *n.* any plant of the leguminous genus *Trifolium,* as clover. [L: triple leaf]

**triforium** /traɪˈfɔriəm/, *n., pl.* **-foria** /-ˈfɔriə/. *Archit.* (in a church) the wall at the side of the nave, choir or transept, corresponding to the space between the vaulting or ceiling and the roof of an aisle, often having a blind arcade or an opening in a gallery. [Anglo-Latin; orig. uncert.]

**triform** /ˈtraɪfɔm/, *adj.* **1.** formed of three parts, or in three divisions. **2.** existing or appearing in three different forms. **3.** combining three different forms. Also, **triformed.** [L *triformis*]

**trifurcate** /ˈtraɪfəkeɪt/, *v.,* **-cated, -cating;** /ˈtraɪfəkət, -keɪt/, *adj. –v.t., v.i.* **1.** to divide into three forks or branches.

*–adj.* **2.** Also, **trifurcated.** divided into three forks or branches. [L *trifurcus* three forked + -ATE[1]] – **trifurcation** /traɪʃəˈkeɪʃən/, *n.*

**trig**[1] /trɪg/, *adj., v.,* **trigged, trigging.** *–adj.* **1.** neat, trim, smart, or spruce. **2.** in good physical condition; sound; well. *–v.t.* **3.** to make trig, trim, or smart (oft. fol. by *up* or *out*). [ME, from Scand; cf. Icel. *tryggr* safe, c. Goth. *triggus* true, faithful. Cf. TRUE]

**trig**[2] /trɪg/, *v.,* **trigged, trigging,** *n.* *–v.t.* **1.** to support or prop, as with a wedge. *–v.i.* **2.** to act as a check on the moving of wheels, vehicles, etc. *–n.* **3.** a wedge or block used to prevent a wheel, cask, or the like from rolling. [? from Scand.; cf. Icel. *tryggja* make fast]

**trig**[3] /trɪg/, *n. Colloq.* →**trig station.**

**trig.,** **1.** trigonometric. **2.** trigonometry.

**trigeminal** /traɪˈdʒɛmənəl/, *adj.* **1.** denoting or pertaining to either of a pair of double-rooted cranial nerves, each dividing into three main branches to supply the face, etc. *–n.* **2.** a trigeminal nerve. [L *trigeminus* threefold + -AL[1]]

**trigesimo-secundo** /traɪˌdʒɛzəmoʊ-səˈkʊndoʊ/, *n., pl.* **-dos,** *adj.* *–n.* **1.** a volume printed from sheets folded to form 32 leaves or 64 pages. *Abbrev.:* 32mo or 32°. *–adj.* **2.** in trigesimo-secundo. Also, **thirty-twomo.** [It.: thirty-second]

**trigger** /ˈtrɪgə/, *n.* **1.** (in firearms) a small projecting tongue which when pressed by the finger liberates the mechanism and discharges the weapon. **2.** a device, as a lever, the pulling or pressing of which releases a detent or spring. **3.** *Electronics.* any circuit which is used to set a system in operation by the application of a single pulse. *–v.t.* **4.** to start or precipitate (something), as a chain of events or a scientific reaction (oft. fol. by *off*). [earlier *tricker,* from D *trekker,* from *trekken* pull] – **triggerless,** *adj.*

**triggerfish** /ˈtrɪgəfɪʃ/, *n., pl.* **-fishes,** (*esp. collectively*) **-fish.** any of various compressed, deep-bodied fishes of the genus *Balistes,* and allied genera, chiefly of tropical seas, having an anterior dorsal fin with three stout spines.

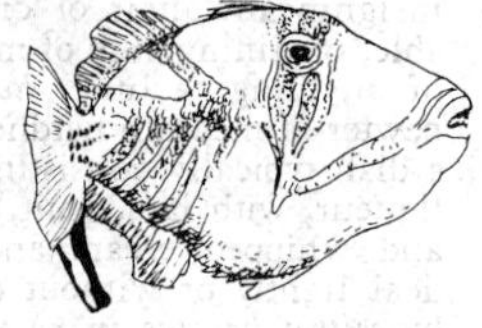
triggerfish

**trigger flower** /ˈtrɪgə flaʊə/, *n.* any species of the large, mostly Australian genus *Stylidium,* characterised by an irritable column (style and two stamens) which dusts the backs of insects with pollen.

**trigger-happy** /ˈtrɪgə-hæpi/, *adj. Colloq.* **1.** ready to fire a gun at the slightest provocation. **2.** reckless, irresponsible, or foolhardy, esp. in matters which could lead to war.

**trigger pressure** /ˈtrɪgə prɛʃə/, *n.* the pressure which must be exerted by a finger on the trigger to fire the gun.

**triglyceride** /traɪˈglɪsəraɪd/, *n.* any ester of glycerol and fatty acids in which each glycerol molecule is combined with three fatty acid molecules.

**triglyph** /ˈtraɪglɪf/, *n.* a structural member of a Doric frieze, separating two consecutive metopes, and consisting typically of a rectangular block with two vertical grooves or glyphs, and two chamfers or half grooves at the sides, together counting as a third glyph, and leaving three flat vertical bands on the face of the block. [L *trīglyphus,* from Gk *tríglyphos* thrice-grooved] – **triglyphic,** *adj.*

**trigon** /ˈtraɪgən/, *n.* the position or aspect of two planets distant 120° from each other. [L *trigōnum* triangle, from Gk *trígōnon,* prop. neut. adj., three-cornered]

**trigon.,** **1.** trigonometric. **2.** trigonometry.

**trigonal** /ˈtrɪgənəl/, *adj.* **1.** triangular. **2.** *Crystall.* having threefold symmetry.

**trigonometer** /trɪgəˈnɒmətə/, *n.* an instrument for solving plane right-angled triangles by inspection. [backformation from TRIGONOMETRY]

**trigonometrical function** /trɪgənəˌmɛtrɪkəl ˈfʌŋkʃən/, *n.* a function relating two sides of a right-angled triangle with one of the acute angles in the triangle, as tangent, sine, cosine, cotangent, secant, cosecant, or any function derived from any of these.

**trigonometry** /trɪgəˈnɒmətri/, *n.* the branch of mathematics that deals with the relations between the sides and angles of triangles (plane or spherical), and the calculations, etc., based on these. [NL *trigōnometria,* from Gk *trígōno(n)* triangle + *-metria* -METRY] – **trigonometric** /trɪgənəˈmɛtrɪk/, **trigonometrical** /trɪgənəˈmɛtrɪkəl/, *adj.* – **trigonometrically** /trɪgənəˈmɛtrɪkli/, *adv.*

**trigonous** /ˈtrɪgənəs/, *adj.* having three angles or corners; triangular, as stems, seeds, etc. [L *trigōnus* triangular, from Gk *trígōnos*]

**trigraph** /ˈtraɪgræf, -graf/, *n.* a group of three letters representing a single speech sound, as *eau* in *beau.* – **trigraphic** /traɪˈgræfɪk/, *adj.*

**trig station** /ˈtrɪg steɪʃən/, *n.* a position of importance in the surveying of a locality, marked by a distinctive fixed post or pole against which bearing may be subsequently taken. Also, **trig point.** [*trig(onometrical) station*]

**trihedral** /traɪˈhidrəl/, *adj.* having, or formed by, three planes meeting in a point: *a trihedral angle.*

**trihedron** /traɪˈhidrən/, *n., pl.* **-drons, -dra** /-drə/. the figure determined by three planes meeting in a point.

**trihydric** /traɪˈhaɪdrɪk/, *adj.* containing three hydroxyl groups. Also, **trihydroxy.**

**trike** /traɪk/, *n. Colloq.* →**tricycle.** [alteration of TRICYCLE]

**trilateral** /traɪˈlætərəl/, *adj.* having three sides. [L *trilaterus* three-sided + -AL[1]] – **trilaterally,** *adv.*

**trilby** /ˈtrɪlbi/, *n., pl.* **-bies.** a man's soft felt hat with an indented crown. Also, **trilby hat.** [named after heroine of *Trilby,* novel by G. Du Maurier, 1834-96, English novelist]

trilby

**trilene** /ˈtraɪlin/, *n.* →**trichlorethylene.**

**trilinear** /traɪˈlɪniə/, *adj.* pertaining to or involving three lines.

**trilingual** /traɪˈlɪŋgwəl/, *adj.* using or involving three languages.

**triliteral** /traɪˈlɪtərəl/, *adj.* **1.** consisting of three letters, as a word. *–n.* **2.** a triliteral word or root.

**triliteralism** /traɪˈlɪtərəlɪzəm/, *n. Gram.* the characteristic presence of triliteral roots in a language, as in the Semitic languages.

**trill** /trɪl/, *v.t.* **1.** to sing with a vibratory effect of voice, esp. in the manner of a shake or trill. **2.** to play with like effect on an instrument. **3.** *Phonet.* to pronounce with rapid vibrations of an elastic organ of speech: *Spanish 'rr' is trilled with the tip of the tongue.* **4.** (of birds, etc.) to sing or give forth in a succession of rapidly alternating or changing sounds. *–v.i.* **5.** to resound vibrantly, or with a rapid succession of sounds, as the voice, song, laughter, etc. **6.** to utter, give forth, or make a sound or a succession of sounds more or less resembling such singing, as a bird, a frog, a grasshopper, a person laughing, etc. **7.** to execute a shake or trill with the voice or on a musical instrument. *–n.* **8.** the act or sound of trilling. **9.** *Music.* a trilled sound, or a rapid alternation of two consecutive notes, in singing or in instrumental music; a shake. **10.** a similar sound, or succession of sounds, uttered or made by a bird, an insect, a person laughing, etc. **11.** *Phonet.* **a.** a trilled articulation. **b.** a trilled consonant, as Spanish *rr.* [It. *trillo,* n., quaver or warble in singing; of Gmc orig.]

**triller** /ˈtrɪlə/, *n.* either of two species of birds of the genus *Lalage,* distinguished by their distinctive trilling call. See **white-winged triller.**

**trillion** /ˈtrɪljən/, *n.* **1.** a million times a billion, or $10^{18}$. **2.** *U.S.* a million times a million, or $10^{12}$. **3.** *Colloq.* a very large amount. *–adj.* **4.** amounting to one trillion in number. [F *tri-* TRI- + *m(illion)* MILLION] – **trillionth,** *n., adj.*

**trillium** /ˈtrɪliəm/, *n.* any of the herbs constituting the genus *Trillium,* characterised by a whorl of three leaves from the centre of which rises a solitary flower. [NL, apparently from Swed. *trilling* triplet + L *-ium* -IUM]

**trilobate** /traɪˈloʊbeɪt, ˈtraɪləbeɪt/, *adj.* having three lobes.

**trilobite** /ˈtraɪləbaɪt/, *n.* any of the Trilobita, a group of extinct arthropods, variously classed with the crustaceans or the arachnids or as intermediate between these, with a flattened oval body varying in length from 3 cm to 60 cm, their remains being found widely distributed in strata of the

Palaeozoic era, and important as being among the earliest known fossils. [NL *Trilobītēs,* from *tri-* TRI- + Gk *lobós* lobe (of ear, etc.) + *-ītēs* -ITE[1]] – **trilobitic** /traɪlə'bɪtɪk/, *adj.*

**trilocular** /traɪ'lɒkjələ/, *adj.* having three loculi, chambers, or cells. [TRI- + L *loculus* small receptacle (diminutive of *locus* place) + -AR[1]]

**trilogy** /'trɪlədʒi/, *n., pl.* **-gies.** **1.** a series or group of three related dramas, operas, novels, etc. **2.** a group of three related things. [Gk *trilogia.* See TRI-, -LOGY]

**trim** /trɪm/, *v.,* **trimmed, trimming,** *n., adj.,* **trimmer, trimmest,** *adv.* *–v.t.* **1.** to reduce to a neat or orderly state by clipping, paring, pruning, etc.: *to trim a hedge.* **2.** to remove by clipping, paring, pruning or the like: (oft. fol. by *off*): *to trim off loose threads from a ragged edge.* **3.** to modify (opinions, etc.) according to expediency. **4.** *Carp.* to bring (a piece of timber, etc.) to the required smoothness or shape. **5.** *Aeron.* to level off (an aircraft in flight). **6.** *Naut.* **a.** to distribute the load of (a vessel) so that it sits well on the water. **b.** to stow or arrange, as cargo. **c.** to adjust (the sails or yards) with reference to the direction of the wind and the course of the ship. **7.** to position a surfboard on a wave. **8.** to decorate or deck with ornaments, etc.: *to trim a Christmas tree.* **9.** to upholster and line the interior of motor cars, etc. **10.** *U.S. Colloq.* to defeat. **11.** to prepare (a lamp, fire, etc.) for burning. **12.** *Obs.* to dress or array (oft. fol. by *up*). **13.** *Obs.* to equip. *–v.i.* **14.** *Naut.* **a.** to assume a particular position or trim in the water, as a vessel. **b.** to adjust the sails or yards with reference to the direction of the wind and the course of the ship. **15.** to pursue a neutral or cautious course or policy between parties. **16.** to accommodate oneself, or adjust one's principles, etc., to the prevailing climate of opinion. *–n.* **17.** proper condition or order: *to find everything out of trim.* **18.** condition or order of any kind. **19.** *Naut.* **a.** the set of a ship in the water, esp. the most advantageous one. **b.** the balance of a ship. **c.** the difference between the draught at the bow of a vessel and that at the stern. **d.** the condition of a ship with reference to her fitness for sailing. **e.** the adjustment of the sails, etc., with reference to the direction of the wind and the course of the ship. **f.** the condition of a submarine as regards buoyancy. **20.** dress, array, or equipment. **21.** material used for decoration; decorative trimming. **22.** *U.S.* window dressing. **23.** a trimming by cutting, clipping, or the like. **24.** a haircut which neatens the appearance of the hair without changing the style. **25.** that which is eliminated or cut off. **26.** *Aeron.* the attitude of an aeroplane with respect to the three axes at which balance occurs in forward flight with free controls. **27.** *Carp.* the visible woodwork of the interior of a building. **28. a.** the upholstery, knobs, handles, and other equipment inside a motor car. **b.** ornamentation on the exterior of a motor car, esp. in chromium or a contrasting colour. *–adj.* **29.** pleasingly neat or smart in appearance: *trim lawns.* **30.** in good condition or order. **31.** *Obs.* properly prepared or equipped. **32.** *Obs.* good, excellent, or fine. *–adv.* **33.** Also, **trimly.** in a trim manner. [OE *trymman, trymian* strengthen, prepare, from *trum,* adj., firm, active] – **trimness,** *n.*

**trimaran** /'traɪməræn/, *n.* a boat with a main middle hull and two outer hulls (usu. smaller) acting as floats to provide transverse stability. [TRI- + (CATA)MARAN]

**trimer** /'traɪmə/, *n.* a substance whose molecules consist of three molecules of a monomer.

**trimerous** /'trɪmərəs/, *adj.* **1.** consisting of or divided into three parts. **2.** *Entomol.* having three segments or parts. [NL *trimerus,* from Gk *trimerḗs* made up of three parts]

**trimester** /traɪ'mɛstə, trə-/, *n.* **1.** a term or period of three months. **2.** a teaching term of approximately three months in some educational institutions which provide teaching over three terms in a year but accept two such terms as a full year's work. [F *trimestre,* from L *trimestris* of three months] – **trimestral, trimestrial,** *adj.*

**trimeter** /'trɪmətə/, *n.* **1.** a verse of three measures or feet. *–adj.* **2.** consisting of three measures or feet. **3.** *Class. Pros.* composed of six feet or three dipodies. [L *trimetrus* having three measures, from Gk *trímetros*]

**trimetric** /traɪ'mɛtrɪk/, *adj.* **1.** pertaining to or consisting of a trimeter or trimeters. **2.** →**orthorhombic.** Also, **trimetrical.**

**trimetric projection** /– prə'dʒɛkʃən/, *n.* three-dimensional projection with three different linear scales at arbitrary angles.

**trimmer** /'trɪmə/, *n.* **1.** one who or that which trims. **2.** a tool or machine for trimming, clipping, paring, or pruning. **3.** a machine for trimming timber. **4.** *Bldg Trades.* a timber or beam into which one of the ends of a joist or rafter is fitted in the framing about an opening, a chimney, etc. **5.** an apparatus for stowing, arranging, or shifting cargo, coal, or the like. **6.** one who has no firm belief, policy, etc., esp. in politics. **7.** one who accommodates himself to one political party or other as expediency may dictate; an opportunist; timeserver. **8.** one employed to upholster and otherwise finish the interior of a vehicle. **9.** *Colloq.* someone or something excellent: *she's a little trimmer.* **10.** →**trimmer condenser.**

**trimmer condenser** /'– kəndɛnsə/, *n.* a small variable capacitor for fine adjustment in a tuned circuit. Also, **trimmer capacitor.**

**trimming** /'trɪmɪŋ/, *n.* **1.** anything used or serving to trim or decorate: *the trimmings of a Christmas tree.* **2.** a decorative fitting or finish; a garnish. **3.** (*pl.*) *Colloq.* agreeable accompaniments or additions to plain or simple dishes or food. **4.** (*pl.*) pieces cut off in trimming, clipping, paring, or pruning. **5.** the act of one who or that which trims. **6.** a rebuking or reproving. **7.** a beating or thrashing. **8.** *U.S. Colloq.* a defeat: *our team took another trimming yesterday.*

**trimolecular** /traɪmə'lɛkjələ/, *adj.* relating to or having three molecules.

**trimonthly** /traɪ'mʌnθli/, *adj.* taking place once each three months.

**trimorph** /'traɪmɔf/, *n.* **1.** a substance existing in three structurally distinct forms; a trimorphous substance. **2.** any one of the three forms.

**trimorphism** /traɪ'mɔfɪzəm/, *n.* **1.** *Zool.* the occurrence of three forms distinct in structure, colouration, etc., among animals of the same species. **2.** *Crystall.* the property of some substances of crystallising in three structurally distinct forms. **3.** the property or condition of occurring in three distinct forms. [Gk *trimorphos* having three forms + -ISM] – **trimorphic, trimorphous,** *adj.*

**trim tab** /'trɪm tæb/, *n.* a small, adjustable airfoil fitted to the trailing edge of the control surface, to aid in balancing or trimming the aircraft.

**trinal** /'traɪnəl/, *adj.* threefold; triple; trine. [LL *trīnālis,* from L *trīnus* threefold + *-ālis* -AL[1]]

**trinary** /'traɪnəri/, *adj.* consisting of three parts, or proceeding by three; ternary.

**trine** /traɪn/, *adj.* **1.** threefold; triple. **2.** *Astrol.* denoting or pertaining to the trigon aspect of two planets distant from each other 120°, or the third part of the zodiac. *–n.* **3.** a set or group of three; a triad. **4.** *Astrol.* the trine aspect of two planets. [ME, from L *trīnus* threefold]

**Trinidad and Tobago,** *n.* a country in the west Indies consisting of the islands of Trinidad and Tobago.

**trinitrine** /traɪ'naɪtrən/, *n.* a nitroglycerine preparation used in the treatment of angina pectoris. Also, **trinitrin.**

**trinitro-,** a combining form meaning 'of three nitro groups', as in *trinitrobenzene.*

**trinitrobenzene** /traɪˌnaɪtroʊ'bɛnzin, -bɛn'zin/, *n.* any of three highly explosive yellow crystalline compounds, $C_6H_3(NO_2)_3$, none of which is produced commercially. *Abbrev.:* TNB, T.N.B.

**trinitrocresol** /traɪˌnaɪtroʊ'krisɒl/, *n.* a yellow crystalline compound, $CH_3C_6H(OH)(NO_2)_3$, used in high explosives.

**trinitron** /'trɪnətrɒn/, *adj.* of or pertaining to a type of picture tube for colour television receivers. [Trademark]

**trinitrotoluene** /traɪˌnaɪtroʊ'tɒljuin/, *n.* a high explosive, $CH_3C_6H_2(NO_2)_3$, exploded by detonators but unaffected by ordinary friction or shock. *Abbrev.:* TNT, T.N.T. Also, **trinitrotoluol** /traɪˌnaɪtroʊ'tɒljuɒl/.

**trinity** /'trɪnəti/, *n., pl.* **-ties.** **1.** a group of three; a triad. **2.** the state of being threefold or triple; threeness. **3.** (*cap.*) the union of three persons (Father, Son, and Holy Ghost) in one Godhead, or the threefold personality of the one Divine Being (**the Holy Trinity** or **Blessed Trinity**). [ME *trinite,* from OF., from L *trinitas* triad, trio, trinity]

**Trinity term** /ˈtrɪnəti tɜm/, *n.* the second term of the academic year at some universities.

**trinket** /ˈtrɪŋkət/, *n.* **1.** any small fancy article, bit of jewellery, or the like, usu. of little value. **2.** anything trifling. [orig. uncert.]

**trinodal** /traɪˈnoudl/, *adj. Bot., etc.* having three nodes or joints. [L *trinōdis* having three knots + -AL[1]]

**trinomial** /traɪˈnoumiəl/, *adj.* **1.** *Alg.* consisting of or pertaining to three terms connected by the sign +, the sign −, or both of these. **2.** *Zool., Bot.* **a.** denoting a name comprising three terms, as of genus, species, and subspecies or variety. **b.** characterised by the use of such names. *–n.* **3.** *Alg.* a trinomial expression, as $a + b - c$. [TRI- + (BI)NOMIAL] **– trinomially,** *adv.*

**trio** /ˈtriou/, *n., pl.* **trios. 1.** a musical composition for three voices or instruments. **2.** a company of three singers or players. **3.** a subordinate division of a minuet, scherzo, march, etc., usu. in a contrasted key and style (perhaps orig. written for three instruments or in three parts). **4.** any group of three persons or things. [It., from *tre* three, modelled after *duo*]

**triode** /ˈtraɪoud/, *n.* a radio valve containing three electrodes, usu. an anode, a grid, and a cathode. [TRI- + -ODE[2]]

**trioecious** /traɪˈiʃəs/, *adj.* having male, female, and hermaphrodite flowers on different plants. Also, *U.S.,* **triecious.** [NL *trioecia* (from *tri-* TRI- + Gk *oikíon* house) + -OUS] **– trioeciously,** *adv.*

**triolein** /traɪˈouliən/, *n.* →**olein.**

**triolet** /ˈtraɪoulɛt/, *n.* a short poem of fixed form, consisting of eight lines using two rhymes: ab aa abab. The first line is repeated as the fourth and seventh lines, and the second line is repeated as the eighth. [F; orig. uncert.]

**trioxide** /traɪˈɒksaɪd/, *n.* an oxide containing three oxygen atoms, as $As_2O_3$. Also, **trioxid** /traɪˈɒksəd/.

**trip** /trɪp/, *n., v.,* **tripped, tripping.** *–n.* **1.** a journey or voyage. **2.** a journey, voyage, or run made by a boat, train, or the like, between two points. **3.** a journey made for pleasure; excursion. **4.** *Colloq.* a quantity of LSD prepared in some form for sale. **5.** *Colloq.* a period under the influence of a hallucinatory drug. **6.** a stumble. **7.** a sudden impeding or catching of a person's foot so as to throw him down, esp. in wrestling. **8.** a slip, mistake, or blunder. **9.** a wrong step in conduct. **10.** an act of stepping lightly; a light or nimble movement of the feet. **11.** *Mach.* **a.** a projecting part, catch, or the like for starting or checking some movement. **b.** a sudden starting or releasing. *–v.i.* **12.** to stumble: *to trip over a child's toy.* **13.** to make a slip or mistake, as in a statement; make a wrong step in conduct. **14.** to step lightly or nimbly; skip; dance. **15.** to go with a light, quick tread. **16.** to tip or tilt. **17.** *Naut.* (of a boom) to roll under water in a seaway. **18.** *Horol.* to move over and beyond the pallet, as a tooth on an escapement wheel. **19.** *Rare.* to make a journey or excursion. **20.** *Colloq.* **a.** to take LSD. **b.** to hallucinate under the influence of LSD or other drugs. **c.** to have an exhilarating experience similar to hallucination. *–v.t.* **21.** to cause to stumble (oft. fol. by *up*): *the rug tripped him up.* **22.** cause to fail; hinder; overthrow. **23.** to cause to make a slip or error (oft. fol. by *up*): *to trip up a witness by artful questions.* **24.** to catch in a slip or error. **25.** to perform with a light or tripping step, as a dance. **26.** to dance upon (ground, etc.). **27.** to tip or tilt. **28.** *Naut.* **a.** to break out (an anchor) by turning it over or lifting it from the bottom by a tripping line. **b.** to tip or turn (a yard) from a horizontal to a vertical position. **c.** to lift (an upper mast) before lowering. **29.** to operate, start, or set free (a mechanism, weight, etc.) by suddenly releasing a catch, clutch, or the like. **30.** *Mach.* to release or operate suddenly (a catch, clutch, etc.). [ME *trippe,* from OF *tripper* strike with the feet, from Gmc; cf. MD *trippen*]

**tripalmitin** /traɪˈpælmətən/, *n.* →**palmitin.**

**triparted** /traɪˈpatəd/, *adj.* divided into three parts.

**tripartite** /traɪˈpataɪt/, *adj.* **1.** divided into or consisting of three parts. **2.** *Bot.* divided into three parts by incisions which extend nearly to the base, as a leaf. **3.** participated in by three parties, as a treaty. [ME, from L *tripartītus* divided into three parts] **– tripartitely,** *adv.* **– tripartism,** *n.*

**tripartition** /traɪpaˈtɪʃən/, *n.* division into three parts.

**trip-check** /ˈtrɪp-tʃɛk/, *n.* a mechanical check of a motor vehicle before a long journey.

**tripe** /traɪp/, *n.* **1.** the first and second divisions of the stomach of a ruminant, esp. of the ox kind, prepared for use as food. **2.** *Colloq.* anything poor or worthless, esp. written work; nonsense; rubbish. **3.** *Colloq.* **beat the tripe out of, a.** to beat up. **b.** to defeat utterly. [ME, from OF, ult. from Ar. *tarb* folds of peritoneum]

**tripedal** /ˈtraɪpɛdl, traɪˈpɛdl/, *adj.* having three feet. [L *tripedālis*]

**tripehound** /ˈtraɪphaund/, *n. Colloq.* (*joc.*) a dog.

**tripeman** /ˈtraɪpmæn/, *n.* a person who handles the processing of tripes in a meatworks.

**tripersonal** /traɪˈpɜsənəl/, *adj.* consisting of or existing in three persons, as the Godhead.

**tripetalous** /traɪˈpɛtələs/, *adj. Bot.* having three petals.

**triphammer** /ˈtrɪphæmə/, *n.* a heavy hammer raised and then let fall by means of some tripping device, as a cam. Also, **trip hammer.**

**triphenylmethane** /traɪˌfɛnəlˈmiθeɪn, -ˌfinəl-/, *n.* a colourless, crystalline organic compound, $(C_6H_5)_3CH$, from which many dyes (the **triphenylmethane dyes**) are derived.

**triphosphopyridine nucleotide** /traɪˌfɒsfəˌpɪrədin ˈnjukliətaɪd/, *n.* a phosphate ester of nicotinamide adenine dinucleotide. *Abbrev.:* TPN

**triphthong** /ˈtrɪfθɒŋ/, *n.* **1.** a union of three vowel sounds pronounced in one syllable. **2.** →**trigraph.** [NL *triphthongus,* from MGk *triphthongos* with three vowels] **– triphthongal** /trɪfˈθɒŋgəl/, *adj.*

**triphyllous** /traɪˈfɪləs/, *adj. Bot.* having three leaves.

**tripinnate** /traɪˈpɪneɪt, -ət/, *adj.* bipinnate, as a leaf, with the divisions also pinnate. Also, **tripinnated. – tripinnately,** *adv.*

**tripl.,** triplicate.

**triplane** /ˈtraɪpleɪn/, *n.* an aeroplane with three supporting wings, one above another.

triplane

**triple** /ˈtrɪpəl/, *adj., n., v.,* **-pled, -pling.** *–adj.* **1.** threefold; consisting of three parts: *a triple knot.* **2.** of three kinds. **3.** three times as great. **4.** *Internat. Law.* tripartite. *–n.* **5.** an amount, number, etc., three times as great as another. **6.** something triple or threefold; a triad. *–v.t.* **7.** to make triple. *–v.i.* **8.** to become triple. [ME, from L *triplus,* from Gk *triploûs* threefold] **– triply** /ˈtrɪpli/, *adv.*

**triple bond** /– ˈbɒnd/, *n.* a chemical linkage between atoms in a molecule consisting of three covalent bonds, often represented in formulas by three lines, as in acetylene, $CH\equiv CH$.

**triple-expansion** /trɪpəl-əkˈspænʃən/, *adj.* denoting or pertaining to a steam-engine in which the steam is expanded in three cylinders in succession, the exhaust steam from the first cylinder being the driving steam for the second, and so on.

**triple jump** /ˈtrɪpəl dʒʌmp/, *n.* an Olympic field event, the object of which is to cover the greatest possible distance by taking in a continuous movement, a hop, a step, and a jump. Also, **hop, step, and jump.**

**triple measure** /– ˈmɛʒə/, *n.* →**triple time.**

**triple-nerved** /ˈtrɪpəl-nɜvd/, *adj.* denoting a leaf in which two prominent nerves emerge from the middle nerve a little above its base.

**triple point** /ˈtrɪpəl pɔɪnt/, *n.* the equilibrium temperature of the solid, liquid and vapour phases of a substance; for water this is 273.16 K.

**triplet** /ˈtrɪplət/, *n.* **1.** one of three children born at one birth. **2.** (*pl.*) three offspring born at one birth. **3.** any group or combination of three. **4.** *Pros.* three successive verses or lines, esp. when rhyming and of the same length; a stanza of three lines. **5.** *Music.* a group of three notes to be performed in the time of two ordinary notes of the same kind. **6.** an assembled imitation gem with three parts, the centre one giving the colour, the top and bottom supplying the wearing qualities. **7.** a thin bar of opal set between two layers of plastic, or one layer of potch and one of crystal. **8.** (*pl.*) (in some card games) three cards of the same denomination. **9.** *Chem.* a chemical bond consisting of three electrons shared between two atoms. [from TRIPLE, modelled after DOUBLET. Cf. F *triplet*]

**tripletail** /ˈtrɪpəlteɪl/, *n.* a large food fish, *Lobotes surinamensis,* of the warmer waters of the Indian, Pacific and Atlantic Oceans and the Mediterranean Sea, with the lobes of its dorsal and anal fins extending backwards and with the caudal fin suggesting a three-lobed tail.

**triple time** /ˈtrɪpəl taɪm/, *n.* time or rhythm characterised by three beats to the bar with an accent on the first beat. Also, **triple measure.**

**triplex** /ˈtrɪplɛks/, *adj.* **1.** threefold; triple. *–n.* **2.** something triple. **3.** →**triple time.** [L: threefold]

**triplicate** /ˈtrɪpləkeɪt/, *v.,* **-cated, -cating;** /ˈtrɪplәkәt/, *adj., n.* *–v.t.* **1.** to make threefold; triple. **2.** to make or produce a third time or in a third instance. *–adj.* **3.** threefold; triple; tripartite. *–n.* **4.** one of three identical things. [L *triplicātus,* pp., tripled] – **triplication** /trɪpləˈkeɪʃən/, *n.*

**triplicity** /trɪˈplɪsәti/, *n., pl.* **-ties. 1.** the state of being triple; triple character. **2.** a group or combination of three; triad. **3.** *Astrol.* a set of three signs of the zodiac.

**triploid** /ˈtrɪplɔɪd/, *adj.* **1.** having or relating to three times the haploid number of chromosomes. *–n.* **2.** a triploid organism. [Gk *triplóos* + (HAP)LOID]

**tripmeter** /ˈtrɪpmitә/, *n.* an odometer which can be manually reset to measure individual journeys.

**tripod** /ˈtraɪpɒd/, *n.* **1.** a stool, pedestal, or the like with three legs. **2.** a three-legged stand, as for a camera. [L *tripūs,* from Gk *trípous* three-footed]

**tripodal** /ˈtrɪpədl/, *adj.* **1.** pertaining to or having the form of a tripod. **2.** having three feet or legs.

**tripodic** /traɪˈpɒdɪk/, *adj.* having or using three feet or legs.

**tripody** /ˈtrɪpədi/, *n., pl.* **-dies.** *Pros.* a group or verse of three feet. [Gk *tripodía*]

**tripos** /ˈtraɪpɒs/, *n., pl.* **triposes.** (at Cambridge University) any of various final honours examinations for the B.A. degree. [L, pseudo-Hellenisation of *tripūs* tripod]

**tripper** /ˈtrɪpә/, *n.* **1.** one who or that which trips. **2.** *Mach.* **a.** a signal device; a trip. **b.** an apparatus causing a signal, or other operating mechanism, to be tripped or activated. **3.** *Colloq.* one who goes on a pleasure trip or excursion.

**trippet** /ˈtrɪpәt/, *n.* a projection, cam, or the like, for striking some other part at regular intervals.

**tripping** /ˈtrɪpɪŋ/, *adj.* **1.** light and quick, as the step, pace, etc. **2.** proceeding with a light, easy movement or rhythm. – **trippingly,** *adv.*

**tripping line** /ˈ– laɪn/, *n.* a line attached to the crown of an anchor to facilitate moving it from the bottom.

**trippy** /ˈtrɪpi/, *adj. Colloq.* exhilarating, as of a hallucinogenic trip; psychedelic.

**tripterous** /ˈtrɪptərəs/, *adj.* three-winged; having three wings or winglike expansions. [TRI- + Gk *pterón* wing + -OUS]

**triptych** /ˈtrɪptɪk/, *n.* **1.** *Art.* a set of three panels or compartments side by side, bearing pictures, carvings, or the like. **2.** a hinged or folding three-leaved writing tablet. [Gk *tríptychos* of three plates]

**trip-wire** /ˈtrɪp-waɪә/, *n.* a concealed wire designed to set off an alarm, explosive device, etc., when touched or pulled.

**triquetral** /traɪˈkwitrәl, -ˈkwɛtrәl/, *adj.* **1.** →**triquetrous.** *–n.* **2.** one of the eight bones of the carpus.

**triquetrous** /traɪˈkwitrәs, -ˈkwɛtrәs/, *adj.* **1.** three-sided; triangular. **2.** having a triangular cross-section. Also, **triquetral.** [L *triquetrus* three-cornered]

**triradiate** /traɪˈreɪdiәt, -eɪt/, *adj.* having, or consisting of, three rays or raylike processes. Also, **triradiated.** – **triradiately,** *adv.*

**trireme** /ˈtraɪrim/, *n.* a galley with three rows or tiers of oars on each side, one above another, used chiefly as a warship. [L *trirēmis*]

**trisaccharide** /traɪˈsækәraɪd/, *n.* a carbohydrate composed of three monosaccharide units, and hydrolysable to a monosaccharide or a mixture of monosaccharides.

**trisect** /traɪˈsɛkt/, *v.t.* to divide into three parts, esp. into three equal parts. [TRI- + L *sectus,* pp., cut] – **trisection,** *n.* – **trisector,** *n.*

**trisepalous** /traɪˈsɛpәlәs/, *adj.* having three sepals.

**triseptate** /traɪˈsɛpteɪt/, *adj.* having three septa.

**triserial** /traɪˈsɪәriәl/, *adj.* arranged in three series or rows.

**triskaidekaphobia** /trɪsˌkaɪdɛkәˈfoubiә/, *n.* fear of the number thirteen.

**triskelion** /trɪsˈkɛliɒn, -әn/, *n., pl.* **-kelia** /-ˈkɛliә/. a symbolic figure consisting of three legs, arms, or branches radiating from a common centre. Also, **triskele** /ˈtrɪskil/. [TRI- + Gk *skélos* leg + *-ion,* diminutive suffix]

**trismus** /ˈtrɪzmәs/, *n.* →**lockjaw.** [NL, from Gk *trismós* a grinding] – **trismic,** *adj.*

**trisoctahedron** /trɪsˌɒktәˈhidrәn/, *n., pl.* **-drons, -dra** /-drә/. a solid bounded by twenty-four equal faces, three corresponding to each face of an octahedron, called (esp. in crystallography) **trigonal trisoctahedron** when the faces are triangles, and **tetragonal trisoctahedron** when the faces are quadrilaterals. [Gk *trís* thrice + OCTAHEDRON] – **trisoctahedral,** *adj.*

**trispermous** /traɪˈspɜmәs/, *adj. Bot.* three-seeded. [TRI- + Gk *-spermos* having seed]

**tristearin** /traɪˈstɪәrәn/, *n.* →**stearin** (def. 1).

**tristichous** /traɪˈstɪkәs/, *adj.* arranged in three rows. [Gk *trístichos* of three rows]

**tristylous** /traɪˈstaɪlәs/, *adj. Bot.* having three styles. [TRI- + Gk *-stylos* columned]

**trisulphide** /traɪˈsʌlfaɪd/, *n.* a sulphide containing three sulphur atoms.

**trisyllable** /ˈtraɪsɪlәbәl/, *n.* a word of three syllables, as *telephone.* – **trisyllabic** /traɪsәˈlæbɪk/, **trisyllabical** /traɪsәˈlæbɪkәl/, *adj.* – **trisyllabically** /traɪsәˈlæbɪkli/, *adv.*

**tritanope** /ˈtraɪtәnoup, ˈtrɪt-/, *n.* one who has tritanopia.

**tritanopia** /traɪtәˈnoupiә, trɪtә-/, *n.* a form of defective colour vision in which hue discrimination is very poor in the green to blue region of the spectrum. [NL, from Gk *trítos* third + *an-* AN-[1] + *opia* -OPIA]

**trite** /traɪt/, *adj.,* **triter, tritest. 1.** hackneyed by constant use or repetition; commonplace: *a trite saying.* **2.** *Archaic.* rubbed or worn by use. [L *trītus,* pp., rubbed, worn] – **tritely,** *adv.* – **triteness,** *n.*

**tritheism** /ˈtraɪθiɪzәm/, *n.* belief in three Gods, esp. in the doctrine that the three persons of the Trinity (Father, Son, and Holy Ghost) are three distinct Gods, each an independent centre of self-consciousness and self-determination. – **tritheist,** *n., adj.* – **tritheistic** /traɪθiˈɪstɪk/, **tritheistical** /traɪθiˈɪstɪkәl/, *adj.*

**tritium** /ˈtrɪtiәm/, *n.* a radioactive isotope of hydrogen containing two neutrons and a proton, with a mass number of 3.

**triton** /ˈtraɪtn/, *n.* **1.** any of various marine gastropods constituting the family Tritonidae (esp. of the genus *Triton*), having a large, spiral, often beautifully coloured shell. **2.** the shell of a triton. **3.** *Physics.* the nucleus of a tritium atom. **4.** a newt. [from *Triton,* in classical mythology, a sea-god represented as having the head and trunk of a man and the tail of a fish, and bearing a conch-shell trumpet]

triton

**tritone** /ˈtraɪtoun/, *n.* an interval consisting of three whole tones. [ML *tritonus,* from Gk *trítonos* having three tones]

**triturable** /ˈtrɪtʃәrәbәl/, *adj.* that may be triturated.

**triturate** /ˈtrɪtʃәreɪt/, *v.,* **-rated, -rating,** *n. –v.t.* **1.** to reduce to fine particles or powder by rubbing, grinding, bruising, or the like; pulverise. *–n.* **2.** a triturated substance. **3.** a trituration. [LL *trītūrātus,* pp., threshed] – **triturator,** *n.*

**trituration** /trɪtʃәˈreɪʃәn/, *n.* **1.** the act of triturating. **2.** the state of being triturated. **3.** *Pharm.* **a.** a mixture of a medicinal substance with milk sugar, triturated to an impalpable powder. **b.** any triturated substance.

**triumph** /ˈtraɪʌmf, ˈtraɪәmf/, *n.* **1.** the act or fact of being victorious, or triumphing; victory; conquest. **2.** a notable achievement; striking success. **3.** the exultation of victory; joy over success. **4.** *Rom. Hist.* the ceremonial entrance into ancient Rome of a victorious commander with his army, spoils, captives, etc., authorised by the senate in honour of an important military or naval achievement. **5.** *Obs.* a public pageant, spectacle, or the like. *–v.i.* **6.** to gain a victory; be victorious. **7.** to gain mastery; prevail. **8.** to achieve success. **9.** to exult over victory; rejoice over success. **10.** to be elated or glad; rejoice proudly; glory. **11.** to celebrate a triumph, as a victorious Roman commander. *–v.t.* **12.** *Obs.* to conquer; triumph over. [ME *triumphe,* OE *triumpha,* from L *triumphus*] – **triumpher,** *n.*

**triumphal** /traɪˈʌmfəl/, *adj.* **1.** of or pertaining to a triumph. **2.** celebrating or commemorating a triumph or victory.

**triumphant** /traɪˈʌmfənt/, *adj.* **1.** having achieved victory or success; victorious; successful. **2.** exulting over victory; rejoicing over success; exultant. **3.** *Rare.* triumphal. **4.** *Obs.* splendid; magnificent. [L *triumphans,* ppr., triumphing] – **triumphantly,** *adv.*

**triumph card** /ˈtraɪʌmf kad/, *n.* one of the 22 cards in the tarot pack which bears a symbolic or mythological character, functioning as trumps in the old game of tarots, and now chiefly used in cartomancy, each card having a particular mystical significance ascribed to it.

**triumvir** /ˈtraɪəmvɪə/, *n.* **1.** *Rom. Hist.* one of three officers or magistrates sharing the same function. **2.** one of three persons associated in any office. [L *triumvirī,* pl., backformation from *trium virōrum* of three men] – **triumviral** /traɪˈʌmvərəl/, *adj.*

**triumvirate** /traɪˈʌmvərət/, *n.* **1.** *Rom. Hist.* the office or magistracy of a triumvir. **2.** the government of three joint officers or magistrates. **3.** a coalition of three magistrates or rulers for joint administration. **4.** any association of three in office or authority. **5.** any group or set of three. [L *triumvirātus*]

**triune** /ˈtraɪjun/, *adj.* **1.** three in one; constituting a trinity, as the Godhead. *–n.* **2.** (*cap.*) the Trinity. [TRI- + L *ūnus* one]

**triunity** /traɪˈjunəti/, *n., pl.* **-ties.** the Trinity.

**trivalent** /traɪˈveɪlənt, ˈtrɪvələnt/, *adj.* having a valency of three. – **trivalence, trivalency,** *n.*

**trivalent carbon** /– ˈkabən/, *n.* a carbon atom which utilises only three of its four valencies.

**trivalve** /ˈtraɪvælv/, *adj.* having three valves, as a shell.

**trivet** /ˈtrɪvət/, *n.* **1.** a small metal plate with short legs put under a hot platter or dish at the table. **2.** a three-footed or three-legged stand or support, esp. one of iron placed over a fire to hold cooking vessels or the like. [ME *trevet,* OE *trefet,* apparently b. L *tripēs* and OE *thrifēte* three-footed (with VL *-e-* for L *-i-*)]

**trivia** /ˈtrɪviə/, *n.pl.* inessential, unimportant, or inconsequential things; trifles; trivialities. [apparently backformation from TRIVIAL]

**trivial** /ˈtrɪviəl/, *adj.* **1.** of little importance; trifling; insignificant. **2.** commonplace; ordinary. **3.** *Biol.* (of names of animals and plants) specific, as distinguished from *generic.* [ME, from L *triviālis* belonging to the crossroads, (hence) common] – **trivially,** *adv.*

**trivialise** /ˈtrɪviəlaɪz/, *v.t.,* **-lised, -lising.** to make trivial or unimportant. Also, **trivialize.** – **trivialisation** /ˌtrɪviəlaɪˈzeɪʃən/, *n.*

**trivialism** /ˈtrɪviəlɪzəm/, *n.* **1.** trivial character. **2.** something trivial.

**triviality** /trɪviˈæləti/, *n., pl.* **-ties.** **1.** something trivial; a trivial matter, affair, remark, etc. **2.** Also, **trivialness.** trivial quality or character.

**trivium** /ˈtrɪviəm/, *n.* (during the Middle Ages) the lower division of the seven liberal arts, comprising grammar, rhetoric, and logic. Cf. **quadrivium.** [ML, special use of L *trivium* public place (lit. place where three roads meet)]

**triweekly** /traɪˈwikli/, *adv., adj., n., pl.* **-lies.** *–adv.* **1.** every three weeks. **2.** three times a week. *–adj.* **3.** occurring or appearing three times a week. **4.** occurring or appearing every three weeks. *–n.* **5.** a triweekly publication.

**-trix,** a suffix of feminine agent-nouns, as in *executrix.* Cf. **-or**[2]. [L]

**trocar** /ˈtroʊka/, *n.* a sharp pointed surgical instrument enclosed in a cannula, used for withdrawing fluid from a cavity, as the abdominal cavity, and to allow for the escape of gas in cases of bloat. [earlier *trocart,* from F, var. of *trois-carts,* lit., three-faced]

**trochaic** /troʊˈkeɪɪk/, *Pros. –adj.* **1.** pertaining to the trochee. **2.** consisting of or employing a trochee or trochees. *–n.* **3.** a trochee. **4.** (*usu. pl.*) a verse or poem consisting of trochees. [L *trochaicus,* from Gk *trochaikós*]

**trochal** /ˈtroʊkəl/, *adj.* resembling a wheel. [Gk *trochós* wheel + -AL[1]]

**trochanter** /trəˈkæntə/, *n.* **1.** *Anat., Zool.* (in many vertebrates) a prominence or process on the upper part of the femur. **2.** *Zool.* (in insects and other arthropods) the lower segment of the leg. [F, from Gk]

**troche** /troʊʃ/, *n.* a small tablet, esp. a circular one, made of some medicinal substance worked into a paste with sugar and mucilage or the like, and dried. [backformation from obs. *trochisk* troche, from L *trochiscus,* from Gk *trochískos*]

**trochee** /ˈtroʊki/, *n.* (in prosody) a metrical foot of two syllables, a long followed by a short, or an accented followed by an unaccented. [L *trochaeus,* from Gk *trochaîos* running]

**trochilus** /ˈtrɒkələs/, *n., pl.* **-li** /-laɪ/. **1.** any of several small Old World warblers, as the willow warbler (*Phylloscopus trochilus*). **2.** →**hummingbird.** **3.** →**crocodile bird.** [L, from Gk *trochîlos*]

**trochlea** /ˈtrɒkliə/, *n., pl.* **-leae** /-lii/. a pulley-like structure or arrangement of parts affording a smooth surface upon which another part glides, as a tendon or bone. [L, from Gk *trochileía* pulley]

**trochlear** /ˈtrɒkliə/, *adj.* **1.** *Anat.* belonging to or connected with a trochlea. **2.** *Physiol., Anat.* pulley-like. Also, **trochleariform** /trɒkliˈærəfɔm/.

**trochlear nerve** /ˈ– nɜv/, *n.* the fourth cranial nerve in vertebrates.

**trochoid** /ˈtroʊkɔɪd/, *n.* **1.** *Geom.* a curve traced by a point rigidly connected with, but not generally on the circumference of, a circle which rolls, without slipping, upon a curve, circle, or straight line. *–adj.* **2.** wheel-like; rotating like a wheel, as a joint. [Gk *trochoeidês* round like a wheel] – **trochoidal** /troʊˈkɔɪdl/, *adj.* – **trochoidally** /troʊˈkɔɪdəli/, *adv.*

**trochophore** /ˈtrɒkəfɔ/, *n.* a ciliate free-swimming larva common to several invertebrate groups.

**trochus** /ˈtroʊkəs/, *n.* a gastropod mollusc of the family Trochidae, having a conical shell.

**trod** /trɒd/, *v.* past tense and past participle of **tread.**

**trodden** /ˈtrɒdn/, *v.* past participle of **tread.**

**trode** /troʊd/, *v. Archaic.* past tense of **tread.**

**troglodyte** /ˈtrɒglədaɪt/, *n.* **1.** a caveman or cave-dweller. **2.** a person living in seclusion. **3.** one unacquainted with affairs of the world. **4.** *Colloq.* anyone thought to be primitive, barbaric, unintelligent, or insensitive. [L *trōglodyta,* from Gk *trōglodýtēs* one who creeps into holes] – **troglodytic** /trɒgləˈdɪtɪk/, **troglodytical** /trɒgləˈdɪtɪkəl/, *adj.*

**trogon** /ˈtroʊgɒn/, *n.* any bird of the family Trogonidae, esp. of the genus *Trogon,* of tropical and subtropical regions, notable for brilliant plumage, as the quetzal. [NL, from Gk: gnawing]

trogon

**trog suit** /ˈtrɒg sut/, *n. Colloq.* an outfit suitable for caving expeditions.

**troika** /ˈtrɔɪkə/, *n.* **1.** a Russian vehicle drawn by a team of three horses abreast. **2.** a team of three horses driven abreast. **3.** any group of three persons acting together for a common purpose. [Russ.]

**Trojan** /ˈtroʊdʒən/, *n. in the phrase,* **work like a Trojan,** to work very hard. [Me, from L *Trōjānus* Trojan, a native or inhabitant of ancient Troy]

**Trojan Horse** /– ˈhɒs/, *n.* one who or that which is designed to subvert or undermine from within. [in classical legend, the gigantic, hollow, wooden figure of a horse, filled with armed Greeks, and brought into Troy, thus ensuring the destruction of the city]

**troll**[1] /troʊl/, *v.t.* **1.** to sing or utter in a full, rolling voice. **2.** to sing in the manner of a round or catch. **3.** to fish by trolling. **4.** to move (the line or bait) in doing this. **5.** to cause to turn round and round; roll. **6.** *Obs.* to pass from one to another, as a bowl of drink at table. *–v.i.* **7.** to sing with a full, rolling voice; give forth full, rolling tones. **8.** to be uttered or sounded in such tones. **9.** to fish with a moving line, as one worked up and down in fishing for pike with a rod, or one trailed behind a boat. **10.** to roll; turn round and round. **11.** *Obs.* to move nimbly, as the tongue in speaking. *–n.* **12.** a song whose parts are sung in succession; a round. **13.** the act of trolling. **14.** a lure used in trolling for fish. **15.** the fishing line containing the lure and hook for use in trolling. [ME *trollen* roll, stroll, from OF *troller,* from MHG *trollen*] – **troller,** *n.*

**troll**[2] /trɒl/, *n.* (in Scandinavian folklore) one of a race of supernatural beings, sometimes conceived as giants and sometimes as dwarfs, inhabiting caves or subterranean dwellings. [Scand.; cf. Icel. *troll*]

**trolley** /'trɒli/, *n., pl.* **-leys,** *v.* *–n.* **1.** any of various kinds of low carts or vehicles. **2.** a small table on castors for carrying dishes, serving food, etc. **3.** a low truck running on rails, used on railways, in factories, mines, etc. **4.** a pulley travelling on an overhead track, or grooved metallic wheel or skid carried on the end of a sprung pole **(trolley pole)** by an electric tram or trolleybus and held in contact with an overhead conductor, usu. a suspended wire **(trolley wire),** from which it collects the current for the propulsion of the vehicle. **5.** a trolleybus. **6.** *U.S.* a tram. **7. off one's trolley,** *Colloq.* crazy; mad; insane. *–v.t.* **8.** to convey by trolley. *–v.i.* **9.** to go by trolley. [probably from TROLL[1]] – **trolleyless,** *adj.*

**trolleybus** /'trɒlibʌs/, *n.* an electric bus, whose motor draws current from two overhead wires by means of twin trolley poles. Also, **trolley-bus, trolley bus.**

**trolley car** /'trɒli ka/, *n. U.S.* a tram.

**trollop** /'trɒləp/, *n.* **1.** an untidy or slovenly woman; a slattern. **2.** an immoral woman; prostitute. [probably from TROLL[1], *v.*]

**trom.,** trombone.

**trombidiasis** /trɒmbə'daɪəsəs/, *n. Vet. Sci.* the condition of being infested with chiggers. [NL, from L *trombidium* red mite + *-iāsis* -IASIS]

**trombone** /trɒm'boun/, *n.* **1.** a musical wind instrument consisting of a cylindrical metal tube expanding into a bell and bent twice in U shape, usu. equipped with a slide. **2.** a variety of gramma which has a long curved fruit, bulbous at one end. [It., from *tromba* trumpet, from OHG *trumba*] – **trombonist,** *n.*

**trommel** /'trɒməl/, *n.* a revolving cylindrical or conical sieve, used for grading rock and ore according to size. [G *Trommel* drum]

**trompe** /trɒmp/, *n.* the apparatus by which the blast is produced in one type of forge. The principle is that water can be made to fall through a pipe in such a way that it will draw in through side openings a considerable amount of air which can be utilised as a constant current or blast. [F: lit., trump]

**trompe l'oeil** /trɒmp 'lɜjə/, *n.* a type of painting intended to deceive the eye; illusionism. [F: trick the eye]

**trona** /'trounə/, *n.* a mineral, greyish, or yellowish hydrous sodium carbonate and bicarbonate, $Na_2CO_3 \cdot NaHCO_3 \cdot 2H_2O$, occurring in dried or partly evaporated lake basins. [Swed., from Ar. *trōn.* Cf. NATRON]

**troop** /trup/, *n.* **1.** an assemblage of persons or things; a company or band. **2.** a great number or multitude. **3.** *Mil.* a body of soldiers being a subdivision of a cavalry regiment. **4.** (*pl.*) a body of soldiers, marines, etc. **5.** a unit of 32 boy scouts, equal to four patrols. **6.** a herd, flock, or swarm. **7.** *Rare.* a band or troupe of actors. *–v.i.* **8.** to gather in a company; flock together. **9.** to go or come in great numbers. **10.** to walk as if on a march. **11.** to go, pass, or march in rank or order. **12.** to associate or consort (fol. by *with*). *–v.t.* **13.** to assemble in, form into, or unite with a troop or troops. **14.** *Mil.* to carry (the flag or colours) in a ceremonial way before troops: *trooping the colour.* [F *troupe,* from LL *troppus* flock, from Gmc]

**troop-carrier** /'trup-kæriə/, *n.* a motorised vehicle, aircraft, or ship, used to transport troops.

**trooper** /'trupə/, *n.* **1.** a cavalry soldier. **2.** a private soldier in a cavalry regiment. **3.** this rank. **4.** (formerly) a mounted policeman. **5.** a cavalry horse. **6.** a troopship. **7. swear like a trooper,** to swear vigorously. [from TROOP. Cf. F *troupier*]

**troopship** /'trupʃɪp/, *n.* a ship for the conveyance of military troops; a transport.

**troostite**[1] /'trustaɪt/, *n.* **1.** the microstructure of hardened steel, consisting of ferrite and finely divided cementite, which is produced on tempering martensite below 450°C. **2.** Also, **troostitic pearlite.** the constituent produced by the decomposition of austenite when cooled at a rate intermediate between that which will produce a martensitic or a sorbitic structure. [named after L. *Troost,* d. 1911, French chemist] – **troostitic** /tru'stɪtɪk/, *adj.*

**troostite**[2] /'trustaɪt/, *n.* a variety of willemite, $Zn_2SiO_4$, occurring in large reddish crystals in which the zinc is partly replaced by manganese. [named after G. *Troost,* 1776-1850, U.S. metallurgist]

**trop.,** tropical.

**tropaeolin** /trou'piələn/, *n.* any of a number of orange or yellow azo dyes of complex composition.

**tropaeolum** /trou'piələm/, *n., pl.* **-lums, -la** /-lə/. any of the pungent herbs constituting the genus *Tropaeolum,* native to tropical America, species of which are well known in cultivation under the name of nasturtium. [NL, diminutive of L *tropaeum* TROPHY]

**-tropal,** an adjective combining form identical in meaning with **-tropic.**

**trope** /troup/, *n.* **1.** *Rhet.* **a.** →**figure of speech. b.** a word or phrase so used. **2.** a phrase, sentence, or verse formerly interpolated in a liturgical text to amplify or embellish. [L *tropus* figure in rhetoric, from Gk *trópos* turn]

**-trope,** a combining form referring to turning, as in *heliotrope.* [Gk *-trópos*]

**trophallaxis** /trɒfə'læksəs/, *n., pl.* **-laxes** /-'læksiz/. (among social insects) a method of feeding and communication by the mutual exchange of regurgitated food. [TROPH(O)- + Gk *állaxis* exchange] – **trophallactic** /trɒfə'læktɪk/, *adj.*

**trophic** /'trɒfɪk/, *adj.* of or pertaining to nutrition; concerned in nutritive processes. [Gk *trophikós* pertaining to food] – **trophically,** *adv.*

**trophied** /'troufid/, *adj.* adorned with trophies.

**tropho-,** a word element referring to nourishment, as in *trophoplasm.* [Gk, combining form of *trophḗ*]

**trophoblast** /'trɒfəblæst/, *n.* the extraembryonic part of a blastocyst, with mainly trophic or nutritive functions, or developing into foetal membranes with trophic functions.

**trophoplasm** /'trɒfəplæzəm/, *n.* that kind of protoplasm which is regarded as forming the nutritive part of a cell.

**trophy** /'troufi/, *n., pl.* **-phies. 1.** anything taken in war, hunting, etc., esp. when preserved as a memento; a spoil or prize. **2.** anything serving as a token or evidence of victory, valour, skill, etc. **3.** a carved, painted, or other representation of objects associated with or symbolical of victory or achievement. **4.** any memento or memorial. [F *trophée,* from L *trop(h)aeum,* from Gk *trópaion,* from *tropḗ* putting to flight, defeat] – **trophyless,** *adj.*

**-trophy,** a word element denoting nourishment, as in *hypertrophy.* [Gk *-trophía* nutrition]

**tropic** /'trɒpɪk/, *n.* **1.** *Geog.* **a.** either of two corresponding parallels of latitude on the terrestrial globe, one **(tropic of Cancer)** about $23\frac{1}{2}°$ north, and the other **(tropic of Capricorn)** about $23\frac{1}{2}°$ south of the equator, being the boundaries of the Torrid Zone. **b. the tropics,** the regions lying between and near these parallels of latitude; the Torrid Zone and neighbouring regions. **2.** *Astron.* **a.** (now) either of two circles on the celestial sphere, parallel to the celestial equator, one **(tropic of Cancer)** about $23\frac{1}{2}°$ north of it, and the other **(tropic of Capricorn)** about $23\frac{1}{2}°$ south of it. **b.** (formerly) either of the two solstitial points, at which the sun reaches its greatest distance north and south of the celestial equator. *–adj.* **3.** pertaining to the tropics; tropical. [ME, from L *tropicus,* from Gk *tropikós* pertaining to a turn]

**-tropic,** an adjective combining form corresponding to *trope, -tropism,* as in *geotropic.*

**tropical** /'trɒpɪkəl/, *adj.* **1.** pertaining to, characteristic of, occurring in, or inhabiting the tropics, esp. the humid tropics: *tropical flowers.* **2.** designed to be used in the tropics: *tropical clothing.* **3.** of or pertaining to the astronomical tropics, or either one of them. **4.** pertaining to, characterised by, or of the nature of a trope or tropes; metaphorical. **5.** *Prison Colloq.* very risky. – **tropically,** *adv.*

**tropical black earth,** *n.* →**regur.**

**tropical climate** /trɒpɪkəl 'klaɪmət/, *n.* a group of climate regions characterised by high temperatures throughout the year and pronounced wet and dry seasons.

**tropical dress** /'– drɛs/, *n.* a uniform worn by members of the armed forces serving in tropical regions.

**tropical medicine** /– 'mɛdəsən/, *n.* the branch of medicine which deals with diseases peculiar to the tropics.

**tropical year** /– 'jɪə/, *n.* See **year** (def. 5).

**tropic bird** /'trɒpɪk bɜd/, *n.* any of several totipalmate seabirds of the family Phaethontidae, found chiefly in tropical regions, having white plumage with black markings and a pair of greatly elongated tail feathers.

**tropine** /'troʊpin, -pən/, *n.* a white crystalline, hygroscopic basic compound, $C_5H_{18}NO$, formed by the hydrolysis of atropine. Also, **tropin** /'troʊpən/. [aphetic var. of ATROPINE]

**tropism** /'troʊpɪzəm/, *n.* the response, usu. an orientation, of a plant or animal, as in growth, to the influences of external stimuli. [separate use of -TROPISM] – **tropistic** /troʊ'pɪstɪk/, *adj.*

**-tropism,** a word element referring to tropism, as in *heliotropism.* [-TROP(E) + -ISM]

**tropo-,** a word element referring to turning or change. [Gk, combining form of *trópos, tropḗ*]

**tropology** /trɒ'pɒlədʒi/, *n., pl.* **-gies.** **1.** the use of tropes or a trope in speech or writing. **2.** the use of a Scripture text so as to give it a moral interpretation or significance apart from its direct meaning. [LL *tropologia,* from Gk. See TROPE] – **tropologic** /trɒpə'lɒdʒɪk/, **tropological** /trɒpə'lɒdʒɪkəl/, *adj.* – **tropologically** /trɒpə'lɒdʒɪkli/, *adv.*

**tropopause** /'trɒpəpɔz/, *n.* the transition layer between the troposphere and the stratosphere.

**tropophilous** /trə'pɒfələs/, *adj.* adapted to a climate with alternate growing and rest periods, as a plant. [TROPO- + Gk *-philos* loving]

**tropophyte** /'trɒpəfaɪt/, *n.* a plant adapted to a climate alternately favourable or unfavourable to growth. – **tropophytic** /trɒpə'fɪtɪk/, *adj.*

**troposphere** /'trɒpəsfɪə/, *n.* the inner layer of atmosphere, varying in height between about 10 kilometres and 19 kilometres, within which there is a steady fall of temperature with increasing altitude of about 2°C per 300 metres, and within which nearly all cloud formations occur and weather conditions manifest themselves.

**-tropous,** a word element synonymous with **-tropal,** as in *heterotropous.* [Gk *-tropos* pertaining to a turn]

**troppo**[1] /'trɒpoʊ/, *adv.* (in musical directions) too much. [It.]

**troppo**[2] /'trɒpoʊ/, *adj. Colloq.* mentally disturbed. [shortened form of TROPICAL from mental illness resulting from long military service in the tropics]

**-tropy,** a word element synonymous with **-tropism.** [Gk *tropḗ* turning]

**trot** /trɒt/, *v.,* **trotted, trotting,** *n.* *–v.i.* **1.** (of a horse, etc.) to go at a gait between a walk and a run, in which the legs move in diagonal pairs, but not quite simultaneously, so that when the movement is slow one foot at least is always on the ground, and when fast all four feet are momentarily off the ground at once. **2.** to go at a quick, steady gait; move briskly, bustle, or hurry. *–v.t.* **3.** to cause to trot. **4.** to ride at a trot. **5.** to lead at a trot. **6. trot out,** *Colloq.* **a.** to bring forward for or as for inspection. **b.** to give voice to in a trite or boring way. *–n.* **7.** the gait of a horse, dog, etc., when trotting. **8.** the sound made. **9.** a jogging gait between a walk and a run. **10.** (*pl.*) races for trotting or pacing horses; a trotting meeting. **11.** (*pl.*) *Colloq.* diarrhoea. **12. a good (bad) trot,** *Colloq.* a run of good (bad) luck. **13.** (in harness racing) a race for trotters. **14. on the trot, a.** in a state of continuous activity. **b.** one after another, in quick succession: *he won three races on the trot.* [ME *trotten,* from OF *trotter,* from MHG *trotten* run, orig. tread]

trot (def. 13): trotting gig

**troth** /troʊθ/, *n. Archaic.* **1.** faithfulness, fidelity, or loyalty: *by my troth.* **2.** truth or verity: *in troth.* **3.** one's word or promise, esp. in engaging oneself to marry. [ME *trowthe, trouthe,* OE *trēowth.* See TRUTH]

**Trotskyism** /'trɒtski,ɪzəm/, *n.* the advocacy of worldwide proletarian revolution. [orig. the political principles of Leon *Trotsky* 1879-1940, Russian revolutionary leader and writer]

**Trotskyite** /'trɒtskiaɪt/, *n.* **1.** a supporter of Trotsky or Trotskyism. *–adj.* **2.** of or pertaining to Trotsky or Trotskyism. Also, **Trotskyist.**

**trotter** /'trɒtə/, *n.* **1.** an animal which trots; a horse bred and trained for harness racing. **2.** one who moves about briskly and constantly. **3.** the foot of an animal, esp. of a sheep or pig, used as food.

**troubadour** /'trubədɔ/, *n.* **1.** one of a class of lyric poets who flourished principally in southern France from the 11th century to the 13th century, and wrote in Provençal, chiefly on courtly love. **2.** a minstrel or ballad singer. [F, from Pr. *trobador,* from *trobar,* ? from LL *tropāre,* from *tropus* song, orig. figure of speech. See TROPE]

**trouble** /'trʌbəl/, *v.,* **-bled, -bling,** *n.* *–v.t.* **1.** to disturb in mind; distress; worry. **2.** to put to inconvenience, exertion, pains, or the like: *may I trouble you to shut the door?* **3.** to cause bodily pain or inconvenience to, as a disease or ailment does. **4.** to annoy, vex, or bother. **5.** to disturb or agitate, or stir up so as to make turbid, as water, etc. *–v.i.* **6.** to put oneself to inconvenience. **7.** to worry. *–n.* **8.** molestation, harassment, annoyance, or difficulty: *to make trouble for someone.* **9.** unfortunate position or circumstances; misfortunes. **10.** disturbance; disorder; unrest: *industrial trouble, political troubles.* **11.** physical derangement or disorder: *heart trouble.* **12.** disturbance of mind, distress, or worry. **13.** inconvenience endured, or exertion or pains taken, in some cause or in order to accomplish something. **14.** something that troubles; a cause or source of annoyance, difficulty, distress, or the like. **15.** a personal habit, characteristic, etc., which is disadvantageous or a source of anxiety or distress. **16. in trouble, a.** suffering or liable to suffer punishment, affliction, etc.; in difficulties. **b.** *Colloq.* pregnant while unmarried. [ME *troublen,* from OF *troubler,* from LL *turbulāre,* replacing L *turbidāre,* influenced by *turbulentus* turbulent] – **troubler,** *n.*

**trouble and strife,** *n. Colloq.* a wife. [rhyming slang]

**troubled waters** /trʌbəld 'wɔtəz/, *n. pl.* a confused or disordered state of affairs; a state of unrest.

**troublemaker** /'trʌbəlmeɪkə/, *n.* one who causes trouble for others, esp. one who does so habitually and deliberately.

**troubleshooter** /'trʌbəlʃutə/, *n.* an expert in discovering and eliminating the cause of trouble in the operation of something, in settling disputes, etc. – **troubleshooting,** *n.*

**troublesome** /'trʌbəlsəm/, *adj.* **1.** causing trouble or annoyance; vexatious. **2.** laborious; difficult. **3.** *Archaic.* full of distress or affliction. – **troublesomely,** *adv.* – **troublesomeness,** *n.*

**trouble spot** /'trʌbəl spɒt/, *n.* an area in which trouble or unrest exists or is liable to develop: *the Middle East is one of the world's trouble spots.*

**troublous** /'trʌbləs/, *adj. Archaic.* **1.** characterised by trouble; disturbed; unsettled. **2.** turbulent; restless. **3.** causing annoyance; troublesome.

**trou-de-loup** /tru-də-'lu/, *n., pl.* **trous-de-loups** /tru-də-'lu/. a conical or pyramidal pit with a pointed stake fixed vertically in the centre, rows of which are dug in front of a position to hinder an enemy's approach, formerly esp. used against cavalry. [F: wolf hole]

**trough** /trɒf/, *n.* **1.** an open, boxlike receptacle, usu. long and narrow, as for containing water or food for animals, or for any of various other purposes. **2.** any receptacle of similar shape. **3.** a channel or conduit for conveying water, as a gutter under the eaves of a building. **4.** any long depression or hollow, as between two ridges or waves. **5.** *Meteorol.* an elongated area of relatively low pressure. [ME; OE *trōh,* c. D, Icel. *trog,* G *Trog*] – **troughlike,** *adj.*

**trounce** /traʊns/, *v.t.,* **trounced, trouncing.** **1.** to beat or thrash severely. **2.** to punish. **3.** *Colloq.* to defeat convincingly. [orig. uncert.]

**troupe** /trup/, *n., v.,* **trouped, trouping.** *–n.* **1.** a troop, company, or band, esp. of actors, singers, or the like. *–v.i.* **2.** to travel as a member of a theatrical company; barnstorm. [F]

**trouper** /'trupə/, *n.* **1.** an actor in a theatrical company. **2.** a veteran actor. **3.** one who shows great devotion to duty, loyalty to a firm, colleagues, etc.

**troupial** /ˈtrupiəl/, *n.* any of the birds of the American family Icteridae, including the American blackbirds, American orioles, etc., esp. one with brilliant plumage, as *I. icterus.* [F *troupiale,* from *troupe* TROOP]

**trouser** /ˈtraʊzə/, *adj.* **1.** of or pertaining to trousers: *trouser leg.* *–n.* **2.** →**trousers.**

**trousered** /ˈtraʊzəd/, *adj.* wearing trousers.

**trousers** /ˈtraʊzəz/, *n. pl.* **1.** an outer garment covering the lower part of the trunk and each leg separately, extending to the ankles. **2. wear the trousers,** *Colloq.* to have control, as of the dominant partner in a marriage.

**trousseau** /ˈtrusoʊ/, *n., pl.* **-seaux, -seaus** /-soʊz/. a bride's outfit of clothes, linen, etc., which she brings with her at marriage. [F: lit., bundle, diminutive of *trousse* truss]

**trout** /traʊt/, *n., pl.* **trouts,** (*esp. collectively*) **trout. 1.** any fish of the genus *Salmo* other than the Atlantic salmon (*S. salar*), including the trout of Europe (*S. trutta*) and the American **rainbow trout** (*S. gairdnerii*), both of which have been introduced into Australia, and the American **cutthroat trout** (*S. clarkii*). **2.** any of various fishes of the salmon family of the genera *Salvelinus* and *Cristivomer,* also known as chars, noted by fishermen for their gameness and prized as food, and including several American species, as the **brook trout,** introduced into New South Wales and Tasmania. **3.** any of several unrelated fishes, such as a bass (*Micropterus salmoides*), a drumfish of the genus *Cynoscion,* or a greenling of the genus *Hexagrammos.* **4.** *Colloq.* a woman of unattractive appearance: *an old trout.* [ME *troute,* OE *truht,* from L *tructa,* from Gk *trṓktēs* gnawer, a sea fish]

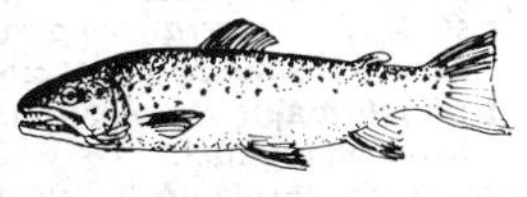
brown trout

**trouvère** /truˈvɛə/, *n.* one of a class of poets who flourished in northern France during the 12th and 13th centuries and composed the chansons de geste and works on courtly love. Also, **trouveur** /truˈvɜ/. [F, from *trouver.* See TROUBADOUR]

**trover** /ˈtroʊvə/, *n.* a common-law action for the recovery of the value of personal property wrongfully converted by another to his own use (originally brought against a finder of such goods). [OF: find, v., from L *turbāre* disturb]

**trow** /troʊ, traʊ/, *v.i. Archaic.* to believe, think, or suppose. [ME *trowen,* OE *trūwian* believe, trust, c. G *trauen*]

**trowel** /ˈtraʊəl/, *n., v.,* **-elled, -elling** or (*esp. U.S.*) **-eled, -eling.** *–n.* **1.** any of various tools consisting of a plate of metal or other material, usu. flat, fitted into a short handle, used for spreading, shaping, or smoothing plaster or the like. **2.** a similar tool with a curved, scooplike blade, used in gardening for taking up plants, etc. *–v.t.* **3.** to apply, shape, or smooth with or as with a trowel. [ME *truel,* from OF *truelle,* from LL *truella,* replacing L *trulla* small ladle] – **troweller;** *esp. U.S.,* **troweler,** *n.*

**troy** /trɔɪ/, *adj.* in or by troy weight. [named after *Troyes,* a town in NE France]

**troy ounce** /– ˈaʊns/, *n.* See **ounce**[1] (def. 2).

**troy weight** /– ˈweɪt/, *n.* an imperial system for measuring the mass of precious metals and gems, in which 24 grams = 1 pennyweight and 20 pennyweights = 1 troy ounce (see **ounce**[1], def. 2).

**truant** /ˈtruənt/, *n.* **1.** a pupil who stays away from school without permission. **2.** one who shirks or neglects his duty. **3. play truant,** to be absent from school, etc., without permission. *–adj.* **4.** staying away from school without permission. **5.** pertaining to or characteristic of a truant. *–v.i.* **6.** to play truant. [ME, from OF, probably of Celtic orig.] – **truancy,** *n.*

**truant officer** /ˈ– ɒfəsə/, *n.* →**attendance officer.**

**truce** /trus/, *n.* **1.** a suspension of hostilities, as between armies, by agreement, for a specified period; an armistice. **2.** an agreement or treaty establishing this. **3.** respite or freedom, as from trouble, pain, etc. [ME, var. of *trewes,* pl. of *trewe,* OE *trēow* treaty, good faith. Cf. TRUE] – **truceless,** *adj.*

**truck**[1] /trʌk/, *n.* **1.** any of various vehicles for carrying goods, etc. **2.** →**goods wagon. 3.** a motor vehicle with cab (def. 3) and tray or compartment for carrying goods; a lorry. **4.** any of various wheeled frames for moving heavy articles, as a barrow with two very low front wheels used to move heavy luggage, etc. **5.** a low rectangular frame on which heavy boxes, etc. are moved. **6.** *Mining.* a wheeled car of various design used for haulage. **7.** a group of two or more pairs of wheels in a frame, for supporting a locomotive body, etc. **8.** a small wooden wheel, cylinder, or roller, as on certain old-style guncarriages. **9.** a circular or square piece of wood fixed on the head of a mast or the top of a flagstaff, and usu. containing small holes for signal halyards. **10. (it) fell off the back of a truck,** *Colloq.* (it) was stolen. *–v.t.* **11.** to transport by a truck or trucks. **12.** to put on a truck. *–v.i.* **13.** to convey articles or goods on a truck. **14.** to drive a truck. **15.** *Colloq.* to walk confidently, jauntily, with somewhat exaggerated movement of the shoulders and arms. [backformation from *truckle* wheel. See TRUCKLE[2]]

**truck**[2] /trʌk/, *n.* **1.** dealings: *to have no truck with a person.* **2.** barter. **3.** a bargain or deal. **4.** the payment of wages in goods, etc., instead of money. **5.** miscellaneous articles; odds and ends. **6.** trash or rubbish. *–v.t.* **7.** to exchange; trade; barter; peddle. *–v.i.* **8.** to exchange commodities; barter; bargain or negotiate. **9.** to traffic; have dealings. [ME *truk(i)e,* from OF *troquer;* orig. uncert.]

**truckage** /ˈtrʌkɪdʒ/, *n.* **1.** conveyance by a truck or trucks. **2.** the charge for this.

**trucker**[1] /ˈtrʌkə/, *n. U.S.* **1.** a truck driver. **2.** one whose business is trucking goods. Also, **truckie.** [TRUCK[1] + -ER[1]]

**trucker**[2] /ˈtrʌkə/, *n. U.S.* one who grows vegetables, etc., for the market; market gardener. [TRUCK[2] + -ER[1]]

**truckie** /ˈtrʌki/, *n. Colloq.* a truck driver.

**trucking**[1] /ˈtrʌkɪŋ/, *n.* the act or business of conveying articles or goods on trucks. [TRUCK[1], *v.* + -ING[1]]

**trucking**[2] /ˈtrʌkɪŋ/, *n.* **1.** commercial bartering. **2.** *U.S.* the growing of vegetables for the market. [TRUCK[2], *v.* + -ING[1]]

**truckle**[1] /ˈtrʌkəl/, *v.i.,* **-led, -ling.** to submit or yield obsequiously or tamely (usu. fol. by *to*). [special use of obs. *truckle,* v., sleep on truckle bed] – **truckler,** *n.* – **trucklingly,** *adv.*

**truckle**[2] /ˈtrʌkəl/, *n.* **1.** →**pulley. 2.** →**truckle bed.** [late ME *trocle,* from L *trochlea,* from Gk *trochileía* pulley]

**truckle bed** /ˈ– bɛd/, *n.* a low bed moving on castors, usu. pushed under another bed when not in use. Also, **trundle bed.**

**truculent** /ˈtrʌkjələnt/, *adj.* **1.** fierce; cruel; brutal; savage. **2.** scathing; harsh; vitriolic. **3.** aggressive; belligerent. [L *truculentus*] – **truculence, truculency,** *n.* – **truculently,** *adv.*

**trudge** /trʌdʒ/, *v.,* **trudged, trudging,** *n.* *–v.i.* **1.** to walk. **2.** to walk laboriously or wearily. *–v.t.* **3.** to walk laboriously or wearily along or over: *he trudged the streets.* [orig. uncert.] – **trudger,** *n.*

**true** /tru/, *adj.,* **truer, truest,** *n., adv., v.,* **trued, truing.** *–adj.* **1.** being in accordance with the actual state of things; conforming to fact; not false: *a true story.* **2.** real or genuine: *true gold.* **3.** free from deceit; sincere: *a true interest in someone's welfare.* **4.** firm in allegiance; loyal; faithful; trusty. **5.** being or indicating the essential reality of something. **6.** agreeing with or conforming to a standard, pattern, rule, or the like: *a true copy.* **7.** exact, correct, or accurate: *a true balance.* **8.** of the right kind; such as it should be; proper: *to arrange things in their true order.* **9.** properly so called; rightly answering to a description: *true statesmanship.* **10.** legitimate or rightful: *the true heir.* **11.** reliable, unfailing, or sure: *a true sign.* **12.** exactly or accurately shaped, formed, fitted, or placed, as a surface, instrument, or part of a mechanism. **13.** *Biol.* belonging to a particular group; conforming to the norm; typical. **14.** *Stock Breeding.* purebred. **15.** *Navig.* (of a bearing) fixed in relation to the earth's axis rather than the magnetic poles: *true north.* **16.** *Archaic.* truthful. **17.** *Archaic.* honest; honourable; upright. *–n.* **18.** exact or accurate formation, position, or adjustment: *to be out of true.* **19. the true,** that which is true. *–adv.* **20.** in a true manner; truly or truthfully. **21.** exactly or accurately. **22.** in agreement with the ancestral type: *to breed true.* **23. to come true,** to happen in reality as desired, expected, dreamt, etc.: *if dreams came true.* *–v.t.* **24.** to make true; shape, adjust, place, etc., exactly or accurately. [ME; OE *trēowe,* c. G *treu*] – **trueness,** *n.*

**true blue** /– ˈblu/, *n.* **1.** a non-fading blue dye or pigment. **2.** one who is true-blue. **3.** a staunch conservative. [orig. the colour adopted by the 17th cent. Covenanters of England and Scotland, in contradistinction to the royal red]

i = peat ɪ = pit ɛ = pet æ = pat a = part ɒ = pot ʌ = putt ɔ = port ʊ = put u = pool ɜ = pert ə = apart aɪ = buy eɪ = bay ɔɪ = boy aʊ = how oʊ = hoe ɪə = here ɛə = hair ʊə = tour g = give θ = thin ð = then ʃ = show ʒ = measure tʃ = choke dʒ = joke ŋ = sing j = you õ = Fr. bon

**true-blue** /'tru-blu/, *adj.* **1.** unchanging; unwavering; staunch; true. **2.** staunchly conservative.

**true-born** /'tru-bɔn/, *adj.* **1.** of pure stock; legitimate; purebred. **2.** having the qualities associated with pure breeding.

**true-bred** /'tru-brɛd/, *adj.* **1.** thoroughbred; purebred. **2.** showing good breeding.

**true-hearted** /'tru-hatəd/, *adj.* **1.** faithful or loyal. **2.** honest or sincere. – **true-heartedness,** *n.*

**true level** /tru 'lɛvəl/, *n.* an imaginary surface everywhere perpendicular to the plumbline, or line of gravity.

**truelove** /'trulʌv/, *n.* **1.** a sweetheart; one truly loving or loved. **2.** the herb Paris, *Paris quadrifolia,* having a whorl of four leaves suggesting a truelove knot.

**truelove knot** /'– nɒt/, *n.* a complicated ornamental knot, esp. one formed of intertwined loops, used as an emblem of true love or interwoven affections. Also, **truelover's knot.**

**true rib** /tru 'rɪb/, *n.* any of the ribs which are attached to the sternum by costal cartilages (the first seven pairs in man).

**true time** /– 'taɪm/, *n.* apparent solar time; the time as shown by a sundial.

**truffle** /'trʌfəl/, *n.* **1.** any of various subterranean edible fungi of the genus *Tuber* of the class Ascomycetes. **2.** any of various similar fungi of other genera. **3.** a chocolate confection resembling this. [F *truffe,* from Pr. *trufa,* or from It. ? *truffa,* from LL *tūfera,* from Osco-Umbrian *tūfer,* c. L *tūber* esculent root] – **truffled,** *adj.*

**trug** /trʌg/, *n.* a shallow, oblong, wooden basket for carrying fruit, vegetables, etc.

**truism** /'truɪzəm/, *n.* a self-evident, obvious truth. – **truistic** /tru'ɪstɪk/, **truistical** /tru'ɪstɪkəl/, *adj.*

**truly** /'truli/, *adv.* **1.** in accordance with fact or truth; truthfully. **2.** exactly; accurately; correctly. **3.** rightly; duly; properly. **4.** legitimately; rightfully. **5.** genuinely; really. **6.** indeed; verily. **7.** *Archaic.* faithfully; loyally; constantly.

**trump**[1] /trʌmp/, *n.* **1.** *Cards.* **a.** any playing card of a suit that for the time outranks the other suits, such a card being able to take any card of another suit. **b.** (*pl., U.S. sometimes sing.*) the suit itself. **c.** a tarot card with a special function or meaning; a major arcanum. *–v.t.* **2.** *Cards.* to take with a trump. **3.** *Prison Colloq.* a senior officer in a prison, or section of a prison. **4.** to excel; surpass; be better than; beat. **5.** **trump up,** to invent deceitfully or dishonestly, as an accusation; fabricate. *–v.i. Cards.* **6.** to play a trump. **7.** to take a trick with a trump. [unexplained var. of TRIUMPH] – **trumpless,** *adj.*

**trump**[2] /trʌmp/, *Archaic or Poetic. –n.* **1.** a trumpet. **2.** its sound. **3.** some similar sound. *–v.i.* **4.** to blow a trumpet. **5.** to make a trumpet-like sound. *–v.t.* **6.** to proclaim, etc., by or as by a trumpet. [ME *trompe,* from F of Gmc orig.]

**trump card** /'– kad/, *n.* **1.** →**trump**[1] (def. 1a). **2.** *Colloq.* a decisive factor; important advantage.

**trumpery** /'trʌmpəri/, *n., pl.* **-ries,** *adj. –n.* **1.** something showy but of little intrinsic value; worthless finery; useless stuff. **2.** rubbish; nonsense. *–adj.* **3.** showy but unsubstantial or useless; of little or no value; trifling; rubbishy. [F *tromperie,* from *tromper* deceive]

**trumpet** /'trʌmpət/, *n.* **1.** *Music.* **a.** any of a family of musical wind instruments with a penetrating, powerful tone, consisting of a tube, now usu. metallic, and commonly once or twice curved round upon itself, having a cup-shaped mouthpiece at one end and a flaring bell at the other. **b.** an organ stop having a tone resembling that of a trumpet. **c.** a trumpeter. **2.** a sound like that of a trumpet. **3.** the loud cry of the elephant or some other animal. **4.** →**ear trumpet.** **5.** (*pl.*) any of several pitcher plants. **6.** **blow one's own trumpet,** to praise oneself. *–v.i.* **7.** to blow a trumpet. **8.** to emit a sound like that of a trumpet, as an elephant. *–v.t.* **9.** to sound on a trumpet. **10.** to utter with a sound like that of a trumpet. **11.** to proclaim loudly or widely. [ME, from OF *trompette,* diminutive of *trompe.* See TRUMP[2]] – **trumpet-like,** *adj.*

**trumpet bird** /'– bɜd/, *n.* →**manucode.**

**trumpeter** /'trʌmpətə/, *n.* **1.** one who sounds or plays a trumpet. **2.** one who proclaims or announces something with a trumpet. **3.** a soldier whose regular duty is to sound trumpet calls at stated hours. **4.** one who proclaims or announces something loudly or widely. **5.** a sport and food fish, *Latris lineata,* principally of New Zealand waters but also occurring off the eastern Australian coast. **6.** any of the large South American birds constituting the family Psophiidae, esp. *Psophia crepitans* (**common trumpeter**), related to the rails. **7.** Also, **trumpeter swan.** a large North American wild swan (*Cygnus buccinator*) having a sonorous cry. **8.** one of a breed of domestic pigeons.

**trumpet-fish** /'trʌmpət-fɪʃ/, *n., pl.* **-fishes,** (*esp. collectively*) **-fish.** any of various long-snouted fish of the family Aulostomidae, esp. *Aulostomus maculatus,* of the southern Atlantic Ocean.

**trumpet flower** /'trʌmpət flaʊə/, *n.* **1.** any of various plants with pendent flowers shaped like a trumpet. **2.** →**trumpet honeysuckle.** **3.** the flower of any of these plants.

**trumpet honeysuckle** /– 'hʌnisʌkəl/, *n.* an American honeysuckle, *Lonicera sempervirens,* with large tubular flowers, deep red outside and yellow within.

**trumpet-major** /trʌmpət-'meɪdʒə/, *n.* the chief trumpeter of a band or regiment.

**truncate** /trʌŋ'keɪt, 'trʌŋkeɪt/, *v.,* **-cated, -cating,** *adj. –v.t.* **1.** to shorten by cutting off a part; cut short; mutilate. *–adj.* **2.** →**truncated.** **3.** *Biol.* **a.** square or broad at the end, as if cut off transversely. **b.** lacking the apex, as certain spiral shells. [L *truncātus,* pp., cut] – **truncation,** *n.*

**truncated** /trʌŋ'keɪtəd/, *adj.* **1.** shortened by the cutting off of a part, or appearing as if so shortened; cut short. **2.** (of a geometrical figure or solid) having the apex, vertex, or end cut off by a plane: *a truncated cone or pyramid.* **3.** *Crystall.* **a.** (of a crystal, etc.) having angles or edges cut off or replaced by a single plane. **b.** (of one of the edges or corners) cut off or replaced by a modifying plane which makes equal angles with the adjacent similar planes. **4.** *Biol.* →**truncate.**

**truncheon** /'trʌnʃən/, *n.* **1.** a short club carried by a policeman. **2.** a baton, or staff of office or authority. **3.** *Archaic.* a club or cudgel. **4.** *Archaic.* the shaft of a spear. *–v.t.* **5.** to beat with a club. [ME *trunchon,* from OF *troncon* piece cut off, from L *truncus* stump]

**trundle** /'trʌndəl/, *v.,* **-dled, -dling,** *n. –v.t.* **1.** to cause (a ball, hoop, etc.) to roll along; roll. **2.** to cause to rotate; twirl; whirl. *–v.i.* **3.** to roll along. **4.** to move or run on a wheel or wheels. **5.** *Colloq.* to walk in a leisurely fashion. *–n.* **6.** the act of trundling or rolling. **7.** a small wheel, roller, or the like. **8.** a small wheel adapted to support a heavy weight, as the wheel of a castor. **9.** →**lantern pinion.** **10.** each of the bars of a lantern pinion. **11.** the impulse which causes something to roll. **12.** *Rare.* a truck or carriage on low wheels. [OE *tryndel* wheel; cf. LG *tründeln* roll]

**trundle bed** /'– bɛd/, *n.* →**truckle bed.**

**trundler** /'trʌndlə/, *n.* **1.** one who or that which trundles. **2.** *N.Z.* →**shopping stroller.** **3.** *N.Z.* →**golf buggy.**

**trunk** /trʌŋk/, *n.* **1.** the main stem of a tree, as distinct from the branches and roots. **2.** a box or chest for holding clothes and other articles, as for use on a journey. **3.** the body of a human being or of an animal, excluding the head and limbs. **4.** *Archit.* **a.** the shaft of a column. **b.** the dado or die of a pedestal. **5.** the main line of a river, railway, or the like. **6.** *Teleph.* **a.** (*pl.*) a trunk call exchange: *give me trunks.* **b.** →**trunk line.** **7.** *Anat.* the main body of an artery, nerve, or the like, as distinct from its branches. **8.** (*pl.*) **a.** shorts, either tight-fitting or loose, worn by swimmers, athletes, etc. **b.** short, tight-fitting breeches, as worn over tights in theatrical use. **c.** *Obs.* →**trunk hose.** **9.** the long, flexible, cylindrical nasal appendage of the elephant. **10.** *Naut.* **a.** a large enclosed passage through the decks or bulkheads of a vessel, for coaling, ventilation, or the like. **b.** any of various watertight casings in a vessel, as the vertical one above the slot for a centre board in the bottom of a boat. **11.** a shaft or chute. **12.** *U.S.* →**boot**[1] (def. 5). **13.** *Obs.* any of various pipes or tubes, as a speaking tube, a blowpipe, or a telescope. *–adj.* **14.** denoting or pertaining to the main line or artery, as of a railway, road, river, etc. [late ME *trunke,* from L *truncus*] – **trunkless,** *adj.*

**trunk call** /'– kɔl/, *n.* a telephone call made by a trunk line.

**trunkfish** /'trʌŋkfɪʃ/, *n., pl.* **-fishes,** (*esp. collectively*) **-fish.** **1.** →**box fish.** **2.** any of the fishes of the genus *Mormyridae* of central and southern Africa, having extended mouthparts forming a trunk. **3.** any of the fishes of the genus *Ostracion*.

**trunk hose** /ˈtrʌŋk hoʊz/, *n.* full, baglike breeches covering the body from the waist to the middle of the thigh or lower, worn in the 16th and 17th centuries.

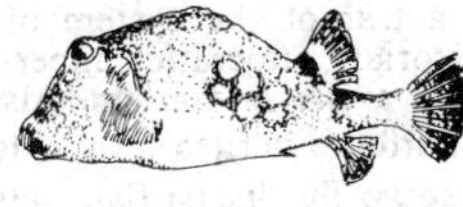

trunkfish

**trunk line** /ˈ– laɪn/, *n.* **1.** *Teleph.* a telephone line or channel between two exchanges in different parts of a country or of the world, which is used to provide connections between subscribers making long-distance calls. **2.** a main railway line. Also, **trunkline.**

**trunk piston** /ˈ– pɪstən/, *n.* a piston with a long skirt to take the side thrust, as in an internal-combustion engine.

**trunk road** /ˈ– roʊd/, *n.* a main road for long-distance travel.

**trunnel** /ˈtrʌnəl/, *n.* →**treenail.**

**trunnion** /ˈtrʌnjən/, *n.* **1.** either of the two cylindrical projections on a cannon, one on each side, which support it on its carriage. **2.** any of various similar supports, gudgeons, or pivots. [F *trognon* trunk, stump, ult. orig. uncert.]

**truss** /trʌs/, *v.t.* **1.** to tie, bind, or fasten. **2.** to make fast with skewers or the like, as the wings of a fowl preparatory to cooking. **3.** *Bldg Trades, etc.* to furnish or support with a truss or trusses. **4.** to confine or enclose, as the body, by something fastened closely around. *–n.* **5.** *Bldg Trades, etc.* **a.** a combination of members, as beams, bars, ties, or the like, so arranged, usu. in a triangle or a collection of triangles, as to form a rigid framework, and used in bridges **(bridge truss),** roofs **(roof truss),** etc., to give support and rigidity to the whole or a part of the structure. **b.** any framework consisting of a number of members connected together and loaded principally at the joints so that the stresses in the members are essentially simple tensions or compressions. **6.** *Med.* an apparatus for maintaining a hernia in a reduced state. **7.** *Hort.* a compact terminal cluster or head of flowers growing upon one stalk. **8.** *Naut.* an iron fitting by which a lower yard is secured to the mast. **9.** a collection of things tied together or packed in a receptacle; a bundle; a pack. **10.** (formerly) a bundle of hay or straw of a specific weight. [ME *trussen,* from OF *trusser,* from L *torca* bundle, replacing *torques* necklace, something twisted] **– trusser,** *n.*

**truss bridge** /ˈ– brɪdʒ/, *n.* a bridge in which the greatest strain is taken by trusses.

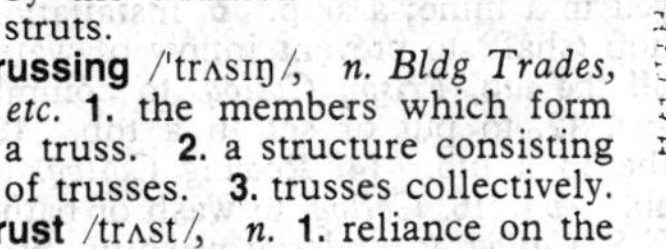

truss bridge

**trussed beam** /ˈtrʌst bim/, *n.* a beam that has been strengthened by the addition of tie rods and struts.

**trussing** /ˈtrʌsɪŋ/, *n. Bldg Trades, etc.* **1.** the members which form a truss. **2.** a structure consisting of trusses. **3.** trusses collectively.

**trust** /trʌst/, *n.* **1.** reliance on the integrity, justice, etc., of a person, or on some quality or attribute of a thing; confidence. **2.** confident expectation of something; hope. **3.** confidence in the ability or intention of a person to pay at some future time for goods, etc.; credit: *to sell goods on trust.* **4.** one on whom or that on which one relies. **5.** the state of being relied on, or the state of one to whom something is entrusted. **6.** the obligation or responsibility imposed on one in whom confidence or authority is placed: *a position of trust.* **7.** the condition of being confided to another's care or guard: *to leave something in trust with a person.* **8.** something committed or entrusted to one, as an office, duty, etc. **9.** *Law.* **a.** a fiduciary relationship in which one person (the trustee) holds the title to property (the **trust estate** or **trust property**) for the benefit of another (the beneficiary). **b.** a fund of securities, cash or other assets, held by trustees on behalf of a number of investors. **10.** *Comm.* **a.** a combination of industrial or commercial companies having a central committee or board of trustees, controlling a majority or the whole of the stock of each of the constituent companies, thus making it possible to manage the concerns so as to economise expenses, regulate production, defeat competition, etc. **b.** a monopolistic organisation or combination in restraint of trade whether in the form of a trust (def. 10a), contract, association or otherwise. **11.** *Rare.* reliability. *–adj.* **12.** *Law.* of or pertaining to trusts or a trust. *–v.i.* **13.** to have or place trust, reliance, or confidence (usu. fol. by *in*). **14.** to have confidence; hope. **15. trust to,** to depend on; rely on. *–v.t.* **16.** to have trust or confidence in; rely on. **17.** to believe. **18.** to expect confidently, hope (usu. fol. by a clause or an infinitive). **19.** to commit or consign with trust or confidence. **20.** to permit to be in some place, position, etc., or to do something, without fear of consequences: *he will not trust it out of his sight.* **21.** to invest with a trust; entrust with something. **22.** to give credit to (a person) for goods, etc., supplied. [ME, from Scand.; cf. Icel. *traust* trust, c. G *Trost* comfort] **– truster,** *n.*

**trust corporation** /ˈ– kɔpəˌreɪʃən/, *n.* a corporation organised to exercise the functions of a trustee.

**trust deed** /ˈ– did/, *n.* the legal document which appoints trustees and defines their power.

**trustee** /trʌsˈti/, *n., v.* **-teed, -teeing.** *Law. –n.* **1.** a person, usu. one of a body of persons, appointed to administer the affairs of a company, institution, etc. **2.** a person who holds the title to property for the benefit of another. *–v.t.* **3.** to place in the hands of a trustee or trustees.

**trusteeship** /trʌsˈtiʃɪp/, *n.* **1.** the office or function of a trustee. **2.** the administrative control of a territory granted to a country by an organ (**Trusteeship Council**) of the United Nations. **3.** →**trust territory.**

**trustful** /ˈtrʌstfəl/, *adj.* full of trust; trusting; confiding. **– trustfully,** *adv.* **– trustfulness,** *n.*

**trusting** /ˈtrʌstɪŋ/, *adj.* that trusts; confiding; trustful. **– trustingly,** *adv.* **– trustingness,** *n.*

**trust instrument** /ˈtrʌst ɪnstrəmənt/, *n.* the document which sets out the trusts upon which the person entitled to the enjoyment of land holds the fee simple.

**trust territory** /ˈ– ˌtɛrətri/, *n.* a territory administered by a country on behalf of the Trusteeship Council of the United Nations.

**trustworthy** /ˈtrʌstwɜði/, *adj.* worthy of trust or confidence; reliable. **– trustworthily,** *adv.* **– trustworthiness,** *n.*

**trusty** /ˈtrʌsti/, *adj.,* **trustier, trustiest,** *n., pl.* **trusties.** *–adj.* **1.** that may be trusted or relied on; trustworthy; reliable. **2.** *Rare.* trustful. *–n.* **3.** one who or that which is trusted. **4.** **a.** well-behaved and trustworthy prisoner to whom special privileges are granted. **b.** an inmate of a hospital or similar institution who has a like status. **– trustily,** *adv.* **– trustiness,** *n.*

**truth** /truθ/, *n.* **1.** that which is true; the true or actual facts of a case: *to tell the truth.* **2.** conformity with fact or reality; verity: *the truth of a statement.* **3.** a verified or indisputable fact, proposition, principle, or the like: *mathematical truths.* **4.** the state or character of being true. **5.** genuineness, reality, or actual existence. **6.** agreement with a standard, rule, or the like. **7.** honesty, uprightness, or integrity. **8.** accuracy, as of position or adjustment. **9. in truth,** in fact; in reality; truly. **10.** *Archaic.* fidelity or constancy. [ME *treuthe,* OE *trēowth,* c. Icel. *tryggdh* faith] **– truthless,** *adj.*

**truth drug** /ˈ– drʌg/, *n. Colloq.* sodium pentothal when used as a mild anaesthetic to render a person incapable of answering questions untruthfully.

**truthful** /ˈtruθfəl/, *adj.* **1.** telling the truth, esp. habitually, as a person. **2.** conforming to truth, as a statement. **3.** corresponding with reality, as a representation. **– truthfully,** *adv.* **– truthfulness,** *n.*

**try** /traɪ/, *v.,* **tried, trying,** *n., pl.* **tries.** *–v.t.* **1.** to attempt to do or accomplish: *it seems easy until you try it.* **2.** to test the effect or result of: *to try a new method.* **3.** to endeavour to ascertain by experiment: *to try one's luck.* **4.** to test the quality, value, fitness, accuracy, etc, of: *to try a new brand of soap powder.* **5.** to attempt to open (a door, window, etc.) in order to find out whether it is locked. **6.** *Law.* to examine and determine judicially, as a cause; determine judicially the guilt or innocence of (a person). **7.** to put to a severe test; strain the endurance, patience, etc., of; subject to grevious experiences, affliction, or trouble. **8.** to melt (fat, etc.) to obtain the oil; render (usu. fol. by *out*). **9.** *Rare.* to ascertain the truth or right of (a matter, etc.) by test (sometimes fol. by *out*). **10.** *Obs.* to show or prove by test or experience.

–*v.i.* **11.** to make an attempt or effort: *try harder next time.* –*v.* **12.** Some special verb phrases are:

**try it on,** *Colloq.* to attempt to hoodwink or test the patience of, esp. impudently.

**try on,** to put on (clothes, etc.) to see if they fit.

**try out,** **1.** to test; experiment with. **2.** to compete (for a position, etc.).

–*n.* **13.** an attempt, endeavour, or effort: *to have a try at something.* **14.** *Rugby Football.* a score of three points earned by a touchdown. [ME *tryen,* from OF *trier* pick, cull] – **trier,** *n.*

**trying** /'traɪɪŋ/, *adj.* annoying; distressing; irritating; testing one's patience. – **tryingly,** *adv.* – **tryingness,** *n.*

**trying plane** /'– pleɪn/, *n.* a very long plane used by carpenters to make the edges of boards straight. [var. of *truing plane.* See TRUE, *v.*]

**tryma** /'traɪmə/, *n., pl.* **-mata** /-mətə/. a drupaceous nut having a fibrous or fleshy epicarp which is ultimately dehiscent, as in the walnut and hickory. [NL, from Gk: hole]

**try-on** /'traɪ-ɒn/, *n. Colloq.* an attempt to hoodwink or test the patience of someone.

**tryout** /'traɪaʊt/, *n. Colloq.* a trial, practice, or test to ascertain fitness for some purpose.

**trypaflavine** /trɪpə'fleɪvən, -vin/, *n.* →**acriflavine.**

**trypanosome** /'trɪpənəsoʊm/, *n.* any of the minute flagellate protozoans constituting the genus *Trypanosoma,* parasitic in the blood or tissues of man and other vertebrates, usu. transmitted by insects, often causing serious diseases, as African sleeping sickness in man, and many diseases in domestic animals. [*trypano-* (combining form of Gk *trýpanon* borer) + -SOME[3]] – **trypanosomic** /trɪpənə'sɒmɪk/, *adj.*

**trypanosomiasis** /ˌtrɪpənoʊsə'maɪəsəs/, *n.* any infection caused by a trypanosome.

**tryparsamide** /trə'pasəmaɪd/, *n.* a synthetic drug, $C_8H_{10}AsN_2O_4Na$, used for the cure of trypanosome infections.

**trypsin** /'trɪpsən/, *n.* **1.** a proteolytic enzyme of the pancreatic juice. [var. of *tripsin,* from Gk *trîpsis* friction + -IN[2]] – **tryptic,** *adj.*

**trypsinogen** /trɪp'sɪnədʒən/, *n.* the inactive precursor of trypsin.

**tryptamine** /'trɪptəmin/, *n.* **1.** a crystalline amine, $C_8H_6NCH_2CH_2NH_2$, occurring naturally as a result of the decomposition of tryptophan. **2.** this substance produced synthetically.

**tryptanol** /'trɪptənɒl/, *n.* an antidepressant drug, $C_{20}H_{23}N \cdot HCl$, which has mild tranquillising effects. [Trademark]

**tryptophan** /'trɪptəfæn/, *n.* a colourless, solid, aromatic, essential amino acid, $C_{11}H_{12}N_2O_2$, necessary to animal life, occurring in proteins and found in the seed of some leguminous plants. Also, **tryptophane.** [*trypto-* (combining form representing Gk *triptós* rubbed) + -PHAN(E)]

**trysail** /'traɪseɪl/; *Naut.* /-səl/, *n.* a small fore-and-aft sail set with or without a gaff, usu. loose-footed, on the foremast or mainmast of a vessel, and used esp. in heavy weather.

**try square** /'traɪ skwɛə/, *n.* two straight edges fastened at right angles to each other, used for testing the squareness of work or for laying out right angles.

**tryst** /trɪst/, *n.* **1.** an appointment, esp. between lovers, to meet at a certain time and place; rendezvous. **2.** an appointed meeting. **3.** an appointed place of meeting. –*v.t.* **4.** *Chiefly Scot.* to make an engagement with (a person) for a meeting. –*v.i.* **5.** *Chiefly Scot.* to make an appointment or agreement. [ME *triste,* from OF; orig. uncert.] – **tryster,** *n.*

**trysting place** /'trɪstɪŋ pleɪs/, *n.* a place where a tryst is kept or is to be kept.

**tsar** /za/, *n.* **1.** an emperor or king. **2.** (*usu. cap.*) the emperor of Russia. **3.** (*oft. cap.*) an autocratic ruler or leader. Also, **czar, tzar.** [Russ., from L *Caesar*] – **tsardom** /'zadəm/, *n.*

**tsarevitch** /'zarəvɪtʃ/, *n.* **1.** the son of a tsar. **2.** (later) the eldest son of a tsar. Also, **czarevitch, tzarevitch.**

**tsarevna** /za'rɛvnə/, *n.* a daughter of a tsar. Also, **czarevna, tzarevna.**

**tsarina** /za'rinə/, *n.* the wife of a tsar; Russian empress. Also, **czarina, tzarina.** [TSAR + *-ina* (Latinisation of G *-in,* fem. suffix, as in *Zarin* wife of tsar)]

**tsarism** /'zarɪzəm/, *n.* dictatorship; autocratic government. Also, **czarism, tzarism.**

**tsarist** /'zarəst/, *adj.* **1.** of, pertaining to, or characteristic of a tsar or the system of government under a tsar. **2.** dictatorial; autocratic; imperious. –*n.* **3.** an adherent or supporter of a tsar or tsarism. Also, **czarist, tzarist.**

**tsaritsa** /za'rɪtsə/, *n.* →**tsarina.** Also, **czaritza, tsaritza, tzaritza.**

**tsetse fly** /'tsɛtsi flaɪ, 'sɛtsi/, *n.* any of the blood-sucking flies of the African genus *Glossina,* some of which transmit protozoan parasites (trypanosomes) which cause sleeping sickness and other serious diseases. Also, **tsetse, tzetze.** [native name]

**T-shirt** /'ti-ʃɜt/, *n.* a lightweight, close-fitting, collarless shirt, with short sleeves. Also, **tee-shirt.**

**tsp.,** teaspoon.

**T square** /'ti skwɛə/, *n.* a T-shaped ruler used in mechanical drawing to make parallel lines, etc., the short crosspiece sliding along the edge of the drawing board as a guide.

**tsunami** /tsu'nami/, *n.* a large, often destructive sea wave caused by an underwater earthquake. [Jap.: tidal wave]

**TT,** telegraphic transfer.

**T.T.,** **1.** teetotal. **2.** teetotaller. **3.** tuberculin tested.

**TTY,** teletype.

**Tu.,** Tuesday.

T square

**tuan** /'tjuən/, *n.* any of certain brush-tailed, carnivorous marsupials, rat-sized and largely arboreal, of the genus *Phascogale;* phascogale; wambenger. [Aboriginal]

**tuart** /'tjuət/, *n.* a large tree, *Eucalyptus gomphocephala,* endemic in south-western Australia on calcareous coastal soil. [Aboriginal]

**tuatara** /tuə'tarə/, *n.* a lizard-like reptile, *Sphaenodon punctatum,* found in a few islands off the coast of New Zealand, the only surviving member of the order Rhynchocephalia. [Maori]

**tub** /tʌb/, *n., v.,* **tubbed, tubbing.** –*n.* **1.** a vessel or receptacle for bathing in; a bathtub. **2.** *Colloq.* a bath in a tub. **3.** a broad, round, open, wooden vessel, usu. made of staves held together by hoops and fitted around a flat bottom. **4.** any of various vessels resembling or suggesting a tub. **5.** as much as a tub will hold. **6.** a large sink installed in a laundry. **7.** *Prison Colloq.* a sanitary bucket in a prison cell. **8.** *Colloq.* a slow, clumsy ship or boat. **9.** *Rowing Colloq.* a heavy boat used for training novices. **10.** *Mining.* **a.** an ore wagon in a mine. **b.** a bucket, box, or the like, in which material is brought from or conveyed in a mine; a skip. **c.** installation of lining in an excavation (shaft) to prevent inflow of water or caving in. **11. go off the tub,** *Prison Colloq.* to commit suicide by hanging. –*v.t.* **12.** to put or set in a tub. **13.** *Colloq.* to wash or bathe in a tub. **14.** *Rowing Colloq.* to coach (oarsmen) in a tub. –*v.i.* **15.** *Colloq.* to wash or bathe oneself in a tub. **16.** *U.S. Colloq.* to undergo washing, esp. without damage, as a fabric. [ME *tubbe,* c. LG *tubbe;* orig. unknown] – **tubbable,** *adj.* – **tubber,** *n.* – **tublike,** *adj.*

**tuba** /'tjubə/, *n., pl.* **-bas, -bae** /-bi/. **1.** a brass wind instrument of low pitch equipped with valves. **2.** an organ reed stop of large scale with notes of exceptional power. **3.** an ancient Roman trumpet. [L: trumpet; akin to TUBE]

tuba

**tubal** /'tjubəl/, *adj.* **1.** of or pertaining to a tube or tubes; tubular. **2.** *Anat.* pertaining to a tube, as the Fallopian tube.

**tubal ligation** /– lɪ'geɪʃən/, *n.* the operation of applying a ligature to the Fallopian tubes, to prevent conception.

**tubate** /'tjubeɪt/, *adj.* forming or having a tube or tubes.

**tubby** /'tʌbi/, *adj.,* **-bier, -biest.** **1.** short and fat: *a tubby man.* **2.** having a dull sound; without resonance. – **tubbiness,** *n.*

**tube** /tjub/, *n., v.,* **tubed, tubing.** –*n.* **1.** a hollow usu. cylindrical body of metal, glass, rubber, or other material, used for conveying or containing fluids, and for other purposes. **2.** a small, collapsible, metal cylinder closed at one end and having the open end provided with a cap, for holding paint, toothpaste, or other semiliquid substance to be squeezed out by pressure. **3.** *Colloq.* a can of beer. **4.** *Anat., Zool.* any hollow, cylindrical vessel or organ: *the bronchial tubes.* **5.** the hollow tube of a wave as it breaks. **6.** (*pl.*) →**Fallopian tubes. 7.** *Bot.* **a.** any hollow, elongated body or part. **b.** the united lower portion of a gamopetalous corolla or a gamosepalous calyx. **8.** *Brit.* the tubular tunnel in which an underground railway runs. **9.** *Brit.* Also, **tube train.** the train itself. **10.** →**valve** (def. 7). **11.** *Archaic.* →**telescope. 12.** *Colloq.* a television set. *–v.t.* **13.** to furnish with a tube or tubes. **14.** to convey or enclose in a tube. **15.** to form in the shape of a tube; make like a tube. [L *tubus* pipe] – **tubeless,** *adj.* – **tubelike,** *adj.*

**tubeless tyre** /tjubləs 'taɪə/, *n.* a pneumatic tyre which is so constructed that the outer cover makes an airtight seal with the wheel rims so that an inner tube is unnecessary.

**tuber**[1] /'tjubə/, *n.* **1.** *Bot.* a fleshy, usu. oblong or rounded thickening or outgrowth (as the potato) of a subterranean stem or shoot, bearing minute scalelike leaves with buds or eyes in their axils, from which new plants may arise. **2.** *Anat., etc.* a rounded swelling or protuberance; a tuberosity; a tubercle. [L: bump, swelling]

**tuber**[2] /'tjubə/, *n.* one who or that which tubes. [TUBE + -ER[1]]

**tubercle** /'tjubəkəl/, *n.* **1.** a small rounded projection or excrescence, as on a bone, on the surface of the body in various animals, or on a plant. **2.** *Pathol.* **a.** a small, firm, rounded nodule or swelling. **b.** such a swelling as the characteristic lesion of tuberculosis. [L *tūbeculum* small swelling]

**tubercle bacillus** /– bə'sɪləs/, *n.* the bacterium, *Myobacterium tuberculosis,* causing tuberculosis. *Abbrev:* T.B., t.b.

**tubercular** /tə'bɜkjələ/, *adj.* **1.** pertaining to tuberculosis; tuberculous. **2.** of, pertaining to, or having the nature of a tubercle or tubercles. **3.** characterised by tubercles. *–n.* **4.** a tuberculous person. – **tubercularly,** *adv.*

**tubercularise** /tə'bɜkjələraɪz/, *v.t., v.i.,* **-rised, -rising.** →**tuberculise.** Also, **tubercularize.** – **tubercularisation** /təˌbɜkjələraɪ'zeɪʃən/, *n.*

**tuberculate** /tə'bɜkjələt/, *adj.* **1.** →**tubercular. 2.** having tubercules. Also, **tuberculose.** [NL *tūberculātus,* from L *tūberculum* tubercle] – **tuberculation** /təbɜkjə'leɪʃən/, *n.*

**tubercule** /'tjubəkjul/, *n.* a nodule, esp. on the roots of certain legumes.

**tuberculin** /tə'bɜkjələn/, *n.* a sterile liquid prepared from cultures of the tubercle bacillus, used in the diagnosis and treatment of tuberculosis.

**tuberculinise** /tə'bɜkjələnaɪz/, *v.t., v.i.,* **-nised, -nising.** →**tuberculise.** Also, **tuberculinize.** – **tuberculinisation** /təˌbɜkjələnaɪ'zeɪʃən/, *n.*

**tuberculise** /tə'bɜkjəlaɪz/, *v.,* **-lised, -lising.** *–v.t.* **1.** to innoculate with tuberculin. **2.** to infect with a tubercle, or with tuberculosis. *–v.i.* **3.** to form tubercles or become tuberculous. Also, **tubercularise, tuberculinise, tuberculize.** – **tuberculisation** /təbɜkjəlaɪ'zeɪʃən/, *n.*

**tuberculo-,** a word element representing **tuberculous, tuberculosis,** or **tubercle bacillus.** [combining form representing L *tūberculum* tubercle]

**tuberculoid** /tə'bɜkjəlɔɪd/, *adj.* resembling a tubercle.

**tuberculose** /tə'bɜkjəloʊs/, *adj.* →**tuberculate.**

**tuberculosis** /təbɜkjə'loʊsəs/, *n.* **1.** an infectious disease affecting any of various tissues of the body, due to the tubercle bacillus, and characterised by the production of tubercles. **2.** this disease when affecting the lungs; pulmonary phthisis; consumption. [NL, from L *tūberculum* TUBERCLE]

**tuberculous** /tə'bɜkjələs/, *adj.* **1.** →**tubercular. 2.** affected with tuberculosis: *several tuberculous patients.*

**tuberose**[1] /tjubə'roʊz, 'tjubəroʊz/, *n.* a bulbous plant, *Polianthes tuberosa,* cultivated for its spike of fragrant, creamy white, lily-like flowers. [L *tūberōsa,* fem. of *tūberōsus* tuberous, popularly confused with TUBE + ROSE[1]]

**tuberose**[2] /'tjubəroʊs/, *adj.* →**tuberous.**

**tuberosity** /tjubə'rɒsəti/, *n., pl.* **-ties.** a rough projection or protuberance of a bone as for the attachment of a muscle.

**tuberous** /'tjubərəs/, *adj.* **1.** covered with or characterised by rounded or wartlike prominences or tubers. **2.** of the nature of such a prominence. **3.** *Bot.* bearing tubers. **4.** having the nature of or resembling a tuber. [L *tūberōsus*]

**tuberous root** /– 'rut/, *n.* a true root so thickened as to resemble a tuber, but bearing no buds or eyes.

**tube train** /'tjub treɪn/, *n. Brit.* →**tube** (def. 9).

**tube worm** /'– wɜm/, *n.* any polychaete worm which constructs and inhabits a protective tube.

**tubing** /'tjubɪŋ/, *n.* **1.** material in the form of a tube: *copper tubing.* **2.** tubes collectively. **3.** a piece of tube.

**tub-thumper** /'tʌb-θʌmpə/, *n. Colloq.* a very vocal enthusiast.

**tubular** /'tjubjələ/, *adj.* **1.** of, or pertaining to a tube or tubes. **2.** characterised by or consisting of tubes. **3.** Also, **tubiform** /'tjubəfɔm/. having the nature or form of a tube; tube-shaped. **4.** *Physiol., Pathol.* denoting a respiratory sound resembling that produced by a current of air passing through a tube. [NL *tubulāris,* from L *tubulus* little tube] – **tubularity** /tjubjə'lærəti/, *n.*

**tubulate** /'tjubjələt/, *adj.;* /'tjubjəleɪt/, *v.,* **-lated, -lating.** *–adj.* **1.** formed into or like a tube; tubular. *–v.t.* **2.** to form into a tube. **3.** to furnish with a tube. – **tubulation** /tjubjə'leɪʃən/, *n.* – **tubulator,** *n.*

**tubule** /'tjubjul/, *n.* a small tube; a minute tubular structure. [L *tubulus* small pipe]

**tubuliflorous** /ˌtjubjulə'flɔrəs/, *adj.* having the corolla tubular in all the perfect flowers of a head, as certain plants of the family Compositae.

**tubulous** /'tjubjələs/, *adj.* **1.** containing or composed of tubes. **2.** having the form of a tube; tubular. [NL *tubulōsus*]

**tubulure** /'tjubjəluə/, *n.* a short tubular opening, as in a glass jar or at the top of a retort. [F, from L *tubulus* little pipe]

**tuck**[1] /tʌk/, *v.t.* **1.** to thrust into some narrow space or close or concealed place: *tuck this in your pocket.* **2.** to thrust the edge or end of (a garment, covering, etc.) closely into place between retaining parts or things (usu. fol. by *in, up,* etc.): *he tucked his napkin under his chin.* **3.** to cover snugly in or as in this manner: *to tuck one up in bed.* **4.** to draw up in folds or a folded arrangement: *to tuck one's legs under a chair.* **5.** *Needlework.* to sew tucks in. **6.** *Colloq.* to eat or drink (usu. fol. by *in, away,* etc.). **7.** *Colloq.* to imprison (usu. fol. by *away*). *–v.i.* **8.** to draw together; contract; pucker. **9.** *Needlework.* to make tucks. **10.** *Colloq.* to eat or drink heartily or greedily (usu. fol. by *in, into, away,* etc.). *–n.* **11.** a tucked piece or part. **12.** *Needlework.* a fold, or one of a series of folds, made by doubling cloth upon itself, and stitching parallel with the edge of the fold. **13.** *Naut.* the part of a vessel where the after ends of the outside planking or plating unite at the sternpost. **14.** *Chiefly Brit. Colloq.* food, esp. sweet delicacies such as cakes, pastries, jam, etc. **15.** *Sport.* (in diving) a dive in which the knees are bent and pulled in close to the chest, the body being straightened again before hitting the water. [ME *t(o)uke(n)* stretch (cloth), torment, OE *tūcian* torment. Cf. MLG *tucken,* G *zucken* tug]

**tuck**[2] /tʌk/, *n. Archaic.* a rapier with a stiff blade. [? sandhi var. of obs. *stock* sword. Cf. G *Stock,* F *estoc*]

**tuckahoe** /'tʌkəhoʊ/, *n.* **1.** the edible underground sclerotium of the fungus *Poria cocos,* found on the roots of trees in the southern U.S. **2.** *U.S.* an inhabitant of Virginia, esp. the eastern part. [Algonquian (Virginia d.) *tockawhouge* it is globular]

**tuckbox** /'tʌkbɒks/, *n.* a box containing food, esp. sweets, cakes etc.

**tucker**[1] /'tʌkə/, *n.* **1.** one who or that which tucks. **2.** *Colloq.* food. [TUCK[1] + -ER[1]]

**tucker**[2] /'tʌkə/, *v.t. Colloq.* to weary; tire; exhaust (oft. fol. by *out*).

**tuckerbag** /'tʌkəbæg/, *n.* any bag used for carrying food.

**tuckerbox** /'tʌkəbɒks/, *n.* any box used to hold food.

**tucket** /'tʌkət/, *n.* a flourish or fanfare on a trumpet.

**tuck-in** /tʌk-'ɪn, 'tʌk-ɪn/, *n. Colloq.* a hearty meal.

**tuck pointing** /'tʌk ˌpɔɪntɪŋ/, *n.* a pointing in which the mortar, often coloured, protrudes beyond the level of the brick or stone work, with square arrises.

**tuckshop** /'tʌkʃɒp/, *n.* a shop, esp. one in a school, where cakes, pastries, etc., are sold.

**-tude,** a suffix forming abstract nouns (generally from Latin adjectives or participles) in words of Latin origin, as in *latitude, fortitude,* but sometimes used directly as an English formative element. [L *-tūdo.* Cf. F *-tude*]

**Tudor** /ˈtjudə/, *adj.* **1.** of, pertaining to, or belonging to the English royal house of Tudor. **2.** of, pertaining to, or characteristic of the period of the reigns of the Tudor monarchs: *Tudor style of architecture.* [orig. the name of the royal family which ruled England from 1485 to 1603, and which was descended from Sir Owen *Tudor,* a Welshman who married the widow of Henry V]

**Tue.,** Tuesday.

**Tues.,** Tuesday.

**Tuesday** /ˈtjuzdeɪ, -di/, *n.* the third day of the week, following Monday. [ME *Tewesday,* OE *Tiwesdæg* Tiw's day (translation of L *Martis dies* day of Mars)]

**tufa** /ˈtjufə/, *n.* a porous mass of mineral calcium carbonate deposited round a spring. [It. *tufo,* from L *tōfus* loose porous stone] – **tufaceous** /tjuˈfeɪʃəs/, *adj.*

**tuff** /tʌf/, *n.* a rock of volcanic origin, comprising compacted or cemented volcanic ash and dust. Also, **volcanic tuff.** [F *tuf,* from It. *tufo* TUFA] – **tuffaceous** /təˈfeɪʃəs/, *adj.*

**tuffet** /ˈtʌfət/, *n.* **1.** a hillock; mound. **2.** a footstool; hassock.

**tuft** /tʌft/, *n.* **1.** a bunch of small, usu. soft and flexible things, as feathers, hairs, etc., fixed at the base with the upper part loose. **2.** a small clump of bushes, trees, etc. **3.** a cluster of short-stalked flowers, leaves, etc., growing from a common point. **4.** any of the bunches of threads sewn through a mattress, quilt, etc., in order to strengthen the padding. **5.** a button through which a tuft is sewn. *–v.t.* **6.** to furnish with a tuft or tufts. **7.** to arrange in a tuft or tufts. **8.** *Upholstery.* to draw together (a cushion, etc.) by passing a thread through at regular intervals, the depressions thus produced being usu. ornamented with tufts or buttons. *–v.i.* **9.** to form a tuft or tufts. [ME *toft;* orig. uncert.]

**tufted** /ˈtʌftəd/, *adj.* **1.** furnished with a tuft or tufts. **2.** formed into a tuft or tufts. **3.** (of carpet) made by a process in which a row of needles sews loops into a backing fabric.

**tufty** /ˈtʌfti/, *adj.* **1.** abounding in tufts. **2.** covered or adorned with tufts. **3.** forming a tuft or tufts.

**tug** /tʌg/, *v.,* **tugged, tugging,** *n.* *–v.t.* **1.** to pull at with force or effort. **2.** to move by pulling forcibly; drag; haul. **3.** to tow (a vessel, etc.) by means of a tugboat. **4. tug someone's head,** *Prison Colloq.* to distract someone's attention. *–v.i.* **5.** to pull with force or effort: *to tug at an oar.* **6.** to strive hard, labour, or toil. *–n.* **7.** the act of tugging; a strong pull. **8.** a struggle; a strenuous contest. **9.** →**tugboat. 10.** that by which something is tugged. **11. a.** a trace of a harness. **b.** any of various pulling or supporting parts of a harness. [ME *toggen,* apparently intensive var. of TOW[1]] – **tugger,** *n.* – **tugless,** *adj.*

**tugboat** /ˈtʌgboʊt/, *n.* a strongly built, heavily powered vessel for towing other vessels.

**tug of war,** *n.* **1.** an athletic contest between two teams at opposite ends of a rope, each team trying to drag the other over a line. **2.** a severe or critical struggle.

**tui** /ˈtui/, *n.* a glossy black honeyeater of New Zealand, *Prosthemadera novaeseelandiae,* which has white markings on the throat, neck and wings, and is an excellent mimic; parson-bird. [Maori]

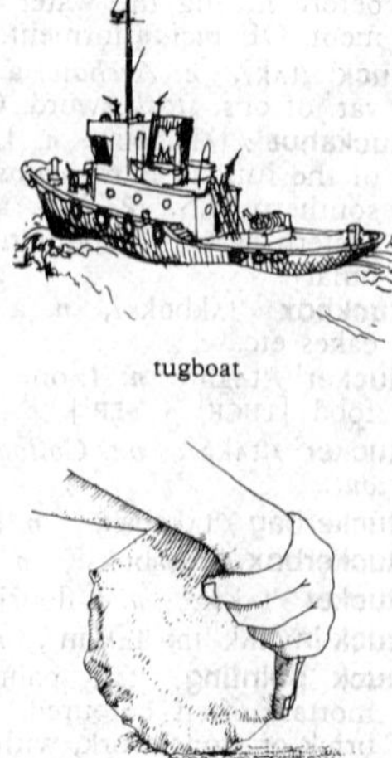

tugboat

tula-adze flake

**tuition** /tjuˈɪʃən/, *n.* **1.** teaching or instruction, as of pupils. **2.** the charge or fee for instruction. **3.** *Archaic.* guardianship or custody. [late ME *tuicion,* from L *tuitio* guardianship] – **tuitional, tuitionary,** *adj.* – **tuitionless,** *adj.*

**tula-adze flake** /tjulə-ædz ˈfleɪk/, *n.* a stone flake which is hafted in resin onto a wooden handle and used by the Aborigines of central Australia for chiselling and scraping wood. Also, **tula, tula adze.**

**tularaemia** /tuləˈrimiə/, *n.* a disease of rabbits, squirrels, etc., caused by a bacterium, *Pasturella tularensis* (or *Bacterium tularense*), transmitted to man by insects or by the handling of infected animals, resembling the plague and taking the form in man of an irregular fever lasting several weeks. Also, *U.S.,* **tularemia.** [*Tulare,* county in California + -AEMIA]

**tulip** /ˈtjuləp/, *n.* **1.** any of the plants constituting the genus, *Tulipa,* cultivated in many varieties, and having large, showy, usu. erect, cup-shaped or bell-shaped flowers of various colours. **2.** a flower or bulb of such a plant. **3.** any of several plants of other genera, as the cape tulip of the genus *Homeria.* [earlier *tulipa(n),* from Turk. *tülbend* TURBAN] – **tulip-like,** *adj.*

**tulip tree** /ˈ– tri/, *n.* **1.** a North American tree, *Liriodendron tulipifera,* with tulip-like flowers and a wood that is used in cabinetwork, etc.; yellow poplar. **2.** a West Indian tree, *Spathodea campanulata,* widely grown for ornament in the tropics.

**tulipwood** /ˈtjuləpwʊd/, *n.* **1.** the wood of the tulip tree. **2.** any of various striped or variegated woods of other trees, as *Harpullia pendula.* **3.** any of these trees.

**tulle** /tjul/, *n.* a thin silk or nylon net, used in millinery, dressmaking, etc. [F, *Tulle,* a town in central France]

tulips

**tum** /tʌm/, *n.* →**tummy.**

**tumatakuru** /ˈtumata,kʊrʊ/, *n.* →**matagouri.** [Maori]

**tumble** /ˈtʌmbəl/, *v.,* **-bled, -bling,** *n.* *–v.i.* **1.** to roll or fall over or down as by losing footing, support, or equilibrium: *to tumble down the stairs.* **2.** to fall rapidly, as stock market prices. **3.** to perform leaps, springs, somersaults, or other feats of bodily agility, as for exhibition or sport. **4.** to roll about by turning one way and another; pitch about; toss. **5.** to stumble or fall (usu. fol. by *over*). **6.** to go, come, get, etc., in a precipitate or hasty way. **7.** *Colloq.* to become suddenly alive to some fact, circumstance, or the like (oft. fol. by *to*). *–v.t.* **8.** to send falling or rolling; throw over or down. **9.** to move or toss about, or turn over, as in handling, searching, etc. **10.** to put in disorder by or as by tossing about. **11.** to throw, cast, put, send, etc., in a precipitate, hasty, or rough manner. **12.** to subject to the action of a tumbling box. *–n.* **13.** an act of tumbling; a fall; a downfall. **14.** tumbled condition; disorder or confusion. **15.** a confused heap. **16. a tumble in the hay,** *Colloq.* sexual intercourse outdoors. **17. take a tumble to (someone),** *Colloq.* to understand the motives of (someone) suddenly. [ME *tum(b)le* (frequentative of *tumben,* OE *tumbian* dance), c. G *tummeln*]

**tumbledown** /ˈtʌmbəldaʊn/, *adj.* dilapidated; ruinous.

**tumble drier** /ˈtʌmbəl draɪə/, *n.* a type of clothes drier in which a rotating barrel tumbles the clothes in warm air.

**tumblehome** /ˈtʌmbəlhoʊm/, *n.* the inward curve of the side of a canoe, boat, etc.

**tumbler** /ˈtʌmblə/, *n.* **1.** a drinking utensil with a flat bottom, without handle or stem, and usu. of glass. **2.** one who or that which tumbles; one who performs leaps, somersaults, and other bodily feats. **3.** (in a lock) any locking or checking part which, when lifted or released by the action of a key or the like, allows the bolt to move. **4.** (in a gunlock) a lever-like piece which by the action of a spring forces the hammer forwards when released by the trigger. **5.** *Mach.* **a.** a part moving a gear into place in a selective transmission. **b.** a single cog or cam on a rotating shaft, transmitting motion to a part with which it engages. **6.** →**tumbling box. 7.** a person who operates a tumbling box. **8.** one of a breed of dogs resembling small greyhounds, formerly used in hunting rabbits. **9.** one of a breed of domestic pigeons having the habit of turning over and over backwards in their flight. **10.** a toy, usu. representing a fat, squatting figure, with a heavy or weighted and rounded base, so as to rock when touched. **11.** a machine in which damp clothes are slowly rotated and subjected to heat in order to dry them.

**tumbler gear** /ˈ– gɪə/, *n.* a transmission having gears actuated by a tumbler.

**tumbler switch** /ˈ– swɪtʃ/, *n.* an electric switch having a quick action; used esp. in lighting circuits.

**tumbleweed** /ˈtʌmbəlwid/, *n.* **1.** any of various plants of North America, as *Amaranthus albus,* whose branching upper part becomes detached from the roots in autumn and is driven about by the wind. **2.** any of various plants in Australia which are similarly blown about by the wind.

tumbleweed

**tumbling box** /ˈtʌmblɪŋ bɒks/, *n.* an apparatus consisting of a box or cylindrical vessel pivoted at each end or at two corners, so that it can be made to revolve, used for polishing objects by allowing them to tumble about with an abrasive substance, for mixing materials, etc. Also, **tumbling barrel.**

**tumbrel** /ˈtʌmbrəl/, *n.* **1.** one of the carts used during the French Revolution to convey victims to the guillotine. **2.** a cart constructed so that the body tilts backwards to empty the load, esp. a dung cart. **3.** *Obs.* a two-wheeled covered cart accompanying artillery in order to carry tools, ammunition, etc. Also, **tumbril.** [ME *tumberell,* from ML *tumberellus,* from OLG *tumben* fall, c. OE *tumbian* dance. Cf. TUMBLE]

**tumefacient** /tjuməˈfeɪʃənt/, *adj.* tumefying; swelling. [L *tumefaciens,* ppr., tumefying]

**tumefaction** /tjuməˈfækʃən/, *n.* the act of making or becoming swollen or tumid. [L *tumefacere*]

**tumefy** /ˈtjuməfaɪ/, *v.t., v.i.,* **-fied, -fying.** to make or become swollen or tumid. [L *tumefacere*]

**tumescent** /tjuˈmɛsənt/, *adj.* swelling; slightly tumid. [L *tumescens* beginning to swell] – **tumescence,** *n.*

**tumid** /ˈtjuməd/, *adj.* **1.** swollen, or affected with swelling, as a part of the body. **2.** pompous, turgid, or bombastic, as language, literary style, etc. [L *tumidus* swollen] – **tumidity** /tjuˈmɪdəti/, **tumidness,** *n.* – **tumidly,** *adv.*

**tummy** /ˈtʌmi/, *n. Colloq.* stomach. Also, **tum.**

**tumour** /ˈtjumə/, *n.* **1.** a swollen part; a swelling or protuberance. **2.** *Pathol.* an abnormal or morbid swelling in any part of the body, esp. a more or less circumscribed morbid overgrowth of new tissue which is autonomous, differs more or less in structure from the part in which it grows, and serves no useful purpose. Also, *U.S.* **tumor.** [L: swollen state] – **tumorous,** *adj.*

**tumular** /ˈtjumjələ/, *adj.* of or like a tumulus or mound. [L *tumulus* mound + -AR[1]]

**tumult** /ˈtjumʌlt/, *n.* **1.** the commotion or disturbance of a multitude, usu. with noise; an uproar. **2.** a popular outbreak or uprising; commotion, disturbance, or violent disorder. **3.** agitation of mind; a mental or emotional disturbance. [ME, from L *tumultus*]

**tumultuary** /tjuˈmʌltʃəri/, *adj.* **1.** tumultuous. **2.** confused; irregular.

**tumultuous** /tjuˈmʌltʃuəs/, *adj.* **1.** full of or marked by tumult or uproar. **2.** making a tumult; disorderly or noisy, as persons, etc. **3.** disturbed or agitated, as the mind, feelings, etc. [L *tumultuōsus*] – **tumultuously,** *adv.* – **tumultuousness,** *n.*

**tumulus** /ˈtjumjələs/, *n., pl.* **-luses, -li** /-laɪ/. **1.** a mound or elevation of earth, etc., esp. of artificial origin and more or less antiquity. **2.** such a mound over a tomb; a barrow. [L: mound]

**tun** /tʌn/, *n., v.,* **tunned, tunning.** *–n.* **1.** a large cask for holding liquids, etc., esp. wine, ale, or beer. **2.** a measure of capacity for wine, etc., equivalent to the volume held by such a cask. *–v.t.* **3.** to put into or store in a tun or tuns. [ME and OE *tunne,* c. G *Tonne*]

**tuna**[1] /ˈtjunə/, *n.* **1.** any of various species of large, fast-swimming, marine food fishes related to and resembling mackerels but with red flesh and warm blood, widely distributed throughout warmer ocean waters, as the bluefin tuna or the yellowfin tuna of the eastern coast of Australia. **2.** any of various fishes of the tuna family as the albacore, bonito, etc. Also, **tunny.** [Amer. Sp., var. of Sp. *atún* (from Ar. *tún*) b. with d. *tun* tunny (from L *thunnus,* from Gk *thýnnos*]

**tuna**[2] /ˈtjunə/, *n.* **1.** any of various prickly pears, esp. the erect, treelike species, *Opuntia tuna* and others, native to Mexico, bearing a sweet, edible fruit. **2.** the fruit. [Sp., from Haitian]

**tuna**[3] /ˈtjunə/, *n. N.Z.* →**eel** (def. 1). [Maori]

**tunable** /ˈtjunəbəl/, *adj.* **1.** capable of being tuned. **2.** *Archaic.* in tune; harmonious; tuneful. Also, **tuneable.** – **tunableness,** *n.* – **tunably,** *adv.*

**tundish** /ˈtʌndɪʃ/, *n.* a conical or cylindrical open-topped receptacle with a tube at its base, forming a funnel through which fluids are led into a larger receptacle. [TUN + DISH]

**tundra** /ˈtʌndrə/, *n.* one of the vast, nearly level, treeless plains of the arctic regions of Europe, Asia, and North America. [Russ.: marshy plain]

**tune** /tjun/, *n., v.,* **tuned, tuning.** *–n.* **1.** a succession of musical sounds forming an air or melody, with or without the harmony accompanying it. **2.** a musical setting of a hymn or psalm, usu. in four-part harmony. **3.** the state of being in the proper pitch: *to be in tune.* **4.** agreement in pitch; unison; harmony. **5.** due agreement, as of radio instruments or circuits with respect to frequency. **6.** accord; agreement. **7.** *Obs.* frame of mind; mood. **8.** *Obs.* a tone or sound. **9. call the tune,** to be in a position to give orders, dictate policy, etc.; command; control. **10. change one's tune, sing another (a different) tune,** to change one's mind; reverse previously held views, attitudes, etc. **11. to the tune of,** to the amount of. *–v.t.* **12.** to adjust (a musical instrument) to a correct or given standard of pitch (oft. fol. by *up*). **13.** to bring into harmony. **14.** to adjust (an engine, machine or the like) for proper or improved running (oft. fol. by *up*). **15.** *Radio.* **a.** to adjust (a circuit, etc.) so as to bring it into resonance with another circuit, a given frequency, or the like. **b.** to adjust (a receiving apparatus) so as to make it in accord in frequency with a sending apparatus whose signals are to be received. **c.** to adjust a receiving apparatus so as to receive (the signals of a sending station). **16.** to put into a proper or a particular condition, mood, etc. **17.** *Rare.* to adapt (the voice, song, etc.) to a particular tone or to the expression of a particular feeling or the like; attune. **18.** *Archaic.* to utter, sound or express musically. **19.** *Archaic.* to play upon (a lyre, etc.). *–v.i.* **20.** to put a musical instrument, etc., in tune (oft. fol. by *up*). **21.** to give forth a musical sound. **22.** to sound or be in harmony. **23. tune in,** to adjust a radio so as to receive signals. **24. tune out,** to adjust a radio so as to avoid the signals of a sending station. [ME; unexplained var. of TONE]

**tuneable** /ˈtjunəbəl/, *adj.* →**tunable.**

**tuned circuit** /tjund ˈsɜkət/, *n.* a circuit consisting of an inductance and a capacitance which can be tuned to resonate at a given frequency by adjusting the values of the inductance or the capacitance; a resonant circuit.

**tuneful** /ˈtjunfəl/, *adj.* **1.** full of melody; melodious: *tuneful compositions.* **2.** producing musical sounds or melody. – **tunefully,** *adv.* – **tunefulness,** *n.*

**tuneless** /ˈtjunləs/, *adj.* **1.** unmelodious; unmusical. **2.** making or giving no music; silent: *in the corner stood a tuneless old piano.* – **tunelessly,** *adv.*

**tuner** /ˈtjunə/, *n.* **1.** one who or that which tunes. **2.** the part of a radio receiver which produces an output suitable for feeding into an amplifier.

**tune-up** /ˈtjun-ʌp/, *n.* a check or adjustment of working order or condition, as an adjustment of the carburettor, ignition timing, etc., of a motor vehicle for maximum efficiency or power.

**tung-oil** /ˈtʌŋ-ɔɪl/, *n.* a drying oil, a valuable ingredient of varnishes, obtained from the seeds of a tree, *Aleurites fordii.* [Chinese *t'ung*]

**tungoo** /ˈtʌŋgu/, *n.* →**boodie rat.** Also, **tungo.** [Aboriginal]

**tungstate** /ˈtʌŋsteɪt/, *n.* a salt of any tungstic acid.

**tungsten** /ˈtʌŋstən/, *n.* a rare metallic element having a bright grey colour, a metallic lustre, and a high melting point (3410°C), found in wolframite, tungstite, and other minerals, and used to make high-speed steel cutting tools, for electric-lamp filaments, etc.; wolfram. *Symbol:* W (for *wolframium*); *at. wt:* 183.85; *at. no.:* 74; *sp. gr.:* 19.3. [Swed.: heavy stone] – **tungstenic** /tʌŋˈstɛnɪk/, *adj.*

**tungsten carbide** /– ˈkabaɪd/, *n.* a grey powder, WC, which has a melting point of 2870°C and which is used as an abrasive, and in forming dies, and in making wear-resistant mechanical parts.

**tungsten lamp** /'– læmp/, *n.* an incandescent electric lamp in which the filament is made of tungsten.

**tungsten steel** /'– stil/, *n.* a hard special steel containing tungsten.

**tungsten trioxide** /– traɪ'ɒksaɪd/, *n.* a yellow insoluble powder, $WO_3$, used in the manfacture of tungstates. Also, **tungstic acid, tungstic anhydride.**

**tungstic** /'tʌŋstɪk/, *adj.* of or containing tungsten, esp. in the pentavalent state or in the hexavalent state.

**tungstic acid** /– 'æsəd/, *n.* **1.** a hydrate of tungsten trioxide, $H_2WO_4.H_2O$, used in the manufacture of tungsten lamp filaments. **2.** any of a group of acids derived from tungsten by polymerisation of tungsten trioxide. **3.** tungsten trioxide.

**tungstite** /'tʌŋstaɪt/, *n.* native tungsten trioxide, $WO_3$, a yellow or yellowish green mineral occurring usu. in a pulverulent form.

**Tungusic** /tʊŋ'gusɪk/, *n.* **1.** a branch of the Altaic family of languages spoken in central and eastern Siberia and Manchuria. *–adj.* **2.** belonging to or pertaining to the Tunguses, a Mongoloid people living in eastern Siberia, or to Tungusic. Also, **Tungusian** /tʊŋ'gusiən/.

**tunic** /'tjunɪk/, *n.* **1.** a coat worn as part of a military or other uniform. **2.** a loose, sleeveless dress, esp. as worn by girls as part of a school uniform. **3.** a similar garment worn by women, as for gymnastics, dancing, etc. **4.** a garment like a shirt or gown, worn by both sexes among the ancient Greeks and Romans. **5.** *Eccles.* a tunicle. **6.** *Anat., Zool.* **a.** any covering or investing membrane or part, as of an organ. **b.** any loose membranous skin not formed from the epidermis. **7.** *Bot.* a natural integument. [OE *tunice,* from L *tunica*]

**tunica** /'tjunɪkə/, *n., pl.* **-cae** /-si/. *Anat., Zool., Bot.* a tunic. [NL, special use of L *tunica* tunic]

**tunicate** /'tjunəkət, -keɪt/, *n.* **1.** *Zool.* any marine chordate of the subphylum Tunicata, having a saclike body enclosed in a thick membrane (tunic) from which protrude two openings or siphons for the ingress and egress of water. *–adj.* Also, **tunicated. 2.** (esp. of the Tunicata) having a tunic or covering. **3.** of or pertaining to the tunicates. **4.** *Bot.* having or consisting of a series of concentric layers, as a bulb. [L *tunicātus,* pp., clothed with a tunic]

**tunicle** /'tjunəkəl/, *n.* a vestment worn over the alb by subdeacons, as at the celebration of the mass, and by bishops. [ME, from L *tunicula,* diminutive of *tunica* tunic]

**tuning** /'tjunɪŋ/, *n.* the configuration of pitches for the individual strings of instruments such as lutes and zithers.

**tuning capacitor** /'– kəpæsətə/, *n.* an adjustable capacitor in a tuned circuit of a radio.

**tuning coil** /'– kɔɪl/, *n.* an inductive coil in an electronic circuit which can be adjusted to tune the circuit.

**tuning fork** /'– fɔk/, *n.* a small steel instrument consisting of two prongs on a stem, designed to produce, when struck, a pure musical note of a definite constant pitch, and thus serving as a standard for tuning musical instruments, in acoustical investigation, etc.

**Tunisia** /tju'nɪziə/, *n.* a republic of northern Africa on the Mediterranean. – **Tunisian,** *adj., n.*

**Tunku** /'tʊŋku/, *n.* a Malayan title of respect before family names as an indication of nobility or rank. Also, **Tuanku.** [Malay: ruler] – **Tengku** /tɛŋku/, **Tenku,** *n. fem.*

**tunnage** /'tʌnɪdʒ/, *n.* →**tonnage.**

**tunnel** /'tʌnəl/, *n., v.,* **-nelled, -nelling** or (*U.S.*) **-neled, -neling.** *–n.* **1.** an underground passage. **2.** a passageway, as for trains, motor vehicles, etc., through or under an obstruction as a hill, mountain, river, town, harbour, etc. **3.** an approximately horizontal passageway or gallery in a mine. **4.** the burrow of an animal. **5.** *Rugby Football.* the space between the opposing front rows of the scrum. **6.** *Obs.* the flue of a chimney. *–v.t.* **7.** to make or form a tunnel through or under. **8.** to make or form as or like a tunnel: *to tunnel a passage under a river.* **9.** to perforate as with tunnels. *–v.i.* **10.** to make a tunnel or tunnels: *to tunnel through the Alps.* [late ME *tonel* funnel-shaped net. Cf. OF *tonel* cask, from *tonne* TON[1]] – **tunneller;** *esp. U.S.,* **tunneler,** *n.*

**tunnel ball** /'– bɔl/, *n.* a team game in which the members stand in a line while the last person takes the ball to the end of the line and bowls it through the tunnel formed by the wide-spread legs of the rest of the team.

**tunnel diode** /– 'daɪoʊd/, *n.* a semiconductor which has a negative resistance over part of its operating range as a result of the tunnel effect.

**tunnel effect** /'– əfɛkt/, *n.* the passage of an electron through a narrow potential barrier in a semiconductor in spite of its energy level being too low to surmount the barrier according to classical mechanics. This is explained in terms of quantum mechanics on the assumption that most of the electron's energy can tunnel through the barrier.

**tunnel vision** /– 'vɪʒən/, *n.* **1.** a disorder in which the field of vision is restricted to 70 per cent or less of the normal field from the straight-ahead position, thereby eliminating everything peripheral. **2.** an impaired ability to plan for the future as a result of an obsession with one particular goal to the exclusion of all other possibilities.

**tunny** /'tʌni/, *n., pl.* **-nies,** (*esp. collectively*) **-ny. 1.** any of a number of widely distributed, important, marine food fishes, genus *Thunnus,* of the mackerel family, esp. *T. thynnus,* occurring in the warmer parts of the Atlantic and Pacific oceans, sometimes reaching a weight of 350kg or more. **2.** →**tuna**[1]. [F *thon,* from Pr. *ton,* from L *thunnus,* from Gk *thýnnos*]

**tup** /tʌp/, *n., v.,* **tupped, tupping.** *–n.* **1.** a male sheep; ram. **2.** the head of a steam hammer or pile-driver. *–v.t.* **3.** (of a ram) to copulate with (a ewe).

**tupelo** /'tjupəloʊ/, *n., pl.* **-los. 1.** any of several trees of the genus *Nyssa,* esp. a large tree, *N. aquatica,* of deep swamps and river bottoms of the southern U.S. **2.** the strong, tough wood of any of these trees, esp. in commercial use. [N. Amer. Ind. (Creek) *ito opelwa* swamp tree]

**Tupi** /tu'pi/, *n., pl.* **-pis. 1.** a member of a widespread group of tribes of South American Indians living along the lower Amazon and in the valleys of other Brazilian rivers. **2.** the language of this group. – **Tupian,** *adj.*

**tupong** /'tupɒŋ/, *n.* →**congolli.** [Aboriginal]

**tuppence** /'tʌpəns/, *n.* (formerly) twopence.

**tuppeny** /'tʌpəni/, *n.* →**twopenny.**

**tuque** /tjuk/, *n.* a kind of knitted cap worn in Canada. [Canadian F, var. of F *toque* cap]

**Turanian** /tju'reɪniən/, *adj.* **1.** belonging or pertaining to a group of Asian peoples or languages comprising all or nearly all those which are neither Indo-European nor Semitic. **2.** *Obs.* Ural-Altaic. *–n.* **3.** a member of any of the races speaking a Turanian (esp. a Ural-Altaic) language. **4.** a member of any of the Ural-Altaic races. [Pers. *Tūrān,* name of district beyond the Oxus + -IAN]

**turban** /'tɜbən/, *n.* **1.** a form of headdress of Muslim origin worn by men chiefly in parts of northern Africa, and south-western and southern Asia, consisting of a scarf of silk, linen, cotton, or the like, wound directly round the head or around a cap. **2.** any headdress resembling this. **3.** a small hat, either brimless or with a brim turned up close against the crown, worn by women. [earlier *turband,* from Turk. *tülbend,* from Ar. *dulband,* from Pers., Hind.] – **turbaned,** *adj.* – **turbanless,** *adj.*

**turbary** /'tɜbəri/, *n., pl.* **-ries. 1.** land, or a piece of land, where turf or peat may be dug or cut. **2.** *Brit. Law.* the right to cut turf or peat on a common or another person's land. [ME *turbarye,* from ML *turbaria,* from *turba* turf]

**turbellarian** /tɜbə'lɛəriən/, *adj.* **1.** belonging to the Turbellaria, a class of platyhelminths or flatworms, mostly aquatic, and characterised by cilia whose motions produce small currents or vortexes in water. *–n.* **2.** a turbellarian platyhelminth. [NL *Turbellāria,* from L *turbella* little crowd + *-āria,* neut. pl. of *-ārius* -ARY[1]]

**turbid** /'tɜbəd/, *adj.* **1.** (of liquids) opaque or muddy with particles of extraneous matter. **2.** not clear or transparent; thick, as smoke or clouds; dense. **3.** disturbed; confused; muddled. [L *turbidus* disturbed] – **turbidity** /tɜ'bɪdəti/, **turbidness,** *n.* – **turbidly,** *adv.*

**turbidimeter** /tɜbə'dɪmətə/, *n.* a device for measuring the turbidity of water or other liquids.

**turbinal** /'tɜbənəl/, *adj.* **1.** turbinate. *–n.* **2.** *Anat.* a turbinate bone. [L *turbo* top + -AL[1]]

**turbinate** /ˈtɜbənət, -neɪt/, *adj.* Also, **turbinated. 1.** scroll-like; whorled; spiral. **2.** *Anat.* denoting or pertaining to certain scroll-like spongy bones of the nasal passages in the higher vertebrates. **3.** inversely conical. *–n.* **4.** a turbinate shell. **5.** *Anat.* a turbinate bone. [L *turbinātus* shaped like a top]

**turbine** /ˈtɜbaɪn/, *n.* **1.** any of a class of hydraulic motors in which a vaned wheel or runner is made to revolve by the impingement of a free jet of fluid (**impulse turbine** or **action turbine**) or by the passage of fluid which completely fills the motor (**reaction** or **pressure turbine**). **2.** any of certain analogous motors using other fluids, as steam (**steam turbine**), products of combustion (**gas turbine**), or air (**air turbine**). [F, from L *turbo* anything that spins]

**turbit** /ˈtɜbət/, *n.* one of a breed of domestic pigeons with a stout, roundish body, a short head and beak, and a ruffled breast and neck. [apparently from L *turbo* a top; so called because of its figure]

**turbo-** /ˈtɜboʊ-/, *adj.* a prefix indicating: **a.** driven by a turbine. **b.** of or pertaining to a turbine.

**turbo-electric** /ˌtɜboʊ-əˈlɛktrɪk/, *adj.* having an electric motor powered by a turbine.

**turbofan** /ˈtɜboʊfæn/, *n.* a turbojet engine incorporating an oversize compressor acting as a ducted fan.

**turbogenerator** /tɜboʊˈdʒɛnəreɪtə/, *n.* an electric generator coupled to a steam turbine.

**turbojet** /ˈtɜboʊdʒɛt/, *n.* **1.** an engine in which the power is developed by a turbine driving a compressor which supplies air to a fuel burner, through the turbine to a thrust-producing exhaust nozzle. **2.** any vehicle propelled by such an engine.

**turboprop** /ˈtɜboʊprɒp/, *n. Aeron.* **1.** a gas-turbine engine coupled to a propeller, forming a propulsive unit of an aircraft. **2.** an aeroplane driven by one or more of such units. Also, **propjet.**

**turbosupercharger** /tɜboʊˈsupətʃadʒə/, *n.* a supercharger which uses an exhaust-driven turbine to maintain air-intake pressure in high-altitude aircraft.

**turbot** /ˈtɜbət/, *n., pl.* **-bots** (*esp. collectively*), **-bot. 1.** a European flatfish, *Psetta maxima,* with a diamond-shaped body. **2.** any of several other flatfishes. **3.** a triggerfish. [ME, from MD (cf. OF *torbot*); orig. uncert.]

turbot

**turbulence** /ˈtɜbjələns/, *n.* **1.** a turbulent state. **2.** *Hydraulics.* the haphazard secondary motion due to eddies within a moving fluid. **3.** *Meteorol.* irregular motion of the atmosphere, as that indicated by gusts and lulls in the wind. Also, **turbulency.**

**turbulent** /ˈtɜbjələnt/, *adj.* **1.** disposed or given to disturbances, disorder, or insubordination; violent; unruly. **2.** marked by or showing a spirit of disorder or insubordination: *a turbulent period.* **3.** disturbed; agitated; troubled; stormy. [L *turbulentus* restless] – **turbulently,** *adv.*

**turbulent flow** /– ˈfloʊ/, *n.* fluid flow in which the motion at any point varies rapidly in magnitude and direction.

**Turco-,** a word element meaning 'Turkish'. [F, from It.]

**turd** /tɜd/, *n. Colloq.* **1.** a piece of excrement. **2.** (*derog.*) an unpleasant person. [ME; OE *tord*]

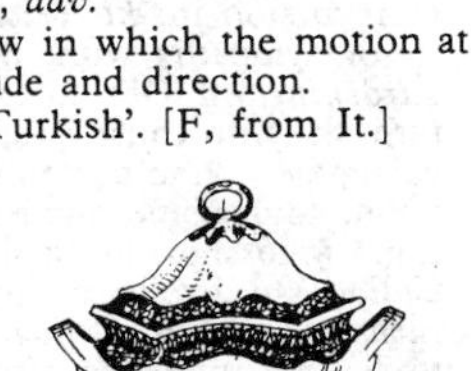

tureen

**turdiform** /ˈtɜdəfɔm/, *adj.* having the form of a thrush. [NL *turdiformis,* from L *turdus* thrush + -(*i*)*formis* -(I)FORM]

**turdine** /ˈtɜdaɪn, -dən/, *adj.* belonging or pertaining to the thrushes, birds of the family Turdidae. [L *turdus* thrush + -INE[1]]

**turd strangler** /ˈtɜd stræŋglə/, *n. Colloq.* a plumber.

**tureen** /təˈrin, tju-/, *n.* a large deep dish with a cover, for holding soup, etc., at the table. [earlier *terrine,* from F: earthenware dish, from L *terra* earth]

**turf** /tɜf/, *n., pl.* **turfs, turves** /tɜvz/, *v.* *–n.* **1.** the covering of grass, etc., with its matted roots, forming the surface of grassland. **2.** a piece cut or torn from the surface of grassland, with the grass, etc., growing on it; a sod. **3.** a block or piece of peat dug for fuel. **4.** peat as a substance for fuel. **5. the turf, a.** the grassy course or other track over which horseraces are run. **b.** the practice or institution of racing horses. **c.** the racing world. *–v.t.* **6.** to cover with turf or sod. **7. turf out,** *Colloq.* to throw out; eject. [ME and OE, c. G *Torf* peat; Latinised, *turba*] – **turfless,** *adj.*

**turf accountant** /ˈ– əkaʊntənt/, *n. Brit.* →**bookmaker.**

**turfman** /ˈtɜfmən/, *n., pl.* **-men.** a man devoted to horseracing.

**turfy** /ˈtɜfi/, *adj.,* **turfier, turfiest. 1.** covered with or consisting of grassy turf. **2.** resembling turf; turf-like. **3.** abounding in, or of the nature of, turf or peat. **4.** pertaining to or characteristic of horseracing. – **turfiness,** *n.*

**turgent** /ˈtɜdʒənt/, *adj. Obs.* swelling; swollen; turgid. [L *turgens,* ppr., swelling] – **turgently,** *adv.*

**turgescent** /tɜˈdʒɛsənt/, *adj.* becoming swollen; swelling. [L *turgescens,* ppr.] – **turgescence, turgescency,** *n.*

**turgid** /ˈtɜdʒəd/, *adj.* **1.** pompous or bombastic, as language, style, etc. **2.** swollen; distended; tumid. [L *turgidus*] – **turgidity** /tɜˈdʒɪdəti/, **turgidness,** *n.* – **turgidly,** *adv.*

**turgor** /ˈtɜgə/, *n.* **1.** the state of being swelled or filled out. **2.** *Plant Physiol.* the normal distension or rigidity of plant cells, resulting from the pressure exerted from within against the cell walls by the cell contents. [L, from *turgēre* swell]

**turinga** /təˈrɪŋgə/, *n.* →**churinga.**

**Turing Machine** /ˈtjurɪŋ məˌʃin/, *n.* a postulated basic computing device consisting of a tape, a scanner, a printer and a table of states in vector form (I,O,N,D), where 'I' is the symbol scanned, 'O' the symbol outputted, 'N' the next state, 'D' the direction of the tape movement. [named after A.M. *Turing,* 1912-54, British mathematician]

turkey

**Turk** /tɜk/, *n.* **1.** a native or inhabitant of Turkey. **2.** (formerly) a native or inhabitant of the Ottoman Empire, esp. a Muslim. **3.** a member of any of the peoples speaking Turkic languages. **4.** a cruel, brutal, tyrannical, or unruly man. **5.** one of a breed of horses allied to the Arab. **6.** any Turkish horse. [ME, from Pers.]

**Turk., 1.** Turkey. **2.** Turkish.

**turkey** /ˈtɜki/, *n., pl.* **-keys,** (*esp. collectively for def. 1*) **-key. 1.** a large gallinaceous bird of the family Meleagrididae, esp. *Meleagris gallopava,* of America, which is domesticated in most parts of the world. **2.** the flesh of this bird, used as food. **3.** *U.S. Colloq.* an unsuccessful theatrical production; flop. **4. talk turkey,** *Colloq.* to talk seriously; talk business.

**Turkey** /ˈtɜki/, *n.* a republic in western Asia and south-eastern Europe.

**turkey bush** /ˈtɜki bʊʃ/, *n.* any of various shrubs having fruits eaten by the bustard, or plain turkey, as the Ellangowan poison-bush.

**turkey buzzard** /ˈ– bʌzəd/, *n.* a vulture, *Cathartes aura,* common in South and Central America and the southern U.S., having a bare reddish head and a dark plumage. Also, **turkey vulture.**

**turkey cock** /ˈ– kɒk/, *n.* **1.** the male of the turkey. **2.** a strutting, pompous, conceited person.

**turkey oak** /ˈ– oʊk/, *n.* an oak tree with deeply cut, hairy leaves, *Quercus cerris,* native to western and southern Europe but often planted and naturalised elsewhere.

turkey buzzard

**turkey quail** /ˈ– kweɪl/, *n.* →**plains wanderer.**

**Turkey red** /tɜki ˈrɛd/, *n.* **1.** a bright red produced in fabrics by madder or alizarin. **2.** cotton cloth of this colour.

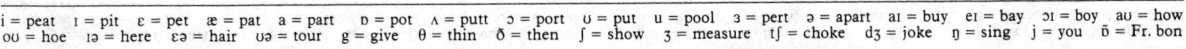

**turkey's-nest tank** /ˈtɜkiz-nɛst ˌtæŋk/, *n.* a tank (def. 2) which is built on flat country where there is no natural run-off; the walls are built up above ground level and the tank filled with water, usu. from a bore or nearby creek. Also, **turkey's-nest dam.**

**turkey trot** /ˈtɜki trɒt/, *n.* a round dance popular during World War I, danced by couples, properly to ragtime, the step being a springy walk with little or no bending of the knees, and accompanied by a swinging motion of the shoulder movements up and down.

**Turkic** /ˈtɜkɪk/, *n.* **1.** a branch of the Altaic family of languages that includes Turkish, Azerbaijani, Turkmen, Uzbeg, Kirghiz, and Yakut. *–adj.* **2.** of or pertaining to Turkic.

**Turkish** /ˈtɜkɪʃ/, *adj.* **1.** pertaining or belonging to or derived from the Turks or Turkey. **2.** of or pertaining to the language of the Turks. *–n.* **3.** the language of Turkey; Ottoman Turkish. **4.** Turkic.

**Turkish bath** /– ˈbaθ/, *n.* a kind of bath introduced from the East, in which, after copious perspiration in a heated room, the body is washed, massaged, etc.

**Turkish delight** /– dəˈlaɪt/, *n.* a cubed, gelatine-stiffened confection covered with icing sugar. Also, **Grecian delight.**

**Turkish towel** /– ˈtaʊəl/, *n.* **1.** a thick cotton towel with a long nap, usu. composed of uncut loops. **2.** candidiasis in turkeys.

**Turkism** /ˈtɜkɪzəm/, *n.* the culture, beliefs, principles, etc., of the Turks.

**Turko-**, variant of **Turco-**.

**Turk's-cap lily** /ˈtɜks-kæp lɪli/, *n.* either of two lilies, *Lilium martagon* and *L. superbum,* having nodding flowers with the perianth segments strongly revolute.

**Turk's-head** /ˈtɜks-hɛd/, *n.* a form of decorative knot made by weaving turns of small cord round a larger rope.

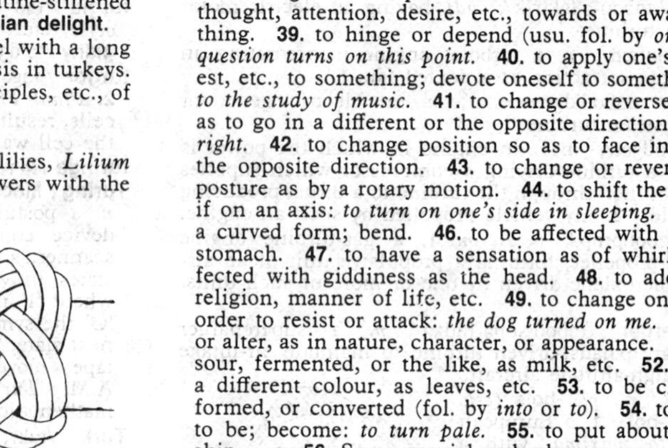
Turk's-head

**Turks' head broom,** *n.* a broom with a very long handle, and a stiff bristled head, used for cleaning cobwebs from ceilings, etc.

**turmaline** /ˈtɜməlin/, *n.* →**tourmaline.**

**turmeric** /ˈtɜmərɪk/, *n.* **1.** the aromatic rhizome of *Curcuma longa,* an East Indian zingiberaceous plant. **2.** a powder prepared from it, used as a condiment (esp. in curry powder), a yellow dye, a medicine, etc. **3.** the plant itself. **4.** any of various similar substances or plants. [earlier *tarmaret,* from ML *terra merita,* lit., deserving earth]

**turmeric paper** /ˈ– peɪpə/, *n.* paper treated with turmeric, used to indicate the presence of alkalis, which turn it brown, or of boric acid, which turns it reddish brown.

**turmoil** /ˈtɜmɔɪl/, *n.* a state of commotion or disturbance; tumult; agitation; disquiet. [apparently from TURN + MOIL]

**turn** /tɜn/, *v.t.* **1.** cause to move round on an axis or about a centre; rotate: *to turn a wheel.* **2.** to cause to move round or partly round, as for the purpose of opening, closing, tightening, etc.: *to turn a key.* **3.** to reverse the position or posture of: *to turn a page.* **4.** to bring the underparts of (sod, soil, etc.) to the surface, as in ploughing. **5.** to change the position of, by, or as by, rotating; to move into a different position. **6.** to change or alter the course of; to divert; deflect. **7.** to change or alter the nature, character, or appearance of. **8.** to change or convert (fol. by *into* or *to*): *to turn water into ice.* **9.** to render or make by some change. **10.** to change the colour of (leaves, etc.). **11.** to cause to become sour, ferment, or the like: *warm weather turns milk.* **12.** to cause (the stomach) to reject food or anything swallowed. **13.** to change from one language or form of expression to another; translate. **14.** to put or apply to some use or purpose: *to turn a thing to good use.* **15.** to go or pass round or to the other side of: *to turn a street corner.* **16.** to get beyond or pass (a certain age, time, amount, etc.): *he has just turned forty.* **17.** to direct, aim or set going towards or away from a specified person or thing, or in a specified direction: *to turn towards the north.* **18.** to direct (the eyes, face, etc.) another way; avert. **19.** to shape (a piece of metal, etc.) into rounded form with a cutting instrument while rotating in a lathe. **20.** to bring into a rounded or curved form in any way. **21.** to shape artistically or gracefully, esp. in rounded form. **22.** to form or express gracefully: *to turn a sentence.* **23.** to direct (thought, desire, etc.) towards or away from something. **24.** to cause to go; send; drive: *to turn a person from one's door.* **25.** to revolve in the mind (oft. fol. by *over*). **26.** to maintain a steady flow or circulation of (money or articles of commerce). **27.** to reverse (a garment, etc.) so that the inner side becomes the outer. **28.** to remake (a garment) by putting the inner side outwards. **29.** to curve, bend, or twist. **30.** to bend back or blunt (the edge of a knife, etc.). **31.** to execute, as a somersault, by rotating or revolving. **32.** to disturb the mental balance of, or make mad, distract; derange. **33.** to throw into disorder or confusion; upset: *the thief turned the room upside down.* *–v.i.* **34.** to move round on an axis or about a centre; rotate. **35.** to move partly round in this manner, as a door on a hinge. **36.** to direct the face or gaze towards or away from something, or in a particular direction. **37.** to direct or set one's course towards or away from something or in a particular direction. **38.** to direct one's thought, attention, desire, etc., towards or away from something. **39.** to hinge or depend (usu. fol. by *on* or *upon*): *the question turns on this point.* **40.** to apply one's efforts, interest, etc., to something; devote oneself to something: *he turned to the study of music.* **41.** to change or reverse the course so as to go in a different or the opposite direction: *to turn to the right.* **42.** to change position so as to face in a different or the opposite direction. **43.** to change or reverse position or posture as by a rotary motion. **44.** to shift the body about as if on an axis: *to turn on one's side in sleeping.* **45.** to assume a curved form; bend. **46.** to be affected with nausea, as the stomach. **47.** to have a sensation as of whirling, or be affected with giddiness as the head. **48.** to adopt a different religion, manner of life, etc. **49.** to change one's position in order to resist or attack: *the dog turned on me.* **50.** to change or alter, as in nature, character, or appearance. **51.** to become sour, fermented, or the like, as milk, etc. **52.** to become of a different colour, as leaves, etc. **53.** to be changed, transformed, or converted (fol. by *into* or *to*). **54.** to change so as to be; become: *to turn pale.* **55.** to put about or tack, as a ship. *–v.* **56.** Some special verb phrases are:

**turn away, 1.** to look or face in a different direction. **2.** to refuse to help; rebuff. **3.** to refuse admission to.

**turn against, 1.** to make hostile towards; cause to be prejudiced against: *to turn a son against his father.* **2.** to take up an attitude of hostility or opposition: *to turn against a person.*

**turn back, 1.** to go back; return. **2.** to cause to go back or return. **3.** to fold back or over.

**turn down, 1.** to fold. **2.** to lessen the intensity of; moderate. **3.** to refuse or reject (a person, request, etc.).

**turn in, 1.** *Colloq.* to go to bed. **2.** *Colloq.* to hand over to; deliver; surrender. **3.** to give back. **4.** to submit; hand in.

**turn it up!** *Colloq.* stop it! shut up!

**turn off, 1.** to stop the flow of (water, gas, etc.) as by closing a valve, etc. **2.** to switch off (a radio, light, etc.). **3.** to branch off; diverge; change direction. **4.** to arouse antipathy or revulsion in: *his teaching turns me off.* **5.** to lose interest in or sympathy with; develop a dislike for: *I've turned off gardening.* **6.** *Obs.* to execute by hanging.

**turn on, 1.** to cause (water, gas, etc.) to flow as by opening a valve, etc. **2.** to switch on (a radio, light, etc.). **3.** Also, **turn upon.** to become suddenly hostile to; attack without warning. **4.** to show or display suddenly: *to turn on the charm.* **5.** *Colloq.* to excite or interest (a person): *that jazz really turns me on!* **6.** *Colloq.* to experience heightened awareness under the influence of a drug (usu. illegal), as marijuana or LSD. **7.** *Colloq.* to take such a drug. **8.** to arouse sexually.

**turn out, 1.** to extinguish or put out (a light, etc.). **2.** to produce as the result of labour; manufacture; make. **3.** to drive out; expel; send away; dismiss; discharge. **4.** to clear or empty (a cupboard, pocket, drawer, etc.) of contents. **5.** to equip; fit out. **6.** to result or issue. **7.** to come to be; become ultimately. **8.** to be found or known; prove. **9.** *Colloq.* to get out of bed. **10.** *Colloq.* to assemble, or cause to assemble; muster; parade; gather.

**turn over, 1.** to move or be moved from one side to another. **2.** to reverse the position of; invert. **3.** to meditate;

ponder; reflect. **4.** to start (an engine). **5.** (of an engine) to start. **6.** hand over; transfer. **7.** *Comm.* to purchase and then sell (goods or commodities). **8.** *Comm.* to do business or sell goods to the amount of (a specified sum). **9.** *Comm.* to invest or recover (capital) in some transaction or in the course of business.
**turn to, 1.** to apply to for help, advice, etc.; appeal to. **2.** to set oneself to a task; attend to.
**turn up, 1.** to fold, esp. so as to shorten, as a garment. **2.** to dig up; bring to the surface by digging; expose. **3.** to find; bring to light; uncover. **4.** to increase the intensity of. **5.** to happen; occur. **6.** to arrive; come. **7.** to come to light; be recovered. **8.** (of a person's nose, or the like) to point slightly upwards at the end. **9.** *Brit. Colloq.* to make (a person) feel sick; nauseate. **10.** *Prison Colloq.* to give evidence that results in an acquittal for (someone).
*–n.* **57.** a movement of rotation, whether total or partial: *a slight turn of the handle.* **58.** the act of changing or reversing position or posture as by a rotary movement: *a turn of the dice.* **59.** the time for action or proceeding which comes in due rotation or order to each of a number of persons, etc.: *it's my turn to pay.* **60.** the act of changing or reversing the course: *to make a turn to the right.* **61.** a place or point at which such a change occurs. **62.** a place where a road, river, or the like turns. **63.** a single revolution, as of a wheel. **64.** the act of turning so as to face or go in a different direction. **65.** direction, drift, or trend: *the conversation took an interesting turn.* **66.** change or a change in nature, character, condition, circumstances, etc. **67.** the point or time of change. **68.** the time during which a workman or a set of workmen is at work in alternation with others. **69.** that which is done by each of a number of persons acting in rotation or succession. **70.** rounded or curved form in general. **71.** shape, form, or mould. **72.** a passing or twisting of one thing round another as of a rope round a mast. **73.** the condition or manner of being twisted. **74.** a single round, as of a wound or coiled rope. **75.** style, as of expression or language. **76.** a distinctive form or style imparted: *a happy turn of expression.* **77.** a short walk, ride, or the like which includes a going and a returning, esp. by different routes. **78.** natural inclination, bent, tendency, or aptitude. **79.** a spell or period of work; shift. **80.** a spell or bout of action. **81.** an attack of illness or the like. **82.** an act of service or disservice (with *good, bad, kind,* etc.). **83.** requirement, exigency, or need: *this will serve your turn.* **84.** *Colloq.* a nervous shock, as from fright or astonishment. **85.** *Stock Exchange.* the difference between the stockjobber's buying and selling price. **86.** *Music.* a melodic embellishment or grace, commonly consisting of a principal note with two auxiliary notes, one above and the other below it. **87.** an individual stage performance, esp. in a music hall, cabaret, etc. **88.** the performer in such an entertainment. **89.** a contest or round; a bout. **90.** Also, **turnout.** a social entertainment; party: *it was a great turn on Friday.* **91.** Some special noun phrases are:
**at every turn,** constantly; in every case.
**by turns,** one after another; alternately; in rotation.
**in turn,** in due order of succession.
**on the turn, 1.** in the process of or about to turn or change. **2.** (of milk) on the point of turning sour.
**out of turn, 1.** out of proper order. **2.** at the wrong time; at an unsuitable moment; indiscreetly; tactlessly.
**take turns,** to do in succession; alternate.
**to a turn,** to just the proper degree; perfectly.
**turn and turn about,** by turns; alternately. [ME; OE *turnian,* from L *tornāre* turn (in a lathe)]
**turnabout** /ˈtɜnəbaʊt/, *n.* **1.** the act of turning in a different or opposite direction. **2.** a change of opinion, loyalty, etc. **3.** →**turnaround.**
**turnaround** /ˈtɜnəraʊnd/, *n.* a reversal in circumstances, as debit to credit, loss to profit.
**turnbuckle** /ˈtɜnbʌkəl/, *n.* a link or sleeve with a swivel at one end and an internal screw thread at the other, or with an internal screw thread at each end, used as a means of uniting or coupling, and of tightening, two parts, as the ends of two rods.
**turncoat** /ˈtɜnkoʊt/, *n.* one who changes his party or principles; a renegade. [TURN + COAT]
**turncock** /ˈtɜnkɒk/, *n.* →**stopcock.**
**turndown** /ˈtɜndaʊn/, *adj.* that is or may be turned down; folded or doubled down.
**turned comma** /tɜnd ˈkɒmə/, *n. Print.* →**quotation mark.**
**turner** /ˈtɜnə/, *n.* **1.** one who or that which turns. **2.** one who fashions objects on a lathe. [ME, from TURN + -ER[1]]
**turnery** /ˈtɜnəri/, *n.* **1.** the art or work of a turner; forming of objects on a lathe. **2.** articles fashioned on a lathe.
**turn-in** /ˈtɜn-ɪn/, *n. Colloq.* a fight.
**turn indicator** /ˈtɜn ɪndəkeɪtə/, *n.* an instrument that indicates the rate of turn of an aircraft about its vertical axis.
**turning** /ˈtɜnɪŋ/, *n.* **1.** the act of one who or that which turns. **2.** a place where one road branches off from another. **3.** the forming of objects on a lathe. **4.** shaping or forming: *the turning of verses.*
**turning-indicator** /ˈtɜnɪŋ-ɪndəˌkeɪtə/, *n.* **1.** →**trafficator. 2.** the device for activating this.
**turning point** /ˈtɜnɪŋ pɔɪnt/, *n.* **1.** a point at which a decisive change takes place; a critical point; a crisis. **2.** *Survey.* a point on which a foresight and a backsight are taken in direct levelling. **3.** a point at which something turns, esp. the high or low point on a graph.
**turnip** /ˈtɜnəp/, *n.* **1.** the thick, fleshy, edible root of the cruciferous plant *Brassica rapa,* the common **white turnip,** or of *B. napus,* the **swedish turnip** or swede. **2.** the plant itself. **3.** the root of this plant used as a vegetable. [earlier *turnepe,* from TURN (with reference to its neatly rounded shape) + ME *nepe* NEEP]

turnip

**turnkey** /ˈtɜnˌki/, *n., pl.* **-keys.** one who has charge of the keys of a prison; a prison keeper.
**turnkey contract** /– ˈkɒntrækt/, *n.* a contract in which the contractor undertakes to complete an installation or building to the point of readiness for operation or occupancy.
**turn-off** /ˈtɜn-ɒf/, *n.* **1.** a branch of a road leading from a major road, esp. an exit from a highway. **2.** the junction of such roads. **3.** an act or instance of turning off. **4.** that which or one who repels.
**turn-on** /ˈtɜn-ɒn/, *n.* that which or one who excites interest, enthusiasm, etc.
**turnout** /ˈtɜnaʊt/, *n.* **1.** the body of persons who come to an assemblage, muster, spectacle, or the like. **2.** the quantity produced; output. **3.** the act of turning out. **4.** the manner or style in which a person or thing is equipped, dressed, etc. **5.** an equipment or outfit. **6.** a short siding or passage which enables vehicles, etc., to pass one another. **7.** *Colloq.* a party, show, entertainment, etc.
**turnover** /ˈtɜnoʊvə/, *n.* **1.** the act or result of turning over; upset. **2.** the aggregate of worker replacements in a given period in a given business or industry. **3.** the ratio of the labour turnover to the average number of employees in a given period. **4.** the number of times that capital is invested and reinvested in a line of merchandise during a specified period of time. **5.** the turning over of the capital or stock of goods involved in a particular transaction or course of business. **6.** the total amount of business done in a given time. **7.** the rate at which items are sold or stock used up and replaced. **8.** a small pastry made by putting fruit, preserves, or some other filling on one half of a circular piece of pastry, folding the other half over, and then baking it. *–adj.* **9.** turned over; that may be turned over. **10.** having a part that turns over.
**turnpike** /ˈtɜnpaɪk/, *n.* **1.** *Hist.* a barrier set across a road to stop passage until toll was paid; a tollgate. **2.** *Hist.* a road on which a turnpike operated. **3.** *U.S.* a road for fast traffic, esp. one maintained by tolls.
**turnplate** /ˈtɜnpleɪt/, *n.* a railway turntable.
**turn-round** /ˈtɜn-raʊnd/, *n.* **1.** the process of preparing a ship in port or a train, etc., at a terminus for the return journey. **2.** the time taken to do this.
**turnspit** /ˈtɜnspɪt/, *n.* **1.** one who turns a spit. **2.** a dog of a breed with long body and short legs formerly used to work

a treadmill which turned a spit.

**turnstile** /ˈtɜnstaɪl/, *n.* a structure usu. consisting of four arms at right angles to each other, revolving horizontally on top of a post, and set in a gateway or opening in a fence, to allow the passage of people one at a time after a fee has been paid.

**turnstone** /ˈtɜnstoʊn/, *n.* any of the small, migratory, limicoline shorebirds constituting the genus *Arenaria,* notable for their habit of turning over stones in search of food, esp. *A. interpres,* common in both Old and New Worlds.

**turntable** /ˈtɜnteɪbəl/, *n.* **1.** the rotating disc on which the record in a gramophone rests. **2.** *Railways.* a rotating, track-bearing platform pivoted in the centre, used for turning round locomotives and other rolling stock.

**turn-up** /ˈtɜn-ʌp/, *n.* **1.** that which is turned up or which turns up. **2.** *Brit.* a trouser-cuff. **3.** *Colloq.* a fight, row, or disturbance. **4.** *Colloq.* Also, **turn-up for the books.** a surprise; an unexpected reversal of fortune. **5.** the attendance at a meeting, sporting event, concert, etc. *–adj.* **6.** that is or may be turned up: *a turn-up sleeve.*

**turophile** /ˈtjurəfaɪl/, *n.* a lover of cheese. [Gk *tȳrós* cheese + -PHILE]

**turophilia** /tjurəˈfɪliə/, *n.* love of cheese. – **turophilic,** *adj.*

**turpentine** /ˈtɜpəntaɪn/, *n., v.,* **-tined, -tining.** *–n.* **1.** an oleoresin exuding from the terebinth, *Pistacia terebinthus.* **2.** any of various oleoresins derived from coniferous trees, esp. the longleaf pine, *Pinus palustris,* and yielding a volatile oil and a resin when distilled. **3.** →**oil of turpentine.** **4.** any of various substitutes for these, esp. white spirit. **5.** a tall rough barked tree common in eastern Australia, *Syncarpia glomulifera.* *–v.t.* **6.** to treat with turpentine; apply turpentine to. **7.** to gather or take crude turpentine from (trees). [ME *ter(e)bentyn(e),* from L *terebinthina,* from Gk *terébinthos*]

**turpentine tree** /ˈ– tri/, *n.* **1.** the mopane, *Colophospermum mopane,* an African leguminous tree of Zambezi forests, having dark, hard wood. **2.** →**turpentine** (def. 5).

**turpeth** /ˈtɜpəθ/, *n.* **1.** a drug obtained from the roots of a plant, *Operculina turpethum,* of the East Indies, formerly used as a purgative. **2.** the plant itself. **3.** its root. [ML *turpethum;* replacing ME *turbit,* from ML *turbith(um),* from Ar. *turbìd*]

**turpitude** /ˈtɜpətʃud/, *n.* **1.** shameful depravity. **2.** a depraved or shameful act. [L *turpitūdo* baseness]

**turps** /tɜps/, *n. Colloq.* **1.** →**turpentine** (def. 4). **2. on the turps,** drinking intoxicating liquor excessively.

**turquoise** /ˈtɜkwɔɪz/, *n.* **1.** a sky blue or greenish blue compact opaque mineral, essentially a hydrous phosphate of aluminium containing a little copper and iron, much used in jewellery. **2.** Also, **turquoise blue.** a greenish blue or bluish green. [F: Turkish (stone), from *Turc* Turk; replacing ME *turkeis,* from OF]

**turret** /ˈtʌrət/, *n.* **1.** a small tower, usu. one forming part of a larger structure. **2.** a small tower at an angle of a building, frequently beginning some distance above the ground. **3.** Also, **turrethead.** a pivoted attachment on a lathe, etc., for holding a number of tools, each of which can be presented to the work in rapid succession by a simple rotating movement. **4.** *Navy, Mil.* a low, tower-like, heavily armoured structure, usu. revolving horizontally, within which guns are mounted. **5.** *Fort.* a tall structure, usu. moved on wheels, formerly employed in breaching or scaling a fortified place, a wall, or the like. [ME *turet,* from OF *touret* diminutive of *tour* TOWER] – **turretless,** *adj.*

**turreted** /ˈtʌrətəd/, *adj.* **1.** furnished with a turret or turrets. **2.** having a turret-like part or parts. **3.** *Zool.* having whorls in the form of a long or towering spiral, as certain shells.

**turret lathe** /ˈtʌrət leɪð/, *n.* a lathe fitted with a turret (def. 3).

**turri-,** a word element meaning 'tower'. [L, combining form of *turris*]

**turrical** /ˈtʌrɪkəl/, *adj.* pertaining to or resembling a turret or turrets.

**turriculate** /təˈrɪkjələt, -leɪt/, *adj.* furnished with or resembling a turret or turrets. [L *turricula* little tower + -ATE[1]]

**turrum** /ˈtʌrəm/, *n.* a large trevally of northern Australian waters; a fine sport fish. [Aboriginal]

**turtle**[1] /ˈtɜtl/, *n., v.,* **-tled, -tling.** *–n.* **1.** any of the Chelonia, an order or group of reptiles having the body enclosed in a shell consisting of a carapace and a plastron, from between which the head, tail, and four legs protrude. **2.** a marine species of turtle, as distinguished from freshwater and terrestrial tortoises, which possess toed feet rather than turtle flippers. **3. turn turtle,** to capsize. *–v.i.* **4.** to catch turtles, esp. as a business. [Sp. *tortuga* (from LL *tortūca,* from *tortus* twisted), influenced by TURTLE[2]]

**turtle**[2] /ˈtɜtl/, *n. Archaic.* a turtledove. [ME and OE, var. of *turtur,* from L]

**turtleback** /ˈtɜtlbæk/, *n.* **1.** Also, **turtledeck.** an arched protection erected over the deck of a ship at the bow, and often at the stern also, to guard against damage from heavy seas. **2.** *Archaeol.* a crude stone implement having one or both faces slightly convex.

**turtledove** /ˈtɜtldʌv/, *n.* **1.** a small, slender Old World dove, *Streptopelia turtur,* having a long, graduated tail which is conspicuous in flight. **2. spotted turtledove,** a turtledove, *S. chinensis,* native to Asia and introduced into Australia, pale brown underneath and dark brown above, with a black nape marked with white spots.

spotted turtledove

**turtleneck** /ˈtɜtlnɛk/, *adj.* **1.** of or pertaining to a sweater, etc., having a high, close-fitting neck. *–n.* **2.** a turtleneck sweater. Also, **turtle neck.**

**turves** /tɜvz/, *n.* a plural of **turf.**

**Tuscan** /ˈtʌskən/, *adj.* **1.** of, pertaining to, or characteristic of Tuscany, its people, or their dialect. **2.** *Archit.* denoting or pertaining to a classical (Roman or Renaissance) order of architecture distinguished by a plain (not fluted) shaft, ring-shaped capital, and a frieze resembling the Doric. *–n.* **3.** the standard literary form of the Italian language. **4.** any Italian dialect of Tuscany. [from *Tuscany,* region in Italy]

**tush**[1] /tʌʃ/, *interj. Archaic.* (used as an exclamation expressing impatience, contempt, etc.).

**tush**[2] /tʌʃ/, *n.* **1.** one of the four canine teeth of the horse. **2.** tusk. [ME; OE *tusc.* See TUSK]

**tusk** /tʌsk/, *n.* **1.** (in certain animals) a tooth developed to great length, usu. as one of a pair, as in the elephant, walrus, wild boar, etc., but singly in the narwhal. **2.** a long, pointed, or protruding tooth. **3.** a projecting part resembling the tusk of an animal. *–v.t., v.i.* **4.** to dig, tear, or gore with the tusks or tusk. [ME *tuske,* metathetic var. of ME and OE *tux,* metathetic var. of OE *tusc;* probably akin to TOOTH] – **tusked** /tʌskt/, *adj.*

**tusker** /ˈtʌskə/, *n.* an animal with tusks, as an elephant or a wild boar.

**tusk fish** /ˈtʌsk fɪʃ/, *n., pl.* **fishes,** *(esp. collectively)* **fish.** any of a number of fishes of the genus *Choerodon,* bearing tusk-like teeth at the front of the jaws, closely related to parrot fish and other wrasses.

**tussah** /ˈtʌsə/, *n.* a coarse silk from India (called shantung in China) of a tan colour, obtained from the cocoon of various undomesticated Asiatic silkworms (*Antheraea mylitta,* etc.). [alteration of TUSSER]

**tussal** /ˈtʌsəl/, *adj.* pertaining to tussis or a cough. [L *tussis* cough + -AL[1]]

**tusser** /ˈtʌsə/, *n.* →**tussore.** [Hind. *tasar* shuttle]

**tussie mussie** /ˈtʌsi mʌsi/, *n.* →**nosegay.** [ME *tuss(e)mose*]

**tussis** /ˈtʌsəs/, *n.* a cough. [L]

**tussive** /ˈtʌsɪv/, *adj.* of or pertaining to a cough.

**tussle** /ˈtʌsəl/, *v.,* **-sled, -sling,** *n.* *–v.i.* **1.** to struggle or fight roughly or vigorously; wrestle; scuffle. *–n.* **2.** a rough struggle as in fighting or wrestling; a scuffle. **3.** any vigorous conflict or contest. [var. of TOUSLE]

**tussock** /ˈtʌsək/, *n.* **1.** a tuft or clump of growing grass or the like. **2.** Also, **tussock grass.** any of various grasses of the genus *Poa.* **3.** any of a number of grass or sedge species as serrated tussock. [apparently akin to MHG *zūsach* thicket, *zūse* lock (of hair), brushwood. See TOUSLE, -OCK]

**tussock moth** /ˈ– mɒθ/, *n.* any of various dull-coloured moths (family Lymantriidae), as the painted applemoth, whose larvae are notorious pests of broad-leaved trees.

**tussocky** /ˈtʌsəki/, *adj.* **1.** abounding in tussocks. **2.** forming tussocks.

**tussocky poa** /– ˈpoʊə/, *n.* a tussocky grass, *Poa caespitosa,* native to Australia, and useful in checking erosion.

**tussore** /ˈtʌsɔ/, *n.* a fabric woven from tussah. Also, **tusser.** [alteration of TUSSER]

**tut**[1] /tʌt/; *or clicked* /t/, *interj., n., v.,* **tutted, tutting.** *–interj.* **1.** (used as an exclamation expressing impatience, contempt, etc.). *–n.* **2.** an exclamation of 'tut'. *–v.i.* **3.** to utter the exclamation 'tut'. Also, **tut-tut.**

**tut**[2] /tʌt/, *v.i.,* **tutted, tutting.** to contract; to perform a piece of work at a given price. [Corn. d.] – **tutworker,** *n.*

**tute** /tjut/, *n. Colloq.* a tutorial.

**tutelage** /ˈtjutəlɪdʒ/, *n.* **1.** the office or function of a guardian; guardianship. **2.** instruction. **3.** the state of being under a guardian or a tutor. [L *tūtēla* watching + -AGE]

**tutelary** /ˈtjutələri/, *adj.* **1.** having the position of guardian or protector of a person, place, or thing: *tutelary saint.* **2.** of or pertaining to a guardian or guardianship. *–n.* **3.** one having tutelary authority, as an angel, saint, or guardian. Also, **tutelar.** [L *tūtēlārius* guardian]

**tutor** /ˈtjutə/, *n.* **1.** one employed to instruct another in some branch or branches of learning, esp. a private instructor. **2.** a university teacher who supervises the studies of certain undergraduates assigned to him. **3.** (in some universities and colleges) a teacher of academic rank lower than lecturer. **4.** a teacher without institutional connections who assists students in preparing for examinations. **5.** *Archaic.* the guardian of a boy or girl below the age of puberty or majority. *–v.t.* **6.** to act as a tutor to; teach or instruct, esp. privately. **7.** to train, school, or discipline. **8.** to admonish or reprove. **9.** to have the guardianship or care of. *–v.i.* **10.** to act as a tutor or private instructor. **11.** to study under a tutor. [ME, from L: protector] – **tutorless,** *adj.* – **tutorship,** *n.*

**tutorage** /ˈtjutərɪdʒ/, *n.* **1.** the office, authority, or care of a tutor; instruction. **2.** the charge for instruction by a tutor.

**tutorial** /tjuˈtɔriəl/, *adj.* **1.** pertaining to or exercised by a tutor: *tutorial functions or authority.* *–n.* **2.** a period of instruction given by a university tutor to an individual student or a small group of students.

**tutorial system** /ˈ– sɪstəm/, *n.* a system of education, esp. in some universities, in which instruction is given personally by tutors, who also act as general supervisors of a small group of students in their charge.

**tutsan** /ˈtʌtsən/, *n.* a shrubby perennial, *Hypericum androsaemum,* occurring in wet woods of Europe and western Asia.

**tutti** /ˈtuti/, *adj., n., pl.* **-tis.** *Music.* *–adj.* **1.** all; all the voices or instruments together (used as a direction). **2.** intended for or performed by all (or most of) the voices or instruments together, as a passage or movement in concerted music (opposed to *solo*). *–n.* **3.** a tutti passage or movement. **4.** the tonal product or effect of tutti performance. [It., pl. of *tutto* TUTTO]

**tutti-frutti** /tutiˈfruti/, *n.* **1.** a preserve of chopped mixed fruits, often with brandy syrup. **2.** a variety of fruits (usu. candied and minced), used in ice-cream, confections, etc. [It., lit., all fruits]

**tutto** /ˈtutoʊ/, *adj.* (a musical direction) all; entire; the whole. [It., from OF *tout*]

**tut-tut** /tʌtˈtʌt/; *or clicked* /t-t/, *interj., n., v.i.,* **-tutted, -tutting.** →**tut**[1].

**tutty** /ˈtʌti/, *n.* an impure oxide of zinc obtained from the flues of smelting furnaces, or a similar substance occurring as a native mineral, used chiefly as a polishing powder. [ME *tutie,* from ML *tūtia,* from Ar. *tūtiyā* oxide of zinc, ? from Pers.]

**tutu**[1] /ˈtutu, ˈtjutju/, *n.* a short, full, ballet skirt, usu. made of several layers of tarlatan or tulle. [F]

tutu[1]

**tutu**[2] /ˈtutu/, *n.* any of many New Zealand shrubs of the genus *Coriaria,* with black berries, the seeds of which contain the poison tutin. Also, **toot.** [Maori]

**tux** /tʌks/, *n. Colloq.* →**tuxedo.**

**tuxedo** /tʌkˈsidoʊ/, *n., pl.* **-dos.** a dinner jacket. [short for *Tuxedo coat,* named after country club at *Tuxedo* Park, in New York State, U.S.]

**tuyère** /ˈtwiɛə, ˈtwaɪə/, *n.* an opening through which the blast of air enters a blast furnace, cupola forge, or the like, to facilitate combustion. Also, **twyere.** [F, from *tuyau* pipe, of Gmc orig.]

**TV** /ti ˈvi/, *n.* television.

**TV dinner** /– ˈdɪnə/, *n.* a pre-packaged meal, esp. one intended to be consumed while watching television.

**twa** /twa/, *n. Scot.* two.

**Twaddell degree** /twəˈdɛl dəgri/, *n.* a unit on an arbitrary scale ranging from 0 to 200 for indicating the specific gravity of liquids; distilled water has a specific gravity of zero. *Abbrev.:* °Tw. [named after W. *Twaddell,* died *c.* 1840, Scottish inventor]

**twaddle** /ˈtwɒdl/, *n., v.,* **-dled, -dling.** *–n.* **1.** trivial, feeble, silly or tedious talk or writing. *–v.i.* **2.** to talk in a trivial, feeble, silly or tedious manner; prate. *–v.t.* **3.** to utter as twaddle. [var. of *twattle,* b. TWIDDLE and TATTLE] – **twaddler,** *n.*

**twain** /tweɪn/, *adj., n. Archaic.* two. [ME *twayn,* OE *twēgen,* c. G (obs.) *Zween*]

**twang**[1] /twæŋ/, *v.i.* **1.** to give out a sharp, ringing sound, as the string of a musical instrument when plucked. **2.** to have a sharp, nasal tone, as the human voice. *–v.t.* **3.** to cause to make a sharp, ringing sound, as a string of a musical instrument. **4.** to produce (music) by plucking the strings of a musical instrument. **5.** to pluck the strings of (a musical instrument). **6.** to speak with a sharp, nasal tone. **7.** to pull or pluck the string of (a bow). **8.** to shoot (an arrow). *–n.* **9.** the sharp, ringing sound produced by plucking or suddenly releasing a tense string. **10.** a sound resembling this. **11.** the act of plucking or picking. **12.** a sharp, nasal tone, as of the human voice. [imitative] – **twangy,** *adj.*

**twang**[2] /twæŋ/, *n.* opium. [orig. unknown]

**'twas** /twɒz/; *unstressed* /twəz/, contraction of *it was.*

**twat** /twɒt/, *n. Colloq.* **1.** the vagina. **2.** a woman considered as a sexual object. **3.** sexual intercourse. **4.** a despicable or unpleasant person. Also, **twot.** [orig. uncert.]

**tweak** /twik/, *v.t.* **1.** to seize and pull with a sharp jerk and twist: *to tweak someone's ear.* *–n.* **2.** an act of tweaking; a sharp pull and twist. [OE *twician* (inferred from *twicere,* n.), var. of *twiccian* catch hold of, pluck, gather. See TWITCH[1]] – **tweaky,** *adj.*

**twee** /twi/, *adj. Colloq.* affected; precious; excessively dainty; coy.

**tweed** /twid/, *n.* **1.** a coarse wool cloth in a variety of weaves and colours, either hand-spun and hand-woven in Scotland, or reproduced, often by machine, elsewhere. **2.** (*pl.*) garments made of this cloth. **3.** (pl.) *Colloq.* trousers. [apparently backformation from Scot. *tweedling* twilling (now obs.), of unexplained orig.]

**Tweedledum and Tweedledee,** any two persons, things, etc., nominally different but practically the same. [humorous imitative coinage, apparently first applied as nicknames to Handel and Bononcini, with reference to their musical rivalry]

**'tween** /twin/, *prep. Poetic.* between.

**tweeny** /ˈtwini/, *n. Obs.* a maidservant who assists other servants. ['TWEEN + -Y[2]]

**tweet** /twit/, *n.* **1.** the weak chirp of a young or small bird. *–v.i.* **2.** to utter a tweet or tweets. [imitative]

**tweeter** /ˈtwitə/, *n.* a small loudspeaker designed for the reproduction of high-frequency sounds.

**tweeter-woofer** /twitəˈwʊfə/, *n.* a loudspeaker, usu. coaxial, in which a tweeter is mounted in and in front of the cone of a woofer.

**tweezers** /ˈtwizəz/, *n.pl.* small pincers or nippers for plucking out hairs, taking up small objects, etc. [pl. of *tweezer,* from *tweeze* case, receptacle (see ETUI) + -ER[1]]

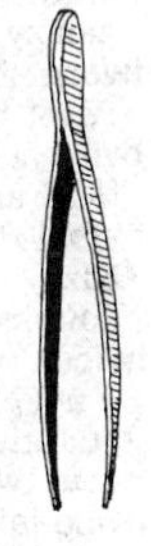

tweezers

**twelfth** /twɛlfθ/, *adj.* **1.** next after the eleventh. **2.** being one of twelve equal parts. *–n.* **3.** a twelfth part, esp. of one ($\frac{1}{12}$). **4.** the twelfth one of a series.

**Twelfth day** /twɛlfθ ˈdeɪ/, *n.* the twelfth day after Christmas, 6 January, on which the festival of the Epiphany is celebrated, formerly observed as the last day of the Christmas festivities.

**twelfth man** /twɛlfθ 'mæn/, *n.* (in cricket) a reserve who may replace any player obliged to leave the ground while his team is fielding, but who may not bowl or bat.

**Twelfth night** /twɛlfθ 'naɪt/, *n.* **1.** the evening before Twelfth day, formerly observed with various festivities. **2.** the evening of Twelfth day itself.

**Twelfthtide** /'twɛlfθtaɪd/, *n.* the season of Twelfth night and Twelfth day.

**twelve** /twɛlv/, *n.* **1.** a cardinal number, ten plus two. **2.** a symbol for this number, as 12 or XII. **3.** a set of this many persons or things. **4. the Twelve,** the twelve apostles chosen by Christ. *–adj.* **5.** amounting to twelve in number. [ME; OE *twelf,* c. G *zwölf*]

**twelve apostle bird,** *n.* →**apostle bird.**

**twelve-bar blues** /ˌtwɛlv-ba 'bluz/, *n.* the characteristic strict form of blues and related genres such as boogie-woogie, consisting of a twelve-bar arrangement of three chords, the tonic seventh, the subdominant seventh and the dominant seventh.

**twelve-mile limit** /twɛlv-maɪl 'lɪmɪt/, *n.* the offshore boundary of a state, extending 12 miles out to sea. Cf. **three-mile limit.**

**twelvemo** /'twɛlvmoʊ/, *n., pl.* **-mos,** *adj.* →**duodecimo.**

**twelvemonth** /'twɛlvmʌnθ/, *n.* a year.

**twelve-string guitar** /ˌtwɛlv-strɪŋ gə'ta/, *n.* a guitar which has six pairs of strings, one member of each pair being tuned at an octave above the other.

**twelve-tone** /'twɛlv-toʊn/, *adj.* based on or incorporating the twelve-tone technique. Also, **twelve-note.**

**twelve-tone technique** /– tɛk'nik/, *n.* a modern system of note relationships in which the 12 notes of an octave are not subjugated to any one key, but are unified by a selected order of notes which form the basis of a given composition. Also, **twelve-note technique.**

**twentieth** /'twɛntiəθ/, *adj.* **1.** next after the nineteenth. **2.** being one of twenty equal parts. *–n.* **3.** a twentieth part, esp. of one ($\frac{1}{20}$). **4.** the twentieth member of a series.

**twentieth man** /– 'mæn/, *n.* (in Australian Rules) the second of the two reserves who may be used to replace any player already on the field.

**twenty** /'twɛnti/, *n., pl.* **-ties,** *adj.* *–n.* **1.** a cardinal number, ten times two. **2.** a symbol for this number, as 20 or XX. **3.** a set of this many persons or things. **4.** (*pl.*) the numbers from 20 to 29 of a series, esp. with reference to the years of a person's age, or the years of a century, esp. the twentieth. *–adj.* **5.** amounting to twenty in number. [ME; OE *twēntig,* akin to G *zwanzig*]

**twenty-eight parrot** /ˌtwɛnti-eɪt 'pærət/, *n.* a predominantly greenish parrot with black head and yellow band at the neck, *Barnardius semitorquatus,* of south-western Australia. [imitative of its call]

**twenty-fourmo** /ˌtwɛnti-'fɔmoʊ/, *n., pl.* **-mos,** *adj.* →**vigesimo-quarto.**

**twentymo** /'twɛntimoʊ/, *n., pl.* **-mos,** *adj.* →**vigesimo.**

**twenty-one** /ˌtwɛnti-'wʌn/, *n.* →**pontoon**[2].

**twenty-one centimetre line,** *n.* electromagnetic radiation with a sharply-defined wavelength of about twenty-one centimetres emitted by neutral hydrogen atoms distributed throughout the galaxy.

**twerp** /twɜp/, *n. Colloq.* an insignificant or stupid person. Also, **twirp.**

**twi-,** a word element meaning 'two', or 'twice', as in *twibill.* [ME and OE, c. G *zwei-,* L *bi-.* See TWO]

**twibill** /'twaɪbɪl/, *n.* **1.** a mattock with one arm like that of an adze and the other like that of an axe. **2.** *Archaic.* a double-bladed battle-axe. [ME and OE. See TWI-, BILL[3]]

**twice** /twaɪs/, *adv.* **1.** two times, as in succession: *write twice a week.* **2.** on two occasions; in two instances. **3.** in twofold quantity or degree; doubly: *twice as much.* [ME *twies,* from *twie* twice (OE *twiga*) + *-s,* adv. gen. suffix]

**twice-laid** /'twaɪs-leɪd/, *adj.* **1.** made from strands of used rope. **2.** made from makeshift or used material.

**twicer** /'twaɪsə/, *n. Colloq.* a crook; double-crosser.

**twice-told** /twaɪs-'toʊld/, *adj.* told twice; told before.

**twiddle** /'twɪdl/, *v.,* **-dled, -dling,** *n.* *–v.t.* **1.** to turn round and round, esp. with the fingers. **2. twiddle one's thumbs** or **fingers, a.** to keep turning one's thumbs or fingers idly about each other. **b.** to do nothing; be idle. *–v.i.* **3.** to play with something idly, as by touching or handling. **4.** to turn round and round; twirl. *–n.* **5.** the act of twiddling; a twirl. [b. TWITCH[1] and FIDDLE] – **twiddler,** *n.*

**twig**[1] /twɪg/, *n.* **1.** a slender shoot of a tree or other plant. **2.** a small offshoot from a branch or stem. **3.** a small dry, woody piece fallen from a branch: *a fire of twigs.* **4.** *Anat.* one of the minute branches of a blood vessel or nerve. [ME and OE *twigge,* akin to G *Zweig* branch] – **twigless,** *adj.* – **twiglike,** *adj.*

**twig**[2] /twɪg/, *v.,* **twigged, twigging.** *Colloq.* *–v.t.* **1.** to look at; observe. **2.** to catch sight of; perceive. **3.** to understand. *–v.i.* **4.** to understand. [orig. uncert.]

**twiggy** /'twɪgi/, *adj.* **1.** abounding in twigs. **2.** consisting of twigs. **3.** twiglike.

**twilight** /'twaɪlaɪt/, *n.* **1.** the light from the sky when the sun is below the horizon, esp. in the evening. **2.** the time during which this light prevails. **3.** a condition or period preceding or succeeding full development, glory, etc. *–adj.* **4.** pertaining to or resembling twilight: *the twilight hour.* **5.** crepuscular, as a bat or moth. [ME, from TWI- + LIGHT[1]; c. G *Zwielicht*] – **twilightless,** *adj.*

**twilight sleep** /'– slip/, *n.* a state of semiconsciousness usu. produced by hypodermic injections of scopolamine and morphine, in order to effect relatively painless childbirth. [translation of G *Dämmerschlaf*]

**twill** /twɪl/, *n.* **1.** a fabric woven with the weft threads so crossing the warp as to produce an effect of parallel diagonal lines, as in serge. **2.** the characteristic weave of such fabrics. *–v.t.* **3.** to weave in the manner of a twill. **4.** to weave in twill construction. [Scot. and North. E var. of *twilly,* ME *twyle,* OE *twili(c),* half translation half adoption of L *bilic(em)* having double thread (acc. sing. of unrecorded *bilix*). See TWI-]

**'twill** /twɪl/, contraction of *it will.*

**twin** /twɪn/, *n., adj., v.,* **twinned, twinning.** *–n.* **1.** (*pl.*) two children or animals brought forth at a birth. **2.** one of two such children or animals. **3.** (*pl.*) two persons or things closely related or connected or closely resembling each other. **4.** either of two such persons or things. **5.** *Crystall.* a compound crystal, consisting of two or more parts or crystals definitely orientated each to the other. **6. the Twins,** the zodiacal constellation or sign Gemini. *–adj.* **7.** being two, or one of two, children or animals born at the same birth: *twin sisters.* **8.** being two persons or things closely related or associated or much alike; forming a pair or couple. **9.** being one of two such persons or things; forming one of a couple or pair: *a twin peak.* **10.** consisting of two similar parts or elements joined or connected: *a twin vase.* **11.** *Bot., Zool.* occurring in pairs; didymous. **12.** *Crystall.* of the nature of a twin (def. 5). **13.** *Obs.* twofold or double. *–v.t.* **14.** to conceive or bring forth as twins. **15.** to pair or couple. **16.** to furnish a counterpart to. **17.** *Crystall.* to form into a twin. *–v.i.* **18.** to bring forth twins. **19.** to be twin-born. **20.** to be paired or coupled. [ME; OE *(ge)twinn,* c. Icel. *tvinnr* double]

**twinborn** /'twɪnbɔn/, *adj.* born at the same birth.

**twine** /twaɪn/, *n., v.,* **twined, twining.** *–n.* **1.** a strong thread or string composed of two or more strands twisted together. **2.** the act of twining. **3.** the state of being twined. **4.** a twined or twisted thing or part; a fold, convolution, or coil. **5.** a twist or turn. **6.** a knot or tangle. *–v.t.* **7.** to twist together; interwind; intertwine. **8.** to form by or as by twisting strands: *to twine a wreath.* **9.** to twist (one strand, thread, or thing) with another. **10.** to bring by or as by twisting or winding (fol. by *in, into,* etc.). **11.** to put or dispose by or as by winding (fol. by *about, around,* etc.). **12.** to encircle or wreathe with something wound about. **13.** to enfold. *–v.i.* **14.** to become twined or twisted together, as two things, or as one thing with another. **15.** to wind itself (fol. by *about, around,* etc.). **16.** to wind in a sinuous or meandering course. **17.** (of plants, stems, etc.) to grow in convolutions about a support. [ME; OE *twin,* c. D *twijn*] – **twiner,** *n.*

**twinflower** /'twɪnflaʊə/, *n.* a slender, creeping, evergreen plant, *Linnaea borealis,* of Europe, or the American *L.*

*americana,* with pink or purplish nodding flowers borne in pairs on threadlike peduncles.

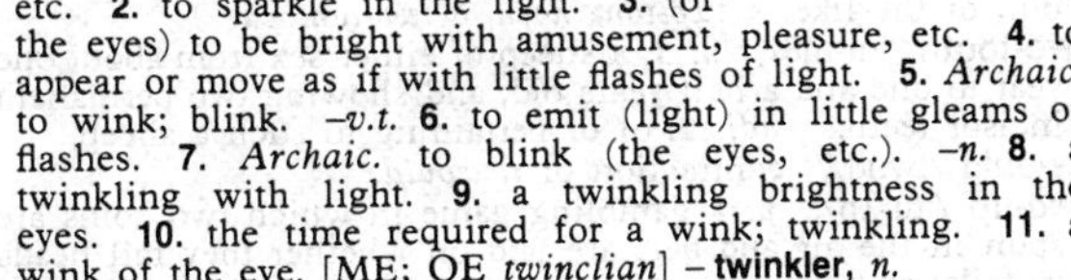
twinflower

**twinge** /twɪndʒ/, *n., v.,* **twinged, twinging.** *–n.* **1.** a sudden, sharp pain (in body or mind): *a twinge of rheumatism, a twinge of remorse.* *–v.t.* **2.** to affect with sudden, sharp pain or pains (in body or mind). **3.** to give (a person, etc.) a twinge or twinges. *–v.i.* **4.** to have or feel a twinge or twinges. **5.** to give a twinge. [ME *twenge(n),* OE *twengan* pinch]

**twinkle** /ˈtwɪŋkəl/, *v.,* **-kled, -kling,** *n.* *–v.i.* **1.** to shine with quick, flickering, gleams of light, as stars, distant lights, etc. **2.** to sparkle in the light. **3.** (of the eyes) to be bright with amusement, pleasure, etc. **4.** to appear or move as if with little flashes of light. **5.** *Archaic.* to wink; blink. *–v.t.* **6.** to emit (light) in little gleams or flashes. **7.** *Archaic.* to blink (the eyes, etc.). *–n.* **8.** a twinkling with light. **9.** a twinkling brightness in the eyes. **10.** the time required for a wink; twinkling. **11.** a wink of the eye. [ME; OE *twinclian*] – **twinkler,** *n.*

**twinkling** /ˈtwɪŋklɪŋ/, *n.* **1.** the act of shining with little gleams of light. **2.** the time required for a wink; an instant. **3.** *Archaic.* winking; a wink.

**twinned** /twɪnd/, *adj.* **1.** born as twins or as a twin. **2.** paired or coupled. **3.** united or combined. **4.** having the nature of a twin.

**twinning** /ˈtwɪnɪŋ/, *n.* **1.** the bearing of twins. **2.** coupling; union. **3.** *Crystall.* the union of crystals to form a twin (def. 5).

**twin-plate process** /ˈtwɪn-pleɪt ˌprouses/, *n.* a process for making polished plate glass in which rolling, annealing, and grinding are carried out on a continuously produced ribbon of glass, both surfaces being ground simultaneously.

**twin-screw** /ˈtwɪn-skru/, *adj.* (of a vessel) having two screw propellers, which usu. revolve in opposite directions.

**twin-set** /ˈtwɪn-sɛt/, *n.* **1.** a cardigan and matching jumper, worn by women. *–adj.* **2. twin-set and pearls,** *Colloq.* (of certain, usu. young, middle-class women) typified by conservative dress, outlook, etc.

**twirl** /twɜl/, *v.t.* **1.** to cause to rotate rapidly; spin; whirl; swing circularly. **2.** to twiddle: *to twirl one's thumbs.* **3.** to wind idly, as about something. *–v.i.* **4.** to rotate rapidly; whirl. **5.** to turn quickly so as to face or point another way. *–n.* **6.** a twirling or a being twirled; a spin; a whirl; a twist. **7.** something twirled; curl; convolution. [b. TWIST and WHIRL] – **twirler,** *n.*

**twirp** /twɜp/, *n.* →**twerp.**

**twist** /twɪst/, *v.t.* **1.** to combine, as two or more strands or threads, by winding together; intertwine. **2.** to combine or associate intimately. **3.** to form by or as by winding strands together. **4.** to entwine (one thing) with or in another; wind or twine (something) about a thing. **5.** to encircle (a thing) with something wound about. **6.** to alter in shape, as by turning the ends in opposite directions, so that parts previously in the same straight line and plane are situated in a spiral curve. **7.** to wring out of shape or place; contort or distort. **8.** to turn sharply and put out of place; sprain: *when she fell she twisted her ankle.* **9.** to change the proper form or meaning; pervert. **10.** to form into a coil, knot, or the like by winding, rolling. etc.: *to twist the hair into a knot.* **11.** to bend tortuously. **12.** to cause to move with a rotary motion, as a ball pitched in a curve. **13.** to turn in another direction. **14. twist (one's) arm,** *Colloq.* to persuade: *you've twisted my arm, I'll do it.* *–v.i.* **15.** to be or become intertwined. **16.** to wind or twine about something. **17.** to writhe or squirm. **18.** to take a spiral form or course; wind, curve, or bend. **19.** to turn or rotate, as on an axis; revolve, as about something. **20.** to turn so as to face in another direction. **21.** to change shape with a spiral or screwing movement of parts. **22.** to move with a progressive rotary motion, as a ball pitched in a curve. **23.** to dance the twist (def. 47). *–n.* **24.** a curve, bend, or turn. **25.** a turning or rotating as on an axis; rotary motion; spin. **26.** anything formed by or as by twisting or twining parts together. **27.** the act or the manner of twisting strands together, as in thread, yarn, or rope. **28.** a wrench. **29.** a twisting awry. **30.** a changing or perverting, of meaning. **31.** spiral disposition, arrangement, or form. **32.** spiral movement or course. **33.** an irregular bend; a crook or kink. **34.** a peculiar bent, bias, or the like, as in the mind or nature. **35.** the altering of the shape of anything by or as by turning the ends in opposite directions. **36.** the stress causing this alteration. **37.** the resulting state. **38.** a sudden, unexpected alteration to the course of events, as in a play. **39.** *Cricket, Baseball, etc.* **a.** a spin given to a ball in pitching, etc. **b.** a ball having such a spin. **40.** a twisting or torsional action, force, or stress. **41.** a kind of strong twisted silk thread, heavier than ordinary sewing silk, used for working buttonholes and for other purposes. **42.** a direction of twisting in weaving yarns, as S twist (left-hand twist), Z twist (right-hand twist). **43.** a loaf or roll of dough twisted and baked. **44.** a kind of tobacco manufactured in the form of a rope or thick cord. **45.** the degree of spiral formed by the grooves in a rifled firearm or cannon. **46.** *Prison Colloq.* a life sentence. **47.** a vigorous dance performed by couples and characterised by strongly rhythmic gyrations of the body and movements of the arms and legs in time to heavily accented music. **48. round the twist,** *Colloq.* insane. [ME *twiste* divide, *twist* divided object, rope, OE *-twist,* c. D *twisten* quarrel. See TWI-] – **twistability,** *n.* – **twistable,** *adj.* – **twistingly,** *adv.*

**twist drill** /ˈ– drɪl/, *n.* a drill with one or more deep spiral grooves in the body.

**twisted pair** /twɪstəd ˈpɛə/, *n.* (in a computer) two insulated conductors twisted together helically and having useful properties for the transmission of digital data.

**twister** /ˈtwɪstə/, *n.* **1.** one who or that which twists. **2.** a ball pitched or moving with a spinning motion. **3.** an untrustworthy, swindling person. **4.** *U.S.* a whirlwind or tornado.

**twist-tie** /ˈtwɪst-taɪ/, *n.* a small piece of paper or plastic encased wire for fastening plastic bags.

**twit**[1] /twɪt/, *v.,* **twitted, twitting,** *n.* *–v.t.* **1.** to taunt, gibe at, or banter by references to anything embarrassing. **2.** to reproach or upbraid. *–n.* **3.** the act of twitting. **4.** a derisive reproach; taunt; gibe. [aphetic var. of obs. *atwite,* ME *atwiten,* OE *ætwītan* taunt, from *æt-* AT + *wītan* blame] – **twitter,** *n.*

**twit**[2] /twɪt/, *n. Colloq.* a fool; twerp. – **twitty,** *adj.*

**twitch**[1] /twɪtʃ/, *v.t.* **1.** to give a short, sudden pull or tug at; jerk. **2.** to pull or draw with a hasty jerk. **3.** to move (a part of the body) with a jerk. **4.** to pinch and pull sharply; nip. *–v.i.* **5.** to move or be moved in a quick, jerky way. **6.** to give a short, sudden pull or tug; tug (fol. by *at*). *–n.* **7.** a quick, jerky movement of the body, or of some part of it. **8. the twitches,** *Colloq.* a state of nerves causing muscular spasms. **9.** a short, sudden pull or tug; a jerk. **10.** a twinge (of body or mind). **11.** a loop or noose, attached to a handle, for drawing tightly about the muzzle of a horse to bring it under control. [ME *twicchen,* akin to OE *twiccian* pluck] – **twitcher,** *n.* – **twitchingly,** *adv.* – **twitchy,** *adj.*

**twitch**[2] /twɪtʃ/, *n.* a pest grass of cultivation and pasture areas, *Agropyron repens,* with underground rhizomes, native to Europe and Asia. [var. *quitch.* See COUCH[2]]

**twitter** /ˈtwɪtə/, *v.i.* **1.** to utter a succession of small, tremulous sounds, as a bird. **2.** to titter; giggle. **3.** to tremble with excitement or the like; be in a flutter. *–v.t.* **4.** to express or utter by twittering. *–n.* **5.** the act of twittering. **6.** a twittering sound. **7.** a state of tremulous excitement. [ME *twiter,* akin to G *zwitschern*] – **twitteringly,** *adv.*

**twitterer** /ˈtwɪtərə/, *n.* **1.** a bird that twitters. **2.** a person who twitters.

**twittery** /ˈtwɪtəri/, *adj.* **1.** given to or characterised by twittering. **2.** tremulous; shaky.

**'twixt** /twɪkst/, *prep. Archaic.* betwixt.

**two** /tu/, *n.* **1.** a cardinal number, one plus one. **2.** a symbol for this number, as 2 or II. **3.** a set of this many persons or things. **4.** a playing card, die face, etc., with two pips. **5. in two,** in two pieces; apart: *to break in two.* **6. put two and two together,** to draw a conclusion from certain circumstances. *–adj.* **7.** amounting to two in number. [ME; OE *twā,* c. G *zwei.* Cf. L *duo,* Gk *dýo*]

**two-blocks** /ˈtu-blɒks/, *adv.* **1.** *Naut.* with the blocks drawn close together, as when a tackle is hauled to the utmost. **2.** →**chock-a-block. 3.** *Naut.* in a close embrace.

**two bob** /tu 'bɒb/, *n. Colloq.* **1.** (formerly) a sum of money of the value of two shillings. **2.** (formerly) a silver coin of this value. **3. have two bob each way,** to support contradictory causes at the same time, often in self-protection. **4. not worth two bob,** insignificant. **5. the full two bob,** that which is genuine and of full value. Also, **two-bob.**

**two-bob** /'tu-bɒb/, *Colloq.* *–adj.* **1.** of poor quality; useless; unreliable: *goes like a two-bob watch.* **2. mad** or **silly as a two-bob watch,** scatty; unpredictable. **3. two-bob boss,** a minor official who delights in exerting his authority in an overbearing manner. **4. two-bob millionaire,** a person temporarily flush with money. **5. two-bob lair,** a person whose clothes are flashy but cheap. *–n.* **6.** →**two bob.**

**two-by-four** /'tu-bi-fɔ/, *adj.* **1.** two units thick and four units wide, esp. in inches. **2.** *U.S. Colloq.* **a.** small in size. **b.** unimportant; insignificant. *–n.* **3.** any length of timber approx. two inches thick and four inches wide.

**two-cycle engine** /ˌtu-saɪkəl 'ɛndʒən/, *n. U.S.* a two-stroke engine.

**two-dimensional** /tu-daɪ'mɛnʃənəl, tu-də-/, *adj.* having two dimensions, as height and width.

**two-edged** /'tu-ɛdʒd/, *adj.* **1.** having two edges, as a sword. **2.** cutting or effective both ways. **3.** having two possible meanings, results, etc., one favourable and one unfavourable.

**two-faced** /'tu-feɪst/, *adj.* **1.** having two faces. **2.** deceitful; hypocritical. – **two-facedly** /tu-'feɪsədli/, *adv.* – **two-facedness,** *n.*

**two-fire stove** /ˌtu-faɪə 'stoʊv/, *n.* →**colonial oven.**

**two-fisted** /'tu-fɪstəd/, *adj.* **1.** having two fists and able to use them. **2.** *U.S. Colloq.* strong and vigorous.

**twofold** /'tufoʊld/, *adj.* **1.** having two elements or parts. **2.** twice as great or as much; double. *–adv.* **3.** in twofold measure; doubly.

**two-four** /tu-'fɔ/, *adj.* (of a musical tempo) characterised by two crotchets to the bar.

**2, 4-D** /tu fɔ-'di/, *n.* dichlorophenoxyacetic acid, usu. used in the form of butyl esters as a weedkiller.

**2, 4, 5-T** /tu fɔ faɪv-'ti/, *n.* trichlorophenoxyacetic acid, usu. used in the form of butyl esters as a weed-killer.

**two-handed** /'tu-hændəd/, *adj.* **1.** having two hands. **2.** using both hands equally well; ambidextrous. **3.** involving or requiring both hands: *a two-handed sword.* **4.** requiring the hands of two persons to operate: *a two-handed saw.* **5.** engaged in by two persons: *a two-handed game.*

**two-ie** /'tu-i/, *v.t.*, **-ied, -iing.** *Qld. Colloq.* to gang up on. [TWO + -IE]

**two-legged** /'tu-lɛgəd, -lɛgd/, *adj.* having two legs.

**two-line brevier** /ˌtu-laɪn-brə'vɪə/, *n.* a printing type (16 point) of a size between English and great primer.

**two-master** /tu-'mastə/, *n.* a vessel rigged with two masts.

**two-party system** /ˌtu-pati 'sɪstəm/, *n.* a system of government in which two major political parties, more or less equal in strength, contend for election to power.

**twopence** /'tʌpəns/, *n.* **1.** (formerly) a sum of money of the value of two pennies. **2.** a British copper coin of this value, issued in the reign of George III. Also, **tuppence.**

**twopenny** /'tʌpəni/, *adj.* **1.** of the amount or value of twopence. **2.** of very little value; trifling; worthless. Also, **tuppenny. 3. not to matter a twopenny damn (dump),** not to be worth any consideration.

**twopenny-halfpenny** /tʌpəni-'heɪpəni/, *adj.* →**twopenny** (def. 2).

**two-phase** /'tu-feɪz/, *adj.* →**quarter-phase.**

**two-piece** /'tu-pis/, *adj.* **1.** consisting of two pieces, usu. matching, as an outfit of clothing. *–n.* **2.** a twopiece outfit.

**two-ply** /'tu-plaɪ/, *adj.* consisting of two thicknesses, layers, strands, or the like.

**two-pot screamer** /tu-pɒt 'skrimə/, *n. Colloq.* someone who gets uproariously drunk after consuming very little alcoholic beverage.

**two-seater** /tu-'sitə/, *n.* a motor vehicle, aeroplane, or the like, able to seat two people.

**twosome** /'tusəm/, *adj.* **1.** consisting of two. **2.** performed or played by two persons. *–n.* **3.** two together or in company. **4.** a match, as in golf, between two persons. [TWO + -SOME[2]]

**twostep** /'tustɛp/, *n., v.*, **-stepped, -stepping.** *–n.* **1.** a dance in duple time, characterised by sliding steps. **2.** a piece of music for, or in the rhythm of, this dance. *–v.i.* **3.** to perform this dance.

**two-stroke** /'tu-stroʊk/, *adj.* **1.** denoting or pertaining to an internal-combustion engine cycle in which one piston stroke out of every two is a power stroke. **2.** powered by such an engine. *–n.* **3.** a two-stroke engine or vehicle.

**twot** /twɒt/, *n. Colloq.* →**twat.**

**two-time** /'tu-taɪm/, *v.*, **-timed, -timing.** *Colloq.* *–v.t.* **1.** to deceive or doublecross. **2.** to deceive (someone) by having a similar relationship with another. *–v.i.* **3.** to deceive or doublecross someone. **4.** to deceive a friend or lover by having a similar relationship with another. – **two-timer,** *n.*

**two-toed anteater** /tu-toʊd 'æntitə/, *n.* →**silky anteater.**

**two-tone** /'tu-toʊn/, *adj.* having two tones, as of sound, colour, or the like: *a two-tone horn, a two-tone car.*

**two-tooth** /'tu-tuθ/, *n.* **1.** a sheep of either sex from about one year to one and a half years old, and showing two permanent incisor teeth. *–adj.* **2.** of or pertaining to such a sheep.

**'twould** /twʊd/, contraction of *it would.*

**two-up** /'tu-ʌp/, *n.* a gambling game in which two coins are spun in the air and bets are laid on whether they fall heads or tails; swy.

**two-up school** /'– skul/, *n.* an organised game of two-up.

**two-way** /'tu-weɪ/, *adj.* **1.** letting persons or vehicles go either way. **2.** having two ways or passages. **3.** capable of having movement in two directions. **4.** *Maths.* having a double mode of variation.

**two-way stretch** /– 'strɛtʃ/, *n.* **1.** (of materials) the ability to stretch in two directions. **2.** a women's girdle made of such material. **3.** a situation which will require compromise on the part of both parties involved.

**twp,** township.

**twyere** /'twiɛə, 'twaɪə/, *n.* →**tuyère.**

**-ty**[1], a suffix of numerals denoting multiples of ten, as *twenty.* [OE *-tig*, c. G *-zig*]

**-ty**[2], a suffix of nouns denoting quality, state, etc., as *unity, enmity.* [ME *-te(e)*, from OF *-te, -tet*, from L *-tas*]

**Ty,** Territory.

**tycoon** /taɪ'kun/, *n.* **1.** a businessman having great wealth and power. **2.** a title used to describe the shogun of Japan to foreigners from 1603 to 1867. [Jap. *taikun*, from Chinese *tai* great (d. var. of *ta*) + *kiun* prince]

**tyke** /taɪk/, *n.* **1.** *Colloq.* a Roman Catholic. **2.** a mischievous or troublesome child. **3.** any small child. **4.** a cur. Also, **tike.** [ME, from Scand.; cf. Icel. *tik* bitch]

**tylomancy** /'taɪləˌmænsi/, *n.* divination from pieces of wood.

**tylosis** /taɪ'loʊsəs/, *n.* balloon-like extensions of the walls of xylem vessels, found esp. in heartwood.

**tymbal** /'tɪmbəl/, *n.* →**timbal.**

**tympan** /'tɪmpən/, *n.* **1.** a sheet or plate of some thin material, in an apparatus. **2.** *Print.* a padlike device interposed between the platen or its equivalent and the sheet to be printed, in order to soften and equalise the pressure. **3.** →**tympanum** (def. 3). [L *tympanum*, from Gk *týmpanon* drum]

**tympanic** /tɪm'pænɪk/, *adj.* pertaining or belonging to a tympanum, esp. the tympanum of the ear.

**tympanic bone** /'– boʊn/, *n.* (in mammals) a bone of the skull, supporting the tympanic membrane and enclosing part of the tympanum or middle ear.

**tympanic membrane** /– 'mɛmbreɪn/, *n.* a membrane separating the tympanum or middle ear from the passage of the external ear; the eardrum.

**tympanist** /'tɪmpənəst/, *n.* a person who plays the kettledrums or other percussion instruments in an orchestra. Also, **timpanist.**

**tympanites** /tɪmpə'naɪtiz/, *n.* distension of the abdomen caused by the presence of air or gas, as in the intestine. [NL, from Gk: pertaining to a drum] – **tympanitic** /tɪmpə'nɪtɪk/, *adj.*

**tympanitis** /tɪmpə'naɪtəs/, *n.* inflammation of the lining membrane of the tympanum or middle ear. [TYMPAN(UM) + -ITIS]

**tympanum** /'tɪmpənəm/, *n., pl.* **-nums, -na** /-nə/. **1.** *Anat., Zool.* the middle ear, comprising that part of the ear situated in a recess of the temporal bone. **2.** →**tympanic membrane. 3.** *Archit.* **a.** the recessed, usu. triangular space enclosed between the horizontal and sloping cornices of a pediment, often adorned with sculpture. **b.** a similar space between an arch and the horizontal head of a door or window below. **4.** *U.S. Elect.* the diaphragm of a telephone. **5.** a drum or similar instrument. **6.** the stretched membrane forming a drumhead. **7.** a scoop wheel for raising water. [L, from Gk *týmpanon* drum]

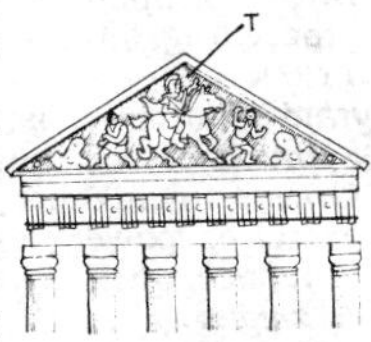

T, tympanum (defs 3a and 3b)

**Tyndall effect** /ˈtɪndl əfɛkt/, *n.* the scattering of light by particles of matter which makes a beam of light visible by illuminating the particles of dust floating in the air. [from John *Tyndall,* 1820-93, English physicist]

**typ.,** **1.** typographer. **2.** typographic. **3.** typographical. **4.** typographically. **5.** typography.

**typal** /ˈtaɪpəl/, *adj.* pertaining to or forming a type.

**type** /taɪp/, *n., v.,* **typed, typing.** *–n.* **1.** a kind, class, or group as distinguished by a particular characteristic. **2.** a person or thing embodying the characteristic qualities of a kind, class, or group; a representative specimen. **3.** the general form, style, or character distinguishing a particular kind, class or group. **4.** *Biol.* **a.** the general form or plan of structure common to a group of animals, plants, etc. **b.** a genus or species which most nearly exemplifies the essential characteristics of a higher group and frequently gives the latter its name. **5.** *Agric.* **a.** the inherited features of an animal or breed favourable for any given purpose: *dairy type.* **b.** a strain, breed, or variety of animals, or a single animal, belonging to a specific kind. **6.** the pattern or model from which something is made. **7.** *Print.* **a.** a rectangular piece or block, now usu. of metal, having on its upper surface a letter or character in relief. **b.** such pieces or blocks collectively. **c.** a similar piece in a typewriter or the like. **d.** such pieces collectively. **e.** a printed character or printed characters: *a headline in large type.* **8.** an image or figure produced by impressing or stamping, as the principal figure or device on either side of a coin or medal. **9.** a prefiguring symbol, as an Old Testament event prefiguring an event in the New Testament. *–v.t.* **10.** to write (a letter, etc.) by means of a typewriter; typewrite. **11.** to reproduce in type or in print. **12.** *Med.* to ascertain the type of (a blood sample). **13.** to be a type or symbol of. **14.** to represent by a symbol; symbolise. *–v.i.* **15.** to write by means of a typewriter; typewrite. [late ME, from L *typus,* from Gk *týpos* blow, impression]

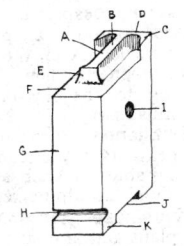

type (def. 7a): A, stem; B, face; C, serif; D, hairline; E, beard or neck; F, shoulder; G, body; H, nick; I, pin mark; J, groove; K, foot

**-type,** a word element representing **type,** as in *prototype,* esp. used of photographic processes, as in *ferrotype.*

**typecast** /ˈtaɪpkast/, *v.,* **-cast, -casting,** *adj. –v.t.* **1.** to cast (an actor, etc.) continually in the same kind of role, esp. because of some physical characteristic. *–adj.* **2.** (of an actor) having acquired a particular image through frequent casting in similar roles.

**typeface** /ˈtaɪpfeɪs/, *n.* →**face** (def. 20b).

**typefounder** /ˈtaɪpfaʊndə/, *n.* one engaged in the making of metallic types for printers.

**type genus** /ˈtaɪp dʒinəs/, *n.* that genus which is formally taken and held to be typical of the family or other higher group to which it belongs.

**type height** /ˈ– haɪt/, *n.* (in printing) the uniform height (0.918 inches or 23.32 mm) at which type is cast and illustrations are mounted so that a uniform impression will be achieved.

**type-high** /ˈtaɪp-haɪ/, *adj.* of the same height as type.

**type metal** /ˈtaɪp mɛtl/, *n.* an alloy for making printing types, etc., consisting chiefly of lead and antimony, and sometimes small quantities of tin, copper, etc.

**typescript** /ˈtaɪpskrɪpt/, *n.* **1.** a typewritten copy of a literary composition, a document, or the like. **2.** typewritten material, as distinguished from handwriting or print.

**typeset** /ˈtaɪpsɛt/, *v.,* **-set, -setting,** *adj. Print. –v.t.* **1.** to set in type, esp. hot metal. *–adj.* **2.** set in type. Cf. **filmset.**

**typesetter** /ˈtaɪpsɛtə/, *n.* **1.** one who sets or composes type; a compositor. **2.** a typesetting machine.

**typesetting** /ˈtaɪpsɛtɪŋ/, *n.* **1.** the process or action of setting type. *–adj.* **2.** used or intended for setting type.

**type species** /ˈtaɪp ˌspisiz/, *n.* that species of a genus which is regarded as the best example of the generic characters, i.e., the species from which a genus is named.

**type specimen** /ˈ– spɛsəmən/, *n.* an individual animal or plant from which the description of a species has been prepared.

**typewrite** /ˈtaɪpraɪt/, *v.t., v.i.,* **-wrote, -written, -writing.** →**type.**

**typewriter** /ˈtaɪpraɪtə/, *n.* **1.** a machine for writing mechanically in letters and characters. **2.** *Print.* a type style which gives the appearance of typewritten copy. **3.** (formerly) a typist.

typewriter

**typewriting** /ˈtaɪpraɪtɪŋ/, *n.* **1.** the act or art of using a typewriter. **2.** work done on a typewriter.

**typhlitis** /təˈflaɪtəs/, *n.* inflammation of the caecum. [Gk *typhl(ón)* caecum + -ITIS] **– typhlitic** /təˈflɪtɪk/.

**typhlology** /tɪfˈlɒlədʒi/, *n.* the sum of scientific knowledge concerning blindness.

**typhlosole** /ˈtɪfləsoʊl/, *n.* an inwardly projecting fold of the intestine of some invertebrates such as the earthworm.

**typho-,** a word element representing **typhus** and **typhoid,** as in *typhogenic.*

**typhogenic** /taɪfoʊˈdʒɛnɪk/, *adj.* producing typhus or typhoid fever.

**typhoid** /ˈtaɪfɔɪd/, *n.* →**typhoid fever.** [TYPH(US) + -OID] **– typhoidal** /taɪˈfɔɪdl/, *adj.*

**typhoid bacillus** /ˈ– bəsɪləs/, *n.* a micro-organism found in the intestinal ulcers and elsewhere in the bodies of sufferers from typhoid fever.

**typhoid fever** /– ˈfivə/, *n.* an infectious, often fatal, febrile disease, usu. of the summer months, characterised by intestinal inflammation and ulceration, due to the typhoid bacillus which is usu. introduced with food or drink.

**typhoidin** /taɪˈfɔɪdən/, *n.* a culture of dead typhoid bacillus used by cutaneous inoculation to detect the presence of a typhoid infection.

**typhomalarial** /ˌtaɪfoʊməˈlɛəriəl/, *adj.* having the character of both typhoid fever and malaria, as a fever.

**typhoon** /taɪˈfun/, *n.* **1.** a tropical cyclone or hurricane of the western Pacific area and the China seas. **2.** a violent storm or tempest of India. [Chinese *tai fung* great wind; influenced by Gk *tŷphōn* violent wind] **– typhonic** /taɪˈfɒnɪk/, *adj.*

**typhus** /ˈtaɪfəs/, *n.* an acute infectious disease characterised by great prostration, severe nervous symptoms, and a peculiar eruption of reddish spots on the body, now regarded as due to a specific micro-organism transmitted by lice and fleas. Also, **typhus fever.** [NL, from Gk *tŷphos* vapour] **– typhous,** *adj.*

**typical** /ˈtɪpɪkəl/, *adj.* **1.** pertaining to, of the nature of, or serving as a type or emblem; symbolic. **2.** of the nature of or serving as a type or representative specimen. **3.** conforming to the type. **4.** *Biol.* exemplifying most nearly the essential characteristics of a higher group in natural history, and forming the type: *the typical genus of a family.* **5.** pertaining or belonging to a representative specimen; characteristic or distinctive. Also, **typic. – typically,** *adv.* **– typicalness,** *n.*

**typify** /ˈtɪpəfaɪ/, *v.t.,* **-fied, -fying.** **1.** to serve as the typical specimen of; exemplify. **2.** to serve as a symbol or emblem of; symbolise; prefigure. **3.** to represent by a type or symbol. [L *typus* TYPE + -IFY] **– typification** /tɪpəfəˈkeɪʃən/, *n.* **– typifier,** *n.*

**typist** /ˈtaɪpəst/, *n.* **1.** one who operates a typewriter. **2.** one whose occupation is typewriting.

**typiste** /taɪˈpist/, *n.* a female typist.

**typog.,** **1.** typographer. **2.** typography.

**typographer** /taɪˈpɒgrəfə/, *n.* one skilled or engaged in typography.

**typographical** /taɪpə'græfɪkəl/, *adj.* pertaining to typography: *typographical errors.* Also, **typographic.** – **typographically,** *adv.*

**typography** /taɪ'pɒgrəfi/, *n.* **1.** the art or process of printing with types. **2.** the work of setting and arranging types and of printing from them. **3.** the general character or appearance of printed matter. [NL *typographia,* from Gk *týpo(s)* type + *graphia* writing]

**typology** /taɪ'pɒlədʒi/, *n.* **1.** the doctrine or study of types or symbols, esp. those of Scripture. **2.** the study of types and classes, esp. as in systematic classification. **3.** *Archaeol.* the study of the shape of artefacts for purposes of classification and comparison. **4.** symbolic significance or representation. – **typological** /taɪpə'lɒdʒɪkəl/, *adj.* – **typologist,** *n.*

**tyramine** /'taɪrəmin, 'tɪ-/, *n.* a colourless, crystalline solid, $HOC_6H_4(CH_2)_2NH_2$, formed by the action of bacteria on tyrosine, esp. in decaying animal products, as cheese.

**tyrannical** /tə'rænɪkəl, taɪ-/, *adj.* arbitrary or despotic; despotically cruel or harsh; severely oppressive. Also, **tyrannic.** [L *tyrannicus* (from Gk *tyrannikós*) + -AL[1]] – **tyrannically,** *adv.* – **tyrannicalness,** *n.*

**tyrannicide** /tə'rænəsaɪd/, *n.* **1.** one who kills a tyrant. **2.** the act of killing a tyrant. [L *tyrannicida* (def. 1), *tyrannicidium* (def. 2). See -CIDE] – **tyrannicidal** /təræ̀nə'saɪdl/, *adj.*

**tyrannise** /'tɪrənaɪz/, *v.,* **-nised, -nising.** *–v.i.* **1.** to exercise power cruelly or oppressively. **2.** to reign as a tyrant. **3.** to rule despotically or cruelly. *–v.t.* **4.** to rule tyrannically. **5.** to act the tyrant to or over. Also, **tyrannize.** – **tyranniser,** *n.* – **tyrannisingly,** *adv.*

**tyrannosaurus** /tərænə'sɔrəs/, *n.* a great carnivorous dinosaur, of the genus *Tyrannosaurus,* of the later Cretaceous period in North America, which walked erect on its powerful hind limbs. Also, **tyrannosaur.**

tyrannosaurus

**tyrannous** /'tɪrənəs/, *adj.* →**tyrannical.** – **tyrannously,** *adv.* – **tyrannousness,** *n.*

**tyranny** /'tɪrəni/, *n., pl.* **-nies. 1.** arbitrary or unrestrained exercise of power; despotic abuse of authority. **2.** the government or rule of a tyrant or absolute ruler. **3.** a state ruled by a tyrant or absolute ruler. **4.** oppressive or unjustly severe government on the part of any ruler. **5.** undue severity or harshness. **6.** a tyrannical act or proceeding. [ME *tirannie,* from ML *tyrannia,* from *tyrannus* TYRANT]

**tyrant** /'taɪrənt/, *n.* **1.** a king or ruler who uses his power oppressively or unjustly. **2.** an absolute ruler, as in ancient Greece, owing his office to usurpation. **3.** any person who exercises power despotically. **4.** a tyrannical or compulsory influence. [ME *tirant,* from OF, from L *tyrannus,* from Gk *týrannos*]

**tyre** /'taɪə/, *n., v.,* **tyred, tyring.** *–n.* **1.** a band of metal or rubber, fitted round the rim of a wheel as a running surface. The inflated rubber **pneumatic tyre** provides good adhesion and resistance to shock. *–v.t.* **2.** to furnish with a tyre or tyres. Also, *U.S.,* **tire.** [late ME; special use of TIRE[3]]

**Tyrian purple** /ˌtɪriən 'pɜpəl/, *n.* highly prized purple dye of classical antiquity, originally obtained at great expense from a certain shellfish. It was later shown to be an indigo derivative and synthesised, and it has been displaced by other synthetic dyes. Cf. **murex.** Also, **Tyrian dye.** [from *Tyre,* an ancient seaport on the E shore of the Mediterranean Sea]

**tyro** /'taɪroʊ/, *n., pl.* **-ros.** a beginner in learning anything; a novice. Also, **tiro.** [L: recruit]

**Tyrolean** /tɪrə'liən/, *adj., n., pl.* **-ese.** *–adj.* **1.** of, or pertaining to the Tyrol, a province in western Austria, or its inhabitants. *–n.* **2.** a native of Tyrol. Also, **Tyrolese** /tɪrə'liz/.

**Tyrolienne** /tɪrə'liən/, *n.* **1.** a dance of the Tyrolese peasants. **2.** a song or melody, characteristically a yodel, suitable for such a dance. [F, fem. of *tyrolien* pertaining to *Tyrol,* an alpine region in W Austria and N Italy]

**tyrosinase** /'taɪrəsəˌneɪz/, *n.* an oxidising enzyme found in plant and animal tissues that catalyses the first stages of the conversion of tyrosine into melanin and other pigments.

**tyrosine** /'taɪrəsin/, *n.* an amino acid, $HO{\cdot}C_6H_4{\cdot}CH_2{\cdot}CH(NH_3^+)COO^-$, occurring in proteins. [Gk *tȳrós* cheese + -INE[2]]

**tzar** /za/, *n.* →**tsar.**

**tzarevitch** /'zarəvɪtʃ/, *n.* →**tsarevitch.**

**tzarevna** /za'rɛvnə/, *n.* →**tsarevna.**

**tzarina** /za'rinə/, *n.* →**tsarina.**

**tzarism** /'zarɪzəm/, *n.* →**tsarism.**

**tzarist** /'zarəst/, *n.* →**tsarist.**

**tzaritza** /za'rɪtsə/, *n.* →**tsaritsa.**

**tzetze fly** /'tsɛtsi flaɪ/, *n.* →**tsetse fly.**

Uu Roman MELIOR  Uu Sans Serif VENUS  Uu Script COPPERPLATE  Uu Decorative ECKMANN

*Although there are numerous typefaces in the world they can be divided into four main classifications. These are:*

*ROMAN or SERIF. This typeface came into being from the technique of the Roman masons who, working in stone, finished off each letter with a serif or small stroke projecting from the top or bottom. This was done to correct any feeling of unevenness or imbalance they may have created in cutting the characters in stone.*

*SANS SERIF (without serif). This typeface is geometric in design and has straight-edged characters and lines of a regular thickness.*

*SCRIPT. Based on the movement of the hand, this typeface is often italicised or slanted, as if drawn by a brush or quill pen.*

*DECORATIVE. Any typeface that exaggerates the characteristics of any of the other three classifications to a degree that places it outside of them.*

*The dictionary entries in this book use a SANS SERIF typeface called Helvetica (set in a bold face for the head words) and a SERIF typeface Plantin (used throughout the body of the entries).*

**U, u** /ju/, *n., pl.* **U's** or **Us, u's** or **us.** a vowel, the 21st letter of the English alphabet.

**u,** atomic mass unit.

**U,** *Chem.* uranium.

**U** /ju/, *adj. Colloq.* appropriate to or characteristic of the upper class. Cf. **non-U.** [initial of UPPER (CLASS)]

**U.,** **1.** Union. **2.** United. **3.** University. **4.** Upper.

**uakari** /wə'kari/, *n.* any of the short-tailed monkeys of the genus *Cacajao,* esp. *C. rubicundus* of the Amazon basin. [Tupi]

**UAR,** United Arab Republic. Also, **U.A.R.**

**UART** /'juat/, *n.* a chip (def. 6) which processes data in a serial form which the computer will accept, and allows the operator to receive data from, and to put data into, the keyboard. [*U(niversal) A(synchronous) R(eceiver-)T(ransmitter)*]

**ubac** /'jubæk/, *n.* a mountain slope shaded from the sun. [d. F, from L *opacus* dark]

**uberrima fidei** /ju,bɛrəmə fɪ'deɪ/, *n. Law.* utmost good faith. [L]

**ubiety** /ju'baɪəti/, *n.* the state of being in a definite place; condition with respect to place; local relation. [NL *ubietas,* from L *ubi* where]

**ubiquinone** /jubi'kwɪnoun/, *n.* any of a group of closely related quinone compounds found widely distributed in living tissues. [UBI(QUITOUS) + QUINONE]

**ubiquitous** /ju'bɪkwətəs/, *adj.* characterised by ubiquity; being everywhere at the same time; present everywhere; omnipresent. Also, *Rare,* **ubiquitary** [UBIQUIT(Y) + -OUS] – **ubiquitously,** *adv.* – **ubiquitousness,** *n.*

**ubiquity** /ju'bɪkwəti/, *n.* **1.** the state or capacity of being everywhere at the same time; omnipresence. **2.** (*cap.*) *Theol.* the omnipresent state of God or Christ. [NL *ubīquitas,* from L *ubīque* everywhere]

**ubi supra** /ubi 'supra/, *adv.* in the page or passage previously referred to. [L: where above]

**U-boat** /'ju-bout/, *n.* a German submarine. [G: half adoption, half translation of *U-boot,* short for *Unterseeboot* undersea boat]

**U-bolt** /'ju-boult/, *n.* a rod of iron bent into the form of the letter U, fitted at both ends with a screw thread which takes a nut.

U-bolt

**u.c.,** **1.** *Music.* 'one string'; soft pedal. [It. *una corda*] **2.** (upper-case letter or letters).

**UCHD,** Usual Childhood Diseases.

**UCV** /ju si 'vi/, Unimproved Capital Value.

**udder** /'ʌdə/, *n.* a mamma or mammary gland, esp. when pendulous and with more than one teat, as in cows. [ME *uddre,* OE *ūder,* c. G *Euter,* akin to L *ūber*] – **udderless,** *adj.* – **udder-like,** *adj.*

**udo** /'udou/, *n.* a plant, *Aralia cordata,* cultivated esp. in Japan and China for its edible shoots. [Jap.]

**udometer** /ju'dɒmətə/, *n.* a rain gauge; a pluviometer. [F *udomètre,* from L *ūdus* wet, damp + *-o-* -O- + *-mètre* -METER[1]] – **udometric** /judə'metrɪk/, *adj.* – **udometry,** *n.*

**UFO** /ju ɛf 'ou, 'jufou/, *n.* unidentified flying object. Also, **U.F.O.**

**ufologist** /ju'fɒlədʒəst/, *n.* one who studies UFOs.

**Uganda** /ju'gændə/, *n.* a republic in eastern Africa between the north-eastern Congo and Kenya. – **Ugandan,** *adj., n.*

**ugari** /'jugəri/, *n.* the eastern Australian pipi, *Plebidonax deltoides,* commonly used for bait.

**ug boot** /'ʌg but/, *n.* a fleecy-lined boot with an untanned upper.

**ugh** /ʌg, əg, ʌ/, *interj.* **1.** (an exclamation expressing disgust, aversion, horror, or the like.) **2.** (a representation of the sound of a cough or grunt.)

**ugli fruit** /'ʌgli frut/, *n.* a large, juicy fruit with a thick yellow skin, a cross between a tangerine, a grapefruit, and a Seville orange.

**uglify** /'ʌgləfaɪ/, *v.t.,* **-fied, -fying.** to make ugly. [UGLY + -FY] – **uglification** /ʌgləfə'keɪʃən/, *n.*

**ugly** /'ʌgli/, *adj.,* **-lier, -liest. 1.** repulsive or displeasing in appearance; offensive to the sense of beauty: *ugly furniture.* **2.** morally revolting: *ugly sin.* **3.** disagreeable; unpleasant; objectionable: *ugly tricks.* **4.** of a troublesome nature; threatening disadvantage or danger: *ugly symptoms.* **5.** unpleasantly or dangerously rough: *ugly weather.* **6.** ill-natured; quarrelsome; vicious: *an ugly disposition.* [ME, from Scand.; cf. Icel. *uggligr* fearful, dreadful] – **uglily,** *adv.* – **ugliness,** *n.*

**ugly duckling** /– 'dʌklɪŋ/, *n.* an unattractive or unpromising child who becomes a beautiful or much admired adult. [name of a story by Hans Christian Andersen, 1805-1875, Danish author]

**Ugrian** /'ugriən, 'ju-/, *adj.* **1.** denoting or pertaining to a race or ethnological group including the Magyars and related peoples of western Siberia and the north-eastern Soviet Union in Europe. *–n.* **2.** a member of any of the Ugrian peoples. **3.** →**Ugric.**

**Ugric** /ˈugrɪk, ˈju-/, *n.* **1.** the group of Finno-Ugric languages that consists of Hungarian and two languages spoken in western Siberia. *–adj.* **2.** →**Ugrian.**

**Ugro-Finnic** /ˌugroʊ-ˈfɪnɪk, jugroʊ-/, *n.* →**Finno-Ugric.**

**u.h.f.** /ju eɪtʃ ˈɛf/, ultra high frequency. Also, **U.H.F.**

**uhlan** /ˈulan, ˈjulən/, *n.* **1.** one of a body of mounted soldiers first known in Europe in Poland, usu. carrying lances. **2.** one of such a body in the former German army, classed as heavy cavalry. Also, **ulan.** [G, from Pol. *ulan,* from Turk *oghlān* boy, lad]

**U-ie** /ˈju-i/, *n. Colloq.* **1.** →**U-turn.** **2. chuck a U-ie,** to do a U-turn.

**uintatherium** /juɪntəˈθɪərɪəm/, *n.* →**dinoceras.**

**U.K.** /ju ˈkeɪ/, *n.* United Kingdom.

**ukase** /juˈkeɪz/, *n.* any absolute or arbitrary order, regulation, or proclamation. [orig. an edict or order of the Tsar of Russia, having the force of law; Russ. *ukaz*]

**Ukraine** /juˈkreɪn/, *n.* a constituent republic of the Soviet Union, in the south-western part.

**Ukrainian** /juˈkreɪnɪən/, *adj.* **1.** of or pertaining to the Ukraine. *–n.* **2.** a native or inhabitant of the Ukraine. **3.** a Slavic language closely related to Russian.

**Ukrainian Soviet Socialist Republic,** *n.* official name of the **Ukraine.**

**ukulele** /jukəˈleɪli/, *n.* a small musical instrument of the guitar kind with a long neck, much used in the Hawaiian Islands. Also, **ukelele.** [Hawaiian: lit., flea]

ukulele

**ulcer** /ˈʌlsə/, *n.* **1.** *Pathol.* a sore open either to the surface of the body or to a natural cavity, and accompanied by the disintegration of tissue and the formation of pus, etc. **2.** a corrupting influence or element. [ME, from L *ulcus,* akin to Gk *hélkos*]

**ulcerate** /ˈʌlsəreɪt/, *v.t., v.i.,* **-rated, -rating.** to affect or be affected with an ulcer; make or become ulcerous. [ME, from L *ulcerātus,* pp.] – **ulceration** /ʌlsəˈreɪʃən/, *n.*

**ulcerative** /ˈʌlsəreɪtɪv/, *adj.* **1.** causing ulceration. **2.** of the nature of or characterised by ulceration.

**ulcerous** /ˈʌlsərəs/, *adj.* **1.** of the nature of an ulcer or ulcers; characterised by the formation of ulcers. **2.** affected with an ulcer or ulcers. **3.** corrupting; corruptive. – **ulcerously,** *adv.* – **ulcerousness,** *n.*

**ule** /ˈuleɪ/, *n.* **1.** a latiferous Central American tree, *Castilla elastica.* **2.** the crude rubber obtained from this tree. [Mex. Sp., from Nahuatl *ulli*]

**-ule,** a diminutive suffix of nouns, as in *globule.* [L *-ulus, -ula, -ulum*]

**-ulent,** an adjective suffix meaning 'abounding in', as in *fraudulent.* [L *-ulentus* full of]

**ulexite** /juˈlɛksaɪt/, *n.* a mineral, hydrous borate of calcium and sodium which occurs in saline crusts in arid regions, esp. in Chile and Nevada, in the form of fine white acicular crystals. [named after G. L. *Ulex,* d. 1883, German chemist; see -ITE[1]]

**ullage** /ˈʌlɪdʒ/, *n., v.,* **-laged, -laging.** *–n.* **1.** the amount by which the contents of a container, tank, ship, etc., fall short of filling it. **2.** the loss of wine or the like from its container by reason of leakage or evaporation. **3.** *Aeron.* the volume of a full tank in excess of the fuel. *–v.i.* **4.** to create an ullage. **5.** to measure an ullage. [late ME, from AF *ulliage* filling up (of a cask), from *aouiller* fill up (a cask), from LL *oculus* bunghole, in L eye]

**ulna** /ˈʌlnə/, *n., pl.* **-nae** /-ni/, **-nas.** **1.** *Anat.* that one of the two bones of the forearm which is on the side opposite to the thumb. **2.** a corresponding bone in the forelimb of other vertebrates. [NL, special use of L *ulna* elbow, arm] – **ulnar,** *adj.*

**-ulose,** variant of **-ulous** in scientific terms, as in *granulose, ramulose.* [L *-ulōsus.* See -ULE, -OSE[1]]

**ulotrichous** /juˈlɒtrəkəs/, *adj.* having woolly hair. [Gk *oûlo(s)* curly + *-trichos* -haired]

**-ulous,** a suffix forming adjectives meaning 'tending to', as in *credulous, populous.* [L *-ulosus,* or *-ulus,* or *-ulus*]

**ulster** /ˈʌlstə/, *n.* a long, loose, heavy overcoat, originally made of cloth from northern Ireland. [from *Ulster* a former province of that name in northern Ireland]

**ult.,** **1.** ultimate. **2.** ultimately. **3.** Also, **ulto.** ultimo.

**ulterior** /ʌlˈtɪəriə/, *adj.* **1.** being beyond what is seen or avowed; intentionally kept concealed: *ulterior motives.* **2.** coming at a subsequent time or stage: *ulterior action.* **3.** being or situated beyond, or on the farther side: *ulterior regions.* [L: farther, compar. adj. akin to *ultrā,* adv., beyond] – **ulteriorly,** *adv.*

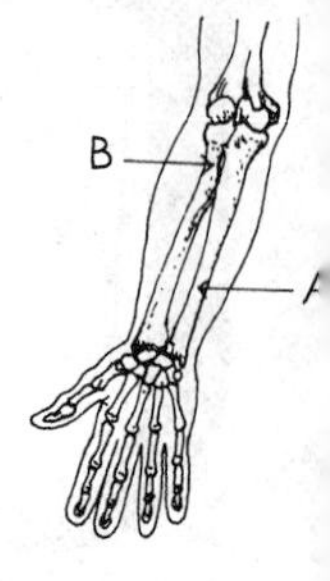


A, ulna; B, radius

**ultima** /ˈʌltəmə/, *n.* the last syllable of a word. [L, fem. of *ultimus* farthest, last]

**ultimate** /ˈʌltəmət/, *adj.* **1.** forming the final aim or object: *his ultimate goal.* **2.** coming at the end, as of a course of action, a process, etc.; final; decisive: *ultimate lot in life.* **3.** beyond which it is impossible to proceed, as by investigation or analysis; fundamental; elemental: *ultimate principles.* **4.** impossible to exceed or override: *ultimate weapon.* **5.** last, as in a series. *–n.* **6.** the final point; final result. **7.** a fundamental fact or principle. **8. the ultimate,** *Colloq.* the most successful, pleasing, handsome, etc. [LL *ultimātus,* pp., ended, from L *ultimus* last] – **ultimately,** *adv.* – **ultimateness,** *n.*

**ultimate load** /– ˈloʊd/, *n.* the maximum load which a structure is designed to withstand.

**ultimate particle** /– ˈpatɪkəl/, *n.* →**elementary particle.**

**ultimate stress** /– ˈstrɛs/, *n.* the load required to fracture a material, divided by the original area of cross-section at the point of fracture. Also, **ultimate tensile stress.**

**ultima Thule** /ʌltəmə ˈθjul/, *n.* **1.** the uttermost degree obtainable. **2.** the farthest limit or point possible. **3.** the farthest north. Also, **Thule.** [L: farthest Thule (supposedly the northernmost point in the world)]

**ultimatum** /ʌltəˈmeɪtəm/, *n., pl.* **-tums, -ta** /-tə/. **1.** the final terms of one of the parties in a diplomatic relationship, the rejection of which by the other party may involve a rupture of relations or lead to a declaration of war. **2.** a final proposal or statement of conditions. [NL, properly neut. of LL *ultimātus* ULTIMATE]

**ultimo** /ˈʌltəmoʊ/, *adv.* in or of the month preceding the present: *on the 12th ultimo. Abbrev.:* ult., ulto. Cf. **proximo.** [L, short for *ultimō mense* in the last month]

**ultimogeniture** /ʌltəmoʊˈdʒɛnətʃə/, *n.* the principle of undivided inheritance or succession by the youngest son (distinguished from *primogeniture*). [*ultimo-* (combining form representing L *ultimus* last) + (PRIMO)GENITURE]

**ulto,** ultimo.

**ultra** /ˈʌltrə/, *adj.* **1.** going beyond what is usual or ordinary; excessive; extreme. *–n.* **2.** one who goes to extremes, as of fashion, etc. [L: beyond, adv., prep.]

**ultra-,** a prefix meaning: **1.** beyond (in space or time) as in *ultraplanetary.* **2.** excessive; excessively, as in *ultraconventional.* [L, combining form of *ultrā,* adv., prep., beyond]

**ultrabasic rock** /ʌltrəˌbeɪsɪk ˈrɒk/, *n.* a rock which contains less silica than basic rock; rock containing less than 45 per cent of silica.

**ultracentrifuge** /ʌltrəˈsɛntrəfjudʒ/, *n., v.,* **-fuged, -fuging.** *–n.* **1.** a high-speed centrifuge capable of separating ultramicroscopic particles. *–v.t.* **2.** to separate in an ultracentrifuge.

**ultracooler** /ʌltrəˈkulə/, *n.* a type of cooling device used during winemaking in which wine is passed in a coil through a bath of refrigerant, as ammonia. [ULTRA- + COOL + -ER[1]]

**ultrafashionable** /ʌltrəˈfæʃənəbəl/, *adj.* →**trendy.**

**ultrafilter** /ʌltrəˈfɪltə/, *n.* **1.** a filter for the separation of colloidal particles consisting of a semipermeable membrane through which the filtrate passes under pressure or suction. *–v.t.* **2.** to separate in an ultrafilter.

**ultra high frequency,** *n.* **1.** any frequency between 300 and 3000 megahertz. *–adj.* **2.** (of a device) designed to transmit or receive such a frequency. *Abbrev.:* u.h.f.

**ultraism** /ˈʌltrəˌɪzəm/, *n.* **1.** extremism. **2.** an extreme view or act. – **ultraist,** *n., adj.* – **ultraistic** /ʌltrəˈɪstɪk/, *adj.*

**ultramafic rock** /ʌltrəˌmæfɪk ˈrɒk/, *n.* →**ultrabasic rock.**

**ultra-marathon** /ˈʌltrə-mærəθɒn/, *n.* any footrace in excess of the marathon distance.

**ultramarine** /ʌltrəməˈrin/, *adj.* **1.** beyond the sea. **2.** of an ultramarine colour; deep blue. *–n.* **3.** a blue pigment consisting of powdered lapis lazuli. **4.** a similar artificial blue pigment. **5.** any of various other pigments. **6.** a deep blue colour. [ML *ultrāmarīnus.* See ULTRA-, MARINE]

**ultramicrobalance** /ʌltrəˈmaɪkroʊbæləns/, *n.* a balance capable of weighing very small quantities of a substance to an accuracy of one hundredth of a microgram.

**ultramicrometer** /ʌltrəmaɪˈkrɒmətə/, *n.* a micrometer calibrated to a very fine scale.

**ultramicroscope** /ʌltrəˈmaɪkrəskoʊp/, *n.* an instrument for detecting, by means of diffractive effects, objects too small to be seen by the ordinary microscope. – **ultramicroscopic** /ˌʌltrəˌmaɪkrəˈskɒpɪk/, **ultramicroscopical,** *adj.*

**ultramicroscopy** /ʌltrəmaɪˈkrɒskəpi/, *n.* the use of the ultramicroscope.

**ultra-modern** /ʌltrə-ˈmɒdən/, *adj.* of or pertaining to an extreme in modern design; avant-garde.

**ultramontane** /ʌltrəˈmɒnteɪn/, *adj.* **1.** beyond the mountains. **2.** south of the Alps; Italian. **3.** pertaining to or supporting the Roman Catholic belief that the pope is the spiritual head of the Church in all countries. **4.** (formerly) north of the Alps; tramontane. *–n.* **5.** one who lives beyond the mountains. **6.** one living south of the Alps. **7.** a member of the ultramontane party in the Roman Catholic Church. **8.** (formerly) one living to the north of the Alps. [ML *ultrāmontānus.* See ULTRA-, MONTANE] – **ultramontanism,** *n.*

**ultramundane** /ʌltrəˈmʌndeɪn/, *adj.* **1.** beyond the limits of the known universe. **2.** *Obs.* beyond the present life. [LL *ultrāmundānus.* See ULTRA-, MUNDANE]

**ultrasonic** /ʌltrəˈsɒnɪk/, *adj.* of or pertaining to ultrasound.

**ultrasonic cleaning** /– ˈklinɪŋ/, *n.* a method of cleaning metallic parts by immersion in a fluid through which ultrasonic waves pass.

**ultrasonics** /ʌltrəˈsɒnɪks/, *n.* the study of ultrasound; supersonics.

**ultrasonic welding** /ʌltrəˌsɒnɪk ˈwɛldɪŋ/, *n.* a method of fusing plastics together by means of ultrasonic waves.

**ultrasound** /ˈʌltrəsaʊnd/, *n.* pressure waves similar in nature to soundwaves but whose frequencies, greater than 20 000 hertz, are above the audible limit.

**ultrastructure** /ˈʌltrəstrʌktʃə/, *n.* the minute structure of a cell as seen only with a very powerful microscope, as an electron microscope.

**ultratropical** /ʌltrəˈtrɒpɪkəl/, *adj.* **1.** outside the tropics. **2.** warmer than the tropics.

**ultraviolet** /ʌltrəˈvaɪələt, -ˈvaɪlət/, *adj.* **1.** beyond the violet, as the invisible rays of the spectrum lying outside the violet end of the visible spectrum. **2.** pertaining to these rays: *ultraviolet light.*

**ultraviolet microscope** /– ˈmaɪkrəskoʊp/, *n.* a microscope in which the object to be viewed is illuminated by ultraviolet radiation.

**ultra vires** /ʌltrə ˈvaɪriz/, going beyond the legal power or authority of an agent, company, tribunal, etc. [L: beyond the power]

**ultravirus** /ʌltrəˈvaɪrəs/, *n.* an ultramicroscopic agent which passes through the finest bacterial filters.

**ultroneous** /ʌlˈtroʊniəs/, *adj. Rare.* spontaneous; voluntary. [L *ultrōneus*] – **ultroneously,** *adv.* – **ultroneousness,** *n.*

**ulu** /ˈulu/, *n.* a type of knife used by Eskimos.

**ululant** /ˈjuljələnt/, *adj.* ululating; howling. [L *ululans,* ppr.; imitative]

**ululate** /ˈjuljəleɪt/, *v.i.,* **-lated, -lating. 1.** to howl, as a dog or wolf. **2.** to utter some similar sound; hoot; wail. **3.** to lament loudly. [L *ululātus,* pp.; imit.] – **ululation** /juljəˈleɪʃən/, *n.*

**-ulus,** a diminutive suffix of nouns, as in *homunculus, calculus.*

**Ulysses butterfly** /juˌlɪsiz ˈbʌtəflaɪ/, *n.* →**mountain blue butterfly.**

**um** /ʌm/ *for defs 1 and 3;* /m, əm/ *for def. 2, interj., v.,* **ummed, umming.** *–interj.* **1.** (an indication of hesitation or inarticulateness). **2.** (an expression of doubt, pensiveness, etc.). *–v.i.* **3. um and ah,** *Colloq.* **a.** to be indecisive. **b.** to prevaricate.

**umbel** /ˈʌmbəl/, *n.* an inflorescence in which a number of flower stalks or pedicels, nearly equal in length, spread from a common centre, called a **simple umbel** when each pedicel is terminated by a single flower, and a **compound umbel** when each pedicel bears a secondary umbel. [L *umbella* sunshade, parasol, diminutive of *umbra* shadow]

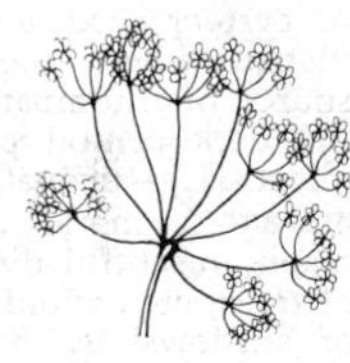
compound umbel

**umbellate** /ˈʌmbələt, -leɪt/, *adj.* having or forming an umbel or umbels. Also, **umbellar** /ʌmˈbɛlə/, **umbellated.** – **umbellately,** *adv.*

**umbelliferous** /ʌmbəˈlɪfərəs/, *adj.* **1.** bearing an umbel or umbels. **2.** belonging or pertaining to the Umbelliferae, a family of plants containing many important umbel-bearing herbs, as the parsley, carrot, etc. [NL *umbellifer* (see UMBEL, -I-, -FER) + -OUS]

**umbellule** /ʌmˈbɛljul, ˈʌmbəljul/, *n.* one of the secondary umbels in a compound umbel. [NL *umbellula,* diminutive of *umbella* UMBEL] – **umbellulate** /ʌmˈbɛljələt, -leɪt/, *adj.*

**umber** /ˈʌmbə/, *n.* **1.** an earth consisting chiefly of a hydrated oxide of iron and some oxide of manganese, used in its natural state **(raw umber)** as a brown pigment, or after heating **(burnt umber)** as a reddish brown pigment. **2.** the colour of such a pigment; dark dusky brown or dark reddish brown. *–adj.* **3.** of such a colour. *–v.t.* **4.** to colour with or as with umber. [It. *(terra di) ombra,* lit., (earth of) shade (see UMBRA); ? properly Umbrian earth]

**umbilical** /ʌmˈbɪləkəl, ʌmbəˈlaɪkəl/, *adj.* **1.** of the umbilicus or umbilical cord. **2.** formed or placed like a naval; central. *–n.* **3.** an umbilical cord (esp. def. 2). [ML *umbilīcālis,* from L *umbilīcus* navel]

**umbilical cord** /ˈ– kɔd/, *n.* **1.** *Anat.* a cord or funicle connecting the embryo or foetus with the placenta of the mother, and transmitting nourishment from the mother. **2.** Also, **umbilical connector, umbilical.** *Aerospace.* **a.** an electrical cable or fluid pipeline conveying supplies and signals from the ground to a rocket before the launch. **b.** an air or oxygen line connecting an astronaut to his spacecraft enabling him to walk in space.

**umbilicate** /ʌmˈbɪləkət/, *adj.* **1.** having the form of an umbilicus or navel. **2.** having an umbilicus. Also, **umbilicated.**

**umbilication** /ʌmˌbɪləˈkeɪʃən/, *n.* **1.** a central navel-like depression. **2.** umbilicate state or formation.

**umbilicus** /ʌmˈbɪləkəs, ʌmbəˈlaɪkəs/, *n., pl.* **-bilici** /-ˈbɪləsaɪ, -bəˈlaɪsaɪ/. **1.** *Anat.* the navel, or central depression in the surface of the abdomen indicating the point of attachment of the umbilical cord. **2.** *Bot., Zool., etc.* a navel-like formation,

---

**ultra-ambitious,** *adj.*
**ultraconfident,** *adj.*
**ultraconservatism,** *n.*
**ultraconservative,** *n., adj.*
**ultracredulous,** *adj.*
**ultracritical,** *adj.*
**ultrafashionable,** *adj.*
**ultraliberal,** *adj., n.*
**ultraloyal,** *adj.*
**ultraloyalist,** *n.*
**ultramodern,** *adj., n.*
**ultramodest,** *adj.*
**ultranationalism,** *n.*
**ultranationalist,** *n., adj.*
**ultraradical,** *adj., n.*
**ultrarapid,** *adj.*
**ultrarational,** *adj.*
**ultrarefined,** *adj.*
**ultrareligious,** *adj.*
**ultraroyalist,** *adj.*

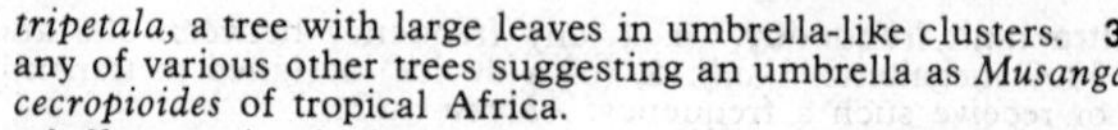

as the hilum of a seed. **3.** a central point or place. **4.** a small, navel-like depression. [L; akin to Gk *omphalós* and NAVEL]

**umbiliform** /ʌm'bɪləfɔm/, *adj.* having the form of an umbilicus or navel. [UMBILI(CUS) + -FORM]

**umble pie** /ʌmbəl 'paɪ/, *n.* →**humble pie.** [orig. spelling of HUMBLE PIE. See UMBLES]

**umbles** /'ʌmbəlz/, *n.pl.* →**numbles.** [var. of NUMBLES]

**umbo** /'ʌmboʊ/, *n., pl.* **umbones** /ʌm'boʊniz/, **umbos. 1.** the boss, knob, or projection at or near the centre of a shield. **2.** any similar boss or protuberance. **3.** the raised centre of the cup of some toadstools. **4.** *Zool.* the beak of a bivalve shell; the protuberance of each valve above the hinge. [L] – **umbonic** /ʌm'bɒnɪk/, *adj.*

**umbonate** /'ʌmbənət, -neɪt/, *adj.* **1.** bosslike. **2.** having an umbo or boss. Also, **umbonal.**

**umbra** /'ʌmbrə/, *n., pl.* **-brae** /-bri/. **1.** shade; shadow. **2.** *Astron.* **a.** the complete or perfect shadow of an opaque body, as a planet, where the direct light from the source of illumination is wholly cut off. **b.** the dark central portion of a sunspot. **3.** ghost. [L] – **umbral,** *adj.*

U, umbra; P, penumbra; S, sun; E, earth; M, moon

**umbrage** /'ʌmbrɪdʒ/, *n.* **1.** offence given or taken; resentful displeasure. **2.** the foliage of trees, etc., affording shade. **3.** *Obs.* shade or shadows, as that cast by trees, etc. **4.** *Rare.* a shadowy appearance or semblance of something. [late ME, from F *ombrage*, from L *umbrāticum*, neut. adj., of or in the shade; def. 1 through obs. meanings 'suspicion', 'disfavour']

**umbrageous** /ʌm'breɪdʒəs/, *adj.* **1.** forming or affording shade; shady; shaded. **2.** *Rare.* apt or disposed to take umbrage or offence, as a person. – **umbrageously,** *adv.* – **umbrageousness,** *n.*

**umbrella** /ʌm'brelə/, *n.* **1.** a portable shade or screen for protection from sunlight, rain, etc., in its modern form consisting of a light circular canopy of silk, cotton, or other material on a folding frame of bars or strips of steel, cane, etc. **2.** the saucer- or bowl-shaped gelatinous body of a jellyfish; the bell. **3.** any general protection or cover. **4.** *Mil.* a covering force of aircraft protecting ground troops. *–adj.* **5.** covering or intended to cover a group or class of things, circumstances, etc.; all-embracing: *winter sports is an umbrella term for skiing, skating, tobogganning, etc.* [It. *ombrella*, from *ombra* shade, from L *umbra*] – **umbrella-like,** *adj.*

**umbrella bird** /'– bɜd/, *n.* **1.** a South American bird, *Cephalopterus ornatus*, family Cotingidae, with an umbrella-like crest above the head. **2.** another bird of this genus, *C. penduliger.*

umbrella bird

**umbrella bush** /'– bʊʃ/, *n.* any of various small trees with a spreading crown, as the nealie.

**umbrella fern** /'– fɜn/, *n.* the fern, *Sticherus flabellatus*, found in moist forests.

**umbrella grass** /'– gras/, *n.* any species of grass with an umbrella-like panicle.

**umbrella mulga** /'– mʌlgə/, *n.* **1.** a mature mulga tree, *Acacia aneura*, branching and leafy. **2.** a closely related species, *A. brachystachya.*

**umbrella organisation** /'– ɔgənaɪ,zeɪʃən/, *n.* a body which coordinates the activities of a number of organisations, companies, etc., which have interests in common, without interfering with their autonomy.

**umbrella stand** /'– stænd/, *n.* a rack or vertical container for walking sticks and closed umbrellas.

**umbrella tree** /'– tri/, *n.* **1.** an Australian tree, *Schefflera actinophylla*, with large digitately compound shining leaves and small raspberry-like clusters of red flowers which are borne at the ends of branches in long radiating spike-like compound umbels. **2.** an American magnolia, *Magnolia tripetala*, a tree with large leaves in umbrella-like clusters. **3.** any of various other trees suggesting an umbrella as *Musanga cecropioides* of tropical Africa.

**umbriferous** /ʌm'brɪfərəs/, *adj.* casting or making shade. [L *umbrifer* shade-bearing + -OUS] – **umbriferously,** *adv.*

**umiak** /'umiæk/, *n.* an open Eskimo boat consisting of a wooden frame covered with skins and provided with several thwarts, for transport of goods and passengers. Also, **umiack, oomiak.** [Eskimo (Eastern d.): large skin boat, or woman's boat]

umiak

**umlaut** /'ʊmlaʊt/, *n.* **1.** (of vowels in Germanic languages) assimilation in which a vowel is influenced by a following vowel or semivowel. **2.** a vowel which has resulted from such assimilation, esp. when written *ä, ö,* or *ü* in German. **3.** two dots as a diacritic over a vowel to indicate a different vowel sound from that of the letter without the diacritic, esp. as so used in German. *–v.t.* **4.** to modify by umlaut. **5.** to write the umlaut over. [G, from *um* about + *Laut* sound]

**ump** /ʌmp/, *n. Colloq.* an umpire.

**umpie** /'ʌmpi/, *n. Colloq.* an umpire. Also, **umpy.**

**umpirage** /'ʌmpaɪərɪdʒ/, *n.* **1.** the office or authority of an umpire. **2.** the decision of an umpire; arbitrament.

**umpire** /'ʌmpaɪə/, *n., v.,* **-pired, -piring.** *–n.* **1.** a person selected to see that a game is played in accordance with the rules. **2.** a person to whose decision a controversy between parties is referred; an arbiter or referee. *–v.t.* **3.** to act as umpire in (a game). **4.** to decide or settle (a controversy, etc.) as umpire; arbitrate. *–v.i.* **5.** to act as umpire. [ME *oumpere*, replacing *noumpere* (*a noumpere* taken as *an oumpere*), from OF *nonper* uneven, odd, from *non* not (from L *nōn*) + *per* (see PEER[1], *n.*)] – **umpireship,** *n.*

**umpteen** /ʌmp'tin, 'ʌmptin/, *adj.* of an indefinite, esp. a very large or immeasurable, number. – **umpteenth,** *adj.*

**umu** /'umu/, *n. N.Z.* →**hangi** (def. 1). [Maori]

**un-**[1], a prefix meaning 'not', freely used as an English formative, giving a negative or opposite force, in adjectives (including participial adjectives) and their derivative adverbs and nouns, as in *unfair, unfairly, unfairness, unfelt, unseen, unfitting, unformed, unheard-of, unget-at-able,* and less freely in certain other nouns, as in *unease, unrest, unemployment.* Note: Of the words in **un-**[1], only a selected number are separately entered, since in most formations of this class, the meaning, spelling, and pronunciation may readily be determined by reference to the simple word from which each is formed. [ME and OE, c. D *on-*, G and Goth. *un-*, Icel. *ú-, ó-;* akin to L *in-*, Gk *an-, a-* (alpha privative)]

**un-**[2], a prefix freely used in English to form verbs expressing a reversal of some action or state, or removal, deprivation, release, etc., as in *unbend, uncork, unfasten,* etc., or to intensify the force of a verb already having such a meaning, as in *unloose.* [ME and OE *un-, on-*, c. D *ont-*, G *ent-*, Goth. *and-;* akin to L *ante* before, Gk *antí* opposite to, against]

**U.N.** /ju 'ɛn/, United Nations.

**unabbreviated** /ʌnə'brivieɪtəd/, *adj.* not shortened; given in full.

**unable** /ʌn'eɪbəl/, *adj.* not able (to do something); lacking ability or power (to do something); weak; impotent.

**unabridged** /ʌnə'brɪdʒd/, *adj.* not abridged or shortened, as a book.

**unaccented** /ʌnæk'sɛntəd/, *adj.* not accented; unstressed.

**unacceptable** /ʌnək'sɛptəbəl/, *adj.* that cannot be accepted; unwelcome; unsuitable. – **unacceptableness,** *n.*

**unaccommodated** /ʌnə'kɒmədeɪtəd/, *adj.* **1.** not satisfied. **2.** not accommodated; not adapted.

**unaccompanied** /ʌnə'kʌmpənid/, *adj.* **1.** not accompanied. **2.** *Music.* without an accompaniment.

**unaccomplished** /ʌnə'kʌmplɪʃt/, *adj.* **1.** not accomplished; incomplete. **2.** without accomplishments.

**unaccountable** /ʌnə'kaʊntəbəl/, *adj.* **1.** not to be accounted for or explained. **2.** not accountable or answerable. – **unaccountability** /ʌnə,kaʊntə'bɪləti/, **unaccountableness,** *n.* – **unaccountably,** *adv.*

**unaccounted-for** /ʌnəˈkaʊntəd-fɔ/, *adj.* not explained, understood, or taken into account.

**unaccustomed** /ʌnəˈkʌstəmd/, *adj.* **1.** not habituated: *to be unaccustomed to hardships.* **2.** unusual; unfamiliar. – **unaccustomedness,** *n.*

**una corda** /unə ˈkɔdə/, *adv.* (a direction in piano music) played with the soft pedal depressed, thus causing the hammers to hit one string only of the three available for each note. [It.: one string]

**unaddressed** /ʌnəˈdrɛst/, *adj.* not bearing an address, as a letter or the like.

**unadmitted** /ʌnədˈmɪtəd/, *adj.* **1.** not stated, said, or conceded. **2.** kept secret. **3.** refused admission, as to a society.

**unadvised** /ʌnədˈvaɪzd/, *adj.* **1.** not advised; without advice. **2.** indiscreet; rash. – **unadvisedly** /ʌnədˈvaɪzədli/, *adv.* – **unadvisedness,** *n.*

**unaesthetic** /ʌnəsˈθɛtɪk/, *adj.* unattractive; offending the aesthetic sense. Also, *U.S.,* **unesthetic.** – **unaesthetically,** *adv.*

**unaffected**[1] /ʌnəˈfɛktəd/, *adj.* free from affectation; sincere; genuine. [UN-[1] + AFFECTED[2]] – **unaffectedly,** *adv.* – **unaffectedness,** *n.*

**unaffected**[2] /ʌnəˈfɛktəd/, *adj.* not affected, acted upon, or influenced. [UN-[1] + AFFECTED[1]]

**unalienable** /ʌnˈeɪliənəbəl/, *adj.* unable or not allowed to be taken away or withheld, as a right. – **unalienably,** *adv.*

**unalive** /ʌnəˈlaɪv/, *adj.* not awake to or conscious of (something) (fol. by *to*): *he was quite unalive to the possibilities.*

**unalterable** /ʌnˈɔltərəbəl, -ˈɒlt-/, *adj.* not able to be changed. Also, **inalterable.** – **unalterably,** *adv.* – **unalterableness,** *n.*

**unaneled** /ʌnəˈnild/, *adj. Archaic.* not having received extreme unction.

**unanimity** /junəˈnɪməti/, *n.* complete accord or agreement.

**unanimous** /juˈnænəməs/, *adj.* **1.** of one mind; in complete accord; agreed. **2.** characterised by or showing complete accord: *a unanimous vote.* [L *ūnanimus*] – **unanimously,** *adv.* – **unanimousness,** *n.*

**unanswerable** /ʌnˈænsərəbəl, -ˈan-/, *adj.* **1.** not able to be refuted or rebutted; conclusive: *an unanswerable accusation.* **2.** not having an answer, as a question. – **unanswerableness,** *n.* – **unanswerably,** *adv.*

**unappealable** /ʌnəˈpiləbəl/, *adj.* **1.** not appealable; that cannot be carried to a higher court by appeal, as a cause. **2.** not to be appealed from, as a judgment or a judge. – **unappealableness,** *n.*

**unappreciative** /ʌnəˈpriʃətɪv/, *adj.* not appreciative; lacking in appreciation. Also, **inappreciative.** – **unappreciatively,** *adv.* – **unappreciativeness,** *n.*

**unapproachable** /ʌnəˈproʊtʃəbəl/, *adj.* **1.** not to be approached; inaccessible. **2.** remote; inaccessible to intimacy. **3.** unrivalled. – **unapproachableness,** *n.* – **unapproachably,** *adv.*

**unappropriated** /ʌnəˈproʊprieɪtəd/, *adj.* **1.** not taken possession of. **2.** not assigned or allotted.

**unapt** /ʌnˈæpt/, *adj.* **1.** unfitted; unsuited. **2.** not disposed, likely, or liable. **3.** not quick to learn; inapt. – **unaptly,** *adv.* – **unaptness,** *n.*

**unarm** /ʌnˈam/, *v.t.* **1.** to disarm. **2.** *Archaic.* to divest or relieve of armour. –*v.i.* **3.** to lay down one's arms. **4.** *Archaic.* to take off one's armour. [ME *unarme.* See UN-[2], ARM[2]]

**unarmed** /ʌnˈamd/, *adj.* **1.** without arms or armour. **2.** defenceless. **3.** not furnished with claws, prickles, scales, or other armature, as animals and plants. **4.** *Mil.* not having a detonator, as a bomb.

**unary** /ˈjunəri/, *adj.* (of a physico-chemical system) containing only one element or component. [L *ūnus* + -ARY[1]]

**unashamed** /ʌnəˈʃeɪmd/, *adj.* **1.** not contrite; not restrained by moral scruples. **2.** unconcealed; unembarrassed: *unashamed gluttony.* – **unashamedly** /ʌnəˈʃeɪmədli/, *adv.*

**unassuming** /ʌnəˈsjumɪŋ/, *adj.* unpretending; modest. – **unassumingly,** *adv.* – **unassumingness,** *n.*

**unassured** /ʌnəˈʃɔd/, *adj.* **1.** not certain; insecure. **2.** not confident. **3.** not having any life assurance.

**unattached** /ʌnəˈtætʃt/, *adj.* **1.** not attached. **2.** not connected or associated with any particular body, group or the like; independent. **3.** not engaged, married, or a partner in a stable relationship.

**unattached participle** /– ˈpatəsɪpəl/, *n.* See **misrelated participle.**

**unattended** /ʌnəˈtɛndəd/, *adj.* **1.** unaccompanied. **2.** alone. **3.** with no-one in charge. **4.** not taken care of. **5.** not heeded or paid attention to.

**unau** /ˈjunaʊ/, *n.* a two-toed sloth, *Choloepus didactylus.* [d. Tupi (Island of Maranhão)]

**unauthentic** /ʌnɔˈθɛntɪk/, *adj.* not authentic.

**unavailing** /ʌnəˈveɪlɪŋ/, *adj.* ineffectual; useless. – **unavailingly,** *adv.*

**unavoidable** /ʌnəˈvɔɪdəbəl/, *adj.* **1.** not to be avoided. **2.** unable to be avoided; inevitable. – **unavoidableness, unavoidability** /ʌnəˌvɔɪdəˈbɪləti/, *n.* – **unavoidably,** *adv.*

**unaware** /ʌnəˈwɛə/, *adj.* **1.** not aware; unconscious, as of something: *to be unaware of any change.* –*adv.* **2.** →**unawares.** – **unawareness,** *n.*

**unawares** /ʌnəˈwɛəz/, *adv.* **1.** while not aware or conscious of a thing oneself; unknowingly or inadvertently. **2.** while another is not aware; unexpectedly: *to come upon someone unawares.*

---

**unabashed,** *adj.*
**unabated,** *adj.*
**unabolished,** *adj.*
**unabrogated,** *adj.*
**unacceptance,** *n.*
**unaccommodating,** *adj.*
**unaccusable,** *adj.*
**unaccused,** *adj.*
**unachievable,** *adj.*
**unacknowledged,** *adj.*
**unacquaintance,** *n.*
**unacquainted,** *adj.*
**unacquaintedness,** *n.*
**unactable,** *adj.*
**unacted,** *adj.*
**unactuated,** *adj.*
**unadaptable,** *adj.*
**unadapted,** *adj.*
**unadjusted,** *adj.*
**unadmired,** *adj.*
**unadmiring,** *adj.*
**unadmonished,** *adj.*
**unadorned,** *adj.*
**unadulterated,** *adj.*
**unadventurous,** *adj.*
**unadvisable,** *adj.*
**unadvisableness,** *n.*
**unafraid,** *adj.*
**unaided,** *adj.*
**unaired,** *adj.*
**unallotted,** *adj.*
**unallowable,** *adj.*
**unalloyed,** *adj.*
**unaltered,** *adj.*
**unambiguous,** *adj.*
**unambitious,** *adj.*
**unambitiously,** *adv.*
**unamenable,** *adj.*
**unamendable,** *adj.*
**unamended,** *adj.*
**unamiability,** *n.*
**unamiable,** *adj.*
**unamiableness,** *n.*
**unamusable,** *adj.*
**unamused,** *adj.*
**unamusingly,** *adv.*
**unanalysable,** *adj.*
**unanalysed,** *adj.*
**unanalytical,** *adj.*
**unanchor,** *v.t., v.i.*
**unanchored,** *adj.*
**unannotated,** *adj.*
**unanticipated,** *adj.*
**unapologetic,** *adj.*
**unapostolic,** *adj.*
**unapostolically,** *adv.*
**unappalled,** *adj.*
**unappealing,** *adj.*
**unappeasable,** *adj.*
**unappeased,** *adj.*
**unappetising,** *adj.*
**unapplauded,** *adj.*
**unapplied,** *adj.*
**unappointed,** *adj.*
**unappreciated,** *adj.*
**unapprehended,** *adj.*
**unapprehensive,** *adj.*
**unapprehensiveness,** *n.*
**unapprised,** *adj.*
**unapproached,** *adj.*
**unapproved,** *adj.*
**unapprovingly,** *adv.*
**unarguable,** *adj.*
**unarmoured,** *adj.*
**unaroused,** *adj.*

**unbacked** /ʌn'bækt/, *adj.* **1.** without backing or support. **2.** not supported by bets. **3.** not endorsed. **4.** never having been mounted by a rider, as a horse.

**unbalance** /ʌn'bæləns/, *v.*, **-anced, -ancing,** *n.* *–v.t.* **1.** to throw out of balance. **2.** to disorder or derange, as the mind. *–n.* **3.** unbalanced condition.

**unbalanced** /ʌn'bælənst/, *adj.* **1.** not balanced, or not properly balanced. **2.** lacking steadiness and soundness of judgment. **3.** mentally disordered or deranged. **4.** (of an account) not adjusted; not brought to an equality of debits and credits.

**unbar** /ʌn'ba/, *v.t.* **-barred, -barring. 1.** to remove a bar or bars from. **2.** to open; unlock.

**unbearable** /ʌn'bɛərəbəl/, *adj.* not bearable; unendurable; intolerable. – **unbearableness,** *n.* – **unbearably,** *adv.*

**unbeatable** /ʌn'bitəbəl/, *adj.* **1.** not able to be beaten or overtaken; unsurpassable. **2.** supremely good or excellent.

**unbeaten** /ʌn'bitn/, *adj.* **1.** not defeated. **2.** untrodden: *unbeaten paths.* **3.** not struck or pounded.

**unbecoming** /ʌnbə'kʌmɪŋ/, *adj.* **1.** not becoming; not appropriate; unsuited. **2.** improper; unseemly. **3.** (of clothing, etc.) unattractively inappropriate. – **unbecomingly,** *adv.* – **unbecomingness,** *n.*

**unbeknown** /ʌnbə'noun/, *adj. Colloq.* unknown; unperceived; without a person's knowledge (usu. fol. by *to*, and oft. used adverbially): *unbeknown to him, she was married already.* Also, **unbeknownst.**

**unbelief** /ʌnbə'lif/, *n.* lack of belief; disbelief, esp. in divine revelation or in the truth of the gospel.

**unbeliever** /ʌnbə'livə/, *n.* **1.** one who does not believe. **2.** one who does not accept any, or some particular, religious belief.

**unbelieving** /ʌnbə'livɪŋ/, *adj.* **1.** not believing; sceptical. **2.** not accepting any, or some particular, religious belief. – **unbelievingly,** *adv.* – **unbelievingness,** *n.*

**unbend** /ʌn'bɛnd/, *v.*, **-bent** or **-bended, -bending.** *–v.t.* **1.** to release from the strain of effort or close application; relax by laying aside formality. **2.** to release from tension, as a bow. **3.** to straighten from a bent form or position. **4.** *Naut.* **a.** to loose or untie, as a sail, rope, etc. **b.** to unfasten from spars or stays, as sails. *–v.i.* **5.** to relax the strictness of formality or ceremony; act in an easy, genial manner. **6.** to become unbent.

**unbending** /ʌn'bɛndɪŋ/, *adj.* **1.** not bending; rigid; unyielding; inflexible. **2.** stern; rigorous; resolute. *–n.* **3.** a relaxing or easing. – **unbendingly,** *adv.* – **unbendingness,** *n.*

**unbent** /ʌn'bɛnt/, *v.* **1.** past tense and past participle of **unbend.** *–adj.* **2.** not bent; unbowed. **3.** not forced to yield or submit.

**unbiased** /ʌn'baɪəst/, *adj.* not biased; unprejudiced; impartial. Also, **unbiassed.** – **unbiasedly,** *adv.* – **unbiasedness,** *n.*

**unbidden** /ʌn'bɪdn/, *adj.* **1.** not commanded; spontaneous. **2.** uninvited. Also, **unbid.**

**unbind** /ʌn'baɪnd/, *v.t.*, **-bound, -binding. 1.** to release from bands or restraint, as a prisoner; free. **2.** to unfasten or loose, as a band or tie. [ME; OE *unbindan*, c. G *entbinden.* See UN-[2], BIND, *v.*]

**unbitted** /ʌn'bɪtəd/, *adj.* **1.** not bitted or bridled. **2.** uncontrolled.

**unblessed** /ʌn'blɛst/, *adj.* **1.** excluded from a blessing. **2.** unhallowed; unholy. **3.** unhappy; wretched. Also, **unblest.** – **unblessedness** /ʌn'blɛsədnəs/, *n.*

**unblinking** /ʌn'blɪŋkɪŋ/, *adj.* **1.** not blinking. **2.** without any show of response. **3.** fearless; undismayed. – **unblinkingly,** *adv.*

**unblushing** /ʌn'blʌʃɪŋ/, *adj.* **1.** shameless. **2.** not blushing. – **unblushingly,** *adv.* – **unblushingness,** *n.*

**unbolt** /ʌn'boult/, *v.t.* **1.** to draw the bolt of (a door, etc.). **2.** to open, dismantle, release, or the like, by the removal of threaded bolts.

**unbolted**[1] /ʌn'boultəd/, *adj.* not fastened, as a door. [UN-[1] + BOLT[1] + -ED[2]]

**unbolted**[2] /ʌn'boultəd/, *adj.* not sifted, as grain. [UN-[1] + BOLT[2] + -ED[2]]

**unboned** /ʌn'bound/, *adj.* **1.** boneless. **2.** not having the bones removed.

**unborn** /ʌn'bɔn/, *adj.* **1.** not yet born; yet to come; future: *ages unborn.* **2.** of a baby, still in the womb.

**unbosom** /ʌn'buzəm/, *v.t.* **1.** to disclose (one's thoughts, feelings, etc.) esp. in confidence. **2. unbosom oneself,** to disclose (one's thoughts, etc., to another person). *–v.i.* **3.** to disclose one's thoughts, feelings, secrets, etc. [UN-[2] + BOSOM, *v.*] – **unbosomer,** *n.*

**unbound** /ʌn'baund/, *v.* **1.** past tense and past participle of **unbind.** *–adj.* **2.** not bound, as a book.

**unbounded** /ʌn'baundəd/, *adj.* **1.** unlimited; boundless. **2.** unrestrained; uncontrolled. – **unboundedly,** *adv.* – **unboundedness,** *n.*

**unbowed** /ʌn'baud/, *adj.* **1.** not bowed or bent. **2.** not yielding or submitting.

**unbrace** /ʌn'breɪs/, *v.t.*, **-braced, -bracing. 1.** to free from tension; relax. **2.** to weaken. **3.** *Obs.* to remove the braces of.

**unbranded** /ʌn'brændəd/, *adj.* (of goods placed on sale) not bearing a manufacturer's label or trademark.

---

**unarranged,** *adj.*
**unarrested,** *adj.*
**unartful,** *adj.*
**unartfully,** *adv.*
**unarticulated,** *adj.*
**unartistic,** *adj.*
**unascendable,** *adj.*
**unascended,** *adj.*
**unascertainable,** *adj.*
**unascertained,** *adj.*
**unaskable,** *adj.*
**unasked,** *adj.*
**unaspiring,** *adj.*
**unassailable,** *adj.*
**unassailably,** *adv.*
**unassailed,** *adj.*
**unassayed,** *adj.*
**unasserted,** *adj.*
**unassertive,** *adj.*
**unassignable,** *adj.*
**unassigned,** *adj.*
**unassimilable,** *adj.*
**unassimilated,** *adj.*
**unassisted,** *adj.*
**unassociated,** *adj.*
**unassuageable,** *adj.*
**unassuaged,** *adj.*
**unastonished,** *adj.*
**unatonable,** *adj.*
**unatoned,** *adj.*
**unattainability,** *n.*
**unattainable,** *adj.*
**unattainableness,** *n.*
**unattainably,** *adv.*
**unattained,** *adj.*
**unattested,** *adj.*
**unattired,** *adj.*
**unattractive,** *adj.*
**unattractively,** *adv.*
**unattractiveness,** *n.*
**unaudited,** *adj.*
**unaugmented,** *adj.*
**unauthenticated,** *adj.*
**unauthenticity,** *n.*
**unauthoritative,** *adj.*
**unauthorised,** *adj.*
**unavailable,** *adj.*
**unavailableness,** *n.*
**unavenged,** *adj.*
**unavertable,** *adj.*
**unavowed,** *adj.*
**unawakened,** *adj.*
**unawed,** *adj.*
**unbag,** *v.t.*
**unbailable,** *adj.*
**unbaited,** *adj.*
**unbaked,** *adj.*
**unbaled,** *adj.*
**unbandage,** *v.t.*
**unbaptised,** *adj.*
**unbarbed,** *adj.*
**unbarbered,** *adj.*
**unbarred,** *adj.*
**unbashful,** *adj.*
**unbathed,** *adj.*
**unbearded,** *adj.*
**unbeauteous,** *adj.*
**unbeautified,** *adj.*
**unbeautiful,** *adj.*
**unbed,** *v.t.*
**unbedded,** *adj.*
**unbefitting,** *adj.*
**unbefriended,** *adj.*
**unbeget,** *v.t.*
**unbegged,** *adj.*

**unbrick** /ʌn'brɪk/, *v.t.* **1.** to remove bricks from, as to set free. **2.** to reveal; free.

**unbridle** /ʌn'braɪdl/, *v.t.*, **-dled, -dling. 1.** to remove the bridle from (a horse, etc.). **2.** to free from restraint.

**unbridled** /ʌn'braɪdld/, *adj.* **1.** unrestrained or uncontrolled. **2.** not having a bridle on, as a horse.

**unbroken** /ʌn'broʊkən/, *adj.* **1.** whole; intact. **2.** not subdued or crushed, as one's spirit. **3.** uninterrupted; continuous. **4.** not tamed. **5.** undisturbed; unimpaired. **6.** (of a record) not improved on. **7.** (of a law) not infringed. Also, *Obs.*, **unbroke.** – **unbrokenly,** *adv.* – **unbrokenness,** *n.*

**unbuckle** /ʌn'bʌkəl/, *v.*, **-led, -ling.** *–v.t.* **1.** to unfasten the buckle or buckles of; remove by unfastening the buckles of. *–v.i.* **2.** to unfasten buckles.

**unbuilt** /ʌn'bɪlt/, *adj.* **1.** not yet built, as a structure. **2.** (fol. by *on* or *upon*) not yet built on, as land.

**unburden** /ʌn'bɜdn/, *v.t.* **1.** to free from a burden. **2.** to relieve (one's mind, conscience, etc., or oneself) by disclosure or confession of something. **3.** to cast off or get rid of, as a burden or something burdensome; disclose; reveal. Also, **unburthen.**

**unbusinesslike** /ʌn'bɪznəsˌlaɪk/, *adj.* not methodical or efficient; vague; unconcerned with the aims or principles of business.

**unbutton** /ʌn'bʌtn/, *v.t.* **1.** to unfasten the button or buttons of. **2.** to unfasten (a button). *–v.i.* **3.** to unfasten one's buttons. **4.** to relax one's formality.

**unbuttoned** /ʌn'bʌtnd/, *adj.* **1.** having the buttons unfastened. **2.** not having a button or buttons. **3.** informal or relaxed.

**uncage** /ʌn'keɪdʒ/, *v.t.*, **-caged, -caging.** to release from or as from a cage.

**uncalculated** /ʌn'kælkjəˌleɪtəd/, *adj.* **1.** not determined by calculation. **2.** not deliberate; unexpected.

**uncalculating** /ʌn'kælkjəˌleɪtɪŋ/, *adj.* **1.** not calculating or scheming. **2.** not planning or trying to achieve a particular aim.

**uncalled-for** /ʌn'kɔld-fɔ/, *adj.* unnecessary and improper; unwarranted.

**uncanny** /ʌn'kæni/, *adj.* **1.** such as to arouse superstitious uneasiness; unnaturally strange. **2.** preternaturally good: *uncanny judgment.* – **uncannily,** *adv.* – **uncanniness,** *n.*

**uncanonical** /ʌnkə'nɒnɪkəl/, *adj.* **1.** not in accordance with canons or rules. **2.** not belonging to the canon of Scripture. **3.** unsuitable for a clergyman. – **uncanonically,** *adv.*

**uncap** /ʌn'kæp/, *v.*, **-capped, -capping.** *–v.t.* **1.** to remove the cap from (the head of a person). **2.** to remove a cap or cover from. *–v.i.* **3.** to remove the cap from the head, as in respect.

**uncase** /ʌn'keɪs/, *v.t.*, **-cased, -casing. 1.** to remove from its case; take the case or casing off. **2.** to strip or bare. **3.** to reveal; make known.

**uncaused** /ʌn'kɔzd/, *adj.* not resulting from a prior cause; self-existent.

**uncensored** /ʌn'sɛnsəd/, *adj.* **1.** not altered by a censor, as a publication or film. **2.** not criticised adversely, disapproved of, or reproved.

**unceremonious** /ˌʌnsɛrə'moʊniəs/, *adj.* not ceremonious; informal; abrupt or rude. – **unceremoniously,** *adv.* – **unceremoniousness,** *n.*

**uncert.,** uncertain.

**uncertain** /ʌn'sɜtn/, *adj.* **1.** not definitely or surely known; doubtful. **2.** not confident, assured, or decided. **3.** not fixed or determined. **4.** doubtful; vague; indistinct. **5.** not to be depended on. **6.** subject to change; variable; capricious. **7.** dependent on chance. **8.** unsteady or fitful, as light. – **uncertainly,** *adv.* – **uncertainness,** *n.*

**uncertainty** /ʌn'sɜtnti/, *n.*, *pl.* **-ties. 1.** an uncertain state or mood. **2.** unpredictability; indefiniteness. **3.** something uncertain.

**uncertainty principle** /'– prɪnsəpəl/, *n.* the principle, that it is not possible to determine simultaneously with complete accuracy both the position and the velocity of an atomic particle, as an electron. Also, **indeterminacy principle.**

**unchain** /ʌn'tʃeɪn/, *v.t.* **1.** to free from chains. **2.** to set free; release.

**uncharitable** /ʌn'tʃærətəbəl/, *adj.* **1.** unforgiving; harsh; censorious. **2.** miserly. – **uncharitableness,** *n.* – **uncharitably,** *adv.*

**uncharted** /ʌn'tʃatəd/, *adj.* not mapped; unexplored; unknown, as a remote region.

**unchartered** /ʌn'tʃatəd/, *adj.* **1.** without a charter. **2.** without regulation; lawless.

**unchaste** /ʌn'tʃeɪst/, *adj.* **1.** not chaste or virtuous, as persons. **2.** marked by lewdness or sexual excess, as life, habits, etc. – **unchastely,** *adv.* – **unchasteness, unchastity** /ʌn'tʃæstəti/, *n.*

**unchristian** /ʌn'krɪstʃən/, *adj.* **1.** not Christian. **2.** unworthy of Christians; uncharitable; improper. – **unchristianly,** *adv.*

**unchurch** /ʌn'tʃɜtʃ/, *v.t.* **1.** to expel (individuals) from a church; excommunicate. **2.** to divest of the status and nature of a church. **3.** to deprive of the authority over, or possession of the building of, or jurisdiction within, a church. **4.** to exclude (an entire group, body, or sect) from membership of the church. [UN-[2] + CHURCH]

**uncial** /'ʌnsiəl/, *adj.* **1.** designating, written in, or pertaining to ancient majuscule letters distinguished from capital majuscules by relatively great roundness, inclination, and ine-

---

**unbeginning,** *adj.*
**unbegotten,** *adj.*
**unbegun,** *adj.*
**unbelievable,** *adj.*
**unbelievably,** *adv.*
**unbelieve,** *v.t., v.i.*
**unbelieved,** *adj.*
**unbelted,** *adj.*
**unbeneficed,** *adj.*
**unbeneficial,** *adj.*
**unbenefited,** *adj.*
**unbenevolent,** *adj.*
**unbetrayed,** *adj.*
**unbetrothed,** *adj.*
**unbetterable,** *adj.*
**unbettered,** *adj.*
**unbevelled,** *adj.*
**unbewildered,** *adj.*
**unbiblical,** *adj.*
**unbiddable,** *adj.*
**unbigoted,** *adj.*
**unbleached,** *adj.*
**unblemished,** *adj.*
**unblended,** *adj.*
**unblinded,** *adj.*
**unblooded,** *adj.*
**unbloodied,** *adj.*
**unbloody,** *adj.*
**unblotted,** *adj.*
**unblown,** *adj.*
**unblunted,** *adj.*
**unboastful,** *adj.*
**unboiled,** *adj.*
**unbooked,** *adj.*
**unbookish,** *adj.*
**unboot,** *v.t., v.i.*
**unbought,** *adj.*
**unbranched,** *adj.*
**unbreakable,** *adj.*
**unbreathable,** *adj.*
**unbreathing,** *adj.*
**unbribable,** *adj.*
**unbribed,** *adj.*
**unbrotherliness,** *n.*
**unbrotherly,** *adj.*
**unbruised,** *adj.*
**unburnished,** *adj.*
**unburnt,** *adj.*
**unburst,** *adj.*
**unbury,** *v.t.*
**unbuttered,** *adj.*
**uncalcined,** *adj.*
**uncalled,** *adj.*
**uncandid,** *adj.*
**uncandidly,** *adv.*
**uncandour,** *n.*
**uncanonised,** *adj.*
**uncanvassed,** *adj.*
**uncapsizable,** *adj.*
**uncaptained,** *adj.*
**uncaptured,** *adj.*
**uncared-for,** *adj.*
**uncaring,** *adj.*
**uncarpeted,** *adj.*
**uncart,** *v.t.*
**uncarved,** *adj.*
**uncashed,** *adj.*
**uncastrated,** *adj.*
**uncatalogued,** *adj.*
**uncatechised,** *adj.*
**uncatholic,** *adj.*
**uncaught,** *adj.*
**unceasing,** *adj.*
**unceasingly,** *adv.*
**uncelebrated,** *adj.*

quality in height. **2.** pertaining to an inch or an ounce. **3.** pertaining to the duodecimal system. *–n.* **4.** an uncial letter. **5.** uncial writing. **6.** a manuscript in uncials. [L *unciālis* pertaining to an inch] – **uncially,** *adv.*

uncials in 8th century Latin

**unciform** /ˈʌnsəfɔm/, *adj.* **1.** hook-shaped. *–n.* **2.** *Anat.* a bone of the carpus with a hooklike process projecting from the palmar surface. [NL *unciformis,* from *unci-* (combining form representing L *uncus* hook) + *-formis* -FORM]

**uncinariasis** /ˌʌnsɪnəˈraɪəsəs/, *n.* →**hookworm disease.** [NL *Uncīnār(ia)* genus of hookworms (from L *uncinus* hook) + *-iāsis* -IASIS]

**uncinate** /ˈʌnsənət, -neɪt/, *adj.* hooked; bent at the end like a hook. Also, **uncinal, uncinated.** [L *uncīnātus*]

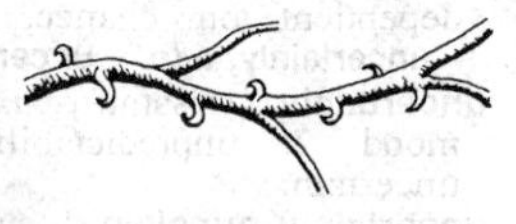

uncinate thorns

**uncinus** /ʌnˈsaɪnəs/, *n., pl.* **uncini** /ʌnˈsaɪnaɪ/. any small hooked structure such as one of the marginal teeth of the radula of a gastropod mollusc. [L: hooked]

**uncircumcised** /ʌnˈsɜkəmsaɪzd/, *adj.* **1.** not circumcised. **2.** not Jewish; gentile. **3.** not spiritually purified; irreligious; heathen.

**uncircumcision** /ˌʌnsɜkəmˈsɪʒən/, *n.* **1.** condition of being uncircumcised. **2.** *Rare.* gentiles collectively.

**uncivil** /ʌnˈsɪvəl/, *adj.* **1.** without good manners; rude; impolite; discourteous. **2.** uncivilised. – **uncivility** /ʌnsəˈvɪləti/, **uncivilness,** *n.* – **uncivilly,** *adv.*

**uncivilised** /ʌnˈsɪvəlaɪzd/, *adj.* barbarous; unenlightened. Also, **uncivilized.**

**unclad** /ʌnˈklæd/, *v.* **1.** past tense and past participle of **unclothe.** *–adj.* **2.** not clad; unclothed.

**unclasp** /ʌnˈklæsp, -ˈklasp/, *v.t.* **1.** to undo the clasp or clasps of; unfasten. **2.** to release from the grasp, as something held. *–v.i.* **3.** to become unclasped, as the hands, etc. **4.** to release or relax the grasp.

**unclassified** /ʌnˈklæsəfaɪd/, *adj.* **1.** not arranged in some order or according to some classification. **2.** (of information) not secret. **3.** any road that is outside the classification system laid down by the relevant authority.

**uncle** /ˈʌŋkəl/, *n.* **1.** a brother of one's father or mother. **2.** an aunt's husband. **3.** *Colloq.* →**pawnbroker. 4.** a familiar title applied to any elderly man. **5. talk like a Dutch uncle,** talk severely to (someone). [ME, from AF, from L *avunculus* mother's brother]

**unclean** /ʌnˈklin/, *adj.* **1.** morally or spiritually impure. **2.** ceremonially or ritually defiled. **3.** (of food) unfit to be eaten; forbidden. **4.** physically defiled or defiling; foul; dirty.

**uncleanly**[1] /ʌnˈklinli/, *adv.* in an unclean manner. [UNCLEAN + -LY]

**uncleanly**[2] /ʌnˈklinli/, *adj.* not cleanly; unclean. [UN-[1] + CLEANLY] – **uncleanliness,** *n.*

**unclench** /ʌnˈklentʃ/, *v.t., v.i.* to open or become opened from a clenched state.

**Uncle Sam** /ʌŋkəl ˈsæm/, *n.* a personification of the government or people of the United States. [extension of the initials *U.S.*]

**Uncle Tom** /– ˈtɒm/, *n.* (*usu. derog.*) a Negro who is openly servile to whites. [after the principal character in *Uncle Tom's Cabin,* a novel by Harriet Beecher Stowe, 1811-96, U.S. writer]

**Uncle Willy** /– ˈwɪli/, *adj. Colloq.* silly. [rhyming slang]

**uncloak** /ʌnˈkloʊk/, *v.t.* **1.** to remove the cloak from. **2.** to reveal; expose. *–v.i.* **3.** to take off the cloak, or the outer garments generally.

**unclog** /ʌnˈklɒg/, *v.t.,* **-clogged, -clogging.** to free from being clogged or from anything that clogs.

**unclose** /ʌnˈkloʊz/, *v.t., v.i.,* **-closed, -closing.** to bring or come out of a closed state; open.

**unclothe** /ʌnˈkloʊð/, *v.t.,* **-clothed** or **-clad, -clothing. 1.** to strip of clothes. **2.** to strip of anything; divest; uncover.

**unco**[1] /ˈʌŋkoʊ/, *adj., adv., n., pl.* **-cos.** *Scot. –adj.* **1.** remarkable; extraordinary. **2.** unknown; strange. **3.** uncanny. *–adv.* **4.** remarkably; extremely. *–n.* **5.** something extraordinary. **6.** (*pl.*) news. **7.** *Obs.* a stranger. [var. of UNCOUTH]

**unco**[2] /ˈʌŋkoʊ/, *Colloq. –adj.* **1.** awkward; clumsy. *–n.* **2.** a clumsy person. [short for UNCOORDINATED]

**uncoil** /ʌnˈkɔɪl/, *v.t.* **1.** to unwind. *–v.i.* **2.** to unwind itself.

**uncome-at-able** /ʌnkʌm-ˈæt-əbəl/, *adj.* inaccessible; unattainable.

**uncomfortable** /ʌnˈkʌmfətəbəl, -ˈkʌmftəbəl/, *adj.* **1.** causing discomfort; disquieting. **2.** in a state of discomfort; uneasy; ill-at-ease. – **uncomfortableness,** *n.* – **uncomfortably,** *adv.*

**uncommercial** /ʌnkəˈmɜʃəl/, *adj.* **1.** not engaged in commerce or trade. **2.** not in accordance with commercial principles or practices. **3.** not likely to be commercially successful. **4.** not profit-seeking.

**uncommitted** /ʌnkəˈmɪtəd/, *adj.* **1.** not committed, esp. not bound by pledge or assurance, as to a course or party. **2.** not having a particular point of view; not partisan.

---

**uncensorious,** *adj.*
**uncertificated,** *adj.*
**uncertified,** *adj.*
**unchallengeable,** *adj.*
**unchallengeably,** *adv.*
**unchangeable,** *adj.*
**unchangeably,** *adv.*
**unchanged,** *adj.*
**unchanging,** *adj.*
**unchangingly,** *adv.*
**unchaperoned,** *adj.*
**uncharacteristic,** *adj.*
**uncharacteristically,** *adv.*
**uncharming,** *adj.*
**uncharred,** *adj.*
**unchastened,** *adj.*
**unchastised,** *adj.*
**uncheckable,** *adj.*
**unchecked,** *adj.*
**uncheered,** *adj.*
**uncheerful,** *adj.*
**uncheerfully,** *adv.*
**uncheerfulness,** *n.*
**uncheering,** *adj.*
**unchildish,** *adj.*
**unchilled,** *adj.*
**unchipped,** *adj.*
**unchiselled,** *adj.*
**unchivalrous,** *adj.*
**unchivalrously,** *adv.*
**unchosen,** *adj.*
**unchristened,** *adj.*
**unchronicled,** *adj.*
**unchronological,** *adj.*
**uncircumscribed,** *adj.*
**uncircumspect,** *adj.*
**uncited,** *adj.*
**unclaimed,** *adj.*
**unclamp,** *v.t.*
**unclarified,** *adj.*
**unclassed,** *adj.*
**unclassical,** *adj.*
**unclassifiable,** *adj.*
**uncleaned,** *adj.*
**uncleansed,** *adj.*
**unclear,** *adj.*
**uncleared,** *adj.*
**unclearly,** *adv.*
**unclearness,** *n.*
**unclerical,** *adj.*
**unclimbable,** *adj.*
**unclimbed,** *adj.*
**unclipped,** *adj.*
**uncloister,** *v.t.*
**uncloistered,** *adj.*
**unclouded,** *adj.*
**uncloudy,** *adj.*
**unclutch,** *v.t.*
**uncoagulated,** *adj.*
**uncoated,** *adj.*
**uncock,** *v.t.*
**uncocked,** *adj.*
**uncoffined,** *adj.*
**uncollated,** *adj.*
**uncollected,** *adj.*
**uncoloured,** *adj.*
**uncomeliness,** *n.*
**uncomely,** *adj.*
**uncommanded,** *adj.*
**uncommendable,** *adj.*
**uncommendably,** *adv.*
**uncommissioned,** *adj.*
**uncommunicable,** *adj.*
**uncommunicably,** *adv.*
**uncommunicated,** *adj.*

**uncommon** /ʌn'kɒmən/, *adj.* **1.** not common; unusual or rare. **2.** unusual in amount or degree; above the ordinary. **3.** exceptional. *–adv.* **4.** very; remarkably. – **uncommonness,** *n.*

**uncommonly** /ʌn'kɒmənli/, *adv.* **1.** in an uncommon or unusual degree; remarkably. **2.** rarely; infrequently.

**uncommunicative** /ʌnkə'mjunəkətɪv/, *adj.* not disposed to impart information, opinions, etc.; reserved; taciturn. – **uncommunicatively,** *adv.* – **uncommunicativeness,** *n.*

**uncompromising** /ʌn'kɒmprə,maɪzɪŋ/, *adj.* not admitting of compromise; unyielding; inflexible. – **uncompromisingly,** *adv.*

**unconcern** /ʌnkən'sɜn/, *n.* lack of concern; freedom from solicitude or anxiety; indifference.

**unconcerned** /ʌnkən'sɜnd/, *adj.* **1.** not concerned; disinterested; free from solicitude or anxiety; uninterested. **2.** not involved (with) or taking part (in). – **unconcernedly** /ʌnkən'sɜnədli/, *adv.* – **unconcernedness,** *n.*

**unconditional** /ʌnkən'dɪʃənəl/, *adj.* not limited by conditions; absolute: *an unconditional promise.* – **unconditionality** /ʌnkən,dɪʃə'næləti/, **unconditionalness,** *n.* – **unconditionally,** *adv.*

**unconditioned** /ʌnkən'dɪʃənd/, *adj.* **1.** not subject to conditions; absolute. **2.** *Psychol.* unlearned; natural; innate.

**unconditioned stimulus** /– 'stɪmjələs/, *n.* a stimulus innately effective in eliciting a specified response.

**unconfessed** /ʌnkən'fɛst/, *adj.* **1.** not admitted, confessed, or avowed. **2.** not having received confession from a priest.

**unconformable** /ʌnkən'fɔməbəl/, *adj.* **1.** not conformable; not conforming. **2.** *Geol.* denoting discontinuity of any type in stratigraphic sequence. – **unconformability** /,ʌnkənfɔmə'bɪləti/, *n.* – **unconformably,** *adv.*

**unconformity** /ʌnkən'fɔməti/, *n., pl.* **-ties. 1.** lack of conformity; incongruity; inconsistency. **2.** *Geol.* **a.** a discontinuity in rock sequence denoting interruption of sedimentation, commonly accompanied by erosion of rocks below the break. **b.** the fault plane separating such strata.

**unconnected** /ʌnkə'nɛktəd/, *adj.* **1.** not connected; separate; distinct (sometimes fol. by *with*). **2.** not internally coherent, as a piece of writing; disunited; broken up. – **unconnectedly,** *adv.* – **unconnectedness,** *n.*

**unconscionable** /ʌn'kɒnʃənəbəl/, *adj.* **1.** unreasonably excessive. **2.** not in accordance with what is just or reasonable: *unconscionable behaviour.* **3.** not guided by conscience; unscrupulous. – **unconscionableness,** *n.* – **unconscionably,** *adv.*

**unconscious** /ʌn'kɒnʃəs/, *adj.* **1.** not conscious; unaware. **2.** temporarily devoid of consciousness. **3.** not endowed with knowledge of one's own existence, etc. **4.** occurring below the level of conscious thought. **5.** unintentional: *an unconscious slight.* **6.** *Psychol.* pertaining to mental processes which the individual cannot bring into consciousness. *–n.* **7. the unconscious,** *Psychol.* an organisation of the mind containing all psychic material not available in the immediate field of awareness. – **unconsciously,** *adv.* – **unconsciousness,** *n.*

**unconsidered** /ʌnkən'sɪdəd/, *adj.* **1.** not considered or thought worthy of consideration; not paid attention to; unimportant. **2.** not resulting from or accompanied by consideration, esp. prior consideration; careless or unthinking.

**unconstitutional** /,ʌnkɒnstə'tjuʃənəl/, *adj.* not constitutional; unauthorised by, contrary to, or inconsistent with the constitution, as of a country. – **unconstitutionality** /,ʌnkɒnstə,tjuʃən'æləti/, *n.* – **unconstitutionally,** *adv.*

**unconventional** /ʌnkən'vɛnʃənəl/, *adj.* not conventional; not bound by or conforming to convention, rule, or precedent; free from conventionality. – **unconventionally,** *adv.*

**unconventionality** /ʌnkən,vɛnʃən'æləti/, *n., pl.* **-ties. 1.** disregard for or freedom from rules and precedents; originality. **2.** something unconventional, as an act.

**unconventional warfare** /,ʌnkənvɛnʃənəl 'wɔfɛə/, *n.* warfare operations, as guerrilla warfare, evasion and escape, and subversion, which do not conform to historical patterns, being conducted within enemy or enemy-controlled territory, usu. by indigenous personnel.

**uncool** /ʌn'kul/, *adj. Colloq.* displaying an unsophisticated level of emotion, as delight, anger, etc.; gauche.

**uncork** /ʌn'kɔk/, *v.t.* to draw the cork from.

**uncounted** /ʌn'kaʊntəd/, *adj.* **1.** not counted. **2.** innumerable.

**uncouple** /ʌn'kʌpəl/, *v.t.,* **-pled, -pling.** to undo from being coupled; disconnect.

**uncourteous** /ʌn'kɜtiəs/, *adj.* discourteous. – **uncourteously,** *adv.* – **uncourteousness,** *n.*

**uncourtly** /ʌn'kɔtli/, *adj.* not courtly; rude. – **uncourtliness,** *n.*

**uncouth** /ʌn'kuθ/, *adj.* **1.** awkward, clumsy, or unmannerly, as persons, behaviour, actions, etc. **2.** strange and ungraceful in appearance or form. **3.** unusual or strange. [ME; OE *uncūth* (from *un-* UN-[1] + *cūth*, pp., known), c. D *onkond*] – **uncouthly,** *adv.* – **uncouthness,** *n.*

**uncovenanted** /ʌn'kʌvənəntəd/, *adj.* **1.** not agreed to or promised by covenant. **2.** not having joined in a covenant.

**uncover** /ʌn'kʌvə/, *v.t.* **1.** to lay bare; disclose; reveal. **2.** to remove the cover or covering from. **3.** to remove (the hat, or other head covering). *–v.i.* **4.** to remove a cover or covering. **5.** to take off one's hat or other head covering, as in respect.

**uncovered** /ʌn'kʌvəd/, *adj.* **1.** having no cover or covering.

---

**uncommunicating,** *adj.*
**uncommuted,** *adj.*
**uncompacted,** *adj.*
**uncompanionable,** *adj.*
**uncompassionate,** *adj.*
**uncompelled,** *adj.*
**uncompensated,** *adj.*
**uncompetitive,** *adj.*
**uncomplaining,** *adj.*
**uncomplainingly,** *adv.*
**uncompliant,** *adj.*
**uncomplicated,** *adj.*
**uncomplimentary,** *adj.*
**uncompounded,** *adj.*
**uncomprehended,** *adj.*
**uncomprehending,** *adj.*
**uncomprehensive,** *adj.*
**uncompressed,** *adj.*
**unconcealed,** *adj.*
**unconceivable,** *adj.*
**unconceivably,** *adv.*
**unconceived,** *adj.*
**unconciliating,** *adj.*
**unconcluded,** *adj.*
**uncondemned,** *adj.*
**uncondensed,** *adj.*
**unconducive,** *adj.*
**unconfident,** *adj.*
**unconfiding,** *adj.*
**unconfinable,** *adj.*
**unconfined,** *adj.*
**unconfirmed,** *adj.*
**unconfused,** *adj.*
**unconfusedly,** *adv.*
**unconfutable,** *adj.*
**unconfuted,** *adj.*
**uncongealed,** *adj.*
**uncongenial,** *adj.*
**uncongeniality,** *n.*
**unconjecturable,** *adj.*
**unconjectured,** *adj.*
**unconquerable,** *adj.*
**unconquerably,** *adv.*
**unconquered,** *adj.*
**unconscientious,** *adj.*
**unconscientiously,** *adv.*
**unconscientiousness,** *n.*
**unconsecrated,** *adj.*
**unconsenting,** *adj.*
**unconsolidated,** *adj.*
**unconstrained,** *adj.*
**unconstrainedly,** *adv.*
**unconstraint,** *n.*
**unconstructive,** *adj.*
**unconsulted,** *adj.*
**unconsumed,** *adj.*
**unconsummated,** *adj.*
**uncontaminated,** *adj.*
**uncontemplated,** *adj.*
**uncontentious,** *adj.*
**uncontestable,** *adj.*
**uncontested,** *adj.*
**uncontracted,** *adj.*
**uncontradictable,** *adj.*
**uncontradictably,** *adv.*
**uncontradicted,** *adj.*
**uncontrollability,** *n.*
**uncontrollable,** *adj.*
**uncontrollably,** *adv.*
**uncontrolled,** *adj.*
**uncontroversial,** *adj.*
**uncontroverted,** *adj.*
**uncontrovertible,** *adj.*
**uncontrovertibly,** *adv.*
**unconversant,** *adj.*

2. having the head bare. 3. not protected by security, as a debt.

**uncritical** /ʌnˈkrɪtɪkəl/, *adj.* 1. disinclined to make critical analysis: *an uncritical reader.* 2. without discrimination or critical perception. 3. not in accordance with the rules of just criticism: *an uncritical estimate.* – **uncritically,** *adv.*

**uncross** /ʌnˈkrɒs/, *v.t.* to remove from a crossed position: *to uncross one's legs.*

**uncrossed** /ʌnˈkrɒst/, *adj.* 1. (of a cheque) not crossed; negotiable. 2. not thwarted.

**uncrown** /ʌnˈkraʊn/, *v.t.* 1. to deprive or divest of a crown. 2. to reduce from dignity or pre-eminence.

**uncrowned** /ˈʌnkraʊnd/, *adj.* 1. not crowned; not having yet assumed the crown. 2. having royal status or power without royal rank. 3. **uncrowned king,** one who is regarded as the unofficial leader of his own particular circle: *he was the uncrowned king of the wharfies.*

**uncrushable** /ʌnˈkrʌʃəbəl/, *adj.* 1. that cannot or cannot easily be crushed. 2. (of textiles) not retaining the creases when crumpled.

**unction** /ˈʌŋkʃən/, *n.* 1. the act of anointing, esp. for medical purposes or as a religious rite. 2. *Relig.* **a.** the act of ceremonial anointing with oil, esp. within the sacrament to strengthen the mortally sick, or at the consecration of a monarch before his coronation, or of an altar or a new church. **b.** the consecrating grace of God bestowed freely on the faithful. 3. something soothing or comforting. 4. a soothing, sympathetic, and persuasive quality in discourse, esp. on religious subjects. 5. a professional, conventional, or affected earnestness or fervour in utterance. [ME, from L *unctio*] – **unctionless,** *adj.*

**unctuous** /ˈʌŋkʃuəs/, *adj.* 1. of the nature of or characteristic of an unguent or ointment; oily; greasy. 2. characterised by religious unction or fervour, esp. of an affected kind; excessively smooth, suave, or bland. 3. having an oily or soapy feel, as certain minerals. [ME, from ML *unctuōsus,* from L *unctum* ointment] – **unctuosity** /ʌŋkʃuˈɒsəti/, **unctuousness,** *n.* – **unctuously,** *adv.*

**uncurl** /ʌnˈkɜl/, *v.t., v.i.* to straighten out, as something curled.

**uncus** /ˈʌŋkəs/, *n., pl.* **unci** /ˈʌnsaɪ/. a hooked piece or projection, as in the human cerebellum. [L: hook]

**uncustomed** /ʌnˈkʌstəmd/, *adj.* on which customs duty has not been paid.

**uncut** /ʌnˈkʌt/, *adj.* 1. not shortened, condensed, or abridged, as a work of literature, by censorship, etc. 2. (of a book) not having its pages trimmed at the edges after printing. 3. (of gems, velvet, etc.) not shaped by cutting. 4. (of a male animal) not castrated; entire. 5. (of drugs, as heroin) not mixed with other substances; unadulterated; pure. 6. not cut.

**undamped** /ʌnˈdæmpt/, *adj.* 1. undiminished, as energy, spirits, etc. 2. *Physics.* (of a vibrating string or other oscillation) having no extrinsic restriction on amplitude.

**undaunted** /ʌnˈdɔntəd/, *adj.* not discouraged; fearless; undismayed. – **undauntedly,** *adv.* – **undauntedness,** *n.*

**undecagon** /ʌnˈdɛkəgɒn/, *n.* a polygon having eleven angles and eleven sides. [L *undec(im)* eleven + (DEC)AGON]

**undeceive** /ʌndəˈsiv/, *v.t.,* **-ceived, -ceiving.** to free from deception, fallacy, or mistake. – **undeceivable,** *adj.* – **undeceiver,** *n.*

**undecided** /ʌndəˈsaɪdəd/, *adj.* 1. not decided or determined. 2. not having one's mind made up; irresolute. – **undecidedly,** *adv.* – **undecidedness,** *n.*

**undecimal** /ʌnˈdɛsəməl/, *adj.* based upon the number eleven.

**undecked** /ʌnˈdɛkt/, *adj.* 1. without a deck, as a ship. 2. not adorned or embellished.

**undefended** /ʌndəˈfɛndəd/, *adj.* 1. without defences or protection; not defended. 2. (of a legal action) not defended by counsel; having no defence put forward.

**undefined** /ʌndəˈfaɪnd/, *adj.* 1. not definitely limited; indefinite. 2. not described by definition or explanation; not explained.

**undemonstrative** /ʌndəˈmɒnstrətɪv/, *adj.* reserved; not inclined to demonstrations of enthusiasm, affection, etc. – **undemonstratively,** *adv.* – **undemonstrativeness,** *n.*

**undeniable** /ʌndəˈnaɪəbəl/, *adj.* 1. not to be refuted; indisputable. 2. that cannot be refused. 3. unquestionably good; unexceptionable. – **undeniableness,** *n.* – **undeniably,** *adv.*

**under** /ˈʌndə/, *prep.* 1. beneath and covered by: *under a table or a tree.* 2. below the surface of: *under the sea.* 3. at a point or position lower than or farther down than: *to stand under a window.* 4. in the position or state of bearing, supporting, sustaining, undergoing, etc.: *to sink under a load, a matter under consideration.* 5. subject to: *under the influence of drink.* 6. bearing as a crop: *land under barley.* 7. beneath (a head, heading, or the like), as in classification. 8. as designated, indicated, or represented by: *under a new name.* 9. below in degree, amount, price, etc.; less than: *under age.* 10. below in rank, dignity, or the like. 11. subject to the rule, direction, guidance, etc., of: *under supervision, to study under a professor.* 12. during the reign or rule of. 13. subject to the influence, conditioning force, etc., of: *under these circumstances, born under Taurus.* 14. with the favour or aid of: *under protection.* 15. authorised, warranted, or attested by: *under one's hand or seal.* 16. in accordance with: *under the provisions of the law.* 17. in the state or process of:

---

**unconverted,** *adj.*
**unconvertible,** *adj.*
**unconvicted,** *adj.*
**unconvinced,** *adj.*
**unconvincedly,** *adv.*
**unconvincing,** *adj.*
**uncooked,** *adj.*
**uncooled,** *adj.*
**uncooperative,** *adj.*
**uncoordinated,** *adj.*
**uncopied,** *adj.*
**uncoquettish,** *adj.*
**uncordial,** *adj.*
**uncordially,** *adv.*
**uncorrected,** *adj.*
**uncorroborated,** *adj.*
**uncorrupted,** *adj.*
**uncorruptedly,** *adv.*
**uncostly,** *adj.*
**uncounselled,** *adj.*
**uncountable,** *adj.*
**uncounteracted,** *adj.*
**uncourted,** *adj.*
**uncovetous,** *adj.*
**uncracked,** *adj.*
**uncramped,** *adj.*
**uncreatability,** *n.*
**uncreatable,** *adj.*
**uncreated,** *adj.*
**uncreative,** *adj.*
**uncreativeness,** *n.*
**uncreditable,** *adj.*
**uncredited,** *adj.*
**uncrippled,** *adj.*
**uncriticised,** *adj.*
**uncriticising,** *adj.*
**uncriticisingly,** *adv.*
**uncropped,** *adj.*
**uncrowded,** *adj.*
**uncrushed,** *adj.*
**uncrystallisable,** *adj.*
**uncrystallised,** *adj.*
**uncultivable,** *adj.*
**uncultivated,** *adj.*
**uncultured,** *adj.*
**uncurbed,** *adj.*
**uncured,** *adj.*
**uncurtailed,** *adj.*
**uncurtain,** *v.t.*
**uncurtained,** *adj.*
**uncustomary,** *adj.*
**undamaged,** *adj.*
**undarned,** *adj.*
**undashed,** *adj.*
**undated,** *adj.*
**undazzled,** *adj.*
**undeadened,** *adj.*
**undealt,** *adj.*
**undebased,** *adj.*
**undebatable,** *adj.*
**undebated,** *adj.*
**undebauched,** *adj.*
**undecidable,** *adj.*
**undecipherable,** *adj.*
**undecipherability,** *n.*
**undeclared,** *adj.*
**undecomposed,** *adj.*
**undecorated,** *adj.*
**undefaced,** *adj.*
**undefeated,** *adj.*
**undefiled,** *adj.*
**undefinable,** *adj.*
**undefinably,** *adv.*
**undeformed,** *adj.*
**undefrayed,** *adj.*

---

*under repair.* –*adv.* **18.** under or beneath something. **19.** beneath the surface. **20.** in a lower place. **21.** in a lower degree, amount, etc. **22.** in a subordinate position or condition. **23.** in or into subjection or submission. **24.** in or into cover or submersion: *to send a boat under.* **25. down under,** in or to Australia and New Zealand. **26. go under,** *Colloq.* **a.** to sink in or as in water. **b.** to fail, esp. of a business. **c.** to be found guilty by a jury. –*adj.* **27.** beneath. **28.** lower in position. **29.** lower in degree, amount, etc. **30.** lower in rank or condition. **31.** facing downwards: *the under fringe of a curtain.* [ME and OE; c. D *onder,* G *unter,* Icel. *undir,* akin to L *infrā* below]

**under-,** a prefixal attributive use of *under,* as to indicate **a.** a place or situation below or beneath, as in *underbrush, undertow,* or lower in grade or dignity, as in *understudy.* **b.** a lesser degree, extent, or amount, as in *undersized.* **c.** an insufficiency, as in *underfeed.*

**underachieve** /ʌndərə'tʃiv/, *v.i.* to fail to perform as well as one's innate ability suggests. – **underachiever,** *n.*

**underact** /ʌndər'ækt/, *v.t.* **1.** to act (a part, as in a play) with a lack of dramatic quality. –*v.i.* **2.** to act in an excessively restrained style.

**under-age** /'ʌndər-eɪdʒ/, *adj.* below the customary or required age, esp. below the legal age, as for entering licensed premises, marrying, etc.

**underage** /'ʌndərɪdʒ/, *n.* shortage; amount of deficiency, as below a set level.

**underarm** /'ʌndəram/, *adj.* **1.** under the arm: *an underarm seam.* **2.** in the armpit: *underarm odour.* **3.** *Cricket, Tennis, etc.* executed with the hand below the shoulder as in bowling, service, etc. –*adv.* **4.** *Cricket, Tennis, etc.* with an underarm action.

**underarmed** /'ʌndəramd/, *adj.* not having sufficient weapons.

**underbelly** /'ʌndəbɛli/, *n.* **1.** the lower part of the belly. **2.** an insufficiently protected area or aspect.

**underbid** /ʌndə'bɪd/, *v.,* **-bid, -bidding.** –*v.t.* **1.** to make a lower bid than (another), as in seeking a contract to be awarded to the lowest bidder. –*v.i.* **2.** to make an unnecessarily low bid. – **underbidder,** *n.*

**underbody** /'ʌndəbɒdi/, *n.* the lower part of the body, as of an animal, vehicle, etc.

**underbred** /'ʌndəbrɛd/, *adj.* **1.** of inferior breeding or manners; vulgar. **2.** not of pure breed, as a horse.

**underbrush** /'ʌndəbrʌʃ/, *n.* shrubs, small trees, etc., growing under large trees.

**underburn** /'ʌndəbɜn/, *v.t.,* **-burnt, -burning.** to burn at less than the normal temperature, as clay, etc.

**underbuy** /ʌndə'baɪ/, *v.t.,* **-bought, -buying.** **1.** to buy more cheaply than (another). **2.** to buy at less than the actual value.

**undercapitalise** /ʌndə'kæpətəlaɪz/, *v.t.,* **-lised, -lising.** to provide insufficient capital for (a business venture). Also, **undercapitalize.**

**undercarriage** /'ʌndəkærɪdʒ/, *n.* **1.** the supporting framework beneath the body of a carriage, etc. **2.** the portions of an aeroplane beneath the body, serving as a support when on the ground or water or when taking off and alighting. Also, *Chiefly U.S.,* **landing gear.**

**undercharge** /ʌndə'tʃadʒ/, *v.,* **-charged, -charging;** /'ʌndətʃadʒ/, *n.* –*v.t.* **1.** to charge (a person, etc.) less than the proper or fair price. **2.** to charge (so much) less than a fair price. **3.** to put an insufficient charge or load into. –*n.* **4.** a charge or price less than is proper or fair. **5.** an insufficient charge or load.

**underclassman** /ʌndə'klasmən/, *n., pl.* **-men.** *U.S.* a fresher or sophomore.

**underclay** /'ʌndəkleɪ/, *n.* a bed of clay underlying a coal seam, representing the soil in which the plants which formed the coal grew.

**underclothes** /'ʌndəkloʊðz/, *n. pl.* →**underwear.** Also, **underclothing.**

**undercoat** /'ʌndəkoʊt/, *n.* **1.** a coat or coats of paint applied to a surface after priming and filling, or after preparation of a previously painted surface, before the application of the finishing coat. **2.** the paint used for this. **3.** a coat worn beneath another. –*v.t.* **4.** to apply an undercoat to.

**undercoating** /'ʌndəkoʊtɪŋ/, *n.* **1.** undercoat. **2.** *U.S.* →**underseal.**

**undercover** /'ʌndəkʌvə/, *adj.* working or done out of public sight; secret: *an undercover agent.*

**undercroft** /'ʌndəkrɒft/, *n.* **1.** the crypt of a church. **2.** a vault or chamber under the ground. **3.** the space below the lowest floor of a building; basement. **4.** the space under a building which is elevated on piers, columns, etc., usu. open on one or more sides. [UNDER- + obs. *croft* vault (from L *crypta* CRYPT)]

**undercurrent** /'ʌndəkʌrənt/, *n.* **1.** a current below the upper currents or below the surface. **2.** an underlying or concealed condition or tendency.

**undercut** /ʌndə'kʌt/, *v.,* **-cut, -cutting;** /'ʌndəkʌt/, *n., adj.* –*v.t.* **1.** to cut under or beneath. **2.** to cut away material from so as to leave a portion overhanging, as in carving or sculpture. **3.** to sell or work at a lower price than. **4.** *Sport.* to hit (the ball) so as to cause a backspin. **5.** to outwit or outmanoeuvre (a rival), thus making his strategy void or his influence ineffectual; undermine. –*v.i.* **6.** to undercut

---

**undegenerate,** *adj.*
**undelayed,** *adj.*
**undelegated,** *adj.*
**undeliberate,** *adj.*
**undeliberated,** *adj.*
**undeliverable,** *adj.*
**undelivered,** *adj.*
**undeluded,** *adj.*
**undemanded,** *adj.*
**undemanding,** *adj.*
**undemocratic,** *adj.*
**undemocratically,** *adv.*
**undemonstrable,** *adj.*
**undemonstrated,** *adj.*
**undenied,** *adj.*
**undenominational,** *adj.*
**undependable,** *adj.*
**undependably,** *adv.*
**undepreciated,** *adj.*
**undepressed,** *adj.*
**underactivity,** *n.*
**under-agent,** *n.*
**underbridge,** *n.*
**underbuild,** *v.t.*
**under-builder,** *n.*
**underbrush,** *n.*
**under-butler,** *n.*
**underclad,** *adj.*
**under-clerk,** *n.*
**undercliff,** *n.*
**underclothe,** *v.t.*
**underclothed,** *adj.*
**undercook,** *v.t.*
**underdeck,** *n.*
**underdrain,** *v.t.*
**underdrain,** *n.*
**underdressed,** *adj.*
**underdrift,** *n.*
**underemployment,** *n.*
**underfed,** *adj.*
**underfloor,** *adj.*
**underframe,** *n.*
**undergardener,** *n.*
**undergrown,** *adj.*
**underhanging,** *adj.*
**underhorsed,** *adj.*
**underkeeper,** *n.*
**underlease,** *n., v.t., v.i.*
**underlessee,** *n.*
**underlid,** *n.*
**underlip,** *n.*
**undermanager,** *n.*
**undermasted,** *adj.*
**undermaster,** *n.*
**undermentioned,** *adj.*
**undernamed,** *adj.*
**undernote,** *n.*
**undernoted,** *adj.*
**underpeopled,** *adj.*
**underpraise,** *v.t., v.i.*
**underprize,** *v.t.*
**underqualified,** *adj.*
**under-represented,** *adj.*
**under-roast,** *v.t.*
**under-robe,** *n.*
**underroof,** *n.*
**undershafted,** *adj.*
**undertaxed,** *adj.*
**under-teacher,** *n.*
**undertenancy,** *n.*
**under-treasurer,** *n.*
**under-utilise,** *v.t.,* **-lised, -lising.**
**under-utilisation,** *n.*
**under-waistcoat,** *n.*

---

material, a competitor, a ball, etc. *–n.* **7.** a cut, or a cutting away, underneath. **8.** *U.S.* a notch cut in a tree to determine the direction in which the tree is to fall and to prevent splitting. **9.** *Sport.* a slice or cut made with an underhand motion. **10.** the tenderloin or fillet of beef or underside of sirloin; fillet. *–adj.* **11.** cut away underneath.

**underdaks** /ˈʌndədæks/, *n.pl. Colloq.* →**underpants.**

**underdamp** /ˈʌndədæmp/, *v.t.* (in physics) to damp (def. 12) so that there is a weak decrease in amplitude of successive oscillations.

**underdamper** /ˈʌndədæmpə/, *n.* (in certain upright pianos) a damping mechanism in which the dampers are below the hammers.

**underdevelop** /ʌndədəˈvɛləp/, *v.t.* to develop short of the required amount: *to underdevelop film.*

**underdeveloped** /ʌndədəˈvɛləpt/, *adj.* **1.** (of a country) →**developing.** **2.** (of film) developed less than normal, producing a lack of contrast. **3.** less fully developed than average. – **underdevelopment,** *n.*

**underdo** /ʌndəˈdu/, *v.t.,* **-did, -done, -doing.** **1.** to do insufficiently or imperfectly. **2.** to cook lightly or insufficiently.

**underdog** /ˈʌndədɒg/, *n.* **1.** a victim of oppression. **2.** the loser or expected loser in a competitive situation, fight, etc. **3.** (in a sawpit) the man who stands in the pit underneath the log and works the bottom end of the saw.

**underdone** /ˈʌndədʌn/, *adj.* (of food, esp. meat) cooked lightly or less than completely.

**underdrainage** /ˈʌndədreɪnɪdʒ/, *n.* drainage of agricultural lands and removal of excess water and alkali by drains buried beneath the surface.

**underdraw** /ʌndəˈdrɔ/, *v.t.* **1.** to depict inadequately. **2.** *Bldg Trades.* to cover (a ceiling) by fixing the plasterwork to the underside of the joists. *–v.i.* **3.** to construct an underdrawn ceiling.

**underdress** /ˈʌndədrɛs/, *n.;* /ʌndəˈdrɛs/, *v.* *–n.* **1.** a dress worn under another. *–v.i.* **2.** to dress too plainly; wear an outfit which is not smart or elaborate enough for the occasion.

**underestimate** /ʌndərˈɛstəmeɪt/, *v.,* **-mated, -mating;** /ʌndərˈɛstəmət/, *n.* *–v.t.* **1.** to estimate at too low a value, rate, or the like. *–n.* **2.** an estimate that is too low. – **underestimation** /ʌndərˌɛstəˈmeɪʃən/, *n.*

**underexpose** /ʌndərəkˈspoʊz/, *v.t.,* **-exposed, -exposing.** to expose to light too little, as in photography.

**underexposure** /ʌndərəkˈspoʊʒə/, *n.* **1.** inadequate exposure to light rays. **2.** a photographic negative or print which has been underexposed. **3.** insufficient exposure to anything, as publicity.

**underfeed** /ʌndəˈfid/, *v.t.,* **-fed, -feeding.** **1.** to feed insufficiently. **2.** to feed with fuel from beneath.

**underfeed stoker** /– ˈstoʊkə/, *n.* an automatic stoker which feeds fuel into a furnace from below the fire.

**underfelt** /ˈʌndəfɛlt/, *n.* a thick felt laid under a carpet to make it more resilient.

**underfoot** /ʌndəˈfʊt/, *adv.* **1.** under the foot or feet; on the ground; underneath or below. **2.** in a state of subjection. *–adj.* **3.** lying under the foot or feet.

**underfur** /ˈʌndəfɜ/, *n.* the fur, or fine, soft, thick, hairy coat, under the longer and coarser outer hair in certain animals, as seals, otters, and beavers.

**undergarment** /ˈʌndəgamənt/, *n.* a garment worn under another garment, esp. next to the skin.

**undergird** /ʌndəˈgɜd/, v.t., **-girt** or **girded, girding.** to make secure from below; to reinforce the bottom of.

**underglaze** /ˈʌndəgleɪz/, *n.* **1.** colouring or decoration applied to pottery or porcelain before it is glazed. *–adj.* **2.** of or pertaining to such colour or decoration.

**undergo** /ʌndəˈgoʊ/, *v.t.,* **-went, -gone, -going.** **1.** to be subjected to; experience; pass through. **2.** to endure; sustain; suffer.

**undergrad** /ˈʌndəgræd/, *n. Chiefly U.S. Colloq.* an undergraduate.

**undergraduate** /ʌndəˈgrædʒuət/, *n.* **1.** a student in a university or college who has not taken his first degree. *–adj.* **2.** having the standing of an undergraduate. **3.** pertaining to, characteristic of, or consisting of undergraduates. – **undergraduateship,** *n.*

**underground** /ˈʌndəgraʊnd/, *adv.* **1.** beneath the surface of the ground. **2.** in concealment or secrecy; not openly. *–adj.* **3.** existing, situated, operating, or taking place beneath the surface of the ground. **4.** used, or for use, underground. **5.** hidden or secret; not open. **6.** not public; not generally known about. *–n.* **7.** the place or region beneath the surface of the ground; the underworld. **8.** a railway running mainly through tunnels laid beneath the roadway or in deeply laid tubes. **9.** a secret organisation fighting the established government or occupation forces, esp. one in the fascist-overrun nations of Europe before and during World War II. *–v.t.* **10.** to put (a pipe, electric cable, etc.) underground.

**underground mutton** /– ˈmʌtn/, *n. Colloq.* rabbit.

**underground water** /– ˈwɔtə/, *n.* all water occurring naturally underground, as artesian water, watertables, etc.

**undergrowth** /ˈʌndəgroʊθ/, *n.* **1.** shrubs or small trees growing beneath or among large trees. **2.** condition of being undergrown or undersized.

**underhand** /ˈʌndəhænd/, *adj.* **1.** not open and aboveboard;

---

**undescribed,** *adj.*
**undescriptive,** *adj.*
**undeserve,** *v.t.*
**undeserved,** *adj.*
**undeservedly,** *adv.*
**undeserving,** *adj.*
**undesigned,** *adj.*
**undesignedly,** *adv.*
**undesired,** *adj.*
**undesiring,** *adj.*
**undesirous,** *adj.*
**undespairing,** *adj.*
**undespairingly,** *adv.*
**undetected,** *adj.*
**undeviating,** *adj.*
**undeviatingly,** *adv.*
**undevout,** *adj.*
**undexterous,** *adj.*
**undexterously,** *adv.*
**undiagnosed,** *adj.*
**undictated,** *adj.*
**undifferentiated,** *adj.*
**undignified,** *adj.*
**undignify,** *v.t.*
**undiligent,** *adj.*
**undiluted,** *adj.*
**undiminished,** *adj.*
**undimmed,** *adj.*
**undiplomatic,** *adj.*
**undipped,** *adj.*
**undiscerned,** *adj.*
**undiscerning,** *adj.*
**undisciplinable,** *adj.*
**undiscipline,** *n.*
**undisclosed,** *adj.*
**undiscourageable,** *adj.*
**undiscouraged,** *adj.*
**undiscoverable,** *adj.*
**undiscovered,** *adj.*
**undiscriminating,** *adj.*
**undiscriminatingly,** *adv.*
**undiscussed,** *adj.*
**undisfigured,** *adj.*
**undisguisable,** *adj.*
**undisguisably,** *adv.*
**undisguised,** *adj.*
**undisguisedly,** *adv.*
**undisheartened,** *adj.*
**undismayed,** *adj.*
**undispersed,** *adj.*
**undisposed,** *adj.*
**undisputed,** *adj.*
**undisputedly,** *adv.*
**undissembled,** *adj.*
**undissembling,** *adj.*
**undissipated,** *adj.*
**undissolved,** *adj.*
**undistinctive,** *adj.*
**undistinguishable,** *adj.*
**undistinguishably,** *adv.*
**undistorted,** *adj.*
**undistracted,** *adj.*
**undistractedly,** *adv.*
**undistributed,** *adj.*
**undisturbed,** *adj.*
**undisturbedly,** *adv.*
**undiversified,** *adj.*
**undiverted,** *adj.*
**undiverting,** *adj.*
**undivulged,** *adj.*
**undock,** *v.t.*
**undoctored,** *adj.*
**undocumented,** *adj.*
**undogmatic,** *adj.*
**undomesticated,** *adj.*

---

secret and crafty or dishonourable. **2.** done or delivered underhand. *–adv.* **3.** with the hand below the shoulder, as in pitching or bowling a ball. **4.** *Tennis.* with the racquet held below the wrist. **5.** secretly; stealthily; slyly.

**underhanded** /ʌndə'hændəd/, *adj., adv.* →**underhand.** – **underhandedly,** *adv.* – **underhandedness,** *n.*

**underhung** /'ʌndəhʌŋ/, *adj.* **1.** *Anat.* **a.** (of the lower jaw) projecting beyond the upper jaw. **b.** having the lower jaw so projecting. **2.** resting on a track beneath, instead of being overhung, as a sliding door.

**underinsure** /ʌndərɪn'ʃɔ/, *v.t.,* **-sured, -suring.** **1.** to insure (possessions) for less than their full value. **2.** to insure (oneself) for less than the full value of one's possessions. – **underinsurance,** *n.*

**underived** /ʌndə'raɪvd/, *adj.* not derived; fundamental, as an axiom.

**underjaw** /'ʌndədʒɔ/, *n.* the lower jaw.

**underlaid** /'ʌndəleɪd/, *adj.* **1.** put beneath. **2.** having an underlay. *–v.* **3.** past tense and past participle of **underlay.**

**underlap** /ʌndə'læp/, *v.t.,* **-lapped, -lapping.** to extend partly under.

**underlay** /ʌndə'leɪ/, *v.,* **-laid, -laying:** /'ʌndəleɪ/, *n.* *–v.t.* **1.** to lay (one thing) under or beneath another. **2.** to provide with something laid underneath; raise or support with something laid underneath. **3.** *Print.* to add (packing material) beneath a printing block in order to give added impression or to bring up to type height. **4.** to extend beneath. *–n.* **5.** something underlaid. **6.** felt, paper, rubber, or the like, laid under a floor-covering to increase its insulation, resilience, etc. **7.** *Print.* a piece or pieces of paper put under types, etc., to bring them to the proper height for printing.

**under-lease** /'ʌndə-lis/, *n.* a lease granted by a lessee (the under-lessor) to another (the under-lessee).

**under-lessee** /ˌʌndə-lɛ'si/, *n.* one to whom a lease is granted by an under-lessor.

**under-lessor** /ˌʌndə-lɛ'sɔ/, *n.* a lessee who grants a lease or who sublets.

**underlet** /ʌndə'lɛt/, *v.t.,* **-let, -letting.** **1.** to let below the true value. **2.** to sublet. – **underletter,** *n.*

**underlie** /ʌndə'laɪ/, *v.t.,* **-lay, -lain, -lying.** **1.** to lie under or beneath; be situated under. **2.** to be at the basis of; form the foundation of. **3.** *Finance.* to support another right or security. [ME *underly,* OE *underlicgan* (see UNDER-, LIE[2])]

**underline** /ʌndə'laɪn/, *v.,* **-lined, -lining;** /'ʌndəlaɪn/, *n.* *–v.t.* **1.** to mark with a line or lines underneath; underscore. **2.** to emphasise or stress the importance of. *–n.* **3.** a line drawn underneath.

**underling** /'ʌndəlɪŋ/, *n.* (*usu. derog.*) a subordinate. [ME and OE; from UNDER, *adv.* + -LING[1]]

**underlying** /'ʌndəlaɪɪŋ/, *adj.* **1.** lying under or beneath (something). **2.** fundamental; existing beneath the apparent aspect of. *–v.* **3.** present tense and participle of **underlie.**

**undermanned** /'ʌndəmænd/, *adj.* lacking a sufficient number of troops, workers, etc.; shorthanded.

**undermanning** /ʌndə'mænɪŋ/, *n.* the fact of being undermanned.

**undermine** /ʌndə'maɪn, 'ʌndəmaɪn/, *v.t.,* **-mined, -mining.** **1.** to form a mine or passage under, as in military operations; make an excavation under. **2.** to render unstable by digging into or wearing away the foundations. **3.** to affect injuriously or weaken by secret or underhand means. **4.** to weaken insidiously; destroy gradually. – **underminer,** *n.*

**undermost** /'ʌndəmoust/, *adj., adv.* lowest.

**underneath** /ʌndə'niθ/, *prep.* **1.** under; beneath. *–adv.* **2.** beneath; below. *–adj.* **3.** lower. *–n.* **4.** the under or lowest part or aspect. [ME *undernethe,* OE *underneothan.* See UNDER, BENEATH]

**undernourish** /ʌndə'nʌrɪʃ/, *v.t.* to provide with less nourishment than is necessary to maintain normal health. – **undernourished,** *adj.* – **undernourishment,** *n.*

**underofficer** /ʌndər'ɒfəsə/, *n.* an officer in a cadet unit.

**underpainting** /'ʌndəˌpeɪntɪŋ/, *n.* **1.** a preliminary painting, usu. in monochrome, done on a canvas or panel to establish the design and tone values of the final composition. **2.** any layer or layers of colour on a painting surface beneath the final coat of paint.

**underpants** /'ʌndəpænts/, *n.pl.* an undergarment, in the form of more or less close-fitting short trousers, with or without legs, and made of light cotton or the like; pants; drawers.

**underpart** /'ʌndəpat/, *n.* the lower part or face.

**underpass** /'ʌndəpas/, *n.* a passage running underneath, esp. a passage for vehicles or pedestrians, or both, crossing under a railway, road, etc.

**underpay** /ʌndə'peɪ/, *v.t.,* **-paid, -paying.** to pay insufficiently. – **underpayment,** *n.*

**underpin** /ʌndə'pɪn/, *v.t.,* **-pinned, -pinning.** **1.** to pin or support underneath; place something under for support or foundation. **2.** to support with masonry, stones, etc., as a building. **3.** to support; prop.

**underpinning** /'ʌndəpɪnɪŋ/, *n.* supports or latticework placed under a completed wall.

**underplay** /ʌndə'pleɪ/, *v.t.* **1.** to act (a part) sketchily. **2.** to act subtly and restrainedly. **3.** to perform or deal with in a subtle or restrained manner. *–v.i.* **4.** to leave out of one's acting all subtlety and enriching detail. **5.** to achieve an effect in acting with a minimum of emphasis. **6.** *Cards.* to

---

**undoubtable,** *adj.*
**undoubting,** *adj.*
**undoubtingly,** *adv.*
**undrainable,** *adj.*
**undrained,** *adj.*
**undreamed,** *adj.*
**undreamed-of,** *adj.*
**undreaming,** *adj.*
**undreamt,** *adj.*
**undried,** *adj.*
**undrinkable,** *adj.*
**undrowned,** *adj.*
**undrunk,** *adj.*
**undug,** *adj.*
**undulled,** *adj.*
**undutiful,** *adj.*
**undutifully,** *adv.*
**undutifulness,** *n.*
**undyed,** *adj.*
**unease,** *n.*
**uneatable,** *adj.*
**uneaten,** *adj.*
**uneclipsed,** *adj.*
**unedified,** *adj.*
**unedifying,** *adj.*
**unedited,** *adj.*
**uneffaced,** *adj.*
**unelaborated,** *adj.*
**unelapsed,** *adj.*
**unelated,** *adj.*
**unelected,** *adj.*
**unemancipated,** *adj.*
**unembellished,** *adj.*
**unembittered,** *adj.*
**unembodied,** *adj.*
**unembraced,** *adj.*
**unemphatic,** *adj.*
**unemphatically,** *adv.*
**unenclosed,** *adj.*
**unencouraged,** *adj.*
**unencumbered,** *adj.*
**unendearing,** *adj.*
**unending,** *adj.*
**unendingly,** *adv.*
**unendingness,** *n.*
**unendorsed,** *adj.*
**unendowed,** *adj.*
**unendurable,** *adj.*
**unendurably,** *adv.*
**unenduring,** *adj.*
**unenforceable,** *adj.*
**unenfranchised,** *adj.*
**unengaged,** *adj.*
**unengaging,** *adj.*
**unenjoyable,** *adj.*
**unenlisted,** *adj.*
**unenlivened,** *adj.*
**unenquiring,** *adj.*
**unenriched,** *adj.*
**unenrolled,** *adj.*
**unentailed,** *adj.*
**unentered,** *adj.*
**unenthusiastic,** *adj.*
**unentitled,** *adj.*
**unenvied,** *adj.*
**unenvious,** *adj.*
**unequable,** *adj.*
**unequalised,** *adj.*
**unequitable,** *adj.*
**uneradicated,** *adj.*
**unescapable,** *adj.*
**unescorted,** *adj.*
**unestablished,** *adj.*
**unevangelical,** *adj.*
**unevaporated,** *adj.*

play a low card while retaining a higher. – **underplayed,** *adj.*

**underplot** /ˈʌndəplɒt/, *n.* **1.** a subplot. **2.** a secret scheme; trick.

**underprice** /ʌndəˈpraɪs/, *v.t.,* **-priced, -pricing.** to price (something offered for sale) below its value or normal price.

**underprivileged** /ʌndəˈprɪvəlɪdʒd/, *adj.* denied the enjoyment of the normal privileges or rights of a society because of poverty and low social status.

**underproduction** /ʌndəprəˈdʌkʃən/, *n.* production that is less than normal, or than the demand.

**underproof** /ˈʌndəpruf/, *adj.* containing a smaller proportion of alcohol than proof spirit does.

**underprop** /ʌndəˈprɒp/, *v.t.,* **-propped, -propping.** to prop underneath; support; uphold.

**underquote** /ʌndəˈkwoʊt/, *v.t.,* **-quoted, -quoting.** **1.** to quote at a price below another price or the market price. **2.** to quote lower prices than (another).

**underrate** /ʌndəˈreɪt/, *v.t.,* **-rated, -rating.** to rate or value too low; underestimate.

**underrun** /ʌndəˈrʌn/, *v.t.,* **-ran, -run, -running.** to run, pass, or go under.

**underscore** /ʌndəˈskɔ/, *v.,* **-scored, -scoring;** /ˈʌndəskɔ/, *n.* *–v.t.* **1.** to mark with a line or lines underneath; underline. *–n.* **2.** a line drawn beneath something written or printed, as for emphasis.

**undersea** /ˈʌndəsi/, *adj.;* /ʌndəˈsi/, *adv.* *–adj.* **1.** submarine. **2.** for use below the surface of the sea. *–adv.* **3.** beneath the surface of the sea.

**underseal** /ˈʌndəsil/, *n.* **1.** a preparation of tar, bitumen, or the like used to protect the underside of a motor vehicle from corrosion, rust, etc. *–v.t.* **2.** to coat with a protective layer of underseal.

**undersecretary** /ʌndəˈsɛkrətri/, *n., pl.* **-taries.** **1.** a secretary subordinate to a principal secretary. **2.** the permanent head in certain government departments. – **undersecretaryship,** *n.*

**undersell** /ʌndəˈsɛl/, *v.t.,* **-sold, -selling.** **1.** to advertise or publicise with restraint. **2.** to sell things at a lower price than (a competitor). **3.** to sell for less than the actual value. **4. undersell oneself,** to lack confidence in one's own worth; underrate oneself. – **underseller,** *n.*

**undersense** /ˈʌndəsɛns/, *n.* an inner or subconscious awareness.

**underservant** /ˈʌndəsɜvənt/, *n.* an inferior or subordinate servant.

**underset** /ˈʌndəsɛt/, *n.;* /ʌndəˈsɛt/, v., **-set, -setting.** *–n.* **1.** an ocean undercurrent. **2.** *Mining.* a lower vein of ore. *–v.t.* **3.** to support from below.

**undersexed** /ˈʌndəsɛkst/, *adj.* having unusually little interest in sex or sexual activity; lacking sexual drive.

**undershirt** /ˈʌndəʃɜt/, *n. U.S.* a singlet.

**undershoot** /ʌndəˈʃut/, *v.,* **-shot, -shooting.** *–v.i.* **1.** *Aeron.* to land an aircraft before it reaches the correct landing strip as a result of insufficient speed or height. **2.** to shoot or launch a projectile so that it falls short of the target. *–v.t.* **3.** *Aeron.* to land short of (a landing strip, etc.). **4.** to shoot or launch a projectile so that it falls short of (a target).

**undershot** /ˈʌndəʃɒt/, *adj.* **1.** underhung; driven by water passing beneath, as a kind of vertical waterwheel. **2.** having the upper jaw shorter than the lower jaw, as a dog, usu. considered to be a malformation.

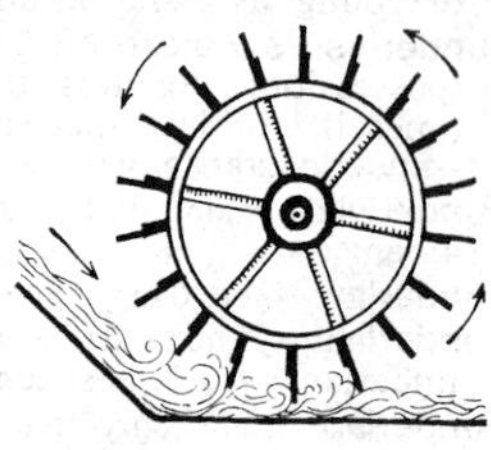
undershot waterwheel

**undershrub** /ˈʌndəʃrʌb/, *n.* a low shrub.

**underside** /ˈʌndəsaɪd/, *n.* the under or lower side.

**undersign** /ʌndəˈsaɪn/, *v.t.* to sign one's name under, or at the end of (a letter or document); to affix one's signature to.

**undersigned** /ˈʌndəsaɪnd/, *adj.* **1.** having signed, as a person, at the end of a letter or document. **2.** signed, as a name. *–n.* **3. the undersigned,** the person or persons undersigning a letter or document.

**undersized** /ˈʌndəsaɪzd/, *adj.* below the usual size. Also, **undersize.**

**underskirt** /ˈʌndəskɜt/, *n.* a skirt worn under an outer skirt or under an overskirt or drapery.

**undersleeve** /ˈʌndəsliv/, *n.* **1.** a sleeve worn under an outer sleeve. **2.** an ornamental inner sleeve extending below the outer sleeve.

**underslung** /ˈʌndəslʌŋ/, *adj.* **1.** attached to the axles from below, as the chassis frame of a car. **2.** having a low centre of gravity. **3.** supported from above.

**undersoil** /ˈʌndəsɔɪl/, *n.* →**subsoil.**

**undersparred** /ˈʌndəspad/, *adj.* having insufficient masts, yards, gaffs, etc., to carry enough sail.

**underspin** /ˈʌndəspɪn/, *n.* →**backspin.**

**understaffed** /ˈʌndəstaft/, *adj.* having too few employees; inadequately staffed.

**understand** /ʌndəˈstænd/, *v.,* **-stood, -standing.** *–v.t.* **1.** to perceive the meaning of; grasp the idea of; comprehend. **2.** to be thoroughly familiar with; apprehend clearly the character or nature of. **3.** to comprehend by knowing the meaning of the words employed, as a language. **4.** to inter-

---

**unevolved,** *adj.*
**unexaggerated,** *adj.*
**unexamined,** *adj.*
**unexcelled,** *adj.*
**unexcitable,** *adj.*
**unexcited,** *adj.*
**unexciting,** *adj.*
**unexclusive,** *adj.*
**unexclusively,** *adv.*
**unexclusiveness,** *n.*
**unexecuted,** *adj.*
**unexemplified,** *adj.*
**unexercised,** *adj.*
**unexhausted,** *adj.*
**unexorcised,** *adj.*
**unexpanded,** *adj.*
**unexpansive,** *adj.*
**unexpended,** *adj.*
**unexplainable,** *adj.*
**unexplainably,** *adv.*
**unexplained,** *adj.*
**unexploited,** *adj.*
**unexplored,** *adj.*
**unexpurgated,** *adj.*
**unextended,** *adj.*
**unextenuated,** *adj.*
**unextinguished,** *adj.*
**unfaded,** *adj.*
**unfallen,** *adj.*
**unfalsified,** *adj.*
**unfaltering,** *adj.*
**unfalteringly,** *adv.*
**unfamed,** *adj.*
**unfamiliarised,** *adj.*
**unfancied,** *adj.*
**unfanciful,** *adj.*
**unfanned,** *adj.*
**unfashioned,** *adj.*
**unfastidious,** *adj.*
**unfathomed,** *adj.*
**unfatigued,** *adj.*
**unfatiguing,** *adj.*
**unfavoured,** *adj.*
**unfeared,** *adj.*
**unfearful,** *adj.*
**unfearfully,** *adv.*
**unfeasibility,** *n.*
**unfeasible,** *adj.*
**unfeathered,** *adj.*
**unfeigning,** *adj.*
**unfelled,** *adj.*
**unfemininity,** *n.*
**unfenced,** *adj.*
**unfertile,** *adj.*
**unfermented,** *adj.*
**unfertilised,** *adj.*
**unfigured,** *adj.*
**unfiled,** *adj.*
**unfilially,** *adv.*
**unfillable,** *adj.*
**unfilled,** *adj.*
**unfilleted,** *adj.*
**unfilmed,** *adj.*
**unfilterable,** *adj.*
**unfiltered,** *adj.*
**unfindable,** *adj.*
**unfinishable,** *adj.*
**unfirm,** *adj.*
**unfirmly,** *adv.*
**unfished,** *adj.*
**unfitted,** *adj.*
**unfitting,** *adj.*
**unfittingly,** *adv.*
**unfixity,** *n.*
**unflanked,** *adj.*

pret, or assign a meaning to; take to mean. **5.** to grasp the significance, implications, or importance of. **6.** to regard or take as a fact, or as settled. **7.** to get knowledge of; learn or hear. **8.** to accept as a fact; believe. **9.** to conceive the meaning of in a particular way: *you are to understand the phrase literally.* **10.** to supply mentally, as a word necessary to complete sense. *–v.i.* **11.** to perceive what is meant. **12.** to have the use of the intellectual faculties. **13.** to have information or knowledge about something: *to understand about a matter.* **14.** to accept sympathetically: *if you go away, I shall understand.* **15.** to be informed; believe. [ME; OE *understondan,* c. D *onderstaan,* G *unterstehen*]

**understandable** /ʌndəˈstændəbəl/, *adj.* that may be understood. – **understandableness,** *n.* – **understandably,** *adv.*

**understanding** /ʌndəˈstændɪŋ/, *n.* **1.** the act of one who understands; comprehension; personal interpretation. **2.** intelligence; wit. **3.** superior intelligence; superior power of recognising the truth: *men of understanding.* **4.** a mutual comprehension of each other's meaning, thoughts, etc. **5.** a state of (good or friendly) relations between persons. **6.** a mutual agreement of a private or unannounced kind. **7.** *Philos.* discursive knowledge based on premises and observations. **8. on the understanding that,** on condition that. *–adj.* **9.** that understands; possessing or showing intelligence or understanding. **10.** sympathetically discerning; tolerant. – **understandingly,** *adv.*

**understate** /ʌndəˈsteɪt/, *v.t.,* **-stated, -stating.** to state or represent less strongly than is desirable or necessary; state with too little emphasis. – **understatement** /ˈʌndəsteɪtmənt/, *n.*

**understeer** /ʌndəˈstɪə/, *v.;* /ʌndəˈstɪə, ˈʌndəstɪə/, *n.* *–v.i.* **1.** (of a motor vehicle) to tend to turn in a wider circle than indicated by the geometry of the wheels. *–n.* **2.** such a tendency.

**understock** /ʌndəˈstɒk/, *v.t.* to supply insufficiently with stock.

**understood** /ʌndəˈstʊd/, *v.* **1.** past tense and past participle of **understand.** *–adj.* **2.** agreed upon by all concerned. **3.** implied; assumed.

**understratum** /ˈʌndəstratəm/, *n., pl.* **-strata** /-stratə/, **-stratums.** →**substratum.**

**understudy** /ˈʌndəstʌdi/, *n., v.,* **-studied, -studying.** *–n.* **1.** an actor or actress who stands by to replace a performer when the latter is unable to appear. *–v.t.* **2.** to act as an understudy to (an actor or actress). **3.** to be the understudy for (a particular role). *–v.i.* **4.** to be an understudy.

**undersurface** /ˈʌndəsɜfəs/, *n.* the surface of the lower part of something; the surface that faces downwards.

**undertake** /ʌndəˈteɪk/, *v.,* **-took, -taken, -taking.** *–v.t.* **1.** to take on oneself (some task, performance, etc.); take in hand; essay; attempt. **2.** to take on oneself by formal promise or agreement; lay oneself under obligation to perform or execute. **3.** to warrant or guarantee (fol. by a clause). **4.** to take in charge; assume the duty of attending to (a person). **5.** *Obs.* to engage with, as in a duel. *–v.i.* **6.** *Archaic.* to take on oneself any task of responsibility. **7.** *Archaic.* to engage oneself by promise (*for*); give a guarantee, or become surety (*for*).

**undertaker** /ʌndəˈteɪkə/ *for def. 1;* /ˈʌndəteɪkə/ *for def. 2, n.* **1.** one who undertakes something. **2.** one whose business it is to prepare the dead for burial and to take charge of funerals; funeral director; mortician.

**undertaking** /ʌndəˈteɪkɪŋ/ *for defs 1-3;* /ˈʌndəteɪkɪŋ/ *for def. 4, n.* **1.** the act of one who undertakes any task or responsibility. **2.** a task, enterprise, etc., undertaken. **3.** a promise; pledge; guarantee. **4.** the business of an undertaker or funeral director.

**undertenant** /ˈʌndətɛnənt/, *n.* →**subtenant.** – **undertenancy,** *n.*

**under-the-counter** /ˈʌndə-ðə-kaʊntə/, *adj.* **1.** pertaining to goods kept hidden for sale in some improper way, as on the black market. *–adv.* **2.** sold illegally, as blackmarket goods. Also, (*esp. in predicative use*), **under the counter** /ʌndə ðə ˈkaʊntə/.

**underthings** /ˈʌndəθɪŋz/, *n. pl.* →**underclothes.**

**undertint** /ˈʌndətɪnt/, *n.* **1.** a subdued tint. **2.** a partly or wholly concealed tint under another.

**undertone** /ˈʌndətoʊn/, *n.* **1.** a low or subdued tone, as of utterance. **2.** an underlying quality, element, or tendency. **3.** a subdued colour; a colour modified by an underlying colour.

**undertook** /ʌndəˈtʊk/, *v.* past tense of **undertake.**

**undertow** /ˈʌndətoʊ/, *n.* **1.** the backward flow or draught of the water, below the surface, from waves breaking on a beach. **2.** any strong current below the surface of a body of water, moving in a direction different from that of the surface current.

**undertrick** /ˈʌndətrɪk/, *n.* (in bridge) a trick lacking from the number needed to make a contract. Cf. **overtrick.**

**undervalue** /ʌndəˈvælju/, *v.t.,* **-ued, -uing.** **1.** to value below the real worth; put too low a value on. **2.** to diminish in value; make of less value. **3.** to esteem too low; esteem lightly; hold in mean estimation. – **undervaluation** /ˌʌndəvæljuˈeɪʃən/, *n.* – **undervaluer,** *n.*

**undervest** /ˈʌndəvɛst/, *n.* a vest.

**underwater** /ˈʌndəwɔtə/, *adj.* **1.** being or occurring under water. **2.** designed to be used under water. **3.** situated below the waterline of a ship.

**underwear** /ˈʌndəwɛə/, *n.* clothes worn under outer clothes,

---

**unflattened,** *adj.*
**unflattered,** *adj.*
**unflattering,** *adj.*
**unflatteringly,** *adv.*
**unflawed,** *adj.*
**unflickering,** *adj.*
**unfloored,** *adj.*
**unfluctuating,** *adj.*
**unflurried,** *adj.*
**unflushed,** *adj.*
**unfluted,** *adj.*
**unforbidden,** *adj.*
**unfordable,** *adj.*
**unforeseeable,** *adj.*
**unforeseeably,** *adv.*
**unforfeitable,** *adj.*
**unforgeable,** *adj.*
**unforged,** *adj.*
**unforgivable,** *adj.*
**unforgivably,** *adv.*
**unforgiven,** *adj.*
**unforgiving,** *adj.*
**unforgivingly,** *adv.*
**unforgotten,** *adj.*
**unformulated,** *adj.*
**unfortified,** *adj.*
**unfossilised,** *adj.*
**unfought,** *adj.*
**unframed,** *adj.*
**unfranchised,** *adj.*
**unfranked,** *adj.*
**unfrequently,** *adv.*
**unfretted,** *adj.*
**unfrightened,** *adj.*
**unfrosted,** *adj.*
**unfrowning,** *adj.*
**unfrozen,** *adj.*
**unfuelled,** *adj.*
**unfulfilled,** *adj.*
**unfunded,** *adj.*
**unfunny,** *adj.*
**unfurnish,** *v.t.*
**unfurred,** *adj.*
**unfurrowed,** *adj.*
**unfused,** *adj.*
**unfussy,** *adj.*
**ungagged,** *adj.*
**ungainful,** *adj.*
**ungallant,** *adj.*
**ungallantly,** *adv.*
**ungallantry,** *n.*
**ungarnered,** *adj.*
**ungarnished,** *adj.*
**ungarrisoned,** *adj.*
**ungartered,** *adj.*
**ungathered,** *adj.*
**ungauged,** *adj.*
**ungear,** *v.t.*
**ungelded,** *adj.*
**ungelt,** *adj.*
**ungeneralisable,** *adj.*
**ungeneralised,** *adj.*
**ungenial,** *adj.*
**ungeniality,** *n.*
**ungenially,** *adv.*
**ungentlemanly,** *adj.*
**ungentlemanliness,** *n.*
**ungifted,** *adj.*
**ungild,** *v.t.*
**ungilded,** *adj.*
**ungilt,** *adj.*
**ungirth,** *v.t.*
**ungirthed,** *adj.*
**ungiven,** *adj.*
**unglamorous,** *adj.*

esp. those worn next to the skin.

**underweight** /ˈʌndəweɪt/, *n.* **1.** deficiency in weight. *–adj.* **2.** lacking usual or required weight.

**underwent** /ʌndəˈwɛnt/, *v.* past tense of **undergo.**

**underwing** /ˈʌndəwɪŋ/, *n.* a hind wing of an insect.

**underwood** /ˈʌndəwʊd/, *n.* **1.** shrubs or small trees growing under larger trees; underbrush. **2.** a growth of underbrush.

**underworld** /ˈʌndəwɜld/, *n.* **1.** the lower, degraded, or criminal part of human society. **2.** the lower or nether world. **3.** the place or region below the surface of the earth. **4.** the opposite side of the earth; the antipodes. **5.** *Archaic.* the world below the skies; the earth.

**underwrite** /ˈʌndəraɪt, ʌndəˈraɪt/, *v.,* **-wrote, -written, -writing.** *–v.t.* **1.** to write (something) under a thing, esp. under other written matter. **2.** to sign one's name to (a document, etc.). **3.** to subscribe to, agree with, or support (a statement, etc.), as by signature. **4.** *Obs.* to agree to give or pay (a certain sum of money) by signing one's name. **5.** to agree to meet the expense of; undertake to finance. **6.** to guarantee the sale of (shares or bonds to be offered to the public for subscription). **7.** *Insurance.* **a.** to write one's name at the end of (a policy of insurance), thereby becoming liable in case of certain losses specified therein. **b.** to insure. **c.** to assume liability to the extent of (a certain sum) by way of insurance. *–v.i.* **8.** to underwrite something. **9.** to carry on the business of an underwriter. [ME; OE *underwrītan* (translation of L *subscrībere*)]

**underwriter** /ˈʌndəraɪtə/, *n.* **1.** one who underwrites policies of insurance, or carries on insurance as a business. **2.** one who underwrites shares or bonds.

**underwritten** /ˈʌndərɪtn, ʌndəˈrɪtn/, *v.* past participle of **underwrite.**

**underwrote** /ˈʌndəroʊt, ʌndəˈroʊt/, *v.* past tense of **underwrite.**

**undescended testicle** /ˌʌndəsɛndəd ˈtɛstɪkəl/, *n.* a testicle that has remained within the inguinal canal and has not descended into the scrotum.

**undesigning** /ʌndəˈzaɪnɪŋ/, *adj.* without underhand or selfish designs.

**undesirable** /ʌndəˈzaɪərəbəl/, *adj.* **1.** objectionable; detrimental. **2.** not desirable. *–n.* **3.** an undesirable person or thing. – **undesirableness,** *n.* – **undesirably,** *adv.*

**undetermined** /ʌndəˈtɜmənd/, *adj.* **1.** not definitely settled or decided; uncertain. **2.** not fixed, limited, or restricted, as in meaning, extent, etc.; indefinite. **3.** undecided, irresolute, or uncertain, as a person.

**undeveloped** /ʌndəˈvɛləpt/, *adj.* **1.** not developed; not fully grown or matured. **2.** (of land) not built on; not made to yield a profit.

**undid** /ʌnˈdɪd/, *v.* past tense of **undo.**

**undies** /ˈʌndiz/, *n.pl. Colloq.* →**underwear.**

**undigested** /ʌndaɪˈdʒɛstəd, -di-, -də-/, *adj.* **1.** (of food) not digested; unassimilated. **2.** (of information, ideas, discourse, etc.) not ordered or arranged in intelligible fashion.

**undine** /ˈʌndin/, *n.* one of a class of mythological female water-sprites. Also, **ondine.** [NL *Undina,* from L *unda* wave]

**undirected** /ʌndəˈrɛktəd, -daɪ-/, *adj.* **1.** not directed; not guided. **2.** bearing no address, as a letter.

**undischarged** /ʌndɪsˈtʃadʒd/, *adj.* **1.** not cleared, as debts. **2.** not performed, as obligations or duties. **3.** not set free or released, as a bankrupt, soldier, etc. **4.** *Archaic.* not fired, as a gun. **5.** not unloaded, as a ship's cargo.

**undisciplined** /ʌnˈdɪsəplənd/, *adj.* **1.** lacking in discipline; unruly; disorderly. **2.** not having been subjected to training or discipline.

**undistinguished** /ʌndəˈstɪŋgwɪʃt/, *adj.* **1.** lacking distinctive features. **2.** not outstanding; mediocre.

**undistributed middle** /ˌʌndəsˌtrɪbjutəd ˈmɪdl/, *n. Logic.* a syllogistic fallacy in which the second premise does not apply to all members of the class in the first premise, and therefore cannot provide the basis for a conclusion.

**undivided** /ʌndəˈvaɪdəd/, *adj.* **1.** not divided, or separated into parts. **2.** not partial; whole; not diluted: *they gave him their undivided loyalty.* – **undividedly,** *adv.* – **undividedness,** *n.*

**undo** /ʌnˈdu/, *v.t.,* **-did, -done, -doing. 1.** to unfasten and open (something closed, locked, barred, etc.). **2.** to untie or loose (strings, etc.). **3.** to open (a parcel, a sealed letter, etc.). **4.** to reverse the doing of; cause to be as if never done. **5.** to do away with; efface. **6.** to bring to ruin or disaster; destroy. [ME; OE *undōn,* c. D *ontdoen;* from UN-[2] + DO[1]] – **undoer,** *n.*

**undoing** /ʌnˈduɪŋ/, *n.* **1.** the reversing of what has been done; annulling. **2.** a bringing to destruction, ruin, or disaster. **3.** a cause of destruction or ruin. **4.** the act or fact of unfastening or opening.

**undone**[1] /ʌnˈdʌn/, *adj.* **1.** not done; not accomplished or completed, or finished. **2.** unfastened. **3.** *Archaic.* neglected or omitted. [UN-[1] + DONE]

**undone**[2] /ʌnˈdʌn/, *v.* **1.** past participle of **undo.** *–adj.* **2.** reversed. **3.** brought to destruction or ruin. **4. come undone,** *Prison Colloq.* to be detected; make a mistake that leads to arrest and conviction. [see UNDO]

**undouble** /ʌnˈdʌbəl/, *v.t., v.i.,* **-bled, -bling.** to unfold; straighten out, as a fist.

**undoubted** /ʌnˈdaʊtəd/, *adj.* not called in question; accepted as beyond doubt; undisputed. – **undoubtedly,** *adv.*

**undramatic** /ʌndrəˈmætɪk/, *adj.* **1.** lacking drama or excite-

---

**unglazed,** *adj.*
**unglorified,** *adj.*
**unglove,** *v.t.*
**ungodlike,** *adj.*
**ungoverned,** *adj.*
**ungraced,** *adj.*
**ungraded,** *adj.*
**ungraduated,** *adj.*
**ungrafted,** *adj.*
**ungranted,** *adj.*
**ungraspable,** *adj.*
**ungraspably,** *adv.*
**ungrasped,** *adj.*
**ungratified,** *adj.*
**ungratifying,** *adj.*
**ungreased,** *adj.*
**ungroomed,** *adj.*
**unground,** *adj.*
**ungrudged,** *adj.*
**unguidable,** *adj.*
**unguided,** *adj.*
**ungum,** *v.t.*
**ungummed,** *adj.*
**unhackneyed,** *adj.*
**unhalting,** *adj.*
**unhampered,** *adj.*
**unhandicapped,** *adj.*
**unhandled,** *adj.*
**unhang,** *v.t.*
**unhardened,** *adj.*
**unharmed,** *adj.*
**unharmonious,** *adj.*
**unharmoniously,** *adv.*
**unharmony,** *n.*
**unharvested,** *adj.*
**unhatched,** *adj.*
**unhazardous,** *adj.*
**unhealable,** *adj.*
**unhealed,** *adj.*
**unhearing,** *adj.*
**unheated,** *adj.*
**unhedged,** *adj.*
**unheeded,** *adj.*
**unheedful,** *adj.*
**unhelmeted,** *adj.*
**unhelped,** *adj.*
**unhelpful,** *adj.*
**unhelpfulness,** *n.*
**unhemmed,** *adj.*
**unheralded,** *adj.*
**unheroic,** *adj.*
**unheroically,** *adv.*
**unhesitating,** *adj.*
**unhesitatingly,** *adv.*
**unhewn,** *adj.*
**unhidden,** *adj.*
**unhindered,** *adj.*
**unhomelike,** *adj.*
**unhomeliness,** *n.*
**unhomely,** *adj.*
**unhonoured,** *adj.*
**unhopeful,** *adj.*
**unhopefully,** *adv.*
**unhoping,** *adj.*
**unhospitable,** *adj.*
**unhulled,** *adj.*
**unhuman,** *adj.*
**unhumanise,** *v.t.*
**unhunted,** *adj.*
**unhurried,** *adj.*
**unhurriedly,** *adv.*
**unhurrying,** *adj.*
**unhurt,** *adj.*
**unhusbanded,** *adj.*
**unidealistic,** *adj.*

---

ment; dull. **2.** not suitable for the theatre.

**undrape** /ʌn'dreɪp/, *v.t.*, **-draped, -draping.** to strip of drapery; bare.

**undress** /ʌn'drɛs/, *v., n.;* /'ʌndrɛs/, *adj.* *–v.t.* **1.** to remove the clothes from; disrobe. **2.** to strip of whatever adorns. **3.** to remove the dressing from (a wound, etc.). **4.** *Colloq.* to shear: *to undress a sheep.* *–v.i.* **5.** to take off one's clothes. *–n.* **6.** the state of having little or no clothes on. **7.** ordinary or informal dress. **8.** *Mil.* a uniform for ordinary occasions (as opposed to *full dress or battledress*). *–adj.* **9.** of or pertaining to ordinary dress. **10.** informal as to dress. **11.** of or pertaining to academic dress for everyday use: *an undress gown.*

**undressed** /ʌn'drɛst/, *adj.* **1.** not dressed; not specially prepared. **2.** without clothes on. **3. a.** (of leather) having a napped finish on the flesh side. **b.** (of textiles, masonry, etc.) not prepared in some way.

**undue** /ʌn'dju/, *adj.* **1.** unwarranted; excessive; too great: *undue haste.* **2.** not proper, fitting, or right; unjustified: *to exert undue influence.* **3.** not yet owing or payable.

**undulant** /'ʌndʒələnt/, *adj.* undulating; waving; wavy. [L *undulans,* ppr.]

**undulant fever** /– 'fivə/, *n.* an irregular, relapsing fever, with swelling of joints, spleen, and rheumatic pains, caused by *Brucella melitensis* ingested in raw milk of diseased cows and goats; Malta fever; Mediterranean fever; brucellosis.

**undulate** /'ʌndʒəleɪt/, *v.,* **-lated, -lating;** /'ʌndʒələt, -leɪt/, *adj.* *–v.i.* **1.** to have a wavy motion; rise and fall or move up and down in waves. **2.** to have a wavy form or surface; bend with successive curves in alternate directions. *–v.t.* **3.** to cause to move in waves. **4.** to give a wavy form to. *–adj.* **5.** Also, **undulated.** wavy; bending with successive curves in alternate directions; having a waved form, surface, margin, etc. [L *undulātus* wavy, from *unda* wave]

**undulation** /ʌndʒə'leɪʃən/, *n.* **1.** the act of undulating; a waving motion. **2.** wavy form or outline. **3.** one of a series of wavelike bends, curves, or elevations. **4.** *Physics.* the motion of waves; a wave; a vibration.

**undulatory** /'ʌndʒəleɪtəri/, *adj.* **1.** moving in undulations. **2.** having the form or appearance of waves. Also, **undulative.**

**unduly** /ʌn'djuli/, *adv.* **1.** excessively. **2.** inappropriately; improperly; unjustifiably.

**undying** /ʌn'daɪɪŋ/, *adj.* deathless; immortal; unending. **– undyingly,** *adv.*

**unearned** /ʌn'ɜnd/, *adj.* **1.** not earned by one's own labour or effort, as income derived from stocks and shares. **2.** not deserved.

**unearned income** /– 'ɪŋkʌm/, *n.* income, from investments, inheritance, property, etc., which is not earned as salary, and is usu. taxed at a higher level than earned income.

**unearned increment** /– 'ɪnkrəmənt/, *n.* the increase in the value of land, etc., due to natural causes, as growth of population, rather than to any labour or expenditure by the owner.

**unearth** /ʌn'ɜθ/, *v.t.* **1.** to dig or get out of the earth; dig up. **2.** to uncover or bring to light by digging, searching, or discovery.

**unearthly** /ʌn'ɜθli/, *adj.* **1.** not of this earth or world. **2.** supernatural; ghostly; unnaturally strange; weird: *an unearthly scream.* **3.** *Colloq.* unreasonable; absurd: *to get up at an unearthly hour.* **– unearthliness,** *n.*

**uneasy** /ʌn'izi/, *adj.,* **-easier, -easiest.** **1.** not easy in body or mind; uncomfortable; restless; disturbed; perturbed. **2.** not easy in manner; constrained. **3.** *Obs.* not conducive to ease; causing bodily discomfort. **– uneasily,** *adv.* **– uneasiness,** *n.*

**uneconomic** /ʌnɛkə'nɒmɪk, -ikə-/, *adj.* not productive of economic benefit.

**uneconomical** /ʌnɛkə'nɒmɪkəl, -ikə-/, *adj.* wasteful, as a method, activity, etc.; unprofitable. **– uneconomically,** *adv.*

**uneducated** /ʌn'ɛdʒəkeɪtəd/, *adj.* **1.** not educated. **2.** not showing signs of education: *an uneducated handwriting.*

**unembarrassed** /ʌnɛm'bærəst/, *adj.* **1.** not embarrassed; not ashamed, constrained, or self-conscious; at ease. **2.** not hampered or obstructed. **– unembarrassedly,** *adv.*

**unemotional** /ʌnə'moʊʃənəl/, *adj.* **1.** (of a person) not subject to strong emotions or reactions; imperturbable; unenthusiastic. **2.** lacking in or unmodified by strong emotion. **– unemotionally,** *adv.*

**unemployable** /ʌnəm'plɔɪəbəl, -ɛm-/, *adj.* **1.** unable to keep a job; not fit to be employed; unusable. *–n.* **2.** a person or thing that is unfit to be employed or used. **– unemployability** /ˌʌnəmplɔɪə'bɪləti, -ɛm-/, *n.*

**unemployed** /ʌnəm'plɔɪd, -ɛm-/, *adj.* **1.** out of work, esp. temporarily and involuntarily; without work or employment. **2.** not employed; not in use; not kept busy or at work. **3.** not in productive or profitable use. *–n.* (*sing. construed as pl.*) **4.** those who are not employed. **5.** those who are out of work, esp. temporarily and involuntarily.

**unemployment** /ʌnəm'plɔɪmənt, -ɛm-/, *n.* **1.** lack of employment; unemployed condition. **2.** the number of people out of work: *unemployment is down this year.* **3.** the excess of unemployed over available jobs.

**unemployment benefit** /'– bɛnəfɪt/, *n.* →**dole** (def. 4.)

**unemployment office** /'– ɒfəs/, *n.* a government office which is responsible for the distribution of unemployment benefits and which acts as an employment agency.

---

**unidentified,** *adj.*
**unidiomatic,** *adj.*
**unignited,** *adj.*
**unilluminated,** *adj.*
**unillustrated,** *adj.*
**unimaginative,** *adj.*
**unimaginatively,** *adv.*
**unimaginativeness,** *n.*
**unimagined,** *adj.*
**unimbued,** *adj.*
**unimpaired,** *adj.*
**unimpeached,** *adj.*
**unimpeded,** *adj.*
**unimpededly,** *adv.*
**unimpressed,** *adj.*
**unimpressible,** *adj.*
**unimpressionable,** *adj.*
**unimpressive,** *adj.*
**unimprisoned,** *adj.*
**unimprovable,** *adj.*
**unimproving,** *adj.*
**unimpugnable,** *adj.*
**unimpulsive,** *adj.*
**uninclined,** *adj.*
**unincreasable,** *adj.*
**unincreased,** *adj.*
**unindebted,** *adj.*
**unindented,** *adj.*
**unindexed,** *adj.*
**unindicated,** *adj.*
**unindulged,** *adj.*
**unindustrious,** *adj.*
**uninfected,** *adj.*
**uninflamed,** *adj.*
**uninflammable,** *adj.*
**uninflammability,** *n.*
**uninflated,** *adj.*
**uninflected,** *adj.*
**uninfluenced,** *adj.*
**uninfluential,** *adj.*
**uninformative,** *adj.*
**uninviting,** *adj.*
**uninvolved,** *adj.*
**unironed,** *adj.*
**unirrigated,** *adj.*
**uninforming,** *adj.*
**uninhabitable,** *adj.*
**uninhabitableness,** *n.*
**uninhabitably,** *adv.*
**uninhabited,** *adj.*
**uninheritable,** *adj.*
**uninitiated,** *adj., n.*
**uninjured,** *adj.*
**uninquiring,** *adj.*
**uninquisitive,** *adj.*
**uninscribed,** *adj.*
**uninstructed,** *adj.*
**uninstructive,** *adj.*
**uninsulated,** *adj.*
**uninsurable,** *adj.*
**uninsurably,** *adv.*
**uninsured,** *adj.*
**unintegrated,** *adj.*
**unintellectual,** *adj.*
**unintended,** *adj.*
**uninteresting,** *adj.*
**uninterestingly,** *adv.*
**unininterestingness,** *n.*
**uninterpretable,** *adj.*
**uninterred,** *adj.*
**unintimidated,** *adj.*
**unintoxicating,** *adj.*
**unintroduced,** *adj.*
**uninured,** *adj.*
**uninvaded,** *adj.*

**unenforceable** /ʌnən'fɔsəbəl/, *adj.* **1.** unable to be put into effect. **2.** *Law.* valid but not enforceable by action in the courts.

**unenlightened** /ʌnən'laɪtnd/, *adj.* **1.** not informed or instructed. **2.** characterised by unreason, prejudice, illiberality, ignorance, superstition, or the like.

**unenterprising** /ʌn'ɛntəpraɪzɪŋ/, *adj.* lacking in adventurousness or initiative. – **unenterprisingly,** *adv.*

**unenviable** /ʌn'ɛnviəbəl/, *adj.* disagreeable: *an unenviable predicament.* – **unenviably,** *adv.*

**unequal** /ʌn'ikwəl/, *adj.* **1.** not equal; not of the same quantity, value, rank, ability, merit, etc.: *unequal size.* **2.** not adequate, as in amount, power, ability, etc. (fol. by *to*): *strength unequal to the task.* **3.** not evenly proportioned or balanced; not having the parts alike or symmetrical: *an unequal leaf.* **4.** not even or regular, as motion, extent, duration, etc. **5.** in which the parties are unevenly matched: *an unequal contest.* **6.** uneven or variable in character, quality, etc. *–n.* **7.** (*pl.*) people or things not equal to one another. – **unequally,** *adv.* – **unequalness,** *n.*

**unequalled** /ʌn'ikwəld/, *adj.* not equalled; unparalleled; matchless. Also, *U.S.,* **unequaled.**

**unequivocal** /ʌni'kwɪvəkəl, -ə'kwɪv-/, *adj.* not equivocal; not ambiguous; clear; plain: *an unequivocal reply.* – **unequivocally,** *adv.* – **unequivocalness,** *n.*

**unerring** /ʌn'ɜrɪŋ/, *adj.* **1.** not erring; not going astray or missing the mark; without error or mistake. **2.** unfailingly right, exact, or sure. – **unerringly,** *adv.* – **unerringness,** *n.*

**UNESCO** /ju'nɛskoʊ/, United Nations Educational, Scientific, and Cultural Organisation. Also, **U.N.E.S.C.O.**

**unessential** /ʌnə'sɛnʃəl/, *adj.* **1.** not of prime importance; not indispensable; inessential. **2.** having no essence or being. *–n.* **3.** an inessential thing; a non-essential. – **unessentially,** *adv.*

**unesthetic** /ʌnəs'θɛtɪk/, *adj.* →**unaesthetic.**

**unethical** /ʌn'ɛθɪkəl/, *adj.* **1.** contrary to moral precept; immoral. **2.** in contravention of some code of professional conduct. – **unethically,** *adv.*

**uneven** /ʌn'ivən/, *adj.* **1.** not level or flat; rough; rugged. **2.** irregular; varying; not uniform. **3.** not equally balanced; not equal: *an uneven contest.* **4.** (of a number) odd; not divisible into two equal integers: *3, 5, and 7 are uneven numbers.* [ME; OE *unefen,* c. G *uneben.* See UN-[1], EVEN[1]] – **unevenly,** *adv.* – **unevenness,** *n.*

**uneventful** /ʌnə'vɛntfəl/, *adj.* not eventful; lacking in important or striking occurrences: *an uneventful day at the office.* – **uneventfully,** *adv.* – **uneventfulness,** *n.*

**unexacting** /ʌnəg'zæktɪŋ/, *adj.* **1.** not exacting; undemanding. **2.** easily satisfied; uncritical.

**unexampled** /ʌnəg'zæmpəld/, *adj.* unlike anything previously known; without parallel; unprecedented: *unexampled kindness, unexampled lawlessness.*

**unexceptionable** /ʌnək'sɛpʃənəbəl/, *adj.* not open or liable to any exception or objection; beyond criticism. – **unexceptionableness,** *n.* – **unexceptionably,** *adv.*

**unexceptional** /ʌnək'sɛpʃənəl/, *adj.* **1.** not exceptional; not unusual or extraordinary. **2.** admitting of no exception. **3.** →**unexceptionable.** – **unexceptionally,** *adv.*

**unexpected** /ʌnək'spɛktəd/, *adj.* unforeseen; surprising. – **unexpectedly,** *adv.* – **unexpectedness,** *n.*

**unexperienced** /ʌnək'spɪəriənst/, *adj.* **1.** not furnished with or taught by experience; inexperienced. **2.** not known by experience, as facts; not having been experienced, as sensations.

**unexpired** /ʌnək'spaɪəd/, *adj.* not having expired, as a period of time, lease, etc.; remaining.

**unexplainable** /ʌnək'spleɪnəbəl/, *adj.* (of events) such that no explanation can be found; mysterious; inexplicable.

**unexposed** /ʌnək'spoʊzd/, *adj.* (of film) not having been exposed to the light; unused.

**unexpressed** /ʌnək'sprɛst/, *adj.* **1.** not expressed, stated, or communicated. **2.** not stated explicitly; tacit.

**unexpressive** /ʌnək'sprɛsɪv/, *adj.* **1.** →**inexpressive.** **2.** *Obs.* →**inexpressible.** – **unexpressively,** *adv.* – **unexpressiveness,** *n.*

**unexpurgated** /ʌn'ɛkspəgeɪtəd/, *adj.* not censored or bowdlerised.

**unfading** /ʌn'feɪdɪŋ/, *adj.* **1.** not diminishing: *unfading enthusiasm.* **2.** not fading, as colour. – **unfadingly,** *adv.* – **unfadingness,** *n.*

**unfailing** /ʌn'feɪlɪŋ/, *adj.* **1.** not failing or giving way; totally dependable: *unfailing good humour.* **2.** never giving out; unceasing; continuous: *an unfailing supply.* **3.** certain; infallible: *an unfailing test.* – **unfailingly,** *adv.* – **unfailingness,** *n.*

**unfair** /ʌn'fɛə/, *adj.* **1.** not fair; biased or partial; not just or equitable; unjust. **2.** marked by deceptive dishonest practices. [ME; OE *unfæger,* c. Icel. *ūfagr.* See UN-[1], FAIR[1]] – **unfairly,** *adv.* – **unfairness,** *n.*

**unfaithful** /ʌn'feɪθfəl/, *adj.* **1.** false to duty or promises; disloyal; perfidious; faithless. **2.** not upright; dishonest. **3.** not faithfully accurate or exact, as a copy or description.

**unfamiliar** /ʌnfə'mɪliə/, *adj.* **1.** not familiar; not acquainted or conversant: *be unfamiliar with a subject.* **2.** not well known; unaccustomed; unusual; strange: *a subject unfamiliar to me.* – **unfamiliarity** /ˌʌnfəˌmɪli'ærəti/, *n.* – **unfamiliarly,** *adv.*

**unfashionable** /ʌn'fæʃnəbəl/, *adj.* **1.** not in accordance with the prevailing fashion or taste. **2.** not in demand, as styles,

---

**uninvented,** *adj.*
**uninventive,** *adj.*
**uninventively,** *adv.*
**uninventiveness,** *n.*
**uninvested,** *adj.*
**uninvestigable,** *adj.*
**uninvestigated,** *adj.*
**uninvited,** *adj.*
**unjaded,** *adj.*
**unjaundiced,** *adj.*
**unjealous,** *adj.*
**unjoyful,** *adj.*
**unjudged,** *adj.*
**unjudging,** *adj.*
**unjudicial,** *adj.*
**unjustifiable,** *adj.*
**unjustifiably,** *adv.*
**unjustified,** *adj.*
**unkindled,** *adj.*
**unlabelled,** *adj.*
**unlaborious,** *adj.*
**unlaboured,** *adj.*
**unladylike,** *adj.*
**unlamented,** *adj.*
**unlaunched,** *adj.*
**unleased,** *adj.*
**unled,** *adj.*
**unlessened,** *adj.*
**unlet,** *adj.*
**unlettable,** *adj.*
**unliberated,** *adj.*
**unlicked,** *adj.*
**unlidded,** *adj.*
**unliquidated,** *adj.*
**unlistened-to,** *adj.*
**unlistening,** *adj.*
**unlit,** *adj.*
**unliterary,** *adj.*
**unlooped,** *adj.*
**unlopped,** *adj.*
**unlosable,** *adj.*
**unlost,** *adj.*
**unlovable,** *adj.*
**unloved,** *adj.*
**unloving,** *adj.*
**unlovingly,** *adv.*
**unlovingness,** *n.*
**unmaidenly,** *adj.*
**unmaintainable,** *adj.*
**unmalleability,** *n.*
**unmalleable,** *adj.*
**unmalted,** *adj.*
**unmanacle,** *v.t.*
**unmanacled,** *adj.*
**unmanfully,** *adv.*
**unmanufacturable,** *adj.*
**unmanured,** *adj.*
**unmapped,** *adj.*
**unmarred,** *adj.*
**unmarriageable,** *adj.*
**unmarried,** *adj.*
**unmartyred,** *adj.*
**unmatchable,** *adj.*
**unmated,** *adj.*
**unmathematical,** *adj.*
**unmediated,** *adj.*
**unmedical,** *adj.*
**unmeditative,** *adj.*
**unmellowed,** *adj.*
**unmelted,** *adj.*
**unmelting,** *adj.*
**unmemorable,** *adj.*
**unmentioned,** *adj.*
**unmercenary,** *adj.*
**unmerchantable,** *adj.*

objects, etc. **3.** (of people) not following the current fashion. **4.** (of people) not concerned with or interested in fashion; continuously out of fashion. – **unfashionability** /ˌʌnfæʃnəˈbɪləti/, **unfashionableness,** *n.* – **unfashionably,** *adv.*

**unfasten** /ʌnˈfasən/, *v.t.* **1.** to loose from, or as from, fastenings. **2.** to undo or open (a fastening). *–v.i.* **3.** to become unfastened.

**unfathered** /ʌnˈfaðəd/, *adj.* **1.** of unknown paternity; bastard. **2.** having no father; deprived of a father; fatherless. **3.** not ascribable to a particular author or responsible person; unauthenticated.

**unfathomable** /ʌnˈfæðəməbəl/, *adj.* **1.** not fathomable; incapable of being fathomed. **2.** impenetrable by the mind; inscrutable; incomprehensible. – **unfathomableness,** *n.* – **unfathomably,** *adv.*

**unfavourable** /ʌnˈfeɪvərəbəl, -vrəbəl/, *adj.* not favourable; not propitious; disadvantageous; adverse. Also, *U.S.,* **unfavorable.** – **unfavourableness,** *n.* – **unfavourably,** *adv.*

**unfeatured** /ʌnˈfitʃəd/, *adj.* **1.** not featured; not given special prominence. **2.** *Obs.* featureless.

**unfeeling** /ʌnˈfilɪŋ/, *adj.* **1.** not feeling; devoid of feeling; insensible or insensate. **2.** unsympathetic; callous; hard-hearted. – **unfeelingly,** *adv.* – **unfeelingness,** *n.*

**unfeigned** /ʌnˈfeɪnd/, *adj.* not feigned; sincere. – **unfeignedly** /ʌnˈfeɪnədli/, *adv.* – **unfeignedness,** *n.*

**unfeminine** /ʌnˈfɛmənən/, *adj.* **1.** (of dress, behaviour, etc.) unsuitable for a woman. **2.** exhibiting such characteristics. – **unfeminineness,** *n.*

**unfetter** /ʌnˈfɛtə/, *v.t.* **1.** to free from fetters. **2.** to free from restraint of any kind.

**unfettered** /ʌnˈfɛtəd/, *adj.* unrestrained; not hindered or restricted.

**unfinished** /ʌnˈfɪnɪʃt/, *adj.* **1.** not finished; incomplete. **2.** lacking some special finish. **3.** not sheared, as cloth.

**unfired** /ʌnˈfaɪəd/, *adj.* **1.** not having been fired, as a gun. **2.** (of pottery, etc.) not baked in a kiln. **3.** not roused or excited.

**unfit** /ʌnˈfɪt/, *adj., v.,* **-fitted, -fitting.** *–adj.* **1.** not fit; not adapted or suited; unsuitable; not deserving or good enough. **2.** unqualified or incompetent. **3.** not physically fit or in due condition. *–v.t.* **4.** to render unfit or unsuitable; disqualify. – **unfitly,** *adv.* – **unfitness,** *n.*

**unfix** /ʌnˈfɪks/, *v.t.* **1.** to render no longer fixed; unfasten; detach; loosen. **2.** to unsettle.

**unflagging** /ʌnˈflægɪŋ/, *adj.* not slackening or weakening, as from fatigue; untiring. – **unflaggingly,** *adv.*

**unflappable** /ʌnˈflæpəbəl/, *adj.* imperturbable; not easily upset. – **unflappably,** *adv.* – **unflappableness,** *n.*

**unfledged** /ʌnˈflɛdʒd/, *adj.* **1.** not fledged; without feathers sufficiently developed for flight, as a young bird. **2.** immature; undeveloped; callow.

**unfleshly** /ʌnˈflɛʃli/, *adj.* not fleshly; not carnal or corporeal; spiritual.

**unflinching** /ʌnˈflɪntʃɪŋ/, *adj.* not flinching; unshrinking: *he faced dangers with unflinching courage.* – **unflinchingly,** *adv.*

**unfold** /ʌnˈfoʊld/, *v.t.* **1.** to bring out of a folded state; spread or open out: *unfold your arms.* **2.** to develop. **3.** to spread out or lay open to view. **4.** to reveal or display. **5.** to reveal or disclose in words; set forth; explain. *–v.i.* **6.** to become unfolded; open out. **7.** to become plain, as by expansion; develop; be revealed: *his story unfolded slowly.* [ME; OE *unfealdan,* c. G *entfalten.* See UN-[2], FOLD[1]] – **unfolder,** *n.* – **unfoldment,** *n.*

**unforced** /ʌnˈfɔst/, *adj.* not compelled; produced without difficulty; spontaneous; natural. – **unforcedly** /ʌnˈfɔsədli/, *adv.* – **unforcedness,** *n.*

**unforeseen** /ʌnfɔˈsin, -fə-/, *adj.* not predicted; unexpected.

**unforgettable** /ʌnfəˈgɛtəbəl/, *adj.* not forgettable; never to be forgotten; remarkable: *scenes of unforgettable beauty.* – **unforgettably,** *adv.*

**unformed** /ʌnˈfɔmd/, *adj.* **1.** not formed; not definitely shaped; shapeless or formless. **2.** undeveloped; crude. **3.** not trained or educated, as the mind. **4.** not made or created.

**unfortunate** /ʌnˈfɔtʃənət/, *adj.* **1.** not lucky; tending to suffer mishaps. **2.** regrettable; disastrous; constituting a misfortune. **3.** unpropitious; likely to have undesirable results: *an unfortunate decision.* **4.** unsuitable; inept: *an unfortunate choice of words.* **5.** deserving of sympathy; sad. *–n.* **6.** an unfortunate person. **7.** *Obs.* a prostitute. – **unfortunately,** *adv.* – **unfortunateness,** *n.*

**unfounded** /ʌnˈfaʊndəd/, *adj.* without foundation; baseless: *unfounded suspicions.* – **unfoundedly,** *adv.* – **unfoundedness,** *n.*

**unfreeze** /ʌnˈfriz/, *v.,* **-froze, -frozen, -freezing.** *–v.t.* **1.** to thaw out; cause to thaw. **2.** to relax restrictions on (prices, incomes, credit, etc.). **3.** to lift controls from the manufacture of or dealing in (a commodity or the like). *–v.i.* **4.** to thaw.

**unfrequented** /ʌnfrəˈkwɛntəd/, *adj.* not frequented, as places; little resorted to or visited; solitary.

**unfriended** /ʌnˈfrɛndəd/, *adj.* without friends; friendless. – **unfriendedness,** *n.*

**unfriendly** /ʌnˈfrɛndli/, *adj.* **1.** not friendly; hostile; inimical; unkindly. **2.** unfavourable, as a climate. *–adv.* **3.** *Rare.* in an unfriendly manner. – **unfriendliness,** *n.*

**unfrock** /ʌnˈfrɒk/, *v.t.* to deprive of priestly status.

**unfruitful** /ʌnˈfrutfəl/, *adj.* not fruitful; unproductive; barren; fruitless. – **unfruitfully,** *adv.* – **unfruitfulness,** *n.*

---

**unmerited,** *adj.*
**unmeritedly,** *adv.*
**unmeritorious,** *adj.*
**unmethodical,** *adj.*
**unmethodically,** *adv.*
**unmilitary,** *adj.*
**unmilked,** *adj.*
**unmilled,** *adj.*
**unminded,** *adj.*
**unmined,** *adj.*
**unmingled,** *adj.*
**unministerial,** *adj.*
**unminted,** *adj.*
**unmissed,** *adj.*
**unmodern,** *adj.*
**unmodernise,** *v.t., v.i.*
**unmodernised,** *adj.*
**unmodifiable,** *adj.*
**unmodulated,** *adj.*
**unmolested,** *adj.*
**unmolestedly,** *adv.*
**unmolesting,** *adj.*
**unmortared,** *adj.*
**unmortgaged,** *adj.*
**unmortified,** *adj.*
**unmotherly,** *adj.*
**unmoulded,** *adj.*
**unmount,** *v.t., v.i.*
**unmourned,** *adj.*
**unmovable,** *adj.*
**unmovably,** *adv.*
**unmown,** *adj.*
**unmuscular,** *adj.*
**unmutilated,** *adj.*
**unnameable,** *adj.*
**unnaturalised,** *adj.*
**unneeded,** *adj.*
**unneedful,** *adj.*
**unneedfully,** *adv.*
**unnegotiable,** *adj.*
**unneighbourly,** *adj.*
**unnoted,** *adj.*
**unnoticeable,** *adj.*
**unnoticed,** *adj.*
**unnourishing,** *adj.*
**unobliterated,** *adj.*
**unobscured,** *adj.*
**unobservable,** *adj.*
**unobservant,** *adj.*
**unobserved,** *adj., adv.*
**unobstructed,** *adj.*
**unobtainable,** *adj.*
**unoffending,** *adj.*
**unoiled,** *adj.*
**unopened,** *adj.*
**unopposed,** *adj.*
**unoppressed,** *adj.*
**unoppressive,** *adj.*
**unordained,** *adj.*
**unordered,** *adj.*
**unorderly,** *adj.*
**unorganisable,** *adj.*
**unoriginal,** *adj.*
**unoriginality,** *n.*
**unoriginated,** *adj.*
**unornamented,** *adj.*
**unorthodox,** *adj.*
**unorthodoxy,** *n.*
**unostentatious,** *adj.*
**unostentatiously,** *adv.*
**unowned,** *adj.*
**unpacified,** *adj.*
**unpaid,** *adj.*
**unpainful,** *adj.*
**unpaintable,** *adj.*

**unfurl** /ʌn'fɜl/, *v.t.* **1.** to spread or shake out from a furled state, as a sail or a flag; unfold. *–v.i.* **2.** to become unfurled.

**unfurnished** /ʌn'fɜnɪʃt/, *adj.* **1.** (of rented living accommodation) not furnished by the landlord; rented without furniture. **2.** not equipped or provided (oft. fol. by *with*).

**unfussed** /ʌn'fʌst/, *adj.* calm; quiet; not easily perturbed.

**ungainly** /ʌn'geɪnli/, *adj.* **1.** not gainly; not graceful or shapely; awkward; clumsy; uncouth. *–adv.* **2.** in an awkward manner. [ME *ungaynly,* adv., from UN-[1] + obs. *gainly* handsome, agile] – **ungainliness,** *n.*

**ungenerous** /ʌn'dʒɛnərəs/, *adj.* not generous; ignoble; illiberal; mean. – **ungenerously,** *adv.* – **ungenerousness, ungenerosity** /ˌʌndʒɛnər'ɒsəti/, *n.*

**ungentle** /ʌn'dʒɛntl/, *adj.* **1.** rough or harsh, as people or their speech or actions. **2.** *Archaic or Rare.* not possessing the attributes of good birth and breeding. – **ungently,** *adv.* – **ungentleness,** *n.*

**unget-at-able** /ʌngɛt-'æt-əbəl/, *adj.* →**inaccessible.** Also, **ungetatable.** – **unget-at-ably,** *adv.*

**ungird** /ʌn'gɜd/, *v.t. Archaic.* **1.** to unfasten or take off the girdle or belt of. **2.** to loosen, or take off, by unfastening a girdle. [UN-[2] + GIRD[1]. Cf. G *entgürten*]

**ungirt** /ʌn'gɜt/, *adj. Archaic.* **1.** having a girdle loosened or removed. **2.** not taut or tightened for use; loose.

**unglue** /ʌn'glu/, *v.t.,* **-glued, -gluing. 1.** to separate or open (something fastened with, or as with, glue). **2.** to separate; dissolve.

**ungodly** /ʌn'gɒdli/, *adj.* **1.** not godly; not conforming to God's laws; irreligious; impious; sinful. **2.** wicked. **3.** *Colloq.* dreadful; outrageous. *–n.* **4. the ungodly,** wicked people. – **ungodlily,** *adv.* – **ungodliness,** *n.*

**ungotten** /ʌn'gɒtn/, *adj.* **1.** not obtained or gained. **2.** *Obs.* not begotten.

**ungovernable** /ʌn'gʌvənəbəl/, *adj.* that cannot be governed, ruled, or restrained; uncontrollable. – **ungovernableness,** *n.* – **ungovernably,** *adv.*

**ungraceful** /ʌn'greɪsfəl/, *adj.* not graceful; lacking grace or elegance; clumsy; awkward. – **ungracefully,** *adv.* – **ungracefulness,** *n.*

**ungracious** /ʌn'greɪʃəs/, *adj.* **1.** not gracious; lacking in gracious courtesy or affability. **2.** unacceptable; unwelcome. **3.** *Obs.* ungraceful; unpleasing. – **ungraciously,** *adv.* – **ungraciousness,** *n.*

**ungrammatical** /ʌngrə'mætɪkəl/, *adj.* **1.** not conforming to the rules of grammar; grammatically clumsy or wrong. **2.** not in accordance with a particular method or set of rules. **3.** not according to native usage, as the language of a foreigner. – **ungrammatically,** *adv.*

**ungrateful** /ʌn'greɪtfəl/, *adj.* **1.** not grateful; not feeling or displaying gratitude; giving no return or recompense. **2.** unpleasant; disagreeable. **3.** (of land) responding badly to cultivation. **4.** thankless; not repaying one's efforts. – **ungratefully,** *adv.* – **ungratefulness,** *n.*

**ungrounded** /ʌn'graʊndəd/, *adj.* baseless; without grounds or justification. – **ungroundedly,** *adv.* – **ungroundedness,** *n.*

**ungrudging** /ʌn'grʌdʒɪŋ/, *adj.* not grudging; willing; hearty; liberal. – **ungrudgingly,** *adv.*

**ungual** /'ʌŋgwəl/, *adj.* of or pertaining to, bearing, or shaped like a nail, claw, or hoof. [L *unguis* nail, claw + -AL[1]]

**unguarded** /ʌn'gadəd/, *adj.* **1.** not guarded; unprotected; undefended. **2.** incautious; imprudent; characterised by carelessness or indiscretion: *a confession made in an unguarded moment.* **3.** open; guileless; candid. **4.** *Chess, Cards, etc.* open to attack by an opponent. **5.** having no guard, screen, or the like. – **unguardedly,** *adv.* – **unguardedness,** *n.*

**unguent** /'ʌŋgwənt/, *n.* any soft preparation or salve, usu. of butter-like consistency, applied to sores, etc.; an ointment. [ME, from L *unguentum*] – **unguentary,** *adj.*

**unguessed** /ʌn'gɛst/, *adj.* **1.** not known or solved by guessing. **2.** unexpected (oft. fol. by *at*).

**unguiculate** /ʌŋ'gwɪkjələt, -leɪt/, *adj.* Also, **unguiculated. 1.** bearing or resembling a nail or claw. **2.** *Zool.* having nails or claws, as distinguished from hoofs. **3.** *Bot.* having a clawlike base, as certain petals. *–n.* **4.** an unguiculate animal. [NL *unguiculātus,* from L *unguiculus* fingernail, diminutive of *unguis* claw]

**unguinous** /'ʌŋgwənəs/, *adj.* consisting of or resembling fat or oil; oily. [L *unguinōsus* oily]

**unguis** /'ʌŋgwəs/, *n., pl.* **-gues** /-gwiz/. **1.** a nail, claw, or hoof. **2.** *Bot.* the clawlike base of certain petals. [L]

**ungula** /'ʌŋgjələ/, *n., pl.* **-lae** /-li/. **1.** *Geom.* a part cut off from a cylinder, cone, or the like, by a plane oblique to the base. **2.** *Zool.* a hoof. [L]

**ungular** /'ʌŋgjələ/, *adj.* pertaining to or of the nature of an ungula; ungual.

**ungulate** /'ʌŋgjələt, -leɪt/, *adj.* **1.** having hoofs. **2.** belonging or pertaining to the Ungulata, a group sometimes set up, though without phylogenetic justification, in order to classify all hoofed mammals together in one category. **3.** hoof-like. *–n.* **4.** a hoofed mammal. [L *ungulātus* having claws]

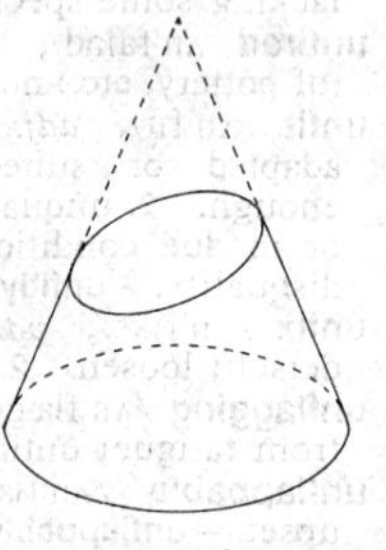
ungula (def. 1)

**unguligrade** /'ʌŋgjələgreɪd/, *adj. Zool.*

---

**unpainted,** *adj.*
**unpaired,** *adj.*
**unpalliated,** *adj.*
**unpampered,** *adj.*
**unpanelled,** *adj.*
**unpapered,** *adj.*
**unparallel,** *adj.*
**unparalysed,** *adj.*
**unpardonable,** *adj.*
**unpardonably,** *adv.*
**unpardoned,** *adj.*
**unpardoning,** *adj.*
**unparticipating,** *adj.*
**unpassable,** *adj.*
**unpassed,** *adj.*
**unpassionate,** *adj.*
**unpassionately,** *adv.*
**unpatented,** *adj.*
**unpathed,** *adj.*
**unpatriotic,** *adj.*
**unpatriotically,** *adv.*
**unpatronised,** *adj.*
**unpatterned,** *adj.*
**unpausing,** *adj.*
**unpaved,** *adj.*
**unpawned,** *adj.*
**unpayable,** *adj.*
**unpaying,** *adj.*
**unpeaceable,** *adj.*
**unpedantic,** *adj.*
**unpeeled,** *adj.*
**unpenetrated,** *adj.*
**unpensioned,** *adj.*
**unpeppered,** *adj.*
**unperceivable,** *adj.*
**unperceived,** *adj.*
**unperceptive,** *adj.*
**unperfected,** *adj.*
**unperforated,** *adj.*
**unperformed,** *adj.*
**unperfumed,** *adj.*
**unperishable,** *adj.*
**unpersuadable,** *adj.*
**unpersuaded,** *adj.*
**unpersuasive,** *adj.*
**unpersuasively,** *adv.*
**unperturbed,** *adj.*
**unperturbedly,** *adv.*
**unperverted,** *adj.*
**unphilosophical,** *adj.*
**unphilosophically,** *adv.*
**unpicked,** *adj.*
**unpierced,** *adj.*
**unpiloted,** *adj.*
**unpitiable,** *adj.*
**unpitied,** *adj.*
**unpitying,** *adj.*
**unpityingly,** *adv.*
**unplanned,** *adj.*
**unplanted,** *adj.*
**unplastered,** *adj.*
**unplayable,** *adj.*
**unplayed,** *adj.*
**unpleasable,** *adj.*
**unpleased,** *adj.*
**unpleasingly,** *adv.*
**unpliable,** *adj.*
**unpliancy,** *n.*
**unpliant,** *adj.*
**unploughed,** *adj.*
**unplucked,** *adj.*
**unplundered,** *adj.*
**unpoetic,** *adj.*
**unpoetically,** *adv.*
**unpointed,** *adj.*

---

walking on hoofs. [*unguli-* (combining form representing UNGULA) + -GRADE]

**unhair** /ʌn'hɛə/, *v.t.* **1.** *Tanning.* to free from hair. *–v.i.* **2.** to become free of hair.

**unhallowed** /ʌn'hæloʊd/, *adj.* **1.** not hallowed or consecrated. **2.** profane; impious or wicked.

**unhand** /ʌn'hænd/, *v.t. Archaic.* to take the hand or hands from; release from a grasp; let go.

**unhandsome** /ʌn'hænsəm/, *adj.* **1.** lacking good looks; plain or ugly. **2.** ungracious; discourteous; unseemly; mean. **3.** ungenerous; illiberal. – **unhandsomely,** *adv.* – **unhandsomeness,** *n.*

**unhandy** /ʌn'hændi/, *adj.* **1.** not handy; not easy to handle or manage, as things. **2.** not skilful in using the hands, as persons. – **unhandily,** *adv.* – **unhandiness,** *n.*

**unhanged** /ʌn'hæŋd/, *adj.* not yet executed by hanging.

**unhappy** /ʌn'hæpi/, *adj.*, **-ier, -iest.** **1.** sad, miserable, or wretched. **2.** unfortunate; unlucky. **3.** unfavourable; inauspicious. **4.** infelicitous: *an unhappy remark.* **5.** *Obs.* of wretched character; objectionable. – **unhappily,** *adv.* – **unhappiness,** *n.*

**unharness** /ʌn'hanəs/, *v.t.* **1.** to strip of harness; free (a horse, etc.) from harness or gear. **2.** to divest of armour.

**unharnessed** /ʌn'hanəst/, *adj.* **1.** (of a horse, etc.) divested of harness. **2.** not under control for industrial exploitation, as a river.

**unhasp** /ʌn'hæsp, -'hasp/, *v.t.* to loose the hasp of.

**unhealthy** /ʌn'hɛlθi/, *adj.*, **-healthier, -healthiest.** **1.** not healthy; not possessing health; not in a healthy or sound condition. **2.** characteristic of or resulting from bad health. **3.** hurtful to health; unwholesome. **4.** morally harmful; noxious. **5.** morbid: *an unhealthy interest in death.* **6.** *Colloq.* dangerous. – **unhealthily,** *adv.* – **unhealthiness,** *n.*

**unheard** /ʌn'hɜd/, *adj.* **1.** not heard; not perceived by the ear. **2.** not given a hearing or audience. **3.** not heard of; unknown.

**unheard-of** /ʌn'hɜd-ɒv/, *adj.* **1.** that was never heard of; unknown. **2.** such as was never known before; unprecedented.

**unheeding** /ʌn'hidɪŋ/, *adj.* not attentive or watchful; unobservant (sometimes fol. by *of*). – **unheedingly,** *adv.*

**unhinge** /ʌn'hɪndʒ/, *v.t.*, **-hinged, -hinging.** **1.** to take (a door, etc.) off the hinges. **2.** to unbalance (the mind, etc.). **3.** to remove the hinges from. **4.** to detach or separate from something. **5.** to deprive of fixity or stability; throw into confusion or disorder. **6.** to upset or discompose (a person). **7.** to unsettle (opinions, etc.).

**unhistorical** /ʌnhɪs'tɒrɪkəl/, *adj.* **1.** not in accordance with historical principles or the accepted methods of historians. **2.** not in history; not having occurred. – **unhistorically,** *adv.*

**unhitch** /ʌn'hɪtʃ/, *v.t.* to free from being hitched or fastened; unfasten.

**unholy** /ʌn'hoʊli/, *adj.*, **-lier, -liest.** **1.** not holy; not sacred or hallowed. **2.** impious; sinful; wicked. **3.** *Colloq.* dreadful; outrageous. [ME; OE *unhālig*, c. D *onheilig*, Icel. *ūheilagr.* See UN-[1], HOLY] – **unholily,** *adv.* – **unholiness,** *n.*

**unhood** /ʌn'hʊd/, *v.t.* to divest of a hood, esp. that of a hawk.

**unhook** /ʌn'hʊk/, *v.t.* **1.** to loose from a hook. **2.** to open or undo by loosening a hook or hooks. *–v.i.* **3.** to become unhooked.

**unhoped-for** /ʌn'hoʊpt-fɔ/, *adj.* not hoped or looked for; unexpected.

**unhorse** /ʌn'hɔs/, *v.t.*, **-horsed, -horsing.** **1.** to throw from a horse, as in battle. **2.** to cause to fall from the saddle. **3.** to dislodge; overthrow.

**unhouse** /ʌn'haʊz/, *v.t.*, **-housed, -housing.** to drive from a house or habitation; deprive of shelter.

**unhung** /ʌn'hʌŋ/, *adj.* (of a picture) not yet publicly exhibited.

**unhusk** /ʌn'hʌsk/, *v.t.* to free from, or as from, a husk.

**uni** /'juni/, *n. Colloq.* a university.

**uni-,** a word element meaning 'one', 'single', as in *unisexual.* [L, combining form of *ūnus* one]

**uni.,** university.

**Uniat** /'juniæt/, *n.* a member of any of various communities of Greek and other Eastern Christians which acknowledge the supremacy of the pope and are in communion with the Church of Rome, but retain their own liturgy, rites, discipline, etc. Also, **Uniate** /'junieɪt/. [Russ.]

**uniaxial** /juni'æksiəl/, *adj.* **1.** having one axis. **2.** (of a crystal) having one direction in which no double refraction occurs. **3.** (of a plant) having a primary stem which does not branch. **4.** (of certain red seaweeds) having a structure in which the main axis is derived from a single filament of cells.

**unicameral** /juni'kæmərəl/, *adj.* having, characterised by, or consisting of a single chamber, as a legislative assembly. – **unicameralism,** *n.* – **unicameralist,** *n.*

**UNICEF** /'junisɛf/, the United Nations International Children's Emergency Fund.

**unicellular** /juni'sɛljələ/, *adj.* pertaining to or consisting of a single cell.

**unicity** /ju'nɪsəti/, *n.* **1.** oneness; the fact of being single. **2.** the fact or state of being unique.

**unicolour** /'juni,kʌlə/, *adj. Zool.* having only one colour.

**unicorn** /'junəkɔn/, *n.* **1.** a mythological animal with a single

---

**unpoised,** *adj.*
**unpolarised,** *adj.*
**unpoliced,** *adj.*
**unpolishable,** *adj.*
**unpolluted,** *adj.*
**unpopulous,** *adj.*
**unportrayable,** *adj.*
**unpossessed,** *adj.*
**unpostponable,** *adj.*
**unpraised,** *adj.*
**unpraiseworthy,** *adj.*
**unpredictable,** *adj.*
**unpreoccupied,** *adj.*
**unprepared,** *adj.*
**unpreparedly,** *adv.*
**unprepossessing,** *adj.*
**unprevailing,** *adj.*
**unpreventable,** *adj.*
**unpreventably,** *adv.*
**unpriestly,** *adj., adv.*
**unprivileged,** *adj.*
**unprized,** *adj.*
**unproclaimed,** *adj.*
**unprocurable,** *adj.*
**unprogressive,** *adj.*
**unprogressively,** *adv.*
**unprolific,** *adj.*
**unprompted,** *adj.*
**unpronounceable,** *adj.*
**unpropitious,** *adj.*
**unpropitiously,** *adv.*
**unprosperous,** *adj.*
**unprosperously,** *adv.*
**unprotected,** *adj.*
**unprotectedness,** *n.*
**unprotesting,** *adj.*
**unprovable,** *adj.*
**unproved,** *adj.*
**unproven,** *adj.*
**unprovocative,** *adj.*
**unprovoked,** *adj.*
**unpruned,** *adj.*
**unpublishable,** *adj.*
**unpublished,** *adj.*
**unpunctual,** *adj.*
**unpunctuality,** *n.*
**unpunctuated,** *adj.*
**unpuncturable,** *adj.*
**unpunishable,** *adj.*
**unpunishably,** *adv.*
**unpunished,** *adj.*
**unpurchaseable,** *adj.*
**unpurchased,** *adj.*
**unpurged,** *adj.*
**unpurified,** *adj.*
**unpursued,** *adj.*
**unquailing,** *adj.*
**unquailingly,** *adv.*
**unqualifiable,** *adj.*
**unquantified,** *adj.*
**unquarried,** *adj.*
**unqueenly,** *adj.*
**unquenchable,** *adj.*
**unquenchably,** *adv.*
**unquenched,** *adj.*
**unquestioning,** *adj.*
**unquickened,** *adj.*
**unquotability,** *n.*
**unquotable,** *adj.*
**unraised,** *adj.*
**unraked,** *adj.*
**unransacked,** *adj.*
**unransomed,** *adj.*
**unrateable,** *adj.*
**unrated,** *adj.*

long horn, said to elude every captor save a virgin. **2.** a conventional and heraldic representation of this animal, in the form of a horse with a lion's tail and with a long, straight, and spirally twisted horn. **3.** (in the Authorised Version of the Bible, Deut. 33:17, and elsewhere) a two-horned animal now usu. identified with the rhinoceros or the aurochs. **4.** (formerly) a carriage drawn by three horses, two abreast behind one leader. **5.** the team of horses. **6.** →**narwhal.** **7.** *Obs.* the rhinoceros. *–adj.* **8.** having one horn. [ME, from L *ūnicornis* having one horn]

unicorn

**unicostate** /juni'kɒsteɪt/, *adj.* having only one costa, rib, or ridge.

**unicum** /'junəkəm/, *n. Rare.* a unique example or thing.

**unicycle** /'juni,saɪkəl/, *n.* a vehicle with only one wheel, esp. a pedal-driven one used by acrobats.

**unideal** /ʌnaɪ'dɪəl/, *adj.* **1.** not having ideals, as a person. **2.** not marked by idealism. **3.** not ideal; not perfect. – **unidealism,** *n.*

unicycle

**unidirectional** /,junidə'rɛkʃənəl/, *adj.* having, or moving in, only one direction.

**unifiable** /'junəfaɪəbəl/, *adj.* that may be unified.

**unific** /ju'nɪfɪk/, *adj.* making one; forming unity; unifying.

**unification** /junəfə'keɪʃən/, *n.* **1.** the act or process of unifying. **2.** the state of being unified.

**unified field theory,** *n.* any theory which is capable of describing the electromagnetic field and the gravitational field in one set of equations.

**unifilar** /juni'faɪlə/, *adj.* having or involving only one thread, wire, or the like.

**uniflorous** /juni'flɔrəs/, *adj.* having or bearing one flower only.

**unifoliate** /juni'fouliət, -eɪt/, *adj.* **1.** one-leafed. **2.** →**unifoliolate.**

**unifoliolate** /,juni'fouliə,leɪt/, *adj.* **1.** compound in structure yet having only one leaflet, as the leaf of the orange. **2.** bearing such leaves, as a plant.

**uniform** /'junəfɔm/, *adj.* **1.** having one form; having always the same form or character; unvarying. **2.** without diversity in appearance, colour, etc.; not discontinuous; unbroken. **3.** regular; even: *a uniform pace.* **4.** consistent in action, opinion, etc., as a person, or as action, etc.; being the same in all places or in all parts of a country: *a uniform divorce law.* **5.** agreeing with one another in form, character, appearance, etc.; alike; of the same form, character, etc., with another or others. *–n.* **6.** a distinctive dress of uniform style, materials, and colour worn by and identifying all the members of a group or organisation, esp. a military body, school, etc. **7.** a single suit of such dress. *–v.t.* **8.** to clothe or furnish with or as with a uniform. **9.** to make uniform. [L *ūniformis*] – **uniformly,** *adv.* – **uniformness,** *n.*

unifoliate leaf

**uniformalise** /junə'fɔməlaɪz/, *v.t.,* **-lised, -lising.** *Rare.* to bring into uniformity. Also, **uniformalize.**

**uniformed** /'junəfɔmd/, *adj.* wearing a uniform.

**uniformitarian** /,junəfɔmə'tɛəriən/, *adj.* **1.** pertaining to uniformity or a doctrine of uniformity, esp. in geological theory. **2.** *Geol.* pertaining to the thesis that early geological processes are not different from those observed now. *–n.* **3.** one who adheres to a doctrine of uniformity. – **uniformitarianism,** *n.*

**uniformity** /junə'fɔməti/, *n., pl.* **-ties.** **1.** the state or character of being uniform; sameness of form or character throughout; absence of variation or diversity. **2.** conformity among several things to each other or to a standard. **3.** regularity or evenness; consistency or agreement of structure or composition. **4.** wearisome sameness; monotony. **5.** conformity of opinions, attitudes, or the like, esp. in religion. **6.** something uniform; an extent or expanse of a uniform character.

**uniform system** /'junəfɔm ,sɪstəm/, *n.* a system for marking the stops on a camera lens in which each stop corresponds to doubling or halving the exposure. On this scale unity is equal to an aperture of f4 on the f number scale. *Abbrev.:* u.s.

**unify** /'junəfaɪ/, *v.t.,* **-fied, -fying.** to form into one; make a unit of; reduce to unity. [ML *ūnificāre,* from L *ūni-* UNI- + *-ficāre* -FY] – **unifier,** *n.*

**unigeniture** /juni'dʒɛnətʃə/, *n.* (of Christ) the state or fact of being the only begotten.

**unijugate** /juni'dʒugət, -geɪt/, *adj.* (of a pinnate leaf) having a single pair of leaflets. [L *ūnijugus* having one yoke + -ATE[1]]

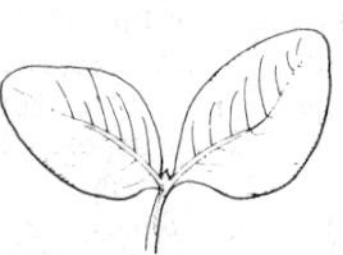
unijugate leaf

**unratified,** *adj.*
**unrationed,** *adj.*
**unravished,** *adj.*
**unrazored,** *adj.*
**unreachable,** *adj.*
**unrealism,** *n.*
**unrealisable,** *adj.*
**unrealised,** *adj.*
**unreaped,** *adj.*
**unrebated,** *adj.*
**unrebuked,** *adj.*
**unrebutted,** *adj.*
**unrecallable,** *adj.*
**unrecalled,** *adj.*
**unreceptive,** *adj.*
**unreceptively,** *adv.*
**unreceptivity,** *n.*
**unreciprocated,** *adj.*
**unreckonable,** *adj.*
**unreclaimed,** *adj.*
**unrecognition,** *n.*
**unrecognisable,** *adj.*
**unrecognisably,** *adv.*
**unrecognising,** *adj.*
**unrecommendable,** *adj.*
**unrecompensed,** *adj.*
**unreconciled,** *adj.*
**unreconstructed,** *adj.*
**unrecorded,** *adj.*
**unrectified,** *adj.*
**unredeemable,** *adj.*
**unredressed,** *adj.*
**unreduced,** *adj.*
**unreducible,** *adj.*
**unreflective,** *adj.*
**unreformable,** *adj.*
**unrefracted,** *adj.*
**unrefreshed,** *adj.*
**unrefreshing,** *adj.*
**unrefreshingly,** *adv.*
**unrefusable,** *adj.*
**unrefuted,** *adj.*
**unregarded,** *adj.*
**unregarding,** *adj.*
**unregistered,** *adj.*
**unregretted,** *adj.*
**unregulated,** *adj.*
**unrehearsed,** *adj.*
**unreined,** *adj.*
**unrelaxed,** *adj.*
**unrelaxing,** *adj.*
**unrelished,** *adj.*
**unremembered,** *adj.*
**unremembering,** *adj.*
**unremittent,** *adj.*
**unremittently,** *adv.*
**unremorseful,** *adj.*
**unremoved,** *adj.*
**unremunerative,** *adj.*
**unremunerativeness,** *n.*
**unrenderable,** *adj.*
**unrenewable,** *adj.*
**unrepaid,** *adj.*
**unrepair,** *n.*
**unrepairable,** *adj.*
**unrepayable,** *adj.*
**unrepelled,** *adj.*
**unrepentance,** *n.*
**unrepentant,** *adj.*
**unrepentantly,** *adv.*
**unrepented,** *adj.*
**unrepenting,** *adj.*
**unreplaceable,** *adj.*
**unreportable,** *adj.*
**unreported,** *adj.*

**unijunction transistor** /ˌjunidʒʌŋkʃən trænˈzɪstə/, *n. Electronics.* a transistor which becomes conducting when the input voltage reaches a certain fraction of the steady voltage across the device, used for oscillator circuits, timing circuits, voltage and current sensing circuits.

**unilabiate** /juniˈlæbiət, -eɪt/, *adj.* one-lipped, as a corolla.

**unilateral** /juniˈlætərəl, -ˈlætrəl, junə-/, *adj.* **1.** pertaining to, occurring on, or affecting one side only. **2.** leaning or tending to one side. **3.** affecting one side, party, or person only. **4.** undertaken or performed by one side only: *unilateral disarmament.* **5.** concerned with or considering but one side of a matter or question; one-sided. **6.** *Law.* (of contracts and obligations) binding one party only; more generally, affecting one party only. **7.** *Bot.* having all the parts disposed on one side of an axis, as an inflorescence. **8.** *Sociol.* indicating line of descent through parents of one sex only. **9.** *Phonet.* produced on one side of the tongue, as *unilateral l.* – **unilaterality** /ˌjunilætəˈræləti/, *n.* – **unilaterally,** *adv.*

**unilingual** /juniˈlɪŋgwəl/, *adj.* knowing, using, concerning, or in only one language.

**unilluminating** /ʌnəˈlumənеɪtɪŋ, -ˈlju-/, *adj.* **1.** failing to clarify or inform. **2.** failing to shed light.

**unilobed** /ˈjunilоʊbd/, *adj.* having, or consisting of, a single lobe.

**unilocular** /juniˈlɒkjələ/, *adj. Bot., Zool.* having, or consisting of, but one loculus, chamber, or cell.

**unimaginable** /ʌnəˈmædʒənəbəl/, *adj.* **1.** impossible to conceive or comprehend. **2.** remarkable, tremendous, or extraordinary. – **unimaginableness,** *n.* – **unimaginably,** *adv.*

**unimpassioned** /ʌnɪmˈpæʃənd/, *adj.* free of strong emotion; unmoved; uninfluenced by emotion.

**unimpeachable** /ʌnɪmˈpitʃəbəl/, *adj.* **1.** that cannot be doubted; beyond question. **2.** irreproachable; blameless. – **unimpeachability** /ˌʌnɪmpitʃəˈbɪləti/, *n.* – **unimpeachably,** *adv.*

**unimportant** /ʌnɪmˈpɔtnt/, *adj.* lacking importance; insignificant. – **unimportance,** *n.*

**unimposing** /ʌnɪmˈpoʊzɪŋ/, *adj.* not imposing or impressive.

**unimproved** /ʌnɪmˈpruvd/, *adj.* **1.** not made better, more useful, more efficient, etc. **2.** (of land) **a.** not built upon or developed. **b.** not cultivated; left in the wild state. **3.** not bred for better quality or productiveness, as crops, domestic animals, etc. **4.** not better, as health.

**unincorporated** /ʌnɪnˈkɔpəreɪtəd/, *adj.* of or pertaining to land which has not been nominated as part of a local government area.

**unincorporated association** /– əsoʊsiˈeɪʃən/, *n.* a company formed for other than business purposes in which each member retains individual liability, even though they are together acting as a group. Also, **unincorporated company.**

**uninformed** /ʌnɪnˈfɔmd/, *adj.* **1.** lacking knowledge in some or any respect; uneducated. **2.** lacking knowledge or information (as to some matter).

**uninhibited** /ʌnɪnˈhɪbətəd/, *adj.* **1.** not restrained by social conventions; informal; free. **2.** not impeded or restricted by inhibitions.

**uninspired** /ʌnɪnˈspaɪəd/, *adj.* dull; lacking inspiration or spiritedness; unimaginative.

**uninspiring** /ʌnɪnˈspaɪərɪŋ/, *adj.* not stimulating or exciting; dreary.

**unintelligent** /ʌnɪnˈtɛlədʒənt/, *adj.* **1.** deficient in intelligence; dull or stupid. **2.** marked by lack of intelligence. **3.** not endowed with intelligence: *plants are an unintelligent form of life.* – **unintelligence,** *n.* – **unintelligently,** *adv.*

**unintelligible** /ʌnɪnˈtɛlədʒəbəl/, *adj.* not intelligible; not capable of being understood. – **unintelligibility** /ˌʌnɪnˌtɛlədʒəˈbɪləti/, **unintelligibleness,** *n.* – **unintelligibly,** *adv.*

**unintentional** /ʌnɪnˈtɛnʃənəl/, *adj.* not intentional; not acting with intention; not done purposely, or not designed. – **unintentionality** /ˌʌnɪnˌtɛnʃəˈnæləti/, *n.* – **unintentionally,** *adv.*

**uninterested** /ʌnˈɪntrəstəd/, *adj.* **1.** having or showing no feeling of interest; indifferent. **2.** not personally concerned in something. **3.** *Colloq.* disinterested. – **uninterestedly,** *adv.* – **uninterestedness,** *n.*

**uninterrupted** /ˌʌnɪntəˈrʌptəd/, *adj.* **1.** unbroken; continuous. **2.** unified; having no divisions between the parts. –*adv.* **3.** without interruption. – **uninterruptedly,** *adv.* – **uninterruptedness,** *n.*

**uninucleate** /juniˈnjukliət/, *adj.* (of a cell) containing only one nucleus.

**union** /ˈjunjən/, *n.* **1.** the act of uniting two or more things into one. **2.** the state of being so united; conjunction; combination. **3.** something formed by uniting two or more things; a combination. **4.** a number of persons, societies, states, or the like, joined together or associated for some common purpose. **5.** the uniting of persons, parties, etc., in general agreement. **6.** a uniting of states or nations into one political body, as that of the American colonies at the time of the War of American Independence. **7.** a device emblematic of union, used in a flag or ensign, sometimes occupying the upper corner next to the staff, or sometimes occupying the entire field. **8.** a uniting or being united in marriage, or some similar relationship. **9.** a trade union. **10.** (*cap.*) *Rugby Union.* **a.** an organisation of Rugby clubs acting as a law-making body for the clubs. **b.** the game, as distinct

---

**unrepresentative,** *adj.*
**unrepresented,** *adj.*
**unrepressed,** *adj.*
**unreproachful,** *adj.*
**unreproducible,** *adj.*
**unreproved,** *adj.*
**unresented,** *adj.*
**unresentful,** *adj.*
**unresentfully,** *adv.*
**unresentfulness,** *n.*
**unresenting,** *adj.*
**unresisting,** *adj.*
**unresistingly,** *adv.*
**unresolvable,** *adj.*
**unrespectable,** *adj.*
**unrespected,** *adj.*
**unresponsive,** *adj.*
**unresponsively,** *adv.*
**unresponsiveness,** *n.*
**unrestful,** *adj.*
**unrestored,** *adj.*
**unrestrainable,** *adj.*
**unrestrained,** *adj.*
**unrestrainedly,** *adv.*
**unrestricted,** *adj.*
**unrestrictedly,** *adv.*
**unretentive,** *adj.*
**unretracted,** *adj.*
**unreturnable,** *adj.*
**unreturning,** *adj.*
**unrevealable,** *adj.*
**unrevealing,** *adj.*
**unrevenged,** *adj.*
**unreverent,** *adj.*
**unreversed,** *adj.*
**unreviewed,** *adj.*
**unrevised,** *adj.*
**unrevoked,** *adj.*
**unrewarding,** *adj.*
**unrhetorical,** *adj.*
**unridden,** *adj.*
**unrideable,** *adj.*
**unrifled,** *adj.*
**unrisen,** *adj.*
**unrivet,** *v.t.*
**unromantic,** *adj.*
**unromantically,** *adv.*
**unromanticised,** *adj.*
**unrope,** *adj.*
**unrouged,** *adj.*
**unroused,** *adj.*
**unroyal,** *adj.*
**unroyally,** *adv.*
**unrubbed,** *adj.*
**unrumpled,** *adj.*
**unsaintliness,** *n.*
**unsaintly,** *adj.*
**unsalaried,** *adj.*
**unsaleable,** *adj.*
**unsalted,** *adj.*
**unsanctified,** *adj.*
**unsanctioned,** *adj.*
**unsanitary,** *adj.*
**unsatisfiable,** *adj.*
**unsatisfied,** *adj.*
**unsatisfying,** *adj.*
**unsayable,** *adj.*
**unscaleable,** *adj.*
**unscaled,** *adj.*
**unscarred,** *adj.*
**unscored,** *adj.*
**unscrutinised,** *adj.*
**unsearched,** *adj.*
**unseaworthiness,** *n.*
**unseaworthy,** *adj.*

from (Rugby) League. **11.** a union house. **12.** any of various contrivances for connecting parts of machinery, etc., esp. a fitting composed of three parts used to connect the ends of two pipes, neither of which can be turned. **13.** a fabric made of two kinds of yarn, of which one is usu. cotton. **14.** (*cap.*) a club offering dining and recreational facilities for the members of certain universities. [late ME, from L *ūnio*]

**union card** /'– kad/, *n.* a card identifying one as a member of a trade union.

**union catalogue** /– 'kætəlɒg/, *n.* a library catalogue listing publications held by cooperating institutions.

**Union Flag** /junjən 'flæg/, *n.* →**Union Jack.**

**unionise** /'junjənaɪz/, *v.*, **-nised, -nising.** *–v.t.* **1.** to organise into a trade union; bring into or incorporate in a trade union. **2.** to subject to the rules of a trade union. **3.** to enforce recognition of trade unions (on an industry, business, etc.). Also, **unionize.** – **unionisation** /ˌjunjənaɪ'zeɪʃən/, *n.*

**un-ionised** /ʌn-'aɪənaɪzd/, *adj. Chem.* not ionised. Also, **un-ionized.**

**unionism** /'junjənɪzəm/, *n.* **1.** the principle of union, esp. trade unionism. **2.** advocacy of this.

**unionist** /'junjənəst/, *n.* **1.** one who promotes or advocates union. **2.** →**trade unionist.** *–adj.* **3.** of or pertaining to unionism, esp. trade unionism, or union. – **unionistic,** *adj.*

**Union Jack** /junjən 'dʒæk/, *n.* **1.** Also, **Union Flag.** the national flag of the United Kingdom, symbolising the union of its component countries. **2.** its design, used as a national symbol and for decoration. **3.** *Naut.* this flag, flown as the jack of a ship. **4.** *U.S.* a flag flown by the U.S. navy which is the same in design as the canton of the U.S. national flag, i.e., white stars on a blue field. **5.** →**double drummer.**

**Union of Soviet Socialist Republics,** *n.* official name of the **Soviet Union.** *Abbrev.:* U.S.S.R.

**uniparous** /ju'nɪpərəs/, *adj.* producing only one at a birth. [NL *ūniparus.* See UNI-, -PAROUS]

**unipartite** /juni'pataɪt/, *adj.* not divided; consisting of or concerning a single part.

**uniped** /'junipɛd/, *adj.* **1.** having a single foot; one-footed; one-legged. *–n.* **2.** a person, animal, or thing having only one foot or leg.

**unipersonal** /juni'pɜsənəl/, *adj.* **1.** consisting of or existing as but one person. **2.** *Gram.* used in only one person, esp. the third person singular, as certain verbs.

**unipetalous** /uni'pɛtələs/, *adj. Bot.* having only one petal.

**uniplanar** /juni'pleɪnə/, *adj.* lying or taking place in one plane: *uniplanar motion.*

**unipolar** /juni'poʊlə/, *adj.* **1.** *Physics.* having or pertaining to one pole only. **2.** *Anat.* denoting a nerve cell in spinal and cranial ganglia in which the incoming and outgoing processes fuse outside the cell body. – **unipolarity** /ˌjunipoʊ'lærəti/, *n.*

**unique** /ju'nik/, *adj.* **1.** of which there is only one; sole. **2.** having no like or equal; standing alone in comparison with others; unequalled. **3.** remarkable, rare or unusual: *a unique experience.* [F, from L *ūnicus;* replacing earlier *unic,* from L *ūnicus*] – **uniquely,** *adv.* – **uniqueness,** *n.*

**uniseptate** /juni'sɛpteɪt/, *adj.* having only one septum or partition, as a silicula.

**uniseriate** /juni'sɛriət/, *adj. Bot.* having, or consisting of, a single row or layer of cells. – **uniseriately,** *adv.*

**unisex** /'junisɛks/, *adj.* of a style of dress, etc., which does not adhere to the traditional differentiations between the sexes.

**unisexer** /'junisɛksə/, *n.* an adherent of the unisex fashion.

**unisexual** /juni'sɛkʃuəl/, *adj.* **1.** of or pertaining to one sex only. **2.** having only male or female organs in one individual, as an animal or a flower. – **unisexuality** /ˌjuniˌsɛkʃu'æləti/, *n.* – **unisexually,** *adv.*

**unison** /'junəsən/, *n.* **1.** coincidence in pitch of two or more notes, voices, etc. **2.** the theoretical interval between any note and a note of exactly the same pitch; a prime. **3.** a sounding together at the same pitch or in octaves, as of different voices or instruments performing the same part. **4.** a sounding together in octaves, esp. of male and female voices or of higher and lower instruments of the same class. **5.** accord or agreement. **6. in unison,** in agreement, concordant; in perfect accord; simultaneously. [LL *ūnisonus* having one sound, from L *ūni-* UNI- + *-sonus* sounding]

**unisonous** /ju'nɪsənəs/, *adj.* according in sound or pitch; being in unison. Also, **unisonal, unisonant.** [LL *ūnisonus*]

**unissued** /ʌn'ɪʃud/, *adj.* not issued, as esp. shares, stock, or the like.

**unit** /'junət/, *n.* **1.** a single thing or person; any group of things or persons regarded as an individual. **2.** one of the individuals or groups making up a whole, or into which a whole may be analysed. **3.** any magnitude regarded as an independent whole; a single, undivided entity. **4.** any specified amount of a quantity, as of length, volume, force, momentum, time, by comparison with which any other quantity of the same kind is measured or estimated. **5.** *Maths.* the lowest positive integer; one. **6.** *Educ.* a quantity of educational instruction, determined usu. by a number of hours of classroom or laboratory work and by the passing of an examination: *he has three units towards his degree.* **7.** *Mil.* **a.** an organised body of soldiers of any size, which is a subdivision of a larger body. **b.** a vessel, vehicle, or large

---

**unseconded,** *adj.*
**unseconded,** *adj.*
**unsectarian,** *adj.*
**unsectarianism,** *n.*
**unsecular,** *adj.*
**unsecularise,** *v.t.*
**unseduced,** *adj.*
**unseeable,** *adj.*
**unseeing,** *adj.*
**unsegmented,** *adj.*
**unseized,** *adj.*
**unselective,** *adj.*
**unselfconscious,** *adj.*
**unselfconsciously,** *adv.*
**unselfconsciousness,** *n.*
**unsensational,** *adj.*
**unsensitised,** *adj.*
**unsensual,** *adj.*
**unsensualise,** *v.t.*
**unsentenced,** *adj.*
**unsentimental,** *adj.*
**unseparated,** *adj.*
**unserved,** *adj.*
**unsexual,** *adj.*
**unshaded,** *adj.*
**unshaken,** *adj.*
**unshaped,** *adj.*
**unshapeliness,** *n.*
**unshapely,** *adv.*
**unshared,** *adj.*
**unshaved,** *adj.*
**unshaven,** *adj.*
**unshed,** *adj.*
**unsheltered,** *adj.*
**unshielded,** *adj.*
**unshifting,** *adj.*
**unshockable,** *adj.*
**unshod,** *adj.*
**unshorn,** *adj.*
**unshortened,** *adj.*
**unshrinkable,** *adj.*
**unshuffled,** *adj.*
**unshutter,** *v.t.*
**unshuttered,** *adj.*
**unsifted,** *adj.*
**unsigned,** *adj.*
**unsigned-for,** *adj.*
**unsignifying,** *adj.*
**unsilenced,** *adj.*
**unsilvered,** *adj.*
**unsinged,** *adj.*
**unsinkability,** *n.*
**unsinkable,** *adj.*
**unsisterliness,** *n.*
**unsisterly,** *adj.*
**unskimmed,** *adj.*
**unskinned,** *adj.*
**unslackened,** *adj.*
**unslackening,** *adj.*
**unsleeping,** *adj.*
**unsleepingly,** *adv.*
**unslept-in,** *adj.*
**unsmart,** *adj.*
**unsmiling,** *adj.*
**unsmilingly,** *adv.*
**unsmilingness,** *n.*
**unsmoked,** *adj.*
**unsmooth,** *v.t.*
**unsmoothed,** *adj.*
**unsmotherable,** *adj.*
**unsmothered,** *adj.*
**unsnubbable,** *adj.*
**unsnuffed,** *adj.*
**unsocial,** *adj.*
**unsociality,** *n.*

---

piece of equipment, as a tank, battleship, etc. **8.** *Mech.* any piece of equipment which has a specific function: *a power unit.* **9.** *Immunol., Pharm.* **a.** the measured amount of a substance necessary to cause a certain effect; a clinical unit used when a substance cannot readily be isolated in pure form and its activity determined directly. **b.** the amount necessary to cause a specific effect upon a specific animal or upon animal tissues. **10.** *N.Z.* a suburban electric multiple-unit train. **11.** →**home unit.** **12.** (in a block of flats or motel) a self-contained suite of rooms. *–adj.* **13.** of, pertaining to, equivalent to, containing, or forming a unit or units. [apparently backformation from UNITY]

**Unit.**, Unitarian.

**unitarian** /junəˈtɛəriən/, *n.* **1.** (*cap.*) one who maintains that God is one being, rejecting the doctrine of the Trinity, and emphasising freedom in religious belief, tolerance of difference in religious opinion, character as the fundamental principle in religion, and the use of all religious history and experience interpreted by reason as a guide to conduct. Cf. **Monarchian.** **2.** (*cap.*) a member of a Christian denomination founded upon the doctrine that God is one being, and giving each congregation complete control over its affairs. **3.** an advocate of some theory of unity or centralisation, as in government. **4.** a member of a non-Christian religion holding monotheistic views, esp. a Muslim. *–adj.* **5.** (*cap.*) pertaining to the Unitarians or their doctrines; accepting Unitarianism; belonging to the Unitarians. **6.** pertaining to a unit or unity; unitary. **7.** advocating or directed towards national or administrative unity or centralisation. – **unitarianism,** *n.*

**unitary** /ˈjunətri/, *adj.* **1.** of or pertaining to a unit or units. **2.** pertaining to, characterised by, or based on unity. **3.** of the nature of a unit; having the individual character of a unit. **4.** serving as a unit, as of measurement or estimation.

**unitary system** /ˈ– sɪstəm/, *n.* a system of government in which legislative responsibility is carried by one set of elected parliamentarians, representing the entire population and fulfilling administrative and executive responsibilities.

**unit character** /ˈjunət kærəktə/, *n.* a characteristic, usu. dependent on a single gene, transmitted according to Mendel's laws.

**unit cost** /– ˈkɒst/, *n.* the cost of a specified unit of a product or service.

**unite** /juˈnaɪt/, *v.,* **united, uniting.** *–v.t.* **1.** to join so as to form one connected whole; join, combine, or incorporate in one; cause to be one. **2.** to cause to hold together or adhere. **3.** to join in marriage. **4.** to associate (persons, etc.) by some bond or tie; join in action, interest, opinion, feeling, etc. **5.** to have or exhibit in union or combination. *–v.i.* **6.** to join together so as to form one connected whole; become one; combine. **7.** to join in marriage. **8.** to enter into alliance or association; join in action; act in concert or agreement; become one in opinion or feeling. [ME, from L *ūnītus,* pp., joined together, made one] – **uniter,** *n.*

**united** /juˈnaɪtəd/, *adj.* **1.** joined or brought together; combined. **2.** of or produced by two or more persons, etc., in combination. **3.** in agreement. **4.** in association for a common purpose. **5.** formed by the union of two or more things, bodies, etc. – **unitedly,** *adv.* – **unitedness,** *n.*

**United Arab Emirates,** *n.pl.* a country on the eastern coast of the Arabian Peninsula.

**United Arab Republic,** *n.* official name of Egypt. *Abbrev.:* UAR, U.A.R.

**United Kingdom** /junaɪtəd ˈkɪŋdəm/, *n.* Great Britain and Northern Ireland. *Abbrev.:* U.K.

**United Kingdom of Great Britain and Northern Ireland,** *n.* official name of **United Kingdom.**

**United Reformed Church,** *n.* the Church which came into being in 1972 with the Union of the Presbyterian and part of the Congregational Churches of England.

**United Republic of Cameroon,** *n.* official name of **Cameroon.**

**United Republic of Tanzania,** *n.* official name of **Tanzania.**

**United States** /junaɪtəd ˈsteɪts/, *n. pl.* a republic in North America. *Abbrev.:* U.S. Also, **America, the States.**

**United States of America,** *n. pl.* official name of **United States.** *Abbrev.:* U.S.A.

**unit factor** /ˈjunət fæktə/, *n.* a gene; a substance which functions as the hereditary unit for a single character.

**Uniting Church** /juˈnaɪtɪŋ tʃɜtʃ/, *n.* an Australian church formed in 1977 drawing membership from the Presbyterian, Methodist and Congregational churches.

**unitised cargo** /ˌjunətaɪzd ˈkagoʊ/, *n.* a quantity of goods consolidated into one unit for loading and unloading.

**unitive** /ˈjunətɪv/, *adv.* serving or tending to unite. –**unitively,** *adv.* [LL *ūnītīvus,* from L *ūnītus,* pp., made one]

**unit organ** /ˈjunət ɔgən/, *n.* an organ in which, to save space, stops of different pitch but the same tone quality are derived from a single rank of pipes.

**unit pole** /ˈ– poʊl/, *n.* a magnetic pole which when placed one centimetre from an identical pole experiences a repulsive force of one dyne.

**unit price** /– ˈpraɪs/, *n.* a price per agreed unit, as per kilogram, per dozen, etc.

**unit process** /ˈ– proʊsɛs/, *n.* any of several operations which are common to many chemical industries and which form part of a sequence of operations, as filtration, distillation,

---

**unsoftened,** *adj.*
**unsoftening,** *adj.*
**unsoiled,** *adj.*
**unsold,** *adj.*
**unsoldierlike,** *adj.*
**unsoldierly,** *adv.*
**unsolemn,** *adj.*
**unsolicitous,** *adj.*
**unsolid,** *adj.*
**unsolidity,** *n.*
**unsolidly,** *adv.*
**unsolvable,** *adj.*
**unsolved,** *adj.*
**unsorted,** *adj.*
**unsought,** *adj.*
**unsoundable,** *adj.*
**unsoured,** *adj.*
**unsovereign,** *adj.*
**unsown,** *adj.*
**unspecialised,** *adj.*
**unspecific,** *adj.*
**unspecified,** *adj.*
**unspectacled,** *adj.*
**unspectacular,** *adj.*
**unspeculative,** *adj.*
**unspellable,** *adj.*
**unspent,** *adj.*
**unspiritualise,** *v.t.*
**unsplinterable,** *adj.*
**unsporting,** *adj.*
**unsportsmanlike,** *adj.*
**unsprayed,** *adj.*
**unspun,** *adj.*
**unspurred,** *adj.*
**unsquared,** *adj.*
**unstack,** *v.t.*
**unstainable,** *adj.*
**unstained,** *adj.*
**unstamped,** *adj.*
**unstarched,** *adj.*
**unstarted,** *adj.*
**unstartled,** *adj.*
**unstartling,** *adj.*
**unstated,** *adj.*
**unstatesmanlike,** *adj.*
**unsteadfast,** *adj.*
**unsteadfastly,** *adv.*
**unsteadfastness,** *n.*
**unsteered,** *adj.*
**unstiffen,** *adj.*
**unstiffened,** *adj.*
**unstifled,** *adj.*
**unstilled,** *adj.*
**unstimulated,** *adj.*
**unstimulating,** *adj.*
**unstinted,** *adj.*
**unstinting,** *adj.*
**unstintingly,** *adv.*
**unstirring,** *adj.*
**unstitch,** *v.t.*
**unstocked,** *adj.*
**unstockinged,** *adj.*
**unstopper,** *v.t.*
**unstoppered,** *adj.*
**unstraightforward,** *adj.*
**unstreaked,** *adj.*
**unstrengthened,** *adj.*
**unstricken,** *adj.*
**unstripped,** *adj.*
**unstruck,** *adj.*
**unstuck,** *adj.*
**unstylish,** *adj.*
**unsubduable,** *adj.*
**unsubdued,** *adj.*
**unsubject,** *adj.*

evaporation, etc. The plant employed is usu. standardised, requiring only minor modifications for specific industries.

**unit trust** /'– trʌst/, *n.* **1.** a trust whose management purchases shares from a number of companies. The portfolio of such shares is divided into equal units for sale to the public, whose interests are served by an independent trustee company. **2.** the units issued for sale by such a trust.

**unity** /'junəti/, *n., pl.* **-ties.** **1.** the state or fact of being one; oneness. **2.** one single thing; something complete in itself, or regarded as such. **3.** the oneness of a complex or organic whole or of an interconnected series; a whole or totality as combining all its parts into one. **4.** the fact or state of being united or combined into one, as of the parts of a whole. **5.** freedom from diversity or variety. **6.** unvaried or uniform character, as of a plan. **7.** oneness of mind, feeling, etc., as among a number of persons; concord, harmony, or agreement. **8.** *Maths.* the number one; a quantity regarded as one. **9.** (in literature and art) a relation of all the parts or elements of a work constituting a harmonious whole and producing a single general effect. **10.** one of the three principles of dramatic structure, esp. in neoclassical drama: **unity of time** (action taking place during twenty-four hours); **unity of place** (no extensive shifts in setting); **unity of action** (a single plot). [ME *unite,* from L *ūnitas*]

**unity ticket** /'junəti tɪkət/, *n.* a how-to-vote card for union elections on which the names of members of the A.L.P. are linked with militant left-wing candidates, as members of the Communist Party.

**univ.,** **1.** universal. **2.** universally. **3.** university.

**Univ.,** **1.** Universalist. **2.** University.

**univalent** /juni'veɪlənt/, *adj.* **1.** *Chem.* →**monovalent.** **2.** *Biol.* one only; applied to a chromosome which does not possess, or does not join, its homologous chromosome in synapsis. [UNI- + -VALENT] – **univalency,** *n.*

**univalve** /'junivælv/, *adj.* Also, **univalved, univalvular.** **1.** having one valve. **2.** (of a shell) composed of a single valve or piece. *–n.* **3.** a univalve mollusc or its shell.

**universal** /junə'vɜsəl/, *adj.* **1.** extending over, including, proceeding from, all or the whole (of something specified or implicit); without exception. **2.** applicable to many individuals or single cases; general. **3.** affecting, concerning, or involving all: *universal military training.* **4.** used or understood by all: *a universal language.* **5.** existing or prevailing in all parts; everywhere: *universal calm of southern seas.* **6.** versed in or embracing many or all subjects, fields, etc.: *universal scholarship.* **7.** given or extended to all: *universal revelation.* **8.** of or pertaining to the universe, all nature, or all existing things: *universal cause.* **9.** *Logic.* pertaining to a proposition that concerns all members of a class: *all men are wealthy* is a universal proposition. Cf. **particular** (def. 8); **singular** (def. 6). **10.** *Mach., etc.* adapted or adaptable for all or various uses, angles, sizes, etc. **11.** (of a joint or the like) allowing free movement in all directions within certain limits. **12.** *Archaic.* comprising all; whole; entire. *–n.* **13.** that which may be applied throughout the universe to many things, usu. thought of as an entity which can be in many places at the same time (distinguished from *particular*). **14.** a trait or characteristic, as distinguished from a particular individual or event, which can be possessed in common by many distinct things, as *mortality.* **15.** *Logic.* a universal proposition. **16.** *Philos.* **a.** a general term or concept, or the generic nature which such a term signifies. **b.** a metaphysical entity which is repeatable and remains unchanged in character in a series of changes or changing relations. **17.** *Mach.* a universal joint, esp. one at the end of the propeller shaft in a motor vehicle. [ME, from L *ūniversālis*] – **universalness,** *n.*

**universal class** /– 'klas/, *n. Logic.* that class which includes all other classes, and has for its members the individuals who are members of any of these subordinate classes.

**universal coupling** /– 'kʌplɪŋ/, *n.* →**universal joint.**

**universal donor** /– 'doʊnə/, *n.* a blood donor whose blood is of a group that may be transfused to persons of other groups.

**universal gas constant,** *n.* →**gas constant.**

**universalise** /junə'vɜsəlaɪz/, *v.t.,* **-lised, -lising.** to make universal. Also, **universalize.** – **universalisation** /ˌjunəˌvɜsəlaɪ'zeɪʃən/, *n.*

**universalism** /junə'vɜsəlɪzəm/, *n.* universal character; universality.

**universalist** /junə'vɜsələst/, *n.* one characterised by universalism, as in knowledge, interests, or activities.

**universalistic** /ˌjunəvɜsə'lɪstɪk/, *adj.* **1.** of, pertaining to, or affecting, the whole of something, esp. mankind; inclined to be universal. **2.** of or pertaining to universalism.

**universality** /junəvɜ'sæləti/, *n., pl.* **-ties.** **1.** the character or state of being universal; existence or prevalence everywhere. **2.** relation, extension, or applicability to all. **3.** very great versatility or range of knowledge, interests, etc.

**universal joint** /junəvɜsəl 'dʒɔɪnt/, *n.* a joint allowing free movement in all directions within certain limits. Also, **universal coupling.**

**universal language** /– 'læŋgwɪdʒ/, *n.* a language understood or intended to be understood everywhere.

**universally** /junə'vɜsəli/, *adv.* in a universal manner; in every instance, part, or place, without exception.

**universal motor** /junəvɜsəl 'moʊtə/, *n.* a series-wound elec-

**unsubjected,** *adj.*
**unsubmerged,** *adj.*
**unsubsidised,** *adj.*
**unsubstantiated,** *adj.*
**unsubtle,** *adj.*
**unsubtlety,** *adj.*
**unsugared,** *adj.*
**unsuit,** *v.t.*
**unsummoned,** *adj.*
**unsunny,** *adj.*
**unsuperstitious** *adj.*
**unsupplied,** *adj.*
**unsupported,** *adj.*
**unsuppressed,** *adj.*
**unsurmised,** *adj.*
**unsurmountable,** *adj.*
**unsurpassable,** *adj.*
**unsurpassably,** *adv.*
**unsurpassed,** *adj.*
**unsurprised,** *adj.*
**unsurveyed,** *adj.*
**unsuspecting,** *adj.*
**unsuspectingly,** *adv.*
**unsuspicious,** *adj.*
**unsuspiciously,** *adv.*
**unsustainable,** *adj.*
**unsustained,** *adj.*
**unsustaining,** *adj.*
**unswallowed,** *adj.*
**unsweet,** *adj.*
**unswept,** *adj.*
**unsworn,** *adj.*
**unsymbolic,** *adj.*
**unsymmetrical,** *adj.*
**unsymmetrically,** *adv.*
**unsystematic,** *adj.*
**unsystematically,** *adv.*
**unsystematised,** *adj.*
**untactful,** *adj.*
**untactfully,** *adv.*
**untainted,** *adj.*
**untaken,** *adj.*
**untameable,** *adj.*
**untameably,** *adv.*
**untamed,** *adj.*
**untanned,** *adj.*
**untarnished,** *adj.*
**untarred,** *adj.*
**untasted,** *adj.*
**untasteful,** *adj.*
**untastefully,** *adv.*
**untaxable,** *adj.*
**untearable,** *adj.*
**untechnical,** *adj.*
**untellable,** *adj.*
**untempered,** *adj.*
**untempted,** *adj.*
**untempting,** *adj.*
**untenantable,** *adj.*
**untenanted,** *adj.*
**untended,** *adj.*
**untender,** *adj.*
**unterminated,** *adj.*
**unterrified,** *adj.*
**untested,** *adj.*
**untether,** *v.t.*
**untethered,** *adj.*
**unthanked,** *adj.*
**unthatched,** *adj.*
**untheological,** *adj.*
**unthickened,** *adj.*
**unthought-of,** *adj.*
**unthought-out,** *adj.*
**unthreatened,** *adj.*
**unthrifty,** *adj.*

trical motor which can be operated on either direct or alternating current.

universal joint

**Universal Product Code,** *n.* a code printed on the label of a product and made up of lines, spaces and numbers which can be read by means of an optical scanner, to enable identification at a checkout counter.

**universal suffrage** /junəvɜsəl 'sʌfrɪdʒ/, *n.* the principle that the right to vote for one's government, etc., should be extended to everyone above a specified age, usu. eighteen.

**universal time** /– 'taɪm/, *n.* a system of time measurement based on Greenwich Mean Time, but counted from 0 hr, which is equivalent to midnight Greenwich Mean Time. *Abbrev.:* U.T.

**universal-wound** /'junəvɜsəl-ˌwaʊnd/, *adj.* (of an electric motor) wound so that it will function with either DC or low frequency AC supply; commonly used in electrical household appliances.

**universe** /'junəvɜs/, *n.* **1.** all of space, and all the matter and energy which it contains; the cosmos. **2.** the whole world; mankind generally: *the whole universe knows it.* **3.** a world or sphere in which something exists or prevails. **4.** a galaxy. **5.** *Logic.* the collection of all the objects to which any discourse refers. [L *ūniversum*]

**universe of discourse,** *n. Logic.* the complex of objects or facts which are capable of being treated by a given technical language or part of a language.

**university** /junə'vɜsəti/, *n., pl.* **-ties. 1.** an institution of higher learning, conducting teaching and research at the undergraduate and postgraduate level. **2.** its members, as teachers, undergraduates, graduate members, etc. **3.** its buildings. **4.** its governing body. **5.** a sports team or crew representing it in competition. **6.** anything considered as a source of learning: *the great university of life.* [ME, from ML *ūniversitas* (*magistrōrum et scholārium*) guild (of teachers and students)]

**university college** /– 'kɒlɪdʒ/, *n.* **1.** an institution (often denominational) within a university offering residential and tutorial facilities. **2.** an institution carrying out the teaching of university courses removed from but controlled by an older-established university which grants the degrees. **3.** *Brit.* →**college** (def. 6).

**university town** /'– taʊn/, *n.* a town dominated by and closely identified with its university, as Armidale.

**univocal** /juni'voʊkəl/, *adj.* having only one possible meaning; unambiguous; unmistakable.

**unjust** /ʌn'dʒʌst/, *adj.* **1.** not just; not acting justly or fairly, as persons. **2.** not in accordance with justice or fairness, as actions. **3.** *Archaic.* unfaithful or dishonest. – **unjustly,** *adv.* – **unjustness,** *n.*

**unjust enrichment** /– ən'rɪtʃmənt/, *n.* the obtaining of money by unjust means, as by capitalising on another's mistake.

**unjustified** /ʌn'dʒʌstəfaɪd/, *adj.* **1.** not justified. **2.** of or pertaining to printed material which has not been regulated in regard to column-width and spacing between letters, etc.

**unkempt** /ʌn'kɛmpt/, *adj.* **1.** not combed, as the hair. **2.** having the hair not combed or cared for. **3.** in an uncared-for, neglected, or untidy state; rough. **4.** crude, coarse, or unpolished, as persons. [var. of *unkembed,* from UN-[2] + *kembed,* pp. of obs. *kemb* (ME *kembe,* OE *cemban*) comb] – **unkemptness,** *n.*

**unkennel** /ʌn'kɛnəl/, *v.t.,* **-nelled, -nelling** or (*esp. U.S.*) **-neled, -neling. 1.** to drive or release from or as from, a kennel; dislodge. **2.** to dislodge a fox from its hole. **3.** to bring to light.

**unkind** /ʌn'kaɪnd/, *adj.* **1.** not kind; harsh; cruel; unmerciful; unfeeling and distressing. **2.** of the weather, soil, etc., harsh; unwelcoming; not mild. – **unkindness,** *n.*

**unkindly** /ʌn'kaɪndli/, *adj.* **1.** not kindly; ill-natured; unkind. **2.** inclement or bleak, as weather, climate, etc.; unfavourable for crops, as soil. *–adv.* **3.** in an unkind manner. – **unkindliness,** *n.*

**unknightly** /ʌn'naɪtli/, *adj.* **1.** unworthy of a knight. **2.** not like a knight. *–adv.* **3.** in a manner unworthy of a knight. – **unknightliness,** *n.*

**unknit** /ʌn'nɪt/, *v.t.,* **-knitted** or **-knit, -knitting. 1.** to untie or unfasten (a knot, etc.); unravel (something knitted). **2.** to dissolve, destroy, unloose, weaken, etc. [ME *unknytte(n),* OE *uncnyttan.* See UN-[2], KNIT, *v.*]

**unknowable** /ʌn'noʊəbəl/, *adj.* **1.** not knowable; incapable of being known; transcending human knowledge. *–n.* **2.** something unknowable. **3. the Unknowable,** *Philos.* the (postulated) reality lying behind all phenomena but not cognisable by any of the processes by which the mind cognises phenomenal objects. –**unknowability** /ʌnˌnoʊə'bɪləti/, *n.* – **unknowableness,** *n.* – **unknowably,** *adv.*

**unknowing** /ʌn'noʊɪŋ/, *adj.* **1.** lacking knowledge; ignorant. **2.** without knowledge (of something). – **unknowingly,** *adv.* – **unknowingness,** *n.*

**unknown** /ʌn'noʊn/, *adj.* **1.** not known; not within the range of one's knowledge, cognisance, or acquaintance; unfamiliar; strange. **2.** not ascertained, discovered, explored, or identified. *–n.* **3.** one who or that which is unknown; an unknown person. **4.** *Maths.* an unknown quantity or a symbol representing this.

---

**untiled,** *adj.*
**untillable,** *adj.*
**untilled,** *adj.*
**untinctured,** *adj.*
**untinned,** *adj.*
**untinted,** *adj.*
**untipped,** *adj.*
**untirable,** *adj.*
**untiring,** *adj.*
**untiringly,** *adv.*
**untoned,** *adj.*
**untormented,** *adj.*
**untorn,** *adj.*
**untraceable,** *adj.*
**untraceably,** *adv.*
**untraced,** *adj.*
**untrainable,** *adj.*
**untrained,** *adj.*
**untransformed,** *adj.*
**untranslatability,** *n.*
**untranslatable,** *adj.*
**untranslatably,** *adv.*
**untreatable,** *adj.*
**untreated,** *adj.*
**untrimmed,** *adj.*
**untrodden,** *adj.*
**untroubled,** *adj.*
**untroublesome,** *adj.*
**untrusting,** *adj.*
**untrustworthiness,** *n.*
**untuneful,** *adj.*
**untunefully,** *adv.*
**untunefulness,** *n.*
**untying,** *adj.*
**untypical,** *adj.*
**ununiformed,** *adj.*
**unusable,** *adj.*
**unuttered,** *adj.*
**unvanquishable,** *adj.*
**unvanquished,** *adj.*
**unvaried,** *adj.*
**unvariegated,** *adj.*
**unvarying,** *adj.*
**unvaryingly,** *adv.*
**unventilated,** *adj.*
**unveracious,** *adj.*
**unverifiable,** *adj.*
**unverified,** *adj.*
**unversed,** *adj.*
**unviolated,** *adj.*
**unvirtuous,** *adj.*
**unvirtuously,** *adv.*
**unvisited,** *adj.*
**unvitiated,** *adj.*
**unvitrifiable,** *adj.*
**unvocal,** *adj.*
**unvulcanised,** *adj.*
**unwandering,** *adj.*
**unwanted,** *adj.*
**unwarlike,** *adj.*
**unwarmed,** *adj.*
**unwarped,** *adj.*
**unwatchful,** *adj.*
**unwatchfully,** *adv.*
**unwatchfulness,** *n.*
**unwatered,** *adj.*
**unwavering,** *adj.*
**unwaveringly,** *adv.*
**unweaned,** *adj.*
**unwearable,** *adj.*
**unwearying,** *adj.*
**unwearyingly,** *adv.*
**unweathered,** *adj.*
**unwebbed,** *adj.*
**unwed,** *adj.*

**Unknown Soldier** /ˌʌnnoʊn 'soʊldʒə/, *n.* (in various countries) an unidentified soldier killed in a war, esp. World War I, and entombed as a memorial to all similar victims of the war. Also, **Unknown Warrior.**

**unlace** /ʌn'leɪs/, *v.t.*, **-laced, -lacing. 1.** to undo the lacing of (a garment, etc.). **2.** to loosen or remove the garments, etc., of by undoing lacing.

**unlade** /ʌn'leɪd/, *v.t.*, **-laded, -lading. 1.** to take the lading, load, or cargo from; unload. **2.** to discharge (the load or cargo). *–v.i.* **3.** to discharge the load or cargo.

**unladen** /ʌn'leɪdn/, *adj.* not carrying any load, as a goods-carrying vehicle, etc.

**unlaid** /ʌn'leɪd/, *adj.* **1.** (of a table) not set for a meal. **2.** (of a ghost) not yet exorcised. **3.** (of paper) not laid; not having the lined texture of laid paper. **4.** untwisted, as a rope.

**unlash** /ʌn'læʃ/, *v.t.* to loosen or unfasten, as something lashed or tied fast.

**unlatch** /ʌn'lætʃ/, *v.t.* **1.** to unfasten or open (a door, etc.) by lifting the latch. *–v.i.* **2.** to become unlatched; open through the lifting of a latch.

**unlawful** /ʌn'lɔfəl/, *adj.* **1.** not lawful; contrary to law; illegal; not sanctioned by law. **2.** contrary to moral rule; immoral; irreligious. **3.** born out of wedlock; illegitimate. – **unlawfully,** *adv.* – **unlawfulness,** *n.*

**unlawful assembly** /– ə'sɛmbli/, *n.* a meeting of three or more persons with intent to commit a crime or breach of the peace.

**unlay** /ʌn'leɪ/, *v.t.*, **-laid, -laying.** to untwist, as a rope into separate strands.

**unleaded** /ʌn'lɛdəd/, *adj.* **1.** not furnished with lead. **2.** *Print.* not separated or spaced with leads, as lines of type or printed matter.

**unlearn** /ʌn'lɜn/, *v.t.* **1.** to put aside from knowledge or memory (something learned); discard or lose knowledge of; forget. *–v.i.* **2.** to put aside knowledge.

**unlearned** /ʌn'lɜnəd/ *for defs 1 and 4;* /ʌn'lɜnt/ *for defs 2 and 3, adj.* **1.** not learned; not scholarly or erudite; uneducated; ignorant. **2.** not acquired by learning; never learned. **3.** known without being learned. **4.** of or pertaining to unlearned persons. Also (*for defs 2 and 3*), **unlearnt.** – **unlearnedly,** *adv.*

**unleash** /ʌn'liʃ/, *v.t.* **1.** to let loose or give vent to (rage, violence, or the like). **2.** to release from or as from a leash; set free to pursue or run at will; let loose.

**unleavened** /ʌn'lɛvənd/, *adj.* **1.** (of bread, etc.) not made to rise by the addition of leaven, as yeast or bicarbonate of soda. **2.** unmodified by the addition of some influence.

**unless** /ʌn'lɛs, ən-/, *conj.* **1.** except on condition that; except if it be, or were, that; except when; if ... not: *I shan't come unless you really want me to. –prep.* **2.** *Obs.* except; but. [ME *onlesse,* from ON, *prep.* + *lesse* LESS, orig. meaning on a lower condition (than)]

**unlettered** /ʌn'lɛtəd/, *adj.* not educated; illiterate; without knowledge of books.

**unlicensed** /ʌn'laɪsənst/, *adj.* **1.** having no licence. **2.** done or undertaken without licence; unauthorised.

**unlike** /ʌn'laɪk/, *adj.* **1.** not like; different or dissimilar; having no resemblance. *–prep.* **2.** otherwise than like; different from. **3.** uncharacteristic of: *it is unlike you to be so cheerful.* – **unlikeness,** *n.*

**unlikelihood** /ʌn'laɪklihʊd/, *n.* the state of being unlikely; improbability.

**unlikely** /ʌn'laɪkli/, *adj.* **1.** not likely to happen or be; improbable; probably not going (to do, be, etc.). **2.** not likely to be true; doubtful. **3.** holding out little prospect of success; unpromising. **4.** *Archaic.* unprepossessing. *–adv.* **5.** improbably. – **unlikeliness,** *n.*

**unlimber** /ʌn'lɪmbə/, *v.t.* **1.** to detach (a gun) from its limber or prime mover. *–n.* **2.** the act of changing a gun from travelling to firing position.

**unlimited** /ʌn'lɪmətəd/, *adj.* **1.** not limited; unrestricted. **2.** boundless; limitless. – **unlimitedly,** *adv.* – **unlimitedness,** *n.*

**unlimited company** /– 'kʌmpəni/, *n.* a company whose members are each liable for its debts to the full extent of their property.

**unlined**[1] /ʌn'laɪnd/, *adj.* not marked or incised with lines.

**unlined**[2] /ʌn'laɪnd/, *adj.* not furnished with a lining, as a garment.

**unlink** /ʌn'lɪŋk/, *v.t.* **1.** to separate the links of (a chain, etc.). **2.** to detach from being linked; to separate or detach by, or as by, undoing a connecting link. *–v.i.* **3.** to become unlinked.

**unlisted** /ʌn'lɪstəd/, *adj.* **1.** not listed; not entered in a list. **2.** (of stock exchange securities) not entered in the official list of those admitted for dealings. **3.** (of a telephone number) not in the directory.

**unlive** /ʌn'lɪv/, *v.t.*, **-lived, -living. 1.** to undo or annul (past life, etc.). **2.** to live down.

**unload** /ʌn'loʊd/, *v.t.* **1.** to take the load from; remove the burden, cargo, or freight from. **2.** to relieve of anything burdensome. **3.** to withdraw the charge from (a firearm). **4.** to remove or discharge (a load, etc.). **5.** to relieve oneself of (something burdensome). **6.** to get rid or dispose of (stock, etc.) by sale. *–v.i.* **7.** to unload something; remove or discharge a load. – **unloader,** *n.*

**unloaded** /ʌn'loʊdəd/, *v.* **1.** past participle of **unload.** *–adj. Colloq.* **2.** knocked over heavily, as in football.

**unlock** /ʌn'lɒk/, *v.t.* **1.** to undo the lock of, esp. with a key. **2.** to open or release by, or as by, undoing a lock. **3.** to open (anything firmly closed or joined): *to unlock the jaws.* **4.** to lay open; disclose. *–v.i.* **5.** to become unlocked.

**unlockable** /ʌn'lɒkəbəl/, *adj.* **1.** that cannot be locked. **2.** that can be unlocked.

**unlooked-for** /ʌn'lʊkt-fɔ/, *adj.* not looked for; unexpected; unforeseen.

**unloose** /ʌn'lus/, *v.t.*, **-loosed, -loosing. 1.** to set or let loose; release from bonds, fastenings, etc.; set free from restraint. **2.** to loose or undo (a bond, fastening, knot, etc.). **3.** to loosen or relax (the grasp, hold, fingers, etc.).

**unlovely** /ʌn'lʌvli/, *adj.* **1.** not lovely; without beauty or charm of appearance; unpleasing to the eye. **2.** unattractive, repellent, or disagreeable in character; unpleasant; objectionable. – **unloveliness,** *n.*

**unlucky** /ʌn'lʌki/, *adj.* not lucky; not having good luck; unfortunate or ill-fated; not attended with good luck. – **unluckily,** *adv.* – **unluckiness,** *n.*

**unmade** /ʌn'meɪd/, *adj.* **1.** not yet made. **2.** not having a maker; not having been made; uncreated.

**unmade road** /– 'roʊd/, *n.* →**unsealed road.**

**unmake** /ʌn'meɪk/, *v.t.*, **-made, -making. 1.** to cause to be as if never made; reduce to the original matter, elements, or state. **2.** to take to pieces; destroy; ruin or undo. **3.** to depose from office or authority. – **unmaker,** *n.*

**unman** /ʌn'mæn/, *v.t.*, **-manned, -manning. 1.** to deprive of the character or qualities of a man or human being. **2.** to deprive of virility; emasculate. **3.** to deprive of manly courage or fortitude; break down the manly spirit of. **4.** to deprive of men: *to unman a ship.*

**unmanageable** /ʌn'mænədʒəbəl/, *adj.* **1.** impossible to govern

---

**unwedded,** *adj.*
**unweeded,** *adj.*
**unweighted,** *adj.*
**unwelcomed,** *adj.*
**unwelcoming,** *adj.*
**unwigged,** *adj.*
**unwinding,** *adj., n.*
**unwiped,** *adj.*
**unwire,** *v.t.*
**unwithdrawn,** *adj.*
**unwitherable,** *adj.*
**unwithered,** *adj.*
**unwithering,** *adj.*
**unwomanliness,** *n.*
**unwomanly,** *adj., adv.*
**unwooded,** *adj.*
**unworkmanlike,** *adj.*
**unworried,** *adj.*
**unwoundable,** *adj.*
**unwounded,** *adj.*
**unwoven,** *adj.*
**unwrinkled,** *adj.*
**unwrought,** *adj.*
**unwrung,** *adj.*
**unyielding,** *adj.*
**unyieldingly,** *adv.*
**unyieldingness,** *n.*
**unyoked,** *adj.*
**unzoned,** *adj.*

---

or control, as a horse, child, etc.; refractory. **2.** incapable of being satisfactorily dealt with or handled, as affairs, objects, etc.; unwieldy. – **unmanageably,** *adv.*

**unmanly** /ʌn'mænli/, *adj.* **1.** not manly; not like or befitting a man; womanish or childish. **2.** ignoble; weak; cowardly. – **unmanliness,** *n.*

**unmanned** /ʌn'mænd/, *adj.* **1.** without a crew, controlled automatically: *an unmanned ship.* **2.** desolate; having no population. **3.** castrated. **4.** (of a falcon) not trained for hunting.

**unmannered** /ʌn'mænəd/, *adj.* **1.** without manners; unmannerly. **2.** not affected or insincere.

**unmannerly** /ʌn'mænəli/, *adj.* **1.** not mannerly; ill-bred; rude; churlish. *–adv.* **2.** *Obs.* with ill manners. – **unmannerliness,** *n.*

**unmarked** /ʌn'makt/, *adj.* **1.** not marked; bearing no marking, stain, etc. **2.** not bearing the marks of blows, punches, etc.; unbruised. **3.** not distinguished; not characterised (by some quality). **4.** unnoticed.

**unmarketable** /ʌn'makətəbəl/, *adj.* incapable of being sold or unsuitable for sale; not finding or likely to find a buyer. – **unmarketability** /ʌnˌmakətə'bɪləti/, *n.* – **unmarketably,** *adv.*

**unmask** /ʌn'mask/, *v.t.* **1.** to strip of a mask or disguise. **2.** to lay open (anything concealed); expose in the true character. **3.** *Mil.* to reveal the presence of (guns, etc.) by firing. *–v.t.* **4.** to put off a mask or disguise. – **unmasker,** *n.*

**unmatched** /ʌn'mætʃt/, *adj.* not matched, rivalled, or equalled; supreme.

**unmeaning** /ʌn'minɪŋ/, *adj.* **1.** not meaning anything; without meaning or significance, as words or actions; meaningless. **2.** expressionless, vacant, or unintelligent, as the face, etc. – **unmeaningly,** *adv.* – **unmeaningness,** *n.*

**unmeant** /ʌn'mɛnt/, *adj.* not intended or deliberate; accidental.

**unmeasured** /ʌn'mɛʒəd/, *adj.* **1.** of undetermined or indefinitely great extent or amount; unlimited; measureless. **2.** unrestrained; intemperate. – **unmeasurable,** *adj.* – **unmeasurably,** *adv.*

**unmechanical** /ʌnmə'kænɪkəl/, *adj.* **1.** not pertaining to or working by means of a mechanism. **2.** (of a person) having little or no mechanical aptitude or inclination. – **unmechanically,** *adv.*

**unmentionable** /ʌn'mɛnʃənəbəl/, *adj.* not mentionable; unworthy or unfit to be mentioned. – **unmentionableness,** *n.* – **unmentionably,** *adv.*

**unmentionables** /ʌn'mɛnʃənəbəlz/, *n. pl.* *(joc.)* trousers, breeches, or undergarments.

**unmerciful** /ʌn'mɜsəfəl/, *adj.* **1.** not merciful; merciless; pitiless; relentless; unsparing. **2.** unsparingly great; unconscionable. – **unmercifully,** *adv.* – **unmercifulness,** *n.*

**unmindful** /ʌn'maɪndfəl/, *adj.* not mindful; regardless; heedless; careless. – **unmindfully,** *adv.* – **unmindfulness,** *n.*

**unmistakable** /ʌnməs'teɪkəbəl/, *adj.* not mistakable; admitting of no mistake; clear; plain; evident. Also, **unmistakeable.** – **unmistakableness,** *n.* – **unmistakably,** *adv.*

**unmitigated** /ʌn'mɪtəgeɪtəd/, *adj.* **1.** not mitigated; not softened or lessened. **2.** unqualified or absolute; utter. – **unmitigatedly,** *adv.*

**unmixed** /ʌn'mɪkst/, *adj.* not mixed; unmingled; pure; unalloyed. Also, **unmixt.** – **unmixedly,** *adv.*

**unmoor** /ʌn'mɔ/, *v.t.* **1.** to loose (a ship, etc.) from moorings or anchorage. *–v.i.* **2.** (of a ship, etc.) to become unmoored.

**unmoral** /ʌn'mɒrəl/, *adj.* non-moral; having no moral aspect, neither moral nor immoral. Cf. **amoral.** – **unmorality** /ʌnmə'ræləti/, *n.* – **unmorally,** *adv.*

**unmounted** /ʌn'maʊntəd/, *adj.* **1.** (of a picture) not having a mount. **2.** not having or riding a horse: *unmounted soldiers.* **3.** not mounted on something, as a stand.

**unmoved** /ʌn'muvd/, *adj.* unaffected; calm; unemotional. – **unmovedly** /ʌn'muvədli/, *adv.*

**unmoving** /ʌn'muvɪŋ/, *adj.* **1.** not moving; motionless. **2.** *Rare.* arousing no feeling.

**unmuffle** /ʌn'mʌfəl/, *v.*, **-fled, -fling.** *–v.t.* **1.** to strip of or free from that which muffles. *–v.i.* **2.** to throw off that which muffles.

**unmurmuring** /ʌn'mɜmərɪŋ/, *adj.* without complaint, grumbling, or demur; willing. – **unmurmuringly,** *adv.*

**unmusical** /ʌn'mjuzɪkəl/, *adj.* **1.** not musical; not melodious or harmonious. **2.** harsh or discordant in sound. **3.** not fond of or skilled in music. – **unmusically,** *adv.* – **unmusicalness,** *n.*

**unmuzzle** /ʌn'mʌzəl/, *v.t.*, **-zled, -zling.** **1.** to free from restraint, as upon speech or expression. **2.** to remove a muzzle from (a dog, etc.).

**unnamed** /ʌn'neɪmd/, *adj.* **1.** having no name; nameless. **2.** not specified or mentioned by name.

**unnatural** /ʌn'nætʃərəl, -'nætʃrəl/, *adj.* **1.** not natural; not proper to the natural constitution or character. **2.** having or showing a lack of natural or proper instincts, feelings, etc. **3.** contrary to the nature of things. **4.** at variance with the ordinary course of nature; unusual, strange, or abnormal. **5.** contrary to accepted or expected modes of behaviour. **6.** artificial or affected; forced or strained. **7.** more than usu. cruel or evil. – **unnaturally,** *adv.* – **unnaturalness,** *n.*

**unnavigable** /ʌn'nævɪgəbəl/, *adj.* not able to be navigated, as because there is insufficient depth of water, lack of room for a vessel to manoeuvre, ice, etc.

**unnecessary** /ʌn'nɛsəsɛri, -səsri/, *adj.* not necessary; superfluous; needless. – **unnecessarily,** *adv.* – **unnecessariness,** *n.*

**unnerve** /ʌn'nɜv/, *v.t.*, **-nerved, -nerving.** to deprive of nerve, strength, or physical or mental firmness; break down the self-control of; upset.

**unnumbered** /ʌn'nʌmbəd/, *adj.* **1.** not numbered; uncounted. **2.** countless; innumerable. **3.** not marked with or bearing a number or numbers.

**U.N.O.,** United Nations Organisation.

**unobjectionable** /ʌnəb'dʒɛkʃənəbəl/, *adj.* that cannot be objected to; acceptable. – **unobjectionableness,** *n.* – **unobjectionably,** *adv.*

**unobtrusive** /ʌnəb'trusɪv, -zɪv/, *adj.* not obvious; discreet. – **unobtrusively,** *adv.* – **unobtrusiveness,** *n.*

**unoccupied** /ʌn'ɒkjəpaɪd/, *adj.* **1.** not occupied; not possessed or held; vacant. **2.** not employed; idle. **3.** not controlled by a foreign army.

**unofficial** /ʌnə'fɪʃəl/, *adj.* **1.** not official; informal. **2.** (of news) not confirmed by official sources. **3.** *Sport.* (of a time or speed, or a record) not confirmed by an official body. – **unofficially,** *adv.*

**unorganised** /ʌn'ɔgənaɪzd/, *adj.* **1.** not organised; without organic structure. **2.** not formed into an organised or systematised whole. **3.** not having membership in a trade union. Also, **unorganized.**

**unpack** /ʌn'pæk/, *v.t.* **1.** to undo or take out (something packed). **2.** to remove the contents packed in (a suitcase, trunk, etc.). **3.** to remove a pack or load from (a horse, etc.); unload (a vehicle, etc.). *–v.i.* **4.** to unpack articles, goods, etc. – **unpacker,** *n.* – **unpacking,** *n.*

**unpaginated** /ʌn'pædʒəneɪtəd/, *adj.* (of a publication) having unnumbered pages.

**unpalatable** /ʌn'pælətəbəl/, *adj.* **1.** disagreeable; distasteful. **2.** not agreeable to the palate; ill-tasting. – **unpalatability** /ˌʌnpælətə'bɪləti/, **unpalatableness,** *n.* – **unpalatable,** *adv.*

**unparalleled** /ʌn'pærəlɛld/, *adj.* not paralleled; having no parallel; unequalled; unmatched.

**unparliamentary** /ˌʌnpalə'mɛntəri, -tri/, *adj.* **1.** not parliamentary; not in accordance with parliamentary practice. **2.** (of language) foul or abusive. – **unparliamentarily,** *adv.* – **unparliamentariness,** *n.*

**unpeg** /ʌn'pɛg/, *v.t.*, **-pegged, -pegging.** **1.** to remove the peg or pegs from. **2.** to open, unfasten, or unfix by removing a peg or pegs. **3.** to permit (wages, prices, etc.) to be increased.

**unpen** /ʌn'pɛn/, *v.t.*, **-penned, -penning.** to release from, or as from, a pen.

**unpeople** /ʌn'pipəl/, *v.t.*, **-pled, -pling.** **1.** to deprive of people; depopulate. **2.** to deprive or divest (of something).

**unpick** /ʌn'pɪk/, *v.t.* to undo the stitches of (something sewn, etc.).

**unpin** /ʌn'pɪn/, *v.t.*, **-pinned, -pinning.** **1.** to remove the pin or pins from. **2.** to unfasten by removing a pin or pins; release from being pinned or pinned down.

**unplaced** /ʌn'pleɪst/, *adj.* **1.** not assigned to, or put in, a particular place. **2.** *Horseracing.* not among the first three (or sometimes four) runners.

**unplait** /ʌnˈplæt/, *v.t.* to bring out of a plaited state; unbraid, as hair.

**unpleasant** /ʌnˈplɛzənt/, *adj.* not pleasant; unpleasing; disagreeable. – **unpleasantly,** *adv.*

**unpleasantness** /ʌnˈplɛzəntnəs/, *n.* **1.** the quality or state of being unpleasant. **2.** something unpleasant; an unpleasant state of affairs. **3.** a disagreement or quarrel.

**unpleasing** /ʌnˈplizɪŋ/, *adj.* distasteful; unwelcome.

**unplug** /ʌnˈplʌg/, *v.t.*, **-plugged, -plugging.** **1.** to disconnect (electrical apparatus) by pulling the plug from it or from a power socket. **2.** to remove the plug from, as to open.

**unplumbed** /ʌnˈplʌmd/, *adj.* **1.** not plumbed; unfathomed; of unknown depth. **2.** not investigated in depth.

**unpolished** /ʌnˈpɒlɪʃt/, *adj.* **1.** not smoothed by polishing. **2.** rough or inelegant in style, language, etc. **3.** not cultured or refined. **4.** (of rice) unmilled, retaining the husk.

**unpolitic** /ʌnˈpɒlətɪk/, *adj. Obs.* →**impolitic.**

**unpolled** /ʌnˈpoʊld/, *adj.* **1.** not polled. **2.** not voting or not cast at the polls. **3.** not consulted by opinion poll.

**unpopular** /ʌnˈpɒpjələ/, *adj.* not popular; not liked by the public or by persons generally or by an individual. – **unpopularity** /ˌʌnpɒpjəˈlærəti/, *n.* – **unpopularly,** *adv.*

**unpractical** /ʌnˈpræktɪkəl/, *adj.* not practical; impractical; lacking practical usefulness or wisdom. – **unpracticality** /ˌʌnpræktɪˈkæləti/, **unpracticalness,** *n.* – **unpractically,** *adv.*

**unpractised** /ʌnˈpræktəst/, *adj.* **1.** not practised; not done habitually or as a practice. **2.** not trained or skilled; inexpert.

**unprecedented** /ʌnˈprɛsədɛntəd, -ˈpri-/, *adj.* having no precedent or preceding instance; never known before; unexampled. – **unprecedentedly,** *adv.*

**unprejudiced** /ʌnˈprɛdʒədəst/, *adj.* **1.** not prejudiced; unbiased; impartial. **2.** *Obs.* not impaired.

**unpremeditated** /ʌnpriˈmɛdəteɪtəd/, *adj.* (of actions, etc.) not planned or decided upon in advance. – **unpremeditatedly,** *adv.*

**unpresentable** /ʌnprəˈzɛntəbəl/, *adj.* not fit to be seen.

**unpretending** /ʌnprəˈtɛndɪŋ/, *adj.* not pretending; unassuming; modest. – **unpretendingly,** *adv.*

**unpretentious** /ʌnprəˈtɛnʃəs/, *adj.* not pretentious; modest; without ostentation. – **unpretentiously,** *adv.* – **unpretentiousness,** *n.*

**unpriced** /ʌnˈpraɪst/, *adj.* **1.** not priced; having no price set or indicated. **2.** *Poetic.* beyond price; priceless.

**unprincipled** /ʌnˈprɪnsəpəld/, *adj.* **1.** lacking sound moral principles, as a person. **2.** showing want of principle, as conduct, etc. **3.** not instructed in the principles of something (fol. by *in*). – **unprincipledness,** *n.*

**unprintable** /ʌnˈprɪntəbəl/, *adj.* **1.** unfit to be printed, as offending against taste, morals, the laws of libel, or the like. **2.** not able to be printed.

**unproductive** /ʌnprəˈdʌktɪv/, *adj.* **1.** not fruitful; producing nothing. **2.** not producing or providing (fol. by *of*). – **unproductively,** *adv.* – **unproductiveness,** *n.*

**unprofessional** /ʌnprəˈfɛʃənəl, -ˈfɛʃnəl/, *adj.* **1.** contrary to professional ethics; unbecoming in members of a profession. **2.** not professional; not pertaining to or connected with a profession. **3.** not belonging to a profession. **4.** not of professional quality; amateur. – **unprofessionally,** *adv.*

**unprofitable** /ʌnˈprɒfətəbəl/, *adj.* **1.** not showing a profit, as a business enterprise. **2.** not beneficial; disadvantageous. – **unprofitably,** *adv.*

**unpromising** /ʌnˈprɒməsɪŋ/, *adj.* not showing signs of future excellence or improvement. – **unpromisingly,** *adv.*

**unprovided** /ʌnprəˈvaɪdəd/, *adj.* **1.** not furnished or supplied with something. **2.** lacking something, esp. the necessities of life (fol. by *for*).

**unpublished work** /ʌnˌpʌblɪʃt ˈwɜk/, *n.* a literary work which, at the time of registration for copyright, has not been reproduced for sale or been publicly distributed.

**unqualified** /ʌnˈkwɒləfaɪd/, *adj.* **1.** not qualified; not fitted; not having the requisite qualifications. **2.** not modified, limited, or restricted in any way: *unqualified praise.* **3.** absolute; out-and-out. – **unqualifiedly,** *adv.* – **unqualifiedness,** *n.*

**unquestionable** /ʌnˈkwɛstʃənəbəl/, *adj.* **1.** not questionable; not open to question; beyond dispute or doubt; indisputable; indubitable. **2.** beyond criticism; unexceptionable. – **unquestionability** /ʌnˌkwɛstʃənəˈbɪləti/, **unquestionableness,** *n.* – **unquestionably,** *adv.*

**unquestioned** /ʌnˈkwɛstʃənd/, *adj.* **1.** not enquired into. **2.** not called in question; undisputed. **3.** not questioned; not interrogated.

**unquiet** /ʌnˈkwaɪət/, *adj.* **1.** not quiet; restless; turbulent; tumultuous. **2.** uneasy; perturbed. **3.** agitated or in commotion; not silent or still. – **unquietly,** *adv.* – **unquietness,** *n.*

**unquote** /ʌnˈkwoʊt, ˈʌnkwoʊt/, *v.i.*, **-quoted, -quoting.** to close a quotation.

**unravel** /ʌnˈrævəl/, *v.*, **-elled, -elling** or (*esp. U.S.*) **-eled, -eling.** –*v.t.* **1.** to free from a ravelled or tangled state; disentangle; disengage the threads or fibres of (a woven or knitted fabric, a rope, etc.). **2.** to take apart (a piece of knitting). **3.** to free from complication or difficulty; make plain or clear; solve. –*v.i.* **4.** to become unravelled. – **unraveller,** *n.* – **unravelment,** *n.*

**unread** /ʌnˈrɛd/, *adj.* **1.** not read or perused, as a book. **2.** not having gained knowledge by reading. **3.** not having read (some subject or matter) (fol. by *in*).

**unreadable** /ʌnˈridəbəl/, *adj.* **1.** not readable; illegible; undecipherable. **2.** not interesting to read; tedious. – **unreadability** /ʌnˌridəˈbɪləti/, **unreadableness,** *n.* – **unreadably,** *adv.*

**unready** /ʌnˈrɛdi/, *adj.* **1.** not ready; not made ready, as for action or use. **2.** not in a state of readiness or preparation, as a person. **3.** not prompt or quick. **4.** *Obs.* not dressed, or not fully dressed. – **unreadily,** *adv.* – **unreadiness,** *n.*

**unreal** /ʌnˈril/, *adj.* **1.** not real; not substantial; imaginary; artificial; unpractical or visionary. **2.** *Colloq.* **a.** unbelievably awful. **b.** unbelievably wonderful. – **unreally,** *adv.*

**unrealistic** /ʌnriəˈlɪstɪk/, *adj.* **1.** not closely or accurately resembling an object or situation depicted. **2.** not practical, hard-headed or clear-sighted.

**unreality** /ʌnriˈæləti/, *n., pl.* **-ties.** **1.** lack of reality; quality of being unreal. **2.** something unreal or without reality.

**unreason** /ʌnˈrizən/, *n.* **1.** lack of reason; inability or unwillingness to think or act rationally, reasonably, or sensibly. **2.** that which is devoid of or contrary to reason.

**unreasonable** /ʌnˈrizənəbəl/, *adj.* **1.** not reasonable; not endowed with reason. **2.** not guided by reason or good sense. **3.** not agreeable to or willing to listen to reason. **4.** not based on or in accordance with reason or sound judgment. **5.** exceeding the bounds of reason; immoderate; exorbitant. – **unreasonableness,** *n.* – **unreasonably,** *adv.*

**unreasoned** /ʌnˈrizənd/, *adj.* worked out or arrived at by some method other than reasoning; irrational.

**unreasoning** /ʌnˈrizənɪŋ/, *adj.* **1.** not employing reason; illogical; unthinking. **2.** irrational, as emotions: *an unreasoning fear.* – **unreasoningly,** *adv.*

**unrecognised** /ʌnˈrɛkəgnaɪzd/, *adj.* **1.** not accorded adequate credit or appreciation. **2.** not recognised. Also, **unrecognized.**

**unredeemed** /ʌnrəˈdimd, -ri-/, *adj.* **1.** unmitigated, unrelieved, or unmodified, as by some good feature. **2.** not recovered from pawn or by ransom.

**unreel** /ʌnˈril/, *v.t., v.i.* to unwind from a reel. – **unreelable,** *adj.*

**unreeve** /ʌnˈriv/, *v.*, **-rove** or **-reeved, -reeving.** –*v.t.* **1.** to withdraw (a rope, etc.) from a block, thimble, etc. –*v.i.* **2.** to unreeve a rope. **3.** (of a rope, etc.) to become unreeved.

**unrefined** /ʌnrəˈfaɪnd/, *adj.* **1.** not refined; not purified, as substances. **2.** coarse or vulgar; lacking nice feeling, taste, etc.

**unreflected** /ʌnrəˈflɛktəd/, *adj.* **1.** not returned by reflection, as by a polished surface. **2.** not considered or thought out (fol. by *on*).

**unreflecting** /ʌnrəˈflɛktɪŋ/, *adj.* not given to the exercise of reflection, meditation, or thought; thoughtless.

**unreformed** /ʌnrəˈfɔmd/, *adj.* **1.** not changed for the better, as persons, their character, etc. **2.** not reformed, as institutions, esp. the Church. **3.** not affected by the Reformation.

**unregenerate** /ʌnrəˈdʒɛnərət/, *adj.* **1.** unreformed; wicked or sinful; unconverted. **2.** not regenerate; not born again spiritually. **3.** remaining at enmity with God. Also, **unregenerated.** – **unregeneracy,** *n.* – **unregenerately,** *adv.*

**unrelated** /ʌnrəˈleɪtəd/, *adj.* **1.** not connected by blood or marriage; not kin. **2.** having no relationship; unconnected. **3.** untold, as a story.

**unrelenting** /ʌnrə'lɛntɪŋ/, *adj.* **1.** not relenting; not yielding to feelings of kindness or compassion. **2.** not slackening in severity or determination. **3.** maintaining speed or rate of advance. – **unrelentingly,** *adv.* – **unrelentingness,** *n.*

**unreliable** /ʌnrə'laɪəbəl/, *adj.* not reliable; not to be relied or depended on. – **unreliability** /ˌʌnrəˌlaɪə'bɪləti/, **unreliableness,** *n.* – **unreliably,** *adv.*

**unrelieved** /ʌnrə'livd/, *adj.* **1.** not varied, moderated, or made less monotonous. **2.** not provided with relief or aid. – **unrelievedly** /ʌnrə'livədli/, *adv.*

**unreligious** /ʌnrə'lɪdʒəs/, *adj.* **1.** irreligious. **2.** having no connection with or relation to religion; neither religious nor irreligious.

**unremarkable** /ʌnrə'makəbəl/, *adj.* ordinary; unexciting; not worthy of note. – **unremarkably,** *adv.*

**unremarked** /ʌnrə'makt/, *adj.* not noticed.

**unremitting** /ʌnrə'mɪtɪŋ/, *adj.* not remitting or slackening; not abating for a time; incessant. – **unremittingly,** *adv.* – **unremittingness,** *n.*

**unrepeatable** /ʌnrə'pitəbəl/, *adj.* **1.** too vulgar, abusive or otherwise unpleasant to be repeated. **2.** unable to be repeated: *an unrepeatable offer of goods on sale.* – **unrepeatability** /ˌʌnrəˌpitə'bɪləti/, *n.* – **unrepeatably,** *adv.*

**unrequited** /ʌnrə'kwaɪtəd/, *adj.* (used esp. of affection) not returned or reciprocated. – **unrequitedly,** *adv.* – **unrequitedness,** *n.*

**unreserve** /ʌnrə'zɜv/, *n.* absence of reserve; frankness.

**unreserved** /ʌnrə'zɜvd/, *adj.* **1.** not reserved; without reservation; full; entire. **2.** free from reserve; frank; open. **3.** not set aside or ordered in advance; not booked. – **unreservedly** /ʌnrə'zɜvədli/, *adv.* – **unreservedness,** *n.*

**unresolved** /ʌnrə'zɒlvd/, *adj.* **1.** (of questions, problems, etc.) not decided or solved. **2.** (of persons) uncertain how to act, or in an opinion. – **unresolvedly** /ʌnrə'zɒlvədli/, *adv.* – **unresolvedness,** *n.*

**unrest** /ʌn'rɛst/, *n.* **1.** lack of rest; restless or uneasy state; inquietude. **2.** strong, almost rebellious, dissatisfaction and agitation.

**unresting** /ʌn'rɛstɪŋ/, *adj.* not stopping or pausing, tireless, seeking or taking no rest. – **unrestingly,** *adv.*

**unrestraint** /ʌnrə'streɪnt/, *n.* absence of or freedom from restraint.

**unrewarded** /ʌnrə'wɔdəd/, *adj.* **1.** (of persons) without appropriate recompense. **2.** (of good or bad actions) not recompensed.

**unrig** /ʌn'rɪg/, *v.t.*, **-rigged, -rigging.** to strip of rigging, as a ship.

**unrighteous** /ʌn'raɪtʃəs/, *adj.* **1.** not righteous; not upright or virtuous; wicked. **2.** not in accordance with right; unjust. *–n.* **3. the unrighteous,** wicked and unjust people collectively. [ME *unrightwyse,* OE *unrihtwīs*] – **unrighteously,** *adv.* – **unrighteousness,** *n.*

**unripe** /ʌn'raɪp/, *adj.* **1.** not ripe; immature; not fully developed. **2.** *Obs.* too early; premature. Also, **unripened.** – **unripeness,** *n.*

**unrivalled** /ʌn'raɪvəld/, *adj.* having no rival or competitor; having no equal; peerless. Also, *U.S.,* **unrivaled.**

**unrobe** /ʌn'roub/, *v.t., v.i.*, **-robed, -robing.** →**disrobe** (def. 1).

**unroll** /ʌn'roul/, *v.t.* **1.** to open or spread out (something rolled, coiled, or folded). **2.** to extend or spread out. **3.** to lay open; display; reveal. *–v.i.* **4.** to become unrolled. **5.** to become visible or apparent.

**unroof** /ʌn'ruf/, *v.t.* to take the roof off.

**unroot** /ʌn'rut/, *v.t.* →**uproot.**

**unround** /ʌn'raund/, *v.t.* to pronounce without rounding the lips; the vowel of *bit* is normally unrounded, the vowel of *put* is often unrounded. – **unrounded,** *adj.*

**unrove** /ʌn'rouv/, *v.* **1.** past tense and past participle of **unreeve.** *–adj.* **2.** withdrawn from a block, thimble, etc.

**unruffled** /ʌn'rʌfəld/, *adj.* **1.** (of a person) calm; undisturbed. **2.** not physically ruffled or disturbed; not choppy, as the sea.

**unruly** /ʌn'ruli/, *adj.* not submissive or conforming to rule; ungovernable; turbulent; refractory; lawless. – **unruliness,** *n.*

**unsaddle** /ʌn'sædl/, *v.*, **-dled, -dling.** *–v.t.* **1.** to take the saddle from. **2.** to cause to fall or dismount from a saddle; unhorse. *–v.i.* **3.** to take the saddle from a horse.

**unsafe** /ʌn'seɪf/, *adj.* **1.** not safe or secure, as a person. **2.** not safe to be in, as a place. **3.** not to be trusted; unreliable. – **unsafely,** *adv.* – **unsafeness,** *n.*

**unsafety** /ʌn'seɪfti/, *n.* the state of being unsafe; exposure to danger or risk; insecurity.

**unsaid** /ʌn'sɛd/, *v.* **1.** past tense and past participle of **unsay.** *–adj.* **2.** not uttered.

**unsatisfactory** /ʌnˌsætəs'fæktri, -təri/, *adj.* not satisfactory; not satisfying specified desires or requirements; inadequate. – **unsatisfactorily,** *adv.* – **unsatisfactoriness,** *n.*

**unsaturated** /ʌn'sætʃəreɪtəd/, *adj.* **1.** not saturated; having the power to dissolve still more of a substance. **2.** *Chem.* capable of taking on an element, etc., by direct chemical combination without the liberation of other elements or compounds, esp. as a result of the presence of a double or triple bond between carbon atoms.

**unsavoury** /ʌn'seɪvəri/, *adj.* **1.** unpleasant in taste or smell. **2.** socially or morally unpleasant or offensive. Also, *esp. U.S.,* **unsavory.** – **unsavourily,** *adv.* – **unsavouriness,** *n.*

**unsay** /ʌn'seɪ/, *v.t.*, **-said, -saying.** to retract (something said).

**unscathed** /ʌn'skeɪðd/, *adj.* not scathed; unharmed; uninjured physically or spiritually.

**unscholarly** /ʌn'skɒləli/, *adj.* not in accordance with principles or standards of scholarship; not learned; inappropriate to a scholar. – **unscholarliness,** *n.*

**unschooled** /ʌn'skuld/, *adj.* **1.** uneducated; having received no schooling. **2.** not disciplined. **3.** not acquired by training; natural.

**unscientific** /ˌʌnsaɪən'tɪfɪk/, *adj.* **1.** not scientific; not in accordance with the requirements of science. **2.** not conforming to the principles or methods of science. – **unscientifically,** *adv.*

**unscramble** /ʌn'skræmbəl/, *v.t.*, **-bled, -bling.** **1.** *Colloq.* to bring out of a scrambled condition; reduce to order. **2.** to restore (a scrambled telephone message, or the like) to intelligibility. – **unscrambler,** *n.*

**unscratched** /ʌn'skrætʃt/, *adj.* **1.** not having been scratched. **2.** having received no injury; totally unharmed.

**unscreened** /ʌn'skrind/, *adj.* **1.** not protected by a screen or screening. **2.** not sifted or separated through or as through a screen. **3.** not yet shown in a cinema. **4.** not investigated for security purposes.

**unscrew** /ʌn'skru/, *v.t.* **1.** to draw the screw or screws from; unfasten by withdrawing screws. **2.** to remove (the lid of a screw-top jar, etc.) by turning. **3.** to loosen or withdraw (a screw, screwlike plug, etc.). *–v.i.* **4.** to permit of being unscrewed. **5.** to become unscrewed.

**unscripted** /ʌn'skrɪptəd/, *adj.* (of a radio or television program, theatrical performance, etc.) performed without a prepared script.

**unscrupulous** /ʌn'skrupjələs/, *adj.* not scrupulous; unrestrained by scruples; conscienceless; unprincipled. – **unscrupulously,** *adv.* – **unscrupulousness,** *n.*

**unseal** /ʌn'sil/, *v.t.* **1.** to break or remove the seal of. **2.** to open, as something sealed or firmly closed: *nothing will unseal my lips on that topic.*

**unsealed** /ʌn'sild/, *adj.* **1.** not closed with or bearing a seal. **2.** not closed, as a letter.

**unsealed road** /– 'roud/, *n.* a road not covered with bitumen or any smooth, weather-resistant surface. Also, **unsurfaced road.**

**unseam** /ʌn'sim/, *v.t.* to open the seam or seams of.

**unsearchable** /ʌn'sɜtʃəbəl/, *adj.* not searchable; not to be searched into or understood by searching; inscrutable; unfathomable. – **unsearchableness,** *n.* – **unsearchably,** *adv.*

**unseasonable** /ʌn'sizənəbəl, -'siznə-/, *adj.* **1.** inappropriate to the time of year or the hour. **2.** untimely; ill-timed; inopportune. – **unseasonableness,** *n.* – **unseasonably,** *adv.*

**unseasoned** /ʌn'sizənd/, *adj.* **1.** (of things) not seasoned; not matured, dried, etc., by due seasoning. **2.** (of persons) not inured to a climate, work, etc.; inexperienced. **3.** (of food) not flavoured with seasoning.

**unseat** /ʌn'sit/, *v.t.* **1.** to throw from a saddle, as a rider. **2.** to depose from an official seat or from office. **3.** to displace from a seat.

**unsecured** /ʌnsə'kjuəd/, *adj.* **1.** not made secure or fastened. **2.** not insured against loss, as by a mortgage, bond, pledge, etc.

**unsecured note** /– 'nout/, *n.* a certificate acknowledging a loan made for a fixed period of time at a fixed rate of interest, not secured by a charge over the company's assets, and ranking after debentures for payment in a winding-up.

**unseeded** /ʌn'sidəd/, *adj.* (of a tennis player) not seeded. See **seed** (def. 20).

**unseemly** /ʌn'simli/, *adj.* **1.** not seemly; unfitting; unbecoming; improper; indecorous. **2.** *Obs.* unattractive. *–adv.* **3.** in an unseemly manner. – **unseemliness,** *n.*

**unseen** /ʌn'sin/, *adj.* **1.** not seen; unperceived; unobserved; invisible. **2.** (of passages of writing or music) not previously seen. *–n.* **3.** an unprepared passage for translation, as in an examination.

**unsegregated** /ʌn'sɛgrəgeɪtəd/, *adj.* not subject to racial segregation.

**unselfish** /ʌn'sɛlfɪʃ/, *adj.* not selfish; disinterested; altruistic. – **unselfishly,** *adv.* – **unselfishness,** *n.*

**unserviceable** /ʌn'sɜvəsəbəl/, *adj.* **1.** not useful, as for its proper purpose. **2.** incapable of being put to use, as through wear or damage. – **unserviceability** /ʌnˌsɜvəsə'bɪləti/, *n.*

**unset** /ʌn'sɛt/, *adj.* **1.** not solidified or become firm. **2.** (of gems) unmounted.

**unsettle** /ʌn'sɛtl/, *v.,* **-tled, -tling.** *–v.t.* **1.** to bring out of a settled state; cause to be no longer firmly fixed or established; render unstable; disturb; disorder. **2.** to shake or weaken (beliefs, feelings, etc.); derange (the mind, etc.). *–v.i.* **3.** to become unfixed or disordered.

**unsettled** /ʌn'sɛtld/, *adj.* **1.** not settled; not fixed in a place or abode. **2.** not populated, as a region. **3.** not fixed or stable, as conditions; without established order, as times. **4.** liable to change, as weather. **5.** wavering or uncertain, as the mind, opinions, etc., or the person. **6.** undetermined, as a point at issue. **7.** not adjusted, closed, or disposed of finally, as an account or an estate. – **unsettledness, unsettlement,** *n.*

**unsex** /ʌn'sɛks/, *v.t.* **1.** to deprive (a person, esp. a woman) of the qualities appropriate to his or her sex. **2.** to castrate.

**unshackle** /ʌn'ʃækəl/, *v.t.,* **-led, -ling.** *v.t.* **1.** to free from restraint. **2.** to free from shackles; unfetter.

**unshadowed** /ʌn'ʃædoud/, *adj.* not shadowed; not darkened or obscured; free from gloom.

**unshakeable** /ʌn'ʃeɪkəbəl/, *adj.* (of opinions, beliefs, positions, etc.) tenaciously held; not open to dissuasion. Also, **unshakable.** – **unshakeably,** *adv.*

**unshapen** /ʌn'ʃeɪpən/, *adj.* not shaped or definitely formed; shapeless; formless; indefinite.

**unsheathe** /ʌn'ʃið/, *v.t.,* **-sheathed, -sheathing.** **1.** to draw from a sheath, as a sword, knife, or the like. **2.** to bring or put forth from a covering, threateningly or otherwise.

**unshell** /ʌn'ʃɛl/, *v.t.* to take out of the shell; remove or release, as from a shell.

**unship** /ʌn'ʃɪp/, *v.t.,* **-shipped, -shipping.** **1.** to put or take off from a ship, as persons or goods. **2.** to remove from the proper place for use, as a mast, oar, tiller, etc.

**unshoulder** /ʌn'ʃouldə/, *v.t.* to remove (a load) from the shoulder.

**unshrinking** /ʌn'ʃrɪŋkɪŋ/, *adj.* not shrinking or drawing back; firm; unyielding. – **unshrinkingly,** *adv.* – **unshrinkingness,** *n.*

**unshriven** /ʌn'ʃrɪvən/, *adj.* not having received the last sacrament; not having received the sacramental grace of penance by confession before a priest.

**unshroud** /ʌn'ʃraud/, *v.t.* to remove the shroud from; divest of something that shrouds; uncover; unveil.

**unsighted** /ʌn'saɪtəd/, *adj.* **1.** (of a gun) not provided with sights. **2.** (of a shot) fired without proper aiming. **3.** not yet in view.

**unsightly** /ʌn'saɪtli/, *adj.* not pleasing to the sight; forming an unpleasing sight. – **unsightliness,** *n.*

**unskilful** /ʌn'skɪlfəl/, *adj.* not skilful; inexpert; awkward; bungling. Also, *U.S.,* **unskillful.** – **unskilfully,** *adv.* – **unskilfulness,** *n.*

**unskilled** /ʌn'skɪld/, *adj.* **1.** of or pertaining to workers lacking specialised training or ability. **2.** not skilled (in some activity). **3.** not requiring or exhibiting skill.

**unslaked lime** /ʌnsleɪkt 'laɪm/, *n.* See **lime**[1] (def. 1).

**unsling** /ʌn'slɪŋ/, *v.t.,* **-slung, -slinging.** **1.** to remove (something) from a position in which it is slung. **2.** *Naut.* to take off the slings of; release from slings.

**unsnap** /ʌn'snæp/, *v.t.,* **-snapped, -snapping.** to release by opening a snap or catch.

**unsnarl** /ʌn'snal/, *v.t.* to bring out of a snarled condition; disentangle.

**unsociable** /ʌn'souʃəbəl/, *adj.* not sociable; having, showing, or marked by a disinclination to friendly social relations. – **unsociability** /ˌʌnsouʃə'bɪləti/, **unsociableness,** *n.* – **unsociably,** *adv.*

**unsolder** /ʌn'sɒldə/, *v.t.* **1.** to separate (something soldered). **2.** to disunite; dissolve.

**unsolicited** /ʌnsə'lɪsətəd/, *adj.* **1.** not asked for: *unsolicited contributions.* **2.** (of persons) not approached or solicited (for some purpose).

**unsophisticated** /ʌnsə'fɪstəkeɪtəd/, *adj.* **1.** not sophisticated; simple; artless. **2.** not complicated, as a mechanism; unsubtle. **3.** unadulterated; pure; genuine. – **unsophisticatedly,** *adv.* – **unsophisticatedness, unsophistication** /ˌʌnsəfɪstə'keɪʃən/, *n.*

**unsound** /ʌn'saund/, *adj.* **1.** not sound; diseased, as the body or mind. **2.** decayed, as timber or fruit; impaired or defective, as goods. **3.** not solid or firm, as foundations. **4.** not well-founded or valid; fallacious. **5.** easily broken; light: *unsound slumber.* **6.** not financially strong; unreliable. – **unsoundly,** *adv.* – **unsoundness,** *n.*

**unsounded**[1] /ʌn'saundəd/, *adj.* not sounded, uttered, or caused to make a noise.

**unsounded**[2] /ʌn'saundəd/, *adj.* not sounded or fathomed.

**unsparing** /ʌn'spɛərɪŋ/, *adj.* **1.** not sparing; liberal or profuse. **2.** unmerciful. – **unsparingly,** *adv.* – **unsparingness,** *n.*

**unspeak** /ʌn'spik/, *v.t.,* **-spoke, -spoken, -speaking.** to retract (something spoken); unsay.

**unspeakable** /ʌn'spikəbəl/, *adj.* **1.** inexpressibly bad or objectionable. **2.** impossible to express in words; unutterable; inexpressible. **3.** not speakable; that may not be spoken. – **unspeakably,** *adv.*

**unspoilt** /ʌn'spɔɪlt/, *adj.* not impaired; not having deteriorated, as the character of a person or place. Also, **unspoiled.**

**unspoken** /ʌn'spoukən/, *adj.* **1.** not spoken; not expressed aloud. **2.** understood without needing to be uttered.

**unspotted** /ʌn'spɒtəd/, *adj.* **1.** not having spots or marks. **2.** (esp. of a reputation) having no moral blemish.

**unsprung** /ʌn'sprʌŋ/, *adj.* not equipped with a spring or springing, as upholstery, vehicles, etc.

**unstable** /ʌn'steɪbəl/, *adj.* **1.** not stable; not firm or firmly fixed; unsteady. **2.** liable to fall, change, or cease. **3.** unsteadfast; inconstant; wavering. **4.** lacking emotional stability. **5.** *Chem.* denoting compounds which readily decompose or change into other compounds. – **unstableness,** *n.* – **unstably,** *adv.*

**unstable equilibrium** /– ikwə'lɪbriəm/, *n.* a state of equilibrium in a body such that any slight displacement will cause the body to move away from its position of equilibrium.

**unstable oscillation** /– ɒsə'leɪʃən/, *n.* a mechanical or electrical oscillation which tends to increase in amplitude with time, esp. in an aircraft structural member, or an electrical circuit.

**unsteady** /ʌn'stɛdi/, *adj.* **1.** not steady; not firmly fixed; not secure or stable. **2.** fluctuating or wavering; unsteadfast. **3.** irregular or uneven. *–v.t.* **4.** to make unsteady. – **unsteadily,** *adv.* – **unsteadiness,** *n.*

**unstep** /ʌn'stɛp/, *v.t.,* **-stepped, -stepping.** to remove (a mast, etc.) from its step.

**unstick** /ʌn'stɪk/, *v.t.,* **-stuck, -sticking.** **1.** to free, as one thing stuck to another. **2. come unstuck,** *Colloq.* **a.** to fail; suffer defeat or disaster, often as a result of questionable practice or being too clever. **b.** to lose mental stability; feel disturbed or insecure.

**unstop** /ʌn'stɒp/, *v.t.,* **-stopped, -stopping.** **1.** to remove the stopper from. **2.** to free from any obstruction; open. **3.** to draw out the stops of (an organ).

**unstoppable** /ʌn'stɒpəbəl/, *adj.* **1.** that cannot be stopped, prevented, or halted; inexorable. **2.** that cannot be stopped up or obstructed. – **unstoppably,** *adv.*

**unstopped** /ʌn'stɒpt/, *adj.* **1.** *Pros.* denoting a line of verse the sense of which continues into the following line. **2.** not stopped up or prevented.

**unstrained** /ʌn'streɪnd/, *adj.* **1.** not under strain or tension. **2.** not separated or cleared by straining.

**unstrap** /ʌn'stræp/, *v.t.*, **-strapped, -strapping.** to take off or slacken the strap of.

**unstratified** /ʌn'strætəfaɪd/, *adj.* not stratified; not arranged in strata or layers: *unstratified rocks* (such as the igneous rocks granite, porphyry, etc.).

**unstressed** /ʌn'strɛst/, *adj.* **1.** not under stress or strain. **2.** not stressed or accented.

**unstring** /ʌn'strɪŋ/, *v.t.*, **-strung, -stringing.** **1.** to deprive of a string or strings. **2.** to take from a string. **3.** to loosen the strings of. **4.** to relax the tension of. **5.** to relax unduly, or weaken (the nerves). **6.** to weaken the nerves of.

**unstriped** /ʌn'straɪpt/, *adj.* not striped; non-striated, as muscular tissue.

**unstructured** /ʌn'strʌktʃəd/, *adj.* **1.** without structural organisation. **2.** not regulated or regimented: *an unstructured playgroup program.* **3.** *Psychol.* having meanings by subjective interpretation only, as ink blot tests; without intrinsic or objective meaning.

**unstrung** /ʌn'strʌŋ/, *v.* **1.** past tense and past participle of **unstring.** *–adj.* **2.** having the string or strings loosened or removed, as a bow or harp. **3.** having the nerves weakened or in bad condition, as a person.

**unstudied** /ʌn'stʌdid/, *adj.* **1.** not premeditated or laboured; natural; unaffected. **2.** not having studied; unversed.

**unsubstantial** /ʌnsəb'stænʃəl/, *adj.* **1.** not substantial; not solid, firm, or strong; flimsy; slight; unreal; insubstantial. **2.** not substantiated; having no foundation in fact. **3.** immaterial; having no substance. – **unsubstantiality** /ˌʌnsəbˌstænʃi'æləti/, *n.* – **unsubstantially,** *adv.*

**unsuccessful** /ʌnsək'sɛsfəl/, *adj.* not successful; without success; unfortunate. – **unsuccessfully,** *adv.* – **unsuccessfulness,** *n.*

**unsuitable** /ʌn'sutəbəl/, *adj.* not suitable; inappropriate; unfitting; unbecoming. – **unsuitability** /ʌnˌsutə'bɪləti/, **unsuitableness,** *n.* – **unsuitably,** *adv.*

**unsuited** /ʌn'sutəd/, *adj.* **1.** not suited or fit; inappropriate: *unsuited to the purpose to which it is put.* **2.** badly matched; incompatible.

**unsullied** /ʌn'sʌlid/, *adj.* **1.** not tarnished or soiled. **2.** blameless.

**unsung** /ʌn'sʌŋ/, *adj.* **1.** not sung; not uttered or rendered by singing. **2.** not celebrated in, or as if in, song.

**unsupported** /ʌnsə'pɔtəd/, *adj.* **1.** not supported. **2.** (of a racehorse) having no backers.

**unsure** /ʌn'ʃɔ/, *adj.* **1.** not certain; not confident. **2.** not to be relied on: *an unsure method.* **3.** precarious; dependent on chance.

**unsurfaced road** /ʌnsɜfəst 'roud/, *n.* →**unselaed road.**

**unsuspected** /ʌnsə'spɛktəd/, *adj.* **1.** clear of or not under suspicion. **2.** not imagined to exist. – **unsuspectedly,** *adv.* – **unsuspectedness,** *n.*

**unswathe** /ʌn'sweɪð/, *v.t.*, **-swathed, -swathing.** to free from that which swathes; take wrappings from.

**unswayed** /ʌn'sweɪd/, *adj.* not influenced or affected.

**unswear** /ʌn'swɛə/, *v.t.*, **-swore, -sworn, -swearing.** to retract (something sworn, or sworn to); recant by a subsequent oath; abjure.

**unswerving** /ʌn'swɜvɪŋ/, *adj.* steady; constant; not turning aside: *unswerving loyalty.* – **unswervingly,** *adv.*

**unsympathetic** /ˌʌnsɪmpə'θɛtɪk/, *adj.* **1.** not offering sympathy; lacking understanding; hostile. **2.** not inspiring sympathy; unpleasing. – **unsympathetically,** *adv.*

**untack** /ʌn'tæk/, *v.t.* to remove the tacking from (a piece of sewing).

**untangle** /ʌn'tæŋgəl/, *v.t.*, **-gled, -gling.** **1.** to bring out of a tangled state; disentangle; unsnarl. **2.** to straighten out or clear up (anything confused or perplexing).

**untapped** /ʌn'tæpt/, *adj.* **1.** not drawn on, as resources, potentialities, etc.: *an untapped fund of money, of enthusiasm.* **2.** not tapped.

**untaught** /ʌn'tɔt/, *v.* **1.** past tense and past participle of **unteach.** *–adj.* **2.** natural or inborn; not acquired by teaching. **3.** not instructed or educated; ignorant; naive.

**untaxed** /ʌn'tækst/, *adj.* **1.** not subjected to taxation. **2.** not under a burden or strain.

**unteach** /ʌn'titʃ/, *v.t.*, **-taught, -teaching.** **1.** to cause to be forgotten or disbelieved, as by contrary teaching. **2.** to cause to forget or disbelieve something previously taught.

**unteachable** /ʌn'titʃəbəl/, *adj.* **1.** (of a subject) unable to be taught or imparted. **2.** (of a person) incapable of being instructed; having no capacity or will to learn. – **unteachably,** *adv.* – **unteachability** /ˌʌntitʃə'bɪləti/, **unteachableness,** *n.*

**untenable** /ʌn'tɛnəbəl/, *adj.* **1.** incapable of being held against attack. **2.** incapable of being maintained against argument, as an opinion, scheme, etc. **3.** not fit to be occupied. – **untenability** /ˌʌntɛnə'bɪləti/, *adv.* – **untenably,** *n.*

**unthankful** /ʌn'θæŋkfəl/, *adj.* **1.** not thankful; ungrateful. **2.** not repaid with thanks; thankless. – **unthankfully,** *adv.* – **unthankfulness,** *n.*

**unthink** /ʌn'θɪŋk/, *v.t.*, **-thought, -thinking.** **1.** to dispel from the mind or thoughts. **2.** to reverse or retract by thinking, as in changing one's mind.

**unthinkable** /ʌn'θɪŋkəbəl/, *adj.* **1.** inconceivable; unimaginable. **2.** not to be considered; utterly out of the question. – **unthinkably,** *adv.*

**unthinking** /ʌn'θɪŋkɪŋ/, *adj.* **1.** not thinking; thoughtless; heedless. **2.** indicating lack of thought or reflection. **3.** not given to reflection; uncritical. **4.** not possessing the faculty of thought. – **unthinkingly,** *adv.* – **unthinkingness,** *n.*

**unthread** /ʌn'θrɛd/, *v.t.* **1.** to draw out or take out the thread from. **2.** to thread one's way out of. **3.** to disentangle; restore from a confused condition.

**untidy** /ʌn'taɪdi/, *adj.*, **-tidier, -tidiest,** *v.t.*, **-tidied, -tidying.** *–adj.* **1.** not tidy or neat; slovenly; disordered. *–v.t.* **2.** to make untidy; disorder. – **untidily,** *adv.* – **untidiness,** *n.*

**untie** /ʌn'taɪ/, *v.*, **-tied, -tying.** *–v.t.* **1.** to loosen or unfasten (anything tied); let or set loose by undoing a knot. **2.** to undo the string or cords of. **3.** to undo, as a cord or a knot. **4.** to free from or as from bonds or restraint. **5.** to resolve, as perplexities. *–v.i.* **6.** to become untied.

**until** /ʌn'tɪl/, *conj.* **1.** up to the time that or when; till. **2.** (with negatives) before: *he did not come until the meeting was half over.* *–prep.* **3.** onward to, or till (a specified time); up to the time of (some occurrence). **4.** (with negatives) before: *he did not go until night.* [ME *untill,* from *un-* (from Scand.; cf. Icel. *unz* up to, as far as) + TILL[1]]

**untimely** /ʌn'taɪmli/, *adj.* **1.** not timely; not occurring at a suitable time or season; ill-timed or inopportune. **2.** premature; not fully mature or ripe. *–adv.* **3.** unseasonably. – **untimeliness,** *n.*

**untinged** /ʌn'tɪndʒd/, *adj.* **1.** not modified or affected: *untinged by sentiment.* **2.** not coloured, as by paint, light, etc.

**untitled** /ʌn'taɪtld/, *adj.* **1.** not titled; without a title, as of nobility. **2.** *Archaic.* having no right or claim.

**unto** /'ʌntu/, *prep. Archaic.* **1.** to (in its various uses, except as the accompaniment of the infinitive). **2.** until; till. [ME; from *un-* (see UNTIL) + TO]

**untold** /ʌn'tould/, *adj.* **1.** not told; not related; not revealed. **2.** more than can be numbered or enumerated; uncounted. **3.** too much to be measured; incalculable. **4.** *Colloq.* unbelievable.

**untouchability** /ˌʌntʌtʃə'bɪləti/, *n.* the defiling character ascribed to low-caste Indians or non-Hindus by high-caste Hindus or Brahmans.

**untouchable** /ʌn'tʌtʃəbəl/, *adj.* **1.** that may not be touched; of a nature such that it cannot be touched; not palpable; intangible. **2.** too distant to be touched. **3.** vile or loathsome to the touch. **4.** unable to be equalled. *–n.* **5.** a member of the lower classes in India, whose touch is believed to defile a high-caste Hindu.

**untouched** /ʌn'tʌtʃt/, *adj.* **1.** not touched or handled. **2.** not harmed or damaged in the least. **3.** not used at all, esp. entirely uneaten or undrunk. **4.** not affected, modified or influenced; innocent. **5.** not discussed or mentioned (sometimes fol. by *upon* or *on*). **6.** not moved or affected in mind; undisturbed; calm.

**untoward** /ʌntəˈwɔd, ʌnˈtouəd/, *adj.* **1.** unfavourable or unfortunate. **2.** unseemly. **3.** *Archaic.* unruly, stubborn, or perverse. [UN-[1] + TOWARD] – **untowardly,** *adv.* – **untowardness,** *n.*

**untrammelled** /ʌnˈtræməld/, *adj.* unrestricted; unhampered. Also, *U.S.,* **untrammeled.**

**untravelled** /ʌnˈtrævəld/, *adj.* **1.** not having travelled, esp. to distant places; not having gained experience by travel. **2.** not travelled through or over; not frequented by travellers. Also, *U.S.,* **untraveled.**

**untried** /ʌnˈtraɪd/, *adj.* **1.** not tried; not tested or put to the proof; not attempted. **2.** not yet tried at law.

**untrue** /ʌnˈtru/, *adj.* **1.** not true, as to a person or a cause, to fact, or to a standard. **2.** unfaithful; false. **3.** incorrect or inaccurate. – **untrueness,** *n.* – **untruly,** *adv.*

**untruth** /ʌnˈtruθ/, *n.* **1.** the state or character of being untrue. **2.** want of veracity; divergence from truth. **3.** something untrue; a falsehood or lie. **4.** *Obs.* unfaithfulness or disloyalty.

**untruthful** /ʌnˈtruθfəl/, *adj.* not truthful; wanting in veracity; diverging from or contrary to the truth; not corresponding with fact or reality. – **untruthfully,** *adv.* – **untruthfulness,** *n.*

**untuck** /ʌnˈtʌk/, *v.t.* to release from or bring out of a tucked condition.

**unturned** /ʌnˈtɜnd/, *adj.* **1.** not having been turned or turned over. **2. leave no stone unturned,** to make an exhaustive search; do everything possible.

**untutored** /ʌnˈtjutəd/, *adj.* not tutored; untaught; uninstructed.

**untwine** /ʌnˈtwaɪn/, *v.t., v.i.,* **-twined, -twining.** to bring or come out of a twined condition.

**untwist** /ʌnˈtwɪst/, *v.t., v.i.* to bring or come out of a twisted condition.

**unused** /ʌnˈjuzd/ *for defs 1 and 2;* /ʌnˈjust/ *for def. 3, adj.* **1.** not used; not put to use. **2.** never having been used. **3.** not accustomed.

**unusual** /ʌnˈjuʒuəl/, *adj.* not usual, common, or ordinary; uncommon in amount or degree; of an exceptional kind. – **unusually,** *adv.* – **unusualness,** *n.*

**unutterable** /ʌnˈʌtərəbəl, -ˈtrəbəl/, *adj.* **1.** not communicable by utterance; incapable of being expressed. **2.** inexpressibly great or remarkable; unspeakable. **3.** incapable of being uttered; unpronounceable. – **unutterably,** *adv.*

**unvalued** /ʌnˈvæljud/, *adj.* **1.** not regarded as of value. **2.** not assessed in a formal valuation. **3.** *Obs.* invaluable. **4.** *Obs.* valueless.

**unvarnished** /ʌnˈvanɪʃt/, *adj.* **1.** (of statements, etc.) not embellished; plain: *the unvarnished truth.* **2.** not covered with varnish.

**unveil** /ʌnˈveɪl/, *v.t.* **1.** to remove a veil from; disclose to view. **2.** to disclose, as if by removing a veil; reveal. *–v.i.* **3.** to remove a veil; reveal oneself; become unveiled.

**unveiling** /ʌnˈveɪlɪŋ/, *n.* **1.** the act of showing a monument or the like for the first time, as in a ceremonial removal of a covering. **2.** the presentation of something for the first time.

**unvoice** /ʌnˈvɔɪs/, *v.t.,* **-voiced, -voicing.** *Phonet.* to pronounce a voiced sound in such a way that vocal cord vibrations are heard during part of its duration only. Before a pause, the end of a voiced fricative is *unvoiced* in English, as in *if you please,* when the final *z* sound ends like *s.*

**unvoiced** /ʌnˈvɔɪst/, *adj.* **1.** not uttered, spoken, or sounded. **2.** →**voiceless** (def. 5).

**unwarrantable** /ʌnˈwɒrəntəbəl/, *adj.* **1.** unable to be justified, confirmed, or proved, as an assertion or argument. **2.** unable to be justified, or vindicated, as an action. – **unwarrantableness,** *n.* – **unwarrantably,** *adv.*

**unwarranted** /ʌnˈwɒrəntəd/, *adj.* **1.** not justified, confirmed, or supported: *an unwarranted supposition.* **2.** not authorised, as actions. – **unwarrantedly,** *adv.*

**unwary** /ʌnˈwɛəri/, *adj.* not wary; not cautious; unguarded. – **unwarily,** *adv.* – **unwariness,** *n.*

**unwashed** /ʌnˈwɒʃt/, *adj.* **1.** (of things) not cleaned by washing. **2.** (of people) not clean; not habitually or usually kept clean by washing. *–n.* **3. the great unwashed,** *Colloq.* (*derog.*) the masses; the rabble.

**unwatched** /ʌnˈwɒtʃt/, *adj.* denoting or pertaining to a construction, as a beacon, which is worked automatically and not normally manned.

**unwearied** /ʌnˈwɪərid/, *adj.* **1.** not wearied; not fatigued. **2.** indefatigable. **3.** (of qualities, actions, etc.) unremitting. – **unweariedly,** *adv.* – **unweariedness,** *n.*

**unweighed** /ʌnˈweɪd/, *adj.* **1.** not weighed; not tested as to weight. **2.** not pondered upon or considered.

**unwelcome** /ʌnˈwɛlkəm/, *adj.* **1.** not welcome, as a person. **2.** not acceptable; unpleasing. – **unwelcomely,** *adv.* – **unwelcomeness,** *n.*

**unwell** /ʌnˈwɛl/, *adj.* not well; ailing; somewhat ill.

**unwept** /ʌnˈwɛpt/, *adj.* **1.** not wept, or wept for; unmourned. **2.** *Rare.* not wept or shed, as tears.

**unwholesome** /ʌnˈhoulsəm/, *adj.* **1.** not wholesome; unhealthy; deleterious to health or well-being, physically or morally. **2.** not sound in health; unhealthy, esp. in appearance; suggestive of disease. – **unwholesomely,** *adv.* – **unwholesomeness,** *n.*

**unwieldy** /ʌnˈwildi/, *adj.* **1.** not wieldy; wielded with difficulty; not readily handled or managed in use or action, as from size, shape, or weight. **2.** ungainly; awkward. – **unwieldily,** *adv.* – **unwieldiness,** *n.*

**unwill** /ʌnˈwɪl/, *v.t.* **1.** to will or determine upon (the reversal of something). **2.** to deprive of will. **3.** to revoke or reverse (one's will or purpose).

**unwilled** /ʌnˈwɪld/, *adj.* not willed; involuntary.

**unwilling** /ʌnˈwɪlɪŋ/, *adj.* **1.** not willing; loath; reluctant. **2.** performed or given reluctantly: *the unwilling admiration of the scornful.* – **unwillingly,** *adv.* – **unwillingness,** *n.*

**unwind** /ʌnˈwaɪnd/, *v.,* **-wound, -winding.** *–v.t.* **1.** to undo (something wound); loose or separate, as what is wound. **2.** to remove the windings from around (something). **3.** to disentangle. *–v.i.* **4.** to become unwound. **5.** to relax or calm down.

**unwinking** /ʌnˈwɪŋkɪŋ/, *adj.* not winking; having a fixed stare; watchful; unsleeping. – **unwinkingly,** *adv.*

**unwisdom** /ʌnˈwɪzdəm/, *n.* **1.** lack of wisdom. **2.** unwise action; folly.

**unwise** /ʌnˈwaɪz/, *adj.* not wise; foolish; imprudent; injudicious. – **unwisely,** *adv.* – **unwiseness,** *n.*

**unwish** /ʌnˈwɪʃ/, *v.t.* **1.** to retract (a wish). **2.** to wish for (something) not to be; desire the cessation of.

**unwished** /ʌnˈwɪʃt/, *adj.* not wished; undesired; unwelcome.

**unwitnessed** /ʌnˈwɪtnəst/, *adj.* **1.** unseen; unobserved. **2.** not attested by a witness, as a signature on a document.

**unwitting** /ʌnˈwɪtɪŋ/, *adj.* **1.** not witting or knowing; ignorant; unaware; unconscious. **2.** performed unintentionally or unknowingly; unpremeditated. – **unwittingly,** *adv.* – **unwittingness,** *n.*

**unwonted** /ʌnˈwountəd/, *adj. Archaic.* **1.** not customary, habitual, or usual. **2.** unused or unaccustomed (to something). – **unwontedly,** *adv.* – **unwontedness,** *n.*

**unworkable** /ʌnˈwɜkəbəl/, *adj.* **1.** incapable of being put into operation, as a system, or into practice, as a theory. **2.** unable to be worked on, or worked. – **unworkability** /ˌʌnwɜkəˈbɪləti/, *n.*

**unworldly** /ʌnˈwɜldli/, *adj.* **1.** not worldly; not seeking material advantage or gain; spiritually minded. **2.** naive; unsophisticated. **3.** not terrestrial; unearthly. – **unworldliness,** *n.*

**unworn** /ʌnˈwɔn/, *adj.* **1.** not damaged or deteriorating, etc., as from use. **2.** (of clothing) never worn; not hitherto worn.

**unworthy** /ʌnˈwɜði/, *adj.* **1.** not worthy; lacking worth or excellence. **2.** not commendable or creditable. **3.** not of adequate merit or character. **4.** of a kind not worthy (with *of,* expressed or understood). **5.** beneath the dignity (*of*). **6.** undeserving. **7.** not deserved or justified. – **unworthily,** *adv.* – **unworthiness,** *n.*

**unwound** /ʌnˈwaund/, *v.* **1.** past tense and past participle of **unwind.** *–adj.* **2.** not wound, or wound up.

**unwrap** /ʌnˈræp/, *v.,* **-wrapped, -wrapping.** *–v.t.* **1.** to bring out of a wrapped condition; unfold or open, as something wrapped. *–v.i.* **2.** to become unwrapped.

**unwrinkle** /ʌnˈrɪŋkəl/, *v.t.*, **-kled, -kling.** to smooth the wrinkles from.

**unwritten** /ʌnˈrɪtn/, *adj.* **1.** not written; not reduced to or recorded in writing. **2.** not actually formulated or expressed; customary. **3.** containing no writing; blank. [ME and OE *unwriten;* from UN-[1] + *writen,* pp. of WRITE]

**unwritten law** /– ˈlɔ/, *n.* **1.** law which rests for its authority on custom, judicial decision, etc., as distinguished from law originating in written command, statute, or decree. **2.** the supposed principle of the right of the individual to avenge wrongs against personal or family honour, esp. in cases involving relations between the sexes (sometimes urged in justification of persons guilty of criminal acts of vengeance). **3.** a custom or social convention.

**unyoke** /ʌnˈjoʊk/, *v.*, **-yoked, -yoking.** *–v.t.* **1.** to free from or as from a yoke. **2.** to part or disjoin, as by removing a yoke. *–v.i.* **3.** to remove a yoke. **4.** to cease work.

**unzip** /ʌnˈzɪp/, *v.t., v.i.*, **-zipped, -zipping.** *–v.t.* **1.** to open the zip of (a garment). *–v.i.* **2.** to become unzipped.

**up** /ʌp/, *adv., prep., adj., n., v.,* **upped, upping,** *interj.* *–adv.* **1.** to, towards, or in a more elevated position: *to climb up to the top of a ladder.* **2.** into the air: *to throw up a ball.* **3.** out of the ground: *to dig up potatoes.* **4.** to or in an erect position: *to stand up.* **5.** out of bed: *to get up.* **6.** above the horizon: *the moon came up.* **7.** to or at any point that is considered higher, as the north, a capital city, or the like. **8.** to or at a source, origin, centre, or the like: *to follow a stream up to its source.* **9.** to or at a higher point or degree in a scale, as of rank, size, value, pitch, etc. **10.** to or at a point of equal advance, extent, etc.: *to catch up in a race.* **11.** ahead; into a leading or more advanced position: *to move up into the lead.* **12.** well advanced or versed, as in a subject: *to keep up in nuclear physics.* **13.** in or into activity, operation, etc.: *to set up vibrations.* **14.** in or into a state of agitation or excitement: *worked up.* **15.** into existence, view, prominence, or consideration: *a problem has cropped up, the lost papers have turned up, his case comes up in court on Thursday.* **16.** to a state of maturity: *to bring up a child.* **17.** into or in a place of safekeeping, storage, retirement, etc.: *to lay up riches.* **18.** to a state of completion; to an end: *to finish something up.* **19.** in or into a state of union, contraction, etc.: *to add up a column of figures, to fold up a blanket.* **20.** to the required or final point: *to pay up one's debts, to burn up rubbish.* **21.** to a standstill: *to rein up, seize up.* **22.** *U.S.* equally; each; apiece; all: *the score was seven points up.* **23.** *Naut.* towards or facing into the wind. **24. up to mud** or **putty,** broken down, worthless. **25. up with,** towards a higher or more favourable position in relation to: *up with the leaders.* *–prep.* **26.** to, towards, or at a higher place on or in: *up the stairs, up a tree.* **27.** to, towards, near, or at a higher station, condition, or rank in. **28.** to, towards, or at a farther or higher point of: *up the street.* **29.** towards the source, origin, etc., of: *up the stream.* **30.** towards or in the interior of (a region, etc.): *the explorers went up the mulga.* **31.** in a course or direction contrary to that of: *to sail up wind.* **32.** *Colloq.* towards or at: *up King's Cross, up the Junction.* **33.** *Colloq.* **a.** engaged in sexual intercourse with: *up her like a lizard up a log.* **b.** angry with: *she was up him for being late.* **34. be up oneself,** *Colloq.* to have an unjustifiably high opinion of oneself; be self-deluding. **35. get up (someone),** to have sexual intercourse with (someone). **36. up a gumtree,** *Colloq.* confused; incorrect. **37. up each other, up one another,** *Colloq.* behaving in a sycophantic or toadying fashion to each other. **38. up the duff,** *Colloq.* pregnant. **39. up you!** *Colloq.* (an exclamation indicating insolent or disgusted dismissal). **40. who's up who (and who's paying the rent),** *Colloq.* **a.** (what are the alliances in a political or business group, etc.). **b.** (what are the alliances and sexual relationships within a particular group of people). *–adj.* **41.** upwards; going or directed upwards. **42.** travelling towards a terminus or centre: *an up train.* **43.** in an upright position or pointing upwards: *the signal is up.* **44.** standing and speaking: *the prime minister was up for three hours.* **45.** out of bed: *I have been up since six o'clock.* **46.** risen above the horizon: *the sun is up.* **47.** at a high point or full: *the tide is up.* **48.** in the air; above the ground: *the aeroplane is 2 000 metres up.* **49.** on horseback; in the saddle. **50.** well informed or advanced, as in a subject: *to be up in mathematics.* **51.** in activity: *the wind is up.* **52.** (esp. of a computer) operational. **53.** under consideration; on offer: *a candidate up for election.* **54.** appearing before a court or the like on some charge: *he is up for speeding again.* **55.** in the process of going on or happening, esp. something amiss: *they wondered what was up.* **56.** in a state of agitation or excitement: *his anger was up.* **57.** impassable to wheeled traffic, as a road under repair. **58.** in a leading or advanced position: *to be up in social standing.* **59.** winning or having won money at gambling or the like: *he was $50 up after an hour in the casino.* **60.** *Games.* winning or ahead of an opponent by a specified number of points, holes, etc. **61. all up.** See **all** (def. 11). **62. up against,** *Colloq.* faced with: *they are up against enormous problems.* **63. up against it,** *Colloq.* in difficulties; in severe straits. **64. up and about,** active; out of bed, esp. after recovering from an illness. **65. up to, a.** engaged in; doing: *what are you up to?* **b.** incumbent upon, as a duty: *it is up to him to make the next move.* **c.** as many as and no more: *I will take up to eight pupils.* **d.** as far as and no farther: *he is up to his knees in water.* **e.** *Colloq.* capable of: *he is not up to the job.* *–n.* **66.** an upward movement; an ascent. **67.** a rise of fortune, mood, etc.: *to have one's ups and downs.* **68. on the up and up,** *Colloq.* **a.** *Chiefly U.S.* honest. frank, or credible. **b.** tending upwards; improving; having increasing success. *–v.t. Colloq.* **69.** to put or take up. **70.** to make larger; step up: *to up output.* **71.** to raise; go better than (a preceding wager). **72.** *Naut.* to turn (the helm) to windward, thus turning the ship's head away from the wind. *–v.i.* **73.** *Colloq.* to get or start up (usu. fol. by *and*). *–interj.* **74.** (a command to rise or stand up). [ME and OE, c. LG *up,* and akin to G *auf*]

**up-,** a prefixal, attributive use of **up,** in its various meanings, as in *upland, upshot, upheaval.* [ME and OE]

**-up,** a suffix denoting the extensiveness or intensity of an activity involving something mentioned; as *beer-up, grog-up, fuck-up.*

**up-and-coming** /ˈʌp-ən-kʌmɪŋ/, *adj.* becoming successful, well-known, fashionable, etc.; promising. Also (*esp. in predicative use*), **up and coming** /ʌp ən ˈkʌmɪŋ/.

**up-and-down** /ˈʌp-ən-daʊn/, *adj.* **1.** taking place, performed, or formed alternately or both upwards and downwards. **2.** inconsistent in performance; erratic. Also (*esp. in predicative use*), **up and down** /ʌp ən ˈdaʊn/.

**up-and-under** /up-ən-ˈʌndə/, *n. Rugby Football.* a short, high punt kick, aimed at enabling the kicker and his team-mates to rush forward and regain possession of the ball; bomb; garryowen.

**Upanishad** /uˈpænɪʃəd, -ˈpʌn-, -ʃæd/, *n.* the chief theological documents of ancient Hinduism, expounding more elaborately the mystical knowledge contained in the earlier Vedas, esp. the pantheistic doctrine that, in all things, but pre-eminently in each human soul, there may be seen manifested the supreme, impersonal Brahma or Atman, the World Soul. – **Upanishadic** /uˌpænəˈʃædɪk, -ˌpʌn-/, *adj.*

**upas** /ˈjupəs/, *n.* **1.** the poisonous milky sap of *Antiaris toxicaria,* a large tree of Java, used for arrow poison. **2.** Also, **upas tree.** the tree. **3.** a destructive or deadly power or influence. [Malay: poison]

**upbear** /ʌpˈbɛə/, *v.t.*, **-bore, -borne, -bearing.** *Rare.* to bear up; raise aloft; support; sustain. – **upbearer,** *n.*

**up-beat** /ˈʌp-bit/, *n.* **1.** *Music.* **a.** the last beat of a bar, esp. when the piece of music or section or phrase starts with a note on that beat. **b.** the introductory beat of a conductor when bringing in the orchestra. *–adj.* **2.** *Colloq.* optimistic; cheerful.

**up-bow** /ˈʌp-boʊ/, *n.* (in bowing on a stringed instrument) a stroke towards the nut of the bow, indicated in scores by the symbol V (opposed to *down-bow*).

**upbraid** /ʌpˈbreɪd/, *v.t.* **1.** to reproach for some fault or offence; reprove severely; chide. **2.** to censure or find fault with (things). *–v.i.* **3.** to utter reproaches. [ME; OE *upbregdan.* See UP-, BRAID, *v.*] – **upbraider,** *n.*

**upbraiding** /ʌpˈbreɪdɪŋ/, *n.* **1.** the act or language of one who upbraids. *–adj.* **2.** reproachful; chiding. – **upbraidingly,** *adv.*

**upbringing** /ˈʌpbrɪŋɪŋ/, *n.* the bringing up or rearing of a person from childhood; care and training devoted to the young while growing up.

**upcast** /ˈʌpkast/, *n.* **1.** the act or an act of casting upwards. **2.** the state of being cast upwards. **3.** something that is cast up. **4.** a shaft or passage up which air passes, as from a mine (opposed to *downcast*); uptake. **5.** *Geol., Mining.* the upthrow of a fault. *–adj.* **6.** cast up; directed upwards.

**up-country** /ˈʌp-kʌntri/, *adj., n.;* /ʌp-ˈkʌntri/, *adv.* *–adj.* **1.** being or living remote from the coast or border; interior: *an up-country town.* **2.** (*derog.*) unsophisticated. *–n.* **3.** the interior of the country. *–adv.* **4.** towards or in the interior of a country.

**update** /ʌpˈdeɪt/, *v.,* **-dated, -dating;** /ˈʌpdeɪt/, *n.* *–v.t.* **1.** to bring up to date. *–n.* **2.** an updated version; revision: *an update on our earlier bulletin.*

**up-end** /ʌp-ˈɛnd/, *v.t.* **1.** to set on end, as a barrel. **2.** to upset or alter drastically. *–v.i.* **3.** to stand on end.

**up-front** /ˈʌp-frʌnt/, *adj.* **1.** placed in a position of leadership or responsibility; placed in a position involving physical activity and stress, as in a battle. **2.** straightforward; open; extroverted. **3.** advance: *the up-front money for the project.*

**upgrade** /ʌpˈgreɪd/, *v.,* **-graded, -grading;** /ˈʌpgreɪd/, *n., adj.;* /ʌpˈgreɪd/, *adv.* *–v.t.* **1.** to assign (a person, job, or the like) to a higher status, usu. with a larger salary. **2.** to improve. *–n.* **3.** *U.S.* an uphill slope. **4. on the upgrade,** improving; up-and-coming. *–adj., adv. U.S.* **5.** →**uphill.**

**upgrowth** /ˈʌpgroʊθ/, *n.* **1.** the process or fact of growing up; development. **2.** something that grows up.

**upheaval** /ʌpˈhivəl/, *n.* **1.** the act of upheaving. **2.** the state of being upheaved. **3.** a thorough, violent, or revolutionary change or disturbance, esp. in a society. **4.** *Geol.* an upward warping of a part of the earth's crust, forcing certain areas into a relatively higher position than before.

**upheave** /ʌpˈhiv/, *v.,* **-heaved** or **-hove, -heaving.** *–v.t.* **1.** to heave or lift up; raise up or aloft. **2.** to disturb or change violently or radically. *–v.i.* **3.** to be lifted up; rise as if thrust up.

**upheld** /ʌpˈhɛld/, *v.* past tense and past participle of **uphold.**

**uphill** /ʌpˈhɪl/, *adv.;* /ˈʌphɪl/, *adj., n.* *–adv.* **1.** up, or as if up, the slope of a hill; upwards. *–adj.* **2.** going or tending upwards on or as on a hill. **3.** at a high place or point. **4.** laboriously fatiguing or difficult. **5. be uphill,** to be in a difficult situation. **6. an uphill battle,** a task to be completed or objective to be reached only with great difficulty. *–n.* **7.** an ascent or rise.

**uphold** /ʌpˈhoʊld/, *v.t.,* **-held, -holding.** **1.** to support, sustain, or preserve unimpaired: *to uphold the old order.* **2.** to keep up, or keep from sinking; support. **3.** to support or maintain, as by advocacy or agreement: *to uphold the decision of a lower court.* – **upholder,** *n.*

**upholster** /ʌpˈhoʊlstə/, *v.t.* **1.** to provide (stools, armchairs, sofas, etc.) with coverings, cushions, stuffing, springs, etc. **2.** to cover or cushion in the manner of upholstery. *–v.i.* **3.** to do upholstery work. [backformation from UPHOLSTERER]

**upholsterer** /ʌpˈhoʊlstərə, -strə/, *n.* one whose business it is to make, finish, or repair the coverings and stuffing of chairs, couches, cushions, etc. [earlier *upholster* (from UPHOLD, *v.* + -STER) + -ER[1]]

**upholstery** /ʌpˈhoʊlstri, -stəri/, *n., pl.* **-ries.** **1.** the cushions, furniture coverings and other material used to stuff and cover furniture and cushions. **2.** the interior padding and lining for the seats, etc., of a car. **3.** the business of an upholsterer.

**uphroe** /ˈjufroʊ/, *n.* →**euphroe.**

**upkeep** /ˈʌpkip/, *n.* **1.** the process of keeping up or maintaining; the maintenance, or keeping in operation, due condition, and repair, of an establishment, a machine, etc. **2.** the cost of this, including operating expenses, cost of renewal or repair, etc.

**upland** /ˈʌplənd/, *n.* **1.** an area of high ground; a stretch of hilly or mountainous country. **2.** the higher ground of a region or district; an elevated region. *–adj.* **3.** of or pertaining to uplands or elevated regions.

**uplift** /ʌpˈlɪft/, *v.;* /ˈʌplɪft/, *n.* *–v.t.* **1.** to lift up; raise; elevate. **2.** to raise socially or morally. **3.** to exalt emotionally or spiritually. *–n.* **4.** the act of lifting up or raising; elevation. **5.** the process or work of improving socially or morally. **6.** emotional or spiritual exaltation. **7.** *Geol.* →**upheaval** (def. 4). – **uplifter,** *n.* – **upliftment,** *n.*

**uplifted** /ʌpˈlɪftəd/, *adj.* **1.** raised up; exalted. **2.** intellectually or spiritually elevated.

**up-lighter** /ˈʌp-laɪtə/, *n.* an electric light which shines upwards, as one which illuminates the leaves of a tree from underneath.

**up-market** /ˈʌp-makət/, *adj.* **1.** of or pertaining to commercial services and goods of superior status, quality and price. **2.** superior in style or production; pretentious. See **down-market.**

**upmost** /ˈʌpmoʊst/, *adj.* uppermost.

**upon** /əˈpɒn/, *prep.* **1.** up and on; upwards so as to get or be on: *to climb upon a table.* **2.** in an elevated position on. **3.** on, in any of various senses (used as an equivalent of *on* with no added idea of ascent or elevation, and preferred in certain cases only for euphonic or metrical reasons). [ME. See UP, *adv.,* ON, *prep.*]

**upper** /ˈʌpə/, *adj.* **1.** higher (than something implied) or highest, as in place, or position, or in a scale: *the upper slopes of a mountain, upper register of a voice.* **2.** occupying or consisting of high or rising ground, or farther into the interior. **3.** forming the higher of a pair of corresponding things or sets. **4.** (of a surface) facing upwards. **5.** superior, as in rank, dignity, or station. **6.** higher or highest in respect of wealth, rank, office, birth, influence, etc.: *the upper classes or orders.* **7.** (*cap.*) *Geol.* denoting a later division of a period, system, or the like: *the Upper Devonian.* *–n.* **8.** anything which is higher (than another, as of a pair) or highest. **9.** the part of a shoe or boot above the sole, comprising the vamp and quarters. **10.** *Colloq.* a stimulant as amphetamine, etc. **11.** *Colloq.* a pleasant or exhilarating experience. **12. be on one's uppers,** *Colloq.* to be reduced to poverty or want.

**upper atmosphere** /ʌpər ˈætməsfɪə/, *n.* that part of the earth's atmosphere which can be reached by rocket or satellite, but not by balloon; the atmosphere from about 30 kilometres upwards.

**upper case** /ʌpə ˈkeɪs/, *n.* the upper half of a pair of cases, which contains the capital letters of the alphabet.

**upper-case** /ˈʌpə-keɪs/, *adj., v.,* **-cased, -casing.** *–adj.* **1.** (of a letter) capital (as opposed to *small*). **2.** *Print.* pertaining to or belonging in the upper case. See **case**[2] (def. 8). *–v.t.* **3.** to print or write with an upper-case letter or letters.

**upper chamber** /ˈʌpə tʃeɪmbə/, *n.* →**upper house.**

**upper circle** /ʌpə ˈsɜkəl/, *n.* one of the sections of seats in the auditorium of a theatre, concert hall, or the like, between the dress circle and the gallery.

**upper class** /– ˈklas/, *n., pl.* **classes.** the class of people socially and conventionally regarded as being higher or highest in the social hierarchy and commonly identified by wealth or aristocratic birth.

**upper-class** /ˈʌpə-klas/, *adj.* belonging, pertaining to, or typical of the upper class.

**upper crust** /ʌpə ˈkrʌst/, *n.* the aristocracy; the higher orders of society.

**uppercut** /ˈʌpəkʌt/, *n., v.,* **-cut, -cutting.** *–n.* **1.** a swinging blow directed upwards, as to an adversary's chin. *–v.t., v.i.* **2.** to strike with an uppercut.

**upper deck** /ʌpə ˈdɛk/, *n.* the highest continuous deck above the main deck.

**upper hand** /– ˈhænd/, *n.* the dominating or controlling position; the advantage.

**upper house** /– ˈhaʊs/, *n.* one of two branches of a legislature, generally smaller and less representative than the lower branch, usu. acting as a house of review, rarely formulating legislation and lacking the constitutional power to initiate any financial legislation, as the Senate in the Australian Parliament. Also, **upper chamber.**

**Upper Karoo** /ʌpə kaˈru/, *n.* **1.** pertaining to the lower Mesozoic period or system in southern Africa roughly equivalent to the Triassic and Lower Jurassic. **2.** a period or system following the Lower Karoo and preceding the Cretaceous in southern Africa. Also, **Upper Karroo.**

**uppermost** /ˈʌpəmoʊst/, *adj.* **1.** highest in place, order; rank, power, etc. **2.** topmost; predominant; foremost. *–adv.* **3.** in the highest or topmost place. **4.** in the foremost place in respect of rank or precedence.

**Upper Volta** /ʌpə ˈvɒltə/, *n.* a republic in western Africa.

**upper works** /ˈʌpə wɜks/, *n.pl.* the structures on the main or freeboard deck, or in any deck above.

**uppish** /ˈʌpɪʃ/, *adj.* **1.** *Cricket.* (of a stroke) hit into the air, increasing the batsman's risk of being caught out. **2.** →**uppity.** [UP, *adv.* + -ISH[1]] – **uppishly,** *adv.* – **uppishness,** *n.*

**uppity** /ˈʌpəti/, *adj. Colloq.* affecting superiority; presumptuous; self-assertive. Also, **uppish.** [UP, *adv.*, from ? (*bigg*)*ity*, U.S. d., conceited, vain, impudent]

**upraise** /ʌpˈreɪz/, *v.t.*, **-raised, -raising.** to raise or elevate; direct upwards; exalt.

**uprear** /ʌpˈrɪə/, *v.t.* to rear up; raise.

**upright** /ˈʌpraɪt/, *adj.* **1.** erect or vertical, as in position or posture. **2.** raised or directed vertically or upward; not inclined or leaning over. **3.** adhering to rectitude; righteous, honest, or just. **4.** in accord with moral rectitude. *–n.* **5.** the state of being upright or vertical. **6.** something standing erect or vertical, as a piece of timber. **7.** an upright piano. **8.** one of the vertical members of a framework, as a goalpost. *–adv.* **9.** in an upright position or direction; vertically. [ME; OE *uppriht*, c. G *aufrecht*] – **uprightly,** *adv.* – **uprightness,** *n.*

**upright piano** /– piˈænoʊ/, *n.* See **piano**[1] (def. 3).

**uprise** /ʌpˈraɪz/, *v.*, **-rose, -risen, -rising;** /ˈʌpraɪz/, *n. Archaic. –v.i.* **1.** to rise; get up, as from a lying or sitting posture. **2.** to come into view. **3.** to come into being or action. **4.** to move upwards; mount up; ascend. **5.** to come above the horizon. **6.** to slope upwards. **7.** to become erect. *–n.* **8.** the act of rising.

**uprising** /ˈʌpraɪzɪŋ, ʌpˈraɪzɪŋ/, *n.* **1.** an insurrection or revolt. **2.** the act of rising. **3.** an ascent or acclivity.

**upriver** /ʌpˈrɪvə/, *adv.*; /ˈʌprɪvə/, *adj.* *–adv.* **1.** along a river in the direction of its source: *he lived five kilometres upriver from us.* *–adj.* **2.** situated farther up the river. **3.** moving or facing upriver. Cf. **downriver.**

**uproar** /ˈʌprɔ/, *n.* **1.** violent and noisy disturbance, as of a multitude; tumultuous or confused noise or din. **2.** an instance of this. [D *oproer* tumult; sense affected by ROAR]

**uproarious** /ʌpˈrɔriəs/, *adj.* **1.** characterised by or in a state of uproar; tumultuous. **2.** making or given to making an uproar, or disorderly and noisy, as an assembly, persons, etc. **3.** confused and loud, as sounds, utterances, etc. **4.** expressed by or producing uproar. **5.** extremely funny. – **uproariously,** *adv.* – **uproariousness,** *n.*

**uproot** /ʌpˈrut/, *v.t.* **1.** to root up; tear up by or as if by the roots. **2.** to eradicate; remove utterly. **3.** to remove (people) from their native environment; displace. – **uprooter,** *n.*

**uprush** /ˈʌprʌʃ/, *n.* a sudden or violent upward flow, movement, etc.

**upsadaisy** /ˈʌpsədeɪzi/, *interj.* (used to encourage or reassure a child when being lifted, climbing, or standing up.) [fanciful reduplication of UP] Also, **upsidaisy, upsydaisy.**

**upset** /ʌpˈsɛt/, *v.*, **-set, -setting;** /ˈʌpsɛt/, *n.*; /ˈʌpsɛt/, *esp. in predicative use* /ʌpˈsɛt/, *adj.* *–v.t.* **1.** to overturn; knock or tip over; capsize. **2.** to spill by knocking over; tip out. **3.** to throw into disorder; disarrange; overthrow or undo. **4.** to disturb (someone) mentally or emotionally; distress. **5.** to disorder physically or make ill, esp. in the digestive system. **6.** to nullify or invalidate: *to upset someone's plans.* **7.** to defeat a competitor or opponent. **8.** *Mach.* to shorten and thicken by hammering on the end, as a heated piece of iron. *–v.i.* **9.** to become overturned or knocked over. *–n.* **10.** a physical upsetting or being upset; overthrow. **11.** the act or fact of disordering or deranging (ideas, plans, patterns, etc.). **12.** a physical disorder; a slight illness, esp. gastric. **13.** an emotional disturbance. **14.** a quarrel. **15.** a defeat, esp. unexpected. **16.** *Mach.* **a.** a tool for upsetting. **b.** something upset, as a bar end. *–adj.* **17.** emotionally disturbed; distressed; affected by emotional disturbance. **18.** affected by slight illness, as the gastric system. **19.** overturned or capsized.

**upset price** /ˈ– praɪs/, *n.* →**reserve price.**

**upsetting** /ʌpˈsɛtɪŋ/, *adj.* causing or tending to cause distress.

**upshot** /ˈʌpʃɒt/, *n.* **1.** the final issue, the conclusion, or the result. **2.** the conclusion (of an argument). [UP- (in sense of termination) + SHOT[1]]

**upside** /ˈʌpsaɪd/, *n.* the upper side or part.

**upside down** /– ˈdaʊn/, *adj.* **1.** with the upper part undermost. **2.** in complete disorder; topsy-turvy. [alteration of ME *up so down*]

**upside-down cake** /ʌpsaɪd-ˈdaʊn keɪk/, *n.* a sponge cake baked with fruit in syrup at the bottom, but turned over before serving.

**upsilon** /ˈʊpsəlɒn/, *n.* the twentieth letter (Υ, υ = English U, u, or Y, y) of the Greek alphabet. [Gk *ŷ psilón* simple or slender *u* or *y*]

**upspring** /ʌpˈsprɪŋ/, *v.i.*, **-sprang** or **-sprung, -sprung, -springing.** to spring up; come into being.

**upstage** /ʌpˈsteɪdʒ/, *adv.*; /ˈʌpsteɪdʒ/, *adj.*; /ʌpˈsteɪdʒ/, *v.*, **-staged, -staging.** *–adv.* **1.** on or to the back of the stage, which was at one time higher in elevation than the front. *–adj.* **2.** of or pertaining to the back of the stage. **3.** haughtily aloof; haughty; supercilious. *–v.t.* **4.** *Theat.* to manoeuvre (an actor) into a less favourable position for holding the audience's attention, as by moving him upstage. **5.** to steal attention (from another) by some manoeuvre.

**upstairs** /ʌpˈstɛəz/, *adv.*; /ˈʌpstɛəz/ *adj.*, *n.* *–adv.* **1.** up the stairs; to or on an upper floor. **2.** *Colloq.* into the air. **3.** to or in a higher rank or office. **4. kick upstairs,** to promote (someone) esp. to a position of diminished power, in order to get him out of the way. *–adj.* **5.** on or pertaining to an upper floor. *–n.* **6.** an upper storey or storeys; that part of a building above the ground floor.

**upstanding** /ˈʌpstændɪŋ/, *esp. in predicative use* /ʌpˈstændɪŋ/, *adj.* **1.** standing erect; erect and tall, esp. of persons or animals; erect, well grown and vigorous in body or form. **2.** straightforward, open, or independent; upright; honourable. **3.** *Colloq.* standing up: *be upstanding and charge your glasses.*

**upstart** /ˈʌpstat/, *n.*, *adj.*; /ʌpˈstat/, *v.* *–n.* **1.** one who has risen suddenly from a humble position to wealth or power, or to assumed consequence; a parvenu. **2.** one who is pretentious and objectionable through being thus exalted. *–adj.* **3.** (of persons, families, etc.) newly or suddenly risen to importance; without pedigree. **4.** lately come into existence or notice. **5.** characteristic of an upstart.

**upstate** /ʌpˈsteɪt/, *n.*; /ˈʌpsteɪt/, *adj.*; /ʌpˈsteɪt/, *adv.* *U.S.* *–n.* **1.** the part of a State farther north or away from the coast, esp. the more northerly part of New York State. *–adj.* **2.** of or coming from the parts of a State farther north or away from the coast. *–adv.* **3.** to or towards such parts of a State. – **upstater,** *n.*

**upstream** /ʌpˈstrim/, *adv.*; /ˈʌpstrim/, *adj.* *–adv.* **1.** towards or in the higher part of a stream; against the current. *–adj.* **2.** situated farther up the stream. **3.** moving or facing upstream.

**upstroke** /ˈʌpstroʊk/, *n.* an upward stroke, esp. of a pen or pencil, or of a piston in a vertical cylinder.

**upsurge** /ʌpˈsɜdʒ/, *v.*, **-surged, -surging;** /ˈʌpsɜdʒ/, *n.* *–v.i.* **1.** to surge up. *–n.* **2.** a surging upwards. – **upsurgeance,** *n.*

**upsweep** /ʌpˈswip/, *v.*, **-swept, -sweeping;** /ˈʌpswip/, *n.* *–v.t.*, *v.i.* **1.** to sweep upwards. *–n.* **2.** a sweeping upwards. **3.** a steep slope.

**upswing** /ˈʌpswɪŋ/, *n.*; /ʌpˈswɪŋ/, *v.*, **-swung, -swinging.** *–n.* **1.** an upward swing or swinging movement, as of a pendulum. **2.** marked advance or increase. *–v.i.* **3.** to make an upward swing.

**upsydaisy** /ˈʌpsədeɪzi/, *interj.* →**upsadaisy.**

**uptake** /ˈʌpteɪk/, *n.* **1.** the action of understanding or comprehension; mental grasp. **2.** the act of taking up. **3.** a pipe or passage leading upwards from below, as for conducting smoke, a current of air, or the like. **4. quick (slow) on the uptake,** quick (slow) to grasp new or complicated ideas, or to learn.

**up-tempo** /ˈʌp-tɛmpoʊ/, *n.* **1.** a fast rhythm. *–adj.* **2.** rhythmic; fast.

**upthrow** /ˈʌpθroʊ/, *n.* **1.** an upheaval. **2.** *Geol., Mining.* that side of a fault where a mass of rock is higher than its continuation on the other side of the fault plane. Also, **upthrow side.**

**upthrust** /ˈʌpθrʌst/, *n.* **1.** a thrust in an upward direction. **2.** *Geol.* an upheaval or uplift.

**uptight** /ˈʌptaɪt/, *adj. Colloq.* **1.** tense, nervous, or irritable.

2. angry. **3.** conforming to established conventions, esp. despised conventions.

**uptilt** /ʌp'tɪlt/, *v.t.* to tilt up.

**up-to-date** /'ʌp-tə-deɪt/, *adj.* **1.** extending to the present time; including the latest facts: *an up-to-date record.* **2.** in accordance with the latest or newest standards, ideas, or style; modern. **3.** (of persons, etc.) keeping up with the times, as in information, ideas, methods, style, etc. Also (*esp. in predicative use*), **up to date** /ʌp tə 'deɪt/. – **up-to-dateness,** *n.*

**up-to-the-minute** /'ʌp-tə-ðə-mɪnət/, *adj.* **1.** most recent or current; extending to the immediate present, as a news report. **2.** entirely modern. Also (*esp. in predicative use*), **up to the minute** /ʌp tə ðə 'mɪnət/.

**uptown** /ʌp'taʊn/, *adv.;* /'ʌptaʊn/, *adj., n.* –*adv.* **1.** to, towards, or in any of various parts of a town or city, esp. one considered to be higher, or away from the centre. –*adj.* **2.** moving towards, situated in, or pertaining to such a part. –*n.* **3.** such a part.

**upturn** /ʌp'tɜn/, *v.;* /'ʌptɜn/, *n.* –*v.t.* **1.** to turn up or over. **2.** to direct upwards. –*v.i.* **3.** to turn upwards. –*n.* **4.** an upward turn, or a changing and rising movement, as in prices, business, etc.

**upturned** /'ʌptɜnd/, *adj.* **1.** turned or directed upwards. **2.** turned over; upside down. **3.** having a turned-up end.

**upvalue** /'ʌpvælju/, *v.t.,* **-ued, -uing.** to revalue (a currency) upwards. – **upvaluation** /ˌʌpvælju'eɪʃən/, *n.*

**upward** /'ʌpwəd/, *adj.* **1.** directed, tending, or moving towards a higher point or level; ascending. –*adv.* **2.** upwards. [ME, OE *upweard,* c. D *opwaart;* from UP- + -WARD] – **upwardly,** *adv.*

**upward mobile** /– 'moʊbaɪl/, *n.* a person moving to a higher social class, a better job or a more prestigious area. – **upwardly mobile,** *adj.*

**upwards** /'ʌpwədz/, *adv.* **1.** towards a higher place or position; in a vertical direction. **2.** towards a higher level, degree, or standard, as of thought, feeling, distinction, rank, age, amount, etc. **3.** towards the source, as of a stream; towards the interior, as of a country; towards the centre, most important part, etc. **4.** so as to be uppermost; in or facing the highest position. **5.** to or into later life. **6. upwards of, a.** more than; above. **b.** approximately. Also, **upward.**

**upwind** /ʌp'wɪnd/, *adv.;* /'ʌpwɪnd/, *adj.* –*adv.* **1.** against the wind; contrary to the course of the wind. **2.** towards or in the direction from which the wind is blowing: *he was standing upwind of us and could be heard clearly.* –*adj.* **3.** tending, facing, or moving towards the direction from which the wind is blowing.

**upya** /'ʌpjə/, *interj. Colloq.* (an offensive exclamation). [contraction of *up you*]

**uracil** /'jurəsɪl/, *n.* a pyrimidine base, $C_4H_4N_2O_2$, present in all living cells, mainly in combined form, as in ribonucleic acids. [UR(O)-[1] + AC(ETIC) + -IL]

**uraemia** /ju'rimiə/, *n.* the morbid condition resulting from the retention of urinary constituents. Also, *U.S.,* **uremia.** [NL. See URO-[1], -AEMIA]

**uraemic** /ju'rimɪk/, *adj.* **1.** pertaining to uraemia. **2.** afflicted with uraemia. Also, *U.S.,* **uremic.**

**uraeus** /ju'riəs/, *n., pl.* **uraei, -ses.** the sacred asp (a cobra, *Naja haje*) as represented upon the headdress of divinities and royal personages of ancient Egypt, usu. directly over the forehead, as an emblem of supreme power. [NL from Gk *ouraîos,* representing Egyptian name of cobra]

**Ural-Altaic** /ˌjurəl-æl'teɪɪk/, *adj.* **1.** of or pertaining to the Urals, on the border between the Soviet Union in Europe and Siberia, and the Altai Mountains, in southern Siberia and north-western Mongolia, or the country or peoples around them. **2.** pertaining to the peoples using Ural-Altaic (def. 3). –*n.* **3.** a supposed, but unproved, linguistic phylum combining the Uralian, Turkic, Tungusic, and Mongolian families of languages.

**Uralian** /ju'reɪliən/, *n.* **1.** a linguistic stock or family comprising the Finno-Ugric and Samoyed languages. –*adj.* **2.** of or pertaining to the Urals or the district around them, or the people living there.

**Uralic** /ju'rælɪk/, *n.* →**Finno-Ugric.**

**uranian** /ju'reɪniən/, *adj.* **1.** of or pertaining to the heavens; celestial. **2.** pertaining to astronomy. [from *Urania,* in Greek mythology, the muse of astronomy; L, from Gk *Ouranía* heavenly one]

**Uranian** /ju'reɪniən/, *adj.* pertaining to the planet Uranus.

**uranic**[1] /ju'rænɪk/, *adj.* **1.** of or containing uranium, esp. in the tetravalent state. **2.** containing uranium in a valency state higher than the corresponding uranous compound. [URAN(IUM) + -IC]

**uranic**[2] /ju'rænɪk/, *adj.* →**uranian** (def. 2). [Gk *ouranós* heaven + -IC]

**uranide** /'jurənaɪd/, *n.* any of the sequence of natural radioactive elements which includes uranium.

**uraninite** /jə'rænənaɪt/, *n.* a mineral, probably originally uranium dioxide ($UO_2$), but altered by radioactive decay, and usu. containing uranium trioxide, lead, radium, and helium, occurring in several varieties including the impure form known as pitchblend; the most important ore of uranium. [URAN(IUM) + -IN[2] + -ITE[1]]

**uranium** /ju'reɪniəm/, *n.* a white, lustrous, radioactive, metallic element, having compounds which are used in photography and in colouring glass. The natural element consists of 99.28 per cent of the isotope U-238 and 0.71 per cent of the isotope U-235. The latter is capable of sustaining a nuclear chain reaction and is the basis of the atomic bomb and nuclear reactors. *Symbol:* U; *at. wt:* 238.03; *at. no.:* 92; *sp. gr.:* 19.05. [NL; see URAN(US), -IUM]

**urano-,** a word element meaning 'heaven', as in *uranography.* [Gk, combining form of *ouranós*]

**uranography** /jurə'nɒgrəfi/, *n.* the branch of astronomy concerned with the description and mapping of the heavens, and esp. of the fixed stars. [Gk *ouranographía.* See URANO-, -GRAPHY] – **uranographer, uranographist,** *n.* – **uranographic** /jurənoʊ'græfɪk/, **uranographical** /jurənoʊ'græfɪkəl/, *adj.*

**uranology** /jurə'nɒlədʒi/, *n. Obs.* astronomy or a treatise on astronomy. – **uranologer,** *n.* – **uranological** /jurənə'lɒdʒɪkəl/, *adj.*

**uranometry** /jurə'nɒmətri/, *n. Obs.* **1.** a treatise on the magnitudes and positions of celestial bodies, esp. the fixed stars. **2.** the measurement of the relative positions of celestial bodies.

**uranoschisis** /jurən'ɒskəsəs/, *n.* →**cleft palate.** [NL, from URANO- + Gk *schísis* fissure, from *schízein* to split]

**uranous** /'jurənəs/, *adj.* containing trivalent uranium.

**Uranus** /ju'reɪnəs/, *n.* the seventh major planet in order from the sun. [in Greek mythology, the personification of Heaven, and the ruler of the world; L, from Gk *Ouranós*]

**uranyl** /'jurənɪl/, *n.* the divalent radical $UO_2$-, which forms salts with acids. [URAN(IUM) + -YL] – **uranylic** /jurə'nɪlɪk/, *adj.*

**urate** /'jureɪt/, *n.* a salt of uric acid. [UR(O)-[1] + -ATE[2]]

**urban** /'ɜbən/, *adj.* **1.** of, pertaining to, or comprising a city or town. **2.** living in a city or cities. **3.** occurring or situated in a city or town. **4.** characteristic of or accustomed to cities; citified. [L *urbānus*]

**urbane** /ɜ'beɪn/, *adj.* **1.** having the refinement and manners considered to be characteristic of city-dwellers; civilised; sophisticated. **2.** smoothly polite; suave or bland. **3.** exhibiting elegance, refinement, or courtesy, as in expression. [L *urbānus*] – **urbanely,** *adv.* – **urbaneness,** *n.*

**urban guerrilla** /ɜbən gə'rɪlə/, *n.* one of a minority group which, to further its aims, uses violence, as bombing, machine gun attack, etc., in an urban situation.

**urbanise** /'ɜbənaɪz/, *v.t.,* **-nised, -nising.** to render urban, as in character. Also, **urbanize.** – **urbanisation** /ɜbənaɪ'zeɪʃən/, *n.*

**urbanity** /ɜ'bænəti/, *n., pl.* **-ties. 1.** the quality of being urbane; refined or elegant courtesy or politeness; suavity. **2.** (*pl.*) civilities; courtesies. [L *urbānitas*]

**urban renewal** /ˌɜbən rə'njuəl/, *n.* the rehabilitation of urban areas, by regeneration, replacement, repair, or renovation, in accordance with comprehensive plans.

**urceolate** /'ɜsiələt, -leɪt/, *adj.* shaped like a pitcher; swelling out like the body of a pitcher and contracted at the orifice, as a corolla. [NL *urceolātus,* from L *urceolus,* diminutive of *urceus* pitcher]

**urchin** /'ɜtʃən/, *n.* **1.** a small boy or youngster, esp. one who is mischievous and impudent, or ragged and shabbily dressed. **2.** →**sea-urchin. 3.** *Archaic* a kind of elf or mischievous sprite. **4.** *Archaic.* →**hedgehog.** *–adj.* **5.** of the nature of or resembling an urchin. [ME *urchone,* from d. OF *hirechon,* from L *ēricius* hedgehog]

**Urdu** /'ɜdu/, *n.* one of the official languages of Pakistan, a dialect used by Muslims derived from Hindustani but using Arabic characters and drawing on Persian and Arabic vocabulary. [Hind.: camp (speech), from Turkic *ordū* camp. See HORDE]

**-ure,** a suffix of abstract nouns indicating action, result, and instrument, as in *legislature, pressure.* [representing F *-ure* and L *-ūra*]

**urea** /ju'riə, 'juriə/, *n.* a colourless crystalline substance, $CO(NH_2)_2$, occurring in wine, used in fertilisers and in making plastics and adhesives; the principal nitrogenous excretory product of mammals, amphibians, elasmobranch fishes, and some reptiles; carbamide. [NL, from Gk *oúrē(sis)* urination + *-a,* noun ending] – **ureal,** *adj.*

**urea cycle** /– 'saɪkəl/, *n.* a series of reactions in animals involving the conversion of ammonia, carbon dioxide and aspartic acid to urea and fumaric acid, for the excretion of urea and the production of arginine.

**urea resin** /– 'rɛzən/, *n.* one of a group of resins formed by the interaction of urea and formaldehyde. Also, **urea-formaldehyde resin.**

**urease** /'jurieɪz, -eɪs/, *n.* an enzyme found in many plants, bacteria, fungi, etc., which catalyses the conversion of urea into ammonia and carbon dioxide. [URE(A) + -ASE]

**uredial stage** /ju'ridiəl ˌsteɪdʒ/, *n.* →**uredostage.**

**uredium** /ju'ridiəm/, *n.* the fructification of the rust-fungi-bearing uredospores. Also, **uredinium** /jurə'dɪniəm/, **uredosorus** /juˌridə'sɔrəs/.

**uredo** /ju'ridoʊ/, *n., pl.* **uredos, uredines** /ju'ridəniz/. a skin irritation; hives; urticaria. [L: rust fungus, itch]

**uredospore** /ju'ridəspɔ/, *n.* the spore of the rust fungi which appears between the aeciospore and the teliospore, commonly the summer spore.

**uredostage** /ju'ridəsteɪdʒ/, *n.* the phase in the life cycle of a rust fungus when the uredospores are formed. Also, **uredial stage.**

**ureide** /'juriaɪd/, *n.* any of several derivations of urea containing an acyl group.

**uremia** /ju'rimiə/, *n. U.S.* →**uraemia.**

**uremic** /ju'rimɪk/, *adj. U.S.* →**uraemic.**

**-uret,** a noun suffix in names of some chemical compounds, having the same force as **-ide,** as in *arseniuret.* [NL *-urētum*]

**ureter** /ju'ritə/, *n.* a muscular duct or tube conveying the urine from a kidney to the bladder or cloaca. [L, from Gk] – **ureteral, ureteric** /jurə'tɛrɪk/, *adj.*

**urethane** /'jurəθeɪn, ju'riθeɪn/, *n.* **1.** any derivative of carbamic acid with the type formula, $NH_2COOR$. **2.** a colourless, crystalline compound, the ethyl ester of carbamic acid, $NH_2COOC_2H_5$, used in the synthesis of organic compounds, esp. in the manufacture of **urethane resins,** and as a mild hypnotic drug. Also, **urethan** /'jurəθən/. [UR(EA) + ETHANE]

**urethr-,** variant of **urethro-** before vowels, as in *urethritis.*

**urethra** /ju'riθrə/, *n., pl.* **-thrae** /-θri/, **-thras.** the membranous tube which extends from the bladder to the exterior. In the male it conveys semen as well as urine. [LL, from Gk] – **urethral,** *adj.*

**urethritis** /jurə'θraɪtəs/, *n.* **1.** inflammation of the urethra; strain. **2.** *Mil.* (*euph.*) venereal disease. – **urethritic** /jurə'θrɪtɪk/, *adj.*

**urethro-,** a word element representing **urethra,** as in *urethroscope.* Also, **urethr-.**

**urethroscope** /ju'riθrəskoʊp/, *n.* a medical apparatus for observing the urethra.

**urethroscopy** /jurə'θrɒskəpi/, *n.* observation of the urethra by a urethroscope.

**urge** /ɜdʒ/, *v.,* **urged, urging,** *n.* *–v.t.* **1.** to endeavour to induce or persuade, as by entreaties or earnest recommendations; entreat or exhort earnestly: *urge a person to take more care.* **2.** to press by persuasion or recommendation, as for acceptance, performance, or use; recommend or advocate earnestly: *urge a plan of action.* **3.** to press (something) upon the attention: *urge a claim.* **4.** to insist on, allege, or assert with earnestness: *urge the need for haste.* **5.** to push or force along; impel with force or vigour: *urge the cause along.* **6.** to drive with incitement to speed or effort: *urge dogs on with shouts.* **7.** to press, push, or hasten (the course, activities, etc.): *urge one's flight.* **8.** to impel, constrain, or move to some action: *urged by necessity.* *–v.i.* **9.** to make entreaties or earnest recommendations. **10.** to exert a driving or impelling force; to give an impulse to haste or action: *hunger urges.* **11.** to press, push, or hasten on (oft. fol. by *on, onwards, along,* etc.). *–n.* **12.** the fact of urging or being urged; impelling action, influence, or force; impulse. **13.** an involuntary, natural, or instinctive impulse. **14. give someone an urge,** *Colloq.* to let someone in ahead of one in a queue. [L *urgēre* press, drive] – **urger,** *n.*

**urgency** /'ɜdʒənsi/, *n., pl.* **-cies. 1.** urgent character; imperativeness; pressing importance. **2.** insistence; importunateness.

**urgency motion** /'– moʊʃən/, *n.* →**urgent bill.**

**urgent** /'ɜdʒənt/, *adj.* **1.** pressing; compelling or requiring immediate action or attention; imperative. **2.** insistent or earnest in solicitation; importunate, as a person. **3.** expressed with insistence, as requests or appeals. [L *urgens,* ppr.] – **urgently,** *adv.*

**urgent bill** /– 'bɪl/, *n.* a parliamentary bill which, because of the urgency of the matter with which it deals, takes precedence over other business before the house. Also, **urgency motion.**

**urger** /'ɜdʒə/, *n. Colloq.* **1.** a racecourse tipster. **2.** one who takes advantage of others.

**-urgy,** a word element meaning 'a technology', as in *metallurgy.* [Gk *-ourgia,* from *érgon* work]

**-uria,** a word element meaning 'urine'. [NL, from Gk *-ouria,* from *oûron* urine]

**uric** /'jurɪk/, *adj.* pertaining to or obtained from urine. [UR(O)-[1] + -IC]

**uric acid** /– 'æsəd/, *n.* a colourless, scaly compound, $C_5H_4N_4O_3$, an oxidised purine, found in the joints in gout; the principal nitrogenous excretory product of birds and most reptiles.

**uridine** /'jurədaɪn/, *n.* a compound of uracil and ribose, present in all living cells, mainly in combined form, as in ribonucleic acids.

**uridylic acid** /jurəˌdɪlɪk 'æsəd/, *n.* the monophosphate of uridine, present in all living cells, mainly in combined form, as in ribonucleic acids.

**urinal** /'jurənəl, ju'raɪnəl/, *n.* **1.** a fixture, room, or building for discharging urine in. **2.** a glass or metallic receptacle for urine. [ME, from L]

**urinalysis** /jurə'næləsəs/, *n., pl.* **-ses** /-siz/. →**urine analysis.** [URIN(E + (AN)ALYSIS]

**urinary** /'jurənri/, *adj., n., pl.* **-naries.** *–adj.* **1.** of or pertaining to urine. **2.** pertaining to the organs secreting and discharging urine. *–n.* **3.** *Archaic.* a reservoir for the reception of urine, etc., for manure. **4.** a urinal.

**urinary calculus** /– 'kælkjələs/, *n.* a calcareous concretion in the urinary tract.

**urinate** /'jurəneɪt/, *v.i.,* **-nated, -nating.** to pass or discharge urine. – **urination** /jurə'neɪʃən/, *n.* – **urinative,** *adj.*

**urine** /'jurən, -aɪn/, *n.* the secretion of the kidneys (in mammals, a fluid), which in most mammals is conducted to the bladder by the ureter, and from there to the exterior by the urethra. [ME, from L *ūrīna,* akin to Gk *oûron*]

**urine analysis** /– ə'næləsəs/, *n.* analysis of urine chemically or microscopically.

**uriniferous** /jurə'nɪfərəs/, *adj.* conveying urine.

**urinogenital** /jurənoʊ'dʒɛnətl/, *adj.* →**urogenital.**

**urinous** /'jurənəs/, *adj.* pertaining to, resembling, or containing urine. Also, **urinose** /'jurənoʊs/.

**urn** /ɜn/, *n.* **1.** a kind of vase, of various forms, esp. one with a foot or pedestal. **2.** such a vase for holding the ashes of the dead after cremation. **3.** *Bot.* the spore-bearing part of the capsule of a moss, between lid and seta. **4.**

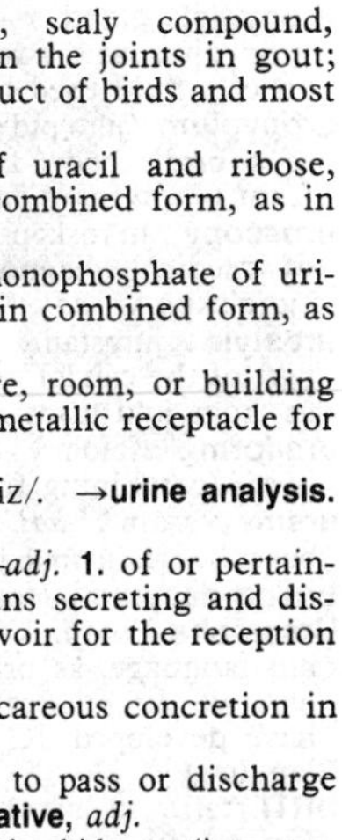

urn: Roman cinerary urn

a vessel or apparatus with a tap, used for heating water, tea, coffee, etc., in quantity. [ME *urne,* from L *urna*] – **urnlike,** *adj.*

**uro-**[1], a word element referring to urine and the urinary tract, as in *urochrome.* [Gk, combining form of *oûron* urine]

**uro-**[2], a word element meaning 'tail', as in *urochord.* [combining form representing Gk *ourá*]

**urochord** /ˈjurəkɔd/, *n.* (in zoology) the notochord of an ascidian or tunicate, found mostly in the larva, or more conspicuous in the larva than in the adult, and confined chiefly to the caudal region. [URO-[2] + CHORD[1]] – **urochordal** /jurəˈkɔdl/, *adj.*

**urochrome** /ˈjurəkroʊm/, *n.* the pigment which gives urine its yellow colour. [URO-[1] + -CHROME]

**urodele** /ˈjurədil/, *adj.* belonging or pertaining to the suborder of the Amphibia, including the newts and salamanders, which retain tails throughout adult life.

**urogenital** /juroʊˈdʒɛnətl/, *adj.* denoting or pertaining to the urinary and genital organs; genito-urinary. [URO-[1] + GENITAL]

**urogenous** /juˈrɒdʒənəs/, *adj.* **1.** secreting or producing urine. **2.** contained in urine.

**urol.,** urology.

**urolith** /ˈjurəlɪθ/, *n.* →**urinary calculus.** [URO-[1] + -LITH] – **urolithic** /jurəˈlɪθɪk/, *adj.*

**urology** /juˈrɒlədʒi/, *n.* the scientific study of the urine and the genito-urinary tract, with special reference to the diagnostic significance of changes in its anatomy and physiology. [URO-[1] + -LOGY] – **urologic** /jurəˈlɒdʒɪk/, **urological** /jurəˈlɒdʒɪkəl/, *adj.* – **urologist,** *n.*

**uroo** /ˈjuru/, *n.* →**wallaroo.** [Aboriginal]

**uropod** /ˈjurəpɒd/, *n.* an abdominal limb of an arthropod, esp. one of those on either side of the telson, as in a lobster. [URO-[2] + -POD]

**uropygial** /jurəˈpɪdʒiəl/, *adj.* of or pertaining to the uropygium. [UROPYGI(UM) + -AL[1]]

**uropygial gland** /– glænd/, *n.* a gland opening on the uropygium at the root of the tail in most birds, and secreting an oily fluid used by the bird in preening its feathers.

**uropygium** /jurəˈpɪdʒiəm/, *n.* the projecting terminal portion of a bird's body, from which the tail feathers spring. [ML, from Gk *ouropygion*]

**uroscopy** /juˈrɒskəpi/, *n.* inspection of the urine as a means of medical diagnosis, etc. [URO-[1] + -SCOPY] – **uroscopic** /jurəˈskɒpɪk/, *adj.* – **uroscopist,** *n.*

**urostyle** /ˈjurəstaɪl/, *n.* a bone formed by the fusion of all or part of the caudal vertebrae in some fish and such amphibians as frogs and toads. [URO-[2] + STYLE (def. 18)]

**ursiform** /ˈɜsəfɔm/, *adj.* having the form of a bear; bearlike. [*ursi-* (combining form of L *ursus* bear) + -FORM]

**ursine** /ˈɜsaɪn/, *adj.* **1.** of or pertaining to a bear or bears. **2.** bearlike. [L *ursīnus*]

**ursine dasyure** /– ˈdæsijuə/, *n.* →**Tasmanian devil.**

**Ursprache** /ˈʊəʃprakə/, *n.* a hypothetically reconstructed parent language, as primitive Germanic (reconstructed by comparative linguistics) from which the Germanic languages have developed. [G, from *ur-* primitive, original + *Sprache* language]

**URTI** /ˈɜti/, *n.* a cold (def. 25). [*U(pper) R(espiratory) T(ract) I(nfection)*]

**urticant** /ˈɜtəkənt/, *adj.* adapted for, or producing, stinging.

**urticaria** /ɜtəˈkɛəriə/, *n.* a skin condition characterised by transient eruptions of itching or weals, usu. due to ingestion or inhalation of an allergen; nettle rash; hives. [NL, from L *urtīca* nettle] – **urticarial, urticarious,** *adj.*

**urticate** /ˈɜtəkeɪt/, *v.,* **-cated, -cating.** *–v.t.* **1.** to sting or whip with or as with nettles. *–v.i.* **2.** to sting as or like a nettle. *–adj.* **3.** characterised by the presence of itching weals. [ML *urticātus,* pp., from L *urtīca* nettle]

**urtication** /ɜtəˈkeɪʃən/, *n.* the action or result of urticating or stinging.

**Uruguay** /ˈjurəgwaɪ/, *n.* a republic in south-eastern South America. – **Uruguayan** /jurəˈgwaɪən/, *adj., n.*

**urus** /ˈjurəs/, *n.* →**aurochs** (def. 1). [L; of Gmc orig.]

**urushiol** /ˈurəʃiɒl, əˈruʃiɒl/, *n.* a toxic, liquid, catechol derivative, the active irritant principle in several species of the plant genus *Rhus,* as poison ivy. [Jap. *urushi* lacquer + -OL[2]]

**us** /ʌs/; *weak forms* /əs, əz/ *pron.* objective case of **we.** [ME and OE, c. G and Goth. *uns*]

**u/s** /ju ˈɛs/, *adj.* unserviceable.

**u.s.,** **1.** ubi supra (in the place above). **2.** ut supra (as above). **3.** unserviceable. **4.** uniform system.

**u.s.** /ju ˈɛs/, *adj. Brit.* →**r.s.**

**U.S.** /ju ˈɛs/, *n.* United States.

**U.S.A.** /ju ɛs ˈeɪ/, *n.* United States of America. Also, **USA.**

**usable** /ˈjuzəbəl/, *adj.* →**useable.** – **usability** /juzəˈbɪləti/, **usableness,** *n.*

**usage** /ˈjusɪdʒ, ˈjuzɪdʒ/, *n.* **1.** customary way of doing; a custom or practice: *the usages of the last fifty years.* **2.** customary manner of using a language or any of its forms, esp. standard practice in a given language: *English usage.* **3.** a particular instance of this: *a usage borrowed from the French.* **4.** the body of rules or customs followed by a particular set of people. **5.** usual conduct or behaviour. **6.** way of using or treating, or treatment: *hard or rough usage.* **7.** habitual or customary use; long-continued practice: *immemorial usage.* **8.** the act or fact of using or employing; use. [ME, from OF, from *us* use, from L *ūsus*]

**usance** /ˈjuzəns/, *n.* **1.** *Comm.* the length of time, exclusive of days of grace, allowed by custom or usage for the payment of foreign bills of exchange. **2.** *Econ.* the income of benefits of every kind derived from the ownership of wealth. **3.** *Archaic.* interest, as on a loan. **4.** *Obs.* custom. **5.** *Obs.* usury. [ME, from OF, from *user* USE, *v.*]

**Usbeg** /ˈʌsbɛg, ˈʌzbɛg/, *n., adj.* →**Uzbek.**

**use** /juz/; *for def. 10 also* /jus/, *v.,* **-used, -using;** /jus/, *n.* *–v.t.* **1.** to employ for some purpose; put into service; turn to account: *use a knife to cut, use a new method.* **2.** to avail oneself of; apply to one's own purposes: *use the front room for a conference.* **3.** to expend or consume in use: *his car uses a lot of oil.* **4.** to act or behave towards, or treat (a person) in some manner. **5.** to exploit (a person) for one's own ends. **6.** to utter (words) or speak (a language). **7.** to operate or put into effect. **8.** *Archaic.* to practise habitually or customarily; make a practice of. **9. use up, a.** to consume completely. **b.** to exhaust; tire out. *–v.i.* **10.** to be accustomed, wont, or customarily found (with an infinitive expressed or understood, and, except in archaic use, now only in the past): *he used to go every day.* **11.** *Archaic.* to resort, stay, or dwell customarily. *–n.* **12.** the act of employing or using, or putting into service: *the use of tools.* **13.** the state of being employed or used: *this book is in use.* **14.** an instance or way of employing or using something: *each successive use of the tool.* **15.** a way of being employed or used; a purpose for which something is used: *the instrument has different uses.* **16.** the power, right, or privilege of employing or using something: *to lose the use of the right eye.* **17.** service or advantage in or for being employed or used; utility or usefulness: *of no practical use.* **18.** help; profit; resulting good: *what's the use of doing that?* **19.** occasion or need, as for something to be employed or used: *have you any use for another calendar?* **20.** continued, habitual, or customary employment or practice; custom; practice: *follow the prevailing use of such occasions.* **21.** way of using or treating; treatment. **22.** consumption, as of food or tobacco. **23.** *Law.* **a.** the enjoyment of property, as by employment, occupation, or exercise of it. **b.** the benefit or profit of property (lands and tenements) in the possession of another who simply holds them for the beneficiary. **c.** the equitable ownership of land the legal title to which is held by another; a passive trust. **24.** *Eccles.* the distinctive form of ritual or of any liturgical observance used in a particular church, diocese, community, etc. **25.** *Obs.* interest; usury. **26.** Some special noun phrases are:

**bring into use,** to introduce so as to become customary or generally employed.

**come into use,** to become customary or generally employed.

**have no use for, 1.** to have no occasion or need for. **2.** to have no liking or tolerance for.

**in use, 1.** occupied; currently employed to some purpose. **2.** in general employment.

**make use of,** to employ; put to use; use for one's own purposes or advantages.

**of no use,** or (elliptically) **no use,** of no service, advantage, or help; useless: *it's no use crying.*

**of use,** useful.
**out of use,** not in current or general employment.
**put to use,** to employ. [ME, from OF *user,* from L *ūsus,* pp.]

**useable** /ˈjuzəbəl/, *adj.* **1.** that is available for use. **2.** that is in condition to be used. Also, **usable.** – **useability** /juzəˈbɪləti/, **useableness,** *n.*

**used**[1] /juzd/, *adj.* **1.** that has been made use of, esp. as showing signs of wear. **2.** →**second-hand.** **3. used up,** completely consumed or exhausted. [pp. of USE]

**used**[2] /just/, *adj.* accustomed; habituated; inured (fol. by *to*). [special use of USE, *v.* See def. 10]

**useful** /ˈjusfəl/, *adj.* **1.** being of use or service; serving some purpose; serviceable, advantageous, helpful, or of good effect. **2.** of practical use, as for doing work; producing material results; supplying common needs: *the useful arts.* **3.** *Colloq.* competent; able. –*n.* **4.** →**bar useful.** – **usefully,** *adv.* – **usefulness,** *n.*

**useless** /ˈjusləs/, *adj.* **1.** of no use; not serving the purpose or any purpose; unavailing or futile. **2.** without useful qualities; of no practical good. – **uselessly,** *adv.* – **uselessness,** *n.*

**user** /ˈjuzə/, *n.* **1.** one who or that which uses. **2.** *Law.* **a.** the right to the enjoyment of property. **b.** the exercise of a right to the enjoyment of property.

**U-shaped** /ˈju-ʃeɪpt/, *adj.* being in the form of a U.

**usher** /ˈʌʃə/, *n.* **1.** one who escorts persons to seats in a church, theatre, etc. **2.** an attendant who keeps order in a law court. **3.** *Brit.* (formerly) a subordinate teacher or assistant in a school. **4.** (formerly) an officer whose business it is to introduce strangers or walk before persons of rank. **5.** *Archaic.* one who goes before; a precursor. **6.** *Obs.* an officer or servant having charge of an entrance door; a doorkeeper. –*v.t.* **7.** to act as an usher to; conduct or show (fol. by *in, into, out,* etc.). **8.** to attend or bring at the coming or beginning. [ME, from AF *usser,* from LL *ustiārius* doorkeeper, replacing L *ostiārius*] – **usherless,** *adj.*

**usherette** /ʌʃəˈrɛt/, *n.* a female attendant, esp. one who shows people to their seats in a cinema or theatre.

**U.S.S.R.** /ju ɛs ɛs ˈa/, Union of Soviet Socialist Republics.

**ustilagineous** /ˌʌstɪləˈdʒɪniəs/, *adj.* of or pertaining to the smut fungi belonging to the family Ustilaginaceae. [LL *ūstilāgo* smut fungus (from L *ūrere* to burn) + -EOUS]

**ustulate** /ˈʌstʃələt, -leɪt/, *adj.* coloured or blackened as if scorched. [L *ūstulātus,* pp., burnt]

**ustulation** /ʌstʃəˈleɪʃən/, *n.* **1.** the act of scorching or burning. **2.** *Pharm.* the roasting or drying of moist substances so as to prepare them for pulverising.

**usu.,** **1.** usual. **2.** usually.

**usual** /ˈjuʒuəl/, *adj.* **1.** habitual or customary: *his usual skill.* **2.** such as is commonly met with or observed in experience; ordinary: *the usual January weather.* **3.** in common use; common: *say the usual things.* **4. as usual,** as is (or was) usual; in the customary or ordinary manner: *he will come as usual.* –*n.* **5.** that which is usual or habitual. [ME, from L *ūsuālis*] – **usually,** *adv.* – **usualness,** *n.*

**usucapion** /juzjuˈkeɪpiən/, *n.* (in law) the acquisition of a thing through long continuance of its use; title by prescription. Also, **usucaption** /juzjuˈkæpʃən/. [L *ūsūcapio*]

**usufruct** /ˈjuzjufrʌkt, ˈjusju-/, *n.* (in Roman and civil law) the right of enjoying all the advantages to be derived from the use of something which belongs to another, so far as compatible with the substance of the thing not being destroyed or injured. [LL *ūsūfructus,* L *ūsusfructus,* for *ūsus et fructus* use and fruit]

**usufructuary** /juzjuˈfrʌktʃuəri, jusju-/, *adj., n., pl.* **-aries.** –*adj.* **1.** of, pertaining to, or of the nature of a usufruct. –*n.* **2.** a person who has a usufruct property. [LL *ūsūfructuārius,* from *ūsūfructus* USUFRUCT]

**usurer** /ˈjuʒərə/, *n.* **1.** one who lends money at an exorbitant rate of interest. **2.** *Obs.* one who lends money at interest. [ME, from AF, from *usure* USURY]

**usurious** /juˈzjuriəs/, *adj.* **1.** practising usury; taking exorbitant interest for the use of money. **2.** pertaining to or of the nature of usury: *usurious interest.* – **usuriously,** *adv.* – **usuriousness,** *n.*

**usurp** /juˈzɜp/, *v.t.* **1.** to seize and hold (an office or position, power, etc.) by force or without right. **2.** to appropriate or make use of (rights, property, etc.) not one's own. –*v.i.* **3.** to commit forcible or illegal seizure of an office, power, etc.; encroach. [ME *usurpe,* from L *ūsūrpāre*] – **usurper,** *n.* – **usurpingly,** *adv.*

**usurpation** /juzɜˈpeɪʃən/, *n.* **1.** the act of usurping; the seizing and holding of the place, power, or the like, of another without right. **2.** the wrongful seizure and occupation of a throne.

**usury** /ˈjuʒəri/, *n., pl.* **-ries.** **1.** an exorbitant amount or rate of interest, esp. in excess of the legal rate. **2.** the lending, or practice of lending money at an exorbitant rate of interest. **3.** *Archaic.* the fact or practice of lending money at interest. **4.** *Obs.* interest paid for the use of money. [ME *usurie,* from ML *ūsūria* interest]

**ut** /ʌt, ʊt/, *n.* the syllable once generally used for the first note or keynote of a scale and sometimes for the note C, now commonly superseded by *do.* [L. See GAMUT]

**U.T.,** universal time. Also, **u.t.**

**utd,** united.

**ute** /jut/, *n.* **1.** →**utility truck.** **2. utility van.**

**utensil** /juˈtɛnsəl/, *n.* **1.** any of the instruments or vessels commonly used in a kitchen, dairy, etc. **2.** any instrument, vessel, or implement. [ME *utensyl(e),* from ML *ūtensile,* prop. neut. of L *ūtensilis* useful]

**uterine** /ˈjutəraɪn/, *adj.* **1.** of or pertaining to the uterus or womb. **2.** related through having the same mother. [ME, from LL *uterinus,* from L *uterus* uterus]

**utero-,** a word element representing **uterus.**

**uterus** /ˈjutərəs/, *n., pl.* **uteri** /ˈjutəraɪ/. that portion of the oviduct in which the fertilised ovum implants itself and develops or rests during prenatal development; the womb of mammals. [L]

**utilise** /ˈjutəlaɪz/, *v.t.,* **-lised, -lising.** to put to use; turn to profitable account: *to utilise water power for driving machinery.* Also, **utilize.** – **utilisable,** *adj.* – **utilisation** /jutəlaɪˈzeɪʃən/, *n.* – **utiliser,** *n.*

**utilitarian** /juˌtɪləˈtɛəriən/, *adj.* **1.** pertaining to or consisting in utility; concerning practical or material things. **2.** having regard to utility or usefulness rather than beauty, ornamentality, etc. **3.** of, pertaining to, or adhering to the doctrine of utilitarianism. –*n.* **4.** an adherent of utilitarianism. **5.** one who is only concerned with practical matters, or who assumes a practical attitude.

**utilitarianism** /ˌjutɪləˈtɛəriəˌnɪzəm/, *n.* the ethical doctrine that virtue is based on utility, and that conduct should be directed towards promoting the greatest happiness of the greatest number of persons.

**utility** /juˈtɪləti/, *n., pl.* **-ties.** **1.** the state or character of being useful. **2.** something useful; a useful thing. **3.** a public service, as a bus or railway service, gas or electricity supply, or the like. **4.** Also, **ute. a.** →**utility truck.** **b.** →**utility van.** **5.** *Econ.* the capacity of an object for satisfying a human want. **6.** well-being or happiness; that which is conducive to the happiness and well-being of the greatest number; the principle and purpose of utilitarianism. **7.** *U.S.* (*pl.*) stocks or shares of public utilities. –*adj.* **8.** provided, designed, bred, or made for usefulness or profitability rather than beauty. [ME *utilite,* from L *ūtilitas*]

**utility player** /ˈ– pleɪə/, *n.* one who can play in a variety of positions in a team sport, as football, hockey, etc.

**utility room** /ˈ– rum/, *n.* a room in a house which serves one or more useful functions as laundry, workshop, storage area, etc.

**utility truck** /ˈ– trʌk/, *n.* a small truck with an enclosed cabin and a rectangular tray which has sides and is sometimes covered by a tarpaulin.

**utility van** /ˈ– væn/, *n.* a utility truck with an enclosed section at the rear, similar to a small van.

**uti possidetis** /jutaɪ pɒsəˈditəs/, *n.* (in international law) the principle which vests in either of the belligerents at the end of a war all territory actually occupied and controlled by them. [L: lit., as you possess]

**utmost** /ˈʌtmoʊst/, *adj.* **1.** of the greatest or highest degree, quantity, or the like; greatest: *of the utmost importance.* **2.** being at the farthest point or extremity; farthest: *the utmost* *boundary of the East.* *–n.* Also, **uttermost. 3.** the greatest degree or amount: *the utmost that can be said.* **4.** the highest, greatest, or best of one's power: *do your utmost.* **5.** the extreme limit or extent. [ME *utmest,* OE *ūtemest,* from *ūte* OUT + *-mest* -MOST]

**Uto-Aztecan** /jutoʊ-'æztɛkən/, *n.* an American Indian linguistic stock, widespread from Idaho to the Isthmus of Tehuantepec, and from the Rocky Mountains to the Pacific; this stock includes Hopi, Ute, Shoshone, Comanche, Nahuatl (Aztec), Piman, and other languages.

**utopia** /ju'toʊpiə/, *n.* (*sometimes cap.*) **1.** a place or state of ideal perfection. **2.** any visionary system of political or social perfection. [from an imaginary island enjoying the utmost perfection in law, politics, etc., described in *'Utopia'* by Sir Thomas More, 1478-1535, English writer and statesman; NL, from Gk *ou* not + *-topia,* from *tópas* place]

**utopian** /ju'toʊpiən/, *adj.* (*sometimes cap.*) **1.** of, pertaining to, or resembling a utopia. **2.** founded upon or involving imaginary or ideal perfection. **3.** given to dreams or schemes of such perfection. *–n.* **4.** an ardent but unpractical political or social reformer; a visionary; an idealist.

**utopianism** /ju'toʊpiə,nɪzəm/, *n.* (*sometimes cap.*) the views or habit of mind of a utopian; impracticable schemes of political or social reform.

**utricle** /'jutrɪkəl/, *n.* **1.** a small sac or baglike body, as an air-filled cavity in a seaweed. **2.** *Bot.* a membranous sheath surrounding the fruit in some members of the Cyperaceae. **3.** *Anat.* the larger of two sacs in the membranous labyrinth of the internal ear and concerned with equilibrium. Cf. **saccule.** [L *ūtriculus,* diminutive of *ūter* bag]

**utricular** /ju'trɪkjələ/, *adj.* **1.** pertaining to or of the nature of a utricle; baglike. **2.** having a utricle or utricles.

**utriculate** /ju'trɪkjələt, -leɪt/, *adj.* having a utricle; utricular; baglike.

**utriculitis** /ju,trɪkjə'laɪtəs/, *n.* inflammation of the utricle bone of the middle ear. [L *ūtriculus* UTRICLE + -ITIS]

**utter**[1] /'ʌtə/, *v.t.* **1.** to give audible expression to (words, etc.); speak or pronounce: *the words were uttered in my hearing.* **2.** to give expression to (a subject, etc.): *unable to utter her opinions.* **3.** to give forth (cries, sounds, etc.) with or as with the voice: *utter a sigh.* **4.** to express or make known in any manner. **5.** to express by written or printed words. **6.** to make publicly known; publish: *utter a libel.* **7.** to put into circulation, as coins, notes, etc., and esp. counterfeit money, forged cheques, etc. **8.** *Rare.* to expel; emit. **9.** *Obs.* to publish, as a book. **10.** *Obs.* to sell. *–v.i.* **11.** to use the faculty of speech. [ME *outre* (frequentative of OUT, *v.*), c. G *äussern* declare] – **utterable,** *adj.* – **utterableness,** *n.*

**utter**[2] /'ʌtə/, *adj.* **1.** complete; total; absolute: *her utter abandonment to grief.* **2.** unconditional; unqualified: *an utter denial.* [ME; OE *ūtera* (compar. of *ūt* OUT), c. G *äusser*]

**utterance**[1] /'ʌtrəns, 'ʌtərəns/, *n.* **1.** the act of uttering; vocal expression. **2.** manner of speaking; power of speaking. **3.** something uttered, as a word or words uttered, a cry, animal's call, or the like. **4.** a putting into circulation. [ME; from UTTER[1], + -ANCE]

**utterance**[2] /'ʌtərəns, 'ʌtrəns/, *n. Obs.* the utmost extremity; death. [ME, from OF *oultrance,* from *oultrer* pass beyond, from L *ultrā* beyond]

**utter barrister** /'ʌtə bærəstə/, *n.* a barrister who is not a Queen's Counsel.

**utterer** /'ʌtərə/, *n.* one who utters; one who puts into circulation, publishes, or expresses audibly.

**uttering** /'ʌtərɪŋ/, *n.* (in criminal law) the crime of knowingly tendering or showing a forged instrument or counterfeit coin to another with intent to defraud.

**utterly** /'ʌtəli/, *adv.* in an utter manner; completely; absolutely.

**uttermost** /'ʌtəmoʊst/, *adj.* **1.** utmost; furthest; extreme. **2.** of the greatest degree, etc.: *uttermost distress.* *–n.* **3.** the extreme limit or extent; the utmost. [ME; from UTTER[2] + -MOST]

**utu** /'utu/, *n. N.Z.* satisfaction; compensation; revenge. [Maori]

**U-turn** /'ju-tɜn/, *n.* a turn executed by the driver of a motor vehicle in which he turns the vehicle sharply to face in the direction from which he was travelling.

**UV,** ultraviolet.

**UV cream** /ju 'vi krim/, *n.* an ointment for application to the face, hands, etc., which offers protection to the skin against ultra-violet radiation from the sun. [*U*(*ltra*) *V*(*iolet*) *cream*]

**uvea** /'juviə/, *n.* the middle tunic of the eye (iris, choroid, and ciliary body, taken collectively). [ML, from L *ūva* grape] – **uveal, uveous,** *adj.*

**uveitis** /juvi'aɪtəs/, *n.* inflammation of the uvea. [NL, from ML *ūvea* UVEA + *-ītis* -ITIS] – **uveitic** /juvi'ɪtɪk/, *adj.*

**uvula** /'juvjələ/, *n., pl.* **-las, -lae** /-li/. the small, fleshy, conical body projecting downwards from the middle of the soft palate. [ME, from ML, diminutive of L *ūva* grape]

**uvular** /'juvjələ/, *adj.* **1.** of or pertaining to the uvula. **2.** *Phonet.* pronounced with the back of the tongue held close to or touching the uvula: *Parisian French uses the uvular 'r'.* *–n.* **3.** *Phonet.* a uvular sound. – **uvularly,** *adv.*

**uvulitis** /juvjə'laɪtəs/, *n.* inflammation of the uvula. [NL, from ML *ūvula* UVULA + *-itis* -ITIS]

**ux.,** wife. [L *uxor*]

**uxorial** /ʌk'sɔriəl/, *adj.* of or pertaining to a wife; typical of or befitting a wife.

**uxoricide** /ʌk'sɔrəsaɪd/, *n.* **1.** one who kills his wife. **2.** the act of killing one's wife. [L *uxori-* wife + -CIDE] – **uxoricidal** /ʌk,sɔrə'saɪdl/, *adj.*

**uxorious** /ʌk'sɔriəs/, *adj.* excessively or foolishly fond of one's wife; doting on a wife. [L *uxōrius*] – **uxoriously,** *adv.* – **uxoriousness,** *n.*

**Uzbek** /'ʌzbɛk/, *n.* **1.** a member of a Turkic people living in central Asia, esp. in Uzbekistan. **2.** the Turkic language of this people. *–adj.* **3.** of or pertaining to this people or their language. Also, **Usbeg, Uzbeg.**

**Vv** Roman SOUVENIR **Vv** Sans Serif CLEARFACE

Script BANK

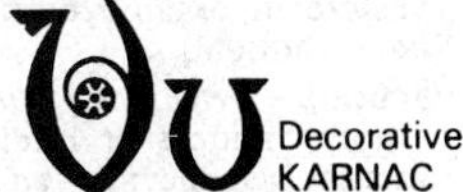

Decorative KARNAC

*Although there are numerous typefaces in the world they can be divided into four main classifications. These are:*

*ROMAN or SERIF. This typeface came into being from the technique of the Roman masons who, working in stone, finished off each letter with a serif or small stroke projecting from the top or bottom. This was done to correct any feeling of unevenness or imbalance they may have created in cutting the characters in stone.*

*SANS SERIF (without serif). This typeface is geometric in design and has straight-edged characters and lines of a regular thickness.*

*SCRIPT. Based on the movement of the hand, this typeface is often italicised or slanted, as if drawn by a brush or quill pen.*

*DECORATIVE. Any typeface that exaggerates the characteristics of any of the other three classifications to a degree that places it outside of them.*

*The dictionary entries in this book use a SANS SERIF typeface called Helvetica (set in a bold face for the head words) and a SERIF typeface Plantin (used throughout the body of the entries).*

**V, v** /vi/, *n., pl.* **V's** or **Vs, v's** or **vs. 1.** a consonant, the 22nd letter of the English alphabet. **2.** (*sometimes l.c.*) the Roman numeral for five. **3.** something shaped like the letter V. **4.** →**V-sign.**

**v, 1.** velocity. **2.** *Elect.* volt.

**v., 1.** *Bot.* variety (of). **2.** vector. **3.** velocity. **4.** verb. **5.** verbal. **6.** verse. **7.** versus (against). **8.** very. **9.** vice-. **10.** violin. **11.** volume.

**V, 1.** *Chem.* vanadium. **2.** *Maths.* vector. **3.** velocity. **4.** *Elect.* volt.

**V-,** a prefix indicating that the cylinders of a specified number in an internal-combustion engine are arranged in a V shape: *V-twin, V-6, V-8.*

**V., 1.** Venerable. **2.** Version. **3.** Vice. **4.** Victoria. **5.** Viscount. **6.** Volunteer.

**Va,** *Music.* viola.

**vac** /væk/, *n. Colloq.* vacation.

**vac., 1.** vacant. **2.** vacancy. **3.** vacation. **4.** vacuum.

**vacancy** /ˈveɪkənsi/, *n., pl.* **-cies. 1.** the state of being vacant; emptiness; unoccupied state. **2.** something vacant; vacant space. **3.** a gap or opening. **4.** an unoccupied office or position: *to fill vacancies by election.* **5.** lack of thought or intelligence; vacuity. **6.** *Crystall.* an irregularity in a lattice caused by a site normally occupied by an atom or ion being vacant. **7.** *Rare.* absence of occupation; idleness or inactivity. **8.** *Obs.* unoccupied or leisure time.

**vacant** /ˈveɪkənt/, *adj.* **1.** having no contents; empty; void. **2.** devoid or destitute (*of*). **3.** having no occupant: *vacant chairs.* **4.** untenanted, as a house, etc. **5.** not in use, as a room. **6.** free from work, business, etc., as time. **7.** characterised by or proceeding from absence of occupation: *a vacant life.* **8.** unoccupied with thought or reflection, as the mind. **9.** characterised by, showing, or proceeding from lack of thought or intelligence. **10.** not occupied by an incumbent, official, or the like, as a benefice, office, etc. **11.** *Law.* **a.** idle or unutilised; open to any claimant, as land. **b.** without an incumbent; abandoned: *a vacant estate* (one having no heir or claimant). [ME, from L *vacans,* ppr.] – **vacantly,** *adv.*

**vacant allotment** /– əˈlɒtmənt/, *n.* an undeveloped building block.

**vacant possession** /– pəˈzɛʃən/, *n.* the right of immediate possession of a house or property, the prior occupant having departed.

**vacate** /vəˈkeɪt, veɪˈkeɪt/, *v.,* **-cated, -cating.** *–v.t.* **1.** to make vacant; cause to be empty or unoccupied. **2.** to give up the occupancy of. **3.** to give up or relinquish (an office, position, etc.). **4.** to render inoperative; deprive of validity; annul: *to vacate a legal judgment.* *–v.i.* **5.** to withdraw from occupancy or possession; leave; quit. [L *vacātus,* pp., freed, emptied]

**vacation** /vəˈkeɪʃən, veɪˈkeɪʃən/, *n.* **1.** a part of the year when law courts, universities, etc., are suspended or closed. **2.** *Chiefly U.S.* a holiday. **3.** the act of vacating. *–v.i.* **4.** *U.S.* to take or have a vacation or holiday. [ME, from L *vacātio*] – **vacationless,** *adj.*

**vaccinal** /ˈvæksənəl/, *adj.* of, pertaining to, or due to vaccine or vaccination.

**vaccinate** /ˈvæksəneɪt/, *v.,* **-nated, -nating.** *–v.t.* **1.** to inoculate with the vaccine of cowpox, so as to render the subject immune to smallpox. **2.** to inoculate with the modified virus of any of various other diseases, as a preventive measure. *–v.i.* **3.** to perform or practise vaccination. [VACCINE + -ATE[1]]

**vaccination** /væksəˈneɪʃən/, *n.* the act or practice of vaccinating; inoculation with vaccine.

**vaccinationist** /væksəˈneɪʃənəst/, *n.* an advocate of vaccination.

**vaccinator** /ˈvæksəneɪtə/, *n.* **1.** one who vaccinates. **2.** an instrument used in vaccination.

**vaccine** /ˈvæksin, vækˈsin/, *n.* **1.** the virus of cowpox, obtained from the vesicles of an affected cow or person, and used in vaccination. **2.** the modified virus of any of various other diseases, used for preventive inoculation. *–adj.* **3.** pertaining to vaccinia or to vaccination. **4.** of, pertaining to, or derived from cows. [L *vaccīnus* pertaining to cows]

**vaccine point** /ˈ– pɔɪnt/, *n.* a thin, pointed, vaccine-coated piece of bone or the like, for use in vaccinating.

**vaccinia** /vækˈsɪniə/, *n.* →**cowpox.** [NL, from L *vaccīnus* VACCINE (def. 4)]

**vaccinisation** /væksənaɪˈzeɪʃən/, *n.* a vaccination produced by a series of virus inoculations. Also, **vaccinization.**

**vacherin** /ˈvæʃərən/, *n.* a sweet made with meringue on a pastry base and filled with ice-cream, cream and sometimes fruit. [F]

**vacillate** /ˈvæsəleɪt/, *v.i.,* **-lated, -lating. 1.** to sway unsteadily; waver; stagger. **2.** to fluctuate. **3.** to waver in mind or opinion; be irresolute or hesitant. [L *vacillātus,* pp.]

**vacillating** /ˈvæsəleɪtɪŋ/, *adj.* **1.** that vacillates; wavering. **2.** characterised by vacillation. Also, **vacillatory.** – **vacillatingly,** *adv.*

**vacillation** /væsəˈleɪʃən/, *n.* **1.** the act of vacillating; wavering in mind or opinion; irresoluteness. **2.** an instance of this. **3.** unsteady movement.

**vacua** /ˈvækjuə/, *n.* a plural of **vacuum.**

**vacuity** /vəˈkjuəti/, *n., pl.* **-ties. 1.** the state of being vacuous or empty; absence of contents; emptiness. **2.** an empty space; a vacuum. **3.** absence or lack of something specified. **4.** vacancy of mind, thought, etc.; mental inactivity. **5.** absence of ideas or intelligence; inanity. **6.** something inane or senselessly stupid. [L *vacuitas*]

**vacuolate** /ˈvækjuələt, -leɪt/, *adj.* provided with or containing a vacuole or vacuoles. Also, **vacuolated.**

**vacuolation** /ˌvækjuəˈleɪʃən/, *n.* **1.** the formation of vacuoles. **2.** the state of being vacuolate. **3.** a system of vacuoles.

**vacuole** /ˈvækjuoʊl/, *n.* **1.** a cavity within a cell, often containing a watery liquid or secretion. **2.** a minute cavity or vesicle in organic tissue. [NL *vacuolum,* diminutive of *vacuum* VACUUM]

**vacuous** /ˈvækjuəs/, *adj.* **1.** empty; without contents. **2.** empty of ideas or intelligence; stupidly vacant. **3.** showing mental vacancy: *a vacuous look.* **4.** purposeless; idle. [L *vacuus*] – **vacuously,** *adv.* – **vacuousness,** *n.*

**vacuum** /ˈvækjum/, *n., pl.* **vacuums, vacua** /ˈvækjuə/ *adj., v.* –*n.* **1.** a space entirely void of matter (**perfect** or **complete vacuum**). **2.** an enclosed space from which air (or other gas) has been removed, as by an air pump (**partial vacuum**). **3.** the state or degree of exhaustion in such an enclosed space. **4.** empty space. –*adj.* **5.** pertaining to, employing, or producing a vacuum. **6.** (of a hollow container) partly exhausted of gas. **7.** pertaining to apparatuses or processes which utilise gas pressures below atmospheric pressure. –*v.t.* **8.** to clean with a vacuum cleaner or treat with any vacuum device. [L, properly neut. of *vacuus* empty]

**vacuum aspiration** /– æspəˈreɪʃən/, *n.* a method of aborting a foetus in which suction is used to abstract it from the uterus.

**vacuum brake** /ˈ– breɪk/, *n.* a type of brake used on railway trains, motor vehicles, etc., operated by a vacuum system.

**vacuum-clean** /ˈvækjum-klin/, *v.t.* to clean by means of a vacuum cleaner.

**vacuum cleaner** /ˈ– klinə/, *n.* an apparatus for cleaning carpets, floors, etc., by suction.

**vacuum crystallisation** /– krɪstəlaɪˈzeɪʃən/, *n.* the process of crystallisation carried out under a reduced pressure at a temperature below that required at normal pressures.

**vacuum distillation** /– dɪstəˈleɪʃən/, *n.* the process of distillation carried out under a reduced pressure, thus depressing the boiling point of the substance to be distilled and enabling the process to be carried out at a reduced temperature.

**vacuum filtration** /– fɪlˈtreɪʃən/, *n.* the process of filtration carried out under a reduced pressure, in order to increase the rate of filtration by sucking the filtrate through the filter.

**vacuum flask** /ˈ– flask/, *n.* →**thermos.** Also, **vacuum bottle.**

**vacuum gauge** /ˈ– geɪdʒ/, *n.* a device for measuring pressures below atmospheric pressure in the receiver of an air pump, in steam condensers, and the like.

**vacuum-packed** /ˈvækjum-pækt/, *adj.* packed with little or no air in an airtight container, so as to maintain freshness, purity, etc. Also, **vacuum-sealed.**

**vacuum pump** /ˈ– pʌmp/, *n.* a pump or device by which a partial vacuum can be produced.

**vacuum tube** /ˈ– tjub/, *n.* **1.** →**valve** (def. 7). **2.** a sealed glass tube containing a partial vacuum or a highly rarefied gas, in which may be observed the effects of a discharge of electricity passed through the tube between electrodes leading into it.

vacuum tube: A, screen grid; B, suppressor grid; C, cathode; D, control grid; E, anode

**vade mecum** /vadeɪ ˈmeɪkʊm/, *n.* **1.** anything a person carries about as being of service. **2.** a book for ready reference; a manual or handbook. [L: go with me]

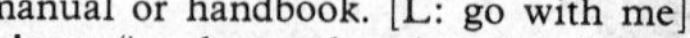

**vadose** /ˈveɪdoʊz, -doʊs/, *adj.* of, pertaining to, or resulting from water found above the watertable: *vadose circulation, vadose deposits.* [L *vadōsus* shallow, from *vadum* ford]

**vag** /væg/, *n., v.,* **vagged, vagging.** –*n.* **1.** *Colloq.* a vagrant. –*v.t.* **2.** to arrest on a vagrancy charge.

**vagabond** /ˈvægəbɒnd/, *adj.* **1.** wandering from place to place without settled habitation; nomadic. **2.** leading an irregular or disreputable life. **3.** good-for-nothing; worthless. **4.** of or pertaining to a vagabond or vagrant: *vagabond habits.* **5.** moving about without certain direction. –*n.* **6.** one who is without a fixed abode and wanders from place to place. **7.** an idle wanderer without visible means of support; a tramp or vagrant. **8.** an idle, worthless fellow; a scamp; a rascal. [ME, from L *vagābundus* strolling about]

**vagabondage** /ˈvægəbɒndɪdʒ/, *n.* **1.** the state or habits of a vagabond; idle wandering. **2.** the class of vagabonds. Also, **vagabondism.**

**vagarious** /vəˈgɛəriəs/, *adj.* **1.** characterised by vagaries; erratic. **2.** wandering; roving; roaming.

**vagary** /ˈveɪgəri/, *n., pl.* **-ries. 1.** an extravagant idea or notion. **2.** a wild, capricious, or fantastic action; a freak. [apparently from L *vagārī* wander]

**vagina** /vəˈdʒaɪnə/, *n., pl.* **-nas, -nae** /-ni/. **1.** *Anat.* **a.** the passage leading from the uterus to the vulva in a female mammal. **b.** a sheathlike part or organ. **2.** *Bot.* the sheath formed by the basal part of certain leaves where they embrace the stem. [L: sheath]

**vaginal** /vəˈdʒaɪnəl/, *adj.* **1.** *Anat., etc.* pertaining to the vagina of a female mammal. **2.** pertaining to or resembling a sheath.

**vaginate** /ˈvædʒənət, -neɪt/, *adj.* furnished with a vagina or sheath; sheathed.

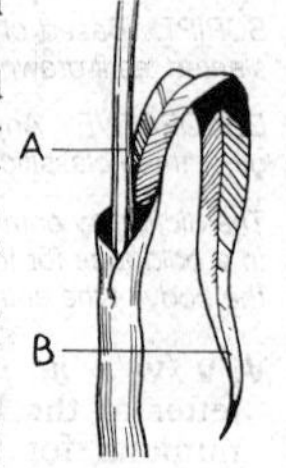


A, vaginate culm; B, vaginate leaf

**vaginectomy** /vædʒənˈɛktəmi/, *n.* **1.** removal by surgery of all or any of the vagina. **2.** removal by surgery of part of the serum-producing sheath of the testis and epididymis.

**vaginismus** /vædʒəˈnɪzməs/, *n.* involuntary contraction of the vagina.

**vaginitis** /vædʒəˈnaɪtəs/, *n.* inflammation of the vagina; colpitis. [NL. See VAGINA, -ITIS]

**vagotomy** /vəˈgɒtəmi/, *n.* a surgical operation for the treatment of severe peptic ulcers in which the vagus nerve is divided, thus limiting gastric secretion.

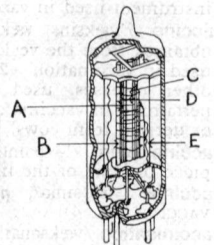

**vagrancy** /ˈveɪgrənsi/, *n., pl.* **-cies. 1.** the state or condition of being a vagrant. **2.** the conduct of a vagrant. **3.** mental wandering; digression in thought.

**vagrant** /ˈveɪgrənt/, *n.* **1.** one who wanders from place to place and has no settled home or means of support; tramp. –*adj.* **2.** wandering or roaming from place to place; nomadic. **3.** living in vagabondage; wandering idly without a settled home or work. **4.** of, pertaining to, or characteristic of a vagrant: *a vagrant life.* **5.** (of plants) straggling in growth. **6.** (of things) not fixed or settled; moving hither and thither. [late ME *vag(a)raunt* wandering (person), from frequentative of ME *vague,* v., wander, from L *vagārī*] – **vagrantly,** *adv.* – **vagrantness,** *n.*

**vague** /veɪg/, *adj.,* **vaguer, vaguest. 1.** not definite in statement or meaning; not explicit or precise: *vague promises.* **2.** of an indefinite or indistinct character, as ideas, feelings, etc. **3.** indistinct to the sight or other sense, or perceptible or recognisable only in an indefinite way: *vague forms seen through mist, vague murmurs.* **4.** not definitely fixed, determined, or known; uncertain. **5.** (of persons, etc.) indefinite in statement; not clear in thought or understanding. **6.** (of the eyes, expression, etc.) showing absence of clear perception or understanding. [L *vagus* wandering] – **vaguely,** *adv.* – **vagueness,** *n.*

**vagus nerve** /ˈveɪgəs nɜv/, *n.* either of two cranial nerves extending through the neck into the thorax and the upper part of the abdomen; a pneumogastric nerve. [*vagus* from L: wandering]

**vain** /veɪn/, *adj.* **1.** without real value or importance; hollow, idle or worthless. **2.** futile; useless; ineffectual. **3.** having an excessive pride in one's own appearance, qualities, gifts, achievements, etc.; conceited. **4.** proceeding from or showing personal vanity: *vain boasts.* **5.** *Archaic.* senseless or foolish. **6. in vain, a.** without effect or avail; to no purpose. **b.** improperly; blasphemously: *to take God's name in vain.* [ME, from OF, from L *vānus* empty, idle] – **vainly,** *adv.* – **vainness,** *n.*

**vainglorious** /veɪn'glɔriəs/, *adj.* **1.** filled with or given to vainglory. **2.** characterised by, showing, or proceeding from vainglory. – **vaingloriously,** *adv.* – **vaingloriousness,** *n.*

**vainglory** /veɪn'glɔri/, *n.* **1.** inordinate elation or pride in one's achievements, abilities, etc. **2.** vain pomp or show. [ME; translation of ML *vāna glōria*]

**vair** /vɛə/, *n.* a kind of fur much used for lining and trimming garments during the 13th and 14th centuries, and generally assumed to have been the skin of a variety of squirrel with a grey back and white belly. [ME, from OF, from L *varius* particoloured]

**valance** /'væləns/, *n.* **1.** a short curtain or piece of dependent drapery, as at the edge of a canopy, from the frame of a bed to the floor, etc. **2.** →**pelmet.** [late ME; ? from OF *avaler* descend, from *à val* down, from L *ad vallem* to the valley] – **valanced,** *adj.*

**vale**[1] /veɪl/, *n. Chiefly Poetic.* a valley. [ME, from OF *val,* from L *vallis*]

**vale**[2] /'valeɪ/, *interj., n.* goodbye; farewell. [L]

**valedict** /'vælədɪkt/, *n.* one who is bidding farewell, esp. a student of a residential university college at the time of his leaving it.

**valediction** /vælə'dɪkʃən/, *n.* **1.** a bidding farewell; a leave-taking. **2.** an utterance, speech, etc., made at the time of or by way of leave-taking. [L *valedictus,* pp., bidden goodbye + -ION]

**valedictorian** /ˌvælədɪk'tɔriən/, *n. U.S.* (in colleges and schools) the student (usu. the one who ranks highest academically) who pronounces the valedictory oration at the commencement exercises.

**valedictory** /vælə'dɪktəri/, *adj., n., pl.* **-ries.** *–adj.* **1.** bidding farewell; farewell. **2.** of or pertaining to an occasion of leave-taking. *–n.* **3.** a valedictory address or oration. **4.** *U.S.* (in colleges and schools) the oration delivered by the valedictorian.

**valence** /'veɪləns/, *n. Chiefly U.S.* →**valency.**

**valenciennes** /vælənsi'ɛnz/, *n.* **1.** a fine bobbin-made lace of which the pattern and the net ground are made together, of the same threads. **2.** a machine-made imitation of it. Also, **valenciennes lace.** [from *Valenciennes,* a city in N France]

**valency** /'veɪlənsi/, *n., pl.* **-cies. 1.** the quality which determines the number of atoms or radicals with which any single atom or radical will unite chemically. **2.** the relative combining capacity of an atom or radical compared with the standard hydrogen atom: *a valency of one* (the capacity to unite with one atom of hydrogen or its equivalent). Also, *Chiefly U.S.,* **valence.** [L *valentia* strength]

**valency band** /'– bænd/, *n.* the range of energies in a semiconductor corresponding to states which can be occupied by the valency electrons which bind the crystal together. Also, *Chiefly U.S.,* **valence band.**

**valency bond** /'– bɒnd/, *n.* a chemical bond between two atoms in a molecule in which electrons are shared between the two atoms.

**valency electron** /'– əˌlɛktrɒn/, *n.* an electron from the outer shell of an atom which can take part in the formation of valency bonds. Also, *Chiefly U.S.,* **valence electron.**

**-valent,** a word element meaning having worth or value, used esp. in scientific terminology to refer to valency, as in *quadrivalent.* [L *valens*]

**valentine** /'væləntaɪn/, *n.* **1.** an amatory or sentimental (sometimes satirical or comic) card or the like, or some token or gift, sent by one person to another on St Valentine's Day. **2.** a sweetheart chosen on St Valentine's Day, 14 February. [named after St *Valentine,* d. A.D. *c.* 270, Christian martyr at Rome]

**valerian** /və'lɛəriən, -'lɪə-/, *n.* **1.** any of the perennial herbs constituting the genus *Valeriana,* as *V. officinalis,* a plant with white or pink flowers and a medicinal root. **2.** a drug consisting of or made from the root, used as a nerve sedative and antispasmodic. [ME, from ML *valeriāna,* fem., from *Valerius,* personal name]

**valeric** /və'lɛərɪk, -'lɪərɪk/, *adj.* pertaining to or derived from valerian. Also, **valerianic** /vælɛəri'ænɪk, -lɪəri'ænɪk/. [VALER(IAN) + -IC]

valerian

**valeric acid** /–'æsəd/, *n.* any of several isomeric organic acids, $C_4H_9COOH$, the common one being a liquid of pungent smell obtained from valerian roots.

**valet** /'vælɛɪ, 'vælət/, *n., v.,* **-leted, -leting.** *–n.* **1.** a manservant who is his employer's personal attendant, caring for his clothing, etc.; manservant. **2.** one who performs similar services for patrons of a hotel, etc. **3.** any of various contrivances, as a rack or stand, for holding coats, hats, etc. *–v.t., v.i.* **4.** to attend or act as valet. [F, var. of MF *vaslet.* See VARLET, VASSAL] – **valetless,** *adj.*

**valeta** /və'litə/, *n.* →**veleta.**

**valet de chambre** /vælɛɪ də 'ʃɒmbrə/, *n., pl.* **valets de chambre.** →**valet** (def. 1). [F]

**valetudinarian** /ˌvælətjudə'nɛəriən/, *n.* **1.** an invalid. **2.** one who is constantly or excessively concerned about the state of his health. *–adj.* **3.** in poor health; sickly; invalid. **4.** constantly or excessively concerned about the state of one's health. **5.** characterised by or pertaining to invalidism: *valetudinarian habits.* [L *valētūdinārius* in poor health + -AN]

**valetudinarianism** /ˌvælətjudə'nɛəriənɪzəm/, *n.* valetudinarian condition or habits.

**valetudinary** /vælə'tjudənəri/, *n., pl.* **-ries.** *adj.* →**valetudinarian.**

**valgus** /'vælgəs/, *n.* **1.** an abnormal position of part of the bone structure of the human body. *–adj.* **2.** of or in such a position. [L: bow-legged]

**valiance** /'væliəns/, *n.* the quality of being valiant; valour; bravery; courage. Also, **valiancy.** [var. of late ME *vailance,* from AF, var. of OF *vaillance,* from *vaillant* VALIANT]

**valiant** /'væliənt/, *adj.* **1.** brave, courageous, or stout-hearted, as persons. **2.** marked by or showing bravery or valour, as deeds, attempts, etc. [ME, from OF *vaillant,* from *valeir* be strong, from L *valēre*] – **valiantly,** *adv.* – **valiantness,** *n.*

**valid** /'væləd/, *adj.* **1.** sound, just, or well-founded: *a valid reason, a valid objection.* **2.** having force, weight, or cogency; authoritative. **3.** legally sound, effective, or binding; having legal force; sustainable in law. **4.** *Logic.* denoting arguments in which the premises imply the conclusion (opposed to *invalid*). **5.** *Archaic.* robust or well. [L *validus* strong] – **validly,** *adv.* – **validness,** *n.*

**validate** /'vælədeɪt/, *v.t.,* **-dated, -dating. 1.** to make valid; confirm; corroborate; substantiate. **2.** to give legal force to; legalise. – **validation** /vælə'deɪʃən/, *n.*

**validity** /və'lɪdəti/, *n., pl.* **-ties. 1.** the state or quality of being valid. **2.** legal soundness or force.

**valine** /'veɪlin/, *n.* a white, crystalline, essential amino acid, $(CH_3)_2\,CHCH(NH_3^+)\,COO^-$, found in proteins.

**valise** /və'liz, -'lis/, *n.* a traveller's case for holding clothes, toilet articles, etc., esp. a small one for carrying by hand; a travelling bag. [F, from It. *valigia;* orig. uncert.]

**Valium** /'væliəm, 'veɪ-/, *n.* a sedative drug with mild tranquillising action used to treat anxiety. [Trademark]

**vallation** /və'leɪʃən/, *n.* **1.** a rampart or entrenchment. **2.** the process or technique of constructing ramparts. [LL *vallātio,* from L *vallum* rampart]

**vallecula** /və'lɛkjələ/, *n., pl.* **-lae** /-li/. *Anat., Bot.* a furrow or depression. [LL, diminutive of L *valles* valley] – **vallecular,** *adj.*

**valleculate** /və'lɛkjəleɪt/, *adj.* having a vallecula or valleculae.

**valley** /'væli/, *n., pl.* **-leys. 1.** an elongated depression, usu. with an outlet, between uplands, hills, or mountains, esp. one following the course of a stream. **2.** an extensive, more or less flat, and relatively low region drained by a great river system. **3.** any hollow or structure likened to a valley. **4.** *Archit.* a depression or angle formed by the meeting of two inclined sides of a roof. **5.** the lower phase of a horizontal wave motion. [ME *valey,* from OF *valee,* from *val,* from L *vallis*] – **valleylike,** *adj.*

**valonia** /və'louniə/, *n.* acorn cups of the **valonia oak,** *Quercus* *aegilops,* used in tanning, dyeing, and making ink. [It. *vallonia,* from Mod. Gk *balánia* acorns]

**valor** /'vælə/, *n. U.S.* →**valour.**

**valorise** /'væləraɪz/, *v.t.,* **-rised, -rising.** *Chiefly U.S.* **1.** to assign a value to. **2.** (of a government) to fix the value or price of (a commercial commodity) and provide for maintaining it against a decline (as to a price below the cost of production), by purchase of the commodity at the fixed price or by other means (esp. with reference to the action of Brazil in fixing the price of coffee). Also, **valorize.** [obs. *valor* worth (see VALOUR) + -ISE[1]] – **valorisation** /ˌvæləraɪ'zeɪʃən/, *n.*

**valorous** /'vælərəs/, *adj.* **1.** having or displaying valour; valiant or brave, as persons. **2.** characterised by valour, as actions, etc. [late ME, from ML *valorōsus*] – **valorously,** *adv.* – **valorousness,** *n.*

**valour** /'vælə/, *n.* boldness or firmness in braving danger; bravery or heroic courage, esp. in battle. Also, *U.S.,* **valor.** [ME, from OF, from LL *valor* (from L *valēre* be strong, be worth)]

**valse** /væls/, *n.* →**waltz**[1]. [F]

**valuable** /'væljuəbəl, 'væljubəl/, *adj.* **1.** of monetary worth. **2.** representing a large market value: *valuable paintings.* **3.** of considerable use, service, or importance: *valuable information, valuable aid.* **4.** capable of having the value estimated. *–n.* **5.** (*usu. pl.*) a valuable article, as of personal property or of merchandise, esp. one of comparatively small size. – **valuableness,** *n.* – **valuably,** *adv.*

**valuable consideration** /– kənsɪdə'reɪʃən/, *n.* something of value given in exchange on the making of a contract.

**valuation** /vælju'eɪʃən/, *n.* **1.** an estimating or fixing of the value of a thing. **2.** a value estimated or fixed; estimated worth. – **valuational,** *adj.*

**valuator** /'væljueɪtə/, *n.* →**appraiser.**

**value** /'vælju/, *n., v.,* **-ued, -uing.** *–n.* **1.** that property of a thing because of which it is esteemed, desirable, or useful, or the degree of this property possessed; worth, merit, or importance: *the value of education.* **2.** material or monetary worth, as in traffic or sale: *even the waste has value.* **3.** the worth of a thing as measured by the amount of other things for which it can be exchanged, or as estimated in terms of a medium of exchange. **4.** equivalent worth or equivalent return: *for value received.* **5.** estimated or assigned worth; valuation. **6.** force, import, or significance: *the value of a word or phrase.* **7.** *Maths.* **a.** the magnitude of a quantity or measurement. **b.** (of a function) the number obtained when particular numbers are substituted for the variables. **8.** (*pl.*) *Sociol.* the things of social life (ideals, customs, institutions, etc.) towards which the people of the group have an affective regard. These values may be positive, as cleanliness, freedom, education, etc., or negative, as cruelty, crime, or blasphemy. **9.** *Ethics.* any object or quality desirable as a means or as an end in itself. **10.** *Painting.* the property of a colour by which it is distinguished as light or dark. **11.** *Music.* the relative length or duration of a note. **12.** *Phonet.* **a.** quality. **b.** the phonetic equivalent of a letter: *one value of the letter 'a' is the vowel sound in 'hat', 'sang', etc.* *–v.t.* **13.** to estimate the value of; rate at a certain value or price; appraise. **14.** to consider with respect to worth, excellence, usefulness, or importance. **15.** to regard or esteem highly. **16. good value,** excellent in one's field; capable. [ME, from OF, pp. of *valeir* be worth, from L *valēre*]

**value added** /– 'ædəd/, *n.* the extent to which the value of a finished product exceeds the cost of its raw material components.

**value added tax,** *n.* a tax on the value added. Also, **V.A.T.**

**valued** /'væljud/, *adj.* **1.** highly regarded or esteemed. **2.** estimated or appraised. **3.** having the value specified.

**valued policy** /'– ˌpɒləsi/, *n.* a form of insurance policy in which the value of the object insured is specified.

**value judgment** /'vælju dʒʌdʒmənt/, *n.* an assessment based on or reflecting one's personal or social values.

**valueless** /'væljuləs/, *adj.* without value; worthless. – **valuelessness,** *n.*

**valuer** /'væljuə/, *n.* **1.** one who estimates or assesses values. **2.** one who values highly.

**valuer general** /– 'dʒɛnrəl/, *n.* a government official in charge of making valuations of property.

**valuta** /və'lutə/, *n.* the value of a currency in terms of another currency. [It.: value]

**valvate** /'vælveɪt/, *adj.* **1.** furnished with or opening by a valve or valves. **2.** serving as or resembling a valve. **3.** *Bot.* **a.** opening by valves, as certain capsules and anthers. **b.** meeting without overlapping, as the parts of certain buds. **c.** composed of or characterised by such parts. [L *valvātus* having folding doors]

**valve** /vælv/, *n., v.,* **valved, valving.** *–n.* **1.** any device for closing or modifying the passage through a pipe, outlet, inlet, or the like, in order to control the flow of liquids, gases, etc. **2.** a hinged lid or other movable part in such a device, which closes or modifies the passage. **3.** *Anat.* a membranous fold or other structure which controls the flow of a fluid, as one which permits blood to flow in one direction only. **4.** (in musical wind instruments of the trumpet class) a device for changing the length of the air column to alter the pitch of a note. **5.** *Zool.* **a.** one of the two or more separable pieces composing certain shells. **b.** either half of the silicified shell of a diatom. **6.** *Bot.* **a.** one of the segments into which a capsule dehisces. **b.** a flap or lidlike part of certain anthers. **7.** *Electronics.* an electrical device consisting of two or more electrodes in an evacuated or gas-filled cylinder of glass or metal, which can be used for controlling a flow of electricity. **8.** *Archaic.* one of the halves or leaves of a double or folding door. *–v.t.* **9.** to provide with a means of control of fluid flow, as gas from a balloon, by inserting a valve. [ME, from L *valva* leaf of a door (pl., folding doors)] – **valveless,** *adj.* – **valvelike,** *adj.*

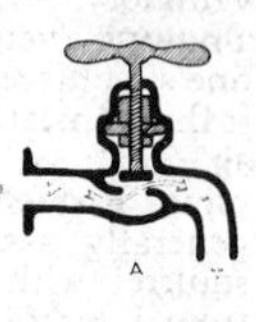


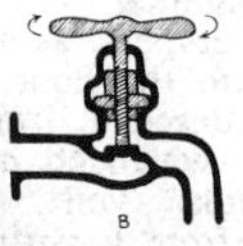


globe valve on domestic tap: A, open; B, closed

**valve base** /'– beɪs/, *n.* **1.** the part of a radio valve envelope from which the connecting pins to the various electrodes project, enabling the valve to be fitted into a valve socket and thus connected to the rest of the circuit. **2.** the specific configuration of these connecting pins.

**valve gear** /'– gɪə/, *n.* the mechanism for opening and closing the valves in an internal-combustion engine.

**valve grind** /'– graɪnd/, *n.* the grinding of the mating surfaces of the valves of an engine and their seats to achieve better fit.

**valve house** /'– haʊs/, *n.* a house or structure at the gate of a dam, reservoir, etc., with apparatus for regulating the flow of water; gatehouse.

**valvelet** /'vælvlət/, *n.* a small valve; a valvule.

**valve socket** /'vælv sɒkət/, *n.* a plastic or ceramic connector, attached to the chassis of an electronic device, into which the pins of the valve base connect, enabling the valve to be connected to the rest of the circuit. Also, **valve-holder.**

**valve spring** /'– sprɪŋ/, *n.* a helical spring used to close a poppet valve, esp. in an internal-combustion engine.

**valvotomy** /væl'vɒtəmi/, *n., pl.* **-mies.** →**valvulotomy.**

**valvular** /'vælvjələ/, *adj.* **1.** having the form of a valve. **2.** furnished with or operating by a valve or valves. **3.** of a valve or valves, esp. of the heart.

**valvule** /'vælvjul/, *n.* a small valve or valvelike part. [NL *valvula,* diminutive of L *valva.* See VALVE]

**valvulitis** /vælvjə'laɪtəs/, *n.* inflammation of the cardiac-valve leaflets, caused by an acute infectious process, usu. rheumatic fever or syphilis. [NL *valvula* valvule + -ITIS]

**valvulotomy** /vælvju'lɒtəmi/, *n., pl.* **-mies.** the opening, slitting, or fracturing of a heart valve along natural lines of cleavage. Also, **valvotomy.** [VALVUL(E) + -O- + -TOMY]

**vamoose** /və'mus/, *v.,* **-moosed, -moosing.** *–v.i. Chiefly U.S.* **1.** to make off; decamp; depart quickly. *–v.t.* **2.** to decamp from; quit hurriedly. Also, **vamose** /və'moʊs/. [Sp. *vamos* let us go]

**vamp**[1] /væmp/, *n.* **1.** the front part of the upper of a shoe or boot. **2.** anything patched up or pieced together. **3.** *Music.* an accompaniment, usu. improvised, consisting of a succession of simple chords. *–v.t.* **4.** to furnish with a vamp, esp. to repair with a new vamp, as a shoe or boot. **5.** to patch up or repair; renovate (oft. fol. by *up*). **6.** to give an appearance of newness to. **7.** *Music.* to improvise (an accompaniment or the like). *–v.i.* **8.** *Music.* to improvise an accompaniment, tune, etc. [ME *vampe,* from OF *avanpie* forepart of the foot, from *avant* before (from L *ab ante* from in front) + *pie* foot, from L *pēs*] – **vamper,** *n.*

**vamp**[2] /væmp/, *Colloq.* *–n.* **1.** a woman who uses her charms to seduce and exploit men. *–v.i.* **2.** to act as a vamp. *–v.t.* **3.** to use one's feminine charms or arts upon (a man). [short for VAMPIRE] – **vamper,** *n.*

**vampire** /ˈvæmpaɪə/, *n.*→**1.** a preternatural being, in the common belief a reanimated corpse of a person improperly buried, supposed to suck blood of sleeping persons at night. **2.** one who preys ruthlessly on others; an extortionist. **3.** Also, **vampire bat. a.** any of various South and Central American bats including *Desmodus rotundus, Diphylla ecaudata* and *Diaemus youngi,* the **true vampires,** which feed on the blood of animals including man. **b.** any large South American bat of the genera *Phyllostomus* and *Vampyrus,* erroneously reputed to suck blood. **c.** any of the false vampires of Asia and Australia. See **false vampire. 4.** *Theat.* a trapdoor on a stage. [F, from G *Vampir,* ? from Turk. *uber* witch] – **vampiric** /væmˈpɪrɪk/, **vampirish,** *adj.*

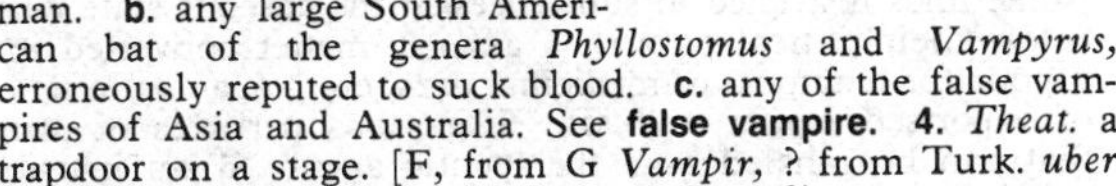

vampire (def. 3): vampire bat

**vampirism** /ˈvæmpaɪəˌrɪzəm/, *n.* **1.** the belief in the existence of preternatural vampires. **2.** acts or practices of vampires. **3.** the unscrupulous exploitation of others.

**van**[1] /væn/, *n.* **1.** (formerly) the foremost division or the front part of an army, a fleet, or any body of individuals advancing, or in order for advancing. **2.** the forefront in any movement, course of progress, or the like. **3.** those who are in the forefront of a movement or the like. [short for VANGUARD]

**van**[2] /væn/, *n.* **1.** a covered vehicle, usu. large in size, for moving furniture, goods, etc. **2.** a closed railway wagon. [short for CARAVAN]

**van**[3] /væn/, *prep.* (*oft. cap.*) from; of (used in Dutch in personal names, originally to indicate place of origin). [D]

**van**[4] /væn/, *n.* **1.** any winnowing device. **2.** *Poetic.* a wing. [var. of FAN[1]]

**van**[5] /væn/, *n.* →**advantage** (def. 5).

**vanad-,** a word element indicating the presence of vanadium, as in *vanadate.*

**vanadate** /ˈvænədeɪt/, *n.* a salt of a vanadic acid. Also, **vanadiate** /vəˈneɪdieɪt/.

**vanadic** /vəˈnædɪk/, *adj.* of or containing vanadium, esp. in the trivalent or pentavalent state.

**vanadic acid** /– ˈæsəd/, *n.* any of certain acids containing vanadium, esp. one with the formula $H_3VO_4$.

**vanadinite** /vəˈnædənaɪt/, *n.* a mineral, lead chlorovanadate, $Pb_5(VO_4)_3Cl$, occurring in yellow, brown, or greenish crystals, an ore of lead and vanadium.

**vanadium** /vəˈneɪdiəm/, *n.* a rare element occurring in certain minerals, and obtained as a light grey powder with a silvery lustre, used as an ingredient of steel to toughen it and increase shock resistance. *Symbol:* V; *at. wt:* 50.942; *at.no.: 23; sp.gr.*: 5.96. [Icel. *Vanad(īs),* epithet of Norse goddess Freya + -IUM; so called because discovered in Sweden]

**vanadium pentoxide** /– pɛnˈtɒksaɪd/, *n.* a brown to red solid, acidic oxide, $V_2O_5$, which reacts with both acid and base to give water solutions of complex anions including vanadates of type $VO_4^{3-}$.

**vanadium steel** /– ˈstil/, *n.* a special steel containing approximately 0.1 to 0.2 per cent vanadium to increase elasticity, etc.

**vanadous** /ˈvænədəs/, *adj.* containing divalent or trivalent vanadium. Also, **vanadious** /vəˈneɪdiəs/.

**Van Allen belt,** *n.* either of two regions above the earth (one at a height of about 4 000 km, another at about 20 000 km) in which charged particles are trapped by the earth's magnetic field. [named after James Alfred *Van Allen,* born 1914, U.S. physicist]

**vandal** /ˈvændl/, *n.* **1.** one who wilfully or ignorantly destroys or damages anything, as property or works of art. *–adj.* **2.** imbued with or characterised by vandalism. [from the *Vandals,* a Germanic people which in the 5th century A.D. ravaged Gaul and Spain, settled in Africa, and in 455 sacked Rome; LL *Vandalus,* Latinisation of native tribal name] – **vandalic** /vænˈdælɪk/, *adj.*

**vandalise** /ˈvændəlaɪz/, *v.t.,* **-lised, -lising.** to destroy or damage by vandalism. Also, **vandalize.**

**vandalism** /ˈvændəlɪzəm/, *n.* **1.** wanton or malicious destruction or damage of property. **2.** wilful or ignorant destruction of artistic or literary treasures. **3.** conduct or spirit characteristic of a vandal.

**Van de Graaff generator** /væn də graf ˈdʒɛnəreɪtə/, *n.* an electrostatic generator in which a high potential is developed in a metal conductor by accumulating the charge from a high-speed belt; often used as a particle accelerator. [named after R.J. *Van de Graaff,* 1901-67, U.S. physicist]

**vandemonian** /vændəˈmoʊniən/, *n.* **1.** (formerly) a convict from Van Diemen's Land, thought of as being an incorrigible. **2.** (formerly) a Tasmanian.

**Van der Waals' equation** /væn də walz əˈkweɪʒən/, *n.* a modification of the gas laws taking into account Van der Waals' forces and the finite size of the atoms or molecules. [named after J. D. *Van der Waals,* 1837-1923, Dutch physicist]

**Van der Waals' forces,** *n.* weak attractive forces between atoms or molecules arising as a result of electrons in neighbouring atoms or molecules moving in sympathy with each other. [see VAN DER WAALS' EQUATION]

**Van Diemen's Land** /væn ˈdimənz lænd/, *n.* former name of Tasmania.

**Vandyke** /vænˈdaɪk/, *n., v.,* **-dyked, -dyking.** *–n.* **1.** (*sometimes l.c.*) →**Vandyke beard. 2.** (*sometimes l.c.*) →**Vandyke collar.** *–v.t.* **3.** (*l.c.*) to cut or shape (material) with deep points. [from Sir Anthony *Vandyke* (also Van Dyct), 1599-1641, Flemish painter living in England]

**Vandyke beard** /– ˈbɪəd/, *n.* a short, pointed beard.

**Vandyke brown** /– ˈbraʊn/, *n.* any of several dark brown pigments consisting of iron oxide admixed with lampblack or similar materials.

**Vandyke collar** /– ˈkɒlə/, *n.* a wide collar with deeply pointed edge.

**vane** /veɪn/, *n.* **1.** a flat piece of metal, or some other device fixed upon a spire or other elevated object in such a way as to move with the wind and indicate its direction; a weathercock. **2.** a similar piece, or sail, in the wheel of a windmill, to be moved by the air. **3.** any plate, blade, or the like, attached to an axis, and moved by or in air or a liquid: *a vane of a screw propeller.* **4.** *Ornith.* the web of a feather. **5.** *Navig., Survey.* a sight on a quadrant or other surveying instrument. [ME; OE *fana* flag, c. G *Fahne*] – **vaned,** *adj.* – **vaneless,** *adj.*

vane

**vang** /væŋ/, *n.* a light tackle passing from near the foot of a mast to the boom somewhat abaft the mast and used to heave the boom down and thus flatten the sail; boom vang. [D: catch]

**vanguard** /ˈvængad/, *n.* **1.** the foremost division or the front part of an army; the van. **2.** the leading position in any field. **3.** the leaders of any intellectual or political movement. [late ME *vandgard,* from OF *avan(t)-garde,* from *avant* before + *garde* guard]

**vanilla** /vəˈnɪlə/, *n.* **1.** any of the tropical climbing orchids constituting the genus *Vanilla,* esp. *V. fragrans,* whose podlike fruit (**vanilla bean**) yields an extract used in flavouring food, in perfumery, etc. **2.** the fruit or bean. **3.** the extract. [NL, from Sp. *vainilla* little pod, from *vaina* sheath, from L *vāgīna*]

vanilla (def. 1)

**vanilla flower** /ˈ– flaʊə/, *n.* any of various herbs of the genera *Sowerbaea* and *Arthropodium,* family Liliaceae, having fragrant flowers. Also, **vanilla-lily.**

i = peat ɪ = pit ɛ = pet æ = pat a = part ɒ = pot ʌ = putt ɔ = port ʊ = put u = pool ɜ = pert ə = apart aɪ = buy eɪ = bay ɔɪ = boy aʊ = how
oʊ = hoe ɪə = here ɛə = hair ʊə = tour g = give θ = thin ð = then ʃ = show ʒ = measure tʃ = choke dʒ = joke ŋ = sing j = you õ = Fr. bon

**vanillic** /və'nɪlɪk/, *adj.* pertaining to, derived from, or resembling vanilla or vanillin.

**vanillin** /və'nɪlən, 'vænələn/, *n.* a white crystalline compound, $C_8H_8O_3$, the active principle of vanilla, now prepared artificially and used as a flavouring agent and a substitute for vanilla. Also, **vanilline** /və'nɪlin, 'vænəlin/.

**vanish** /'vænɪʃ/, *v.i.* **1.** to disappear from sight, or become invisible, esp. quickly. **2.** to disappear by ceasing to exist; come to an end; cease. **3.** *Maths.* (of a number or quantity) to become zero. *–n.* **4.** *Phonet.* the last part of a vowel sound when it differs noticeably in quality from the main sound. [ME *vanisshen,* from OF *evaniss-,* stem of *evanir.* See EVANESCE] – **vanisher,** *n.*

**vanishing cream** /'vænəʃɪŋ krim/, *n.* a white foundation cream which becomes colourless on application.

**vanishing point** /'– pɔɪnt/, *n.* **1.** a point of disappearance. **2.** (in perspective) that point towards which receding parallel lines appear to converge.

**vanity** /'vænəti/, *n., pl.* **-ties. 1.** the quality of being personally vain; excessive pride in one's own appearance, qualities, gifts, achievements, etc. **2.** an instance or display of this quality or feeling. **3.** something about which one is vain. **4.** vain or worthless character; want of real value; hollowness or worthlessness. **5.** something vain or worthless. **6.** →**vanity unit.** [ME *vanite,* from OF, from L *vānitas* emptiness]

**vanity case** /'– keɪs/, *n.* a small case or bag for holding cosmetics, toilet articles, etc., carried by a woman. Also, **vanity box, vanity bag.**

**vanity edition** /'– ədɪʃən/, *n.* an edition of a book which is published with the financial backing of the author.

**Vanity Fair** /vænəti 'fɛə/, *n.* (*oft. l.c.*) any place or group, as the world, a great city, fashionable society, etc., regarded as given over to vain pleasure or empty show. [orig., in Bunyan's *Pilgrim's Progress,* a fair, symbolising worldly ostentation and frivolity, in the town of Vanity]

**vanity publishing** /'vænəti ˌpʌblɪʃɪŋ/, *n.* the publishing of unprofitable books with the financial backing of the author.

**vanity unit** /'– junət/, *n.* an item of bathroom furniture consisting of a cabinet with a bench top and an inset basin. Also, **vanity table.**

**vanquish** /'væŋkwɪʃ/, *v.t.* **1.** to conquer or defeat in battle or conflict; reduce to subjection by superior force. **2.** to defeat in any contest. **3.** to overcome or overpower. [ME *vencusche,* from OF *vencus,* pp. of *veintre,* from L *vincere*] – **vanquishable,** *adj.* – **vanquisher,** *n.* – **vanquishment,** *n.*

**vantage** /'væntɪdʒ, 'van-/, *n.* **1.** position or condition affording superiority, as for action. **2.** opportunity likely to give superiority. **3.** *Tennis.* advantage. [ME, aphetic modification of *avantage* ADVANTAGE]

**vantage ground** /'– graʊnd/, *n.* a position which gives one an advantage, as for action of defence; favourable position.

**vantage point** /'– pɔɪnt/, *n.* a position or place affording an advantageous or clear view or perspective.

**Van't Hoff's law** /vant 'hɔfs lɔ/, *n.* the law which states that the osmotic pressure of a dilute solution is equal to the pressure which the solute would exert in the gaseous state, if it occupied a volume equal to the volume of the solution, at the same temperature. [named after J. H. *Van't Hoff,* 1852-1911, Dutch chemist]

**Vanuatu** /vænu'atu/, *n.* an island state in the South Pacific. Formerly, **New Hebrides.**

**vanward** /'vænwəd/, *adj.* towards or in the van or front (opposed to *rearward*).

**vapid** /'væpəd/, *adj.* **1.** having lost life, sharpness, or flavour; insipid; flat. **2.** without animation or spirit; dull, uninteresting or tedious, as talk, writings, persons, etc. [L *vapidus*] – **vapidity** /və'pɪdəti/, **vapidness,** *n.* – **vapidly,** *adv.*

**vapor** /'veɪpə/, *n., v.t., v.i. U.S.* →**vapour.** – **vaporability** /veɪpərə'bɪləti/, *n.* – **vaporable,** *adj.* – **vaporer,** *n.* – **vaporless,** *adj.* – **vapor-like,** *adj.*

**vaporescence** /veɪpə'rɛsəns/, *n.* a changing into vapour. [VAPO(U)R + -ESCENCE] – **vaporescent,** *adj.*

**vaporific** /veɪpə'rɪfɪk/, *adj.* **1.** producing vapour, or connected with the production of vapour; tending towards vapour. **2.** pertaining to or of the nature of vapour. [NL *vaporificus*]

**vaporimeter** /veɪpə'rɪmətə/, *n.* an instrument for measuring vapour pressure or volume.

**vaporing** /'veɪpərɪŋ/, *adj., n. U.S.* →**vapouring.** – **vaporingly,** *adv.*

**vaporisation** /ˌveɪpəraɪ'zeɪʃən/, *n.* **1.** the process by which a liquid is converted into a vapour. **2.** the rapid change of water into steam, esp. in a boiler. **3.** *Med.* a vapour therapy. Also, **vaporization.**

**vaporise** /'veɪpəraɪz/, *v.,* **-rised, -rising.** *–v.t.* **1.** to cause to pass into the gaseous state. *–v.i.* **2.** to become converted into vapour. Also, **vaporize.** – **vaporisable,** *adj.*

**vaporiser** /'veɪpəraɪzə/, *n.* **1.** one who or that which vaporises. **2.** a form of atomiser. Also, **vaporizer.**

**vaporish** /'veɪpərɪʃ/, *adj. U.S.* →**vapourish.** – **vaporishness,** *n.*

**vaporous** /'veɪpərəs/, *adj.* **1.** full of or abounding in vapour; foggy or misty. **2.** dimmed or obscured with vapour. **3.** of the form of vapour; unsubstantial. **4.** given to fanciful or foolish ideas or discourse. – **vaporously,** *adv.* – **vaporousness, vaporosity** /veɪpə'rɒsəti/, *n.*

**vapory** /'veɪpəri/, *adj. U.S.* →**vapoury.**

**vapour** /'veɪpə/, *n.* **1.** a visible exhalation, as fog, mist, condensed steam, smoke, etc. **2.** a substance in the gaseous state (sometimes restricted to substances in the gaseous state when below their critical points); a gas. **3.** matter converted into vapour for technical or medicinal uses, etc. **4.** a combination of vaporised matter and air. **5.** gaseous particles of drugs that can be inhaled as a therapeutic agent. **6.** an invisible exhalation, as of moisture, noxious gases, etc. **7.** *Archaic.* something unsubstantial or transitory. **8.** (*pl.*) *Archaic.* hypochondria, low spirits. **9.** (*pl.*) *Obs.* injurious exhalations formerly supposed to be produced within the body, esp. the stomach. *–v.t.* **10.** to cause to rise or pass off in, or as in, vapour. **11.** *Archaic.* to affect with vapours. *–v.i.* **12.** to rise or pass off in the form of vapour. **13.** to emit vapour or exhalations. **14.** to talk or act grandiloquently or boastfully; bluster. Also, *U.S.,* **vapor.** [ME, from AF, from L *vapor* steam] – **vapourability** /veɪpərə'bɪləti/, *n.* – **vapourer,** *n.* – **vapourable,** *adj.* – **vapourless,** *adj.* – **vapour-like,** *adj.*

**vapour concentration** /– kɒnsən'treɪʃən/, *n.* →**humidity** (def. 2c).

**vapour density** /'– ˌdɛnsəti/, *n.* **1.** the mass which a unit volume of a vapour would possess if it could exist as an ideal gas at 0°C at a pressure of 760mm of mercury. **2.** the ratio of the mass of a given volume of a gas to an equal volume of hydrogen under the same conditions of temperature and pressure.

**vapouring** /'veɪpərɪŋ/, *adj.* **1.** that vapours. **2.** foolishly boastful. *–n.* **3.** the act of bragging or blustering; windy talk. Also, *U.S.,* **vaporing.** – **vapouringly,** *adv.*

**vapourish** /'veɪpərɪʃ/, *adj.* **1.** of the nature of vapour. **2.** abounding in vapour. **3.** *Archaic.* inclined to or affected by the vapours or low spirits; depressed. Also, *U.S.,* **vaporish.** – **vapourishness,** *n.*

**vapour lock** /'veɪpə lɒk/, *n.* a blockage in the fuel line of an internal combustion engine, usu. caused by over-heating of the petrol.

**vapour-phase chromatography** /ˌveɪpə-feɪz kroumə'tɒgrəfi/, *n.* →**gas chromatography.**

**vapour pressure** /'veɪpə prɛʃə/, *n.* **1.** the pressure exerted by the molecules of a liquid which escape from the surface of that liquid as a vapour. **2.** the maximum pressure that this vapour can exert, at a given temperature, in a system consisting of a liquid (or solid) in equilibrium with its vapour; saturated vapour pressure.

**vapour trail** /'– treɪl/, *n.* a trail of condensed vapour left by high-flying aeroplanes, rockets, etc.

**vapoury** /'veɪpəri/, *adj.* **1.** →**vaporous. 2.** →**vapourish.** Also, *U.S.,* **vapory.**

**vaquero** /væ'kɛərou/, *n., pl.* **-ros** /-rouz/. *U.S.* a herdsman or cowboy. [Sp., from *vaca* cow, from L *vacca*]

**var.,** **1.** variant. **2.** variation. **3.** variety.

**varactor** /'vɛəræktə/, *n.* a semiconductor device with variable capacitance.

**varan** /'værən/, *n.* →**goanna**[1]. [NL *Varanus.* See VARANID]

**varanid** /'værənəd/, *adj.* belonging to or characteristic of the Varanidae, a family of carnivorous lizards having elongated necks and heads, strong, well developed limbs and long, powerful tails, as the goannas or the komodo dragon. [NL *Varanidae,* from *Varanus,* typical genus (from Ar. *waran, waral* monitor lizard) + -IDAE]

**varec** /ˈværɛk/, *n.* the ash of kelp. [F, from Gmc; cf. ME, MD, MLG *wrak* WRACK]

**varia** /ˈvɛəriə/, *n.* a miscellaneous collection, esp. of literary works. [L]

**variable** /ˈvɛəriəbəl/, *adj.* **1.** apt or liable to vary or change; changeable. **2.** capable of being varied or changed; alterable. **3.** inconsistent or fickle, as a person. **4.** *Biol.* deviating from the usual type, as a species or a specific character. **5.** *Elect.* (of a circuit component) being so constructed that the characteristic value of the component may be continuously varied. **6.** *Astron.* (of a star) changing in brightness. **7.** *Meteorol.* (of wind) tending to change in direction. **8.** (of a gaol or similar institution) not guarded by manned watchtowers, but fenced. *–n.* **9.** something variable. **10.** *Maths.* a symbol, or the quantity or function which it signifies, which may represent any one of a given set of numbers and other objects. **11.** *Astron.* a star whose light varies in intensity. **12.** *Meteorol.* a shifting wind, esp. as opposed to a trade wind. **13.** (*pl.*) a region where such winds occur. [L *variābilis*] **– variability** /ˌvɛəriəˈbɪləti/, **variableness,** *n.* **– variably,** *adv.*

**variable geometry** /– dʒiˈɒmətri/, *n.* the principle upon which swing-wing aircraft are designed.

**variable groundsel** /– ˈgraʊnsəl/, *n.* →**fireweed** (def. 1).

**variable time fuse,** *n.* →**proximity fuse.**

**Variable Zone** /ˈvɛəriəbəl zoʊn/, *n.* →**Temperate Zone.**

**varia lectio** /vɛəriə ˈlɛktioʊ/, *n., pl.* **variae lectiones** /vɛərii lɛktiˈoʊniz/. a variant reading. [L]

**variance** /ˈvɛəriəns/, *n.* **1.** the state or fact of varying; divergence or discrepancy. **2.** an instance of this; difference. **3.** *Statistics.* the square of the standard deviation. **4.** *Law.* **a.** a difference or discrepancy, as between two statements or documents in law which should agree. **b.** a departure from the cause of action originally stated in the complaint. **5.** a disagreement, dispute, or quarrel. **6.** **at variance, a.** in a state of difference, discrepancy, or disagreement, as things. **b.** in a state of controversy or of dissension, as persons. [ME, from OF]

**variant** /ˈvɛəriənt/, *adj.* **1.** exhibiting diversity; varying; tending to change or alter. **2.** being an altered or different form of something: *a variant spelling of a word.* *–n.* **3.** a variant form. **4.** a different form or spelling of the same word: *'lanthorn' is an old variant of 'lantern'.* **5.** a different reading of a passage. **6.** *Statistics.* →**variate.** [ME, from L *varians,* ppr., varying]

**variate** /ˈvɛəriət/, *n.* the numerical value of an attribute belonging to a statistical item. Also, **variant.**

**variation** /vɛəriˈeɪʃən/, *n.* **1.** the act or process of varying; change in condition, character, degree, etc. **2.** an instance of this. **3.** amount or rate of change. **4.** a different form of something; a variant. **5.** *Music.* **a.** the transformation of a melody or theme with changes or elaborations in harmony, rhythm, and melody. **b.** a varied form of a melody or theme, esp. one of a series of such forms developing the capacities of the subject. **6.** *Astron.* **a.** any deviation from the mean orbit of a heavenly body, esp. of a planetary or satellite orbit. **b.** an inequality in the moon's motion having a period of half a synodic month. **7.** →**declination** (def. 2). **8.** *Biol.* **a.** a deviation in the structure or character of an organism from that of others of the same species or group, or that of the parents. **b.** an organism exhibiting such deviation; variety. **9.** *Ballet.* a solo dance. **10.** **variations on a theme,** the same thing presented in many different ways. [ME *variacio(u)n,* from L *variātio*] **– variational,** *adj.*

**varic-,** variant of **varico-** before vowels.

**varicella** /væriˈsɛlə/, *n.* →**chickenpox.** [NL, from *vari(ola)* VARIOLA + *-cella,* diminutive suffix]

**varicellate** /væriˈsɛlət, -eɪt/, *adj.* having small varices, as certain shells. [NL *varicella* (alteration of L *varicula,* diminutive of *varix* varicose vein) + -ATE[1]]

**varicelloid** /væriˈsɛlɔɪd/, *adj.* resembling varicella.

**varices** /ˈværəsiz/, *n.* plural of **varix.**

**varico-,** a word element meaning 'varicose veins', as in *varicocele.* Also, before vowels, **varic-.** [combining form representing L *varix* VARIX]

**varicocele** /ˈværəkoʊsil/, *n.* a varicose condition of the spermatic veins of the scrotum.

**varicoloured** /ˈvɛərikʌləd/, *adj.* **1.** having various colours; variegated in colour; motley. **2.** varied; assorted. Also, *U.S.,* **varicolored.**

**varicose** /ˈværəkoʊs, -kəs/, *adj.* **1.** abnormally or unusually enlarged, swollen, or dilated. **2.** pertaining to or affected with varices or varicose veins, which often affect the superficial portions of the lower limbs. [L *varicōsus.* See VARIX]

**varicosis** /værəˈkoʊsəs/, *n. Pathol.* **1.** the formation of varices. **2.** →**varicosity.** [VARIC(O)- + -OSIS]

**varicosity** /værəˈkɒsəti/, *n., pl.* **-ties. 1.** the state or condition of being varicose. **2.** →**varix.**

**varicotomy** /værəˈkɒtəmi/, *n.* a surgical operation in which a varicose vein is removed.

**varied** /ˈvɛərid/, *adj.* **1.** made various, diversified; characterised by variety: *a varied assortment.* **2.** changed or altered: *a varied form of a word.* **3.** variegated, as in colour, as an animal. **– variedly,** *adv.* **– variedness,** *n.*

**variegate** /ˈvɛəriəgeɪt, ˈvɛərə-/, *v.t.,* **-gated, -gating. 1.** to make varied in appearance; mark with different colours, tints, etc. **2.** to give variety to; diversify. [LL *variegātus,* pp. (def. 1)]

**variegated** /ˈvɛəriəgeɪtəd, ˈvɛərə-/, *adj.* **1.** varied in appearance or colour; marked with patches or spots of different colours. **2.** varied; diversified; diverse.

**variegated thistle** /– ˈθɪsəl/, *n.* an erect, glabrous, prickly biennial, *Silybum marianum,* with large purple flowers and mottled, white-veined leaves, reaching three metres in height and proving a troublesome weed.

**variegation** /ˌvɛəriəˈgeɪʃən, ˌvɛərə-/, *n.* **1.** the act of variegating. **2.** the state or condition of being variegated; varied colouration.

**varietal** /vəˈraɪətl/, *adj.* **1.** of, pertaining to, or characteristic of a variety. **2.** constituting a variety. **– varietally,** *adv.*

**variety** /vəˈraɪəti/, *n., pl.* **-ties,** *adj.* *–n.* **1.** the state or character of being various or varied; diversity, or absence of uniformity or monotony. **2.** difference or discrepancy. **3.** a number of things of different kinds. **4.** a kind or sort. **5.** a different form, condition, or phase of something. **6.** a category within a species, based on some hereditary difference not considered great enough to distinguish species. **7.** a group or type of animals or plants produced by artificial selection. **8.** *Theat.* entertainment of mixed character, consisting of a number of individual performances or acts, as of singing, dancing, comic turns, acrobatics, etc. *–adj.* **9.** *Theat.* of, pertaining to, or characteristic of a variety. **10.** *Viticulture.* a type of grape grown to produce a particular type of wine: *a red table wine variety.* [L *varietas*]

**variety meat** /ˈ– mit/, *n.* →**fancy meat.**

**variform** /ˈvɛərəfɔm/, *adj.* varied in form; having various forms. [L *varius* various + -FORM]

**variola** /vəˈraɪələ/, *n.* →**smallpox.** [ML, from L *varius* various, spotted]

**variolar** /vəˈraɪələ/, *adj.* →**variolous.**

**variolate** /ˈvɛəriəleɪt/, *v.t.,* **-lated, -lating.** to inoculate with virus of variola. **– variolation** /ˌvɛəriəˈleɪʃən/, *n.*

**variole** /ˈvɛərioʊl/, *n.* **1.** a shallow pit or depression like the mark left by a smallpox pustule; a foveola. **2.** *Geol.* any of the spherules of variolite.

**variolite** /ˈvɛəriəlaɪt/, *n.* any of certain fine-grained, basic igneous rocks containing light-coloured spherules, which, esp. on weathered surfaces, give them a pockmarked appearance. [VARIOL(A) + -ITE[1]]

**variolitic** /ˌvɛəriəˈlɪtɪk/, *adj.* **1.** *Geol.* of or resembling variolite, esp. in texture. **2.** spotted; speckled.

**varioloid** /ˈvɛəriəlɔɪd/, *adj.* **1.** resembling variola or smallpox. **2.** of or pertaining to a mild case of smallpox. *–n.* **3.** a mild smallpox, esp. as occurring in persons who have been vaccinated or have previously had smallpox.

**variolous** /vəˈraɪələs/, *adj.* **1.** pertaining to variola or smallpox. **2.** affected with smallpox. **3.** having pits like those left by smallpox. Also, **variolar.**

**variometer** /vɛəriˈɒmətə/, *n.* **1.** *Elect.* an instrument for comparing the intensity of magnetic forces, esp. the magnetic force of the earth, at different points. **2.** *Elect.* an instrument for varying inductance, consisting of a fixed coil and a movable coil connected in series (used as a tuning device). **3.** *Aeron.* an instrument for measuring the rate of climb or descent of an aircraft. [*vario-* (combining form representing L *varius* various) + -METER[1]]

**variorum** /vɛəri'ɔrəm/, *adj.* **1.** (of an edition, etc.) characterised by various versions of the text or commentaries by various editors: *a variorum edition of Shakespeare.* *–n.* **2.** a variorum edition, text, etc. [short for L *ēditio cum notīs variōrum* edition with notes of various persons]

**various** /'vɛəriəs/, *adj.* **1.** differing one from another, or of different kinds, as two or more things. **2.** divers, several, or many: *in various parts of the world.* **3.** exhibiting or marked by variety or diversity. **4.** differing in different parts, or presenting differing aspects. [L *varius*] – **variously,** *adv.* – **variousness,** *n.*

**varix** /'vɛərɪks/, *n., pl.* **varices** /'værəsiz/. **1.** *Pathol.* a permanent abnormal dilation and lengthening of a vein, usu. accompanied by some tortuosity; a varicose vein. **2.** *Zool.* a mark or scar on the surface of a shell at a former position of the lip of the aperture. [ME, from L: dilated vein]

**varlet** /'valət/, *n. Archaic.* **1.** an attendant. **2.** a page attached to a knight. **3.** a low fellow or a rascal. [ME, from OF, var. of *va(s)let* VALET. See VASSAL]

**varletry** /'valətri/, *n. Archaic.* **1.** varlets collectively. **2.** the mob or rabble.

**varmint** /'vamənt/, *n.* **1.** →**vermin.** **2.** an objectionable or undesirable animal. **3.** an objectionable or undesirable person. Also, **varment.**

**varnish** /'vanɪʃ/, *n.* **1.** a preparation which consists of resinous matter (as copal, lac, etc.) dissolved in an oil (**oil varnish**) or in alcohol (**spirit varnish**) or other volatile liquid, and which, when applied to the surface of wood, metal, etc., dries and leaves a hard, more or less glossy, usu. transparent coating. **2.** the sap of certain trees, used for the same purpose (**natural varnish**). **3.** any of various other preparations similarly used, as one having indiarubber, pyroxylin, or asphalt for the chief constituent. **4.** a coating or surface of varnish. **5.** something resembling a coating of varnish; a gloss. **6.** a merely external show, or a veneer. *–v.t.* **7.** to lay varnish on. **8.** to invest with a glossy appearance. **9.** to give an improved appearance to; embellish; adorn. **10.** to cover with a specious or deceptive appearance. [ME *vernisshe(n)*, from OF *vernisser,* from *vernis* varnish, n., from ML *vernicium* sandarac, sweet-smelling resin, from MGk *berníkē,* Gk *Bereníkē,* a city in Cyrenaica] – **varnisher,** *n.*

**varnish tree** /'– tri/, *n.* any of various trees yielding sap or other substances used for varnish, as *Rhus verniciflua* of Japan. See **lacquer.**

**varsity** /'vasəti/, *n., pl.* **-ties.** *Colloq.* university. [var. of (UNI)VERSITY]

**varus** /'vɛərəs/, *n.* abnormal angulation of a bone or joint, with the angle pointing away from mid-line. [L: bandy-legged]

**varve** /vav/, *n.* the layer of sediment deposited during a year particularly in a melt-water lake, consisting of a lower layer of sand deposited in spring and an upper layer of silt deposited in the summer. [Swed. *varv,* lit., full circle]

**vary** /'vɛəri/, *v.,* **-ried, -rying.** *–v.t.* **1.** to change or alter, as in form, appearance, character, substance, degree, etc. **2.** to cause to be different, one from another. **3.** to diversify (something); relieve from uniformity or monotony. **4.** *Music.* to alter (a melody or theme) by modification or embellishments, without changing its identity. *–v.i.* **5.** to be different, or show diversity. **6.** to undergo change in form, appearance, character, substance, degree, etc. **7.** *Maths.* to be subject to change. **8.** to change in succession, follow alternately, or alternate. **9.** to diverge; deviate (usu. fol. by *from*). **10.** *Biol.* to exhibit variation. [ME, from L *variāre,* from *varius* various] – **varier,** *n.* – **varyingly,** *adv.*

**vas** /væs/, *n., pl.* **vasa** /'veɪsə/. *Anat., Zool., Bot.* a vessel or duct. [L: vessel]

**vascular** /'væskjələ/, *adj.* pertaining to, composed of, or provided with vessels or ducts which convey fluids, as blood, lymph, or sap. Also, **vasculose, vasculous.** [NL *vāsculāris,* from L *vāsculum* little vessel] – **vascularity** /væskjə'lærəti/, *n.* – **vascularly,** *adv.*

**vascular bundle** /– 'bʌndl/, *n.* →**bundle** (def. 4).

**vascular cambium** /– 'kæmbiəm/, *n.* a cambium which gives rise to secondary vascular tissues, usu. a large quantity of xylem and a small amount of phloem.

**vascular tissue** /– 'tɪʃu/, *n.* plant tissue consisting of ducts or vessels which, in highly developed plants, form the system by which sap is conveyed through the plant.

**vasculum** /'væskjələm/, *n., pl.* **-la** /-lə/, **-lums.** a kind of case or box used by botanists for carrying specimens as they are collected. [L, diminutive of *vās* vessel]

**vas deferens** /væs 'dɛfərɛnz/, *n. pl.* **vasa deferentia** /ˌveɪsə dɛfə'rɛnʃiə/. the deferent duct of the testicle which transports the sperm from the epididymus to the penis. [L: vessel carrying down]

**vase** /vaz/, *n.* a hollow vessel, generally higher than it is wide, made of glass, earthenware, porcelain, etc., now chiefly used as a flower container or for decoration. [F, from L *vās* vessel] – **vaselike,** *adj.*

Worcester china covered vase

**vasectomy** /və'sɛktəmi/, *n., pl.* **-mies.** excision of the vas deferens, or of a portion of it.

**vaseline** /'væsəlin, væsə'lin/, *n.* a translucent, yellow or whitish, semisolid petroleum product (a form of petrolatum), used as a remedial ointment and internal remedy, and in various medicinal and other preparations. [Trademark; from *vas* (from G *Wasser* water) + *-el-* (from Gk *élaion* oil) + -INE[2]]

**VASIS** /'veɪsəs/, *n.* a system of lights that provides approach guidance to the pilot of a landing aircraft. [*V(isual) A(pproach) S(lope) I(ndicator) S(ystem)*]

**vaso-,** a word element meaning 'vessel', as in *vasoconstrictor.* [combining form representing L *vās* vessel]

**vasoconstriction** /ˌveɪzoʊkən'strɪkʃən/, *n.* constriction of the blood vessels, as by the action of a nerve.

**vasoconstrictor** /ˌveɪzoʊkən'strɪktə/, *adj.* **1.** serving to constrict blood vessels. *–n.* **2.** a nerve or drug that causes vasoconstriction.

**vasodilatation** /ˌveɪzoʊˌdaɪlə'teɪʃən/, *n.* dilatation of the blood vessels, as by the action of a nerve.

**vasodilator** /ˌveɪzoʊdaɪ'leɪtə/, *adj.* **1.** serving to dilate or relax blood vessels. *–n.* **2.** a nerve or drug that causes vasodilatation.

**vasoinhibitor** /ˌveɪzoʊɪn'hɪbətə/, *n.* an agent or drug that inhibits the action of the vasomotor nerves. – **vasoinhibitory** /ˌveɪzoʊɪn'hɪbətri, -'hɪbətəri/, *adj.*

**vasomotor** /'veɪzoʊmoʊtə/, *adj. Physiol.* serving to regulate the diameter of blood vessels, as certain nerves.

**vasopressin** /'veɪzəˌprɛsən/, *n.* a hormone produced by the neurophypophysis acting on arterioles to control blood pressure and on kidney tubules to control water reabsorption.

**vassal** /'væsəl/, *n.* **1.** (in the feudal system) a person holding lands by the obligation to render military service or its equivalent to his superior. **2.** a feudatory tenant. **3.** a person holding some similar relation to a superior; a subject, follower, or retainer. **4.** *Archaic.* a servant or slave. *–adj.* **5.** pertaining to or characteristic of a vassal. **6.** being a vassal or in vassalage. [ME, from OF, from LL *vassallus,* from *vassus* servant; of Celtic orig.] – **vassalless,** *adj.*

**vassalage** /'væsəlɪdʒ/, *n.* **1.** the state of being a vassal; the status of a vassal. **2.** homage or service due from a vassal. **3.** a territory held by a vassal. **4.** dependence, subjection, or servitude.

**vast** /vast/, *adj.* **1.** of very great extent or area; very extensive, or immense. **2.** of very great size or proportions; huge; enormous. **3.** very great in number, quantity, or amount, etc.: *a vast army, a vast sum.* **4.** very great in degree, intensity, etc.: *in vast haste, vast importance.* [L *vastus*] – **vastly,** *adv.* – **vastness,** *n.*

**vastitude** /'vastətjud/, *n.* **1.** vastness or immensity. **2.** a vast expanse or space.

**vasty** /'vasti/, *adj. Poetic.* vast; immense.

**vat** /væt/, *n., v.,* **vatted, vatting.** *–n.* **1.** a large container for liquids. *–v.t.* **2.** to put into or treat in a vat. [ME; OE *fæt,* c. G *Fass* keg]

**V.A.T.** /vi eɪ 'ti/, value added tax.

**vat dye** /'væt daɪ/, *n.* any of a group of insoluble dyes which are applied to fabrics by first reducing them to alkali-soluble leuco bases. After dyeing, the insoluble dye is regenerated in the fibres of the material by oxidisation.

**vatic** /'vætɪk/, *adj.* of, pertaining to, or characteristic of a prophet. Also, **vatical.** [apparently backformation from VATICINAL]

**Vatican City** /ˌvætɪkən 'sɪti/, *n.* the independent papal city within the city of Rome.

**Vatican roulette** /– ru'lɛt/, *n. Colloq.* →**rhythm method.**

**vaticinal** /və'tɪsənəl/, *adj.* of, pertaining to, or characterised by prophecy; prophetic. [L *vāticinus* prophetic + -AL[1]]

**vaticinate** /və'tɪsəneɪt/, *v.t., v.i.,* **-nated, -nating.** to prophesy. [L *vāticinātus,* pp.] – **vaticinator,** *n.*

**vaticination** /vætəsə'neɪʃən/, *n.* **1.** the act of prophesying. **2.** a prophecy.

**vaudeville** /'vɔdvɪl, 'vɔdəvɪl/, *n.* **1.** variety entertainment. **2.** a theatrical piece of light or amusing character, interspersed with songs and dances. [F, alteration of *chanson du Vau de Vire,* a type of satirical song popular in the 15th century in the Valley of Vire, a region in Normandy, France]

**vault**[1] /vɔlt, vɒlt/, *n.* **1.** an arched structure, commonly made of stones, concrete, or bricks, forming a ceiling or roof over a hall, room, sewer, or other wholly or partially enclosed construction. **2.** an arched space, chamber, or passage, esp. one underground. **3.** an underground chamber, as a cellar or a division of a cellar. **4.** a burial chamber. **5.** a strongroom for storing and safeguarding valuables. **6.** *Anat.* an arched roof of a cavity. **7.** something resembling an arched roof: *the vault of heaven.* *–v.t.* **8.** to construct or cover with a vault. **9.** to make in the form of a vault; arch. [ME *vaute,* from OF *voute,* from Rom. *volta,* from *vol(vi)tus,* replacing L *volūtus,* pp., turned, rolled] – **vaultlike,** *adj.*

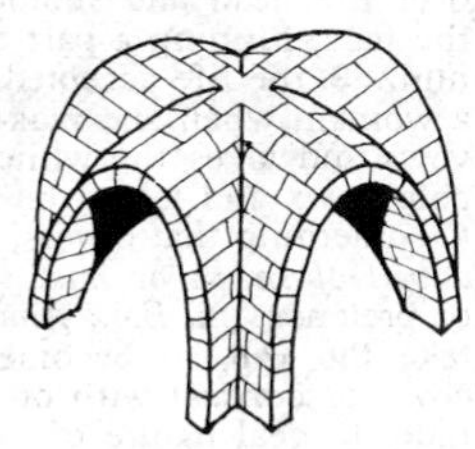

groin vault

**vault**[2] /vɔlt, vɒlt/, *v.i.* **1.** to leap or spring, as to or from a position or over something. **2.** to leap with the aid of the hands supported on something, sometimes on a pole: *to vault over a fence or a bar.* *–v.t.* **3.** to leap or spring over: *to vault a fence.* *–n.* **4.** the act of vaulting. [OF *volter,* from It. *voltare,* from frequentative of L *volvere* roll] – **vaulter,** *n.*

**vaulted** /'vɔltəd/, *adj.* **1.** constructed or covered with a vault, as a building, chamber, etc. **2.** provided with a vault or vaults, as below the ground.

**vaulting**[1] /'vɔltɪŋ/, *n.* **1.** the act or process of constructing vaults. **2.** the structure forming a vault or vaults. **3.** a vault, vaulted ceiling, or the like, or such structures collectively. [VAULT[1] + -ING[1]]

**vaulting**[2] /'vɔltɪŋ/, *adj.* **1.** that vaults. **2.** used in vaulting: *a vaulting pole.* **3.** exaggerated: *vaulting conceit.* [VAULT[2] + -ING[2]]

**vaulting horse** /'– hɔs/, *n.* →**horse** (def. 6).

**vault light** /'vɔlt laɪt/, *n.* →**pavement light.**

**vaunt** /vɔnt/, *v.t.* **1.** to speak vaingloriously or boastfully of. *–v.i.* **2.** *Archaic or Literary.* to talk vaingloriously or boastfully; boast; brag. *–n.* **3.** vainglorious or boastful utterance. [ME *vaunt(en),* from MF *vanter,* from LL *vānitāre,* from L *vānus* vain] – **vaunter,** *n.* – **vauntingly,** *adv.*

**vaunt-courier** /vɔnt-'kʊriə/, *n. Archaic.* one who goes in advance, as a herald. [OF *avaunt-courrier* fore-runner]

**vavasor** /'vævəsɔ/, *n.* (in the feudal system) a vassal, or feudal tenant, next in rank to a baron. Also, **vavasour.** [ME, from OF, from ML *vassus vassōrum* vassal of vassals]

**vb,** verb.

**V-box** /'vi-bɒks/, *n.* →**banjo** (def. 5b).

**V.C.** /vi 'si/, **1.** Vice-Chairman. **2.** Vice-Chancellor. **3.** Vice-Consul. **4.** Victoria Cross.

**V.D.** /vi 'di/, *n.* venereal disease.

**V.D.T.** /vi di 'ti/, *n.* →**visual display unit.**

**VDU** /vi di 'ju/, *n.* →**visual display unit.**

**'ve,** /v/, *v.* a contraction of have: *I've, you've.*

**veal** /vil/, *n.* the flesh of the calf as used for food. [ME *veel,* from OF, from L *vitellus* little calf]

**vealer** /'vilə/, *n.* a calf in fat condition, eight to nine months of age.

**vector** /'vɛktə/, *n.* **1.** *Maths.* a quantity which possesses both magnitude and direction. Two such quantities acting on a point may be represented by the two sides of a parallelogram, so that their resultant is represented in magnitude and direction by the diagonal of the parallelogram. **2.** *Computers.* the address of an entry in a memory which is conceptually organised into position-dependent entries of fixed length. **3.** *Biol.* an insect or other organism transmitting germs or other agents of disease. [L: carrier] – **vectorial** /vɛk'tɔriəl/, *adj.*

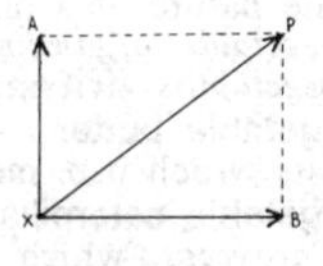


XA, XB, vectors; XP, resultant

**vectored thrust** /vɛktəd 'θrʌst/, *n.* a method of jet propulsion efflux of which can be directed downward or forward to obtain VTOL or STOL performance.

**vector field** /'vɛktə fild/, *n.* a region, each point of which is characterised by a definite value of some vector quantity; a field of force.

**Veda** /'veɪdə, 'vidə/, *n.* (*sometimes pl.*) the entire sacred scriptures of Hinduism, esp. as comprising the four Books of Wisdom which have the word 'Veda' in their titles: **Rig-Veda** or The Veda of Psalms or Verses, the **Yajur-Veda** or The Veda of Sacred Formulas, **Sama-Veda** or The Veda Chants, and the **Atharva-Veda** or The Veda of Charms. [Skt: lit., knowledge] – **Vedaic** /və'deɪɪk/, *adj.* – **Vedaism,** *n.*

**vedalia** /və'deɪliə/, *n.* an Australian ladybird, *Rodolia cardinalis,* used elsewhere to control citrus fruit pests. [NL]

**Vedanta** /və'dæntə, -'dan-/, *n.* the chief philosophy among the Hindus, a system of idealistic monism, chiefly as expounded by the philosopher S(h)ankara about 800 A.D., with some varieties occurring later. It is concerned with the end of the Vedas, both chronologically and teleologically. [Skt, from *Veda* VEDA + *anta* end] – **Vedantic,** *adj.* – **Vedantism,** *n.* – **Vedantist,** *n.*

**vedette** /və'dɛt/, *n.* **1.** Also, **vedette boat.** a small naval launch used for scouting. **2.** a mounted sentry in advance of the outposts of an army. Also, **vidette.** [F, from It. *vedetta,* from *vedere* see, from L *vidēre*]

**Vedic** /'veɪdɪk/, *adj.* **1.** of or pertaining to the Veda or Vedas. *–n.* **2.** the language of the Veda, closely related to classical Sanskrit.

**veduta** /və'dutə/, *n.* a drawing or painting of a town or city. [It.: view]

**vee** /vi/, *n.* the shape of a V.

**veer**[1] /vɪə/, *v.i.* **1.** to turn or shift to another direction; change from one direction or course to another. **2.** to change; alter; be variable or changeable; pass from one state to another. **3.** (of the wind) **a.** to change direction by moving clockwise round the points of the compass. See **back**[1] (def. 23). **b.** *Naut.* to shift more aft in relation to the vessel's course (opposed to *haul*). *–n.* **4.** a change of direction. [F *virer,* from LL *gīrāre* turn, (from *gȳrus* a turn, from Gk *gŷros*) b. with L *vertere* turn] – **veeringly,** *adv.*

**veer**[2] /vɪə/, *v.t. Naut.* to slacken or let out: *to veer chain.* [late ME *vere,* from MD *vieren* let out]

**veg.,** vegetable.

**vegan** /'vigən/, *n.* a person who follows a strict vegetarian diet which excludes any animal product.

**vegemite** /'vɛdʒəmaɪt/, *n.* a vegetable extract used as a spread. [Trademark]

**vegetable** /'vɛdʒtəbəl/, *n.* **1.** any herbaceous plant, annual, biennial, or perennial, whose fruits, seeds, roots, tubers, bulbs, stems, leaves, or flower parts are used as food, as tomato, bean, beet, potato, asparagus, cabbage, etc. **2.** the edible part of such plants, as the fruit of the tomato or the tuber of the potato. **3.** any member of the vegetable kingdom; a plant. **4.** *Colloq.* a dull or uninspiring person. **5.** *Colloq.* a person who, due to physical injury or mental deficiency, is entirely dependent on the agencies of others for subsistence. *–adj.* **6.** of, consisting of, or made from edible vegetables: *a vegetable diet, a vegetable dinner.* **7.** of, pertaining to or characteristic of plants: *vegetable life or processes.* **8.** derived from plants or some part of plants: *vegetable fibre, vegetable oils.* **9.** consisting of or containing the substance or remains of plants: *vegetable matter.* **10.** of the nature of a plant; consisting of or comprising plants: *a vegetable organism, the vegetable kingdom.* [ME, from LL *vegetābilis* vivifying]

**vegetable butter** /'– bʌtə/, *n.* any of various fixed vegetable fats which usu. melt at or below body temperature.

**vegetable caterpillar** /– 'kætəpɪlə/, *n.* a fungus of the genus *Cordyceps,* which parasitises insect bodies and leaves them solidified.

**vegetable garden** /'– gadn/, *n.* a garden in which vegetables and fruit for the table are grown; kitchen garden.

**vegetable ivory** /– 'aɪvəri/, *n.* See **ivory** (def. 8).

**vegetable kingdom** /'– kɪŋdəm/, *n.* →**plant kingdom.**

**vegetable marrow** /'– mæroʊ/, *n.* See **marrow** (def. 5).

**vegetable oil** /'– ɔɪl/, *n.* any of a group of oils which are obtained from plants or their seeds or fruits, usu. consisting of esters of fatty acids and glycerol.

**vegetable oyster** /– 'ɔɪstə/, *n.* →**salsify.**

**vegetable sheep** /– 'ʃip/, *n. N.Z.* a whitish sub-alpine cushion plant, as *Haastia pulvinaris,* which from a distance resembles sheep.

**vegetable silk** /– 'sɪlk/, *n.* a fine, glossy fibre, similar to silk cotton, from the seeds of a Brazilian tree, *Chorisia speciosa.*

**vegetable tallow** /– 'tæloʊ/, *n.* any of several tallow-like substances of vegetable origin, used in making candles, soap, etc., and as lubricants.

**vegetable wax** /'– wæks/, *n.* a wax or waxlike substance obtained from various plants, as the wax-palm.

**vegetal** /'vɛdʒətl/, *adj.* **1.** pertaining to or of the nature of plants or vegetables; vegetable. **2.** →**vegetative** (def. 3).

**vegetarian** /vɛdʒə'tɛəriən/, *n.* **1.** one who on moral principle or from personal preference lives on vegetable food (refusing meat, fish, etc.), or maintains that vegetables and farinaceous substances constitute the only proper food for man. *–adj.* **2.** of or pertaining to the practice or principle of living solely or chiefly on vegetable food. **3.** devoted to or advocating this practice. **4.** consisting solely of vegetables.

**vegetarianism** /vɛdʒə'tɛəriənɪzəm/, *n.* the beliefs and practices of a vegetarian.

**vegetate** /'vɛdʒəteɪt/, *v.i.,* **-tated, -tating. 1.** to grow in the manner of plants; increase as if by vegetable growth. **2.** to live like vegetables, in an inactive, passive, or unthinking way. **3.** *Pathol.* to grow, or increase by growth, as an excrescence. [L *vegetātus,* pp., enlivened]

**vegetation** /vɛdʒə'teɪʃən/, *n.* **1.** plants collectively; the plant life of a particular region considered as a whole. **2.** the act or process of vegetating. **3.** *Pathol.* a morbid growth or excrescence. – **vegetational,** *adj.*

**vegetative** /'vɛdʒəteɪtɪv/, *adj.* **1.** growing or developing as or like plants; vegetating. **2.** of, pertaining to, or connected with vegetation or vegetable growth. **3.** denoting the parts of a plant not specialised for reproduction. **4.** (of reproduction) asexual. **5.** denoting or pertaining to those bodily functions which, being performed unconsciously or involuntarily, are likened to the processes of vegetable growth. **6.** having the power to produce or support growth in plants: *vegetative mould.* Also, **vegetive.** – **vegetatively,** *adv.* – **vegetativeness,** *n.*

**vegies** /'vɛdʒiz/, *n. pl. Colloq.* vegetables.

**vehemence** /'viəməns/, *n.* **1.** the quality of being vehement; violent ardour; fervour; fire. **2.** impetuosity; violence; fury. Also, **vehemency.**

**vehement** /'viəmənt/, *adj.* **1.** eager, impetuous, or impassioned. **2.** characterised by anger, bitterness, or rancour: *vehement opposition.* **3.** passionate, as feeling; strongly emotional: *vehement desire, vehement dislike.* **4.** (of actions) marked by great energy, exertion, or unusual force. [late ME, from L *vehemens*] – **vehemently,** *adv.*

**vehicle** /'viɪkəl, 'viəkəl/, *n.* **1.** any receptacle, or means of transport, in which something is carried or conveyed, or travels. **2.** a carriage or conveyance moving on wheels or runners. **3.** *Astronautics.* a rocket excluding the payload or spacecraft. **4.** a means of conveyance, transmission, or communication: *air is the vehicle of sound.* **5.** a medium by which ideas or effects are communicated: *language is a vehicle for the conveyance of thought.* **6.** *Pharm.* a substance, usu. fluid, possessing little or no medicinal action, used as a medium for active remedies. **7.** *Painting.* the liquid portion of a paint, in which the pigment is dispersed. [L *vehiculum* conveyance]

**vehicle deck** /'– dɛk/, *n.* a long deck within a ship intended for direct access of vehicles to the shore via a ramp.

**vehicular** /və'hɪkjələ/, *adj.* **1.** of, pertaining to, or associated with vehicles. **2.** serving as a vehicle. **3.** carried or transported by means of a vehicle or vehicles.

**V8** /vi 'eɪt/, *adj.* **1.** of or pertaining to a reciprocating engine whose eight cylinders are in a V formation. A variation in the number, as V6, V12, indicates a similar engine with the corresponding number of cylinders. *–n.* **2. a.** such an engine. **b.** a vehicle, etc., esp. a motor car, powered by such an engine.

**veil** /veɪl/, *n.* **1.** a piece of material, usu. light and more or less transparent, worn, esp. by women, over the head or face, as to conceal the face or to protect it from the sun or wind. **2.** a piece of material worn so as to fall over the head and shoulders on each side of the face, forming a part of the headdress of a nun. **3.** the life accepted or the vows made by a woman, when she makes either her novice's vows and takes the white veil, or her irrevocable vows and takes the black veil of a nun. **4.** something that covers, screens, or conceals: *a veil of smoke or mist.* **5.** a mask, disguise, or pretence. **6.** *Bot., Anat., Zool.* →**velum. 7. take the veil,** to become a nun. *–v.t.* **8.** to cover or conceal with or as with a veil. **9.** to hide the real nature of; mask; disguise. [ME, from AF, from L *vēlum* sail, covering] – **veiled,** *adj.* – **veilless,** *adj.* – **veil-like,** *adj.*

veil: veiled Muslim woman

**veiled** /veɪld/, *adj.* **1.** covered with or wearing a veil. **2.** concealed or covered, with or as with a veil. **3.** not openly expressed or declared; disguised. **4.** lacking distinctness or clarity; muffled.

**veiling** /'veɪlɪŋ/, *n.* **1.** a veil. **2.** a thin net used in making veils. Also, **nun's veiling.**

**vein** /veɪn/, *n.* **1.** one of the system of branching vessels or tubes conveying blood from various parts of the body to the heart. **2.** (loosely) any blood vessel. **3.** one of the tubular, riblike thickenings that ramify in an insect's wing. **4.** one of the strands or bundles of vascular tissue forming the principal framework of a leaf. **5.** any body or stratum of ore, coal, etc., clearly separated or defined. **6.** a body or mass of igneous rock, deposited mineral, or the like, occupying a crevice or fissure in rock; a lode. **7.** a small natural channel or watercourse under the surface of the earth. **8.** the water running through it. **9.** a streak or marking, as of a different shade or colour, running through marble, wood, etc. **10.** mood; temper; disposition. **11.** a strain or quality traceable in character or conduct, writing, etc.: *a vein of stubbornness, to write in a poetic vein.* *–v.t.* **12.** to furnish with veins. **13.** to mark with lines or streaks suggesting veins. **14.** to extend over or through (something) in the manner of veins. [ME *veine,* from OF, from L *vēna*] – **veined,** *adj.* – **veinless,** *adj.* – **veinlike,** *adj.*

**veining** /'veɪnɪŋ/, *n.* **1.** the act or process of forming veins or veinlike markings. **2.** a pattern of veins or veinlike markings.

**veinlet** /'veɪnlət/, *n.* a small vein.

**veinstone** /'veɪnstoʊn/, *n.* →**gangue.**

**veinule** /'veɪnjul/, *n.* →**venule** (def. 2). [F, from L *vēnula* little vein]

**veiny** /'veɪni/, *adj.,* **-nier, -niest.** full of veins; veined.

**vel.,** velocity.

**vela** /'vilə/, *n.* plural of **velum.**

**velamen** /və'leɪmən/, *n., pl.* **-lamina** /-'læmənə/. **1.** *Anat.* a membranous covering; a velum. **2.** *Bot.* the thick, spongy integument or epidermis covering the aerial roots of epiphytic orchids. [L: covering]

**velar** /'vilə/, *adj.* **1.** of or pertaining to a velum or veil, esp. that of the palate. **2.** *Phonet.* with the back of the tongue held close to or touching the soft palate. *–n.* **3.** a velar sound. [L *vēlāris,* from *vēlum* curtain]

**velarise** /'vilәraɪz/, *v.t.,* **-rised, -rising.** to pronounce with velar articulation. Also, **velarize.** – **velarisation** /ˌvilәraɪ'zeɪʃәn/, *n.*

**velate** /'vilәt, -leɪt/, *adj., v.,* **-lated, -lating.** *–adj.* **1.** *Bot., Zool.* having a velum. *–v.t.* **2.** *Phonet.* to velarise. [L *vēlātus* veiled]

**velation** /vә'leɪʃәn/, *n.* pronunciation with velar articulation. [LL *vēlātio*]

**veldt** /vɛlt/, *n.* the open country, bearing grass, bushes, or shrubs, or thinly forested, characteristic of parts of southern Africa. Also, **veld.** [Afrikaans, from D: FIELD]

**veldt grass** /'– gras/, *n.* any grass of the southern African genus *Ehrharta,* esp. perennial veldt, *E. calycia,* sometimes used as a pasture grass in Australia.

**velella** /vә'lɛlә/, *n.* a small, blue hydrozoan related to the bluebottle (def. 1), having a flattened, oval float and a thin, transparent, vertical sail; by-the-wind sailor; sallee rover.

**veleta** /vә'litә/, *n.* a ballroom dance in waltz time. Also, **valeta.** [Sp.: weathercock]

**veliger** /'vɛlәdʒә/, *n.* the free-swimming, larval stage in the development of a mollusc. [NL. See VELUM, -I-, -GEROUS]

**velleity** /vә'liәti/, *n., pl.* **-ties. 1.** volition in its weakest form. **2.** a mere wish, unaccompanied by an effort to obtain it. [ML *velleitas,* from L *velle* wish]

**vellicate** /'vɛlәkeɪt/, *v.t.,* **-cated, -cating.** to pluck; nip; pinch. [L *vellicātus,* pp., from *vellere*] – **vellication** /vɛlә'keɪʃәn/, *n.* – **vellicative,** *adj.*

**vellum** /'vɛlәm/, *n.* **1.** a sheet of calfskin prepared as parchment for writing or bookbinding. **2.** a manuscript or the like on such parchment. **3.** a texture of paper or cloth resembling that of such parchment. *–adj.* **4.** made of or resembling vellum. **5.** bound in vellum. [ME *velym,* from OF *velin,* from *veel* VEAL]

**veloce** /vә'loʊtʃeɪ/, *adv.* (a musical direction) at a quick tempo. [It.: quick, from L *vēlox*]

**velocipede** /vә'lɒsәpid/, *n.* **1.** a bicycle-like vehicle, usu. with two or three wheels, propelled by the rider. **2.** an early kind of bicycle or tricycle. **3.** *N.Z.* a small, hand-propelled railway car used by maintenance personnel. [F *vélocipède,* from L *vēlōci-* swift + *pēs* foot]

velocipede

**velocitator** /vә'lɒsәteɪtә/, *n.* (in filming) a form of dolly incorporating a small crane for the camera and seats for the technical operators.

**velocity** /vә'lɒsәti/, *n., pl.* **-ties. 1.** rapidity of motion or operation; swiftness; quickness. **2.** *Physics.* rate of motion, esp. when the direction of motion is also specified. [L *vēlōcitas* swiftness]

**velocity modulation** /– mɒdʒә'leɪʃәn/, *n.* the process of altering the velocity of a beam of electrons in proportion to the strength of a control signal.

**velocity of light,** *n.* a universal constant defining the rate of propagation of any electromagnetic radiation in vacuo, equal to $2.998 \times 10^8$ metres per second. *Symbol:* c

**velocity ratio** /vә'lɒsәti ˌreɪʃioʊ/, *n.* (of a machine) the ratio of the distance through which the point of application of the applied force moves, to the distance through which the point of application of the load moves in the same time.

**velodrome** /'vɛlәdroʊm/, *n.* an arena with a suitably banked track for cycle races.

**velour** /vә'lʊә/, *n.* any of various fabrics with a fine, raised finish. Also, **velours.** [F *velours* velvet, earlier *velous,* from Pr. *velos,* from L *villus* hair]

**velouté** /vɛlu'teɪ/, *n.* a white sauce made from chicken, veal, fish or vegetable stock, thickened with a roux of butter and flour. Also, **velouté sauce, velvet sauce.** [F, from *velours* velvet]

**velum** /'vilәm/, *n., pl.* **-la** /-lә/. **1.** *Biol.* any of various veil-like or curtain-like membranous partitions. **2.** *Anat.* →**soft palate.** [L: sail, covering]

**velure** /vә'lʊә/, *n., v.,* **-lured, -luring.** *–n.* **1.** velvet or a substance resembling it. **2.** a hatter's pad of velvet, plush, or the like, for smoothing or dressing silk hats. *–v.t.* **3.** to smooth or dress (a hat) with a velure. [var. of VELOUR]

**velutinous** /vә'lutәnәs/, *adj.* having a soft, velvety surface, as certain plants. [NL *velūtinus,* from ML *velutum* velvet]

**velvet** /'vɛlvәt/, *n.* **1.** a fabric of silk, silk and cotton, cotton, etc., with a thick, soft pile formed of loops of the warp thread either cut at the outer end (as in ordinary velvet) or left uncut (as in uncut or terry velvet). **2.** something likened to the fabric velvet in softness, etc. **3.** the soft, deciduous covering of a growing antler. **4.** *Colloq.* a very agreeable or desirable position or situation. **5.** *Colloq.* money gained through gambling or speculation. **6.** *Colloq.* clear gain or profit. *–adj.* **7.** Also, **velveted.** made of velvet or covered with velvet. **8.** resembling velvet; velvety; smooth and soft. [ME, from ML *velvetum,* from L *villus* shaggy hair] – **velvet-like,** *adj.*

**velvet carpet** /– 'kapәt/, *n.* a carpet or rug of pile weave resembling Wilton.

**velveteen** /vɛlvә'tin/, *n.* **1.** a cotton pile fabric with short pile. **2.** (*pl.*) trousers or knickerbockers made of velveteen. *–adj.* **3.** Also, **velveteened.** made of velveteen.

**velvet glove** /vɛlvәt 'glʌv/, *n.* a superficially pleasant manner concealing ruthless determination, esp. in the phrase **an iron hand in a velvet glove.**

**velvet sauce** /– 'sɔs/, *n.* →**velouté.**

**velvety** /'vɛlvәti/, *adj.* **1.** like or suggestive of velvet; smooth and soft. **2.** (of wines, spirits, etc.) having no harshness; smooth. **3.** gentle and smooth in contact. – **velvetiness,** *n.*

**Ven.,** Venerable.

**vena** /'vinә/, *n., pl.* **-nae** /-ni/. (in anatomy) a vein. [L]

**vena cava** /– 'keɪvә/, *n., pl.* **venae cavae** /ˌvinә 'keɪvi/. *n.* either of two large veins discharging into the right auricle of the heart. [L: hollow vein]

**venal** /'vinәl/, *adj.* **1.** ready to sell one's services or influence unscrupulously; accessible to bribery; corruptly mercenary. **2.** purchasable like mere merchandise, as things not properly bought and sold. **3.** characterised by venality: *a venal period, a venal agreement.* [L *vēnālis* for sale] – **venally,** *adv.*

**venality** /vi'nælәti/, *n., pl.* **-ties.** the quality of being venal; prostitution of talents or principles for money or reward.

**venatic** /vi'nætɪk/, *adj.* of or pertaining to hunting. Also, **venatical.** [L *vēnāticus*] – **venatically,** *adv.*

**venation** /vә'neɪʃәn/, *n.* **1.** the arrangement of veins, as in a leaf or an insect's wing. **2.** these veins collectively. [NL *vēnātio,* from L *vēna* vein] – **venational,** *adj.*

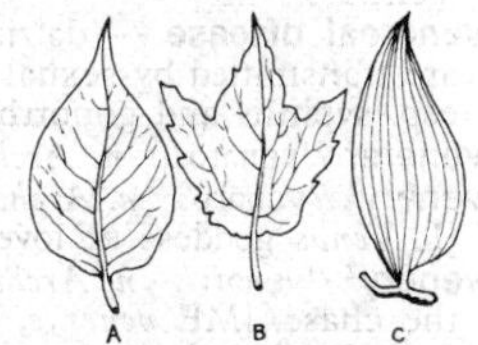

venations of leaves: A, pinnate; B, palmate; C, parallel

**vend** /vɛnd/, *v.t.* **1.** to dispose of by sale; peddle. **2.** to give utterance to (an opinion, etc.). *–v.i.* **3.** to vend something. **4.** to be disposed of by sale. [L *vendere* sell]

**vendace** /'vɛndeɪs/, *n.* either of two species of whitefish of the genus *Corogenus, C. vandesius* or *C. gracilior.* [OF *vendese,* ? from Celtic **vindasia,* from **vindos* white (cf. OIrish *find* white), influenced by DACE]

**vendee** /vɛn'di/, *n.* (in law) the person to whom a thing is vended or sold.

**vender** /'vɛndә/, *n.* →**vendor.**

**vendetta** /vɛn'dɛtә/, *n.* **1.** a private feud in which the relatives of a murdered person seek to obtain vengeance by killing the murderer or a member of his family, esp. as existing in Corsica and parts of Italy; blood feud. **2.** any prolonged or persistent quarrel, rivalry, etc. **3.** *Colloq.* a firm stand taken on a particular issue, and strictly enforced: *the police conducted a vendetta against drunken driving.* [It., from L *vindicta* vengeance] – **vendettist,** *n.*

**vendible** /'vɛndәbәl/, *adj.* **1.** capable of being vended or sold; saleable. *–n.* **2.** a vendible article. – **vendibility** /vɛndә'bɪlәti/, **vendibleness,** *n.* – **vendibly,** *adv.*

**vending machine** /ˈvɛndɪŋ məʃin/, *n.* a coin-operated machine for selling goods.

**vendition** /vɛnˈdɪʃən/, *n.* the act of vending; sale.

**vendor** /ˈvɛndə/, *n.* one who vends or disposes of a thing by sale. Also, **vender.** [VEND + -OR[2]]

**vendor's shares** /vɛndəz ˈʃɛəz/, *n. pl.* shares created in order to remunerate a person who has sold assets or property to a company.

**vendue** /vɛnˈdju/, *n.* a public auction. [D *vendu,* from OF *vendue* sale, from *vendre* sell]

**veneer** /vəˈnɪə/, *n.* **1.** a thin layer of wood or other material used for facing or overlaying wood. **2.** one of the several layers of plywood. **3.** a superficially pleasing appearance or show: *a veneer of good manners.* –*v.t.* **4.** to overlay or face (wood) with thin sheets of some material, as a fine wood, ivory, tortoiseshell, etc. **5.** to cover (an object) with a thin layer of costly material to give an appearance of superior quality. **6.** to cement (layers of wood veneer) to form plywood. **7.** to give a superficially pleasing appearance to. [G *furniren,* from F *fournir.* See FURNISH] – **veneerer,** *n.*

**veneering** /vəˈnɪərɪŋ/, *n.* **1.** the process, work, or craft of applying veneers. **2.** material applied as a veneer. **3.** the surface thus formed. **4.** a merely superficial show or outward display: *a veneering of civilisation.*

**venenose** /ˈvɛnənoʊs/, *adj. Rare.* poisonous.

**venerable** /ˈvɛnrəbəl, -nərəbəl/, *adj.* **1.** worthy of veneration or reverence, as on account of high character or office. **2.** commanding respect by reason of age and dignity of appearance. **3.** (of places, buildings, etc.) hallowed by religious, historic, or other lofty associations. **4.** impressive or interesting from age, antique appearance, etc. **5.** ancient: *a venerable error.* [ME, from L *venerābilis*] – **venerability** /vɛnrəˈbɪləti, -nərəˈbɪləti/, **venerableness,** *n.* – **venerably,** *adv.*

**venerate** /ˈvɛnəreɪt/, *v.t.,* **-rated, -rating.** to regard with reverence, or revere. [L *venerātus,* pp., having reverenced] – **venerator,** *n.*

**veneration** /vɛnəˈreɪʃən/, *n.* **1.** the act of venerating. **2.** the state of being venerated. **3.** the feeling of one who venerates; reverence: *filled with veneration for the traditions of one's country.* **4.** the outward expression of reverent feeling.

**venereal** /vəˈnɪəriəl/, *adj.* **1.** arising from or connected with sexual intercourse with an infected person: *venereal disease.* **2.** pertaining to diseases so arising. **3.** infected with or suffering from venereal disease. **4.** adapted to the cure of such disease: *a venereal remedy.* **5.** of or pertaining to sexual desire or intercourse. [ME, from L *venereus* pertaining to Venus + -AL[1]]

**venereal disease** /– dəˈziz/, *n.* any of those diseases which are transmitted by sexual intercourse with an infected person, esp. syphilis and gonorrhoea.

**venerer** /ˈvɛnərə/, *n. Archaic.* a huntsman.

**venery**[1] /ˈvɛnəri/, *n. Archaic.* the gratification of sexual desire. [L *Venus* goddess of love + -Y[3]]

**venery**[2] /ˈvɛnəri/, *n. Archaic.* the practice or sport of hunting; the chase. [ME *venerye,* from OF *venerie,* from *vener* hunt, from L *vēnārī*]

**venesection** /vɛnəˈsɛkʃən/, *n.* →**phlebotomy.** [ML *vēnae sectio* cutting of a vein. See VEIN, SECTION]

**venetian** /vəˈniʃən/, *n.* **1.** *Colloq.* →**venetian blind.** **2.** (*pl.*) a tape or braid for holding the slats of venetian blinds in place. **3.** a cotton or wool cloth of superior quality, used for linings. [orig. with ref. to *Venice,* a seaport in NE Italy]

**venetian blind** /– ˈblaɪnd/, *n.* a blind, as for a window, having overlapping horizontal slats that may be opened or closed, esp. one in which the slats may be raised and drawn together above the window by pulling a cord.

**Venetian glass** /vəniʃən ˈglas/, *n.* ornamental glassware made at or near Venice.

**Venetian red** /– ˈrɛd/, *n.* **1.** a red pigment, originally prepared from a natural oxide of iron, but now usu. made by calcining a mixture of lime and iron sulphate. **2.** a dark shade of orangy red.

**Venetian white** /– ˈwaɪt/, *n.* a mixture of white lead and barium sulphate in equal parts, used as a pigment.

**Venezuela** /vɛnəˈzweɪlə/, *n.* a republic in northern South America. – **Venezuelan,** *adj., n.*

**venge** /vɛndʒ/, *v.t.,* **venged, venging.** *Archaic.* to avenge. [ME, from OF *venger,* from L *vindicāre*]

**vengeance** /ˈvɛndʒəns/, *n.* **1.** the avenging of wrong, injury, or the like, or retributive punishment. **2.** infliction of injury or suffering in requital for wrong done or other cause of bitter resentment. **3. with a vengeance, a.** with force or violence. **b.** extremely. **c.** to a surprising or unusual degree. [ME, from OF, from *venger* VENGE]

**vengeful** /ˈvɛndʒfəl/, *adj.* **1.** desiring or seeking vengeance, as persons; vindictive. **2.** characterised by or showing a vindictive spirit: *a vengeful sort of person.* **3.** taking or executing vengeance. – **vengefully,** *adv.* – **vengefulness,** *n.*

**venial** /ˈviniəl/, *adj.* **1.** that may be forgiven or pardoned; not seriously wrong, as a sin (opposed to *mortal*). **2.** excusable, as an error or slip. [ME, from L *veniālis,* from *venia* pardon] – **veniality** /viniˈæləti/, **venialness,** *n.* – **venially,** *adv.*

**venial sin** /– ˈsɪn/, *n.* **1.** *Rom. Cath. Ch.* a voluntary transgression of God's law, which without destroying charity or union with God, retards man in attaining final union with Him. **2.** any misdeed of a minor nature.

**venin** /ˈvɛnən/, *n.* any of various toxic components of venom. [VEN(OM) + -IN[2]]

**venipuncture** /ˈvɛnəpʌŋktʃə/, *n.* the puncture of a vein for surgical or therapeutic purposes. [*veni-* (combining form representing L *vēna* vein) + PUNCTURE]

**venison** /ˈvɛnəsən, ˈvɛnzən/, *n.* the flesh of a deer or similar animal. [ME, from OF *veneson,* from L *vēnātio* hunting]

**Venn diagram** /ˈvɛn daɪəgræm/, *n. Maths, Logic.* a diagram which represents sets of elements as circles whose overlap indicates the overlap of the sets. [named after John *Venn,* 1834-1923, English logician]

**venom** /ˈvɛnəm/, *n.* **1.** the poisonous fluid which some animals, as certain snakes, spiders, etc., secrete, and introduce into the bodies of their victims by biting, stinging, etc. **2.** something resembling or suggesting poison in its effect; spite or malice. **3.** *Rare.* poison in general. –*v.t.* **4.** *Archaic.* to infect with venom; make venomous; envenom. [ME *venim,* from OF, var. of *venin,* from L *venēnum* poison] – **venomer,** *n.* – **venomless,** *adj.*

**venomous** /ˈvɛnəməs/, *adj.* **1.** (of an animal) having a gland or glands for secreting venom; inflicting a poisoned bite, sting, or wound. **2.** full of venom; poisonous. **3.** spiteful or malignant: *a venomous disposition, a venomous attack.* – **venomously,** *adv.* – **venomousness,** *n.*

**venose** /ˈvinoʊs/, *adj.* **1.** having many or prominent veins. **2.** venous. [L *vēnōsus*]

**venosity** /vəˈnɒsəti/, *n.* venous or venose state, quality, or characteristic.

**venous** /ˈvinəs/, *adj.* **1.** of, pertaining to, or of the nature of a vein or veins. **2.** pertaining to the blood of the veins which has given up oxygen and become charged with carbon dioxide, and, in the higher animals, is dark red in colour. [L *vēnōsus*] – **venously,** *adv.* – **venousness,** *n.*

**vent**[1] /vɛnt/, *n.* **1.** an opening or aperture serving as an outlet for air, smoke, fumes, etc. **2.** the small opening at the breech of a gun by which fire is communicated to the charge. **3.** *Zool.* the anal or excretory opening of animals, esp. of those below mammals, as birds and reptiles. **4.** a means of escaping or passing out; an outlet, as from confinement. [apparently coalescence of VENT[2] and VENT[3]] – **ventless,** *adj.*

**vent**[2] /vɛnt/, *n.* **1.** expression or utterance: *to give vent to emotions, to complaints.* **2.** *Obs.* the act or fact of venting; emission or discharge; issue. –*v.t.* **3.** to give free course or expression to (an emotion, passion, etc.): *glad of any excuse to vent her pique.* **4.** to give utterance to; publish or spread abroad. **5.** to relieve by giving vent to something. **6.** to let out or discharge (liquid, smoke, etc.). **7.** to furnish with a vent or vents. [ME *venten,* from OF *esventer* let out air, from VL **exventāre,* from L *ex-* EX-[1] + *ventus* wind] – **venter,** *n.*

**vent**[3] /vɛnt/, *n.* the slit in the back or sides of a coat. [ME, var. of *fente,* from OF: slit]

**ventage** /ˈvɛntɪdʒ/, *n.* a small hole or vent, as one of the finger holes of a flute.

**venter** /ˈvɛntə/, *n.* **1.** *Anat., Zool.* the abdomen or belly. **2.** a belly-like cavity or concavity. **3.** a belly-like protuberance. **4.** *Law.* the womb, or a wife or mother, as a source of offspring. [L: belly, womb]

**ventiduct** /ˈvɛntədʌkt/, *n.* a duct, pipe or passage for wind or air, as for ventilating an apartment or room. [*venti-* (combining form representing L *ventus* wind) + DUCT]

**ventilate** /ˈvɛntəleɪt/, *v.t.*, **-lated, -lating. 1.** to provide (a room, mine, etc.) with fresh air in place of air which is vitiated. **2.** to introduce fresh air: *the lungs ventilate the blood.* **3.** (of air, wind, etc.) to circulate through, blow on, etc., so as to freshen. **4.** to expose (substances, etc.) to the action of air or wind. **5.** to submit (a question, etc.) to free examination and discussion. **6.** to give utterance or expression to (an opinion, etc.). **7.** to furnish with a vent or opening, as for the escape of air or gas. [L *ventilātus*, pp., fanned]

**ventilation** /vɛntəˈleɪʃən/, *n.* **1.** the act of ventilating. **2.** the state of being ventilated. **3.** any means of or device for ventilating.

**ventilative** /ˈvɛntəleɪtɪv/, *adj.* **1.** promoting or producing ventilation. **2.** of or pertaining to ventilation.

**ventilator** /ˈvɛntəleɪtə/, *n.* **1.** one who or that which ventilates. **2.** any contrivance for replacing foul or stagnant air by fresh air.

**ventolin** /ˈvɛntələn/, *n.* (*also cap.*) →**salbutamol.** [Trademark]

**ventral** /ˈvɛntrəl/, *adj.* **1.** of or pertaining to the venter or belly; abdominal. **2.** situated on the abdominal side of the body. **3.** of, pertaining to, or situated on the anterior or lower side or surface, as of an organ or part. **4.** *Bot.* of or designating the lower or inner surface, as of a petal, etc. *–n.* **5.** a ventral fin. [L *ventrālis*] – **ventrally,** *adv.*

**ventral fin** /– ˈfɪn/, *n.* (in fishes) either of a pair of fins on the lower surface of the body, and corresponding to the hind limbs of higher vertebrates.

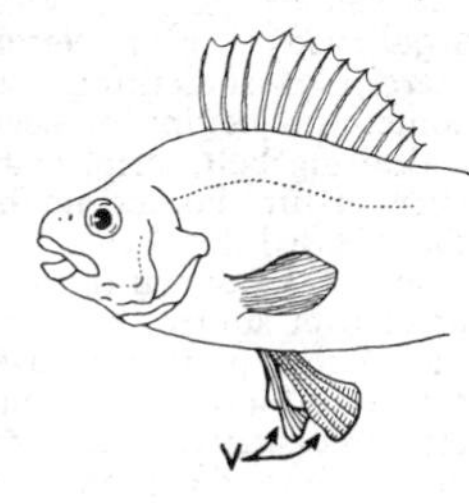
V, ventral fin

**ventricle** /ˈvɛntrɪkəl/, *n.* **1.** any of various hollow organs or parts in an animal body. **2.** one of the two main cavities of the heart which receive the blood from the auricles and propel it into the arteries. **3.** one of a series of connecting cavities of the brain. [ME, from L *ventriculus*, diminutive of *venter* belly]

**ventricose** /ˈvɛntrəkoʊs/, *adj.* **1.** swelling out, esp. on one side or unequally; protuberant. **2.** having a large abdomen. [NL *ventricōsus*, from L *venter* belly] – **ventricosity** /vɛntrəˈkɒsəti/, *n.*

**ventricular** /vɛnˈtrɪkjələ/, *adj.* **1.** of, pertaining to, or of the nature of a ventricle. **2.** swelling out; distended.

**ventricular fibrillation** /– fɪbrəˈleɪʃən/, *n.* a cardiac arrhythmia, in which the ventricles of the heart are fibrillating, thus causing ineffective contraction; fatal unless normal rhythm is restored.

**ventriculus** /vɛnˈtrɪkjələs/, *n.* **1.** the stomach of an insect, the part of the food tract where digestion and absorption take place. **2.** the muscular portion of a bird's stomach. [L, diminutive of *venter* belly]

**ventriloquial** /vɛntrəˈloʊkwiəl/, *adj.* of, pertaining to, or using ventriloquism. Also, **ventriloqual** /vɛnˈtrɪləkwəl/. – **ventriloquially,** *adv.*

**ventriloquise** /vɛnˈtrɪləkwaɪz/, *v.i., v.t.*, **-quised, -quising.** to speak or produce sounds in the manner of a ventriloquist. Also, **ventriloquize.**

**ventriloquism** /vɛnˈtrɪləkwɪzəm/, *n.* the art or practice of speaking or of uttering sounds with little or no lip movement, in such a manner that the voice appears to come not from the speaker but from some other source, as a dummy. Also, **ventriloquy.** [LL *ventriloquus* one who apparently speaks from the belly + -ISM]

**ventriloquist** /vɛnˈtrɪləkwəst/, *n.* one who performs or is expert in ventriloquism. – **ventriloquistic** /ˌvɛntrɪləˈkwɪstɪk/, *adj.*

**venture** /ˈvɛntʃə/, *n., v.*, **-tured, -turing.** *–n.* **1.** a hazardous or daring undertaking; any undertaking or proceeding involving uncertainty as to the outcome. **2.** a business enterprise or proceeding in which loss is risked in the hope of profit; a commercial or other speculation. **3.** that on which risk is taken in a business enterprise or speculation, as a ship, cargo, merchandise, etc. **4.** *Archaic.* hazard or risk. **5. at a venture,** according to chance; at random. *–v.t.* **6.** to expose to hazard; risk. **7.** to take the risk of; brave the dangers of. **8.** to dare; presume; be so bold as; go so far as. **9.** *Archaic.* to take the risk of sending. *–v.i.* **10.** to make a venture; risk oneself. **11.** to take a risk; dare or presume (oft. fol. by *on* or *upon* or an infinitive): *to venture on an ambitious project.* [ME, aphetic var. of *aventure*, earlier form of ADVENTURE] – **venturer,** *n.*

**venturesome** /ˈvɛntʃəsəm/, *adj.* **1.** having or showing a disposition to venture or take risks, often rashly; daring. **2.** attended with risk; hazardous. – **venturesomely,** *adv.* – **venturesomeness,** *n.*

**venturi** /vɛnˈtjuri/, *n.* a device for draining the hull of a boat, which operates on the same principle as a Venturi meter.

**Venturi meter** /ˈ– mitə/, *n.* a device for measuring the rate of flow of fluids, consisting of a narrow tube, in the centre of which is a constriction, means being provided for measuring the drop in pressure across this constriction. The drop in pressure is directly related to the rate of fluid flow. [named after G.B. *Venturi*, 1746-1822, Italian physicist]

**venturous** /ˈvɛntʃərəs/, *adj.* **1.** disposed to venture; bold; daring; adventurous. **2.** hazardous; risky. – **venturously,** *adv.* – **venturousness,** *n.*

**venue** /ˈvɛnju/, *n.* **1.** the scene of any action or event, as a hall for a concert, meeting, etc. **2.** *Law.* **a.** the place of a crime or cause of action. **b.** the county or place where the jury is gathered and the cause tried. **c.** the designation, in the pleading, of the jurisdiction where trial will be held. **d.** the statement naming the place and person before whom an affidavit was sworn. [ME, from OF: coming]

**venule** /ˈvɛnjul/, *n.* **1.** a small vein. **2.** one of the branches of the veins in an insect's wing. Also, **veinule.** [L *vēnula*, diminutive of *vēna* vein] – **venular,** *adj.*

**venulose** /ˈvɛnjəloʊs/, *adj.* having veinlets. Also, **venulous.**

**Venus** /ˈvinəs/, *n.* **1.** a beautiful woman. **2.** *Astron.* the most brilliant planet, having an orbit next inside the earth's and second from the sun. **3.** *Chem. Obs.* copper. **4. mount of Venus, a.** the elevation at the base of the thumb. **b.** (in women) the fleshy pad over the pubic bone. [from *Venus*, Roman goddess of love and beauty]

**Venusian** /vəˈnjuziən/, *adj.* **1.** of or pertaining to the planet Venus. *–n.* **2.** a supposed inhabitant of Venus.

**Venus's flower basket,** *n.* a deep-sea sponge of the genus *Euplectella*, having an intricate skeleton of siliceous spicules.

**Venus's flytrap** /vinəsəz ˈflaɪtræp/, *n.* a plant, *Dionæa muscipula*, native to the south-eastern U.S., whose leaves have two lobes which close like a trap when certain delicate hairs on them are irritated, as by a fly. Also, **Venus flytrap.**

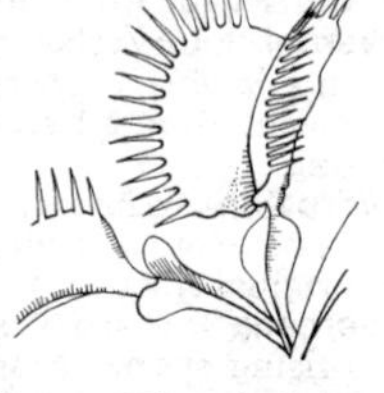
leaves of Venus's flytrap

**Venus's girdle** /– ˈgɜdl/, *n.* a pelagic ctenophore of the Mediterranean, *Cestus veneris*, with a flattened, ribbon-like shape.

**Venus's hair** /– ˈhɛə/, *n.* a delicate maidenhair fern, *Adiantum capillus-veneris.*

**ver.,** **1.** verse; verses. **2.** version.

**veracious** /vəˈreɪʃəs/, *adj.* **1.** speaking truly; truthful or habitually observant of truth: *a veracious witness.* **2.** characterised by truthfulness; true: *a veracious statement or account.* [VERACI(TY) + -OUS] – **veraciously,** *adv.* – **veraciousness,** *n.*

**veracity** /vəˈræsəti/, *n., pl.* **-ties. 1.** truthfulness in speaking or statement; habitual observance of truth. **2.** conformity to truth or fact, as of statements. **3.** correctness or accuracy, as of the senses, a scientific instrument, etc. **4.** something veracious; a truthful statement; a truth. [ML *vērācitas*, from L *vērus* true]

veranda, Australian style

**veranda** /vəˈrændə/, *n.* an open or partly open portion of a house or other building, outside its principal rooms, but roofed usu. by the main structure. Also, **verandah.** [apparently from Pg. and OSp. *varanda* railing, from L *vāra* rod; related to Hindi *varandā* railing]

**veratric acid** /vəˌrætrɪk 'æsəd/, *n.* a white crystalline acid, $(CH_3O)_2C_6H_3COOH$, obtained by the decomposition of veratrine and in other ways. [*veratric,* from L *vērātrum* hellebore + -IC]

**veratridine** /və'rætrədin/, *n.* a soluble amorphous alkaloid, $C_{36}H_{51}NO_{11}$, occurring with veratrine in the seeds of the sabadilla. Also, **veratridin** /və'rætrədən/.

**veratrine** /'vɛrətrin/, *n.* a slightly soluble, crystalline alkaloid, $C_{32}H_{49}NO_9$, obtained from the seeds of the sabadilla, formerly used in medicine, chiefly in the local treatment of rheumatism, neuralgia, etc., and causing prolonged contraction of voluntary muscle. Also, **veratria** /və'reɪtriə, -'rætriə/, **veratrin** /'vɛrətrən/, **veratrina** /vɛrə'traɪnə/.

**verb** /vɜb/, *n.* **1.** one of the major form classes, or parts of speech, comprising words which express the occurrence of an action, existence of a state, and the like, and such other words as show similar grammatical behaviour, as English *discover, remember, write, be.* **2.** any such word. **3.** any word or construction of similar function or meaning. [ME, from L *verbum* word, verb] – **verbless,** *adj.*

**verbal** /'vɜbəl/, *adj., n., v.,* **-balled, -balling.** *–adj.* **1.** of or pertaining to words: *verbal symbols.* **2.** consisting of or in the form of words: *a verbal picture of a scene.* **3.** expressed in spoken words; oral rather than written: *verbal tradition, a verbal message.* **4.** pertaining to or concerned with words only, rather than ideas, facts, or realities: *a purely verbal distinction.* **5.** corresponding word for word; verbatim: *a verbal copy or quotation.* **6.** *Gram.* **a.** of, pertaining to, or derived from a verb. **b.** used in a sentence as or like a verb, as participles and infinitives. *–n.* **7.** *Gram.* a word, particularly a noun or adjective, derived from a verb. **8.** a verbal confession, usu. made to police and recorded by them, and sometimes alleged to be fabricated. *–v.t.* **9.** (of the police) to insert into a prisoner's statement admissions which he did not make, and present it to a court as evidence. [late ME, from L *verbālis,* from *verbum* word] – **verbally,** *adv.*

**verbalise** /'vɜbəlaɪz/, *v.,* **-lised, -lising.** *–v.t.* **1.** to express in words. **2.** *Gram.* to convert into a verb: *to verbalise 'butter' into 'to butter'.* *–v.i.* **3.** to use many words; be verbose. **4.** to express in words. Also, **verbalize.** – **verbalisation** /ˌvɜbəlaɪ'zeɪʃən/, *n.* – **verbaliser,** *n.*

**verbalism** /'vɜbəlɪzəm/, *n.* **1.** a verbal expression; a word or phrase. **2.** a formal phrase or sentence, with little or no meaning. **3.** predominance of mere words, as over ideas or realities.

**verbalist** /'vɜbələst/, *n.* **1.** one skilled in words. **2.** one who deals with words merely, rather than ideas or realities.

**verbal noun** /vɜbəl 'naʊn/, *n.* a noun derived from a verb, esp. in a language where nouns are derived by the same or similar means from all or nearly all verbs, as (in English) by adding *-ing.*

**verbatim** /vɜ'beɪtəm/, *adv.* **1.** word for word, or in exactly the same words. *–adj.* **2.** corresponding word for word to an original. [ML, from L *verbum* word]

**verbena** /vɜ'binə/, *n.* any plant of the genus *Verbena,* comprising species characterised by elongated or flattened spikes of sessile flowers, some of which are much cultivated as garden plants. [L: foliage]

**verbenaceous** /vɜbə'neɪʃəs/, *adj.* belonging to the Verbenaceae, or verbena family of plants, which includes also the lantana, teak, etc.

**verbiage** /'vɜbiɪdʒ/, *n.* abundance of useless words, as in writing or speech; wordiness. [F, from *verbier* gabble, from L *verbum* word. See -AGE]

**verbid** /'vɜbɪd/, *n. Gram.* a non-finite verb form; an infinitive or participle.

**verbose** /vɜ'boʊs/, *adj.* expressed in, characterised by the use of, or using many or too many words; wordy. [L *verbōsus* full of words] – **verbosely,** *adv.* – **verboseness,** *n.*

**verbosity** /vɜ'bɒsəti/, *n.* the quality of being verbose; wordiness; superfluity of words.

**verdant** /'vɜdnt/, *adj.* **1.** green with vegetation; covered with growing plants or grass: *a verdant valley.* **2.** of a green colour. **3.** inexperienced; unsophisticated. [VERD(URE) + -ANT] – **verdancy,** *n.* – **verdantly,** *adv.*

**verd antique** /vɜd æn'tik/, *n.* **1.** a green, mottled or impure serpentine, used for decorative purposes. **2.** any of various similar greenish stones. [OF: antique green]

**Verdelho** /vɜ'dɛloʊ/, *n.* a white wine grape variety grown for producing both table wines and sweet white fortified wines.

**verdict** /'vɜdɪkt/, *n.* **1.** *Law.* the finding or answer of a jury given to the court concerning a matter submitted to their judgment. **2.** a judgment or decision: *the verdict of the public.* [b. ML *vērēdictum* verdict (lit., truly said) and ME *verdit* (from OF: lit., true saying)]

**verdigris** /'vɜdəgri, 'vɜdəgris/, *n.* a green or bluish patina formed on copper, brass, or bronze surfaces exposed to the atmosphere for long periods of time, consisting principally of basic copper sulphate. [ME *verdegres(e),* from AF *vert de Grece,* lit., green of Greece]

**verditer** /'vɜdɪtə/, *n.* **1.** either of two pigments, consisting usu. of carbonate of copper prepared by grinding either azurite (**blue verditer**) or malachite (**green verditer**). **2.** *Obs.* →**verdigris.** [F *vert de terre,* lit., green of earth]

**verdure** /'vɜdʒuə/, *n.* **1.** greenness, esp. of fresh, flourishing vegetation. **2.** green vegetation, esp. grass or herbage. **3.** freshness in general; flourishing condition. [ME, from OF, from *verd* green (from L *viridis*) + *-ure* -URE] – **verdureless,** *adj.*

**verdurous** /'vɜdʒərəs/, *adj.* **1.** rich in verdure or fresh greenness, as vegetation. **2.** covered with verdure or green vegetation, as places. **3.** consisting of verdure. **4.** pertaining to or characteristic of verdure. – **verdurousness,** *n.*

**verecund** /'vɛrikʌnd/, *adj. Rare.* bashful; modest. [L *verēcundus*]

**verge**[1] /vɜdʒ/, *n., v.,* **verged, verging.** *–n.* **1.** the edge, rim, or margin of something. **2.** the limit or point beyond which something begins or occurs: *to be on the verge of tears.* **3.** a limiting belt, strip, or border of something. **4. a.** a narrow strip of turf bordering the edge of a road, pathway, etc. **b.** the cleared levelled space bordering the edge of a sealed road. **5.** space within boundaries; room or scope. **6.** an area or district subject to a particular jurisdiction. **7.** the edge of the roofing projecting over the gable. **8.** *Archit.* the shaft of a column; a small ornamental shaft. **9.** a rod, wand, or staff esp. one carried as an emblem of authority or ensign of office of a bishop, dean, and the like. **10.** *Horol.* a lever with lips or projections, in a clock, which intermittently lock the escape wheel and transmit impulses from the escape wheel to the pendulum. *–v.i.* **11.** to be on the verge or border, or touch at the border. **12.** to come close to, approach, or border on some state or condition (usu. fol. by *on* or *upon*). [ME, from F, from L *virga* rod]

**verge**[2] /vɜdʒ/, *v.i.,* **verged, verging.** to incline or tend; slope (usu. fol. by *to* or *towards*). [L *vergere* turn, incline]

**verger** /'vɜdʒə/, *n.* **1.** an official who takes care of the interior of a church and acts as attendant. **2.** an official who carries the verge or other symbol of office before a bishop, dean, or other dignitary. [late ME, from F (obs.), from *verge* rod. See VERGE[1]]

**veridical** /və'rɪdɪkəl/, *adj.* truth-telling; truthful; veracious. Also, **veridic.** [L *vēridicus* truth-telling + -AL[1]] – **veridicality** /vərɪdə'kæləti/, *n.* – **veridically,** *adv.*

**veriest** /'vɛriəst/, *adj.* utmost; thoroughgoing: *the veriest stupidity.*

**verification** /vɛrəfə'keɪʃən/, *n.* **1.** the act of verifying. **2.** the state of being verified. **3.** formal assertion of the truth of something. – **verificative,** *adj.*

**verifier** /'vɛrəfaɪə/, *n.* **1.** one who or that which verifies. **2.** *Computers.* a machine which checks that punched cards have been punched correctly.

**verify** /'vɛrəfaɪ/, *v.t.,* **-fied, -fying.** **1.** to prove (something) to be true, as by evidence or testimony; confirm or substantiate. **2.** to ascertain the truth or correctness of, esp. by examination or comparison: *to verify dates, spelling, or a quotation.* **3.** to state to be true, esp., in legal use, formally or upon oath. [ME *verifie,* from OF *verifier,* from LL *vērificāre,* from L *vērus* true] – **verifiable,** *adj.*

**verily** /'vɛrəli/, *adv. Archaic.* in very truth; truly; really; indeed. [ME; from VERY + -LY]

**verisimilar** /vɛri'sɪmələ/, *adj.* having the appearance of truth; likely or probable. [L *vērisimilis,* modelled on SIMILAR] – **verisimilarly,** *adv.*

**verisimilitude** /ˌvɛrisəˈmɪlətʃud/, *n.* **1.** appearance or semblance of truth; probability. **2.** something having merely the appearance of truth. [L *vērī similitūdo* likeness of truth]

**verism** /ˈvɛrɪzəm/, *n.* the theory that rigid representation of truth and reality is essential to art and literature and therefore the ugly and vulgar must be included. [L *vērus* true + -ISM] – **verist,** *n., adj.* – **veristic** /vəˈrɪstɪk/, *adj.*

**veritable** /ˈvɛrətəbəl/, *adj.* **1.** being truly such; genuine or real: *a veritable triumph.* **2.** *Rare.* true, as statements, etc. [late ME, from AF, from *verite,* from L *vēritas* truth] – **veritableness,** *n.* – **veritably,** *adv.*

**verity** /ˈvɛrəti/, *n., pl.* **-ties. 1.** quality of being true, or in accordance with fact or reality. **2.** a truth, or true statement, principle, belief, idea, or the like. [ME *verite,* from L *vēritas*]

**verjuice** /ˈvɜdʒus/, *n.* **1.** an acid liquor made from the sour juice of crab apples, unripe grapes, etc., formerly much used for culinary and other purposes. **2.** sourness, as of temper or expression. *–adj.* Also, **verjuiced. 3.** of or pertaining to verjuice. **4.** sour in temper, expression, etc. [ME *verjous,* from OF *vertjus,* from *vert* green + *jus* juice]

**vermeil** /ˈvɜmeɪl/, *n.* **1.** vermilion red. **2.** metal, as silver or bronze, coated with gilt. *–adj.* **3.** of the colour vermilion. [ME *vermaile,* from OF *vermail* bright red, from L *vermiculus* little worm, applied to cochineal]

**vermi-,** a word element meaning 'worm', as in *vermiform.* [L, combining form of *vermis*]

**vermicelli** /vɜməˈsɛli, -ˈtʃɛli/, *n.* a kind of pasta of Italian origin in the form of long, slender, solid threads (thinner than spaghetti), to be cooked for food. [It., pl. of *vermicello* little worm, from *verme* worm, from L *vermis*]

**vermicide** /ˈvɜməsaɪd/, *n.* any agent that kills worms, esp. a drug used to kill parasitic intestinal worms. – **vermicidal** /vɜməˈsaɪdl/, *adj.*

**vermicular** /vɜˈmɪkjələ/, *adj.* **1.** consisting of or characterised by sinuous or wavy outlines or markings, resembling the tracks of worms. **2.** of, pertaining to, or characteristic of a worm or worms. [ML *verniculāris,* from L *vermiculus* little worm] – **vermicularly,** *adv.*

**vermiculate** /vɜˈmɪkjəleɪt/, *v.,* **-lated, -lating;** /vɜˈmɪkjələt, -leɪt/, *adj.* *–v.t.* **1.** to work or ornament with winding or wavy outlines or markings, resembling the tracks of worms. *–adj.* **2.** worm-eaten, or appearing as if worm-eaten; vermiculated. **3.** →**vermicular. 4.** (of thought processes) subtly sinuous. [L *vermiculātus,* pp., worm-eaten] – **vermiculation** /vɜˌmɪkjəˈleɪʃən/, *n.*

**vermicule** /ˈvɜməkjul/, *n.* any small worm.

**vermiculite** /vɜˈmɪkjəlaɪt/, *n.* any of various micaceous minerals, usu. formed by alteration of the common micas, occurring in yellow to brown foliated masses with inelastic laminae. They exfoliate and expand after heating and in the exfoliated form are used extensively as insulating material. [L *vermiculus* little worm + -ITE[1]]

**vermiform** /ˈvɜməfɔm/, *adj.* like a worm in form; long and slender. [ML *vermiformis.* See VERMI-, -FORM]

**vermiform appendix** /– əˈpɛndɪks/, *n.* a narrow, blind tube protruding from the caecum, situated in the lower right-hand part of the abdomen in man, and having no known useful function, its diameter being about that of a pencil and its length approximately 10 cm. Also, **appendix.**

**vermiform process** /– ˈprousɛs/, *n.* **1.** the median lobe or division of the cerebellum. **2.** the vermiform appendix.

**vermifuge** /ˈvɜməfjudʒ/, *adj.* **1.** serving to expel worms or other animal parasites from the intestines, as a medicine. *–n.* **2.** a vermifuge medicine or agent.

**vermilion** /vəˈmɪljən/, *n.* **1.** brilliant scarlet red. **2.** a bright red pigment consisting of mercuric sulphide; cinnabar. *–adj.* **3.** of the colour of vermilion. *–v.t.* **4.** to colour with or as with vermilion. [ME *vermilioun,* from OF *vermillon* bright red, from *vermeil* VERMEIL]

**vermin** /ˈvɜmən/, *n.pl. or sing.* **1.** noxious, troublesome, or objectionable animals collectively, esp. troublesome or disgusting insects or other minute animals, more particularly creeping ones parasitic on living animals or plants. **2.** *Obs.* a single animal of this kind. **3.** obnoxious persons collectively. **4.** a single person of this kind. [ME *vermyne,* from OF *vermin,* from *verm* worm, from L *vermis*]

**vermination** /vɜməˈneɪʃən/, *n.* **1.** the breeding of vermin. **2.** the fact of being infested with vermin, esp. parasitic vermin.

**verminous** /ˈvɜmənəs/, *adj.* **1.** of the nature of or resembling vermin. **2.** pertaining to or caused by vermin. **3.** infested with vermin, esp. parasitic vermin. – **verminously,** *adv.* – **verminousness,** *n.*

**vermis** /ˈvɜməs/, *n., pl.* **-mes** /-miz/. the median lobe of the cerebellum.

**vermivorous** /vɜˈmɪvərəs/, *adj.* worm-eating.

**vermouth** /ˈvɜməθ, vəˈmuθ/, *n.* an aromatised white wine in which herbs, roots, barks, bitters, and other flavourings have been steeped. [F *vermout,* from G *Wermuth* wormwood]

**vernacular** /vəˈnækjələ/, *adj.* **1.** native or originating in the place of its occurrence or use, as language or words (oft. as opposed to *literary* or *learned* language). **2.** expressed or written in the native language of a place, as literary works. **3.** using such a language, as a speaker or a writer. **4.** pertaining to such a language. **5.** denoting or pertaining to the common name for a plant or animal. **6.** native or peculiar to popular taste, as a style of architecture. **7.** *Obs.* endemic, as a disease. *–n.* **8.** the native speech or language of a place. **9.** the language or phraseology peculiar to a class or profession. **10.** a vernacular word or expression. **11.** the common name for a plant or animal rather than the scientific term which gives genus and species. [L *vernāculus* native + -AR[1]] – **vernacularly,** *adv.*

**vernacularise** /vəˈnækjələraɪz/, *v.t.,* **-rised, -rising.** to translate into the native speech of a people. Also, **vernacularize.** – **vernacularist,** *n.* – **vernacularisation** /vəˌnækjələraɪˈzeɪʃən/, *n.*

**vernacularism** /vəˈnækjələrɪzəm/, *n.* **1.** a vernacular word or expression. **2.** the use of the vernacular.

**vernal** /ˈvɜnəl/, *adj.* **1.** of or pertaining to spring. **2.** appearing or occurring in spring. **3.** appropriate to or resembling spring. **4.** belonging or pertaining to youth. [L *vernālis*] – **vernally,** *adv.*

**vernal equinox** /– ˈikwənɒks/, *n.* See **equinox.** Also, **vernal point.**

**vernalise** /ˈvɜnəlaɪz/, *v.t.,* **-lised, -lising.** to shorten the growth period before blossoming and fruit or seed bearing of (a plant), as by chilling its seed or bulb. Also, **vernalize.** – **vernalisation** /vɜnəlaɪˈzeɪʃən/, *n.*

**vernation** /vɜˈneɪʃən/, *n.* the disposition of the foliage leaves within the bud. [L *vernātio* shedding of the skin of snakes, from *ver* spring]

**Verner's law** /ˈvɜnəz lɔ/, *n.* (in the history of Indo-European languages) the statement by Verner of some hitherto unexplained features in the system formulated by Grimm's law, showing the continuance into later languages of the effects of the primitive Indo-European word accent. [named after Karl Adolph *Verner,* 1846-96, Danish philologist] – **Vernerian** /vɜˈnɛəriən/, *adj.*

**vernicle** /ˈvɜnɪkəl/, *n.* →**veronica**[1] (defs 2-4).

**vernier** /ˈvɜniə/, *n.* **1.** Also, **vernier scale.** a small, movable, graduated scale running parallel with the fixed graduated scale of a sextant, theodolite, barometer, or other graduated instrument, and used for measuring a fractional part of one of the divisions of the fixed scale. *–adj.* **2.** equipped with a vernier: *a vernier barometer.* **3.** *Aerospace.* denoting or pertaining to a low-thrust rocket engine used to achieve fine adjustments of the velocity or attitude of a spacecraft. [F; named after Pierre *Vernier,* 1580-1637, French mathematician]

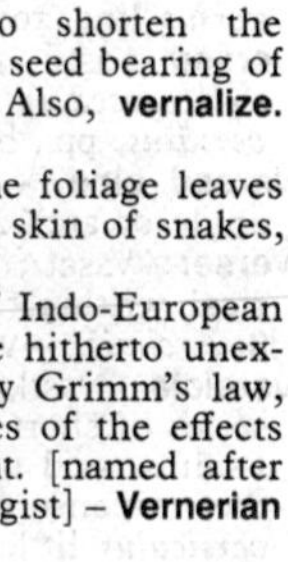

vernier

**vernier rocket** /ˈ– rɒkət/, *n.* →**thruster** (def. 2).

**veronal** /ˈvɛrənəl/, *n.* (*also cap.*) →**barbitone.** [Trademark, from G, said to have been named after *Verona,* a city in N Italy]

**veronica**[1] /vəˈrɒnɪkə/, *n.* **1.** any plant of the genus *Veronica,* as the speedwell, and of related genera, esp. *Hebe.* **2.** the representation of the face of Christ which, according to a legend, was miraculously impressed on a cloth which St Veronica offered to him to wipe his brow as he carried his cross to Calvary. **3.** the cloth itself. Cf. **sudarium. 4.** any similar picture of Christ's face, as on a garment. Also, (defs 2-4), **vernicle.** [ML, apparently named after St *Veronica*]

**veronica**[2] /vəˈrɒnɪkə/, *n.* (in bullfighting) a pass in which the matador, standing immobile, swings the cape in front of the charging bull. [Sp., from the name *Veronica*]

**verruca** /vəˈrukə/, *n., pl.* **-cae** /-si/. **1.** *Med.* a wart. **2.** *Zool.* a small, flattish, wartlike prominence. [L]

**verrucose** /ˈvɛrəkoʊs/, *adj.* studded with wartlike excrescences or elevations. Also, **verrucous** /ˈvɛrəkəs, vəˈrukəs/. – **verrucosity** /vɛrəˈkɒsəti/, *n.*

**vers.,** *Trig.* versed sine.

**versant** /ˈvɜsənt/, *n.* **1.** a slope of a mountain or mountain chain. **2.** the general slope of a country or region. [F, ppr. of *verser* turn, from L *versāre,* from *vertere*]

**versatile** /ˈvɜsətaɪl/, *adj.* **1.** capable of or adapted for turning with ease from one to another of various tasks, subjects, etc.; many-sided in abilities. **2.** *Bot.* attached at or near the middle so as to swing freely, as an anther. **3.** *Zool.* turning either forwards or backwards: *a versatile toe.* **4.** variable or changeable, esp. in feeling, purpose, policy, etc. [L *versātilis* turning about] – **versatilely,** *adv.* – **versatility** /vɜsəˈtɪləti/, **versatileness,** *n.*

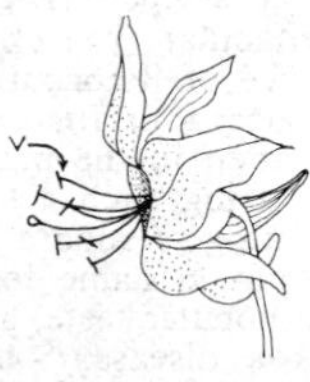

V, versatile anthers

**verse** /vɜs/, *n.* **1.** (not in technical use) a stanza or other subdivision of a metrical composition: *the first verse of a hymn.* **2.** a succession of metrical feet written or printed or orally composed as one line; one of the lines of a poem. **3.** a particular type of metrical line: *a hexameter verse.* **4.** a poem, or piece of poetry. **5.** metrical composition; poetry, esp. as involving metrical form. **6.** a particular type of metrical composition: *iambic verse, elegiac verse.* **7.** the metrical compositions of an author, period, or the like, considered collectively: *Elizabethan verse.* **8.** *Obs.* a line of prose, esp. a sentence, or part of a sentence, written as one line; a stich. **9.** a short division of a chapter in the Bible, usu. one sentence, or part of a long sentence. *–adj.* **10.** written in poetry: *a verse drama.* [ME and OE *vers,* from L *versus* line, row]

**versed** /vɜst/, *adj.* experienced; practised; skilled (fol. by *in*): *well versed in a subject.* [half adoption, half translation of L *versātus,* pp., busied, engaged]

**versed sine** /– ˈsaɪn/, *n.* one minus the cosine (of a given angle or arc). *Abbrev.:* vers.

**verset** /ˈvɜsɛt/, *n. Archaic.* **1.** a short verse or scrap of metrical writing. **2.** *Music.* a short organ prelude or interlude. **3.** *Archaic.* →**versicle.**

**versicle** /ˈvɜsɪkəl/, *n.* **1.** a little verse. **2.** *Eccles.* one of a series of short sentences, or parts of sentences, usu. from the Psalms, said or sung by the officiant, as distinguished from the response of the choir or congregation. [ME, from L *versiculus* little verse]

**versicolour** /ˈvɜsəkʌlə/, *adj.* **1.** changeable in colour. **2.** of various colours; particoloured. Also, **versicoloured;** *U.S.,* **versicolor.** [L *versicolor*]

**versicular** /vɜˈsɪkjələ/, *adj.* of or consisting of versicles or verses. [L *versiculus* little verse + -AR[1]]

**versification** /vɜsəfəˈkeɪʃən/, *n.* **1.** the act of versifying. **2.** form or style of verse; metrical structure. **3.** a metrical version of something. **4.** the rules or customs of verse-making.

**versify** /ˈvɜsəfaɪ/, *v.,* **-fied, -fying.** *–v.t.* **1.** to relate or describe in verse; treat as the subject of verse. **2.** to turn into verse or metrical form. *–v.i.* **3.** to compose verses. [ME *versifie,* from L *versificāre* put into verse] – **versifier,** *n.*

**version** /ˈvɜʒən/, *n.* **1.** a particular account of some matter, as from one person or source, as contrasted with some other account or accounts. **2.** a translation. **3.** a particular form or variant of anything. **4.** (*oft. cap.*) a translation of the Bible or a part of it: *the King James Version.* **5.** *Med.* the act of turning a child in the uterus so as to bring it into a more favourable position for delivery. **6.** *Pathol.* an abnormal direction of the axis of the uterus. [L *versio* turning] – **versional,** *adj.*

**vers libre** /vɛə ˈlibrə/, *n.* →**free verse.** [F] – **vers librist.**

**verso** /ˈvɜsoʊ/, *n., pl.* **-sos. 1.** *Print.* Also, **reverso.** a lefthand page of a book or manuscript. **2.** the reverse, back, or other side of some object, as a coin or medal. [L, short for *versō foliō,* lit., on the turned leaf]

**verst** /vɜst/, *n.* a Russian measure of distance equivalent to approx. one kilometre. [Russ. *versta*]

**versus** /ˈvɜsəs/, *prep.* against (used esp. in law to indicate an action brought by one party against another, and in sport to denote a contest between two teams or players). *Abbrev.:* v., vs. [L]

**vert**[1] /vɜt/, *n.* **1.** *Brit. Forest Law.* **a.** vegetation bearing green leaves in a forest and capable of serving as a cover for deer. **b.** the right to cut such green trees or shrubs. **2.** *Her.* green. *–adj.* **3.** *Her.* of the colour green. [late ME, from AF: green]

**vert**[2] /vɜt/, *v.t.* to turn (a foetus) by application of pressure on the abdomen. [L *vertere*]

**vert.,** **1.** vertical. **2.** vertebrate.

**vertebra** /ˈvɜtəbrə/, *n., pl.* **-brae** /-bri/, **-bras.** any of the bones or segments composing the spinal column, consisting typically in man and the higher animals of a more or less cylindrical body (centrum) and an arch (neural arch) with various processes, forming a foramen through which the spinal cord passes. [L]

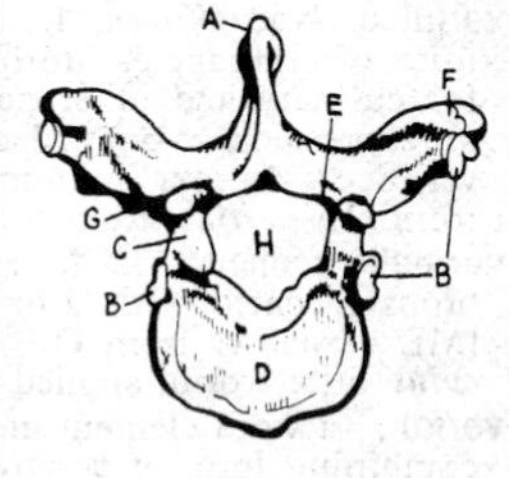

vertebra: A, spine; B, facet of rib; C, pedicel; D, body; E, lamina; F, transverse process; G, articular process; H, spinal canal

**vertebral** /ˈvɜtəbrəl/, *adj.* **1.** of or pertaining to a vertebra or the vertebrae; spinal. **2.** of the nature of a vertebra. **3.** composed of vertebrae. **4.** having vertebrae. – **vertebrally,** *adv.*

**vertebral column** /– ˈkɒləm/, *n.* →**spinal column.**

**vertebrate** /ˈvɜtəbreɪt, -brət/, *n.* **1.** a vertebrate animal. *–adj.* **2.** having vertebrae; having a backbone or spinal column. **3.** belonging or pertaining to the Vertebrata, a subphylum of the phylum Chordata, all members of which have backbones. [L *vertebrātus* jointed]

**vertebrated** /ˈvɜtəbreɪtəd/, *adj.* **1.** having vertebrae; vertebrate. **2.** consisting of vertebrae.

**vertebration** /vɜtəˈbreɪʃən/, *n.* vertebrate formation.

**vertex** /ˈvɜtɛks/, *n., pl.* **-tices** /-təsiz/, **-texes. 1.** the highest point of something; the apex; the top; the summit. **2.** *Anat., Zool.* the crown or top of the head. **3.** *Astron., etc.* a point in the celestial sphere towards which or from which the common motion of a group of stars is directed. **4.** *Maths.* the point farthest from the base. **5.** *Geom.* **a.** a point in a plane figure common to two or more sides. **b.** a point in a solid common to three or more sides. [L: whirl, crown of the head, summit]

**vertical** /ˈvɜtɪkəl/, *adj.* **1.** being in a position or direction perpendicular to the plane of the horizon; upright; plumb. **2.** of, pertaining to, or situated at the vertex. **3.** *Bot.* **a.** (of a leaf) having the blade in a perpendicular plane, so that neither of the surfaces can be called upper or under. **b.** in the same direction as the axis; lengthways. **4.** of or pertaining to the consolidation of businesses or industries that are closely related in the manufacture or sale of a certain commodity. *–n.* **5.** a vertical line, plane, or the like. **6.** vertical or upright position. **7.** (in a truss) a vertical member. [LL *verticālis,* from *vertex* VERTEX] – **verticality** /vɜtəˈkæləti/, **verticalness,** *n.* – **vertically,** *adv.*

**vertical angle** /– ˈæŋgəl/, *n.* **1.** *Geom.* **a.** either of the two opposite angles formed by two intersecting lines or planes; vertically opposite angle. **b.** the angle at the vertex of a triangle or polygon. **2.** *Astron.* an angle measured on a vertical circle.

**vertical circle** /– ˈsɜkəl/, *n.* **1.** *Astron.* a great circle on the celestial sphere which passes through the zenith and cuts the horizon at right angles. **2.** *Survey.* the graduated circular plate of a theodolite used for measuring vertical angles.

**vertical mobility** /– moʊˈbɪləti/, *n.* the movement of a person to a social class above or below that into which he was born.

**vertices** /ˈvɜtəsiz/, *n.* a plural of **vertex.**

**verticil** /ˈvɜtəsɪl/, *n.* a whorl or circle, as of leaves, hairs, etc., arranged round a point on an axis. [L *verticillus,* diminutive of *vertex* whorl (of a spindle)]

**verticillaster** /ˌvɜtəsəˈlæstə/, *n.* an inflorescence in which the flowers are arranged in a seeming whorl, consisting in fact of a pair of opposite axillary, usu. sessile, cymes, as in many mints. [NL, from L *verticillus* whorl + *-aster* -ASTER[2]]

verticil

**verticillate** /vɜ'tɪsələt, -leɪt/, *adj.* **1.** disposed in or forming verticils or whorls, as flowers, etc. **2.** (of plants) having flowers, etc., so arranged or disposed. Also, **verticillated.** – **verticillately,** *adv.* – **verticillation** /vɜˌtɪsə'leɪʃən/, *n.*

**verticillium** /vɜtə'sɪliəm/, *n.* a disease of plants caused by fungi of the genus *Verticillium;* wilt.

**vertiginous** /vɜ'tɪdʒənəs/, *adj.* **1.** whirling or rotary. **2.** affected with vertigo. **3.** liable to cause vertigo. **4.** apt to change quickly; unstable. [L *vertīginōsus* suffering from giddiness] – **vertiginously,** *adv.* – **vertiginousness,** *n.*

**vertigo** /'vɜtəgoʊ/, *n., pl.* **vertigos, vertigines** /vɜ'tɪdʒəniz/. a disordered condition in which an individual, or whatever is around him, seems to be whirling about; dizziness. [L: lit., whirling round]

**vertrep** /'vɜtrɛp/, *n.* vertical replenishment of one ship by another by means of helicopter transferred loads.

**vertu** /vɜ'tu/, *n.* →**virtu.**

**vervain** /'vɜveɪn/, *n.* any plant of the genus *Verbena* (see **verbena**), esp. one of the species with small spicate flowers, as *V. officinalis.* [ME *verveine,* from OF, from L *verbēna* green bough]

**verve** /vɜv/, *n.* **1.** enthusiasm or energy, as in literary or artistic work; spirit, liveliness, or vigour: *her novel lacks verve.* **2.** *Rare.* talent. [F: enthusiasm, fancy; orig. uncert.]

**vervet** /'vɜvət/, *n.* an African monkey, *Cercopithecus aethiops pygerythrus,* allied to the green monkey and the grivet, but distinguished by a rusty patch at the root of the tail. [F, b. *ver(t)* green and *(gri)vet* grivet]

**very** /'vɛri/, *adv., adj.,* **-rier, -riest.** *–adv.* **1.** in a high degree, extremely, or exceedingly. **2.** (used as an intensive emphasising superlatives or stressing identity or oppositeness): *the very best thing to be done, in the very same place.* *–adj.* **3.** precise or identical: *the very thing you should not have done.* **4.** even (what is specified): *they grew to dread his very name.* **5.** mere: *the very thought is distressing.* **6.** sheer: *to weep for very joy.* **7.** actual: *caught in the very act.* **8.** (with emphatic or intensive force) being such in the true or full sense of the term: *the very heart of the matter.* **9.** true, genuine, or real: *the very God.* **10.** *Archaic.* rightful or legitimate. [ME, from OF *verai,* from L *vērus* true]

**very high frequency,** *n.* any radio frequency between 30 and 300 megahertz. *Abbrev.:* v.h.f.

**Very light** /'vɛri laɪt, 'vɪəri/, *n.* a small coloured flare which is fired from a special pistol (**Very pistol**) for the purposes of illumination or signalling. [named after E. W. *Very,* 1847-1907, American inventor]

**very low frequency,** *n.* any radio frequency below 30 kilohertz. *Abbrev.:* v.l.f.

**vesica** /'vɛsɪkə/, *n., pl.* **-cae** /-si/. **1.** a bladder; a sac. **2.** the urinary bladder, *Vesica urinaria,* or gall bladder, *V. fellea.* [L: bladder, blister]

**vesical** /'vɛsɪkəl/, *adj.* **1.** of or pertaining to a vesica or bladder, esp. the urinary bladder. **2.** having the shape of a vesica, esp. elliptical.

**vesicant** /'vɛsəkənt/, *adj.* **1.** vesicating; producing a blister or blisters, as a medicinal substance. *–n.* **2.** a vesicant agent or substance. **3.** *Chem. Warfare.* a chemical agent that causes burns and destruction of tissue both internally and externally. [NL *vēsīcans* blistering]

**vesicate** /'vɛsəkeɪt/, *v.t.,* **-cated, -cating.** to raise vesicles or blisters on; blister. – **vesication** /vɛsə'keɪʃən/, *n.*

**vesicatory** /'vɛsəkeɪtəri/, *adj., n., pl.* **-ries.** →**vesicant.**

**vesicle** /'vɛsɪkəl/, *n.* **1.** a little sac or cyst. **2.** *Anat., Zool.* a small bladder-like cavity, esp. one filled with fluid. **3.** *Pathol.* a circumscribed elevation of the epidermis containing serous fluid. **4.** *Bot.* a small bladder, or bladder-like air cavity, esp. one present in plants which float on water. **5.** *Geol.* a small, usu. spherical cavity in a rock or mineral, due to gas or vapour. [L *vēsīcula,* diminutive of *vēsīca* bladder, blister]

**vesicular** /və'sɪkjələ/, *adj.* **1.** of or pertaining to vesicles. **2.** having the form of a vesicle. **3.** characterised by or consisting of vesicles. – **vesicularly,** *adv.*

**vesicular exanthema** /– ˌɛksæn'θimə/, *n.* a specific infectious disease of pigs, closely resembling foot-and-mouth disease.

**vesiculate** /və'sɪkjələt, -leɪt/, *adj.;* /və'sɪkjəleɪt/, *v.,* **-lated, -lating.** *–adj.* **1.** characterised by or covered with vesicles. **2.** of the nature of a vesicle. *–v.t., v.i.* **3.** to make or become vesiculate or vesicular. – **vesiculation** /vəsɪkjə'leɪʃən/, *n.*

**vesper** /'vɛspə/, *n.* **1.** evening. **2.** *(cap.)* the evening star, esp. Venus; Hesperus. **3.** an evening prayer, service, song, etc. **4.** a vesper bell; a bell rung at evening. *–adj.* **5.** of, pertaining to, appearing in, or proper to the evening. **6.** of or pertaining to vespers. [ME, from L]

**vesperal** /'vɛspərəl/, *n.* **1.** that part of the antiphonary which contains the chants for vespers. **2.** a cloth used between offices to cover the altar cloth.

**vespers** /'vɛspəz/, *n. pl. (sometimes cap.)* **1.** a religious service held in the late afternoon or the evening. **2.** the sixth of the seven canonical hours, or the service for it, occurring in the late afternoon or evening. **3.** *Rom. Cath. Ch.* a part of the office to be said in the evening by those in major orders, frequently made a public ceremony in the afternoons or evenings of Sundays and holy days. **4.** →**Evensong.** [ML *vesperae,* pl., vespers, special use of L *vespera* evening]

**vespertilionine** /vɛspə'tɪliənaɪn, -nən/, *adj.* of or pertaining to the bats of the subfamily Vespertilioninae, common in temperate regions and including many well-known species. [L *vespertīlio* bat + -INE[1]] – **vespertilionid,** *n., adj.*

**vespertine** /'vɛspətaɪn/, *adj.* **1.** of, pertaining to, or occurring in the evening. **2.** *Bot.* opening or expanding in the evening, as certain flowers. **3.** *Zool.* appearing or flying in the early evening; crepuscular. Also, **vespertinal** /vɛspə'taɪnəl/. [L *vespertīnus* of the evening]

**vespiary** /'vɛspjəri/, *n., pl.* **-ries.** a wasp's nest. [L *vespa* wasp + *-iary* as in APIARY]

**vespid** /'vɛspəd/, *n.* **1.** any member of the Vespidae, a widely distributed family of social wasps, including the hornets, which live in communities composed of males (drones), females (queens), and workers. *–adj.* **2.** belonging or pertaining to the Vespidae. [NL *Vespidae,* from L *vespa* wasp]

**vespine** /'vɛspaɪn/, *adj.* **1.** of or pertaining to wasps. **2.** wasp-like.

**vessel** /'vɛsəl/, *n.* **1.** a craft for travelling on water, now esp. one larger than an ordinary rowing boat; a ship or boat. **2.** a hollow or concave article, as a cup, bowl, pot, pitcher, vase, bottle, etc., for holding liquid or other contents. **3.** *Anat., Zool.* a tube or duct, as an artery, vein, or the like, containing or conveying blood or some other body fluid. **4.** *Bot.* a duct formed of connected cells which have lost their intervening partitions, containing or conveying sap, etc. **5.** a person regarded as a receptacle or container (chiefly in or after biblical expressions). [ME, from OF, from L *vascellum* small vase. See VASE]

**vest** /vɛst/, *n.* **1.** a short, warm undergarment with sleeves, usu. worn next to the skin under a shirt; a singlet. **2.** a waistcoat. **3.** a similar garment, or a part or trimming simulating the front of such a garment, worn by women. **4.** a long garment resembling a cassock, worn by men in the times of Charles II. **5.** *Archaic.* dress, apparel, or vesture. **6.** *Archaic.* an outer garment, robe, or gown. **7.** *Rare.* an ecclesiastical vestment. [It. *veste,* from L *vestis* garment] *–v.t.* **8.** to clothe, dress, or robe. **9.** to dress in ecclesiastical vestments. **10.** to cover or drape (an altar). **11.** to place or settle (something, esp. property, rights, powers, etc.) in the possession or control of a person or persons (usu. fol. by *in*): *to vest an estate or a title in a person.* **12.** to invest or endow (a person, etc.) with something, esp. with powers, functions, etc. *–v.i.* **13.** to put on vestments. **14.** to become vested in a person or persons, as a right. **15.** to pass into possession; to devolve upon a person as possessor. [ME, from OF *vestir,* from L *vestīre* clothe] – **vestless,** *adj.* – **vestlike,** *adj.*

**vesta** /'vɛstə/, *n.* a short match with a wood or wax stem which can be struck on any rough surface. [from *Vesta,* the Roman goddess of the hearth and hearth fire]

**vestal** /'vɛstl/, *adj.* **1.** pertaining to, characteristic of, or resembling a virgin; virgin; chaste. *–n.* **2.** a virgin; a chaste, unmarried woman. **3.** a nun. [from the four (later six) virgins, consecrated by the ancient Romans to *Vesta,* goddess of the hearth and hearth fire, and to the service of watching the sacred fire kept burning perpetually on her altar]

**vested** /ˈvɛstəd/, *adj.* **1.** settled or secured in the possession of a person or persons, as a complete or fixed right, an interest sometimes possessory, sometimes future, which has substance because of its relative certainty. **2.** clothed or robed, esp. in ecclesiastical vestments: *a vested choir.*

**vested interests** /– ˈɪntrəsts/, *n.pl.* **1.** personal interests or rights in a system, institution, or the like, usu. protected by law or custom. **2.** the persons, groups, etc., who have acquired rights or powers by which they are able to further or maintain their position of dominance in some sphere of a country's activities, as business or finance.

**vested remainder** /– rəˈmeɪndə/, *n.* (in law) an interest, property, etc., to which a person is presently entitled but which will not come into his possession until some future event, as a remainder contingent on the death of a relative.

**vestiary** /ˈvɛstʃəri/, *adj.* of or pertaining to garments or dress. [L *vestiārius*]

**vestibular** /vɛsˈtɪbjələ/, *adj.* of, pertaining to, or resembling a vestibule.

**vestibule** /ˈvɛstəbjul/, *n., v.,* **-buled, -buling.** *–n.* **1.** a passage, hall, or antechamber between the outer door and the interior parts of a house or building. **2.** *Anat., Zool.* any of various cavities or hollows regarded as forming an approach or entrance to another cavity or space: *the vestibule of the ear.* **3.** an enclosed space at the end of a railway carriage, affording entrance to the carriage from outside and from the next carriage. *–v.t.* **4.** to provide with a vestibule or vestibules, as a railway carriage. [L *vestibulum*]

**vestige** /ˈvɛstɪdʒ/, *n.* **1.** a mark, trace, or visible evidence of something which is no longer present or in existence. **2.** a surviving evidence or memorial of some condition, practice, etc. **3.** a very slight trace or amount of something. **4.** *Biol.* a degenerate or imperfectly developed organ or structure having little or no utility, but which in an earlier stage of the individual or in preceding organisms performed a useful function. **5.** *Archaic.* a footprint or track. [F, from L *vestīgium* footprint]

**vestigial** /vɛsˈtɪdʒəl/, *adj.* pertaining to or of the nature of a vestige. – **vestigially,** *adv.*

**vestigium** /vɛsˈtɪdʒiəm/, *n., pl.* **-tigia** /-ˈtɪdʒiə/. a vestige; a vestigial structure of any kind. [L]

**vesting** /ˈvɛstɪŋ/, *n. Chiefly U.S.* any of various medium or heavy cloths used for making waistcoats, etc.

**vestment** /ˈvɛstmənt/, *n.* **1.** a garment, esp. an outer garment, robe, or gown. **2.** an official or ceremonial robe. **3.** *Eccles.* **a.** one of the garments worn by the clergy and their assistants, choristers, etc., during divine service and on other occasions. **b.** one of the garments worn by the celebrant, deacon, and subdeacon during the celebration of the Eucharist. **4.** something that covers like a garment. [ME *vestement,* from OF, from L *vestīmentum* clothing] – **vestmental** /vɛstˈmɛntl/, *adj.*

**vestry** /ˈvɛstri/, *n., pl.* **-tries.** **1.** a room in or a building attached to a church, in which the vestments, and sometimes also the sacred vessels, etc., are kept; a sacristy. **2.** (in some churches) a room in or a building attached to a church, used as a chapel, for prayer meetings, for the Sunday school, etc. **3.** (in parishes of the Church of England) **a.** a meeting of all the parishioners, or of a committee of parishioners, held in the vestry for the dispatch of the official business of the parish. **b.** the body of parishioners so meeting; parish council. [ME, from VEST, *v.* + -RY]

**vestry book** /ˈ– bʊk/, *n.* →**parish register.**

**vestryman** /ˈvɛstrimən/, *n., pl.* **-men.** a member of a church vestry.

**vesture** /ˈvɛstʃə/, *n., v.,* **-tured, -turing.** *–n.* **1.** *Law.* **a.** everything growing on and covering the land, with the exception of trees. **b.** any such product, as grass or wheat. **2.** *Archaic.* clothing; garments. **3.** *Archaic.* something that covers like a garment; a covering. *–v.t.* **4.** *Archaic.* to clothe, as with vesture. [ME, from OF, from *vestir* clothe, influenced by ML *vestītūra* clothing] – **vestural,** *adj.*

**vesuvianite** /vəˈsuviənaɪt/, *n.* a mineral, a hydrous silicate of calcium and aluminium chiefly, commonly in prismatic crystals and usu. of a brown to green colour; common in contact-metamorphosed limestones; idocrase.

**vet**[1] /vɛt/, *n., v.,* **vetted, vetting.** *Colloq.* *–n.* **1.** a veterinary surgeon. *–v.t.* **2.** to examine or treat as a veterinary surgeon does. **3.** to examine (a person): *the applicants were well vetted.* **4.** to examine (a product, proposal, or the like) with a view to acceptance, rejection, or correction. *–v.i.* **5.** to work as a veterinary surgeon. [short for VETERINARY]

**vet**[2] /vɛt/, *n. U.S. Colloq.* a veteran.

**vetch** /vɛtʃ/, *n.* **1.** any of various leguminous plants, mostly climbing herbs, of the genus *Vicia,* as *V. sativa,* the common vetch, cultivated for forage and soil improvement. **2.** any of various allied plants, as *Lathyrus sativus,* of Europe, cultivated for its edible seeds and as a forage plant. **3.** the beanlike seed or fruit of any such plant. [ME *veche,* from d. OF, from L *vicia*]

**vetchling** /ˈvɛtʃlɪŋ/, *n.* any of the plants constituting the leguminous genus *Lathyrus,* as *L. pratensis,* common in meadows of the northern temperate regions.

vetch

**veteran** /ˈvɛtərən, ˈvɛtrən/, *n.* **1.** one who has seen long service in any occupation or office. **2.** a soldier who has seen active service: *a veteran of the desert war.* **3.** anyone who has had any experience in some field, esp. a soldier. *–adj.* **4.** experienced through long service or practice; having served for a long period; grown old in service. **5.** of, pertaining to, or characteristic of veterans. **6.** denoting or pertaining to cars built before 1918. **7.** (of soldiers) having had service or experience in warfare: *veteran troops.* [L *veterānus,* from *vetus* old]

**veterinarian** /vɛtərəˈnɛəriən, vɛtrə-/, *n. Chiefly U.S.* a veterinary surgeon.

**veterinary** /ˈvɛtənri, ˈvɛtərənri/, *n., pl.* **-ries** *adj.* *–n.* **1.** a veterinary surgeon. *–adj.* **2.** of the medical and surgical treatment of animals, esp. domesticated ones. [L *veterīnārius,* from *veterinus* pertaining to cattle]

**veterinary science** /– ˈsaɪəns/, *n.* that branch of medicine that concerns itself with the study, prevention, and treatment of animal diseases. Also, **veterinary medicine.**

**veterinary surgeon** /– ˈsɜdʒən/, *n.* one who practises veterinary science or surgery.

**vetiver** /ˈvɛtɪvə/, *n.* **1.** the long, fibrous, aromatic roots of an Indian grass, *Vetiveria zizanioides,* used for making hangings and screens, and yielding vetiver oil, used in perfumery. **2.** the grass itself. [Tamil *vettivēru*]

**veto** /ˈvitoʊ/, *n., pl.* **-toes,** *v.,* **-toed, -toing.** *–n.* **1.** the power or right of preventing action by a prohibition. **2.** a prohibition directed against some proposed or intended act. *–v.t.* **3.** to prevent (a proposal, legislative bill, etc.) being put into action by exercising the right of veto. **4.** to refuse to consent to. [L: I forbid] – **vetoer,** *n.* – **vetoless,** *adj.*

**vet. sci.,** veterinary science.

**ve-tsin** /vi-ˈtsɪn/, *n.* →**monosodium glutamate.**

**vex** /vɛks/, *v.t.* **1.** to irritate; annoy; provoke; make angry: *enough to vex a saint.* **2.** to torment; plague; worry: *want of money vexes many.* **3.** *Archaic.* to disturb by motion; stir up; toss about. **4.** *Archaic.* to trouble or afflict physically. [ME *vexe(n),* from L *vexāre* agitate] – **vexer,** *n.* – **vexingly,** *adv.*

**vexation** /vɛkˈseɪʃən/, *n.* **1.** the act of vexing. **2.** the state of being vexed. **3.** something that vexes.

**vexatious** /vɛkˈseɪʃəs/, *adj.* **1.** causing vexation; vexing; annoying. **2.** *Law.* (of legal actions) instituted without sufficient grounds, and serving only to cause annoyance. – **vexatiously,** *adv.* – **vexatiousness,** *n.*

**vexed** /vɛkst/, *adj.* **1.** disturbed; troubled; annoyed. **2.** much discussed or disputed: *a vexed question.* **3.** tossed about, as waves. – **vexedly** /ˈvɛksədli/, *adv.* – **vexedness,** *n.*

**vexillate** /ˈvɛksələt, -leɪt/, *adj.* having a vexillum or vexilla.

**vexillology** /vɛksəˈlɒlədʒi/, *n.* the study of flags and their meanings, history, etc.

**vexillum** /vɛkˈsɪləm/, *n., pl.* **-vexilla** /-lə/. **1.** a military standard or flag carried by ancient Roman troops. **2.** a body of men serving under such a standard. **3.** Also, **vexil.** *Bot.* the large upper petal of a flower of the family Papilionaceae. **4.** *Ornith.* the web or vane of a feather. [L: standard]

**VF,** video frequency.

**v.g.,** very good.

**V.G.,** Valuer-General.

**V.G.** /vi 'dʒi/, *n. Colloq.* a valuation authorised by the Valuer-General.

**v.h.f.** /vi eɪtʃ 'ɛf/, *Radio.* very high frequency. Also, **V.H.F.**

**v.i.,** **1.** verb intransitive. **2.** vide infra.

**via** /'vaɪə/, *prep.* **1.** by way of; by a route that passes through: *go to Italy via Singapore.* **2.** by means of: *to reach a conclusion via three logical steps.* [L, abl. of *via* way]

**viable** /'vaɪəbəl/, *adj.* **1.** capable of living. **2.** practicable; workable. **3.** *Physiol.* **a.** physically fitted to live. **b.** (of a foetus) having reached such a stage of development as to permit continued existence, under normal conditions, outside the womb. **4.** *Bot.* able to live and grow. [F, from *vie* life, from L *vīta*] – **viability** /vaɪə'bɪləti/, *n.*

**viaduct** /'vaɪədʌkt/, *n.* **1.** a bridge consisting of a series of narrow masonry arches with high supporting piers, for carrying a road, railway, etc., over a valley, ravine, or the like. **2.** a similar bridge of steel girders. [L *via* way + *-duct* as in AQUEDUCT]

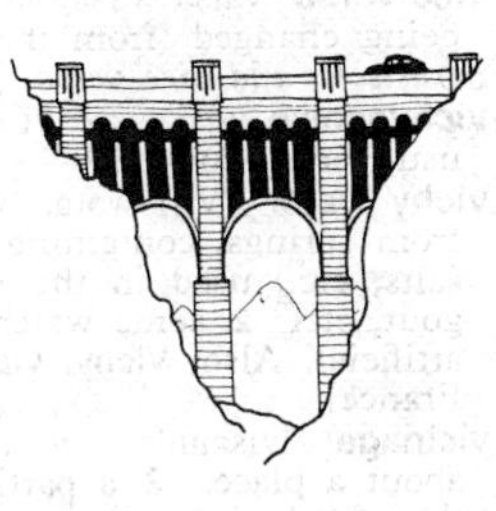
viaduct (def. 1)

**vial** /'vaɪəl/, *n.* →**phial** (def. 1). [ME *viole,* var. of *fiole* PHIAL]

**viand** /'vaɪənd, 'viənd/, *n.* **1.** an article of food. **2.** (*pl.*) articles or dishes of food, now usu. of a choice or delicate kind. [ME *vyaunde,* from OF *viande,* from L *vīvenda* things to be lived on]

**viaticum** /vaɪ'ætɪkəm, vi-/, *n., pl.* **-ca** /-kə/, **-cums.** **1.** *Eccles.* the Eucharist or communion as given to a person dying or in danger of death. **2.** (among the ancient Romans) a provision or allowance for travelling, originally of transport and supplies, later of money, made to officials on public missions. **3.** money or necessities for any journey. [L]

**vibes**[1] /vaɪbz/, *n.pl. Colloq.* →**vibraphone.**

**vibes**[2] /vaɪbz/, *n.pl. Colloq.* the quality, mood or atmosphere of a place or person, thought of as producing vibrations to which one unconsciously responds: *the vibes of that town were all wrong.*

**vibist** /'vaɪbəst/, *n.* a vibraphone player.

**vibraculum** /vaɪ'brækjələm/, *n., pl.* **-la** /-lə/. one of the long, tapering, whip-like, movable appendages possessed by certain polyzoans. [NL, from L *vibrāre* shake] – **vibracular,** *adj.*

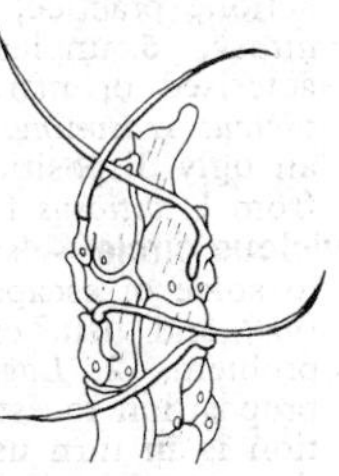
vibracula

**vibraharp** /'vaɪbrəhap/, *n. U.S.* a vibraphone.

**vibrant** /'vaɪbrənt/, *adj.* **1.** moving to and fro rapidly; vibrating. **2.** vibrating so as to produce sound, as a string. **3.** (of sounds) characterised by perceptible vibration, or resonant. **4.** pulsating with energy. **5.** full of vigour; energetic; powerful; forceful. **6.** exciting; producing a thrill. **7.** *Phonet.* voiced. *–n.* **8.** *Phonet.* a voiced sound. [L *vibrans,* ppr.] – **vibrancy,** *n.* – **vibrantly,** *adv.*

**vibraphone** /'vaɪbrəfoun/, *n.* a xylophone-like musical instrument with electronically operated resonators controlled by a pedal. Also, *U.S.,* **vibraharp.** [L *vibrā(re)* shake, vibrate + -PHONE] – **vibraphonist,** *n.*

**vibrate** /vaɪ'breɪt/, *v.,* **-brated, -brating.** *–v.i.* **1.** to move to and fro, as a pendulum; oscillate. **2.** to move to and fro or up and down quickly and repeatedly; quiver; tremble. **3.** (of sounds) to produce or have a quivering or vibratory effect; resound. **4.** to thrill, as in emotional response. **5.** to move between extremes; fluctuate; vacillate. *–v.t.* **6.** to cause to move to and fro, swing, or oscillate. **7.** to cause to move to and fro or up and down quickly and repeatedly; cause to quiver or tremble. **8.** to give forth or emit (sound, etc.) by or as by vibratory motion. [L *vibrātus,* pp., shaken]

**vibratile** /'vaɪbrətaɪl/, *adj.* **1.** capable of vibrating or of being vibrated. **2.** having a vibratory motion. **3.** pertaining to or of the nature of vibration. – **vibratility** /vaɪbrə'tɪləti/, *n.*

**vibration** /vaɪ'breɪʃən/, *n.* **1.** the act of vibrating; oscillation. **2.** the state of vibrating; tremulous effect. **3.** *Physics.* the oscillating or periodic motion of a particle, group of particles, or solid object about its equilibrium position. **4.** a single vibrating motion; an oscillation; a quiver or tremor. **5.** (*pl.*) *Colloq.* →**vibes**[2]. – **vibrational,** *adj.* – **vibrationless,** *adj.*

vibraphone

**vibrative** /vaɪ'breɪtɪv/, *adj.* vibratory.

**vibrato** /və'bratoʊ/, *n., pl.* **-tos.** a pulsating effect produced in the singing voice or in an instrumental tone by rapid small oscillations in pitch about the given note. [It., pp. of *vibrare* vibrate, from L]

**vibrator** /vaɪ'breɪtə, 'vaɪbreɪtə/, *n.* **1.** one who or that which vibrates. **2.** any of various instruments or devices causing a vibratory motion or action. **3.** an appliance with a rubber or other tip of variable shape, made to oscillate very rapidly, used in vibratory massage, sometimes for the purpose of erotic stimulation. **4.** *Elect.* **a.** a device containing a vibrating member for converting a direct current into an oscillating current. **b.** a device for producing electrical oscillations.

**vibratory** /vaɪ'breɪtəri, 'vaɪbrətəri, -tri/, *adj.* **1.** producing vibration. **2.** vibrating, or admitting of vibration. **3.** of the nature of or inherent in vibration. **4.** pertaining to vibration. Also, **vibrative.**

**vibrio** /'vɪbrioʊ/, *n., pl.* **-rios.** any bacterium of the genus *Vibrio,* made up of comma-shaped organisms, the most important of which is *V. comma,* the causative agent of Asiatic cholera. [NL, from L *vibrāre* shake] – **vibrioid** /'vɪbriɔɪd/, *adj.*

**vibrionic** /vɪbri'ɒnɪk/, *adj.* of, pertaining to, or caused by an infection by any bacterium of the genus *Vibrio.*

**vibrissa** /vaɪ'brɪsə/, *n., pl.* **-brissae** /-'brɪsi/. **1.** one of the stiff, bristly hairs growing about the mouth of certain animals, as a cat's whisker. **2.** one of the long, slender, bristle-like feathers growing along the side of the mouth in many birds. [L: hair in the nostrils]

**vibronic** /vaɪ'brɒnɪk/, *adj.* of, pertaining to, or having both vibratory and electronic energy. [VIBR(ATORY) + (ELECTR)ONIC]

**viburnum** /və'bɜnəm/, *n.* **1.** any of the shrubs or small trees constituting the genus *Viburnum,* species of which, as *V. opulus,* the snowball tree, are cultivated for ornament. **2.** the dried bark of various species of *Viburnum,* used in medicine. [L: the wayfaring tree]

viburnum

**Vic.,** Victoria.

**vicar** /'vɪkə/, *n.* **1.** *C. of E.* a clergyman acting as priest of a parish. **2.** *Rom. Cath. Ch.* **a.** an ecclesiastic representing the pope or a bishop. **b.** the pope as the representative on earth of God or Christ. **3.** one acting in place of another. **4.** a person authorised to perform the functions of another; a deputy. [ME *vicare,* from AF, from L *vicārius* substitute] – **vicarship,** *n.*

**vicarage** /'vɪkərɪdʒ/, *n.* **1.** the residence of a vicar. **2.** the benefice of a vicar. **3.** the office or duties of a vicar.

**vicar apostolic** /ˌvɪkər æpə'stɒlɪk/, *n. Rom. Cath. Ch.* **1.** a missionary or titular bishop stationed either in a country where no episcopal see has yet been established, or in one where the succession of bishops has been interrupted. **2.** (formerly) an archbishop, bishop, or other ecclesiastic to whom the pope delegated a portion of his jurisdiction.

**vicarate** /'vɪkərət/, *n.* →**vicariate.**

**vicar choral** /vɪkə 'kɒrəl/, *n. Brit.* a cleric or layman who sings in an Anglican cathedral choir.

**vicar forane** /– fɒ'reɪn/, *n.* (in the Roman Catholic Church) an ecclesiastical dignitary appointed by the bishop to exercise a limited jurisdiction in a particular town or district of his diocese; a rural dean. [VICAR + L *foraneus* living outside; see FOREIGN]

**vicar-general** /vɪkə-'dʒɛnrəl/, *n.*, *pl.* **vicars-general.** **1.** *Rom. Cath. Ch.* a priest appointed by a bishop to assist him in the administration of a diocese. **2.** *C. of E.* an ecclesiastical officer, usu. a layman, who assists a bishop or an archbishop in the discharge of his judicial or administrative duties.

**vicarial** /vaɪ'kɛəriəl/, *adj.* **1.** of or pertaining to a vicar or vicars. **2.** acting as or holding the office of a vicar. **3.** delegated or vicarious, as powers.

**vicariate** /vaɪ'kɛəriət/, *n.* **1.** the office or authority of a vicar. **2.** a district under a vicar. Also, **vicarate.**

**vicarious** /və'kɛəriəs, vaɪ-/, *adj.* **1.** performed, exercised, received, or suffered in place of another: *vicarious pleasure.* **2.** taking the place of another person or thing; acting or serving as a substitute. **3.** pertaining to or involving the substitution of one for another. **4.** *Physiol.* pertaining to or denoting the performance by one organ of part of the functions normally performed by another. [L *vicārius* substituted] – **vicariously,** *adv.* – **vicariousness,** *n.*

**vicarly** /'vɪkəli/, *adj.* pertaining to, resembling, or suggesting a vicar.

**vice**[1] /vaɪs/, *n.* **1.** an immoral or evil habit or practice; a grave moral fault. **2.** immoral conduct or life; indulgence in impure or degrading practices. **3.** a particular form of depravity. **4.** a fault, defect, or imperfection: *a vice of literary style.* **5.** a physical defect or infirmity: *a constitutional vice.* **6.** a bad habit, as in a horse. **7.** (*cap.*) a character in the English morality plays, a personification of general vice or of a particular vice, serving as the buffoon. [ME, from OF, from L *vitium* fault]

**vice**[2] /vaɪs/, *n.*, *v.*, **viced, vicing.** –*n.* **1.** any of various devices, usu. having two jaws which may be brought together or separated by means of a screw, lever, or the like, used to hold an object firmly while work is being done upon it. –*v.t.* **2.** to hold, press, or squeeze with or as with a vice. Also, *U.S.*, **vise.** [ME *vyse,* from OF *vis* screw, from L *vītis* vine] – **vice-like,** *adj.*

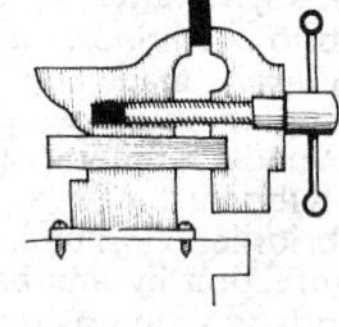
vice[2]

**vice**[3] /'vaɪsi/, *prep.* instead of; in the place of. [L, abl. of *vicis* turn]

**vice-,** a prefix denoting a substitute, deputy, or subordinate: *vice-chairman, viceroy, viceregent.* [see VICE[3]]

**vice-admiral** /vaɪs-'ædmərəl/, *n.* a naval officer next in rank below an admiral. – **vice-admiralty,** *n.*

**vice-chairman** /vaɪs-'tʃɛəmən/, *n.*, *pl.* **-men.** a member of a board, committee, or the like, immediately below the chairman in rank, and taking the place of the chairman in his absence. – **vice-chairmanship,** *n.*

**vice-chancellor** /vaɪs-'tʃænsələ, -'tʃan-/, *n.* **1.** the executive head of a university. **2.** a substitute, deputy, or subordinate chancellor. – **vice-chancellorship,** *n.*

**vice-consul** /vaɪs-'kɒnsəl/, *n.* a consular officer of a grade below that of consul. – **vice-consular** /vaɪs-'kɒnsjələ/, *adj.* – **viceconsulate** /vaɪs-'kɒnsjələt/, *n.* – **vice-consulship,** *n.*

**vicegeral** /vaɪs'dʒɛrəl/, *adj.* of a vicegerent or his position.

**vicegerency** /vaɪs'dʒɛrənsi/, *n.*, *pl.* **-cies.** **1.** the position, government, or office of a vicegerent. **2.** the territory or district under a vicegerent.

**vicegerent** /vaɪs'dʒɛrənt/, *n.* **1.** an officer deputed by a ruler or supreme head to exercise the powers of the ruler or head. **2.** any deputy. –*adj.* **3.** exercising delegated powers. **4.** characterised by delegation of powers. [ML *vicegerens,* ppr., place-holding, substituting]

**viceless** /'vaɪsləs/, *adj.* free from vices or vice.

**vicenary** /'vɪsənəri/, *adj.* pertaining to or consisting of twenty. [L *vīcēnārius*]

**vicennial** /və'sɛniəl/, *adj.* **1.** of or for twenty years. **2.** occurring every twenty years. [L *vicennium* period of twenty years + -AL[1]]

**Vice-Pres.,** Vice-President.

**vice-president** /vaɪs-'prɛzədənt/, *n.* an officer next in rank to a president and taking his place under certain conditions. – **vice-presidency,** *n.* – **vice-presidential** /ˌvaɪs-prɛzə'dɛnʃəl/, *adj.*

**viceregal** /vaɪs'rigəl/, *adj.* of or pertaining to a viceroy. – **viceregally,** *adv.*

**vice-regent** /vaɪs-'ridʒənt/, *n.* **1.** a deputy regent; one who acts in the place of a ruler, governor, or sovereign. –*adj.* **2.** of, pertaining to, or occupying the position of a vice-regent. – **vice-regency,** *n.*

**vicereine** /vaɪs'reɪn/, *n.* a viceroy's wife. [F, equivalent to *vice-* VICE- + *reine* queen]

**viceroy** /'vaɪsrɔɪ/, *n.* **1.** one appointed to rule a country or province as the deputy of the sovereign: *the viceroy of India.* **2.** anyone to whom rank or authority has been delegated. [F, from *vice-* VICE- + *roi* king] – **viceroyship,** *n.*

**viceroyalty** /vaɪs-'rɔɪəlti/, *n.*, *pl.* **-ties.** **1.** the dignity, office, or period of office of a viceroy. **2.** a country or province ruled by a viceroy.

**vice squad** /'vaɪs skwɒd/, *n.* that section of the police force concerned with enforcement of laws relating to prostitution, gambling, etc.

**vice versa** /vaɪsə 'vɜsə, vaɪs, vaɪsi/, *adv.* conversely; the order being changed (from that of a preceding statement): *A distrusts B, and vice versa.* [L]

**vichyssoise** /vɪʃi'swaz, vi-/, *n.* a creamy potato and leek soup, usu. served cold. [F]

**vichy water** /'vɪʃi wɔtə, 'viʃi/, *n.* **1.** a natural mineral water from springs, containing sodium bicarbonate, other alkaline salts, etc., used in the treatment of digestive disturbances, gout, etc. **2.** some water of similar composition, natural or artificial. Also, **Vichy, vichy.** [from *Vichy,* a town in central France]

**vicinage** /'vɪsənɪdʒ/, *n.* **1.** the vicinity; the region near or about a place. **2.** a particular neighbourhood or district, or the people belonging to it. **3.** proximity. [ME, from OF, from L *vīcīnus* near]

**vicinal** /'vɪsənəl/, *adj.* **1.** belonging to a neighbourhood or district. **2.** neighbouring; adjacent. **3.** *Crystall.* denoting planes whose position varies very little from planes of much simpler indices which they replace. **4.** *Chem.* denoting a compound in which adjacent carbon atoms have been substituted. [L *vīcīnālis* neighbouring]

**vicinity** /və'sɪnəti/, *n.*, *pl.* **-ties.** **1.** the region near or about a place; the neighbourhood or vicinage. **2.** the state or fact of being near in place; proximity; propinquity. [L *vīcīnitas*]

**vicious** /'vɪʃəs/, *adj.* **1.** addicted to or characterised by vice or immorality; depraved; profligate. **2.** given or disposed to evil; bad. **3.** reprehensible, blameworthy, or wrong, as an action, practice, etc. **4.** spiteful or malignant: *a vicious attack.* **5.** unpleasantly severe: *a vicious headache.* **6.** characterised or marred by faults or defects; faulty; defective: *vicious reasoning.* **7.** (of a horse, etc.) having bad habits or an ugly disposition. **8.** *Obs.* morbid, foul, or noxious. [ME, from L *vitiōsus* faulty] – **viciously,** *adv.* – **viciousness,** *n.*

**vicious circle** /– 'sɜkəl/, *n.* **1.** a situation in which an attempt to solve or escape from one problem creates further difficulties, and usu. exacerbates or makes chronic the original problem. **2.** *Logic.* **a.** (in demonstration) the use of one proposition to establish a second, when the second proposition is in turn used to establish the first. **b.** (in definition) the use of one term in defining a second, the second in turn being used to define the first. **3.** *Pathol.* a series of unhealthy changes in which the first change produces the second which in turn affects the first.

**vicissitude** /və'sɪsətjud/, *n.* **1.** a change or variation, or something different, occurring in the course of something. **2.** interchange or alteration, as of states or things. **3.** (*pl.*) changes, variations, successive or alternating phases or conditions, etc., in the course of anything. **4.** regular change or succession of one state or thing to another. **5.** change, mutation, or mutability. [L *vicissitūdo* change] – **vicissitudinary** /vəsɪsə'tjudənəri/, **vicissitudinous** /vəsɪsə'tjudənəs/, *adj.*

**victim** /'vɪktəm/, *n.* **1.** a sufferer from any destructive, injurious, or adverse action or agency: *victims of disease or oppression.* **2.** a dupe, as of a swindler. **3.** a person or animal sacrificed, or regarded as sacrificed. **4.** a living creature sacrificed in religious rites. [L *victima* beast for sacrifice]

**victimise** /'vɪktəmaɪz/, *v.t.*, **-mised, -mising.** **1.** to make a victim of. **2.** to discipline or punish selectively, esp. as a result of an industrial dispute: *four men were victimised by management after the strike.* **3.** to punish unfairly. **4.** to dupe, swindle, or cheat: *to victimise poor widows.* **5.** to slay as or like a sacrificial victim. Also, **victimize.** – **victimisation** /ˌvɪktəmaɪˈzeɪʃən/, *n.* – **victimiser,** *n.*

**victimless crime** /vɪktəmləs ˈkraɪm/, *n.* behaviour which has been made illegal because it offends against the mores of a society even though it involves no threat to the property or person of another, as drunkenness, vagrancy, homosexuality, etc.

**victor** /ˈvɪktə/, *n.* **1.** one who has vanquished or defeated an adversary; a conqueror. **2.** a winner in any struggle or contest. [ME, from L]

**victoria** /vɪkˈtɔriə/, *n.* **1.** a low, light, four-wheeled carriage with a folding hood, a seat for two passengers, and a perch in front for the driver. **2.** Also, **victoria plum.** a large, sweet, pinkish red variety of plum. **3.** a waterlily, *Victoria regia* (or *amazonica*), native to still waters from Paraguay to Venezuela, with leaves 1.80 m and flowers 30-45 cm across. **4.** (*cap.*) a State in south-eastern Australia, one of the six States of Australia. *Abbrev.:* Vic.

Victoria (def. 4): coat of arms

**Victoria** /vɪkˈtɔriə/, *n.* a state in south-eastern Australia. *Abbrev.:* Vic.

**Victorian** /vɪkˈtɔriən/, *adj.* **1.** of or pertaining to Queen Victoria (1819-1901, Queen of Great Britain and Ireland, 1837-1901) or her reign or period: *the Victorian age.* **2.** having the characteristics usu. attributed to the Victorians, as prudishness. **3.** of or pertaining to the State of Victoria. –*n.* **4.** a person living in the Victorian period. **5.** a person having the characteristics usu. attributed to the Victorians; a prude. **6.** one who was born in Victoria or who has come to regard it as his home State.

**Victoriana** /vɪkˌtɔriˈanə/, *n.* ornaments, bric-a-brac, etc., of the Victorian period.

**Victorianism** /vɪkˈtɔriənɪzəm/, *n.* the distinctive character, thought, tendencies, etc., of the Victorian period.

**victoria sandwich** /vɪkˌtɔriə ˈsænwɪtʃ/, *n.* a type of sponge cake made with equal quantities of fat and sugar.

**victorine** /ˈvɪktərin/, *n.* a fur tippet with long ends.

**victorious** /vɪkˈtɔriəs/, *adj.* **1.** having achieved a victory. **2.** characterised by or pertaining to victory. **3.** conquering; triumphant. – **victoriously,** *adv.* – **victoriousness,** *n.*

**victory** /ˈvɪktəri, -tri/, *n., pl.* **-ries. 1.** the ultimate and decisive superiority in a battle or any contest. **2.** a success or triumph won over the enemy in battle or war, or an engagement ending in such a triumph: *naval victories.* **3.** any success or successful performance achieved over an adversary or opponent, opposition, difficulties, etc. [ME *victorie,* from L *victōria*] – **victoryless,** *adj.*

**victress** /ˈvɪktrəs/, *n.* a female victor.

**victual** /ˈvɪtl/, *n., v.,* **-ualled, -ualling** or (*U.S.*) **-ualed, -ualing.** –*n.* **1.** (*pl.*) *Colloq.* articles of food prepared for use. **2.** *Archaic.* food or provisions, usu. for human beings. –*v.t.* **3.** to supply or store with victuals. –*v.i.* **4.** to take or obtain victuals. **5.** *Archaic.* to eat or feed. [ME *vitaile,* from OF, from LL *victuālia* provisions] – **victualless,** *adj.*

**victualler** /ˈvɪtələ, ˈvɪtlə/, *n.* **1.** one who furnishes victuals or provisions; a sutler. **2.** a supply ship. **3.** a licensed victualler. Also, *U.S.,* **victualer.**

vicuña

**vicuña** /vəˈkjunə/, *n.* **1.** a wild South American ruminant, *Lama vicugna,* of the Andes, related to the guanaco but smaller, and having a soft, delicate wool. **2.** a fabric made of this wool, or of some substitute, usu. twilled and finished with a soft nap. **3.** a garment of this fabric. [Sp., from Quechua *vicunna*]

**vid.,** see. [L *vide*]

**vide** /ˈvideɪ, ˈvaɪdi/, *v.* see (used esp. in making reference to parts of a text). [L, impv. of *vidēre* to see]

**vide ante** /– ˈænteɪ, -ti/, *v.* see before (used to direct a reader's attention to preceding material). [L]

**vide infra** /– ˈɪnfrə/, *v.* see below (used to direct a reader's attention to subsequent material). *Abbrev.:* v. inf. [L]

**videlicet** /vəˈdiləsɛt/, *adv.* namely; that is to say (used to introduce examples, details, lists, etc.). *Abbrev.:* viz. [L, for *vidēre licet* it is permitted to see]

**video** /ˈvɪdioʊ/, *adj.* **1.** *Television.* pertaining to or employed in the transmission or reception of a televised image, or to images displayed on television screens as in the video terminal of a computer. –*n.* **2.** *U.S. Colloq.* television. [L: I see]

**videoart** /ˈvɪdioʊˌat/, *n.* an art form using video equipment.

**video frequency** /vɪdioʊ ˈfrikwənsi/, *n.* the frequency of the signal which conveys the image and synchronising pulses in a television broadcasting system. *Abbrev.:* VF

**video game** /ˈ– geɪm/, *n.* an electronic game which is played on a display screen, as a television screen.

**videophone** /ˈvɪdioʊfoʊn/, *n.* a telephone which allows visual, as well as verbal, communication.

**videotape** /ˈvɪdioʊteɪp/, *n., v.,* **-taped, -taping.** –*n.* **1.** magnetic tape upon which a video-frequency signal is recorded; used for storing a television program or film. –*v.t.* **2.** to record on videotape.

**video tape recorder,** *n.* a tape recorder which records both images and sounds. Also, **video recorder.**

**video terminal** /ˈvɪdioʊ tɜmənəl/, *n.* a computer terminal in which information is displayed on a television screen.

**videotex** /ˈvɪdioʊtɛks/, *n.* any of various cable and broadcast alphanumeric and graphic data systems using video displays.

**vide post** /videɪ ˈpoʊst/, *v.* see after or afterwards (used to direct a reader's attention to later material). [L]

**vide supra** /– ˈsuprə/, *v.* see as above (used to direct the reader's attention to preceding material). *Abbrev.:* v. sup. [L]

**vidette** /vəˈdɛt/, *n.* →**vedette.**

**vidicon** /ˈvɪdikɒn/, *n.* a television camera pick-up tube in which the image is focussed on a photoconductive antimony trisulphate plate.

**vidual** /ˈvɪdʒuəl/, *adj.* of or pertaining to a widow or the state of widowhood. [L *viduālis*]

**viduity** /vəˈdjuəti/, *n.* the state of being a widow; widowhood. [ME (Scot.) *viduite,* from OF, from L *viduitas*]

**vie** /vaɪ/, *v.,* **vied, vying.** –*v.i.* **1.** to strive in competition or rivalry with another; to contend for superiority. –*v.t.* **2.** *Archaic.* to put forward or offer in competition or rivalry. **3.** *Obs.* to stake in card playing. [F *envier* challenge, from L *invītāre* invite]

**vienna** /viˈɛnə/, *n.* **1.** a smoked sausage, eaten boiled, usu. made of beef or pork. **2.** Also, **vienna loaf.** a cigar-shaped loaf of white bread. **3.** espresso coffee with whipped cream on top. [from *Vienna,* the capital of Austria]

**Viet Nam** /ˈvjɛt nam, vjɛt ˈnam/, *n.* a republic in south-east Asia. Also, **Vietnam.**

**Vietnamese** /vjɛtnəˈmiz/, *adj., n., pl.* **-ese.** –*adj.* **1.** of or pertaining to Vietnam or its inhabitants. –*n.* **2.** a native or inhabitant of Vietnam. **3.** Formerly, **Annamese, Annamite.** the official language of Vietnam. **4.** the Annamese linguistic family.

**Vietnamese matting** /– ˈmætɪŋ/, *n.* →**seagrass matting.**

**view** /vju/, *n.* **1.** a seeing or beholding; an examination by the eye. **2.** sight or vision: *exposed to view.* **3.** range of sight or vision: *objects in view.* **4.** a sight or prospect of some landscape, scene, etc. **5.** a picture of a scene. **6.** the aspect, or a particular aspect, of something. **7.** mental contemplation or examination; a mental survey. **8.** contemplation or consideration of a matter with reference to action: *a project in view.* **9.** aim, intention, or purpose. **10.** prospect or expectation: *with no view of success.* **11.** a general account or description of a subject. **12.** a particular way of regarding something. **13.** a conception, notion, or idea of a thing; an opinion or theory. **14.** a survey or inspection. **15. a dim view,** an unfavourable opinion. **16. in view, a.** within range of vision. **b.** under consideration. **c.** near to realisation. **17. in view of, a.** in sight of. **b.** in prospect or anticipation of. **c.** in consideration of. **d.** on account of. **18. on view,** in a place for public inspection; on exhibition. **19. with a view to, a.** with an aim or intention directed to. **b.** with an expectation or hope of. **c.** in consideration of. **d.** with regard to. *–v.t.* **20.** to see or behold. **21.** to watch (a television program). **22.** to look at, survey, or inspect. **23.** to contemplate mentally; consider. **24.** to regard in a particular light or as specified. **25.** *Hunting.* to sight (a hunted animal). *–v.i.* **26.** to inspect a prospective purchase or the like. **27.** to watch television or a television program. [ME *vewe,* from AF, var. of *veue,* pp. of *veoir* see, from L *vidēre*]

**viewable** /'vjuəbəl/, *adj.* **1.** able to be viewed; visible. **2.** ready to be inspected: *the house is viewable now.*

**viewdata** /'vjudeɪtə/, *n.* a one-way or interactive data service delivered by telephone cable.

**viewer** /'vjuə/, *n.* **1.** one who or that which views. **2.** one who watches television or a television program. **3.** a device for viewing photographic transparencies.

**viewfinder** /'vjufaɪndə/, *n.* an attachment to a camera enabling the photographer to determine what will be included in his picture.

**viewless** /'vjuləs/, *adj.* **1.** that cannot be viewed or seen; invisible. **2.** without views or opinions. **3.** not having a pleasant view, or having no view at all. **– viewlessly,** *adv.*

**viewpoint** /'vjupɔɪnt/, *n.* **1.** a place affording a view of something. **2.** a point of view; an attitude of mind: *the viewpoint of an artist.*

**vigesimal** /vaɪ'dʒɛsəməl/, *adj.* **1.** pertaining to or based upon twenty. **2.** twentieth. **3.** proceeding by twenties. [L *vīgēsimus* twentieth + -AL[1]]

**vigesimo** /vaɪ'dʒɛsəmoʊ/, *n., pl.* **-mos,** *adj. Bookbinding.* *–n.* **1.** a volume printed from sheets folded to form 20 leaves or 40 pages, approximately 7 × 13 cm. *Abbrev.:* 20mo or 20°. *–adj.* **2.** in vigesimo. Also, **twentymo.** [L, abl. sing. of *vīgēsimus* twentieth]

**vigesimo-quarto** /vaɪˌdʒɛsəmoʊ-'kwɔtoʊ/, *n., pl.* **-tos,** *adj. Bookbinding. –n.* **1.** a volume printed from sheets folded to form 24 leaves or 48 pages. *Abbrev.:* 24mo or 24°. *–adj.* **2.** in vigesimo-quarto. Also, **twenty-fourmo.** [L, abl. sing. of *vīgēsimus-quartus* twenty-fourth]

**vigia** /və'dʒɪə/, *n. Naut.* **1.** a mark on a navigational chart indicating a hazard or supposed hazard, the precise location and nature of which is uncertain. **2.** an unidentified object sighted in the water and regarded as a possible hazard to navigation. [Sp.: lookout, reef; akin to VIGILANT]

**vigil** /'vɪdʒəl/, *n.* **1.** a keeping awake for any purpose during the normal hours of sleep. **2.** a watch kept by night or at other times; a course or period of watchful attention. **3.** a period of wakefulness from inability to sleep. **4.** *Eccles.* **a.** a devotional watching, or keeping awake, during the customary hours of sleep. **b.** (*oft. pl.*) a nocturnal devotional exercise or service, esp. on the eve before a church festival. **c.** the eve, or day and night, before a church festival, esp. an eve which is a fast. [ME *vigile,* from AF, from L *vigilia* watch]

**vigilance** /'vɪdʒələns/, *n.* **1.** the quality or fact of being vigilant; watchfulness. **2.** *Pathol.* insomnia.

**vigilance committee** /'– kəˌmɪti/, *n.* **1.** a committee of a trade union organised to ensure that award conditions of employment are maintained. **2.** *Chiefly U.S.* an unauthorised committee of citizens organised for the maintenance of order and the summary punishment of crime in the absence of regular or efficient courts.

**vigilance man** /'– mæn/, *n. U.S.* →**vigilante.**

**vigilant** /'vɪdʒələnt/, *adj.* **1.** keenly attentive to detect danger; wary: *a vigilant sentry.* **2.** ever awake and alert; sleeplessly watchful. [late ME, from L *vigilans* watching] **– vigilantly,** *adv.* **– vigilantness,** *n.*

**vigilante** /vɪdʒə'lænti/, *n. Chiefly U.S.* a member of a vigilance committee. [Sp.: vigilant]

**vigneron** /'vɪnjərən/, *n.* a wine-grower. [F]

**vignette** /vɪn'jɛt/, *n., v.,* **-gnetted, -gnetting.** *–n.* **1.** a decorative design or small illustration used on the title-page of a book, or at the beginning or end of a chapter. **2.** an engraving, drawing, photograph, or the like, shading off gradually at the edges; a design without a borderline. **3.** decorative work representing meandering branches, leaves, or tendrils, as in architecture or in manuscripts. **4.** any small, pleasing picture or view. **5.** a small, graceful literary sketch. *–v.t.* **6.** to finish (a picture, photograph, etc.) in the manner of a vignette. [F, diminutive of *vigne* vine] **– vignettist,** *n.*

**vignetter** /vɪn'jɛtə/, *n.* a device for shading off the edges of a photographic print into a plain margin.

**vignetting** /vɪn'jɛtɪŋ/, *n.* a reduction in intensity of the light transmitted through an optical system at the edges of the field of view, because of the interference by the aperture with light rays which are not axial. In photography, it may cause gradual shading off at the edges of the print.

**vigoro** /'vɪgəroʊ/, *n.* a team game with 12 players a side, combining elements of baseball and cricket. [? from VIGOUR]

**vigoroso** /vɪgə'roʊsoʊ/, *adj.* (in music) vigorous or spirited in manner. [It.]

**vigorous** /'vɪgərəs/, *adj.* **1.** full of or characterised by vigour. **2.** strong and active; robust. **3.** energetic or forcible. **4.** powerful in action or effect. **5.** growing well, as a plant. [ME, from ML *vigorōsus*] **– vigorously,** *adv.* **– vigorousness,** *n.*

**vigour** /'vɪgə/, *n.* **1.** active strength or force, as of body or mind. **2.** healthy physical or mental energy or power. **3.** energy; energetic activity. **4.** force of healthy growth in any living matter or organism, as a plant. **5.** active or effective force. Also, *U.S.,* **vigor.** [ME, from OF, from L *vigor*]

**Viking** /'vaɪkɪŋ/, *n.* (*sometimes l.c.*) a Scandinavian rover or sea-robber of the type that infested the seas about northern and western Europe during the 8th, 9th, and 10th centuries, making raids upon the coasts. [Icel. *víkingr* free-booter, pirate, c. OE *wīcing*]

**vile** /vaɪl/, *adj.,* **viler, vilest. 1.** wretchedly bad: *vile weather.* **2.** highly offensive, obnoxious, or objectionable. **3.** repulsive or disgusting, as to the senses or feelings; despicably or revoltingly bad. **4.** morally base, depraved, or despicable, as persons or the mind, character, actions, etc.: *vile thoughts.* **5.** foul, as language. **6.** poor or wretched, as in quality or state. **7.** of mean or low condition, as a person. **8.** mean or menial, as tasks, etc. **9.** low, degraded, or ignominious, as a condition, etc.: *vile servitude.* **10.** of little value or account; paltry. [ME, from AF, from L *vīlis* cheap, base] **– vilely,** *adv.* **– vileness,** *n.*

**vilify** /'vɪləfaɪ/, *v.t.,* **-fied, -fying. 1.** to speak evil of; defame; traduce. **2.** *Obs.* to make vile. [ME, from LL *vīlificāre*] **– vilification** /vɪləfə'keɪʃən/, *n.* **– vilifier,** *n.*

**vilipend** /'vɪləpɛnd/, *v.t.* **1.** to regard or treat as of little value or account. **2.** to vilify. [late ME, from L *vīlipendere,* from *vīli(s)* vile + *pendere* consider] **– vilipender,** *n.*

**villa** /'vɪlə/, *n.* **1.** a country residence, usu. of some size and pretensions, esp. one in a Mediterranean country. **2.** a suburban house of pseudo-Spanish style. **3.** a large house in the suburbs or at a resort. **4.** an ancient Roman rural dwelling associated with agriculture, usu. one built round a courtyard. **5.** *Chiefly Brit.* a detached or semidetached dwelling house, usu. suburban. [L or It.: country house]

**village** /'vɪlɪdʒ/, *n.* **1.** a small assemblage of houses in a country district, larger than a hamlet and smaller than a town. **2.** the inhabitants collectively. **3.** an assemblage of animal dwellings or the like, resembling a village. **4.** a group of small, sometimes fashionable and exclusive shops, servicing a suburb. **5.** *U.S.* a small municipality. *–adj.* **6.** of, belonging to, or characteristic of a village; rustic. [ME, from OF, from *ville,* from L *villa* villa] **– villageless,** *adj.*

**village community** /– kə'mjunəti/, *n.* an early form of organisation, in which the land belonged to the village, the arable land being allotted by it to the members or households of the community, by more or less permanent arrangements, the waste or common land remaining undivided.

**villager** /'vɪlədʒə/, *n.* **1.** an inhabitant of a village. **2.** a rustic.

**villa home** /'vɪlə hoʊm/, *n.* a house of the terrace type, usu. single storey and built down the depth of the allotment, joined to the next villa by a garage. Also, **villa unit.**

**villain** /ˈvɪlən/, *n.* **1.** a wicked person; scoundrel. **2.** a character in a play, novel, or the like, who constitutes an important evil agency in the plot. **3.** *Colloq.* a criminal. **4.** a villein. [ME, from OF, from L *villānus* farm servant] – **villainess** /vɪləˈnɛs/, *n. fem.*

**villainage** /ˈvɪlənɪdʒ/, *n.* →**villeinage.** Also, **villanage.**

**villainous** /ˈvɪlənəs/, *adj.* **1.** having the character of a villain. **2.** pertaining to or befitting a villain. **3.** base; wicked; vile. **4.** very bad or unpleasant: *villainous weather.* – **villainously,** *adv.* – **villainousness,** *n.*

**villainy** /ˈvɪləni/, *n., pl.* **-nies. 1.** the action or conduct of a villain or scoundrel. **2.** a villainous act or deed. **3.** *Obs.* →**villeinage.**

**villanella** /vɪləˈnɛlə/, *n.* an Italian rustic part-song without accompaniment. [It.: rustic, diminutive of *villano* peasant, from *villa* villa]

**villanelle** /vɪləˈnɛl/, *n.* a short poem of fixed form, written in tercets (usu. five) with a final quatrain, all based on two rhymes. [F, from It. See VILLANELLA]

**Villanovan** /vɪləˈnoʊvən/, *adj.* **1.** denoting or pertaining to an early Iron Age culture in northern Italy, characterised by lake dwellings and the primitive use of iron and extensive use of bronze in the 9th century B.C. *–n.* **2.** this culture. **3.** a member of the people which founded this culture. [named after *Villanova,* near Bologna, Italy, where the first remains were found in 1853]

**villatic** /vəˈlætɪk/, *adj.* of or pertaining to a farm; rural. [L *villāticus,* from *villa* villa]

**villa unit** /ˈvɪlə junət/, *n.* →**villa home.**

**-ville,** *Chiefly U.S.* a combining form indicating a fictitious city, usu. specified as to type or kind, as *dullsville.*

**villein** /ˈvɪlən/, *n.* a member of a class of half-free persons under the feudal system who were serfs with respect to their lord but had the rights and privileges of freemen with respect to others. Also, **villain.** [var. of VILLAIN]

**villeinage** /ˈvɪlənɪdʒ/, *n.* **1.** the tenure by which a villein held land and tenements from his lord. **2.** the condition or status of a villein. Also, **villainage, villanage, villenage.** [ME, from OF. See VILLAIN, -AGE]

**villi** /ˈvɪlaɪ/, *n.* plural of **villus.**

**villiform** /ˈvɪləfɔm/, *adj.* **1.** having the form of a villus. **2.** so shaped and closely set as to resemble the pile of velvet, as the teeth of certain fishes. [NL *villiformis.* See VILLUS, -FORM]

**villosity** /vəˈlɒsəti/, *n., pl.* **-ties. 1.** a villous surface or coating. **2.** a number of villi together. **3.** a villus.

**villous** /ˈvɪləs/, *adj.* **1.** covered with or of the nature of villi. **2.** abounding in villiform processes. **3.** *Bot.* pubescent with long and soft hairs which are not interwoven. Also, **villose.** [L *villōsus* hairy] – **villously,** *adv.*

**villus** /ˈvɪləs/, *n., pl.* **villi** /ˈvɪlaɪ/. **1.** *Anat.* one of the minute, wormlike, vascular processes on certain animal membranes, esp. on the mucous membrane of the small intestine, where they serve in absorbing nutriment. **2.** *Bot.* one of the long, soft, straight hairs covering the fruit, flowers, and other parts of certain plants. [L: tuft of hair, shaggy hair]

**vim** /vɪm/, *n. Colloq.* force; energy; vigour in action. [L, acc. of *vīs*]

**vimen** /ˈvaɪmən/, *n., pl.* **vimina** /ˈvɪmənə/. a long, flexible shoot of a plant. [L: twig] – **viminal** /ˈvɪmənəl/, *adj.*

**vimineous** /vəˈmɪniəs/, *adj. Bot.* **1.** of, like, or producing long, flexible shoots. **2.** of or made of twigs. [L *vīmineus* made of twigs]

**v. imp.,** verb impersonal.

**vina** /ˈvinə/, *n.* an Indian musical instrument with numerous strings stretched over a long, sticklike fingerboard with movable frets, to which up to three gourds are attached to increase resonance. [Skt]

**vinaceous** /vaɪˈneɪʃəs, və-/, *adj.* **1.** relating to, or resembling, wine or grapes. **2.** wine-coloured. [L *vīnāceus*]

**vinaigrette** /vɪnəˈgrɛt/, *n.* **1.** Also, **vinegarette.** a small ornamental bottle or box for holding aromatic vinegar, smelling salts, or the like. *–adj.* **2.** served with a vinaigrette sauce. [F, from *vinaigre* VINEGAR + *-ette* -ETTE]

**vinaigrette sauce** /– ˈsɔs/, *n.* a cold, tart sauce of oil, vinegar, seasonings, and herbs.

**vinasse** /vəˈnæs/, *n.* the residuum in a still after distillation, esp. the residual liquid obtained after the distillation of beetroot molasses which is used as a source of potassium carbonate. [F, from Pr. *vinassa,* from L *vīnācea* grapeskin]

**Vincent's angina** /ˌvɪnsənts ænˈdʒaɪnə/, *n.* a disease characterised by ulceration of the mucosa of the tonsils, pharynx, and mouth, and the development of a membrane, caused by a bacillus and a spirillum; trench mouth. Also, **Vincent's infection.** [named after J.H. *Vincent,* 1862-1950, French physician]

**vincible** /ˈvɪnsəbəl/, *adj. Rare.* capable of being conquered or overcome. [L *vincibilis*] – **vincibility** /vɪnsəˈbɪləti/, **vincibleness,** *n.*

**vinculum** /ˈvɪŋkjələm/, *n., pl.* **-la** /-lə/. **1.** a bond or union; a tie. **2.** *Maths.* a stroke or brace drawn over a quantity consisting of several members or terms, as $\overline{a+b}$, in order to connect them and show that they are to be considered together. [L: fetter]

**vindaloo** /vɪndəˈlu/, *adj.* **1.** of or pertaining to a sour Indian dish flavoured with hot indigenous spices of India, esp. vinegar: *chicken vindaloo.* *–n.* **2.** such a dish.

**vindicable** /ˈvɪndəkəbəl/, *adj.* that may be vindicated. – **vindicability** /vɪndəkəˈbɪləti/, *n.*

**vindicate** /ˈvɪndəkeɪt/, *v.t.,* **-cated, -cating. 1.** to clear, as from a charge, imputation, suspicion, or the like. **2.** to afford justification for: *subsequent events vindicated his policy.* **3.** to uphold or justify by argument or evidence. **4.** to assert, maintain, or defend (a right, cause, etc.) against opposition. **5.** to lay claim to, for oneself or another. **6.** *Rom. and Civil Law.* to regain possession, under claim of title of property through legal procedure or to assert one's right to its possession. **7.** *Obs.* to deliver from something. **8.** *Obs.* to avenge, revenge, or punish. [L *vindicātus,* pp., set free, punished] – **vindicator,** *n.*

**vindication** /vɪndəˈkeɪʃən/, *n.* **1.** the act of vindicating. **2.** the state of being vindicated. **3.** defence or justification. **4.** something that vindicates: *the success of his plan was the real vindication.*

**vindicatory** /vɪndəˈkeɪtəri, ˈvɪndəkətri/, *adj.* **1.** serving to vindicate. **2.** justificatory. **3.** punitive; retributive. Also, **vindicative** /vɪnˈdɪkətɪv/.

**vindictive** /vɪnˈdɪktɪv/, *adj.* **1.** disposed or inclined to revenge; revengeful: *a vindictive person.* **2.** proceeding from or showing a revengeful spirit. [L *vindicta* vengeance + -IVE] – **vindictively,** *adv.* – **vindictiveness,** *n.*

**vine** /vaɪn/, *n.* **1.** a long, slender stem that trails or creeps on the ground or climbs by winding itself about a support or holding fast with tendrils or claspers. **2.** a plant bearing such a stem. **3.** any of the climbing plants constituting the genus *Vitis,* having a woody stem and bearing grapes, esp. *V. vinifera,* the common European species; a grapevine. [ME, from OF, from L *vinea*] – **vineless,** *adj.* – **vinelike,** *adj.*

**vinedresser** /ˈvaɪndrɛsə/, *n.* one who dresses, trims, or cultivates vines, esp. grapevines.

**vinegar** /ˈvɪnɪgə, -nə-/, *n.* **1.** a sour liquid consisting of dilute and impure acetic acid, obtained by acetous fermentation from wine, cider, beer, ale, or the like, and used as a condiment, preservative, etc. **2.** *Pharm.* a solution of a medicinal substance in dilute acetic acid, or vinegar. **3.** sour or crabbed speech, temper, or countenance. *–v.t.* **4.** to apply vinegar to. [ME *vinegre,* from OF, from *vin* wine + *egre* sour] – **vinegar-like,** *adj.*

**vinegar eel** /ˈvɪnɪgər il/, *n.* a minute nematode worm, *Anguillula aceti,* found in vinegar, etc. Also, **vinegar worm.**

**vinegarette** /vɪnɪgəˈrɛt, -nə-/, *n.* →**vinaigrette.**

**vinegar fly** /ˈvɪnɪgə flaɪ/, *n.* any fly of the genus *Drosophila,* esp. *D. melanogaster;* fruit-fly.

**vinegarish** /ˈvɪnɪgərɪʃ, -nə-/, *adj.* slightly sour; resembling vinegar.

**vinegar-plant** /ˈvɪnɪgə-plænt, -nə-/, *n.* a bacterium, *Acetobacter xylinum,* causing acetic fermentation.

**vinegarroon** /vɪnɪgəˈrun, -nə-/, *n.* a large whip scorpion, *Thelyphonus giganteus,* of the southern U.S., etc., which emits a vinegar-like smell when alarmed. [Sp. *vinagrón,* from *vinagre* vinegar]

**vinegary** /ˈvɪnɪgəri, -nə-/, *adj.* **1.** of the nature of or resembling vinegar; sour. **2.** ill-natured, as a person.

**vinery** /ˈvaɪnəri/, *n., pl.* **-eries.** **1.** a vineyard. **2.** *U.S.* vines collectively.

**vineyard** /ˈvɪnjəd/, *n.* a plantation of grapevines, for producing grapes for wine-making, etc. [ME; from VINE + YARD²] – **vineyardist,** *n.*

**vingt-et-un** /vænt-eɪ-ˈɜn/, *n.* →**pontoon**². [F: lit., twenty-one]

**vinic** /ˈvaɪnɪk, ˈvɪnɪk/, *adj.* of, pertaining to, found in, or extracted from wine. [L *vīnum* wine + -IC]

**viniculture** /ˈvɪnikʌltʃə/, *n.* **1.** the cultivation of the vine. **2.** the study or science of wine-making. [*vini-* (combining form of L *vīnum* wine) + CULTURE] – **vinicultural** /vɪniˈkʌltʃərəl/, *adj.* – **viniculturist** /vɪniˈkʌltʃərəst/, *n.*

**viniferous** /vəˈnɪfərəs/, *adj.* producing wine.

**vinification** /vɪnəfəˈkeɪʃən/, *n.* the process of wine making.

**vinificator** /ˈvɪnəfəkeɪtə/, *n.* a condenser for alcohol vapours escaping from fermenting wine. [*vini-* (combining form of L *vīnum* wine) + L *-ficātor* maker]

**vino** /ˈvinoʊ/, *n. Colloq.* wine. [It.]

**vinometer** /vəˈnɒmətə, vaɪ-/, *n.* a hydrometer for measuring the percentage of alcohol in wine. [*vino-* (combining form representing L *vīnum* wine) + -METER¹]

**vin ordinaire** /væn ɔdəˈnɛə/, *n.* a cheap wine generally for popular consumption. [F: common wine]

**vinosity** /vəˈnɒsəti, vaɪ-/, *n.* the essential quality or heart of the wine.

**vinous** /ˈvaɪnəs/, *adj.* **1.** having the nature of or resembling wine. **2.** pertaining to or characteristic of wine. **3.** produced by, indicative of, or given to indulgence in wine. **4.** wine-coloured; wine-red. [L *vīnōsus*]

**vintage** /ˈvɪntɪdʒ/, *n., adj., v.,* **-taged, -taging.** *–n.* **1.** the wine from a particular harvest or crop. **2.** the annual produce of the grape harvest, esp. with reference to the wine obtained: *a luxuriant vintage.* **3.** an exceptionally fine wine from the crop of a good year, designated and sold as the produce of that year. **4.** wine, esp. good wine. **5.** the act of gathering ripe grapes. **6.** the season of gathering grapes, or of wine-making. **7.** wine-making. **8.** *Colloq.* the crop or output of anything: *a hat of last year's vintage.* *–adj.* **9.** of or pertaining to wine or wine-making. **10.** (of wines) designated and sold as the produce of a specified year. **11.** of high quality; exceptionally fine: *the actor gave a vintage performance last night.* **12.** denoting or pertaining to a motor vehicle built between 1918 and 1930, or a racing car more than ten years old. **13.** old-fashioned; out of date. *–v.t.* **14.** to gather (grapes) for wine-making. **15.** to make (wine, esp. vintage wine) from grapes gathered. [late ME, from AF, b. *vinter* VINTNER and *vendage,* OF *vendange* (from L *vindēmia* grape gathering)]

**vintager** /ˈvɪntɪdʒə/, *n.* one who gathers harvest grapes.

**vintner** /ˈvɪntnə/, *n.* a dealer in wine; a wine merchant. [late ME *vyntenere,* alteration of ME *viniter,* from AF. Cf. ML *vīnetārius* wine-seller]

**vinum** /ˈvaɪnəm/, *n.* a solution of a medicinal substance in wine. [special use of L *vīnum* wine]

**viny** /ˈvaɪni/, *adj.,* **-nier, -niest.** **1.** pertaining to, of the nature of, or resembling vines. **2.** abounding in or producing vines.

**vinyl** /ˈvaɪnəl/, *n.* **1.** *Chem.* the univalent radical $CH_2$:CH, derived from ethylene, compounds of which undergo polymerisation to form high-molecular-weight plastics and resins. **2.** →**vinylite.** [L *vinum* wine + -YL]

**vinyl acetate** /– ˈæsəteɪt/, *n.* a colourless, easily polymerised fluid, $CH_3COOCH{=}CH_2$, used in the plastics industry.

**vinyl chloride** /– ˈklɔraɪd/, *n.* an inflammable gas, $CH_2CHCl$, widely used in the plastics industry.

**vinylidene** /vaɪˈnɪlədin/, *n.* the bivalent radical $CH_2$:C:, derived from ethylene, polymerised compounds of which are used in plastics and resins. [VINYL + -ID³ + -ENE]

**vinylidene chloride** /– ˈklɔraɪd/, *n.* a colourless liquid, $CH_2{=}CCl_2$, which is widely used in the plastics industry to form a copolymer, esp. with vinyl chloride.

**vinylite** /ˈvaɪnəlaɪt/, *n.* **1.** a synthetic, thermoplastic substance used in the manufacture of moulded plastic ware, esp. gramophone records. **2.** (*cap.*) a trademark for this substance. Also, **vinyl.**

**vinyl polymers** /vaɪnəl ˈpɒləməz/, *n.pl.* a group of compounds derived from vinyl compounds such as vinyl acetate, styrene, etc., by polymerisation.

**vinyl tile** /– ˈtaɪl/, *n.* a tile made out of vinyl, used in kitchens, bathrooms, etc.

**viol** /ˈvaɪəl/, *n.* a bowed musical instrument, differing from the violin in having deeper ribs, sloping shoulders, a greater number of strings (usu. 6) and frets, common in the 16th and 17th centuries in various sizes from the **treble viol** to the **bass viol.** [earlier *viole,* from F; replacing late ME *vyell,* from F *vielle;* ? both from ML *vitula, vidula*]

**viola**¹ /viˈoʊlə/, *n.* **1.** a four-stringed musical instrument of the violin family, slightly larger than the violin; a tenor or alto violin. **2.** a labial organ stop of 8-foot or 4-foot pitch, giving notes of a penetrating stringlike quality. [It. See VIOL]

**viola**² /ˈvaɪələ, vaɪˈoʊlə/, *n.* **1.** any of a genus of plants, *Viola,* including the violet and the pansy, bearing irregular flowers on axillary peduncles. **2.** a pansy, *V. cornuta,* cultivated as a garden plant. [L: violet]

**violable** /ˈvaɪələbəl/, *adj.* that may be violated. [L *violābilis*] – **violability** /vaɪələˈbɪləti/, **violableness,** *n.* – **violably,** *adv.*

**violaceous** /vaɪəˈleɪʃəs/, *adj.* **1.** belonging to the Violaceae, or violet family of plants. **2.** of a violet colour; bluish purple. [L *violāceus* violet-coloured]

**viola da braccio** /vioʊlə də ˈbratʃioʊ/, *n.* an old musical instrument of the viol family, held against the shoulder like a violin, superseded by the modern viola. [It.: lit., viol for the arm]

**viola da gamba** /vioʊlə də ˈgæmbə/, *n.* **1.** an old musical instrument of the viol family, superseded by the modern cello, held between the knees and having a range approximately that of the cello; bass viol. **2.** an organ stop of 8-foot pitch giving a stringlike tone. [It.: lit., viol for the leg]

**viola d'amore** /vioʊlə dˈəˈmɔreɪ/, *n.* a viol with numerous sympathetic strings (in addition to several gut strings), producing a characteristic silvery tone. [It.: lit., viol of love]

viola da gamba

**violate** /ˈvaɪəleɪt/, *v.,* **-lated, -lating,** *adj.* *–v.t.* **1.** to break, infringe, or transgress (a law, rule, agreement, promise, instructions, etc.). **2.** to break in upon or disturb rudely: *to violate privacy, peace, or a peaceful spot.* **3.** to break through or pass by force or without right: *to violate a frontier.* **4.** to do violence to. **5.** to deal with or treat in a violent or irreverent way; desecrate or profane: *to violate a temple or an altar.* **6.** to rape (esp. a woman). *–adj.* **7.** *Archaic.* defiled; violated. [late ME, from L *violātus,* pp.] – **violator,** *n.*

**violation** /vaɪəˈleɪʃən/, *n.* **1.** the act of violating. **2.** the state of being violated. **3.** a breach, infringement, or transgression, as of a law, promise, etc. **4.** desecration. **5.** ravishment or rape. **6.** *Obs.* the act of treating with violence. [ME, from L *violātio*]

**violative** /ˈvaɪələtɪv/, *adj. Chiefly U.S.* pertaining to or involving violation.

**violence** /ˈvaɪələns/, *n.* **1.** rough force in action: *the violence of the wind.* **2.** rough or injurious action or treatment: *to die of violence.* **3.** any unjust or unwarranted exertion of force or power, as against rights, laws, etc.; injury; wrong; outrage. **4.** a violent act or proceeding. **5.** rough or immoderate vehemence, as of feeling or language; fury; intensity; severity. **6.** a distortion of meaning or fact. [ME, from OF, from L *violentia* vehemence]

**violent** /ˈvaɪələnt/, *adj.* **1.** acting with or characterised by uncontrolled, strong, rough force: *a violent blow, explosion, tempest, etc.* **2.** acting with, characterised by, or due to injurious or destructive force: *violent measures, a violent death.* **3.** intense in force, effect, etc.; severe; extreme: *violent heat, pain, contrast, etc.* **4.** roughly or immoderately vehement, ardent, or passionate: *violent feeling.* **5.** furious in impetuosity, energy, etc.: *violent haste.* [ME, from L *violentus*] – **violently,** *adv.*

**violent storm** /– ˈstɔm/, *n. Meteorol.* a wind of Beaufort scale force 11, i.e. with average windspeed of 103-117 km/h.

**violescent** /vaɪəˈlɛsənt/, *adj.* tending to a violet colour. [L *viola* violet + -ESCENT]

**violet** /ˈvaɪələt/, *n.* **1.** any plant of the genus *Viola,* comprising chiefly low, stemless or leafy-stemmed herbs with purple, blue, yellow, white, or variegated flowers, as *V. hederacea,* and *V. odorata,* the much cultivated **English violet. 2.** any of various similar plants of other genera, as the fringed violet. **3.** a bluish purple colour. **4. shrinking violet,** *Colloq.* a shy or retiring person. *–adj.* **5.** of the colour called violet; bluish purple. [ME, from OF *violete,* from L *viola*] – **violet-like,** *adj.*

violet

**violet ray** /– ˈreɪ/, *n.* light of the shortest visible wavelength.

**violet wood** /– ˈwʊd/, *n.* →**kingwood.**

**violin** /vaɪəˈlɪn/, *n.* **1.** the treble of the family of modern bowed instruments, which is held nearly horizontal by the player's arm, with the lower part supported against the collarbone or shoulder; a fiddle. **2.** a violinist. [It. *violino,* diminutive of *viola* viol] – **violinless,** *adj.*

**violinist** /vaɪəˈlɪnəst/, *n.* a player on the violin.

**violin-maker** /vaɪəˈlɪn-meɪkə/, *n.* one who designs and builds violins and instruments of the violin family.

violin

**violist** /ˈvaɪələst/, *n.* a player on the viol.

**violoncellist** /vaɪələnˈtʃɛləst/, *n.* →**cellist.**

**violoncello** /vaɪələnˈtʃɛloʊ/, *n., pl.* **-los, -li** /-li/. →**cello.** [It., diminutive of *violone* bass viol]

**violone** /ˈvaɪəloʊn/, *n.* **1.** a member of the viol family played in the 18th century, intermediate between the double bass viol and the modern double bass. **2.** a sixteen-foot organ pedal stop, resembling the cello. [It., augmentative of *viola* viol]

**V.I.P.** /vi aɪ ˈpi/, *n. Colloq.* very important person.

**viper** /ˈvaɪpə/, *n.* **1.** any of the Old World venomous snakes of the genus *Vipera,* esp. *V. berus,* a small European species; the adder. **2.** any snake of the highly venomous family Viperidae, confined to the Old World and including the common vipers, the puff adder, and various other types, all characterised by erectile venom-conducting fangs. **3.** any of various venomous or supposedly venomous snakes of allied or other genera, as the **horned viper,** *Cerastes cornutus,* a venomous species of Egypt, Palestine, etc., with a horny process above each eye. **4.** a venomous, malignant, or spiteful person. **5.** a false or treacherous person. [L *vīpera,* for *vīvipera,* from *vīvi-* (combining form of *vīvus*) + *-pera* bringing forth (vipers were formerly thought to be viviparous)] – **viper-like,** *adj.*

**viperine** /ˈvaɪpəraɪn/, *adj.* of or like a viper.

**viperish** /ˈvaɪpərɪʃ/, *adj.* viper-like; viperous.

**viperous** /ˈvaɪpərəs/, *adj.* **1.** of the nature of a viper or vipers; viper-like. **2.** pertaining to vipers. **3.** characteristic of vipers. **4.** venomous or malignant. – **viperously,** *adv.*

**viper's bugloss** /vaɪpəz ˈbjuglɒs/, *n.* a bristly weed, *Echium vulgare,* with showy blue flowers; blueweed, blue borage.

**virago** /vəˈragoʊ/, *n., pl.* **-goes, -gos. 1.** a turbulent, violent, or ill-tempered, scolding woman; a shrew. **2.** a woman of masculine strength or spirit. [ME and OE, from L: manlike woman] – **viraginous** /vəˈrædʒənəs/, *adj.* – **virago-like,** *adj.*

**viral** /ˈvaɪrəl/, *adj.* pertaining to or caused by a virus.

**viral meningitis** /– mɛnənˈdʒaɪtəs/, *n.* meningitis associated with a viral infection.

**virelay** /ˈvɪrəleɪ/, *n.* **1.** an old French form of short poem, with short lines running on two rhymes, and having two opening lines recurring at intervals. **2.** any of various similar or other forms of poem, as one consisting of stanzas made up of longer and shorter lines, the lines of each kind rhyming together in each stanza, with the rhyme of the shorter lines of one stanza forming the rhyme of the longer lines of the next stanza. Also, *French,* **virelai.** [ME, from OF, from *virel(i)* dance + *lai* song]

**virescence** /vəˈrɛsəns/, *n.* the state of becoming green,

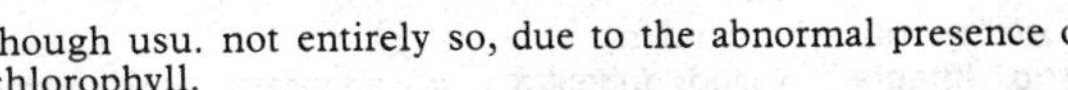

though usu. not entirely so, due to the abnormal presence of chlorophyll.

**virescent** /vəˈrɛsənt/, *adj.* **1.** turning green. **2.** tending to a green colour; slightly greenish. [L *virescens,* ppr.]

**virga** /ˈvɜgə/, *n.* rain or snow that is dissipated in falling and does not reach the ground, commonly appearing in trails descending from a cloud layer. [L: twig, streak]

**virgate**[1] /ˈvɜgət, -geɪt/, *adj.* shaped like a rod or wand; long, slender, and straight. [L *virgātus*]

**virgate**[2] /ˈvɜgət, -geɪt/, *n.* an early English measure of land of varying extent, generally regarded as having been equivalent to a quarter of a hide, or about 12 hectares. [ML *virgāta,* short for *virgāta terrae* (translation of OE *geard landes,* lit., yard of land)]

**virgin** /ˈvɜdʒən/, *n.* **1.** a woman, esp. a young woman, who has had no sexual intercourse. **2.** a girl, young woman, or unmarried woman. **3.** *Eccles.* (usu. of saints) an unmarried religious woman. **4. the Virgin,** Mary, the mother of Christ (often called **the Blessed Virgin**). **5.** (*cap.*) any representation of the Virgin, esp. a statue or statuette. **6.** any female animal that has not copulated. **7.** a youth or man who has not had sexual intercourse. **8.** an unfertilised insect. **9.** (*cap.*) the zodiacal constellation or sign Virgo. *–adj.* **10.** being a virgin: *Virgin Mother.* **11.** consisting of virgins. **12.** pertaining to, characteristic of, or befitting a virgin. **13.** resembling or suggesting a virgin; pure; unsullied; undefiled: *virgin snow.* **14.** without admixture, alloy, or modification: *virgin gold.* **15.** untouched, untried, or unused: *virgin bush, virgin soil.* **16.** *Zool.* unfertilised. **17.** *Metall.* made directly from ore or from first smelting. **18.** denoting the oil obtained as from olives, etc., by the first pressing without the application of heat. **19.** *Physics.* (of a neutron) not having experienced a collision of any kind. [ME *virgine,* from OF, from L *virgo* maiden]

**virginal**[1] /ˈvɜdʒənəl/, *adj.* **1.** of, pertaining to, characteristic of, or befitting a virgin. **2.** continuing in a state of virginity. **3.** pure or unsullied; untouched; fresh. **4.** *Zool.* unfertilised. [L *virginālis* maidenly] – **virginally,** *adv.*

**virginal**[2] /ˈvɜdʒənəl/, *n.* Also, **virginals, pair of virginals. 1.** a small harpsichord of rectangular shape, with the strings stretched parallel to the keyboard, the earlier types placed on a table, common in the 16th and 17th centuries. **2.** (loosely) any harpsichord. [apparently special use of VIRGINAL[1]] – **virginalist,** *n.*

virginal[2]

*n.*

**virgin birth** /vɜdʒən ˈbɜθ/, *n.* **1.** *Theol.* the doctrine or dogma that the birth of Christ did not, by the miraculous agency of God, impair or prejudice the virginity of Mary. Cf. **Immaculate Conception. 2.** *Zool.* parthenogenesis; a birth resulting from a female who has not copulated.

**Virginia creeper** /vəˌdʒɪniə ˈkripə/, *n.* a climbing plant, *Parthenocissus quinquefolia,* and other species of *Parthenocissus,* of North America and elsewhere, having palmate leaves, usu. with five leaflets, and bluish-black berries.

**Virginia deer** /– ˈdɪə/, *n.* **1.** the common white-tailed deer, *Odocoileus virginianus,* of eastern North America. **2.** any related variety of white-tailed deer.

**Virginia stock** /– ˈstɒk/, *n.* a commonly cultivated annual, *Malcolmia maritima,* native to the Mediterranean region.

**virginity** /vəˈdʒɪnəti/, *n.* **1.** the condition of being a virgin; virginal chastity; maidenhood. **2.** the condition of being unsullied or unused.

**virgin's-bower** /vɜdʒənz-ˈbaʊə/, *n.* any of several climbing varieties of clematis with small white flowers in large panicles, as *Clematis virginiana,* of the U.S.

**virgin wool** /vɜdʒən ˈwʊl/, *n.* wool which has not been treated or processed in any way.

**Virgo** /ˈvɜgoʊ/, *n.* **1.** the Virgin, a constellation and sign of the zodiac. **2.** a person born under the sign of Virgo, and (according to tradition) exhibiting the typical Virgo personality traits in some degree. *–adj.* **3.** of or pertaining to Virgo. **4.** of or pertaining to such a person or such a personality trait. [L: maiden]

**virgo intacta** /ˌvɜgoʊ ɪnˈtæktə/, *n.* a virgin with hymen unbroken. [L: untouched virgin]

**virgulate** /ˈvɜgjələt, -leɪt/, *adj.* rod-shaped; virgate.

**virgule** /ˈvɜgjul/, *n.* **1.** a short oblique stroke (/) between two words, designating that the interpretation may be made in either sense: *and/or.* **2.** such a stroke used as a mark of division. [L *virgula* little rod]

**viridescent** /vɪrəˈdɛsənt/, *adj.* slightly green or greenish. [LL *viridescens* becoming green] – **viridescence,** *n.*

**viridian** /vəˈrɪdiən/, *n.* a bluish green pigment of great permanency, consisting of a hydrated oxide of chromium. [L *viridi(s)* green + -AN]

**viridity** /vəˈrɪdəti/, *n.* **1.** greenness; verdancy; verdure. **2.** inexperience or simplicity. [late ME, from L *viriditas* greenness]

**virile** /ˈvɪraɪl/, *adj.* **1.** of, pertaining to, or characteristic of a man, as opposed to a woman or a child; masculine or manly; natural to or befitting a man. **2.** having or exhibiting in a marked degree masculine strength, vigour, or forcefulness. **3.** characterised by a vigorous masculine spirit: *a virile literary style.* **4.** pertaining to or capable of procreation. [L *virilis,* from *vir* man]

**virilism** /ˈvɪrəlɪzəm/, *n.* hermaphroditism in which a female has certain minor sexual characteristics resembling those of a male, as a deep voice, etc.

**virility** /vəˈrɪləti/, *n., pl.* **-ties. 1.** the state or quality of being virile; manhood; masculine or manly character, vigour, or spirit. **2.** the power of procreation.

**viroid** /ˈvɪrɔɪd/, *n.* a virus-like particle.

**virology** /vaɪˈrɒlədʒi/, *n.* the study of viruses and the diseases caused by them. [*viro-* (combining form of VIRUS) + -LOGY] – **virological** /vaɪrəˈlɒdʒɪkəl/, *adj.* – **virologically** /vaɪrəˈlɒdʒɪkli/, *adv.* – **virologist,** *n.*

**virtu** /vɜˈtu/, *n.* **1.** excellence or merit in objects of art, curios, and the like. **2.** (*construed as pl.*) such objects or articles collectively. **3.** a taste for or knowledge of such objects or articles. Also, **vertu.** [It., from L *virtūs* VIRTUE]

**virtual** /ˈvɜtʃuəl/, *adj.* **1.** being such in power, force, or effect, although not actually or expressly such: *he was reduced to virtual poverty.* **2.** *Optics.* **a.** denoting an image formed by the apparent convergence of rays geometrically (but not actually) prolonged, as the image in a mirror (opposed to *real*). **b.** denoting a focus of a corresponding nature. **3.** *Archaic.* having virtue or inherent power to produce effects. [ME *vertual,* from ML *virtuālis*] – **virtuality,** *n.*

**virtually** /ˈvɜtʃuəli, ˈvɜtʃəli/, *adv.* **1.** in effect, although not in name or in fact: *a licence for a television station is virtually a licence to print money.* **2.** *Colloq.* almost.

**virtual work** /ˈvɜtʃuəl wɜk/, *n.* the work done by a set of forces acting on a body, when the body is imagined to undergo a small displacement. The principle is used to calculate the equilibrium position of a body, or system of bodies, under the action of a given set of forces.

**virtue** /ˈvɜtʃu/, *n.* **1.** moral excellence or goodness. **2.** conformity of life and conduct to moral laws; uprightness; rectitude. **3.** a particular moral excellence: *the cardinal virtues* (justice, prudence, temperance, and fortitude), *the theological virtues* (faith, hope, and charity). **4.** an excellence, merit, or good quality: *brevity is often a virtue.* **5.** chastity, esp. in women. **6.** effective force: *there is no virtue in such measures.* **7.** a power or property of producing a particular effect. **8.** inherent power to produce effects; potency or efficacy: *a medicine of sovereign virtue.* **9.** (*pl.*) an order of angels. See **angel** (def. 1). **10.** *Obs.* manly excellence, spirit, or valour. **11. by** or **in virtue of,** by reason of: *to act by virtue of authority conferred.* [ME *virtu,* from L *virtūs* manliness (from *vir* man); replacing ME *vertu,* from OF]

**virtuosity** /vɜtʃuˈɒsəti/, *n., pl.* **-ties. 1.** the character or skill of a virtuoso. **2.** a fondness for or interest in virtu.

**virtuoso** /vɜtʃuˈoʊsoʊ, -ˈoʊzoʊ/, *n., pl.* **-sos, -si** /-si, -zi/, *adj.* –*n.* **1.** one who has special knowledge or skill in any field, as in music. **2.** one who excels in musical technique or execution. **3.** one who has a cultivated appreciation of artistic excellence; a connoisseur of works or objects of art; a student or collector of objects of art, curios, antiquities, etc. **4.** *Obs.* one who has special interest or knowledge in art and science. –*adj.* **5.** characteristic of a virtuoso. [It.: learned, skilful]

**virtuous** /ˈvɜtʃuəs/, *adj.* **1.** morally excellent or good; conforming or conformed to moral laws; upright; righteous; moral. **2.** *Archaic.* having effective virtue; potent; efficacious. [ME, from LL *virtuōsus;* replacing ME *vertuous,* from OF, from *vertu* VIRTUE] – **virtuously,** *adv.* – **virtuousness,** *n.*

**virulence** /ˈvɪrələns/, *n.* **1.** the quality of being virulent; actively poisonous or malignant quality. **2.** venomous hostility. **3.** intense acrimony. Also, **virulency.**

**virulent** /ˈvɪrələnt/, *adj.* **1.** actively poisonous, malignant, or deadly: *a virulent poison, a virulent form of a disease.* **2.** *Med.* highly infective; malignant or deadly. **3.** *Bacteriol.* of the nature of an organism causing specific or general clinical symptoms. **4.** violently or venomously hostile. **5.** intensely bitter, spiteful, or acrimonious. [ME, from L *virulentus* poisonous. See VIRUS] – **virulently,** *adv.*

**virus** /ˈvaɪrəs/, *n.* **1.** an infective agent; in a restricted sense, an infective agent smaller than a common micro-organism, and requiring living cells for multiplication. Cf. **filterable** (def. 2). **2.** any disease caused by a virus. **3.** the venom of a poisonous animal. **4.** a moral or intellectual poison; a corrupting influence. [L: slimy liquid, poison] – **virus-like,** *adj.*

**Vis.,** **1.** Viscount. **2.** Viscountess.

**visa** /ˈvizə/, *n., v.,* **-saed, -saing.** –*n.* **1.** an endorsement made by an authorised representative of a country upon the passport of a citizen of another country, testifying that the passport has been examined and found in order, and permitting passage to the country making the endorsement. –*v.t.* **2.** to put a visa on; examine and endorse, as a passport. [L, short for *carta vīsa* paper (has been) seen]

**visage** /ˈvɪzɪdʒ/, *n.* **1.** the face, esp. of a human being, and commonly with reference to shape, features, expression, etc.; the countenance. **2.** aspect; appearance. [ME, from AF and OF, from *vis* face (from L *vīsus*). See -AGE] – **visaged,** *adj.*

**visard** /ˈvɪzəd/, *n.* →**vizard.**

**vis-a-vis** /viz-a-ˈvi/, *adv., adj., prep., n., pl.* **-vis.** –*adv.* **1.** face to face. –*adj.* **2.** face to face; opposite. –*prep.* **3.** face to face with; opposite. **4.** regarding; with relation to: *discussions with the treasurer vis-a-vis the finances of a proposal.* –*n.* **5.** one face to face with or situated opposite to another. **6.** a person corresponding in status or function to another; opposite number. **7.** →**tete-a-tete** (def. 3). **8.** (formerly) a carriage in which the occupants sit face to face. Also, *French,* **vis-à-vis.** [F: face to face]

**Visc.,** **1.** Viscount. **2.** Viscountess.

**viscacha** /vɪsˈkætʃə/, *n.* **1.** a burrowing rodent, *Lagostomus maximus,* about the size of a domestic cat, inhabiting the pampas of Paraguay and Argentina, related to the chinchilla. **2.** a rodent of a related genus, *Lagidium,* of the Andes (**alpine** or **mountain viscacha**), about the size of a grey squirrel, having long rabbit-like ears and a squirrel-like tail. Also, **vizcacha.** [Sp., from Quechua]

**viscera** /ˈvɪsərə/, *n. pl., sing.* **viscus. 1.** the soft interior organs in the cavities of the body, including the brain, lungs, heart, stomach, intestines, etc., esp. such of these as are confined to the abdomen. **2.** (in popular use) the intestines or bowels. [L]

**visceral** /ˈvɪsərəl/, *adj.* **1.** of the viscera. **2.** affecting the viscera. **3.** having the character of viscera.

**viscid** /ˈvɪsəd/, *adj.* **1.** sticky, adhesive, or glutinous; of a glutinous consistency; viscous. **2.** *Bot.* covered by a sticky substance, as a leaf. [LL *viscidus,* from L *viscum* birdlime] – **viscidity** /vəˈsɪdəti/, **viscidness,** *n.* – **viscidly,** *adv.*

**viscoid** /ˈvɪskɔɪd/, *adj.* somewhat viscous. Also, **viscoidal** /vɪsˈkɔɪdl/. [VISC(OUS) + -OID]

**viscometer** /vɪsˈkɒmətə/, *n. Physics.* any instrument used to measure the viscosity of a liquid. Also, **viscosimeter.** – **viscometrical** /vɪskəˈmɛtrɪkəl/, *adj.* – **viscometry,** *n.*

**viscose** /ˈvɪskoʊz, -oʊs/, *Chem.* –*n.* **1.** a viscous solution prepared by treating cellulose with caustic soda and carbon bisulphide; used in manufacturing regenerated cellulose fibres, sheets, or tubes, as rayon or cellophane. –*adj.* **2.** relating to or made from viscose. [L *viscōsus.* See VISCOUS]

**viscosity** /vɪsˈkɒsəti/, *n., pl.* **-ties. 1.** the state or quality of being viscous. **2.** *Physics.* a property of a fluid in resisting change in the shape or arrangement of its elements during flow, and the degree to which this property exists in a particular fluid.

**viscount** /ˈvaɪkaʊnt/, *n.* **1.** a nobleman next below an earl or count and next above a baron. **2.** the son or younger brother of an earl or a count. **3.** (formerly) a deputy of a count or earl. **4.** *Hist.* a sheriff. [ME, from AF *viscounte,* from *vis* VICE- + *counte* COUNT[2]]

**viscountcy** /ˈvaɪkaʊntsi/, *n., pl.* **-cies.** the rank or dignity of a viscount. Also, **viscountship.**

**viscountess** /ˈvaɪkaʊntɛs/, *n.* **1.** the wife or widow of a viscount. **2.** a woman holding in her own right a rank equivalent to that of a viscount.

**viscounty** /ˈvaɪkaʊnti/, *n., pl.* **-ties. 1.** →**viscountcy. 2.** *Hist.* the jurisdiction of a viscount, or the territory under his authority.

**viscous** /ˈvɪskəs/, *adj.* **1.** sticky, adhesive, or glutinous; of a glutinous character or consistency; thick. **2.** having the property of viscosity. [ME *viscouse,* from L *viscōsus,* from *viscum* birdlime] – **viscously,** *adv.* – **viscousness,** *n.*

**viscus** /ˈvɪskəs/, *n.* singular of **viscera.**

**vise** /vaɪs/, *n., v.,* **vised, vising.** *U.S.* →**vice**[2].

**Vishnu** /ˈvɪʃnu/, *n.* **1.** 'the Pervader', one of a halfdozen solar deities in the Rig-Veda, daily traversing the sky in three strides, morning, noon, and night. **2.** (in popular Hinduism) a deity believed to have descended from heaven to earth in several incarnations, or avatars, varying in number from nine to twenty-two, but always including animals. His most important human incarnation is the Krishna of the Bhagavad-gita. **3.** (in later Hinduism) 'the Preserver', the second member of an important trinity, together with Brahma the Creator and Shiva the Destroyer. [Skt]

**visibility** /vɪzəˈbɪləti/, *n., pl.* **-ties. 1.** the state or fact of being visible; capability of being seen. **2.** the relative capability of being seen under given conditions of distance, light, atmosphere, etc.: *low or high visibility.* **3.** *Meteorol.* the greatest distance at which an object of specified characteristics can be seen and identified; visual range. **4.** *Photog.* the ratio of the luminous flux, in lumens, to the corresponding energy flux in watts. **5.** something visible; a visible thing.

**visibility meter** /ˈ– mitə/, *n.* a meter for measuring and giving a standardised scale value to visibility through the atmosphere.

**visible** /ˈvɪzəbəl/, *adj.* **1.** capable of being seen; perceptible by the eye; open to sight or view. **2.** *Physics.* (of electromagnetic radiation) having a wavelength between 380 and 780 nanometres. **3.** perceptible by the mind. **4.** apparent; manifest; obvious. **5.** represented visually; prepared or converted for visual presentation: *visible sound* (an oscillograph of a soundwave). [ME, from L *vīsibilis*] – **visibleness,** *n.* – **visibly,** *adv.*

**visible horizon** /– həˈraɪzən/, *n.* See **horizon** (def. 1).

**visible speech** /– ˈspitʃ/, *n.* a system of notation in which each symbol shape is designed to indicate diagrammatically the articulatory position of the sound it stands for and in which phonetically related sounds are represented by related symbol shapes.

**visile** /ˈvɪzaɪl/, *n.* one in whose mind visual images are especially distinct.

**vision** /ˈvɪʒən/, *n.* **1.** the act of seeing with the eye; the power, faculty, or sense of sight. **2.** the act or power of perceiving what is not actually present to the eye, whether by some supernatural endowment or by natural intellectual acuteness: *to lack vision in dealing with great problems.* **3.** something seen or presented to the mind otherwise than by natural, ordinary sight in the normal waking state. **4.** a mental view or image, whether of supernatural origin or merely imaginative, of what is not actually present in place or time: *visions of the past or the future.* **5.** a vivid imaginative conception or anticipation: *visions of wealth or glory.* **6.** something seen; an object of sight. **7.** a sight seen in a dream, ecstasy, trance, or the like. **8.** a sight such as might be seen in a vision, dream, etc.: *a vision of loveliness.* **9.** a scene, person, etc., of extraordinary beauty. *–v.t.* **10.** to show, or to see, in or as in a vision. [ME, from L *vīsio* sight] – **visionless,** *adj.*

**visional** /ˈvɪʒənəl/, *adj.* **1.** of or pertaining to visions. **2.** belonging to or seen in a vision. – **visionally,** *adv.*

**visionary** /ˈvɪʒənri/, *adj., n., pl.* **-ries.** *–adj.* **1.** given to or characterised by radical, often unpractical ideas, views, or schemes: *a visionary enthusiast.* **2.** given to or concerned with seeing visions. **3.** belonging to or seen in a vision. **4.** unreal or imaginary: *visionary evils.* **5.** purely ideal or speculative; unpractical. **6.** proper only to a vision. *–n.* **7.** one who sees visions. **8.** one who is given to novel ideas or schemes which are not immediately practicable; an unpractical theorist or enthusiast: *although a visionary, he was an excellent economist.* – **visionariness,** *n.*

**vision mixer** /ˈvɪʒən mɪksə/, *n.* a television technician responsible for switching transmission from one camera to another, from camera to film, etc. at the discretion of the director.

**visit** /ˈvɪzət/, *v.t.* **1.** to go to see (a person, place, etc.) in the way of friendship, ceremony, duty, business, curiosity, or the like. **2.** to call upon (a person, family, etc.) for social or other purposes. **3.** to make a stay or sojourn with, as a guest. **4.** (in general) to come or go to. **5.** to go to for the purpose of official inspection or examination; inspect or examine. **6.** to come to in order to comfort or aid. **7.** to come upon or assail: *the plague visited London in 1665.* **8.** to afflict with suffering, trouble, etc. **9.** *Obs.* to inflict punishment for. *–v.i.* **10.** to make a visit or visits. **11.** *U.S.* to talk casually; chat. **12.** *Obs.* to inflict punishment. *–n.* **13.** an act of visiting. **14.** a going to see a person, place, etc. **15.** a call paid to a person, family, etc. **16.** a stay or sojourn as a guest. **17.** a going to a place to make an official inspection or examination. **18.** the visiting of a vessel, as at sea, by an officer of a hostile state, to ascertain its nationality, the nature of its cargo (whether contraband), etc.: *the right of visit and search.* [ME, from L *vīsitāre* go to see]

**visitable** /ˈvɪzətəbəl/, *adj.* **1.** capable of or suitable for being visited. **2.** liable or subject to official visitation.

**visitant** /ˈvɪzətənt/, *n.* **1.** a visitor; a guest; a temporary resident. **2.** a supernatural visitor; an apparition; a ghost. **3.** one who visits a place of interest, a shrine, etc., for sightseeing, on a pilgrimage, or the like. **4.** a migratory bird, or other animal, at a temporary feeding place, etc., or on its nesting-ground **(summer visitant)** or wintering ground **(winter visitant).** *–adj.* **5.** visiting; paying a visit.

**visitation** /vɪzəˈteɪʃən/, *n.* **1.** the act of visiting; a visit. **2.** a visiting or a visit for the purpose of making an official inspection or examination. **3.** (*cap. or l.c.*) the visit of the Virgin Mary to her cousin Elizabeth. (See Luke 1: 39-56). **4.** a visiting with comfort or aid, or with affliction or punishment, as by God. **5.** a special dispensation from heaven, whether of favour or of affliction. **6.** any experience or event, esp. an unpleasant one, regarded as occurring by divine dispensation. **7.** an affliction or punishment from God. – **visitational,** *adj.*

**visitatorial** /vɪzətəˈtɔriəl/, *adj.* **1.** pertaining to an official visitor or to official visitation. **2.** having the power of visitation.

**visiting card** /ˈvɪzətɪŋ ˌkad/, *n.* **1.** a small card bearing one's name, used on various social or business occasions. **2.** *Colloq.* any article or thing, esp. a recognisable one, which serves to announce its owner.

**visiting fireman** /– ˈfaɪəmən/, *n. Colloq.* a visiting member of high status in an organisation, such as a visiting professor in academic circles, a visiting director of a multinational company, etc.

**visiting medical officer,** *n.* a specialist who provides services under contract to a hospital; honorary. Also, **V.M.O.**

**visiting professor** /– prəˈfɛsə/, *n.* a university professor invited to teach at a university not his own for a short period, usu. an academic year.

**visitor** /ˈvɪzətə/, *n.* one who visits, or makes a visit, as for friendly, business, official, or other purposes. – **visitress** /ˈvɪzətrəs/, *n. fem.*

**visitorial** /vɪzəˈtɔriəl/, *adj.* of or pertaining to a visitor; visitatorial.

**visitors' book** /ˈvɪzətəz bʊk/, *n.* a book kept at a private home, a place of interest, a hotel, etc., in which visitors sign their names and sometimes write comments about their visit.

**vis major** /vɪs ˈmeɪdʒə/, *n.* →**force majeure.** [L: lit., greater force]

**visor** /ˈvaɪzə/, *n.* **1.** the movable front parts of a helmet, covering the face, esp. the uppermost part which protects the eyes. **2.** any disguise or means of concealment. **3.** *Chiefly U.S.* the projecting forepiece of a cap, for protecting the eyes. **4.** a small shield attached to the inside roof of a car, which may be swung down to protect the driver's eyes from glare or sunlight. *–v.t.* **5.** to protect or mask with a visor; shield. Also, **vizor.** [ME *viser*, from AF, from *vis* face] – **visored,** *adj.* – **visorless,** *adj.*

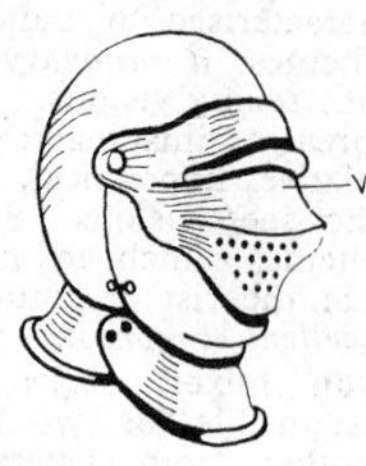


V, visor (def. 1)

**vista** /ˈvɪstə/, *n.* **1.** a view or prospect, esp. one seen through a long, narrow avenue or passage, as between rows of trees, houses, or the like. **2.** such an avenue or passage. **3.** a mental view of a far-reaching kind: *vistas of thought.* **4.** a mental view extending over a long time or a stretch of remembered, imagined, or anticipated experiences, etc.: *dim vistas of the past or the future.* [It.: sight, view; fem. of *visto*, pp. of *vedere* see, from L *vidēre*] – **vistaed** /ˈvɪstəd/, *adj.* – **vistaless,** *adj.*

**vista-vision** /vɪstə-ˈvɪʒən/, *n.* a system of wide-screen cinematography depending on the use of an image whose horizontal axis runs parallel to the length of the film instead of across it.

**visual** /ˈvɪʒuəl/, *adj.* **1.** of or pertaining to sight. **2.** *Optics.* optical. **3.** perceptible by the sight; visible. **4.** perceptible by the mind; of the nature of a mental vision. *–n.* **5.** (in advertising) the preliminary sketch of a layout showing the arrangement of copy. **6.** (*pl.*) visual items, as photographs, films, slides, etc. [ME, from LL *vīsuālis* belonging to sight]

**visual aid** /– ˈeɪd/, *n.* a device, technique, or the like, which uses the student's sense of sight in carrying on or assisting the learning process: *television and photographs are good visual aids.*

**visual arts** /vɪʒuəl ˈats/, *n.pl.* painting, sculpture, etc., esp. as opposed to the literary arts of drama, music, etc.

**visual display unit,** *n.* a computer terminal which displays information on a screen. Also, **visual display terminal.**

**visual flight rules,** *n.pl.* the aviational code of regulations for visual flying which specifies minimum horizontal visibility, etc.

**visualise** /ˈvɪʒuəlaɪz/, *v.,* **-lised, -lising.** *–v.i.* **1.** to call up or form mental images or pictures. *–v.t.* **2.** to make visual or visible. **3.** to form a mental image of. **4.** to make perceptible to the mind or to the imagination. Also, **visualize.** – **visualisation** /ˌvɪʒuəlaɪˈzeɪʃən/, *n.* – **visualiser,** *n.*

**visually** /ˈvɪʒuəli/, *adv.* in a visual manner or respect; by sight.

**visual purple** /ˌvɪzjuəl ˈpɜpəl/, *n.* the substance in the rod cells of the retina of the eye which is photosensitive to dim light; rhodopsin.

**visual range** /– ˈreɪndʒ/, *n.* →**visibility** (def. 3).

**vis viva** /vɪs ˈvivə/, *n. Physics. Obs.* the force of a moving body, equal to the product of its mass and the square of its velocity. [L: living force]

**vitaceous** /vaɪˈteɪʃəs/, *adj.* belonging to the Vitaceae, or grape family of plants, many of which are climbers, as the ampelopsis, Japanese ivy, Virginia creeper, etc. [NL *Vītāceae* the grape family (from L *vītis* vine) + -OUS]

**vital** /ˈvaɪtl/, *adj.* **1.** of or pertaining to life: *vital functions or processes.* **2.** having life, or living. **3.** having remarkable energy, enthusiasm, vivacity: *he has a very vital personality.* **4.** being the seat or source of life: *the vital parts or organs.* **5.** necessary to life. **6.** necessary to the existence, continuance, or well-being of something; indispensable; essential: *a vital necessity.* **7.** affecting the existence, wellbeing, truth, etc., of something: *a vital error.* **8.** of critical importance: *vital problems.* **9.** imparting life or vigour; vitalising, or invigorating. **10.** affecting life; destructive to life: *a vital wound.* *–n.* **11.** (*pl.*) those bodily organs which are essential to life, as the brain, heart, lungs, and stomach. **12.** (*pl.*) the essential parts of anything. [ME, from L *vītālis*] – **vitally,** *adv.* – **vitalness,** *n.*

**vital dye** /– ˈdaɪ/, *n.* a dye capable of penetrating living cells without any immediate adverse effects, thus facilitating observation with a microscope. Also, **vital stain.**

**vital force** /– ˈfɔs/, *n.* the animating force in animals and plants. Also, **vital principle.**

**vitalise** /ˈvaɪtəlaɪz/, *v.t.,* **-lised, -lising. 1.** to make vital or living, or give life to. **2.** to give vitality or vigour to; animate. Also, **vitalize.** – **vitalisation** /vaɪtəlaɪˈzeɪʃən/, *n.*

**vitalism** /ˈvaɪtəlɪzəm/, *n.* **1.** the doctrine that phenomena are only partly controlled by mechanical forces and that they are in some measure self-determining (opposed to *mechanism*). **2.** *Biol.* the doctrine that ascribes the functions of a living organism to a vital principle distinct from chemical and other forces. – **vitalist,** *n., adj.* – **vitalistic** /vaɪtəˈlɪstɪk/, *adj.*

**vitality** /vaɪˈtæləti/, *n., pl.* **-ties. 1.** exuberant physical vigour; energy; enthusiastic vivacity: *of terrific vitality.* **2.** vital force. **3.** the principle of life. **4.** power to live, or physical strength as a condition of life. **5.** power of continued existence, as of an institution, a book, etc. **6.** something having vital force.

**vital stain** /vaɪtl ˈsteɪn/, *n.* →**vital dye.**

**vital statistics** /vaɪtl stəˈtɪstɪks/, *n.pl.* **1.** statistics concerning human life or the conditions affecting human life and the maintenance of population. **2.** *Colloq.* the measurements of a woman's figure, as at the bust, waist, and hips.

**vitamin** /ˈvaɪtəmən, ˈvɪt-/, *n.* any of a group of food factors essential in small quantities to maintain life, but not themselves employing energy. The absence of any one of them results in a characteristic deficiency disease. [L *vīt(a)* life + AMIN(E)]

**vitamin A** /– ˈeɪ/, *n.* a fat-soluble yellow unsaturated alcohol found in green and yellow vegetables, butter, egg yolk and fish-liver oil, essential for the prevention of night blindness and the protection of epithelial tissue. Also, **vitamin** $\mathbf{A_1}$.

**vitamin** $\mathbf{A_2}$ /– eɪtu/, *n.* a vitamin found in the tissues of freshwater fish, with a function similar to that of vitamin A.

**vitamin** $\mathbf{B_1}$ /– bi ˈwʌn/, *n.* →**thiamine.**

**vitamin** $\mathbf{B_2}$ /– bi ˈtu/, *n.* →**riboflavin.**

**vitamin B complex,** *n.* an important group of water-soluble vitamins containing vitamin $B_1$, vitamin $B_2$, etc.

**vitamin** $\mathbf{B_{12}}$ /vaɪtəmən biˈtwɛlv/, *n.* →**cobalamin.**

**vitamin C** /vaɪtəmən ˈsi/, *n.* →**ascorbic acid.**

**vitamin D** /– ˈdi/, *n.* any of the several fat-soluble antirachitic vitamins $D_1$, $D_2$, $D_3$, found in milk and fish-liver oils, esp. cod and halibut, or obtained by irradiating provitamin D with ultraviolet light.

**vitamin** $\mathbf{D_1}$ /– diˈwʌn/, *n.* a mixture of lumisterol and calciferol, obtained by ultraviolet irradiation of ergosterol.

**vitamin** $\mathbf{D_2}$ /– diˈtu/, *n.* →**calciferol.**

**vitamin** $\mathbf{D_3}$ /– diˈθri/, *n.* the naturally occurring D-vitamin, found in fish-liver oils, differing from vitamin $D_2$ by slight structural differences in the molecule.

**vitamin E** /– ˈi/, *n.* a pale yellow viscous fluid, found in wheat-germ oil, which promotes fertility in mammals and prevents human abortions. See **tocopherol.**

**vitamin H** /– ˈeɪtʃ/, *n.* →**biotin.**

**vitamin K** /– ˈkeɪ/, *n.* a group of compounds, esp. menadione, involved in blood clotting.

**vitamin** $\mathbf{K_1}$ /– keɪˈwʌn/, *n.* a fat-soluble vitamin found in leafy vegetables, rice, bran, pig's liver, etc., and obtained from alfalfa oil or putrefied sardine meat, which promotes blood clotting by increasing the prothrombin content of the blood; menadione.

**vitamin** $\mathbf{K_2}$ /– keɪˈtu/, *n.* a compound similar in activity to vitamin $K_1$; menaquinone.

**vitamin P** /– ˈpi/, *n.* any of a group of water-soluble crystalline substances, found mainly in citrus fruits, esp. in their peel, blackcurrants, and rosehips, which regulate the permeability of the blood capillaries.

**vitamise** /ˈvaɪtəmaɪz/, *v.t.,* **-ised, -ising.** to prepare food using a vitamiser or blender.

**vitamiser** /ˈvaɪtəmaɪzə/, *n.* →**blender** (def. 2). [Trademark]

**vitellin** /vəˈtɛlən/, *n.* a phosphoprotein in the yolk of eggs. [VITELL(US) + -IN[2]]

**vitelline** /vəˈtɛlən, -aɪn/, *adj.* **1.** pertaining to the egg yolk. **2.**

having a yellow colour.

**vitelline membrane** /'– ˌmɛmbreɪn/, *n.* the membrane surrounding the egg yolk.

**vitellus** /və'tɛləs/, *n.* the yolk of an egg. [L]

**vitex** /'vaɪtɛks/, *n.* a widespread genus of the family Verbenaceae with many species, some ornamental, and some yielding useful timber.

**vitiable** /'vɪʃiəbəl/, *adj.* subject to being vitiated.

**vitiate** /'vɪʃieɪt/, *v.t.*, **-ated, -ating.** **1.** to impair the quality of; make faulty; mar. **2.** to contaminate; corrupt; spoil. **3.** to make legally defective or invalid; invalidate. [L *vitiātus*, pp., spoiled] – **vitiation** /vɪʃi'eɪʃən/, *n.* – **vitiator,** *n.*

**vitiated** /'vɪʃieɪtəd/, *adj.* spoiled; corrupted; rendered invalid.

**viticulture** /'vɪtikʌltʃə/, *n.* **1.** the culture or cultivation of the grapevine; grape-growing. **2.** the study or science of grapes and their culture. [*viti-* (from L, combining form of *vītis* vine) + CULTURE] – **viticultural** /vɪti'kʌltʃərəl/, *adj.* – **viticulturer** /vɪti'kʌltʃərə/, **viticulturist** /vɪti'kʌltʃərəst/, *n.*

**vitiligo** /vɪtə'laɪgoʊ/, *n.* a disease in which smooth white patches are formed on various parts of the body, owing to loss of the natural pigment. [L: tetter]

**vitreous** /'vɪtriəs/, *adj.* **1.** of the nature of glass; resembling glass, as in transparency, brittleness, hardness, etc.; glassy: *vitreous china.* **2.** of or pertaining to glass. **3.** obtained from glass. [L *vitreus*, from *vitrum* glass] – **vitreously,** *adv.* – **vitreousness, vitreosity** /vɪtri'ɒsəti/, *n.*

**vitreous electricity** /– əlɛk'trɪsəti/, *n.* positive electricity; electricity produced on glass by rubbing with silk.

**vitreous enamel** /– ə'næməl/, *n.* a coloured glassy coating, stoved on to metal articles, as baths, signs, etc., giving resistance to heat, corrosion, etc.

**vitreous humour** /– 'hjumə/, *n.* the transparent gelatinous substance filling the eyeball behind the crystalline lens.

**vitreous silica** /– 'sɪləkə/, *n.* →**silica glass.**

**vitrescent** /və'trɛsənt/, *adj.* **1.** turning into glass. **2.** tending to become glass. **3.** capable of being formed into glass. [L *vitrum* glass + -ESCENT] – **vitrescence,** *n.*

**vitri-**, a word element meaning 'glass', as in *vitriform.* [combining form representing L *vitrum*]

**vitric** /'vɪtrɪk/, *adj.* **1.** of or pertaining to glass. **2.** of the nature of glass; glasslike. [L *vitrum* glass + -IC]

**vitrification** /vɪtrəfə'keɪʃən/, *n.* **1.** the act or process of vitrifying. **2.** the state of being vitrified. **3.** something vitrified. Also, **vitrifaction** /vɪtrə'fækʃən/.

**vitriform** /'vɪtrəfɔm/, *adj.* having the form or appearance of glass.

**vitrify** /'vɪtrəfaɪ/, *v.t., v.i.*, **-fied, -fying.** **1.** to convert or be converted into glass. **2.** to make or become vitreous. – **vitrifiable,** *adj.* – **vitrifiability** /ˌvɪtrəfaɪə'bɪləti/, *n.*

**vitriol** /'vɪtriɒl/, *n., v.*, **-olled, -olling** or (*U.S.*) **-oled, -oling.** –*n.* **1.** *Chem.* any of certain metallic sulphates of glassy appearance, as of copper (blue vitriol), or iron (green vitriol), or zinc (white vitriol), etc. **2.** sulphuric acid. **3.** something highly caustic, or severe in its effects, as criticism. –*v.t.* **4.** to injure or burn with vitriol or sulphuric acid; vitriolise. [ME, from ML *vitriolum*, from L *vitrum* glass]

**vitriolic** /vɪtri'ɒlɪk/, *adj.* **1.** of, resembling, or pertaining to vitriol. **2.** obtained from vitriol; resembling vitriol. **3.** severely caustic or scathing: *vitriolic criticism.*

**vitriolise** /'vɪtriəlaɪz/, *v.t.*, **-lised, -lising.** **1.** to treat with or change into vitriol. **2.** to injure or burn with vitriol or sulphuric acid, as by throwing it in one's face. Also, **vitriolize.** – **vitriolisation** /ˌvɪtriəlaɪ'zeɪʃən/, *n.*

**vitrolite** /'vɪtrəlaɪt/, *n.* (*also cap.*) an opaque type of glass with a fire-finished surface. [Trademark]

**vitta** /'vɪtə/, *n., pl.* **vittae** /'vɪti/. **1.** *Bot.* a tube or receptacle for oil, found in the fruits of most umbelliferous plants. **2.** *Zool., Bot.* a streak or stripe, as of colour. [L: ribbon, fillet]

A B C

vitta (def. 1) black dots represent the vittae in the fruits (section): A, spotted cowbane; B, celery; C, parsley

**vittate** /'vɪteɪt/, *adj.* **1.** provided with or having a vitta or vittae. **2.** striped longitudinally.

**vituline** /'vɪtʃəlaɪn, -lən/, *adj.* of, pertaining to, or resembling a calf or veal. [L *vitulīnus*]

**vituperate** /və'tjupəreɪt, vaɪ-/, *v.*, **-rated, -rating.** –*v.t.* **1.** to find fault with abusively. **2.** to address abusive language to; revile; objurgate. –*v.i.* **3.** to use abusive language. [L *vituperātus*, pp.] – **vituperator,** *n.*

**vituperation** /vəˌtjupə'reɪʃən, vaɪ-/, *n.* **1.** the act of vituperating. **2.** verbal abuse.

**vituperative** /və'tjuprətɪv, vaɪ-/, *adj.* characterised by or of the nature of vituperation; abusive. – **vituperatively,** *adv.*

**viva**[1] /'vivə/, *interj.* **1.** (used in phrases of acclamation) long live (the person or idea named)! –*n.* **2.** a shout of 'viva!' [It.: lit., may he live, subj. of *vivere* live]

**viva**[2] /'vaɪvə/, *n. Colloq.* →**viva voce** (def. 2).

**vivace** /və'vatʃeɪ/, *adj. Music.* vivacious; lively. [It., from L *vīvax*]

**vivacious** /və'veɪʃəs/, *adj.* **1.** lively, animated, or sprightly: *a vivacious manner or style, vivacious conversation.* **2.** *Archaic.* long-lived, or tenacious of life. [VIVACI(TY) + -OUS] – **vivaciously,** *adv.* – **vivaciousness,** *n.*

**vivacity** /və'væsəti/, *n., pl.* **-ties.** **1.** the quality of being vivacious. **2.** liveliness; animation; sprightliness. **3.** a vivacious act or speech; a lively sally. [late ME, from L *vīvācitas*]

**vivarium** /və'vɛəriəm/, *n., pl.* **-riums, -ria** /-riə/. a place where animals are kept alive in conditions simulating their natural state. Cf. **terrarium** and **aquarium.** [L: enclosure for live game]

**viva voce** /vaɪvə 'voʊtʃeɪ/, *adv.* **1.** by word of mouth; orally. –*n.* **2.** an examination where questions are asked and answered orally rather than by a written paper. Also, **viva.** [ML: lit., with the living voice] – **viva-voce,** *adj.*

**vive** /viv/, *interj.* (used in phrases of acclamation) long live (the person or idea named)! [F]

**viverrine** /vaɪ'vɛraɪn/, *adj.* **1.** of or pertaining to the Viverridae, a family of small carnivorous mammals including the civets, genets, palm civets, etc. –*n.* **2.** a viverrine animal. [NL *viverrīnus*, from L *viverra* ferret]

**vivianite** /'vɪviənaɪt/, *n.* a rare, blue, crystalline mineral phosphate of iron, $Fe_3(PO_4)_2 \cdot 8H_2O$. [named after J. G. *Vivian*, 19th-cent. English mineralogist]

**vivid** /'vɪvəd/, *adj.* **1.** strikingly bright, as colour, light, objects, etc.: *a vivid green.* **2.** strikingly alive; full of life: *a vivid personality.* **3.** lively or intense, as feelings, etc. **4.** vigorous, as activities, etc. **5.** lively, or presenting the appearance, freshness, spirit, etc., of life, as a picture. **6.** clearly perceptible to the eye or mind. **7.** strong and distinct, as an impression or recollection. **8.** forming distinct and striking mental images, as the imagination. **9.** lively in operation. [L *vīvidus* animated] – **vividly,** *adv.* – **vividness,** *n.*

**vivify** /'vɪvəfaɪ/, *v.t.*, **-fied, -fying.** **1.** to give life to; quicken. **2.** to enliven; render lively or animated; brighten. [L *vīvificāre*] – **vivification** /vɪvəfə'keɪʃən/, *n.* – **vivifier,** *n.*

**vivipara** /və'vɪpərə/, *n. pl.* viviparous animals.

**viviparous** /və'vɪpərəs/, *adj.* **1.** *Zool.* bringing forth living young (rather than eggs), as most mammals and some reptiles and fishes. **2.** *Bot.* producing seeds that germinate on the plant. [L *vīviparus* bringing forth living young] – **viviparity** /vɪvə'pærəti/, **viviparousness,** *n.* – **viviparously,** *adv.*

**vivisect** /'vɪvəsɛkt, vɪvə'sɛkt/, *v.t.* **1.** to dissect the living body of. –*v.i.* **2.** to practise vivisection. [*vīvi-* (from L, combining form of *vīvus* alive) + -SECT] – **vivisector,** *n.*

**vivisection** /vɪvə'sɛkʃən/, *n.* **1.** the action of cutting into or dissecting a living body. **2.** the practice of subjecting living animals to cutting operations, esp. in order to advance physiological and pathological knowledge. – **vivisectional,** *adj.*

**vivisectionist** /vɪvə'sɛkʃənəst/, *n.* **1.** one who practises vivisection. **2.** one who favours or defends the practice of vivisection.

**vivo** /'vivoʊ/, *adv.* (a musical direction) in a lively, spirited manner. [It.]

**vixen** /'vɪksən/, *n.* **1.** a female fox. **2.** an ill-tempered or quarrelsome woman; a spitfire. [southern d. var. of ME *fixen* she-fox, from OE *fyxe* she-fox + *-en*, obs. fem. suffix] – **vixenish, vixenly,** *adj.* – **vixenishly,** *adv.* – **vixenishness,** *n.*

**viyella** /vaɪ'ɛlə/, *n.* (*also cap.*) a soft fabric made of cotton and wool, used esp. for blouses, shirts, and children's clothing. [Trademark]

**viz.,** videlicet.

**vizard** /ˈvɪzəd/, *n.* **1.** a mask. **2.** *Obs.* a visor. Also, **visard.** [alteration of VISOR] – **vizarded,** *adj.*

**vizcacha** /vɪsˈkætʃə/, *n.* →**viscacha.**

**vizier** /vəˈzɪə/, *n.* **1.** a high official in various Muslim countries. **2.** a minister of state. Also, **vizir.** [Turk. *vezīr,* from Ar. *wazīr* bearer of burdens] – **vizierate** /vəˈzɪərət, -reɪt/, **viziership,** *n.* – **vizierial,** *adj.*

**vizor** /ˈvaɪzə/, *n., v.t.* →**visor.** – **vizored,** *adj.* – **vizorless,** *adj.*

**V.J.** /vi ˈdʒeɪ/, *n.* a type of small yacht. [*V*(*aucluse*) *J*(*unior*)]

**vl.,** violin.

**v.l.,** varia lectio.

**VL,** Vulgar Latin.

**v.l.f.** /vi ɛl ˈɛf/, very low frequency.

**V.M.O.** /vi ɛm ˈoʊ/, *n.* →**visiting medical officer.**

**V-neck** /vi-ˈnɛk/, *n.* a neckline shaped in front like a V. – **V-necked,** *adj.*

**vo,** verso.

**voc.,** vocative.

**vocab** /ˈvoʊkæb/, *n. Colloq.* vocabulary.

**vocable** /ˈvoʊkəbəl/, *n.* **1.** a word; a term. **2.** a word considered merely as composed of certain sounds or letters, without regard to meaning. *–adj.* **3.** that may be spoken. [L *vocābulum* name, term]

**vocabulary** /vəˈkæbjələri/, *n., pl.* **-ries. 1.** the stock of words used by a people, or by a particular class or person. **2.** a list or collection of the words of a language, book, author, branch of science, or the like, usu. in alphabetical order and defined; a wordbook, glossary, dictionary, or lexicon. **3.** the words of a language. **4.** a range of stylised artistic forms, as in music, architecture, etc.: *she is a versatile composer with a large musical vocabulary.* [ML *vocābulārius,* from L *vocābulum* vocable]

**vocal** /ˈvoʊkəl/, *adj.* **1.** of or pertaining to the voice; uttered with the voice; oral: *the vocal organs.* **2.** rendered by or intended for singing, as music. **3.** having a voice: *a vocal being.* **4.** giving forth sound with or as with a voice. **5.** inclined to express oneself in speech; stridently insistent. **6.** *Phonet.* **a.** →**vocalic** (def. 1). **b.** voiced. *–n.* **7.** a vocal sound. **8.** (in pop, rock, etc.) a piece of music performed by a singer. **9.** (*pl.*) (in pop, rock etc.) the vocal part or track. [ME, from L *vōcālis,* from *vox* voice] – **vocality** /voʊˈkæləti/, **vocalness,** *n.* – **vocally,** *adv.*

**vocal cords** /ˈ– kɔdz/, *n.pl.* folds of mucous membrane projecting into the cavity of the larynx, the edges of which can be drawn tense and made to vibrate by the passage of air from the lungs, thus producing vocal sound.

**vocalic** /voʊˈkælɪk/, *adj.* **1.** of or pertaining to a vowel or vowels; vowel-like. **2.** containing many vowels.

**vocalise**[1] /ˈvoʊkəlaɪz/, *v.,* **-lised, -lising.** *–v.t.* **1.** to make vocal; form into voice; utter or articulate; sing. **2.** to endow with voice or utterance. **3.** *Phonet.* **a.** to use as a vowel, as the *l* of *bottle.* **b.** to change into a vowel. **c.** to voice. **4.** (of Hebrew, Arabic, and similar systems of writing) to furnish with vowels or vowel points. *–v.i.* **5.** to use the voice, as in speech or song. **6.** to sing on a vowel or vowel sounds. Also, **vocalize.** – **vocalisation** /voʊkəlaɪˈzeɪʃən/, *n.* – **vocaliser,** *n.*

**vocalise**[2] /voʊkəˈliz/, *n.* a piece of music to be sung on vowel sounds without words; often a training exercise. [F, from *vocaliser* to vocalise]

**vocalism** /ˈvoʊkəlɪzəm/, *n.* **1.** *Phonet.* **a.** the system of vowels of a particular language. **b.** the nature of one or more given vowels. **2.** the use of the voice, as in speech or song. **3.** the act, principles, or art of singing.

**vocalist** /ˈvoʊkələst/, *n.* a singer.

**vocal score** /ˈvoʊkəl skɔ/, *n.* a musical score for singers, which shows the voice part in full and the orchestral part as a piano transcription only.

**vocal tract** /voʊkəl ˈtrækt/, *n.* the part of the vocal system above the vocal cords.

**vocat.,** vocative.

**vocation** /voʊˈkeɪʃən/, *n.* **1.** a particular occupation, business, or profession; a trade or calling. **2.** a calling or summons, as to a particular activity or career. **3.** a divine call to God's service or to the Christian life. **4.** a function or station to which one is called by God. [late ME *vocacion,* from L *vocātio* calling]

**vocational** /voʊˈkeɪʃənəl/, *adj.* of or pertaining to a vocation or occupation: **1. vocational schools,** schools that train people for various trades or occupations. **2. vocational guidance,** the process of helping pupils and students choose their future careers. – **vocationally,** *adv.*

**vocative** /ˈvɒkətɪv/, *adj.* **1.** *Gram.* **a.** (in some inflected languages) designating a case that indicates the person or thing addressed. **b.** similar to such a case form in function or meaning. **2.** pertaining to or used in calling. *–n.* **3.** *Gram.* **a.** the vocative case. **b.** any other formation of vocative meaning. **c.** a word therein, as Latin *Paule,* 'Paul' (nominative *Paulus*). [late ME, from L *vocātīvus,* from *vocāre* call] – **vocatively,** *adv.*

**vociferance** /vəˈsɪfərəns/, *n.* vociferant utterance; vociferation.

**vociferant** /vəˈsɪfərənt/, *adj.* **1.** vociferating. *–n.* **2.** one who vociferates.

**vociferate** /vəˈsɪfəreɪt/, *v.i., v.t.,* **-rated, -rating.** to cry out loudly or noisily; shout; bawl. [LL *vōciferātus,* pp.] – **vociferator,** *n.*

**vociferation** /vəsɪfəˈreɪʃən/, *n.* noisy outcry; a clamour.

**vociferous** /vəˈsɪfərəs/, *adj.* **1.** crying out noisily; clamorous. **2.** of the nature of vociferation; uttered with clamour. [VOCIFER(ATE) + -OUS] – **vociferously,** *adv.* – **vociferousness,** *n.*

**vodka** /ˈvɒdkə/, *n.* an alcoholic drink of Russian origin, distilled originally from wheat, but now from corn, other cereals, and potatoes. [Russ., diminutive of *voda* water]

**vogue** /voʊg/, *n.* **1.** the fashion, as at a particular time: *a style in vogue fifty years ago.* **2.** popular currency, acceptance, or favour: *the book had a great vogue in its day.* [F, from *voguer* row, from It. *vogare,* ? from L *vocāre* call (through use in sailors' shanties)]

**voice** /vɔɪs/, *n., v.,* **voiced, voicing.** *–n.* **1.** the sound or sounds uttered through the mouth of living creatures, esp. of human beings in speaking, shouting, singing, etc. **2.** the sounds naturally uttered by a single person in speech or vocal utterance, often as characteristic of the utterer. **3.** such sounds considered with reference to their character or quality: *a manly voice, a sweet voice.* **4.** the condition of the voice for speaking or singing, esp. effective condition: *she was in poor voice.* **5.** the ability to sing well: *she has a wonderful voice.* **6.** any sound likened to vocal utterance: *the voice of the wind.* **7.** anything likened to speech as conveying impressions to the mind: *the voice of nature.* **8.** the faculty of uttering sounds through the mouth, esp. articulate sounds; utterance; speech. **9.** expression in spoken or written words, or by other means: *to give voice to one's disapproval by a letter.* **10.** expressed opinion or choice: *his voice was for compromise.* **11.** the right to express an opinion or choice; vote; suffrage: *have no voice in a matter.* **12.** expressed wish or injunction: *obedient to the voice of God.* **13.** the person or other agency by which something is expressed or revealed. **14.** musical sound created by the vibration of the vocal cords and amplified by oral and other throat cavities; tone produced in singing. **15.** *Phonet.* the sound produced by vibration of the vocal cords, as air from the lungs is forced through between them. **16.** *Gram.* **a.** (in some languages, as Latin) a group of categories of verb inflection denoting the relationship between the action expressed by the verb and the subject of the sentence (e.g., as acting or as acted upon). **b.** (in some other languages) one of several contrasting constructions with similar functions. **c.** any one of such categories or constructions in a particular language, as the *active* and *passive* voices in Latin. **17.** the finer regulation, as of intensity and colour, in tuning, esp. of a piano or organ. **18.** a singer. **19.** a voice part. **20. with one voice,** in chorus; unanimously. *–v.t.* **21.** to give voice, utterance, or expression to (an emotion, opinion, etc.); express; declare; proclaim: *to voice one's discontent.* **22.** *Music.* **a.** to regulate the tone of, as the pipes of an organ. **b.** to write the voice parts for (music). **23.** *Phonet.* to utter with vibration of the vocal cords. [ME, from AF, from L *vox*] – **voicer,** *n.*

**voice box** /ˈ– bɒks/, *n.* →**larynx.**

**voiced** /vɔɪst/, *adj.* **1.** having a voice of a specified kind: *low-voiced.* **2.** expressed vocally. **3.** *Phonet.* having voice (def. 15).

**voice frequency** /'vɔɪs ˌfrikwənsi/, *n.* a frequency within the range suitable for the transmission of intelligible speech; a frequency in the range 200 to 3500 hertz. *Abbrev.:* VF

**voiceful** /'vɔɪsfəl/, *adj.* having a voice, esp. a loud voice; sounding; sonorous.

**voiceless** /'vɔɪsləs/, *adj.* **1.** having no voice; mute; dumb. **2.** uttering no speech or words; silent. **3.** having an unmusical voice. **4.** unspoken or unuttered. **5.** *Phonet.* uttered without tonal vibration of the vocal cords: *p, f,* and *s* are *voiceless;* surd; unvoiced. **6.** having no voice or vote. **– voicelessly,** *adv.* **– voicelessness,** *n.*

**voice-over** /'vɔɪs-oʊvə/, *n.* a spoken commentary to a film, documentary, etc., which accompanies action filmed.

**voice part** /'vɔɪs pat/, *n.* the melody or succession of notes for one of the voices or instruments in a harmonic or concerted composition.

**voiceprint** /'vɔɪsprɪnt/, *n.* a representation of a person's voice, as in spectographic or other display, revealing a pattern unique to that person. [VOICE + (FINGER)PRINT]

**void** /vɔɪd/, *adj.* **1.** *Law.* without legal force or effect; not legally binding or enforceable. **2.** useless; ineffectual; vain. **3.** completely empty; devoid; destitute (fol. by *of*). **4.** without contents. **5.** without an incumbent, as an office. *–n.* **6.** an empty space: *the void of heaven.* **7.** a place without the usual or desired occupant: *his death left a void among us.* **8.** a gap or opening, as in a wall. **9.** emptiness; vacancy. *–v.t.* **10.** to make void or of no effect; invalidate; nullify. **11.** to empty or discharge (contents); evacuate (excrement, etc.). **12.** *Archaic.* to make empty or vacant. **13.** *Archaic.* to clear or rid (fol. by *of*). **14.** *Archaic.* to leave, as a place. [ME, from OF *voide,* from LL *vocitus,* from *vocuus,* replacing L *vacuus* empty] **– voider,** *n.* **– voidness,** *n.*

**voidable** /'vɔɪdəbəl/, *adj.* **1.** capable of being voided. **2.** *Law.* capable of being made or adjudged void. **– voidableness,** *n.*

**voidance** /'vɔɪdns/, *n.* **1.** the act of voiding. **2.** annulment, as of a contract. **3.** ejection from a benefice. **4.** vacancy, as of a benefice.

**voile** /vɔɪl/, *n.* a semitransparent dress fabric of wool, silk, rayon, or cotton, with an open weave. [F: veil. See VEIL]

**voir dire** /vwa 'dɪə/, *n.* **1.** an oath administered to a proposed witness or juror by which he is sworn to speak the truth in an examination to ascertain his competence. **2.** the preliminary examination of a prospective witness or juror touching his competence. **3.** *Criminal Law.* statements made to a judge as to the character or previous convictions of a prisoner, after he has been convicted or pleaded guilty. [AF, from *voir* true, truly + *dire* say]

**voix céleste** /vwa sɛ'lɛst/, *n.* an organ stop having two pipes for each note tuned to very slightly different pitches and producing a wavering, gentle sound. [F: heavenly voice]

**vol.,** volume.

**volant** /'voʊlənt/, *adj.* **1.** flying; having the power of flight. **2.** *Poetic.* moving lightly; nimble. **3.** *Her.* represented as flying. [L *volans,* ppr. of *volāre* fly]

bird volant (def. 3)

**volante** /və'lænti/, *adv., adj.* moving quickly and lightly. [It.: flying]

**volar** /'voʊlə/, *adj.* of or pertaining to the palm of the hand or the sole of the foot. [L *vola* hollow of the hand or foot + -AR[1]]

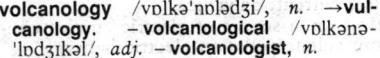

**volatile** /'vɒlətaɪl/, *adj.* **1.** evaporating rapidly; passing off readily in the form of vapour; *a volatile oil.* **2.** light and changeable of mind; frivolous; flighty. **3.** fleeting; transient. **4.** *Archaic.* able or accustomed to fly as winged creatures. **5.** (of wine) pricked; vinegary. **6.** pertaining to information in the memory bank of a computer which is lost when power is disconnected. [ME *volatil,* from L *volātilis* flying] **– volatility** /vɒlə'tɪləti/, **volatileness,** *n.*

**volatile oil** /– 'ɔɪl/, *n.* a distilled oil, esp. an essential oil distilled from plant tissue. Such oils are distinguished from glyceride oils by their volatility and failure to saponify.

**volatile salt** /– 'sɒlt/, *n.* **→sal volatile.**

**volatilise** /və'lætəlaɪz/, *v.,* **-lised, -lising.** *–v.i.* **1.** to become volatile; pass off as vapour. *–v.t.* **2.** to make volatile; cause to pass off in the form of vapour. Also, **volatilize. – volatilisable,** *adj.* **– volatilisation** /vəlætəlaɪ'zeɪʃən/, *n.* **– volatiliser,** *n.*

**vol-au-vent** /vɒl-oʊ-'võ/, *n.* a pastry case, often filled with meat in a sauce, or with fruit, or the like. [F: flight on the wind]

**volcanic** /vɒl'kænɪk/, *adj.* **1.** of or pertaining to a volcano or volcanoes: *a volcanic eruption.* **2.** discharged from or produced by volcanoes: *volcanic mud.* **3.** characterised by the presence of volcanoes. **4.** suggestive of a volcano, or its eruptive violence, etc. **5.** *Geol.* denoting a class of igneous rocks which have solidified on the earth's surface. **6. →mud volcano. – volcanically,** *adv.* **– volcanicity** /vɒlkə'nɪsəti/, *n.*

**volcanic glass** /– 'glas/, *n.* a natural glass produced when molten lava cools very rapidly; obsidian.

**volcanic neck** /– 'nɛk/, *n.* the eroded vent of a dead volcano, forming a topographic depression.

**volcanic plug** /– 'plʌg/, *n.* the eroded vent of a dead volcano, commonly forming a topographic high point.

**volcanic tuff** /– 'tʌf/, *n.* See **tuff.**

**volcanism** /'vɒlkənɪzəm/, *n.* the phenomena connected with volcanoes and volcanic activity.

**volcano** /vɒl'keɪnoʊ/, *n., pl.* **-noes, -nos. 1.** an opening in the earth's crust through which molten rock (lava), steam, ashes, etc., are expelled from within, either continuously or at irregular intervals, gradually forming a conical heap (or in time a mountain), commonly with a cup-shaped hollow (crater) about the opening. **2.** a mountain or hill having such an opening and formed wholly or partly of its own lava. [It., from L *Volcānus* Vulcan, god of fire]

volcano: A, main vent; B, cone; C, lava flow; D, rock strata; E, magma

**volcanology** /vɒlkə'nɒlədʒi/, *n.* **→vulcanology. – volcanological** /vɒlkənə'lɒdʒɪkəl/, *adj.* **– volcanologist,** *n.*

**vole** /voʊl/, *n.* any of the rodents of the genus *Microtus* and allied genera, resembling and belonging to the same family as the common rats and mice, and usu. of heavy build and having short limbs and tail. [short for *vole-mouse* field mouse; *vole,* from Scand.; cf. Norw. *voll* field, c. OE *weald* forested area]

vole

**volitant** /'vɒlətənt/, *adj.* **1.** flying; having the power of flight; volant. **2.** active; moving. [L *volitans,* ppr., flying to and fro]

**volitation** /vɒlə'teɪʃən/, *n.* the act or power of flying; flight. [ML *volitātio,* from *volitāre,* frequentative of *volāre* fly] **– volitational,** *adj.*

**volition** /və'lɪʃən/, *n.* **1.** the act of willing; exercise of choice to determine action. **2.** a determination by the will. **3.** the power of willing; will. [ML *volitio,* from L *volo* I wish] **– volitional, volitionary,** *adj.* **– volitionally,** *adv.*

**volitive** /'vɒlətɪv/, *adj.* **1.** characterised by or pertaining to volition. **2.** *Gram.* expressing a wish or permission: *a volitive construction.* [VOLIT(ION) + -IVE]

**Volkslied** /'foʊkslid/, *n., pl.* **-lieder.** a folksong. [G]

**volley** /'vɒli/, *n., pl.* **-leys,** *v.,* **-leyed, -leying.** *–n.* **1.** the flight of a number of missiles together. **2.** the discharge of a number of missiles or firearms simultaneously. **3.** a burst or outpouring of many things at once or in quick succession. **4.** *Tennis, etc.* **a.** a flight of a ball in play before striking the ground. **b.** a return of the ball before it touches the ground. **c.** a succession of such returns. **5.** *Cricket.* a ball so bowled that it reaches the batsman before it touches the ground; full toss. **6.** *Mining.* the explosion of several blasts in the rock at one time. *–v.t.* **7.** to discharge in or as in a volley. **8.** *Tennis, Soccer, etc.* to return, kick, etc., (the ball) before it strikes the ground. **9.** *Cricket.* to bowl (a ball) in such a manner that it is pitched near the top of the wicket. *–v.i.* **10.** to fly or be discharged together, as missiles. **11.** to move or proceed with great rapidity, as in a volley. **12.** to fire a volley or sound together, as firearms. **13.** to emit or produce loud sounds simultaneously or continuously. [F *volée* flight, from *voler* fly, from L *volāre*] – **volleyer,** *n.*

**volleyball** /'vɒlibɔl/, *n.* **1.** a game, played outdoors or in a gymnasium, the object of which is to prevent a large ball from touching the ground by striking it from side to side over a high net with the hands or arms. **2.** the ball used in this game.

**volplane** /'vɒlpleɪn/, *v.i.,* **-planed, -planing.** to glide towards the earth in an aeroplane, with no engine power or with the engine shut off. [F *vol plané* glided flight]

**vols,** volumes.

**volt**[1] /voult/, *n.* the derived SI unit of electric potential or electromotive force, defined as the difference of potential between two points of a conducting wire carrying a constant current of one ampere, when the power dissipated between these points is one watt. *Symbol.:* V [named after Alessandro *Volta,* 1745-1827, Italian physicist]

**volt**[2] /vɒlt/, *n.* →**volte.**

**volta** /'vɒltə/, *n., pl.* **-te** /-teɪ/. *Music.* turn; time (used in phrases): *una volta* (once), *due volte* (twice), *prima volta* (first time), *etc.* [It.: turn]

**volta-,** combining form of **voltaic,** as in *voltameter.*

**voltage** /'voultɪdʒ/, *n.* electromotive force or potential expressed in volts.

**voltage divider** /'– dəvaɪdə/, *n.* a resistor (or series of resistors) with either a fixed or adjustable tapping allowing a voltage to be obtained which is a fraction of the total voltage across the resistor (or series of resistors). Also, **potential divider, potentiometer.**

**voltage drop** /'– drɒp/, *n.* →**potential difference.**

**voltaic** /vɒl'teɪɪk/, *adj.* denoting or pertaining to the electricity or electric currents produced by chemical action, or, more broadly, to any electric current; galvanic.

**voltaic battery** /– 'bætri/, *n.* a source of electric current consisting of one or more voltaic cells; an electric battery.

**voltaic cell** /– 'sɛl/, *n.* See **cell** (def. 7).

**voltaic couple** /– 'kʌpəl/, *n.* (in a voltaic cell) the substances (commonly two metallic plates) in the dilute acid or other electrolyte, giving rise to the electric current.

**voltaic pile** /– 'paɪl/, *n.* an early form of voltaic battery consisting of a number of voltaic cells joined in series, each one containing a sheet of copper and a sheet of zinc separated by a piece of cloth moistened with dilute sulphuric acid. [named after Alessandro *Volta,* 1745-1827, Italian physicist]

**voltaism** /'vɒltə,ɪzəm/, *n.* the branch of electrical science that deals with the production of electricity or electric currents by chemical action.

**voltameter** /vɒl'tæmətə/, *n.* a device for measuring the quantity of electricity passing through a conductor by the amount of electrolytic decomposition it produces, or for measuring the strength of a current by the amount of such decomposition in a given time; coulometer. – **voltametric** /vɒltə'mɛtrɪk/, *adj.*

**voltammeter** /voult'æmətə/, *n.* an instrument which can be used for measuring either volts or amperes.

**volt-ampere** /voult-'æmpɛə/, *n.* an electrical unit equal to the product of one volt and one ampere, which with direct current circuits is equivalent to one watt.

**volte** /vɒlt/, *n.* **1.** *Fencing.* a sudden movement or leap to avoid a thrust. **2.** *Manège.* **a.** a circular or turning movement of a horse. **b.** a gait in which a horse going sideways turns around a centre, with the head turned outward. Also, **volt.** [F *volte,* from It. *volta* turn, from L *volvere* turn]

**volte-face** /vɒlt-'fas/, *n.* **1.** a turning so as to face in the opposite direction. **2.** a reversal of opinion or policy. [F, from It. *volta-faccia,* from *volta* turn + *faccia* face (from L *facies*)]

**volti** /'vɒlti/, *v. Music.* turn; turn over (a direction to turn the page). [It.]

**voltmeter** /'voultmitə/, *n.* an instrument for measuring the voltage between two points.

**voluble** /'vɒljəbəl/, *adj.* characterised by a ready and continuous flow of words, as a speaker or his tongue or speech; glibly fluent: *a voluble talker.* [L *volūbilis,* from *volvere* roll, turn] – **volubility** /vɒljə'bɪləti/, **volubleness,** *n.* – **volubly,** *adv.*

**volume** /'vɒljum/, *n.* **1.** a collection of written or printed sheets bound together and constituting a book. **2.** a book forming one of a related set or series. **3.** *Hist.* a roll of papyrus, parchment, or the like, or of manuscript. **4.** the size, measure, or amount of anything in three dimensions; the space occupied by a body or substance in cubic units; the SI unit of volume is the cubic metre ($m^3$). **5.** a mass or quantity, esp. a large quantity, of anything: *a volume of sound, to pour out volumes of abuse.* **6.** amount: *the volume of travel on a railway for a given period.* **7.** loudness or softness. **8.** fullness or quantity of tone or sound. [ME *volym,* from OF *volum,* from L *volūmen* roll (of papyrus or parchment); def. 4, etc., developed from meaning 'dimensions of a book']

**volume control** /'– kən,troul/, *n.* a manually operated potentiometer for controlling the output of an electronic circuit, esp. of the sound of a radio, television, or gramophone.

**volumed** /'vɒljumd/, *adj.* **1.** consisting of a volume or volumes (usu. with a qualifying adverb): *a many-volumed work.* **2.** in volumes of rolling or rounded masses, as smoke.

**volumeter** /vɒl'jumətə/, *n.* any of various instruments or devices for measuring volume, as of gases, liquids, or solids.

**volumetric** /vɒljə'mɛtrɪk/, *adj.* denoting, pertaining to, or depending upon measurement by volume. Also, **volumetrical.** – **volumetrically,** *adv.* – **volumetry** /vɒl'jumətri/, *n.* – **volumetrics,** *n.*

**volumetric analysis** /– ə'næləsəs/, *n.* **1.** chemical analysis by volume, esp. by titration. **2.** determination of the volume of gases or changes in their volume during combination.

**voluminous** /və'lumənəs/, *adj.* **1.** forming, filling, or writing a large volume or book, or many volumes: *a voluminous author.* **2.** sufficient to fill a volume or volumes: *a voluminous correspondence.* **3.** of great volume, size, or extent; in great volumes: *a voluminous flow of lava.* **4.** of ample size, extent, or fullness, as garments, draperies, etc. **5.** *Obs.* having many coils, convolutions, or windings. [LL *volūminōsus* full of folds. See VOLUME] – **voluminously,** *adv.* – **voluminousness, voluminosity** /vəlumə'nɒsəti/, *n.*

**voluntarism** /'vɒləntərɪzəm/, *n.* any theory regarding the will rather than the intellect as the fundamental agency or principle. – **voluntarist,** *n., adj.* – **voluntaristic** /vɒləntə'rɪstɪk/, *adj.*

**voluntary** /'vɒləntri, -ləntəri/, *adj., n., pl.* **-taries.** *–adj.* **1.** done, made, brought about, undertaken, etc., of one's own accord or by free choice: *a voluntary contribution.* **2.** acting of one's own will or choice: *a voluntary substitute.* **3.** pertaining to or depending on voluntary action or contribution. **4.** *Law.* **a.** acting or done without compulsion or obligation. **b.** done by intention, and not by accident: *voluntary manslaughter.* **c.** made without valuable consideration: *a voluntary conveyance or settlement.* **5.** *Physiol.* subject to or controlled by the will: *voluntary muscles.* **6.** having the power of willing or choosing: *a voluntary agent.* **7.** proceeding from a natural impulse; spontaneous: *voluntary faith.* *–n.* **8.** something done voluntarily. **9.** a piece of music, frequently spontaneous and improvised, performed as a prelude to a larger work, esp. a piece of organ music performed before, during, or after an office of the church. [ME, from L *voluntārius*] – **voluntarily,** *adv.* – **voluntariness,** *n.*

**voluntaryism** /'vɒləntriɪzəm, -təri-/, *n.* the principle or system of supporting churches, schools, etc., by voluntary contributions or aid, independently of the state. – **voluntaryist,** *n.*

**volunteer** /vɒlən'tɪə/, *n.* **1.** one who enters into any service of his own free will, or who offers himself for any service or undertaking. **2.** *Mil., etc.* one who enters one of the armed services voluntarily (rather than through conscription), specifically for special or temporary service (rather than as a member of the regular or permanent army). **3.** *Law.* **a.** a person whose actions are not founded on any legal obligation to so act. **b.** one to whom a conveyance is made or promise given without valuable consideration. *–adj.* **4.** entering voluntarily into any service; being a volunteer; consisting of volunteers. **5.** *Agric.* springing up spontaneously, or without being planted. *–v.i.* **6.** to offer oneself for some service or undertaking. **7.** to enter service or enlist as a volunteer. *–v.t.* **8.** to offer (one's services, etc. or oneself) for some duty or purpose. **9.** to offer to undertake or undergo: *volunteer a dangerous duty.* **10.** to offer to give, or to give, bestow, show, etc., voluntarily: *volunteer advice* (without being asked). **11.** to offer in speech; communicate, tell, or say voluntarily: *to volunteer an explanation.* [F *volontaire,* from L *voluntārius* VOLUNTARY]

**voluptuary** /və'lʌptʃuəri/, *n., pl.* **-aries,** *adj.* *–n.* **1.** one given up to luxurious or sensuous pleasures. *–adj.* **2.** pertaining to or characterised by luxurious or sensuous pleasures: *voluptuary habits.* [L *voluptuārius,* var. of *voluptārius,* from *voluptas* pleasure]

**voluptuous** /və'lʌptʃuəs/, *adj.* **1.** full of, characterised by, or ministering to pleasure or luxurious or sensuous enjoyment: *a voluptuous life.* **2.** derived from luxurious or full gratification of the senses: *voluptuous pleasure.* **3.** directed towards luxurious or sensuous enjoyment: *voluptuous desires.* **4.** given or inclined to luxurious enjoyment of the pleasures of the senses: *a voluptuous woman.* **5.** suggestive of an inclination to sensuous pleasure: *a voluptuous mouth.* **6.** sensuously pleasing or delightful: *voluptuous beauty.* **7.** (of the female figure) curvaceous. [ME, from L *voluptuōsus,* from *voluptas* pleasure] – **voluptuously,** *adv.* – **voluptuousness, voluptuosity,** *n.*

**volute** /və'ljut/, *n.* **1.** a spiral or twisted formation or object. **2.** *Archit.* a spiral scroll-like ornament, esp. one forming the distinctive feature of the Ionic capital or a more or less important part of the Corinthian and Composite capitals. **3.** *Zool.* **a.** a turn or whorl of a spiral shell. **b.** any of the Volutidae, a family of tropical marine gastropods, many species of which have shells prized for their beauty. *–adj.* **4.** in the form of a volute; rolled up. **5.** *Mach.* **a.** spirally shaped or having a part so shaped. **b.** moving in a circular way, esp. if combined with a lateral motion. [L *volūta* scroll] – **volution** /və'ljuʃən/, *n.*

volute (def. 2)

**volva** /'vɒlvə/, *n.* a cuplike membranous sheath at the base of the stalk in some toadstools and mushrooms. [L: covering]

**volvulus** /'vɒlvjələs/, *n.* a torsion or twisting of the intestine causing intestinal obstruction. [NL, from L *volvere* turn]

**vomer** /'voumə/, *n.* a bone of the skull in most vertebrates, in man being shaped like a ploughshare, and forming a large part of the nasal septum, or partition between the right and left nasal cavities. [L: ploughshare] – **vomerine** /'voumәraɪn, -әrәn/, *adj.*

**vomica** /'vɒməkə/, *n., pl.* **-cae** /-si/. **1.** a cavity, usu. in the lungs, containing pus. **2.** the pus content of such a cavity. [L: ulcer]

**vomit** /'vɒmət/, *v.i.* **1.** to eject the contents of the stomach by the mouth; spew; be sick. **2.** to be ejected or come out with force or violence. *–v.t.* **3.** to throw up or eject from the stomach through the mouth; spew. **4.** to cast out or eject as if in vomiting; to send out with force or copiously. *–n.* **5.** the act of vomiting. **6.** matter ejected in vomiting. [late ME *vomyte,* from L *vomitāre*] – **vomiter,** *n.* – **vomitive,** *adj.*

**vomitory** /'vɒmətri, -ətəri/, *adj., n., pl.* **-ries.** *–adj.* **1.** inducing vomiting; emetic. **2.** pertaining to vomiting. *–n.* **3.** an emetic. **4.** an opening through which something is ejected or discharged.

**vomiturition** /vɒmətʃə'rɪʃən/, *n.* **1.** ineffectual efforts to vomit. **2.** the vomiting of a little matter. **3.** *Obs.* vomiting with little effort.

**vomitus** /'vɒmətəs/, *n.* →**vomit.** [L]

**von** /fɒn, vɒn/, *prep.* from; of (much used in German personal names, originally before names of places or estates, and later before family names as an indication of nobility or rank). [G]

**voodoo** /'vudu/, *n., pl.* **-doos,** *adj., v.,* **-dooed, -dooing.** *–n.* **1.** a class of mysterious rites or practices, of the nature of sorcery, witchcraft, or conjuration, prevalent among the Negroes of the West Indies and the southern U.S., and probably of African origin. **2.** one who practises such rites. **3.** a fetish or other object of voodoo worship. *–adj.* **4.** pertaining to, associated with, or practising voodoo or voodooism. *–v.t.* **5.** to affect by or as by voodoo sorcery or conjuration. [Haitian Creole *vodu,* from an African language. See HOODOO]

**voodooism** /'vuduɪzəm/, *n.* the voodoo rites or practices; voodoo sorcery; the voodoo superstition. – **voodooist,** *n.* – **voodooistic** /vudu'ɪstɪk/, *adj.*

**voracious** /və'reɪʃəs/, *adj.* **1.** devouring or craving food in large quantities: *a voracious appetite.* **2.** greedy in eating; ravenous. **3.** eager and indefatigable: *she is a voracious reader.* [*voraci(ty)* (from L *vorācitas* greediness) + -OUS] – **voraciously,** *adv.* – **voracity** /və'ræsəti/, **voraciousness,** *n.*

**Vorlage** /'fɔlagə/, *n.* (in skiing) a position in which the skier leans forward but keeps his heels in contact with the skis. [G: forward position]

**-vorous,** a word element meaning 'eating', as in *carnivorous, herbivorous, omnivorous.* [L *-vorus* devouring]

**vortex** /'vɔtɛks/, *n., pl.* **-texes, -tices** /-təsiz/. **1.** a whirling movement or mass of water, as a whirlpool. **2.** a whirling movement or mass of air, as a whirlwind. **3.** a whirling mass of fire, flame, etc. **4.** a state of affairs likened to a whirlpool for violent activity, irresistible force, etc. **5.** something looked upon as drawing into its powerful whirl or current everything that is near it. **6.** (in old theories, as in the Cartesian philosophy) a rapid rotatory movement of cosmic matter about a centre, regarded as accounting for the origin or phenomena of bodies or systems of bodies in space. [L, var. of *vertex* VERTEX]

**vortical** /'vɔtɪkəl/, *adj.* **1.** of or pertaining to a vortex. **2.** resembling a vortex. **3.** moving in a vortex. – **vortically,** *adv.*

**vorticella** /vɔtə'sɛlə/, *n., pl.* **-cellae** /-'sɛli/. a transparent, bell-shaped animalcule on a fine elastic stem.

**vortices** /'vɔtəsiz/, *n.* a plural of **vortex.**

**vorticism** /'vɔtəsɪzəm/, *n.* (*sometimes cap.*) an English modern art movement initiated in 1914 and inspired by cubism and futurism. – **vorticist,** *n.*

**vorticose** /'vɔtəkous/, *adj.* vortical; whirling. [L *vorticōsus,* from *vortex* VORTEX]

**vortiginous** /vɔ'tɪdʒənəs/, *adj.* whirling; vortical. [var. of VERTIGINOUS]

**votable** /'voutəbəl/, *adj.* subject to a vote. Also, **voteable.**

**votary** /'voutəri/, *n., pl.* **-ries,** *adj.* *–n.* Also, **votarist. 1.** one who is bound by a vow, esp. one bound by vows to a religious life; a monk or a nun. **2.** a devotee of some form of religious worship; a devoted worshipper, as of God, a saint, etc. **3.** one devoted to some pursuit, study, etc. **4.** a devoted follower or admirer. *–adj. Obs.* **5.** consecrated by a vow. **6.** →**votive.** [L *vōtum* VOW + -ARY[1]] – **votaress, votress,** *n. fem.*

**vote** /vout/, *n., v.,* **voted, voting.** *–n.* **1.** a formal expression of will, wish, or choice in some matter, whether of a single individual, as one of a number interested in common, or of a body of individuals, signified by voice, by ballot, etc. **2.** the means by which such expression is made, as a ballot, ticket, etc. **3.** the right to such expression; suffrage. **4.** the decision reached by voting, as by a majority of ballots cast. **5.** a number of votes (or expressions of will) collectively: *the Labor vote, a light vote was polled.* **6.** an expression of feeling, as approval, or the like: *they gave him a vote of confidence.* **7.** an award, grant, or the like, voted: *a vote of $100 000 for a new building.* **8.** *Obs.* a vow. *–v.i.* **9.** to express or signify choice in a matter undergoing decision, as by a voice, ballot, or otherwise; give or cast a vote or votes: *for whom will you vote at the election?* **10. vote with one's feet,** *Colloq.* to express one's disapproval by leaving. *–v.t.* **11.** to enact, establish, or determine by vote; bring or put (*in, out, down,* etc.) by vote; grant by vote: *to vote an appropriation for a new school.* **12.** to support by one's vote: *to vote Liberal.* **13.** to advocate by or as by one's vote: *to vote that the report be accepted.* **14.** to declare by general consent: *they voted the trip a success.* [late ME, from L *vōtum* vow, wish]

**voter** /'voutə/, *n.* **1.** one who votes. **2.** one who has a right to vote; an elector.

**voting machine** /'voutɪŋ məʃin/, *n. U.S.* a mechanical substitute for the ballot-paper which automatically registers and counts votes.

**voting paper** /'– peɪpə/, *n.* →**ballot-paper.**

**votive** /'voutɪv/, *adj.* **1.** offered, given, dedicated, etc., in accordance with a vow: *a votive offering.* **2.** performed, undertaken, etc., in consequence of a vow. **3.** of the nature of or expressive of a wish or desire. **4.** *Rom. Cath. Ch.* optional; not prescribed: *a votive mass* (a mass which does not correspond with the office of the day, but is said at the choice of the priest). [L *vōtīvus* pertaining to a vow] – **votively,** *adv.* – **votiveness,** *n.*

**vouch** /vaʊtʃ/, *v.i.* **1.** to answer (*for*) as being true, certain, reliable, justly asserted, etc. **2.** to give warrant or attestation; give one's own assurance, as surety or sponsor (fol. by *for*): *I can vouch for him.* –*v.t.* **3.** to warrant; attest; confirm. **4.** to sustain or uphold by some practical proof or demonstration, or as such proof does. **5.** to affirm or declare as with warrant; vouch for. **6.** to adduce or quote in support, as extracts from a book or author; cite in warrant or justification, as authority, instances, facts, etc. **7.** to support or authenticate with evidence. **8.** *Law.* (formerly) to call or summon (a person) into court to make good a warranty of title. **9.** *Obs.* to call or take to witness, as a person. –*n. Obs.* **10.** a vouching. **11.** a supporting warrant or attestation. [ME *vouche,* from AF *voucher;* akin to L *vocāre* call]

**voucher** /'vaʊtʃə/, *n.* **1.** one who or that which vouches, as for something. **2.** a document, receipt, stamp, or the like, which proves the truth of a claimed expenditure. **3.** a ticket used as a substitute for cash, as a gift voucher, luncheon voucher, etc.

**vouchsafe** /vaʊtʃ'seɪf/, *v.,* **-safed, -safing.** –*v.t.* **1.** to grant or give, by favour, graciousness, or condescension: *to vouchsafe a reply.* **2.** to allow or permit, by favour or graciousness. –*v.i.* **3.** to condescend; deign; have the graciousness (to do something). [ME *vouche sauf,* lit., guarantee as safe. See VOUCH] – **vouchsafement,** *n.*

**vouge** /vuʒ/, *n.* a long-handled weapon with a kind of axe blade prolonged to a point at the top, used by foot soldiers in the 14th century and later.

**voussoir** /'vuswa/, *n.* any of the pieces, in the shape of a truncated wedge, which form an arch or vault. [ME, from F, from L *volvere* turn]

**vow** /vaʊ/, *n.* **1.** a solemn promise, pledge, or personal engagement: *marriage vows, a vow of secrecy.* **2.** a solemn or earnest declaration. **3.** a solemn, religiously binding promise made to God or to any deity or saint, as to perform some act, make some offering or gift, or enter some service or condition. **4.** a promise, limited in duration and in subject, made at the novitiate by one seeking to become a member of a religious community (**simple vow**). **5.** a promise, binding for life, and usu. undertaking absolute chastity, total poverty, and unquestioning obedience, made at the profession of a religious when the habit is taken (**solemn vow**). **6. take vows,** to enter a religious order or house. –*v.t.* **7.** to make a vow of; promise by a vow, as to God or a saint: *to vow a crusade or a pilgrimage.* **8.** to pledge oneself to do, make, give, observe, etc.; make a solemn threat or resolution of: *I vowed revenge.* **9.** to declare solemnly or earnestly; assert emphatically, or asseverate (oft. with a clause as object): *she vowed she would go to law.* **10.** to make (a vow). **11.** to dedicate or devote by a vow: *to vow oneself to the service of God.* –*v.i.* **12.** to make a solemn or earnest declaration; bind oneself by a vow. [ME *vou,* from AF, from L *vōtum*] – **vower,** *n.* – **vowless,** *adj.*

**vowel** /'vaʊəl/, *n.* **1.** *Phonet.* a voiced speech sound during the articulation of which air from the lungs is free to pass out through the middle of the mouth without causing undue friction. **2.** *Gram.* a letter which usually represents a vowel, as in English, *a, e, i, o,* and *u,* and sometimes *y.* –*adj.* **3.** pertaining to a vowel. [ME, from OF *vouel,* from L *vōcālis* (*littera*) vocal (letter)] – **vowelless,** *adj.*

**vowelise** /'vaʊəlaɪz/, *v.t.,* **-lised, -lising.** to provide (a Hebrew, Arabic, etc., text) with vowel points. Also, **vowelize.** – **vowelisation** /ˌvaʊəlaɪ'zeɪʃən/, *n.*

**vowel point** /'vaʊəl pɔɪnt/, *n.* (in Hebrew and Arabic writing and systems derived from them) any of certain marks placed above or below consonant letters to indicate vowels.

**vox** /vɒks/, *n., pl.* **voces** /'voʊsiz/. voice; sound. [L]

**vox angelica** /– æn'dʒɛlɪkə/, *n.* an organ stop producing delicate tones, and having two pipes for each digital, one of which is tuned slightly sharp, so that by their dissonance a wavy effect is produced. Also, **vox caelestis** /sə'lɛstɪs/. [L: angelic voice]

**vox barbara** /– 'babərə/, *n.* a word or term not conforming to classical standards or accepted usage (applied esp. to Neo-Latin terms in botany, zoology, etc., formed from elements that are neither Latin nor Greek). [L]

**vox humana** /– hju'manə/, *n.* an organ stop designed to produce tones resembling those of the human voice. [L: human voice]

**vox pop** /– 'pɒp/, *n. Chiefly Brit.* (in radio) a series of brief statements from a number of people, which are tightly edited and designed to give an indication of public opinion on a current issue, event, etc. [shortened form of VOX POPULI]

**vox populi** /– 'pɒpəli/, *n.* the voice or opinion of the people. [L]

**voyage** /'vɔɪɪdʒ/, *n., v.,* **-aged, -aging.** –*n.* **1.** a passage, or course of travel, by sea or water, esp. to a distant place. **2.** a flight through air or space, as a journey in an aeroplane. **3.** (formerly) a journey or passage from one place to another by land. **4.** (*oft. pl.*) a voyage as the subject of a written account, or the account itself. **5.** *Obs.* an enterprise or undertaking. –*v.i.* **6.** to make or take a voyage; travel by sea or water. –*v.t.* **7.** to traverse by a voyage. [F; replacing ME *viage,* from OF, from L *viāticum* provision for a journey] – **voyager,** *n.*

**voyeur** /vɔɪ'ɜ, vwa'jɜ/, *n.* one who attains sexual gratification by looking at sexual objects or situations. [F, from *voir* see]

**voyeurism** /'vɔɪərɪzəm, vwa'jɜrɪzəm/, *n.* a deviation in which sexual gratification is obtained by looking at sexual objects or situations; the condition of a voyeur. – **voyeuristic** /vɔɪə'rɪstɪk, vwajə-/, *adj.*

**v.p.,** verb passive.

**V.P.,** Also, **V. Pres.** Vice-President.

**VPC,** *Chem.* vapour-phase chromatography.

**v.r.,** verb reflexive.

**V.R.,** **1.** Vice-Regent. **2.** Queen Victoria. [L *Victoria regina*]

**V. Rev.,** Very Reverend.

**vs.,** **1.** verse. **2.** versus.

**v.s.,** vide supra.

**V.S.,** Veterinary Surgeon.

**V.S.** /vi 'ɛs/, *n.* a type of large yacht. [*V*(*aucluse*) *S*(*enior*)]

**V-shaped** /'vi-ʃeɪpt/, *adj.* in the shape of the letter V.

**V-sign** /'vi-saɪn/, *n.* **1.** a gesture made by holding up the first and second fingers spread apart with the palm facing outwards, symbolising victory. **2.** a similar obscene gesture made with the palm facing inwards usu. done with a thrusting motion, and indicating contempt.

**v.t.,** verb transitive.

**Vte,** Vicomte.

**Vtesse,** Vicomtesse.

**VTO,** vertical take-off.

**VTOL** /'vitɒl, vi ti oʊ 'ɛl/, *n.* an aircraft capable of taking off and landing vertically. [*V*(*ertical*) *T*(*ake*) *O*(*ff and*) *L*(*anding*)]

**VTR,** video tape recorder. Also, **V.T.R.**

**vugh** /vʌg/, *n. Mining.* a small cavity in a rock or lode, often lined with crystals. Also, **vug, vugg.** [Cornish *vooga* cave] – **vuggy,** *adj.*

**Vul.,** Vulgate.

**Vulcan** /'vʌlkən/, *n.* an imaginary planet with a smaller orbit than that of Mercury, which was believed to exist in the 19th century but whose existence has now been disproved. [named after *Vulcan,* the Roman god of fire and metal-working]

**vulcanian** /vʌl'keɪniən/, *adj.* **1.** volcanic. **2.** of metalworking.

**vulcanise** /'vʌlkənaɪz/, *v.t.,* **-nised, -nising.** **1.** to treat (indiarubber) with sulphur or some compound of sulphur, and subject to a moderate heat (110°-140°C), in order to render it non-plastic and give greater elasticity, durability, etc., or when a large amount of sulphur and a more extensive heat treatment are employed, in order to make it very hard, as in the case of vulcanite. **2.** to treat (indiarubber) similarly with sulphur or sulphur compounds but without heat, in which case the effects are only superficial. **3.** to subject (substances other than indiarubber) to some analogous process, as to harden. Also, **vulcanize.** – **vulcanisable** /vʌlkə'naɪzəbəl/, *adj.* – **vulcanisation** /vʌlkənaɪ'zeɪʃən/, *n.* – **vulcaniser,** *n.*

**vulcanised fibre** /ˌvʌlkənaɪzd 'faɪbə/, *n.* a fibre obtained by treating paper pulp with zinc chloride solution and used as a low-voltage electrical insulator.

**vulcanism** /ˈvʌlkənɪzəm/, *n.* the phenomena connected with the genesis and movement of molten rock material within and at the surface of the earth (including those phenomena connected with plutonic rocks as well as volcanism). Also, **vulcanicity** /vʌlkəˈnɪsəti/.

**vulcanite** /ˈvʌlkənaɪt/, *n.* a hard rubber, readily cut and polished, used for making combs, buttons, etc., and for electrical insulation, and obtained by vulcanising indiarubber with a large amount of sulphur; ebonite.

**vulcanology** /vʌlkəˈnɒlədʒi/, *n.* the scientific study of volcanoes and volcanic phenomena. Also, **volcanology.** – **vulcanological** /vʌlkənəˈlɒdʒɪkəl/, *adj.* – **vulcanologist,** *n.*

**Vulg.,** Vulgate.

**vulgar** /ˈvʌlgə/, *adj.* **1.** marked by ignorance of or want of good breeding or taste, as manners, actions, language, dress, display, etc.: *her appearance and manners were very vulgar.* **2.** crude; coarse; unrefined. **3.** obscene; indecent: *a vulgar joke.* **4.** ostentatious; unsubtle; lacking in good taste, as works: *a vulgar piece of architecture.* **5.** belonging to or constituting the common people of society: *the vulgar herd.* **6.** of, pertaining to, or current among the multitude or general mass of the people: *vulgar errors or superstitions.* **7.** spoken by or being in the language spoken by the people generally; vernacular: *a vulgar translation of the Greek text of the New Testament.* **8.** common or ordinary: *a vulgar fraction.* –*n.* **9.** *Archaic.* the common people. **10.** *Obs.* the vernacular. [ME, from L *vulgāris* pertaining to the common people] – **vulgarly,** *adv.* – **vulgarness,** *n.*

**vulgar fraction** /– ˈfrækʃən/, *n.* →**common fraction.**

**vulgarian** /vʌlˈgɛəriən/, *n.* a vulgar person, esp. one whose vulgarity is the more conspicuous for his wealth, prominence, or pretensions to good breeding.

**vulgarise** /ˈvʌlgəraɪz/, *v.t.,* **-rised, -rising.** **1.** to make vulgar, common or commonplace; to lower; debase: *to vulgarise manners or taste.* **2.** to put into general use; make known to the general public. Also, **vulgarize.** – **vulgarisation** /vʌlgəraɪˈzeɪʃən/, *n.* – **vulgariser,** *n.*

**vulgarism** /ˈvʌlgərɪzəm/, *n.* **1.** vulgar character or action; vulgarity. **2.** a vulgar expression; a word or phrase used only in common colloquial, and esp. in coarse, speech.

**vulgarity** /vʌlˈgærəti/, *n., pl.* **-ties.** **1.** the state or quality of being vulgar; commonness; plebeian character; want of good breeding, manners, or taste; coarseness. **2.** something vulgar; a vulgar act or speech; a vulgar expression; vulgarism.

**Vulgar Latin** /vʌlgə ˈlætn/, *n.* popular Latin, as opposed to literary or standard Latin, esp. those forms of popular Latin speech from which sprang the Romance languages of later times.

**Vulgate** /ˈvʌlgeɪt, -gət/, *n.* **1.** the Latin version of the Scriptures, accepted as the authorised version of the Roman Catholic Church. It was prepared mainly by Jerome near the end of the 4th century. **2.** (*l.c.*) any vulgate text or version. –*adj.* **3.** of or pertaining to the Vulgate. **4.** (*l.c.*) common, or in common use. [ML *Vulgāta,* short for LL *vulgāta ēditio* popular edition]

**vulnerable** /ˈvʌlnrəbəl, -nərəbəl/, *adj.* **1.** susceptible to being wounded; liable to physical hurt. **2.** not protected against emotional hurt; highly sensitive. **3.** not immune to moral attacks, as of criticism or calumny, or against temptations, influences, etc. **4.** (of a place, fortress, etc.) open to attack or assault; weak in respect of defence. **5.** *Contract Bridge.* exposed to greater than usual penalties (applied to the partners who have won one game towards a rubber). [LL *vulnerābilis* wounding] – **vulnerability** /vʌlnrəˈbɪləti, -nərə-/, **vulnerableness,** *n.* – **vulnerably,** *adv.*

**vulnerary** /ˈvʌlnərəri/, *adj., n., pl.* **-ries.** –*adj.* **1.** used or useful for healing wounds, as plants or remedies. –*n.* **2.** a remedy for wounds.

**vulpecular** /vʌlˈpɛkjələ/, *adj.* pertaining to or of the nature of a young fox or any fox; vulpine.

**vulpine** /ˈvʌlpaɪn/, *adj.* pertaining to, like, or characteristic of a fox. [L *vulpīnus*]

**vulture** /ˈvʌltʃə/, *n.* **1.** any of various large, carrion-eating birds related to the eagles, kites, hawks, falcons, etc., but having less powerful toes and straighter claws and usu. a naked head, esp. the species of the Old World family Vulturidae, as the **Egyptian vulture** (*Neophron percnopterus*), and those of the New World family Cathartidae, as the **turkey vulture** (*Cathartes aura*). **2.** a person or thing that preys ravenously and ruthlessly. [ME *vultur,* from L] – **vulture-like,** *adj.*

**vulturine** /ˈvʌltʃəraɪn/, *adj.* **1.** pertaining to or characteristic of vultures. **2.** resembling a vulture. Also, **vulturous.** [L *vulturīnus*]

**vulva** /ˈvʊlvə/, *n., pl.* **-vae** /-vi/, **-vas.** the external female genitalia, specifically, the two pairs of labia and the cleft between them. [L: wrapper] – **vulval, vulvar,** *adj.* – **vulviform,** *adj.*

vulture

**vulvitis** /vʌlˈvaɪtəs/, *n.* inflammation of the vulva.

**VU meter** /vi ˈju mitə/, *n.* a meter on devices which process audio signals, such as a tape-recorder or a mixer, which indicates the energy level of the signal to assist the operator in preventing overload while achieving optimum signal-to-noise ratio. [*V*(*olume*) *U*(*nit*) *meter*]

**vv.,** verses.

**v.v.,** vice versa.

**vv-ll.,** variae lectiones. See **varia lectio.** Also, **vv. ll.**

**vying** /ˈvaɪɪŋ/, *adj.* that vies; competing: *men vying with one another for attention.* – **vyingly,** *adv.*

Ww Roman SERIF GOTHIC

Ww Sans Serif MILLENIUM

Ww Script STUDIO

Ww Decorative DATA

*Although there are numerous typefaces in the world they can be divided into four main classifications. These are:*

*ROMAN or SERIF. This typeface came into being from the technique of the Roman masons who, working in stone, finished off each letter with a serif or small stroke projecting from the top or bottom. This was done to correct any feeling of unevenness or imbalance they may have created in cutting the characters in stone.*

*SANS SERIF (without serif). This typeface is geometric in design and has straight-edged characters and lines of a regular thickness.*

*SCRIPT. Based on the movement of the hand, this typeface is often italicised or slanted, as if drawn by a brush or quill pen.*

*DECORATIVE. Any typeface that exaggerates the characteristics of any of the other three classifications to a degree that places it outside of them.*

*The dictionary entries in this book use a SANS SERIF typeface called Helvetica (set in a bold face for the head words) and a SERIF typeface Plantin (used throughout the body of the entries).*

**W, w** /ˈdʌbəlju/, *n., pl.* **W's** or **Ws, w's** or **ws. 1.** the 23rd letter of the English alphabet. **2.** the twenty-third in order or of a series.

**w., 1.** weight. **2.** west. **3.** western. **4.** weekly. **5.** wide. **6.** width. **7.** widow. **8.** widower.

**W, 1.** *Elect.* watt; watts. **2.** west. **3.** western. **4.** *Chem.* **a.** wolfram. **b.** wolframium.

**W., 1.** Warden. **2.** Wednesday. **3.** West.

**W.A.** /ˌdʌbəlju ˈeɪ/, Western Australia. Also, **WA.**

**W.A.A.A.F.** /wæf/, Women's Auxiliary Australian Air Force.

**wabble** /ˈwɒbəl/, *v.i., v.t.,* **-bled, -bling,** *n.* →**wobble.** – **wabbler,** *n.* – **wabbling,** *adj.* – **wabblingly,** *adv.* – **wabbly,** *adj., adv.*

**wack** /wæk/, *n. Colloq.* an erratic, irrational, or unconventional person.

**wacke** /ˈwækə/, *n.* a soft rock of fine texture, derived from disintegrated basaltic rocks. [G: kind of stone]

**wacko** /wækˈoʊ/, *interj.* →**whacko.**

**wacky** /ˈwæki/, *adj.,* **wackier, wackiest.** *Chiefly U.S. Colloq.* erratic, irrational, or unconventional; crazy. Also, **whacky.**

**wad**[1] /wɒd/, *n., v.,* **wadded, wadding.** *–n.* **1.** a small mass or lump of anything soft. **2.** a small mass of cotton, wool, or other fibrous or soft material, used for stuffing, padding, packing, etc. **3.** a ball or mass of something squeezed together: *a wad of folded paper.* **4.** a roll or bundle, esp. of banknotes. **5.** a large quantity of something, esp. money. **6.** a plug of cloth, tow, paper, or the like, used to hold the powder or shot, or both, in place in a gun or cartridge. *–v.t.* **7.** to form into a wad. **8.** to hold in place by a wad, as powder or shot. **9.** to put a wad into (a gun, etc.). **10.** to fill out with or as with wadding; stuff; pad. [orig. uncert.; akin to Swed. *wadd,* G *Watte* wadding] – **wadder,** *n.*

**wad**[2] /wɒd/, *n.* a soft, earthy, black to dark brown mass of manganese oxide minerals. [orig. uncert.]

**wadding** /ˈwɒdɪŋ/, *n.* **1.** any fibrous or soft material for stuffing, padding, packing, etc., esp. carded cotton in specially prepared sheets. **2.** material for wads for guns, etc. **3.** a wad or lump.

**waddle** /ˈwɒdl/, *v.,* **-dled, -dling,** *n. –v.i.* **1.** to walk with short steps and swaying or rocking from side to side, as a duck. **2.** to move with a similar movement. *–n.* **3.** the act of waddling; a waddling gait. [frequentative of WADE] – **waddler,** *n.* – **waddlingly,** *adv.*

**waddy** /ˈwɒdi/, *n., pl.* **-dies,** *v.,* **-died, -dying.** *–n.* **1.** an Aboriginal heavy wooden war club. **2.** a heavy stick or club of any kind. *–v.t.* **3.** to beat or strike with a waddy. [Aboriginal]

waddy

**waddy-wood** /ˈwɒdi-wʊd/, *n.* a tree, *Acacia peuce,* with very hard dark wood, found in the dry interior of Australia.

**wade** /weɪd/, *v.,* **waded, wading,** *n. –v.i.* **1.** to walk through any substance, as water, snow, sand, etc., that impedes free motion: *wading in mud, wading through high grass.* **2.** to make one's way with labour or difficulty: *to wade through a dull book.* **3.** *Obs.* to go or proceed. **4. wade in** or **into,** *Colloq.* **a.** to begin energetically. **b.** to attack strongly. *–v.t.* **5.** to pass through or cross by wading; ford: *to wade a stream.* *–n.* **6.** the act of wading. [ME; OE *wadan* go, c. G *waten,* L *vādāre*]

**wader** /ˈweɪdə/, *n.* **1.** one who or that which wades. **2.** any of various long-legged birds, as cranes, herons, storks, sandpipers, plovers, etc., that wade in water in search of food. **3.** (*pl.*) high waterproof boots used for wading.

**wadi** /ˈwɒdi/, *n., pl.* **-ies.** (in Arabia, Syria, northern Africa, etc.) **1.** the channel of a watercourse which is dry except during periods of rainfall. **2.** the stream or watercourse itself. [Ar.]

**wading bird** /ˈweɪdɪŋ bɜd/, *n.* →**wader** (def. 2).

**Wadjuk** /ˈwɒdʒʊk/, *n.* an Australian Aboriginal language, now probably extinct, but originally spoken in the region of Perth, Western Australia.

**wady** /ˈwɒdi/, *n., pl.* **-ies.** →**wadi.**

**wafer** /ˈweɪfə/, *n.* **1.** a thin, crisp cake or biscuit, variously made, and often sweetened and flavoured, usu. eaten with ice-cream. **2.** a thin disc of unleavened bread, used in the Eucharist, as in the Roman Catholic Church. **3.** any of various other thin, flat cakes, sheets, or the like. **4.** a thin disc of dried paste, gelatine, adhesive paper, or the like, used for sealing letters, attaching paper, etc. **5.** *Med.* a thin, circular sheet of dry paste or the like, or a pair of such sheets, used upon moistening to wrap about or enclose a powder to be swallowed. *–v.t.* **6.** to seal, close, or attach by means of a wafer or wafers: *to wafer a letter.* [ME *wafre,* from OF *waufre,* from MLG *wafel* honeycomb. Cf. WAFFLE[1]] – **waferlike, wafery,** *adj.*

**wafer-thin** /ˈweɪfə-θɪn/, *adj.* very thin.

**waffle**[1] /ˈwɒfəl/, *n.* a batter cake with deep indentations formed by baking it in a waffle iron. [D *wafel.* Cf. WAFER]

**waffle**[2] /ˈwɒfəl/, *v.,* **-fled, -fling.** *Colloq.* *–v.i.* **1.** to speak or write vaguely, pointlessly, and at considerable length. **2.** to talk or write nonsense. *–n.* **3.** verbosity in the service of superficial thought. **4.** nonsense; twaddle. Also, **woffle.** [frequentative of Brit. d. *waff* to yelp]

**waffle-iron** /ˈwɒfəl-aɪən/, *n.* a metal appliance with two hinged parts, and a grid which leaves deep impressions on the batter baked inside it.

**waffle-weave** /ˈwɒfəl-wiv/, *adj.* **1.** of or pertaining to a fabric, etc., woven to resemble a waffle. *–n.* **2.** such a fabric.

**waft** /wɒft/, *v.t.* **1.** to bear or carry through the air or over water: *the gentle breeze wafted the sound of voices.* **2.** to bear or convey lightly as if in flight: *he wafted her away.* *–v.i.* **3.** to float or be carried, esp. through the air. *–n.* **4.** a sound, smell, etc., carried through the air: *a waft of bells.* **5.** a wafting movement; current or gust: *a waft of wind.* **6.** the act of wafting. **7.** *Naut.* →**waif** (def. 4). [backformation from obs. *wafter,* late ME *waughter* armed escort vessel, from D or LG *wachter* guard.] – **wafter,** *n.*

**wafture** /ˈwɒftʃə/, *n.* **1.** the act of wafting. **2.** something wafted: *waftures of incense.*

**wag**[1] /wæg/, *v.,* **wagged, wagging,** *n.* *–v.t.* **1.** to move from side to side, forwards and backwards, or up and down, esp. rapidly and repeatedly: *a dog wagged his tail.* **2.** to move (the tongue) in talking. **3.** to shake (a finger) at someone, esp. in reproval, reproach, or admonition. **4.** to be absent from (school, etc.) without permission. **5. wag it,** *Colloq.* to deliberately stay away from school, work, etc., without permission. *–v.i.* **6.** to be moved from side to side or one way and the other, esp. rapidly and repeatedly, as the head or the tail. **7.** (of the tongue) to move busily, esp. in idle or indiscreet talk. **8.** to get along; travel; proceed: *how the world wags.* **9.** to totter or sway. *–n.* **10.** the act of wagging. **11. play the wag,** to wag school. [ME *wagge,* from Scand.; cf. Icel. *vaga* to rock]

**wag**[2] /wæg/, *n.* **1.** a humorous person; joker. **2. play the wag,** to entertain with jokes, silly antics, etc. [orig. unknown]

**wage** /weɪdʒ/, *n., v.,* **waged, waging.** *–n.* **1.** (*oft. pl.*) that which is paid for work or services, as by the day or week; hire; pay. **2.** (*pl.*) *Econ.* the share of the products of industry received by labour for its work, as distinct from the share going to capital. **3.** (*usu. pl., sometimes construed as sing.*) recompense or result: *the wages of sin is death.* **4.** *Obs.* a pledge or security. *–v.t.* **5.** to carry on (a battle, war, conflict, etc.): *to wage war against a nation.* **6.** *Obs.* **a.** to stake or wager. **b.** to pledge. *–v.i.* **7.** *Obs.* to contend; battle. [ME, from OF *wagier,* from *wage* pledge. See GAGE[1]] – **wageless,** *adj.*

**wage-earner** /ˈweɪdʒ-ɜnə/, *n.* one who works for wages (as opposed to *salary).*

**wage freeze** /ˈweɪdʒ friz/, *n.* →**freeze** (def. 30).

**wage increment** /ˈ– ɪŋkrəmənt/, *n.* →**increment** (def. 4).

**wage-price-freeze** /weɪdʒ-ˈpraɪs-friz/, *n.* a simultaneous freeze on both wages and prices.

**wager** /ˈweɪdʒə/, *n.* **1.** something staked or hazarded on an uncertain event; a bet. **2.** the act of betting. **3.** the subject of a bet. **4.** *Archaic.* a pledge to make good one's cause. **5.** →**wagering contract.** *–v.t.* **6.** to hazard (something) on the issue of a contest or any uncertain event or matter; stake; bet. **7.** *Hist.* to pledge oneself to (battle) for the decision of a case. *–v.i.* **8.** to make or offer a wager; bet. [ME, from AF *wageure.* See WAGE] – **wagerer,** *n.*

**wagering contract** /ˌweɪdʒərɪŋ ˈkɒntrækt/, *n.* a contract in which mutual promises are made between two persons, that one will pay the other a certain sum of money if a certain event is ascertained to have happened. Also, **wager.**

**wager of law,** *n. Old Eng. Law.* a proceeding by which a defendant discharged himself on his own oath, bringing eleven neighbours to support his denial of the charge of claim.

**wage-sharing** /ˈweɪdʒ-ʃɛərɪŋ/, *n.* an industrial strategy to reduce unemployment, whereby more than one person is employed on a job but no more in wages are paid overall than if only one had been employed.

**wagga** /ˈwɒgə/, *n.* a blanket made from hessian bags or similar material. Also, **Wagga blanket, Wagga rug.** [from *Wagga Wagga,* town in N.S.W.]

**waggery** /ˈwægəri/, *n., pl.* **-geries. 1.** the action, spirit, or language of a wag. **2.** a waggish act; a jest.

**waggish** /ˈwægɪʃ/, *adj.* **1.** like a wag; roguish in merriment and good humour; jocular. **2.** characteristic of or befitting a wag: *waggish humour.* – **waggishly,** *adv.* – **waggishness,** *n.*

**waggle** /ˈwægəl/, *v.,* **-gled, -gling,** *n.* *–v.t., v.i.* **1.** to wag with short, quick movements. *–n.* **2.** a waggling motion. [frequentative of WAG[1]. Cf. G *wackeln* stagger] – **wagglingly,** *adv.*

**waggly** /ˈwægli/, *adj.* waggling; unsteady.

**waggon** /ˈwægən/, *n.* →**wagon.** – **waggonage,** *n.* – **waggoner,** *n.* – **waggonette,** *n.*

**waggon-headed** /ˈwægən-hɛdəd/, *adj.* →**wagon-headed.**

**Wagnerian** /vagˈnɪəriən/, *adj.* **1.** of, pertaining to, or like the composer Richard Wagner (1813-1883), or his works. **2.** of a singer, suited to singing in Wagnerian operas. **3.** (*joc.*) a woman of large proportions. *–n.* **4.** Also, **Wagnerite.** a follower or admirer of the music or theories of Richard Wagner.

**Wagnerism** /ˈvagnərɪzəm/, *n.* **1.** Richard Wagner's theory of method as exemplified in his music dramas, which, departing from the conventional methods of earlier (esp. Italian) opera, shows constant attention to dramatic and emotonal effect, and the abundant use of the leitmotiv. **2.** the study, imitation, or influence of the music of Richard Wagner. – **Wagnerist,** *n.*

**Wagnerite** /ˈvagnəraɪt/, *n.* a person who has an enthusiasm for Wagnerian opera.

**Wagner tuba** /vagnə ˈtjubə/, *n.* **1.** either of two modified French horns, designed by Richard Wagner, of tenor and bass range. **2.** a double-bass tuba.

**wagon** /ˈwægən/, *n.* **1.** any of various kinds of four-wheeled vehicles, esp. one designed for the transport of heavy loads, delivery, etc. **2.** a railway truck. **3.** →**paddy-wagon. 4.** *Obs.* a chariot. **5.** *Colloq.* a tea-trolly. **6. on the (water) wagon,** *Colloq.* abstaining from alcoholic drink. *–v.t.* **7.** to transport or convey by wagon. Also, **waggon.** [D *wagen,* c. OE *wægn* WAIN] – **wagonless,** *adj.*

**wagonage** /ˈwægənɪdʒ/, *n. Archaic.* **1.** transport or conveyance by wagon. **2.** money paid for this. **3.** a collection of wagons; wagons collectively. Also, **waggonage.**

**wagoner** /ˈwægənə/, *n.* one who drives a wagon. Also, **waggoner.**

**wagonette** /wægəˈnɛt/, *n.* a four-wheeled horse-drawn vehicle, with or without a top, having a crosswise seat in front and two lengthwise seats facing each other at the back. Also, **waggonette.**

wagonette

**wagon-headed** /ˈwægən-hɛdəd/, *adj.* of the form of a round arch or semicylinder, like the cover of a wagon when stretched over the bows, as a ceiling, roof, etc. Also, **waggon-headed.**

**wagon-lit** /vagõ-ˈli/, *n.* (in French and other Continental use) a railway sleeping-car. [F, from *wagon* railway coach, WAGON + *lit* bed]

**wagonload** /ˈwægənloʊd/, *n.* the load carried by a wagon.

**wagon train** /ˈwægən treɪn/, *n. U.S.* (formerly) a train of wagons and horses, esp. one carrying military supplies.

**wagtail** /ˈwægteɪl/, *n.* **1.** any of numerous small, chiefly Old World birds of the family Motacillidae, having a slender body with a long, narrow tail which is habitually wagged up and down. **2.** any of various fantails, as the Willie wagtail.

**wahine** /waˈhini/, *n. N.Z.* a girl or woman, usu. Maori. [Maori]

**wahoo** /waˈhu, ˈwahu/, *n., pl.* **-hoos.** a large, swift game fish, *Acanthocybium solandri,* found in tropical seas. [Amer. Ind.]

**wah wah pedal,** *n.* a pedal which can be attached to a musical instrument, and is used to alternate the bass and treble levels of the sound output, thus producing a 'wah wah' effect. Also, **wah-wah pedal.**

**waiata** /ˈwaɪatə/, *n. N.Z.* a Maori song. [Maori]

**waif** /weɪf/, *n.* **1.** a person without home or friends, esp. a child. **2.** a stray thing or articles. **3.** something found, of which the owner is not known, as an animal. **4.** Also, **waft.** *Naut.* a signalling, or a signal given, by a flag rolled and stopped or fastened. [ME, from AF, probably from Scand.; cf. Icel. *veif* oscillation]

**wail** /weɪl/, *v.i.* **1.** to utter a prolonged, inarticulate, mournful cry, usu. high-pitched or clear-sounding, as in grief or suffering: *the child wailed when he fell over.* **2.** to sound mournfully, as music, the wind, etc. **3.** to lament or mourn bitterly. *–v.t.* **4.** to wail over; bewail; lament: *to wail the dead.* **5.** to cry or say in lamentation. *–n.* **6.** the act of wailing. **7.** a wailing cry, as of grief, pain, etc. **8.** any similar mournful sound: *the wail of an old tune.* [ME *weile,* from Scand.; cf. Icel. *vǣla* wail, from *vǣ,* var. of *vei* woe] **– wailer,** *n.* **– wailingly,** *adv.*

**Wailbri** /'walbri/, *n.* →**Walbiri.**

**wailful** /'weɪlfəl/, *adj.* mournful; plaintive. **– wailfully,** *adv.*

**wailsome** /'weɪlsəm/, *adj.* wailing.

**wain** /weɪn/, *n. Chiefly Poetic.* a wagon or cart. [ME; OE *wægn,* c. D *wagen,* G *Wagen.* Cf. OE *wegan* carry]

**wainscot** /'weɪnskət, -koʊt/, *n., v.,* **-scoted, -scoting** or **-scotted, -scotting.** *–n.* **1.** oak or other wood, usu. in panels, serving to line the walls of a room, etc. **2.** a dado, or a facing of any material on interior walls, etc. **3.** the lower portion of a wall surfaced in a different manner or material from the upper portion. **4.** (originally) a superior quality of oak imported into England for fine panelled work and the like. *–v.t.* **5.** to line (a room, walls, etc.) with wainscot or wood: *a room wainscoted in oak.* [ME *waynscot,* half translation, half adoption of MLG *wagenschot,* from *wagen* WAIN + *schot,* of doubtful meaning]

**wainscoting** /'weɪnskətɪŋ, -koʊt-/, *n.* **1.** panelling or woodwork with which walls, etc., are wainscoted. **2.** wainscots collectively. Also, **wainscotting.**

**wainwright** /'weɪnraɪt/, *n.* a wagon maker and repairer.

**waipiro** /waɪ'piroʊ/, *n. N.Z. Colloq.* strong alcoholic drink. [Maori *wai* water, + *piro* stinking]

**waist** /weɪst/, *n.* **1.** the part of the human body between the ribs and the hips. **2.** the part of a garment covering the waist. **3.** that part of an object, esp. a central or middle part, which bears some analogy to the human waist: *the waist of a violin.* **4.** *Naut.* the central part of a ship; that part of the deck between the forecastle and the quarterdeck. **5.** the narrow part or petiole of the abdomen of certain insects, as the wasp. [ME *wast,* c. Icel. *vöxtr,* OHG *wahst* growth. See WAX[2], *v.,* grow] **– waistless,** *adj.*

**waistband** /'weɪstbænd/, *n.* a band encircling the waist, esp. as a part of a skirt, trousers, etc.

**waistcloth** /'weɪstklɒθ/, *n.* →**loincloth.**

**waistcoat** /'weɪstkoʊt/, *n.* **1.** a close-fitting, sleeveless garment for men which reaches to the waist and buttons down the front, and is designed to be worn under a jacket. **2.** a similar garment sometimes worn by women. **3.** a body garment for men, formerly worn under the doublet. **– waistcoated,** *adj.*

**waisted** /'weɪstəd/, *adj.* shaped like or so as to form a waist.

**waist-high** /'weɪst-haɪ/, *adj.* reaching as high as the waist. Also, **waist-deep.**

**waistline** /'weɪstlaɪn/, *n.* **1.** a line around the body at the smallest part of the waist. **2.** that part of a woman's dress, coat, etc., which lies at or close to the waist. **3. watch one's waistline,** to take care with one's diet, so as not to put on weight; to be on a diet.

**wait** /weɪt/, *v.i.* **1.** to stay or rest in expectation; remain in a state of quiescence or inaction, as until something expected happens (oft. fol. by *for, till,* or *until*): *waiting for him to go.* **2.** (of things) to be in readiness: *a letter waiting for you.* **3.** to remain neglected for a time: *a matter that can wait.* **4.** to postpone or delay something or to be postponed or delayed. **5. wait on** or **upon, a.** to perform the duties of an attendant or servant for. **b.** to supply the wants of (a person) at table. **c.** to call upon or visit (a person, esp. a superior): *to wait on the emperor in his palace.* **d.** to attend as an accompaniment or consequence. **6. to wait up,** to delay going to bed to await someone's arrival. *–v.t.* **7.** to continue stationary or inactive in expectation of; await: *to wait one's turn in a queue.* **8.** (of things) to be in readiness for; be reserved for: *glory waits thee.* **9.** *Colloq.* to defer or postpone in expectation of the arrival of someone: *to wait dinner for the guests.* **10.** *Obs.* to attend upon or escort, esp. as a sign of honour. **11. wait table,** to wait at table; serve. *–n.* **12.** the act of waiting or awaiting; delay; halt. **13.** a period or interval of waiting. **14.** *Theat.* the time between two acts or the like. **15.** (*usu. pl.*) one of a band of singers and musicians who go about the streets by night at Christmas singing and playing carols, etc. **16.** *Obs.* the hourly calls of the watchman. **17. lie in wait,** to wait in ambush. [ME *waite(n),* from OF *waitier,* from OHG *wahtēn* watch; akin to WATCH]

**wait-a-bit** /'weɪt-ə-bɪt/, *n.* any of various plants bearing thorns or prickly appendages, as a procumbent herb, *Harpagophytum procumbens,* of southern Africa, or **wait-a-while,** *Acacia colletioides,* of Australia. [translation of Afrikaans *wacht-een-beetje* from the thorns which caught the clothing of the passer-by]

**waiter** /'weɪtə/, *n.* **1.** a man who waits at table, as in a restaurant, hotel, etc. **2.** a tray on which dishes, etc., are carried; salver. **3.** one who waits or awaits. **4.** *Obs.* an attendant.

**waiting** /'weɪtɪŋ/, *n.* **1.** a period of waiting. **2. in waiting,** in attendance, as upon a king, queen, prince, etc. *–adj.* **3.** that serves or attends: *a waiting man, waiting maid.*

**waiting game** /'– geɪm/, *n.* **1.** the postponement of action on a particular matter for the time being in order to have an opportunity for more effective action later on. **2. play a waiting game,** *Colloq.* to avoid any definite action in the belief that the passage of time will alter circumstances to one's advantage.

**waiting list** /'– lɪst/, *n.* a list of persons waiting for something to become available, as applicants for housing accommodation, etc.

**waiting room** /'– rum/, *n.* a room for the use of persons waiting, as in a railway station or a doctor's surgery.

**waitlist** /'weɪtlɪst/, *n.* **1.** a list of persons waiting for a seat or berth to become available on an aeroplane, ship, etc. *–v.t.* **2.** to place the name of (a person) on such a list.

**waitress** /'weɪtrəs/, *n.* a woman who waits at table, as in a restaurant, hotel, etc.

**waive** /weɪv/, *v.t.,* **waived, waiving. 1.** to forbear to insist on; relinquish; forgo: *to waive one's rank, to waive honours.* **2.** *Law.* to relinquish (a known right, etc.) intentionally. **3.** to put aside for the time; defer. **4.** to put aside or dismiss from consideration or discussion: *waiving my attempts to explain.* [ME *weyven,* from AF *weyver* abandon. See WAIF]

**waiver** /'weɪvə/, *n.* **1.** (in law) an intentional relinquishment of some right, interest, or the like. **2.** an express or written statement of such relinquishment. [AF *weyver.* See WAIVE]

**wake**[1] /weɪk/, *v.,* **woke, woken, waking** or (*Chiefly U.S.*) **waked, waken, waking,** *n.* *–v.i.* **1.** to become roused from sleep; awake (oft. fol. by *up*). **2.** to be or continue awake. **3.** to remain awake for some purpose, duty, etc. **4.** to become roused from a quiescent or inactive state. **5.** to become alive, as to something perceived; become aware of. **6.** *Archaic.* to keep watch or vigil. **7. wake up to (oneself),** *Colloq.* to adopt a more sensible and responsible attitude. *–v.t.* **8.** to rouse from sleep; awake (oft. fol. by *up*). **9.** to rouse from quiescence, inactivity. lethargy, unconsciousness, etc. (oft. fol. by *up*). **10.** *Archaic.* to keep watch or vigil. *–n.* **11.** a watching, or a watch kept, esp. for some solemn or ceremonial purpose. **12.** a watch, esp. at night, near the body of a dead person before burial, often accompanied by drinking and feasting. **13.** the state of being awake: *between sleep and wake.* [ME *wake(n),* OE *wacian,* c. D *waken,* G *wachen,* Icel. *vaka* wake, watch; ME *woke,* OE *wōc* (past tense)] **– waker,** *n.*

**wake**[2] /weɪk/, *n.* **1.** the track left by a ship or other object moving in the water. **2.** the path or course of anything that has passed or preceded. **3. in the wake of, a.** following behind. **b.** following as a result or consequence of. [Scand.; cf. Icel. *vök* hole in the ice]

**wakeful** /'weɪkfəl/, *adj.* **1.** indisposed or unable to sleep, as a person. **2.** characterised by absence of sleep: *a wakeful night.* **3.** watchful or vigilant: *a wakeful foe.* **– wakefully,** *adv.* **– wakefulness,** *n.*

**waken** /'weɪkən/, *v.t.* **1.** to rouse from sleep; awake. **2.** to rouse from inactivity; stir up or excite; arouse. *–v.i.* **3.** to wake, or become awake; awaken. [ME; OE *wæcnan,* c. Icel.

*vakna.* See WAKE[1]] – **wakener,** *n.*

**wake-robin** /ˈweɪk-rɒbən/, *n.* **1.** →**cuckoopint.** **2.** any of various other arums or other genera of the family Araceae. **3.** any of various plants of North America of the genus *Trillium,* as *T. erectum,* a species with ill-scented purple, pink, or white flowers.

**wake-up** /ˈweɪk-ʌp/, *n. Colloq.* **1.** one who is fully aware: *he's a real wake-up.* **2. take a wake-up,** to understand; perceive meaning or purpose of (fol. by *to*).

**wakey-wakey** /ˈweɪki-weɪki/, *Colloq.* –*n.* **1.** the time to rise from bed. –*interj.* **2.** wake up!

**Walbiri** /ˈwalbri/, *n.* an Australian Aboriginal language from the north of Central Australia, still in full tribal use with an estimated 1400 speakers. Also, **Wailbri.**

**waldorf salad** /ˌwɔldɔf ˈsæləd/, *n.* a crisp, chopped salad including apples, celery and walnuts in a light dressing.

**wale** /weɪl/, *n., v.,* **waled, waling.** –*n.* **1.** a streak, stripe, or ridge produced on the skin by the stroke of a rod or whip; a welt. **2.** a ridge or raised line formed in the weave of cloth. **3.** the texture of a fabric; the kind of weave. **4.** a ledger, esp. one used to support the planking in a trench. **5.** *Naut.* **a.** any of certain strakes of thick outside planking on the sides of a wooden ship. **b.** the gunwale. –*v.t.* **6.** to mark with wales. **7.** to weave with wales. [ME; OE *walu* weal, ridge, probably akin to Icel. *völr,* Goth *walus* rod, wand]

**Wales** /weɪlz/, *n.* a division of the United Kingdom, a principality forming the south-western part of the island of Britain.

**waling** /ˈweɪlɪŋ/, *n.* a set or row of wales or planks.

**walk** /wɔk/, *v.i.* **1.** to go or travel on foot at a moderate pace; to proceed by steps, or by advancing the feet in turn, at a moderate pace (in bipedal locomotion, so that there is always one foot on the ground, and in quadrupedal locomotion, so that there are always two or more feet on the ground). **2.** to go about or travel on foot for exercise or pleasure. **3.** to go about on the earth, or appear to living persons, as a ghost. **4.** (of things) to move in a manner suggestive of walking, as through repeated vibrations or the effect of alternate expansion and contraction. **5.** to conduct oneself in a particular manner, or pursue a particular course of life: *to walk humbly with thy God.* **6.** *Baseball, Softball.* to go to first base after the pitcher has thrown four balls (def. 5). **7.** *Obs.* to be in motion or action. –*v.t.* **8.** to proceed through, over, or upon by walking: *walking Sydney streets by night.* **9.** to cause to walk; lead, drive, or ride at a walk, as an animal: *walking their horses towards us.* **10.** to force or help to walk, as a person. **11.** to conduct or accompany on a walk: *he walked them about the park.* **12.** to move (an object, as a box or a trunk) in a manner suggestive of walking, as by a rocking motion. **13.** to examine, measure, etc., by traversing on foot: *to walk a track.* –*v.* **14.** Some special verb phrases are:

**walk all over (someone),** *Colloq.* to behave in a domineering and aggressive fashion towards (someone).

**walk away with,** to win easily.

**walk into,** to encounter unwittingly: *he walked into my trap.*

**walk off,** to get rid of by walking: *to walk off a headache.*

**walk off with, 1.** to remove without permission; steal. **2.** to win, as in a competition. **3.** to outdo one's competitors; win easily.

**walk out, 1.** to go on strike. **2.** to leave in protest; leave angrily.

**walk out on,** to abandon; forsake; desert.

**walk out with,** to court, woo, or be courted or wooed by.

**walk over, 1.** (of an unopposed contestant) to go over (the course) at walking pace and thus be judged the winner. **2.** to win easily.

**walk the board,** *Surfing.* to walk along the board while riding a wave, usu. as a means of controlling the board's performance.

**walk the streets, 1.** to wander about the streets, esp. as a result of being homeless. **2.** to be a prostitute, esp. one who solicits on the streets.

**walk up, 1.** to ascend; go upstairs. **2.** to approach on foot; draw near.

–*n.* **15.** the act or course of walking, or going on foot. **16.** a spell of walking for exercise or pleasure: *to take a walk.* **17.** a distance walked or to be walked, often in terms of the time required: *ten minutes' walk from the station.* **18.** the gait or pace of a person or animal that walks. **19.** manner of walking: *impossible to mistake her walk.* **20.** a department or branch of activity, or a particular line of work: *they found every walk of life closed against them.* **21.** *Athletics.* a walking race. **22.** a way for pedestrians at the side of a street or road; a path or pavement. **23.** a place prepared or set apart for walking. **24.** a path in a garden or the like. **25.** a passage between rows of trees. **26.** an enclosure in which poultry may run about freely. **27.** →**sheepwalk.** **28.** →**ropewalk.** **29.** a plantation of coffee or other trees, as in the West Indies. **30.** *Baseball, Softball.* an instance of walking. [ME; OE *wealcan* roll, toss, *gewealcan* go, c. D and G *walken* to full (cloth), Icel. *vālka* toss] – **walkable,** *adj.* – **walker,** *n.*

**walkabout** /ˈwɔkəbaʊt/, *n.* **1.** a period of wandering as a nomad, often as undertaken by Aborigines who feel the need to leave the place where they are in contact with white society, and return for spiritual replenishment to their traditional way of life. **2. go walkabout, a.** to wander around the country in a nomadic manner. **b.** to be misplaced or lost.

**walkathon** /ˈwɔkəθɒn/, *n.* a charity drive (def. 26) in which participants are guaranteed a donation in proportion to the distance walked.

**walkaway** /ˈwɔkəweɪ/, *n.* an easy victory or conquest.

**walkie-talkie** /wɔki-ˈtɔki/, *n.* a combined radio transmitter and receiver, light enough to be carried by one man, developed originally for military use in World War II and subsequently widely used by police, medical services, etc.

**walking** /ˈwɔkɪŋ/, *adj.* **1.** that walks; able to walk. **2.** used for or in walking: *walking shoes.* **3.** characterised by or consisting of walking: *a walking holiday.* **4.** of or pertaining to an implement, machine, etc., drawn by an animal and operated by a person on foot: *a walking plough.* **5. give (one) one's walking papers,** *Colloq.* to sack; dismiss. –*n.* **6.** the act of one who or that which walks: *walking was the best exercise for him.* **7.** manner or style of walking. **8.** the state of the grass, paths, etc. on which one walks: *dry walking in the garden.*

**walking bass** /– ˈbeɪs/, *n.* a bass part which consists of scale-like patterns played in a simple rhythm, as in baroque music or swing music.

**walking fern** /ˈ– fɜn/, *n.* a fern of the family Polypodiaceae, *Camptosorus rhizophyllus,* with simple fronds tapering into a prolongation which often takes root at the apex.

**walking race** /ˈ– reɪs/, *n.* a race in which the winner is the one who walks the fastest.

**walking-stick** /ˈwɔkɪŋ-stɪk/, *n.* **1.** a stick used to aid in walking; a cane. **2.** *N.Z.* →**stick insect.**

**walking-stick palm** /– ˈpam/, *n.* a slender, erect palm, *Bacularia monostachya,* of northern New South Wales and southern Queensland.

**walking ticket** /ˈwɔkɪŋ tɪkət/, *n. Colloq.* dismissal from one's place of work; the sack: *he was given a walking ticket.* Also, **walking papers.**

**walking track** /ˈ– træk/, *n.* a track made in the bush for the use of bushwalkers.

**walk-in, walk-out sale,** *n.* a sale of a shop, house, etc., in which the buyer takes over the property with all its furnishings, fixtures, etc.

**walk of life,** *n.* occupation, profession, or social position.

**walk-on** /ˈwɔk-ɒn/, *n.* a small part in a play, esp. one in which the actor does not speak at all. Also, **walking part, walk-on part.**

**walkout** /ˈwɔkaʊt/, *n.* **1.** a strike by workers. **2.** the act of leaving or boycotting a conference, meeting, etc., esp. as an act of protest.

**walkover** /ˈwɔkoʊvə/, *n. Colloq.* **1.** *Racing.* a going over the course at a walk or otherwise by a contestant who is the only starter. **2.** an unopposed or easy victory.

**walk-through** /ˈwɔk-θru/, *n.* a theatrical rehearsal in which the actors consider the form and content of a play, without concerning themselves with projecting to an audience.

**walk-up** /ˈwɔk-ʌp/, *n.* a block of home units, flats, etc., not provided with a lift: *a three-storey walk-up.*

**walk-up start** /ˈwɔk-ʌp stat/, *n. Colloq.* something easily taken or achieved.

**walkway** /ˈwɔkweɪ/, *n.* an area, space, or path for pedestrian traffic.

**wall** /wɔl/, *n.* **1.** an upright work or structure of stone, brick, or similar material, serving for enclosure, division, support, protection, etc., as one of the upright enclosing sides of a building or a room, or a solid fence of masonry. **2.** (*usu. pl.*) a rampart raised for defensive purposes. **3.** anything which resembles or suggests a wall: *a wall of prejudice.* **4.** a wall-like enclosing part, thing, mass, etc.: *a wall of fire; a wall of troops.* **5.** an embankment to prevent flooding. **6.** the external layer of structural material surrounding an object, as an organ of the body or a plant or animal cell. **7.** *Mountaineering.* a vertical or nearly vertical stretch of unbroken rock. **8. go to the wall, a.** to give way or suffer defeat in a conflict or competition. **b.** to fail in business, or become bankrupt. **9. up the wall,** *Colloq.* in or into a state of exasperation, confusion, etc.: *washing dishes drives me up the wall.* **10. with one's back to the wall,** in a very difficult predicament. *–adj.* **11.** of or pertaining to a wall. **12.** growing against or on a wall. **13.** situated or placed in or on a wall. *–v.t.* **14.** to enclose, shut off, divide, protect, etc., with or as with a wall (oft. fol. by *in* or *off*). **15.** to fill up (a doorway, etc.) with a wall. **16.** to shut up within walls; entomb; immure (usu. fol. by *up*). [ME and OE, from L *vallum*] – **walled,** *adj.* – **wall-less,** *adj.* – **wall-like,** *adj.*

**walla** /ˈwɒlə/, *n.* →**wallah.**

**wallaby** /ˈwɒləbi/, *n., pl.* **-bies,** (*esp. collectively*) **-by. 1.** any of various smaller members of the family Macropodidae, many resembling kangaroos, others more possum-like in size and appearance, belonging to a number of different genera, as *Macropus* (as the tammar and parma), *Thylogale* (as the smaller pademelons), *Setonix* (as the quokka), *Onychogalea* (as the nail-tailed wallabies), *Lagorchestes* and *Lagostrophus* (as the hare-wallabies), *Petrogale* (as the rock-wallabies). **2. on the wallaby (track),** *Colloq.* on the move as a swagman. **3.** (*cap. pl.*) the Australian Rugby Union international touring team. [Aboriginal]

wallaby

**wallaby grass** /ˈ– gras/, *n.* any of various hardy native perennials of the genus *Danthonia,* used as winter fodder; it grows in tussocks, usu. with straw-coloured spikelets, and is abundant in southern parts of the continent.

**Wallace's line** /ˈwɒləsəz laɪn/, *n.* an imaginary line passing between the islands of Bali and Lombak, through the Macassar Straits to east of the Philippines. It separates the Australian and oriental biogeographical realms. [named after A. R. *Wallace,* 1823-1913, British naturalist, who first pointed out the sharp break between the two realms]

**wallah** /ˈwɒlə/, *n. Colloq.* a person employed at or concerned with a particular thing (used esp. in combination with another word): *laundry wallah; cleaning wallah.* Also, **walla.** [Hind. *-wālā*]

**wallaroo** /wɒləˈru/, *n.* a stocky, coarse-haired kangaroo, *Macropus robustus,* widely distributed throughout mainland Australia in rocky ranges and gullies; euro; biggada; uroo. [Aboriginal]

**wall bars** /ˈwɔl baz/, *n.pl.* a gymnasium apparatus consisting of rows of vertical wooden bars attached to a wall and used for various exercises.

**wallboard** /ˈwɔlbɔd/, *n.* an artificial sheet material for use in making or covering walls, ceilings, etc., as a substitute for wooden boards or plaster.

**wall creeper** /ˈwɔl kripə/, *n.* a small grey and crimson Old World bird, *Tichodroma muraria,* which makes its home among precipitous rocks.

**walled plain** /wɔld ˈpleɪn/, *n.* one of a number of large ring mountains or craters on the surface of the moon, whose diameters vary between about 50 and 320 km.

**wallet** /ˈwɒlət/, *n.* **1.** a small, booklike folding case for carrying papers, paper money, etc., in the pocket. **2.** a bag for holding food, clothing, toilet articles, or the like, as for use on a journey. [ME *walet;* orig. uncert.]

**walleye** /ˈwɔlaɪ/, *n.* **1.** any of various North American fishes with large staring eyes, esp. the **walleyed pike,** a pike-perch, *Stizostedion vitreum.* **2.** an eye such as is seen in a walleyed person or animal.

**walleyed** /ˈwɒlaɪd/, *adj.* **1.** having eyes in which there is an abnormal amount of the white showing, because of divergent strabismus. **2.** having an eye or the eyes presenting little or no colour, as the result of a light-coloured or white iris or of white opacity of the cornea. **3.** having large, staring eyes, as some fishes. [ME *wawileghed,* from Scand.; cf. Icel. *vagl-eygr,* from *vagl* film over eye + *-eygr* -eyed]

**wallflower** /ˈwɔlflaʊə/, *n.* **1.** a European perennial, *Cheiranthus cheiri,* growing wild on old walls, cliffs, etc., and also cultivated in gardens, with sweet-scented flowers, commonly yellow or orange but in cultivation varying from pale yellow to brown, red, or purple. **2.** any plant of the brassicaceous genera *Cheiranthus* and *Erysimum.* **3.** *Colloq.* a person, esp. a woman, who looks on at a dance, esp. from failure to obtain a partner.

**Walloon** /wəˈlun/, *n.* **1.** one of a people inhabiting chiefly the southern and south-eastern parts of Belgium and adjacent regions in France. **2.** the French dialect of Belgium, esp. of the south-east. *–adj.* **3.** of or pertaining to the Walloons or their language. [F *Wallon,* from ML *Wallo,* from Gmc.; cf. OHG *walh* foreigner]

**wallop** /ˈwɒləp/, *Colloq. –v.t.* **1.** to beat soundly; thrash. **2.** to strike with a vigorous blow. **3.** to defeat thoroughly, as in a game. *–n.* **4.** a vigorous blow. **5.** (in boxing, etc.) an ability to deliver such blows. **6.** a forceful impression or impact. **7.** beer; any alcoholic drink. [ME *walop,* from OF, akin to F *galoper* GALLOP]

**walloper** /ˈwɒləpə/, *n. Colloq.* **1.** one who or that which wallops. **2.** a policeman.

**walloping** /ˈwɒləpɪŋ/, *Colloq. –n.* **1.** a sound beating or thrashing. **2.** a thorough defeat. *–adj.* **3.** of large size; whopping.

**wallow** /ˈwɒloʊ/, *v.i.* **1.** to roll the body about, or lie, in water, snow, mud, dust, or the like, as for refreshment: *pigs wallowing in the mud.* **2.** to live self-indulgently or luxuriously: *to wallow in wealth, to wallow in sensuality.* **3.** to flounder about clumsily or with difficulty: *the gunboat wallowing in the water.* **4.** to surge up, as smoke, heat, etc. *–n.* **5.** the act of wallowing. **6.** a place to which animals, as buffaloes, resort to wallow. **7.** the indentation produced by their wallowing. [ME *walwe,* OE *wealwian* roll, akin to Goth. *walwjan,* L *volvere* roll] – **wallower,** *n.*

**wallpaper** /ˈwɔlpeɪpə/, *n.* **1.** paper, commonly with printed decorative patterns in colour, for pasting on and covering the walls or ceilings of rooms, etc. *–v.t.* **2.** to put wallpaper on; furnish with wallpaper.

**wall pellitory** /wɔl ˈpɛlətri/, *n.* a small, bushy, Old World plant, *Parietaria officinalis,* growing on walls, and said to be a diuretic and refrigerant.

**wall pepper** /– ˈpɛpə/, *n.* a small, perennial herb, *Sedum acre,* having fleshy leaves with a hot peppery taste, occurring in dry places in Europe and western Asia.

**wall plate** /ˈ– pleɪt/, *n.* **1.** *Bldg Trades.* a plate or timber placed horizontally in or on a wall, under the ends of girders, joists, or other timbers, in order to distribute pressure. **2.** *Mach.* a vertical metal plate secured against a wall or the like, as to attach a bracket.

**wall rock** /ˈ– rɒk/, *n.* the rock forming the walls of a mineral vein, fault or igneous intrusion.

**wall rocket** /ˈ– rɒkət/, *n.* a European plant, *Diplotaxis muralis,* growing along old walls, etc.

**wall rue** /ˈ– ru/, *n.* a small delicate fern, *Asplenium ruta-muraria,* growing on walls and cliffs.

**wall-to-wall** /ˈwɔl-tə-wɔl/, *adj.* covering the entire floor space of a room, as a carpet.

**wallum** /ˈwɒləm/, *n.* **1.** a small shrubby tree, *Banksia aemula,* of coastal eastern Australia, mainly Queensland. **2.** the sandy heath-land country in which this species grows. [Aboriginal]

**wall unit** /ˈwɔl junət/, *n.* a set of cupboards standing against a wall.

**wall-washer** /ˈwɔl-wɒʃə/, *n.* an electric light which casts an even radiance on to the walls of a room.

**wally** /ˈwɒli/, *n. Brit. Colloq.* **1.** a fool; a stupid person. *–adj.* **2.** angry; annoyed. [contraction of *Walter,* man's name]

**walnut** /ˈwɔlnʌt/, *n.* **1.** the edible nut of trees of the genus *Juglans,* of the North Temperate zone. **2.** a tree bearing this nut, as *J. regia* **(common walnut),** or *J. nigra* **(black walnut),** which yields both a valuable timber and a distinctively flavoured nut. **3.** the wood of such a tree. **4.** any of various fruits or trees resembling the walnut, as those of the genus *Beilschmiedia.* **5.** a shade of brown, as that of the heartwood of the black walnut tree. [ME *walnotte,* OE *walhhnutu,* lit., foreign nut]

walnut

**walrus** /ˈwɔlrəs, ˈwɒlrəs/, *n., pl.* **-ruses,** *(esp. collectively)* **-rus.** either of two large marine mammals of the genus *Odobenus,* of arctic seas, related to the seals, and having flippers, a pair of large tusks, and a thick, tough skin. [D: lit., whalehorse. Cf. G *Walross,* Dan. *hvalros;* also OE *horshwæl* horse-whale]

Atlantic walrus

**walrus moustache** /ˈ– məstaʃ/, *n.* a thick moustache hanging down loosely at both ends.

**waltz**[1] /wɔls/, *n.* **1.** a ballroom dance in moderately fast triple time, in which the dancers move in a series of circles, taking one step to each beat. **2.** a slower dance, also in triple time. **3.** a piece of music for, or in the rhythm of, this dance. *–adj.* **4.** of, pertaining to, or characteristic of the waltz, as music, rhythm, or dance. *–v.i.* **5.** to dance or move in the movement or step of a waltz. **6.** *Colloq.* to take away with great ease: *he waltzed off with the first prize.* **7.** *Colloq.* to move nimbly or quickly. *–v.t.* **8.** to cause to waltz; accompany in a waltz. [G *walzer,* from *walzen* roll, dance a waltz] **– waltzer,** *n.*

waltz²: waltzing Matilda

**waltz**[2] /wɔls/, *v.t. in the phrase,* **waltz Matilda,** *Colloq.* to wander about as a tramp with a swag. [? G *walzen* to move in a circular fashion, as of apprentices travelling from master to master + G *Mathilde,* female travelling companion, bed-roll, from the girl's name; ? taken to goldfields by German speakers from S.A.]

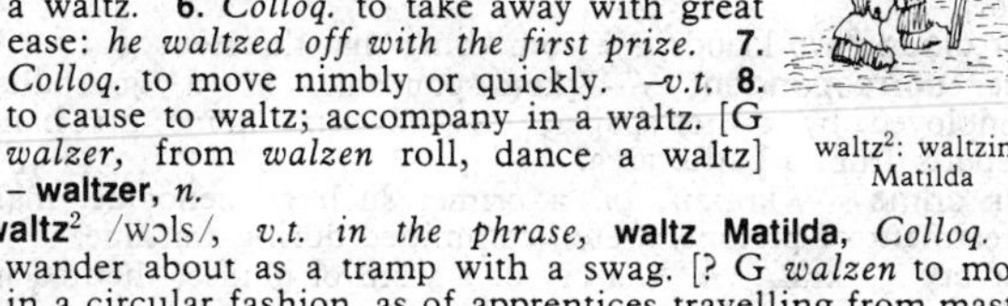

**waltzing mouse** /wɔlsɪŋ ˈmaʊs/, *n.* a mouse born with a genetic peculiarity or of a breed believed to have originated in Japan, which is distinguished by its inability to walk in a straight line and a tendency to go round in small circles.

**wambenger** /wɒmˈbɛŋə/, *n.* →**tuan.** [Aboriginal]

**wampum** /ˈwɒmpəm/, *n.* **1.** cylindrical beads made from shells, pierced and strung, used by North American Indians as money and for ornament, properly denoting a white variety but applied also to a black or dark purple variety commonly considered more valuable than the white; peag. **2.** *U.S. Colloq.* money. [short for *wompanpeag,* from Algonquian *wanpanpiak* string of shell beads, from *wap* white + *anpi* string of shell beads + *-ak,* animate pl. suffix]

**wan** /wɒn/, *adj.,* **wanner, wannest,** *v.,* **wanned, wanning.** *–adj.* **1.** of an unnatural or sickly pallor; pallid: *his wan face flushed.* **2.** pale in colour or hue: *cowslips wan.* **3.** showing or suggesting ill health, worn condition, unhappiness, etc.: *a wan look, a wan smile.* **4.** *Archaic.* dark or gloomy. *–v.i., v.t.* **5.** *Poetic.* to become or make wan. [ME; OE *wann* dark, gloomy] **– wanly,** *adv.* **– wanness,** *n.*

**wand** /wɒnd/, *n.* **1.** a slender stick or rod, esp. one used by a conjurer, or supposedly by a magician or fairy to work magic. **2.** a rod or staff borne as an ensign of office or authority. **3.** a slender shoot, stem, or branch of a shrub or tree: *lissom as a hazel wand.* [ME, from Scand.; cf. Icel. *vöndr,* c. Goth. *wandus*] **– wand-like,** *adj.*

**wanda** /ˈwɒndə/, *n. Colloq.* a white man. [Aboriginal: white ghost]

**wander** /ˈwɒndə/, *v.i.* **1.** to ramble without any certain course or object in view; roam, rove, or stray: *to wander over the earth.* **2.** to go aimlessly or casually: *wandering into the adjoining room.* **3.** to pass or extend in an irregular course or direction: *off to the south wandered the purple hills.* **4.** to move, pass, or turn idly, as the hand, the pen, the eyes, etc. **5.** (of the mind, thoughts, desires, etc.) to take one direction or another without intention or control. **6.** to stray from a path, place, companions, etc. **7.** to deviate in conduct, belief, etc.; err; go astray: *let me not wander from thy commandments.* **8.** to think or speak confusedly or incoherently. *–v.t.* **9.** *Poetic.* to wander over or through. *–n.* **10.** →**ramble** (def. 5). [ME *wandre(n),* OE *wandrian,* c. MD *wanderen,* G *wandern*] **– wanderer,** *n.* **– wanderingly,** *adv.*

**wanderer** /ˈwɒndərə/, *n.* **1.** one who or that which wanders. **2.** →**monarch** (def. 4).

**wandering albatross** /ˌwɒndərɪŋ ˈælbətrɒs/, *n.* a large albatross, *Diomedea exulans,* of southern waters, having the plumage mostly white with dark markings on the upper parts.

**Wandering Jew** /wɒndərɪŋ ˈdʒu/, *n.* **1.** a legendary character condemned to roam without rest because he struck or mocked Christ on the day of Crucifixion. **2.** Also, **wandering Jew.** any of various trailing or creeping plants, as *Zebrina pendula* or *Tradescantia albiflora.*

**wanderlust** /ˈwɒndəlʌst/, *n.* an instinctive impulse to rove or travel about. [G]

**wanderoo** /wɒndəˈru/, *n.* **1.** any of several langurs, of Sri Lanka. **2.** a macaque, *Macacus silenus,* of southern India. [Singhalese *wanderu* monkey]

**wanderrie** /wɒnˈdɪəri/, *n.* any of various plant species of the genus *Eriachne,* which are native to inland Australia and which range from slender annuals to tussocky perennials, with purple or straw-coloured spikelets.

**wandoo** /wɒnˈdu/, *n.* **1.** a large white-barked tree endemic in western Australia, *Eucalyptus wandoo.* **2.** a spirit; ghost. **3.** a white man. [Aboriginal]

**wane** /weɪn/, *v.,* **waned, waning,** *n. –v.i.* **1.** (of the moon) to decrease periodically in the extent of its illuminated portion after the full moon (opposed to *wax*). **2.** to decline in power, importance, prosperity, etc. **3.** to decrease in strength, intensity, etc.: *daylight waned, and night came on.* **4.** to draw to a close. *–n.* **5.** gradual decline in strength, intensity, power, etc. **6.** the drawing to a close of life, a time, etc.: *the wane of life.* **7.** the waning of the moon. **8.** a period of waning. **9.** a bevelled edge of a plank or board as sawn from an unsquared log, due to the curvature of the log. **10. on the wane,** decreasing; diminishing. [ME; OE *wanian* lessen, c. MD and MHG *wanen*]

**wangle** /ˈwæŋgəl/, *v.,* **-gled, -gling,** *n. Colloq. –v.t.* **1.** to bring about, accomplish, or obtain by contrivance, scheming, or often, indirect or insidious methods. **2.** to fake; falsify; manipulate. *–v.i.* **3.** to use contrivance, scheming, or indirect methods to accomplish some end. **4.** to manipulate or continue something for dishonest purposes. *–n.* **5.** an act or instance of wangling. [b. WAG[1] and DANGLE] **– wangler,** *n.*

**waning moon** /weɪnɪŋ ˈmun/, *n.* See **moon** (def. 2f).

**wank** /wæŋk/, *Colloq. –v.i.* **1.** to masturbate. *–v.t.* **2. wank oneself,** to maintain an illusion; deceive oneself. *–n.* **3.** an act or instance of masturbation. **4.** a hobby: *flying is his wank.* **5.** behaviour which is self-indulgent or egotistical. [orig. uncert.] **– wanker,** *n.*

**Wankel engine** /ˈwæŋkəl ɛndʒən/, *n.* an internal-combustion engine with one or more combustion chambers, each shaped like an ellipse with its longer sides slightly indented and within each of which a triangular-shaped piston rotates eccentrically and in so doing encloses varying volumes between its sides and the chamber walls which provide the same cycle as a reciprocating engine. [named after Dr Felix *Wankel,* born 1902, German engineer]

**wannish** /ˈwɒnɪʃ/, *adj.* somewhat wan.

**want** /wɒnt/, *v.t.* **1.** to feel a need or a desire for; wish for: *to want one's dinner; always wanting something new.* **2.** to wish or desire (oft. fol. by infinitive): *I want to see you, he wants to be notified.* **3.** to be without or be deficient in: *to want judgment or knowledge.* **4.** to fall short by (a specified amount): *it wants a few minutes of twelve.* **5.** to require or need: *the car wants cleaning.* *–v.i.* **6.** to wish; like; feel inclined to (oft. fol. by *to*): *they can go out if they want.* **7.** to be deficient by the absence of some part or thing, or fall short (sometimes fol. by *for*): *he did not want for abilities.* **8.** to have need (usu. fol. by *for*): *if you want for anything, let him know.* **9.** to be in a state of destitution or poverty. **10.** to be lacking or absent, as a part or thing necessary to completeness. **11. want out,** to wish to withdraw from a difficult situation, obligation, etc. (fol. by *of*). *–n.* **12.** something wanted or needed; a necessity. **13.** a need or requirement: *the wants of mankind.* **14.** absence or deficiency of something desirable or requisite; lack: *plants dying for want of rain.* **15.** the state of being without something desired or needed; need: *to be in want of an assistant.* **16.** the state of being without the necessities of life; destitution; poverty. **17.** a sense of lack or need of something. [ME *wante,* from Scand.; cf. Icel. *vanta* lack] – **wanter,** *n.* – **wantless,** *adj.*

**want ad** /'– æd/, *n.* a classified advertisement for something wanted, as a job, car, etc.

**wantage** /'wɒntɪdʒ/, *n. U.S.* that which is wanting or lacking; an amount lacking.

**wanted** /'wɒntəd/, *adj.* (of a suspected criminal, etc.) sought by the police.

**wanted poster** /'– poustə/, *n.* a poster identifying a criminal, and advertising reward money for his capture.

**wanting** /'wɒntɪŋ/, *adj.* **1.** lacking or absent: *an apparatus with some of the parts wanting.* **2.** deficient in some part, thing, or respect: *to be wanting in courtesy.* *–prep.* **3.** lacking; without. **4.** less; minus: *a century, wanting three years.*

**wanton** /'wɒntən/, *adj.* **1.** done, shown, used, etc., maliciously or unjustifiably: *a wanton attack, injury, or affront; wanton cruelty.* **2.** deliberate and uncalled for: *why ruin your career in this wanton way?* **3.** reckless or disregardful of right, justice, humanity, etc., as persons: *a wanton disturber of men's religious convictions.* **4.** lawless or unbridled with respect to sexual behaviour; loose, lascivious, or lewd. **5.** extravagantly luxurious or self-indulgent, as a person, way of life, etc. **6.** *Poetic.* sportive or frolicsome, as children, young animals, etc. **7.** *Chiefly Poetic.* having free play: *wanton breezes, a wanton brook.* **8.** *Poetic.* luxuriant, as vegetation. *–n.* **9.** a wanton or lascivious person, esp. a woman. *–v.i.* **10.** to act, grow, etc., in a wanton manner. *–v.t.* **11.** to squander (away), as in pleasure. [ME *wantowen,* lit., undisciplined, from *wan-* not + OE *togen* disciplined] – **wantonly,** *adv.* – **wantonness,** *n.*

**wapiti** /'wɒpəti/, *n., pl.* **-tis,** (*esp. collectively*) **-ti.** a North American species of deer, *Cervus canadensis,* with long, slender antlers; elk. [Algonquian (Shawnee): white rump]

**war** /wɔ/, *n., v.,* **warred, warring,** *adj.* *–n.* **1.** a conflict carried on by force of arms, as between nations or states, or between parties within a state; warfare (by land, by sea, or in the air). **2.** a contest carried on by force of arms, as in a series of battles or campaigns. **3.** active hostility or contention; conflict; contest: *a war of words.* **4.** armed fighting, as a department of activity, a profession, or an art: *war is our business.* **5.** *Obs. Poetic.* a battle; engagement. **6. at war,** in a state of hostility or active military operations. **7. in the wars,** *Colloq.* involved in a series of misfortunes or minor injuries. *–v.i.* **8.** to make or carry on war; fight. **9.** to carry on active hostility or contention: *to war with evil.* **10.** to be in a state of strong opposition: *warring principles.* *–adj.* **11.** of, belonging to, used in, or due to war. [ME *werre,* from OF, from OHG *werra* strife] – **warless,** *adj.*

waratah

**waratah** /wɒrə'ta, 'wɒrəta/, *n.* a shrub or small tree of the eastern Australian genus *Telopea,* esp. *T. speciosissima,* the floral emblem of New South Wales, which has a dense globular head of red flowers surrounded by red bracts. [Aboriginal]

**waratah anemone** /– ə'nɛməni/, *n.* a small, brownish-red sea anemone, *Actinia tenebrosa,* with vivid light red tentacles, widespread and common along the Australian coastline; bloodsucker. Also, **sea waratah.**

**warb** /wɔb/, *n. Colloq.* a dirty or unkempt person. [backformation from WARBY]

**war baby** /'wɔ beɪbi/, *n.* a baby conceived in wartime, esp. as the unplanned or illegitimate child of a serviceman.

**warble**[1] /'wɔbəl/, *v.,* **-bled, -bling,** *n.* *–v.i.* **1.** to sing with trills, quavers, or melodic embellishments. **2.** *U.S.* to yodel. *–v.t.* **3.** to sing with trills, quavers, or melodious turns; carol. **4.** to express or celebrate in song. *–n.* **5.** a warbled song. **6.** the act of warbling. [ME *werblen,* from OF *werbler* quaver, from Gmc; cf. OHG *werbel* something that revolves]

waratah anemone

**warble**[2] /'wɔbəl/, *n.* **1.** a small, hard tumour on a horse's back, produced by the galling of the saddle. **2.** a lump in the skin of an animal's back, containing the larva of a warble fly. [orig. uncert. Cf. obs. Swed. *varbulde* boil] – **warbled,** *adj.*

**warble fly** /'– flaɪ/, *n.* any of various flies of the family Hypodermatidae, whose larvae produce warbles.

**warbler** /'wɔblə/, *n.* **1.** one who or that which warbles. **2.** any of the small, chiefly Old World songbirds constituting the family Sylviidae, represented in Australia by a few species, as the reedwarbler. **3.** any of numerous small birds of the family Maluridae found in Australia, New Zealand and islands to the north, as the white-throated warbler. **4.** any of various small, insectivorous New World birds of the family Parulidae, many of which are brightly coloured. **5.** *Elect.* any device, as a rotating capacitor, for rapidly varying the carrier frequency in a radiotelephone system to ensure secrecy.

**war bride** /'wɔ braɪd/, *n.* a woman who was married during a war to a soldier, esp. from another country.

**warby** /'wɔbi/, *adj. Colloq.* **1.** unkempt; decrepit. **2.** of dubious worth. **3.** unwell; squeamish. [Brit. d. *warbie* maggot]

**war cloud** /'wɔ klaud/, *n.* something that threatens war.

**war correspondent** /'– kɒrə,spɒndənt/, *n.* a journalist employed by a newspaper, etc., to send home first-hand reports from a battle area.

**war crime** /'– kraɪm/, *n.* a crime, such as genocide, maltreatment of prisoners, etc., committed during wartime.

**war cry** /'– kraɪ/, *n.* **1.** a cry or a word or phrase, shouted in charging or in rallying to attack; a battle cry. **2.** a party cry or slogan in any contest.

**ward** /wɔd/, *n.* **1.** a division or district of a municipality, city or town, as for administrative or representative purposes. **2.** a division of a hospital or the like, as for a particular class of patients: *a convalescent ward.* **3.** each of the separate divisions of a prison. **4.** *Fort.* an open space within walls, or between lines of walls, of a castle or fortified place: *the castle's lower ward.* **5.** *Law.* **a.** a person, esp. a minor, who has been legally placed under the care or control of a legal guardian. **b.** the state of being under the care or control of a legal guardian. **c.** guardianship over a minor or some other person legally incapable of managing his own affairs. **6.** the state of being under restraining guard or in custody. **7.** one who is under the protection or control of another. **8.** a movement or posture of defence, as in fencing. **9.** a curved ridge of metal inside a lock, forming an obstacle to the passage of a key which does not have a corresponding notch. **10.** the notch or slot in the bit of a key, into which such a ridge fits. **11.** the act of keeping guard or protective watch: *watch and ward.* *–v.t.* **12.** to avert, repel, or turn aside, as danger, an attack, assailant, etc. (usu. fol. by *off*): *to ward off a blow.* **13.** to place in a ward, as of a hospital. **14.** *Archaic.* to guard. [ME; OE *weardian,* G *warten.* See GUARD, *v.*] – **wardless,** *adj.*

**-ward,** an adjectival and adverbial suffix indicating direction, as in *onward, seaward, backward.* [ME; OE *-weard* towards]

**war dance** /ˈwɔ dæns/, *n.* **1.** (among primitive people) a dance preliminary to a warlike excursion or in celebration of a victory. **2.** *Sport.* a morale-raising dance, etc., performed before commencement of play or in celebration of victory.

**war dead** /ˈ– dɛd/, *n.* those killed in a war.

**warded** /ˈwɔdəd/, *adj.* having notches, slots, or wards, as in locks and keys.

**warden**[1] /ˈwɔdn/, *n.* **1.** one charged with the care or custody of something; a keeper. **2.** any of various public officials charged with superintendence, as over a port, etc. **3.** *Chiefly U.S.* the chief administrative officer in charge of a prison. **4.** (formerly) the principal official in a region, town, etc. **5.** the government official, with magisterial and executive powers, in charge of a mineral field. **6.** the head of certain colleges, schools, hospitals, youth hostels, etc. **7.** a member of the governing body of a guild. **8.** a churchwarden. **9.** *Rare.* a gatekeeper. [ME *wardein,* from OF. See GUARDIAN] – **wardenship,** *n.*

**warden**[2] /ˈwɔdn/, *n.* one of a group of cooking pears, distinguished for crisp, firm flesh. [orig. uncert.]

**wardenry** /ˈwɔdnri/, *n., pl.* **-ries.** the office, jurisdiction, or district of a warden.

**warder**[1] /ˈwɔdə/, *n.* **1.** an official having charge of prisoners in a gaol; prison officer. **2.** one who wards or guards something. [ME, from WARD, *v.*] – **wardership,** *n.*

**warder**[2] /ˈwɔdə/, *n.* a truncheon or staff of office or authority, used in giving signals. [late ME; orig. uncert.]

**wardress** /ˈwɔdrəs/, *n.* a female warder.

**wardrobe** /ˈwɔdroʊb/, *n.* **1.** a stock of clothes or costumes, as of a person or of a theatrical company. **2.** a piece of furniture for holding clothes, now usu. a tall, upright, movable cupboard fitted with hooks, shelves, etc. **3.** a room or place for keeping clothes or costumes in. **4.** the department of a royal or other great household charged with the care of wearing apparel. [ME *warderobe,* from OF. See WARD, ROBE[2]]

**wardroom** /ˈwɔdrum/, *n.* (in a warship) **1.** the mess room for naval officers other than midshipmen and not including the commanding officer or flag officer. **2.** these officers collectively.

**-wards,** an adverbial suffix indicating direction, as in *onwards, seawards, backwards.* Also, *Chiefly U.S.,* **-ward.** [ME *-wardes;* OE *-weardes,* adv. genitive of *-weard* -WARD; cf. D *-waarts,* OHG *-wartes*]

**wardship** /ˈwɔdʃɪp/, *n.* **1.** guardianship; custody. **2.** *Law.* the guardianship over a minor or ward.

**ware**[1] /wɛə/, *n.* **1.** (*usu. pl.*) articles of merchandise or manufacture, or goods: *a pedlar selling his wares.* **2.** a particular kind or class of articles of merchandise or manufacture (now chiefly in composition): *tinware, silverware.* **3.** pottery, or a particular kind of pottery: *Delft ware.* [ME; OE *waru,* c. G *Ware*]

**ware**[2] /wɛə/, *adj., v.,* **wared, waring.** *Archaic.* *–adj.* **1.** watchful, wary, or cautious. **2.** aware or conscious. *–v.t.* **3.** (*usu. used in the imperative*) to beware of. [ME; OE *wær,* c. Icel. *varr,* Goth. *wars*]

**ware**[3] /ˈwari/, *n.* →**Murray tortoise.** [Aboriginal]

**war effort** /ˈwɔr ɛfət/, *n.* a program designed to raise money, food or clothing for soldiers.

**warehouse** /ˈwɛəhaʊs/, *n.;* /ˈwɛəhaʊz, -haʊs/, *v.,* **-housed, -housing.** *–n.* **1.** a storehouse for wares or goods. **2.** the building in which a wholesale dealer keeps his stock of merchandise. *–v.t.* **3.** to deposit or store in a warehouse. **4.** to place in a government or bonded warehouse, to be kept until duties are paid.

**warehouseman** /ˈwɛəhaʊsmən/, *n., pl.* **-men.** **1.** one who is employed in or has charge of a warehouse. **2.** a wholesale merchant who has a warehouse for the storing of merchandise.

**warfare** /ˈwɔfɛə/, *n.* **1.** the act of waging war. **2.** armed conflict. **3.** military operations.

**war footing** /ˈwɔ fʊtɪŋ/, *n.* readiness for war, as in a state, nation, etc. Also, **wartime footing.**

**war game** /ˈwɔ geɪm/, *n.* **1.** a training exercise that imitates war, in which commanders, staffs, and assistants perform war duties, but no troops are used. **2.** a military exercise which is a practical training exercise for troops. **3.** a game in which famous battles are re-created using toy soldiers and miniature battlefields.

**warhead** /ˈwɔhɛd/, *n.* the forward section of a self-propelled missile, bomb, torpedo, etc., containing explosives, chemical or biological agents or inert materials intended to inflict damage.

**warhorse** /ˈwɔhɔs/, *n.* **1.** a horse used in war; a charger. **2.** a veteran soldier, politician, etc., esp. an aggressive one.

**warily** /ˈwɛərəli/, *adv.* in a wary manner.

**wariness** /ˈwɛərinəs/, *n.* the state or quality of being wary.

**warlike** /ˈwɔlaɪk/, *adj.* **1.** fit, qualified, or ready for war; martial: *warlike fleet, warlike tribes.* **2.** threatening or betokening war: *a warlike tone.* **3.** of or pertaining to war: *a warlike expedition, warlike deeds.* – **warlikeness,** *n.*

**war loading** /ˈwɔ loʊdɪŋ/, *n.* (formerly) a loading (def. 3) paid to an employee during the Second World War and in some cases beyond it, in recognition of the special demands made on him by wartime production.

**warlock** /ˈwɔlɒk/, *n.* **1.** one who practises magic arts by the aid of the devil; a sorcerer or wizard. **2.** a fortune-teller, conjurer, or the like. [ME *warloghe,* OE *wǣrloga* oath-breaker, devil]

**war lord** /ˈwɔ lɔd/, *n.* **1.** a military commander or commander-in-chief, esp. of a warlike country. **2.** a military leader, esp. one who has seized power in part of a country: *the Chinese war lords.*

**warm** /wɔm/, *adj.* **1.** having or communicating a moderate degree of heat, as perceptible to the senses. **2.** of or at a moderately high temperature; characterised by comparatively high temperature: *a warm climate.* **3.** having a sensation of bodily heat: *to be warm from fast walking.* **4.** keeping or maintaining warmth: *warm clothes.* **5.** (of colour, effects of colour, etc.) suggestive of warmth; inclining towards red or orange, as yellow (rather than towards green or blue). **6.** characterised by or showing lively feelings, passions, emotions, sympathies, etc.: *a warm heart, warm interest.* **7.** strongly attached, or intimate: *warm friends.* **8.** cordial or hearty: *a warm welcome.* **9.** heated; irritated, or angry: *to become warm when contradicted.* **10.** animated, lively, brisk, or vigorous: *a warm debate.* **11.** strong or fresh: *a warm scent.* **12.** *Colloq.* relatively close to something sought, as in a game. **13.** *Colloq.* uncomfortable or unpleasant. *–v.t.* **14.** to make warm; heat (oft. fol. by *up*): *to warm one's feet, warm up a room.* **15.** to heat, as cooked food for reuse. **16.** to excite ardour, enthusiasm, or animation in. **17.** to inspire with kindly feeling; affect with lively pleasure. **18. warm a seat,** *Colloq.* to occupy a position, usu. in a temporary capacity, and without actively discharging its responsibilities. *–v.i.* **19.** to become warm (oft. fol. by *up*). **20.** to become ardent, enthusiastic, animated, etc. (oft. fol. by *up* or *to*). **21.** to grow kindly, friendly, or sympathetically disposed (oft. fol. by *to* or *towards*): *my heart warms towards him.* **22. warm up,** to prepare for a sporting event, musical or theatrical performance, etc. [ME; OE *wearm,* c. D, G *warm*] – **warmer,** *n.* – **warmish,** *adj.* – **warmly,** *adv.* – **warmness,** *n.*

**warm-blooded** /ˈwɔm-blʌdəd/, *adj.* **1.** denoting or pertaining to animals, as mammals and birds, whose blood ranges in temperature from about 36° to 44° C, and remains relatively constant, irrespective of the temperature of the surrounding medium. **2.** ardent, impetuous, or passionate: *young and warm-blooded valour.*

**war memorial** /ˈwɔ məˌmɔriəl/, *n.* a monument or building commemorating those who died in a war.

**warm front** /ˈwɔm frʌnt/, *n. Meteorol.* **1.** the contact surface between two air masses where the warmer mass is advancing against and over the cooler mass. **2.** the line of intersection of this surface with the surface of the earth.

**warm-hearted** /ˈwɔm-hatəd/, *adj.* having or showing sympathy, cordiality, etc. – **warm-heartedly,** *adv.* – **warm-heartedness,** *n.*

**warming pan** /ˈwɔmɪŋ pæn/, *n.* a long-handled, covered, flat vessel, as of brass, for holding hot coals or the like, formerly in common use for warming beds before they were to be occupied.

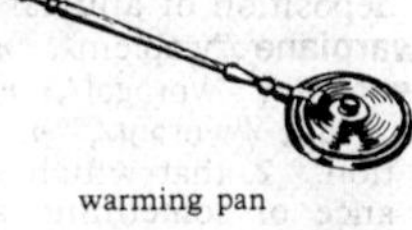
warming pan

**warmonger** /ˈwɔmʌŋgə/, *n.* one

who advocates war or seeks to bring it about.

**warmongering** /ˈwɔmʌŋgərɪŋ/, *n.* the principles and practices of a warmonger.

**warm sector** /ˈwɔm sɛktə/, *n.* a body of warm air found in a recently formed active depression, bounded by the cold and warm fronts.

**warmth** /wɔmθ/, *n.* **1.** the state of being warm; moderate or gentle heat. **2.** the sensation of moderate heat. **3.** liveliness of feelings, emotions, or sympathies; ardour or fervour; cordiality; enthusiasm or zeal. **4.** rising emotion; anger.

**warm-up** /ˈwɔm-ʌp/, *n.* the act or instance of warming up.

**warn** /wɔn/, *v.t.* **1.** to give notice or intimation to (a person, etc.) of danger, impending evil, possible harm, or anything unfavourable: *to warn a person of a plot against him, warned that he was in danger.* **2.** to urge or advise to be on one's guard; caution: *to warn a foolhardy person.* **3.** to admonish or exhort as to action or conduct: *to warn a person to be on time.* **4.** to notify, apprise, or inform: *to warn a person of an intended visit.* **5.** to give notice to (a person, etc.) to go, stay, or keep (away, off, etc.): *to warn trespassers off private grounds.* **6.** to give authoritative or formal notice to, order, or summon. *–v.i.* **7.** to give a warning: *to warn of impending disaster.* [ME; OE *warnian*, c. G *warnen.* Cf. WARE[2]] – **warner,** *n.*

**warning** /ˈwɔnɪŋ/, *n.* **1.** the act of warning, giving notice, or cautioning. **2.** something serving to warn, give notice, or caution. *–adj.* **3.** that warns. – **warningly,** *adv.*

**war nose** /ˈwɔ noʊz/, *n.* a device in the front end of a projectile, as a torpedo, for detonating the explosive charge.

**war of nerves,** *n.* a conflict in which the aim is to intimidate or demoralise the enemy by using psychological methods such as threats, propaganda, etc.

**warp** /wɔp/, *v.t.* **1.** to bend or twist out of shape, esp. from a straight or flat form, as timbers, flooring, etc. **2.** to bend or turn from the natural or true direction or course. **3.** to distort from the truth, fact, true meaning, etc.; bias or pervert: *prejudice warps the mind, warped in his political principles.* **4.** *Aeron.* to bend (a wing, plane or aerofoil) at the end or ends, to promote equilibrium or to secure lateral control. **5.** *Naut.* to move (a ship, etc.) into some desired place or position by hauling on a rope or warp which has been fastened to something fixed, as a buoy, anchor, or the like. **6.** *Agric.* to treat (land) by inundation with water that deposits alluvial matter. *–v.i.* **7.** to become bent or twisted out of shape, esp. out of a straight or flat form: *the wood has warped in drying.* **8.** to turn or change from the natural or proper course, state, etc. **9.** *Geol.* (of the earth's crust) to undergo a slow bending process without forming pronounced folds or dislocations. **10.** *Naut.* **a.** to warp a ship or the like along. **b.** to move by being warped, as a ship. *–n.* **11.** a bend or twist in something, as in wood that has dried unevenly. **12.** a mental twist or bias. **13.** yarns placed lengthwise in the loom, across the weft or woof, and interlaced. **14.** *Naut.* a rope, cable, etc., for warping or hauling a ship or the like along or into a position. **15.** a type of wool which is strong and of a specified minimum length, suitable for warp yarns. **16.** alluvial matter deposited by water, esp. water let in to inundate low land so as to enrich it. [ME *warpe*, OE *wearp*, c. G *Warf*] – **warper,** *n.*

**war paint** /ˈwɔ peɪnt/, *n.* **1.** paint once applied to the face and body by certain North American Indians upon going to war. **2.** *Colloq.* make-up; cosmetics. **3.** *Colloq.* full dress; finery.

**warpath** /ˈwɔpaθ/, *n.* **1.** the path or course taken by North American Indians on a warlike expedition. **2. on the warpath, a.** engaging in, seeking, or preparing for war. **b.** in a state of wrath; angry; indignant.

**warped** /wɔpt/, *adj.* twisted; distorted; perverted.

**warp knitted** /ˈwɔp nɪtəd/, *adj.* (of textiles) knitted on a warp loom to a close pattern and often in a locknit.

**warpland** /ˈwɔplænd/, *n.* an area of land subject to the deposition of alluvial sediment in flooding.

**warplane** /ˈwɔpleɪn/, *n. U.S.* an aeroplane for warfare.

**warragul** /ˈwɒrəgəl/, *n.* →**warrigal.**

**warrant** /ˈwɒrənt/, *n.* **1.** authorisation, sanction, or justification. **2.** that which serves to give reliable or formal assurance of something; a guarantee. **3.** something having the force of a guarantee or positive assurance of a thing. **4.** a writing or document certifying or authorising something, as a certificate, receipt, licence, or commission. **5.** *Law.* an instrument, issued by a magistrate, authorising an officer to make an arrest, seize property, make a search, or carry a judgment into execution. **6.** (in the army and navy) the certificate of authority or appointment issued to an officer below the rank of a commissioned officer. **7.** a warehouse receipt. **8.** a written authorisation for the payment or receipt of money: *a treasury warrant; dividend warrant.* *–v.t.* **9.** to give authority to; authorise. **10.** to afford warrant or sanction for, or justify: *the circumstances warrant such measures.* **11.** to give one's word for; vouch for (oft. used with a clause in mere emphatic assertion): *I'll warrant he did!* **12.** to give a formal assurance, or a guarantee or promise, to or for; guarantee: *to warrant payment; to warrant safe delivery.* **13.** to guarantee the quantity, quality, and other representations made to a purchaser of goods. **14.** to guarantee or secure title to (the purchaser of goods); assure indemnification against loss to. **15.** *Law.* to guarantee title of an estate or other granted property (to a grantee). [ME *warant*, from OF, var. of *guarant* defender, from Gmc; cf. MHG *warend* warranty] – **warrantable,** *adj.* – **warrantably,** *adv.* – **warrantless,** *adj.*

**warrantee** /wɒrənˈti/, *n.* one to whom a warranty is made.

**warranter** /ˈwɒrəntə/, *n.* one who warrants.

**warrant officer** /ˈwɒrənt ɒfəsə/, *n.* a member of the armed forces holding, by warrant, an intermediate rank between that of commissioned and non-commissioned officers, as a sergeant-major.

**warrantor** /ˈwɒrəntɔ/, *n.* one who warrants, or makes a warranty.

**warranty** /ˈwɒrənti/, *n., pl.* **-ties. 1.** the act of warranting; warrant; assurance. **2.** *Law.* **a.** an engagement, express or implied, in assurance of some particular in connection with a contract, as of sale: *an express warranty of the quality of goods.* **b.** a covenant in a deed to land by which the party conveying assures the grantee that he will enjoy the premises free from interference by any person claiming under a superior title. A **warranty deed** is a deed containing such a covenant, as distinguished from a *quit claim deed,* which conveys without any assurances only such title as the grantor may have. **c.** (in the law of insurance) a statement or promise, made by the party insured, and included as an essential part of the contract, falsity or nonfulfilment of which renders the policy void. **d.** a judicial document, as a warrant or writ. [ME *warantie*, from OF. Cf. GUARANTEE, WARRANT]

**warregal** /ˈwɒrəgəl/, *n.* →**warrigal.**

**warren** /ˈwɒrən/, *n.* **1.** a place where rabbits breed or abound. **2.** a building, district, etc., containing many poor people living in overcrowded conditions. [ME, from AF *warenne* game park; akin to GUARD, WARD]

**warrener** /ˈwɒrənə/, *n.* the keeper of a rabbit warren.

**warrigal** /ˈwɒrəgəl/, *n.* **1.** the dingo. *–adj.* **2.** wild; untamed. Also, **warragul, warregal.** [Aboriginal]

**warrior** /ˈwɒriə/, *n.* a man engaged or experienced in warfare; soldier. [ME *werreour*, from ONF *werreieor.* See WAR] – **warrior-like,** *adj.*

**warrior bush** /ˈ– bʊʃ/, *n.* a small tree, leafless but with green branchlets, *Apophyllum anomalum,* common on the plains of eastern Australia.

**warship** /ˈwɔʃɪp/, *n.* a ship built or armed for use in war.

**wart** /wɔt/, *n.* **1.** a small, usu. hard, abnormal elevation on the skin, caused by a filterable virus. **2.** a small protuberance. [ME; OE *wearte,* c. G *Warze*]

**wartcress** /ˈwɔtkrɛs/, *n.* →**swinecress.**

**wart-hog** /ˈwɔt-hɒg/, *n.* an African wild swine, *Phacochoerus aethiopicus,* having large tusks, and warty excrescences on the face.

wart-hog

**wartime** /ˈwɔtaɪm/, *n.* **1.** a time or season of war. *–adj.* **2.** of, pertaining to, or occurring during war: *wartime conferences.*

**warty** /ˈwɔti/, *adj.,* **wartier, wartiest. 1.** having warts; covered with or as with warts. **2.** like a wart.

**war-weary** /ˈwɔ-wɪəri/, *adj.* completely exhausted by war, esp. after a long conflict.

**warwicks** /ˈwɒrɪks/, *n.pl. Colloq.* the arms. [rhyming slang, *Warwick Farm,* racecourse in Sydney]

**wary** /ˈwɛəri/, *adj.,* **warier, wariest. 1.** watchful, or on one's guard, esp. habitually; on the alert; cautious; careful. **2.** characterised by caution. [WARE², *adj.* + -Y¹] – **warily,** *adv.* – **wariness,** *n.*

**was** /wɒz/, *v.* first and third person singular past tense indicative of **be.** [ME; OE *wæs,* c. G *war*]

**wash** /wɒʃ/, *v.t.* **1.** to apply water or some other liquid to for the purpose of cleansing; cleanse by dipping, rubbing, or scrubbing in water, etc. **2.** to remove (dirt, stains, paint, or any matter) by or as by the action of water, or as water does (fol. by *out, off,* etc.). **3.** to free from spiritual defilement, or from sin, guilt, etc. **4.** to wet with water or other liquid, or as water does. **5.** to flow over or against: *a shore or cliff washed by waves.* **6.** to carry or bring with water or any liquid, or as the water or liquid does (oft. fol. by *up, down,* or *along*): *the storm washed seaweed high on the beach.* **7.** to wear, as water does, by flowing over or against a surface (oft. fol. by *out* or *away*). **8.** to form (a channel, etc.), as flowing water does. **9.** *Mining, etc.* **a.** to subject (earth, etc.) to the action of water in order to separate valuable material. **b.** to separate (valuable material, as gold) thus. **10.** to purify (a gas or gaseous mixture) by passage through or over a liquid. **11.** to cover with a watery or thin coat of colour. **12.** to overlay with a thin coat or deposit of metal: *to wash brass with gold.* **13. wash down, a.** to clean completely by washing. **b.** to swallow (food) with the aid of liquid. **14. wash out, a.** to remove or get rid of by washing. **b.** to cancel or abandon (an arrangement, sporting event, etc.). **15. wash up,** to wash (dishes, saucepans, etc.) after a meal. *–v.i.* **16.** to wash oneself: *time to wash for supper.* **17.** to wash clothes. **18.** to cleanse anything with or in water or the like. **19.** to undergo washing, esp. without injury. **20.** *Colloq.* to stand being put to the proof; bear investigation: *that excuse might wash with some people.* **21.** to be carried or driven (along, ashore, etc.) by water. **22.** to flow or beat with a lapping sound, as waves on a shore. **23.** to move along in or as in waves, or with a rushing movement, as water. **24.** to be eroded, as by a stream, rainfall, etc.: *a hillside that washes frequently.* **25.** to be worn by the action of water, as a hill (oft. fol. by *away*). **26. wash out,** *Rowing.* to allow the blade to rise wholly or partly out of the water before a stroke is properly finished. *–n.* **27.** the act of washing with water or other liquid. **28.** a quantity of clothes, etc., washed, or to be washed, at one time. **29.** a liquid with which something is washed, wetted, coloured, overspread, etc. **30.** the flow, sweep, dash, or breaking of water. **31.** the sound made by this: *listening to the wash of the Atlantic.* **32.** water moving along in waves or with a rushing movement. **33.** the rough or broken water left behind a moving ship, etc. **34.** *Aeron.* the disturbance in the air left behind by a moving aeroplane or any of its parts. **35.** any of various liquids for toilet purposes: *a hair wash.* **36.** a medicinal lotion. **37.** earth, etc., from which gold or the like can be extracted by washing. **38.** the wearing away of the shore by breaking waves. **39.** a tract of land washed by the action of the sea or a river. **40.** a fen, marsh, or a bog. **41.** a small stream or shallow pool. **42.** a shallow arm of the sea or a shallow part of a river. **43.** a depression or channel formed by flowing water. **44.** alluvial matter transferred and deposited by flowing water. **45.** a broad, thin layer of colour applied by a continuous movement of the brush, as in watercolour painting. **46.** a thin coat of metal applied in liquid form. **47.** waste liquid matter, refuse food, etc., from the kitchen, as for pigs. **48.** washy or weak drink or liquid food. **49.** the fermented wort from which the spirit is extracted in distilling. **50. come out in the wash,** *Colloq.* to be revealed eventually; become known. [ME; OE *wascan,* G *waschen,* Icel. *vaska*]

**washable** /ˈwɒʃəbəl/, *adj.* capable of being washed, esp. without injury: *a washable fabric.*

**wash-and-wear** /ˈwɒʃ-ən-wɛə/, *adj.* treated so as to be easily washed and need no ironing: *a wash-and-wear shirt.*

**washaway** /ˈwɒʃəweɪ/, *n.* →**wash-out** (def. 1).

**washbasin** /ˈwɒʃbeɪsən/, *n.* a large basin or bowl for washing face and hands, etc. Also, **washbowl** /ˈwɒʃboʊl/.

**washboard** /ˈwɒʃbɔd/, *n.* **1.** a board or frame with a corrugated metallic or other surface, on which clothes are scrubbed in the process of washing. **2.** such a board or frame used as a rhythm instrument in certain types of folk music. **3.** *U.S.* a skirting board. **4.** *Naut.* **a.** a thin broad plank fastened to and projecting above the gunwale or side of a boat to keep out the spray and sea. **b.** a similar board on the sill of a port.

**washcloth** /ˈwɒʃklɒθ/, *n.* →**washer** (defs 4 and 5).

**washday** /ˈwɒʃdeɪ/, *n.* the day set apart in a household for washing clothes. Also, **washing day.**

**washed-out** /ˈwɒʃt-aʊt/, *adj.* **1.** faded, esp. during washing. **2.** *Colloq.* **a.** utterly fatigued; exhausted. **b.** tired-looking; pale; wan.

**washed-up** /wɒʃt-ˈʌp/, *adj. Colloq.* **1.** having failed completely; finished; ruined. **2.** exhausted.

**washer** /ˈwɒʃə/, *n.* **1.** one who or that which washes. **2.** a machine or apparatus for washing something. **3.** a flat ring or perforated piece of leather, rubber, metal, etc., used to give tightness to a joint, to prevent leakage, and to distribute pressure (as under the head of a bolt, under a nut, etc.). **4.** Also, **facecloth, flannel, washrag.** a small piece of towelling or similar material used for washing the face or body. **5.** Also, **washrag.** a cloth used for washing dishes, etc.

**washerman** /ˈwɒʃəmən/, *n., pl.* **-men.** a man who washes clothes, etc., for hire.

**washerwoman** /ˈwɒʃəwʊmən/, *n., pl.* **-women.** a woman who washes clothes, etc., for hire.

**washhouse** /ˈwɒʃhaʊs/, *n.* a house or building, as an outhouse, where clothes are washed; laundry.

**washing** /ˈwɒʃɪŋ/, *n.* **1.** the act of one who or that which washes; ablution. **2.** clothes, etc., washed or to be washed, esp. those washed at one time. **3.** matter removed in washing something. **4.** material, as gold dust, obtained by washing earth, etc. **5.** a placer or other superficial deposit so washed. **6.** a thin coating or covering applied in liquid form.

**washing blue** /ˈ– blu/, *n.* →**blue** (def. 3).

**washing day** /ˈ– deɪ/, *n.* →**washday.**

**washing dolly** /ˈ– dɒli/, *n.* →**dolly**² (def. 5a).

**washing machine** /ˈ– məʃin/, *n.* an apparatus for washing clothing, etc.

**washing powder** /ˈ– paʊdə/, *n.* a powdered preparation, usu. a detergent, used for washing clothes.

**washing soda** /ˈ– soʊdə/, *n.* crystalline sodium carbonate, or sal soda, used as a cleansing agent.

**Washington palm** /ˌwɒʃɪŋtən ˈpam/, *n.* either of two fan palms of south-western North America, *Washingtonia filifera* and *W. robusta.*

**washing-up** /wɒʃɪŋ-ˈʌp/, *n.* **1.** the washing of kitchen utensils, crockery, etc., esp. after a meal. **2.** the kitchen utensils, crockery, etc., waiting to be washed.

**wash-leather** /ˈwɒʃ-lɛðə/, *n.* a soft leather, usu. sheepskin, prepared in imitation of chamois leather, used for gloves, etc., and polishing surfaces as glass.

**wash-out** /ˈwɒʃ-aʊt/, *n.* **1.** Also, **washaway.** a washing out of earth, etc., by water, as from an embankment or a roadway by heavy rain or a freshet. **2.** the hole or break produced. **3.** *Colloq.* a failure or fiasco. **4.** *Med.* lavage of the bowels or bladder.

**washrag** /ˈwɒʃræg/, *n.* →**washer** (defs 4 and 5).

**washroom** /ˈwɒʃrum/, *n.* a room having washbasins and other toilet facilities.

**washstand** /ˈwɒʃstænd/, *n.* **1.** a piece of furniture for holding a basin, a ewer, etc., for use in washing one's hands and face. **2.** a stationary fixture having taps with running water, for the same purpose.

**washtub** /ˈwɒʃtʌb/, *n.* a tub for use in washing something, esp. clothes, etc.

**washwoman** /ˈwɒʃwʊmən/, *n., pl.* **-women.** →**washerwoman.**

**washy** /ˈwɒʃi/, *adj.,* **washier, washiest. 1.** overdiluted; weak: *washy coffee.* **2.** weak, thin, or poor, as if from excessive dilution: *washy colouring.* Also, **wishy-washy.** – **washiness,** *n.*

**wasn't** /ˈwɒzənt/, *v.* contraction of *was not.*

**wasp** /wɒsp/, *n.* **1.** any of numerous hymenopterous, stinging insects, included for the most part in two superfamilies, Sphecoidea and Vespoidea. Their habits vary from a solitary life to colonial organisation. **2.** a waspish person. [ME *waspe,* OE *wæsp,* akin to D. *wesp,* G *Wespe,* L *vespa*] – **waspike, waspy,** *adj.*

**WASP** /wɒsp/, *n. Orig. U.S.* **1.** a member of the establishment conceived as being white, Anglo-Saxon and Protestant. *–adj.* **2.** of or pertaining to this establishment. [*W(hite) A(nglo)-S(axon) P(rotestant)*] – **WASP-ishness,** *n.*

**waspish** /ˈwɒspɪʃ/, *adj.* **1.** like or suggesting a wasp. **2.** quick to resent a trifling affront or injury; snappish. **3.** showing irascibility or petulance: *waspish writing.* **4.** having a slender waist, like a wasp. – **waspishly,** *adv.* – **waspishness,** *n.*

wasp

**wasp waist** /ˈwɒsp weɪst/, *n.* a slender, or tightly laced, waist. – **wasp-waisted,** *adj.*

**wassail** /ˈwɒsəl, -seɪl/, *n.* **1.** *Hist.* a salutation wishing health to a person, used when presenting a cup of drink or when drinking to the person. **2.** a festivity or revel with drinking of healths. **3.** alcoholic drink for toasting on festive occasions, esp. spiced ale, as on Christmas Eve and Twelfthnight. **4.** *Obs.* a song sung in wassailing. *–v.i.* **5.** to drink healths; revel with drinking. *–v.t.* **6.** to drink to the health or success of. [early ME *wes hail,* from Scand.; cf. early Icel. *ves heill,* c. OE *wes hāl* be hale or whole] – **wassailer,** *n.*

**Wassermann reaction** /ˈvasəmən rɪˌækʃən/, *n.* a diagnostic test for syphilis using the fixation of a complement by the serum of a syphilitic individual. Also, **Wassermann test.** [named after A. von *Wassermann,* 1866-1925, German physician and bacteriologist]

wasp waist

**wast** /wɒst/, *v. Archaic.* 2nd person singular past tense indicative of **be.**

**wastage** /ˈweɪstɪdʒ/, *n.* loss by use, wear, decay, wastefulness, etc.

**waste** /weɪst/, *v.,* **wasted, wasting,** *n., adj. –v.t.* **1.** to consume, spend, or employ uselessly or without adequate return; use to no avail; squander: *to waste money, time, effort, or words.* **2.** to fail or neglect to use, or let go to waste: *to waste an opportunity.* **3.** to destroy or consume gradually, or wear away. **4.** to wear down or reduce in bodily substance, health, or strength; emaciate; enfeeble: *to be wasted by disease or hunger.* **5.** to destroy, devastate, or ruin: *a country wasted with fire and sword.* **6.** *Chiefly U.S. Colloq.* to murder. *–v.i.* **7.** to be consumed or spent uselessly or without being fully utilised. **8.** to become gradually consumed, used up, or worn away: *a candle wastes in burning.* **9.** to become physically wasted, lose flesh or strength, or become emaciated or enfeebled (oft. fol. by *away*). **10.** to diminish gradually, or dwindle, as wealth, power, etc. (oft. fol. by *away*). **11.** to pass gradually, as time. *–n.* **12.** useless consumption or expenditure, or use without adequate return: *waste of material, money, or time.* **13.** neglect, instead of use: *waste of opportunity.* **14.** gradual destruction, impairment, or decay: *the waste and repair of bodily tissue.* **15.** devastation or ruin, as from war, fire, etc. **16.** a region or place laid waste or in ruins. **17.** anything unused, unproductive, or not properly utilised. **18.** an uncultivated tract of land. **19.** a tract of wild land, desolate country, or desert. **20.** *Law.* positive damage to, or neglect of land by a tenant. **21.** an empty, desolate, or dreary tract or extent: *a waste of snow.* **22.** anything left over or superfluous, as excess material, by-products, etc., not of use for the work in hand. **23.** remnants from the working of cotton, etc., used for wiping machinery, absorbing oil, etc. **24.** *Bldg Trades.* **a.** sullage. **b.** a pipe or conduit for draining sullage from a fitting or a floor, as floor waste. **25.** *Phys. Geog.* material derived by mechanical and chemical disintegration of rock, as the detritus transported by streams, etc. **26. go to waste,** to be wasted; fail to be used. **27. lay waste,** to destroy; devastate; ruin. *–adj.* **28.** not used or in use: *waste energy.* **29.** (of land, regions, etc.) uninhabited and wild, desolate and barren, or desert. **30.** (of regions, towns, etc.) in a state of desolation and ruin, as from devastation or decay. **31.** left over or superfluous: *to utilise waste products of manufacture.* **32.** having served a purpose and no longer of use. **33.** rejected as useless or worthless, or refuse: *waste products.* **34.** *Physiol.* pertaining to material unused by or unusable to the organism. **35.** intended to receive, hold, or carry away refuse or surplus material, etc.

**wastebasket** /ˈweɪstbaskət/, *n.* →**wastepaper basket.**

**wasted** /ˈweɪstəd/, *adj.* **1.** worn; emaciated. **2.** *Colloq.* lethargic, exhausted, as a result of taking drugs.

**wasteful** /ˈweɪstfəl/, *adj.* **1.** given to or characterised by useless consumption or expenditure: *wasteful methods of living.* **2.** squandering, or grossly extravagant. **3.** devastating or destructive: *wasteful war.* – **wastefully,** *adv.* – **wastefulness,** *n.*

**wasteland** /ˈweɪstlænd/, *n.* **1.** land which lies waste, barren and uncultivated. **2.** a place, or era, considered devoid of intellectual, artistic, or spiritual cultivation: *a cultural wasteland.*

**wasteness** /ˈweɪstnəs/, *n.* the state of being waste or desolate.

**wastepaper** /weɪstˈpeɪpə/, *n.* paper thrown away or otherwise disposed of as useless.

**wastepaper basket** /ˈ– ˌbaskət/, *n.* a basket for wastepaper, or papers, scraps of paper, etc., to be disposed of as refuse. Also, **wastebasket.**

**wastepipe** /ˈweɪstpaɪp/, *n.* **1.** a pipe for conveying away water, etc. **2.** *Plumbing.* a pipe carrying liquid wastes from all fixtures except water closets. Cf. **soil pipe.**

**waste product** /ˈweɪst ˌprɒdʌkt/, *n.* material produced in a process, as manufacture, and discarded as useless when the process is completed.

**waster** /ˈweɪstə/, *n.* **1.** one who or that which wastes. **2.** a spendthrift. **3.** an idler or good-for-nothing. **4.** something rejected as waste, esp. an inferior or badly made article. **5.** one who destroys or lays waste.

**wasting** /ˈweɪstɪŋ/, *adj.* **1.** gradually reducing the fullness and strength of the body: *a wasting disease.* **2.** laying waste; devastating; despoiling.

**wastrel** /ˈweɪstrəl/, *n.* **1.** a wasteful person; spendthrift. **2.** an idler, or good-for-nothing. [WAST(E) + -REL]

**watch** /wɒtʃ/, *v.i.* **1.** to be on the lookout, look attentively, or be closely observant, as to see what comes, is done, happens, etc.: *to watch while an experiment is performed.* **2.** to look or wait attentively and expectantly (usu. fol. by *for*): *to watch for a signal, an opportunity.* **3.** to be careful or cautious. **4.** to keep awake, esp. for a purpose; keep a vigilant watch as for protection or safekeeping. **5.** to keep vigil, as for devotional purposes. **6.** to keep guard. **7. watch it! a.** look out! **b.** be warned! **8. watch out,** to be on one's guard; be alert or cautious. **9. watch out for, a.** to beware of; avoid. **b.** to look for with anticipation. **10. watch over,** to guard; protect. *–v.t.* **11.** to keep under attentive view or observation, as in order to see or learn something; view attentively or with interest: *to watch a game of cricket.* **12.** to contemplate or regard mentally: *to watch his progress.* **13.** to look or wait attentively and expectantly for: *to watch one's chance or opportunity.* **14.** to guard for protection or safekeeping. **15.** to be careful of; pay attention to: *watch what you're doing.* *–n.* **16.** close, constant observation for the purpose of seeking or discovering something. **17.** a lookout, as for something expected: *to be on the watch.* **18.** vigilant guard, as for protection, restraint, etc. **19.** a keeping awake for some special purpose: *a watch beside a sickbed.* **20.** a period of time for watching or keeping guard. **21.** something that measures and indicates the progress of time. **22.** a small, portable timepiece. **23.** *Naut.* **a.** a period of time (usu. four hours) during which one part of a ship's crew is on duty, taking turns with another part. **b.** a certain part (usu. half) of the officers and crew of a vessel who together attend to working it for an allotted period of time. **24.** one of the periods into which the night was divided by the ancients: *the fourth watch of the night.* **25.** a watchman, or a body of watchmen. [ME *wacche,* OE *wæcca* (North.), var. of *wacian* WAKE[1]] – **watcher,** *n.*

**watchband** /ˈwɒtʃbænd/, *n.* →**watchstrap.**

**watchcase** /ˈwɒtʃkeɪs/, *n.* the case or outer covering for the works of a watch.

**watch-chain** /ˈwɒtʃ-tʃeɪn/, *n.* a chain for securing a pocket watch to the clothing.

**watchdog** /ˈwɒtʃdɒg/, *n.* **1.** a dog kept to guard property. **2.** a watchful guardian as of morals, standards, etc.

**watch-fire** /ˈwɒtʃ-faɪə/, *n.* a fire maintained during the night as a signal and for a watching party.

**watchful** /ˈwɒtʃfəl/, *adj.* **1.** vigilant or alert; closely observant. **2.** characterised by vigilance or alertness. **3.** *Archaic.* wakeful or sleepless. – **watchfully,** *adv.* – **watchfulness,** *n.*

**watch-glass** /ˈwɒtʃ-glas/, *n.* a transparent cover for the face of a watch.

**watch-guard** /ˈwɒtʃ-gad/, *n.* a chain, cord, or ribbon for securing a watch when worn on the person.

**watch-house** /ˈwɒtʃ-haʊs/, *n.* **1.** (in some States) a place where people are held under temporary arrest. **2.** *Chiefly Brit.* a house in which a guard is stationed.

**watchmaker** /ˈwɒtʃmeɪkə/, *n.* one whose occupation it is to make and repair watches. – **watchmaking,** *n.*

**watchman** /ˈwɒtʃmən/, *n., pl.* **-men. 1.** one who keeps guard over a building usu. at night, to protect it from fire or thieves. **2.** (formerly) one who guarded or patrolled the streets at night.

**watchnight service** /ˈwɒtʃnaɪt sɜvəs/, *n.* (in Protestant churches) a service held on New Year's Eve.

**watchout** /ˈwɒtʃaʊt/, *n.* the act of looking out for something; lookout.

**watchstrap** /ˈwɒtʃstræp/, *n.* a strap for attaching a watch to the wrist. Also, **watchband.**

**watchtower** /ˈwɒtʃtaʊə/, *n.* a tower on which a sentry keeps watch.

**watchword** /ˈwɒtʃwɜd/, *n.* **1.** a word or short phrase to be communicated, on challenge, to a sentinel or guard; a password; a countersign. **2.** a word or phrase expressive of a principle or rule of action. **3.** a rallying cry of a party, etc.; a slogan.

**water** /ˈwɔtə/, *n.* **1.** the liquid which in a more or less impure state constitutes rain, oceans, lakes, rivers, etc., and which in a pure state is a transparent, odourless, tasteless liquid, a compound of hydrogen and oxygen, $H_2O$, freezing at 32°F or 0°C, and boiling at 212°F or 100°C. It contains 11.188 per cent hydrogen and 88.812 per cent oxygen, by weight. **2.** a special form or variety of this liquid, as rain. **3.** (*oft. pl.*) the liquid obtained from a mineral spring. **4.** the water of a river, etc., with reference to its relative height, esp. as dependent on tide: *high or low water.* **5.** that which enters a vessel through leaks: *the ship is taking water.* **6.** the surface of water: *above, below,* or *on the water.* **7.** (*pl.*) flowing water, or water moving in waves. **8.** (*pl.*) a body of water as a sea or seas bordering a particular country or situated in a particular region. **9.** a liquid solution or preparation: *toilet water.* **10.** any of various solutions of volatile or gaseous substances in water: *ammonia water.* **11.** any liquid or aqueous organic secretion, exudation, humour, or the like, as tears, perspiration, urine, the amniotic fluids, etc. **12.** a wavy, lustrous pattern or marking, as on silk fabrics, metal surfaces, etc. **13.** the degree of transparency and brilliancy of a diamond or other precious stone. **14. above water,** out of embarrassment or trouble, esp. of a financial nature. **15. by water,** by ship or boat. **16. go to water,** to lose courage; abandon one's resolve. **17. in deep (hot) water, a.** in trouble; in a difficult situation. **b.** touching on an area of consideration which is contentious. **18. like water,** abundantly; freely: *to spend money like water.* **19. of the first water,** of the finest quality or rank: *a literary critic of the first water.* **20. throw cold water on,** to discourage. *–v.t.* **21.** to sprinkle, moisten, or drench with water: *to water a road or street.* **22.** to supply (animals) with water for drinking. **23.** to furnish with a supply of water, as a ship. **24.** to furnish water to (a region, etc.), as by streams; supply (land, etc.) with water, as by irrigation. **25.** to dilute or adulterate with water (oft. fol. by *down*): *to water soup.* **26.** (*fig.*) to weaken (fol. by *down*): *to water down an argument.* **27.** *Finance.* to issue (shares of stock) without receiving a corresponding amount of cash or property. **28.** to produce a wavy lustrous pattern, marking, or finish on (fabrics, metals, etc.). **29. water the horse,** *Colloq.* to urinate. *–v.i.* **30.** to discharge, fill with, or secrete water or liquid, as the eyes, or as the mouth at the sight or thought of tempting food. **31.** to drink water, as an animal. **32.** to take in a supply of water, as a ship. *–adj.* **33.** of or pertaining to water in any way. **34.** holding water: *a water bucket.* **35.** worked or powered by, or treating, water: *a water mill.* **36.** used in or on water: *a water vehicle.* **37.** prepared with water for hardening, dilution, etc.: *water mortar.* **38.** residing by or in, or ruling over, water: *water people, water deity.* [ME; OC *wæter,* c. D *water,* G *Wasser;* akin to Icel. *vatn,* Goth. *wato*] – **waterer,** *n.* – **waterless,** *adj.* – **waterlike,** *adj.*

**waterage** /ˈwɔtərɪdʒ/, *n.* **1.** delivery of goods over water routes. **2.** the cost of this.

**water-baby** /ˈwɔtə-beɪbi/, *n. Colloq.* a person, esp. a child, who finds no difficulty in learning to swim and enjoys playing in water.

**water-back** /ˈwɔtə-bæk/, *n.* a reservoir, set of pipes, or the like, at the back of a stove or fireplace, providing a supply of hot water.

**waterbag** /ˈwɔtəbæg/, *n.* a bag made of canvas or similar material, for carrying water, esp. in dry areas.

**water bath** /ˈwɔtə baθ/, *n.* a vessel filled with water used to transfer heat uniformly and at temperatures below the boiling point of water.

**Water-bearer** /ˈwɔtə-bɛərə/, *n.* the zodiacal constellation or sign Aquarius.

**waterbed** /ˈwɔtəbɛd/, *n.* a heavy durable plastic bag filled with water, used as a mattress often in a supporting wooden frame.

**water-beetle** /ˈwɔtə-bitl/, *n.* any of the aquatic beetles of the families Dytiscidae (diving beetles) or Hydrophilidae.

**water-betony** /wɔtə-ˈbɛtəni/, *n.* a perennial herb, *Scrophularia aquatica,* common in wet places in Europe.

**waterbird** /ˈwɔtəbɜd/, *n.* an aquatic bird, or bird that frequents the water; a swimming or wading bird.

**water blinks** /ˈwɔtə blɪŋks/, *n.* a weak, tufted annual plant, *Montia verna,* found in or near shallow fresh water in south-eastern Australia.

**water-biscuit** /ˈwɔtə-bɪskət/, *n.* a thin, crisp biscuit prepared from flour and water.

**water-blister** /ˈwɔtə-blɪstə/, *n.* a blister which contains a clear, serous fluid, as distinguished from a blood blister, in which the fluid is sanguineous.

**water-boatman** /wɔtə-ˈboʊtmən/, *n., pl.* **-men. 1.** a hemipterous insect of the family Corixidae, members of which swim in fresh water, using their long legs. **2.** →**water-strider.**

waterbuck

**waterborne** /ˈwɔtəbɔn/, *adj.* **1.** supported by the water; carried by the water. **2.** conveyed by ship or boat. **3.** transmitted by water, as a disease.

**water-bottle** /ˈwɔtə-bɒtl/, *n.* a flask or vessel of leather, glass, etc., for holding drinking water, esp. as used by soldiers, travellers, etc.

**waterbrain** /ˈwɔtəbreɪn/, *n.* →**gid.**

**waterbrash** /ˈwɔtəbræʃ/, *n.* →**heart-burn.**

**waterbuck** /ˈwɔtəbʌk/, *n., pl.* **-bucks,** (*esp. collectively*) **-buck.** any of various African antelopes of the genus *Kobus,* frequenting marshes and reedy places, esp. *K. ellipsiprymnus,* a large species of southern and central Africa. [D *waterbok*]

water-buffalo

**water-buffalo** /ˈwɔtə-bʌfəloʊ/, *n.* a large buffalo, *Bubalus bubalis,* originally from India but now domesticated and widely used as a draught animal. Also, **water-ox.**

**water-butt** /ˈwɔtə-bʌt/, *n.* an open-ended barrel or container for collecting and storing rain-water.

**waterbuttons** /ˈwɔtəbʌtnz/, *n.* a low growing herb, *Cotula coronopifolia,* family Compositae, with small yellow disc-shaped flower heads, found in wet situations.

**water-carrier** /ˈwɔtə-kæriə/, *n.* **1.** a person who or an animal which carries water. **2.** a container for carrying water. **3.** *Railways.* a freight carriage of cylindrical shape, designed for the transportation of water or other liquids.

**water-cart** /ˈwɔtə-kat/, *n.* a vehicle that carries water, esp. one which waters the roads.

**water-chestnut** /ˈwɔtə-ˌtʃɛsnʌt/, *n.* **1.** any of the aquatic plants constituting the genus *Trapa,* bearing an edible, nut-like fruit, esp. *T. natans* of the Old World. **2.** the fruit. Also, **water-caltrop** /ˈwɔtə-kæltrəp/.

**water-chickweed** /wɔtə-ˈtʃɪkwid/, *n.* a slender perennial herb, *Mysoton aquaticum,* common in wet places in Europe and temperate Asia.

**water-clock** /ˈwɔtə-klɒk/, *n.* a device, as a clepsydra, for measuring time by the flow of water.

**water-closet** /ˈwɔtə-klɒzət/, *n.***1.** a receptacle in which human excrement is flushed down a drain by water from a cistern. **2.** a room fitted with a water-closet. *Abbrev.:* WC.

**watercolour** /ˈwɔtəkʌlə/, *n.* **1.** a pigment dispersed in water-soluble gum. **2.** the art or method of painting with such pigments. **3.** a painting or design executed by this method. *–adj.* **4.** of or pertaining to watercolour or a watercolour painting. Also, *U.S.,* **watercolor.** – **watercolourist,** *n.*

**water-column** /ˈwɔtə-kɒləm/, *n.* the sea viewed as the habitat of marine creatures, as opposed to the bottom of the ocean, the surface of the water, etc.

**water-cool** /ˈwɔtə-kul/, *v.t.* to cool by means of water, esp. by water circulating in pipes or a jacket. – **water-cooled,** *adj.*

**water-cooler** /ˈwɔtə-kulə/, *n.* a vessel for holding drinking water which is cooled and drawn off for use by a tap.

**water couch** /ˈwɔtə kutʃ/, *n.* a native perennial grass, *Paspalum distichum,* having coarse stems and leaves, with spreading runners, and found in wet-soil areas of Australia.

**watercourse** /ˈwɔtəkɔs/, *n.* **1.** a stream of water, as a river or brook. **2.** the bed of such a stream. **3.** a natural channel conveying water. **4.** a channel or canal made for the conveyance of water.

**watercraft** /ˈwɔtəkraft/, *n.* **1.** skill in boating and water sports. **2.** any boat or ship. **3.** boats and ships collectively.

**water-crake** /ˈwɔtə-kreɪk/, *n.* **1.** →**spotted crake.** **2.** the Old World water-ouzel, *Cinclus aquaticus.*

**watercress** /ˈwɔtəkrɛs/, *n.* **1.** a perennial cress, *Rorippa nasturtium-aquaticum,* usu. growing in clear, running water, and bearing pungent leaves. **2.** the leaves, used for salads, soups, and as a garnish.

**water cure** /ˈwɔtə kjuə/, *n.* **1.** hydropathy or hydrotherapy. **2.** *Colloq.* torture by means of forcing water in great quantities into the victim's stomach.

**water cycle** /ˈ– saɪkəl/, *n.* the circulation of water on earth, as it evaporates from the sea, condenses into clouds and precipitates.

**water-diviner** /ˈwɔtə-dəvaɪnə/, *n.* one who uses a divining rod to discover water in the ground. Also, **waterfinder.**

**water-dog** /ˈwɔtə-dɒg/, *n.* a dog accustomed to or delighting in the water, or trained to go into the water to retrieve game.

**water dragon** /ˈwɔtə drægən/, *n.* any of various species of robust, agamid lizards of genus *Physignathus,* found throughout Australia, generally close to water. Also, **water goanna.**

**water-dropwort** /ˈwɔtə-ˌdrɒpwɜt/, *n.* any of several perennial umbelliferous herbs of the genus *Oenanthe,* as *O. fistulosa,* a plant of wet places in Europe and south-west Asia.

waterfall

**watered-down** /wɔtəd-ˈdaʊn/, *adj.* made weaker, less effective, by or as by the addition of water.

**water equivalent** /ˈwɔtər əkwɪvələnt/, *n.* →**heat capacity.**

**waterfall** /ˈwɔtəfɔl/, *n.* a steep fall or flow of water from a height; a cascade.

**waterfern** /ˈwɔtəfɜn/, *n.* any fern belonging to the families Marsiliaceae, Azollaceae and Salviniaceae which grows in or floats on water.

**waterfinder** /ˈwɔtəfaɪndə/, *n.* →**water-diviner.**

**water-flea** /ˈwɔtə-fli/, *n.* any of various small aquatic crustaceans of the order Cladocera, as the *C. daphnia,* which swim with characteristically jerky movements.

**waterfowl** /ˈwɔtəfaʊl/, *n.* **1.** a waterbird, esp. a swimming bird. **2.** such birds collectively, esp. swimming game birds.

**waterfront** /ˈwɔtəfrʌnt/, *n.* **1.** land abutting on a body of water. **2.** a part of a city or town so abutting. **3.** workers in industries using wharf facilities: *industrial unrest on the waterfront.* – **waterfrontage,** *n.*

**water-gap** /ˈwɔtə-gæp/, *n.* a transverse gap in a mountain ridge, cut by and giving passage to a stream.

**water-gas** /ˈwɔtə-gæs/, *n.* a poisonous gas used for lighting, etc., made by passing steam over incandescent coal or other carbon fuel, and consisting of a mixture of various gases, chiefly carbon monoxide and hydrogen.

**water-gate** /ˈwɔtə-geɪt/, *n.* **1.** →**floodgate.** **2.** a gateway giving access to a body of water.

**watergate** /ˈwɔtəgeɪt/, *n., v.,* **-gated, -gating.** *Colloq.* *–n.* **1.** a scandal involving charge of corruption against a political leader. **2.** a downfall of a political leader, caused by a scandal. *–v.t.* **3.** to conceal; cover up. [from *Watergate,* hotel in Washington, the bugging of which led to a political scandal, and the resignation of the U.S. President, Richard Nixon]

**water-gauge** /ˈwɔtə-geɪdʒ/, *n.* any device for indicating the height of water in a reservoir, tank, boiler, or other vessel.

**waterglass** /ˈwɔtəglas/, *n.* **1.** a glass or goblet for drinking. **2.** a vessel of glass to hold water. **3.** a glass tube used to indicate water-level, as in a boiler. **4.** a device for observing objects beneath the surface of the water, consisting essentially of an open tube or box with a glass bottom. **5.** →**sodium silicate.**

**water goanna** /ˈwɔtə goʊˌænə/, *n.* →**water dragon.**

water-gauge in a boiler: A, water-level; B, upper cock; C, lower cock

**watergum** /ˈwɔtəgʌm/, *n.* **1.** any of several myrtaceous trees growing near water, as species of the genus *Tristania.* **2.** (in the U.S.) a tupelo, *Nyssa sylvatica,* of the southern states.

**water-hammer** /ˈwɔtə-hæmə/, *n.* the concussion which results when a moving volume of water in a pipe is suddenly arrested.

**water harvesting** /wɔtə ˈhavəstɪŋ/, *n.* the collection of surplus water to be stored for later use, usu. in a dry period.

**water-hemlock** /ˈwɔtə-ˌhɛmlɒk/, *n.* any of the poisonous plants constituting the umbelliferous genus *Cicuta,* as *C. virosa* of Europe, and *C. maculata* of North America, growing in swamps and marshy places.

**waterhen** /ˈwɔtəhɛn/, *n.* →**gallinule.**

**waterhole** /ˈwɔtəhoʊl/, *n.* a natural hole or hollow in which water collects, as a spring in a desert, a cavity in the dried-up course of a river, etc.

**water hyacinth** /wɔtə ˈhaɪəsɪnθ/, *n.* a floating plant of Central and South America, *Eichhornia crassipes,* which has become a serious pest of water courses in warm countries.

**water-ice** /ˈwɔtər-aɪs/, *n.* **1.** ice formed by direct freezing of fresh or salt water, and not by compacting of snow. **2.** *Chiefly Brit.* a frozen confection made with fruit juice and sugar syrup.

**wateriness** /ˈwɔtərinəs/, *n.* a watery state.

**watering** /ˈwɔtərɪŋ/, *n.* **1.** the act of one who or that which waters. **2.** a watered appearance on silk, etc. *–adj.* **3.** that waters. **4.** pertaining to medicinal springs or a sea-bathing resort.

**watering-can** /ˈwɔtərɪŋ-kæn/, *n.* a vessel, esp. with a spout having a perforated nozzle, for watering or sprinkling plants, etc.

**watering hole** /ˈwɔtərɪŋ hoʊl/, *n.* **1.** a waterhole where animals drink. **2.** *Colloq.* a hotel.

**watering-place** /ˈwɔtərɪŋ-pleɪs/, *n.* **1.** a health resort with mineral springs; spa. **2.** *Brit.* a seaside resort. **3.** a place where drinking water may be obtained. **4.** *Colloq.* a hotel.

**waterish** /ˈwɔtərɪʃ/, *adj.* watery.

**water-jacket** /ˈwɔtə-dʒækət/, *n.* a casing or compartment containing water, placed about something to keep it cool or otherwise regulate its temperature, as round the cylinder or cylinders of an internal-combustion engine.

**water-jump** /ˈwɔtə-dʒʌmp/, *n.* any small body of water which a horse must jump over, as in a steeplechase.

**water-level** /ˈwɔtə-lɛvəl/, *n.* **1.** the surface level of any body of water. **2.** *Naut.* →**waterline.**

**waterlily** /ˈwɔtəlɪli/, *n.* **1.** any of the aquatic plants constituting the genus *Nymphaea,* having floating leaves and showy, often fragrant, flowers as *N. gigantea.* **2.** any plant of the genus *Nuphar* of the same family **(yellow waterlily** or **yellow pond-lily). 3.** any member of the family Nymphaeaceae. **4.** the flower of any such plant.

waterlily

**waterline** /ˈwɔtəlaɪn/, *n.* **1.** *Naut.* **a.** that part of the outside of the hull of a ship that is just at the water-level. **b.** any of several lines marked on the hull of a ship, showing the depth to which it sinks when unloaded and when partially or fully loaded. **2.** →**water-level. 3.** the line in which water at its surface borders upon a floating body.

**waterlog** /ˈwɔtəlɒg/, *v.t.,* **-logged, -logging. 1.** to cause (a ship, etc.) to become unmanageable as a result of flooding. **2.** to soak or saturate with water.

**waterlogged** /ˈwɔtəlɒgd/, *adj.* **1.** so filled with water, by leakage or overflow, as to be heavy or unmanageable, as a ship, etc. **2.** excessively saturated with water: *waterlogged ground.*

**waterloo** /wɔtəˈlu/, *n.* a decisive or crushing defeat: *to meet one's waterloo.* [from *Waterloo,* village in central Belgium where Napoleon (Bonaparte), Emperor of France, was defeated on 18 June, 1815]

**water main** /ˈwɔtə meɪn/, *n.* a main or principal pipe or conduit in a system for conveying water.

**waterman** /ˈwɔtəmən/, *n., pl.* **-men. 1.** a man who manages, or works on, a boat; boatman. **2.** one skilled in rowing or boating.

**watermanship** /ˈwɔtəmənʃɪp/, *n.* **1.** the function of a waterman. **2.** skill in rowing, etc.

**watermark** /ˈwɔtəmak/, *n.* **1.** a mark indicating the height to which water rises or has risen, as in a river, etc. **2.** a figure or design impressed in the fabric in the manufacture of paper and visible when the paper is held to the light. *–v.t.* **3.** to mark (paper) with a watermark. **4.** to impress (a design, etc.) as a watermark.

**water-meadow** /ˈwɔtə-mɛdoʊ/, *n.* a meadow kept fertile by flooding from a stream.

**water meadow grass,** *n.* an aquatic perennial, *Glyceria maxima,* originally from Europe; useful for fodder in swampy areas.

**watermelon** /ˈwɔtəmɛlən/, *n.* **1.** the large, roundish or elongated fruit of a trailing vine, *Citrullus lanatus,* having a hard, green rind and a (usu.) pink or red pulp which abounds in a sweetish, watery juice. **2.** the plant or vine.

**water-meter** /ˈwɔtə-mitə/, *n.* a device for measuring and registering the quantity of water that passes through a pipe, etc.

**water-milfoil** /wɔtə-ˈmɪlfɔɪl/, *n.* any of various aquatic plants, chiefly of the genus *Myriophyllum,* the submersed leaves of which are very finely divided.

**watermill** /ˈwɔtəmɪl/, *n.* a mill with machinery driven by water.

**water moccasin** /ˈwɔtə mɒkəsən/, *n.* a venomous snake, *Ancistrodon piscivorus,* of the rattlesnake family, inhabiting swamps of the southern U.S.; cottonmouth.

**water mole** /ˈ– moʊl/, *n.* →**platypus.**

**water-monkey** /ˈwɔtə-mʌŋki/, *n.* **1.** a carafe of drinking water held in a special bracket on the wall of a railway carriage. **2.** a flask-shaped piece of pottery.

**water-motor** /ˈwɔtə-moʊtə/, *n.* any form of prime mover, or motor, that is operated by the kinetic energy, pressure, or weight of water, esp. a small turbine or waterwheel fitted to a pipe supplying water.

**water-nymph** /ˈwɔtə-nɪmf/, *n.* **1.** a nymph of the water, as a naiad or a nereid. **2.** →**waterlily. 3.** any of the aquatic plants constituting the genus *Naias.*

**water-oak** /ˈwɔtər-oʊk/, *n.* **1.** an oak, *Quercus nigra,* of the southern U.S., growing chiefly along streams and swamps. **2.** any of several other American oaks.

**water of constitution,** *n. Obs.* →**coordinated water.**

**water of crystallisation,** *n.* water of hydration, formerly thought necessary to crystallisation, but now usu. regarded as affecting crystallisation only as it forms new molecular combinations.

**water of hydration,** *n.* that portion of a hydrate which is represented as, or can be driven off as, water, now usu. regarded as being in true molecular combination with the other atoms of the compound, and not existing in the compound as water.

**water-ouzel** /ˈwɔtər-uzəl/, *n.* any of several plump, thick-plumaged, aquatic birds of the family Cinclidae, allied to the thrushes, esp. *Cinclus cinclus* of Europe, and *C. mexicanus* of western North America, having the habit of jerking the body or 'dipping' as they perch, walk, etc; a dipper.

water-ouzel

**water-ox** /ˈwɔtər-ɒks/, *n.* →**water-buffalo.**

**water-paint** /ˈwɔtə-peɪnt/, *n.* any paint in which the volatile portion is mainly water, esp. an emulsion paint in which the binder is, or becomes, insoluble in water.

**water-parsnip** /wɔtə-ˈpasnɪp/, *n.* a large, perennial, umbelliferous herb, *Sium latifolium,* occurring in wet places.

**water-parting** /ˈwɔtə-patɪŋ/, *n.* a watershed or divide.

**waterpepper** /ˈwɔtəpɛpə/, *n.* any of various plants of the genus *Polygonum,* growing in wet places, esp. *P. hydropiper.*

**water pipe** /ˈwɔtə paɪp/, *n.* →**hookah.**

**water-pipit** /ˈwɔtə-pɪpət/, *n.* →**pipit.**

**water-pistol** /ˈwɔtə-pɪstl/, *n.* a toy gun that squirts a jet of water or other liquid.

**water-plantain** /ˈwɔtə-plænteɪn/, *n.* any of the aquatic herbs of the genus *Alisma,* esp. *A. plantago-aquatica,* a species growing in shallow water and having leaves suggesting those of the common plantain.

**water point** /ˈwɔtə pɔɪnt/, *n.* a place such as a dam, a bore or a creek where animals may drink.

**water-polo** /ˈwɔtə-poʊloʊ/, *n.* a water game played by two teams, each having seven swimmers, in which the object is to carry or pass the ball over the opponent's goal line.

**water-power** /ˈwɔtə-paʊə/, *n.* **1.** the power of water used, or capable of being used, to drive machinery, etc. **2.** a fall or descent in a stream, capable of being so used. **3.** a water right possessed by a mill.

**waterpox** /ˈwɔtəpɒks/, *n.* →**chickenpox.**

**waterproof** /ˈwɔtəpruf/, *adj.* **1.** impervious to water. **2.** rendered impervious to water by some special process, as coating or treating with rubber or the like. *–n.* **3.** any of several coated or rubberised fabrics which will hold water. **4.** an outer garment of waterproof material. *–v.t.* **5.** to make waterproof.

**waterproofing** /ˈwɔtəprufɪŋ/, *n.* **1.** the material used to make something waterproof. **2.** the act or process of making something waterproof.

**water rail** /ˈwɔtə reɪl/, *n.* **1.** a brown and grey bird, *Rallus pectoralis,* 20-23 cm long, inhabiting swamps and lagoons and found in the southern and eastern coastal districts of Australia. **2.** a similar bird, *Rallus aquaticus,* of the coot family, about 30 cm long, inhabiting marshes and rivers of Europe and Asia.

**water-rat** /ˈwɔtə-ræt/, *n.* **1.** a large, aquatic, native rat, *Hydromys chrysogaster,* having soft dense fur and webbed hind feet, found near rivers and streams throughout Australia. **2.** any of several different rodents of aquatic habits, as the water-vole, *Arvicola amphibius.* **3.** the American muskrat, *Fiber zibethicus.* **4.** *U.S. Colloq.* a vagrant or thief who frequents a waterfront. **5.** *Colloq.* →**water-baby.**

**water-repellent** /wɔtə-rəˈpɛlənt, -ri-/, *adj.* having a finish which is resistant to water.

**water-resistant** /ˈwɔtə-rəzɪstənt/, *adj.* having some resistance to water but not waterproof, as a watch, overcoat, etc.

**water ribbons** /ˈwɔtə rɪbənz/, *n.* the water or marsh plant *Triglochin procera.*

water ribbons

**water right** /ˈ– raɪt/, *n.* the right to make use of the water from a particular stream, lake, or canal.

**water-sapphire** /ˌwɔtə-ˈsæfaɪə/, *n.* a transparent variety of cordierite, found in Sri Lanka, Madagascar, and elsewhere, sometimes used as a gem. [translation of F *saphir d'eau*]

**waterscape** /ˈwɔtəskeɪp/, *n.* a picture or view of the sea or other body of water. [WATER + *-scape,* modelled on LANDSCAPE]

**water-scorpion** /ˈwɔtə-skɔpiən/, *n.* any of the aquatic hemipterous insects constituting the family Nepidae (genera *Nepa, Ranatra,* etc.), having a tail-like process through which respiration is effected.

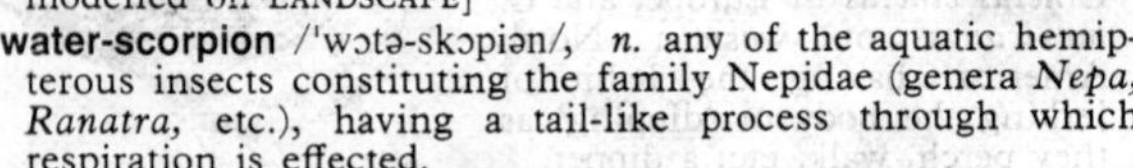

**watershed** /ˈwɔtəʃɛd/, *n.* **1.** the ridge or crest line dividing two drainage areas; water-parting; divide. **2.** a turning point; a crucial event or time in a career, venture, etc. **3.** *U.S.* the region or area drained by a river, etc.; a drainage area. [WATER + SHED[2]]

**water-shield** /ˈwɔtə-ʃild/, *n.* any of the aquatic plants of the genera *Brasenia* and *Cabomba,* with peltate floating leaves.

**water-shrew** /ˈwɔtə-ʃru/, *n.* either of two small aquatic shrews of the genus *Neomys,* inhabiting Europe and parts of Asia.

**water-sick** /ˈwɔtə-sɪk/, *adj.* excessively watered, esp. by irrigation, so that tilling and planting cannot be done.

**waterside** /ˈwɔtəsaɪd/, *n.* **1.** the margin, bank, or shore of the sea, a river, a lake, etc. *–adj.* **2.** of, relating to, or situated at the waterside: *waterside insects.* **3.** working by the waterside: *waterside police.*

**waterside worker** /ˈ– ˌwɜkə/, *n.* wharf labourer. Also, **watersider.**

**water-ski** /ˈwɔtə-ski/, *n., v.,* **-ski'd** or **-skied, -skiing.** *–n.* **1.** a type of ski used for gliding over water. *–v.i.* **2.** to glide over water on water-skis by grasping a rope towed by a speedboat.

**water-snake** /ˈwɔtə-sneɪk/, *n.* **1.** any of the harmless colubrine snakes of the genus *Natrix,* found in or near fresh water. **2.** any of various other snakes living in or frequenting water.

**water-soak** /ˈwɔtə-soʊk/, *v.t.* to soak with water.

**water-softener** /ˈwɔtə-sɒfənə/, *n.* any substance or device for destroying the hardness of water, usu. by causing the precipitation, or removal from solution, of the metals whose salts cause the hardness.

**water-soldier** /ˈwɔtə-soʊldʒə/, *n.* a floating aquatic herb, *Stratiotes aloides* (family Hydrocharitaceae), with rosettes of fleshy, serrated leaves, occurring in ponds in Europe and north-western Asia.

**water-soluble** /ˈwɔtə-sɒljəbəl/, *adj.* able to dissolve in water: *water-soluble vitamins B and C.*

**water-spaniel** /ˈwɔtə-spænjəl/, *n.* a curly-haired spaniel of either of two varieties, taking to water and readily trained for hunting.

Irish water-spaniel

**water-speedwell** /ˈwɔtə-ˌspidwɛl/, *n.* a speedwell, *Veronica anagallis-aquatica,* found esp. in marshes.

**water-spider** /ˈwɔtə-spaɪdə/, *n.* an aquatic spider, *Argyroneta aquatica,* of Europe and northern Asia which lives under water in an air bubble trapped by a web.

**waterspout** /ˈwɔtəspaʊt/, *n.* **1.** a pipe running down the side of a house to take away water from the gutter of the roof. **2.** a spout, nozzle, or orifice from which water is discharged. **3.** *Meteorol.* **a.** a tornado-like storm or whirlwind over the ocean or other body of water, which takes the form of a progressive gyrating mass of air laden with mist and spray, presenting the appearance of a solid column of water reaching upwards to the clouds. **b.** a sudden and violent downpour of rain; cloudburst.

**water-sprite** /ˈwɔtə-spraɪt/, *n.* a sprite or spirit inhabiting the water.

**water-starwort** /wɔtə-ˈstawɜt/, *n.* any plant of the genus *Callitriche,* of aquatic herbs.

**water-strider** /ˈwɔtə-straɪdə/, *n.* any of the hemipterous insects constituting the family Gerridae, having long, slender legs, and darting about on the surface of water; pond-skater.

**water supply** /ˈwɔtə səplaɪ/, *n.* **1.** the system of dams, pipes, etc., by which water is supplied to a community. **2.** the supply of water to a community or region.

**watertable** /ˈwɔtəteɪbəl/, *n.* **1.** in an aquifer, the upper limit of the portion of ground saturated with water. **2.** *Archit.* a projecting string-course or similar member placed to throw off or divert water. **3.** *Colloq.* a ditch, esp. one at the side of the road: *I fell off my bike and rolled into the watertable.*

**water thyme** /ˈwɔtə taɪm/, *n.* a native freshwater perennial, *Hydrilla verticillata,* growing totally submerged in still or slow-flowing water.

**watertight** /ˈwɔtətaɪt/, *adj.* **1.** impervious to water. **2.** without fault; irrefutable; flawless: *a watertight argument or alibi.* **– watertightness,** *n.*

**water tortoise** /ˈwɔtə tɔtəs/, *n.* any of the indigenous side-necked tortoises of Australia which are essentially aquatic but have webbed feet rather than turtle flippers and are capable of moving considerable distances overland.

**water torture** /ˈ– tɔtʃə/, *n.* →**Chinese water torture.**

**water-tower** /ˈwɔtə-taʊə/, *n.* **1.** a vertical pipe or tower into which water is pumped to obtain a required head; a standpipe. **2.** a fire-extinguishing apparatus throwing a stream of water on the upper parts of a tall burning building.

**water-tube boiler** /ˈwɔtə-tjub ˌbɔɪlə/, *n.* a boiler in which the water passes through tubes in the combustion zone; fire-tube boiler.

**water-tunnel** /ˈwɔtə-tʌnəl/, *n.* a device similar to a wind-tunnel, except that water is the circulating fluid instead of air, used for aerodynamic tests at slow stream velocities.

**water-vapour** /ˈwɔtə-veɪpə/, *n.* gaseous water, esp. when diffused and below the boiling point, distinguished from steam.

**watervine** /ˈwɔtəvaɪn/, *n.* any of several large rainforest vines of eastern Australia esp. of the grape family, as species of the genera *Cissus,* and *Entada,* family Papilionaceae, so named because broken stems give drinkable water.

**water-violet** /ˈwɔtə-vaɪələt/, *n.* a floating, aquatic, perennial herb, *Hottonia palustris,* with projecting pale mauve flowers, occurring in ponds in Europe.

**water-vole** /ˈwɔtə-voʊl/, *n.* a large dark brown vole, *Arvicola amphibius,* of western Europe, which infests river banks in Britain.

**water wagon** /ˈwɔtə wægən/, *n.* **1.** →**water-cart. 2. on the water wagon,** *Colloq.* teetotal.

**water-wagtail** /ˈwɔtə-wægteɪl/, *n.* a long-tailed, grey and white bird, *Motacilla alba,* of Europe, including Britain.

**water-wave** /ˈwɔtə-weɪv/, *n., v.,* **-waved, -waving.** *–n.* **1.** a wave on the surface of a body of water. **2.** a wave set into lotioned hair with combs and then allowed to dry by the application of heat from a drier. *–v.t.* **3.** to set (hair) in a water-wave.

**waterway** /ˈwɔtəweɪ/, *n.* **1.** a river, canal, or other body of water as a route or way of travel or transport. **2.** a channel for vessels, esp. a fairway in a harbour, etc. **3.** *Naut.* a drainage gutter on the deck of a ship which carries water to the scuppers.

**waterweed** /ˈwɔtəwid/, *n.* **1.** any aquatic plant without special use or beauty, as *Elodea canadensis.* **2.** →**duckweed** (def. 2). Also, **water weed.**

**waterwheel** /ˈwɔtəwil/, *n.* **1.** a wheel turned by water and used to perform mechanical work; a water turbine. **2.** a wheel with buckets for raising water, as a noria.

**water-wings** /ˈwɔtə-wɪŋz/, *n.pl.* a device shaped like a pair of wings and inflated with air, usu. worn under the arms to keep the body afloat while learning to swim.

**water-witch** /ˈwɔtə-wɪtʃ/, *n. U.S.* →**water-diviner.** – **water-witching,** *n.*

**waterworks** /ˈwɔtəwɜks/, *n. pl.* **1.** (*oft. construed as sing.*) an aggregate of apparatus and structures by which water is collected, preserved, and distributed for domestic and other purposes, as for a town. **2.** *Colloq.* tears, or the source of tears. **3.** *Colloq.* the bladder or its functioning. **4. turn on the waterworks,** to cry loudly and profusely, often for the sake of gaining sympathy or getting one's own way.

**waterworn** /ˈwɔtəwɔn/, *adj.* worn by the action of water; smoothed by water in motion.

**watery** /ˈwɔtəri/, *adj.* **1.** pertaining to or connected with water: *watery Neptune.* **2.** full of or abounding in water, as soil, a region, etc. **3.** containing much or too much water. **4.** soft or soggy as a result of too much water or overcooking: *watery cabbage.* **5.** tearful. **6.** of the nature of water: *watery vapour.* **7.** resembling water in appearance or colour: *a watery blue.* **8.** resembling water in consistency: *a watery fluid.* **9.** weak, thin, washy, vapid, or poor: *watery writing.* **10.** consisting of water: *a watery grave.* **11.** discharging, filled with, or secreting a waterlike morbid discharge.

**watsonia** /wɒtˈsoʊniə/, *n.* any herb of a large southern African genus, *Watsonia,* family Iridaceae, many species of which are cultivated for their tall spikes of tubular white or pink flowers.

**watt** /wɒt/, *n.* the derived SI unit of power, defined as one joule per second. *Symbol:* W [named after James *Watt,* 1736-1819, Scottish engineer and inventor]

**wattage** /ˈwɒtɪdʒ/, *n.* **1.** *Elect.* power, in watts. **2.** the watts required to operate an electrical device.

**wattle** /wɒtl/, *n., v.,* **-tled, -tling,** *adj.* –*n.* **1.** (*pl.* or *sing.*) rods or stakes interwoven with twigs or branches of trees, used for making fences, walls, roofs, etc. **2.** (*pl.*) the poles forming the framework of a thatched roof. **3.** any of the very numerous Australian species of the genus *Acacia,* shrubs or trees with spikes or globular heads of yellow or cream flowers. **4.** the huilbos of southern Africa, *Peltophorum africanum.* **5.** a fleshy lobe or appendage hanging down from the throat or chin of certain birds, etc., as the domestic fowl, the turkey, etc., or from the neck of certain breeds of pigs, sheep, goats and from the necks of some humans. –*v.t.* **6.** to bind, wall, fence, or otherwise fit with wattles. **7.** to roof or frame with wattles or in similar fashion. **8.** to form into a basketwork; interweave; interlace. **9.** to form by interweaving twigs or branches: *to wattle a fence.* –*adj.* **10.** built or roofed with wattles. [ME *wattel,* OE *watul* covering, var. of *wætla* bandage] – **wattled,** *adj.*

wattle (def. 5) of domestic turkey

**wattle and daub,** *n.* **1.** wattles plastered with mud or clay and used as a building material. **2.** a dwelling made from such material.

wattle-and-daub hut

**wattlebark** /ˈwɒtlbak/, *n.* the bark of various wattle trees, containing tannin.

**wattlebird** /ˈwɒtlbɜd/, *n.* **1.** any of several large honeyeaters of the genus *Anthochaera* having pendulous wattles on each side of the throat, as the **red wattlebird,** *A. carunculata.* **2.** any of several New Zealand birds of the family Callaeidae, as the kokako.

**wattless** /ˈwɒtləs/, *adj.* with no dissipation of energy: *a wattless alternating current* (one differing in phase by 90 degrees from the associated emf); *a wattless electro-motive force* (one differing in phase by 90 degrees from the current).

**wattmeter** /ˈwɒtmitə/, *n.* an instrument for measuring electric power in watts.

**waul** /wɔl/, *v.i.* to cry as a cat or a newborn baby; squall. Also, **wawl.**

**wave** /weɪv/, *n., v.,* **waved, waving.** –*n.* **1.** a disturbance of the surface of a liquid body, as the sea or a lake, in the form of a ridge or swell. **2.** any surging or progressing movement or part resembling a wave of the sea: *a wave of the pulse.* **3.** a swell, surge, or rush, as of feeling, excitement, prosperity, etc.: *a wave of anger swept over him.* **4.** a widespread movement, feeling, opinion, tendency, etc.: *a wave of anti-Americanism.* **5.** one of a succession of movements of people migrating into a region, country, etc. **6.** a line of soldiers advancing or attacking. **7.** a movement of migrating birds, animals, etc. **8.** an outward curve, or one of a series of such curves, in a surface or line; an undulation. **9.** *Physics.* a progressive vibrational disturbance propagated through a medium, as air, without corresponding progress or advance of the parts or particles themselves, as in the transmission of sound or electromagnetic energy. **10.** the act of waving, as a flag or the hand. **11.** a sign made with a wave of the hand, a flag, etc. **12.** a period or spell of exceptionally hot or cold weather. **13.** *Archaic.* water; a body of water; the sea. –*v.i.* **14.** to move loosely to and fro or up and down; flutter. **15.** to curve alternately in opposite directions; have an undulating form. **16.** to bend or sway up and down or to and fro, as branches or plants in the wind. **17.** to be moved, esp. alternately in opposite directions: *the lady's handkerchief waved in token of encouragement.* **18.** to give a signal by waving something: *she waved to me as I left.* –*v.t.* **19.** to cause to move loosely to and fro or up and down. **20.** to cause to bend or sway up and down or to and fro. **21.** to give an undulating form to; cause to curve up and down or in and out. **22.** to give a wavy appearance or pattern to, as silk. **23.** to impart a wave to (the hair). **24.** to move, esp. alternately in opposite directions: *to wave the hand.* **25.** to signal to by waving a flag or the like; direct by a waving movement: *to wave a train to a halt.* **26.** to signify or express by a waving movement: *to wave a last goodbye.* [ME; OE *wafian,* akin to Icel. *vāfa* swing] – **waver,** *n.* – **waveless,** *adj.* – **wavelike,** *adj.*

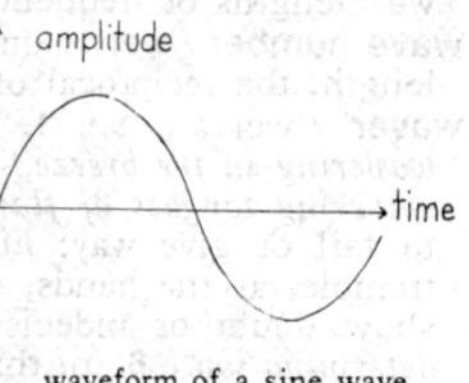

waveform of a sine wave

**waveband** /ˈweɪvbænd/, *n.* a range of radio wavelengths or frequencies in which the waves have similar propagation characteristics.

**wavecut platform** /ˈweɪvkʌt plætfɔm/, *n.* a platform cut in rock by the action of the waves upon it.

**wave equation** /ˈweɪv əkweɪʒən/, *n.* any equation, based on quantum theory, in which a wave motion is described in terms of a wave-function, or the solution to which is a wave-function.

**waveform** /ˈweɪvfɔm/, *n.* the trace or shape of a wave, the shape of the graph obtained by plotting the instantaneous values of a function, which varies periodically, against time.

**wavefront** /ˈweɪvfrʌnt/, *n.* an imaginary surface that is the locus of all adjacent points at which the phase of vibration is the same. The locus of all adjacent points at which the phase of the wave is the same (as the crest of a wave).

**wave function** /ˈweɪv fʌŋkʃən/, *n.* **1.** a function used in wave-mechanics to define the three-dimensional stationary wave system which represents the orbital electrons around an atomic nucleus. **2.** a solution of a wave-equation in wave-mechanics.

**waveguide** /ˈweɪvgaɪd/, *n.* a piece of hollow, conducting tubing, usu. rectangular or circular in cross-section, used as a conductor or directional transmitter for microwaves which are propagated through its interior.

**wavelength** /ˈweɪvlɛŋθ/, *n.* **1.** *Physics.* the distance, measured in the direction of propagation of a wave, between two successive points that are characterised by the same phase of vibration. **2.** *Radio.* the wavelength (def. 1) of the carrier wave of a particular radio transmitter or station. **3.** a mode of thinking or understanding: *the teacher was obviously not on the same wavelength as his pupils.*

**wavelet** /ˈweɪvlət/, *n.* a small wave; ripple.

**wavellite** /ˈweɪvəlaɪt/, *n.* a white to yellowish green or brown mineral, a hydrous aluminium fluophosphate. [named after its discoverer, W. *Wavell,* died 1829, English physician]

**wave mechanics** /weɪv mə'kænɪks/, *n.* an early development of quantum mechanics where wave properties are associated with material particles.

**wavemeter** /'weɪvmitə/, *n.* an instrument for measuring radio wavelengths or frequencies.

**wave number** /'weɪv nʌmbə/, *n.* the number of waves per unit length; the reciprocal of wavelength.

**waver** /'weɪvə/, *v.i.* **1.** to sway to and fro; flutter: *leaves wavering in the breeze.* **2.** to flicker or quiver, as light, etc.: *wavering tongues of flame.* **3.** to become unsteady or begin to fail or give way: *his mind is wavering.* **4.** to shake or tremble, as the hands, etc.: *his voice wavered.* **5.** to feel or show doubt or indecision, or vacillate: *he wavered in his determination.* **6.** (of things) to fluctuate or vary. **7.** to totter. [ME, frequentative of OE *wafian* WAVE; c. d. G *wabern* move about. Icel. *vafra* toddle] – **waverer,** *n.* – **waveringly,** *adv.*

**wave theory** /'weɪv θɪəri/, *n.* the theory, proposed by Christian Huygens, 1629-95, Dutch physicist, that light travels in waves.

**wave-train** /'weɪv-treɪn/, *n.* a group or series of successive waves sent out along the same path or course by a vibrating body, a radio aerial, or the like.

**wavy** /'weɪvi/, *adj.*, **-vier, -viest. 1.** curving alternately, in opposite directions in movement or form: *a wavy course, wavy hair.* **2.** abounding in or characterised by waves: *the wavy sea.* **3.** resembling or suggesting waves. **4.** *Bot.* **a.** bending with successive curves in opposite directions, as a margin. **b.** having such a margin, as a leaf. **5.** vibrating or tremulous; unsteady; wavering. – **wavily,** *adv.* – **waviness,** *n.*

**wawl** /wɔl/, *v.i.* →**waul.**

**wax**[1] /wæks/, *n.* **1.** any of a group of amorphous solid materials consisting of esters of monohydric alcohols and the higher homologues of fatty acids, as beeswax, an ester of palmitic acid, $C_{30}H_{61}OCOC_{15}H_{31}$. **2.** any of various other similar substances, as spermaceti, the secretions of certain insects (wax insects), and the secretions (vegetable wax) of certain plants. **3.** any of a group of solid, non-greasy, insoluble substances which have a low melting or softening point, esp. mixtures of the higher hydrocarbons, as paraffin wax. **4.** →**cerumen. 5.** a resinous substance used by shoemakers for rubbing their thread. **6.** →**sealing wax. 7.** Also, **waxflower.** any of various shrubs of the genus *Chamelaucium,* family Myrtaceae, of Western Australia, having waxy flowers, as Esperance wax and Geraldton wax. **8.** something suggesting wax as being readily moulded, worked upon, handled, managed, etc.: *helpless wax in their hands.* –*v.t.* **9.** to rub, smear, stiffen, polish, etc., with wax; treat with wax: *waxed moustaches, a waxed floor.* –*adj.* **10.** made of or resembling wax. [ME; OE *weax,* c. D *was,* G *Wachs,* Icel. *vax*] – **waxer,** *n.* – **waxlike,** *adj.*

**wax**[2] /wæks/, *v.i.*, **waxed; waxed** or (*Poetic*) **waxen; waxing. 1.** to increase in extent, quantity, intensity, power, etc.: *discord waxed daily.* **2.** (of the moon) to increase in the extent of its illuminated portion before the full moon (opposed to *wane.*) **3.** to grow or become (as stated). **4. wax lyrical,** to speak in an enthusiastic and sometimes exaggeratedly poetic manner, in praise or in support of a person, scheme etc.

**wax**[3] /wæks/, *n. Colloq.* a fit of anger. [orig. uncert.; ? from phrase *to wax angry* (see WAX[2], def. 3)]

**wax-bean** /'wæks-bin/, *n. U.S.* any variety of snap-bean with a yellowish colour and waxy appearance.

**waxberry** /'wæksbɛri/, *n.* →**snowberry** (def. 2).

**waxbill** /'wæksbɪl/, *n.* any of various weaverbirds, esp. of the genus *Estrilda,* having white, pink, or red bills of waxlike appearance, and including many well-known cagebirds, as an African species, *Estrilda astrild,* the amadavat, and the Java sparrow.

**waxen** /'wæksən/, *adj.* **1.** made of or covered with wax. **2.** resembling or suggesting wax: *his face had an unhealthy waxen appearance.* **3.** weak or impressionable, as a person or his characteristics. –*v.* **4.** *Poetic.* past participle of **wax**[2].

**wax-eye** /'wæks-aɪ/, *n.* →**silver-eye.**

**waxflower** /'wæksflaʊə/, *n.* **1.** any of various Australian shrubs of the genus *Eriostemon,* family Rutaceae, as Bendigo waxflower, *E. obovalis,* of south-eastern Australia. **2.** →**wax**[1] (def. 7).

**waxing moon** /ˌwæksɪŋ 'mun/, *n.* →**moon** (def. 2e).

**wax-insect** /'wæks-ɪnsɛkt/, *n.* any of various homopterous insects which secrete a wax or waxlike substance, as a Chinese scale insect, *Ericerus pela.*

**wax-moth** /'wæks-mɒθ/, *n.* →**bee-moth.**

**wax-myrtle** /'wæks-mɜtl/, *n.* a shrub or tree of the genus *Myrica,* as *M. cerifera,* which bears small berries coated with wax (sometimes used in making candles, etc.), or *M. pensylvanica.* Cf. **bayberry.**

**wax-palm** /'wæks-pam/, *n.* **1.** a tall pinnate-leaved palm, *Ceroxylon alpinum,* of the Andes, whose stem and leaves yield a resinous wax. **2.** a palmate-leaved palm, *Copernicia cerifera,* of Brazil, whose young leaves are coated with a hard wax; carnauba.

**wax-paper** /'wæks-peɪpə/, *n.* paper made moistureproof by coating with paraffin wax.

**waxplant** /'wæksplænt, -plant/, *n.* **1.** any of the climbing or trailing plants of the genus *Hoya,* natives of tropical Asia and Australia, having glossy leaves and umbels of pink, white, or yellowish waxy flowers. **2.** any of several Western Australian species of the genus *Chamelaucium,* esp. *C. uncinatum,* Geraldton wax. **3.** any of the shrubs of the genus *Eriostemon* of eastern Australia, esp. *E. australasicum.*

**wax tree** /'wæks tri/, *n.* →**rhus tree.** Also, **Chinese wax tree.**

**waxwing** /'wækswɪŋ/, *n.* any bird of the passerine family Bombycillidae, having a showy crest and small red appendages at the tips of the secondary wing feathers and sometimes the tail feathers, as *Bombycilla garrula* of the northern hemisphere.

**waxwork** /'wækswɜk/, *n.* **1.** figures, ornaments, etc., made of wax, or one such figure. **2.** (*pl. construed as sing.*) an exhibition of wax figures, ornaments, etc.

**waxy** /'wæksi/, *adj.*, **-ier, -iest. 1.** resembling wax, as in substance or appearance. **2.** abounding in, covered with, or made of wax. **3.** *Pathol.* pertaining to or suffering from a degeneration caused by deposits of a waxlike insoluble material in an organ. **4.** pliable, yielding, or impressionable. – **waxiness,** *n.*

**way** /weɪ/, *n.* **1.** manner, mode, or fashion: *a new way of looking at a matter, to reply in a polite way.* **2.** characteristic or habitual manner: *that is only his way.* **3.** a course, plan, or means for attaining an end: *to find a way to reduce friction.* **4.** respect or particular: *a plan defective in several ways.* **5.** direction: *look this way.* **6.** passage or progress on a course: *to make one's way on foot, to lead the way.* **7.** distance: *a long way off.* **8.** a path or course leading from one place to another. **9.** a road, route, passage, or channel (usu. used in combination): *a highway, waterway, doorway.* **10.** *Law.* a right of way. **11.** any line of passage or travel used or available: *blaze a way through dense woods.* **12.** space for passing or advancing: *he cleared a way through the throng of people.* **13.** (*oft. pl.*) a habit or custom: *I don't like his ways at all.* **14.** the course of mode or action which one prefers or upon which one is resolved: *to have one's own way, the local Don Juan was reputed to have had his way with numerous young women.* **15.** *Colloq.* condition, as to health, prosperity, etc.: *to be in a bad way.* **16.** range of experience or notice: *the best device that ever came my way.* **17.** course of life, action, or experience: *the way of transgressors is hard.* **18.** (*pl.*) (in shipbuilding) the timbers on which a ship is launched. **19.** *Mach.* a longitudinal strip, as in a planer, guiding a moving part along a surface. **20.** *Naut.* movement or passage through the water. **21.** Some special noun phrases are:

**by the way,** incidentally; in the course of one's remarks: *by the way, have you received that letter yet?*

**by way of, 1.** by the route of; via; through. **2.** as a method or means of: *to number articles by way of distinguishing them.* **3.** having a reputation for; ostensibly (being, doing, etc.): *he is by way of being an authority on the subject.*

**come one's way,** to come to one; happen to one.

**give way, 1.** to withdraw; retreat. **2.** to yield; break down; collapse.

**give way to, 1.** to yield to. **2.** to lose control of (one's emotions, etc.).

**go out of one's way,** to make a special effort; inconvenience oneself.

**have a way with,** to have a skill in dealing with: *she has a way with children.*
**have a way with one,** to have a charming or persuasive manner.
**have it both ways,** to gain or succeed by each of two contrary means, situations, etc.
**in a way,** to a certain extent; after a fashion: *in a way he's a pleasant person.*
**in the way,** forming an obstruction or hindrance.
**lead the way, 1.** to proceed in advance of others. **2.** to take the initiative; show by example.
**make one's way, 1.** to proceed. **2.** to achieve advancement, recognition, or success: *to make one's way in the world.*
**make way, 1.** to allow to pass. **2.** to give up or retire in favour of: *the manager resigned to make way for a younger man.*
**no way,** not at all; never.
**on the way out, 1.** becoming obsolete; ready for rest or retirement. **2.** losing popularity.
**out of the way, 1.** so as not to obstruct or hinder. **2.** disposed of; dealt with. **3.** murdered: *to put a person out of the way.* **4.** out of the frequented way; off the beaten track. **5.** unusual; extraordinary.
**pay one's** or **its way,** to remain solvent or financially self-supporting.
**under way, 1.** in motion or moving along, as a ship that has weighed anchor. **2.** in progress, as an enterprise.
[ME; OE *weg,* c. D *weg,* G *Weg,* Icel. *vegr,* Goth. *wigs*]

**wayang** /ˈwaɪæŋ/, *n.* a ritual performance, as with dances or puppet plays, of the religious epics of Java and Bali. [Javanese *wayang* shadow]

**wayback** /ˈweɪbæk/, *adv.* **1.** a long way behind. *–n.* **2.** the outback. **3. the waybacks,** *N.Z.* remote rural districts. *–adj.* **4.** remote.

**waybill** /ˈweɪbɪl/, *n.* **1.** a list of goods sent by a common carrier, as a railway, with directions. **2.** (on a bus, etc.) a list showing the number of passengers carried or tickets sold.

**waybung** /ˈweɪbʌŋ/, *n.* →**white-winged chough.** [Aboriginal]

**wayfarer** /ˈweɪfɛərə/, *n.* a traveller, esp. on foot.

**wayfaring** /ˈweɪfɛərɪŋ/, *adj., n.* travelling, esp. on foot.

**wayfaring tree** /ˈ– tri/, *n.* a deciduous shrub, *Viburnum lantana,* having hairy leaves and black fruits, occurring on calcareous soils in Europe and western Asia.

**waylaid** /weɪˈleɪd/, *v.* past tense and past participle of **waylay.**

**waylay** /weɪˈleɪ/, *v.t.,* **-laid, -laying. 1.** to fall upon or assail from ambush, as in order to rob, seize, or slay. **2.** to await and accost unexpectedly. [WAY + LAY[1]. Cf. MLG *wegelagen*] **– waylayer,** *n.*

**way-out** /ˈweɪ-aʊt/, *adj. Colloq.* **1.** advanced in technique, style, etc. **2.** unusual; odd; eccentric.

**-ways,** a suffix of manner creating adverbs, as in *sideways, lengthways.* See **-wise.** [orig. gen. of WAY]

**ways and means,** *n.* **1.** legislation, methods, and means of raising revenue for the use of the government. **2.** methods of accomplishing something.

**wayside** /ˈweɪsaɪd/, *n.* **1.** the side of the way; the border or edge of the road or highway. *–adj.* **2.** being, situated, or found at or along the wayside: *a wayside inn.*

**way station** /ˈweɪ steɪʃən/, *n. U.S.* a station intermediate between principal stations, as on a railway.

**wayward** /ˈweɪwəd/, *adj.* **1.** turned or turning away from what is right or proper; perverse: *a wayward son.* **2.** swayed or prompted by caprice, or capricious: *a wayward fancy or impulse.* **3.** turning or changing irregularly; irregular: *a wayward stream or breeze.* [ME; aphetic var. of *awayward*] **– waywardly,** *adv.* **– waywardness,** *n.*

**wayworn** /ˈweɪwɔn/, *adj.* worn or wearied by travel.

**w/b,** weatherboard.

**w.b., 1.** westbound. **2.** weatherboard.

**Wb,** weber.

**w'board,** weatherboard.

**w.c.,** without charge.

**WC** /dʌbəlju ˈsi/, *n. Colloq.* a toilet. Also, **wc.** [*w(ater)-c(loset)*]

**wd, 1.** ward. **2.** word. **3.** would.

**we** /wi/; *Brit. weak form* /wɪ/, *pron., pl.; poss.* **our** or **ours;** *obj.* **us. 1.** nominative plural of 'I'. **2.** (used by a speaker or writer to denote people in general, including himself): *we usually take our holidays in August.* **3.** (used by a sovereign when alluding to himself or herself in formal speech): *we are not amused.* **4.** (used by an editor or other writer to avoid any appearance of egotism from the use of *I*): *we deplore the present economic situation.* **5.** (used as a term of encouragement or cajolery where the 2nd person sing. is meant): *we really should work a little harder.* [ME and OE, c. D *wij,* G *wir,* Icel. *vēr* Goth. *weis*]

**W.E.A.** /ˌdʌbəlju i ˈeɪ/, Workers' Educational Association.

**weak** /wik/, *adj.* **1.** liable to yield, break, or collapse under pressure or strain; fragile; frail; not strong: *a weak fortress, a weak spot in armour.* **2.** deficient in bodily strength or healthy vigour, as from age, sickness, etc.; feeble; infirm: *a weak old man; weak eyes.* **3.** deficient in political strength, governing power, or authority: *a weak nation or ruler.* **4.** lacking in force, potency, or efficacy; impotent, ineffectual, or inadequate: *weak prayers.* **5.** lacking in rhetorical force or effectiveness: *a weak style.* **6.** lacking in logical or legal force or soundness: *a weak argument.* **7.** deficient in mental power, intelligence, or judgment: *a weak mind.* **8.** deficient in moral strength or firmness, resolution, or force of character: *prove weak under temptation, weak compliance.* **9.** deficient in amount, volume, loudness, intensity, etc.; faint; slight: *weak vibrations, a weak current of electricity.* **10.** deficient, wanting, or poor in something specified: *a hand weak in trumps, weak in spelling.* **11.** deficient in the essential or desirable properties or ingredients: *weak tea, a weak infusion.* **12.** inconclusive; anticlimactic or logically unsatisfactory, as the ending of a book, play, or the like. **13.** unstressed, as a syllable, word, etc. **14.** (of Germanic verbs) inflected with suffixes, without inherited change of the root vowel, as English *work, worked* or *keep, kept* (in which the vowel change is not inherited). **15.** (of Germanic nouns and adjectives) inflected with endings originally appropriate to stems terminating in *-n. Alte* in German *der alte Mann* 'the old man' is a weak adjective. **16.** pertaining to a flour or wheat which has a low gluten content. **17.** *Photog.* thin; not dense. **18.** *Comm.* characterised by falling prices. [ME *weik,* from Scand.; cf. Icel. *veikr,* c. OE *wāc,* G *weich*] **– weakish,** *adj.*

**weaken** /ˈwikən/, *v.t., v.i.* to become or make weak or weaker. **– weakener,** *n.*

**weak ending** /wik ˈɛndɪŋ/, *n.* a verse ending in which the metrical stress falls on a word or syllable which would not be stressed in natural utterance, as a preposition whose object is carried over to the next line.

**weaker sex** /ˈwikə sɛks/, *n. Colloq.* the female sex.

**weakie** /ˈwiki/, *n. Colloq.* a weak or cowardly person. Also, **weaky.**

**weak-kneed** /ˈwik-nid/, *adj.* yielding readily to opposition, intimidation, etc.

**weakling** /ˈwiklɪŋ/, *n.* **1.** a weak or feeble creature (physically or morally). *–adj.* **2.** weak; not strong.

**weakly** /ˈwikli/, *adj.,* **-lier, -liest,** *adv.* *–adj.* **1.** weak or feeble in constitution; not robust; sickly. *–adv.* **2.** in a weak manner. **– weakliness,** *n.*

**weak-minded** /ˈwik-maɪndəd/, *adj.* **1.** having or showing a want of firmness of mind. **2.** having or showing a weak or feeble mind. **– weak-mindedness,** *n.*

**weakness** /ˈwiknəs/, *n.* **1.** the state or quality of being weak; feebleness. **2.** a weak point, as in a person's character; slight fault or defect. **3.** a self-indulgent inclination or liking, as for a person, object, etc.

**weak nuclear interaction,** *n.* an interaction of the type responsible for the decay of all elementary particles except protons, electrons, neutrons, and photons. Also, **weak interaction.**

**weak-willed** /ˈwik-wɪld/, *adj.* **1.** lacking strength of will; easily swayed, persuaded, etc. **2.** vacillating.

**weal**[1] /wil/, *n.* **1.** *Archaic.* well-being, prosperity, or happiness: *in weal or woe, zealous only for the public weal.* **2.** *Obs.* wealth or riches. [ME *wele,* OE *wela.* See WELL[1]]

**weal**[2] /wil/, *n.* **1.** a small burning or itching swelling on the skin, as from a mosquito bite or from urticaria. **2.** a wale or welt. [var. of WALE]

**weald** /wild/, *n. Archaic.* open or wooded country. [ME *weeld,*

OE *weald* forest, var. of *wald* WOLD[1]]

**wealth** /wɛlθ/, *n.* **1.** a great store of valuable possessions, property, or riches: *the wealth of a city.* **2.** a rich abundance or profusion of anything: *a wealth of imagery.* **3.** *Econ.* **a.** all things having a value in money, in exchange, or in use. **b.** anything having utility and capable of being appropriated or exchanged. **4.** rich or valuable contents or produce: *the wealth of the soil.* **5.** the state of being rich; affluence: *persons of wealth and standing.* **6.** *Obs. or Archaic.* well-being or prosperity. [ME *welth,* from *wel* WELL[1] + -TH[1]]

**wealth tax** /'– tæks/, *n.* a tax on personal goods and property.

**wealthy** /'wɛlθi/, *adj.*, **-thier, -thiest. 1.** possessed of wealth; rich: *a wealthy person or nation.* **2.** characterised by, pertaining to, or suggestive of wealth: *a wealthy appearance.* **3.** rich in character, quality, or amount; abundant or ample. – **wealthily,** *adv.* – **wealthiness,** *n.*

**wean** /win/, *v.t.* **1.** to accustom (a child or animal) to food other than its mother's milk. **2.** to withdraw from any object or form of habit or enjoyment (usu. fol. by *from*). [ME *wene,* OE *wenian,* c. D *wennen* accustom, G *gewöhnen,* Icel. *venja*] – **weaner,** *n.*

**weaner** /'winə/, *n.* a young animal which has been weaned from its mother's milk, to live wholly on grass.

**weanling** /'winlıŋ/, *n.* **1.** a child or animal newly weaned. *–adj.* **2.** newly weaned.

**weapon** /'wɛpən/, *n.* **1.** any instrument for use in attack or defence in combat, fighting, or war, as a sword, rifle, cannon, etc. **2.** anything serving as an instrument for making or repelling an attack: *the deadly weapon of meekness.* **3.** *Zool.* any part or organ serving for attack or defence, as claws, horns, teeth, stings, etc. [ME *wepen,* OE *wǣpen,* c. G *Waffe*] – **weaponed,** *adj.* – **weaponless,** *adj.*

**weapon debris** /– də'bri/, *n.* the residue of a nuclear weapon after it has exploded, that is, the materials used for the casing, and other components of the weapon, plus unexpended plutonium or uranium, together with fission products.

**weaponry** /'wɛpənri/, *n.* weapons collectively.

**wear**[1] /wɛə/, *v.*, **wore, worn, wearing,** *n.* *–v.t.* **1.** to carry or have on the body or about the person as a covering, equipment, ornament, or the like: *wear a coat, a watch, wear a disguise.* **2.** to have or use on a person habitually: *to wear a beard.* **3.** to bear or have in the aspect or appearance: *to wear a smile, or an air of triumph.* **4.** to show or fly: *the ship wore its colours.* **5.** to impair (garments, etc.) by wear: *gloves worn at the fingertips.* **6.** to impair, deteriorate, or consume gradually by use or any continued process: *a well-worn volume.* **7.** to waste or diminish gradually by rubbing, scraping, washing, etc.; *rocks worn by the waves.* **8.** to make (a hole, channel, way, etc.) by such action. **9.** to bring, reduce, make, take, etc. (as specified), by wear or any gradual change: *to wear clothes to rags or a person to a shadow.* **10.** to weary or exhaust: *worn with toil or care.* **11.** to pass (time, etc.) gradually or tediously (commonly fol. by *away or out*). **12.** *Colloq.* to accept, tolerate, or be convinced by: *he told me a lie but I wouldn't wear it.* **13. wear clothes well,** to wear clothes so that they seem to suit the wearer and inpart grace and flair. **14. wear out, a.** to wear or use until no longer fit for use: *to wear out clothes or tools.* **b.** to use up. **c.** to exhaust by continued use, strain, or any gradual process: *to wear out patience.* *–v.i.* **15.** to undergo gradual impairment, diminution, reduction, etc., from wear, use, attrition, or other causes (often fol. by *away, down, out,* or *off*). **16.** to hold out or last under wear, use, or any continued strain: *materials or colours that will wear, or wear well.* **17.** to become; grow gradually: *my patience is wearing thin.* **18.** to pass, as time, etc., esp. slowly or tediously (often fol. by *away* or *on*). *–n.* **19.** the act of wearing; use as of a garment: *I have had very good wear from this dress.* **20.** the state of being worn, as on the person. **21.** clothing, garments, or other articles for wearing. **22.** style of dress, adornment, etc., esp. for a particular time, activity, etc.: *evening wear; beach wear.* **23.** gradual impairment, wasting, diminution, etc., as from use: *the carpet shows wear.* [ME *were,* OE *werian,* c. Icel. *verja,* Goth. *wasjan* clothe] – **wearer,** *n.*

**wear**[2] /wɛə/, *v.*, **wore, wearing,** *n.* *Naut.* *–v.t.* **1.** to bring (a vessel) on another tack by turning her head away from the wind until the wind is on her stern, and then bringing her head up towards the wind on the other side. *–n.* **2.** a tactical manoeuvre by which a sailing vessel is changed from one tack to another. [orig. uncert.]

**wearability** /wɛərə'bıləti/, *n.* the ability to withstand the wear and stress of normal use.

**wearable** /'wɛərəbəl/, *adj.* **1.** that may be worn. *–n.* **2.** (*chiefly pl.*) that which may be worn, esp. clothing.

**wear and tear,** *n.* diminution, decay, damage, or injury sustained by ordinary use.

**weariful** /'wıərifəl/, *adj.* **1.** wearisome; tedious. **2.** full of weariness. – **wearifully,** *adv.* – **wearifulness,** *n.*

**weariless** /'wıəriləs/, *adj.* unwearying; tireless.

**wearing** /'wɛərıŋ/, *adj.* **1.** relating to or made for wear. **2.** gradually impairing or wasting. **3.** wearying or exhausting. – **wearingly,** *adv.*

**wearing apparel** /'– əpærəl/, *n.* dress in general; garments.

**wearisome** /'wıərisəm/, *adj.* **1.** causing weariness; fatiguing: *a difficult and wearisome march.* **2.** tiresome or tedious: *a wearisome person, day, or book.* – **wearisomely,** *adv.* – **wearisomeness,** *n.*

**weary** /'wıəri/, *adj.*, **-rier, -riest,** *v.*, **-ried, -rying.** *–adj.* **1.** exhausted physically or mentally by labour, exertion, strain, etc.; fatigued; tired: *weary eyes, feet, or brain.* **2.** characterised by or causing fatigue: *a weary journey.* **3.** impatient or dissatisfied at excess or overlong continuance (oft. fol. by *of*): *weary of excuses.* **4.** characterised by or causing such impatience or dissatisfaction; tedious; irksome: *a weary wait.* *–v.t., v.i.* **5.** to make or become weary; fatigue or tire. **6.** to make or grow impatient or dissatisfied at having too much of something (oft. fol. by *of*). [ME *wery,* OE *wērig*] – **wearily,** *adv.* – **weariness,** *n.*

**weasel** /'wizəl/, *n.* **1.** any of certain small carnivores of the genus *Mustela* (family Mustelidae), esp. *M. nivalis,* common in Europe and much of northern Asia, having a long, slender body, and feeding largely on small rodents. **2.** any of various similar animals of the Mustelidae. **3.** a cunning, sneaking fellow. **4.** a tracked vehicle used in snow; a kind of tractor. *–v.i.* **5.** *Chiefly U.S.* to go back on one's word; evade, as an obligation (oft. fol. by *out*). [ME *wesel,* OE *weosul,* c. G *Wiesel*] – **weaselly,** *adj.*

weasel

**weather** /'wɛðə/, *n.* **1.** the state of the atmosphere with respect to wind, temperature, cloudiness, moisture, pressure, etc. **2.** windy or stormy weather. **3. keep one's weather eye open,** *Colloq.* to be on one's guard; keep a sharp lookout. **4. make heavy weather of,** to have a lot of difficulty coping with (something). **5. under the weather,** *Colloq.* **a.** indisposed; ill; ailing. **b.** drunk. *–v.t.* **6.** to expose to the weather; to dry, season, or otherwise affect by exposure to the air or atmosphere. **7.** to discolour, disintegrate, or affect injuriously, as by atmospheric agencies. **8.** to bear up against and come safely through (a storm, danger, trouble, etc.). **9.** *Naut.* (of a ship, mariner, etc.) to pass or sail to the windward of: *to weather a cape.* **10.** *Archit.* to cause to slope, so as to shed water. *–v.i.* **11.** to undergo change, as discolouration or disintegration, as the result of exposure to atmospheric conditions. **12.** to endure or resist exposure to the weather. **13.** to go or come safely through a storm, danger, trouble, etc. (fol. by *through*). *–adj.* **14.** of or pertaining to the side or part, as of a ship, that is exposed to the wind: *the weather bow.* [ME and OE *weder,* c. D *weder,* G *Wetter,* Icel. *vedhr*]

**weather-beaten** /'wɛðə-bitn/, *adj.* **1.** bearing evidences of exposure to the weather. **2.** seasoned or hardened by exposure to weather: *a weather-beaten face.*

**weatherboard** /'wɛðəbɔd/, *n.* **1.** one of a series of thin boards, usu. thicker along one edge than the other, nailed on an outside wall or a roof in overlapping fashion to form a protective covering which will shed water. **2.** a building whose exterior walls are constructed from weatherboards. **3.** *Naut.* the side of a vessel towards the wind. *–v.t.* **4.** to cover or furnish with weatherboards. – **weather-boarded,** *adj.*

**weatherboarding** /'wɛðəbɔdıŋ/, *n.* **1.** a covering or facing of weatherboards or the like. **2.** weatherboards collectively.

**weatherbound** /ˈwɛðəbaʊnd/, *adj.* delayed by bad weather.

**weather bureau** /ˈwɛðə bjuroʊ/, *n.* the place where meteorological data is collected and processed, and from which weather forecasts are issued.

**weathercock** /ˈwɛðəkɒk/, *n.* **1.** a weathervane in the shape of a cock. **2.** any weathervane. **3.** a fickle or inconstant person or thing. *–v.i.* **4.** (of an aeroplane or missile) to tend to turn into the relative wind.

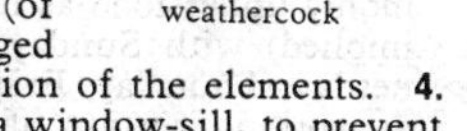

weathercock

**weather deck** /ˈwɛðə dɛk/, *n.* a ship's deck which is exposed to the weather.

**weathered** /ˈwɛðəd/, *adj.* **1.** seasoned or otherwise affected by exposure to the weather or elements. **2.** (of wood) discoloured or stained by the action of air, rain, etc., or by artificial means. **3.** (of rocks) worn, disintegrated, or changed in colour or composition, by the action of the elements. **4.** *Archit.* made sloping or inclined, as a window-sill, to prevent the lodgment of water.

**weather eye** /ˈwɛðər aɪ/, *n. Colloq.* **1.** ability to forecast the weather: *old Giles has a good weather eye.* **2. keep a weather eye open,** to be on the lookout (fol. by *for*).

**weather forecast** /ˈwɛðə ˌfɔkast/, *n.* a description of the prevailing weather conditions and a forecast of those of the immediate future, based on meteorological observation.

**weatherglass** /ˈwɛðəglas/, *n.* any of various instruments, as a barometer or a hygroscope, designed to indicate the state of the atmosphere.

**weatherly** /ˈwɛðəli/, *adj.* (of a boat) making very little leeway when close-hauled. – **weatherliness,** *n.*

**weatherman** /ˈwɛðəmæn/, *n., pl.* **-men.** *Colloq.* **1.** one who foretells weather. **2.** one who is employed in a meteorological office.

**weather map** /ˈwɛðə mæp/, *n.* a map or chart showing meteorological conditions over a wide area at a particular time, compiled from simultaneous observations at different places.

**weatherproof** /ˈwɛðəpruf/, *adj.* **1.** proof against the weather; able to withstand exposure to all kinds of weather. *–v.t.* **2.** to make proof against the weather.

**weather shield** /ˈwɛðə ʃild/, *n.* a plastic hood over the driver's window of a motor car, providing protection from rain or excessive sun.

**weathership** /ˈwɛðəʃɪp/, *n.* a ship that goes to sea specifically to make meteorological observations.

**weatherside** /ˈwɛðəsaɪd/, *n.* the windward side.

**weather station** /ˈwɛðə steɪʃən/, *n.* an installation equipped and used for the making of meteorological observations.

**weather strip** /ˈ– strɪp/, *n.* a narrow strip, as of rubber, metal, wood, etc., covering the joint between a door, window sash, or the like, and the jamb, casing, etc., to exclude wind, rain, etc.

**weather-strip** /ˈwɛðə-strɪp/, *v.t.,* **-stripped, -stripping.** to fit with weather strips.

**weather-stripping** /ˈwɛðə-strɪpɪŋ/, *n.* **1.** a weather strip. **2.** weather strips collectively.

**weathervane** /ˈwɛðəveɪn/, *n.* a vane for indicating the direction of the wind; a weathercock.

**weatherwise** /ˈwɛðəwaɪz/, *adj.* **1.** skilful in predicting weather. **2.** skilful in predicting reactions, opinions, etc.

**weatherworn** /ˈwɛðəwɔn/, *adj.* weather-beaten.

**weave** /wiv/, *v.,* **wove** or (*esp. for defs 5 and 9*) **weaved; woven** or **wove; weaving;** *n. –v.t.* **1.** to interlace (threads, yarns, strips, fibrous material, etc.) so as to form a fabric or texture. **2.** to form by interlacing threads, yarns, strands, or strips of some material: *to weave a basket, to weave cloth.* **3.** to form by combining various elements or details into a connected whole: *to weave a tale or a plot.* **4.** to introduce as an element or detail into a connected whole: *to weave a melody into a musical composition.* **5.** to follow in a winding course; to move from side to side: *to weave one's way through traffic. –v.i.* **6.** to weave cloth, etc. **7.** to become woven or interwoven. **8.** to move from side to side. **9.** to wind in and out of or through: *she weaved through the crowd.* **10. get weaving,** *Colloq.* to make a start, esp. hurriedly, enthusiastically, etc. *–n.* **11.** a manner of interlacing yarns: *plain, twill, or satin weave.* [ME *weve,* OE *wefan,* c. G *weben*]

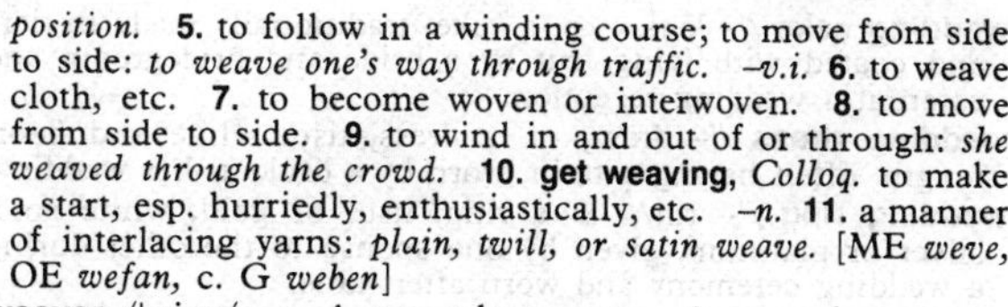



weave: A, weft; B, warp

**weaver** /ˈwivə/, *n.* **1.** one who weaves. **2.** one whose occupation is weaving. **3.** →**weaverbird.**

**weaverbird** /ˈwivəbɜd/, *n.* any of numerous (chiefly African and Asiatic) passerine birds of the family Ploceidae related to the finches and building elaborately woven nests. Also, **weaver-finch.**

**weaver's knot** /wivəz ˈnɒt/, *n.* →**sheet bend.** Also, **weaver's hitch.**

**web** /wɛb/, *n., v.,* **webbed, webbing.** *–n.* **1.** something formed as by weaving or interweaving. **2.** a thin silken fabric spun by spiders, and also by the larvae of some insects, as the tent caterpillars, etc.; cobweb. **3.** a woven fabric, esp. a whole piece of cloth in the course of being woven or after it comes from the loom. **4.** anything resembling this, as seeming to be interlaced, tightly woven, or closely linked. **5.** a tangled intricate state of circumstances, events, etc.: *the web of intrigue.* **6.** *Zool.* **a.** a membrane which connects the digits of an animal. **b.** that which connects the toes of aquatic birds and aquatic mammals. **7.** *Ornith.* **a.** the series of barbs on each side of the shaft of a feather. **b.** the series on both sides, collectively. **8.** the vertical member in a rolled or fabricated beam. **9.** *Mach.* the radius portion of a crank, connecting the axle and the crankpin. **10.** →**cell** (def. 10). **11.** a large reel of paper, esp. as used in certain types of printing. *–v.t.* **12.** to cover with or as with a web; envelop. [ME and OE, c. D and LG *webbe,* Icel. *vefr;* akin to WEAVE] – **webless,** *adj.* – **weblike,** *adj.*

**webbed** /wɛbd/, *adj.* **1.** having the digits connected by a web, as the foot of a duck or a beaver. **2.** (of the digits) connected thus. **3.** formed like or with a web.

**webbing** /ˈwɛbɪŋ/, *n.* **1.** woven material of hemp, cotton, or jute, in bands of various widths, for use where strength is required. **2.** such woven bands nailed on furniture under springs or upholstery, for support. **3.** *Zool.* the membrane forming a web or webs.

**webby** /wɛbi/, *adj.* **1.** pertaining to, of the nature of, or resembling a web. **2.** webbed.

**weber** /ˈveɪbə, ˈweɪbə/, *n.* the derived SI unit of magnetic flux, defined as the flux which, linking a circuit of one turn, produces in it an electromotive force of one volt as it is reduced to zero at a uniform rate in one second. *Symbol:* Wb [named after Wilhelm *Weber,* 1804-91, German physicist]

**webfoot** /ˈwɛbfʊt/, *n., pl.* **-feet.** a foot with the toes joined by a web. – **web-footed,** *adj.*

**web-offset** /ˌwɛb-ˈɒfsɛt/, *n.* **1.** the offset lithographic printing process adapted for printing a continuous reel in one or several colours on both sides of the paper. *–adv., adj.* **2.** (printed) by this process.

**web-toed** /ˈwɛb-toʊd/, *adj.* web-footed.

**wed** /wɛd/, *v.,* **wedded** or **wed, wedding.** *–v.t.* **1.** to bind oneself to (a person) in marriage; take for husband or wife. **2.** to unite (a couple) or join (one person to another) in marriage or wedlock; marry. **3.** to bind by close or lasting ties; attach firmly: *to be wedded to a theory. –v.i.* **4.** to contract marriage; marry. **5.** to become united as if in wedlock. [ME; OE *weddian* pledge, c. G *wetten* bet, Icel. *vedhja* pledge]

**we'd** /wid/, contraction of *we had, we should* or *we would.*

**Wed.,** Wednesday.

**wedded** /ˈwɛdəd/, *adj.* **1.** united in matrimony; married. **2.** joined. **3.** joined by devotion: *he was wedded to the cause.*

**wedding** /ˈwɛdɪŋ/, *n.* **1.** the act or ceremony of marrying; marriage; nuptials. **2.** a celebration of an anniversary of a marriage, as a silver wedding, celebrated on the 25th anniversary of a marriage. [ME; OE *weddung.* See WED]

**wedding breakfast** /ˈ– brɛkfəst/, *n.* a meal taken after a wedding ceremony in celebration of the event.

**wedding bush** /ˈ– bʊʃ/, *n.* **1.** any species of the genus *Ricinocarpos,* esp. *R. pinifolius* of New South Wales. **2.** the tree, *Dombeya natalensis,* of South Africa.

**wedding cake** /ˈ– keɪk/, *n.* a cake, traditionally made in tiers and coated with icing, cut by a bride and bridegroom and eaten at a wedding reception.
**wedding dress** /ˈ– drɛs/, *n.* a dress, usu. white and floor-length, often having a train, worn by a bride at her wedding.
**wedding ring** /ˈ– rɪŋ/, *n.* a ring, usu. of gold, white gold, silver or platinum, given by one spouse to the other during a wedding ceremony and worn afterwards.
**wedeling** /ˈveɪdəlɪŋ/, *n.* (in skiing, skateboarding, etc.) a series of turns made at high speed. [G *wedeln* to wag]
**wedge** /wɛdʒ/, *n., v.,* **wedged, wedging.** *–n.* **1.** a device (one of the so-called simple machines) consisting of a piece of hard material with two principle faces meeting in a sharply acute angle. **2.** a piece of anything of like shape: *a wedge of pie or cheese.* **3.** *Meteorol.* a region of relatively high pressure, extending from an anticyclone, with isobars in the shape of a wedge. **4.** a wedge-shaped cuneiform character or stroke. **5.** something that serves to part, divide, etc.: *a disrupting wedge divided the loyalties of party members.* **6.** *Mil.* (formerly) a tactical formation generally in the form of a V with the point towards the enemy. **7.** →**sand wedge. 8. thin end of the wedge,** something small or insignificant which is likely to lead to something large and important. *–v.t.* **9.** to cleave or split with or as with a wedge. **10.** to pack or fix tightly by driving in a wedge or wedges. **11.** to thrust, drive, or fix (in, between, etc.) like a wedge: *to wedge oneself through a narrow opening.* **12.** to knead (clay) so as to gain a uniform consistency. *–v.i.* **13.** to force a way (in, etc.) like a wedge. [ME; OE *wecg,* c. d. G *Weck*] **– wedgelike, wedgy,** *adj.*
**wedgebill** /ˈwɛdʒbɪl/, *n.* a small, brownish, crested, Australian songbird, *Sphenostoma cristatum.*
**wedge heel** /wɛdʒ ˈhil/, *n.* a solid wedge-shaped piece on a woman's shoe, deepest at the back of the sole, tapering to nothing at the front.
**wedge-pea** /wɛdʒ-ˈpi/, *n.* any shrub of the endemic Australian genus *Gompholobium,* family Papilionaceae, with yellow or occasionally reddish pea-shaped flowers.
**wedge-tailed eagle** /ˌwɛdʒ-teɪld ˈigəl/, *n.* a very large, dark, long-tailed eagle, *Aquila audax,* of plains and forests throughout Australia and New Guinea; the largest of Australian birds of prey. Also, **wedgetail eagle, wedgie.**

wedge-tailed eagle

**wedgie** /ˈwɛdʒi/, *n.* →**wedge-tailed eagle.**
**Wedgwood** /ˈwɛdʒwʊd/, *n.* **1.** a type of artistic pottery with tinted (usu. blue) ground and white decoration in relief in designs based on Greek and Roman models. *–adj.* **2.** pertaining to Wedgwood pottery. [orig. with ref. to Josiah *Wedgwood,* 1730-95, English potter]
**Wedgwood blue** /– ˈblu/, *n.* a light shade of greyish blue, characteristic of that used on Wedgwood pottery.
**wedlock** /ˈwɛdlɒk/, *n.* the state of marriage; matrimony. [ME *wedlok,* OE *wedlāc,* from *wed* pledge + *-lāc,* suffix making neut. nouns]
**Wednesday** /ˈwɛnzdeɪ, -di, ˈwɛdn-/, *n.* the fourth day of the week, following Tuesday. [ME *Wednesdai,* OE *Wōdnes dæg* Woden's day, c. D*Woensdag,* Dan. *Onsdag;* translation of L *Mercuriī diēs*]
**wee** /wi/, *adj.,* **weer, weest,** *n. –adj.* **1.** little; very small. *–n.* **2.** Also, **wees.** →**wee-wee.** [ME *we,* var. of *wei* (small) quantity, OE *wēg* weight, amount]
**weed**[1] /wid/, *n.* **1.** a plant growing wild, esp. in cultivated ground to the exclusion or injury of the desired crop. **2.** any useless, troublesome, or noxious plant, esp. one that grows profusely. **3.** *Colloq.* a cigar or cigarette. **4.** *Colloq.* a marijuana cigarette. **5.** a thin or weakly person, esp. one regarded as stupid or infantile. **6.** a sorry animal, esp. a horse unfit for racing or breeding purposes. **7. the weed,** *Colloq.* **a.** tobacco. **b.** marijuana. *–v.t.* **8.** to free from weeds or troublesome plants: *to weed a garden.* **9.** to root out or remove (a weed) (oft. fol. by *out*). **10.** to remove as being undesirable or superfluous (oft. fol. by *out*): *to weed out undesirable members.* **11.** to rid of what is undesirable or superfluous. *–v.i.* **12.** to remove weeds or the like. [ME *wede,* OE *wēod*] **– weeder,** *n.* **– weedless,** *adj.* **– weedlike,** *adj.*
**weed**[2] /wid/, *n.* **1.** (*pl.*) mourning garments: *widow's weeds.* **2.** a mourning band of black crepe or cloth, as on a man's hat or coat sleeve. **3.** *Archaic* a garment or clothing or dress: *clad in rustic weeds.* [ME *wede,* OE *wǣd,* var. of *wǣd* garment, c. Icel. *vādh* cloth]
**weedicide** /ˈwidəsaɪd/, *n.* →**weedkiller.**
**weedkiller** /ˈwidkɪlə/, *n.* a substance or preparation used for killing weeds.
**weedy** /ˈwidi/, *adj.,* **-dier, -diest. 1.** abounding in weeds. **2.** consisting of or pertaining to weeds. **3.** of a poor, straggling growth, as a plant. **4.** thin and weakly, as a person or animal. **– weediness,** *n.*
**wee juggler** /wi ˈdʒʌglə/, *n.* →**Major Mitchell.**
**week** /wik/, *n.* **1.** a period of seven successive days, commonly understood as beginning (unless otherwise specified or implied) with Sunday, followed by Monday, Tuesday, Wednesday, Thursday, Friday, and Saturday. **2.** the working days or working portion of the seven-day period: *a working week of 40 hours.* **3.** seven days after a specified day: *I shall come Tuesday week.* **4. week in, week out,** continuously; incessantly. [ME *weke,* OE *wice,* c. D *week,* akin to G *Woche*]
**weekday** /ˈwikdeɪ/, *n.* **1.** any day of the week except Saturday and Sunday. *–adj.* **2.** of or on a weekday: *weekday occupations.*
**weekend** /wikˈɛnd/, *n.;* /ˈwikɛnd/, *adj., v. –n.* **1.** the end of the working week, esp. the period from Friday night or Saturday to Monday, as a time for recreation, visiting, etc. *–adj.* **2.** of, for, or on a weekend. *–v.i.* **3.** to pass the weekend, as at a place.
**weekender** /wikˈɛndə/, *n.* **1.** a person who regularly visits a certain place at weekends. **2.** a periodic detainee. **3.** a holiday cottage.
**weekend penalty rate,** *n.* an additional rate for weekend work which employers are obliged to pay and which is intended to discourage their use of labour at weekends.
**weekend revolutionary** /wikˌɛnd rɛvəˈluʃənri/, *n.* (*derog.*) one who advocates revolution while enjoying the life-style of the established society under attack.
**weekly** /ˈwikli/, *adj., adv., n., pl.* **-lies.** *–adj.* **1.** pertaining to a week, or to each week. **2.** done, happening, appearing, etc., once a week, or every week. **3.** continuing or staying for a week: *a weekly boarder.* *–adv.* **4.** once a week. **5.** by the week. *–n.* **6.** a periodical appearing once a week. **7.** Also, **weekly ticket.** a commuter's ticket bought to cover his transport fares to and from work for the following week.
**weeknight** /ˈwiknaɪt/, *n.* a weekday night or evening.
**ween** /win/, *v.i., v.t. Archaic.* to think or suppose. [ME *wene,* OE *wēnan* expect, c. G *wähnen imagine*]
**weeny** /ˈwini/, *adj. Colloq.* very small; tiny.
**weeny-bopper** /ˈwini-bɒpə/, *n.* a youngster (8-12 years) who conforms to the style of dress, music, etc., of current pop groups. [formed on the model of TEENY-BOPPER]
**weep**[1] /wip/, *v.,* **wept, weeping,** *n. –v.i.* **1.** to manifest grief or anguish, originally by outcry, now by tears; shed tears, as from sorrow, unhappiness, or any overpowering emotion; cry: *to weep for joy or rage.* **2.** to let fall drops of water or liquid; drip. **3.** to exude water or liquid, as soil, rock, a plant stem, a sore, etc. *–v.t.* **4.** to weep for; mourn with tears or other expression of sorrow: *he wept his dead brother.* **5.** to shed (tears, etc.). **6.** to let fall or give forth in drops: *trees weeping odorous gums.* **7.** to pass, bring, put, etc., with the shedding of tears (fol. by *away, out,* etc.): *to weep one's eyes out.* *–n.* **8.** *Colloq.* weeping, or a fit of weeping. **9.** exudation of water or liquid. [ME *wepe,* OE *wēpan* wail, c. Goth. *wōpjan* call]
**weep**[2] /wip/, *n.* the lapwing, *Vanellus vanellus,* of Europe, so called from its cries.
**weeper** /ˈwipə/, *n.* **1.** one who weeps. **2.** a hired mourner at a funeral. **3.** something worn as a symbol of mourning.
**weephole** /ˈwiphoʊl/, *n.* a small gap left between bricks at the foot of a cavity wall to allow water to drain out.
**weepie** /ˈwipi/, *n. Colloq.* a sentimental film or play. [WEEP[1] + -IE]
**weeping** /ˈwipɪŋ/, *adj.* **1.** that weeps. **2.** expressing sorrow by shedding tears. **3.** (of trees, etc.) having slender, drooping branches.

**weeping myall** /– ˈmaɪəl/, *n.* a wattle tree, *Acacia pendula,* with drooping branches and hard sweet-scented purple-brown wood, used for fencing.

**weeping willow** /– ˈwɪloʊ/, *n.* a commonly cultivated willow, *Salix babylonica,* with long pendulous branches.

**weepy** /ˈwipi/, *adj.* **1.** tearful; likely to burst into tears for the slightest reason. **2.** exuding moisture or the like.

**weever** /ˈwivə/, *n.* **1.** either of two small marine fishes of the genus *Trachinus, T. vipera* (**lesser weever**), common in British waters, and the rarer *T. draco* (**greater weever**), notable for their poison glands at the base of certain spinous fins. **2.** any fish of the same family (Trachinidae). [? OE *wifer* dart (c. Icel. *vifr* sword); modern meaning by association with obs. *wyver* WYVERN]

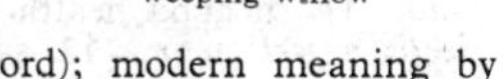
weeping willow

**weevil** /ˈwivəl/, *n.* **1.** any of the numerous beetles of the family Curculionidae, many of which are economically important, being destructive to nuts, grain, fruit, the stems of leaves, the pitch of trees, etc.; a snout-beetle. **2.** any of the beetles of the family Lariidae, known as **seed-weevils** or **bean-weevils.** [ME *wevel,* OE *wifel;* akin to WAVE or WEAVE]

weevil

**weevilly** /ˈwivəli/, *adj.* infested with weevils. Also, **weevilled** /ˈwivəld/; *Chiefly U.S.,* **weevily, weeviled.**

**wee-wee** /ˈwi-wi/, (*in children's speech*) *n.* **1.** urine. *–v.i.* **2.** to urinate. Also, **wee-wees.**

**weft** /wɛft/, *n.* **1.** woof or filling yarns which interlace with warp running from selvage to selvage. **2.** a woven piece. [ME and OE. See WEAVE]

**weigela** /waɪˈdʒilə, -ˈgi-/, *n.* any of various shrubby plants of the genus *Weigela,* native to eastern Asia, including species or varieties familiar in cultivation, with funnel-shaped white, pink, or crimson flowers. [NL, after G. E. *Weigel,* 1748-1831, German physician]

**weigh**[1] /weɪ/, *v.t.* **1.** to ascertain the weight of by means of a balance, scale, or other mechanical device: *to weigh gold, gases, persons, etc.* **2.** to hold up or balance, as in the hand, in order to estimate the weight. **3.** to measure (a certain quantity of something) according to weight (usu. fol. by *out*): *to weigh out 5 kg of sugar.* **4.** to bear (down) by weight, heaviness, oppression, etc.: *weighed down with care, a bough weighed down by fruit.* **5.** to balance in the mind; consider carefully in order to reach an opinion, decision, or choice (sometimes fol. by *up*): *to weigh facts or a proposal; to weigh up the pros and cons.* **6.** to raise or lift (now chiefly in the phrase *to weigh anchor*). **7.** *Obs.* to regard or esteem. **8. weigh one's words,** to consider and choose one's words carefully in speaking or writing. *–v.i.* **9.** to have weight or heaviness: *to weigh little or less, to weigh a lot.* **10.** to have importance, moment, or consequence: *wealth weighs little in this case.* **11.** to bear down as a weight or burden: *such responsibility weighed upon him.* **12. weigh in, a.** (of a boxer or wrestler) to be weighed before a fight. **b.** (of a jockey) to be weighed after a race. **13. weigh into, a.** to attack, physically or verbally. **b.** to begin to eat with hearty appetite. **14. weigh in with,** *Colloq.* to offer an opinion. [ME *weghe,* OE *wegan* carry, weigh, c. D *wegen,* G *wägen,* Icel. *vega*] **–weighable,** *adj.* **–weigher,** *n.*

**weigh**[2] /weɪ/, *n. in the phrase* **under weigh,** *Naut.* in motion, as a ship that has weighed anchor. [special use of WEIGH[1]]

**weighbridge** /ˈweɪbrɪdʒ/, *n.* a road-level weighing machine for vehicles; used esp. to determine the weight of their loads.

**weigh-in** /ˈweɪ-ɪn/, *n.* the checking of a contestant's weight, as before a boxing or wrestling match, or a jockey's weight after a horserace.

**weight** /weɪt/, *n.* **1.** amount of heaviness; amount a thing weighs. **2.** the force which gravitation exerts upon a material body, varying with altitude and latitude. It is often taken as a measure of the mass, which does not vary, and is equal to the mass times the acceleration due to gravity. **3.** a system of units for expressing weight or mass: *avoirdupois weight.* **4.** a unit of weight or mass. **5.** a body of determinate mass, as of metal, for using on a balance or scale in measuring the weight or mass of (or weighing) objects, substances, etc. **6.** one of a series of standard divisions within which boxers or wrestlers fight, according to how much they weigh. **7. top weight,** *Horseracing.* the maximum handicap. **8.** a quantity of a substance determined by weighing: *a gram weight of gold dust.* **9.** any heavy mass or object, esp. an object used because of its heaviness: *the weights of a clock.* **10.** pressure or oppressive force, as of something burdensome: *the weight of cares, sorrows.* **11.** a heavy load or burden: *that is such a weight I can't lift it.* **12.** a burden, as of care or responsibility: *to remove a weight from my mind.* **13.** importance, moment, consequence, or effective influence: *an opinion of great weight, men of weight.* **14.** →**stress** (def. 7). **15.** a measure of the relative importance of an item in a statistical population. **16.** (of clothing) the relative thickness as determined by the weather. **17.** *Print.* the degree of blackness of a typeface; the extent to which a bold typeface is heavier than its roman equivalent. **18. by weight,** according to weight measurement. **19. carry weight,** to have influence or importance. **20. correct weight,** *Horseracing.* the confirmation that the contestants in a race did in fact carry the handicap weight allotted to them. **21. pull one's weight,** to do one's fair share of work. **22. put (a person's) weights up,** *N.Z. Colloq.* to inform on (someone). **23. throw one's weight around** or **about, a.** to behave in an aggressive or selfish fashion. **b.** to use one's influence, personality, etc., to gain one's own ends without regard for others. *–v.t.* **24.** to add weight to; load with additional weight. **25.** to load (fabrics, threads, etc.) with mineral or other matter to increase the weight or bulk. **26.** to burden with or as with weight: *to be weighted with years.* **27.** *Statistics.* to give a (statistical) weight to. [ME; OE *wiht,* c. D *wicht,* G *Wucht.* See WEIGH[1]]

**weight-belt** /ˈweɪt-bɛlt/, *n.* a belt with weights attached worn by divers to counteract buoyancy.

**weight density** /ˈweɪt ˌdɛnsəti/, *n.* the weight per unit volume.

**weight-for-age** /weɪt-fər-ˈeɪdʒ/, *adj.* of a race, etc., in which the contestants are handicapped according to their age.

**weighting** /ˈweɪtɪŋ/, *n.* an increased amount, as of salary or the like, to balance the higher cost of living in a particular area.

**weightlessness** /ˈweɪtləsnəs/, *n.* the state of being without apparent weight as experienced in free fall, due to the absence of any apparent gravitational pull; zero gravity.

**weight-lifting** /ˈweɪt-lɪftɪŋ/, *n.* the sport of lifting barbells of specified weights, in competition or for exercise. **–weight-lifter,** *n.*

**weight watcher** /ˈweɪt wɒtʃə/, *n.* one who diets constantly to reduce weight.

**weighty** /ˈweɪti/, *adj.,* **-tier, -tiest. 1.** having considerable weight; heavy; ponderous. **2.** burdensome or onerous: *the weighty cares of sovereignty.* **3.** important or momentous: *weighty negotiations.* **4.** influential: *a weighty financier.* **–weightily,** *adv.* **–weightiness,** *n.*

**weir** /wɪə/, *n.* **1.** a dam in a river or stream to stop and raise the water, as for conducting it to a mill, for purposes of irrigation, etc. **2.** an obstruction placed across a stream thereby causing the water to pass through a particular opening or notch, thus measuring the quantity flowing. **3.** a fence, as of brush, narrow boards, or a net, set in a stream, channel, etc., for catching fish. [ME and OE *wer,* c. G *Wehr*]

**weird** /wɪəd/, *adj.* **1.** involving or suggesting the supernatural; unearthly or uncanny: *a weird scene, light, or sound.* **2.** *Colloq.* startlingly or extraordinarily singular, odd, or queer: *a weird get-up.* **3.** concerned with fate or destiny. [ME *werd,* n., OE *wyrd* fate; akin to WORTH[2], *v.*] **–weirdly,** *adv.* **–weirdness,** *n.*

**weirdo** /ˈwɪədoʊ/, *n. Colloq.* one who behaves in a strange, abnormal, or eccentric way. Also, **weirdie, weirdy.**

**Weismanism** /ˈvaɪsmənɪzəm/, *n.* the theories and teachings of the German biologist August Weismann, 1834-1914, esp. his theory respecting the continuity of the germ plasm and its isolation from the body plasm, with the accompanying doctrine that acquired characters in the latter are not and cannot be inherited.

**weka** /'wɛkə/, *n.* any of several large, flightless New Zealand rails of genus *Gallirallus;* Maori hen; woodhen.

**WEL** /wɛl/, Women's Electoral Lobby.

**welch** /wɛlʃ/, *v.t., v.i. Colloq.* →**welsh.** – **welcher,** *n.*

**welcome** /'wɛlkəm/, *interj., n., v.,* **-comed, -coming,** *adj.* –*interj.* **1.** (a word of kindly greeting as to one whose coming gives pleasure): *welcome, friends!* –*n.* **2.** a kindly greeting or reception, as of one whose coming gives pleasure: *to give one a warm welcome.* –*v.t.* **3.** to greet the coming of (a person, etc.) with pleasure or kindly courtesy. **4.** to receive or regard as welcome: *to welcome a change.* **5.** to receive or greet the arrival (of a person) with displeasure, or the like: *they welcomed the leader with silence.* –*adj.* **6.** gladly received, as one whose coming gives pleasure: *a welcome visitor.* **7.** agreeable, as something coming, occurring, or experienced: *a welcome letter, a welcome rest.* **8.** given full right by the cordial consent of others: *welcome to anything he can find.* **9.** free to enjoy courtesies, etc., without being under obligation (used in conventional response to thanks): *you are quite welcome.* [ME; OE *wilcuma,* from *wil-* pleasure + *cuma* guest] – **welcomeless,** *adj.* – **welcomely,** *adv.* – **welcomeness,** *n.* – **welcomer,** *n.*

**welcome swallow** /– 'swɒloʊ/, *n.* a swallow, *Hirundo neoxena,* with a swift, swooping flight, widely distributed throughout Australia, except in the north-west and the Northern Territory.

**weld**[1] /wɛld/, *v.t.* **1.** to unite or fuse (pieces of metal, etc.) by hammering, compression, or the like, esp. after rendering soft or pasty by heat, and sometimes with the addition of fusible material like or unlike the pieces to be united. **2.** to bring into complete union. –*v.i.* **3.** to undergo welding; be capable of being welded. –*n.* **4.** a welded junction or joint. **5.** the act of welding. [var. of WELL[2], *v.*] – **weldable,** *adj.* – **welder,** *n.*

**weld**[2] /wɛld/, *n.* **1.** a mignonette, *Reseda luteola,* a native of southern Europe, yielding a yellow dye. **2.** the dye. Also, **wold, woald.** [ME *welde,* c. MLG *walde*]

**weldmesh** /'wɛldmɛʃ/, *n.* a wire mesh made by welding horizontal wires onto vertical wires, designed for fencing.

**welfare** /'wɛlfɛə/, *n.* **1.** the state of faring well; well-being: *one's welfare, the physical or moral welfare of society.* **2.** →**welfare work. 3.** →**social services.** [ME; see WELL[1], FARE]

**welfare state** /'– steɪt/, *n.* a state (def. 8) in which the welfare of the people in such matters as social security, health and education, housing, and working conditions is the responsibility of the government.

**welfare work** /'– wɜk/, *n.* work devoted to the welfare of persons in a community, esp. the aged, sick, poor, etc.

**welkin** /'wɛlkən/, *n. Archaic.* the sky; the vault of heaven. [ME *welken(e),* OE *wolcen* cloud, c. G *Wolke*]

**well**[1] /wɛl/, *adv., adj., compar.* **better,** *super.* **best,** *interj.* –*adv.* **1.** in a satisfactory, favourable, or advantageous manner; fortunately or happily: *affairs are going well, to be well supplied, well situated.* **2.** in a good or proper manner: *he behaved very well.* **3.** commendably, meritoriously, or excellently: *to act, write, or reason well, a good work well done.* **4.** with propriety, justice, or reason: *I could not well refuse.* **5.** in satisfactory or good measure; adequately or sufficiently: *think well before you act.* **6.** thoroughly or soundly: *shake well before using; beat well.* **7.** easily; clearly: *I can see it very well.* **8.** to a considerable extent or degree: *a sum well over the amount fixed, dilute the acid well.* **9.** personally; to a great degree of intimacy: *to know a person well.* **10.** Some special adverbial phrases are:

**as well,** in addition: *she is bringing a friend as well.*

**as well as,** in addition to; no less than: *he was handsome as well as rich.*

**just as well,** preferable; more favourable; advisable: *it would be just as well if you went.*

**very well 1.** with certainty; undeniably: *you know very well you are late.* **2.** (a phrase used to indicate consent, often with reluctance): *very well, you may go out, but not for long.* **3.** (*ironic*) satisfactory; pleasing: *it's all very well for you, you don't have to worry about money.*

–*adj.* **11.** in good health, or sound in body and mind: *I am well; a well man.* **12.** satisfactory or good: *all is well with us.* **13.** proper or fitting. **14.** in a satisfactory position; well-off: *I am very well as I am.* –*interj.* **15.** (used to express surprise, agreement): *well, who would have thought it?* **16.** (used as a preliminary to further speech): *well, as I was saying.* [ME and OE *wel(l),* c D *wel,* G *wohl,* Icel. *vel,* Goth. *waila*]

**well**[2] /wɛl/, *n.* **1.** a hole drilled into the earth, generally by boring, for the production of water, petroleum, natural gas, brine, or sulphur. **2.** a spring or natural source of water. **3.** a fountain, fountainhead, or source: *Chaucer, well of English undefiled.* **4.** a vessel, receptacle, or reservoir for a liquid: *an inkwell.* **5.** any sunken or deep enclosed space, as a shaft for air or light, or for stairs, a lift, or the like, extending vertically through the floors of a building. **6.** a compartment or enclosure around a ship's pumps to render them easy of access and protect them from being injured by the cargo. –*v.i.* **7.** to rise, spring, or gush, as water, from the earth or some source (oft. fol. by *up, out,* or *forth*): *tears well up in the eyes.* –*v.t.* **8.** to send welling up or forth: *a fountain welling its pure water.* [ME *welle,* OE *wellan* (c. D *wellen,* Icel. *vella*), var. of *wiellan,* causative of *weallan* boil]

**we'll** /wil/, contraction of *we will* or *we shall.*

**well-advised** /'wɛl-ədvaɪzd/, *adj.* prudent; acting with care and wisdom. Also (*esp. in predicative positions*), **well advised** /wɛl əd'vaɪzd/.

**well-appointed** /'wɛl-əpɔɪntəd/, *adj.* comfortably and adequately equipped, decorated, furnished, etc., as a hotel, house, or the like. Also (*esp. in predicative positions*), **well appointed** /wɛl ə'pɔɪntəd/.

**wellaway** /wɛlə'weɪ/, *interj. Archaic.* (an exclamation of sorrow.) Also, **welladay** /wɛlə'deɪ/. [ME *welawei,* replacing ME and OE *weilāwei* (*wei* from Scand.; cf. Icel. *vei* woe), replacing OE *wā lā wā* woe! la! woe!]

**well-balanced** /'wɛl-bælənst/, *adj.* **1.** rightly balanced, adjusted, or regulated. **2.** sensible; sane. Also (*esp. in predicative positions*), **well balanced** /wɛl 'bælənst/.

**well-behaved** /'wɛl-bəheɪvd/, *adj.* characterised by good behaviour or conduct. Also (*esp. in predicative positions*), **well behaved** /wɛl bə'heɪvd/.

---

**well-acted,** *adj.*
**well-aimed,** *adj.*
**well-argued,** *adj.*
**well-armed,** *adj.*
**well-arranged,** *adj.*
**well-bound,** *adj.*
**well-conditioned,** *adj.*
**well-conducted,** *adj.*
**well-considered,** *adj.*
**well-covered,** *adj.*
**well-cut,** *adj.*
**well-defended,** *adj.*
**well-defined,** *adj.*
**well-deserved,** *adj.*
**well-developed,** *adj.*
**well-directed,** *adj.*
**well-disguised,** *adj.*
**well-drawn,** *adj.*
**well-dried,** *adj.*
**well-drilled,** *adj.*
**well-equipped,** *adj.*
**well-fashioned,** *adj.*
**well-feathered,** *adj.*
**well-filled,** *adj.*
**well-finished,** *adj.*
**well-fitting,** *adj.*
**well-formed,** *adj.*
**well-fortified,** *adj.*
**well-fought,** *adj.*
**well-furnished,** *adj.*
**well-governed,** *adj.*
**well-grown,** *adj.*
**well-horsed,** *adj.*
**well-instructed,** *adj.*
**well-intended,** *adj.*
**well-intentional,** *adj.*
**well-judged,** *adj.*
**well-kept,** *adj.*
**well-liked,** *adj.*
**well-looking,** *adj.*
**well-made,** *adj.*
**well-managed,** *adj.*
**well-marked,** *adj.*
**well-matched,** *adj.*
**well-mounted,** *adj.*

**well-being** /ˈwɛl-biɪŋ/, *n.* good or satisfactory condition of existence; welfare.

**well-beloved** /ˈwɛl-bəlʌvd/, *adj.* dearly loved; very dear. Also (*esp. in predicative positions*), **well beloved** /wɛl bəˈlʌvd/.

**well-born** /ˈwɛl-bɔn/, *adj.* of good birth or family. Also (*esp. in predicative positions*), **well born** /wɛl ˈbɔn/.

**well-bred** /ˈwɛl-brɛd/, *adj.* **1.** well brought up, as persons. **2.** showing good breeding, as behaviour, manners, etc. **3.** of good breed, as a domestic animal. Also (*esp. in predicative positions*), **well bred** /wɛl ˈbrɛd/.

**well-built** /ˈwɛl-bɪlt/, *adj.* **1.** that has been built soundly: *a well-built house.* **2.** (of a person) strongly built; broad. Also (*esp. in predicative positions*), **well built** /wɛl ˈbɪlt/.

**well-chosen** /ˈwɛl-tʃoʊzən/, *adj.* chosen with care, consideration, and aptness: *her speech centred round a few well-chosen topics.* Also (*esp. in predicative positions*), **well chosen** /wɛl ˈtʃoʊzən/.

**well-connected** /ˈwɛl-kənɛktəd/, *adj.* **1.** having important, powerful, or influential relatives. **2.** having useful connections with influential people. Also (*esp. in predicative positions*), **well connected** /wɛl kəˈnɛktəd/.

**welldeck** /ˈwɛldɛk/, *n.* a deck on a ship lying between two raised decks and forming a well below their level.

**well-disposed** /ˈwɛl-dəspoʊzd/, *adj.* **1.** rightly or properly disposed; well-meaning. **2.** favourably or kindly disposed: *well-disposed hearts.* Also (*esp. in predicative positions*), **well disposed** /wɛl dəsˈpoʊzd/.

**welldoer** /ˈwɛlduə/, *n.* **1.** one who does well or acts rightly. **2.** a doer of good deeds.

**welldoing** /ˈwɛlduɪŋ/, *n.* good conduct or action.

**well-done** /ˈwɛl-dʌn/, *adj.* **1.** cooked thoroughly, esp. of beef. **2.** performed satisfactorily, or excellently. Also, (*in predicative use*) **well done** /wɛl ˈdʌn/.

**well-dressed** /ˈwɛl-drɛst/, *adj.* wearing clothes that are smart, fit well, and are suitable for the occasion. Also (*esp. in predicative positions*), **well dressed** /wɛl ˈdrɛst/.

**well-earned** /ˈwɛl-ɜnd/, *adj.* well deserved, as after much effort, hard work, etc.: *a well-earned rest.* Also (*esp. in predicative positions*), **well earned** /wɛl ˈɜnd/.

**well-educated** /ˈwɛl-ɛdʒəkeɪtəd/, *adj.* **1.** having had a good education. **2.** apparently cultured and refined. Also (*esp. in predicative positions*), **well educated** /wɛl ˈɛdʒəkeɪtəd/.

**well-endowed** /ˈwɛl-əndaʊd/, *adj. Colloq.* **1.** (of a college, institution, etc.) well provided with monies. **2.** (of a woman) bosomy. **3.** (of a man) with big genitals. Also, (*esp. in predicative positions*), **well endowed** /wɛl ənˈdaʊd/.

**well-established** /ˈwɛl-əstæblɪʃt/, *adj.* **1.** having a reliable reputation, often of some years' standing, and an apparently stable and successful future: *a well-established bank.* **2.** firmly set and unlikely to change: *a well-established fashion.* Also (*esp. in predicative positions*), **well established** /wɛl əsˈtæblɪʃt/.

**well-favoured** /ˈwɛl-feɪvəd/, *adj.* of pleasing appearance; good-looking. Also (*esp. in predicative positions*), **well favoured** /wɛl ˈfeɪvəd/.

**well-fed** /ˈwɛl-fɛd/, *adj.* **1.** having a plentiful, balanced diet. **2.** fat; plump. Also (*esp. in predicative positions*), **well fed** /wɛl ˈfɛd/.

**well-fixed** /ˈwɛl-fɪkst/, *adj. Colloq.* well-off. Also (*esp. in predicative positions*), **well fixed** /wɛl ˈfɪkst/.

**well-found** /ˈwɛl-faʊnd/, *adj.* well furnished with supplies, necessaries, etc. Also (*esp. in predicative positions*), **well found** /wɛl ˈfaʊnd/.

**well-founded** /ˈwɛl-faʊndəd/, *adj.* rightly or justly founded, as on good grounds: *well-founded suspicions.* Also (*esp. in predicative positions*), **well founded** /wɛl ˈfaʊndəd/.

**well-groomed** /ˈwɛl-grumd/, *adj.* **1.** having a fresh, clean, tidy appearance; neatly dressed. **2.** tended, cleaned, curried, etc., with great care, as a horse. Also (*esp. in predicative positions*), **well groomed** /wɛl ˈgrumd/.

**well-grounded** /ˈwɛl-graʊndəd/, *adj.* **1.** based on good grounds or reasons; well-founded. **2.** well or thoroughly instructed in the first principles of a subject. Also (*esp. in predicative positions*), **well grounded** /wɛl ˈgraʊndəd/.

**wellhead** /ˈwɛlhɛd/, *n.* a fountainhead; source.

**well-heeled** /ˈwɛl-hild/, *adj. Colloq.* wealthy; prosperous. Also (*esp. in predicative positions*), **well heeled** /wɛl ˈhild/.

**well-hung** /ˈwɛl-hʌŋ/, *adj. Colloq.* (of a man) with big genitals. Also (*esp. in predicative positions*), **well hung** /wɛl ˈhʌŋ/.

**wellies** /ˈwɛliz/, *n.pl. Colloq.* wellington boots.

**well-in** /ˈwɛl-ɪn/, *adj. Colloq.* having influential friends; well-connected. Also (*esp. in predicative positions*), **well in** /wɛl ˈɪn/.

**well-informed** /ˈwɛl-ɪnfɔmd/, *adj.* **1.** having reliable or full information on a subject. **2.** having information on a variety of subjects: *a well-informed man.* Also (*esp. in predicative positions*), **well informed** /wɛl ɪnˈfɔmd/.

**wellington boot** /ˈwɛlɪŋtən but/, *n.* **1.** Also, **wellington.** a waterproof boot made of rubber, stretching up to the knee; a gum boot. **2.** originally, a leather boot with the front stretching up to above the knee. [named after the Duke of *Wellington*, 1769-1852, British general and statesman, Prime Minister 1828-30]

**well-knit** /ˈwɛl-nɪt/, *adj.* firmly and compactly built.

**well-known** /ˈwɛl-noʊn/, *adj.* **1.** clearly or fully known. **2.** familiarly known, or familiar: *his well-known face.* **3.** generally or widely known: *the well-known sculptor.* Also (*esp. in predicative positions*), **well known** /wɛl ˈnoʊn/.

**well-lined** /ˈwɛl-laɪnd/, *adj.* (of a purse, pocket, etc.) full of money. Also (*esp. in predicative positions*), **well lined** /wɛl ˈlaɪnd/.

**well-mannered** /ˈwɛl-mænəd/, *adj.* polite; courteous. Also (*esp. in predicative positions*), **well mannered** /wɛl ˈmænəd/.

**well-meaning** /ˈwɛl-minɪŋ/, *adj.* **1.** meaning or intending well: *a well-meaning but tactless person.* **2.** proceeding from good intentions. Also (*esp. in predicative positions*), **well meaning** /wɛl ˈminɪŋ/.

**well-meant** /ˈwɛl-mɛnt/, *adj.* →**well-meaning** (def. 2). Also (*esp. in predicative positions*), **well meant** /wɛl ˈmɛnt/.

**wellnigh** /ˈwɛlnaɪ/, *adv.* very nearly; almost.

**well-off** /ˈwɛl-ɒf/, *adj.* **1.** in a satisfactory, favourable, or good position or condition. **2.** in good or easy circumstances as to money or means; moderately rich. Also (*esp. in predicative positions*), **well off** /wɛl ˈɒf/.

**well-oiled** /ˈwɛl-ɔɪld/, *adj. Colloq.* drunk. Also (*esp. in predicative positions*), **well oiled** /wɛl ˈɔɪld/.

---

**well-named**, *adj.*
**well-organised**, *adj.*
**well-paid**, *adj.*
**well-painted**, *adj.*
**well-placed**, *adj.*
**well-planned**, *adj.*
**well-planted**, *adj.*
**well-polished**, *adj.*
**well-printed**, *adj.*
**well-reasoned**, *adj.*
**well-regulated**, *adj.*
**well-remembered**, *adj.*
**well-respected**, *adj.*
**well-rigged**, *adj.*
**well-seasoned**, *adj.*
**well-served**, *adj.*
**well-set**, *adj.*
**well-set-up**, *adj.*
**well-sharpened**, *adj.*
**well-shod**, *adj.*
**well-spent**, *adj.*
**well-stacked**, *adj.*
**well-stocked**, *adj.*
**well-tailored**, *adj.*
**well-tanned**, *adj.*
**well-taught**, *adj.*
**well-tempered**, *adj.*
**well-thumbed**, *adj.*
**well-timbered**, *adj.*
**well-told**, *adj.*
**well-trained**, *adj.*
**well-travelled**, *adj.*
**well-trimmed**, *adj.*
**well-trodden**, *adj.*
**well-tuned**, *adj.*
**well-ventilated**, *adj.*
**well-warmed**, *adj.*
**well-watered**, *adj.*
**well-wooded**, *adj.*
**well-worded**, *adj.*
**well-worked-out**, *adj.*
**well-written**, *adj.*

**well-ordered** /ˈwɛl-ɔdəd/, *adj.* properly or efficiently regulated or arranged. Also (*esp. in predicative positions*), **well ordered** /wɛl ˈɔdəd/.

**wellpoint** /ˈwɛlpɔɪnt/, *n.* one of a series of pipes with perforated tips, driven into the ground around an excavation site in order to pump the ground-water level below that of the excavation.

**well-preserved** /ˈwɛl-prəzɜvd/, *adj.* **1.** having been kept in good condition. **2.** preserving a young or youthful appearance. Also (*esp. in predicative positions*), **well preserved** /wɛl prəˈzɜvd/.

**well-proportioned** /ˈwɛl-prəpɔʃənd/, *adj.* **1.** having pleasing proportions, esp. as regards size and shape. **2.** (of a person) having a good figure. Also (*esp. in predicative positions*), **well proportioned** /wɛl prəˈpɔʃənd/.

**well-read** /ˈwɛl-rɛd/, *adj.* **1.** having read much: *well-read in science.* **2.** having an extensive and intelligent knowledge of books or literature. Also (*esp. in predicative positions*), **well read** /wɛl ˈrɛd/.

**well-rounded** /ˈwɛl-raʊndəd/, *adj.* **1.** having an agreeable rounded shape. **2.** full and varied, as a person's life. **3.** sonorous and well constructed, as a phrase or sentence. Also (*esp. in predicative positions*), **well rounded** /wɛl ˈraʊndəd/.

**well-spoken** /ˈwɛl-spoʊkən/, *adj.* **1.** having a cultured, refined accent. **2.** speaking well, fittingly, or pleasingly. **3.** polite in speech. **4.** spoken well, appropriately, etc. Also (*esp. in predicative positions*), **well spoken** /wɛl ˈspoʊkən/.

**wellspring** /ˈwɛlsprɪŋ/, *n.* **1.** a fountainhead. **2.** a source of anything.

**well sweep** /ˈwɛl swip/, *n.* →**sweep**[1] (def. 33).

**well-thought-of** /wɛl-ˈθɔt-ɒv/, *adj.* having a good reputation; held in estimation. Also (*esp. in predicative positions*), **well thought of.**

**well-timed** /ˈwɛl-taɪmd/, *adj.* fittingly timed; opportune; timely: *a well-timed attack.* Also (*esp. in predicative positions*), **well timed** /wɛl ˈtaɪmd/.

**well-to-do** /ˈwɛl-tə-du/; *esp. in predicative use* /wɛl-tə-ˈdu/, *adj.* **1.** having a sufficiency of means for comfortable living, well-off, or prosperous. **2.** characterised by or showing a comfortable sufficiency of means, or prosperity: *well-to-do circumstances.*

**well-tried** /ˈwɛl-traɪd/, *adj.* **1.** thoroughly tried or tested. **2.** (of a person) refined and proper in one's manner of speech and its content. Also (*esp. in predicative positions*), **well tried** /wɛl ˈtraɪd/.

**well-turned** /ˈwɛl-tɜnd/, *adj.* **1.** having a pleasing shape: *a well-turned ankle.* **2.** aptly and pleasingly expressed: *a well-turned compliment.* Also (*esp. in predicative positions*), **well turned** /wɛl ˈtɜnd/.

**well-wisher** /ˈwɛl-wɪʃə/, *n.* one who wishes well to a person, a cause, etc. – **well-wishing,** *adj., n.*

**well-worn** /ˈwɛl-wɔn/, *adj.* **1.** much worn or affected by use: *well-worn garments or carpets, a well-worn volume.* **2.** trite, hackneyed, or stale: *a well-worn saying or theme.* **3.** *Archaic.* fittingly or becomingly worn or borne: *well-worn reserve.* Also (*esp. in predicative positions*), **well worn** /wɛl ˈwɔn/.

**Welsbach burner** /wɛlzbæk ˈbɜnə/, *n.* a gas burner, consisting essentially of a Bunsen burner, about the flame of which is placed an incombustible mantle (**Welsbach mantle**) composed of thoria and some ceria, which becomes brilliantly incandescent. [named after Karl Auer von *Welsbach,* 1858-1929, Austrian chemist who devised it]

**welsh** /wɛlʃ/, *v.t., v.i. Colloq.* **1.** to cheat by evading payment, esp. of a gambling debt (sometimes fol. by *on*). **2.** to inform or tell on someone. Also, **welch.** [orig. obscure] – **welsher,** *n.*

**Welsh** /wɛlʃ/, *adj.* **1.** of or pertaining to Wales, its people, or their language. *–n.* **2.** the people of Wales. **3.** the Celtic language of Wales. [ME *Welische,* OE *Welisc,* from *Walh* Briton, foreigner]

**Welsh corgi** /– ˈkɔgi/, *n.* See **corgi.**

**Welsh dresser** /– ˈdrɛsə/, *n.* a sideboard having drawers or compartments below and open shallow shelves above.

**Welshman** /ˈwɛlʃmən/, *n., pl.* **-men.** a native or inhabitant of Wales.

**Welsh pony** /wɛlʃ ˈpoʊni/, *n.* one of a breed of very small, stocky ponies, originally from Wales.

**Welsh poppy** /– ˈpɒpi/, *n.* a perennial herb with yellow flowers, *Meconopsis cambrica,* occurring in shady places in western Europe.

**Welsh rarebit** /– ˈrɛəbɪt/, *n.* melted cheese, sometimes mixed with beer, milk, etc., eaten on toast. Also, **Welsh rabbit.** [var. of *Welsh rabbit,* probably of jocular orig.]

**Welsh springer spaniel,** *n.* one of the two breeds of springer spaniel, slightly smaller than the English springer spaniel, and having a distinctive red-and-white coat.

**Welsh terrier** /wɛlʃ ˈtɛriə/, *n.* a black-and-tan terrier of a breed developed in Wales as a hunting dog.

Welsh terrier

**welt** /wɛlt/, *n.* **1.** a ridge or wale on the surface of the body, as from the stroke of a stick or whip. **2.** a stroke of this kind. **3.** a strip of leather set in between the edges of the inner sole and upper and the outer sole of a shoe. **4.** a strengthening or ornamental finish along a seam, the edge of a garment, etc. **5.** a type of seam in which one edge is cut close to the stitching line and covered by the other edge which is stitched over it. *–v.t.* **6.** to beat soundly, as with a stick or whip. **7.** to furnish with a welt or welts. [ME *welte, walt;* cf. OE *wæltan, weltan* roll]

**Weltanschauung** /ˈvɛltanʃaʊʊŋ/, *n.* →**world view.** [G.]

**welter** /ˈwɛltə/, *v.i.* **1.** *Archaic.* to roll, toss, or heave, as waves, the sea, etc. **2.** *Archaic.* to lie bathed or be drenched in something, esp. blood. **3.** *Obs.* to roll or tumble about, or wallow, as animals. *–n.* **4.** a rolling or tumbling about: *in the welter of the sea.* **5.** commotion, turmoil, or chaos: *the welter of our mutable world.* **6.** a race in which the horses carry weights which are not less than 51 kg. **7. make a welter of it,** *Colloq.* to indulge in to excess. [ME, frequentative of obs. *welt* roll, OE *weltan.* Cf. MD *welteren,* LG *weltern* roll]

**welterweight** /ˈwɛltəweɪt/, *n.* a boxer weighing between 63.5 and 67 kg (in the amateur ranks) and 63.503 and 66.678 kg (in the professional ranks). [*welter* heavyweight rider or boxer (lit. beater, from WELT, *v.*) + WEIGHT]

**Weltschmerz** /ˈvɛltʃmɛəts/, *n.* sorrow felt and accepted as the necessary portion of the world; sentimental pessimism. [G: world-pain]

**welwitschia** /wɛlˈwɪtʃiə/, *n.* a plant, *Welwitschia bainesii,* of desert regions of southern Africa, having an extremely long taproot, and a life of several centuries. [named after Friedrich Martin Josef *Welwitsch,* 1807-1872, Portuguese botanist born in Austria]

**wen** /wɛn/, *n.* a benign encysted tumour of the skin, esp. on the scalp, containing sebaceous matter; a sebaceous cyst. [ME and OE *wenn,* c. D *wen*]

**wench** /wɛntʃ/, *n.* **1.** a girl, or young woman. **2.** a rustic or working girl. **3.** *Archaic.* a prostitute or promiscuous woman. *–v.i.* **4.** to consort with promiscuous women or prostitutes. [ME, var. of *wenchel,* OE *wencel* child. Cf. OE *wancol* weak] – **wencher,** *n.*

**wend** /wɛnd/, *v.,* **wended** or (*Archaic*) **went; wending.** *–v.t.* **1.** to direct or pursue (one's way, etc.): *he wended his way to the riverside.* *–v.i.* **2.** *Archaic.* to proceed or go. [ME; OE *wendan,* c. D and G *wenden*]

**Wendy house** /ˈwɛndi haʊs/, *n.* a cubbyhouse.

**wensleydale** /ˈwɛnzlideɪl/, *n.* an English white cheese with a subtle flavour and flaky texture. [from *Wensleydale,* England]

**went** /wɛnt/, *v.* **1.** past tense of **go. 2.** archaic past tense and past participle of **wend.**

**wentletrap** /ˈwɛntltræp/, *n.* any of the handsome, usu. white, spiral-shelled marine gastropods constituting the genus Scalaria or the family Scalariidae. [D *wenteltrap* winding stair, spiral shell]

wentletrap

**wept** /wɛpt/, *v.* past tense and past participle of **weep.**

**were** /wɜ/, *v.* past tense indicative plural and subjunctive singular and plural of **be.** [ME; OE *wǣron, wǣre(n)*, c G *waren.* See WAS]

**we're** /wɪə, wɜ, wɛə/, contraction of *we are.*

**weren't** /wɜnt/, contraction of *were not.*

**werewolf** /ˈwɪəwʊlf, ˈwɜ-, ˈwɛə-/, *n., pl.* **-wolves** /-wʊlvz/. (in old superstition) a human being turned preternaturally into a wolf, or capable of assuming the form of a wolf, while retaining human intelligence; loup-garou; lycanthrope. Also, **werwolf.** [ME *werwolf,* OE *wer(e)wulf,* from *wer* man (c. L *vir*) + WOLF]

**wernerite** /ˈwɜnəraɪt/, *n.* →**scapolite.**

**werris** /ˈwɛrəs/, *n.* an act of passing water; urination. [rhyming slang, *Werris Creek* leak]

**wert** /wɜt/, *v. Archaic.* 2nd person singular past tense indicative and subjunctive of **be.**

**weskit** /ˈwɛskət/, *n.* →**waistcoat.**

**Wesleyan** /ˈwɛzliən/, *adj.* **1.** of or pertaining to Methodism. *–n.* **2.** a Methodist. [from Charles *Wesley,* 1707-88, English preacher and hymnwriter, and John *Wesley,* his brother, 1703-91, preacher, founder of Methodism] – **Wesleyanism,** *n.*

**Wessex saddleback** /wɛsəks ˈsædlbæk/, *n.* a breed of pig, black with a white saddle over its shoulder, reared for pork and bacon.

**west** /wɛst/, *n.* **1.** a cardinal point of the compass (90° to the left of north) corresponding to the point where the sun is seen to set. **2.** the direction in which this point lies. **3.** (*l.c.* or *cap.*) a quarter or territory situated in this direction. **4. the West, a.** the western part of the world as distinct from the East or Orient; the Occident. **b.** the countries of Western Europe and the Americas not under Communist government. **c.** Western Australia. *–adj.* **5.** direct or proceeding towards the west. **6.** coming from the west: *a west wind.* **7.** lying towards or situated in the west: *the west side.* **8.** *Eccles.* designating lying towards, or in that part of a church opposite to and farthest from the altar. *–adv.* **9.** in the direction of the sunset; towards or in the west. **10.** from the west (as of wind). **11. go west,** *Colloq.* **a.** to die. **b.** to disappear; be lost. [ME and OE, c. D *west,* G *West,* Icel. *vestr*]

**West Australian** /wɛst əsˈtreɪljən/, *n.* **1.** one who was born in Western Australia or who has come to regard it as his home State. *–adj.* **2.** of or pertaining to the State of Western Australia.

**westbound** /ˈwɛstbaʊnd/, *adj.* travelling towards the west.

**west by north,** *n. Navig., Survey.* 11°15′ (one point) north of west; 281°15′ from due north. *Abbrev.:* W by N.

**west by south,** *n. Navig., Survey.* 11°15′ (one point) south of west; 258°45′ from due north. *Abbrev.:* W by S.

**wester** /ˈwɛstə/, *v.i.* to move or tend westwards.

**westering** /ˈwɛstərɪŋ/, *adj.* moving towards the west.

**westerly** /ˈwɛstəli/, *adj., adv., n., pl.* **-lies.** *–adj.* **1.** moving, directed, or situated towards the west. **2.** coming from the west: *a westerly gale.* *–adv.* **3.** towards the west. **4.** from the west. *–n.* **5.** a westerly wind.

**western** /ˈwɛstən/, *adj.* **1.** lying towards or situated in the west. **2.** directed or proceeding towards the west. **3.** coming from the west, as a wind. **4.** (*usu. cap.*) of or pertaining to the west: *the Western Church.* **5.** (*cap.*) →**occidental.** *–n.* **6.** (*usu. cap.*) **a.** a story or film about frontier life in the American west during the latter half of the nineteenth century. **b.** a story or film, often, but not always, set in a lawless society, in which the hero is in conflict either with the society in which he lives, as in the traditional western, or with himself. [ME and OE *westerne*]

**Western Australia** /wɛstən əsˈtreɪliə/, *n.* a State in western Australia, one of the six States of Australia. *Abbrev.:* WA, W.A.

Western Australia: coat of arms

**western catalpa** /wɛstən kəˈtælpə/, *n.* See **catalpa.**

**Western Church** /wɛstən ˈtʃɜtʃ/, *n.* **1.** the Roman Catholic Church, sometimes with the Anglican Church, or, more broadly, the Christian Churches of western Europe and those churches elsewhere which are connected with or have sprung from them. **2.** the Christian Church in the countries once comprised in the Western Empire and in countries evangelised from these countries, or that part of the Christian Church which acknowledged the popes after the split between Greek and Latin Christianity.

**westerner** /ˈwɛstənə/, *n.* (*oft. cap.*) a native or inhabitant of a western area, esp. of Western Australia.

**western grey kangaroo,** *n.* the species of kangaroo, *Macropus fuliginosus,* characteristic of the western and southern areas of Australia. It overlaps with the great grey kangaroo in the south-west of New South Wales. Also, **western forester kangaroo, black-faced kangaroo, mallee kangaroo.**

**Western Hemisphere** /wɛstən ˈhɛməsfɪə/, *n.* **1.** a hemisphere of the earth cut along a meridian so chosen as to include all of North and South America, but no part of any other continent. **2.** that half of the earth traversed in passing westwards from the prime meridian to 180° longitude.

**western hemlock** /wɛstən ˈhɛmlɒk/, *n.* a coniferous tree, *Tsuga heterophylla,* a native of north America but frequently planted for forestry elsewhere.

**Westernise** /ˈwɛstənaɪz/, *v.t.,* **-nised, -nising.** to make Western in ideas, character, ways, etc. Also, **Westernize.** – **Westernisation** /ˌwɛstənaɪˈzeɪʃən/, *n.*

**westernmost** /ˈwɛstənmoʊst/, *adj.* farthest west.

**Western red cedar,** *n.* →**red cedar.**

**western roll** /wɛstən ˈroʊl/, *n.* a style of high jumping in which the competitor takes off with the leg nearest the bar, rolling towards the bar as he clears it horizontally, and face down.

**Western Samoa** /wɛstən səˈmoʊə/, *n.* the Western section of the Samoa island group in the south Pacific; an independent state.

**Western Standard Time,** *n.* a time zone lying on the 120th meridian in Western Australia eight hours ahead of Greenwich Mean Time, two hours behind Eastern Standard Time, and one and a half hours behind Central Standard Time.

**West Germany** /wɛst ˈdʒɜməni/, *n.* a republic in central Europe, formed after World War II as the British, French, and U.S. zones of occupation. Official name: **Federal Republic of Germany.**

**westie** /ˈwɛsti/, *n. Colloq.* someone from the western suburbs of Sydney.

**West Indies** /– ˈɪndiz/, *n.* an archipelago in the North Atlantic between North and South America, enclosing the Caribbean Sea and the Gulf of Mexico.

**westing** /ˈwɛstɪŋ/, *n.* **1.** westward movement or deviation. **2.** the distance due west made on any course tending westwards.

**Westminster system** /ˈwɛstmɪnstə sɪstəm/, *n.* a system of government originating in Britain, the major characteristics of which are the collective and individual responsibility of ministers to parliament, a head of state who is not also head of government, and a judiciary independent of the executive and legislature. [so named because the British Houses of Parliament are situated in the borough of *Westminster,* London]

**west-north-west** /wɛst-nɔθ-ˈwɛst/, *n.* **1.** the point of the compass midway between west and north-west; 290°30′ from north. *–adj.* **2.** lying or situated in this direction. *–adv.* **3.** to, in or from this direction. *Abbrev.:* WNW. Also, *esp. Naut.,* **west-nor'-west** /wɛst-nɔ-ˈwɛst/.

**Weston cell** /wɛstən ˈsɛl/, *n.* a type of primary cell used as a standard of electromotive force, consisting of mercury and cadmium electrodes in a saturated solution of cadmium sulphate; produces 1.0183 volts at 20°C. Also, **cadmium cell.**

**Westralian** /wɛsˈtreɪljən/, *n., adj.* →**West Australian.**

**westringia** /wəˈstrɪndʒiə/, *n.* any of the shrubs of the genus *Westringia,* family Labiatae, with white flowers and narrow leaves, as *W. fruticosa,* a plant found on sea cliffs and commonly planted as an ornamental.

**west-south-west** /wɛst-saʊθ-ˈwɛst/, *n.* **1.** the point of the compass midway between west and south-west; 247°30′ from north. *–adj.* **2.** lying or situated in this direction. *–adv.* **3.** to, in, or from this direction. *Abbrev.:* WSW. Also, *esp. Naut.,* **west-sou'-west** /wɛst-saʊ-ˈwɛst/.

**westward** /ˈwɛstwəd/, *adj.* **1.** moving, bearing, facing, or situated towards the west. *–adv.* **2.** westwards. *–n.* **3.** the westward part, direction, or point.

**westwardly** /ˈwɛstwədli/, *adj.* **1.** having a westward direction or situation. **2.** coming from the west, as a wind. *–adv.* **3.** towards the west. **4.** from the west.

**westwards** /ˈwɛstwədz/, *adv.* towards the west; west. Also, **westward.**

**wet** /wɛt/, *adj.*, **wetter, wettest,** *n.*, *v.*, **wet** or **wetted, wetting.** *–adj.* **1.** covered or soaked, wholly or in part, with water or some other liquid: *wet hands, a wet sponge.* **2.** moist, damp, or not dry: *wet ink or paint.* **3.** characterised by the presence or use of water or other liquid: *the wet of chemical analysis.* **4.** rainy; having a rainy climate. **5.** characterised by or favouring allowance of the manufacture and sale of alcoholic beverages. **6.** *Colloq.* weak; feeble; spiritless. **7. wet behind the ears,** *Colloq.* naive, lacking maturity, experience, or the like. *–n.* **8.** that which makes wet, as water or other liquid; moisture. **9.** a wet state, condition, or place. **10.** rain. **11.** *U.S.* one who favours allowance of the manufacture and sale of alcoholic beverages. **12. the wet,** the rainy season in central and northern Australia, from December to March. *–v.t.* **13.** to make wet. **14.** to make wet, as by urinating: *the child wet the bed.* **15. wet one's whistle,** *Colloq.* to take a drink. *–v.i.* **16.** to become wet. [ME *wett,* properly pp. of *wete,* OE *wǣtan* to wet; replacing ME *weet,* OE *wǣt,* c. Icel. *vātr*] – **wetly,** *adv.* – **wetness,** *n.* – **wetter,** *n.* – **wettish,** *adj.*

**weta** /ˈwɛtə/, *n.* one of several large, long-horned, somewhat scorpion-like but non-venomous insects of New Zealand; sawyer. [Maori]

**wet and dry,** *n.* fine emery paper used either with a lubricant to reduce clogging or in a dry state, for producing a good finish on metal or the like.

**wet-and-dry bulb hygrometer,** *n.* →**psychrometer.**

**wetback** /ˈwɛtbæk/, *n.* **1.** *N.Z.* a fuel stove with a hot-water heater behind it. **2.** *U.S.* an illegal Mexican immigrant.

**wetbike** /ˈwɛtbaɪk/, *n.* a motorised, steerable machine similar to a motorbike but with a large ski instead of wheels, and designed to be ridden over water.

**wet blanket** /wɛt ˈblæŋkət/, *n.* a person or thing that dampens ardour or has a discouraging or depressing effect.

**wet-blanket** /wɛt-ˈblæŋkət/, *v.t.* to dampen the ardour of.

**wet cell** /ˈwɛt sɛl/, *n.* an electric cell whose electrolyte is in liquid form and free to flow.

**wet dock** /ˈ– dɒk/, *n.* a basin into which vessels enter and in which the water is kept at one level by dock gates, irrespective of outside tides.

**wet dream** /– ˈdrim/, *n.* a sexually exciting dream, resulting in an emission while or just after being asleep.

**wet fly** /wɛt ˈflaɪ/, *n.* a fisherman's lure resembling a fly which floats below the water level. – **wet-fly** /ˈwɛt-flaɪ/, *adj.*

**wet ground** /– ˈgraʊnd/, *n.* ground that is constantly wet, so that special mining methods have to be used to remove the water while mining.

**wether** /ˈwɛðə/, *n.* a ram castrated when young. [ME and OE, c. G *Widder*; akin to L *vitulus* calf]

**wet-look** /ˈwɛt-lʊk/, *adj.* of or pertaining to the shiny finish given to some materials, esp. leather or P.V.C., or the articles made from such a material.

**wet nurse** /wɛt ˈnɜs/, *n.* a woman hired to suckle another's infant.

**wet-nurse** /ˈwɛt-nɜs/, *v.t.*, **-nursed, -nursing. 1.** to act as wet nurse to. **2.** *Colloq.* to cosset or pamper.

**wet pack** /ˈwɛt pæk/, *n.* a type of bath in which wet sheets are applied to the patient.

**wet place** /ˈ– pleɪs/, *n.* a workplace where clothing or footwear are likely to become saturated and for working in which employees are either supplied with protective clothing or are paid an extra rate.

**wet rot** /– ˈrɒt/, *n.* a state of decay in timber caused by alternate wetting and drying.

**wet sheep** /– ˈʃip/, *n.* **1.** a sheep the fleece of which is wet. **2.** a ewe rearing a lamb.

**wet sinking** /ˈ– sɪŋkɪŋ/, *n.* the act of sinking a shaft in wet ground.

**wet steam** /– ˈstim/, *n.* a mixture of steam and water resulting from the cooling of dry saturated steam.

**wetsuit** /ˈwɛtsut/, *n.* a set of tight-fitting upper and lower garments made of rubber worn by scuba divers, canoeists, etc., to retain body heat while immersed in water.

**wettex** /ˈwɛtɛks/, *n.* a small cloth of spongy, absorbent material used for cleaning. [Trademark]

**wetting agent** /ˈwɛtɪŋ eɪdʒənt/, *n.* any substance added to a liquid to increase its penetrating, spreading, or wetting properties.

**wet-weather clause** /wɛt-ˈwɛðə klɔz/, *n.* a clause in an industrial award or agreement providing for the payment of workers stood down because of wet weather and/or for the supplying of protective clothing or an allowance to buy it.

**we've** /wiv/; *unstressed* /wəv/, contraction of *we have.*

**wf,** *Print.* wrong font. Also, **w.f.**

**W Gmc,** West Germanic.

**wh.,** watt-hour.

**whack** /wæk/, *Colloq.* *–v.t.* **1.** to strike with a smart, resounding blow or blows. **2. whack down,** put down quickly: *whack it down here.* **3. whack in,** put in; insert. **4. whack up,** to divide up; share. *–v.i.* **5.** to strike a smart, resounding blow or blows. **6. whack off,** *Colloq.* to masturbate. *–n.* **7.** a smart, resounding blow: *a whack with his hand.* **8.** a trial or attempt: *to take a whack at a job.* **9.** a portion or share. [? imitative; ? var. of THWACK] – **whacker,** *n.*

**whacked** /wækt/, *adj. Colloq.* exhausted; defeated: *I am whacked from all that work.*

**whacking** /ˈwækɪŋ/, *adj. Colloq.* large.

**whacko** /wæˈkoʊ/, *interj.* (an expression denoting pleasure, delight, etc.) Also, **whacko-the-diddle-oh** /wækoʊ-ðə-ˈdɪdl-oʊ/, **whacko-the-did.**

**whacky** /ˈwæki/, *adj.*, **-ier, -iest.** →**wacky.**

**whale**[1] /weɪl/, *n.*, *pl.* **whales,** (*esp. collectively*) **whale,** *v.*, **whaled, whaling.** *–n.* **1.** *Zool.* any of the larger marine mammals of the order Cetacea, which includes the large sperm and whalebone whales, and the smaller dolphins and porpoises. All have fishlike bodies, modified foreflippers, and a horizontally flattened tail. **2.** *Colloq.* something extraordinarily big, great, or fine of its kind: *a whale of a lot, a whale of a time.* **3.** *Colloq.* a Murray cod. *–v.i.* **4.** to carry on the work of taking whales. **5.** *Colloq.* to fish for Murray cod. [ME; OE *hwæl,* c. MHG *wal,* Icel. *hvalr*]

**whale**[2] /weɪl/, *v.*, **whaled, whaling.** *Colloq.* *–v.t.* **1.** to whip, thrash, or beat soundly. *–v.i.* **2.** to throw oneself into something energetically (fol. by *into*). **3. a.** to beat up, bash. **b.** to attack verbally, berate (fol. by *into*). [orig. uncert.; ? var. of WALE]

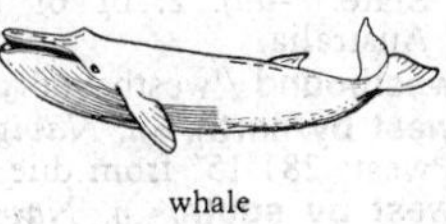
whale

**whaleboat** /ˈweɪlboʊt/, *n.* a type of very handy boat designed for quick turning and use in rough sea; formerly used in whaling, now mainly for sea rescue.

**whalebone** /ˈweɪlboʊn/, *n.* **1.** an elastic horny substance growing in place of teeth in the upper jaw of certain whales, and forming a series of thin, parallel plates on each side of the palate; baleen. **2.** a thin strip of this material, used for stiffening corsets.

**whaleman** /ˈweɪlmən/, *n.*, *pl.* **-men.** a man engaged in whaling.

**whaler** /ˈweɪlə/, *n.* **1.** a person or vessel engaged in whaling. **2.** one who fishes for Murray cod. **3.** →**Murrumbidgee whaler.**

**whaler shark** /ˈ– ʃak/, *n.* a large dangerous shark, *Galeolamna macrurus,* of eastern Australian waters.

**whale shark** /ˈweɪl ʃak/, *n.* a huge, plankton-feeding shark, *Rhincodon typus,* of tropical and warm temperate oceans, growing to about eighteen metres.

**whaling** /ˈweɪlɪŋ/, *n.* the work or industry of taking whales; whale fishing.

**whaling station** /ˈ– steɪʃən/, *n.* a centre, usu. a small port, devoted to the whaling industry.

**wham** /wæm/, *n.*, *v.*, **whammed, whamming,** *adv.* *–n.* **1.** a forceful stroke or blow. **2.** the sound of this. *–v.i., v.t.* **3.** to hit forcefully, esp. with a single loud noise. *–adv.* **4.** with force, suddenness, and often a loud noise.

**whammy** /ˈwæmi/, *n. Colloq.* a forceful influence, blow, spell, etc.: *the witch's whammy immobilised him.*

**whang** /wæŋ/, *n.* **1.** a resounding, clanging blow, as to a sheet of metal, etc. **2.** the noise of such a blow. *–v.t.* **3.** to strike with such a blow. [partly imitative, partly var. of ME *thwang* THONG]

**whangee** /wæŋ'i/, *n.* **1.** one of the species of the bamboo genus *Phyllostachys,* native to China. **2.** a cane made from the stem of one of these. [Chinese, alteration of *huang* hard bamboo]

**whare** /'wɒri/, *n. N.Z.* **1.** a Maori hut. **2.** any hut or make-shift home; a bach. [Maori]

**wharf** /wɔf/, *n., pl.* **wharves, wharfs,** *v. –n.* **1.** a structure built on the shore of, or projecting out into, a harbour, stream, etc., so that vessels may be moored alongside to load or unload or to lie at rest; a quay; a pier. **2.** *Obs.* a bank or shore. *–v.t.* **3.** to provide with a wharf or wharves. **4.** to place or store on a wharf. [ME; OE *hwearf* dam, akin to G *Werft* wharf] – **wharfless,** *adj.*

**wharfage** /'wɔfɪdʒ/, *n.* **1.** the use of a wharf. **2.** storage of goods at a wharf. **3.** the charge or payment for the use of a wharf. **4.** wharves collectively.

**wharfie** /'wɔfi/, *n. Colloq.* →**wharf labourer.** Also, **wharfy.**

**wharfinger** /'wɔfəndʒə/, *n.* one who owns, or has charge of, a wharf. [WHARFAGE + -ER[1], with n-infix as in *passenger,* etc.]

**wharf labourer** /'wɔf leɪbərə/, *n.* a labourer employed to load and unload vessels in port; lumper.

**wharve** /wɔv/, *n.* a wheel or round piece of wood on a spindle, serving as a flywheel or as a pulley. [ME *wherve,* OE *hweorfa*]

**wharves** /wɔvz/, *n.* **1.** plural of **wharf. 2.** plural of **wharve.**

**what** /wɒt/, *pron. (sing. and pl.), adv. –interrog. pron.* **1.** (asking for the specifying of some impersonal thing): *what is your name? what did he do?* **2.** (enquiring as to the nature, character, class, origin, etc., of a thing or person): *what is that animal?* **3.** (enquiring as to the worth, usefulness, force, or importance of something): *what is wealth without health?* **4.** (asking, often elliptically, for repetition or explanation of some word or words used, as by a previous speaker): *you need five what? you claim to be what?* **5.** how much?: *what did it cost?* **6.** *Brit. Colloq.* (used with a general or vague interrogative force, esp. at the end of a sentence): *a sort of anarchical fellow, what?* **7.** (used adjectively, before a noun (whether thing or person)): *what news? what men?* **8.** (often used interjectionally to express surprise, disbelief, indignation, etc.). **9.** (often used with intensive force in exclamatory phrases, preceding an indefinite article, if one is used): *what luck! what an idea!* **10. and what not** (Also, **and what have you**), and anything whatever; and anything else that there may be; et cetera. **11. so what?** (an exclamation of contempt, dismissal, or the like). **12. what for?** for what reason or purpose. **13. what of it?** what does it matter? (an exclamation of dismissal, etc.). *–rel. pron.* **14.** (as a compound relative) that which: *this is what he says, I will send what was promised.* **15.** the kind of thing or person that, or such: *the book is just what it professes to be, the old man is not what he was.* **16.** anything that, or whatever: *say what you please, come what may.* **17.** (in parenthetic clauses) something that: *but he went, and, what is more surprising, gained a hearing.* **18.** (as a simple relative) that, which, or who (now regarded as non-standard English). **19.** (used adjectively) that or any ... which; such ... as: *take what time and what assistants you need.* **20. know what it is to,** to have experience of. **21. what for,** *Colloq.* severe treatment, punishment, or violence: *he hit me, so I gave him what for.* **22. what it takes,** the necessary ability, personality, or the like: *he may look stupid, but he's got what it takes to hold the job down.* **23. what's what,** the true position. *–adv.* **24.** to what extent or degree, or how much?: *what does it matter?* **25.** (in certain expressions) in what or some manner or measure, or partly: *what with storms and sickness his return was delayed.* **26.** *Obs.* in what respect or how?: *what are men better than sheep?* **27.** *Obs.* for what reason or purpose or why? [ME; OE *hwæt,* c. D *wat,* G *was,* Icel. *hvat,* Goth. *hwa*]

**whata** /'wɒtə/, *n. N.Z.* a Maori storehouse on raised posts. [Maori]

**what-d'ye-call-it** /'wɒt-dʒə-kɔl-ət/, *n.* (a name used in place of one temporarily forgotten): *please pass me the what-d'ye-call it.* Also, **what-d'ye-m'-call-it** /'wɒt-dʒə-mə-kɔl-ət/.

**whatever** /wɒt'ɛvə/, *pron.* **1.** *indef. rel. pron.* **a.** anything that: *do whatever you like.* **b.** any amount or measure (of something) that: *whatever of time or energy may be mine.* **c.** no matter what: *do it, whatever happens.* **2.** *interrog. pron. Colloq.* what ever? what? (used emphatically): *whatever do you mean?* **3.** *Colloq.* anything or anyone: *bring friends, family –whatever. –adj.* **4.** any ... that: *whatever merit the work has.* **5.** no matter what: *whatever rebuffs he might receive.* **6.** being what or who it may be: *for whatever reason he is unwilling, any person whatever.* Also, *Poetic,* **whate'er.**

**whatnot** /'wɒtnɒt/, *n.* **1.** a stand with shelves for bric-a-brac, books, etc. **2.** *Colloq.* anything; no matter what; what you please: *a chronicler of whatnots.* **3.** an insignificant or unspecified article. **4.** (a name for a person, used esp. in contempt): *the examiner was such a whatnot.*

**what's** /wɒts/, contraction of *what is.*

**what's-his-name** /'wɒts-ɪz-neɪm/, *n.* (a name of a person substituted for one temporarily forgotten): *I met what's-his-name in the library.*

**whatsit** /'wɒtsət/, *n. Colloq.* →**what-d'ye-call-it.** [contraction of *what is it*]

**whatsoever** /wɒtsoʊ'ɛvə/, *pron., adj.* intensive form of **whatever:** *whatsoever it be, in any place whatsoever.* Also, *Poetic,* **whatsoe'er** /wɒtsoʊ'ɛə/.

**whau** /waʊ/, *n.* a shrub or tree, *Entelea arborescens,* of coastal and lowland forest in New Zealand. [Maori]

**wheal**[1] /wil/, *n.* a mine. [Cornish *huel*]

**wheal**[2] /wil/, *n.* →**weal**[2] [ME *whele,* akin to obs. *wheal* v., OE *hwelian* suppurate]

**wheat** /wit/, *n.* **1.** the grain of a widely distributed cereal grass, genus *Triticum,* esp. *T. aestivum* (*T. sativum*), used extensively in the form of flour for white bread, cakes, pastry, etc. **2.** the plant, which bears the edible grain in dense spikes that sometimes have awns (**bearded wheat**) and sometimes do not (**beardless wheat** or **bald wheat**). [ME *whete,* OE *hwǣte,* c. D *weit,* G *Weizen*] – **wheatless,** *adj.*

wheat

**wheat-belt** /'wit-bɛlt/, *n.* that part of the country, usu. a long, broad strip, in which conditions are ideal for growing wheat.

**wheat-cocky** /'wit-kɒki/, *n.* a wheat farmer on a small scale of operation.

**wheaten** /'witn/, *adj.* **1.** made of the grain or flour of wheat: *wheaten bread.* **2.** of or pertaining to wheat.

**wheat germ** /'wit dʒɜm/, *n.* that part of the wheat kernel which is removed when the wheat is milled.

**wheat grass** /'wit gras/, *n.* any of various native pasture grasses of the genus *Agropyron,* similar in appearance to wheat.

**wheatmeal** /'witmil/, *n.* meal (def. 2) made from wheat; ground wheat grains.

**Wheatstone bridge** /ˌwitstoʊn 'brɪdʒ/, *n.* an instrument designed for measuring the electrical resistance of a circuit or a circuit component. Also, **Wheatstone's bridge.** [named after Sir Charles *Wheatstone,* 1802-75, English physicist and inventor]

**wheatworm** /'witwɜm/, *n.* a small nematode worm, *Anguina tritici,* causing disease in wheat.

**whee** /wi/, *interj.* an expression of delight or thrill, esp. at fast movement, as on a slippery-dip, or merry-go-round.

**wheedle** /'widl/, *v.,* **-dled, -dling.** *–v.t.* **1.** to endeavour to influence (a person) by smooth, flattering, or beguiling words. **2.** to get by artful persuasions: *wheedling my money from me. –v.i.* **3.** to use beguiling or artful persuasions. [orig. obscure. Cf. OE *wǣdlian* beg] – **wheedler,** *n.* – **wheedlingly,** *adv.*

**wheel** /wil/, *n.* **1.** a circular frame or solid disc arranged to turn on an axis, as in vehicles, machinery, etc. **2.** any instrument, machine, apparatus, etc., shaped like this, or having such a frame or disc as an essential feature: *a potter's wheel.* **3.** a circular frame with or without projecting handles and an axle connecting with the rudder, for steering a ship. **4.** an old instrument of torture in the form of a circular frame on which the victim was stretched while his limbs were broken with an iron bar. **5.** anything resembling or suggesting a wheel (in first sense) in shape, movement, etc., as a decoration, or the trochal disc of a rotifer. **6.** a circular firework which revolves while burning. **7.** Also, **wheel of Fortune.** a rotating instrument which Fortune is represented as turning in order to bring about changes or reverses in human affairs. **8.** *Poetry.* a set of rhyming lines, usu. four, forming the conclusion of a stanza of Middle English alliterative poetry. **9.** (*pl.*) moving, propelling, or animating agencies: *the wheels of trade or of thought.* **10.** (*pl.*) *Colloq.* a motor vehicle. **11.** a wheeling or circular movement: *merrily whirled the wheels of the dizzying dances.* **12.** *Mil.* a change of direction. **13.** (formerly) a movement of troops, ships, etc., drawn up in line, as if turning on a pivot. **14.** *Colloq.* a person of considerable importance or influence: *a big wheel.* **15. at the wheel, a.** at the steering wheel of a motor car, ship, etc. **b.** in command or control. **16. wheels within wheels,** a complicated situation in which many different factors are involved. **17. put one's shoulder to the wheel,** to exert oneself greatly, as in a combined effort to achieve some end. *–v.t.* **18.** to cause to turn, rotate, or revolve, as on an axis. **19.** to perform in a circular or curving direction or to cause (troops, etc.) to change direction. **20.** to move, roll, or convey on wheels, castors, etc.: *the maid wheels in the trolley.* **21.** to provide (a vehicle, etc.) with a wheel or wheels. *–v.i.* **22.** to turn on or as on an axis or about a centre; rotate, revolve. **23.** *Mil.* to change direction while marching: *to wheel left.* **24.** to move in a circular or curving course: *pigeons wheeling above.* **25.** to turn or change in procedure or opinion (oft. fol. by *about* or *round*). **26.** to roll along on, or as on, wheels; to travel along smoothly. **27. wheel and deal,** to act as a wheeler-dealer. [ME; OE *hwēol, hweogol,* c. D *wiel,* Icel. *hjōl*] – **wheeled,** *adj.*

**wheel and axle,** *n.* a device (one of the so-called simple machines) consisting, in its typical form, of a cylindrical drum to which a wheel concentric with the drum is firmly fastened. Ropes are so applied that as one unwinds from the wheel the other is wound on to the drum.

**wheel animalcule** /ˌwil ænəˈmælkjul/, *n.* →**rotifer.**

**wheelbarrow** /ˈwilbæroʊ/, *n.* **1.** a frame or box for conveying a load, usu. supported at one end by a wheel and at the other by two vertical legs above which are two horizontal shafts used in lifting the legs from the ground when the vehicle is pushed or pulled. **2.** a similar vehicle with more than one wheel. *–v.t.* **3.** to move or convey in a wheelbarrow.

wheelbarrow

**wheelbarrow race** /ˈ– reɪs/, *n.* a race in which the contestants walk on their hands, their legs being supported by a person at the rear.

**wheelbase** /ˈwilbeɪs/, *n.* the distance between the front and rear axles of a vehicle.

**wheelchair** /ˈwiltʃɛə/, *n.* a chair mounted on large wheels, and used by invalids.

**wheeler** /ˈwilə/, *n.* **1.** one who or that which wheels. **2.** something provided with a wheel or wheels: *a side-wheeler, a stern-wheeler.* **3.** that one of a team of horses which is harnessed nearest the front wheels of a vehicle.

**wheeler-dealer** /wilə-ˈdilə/, *n. Colloq.* **1.** *Chiefly U.S.* one in a position of power who controls and directs the actions of others. **2.** one who actively pursues his own advancement by moving constantly from one profitable business transaction to another. [shaped by euphony, from *wheel and deal* (WHEEL def. 27)]

**wheelhop** /ˈwilhɒp/, *n.* an uncontrolled sideways bounce of the wheel of a motor vehicle, usu. when cornering.

**wheel-horse** /ˈwil-hɔs/, *n.* **1.** →**wheeler** (def. 3). **2.** *U.S. Colloq.* →**workhorse** (def. 2).

**wheelhouse** /ˈwilhaʊs/, *n.* →**pilot house.**

**wheelie** /ˈwili/, *n. Colloq.* **1.** a violent, usu. noisy skidding of the driving wheels of a motor car while accelerating as around a corner or from a standing start: *to do a wheelie.* **2.** a manoeuvre performed on a bicycle, motorbike, etc., in which the rider maintains his balance while lifting the front wheel off the ground.

**wheel-lock** /ˈwil-lɒk/, *n.* an old type of gunlock in which sparks are produced by the friction of a small steel wheel against a piece of iron pyrites.

**wheelman** /ˈwilmən/, *n., pl.* **-men.** **1.** *U.S.* Also, **wheelsman.** →**helmsman.** **2.** *Colloq.* the driver of a getaway car. **3.** a professional cyclist. Also, **wheelsman.**

**wheel of life,** *n.* →**zoetrope.**

**wheel ore** /ˈwil ɔ/, *n.* →**bournonite.**

**wheel stand** /ˈwil stænd/, *n.* (of motorcycles) a movement in which the front wheel leaves the ground while accelerating.

**wheelwork** /ˈwilwɜk/, *n.* a train of gears.

**wheelwright** /ˈwilraɪt/, *n.* one whose trade it is to make or repair wheels, wheeled carriages, etc.

**wheeze** /wiz/, *v.,* **wheezed, wheezing,** *n.* *–v.i.* **1.** to breathe with difficulty and with a whistling sound: *wheezing with asthma.* *–v.t.* **2.** to utter such a sound. *–n.* **3.** a wheezing breath or sound. **4.** a theatrical gag. **5.** *Brit. Colloq.* a trick, dodge, or idea, esp. a cunning or artful one. [ME *whese,* probably from Scand.; cf. Icel. *hvæsa* hiss] – **wheezer,** *n.* – **wheezingly,** *adv.*

**wheezy** /ˈwizi/, *adj.,* **-zier, -ziest.** affected with or characterised by wheezing. – **wheezily,** *adv.* – **wheeziness,** *n.*

**whelk**[1] /wɛlk/, *n.* any of various large spiral-shelled marine gastropods of the family Buccinidae, as the giant whelk *Verconella maxima* found along the continental shelf from South Australia to New South Wales. [ME *welke,* OE *weoloc;* orig. uncert.]

whelk[1]

**whelk**[2] /wɛlk/, *n.* a pimple or pustule. [ME *whelke,* OE *hwylca.* See WHEAL[2]]

**whelm** /wɛlm/, *v.t. Archaic.* **1.** to submerge; engulf. **2.** to overcome utterly, or overwhelm: *sorrow whelmed him.* [ME, apparently b. obs. *whelve* (OE *gehwelfan* bend over) and *helm* (OE *helmian* cover)]

**whelp** /wɛlp/, *n.* **1.** the young of the dog, or of the wolf, bear, lion, tiger, seal, etc. **2.** (*derog.*) a youth. **3.** *Mach.* **a.** any of a series of longitudinal projections or ridges of iron or the like on the barrel of a capstan, windlass, etc. **b.** one of the teeth of a sprocket wheel. *–v.t., v.i.* **4.** (of a bitch, lioness, etc.) to bring forth (young). [ME; OE *hwelp,* c. G *Welf*]

**when** /wɛn/, *adv.* **1.** at what time: *when are you coming?* **2. say when,** to tell one when to stop, esp. in pouring a drink. *–conj.* **3.** at what time: *to know when to be silent.* **4.** at the time that: *when we were young, when the noise stopped.* **5.** at any time, or whenever: *he is impatient when he is kept waiting.* **6.** *Obsolesc.* upon or after which; and then. **7.** while on the contrary, or whereas: *you cover up the wound when you should clean it first.* *–pron.* **8.** what time: *since when have you known this?* **9.** which time: *they left on Monday, since when we have heard nothing.* *–n.* **10.** the time of anything: *the when and the where of an act.* [ME *when(ne),* OE *hwenne,* c. G *wann* when, *wenn* if, Goth. *hwan* when, how; akin to WHO, WHAT]

**whenas** /wɛnˈæz/, *conj. Archaic.* when; whereas.

**whence** /wɛns/, *adv. Archaic.* **1.** from what place?: *whence comest thou?* **2.** from what source, origin or cause?: *whence hath he wisdom?* *–conj.* **3.** from what place, source, cause, etc.: *he told whence he came.* [ME *whennes,* from *whenne* (OE *hwanone* whence) + *-s,* adv. gen. suffix]

**whencesoever** /wɛnsoʊˈɛvə/, *adv., conj. Archaic.* from whatsoever place, source, or cause.

**whenever** /wɛnˈɛvə/, *conj.* **1.** at whatever time; at any time when: *come whenever you like.* *–adv.* **2.** *Colloq.* when ever? when? (used emphatically): *whenever did he say that?* Also, *Poetic,* **whene'er.**

**whensoever** /wɛnsoʊˈɛvə/, *adv., conj. Archaic.* at whatsoever time.

**where** /wɛə/, *adv.* **1.** in or at what place?: *where is he?, where do you live?* **2.** in what position or circumstances?: *where do you stand on this question? without money where are you?* **3.** in what particular, respect, way, etc.?: *where does this affect us?* **4.** to what place, point, or end, or whither?: *where are you going?* **5.** from what source, or whence: *where did you get such a notion?* *–conj.* **6.** in or at what place, part, point, etc.: *find where he is, or where the trouble is.* **7.** in or at the place, part, point, etc., in or at which: *the book is where you left it.* **8.** in a position, case, etc., in which: *where ignorance is bliss, 'tis folly to be wise.* **9.** in any place, position, case, etc., in which, or wherever: *use the lotion where pain is felt.* **10.** to what or whatever place, or to the or any place to which: *go where you will, I will go where you go.* **11.** in or at which place; and there: *they came to the town, where they lodged for the night.* *–pron.* **12.** what place: *from where, where from?* **13.** the place in which: *this is where we live.* *–conj. Colloq.* **14.** that: *I read where they are going to increase taxes.* [ME *wher,* OE *hwǣr,* c. D *waar;* akin to Icel. *hvar,* Goth. *hwar*]

**where-,** a word element meaning 'what' or 'which'. [special use of WHERE]

**-where,** suffixal use of 'where', as in *somewhere.*

**whereabouts** /ˈwɛərəbaʊts/, *interrogatively* /wɛərəˈbaʊts/, *adv.* **1.** Also, *Rare,* **whereabout.** about where? where? *–conj.* **2.** near or in what place: *seeing whereabouts in the world we were.* *–n.pl.* **3.** (sometimes construed as sing.) the place where a person or thing is; the locality of a person or thing: *no clue as to his whereabouts.*

**whereas** /wɛərˈæz/, *conj., n., pl.* **whereases.** *–conj.* **1.** while on the contrary: *one came, whereas the others didn't.* **2.** it being the case that, or considering that (esp. used in formal preambles). *–n.* **3.** a statement having 'whereas' as the first word: *to read the whereases in the will.*

**whereat** /wɛərˈæt/, *adv., conj.* at what or at which.

**whereby** /wɛəˈbaɪ/, *adv., conj.* **1.** by what or by which. **2.** *Obs.* by what? how?

**where'er** /wɛərˈɛə/, *conj., adv. Poetic.* →**wherever.**

**wherefore** /ˈwɛəfɔ/, *adv.* **1.** for what? why? *–conj.* **2.** for what or which cause or reason. *–n.* **3.** the cause or reason. [ME; from WHERE + *fore* because of, FOR]

**wherefrom** /wɛəˈfrɒm/, *adv., conj. Archaic.* from which; whence.

**wherein** /wɛərˈɪn/, *adv., conj.* in what or in which.

**whereinto** /wɛərˈɪntu/, *adv., conj.* into what or into which.

**whereof** /wɛərˈɒv/, *adv., conj.* of what, which or whom.

**whereon** /wɛərˈɒn/, *adv., conj.* on what or on which.

**wheresoever** /wɛəsoʊˈɛvə/, *adv., conj.* in or to whatsoever place; wherever. Also, *Poetic,* **wheresoe'er** /wɛəsoʊˈɛə/.

**whereto** /wɛəˈtu/, *adv., conj.* to what or to which. Also, *Archaic,* **whereunto** /wɛərˈʌntu/.

**whereupon** /wɛərəˈpɒn/, *adv.* **1.** *Archaic.* upon what? whereon? *–conj.* **2.** at or after which. **3.** upon what or upon which.

**wherever** /wɛərˈɛvə/, *conj.* **1.** in, at, or to whatever place. **2.** in any case or condition: *wherever it is heard of.* *–adv.* **3.** *Colloq.* where ever? where? (used emphatically): *wherever did you find that?* Also, *Poetic,* **where'er.**

**wherewith** /wɛəˈwɪð, -ˈwɪθ/, *adv., conj.* **1.** with what? **2.** with what or which. **3.** (by ellipsis) that with which: *I shall have wherewith to answer him.*

**wherewithal** /ˈwɛəwɪðɔl, -θɔl/, *n.* that wherewith to do something; means or supplies for the purpose or need, esp. money: *the wherewithal to pay my rent.*

**wherry** /ˈwɛri/, *n., pl.* **-ries,** *v.,* **-ried, -rying.** *–n.* **1.** any of certain larger boats (fishing vessels, barges, etc.) used locally in Britain. **2.** a kind of light rowing boat used chiefly in England for carrying passengers and goods on rivers. **3.** *U.S.* →**skiff.** *–v.t., v.i.* **4.** to use, or transport in, a wherry. [late ME; orig. uncert.] – **wherryman,** *n.*

**whet** /wɛt/, *v.,* **whetted, whetting,** *n.* *–v.t.* **1.** to sharpen (a knife, tool, etc.) by grinding or friction. **2.** to make keen or eager: *to whet the appetite or the curiosity.* *–n.* **3.** the act of whetting. **4.** something that whets; an appetiser. [ME *whette,* OE *hwettan,* c. G *wetzen*] – **whetter,** *n.*

**whether** /ˈwɛðə/, *conj.* **1.** a word introducing, in dependent clauses or the like, the first of two or more alternatives, and sometimes repeated before the second or later alternative (used in correlation with *or*): *it matters little whether we go or whether we stay.* **2.** used to introduce a single alternative (the other being implied or understood), and hence some clause or element not involving alternatives: *see whether he has come (or not), I doubt whether we can do any better.* **3.** **whether or no,** under whatever circumstances: *he threatens to go, whether or no.* *–pron. Archaic.* **4.** which (of two)? **5.** a word introducing a question presenting alternatives (usu. with the correlative *or*). [ME; OE *hwether, hwæther,* c. Icel. *hvadharr,* Goth. *hwathar*]

**whetstone** /ˈwɛtstoʊn/, *n.* **1.** a stone for sharpening cutlery or tools by friction. **2.** anything that sharpens: *a whetstone for dull wits.*

**whew** /hwju/, *interj.* **1.** (a whistling exclamation or sound expressing astonishment, dismay, etc.) *–n.* **2.** an utterance of 'whew'.

**whey** /weɪ/, *n.* milk serum, separating as a watery liquid from the curd after coagulation, as in cheese-making. [ME *wheye,* OE *hwæg,* c. D and LG *wei*] – **wheyish, wheylike,** *adj.*

**wheyey** /ˈweɪi/, *adj.* of, like, or containing whey.

**wheyface** /ˈweɪfeɪs/, *n.* a face or a person that is pallid, as from fear. – **wheyfaced,** *adj.*

**whf,** wharf.

**which** /wɪtʃ/, *interrog. pron.* **1.** what one (of a certain number mentioned or implied)?: *which of these, or which, do you want?* *–rel. pron.* **2.** as a simple relative with antecedent (a thing, body of persons, formerly a person) expressed: **a.** in clauses conveying an additional idea: *I read the book, which was short; five sons, of which he was the eldest.* **b.** used in clauses defining or restricting the antecedent, regularly after that (*that which must be will be*), or after a preposition (*the horse on which I rode*), or otherwise in place of the restrictive that (*the book which I gave you*). **c.** used adjectivally: *be careful which way you turn.* **3.** (as a compound relative representing both antecedent and consequent (either thing or person), what particular one, or the or any one that: *choose which you like.* **4.** (in parenthetic clauses) a thing that: *and, which is worse, all you have done is wrong.* *–adj.* **5.** what one of (a certain number mentioned or implied): *which book do you want?* **6.** no matter what; any that: *go which way you please, you'll end up here.* **7.** being previously mentioned: *it stormed all day, during which time the ship broke up.* [ME; OE *hwilc,* c. D *welk,* G *welch,* Goth. *hwileiks,* lit., of what form, like whom or what. See WHO, WHAT, LIKE[1]]

**whichever** /wɪtʃˈɛvə/, *pron.* **1.** any one (of those in question) that: *take whichever you like.* **2.** no matter which: *whichever you choose, the others will be offended.* *–adj.* **3.** no matter which: *whichever day, whichever person.*

**whichsoever** /wɪtʃsoʊˈɛvə/, *pron.* intensive form of **whichever.**

**whicker** /ˈwɪkə/, *v.i.* (of a horse) to neigh or whinny. [OE **hwican* (in *hwicung* squeaking) + -ER[6], akin to G *wiehern* neigh]

**whidah** /ˈwɪdə/, *n.* →**whydah.** Also, **whidah-bird.**

**whiff** /wɪf/, *n.* **1.** a slight blast or puff of wind or air: *a whiff of fresh air.* **2.** a puff or waft of scent or smell: *a whiff of honeysuckle.* **3.** a puff of vapour, smoke, etc. **4.** a single inhalation or exhalation of air, tobacco smoke, or the like. **5.** a slight outburst: *a little whiff of temper.* **6.** a light clinker boat with outriggers, for one sculler. *–v.i.* **7.** to blow or come in whiffs or puffs, as wind, smoke, etc. **8.** to inhale or exhale whiffs, as in smoking tobacco. **9.** to have an unpleasant smell. *–v.t.* **10.** to blow or drive with a whiff or puff, as the wind. **11.** to inhale or exhale (air, tobacco smoke, etc.) in whiffs. **12.** to smoke (a pipe, cigar, etc.). [? b. WHIP and PUFF] – **whiffer,** *n.*

**whiffle** /ˈwɪfəl/, *v.,* **-fled, -fling.** *–v.i.* **1.** to blow in light or shifting gusts or puffs, as the wind; veer irregularly (about). **2.** to shift about; vacillate. *–v.t.* **3.** to blow with light, shifting gusts. [frequentative of WHIFF, *v.*] – **whiffler,** *n.*

**whiffletree** /ˈwɪfəlˌtri/, *n.* →**whippletree.**

**whiffy** /ˈwɪfi/, *adj. Colloq.* smelly.

**while** /waɪl/, *n., conj., v.,* **whiled, whiling.** *–n.* **1.** a space of time: *a long while, a while ago.* **2.** **once in a while,** occasionally. **3.** **the while,** during this time. **4.** **worth one's while,**

worth time, pains, or expense. *–conj.* Also, **whilst. 5.** during or in the time that. **6.** throughout the time that, or as long as. **7.** at the same time that (implying opposition or contrast): *while he appreciated the honour, he could not accept the position.* *–v.t.* **8.** to cause (time) to pass, esp. in some easy or pleasant manner (usu. fol. by *away*). [ME; OE *hwīl,* c. D *wijl,* G *Weile,* Goth. *hweila*]

**whiles** /waɪlz/, *adv.* **1.** *Archaic.* at times. **2.** *Obs.* in the meantime. *–conj.* **3.** *Archaic.* while.

**whilom** /ˈwaɪləm/, *Archaic.* *–adv.* **1.** at one time; formerly. *–adj.* **2.** former. [ME; OE *hwīlum* at times, dat. pl. of *hwīl* WHILE, *n.*]

**whilst** /waɪlst/, *conj.* while. [earlier *whilest,* from WHILES + inorganic *-t,* as in AMONGST]

**whim** /wɪm/, *n.* **1.** an odd or fanciful notion; a freakish or capricious fancy or desire. **2.** capricious humour: *to be swayed by whim.* **3.** *Mining.* a large capstan or vertical drum turned by horse-power for raising coal, water, etc., from a mine. [probably from Scand.; cf. Icel. *hvim* unsteady look. In some senses short for *whim-wham,* itself from *whim,* modelled on *trim-tram* gewgaw]

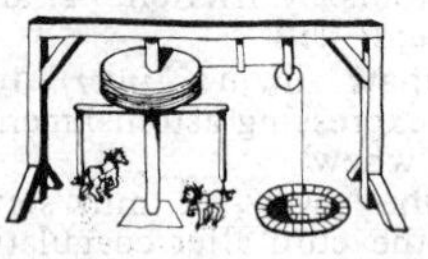
whim (def. 3)

**whimbrel** /ˈwɪmbrəl/, *n.* either of two medium-sized birds of the genus *Numenius,* as: **a.** *Numenius phaeopus,* a light brown shorebird with a long down-curved bill, which breeds in the far north of America, Asia and Europe, and migrates as far as South America, Australasia and Africa. **b. little whimbrel,** *Numenius minutus,* a dark brown bird with a slightly down-curved bill, found on coastal black soil plains and open dry country, which breeds in the Arctic tundra.

**whimper** /ˈwɪmpə/, *v.i.* **1.** to cry with low, plaintive, broken sounds, as a child, a dog, etc. *–v.t.* **2.** to utter in a whimper. *–n.* **3.** a whimpering cry or sound. [frequentative of *whimp* (now Brit. d.) whine, orig. uncert.; cf. Icel. *hvimpinn* shy (said of horse)] **– whimperer,** *n.* **– whimperingly,** *adv.*

**whimsey** /ˈwɪmzi/, *n., pl.* **-seys.** →**whimsy.**

**whimsical** /ˈwɪmzɪkəl/, *adj.* **1.** given to whimsies or odd notions. **2.** of the nature of or proceeding from a whimsy, as thoughts, actions, etc. **3.** of an odd, quaint, or comical kind. **– whimsically,** *adv.* **– whimsicalness,** *n.*

**whimsicality** /wɪmzəˈkæləti/, *n., pl.* **-ties. 1.** whimsical character. **2.** a whimsical notion, speech, or act.

**whimsy** /ˈwɪmzi/, *n., pl.* **-sies. 1.** an odd or fanciful notion. **2.** anything odd or fanciful; a product of playful fancy, as a literary trifle. Also, **whimsey.**

**whim-wham** /ˈwɪm-wæm/, *n.* any odd or fanciful object or thing; a gimcrack.

**whin**[1] /wɪn/, *n.* gorse, furze. [late ME *whynne,* apparently from Scand.; cf. Icel. *hvingras* bent grass]

**whin**[2] /wɪn/, *n.* **1.** →**whinstone. 2.** any of various other dark-coloured rocks. [orig. uncert.]

**whine** /waɪn/, *v.,* **whined, whining,** *n.* *–v.i.* **1.** to utter a nasal, complaining cry or sound, as from uneasiness, discontent, peevishness, etc. **2.** to complain in a feeble, plaintive way. **3.** to emit a high-pitched, monotonous sound, as of machinery, etc. *–v.t.* **4.** to utter with a whine. *–n.* **5.** a whining utterance, sound, or tone. **6.** a feeble, peevish complaint. [ME; OE *hwīnan,* c. Icel. *hvina* whiz] **– whiner,** *n.* **– whiningly,** *adv.* **– whiny,** *adj.*

**whinge** /wɪndʒ/, *v.,* **whinged, whingeing,** *n.* *–v.i.* to complain; whine. **– whinger,** *n.*

**whingeing Pom** /ˌwɪndʒɪŋ ˈpɒm/, *n.* (*derog.*) an Englishman thought to be always criticising and complaining about life in Australia.

**whinny** /ˈwɪni/, *v.,* **-nied, -nying,** *n., pl.* **-nies.** *–v.i.* **1.** (of a horse) to utter its characteristic cry; neigh. *–v.t.* **2.** to express by whinnying. *–n.* **3.** a neigh. [alteration of WHINE in (now obs.) sense 'whinny']

**whinstone** /ˈwɪnstoʊn/, *n.* any of the dark-coloured fine-grained rocks such as dolerite and basalt trap.

**whip** /wɪp/, *v.,* **whipped** or **whipt, whipping,** *n.* *–v.t.* **1.** to strike with quick, repeated strokes of something slender and flexible; lash. **2.** to beat with a whip or the like, esp. by way of punishment or chastisement; flog; thrash. **3.** to lash or castigate with words. **4.** to drive (*on, out, in,* etc.) by strokes or lashes. **5.** to spin (a top) by whipping. **6.** to bring (*in, into line, together,* etc.) as a party whip. **7.** *Chiefly U.S. Colloq.* to beat, outdo, or defeat, as in a contest. **8.** *Naut.* to hoist or purchase by means of a whip. **9.** to move quickly and suddenly; pull, jerk, snatch, seize, put, etc., with a sudden movement (fol. by *away, out, up, into,* etc.). **10.** to take, steal (fol. by *off*). **11.** to fish (a stream, etc.) with a rod and line. **12.** to overlay or cover (cord, etc.) with cord, thread or the like wound about it. **13.** to wind (cord, twine, thread, etc.) about something. **14.** to gather, or form into pleats by overcasting the turned edge with small stitches and then drawing up the thread. **15. whip (flog) the cat,** to reproach oneself. **16.** to beat (eggs, cream, etc.) to a froth with a whisk, fork, or other implement in order to incorporate air and produce expansion. **17. whip up, a.** to create quickly: *I whipped up a meal when I heard he was coming.* **b.** to arouse to fury, intense excitement, etc.: *his speech soon whipped up the crowd.* *–v.i.* **18.** to move or go quickly and suddenly (*away, off, out, in,* etc.); dart; whisk. **19.** to beat or lash about, as a pennant in the wind. **20.** to fish with a rod and line. **21. whip in,** *Hunting.* to prevent from wandering, as hounds. **22. whip round,** to make a collection of money. *–n.* **23.** an instrument to strike with, as in driving animals or in punishing, typically consisting of a lash or other flexible part with a more rigid handle. **24.** a whipping or lashing strike or motion. **25.** a windmill vane. **26.** one who handles a whip; a driver of horses, a coach, etc. **27.** one who has charge of the hounds in hunting. **28.** a party manager in a legislative body, who supplies information to members about the government business, secures their attendance for voting, supplies lists of members to serve on committees and keeps the leaders informed as to the trend of party opinion. **29. follow a whip,** *Parl. Proc.* to vote in accordance with a party decision as conveyed by the parliamentary whip. **30.** a contrivance for hoisting, consisting essentially of a rope and pulley. **31. crack the whip,** *Colloq.* to urge to greater effort. **32. fair crack of the whip!** *Colloq.* (an exhortation to be fair). **33.** a wooden percussion instrument imitating the crack of a whip. **34.** a dish made of cream or eggwhites whipped to a froth with flavouring, etc., often with fruit pulp or the like: *prune whip.* **35. whips of,** *Colloq.* great quantities of. [ME *whippe,* earlier *(h)wippen,* c. D *wippen* wing, oscillate] **– whipper,** *n.*

whip

**whipbird** /ˈwɪpbɜd/, *n.* any of a number of birds the terminal note of whose call resembles the crack of a whip, esp. the **eastern whipbird,** *Psophodes olivaceus,* of coastal and mountain forests and gullies from northern Queensland to Victoria; coachman. Also, **coachman's whipbird, coach-whip bird.**

**whipcord** /ˈwɪpkɔd/, *n.* **1.** a worsted fabric with a diagonally ribbed surface. **2.** a kind of strong, hard-twisted cord, sometimes used for the lashes of whips.

**whip graft** /ˈwɪp graft/, *n.* a graft prepared by cutting both the scion and the stock in a sloping direction and inserting a tongue in the scion into a slit in the stock. Also, **tongue graft, whip grafting, whip graftage.**

**whip hand** /ˈ– hænd/, *n.* **1.** the hand that holds the whip, in driving. **2.** the position of control, or the advantage.

**whiplash** /ˈwɪplæʃ/, *n.* **1.** the lash of a whip. **2.** an injury to the spine, usu. in the cervical area, caused by sudden movement forwards or backwards, as in a motor accident.

**whipper-in** /wɪpər-ˈɪn/, *n., pl.* **whippers-in.** one who whips in hounds.

**whippersnapper** /ˈwɪpəsnæpə/, *n.* a petty or insignificant person, often young, who affects importance.

**whippet** /ˈwɪpət/, *n.* a dog of an English breed, probably a cross between the greyhound and the terrier, used esp. in rabbit coursing and racing. [n. use of obs. v., to frisk, orig. the phrase *whip it* move briskly]

**whipping** /ˈwɪpɪŋ/, *n.* **1.** a beating administered with a whip or the like, as for punishment; a flogging. **2.** an arrangement of cord, twine, or the like, whipped or wound about a thing. **3.** *Sewing.* →**overcasting.**

whippet

**whipping boy** /ˈ– bɔɪ/, *n.* **1.** →**scapegoat** (def. 1). **2.** (formerly) a boy educated with and taking punishment in place of a young prince or nobleman.

**whipping post** /ˈ– poust/, *n.* (formerly) a post to which persons were fastened to undergo whipping as a legal penalty.

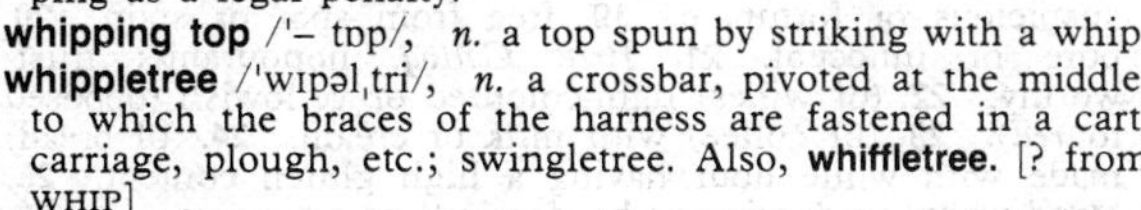

**whipping top** /ˈ– tɒp/, *n.* a top spun by striking with a whip.

**whippletree** /ˈwɪpəlˌtri/, *n.* a crossbar, pivoted at the middle, to which the braces of the harness are fastened in a cart, carriage, plough, etc.; swingletree. Also, **whiffletree.** [? from WHIP]

**whippoorwill** /ˈwɪpəwɪl/, *n.* a nocturnal North American goatsucker (bird), *Caprimulgus vociferus,* having a variegated plumage of grey, black, white, and tawny. [imitative, from its cry]

**whippy** /ˈwɪpi/, *n.* **1.** *Colloq.* a wallet. **2.** (in games) the goal; finishing post, base. **3. all in, the whippy's taken,** (an expression used to signal the end of a round in certain games of hide-and-seek). *–adj.* **4.** *Colloq.* speedy, nimble. **5.** of or pertaining to a shaft, branch, etc., which is flexible as of a riding crop, certain golf clubs, etc.

**whip-round** /wɪp-ˈraund/, *n. Colloq.* an impromptu collection of money.

**whips** /wɪps/, *n.pl. Colloq.* plenty; lots (fol. by *of*): *whips of money.* [cf. LASHING[1] (def. 4)]

**whipsaw** /ˈwɪpsɔ/, *n.* **1.** any flexible saw, as a bandsaw. *–v.t.* **2.** to cut with a whipsaw. **3.** *U.S.* to win two bets from (a person) at one turn or play, as in faro. **4.** *U.S.* to defeat or worst in two ways at once.

**whip scorpion** /wɪp ˈskɔpiən/, *n.* any of various arachnids of the order Uropygi, resembling the true scorpions, but having (in the typical members) an abdomen ending in a slender whiplike part.

**whip snake** /ˈ– sneɪk/, *n.* any of various slender snakes in which the scaling of the tail resembles a braided whip, as the **Yellow-faced whip snake,** *Demansia psammophis,* an olive brown snake with a yellow border round the eye, widely distributed throughout Australia.

**whipstall** /ˈwɪpstɔl/, *n. Aeron.* **1.** a stall during a vertical climb in which there is often a momentary slide of the aircraft tail first, the nose then pitching violently forward and down in a whiplike movement. *–v.t.* **2.** to cause (an aircraft) to perform a whipstall. *–v.i.* **3.** to perform a whipstall.

**whipstick** /ˈwɪpstɪk/, *n.* a slender woody plant stem, usu. found where numerous upright stems grow close together, as whipstick mulga and whipstick mallee.

**whipstitch** /ˈwɪpstɪtʃ/, *v.t.* **1.** to sew with stitches passing over an edge, in joining, finishing, or gathering. *–n.* **2.** one such stitch. **3.** *U.S. Colloq.* an instant.

**whipstock** /ˈwɪpstɒk/, *n.* the handle of a whip.

**whiptail wallaby** /ˌwɪpteɪl ˈwɒləbi/, *n.* a wallaby, *Macropus parryi,* with long slender tail and distinctive face markings, found in eastern New South Wales and Queensland. Also, **pretty-face wallaby.**

**whipworm** /ˈwɪpwɜm/, *n.* any of certain parasitic nematode worms of the genus *Trichuris,* having a long, slender anterior end, giving a whiplike shape.

**whir** /wɜ/, *v.i., v.t., n.* →**whirr.**

**whirl** /wɜl/, *v.i.* **1.** to turn round, spin, or rotate rapidly. **2.** to turn about or aside quickly. **3.** to move, travel, or be carried rapidly along on wheels or otherwise. **4.** to have the sensation of turning round rapidly. *–v.t.* **5.** to cause to turn round, spin, or rotate rapidly. **6.** to send, drive, or carry in a circular or curving course. **7.** to drive, send, or carry along with great or dizzying rapidity. **8.** *Obs.* to hurl. *–n.* **9.** the act of whirling; rapid rotation or gyration. **10.** a whirling movement; a quick turn or swing. **11.** a short drive, run, walk, or the like, or a spin. **12.** something that whirls; a whirling current or mass. **13.** a rapid round of events, affairs, etc. **14.** a state marked by a dizzying succession or mingling of feelings, thoughts, etc. **15. give it a whirl,** *Colloq.* to make an attempt. [ME *whirle,* from Scand.; cf. Icel. *hvirfla*] – **whirler,** *n.*

**whirlabout** /ˈwɜləbaut/, *n.* **1.** a whirling about. **2.** a whirligig. *–adj.* **3.** whirling about. Also, **whirlaround.**

**whirligig** /ˈwɜligɪg/, *n.* **1.** something that whirls, revolves, or goes round; a revolving agency or course. **2.** a continuous round or succession. **3.** a giddy or flighty person. **4.** a merry-go-round. **5.** a toy for whirling or spinning, as a top. [from WHIRL. See GIG[1]]

**whirligig beetle** /– ˈbitl/, *n.* any of the aquatic beetles of the family Gyrinidae, commonly seen circling rapidly about in large numbers on the surface of the water.

**whirlpool** /ˈwɜlpul/, *n.* a whirling eddy or current, as in a river or the sea, produced by irregularity in the channel or stream banks, by the meeting of opposing currents, by the interaction of winds and tides, etc.; a vortex of water.

**whirlwind** /ˈwɜlwɪnd/, *n.* **1.** a mass of air rotating rapidly round and towards a more or less vertical axis, and having at the same time a progressive motion over the surface of the land or sea. **2.** anything resembling a whirlwind, as in violent activity. **3.** any circling rush or violent onward course. [ME, from Scand.; cf. Icel. *hvirfilvindr.* See WHIRL, WIND[1]]

**whirlybird** /ˈwɜlibɜd/, *n. U.S. Colloq.* a helicopter.

**whirly-whirly** /ˈwɜli-ˌwɜli/, *n. Colloq.* →**willy-willy.**

**whirr** /wɜ/, *v.,* **whirred, whirring,** *n.* *–v.i.* **1.** to go, fly, dart, revolve, or otherwise move quickly with a vibratory or buzzing sound. *–n.* **2.** the act or sound of whirring: *the whirr of wings.* Also, **whir.** [ME, from Scand.; cf. Dan. *hvirre;* akin to WHIRL]

**whish** /wɪʃ/, *v.i.* **1.** to make, or move with, a whiz or swish. *–n.* **2.** a whishing sound.

**whisht** /wɪst/, *interj., adj. Obs.* →**whist**[1].

**whisk**[1] /wɪsk/, *v.t.* **1.** to sweep (dust, crumbs, etc.) or a surface with a brush, or the like. **2.** to move with a rapid, sweeping stroke. **3.** to draw, snatch, carry, etc., lightly and rapidly. *–v.i.* **4.** to sweep, pass, or go lightly and rapidly. *–n.* **5.** the act of whisking. **6.** a rapid, sweeping stroke; light, rapid movement. [late ME, from Scand.; cf. Dan. *viske* wipe]

**whisk**[2] /wɪsk/, *v.t.* **1.** to whip (eggs, cream, etc.) to a froth with a whisk or beating implement. *–n.* **2.** a small bunch of grass, straw, hair, or the like, esp. for use in brushing. **3.** an implement, in one form a bunch of loops of wire held together in a handle, for beating or whipping eggs, cream, etc. [ME *wisk,* Scand.; cf. Icel. *visk* wisp, c. G *Wisch* wisp of straw]

**whisker** /ˈwɪskə/, *n.* **1.** (*pl.*) the beard generally. **2.** a single hair of the beard. **3.** (*pl.*) a moustache. **4.** one of the long, stiff, bristly hairs growing about the mouth of certain animals, as the cat, rat, etc.; a vibrissa. **5.** Also, **whisker boom.** *Naut.* either of two bars of wood or iron projecting laterally one from each side of the bowsprit to give more spread to the guys which support the jib boom. **6.** *Obs.* one who or that which whisks. **7.** *Colloq.* a very small quantity or distance: *he won the race by a whisker.* **8.** *Chem., Crystall.* a single axially oriented crystal filament of metals, as iron, cobalt, etc., of refractory materials, as sapphire, silicon carbide, of carbon, boron, etc., having very high tensile strength and elastic modulus. **9. have whiskers on it,** *Colloq.* to be old-fashioned or useless: *that idea has whiskers on it.* [ME; from **whisk**[2]. Cf. LG *wisker* duster] – **whiskered, whiskery,** *adj.*

**whisky** /ˈwɪski/, *n., pl.* **-kies.** *–n.* **1.** a distilled spirit made from grain, as barley, rye, oats, etc. **2.** a drink of whisky. *–adj.* **3.** made of, relating to, or resembling, whisky. Also, *U.S. and Irish,* **whiskey.** [short for *whiskybae,* from Gaelic *uisgebeatha* water of life]

**whisky drinker** /ˈ– drɪŋkə/, *n. Colloq.* →**cherry nose.**

**whisper** /ˈwɪspə/, *v.i.* **1.** to speak with soft, low sounds, using the breath, lips, etc., without vibration of the vocal cords. **2.** to talk softly and privately (often with implication of gossip, slander, or plotting). **3.** (of trees, water, breezes, etc.) to make a soft, rustling sound. *–v.t.* **4.** to utter with soft, low sounds, using the breath, lips, etc. **5.** to say or tell in a whisper; to tell privately. **6.** to utter as a rumour, gossip, etc. **7.** to speak to or tell (a person) in a whisper, or privately. *–n.* **8.** the mode of utterance, or the voice, of one who whispers: *to speak in a whisper.* **9.** a sound, word, remark, or the like, uttered by whispering; something said or repeated privately: *low whispers.* **10.** a soft, rustling sound, as of leaves moving in the wind. **11.** confidential information; rumour. [ME *whysper,* OE *hwisprian,* c. G *wispern*] – **whisperer,** *n.*

**whispering** /ˈwɪspərɪŋ/, *n.* **1.** whispered talk or conversation; a whisper or whispers. *–adj.* **2.** that whispers; making a sound like a whisper. – **whisperingly,** *adv.*

**whispering gallery** /ˈ– gæləri/, *n.* a gallery or dome in which sounds, however soft, are reflected and can be heard at a considerable distance.

**whist**[1] /wɪst/, *interj.* hush! silence! be still! Also, **whisht.** [cf. SHUSH, etc.]

**whist**[2] /wɪst/, *n.* a card game played by four players, two against two, with 52 cards. [earlier *whisk,* ? special use of WHISK[1], altered by confusion with WHIST[1]]

**whist-drive** /ˈwɪst-draɪv/, *n.* a series of games of whist played by a number of sets of partners at different tables, winning pairs moving to the next table at the end of each game.

**whistle** /wɪsl/, *v.,* **-tled, -tling,** *n.* *–v.i.* **1.** to make a kind of clear musical sound, or a series of such sounds, by the forcible expulsion of the breath through a small orifice formed by contracting the lips, or through the teeth, together with the aid of the tongue. **2.** to make such a sound or series of sounds otherwise, as by blowing on a particular device. **3.** to produce a more or less similar sound by an instrument operated by steam or the like, or as such an instrument does. **4.** to emit somewhat similar sounds from the mouth, as birds. **5.** to move, go, pass, etc., with a high-pitched sound, as a bullet. *–v.t.* **6.** to produce or utter by whistling. **7.** to call, direct, or signal by or as by whistling. **8.** to send with a whistling or whizzing sound. **9. whistle for,** to ask or wish for (something) in vain. **10. whistle in (against) the wind,** to protest in vain. *–n.* **11.** an instrument for producing whistling sounds as by the breath, steam, etc., as a small wooden or tin tube or a small pipe. **12.** →**fipple flute. 13.** a sound produced by or as by whistling: *a long-drawn whistle of astonishment.* **14. blow the whistle on,** *Colloq.* to betray, esp. to the authorities. **15. wet one's whistle,** *Colloq.* to satisfy one's thirst, usu. with an alcoholic drink. [ME; OE *hwistlian*]

**whistler** /ˈwɪslə/, *n.* **1.** one who or that which whistles. **2.** something that sounds like a whistle. **3.** *Radio.* a whistling sound sometimes heard on radio receivers due to atmospherics. **4.** any of a large number of birds of the family Pachycephalidae, found in Australia, having loud melodious calls. **5.** any of various birds whose wings whistle in flight. **6.** a horse affected with whistling.

**whistlestop** /ˈwɪsəlstɒp/, *v.,* **-stopped, -stopping,** *n., adj.* *–v.i.* **1.** to travel about the country, esp. by train, in campaigning for political office, stopping at small communities to reach voters in small groups. *–n.* **2.** *U.S.* a small unimportant community, esp. one on a railway line. **3.** a brief appearance, speech, or the like, in a small community, as during a political campaign. *–adj.* **4.** denoting or pertaining to whistlestopping or a whistlestop: *a whistlestop tour; whistlestop speeches.*

**whistling** /ˈwɪstlɪŋ/, *n.* **1.** the act of one who or that which whistles. **2.** the sound produced. **3.** *Vet. Sci.* a form of roaring characterised by a peculiarly shrill sound. [ME; OE *hwistlung,* from *hwistlian* WHISTLE, *v.*]

**whistling moth** /– ˈmɒθ/, *n.* an Australian agaristid moth of genera *Hecatesia* or *Idalima,* the male of which can produce a whistling sound by means of a special mechanism on the wings.

**whistling swan** /– ˈswɒn/, *n.* a large North American swan, *Cygnus columbianus,* which in its adult form is pure white with black bill and feet, and has a small yellow spot on the bill in front of the eye.

**whit** /wɪt/, *n.* (*used esp. in negative phrases*) a particle; bit; jot: *not a whit better.* [unexplained alteration of WIGHT]

**white** /waɪt/, *adj.,* **whiter, whitest,** *n., v.,* **whited, whiting.** *–adj.* **1.** of the colour of pure snow, reflecting all or nearly all the rays of sunlight (see def. 26). **2.** light or comparatively light in colour. **3.** lacking colour; transparent. **4.** having a light skin; marked by comparatively slight pigmentation of the skin. **5.** denoting or pertaining to the Caucasian race. **6.** dominated by or exclusively for only members of the white race. **7.** pallid or pale, as from fear or other strong emotion, or pain or illness. **8.** silvery, grey, or hoary: *white hair.* **9.** *Archaic.* blond or fair. **10.** snowy: *a white Christmas.* **11.** (in some European countries) royalist, reactionary, or politically extremely conservative (opposed to *red*). **12.** blank, as an unoccupied space in printed matter. **13.** (of silverware) not burnished. **14.** *Armour.* composed of polished steel plates without fabric covering or the like. **15.** wearing white clothing: *a white friar.* **16.** *Electronics.* (of a signal) containing components of all frequencies at random: *white noise.* **17.** benevolent, beneficent, or good: *white magic.* **18.** auspicious or fortunate. **19.** free from spot or stain. **20.** pure or innocent. **21.** *Brit. Colloq.* honourable; trustworthy. **22.** (of wines) light-coloured or yellowish (opposed to *red*). **23.** (of coffee) with milk or cream. **24.** (of bread) made with white flour having a high gluten content. **25. bleed white,** to deprive or be deprived of resources. *–n.* **26.** an achromatic visual sensation of relatively high luminosity. A white surface reflects light of all hues completely and diffusely. Most so-called whites are very light greys: fresh snow, for example, reflects about 80 per cent of the incident light, but to be strictly white, snow would have to reflect 100 per cent of the incident light. It is the ultimate limit of a series of progressively lightening tints of any colour, as black is the ultimate limit of a series of darkening shades of any colour. **27.** the quality or state of being white. **28.** lightness of skin pigment. **29.** (*sometimes cap.*) a member of the white or Caucasian race. **30.** something white, or a white part of something. **31.** a pellucid viscous fluid which surrounds the yolk of an egg; albumen. **32.** the white part of the eyeball. **33.** (*pl.*) *Pathol.* leucorrhoea. **34.** white wine. **35.** a type or breed which is white in colour. **36.** any of several white-winged butterflies of the family Pieridae, as the cabbage white. **37.** (*cap.*) a pig of a white-haired breed. **38.** white fabric. **39.** (*pl.*) *Brit.* household goods as sheets, tablecloths, and sometimes underclothes, esp. goods made of cotton or linen and usu. but not necessarily coloured white. **40.** (*pl.*) white or off-white clothing worn for sports, esp. cricket. **41.** a blank space in printing. **42.** *Archery.* **a.** the outermost ring of the butt (target). **b.** an arrow that hits this portion of the butt. **c.** the central part of the butt formerly painted white, but now painted gold or yellow. **d.** *Archaic.* a target painted white. **43.** *Chess, Draughts.* the men or pieces which are light-coloured. **44.** a member of a royalist or reactionary party. **45. in the white,** (of furniture or wood) unvarnished or unpainted. *–v.t.* **46.** *Print.* to make white by leaving blank spaces (oft. fol. by *out*). **47.** *Obs.* to make white; whiten. **48.** to reduce the daylight visibility of, as a result of snow or fog (fol. by *out*). [ME; OE *hwīt,* c. G *weiss,* Icel, *hvītr,* Goth. *hweits*]

**white admiral** /– ˈædmərəl/, *n.* a butterfly, *Limenitis camilla,* with brown wings with prominent white markings, inhabiting Europe and much of Asia.

**white alkali** /– ˈælkəlaɪ/, *n.* a whitish layer of mineral salts, esp. sodium sulphate, sodium chloride, and magnesium sulphate, often found on top of soils under low rainfall.

**white angel** /– ˈeɪndʒəl/, *n. Colloq.* a drink made by mixing methylated spirits and white shoe polish.

**white ant** /ˈ– ænt/, *n.* an of various species of wood-eating isopterous insects which, like ants, exhibit social organisation and often form enormous moist colonies; destructive of trees, wooden fences, houses, etc.; termite.

**white-ant** /ˈwaɪt-ænt/, *v.t. Colloq.* to subvert or undermine from within (an organisation or enterprise).

**white arsenic** /– ˈasənɪk/, *n.* arsenic trioxide. See **arsenic** (def. 2).

**white Australia policy,** *n.* any immigration policy designed to restrict the entry of coloured people into Australia.

**whitebait** /ˈwaɪtbeɪt/, *n., pl.* **-bait.** any small delicate fish cooked whole without being cleaned, as the Derwent smelt or the inanga.

**white beam** /waɪt ˈbim/, *n.* a variable, deciduous tree, *Sorbus* *aria,* the leaves of which are densely hairy underneath, occurring on calcareous soil in western and southern Europe.

**white bean** /'– bin/, *n.* **1.** See **haricot.** **2.** a tree, *Ailanthus imberbiflora,* of temperate eastern Australia, having long beanlike pods.

**white bear** /– 'bɛə/, *n.* →**polar bear.**

**whitebeard** /'waɪtbɪəd/, *n.* a man having a white or grey beard; an old man.

**white beech** /waɪt 'bitʃ/, *n.* **1.** a tree, *Gmelina leichhardtii,* family Verbenaceae, of temperate eastern Australia, felled for its timber. **2.** any of various other trees having useful timber thought to resemble that of beech. **3.** the wood of any such tree.

**white birch** /– 'bɜtʃ/, *n.* **1.** the European birch, *Betula pendula,* having a hard wood of many uses. **2.** →**paper birch.**

**white blood cell,** *n.* →**leucocyte.**

**whiteboard** /'waɪtbɔd/, *n.* a type of blackboard made from white plastic on which one writes with a special felt pen.

**white-breasted finch** /waɪt-brɛstəd 'fɪntʃ/, *n.* →**pictorella mannikin.**

**white-breasted sea-eagle** /– 'si-igəl/, *n.* a fish-eating and scavenging eagle, *Haliaetus leucogaster,* of the Australian coasts and some inland waters, and certain areas of Asia.

**white-browed babbler** /waɪt-braʊd 'bæblə/, *n.* a grey bird with a white stripe over the eye and a white breast, *Pomatostomus superciliosus,* found in dry woodlands and scrub country in southern Australia, and having a cry similar to the catbird.

**white bryony** /waɪt 'braɪəni/, *n.* a European bryony, *Bryonia dioica.*

**whitecap** /'waɪtkæp/, *n.* a wave with a broken white crest.

**white cast iron,** *n.* cast iron which shows a white fracture when broken; the carbon is present predominantly as iron carbide.

**white cedar** /waɪt 'sidə/, *n.* **1.** a large deciduous rainforest tree of eastern Australia, *Melia azedarach,* frequently planted in dry inland areas. **2.** a coniferous tree, *Chamaecyparis thyoides,* of the swamps of the eastern U.S. **3.** its wood, from which wooden utensils and building articles are often made. **4.** the timber of these trees.

**Whitechapel** /'waɪtˌtʃæpəl/, *n.* **1.** *Whist, etc.* a lead of a one-card suit with a view to subsequent trump. **2.** *Billiards.* the intentional pocketing of an opponent's ball.

**white clover** /waɪt 'kloʊvə/, *n.* a valuable pasture plant, *Trifolium repens,* widely naturalised in temperate regions.

**white cockatoo** /– kɒkə'tu/, *n.* →**sulphur-crested cockatoo.**

**white-collar** /'waɪt-kɒlə/, *adj.* belonging or pertaining to non-manual workers, as those in professional and clerical work, who traditionally wore a suit, white shirt and tie.

**white currant** /waɪt 'kʌrənt/, *n.* a variety of the redcurrant, *Ribes sativum,* having white berries.

**whitedamp** /'waɪtdæmp/, *n.* →**carbon monoxide.**

**whited sepulchre** /waɪtəd 'sɛpəlkə/, *n.* a specious hypocrite.

**white dwarf** /waɪt 'dwɔf/, *n.* a small dying star which becomes cold and dense and usu. has a mass similar to that of the earth.

**white elder** /– 'ɛldə/, *n.* →**native elder.**

**white elephant** /– 'ɛləfənt/, *n.* **1.** an abnormally whitish or pale elephant, found usu. in Thailand; an albino elephant. **2.** an annoyingly useless possession. **3.** a possession of great value but entailing even greater expense.

**white ensign** /– 'ɛnsən/, *n.* **1.** the flag borne by ships of the Royal Australian Navy consisting of five blue stars of the Southern Cross and a blue Commonwealth star on a white background with a Union Jack in canton. **2.** *Brit.* a flag borne by ships of the British navy consisting of a red cross on a white background with a Union Jack in canton.

**white-eye** /'waɪt-aɪ/, *n.* any of the numerous small, chiefly tropical, singing birds of Australia, the Old World and some Pacific islands, constituting the family Zosteropidae, most species of which have a ring of white feathers round the eye, as the silver-eye.

**white-eyed duck** /waɪt-aɪd 'dʌk/, *n.* a dark brown duck, with white eyes and a black bill with a slate-blue bar at the tip and black tail, *Aythya australis,* found in swamps and lagoons throughout eastern and south-western Australia.

**whiteface** /'waɪtfeɪs/, *n.* any of various small birds of the genus *Aphelocephala* with a white forehead, found in central and southern Australia.

**white-faced** /'waɪt-feɪst/, *adj.* **1.** having a white or pale face. **2.** marked with white on the front of the head, as a horse. **3.** having a white front or surface.

**white-faced heron** /ˌwaɪt-feɪst 'hɛrən/, *n.* a medium-sized grey heron with a white face and throat, *Ardea novaehollandiae,* common in shallow-water areas of coastal and inland Australasia, often erroneously called the blue 'crane'.

**white feather** /waɪt 'fɛðə/, *n.* a symbol of cowardice, originally from a white feather in a gamecock's tail taken as a sign of inferior breeding and hence of poor fighting qualities.

**white feather orchid,** *n.* an epiphytic orchid, *Dendrobium aemulum,* with linear perianth segments and fragrant flowers, found on tree trunks in coastal forests of Queensland and New South Wales.

**whitefish** /'waɪtfɪʃ/, *n., pl.* **-fishes,** (*esp. collectively*) **-fish.** **1.** any fish of the family Coregonidae, similar to the trout but with smaller mouths and larger scales, esp. *Coregonus clupeaformis,* the common whitefish, a highly valued and important food fish. **2.** an edible sea fish of any kind except herring, any of the salmon species or any species of migratory trout, including all shellfish.

**white flag** /waɪt 'flæg/, *n.* an all-white flag, used as a symbol of surrender, etc.

**white-fronted chat** /ˌwaɪt-frʌntəd 'tʃæt/, *n.* a small, sprightly Australian bird, *Epthianura albifrons,* with pure white face and underparts, a broad black band across the back of the head and breast, and a metallic call; baldyhead; banded tintac; moonbird; nun; tang.

**white frost** /waɪt 'frɒst/, *n.* →**frost** (def. 3).

**white gold** /– 'goʊld/, *n.* any of several gold alloys possessing a white colour due to the presence of nickel or platinum. Commercial alloys contain gold, nickel, copper, and zinc.

**whitegoods** /'waɪtgʊdz/, *n. pl.* **1.** electrical goods as fridges, washing machines, etc., which have a white enamel surface. *–adj.* **2.** of or pertaining to such goods: *the whitegoods industry.*

**white gum** /'waɪt gʌm/, *n.* any of various eucalypts with smooth white bark.

**white-haired** /'waɪt-hɛəd/, *adj.* **1.** having grey hair, esp. as a mark of old age. **2.** *Colloq.* favourite; darling: *a white-haired boy.*

**white-handed** /waɪt-'hændəd/, *adj.* **1.** having white hands. **2.** innocent; guiltless.

**white-headed** /waɪt-'hɛdəd/, *adj.* **1.** having white hair. **2.** having fair or flaxen hair. **3.** (of an animal) having the head wholly or partly white. **4.** *Colloq.* →**white-haired.**

**whiteheart** /'waɪthat/, *n.* a kind of cherry bearing a large, sweet, soft-fleshed fruit.

**white heat** /waɪt 'hit/, *n.* **1.** an intense heat at which a substance glows with white light. **2.** a stage of intense activity excitement, feeling, etc.: *to work at a white heat.*

**white hope** /– 'hoʊp/, *n.* one who is expected to bring glory, etc., to a country, team, or other group which he represents.

**white horse** /– 'hɔs/, *n.* a white-topped wave; a whitecap.

**white-hot** /waɪt-'hɒt/, *adj.* **1.** very hot. **2.** showing white heat.

**white lady** /waɪt 'leɪdi/, *n.* **1.** a cocktail made from gin, Cointreau liqueur, lemon juice, sometimes with white of egg, shaken with crushed ice and strained before serving. **2.** *Colloq.* methylated spirits mixed with shoe polish or other additive as a drink.

**white lead** /– 'lɛd/, *n.* **1.** basic lead carbonate, $2PbCO_3 \cdot Pb(OH)_2$, a white, heavy powder used as a pigment, in putty, and in medicinal ointments for burns. **2.** the putty made from this substance in oil.

**white lead ore,** *n.* →**cerussite.**

**white leather** /waɪt 'lɛðə/, *n.* →**whitleather.**

**white leg** /'– lɛg/, *n.* →**milk leg.**

**white leghorn** /– 'lɛghɔn/, *n.* **1.** a pure white domestic fowl, which is a variety of leghorn. **2.** *Colloq.* a woman who plays lawn bowls.

**white lie** /– 'laɪ/, *n.* a lie uttered from polite, amiable, or pardonable motives; a harmless fib.

**white light** /– 'laɪt/, *n.* light which contains all the wavelengths of the visible spectrum at approximately the same intensity, as light from an incandescent white-hot solid.

**white line** /– 'laɪn/, *n.* **1.** any blank or white part or margin. **2.** *Print.* a line of space. **3.** a line of white paint or the like, either continuous or interrupted, laid along the centre of a road to separate traffic lanes. **4.** a white layer in a horse's hoof.

**white-livered** /waɪt-'lɪvəd/, *adj.* **1.** pale or unhealthy. **2.** cowardly.

**whitely** /'waɪtli/, *adv.* with a white hue or colour.

**white magic** /waɪt 'mædʒɪk/, *n.* magic used for benevolent or good purposes.

**white man** /'– mæn/, *n.* **1.** a member of the white race. **2.** *Brit. Colloq.* an honest, straightforward, or reliable person.

**white man's burden,** *n.* the supposed duty of the white race to care for and educate peoples of other races in the colonies. [coined by Rudyard Kipling, 1865-1936, English novelist and poet]

**white matter** /'waɪt ˌmætə/, *n.* nervous tissue, esp. of the brain and spinal cord, containing fibres only, and nearly white in colour.

**white meat** /'– mit/, *n.* any light-coloured meat, as veal, the breast of chicken, etc., (distinguished from *red meat*).

**white metal** /– 'mɛtl/, *n.* **1. a.** any of various light-coloured alloys containing a high proportion of tin, as babbitt metal, britannia metal, etc., used for bearings, light castings, and domestic articles. **b.** any of various similar alloys containing a high proportion of lead instead of tin. **2.** the intermediate metal in the conversion of copper matter.

**white mundic** /– 'mʌndɪk/, *n.* →**arsenopyrite.**

**whiten** /'waɪtn/, *v.t.* **1.** to make white. *–v.i.* **2.** to become white. **– whitener,** *n.*

**white-naped honeyeater** /waɪt-neɪpt 'hʌniitə/, *n.* a honeyeater, *Melithreptus lunatus,* olive-brown in colour, with a black head and white crescent on the nape, found on the east coast and around Perth in wet and dry sclerophyll forests; blackcap.

**whiteness** /'waɪtnəs/, *n.* **1.** the quality or state of being white. **2.** paleness. **3.** purity. **4.** a white substance.

**white nickel** /waɪt 'nɪkəl/, *n.* →**chloanthite.**

**whitening** /'waɪtnɪŋ/, *n.* **1.** the act or process of making or turning white. **2.** a preparation for making something white; whiting.

**white noise** /waɪt 'nɔɪz/, *n.* an electronically produced noise used for experimental purposes as sound masking, etc., in which all frequencies are represented with equal energy in each equal range of frequencies, that is, with as much energy between 100 Hz and 200 Hz as between 200 Hz and 300 Hz, 1000 Hz and 1100 Hz, etc. Cf. **pink noise.**

**white oak** /– 'oʊk/, *n.* **1.** an oak, *Quercus alba,* of eastern North America, having a light grey to white bark and a hard, durable wood. **2.** the wood of this or any of several other related oaks.

**white-out** /'waɪt-aʊt/, *n.* **1.** an arctic weather condition caused by heavy cloud cover over the snow so that light reflected from below is approximately equal to light from above, so that there is an absence of shadow and the horizon is invisible. **2.** →**correction fluid.**

**white paper** /'waɪt peɪpə/, *n.* **1.** paper bleached white. **2.** an official report or policy proposal of a government on a specific subject.

**white pepper** /– 'pɛpə/, *n.* a condiment prepared from the husked dried berries of the pepper plant, used either whole or ground. See **pepper.**

**white pine** /– 'paɪn/, *n.* **1.** the Australian cypress pine, *Callitris hugelli.* **2.** the New Zealand tree, kahikatea. **3.** a pine, *Pinus strobus,* of eastern North America. **4.** the valuable timber of these trees. **5.** any of various other similar species or timbers.

**white plague** /– 'pleɪg/, *n.* tuberculosis, esp. pulmonary tuberculosis.

**white pointer** /– 'pɔɪntə/, *n.* →**white shark.**

**white poplar** /– 'pɒplə/, *n.* **1.** an Old World poplar, *Populus alba,* having the underside of the leaves covered with a dense silvery white down. **2.** the soft, straight-grained wood of the tulip tree.

**white potato** /– pə'teɪtoʊ/, *n.* See **potato** (def. 1).

**white-quilled rock pigeon,** *n.* a handsome pigeon of the Kimberley district of Western Australia, *Petrophassa albipennis.*

**white race** /'waɪt reɪs/, *n.* →**Caucasian.**

**white rat** /– 'ræt/, *n.* an albino variety of the common rat, *Rattus norvegicus,* used in biological experiments.

**white rhinoceros** /– raɪ'nɒsərəs/, *n.* a two-horned rhinoceros, *Rhinoceros simus,* of Africa, characterised by wide square lips. [*white* from Afrikaans *wyd* WIDE (so called on account of its broad lips), influenced by WHITE]

**white-root** /'waɪt-rut/, *n.* a prostrate white-flowered herb, *Pratia purpurascens,* found in damp places and common in forests of eastern Australia.

**White Russian** /waɪt 'rʌʃən/, *n.* a member of a division of the Russian people dwelling in the republic of White Russia, a constituent of the Soviet Union, and its adjacent parts.

**white sapphire** /waɪt 'sæfaɪə/, *n.* a white variety of corundum, used as a gem.

**white sauce** /– 'sɔs/, *n.* a sauce made of butter, flour, seasoning, and milk or sometimes chicken or veal stock.

**white shark** /– 'ʃak/, *n.* a very large dangerous shark, *Carcharodon albimors.* Also, **white pointer.**

**white slave** /– 'sleɪv/, *n.* a white woman who is sold or forced to serve as a prostitute, esp. outside her native land.

**white-slaver** /waɪt-'sleɪvə/, *n.* a person engaged in the traffic in white slaves.

**white slavery** /waɪt 'sleɪvəri/, *n.* the condition of or the traffic in white slaves.

**white-slaving** /waɪt-'sleɪvɪŋ/, *n.* traffic in white slaves.

**whitesmith** /'waɪtsmɪθ/, *n.* →**tinsmith.**

**white spirit** /– 'spɪrət/, *n.* a mixture of petroleum hydrocarbons in the boiling range 150°-200°C, used as a solvent for paints and varnishes as a substitute for turpentine.

**white spruce** /– 'sprus/, *n.* See **spruce**[1] (def. 1).

**white squall** /– 'skwɔl/, *n.* a whirlwind or violent disturbance of small radius, occurring in tropical or sub-tropical waters, which is not accompanied by the usual clouds, but is indicated merely by the whitecaps and turbulent water beneath it.

**white supremacist** /– su'prɛməsəst/, *n.* a believer in white supremacy.

**white supremacy** /– su'prɛməsi/, *n.* the belief or theory that white men have a natural or god-given supremacy over people of other races.

**white-tailed deer** /ˌwaɪt-teɪld 'dɪə/, *n.* a common deer of North America, *Odocoileus virginianus,* and related species, whose tail is white on the underside. Also, **whitetail.**

**white-tailed spider** /'– spaɪdə/, *n.* a nocturnal spider, *Lampona cylindrata,* found in dark places, whose bite causes illness followed by a slow-healing lesion.

**whitethorn** /'waɪtθɔn/, *n.* a white-flowering hawthorn.

**whitethroat** /'waɪtθroʊt/, *n.* **1.** a small Old World songbird, *Sylvia communis,* reddish brown above, with white throat, and distinguishable from its closest allies by the white marks on its outer tail feathers. **2.** any of several other Old World birds of the same genus.

**white-throated warbler** /ˌwaɪt-θroʊtəd 'wɔblə/, *n.* a small Australian bird, *Gerygone olivacea,* with bright yellow underparts and a white throat, having a distinctive and beautiful voice.

**white tie** /waɪt 'taɪ/, *n.* **1.** a white bow tie for men, worn with the most formal style of evening dress. **2.** the most formal style of evening dress for men, of which the characteristic garments are a white bow tie and a tail coat (distinguished from *black tie*).

**white trash** /– 'træʃ/, *n.* (*derog.*) **1.** poor white people collectively, esp. in the southern U.S. **2.** one such person.

**white vitriol** /– 'vɪtriɒl/, *n.* zinc sulphate heptahydrate, $ZnSO_4 \cdot 7H_2O$, a white crystalline compound, used as an antiseptic, mordant, preservative, etc.

**whitewall** /'waɪtwɔl/, *n.* **1.** a vehicle tyre having a white sidewall. *–adj.* **2.** of or pertaining to such a tyre.

**whitewash** /'waɪtwɒʃ/, *n.* **1.** a composition, as of lime and water or of whiting, size, and water, used for whitening walls, woodwork, etc. **2.** anything used to cover up defects, gloss over faults or errors, or give a specious semblance of respectability, honesty, etc. **3.** *Colloq.* (in various games) a defeat in which the loser fails to score. *–v.t.* **4.** to whiten with whitewash. **5.** to cover up or gloss over the defects, faults, errors, etc., of by some means. **6.** *Colloq.* (in various games) to subject to a whitewash. – **whitewasher,** *n.*

**white water** /waɪt 'wɔtə/, *n.* water in which air bubbles are suspended and which indicates the presence of fish, or any stretch of water in which the surface is broken as in breakers, due to movement over a shallow bottom.

**white wax** /– 'wæks/, *n.* any of various waxes, as paraffin wax or beeswax, that are naturally white or artificially whitened.

**white whale** /– 'weɪl/, *n.* →**beluga** (def. 1).

**white-winged chough** /waɪt-wɪŋd 'tʃʌf/, *n.* →**chough** (def. 2).

**white-winged triller** /– 'trɪlə/, *n.* a medium sized bird, *Lalage sueurii,* which migrates from northern to southern Australia for spring and summer, the male of the species being noted for its singing in the breeding season; caterpillar-eater.

**white witch** /'waɪt wɪtʃ/, *n.* a witch who employs her magic powers only to do good deeds. Cf. **black witch.**

**whitewood** /'waɪtwʊd/, *n.* a name given to a number of trees with pale timber, as *Atalaya hemiglauca* of inland Australia, and the tulip tree and cottonwood of North America.

**whitewood furniture** /– 'fɜnətʃə/, *n.* furniture made from unstained and unpolished whitewood, esp. pine.

**whitey** /'waɪti/, *n. Colloq.* (*derog.*) a white man.

**whiteywood** /'waɪtiwʊd/, *n. N.Z.* →**mahoe.**

**whither** /'wɪðə/, *Archaic; now replaced by* **where.** *–adv.* **1.** to what place? **2.** to what point, end, course, etc., or to what? *–conj.* **3.** to what, whatever, or which place, point, end, etc. [ME and OE *hwider,* alteration of *hwæder* (c. Goth. *hwadrē*) on model of *hider* HITHER]

**whithersoever** /wɪðəsoʊ'ɛvə/, *adv. Archaic.* to whatsoever place.

**whitherward** /'wɪðəwəd/, *adv. Archaic.* towards what place; in what direction. Also, **whitherwards.**

**whiting**[1] /waɪtɪŋ/, *n.* **1.** in Australia, any of numerous species of estuarine and surf fishes of the family Sillanginidae, highly prized for sport and table. **2.** elsewhere, **a.** any of several European species of the cod family, esp. *Merlangus merlangus.* **b.** the American Atlantic hake (*Merluccins bilinearis*). **c.** a slender Atlantic shore fish of the genus *Menticirrhus,* of the croaker family (Sciaenidae). [late ME *whytynge,* ? alteration of OE *hwītling* kind of fish. Cf. D *wijting*]

**whiting**[2] /'waɪtɪŋ/, *n.* pure white chalk (calcium carbonate) which has been ground and washed, used in making putty, whitewash, etc., and for cleaning silver, etc. [WHITE + -ING[1]]

**whitish** /'waɪtɪʃ/, *adj.* somewhat white; tending to white. – **whitishness,** *n.*

**whitleather** /'wɪtlɛðə/, *n.* leather dressed with alum, salt, or other chemicals; white leather.

**whitlow** /'wɪtloʊ/, *n.* an inflammation of the deeper tissues of a finger or toe, esp. of the terminal phalanx, usu. terminating in suppuration. [ME *whitflawe, whitflowe,* from WHITE + FLAW[1]]

**whitlow grass** /'wɪtloʊ gras/, *n.* any of several small herbaceous plants as **Vernal Whitlow grass,** *Erophila verna,* and **Chilean Whitlow grass,** *Paronychia brasiliana,* a troublesome weed of lawns. [so called because once believed to cure whitlows]

**Whit Sunday** /wɪt 'sʌndeɪ/, *n.* the seventh Sunday after Easter, celebrated as a festival in commemoration of the descent of the Holy Spirit on the day of Pentecost. [ME *whytsonenday,* OE *Hwīta Sunnandæg,* lit., white Sunday, from the white (baptismal) robes worn on that day]

**whittle** /'wɪtl/, *v.,* **-tled, -tling,** *n.* *–v.t.* **1.** to cut, trim, or shape (a stick, piece of wood, etc.) by taking off bits with a knife. **2.** to cut off (a bit or bits). **3.** to cut by way of reducing amount (esp. fol. by *down*): *to whittle down expenses.* *–v.i.* **4.** to cut bits or chips from wood or the like with a knife, as in shaping something or as a mere aimless diversion. [alteration of *thwittle,* ME *thwitel* knife, from OE *thwītan* whittle] – **whittler,** *n.*

**whittling** /'wɪtlɪŋ/, *n.* **1.** the act of one who whittles. **2.** (*usu. pl.*) a bit or chip whittled off.

**whity** /'waɪti/, *adj.* →**whitish.**

**whiz**[1] /wɪz/, *v.,* **whizzed, whizzing,** *n.* *–v.i.* **1.** to make a humming or hissing sound, as an object passing rapidly through the air. **2.** to move or rush with such a sound. *–v.t.* **3.** to cause to whiz. **4.** to treat with a whizzer. *–n.* **5.** the sound of a whizzing object. **6.** a swift movement producing such a sound. Also, **whizz.** [imitative]

**whiz**[2] /wɪz/, *n.* a person who shows outstanding ability in a particular field or who is notable in some way; expert. [? abbreviation of WIZARD]

**whiz-bang** /'wɪz-bæŋ/, *n.* **1.** *Mil.* a small shell which travels through the air at or near the speed of sound, so that it explodes at the same time as or shortly before the sound of its flight is heard. **2.** a firework making such a sound. **3.** the sound itself. *–v.i.* **4.** to make such a sound. Also, **whizz-bang.**

**whiz-kid** /'wɪz-kɪd/, *n. Colloq.* a person, esp. young, who achieves spectacular success in a given enterprise.

**whizzer** /'wɪzə/, *n.* **1.** something that whizzes. **2.** a centrifugal machine for drying sugar, grain, clothes, etc.

**who** /hu/, *pron.; poss.* **whose;** *obj.* **whom.** *–interrog. pron.* **1.** what person?: *who told you so? whose book is this? of whom are you speaking?* **2.** (of a person) what as to character, origin, position, importance, etc.: *who is the man in uniform?* *–rel. pron.* **3.** (as a compound relative): **a.** the or any person that; any person, be it who it may. **b.** *Archaic.* one that (after *as*). **4.** (as a simple relative, with antecedent (a person, or sometimes an animal or a personified thing) expressed): **a.** in clauses conveying an additional idea: *we saw men who were at work.* **b.** used in clauses defining or restricting the antecedent: *one on whose word we rely, the man to whom it was told.* **5. who's who,** the people who carry influence or importance. [ME; OE *hwā,* c. D *wie,* G *wer,* Goth. *hwas*]

**W.H.O.** /dʌbəlju eɪtʃ 'oʊ/, World Health Organisation. Also, **WHO.**

**whoa** /woʊ/, *interj.* stop! (used esp. to horses).

**who'd** /hud/, contraction of *who would.*

**whodunit** /hu'dʌnət/, *n. Colloq.* a novel, play, etc., dealing with a murder or murders and the detection of the criminal.

**whoever** /hu'ɛvə/, *pron.; possessive* **whosever;** *objective* **whomever.** *–indef. rel. pron.* **1.** whatever person, or anyone that: *whoever wants it may have it.* *–interrog. pron.* **2.** *Colloq.* who ever? who? (used emphatically): *whoever is that?* Also, *Poetic,* **whoe'er** /hu'ɛə/.

**whole** /hoʊl/, *adj.* **1.** comprising the full quantity, amount, extent, number, etc., without diminution or exception; entire, full, or total. **2.** containing all the elements properly belonging; complete: *a whole set.* **3.** undivided, or in one piece: *to swallow a thing whole.* **4.** *Maths.* integral, or not fractional: *a whole number.* **5.** uninjured, undamaged, or unbroken; sound; intact: *to get off with a whole skin.* **6.** sound; healthy. **7.** fully developed and balanced, in all aspects of one's nature: *educated to be a whole man.* **8.** being fully or entirely such: *whole brother.* **9. out of whole cloth,** *U.S. Colloq.* without foundation in fact: *a story made out of whole cloth.* *–n.* **10.** the whole assemblage of parts or elements belonging to a thing; the entire quantity, account, extent, or number. **11.** a thing complete in itself, or comprising all its parts or elements. **12.** an assemblage of parts associated or viewed together as one thing; a unitary system. **13. as a whole,** all things included or considered. **14. on** or **upon the whole, a.** on consideration of the whole matter, or in view of all the circumstances. **b.** as a whole or in general, without regard to exceptions. [ME *hole,* OE *hāl,* c. D *heel,* G *heil,* Icel. *heill;* spelling *wh-* (15th C) from d. pronunciation. Cf. HALE[1], HEAL] – **wholeness,** *n.*

**whole brother** /– 'brʌðə/, *n.* →**full brother.**

**wholefood** /'hoʊlfud/, *n.* food eaten in as near as possible to the natural state, with the minimum of processing or cooking.

**whole gale** /– 'geɪl/, *n.* a wind of Beaufort scale force 10 with an average speed of 48 to 55 knots, or 89 to 102 km/h.

**wholegrain** /'hoʊlgreɪn/, *adj.* →**wholemeal.**

**wholehearted** /'hoʊlhatəd/, *adj.* hearty; cordial; earnest; sincere. – **wholeheartedly,** *adv.* – **wholeheartedness,** *n.*

**whole hog** /hoʊl 'hɒg/, *n. Colloq.* **1.** entireness; completeness. **2. go the whole hog,** to involve oneself to the fullest extent; do something thoroughly or completely. – **wholehogger,** *n.*

**whole-length** /'hoʊl-lɛŋθ/, *adj.* →**full-length.**

**whole-life insurance** /hoʊl-ˌlaɪf ɪn'ʃɔrəns/, *n.* a life insurance contract where the capital sum is only payable on the death of the insured. Also, **whole-of-life insurance.**

**wholemeal** /'hoʊlmil/, *adj.* prepared with the complete wheat kernel, as flour or the bread baked with it; whole-wheat.

**whole milk** /'hoʊl mɪlk/, *n.* milk containing all its constituents as received from the cow, or other milk-giving animal.

**whole note** /– 'noʊt/, *n. U.S.* →**semibreve.**

**whole number** /– 'nʌmbə/, *n.* an integer as 0, 1, 2, 3, 4, 5, etc.

**wholesale** /'hoʊlseɪl/, *n., adj., adv., v.,* **-saled, -saling.** *–n.* **1.** the sale of commodities in large quantities, as to retailers or jobbers rather than to consumers directly (distinguished from *retail*). **2. by wholesale, a.** in large quantities, as in the sale of commodities. **b.** on a large scale and without discrimination: *slaughter by wholesale.* *–adj.* **3.** of, pertaining to, or engaged in sale by wholesale. **4.** extensive and indiscriminate: *wholesale discharge of workers.* *–adv.* **5.** in a wholesale way. **6.** on wholesale terms. *–v.t., v.i.* **7.** to sell by wholesale. – **wholesaler,** *n.*

**whole sister** /hoʊl 'sɪstə/, *n.* →**full sister.**

**wholesome** /'hoʊlsəm/, *adj.* **1.** conducive to moral or general well-being; salutary; beneficial: *wholesome advice.* **2.** conducive to bodily health; healthful; salubrious: *wholesome food, air, or exercise.* **3.** suggestive of health (physical or moral), esp. in appearance. **4.** healthy or sound. [ME *holsum,* from *hol* WHOLE + *-sum* -SOME[1]] – **wholesomely,** *adv.* – **wholesomeness,** *n.*

**whole tone** /'hoʊl toʊn/, *n.* a musical interval of two semitones, as A-B or C-D; a major second. Also, *U.S.,* **whole step.**

**whole-tone scale** /ˌhoʊl-toʊn 'skeɪl/, *n.* a musical scale entirely constructed from whole tones.

**whole-wheat** /'hoʊl-wit/, *adj. U.S.* →**wholemeal.**

**wholism** /'hoʊlɪzəm/, *n.* →**holism.** – **wholist,** *n.* – **wholistic** /hoʊ'lɪstɪk/, *adj.*

**who'll** /hul/, contraction of *who will* or *who shall.*

**wholly** /'hoʊlli, 'hoʊli/, *adv.* **1.** entirely; totally; altogether; quite. **2.** to the whole amount, extent, etc. **3.** so as to comprise or involve all.

**whom** /hum/, *pron.* objective case of **who.** [ME; OE *hwām,* dat. of *hwā* WHO]

**whomever** /hum'ɛvə/, *pron.* objective case of **whoever, whomever.** *–indef. rel. pron.* **1.** whatever person, or anyone that: *whoever wants it may have it.* **2.** no matter who. *–interrog. pron.* **3.** *Colloq.* who ever? who? (used emphatically): *whoever is that?* Also, *Poetic,* **whoe'er.**

**whomsoever** /humsoʊ'ɛvə/, *pron.* objective case of **whosoever.**

**whoop** /wup, wʊp, hup/, *n.* **1.** a loud cry or shout, as one uttered by children or warriors. **2.** the whooping sound characteristic of whooping cough. **3. not worth a whoop,** *Colloq.* not worth a thing; utterly valueless. *–v.i.* **4.** to utter a loud cry or shout (originally the syllable whoop, or hoop), as a call, or in enthusiasm, excitement, frenzy, etc. **5.** to cry as an owl, crane, or certain other birds. **6.** to make the characteristic sound accompanying the deep indrawing of breath after a series of coughs in whooping cough. *–v.t.* **7.** to utter with or as with a whoop or whoops. **8.** to whoop to or at. **9.** to call, urge, pursue, or drive with whoops: *to whoop dogs on.* **10. whoop it (or things) up,** *Colloq.* **a.** to raise an outcry or disturbance. **b.** to have a party or celebration. *–interj.* **11.** (a cry to show excitement, encouragement, enthusiasm, etc.) [ME *whope,* OE *hwōpan* threaten, c. Goth. *hwōpan* boast]

**whoopee** /'wʊpi/ *for defs 1 and 2;* /wʊ'pi/ *for def. 3 Colloq.* *–n.* **1.** uproarious festivity. **2. make whoopee,** to engage in uproarious merry-making. *–interj.* **3.** (a shout of 'whoopee'.) [extended var. of WHOOP]

**whooper** /'hupə/, *n.* **1.** one who or that which whoops. **2.** Also, **whooper swan.** a common Old World swan, *Cygnus cygnus,* notable for its whooping cry.

**whooping cough** /'hupɪŋ kɒf/, *n.* an infectious disease of the respiratory mucous membrane, esp. of children, characterised by a series of short, convulsive coughs followed by a deep inspiration accompanied by a whooping sound; pertussis.

**whoops** /wʊps/, *interj.* (an exclamation of mild surprise, dismay, etc.). Also, **whoops-a-daisy.**

**whoosh** /wʊʃ/, *n.* **1.** a loud rushing noise, as of water or air. *–v.i.* **2.** to move with a loud rushing noise.

**whop** /wɒp/, *v.,* **whopped, whopping,** *n. Colloq.* *–v.t.* **1.** to throw with force, pitch, or dash. **2.** to strike forcibly. **3.** to defeat soundly, as in a contest. **4.** to strike out or move suddenly. *–v.i.* **5.** to plump suddenly down; flop. *–n.* **6.** a forcible blow or impact. **7.** the sound made by it. **8.** a bump; a heavy fall. [orig. uncert.]

**whopper** /'wɒpə/, *n. Colloq.* **1.** something uncommonly large of its kind. **2.** a big lie. **3.** one who or that which whops. [WHOP + -ER[1]]

**whopping** /'wɒpɪŋ/, *adj. Colloq.* very large of its kind; huge.

**whore** /hɔ/, *n., v.,* **whored, whoring.** *–n.* **1.** a prostitute. *–v.i.* **2.** to act as a whore. **3.** to consort with whores. *–v.t.* **4.** to make a whore of; debauch. [ME and OE *hōre,* c. G *Hure;* akin to L *cārus* dear]

**who're** /'huə/, contraction of *who are.*

**whoredom** /'hɔdəm/, *n.* **1.** prostitution. **2.** (in biblical use) idolatry.

**whorehouse** /'hɔhaʊs/, *n., pl.* **-houses** /-haʊzəz/. a brothel; house of prostitution.

**whoremonger** /'hɔmʌŋgə/, *n.* one who consorts with whores. Also, **whoremaster** /'hɔmastə/.

**whoreson** /'hɔsən/, *Obs.* *–n.* **1.** the son of a whore; a bastard. **2.** (*derog.*) a person. *–adj.* **3.** being a bastard. **4.** mean; wretched; contemptible. [WHORE + SON]

**whorish** /'hɔrɪʃ/, *adj.* being or having the character of a whore; lewd; unchaste. – **whorishly,** *adv.* – **whorishness,** *n.*

**whorl** /wɜl/, *n.* **1.** a circular arrangement of like parts, as leaves, flowers, etc., round a point on an axis; a verticil. **2.** one of the turns or volutions of a spiral shell. **3.** one of the principal ridge-shapes of a fingerprint, forming at least one complete circle (distinguished from *loop* and *arch*). **4.** *Anat.* one of the turns in the cochlea of the ear. **5.** anything shaped like a coil. [ME *whorvil,* from *whorve* (OE *hweorfa* whorl) + *-l,* suffix]

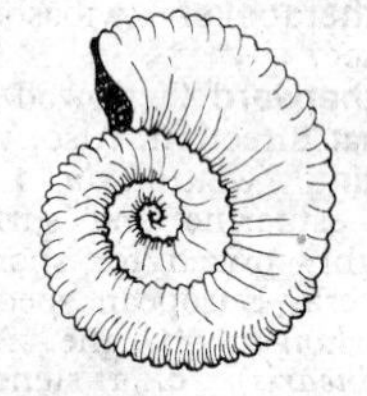
whorls of ammonite

**whorled** /wɜld/, *adj.* **1.** having a whorl or whorls. **2.** disposed in the form of a whorl, as leaves.

**whortleberry** /'wɜtlbəri, -bri/, *n., pl.* **-ries. 1.** the edible, black berry of the shrub, *Vaccinium myrtillus,* of Europe and Siberia. **2.** the shrub itself. [d. var. of hurtleberry, from hurtle (from hurt, OE *horta* whortleberry) + BERRY]

**who's** /huz/, contraction of *who is* or *who has.*

**whose** /huz/, *pron.* **1.** possessive case of the relative and interrogative pronoun **who:** *the man whose book I borrowed, whose is this book?* **2.** possessive case of the relative pronoun **which** (historically, of **what**): *a pen whose point is broken.* [ME *whos,* OE *hwæs,* gen. of *hwā* who]

**whosesoever** /huzsoʊ'ɛvə/, *pron.* possessive case of **whosoever.**

**whosever** /huz'ɛvə/, *pron.* possessive case of **whoever.**

**whoso** /'husoʊ/, *pron.* whosoever; whoever.

**whosoever** /husoʊ'ɛvə/, *pron., possessive* **whosesoever;** *objective* **whomsoever.** whoever; whatever person.

**who've** /huv/, contraction of *who have.*

**whr,** watt-hour.

**why** /waɪ/, *adv., conj., n., pl.* **whys,** *interj.* *–adv.* **1.** for what? for what cause, reason, or purpose? *–conj.* **2.** for what cause or reason. **3.** for which, or on account of which (after *reason,* etc., to introduce a relative clause): *the reason why he refused.* **4.** the reason for which: *that is why I raised this question again.* *–n.* **5.** the cause or reason. *–interj.* **6.** (an expression of surprise, hesitation, etc., or sometimes a mere expletive): *Why, it is all gone!* [ME; OE *hwī, hwȳ,* instrumental case of *hwæt* WHAT]

**whydah** /'wɪdə/, *n.* **1.** any of the small African birds which constitute the subfamily Viduinae, comprising species of weaverbirds the males of which have elongated drooping tail feathers. **2.** any of the birds of the genera *Coliuspasser, Drepanoplectes,* and *Diatropura.* Also, **whidah, whidahbird, widowbird, wydah.** [alteration of *widow bird* to agree with name of town in Dahomey, W Africa, one of its haunts]

whydah

**W-I,** walk-in.

**wick**[1] /wɪk/, *n.* **1.** a bundle or loose twist or braid of soft threads, or a woven strip or tube, as of cotton, which in a candle, lamp, oilstove, or the like serves to draw up the melted tallow or wax or the oil or other inflammable liquid to be burned at its top end. **2.** *Colloq.* a penis. **3.** *Colloq.* **get on one's wick,** to irritate. **4. dip one's wick,** *Colloq.* (of a man) to have sexual intercourse. [ME *wicke, weke,* OE *wice, wēoc(e)* c. MD *wiecke,* OHG *wiohha*] – **wickless,** *adj.*

**wick**[2] /wɪk/, *n. Curling.* a narrow opening in the field, bounded by other players' stones. [n. use of v., to drive a stone through an opening]

**wicked** /'wɪkəd/, *adj.* **1.** evil or morally bad in principle or practice; iniquitous; sinful. **2.** mischievous or playfully malicious. **3.** *Colloq.* distressingly severe, as cold, pain, wounds, etc. **4.** *Colloq.* ill-natured, savage, or vicious: *a wicked horse.* **5.** *Colloq.* extremely trying, unpleasant, or troublesome. [ME, from *wick(e)* wicked (now d.) + -ED[2]. Cf. OE *wicca* wizard] – **wickedly,** *adv.*

**wickedness** /'wɪkədnəs/, *n.* **1.** the quality or state of being wicked. **2.** wicked conduct or practices. **3.** a wicked act or thing.

**wicker** /'wɪkə/, *n.* **1.** a slender, pliant twig; an osier; a withe. **2.** →**wickerwork** (def. 1). **3.** *Obs.* something made of wickerwork, as a basket. *–adj.* **4.** consisting or made of wicker: *a wicker basket.* **5.** covered with wicker. [ME, from Scand.; cf. d. Swed. *vikker* willow]

**wickerwork** /'wɪkəwɜk/, *n.* **1.** work consisting of plaited or woven twigs or osiers; articles made of wicker. *–adj.* **2.** →**wicker.**

**wicket** /'wɪkət/, *n.* **1.** a small door or gate, esp. one beside, or forming part of, a larger one. **2.** a window or opening, often closed by a grating or the like, as in a door, or forming a place of communication in a ticket office or the like. **3.** →**turnstile.** **4.** a small gate by which a canal lock is emptied. **5.** a gate by which a flow of water is regulated, as to a waterwheel. **6.** *Cricket.* **a.** either of the two frameworks, each consisting of three stumps with two bails in grooves across their tops, at which the bowler aims the ball. **b.** the area between the wickets, esp. with reference to the state of the ground. **c.** one end of the pitch, esp. the area between the stumps and the popping crease. **d.** one batsman's turn at the wicket. **e.** the period during which two men bat together. **f.** the achievement of a batsman's dismissal by the fielding side. **7. sticky wicket, a.** a wet or muddy wicket. **b.** *Colloq.* a difficult or disadvantageous situation or set of circumstances. **8. a good wicket,** *Colloq.* an advantageous situation or set of circumstances. [ME, from AF, from Scand.; cf. Icel. *vikja* move]

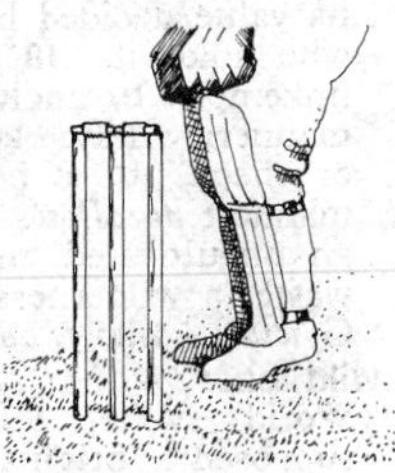
wicket (def. 6)

**wicket-keeper** /'wɪkət-kipə/, *n. Cricket.* the player on the fielding side who stands immediately behind the wicket to stop balls that pass it.

**wicket maiden** /wɪkət 'meɪdn/, *n.* (in cricket) a maiden over in which at least one wicket is taken by the bowler.

**wicking** /'wɪkɪŋ/, *n.* material for wicks.

**wicopy** /'wɪkəpi/, *n., pl.* **-pies.** *U.S.* **1.** the leatherwood, *Dirca palustris.* **2.** any of various willow herbs, as *Chamaenerion angustifolium.* **3.** →**basswood.** [Algonquian *wik'pi, wighebi,* etc., inner bark]

**widdershins** /'wɪdəʃɪnz/, *adv. Archaic.* in a direction contrary to the apparent course of the sun; anticlockwise. Also, **withershins.** [MLG *weddersins* in an opposite direction]

**wide** /waɪd/, *adj.,* **wider, widest,** *adv., n.* *–adj.* **1.** having considerable or great extent from side to side; broad; not narrow. **2.** having a certain or specified extent from side to side: *three metres wide.* **3.** of great horizontal extent; extensive; vast; spacious. **4.** of great range or scope; embracing a great number or variety of subjects, cases, etc.: *wide reading, experience, etc.* **5.** open to the full or a great extent; expanded; distended: *to stare with wide eyes, or a wide mouth.* **6.** full, ample, or roomy, as clothing. **7.** apart or remote from a specified point or object: *a guess wide of the truth.* **8.** too far or too much to one side: *a wide ball in cricket.* **9.** *Horseracing.* away from the inside fence of a racetrack: *the horse drawn wide faces a disadvantage.* *–adv.* **10.** to a great, or relatively great, extent from side to side. **11.** over an extensive space or region, or far abroad: *scattered far and wide.* **12.** to the full extent of opening: *to open the eyes or mouth wide.* **13.** to the utmost, or fully: *to be wide awake.* **14.** away from or to one side of a point, mark, purpose, or the like; aside; astray: *the shot went wide.* *–n.* **15.** *Cricket.* a bowled ball that passes outside the batsman's reach, and counts as a run for the side batting. **16.** *Bowls.* a delivery making too great an allowance for the bias of the bowl, and thus not curving inward sufficiently. [ME; OE *wīd,* c. D *wijd,* G *weit*] – **wideness,** *n.* – **widish,** *adj.*

**wide-angle** /'waɪd-æŋgəl/, *adj.* (in photography) denoting or pertaining to a camera lens with a wide angle of view (up to 100°) and a short focal length.

**wide-awake** /waɪd-ə'weɪk/, *adj.* **1.** fully awake; with the eyes wide open. **2.** alert, keen, or knowing. **3.** a soft wide-brimmed felt hat as worn by a country man.

**wide-band** /'waɪd-bænd/, *adj.* denoting or pertaining to electronic equipment which can respond to a wide range of frequencies.

**wide-eyed** /waɪd-'aɪd/, *adj.* **1.** having the eyes habitually or temporarily wide open, as from innocence, amazement, wakefulness, or the like. **2.** innocent or naive.

**widely** /'waɪdli/, *adv.* **1.** to a wide extent. **2.** over a wide space or area: *a widely distributed plant.* **3.** throughout a large number of persons: *a man who is widely known.* **4.** in many or various subjects, cases, etc.: *to be widely read.* **5.** greatly, very much, or very: *two widely different accounts of an affair.*

**widen** /'waɪdn/, *v.t., v.i.* to make or become wide or wider; expand. – **widener,** *n.*

**wide-open** /'waɪd-oupən/, *adj.* **1.** opened to the full extent. **2.** open to attack or dispute: *a wide-open statement.* **3.** *U.S.* denoting the loose or irregular enforcement or the non-enforcement of laws concerning the consumption of alcoholic drinks, vice, gambling, etc.

**wide-screen** /'waɪd-skrin/, *adj.* denoting films projected on to a screen having greater width than height, intended to give the audience a greater sense of actuality.

**widespread** /'waɪdsprɛd/, *adj.* **1.** spread over or occupying a wide space. **2.** distributed over a wide region, or occurring in many places or among many persons or individuals. Also, **widespreading.**

**widey** /'waɪdi/, *n. Colloq.* a wide motor car tyre.

**widgeon** /'wɪdʒən/, *n.* **1.** any of several Old World and New World freshwater ducks between the mallard and teal in size, esp. the white-eyed duck. **2.** *Obs.* a fool. Also, **wigeon.** [orig. obscure]

**widgie** /'wɪdʒi/, *n. Colloq.* a female bodgie.

**widow** /'wɪdou/, *n.* **1.** a woman who has lost her husband by death and has not married again. **2.** (used in combination) a woman whose husband is often absent, devoting his attention to some sport or other activity: *a golf widow.* **3.** *Cards.* an additional hand or part of a hand, as one dealt to the table. **4.** *Print.* a short line at the end of a paragraph, esp. one which makes less than half the full width. *–v.t.* **5.** to make (one) a widow (chiefly in pp.). **6.** to deprive of anything valued, or bereave. **7.** *Obs.* **a.** to endow with a widow's right. **b.** to survive as the widow of. [ME; OE *widuwe,* c. G *Witwe;* akin to L *vidua* widow (fem. of *viduus* deprived of)]

**widowbird** /'wɪdoubɜd/, *n.* →**whydah.**

**widower** /'wɪdouə/, *n.* a man who has lost his wife by death and has not married again.

**widowhood** /'wɪdouhʊd/, *n.* the state or period of being a widow (or, sometimes, a widower).

**widow's hump** /wɪdoʊz 'hʌmp/, *n.* a hump at the base of the back of the neck, occurring in elderly women. Also, **dowager's hump.**

**widow's mite** /– 'maɪt/, *n.* a small gift of money given in good spirit by one who can ill afford it.

**widow's peak** /– 'pik/, *n.* a point formed by the hair growing down in the middle of the forehead.

**width** /wɪdθ/, *n.* **1.** extent from side to side; breadth; wideness. **2.** a piece of the full wideness, as of cloth.

**widthwise** /'wɪdθwaɪz/, *adv.* in the direction of the width. Also, **widthways** /'wɪdθweɪz/.

**wield** /wild/, *v.t.* **1.** to exercise (power, authority, influence, etc.), as in ruling or dominating. **2.** to manage (a weapon, instrument, etc.) in use; handle or employ in action. **3.** *Archaic.* to guide or direct. [ME *welde(n)*, OE *wieldan* control, from *wealdan* rule, govern, c. G *walten*] – **wieldable,** *adj.* – **wielder,** *n.*

**wieldy** /'wildi/, *adj.*, **wieldier, wieldiest.** readily wielded or managed, as in use or action.

**wiener** /'winə/, *n. U.S.* →**frankfurt.** Also, **wienerwurst** /'winəwɜst/. [G; short for *weinerwurst* Viennese sausage]

**Wiener schnitzel** /vinə 'ʃnɪtsəl/, *n.* a breaded veal cutlet or escalope, variously seasoned or garnished. [G: Viennese cutlet]

**wife** /waɪf/, *n.*, *pl.* **wives** /waɪvz/. **1.** a woman joined in marriage to a man as husband. **2.** a woman (*archaic* except in compounds): *housewife, midwife.* [ME; OE *wīf* woman, wife, c. D *wijf*, G *Weib*, Icel. *vīf*] – **wifedom,** *n.* – **wifeless,** *adj.* – **wifelessness,** *n.*

**wife-beater** /'waɪf-bitə/, *n.* a very long, narrow, loaf of bread. Also, **husband-beater.**

**wifehood** /'waɪfhʊd/, *n.* **1.** the position or relation of a wife. **2.** wifely character.

**wifely** /'waɪfli/, *adj.*, **-lier, -liest.** of, like, or befitting a wife. Also, **wifelike** /'waɪflaɪk/. – **wifeliness,** *n.*

**wifey** /'waɪfi/, *n. Colloq.* wife.

**wig**[1] /wɪg/, *n.*, *v.*, **wigged, wigging.** *–n.* **1.** an artificial covering of hair for the head, worn to conceal baldness, for disguise, theatricals, etc., or formerly as an ordinary head covering. **2.** real or synthetic hair worn by women over their own hair, attached to a base or entwined with it, to create a new hairstyle, for a change of hair colour, etc. **3.** the wool on a sheep's face and head. *–v.t.* **4.** to furnish with a wig or wigs. **5.** *Brit. Colloq.* to reprimand or reprove severely. **6.** *Agric.* to remove wool from around the eyes of a sheep so that it does not become wool blind. *–v.i.* **7.** *Brit. Colloq.* to scold. [short for PERIWIG] – **wigged,** *adj.* – **wigless,** *adj.* – **wiglike,** *adj.*

**wig**[2] /wɪg/, *n.* **1.** the male of the Australian fur seal. **2.** the fur on the shoulders of a male hooded seal of large size.

**wigan** /'wɪgən/, *n.* a stiff, canvas-like fabric used for stiffening parts of garments. [named after *Wigan,* town in Lancashire, England, where it was first made]

**wigeon** /'wɪdʒən/, *n.* →**widgeon.**

**wiggery** /'wɪgəri/, *n.*, *pl.* **-geries.** **1.** wigs or a wig; false hair. **2.** the wearing of wigs.

**wigging** /'wɪgɪŋ/, *n.* **1.** *Brit. Colloq.* a scolding or reproof. **2.** *Agric.* the cutting of wool from around the eyes of a sheep, to prevent wool blindness.

**wiggle** /'wɪgəl/, *v.*, **-gled, -gling,** *n.* *–v.i.* **1.** to move or go with short, quick, irregular movements from side to side; wriggle. *–v.t.* **2.** to cause to wiggle; move quickly and irregularly from side to side. *–n.* **3.** a wiggling movement or course. **4.** a wiggly line. [ME *wigle(n)*, frequentative of *wig* (now Brit. d.) wag. Cf. Norw. *vigla* totter, frequentative of *vigga* rock oneself, and D and LG *wiggelen*] – **wiggler,** *n.*

**wiggly** /'wɪgli/, *adj.* **1.** undulating; wavy: *a wiggly line.* **2.** wriggly.

**wight** /waɪt/, *n. Archaic.* **1.** a human being or person. **2.** a supernatural being. **3.** a living being or creature. [ME; OE *wiht*, c. G *Wicht*]

**wigmaker** /'wɪgmeɪkə/, *n.* one who makes wigs.

**wigwag** /'wɪgwæg/, *v.*, **-wagged, -wagging,** *n.*, *adj.* *–v.t., v.i.* **1.** to move to and fro. **2.** *Navy, etc.* to signal by movements of two flags or the like waved according to a code. *–n. Navy, etc.* **3.** wigwagging, or signalling by movements of flags or the like. **4.** a message so signalled. *–adj.* **5.** *Navy, etc.* signalled in this manner. [contraction of phrase *wig and wag.* See WIGGLE, WAG[1]] – **wigwagger,** *n.*

**wigwam** /'wɪgwɒm/, *n.* **1.** an American Indian hut or lodge, usu. of rounded or oval shape, formed of poles overlaid with bark, mats, or skins. **2.** *U.S. Colloq.* a structure, esp. of large size, used for political conventions, etc. **3. a wigwam for a goose's bridle,** *Colloq.* a jocular name given to an object which one is unable to identify. [Algonquian (Abnaki): dwelling]

wigwam showing structural details

**Wik-Munkan** /wɪk-'mʊŋkən/, *n.* an Australian Aboriginal language of Cape York in Queensland, spoken mainly near Aurukun.

**Wilcannia shower** /wɪl,kænjə 'ʃaʊə/, *n.* a dust storm. [from *Wilcannia,* town in W N.S.W.]

**wilco** /wɪl'koʊ/, *interj.* message received and will be complied with (used in signalling and telecommunications). [shortened form of *will comply*]

**wild** /waɪld/, *adj.* **1.** living in a state of nature, as animals that have not been tamed or domesticated. **2.** growing or produced without cultivation or the care of man, as plants, flowers, fruit, honey, etc. **3.** uncultivated, uninhabited, or waste, as land. **4.** uncivilised or barbarous, as tribes or savages. **5.** of unrestrained violence, fury, intensity, etc.; violent; furious: *wild fighting, wild storms.* **6.** characterised by or indicating violent excitement, as actions, the appearance, etc. **7.** frantic; distracted, crazy, or mad: *to drive someone wild.* **8.** violently excited: *wild with rage, fear, or pain.* **9.** undisciplined, unruly, lawless, or turbulent: *wild boys, a wild crew.* **10.** unrestrained, untrammelled, or unbridled: *wild gaiety, wild orgies.* **11.** disregardful of moral restraints as to pleasurable indulgence. **12.** unrestrained by reason or prudence: *wild schemes.* **13.** extravagant or fantastic: *wild fancies.* **14.** disorderly or dishevelled: *wild locks.* **15.** wide of the mark: *a wild throw.* **16.** *Colloq.* intensely eager or enthusiastic. **17.** *Cards.* (of a card) having its value decided by the wishes of the players or the player who holds it. **18. wild and woolly,** *Colloq.* **a.** rough; untidy; unkempt. **b.** uncivilised; unrestrained. *–adv.* **19.** in a wild manner; wildly. **20. run wild, a.** to grow without cultivation or check. **b.** to behave in an unrestrained or uncontrolled manner: *he allows his children to run wild.* *–n.* **21.** (*oft. pl.*) an uncultivated, uninhabited, or desolate region or tract; a waste; a wilderness; a desert. [ME and OE *wilde,* c. D and G *wild*] – **wildly,** *adv.* – **wildness,** *n.*

**wild boar** /– 'bɔ/, *n.* a wild Old World swine, *Sus scrofa,* the supposed original of most domestic pigs.

**wild carrot** /– 'kærət/, *n.* a biennial umbelliferous herb with white flowers and hooked fruits, *Daucus carota,* widespread in temperate regions, esp. near the coast, and the original of the cultivated carrot.

wild boar

**wildcat** /'waɪldkæt/, *n.*, *adj.*, *v.*, **-catted, -catting.** *–n.* **1.** a forest-dwelling European feline, *Felis sylvestris,* somewhat larger than, but very much like, the domestic cat, to which it is closely related and with which it interbreeds freely. **2.** a similar North African species, *Felis libyca,* probably the main source of the domesticated cat. **3.** any of several North American felines of the genus *Lynx,* esp. *L. rufus* and *L. canadensis,* the former widely distributed, the latter largely restricted to Canada. **4.** any of several other of the smaller felines, as the serval, ocelot, etc. **5.** a quick-tempered or savage person. **6.** an exploratory well drilled in an effort to discover deposits of oil or gas; a prospect well. *–adj.* **7.** characterised by or proceeding from reckless or unsafe business methods: *wildcat companies or shares.* **8.** of or pertaining to an illicit enterprise or product. *–v.i.* **9.** to search for oil, ore, or the like, as an independent prospector. – **wildcatting,** *n.*, *adj.*

**wildcat strike** /– 'straɪk/, *n.* a strike which has not been called or sanctioned by officials of a trade union; unofficial strike.

**wildcatter** /'waɪldkætə/, *n. U.S. Colloq.* one who prospects for oil or ores; a prospector.

**wild cherry** /waɪld 'tʃɛri/, *n.* →**gean.**

**wildebeest** /'wɪldəbist/, *n., pl.* **-beests.** →**gnu.** [Afrikaans: lit., wild beast]

**wilder** /'wɪldə/, *Archaic.* –*v.t.* **1.** to cause to lose one's way. **2.** to bewilder. –*v.i.* **3.** to lose one's way. **4.** to be bewildered. – **wilderment,** *n.*

**wilderness** /'wɪldənəs/, *n.* **1.** a wild region, as of forest or desert; a waste; a tract of land inhabited only by wild animals. **2.** any desolate tracts, as of water. **3.** a part of a garden set apart for plants growing with unchecked luxuriance. **4.** a bewildering mass or collection. **5. in the wilderness,** *Colloq.* **a.** in a state or place of isolation; away from the centre of things. **b.** out of political office. [ME, from *wilder(n)* wild (OE *wilddēoren* of wild beasts) + -NESS]

**wilderness area** /'– ɛəriə/, *n.* a wilderness (def. 1) in which the ecology is undisturbed.

**wild-eyed** /'waɪld-aɪd/, *adj.* glaring in an angry or wild manner.

**wildfire** /'waɪldfaɪə/, *n.* **1.** a highly inflammable composition, as Greek fire, difficult to extinguish when ignited, formerly used in warfare. **2.** something that runs or spreads with extraordinary rapidity: *the news spread like wildfire.* **3.** sheet lightning, unaccompanied by thunder. **4.** the will-o'-the-wisp or ignis fatuus. **5.** *Obs. Pathol.* erysipelas or some similar disease. **6.** *Obs. Vet. Sci.* an inflammatory disease of the skin of sheep; scabies.

**wild flooding** /ˌwaɪld 'flʌdɪŋ/, *n.* a method of flood irrigation where water is released on to land which is ungraded or partially graded.

**wild flower** /'waɪld flaʊə/, *n.* **1.** the flower of an uncultivated plant. **2.** such a plant. Also, **wildflower.**

**wildfowl** /'waɪldfaʊl/, *n.* **1.** a game bird, esp. a wild duck or wild goose. **2.** game birds collectively. – **wildfowler,** *n.* – **wildfowling,** *n., adj.*

**wild goose** /waɪld 'gus/, *n.* **1.** any undomesticated goose, esp. the European greylag and the Canada goose. **2.** *Colloq.* a foolish person.

**wild-goose chase** /waɪld-'gus tʃeɪs/, *n.* **1.** a wild or absurd chase, as after something non-existent or unobtainable. **2.** any senseless pursuit of an object or end.

**wild indigo** /waɪld 'ɪndɪgoʊ/, *n.* any of the American leguminous plants constituting the genus *Baptisia,* esp. *B. tinctoria,* a species with yellow flowers.

**wilding** /'waɪldɪŋ/, *n.* **1.** any plant that grows wild. **2.** an escape (plant). **3.** a wild animal. –*adj.* **4.** *Archaic.* not cultivated or domesticated; wild.

**wild Irishman** /waɪld 'aɪrɪʃmən/, *n.* →**matagouri.**

**wildish** /'waɪldɪʃ/, *adj.* somewhat wild.

**wild lettuce** /waɪld 'lɛtəs/, *n.* any of various uncultivated species of lettuce of the genus *Lactuca,* growing as weeds in waste places, as *L. saligna.*

**wildlife** /'waɪldlaɪf/, *n.* animals living in their natural habitat.

**wildling** /'wɪldlɪŋ/, *n.* a wild plant, flower, or animal.

**wild mustard** /waɪld 'mʌstəd/, *n.* any of various cruciferous weeds related to mustard.

**wild oat** /– 'oʊt/, *n.* **1.** Also, **black oat.** any uncultivated species of the genus *Avena,* esp. *A. fatua,* a common grass or weed resembling the cultivated oat. **2.** (*pl.*) dissolute life in one's youth. **3. sow one's wild oats,** to live a dissolute life, esp. to be promiscuous in youth.

**wild onion** /– 'ʌnjən/, *n.* a perennial, onion-like plant, *Asphodelus fistulosus,* native to the Mediterranean region but common in parts of southern Australia. Also, **onion weed.**

**wild parsley** /– 'pasli/, *n.* any of numerous umbelliferous plants resembling the parsley in shape and structure.

**wild parsnip** /– 'pasnɪp/, *n.* **1.** an umbelliferous weed, *Pastinaca sativa,* having an inedible acrid root, common in fields and waste places, and regarded as the original of the cultivated parsnip. **2.** any of several Australian species of the genus *Trachymene.*

**wild rose** /'– roʊz/, *n.* any uncultivated species of rose, usu. having a single flower with the corolla consisting of one circle of roundish spreading petals.

**wild rubber** /– 'rʌbə/, *n.* caoutchouc from trees growing wild.

**wild silk** /– 'sɪlk/, *n.* any silk having a rough texture, as tussah.

**wild sorghum** /– 'sɔgəm/, *n.* a pasture grass, *Sorghum leiocladum,* with reddish-brown seed heads, native to Australia.

**wild thyme** /– 'taɪm/, *n.* a thyme, *Thymus serpyllum.*

**wild track** /'– træk/, *n.* a soundtrack recorded quite independently of any picture with which it may subsequently be combined.

**Wild West** /waɪld 'wɛst/, *n.* the western frontier region of the U.S. before the establishment of stable government, esp. as a setting or background for cowboy films and stories or the like.

**wildwood** /'waɪldwʊd/, *n. Archaic.* a wood growing in the wild or natural state; a forest.

**wile** /waɪl/, *n., v.,* **wiled, wiling.** –*n.* **1.** a trick, artifice, or stratagem. **2.** (*oft. pl.*) an artful or beguiling procedure. **3.** deceitful cunning; trickery. –*v.t.* **4.** to beguile, entice, or lure (*away, from, into,* etc.). **5. wile away,** while away. [ME *wil(e),* probably from Scand.; cf. Icel. *vēl* craft, fraud, *vēla* defraud]

**wilful** /'wɪlfəl/, *adj.* **1.** willed, voluntary, or intentional: *wilful murder.* **2.** self-willed or headstrong; perversely obstinate or intractable. Also, *U.S.,* **willful.** [ME; OE *wilful-* willing (in *wilful-līce* willingly). See WILL², -FUL] – **wilfully,** *adv.* – **wilfulness,** *n.*

**wilga** /'wɪlgə/, *n.* a small shapely tree, *Geijera parviflora,* of inland eastern Australia, valuable as fodder in drought. [Aboriginal]

**wilkintie** /wɪl'kɪnti/, *n.* the dusky hopping-mouse, *Notomys fuscus,* of central Australia. [Aboriginal]

**will**[1] /wɪl/; *weak forms* /wəl, l/, *v.; pres. sing.* 1 **will;** 2 **will** or (*Archaic*) **wilt;** 3 **will;** *pl.* **will;** *pt.* 1 **would;** 2 **would** or (*Archaic*) **wouldst;** 3 **would;** *pl.* **would;** *pp.* (*Obs.*) **would;** *imperative and infinitive lacking.* –*aux. v.* **1.** am (is, are, etc.) about or going to (in future constructions, denoting in the first person promise or determination, in the second and third persons mere futurity). **2.** am (is, are, etc.) disposed or willing to. **3.** am expected or required to. **4.** may be expected or supposed to: *you will not have forgotten him, this will be right.* **5.** am (is, are, etc.) determined or sure to (used emphatically): *you would do it, people will talk.* **6.** am (is, are, etc.) accustomed to, or do usually or often: *he would write for hours at a time.* –*v.t., v.i.* **7.** to wish; desire; like: *as you will, would it were true.* [ME; OE *wyllan,* c. D *willen,* Icel. *vilja,* Goth. *wiljan;* akin to G *wollen,* L *velle* wish]

**will**[2] /wɪl/, *n., v.,* **willed, willing.** –*n.* **1.** the faculty of conscious and esp. of deliberate action: *the freedom of the will.* **2.** the power of choosing one's own actions: *to have a strong or a weak will.* **3.** the act of using this power. **4.** the process of willing, or volition. **5.** wish or desire: *to submit against one's will.* **6.** purpose or determination, often hearty determination: *to have the will to succeed.* **7.** the wish or purpose as carried out, or to be carried out: *to work one's will.* **8.** disposition (good or ill) towards another. **9.** *Law.* **a.** a legal declaration of a person's wishes as to the disposition of his (real) property, etc., after his death, usu. in writing, and either signed by the testator and attested by witnesses or, in Scotland, holographic. **b.** the document containing such a declaration. **10. at will,** at one's discretion or pleasure: *to wander at will.* **11. a will of one's own,** a strong power of asserting oneself. **12. with a will,** willingly; readily; eagerly. **13. work one's will,** to do as one chooses. –*v.t.* **14.** to give by will or testament; to bequeath or devise. **15.** to influence by exerting willpower. **16.** to wish or desire. **17.** to decide by act of will. **18.** to purpose, determine on, or elect, by act of will. –*v.i.* **19.** to exercise the will. **20.** to determine, decide, or ordain, as by act of will. [ME and OE (also ME *wille,* OE *willa*); c. D *wil,* G *Wille,* Icel. *vili,* Goth. *wilja*] – **willer,** *n.*

**willable** /'wɪləbəl/, *adj.* capable of being willed, or fixed by will.

**willaroo** /wɪlə'ru/, *n.* →**southern stone curlew.** [imitative]

**willed** /wɪld/, *adj.* having a will of the kind specified (used in combination): *strong-willed.*

**willemite** /'wɪləmaɪt/, *n.* a mineral, a zinc silicate, $Zn_2SiO_4$, sometimes containing manganese, occurring in prismatic

W–Z

crystals or granular masses, usu. greenish, sometimes white, brown, or red; a minor ore of zinc. [D *Willemit,* named after King *Willem* I of the Netherlands]

**willet** /ˈwɪlət/, *n.* a large North American semipalmate shorebird, *Catoptrophorus semipalmatus,* with striking black-and-white wing pattern. [short for *pill-will-willet,* imitative of cry of bird]

**willful** /ˈwɪlfəl/, *adj. U.S.* →**wilful.** – **willfully,** *adv.* – **willfulness,** *n.*

**willie** /ˈwɪli/, *n. Colloq.* (*esp. in children's speech*) a penis.

**willies** /ˈwɪliz/, *n. pl. Colloq.* feelings of uneasiness or fear: *that creaking door is giving me the willies.*

**Willie wagtail** /wɪli ˈwægteɪl/, *n.* a common black and white Australian fantail, *Rhipidura leucophrys.* Also, **Willy wagtail.**

Willie wagtail

**willing** /ˈwɪlɪŋ/, *adj.* **1.** disposed or consenting (without being particularly desirous): *willing to take what one can get.* **2.** cheerfully consenting or ready: *a willing worker.* **3.** done, given, borne, used, etc., with cheerful readiness. **4.** of or pertaining to someone who overcharges or makes excessive demands: *that salesman is a bit willing.* **5.** of or pertaining to a situation in which such excessive demands are made: *that's a bit willing.* – **willingly,** *adv.* – **willingness,** *n.*

**williwaw** /ˈwɪliwɔ/, *n. N.Z.* a whirlwind, esp. at sea.

**will-o'-the-wisp** /ˈwɪl-ə-ðə-wɪsp/, *n.* **1.** →**ignis fatuus. 2.** anything that deludes or misleads by luring on.

**willow** /ˈwɪloʊ/, *n.* **1.** any of the trees or shrubs constituting the genus *Salix,* many species of which have tough, pliable twigs or branches which are used for wickerwork, etc. **2.** the wood of the willow. **3.** *Colloq.* something made of this, as a cricket bat. **4.** a machine consisting essentially of a cylinder armed with spikes revolving within a spiked casing, for opening and cleaning cotton or other fibre. *–v.t.* **5.** to treat (cotton, etc.) with a willow. [ME *wilwe,* var. of *wilghe,* OE *welig,* c. D *wilg,* LG *wilge*]

**willower** /ˈwɪloʊə/, *n.* **1.** a person or a thing that willows. **2.** →**willow** (def. 4).

**willowherb** /ˈwɪloʊhɜb/, *n.* **1.** a plant, *Chamaenerion angustifolium,* with narrow, willow-like leaves and racemes of purple flowers. **2.** any plant of the related genus *Epilobium.*

**willowish** /ˈwɪloʊɪʃ/, *adj.* →**willowy.**

**willow myrtle** /wɪloʊ ˈmɜtəl/, *n.* →**agonis.**

**willow pattern** /ˈ– pætn/, *n.* a pattern used on china, employing the design of the willow tree, and originated in approximately 1780 by Thomas Turner in England.

**willow warbler** /ˈ– wɔblə/, *n.* a small brown bird of the family Sylviidae, *Phylloscopus trochilus,* of Europe and northern Asia.

**willow-ware** /ˈwɪloʊ-wɛə/, *n.* china using willow pattern.

**willowy** /ˈwɪloʊi/, *adj.* **1.** pliant; lithe. **2.** gracefully slender and supple. **3.** abounding with willows.

**willpower** /ˈwɪlpaʊə/, *n.* **1.** control over one's impulses and actions. **2.** strength of will: *he has great willpower.*

**willy**[1] /ˈwɪli/, *n. Colloq.* a wallet.

**willy**[2] /ˈwɪli/, *n. Colloq.* **1.** a sudden outburst of emotion, as enthusiasm, annoyance, etc. **2. have (take) a willy,** to be very upset or alarmed. **3. throw a willy,** to become heated or excited. [? short for WILLY-WILLY]

**willy-nilly** /wɪli-ˈnɪli/, *adv.* **1.** willingly or unwillingly. **2.** in random order; in disarray. *–adj.* **3.** shilly-shallying; vacillating. [from phrase *will I* (*he, ye*)*, nill I* (*he, ye*); *nill* be unwilling]

**willy-willy** /ˈwɪli-wɪli/, *n.* **1.** a spiralling wind, often collecting dust, refuse, etc. *n.* **2.** a cyclonic storm. [Aboriginal]

**Wilson's petrel** /wɪlsənz ˈpɛtrəl/, *n.* a small petrel, *Oceanites oceanicus,* black with white rump, of antarctic and tropical oceans, and occasionally found farther north.

**wilt**[1] /wɪlt/, *v.i.* **1.** to become limp and drooping, as a fading flower; wither. **2.** to lose strength, vigour, assurance, etc. *–v.t.* **3.** to cause to wilt. *–n.* **4.** the act of wilting. **5.** a spell of depression, lassitude, or dizziness. [d. var. of *wilk* wither itself var. of *welk,* ME *welken.* Cf. D and G *welken* wither]

**wilt**[2] /wɪlt/, *Archaic.* second pers. sing. pres. ind. of **will**[1].

**wilt**[3] /wɪlt/, *n.* **1.** *Bot.* any of various plant diseases in which the leaves droop, become flaccid and then dry, usu. because water cannot pass through the plant, as that caused by fungus of the genus *Verticillium* in potatoes. **2.** a highly infectious disease in certain caterpillars, which causes their bodies to liquefy. Also, **wilt disease.** [special use of WILT[1]]

**Wilton carpet** /wɪltən ˈkapət/, *n.* a kind of carpet, woven on a Jacquard loom like Brussels carpet, but having the loops cut to form a velvet pile. Also, **Wilton.** [named after *Wilton,* town in England]

**wily** /ˈwaɪli/, *adj.,* **-lier, -liest.** full of, marked by, or proceeding from wiles; crafty; cunning. [ME, from WIL(E) + -Y[1]] – **wilily,** *adv.* – **wiliness,** *n.*

**wimble** /ˈwɪmbəl/, *n., v.,* **-bled, -bling.** *–n.* **1.** a device in mining, etc., for extracting the rubbish from a bored hole. **2.** a brace for drilling marble, etc. **3.** any of various other instruments for boring, etc. *–v.t.* **4.** to bore or perforate with or as with a wimble. [ME, from AF. Cf. GIMLET]

**Wimmera rye** /wɪmərə ˈraɪ/, *n.* a frost-resistant annual, *Lolium rigidum,* native to Europe widely grown as a pasture grass in cold dry areas, introduced into Australia in the Wimmera district, Victoria.

**Wimmera shower** /– ˈʃaʊə/, *n.* →**Wilcannia shower.** [from *Wimmera,* district in W Vic.]

**wimple** /ˈwɪmpəl/, *n., v.,* **-pled, -pling.** *–n.* **1.** a woman's headcloth drawn in folds about the chin, formerly worn out of doors, and still in use by some nuns. *–v.t.* **2.** to cover or muffle with or as with a wimple. **3.** to cause to ripple or undulate, as water. **4.** *Archaic.* to lay in folds, as a veil. *–v.i.* **5.** to ripple, as water. **6.** *Archaic.* to lie in folds, as a veil. [ME; var. of ME and OE *wimpel,* c. D and LG *wimpel*]

wimple

**Wimshurst machine** /ˈwɪmzhɜst məˌʃin/, *n.* a laboratory apparatus for generating and storing at high potential the static electricity produced by the friction between two coaxial, counter-revolving, insulating discs; a static machine. [named after J. *Wimshurst,* died 1903, English scientist]

**win**[1] /wɪn/, *v.,* **won, winning,** *n. –v.i.* **1.** to succeed by striving or effort (sometimes fol. by *out*). **2.** to gain the victory. **3.** to be placed first in a race or the like. **4.** to get (*in, out, through, to,* etc., *free, loose,* etc.). *–v.t.* **5.** to get by effort, as through labour, competition, or conquest. **6.** to gain (a prize, fame, etc.). **7.** to be successful in (a game, battle, etc.). **8.** to make (one's way), as by effort, ability, etc. **9.** to attain or reach (a point, goal, etc.): *to win the shore in a storm.* **10.** to gain (favour, love, consent, etc.) as by qualities or influence. **11.** to gain the favour, regard, or adherence of. **12.** to bring (*over*) to favour, consent, etc.; persuade. **13.** to persuade to love or marriage, or gain in marriage. **14.** *Mining.* **a.** to obtain (ore, coal, etc.). **b.** to prepare (a vein, bed, mine, etc.) for working, by means of shafts, etc. *–n.* **15.** an act of winning; a success; a victory. **16.** the act or fact of finishing first, esp. in a horserace. [ME *winne(n),* OE *winnan* work, fight, bear, c. G *gewinnen*]

**win**[2] /wɪn/, *v.t.,* **won** or **winned, winning.** *Scot.* to dry (hay, seed, turf, or the like) by exposure to air or heat. [special use of WIN[1] (obs. sense, to harvest), influenced by WINNOW]

**wince** /wɪns/, *v.,* **winced, wincing,** *n. –v.i.* **1.** to shrink, as in pain or from a blow; start; flinch. *–n.* **2.** a wincing or shrinking movement; a slight start. [ME *wynse.* Cf. OF *guenchir* turn aside] – **wincer,** *n.*

**wincey** /ˈwɪnsi/, *n.* a plain or twilled cloth, usu. with a linen or cotton warp and woollen filling. Also, **winsey.** [orig. Scot. d.]

**winceyette** /wɪnsiˈɛt/, *n.* a plain lightweight cotton cloth raised slightly on both sides. [WINCEY + -ETTE]

**winch** /wɪntʃ/, *n.* **1.** the crank or handle of a revolving machine. **2.** a windlass turned by a crank, for hoisting, etc. **3.** any one of a number of contrivances to crank objects by. *–v.t.* **4.** to hoist or haul by means of a winch. [ME *wynch,* OE *wince*] – **wincher,** *n.*

**Winchester gallon** /ˈwɪntʃɛstə gælən/, *n.* →**gallon** (def. 2).

**Winchester rifle** /ˈ– raɪfəl/, *n.* a type of magazine rifle, first made about 1866. Also, **Winchester.** [named after Oliver F. *Winchester,* 1810-80, U.S. manufacturer]

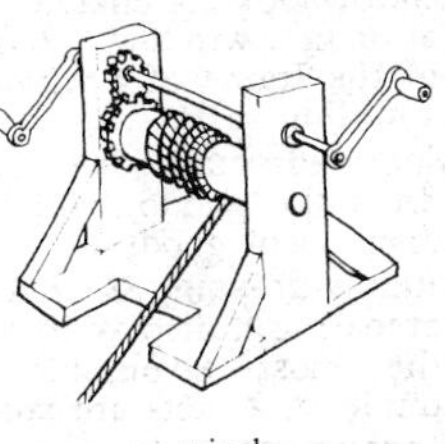
winch

**wind**[1] /wɪnd/, *n.* **1.** air in natural motion, as along the earth's surface. **2.** a gale; storm; hurricane. **3.** any stream of air, as that produced by a bellows, a fan, etc. **4.** air impregnated with the scent of an animal or animals. **5.** a hint or intimation: *get wind of the scandal.* **6.** any tendency or likely course: *the wind of public opinion, wind of change.* **7.** breath or breathing; power of breathing freely, as during continued exertion. **8.** empty talk; mere words. **9.** vanity; conceitedness. **10.** gas generated in the stomach and bowels. **11.** *Colloq.* the solar plexus, where a blow may cause shortness of breath. **12.** See **second wind. 13.** *Music.* **a.** a wind instrument or wind instruments collectively. **b.** (*oft. pl.*) the players on such instruments collectively. **14.** *Naut.* the point or direction from which the wind blows. **15.** a point of the compass, esp. a cardinal point: *the four winds of heaven.* **16.** Some special noun phrases are:

**before the wind,** carried along by the wind; (of a ship) running with the wind astern.

**between wind and water, 1.** *Naut.* denoting the part of a ship, esp. the deck of a heavily laden ship, which the waves wash over. **2.** in a vulnerable or precarious position.

**break wind,** to expel flatus through the anus.

**cast, fling,** or **throw to the wind** or **winds,** to throw off or discard recklessly or in an abandoned manner: *throw all caution to the winds.*

**close to the wind, 1.** *Naut.* sailing as near as possible to the direction from which the wind is blowing. **2.** taking a calculated risk. **3.** transgressing or nearly transgressing conventions of taste, propriety, or the like.

**get the wind up,** *Colloq.* to take fright.

**how the wind blows** or **lies,** what the tendency or likelihood is. Also, **which way the wind blows** or **lies.**

**in the teeth of the wind, 1.** *Naut.* sailing directly against the wind. **2.** against opposition.

**in the wind, 1.** likely to happen; imminent. **2.** circulating as a rumour.

**put the wind up,** *Colloq.* to frighten.

**raise the wind,** *Colloq.* to obtain the necessary finances.

**take the wind out of one's sails,** to frustrate, disconcert, or deprive of an advantage.

*–v.t.* **17.** to expose to wind or air. **18.** to follow by the scent. **19.** to make short of wind or breath, as by vigorous exercise. **20.** to deprive momentarily of breath, as by a blow. **21.** to let recover breath, as by resting after exertion. [ME and OE, c. D *wind* and G *Wind,* Icel. *vindr,* Goth. *winds,* L *ventus*]

**wind**[2] /waɪnd/, *v.,* **wound, winding,** *n.* *–v.i.* **1.** to change direction; bend; turn; take a frequently bending course; meander. **2.** to have a circular or spiral course or direction. **3.** to coil or twine about something. **4.** to be twisted or warped, as a board. **5.** to proceed circuitously or indirectly. **6.** to undergo winding, or winding up. **7. wind down, a.** to relax after a period of tension or activity. **b.** (of a clock) to run down. **8. wind up,** *Colloq.* **a.** to conclude action, speech, etc. **b.** to end: *wind up in the poorhouse.* *–v.t.* **9.** to encircle or wreathe, as with something twined, wrapped, or placed about. **10.** to roll or coil (thread, etc.) into a ball or on a spool or the like (oft. fol. by *up*). **11.** to remove or take off by unwinding (fol. by *off*). **12.** to twine, fold, wrap, or place about something. **13.** to adjust (a mechanism, etc.) for operation by some turning or coiling process (oft. fol. by *up*): *to wind a clock.* **14.** to haul or hoist by means of a winch, windlass, or the like (oft. fol. by *up*). **15.** to make (one's or its way) in a winding or frequently bending course. **16.** to make (the way) by indirect or insidious procedure. **17. wind down, a.** to reduce the scope, intensity of (an operation). **b.** to lower by winding, as by a crank. **18. wind up, a.** to bring to a state of great tension; key up; excite. **b.** to conclude (action, affairs, etc.). *–n.* **19.** a winding; a bend or turn. **20.** a twist producing an uneven surface. [ME; OE *windan* c. D and G *winden,* Icel. *vinda,* Goth. *-windan*]

**wind**[3] /waɪnd/, *v.t.,* **winded** or **wound, winding. 1.** to blow (a horn, a blast, etc.). **2.** to sound by blowing. **3.** to signal or direct by blasts of the horn or the like. [special use of WIND[1]]

**windable** /ˈwaɪndəbəl/, *adj.* that can be wound.

**windage** /ˈwɪndɪdʒ/, *n.* **1.** the influence of the wind in deflecting a missile. **2.** the amount of such deflection. **3.** the amount of movement of a gunsight necessary to compensate for this deflection. **4.** a difference between the diameter of a projectile and that of the gun bore, for the escape of gas and the preventing of friction. **5.** the friction between any rotating part of a machine and the air within the casing which encloses it. **6.** *Naut.* that portion of a vessel's surface upon which the wind acts.

**windbag** /ˈwɪndbæg/, *n.* **1.** *Colloq.* an empty, voluble, pretentious talker. **2.** the bag of a bagpipe.

**wind band** /ˈwɪnd bænd/, *n.* **1.** a military band. **2.** *Music.* a company of performers on wind instruments, as the wind players of a symphony orchestra or a group of them.

**windblown** /ˈwɪndbloʊn/, *adj.* **1.** blown by the wind. **2.** (of trees) growing in a certain shape because of strong prevailing winds. **3.** (of hair) windswept.

**windborne** /ˈwɪndbɔn/, *adj.* carried by the wind, as pollen or seed.

**windbound** /ˈwɪndbaʊnd/, *adj.* (of a sailing ship) prevented from sailing by a contrary or high wind.

**windbreak** /ˈwɪndbreɪk/, *n.* a growth of trees, a structure of boards, or the like, serving as a shelter from the wind.

**wind-broken** /ˈwɪnd-broʊkən/, *adj.* (of horses, etc.) having the breathing impaired; affected with heaves.

**windburn** /ˈwɪndbɜn/, *n.* inflammation of the face, hands, etc., caused by excessive exposure to the wind.

**wind cap** /ˈwɪnd kæp/, *n.* the mouthpiece of a crumhorn, etc., which is extended to form a chamber in which a double reed is enclosed, and which is blown into to set the reed vibrating.

**wind-capped** /ˈwɪnd-kæpt/, *adj.* of or pertaining to a musical instrument which has a windcap.

**windcheater** /ˈwɪntʃitə/, *n.* any close-fitting garment for the upper part of the body designed to give protection against the wind.

**windchest** /ˈwɪntʃɛst/, *n.* a box or reservoir that supplies air under pressure to the pipes or reeds of an organ.

**wind cone** /ˈwɪnd koʊn/, *n.* →**windsock.**

**winded** /ˈwɪndəd/, *adj.* **1.** having wind or breath: *short-winded.* **2.** out of breath. **3.** momentarily unable to breathe, as after a blow in the solar plexus. – **windedness,** *n.*

**winder** /ˈwaɪndə/, *n.* **1.** one who or that which winds (bends, turns, etc.) or is wound. **2.** a tread of triangular or wedge shape which changes the direction of a stair. **3.** a plant that coils or twines itself about something. **4.** an instrument or a machine for winding thread, etc. **5.** a small knob on a watch for winding it up. **6.** *Mining.* a winding engine for raising cages in a mineshaft.

**windfall** /ˈwɪndfɔl/, *n.* **1.** something blown down by the wind, as fruit. **2.** an unexpected piece of good fortune.

**windfall profits** /ˈ– prɒfəts/, *n. pl.* profits made unexpectedly as a result of events not directly related to the company, as fluctuations in the currency or on the stock exchange, changes in government policy affecting the market, etc. Also, **windfall gains.**

**windflower** /ˈwɪndflaʊə/, *n.* any plant of the genus *Anemone.* [translation of Gk *anemṓnē* ANEMONE]

**windgall** /ˈwɪndgɔl/, *n.* a puffy distension of the synovial bursa at the fetlock joint. – **windgalled,** *adj.*

**wind-gap** /ˈwɪnd-gæp/, *n.* a gap in a mountain ridge where a stream once flowed, usu. higher than a water-gap.

**wind gauge** /ˈwɪnd geɪdʒ/, *n.* **1.** →**anemometer. 2.** an appliance attached to a gun to enable allowance to be made for the force of the wind on the projectile when sighting. **3.** a gauge for measuring the pressure of the wind in an organ.

**wind harp** /ˈ– hap/, *n.* →**aeolian harp.**

**windhover** /ˈwɪndhɒvə/, *n.* **1.** →**nankeen kestrel. 2.** the

European kestrel, *Falco tinnunculus.* [WIND[1], *n.* + HOVER]

**Windies** /ˈwɪndiz/, *n. pl. Colloq.* members of touring cricket teams from the West Indies. [contraction of *W(est) Indies*]

**winding** /ˈwaɪndɪŋ/, *n.* **1.** the act of one who or that which winds. **2.** a bend, turn, or flexure. **3.** a coiling, folding, or wrapping, as of one thing about another. **4.** something that is wound or coiled, or a single round of it. **5.** *Elect.* **a.** a symmetrically laid, electrically conducting current path in any device. **b.** the manner of such coiling: *a series winding.* *–adj.* **6.** bending or turning; sinuous. **7.** spiral, as stairs. – **windingly,** *adv.*

**winding sheet** /ˈ– ʃit/, *n.* **1.** a sheet in which a corpse is wrapped for burial. **2.** a mass of tallow or wax that has run down and hardened on the side of a candle.

**winding strip** /ˈ– strɪp/, *n.* one of a pair of parallel battens which are looked through to examine a piece of wood for twist.

**winding-up** /waɪndɪŋ-ˈʌp/, *n.* **1.** a concluding, esp. the stopping of a business operation with the realising of assets, discharging of liabilities, etc. *–adj.* **2.** of or pertaining to such a concluding: *the winding-up period was difficult.*

**wind instrument** /ˈwɪnd ɪnstrəmənt/, *n.* a musical instrument sounded by the player's breath or any current of air.

**windjammer** /ˈwɪndʒæmə/, *n.* **1.** any vessel propelled wholly by sails. **2.** a member of its crew. **3.** →**windcheater.**

**windlass** /ˈwɪndləs/, *n.* **1.** a device for raising weights, etc., usu. consisting of a horizontal cylinder or barrel turned by a crank, lever, or the like, upon which a cable or the like winds, the outer end of the cable being attached directly or indirectly to the weight to be raised or the thing to be hauled or pulled. *–v.t.* **2.** to raise, haul, or move by means of a windlass. [ME *windelas,* from *windel* to wind (frequentative of WIND[2]) + *-as* pole (from Scand.; from Icel. *āss*)]

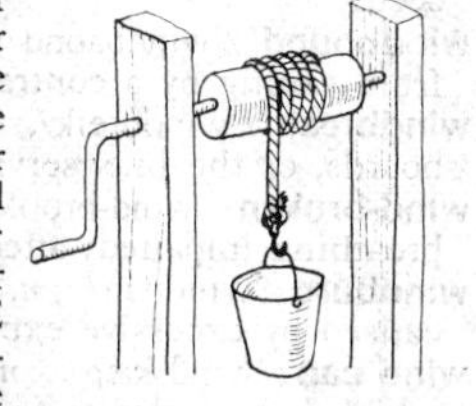
windlass (hand-operated)

**windless** /ˈwɪndləs/, *adj.* **1.** free from wind; calm. **2.** out of breath.

**wind-machine** /ˈwɪnd-məʃin/, *n.* a device for producing a sound resembling a howling gale, usu. consisting of a ribbed drum revolved against a silk or canvas sheet.

**windmill** /ˈwɪndmɪl, ˈwɪn-/, *n.* **1.** a mill or machine, as for grinding or pumping, operated by the wind, usu. by the wind acting on a set of arms, vanes, sails, or slats attached to a horizontal axis so as to form a vertical revolving wheel. **2.** the wheel itself. **3.** *Aeron.* a small air turbine with blades, like those of an aeroplane propeller, exposed on a moving aircraft and driven by the air, used to operate fuel pumps, radio apparatus, etc. **4.** an imaginary opponent, wrong, etc. (in allusion to Cervantes' *Don Quixote*): *to fight windmills.* *–v.i.* **5.** *Aeron. Colloq.* (of an aeroplane propeller or turbojet) to rotate freely under the influence of a passing airstream.

**windmill grass** /ˈ– gras/, *n.* one of the most plentiful summer-growing native species, *Chloris truncata,* whose seedheads radiate out from the stem like windmills, and found in low rainfall areas of New South Wales.

**window** /ˈwɪndoʊ/, *n.* **1.** an opening in the wall or roof of a building, the cabin of a boat, etc., for the admission of air or light, or both, commonly fitted with a frame in which are set movable sashes containing panes of glass. **2.** such an opening with the frame, sashes, and panes of glass, or any other device, by which it is closed. **3.** the frame, sashes, and panes of glass, or the like, intended to fit such an opening. **4.** a windowpane. **5.** anything likened to a window in appearance or function, as a transparent section in an envelope, displaying the address. **6.** any area, interval, or range of frequencies whose existence permits a particular event or phenomenon to be observed or accomplished, as the launching of a spacecraft aimed at a particular target. **7.** a period of time in which there is a lessening of some disturbing or disagreeable activity: *a window in city traffic after peak hour.* **8.** strips of metal foil which when dropped from an aircraft give confusing reflections on enemy radar screens. *–v.t.* **9.** to furnish with a window or windows. [ME, from Scand.; cf. Icel. *vindauga,* from *vind(r)* WIND[1] + *auga* eye] – **windowless,** *adj.*

**window box** /ˈ– bɒks/, *n.* **1.** a box for growing plants, placed at or in a window. **2.** one of the vertical hollows at the sides of the frame of a window, for the weights counterbalancing a sliding sash.

**window-dresser** /ˈwɪndoʊ-drɛsə/, *n.* a person employed to dress the windows of a shop, or arrange in them attractive displays of goods for sale.

**window-dressing** /ˈwɪndoʊ-drɛsɪŋ/, *n.* **1.** the act or fact of preparing a display in a shopwindow. **2.** the presentation of the most favourable aspect of something, esp. when unpleasant facts are concealed. – **window-dress,** *n.*

**windowpane** /ˈwɪndoʊpeɪn/, *n.* a plate of glass used in a window.

**window sash** /ˈwɪndoʊ sæʃ/, *n.* the frame holding the pane or panes of a window.

**window seat** /ˈ– sit/, *n.* **1.** a seat built beneath the sill of a recessed or other window. **2.** any passenger seat in a train, aeroplane, etc., which is next to a window and affords a view out.

**window shade** /ˈ– ʃeɪd/, *n. Chiefly U.S.* a blind or awning for a window.

**window-shop** /ˈwɪndoʊ-ʃɒp/, *v.i.,* **-shopped, -shopping.** to look at articles in shopwindows instead of actually buying. – **window-shopper,** *n.* – **window-shopping,** *adj., n.*

**windowsill** /ˈwɪndoʊsɪl/, *n.* the sill under a window.

**windpipe** /ˈwɪndpaɪp, ˈwɪn-/, *n.* the trachea of an air-breathing vertebrate.

**wind-pollinated** /wɪnd-ˈpɒləneɪtəd/, *adj.* pollinated by airborne pollen. – **wind-pollination** /ˌwɪnd-pɒləˈneɪʃən/, *n.*

**windproof** /ˈwɪndpruf/, *adj.* resisting penetration by the wind.

**windpump** /ˈwɪndpʌmp/, *n.* a pump operated by a windmill.

**windrode** /ˈwɪndroʊd/, *adj.* (of a vessel) riding at anchor with her head to the wind, and the tide running approximately the opposite way.

**wind rose** /ˈwɪnd roʊz/, *n.* a diagram which shows for a given locality or area the frequency and strength of the wind from various directions.

**windrow** /ˈwɪndroʊ, ˈwɪnroʊ/, *n.* **1.** a row or line of hay raked together to dry before being made into cocks or heaps. **2.** any similar row, as of sheaves of grain or stacks of peat, made for the purpose of drying. **3.** a row of dry leaves, dust, etc., swept together by the wind. **4.** *Agric.* timber and bush bulldozed or put into long ridges after the clearing of land and left to dry before burning. *–v.t.* **5.** to arrange in a windrow or windrows. [WIND[1] + ROW[1]] – **windrower,** *n.*

**windsail** /ˈwɪndseɪl, ˈwɪn-/, *n.* a canvas funnel facing into the wind used to ventilate a ship's hold.

**wind scale** /ˈwɪnd skeɪl/, *n.* a numerical scale, like the Beaufort scale, for designating relative wind intensities.

**windscreen** /ˈwɪndskrin, ˈwɪn-/, *n.* the sheet of glass which forms the front window of a motor vehicle. Also, *Chiefly U.S.,* **windshield.**

**windscreen-wiper** /ˈwɪndskrin-waɪpə, ˈwɪn-/, *n.* a mechanically operated, rubber-bladed wiper for keeping the windscreen of a motor vehicle clear of rain, snow, etc.

**wind shadow** /ˈwɪnd ʃædoʊ/, *n.* the calmer area to the lee of a large ship, etc., in the path of the wind: *the racing yacht was becalmed in the wind shadow of a freighter.*

**wind shake** /ˈwɪnd ʃeɪk/, *n.* **1.** a flaw in wood supposed to be caused by the action of strong winds upon the trunk of the tree. **2.** such flaws collectively.

**wind-shaken** /ˈwɪnd-ʃeɪkən, ˈwɪn-/, *adj.* **1.** affected by wind-shake. **2.** shaken by the wind.

**windshear** /ˈwɪndʃɪə, ˈwɪn-/, *n.* a change of wind velocity with distance along an axis at right angles to the wind direction.

**windshield** /ˈwɪndʃild, ˈwɪn-/, *n. Chiefly U.S.* →**windscreen.**

**windsock** /ˈwɪndsɒk, ˈwɪn-/, *n.* a wind-direction indicator, installed at airports and elsewhere, consisting of an elongated truncated cone of textile material, flown from a mast. Also, **airsock, wind cone, wind sleeve.**

Windsor chair

**Windsor chair** /wɪnzə 'tʃɛə/, *n.* a wooden chair of many varieties, having a spindle back and legs slanting outwards, common in 18th-century England.

**Windsor knot** /'– nɒt/, *n.* a wide, triangular knot in a tie produced by extra turns when tying.

**Windsor sausage** /wɪnzə 'sɒsɪdʒ/, *n.* →**devon** (def. 3).

**Windsor soap** /– 'soʊp/, *n.* a kind of perfumed toilet soap, usu. coloured brown.

**Windsor tie** /– 'taɪ/, *n.* a wide, soft, silk tie in a loose bow.

**windstorm** /'wɪndstɔm, 'wɪn-/, *n.* a storm with heavy wind, but little or no precipitation.

**windsucker** /'wɪndsʌkə, 'wɪn-/, *n.* a horse afflicted with cribbing.

**wind-sucking** /'wɪnd-sʌkɪŋ, 'wɪn-/, *adj.* →**cribbing** (def. 1).

**windsurf** /'wɪndsɜf/, *v.i.* to ride a windsurfer.

**windsurfer** /'wɪndsɜfə/, *n.* **1.** →**sailboard.** **2.** a person who windsurfs. [Trademark]

**windswept** /'wɪndswɛpt, 'wɪn-/, *adj.* **1.** open or exposed to the wind. **2.** (of hair) blown about by the wind, or styled to give such an effect.

**windtight** /'wɪndtaɪt, 'wɪn-/, *adj.* so tight as to prevent passage of wind or air.

**wind-tunnel** /'wɪnd-tʌnəl, 'wɪn-/, *n.* a tunnel-like device through which a controlled airstream can be drawn at various speeds, in order to subject scale models of aircraft, parts of aircraft, or complete aircraft, to aerodynamic tests.

**wind-up** /'waɪnd-ʌp/, *n.* **1.** the conclusion of any action, etc.; the end or close. **2.** a final act or part.

**windvane** /'wɪndveɪn/, *n.* a device using a pivoted arm with a vertical vane to indicate the direction of the wind.

**windward** /'wɪndwəd/, *adv.* **1.** towards the wind; towards the point from which the wind blows. *–adj.* **2.** pertaining to, situated in, or moving towards the quarter from which the wind blows (opposed to *leeward*). *–n.* **3.** the point or quarter from which the wind blows. **4.** the side towards the wind. **5. get to the windward of,** to get the advantage of.

**windy** /'wɪndi/, *adj.*, **windier, windiest. 1.** accompanied or characterised by wind: *windy weather.* **2.** exposed to or swept by the wind: *a windy hill.* **3.** consisting of or resembling wind: *the windy tempest of my heart.* **4.** towards the wind, or windward. **5.** unsubstantial or empty. **6.** of the nature of, characterised by, or given to prolonged, empty talk; voluble. **7.** characterised by or causing flatulence. **8.** *Colloq.* frightened; nervous. [ME; OE *windig,* from *wind* WIND[1] + *-ig* -Y[1]] – **windily,** *adv.* – **windiness,** *n.*

**windy woof** /'– wʊf/, *n. Colloq.* (in cricket) a wild swing by a batsman, usu. missing the ball.

**wine** /waɪn/, *n., v.,* **wined, wining.** *–n.* **1.** the fermented juice of the grape, in many varieties (red, white, sweet, dry, still, sparkling, etc.) used as a beverage and in cookery, religious rites, etc. **2.** a particular variety of such fermented grape juice: *port and sherry wines.* **3.** the juice, fermented or unfermented, of various other fruits or plants, used as a beverage, etc.: *gooseberry wine, currant wine.* **4.** a dark reddish colour, as of red wines. **5.** something that invigorates, cheers, or intoxicates like wine. *–adj.* **6.** wine-coloured; dark purplish red. *–v.t.* **7.** to entertain with wine. **8.** to supply with wine. *–v.i.* **9.** to drink wine. [ME; OE *wīn,* c. D *wijn,* G *Wein,* Icel. *vīn,* Goth. *wein,* all from a prehistoric Gmc word from L *vīnum*]

**wine bar** /'– ba/, *n.* a place which is licensed to serve only wine to drink.

**wineberry** /'waɪnbɛri/, *n.* →**makomako** (def. 1).

**winebibber** /'waɪnbɪbə/, *n.* one who drinks much wine; a drunkard. – **winebibbing,** *n., adj.*

**wine biscuit** /'waɪn bɪskət/, *n.* a semisweet biscuit originally intended to be eaten with wine.

**wine cellar** /'– sɛlə/, *n.* **1.** a cellar for the storage of wine. **2.** the wine stored there; a store or stock of wines.

**wine-cooler** /'waɪn-kulə/, *n.* a bucket with ice for cooling wine in bottles to be served at table.

**winedot** /'waɪndɒt/, *n.* an alcohol addict. [pun on *Wyandotte* an American breed of fowl]

**wineglass** /'waɪnglas/, *n.* a small drinking glass for wine.

**wineglassful** /'waɪnglasfʊl/, *n., pl.* **-fuls.** the capacity of a wineglass, commonly considered as equal to 55 ml.

**winegrower** /'waɪn-groʊə/, *n.* one who owns or works in a vineyard or wine-making business.

**winegrowing** /'waɪn-groʊɪŋ/, *n.* the act or business of a wine-grower.

**winemaking** /'waɪn-meɪkɪŋ/, *n.* the process of preparing wine from grapes or other fruit.

**wine measure** /'waɪn mɛʒə/, *n.* a former English system of measurement for wine, etc., in which the gallon (wine gallon) was equal to 231 cu.ins (3.78 L approx.).

**wine palm** /'– pam/, *n.* any of various palms yielding toddy (def. 2).

**winepress** /'waɪnprɛs/, *n.* a machine in which the juice is pressed from grapes for wine.

**winery** /'waɪnəri/, *n., pl.* **-eries.** an establishment for making wine.

**wineshop** /'waɪnʃɒp/, *n.* a shop where wine is sold.

**wineskin** /'waɪnskɪn/, *n.* **1.** a vessel made of the nearly complete skin of a goat, or the like, used, esp. in the East, for holding wine. **2.** *Colloq.* one who drinks great or excessive quantities of wine.

**wine stone** /'waɪn stoʊn/, *n.* cream of tartar deposited in wine tanks and casks.

**wine-taster** /'waɪn-teɪstə/, *n.* one whose occupation is to sample wines to examine their quality.

**wine-tasting** /'waɪn-teɪstɪŋ/, *n.* **1.** the occupation of a wine-taster. **2.** a social or other gathering to sample various wines.

**wine waiter** /'waɪn weɪtə/, *n.* →**drink waiter.** Also, **wine steward.**

**winey** /'waɪni/, *adj.,* **winier, winiest.** →**winy.**

**wing** /wɪŋ/, *n.* **1.** either of the two anterior extremities, or appendages of the scapular arch or shoulder girdle, of most birds and of bats, which constitute the forelimbs and correspond to the human arms, but are adapted for flight. **2.** either of two corresponding but rudimentary or functionless parts in certain other birds, as ostriches and penguins. **3.** any of certain other winglike structures of other animals, as the patagium of a flying squirrel. **4.** (in insects) one of the thin, flat, movable, lateral extensions from the back of the mesothorax and the metathorax by means of which the insects fly. **5.** a similar structure with which gods, angels, demons, etc., are conceived to be provided for the purpose of flying. **6.** *Colloq.* an arm of a human being. **7.** a means or instrument of flight, travel, or progress. **8.** the act or manner of flying. **9.** flight; departure: *to take wing.* **10.** something resembling or likened to a wing, as a vane or sail of a windmill. **11.** *Aeron.* **a.** that portion of a main supporting surface confined to one side of an aeroplane. **b.** any complete winglike structure; plane. **12.** the mudguard of a motor vehicle. **13.** *Archit.* a part of a building projecting on one side of, or subordinate to, a central or main part. **14.** *Furnit.* an extension on the side of the back of an armchair above the arms. **15.** *Navy.* either of the two side portions of fleet (usu. called right wing and left wing, and distinguished from the centre); flank unit. **16. a.** (in fighter command of the RAAF and certain other airforces) a number of squadrons, usu. three, four, or five, operating together as a tactical unit. **b.** (in the U.S. Air Force) an administrative and tactical unit consisting of two or more groups, a headquarters, and certain supporting and service units. **17.** (*pl.*) the insignia or emblem worn by a qualified pilot. **18.** *Fort.* either of the longer sides of a crownwork, uniting it to the main work. **19. a.** *Aus. Rules.* either of the two centre-line positions on each side of the centre. **b.** *Hockey, Rugby, Soccer, etc.* either of the two areas of the pitch near the touchline and ahead of the halfway line, known as the left and right wings respectively, with reference to the direction of the opposing goal. **c.** a player in one of these positions. **20.** *Theat.* **a.** the platform or space on the right or left of the stage proper. **b.** one of the long, narrow side pieces of scenery. **21.** *Anat.* an ala: *the wings of the sphenoid.* **22.** *Bot.* **a.** any leaf-like expansion, as of a samara. **b.** one of the two side petals of a papilionaceous flower. **23.** either of the

upper surface of a bird's wing

parts of a double door, etc. **24.** the feather of an arrow. **25.** a group within a political party: *right wing, left wing.* **26.** *Naut.* **a.** the side part of a ship's hold. **b.** a side piece of an awning. **27. clip one's wings,** to restrict the independence or freedom of action of. **28. in the wings,** unobtrusively ready to take action when required; in reserve. **29. on the wing, a.** in flight; flying. **b.** in motion; travelling; active. **c.** *Football, Hockey, etc.* playing in the position on the left or right extreme of the forward line. **30. take wing, a.** to fly off. **b.** to leave hastily. **31. under one's wing,** in or into one's care or protection. *–v.t.* **32.** to equip with wings. **33.** to enable to fly, move rapidly, etc.; lend speed or celerity to. **34.** to supply with a winglike part, a side structure, etc. **35.** to transport on or as on wings. **36.** to perform or accomplish by wings. **37.** to traverse in flight. **38.** to wound or disable (a bird, etc.) in the wing. **39.** to wound (a person) in an arm or other non-vital part. **40.** to bring down (an aeroplane, etc.) by a shot. **41.** to brush or clean with a wing. **42.** *Theat. Colloq.* to perform (a part, etc.) relying on prompters in the wings. *–v.i.* **43.** to travel on or as on wings; fly; soar. [ME *wenge,* pl., from Scand.; cf. Icel. *vængir,* pl.] – **winglike,** *adj.*

**wing-and-wing** /wɪŋ-ən-ˈwɪŋ/, *adj.* →**goosewinged** (def. 2).

**wing-case** /ˈwɪŋ-keɪs/, *n.* →**elytron.** Also, **wing-cover.**

**wing chair** /ˈwɪŋ tʃɛə/, *n.* a large upholstered chair, with winglike parts projecting from the back above the arms.

**wing collar** /ˈ– kɒlə/, *n.* a stand-up collar with the corners turned down above the tie, formerly worn with formal dress.

**wing-commander** /ˈwɪŋ-kəmændə, -mandə/, *n.* **1.** a commissioned officer in the Royal Australian Air Force ranking above a squadron leader and below group captain. **2.** an officer of equivalent rank in any of various other airforces.

**wing-coverts** /wɪŋ-ˈkʌvəts/, *n.* the feathers which cover the bases of the quill feathers of the wing in birds, divided into greater, middle, lesser, and primary coverts.

**wing dam** /ˈwɪŋ dæm/, *n. U.S.* →**spur** (def. 10).

**wing-ding** /ˈwɪŋ-dɪŋ/, *n. Colloq.* a wild party.

**winged** /wɪŋd/ *or, esp. Poetic.,* /ˈwɪŋəd/ *adj.* **1.** having wings. **2.** having a winglike part or parts: *a winged bone, a winged seed.* **3.** moving or passing on or as if on wings: *winged words.* **4.** rapid or swift. **5.** elevated or lofty: *winged sentiments.* **6.** disabled in the wing, as a bird. **7.** wounded in an arm or other non-vital part. **8.** *Archaic.* abounding with wings or winged creatures.

**winger** /ˈwɪŋə/, *n.* (in football, hockey, etc.) a player on the wing.

**wing-footed** /ˈwɪŋ-fʊtəd/, *adj. Archaic.* having winged feet; rapid; swift.

**wing-forward** /wɪŋ-ˈfɔwəd/, *n.* **1.** *Soccer, etc.* either of the two players at the ends of the forward line. **2.** *Rugby Union. Brit.* a breakaway.

**wing-half** /wɪŋ-ˈhaf/, *n. Soccer, etc.* a left half or right half.

**wingless** /ˈwɪŋləs/, *adj.* **1.** having no wings. **2.** having only rudimentary wings, as an apteryx. – **winglessness,** *n.*

**wingless grasshopper** /– ˈgrashɒpə/, *n.* any of various species of flightless grasshoppers, sometimes found in plague proportions.

**winglet** /ˈwɪŋlət/, *n.* **1.** a little wing. **2.** →**alula.**

**wing-loading** /ˈwɪŋ-loʊdɪŋ/, *n.* See **loading** (def. 5).

**wingman** /ˈwɪŋmæn/, *n. Aus. Rules.* a player in the wing position on the field; winger.

**wing nut** /ˈwɪŋ nʌt/, *n.* a nut which incorporates two flat projecting wings enabling it to be turned by thumb and forefinger. Also, **butterfly nut.**

wing nut

**wingover** /ˈwɪŋoʊvə/, *n.* a flight manoeuvre in which a plane reverses direction by being put into a climbing turn until nearly stalled, the nose then being allowed to drop until normal flight is resumed.

**wing-sheath** /ˈwɪŋ-ʃiθ/, *n.* →**elytron.**

**wingspan** /ˈwɪŋspæn/, *n.* the distance between the wingtips of an aeroplane, bird, or insect. Also, **wingspread.**

**wing-three-quarter** /ˌwɪŋ-θri-ˈkwɔtə/, *n. Rugby Football.* either of the two outside players in the three-quarter line; left wing or right wing.

**wingtip** /ˈwɪŋtɪp/, *n.* the extreme outer edge of the wing of an aeroplane, bird, or insect.

**wingy** /ˈwɪŋi/, *adj.* **1.** having wings. **2.** rapid; swift.

**wink**[1] /wɪŋk/, *v.i.* **1.** to close and open the eyes quickly. **2.** (of the eyes) to close and open thus; blink. **3.** to close and open one eye quickly as a hint or signal or with some sly meaning (oft. fol. by *at*). **4.** to be purposely blind to a thing, as if to avoid the necessity of taking action (usu. fol. by *at*): *to wink at petty offences.* **5.** to shine with little flashes of light, or twinkle. *–v.t.* **6.** to close and open (the eyes or an eye) quickly; execute or give (a wink). **7.** to drive or force (away, back, etc.) by winking: *to wink back one's tears.* **8.** to signal or convey by a wink. *–n.* **9.** the act of winking. **10.** a winking movement, esp. of one eye as in giving a hint or signal. **11.** a hint or signal given by winking. **12.** the time required for winking once; an instant or twinkling. **13.** a little flash of light; a twinkle. **14.** *Colloq.* a bit: *I didn't sleep a wink.* **15. forty winks,** *Colloq.* a short sleep or nap. **16. tip (someone) the wink,** *Colloq.* to give information or a vital hint to (someone). [ME; OE *wincian,* c. G *winken*]

**wink**[2] /wɪŋk/, *n.* one of the discs used in tiddlywinks.

**winker** /ˈwɪŋkə/, *n.* **1.** one who or that which winks. **2.** a blinker for a horse. **3.** the nictitating membrane of a bird's eye. **4.** *Colloq.* a trafficator on a vehicle. **5.** *Colloq.* an eyelash or an eye.

**winkle** /ˈwɪŋkəl/, *n., v.,* **-kled, -kling.** *–n.* **1.** any of various marine gastropods; a periwinkle. *–v.t.* **2.** *Colloq.* to prise or extract (something) out of, as a winkle from its shell with a pin (fol. by *out*). [short for PERIWINKLE[1]]

**winner** /ˈwɪnə/, *n.* **1.** one who or that which wins. **2.** *Colloq.* something successful or highly valued: *this song is a real winner.*

**winning** /ˈwɪnɪŋ/, *n.* **1.** the act of one who or that which wins. **2.** (*usu. pl.*) that which is won. **3.** *Mining.* **a.** an opening of any kind by which coal is being, or has been, won. **b.** a bed of coal ready for mining. *–adj.* **4.** that wins; successful or victorious, as in a contest. **5.** taking, engaging, or charming, as a person or the manner, qualities, ways, etc. – **winningly,** *adv.* – **winningness,** *n.*

**winning gallery** /ˈ– ˌgæləri/, *n. Royal Tennis.* the opening that is farthest from the spectators' gallery (so named because any ball struck into it is called a winning ball).

**winning opening** /– ˈoʊpənɪŋ/, *n. Royal Tennis.* the dedans, winning gallery, or the grille (so named because it is a winning stroke to hit a ball into any of them).

**winning post** /ˈ– poʊst/, *n.* a post on a racecourse, forming the goal or finishing point of a race.

**winnow** /ˈwɪnoʊ/, *v.t.* **1.** to free (grain, etc.) from chaff, refuse particles, etc., by means of wind or driven air; fan. **2.** to blow upon, as the wind does upon grain in this process. **3.** to drive or blow (chaff, etc.) away by fanning. **4.** to subject to some process of separating or distinguishing; analyse critically; sift: *to winnow a mass of statements.* **5.** to separate or distinguish: *to winnow truth from falsehood.* **6.** to pursue (a course) with flapping wings in flying. **7.** *Archaic.* to fan or stir (the air) as with the wings in flying. *–v.i.* **8.** to free grain from chaff by wind or driven air. **9.** to fly with flapping wings; flutter. *–n.* **10.** a device or contrivance for winnowing grain, etc. **11.** the act of winnowing. [ME *win(d)we,* OE *windwian* (from WIND[1], *n.*). Cf. L *ventilāre*] – **winnower,** *n.*

**winnowing machine** /ˈwɪnəwɪŋ məʃin/, *n.* a machine for cleaning grain by the action of riddles and sieves and an air blast. Also, *U.S.,* **fanning mill.**

**wino** /ˈwaɪnoʊ/, *n. Colloq.* one addicted to drinking wine. [WIN(E) + -O]

**winsey** /ˈwɪnsi/, *n.* →**wincey.**

**winsome** /ˈwɪnsəm/, *adj.* winning, engaging, or charming: *a winsome smile.* [ME *winsom,* OE *wynsum,* from *wyn* joy + *-sum* -SOME[1]] – **winsomely,** *adv.* – **winsomeness,** *n.*

**wintarro** /wɪnˈtaroʊ/, *n.* a short-nosed bandicoot, *Isoodon auratus,* of central Australia, distinguished by the golden brown fur on its back; golden bandicoot. [Aboriginal]

**winter** /ˈwɪntə/, *n.* **1.** the coldest season of the year. **2.** a period of cold weather associated with this season. **3.** a whole year as represented by this season: *a man of sixty winters.* **4.** a period like winter, as the last or final period of life, a period of decline, decay, inertia, dreariness, or adversity. *–adj.* **5.** of, pertaining to, or characteristic of winter.

**6.** suitable for wear or use in winter. **7.** (of fruit and vegetables) of a kind that may be kept for use during the winter. **8.** *Agric.* designating varieties of grain, esp. wheat, oats, and barley, which are sown before winter to be harvested the following spring or summer. *–v.i.* **9.** to spend or pass the winter: *planning to winter in Queensland.* *–v.t.* **10.** to keep, feed, or manage during the winter, as plants or cattle. [MW and OE, c. D *winter* and G *Winter,* Icel. *vetr,* Goth. *wintrus*] **– winterer,** *n.* **– winterless,** *adj.* **– winter-like, winterish,** *adj.*

**winter aconite** /wɪntər 'ækənaɪt/, *n.* a small herb, *Eranthis hyemalis,* a native of the Old World, often cultivated for its bright yellow flowers, which appear very early in the spring.

**winterbourne** /'wɪntəbɔn/, *n.* a channel filled only at a time of excessive rainfall.

**winter cress** /wɪntə 'krɛs/, *n.* **1.** a small herb, *Barbarea vulgaris,* formerly grown for salad. **2.** any of certain other species of the genus *Barbarea.*

**winterfeed** /'wɪntəfid/, *v.t.,* **-fed, -feeding.** to feed in the winter, as cattle.

**wintergarden** /'wɪntəgadn/, *n.* **1.** an ornamental garden of evergreen plants, etc. **2.** a conservatory in which flowers are cultivated to bloom in the winter.

**winter grass** /'wɪntə gras/, *n.* any of several grasses which become garden weeds in winter, esp. *Poa annua,* a tufted annual which infests lawns.

**wintergreen** /'wɪntəgrin/, *n.* **1.** a small, creeping evergreen ericaceous shrub, *Gaultheria procumbens,* common in eastern North America, with white bell-shaped flowers, a bright red berry-like fruit, and aromatic leaves which yield a volatile oil. **2.** this oil **(oil of wintergreen).** **3.** the flavour of oil of wintergreen or something flavoured with it. **4.** any of various other plants of the same genus. **5.** any of various small evergreen herbs of the genera *Pyrola* and *Chimaphila.*

**winter heliotrope** /wɪntə 'hɛliətroup, 'hil-/, *n.* a rhizomatous herb with pale mauve, scented capitula, *Petasites fragrans,* native to the Mediterranean region but frequently cultivated and sometimes naturalised elsewhere.

**winterise** /'wɪntəraɪz/, *v.t.,* **-rised, -rising.** *U.S., Canada, etc.* to prepare (a motor vehicle, house, etc.) for cold weather by (in motor vehicles) adding antifreeze and changing weight of oil, (in houses) adding insulation, heating units, etc.

**winterkill** /'wɪntəkɪl/, *v.t., v.i. U.S.* to kill by or die from exposure to the cold of winter, as wheat. **– winterkilling,** *adj., n.*

**winter quarters** /'wɪntə kwɔtəz/, *n.* **1.** the quarters of an army during winter. **2.** a winter residence.

**winter solstice** /'– sɒlstəs/, *n.* See **solstice** (def. 1).

**winter sports** /'– spɔts/, *n.pl.* sports which take place on snow and ice, esp. skiing, skating, and bobsleighing.

**wintersweet** /'wɪntəswit/, *n.* a winter-flowering shrub with scented flowers, *Chimonanthus praecox,* native to China and Japan.

**wintertime** /'wɪntətaɪm/, *n.* the season of winter. Also, *Archaic,* **wintertide.**

**wintry** /'wɪntri/, *adj.,* **-trier, -triest.** **1.** of or characteristic of winter. **2.** having the season, storminess, or cold of winter. **3.** suggestive of winter, as in lack of warmth or cheer. Also, **wintery, winterly.** **– wintrily,** *adv.* **– wintriness,** *n.*

**winy** /'waɪni/, *adj.,* **winier, winiest.** **1.** of, like, or characteristic of wine. **2.** affected by or intoxicated with wine. Also, **winey.**

**winze** /wɪnz/, *n. Mining.* a small underground shaft, esp. one sunk from one level to another to connect one work face with another. [earlier *winds,* apparently from WIND[1], *n.*]

**wipe** /waɪp/, *v.,* **wiped, wiping,** *n.* *–v.t.* **1.** to rub lightly with or on a cloth, towel, paper, the hand, etc., in order to clean or dry. **2.** to remove by rubbing with or on something (usu. fol. by *away, off, out,* etc.) **3.** to remove as if by rubbing: *wipe the smile off your face.* **4.** to destroy or eradicate, as from existence or memory. **5.** *Colloq.* to refuse to have anything to do with. **6.** to rub or draw (something) over a surface, as in cleaning or drying. **7.** *Plumbing.* **a.** to apply (solder in a semi-fluid state) by spreading with leather or cloth over the part to be soldered. **b.** to form (a joint) in this manner. **8. wipe out,** to destroy completely. **9. wipe the floor with,** *Colloq.* to defeat utterly; overcome completely. *–n.* **10.** the action of wiping. **11.** a rub, as of one thing over another. **12.** *Films.* a technique in film editing by which the projected image of a scene appears to be pushed or wiped off the screen by the image that follows. [ME; OE *wipian,* c. OHG *wifan* wind round, Goth. *weipan* crown; akin to VIBRATE]

**wipe-out** /'waɪp-aʊt/, *n. Colloq.* **1.** *Surfing.* a fall from a surfboard because of loss of balance. **2.** a failure; fiasco. **3.** a blotting out of radio signals by atmospherics, jamming, etc.

**wiper** /'waɪpə/, *n.* **1.** one who or that which wipes. **2.** that with which anything is wiped, as a towel or a handkerchief. **3.** *Elect.* that portion of the moving member of a selector, or other similar device, which makes contact with the terminals of a bank; a type of brush (def. 9a). **4.** *Mach.* a projecting piece, as on a rotating axis, acting on another part, as a stamper, esp. to raise it so that it may fall by its own weight. **5.** →**windscreen-wiper.**

**wire** /'waɪə/, *n., adj., v.,* **wired, wiring.** *–n.* **1.** a piece of slender, flexible metal, ranging from a thickness that can be bent by the hand only with some difficulty down to a fine thread, and usu. circular in section. **2.** such pieces as a material. **3.** a length of such material used as a conductor of electricity, usu. insulated in a flex. **4.** a crosswire or crosshair. **5.** a barbed-wire fence. **6.** a long wire or cable used in a telegraph, telephone, or cable system. **7.** *Orig. U.S. Colloq.* a telegram. **8.** *Orig. U.S. Colloq.* the telegraphic system: *to send a message by wire.* **9.** *(pl.)* a system of wires by which puppets are moved. **10.** a metallic string of a musical instrument. **11.** *Ornith.* one of the extremely long, slender, wirelike filaments or shafts of the plumage of various birds. **12.** a metal device used to snare rabbits, etc. **13. have (get) one's wires crossed,** *Colloq.* to become confused; misunderstand. **14. pull wires,** *Chiefly U.S.* to exert hidden influence; pull strings. **15.** *Horseracing. Colloq.* the finishing post. *–adj.* **16.** made of wire; consisting of or constructed with wires. **17.** wirelike. *–v.t.* **18.** to furnish with a wire or wires. **19.** to install an electric system of wiring, as for lighting, etc. **20.** to fasten or bind with wire. **21.** to put on a wire, as beads. **22.** *Colloq.* to send by telegraph, as a message. **23.** *Colloq.* to send a telegraphic message to. **24.** to snare by means of a wire or wires. **25.** *Croquet.* to arrange (a ball) in such a manner that it will rest behind an arch and thus prevent a shot which would be successful. *–v.i.* **26.** *Colloq.* to send a telegraphic message; telegraph. [ME and OE *wir,* c. LG *wir,* Icel. *virr*] **– wirelike,** *adj.*

**wire brush** /– 'brʌʃ/, *n.* a brush with bristles of stiff wire, used for cleaning, esp. for removal of rust.

**wire closure** /waɪə 'klouʒə/, *n.* →**twist-tie.**

**wirecloth** /'waɪəklɒθ/, *n.* **1.** a mesh made of wires of moderate fineness, used for strainers, or in the manufacture of paper, etc. *–adj.* **2.** made of this material or mesh.

**wire-cutter** /'waɪə-kʌtə/, *n.* a tool designed to cut wire.

**wiredancer** /'waɪədænsə/, *n.* one who dances or performs other feats upon a high wire. **– wiredancing,** *n.*

**wired glass** /waɪəd 'glas/, *n.* sheet glass having wire netting embedded within it to increase its strength.

**wiredraw** /'waɪədrɔ/, *v.t.,* **-drew, -drawn, -drawing.** **1.** to draw (metal) out into wire, esp. by pulling forcibly through a series of holes gradually decreasing in diameter. **2.** to draw out to great length, in quantity or time; stretch out to excess. **3.** to strain unwarrantably, as in meaning. **– wiredrawer,** *n.* **– wiredrawing,** *n.*

**wire entanglement** /,waɪər ɛn'tæŋgəlmənt/, *n.* heavy barbed-wire erected to impede the advance of the enemy.

wire-gauge

**wire-gauge** /'waɪə-geɪdʒ/, *n.* a gauge calibrated for standard wire diameters.

**wire gauze** /waɪə 'gɔz/, *n.* a gauzelike mesh woven of very fine wires.

**wire grass** /'– gras/, *n.* any species of the widespread genus *Aristida,* a wiry grass characterised by a trifid awn; three-awned spear grass.

**wire-haired** /'waɪə-hɛəd/, *adj.* having coarse, stiff, wirelike hair.

i = peat  ɪ = pit  ɛ = pet  æ = pat  a = part  ɒ = pot  ʌ = putt  ɔ = port  ʊ = put  u = pool  ɜ = pert  ə = apart  aɪ = buy  eɪ = bay  ɔɪ = boy  aʊ = how
oʊ = hoe  ɪə = here  ɛə = hair  ʊə = tour  g = give  θ = thin  ð = then  ʃ = show  ʒ = measure  tʃ = choke  dʒ = joke  ŋ = sing  j = you  õ = Fr. bon

**wire-haired terrier** /– 'tɛriə/, *n.* a fox-terrier having a wiry coat. Also, *Chiefly U.S.,* **wirehair.**

**wireless** /'waɪələs/, *adj.* **1.** having no wire. **2.** denoting or pertaining to any of various devices which are operated with or set in action by electromagnetic waves. **3.** radio. *–n.* **4.** radio. **5.** wireless telegraphy or telephony. **6.** a wireless telegraph or telephone, or the like. *–v.t., v.i.* **7.** to telegraph or telephone by wireless.

**wireless set** /'– sɛt/, *n.* a radio receiver, or a radio receiver and transmitter.

**wireline drilling** /ˌwaɪəlaɪn 'drɪlɪŋ/, *n.* the drilling of boreholes with a steel cable attached to the core barrel; the cable or wireline enables the rock core to be extracted without removing the drill rods.

**wire netting** /waɪə 'nɛtɪŋ/, *n.* a texture or area of wire woven in the form of a net.

**wirephoto** /'waɪəˌfoutou/, *n.* **1.** a method of sending photographs by telegraphy. **2.** a photograph sent by this method.

**wire-pulling** /'waɪə-pulɪŋ/, *n. Chiefly U.S.* →**string-pulling.** – **wire-puller,** *n.*

**wirer** /'waɪərə/, *n.* **1.** one who wires. **2.** one who uses wire to snare game.

**wire recorder** /'waɪə rəkɔdə/, *n.* (formerly) a device to record sound on a steel wire by magnetising the wire as it passes an electromagnet, the sound being reproduced by the motion of the wire past a receiver.

**wire rope** /– 'roup/, *n.* a rope made of strands of wire.

**wire-tapper** /'waɪə-tæpə/, *n.* **1.** one who illicitly taps telegraph or telephone wires to learn the nature of messages passing over them. **2.** *U.S. Colloq.* a swindler who professes to secure by this or some similar means advance information for betting or the like. – **wire-tapping,** *n., adj.*

**wirewalker** /'waɪəwɔkə/, *n. Chiefly U.S.* →**tightrope-walker.**

**wireweed** /'waɪəwid/, *n.* any of various plants of the genus *Polygonum,* esp. *Polygonum aviculare,* a low-growing annual with nodose stems, small pink or white flowers, and black fruit. Also, **knotweed.**

**wire wheel** /'waɪə wil/, *n.* a wheel having wire spokes, as used on high-speed sports cars.

**wire wool** /'– wul/, *n.* →**steel wool.**

**wirework** /'waɪəwɜk/, *n.* **1.** work consisting of wire. **2.** fabrics or articles made of wire.

**wireworker** /'waɪəwɜkə/, *n.* one who works with wire, esp. in industrial use.

**wireworks** /'waɪəwɜks/, *n.pl. or sing.* an establishment where wire is made, or is put to some industrial use.

**wireworm** /'waɪəwɜm/, *n.* **1.** any of the slender, hardbodied larvae of click beetles, which in many species live underground and feed on the roots of plants. **2.** any of various small myriapods. **3.** →**stomach worm.**

**wire-wound** /'waɪə-waund/, *adj.* wound with wire, as a resistor or armature.

**wirewove** /'waɪəwouv/, *adj.* **1.** made of woven wire. **2.** denoting fine glazed paper used esp. for letter paper.

**wire-wrap** /'waɪə-ræp/, *n.* **1.** a technique of construction for electronic equipment in which the junction of wires is effected by winding one around the other. *–adj.* **2.** of or pertaining to this technique.

**wirey** /'waɪəri/, *adj.,* **wirier, wiriest,** *n.* →**wiry.**

**wirilda** /wə'rɪldə/, *n.* a wattle of south-eastern Australia *Acacia retinoides,* which flowers almost all year round and which has edible seeds.

**wiring** /'waɪərɪŋ/, *n.* **1.** the act of one who wires. **2.** *Elect.* the aggregate of wires, in a lighting system, switchboard, radio, etc. *–adj.* **3.** that installs, or is used in, wiring.

**wirra** /'wɪrə/, *n.* →**kelpfish.** Also, **wirrah.** [Aboriginal]

**wirrah** /'wɪrə/, *n.* an Australian rock fish, *Acanthistius serratus,* usu. dull brown with blue spots, sometimes transversely banded. Also, **peppermint cod.** [Aboriginal]

**wiry** /'waɪəri/, *adj.,* **wirier, wiriest,** *n. –adj.* **1.** made of wire. **2.** in the form of wire. **3.** resembling wire, as in form, stiffness, etc.: *wiry grass.* **4.** lean and sinewy. **5.** produced by or resembling the sound of a vibrating wire: *wiry tones.* *–n.* **6.** a beachworm, *Onuphis mariahirsuta,* growing up to 100 cm long and 1 cm wide, sometimes with dark brown pigment on its back, and with antennae longer than those of the kingworm or slimy. It prefers a sheltered habitat such as between breakwater or on headlands, and is found from northern New South Wales to Yeppoon in Queensland. – **wirily,** *adv.* – **wiriness,** *n.*

**wis** /wɪs/, *v.t., v.i. Archaic.* to know. [abstracted from *iwis* certainly (OE *gewiss*), misread as *I wis* I know]

**wisdom** /'wɪzdəm/, *n.* **1.** the quality or state of being wise; knowledge of what is true or right coupled with just judgment as to action; sagacity, prudence, or common sense. **2.** scholarly knowledge, or learning: *the wisdom of the schools.* **3.** wise sayings or teachings. **4.** a wise act or saying. [ME and OE, c. Icel. *vīsdōmr.* See WISE[1], -DOM]

**wisdom tooth** /'– tuθ/, *n.* the third molar tooth; the last tooth in each quadrant of the jaw; the last tooth to erupt (usu. between the ages of 17-25).

**wise**[1] /waɪz/, *adj.,* **wiser, wisest. 1.** having the power of discerning and judging properly as to what is true or right. **2.** characterised by or showing such power; shrewd, judicious, or prudent. **3.** possessed of or characterised by scholarly knowledge or learning; learned; erudite: *wise in the law.* **4.** having knowledge or information as to facts, circumstances, etc.: *we are wiser for his explanations.* **5.** *Colloq.* in the know (about something implied); alerted; cognisant (oft. fol. by *to*): *they tried to keep it secret, but he was wise, I'm wise to your tricks.* **6. get wise,** *Colloq.* **a.** to face facts or realities. **b.** to learn something. **7. none the wiser,** still in ignorance or confusion. **8. put wise,** *Colloq.* **a.** to explain something (to someone, esp. a naive person). **b.** to warn. **9. wise up,** *Colloq.* to make aware; inform; alert. *–v.i.* **10. wise up,** *Colloq.* to become aware, informed, or alerted; face the realities. [ME and OE *wīs,* c. D *wijs,* G *weise*] – **wisely,** *adv.*

**wise**[2] /waɪz/, *n. Archaic.* **1.** way of proceeding; manner; fashion. **2.** respect; degree (now usu. in composition or in certain phrases): *in no wise* (in no way, respect, or degree). [ME and OE; c. D *wijze,* G *Weise* manner, tune]

**-wise,** a suffixal use of **wise**[2] in adverbs denoting: **1.** attitude or direction: *lengthwise, clockwise.* **2.** with reference to; in respect of: *moneywise.* **3.** *U.S.* var. of **-ways:** *sidewise.*

**wiseacre** /'waɪzeɪkə/, *n.* **1.** (*ironic*) one who possesses or affects to possess great wisdom. **2.** a know-all. [MD *wijsseggher* soothsayer]

**wisecrack** /'waɪzkræk/, *Colloq. –n.* **1.** a smart, pungent, or facetious remark. *–v.i.* **2.** to make wisecracks. *–v.t.* **3.** to say as a wisecrack. – **wisecracker,** *n.*

**wise guy** /'waɪz gaɪ/, *n. Chiefly U.S. Colloq.* a cocksure or impertinent person of either sex.

**wisent** /'vizɛnt/, *n.* a European bison, *Bison bonasus;* aurochs. [G, from OHG *wisunt*]

**wish** /wɪʃ/, *v.t.* **1.** to want; desire; long for (oft. with an infinitive or a clause as object): *I wish to see him, I wish that he would come.* **2.** to desire (a person or thing) to be (as specified): *to wish oneself elsewhere.* **3.** to entertain wishes of something, favourable or otherwise, for: *to wish one well or ill.* **4.** to bid, as in greeting or leave-taking: *to wish one a good morning.* **5.** to command, request, or entreat: *I wish him to come.* **6.** to force or impose (fol. by *on*): *to wish a hard job on someone.* *–v.i.* **7.** to have a desire, longing, or yearning. **8.** to express a desire (for something), as in a magic ritual: *blow out the candles and wish.* **9. wish on** or **upon,** to perform such a ritual, using something as a talisman or charm: *to wish upon a forked hazel twig.* *–n.* **10.** a distinct mental inclination towards the doing, obtaining, attaining, etc., of something; a desire, felt or expressed: *disregard the wishes of others.* **11.** an expression of a wish, often one of a kindly or courteous nature: *send one's best wishes.* **12.** that which is wished: *get one's wish.* **13.** an act of ritual wishing: *to make a wish.* [ME *wisshe,* OE *wȳscan,* c. G *wünschen,* Icel. *æskja*] – **wisher,** *n.*

**wishbone** /'wɪʃboun/, *n.* **1.** the forked bone (a united pair of clavicles) in front of the breastbone in most birds; the furcula. **2.** something which resembles the wishbone of a bird, as a piece of machinery, electrical fitting, etc. [so called from the superstition that when two people pull the bone apart, the one getting the longer piece will have his wish fulfilled]

**wishful** /'wɪʃfəl/, *adj.* **1.** having or showing a wish; desirous; longing. **2. wishful thinking,** a belief that a thing will happen or is so, based on one's hopes rather than on reality.

**wish fulfilment** /ˌwɪʃ fʊlˈfɪlmənt/, *n.* (in psychology) the satisfaction of conscious or unconscious desires, esp. through realistic or symbolic gratification in dreams.

**wishy-washy** /ˈwɪʃi-wɒʃi/, *adj.* **1.** washy or watery, as a liquid; thin and weak. **2.** lacking in substantial qualities; without strength or force; weak, feeble, or poor. [reduplication of WASHY]

**wisp** /wɪsp/, *n.* **1.** a handful or small bundle of straw, hay, or the like. **2.** any small or thin tuft, lock, mass, etc.: *wisps of hair.* **3.** anything small or thin, as a shred, bundle, or slip of something, sometimes used as a brush or whisk. **4.** a small or slight person. **5.** a flock (of birds, esp. snipe). *–v.t.* **6.** to rub (a horse) down with a wisp of straw. **7.** *Rare.* to twist into a wisp. [ME *wisp, wips;* akin to WIPE] – **wisplike,** *adj.*

**wispy** /ˈwɪspi/, *adj.*, **wispier, wispiest.** being a wisp or in wisps; wisplike; thin, weak-looking, or pale: *a wispy plant.* Also, **wispish.**

**wist** /wɪst/, *v.* past tense and past participle of **wit**[2].

**wisteria** /wɪsˈtɪəriə/, *n.* any of the climbing shrubs, with handsome pendent racemes of purple flowers, which constitute the leguminous genus *Wisteria,* as *W. chinensis* (**Chinese wisteria**), much used to cover verandas and walls. Also, **wistaria** /wɪsˈtɛəriə/. [after Caspar *Wistar,* 1761-1818, U.S. anatomist]

**wistful** /ˈwɪstfəl/, *adj.* **1.** pensive or melancholy. **2.** showing longing tinged with melancholy; regretful; sad. [obs. *wist* attentive (backformation from *wistly* attentively, var. of *whistly;* see WHIST[1]) + -FUL] – **wistfully,** *adv.* – **wistfulness,** *n.*

**wit**[1] /wɪt/, *n.* **1.** keen perception and cleverly apt expression of connections between ideas which may arouse pleasure and especially amusement. **2.** speech or writing showing such perception and expression. **3.** a person endowed with or noted for such wit. **4.** understanding, intelligence, or sagacity: *wit enough to come in out of the rain.* **5.** (*pl.*) mental abilities, or powers of intelligent observation, keen perception, ingenious contrivance, etc.: *to have one's wits about one.* **6.** (*pl.*) mental faculties, or senses: *to lose or regain one's wits.* **7.** *Archaic.* mental capacity; reason; intellect. **8.** *Archaic.* a clever or learned person. **9. at one's wits'** (or **wit's**) **end,** at the end of one's powers of knowing, thinking, etc.; utterly at a loss or perplexed. **10. five wits,** the five senses, or the perceptions generally. **11. live by one's wits,** to gain a livelihood by resourcefulness and quick-wittedness rather than by hard work. **12. out of one's wits,** in or into a state of great fear or incoherence: *to frighten someone out of his wits.* [ME and OE, c. G *Witz,* Icel. *vit*]

**wit**[2] /wɪt/, *v., pres.* 1 **wot,** 2 **wost,** 3 **wot,** *pl.* **wit;** *pt.* and *pp.* **wist;** *pres. p.* **witting.** *–v.t., v.i. Archaic.* **1.** to know. **2. God wot,** *Archaic.* God knows (used to emphasise a statement). **3. to wit,** that is to say; namely. [ME; OE *witan,* c. D *weten,* G *wissen*]

**witan** /ˈwɪtən/, *n.pl. Early Eng. Hist.* **1.** the members of the national council or witenagemot. **2.** (*construed as sing.*) the witenagemot. [OE, pl. of *wita* man of knowledge, councillor]

**witch**[1] /wɪtʃ/, *n.* **1.** a person, now esp. a woman, who professes or is supposed to practise magic, esp. black magic or the black art; a sorceress. **2.** an ugly or malignant old woman; a hag. **3.** a fascinatingly attractive woman. *–v.t.* **4.** to affect by or as by witchcraft; bewitch; charm. **5.** to change by or as by witchcraft (fol. by *into, to,* etc.). **6.** to fascinate. [ME *wiche,* OE *wicce,* from *wiccian* practise sorcery] – **witchlike,** *adj.*

**witch**[2] /wɪtʃ/, *n.* a flatfish of the northern Atlantic, *Pleuronectes cynoglossus,* resembling the lemon sole.

**witchcraft** /ˈwɪtʃkraft/, *n.* **1.** the art or practices of a witch; sorcery; magic. **2.** magical influence; witchery.

**witchdoctor** /ˈwɪtʃdɒktə/, *n.* (in various primitive societies) **1.** a person possessing or supposed to possess magical powers of healing or of harming; medicine man. **2.** a person thought to have the power of detecting witches.

**witch-elm** /wɪtʃ-ˈɛlm/, *n.* →**wych-elm.**

**witchery** /ˈwɪtʃəri/, *n., pl.* **-eries.** **1.** the use or practice of witchcraft; magic. **2.** magical influence; fascination; charm: *the witchery of her beauty.*

**witches'-broom** /ˈwɪtʃəz-brum/, *n.* a dense mass of small thin branches frequently emerging from a swelling on a tree branch, as on cherry (caused by fungus of the genus *Taphrina*) and on conifers (caused by various mistletoes). Also, **witches'-besom** /ˈwɪtʃəz-bizəm/.

**witchetty** /ˈwɪtʃəti/, *n.* any of various large, white, edible, wood-boring grubs that are the larvae of certain Australian moths and beetles. [Aboriginal]

witchetty grub

**witch-hazel** /ˈwɪtʃ-heɪzəl/, *n.* **1.** a shrub, *Hamamelis virginiana,* of eastern North America, whose bark and leaves afford medicinal preparations used for inflammation, bruises, etc. **2.** a liquid medicinal preparation used externally for inflammation and bruises. Also, **wych-hazel.**

**witch-hunt** /ˈwɪtʃ-hʌnt/, *n.* **1.** *Chiefly Hist.* the searching out of people to be accused of, and executed for, witchcraft. **2.** an intensive effort to discover and expose disloyalty, subversion, dishonesty, or the like, usu. based on slight, doubtful, or irrelevant evidence. – **witch-hunter,** *n.* – **witch-hunting,** *n., adj.*

**witching** /ˈwɪtʃɪŋ/, *n.* **1.** the use of witchcraft. **2.** fascination. *–adj.* **3.** characterised by or suitable for sorcery, etc. **4.** enchanting. **5. witching hour,** (usu.) midnight. – **witchingly,** *adv.*

**witchweed** /ˈwɪtʃwid/, *n.* any of the semiparasitic plants of the genus Striga, family Scrophulariaceae, of Asia, Africa, and northern Australia.

**witenagemot** /ˌwɪtənəgəˈmoʊt/, *n. Early Eng. Hist.* the assembly of the witan; the national council attended by the king, aldermen, bishops, and nobles. [OE: councillors' assembly. See WITAN, MOOT]

**with** /wɪð, wɪθ/, *prep.* **1.** accompanied by or accompanying: *I will go with you.* **2.** in some particular relation to (esp. implying interaction, company, association, conjunction, or connection): *to deal, talk, sit, side, or rank with; to mix, compare, or agree with.* **3.** visiting; at the house of or in the company of: *he is with the doctor at the moment; she is with her cousin in the country.* **4.** (expressing similarity or agreement): *in harmony with.* **5.** (expressing equality or identity): *to be level with someone.* **6.** on the side of; in favour of; of the same opinion as: *are you with us or against us?* **7.** *Colloq.* comprehending of: *are you with me?* **8.** of the same opinion as: *I'm with you on that subject.* **9.** in the same direction as: *with the stream, to cut timber with the grain.* **10.** in the same way as: *let us, with Solomon, be judicious.* **11.** characterised by or having: *a man with long arms.* **12.** carrying (a child or young), as a pregnant female. **13.** (of means or instrument) by the use of: *to line a coat with silk, to cut with a knife.* **14.** (of manner) using or showing: *to work with diligence.* **15.** in correspondence or proportion to: *their power increased with their number.* **16.** on the occasion or occurrence of; at the same time as, or immediately after: *to rise with the dawn, he swayed with every step he took.* **17.** in consequence of (the passage of time): *to alter with the years.* **18.** in regard to: *to be pleased with a thing.* **19.** in the estimation or view of: *if that's all right with you.* **20.** in the practice or experience of, or according to: *it's always the way with him.* **21.** (expressing power or influence over): *to prevail with someone.* **22.** (expressing subjection to power or influence): *to sway with the wind.* **23.** (of cause) owing to: *racked with pain.* **24.** in the region, sphere, or view of: *it is day with us while it is night with the British.* **25.** (of separation, etc.) from: *to part with a thing.* **26.** against, as in opposition or competition: *to fight or vie with.* **27.** in the hands, care, keeping or service of: *leave it with me.* **28. be (get) with it,** *Colloq.* **a.** to be (become) aware of a situation. **b.** to concentrate. **c.** to be able to cope. **d.** to be (become) fashionable or up-to-date. [ME and OE, c. Icel. *vidh*]

**with-,** limited prefixal use of *with,* separative or opposing, as in *withdraw, withstand.* [ME and OE. See WITH]

**-with,** a suffix indicating conjunction: *herewith, therewith.*

**withal** /wɪðˈɔl, wɪθ-/, *Archaic. –adv.* **1.** with it all; also; as well; besides. **2.** nevertheless. **3.** therewith. *–prep.* **4.** with (used after its object). [WITH + AL(L)]

**withdraw** /wɪðˈdrɔ, wɪθ-/, *v.,* **-drew, -drawn, -drawing.** *–v.t.* **1.** to draw back or away; take back; remove. **2.** to retract or recall: *to withdraw a charge.* *–v.i.* **3.** to retire; retreat; go apart or away. **4.** to retract a statement or expression. **5.** *Parl. Proc.* to remove an amendment, motion, etc., from consideration. – **withdrawer,** *n.*

**withdrawal** /wɪð'drɔəl, wɪθ-/, *n.* the act of withdrawing. Also, **withdrawment.**

**withdrawal symptom** /'– sɪmptəm/, *n.* any distressing or painful symptom experienced by an addict due to the withdrawal of the drug of his addiction, as alcohol or heroin.

**withdrawn** /wɪð'drɔn, wɪθ-/, *v.* **1.** past participle of **withdraw.** *–adj.* **2.** shy, retiring, or modest. **3.** secluded, as a place.

**withdrew** /wɪð'dru, wɪθ-/, *v.* past tense of **withdraw.**

**withe** /wɪθ/, *n., v.,* **withed, withing.** *–n.* **1.** a willow twig or osier. **2.** any tough, flexible twig or stem suitable for binding things together. **3.** an elastic handle for a tool, to lessen shock in using. **4.** a thin brick partition dividing the flues in a chimney. *–v.t.* **5.** to bind with withes. [ME and OE *withthe,* c. LG *wedde*]

**wither** /'wɪðə/, *v.i.* **1.** to shrivel; fade; decay. **2.** to deteriorate or lose freshness (also fol. by *away*). *–v.t.* **3.** to make flaccid, shrunken, or dry, as from loss of moisture; cause to lose freshness, bloom, vigour, etc. **4.** to affect harmfully; blight: *reputations withered by scandal.* **5.** to abash, as by a scathing glance. [ME; ? var. of WEATHER, *v.*]

**withered** /'wɪðəd/, *adj.* faded, dry, or wizened.

**withering** /'wɪðərɪŋ/, *adj.* **1.** scathing, contemptuous, or crushing, as a remark, look, etc. **2.** causing to become withered. – **witheringly,** *adv.*

**witherite** /'wɪðəraɪt/, *n.* a white to greyish mineral, barium carbonate ($BaCO_3$), occurring in crystals and masses, a minor ore of barium. [named after W. *Withering,* 1741-99, English physician]

**withers** /'wɪðəz/, *n. pl.* the highest part of a horse's or other animal's back, behind the neck. [orig. uncert.]

**withershins** /'wɪðəʃɪnz/, *adv.* →**widdershins.**

**withhold** /wɪð'hoʊld, wɪθ-/, *v.,* **-held, -holding.** *–v.t.* **1.** to hold back; restrain or check. **2.** to refrain from giving or granting: *to withhold payment.* *–v.i.* **3.** *Obs.* to hold back; refrain. [ME *withholde(n).* See WITH-, HOLD[1], *v.*] – **withholder,** *n.*

**withholding tax** /wɪð'hoʊldɪŋ tæks, wɪθ-/, *n.* that part of one's tax liability withheld by the employer and paid directly to the government.

**within** /wɪð'ɪn, wɪθ'ɪn/, *adv.* **1.** in or into the interior or inner part, or inside. **2.** in or into a house, building, etc., or indoors. **3.** in or into an inner or farther room. **4.** on, or as regards, the inside, or internally. **5.** in the mind, heart, or soul; inwardly. *–prep.* **6.** in or into the interior of or the parts or space enclosed by: *within a city or its walls.* **7.** inside; in. **8.** in the compass or limits of; not beyond: *within view, to live within one's income.* **9.** at or some point not beyond, as in length or distance; not farther than: *within a radius of a kilometre.* **10.** at or to some amount or degree not exceeding: *within two degrees of freezing.* **11.** in the course or period of, as in time: *within one's lifetime or memory.* **12.** inside the limits fixed or required by; not transgressing: *within the law, within reason.* **13.** in the field, sphere, or scope of: *within the family, within one's power.* *–n.* **14.** the inside of a building, enclosed space, etc. [ME; OE *withinnan*]

**withindoors** /wɪðɪn'dɔz, wɪθ-/, *adv. Obs.* indoors.

**with-it** /'wɪð-ət, 'wɪθ-/, *adj.* trendy, sophisticated, up to date: *with-it gear.*

**without** /wɪð'aʊt, wɪθ-/, *prep.* **1.** not with; with no; with absence, omission, or avoidance of; lacking (as opposed to *with*). **2.** free from; excluding. **3.** *Archaic* at, on, or to the outside of; outside of: *both within and without the house or the city.* **4.** beyond the compass, limits, range, or scope of (now used chiefly in opposition to *within*): *whether within or without the law.* *–adv.* **5.** in or into space without, or outside. **6.** outside a house, building, etc. **7.** without, or lacking, something implied or understood: *we must take this or go without.* **8.** as regards the outside, or externally. **9.** as regards external acts, or out-outwardly. **10.** *Brit. Colloq.* unless. *–adj.* **11.** lacking means, possessions, etc.; destitute: *to be without.* [ME; OE *withūtan*]

**withoutdoors** /wɪðaʊt'dɔz, wɪθ-/, *adv. Obs.* out of doors.

**withstand** /wɪð'stænd, wɪθ-/, *v.,* **-stood, -standing.** *–v.t.* **1.** to stand or hold out against; resist or oppose, esp. successfully. *–v.i.* **2.** to stand in opposition. [ME *withstande,* OE *withstandan,* c. Icel. *vidhstanda.* See WITH-, STAND] – **withstander,** *n.*

**withy** /'wɪði/, *n., pl.* **withies,** *adj.* *–n.* **1.** a willow, esp. an osier. **2.** a flexible twig, or withe. **3.** a band or halter made of a willow twig, or the like. *–adj. Rare.* **4.** like a withe, as in slenderness, flexibility, etc. [ME *withie,* OE *wīthig.* See WITHE]

**witless** /'wɪtləs/, *adj.* lacking wits or intelligence; stupid; foolish. – **witlessly,** *adv.* – **witlessness,** *n.*

**witling** /'wɪtlɪŋ/, *n. Archaic.* a petty or would-be wit.

**witness** /'wɪtnəs/, *v.t.* **1.** to see or know by personal presence and perception. **2.** to be present at (an occurrence) as a formal witness or otherwise. **3.** to bear witness to; testify to; give or afford evidence of. **4.** to attest by one's signature. **5.** to be the scene of. *–v.i.* **6.** to bear witness; testify; give or afford evidence (also fol. by *to*). *–n.* **7.** one who, being present, personally sees or perceives a thing; a beholder, spectator, or eyewitness. **8.** a person or thing that affords evidence. **9.** one who gives testimony, as in a court of law. **10.** one who signs a document in attestation of the genuineness of its execution. **11.** testimony or evidence: *to bear witness to the truth of a statement.* [ME and OE *witnes.* See WIT[1], *n.,* -NESS] – **witnesser,** *n.*

**witness box** /'– bɒks/, *n.* the place occupied by one giving evidence in a court. Also, *U.S.,* **witness stand.**

**witness mark** /'– mak/, *n.* a mark or stake set to identify a property corner or a survey point.

**witted** /'wɪtəd/, *adj.* having wit or wits (only used in combination): *quick-witted, slow-witted.*

**witticism** /'wɪtəsɪzəm/, *n.* a witty remark; a joke. [from WITTY; modelled on CRITICISM]

**witting** /'wɪtɪŋ/, *adj. Archaic.* knowing; aware; conscious. – **wittingly,** *adv.*

**wittol** /'wɪtl/, *n. Obs.* a man who knows and tolerates his wife's infidelity. [ME *wetewold,* from *wete* WIT[2], *v.* + *-wold,* modelled on *cokewold* CUCKOLD]

**witty** /'wɪti/, *adj.,* **-tier, -tiest.** **1.** possessing wit in speech or writing; amusingly clever in perception and expression. **2.** characterised by wit: *a witty remark.* **3.** *Obs.* wise; intelligent. [ME; OE *wittig,* from *witt* WIT[1] + *-ig* -Y[1]] – **wittily,** *adv.* – **wittiness,** *n.*

**wive** /waɪv/, *v.,* **wived, wiving.** *Rare.* *–v.i.* **1.** to take a wife; marry. *–v.t.* **2.** to take as wife; marry. **3.** to marry off. **4.** to provide with a wife. [ME; OE *wīfian.* See WIFE]

**wivern** /'waɪvən/, *n.* →**wyvern.**

**wives** /waɪvz/, *n.* plural of **wife.**

**wizard** /'wɪzəd/, *n.* **1.** one who professes to practise magic; a magician or sorcerer. **2.** a person of exceptional or prodigious accomplishment (esp. in a specified field). **3.** *Archaic.* a sage; wise man. *–adj.* **4.** of or pertaining to a wizard. **5.** *Chiefly Brit. Colloq.* superb; marvellous. [ME *wysard, wys* WISE[1] + -ARD]

wizard

**wizardly** /'wɪzədli/, *adj.* **1.** of, like, or befitting a wizard. *–adv.* **2.** *Chiefly Brit. Colloq.* extremely well.

**wizardry** /'wɪzədri/, *n.* the art or practices of a wizard; sorcery; magic.

**wizen** /'wɪzən/, *v.i., v.t.* **1.** to wither; shrivel; dry up. *–adj.* **2.** wizened. [ME *wisen,* OE *wisnian,* c. Icel. *visna* wither]

**wizened** /'wɪzənd/, *adj.* dried-up; withered; shrivelled.

**wk,** *pl.* **wks.** **1.** week. **2.** work.

**wkly,** weekly.

**wkt,** *pl.* **wkts.** wicket.

**WNW,** west-north-west. Also, **W.N.W.**

**wo** /woʊ/, *n., interj.* **1.** →**whoa.** **2.** →**woe.**

**W.O.,** **1.** warrant officer. **2.** wireless operator.

**woad** /woʊd/, *n.* **1.** a European plant, *Isatis tinctoria,* formerly much cultivated for a blue dye extracted from its leaves. **2.** the dye. [ME *wode,* OE *wād,* c. G *Waid*]

**woaded** /ˈwoʊdəd/, *adj.* dyed or coloured blue with woad.

**woald** /woʊld/, *n.* →**weld**[2].

**wobbegong** /ˈwɒbigɒŋ/, *n.* a shark, *Orectolobus maculatus,* of the eastern Australian coast, having a flattened body and mottled skin and living on the bottom of the sea. [Aboriginal]

**wobble** /ˈwɒbəl/, *v.,* **-bled, -bling,** *n.* *–v.i.* **1.** to incline to one side and to the other alternately, as a wheel, top, or other rotating body, when not properly balanced. **2.** to move unsteadily from side to side. **3.** to show unsteadiness; tremble; quaver: *his voice wobbled.* **4.** to vacillate; waver. *–v.t.* **5.** to cause to wobble. *–n.* **6.** the act or fact of wobbling; a wobbling motion. **7.** (*pl.*) *Colloq.* locomotive ataxia in horses and cattle, usu. held to be a recessive hereditary trait, but also caused by eating the leaves of certain palm trees. Also, **wabble.** [LG *wabbeln,* c. Icel. *vafla* toddle] – **wobbler,** *n.*

**wobble board** /ˈ– bɔd/, *n.* a thin rectangular sheet of masonite approximately 90 cm by 60 cm which is held lengthways and shaken so that the middle bulges back and forth, producing a low-pitched booming sound.

**wobbler** /ˈwɒblə/, *n.* a lure used in fishing, which wobbles with a fish-like action when moving through the water.

**wobbling** /ˈwɒblɪŋ/, *adj.* that wobbles, or causes to wobble. Also, **wabbling.** – **wobblingly,** *adv.*

**wobbly**[1] /ˈwɒbli/, *adj.* Also, **wabbly.** shaky; unsteady. – **wobbliness,** *n.*

**wobbly**[2] /ˈwɒbli/, *n. N.Z. Colloq.* a tantrum.

**Wobbly** /ˈwɒbli/, *n., pl.* **-blies.** *Colloq.* a member of the Industrial Workers of the World (trade union).

**wobulator** /ˈwɒbjəleɪtə/, *n.* →**swept frequency oscillator.**

**woe** /woʊ/, *n.* **1.** grievous distress, affliction, or trouble. **2.** an affliction. *–interj.* **3.** (an exclamation of grief, distress, or lamentation). Also, **wo.** [ME *wo,* OE *wā,* interj., c. D *wee,* G *Weh,* L *vae*]

**woebegone** /ˈwoʊbəgɒn/, *adj.* **1.** beset with woe; mournful or miserable; affected by woe, esp. in appearance. **2.** showing or indicating woe: *he had a perpetual woebegone look on his face.* Also, **wobegone.**

**woeful** /ˈwoʊfəl/, *adj.* **1.** full of woe; wretched; unhappy. **2.** affected with, characterised by, or indicating woe: *her poetry is a conglomeration of woeful ditties.* **3.** of wretched quality; sorry; poor. Also, **woful.** – **woefully,** *adv.* – **woefulness,** *n.*

**woffle** /ˈwɒfəl/, *v.i.* →**waffle**[2].

**wog**[1] /wɒg/, *n. Colloq.* (*derog.*) **1.** a native of North Africa or the Middle East, esp. an Arab. **2.** a person of Mediterranean extraction, or of similar complexion and appearance. [? short for GOLLIWOG[1]]

**wog**[2] /wɒg/, *n. Colloq.* **1.** a small insect or germ, esp. a germ leading to a minor disease such as a cold or a stomach upset. **2.** such as a cold, stomach upset, etc. [orig. uncert.]

**wogball** /ˈwɒgbɔl/, *n. Colloq.* →**soccer.** [WOG[1] + (FOOT)BALL]

**woggle** /ˈwɒgəl/, *n.* a small ring, usu. of plaited leather, through which the ends of the neck scarf of a Boy Scout or Girl Guide are passed so as to secure it about the neck.

**wogoit** /ˈwoʊgɔɪt/, *n.* the rock-haunting ringtail possum, *Petropseudes dahli,* of north western Australia; rock possum. [Aboriginal]

**wok** /wɒk/, *n.* a large, shallow, round-bottomed, metal bowl used for frying, esp. in Chinese cooking. [Cantonese: cooking pot]

**woke** /woʊk/, *v.* a past tense of **wake.**

**woken** /ˈwoʊkən/, *v.* past participle of **wake.**

**wold**[1] /woʊld/, *n.* an open, elevated tract of country. [ME; OE *wald* forest, c. G *Wald.* Cf. Icel. *völlr* plain]

**wold**[2] /woʊld/, *n.* →**weld**[2].

**wolf** /wʊlf/, *n., pl.* **wolves** /wʊlvz/, *v.* *–n.* **1.** a large, wild carnivore, *Canis lupus,* of Europe, Asia, and North America, belonging to the dog family, a swift-footed, cunning, rapacious animal, destructive to game, sheep, etc. **2.** the fur of such an animal. **3.** some wolf-like animal not of the dog family, as the Tasmanian wolf. **4.** *Entomol.* the larva of any of various small insects infesting granaries. **5.** any of various rapacious fishes, as the pike. **6.** a cruelly rapacious person. **7.** *Colloq.* a man who is boldly flirtatious or amorous towards many women. **8.** *Music.* **a.** the harsh discord heard in certain chords of keyboard instruments, esp. the organ, when tuned to some system of unequal temperament. **b.** a chord or interval in which such a discord appears. **c.** Also, **wolf note.** (in bowed instruments) a discordant or false vibration in a string due to a defect in structure or adjustment of the instrument. **9. cry wolf,** to give false alarms habitually. **10. keep the wolf from the door,** to ward off or keep away poverty or hunger. **11. lone wolf,** a person or animal who prefers to be and act alone. **12. wolf in sheep's clothing,** one who hides hostile or malicious intentions behind a harmless appearance. *–v.t.* **13.** *Colloq.* to eat ravenously. *–v.i.* **14.** to hunt for wolves. [ME; OE *wulf,* c. D *wolf,* G *Wolf,* Icel. *ulfr*]

wolf

**wolf cub** /ˈ– kʌb/, *n.* **1.** a young wolf. **2.** →**cub** (def. 4).

**wolf-dog** /ˈwʊlf-dɒg/, *n. Chiefly U.S.* **1.** any of various dogs of different breeds used for hunting wolves. See **wolfhound. 2.** a cross between a wolf and a domestic dog. **3.** an Eskimo dog.

**wolfer** /ˈwʊlfə/, *n.* →**wolver.**

**wolf-fish** /ˈwʊlf-fɪʃ/, *n.* **1.** a large fish of the genus *Anarhichas,* as *A. lupus* of the northern Atlantic, allied to the blenny, and noted for its ferocious aspect and habits. **2.** →**lancet fish.**

**wolfhound** /ˈwʊlfhaʊnd/, *n.* a dog of various breeds formerly much used in hunting wolves, as the borzoi.

**wolfish** /ˈwʊlfɪʃ/, *adj.* **1.** resembling a wolf, as in form or characteristics. **2.** characteristic of or befitting a wolf. – **wolfishly,** *adv.* – **wolfishness,** *n.*

**wolf note** /ˈwʊlf noʊt/, *n.* →**wolf** (def. 8c).

**wolfram** /ˈwʊlfrəm/, *n.* **1.** →**tungsten. 2.** →**wolframite.** [G; ? orig. proper name]

**wolframite** /ˈwʊlfrəmaɪt/, *n.* a mineral, iron manganese tungstate, $(Fe, Mn)WO_3$, occurring in heavy, greyish to brownish black tabular or bladed crystals (*sp. gr.:* 7.0-7.5), an important ore of tungsten. Also, **wolfram.** [G *Wolframit,* from *Wolfram* + *-it* -ITE[1]]

**wolframium** /wʊlˈfreɪmiəm/, *n.* →**tungsten.**

**wolf's-bane** /ˈwʊlfs-beɪn/, *n.* a plant of the genus *Aconitum,* esp. a yellow-flowered species, *A. lycoctonum.* See **aconite** (def. 1). Also, **wolfsbane.**

**wolf spider** /ˈwʊlf spaɪdə/, *n.* **1.** the most common ground tunnelling Australian spider, *Lycosa godeffroyi,* often mistaken for a funnel-web spider but regarded as harmless to man. **2.** any spider of the family Lycosidae, members of which do not spin webs, but pursue their prey.

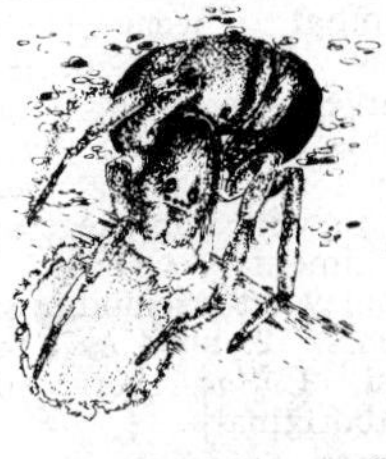

wolf spider

**wolf-whistle** /ˈwʊlf-wɪsəl/, *n., v.,* **-led, -ling.** *–n.* **1.** a whistle in appreciation of an attractive woman, typically sliding up to a high note and then sliding down to a low one. *–v.t.* **2.** to make such a whistle at (someone). *–v.i.* **3.** to whistle in this manner.

**wollastonite** /ˈwʊləstənaɪt/, *n.* a mineral, calcium silicate, $CaSiO_3$, occurring usu. in fibrous white masses. [named after W. H. *Wollaston,* 1766-1828, English chemist]

**Wollaston prism** /wʊləstən ˈprɪzəm/, *n.* a quartz prism for obtaining plane-polarised light, which is suitable for use with ultraviolet radiation. [See WOLLASTONITE]

**wollomai** /ˈwɒləmaɪ/, *n.* →**snapper** (def. 1). [Aboriginal]

**wolver** /ˈwʊlvə/, *n.* one who hunts for wolves. Also, **wolfer.**

**wolverine** /ˈwʊlvərin/, *n.* the glutton, *Gulo gulo,* of America. Also, **wolverene.** [earlier *wolvering,* from *wolver* wolf-like

wolverine

creature + -ING[1]]

**wolves** /wʊlvz/, *n.* plural of **wolf.**

**woma** /ˈwoʊmə/, *n.* a non-venomous snake of eastern Australia, of genus *Aspidites,* closely related to the black-headed python, but lacking the latter's distinctive head colouring. [Aboriginal]

**woman** /ˈwʊmən/, *n., pl.* **women** /ˈwɪmən/ *v., adj.* *–n.* **1.** the female human being (distinguished from *man*). **2.** an adult female person (distinguished from *girl*). **3.** a mistress or paramour. **4.** a female servant, esp. one who does domestic chores, as cleaning, cooking, etc. **5.** (formerly) a female personal maid. **6.** feminine nature, characteristics, or feelings. **7.** a wife. **8. kept woman,** a girl or woman maintained as a mistress by one man. **9. old woman,** a man who is pedantic or tends to fuss, gossip, etc. **10. scarlet woman, a.** a prostitute. **b.** a woman whose sexual relations with men are considered scandalous. *–v.t.* **11.** *Obs.* to cause to act or be like a woman; make effeminate. *–adj.* **12.** female: *a woman doctor.* **13.** of, characteristic of, or belonging to women: *woman talk.* [ME; OE *wifman,* from *wif* female + *man* human being] – **womanless,** *adj.*

**womanhood** /ˈwʊmənhʊd/, *n.* **1.** the state of being a woman. **2.** womanly character or qualities. **3.** the state of being a grown woman (as opposed to a *girl*). **4.** women collectively.

**womanise** /ˈwʊmənaɪz/, *v.* **-nised, -nising.** *–v.i.* **1.** (of a man) to have numerous casual affairs; philander. *–v.t.* **2.** to cause to act or be like a woman; make effeminate. Also, **womanize.** – **womaniser,** *n.*

**womanish** /ˈwʊmənɪʃ/, *adj.* **1.** weakly feminine; effeminate. **2.** womanlike or feminine. – **womanishly,** *adv.* – **womanishness,** *n.*

**womankind** /wʊmənˈkaɪnd/, *n.* women, as distinguished from men; the female sex.

**womanlike** /ˈwʊmənlaɪk/, *adj.* **1.** like a woman; womanly. *–adv.* **2.** in a manner characteristic of or befitting a woman.

**womanly** /ˈwʊmənli/, *adj.* **1.** like or befitting a woman; feminine; not masculine or girlish. *–adv.* **2.** *Obs.* in the manner of, or befitting, a woman. – **womanliness,** *n.*

**woman of the world,** *n.* a sophisticated woman, versed in the ways and usages of the world and society.

**womb** /wum/, *n.* **1.** the uterus of the human female and some of the higher mammalian quadrupeds. **2.** a hollow space. **3.** a place of origin, conception, etc. **4.** *Obs.* the belly. [ME and OE, c. D *wam,* G *Wamme,* Goth. *wamba* belly]

**wombat** /ˈwɒmbæt/, *n.* **1.** any of several species of large, burrowing marsupials constituting the family Vombatidae, heavily built with short legs and a rudimentary tail, and somewhat resembling small bears. **2. blind as a wombat,** *Colloq.* very blind. [Aboriginal]

wombat

**women** /ˈwɪmən/, *n.* plural of **woman.**

**womenfolk** /ˈwɪmənfoʊk/, *n. pl.* **1.** women in general; all women. **2.** a particular group of women, esp. those of one's family.

**women's lib** /wɪmənz ˈlɪb/, *n.* →**women's liberation.**

**women's libber** /– ˈlɪbə/, *n.* a member or advocate of the woman's liberation movement.

**women's liberation** /– lɪbəˈreɪʃən/, *n.* the movement which seeks to free women from sexist discrimination and make available to them the opportunity to play any role in society. Also, **women's lib** /wɪmənz ˈlɪb/.

**womera** /ˈwʊmərə/, *n.* →**woomera.**

**wompoo pigeon** /wɒmpu ˈpɪdʒən/, *n.* a large, strikingly coloured pigeon of eastern Australia and New Guinea, having deep gurgling notes in its call; bubbly Jock; bubbly Mary. [Aboriginal]

wompoo pigeon

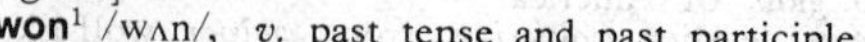

**won**[1] /wʌn/, *v.* past tense and past participle of **win.**

**won**[2] /wʌn, wɒn, woʊn/, *v.i.,* **wonned, wonning.** *Archaic.* to dwell, abide, or stay. [ME *wone,* OE *wunian,* c. G *wohnen*]

**wonder** /ˈwʌndə/, *v.i.* **1.** to think or speculate curiously: *to wonder about a thing.* **2.** to be affected with wonder; marvel (oft. fol. by *at*). **3.** to doubt (that something will or will not happen): *I wonder if she will come after all; I wonder if she'll really come.* *–v.t.* **4.** to be curious about; be curious to know (fol. by a clause): *to wonder what happened.* **5.** to feel wonder at (now only fol. by a clause as object): *I wonder that you went.* *–n.* **6.** something strange and surprising; a cause of surprise, astonishment, or admiration: *it is a wonder he declined such an offer.* **7.** the emotion excited by what is strange and surprising; a feeling of surprised or puzzled interest, sometimes tinged with admiration. **8.** a miracle, or miraculous deed or event. **9. nine day wonder,** a subject of general surprise and interest for a short time. **10. no wonder,** (it is) not at all surprising (that). **11. small wonder,** (it is) hardly surprising (that). [ME; OE *wundor,* c. D *wonder,* G *Wunder*] – **wonderer,** *n.*

**wonderful** /ˈwʌndəfəl/, *adj.* **1.** excellent; delightful; extremely good or fine. **2.** of a kind to excite wonder; marvellous; extraordinary; remarkable. [OE *wundorfull.* See WONDER, -FUL] – **wonderfully,** *adv.* – **wonderfulness,** *n.*

**wondering** /ˈwʌndərɪŋ/, *adj.* **1.** expressing admiration or amazement; marvelling. *–n.* **2.** the act or process of expressing amazement or curiosity. – **wonderingly,** *adv.*

**wonderland** /ˈwʌndəlænd/, *n.* **1.** an imaginary land or place of wonders or marvels. **2.** a wonderful country or region: *a wonderland of snow, a winter wonderland.*

**wonderment** /ˈwʌndəmənt/, *n.* **1.** wondering or wonder. **2.** a cause or occasion of wonder.

**wonderstruck** /ˈwʌndəstrʌk/, *adj.* struck or affected with wonder. Also, **wonder-stricken** /ˈwandəstrɪkən/.

**wonderwork** /ˈwʌndəwɜk/, *n.* a wonderful work; a marvel; a miracle. [ME *wonderworc,* OE *wundor weorc.* See WONDER, WORK]

**wonder-worker** /ˈwʌndə-wɜkə/, *n.* a worker or performer of wonders or marvels. – **wonder-working,** *adj.*

**wondrous** /ˈwʌndrəs/, *adj.* **1.** wonderful; marvellous. *–adv.* **2.** in a wonderful or surprising degree; remarkably. [metathetic var. of ME *wonders* (gen. of WONDER) wonderful; spelling conformed to -OUS] – **wondrously,** *adv.* – **wondrousness,** *n.*

**Wonga bluey** /wɒŋgə ˈblui/, *n.* **1.** a blue woollen cloth, warm and waterproof, from which articles of clothing for bushmen, farmers, etc., are made. **2.** such an article of clothing. [manufactured in *Wonga,* town in Vic.]

**wonga pigeon** /wɒŋgə ˈpɪdʒən/, *n.* a large ground-dwelling bird, *Leucosarcia melanoleuca,* inhabiting heavily timbered areas of eastern Australia. Also, **wonga-wonga.** [Aboriginal]

wonga pigeon

**wonga-wonga** /ˈwɒŋgə-wɒŋgə/, *n.* **1.** →**wonga pigeon.** **2.** Also, **wonga-vine.** a climbing plant, *Pandorea pandorana,* family Bignoniaceae, with cream spotted flowers found in eastern Australia. [Aboriginal]

**wongi** /ˈwɒŋgi/, *Colloq.* *–n.* **1.** a talk, a chat. *–v.i.* **2.** to talk. [Aboriginal]

**wonk** /wɒŋk/, *n.* *Colloq.* (*derog.*) a white man.

**wonky** /ˈwɒŋki/, *adj.* *Colloq.* **1.** shaky; unsound. **2.** askew; awry. **3.** unwell; upset. [var. of Brit. d. *wanky,* itself alteration of *wankle,* ME *wankel,* OE *wancol* shaky, unsteady]

**wont** /woʊnt/, *adj., n., v.,* **wont, wont** or **wonted, wonting.** *–adj.* **1.** accustomed; used (commonly followed by an infinitive). *–n.* **2.** custom; habit; practice. *–v.t.* **3.** to accustom (a person), as to a thing. **4.** to render (a thing) customary or usual (commonly in the passive). *–v.i.* **5.** to be wont or accustomed. [ME *woned,* OE *gewunod,* pp. of *gewunian* be accustomed]

**won't** /woʊnt/, *v.* contraction of *will not.*

**wonted** /ˈwoʊntəd/, *adj.* *Archaic.* **1.** accustomed; habituated; used. **2.** rendered customary; habitual or usual: *the old man was in his wonted place.* – **wontedly,** *adv.* – **wontedness,** *n.*

**won ton** /ˈwɒn tɒn/, *n.* **1.** a ball of noodle dough filled with spicy minced pork, usu. boiled and served in soup. **2.** soup containing won tons. [Chinese (cantonese) *wan t'an* pastry]

**woo** /wu/, *v.t.* **1.** to seek the favour, affection, or love of, esp. with a view to marriage. **2.** to seek to win: *to woo fame.* **3.** to invite (consequences, good or bad) by one's own action: *to woo one's own destruction.* **4.** to seek to persuade (a person, etc.), as to do something; solicit; importune. *–v.i.* **5.** to pay court to someone (usu. of a man to a woman). [ME *wowe*, OE *wōgian*] – **wooer,** *n.* – **wooingly,** *adv.*

**wood**[1] /wʊd/, *n.* **1.** the hard, fibrous substance composing most of the stem and branches of a tree or shrub, and lying beneath the bark; the xylem. **2.** the trunks or main stems of trees as suitable for architectural and other purposes; timber or lumber. **3.** firewood. **4.** the cask, barrel, or keg in which wine, beer, or spirits are stored, as distinguished from the bottle: *aged in the wood.* **5.** *Print.* a woodblock (def. 1). **6.** *Music.* **a.** a wooden wind instrument. **b.** such instruments collectively in a band or orchestra; woodwind. **7.** (*oft. pl.*) a large and thick collection of growing trees, usu. less extensive than a forest. **8.** *Golf.* a club with a wooden head. **9.** *Tennis, etc.* the frame part of a racquet, usu. made of wood. **10.** *Bowls.* →**bowl**[2] (def. 1). **11. out of the wood,** disengaged or escaped from a series of difficulties or dangers. **12. can't see the wood for the trees,** to be unable to distinguish the essential or cardinal points of a problem, situation, or the like, from the mass of detail. **13. have the wood on (someone),** *Colloq.* to be in possession of evidence or information which can be used to damage (someone). *–adj.* **14.** made of wood; wooden. **15.** used to store or carry wood. **16.** used to cut, carve, or otherwise shape wood. **17.** dwelling or growing in woods: *a wood owl.* *–v.t.* **18.** to cover or plant with trees. **19.** to supply with wood; get supplies of wood for. *–v.i.* **20.** to take in or get supplies of wood. [ME; OE *wudu*, earlier *widu*, c. Icel. *vidhr*, OHG *witu*, OIrish *fid*]

**wood**[2] /wʊd/, *adj. Obs.* mad or wild, as with rage or excitement. [ME; OE *wōd*, c. Icel. *odhr;* akin to G *Wut* rage, OE *wōth* song, L *vātes* seer]

**wood alcohol** /– ˈælkəhɒl/, *n.* **1.** the product of the destructive distillation of wood, consisting principally of methyl alcohol. **2.** →**methyl alcohol.**

**wood-and-water joey** /wʊd-ən-ˈwɔtə dʒoʊi/, *n.* a station hand, usu. very young, performing menial tasks; an odd-job man; rouseabout. [from JOEY[1]]

**wood ant** /ˈwʊd ænt/, *n.* a large ant, *Formica ruta*, of woodlands of Europe.

**woodbin** /ˈwʊdbɪn/, *n.* a box for wood fuel. Also, **woodbox.**

**woodbine** /ˈwʊdbaɪn/, *n.* **1.** the common European honeysuckle, *Lonicera periclymenum.* **2.** any of various other honeysuckles, as *L. caprifolium* (**American woodbine**). [ME *wodebinde*, OE *wudubind*, from *wudu* WOOD[1] + *-bind* binding]

**woodblock** /ˈwʊdblɒk/, *n.* **1.** *Print.* **a.** a block of wood engraved in relief, for printing from; a woodcut. **b.** a print or impression from such a block. **2.** a wooden block or sett, as used for flooring, road making, etc. **3.** *Music.* a hollow block used in the percussion section of an orchestra. *–adj.* **4.** printed with or made from a woodblock or blocks.

**wood-borer** /ˈwʊd-bɔrə/, *n.* any animal that bores wood, as some marine molluscs, some crustaceans, and certain insect larvae.

**woodcarving** /ˈwʊdkavɪŋ/, *n.* **1.** the art, craft, or activity of carving wood into useful or ornamental forms. **2.** a carved wooden object, esp. as a work of art. **3.** such objects collectively.

**woodchat** /ˈwʊdtʃæt/, *n.* **1.** Also, **woodchat shrike.** a shrike or butcher-bird, *Lanius senator*, of Europe and North Africa, having black forehead and chestnut crown, nape, and upper mantle. **2.** any of various Asiatic thrushes, esp. of the genus *Larvivora.*

**woodchip** /ˈwʊdtʃɪp/, *n.* **1.** (*pl.*) small pieces of wood, made by mechanically reducing trees to fragments for subsequent industrial use. *–adj.* **2.** of or pertaining to an industry, company, etc., which deals in woodchips.

**woodchop** /ˈwʊdtʃɒp/, *n.* a formalised competition amongst axemen in which the winner is the one who cuts through a standard size log in the fastest time.

**woodchuck** /ˈwʊdtʃʌk/, *n.* a common North American marmot, *Marmota monax*, of stout, heavy form, that burrows in the ground and hibernates in the winter; the ground hog. [alteration of Algonquian (Cree or Chippewa) *otchek, otchig, odjik* fisher, weasel]

**wood coal** /ˈwʊd koʊl/, *n.* →**lignite.**

woodchuck

**woodcock** /ˈwʊdkɒk/, *n., pl.* **-cocks,** (*esp. collectively*) **-cock.** an Old World snipelike game bird, *Scolopax rusticula*, with long bill, short legs and large eyes placed far back in the head. [ME *wodecok*, OE *wuducoc.* See WOOD[1], *n.*, COCK[1], *n.*]

**woodcraft** /ˈwʊdkraft/, *n. Chiefly U.S.* **1.** skill in anything which pertains to the woods or forest, esp. in making one's way through the woods, or in hunting, trapping, etc. **2.** forestry. **3.** the art of making or carving wooden objects. – **woodcraftsman,** *n.*

**woodcut** /ˈwʊdkʌt/, *n.* **1.** a carved or engraved block of wood for printing from. **2.** a print or impression from such a block.

**woodcutter** /ˈwʊdkʌtə/, *n.* **1.** one who cuts wood, fells trees, etc. **2.** an engraver in wood, or maker of woodcuts. – **woodcutting,** *n.*

**wooded** /ˈwʊdəd/, *adj.* covered with or abounding in woods or trees.

**wooden** /ˈwʊdn/, *adj.* **1.** consisting or made of wood. **2.** stiff, ungainly, or awkward. **3.** without spirit or animation: *a wooden stare.* **4.** dull or stupid: *wooden wits.* **5.** (of a sound) as if issuing from a hollow wooden object when struck. **6.** indicating the fifth event of a series, as a wedding anniversary. *–v.t.* **7.** to knock out; bring down to the ground. – **woodenly,** *adv.* – **woodenness,** *n.*

**woodener** /ˈwʊdənə/, *n. Colloq.* a knock-out blow.

**wood engraving** /ˈwʊd ɛnˌgreɪvɪŋ/, *n.* **1.** the art or process of engraving designs in relief with a burin on the end grain of wood, for printing. **2.** a block of wood so engraved. **3.** a print or impression from it. – **wood engraver,** *n.*

**woodenhead** /ˈwʊdnhɛd/, *n. Colloq.* a blockhead; a dull or stupid person.

**wooden-headed** /wʊdn-ˈhɛdəd/, *adj. Colloq.* thick-headed; dull; stupid. – **wooden-headedness,** *n.*

**wooden leg** /wʊdn ˈlɛg/, *n.* an artificial leg, esp. (formerly) one made of wood.

**wooden pear** /– ˈpɛə/, *n.* →**woody pear.**

**wooden spoon** /– ˈspun/, *n.* **1.** a spoon made out of wood, as used in cooking. **2.** *Colloq.* the fictitious prize awarded to the individual or team coming last in a sporting competition. **3. win (get) the wooden spoon,** *Colloq.* to come last in a contest.

**wooden spooner** /– ˈspunə/, *n. Colloq.* the individual or team coming last in a sporting competition. Also, **wooden spooners.**

**woodenware** /ˈwʊdnwɛə/, *n.* vessels, utensils, etc., made of wood.

**wood flour** /ˈwʊd flaʊə/, *n.* waste wood reduced to a flourlike consistency, used as a filler, as a constituent of many synthetic materials, etc.

**woodgrouse** /ˈwʊdgraʊs/, *n.* →**capercailzie.**

**woodheap** /ˈwʊdhip/, *n.* a pile of wood collected or cut in readiness for use in a fire, wood stove, etc.

**woodhen** /ˈwʊdhɛn/, *n. N.Z.* →**weka.**

**woodhouse** /ˈwʊdhaʊs/, *n. Chiefly Brit.* →**woodshed.**

**wood hyacinth** /wʊd ˈhaɪəsənθ/, *n.* See **bluebell** (def. 3).

**wood ibis** /ˈ– aɪbəs/, *n.* a large naked-headed wading bird, *Mycteria americana*, of the family Threskiornithidae, of the wooded swamps of the southern U.S. and regions southwards.

wood ibis

**woodland** /ˈwʊdlənd, -lænd/, *n.* **1.** land covered with woods or trees. *–adj.* **2.** of, pertaining to, or inhabiting the woods; sylvan.

**woodlander** /ˈwʊdləndə, -lændə/, *n.* an inhabitant of the woods.

**woodlark** /ˈwʊdlak/, *n.* a small European songbird, *Lullula arborea,* less famous than the skylark but equally gifted as an aerial songster.

**wood lot** /ˈwʊd lɒt/, *n.* a tract, esp. on a farm, set aside for trees.

**woodlouse** /ˈwʊdlaʊs/, *n., pl.* **-lice** /-laɪs/. →**slater.**

**woodman** /ˈwʊdmən/, *n., pl.* **-men. 1.** one who tends trees or fells them for timber. **2.** *Hist.* an officer having charge of the king's woods. **3.** *Obs.* a hunter of forest game.

**wood naphtha** /wʊd ˈnæfθə/, *n.* →**wood alcohol.**

**woodnote** /ˈwʊdnoʊt/, *n.* a wild or natural musical note, as that of a forest bird.

**wood nymph** /ˈwʊd nɪmf/, *n.* a nymph of the woods, or a dryad.

**woodpecker** /ˈwʊdpɛkə/, *n.* any of numerous scansorial birds constituting the family Picidae, having a hard, chisel-like bill for boring into wood after insects, stiff tail feathers to assist in climbing, and usu. a more or less boldly patterned plumage.

woodpecker

**woodpeckers' day** /ˈwʊdpɛkəz ˌdeɪ/, *n. Prison Colloq.* the day reserved for hearing the cases of people who are pleading guilty. [the majority of criminals appearing in court on this day are 'nodding the head' that is, pleading guilty]

**woodpigeon** /ˈwʊdpɪdʒən/, *n.* **1.** a large wild pigeon, *Columba palumbus,* of Europe; the ringdove. **2.** →**kuku.**

**woodpile** /ˈwʊdpaɪl/, *n.* a pile or stack of wood, esp. wood for fuel.

**wood pitch** /ˈwʊd pɪtʃ/, *n.* See **wood tar.**

**wood pulp** /ˈ– pʌlp/, *n.* wood reduced to pulp through mechanical and chemical treatment and used in the manufacture of paper.

**wood rat** /ˈ– ræt/, *n.* →**pack rat.**

**woodruff** /ˈwʊdrʌf/, *n.* any of the low herbaceous plants belonging to the genus *Galium,* having small sweet-scented white flowers. [ME *woderove,* OE *wudurōfe,* from *wudu* WOOD[1] + *rōfe* (c. MLG *rōve* carrot)]

**woodrush** /ˈwʊdrʌʃ/, *n.* any plant of the genus *Luzula,* family Juncaceae, as *L. campestris* widespread in temperate areas.

**woodscrew** /ˈwʊdskru/, *n.* a metal screw used in carpentry.

**woodshed** /ˈwʊdʃɛd/, *n.* a shed, esp. one for firewood.

**woodsman** /ˈwʊdzmən/, *n., pl.* **-men. 1.** one accustomed to life in the woods and skilled in the arts of the woods, as hunting, trapping, etc. **2.** one who works in the woods, esp. a timbergetter.

**wood sorrel** /ˈwʊd sɒrəl/, *n.* any of a number of species of *Oxalis* as yellow wood sorrel.

**wood spirit** /ˈ– spɪrət/, *n.* **1.** Also, **wood alcohol.** →**methyl alcohol. 2.** a supernatural being supposed to inhabit woods.

**wood stove** /ˈ– stoʊv/, *n.* a type of fuel stove designed to burn wood.

**wood swallow** /ˈ– swɒloʊ/, *n.* any insectivorous bird of the family Artamidae, of Australia.

**woodsy** /ˈwʊdzi/, *adj. U.S.* of, like, suggestive of, or associated with the woods: *a woodsy fragrance.*

**wood tar** /ˈwʊd ta/, *n.* a dark viscid product obtained from wood by distillation or burning slowly without flame, used in its natural state to preserve timber, etc., or subjected to further distillation, when it yields creosote, oils, and a final residuum called **wood pitch.**

**wood-turning** /ˈwʊd-tɜnɪŋ/, *n.* **1.** the forming of wood articles upon a lathe. *–adj.* **2.** used for or pertaining to wood-turning. – **wood-turner,** *n.*

**wood vinegar** /ˈ– vɪnəgə/, *n.* **1.** an impure acetic acid obtained by the distillation of wood. **2.** →**pyroligneous acid.**

**woodwind** /ˈwʊdwɪnd/, *n.* **1.** (*sing., sometimes construed as pl.*) the group of wind instruments which comprises the flutes, clarinets, oboes, and bassoons. **2.** this group considered as a section of an orchestra. **3.** an instrument of this group. *–adj.* **4.** of or pertaining to wind instruments of this group.

**woodwool** /ˈwʊdwʊl/, *n.* fine wood shavings used as a packing material for fragile or delicate objects and as a filler for plaster.

**woodwork** /ˈwʊdwɜk/, *n.* **1.** objects or parts made of wood. **2.** the interior wooden fittings of a house or the like. **3.** the art or craft of working in wood; carpentry.

**woodworker** /ˈwʊdwɜkə/, *n.* a worker in wood, as a carpenter, joiner, or cabinetmaker.

**woodworking** /ˈwʊdwɜkɪŋ/, *n.* **1.** the art or craft of one who works in wood. *–adj.* **2.** pertaining to or used for shaping wood: *woodworking tools.*

**woodworm** /ˈwʊdwɜm/, *n.* a worm or larva that is bred in or bores in wood, esp. the larva of the beetle *Anobium striatum,* which attacks domestic woodwork.

**woody** /ˈwʊdi/, *adj.,* **woodier, woodiest. 1.** abounding with woods; wooded. **2.** belonging or pertaining to the woods; sylvan. **3.** situated in a wood. **4.** consisting of or containing wood; ligneous. **5.** resembling wood, as in hardness, texture, etc. **6.** (of wine) tasting of wood. – **woodiness,** *n.*

**woody nightshade** /– ˈnaɪt-ʃeɪd/, *n.* →**bittersweet** (def. 1).

**woody pear** /– ˈpɛə/, *n.* **1.** a shrub or small tree, *Xylomelum pyriforme,* found growing on sandstone in eastern Australia. **2.** the hard, beaked wooden fruit of this plant. Also, **wooden pear.**

**woof**[1] /wʊf/, *n.* **1.** yarns which travel from selvage to selvage in a loom, interlacing with the warp; weft; filling. **2.** texture; fabric. [ME *oof,* OE *ōwef.* See WEB, WEAVE]

**woof**[2] /wʊf/, *n.* **1.** the sound of a dog barking, esp. deeply and loudly. **2.** a sound in imitation of this; a deep, resonant sound. *–v.i.* **3.** to make any such sound. [imitative]

**woofer** /ˈwʊfə/, *n.* a loudspeaker designed for the reproduction of low-frequency sounds.

**wool** /wʊl/, *n.* **1.** the fine, soft, curly hair, characterised by minute, overlapping surface scales, to which its felting property is mainly due, that forms the fleece of sheep and certain other animals, that of sheep constituting one of the most important materials of clothing. **2.** a fibre produced from sheep's fleece or the like, that may be spun into yarn, or made into felt, upholstery materials, etc. **3.** any of various types of yarn spun from this, as worsted, tweed, etc. **4.** fabric made from sheep's wool. **5.** woollen yarn used for knitting, crocheting, ornamental needlework, etc. **6.** any of various substances used commercially as substitutes for the wool of sheep, etc. **7.** a kind of wool-like yarn or material made from cellulose by a process similar to that used in manufacturing rayon or artificial silk. **8.** any of certain vegetable fibres, such as cotton, flax, etc., so used, esp. after preparation by special process (**vegetable wool**). **9.** any finely fibrous or filamentous matter suggestive of the wool of sheep: *glass wool.* **10.** *Colloq.* the human hair, esp. when short, thick, and curly. **11. all wool and a yard wide,** *Colloq.* (formerly) genuine; completely honest. **12. dyed in the wool,** inveterate. **13. in the wool,** (of sheep) ready or nearly ready for shearing. **14. keep** (or **lose**) **one's wool,** to keep (or lose) one's temper; not become (or become) angry. **15. pull the wool over one's eyes,** to deceive or delude one. [ME *wole,* OE *wull,* c. D *wol,* G *Wolle,* Icel. *ull,* Goth. *wulla*]

**wool-blind** /ˈwʊl-blaɪnd/, *adj.* (of sheep) with excessive growth of wool around the eyes, affecting the sight, so that wigging is necessary.

**wool cheque** /ˈwʊl tʃɛk/, *n.* money received for a woolclip.

**wool classing** /ˈwʊlklasɪŋ/, *n.* the trade or occupation of grading wool. – **wool classer,** *n.*

**woolclip** /ˈwʊlklɪp/, *n.* the amount of wool yielded from the annual shearing season (by a station, district, etc.). Also, **clip.**

**wool count** /ˈwʊl kaʊnt/, *n.* a quality number used to indicate fineness in raw wool.

**wool fat** /ˈ– fæt/, *n.* →**lanolin.**

**woolfell** /ˈwʊlfɛl/, *n. Obs.* the skin of a wool-bearing animal with the fleece still on it. [WOOL + FELL[4]]

**wool-gathering** /ˈwʊl-gæðərɪŋ/, *n.* **1.** indulgence in desultory fancies or a fit of abstraction. **2.** gathering of the tufts of wool as caught on bushes, etc., by passing sheep. **3.** idle speculation; undirected thought. *–adj.* **4.** inattentive;

abstracted. – **wool-gatherer,** *n.*

**woolgrower** /'wʊlgroʊə/, *n.* one who raises sheep or other wool-bearing animals for the production of wool. – **wool-growing,** *n.*

**woollen** /'wʊlən/, *n.* **1.** a fabric made from wool, esp. a soft loose one. **2.** (*pl.*) knitted woollen clothing, esp. jerseys. *–adj.* **3.** made or consisting of wool. **4.** of or pertaining to wool, or products made of wool, or their manufacture. Also, *U.S.,* **woolen.**

**wool lien** /'wʊl liən/, *n.* a lien given over the ensuing clip of wool as security for an advance.

**woollies** /'wʊliz/, *n.pl. Colloq.* woollen clothing.

**woolly** /'wʊli/, *adj.,* **-lier, -liest,** *n., pl.* **-lies.** *–adj.* **1.** consisting of wool. **2.** resembling wool. **3.** clothed or covered with wool or something resembling it. **4.** not clear or firm, as thinking, expression, depiction, etc.; blurred, confused, or indistinct. **5.** *Bot.* covered with a pubescence of soft hairs resembling wool. **6.** *U.S. Colloq.* like the rough atmosphere of the early West: *the wild and woolly West.* *–n.* **7.** *Colloq.* an article of clothing made of wool. **8.** a sheep. – **woollily,** *adv.* – **woolliness,** *n.*

**woolly bear** /– 'bɛə/, *n.* the caterpillar of any of various moths, as tiger moths, covered with a dense coat of woolly hairs.

**woolly butt** /'– bʌt/, *n.* **1.** any of several species of *Eucalyptus* with thick fibrous bark present only on the lower part of the trunk, esp. *E. longifolia* of New South Wales. **2.** any of several species of the genus *Eragrostis,* esp. *E. eriopoda,* a tussocky native perennial, with bristly stems and a woolly covering on the roots and butt, growing in low rainfall areas.

**woolly-minded** /wʊli-'maɪndəd/, *adj.* forgetful; vague; confused.

**woollynose** /'wʊlinoʊz/, *n. Colloq.* a fettler.

**woolmark** /'wʊlmak/, *n.* a mark placed on sheep for their identification.

**Wooloomooloo Yank** /wʊləmə'lu 'jæŋk/, *n.* an Australian who modelled his behaviour on that of American soldiers on leave in Sydney during World War II; a flashy character who would like to be taken for an American. [from *Wooloomooloo,* an inner Sydney suburb]

**woolpack** /'wʊlpæk/, *n.* **1.** the bale in which wool was formerly done up, as for transporting. **2.** *Meteorol.* a cumulus cloud of fleecy appearance.

**wool press** /'wʊl prɛs/, *n.* a hydraulic press set in a strong frame, designed to ram wool into a wool pack. Also, **wool screw.**

**woolroller** /'wʊlroʊlə/, *n.* →**roller** (def. 11). Also, **fleeceroller.**

**woolsack** /'wʊlsæk/, *n.* **1.** (in England) the seat of the Lord Chancellor in the House of Lords, made of a large, square, cloth-covered bag of wool. **2.** the office of the Lord Chancellor. **3. sit on the woolsack,** to occupy the office of Lord Chancellor. **4.** a sack or bag of wool.

**wool-shears** /'wʊl-ʃɪəz/, *n.* large shears specially designed for shearing sheep.

**woolshed** /'wʊlʃɛd/, *n.* a large shed for shearing and baling of wool.

**woolshed hop** /– 'hɒp/, *n. Colloq.* →**barn-dance** (def. 1.)

**wool sorter** /'wʊl sɔtə/, *n.* one who classifies wool into various classes.

**wool-sorters' disease** /ˌwʊl-sɔtəz də'ziz/, *n.* pulmonary anthrax in man caused by inhaling the spores of *Bacillus anthracis.*

**wool-stapler** /'wʊl-steɪplə/, *n.* a dealer in wool, esp. one who sorts it according to the staple or fibre, before selling it to the manufacturer. – **wool-stapling,** *adj.*

**wool table** /'wʊl teɪbəl/, *n.* a table, the top of which is made from ridged slats with spaces between, on which the fleece is rolled and skirted.

**woomera** /'wʊmərə/, *n.* a type of throwing stick with a notch at one end for holding a dart or spear, thus giving increased leverage in throwing, used by Australian Aborigines. Also, **womera.** [Aboriginal]

**woops** /wʊps, wups/, *interj.* (an exclamation indicating surprise, dismay, etc.).

**Woop Woop** /'wʊp wʊp/, *n.* (*joc.*) any remote or backward town or district. Also, **woop woop.**

**woozy** /'wuzi/, *adj. Colloq.* **1.** muddled, or stupidly confused. **2.** out of sorts physically, as with dizziness, nausea, or the like. **3.** slightly or rather drunk. [? from *wooze,* var. of OOZE[2]] – **woozily,** *adv.* – **wooziness,** *n.*

**wop** /wɒp/, *Colloq.* (*usu. derog.*). *–n.* **1.** an Italian or any foreigner thought to be of Italianate appearance. *–adj.* **2.** of or pertaining to any Latin country, its culture, or inhabitants. [? from It. (Neapolitan d.) *guapo* dandy]

**wop-wops** /'wɒp-wɒps/, *n. pl.* (*sometimes sing.*) *N.Z.* any remote town or district: *I live out in the wop-wops.*

**Worcestershire sauce** /ˌwʊstəʃɪə 'sɔs/, *n.* a sharp sauce made with soya, vinegar, spices, etc. Also, **worcester sauce.** [from *Worcestershire,* England, where it was first made]

**word** /wɜd/, *n.* **1.** a sound or a combination of sounds, or its written or printed representation, used in any language as the sign of a concept. **2.** *Gram.* an element which can stand alone as an utterance, not divisible into two or more parts similarly characterised; thus *boy* and *boyish,* but not *-ish* or *boy scout,* the former being less than a word, the latter more. **3.** a speech element which signifies; a term used to describe or refer: *'blue' is not an accurate word for the sea.* **4.** (*oft. pl.*) speech or talk: *to have a word with someone.* **5.** an utterance or expression, usu. brief: *a word of praise, or of warning.* **6.** (*pl.*) the text or lyrics of a song as distinguished from the music. **7.** (*pl.*) contentious or angry speech; a quarrel. **8.** warrant, assurance, or promise: *to give or keep one's word.* **9.** intelligence or tidings: *to get word of an occurrence.* **10.** a verbal signal, as a password, watchword, or countersign. **11.** an authoritative utterance, or command: *his word was law.* **12.** a rumour; hint. **13.** (*cap.*) *Theol.* **a.** the Scriptures, or Bible (often **the Word of God**). **b.** the Logos; the concept of the second person of the Trinity (often, **the Word made Flesh.**) **14.** *Computers.* a unit of information, usu. consisting of a number or of a group of alphanumeric characters, in the memory of a computer. **15.** *Obs.* a proverb; motto. **16.** Some special noun phrases are:

**as good as one's word,** dependable; reliable; true to one's promises or stated intentions.

**eat one's words,** *Colloq.* to retract something said or written.

**have a word with,** to speak briefly to.

**have words with,** to remonstrate with; to argue.

**in a word, 1.** in short; briefly. **2.** by way of summing up.

**in so many words,** explicitly; unequivocally; without prevarication.

**my word!, 1.** (an expression of agreement). **2.** (an expression of surprise, mild annoyance, etc.)

**of few words,** taciturn or laconic; disinclined to talk.

**of many words,** loquacious.

**of one's word,** reliable; dependable: *he is a man of his word.*

**play on words,** a verbal construction making use of the peculiarities of words, esp. ambiguities of spelling or pronunciation, as a pun.

**put in a (good) word for,** to recommend (someone); mention in a favourable way.

**suit the action to the word,** to do what one has said one would do.

**take one at one's word,** to act on the assumption that someone means what he says literally.

**take the words out of one's mouth,** to say exactly what another was about to say.

**the last word, 1.** the closing remark, as of an argument. **2.** the very latest, most modern, or most fashionable; the best, or most sophisticated: *this machine is the last word in automation.*

**word for word, 1.** (of a repetition, report, etc.) using exactly the same words as the original; verbatim. **2.** translated by means of exact verbal equivalents rather than by general sense.

**word of honour,** a promise.

**word perfect,** knowing (a lesson, part in a play, formula, etc.) completely and correctly; by rote: *study this until you are word perfect.*

*–v.t.* **17.** to express in words, or phrase; select words to express: *he words his speeches carefully to avoid causing offence.* **18.** *Colloq.* (oft. fol. by *up*) to speak to esp. when informing beforehand: *he worded up the magistrate.* [ME and OE, c. D *woord,* G *Wort,* Icel. *ordh,* Goth. *waurd*]

**wordage** /ˈwɜdɪdʒ/, *n.* **1.** words collectively. **2.** quantity of words.

**word association** /ˈwɜd əsousieɪʃən/, *n.* **1.** a method of psychoanalysis in which the subject responds to a key word by the first word that comes to mind. **2.** a party game in which each member of the group in turn gives a word associated with the previous one.

**word-blind** /ˈwɜd-blaɪnd/, *adj.* suffering from alexia.

**word blindness** /ˈwɜd blaɪndnəs/, *n.* →**alexia.**

**wordbook** /ˈwɜdbʊk/, *n.* **1.** a book of words, usu. with explanations, etc.; a dictionary. **2.** the libretto of an opera.

**wordbreak** /ˈwɜdbreɪk/, *n.* the point of division in a word which runs over from one line to the next. The exact placing of the division is usu. determined according to certain rules of sound, as not breaking words of one syllable, and of sense, as breaking words after a prefix.

**worded** /ˈwɜdəd/, *adj.* expressed by words selected in a specified way: *a carefully worded report.*

**word game** /ˈwɜd geɪm/, *n.* any game based on skill in the formation and use of words.

**wording** /ˈwɜdɪŋ/, *n.* **1.** the act or manner of expressing in words; phrasing. **2.** the form of words in which a thing is expressed.

**wordless** /ˈwɜdləs/, *adj.* **1.** speechless, silent, or mute. **2.** not put into words; unexpressed.

**word order** /ˈwɜd ɔdə/, *n.* the arrangement in a sequence of the words of a sentence or smaller construction, usu. to show meaning, as *Jack ate the beef* compared with *the beef Jack ate.*

**word-painting** /ˈwɜd-peɪntɪŋ/, *n.* the art or practice of verbal description.

**word picture** /ˈwɜd pɪktʃə/, *n.* a verbal description, esp. a vivid one.

**word play** /ˈ– pleɪ/, *n.* verbal witticisms, quips, puns, etc.

**word processor** /ˈ– prousɛsə/, *n.* a computer usu. with keyboard and visual display unit, designed esp. for storing and editing text.

**word-square** /ˈwɜd-skwɛə/, *n.* a set of words such that when arranged one beneath another in the form of a square they read alike horizontally and vertically.

**wordy** /ˈwɜdi/, *adj.*, **wordier, wordiest.** **1.** characterised by or given to the use of many, or too many, words; verbose. – **wordily,** *adv.* – **wordiness,** *n.*

**wore** /wɔ/, *v.* past tense of **wear.**

**work** /wɜk/, *n., adj., v.,* **worked** or **wrought, working.** *–n.* **1.** exertion directed to produce or accomplish something; labour; toil. **2.** that on which exertion or labour is expended; something to be made or done; a task or undertaking. **3.** productive or operative activity. **4.** manner of working or quality of workmanship. **5.** *Physics.* **a.** the product of the force acting upon a body and the distance through which the point of application of force moves. The derived SI unit of work is the joule. **b.** the transference of energy from one body or system to another. **6.** employment; a job, esp. that by which one earns a living. **7.** materials, things, etc., on which one is working, or is to work. **8.** the result of exertion, labour, or activity; a deed or performance. **9.** a product of exertion, labour, or activity: *a work of art, literary or musical works.* **10.** an engineering structure, as a building, bridge, dock, or the like. **11.** (*usu. pl.*) a building, wall, trench, or the like, constructed or made as a means of fortification. **12.** (*pl. oft. construed as sing.*) a place or establishment for carrying on some form of labour or industry: *iron works.* **13.** (*pl.*) the working parts of a mechanical contrivance. **14.** the piece being cut, formed, ground, or otherwise processed in a machine tool, grinder, punching machine, etc. **15.** (*pl.*) *Theol.* acts performed in obedience to the law of God, or righteous deeds. **16.** Some special noun phrases are:

**at work, 1.** at one's place of work. **2.** engaged in working: *danger, men at work.* **3.** operating; functioning: *strange forces have been at work in the neighbourhood.*

**have one's work cut out,** to be pressed; have a difficult task.

**make short work of,** to dispose or deal with quickly.

**out of work,** unemployed.

**set to work,** to start; begin.

**the works, 1.** everything there is; the whole lot. **2.** *Colloq.* a violent assault. **3.** *N.Z.* →**freezing works.**

*–adj.* **17.** of, for, or concerning work: *work clothes.* [ME *worke,* n., OE *worc* (v. ME *werk,* OE *Weorc*), c. D *werk,* G *werk,* Icel. *verk,* Gk *érgon*]

*–v.i.* **18.** to do work, or labour; exert oneself (contrasted with *play*). **19.** to be employed, as for one's livelihood: *he works in a laundry.* **20.** to be in operation, as a machine. **21.** to act or operate effectively: *the pump will not work, the plan works.* **22.** to get (*round, loose,* etc.), as if by continuous effort. **23.** to move (*into, round, through,* etc.) gradually, carefully, or with effort: *to work carefully through a subject.* **24.** to have an effect or influence, as on a person or on the mind or feelings. **25.** to move in agitation, as the features under strong feeling. **26.** to make way with effort or difficulty: *a ship works to windward.* **27.** *Naut.* to give slightly at the joints, as a vessel under strain at sea. **28.** *Mach.* to move improperly, as from defective fitting of parts or from wear. **29.** to undergo treatment by labour in a given way: *this dough works slowly.* **30.** to ferment, as a liquid. *–v.t.* **31.** to use or manage (an apparatus, contrivance, etc.) in operation. **32.** to bring, put, get, render, etc., by work, effort, or action (fol. by *in, off, out,* or other completive words): *to work off a debt, to work up a case.* **33.** to get, or cause (something or someone) to go or be (*in, into, up,* etc.) gradually, carefully, or with difficulty: *to work a broom up the chimney.* **34.** to bring about (any result) by or as by work or effort: *to work a change.* **35.** to effect, accomplish, cause, or do. **36.** to expend work on; manipulate or treat by labour: *to work butter.* **37.** to put into effective operation. **38.** to operate (a mine, farm, etc.) for productive purposes. **39.** to carry on operations in (a district or region). **40.** to make, fashion, or execute by work. **41.** to achieve, win, or pay for by work or effort: *to work one's way through college.* **42.** to arrange or contrive: *it'll be difficult but I think I can work you a day off.* **43.** to keep (a person, a horse, etc.) at work. **44.** to move, stir, or excite in feeling, etc. (oft. fol. by *up*): *he worked himself into a frenzy.* **45.** to make or decorate by needlework or embroidery. **46.** to cause (a liquid, etc.) to ferment. *–v.* **47.** Some special verb phrases are:

**work a point,** *Colloq.* to take an unfair advantage.

**work at,** to attempt to achieve or master (something) with application and energy: *skating isn't easy; you've got to work at it.*

**work back,** to remain at one's place of employment to work after hours.

**work in, 1.** to introduce, insert, or cause to penetrate, esp. gradually: *work in the butter and sugar; he managed to work in the question of money.* **2.** to find room for or fit in, as into a program.

**work into, 1.** to make (one's) way gradually into; penetrate slowly. **2.** to introduce or cause to mingle gradually, with care, etc. **3.** to get (something) into (somewhere) slowly, or with difficulty: *he worked his feet into his boots.*

**work off, 1.** to get rid of by working. **2.** to discharge (a debt) by one's labour.

**work one's passage,** to pay for one's fare on a sea trip, or the like, by working as a member of the crew.

**work out, 1.** to effect or achieve by labour: *to work out one's own salvation.* **2.** to discharge (a debt, etc.) by one's labour. **3.** to solve (a problem) by a reasoning process. **4.** to find (the answer to a problem) by reasoning. **5.** to calculate (the best way of doing something, etc.): *to work out a plan of campaign.* **6.** to amount to a total or calculated figure: *it works out at $10 a metre.* **7.** to cause to finish up, turn out, or culminate (satisfactorily, unless otherwise specified): *to work out one's difficulties.* **8.** to turn out; prove (effective or suitable, unless otherwise specified). **9.** to develop; elaborate: *he doesn't always work out his plots.* **10.** to exhaust (a mine, or the like). **11.** to expiate by or as by one's effort or labour. **12.** to undergo training or practice, esp. intensively, as an athlete.

**work to rule, work to regulations,** to operate or take part in a go-slow.

**work up, 1.** to excite or arouse (as feelings in oneself or others): *to work up an appetite.* **2.** to expand or elaborate (something). **3.** to move or cause to move gradually upwards. **4.** to rise gradually, as in intensity: *to work up to a climax.* **5.** to get gradually to something considered as higher, more important, etc.: *I was working up to that topic.*

[ME *worke* (v. use of *worke,* n.) replacing ME *wyrche,* OE *wyrcean,* c. G *wirken,* Icel. *verkja,* Goth. *waurkjan*] **–workless,** *adj.*

**workable** /ˈwɜkəbəl/, *adj.* **1.** practicable or feasible. **2.** capable of or suitable for being worked. **–workability** /wɜkəˈbɪləti/, **workableness,** *n.*

**workaday** /ˈwɜkədeɪ/, *adj.* **1.** of or befitting working days; working; practical; everyday. **2.** commonplace; humdrum.

**workaholic** /wɔkəˈhɒlɪk/, *n.* a person who is addicted to work. [modelled on ALCOHOLIC]

**workbag** /ˈwɜkbæg/, *n.* a bag for holding implements and materials for work, esp. needlework.

**workbasket** /ˈwɜkbaskət/, *n.* a small basket for holding equipment for needlework or the like.

**workbench** /ˈwɜkbɛntʃ/, *n.* a bench or table at which someone works.

**workbook** /ˈwɜkbʊk/, *n.* **1.** a manual of operating instructions. **2.** a book designed to guide the work of a student by inclusion of some instructional material, and usu. providing questions, etc. **3.** a book in which a record is kept of work completed or planned.

**workbox** /ˈwɜkbɒks/, *n.* a box to hold instruments and materials for work, esp. needlework.

**workday** /ˈwɜkdeɪ/, *n.* **1.** working day. *–adj.* **2.** workaday.

**worked** /wɜkt/, *adj.* that has undergone working; wrought; ornamented; embroidered: *a prettily worked handbag.*

**worker** /ˈwɜkə/, *n.* **1.** one who or that which works: *he's a good steady worker.* **2.** one employed in manual or industrial labour. **3.** an employee, esp. as contrasted with a capitalist or a manager. **4.** one who works in a specified occupation: *office workers, research workers.* **5.** (in the U.S.S.R.) a citizen, excluding the peasants and members of the army or navy. **6.** *Entomol.* the sterile or infertile female of bees, wasps, ants, or termites, which does the work of the colony. **7.** Also, **working girl.** *Colloq.* a prostitute. **–workerless,** *adj.*

**worker participation** /– patɪsəˈpeɪʃən/, *n.* a formal arrangement whereby the workers in a factory, office, etc., have a role in making decisions on questions of policy, management, etc.

**workers' compensation** /wɜkəz kɒmpənˈseɪʃən/, *n.* payments by employers to employees as compensation for injuries incurred while engaged in the employers' business.

**workface** /ˈwɛkfeɪs/, *n.* →**face** (def. 19).

**workfellow** /ˈwɜkfɛloʊ/, *n.* one who works in the same place or at the same job as another.

**workfolk** /ˈwɜkfoʊk/, *n.pl.* →**workpeople.** Also, *U.S. Colloq.* **workfolks.**

**work force** /ˈwɜk fɔs/, *n.* the total of all those engaged in employment.

**work function** /– fʌŋkʃən/, *n.* the energy required to free an electron from the surface of a metal.

**work-hardening** /ˈwɜk-hadnɪŋ/, *n.* →**strain-hardening.**

**workhorse** /ˈwɜkhɔs/, *n.* **1.** a horse used for draught or riding purposes, rather than recreation or sport. **2.** *Colloq.* a person who works very hard.

**workhouse** /ˈwɜkhaʊs/, *n.* **1.** *Hist.* a publicly supported institution for the maintenance of able-bodied paupers who performed unpaid work. **2.** *U.S.* a house of correction.

**working** /ˈwɜkɪŋ/, *n.* **1.** the act of a person or thing that works. **2.** operation; action. **3.** the process of skilful working of something into a shape. **4.** the act of manufacturing or building a thing. **5.** the act of solving a problem. **6.** (*usu. pl.*) a part of a mine, quarry, or the like, in which work is being or has been carried on. **7.** (*pl.*) the intermediate stages of a calculation, esp. in mathematics. **8.** the process of fermenting, as of yeasts. **9.** a slow advance involving exertion. **10.** disturbed or twisting motions. *–adj.* **11.** that performs work or labour, esp. of a manual, mechanical or industrial kind. **12.** that performs the work of a business or the like, as against providing the capital or administration. **13.** that is functional or operative, as a machine. **14.** that is sufficient to permit work of a particular kind to proceed: *a working majority, working knowledge.* **15.** of a theory, arrangement, etc., providing a basis to work on (esp. for the time being, to prevent work from being delayed, etc.). **16.** pertaining to, connected with, or used in operating or working. **17.** that moves with jerks or twists, as the face when chewing or under emotional stress.

**working bee** /– bi/, *n.* →**bee**[1] (def. 3).

**working capital** /– ˈkæpətl/, *n.* **1.** the amount of capital needed to carry on a business. **2.** *Accounting.* current assets minus current liabilities. **3.** *Finance.* liquid as distinguished from fixed capital assets.

**working class** /– klas/, *n., pl.* **classes.** the class of people composed chiefly of manual workers and labourers; the proletariat.

**working-class** /ˈwɜkɪŋ-klas/, *adj.* belonging or pertaining to, or characteristic of the working class; proletarian.

**working day** /ˈwɜkɪŋ deɪ/, *n.* **1.** the amount of time that a worker must work for an agreed daily wage. **2.** a day ordinarily given to working (opposed to *holiday*). **3.** the daily period of hours for working.

**working-day** /ˈwɜkɪŋ-deɪ/, *adj.* workaday; everyday.

**working drawing** /ˈwɜkɪŋ ˌdrɔ-ɪŋ/, *n.* a drawing, as of the whole or part of a structure or machine, made to scale and in such detail with regard to dimensions, etc., as to form a guide for the workmen in the construction of the object.

**working edge** /– ɛdʒ/, *n.* an edge of a piece of wood trued square with the working face to assist in truing the other surfaces square; face edge.

**working face** /– feɪs/, *n.* that face of a piece of wood or the like which is first trued and then used as a basis for truing the other surfaces; face side.

**working girl** /– gɜl/, *n.* **1.** a girl or woman who is employed. **2.** *Colloq.* a prostitute.

**working load** /– loʊd/, *n.* the maximum load in normal conditions.

**workingman** /ˈwɜkɪŋmæn/, *n., pl.* **-men.** a man of the working class; a man (skilled or unskilled) who earns his living at some manual or industrial work.

**working memory** /ˈwɜkɪŋ ˌmɛməri, -ˌmɛmri/, *n. Computers.* a high-speed memory unit used to hold intermediate results during a calculation.

**working model** /– mɒdl/, *n.* a model, as of a machine, having a moving mechanism which reproduces that of the original.

**working order** /– ɔdə/, *n.* the state of something, as a mechanism, when it is functioning properly.

**working papers** /– peɪpəz/, *n.pl.* legal papers giving information often required for employment.

**working party** /– pati/, *n.* **1.** a group, committee, etc., appointed to study a problem in detail, solve a difficulty, conduct an investigation, etc. **2.** a group of soldiers, prisoners, etc., who are detailed to carry out a special task.

**working substance** /– sʌbstəns/, *n.* the substance, as a working fluid, which operates a prime mover.

**workload** /ˈwɜkloʊd/, *n.* the amount of work done or to be done in a specified time: *I have a very heavy workload this month.*

**workman** /ˈwɜkmən/, *n., pl.* **-men. 1.** a man employed or skilled in some form of manual, mechanical, or industrial work. **2.** a male worker. **–workmanless,** *adj.*

**workmanlike** /ˈwɜkmənlaɪk/, *adj.* **1.** like or befitting a good workman; skilful; well executed. **2.** efficient, smart, or businesslike. *–adv.* **3.** in a manner characteristic of a good workman. Also, **workmanly.**

**workmanship** /ˈwɜkmənʃɪp/, *n.* **1.** the art or skill of a workman; skill in working or execution. **2.** quality or mode of execution, as of a thing made. **3.** the product or result of the labour and skill of a workman; work executed.

**work of art,** *n.* **1.** a piece of creative work in the arts, esp. a painting or a piece of sculpture. **2.** anything executed extremely well or in particularly good taste.

**work-out** /ˈwɜk-aʊt/, *n.* **1.** a trial at running, boxing, a game, or the like, usu. preliminary to and in preparation for a contest, exhibition, etc. **2.** any performance for practice or training, or as a trial or test. **3.** physical exercise.

**workpeople** /ˈwɜkpipəl/, *n. pl.* people employed at work or labour, esp. manual or industrial workers.

**workplace** /ˈwɜkpleɪs/, *n.* a place of employment.

**workroom** /ˈwɜkrum/, *n.* a room in which work is carried on.

**works committee** /ˈwɜks kəˌmɪti/, *n.* **1.** an elected body of employee representatives which deals with management regarding grievances, working conditions, wages, etc., and which is consulted by management in regard to labour matters. **2.** a joint council or committee representing employer and employees which discusses working conditions, wages, etc., within a factory or office. Also, **works council.**

**work sheet** /ˈwɜk ʃit/, *n.* **1.** a prepared sheet of paper with diagrams, instructions, etc., from which one works. **2.** a sheet of paper on which to record work being done or to be done.

**workshop** /ˈwɜkʃɒp/, *n.* **1.** a room or building in which work, esp. mechanical work, is carried on (considered as smaller than a factory). **2.** a group meeting to exchange ideas and study techniques, skills, etc.: *theatre workshop.*

**work-shy** /ˈwɜk-ʃaɪ/, *adj.* disliking and tending to avoid work or effort of any kind; lazy.

**work-table** /ˈwɜk-teɪbl/, *n.* a table for working at; often with drawers or receptacles for materials, etc., as for sewing.

**work the oracle,** *n. Colloq.* to achieve (often secretly and with cunning) a desired end.

**work-to-rule** /wɜk-tə-ˈrul/, *n.* **1.** a deliberate curtailment of output by workers, by meticulous observation of rules, as an industrial sanction. **2.** →**go-slow.**

**world** /wɜld/, *n.* **1.** the earth or globe. **2.** a particular division of the earth: *the New World.* **3.** the earth, with its inhabitants, affairs, etc., during a particular period: *the ancient world.* **4.** a particular section of the world's inhabitants: *the Third World.* **5.** mankind; humanity. **6.** the public generally: *the whole world knows it.* **7.** the class of persons devoted to the affairs, interests, or pursuits of this life: *the world worships success.* **8.** society; secular, social, or fashionable life, with its ways and interests: *to withdraw from the world.* **9.** a particular class of mankind, with common interests, aims, etc.: *the fashionable world.* **10.** any sphere, realm, or domain, with all that pertains to it: *woman's world, the world of dreams, the insect world.* **11.** the totality of a person's immediate environment or context; one's physical and spiritual surroundings: *the world of high finance.* **12.** the entire system of created things; the universe; the macrocosm. **13.** any complex whole conceived as resembling the universe (cf. **microcosm**). **14.** one's life, conceived of as complete and separate from the rest of society; one's private mental universe. **15.** one of the three general groupings of physical nature, as the **animal world, mineral world, vegetable world.** **16.** any period, state, or sphere of existence: *this world, the world to come.* **17.** a very great quantity or extent: *to do a world of good.* **18.** any indefinitely great expanse or amount. **19.** *Colloq.* all that is important, agreeable, or necessary to one's happiness: *you're the world to me.* **20.** any heavenly body: *the starry worlds.* **21.** Some special noun phrases are:

**a world of one's own,** a state of being out of touch with other people.

**bring into the world, 1.** to bear (a child), as a mother. **2.** to deliver (a child), as a midwife.

**come into the world,** to be born.

**dead to the world,** *Colloq.* **1.** unaware of one's surroundings; sleeping heavily. **2.** totally drunk. **3.** utterly tired; exhausted.

**for all the world, 1.** for any consideration, no matter how great: *he wouldn't come for all the world.* **2.** in every respect, or precisely: *he looks for all the world like a drug addict.*

**for the world** or **for worlds,** on any account.

**in the world, 1.** in the universe, or on earth anywhere. **2.** at all; ever: *nothing in the world will make me change my mind, where in the world did you get that hat?*

**on top of the world,** elated; delighted; exultant.

**out of this world,** excellent; supremely or sublimely good.

**set the world on fire,** to be a great success.

**think the world of,** to esteem very highly.

**world without end,** through all eternity; for ever. [ME and OE, var. of OE *weorold,* c. D *wereld,* G *Welt,* Icel. *veröld,* all g. Gmc **wer-ald,* lit., man-age]

**world-beater** /ˈwɜld-bitə/, *n.* a surpassingly good thing, person, etc. – **world-beating,** *adj., n.*

**world-class** /ˈwɜld-klas/, *adj.* sufficiently good to be acceptable anywhere in the world.

**worldling** /ˈwɜldlɪŋ/, *n.* one devoted to the interests and pleasures of this world; a worldly person.

**worldly** /ˈwɜldli/, *adj.,* **-lier, -liest,** *adv.* –*adj.* **1.** earthly or mundane (as opposed to *heavenly, spiritual,* etc.). **2.** devoted to, directed towards, or connected with the affairs, interests, or pleasures of this world. **3.** secular (as opposed to *ecclesiastic, religious,* etc.). **4.** *Obs.* of or pertaining to this world. –*adv.* **5.** in a worldly manner. – **worldliness** /ˈwɜldlinəs/, *n.*

**worldly-minded** /wɜldli-ˈmaɪndəd/, *adj.* having or showing a worldly mind, or devotion to the affairs and interests of this world. – **worldly-mindedly,** *adv.* – **worldly-mindedness,** *n.*

**worldly-wise** /ˈwɜldi-waɪz/, *adj.* wise as to the affairs of this world.

**world power** /wɜld ˈpaʊə/, *n.* a nation so powerful that it is capable of influencing or changing the course of world events.

**world-shaking** /ˈwɜld-ʃeɪkɪŋ/, *adj.* remarkable; of great importance or significance. Also, **world-shattering.**

**world view** /ˈwɜld vju/, *n.* the philosophy of an individual, a group or a race, with an interpretation of world history or civilisation; weltanschauung.

**world war** /wɜld ˈwɔ/, *n.* a war involving a large number of countries, esp. the most powerful ones, and waged in many parts of the world.

**world-weary** /ˈwɜld-wɪəri/, *adj.* weary of the world or of existence and its pleasures; blasé.

**worldwide** /ˈwɜldwaɪd/, *adj.* extending or spread throughout the world.

**worm** /wɜm/, *n.* **1.** *Zool.* any of the long, slender, soft-bodied bilateral invertebrates including the flatworms, roundworms, acanthocephalans, nemerteans, and annelids. **2.** (in popular language) any of numerous small creeping animals with more or less slender, elongated bodies, and without limbs or with very short ones, including individuals of widely differing kinds, as earthworms, tapeworms, insect larvae, adult forms of some insects, etc. **3.** woodworm, or its presence, as indicated by wormholes, etc. **4.** something resembling or suggesting a worm in appearance, movement, etc. **5.** the spiral pipe in a still, in which the vapour is condensed. **6.** a screw or screw thread. **7.** an endless screw (shaft on which one or more helical grooves are cut), or a device in which this is the principal feature. **8.** the endless screw which engages with a worm wheel or worm gear. **9.** a grovelling, abject, or contemptible person. **10.** a downtrodden or miserable person. **11.** something that penetrates, injures, or consumes slowly or insidiously, like a gnawing worm. **12.** (*pl.*) *Pathol.* any disease or disorder arising from the presence of parasitic worms in the intestines or other tissues. **13.** the lytta of a dog, etc. **14.** (*pl.*) **a can of worms,** *Colloq.* a difficult and complicated situation. –*v.i.* **15.** to move or act like a worm; creep, crawl, or advance slowly or stealthily. **16.** to get by insidious procedure (fol. by *into,* etc.). –*v.t.* **17.** to make, cause, bring, etc., along by creeping or crawling, or by stealthy or devious advances. **18.** to get by persistent, insidious efforts (esp. fol. by *out* or *from*): *to worm a secret out of a person.* **19.** to free from worms. **20.** *Naut.* to wind yarn or the like spirally round (a rope) so as to fill the spaces between the strands and render the surface smooth. [ME; OE *wyrm* worm, serpent, c. D *worm,* G *Wurm,* Icel. *ormr,* akin to L *vermis*] – **wormer,** *n.* – **wormless,** *adj.* – **wormlike,** *adj.*

**wormcast** /ˈwɜmkast/, *n.* an irregular coil of compacted soil or sand voided on the surface by some annelid worms, as earthworms and lugworms.

**worm-eaten** /ˈwɜm-itn/, *adj.* **1.** eaten into or gnawed by worms. **2.** impaired by time, decayed, or antiquated.

**worm fence** /ˈwɜm fɛns/, *n. Chiefly U.S.* a fence of zigzag outline made of rails laid horizontally with the ends resting one across another at an angle; snake fence.

worm fence

**worm gear** /ˈ– gɪə/, *n. Mach.* **1.** →**worm wheel.** **2.** such a worm wheel together with the endless screw forming a device by which the rotary motion of one shaft can be transmitted to another shaft at right angles to it.

**wormhole** /ˈwɜmhoʊl/, *n.* a hole made by a burrowing or

gnawing worm, as in timber, nuts, etc.

**worm pump** /'wɜm pʌmp/, *n.* a pump for collecting worms through which mud and water can pass while the worms are retained in a sieve.

**wormseed** /'wɜmsid/, *n.* **1.** the dried unexpanded flower heads of santonica, *Artemisia cina* **(Levant worm-seed),** or the fruit of certain goosefoots, esp. *Chenopodium anthelminticum* **(American wormseed),** used as an anthelmintic drug. **2.** any of these plants. **3.** any plant with anthelmintic properties.

**worm's eye view,** *n.* **1.** a picture or view from below. **2.** a meek or lowly outlook.

**worm snake** /'wɜm sneɪk/, *n.* →**blind snake.**

**worm wheel** /'– wil/, *n. Mach.* a toothed wheel which engages with a revolving worm, or endless screw, in order to receive or impart motion. Cf. **worm gear.**

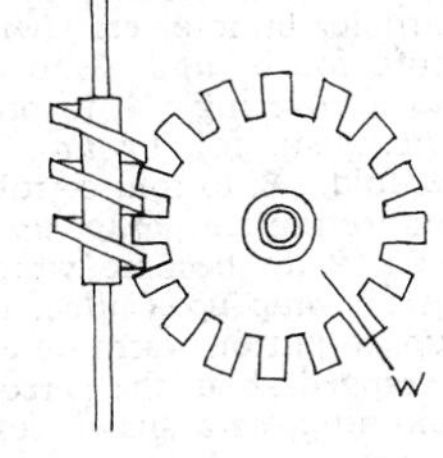

W, worm wheel

**wormwood** /'wɜmwʊd/, *n.* **1.** any plant of the genus *Artemisia,* as santonica and moxa. **2.** a bitter, aromatic herb, *Artemisia absinthium,* native to the Old World, formerly much used as a vermifuge and a tonic, but now chiefly in making absinth. **3.** something bitter, grievous, or extremely unpleasant; bitterness. [WORM + WOOD[1]; replacing ME *wermode,* OE *wermōd,* c. G *Wermut.* See VERMOUTH]

**wormy** /'wɜmi/, *adj.,* **wormier, wormiest. 1.** containing a worm or worms; infested with worms. **2.** worm-eaten. **3.** wormlike; grovelling; low. – **worminess,** *n.*

**worn** /wɔn/, *v.* **1.** past participle of **wear.** *–adj.* **2.** impaired by wear or use: *worn clothing.* **3.** wearied or exhausted. – **wornness,** *n.*

**worn-out** /wɔn-'aʊt/, *adj.* **1.** worn or used until no longer fit for use. **2.** exhausted by use, strain, etc.

**worried** /'wʌrid/, *adj.* **1.** affected by worry; anxious; troubled; distressed. **2.** indicating or expressing worry.

**worriment** /'wʌrimənt/, *n. Colloq.* **1.** trouble; harassing annoyance. **2.** worry, anxiety.

**worrisome** /'wʌrisəm/, *adj.* **1.** worrying, annoying, or disturbing; causing worry. **2.** inclined to worry. – **worrisomely,** *adv.*

**worry** /'wʌri/, *v.,* **-ried, -rying,** *n., pl.* **-ries.** *–v.i.* **1.** to feel uneasy or anxious; fret; torment oneself with or suffer from disturbing thoughts. **2. worry along** or **through,** to progress by constant effort, in spite of difficulties. *–v.t.* **3.** to cause to feel uneasy or anxious; trouble; torment with annoyances, cares, anxieties, etc.; plague, pester, or bother. **4.** to seize (originally by the throat) with the teeth and shake or mangle, as one animal does another. **5.** to harass by repeated biting, snapping, etc. **6.** to cause to move, etc., by persistent efforts, in spite of difficulties. *–n.* **7.** worried condition or feeling; uneasiness or anxiety. **8.** a cause of uneasiness or anxiety, or a trouble. **9.** the act of worrying. [ME *wory,* var. of *wery, wiry,* OE *wyrgan* strangle, c. G *würgen*] – **worrier,** *n.*

**worry beads** /'– bidz/, *n.pl.* a set of beads fingered to allay nervousness or tension.

**worrywart** /'wʌriwɔt/, *n. Colloq.* one who constantly worries unnecessarily.

**worse** /'wɜs/, *adj., used as compar. of* **bad. 1.** bad or ill in a greater or higher degree; inferior in excellence, quality, or character. **2.** more unfavourable or injurious. **3.** in less good condition; in poorer health. **4. none the worse for, a.** not harmed by. **b.** *Colloq.* positively benefited by. **5. the worse for wear, a.** showing signs of considerable wear; shabby or worn out. **b.** *Colloq.* drunk. *–n.* **6.** that which is worse. **7. for the worse,** so as to deteriorate: *a change for the worse.* **8. go from bad to worse,** to deteriorate. *–adv.* **9.** in a more disagreeable, evil, wicked, severe, or disadvantageous manner. **10.** with more severity, intensity, etc.; in a greater degree. **11.** in a less effective manner. **12. worse off,** in worse circumstances; poorer; less fortunate or well placed. [ME; OE *wyrsa,* c. Icel. *verri,* Goth. *wairsiza*] – **worseness,** *n.*

**worsen** /'wɜsən/, *v.t.* **1.** to make worse. *–v.i.* **2.** to become worse.

**worship** /'wɜʃəp/, *n., v.,* **-shipped, -shipping** or (*U.S.*) **-shiped, -shiping.** *–n.* **1.** reverent honour and homage paid to God, a god, or a sacred personage, or to any object regarded as sacred. **2.** formal or ceremonious rendering of such honour and homage. **3.** adoring reverence or regard: *hero worship.* **4.** (with *your, his,* etc.) a title of honour used in addressing or mentioning certain magistrates and others of rank or station. **5.** *Archaic.* honourable character or standing: *men of worship.* *–v.t.* **6.** to render religious reverence and homage to. **7.** to feel an adoring reverence or regard for (any person or thing). *–v.i.* **8.** to render religious reverence and homage, as to a deity. **9.** to attend services of divine worship. **10.** to feel an adoring reverence or regard. [ME; OE *worthscip,* northern var. of *weorthscipe,* from *weorth* WORTH[1] + *-scipe* -SHIP] – **worshipable,** *adj.* – **worshipper;** *U.S.* **worshiper,** *n.*

**worshipful** /'wɜʃəpfəl/, *adj.* **1.** given to the worship of something. **2.** *Chiefly Brit.* (an honorific title for persons or bodies of distinguished rank, as civil dignitaries, etc.). – **worshipfully,** *adv.* – **worshipfulness,** *n.*

**worst** /wɜst/, *adj., used as superl. of* **bad. 1.** bad or ill in the greatest or highest degree. **2.** most faulty, unsatisfactory, or objectionable. **3.** most unfavourable or injurious. **4.** in the poorest condition. **5.** most unpleasant or disagreeable. **6.** most unsuccessful, ineffective, or unskilful. *–n.* **7.** that which or one who is worst or the worst part. **8. come off worst** or **get the worst (of),** to be defeated (in a contest). **9. if (the) worst comes to (the) worst,** if the very worst happens. **10. one's worst,** the utmost, esp. the utmost harm, that a person is capable of: *to do one's worst to someone.* *–adv.* **11.** in the most evil, wicked, or disadvantageous manner. **12.** with the most severity, intensity, etc.; in the greatest degree. **13.** in the least satisfactory, complete or effective manner: *the worst-dressed girl in the room.* *–v.t.* **14.** to give (one) the worst of a contest or struggle; defeat; beat. [ME; OE *wurresta,* northern var. of *wyr(re)sta, wer(re)sta,* c. Icel. *verstr*]

**worsted**[1] /'wʊstəd/, *n.* **1.** firmly twisted yarn or thread spun from combed long-staple wool, used for weaving, etc. **2.** wool cloth woven from such yarns, having a hard, smooth surface, and no nap. *–adj.* **3.** consisting or made of worsted. [named after ME *Worsted,* parish in Norfolk, England (now Worstead)]

**worsted**[2] /'wɜstəd/, *v.* past participle of **worst.**

**wort**[1] /wɜt/, *n.* the unfermented or fermenting infusion of malt which after fermentation becomes beer or mash. [ME; OE *wyrt,* c. G *Würze* spice. See WORT[2]]

**wort**[2] /wɜt/, *n.* a plant; herb; vegetable (now used chiefly in combination, as in *liverwort, figwort,* etc.). [ME; OE *wyrt* root, plant, c. G *Wurz;* akin to ROOT[1]]

**worth**[1] /wɜθ/, *adj.* **1.** good or important enough to justify (what is specified): *advice worth taking, a place worth visiting.* **2.** having a value of, or equal in value to, as in money. **3.** having property to the value or amount of. *–n.* **4.** excellence of character or quality as commanding esteem: *men of worth.* **5.** usefulness or importance, as to the world, to a person, or for a purpose. **6.** value, as in money. **7.** a quantity of something, of a specified value. **8.** wealth; the value of one's property. **9. for all one's worth,** with all one's might; to one's utmost. **10. for what it is worth,** in spite of possible doubts about the accuracy or veracity of what is said: *I tell you this for what it is worth.* [ME and OE; c. G *wert*]

**worth**[2] /wɜθ/, *v.i. Archaic.* to happen or betide: *woe worth the day.* [ME; OE *weorthan,* c. G *werden*]

**worthless** /'wɜθləs/, *adj.* without worth; of no use, importance, or value; good-for-nothing; useless; valueless. – **worthlessly,** *adv.* – **worthlessness,** *n.*

**worthwhile** /wɜθ'waɪl/, *adj.* such as to repay one's time, attention, interest, work, trouble, etc.: *a worthwhile book.*

**worthy** /'wɜði/, *adj.,* **-thier, -thiest,** *n., pl.* **-thies.** *–adj.* **1.** of adequate merit or character. **2.** of commendable excellence or merit; deserving (oft. fol. by *of,* an infinitive, or occasionally a clause). *–n.* **3.** a person of eminent worth or merit or of social importance. **4.** (*oft. joc.*) a person. – **worthily,** *adv.* – **worthiness,** *n.*

**wortle** /'wɜtl/, *n., v.,* **wortled, wortling.** *–n.* **1.** a perforated plate through which metal is drawn to produce wire or tubing. *–v.t.* **2.** to produce (wire or tubing) by this means.

**wot** /wɒt/, *v. Archaic.* first and third person singular present of **wit**[2]. [ME *woot,* OE *wāt,* c. G *weiss*]

**would** /wʊd/, *weak forms* /wəd, d/ *v.* past tense of **will**[1] used: **1.** specially in expressing a wish: *I would it were true.* **2.** often in place of *will,* to make a statement or question less direct or blunt: *that would scarcely be fair, would you be so kind?* [ME and OE *wolde.* See WILL[1]]

**would-be** /ˈwʊd-bi/, *adj.* **1.** wishing or pretending to be: *a would-be wit.* **2.** intended to be: *a would-be kindness.*

**wouldn't** /ˈwʊdənt/, *v.* **1.** contraction of *would not.* **2.** **wouldn't it!,** (an exclamation indicating dismay, disapproval, disgust, etc.).

**wouldst** /wʊdst/, *v. Archaic and Poetic.* second person singular past tense of **will**[1].

**wound**[1] /wund/, *n.* **1.** an injury to an organism, usu. one involving division of tissue or rupture of the integument or mucous membrane, due to external violence or some mechanical agency rather than disease. **2.** a similar injury to the tissue of a plant. **3.** an injury or hurt to feelings, sensibilities, reputation, etc. *–v.t.* **4.** to inflict a wound upon; injure; hurt. *–v.i.* **5.** to inflict a wound or wounds. [ME; OE *wund,* c. G *Wunde*] – **woundable,** *adj.* – **wounder,** *n.* – **woundless,** *adj.*

**wound**[2] /waʊnd/, *v.* past tense and past participle of **wind**[2] and **wind**[3].

**wounded** /ˈwundəd/, *adj.* **1.** injured; suffering bodily harm. **2.** damaged, marred, or impaired. *–n.* **3.** wounded people collectively. **4. the walking wounded, a.** soldiers who, though injured, can walk from the battlefield. **b.** people who, though emotionally or physically distressed in some way, nevertheless continue with the normal conduct of their lives.

**woundwort** /ˈwundwɜt/, *n.* any of several herbs of the genus *Stachys,* the soft leaves of which have been used to dress wounds.

**wove** /woʊv/, *v.* past tense and occasional past particple of **weave.**

**woven** /ˈwoʊvən/, *v.* past participle of **weave.**

**wove paper** /woʊv ˈpeɪpə/, *n.* paper having no pattern impressed into its surface by the dandy-roller, as opposed to *laid paper,* which has such patterns.

**wow** /waʊ/, *n.* **1.** *Colloq.* something that proves an extraordinary success. **2.** a slow variation in pitch fidelity resulting from fluctuations in the speed of a recording. *–v.t.* **3.** to win approval, admiration from. *–interj.* **4.** *Colloq.* (an exclamation of surprise, wonder, pleasure, dismay, etc.).

**wowser** /ˈwaʊzə/, *n. Colloq.* a prudish teetotaller; a killjoy. [? Brit. d. *wow* to make a complaint; whine; popularly supposed to be an acronym of *W(e) O(nly) (W)ant S(ocial) E(vils) R(emedied),* a slogan invented by John Norton, Australian journalist and politician, 1862-1916]

**woylie** /ˈwɔɪli/, *n.* a small bettong, *Bettongia penicillata,* of central and southern Australia, having a long prehensile tail covered with black hairs on the upper surface towards the tip. Also, **brush-tailed bettong.** [Aboriginal]

**W.P.,** Workers' Party.

**w.p.b.** /ˌdʌbəlju pi ˈbi/, *n. Colloq.* a wastepaper basket.

**w.p.b. file** /ˈ– faɪl/, *n. Colloq.* (*joc.*) the wastepaper basket, viewed as a place for filing useless or unwanted material.

**wpm,** words per minute. Also, **w.p.m.**

**W.R.A.A.C.,** Women's Royal Australian Army Corps.

**W.R.A.A.F.,** Women's Royal Australian Air Force.

**wrack** /ræk/, *n.* **1.** any brown seaweed of the genus *Fucus,* as the **serrated wrack,** *F. serratus,* and the **bladderwrack,** *F. vesiculosus.* **2.** any seaweed or marine vegetation cast ashore. **3.** wreck or wreckage. **4.** ruin or destruction; disaster; rack. [ME *wrak* wreck, from MD or MLG]

**wraith** /reɪθ/, *n.* **1.** an apparition of a living person, or one supposed to be living, reputed to portend or indicate his death. **2.** a visible spirit. **3.** an insubstantial copy or replica of something. **4.** something pale, thin, and insubstantial, as a plume of vapour, smoke, or the like. [orig. uncert.] – **wraithlike,** *adj.*

**Wran** /ræn/, *n.* a member of the Women's Royal Australian Naval Service.

**wrangle** /ˈræŋgəl/, *v.,* **-gled, -gling,** *n.* *–v.i.* **1.** to argue or dispute, esp. in a noisy or angry manner. **2.** to engage in argument, debate, or disputation. *–v.t.* **3.** to influence, persuade, or otherwise affect by arguing. **4.** *U.S.* to tend (horses). *–n.* **5.** a noisy or angry dispute; altercation. [LG *wrangeln,* frequentative of *wrangen* struggle, make uproar. Cf. WRING]

**wrangler** /ˈræŋglə/, *n.* **1.** one who wrangles or disputes. **2.** (formerly, at Cambridge University) one of those who attained first-class honours in mathematics. **3.** *U.S.* one who tends or wrangles horses.

**W.R.A.N.S.,** Womens Royal Australian Naval Service.

**wrap** /ræp/, *v.,* **wrapped** or **wrapt, wrapping,** *n.* *–v.t.* **1.** to enclose, envelop, or muffle in something wound or folded about (oft. fol. by *up*). **2.** to enclose and make fast (an article, bundle, etc.) within a covering of paper or the like (oft. fol. by *up*). **3.** to wind, fold, or bind (something) about as a covering. **4.** to protect with coverings, outer garments, etc. (usu. fol. by *up*). **5.** to surround, envelop, shroud, or enfold. **6.** to fold or roll up. **7. wrap up,** *Colloq.* to conclude or settle: *to wrap up a financial transaction.* **8.** →**rap**[1]. *–v.i.* **9.** to become wrapped, as about something; fold. **10.** Also, **wrap up,** *Colloq.* to conclude; finish off. *–n.* **11. wrap up,** to put on warm outer garments. *–n.* **12.** something to be wrapped about the person, esp. in addition to the usu. indoor clothing, as a shawl, scarf, or mantle. **13.** (*pl.*) outdoor garments, or coverings, furs, etc. [b. obs. *wry,* v., cover and LAP[2]]

**wraparound** /ˈræpəraʊnd/, *adj., n.* →**wrapround.**

**wrapped** /ræpt/, *adj.* **1.** enthused (about): *I'm wrapped in Mahler.* **2. wrapped up in, a.** engrossed or absorbed in. **b.** *Colloq.* involved or implicated in.

**wrapper** /ˈræpə/, *n.* **1.** that in which something is wrapped; a covering or cover. **2.** a long, loose outer garment. **3.** a book jacket. **4.** one who or that which wraps. **5.** the tobacco leaf used for covering a cigar.

**wrapping** /ˈræpɪŋ/, *n.* (*usu. pl.*) that in which something is wrapped.

**wrapround** /ˈræpraʊnd/, *adj.* **1.** curved so as to follow the contours of what it covers, as a windscreen, sunglasses, etc. **2.** that wraps around or overlaps, as a skirt. *–n.* **3.** something that is wrapped round. **4.** *Print.* a sheet of colour plates or the like which is printed separately and wrapped round a signature in binding. Also, **wraparound.**

**wrapt** /ræpt/, *v. Obs.* a past tense and past participle of **wrap.**

**wrap-up** /ˈræp-ʌp/, *n. Colloq.* an enthusiastic approval or recommendation: *he gave the new product a good wrap-up.*

**wrasse** /ræs/, *n.* any of various marine fishes of the family Labridae, having thick, fleshy lips, powerful teeth, and usu. a brilliant colour, certain species being valued as food fishes, as the **hump-headed wrasse,** *Cheilinus undulatus,* of the Great Barrier Reef. [Cornish *wrach,* var. of *gwrach*]

**wrath** /rɒθ/, *n.* **1.** strong, stern, or fierce anger; deeply resentful indignation; ire. **2.** vengeance or punishment, as the consequence of anger. *–adj.* **3.** *Archaic.* wroth; angry. [ME; OE *wrǣththo,* from *wrāth* WROTH. See -TH[1]] – **wrathless,** *adj.*

**wrathful** /ˈrɒθfəl/, *adj.* **1.** full of wrath, very angry, or ireful. **2.** characterised by or showing wrath: *wrathful words.* – **wrathfully,** *adv.* – **wrathfulness,** *n.*

**wreak** /rik/, *v.t.* **1.** to inflict or execute (vengeance, etc.). **2.** to carry out the promptings of (one's rage, ill humour, will, desire, etc.), as on a victim or object. [ME *wreke(n),* OE *wrecan,* c. G *rächen*] – **wreaker,** *n.*

**wreath** /riθ/, *n., pl.* **wreaths** /riðz/. **1.** something twisted or bent into a circular form; a circular band of flowers, foliage, or any ornamental work, for adorning the head or for any decorative purpose; a garland or chaplet. **2.** a garland of flowers, laurel leaves, etc., worn on the head as a mark of honour. **3.** such a circular band of flowers, foliage, etc., left at a grave, tomb, or memorial as a mark of respect or affection for the dead. **4.** any ringlike, curving, or curling mass or formation. **5.** any object having a helical path, as a rising curve in the handrail of a staircase. **6.** a defect in glass having a circular shape. [ME *wrethe,* OE *wrǣth;* akin to WRITHE] – **wreathless,** *adj.* – **wreathlike,** *adj.*

**wreathe** /rið/, *v.,* **wreathed; wreathed** or (*Archaic*) **wreathen; wreathing.** *–v.t.* **1.** to encircle or adorn with or as with a wreath or wreaths. **2.** to form as a wreath, by twisting, twining, or otherwise. **3.** to surround in curving or curling masses or form. **4.** to envelop: *a face wreathed in smiles.* *–v.i.* **5.** to take the form of a wreath or wreaths. **6.** to move in curving or curling masses, as smoke.

**wreck** /rɛk/, *n.* **1.** the ruin or destruction of a vessel in the course of navigation; shipwreck. **2.** a vessel in a state of ruin from disaster at sea, on rocks, etc. **3.** any building, structure, or thing reduced to a state of ruin. **4.** the ruin or destruction of anything: *the wreck of one's hopes.* **5.** that which is cast ashore by the sea, as the remains of a ruined vessel or of its cargo; shipwrecked property, or wreckage, cast ashore or (less strictly) floating on the sea. **6.** a broken-down or debilitated person; someone in poor physical or mental health. *–v.t.* **7.** to cause the wreck of (a vessel), as in navigation; shipwreck. **8.** to involve in a wreck. **9.** to cause the ruin or destruction of; spoil. *–v.i.* **10.** to suffer wreck. [ME *wrek,* from Scand.; cf. Icel. *rek;* akin to WREAK, WRACK]

**wreckage** /ˈrɛkɪdʒ/, *n.* **1.** remains or fragments of something that has been wrecked. **2.** the act of wrecking. **3.** the state of being wrecked.

**wrecked** /rɛkt/, *v.* **1.** past tense and past participle of wreck. *–adj.* **2.** exhausted; ill or weak because of fatigue or overindulgence in food, drink, etc.

**wrecker** /ˈrɛkə/, *n.* **1.** one who or that which wrecks. **2.** one whose business it is to tear down buildings as in clearing sites for other uses; a demolition worker. **3.** one who causes shipwrecks, as by false lights on shore, to secure wreckage, or who makes a business of plundering wrecks.

**wreckful** /ˈrɛkfəl/, *adj. Archaic.* causing wreckage.

**wren** /rɛn/, *n.* **1.** any of a large number of small passerine birds with long legs and long, almost upright tails, of the family Maluridae, esp. the brightly coloured birds of the genus *Malurus,* as the superb blue wren, and those of related genera, as the emu-wrens (*Stipiturus*) and the grass-wrens (*Amytornis*). **2.** any of numerous small, active, oscinine passerine birds constituting the family Troglodytidae, esp. *Troglodytes troglodytes,* known as the wren in England and as the **winter wren** in America; and the common **house wren** (*T. aedon*) of North America. **3.** any of various similar birds of other families, as the **golden-crested wren** (*Regulus regulus*). [ME *wrenne,* OE *wrenna.* Cf. Icel. *rindill*]

**Wren** /rɛn/, *n. Brit. Colloq.* a member of the Women's Royal Naval Service.

**wrench** /rɛntʃ/, *v.t.* **1.** to twist suddenly and forcibly; pull, jerk, or force by a violent twist. **2.** to overstrain or injure (the ankle, etc.) by a sudden, violent twist. **3.** to affect distressingly as if by a wrench. **4.** to wrest, as from the right use or meaning: *to wrench facts or statements.* *–v.i.* **5.** to twist, turn, or move suddenly aside. **6.** to give a wrench or twist at something. *–n.* **7.** a wrenching movement; a sudden, violent twist. **8.** a painful, straining twist, as of the ankle or wrist. **9.** a sharp, distressing strain, as to the feelings, esp. on parting or separation. **10.** a wrestling, as of meaning; a forced interpretation. **11.** an adjustable spanner. **12.** a spanner. [ME *wrenche(n),* OE *wrencan* twist, turn, c. G *renken*]

wrench (def. 11)

**wrest** /rɛst/, *v.t.* **1.** to twist or turn; pull, jerk, or force by a violent twist. **2.** to take away by force. **3.** to get by effort: *to wrest a living from the soil.* **4.** to twist or turn from the proper course, application, use, meaning, or the like. *–n.* **5.** a wresting; a twist or wrench. **6.** a key or small wrench for tuning stringed musical instruments, as the harp or piano, by turning the pins to which the strings are fastened. [ME *wreste(n),* OE *wrǣstan,* c. Icel. *reista;* akin to WRIST] – **wrester,** *n.*

wren

**wrestle** /ˈrɛsəl/, *v.,* **-tled, -tling,** *n.* *–v.i.* **1.** to engage in wrestling. **2.** to contend, as in a struggle for mastery; grapple. **3.** to deal (with a subject) as a difficult task or duty. *–v.t.* **4.** to contend with in wrestling. **5.** to force by or as if by wrestling. **6.** *U.S.* to throw (an animal) for the purpose of branding. *–n.* **7.** an act of or a bout at wrestling. **8.** a struggle. [ME, frequentative of WREST] – **wrestler,** *n.*

**wrestling** /ˈrɛslɪŋ/, *n.* **1.** an exercise or sport, subject to special rules, in which two persons struggle hand to hand, each striving to throw or force the other to the ground. **2.** the act of one who wrestles.

**wretch** /rɛtʃ/, *n.* **1.** a deplorably unfortunate or unhappy person. **2.** a person of despicable or base character. [ME *wretche,* OE *wrecca* exile, adventurer, c. G *Recke* warrior, hero, Icel. *rekkr* man]

**wretched** /ˈrɛtʃəd/, *adj.* **1.** very unfortunate in condition or circumstances; miserable; pitiable. **2.** characterised by or attended with misery. **3.** despicable, contemptible, or mean. **4.** poor, sorry, or pitiful; worthless: *a wretched blunderer, wretched little daubs.* – **wretchedly,** *adv.* – **wretchedness,** *n.*

ancient Greek wrestling

**wrick** /rɪk/, *v.t.* **1.** to wrench or strain; rick. *–n.* **2.** a strain. [ME *wrikke(n)* jerk; ? akin to WRENCH, WRINKLE[1]]

**wrier** /ˈraɪə/, *adj.* comparative of **wry.**

**wriest** /ˈraɪəst/, *adj.* superlative of **wry.**

**wriggle** /ˈrɪgl/, *v.,* **-gled, -gling,** *n.* *–v.i.* **1.** to twist to and fro, writhe, or squirm. **2.** to move along by twisting and turning the body, as a worm or snake. **3.** to make one's way by shifts or expedients: *to wriggle out of a difficulty.* **4.** to insinuate oneself into a position of advantage; wheedle. *–v.t.* **5.** to cause to wriggle. **6.** to bring, get, make, etc., by wriggling. *–n.* **7.** an act of wriggling; a wriggling movement. **8.** a sinuous formation or course. **9. get a wriggle on,** to hurry. [MLG *wriggeln,* c. D *wriggelen*] – **wriggler,** *n.* – **wriggly,** *adj.*

**wright** /raɪt/, *n.* a workman, esp. a constructive workman (now chiefly in *wheelwright, playwright,* etc.). [ME; OE *wryhta,* metathetic var. of *wyrhta* worker. See WORK]

**wring** /rɪŋ/, *v.,* **wrung** or (*Rare*) **wringed; wringing;** *n.* *–v.t.* **1.** to twist forcibly, as something flexible. **2.** to twist and compress, or compress without twisting, in order to force out moisture (oft. fol. by *out*): *to wring one's clothes out.* **3.** to extract or expel by twisting or compression (usu. fol. by *out* or *from*). **4.** to affect painfully by or as if by some contorting or compressing action; pain, distress, or torment. **5.** to clasp (another's hand) fervently. **6.** to clasp (one's hands) together, as in grief, etc. **7.** to force (*off,* etc.) by twisting. **8.** to extract or extort as if by twisting. *–v.i.* **9.** to perform the action of wringing something. **10.** to writhe, as in anguish. *–n.* **11.** a wringing; forcible twist or squeeze. [ME; OE *wringan,* c. G *ringen*]

**wringer** /ˈrɪŋə/, *n.* **1.** one who or that which wrings. **2.** an apparatus or machine which wrings water or the like out of anything wet; a mangle.

**wringing** /ˈrɪŋɪŋ/, *v.* **1.** present participle of **wring.** *–adv.* **2. wringing wet,** very wet; soaked.

**wrinkle**[1] /ˈrɪŋkəl/, *n., v.,* **-kled, -kling.** *–n.* **1.** a ridge or furrow on a surface, due to contraction, folding, rumpling, or the like; corrugation; slight fold; crease. *–v.t.* **2.** to form a wrinkle or wrinkles in; corrugate; crease. *–v.i.* **3.** to become contracted into wrinkles; become wrinkled. [late ME *wrynkle;* backformation from *wrinkled,* OE *gewrinclod* serrate] – **wrinkleless,** *adj.* – **wrinkly,** *adj.*

**wrinkle**[2] /ˈrɪŋkəl/, *n. Colloq.* an ingenious, indirect or artful procedure or method; a novel or clever trick or device. [ME *wrink,* from OE *wrenc* trick]

**wrinklie** /ˈwɪŋkli/, *n. Colloq.* anyone as old as or older than one's parents. Also, **wrinkly.**

**wrist** /rɪst/, *n.* **1.** the part of the arm between the forearm and the hand; technically, the carpus. **2.** the joint between the radius and the carpus **(wrist joint).** **3.** that part of an article of clothing which fits round the wrist. **4.** *Mach.* →**wristpin.** [ME and OE, c. G *Rist* back of hand, Icel. *rist* instep; akin to WRITHE]

**wristband** /ˈrɪstbænd/, *n.* the band or part of a sleeve, as of a shirt, which covers the wrist.

**wrist drop** /ˈrɪst drɒp/, *n.* paralysis of the extensor muscles of the hand causing it to droop, due to injuries or some poisons, as lead or arsenic.

**wristlet** /ˈrɪstlət/, *n.* **1.** a band worn round the wrist, esp. to protect it from cold. **2.** a bracelet.

**wristlock** /ˈrɪstlɒk/, *n.* a wrestling hold by which the opponent is made defenceless by a wrenching grasp on the wrist.

**wristpin** /ˈrɪstpɪn/, *n.* a stud or pin projecting from the side of a crank, wheel, or the like, and attaching it to a connecting rod leading to some other part of the mechanism.

**wrist shot** /ˈrɪst ʃɒt/, *n.* a short chopping golf stroke pivoting from the wrists with the arms held almost still.

**wristwatch** /ˈrɪstwɒtʃ/, *n.* a watch attached to a strap or band worn about the wrist.

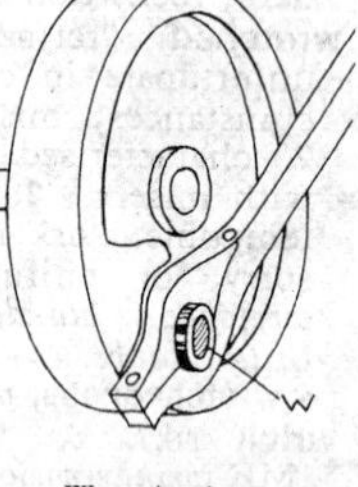

W, wristpin

**wristwork** /ˈrɪstwɜk/, *n.* skilful use of the flexibility of the wrist, as in sport.

**wristy** /ˈrɪsti/, *adj.* using very flexible wrist movements, as in cricket or similar sports.

**writ**[1] /rɪt/, *n.* **1.** *Law.* **a.** a formal order under seal, issued in the name of a sovereign, government, court, or other competent authority, enjoining the officer or other person to whom it is issued or addressed, to do or refrain from some specified act. **b.** (in early English law) any formal document in letter form, under seal, and in the king's name. **2.** *Archaic.* something written: *Holy Writ* (the Bible). [ME and OE, c. Icel. *rit* writing. See WRITE]

**writ**[2] /rɪt/, *v.* **1.** *Archaic.* past tense and past participle of **write.** **2. writ large,** substantially the same, if on a large or larger scale.

**write** /raɪt/, *v.*, **wrote** or (*Archaic*) **writ; written, writing.** *–v.t.* **1.** to trace or form (characters, letters, words, etc.) on the surface of some material, as with a pen, pencil, or other instrument or means; inscribe. **2.** to express or communicate in writing; give a written account of. **3.** to fill in the blank spaces of (a form, etc.) with writing: *to write a cheque.* **4.** to execute or produce by setting down words, etc.: *to write two copies of a letter.* **5.** to compose and produce in words or characters duly set down: *to write a letter to a friend.* **6.** to produce as author or composer. **7.** to trace significant characters on, or mark or cover with writing. **8.** to impress the marks or indications of: *honesty is written in his face.* **9.** *U.S.* to write a letter to (someone). **10.** *Computers.* to store (information) on a medium, esp. magnetic tape. *–v.i.* **11.** to trace or form characters, words, etc., with a pen, pencil, or other instrument or means, or as a pen or the like does. **12.** (of a writing implement) to produce characters, words, etc., in a specified manner: *this pen writes well.* **13.** to be a writer, journalist, or author for one's living. **14.** to express ideas in writing. **15.** to write a letter or letters, or communicate by letter. *–v.* **16.** Some special verb phrases are:

**write down, 1.** to set down in writing. **2.** to write in deprecation of; injure as by writing against. **3.** to write in consciously simple terms for a supposedly ignorant readership (fol. by *to*). **4.** *Comm.* to reduce the book value of.

**write for,** to request or apply for by letter.

**write in, 1.** to write a letter to a newspaper, business firm, or the like. **2.** *U.S. Politics.* (in a ballot) to add the name of a candidate not listed in the printed ballot.

**write off, 1.** to cancel, as an entry in an account, as by an offsetting entry. **2.** to treat as an irreparable or nonrecoverable loss. **3.** to consider as dead.

**write out, 1.** to put into writing. **2.** to write in full form. **3.** to exhaust the capacity or resources of by excessive writing: *an author who has written himself out.*

**write up, 1.** to write out in full or in detail. **2.** to bring up to date or to the latest fact or transaction in writing. **3.** to present to public notice in a written description or account. **4.** to commend to the public by a favourable written description or account. **5.** *Accounting.* to make an excessive valuation of (an asset).

**write oneself off,** *Colloq.* **1.** to get very drunk. **2.** to have a motor accident. **3.** to give a poor account of oneself. [ME; OE *wrītan,* c. G *reissen* tear, draw, akin to Icel. *rīta* write]

**write-off** /ˈraɪt-ɒf/, *n.* **1.** *Accounting.* something written off from the books. **2.** *Colloq.* something irreparably damaged, as an aircraft, car, etc. **3.** *Colloq.* a person who is incapacitated through drunkenness, injury, etc. **4.** *Colloq.* an incompetent person; a no-hoper.

**writer** /ˈraɪtə/, *n.* **1.** one who expresses ideas in writing. **2.** one engaged in literary work. **3.** one whose occupation is writing, as a journalist or author. **4.** a composer of music. **5.** one who paints or draws lettering; sign-writer. **6.** *Obs.* a manual for teaching how to write: *a letterwriter.* **7. the writer,** he who is writing this (referring to oneself in a piece of writing).

**writer's cramp** /ˈraɪtəz kræmp/, *n.* muscular incapacity of the thumb and fore finger affecting those who constantly write.

**write-up** /ˈraɪt-ʌp/, *n.* **1.** a written description or account, as in a newspaper or magazine. **2.** *U.S. Finance.* an illegally excessive statement of corporate assets.

**writhe** /raɪð/, *v.*, **writhed; writhed** or (*Obs. except Poetic*), **writhen; writhing;** *n.* *–v.i.* **1.** to twist the body about, or squirm, as in pain, violent effort, etc. **2.** to shrink mentally, as in acute discomfort, embarrassment, etc. *–v.t.* **3.** to twist or bend out of shape or position; distort; contort. **4.** to twist (oneself, the body, etc.) about, as in pain. *–n.* **5.** a writhing movement; a twisting of the body, as in pain. [ME; OE *wrīthan* twist, wind, c. Icel. *rīdha* knit, twist] **–writher,** *n.* **–writhingly,** *adv.*

**writhen** /ˈrɪðən/, *adj. Obs.* twisted.

**writing** /ˈraɪtɪŋ/, *n.* **1.** the act of one who or that which writes. **2.** the state of being written; written form: *to commit one's thoughts to writing.* **3.** that which is written; characters or matter written with a pen or the like. **4.** such characters or matter with respect to style, kind, quality, etc. **5.** handwriting. **6.** an inscription. **7.** a letter. **8.** any written or printed paper, document, or the like. **9.** literary matter or work, esp. with respect to style, kind, quality, etc. **10.** a literary composition or production. **11. writing on the wall,** an event presaging disaster, etc.

**writing case** /ˈ– keɪs/, *n.* a portable case containing writing materials.

**writing desk** /ˈ– dɛsk/, *n.* **1.** a piece of furniture with a surface for writing upon, usu. with drawers and pigeonholes to hold writing materials, etc. **2.** a portable case for holding writing materials and affording, when opened, a surface for writing upon.

**writing pad** /ˈ– pæd/, *n.* →**pad**[1] (def. 4). Also, **writing block.**

**writing paper** /ˈ– peɪpə/, *n.* paper for writing letters on.

**writing table** /ˈ– teɪbəl/, *n.* a table fitted or used for writing on.

**writ of execution,** *n.* a writ granted to enforce a judgment.

**writ of prohibition,** *n. Law.* (formerly) a command by a higher court that a lower court shall not exercise jurisdiction in a particular case, now replaced by a prerogative order.

**writ of right,** *n. Law.* **1.** (formerly) one of two writs issued by a manorial court in a dispute between feudal tenants as to ownership or extent of a freehold. **2.** *U.S.* a similar writ, now supplanted by ejectment actions.

**written** /ˈrɪtn/, *v.* past participle of **write.**

**wrong** /rɒŋ/, *adj.* **1.** not in accordance with what is morally right or good. **2.** deviating from truth or fact; erroneous. **3.** not correct in action, judgment, opinion, method, etc., as a person; in error. **4.** not in accordance with a code, convention or set of rules; not proper: *the wrong way to talk to one's betters.* **5.** not in accordance with needs or expectations: *to take the wrong road, the wrong way to hold a golf club.* **6.** out of order, awry, or amiss: *something is wrong with the machine.* **7.** not suitable or appropriate: *to say the wrong thing.* **8.** (of a fabric, etc.) pertaining to or constituting the side that is less finished, which forms the inner side of a garment, etc. **9. get on the wrong side of,** to incur the hostility of. **10. get the wrong end of the stick,** to misunderstand. **11. get up on the wrong side (of bed),** to be bad-tempered. **12. wrong in the head,** *Colloq.* crazy; mad. *–n.* **13.** that which is wrong, or not in accordance with morality, goodness, justice, truth, or the like; evil. **14.** an unjust act; injury. **15.** *Law.* an invasion of right, to the damage of another person. **16. in the wrong, a.** responsible for some error or accident; guilty; to blame. **b.** mistaken; in error. **17. in wrong with,** in disfavour with. *–adv.* **18.** in a wrong manner; not rightly; awry or amiss. **19. get (someone) wrong,**

to misunderstand (someone). *–v.t.* **20.** to do wrong to; treat unfairly or unjustly; injure or harm. **21.** impute evil to unjustly. **22.** to seduce. [ME; OE *wrang,* from Scand.; cf. Icel. *rangr* awry, c. D *wrang* acid, tart; akin to WRING]

**wrongdoer** /ˈrɒŋduə/, *n.* one who does wrong.

**wrongdoing** /ˈrɒŋduɪŋ/, *n.* blameworthy action; evil behaviour.

**wrong-foot** /rɒŋ-ˈfʊt/, *v.t.* (in various sports, as football, tennis, etc.,) to trick (an opponent) into moving the wrong way.

**wrong font** /rɒŋ ˈfɒnt/, *n. Print.* the incorrect font, or size and style, for its place. *Abbrev.:* wf *or* w.f.

**wrongful** /ˈrɒŋfəl/, *adj.* **1.** full of or characterised by wrong. **2.** having no legal right; unlawful. **–wrongfully,** *adv.* **–wrongfulness,** *n.*

**wrong-headed** /rɒŋ-ˈhɛdəd/, *adj.* wrong in judgment or opinion; misguided and stubborn; perverse. **–wrong-headedly,** *adv.* **–wrong-headedness,** *n.*

**wrong 'un** /ˈrɒŋ ən/, *n. Colloq.* **1.** a dishonest person. **2.** *Cricket.* →**googly.**

**wrote** /roʊt/, *v.* past tense of **write.**

**wroth** /roʊθ, rɒθ/, *adj.* angry; wrathful (used predicatively). Also, *Archaic,* **wrath.** [ME; OE *wrāth,* c. D *wreed* cruel, Icel. *reidhr* angry. See WRITHE]

**wrought** /rɔt/, *v.* **1.** *Archaic.* a past tense and past participle of **work.** *–adj.* **2.** fashioned or formed; resulting from or having been subjected to working or manufacturing. **3.** produced or shaped by beating with a hammer, etc., as iron or silver articles. **4.** ornamented or elaborated. **5.** not rough or crude.

**wrought iron** /– ˈaɪən/, *n.* a comparatively pure form of iron (as that produced by puddling pig-iron) which contains practically no carbon, and which is easily forged, welded, etc., and does not harden when suddenly cooled.

**wrought-iron** /ˈrɔt-aɪən/, *adj.* made of, or used in the working or manufacture of, wrought iron.

**wrought-iron casting** /– ˈkastɪŋ/, *n.* **1.** casting with mitis. **2.** a casting made from mitis.

**wrought timber** /rɔt ˈtɪmbə/, *n.* timber which has been planed or sanded to a smooth finish.

**wrought-up** /rɔt-ˈʌp/, *adj.* excited; perturbed.

**wrung** /rʌŋ/, *v.* past tense and past participle of **wring.**

**wrung-out** /rʌŋ-ˈaʊt/, *adj.* exhausted.

**wry** /raɪ/, *adj.* **wryer, wryest** or **wrier, wriest. 1.** produced by the distortion of the facial features, usu. to indicate dislike, dissatisfaction, or displeasure. **2.** ironically or bitterly amusing. **3.** abnormally bent or turned to one side; twisted or crooked: *a wry nose.* **4.** devious in course or purpose; misdirected. **5.** distorted or perverted, as in meaning. **6.** wrong, unsuitable, or ill-natured, as thoughts, words, etc. [adj. use of v., ME *wrye(n)*; OE *wrīgian* go forward, swerve] **–wryly,** *adv.* **–wryness,** *n.*

**wrybill** /ˈraɪbɪl/, *n.* a shorebird, *Anarhynchus frontalis,* of New Zealand, related to the plovers, and having its bill twisted to the right.

**wryneck** /ˈraɪnɛk/, *n.* **1.** either of two species of small Old World scansorial birds constituting the family Jynginae, allied to the woodpeckers, and notable for their peculiar manner of twisting the neck and head. **2.** *Colloq.* **a.** →**torticollis. b.** a person having torticollis.

**wry-necked** /ˈraɪ-nɛkt/, *adj.* afflicted with wryneck (def. 2).

**wry-tail** /ˈraɪ-teɪl/, *n. Vet. Sci. Colloq.* a hereditary disease of turkeys and other birds and animals whereby the tail is malformed.

**WST,** Western Standard Time.

**WSW,** west-south-west. Also, **W.S.W.**

**wt,** weight.

**W.T., 1.** wireless telegraphy. **2.** wireless telephony.

wurley

**wuhl-wuhl** /ˈwʊl-wʊl/, *n.* →**pitchi-pitchi.** [Aboriginal]

**wulfenite** /ˈwʊlfənaɪt/, *n.* a mineral consisting of lead molybdate, occurring usu. in tabular crystals, and varying in colour from greyish to bright yellow or red. [named after F.X. von *Wulfen,* 1728-1805, Austrian mineralogist]

**wunderkind** /ˈvʊndəkɪnt/, *n.* **1.** a child prodigy. **2.** one who attains great success in a competitive field at a relatively early age. [G: wonder child]

**wurley** /ˈwɜli/, *n.* an Aboriginal hut or shelter made of boughs, leaves and plaited grass. Also, **wurlie.** [Aboriginal]

**wurlitzer** /ˈwɜlɪtsə/, *n.* a large organ, originally a pipe organ but now electric, designed primarily for theatres, etc., and having a large number of sound effects which attempt to reproduce the sounds of an orchestra. [Trademark]

**wurrung** /ˈwʌrʌŋ/, *n.* the crescent nail-tailed wallaby of central and southern Australia, *Onychogalea lunata.* [Aboriginal]

**wurrup** /ˈwʌrəp/, *n.* the western hare-wallaby, *Lagorchestes hirsutus,* of central Australia. [Aboriginal]

**wurst** /wɜst, vɜst/, *n.* sausage, esp. of a Continental type. [G: lit., mixture; akin to WORSE]

**wurtzite** /ˈwɜtsaɪt/, *n.* a mineral sulphide of zinc which crystallises in the hexagonal system. [named after Charles *Wurtz,* 1817-84, French chemist]

**ww,** wall to wall. Also, **w.w., W.W.**

**Wyandotte** /ˈwaɪəndɒt/, *n.* one of an American breed of medium-sized domestic fowls, valuable for eggs and for the table. [name of an American Indian tribe]

**wych-elm** /ˈwɪtʃ-ɛlm/, *n.* an elm, *Ulmus glabra,* of northern and western Europe. Also, **witch-elm.** [*wych* (ME *wyche,* OE *wice* wych-elm) + ELM]

**wych-hazel** /ˈwɪtʃ-heɪzəl/, *n.* →**witch-hazel.**

**wydah** /ˈwɪdə/, *n.* →**whydah.**

**wye** /waɪ/, *n., pl.* **wyes. 1.** the letter Y, or something having a similar shape. **2.** →**star connection.**

**wye level** /ˈ– lɛvəl/, *n.* a surveying instrument consisting of a spirit level mounted under and parallel to a telescope which can be rotated in its supports (Y's) for adjustment. Also, **Y level.**

**wyvern** /ˈwaɪvən/, *n. Her.* a two-legged, winged dragon having the hinder part of a serpent with a barbed tail. Also, **wivern.** [obs. *wiver* viper (from OF) + *in,* of obscure orig. and sense]

Roman WEISS

Sans Serif OLIVE

Script OLD ENGLISH

Decorative SPEAK EASY

*Although there are numerous typefaces in the world they can be divided into four main classifications. These are:*

*ROMAN or SERIF. This typeface came into being from the technique of the Roman masons who, working in stone, finished off each letter with a serif or small stroke projecting from the top or bottom. This was done to correct any feeling of unevenness or imbalance they may have created in cutting the characters in stone.*

*SANS SERIF (without serif). This typeface is geometric in design and has straight-edged characters and lines of a regular thickness.*

*SCRIPT. Based on the movement of the hand, this typeface is often italicised or slanted, as if drawn by a brush or quill pen.*

*DECORATIVE. Any typeface that exaggerates the characteristics of any of the other three classifications to a degree that places it outside of them.*

*The dictionary entries in this book use a SANS SERIF typeface called Helvetica (set in a bold face for the head words) and a SERIF typeface Plantin (used throughout the body of the entries).*

**X, x** /ɛks/, *n., pl.* **X's** or **Xs, x's** or **xs.** **1.** the 24th letter of the English alphabet. **2.** a term often used to designate a person, thing, agency, factor, or the like, whose true name is unknown or withheld. **3.** the Roman numeral for 10.

**x** /ɛks/, **1.** *Maths.* **a.** →**abscissa. b.** an unknown quantity or a variable. **2.** *Comm.* without or not including.

**x.,** **1.** extra. **2.** xylonite.

**X.,** cross.

**xanth-,** variant of **xantho-**, before vowels, as in *xanthine.*

**xanthate** /ˈzænθeɪt/, *n.* a salt or ester of xanthic acid. [XANTH- + -ATE[2]]

**xanthein** /ˈzænθiən/, *n.* that part of the yellow colouring matter in yellow flowers soluble in water. Cf. **xanthin** (def. 1). [F *xanthéine,* from *xanth-* yellow + *-éine,* to distinguish it from *xanthine* XANTHIN]

**xanthene** /ˈzænθin/, *n.* a colourless crystalline solid, $C_6H_4OC_6H_4CH_2$, which forms the basis for a group of dyestuffs.

**xanthic** /ˈzænθɪk/, *adj.* **1.** *Chiefly Bot.* yellow. **2.** *Chem.* of or derived from xanthine or xanthic acid.

**xanthic acid** /– ˈæsəd/, *n.* an unstable organic acid with the type formula ROCSSH, the methyl and ethyl esters of which are colourless, oily liquids with a penetrating smell. Its copper salts are bright yellow. [F *xanthique.* See XANTHO-, -IC]

**xanthin** /ˈzænθən/, *n.* **1.** that part of the yellow colouring matter in yellow flowers which is insoluble. **2.** a yellow colouring matter in madder. [F *xanthine,* or from G. See XANTHO-, -IN[2]]

**xanthine** /ˈzænθin, -θaɪn/, *n.* a crystalline nitrogenous compound, $C_5H_4N_4O_2$, related to uric acid, found in urine, blood, and certain animal and vegetable tissues. [F. See XANTHO-, -INE[2]]

**xanthippe** /zænˈθɪpi/, *n.* a scolding or ill-tempered wife; a shrewish woman. Also, **xantippe.** [orig. with ref. to *Xanthippe,* wife of Socrates, proverbial as a scold]

**xanthium** /ˈzænθiəm/, *n.* any plant of the genus *Xanthium,* which includes troublesome burr-bearing weeds as the Noogoora burr, *X. chinense,* and the Bathurst burr, *X. spinosum.*

Xanthium; Noogoora burr

**xantho-,** a word element meaning 'yellow', as in *xanthochroid.* Also, **xanth-.** [Gk, combining form of *xanthós*]

**xanthochroid** /ˈzænθoʊkrɔɪd/, *Ethnol. –adj.* **1.** belonging or pertaining to the light-complexioned or light-haired white peoples. *–n.* **2.** one having xanthochroid characteristics. [NL *xanthochroi* yellow-pale ones, from Gk *xanth-* XANTH- + *ōchroí* (pl. of *ōchrós* pale)]

**xanthophyll** /ˈzænθoʊfɪl/, *n.* a yellow vegetable pigment, $C_{40}H_{56}O_2$, occurring in grain or leaves; oxygenated derivatives of carotene hydrocarbons. Also, *U.S.,* **xanthophyl.** [F *xanthophylle,* from *xantho-* XANTHO- + Gk *phýllon* leaf] **–xanthophyllous** /zænˈθoʊfɪləs/, *adj.*

**xanthoproteic acid** /ˌzænθoʊproʊˌtiɪk ˈæsəd/, *n.* a yellow substance of unknown structure formed by the action of nitric acid on proteins. [XANTHO- + PROTE(IN) + -IC]

**xanthous** /ˈzænθəs/, *adj.* **1.** yellow. **2.** denoting or pertaining to the peoples with a yellow complexion (the Mongolians). [Gk *xanthós* yellow]

**X-axis** /ˈɛks-æksəs/, *n.* the horizontal reference axis in a two-dimensional Cartesian coordinate system.

**X chromosome** /ˈɛks ˌkroʊməsoʊm/, *n.* the sex chromosome having major control in sex determination, often paired with an unlike or Y chromosome. In humans and most mammals the XX condition controls femaleness and XY maleness; in poultry and some insects the reverse is true, the female being the heterozygous sex. See **sex chromosome.**

**x-div.,** *Comm.* ex dividend.

**Xe,** *Chem.* xenon.

**xenia** /ˈziniə/, *n.* the immediate influence or effect on the seed or fruit by the pollen other than on the embryo. [NL, from Gk, from *xénos* guest]

**xeno-,** a word element meaning 'alien', 'strange', 'foreign', as in *xenogenesis.* Also, (before a vowel), **xen-.** [Gk, combining form of *xénos,* n., stranger, guest and *xénos,* adj., foreign, alien]

**xenocryst** /ˈzɛnəkrɪst/, *n.* a crystal which becomes included in a magma as it rises and is not formed by the magma itself. [XENO- + CRYST(AL)]

**xenodiagnosis** /ˌzɛnədaɪəgˈnoʊsəs/, *n.* a method of diagnosing certain diseases having insects, ticks, etc., as vectors, by feeding uninfected vectors on the patient and later examining them for infection.

**xenogamy** /zɛˈnɒgəmi/, *n. Bot.* →**cross-fertilisation.**

**xenogenesis** /zɛnəˈdʒɛnəsəs/, *n.* the supposed generation of offspring completely and permanently different from the parent. Also, **xenogeny** /zəˈnɒdʒəni/. – **xenogenetic** /ˌzɛnoudʒəˈnɛtɪk/, **xenogenic**, *adj.*

**xenoglossia** /zɛnəˈglɒsiə/, *n.* the supposed ability of a person, as a psychic medium, to speak a language which he has not previously learned. [Gk *xéno-* XENO- + *glôss(a)* language + *-ia* -IA]

**xenolith** /ˈzɛnəlɪθ/, *n.* a rock fragment foreign to the igneous rock in which it is embedded.

**xenomorphic** /zɛnəˈmɔfɪk/, *adj.* denoting or pertaining to a mineral constituent of a rock, which does not have its characteristic crystalline form, but one forced upon it by other constituents. – **xenomorphically**, *adv.*

**xenon** /ˈzinɒn/, *n.* a heavy, colourless, chemically unreactive but not completely inert monatomic gaseous element present in the atmosphere, one volume in 170 000 000 volumes of air. *Symbol:* Xe; *at. wt:* 131.3; *at. no.:* 54. [Gk, neut. of *xénos* strange]

**xenophile** /ˈzɛnəfaɪl/, *n.* a lover of foreign people, things, customs, etc. [Gk *xénos* strange + -PHILE]

**xenophobe** /ˈzɛnəfoub/, *n.* one who fears or hates foreigners or things foreign.

**xenophobia** /zɛnəˈfoubiə/, *n.* fear or hatred of foreigners. – **xenophobic**, *adj.*

**xenopus** /ˈzɛnəpəs/, *n.* any frog of the African clawed genus *Xenopus*, used in pregnancy testing.

**xenotime** /ˈzɛnətaɪm/, *n.* a mineral, yttrium phosphate, $YPO_4$, often containing cerium, erbium, and thorium, of which it is a source.

**xeric** /ˈzɪərɪk/, *adj.* pertaining to an environment containing or characterised by little moisture. Cf. **hydric** (def. 2), **mesic.**

**xero-**, a word element meaning 'dry', as in *xeroderma.* Also, before a vowel, **xer-**. [combining form representing Gk *xērós*]

**xeroderma** /zɪərouˈdɜmə/, *n.* a disease in which the skin becomes dry and hard, and usu. scaly. Also, **xerodermia.**

**xerography** /zɪəˈrɒgrəfi/, *n.* a method of photographic copying in which an electrostatic image is formed on a surface coated with selenium when it is exposed to an optical image. A dark resinous powder is dusted onto this surface after exposure so that the particles adhere to the charged regions; the image so formed is transferred to a sheet of charged paper and fixed by heating. [Gk *xērō(s)* dry + *graphḗ* writing. See -GRAPHY] – **xerograph** /ˈzɪərəgræf, -graf/, *n.* – **xerographic** /zɪərəˈgræfɪk/, *adj.*

**xerophilous** /zəˈrɒfələs/, *adj.* **1.** *Bot.* growing in or adapted to dry, esp. dry and hot regions. **2.** *Zool.* living in dry situations. – **xerophily**, *n.*

**xerophthalmia** /zɪərɒfˈθælmiə/, *n.* abnormal dryness of the eyeball, usu. due to long-continued conjunctivitis.

**xerophyte** /ˈzɪərəfaɪt/, *n.* a plant adapted for growth under dry conditions. – **xerophytic** /zɪərəˈfɪtɪk/, *adj.*

**xerox** /ˈzɪərɒks/, *n.* **1.** a xerographic process. **2.** a copy obtained by this process. *–v.t., v.i.* **3.** to obtain copies (of) by this process. [Trademark]

**Xhosa** /kɔsə/, *n.* **1.** a Bantu language of Cape Province in the Republic of South Africa, related to Zulu. **2.** a member of the people speaking this language.

**xi** /saɪ/, *n.* the fourteenth letter (Ξ, ξ, = English X, x) of the Greek alphabet.

**x-int.**, *Comm.* without interest.

**-xion**, variant of **-tion**, as in *inflexion, flexion.*

**xiphisternum** /zɪfəˈstɜnəm/, *n., pl.* **-na** /-nə/. *Anat., Zool.* the hindmost (or, in man, the lowermost) segment or division of the sternum. [*xiphi-* (combining form representing Gk *xíphos* sword) + STERNUM] – **xiphisternal** /zɪfəˈstɜnəl/, *adj.*

**xiphoid** /ˈzɪfɔɪd/, *Anat., Zool.* *–adj.* **1.** sword-shaped; ensiform. *–n.* **2.** →**xiphisternum.** [NL *xiphoīdēs,* from Gk *xiphoeidḗs* swordlike]

**xiphosuran** /zɪfəˈsjurən/, *adj.* **1.** of or pertaining to the horseshoe crabs (order Xiphosura). *–n.* **2.** a member of the order Xiphosura; a horseshoe crab. [NL *Xiphosūra* (irregularly from Gk *xíphos* sword + *ourá* tail) + -AN]

**XL** /ɛks ˈɛl/, *adj.* extra large.

**Xmas** /ˈɛksməs/, Christmas.

**Xn**, Christian.

**x-new**, *Comm.* without the right to new shares.

**XP** /kaɪˈrou/, *n.* the Christian monogram made from the first two letters of the Greek word for Christ. Also, χρ. [Gk, representing *chi* and *rho*]

**X-radiation** /ˌɛks-reɪdiˈeɪʃən/, *n.* →**X-ray.**

**X-ray** /ˈɛks-reɪ, ɛks-ˈreɪ/, *n.* **1.** *Physics.* (*oft. pl.*) electromagnetic radiation of shorter wavelength than light ($5 \times 10^{-9}$ to $6 \times 10^{-12}$ m) which are able to penetrate solids, ionise gases, and expose photographic plates; roentgen ray. **2.** an examination of the interior of a person or an opaque substance by means of an apparatus using X-rays. **3.** →**radiograph.** *–v.t.* **4.** to examine by means of X-rays. **5.** to make an X-ray radiograph of. See **roentgenise.** **6.** to treat with X-rays. [G: translation of *X-strahlen,* so called because their nature was not known]

**X-ray crystallography** /– krɪstəˈlɒgrəfi/, *n.* the study of a crystalline substance by observing the diffraction patterns which occur when a beam of X-rays is passed through it.

**X-ray image** /– ˈɪmɪdʒ/, *n.* an image, as of a broken bone, etc., produced by the action of X-rays which can be viewed on a television screen, or permanently recorded on a photographic film.

**X-ray star** /– ˈsta/, *n.* an astronomical object which emits X-rays.

**X-ray therapy** /– ˈθɛrəpi/, *n.* treatment of a disease, such as cancer, using controlled quantities of X-rays.

**X-ray tube** /ˈ– tjub/, *n.* *Physics.* an evacuated tube for the production of X-rays in which a heavy metal target is bombarded with a high-velocity stream of electrons.

**X ref.**, cross reference.

**X roads**, crossroads.

**x-rts**, *Comm.* without rights.

**X unit** /ˈɛks junət/, *n.* a non-SI unit which was used to express wavelengths of X-rays, equal to $1.002 \times 10^{-15}$m.

**xyl-**, variant of **xylo-**, before vowels, as in *xylem.*

**xylan** /ˈzaɪlən/, *n.* the pentosan occurring in woody tissue which hydrolyses to xylose, used as the source of furfural. [XYL- + -AN]

**xylem** /ˈzaɪləm/, *n.* that part of a vascular bundle which consists of tracheids and immediately associated cells, forming the woody portion; woody tissue. See **phloem.** [XYL- + *-em* (from Gk *-ēma* noun suffix)]

**xylene** /ˈzaɪlin/, *n.* any of three isomeric hydrocarbons, $C_6H_4(CH_3)_2$, of the benzene series, occurring as oily, colourless liquids obtained chiefly from coal tar, and used in making dyes, etc. Also, **xylol.**

**xylenol** /ˈzaɪlənɒl/, *n.* any of six isomeric phenols derived from xylene, $(CH_3)_2C_6H_3OH$, used in the manufacture of plastics, and derivatives of which are used in antiseptics.

**xylenol resin** /– ˈrɛzən/, *n.* a synthetic resin produced by the condensation of a xylenol with an aldehyde.

**xylic acid** /ˌzaɪlɪk ˈæsəd/, *n.* any of six isomeric acids derived from xylene, $(CH_3)_2C_6H_3COOH$.

**xylidine** /ˈzaɪlədin, -daɪn, ˈzɪlə-/, *n.* **1.** any of six isomeric compounds, $(CH_3)_2C_6H_3NH_2$, derived from xylene and resembling aniline, used in dye manufacture. **2.** an oily liquid consisting of a mixture of certain of these compounds, used commercially in making dyes. Also, **xylidin.** [XYL(ENE) + -id[3] + -ine[2]]

**xylo-**, a word element meaning 'wood', as in *xylograph.* Also, **xyl-**. [Gk, combining form of *xýlon*]

**xylo.**, xylophone.

**xylocarp** /ˈzaɪləkap/, *n.* any fruit having a hard woody pericarp.

**xylograph** /ˈzaɪləgræf, -graf/, *n.* an engraving on wood. – **xylographer** /zaɪˈlɒgrəfə/, *n.*

**xylography** /zaɪˈlɒgrəfi/, *n.* the art of engraving on wood, or of printing from such engravings. [F *xylographie.* See XYLO-, -GRAPHY] – **xylographic** /zaɪləˈgræfɪk/, **xylographical** /zaɪləˈgræfɪkəl/, *adj.*

**xyloid** /ˈzaɪlɔɪd/, *adj.* resembling wood; ligneous. [Gk *xyloeidḗs*, from *xylo-* XYLO- + *-eidḗs* -OID]

**xylol** /ˈzaɪlɒl/, *n.* →**xylene.**

**xylonite** /ˈzaɪlənaɪt/, *n.* a thermoplastic material of the cellulose nitrate type. [Trademark]

**xylophage** /ˈzaɪləfeɪdʒ/, *n.* *Obs.* a wood-eating insect.

**xylophagous** /zaɪˈlɒfəgəs/, *adj.* **1.** eating wood, as the larvae of certain insects. **2.** perforating or destroying timber, as certain molluscs and crustaceans.

**xylophone** /ˈzaɪləfoʊn/, *n.* a musical instrument consisting of a graduated series of wooden bars, usu. sounded by striking with small wooden hammers. – **xylophonic** /zaɪləˈfɒnɪk/, *adj.* – **xylophonist** /zaɪˈlɒfənəst/, *n.*

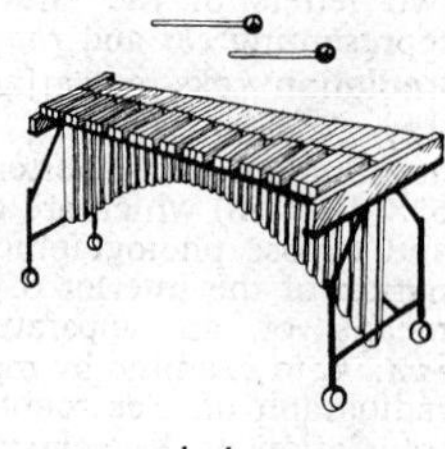
xylophone

**xylose** /ˈzaɪloʊz, -oʊs/, *n.* a colourless crystalline aldopentose, $C_5H_{10}O_5$, derived from xylan, straw, corncobs, etc., by treating with heated dilute sulphuric acid, and dehydrating to furfural if stronger acid is used.

**xylotomous** /zaɪˈlɒtəməs/, *adj.* boring into or cutting wood, as certain insects.

**xylotomy** /zaɪˈlɒtəmi/, *n.* the art of cutting sections of wood, as with a microtome, for microscopic examination. – **xylotomist,** *n.*

**xylyl** /ˈzaɪləl/, *adj.* denoting any of the univalent radicals, $CH_3C_6H_4CH_2-$, derived from xylene.

**xyster** /ˈzɪstə/, *n.* a surgical instrument for scraping bones. [Gk: scraping tool]

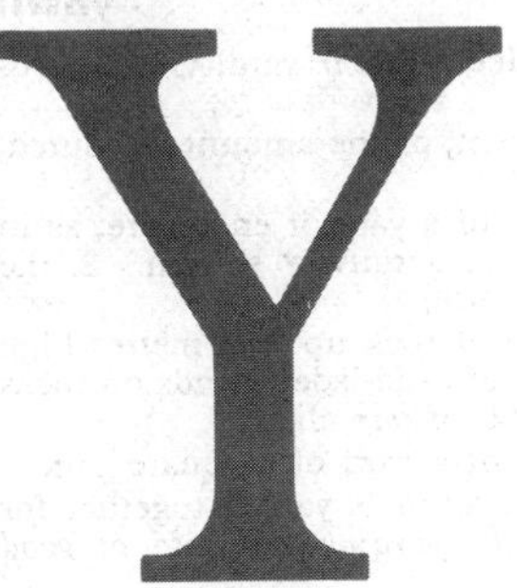

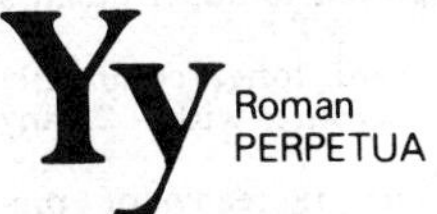 Roman PERPETUA

Yy Sans Serif BURKO

 Script HAUSER

yy Decorative RITMO

*Although there are numerous typefaces in the world they can be divided into four main classifications. These are:*

*ROMAN or SERIF. This typeface came into being from the technique of the Roman masons who, working in stone, finished off each letter with a serif or small stroke projecting from the top or bottom. This was done to correct any feeling of unevenness or imbalance they may have created in cutting the characters in stone.*

*SANS SERIF (without serif). This typeface is geometric in design and has straight-edged characters and lines of a regular thickness.*

*SCRIPT. Based on the movement of the hand, this typeface is often italicised or slanted, as if drawn by a brush or quill pen.*

*DECORATIVE. Any typeface that exaggerates the characteristics of any of the other three classifications to a degree that places it outside of them.*

*The dictionary entries in this book use a SANS SERIF typeface called Helvetica (set in a bold face for the head words) and a SERIF typeface Plantin (used throughout the body of the entries).*

**Y, y** /waɪ/, *n., pl.* **Y's** or **Ys, y's** or **ys. 1.** the 25th letter of the English alphabet. **2.** something resembling the letter Y in shape.

**y** /waɪ/, *Maths.* **1.** an ordinate. (See **abscissa). 2.** an unknown quantity, or a variable.

**y-**, *Obs.* an inflective prefix used in past participles, as in *y-clept* 'named'.

**-y**[1], a suffix of adjectives meaning 'characterised by or inclined to' the substance or action of the word or stem to which the suffix is attached, as in *juicy, dreamy, chilly.* Also, **-ey**[1]. [OE *-ig.* Cf. G *-ig*]

**-y**[2], a diminutive suffix, often affectionate, common in names, as in *Billy, pussy.* Also, **-ey**[2], **-ie.** [ME; often through Scot. influence]

**-y**[3], a suffix forming action nouns from verbs, as in *enquiry,* also found in other abstract nouns, as *carpentry, infamy.* [representing L *-ia, -ium,* Gk *-ia, -eia, -ion,* F *-ie,* G *-ie*]

**y., 1.** yacht. **2.** yard. **3.** year. **4.** young. **5.** younger. **6.** youngest.

**Y,** *Chem.* **yttrium.**

**yabber** /ˈjæbə/, *Colloq. –v.i.* **1.** to talk; converse. *–n.* **2.** talk; conversation. [Aboriginal] **– yabberer,** *n.*

yabby

**yabby** /ˈjæbi/, *n.* **1.** an Australian freshwater crayfish, of genus *Cherax.* *–v.i.* **2.** to catch yabbies. Also, **yabbie.** [Aboriginal] **– yabbying,** *n.*

**yabby pump** /ˈ– pʌmp/, *n.* a type of worm pump for catching yabbies.

**yacht** /jɒt/, *n.* **1.** a sailing vessel used for private cruising, racing, or other like non-commercial purposes. *–v.i.* **2.** to sail, voyage, or race in a yacht. [earlier *yaught,* from early mod. D *jaght,* short for *jaghtschip* ship for chasing. Cf. G *Jacht, Jagd* hunting]

**yachting** /ˈjɒtɪŋ/, *n.* the practice or sport of sailing or voyaging in a yacht.

**yachtsman** /ˈjɒtsmən/, *n., pl.* **-men.** one who owns or sails a yacht. **– yachtsmanship, yachtmanship,** *n.* **– yachtswoman,** *n. fem.*

**yachty** /ˈjɒti/, *n. Colloq.* a yachtsman. Also, **yachtie.**

**yack-ai** /ˈjæk-aɪ/, *interj.* (an exclamation drawing attention or expressing enthusiasm). [? Aboriginal]

**yager** /ˈjeɪgə/, *n.* →**jaeger.**

**Yagi aerial** /ˈjagi ˌɛəriəl/, *n.* a directional aerial used in television and radio astronomy. [named after H. *Yagi,* born 1886, Japanese electrical engineer]

**yah** /ja/, *interj.* (an exclamation of impatience or derision.)

**yahoo** /ˈjahu, jaˈhu/, *n.* **1.** a rough, coarse, or uncouth person. *–v.i.* **2.** to behave in a rough, uncouth manner (fol. by *around*). *–interj.* **3.** (an exclamation expressing enthusiasm or delight). [from *Yahoo,* one of a race of brutes having the form of man and all his degrading passions, in *Gulliver's Travels* (1726) by Jonathan Swift, 1667-1745, Anglo-Irish satirist]

**Yahweh** /ˈjaweɪ/, *n.* a name of God in the Hebrew text of the Old Testament, commonly transliterated Jehovah. See **Tetragrammaton.** Also, **Yahve, Yahveh** /ˈjaveɪ/, **Jahveh, Jahve.**

**Yahwism** /ˈjawɪzəm/, *n.* **1.** the religion of the ancient Hebrews, as based on the worship of Yahweh as the national deity. **2.** the use of Yahweh as the name of God. Also, **Yahvism** /ˈjavɪzəm/.

**yair** /jɛə/, *adv. Colloq.* yes. Also, **yeah.**

**Yajur-Veda** /ˌjʌdʒuə-ˈveɪdə/, *n.* See **Veda.**

**yak**[1] /jæk/, *n.* **1.** the long-haired wild ox, *Poephagus grunniens,* of the Tibetan highlands. **2.** a domesticated variety of the same species. [Tibetan *gyag*]

yak[1]

**yak**[2] /jæk/, *n., v.,* **yakked, yakking.** *Colloq. –n.* **1.** empty conversation. *–v.i.* **2.** to talk or chatter, esp. pointlessly and continuously. [imitative]

**yakety-yak** /jækəti-ˈjæk/, *n., v.i.,* **-yakked, -yakking.** →**yak**[2]. Also, **yackety-yak.** [reduplicative of YAK[2]]

**yakka**[1] /ˈjækə/, *n. Colloq.* work. Also, **yacker, yakker.** [Aboriginal]

**yakka**[2] /ˈjækə/, *n.* →**grasstree.** Also, **yacca.** [Aboriginal]

**yakka grass** /ˈ– gras/, *n.* →**fairy grass.**

**yale lock** /ˈjeɪl lɒk/, *n.* a type of cylinder lock. [Trademark; named after Linus *Yale,* 1821-68, U.S. locksmith]

**yallara** /jəˈlarə/, *n.* the lesser rabbit-eared bandicoot, *Macrotis leucura,* which inhabits the sand dunes of central Australia. [Aboriginal]

**yam** /jæm/, *n.* **1.** the starchy, tuberous root of any of various climbing vines of the genus *Dioscorea,* much cultivated for food in the warmer regions of both hemispheres. **2.** any of these plants. **3.** *Southern U.S.* →**sweet potato. 4.** any of other plants with edible tubers as *Microseris scapigera,* blackfellow's yam. [Sp. *(i)ñame;* ultimately of African orig.; cf. Senegalese *nyami* eat]

yam

**yam daisy** /– 'deɪzi/, *n.* →**blackfellow's yam.**

**yammer** /'jæmə/, *Colloq.* *–v.i.* **1.** to whine or complain. **2.** to make an outcry or clamour; talk loudly and persistently. *–v.t.* **3.** to utter or say in complaint. *–n.* **4.** the act of yammering. [ME *yamur,* var. of *yomer,* OE *geōmrian* complain; akin to G *Jammer* lamentation] – **yammerer,** *n.*

**yam stick** /'jæm stɪk/, *n.* a long, pointed stick used by Aboriginals in digging for yams.

**yandy** /'jændi/, *n.* **1.** a long, shallow dish in which mineral is separated from alluvial by means of a rocking motion. *–v.i.* **2.** to operate a yandy. **3.** to winnow grass seeds from husks. [Aboriginal]

**Yang** /jæŋ/, *n.* one of the two fundamental principles of the universe in Chinese philosophy, regarded as masculine, active, and assertive. Cf. **Yin.**

**yank** /jæŋk/, *Colloq.* *–v.t., v.i.* **1.** to pull or move with a sudden jerking motion; tug sharply. *–n.* **2.** a jerk or tug. [orig. uncert.]

**Yank** /jæŋk/, *n., adj. Colloq.* American. [short for YANKEE]

**Yankee** /'jæŋki/, *n.* **1.** a native or inhabitant of New England. **2.** a native or inhabitant of a northern state of the U.S. **3.** a native or inhabitant of the U.S. **4.** a Federal soldier in the American Civil War. *–adj.* **5.** of, pertaining to, or characteristic of the Yankees. [? backformation from D *Jan Kees* John Cheese, nickname (mistaken for plural)]

**Yankee Doodle** /– 'dudl/, *n.* an English song taken over by the American troops during the American War of Independence.

**Yankeeism** /'jæŋkiɪzəm/, *n.* **1.** Yankee character or characteristics. **2.** a Yankee peculiarity, as of speech.

**Yankeeland** /'jæŋkilænd/, *n. Colloq.* **1.** the United States. **2.** *Chiefly Southern U.S.* the northern states of the U.S. **3.** *Chiefly Northern U.S.* New England.

**yank tank** /'jæŋk tæŋk/, *n. Colloq.* (*usu. derog.*) a large car of American manufacture.

**yap** /jæp/, *v.,* **yapped, yapping,** *n.* *–v.i.* **1.** to yelp; bark snappishly. **2.** *Colloq.* to talk snappishly, noisily, or foolishly. *–v.t.* **3.** to utter by yapping. *–n.* **4.** a yelp: a snappish bark. **5.** *Colloq.* snappish, noisy, or foolish talk. **6.** *Colloq.* the mouth. [imitative]

**yapok** /jə'pɒk/, *n.* a small South and Central American aquatic opossum, *Chironectes minimus,* with webbed hind feet and variegated fur. [named after *Oyapok,* river in Brazil and French Guiana]

**yapp** /jæp/, *n.* **1.** a style of bookbinding in limp leather or the like with projecting flaps overlapping the edges of the pages, used esp. on Bibles. *–adj.* **2.** of or pertaining to this style of binding.

**Yarborough** /'jabərə/, *n. Whist, Bridge.* a hand of cards, none of which is higher than a nine. [named after the 2nd Earl of *Yarborough,* died 1897]

**yard**[1] /jad/, *n.* **1.** a common unit of linear measure in the imperial system equal to 3ft or 36 in., defined as 0·9144 metres. **2.** *Naut.* a long cylindrical spar with a taper towards each end, slung crosswise to a mast and suspending a square sail, lateen sail, etc. [ME *yerd(e),* OE *gerd* (Anglian), c. D *gard,* G *Gerte* rod; cf. GAD[2]]

**yard**[2] /jad/, *n.* **1.** a piece of enclosed ground adjoining or surrounding a house or other building, or surrounded by it. **2.** a piece of enclosed ground for use as a garden, for animals, or for some other purpose. **3.** an enclosure within which any work or business is carried on: *a brickyard, a shipyard.* **4.** *Railways.* **a.** →**goods yard. b.** →**marshalling yard. 5.** *U.S.* the winter pasture or browsing ground of moose and deer. *–v.t.* **6.** to put into or enclose in a yard. [ME *yerd,* OE *geard* enclosure, c. D *gaard* garden, Icel. *gardhr* yard, Goth. *gards* house]

**yardage**[1] /'jadɪdʒ/, *n.* measurement, or the amount measured, in yards. [YARD[1] + -AGE]

**yardage**[2] /'jadɪdʒ/, *n.* **1.** the use of a yard or enclosure, as in lading or unlading cattle, etc., at a railway station. **2.** the charge for such use. [YARD[2] + -AGE]

**yardang** /'jadæŋ/, *n.* a sharp rib of rock up to 6 metres high formed in a desert by the action of sand-laden winds on rocks of varying hardness. [Turkic, abl. of *yar* cliff]

**yardarm** /'jadam/, *n.* either end of a yard of a square sail.

**yarding** /'jadɪŋ/, *n.* a number of animals yarded together for sale or treatment: *the bulk of the yarding was sold at good prices.*

**yardman** /'jadmən/, *n.* a general assistant in a hotel.

**yardmaster** /'jadmastə/, *n.* a man employed to superintend a railway yard.

**yardstick** /'jadstɪk/, *n.* **1.** a stick a yard long, commonly marked with subdivisions, used to measure with. **2.** any standard of measurement.

**yare** /jɛə/, *adj.,* **yarer, yarest.** *Archaic.* **1.** ready or prepared. **2.** prompt; brisk or quick. **3.** easily handled or manageable. [ME; OE *gearu, gearo,* c. D *gaar,* G *gar* done, dressed (as meat)] – **yarely,** *adv.*

**yarn** /jan/, *n.* **1.** thread made by twisting fibres, as nylon, cotton or wool, and used for knitting and weaving. **2.** the thread, in the form of a loosely twisted aggregate of fibres, as of hemp, of which rope is made (rope yarn). **3.** *Colloq.* a story or tale of adventure, esp. a long one about incredible events. **4.** a talk, chat. *–v.i.* **5.** *Colloq.* to spin a yarn; tell stories. **6.** to talk, chat. [ME; OE *gearn,* c. G *Garn;* akin to Icel. *görn* gut]

**yarn-dyed** /'jan-daɪd/, *adj.* (of fabrics) woven from yarns previously dyed.

**yarra** /'jærə/, *adj. Colloq.* mad. Also, **yarrah.** [orig. uncert.]

**Yarra banker** /jærə 'bæŋkə/, *n.* a man addressing passers-by from a soapbox on the banks of the Yarra; an agitator.

**Yarra herring** /– 'hɛrɪŋ/, *n.* →**grayling** (def. 1).

**yarraman** /'jærəmən/, *n.* a horse. [Aboriginal]

**yarran** /'jærən/, *n.* **1.** a small tree, *Acacia homalophylla,* found in inland eastern Australia, useful as fodder, and for firewood and fence posts. **2.** Also, **bastard myall.** a wattle, *A. glaucescens,* which is chiefly coastal and has silvery foliage and fluffy spikes of flowers. [Aboriginal]

**Yarrasider** /'jærəsaɪdə/, *n. Colloq.* →**Melburnian.** [from the *Yarra* river which flows into Port Philip Bay at Melbourne]

**yarrow** /'jæroʊ/, *n.* →**milfoil** (def. 1). [ME *yarowe, yarwe,* OE *gearwe,* c. G *Garbe*]

**yashmak** /'jæʃmæk/, *n.* the veil worn by Muslim women in public. Also, **yashmac.** [Ar.]

**Yass river tussock,** *n.* →**serrated tussock.**

**yataghan** /'jætəgən/, *n.* a Turkish sabre with a curved blade, having an eared pommel and lacking a guard. Also, **ataghan, yatagan.** [Turk.]

**yate** /jeɪt/, *n.* any of several species of *Eucalyptus,* native to western Australia, esp. *E. cornuta* of the south coastal region. [Aboriginal]

**yaup** /jɔp/, *v.i., n.* →**yawp.** – **yauper,** *n.*

**yaupon** /'jɔpən/, *n.* a shrub or small tree, *Ilex vomitoria,* a species of holly, of the southern U.S., with leaves which are sometimes used as a substitute for tea.

**yaw** /jɔ/, *v.i.* **1.** to deviate temporarily from the straight course, as a ship. **2.** (of an aircraft, rocket, etc.) to have a motion about its vertical axis. *–v.t.* **3.** to cause to yaw. *–n.* **4.** a movement of deviation from the direct course, as of a vessel. **5.** a motion of an aircraft, etc., about its vertical axis. [orig. uncert.]

yawl (def. 1)

**yawl** /jɔl/, *n.* **1.** a fore-and-aft-rigged vessel with a large mainmast forward and a much smaller mast set far aft, usu. abaft the rudderpost. **2.** *Obs.* a jolly-boat. Cf. **ketch.** [D *jol* kind of boat; orig. unknown]

**yawn** /jɔn/, *v.i.* **1.** to open the mouth involuntarily with a prolonged, deep intake of breath, as from drowsiness or weariness. **2.** to open wide like a mouth. **3.** to extend or stretch wide, as an open (and usu. deep) space. *–v.t.* **4.** to say with a yawn. **5.** *Archaic.* to open wide, or lay open, as if by yawning. *–n.* **6.** the act of yawning. **7.** an opening, open space, or chasm. **8.** *Colloq.* a boring event; a bore. [ME *yane, yone,* OE *geonian;* akin to OE *gānian, gīnan,* G *gähnen*] – **yawner,** *n.* – **yawningly,** *adv.*

**yawp** /jɔp/, *Colloq. –v.i.* **1.** to utter a loud, harsh cry or sound; bawl. **2.** to talk noisily and foolishly. *–n.* **3.** a yawping cry. **4.** any harsh or raucous sound. **5.** a noisy, foolish utterance. Also, **yaup.** [imitative] – **yawper,** *n.*

**yaws** /jɔz/, *n. pl.* a contagious disease resembling syphilis, caused by the spirochaete, *Treponema pertenue,* prevalent in certain tropical regions and characterised by an eruption of raspberry-like excrescences. Also, **framboesia.**

**Y-axis** /ˈwaɪ-æksəs/, *n.* the vertical reference axis in a two-dimensional Cartesian coordinate system.

**Yb,** *Chem.* ytterbium.

**Y.B.,** yearbook.

**Y chromosome** /ˈwaɪ ˌkroʊməsoʊm/, *n.* the mate of the X chromosome in one sex of species having differentiated sex chromosomes.

**y-clad** /ɪ-ˈklæd/, *v. Archaic.* past participle of **clothe.**

**y-clept** /ɪ-ˈklɛpt/, *v., pp. Archaic.* called; named; styled. Also, **y-cleped.** [ME; OE *geclypod,* pp. See CLEPE]

**yd,** yard; yards.

**yds,** yards.

**ye**[1] /ji/, *pron. Archaic* **1.** (nominative or objective plural of **thou**) you. **2.** (nominative singular) you. [ME; OE *gē,* c. D *gij,* G *ihr,* Icel. *ēr,* Goth. *jus*]

**ye**[2] /ði/; *spelling pron.* /ji/, *def. art.* an archaic spelling of **the**[1]. [var. of THE[1] due to misreading of ME symbol þ (see THORN, def. 5)]

**yea** /jeɪ/, *adv.* **1.** yes (used in affirmation or assent). **2.** *Archaic.* indeed or truly (used to introduce a sentence or clause). **3.** *Archaic.* not only so, but also (used in adding something which intensifies and amplifies). *–n.* **4.** an affirmation; an affirmative reply or vote. **5.** one who votes in the affirmative. [ME *ye, ya,* OE *gēa,* c. D, G, Icel., and Goth. *ja*]

**yeah** /jɛə/, *adv. Colloq.* yes. Also, **yair.**

**yean** /jin/, *v.t.* **1.** (of a sheep or goat) to bring forth (a lamb or a kid). *–v.i.* **2.** to bring forth young. [ME *yene,* OE *geēanian* bring forth (young)]

**yeanling** /ˈjinlɪŋ/, *n.* **1.** the young of a sheep or a goat; a lamb or a kid. *–adj.* **2.** just born; infant.

**year** /jɪə/, *n.* **1.** a period of 365 or 366 days, divided into 12 calendar months, now reckoned as beginning 1 January and ending 31 December (**calendar year**). **2.** a period of approximately the same length in other calendars. **3.** a space of 12 calendar months reckoned from any point: *he left on 15 May and he'll be away for a year.* **4.** a period consisting of 12 lunar months (**lunar year**). **5.** (in scientific use) the time interval between one vernal equinox and the next, or the period of one complete apparent circuit of the ecliptic by the sun, being equal to about 365 days, 5 hours, 48 minutes, 46 seconds (**tropical year, solar year, astronomical year**). **6.** the true period of the earth's revolution round the sun; the time it takes for the apparent travelling of the sun from a given star back to it again, being about 20 minutes longer than the tropical year, which is affected by the precession of the equinoxes (**sidereal year**). **7.** the time in which any planet completes a revolution round the sun. **8.** a full round of the seasons. **9.** a period out of every 12 months, devoted to a certain pursuit, activity, or the like: *the academic year.* **10.** a level or grade in an academic program, usu. indicating one full year's study: *he's in fourth year science; she's in fifth year medicine.* **11.** the group of pupils in a high school who enrolled at the beginning of the same year and who are variously referred to in different schools in terms of numbers which change as they move up the school, as second year, fourth year, year ten, year eleven, etc.: *she was in my year.* **12.** (*pl.*) age, esp. of a person. **13.** (*pl.*) old age: *his years are beginning to tell.* **14.** (*pl.*) time, esp. a long time. **15. a year and a day,** a period specified as the limit of time in various legal matters, as in determining a right or a liability, to allow for a full year by any way of counting. **16. year in, year out,** occurring regularly year after year; continuously. [ME *yeer,* OE *gēar,* c. D *jaar,* G *Jahr,* Icel. *ār,* Goth. *jēr*]

**yearbook** /ˈjɪəbʊk/, *n.* a book published annually, containing information, statistics, etc., about the year.

**yearling** /jɪəlɪŋ/, *n.* **1.** an animal one year old or in the second year of its age. **2.** *Horseracing.* a horse one year old, dating from August 1st of the year of foaling, but not yet two. [YEAR + -LING[1]. Cf. G *Jährling*]

**yearlong** /ˈjɪəlɒŋ/, *adj.* lasting for a year.

**yearly** /ˈjɪəli/, *adj., adv., n., pl.* **-lies.** *–adj.* **1.** pertaining to a year, or to each year. **2.** done, made, happening, appearing, coming, etc., once a year, or every year. **3.** continuing for a year. **4.** lasting only a year. *–adv.* **5.** once a year; annually. *–n.* **6.** a publication appearing once a year.

**yearn** /jɜn/, *v.i.* **1.** to have an earnest or strong desire; long. **2.** to be moved or attracted tenderly. [ME *yerne,* OE *giernan,* c. Icel. *girna*]

**yearning** /ˈjɜnɪŋ/, *n.* **1.** deep longing, esp. when tinged with tenderness or sadness. **2.** an instance of it. – **yearningly,** *adv.*

**year of grace,** *n.* the year as reckoned from the birth of Christ; A.D.

**year-round** /ˈjɪə-raʊnd/, *adj.* open, effective, employed, etc., for the whole year; not seasonal.

**yeast** /jist/, *n.* **1.** a yellowish, somewhat viscid, semifluid substance consisting of the aggregated cells of certain minute fungi, which appears in saccharine liquids (fruit juices, malt worts, etc.), rising to the top as a froth (**top yeast** or **surface yeast**) or falling to the bottom as a sediment (**bottom yeast** or **sediment yeast**), employed to induce fermentation in the manufacture of alcoholic drink, esp. beer, and as a leaven to render bread, etc., light and spongy, and also used in medicine. **2.** a commercial substance made of living yeast cells and some meal-like material, used in raising dough for bread, etc. **3.** a yeast plant. **4.** spume or foam. **5.** ferment or agitation. *–v.i.* **6.** to ferment. **7.** to be covered with froth. [ME *yeest,* OE *gist,* c. G *Gischt*]

bud vacuole

yeast: bud and vacuole of yeast cell

**yeast cake** /ˈ– keɪk/, *n.* living yeast cells compressed with a little starch into a small cake. In **dried yeast cake,** yeasts are inactive; in a **compressed yeast cake** they are active and the product is perishable.

**yeast plant** /ˈ– plænt/, *n.* any of the minute, unicellular ascomycetous fungi constituting the genus *Saccharomyces,* and related genera.

**yeasty** /ˈjisti/, *adj.,* **yeastier, yeastiest. 1.** of, containing, or resembling yeast. **2.** frothy or foamy. **3.** trifling or frivolous. – **yeastily,** *adv.* – **yeastiness,** *n.*

**yecch** /jɛk/, *interj.* (an exclamation of disgust, aversion, horror, or the like).

**yegg** /jɛg/, *n. U.S. Colloq.* **1.** a burglar, esp. a petty one. **2.** a thug. Also, **yeggman.** [orig. obscure; ? var. of *yekk* beggar, a term once popular in California Chinatowns]

**yeggman** /ˈjɛgmən/, *n., pl.* **-men.** →**yegg.**

**yell** /jɛl/, *v.i.* **1.** to cry out with a strong, loud, clear sound. **2.** to scream with pain, fright, etc. *–v.t.* **3.** to utter or tell by yelling. *–n.* **4.** a cry uttered by yelling. **5.** *U.S.* a cry or shout of fixed sounds or words, as one adopted by a school or college. [ME *yelle,* OE *gellan, giellan,* c. G *gellen* resound] – **yeller,** *n.*

**yellow** /ˈjɛloʊ/, *adj.* **1.** of a bright colour like that of butter, lemons, etc.; between green and orange in the spectrum. **2.** having the yellowish skin characteristic of the Mongoloid peoples. **3.** denoting or pertaining to the Mongoloid race. **4.** *U.S. Colloq.* (*oft. derog.*) having the yellowish skin characteristic of mulattos or dark-skinned quadroons. **5.** of sallow complexion. **6.** *Colloq.* cowardly; mean or contemptible. **7.** *Colloq.* (of newspapers, etc.) sensational, esp. morbidly or offensively sensational. *–n.* **8.** a hue between green and orange in the spectrum. **9.** the yolk of an egg. **10.** a yellow pigment or dye. *–v.t.* **11.** to make yellow. *–v.i.* **12.** to become yellow. [ME *yelou,* OE *geolu,* c. G *gelb,* L *helvus*] – **yellowish,** *adj.* – **yellowness,** *n.*

**yellowback** /ˈjɛloʊbæk/, *n.* a pornographic paperback.

**yellow-bellied** /ˈjɛlə-bɛlid/, *adj. Colloq.* cowardly.

i = peat ɪ = pit ɛ = pet æ = pat a = part ɒ = pot ʌ = putt ɔ = port ʊ = put u = pool ɜ = pert ə = apart aɪ = buy eɪ = bay ɔɪ = boy aʊ = how oʊ = hoe ɪə = here ɛə = hair ʊə = tour g = give θ = thin ð = then ʃ = show ʒ = measure tʃ = choke dʒ = joke ŋ = sing j = you õ = Fr. bon

**yellow-bellied glider** /jɛloʊ-bɛlid 'glaɪdə/, *n.* →**fluffy glider.**

**yellow-belly** /'jɛlə-bɛli/, *n.* **1.** *Colloq.* a coward. **2.** →**golden perch.** Also, **yellowbelly.**

**yellowbird** /'jɛloʊbɜd/, *n.* **1.** any of various yellow or golden birds, as the golden oriole of Europe. **2.** any of several American goldfinches.

**yellow box** /jɛloʊ 'bɒks/, *n.* a large spreading tree, *Eucalyptus melliodora,* common on the western slopes in eastern Australia, and valued as a source of honey.

**yellowcake** /'jɛloʊkeɪk/, *n.* uranium oxide in an unprocessed form, which has low radioactivity.

**yellow fever** /jɛloʊ 'fivə/, *n.* a dangerous, often fatal, infectious febrile disease of warm climates, due to a filterable virus transmitted by a mosquito, *Aëdes* (or *Stegomyia*) *calopus,* and characterised by jaundice, vomiting, haemorrhages, etc.

**yellowfin tuna** /ˌjɛloʊfɪn 'tjunə/, *n.* an important Pacific food fish, *Neothunnus macropterus.*

**yellow flag** /jɛloʊ 'flæg/, *n.* a flag indicating a state of quarantine, esp. on a ship.

**yellow-flowered oxalis** /ˌjɛloʊ-flaʊəd ɒk'saləs/, *n.* a garden and lawn weed, *Oxalis pes-caprae,* with yellow flowers and leaves marked with small purple spots, native to South Africa; soursob.

**yellow-green** /jɛloʊ-'grin/, *n.* **1.** a colour about midway between green and yellow in the spectrum.

**yellowhammer** /'jɛloʊhæmə/, *n.* a yellow bird, *Emberiza citrinella,* of Europe, the male of which is marked with bright yellow. [earlier *yelambre,* from OE *geolu* YELLOW + *omer* kind of bird (? bunting); *-h-* ? from obs. *yellow-ham,* representing OE *geolu* YELLOW + *hama* covering (i.e. yellow-feathered bird)]

**yellowhead** /'jɛloʊhɛd/, *n.* →**bush canary** (def. 2).

**yellowish** /'jɛloʊɪʃ/, *adj.* somewhat yellow.

**yellow jack** /jɛloʊ 'dʒæk/, *n.* **1.** the (yellow) flag of quarantine. **2.** →**yellow fever. 3.** any carangoid fish, esp. a Caribbean food fish, *Caranx bartholomaei.* **4.** →**yellow jacket** (def. 2).

**yellow jacket** /'– dʒækət/, *n.* **1.** any of several social wasps of the family Vespidae, having the body marked with bright yellow. **2.** Also, **yellow jack.** any of various species of eucalypt of the bloodwood group with yellowish bark.

**yellow jasmine** /– 'dʒæzmən/, *n.* →**Carolina jasmine.**

**yellow metal** /– 'mɛtl/, *n.* **1.** a yellow alloy consisting of approximately three parts of copper and two of zinc. **2.** gold.

**yellow Monday** /– 'mʌndeɪ/, *n. Colloq.* a large, yellow cicada, *Cyclochila australasiae;* a colour variant of the greengrocer.

**yellow mullet** /– 'mʌlət/, *n.* the cool-water species *Aldrichetta forsteri,* the principal commercial mullet of Victoria and South Australia.

**yellow pages** /– 'peɪdʒəz/, *n.pl.* (*sometimes construed as sing.*) a telephone directory listing businesses, professional people, organisations, etc.

**yellow peril** /– 'pɛrəl/, *n. Colloq.* **1.** the alleged danger of a predominance of the yellow race, with its enormous numbers, over the white race and Western civilisation generally. **2.** the putative danger of a Chinese invasion of Australia.

**yellow poplar** /– 'pɒplə/, *n.* →**tulip tree** (def. 1).

**yellow press** /– 'prɛs/, *n.* publications that exploit, distort or exaggerate news to create sensations and attract readers. [said to be an allusion to the *Yellow Kid,* a cartoon (1895) in the *New York World,* which was noted for sensationalism and vulgarity]

**yellow quartz** /– 'kwɔtz/, *n.* →**citrine** (def. 3).

**yellows** /'jɛloʊz/, *n.* **1.** *Bot.* one of various plant diseases such as **peach yellows, cabbage yellows,** and **aster yellows,** whose most prominent symptom is a loss of green pigment in the leaves. **2.** jaundice, esp. in animals. **3.** *Obs.* jealousy.

**yellow sassafras** /jɛloʊ 'sæsəfræs/, *n.* →**canary sassafras.**

**yellow satin** /– 'sætn/, *n. Colloq.* a Chinese woman considered as a sex object. Cf. **black velvet.**

**yellow sorrel** /– 'sɒrəl/, *n.* any of several oxalidaceous herbs of the genus *Oxalis,* as *O. corniculata,* the procumbent yellow sorrel, a worldwide garden weed.

**yellow spot** /'– spɒt/, *n.* a small, circular, yellowish area on the retina, opposite the pupil.

**yellow streak** /'– strik/, *n.* a cowardly trait in a person's character.

**yellowtail** /'jɛloʊteɪl/, *n.* **1.** →**yellowtail kingfish. 2.** a small carangid fish, *Trachurus declivis,* with yellowish fins and prominent scutes found in southern Australian and New Zealand waters. **3.** any of several fishes with a yellow caudal fin, as *Ocyurus chrysurus,* a small snapper of the Caribbean.

**yellowtail kingfish** /– 'kɪŋfɪʃ/, *n.* a large carangid fish, *Seriola grandis,* of southern Australian waters.

**yellow waterlily** /ˌjɛloʊ 'wɔtəlɪli/, *n.* a European waterlily, *Nuphar lutea,* with deep yellow, globular flowers and green bottle-shaped fruits.

**yellowwood** /'jɛloʊwʊd/, *n.* any of various trees with yellow wood, as *Podocarpus falcatus* of southern Africa and *Flindersia oxleyana* of Australia.

**yellow wood sorrel,** *n.* a perennial lawn weed, *Oxalis corniculata,* with creeping branches, small leaves and small, yellow flowers, native to North America; creeping oxalis.

**yellowy** /'jɛloʊi/, *adj.* somewhat yellow.

**yelp** /jɛlp/, *v.i.* **1.** to give a quick, sharp, shrill cry, as dogs, foxes, etc. **2.** to call or cry out sharply. *–v.t.* **3.** to utter or express by, or as by, yelps. *–n.* **4.** a quick, sharp bark or cry. [ME *yelpe,* OE *gelpan* boast; akin to LG *galpen* croak] **–yelper,** *n.*

**Yemen** /'jɛmən/, *n.* **1.** Official name: **Yemen Arab Republic.** a country on the southern Arabian Peninsula. **2.** See **Democratic Yemen.**

**yen**[1] /jɛn/, *n., pl.* **yen.** the monetary unit of Japan. [Jap., from Chinese *yüan* a round thing, a dollar]

**yen**[2] /jɛn/, *n., v.,* **yenned, yenning.** *Colloq.* *–n.* **1.** desire; longing. *–v.i.* **2.** to desire. [? alteration of YEARN]

**yeo** /joʊ/, *n. Colloq.* ewe: *bare-bellied yeo.* [Brit. d. var. of EWE]

**yeoman** /'joʊmən/, *n., pl.* **-men. 1.** *Brit.* a countryman, esp. one of some social standing, who cultivates his own land. **2.** a petty officer in the Royal Australian Navy. **3.** *Archaic.* a servant, attendant, or subordinate official in a royal or other great household. **4.** *Archaic.* a subordinate or assistant, as of a sheriff or other official or in a craft or trade. *–adj.* **5.** of, pertaining to, or characteristic of a yeoman. [ME *yeman, yoman,* from *ye, yo* (of uncert. orig.) + MAN]

**yeomanly** /'joʊmənli/, *adj.* **1.** of the condition or rank of a yeoman. **2.** pertaining to or befitting a yeoman. *–adv.* **3.** like or as befits a yeoman.

**yeoman service** /joʊmən 'sɜvəs/, *n.* good, useful, or substantial service. Also, **yeoman's service.**

**yep** /jɛp/, *interj. Colloq.* →**yes.**

**yertchuk** /'jɜtʃək/, *n.* a species of Eucalypt, *E. consideniana,* with a close rough bark, found on poor soils in Victoria and New South Wales. [Aboriginal]

**yes** /jɛs/, *adv., n., pl.* **yeses.** *–adv.* **1.** (used to express affirmation or assent or to mark the addition of something emphasising and amplifying a previous statement.) *–n.* **2.** an affirmative reply. [ME; OE *gēse;* apparently from *gēa* yes + *sī* be it]

**yes-man** /'jɛs-mæn/, *n. Colloq.* one who always agrees with his superiors; an obedient or sycophantic follower.

**yester** /'jɛstə/, *adj. Archaic.* being that preceding the present: *yester sun.*

**yester-,** a word element meaning: **1.** being, or belonging to, the day next before the present: *yesterevening, yesternight, yestermorning.* **2.** being that preceding the present: *yesterweek.* [backformation from YESTERDAY]

**yesterday** /'jɛstədeɪ, -di/, *adv.* **1.** on the day preceding this day. **2.** a short time ago. *–n.* **3.** the day preceding this day. **4.** time in the immediate past. *–adj.* **5.** belonging or pertaining to the day before or to a time in the immediate past. [ME; OE *geostrandæg,* from *geostran* (c. G *gestern* yesterday) + *dæg* day]

**yesteryear** /'jɛstəjɪə/, *adv., n. Chiefly Poetic.* **1.** last year. **2.** previous years; former times.

**yet** /jɛt/, *adv.* **1.** at the present time: *don't go yet.* **2.** up to a particular time, or thus far: *he had not yet come.* **3.** in the time still remaining, or before all is done: *there is yet time.* **4.** now or then as previously; still: *he is here yet.* **5.** in addition, or again: *yet once more.* **6.** moreover: *he won't do it for you nor yet for me.* **7.** even or still (with comparatives):

*a yet milder tone.* **8.** though the case be such; nevertheless: *strange and yet true.* **9. as yet,** up to the present time. *–conj.* **10.** and yet, but yet, nevertheless: *it is good, yet it could be improved.* [ME; OE *giet(a),* c. MHG *ieze* yet, now (whence G *jetzt*)]

**yeti** /ˈjɛti/, *n.* →**abominable snowman.** [Tibetan]

**yew** /ju/, *n.* **1.** an evergreen coniferous tree, of the genus *Taxus,* of moderate height, native to the Old World, western North America, and Japan, having a thick, dark foliage and a fine-grained elastic wood. **2.** the wood of such a tree. **3.** a bow for shooting, made of this wood. [ME *ew,* OE *īw, ēow,* c. G *Eibe,* Icel. *ȳr*]

**Y-fronts** /ˈwaɪ-frʌnts/, *n.pl.* men's underpants with two overlapping layers of cloth at the bottom front which, with a vertical seam at the top front, form an inverted Y. [Trademark]

**yickadee** /jɪkəˈdi/, *interj. N.T.* (an exclamation of greeting or farewell). [Aboriginal]

**Yid** /jɪd/, *n. (derog.)* a Jew. [shortened form of YIDDISH]

**Yiddish** /ˈjɪdɪʃ/, *n.* **1.** a language consisting of a group of closely similar High German dialects, with vocabulary admixture from Hebrew and Slavic, written in Hebrew letters, spoken mainly by Jews in countries east of Germany and by Jewish emigrants from these regions, and now the official language of Birobidzhan, an autonomous Jewish region in the south-eastern Soviet Union in Asia. *–adj.* **2.** Jewish. [G *jüdisch* Jewish]

**yiddisher** /ˈjɪdɪʃə/, *n.* **1.** a Jew. *–adj.* **2.** of or pertaining to a Jew; Jewish.

**yield** /jild/, *v.t.* **1.** to give forth or produce by a natural process or in return for cultivation. **2.** to produce or furnish as payment, profit, or interest. **3.** to give up, as to superior power or authority. **4.** to give up or surrender (oneself) (oft. fol. by *up*). **5.** to give up or over, relinquish, or resign. *–v.i.* **6.** to give a return, as for labour expended; produce or bear. **7.** to surrender or submit, as to superior power. **8.** to give way to influence, entreaty, argument, or the like. **9.** to give place or precedence (fol. by *to*). **10.** to give way to force, pressure, etc., so as to move, bend, collapse, or the like. *–n.* **11.** the action of yielding or producing. **12.** that which is yielded. **13.** the quantity or amount yielded. **14.** *Chem.* the ratio of the product actually formed in a chemical process to that theoretically possible, usu. expressed as a percentage. **15.** *Stock Exchange.* dividend return on investment outlet, usu. expressed as a percentage. **16.** *Mil.* the explosive force of a nuclear weapon. [ME *yelde(n),* OE *g(i)eldan* pay, c. G *gelten* be worth, apply to]

**yielding** /jildɪŋ/, *adj.* submissive or compliant. – **yieldingly,** *adv.* – **yieldingness,** *n.*

**yield point** /ˈjild pɔɪnt/, *n.* the stress at which an elongation of the test piece of metal in a tensile test first occurs without increase of load. Also, **yield stress.**

**yiel-yiel** /ˈjil-jil/, *n.* a small tree of eastern Australian rainforests, *Grevillea hilliana,* the wood of which is used in cabinet-making.

**yike** /jaɪk/, *n. Colloq.* a brawl, argument.

**yikes** /jaɪks/, *interj.* (a mild exclamation of surprise or concern).

**Yin** /jɪn/, *n.* one of the two fundamental principles of the universe in Chinese philosophy, regarded as feminine, passive, and yielding. Cf. **Yang.**

**yip** /jɪp/, *v.i.,* **yipped, yipping,** *n. Chiefly U.S.* yap, as a small dog. [imitative]

**yippee** /jɪˈpi/, *interj.* (an exclamation used to express joy, pleasure, or the like.)

**-yl,** a word element used in names of chemical radicals, as in *ethyl.* [combining form representing Gk *hýlē* wood, matter]

**ylang-ylang** /ilæŋ-ˈilæŋ/, *n.* **1.** an aromatic Asian tree, *Cananga odorata,* bearing fragrant drooping flowers which yield a volatile oil used in perfumery. **2.** the oil or perfume. Also, **ilang-ilang.** [Tagalog]

**ylem** /ˈaɪləm/, *n.* a proposed name for the hypothetical substance out of which all atomic nuclei may have been formed. It would consist chiefly of neutrons and have a density of about $10^{13}$ grams per cc. [ME, from OF *ilem,* probably from ML *hȳlem,* acc. of L *hȳlē,* from Gk: matter, wood]

**Y level** /ˈwaɪ lɛvəl/, *n.* →**wye level.**

**ylid** /ˈɪləd/, *n.* a substance in which a carbanion is covalently linked to a heteroatomic molecule which has a high positive charge.

**Y.M.C.A.** /ˌwaɪ ɛm si ˈeɪ/, Young Men's Christian Association.

**y.o.,** year old.

**yob** /jɒb/, *n. Colloq.* a loutish, aggressive, or surly youth. Also, **yobbo** /ˈjɒboʊ/. [? *boy* spelt backwards]

**yodel** /ˈjoʊdl/, *v.,* **-delled, -delling** or *(U.S.)* **-deled, -deling,** *n.* *–v.t., v.i.* **1.** to sing with frequent changes from the natural voice to falsetto and back again, in the manner of the Swiss and Tyrolean mountaineers. *–n.* **2.** a song, refrain, etc., so sung. Also, **yodle.** [G *jodeln*] – **yodeller,** *n.*

**yodle** /ˈjoʊdl/, *v.t., v.i.,* **-dled, -dling,** *n.* →**yodel.** – **yodler,** *n.*

**yoga** /ˈjoʊgə/, *n. (also l.c.)* (in Hindu religious philosophy) the union of the human soul with the Universal Spirit; ascetic practice aiming to effect such union through the withdrawal of the senses from all external objects, often for this purpose employing unfamiliar movements or postures. [Hind., from Skt: lit., union; akin to YOKE] – **yogic,** *adj.*

**yoggy** /ˈjɒgi/, *n. Colloq.* a young criminal.

**yogh** /jɒg/, *n.* the name of the Middle English letter (ʒ), used to represent a a voiced or voiceless fricative made against the roof of the mouth; the voiced fricative eventually became *y* or *x* according to whether it was palatal or velar; the voiceless fricative finally came to be written *gh* and this is kept in current spelling, though the old fricative has been lost (as in *light*) or has become an *f* (as in *tough*).

**yoghurt** /ˈjoʊgət, ˈjɒgət/, *n.* a prepared food of custard-like consistency, sometimes sweetened or flavoured, made from milk that has been curdled by the action of enzymes or other cultures. Also, **yoghourt, yogurt.** Cf. **kumis.** [Turk.]

**yogi** /ˈjoʊgi/, *n., pl.* **-gis** /-giz/. one who practises yoga.

**yogini** /joʊˈgini/, *n.* a female yogi.

**yogism** /ˈjoʊgɪzəm/, *n.* the teachings or practice of yoga. [YOGA + -ISM]

**yo-heave-ho** /joʊ-hiv-ˈhoʊ/, *interj.* (a chant formerly shouted by sailors when hauling together.)

**yo-ho** /joʊ-ˈhoʊ/, *interj., v.,* **-hoed, -hoing.** *–interj.* **1.** (used as a call or shout to attract attention, accompany effort, etc.) *–v.i.* **2.** to shout 'yo-ho!'

**yoicks** /jɔɪks/, *interj.* (a cry used to urge on the hounds in fox-hunting ) [cf. HOICKS]

**yoke** /joʊk/, *n., v.,* **yoked, yoking.** *–n.* **1.** a contrivance for joining a pair of draught animals, esp. oxen, usu. consisting of a crosspiece with two bow-shaped pieces (oxbow) beneath, one at each end, each bow enclosing the head of an animal. **2.** a pair of draught animals fastened together by a yoke (*pl.* after a numeral, **yokes** or **yoke**): *five yoke of oxen.* **3.** something resembling a yoke or a bow of a yoke in form or use. **4.** a frame fitting the neck and shoulders of a person, for carrying a pair of buckets or the like, one at each end. **5.** *Mach.* a vicelike piece gripping two parts firmly together. **6.** a crosshead attached to the upper piston of an opposed piston engine with rods to transmit power to the crankshaft. **7.** a crossbar on the head of a boat's rudder. **8.** a shaped piece in a garment, fitted about or below the neck, shoulders, or about the hips, from which the rest of the garment hangs. **9.** an emblem or token of subjection, servitude, slavery, etc., as one under which prisoners of war were compelled to pass by the ancient Romans and others. **10.** something that couples or binds together, or a bond or tie. *–v.t.* **11.** to put a yoke on; join or couple by means of a yoke. **12.** to attach (a draught animal) to a plough or vehicle; harness a draught animal to (a plough or vehicle). **13.** to join, couple, link, or unite. **14.** *Obs.* to bring into subjection or servitude. *–v.i.* **15.** to be or become joined, linked, or united. [ME *yok,* OE *geoc,* c. D *juk,* G *Joch,* Icel. *ok,* L *jugum*] – **yokeless,** *adj.*

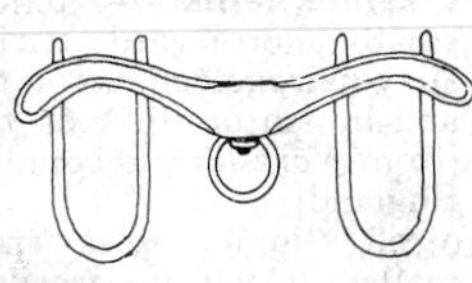

yoke (def. 1)

**yokefellow** /ˈjoʊkfɛloʊ/, *n.* **1.** an intimate associate; a partner. **2.** a spouse. Also, **yokemate.**

**yokel** /ˈjoʊkəl/, *n.* a countryman or rustic; a country bumpkin.

[orig. uncert.]

**yolk** /joʊk/, *n.* **1.** the yellow and principal substance of an egg, as distinguished from the white. **2.** *Biol.* that part of the contents of the egg of an animal which enters directly into the formation of the embryo (**formative yolk,** or archiblast), together with any material which nourishes the embryo during its formation (**nutritive yolk,** deutoplasm, or parablast): distinguished from a mass of albumen (the white of the egg) which may surround it, and from the membrane or shell enclosing the whole. **3.** the essential part; the inner core. **4.** a natural grease exuded from the skin of sheep. [ME *yolke, yelke,* OE *geolca,* from *geolu* yellow] – **yolkless,** *adj.* – **yolky,** *adj.*

**Yom Kippur** /jɒm ˈkɪpə/, *n.* the Day of Atonement, an annual Jewish fast day. [Heb.: Day of Atonement]

**yon** /jɒn/, *Archaic.* –*adj., adv.* **1.** yonder. –*pron.* **2.** that or those yonder. [ME; OE *geon;* akin to G *jener* that]

**yond** /jɒnd/, *adv., adj. Archaic.* yonder. [ME; OE *geond,* c. D *ginds.* Cf. YON, YONDER]

**yonder** /ˈjɒndə/, *adj.* **1.** being the more distant, or farther. **2.** being in that place or over there, or being that or those over there. –*adv.* **3.** at, in, or to that place (specified or more or less distant); over there. [ME; cf. Goth. *jaindre* there]

**yoni** /ˈjoʊni/, *n.* a symbol for the external female genitalia, in the Hindu religion. [Skt]

**yonnie** /ˈjɒni/, *n. Colloq.* a stone, esp. one for throwing.

**yoo-hoo** /ˈju-hu/, *interj.* **1.** a call used to attract someone's attention. –*v.t.* **2.** to attract someone's attention by, or as if by, calling yoo-hoo: *we yoo-hooed but he didn't hear.*

**yore** /jɔ/, *n.* time long past, now only in the phrase **of yore:** *the knights of yore.* [ME; OE *geāra,* apparently from *gēar* YEAR]

**yorker** /ˈjɔkə/, *n.* (in cricket) a ball so bowled that it pitches directly under the bat. [? from *Yorkshire,* a county in NE england]

**york-road poison** /ˌjɔk-roʊd ˈpɔɪzən/, *n.* a poisonous shrub, *Gastrolobium calycinum,* of western Australia.

**Yorkshire fog** /jɔkʃə ˈfɒg/, *n.* a widespread, tufted perennial grass, *Holcus lanatus;* softgrass. [from *Yorkshire,* a county in NE England]

**Yorkshire pudding** /– ˈpʊdɪŋ/, *n.* a baked pudding made from batter and served with gravy before or with roast beef. [from *Yorkshire,* a county in NE England]

**Yorkshire terrier** /– ˈtɛriə/, *n.* a small short-legged terrier with silky hair, golden tan on the head, and bluish or silver on the body. [from *Yorkshire,* a county in NE England]

Yorkshire terrier

**yorrell** /ˈjɒrəl/, *n.* a species of mallee, *Eucalyptus gracilis,* found in dry areas of southern inland Australia.

**you** /ju/; *weak form* /jə/, *pron., poss.* **your** or **yours,** *obj.* **you,** *n.* –*pron.* **1.** the ordinary pronoun of the second person, originally the objective (plural) of *ye,* but now used regularly as either objective or nominative, and with either plural or singular meaning. **2.** one; anyone; people in general. –*n.* **3.** *Colloq.* something resembling or closely identified with the person addressed: *that dress simply isn't you.* [ME; OE *ēow,* c. D *u*]

**you-beaut** /ju-ˈbjut/, *adj. Colloq.* wonderful; amazing; excellent.

**you-beaut country** /ˈ– kʌntri/, *n. Colloq.* Australia.

**you'd** /jud/; *weak form* /jəd/, contraction of *you had* or *you would.*

**you'll** /jul/; *weak form* /jəl/, contraction of *you will* or *you shall.*

**you'lldo** /ˈjuldu/, *n. Colloq.* a bribe.

**young** /jʌŋ/, *adj.* **1.** being in the first or early stage of life, or growth; youthful; not old. **2.** having the appearance, freshness, vigour, or other qualities of youth. **3.** of or pertaining to youth: *in one's young days.* **4.** inexperienced. **5.** not far advanced in years in comparison with another or others. **6.** junior (applied to the younger of two persons of the same name). **7.** being in an early stage generally, as of existence, progress, operation, etc.; new; early. **8.** representing or advocating recent or progressive tendencies, policies, or the like. –*n.* **9.** young offspring. **10.** young people collectively. **11. with young,** pregnant. [ME *yong,* OE *geong,* c. G *jung*] – **youngish,** *adj.*

**youngberry** /ˈjʌŋbəri, -bri/, *n., pl.* **-ries.** the large, dark purple, sweet fruit of a trailing blackberry in the south-western U.S., a cross between several blackberries. [named after B. M. *Young,* 20th cent. U.S. fruitgrower, who developed it]

**young blood** /ˈjʌŋ blʌd/, *n.* youthful people who introduce fresh ideas, practices, etc.

**young-eyed** /ˈjʌŋ-aɪd/, *adj.* **1.** clear-eyed; bright-eyed. **2.** having a youthful outlook; enthusiastic; fresh.

**youngie** /ˈjʌŋi/, *n. Colloq.* a child.

**youngling** /ˈjʌŋlɪŋ/, *n.* **1.** a young person. **2.** anything young, as a plant, etc. **3.** a novice; a beginner. –*adj.* **4.** young; youthful. [ME *yongling,* OE *geongling,* c. G *Jüngling.* See YOUNG, -LING[1]]

**Young's modulus** /jʌŋz ˈmɒdʒələs/, *n.* the modulus of elasticity of a material in tension or compression, equal to the ratio of the stress applied to a wire or rod of the material to the longitudinal strain produced. [named after Thomas *Young,* 1773-1829, English physicist]

**youngster** /ˈjʌŋstə/, *n.* **1.** a child. **2.** a young person. **3.** a young horse or other animal.

**Young Turk** /jʌng ˈtɜk/, *n.* **1.** any person who agitates for radical reforms. **2.** *Colloq.* an impudent child. [orig. a member of a Turkish reformist and nationalist party founded in the latter half of the 19th cent.]

**younker** /ˈjʌŋkə/, *n.* **1.** *Archaic.* a youngster. **2.** *Obs.* a young gentleman or knight. [MD *jonchere* (from *jonc* young + *here* master), c. G *Junker*]

**your** /jɔ/, *pron.* **1.** the possessive form of *you, ye,* used before a noun. **2.** (used to indicate all members of a particular group): *your suburban housewife; your typical old-age pensioner.* Cf. **yours.** [ME; OE *ēower* (gen. of *gē* YE[1]), c. G *euer*]

**you're** /jɔ/, contraction of *you are.*

**yours** /jɔz/, *pron.* form of *your* used predicatively or without a noun following.

**yourself** /jɔˈsɛlf/, *pron., pl.* **-selves. 1.** a reflexive form of *you: you've cut yourself.* **2.** an emphatic form of *you* or *ye* used **a.** as object: *you took it for yourself.* **b.** in apposition to a subject or object: *you yourself did it.* **3.** your proper or normal self: *you'll soon be yourself again.*

**yours truly** /jɔz ˈtruli/, *n.* **1.** (a conventional phrase used at the end of a letter.) **2.** *Colloq.* I, myself, or me.

**youse** /juz/, *pron. Colloq.* (*in non-standard use*) plural form of **you.**

**youth** /juθ/, *n., pl.* **youths** /juðz/, (*collectively*) **youth. 1.** the condition of being young; youngness. **2.** the appearance, freshness, vigour, spirit, etc., characteristic of one that is young. **3.** the time of being young; early life. **4.** the period of life from puberty to the attainment of full growth; adolescence. **5.** the first or early period of anything. **6.** young persons collectively. **7.** a young person, esp. a young man. [ME *youthe,* OE *geoguth,* c. G *Jugend*]

**youthful** /ˈjuθfəl/, *adj.* **1.** characterised by youth; young. **2.** of, pertaining to, or befitting youth. **3.** having the appearance, freshness, vigour, etc., of youth. **4.** early in time. **5.** *Phys. Geog.* (of topographical features) having advanced in reduction of the land surface by erosion, etc., to a slight extent only. – **youthfully,** *adv.* – **youthfulness,** *n.*

**youth hostel** /ˈjuθ hɒstl/, *n.* a simple lodging place for young travellers.

**you've** /juv/, contraction of *you have.*

**yow** /jaʊ/, *interj.* (a shout of pain, dismay, etc.)

**yowie** /ˈjaʊi/, *n.* an ape-like man, two to two and a half metres tall, believed by some to roam in certain parts of Australia, esp. southern New South Wales.

**yowl** /jaʊl/, *v.i.* **1.** to utter a long distressful or dismal cry, as an animal or a person; howl. –*n.* **2.** a yowling cry; a howl. [ME *yowle,* earlier *yuhele,* apparently from OE *gēoh-* in *gēohthu* care, sorrow]

**yoyo** /ˈjoʊjoʊ/, *n., pl.* **-yos.** a toy, consisting of a round, flat-sided block of wood, plastic, etc., with a groove round the edge, in which a string is wound. The yoyo is spun out and reeled in by the string, one end of which remains attached to the finger. [Trademark]

**yperite** /ˈipəraɪt/, *n.* →**mustard gas.** [named after *Ypres,* a town in Belgium, the scene of many battles, 1914-18]

**yr,** **1.** year. **2.** your.

**yrs,** **1.** years. **2.** yours.

**Yt,** *Chem.* yttrium.

**ytterbia** /ɪˈtɜbiə/, *n.* ytterbium oxide, $Yb_2O_3$, which is white and forms colourless salts. [NL, from *Ytterb(y)* in Sweden, where found + -IA. Cf. ERBIUM, TERBIUM, TERBIA, YTTRIA]

**ytterbite** /ɪˈtɜbaɪt/, *n.* →**gadolinite.**

**ytterbium** /ɪˈtɜbiəm/, *n.* a rare metallic element found in the mineral gadolinite, and forming compounds resembling those of yttrium. *Symbol:* Yb; *at. wt:* 173.04; *at. no.:* 70. [NL, from YTTERB(ITE) + -IUM] – **ytterbic,** *adj.*

**yttria** /ˈɪtriə/, *n.* a white insoluble oxide of yttrium, $Y_2O_3$, used in making incandescent mantles. [NL, from *Ytt(e)r(by)* in Sweden + -IA]

**yttriferous** /ɪˈtrɪfərəs/, *adj.* yielding or containing yttrium.

**yttrium** /ˈɪtriəm/, *n.* a rare trivalent metallic element, found in gadolinite and other materials. *Symbol:* Y or Yt; *at. wt:* 88.905; *at. no.:* 39; *sp. gr.:* 4.34. See **rare-earth elements.** [NL, from YTTR(IA) + -IUM] – **yttric,** *adj.*

**yttrocerite** /ɪtrəˈsɛraɪt/, *n.* a blue mineral, calcium fluoride, which contains metals of the yttrium and cerium groups.

**yttrotantalite** /ɪtrəˈtæntəlaɪt/, *n.* a dark brown mineral, tantalite of yttrium, which also contains iron, cerium, and niobates.

**yuan** /ˈjuən/, *n.* the unit of currency of China. [see YEN[1]]

**yucca** /ˈjʌkə/, *n.* any plant of the genus *Yucca,* of the warmer regions of America, having pointed, usu. rigid leaves, and whitish flowers in terminal central racemes. [NL, from Sp. *yuca,* from Arawak]

**yucky** /ˈjʌki/, *adj.* disgusting; unpleasant; repulsive. Also, **yukky.**

**Yuga** /ˈjugə/, *n.* (in Hindu) **1.** an age of time. **2.** one of four ages distinguished in a period of the world's existence, the first being a golden age, with deterioration in those following. [Skt: age, orig., yoke]

**Yugoslav** /ˈjugəslav/, *n.* **1.** a native or inhabitant of Yugoslavia. **2.** a southern Slav; a member of the southern group of Slavic peoples. *–adj.* **3.** of or pertaining to the Yugoslavs. Also, **Jugoslav, Jugo-Slav.**

**Yugoslavia** /jugəˈslaviə/, *n.* a republic in southern Europe, formed in 1918 from the kingdoms of Serbia and Montenegro and part of Austria-Hungary. – **Yugoslavian,** *adj., n.* – **Yugoslavic,** *adj.*

**yuk** /jʌk/, *interj.* **1.** (*esp. in children's speech*) (an expression of disgust). *–adj.* **2.** repulsive; disgusting.

**yule** /jul/, *n.* Christmas, or the Christmas season. [ME *yole,* OE *geōl(a)* Christmastide, c. Icel. *jōl*]

**yule log** /ˈ– lɒg/, *n.* a large log of wood which traditionally formed the foundation of the fire at Christmas. Also, **yule block, yule clog.**

**yuletide** /ˈjultaɪd/, *n.* the Christmas season.

**Yuman** /ˈjumən/, *n.* **1.** a North American Indian linguistic stock of the south-western U.S. *–adj.* **2.** of or pertaining to the Yuman.

**yummy** /ˈjʌmi/, *adj. Colloq.* (esp. of food) very good. Also, **yum.**

**yum yum** /jʌm ˈjʌm/, *interj.* delicious!

**Y.W.C.A.** /ˌwaɪ dʌbəlju si ˈeɪ/, Young Women's Christian Association.

**ywis** /ɪˈwɪs/, *adv. Obs.* →**iwis.**

# Z

Zz Roman ZAPF Zz Sans Serif KABEL Zz Script MANDATE Zz Decorative UNICAL

*Although there are numerous typefaces in the world they can be divided into four main classifications. These are:*

*ROMAN or SERIF. This typeface came into being from the technique of the Roman masons who, working in stone, finished off each letter with a serif or small stroke projecting from the top or bottom. This was done to correct any feeling of unevenness or imbalance they may have created in cutting the characters in stone.*

*SANS SERIF (without serif). This typeface is geometric in design and has straight-edged characters and lines of a regular thickness.*

*SCRIPT. Based on the movement of the hand, this typeface is often italicised or slanted, as if drawn by a brush or quill pen.*

*DECORATIVE. Any typeface that exaggerates the characteristics of any of the other three classifications to a degree that places it outside of them.*

*The dictionary entries in this book use a SANS SERIF typeface called Helvetica (set in a bold face for the head words) and a SERIF typeface Plantin (used throughout the body of the entries).*

**Z, z** /zɛd/ *U.S.* /zi/ *n., pl.* **Z's** or **Zs, z's** or **zs.** a consonant, the 26th letter of the English alphabet.

**z,** *Maths.* **1.** an unknown quantity or a variable. **2.** a complex number or variable.

**z.,** **1.** *Astron.* zenith. **2.** zero. **3.** zone.

**Z,** **1.** *Chem.* atomic number. **2.** *Astron.* zenith. **3.** zone. **4.** zero.

**zabaglione** /zæbəˈljoʊni/, *n.* a cream mousse of Italian origin composed of egg yolks, sugar, and wine, usu. marsala. Also, **zabaione** /zæbaˈjoʊni/.

**zack** /zæk/, *n. Colloq.* **1.** (formerly) a sixpence. **2.** a five cent piece. **3.** *Prison.* a prison sentence of six months' duration.

**zaffre** /ˈzæfə/, *n.* an artificial mixture containing cobalt oxide and usu. silica, used to produce a blue colour in glass and other ceramic products (related to *smalt*). Also, **zaffer.** [F *zafre,* from Ar. *sufr* yellow copper, influenced by *za'farān* saffron. Cf. SAPPHIRE]

**Zaire** /zaɪˈɪə/, *n.* a republic in western central Africa.

**Zambia** /ˈzæmbiə/, *n.* an independent state in central Africa. – **Zambian,** *adj., n.*

**zambuck** /ˈzæmbʌk/, *n. Colloq.* a St John ambulance man. [from *Zambuck,* tradename of ointment in a black and white container, calling to mind the black and white uniform worn by St John ambulance men]

**zamia** /ˈzeɪmiə/, *n.* **1.** any of the plants constituting the primitive cycad family esp. the genus *Macrozamia,* having a crown of palm-like leaves. **2.** →**burrawang.** Also, **zamia palm.** [NL, misreading of L *azānia* pine-nut (Pliny)]

**zanthoxylum** /zænˈθɒksələm/, *n.* the barks of various shrubs or trees of the genus *Zanthoxylum,* esp. *Z. americanum* and *Z. clavaherculis,* used in medicine.

**zany** /ˈzeɪni/, *adj.,* **-nier, -niest,** *n., pl.* **-nies.** *–adj.* **1.** extremely comical; clownish. **2.** slightly crazy; fantastic or ludicrous. *–n.* **3.** an apish buffoon; clown. **4.** a silly person; simpleton. [F *zani,* from d. It. (Venetian) *zanni* clown, lit., Johnny, c. It. *Giovanni* John] – **zanyism,** *n.*

**zap** /zæp/, *v.,* **zapped, zapping,** *n. Colloq. –v.t.* **1.** to destroy with a sudden burst of violence; annihilate. **2.** to move quickly. **3. zap up,** to make livelier and more interesting. *–n.* **4.** vitality; force.

**zapateado** /zæpəteɪˈadoʊ/, *n.* a vigorous Spanish dance for a solo performer, accompanied by much tapping of the heels.

**zapped** /ˈzæpt/, *Colloq. –v.* **1.** past participle of **zap.** *–adj.* **2.** tired to the point of exhaustion.

**zarf** /zaf/, *n.* a cuplike holder, usu. of ornamental metal, for a coffee cup without a handle, as used in the Levant. [Ar.: vessel]

Z, zarf

**zeal** /zil/, *n.* ardour for a person, cause, or object; eager desire or endeavour; enthusiastic diligence. [ME *zele,* from L *zēlus,* from Gk *zêlos,* from *zéein* boil]

**zealot** /ˈzɛlət/, *n.* **1.** one who displays zeal. **2.** one carried away by excess of zeal. **3.** *Colloq.* a religious fanatic. [LL *zēlōtēs,* from Gk, from *zêlos* zeal]

**zealotry** /ˈzɛlətri/, *n.* undue or excessive zeal; fanaticism.

**zealous** /ˈzɛləs/, *adj.* full of, characterised by, or due to zeal; ardently active, devoted, or diligent. – **zealously,** *adv.* – **zealousness,** *n.*

**zebra** /ˈzɛbrə/, *U.S.* /ˈzibrə/, *n.* a wild, horselike animal, fully and regularly striped with dark bands on a light ground, or with alternating dark and light bands, occurring in three species, each with its own characteristic pattern of markings: the **mountain zebra,** *Equus zebra,* of southern Africa; the **common zebra,** *E. burchelli,* of southern, central, and eastern Africa; and **Grevy's zebra,** *E grevyi,* of north-eastern Africa. [It. or Pg.; orig. uncert.] – **zebrine** /ˈzɛbraɪn, ˈzibraɪn/, *adj.*

zebra

**zebra crossing** /– ˈkrɒsɪŋ/, *n.* a pedestrian crossing marked with broad black and white or black and yellow stripes parallel to the kerb.

**zebra finch** /ˈ– fɪntʃ/, *n.* a small finch *Taeniopygia guttata,* having black and white banded rump feathers.

**zebra-fish** /ˈzɛbrə-fɪʃ/, *n., pl.* **-fishes,** (*esp. collectively*) **-fish.** a popular egg-laying aquarium fish, *Brachydanio rerio,* with zebra-like stripes.

**zebra parrot** /ˈzɛbrə pærət/, *n.* →**budgerigar.**

**zebra shark** /ˈ– ʃak/, *n.* a bottom-dwelling, harmless, elongate shark, *Stegostoma fasciatum,* zebra-patterned when young but spotted at maturity. Also, **leopard shark.**

**zebrawood** /ˈzɛbrəwʊd/, *n.* **1.** the striped hardwood of a tropical American tree, *Connarus guianensis,* used for cabinetwork, etc. **2.** the tree itself. **3.** any of various similar woods or trees.

**Zebu** /'zibu/, *n.* a bovine animal, *Bos indicus,* varying greatly in size and colour in different breeds, but having a characteristic large hump (sometimes double) over the shoulders and a very large dewlap; widely domesticated in India, China, eastern Africa, etc. and used for cross-breeding in Australia. [F; orig. uncert.]

Zebu

**Zech.,** *Bible.* Zechariah.

**zed** /zɛd/, *n.* **1.** a name for the letter Z. **2.** *Colloq.* a nonentity; cipher. **3. push up** or **stack zeds,** *Colloq.* to go to sleep. [ME, from F *zède,* from L *zēta,* from Gk]

**zedoary** /zə'douəri/, *n.* an East Indian drug consisting of the rhizome of either of two species of curcuma, *Curcuma zedoaria* or *C. aromatica,* used as a stimulant. [late ME, from ML *zedoārium,* from Ar. *zedwār*]

**zee** /zi/, *n. Chiefly U.S.* a name for the letter Z.

**Zeeman effect** /'zimən əfɛkt/, *n.* the splitting of spectral lines into components when the light source is operated in a magnetic field. [named after P. *Zeeman,* 1865-1943, Dutch physicist]

**zein** /'ziən/, *n.* a protein found in maize, used in the manufacture of textiles, plastics, lacquers and adhesives. [NL *zē(a)* maize (in L: spelt) + -IN[2]]

**Zeitgeist** /'tsaɪtgaɪst/, *n.* the spirit of the time; general drift of thought or feeling characteristic of a particular period of time. [G: time-spirit]

**Zen** /zɛn/, *n.* a Buddhist sect, popular in Japan (where it was introduced from China in the 12th century), advocating self-contemplation as the key to the understanding of the universe. [Jap., from Chinese *ch'an,* from Pali *jhāna,* Skt *dhyāna* religious meditation]

**Zener diode** /zɛnə 'daɪoud/, *n.* a diode which has a stable Zener voltage which is used for a reference. [named after Clarence Melvin *Zener,* born 1905, U.S. physicist]

**Zener voltage** /– voultɪdʒ/, *n.* the voltage at which the insulating properties of a semiconductor break down.

**zenith** /'zɛnəθ/, *n.* **1.** the point of the celestial sphere vertically above any place or observer, and diametrically opposite to the nadir. **2.** highest point or state; culmination. [ME *senyth,* from ML *cenit,* from Ar. *samt* path, way in *samt ar-rās,* lit., way over the head] – **zenithal,** *adj.*

**zenithal projection** /ˌzɛnəθəl prə'dʒɛkʃən/, *n.* →**azimuthal projection.**

**zenith tube** /'zɛnəθ tjub/, *n.* a telescope mounted to point only at the zenith, used at observatories for taking time from the stars.

**zeolite** /'ziəlaɪt/, *n.* **1.** any of a group of hydrated silicates of aluminium with alkali metals, commonly occurring as secondary minerals in cavities in igneous rocks. **2.** any similar artificial substance used in water softening by the ion-exchange method. [*zeo-* (combining form representing Gk *zeeín* boil) + -LITE] – **zeolitic** /ziə'lɪtɪk/, *adj.*

**Zeph.,** *Bible.* Zephaniah.

**zephyr** /'zɛfə/, *n.* **1.** a soft, mild breeze. **2.** (*cap.*) *Poetic.* the west wind personified. **3.** any of various things of fine, light quality, as a fabric, yarn, etc. [L *zephyrus,* from Gk *zéphyros*]

**zephyr cloth** /'– klɒθ/, *n.* a light type of material used for women's clothing.

**Zephyrus** /'zɛfərəs/, *n.* the west wind personified.

**zephyr yarn** /'zɛfə jan/, *n.* a soft worsted yarn used in embroidery and knitting. Also, **zephyr worsted.**

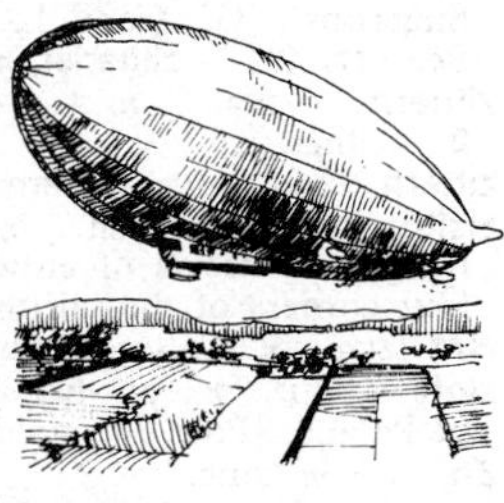
zeppelin

**zeppelin** /'zɛpələn/, *n.* a large dirigible consisting of a long, cylindrical, covered framework containing compartments or cells filled with gas, and of various structures for holding the engines, passengers, etc. [named after F. von *Zeppelin,* 1838-1917, German general and airship builder]

**zero** /'zɪərou/, *n., pl.,* **-ros, -roes,** *v.,* **-roed, -roing.** *–n.* **1.** the figure or symbol 0, which stands for the absence of quantity in the Arabic notation for numbers; a cipher. **2.** the origin of any kind of measurement; line or point from which all divisions of a scale (as a thermometer) are measured in either a positive or a negative direction. **3.** naught or nothing. **4.** the lowest point or degree. **5.** *Gram.* a hypothetical affix or other alteration of an underlying form to derive a complex word, not present in the phonemic shape of the word but functioning in the same way as other affixes or alterations in the language, for example, the plural of *deer* is formed by adding a zero ending (that is, by adding nothing). **6.** *Ordn.* a sight setting for both elevation and windage for any given range. *–v.t.* **7.** *Chiefly U.S.* to adjust (any instrument or apparatus) to a zero point or to an arbitrary reading from which all other readings are to be measured. **8. zero in,** to adjust the sight settings of (a rifle) by calibrated firing on a standard range with no wind blowing. *–v.i.* **9. zero in, a.** to focus attention (fol. by *on*). **b.** to arrive at by a process of elimination (fol by *on*): *they zeroed in on the conservatory as the site of the murder.* [It., from Ar. *sifr* CIPHER]

**zero gravity** /– 'grævəti/, *n.* →**weightlessness.**

**zero grazing** /– 'greɪzɪŋ/, *n.* the feeding on green feed, grain or hay, of an animal which has no access to pasture.

**zero hour** /'– auə/, *n.* **1.** *Mil.* the time set for the beginning of an attack. **2.** *Colloq.* the time at which any contemplated move is to begin.

**zero length launching,** *n.* a technique in which the first motion of the missile or aircraft removes it from the launcher.

**zero point energy,** *n.* the energy possessed by the atoms or molecules of a substance at the absolute zero of temperature.

**zero population growth,** *n.* the doctrine which advocates that population increase be limited to the number of children needed to maintain the existing population, calculated to be 2.11 children per family.

**zest** /zɛst/, *n.* **1.** anything added to impart flavour or cause relish. **2.** an agreeable or piquant flavour imparted. **3.** piquancy, interest, or charm. **4.** keen relish, hearty enjoyment, or gusto. **5.** the thin outer skin of citrus fruits. *–v.t.* **6.** to give zest, relish, or piquancy to. [F *zeste* orange or lemon peel (used for flavouring); orig. unknown] – **zestless,** *adj.* – **zesty,** *adj.*

**zestful** /'zɛstfəl/, *adj.* **1.** full of zest. **2.** characterised by keen relish or hearty enjoyment. – **zestfully,** *adv.* – **zestfulness,** *n.*

**zeta** /'zitə/, *n.* the sixth letter (Z, ζ, = English Z, z) of the Greek alphabet.

**ZETA** /'zitə/, *n.* a torus-shaped apparatus for studying controlled thermonuclear reactions. [*Z*(*ero*) *E*(*nergy*) *T*(*hermonuclear*) *A*(*pparatus*)]

**zetapotential** /zitəpə'tɛnʃəl/, *n.* the potential across the interface of all solids and liquids (specifically, the potential across the diffuse layer of ions surrounding a charged colloidal particle) largely responsible for colloidal stability; electrokinetic potential.

**zeuge** /'zjugə, 'zugə/, *n., pl.* **zeugen.** a tabular mass of rock, two to forty-five metres high, standing up from a stratum of softer rock, formed in a desert by the action of sand-laden winds. [G: lit., witness]

**zeugma** /'zjugmə/, *n.* a figure in which a verb is associated with two subjects or objects, or an adjective with two nouns, although appropriate to only one of the two, as in 'to wage war and peace'. [NL, from Gk: yoking] – **zeugmatic** /zjug'mætɪk/, *adj.*

**zibeline** /'zɪbəlaɪn, -lən/, *adj.* **1.** of or pertaining to the sable. *–n.* **2.** the fur of the sable. **3.** a thick woollen cloth with a flattened hairy nap. Also, **zibelline.** [F, from It. *zibellino,* from ML *sabellīnus,* from *sabellum* sable, of Slavic orig. Cf. SABLE]

**zibet** /'zɪbət/, *n.* a civet, *Viverra zibetha,* of India, the Malay Peninsula, etc. [ML *zibethum.* See CIVET]

**Ziegler catalysts** /'ziglə kætələsts/, *n.pl.* catalysts which promote the polymerisation of ethylene and propylene at normal temperatures and pressures, as titanium trichloride. [named after Carl *Ziegler,* 1898-1973, German chemist]

**ziff** /zɪf/, *n. Colloq.* a (short) beard.

**ziggurat** /ˈzɪgəræt/, *n.* (among the ancient Babylonians and Assyrians) a temple (of Sumerian origin) in the form of a pyramidal tower consisting of a number of storeys, and having about the outside a broad ascent winding round the structure and presenting the appearance of a series of terraces. Also, **zikkurat, zikurat.** [Assyrian *ziqquratu* pinnacle]

**zigzag** /ˈzɪgzæg/, *n., adj., adv., v.,* **-zagged, -zagging.** *–n.* **1.** a line, course, or progression characterised by sharp turns first to one side and then to the other. **2.** one of a series of such turns, as in a line or path. **3.** anything in the form of a zigzag. *–adj.* **4.** proceeding or formed in a zigzag. *–adv.* **5.** with frequent sharp turns from side to side. *–v.t.* **6.** to make zigzag, as in form or course; move in a zigzag direction. *–v.i.* **7.** to proceed in a zigzag line or course. [F, from G *Zickzack,* reduplication of *Zacke* point, tooth]

zigzag lines

**zilch** /ˈzɪltʃ/, *n. Chiefly U.S. Colloq.* nothing. [orig. uncert.]

**zillion** /ˈzɪljən/, *n. Colloq.* an unimaginably large amount. [the letter *z,* the last in the alphabet + *(m)illion*]

**Zimbabwe** /zɪmˈbabweɪ/, *n.* a republic in southern Africa; an independent member of the British Commonwealth. Official name: **Republic of Zimbabwe.**

**zinc** /zɪŋk/, *n., v.,* **zincked, zincking** or **zinced** /zɪŋkt/, **zincing** /ˈzɪŋkɪŋ/. *–n.* **1.** *Chem.* a bluish-white metallic element occurring combined as the sulphide, oxide, carbonate, silicate, etc., resembling magnesium in its chemical relations, and used in making galvanised iron, alloys such as brass and die-casting metal, etc., as an element in voltaic cells, and, when rolled out into sheets, as a protective covering for roofs, etc. *Symbol:* Zn; *at. wt.:* 65.37; *at. no.:* 30; *sp. gr.:* 7.14 at 20°C. **2.** a piece of this metal used as an element in a voltaic cell. *–v.t.* **3.** to coat or cover with zinc. [G *Zink;* orig. uncert.] – **zincic** /ˈzɪŋkɪk/, **zincky,** *adj.*

**zincate** /ˈzɪŋkeɪt/, *n.* a salt formed from anions such as $Zn(OH)_4^{2-}$ or $Zn\ (OH)_3^-$.

**zinc blende** /zɪŋk ˈblɛnd/, *n.* →**sphalerite.**

**zinc chloride** /– ˈklɔraɪd/, *n.* a white crystalline soluble solid, $ZnCl_2$, used as a wood preservative, disinfectant, and for various industrial purposes.

**zinc chromate** /– ˈkroʊmeɪt/, *n.* See **zinc yellow.**

**zinc chrome** /– ˈkroʊm/, *n.* →**zinc yellow.**

**zinc dust** /ˈ– dʌst/, *n.* finely divided zinc used as a pigment in protective paints for iron and steel.

**zinciferous** /zɪŋkˈɪfərəs/, *adj.* yielding or containing zinc.

**zincify** /ˈzɪŋkəfaɪ/, *v.t.,* **-fied, -fying.** to cover or impregnate with zinc. – **zincification** /zɪŋkəfəˈkeɪʃən/, *n.*

**zincite** /ˈzɪŋkaɪt/, *n.* native zinc oxide, ZnO, a brittle deep red to orange-yellow mineral, usu. massive or granular, and an important ore of zinc.

**zinckenite** /ˈzɪŋkənaɪt/, *n.* →**zinkenite.**

**zincograph** /ˈzɪŋkəgræf, -graf/, *n.* **1.** a zinc plate produced by zincography. **2.** a print from such a plate.

**zincography** /zɪŋkˈɒgrəfi/, *n.* the art or process of producing a printing surface on a zinc plate, esp. of producing one in relief by etching away unprotected parts with acid. – **zincographer,** *n.* – **zincographic** /zɪŋkəˈgræfɪk/, **zincographical** /zɪŋkəˈgræfɪkəl/, *adj.*

**zinc ointment** /ˈzɪŋk ɔɪntmənt/, *n.* a skin ointment composed of paraffin, white petroleum, and 20 per cent of zinc oxide.

**zincous** /ˈzɪŋkəs/, *adj.* pertaining to zinc.

**zinc oxide** /zɪŋk ˈɒksaɪd/, *n.* a compound of zinc and oxygen, ZnO, having a mild antiseptic and astringent action, used for the treatment of certain skin diseases, and as a pigment.

**zinc pyridinethione** /– ˌpaɪrədəˈniθioʊn/, *n.* an organic complex of zinc used to treat dandruff.

**zinc-spinel** /ˈzɪŋk-spɪnəl/, *n.* →**gahnite.**

**zinc white** /zɪŋk ˈwaɪt/, *n.* a white pigment consisting of zinc oxide, used in paints.

**zinc yellow** /– ˈjɛloʊ/, *n.* a yellow pigment consisting of **zinc chromate,** $ZnCrO_4$, used in paints. Also, **zinc chrome.**

**zing** /zɪŋ/, *n.* **1.** a sharp singing sound. **2.** *Colloq.* vitality; enthusiasm: *she has lots of zing.* *–interj.* **3.** (used to imitate a sharp singing sound.) [imitative] – **zingy,** *adj.*

**zingara sauce** /ˌzɪŋgarə ˈsɔs/, *n.* a rich sauce for meat or poultry, made with tomato and mushroom, and flavoured with madeira. Also, **gipsy sauce.** [It., fem. of *zingaro* gipsy]

**zinkenite** /ˈzɪŋkənaɪt/, *n.* a steel grey mineral with metallic lustre, lead antimony sulphide ($PbSb_2S_4$). Also, **zinckenite.** [G *Zinkenit,* named after J.K.L. *Zincken,* 1790-1862, German mineralogist]

**zinnia** /ˈzɪniə/, *n.* any of the annual plants of the genus *Zinnia,* esp. the colourful, cultivated varieties of *Z. elegans,* native to Mexico. [NL, named after J.G. *Zinn,* 1727-59, German botanist]

**Zion** /ˈzaɪən/, *n.* **1.** a hill or mount of Jerusalem, the site of the Temple. **2.** the Israelites. **3.** the Jewish people. **4.** Israel as the national home of the Jews. **5.** the theocracy, or Church of God. **6.** heaven as the final gathering place of true believers. Also, **Sion.** [ME and OE *Sion,* from LL (Vulgate), from Gk (Septuagint), from Heb. *tsīyōn*]

**Zionism** /ˈzaɪənɪzəm/, *n.* a worldwide movement founded with the purpose of establishing a national home for the Jews in Palestine, which now provides support to the state of Israel. – **Zionist,** *n., adj.* – **Zionistic** /zaɪənˈɪstɪk/, *adj.*

**zip** /zɪp/, *n., v.,* **zipped, zipping.** **1.** Also, **zip-fastener.** a fastener consisting of an interlocking device set along two edges to unite (or separate) them when an attached piece sliding between them is pulled, and used in place of buttons, hooks, or the like, on clothing, bags, etc. **2.** *Colloq.* a sudden, brief hissing sound, as of a bullet. **3.** energy or vim. *–v.i.* **4.** *Colloq.* to make or move with a zip. **5.** to proceed with energy. *–v.t.* **6.** to fasten with a zip (fol. by *up*). [imitative]

**zipcode** /ˈzɪpkoʊd/, *n. U.S.* →**postcode.**

**zip-fastener** /zɪp-ˈfasnə/, *n.* →**zip** (def. 1).

**zipper** /ˈzɪpə/, *n.* **1.** →**zip** (def. 1). *–v.t.* **2.** to provide with a zipper.

**zippy** /ˈzɪpi/, *adj.,* **-pier, -piest.** *Colloq.* lively; bright.

**zircon** /ˈzɜkɒn/, *n.* a common mineral, zirconium silicate, $ZrSiO_4$, occurring in square prismatic crystals or grains of various colours, usu. opaque, used as a refractory when opaque and as a gem when transparent. [earlier *cicon,* var. of JARGON[2], ? from Pers. *zargūn* gold-coloured]

**zirconate** /ˈzɜkəneɪt/, *n.* any of various compounds formed by combining oxides, hydroxides, nitrates, etc., of other metals with similar zirconium compounds at high temperatures.

**zirconia** /zɜˈkoʊniə/, *n.* an oxide of zirconium, $ZrO_2$, notable for its infusibility, used as a pigment, abrasive and refractory. [NL. See ZIRCON]

**zirconium** /zɜˈkoʊniəm/, *n.* a metallic element found combined in zircon, etc., resembling titanium chemically, used in steel metallurgy, as a scavenger, as a refractory, and to create opacity in vitreous enamel. *Symbol:* Zr; *at. wt:* 91.22; *at. no.:* 40; *sp. gr.:* 6.4 at 20°C. [NL. See ZIRCON] – **zirconic** /zɜˈkɒnɪk/, *adj.*

**zirconyl** /ˈzɜkənɪl/, *adj.* containing the radical ZrO.

**zit** /zɪt/, *n. Colloq.* **1.** a pimple. **2.** (*pl.*) acne.

**zither** /ˈzɪðə/, *n.* a musical folk instrument consisting of a flat soundbox with numerous strings stretched over it, which is placed on a horizontal surface and played with a plectrum and the fingertips. [G, from L *cithara.* See CITHARA] – **zitherist,** *n.*

zither

**zithern** /ˈzɪθən/, *n.* **1.** →**cittern.** **2.** →**zither.**

**zittern** /ˈzɪtn/, *n.* →**cittern.**

**zizith** /ˈtsɪtsɪs, ˈtsitsit/, *n.pl.* the fringes or tassels of entwined blue and white threads at the four corners of the tallith. [Heb.]

**zizz** /zɪz/, *n. Colloq.* a nap; sleep.

**zloty** /ˈzlɒti/, *n., pl.* **-tys,** (*collectively*) **-ty.** the monetary unit of Poland. [Pol.: lit., golden]

**Zn,** *Chem.* zinc.

**-zoa,** plural combining form naming zoological groups as in *Protozoa.* [NL, pl. See ZOON]

**zod.**, zodiac.

**zodiac** /ˈzoʊdiæk/, *n.* **1.** an imaginary belt of the heavens, extending about 8° on each side of the ecliptic, within which are the apparent paths of the sun, moon, and principal planets. It contains twelve constellations and hence twelve divisions (called *signs*), each division, however, because of the precession of the equinoxes, now containing the constellation west of the one from which it took its name. **2.** a circular or elliptical diagram representing this belt, and usu. containing pictures of the animals, etc., which are associated with the constellations and signs. **3.** *Rare.* a circuit or round. [ME, from L *zōdiacus,* from Gk *zōidiakós* (*kýklos*) circle of the signs, from *zôion* animal] – **zodiacal** /zoʊˈdaɪəkəl/, *adj.*

zodiac(def. 2)

**zodiacal light** /zoʊˌdaɪəkəl ˈlaɪt, ˌzoʊdiækəl/, *n.* a luminous tract in the sky, seen in the west after sunset or in the east before sunrise and supposed to be the light reflected from a cloud of meteoric matter revolving round the sun. A faint extension of this light along the ecliptic is called the **zodiacal band.**

**zoetrope** /ˈzoʊitroʊp/, *n.* an optical device consisting of a drum with a sequence of pictures on the inside and slits through which the viewer looks. When the drum is spun an illusion of a single moving picture is obtained; wheel of life. [Trademark]

**zoisite** /ˈzɔɪsaɪt/, *n.* a mineral, aluminium silicate of calcium, which crystallises in the orthorhombic system. [named after the discoverer, Baron *Zois* von Edelstein, 1747-1819, Slovenian mineralogist]

**Zollner's lines** /ˈzɒlnəz laɪnz/, *n.pl.* parallel lines, intersected by short oblique lines, which appear to converge or diverge. [named after J.K.F. *Zöllner,* 1834-82, German physicist]

**Zollverein** /ˈtsɒlfəraɪn/, *n.* a customs or similar trading union or arrangement between a number of states. [G, from *Zoll* tax, TOLL[2] + *Verein* union; orig. with ref. to a union which by 1844 included practically all German states]

**zombie** /ˈzɒmbi/, *n.* **1.** the python god among certain West Africans. **2.** the snake god worshipped in the voodoo ceremonies in the West Indies and certain parts of the southern U.S. **3.** a supernatural force which brings a corpse to physical life. **4.** a dead body brought to life in this way. **5.** a person thought to resemble the walking dead. **6.** (*derog.*) a person having no independent judgment, intelligence, etc. Also, **zombi.** [West African (Kongo) *zumbi* good-luck fetish] – **zombiism,** *n.*

**zonal** /ˈzoʊnəl/, *adj.* **1.** pertaining to a zone or zones. **2.** of the nature of a zone. Also, **zonary.** – **zonally,** *adv.*

**zonal soil** /– ˈsɔɪl/, *n.* one of a group of mature soils in the formation of which climate and vegetation have played a dominant part.

**zonate** /ˈzoʊneɪt/, *adj.* **1.** marked with a zone or zones, as of colour, texture, or the like. **2.** arranged in a zone or zones. Also, **zonated.**

**zonation** /zoʊnˈeɪʃən/, *n.* **1.** zonate state or condition. **2.** arrangement or distribution in zones.

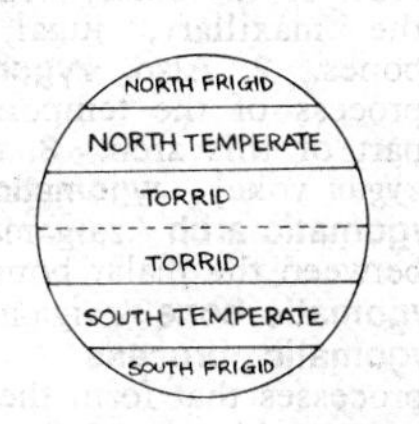

zones (def. 2)

**zone** /zoʊn/, *n., v.,* **zoned, zoning.** –*n.* **1.** any continuous tract or area, which differs in some respect, or is distinguished for some purpose, from adjoining tracts or areas, or within which certain distinguishing circumstances exist or are established. **2.** *Geog.* any of five divisions of the earth's surface, bounded by lines parallel to the equator, and named according to the prevailing temperature (as the Torrid Zone, extending from the tropic of Cancer to the tropic of Capricorn; the North Temperate Zone, extending from the tropic of Cancer to the Arctic Circle; the South Temperate Zone, extending from the tropic of Capricorn to the Antarctic Circle; the North Frigid Zone, extending from the Arctic Circle to the North Pole; the South Frigid Zone, extending from the Antarctic Circle to the South Pole). **3.** *Ecol.* an area characterised by a particular set of organisms, which are determined by a particular set of environmental conditions, as an altitudinal belt on a mountain such as the alpine zone. **4.** *Geol.* a geological horizon. **5.** *Geom.* a part of the surface of a sphere included between two parallel planes. **6.** a ringlike or surrounding area, or one of a series of such areas, about a particular place, to all points within which a uniform charge is made for transport or some similar service. **7.** *U.S.* the total number of available railway terminals within a given circumference round a given shipping centre. **8.** an area or district under special restrictions or where certain conditions or circumstances prevail: *a military zone; parking-meter zone.* **9.** *Chiefly Poetic.* a girdle, belt, or cincture. –*v.t.* **10.** to encircle with or surround like a zone, girdle, or belt. **11.** to mark with zones or bands. **12.** to divide into zones, tracts or areas, as according to existing characteristics, or as distinguished for some purpose. [L *zōna,* from Gk *zṓnē* girdle]

**zone allowance** /ˈ– əlaʊəns/, *n.* an allowance paid to employees as an inducement to work in remote areas.

**zone-melting** /ˈzoʊn-mɛltɪŋ/, *n.* a process of purifying solids whereby a small portion is heated for a short time by moving it through a heated zone or by moving the zone along the solid. The process is employed to obtain very pure metals for use in transistors. Also, **zone-refining.**

**zoning** /ˈzoʊnɪŋ/, *n.* (of land) the marking out of an area of land with respect to its use.

**zonked** /zɒŋkt/, *adj. Colloq.* exhausted; faint with fatigue. Also, **zonked-out.**

**zonule** /ˈzoʊnjul/, *n.* a little zone, belt, or band. [NL *zōnula,* diminutive of L *zōna* girdle]

**zoo** /zu/, *n.* a park or other large enclosure in which live animals are kept for public exhibition; a zoological garden.

**zoo-,** a word element meaning 'living being', as in *zoochemistry.* [Gk *zōio-,* combining form of *zôion* animal]

**zoochemistry** /zoʊəˈkɛməstri/, *n.* the chemistry of the constituents of the animal body; animal chemistry. – **zoochemical** /zoʊəˈkɛmɪkəl/, *adj.*

**zoogamy** /zoʊˈɒgəmi/, *n.* reproduction by means of gametes; sexual reproduction. – **zoogamous,** *adj.*

**zoogeog.,** zoogeography.

**zoogeographic** /ˌzoʊədʒiəˈgræfɪk/, *adj.* of or pertaining to zoogeography. – **zoogeographical,** *adj.* – **zoogeographically,** *adv.*

**zoogeography** /zoʊədʒiˈɒgrəfi/, *n.* **1.** the science of the geographical distribution of animals. **2.** the study of the causes, effects, and other relations involved in such distributions. – **zoogeographer,** *n.*

**zoogloea** /zoʊəˈgliə/, *n.* a jelly-like mass or aggregate of bacteria formed when the cell walls swell through absorption of water and become contiguous. [ZOO- + *gloea* (Latinisation of Gk *gloía* glue)] – **zoogloeal,** *adj.*

**zoographic** /zoʊəˈgræfɪk/, *adj.* of or pertaining to zoography. – **zoographical,** *adj.* – **zoographically,** *adv.*

**zoography** /zoʊˈɒgrəfi/, *n.* that branch of zoology which deals with the description of animals.

**zooid** /ˈzoʊɔɪd/, *n.* **1.** *Biol.* any organic body or cell which is capable of spontaneous movement and of an existence more or less apart from or independent of the parent organism. **2.** *Zool.* **a.** any animal organism or individual capable of separate existence, and produced by fission, gemination or some method other than direct sexual reproduction. **b.** one of the individuals, as certain free-swimming medusas, which intervene in the alternation of generations between the products of proper sexual reproduction. **c.** any one of the recognisably distinct individuals or elements of a compound or colonial animal, whether detached or detachable or not. –*adj.* **3.** Also, **zooidal** /zoʊˈɔɪdl/. resembling or of the nature of an animal. [ZO(O)- + -OID]

**zool.,** **1.** zoological. **2.** zoologist. **3.** zoology.

**zoolatry** /zoʊˈɒlətri/, *n.* **1.** worship of animals. **2.** excessive attention to a domestic pet. – **zoolatrous,** *adj.*

**zoological** /zoʊə'lɒdʒɪkəl/, *adj.* **1.** of or pertaining to zoology. **2.** relating to or concerned with animals. Also, **zoologic.** – **zoologically,** *adv.*

**zoological garden** /– 'gadn/, *n.* (*oft. pl.*) a zoo.

**zoologist** /zoʊ'ɒlədʒəst/, *n.* one versed in zoology.

**zoology** /zoʊ'ɒlədʒi/, *n., pl.* **-gies. 1.** the science that treats of animals or the animal kingdom. **2.** a treatise on this subject. **3.** the animals existing in a particular region. [NL *zōologia* or NGk *zōiología.* See ZOO-, -LOGY]

**zoom** /zum/, *v.i.* **1.** to make a continuous humming sound. **2.** to move with this sound: *he zooms along in his new car.* **3.** (of prices) to rise rapidly. **4.** *Aeron.* to gain height in an aircraft, in a sudden climb, using the kinetic energy of the aircraft. **5.** *Films, Television, etc.* to use a zoom lens so as to make an object appear to approach (oft. fol. by *in*) or recede from the viewer. *–v.t.* **6.** to cause (an aeroplane) to zoom. **7.** to fly over (an obstacle) by zooming. *–n.* **8.** the act of zooming. [imitative]

**zoometry** /zoʊ'ɒmətri/, *n.* measurement of the proportionate lengths or sizes of the parts of animals. – **zoometric** /zoʊə'mɛtrɪk/, *adj.*

**zoomie** /'zumi/, *n. Colloq.* a fancy exhaust pipe on a motor car.

**zoom lens** /zum 'lɛnz/, *n.* (in a camera or projector) a lens system which can be adjusted so as to give continuously varying magnification of an image without loss of focus.

**zoomorphic** /zoʊə'mɔfɪk/, *adj.* **1.** ascribing animal form or attributes to beings or things not animal; representing a deity in the form of an animal. **2.** characterised by or involving such ascription or representation. **3.** representing or using animal forms.

**zoomorphism** /zoʊə'mɔfɪzəm/, *n.* **1.** zoomorphic representation, as in ornament. **2.** zoomorphic conception, as of a deity.

**zoon** /'zoʊɒn/, *n., pl.* **zoa** /'zoʊə/, **zoons.** any of the individuals of a compound organism. [NL, from Gk *zôion* animal]

**-zoon,** a combining form of **zoon.**

**zoonosis** /zoʊə'noʊsəs/, *n., pl.* **-noses** /-'noʊsiz/. any disease which is communicable to man from another animal species.

**zoophile** /'zoʊəfaɪl/, *n.* one who loves animals, esp. one who is opposed to vivisection or other such experimentation. – **zoophilism** /zoʊ'ɒfəlɪzəm/, *n.*

**zoophilous** /zoʊ'ɒfələs/, *adj.* **1.** *Bot.* adapted to pollination by the agency of animals. **2.** loving animals. **3.** (of insects) feeding on animals.

**zoophobia** /zoʊə'foʊbiə/, *n.* morbid fear of animals.

**zoophyte** /'zoʊəfaɪt/, *n.* any of various animals resembling a plant, as a coral, a sea-anemone, etc. [NL *zōophyton,* from Gk. See ZOO-, -PHYTE] – **zoophytic** /zoʊə'fɪtɪk/, **zoophytical** /zoʊə'fɪtɪkəl/, *adj.*

**zooplankton** /zoʊə'plæŋktən/, *n.* animal plankton.

**zooplasty** /'zoʊəplæsti/, *n.* the transplanting of living tissue from a lower animal to the human body. – **zooplastic** /zoʊə'plæstɪk/, *adj.*

**zoosporangium** /zoʊəspə'rændʒiəm/, *n., pl.* **-gia** /-dʒiə/. a sporangium or spore case in which zoospores are produced. – **zoosporangial,** *adj.*

**zoospore** /'zoʊəspɔ/, *n.* **1.** *Bot.* an asexual spore, produced by certain algae and some fungi, capable of moving about by means of flagella. **2.** *Zool.* any of the minute motile flagelliform or amoeboid bodies which issue from the sporocyst of certain protozoans. – **zoosporic** /zoʊə'spɔrɪk/, **zoosporous** /zoʊ'ɒspərəs, zoʊə'spɔrəs/, *adj.*

**zootomy** /zoʊ'ɒtəmi/, *n.* the dissection or the anatomy of animals. [NL *zōotomia.* See ZOO-, -TOMY] – **zootomic** /zoʊə'tɒmɪk/, **zootomical** /zoʊə'tɒmɪkəl/, *adj.* – **zootomically** /zoʊə'tɒmɪkli/, *adv.* – **zootomist,** *n.*

**zootoxin** /zoʊə'tɒksən/, *n.* any poison excreted by an animal, as snake venom. – **zootoxic,** *adj.*

**zori** /'zɔri/, *n.* a low, flat Japanese sandal having thongs passing between the two inner toes. [Jap.]

**zoril** /'zɒrəl/, *n.* a weasel-like animal of southern Africa, *Ictonyx striatus,* resembling a skunk, and capable of emitting a fetid odour. Also, **zorilla** /zɒ'rɪlə/. [F *zorille,* from Sp. *zorrilla,* diminutive of *zorra* fox]

**Zoroastrian** /zɒroʊ'æstriən/, *adj.* **1.** pertaining to Zoroastrianism. *–n.* **2.** one of the followers of Zoroastrianism.

**Zoroastrianism** /zɒroʊ'æstriənɪzəm/, *n.* a strongly ethical code which teaches a continuous struggle between Good (Ormazd), and Evil (Angra Mainyu). Also, **Zoroastrism.** [after *Zoroaster* (also Zarathustra), fl. *c.* 600 B.C., Persian religious teacher]

**zoster** /'zɒstə/, *n.* →**shingles.** [L, from Gk: girdle]

**zot** /zɒt/, *v.,* **zotted, zotting.** *Colloq. –v.i.* **1.** to depart quickly (usu. fol. by *off*). *–v.t.* **2.** to knock, or kill: *quickly, zot that fly.* **3.** *interj.* (an exclamation expressing suddenness): *when suddenly, zot, out jumped a red kangaroo.*

**zounds** /zaʊndz, zundz/, *interj. Archaic.* (a minced oath, often used as a mere emphatic exclamation, as of surprise, indignation, or anger.) [short for *by God's wounds*]

**ZPG** /zɛd pi 'dʒi/, zero population growth.

**Zr,** *Chem.* zirconium.

**zucchetto** /tsu'kɛtoʊ, zu-/, *n., pl.* **-tos.** a small, round skullcap worn by Roman Catholic ecclesiastics, a priest's being black, a bishop's violet, a cardinal's red, and the pope's white. [incorrect var. of It. *zucchetta* cap, diminutive of *zucca* gourd, head]

**zucchini** /zə'kini, zu-/, *n., pl.* **-ni, -nis.** a small vegetable marrow, usu. harvested when very young; baby marrow; courgette. [It., pl. of *zucchino*]

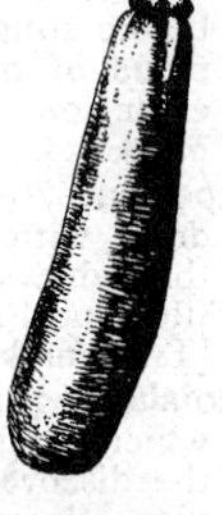
zucchini

**Zulu** /'zulu/, *n., pl.* **-lus, -lu,** *adj. –n.* **1.** a Bantu people of south-eastern Africa, occupying the coastal region between Natal and Lourènço Marques. **2.** a member of the Zulu nation. **3.** their language. *–adj.* **4.** of or pertaining to the Zulus or their language.

**zulu time** /'zulu taɪm/, *n. Mil. Colloq.* →**Greenwich Mean Time.**

**zwieback** /'zwaɪbæk, 'zwi-/, *n.* a kind of bread cut into slices and dried in the oven. [G: twice-baked. Cf. BISCUIT]

**zwitterion** /'tsvɪtəraɪən/, *n.* an ion carrying both a positive and a negative charge. [G *Zwitter* half-breed + ION] – **zwitterionic** /tsvɪtəraɪ'ɒnɪk/, *adj.*

**zygapophysis** /zɪgə'pɒfəsəs, zaɪgə-/, *n., pl.* **-ses** /-siz/. one of the articular processes upon the neural arch of a vertebra, usu. occurring in two pairs, one anterior and the other posterior, and serving to interlock each vertebra with the one above and below. [ZYGO- + APOPHYSIS] – **zygapophyseal** /ˌzɪgæpə'fɪziəl/, **zygapophysial,** *adj.*

**zygo-,** a word element meaning 'yoke', esp. referring to shape, as in *zygodactyl.* Also, before vowels, **zyg-.** [Gk, combining form of *zygón*]

**zygodactyl** /zaɪgə'dæktl, zɪgə-/, *adj.* **1.** Also, **zygodactylous.** (of a bird or bird's foot) having the toes disposed in pairs, one pair before and one pair behind on each foot. *–n.* **2.** a zygodactyl bird. – **zygodactylism,** *n.*

zygodactyl foot

**zygoma** /zaɪ'goʊmə, zɪ-/, *n., pl.* **-mata** /-mətə/. **1.** the bony arch below the orbit of the skull, which is formed by the maxillary, jugal, and temporal bones. **2.** Also, **zygomatic process.** a process of the temporal bone forming part of this arch. **3.** the jugal bone. [NL, from Gk, from *zygón* yoke] – **zygomatic** /zaɪgoʊ'mætɪk, zɪgoʊ-/, *adj.*

**zygomatic arch** /ˌzaɪgəmætɪk 'atʃ/, *n.* the narrow arch of bone between the malar bone and the temporal bone of mammals.

**zygomatic bone** /zaɪgəˌmætɪk 'boʊn/, *n.* →**malar** (def. 2.)

**zygomatic process** /– 'proʊsɛs/, *n.* any of several bony processes that form the zygomatic arch.

**zygomorphic** /zaɪgoʊ'mɔfɪk, zɪgoʊ-/, *adj.* (of flowers, etc.) divisible into similar or symmetrical halves by one plane only. Cf. **actinomorphic.** Also, **zygomorphous.** – **zygomorphism, zygomorphy,** *n.*

**zygophyte** /'zaɪgəfaɪt, 'zɪgə-/, *n.* a plant which is reproduced by means of zygospores.

**zygopteran** /zaɪ'gɒptərən/, *adj.* **1.** of or pertaining to the suborder Zygoptera, containing the smaller dragonflies. *–n.* **2.** a member of the Zygoptera.

**zygosis** /zaɪˈgoʊsəs, zɪ-/, *n.* the coming together of two apparently identical cells as a prelude to the fusion of two similar gametes; conjugation.

**zygospore** /ˈzaɪgəspɔ, ˈzɪgə-/, *n.* a cell formed by fusion of two similar gametes, as in certain algae and fungi.

**zygote** /ˈzaɪgoʊt, ˈzɪgoʊt/, *n.* **1.** the cell produced by the union of two gametes. **2.** the individual developing from such a cell. [Gk *zygōtós* yoked] – **zygotic** /zaɪˈgɒtɪk, zɪ-/, *adj.*

**zygotene** /ˈzaɪgətin/, *n.* a phase of meiotic cell division in which the chromosomes come together in pairs.

**zymase** /ˈzaɪmeɪz, -meɪs/, *n.* an extract obtained from yeast that is capable of fermenting sugar to alcohol and carbon dioxide. It was originally thought to contain a single enzyme, but it is now known that more than a dozen enzymes are involved in the fermentation process. [F, from Gk *zýmē* leaven; modelled on DIASTASE]

**zyme** /zaɪm/, *n. Obs.* the specific principle regarded as the cause of a zymotic disease. Cf. **zymosis.** [Gk: leaven]

**zymo-**, a word element meaning 'leaven', as in *zymogen.* Also, before vowels, **zym-**. [combining form representing Gk *zŷmē*]

**zymogen** /ˈzaɪmədʒən/, *n.* **1.** *Biochem.* the inactive form in which many enzymes, particularly proteolytic enzymes, are made and stored. **2.** *Biol.* any of various bacterial organisms which produce enzymes. Also, **zymogene.** [G. See ZYMO-, -GEN]

**zymogenesis** /zaɪmoʊˈdʒɛnəsəs/, *n.* the conversion of a zymogen into an enzyme.

**zymogenic** /zaɪmoʊˈdʒɛnɪk/, *adj.* of or pertaining to a zymogen.

**zymogenic organism** /– ˈɔgənɪzəm/, *n.* any micro-organism producing an enzyme which causes fermentation.

**zymometer** /zaɪˈmɒmətə/, *n.* an instrument for ascertaining the degree of fermentation.

**zymosis** /zaɪˈmoʊsəs/, *n., pl.* **-ses** /-siz/. **1.** an infectious or contagious disease. **2.** *Obs.* a process analogous to fermentation, by which certain infectious and contagious diseases were supposed to be produced. [NL, from Gk: fermentation]

**zymotic** /zaɪˈmɒtɪk/, *adj.* **1.** pertaining to, or caused by or as if by fermentation. Cf. **zymosis.** **2.** pertaining to a zymotic disease. [Gk *zymōtikós* causing fermentation]

**zymotic disease** /ˈ– dəziz/, *n.* an infectious disease, as smallpox, typhoid fever, etc., which was regarded as due to the presence in the body of a morbific principle acting in a manner analogous to fermentation.

**zymurgy** /ˈzaɪmɜdʒi/, *n.* that branch of chemistry which deals with fermentation, as in winemaking, brewing, distilling, the preparation of yeast, etc. [ZYM(O)- + -URGY]

**zzz** /zəz/, *n. Colloq.* a sleep. [from the convention used, esp. by cartoonists, to represent sleep or the sound of snoring]

# Appendixes


Guide to Usage 2027

Signs and Symbols 2035

- Astrology 2035
- Astronomy 2035
- Biology 2036
- Chemistry 2036
- Language 2037
- Mathematics 2038
- Miscellaneous 2039
- Roman Numerals 2039

Proofreaders' Marks 2040

Weights and Measures 2041

- Metric Conversion Table 2041
- Fraction Conversion Table 2042
- International System of Units 2043
- Paper Sizes 2044
- Meat Cuts 2045

Foreign Alphabets 2046

Ancient Alphabets 2047

Indo-European Languages 2048

Abbreviations used in Etymologies 2049

# Guide to Usage

## I. Full stop or period (.)

1. The full stop is used to indicate the end of any sentence other than an exclamation or question. Sentences which for politeness or other reasons are worded as exclamations or questions may also end in a full stop:

That is a good idea.
Would you pass me that book please.

A declarative sentence which contains an indirect question ends in a full stop, not a question mark:

He wanted to know when I would arrive.

2. The full stop is also used after an abbreviated word:

abbrev. (abbreviation) Brit. (British)
cf. (Latin *confer* compare)

The Commonwealth *Style Manual* distinguishes between abbreviations and contractions, and does not place a full stop after a contraction. A contraction is any shortened form of a word in which the last letter of the full word is shown:

Mr ( [originally] master) Dr (doctor)

Abbreviations do not take a full stop if they are regarded as symbols:

N (north) m (metre) H (hydrogen)

There is an increasing tendency to omit full stops in abbreviations of widely-known organisations:

ACTU UNESCO

## II. Question mark or mark of interrogation (?)

1. The question mark is used to end an interrogative sentence, phrase, or word standing alone:

What do you mean? Under there?

It is not used after an interrogative subordinate clause:

I asked what you meant.

2. The question mark is also used to indicate uncertainty about stated facts:

Captain William Bligh 1753? – 1817

## III. Exclamation mark (!)

1. The exclamation mark is used to end an emphatic utterance of surprise, admiration, disgust, or other strong feeling. The utterance need not necessarily be a finite sentence:

Good heavens! What a hot day!

2. The exclamation mark may also be used to lend emphasis to a command (imperative sentence). It is not necessary to place an exclamation mark after every imperative sentence:

'Come here this instant!' he cried.
Please give me that book.

## IV. Comma (,)

The comma is the most frequent mark of punctuation. Its basic function is to separate or set off within a sentence. We may consider this function under three headings.

1. Uses of the comma to separate off introductory matter.

a. The comma is used to separate introductory words of address, hesitation, transition, interjection or the like from the main sentence:

John, what are you doing?
Ah, here's the train.

In some cases where the introductory or transitional word is very closely linked with the phrase, clause or sentence that follows, the comma may be omitted:

Nevertheless I dislike it, I tell you.

In such cases the whole phrase, clause or sentence may be regarded as forming part of a transition or introduction.

b. It is also used to separate off a word or phrase which has been placed first for emphasis or for some other reason:

Scientifically, what he said had no basis in fact.
Hopeful about the outcome of the negotiations, he asked for a summit conference.

c. It may be used as a convenience to the reader to show where one phrase or clause ends and the next begins:

If, after hearing the delegate speak, the ACTU conference remains unconvinced, you may count on me, as your representative, to press for militant action.

There is, however, no need to use a comma after a short introductory phrase or clause:

If you like we'll go soon.

2. Use of the comma in lists, sets and groups.

a. The comma is used to separate three or more items in a series:

In this class the children are taught English, Mathematics, History and Art.

Although some writers insert a comma before the final conjunction (*and*, *or*), the modern tendency is to leave it out.

b. Groups of adjectives preceding the noun they modify are separated by commas only if they form a series of separate ideas:

yellow, white, purple, and pink flowers

But:

interesting colonial buildings

In the latter example the adjective 'interesting' may be said to modify not only the noun 'buildings' but also the phrase 'colonial buildings'. Mixtures of both types of groups of adjectives may occur:

yellow, white, purple, and pink little flowers

A rule of thumb is that if the word 'and' could be meaningfully placed between two adjectives, then a comma is appropriate.

c. A comma may be used to divide two independent main clauses linked by a coordinating conjunction:

A large number of people are concerned about pollution, but very few are prepared to take active steps to combat it.

The comma in such cases is optional, and should be used only as an aid to sense or clarity.

3. Restrictive and non-restrictive.

a. One of the most important functions of the comma is to set off a non-restrictive phrase or clause. Its absence from a restrictive phrase or clause is equally significant. A restrictive phrase or clause is one whose meaning restricts or forms an essential part of the rest of the sentence and which should therefore not be divided from the rest of the sentence by commas. The relative clause in:

My daughter who is six has blonde hair

is restrictive in that it implies that I have other daughters who are not six, and this sentence is restricted to the one who is. On the other hand:

My daughter, who is six, has blonde hair

does not restrict, but merely gives further information about my daughter.

In non-restrictive clauses and phrases commas should be placed before and after the clause or phrase:

Phillip and Hunter, who were capable administrators, ruled the early colony well.

But:

Governors who were capable administrators became increasingly rare as the nineteenth century advanced.

b. Words and phrases in apposition, which are by definition non-restrictive, should be preceded and followed by commas:

Cairns, one of Australia's most northerly cities, is a popular tourist centre.

c. Words, phrases and clauses introduced parenthetically into a sentence may be set off by commas:

That is, however, not completely accurate.

d. See also section XIII 1 (a) on quotes.

## V. Semicolon (;)

The semicolon is a mark of punctuation midway in function between the full stop and the comma. Its function, like theirs, is to separate. It is used to separate main clauses not joined by a conjunction:

Hitler expected to defeat Russia within six months; in this expectation he was disappointed.

2. It is also used to separate main clauses linked by a conjunctive adverb such as *nevertheless*, *therefore*, *moreover* and conjunctive adverbial phrases such as *all the same*.

The plan has not worked; all the same, it was worth trying.

3. A semicolon is also used to separate items in a series when there are already series within the items:

> This book contains information about distribution and habitat; form, dimensions and colouring; life-cycle; and economic significance.

In such cases the use of the semicolon avoids ambiguity.

VI. **Colon** (:)

The main function of the colon is to introduce.

1. It is used to introduce a series or list of items or examples:

> Four named trains are better known to Melburnians than any others: the *Overland*, the *Southern Aurora*, the *Spirit of Progress* and *Puffing Billy*.

The colon is used where there is a grammatical hiatus, and should not be placed before a list of items forming the direct or indirect object of a verb, the complement of the verb to be, or some other integral part of a sentence structure:

> The best-known named trains in Melbourne are the *Overland*, the *Southern Aurora*, the *Spirit of Progress* and *Puffing Billy*.

2. The colon is commonly used after some introductory form of words such as the phrase 'as follows', whether before speech, a list of items, a formal statement or the like:

> His precise words were as follows: 'I wish to place on record my dissent.'
> The following men are to parade at 0930 hours: Adams, Jones, Schulz, Williamson.

Some writers use a capital letter after a colon if what follows is a complete sentence. We recommend, however, that a lower-case letter be preferred after a colon except in direct quotations.

3. A colon is used to mark off that part of the sentence which enlarges on or summarises that which preceded it. It is also used to separate two contrastive clauses:

> His life was short: he was born in 1902, was a healthy boy, but was killed in 1908.
> Wealth is good: health is better.

4. A colon is also used in dialogue, in verbatim court reports, plays, etc., following the name of the speaker:

> Macduff: Your royal father's murder'd.
> Malcolm: O, by whom?

VII. **Parentheses** or **round brackets** ( )

1. Parentheses are used to enclose matter which does not form part of the flow of thought in the sentence or paragraph in which it occurs:

> Hugo Wolf wrote his *Italian Song Book* in the year 1891. (The text is not in Italian, but is a German translation of some Italian poems.) This is considered by many musicians to be the culmination of the art of *Lieder*.
>
> The comma, as I have said (see above), is easily misused.

Note that other punctuation may accompany parentheses. If the mark of punctuation applies only to the matter inside the parentheses then it comes before the close parenthesis. If it applies to the text outside the part in parentheses it is placed after the close parenthesis.

2. Series of numbers or letters enumerating parts of a list or series are placed within parentheses:

> The aims of a good teacher are (1) to help his pupils grow into integrated adults, (2) to give them an understanding of the subject he is teaching, (3) to extend human understanding of his own subject.

3. Parentheses are also used to enclose explanatory matter within the sentence which does not form part of the sentence itself:

> When he arrived at Manly (Brisbane), he decided to stay the night.

4. Parentheses are placed round an *-s* plural marker to avoid a cumbrous circumlocution, showing that a noun may or may not be plural, depending on context.

> A teacher must aim to impart an understanding of the subject(s) he is teaching.

VIII. **Square brackets** [ ]

Square brackets are used to indicate a deliberate interpolation in a text. The interpolation may be one of the following:

1. Correction or comment on a text that is for some reason reproduced verbatim:

Mussolini was killed in 1944 [1945—ed.].

2. Indication that the matter within the brackets is substituted for other words in the original version:

And [God] was made flesh.

3. The addition of some explanatory words:

This failing [making misleading statements in public] destroyed his political career.

4. The addition of some comment within the text of a verbatim transcript:

The Witness: Your Honour, I don't know what the word 'obscene' means. [Laughter in Court.]

5. Square brackets are used as 'brackets within brackets', as a substitute for parentheses:

$3x(24y - [2x + 3]) = 119$.
Their behaviour, which suggested arrogance (some people [in Fremantle especially] would put it more strongly), surprised him.

### IX. Dash or em rule (—)

The dash is used mainly to indicate interruption.

1. It is used, especially in writing direct speech, to show that a sentence remains unfinished:

'Now George, I don't want you to—'
'I shall do what I please,' he cut in.

2. It is used to indicate an interruption in the grammatical flow of a sentence, or an abrupt change of idea, subject, etc.

'Last Tuesday I was at the—but I don't think I ought to tell you about that.'

3. It is used to indicate hesitation or indistinctness in speech:

'I—er—um—well, frankly, I can't help you.'

Ellipsis may also be used to indicate hesitation. See section XI below.

4. It is used to show that a sentence is interrupted by some parenthetical observation. Enclosing such an observation in dashes rather than commas or parentheses lends more emphasis to it.

The American president John F. Kennedy—the product of the great Kennedy political machine—was a victim of his own image.

5. A dash may be used to replace a word or part of a word which is taboo:

'What the — are you doing?'

6. Another use of the dash is to join two ends or points of a route, date, or the like:

the Fremantle—Rottnest Island ferry
I shall be flying Sydney—Bahrein—London.

In such cases a dash is always appropriate; a hyphen may be confusing. However, in such cases and in giving dates and other numerals the convention in printing is to use a slightly shorter dash (en rule):

1797–1805 15–27 May

### X. Hyphen (-)

The principal function of the hyphen is to join two words or parts of words together. It is often used excessively and inconsistently. The current trend is to avoid using the hyphen except where there is a real justification for it. The functions of the hyphen are considered here under three headings: joining for syntactical reasons, joining for morphological reasons, and use of the hyphen as a separator.

1. Use of the hyphen to join two words or word elements for syntactical reasons.

The hyphen is used to join two or more words in order to make them function syntactically as a single word.

a. Attributive phrases take a hyphen where the second (or main) element is a noun. The same phrases used predicatively or independently do not take a hyphen. Thus:

a white-goods salesman
a machine-tool minder

But:

a salesman for white goods
a man who minds a machine tool

The purpose of the hyphen in the first pair of examples is to make clear that what is meant is not a 'goods salesman who is white', or a 'tool-minder that is a machine'. In other words, the phrases 'white-goods' and 'machine-tool' have precisely the same syntactic function as an attributive adjective.

b. Phrases consisting of noun plus modifier take a hyphen whatever their position in the sentence:

a computer-readable tape
a human-eye-readable print-out

The reason for using a hyphen in such positions is to make clear that the noun is subordinate to the modifier—a reversal of the usual pattern of English.

c. Adverbs should never be hyphenated with adjectives:

beautifully made shoes

d. However, there is an exception. The adverbs 'ill' and 'well' (also 'better', 'best', 'worse', 'worst') are commonly hyphenated with adjectives, but only in attributive positions:

A well-known person is coming to see you.

A worse-shaped handle I have never known.

But:

He is very well known.
This handle is worse shaped than the others.

'Well' and 'ill' are not hyphenated to nouns which they may modify:

Ill feeling arose between them.

e. Some other compounds take hyphens if placed before the noun they modify (i.e., in attributive positions):

a hand-to-mouth existence

But:

They lived hand to mouth.

f. The common names of certain plants are composed of phrases which in another context would have a quite different meaning. Such names are hyphenated:

Bacon-and-eggs is a name for a number of Australian plants.
Wait-a-while is a creeper with many jagged thorns.

2. Use of the hyphen to join two or more words or word elements for morphological reasons.

a. Certain compound nouns are customarily hyphenated, although other compounds of the same grammatical type are customarily written or printed as one word (set solid). Thus:

has-been march-past

But:

newsreel eyelid lyrebird

b. Agentive and gerundive compounds are normally hyphenated:

marble-worker stone-quarrying

but:

engineering worker, etc.

are not, for they are not agent compounds; nor are:

watchmaker bookbinder

on the grounds of common usage. The more common the compound, the more likely it is to be set solid. Compounds consisting of single-syllabled elements are more likely to be hyphenated than those made up of polysyllabic words.

c. Nouns and adjectives formed from prepositional verbs take a hyphen:

to go ahead give the go-ahead
a go-ahead young man

There are a number of exceptions, in which the noun or adjective compound is set solid in common usage—usually because the word is a very common one:

breakthrough changeover

d. The following prefixes are customarily hyphenated to the word with which they are compounded:

ex-: ex-directory, ex-serviceman, ex-wife
non-: non-restrictive, non-swimmer
self-: self-assurance, self-discipline

The following prefixes are customarily set solid with the main word element, unless the latter begins with a capital letter, in which case a hyphen is used:

anti: anti-American feeling, anticorrosive
co: coaxial, copilot
counter: counteract, counterproposal
neo: neo-Gothic, neoclassicism
pan: pan-Slavism, panplegia

The hyphen is used when it is necessary to distinguish between pairs of words whose form would otherwise give rise to ambiguity:

recover (to regain health)

and

re-cover (to cover again)

As a general rule, suffixes are set solid with the rest of the word. Some adjectives which follow the noun are regarded by some writers as suffixes and hyphenated to the main noun—e.g. 'president-elect', 'secretary-designate'.

e. Hyphens are used to avoid awkward juxtapositions of the same letter:

damp-proof counter-revolutionary

or misleading combinations of letters:

infra-red re-election

3. Use of the hyphen as a separator.

a. In spelling out a compound number from 21 to 99, a hyphen is used:

twenty-one one hundred and ninety-two

b. In spelling out a fraction, a hyphen is sometimes used between the numerator and the denominator:

two-thirds eight-seventeenths

The hyphen should never be used between numerator and denominator if one or other is a compound number:

one thirty-second forty-four fiftieths

c. The hyphen is used to divide part of a long word which falls at the end of a line from its continuation on the next line. The rules for the division of words are many and various. They usually take into account the etymological structure and the pronunciation of a word. Words consisting of one syllable only, such as 'stroked', should not be divided.

XI. **Leaders or Ellipsis** (. . .)

Leaders are used to indicate an omission in some quoted matter.

1. If the omission occurs at the beginning or in the middle of a sentence, the leaders consist of three full points:

Shaw wrote, '. . . this is a brilliant . . . book.'

2. Even if the omission occurs at the end of a sentence, three dots only are required:

Down with all traitors . . .

When the ellipsis is not part of quoted matter it should be placed outside the quotes:

'Down with all traitors'. . .

XII. **Apostrophe** (')

The apostrophe is used to indicate the omission of letters or figures, and to distinguish in writing the possessive case of nouns.

1. It is used to indicate the omission of a vowel and certain other letters where two words have been run together to form a single word:

he'll John'll come

Frequently the apostrophe distinguishes between two quite different pronunciations and senses of the same group of letters as *he'll* and *hell* or *I'll* and *ill*. The distinction in writing between *it's* (a contraction of *it is*) and *its* (possessive case of *it*) should be carefully observed.

2. Certain conventions are observed in the placing of the apostrophe in contractions derived from the negative adverb *not*:

can't couldn't ain't etc.

3. In certain contractions an apostrophe may be used to show where letters are omitted. This is done especially where the contracted form might be unclear or confused with another word, or where it is particularly desired to draw attention to the fact that the form given is a contraction:

e'er e'en m'f'g chemists

4. An apostrophe is also used to indicate the omission of numerals, especially of the century in a date:

the gay '90s back in '43

5. a. The addition of an apostrophe and an *s* is the regular way of forming the possessive of singular nouns, and certain indefinite pronouns:

a gentleman's gentleman anyone's guess

b. In the case of singular nouns which end in *-s*, the most usual practice is to add an *'s* as with other nouns.

Frances's meeting Idriess's books

But where obvious awkwardness would occur, and with certain Biblical and monosyllabic words, *s'* may be preferred.

Thucydides' history    Jesus' teachings
Keats' poetry

c. Plural nouns ending in *-s* form their possessive by the addition of an apostrophe alone:

the horses' hoofs    politicians' arguments

A few plural nouns, those which form their plural in some way other than the addition of *-s*, form their possessive plural by adding an apostrophe and an *s*:

the men's room    geese's wings

d. In indicating joint possession by more than one person or other proper noun, an apostrophe and *s* are added to the last name:

Paul and Anne's house

e. However, if the several individuals are all in individual possession of the named objects, an apostrophe and *s* are added to all nouns:

Paul's and Anne's clothes

6. An apostrophe is sometimes used before a plural *s* in forming plurals of figures and abbreviations, especially where there is possibility of confusion with other words:

8's and 9's    a's, e's, i's, o's, and u's

However, as long as there is no possibility of confusion, no apostrophe should be shown:

the 1940s    M.P.s    pros and cons

**XIII. Quotes, Quotation Marks, or Inverted Commas** (' ' or " ")

The primary use of quotes is to set off spoken words from the rest of the text. The modern practice is to prefer single quotes (' ') to double (" "), and this is the practice recommended here. This section will consider not only the use of quotes but also the conventions of all punctuation surrounding quoted matter.

1. In reporting speech, quotes are placed before and after the paragraph, sentence, phrase, or word quoted. If the quoted matter consists of more than one paragraph, a raised turned comma (') is placed at the beginning of each new paragraph, but a raised unturned comma (') is placed only at the end of the whole quotation.

a. A comma is placed at the end of quoted matter before the raised comma if what follows is a verb or expression of speech such as 'I said', 'he explained', 'they asked' and the word following the quotation begins with a lower-case letter, unless it is a proper noun:

'I've got indigestion,' said John.

b. However, if the last sentence in the quoted matter is a question or an exclamation, a question mark or exclamation mark is the point used, although the following word still begins with a lower-case letter:

'What are you doing?' he demanded.

c. If the verb of saying precedes quoted matter, it is followed by a comma, but the first word of the quoted matter begins with a capital:

He exclaimed, 'That is a very good idea.'

d. If the verb of saying falls in the middle of a sentence in the quoted matter, there is a comma before the first raised comma, and another one before the second raised turned comma, and both are followed by a lower-case letter:

'That,' said John, 'is a very good idea.'

If the punctuation following the quoted matter is applicable to the whole of the sentence and not just the quoted part, the punctuation is placed after the final raised comma:

What do you mean by 'I don't like it'?

In all other cases the punctuation is placed before the final raised comma:

'I believe . . .'

e. To give a quotation within a quotation, double quotes are used:

He asked, 'What do you mean by "no"?'

2. Quotes are also used to surround short passages quoted from a text, especially in the middle of a sentence:

> The words of Alfred Hill's song 'Ah, leave me not' may have been set to music more than once.

Longer quotes are generally preceded by a colon and set off in a new, indented paragraph.

3. Titles of essays, articles, chapters, etc., within a publication are usually placed within quotes, the name of the publication being italicised in print or underlined in type. Quotes may also be used to mark names of works of art, pieces of music, radio and television programs, and other works, especially if they are referred to as part of a larger collection:

Nancy Keesing's article 'Australia's "Unlucky" Novelists' appeared in *Southerly* in 1962.

4. Quotes may be used to denote the names of aeroplanes, vehicles, etc.:

Kingsford Smith's 'Southern Cross' may still be seen in Brisbane.

5. Quotes may be placed round a letter, word or phrase to which the writer wishes to draw special attention. This may be because the word itself is the subject of special discussion, or because the word is used in an unusual, new or special sense, or is a newly coined word or expression, or because the word is used ironically or is a colloquial, dialectal or other non-standard expression.

The word 'ocker' need not be used with pejorative sense.

XIV. **Capital Letters**

1. A capital letter is used for the first letter of the first word of any sentence:

That is quite right.
Now is the winter of our discontent. . .

See also section XIII 1 (c) and (d) on quotes.

2. All proper nouns and adjectives begin with a capital letter:

| | |
|---|---|
| Charles | the New Zealanders |
| Charles the Bold | New Zealand people |

3. Names of particular regions, as opposed to points of the compass, are capitalised:

the Deep North    the Far East

But:

The sun rises in the east and sets in the west.

4. In names of geographical features, words such as 'river', 'islands', 'street', etc., are capitalised if they form an integral part of the name:

the Swan River    *but*:    the river Murray
Those blue mountains are not the Blue Mountains.

5. Except in some modern poetry, where the poet may specifically direct otherwise, each line of a piece of verse begins with a capital letter:

I love a sunburnt country
A land of sweeping plains,
Of rugged mountain ranges,
Of droughts and flooding rains.

6. In titles of works of literature, art, music, etc., some writers capitalise all words except articles, prepositions and conjunctions. Others capitalise only the first word, nouns and adjectives, and this is the practice recommended here:

*All's well that ends well*    *The Sentimental Bloke*

7. In expressions of time, the abbreviations A.D., B.C. are usually capitalised. B.C. follows the year, but **A.D.** normally precedes it:

436 B.C.    A.D. 1914

XV. **Italics**

Italics are useful for highlighting certain words in a text. In manuscript or typewriting, italics are indicated by underlining.

1. Names of publications, titles or works of literature, art, music, etc., are usually set in italics:

White's *Voss*    the Melbourne *Age*

2. Certain names, as names of ships or vehicles, may be placed in italics or surrounded by inverted commas:

the *Bass Strait Trader*    the *Sunlander*
the 'Lady Denman'

3. Italics are used to show that a word is emphasised, or particularly stressed:

'Can't you see? I *want* to come,' she said.

4. In quoting the words of another writer or speaker, attention may be drawn to a particular word or phrase by italicising it. In such cases it is customary to place the words '[my italics]' in square brackets after the quoted matter:

Some of our words will be harsh, fierce, destructive words, aimed in defiance *and contempt* at men and policies we detest [my italics].

5. Italics may be used to indicate that a letter, word or phrase is itself the subject of discussion. However, we recommend inverted commas for this purpose.

6. Foreign words and phrases are placed in italics:

A significant period in European thought and literature was the *Aufklärung* in Germany.

# Signs and Symbols

## Astrology

### Signs of the Zodiac

A. SPRING SIGNS

♈ Aries, the Ram.
♉ Taurus, the Bull.
♊, Π Gemini, the Twins.

B. SUMMER SIGNS

♋, ♋ Cancer, the Crab.
♌ Leo, the Lion.
♍ Virgo, the Virgin.

C. AUTUMN SIGNS

♎ Libra, the Balance.
♏ Scorpio, the Scorpion.
♐ Sagittarius, the Archer.

D. WINTER SIGNS

♑ ♑ Capricorn, the Goat.
♒ Aquarius, the Water Bearer.
♓ Pisces, the Fishes.

## Astronomy

### 1. Astronomical Bodies

☉ **a.** the sun. **b.** Sunday.
⊖ centre of sun.
☉̄ upper limb of sun.
☉̲ lower limb of sun.
☿ **a.** Mercury. **b.** Wednesday.
♀ **a.** Venus. **b.** Friday.
⊕, ♁, ⊖ the earth.
☾, ☽ **a.** the moon. **b.** Monday.
● new moon.
☽, ☽, ◐, ☽ the moon, first quarter.
○ full moon.
☾, ☾, ◑, ☾ the moon, last quarter.
☾ upper limb of moon.
☾ lower limb of moon.
♂ **a.** Mars. **b.** Tuesday.
①, ②, ③, etc. asteroids. Each of the known asteroids is designated by a number within a circle, as ① for Ceres, ② for Pallas, etc.
♃ **a.** Jupiter. **b.** Thursday.
♄ **a.** Saturn. **b.** Saturday.
♅, ♅ Uranus.
♆ Neptune.
P Pluto.
☄ comet.
✱, ∗ star.
α, β, etc. the first, second, etc., brightest star in a specified constellation (fol. by the Latin name of the constellation in the genitive).

### 2. Signs of Position

☌ in conjunction; having the same longitude or right ascension. Thus, ☌♀☉ signifies the conjunction of Venus and the sun.
∗ sextile; 60° apart in longitude or right ascension.
□ quadrature; 90° apart in longitude or right ascension.
△ trine; 120° apart in longitude or right ascension.
☍ in opposition; 180° apart in longitude or right ascension. Thus, ☍♂☉ signifies the opposition of Mars and the sun.
☊ ascending node. See **node**.
☋ descending node. See **node**.
♈ vernal equinox.
♎ autumnal equinox.
α, RA, AR right ascension.
β celestial latitude.
δ, Decl. declination.
θ sidereal time.
λ celestial (or geographical) longitude.

# Biology

♂ a male organism, organ, cell, etc.

♀ a female organism, organ, cell, etc.

⚥ an organism having both male and female organs—hermaphrodite.

□ an individual organism, esp. a male.

○ an individual organism, esp. a female.

× (of a hybrid organism) crossed with.

P parent or parental generation; the first generation in a specified line of descent.

F filial generation; any generation following a parental generation.

$F_1$, $F_2$, $F_3$, etc. the first, second, third, etc., filial generations.

\+ **1.** denoting the presence of a specified trait or characteristic. **2.** used to indicate computable mating strains of heterothallic fungi which show no morphological differences.

— **1.** denoting the absence of a specified trait or characteristic. **2.** used to indicate computable mating strains of heterothallic fungi which show no morphological differences.

n haploid number of chromosomes.

2n, 3n, 4n, etc. diploid, triploid, tetraploid, etc., chromosomes, i.e. having 2, 3, 4, etc., haploid sets.

⊙ annual plant.

⊙⊙ biennial plant.

♃ a perennial herb or plant.

△ an evergreen.

✱̲ Northern Hemisphere.

✱̅ Southern Hemisphere.

|✱ Old World.

✱| New World.

# Chemistry

**1. Elements**

Each of the chemical elements is represented by a letter or combination of letters, consisting of the initial or an abbreviation of the English or Latin name of the element.

| Symbol | Name | Atomic Number |
|---|---|---|
| Ac | Actinium | 89 |
| Ag | Silver (L *argentum*) | 47 |
| Al | Aluminium | 13 |
| Am | Americium | 95 |
| Ar | Argon | 18 |
| As | Arsenic | 33 |
| At | Astatine | 85 |
| Au | Gold (L *aurum*) | 79 |
| B | Boron | 5 |
| Ba | Barium | 56 |
| Be | Beryllium | 4 |
| Bi | Bismuth | 83 |
| Bk | Berkelium | 97 |
| Br | Bromine | 35 |
| C | Carbon | 6 |
| Ca | Calcium | 20 |
| Cd | Cadmium | 48 |
| Ce | Cerium | 58 |
| Cf | Californium | 98 |
| Cl | Chlorine | 17 |
| Cm | Curium | 96 |
| Co | Cobalt | 27 |
| Cr | Chromium | 24 |
| Cs | Caesium | 55 |
| Cu | Copper (L *cuprum*) | 29 |
| Dy | Dysprosium | 66 |
| Er | Erbium | 68 |
| Es | Einsteinium | 99 |
| Eu | Europium | 63 |
| F | Fluorine | 9 |
| Fe | Iron (L *ferrum*) | 26 |
| Fm | Fermium | 100 |
| Fr | Francium | 87 |
| Ga | Gallium | 31 |
| Gd | Gadolinium | 64 |
| Ge | Germanium | 32 |
| H | Hydrogen | 1 |
| He | Helium | 2 |
| Hf | Hafnium | 72 |
| Hg | Mercury (L *hydrargyrum*) | 80 |
| Ho | Holmium | 67 |
| I | Iodine | 53 |
| In | Indium | 49 |
| Ir | Iridium | 77 |
| K | Potassium (L *kalium*) | 19 |
| Kr | Krypton | 36 |
| La | Lanthanum | 57 |
| Li | Lithium | 3 |
| Lu | Lutetium | 71 |
| Lw | Lawrencium | 103 |
| Md | Mendelevium | 101 |
| Mg | Magnesium | 12 |
| Mn | Manganese | 25 |
| Mo | Molybdenum | 42 |
| N | Nitrogen | 7 |
| Na | Sodium (L *natrium*) | 11 |
| Nb | Niobium | 41 |
| Nd | Neodymium | 60 |
| Ne | Neon | 10 |
| Ni | Nickel | 28 |
| No | Nobelium | 102 |
| Np | Neptunium | 93 |
| O | Oxygen | 8 |
| Os | Osmium | 76 |
| P | Phosphorus | 15 |
| Pa | Protactinium | 91 |
| Pb | Lead (L *plumbum*) | 82 |
| Pd | Palladium | 46 |
| Pm | Promethium | 61 |
| Po | Polonium | 84 |
| Pr | Praseodymium | 59 |
| Pt | Platinum | 78 |
| Pu | Plutonium | 94 |
| Ra | Radium | 88 |
| Rb | Rubidium | 37 |
| Re | Rhenium | 75 |
| Rh | Rhodium | 45 |
| Rn | Radon | 86 |
| Ru | Ruthenium | 44 |
| S | Sulphur | 16 |
| Sb | Antimony (L *stibium*) | 51 |
| Sc | Scandium | 21 |
| Se | Selenium | 34 |
| Si | Silicon | 14 |
| Sm | Samarium | 62 |
| Sn | Tin (L *stannum*) | 50 |
| Sr | Strontium | 38 |
| Ta | Tantalum | 73 |
| Tb | Terbium | 65 |
| Tc | Technetium | 43 |
| Te | Tellurium | 52 |
| Th | Thorium | 90 |
| Ti | Titanium | 22 |
| Tl | Thallium | 81 |
| Tm | Thulium | 69 |
| U | Uranium | 92 |
| V | Vanadium | 23 |
| W | Tungsten (G *Wolfram*) | 74 |
| Xe | Xenon | 54 |
| Y | Yttrium | 39 |
| Yb | Ytterbium | 70 |
| Zn | Zinc | 30 |
| Zr | Zirconium | 40 |

### 2. Compounds

Compounds are represented by combinations of the symbols of their constituent elements, with an inferior numeral to the right of each symbol indicating the number of atoms of the element entering into the compound (number 1 is, however, omitted). Thus, in some simple cases, NaCl (sodium chloride, or common salt) is a compound containing one atom of sodium and one of chlorine, $H_2O$ (water) contains two atoms of hydrogen and one of oxygen, $H_2O_2$ (hydrogen peroxide, or common peroxide) contains two atoms apiece of hydrogen and oxygen. A molecule may also consist entirely of atoms of a single element, as $O_3$ (ozone), which consists of three atoms of oxygen. Other symbols used in the formulas of molecules and compounds are:

· **a.** denoting radicals, as in $CH_3\cdot$-COOH. **b.** denoting water of crystallisation (or hydration) as in $Na_2CO_3\cdot10H_2O$ (washing soda).

( ) denoting a radical within a compound, as $(C_2H_5)_2O$ (ether).

1, 2, 3, etc. (before a symbol or formula) denoting a multiplication of the symbol or formula. Thus 3H = three atoms of hydrogen; $6H_2O$ = six molecules of water, etc.

1-, 2-, 3-, etc. (in names of compounds) denoting one of several possible positions of substituted atoms or groups.

α, β, etc. (in names of compounds) denoting one of several possible positions of substituted atoms or groups.

+ denoting dextrorotation, as +120°.

− denoting laevorotation, as −120°.

### 3. Valency and Electric Charge

−, =, ≡, etc. **a.** denoting a negative charge of one, two, three, etc., as $(OH)^-$, $(SO_4)^=$. **b.** denoting a single, double, triple, etc., bond, as H−O−H.

$^{-1}$, $^{-2}$, $^{-3}$, etc. Same as −, =, ≡, etc. (def. **a**); as $(OH)^{-1}$; $(SO_4)^{-2}$.

$^+$, $^{++}$, $^{+++}$, etc. denoting a positive charge of one, two, three, etc., as $K^+$, $Ca^{++}$.

$^{+1}$, $^{+2}$, $^{+3}$, etc. Same as $^+$, $^{++}$, $^{+++}$, etc., as $K^{+1}$, $Ca^{+2}$.

/, //, ///, etc. **a.** denoting a valency of one, two, three, etc. **b.** denoting a charge, esp. a negative charge, of one, two, three, etc.

·, :, ⁝, etc. denoting a single, double, triple, etc., bond.

### 4. Chemical Reactions

+ added to; together with.

= form; are equal to; as H + H + O = $H_2O$.

→, ← denoting a reaction in the direction specified.

⇄ denoting a reversible reaction, i.e. a reaction which proceeds simultaneously in both directions.

↓ (after a symbol or formula) denoting the precipitation of a specified substance.

↑ (after a symbol or formula) denoting the appearance of a specified substance as a gas.

≡, ⇋ (in a quantitative equation) denoting the quantities of specified substances which will enter completely into a reaction, without leaving excess material.

# Language

^ circumflex accent; as in *s'il vous plaît.*

¸ (with c) cedilla; as in *Alençon.*

´ acute accent; as in *passé.*

` grave accent; as in *à la mode.*

~ tilde; as in *São Paulo.*

¨ **1.** dieresis; as in *Laocoön.* **2.** umlaut; as in *Aufklärung.*

¯ macron.

˘ breve.

' smooth breathing.

ʽ rough breathing.

* denoting a hypothetical or reconstructed form: used esp. in etymologies.

# Mathematics

## 1. Arithmetic and Algebra

$+$ **a.** plus. **b.** positive. **c.** denoting approximate accuracy, with some figures omitted at the end; as in $\pi = 3{\cdot}141592+$.

$-$ **a.** minus. **b.** negative. **c.** denoting approximate accuracy, with some figures omitted at the end. Cf. + (def. **c**).

$\pm, \mp, \pm, \mp$ **a.** plus or minus: $4 \pm 2 = 6$ or 2. **b.** positive or negative: $\pm a = +a$ or $-a$. **c.** denoting the probable error associated with a figure derived by experiment and observation, approximate calculation, etc.

$\times, \cdot$ times; multiplied by: $3 \times 3 = 9$; $3 \cdot 3 = 9$. NOTE: multiplication may also be indicated by writing the algebraic symbols for multiplicand(s) and multiplier(s) consecutively; as in: xy; $a(a+b) = a^2 + ab$.

$\div$, /, $-$,: divided by; denoting the ratio of; as in $8 \div 2 = 8/2 = \frac{8}{2} = 8:2 = 4$.

$=$ equals; is equal to.

$\equiv$ is identical with.

$\neq$ $\neq$ is not equal to.

$\sim, \backsim$ **a.** is equivalent to. **b.** is similar to.

$>$ is greater than.

$<$ is less than.

$\geqq$ $\geq$ is equal to or greater than.

$\leqq$ $\leq$ is equal to or less than.

$^1, ^2, ^3$, etc. (at the right of a symbol, figure, etc.) exponents, indicating the raising of a power to the first, second, third, etc., power: $(ab)^2 = a^2b^2$; $4^3 = 64$.

$\surd$ $\sqrt{}$ the radical sign, indicating the square root of, as in: $\sqrt{81} = 9$.

$\sqrt[3]{}, \sqrt[4]{}, \sqrt[5]{}$, etc. the radical sign used with indices, indicating the third, fourth, etc., root of; as in: $\sqrt[3]{125} = 5$.

$^{\frac{1}{2}}, ^{\frac{1}{3}}, ^{\frac{1}{4}}$, etc. fractional exponents used to indicate roots, and equal to $\sqrt{}, \sqrt[3]{}, \sqrt[4]{}$, etc.; as. $9^{\frac{1}{2}} = \sqrt{9} = 3$; $a^{\frac{3}{8}} = (a^{\frac{1}{8}})^3 = (a^3)^{\frac{1}{8}} = \sqrt[8]{a^3}$.

$^{-1}, ^{-2}, ^{-3}$, etc. negative exponents, used to indicate the reciprocal of the same quantity with a positive exponent; as in: $9^{-2} = \frac{1}{9^2} = \frac{1}{81}$; $a^{-\frac{1}{2}} = \frac{1}{\sqrt{a}}$.

( ) parentheses; as in: $2(a+b)$.

[ ] brackets; as in: $4+[3(a-b)]$.

{ } braces; as in: $5+\{6[2-(a+2)+4]\}$.

$\overline{\quad}$ vinculum; as in: $\overline{a+b}$.

NOTE: Parentheses, brackets, braces, and vinculum are usually applied to quantities consisting of more than one member or term, to connect them and show that they are to be considered together.

$\propto$ varies directly as; is directly proportional to: $x \propto y$.

!, $\lfloor$ factorial of: $4! = \lfloor 4 = 1 \times 2 \times 3 \times 4 = 24$.

$f$, F, $\phi$, etc. function of; as in: $f(x)$ = a function of x.

NOTE: In addition to $\phi$, other symbols (esp. letters from the Greek alphabet) may be used to indicate functions, as $\psi, \gamma$, etc.

$'$, $''$, $'''$, etc. prime, double prime, triple prime, etc., used to indicate: **a.** first, second, third, etc., derivatives of a function, as in: $f'(x)$; $f''(x)$; etc. **b.** constants, as distinguished from the variable denoted by a letter alone. **c.** different variables using the same letters, as in y, $y'$, $y''$, etc.

$\sigma$ standard deviation.

$r$ correlation coefficient.

$e$, $\in$. Same as **e** (def. 1).

$\infty$ infinity.

## 2. Geometry

$\angle$, *pl.* $\angle$s angle; as in: $\angle ACB$.

$\perp$ **a.** a perpendicular (*pl.* $\perp$s). **b.** is perpendicular to; as in: $AB \perp CD$.

$\|$ **a.** a parallel (*pl.* $\|$s). **b.** is parallel to; as in: $AB \| CD$.

$\triangle$, *pl.* $\triangle$s triangle, as in: $\triangle ABC$.

$\square$ parallelogram, as in: $\square ABCD$.

$\square$ square, as in: $\square ABCD$.

$\bigcirc$, *pl.* Ⓢ circle.

$\pi$ the Greek letter pi, representing the ratio ($3{\cdot}141592+$) of the circumference of a circle to its diameter.

$\frown$ arc.

$^\circ$ degree(s), esp. of arc or (in physics, etc.) of temperature; as in: $60^\circ$.

$'$ minute(s); as in: $60^\circ\ 20'$.

$''$ second(s); as in: $60^\circ\ 20'\ 5''$

$\cong$, $\equiv$ is congruent to.

$\therefore$ therefore; hence.

$\because$ since; because.

## 3. Calculus

$\frac{d}{d}$ derivative; as in: $\frac{dy}{dx}$ = the derivative of y with respect to x.

$\Delta$, $\delta$ an increment; as $\Delta$ y or $\delta$ y = an increment of y.

$d$ differential, as $dy$ = differential y.

$\sum_1^n$ sum of $n$ terms.

$\Sigma$ sum of an infinite number of terms.

$\prod_1^n$ product of $n$ terms.

$\Pi$ product of an infinite number of terms.

lim, limit. An example of the use of this abbreviation is: $\lim_{y \to b} (x) = a$; i.e. the limit of x as y approaches b is a.

$\int$ integral. An example of the use of this symbol is: $\int f(x)dx$; i.e. the integral of $f(x)$ with respect to x.

$\int_a^b$ definite integral, giving limits. Thus, $\int_a^b f(x)dx$ is the definite integral of $f(x)$ between limits a and b.

# Miscellaneous

@ at: material @ $2 per metre.
& the ampersand meaning *and.* Cf. **ampersand.**
&c. et cetera; and others; and so forth; and so on. Cf. et cetera.
© copyright; copyrighted.
' foot; feet; as in: 6' = six feet.
" inch(es); as in: 6' 2" = six feet, two inches.

× 1. by: used in stating dimensions, as in: a vat that is 2m × 4m × 1m; a 2cm × 4cm board. 2. a sign (the cross) made in place of a signature by a person who cannot write; as in:

his
John × Jones
mark.

% per cent.
♠ *Cards.* spade.
♥ *Cards.* heart.
♦ *Cards.* diamond.
♣ *Cards.* club.
† died: used esp. in genealogical tables.

# Roman Numerals

| NUMBER | ROMAN NUMERAL | NUMBER | ROMAN NUMERAL |
|---|---|---|---|
| 1 | I | 43 | XLIII |
| 2 | II | 50 | L |
| 3 | III | 54 | LIV |
| 4 | IV | 60 | LX |
| 5 | V | 65 | LXV |
| 6 | VI | 70 | LXX |
| 7 | VII | 76 | LXXVI |
| 8 | VIII | 80 | LXXX |
| 9 | IX | 87 | LXXXVII |
| 10 | X | 90 | XC |
| 11 | XI | 98 | XCVIII |
| 12 | XII | 100 | C |
| 13 | XIII | 101 | CI |
| 14 | XIV | 115 | CXV |
| 15 | XV | 150 | CL |
| 16 | XVI | 200 | CC |
| 17 | XVII | 300 | CCC |
| 18 | XVIII | 400 | CD |
| 19 | XIX | 500 | D |
| 20 | XX | 600 | DC |
| 21 | XXI | 700 | DCC |
| 30 | XXX | 800 | DCCC |
| 32 | XXXII | 900 | CM |
| 40 | XL | 1,000 | M |

# Proofreaders' Marks

| Instruction | Textual mark | Marginal mark |
|---|---|---|
| Insert in text the matter indicated in margin | ⅄ | *New matter followed by* / |
| Delete | Strike through characters to be deleted | ꝺ |
| Delete and close up | Strike through characters to be deleted and use linking marks | ꝺ (with linking marks) |
| Leave as printed | .... under characters to remain | *stet* |
| Change to italic | — under characters to be altered | *ital* |
| Change to even small capitals | ═ under characters to be altered | *s.c.* |
| Change to capital letters | ≡ under characters to be altered | *caps* |
| Use capital letters for initial letters and small capitals for rest of words | ≡ under initial letters and ═ under the rest of the words | *c.&s.c.* |
| Change to bold type | ∿ under characters to be altered | *bold* |
| Change to lower case | Encircle characters to be altered | *l.c.* |
| Change to roman type | Encircle characters to be altered | *rom* |
| Underline word or words | — under words affected | *underline* |
| Substitute or insert character(s) under which this mark is placed, in 'superior' position | / through character or ⅄ where required | ⁊ *under character* (e.g. ⁊) |

| Instruction | Textual mark | Marginal mark |
|---|---|---|
| Substitute or insert character(s) over which this mark is placed, in 'inferior' position | / through character or ⅄ where required | ^ *over character* (e.g. ^) |
| Change damaged character(s) | Encircle character(s) to be altered | × |
| Close up—delete space between characters | ⊂ linking characters | ⊂ |
| Insert space | ⅄ | # |
| Transpose | ⊔⊓ between characters or words, | *trs* |
| Move matter to right | ⊏ at left side of group to be moved | ⊏ |
| Move matter to to left | ⊐ at right side of group to be moved | ⊐ |
| Raise lines | ⊤ over lines to be moved ⊥ under lines to be moved | *raise* |
| Lower lines | ⊓ over lines to be moved ⊥ under lines to be moved | *lower* |
| Correct the vertical alignment | \|\| | \|\| |
| Straighten lines | ═ through lines to be straightened | ═ |
| Begin a new paragraph | ⊏ before first word of new paragraph | *n.p.* |
| No fresh paragraph here | ⌒ between paragraphs | *run on* |
| Insert en (half-em) rule | ⅄ | *en* |
| Insert one-em rule | ⅄ | *em* |

# Weights and Measures

## Metric Conversion Table

| Quantity | Metric Unit | Imperial Unit | Conversion Factors (Approximate): Metric to Imperial Units | Conversion Factors (Approximate): Imperial to Metric Units |
|---|---|---|---|---|
| LENGTH | millimetre (mm) or centimetre (cm) | inch (in) | 1 cm = 0.394 in | 1 in = 25.4 mm |
| | centimetre (cm) or metre (m) | foot (ft) | 1 m = 3.28 ft | 1 ft = 30.5 cm |
| | metre (m) | yard (yd) | 1 m = 1.09 yd | 1 yd = 0.914 m |
| | kilometre (km) | mile | 1 km = 0.621 mile | 1 mile = 1.61 km |
| MASS | gram (g) | ounce (oz) | 1 g = 0.0353 oz | 1 oz = 28.3 g |
| | gram (g) or kilogram (kg) | pound (lb) | 1 kg = 2.20 lb | 1 lb = 454 g |
| | tonne (t) | ton | 1 tonne = 0.984 ton | 1 ton = 1.02 tonne |
| AREA | square centimetre ($cm^2$) | square inch ($in^2$) | 1 $cm^2$ = 0.155 $in^2$ | 1 $in^2$ = 6.45 $cm^2$ |
| | square centimetre ($cm^2$) or square metre ($m^2$) | square foot ($ft^2$) | 1 $m^2$ = 10.8 $ft^2$ | 1 $ft^2$ = 929 $cm^2$ |
| | square metre ($m^2$) | square yard ($yd^2$) | 1 $m^2$ = 1.20 $yd^2$ | 1 $yd^2$ = 0.836 $m^2$ |
| | hectare (ha) | acre (ac) | 1 ha = 2.47 ac | 1 ac = 0.405 ha |
| | square kilometre ($km^2$) | square mile (sq. mile) | 1 $km^2$ = 0.386 sq. mile | 1 sq. mile = 2.59 $km^2$ |
| VOLUME | cubic centimetre ($cm^3$) | cubic inch ($in^3$) | 1 $cm^3$ = 0.0610 $in^3$ | 1 $in^3$ = 16.4 $cm^3$ |
| | cubic decimetre ($dm^3$) or cubic metre ($m^3$) | cubic foot ($ft^3$) | 1 $m^3$ = 35.3 $ft^3$ | 1 $ft^3$ = 28.3 $dm^3$ |
| | cubic metre ($m^3$) | cubic yard ($yd^3$) | 1 $m^3$ = 1.31 $yd^3$ | 1 $yd^3$ = 0.765 $m^3$ |
| | cubic metre ($m^3$) | bushel (bus) | 1 $m^3$ = 27.5 bus | 1 bus = 0.0364 $m^3$ |
| VOLUME (fluids) | millilitre (mL) | fluid ounce (fl oz) | 1 mL = 0.0352 fl oz | 1 fl oz = 28.4 mL |
| | millilitre (mL) or litre (L) | pint (pt) | 1 litre = 1.76 pint | 1 pint = 568 mL |
| | litre (L) or cubic metre ($m^3$) | gallon (gal) | 1 $m^3$ = 220 gallons | 1 gal = 4.55 litre |
| FORCE | newton (N) | pound-force (lbf) | 1 N = 0.225 lbf | 1 lbf = 4.45 N |
| PRESSURE | kilopascal (kPa) | pound per square inch (psi) | 1 kPa = 0.145 psi | 1 psi = 6.89 kPa |
| *(for meteorology)* | millibar (mb) | inch of mercury (inHg) | 1 mb = 0.0295 inHg | 1 inHg = 33.9 mb |
| ANGULAR VELOCITY | radian per second (rad/s) | revolution per minute (r/min, rpm) | 1 rad/s = 9.55 r/min | 1 r/min = 0.105 rad/s |
| VELOCITY | kilometre per hour (km/h) | mile per hour (mph) | 1 km/h = 0.621 mph | 1 mph = 1.61 km/h |
| TEMPERATURE | Celsius temp (°C) | Fahrenheit temp (°F) | $°F = (\frac{9}{5} \times °C) + 32$ | $°C = \frac{5}{9} \times (°F - 32)$ |
| ENERGY | kilojoule (kJ) | British thermal unit (Btu) | 1 kJ = 0.948 Btu | 1 Btu = 1.06 kJ |
| | megajoule (MJ) | therm | 1 MJ = $9.48 \times 10^{-3}$ therm | 1 therm = 106 MJ |
| POWER | kilowatt (kW) | horsepower (hp) | 1 kW = 1.34 hp | 1 hp = 0.746 kW |

# Decimal and Percentage Equivalents of Common Fractions

| FRACTION | DECIMAL EQUIVALENT | | PERCENT EQUIVALENT |
|---|---|---|---|
| 1/2 | .5 | | 50% |
| 1/3 | .33. . . | | $33\frac{1}{3}$% |
| 2/3 | .66. | | $66\frac{2}{3}$% |
| 1/4 | .25 | | 25% |
| 2/4 | .5 | | 50% |
| 3/4 | .75 | | 75% |
| 1/5 | .2 | | 20% |
| 2/5 | .4 | | 40% |
| 3/5 | .6 | | 60% |
| 4/5 | .8 | | 80% |
| 1/6 | .166. . . | | $16\frac{2}{3}$% |
| 2/6 | .33. . . | | $33\frac{1}{3}$% |
| 3/6 | .5 | | 50% |
| 4/6 | .66. . . | | $66\frac{2}{3}$% |
| 5/6 | .833. . . | | $83\frac{1}{3}$% |
| 1/7 | .1429 | (nearest ten-thousandth) | $14\frac{2}{7}$% |
| 2/7 | .2857 | " | $28\frac{4}{7}$% |
| 3/7 | .4286 | " | $42\frac{6}{7}$% |
| 4/7 | .5714 | " | $57\frac{1}{7}$% |
| 5/7 | .7143 | " | $71\frac{3}{7}$% |
| 6/7 | .8571 | " | $85\frac{5}{7}$% |
| 1/8 | .125 | | $12\frac{1}{2}$% |
| 2/8 | .25 | | 25% |
| 3/8 | .375 | | $37\frac{1}{2}$% |
| 4/8 | .5 | | 50% |
| 5/8 | .625 | | $62\frac{1}{2}$% |
| 6/8 | .75 | | 75% |
| 7/8 | .875 | | $87\frac{1}{2}$% |
| 1/9 | .11. . . | | $11\frac{1}{9}$% |
| 2/9 | .22. . . | | $22\frac{2}{9}$% |
| 3/9 | .33. . . | | $33\frac{1}{3}$% |
| 4/9 | .44. . . | | $44\frac{4}{9}$% |
| 5/9 | .55. . . | | $55\frac{5}{9}$% |
| 6/9 | .66. . . | | $66\frac{2}{3}$% |
| 7/9 | .77. . . | | $77\frac{7}{9}$% |
| 8/9 | .88. . . | | $88\frac{8}{9}$% |
| 1/10 | .1 | | 10% |
| 2/10 | .2 | | 20% |
| 3/10 | .3 | | 30% |
| 4/10 | .4 | | 40% |
| 5/10 | .5 | | 50% |
| 6/10 | .6 | | 60% |
| 7/10 | .7 | | 70% |
| 8/10 | .8 | | 80% |
| 9/10 | .9 | | 90% |
| 1/11 | .0909. . . | | $9\frac{10}{11}$% |
| 1/12 | .0833. . . | | $8\frac{1}{3}$% |
| 1/20 | .05 | | 5% |
| 1/32 | .03125 | | $3\frac{1}{8}$% |
| 1/64 | .015625 | | $1\frac{9}{16}$% |

# The International System of Units (SI)

## 1. Base SI Units

| BASIC PHYSICAL QUANTITY | SI UNIT | SYMBOL |
|---|---|---|
| length | metre | m |
| mass | kilogram | kg |
| time | second | s |
| electric current | ampere | A |
| thermodynamic temperature | kelvin | K |
| amount of substance | mole | mol |
| luminous intensity | candela | cd |

## 2. Supplementary Units

| | | |
|---|---|---|
| plane angle | radian | rad |
| solid angle | steradian | sr |

## 3. Some Derived SI Units with Special Names

| PHYSICAL QUANTITY | SI UNIT | SYMBOL |
|---|---|---|
| frequency | hertz | Hz |
| energy | joule | J |
| force | newton | N |
| power | watt | W |
| electric charge | coulomb | C |
| potential difference | volt | V |
| resistance | ohm | Ω |
| capacitance | farad | F |
| conductance | siemens | S |
| magnetic flux | weber | Wb |
| inductance | henry | H |
| magnetic flux density | tesla | T |
| luminous flux | lumen | lm |
| illumination | lux | lx |

## 4. Prefixes for SI Units

| FRACTION | PREFIX | SYMBOL | MULTIPLE | PREFIX | SYMBOL |
|---|---|---|---|---|---|
| $10^{-1}$ | deci | d | 10 | deka | da |
| $10^{-2}$ | centi | c | $10^{2}$ | hecto | h |
| $10^{-3}$ | milli | m | $10^{3}$ | kilo | k |
| $10^{-6}$ | micro | $\mu$ | $10^{6}$ | mega | M |
| $10^{-9}$ | nano | n | $10^{9}$ | giga | G |
| $10^{-12}$ | pico | p | $10^{12}$ | tera | T |
| $10^{-15}$ | femto | f | $10^{15}$ | peta | P |
| $10^{-18}$ | atto | a | $10^{18}$ | exa | E |

# Paper Sizes

| *Parent sizes (untrimmed)* | | *Equivalent imperial sizes* |
|---|---|---|
| Printing and writing ..... | 530 mm × 840 mm | Double Large Post |
| | 570 mm × 890 mm | Double Demy |
| | 580 mm × 910 mm | Double Medium |
| | 690 mm × 860 mm | Quad Foolscap |
| | 640 mm × 1020 mm | Double Royal |
| | 760 mm × 1020 mm | Quad Crown |
| ISO RA1 .................. | 610 mm × 860 mm | (ISO size) |
| ISO SRA1 ................ | 640 mm × 900 mm | (ISO size) |
| Ledger and account book | 510 mm × 790 mm | Double Ledger Demy |
| | 580 mm × 940 mm | (additional size) |
| Drawing cartridge ........ | 510 mm × 640 mm | Royal |
| | 560 mm × 760 mm | Imperial |
| System board ............. | 650 mm × 780 mm | Index Royal and a half |

| *Cut sizes (trimmed)* | |
|---|---|
| Quarto ...................... | 260 mm × 206 mm (formerly Large Post Quarto) |
| Foolscap .................... | 337 mm × 206 mm (formerly Foolscap Folio) |
| A4 ........................... | 297 mm × 210 mm |

| *International sizes—Trimmed page sizes* | |
|---|---|
| A4 ........................... | 297 mm × 210 mm |
| B5 ........................... | 250 mm × 176 mm |
| A5 ........................... | 210 mm × 148 mm |
| B6 ........................... | 176 mm × 125 mm |
| A6 ........................... | 148 mm × 105 mm |
| B7 ........................... | 125 mm × 88 mm |

| *Imperial sizes* | |
|---|---|
| Foolscap folio ............ | 333 mm × 210 mm |
| Demy quarto .............. | 273 mm × 216 mm |
| Crown quarto ............ | 242 mm × 184 mm |
| Royal octavo .............. | 242 mm × 152 mm |
| Foolscap quarto .......... | 207 mm × 165 mm |
| Demy octavo .............. | 213 mm × 137 mm |
| Crown octavo ............ | 181 mm × 121 mm |

# Australian Standard Meat Cuts

The Macquarie Dictionary conforms in headwords and definitions to the industry code of practice prepared in 1980 at the request of the Food Standards Committee of the National Health and Medical Research Council.

The major terms in common use are illustrated in the diagrams below.

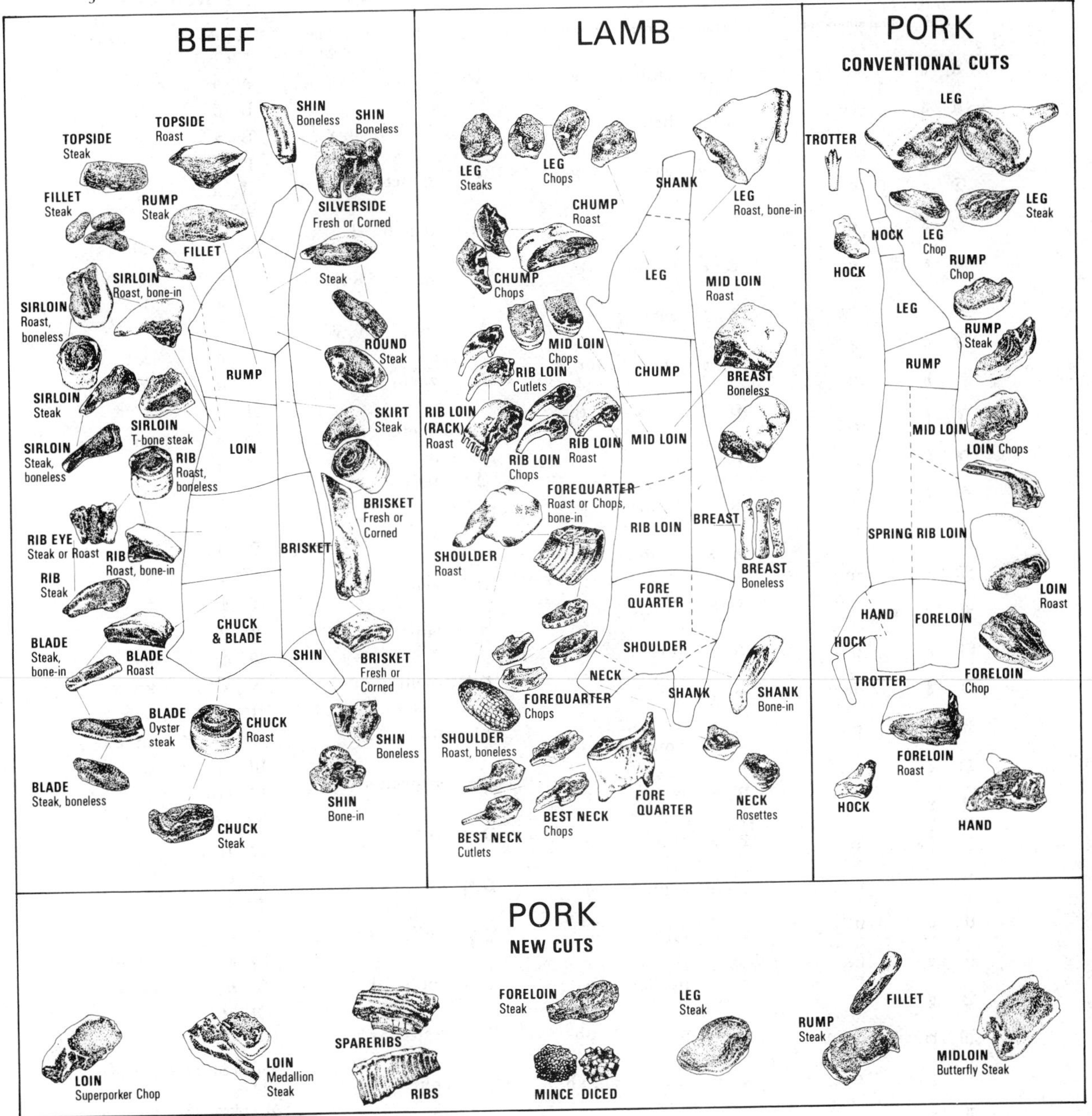

# Foreign Alphabets

## GERMAN

| Letter | | Transliteration |
|---|---|---|
| 𝔄 | 𝔞 | a |
| 𝔄̈ | 𝔞̈ | ae |
| 𝔅 | 𝔟 | b |
| ℭ | 𝔠 | c |
| 𝔇 | 𝔡 | d |
| 𝔈 | 𝔢 | e |
| 𝔉 | 𝔣 | f |
| 𝔊 | 𝔤 | g |
| ℌ | 𝔥 | h |
| ℑ | 𝔦 | i |
| 𝔍 | 𝔧 | j |
| 𝔎 | 𝔨 | k |
| 𝔏 | 𝔩 | l |
| 𝔐 | 𝔪 | m |
| 𝔑 | 𝔫 | n |
| 𝔒 | 𝔬 | o |
| 𝔒̈ | 𝔬̈ | oe |
| 𝔓 | 𝔭 | p |
| 𝔔 | 𝔮 | q |
| ℜ | 𝔯 | r |
| 𝔖 | ſ 𝔰[1] | s |
| 𝔗 | 𝔱 | t |
| 𝔘 | 𝔲 | u |
| 𝔘̈ | 𝔲̈ | ue |
| 𝔙 | 𝔳 | v |
| 𝔚 | 𝔴 | w |
| 𝔛 | 𝔵 | x |
| 𝔜 | 𝔶 | y |
| ℨ | 𝔷 | z |

[1] At end of syllable.

## GREEK

| Letter | | Name | Transliteration |
|---|---|---|---|
| Α | α | alpha | a |
| Β | β | beta | b |
| Γ | γ | gamma | g |
| Δ | δ | delta | d |
| Ε | ε | epsilon | e |
| Ζ | ζ | zeta | z |
| Η | η | eta | e (or ē) |
| Θ | θ | theta | th |
| Ι | ι | iota | i |
| Κ | κ | kappa | k |
| Λ | λ | lambda | l |
| Μ | μ | mu | m |
| Ν | ν | nu | n |
| Ξ | ξ | xi | x |
| Ο | ο | omicron | o |
| Π | π | pi | p |
| Ρ | ρ | rho | r |
| Σ | σ, ς[1] | sigma | s |
| Τ | τ | tau | t |
| Υ | υ | upsilon | y |
| Φ | φ | phi | ph |
| Χ | χ | chi | ch, kh |
| Ψ | ψ | psi | ps |
| Ω | ω | omega | o (or ō) |

[1] At end of word.

## HEBREW

| Letter | Name | Transliteration |
|---|---|---|
| א | aleph | – or ʼ |
| ב | beth | b, v |
| ג | gimel | g |
| ד | daleth | d |
| ה | he | h |
| ו | vav | v, w |
| ז | zayin | z |
| ח | cheth | ḥ |
| ט | teth | ṭ |
| י | yod | y, j, i |
| כ ך[1] | kaph | k, kh |
| ל | lamed | l |
| מ ם[1] | mem | m |
| נ ן[1] | nun | n |
| ס | samekh | s |
| ע | ayin | ʻ |
| פ ף[1] | pe | p, f |
| צ ץ[1] | sadi | ṣ |
| ק | koph | ḳ |
| ר | resh | r |
| שׁ | shin | sh, š |
| שׂ | śin | ś |
| ת | tav | t |

[1] At end of word.

## RUSSIAN

| Letter | | Transliteration |
|---|---|---|
| А | а | a |
| Б | б | b |
| В | в | v |
| Г | г | g |
| Д | д | d |
| Е | е | e, ye |
| Ж | ж | zh |
| З | з | z |
| И | и | i |
| І[1] | і[1] | |
| Й | й | ĭ, i |
| К | к | k |
| Л | л | l |
| М | м | m |
| Н | н | n |
| О | о | o |
| П | п | p |
| Р | р | r |
| С | с | s |
| Т | т | t |
| У | у | u |
| Ф | ф | f |
| Х | х | kh, x |
| Ц | ц | ts, c |
| Ч | ч | ch, č |
| Ш | ш | sh, š |
| Щ | щ | shch, šč |
| Ъ[2] | ъ[2] | |
| Ы | ы | i |
| Ь | ь | ʼ |
| Ѣ[3] | ѣ[3] | |
| Э | э | e |
| Ю | ю | yu, ju |
| Я | я | ya, ja |
| Ѳ[4] | ѳ[4] | |
| Ѵ[1] | ѵ[1] | |

[1] Abolished (1918) in favour of и.

[2] Abolished (1918) except in middle of words as sign of division (where it often is replaced by ').

[3] Abolished (1918) in favour of e.

[4] Abolished (1918) in favour of ф.

# Ancient Alphabets

| PHOENICIAN | EARLY GREEK | LATIN (Early Monumental) | EARLY ETRUSCAN | RUNIC (Anglo Saxon) | MODERN ROMAN CAPITALS |
|---|---|---|---|---|---|
| (1) | | | | | A |
| | | | | | B |
| (2) | (2) | (3) | | | C |
| | | | | | D |
| (4) | | | | | E |
| (5) | (5) | | | | F |
| | | | | | G |
| (6) | (6) | | (6) | | |
| | | | | | H |
| (7) | (8) | | (8) | | |
| (9) | | | | | I |
| | | | | | J |
| | | | | | K |
| | | | | | L |
| | | | | | M |
| | | | | | N |
| (10) | | | (10) | | |
| (11) | | | | | O |
| | | | | | P |
| (12) | | | (10) | | |
| | | | | | Q |
| | | | | | R |
| (13) | | | | | S |
| | | | | | T |
| | | | | | U |
| | | | | | V |
| | | | | | W |
| | | | | | X |
| | | | | | Y |
| | | | | | Z |
| | | | (14) | | |

| RUNIC | Phonetic Value |
|---|---|
| | þ |
| | ā |
| | ċ |
| | ng |
| | ae |
| | ea |
| | io |

(1) = ʾ (5) = w (8) = th (11) = ʿ

(2) = g (6) = z (9) = y (12) = ṣ

(3) = k (7) = ṭ (10) = s (13) = š

(4) = h (14) = kh

# Indo-European Languages

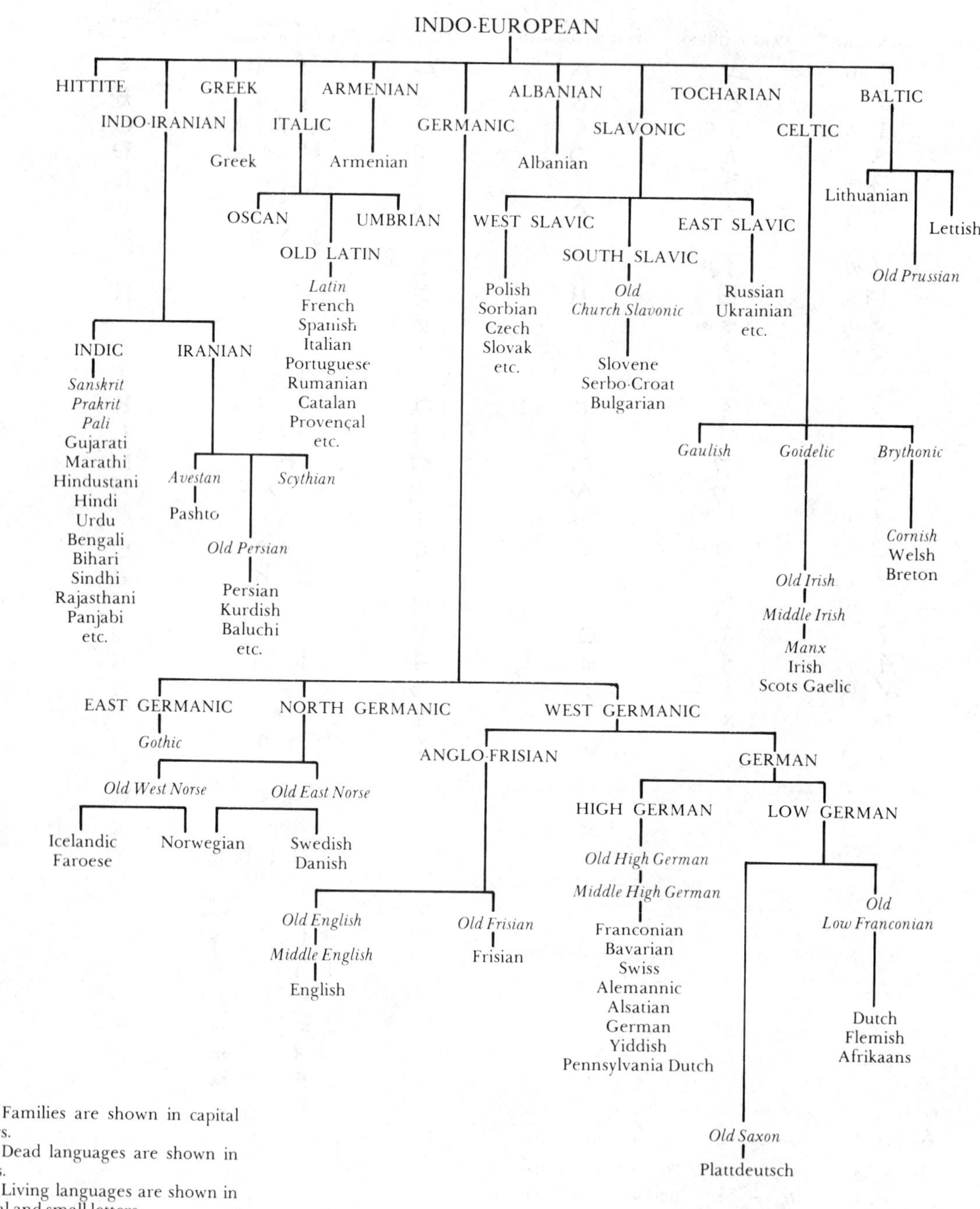


KEY

1. Families are shown in capital letters.
2. Dead languages are shown in italics.
3. Living languages are shown in capital and small letters.

# Abbreviations used in Etymologies

| | |
|---|---|
| abbrev. | abbreviation |
| b. | blend of, blended |
| c. | cognate with |
| cf. | compare |
| d. | dialect, dialectal |
| fig. | figurative |
| lit. | literally |
| obs. | obsolete |
| orig. | origin, original, originally |
| ult. | ultimate, ultimately |
| uncert. | uncertain |
| var. | variant |
| ? | perhaps |
| * | hypothetical form |

A colon indicates that the form of a word in a foreign language is the same as the headword or as the immediately preceding form in the etymology.

Commonly used abbreviations for gender (e.g. fem. for feminine), parts of speech (e.g. ppr. for present participle), etc., may be found in the body of the dictionary.

## Languages

| | |
|---|---|
| **AF** | Anglo-French |
| **Amer. Ind.** | American Indian |
| **Ar.** | Arabic |
| **Aram.** | Aramaic |
| **D** | Dutch |
| **Dan.** | Danish |
| **E** | English |
| **Egypt.** | Egyptian |
| **F** | French |
| **Fris.** | Frisian |
| **G** | German |
| **Gk** | Greek |
| **Gmc** | Germanic |
| **Goth.** | Gothic |
| **Heb.** | Hebrew |
| **HG** | High German |
| **Hind.** | Hindustani |
| **Hung.** | Hungarian |
| **Icel.** | Icelandic |
| **IE** | Indo-European |
| **It.** | Italian |
| **Jap.** | Japanese |
| **L** | Latin |
| **LG** | Low German |
| **LGk** | Late Greek (300–700) |
| **LHeb.** | Late Hebrew |
| **LL** | Late Latin (300–700) |
| **M** | 1. Middle 2. Medieval |
| **ME** | Middle English (1100–1500) |
| **Mex.** | Mexican |
| **MF** | Middle French (1400–1600) |
| **MGk** | Medieval Greek (700–1500) |
| **ML** | Medieval Latin (700–1500) |
| **NL** | Neo-Latin (after 1500) |
| **Norw.** | Norwegian |
| **O** | Old |
| **OE** | Old English (before 1100) |
| **OF** | Old French (before 1400) |
| **OS** | Old Saxon |
| **Pers.** | Persian |
| **Pg.** | Portuguese |
| **Pol.** | Polish |
| **Pr.** | Provençal |
| **Rom.** | Romance, Romanic |
| **Russ.** | Russian |
| **Scand.** | Scandinavian |
| **Scot.** | Scottish |
| **Skt** | Sanskrit |
| **Sp.** | Spanish |
| **Swed.** | Swedish |
| **Turk.** | Turkish |
| **VL** | Vulgar Latin |
| **WGmc** | West Germanic |

# The Macquarie Supplement

*Since the first edition of The Macquarie Dictionary was published, research into new material for the dictionary has proceeded, research which has been boosted by the contributions of interested readers.*

*The following pages contain some of the material which in the short time available could be prepared for publication.*

*The asterisk (*) indicates that the definition supplements the entry given under an existing headword in the body of the dictionary.*

# Aa

**Aborig.,** Aboriginal.

**accent,**
**n.* emphasis: *this school puts a lot of accent on discipline.*

**accommodate,**
**v.i.* to adapt: *his eyes had not accommodated to the glare.*

**account,**
**n.* a bill, as for service rendered or goods purchased: *the grocery account was due.*
**n.* a relationship between a person and a bank which implies regularity of trading between the two and the keeping of formal records of this trading by the bank: *I have an account with the Commonwealth Bank.*
**n.* such a relationship with a department store, garage, etc., which allows the provision of goods and services without immediate cash payment and sometimes with special privileges.
**n.* **on (someone's) account,** on (someone's) behalf: *I was acting on her account at the time.*
**adj.* of or pertaining to a person with an account: *the garage sells petrol to account customers only.*

**acker** /'ækə/, *n. S.A.* →**alley**[2] (def. 1).

**acquisitive prize** /ə'kwɪzətɪv ˌpraɪz/, *n.* a cash prize, offered in art competitions and the like, the award and acceptance of which entitles the donor to ownership of the winning work.

**adapt,**
**v.i.* to adjust, change appropriately.

**aetiology,**
**n. Med.* cause or origin: *a disease of unknown aetiology.*

**affrication** /æfrə'keɪʃən/, *n.* the less than rapid release of a consonant articulation so that a fricative is heard towards the end of the release, as in the first consonant of 'joke'.

**afternoon shift** /aftə'nun ʃɪft/, *n.* (in a factory, shipyard, etc., where continuous shifts are worked) the shift which is neither day shift nor night shift, and typically runs from early afternoon to some time before midnight.

**aggro,**
**n.* aggression; violence.

**ailurophobe** /aɪ'lurəfoub/, *n.* a hater of cats. [Gk *aílouros* cat + -PHOBE] – **ailurophobia** /aɪˌlurə'foubiə/, *n.*

**ailurophile** /aɪ'lurəfaɪl/, *n.* a lover of cats. [Gk *aílouros* cat + -PHILE] – **ailurophilia** /aɪˌlurə'fɪliə/, *n.*

**airing,**
**n.* a promulgation of an idea, proposal, etc., usu. to evoke response and evaluation.

**all clear,**
**n.* an indication that hazards, impediments, etc., have been removed and it is safe to embark on or continue a journey, project, etc.

**allen key** /'ælən ki/, *n.* one of a number of variously-sized, small, hexagonal metal bars bent to form a right angle, the ends of which may be slotted into the matching recess in the heads of grub screws or certain bolts so as to tighten or loosen them.

**along,**
**prep.* in accordance with: *along the lines suggested.*

**alphabet block** /'ælfəbɛt ˌblɒk/, *n.* a block (def. 2) with a letter of the alphabet on each face.

**Am,** *Chem.* americium.

**anacrusis,**
**n. Music.* a note or group of notes which comes immediately before the first strong beat of a phrase of music.

**ancillary,**
**n., pl.* **-aries.** an accessory, subsidiary or helping thing or person.

**angel dust** /'eɪndʒəl dʌst/, *n.* →**phencyclidine.**

**APC,**
**Mil.* Armoured Personnel Carrier.

**Arab bread** /'ærəb brɛd/, *n.* →**Lebanese bread.**

**ark,**
**n.* Also, **holy ark.** a wooden chest in the synagogue holding scrolls of Jewish law.

**arouse,**
**v.t.* to awaken sexual excitement and readiness in.

**astral body** /'æstrəl bɒdi/, *n. Theosophy.* a body separate from, but corresponding to, the human body and surviving it in death, but made of astral (def. 3) substance.

**auditory nerve** /'ɔdətri nɜv/, *n.* the nerve which transmits the sensation of sound, running from the cochlea towards the brain.

**Australian arbo-encephalitis** /ɒsˌtreɪljən ˌabou-ɛnsɛfə'laɪtəs/, *n.* a mosquito-transmitted viral disease of the brain, formerly known as Murray Valley encephalitis; Australian X disease.

**australwink** /ˈɒstrəl,wɪŋk/, *n.* a small periwinkle-like shell, family Littorinidae, found in great numbers on the Australian coast.

**auteur** /oʊˈtɜ/, *adj. Films.* of or pertaining to a type of film where the director is also largely the author.

**axebird** /ˈæksbɜd/, *n.* a large-tailed nightjar of northern Queensland and New Guinea, the call of which resembles the sound of chopping.

# Bb

**backmarker** /ˈbækmakə/, *n.* the competitor in a handicap race who starts in the rearmost position; the competitor on scratch (def. 19).

**badly,**
**adv.* **badly off, a.** poor; impoverished: *the Smiths are very badly off.* **b.** badly supplied with (fol. by *for*): *the school is badly off for money.*

**balance of power,**
**n.* a distribution of forces among members of a committee, political group, etc., so that no one member or group of members has an advantage or majority.
**n.* **hold the balance of power,** to be in a position to influence (a vote, decision, etc.) by supporting either of two more or less evenly divided sides.

**balanda** /bəˈlændə/, *n.* a white man. [Aboriginal (Northern Australian); ? from *Hollander*]

**baldy** /ˈbɔldi/, *n. Colloq.* **1.** (*oft. derog.*) a bald person: *Hey! Baldy!* **2.** →**Hereford.**

**bank engine** /ˈbæŋk ɛndʒən/, *n. Railways.* a locomotive coupled to a train to help pull it up steep inclines. Also, **banker.**

**banquet,**
**n.* in a Chinese restaurant, a meal consisting of a fixed number of set dishes eaten communally.

**bareboat charter** /ˈbɛəboʊt ˌtʃatə/, *n.* the charter of a boat equipped for sailing but not provided with skipper or crew.

**bash,**
**n.* the longitudinal dent in the crown of a slouch hat.

**bashing** /ˈbæʃɪŋ/, *n. Colloq.* **1.** excessive attention, exposure or use: *that song's had a bashing on air lately.* **2.** such activity evincing hostility.

**basilar membrane** /ˌbæsələ ˈmɛmbreɪn/, *n.* a membrane in the spiral canal of the cochlea and supporting the organ of corti.

**basilisk,**
**n.* a legendary reptile, the glance and breath of which could kill.

**bat**[2]**,**
**n.* **blind as a bat,** *Colloq.* very blind.

**batch processing** /ˈbætʃ ˌproʊsɛsɪŋ/, *n. Computers.* a method of processing whereby a large amount of data is collected for handling as a single unit or a number of programs are accumulated ready to be processed at the one time. Cf. **real-time.**

**bath,**
**n.* **in everything bar (but) a bath,** (*usu. derog.*) officiously busy in a multitude of activities.

**baud** /bɔd/, *n.* a unit for measuring the speed with which electronic data is transmitted, esp. in computers. [named after J. M. E. *Baudet,* 1845-1903, French engineer]

**beam,**
**n.* **broad in the beam,** *Colloq.* (of a person, usu. female) very wide across the buttocks.

**beanstalk,**
**n.* →**beanpole** (def. 2).

**bingle,**
**v.t.,* **-gled, -gling.** to cause a bingle in a motor vehicle, surfboard, etc.

**billy boulder** /ˈbɪli ˌboʊldə/, *n.* a smooth, rounded stone about as large as a pumpkin.

**bio-box** /ˈbaɪoʊ-bɒks/, *n. Colloq.* →**projection room.** [BIO(SCOPE) + BOX]

**biomass** /ˈbaɪoʊmæs/, *n.* the quantity of living matter contributed to a given habitat by one or several kinds of organism, and usu. expressed as weight for unit area or volume.

**biotechnology** /ˌbaɪoʊtɛkˈnɒlədʒi/, *n.* →**ergonomics.** – **biotechnological** /ˌbaɪoʊtɛknəˈlɒdʒɪkəl/, *adj.* – **biotechnologically** /ˌbaɪoʊtɛknəˈlɒdʒɪkli/, *adv.* – **biotechnologist,** *n.*

**bird**[1]**,**
**n.* **bird in the hand,** that which is sure though perhaps not entirely satisfactory. [from proverb, *a bird in the hand is worth two in the bush*]
**n.* **bird of passage,** a person whose stay in a given place is short.

**bit,**
**n.* *Colloq.* sexual intercourse: *did you get a bit?*

**Black Poll** /blæk ˈpoʊl/, *n.* →**Aberdeen Angus.**

**blooper,**
**n.* a sail, additional to the usual working sails, and used as an extra spinnaker.

**blouson** /ˈbluzɒn, ˈblaʊzɒn/, *adj.* (of a dress, jacket, etc.) having a loose-fitting top gathered in at the waist. [F]

**BMX** /bi ɛm ˈɛks/, *adj.* **1.** of or pertaining to the racing of small sturdily-built pushbikes on circuits presenting a variety of surfaces and terrain. *–n.* **2.** any pushbike designed for such a use. [short for Bike Motocrosse]

**boatshed** /ˈboʊt,ʃɛd/, *n.* a place where boats may be bought, hired, refuelled, or repaired.

**body,**
**n.* **body and soul,** entirely; completely: *she owned him body and soul.*

**body shop,**
**n.* a workshop where motor vehicle bodies are repaired.

**bone,**
**n.* a white colour with a touch of yellowish beige; the colour of dry bones.
**n.* **bare bones,** the essentials without any trimming: *these are the bare bones of the argument.*
**n.* **have a bone to pick with,** have a quarrel with (someone) and

a wish to resolve it straightaway.
*n. **close to (near) the bone,** indecent; risqué.
*n. **not make old bones,** (of a person or animal) to be unlikely to reach a great age.

**boo,**
*n. **wouldn't say boo to a goose,** (of a person) to be timid or shy.

**boom arm** /'bum am/, *n.* →**boom**[2] (def. 5).

**boot**[1],
*n. **be too big for one's boots,** to hold too high an opinion of oneself; be conceited.

**bop,**
*v.t. *Colloq.* to hit: *Jack bopped him on the head.*

**bore drain** /'bɔ dreɪn/, *n.* (in outback areas) a drain carrying water from an artesian bore to wherever it may be needed for sheep, cattle, irrigation, etc. Also, **boredrain, bore-drain.**

**Botany Bay greens,** *n. pl. Obs.* certain weeds used as green vegetables in the early colony when the food supply was short.

**British bulldog** /ˌbrɪtɪʃ 'bʊldɒg/, *n.* a children's game resembling cockylora.

**brush-tailed possum** /ˌbrʌʃ-teɪld 'pɒsəm/, *n.* any of various strongly-built, medium-sized possums of the genus *Trichosurus,* widely distributed in many parts of Australia. Also, **brush-tail possum.**

**bug-eyed** /'bʌg-aɪd/, *adj. Colloq.* popeyed; with eyes protruding like those of a bug, as a sign of surprise, tiredness, etc.

**building block,**
*n. →**brick** (def. 4).

**bull-head shark** /'bʊl-hɛd ʃak/, *n.* →**Port Jackson shark.**

**bump cap** /'bʌmp kæp/, *n.* a type of safety helmet of light construction, as used in the meat industry.

**bumzack** /'bʌmzæk/, *n. W.A. Colloq.* a cadger, esp. of drinks. [BUM + ZACK]

**bundy**[1],
*v.i., **-died, -dying. bundy on,** to start work by putting one's card into the bundy.
*v.i. **bundy off,** to finish work in the same way.

**bungarra** /bʌn'gærə/, *n. W.A.* →**Gould's goanna.**

**bunting tosser** /'bʌntɪŋ ˌtɒsə/, *n. Navy Colloq.* (formerly) a signalman.

**bus,**
*v.t. *Chiefly U.S.* to transport (people) by bus, esp. to transport school children to a school distant from their home.

**bust**[2],
*v.t. (of the police) to carry out a raid on (a place): *they busted the club again last night.*

**butcher's canary** /ˌbʊtʃəz kə'nɛəri/, *n. Colloq. (joc.)* a blowfly.

**buttinski,**
*n. *Colloq.* a telephone device enabling a technician to cut into a local cable and speak to a subscriber, as when a fault is being repaired.

# Cc

**cake,**
*n. **have one's cake and eat it,** to have the advantages, and be free of the disadvantages, of a situation.

**calcitonin** /kælsə'toʊnən/, *n.* a hormone secreted by the thyroid gland which inhibits the release of calcium from the skeleton into the blood.

**calendar,**
*n. the handbook of an educational institution, giving information on courses, rules, etc.

**call,**
**special verb phrase.* **call back,** to telephone a further time or in reply.

**cane,**
*v.t. to drive (def. 2): *he's really caning the car along.*

**canvas work** /'kænvəs wɜk/, *n.* →**needle point.**

**carbon chain** /'kabən tʃeɪn/, *n.* (within a molecule of an organic substance) a number of carbon atoms each linked to its adjacent neighbours.

**carer** /'kɛərə/, *n.* one who looks after other people, as children in child-care or aged relatives.

**castor**[3] /'kastə/, *adj. Colloq.* pleasing; excellent: *she'll be castor!* [orig. uncert.]

**cattle ramp,**
*n. a ramp (def. 1) by which cattle are loaded into trucks.

**chaise lounge** /ʃeɪz 'laʊndʒ/, *n.* →**chaise longue.**

**charge nurse** /'tʃadʒ nɜs/, *n.* →**sister** (def. 6).

**chaser**[1],
*n. a theme, usu. short, played by a band to signify the end of a bracket (def. 8).

**checkout,**
*adj. **checkout chick,** *Colloq.* a young girl serving at a checkout.

**child abuse** /'tʃaɪld əbjus/, *n.* →**child bashing.**

**chlorobenzene** /ˌklɔroʊbɛn'zin/, *n.* a colourless, insoluble liquid, $C_6H_5Cl$, which is volatile and flammable, made from chlorine and benzene; used in the preparation of many organic compounds, as DDT.

**C.H.O.G.M.** /'tʃɒgəm/, Commonwealth Heads of Government Meeting.

**chopping board** /'tʃɒpɪŋ bɔd/, *n.* a board, usu. wooden, on which meat or vegetables are chopped.

**cityite** /'sɪtiaɪt/, *n.* →**townie** (def. 3). [CITY + -ITE]

**classical conditioning** /ˌklæsɪkəl kən'dɪʃənɪŋ/, *n.* (in psychology) a procedure by which stimuli are paired so that an organism is trained to respond to the second stimulus alone in the way it originally responded to the first stimulus.

**clearing sale** /'klɪərɪŋ seɪl/, *n.* the sale, usu. by auction, of some or all of the household effects, agricultural equipment and stock from a farm or station (def. 8b).

**click,**
**n. (pl.)* Also, **klick.** *Colloq.* kilometres.

**close,**
**v.i.* **close down,** to cease operation.

**clout,**
**n.* →**clout nail.**

**cohort,**
**n.* a member of a cohort (def. 3); an individual supporter.

**coin,**
**v.t.* **coin a phrase,** (*joc.*) to use an acknowledged cliché.

**cold,**
**adj.* unprepared: *he started cold in the race.*

**cold change** /kould 'tʃeɪndʒ/, *n.* a drop in the temperature of the atmosphere, usually associated with the arrival of a cold front.

**colossal,**
**adj. Colloq.* →**mighty** (def. 3).

**colour,**
**v.t.* **colour in,** to colour an outline drawing, with paint, crayon, etc.

**colouring,**
**n.* **colouring in,** the activity of colouring an outline drawing with paint, crayon, etc.

**colouring-in book** /kʌlərɪŋ-'ɪn bʊk/, *n.* a book of outline designs or drawings for children to colour in.

**corpus,**
**n.* a body of data: *the linguist analysed the corpus of sentences.*

**cow juice** /'kaʊ dʒus/, *n. Colloq.* milk.

**crab stick** /'kræb stɪk/, *n.* a stick-shaped piece of prepared and compacted seafood, with a crab flavour.

**crash trolley** /'kræʃ trɒli/, *n.* →**crash cart.**

**credit,**
**n.* Also, **pass with credit.** (in some educational institutions) a result in an examination which indicates performance higher than necessary to pass.

**creeper,**
**n.* →**cradle** (def. 6).

**crook**², 
**adj.* broken; damaged.

**cue card** /'kju kad/, *n.* →**idiot board.**

**cyesis** /saɪ'isəs/, *n., pl.* **-es.** pregnancy; gestation. [NL, from Gk *kyésis* pregnancy]

# Dd

**Dad's army** /dædz 'ami/, *n. Colloq.* a body of retired or unfit men or mothballed plant or machinery brought back into service: *a Dad's army of old power stations.* [with reference to the British Home Guard, and made popular by the television series of the same name]

**daisy wheel** /'deɪzi wil/, *n.* a disc with multiple segments bearing raised characters on its circumference, used to produce high quality printing on some typewriters, printers, etc. [from the fancied likeness to the petals of a daisy]

**debark**² /di'bak/, *v.t.* to remove bark from (logs, etc.). [DE + BARK²]

**default,**
**n. Computers.* a course which a program automatically follows in the absence of any specific alternative instruction.

**dinnyhayser,**
**n.* a spectacular fall.

**diskette** /dɪs'kɛt/, *n.* →**floppy disc.**

**divorce,**
**v.t.* to legally separate from (one's spouse): *she divorced him last year.*
**v.i.* to be separated by divorce: *we divorced last year.*

**dook** /duk/, *n.* (*chiefly pl.*) →**duke** (def. 4).

**dope,**
**n. Colloq.* marijuana.

**dot**¹,
**n.* **the dots,** *Jazz Colloq.* musical notation.

**double-gee** /dʌbəl-'dʒi/, *n. W.A.* →**cat's head.**

**down time** /'daʊn taɪm/, *n.* time during which equipment is out of order or otherwise not able to be used productively.

**draw,**
**special verb phrase.* **draw a bead on,** to take aim at.

**drott** /drɒt/, *n.* **1.** a multipurpose implement for use as a scoop, hoe, jaws, etc., for attachment to an excavator. **2.** an excavator with such an attachment.

**DSE** /di ɛs 'i/, *n.* a measure of the carrying capacity of land in terms of the number of sheep it can support. [*D(ry) S(heep) E(quivalent)*]

**dumbbell,**
**n. Colloq.* →**dumbcluck.**

**dump**²,
**n.* **not give a twopenny dump,** *Colloq.* →**damn** (def. 8).

**duplex,**
**n. Qld.* two semidetached cottages.

# Ee

**echo,**
**n. S.A.* a small returnable bottle of beer; stubby.

**economies of scale,** *n. pl.* savings made when expansion of productive capacity permits a lower unit cost.

**eight ball** /'eɪt bɔl/, *n. in the phrase* **behind the eight ball,** *Colloq.* in an awkward or disadvantageous position. [from the game of eight ball; see POOL² (def. 8.)]

**electrified fence** /ə,lɛktrəfaɪd 'fɛns/, *n.* →**electric fence.**

**element,**
**n. Mil.* a group of soldiers not corresponding to one of the regular groups of platoon, company, battalion, etc.

**embattled** /ɛm'bætld/, *adj.* involved in a battle or argument.

**enate** /'ineɪt/, *adj.* **1.** pertaining to that which grows outwards. **2.** Also, **enatic** /i'nætɪk/. related on the mother's side. – *n.* **3.** one who is related on the mother's side. [L *ēnātus,* from *nāsci* to be born]

**encapsulate,**
**v.t.* to put in shortened form; condense; abridge.

**endemic,**
**adj.* native to a country or locality, as a plant.

**endorphin** /ɛn'dɔfən/, *n.* an opiate-like substance manufactured in the human brain which apparently enables the body to withstand pain. [ENDO- + (MOR)PHIN(E)]

**erasure,**
**n.* the word or mark erased.

**erlang** /'ɜlæŋ/, *n. Telecom.* a measure of occupancy of a circuit or set of circuits; one circuit occupied full-time has a rating of one erlang.

**explosive bolt** /əksplouzɪv 'boult/, *n.* a bolt used, esp. in space technology, to hold components together temporarily, and which is designed to explode when the parts are to be separated.

# Ff

**father confessor,**
**n. Colloq.* someone who listens willingly to another and is ready to give help, advice, etc.

**federation,**
**adj.* of the style common at and about the time of the federation of the six original Australian States: *federation house, federation architecture.*

**feel,**
**n. Colloq.* the precise manner of doing, using, etc.: *you'll soon get the feel of it.*

**fenced-in,**
**adj.* trapped; limited in scope of action or choice.
**adj.* claustrophobic.

**fiche** /fiʃ/, *n.* →**microfiche.**

**fifth wheel,**
**n.* an extra wheel attached to a vehicle and used with a recording device to accurately measure distance travelled.

**fill,**
**special verb phrase.* **fill in,** to give all necessary information, etc.

**film-maker** /'fɪlm-meɪkə/, *n.* a person who initiates the production of a film, esp. by arranging the financial backing, and who supervises its production; producer.

**f.i.s.,**
*free into store.

**fishbowl,**
**n.* any place or way of life which is open to the public gaze: *to live in a fishbowl.*

**fishtail,**
**v.i.* (of a car) to skid with side to side movement of the rear wheels.
**n.* a section at the back of a full-length skirt, shaped like a fish's tail and forming a short train.

**fixer** /'fɪksə/, *n.* **1.** *Photog.* a chemical solution used to remove the light-sensitive silver halides from a photographic image, rendering it permanent. **2.** a mason who sets stones in walls.

**flag,**
**n.* any signal or indicator.
**n.* **raise the flags, a.** to score a goal. **b.** to accomplish something.

**flair,**
**n.* elegance; stylishness: *to dress with flair.*

**flick,**
**n. S.A.* **give the flick,** to reject or dismiss. [? from pest exterminator advertisement *One Flick and They're Gone*]

**float valve** /'flout vælv/, *n.* →**ballcock.**

**flown scenery** /floun 'sinəri/, *n.* (in a theatre) scenery which, when not in use, can be lifted up out of sight into the flies.

**food processor** /'fud prousɛsə/, *n.* a kitchen implement used to shred, slice, juice, mash, etc.

**foots** /fʊts/, *n. pl.* →**footlights.**

**foxing** /'fɒksɪŋ/, *n.* spotting or staining on prints, drawings, etc., caused by the growth of mildew.

**franking machine** /'fræŋkɪŋ məʃin/, *n.* a machine bought or rented from the postal service, which stamps an item of mail to indicate that postage has been or will be paid, and which keeps a record of accumulated postage.

**fresh,**
**adj.* **fresh out of,** *Chiefly U.S.* completely lacking in (a commodity, ideas, etc.): *we are fresh out of coffee.*

**fry,**
**n. Chiefly Brit.* various internal organs of specified animals, usu. eaten fried: *calf's fry.* Cf. **lamb's fry.**

**full-bodied,**
**adj.* (of a woman) buxom; full-bosomed.

**functor** /'fʌŋktə/, *n.* a factor among others which brings about a certain condition; a parameter. [FUNC(TION) + -OR[2]]

**fundamentalism,**
**n.* any religious movement which stresses the authority and literal application of its founding tenets: *Muslim fundamentalism.*

**furrow,**
**v.i.* (of the face, brow, etc.) to wrinkle; crease.

**Galloway,**
**n.* a small horse of between fourteen and fifteen hands.

**gazette,**
*v.t. to make official by listing in a government gazette: *the new regulations will be gazetted next week.*

**gemfish** /ˈdʒɛmfɪsh/, *n.* a food fish with delicate flavour, *Rexea solandri,* plentiful in waters of south-eastern Australia; hake.

**ghittoe** /ˈgɪtoʊ/, *n.* either of two species of trees used for their strong, resilient timber which is known as saffronheart: **1.** *Halfordia scleroxyla* of northern Queensland; kerosene-wood. **2.** *Halfordia kendack* of Queensland and New South Wales; greenheart.

**gibberellin** /dʒɪbəˈrɛlən/, *n.* any of several plant hormones which cause elongation of the plant stem. [first isolated from the fungus *Gibberella fujikuroi;* NL *Gibberella,* from L *gibber* hump + -IN[2]]

**give,**
*special verb phrase.* **give away,** to abandon; give up: *times were hard so I gave farming away.*

**godfather,**
*n. one who exercises power and dispenses protection while keeping in the background; grey eminence.

**goolie,**
*n. a gob of phlegm.

**grab,**
*n. **up for grabs,** ready for the taking; available for anyone to claim.

**grading** /ˈgreɪdɪŋ/, *n.* →**grade** (def. 6).

**granulose** /ˈgrænjəloʊs/, *adj.* →**granular.**

**gravel rash,**
*n. **get gravel rash,** *Colloq.* to act in a sycophantic fashion.

**greenheart,**
*n. →**ghittoe** (def. 2).

**gross,**
*v.t. to amplify; enlarge; fill out the details of (fol. by *up*).

**gross motor skills,** *n.* **1.** those physical skills considered basic to human activity, as locomotion, balance, spatial orientation, etc. **2.** Also, **gross motor.** a program designed to foster such skills, esp. in school children.

**guiding** /ˈgaɪdɪŋ/, *n.* the activities of a guide or guides.

# Hh

**Ha,** *Chem.* hahnium.

**ha-ha[1],**
*n. **have the ha-has,** *Colloq.* to be insane.

**hair cell** /ˈhɛə sɛl/, *n.* a cell with a hair-like process, the mechanical stimulation of which often triggers some form of response in nerve fibres running from the cell.

**hake,**
*n. →**gemfish.**

**handfeed,**
*v.t. *Colloq.* to give people, as students, more help than they need or should have.

**hands-on** /hændz-ˈɒn/, *adj.* **1.** practical, as opposed to theoretical: *hands-on experience in teaching.* **2.** requiring or encouraging manual contact or operation: *participatory playgrounds with hands-on exhibits.*

**handyman,**
*n. a person who enjoys or is skilled at doing small repairs, etc., esp. around the house.

**hat,**
*n. **throw one's hat in the door,** to test the warmth of one's reception in company, as when arriving late.

**have,**
*v.t. to entertain; accept as a welcome visitor: *thank you for having me.*

**heap,**
*n. *(pl.)* (used as intensifier): *Bill's pile is heaps bigger than mine.*

**hendeca-,** a prefix meaning eleven. [Gk *hendeka*]

**heresy,**
*n. any opinion or belief contrary to established theory.

**hispanic,**
*n. a person of hispanic antecedents.

**homogenous,**
*adj. →**homogeneous** (defs. 1 and 2).

**hop,**
*v.i. *Colloq.* to go, come, move, etc.: *hop into the car and we'll go.*

**hopper window** /ˈhɒpə wɪndoʊ/, *n.* a window, usu. wider than it is tall, which is hinged either from the top or the two sides so that it is opened by pushing the bottom edge outwards.

**hurling** /ˈhɜlɪŋ/, *n.* an Irish game resembling hockey in which teams of 15 players, using sticks, attempt to score by getting the ball through their opponent's goal.

**hot spot,**
*n. a spot in the inlet manifold of an internal combustion engine which is heated by exhaust gases to vaporise the fuel.
*n. a sharp metal spike or piece of carbon in the combustion chamber which becomes hot and causes pre-ignition.

**hyponym** /ˈhaɪpənɪm/, *n.* a word whose sense is included in that of a more general word: *'chair' is a hyponym of 'furniture'.*

**hyponymy** /haɪˈpɒnəmi/, *n.* the relation that holds between a hyponym and its more general term.

# Ii

**ILO** /ˌaɪ ɛl ˈoʊ/, International Labour Organisation.

**incompatibility** /ɪnkəmpætəˈbɪləti, ɪŋ-/, *n.* inability to exist together in harmony.

**incomputerate** /ɪnkəm'pjutərət, ɪŋ-/, *n.* lacking any knowledge or understanding of computers or computer systems.

**independent,**
**n. Politics.* a candidate for election or an elected representative in parliament who is not formally affiliated with a political party.

**iridology** /ɪrə'dɒlədʒi/, *n.* the examination of the iris to detect evidence of pathological changes in the body. – **iridologist,** *n.*

**ISD** /aɪ ɛs 'di/, International Subscriber Dialling. Also, **I.S.D.**

**itchy,**
**adj.* **have itchy feet,** to have the desire to travel.

# Jj

**jackpot,**
**v.i.* **-potted, -potting.** to accumulate by the amount of the previous unclaimed prize.

**jaspilite** /'dʒæspəlaɪt/, *n.* one name given to rocks of banded iron formation abundant in Western Australia, principally consisting of layers of red jasper and black haematite; such formations are often the host rocks of important mineral deposits.

**judgmental** /dʒʌdʒ'mɛntəl/, *adj.* inclined to pass judgment, esp. in a dogmatic fashion.

**juice,**
**v.t.* **juiced, juicing.** to extract juice from (fruit or vegetables).

# Kk

**k** /keɪ/, *n. Colloq.* kilometres: *we were only doing 100 k.* Also, **k's.**

**kapok bush** /'keɪpɒk bʊʃ/, *n.* any of various small trees of the genus *Cochlospermum* found in northern Australia, which have bright yellow flowers yielding a floss like kapok.

**kerosene-wood** /kərə'sin-wʊd/, *n.* →**ghittoe** (def. 1).

**kiddiewinks** /'kɪdiwɪŋks/, *n. pl. Colloq. (joc.)* very young children viewed affectionately.

**kiss-and-ride commuter** /kɪs-ən-ˌraɪd kə'mjutə/, *n. Colloq.* a commuter who is driven to and from the point of contact with the public transport system, usu. by the partner, spouse, etc.

**knapsack spray** /'næpsæk spreɪ/, *n.* a spraying device consisting of a tank and pump carried on the back and a hand-held spray, used for dispensing insecticides and weed-killers, and esp. for fighting bushfires.

**knickers,**
**n. pl.* **get one's knickers in a twist (knot),** *Orig. Brit. Colloq.* to become agitated or flustered.

**knobbly,**
**n.* a tyre with large rubber knobs on its tread, suitable for trail bikes.

**kombi** /'kɒmbi/, *n.* a light, multi-purpose motor van for family or small business use. Also, **kombivan, combi.** [Trademark]

**krill** /krɪl/, *n.pl.* a number of shrimp-like crustaceans of the order Euphausiacea, esp. those occurring in immense swarms in antarctic waters; the main food source of whalebone (baleen) whales. [Norw. *kril* young fish]

# Ll

**layside** /'leɪsaɪd/, *adj.* of or pertaining to non-uniformed members or groups in the Scout Association of Australia.

**league,**
**n.* a society or association, esp. one with a national or state-wide structure and local branches.

**Lebanese bread** /lɛbəniz 'brɛd/, *n.* unleavened bread in large flat discs. Also, **Arab bread.**

**lend,**
**n.* often used erroneously to mean 'loan': *give me a lend of your pen.*

**loan,**
**n.* **have a loan (lend) of (someone),** *Colloq.* to practise a deception on or tease (someone).

**let**[1]**,**
**special verb phrase.* **let fly,** to express one's anger without restraint.

**level,**
**adj.* used as a measure of the density of a rainforest: *a seven-level forest* (very dense).

**life,**
**n.* **life of Riley,** a life of ease and luxury: *after I won the pools it was just a life of Riley.*

**lime**[1]**,**
**n. Films.* a carbon-arc projector (formerly limelight was used).

**lobster,**
**n. Hist. Colloq.* a trooper; redcoat.

**lock**[1]**,**
**v.t. Hist.* **lock up the land,** to make the land unavailable to all but very few people (by giving out only large parcels of it by grant or to squatters).

**Logie** /'loʊgi/, *n.* a statuette awarded annually by the Australian television industries to outstanding television practitioners. [after John *Logie* Baird, inventor of television, and coined by Graham Kennedy when in 1958 he received the first award]

**lollipop lady** /'lɒlipɒp ˌleɪdi/, *n.* a woman, often a parent, who supervises children crossing roads outside schools.

**lollipop man** /'lɒlipɒp mæn/, *n.* a man, often retired, who supervises children crossing roads outside schools.

**louvre window** /'luvə ˌwɪndoʊ/, *n.* a window made from a number of narrow panes of glass, each just overlapping the next like louvre-boards and all being opened or shut by the one lever.

**lovey-dovey** /'lʌvi-dʌvi/, *adj. Colloq. (derog.)* affectionate, often noticeably in public.

**lowblocked** /ˈloʊblɒkt/, *adj.* (in the northern parts of Australia) pertaining to a house which stands on low foundations.

**lowset** /ˈloʊsɛt/, *adj.* **1.** →**lowblocked. 2.** (in the northern parts of Australia) pertaining to a house built on a concrete slab set into the earth.

**lyre,**
**n.* a lyre-shaped clamp fitting onto a musical instrument to hold a piece of music, esp. used by musicians in a marching band.

# Mm

**mallee,**
**n.* **strong as a mallee bull,** *Colloq.* very strong.

**makarrata** /makəˈratə, mækəˈratə/, *n.* **1.** (in certain Aboriginal tribes) a peacemaking ceremony marking a resumption of normal relations after a cessation of hostilities. **2.** a movement to attain such a situation between Aborigines and other Australians. [Aboriginal]

**Manila folder** /mənɪlə ˈfoʊldə/, *n.* →**folder** (def. 3).

**milk run,**
**n.* any routine trip involving a number of stops.

**minor,**
**n. Aus. Rules.* Also, **minor score.** a behind.

**mirror dory** /ˈmɪrə dɔri/, *n.* a fish, *Zenopsis nebulosus,* similar to the John Dory, found in N.S.W. coastal waters.

**mogul**[2] /ˈmoʊgəl/, *n. Skiing.* a bump or mound on a ski run.

**monetarist** /ˈmʌnətərəst/, *adj.* **1.** of or pertaining to policies which or persons who seek to control the economy of a country by adjustments to the money supply. – *n.* **2.** such a person.

**monkey,**
**n.* **a monkey on one's back,** any obsession, compulsion, or addiction, seen as a burden, as a compulsion to work or an addiction to drugs.

**Moonie** /ˈmuni/, *n. Colloq.* a follower of the Unification Church founded by the Rev. Sun Myung Moon.

**murri** /ˈmʌri/, *n.* an Aborigine.

# Nn

**natural justice** /nætʃərəl ˈdʒʌstəs/, *n.* that justice which responds to fundamental logic and absolute fairness rather than to the laws of a particular place and time.

**naturopathy** /nætʃəˈrɒpəθi/, *n.* a system of treating disease and disorders based on assistance to nature, esp. by use of herbs, natural foods, exercise and sunlight. –**naturopath** /ˈnætʃərəˌpæθ/, *n.*

**no-frills** /ˈnoʊ-frɪlz/, *adj.* plain; providing basic necessities but not luxuries: *a no-frills package tour.*

**no-name** /ˈnoʊ-neɪm/, *adj.* →**generic** (def. 3).

**north-south** /nɔθ-ˈsaʊθ/, *adj.* of or pertaining to discussions, relations, etc., between the richer and better developed countries, most of which are in the Northern Hemisphere, and the poorer, less developed countries, most of which are in the Southern Hemisphere.

**nose,**
**n.* **keep one's nose clean,** to follow rules and regulations meticulously so as to avoid any blame.

# Oo

**off,**
**adj. Theat.* off stage: *I sacked my dresser as soon as I was off.*

**off-peak,**
**adj.* (of a hot-water or other electrical system) set to operate only during an off-peak period, normally during the night.

**on,**
**adj. Theat.* on stage: *you'll be on in five minutes.*

**O.P.,**
**n. Theat.* opposite prompt.

**open order,**
**n.* permission to make any purchase on account.

**opposite prompt** /ˈɒpəsət prɒmpt/, *n. Theat.* the side of the stage opposite to prompt-side.

**optical character reader,** *n.* a device which uses optical character recognition to read information. Cf. **OCR.**

**oracy** /ˈɒrəsi/, *n.* basic competence in oral communication.

**oral history** /ɒrəl ˈhɪstri/, *n.* an account of past events assembled from the spoken reminiscences of those who lived through them.

**organ of corti** /ˌɔgən əv ˈkɔti/, *n.* the large number of hair cells and nerve cells with their supporting structures which convert the mechanical vibrations of the basilar membrane of the cochlea into nerve impulses for the auditory nerve. [named after Alfonso *Corti*]

**ort** /ɔt/, *n. Colloq.* anus: *in your ort, sport.*

**orthosis** /ɔˈθoʊsəs/, *n., pl.* **-ses** /-siz/. a device applied to the body to modify position or motion, as a supporting collar, plaster cast, etc. – **orthotic,** *adj.*

**orthotics** /ɔˈθɒtɪks/, *n. Med.* the study of the application of orthoses.

**othersider** /ˈʌðəsaɪdə/, *n. W.A. Colloq.* →**t'othersider.**

**out,**
**adj. Theat.* up (of flown scenery).

# Pp

**package tour** /ˈpækɪdʒ ˌtʊə/, *n.* a tour for which the travel, accommodation and certain varying but specified other costs, as for meals, use of a car, etc., are all paid for at the one time, usu. with considerable saving to the purchaser.

**paraflier** /ˈpærəflaɪə/, *n.* one who, while suspended from a parachute, is kept aloft by the speed of a boat to which he or she is attached by a rope. – **paraflying,** *n.*

**party room** /ˈpati rum/, *n.* a room, usu. in a house of parliament, in which the members of one politcal party meet for private discussions, decision-making, election of officers, etc.

**paintwork** /ˈpeɪntwɜk/, *n.* **1.** the application of paint to a surface. **2.** a painted surface: *mind the paintwork.*

**part work** /ˈpat wɜk/, *n.* a series of magazines, or supplements to magazines, issued at intervals but intended to be bound together when the set is complete.

**parental,**
**n. Genetics.* a stage in the sequence of generations.

**park,**
**v.t.* **park oneself,** *Colloq.* to be seated.

**partisan**[1],
**adj.* excessively dedicated to a cause or party.
**adj.* biased; prejudiced.

**patch,**
**v.t.* **patch in,** to join to, esp. to join (an electronic circuit) to an existing set of circuits, usu. on a temporary basis.

**PCP** /pi si ˈpi/, *n.* →**phencyclidine.**

**pea eater** /ˈpi itə/, *n. Colloq.* a foolish person. [with reference to cattle who have eaten the DARLING PEA and gone mad]

**people,**
**n.* **go to the people,** to hold an election.

**pet**[1],
**n.* a term of endearment or affection.

**phencyclidine** /fɛnˈsaɪklədin/, *n.* a combined depressant and hallucinogen, orig. manufactured as a veterinary anaesthetic, now considered highly dangerous. Also, **PCP, angel dust.**

**phragmosis** /frægˈmousəs/, *n.* the use by some insects of a part of their body to protect themselves and their nests. [NL, from Gk *phragmós* fence + -OSIS]

**physique,**
**n. Colloq.* →**figure** (def. 6).

**pigsty,**
**n.* any dirty, messy or untidy place: *this room is a veritable pigsty.*

**pinch,**
**n.* the steepest or most difficult section of a path or road.

**pintail,**
**n.* →**rainbow bee-eater.**

**pissaphone** /ˈpɪsəfoun/, *n. Mil. Colloq.* (in World War II, esp. in tropical areas) a large funnel resembling the mouthpiece of a wall telephone, set into the ground for use as a urinal.

**pit stop,**
**n. Colloq.* any stop made on a journey in a motor car, for refuelling, refreshment, etc.

**pitta**[2] /ˈpɪtə/, *n.* →**pocket bread.**

**plissé** /ˈplɪseɪ/, *n.* a lightweight fabric with a permanent stripe produced by treating with caustic soda.

**plod,**
**n. W.A. Mining.* instructions left for a worker on the following shift.
**n. Colloq.* a long, rambling narrative.

**ploughman's lunch** /ˈplaumənz ˌlʌntʃ/, *n. Orig. Brit.* a simple lunch of beer, bread and cheese, usu. as served in a hotel.

**plunge,**
**n. Qld.* Also, **plunge bath.** a bath.

**POA,** price on application.

**pocket bread** /ˈpɒkət brɛd/, *n.* a flat, round, usu. unleavened bread forming a pocket, which, when opened, can be filled with food.

**point,**
**v.t.* **point up,** to highlight.

**Poll Hereford** /poul ˈhɛrəfəd/, *n.* Hereford cattle which have been polled (def. 22).

**polony** /pəˈlouni/, *n. W.A.* bologna sausage. [Trademark]

**populism** /ˈpɒpjəlɪzəm/, *n.* a political philosophy concerned with the needs of the common people. [orig. advocated by U.S. Populist Party formed in 1891]

**populist** /ˈpɒpjələst/, *n.* a political advocate of the needs of the common people.

**potato cake** /pəˈteɪtou keɪk/, *n.* **1.** a fried ball or cake of grated potato, onion, etc. **2.** *Vic.* a potato scallop.

**prawn,**
**n. Colloq.* a weak, spiritless, insignificant person: *he's a bit of a prawn.*

**prawn cocktail** /ˌprɔn ˈkɒkteɪl/, *n.* a cold entree of cooked prawns, served on a lettuce leaf with a spiced mayonnaise. Cf. **seafood cocktail.**

**prepubescent** /ˌpripjuˈbɛsənt/, *adj.* before the age of puberty.

**projection room** /prəˈdʒɛkʃən ˌrum/, *n.* (in a cinema or theatre) the room containing the equipment for the projection of films or slides, and often the lighting controls; bio-box.

**prompt,**
**n. Theat.* one who prompts (def. 7).

**prosopography** /ˌprɒsəˈpɒgrəfi/, *n.* **1.** the study of an individual by means of such records as may exist in official records, newspapers, etc., of his or her offices, honours, relations and achievements; the assembling of a biography. **2.** the biography itself. [Gk *prosōpon* face + -GRAPHY]

**provost,** /ˈprouvou/
**n.* a military policeman.

**public sector** /pʌblɪk ˈsɛktə/, *n.* that sector of a community's activities or enterprises under state ownership or control (as opposed to the *private sector*).

**pull,**
**v.t.* **pull the plug on,** to prevent (someone) from continuing their present activities as by making some damning revela-

tion, issuing an order, etc. [analogy with pulling out the plug of an electric appliance]

# Qq

**queen's guide** /kwinz 'gaɪd/, *n.* a girl guide who has achieved the greatest degree of proficiency in guiding.

**quince,**
**n.* **do one's quince,** *Colloq.* to lose one's temper.

# Rr

**ratbag,**
**n.* a person whose preoccupation with a particular theory or belief is seen as obsessive or discreditable: *that Marxist ratbag.*

**rave,**
**n.* *Colloq.* a long and animated conversation.

**recording studio** /rə'kɔdɪŋ ˌstjudioʊ/, *n.* a studio (def. 3) for recording sound, as music, speech, etc.

**recuperator,**
**n.* (in weaponry) an assembly which forms part of the recoil system of a weapon.

**repiano** /rɛpi'anoʊ/, *n.* (in brass bands) the part written for cornet supplementing the solo cornet part. [from It. *ripieno,* by distortion]

**rheumatology** /rumə'tɒlədʒi/, *n.* the branch of medicine dealing with rheumatic diseases.

**ridge**[1]**,**
**n.* **round the ridges,** →**trap**[1] (def. 13).
**n.* **have been (a)round the ridges,** to be expert, experienced.

**road plant** /'roʊd plænt/, *n.* a group of machines working together to repair or construct a road.

**Rockie** /'rɒki/, *n.* *Colloq.* a member of the Royal Australia Naval Reserve. [one from the 'rocks', i.e. the shore]

**rogaining** /roʊ'geɪnɪŋ/, *n.* a competitive sport involving cross-country navigation over long distances and entailing movement both by day and night.

**round robin,**
**n.* a sporting competition in which each player or team plays against all other participants.
**n.* any procedure involving the circulation of data, samples, etc., so that comparisons may be made.

**Rubik's cube** /rubɪks 'kjub/, *n.* a puzzle in the shape of a cube whose faces are divided into separable coloured squares which may be moved to form patterns, or to return to the original state of solid-coloured faces. [named after its inventor]

**rude,**
**adj.* *Colloq.* inconsiderate; unfair; dismissive: *that's a bit rude.*

# Ss

**SAA,** Standards Association of Australia.

**saffronheart** /'sæfrənhat/, *n.* the timber of the ghittoe.

**schnitzel** /'ʃnɪtsəl/, *n.* a thin slice of meat, usu. veal, pounded flat and pan-fried. Cf. **Wiener Schnitzel.**

**scoot,**
**v.i.* →**scram.**

**selection act** /sə'lɛkʃən ækt/, *n.* one of a number of acts of parliament, esp. in New South Wales and Victoria, which sought to break up the very large land holdings of the squatters after the middle of the nineteenth century and make land available to free selectors.

**set,**
**n.* (in popular music, jazz, etc.) a bracket (def. 8).

**shandy,**
**n.* a mixture: *a shandy of fish.*
**v.i.,* **-died, -dying.** to mix with (fol. by *in*): *let's shandy in some sand.*

**shirt-lifter** /'ʃɜt-lɪftə/, *n.* *Colloq.* a male homosexual.

**short-circuit,**
**v.t.* *Colloq.* to abbreviate procedures, esp. in relation to paperwork; bypass procedural steps: *I can short-circuit the system.*

**show,**
**n.* →**colour** (def. 19).
**n.* *Colloq.* a party.

**show pony** /'ʃoʊ poʊni/, *n.* an animal or person who displays elan but whose performance lacks substance.

**shrink-fit** /ʃrɪŋk-'fɪt/, *v.t.* to fit two components of a manufactured object together by heating or cooling one of them, so that as it returns to a natural temperature it fits more snugly with the other.

**shrink-wrap** /ʃrɪŋk-'ræp/, *v.t.* to enclose an object in a flexible plastic wrapping which shrinks to the shape of the object, sealing it in.

**silky**[2] /'sɪlki/, *n.* →**Australian silky terrier.**

**simulcast** /'sɪməlkast/, *n.* the broadcasting at the same time of a program on television and stereo radio with the object of enhancing the effect of the television viewing by means of superior sound.

**slaw** /slɔ/, *n.* →**coleslaw.**

**small businessman** /smɔl 'bɪznəsmən/, *n.* one who engages in business in a small way, as an independent shopkeeper.

**snatch,**
**v.t.* **snatch one's time,** *Colloq.* to leave a job.

**snow,**
**n.* *Colloq.* Also, **snowie.** (a nickname for a fair-haired person, usu. male).

**snow pea** /'snoʊ pi/, *n.* a variety of pea, the pods of which may be cooked and served whole.

**s.o.l.** /ɛs oʊ 'ɛl/, *adj.* →**shitty-livered.** [*s(hit) o(n the) l(iver)*]

**sound studio** /'saʊnd stjudioʊ/, *n.* →**recording studio.**

**sound stage** /'saʊnd steɪdʒ/, *n.* a building, usu. large and like a hangar, in which motion pictures are made and which has provision for the setting up of scenery and the recording of the actors' voices.

**sphairee** /sfaɪ'ri/, *n.* a game played on a small hard court with a perforated plastic ball; a reduced derivative of tennis. [from Gk *sphâira* a ball]

**spoiler,**
**n.* (on a motor vehicle) a surface, plane or shaped, attached either at the front of the vehicle or the rear, which seeks to gain advantage in traction or handling from the aerodynamic forces created by the air rushing past it at speed.

**squat,**
**n.* a building inhabited by squatters (def. 4): *he lives in a squat.*

**squitters** /'skwɪtəz/, *n. Colloq.* →**diarrhoea.**

**starter,**
**n.* *(pl.)* the first course of a large meal.
**n.* **for starters,** in the first place: *Well, for starters, he's a crook.*

**stay stitching** /'steɪ stɪtʃɪŋ/, *n.* a row of stitching used to reinforce a seam during the making of a garment.

**storeman** /'stɔmən/, *n.* one who has charge of a stock of goods.

**storm signals,**
**n. pl.* signs of impending trouble.

**storm warning** /'stɔm wɔnɪŋ/, *n.* **1.** →**storm signals. 2.** →**weather alert.**

**stroller,**
**n.* →**shopping stroller.**

**stu vac** /'stju væk/, *n.* (in a school, college, etc.) the period between the end of classes and the commencement of examinations, in which students are free to study for the examinations. Also, **swot vac.**

**sugar pea** /'ʃʊgə pi/, *n.* →**snow pea.**

**supercargo,**
**n.* →**supernumerary** (def. 3).

**supplementary,**
**n.* an examination held at some universities, etc., after the time of the regular examinations because of a candidate's illness or misadventure.

**swot vac** /'swɒt væk/, *n.* →**stu vac.**

# Tt

**tabouli** /tə'buli/, *n.* a salad of cracked wheat, chopped parsley, mint, tomato, oil, lemon juice, etc. Also, **tabouleh, tabbouli.**

**tacking** /'tækɪŋ/, *n.* a row of temporary stitching used to hold pieces of a garment together while it is being sewn.

**take,**
**special verb phrase.* **take to,** *Colloq.* to attack: *he took to his brother with a hairbrush.*

**tapestry,**
**n.* →**needle point.**

**TEAS** /tis, tiz/, *n.* **1.** Tertiary Education Assistance Scheme. **2. on TEAS,** in receipt of a Tertiary Education Assistance Scheme award.

**telephone pea** /'tɛləfoʊn pi/, *n.* a variety of climbing pea.

**thank,**
**n.* **thanks a million (a bunch),** (sarcastic thanks for something not wanted or disadvantageous to the speaker).

**three-corner jack** /'θri-kɔnə dʒæk/, *n.* →**cat's head.**

**time series** /'taɪm sɪəriz/, *n. Maths.* a sequence of numbers representing the values of a variable taking part in a continuing process, usu. at equally spaced points in time.

**tit,**
**n. Colloq.* →**push-button.**

**titch** /'tɪtʃ/, *n.* a small person. [Brit. dial. from OE *ticcen* kid]

**tofu** /'toʊfu/, *n.* →**beancurd.** [Jap. *tofu*]

**tram,**
**n. Obs.* a Queensland cane train.

**trick cyclist** /trɪk 'saɪkləst/, *n. Colloq.* a psychiatrist.

**trip,**
**n. Colloq.* a period of activity engaging a person's full energies: *into a money-making trip now.*

**trog** /trɒg/, *n. Colloq.* →**troglodyte** (def. 4).

**turn,**
**special verb phrase.* **turn up one's toes,** *Colloq.* to die.

**two,**
**adj.* **two men and a dog,** *Colloq.* very few people.

# Uu

**UF** /ju 'ɛf/, urea formaldehyde.

**UFFI** /ju ɛf ɛf 'aɪ/, urea formaldehyde foam insulation.

**unfaithful,**
**adj.* having sexual intercourse with person other than one's spouse or partner.

**union bashing** /'junjən bæʃɪŋ/, *n.* activity perceived as evincing hostility to trade unions. See **bashing.**

**unlock,**
**v.t. Hist.* **unlock the land,** to make the land available to many people (by the selection acts).

**urea formaldehyde** /juˌriə fɔ'mældəhaɪd/, *n.* a chemical used in the production of rigid plastics of many uses, as in particle board, adhesives, house insulation, etc.

# Vv

**VCR** /vi si 'a/, *n.* video cassette recorder.

**V.D.C.** /vi di 'si/, Volunteer Defence Corps.

**vertical integration** /vɜtɪkəl ɪntə'greɪʃən/, *n.* the linking up via a single organisation of a number of business concerns each operating successive stages in the production of a certain commodity.

**video cassette recorder,** *n.* a video tape recorder in which the tape is held in a cassette.

**videodisc** /'vɪdioʊ,dɪsk/, *n.* a videorecording made on a plastic disc superficially resembling an L.P. record. [Trademark]

**videorecord** /'vɪdioʊrə,kɔd/, *v.t.* to record images and usu. sounds either on videotape or videodisc.

**violist**² /vi'oʊləst/, *n.* a player of the viola.

# Ww

**walk-in, walk-out,** *adj.* pertaining to the sale of a house, etc., in which the sellers leave the house as it is and the buyers accept it in this condition asking for no repairs, improvements, etc.

**watered-down,**
**adj.* made less strong, as of successive versions of reports, etc.

**wave,**
**n.* →**permanent wave.**

**weather alert** /'wɛðər əlɜt/, *n.* a warning broadcast on radio or television of an approaching storm or gale, or of an impending cold change.

**Westralia** /wɛs'treɪljə/, *n. Colloq.* Western Australia. [shortened form]

**whistling duck** /'wɪslɪŋ dʌk/, *n.* either of two ducks, *Dendrocygna arcuata* or *D. eytoni,* found mainly in northern Australia, and characterised by making a whistling sound.

**wineglass,**
**n. Sailing.* a twisted spinnaker.

**wither,**
**v.i.* **wither on the vine,** to disappear because of lack of use.

**w.i., w.o.,** walk-in, walk-out.

**wood duck** /'wʊd dʌk/, *n.* a customer, as at a used-car saleyard, who is seen as having little or no likelihood of making a purchase. Also **woodie.**

**worry,**
**n.* **no worries,** *Colloq.* (an expression of confidence that everything will go well.)

**wrap,**
**n.* a wrapper, esp. a plastic one: *the sausages were in a plastic wrap.*

# Yy

**yum cha** /jʌm 'tʃa/, *n.* a form of Chinese meal in which diners choose individual serves from selections arranged on trolleys.

# Zz

**zigzag,**
**adj.* (of a railway track) following a zigzag course in order to take in an extremely steep slope.

# NOTES

# NOTES